VARIETY
MOVIE GUIDE

VARIETY ®
MOVIE GUIDE

Foreword by
Richard Attenborough

Editor
Derek Elley

HAMLYN

ACKNOWLEDGEMENTS

This guide has been the work of many hands, often labouring well
beyond the call of duty. For their help with editing the enormous
original manuscript and compiling credits, I would like to thank (in
order of workload) Alan Stanbrook, Miles Smith-Morris, Allen Eyles,
Sally Hibbin, Ingrid Aaroe, David Pilling, and David McGillivray.
Graham Berry provided invaluable help at a late stage with extra
credits, and Jack Pitman of *Variety*'s London bureau kindly cast a
veteran's eye over the Glossary. Last but not least, I would like to thank
Peter Cowie, European Publishing Director of *Variety*, for his overall
support, and Julian Brown, Commissioning Editor at Reed Consumer
Books, for all his understanding and calmness under fire.

DEREK ELLEY has written for and edited a wide variety of film
publications in the past twenty odd years as well as arranging
programmes for London's National Film Theatre and advising for
international festivals. His books include *The Epic Film: Myth and
History* (1984) and *Chronicle of the Movies* (Ed., 1991). He currently
works as an associate editor and reviewer for *Variety*.

First published in Great Britain 1993
by Hamlyn
an imprint of Reed Consumer Books Limited
Michelin House, 81 Fulham Road, London SW3 6RB
and Auckland, Melbourne, Singapore and Toronto

Copyright © 1993 Variety Inc.

ISBN 0 600 57898 4

A catalogue record for this book is available from the
British Library

Printed by Clowes in Great Britain

Commissioning Editor: Julian Brown   *Assistant Editor:* Katie Piper
Executive Art Editor: Bryan Dunn   *Designer:* David Rowley
Production Controller: Michelle Thomas

CONTENTS

FOREWORD

As any moviemaker like myself knows, critical fashions
wax and wane but *Variety* never changes – hard-nosed,
dedicated to the business (as well as the art) of cinema
and unsparing in both its brickbats and bouquets. That
is why we treasure it, even though – when directed at our
own performances or productions – its wrath may
distress us profoundly.

As the world's longest-running newspaper dedicated to
the entertainment industry, *Variety* is itself a crucial part
of the history it has charted. The 5000 plus reviews
extracted here from the past 80 years do not reflect the
opinions of critics looking back from the present but, far
more revealing, reflect the views of reporters who were
there at the time. Some of them may surprise now; but
they never fail to give a valuable insight into how these
movies were regarded during their age.

And one of the great pleasures of reading *Variety* is, of
course, its language. Trade paper it may be, but dry it
never is. Colourful jargon like 'oater', 'helmer', 'lensing',
'pic' and 'thesping' makes its prose leap off the page with
an immediacy that remains unequalled by any other
movie publication. Indeed, many of these expressions
have passed into the language without people being
aware of their origin.

Reading this new guide, I am reminded of my own first
notice in *Variety* which appeared in 1947. The film,
adapted from a Graham Greene novel and my seventh as
a screen actor, was called *The Man Within*. It was the first
Technicolor movie to be made at Shepherd's Bush
studios and I, still a rookie in my mid-20s, was fourth-
billed. I opened the paper and there, way down in the
fifth paragraph of the review, were the words:
'Attenborough, as the coward who finds courage, has his
moments'. Rightly or wrongly, I felt that Hollywood
must surely be just around the corner!

Richard Attenborough

INTRODUCTION

Welcome to the third annual edition of *Variety Movie Guide*, the only one of its kind to combine a you-were-there-at-the-time feel with an unrivalled 'trade' orientation to the reviews.

The current volume contains over 6,500 entries (some 500 more than the last edition) selected from the 50,000-plus reviews published by *Variety* over the past 86 years, from January 1907 to July 1993. The earliest review included is of D.W. Griffith's *Judith of Bethulia* (1914); the most recent, *In the Line of Fire*. Although *Variety* stopped publishing film reviews for a short spell – between March 1911 and January 1913 – the paper is still the longest unbroken source of film criticism still in existence.

The *Guide* does not pretend to supplant the 21-volume *Variety Film Reviews* (1907-1990) which reprints the original texts in full. What it does do, in the space of a single handy volume, is to provide the guts of the original reviews (by cutting, not rewriting) along with key technical and creative credits. As such, it's a practical guide first, not a pure reference work for scholars or archivists. And, one hopes, a fascinating browse.

The present edition has been extensively corrected as part of the ongoing process of checking all credits against actual prints of the movies. (Uncredited personnel are listed in square brackets.) As anyone involved in film research knows, this is an endless chore; corrections from readers for future editions are more than welcome. For space reasons, the selection of movies has been limited to those films made in the English language – or in English versions, as opposed to those 100 per cent revoiced from a foreign language ('dubbed', as it is popularly known). For this edition we have also started to include alternative English titles as well as more information on Oscar awards.

Reviewers' now-meaningless box-office predictions ('Fort Knox, move over' – *A Star Is Born*) have been cut out, as well as plot revelations. Minor changes to tenses have been made so that the reviews 'read' from a modern viewpoint, and any obscure contemporary references or pointless prejudices (especially during the two world wars and the McCarthy period) have been toned down or deleted. Until the mid-1930s, when *Variety* reviews began to take on their current shape, editing has had to be considerably heavier. (Early reviews were more like scattergun essays; 'film criticism' as we now know it did not arrive until the 1930s.)

American spellings and *Variety* 'slanguage' have been retained (see Glossary on page XI); any annotations to the reviews have been put in square brackets. Although *Variety* has occasionally included accents on foreign names, this book adheres to tradition by omitting them.

Assembling credits for each film has often involved extra research, and this in turn has been limited by the usual constraints of time and money. *Variety* only started regularly to publish cast lists and limited technical credits in the mid-1920s; fuller credits began from the late 1930s. Mistakes and misprints have been corrected where possible; real names put in square brackets after pseudonyms; and the latest version of people's names used throughout for consistency in the present format. The following are the main criteria used.

■ **Film title.** The original title in country of origin ('majority' country, in the case of co-productions) or, for foreign productions shot in English, the English title (e.g. Bergman's *The Touch*). When a film has subsequently had a title change, and is now better known under that title, the latter is used (e.g. *Murder My Sweet*, originally released out-of-town in 1944 as *Farewell, My Lovely*). The form of the title is that used on the print itself, not the officially registered one nor that on secondary material like posters or press handouts. So-called 'possessory credits' are omitted (e.g. *Billy Rose's Jumbo* is listed as *Jumbo*). A film's subsidiary title ('handle'), a growing trend since the 1980s, is put on a separate line. A.k.a. ('also known as') is a general dumping ground for other release titles, video titles and TV titles, but not production titles. The book is self-indexing, with entries in strict letter-by-letter A-Z order; those starting with numerals are positioned as if the figures were spelt out. All films included have received a theatrical showing somewhere at some time in their life.

■ **Year.** The year of first public release in its country of origin (or, with co-productions, 'majority' country). Sneaks, out-of-town tryouts and festival screenings don't count; end-of-year Oscar-qualifying runs do. Establishing some films' opening dates is still problematical.

■ **Running time.** The hardest nut to crack. Except when it's obvious the reviewer has been shown a rough-cut, *Variety's* original running times are used. For silent films a *very* approximate conversion has been made, based on the number of reels or on information contained in the review. Films tend to get shorter over the years as they're trimmed, cut for TV and generally mangled; more recently there has been a trend towards issuing longer versions for TV or video. No running time should be taken as gospel.

■ **Country of origin.** The second hardest nut. The rule here has been where the money actually came from, rather than where a film was shot, what passport the director had, or what language the cast spoke in.

With co-productions, the first country listed is the 'majority' one (which decides its official title – see above). In the case of many British and American movies, especially since the 1950s, deciding whether some are UK/US, US/UK, or even UK or US is virtually impossible.

■ **Colour.** All films in colour, partly in colour, or originally tinted carry the symbol ◇. Some in the last two categories are now only shown wholly in black-and-white (e.g. *The Picture of Dorian Gray*, *Portrait of Jennie*, many silents) but still carry the colour symbol as this denotes their original form.

■ **Silent.** Films originally shown without a synchronised soundtrack are indicated with the symbol ⊗.

■ **Video.** A nightmare. Films which have been released on video (at one time or another) carry the following symbols:

🅥 = available in both the US and UK;
🅥 = available in the US only; and
🅥 = available in the UK only.

But given the rapid pace of deletions, don't necessarily expect to find a copy in your local store. Catalogue numbers are of little practical use, so have not been included.

■ **Laserdisc.** ⊙ denotes the film has been released on lazerdisc, either in the US or UK.

■ **Director.** The film's officially credited director or co-directors. Some productions are in fact the work of several hands (especially during Hollywood's studio era); only well-known uncredited contributions are noted in square brackets. Second unit or dance-number directors are occasionally included if their contribution merits it.

■ **Producer.** This does not include co-producers, associate, executive or line producers. If no producer is credited on a film's print, the executive or associate producer is included instead (and noted as such).

■ **Script.** The official scriptwriters or dialogue writers; not adaptors, story writers or authors of the original novel, play or musical (their names generally appear in the review, or have been added in square brackets). Because of changes in terminology over the years, deciding the scriptwriter credit for films up to the early 1930s is especially difficult; when in doubt, a name has been included. Also includes additional dialogue writers.

■ **Photography.** The director of photography, also known as 'lighting cameraman'. Occasionally includes those credited with 'additional photography' but not camera operators or (apart from rare instances) second-unit directors of photography.

■ **Editor.** Also includes supervising editor, if there is one, but not assistants or assembly editors.

■ **Music.** A thorny problem. The general rule has been to include composers who actually contributed a dramatic score to the movie. With musicals/song movies, the musical director/arranger/adapter is listed rather than those who wrote the original musical or songs (their names generally appear in the review, or have been added in square brackets). Dates against names of musicals in the text are those of their first stage production.

■ **Art director.** When a film carries a production designer as well as an art director credit, the former is chosen. In productions from the studio era, 'associates' are also included as these, rather than the first-listed heads of department, did most of the actual work. Does not include set decorators, costume designers or any other artistic types. *Variety* only began regularly to credit art directors from the late 1960s; prior to that they were sometimes mentioned in the reviews themselves, if notable.

■ **Cast lists.** For space reasons, these have been limited to a maximum of six, not necessarily in their original order of billing. Early appearances by later stars are often included for interest's sake, even though they may only be bit-parts. For consistency, actors who later changed names are listed by their latest moniker.

■ **Production company.** More and more difficult thanks to the growing complexity of production credits. The general rule, as in deciding the country of origin, has been to list those companies which actually stumped up the cash, but that too is often difficult to ascertain. For space reasons, the shortest forms possible are used. Companies that simply distributed the finished product are not included; nor are those credited as 'in association with'.

■ **Academy awards/nominations.** Includes winners and nominations in all categories. The date is that of the Oscar award, not of the ceremony (generally held the following spring).

DEREK ELLEY London 1993

GLOSSARY

The following is a guide to 80 years of *Variety* 'slanguage' as occurs in the reviews selected; it is not exhaustive and is intended especially for non-American and more general readers.

Variety's snazzy coinages are a goulash of publishing and showbiz/movie jargon, foreign words, Yiddish, street slang, contractions and acronyms that since the mid-1930s (when the reviews took on a recognisable style) have since acquired a reputation and life of their own.

Many of the words have long vanished from use in the paper (along with the slang that inspired them); new ones are still being invented by writers. The only rule is that they sound 'right' and carry on the tradition of sharp, tabloid, flavourful prose. As a further aid for general readers we have also included some words that are simple movie jargon or archaic slang rather than pure *Variety* slanguage.

a.k.	ass-kisser	dualer	double-billed feature film	legit(imate)	theatrical, theatre, stage
a.k.a.	also known as			legiter	stage play
alky	alcoholic			legituner	stage musical
ankle	leave, quit	femme	female; woman	lense(r)	photograph(r)
anent	regarding	flap	flapper	limn	portray
avoirdupois	weight	flivver	car	lingo	dialogue; language
				longhair	intellectual; highbrow
back-to-back	(two or more films shot) at the same time or without a break between	G	$1,000	lower case	minor (quality)
		gat	gun	LST	landing ship tank (a WWII landing craft)
		g.f.	girlfriend		
		gob	sailor		
b.b.	big business	Gotham	New York	manse	mansion
beer stube	bar	gyp	swindler; cheat	medico	doctor
belter	boxer			meg(aphoner)	direct(or)
b.f.	boyfriend	habiliments	clothing	megger	director
Big Apple	New York	helm(er)	direct(or)	meller	melodrama(tic)
burley	burlesque, music hall	histrionics	performance(s)	milquetoast	meek man
b.o.	box office	histrionically	performance-wise	m.o.	modus operandi
bow	debut; praise	hoke	hokum	moppet	child
b.r.	bankroll; sum of money	hoke up	over-act		
		hoofology	dancing	nabes	suburbs
cannon	gun	hotcha	excellent	negative cost	production cost
carny	carnival	hoyden(ish)	tomboy(ish)	nitery	nightclub
Chi	Chicago				
chick	girl	indie	independent (production or company), i.e. not by an established major studio	oater	Western
chili	Mexican			ofay	white man
chirp(er)	sing(er)			oke	okay
chopsocky	martial arts (film)			one-shot	one-off
chore	job; routine assignment			o.o.	once-over
chump	crazy (in love)	ink	sign	opp	opposite
cleff(er)	compose(r)	i.r.	inquiring reporter; investigative reporter	org	organization
click	hit; success			ozoner	drive-in theatre
coin	money; finance				
contempo	contemporary	j.d.	juvenile deliquent	p.a.	press agent
		jitterbug	(1940s) jazz dance(r); nervous person	pactee	contract player
d.a.	district attorney			Par	Paramount
dick	detective			pen	penitentiary; prison
doughboy	infantry soldier	kayo	knockout	Pennsy	Pennsylvania

photog	photographer	sock(eroo)	excellent; powerful	topline(r)	star
pic	picture; movie	solon	lawmaker	trick work	special effects
plat	platinum blonde	speak	speakeasy	troubadour	singer
p.m.	professional model	spec	spectacle	trouping	acting
p.o.v.	point of view	stepping	dancing	tube	TV
p.r.	public relations	stew	drinking bout	20th	20th Century-Fox
prexy	(company) president	stock	repertory theatre		
profesh	profession	sudser	soap opera	U	Universal
programmer	B-movie fodder	super	super-production	unreel	play
pug	boxer	switcheroo	(plot) twist	unspool	play
				upper case	major (quality)
quondam	one time	tab	tabloid		
		tapster	tap-dancer	vaude	vaudeville
ridic	ridiculous	tech credits	technical credits, i.e.	vet	veteran
rod-man	gunman		photography, editing, art	vignetting	describing
RR	railroad; railway		direction etc.	vis-a-vis	(romantic/sexual/billing)
		ten-twent-thirt/			partner
s.a.	sex appeal	10-20-30	amateurish (acting)		
sagebrush saga	Western	terp(ing)	danc(ing)	warbling	singing
sauce	alcohol	terpsichore	dancing	WB	Warner Bros.
schtick	comic routine(s)	thesp(ing)	actor, act(ing)	w.k.	well-known
scripter	scriptwriter	thespically	performance-wise		
sec	secretary	thespics	acting	yahoo	redneck
sheet	screen; newspaper	tint(ed)	colour(ed)	yak	joke
shutterbug	photographer	tintuner	showbiz musical	yclept	played by
slugfest	fight	topkick	boss	yock	joke
smokeater	fireman	topper	boss		

THE MOVIE GUIDE A-Z

A&BA THE MOVIE

1977, 94 MINS, SWEDEN/AUSTRALIA ◇ Ⓥ
Dir Lasse Hallstrom   *Prod* Stig Anderson, Reg Grundy
Scr Lasse Hallstrom, Bob Caswell   *Ph* Jack Churchill, Paul
Onorato   *Ed* Lasse Hallstrom, Malou Hallstrom, Ulf
Neidemar
● Anni-Frid Lyngstad, Agnetha Faltskog, Benny
Andersson, Bjorn Ulvaeus, Bruce Barry, Robert Hughes
(Polar Music/Grundy)

A&BA The Movie is a handsomely-produced,
smooth, fast and wittily-edited musical entertainment that, in Lasse Hallstrom's script
and direction, is both a bit of a documentary
of Swedish group A&BA's Australian tour and
of its four personable performers' background
and work methods. There's also a slight but
funny story about an Aussie disk-jockey's
chasing of the group and being most of the
way thwarted in his attempts to do a taped in-
depth interview with the Swedes.

The Australian actors perform with obvious
gusto. So does A&BA as a group whereas they
have not wished to attempt any acting.

Apart from glimpses of them receiving
adoring crowds of fans, they are seen mostly
doing their stage work.

ABBOTT AND COSTELLO IN HOLLYWOOD

1945, 83 MINS, US Ⓥ
Dir S. Sylvan Simon   *Prod* Martin A. Gosch   *Scr* Nat
Perrin, Lou Breslow   *Ph* Charles Schoenbaum   *Ed* Ben
Lewis   *Mus* George Bassman (dir.)   *Art Dir* Cedric
Gibbons, Wade B. Rubottom
● Bud Abbott, Lou Costello, Frances Rafferty, Robert
Stanton, Jean Porter, Warner Anderson (M-G-M)

An Abbott and Costello picture may not be an
artistic triumph, but the duo certainly try
hard enough to make audiences laugh. *Abbott
and Costello in Hollywood* is no exception.

Duo portrays the role of barber and
shineboy in a tonsorial establishment, who
get the yen to be actor's agents when they see
the easy life one of the latter has. When the
agent turns down a youngster with a nice
voice, they take him on, and before the film
unwinds they have him set in a picture, but
not before they almost wreck the studio and
upset the personnel therein.

Despite the 83 minutes running time, this
one [from a story by Nat Perrin and producer
Martin A. Gosch] moves rapidly, aided by
direction of S. Sylvan Simon.

ABBOTT AND COSTELLO MEET DR. JEKYLL AND MR. HYDE

1953, 76 MINS, US Ⓥ
Dir Charles Lamont   *Prod* Howard Christie   *Scr* Lee
Loeb, John Grant   *Ph* George Robinson   *Ed* Russell
Schoengarth   *Mus* Joseph Gershenson   *Art Dir* Bernard
Herzbrun, Eric Orbom
● Bud Abbott, Lou Costello, Boris Karloff, Craig Stevens,
Helen Westcott, Reginald Denny (Universal)

A rousing good time for Abbott & Costello
fans is contained in this spoof on fiction's
classic bogeyman [from stories by Sidney
Fields and Grant Garrett]. The fat & thin
comics combat Boris Karloff as the fictional
dual personality in the very broad doings, and
Karloff's takeoff on the character adds to the
chuckles dished out by A & C.

Helen Westcott, ward of, and coveted by,
the good Dr. Jekyll, supplies excellent femme
appeal in a romance with Craig Stevens, a reporter, while Reginald Denny, harassed

Scotland Yard inspector, and John Dierkes,
the doctor's zombie-like assistant, help the
fun.

Bounced off Denny's police force because of
their bungling, Abbott & Costello figure they
might be able to get their jobs back if they
catch the monster that is terrorizing Hyde
Park. Comedic chills and thrills ensue as the
pair track down the monster and wind up
with its alter ego, Dr. Jekyll.

ABBOTT AND COSTELLO MEET FRANKENSTEIN

(UK: Abbott and Costello Meet the Ghosts)

1948, 82 MINS, US Ⓥ ⊙
Dir Charles T. Barton   *Prod* Robert Arthur   *Scr* Robert
Lees, Frederic I. Rinaldo, John Grant   *Ph* Charles Van
Enger   *Ed* Frank Gross   *Mus* Frank Skinner
Art Dir Bernard Herzbrun, Hilyard Brown
● Bud Abbott, Lou Costello, Lon Chaney, Bela Lugosi,
Glenn Strange, Lenore Aubert (Universal)

The comedy team battles it out with the studio's roster of bogeymen in a rambunctious
fracas that is funny and, at the same time,
spine-tingling. Stalking through the piece to
add menace are such characters as the
Frankenstein Monster, the Wolf Man and
Dracula.

Loosely-knit script depicts the Monster
growing weak. His master, Dracula, decides
to transfer Costello's brain to the
Frankenstein creation. As a lure, the batman
uses wiles of Lenore Aubert to soften the fat
man and maneuver him into a proper setup.

Through it all runs the Wolf Man as a sympathetic character who tries to warn the heroes against the plot but, unfortunately,
proves a bit of a menace himself whenever
the moon rises and changes him into a killer.

ABBOTT AND COSTELLO MEET THE GHOSTS

See: Abbott and Costello Meet Frankenstein

ABBOTT AND COSTELLO . . . MEET THE INVISIBLE MAN

1951, 82 MINS, US
Dir Charles Lamont   *Prod* Howard Christie   *Scr* Robert
Lees, Frederic I. Rinaldo, John Grant   *Ph* George
Robinson   *Ed* Virgil Vogel   *Mus* Joseph Gershenson
(dir.)   *Art Dir* Bernard Herzbrun, Richard H. Riedel
● Bud Abbott, Lou Costello, Nancy Guild, Arthur Franz,
Adele Jergens, Sheldon Leonard (Universal)

Team's stock double-takes and bewhiskered
gags are still fulsome, but the hackneyed
quips achieve a new gloss in this entry. Credit
for the comics' renaissance goes primarily to
the story that Hugh Wedlock Jr and Howard
Snyder fashioned from H.G. Wells' *The
Invisible Man*.

With three other writers screenplaying, the
yarn is tied around the efforts of fighter
Arthur Franz to clear himself of a murder
rap. He hires private eyes Abbott and
Costello to help him in his mission. When
Franz injects himself with a serum possessing
powers of invisibility, a flock of amusing sequences are touched off. Best of these is a
scene in which Costello kayoes the champ
(with the invisible man's help).

Franz does a crisp job as the 'invisible' boxer,
while Sheldon Leonard is well cast as the
heavy. Nancy Guild portrays Franz's girl with
a tender affection and, in contrast to her de-
mureness, is the blowziness Adele Jergens injects into her role as a come-on for the fixers.

ABDICATION, THE

1974, 103 MINS, UK ◇
Dir Anthony Harvey   *Prod* Robert Fryer, James Cresson
Scr Ruth Wolff   *Ph* Geoffrey Unsworth   *Ed* John Bloom
Mus Nino Rota   *Art Dir* Alan Tomkins

● Liv Ullmann, Peter Finch, Cyril Cusack, Graham
Crowden, Michael Dunn, Paul Rogers (Warner)

The Abdication is a period film in more ways
than one. The Ruth Wolff script from her
play, based on the 17th-century abdication of
Queen Christina of Sweden, has been directed by Anthony Harvey, like a trite 1930s
sob-sister meller, with dainty debauchery and
titillating tease straight from 1920s women's
pulp magazines.

Peter Finch plays a Vatican-based Cardinal
assigned to investigate the background and
the motivations of Liv Ullmann, who has quit
her throne after converting to Roman
Catholicism late in 1655.

Ullmann's early life was a mess: her kindly
father (Edward Underdown) died when she
was six: her mother (Kathleen Byron) was a
horror; she was reared as a boy; and chancellor Cyril Cusack keeps chiding her on her
queenly duties.

Michael Dunn, engaged as queen
Ullmann's dwarf companion, died during
Pinewood Studios shooting, and the covering
substitute is too different to escape casual
notice.

ABIE'S IRISH ROSE

1946, 96 MINS, US
Dir A. Edward Sutherland   *Prod* Bing Crosby   *Scr* Anne
Nichols   *Ph* William Mellor   *Mus* John Scott Trotter
Art Dir William Flannery
● Joanne Dru, Richard Norris, Michael Chekhov, J.M.
Kerrigan (United Artists/Crosby)

The essence of film fare is obviously to entertain. This one doesn't. It can't, when the fundamentals are as meretricious as unwind in
these hokey 96 minutes.

Fundamentally the story is a topical misfit.
It opens with ultra-modern young Abie Levy
meeting USO-Camp Shows entertainer
Rosemary Murphy in a V-E Day London
mixup, resulting in their marriage by an
army chaplain (incidentally Protestant, so as
to get in all the three faiths, which didn't exist in the original play by Anne Nichols).

Papa Levy is patently a prosperous Bronx
department store owner; his place of business, his household and his friends bespeak
prosperity. But thereafter this premise falls
apart for he has the prejudices of a pushcart
peddler, and barrister Isa Cohen (George E.
Stone) and Mrs Levy (Vera Gordon who,
somehow, manages a slightly more restrained
characterization) are depicted as narrow-
minded nitwits.

ABOMINABLE DOCTOR PHIBES, THE

1971, 94 MINS, UK ◇ Ⓥ ⊙
Dir Robert Fuest   *Prod* Louis M. Heyward, Ronald S.
Dunas   *Scr* James Whiton, William Goldstein
Ph Norman Warwick   *Ed* Tristam Cones   *Mus* Basil
Kirchen, Jack Nathan   *Art Dir* Brian Eatwell
● Vincent Price, Joseph Cotten, Virginia North, Terry-
Thomas, Hugh Griffith, Peter Jeffrey (American
International)

The Abominable Doctor Phibes stars Vincent
Price as a living corpse, out for revenge on
the nine medics in attendance when his wife
died in surgery. Anachronistic period horror
musical camp fantasy is a fair description,
loaded with comedic gore of the type that
packs theatres and drives child psychologists
up the walls. Joseph Cotten also stars as an
intended victim who foils the plot.

James Whiton and William Goldstein wrote
a well-structured screenplay which starts in
motion a series of inventive murders, and
later drops the requisite expository clues.
Price, presumed dead until Cotten and
gumshoe Peter Jeffrey discover his and the
wife's coffins bare, concocts revenge on nine
doctors according to the pattern of 10 curses
upon the Pharaoh, from the Old Testament.

Terry-Thomas is one of the victims, all of whom die from some bizarre use of rats, bees, bats, boils, etc. Assisting Price is the silent Virginia North. Price's makeup, by Trevor Crole-Rees, is outstanding in depicting without revulsion the look of a living corpse covered with scars.

• •

■ **ABOUT LAST NIGHT. . .**

1986, 113 MINS, US ◇ ⓦ ⊙
Dir Edward Zwick *Prod* Jason Brett, Stuart Oken
Scr Tim Kazurinsky, Denise DeClue *Ph* Andrew
Dintenfass *Ed* Harry Keramidas *Mus* Miles Goodman
Art Dir Ida Random
● Rob Lowe, Demi Moore, James Belushi, Elizabeth
Perkins, George DiCenzo, Michael Alldredge (TriStar-
Delphi IV & V)

About Last Night . . . has little to do with perversity, let alone *Sexual Perversity in Chicago*, the David Mamet play on which it ostensibly is based. Film lacks much of Mamet's grittiness, but is likable in its own right.

Film presents a look at the mating habits of young Americans, the ones who frequent singles bars and regard commitment as a lifelong disease.

Focus of the story is on Danny (Rob Lowe) and Debbie (Demi Moore) who meet, move in together, separate and get back together with an ease and casualness that makes it both appealing and disturbing. Ups and downs of the relationship are delivered in a series of montages that look like soft-drink commercials for the now generation.

As the sour note, James Belushi is probably the high point of the film. Performance borrows much from his late brother (John) in its outrageousness and unpredictability.

• •

■ **ABOVE SUSPICION**

1943, 90 MINS, US ⓦ
Dir Richard Thorpe *Prod* Victor Saville *Scr* Keith
Winter, Melville Baker, Patricia Coleman *Ph* Robert
Planck *Ed* George Hively *Mus* Bronislau Kaper
● Joan Crawford, Fred MacMurray, Conrad Veidt, Basil
Rathbone, Reginald Owen, Richard Ainley (M-G-M)

After establishing Fred MacMurray and Joan Crawford as newlywed Americans in England, planning honeymoon in south of Germany just prior to outbreak of the war, yarn has British secret service drafting them for mission to secure vital confidential plans for the secret weapon – a magnetic mine. Pair pick up the trail in Paris and then hop to Salzburg, where it becomes a mysterious chase with various and sundry characters peering out of shadows and suddenly turning up in the most approved spy fashion.

Picture is filled with various incidents that crop up and then vanish, with no reason for their inclusion except to confuse the audience and by-pass straight-line exposition of the tale.

Both MacMurray and Crawford competently handle their roles, despite drawbacks of script material. Conrad Veidt clicks solidly in major supporting spot, along with brief appearances of Basil Rathbone as a Gestapo leader.

• •

■ **ABOVE THE LAW**

1988, 99 MINS, US ◇ ⓦ ⊙
Dir Andrew Davis *Prod* Steven Seagal, Andrew Davis
Scr Steven Pressfield, Ronald Shusett, Andrew Davis
Ph Robert Steadman *Ed* Michael Brown *Mus* David M.
Frank *Art Dir* Maher Ahmad
● Steven Seagal, Pam Grier, Henry Silva, Ron Dean,
Daniel Faraldo, Sharon Stone (Warner)

Above the Law is an ultraviolent actioner with Steven Seagal playing an aikido-chopping cop on a one man crusade to clean up Chi streets. [Screen story by Seagal and director Andrew Davis.]

As Nico Toscani, Seagal is a no-nonsense cop with cynical eye towards authority. When he's taken off the trail of a suspected drug dealer, he smells a rat or two at the top of his chain of command.

With a couple dozen stunt persons and an earthy, warm and supportive partner (Pam Grier), Seagal kicks, kills and crushes with his skillful hands one handful after another of street hoods who try and thwart his mission.

Somehow is worked in an assassination plot against the US senator who's about ready to expose a drug trafficking trade in Central America and a group of Salvadoran refugees hiding out in the basement of Seagal's neighborhood Catholic church.

Henry Silva is a sicko sadist who gets off threatening to chop his victims' limbs off one by one until they talk. Quiet moments like the ones with Seagal and his emotional wife (Sharon Stone) comprise about 1% of the film.

• •

■ **ABRAHAM LINCOLN**

1930, 93 MINS, US ⓦ ⊙
Dir D.W. Griffith *Scr* Stephen Vincent Benet *Ph* Karl
Struss *Ed* James Smith, Hal C. Kern *Mus* Hugo
Riesenfeld *Art Dir* William Cameron Menzies, Park
French
● Walter Huston, Una Merkel, Kay Hammond, Jason
Robards, Ian Keith, Hobart Bosworth (United Artists)

Abraham Lincoln is a startlingly superlative accomplishment. Next to the direction by D.W. Griffith, with only a tiny margin separating, is Walter Huston's Abraham Lincoln. Young, aging and aged; playful, fighting, grief-stricken; commanding, pleading.

A vivid prolog, with camera sweeping through dark-lit forests, hazy fields and clouded cities, brings the opening to the little log cabin and the birth of Abe. Romance of Lincoln and Ann Rutledge (Una Merkel) is slightly unconvincing parts.

From the first fight in the country store and the passing of Ann, Huston then begins to make the personality of Lincoln heighten in realism.

The scenes at Springfield where he meets the haughty Mary Todd (Kay Hammond) have considerable comedy. The assassination of Lincoln is classically melodramatic.

• •

■ **ABSENCE OF MALICE**

1981, 116 MINS, US ◇ ⓦ ⊙
Dir Sydney Pollack *Prod* Sydney Pollack *Scr* Kurt
Luedtke *Ph* Owen Roizman *Ed* Sheldon Kahn
Mus Dave Grusin *Art Dir* Terence Marsh
● Paul Newman, Sally Field, Bob Balaban, Melinda
Dillon, Luther Adler, Barry Primus (Columbia)

Absence of Malice is the flipside of *All The President's Men*, a splendidly disturbing look at the power of sloppy reporting to inflict harm on the innocent.

Tackling a long-standing public issue that has no resolution, producer-director Sydney Pollack neatly keeps all the points in focus while sustaining traditional entertainment values. This is, quite simply, a whale of a good story with something important to say. For that, much of the credit undoubtedly should go to writer Kurt Luedtke, a veteran newsman himself.

More typical of her trade than a Woodward or Bernstein, Sally Field is a workaday reporter on a Miami paper, trying to stay on top of a breaking story about the mysterious disappearance of a local longshore labor leader.

Paul Newman is the son of a mobster whose late father kept him straight and out of the rackets, running a legitimate business. But he still has unsavory family ties, particularly uncle Luther Adler, and Bob Balaban the head of a federal task force investigating the case, believes a little pressure on Newman might force his help in solving the disappearance.

Though Newman has no connection with a crime, Balaban suckers Field into printing a story identifying him – with editor Josef Sommer's zealous encouragement – as a prime suspect.

Not surprisingly, the story produces tragedy, finally shaking Field's faith in her calling. It also outrages Newman and his grievous, angry confrontation with Field may be the best single scene the actor has ever performed.

☐ 1981: Nominations: Best Actor (Paul Newman), Supp. Actress (Melinda Dillon), Original Screenplay

• •

■ **ABSENT MINDED PROFESSOR, THE**

1961, 90 MINS, US ⓦ ⊙
Dir Robert Stevenson *Prod* Bill Walsh (assoc.) *Scr* Bill
Walsh *Ph* Edward Colman *Ed* Cotton Warburton
Mus George Bruns *Art Dir* Carroll Clark
● Fred MacMurray, Nancy Olson, Keenan Wynn,
Tommy Kirk, Leon Ames, Ed Wynn (Walt Disney)

On the surface, Walt Disney's *The Absent Minded Professor* is a comedy-fantasy of infectious absurdity, a natural follow-up to the studio's *Shaggy Dog*. But deeply rooted within the screenplay [from a story by Samuel W. Taylor] is a subtle protest against the detached, impersonal machinery of modern progress.

The Professor (Fred MacMurray) is an easygoing, likeable smalltown practical chemist who comes up with a practical discovery – a gooey substance endowed with the elusive quality of anti-gravity. He dubs it 'flubber' (flying rubber) and proceeds to put it to use in incongruous ways.

In the film's most hilarious passage, he applies it at half time to the gym shoes of a basketball team hopelessly outclassed by its opponents' height, whereupon the beaten boys promptly stage a bouncy aerial second half ballet.

MacMurray is ideally cast as the car-hopping prof, and plays the role with warmth and gusto. Nancy Olson attractively supplies romantic interest. Keenan Wynn is a delight in a delicious satirical role – that of a money-man loan tycoon who would sell his own alma mater for a buck.

☐ 1961: Nominations: Best B&W Cinematography, B&W Art Direction, Special Effects

• •

■ **ABSOLUTE BEGINNERS**

1986, 107 MINS, UK ◇ ⓦ ⊙
Dir Julien Temple *Prod* Stephen Woolley, Chris Brown
Scr Richard Burridge, Christopher Wicking, Don
MacPherson *Ph* Oliver Stapleton *Ed* Michael Bradsell,
Gerry Hambling, Richard Bedford, Russell Lloyd *Mus* Gil
Evans (arr.) *Art Dir* John Beard
● Eddie O'Connell, Patsy Kensit, David Bowie, James
Fox, Ray Davies, Steven Berkoff
(Virgin/Goldcrest/Palace)

Absolute Beginners is a terrifically inventive original musical for the screen. Daring attempt to portray the birth of teenagedom in London, 1958, almost exclusively through song is based upon Colin MacInnes' cult novel about teen life and pop fashion in the percolating moments just before the youth cultural explosion in the early 1960s.

Tenuous storyline is a typical one of teen love achieved, lost and regained, and is used as a mere string to which a constant parade of musical numbers and flights of fancy are attached.

Aspiring photographer Colin (Eddie O'Connell) and tyro fashion designer Suzette (Patsy Kensit) seem a perfect match, but when the latter begins getting ahead and becomes engaged to a snooty couturier played by James Fox, Colin decides to sell out and make the most of his connections in a last-ditch effort to win back his lady love.

A

In creating a stylized view of 1950s culture, director Julien Temple and lenser Oliver Stapleton have made great use of fabulous sets fashioned by production designer John Beard. An astonishing moving camera take throughout the Soho set in the early going represents a fully worthy homage to the opening shot of Orson Welles' *Touch of Evil*.

....

■ ABSOLUTION

1981, 95 MINS, UK ◇ ⓥ ⊙
Dir Anthony Page   *Prod* Elliott Kastner, Danny O'Donovan   *Scr* Anthony Shaffer   *Ph* John Coquillon   *Ed* John Victor Smith   *Mus* Stanley Myers   *Art Dir* Natasha Kroll
● Richard Burton, Dominic Guard, Billy Connolly, Dai Bradley, Andrew Keir, Willoughby Gray (Kastner-O'Donovan)

Absolution is a dull, gloomy, nasty, contrived marketplace misfit, apparently designed to ride on Richard Burton's shirttails.

Or in this case his cassock since the actor portrays a stern, super devout priest-teacher in a Catholic boarding school for boys. Gist of Anthony Shaffer's melodramatic plot has to do with a catch-22 test of Burton's faith as two embittered students, taking advantage of the secrecy of the confessional box, conspire to drive him round the bend and to an unwitting killing.

It's heavy, artless going, with an abrupt, embarrassing (for Burton) conclusion. Anthony Page's direction is routine, perhaps unavoidably.

....

■ ABYSS, THE

1989, 140 MINS, US ◇ ⓥ ⊙
Dir James Cameron   *Prod* Gale Anne Hurd   *Scr* James Cameron   *Ph* Mikael Salomon   *Ed* Joel Goodman   *Mus* Alan Silvestri   *Art Dir* Leslie Dilley
● Ed Harris, Mary Elizabeth Mastrantonio, Michael Biehn, Leo Burmester, Todd Graff, Kimberly Scott (20th Century-Fox)

A firstrate underwater suspenser with an otherworldly twist, *The Abyss* suffers from a payoff unworthy of its buildup. Same sensibilities that enable writer-director James Cameron to deliver riveting, supercharged action segments get soggy when the 'aliens' turn out to be friendly.

Action is launched when a navy nuclear sub suffers a mysterious power failure and crashes into a rock island. Bud Brigman (Ed Harris) and his gamy crew of undersea oil-rig workers are hired to dive for survivors.

At the last minute Brigman's flinty estranged wife, Lindsey (Mary Elizabeth Mastrantonio), who designed their submersible oil rig, insists on coming aboard to lend an uninvited hand.

Crew finds nothing but a lot of corpses floating eerily in the water-filled sub, but meanwhile, Lindsey has a close encounter with a kind of swift-moving neon-lit jellyfish she's convinced is a friendly alien.

When turbulence from a hurricane rocking the surface cuts off the crew's ties to their command ship, their underwater stay is perilously extended.

The Abyss has plenty of elements in its favor, not least the performances by Harris as the compassionate crewleader and Mastrantonio as his steel-willed counterpart. Not even the $50 million-plus pic's elaborate technical achievements can overshadow these two.

[In 1993 a 171-min. version, *The Abyss: Special Edition* was released. Restored footage was spread throughout the pic but primarily during the final two reels, including the original ending.]
□ 1989: Best Visual Effects.
□ Nominations: Best Cinematography, Art Direction, Sound

....

■ ACCIDENT

1967, 105 MINS, UK ◇ ⓥ
Dir Joseph Losey   *Prod* Joseph Losey, Norman Priggen   *Scr* Harold Pinter   *Ph* Gerry Fisher   *Ed* Reginald Beck   *Mus* John Dankworth   *Art Dir* Carmen Dillon
● Dirk Bogarde, Stanley Baker, Jacqueline Sassard, Michael York, Vivien Merchant, Harold Pinter (London)

The team that turned *The Servant* into a success took another novel as their plot material – Nicholas Mosley's *Accident* – and jacked it into a haunting study in relationships, with Harold Pinter's flair for spare, suggestive dialog getting full scope in an adaptation which stays remarkably faithful to the book.

It starts with a car crash splitting that night air of the quiet countryside outside Oxford. A male student has been killed, and his female companion, a campus gal, is taken into the neighboring mansion, occupied by the university teacher (Dirk Bogarde) who has been instructing them both in philosophy.

The accident sparks the prolonged flashback that explores the tight-knit relationship of this enclosed community.

A firstrate cast is headed by Bogarde, who wins sympathy for his superficially cold character, and his contained way with emotion is superbly right. But the main acting surprise is contributed by Stanley Baker, unusually bespectacled as the amorous Charlie, and wittily suggesting the man's self-esteem and his lonely search for horizontal satisfaction.

....

■ ACCIDENTAL HERO

See: Hero

....

■ ACCIDENTAL TOURIST, THE

1988, 121 MINS, US ◇ ⓥ ⊙
Dir Lawrence Kasdan   *Prod* Lawrence Kasdan, Charles Okun, Michael Grillo   *Scr* Frank Galati, Lawrence Kasdan   *Ph* John Bailey   *Ed* Carol Littleton   *Mus* John Williams   *Art Dir* Bo Welch
● William Hurt, Kathleen Turner, Geena Davis, Amy Wright, Bill Pullman, Ed Begley Jr (Warner)

The Accidental Tourist is a slow, sonorous and largely satisfying adaptation of Anne Tyler's bestseller of one man's intensely self-contained passage from a state of grief to one of newfound love.

William Hurt is an uptight, travel book writer from the slightly eccentric, financially comfortable Leary family of unmarried middle-aged siblings in this essentially simple narrative story awash in warmth and wisdom about the emotional human animal.

Weighty tone is set from the opening scene where Kathleen Turner, having just made tea for Hurt upon his return from a travel-writing excursion, calmly informs him she's moving out. Then, in a series of strange, unpredictable and out-of-character encounters with his unruly dog's trainer (Geena Davis), Hurt finds himself in another, vastly different, relationship. Davis is unabashedly forward, poor, openly vulnerable, a flamboyant dresser and most importantly, has a sickly son (Robert Gorman) who fills the parental void in Hurt's life.

That Hurt remains expressionless and speaks in a monotone, except at the very end, puts a damper on the hopefulness of his changing situation. Davis is the constant, upbeat force in the proceedings. Turner is equally compelling and sympathetic throughout.
□ 1988: Best Supp. Actress (Geena Davis).
□ Nominations: Best Picture, Score, Adapted Screenplay

....

■ ACCUSED, THE

1949, 101 MINS, US ⓥ
Dir William Dieterle   *Prod* Hal B. Wallis   *Scr* Ketti Frings, [Leonard Spigelgass, Barre Lyndon, Jonathan Latimer, Allen Rivkin, Charles Schnee]   *Ph* Milton Krasner   *Ed* Warren Low   *Mus* Victor Young   *Art Dir* Hans Dreier, Earl Hedrick
● Loretta Young, Robert Cummings, Wendell Corey, Sam Jaffe, Douglas Dick, Sara Allgood (Paramount)

The Accused exploits fear and emotional violence into a high grade melodrama. The screenplay is based on a novel [*Be Still, My Love*] by June Truesdell and is class scripting. Director William Dieterle, with a solid story foundation and ace cast upon which to build, marches the melodrama along with a touch that keeps punching continually at audience emotions.

An unbalanced but attractive student is on the make for his professor. By guile he induces her to ride with him to the beach. He attempts to attack her and she, in a moment of surrender to violence, bashes his head in with a tire iron. The crime is concealed to make it look like he had died in a dive over the sea cliff.

Loretta Young's portrayal of the distraught professor plays strongly for sympathy. It's an intelligent delineation, gifting the role with life. She gets under the skin in bringing out the mental processes of an intelligent woman who knows she has done wrong but believes that her trail is so covered that murder will never out.

....

■ ACCUSED, THE

1988, 110 MINS, US ◇ ⓥ ⊙
Dir Jonathan Kaplan   *Prod* Stanley R. Jaffe, Sherry Lansing   *Scr* Tom Topor   *Ph* Ralf Bode   *Ed* Jerry Greenberg, O. Nicholas Brown   *Mus* Brad Fiedel   *Art Dir* Richard Kent Wilcox
● Kelly McGillis, Jodie Foster, Bernie Coulson, Leo Rossi, Ann Hearn, Carmen Argenziano (Paramount)

The Accused is a dry case study of a rape incident whose only impact comes from the sobering crime itself, not the dramatic treatment.

Inspired by, but not based upon the 1983 barroom pooltable gang rape in New Bedford, Mass, screenplay is designed to pose questions about the thin line between sexual provocation and assault, seduction and force, and observation of and participation in a crime.

Pic begins with a bloodied, dishevelled Jodie Foster stumbling out of a roadhouse. A young patron calls the police to report an incident, and in short order three men plead guilty to the reduced charge of 'reckless endangerment' (the film's original title) rather than rape.

All this takes place without the participation of the victim, who becomes furious with her lawyer (Kelly McGillis) when she learns via television of the legal deal. McGillis abruptly decides to pursue the matter much further by prosecuting some of the onlookers in the bar for criminal solicitation.

Foster is edgy and spunky but McGillis' role, as conceived, is a joke, since she exists only as a stick figure with no psychology or background offer up over the course of nearly two hours.

With British Columbia standing in for Washington State, pic looks only okay.
□ 1988: Best Actress (Jodie Foster)

....

■ ACE IN THE HOLE

(Aka: The Big Carnival)

1951, 111 MINS, US ⓥ
Dir Billy Wilder   *Prod* Billy Wilder   *Scr* Billy Wilder, Lesser Samuels, Walter Newman   *Ph* Charles B. Lang Jr   *Ed* Doane Harrison, Arthur Schmidt   *Mus* Hugo Friedhofer   *Art Dir* Hal Pereira, Earl Hedrick
● Kirk Douglas, Jan Sterling, Bob Arthur, Porter Hall, Frank Cady, Richard Benedict (Paramount)

The grim story of an unscrupulous reporter who wins brief fame at the expense of a

3

cave-in victim is rather graphically unfolded in *Ace in the Hole*.

Kirk Douglas is the reportorial opportunist. He has been exiled to a small New Mexico daily after being kicked off top eastern sheets for dishonesty, drinking and a variety of insubordination. One day he accidentally stumbles on a story that he believes can get him back in the big leagues, if he plays the yarn long enough and can keep it himself.

A dealer in Indian curios has become trapped by a cave-in in an ancient cliff dwelling. Douglas is the first to reach the victim (Richard Benedict), sees the story possibilities and makes a deal with a crooked sheriff and a contractor delay the rescue as long as possible while he arranges exclusive coverage.

The performances are fine. Douglas enacts the heel reporter ably, giving it color to balance its unsympathetic character. Jan Sterling also is good in a role that has no softening touches, and Benedict's victim portrayal is first-rate. Billy Wilder's direction captures the feel of morbid expectancy that always comes out in the curious that flock to scenes of tragedy.

□ 1951: Nomination: Best Story & Screenplay

● ●

■ ACES HIGH

1976, 114 MINS, UK/FRANCE ◇ ▽
Dir Jack Gold *Prod* S. Benjamin Fisz *Scr* Howard Barker *Ph* Gerry Fisher *Ed* Anne V. Coates *Mus* Richard Hartley *Art Dir* Syd Cain
● Malcolm McDowell, Christopher Plummer, Simon Ward, Peter Firth, John Gielgud, Trevor Howard (EMI/Fisz)

Pic is based on R. C. Sheriff's 1929 London and Broadway stageplay, *Journey's End*, a classic on the theme of the futility and boredom of trench warfare in which some men cracked up while others found ways – like the bottle – of averting crackup. *Aces High* packs little of the involving emotional credibility and impact of the play.

Characterization in the film is without sufficient ambiguity and dimension. Thus, the young British airmen of 76 Squadron are either bushy-tail rookies (Peter Firth), disciplined but emotionally soft (Christopher Plummer), or scared stiff and bucking for medical discharge (Simon Ward). As their squadron leader, Malcolm McDowell is both brave and scared – and dependent on whisky to sustain him as a credible leader of machine-gun fodder.

● ●

■ ACES IRON EAGLE III

1992, 98 MINS, US ◇ ▽ ⊙
Dir John Glen *Prod* Ron Samuels *Scr* Kevin Elders *Ph* Alec Mills *Ed* Bernard Gribble *Mus* Harry Manfredini *Art Dir* Robb Wilson King
● Louis Gossett Jr, Rachel McLish, Paul Freeman, Horst Buchholz, Christopher Cazenove, Sonny Chiba (Seven Arts/Carolco)

Aces is an action-packed, campy entry in Lou Gossett's *Iron Eagle* series. Best in its cartoonish moments, this followup helmed by James Bond director John Glen notably introduces the beautiful bodybuilder Rachel McLish.

Air Force pilot Gossett rounds up a group of fellow veteran fighter aces to fly to Peru and blow up a cocaine factory. The US government won't support this mission so the guys use vintage World War II era planes they've been flying in air shows.

Gossett fights the drug lords because a friend was killed by them and his sister (McLish) captured and tortured. He frees McLish, who turns out to be more than the equal of any of the male combatants.

When not making corny patriotic speeches

Gossett is steadying force here. McLish is terrific in action scenes and merely needs intensive coaching on her acting.

● ●

■ ACROSS 110TH STREET

1972, 102 MINS, US ◇ ▽
Dir Barry Shear *Prod* Ralph Serpe, Fouad Said *Scr* Luther Davis *Ph* Jack Priestley *Ed* Byron Brandt *Mus* J.J. Johnson *Art Dir* Perry Watkins
● Anthony Quinn, Yaphet Kotto, Anthony Franciosa, Paul Benjamin, Ed Bernard, Richard Ward (Film Guarantors/United Artists)

Across 110th Street is not for the squeamish. From the beginning it is a virtual bloodbath. Those portions of it which aren't bloody violent are filled in by the squalid location sites in New York's Harlem or equally unappealing ghetto areas leaving no relief from depression and oppression. Based upon the novel *Across 110th* by Wally Ferris, it is strong and relentless in its pursuit of violence.

With the knock-over by three Harlem blacks (Paul Benjamin, Ed Bernard, Antonio Fargas) of 'the family's' $300,000 take from the streets, Anthony Franciosa, uncool son-in-law of org's head, goes out to 'teach them a lesson'.

Quinn's performance is controlled, but the character is not clearly defined.

● ●

■ ACROSS THE BRIDGE

1957, 103 MINS, UK
Dir Ken Annakin *Prod* John Stafford *Scr* Guy Elmes, Denis Freeman *Ph* Reginald Wyer *Ed* Alfred Roome *Mus* James Bernard *Art Dir* Cedric Dawe
● Rod Steiger, David Knight, Marla Landi, Noel Willman, Bernard Lee, Eric Pohlmann (Rank)

Across the Bridge, based on Graham Greene's story, unfolds slowly. But this is strong on situation and acting stints and winds up with a sure-fire climax. In essence, it is a gripping character study of an arrogant man who, through his own crooked folly and greed, topples from power to degrading death as a gutter outcast.

Rod Steiger is a shady international financier who is on the lam from Scotland Yard and the FBI. On the train he meets up with a gabby Mexican stranger and, by skullduggery, assumes the stranger's identity and acquires his passport. In Mexico, he is caught between the Scotland Yard man, trying to lure him into American territory, and the Mexican police chief, who withholds Steiger's own passport in order to indulge in a spot of astute blackmail.

These complicated goings-on are background to a remarkable study of mental and physical decay by Steiger. At times it is irritatingly over-fussy and mannered, but he dominates the screen.

Aided by skillful lensing, director Ken Annakin has excellently built up the atmosphere of a sleepy, brooding Mexican bordertown. Exteriors were shot in Spain.

As the Mexican police chief Noel Willman gives a wily, subtle performance which, because of its very restraint, contrasts admirably with the Steiger technique. The scenes between the two are filmic highlights.

● ●

■ ACROSS THE PACIFIC

1942, 86 MINS, US ▽
Dir John Huston *Prod* Jerry Wald, Jack Saper *Scr* Richard Macauley *Ph* Arthur Edeson *Ed* Frank Magee *Mus* Adolph Deutsch
● Humphrey Bogart, Sydney Greenstreet, Mary Astor, Victor Sen Yung, Keye Luke, Richard Loo (Warner)

Warners had a problem in transferring the Robert Carson *Sat Eve Post* serial to the screen. Original, under title of *Aloha Means Goodbye*, depicted a spy melodrama on ship

that finally reached Hawaii – but after the war's start and studio purchase scripter Richard Macauley had to change things around.

Result is switch of locale from the west to east coast – and the yarn never gets into the Pacific Ocean, despite the title.

After Humphrey Bogart is court-martialed out of the army coast artillery, he shifts to Canada in attempt to enlist in the Dominion artillery. Turned down, he gets passage on a Jap freighter bound for Panama and the Orient.

Although picture does not quite hit the edge-of-seat tension engendered by *Maltese Falcon*, it's a breezy and fast-paced melodrama. Huston directs deftly from thrill-packed script by Macauley.

● ●

■ ACROSS THE WIDE MISSOURI

1951, 78 MINS, US ◇ ▽
Dir William A. Wellman *Prod* Robert Sisk *Scr* Talbot Jennings *Ph* William C. Mellor *Ed* John Dunning *Mus* David Raksin *Art Dir* Cedric Gibbons, James Basevi
● Clark Gable, Ricardo Montalban, John Hodiak, Adolphe Menjou, Maria Elena Marques, J. Carrol Naish (M-G-M)

There's much that will seize audience attention in *Missouri*. The color lensing of the rugged outdoor locations backgrounding the story of beaver trappers and Indians in the early west brings the sites to the screen with breathtaking beauty. Critically, though, the presentation is choppy and episodic, and the device of having the Indian dialog lengthily translated, is dull and boring.

Story is narrated by an unseen voice (Howard Keel) identified as the son of Clark Gable and his Indian wife, played by Mexican film star Maria Elena Marques.

Plot finds Gable, a rough and ready trapper, taking Marques as a bride because he believes it will help him get into some untouched beaver country controlled by an Indian tribe led by the bride's grandfather (Jack Holt). Gable, the wife and other trappers make the long trek and, upon arrival, are temporarily repulsed by young Indians led by Ricardo Montalban.

Wellman's direction clicks when he has the story on the move in the battle and trekking sequences. He's not able to do much when the script requires the actors to sit down and talk out the long translations.

● ●

■ ACT OF VIOLENCE

1949, 82 MINS, US
Dir Fred Zinnemann *Prod* William H. Wright *Scr* Robert L. Richards *Ph* Robert Surtees *Ed* Conrad A. Nervig *Mus* Bronislau Kaper *Art Dir* Cedric Gibbons, Hans Peters
● Van Heflin, Robert Ryan, Janet Leigh, Phyllis Thaxter, Mary Astor, Berry Kroeger (M-G-M)

The grim melodrama implied by its title is fully displayed in *Act of Violence*. It is strong meat for the heavy drama addicts, tellingly produced and played to develop tight excitement.

Story concerns two vets. Van Heflin has come out of the war with honors while his comrades, all but one, were killed in a Nazi prison camp. Robert Ryan, crippled and vengeful, pursues Heflin to make him answer for betraying his buddies.

The playing and direction catch plot aims and the characterizations are all topflight thesping. Heflin and Ryan deliver punchy performances that give substance to the menacing terror of the Robert L. Richards script, taken from a story by Collier Young.

It's grim business, unrelieved by lightness, and the players belt over their assignments under Zinnemann's knowing direction. Janet Leigh points up her role as Heflin's worried

A

but courageous wife, while Phyllis Thaxter does well by a smaller part as Ryan's girl. A standout is the brassy, blowzy femme created by Mary Astor – a woman of the streets who gives Heflin shelter during his wild flight from fate.

■ ACTORS AND SIN

1952, 85 MINS, US Ⓥ
Dir Ben Hecht *Prod* Sid Kuller *Scr* Ben Hecht *Ph* Lee Garmes *Ed* Otto Ludwig *Mus* George Antheil *Art Dir* Howard Bristol
● Edward G. Robinson, Marsha Hunt, Dan O'Herlihy, Eddie Albert, Tracey Roberts, Jenny Hecht (Hecht/United Artists)

Written, produced and directed by Ben Hecht, *Actors and Sin* is an overall title for two stories separately tagged *Actor's Blood* and *Woman of Sin*. First is a creaky yarn while the second is a racy, tradey satire on Hollywood.

Actor's Blood largely wastes the talents of Edward G. Robinson and Marsha Hunt. At the peak of her stage career, Hunt is shown slipping downward on a rope of poor plays, an uneven temperament and a variety of pointless affairs with male acquaintances. Robinson, her doting father and an actor of the old school, decides to take revenge upon those who have cast his daughter aside by making her suicide appear as murder.

Woman of Sin is a genuinely, amusing burlesque of prewar Hollywood.

■ ACTRESS, THE

1953, 89 MINS, US
Dir George Cukor *Prod* Lawrence Weingarten *Scr* Ruth Gordon *Ph* Harold Rosson *Ed* George Boemler *Mus* Bronislau Kaper *Art Dir* Cedric Gibbons, Arthur Lonergan
● Spencer Tracy, Jean Simmons, Teresa Wright, Anthony Perkins, Ian Wolfe, Kay Williams (M-G-M)

A warm, humorous motion picture has been made from Ruth Gordon's chronicle of her New England girlhood and burning desire for a legit career. Presented on the stage as *Years Ago*, it engagingly puts over the characters taken from real life, as well as the feel of the early 1900 period in which the plot is laid.

Jean Simmons plays the title role, and portrays perfectly the teenage agonies and joys of a girl who must become an actress at all cost, yet stands in awe of a papa who, though seeming to have no sympathy for such youthful ambitions, is the one who comes through to make them possible at the finale.

Spencer Tracy is fine as the father, a man who easily becomes a bore at times, who lives quite a bit in his seafaring past, and desires better things for his family than he can provide on the miserly stipend he makes as a clerk. As a balance wheel in the family, Teresa Wright's mother is topnotch.

Actually, the script is a series of incidents establishing Miss Simmons' stage yen and it's told with solid heart, some drama and humor that spills honestly from the family types seen.

Anthony Perkins impresses as Simmons' swain, and their scenes together have a nostalgic flavor.
☐ 1950: Nomination: B&W Costume Design

■ ADAM HAD FOUR SONS

1941, 108 MINS, US Ⓥ
Dir Gregory Ratoff *Prod* Robert Sherwood *Scr* William Hurlbut, Michael Blankfort *Ph* Peverell Marley *Ed* Francis D. Lyon *Mus* W. Franke Harling
● Ingrid Bergman, Warner Baxter, Susan Hayward, Fay Wray (Columbia)

This is a film version of Charles Bonner's novel, *Legacy*, which details the decade history of a typical American family kept intact by

the father through the panic of 1907 and the World War. The unanimous loyalties of the group, through prosperity and vicissitudes, are broadly etched to result in moderately satisfactory entertainment.

Under able guidance of Gregory Ratoff, Ingrid Bergman turns in a persuasive and sympathetic performance. Warner Baxter does well as the head of the household, steeped in good old American tradition that family bonds are unbreakable.

In 1907, young Bergman arrives from abroad to assume charge of the four young boys as governess. She soon becomes one of the family, but sudden death of the wife, followed by family's financial collapse necessitate the girl returning home.

Ten years later Baxter recoups his fortunes, reacquires the old home, and sends for Bergman to return. With the boys grown to near-manhood, and all enlisting in various branches of the service, she is pitted against the attempts of unscrupulous Susan Hayward to disrupt the family happiness.

■ ADAM'S RIB

1950, 103 MINS, US Ⓥ ☉
Dir George Cukor *Prod* Lawrence Weingarten *Scr* Ruth Gordon, Garson Kanin *Ph* George J. Folsey *Ed* George Boemler *Mus* Miklos Rozsa *Art Dir* Cedric Gibbons, William Ferrari
● Spencer Tracy, Katharine Hepburn, Judy Holliday, Tom Ewell, David Wayne, Jean Hagen (M-G-M)

Adam's Rib is a bright comedy success, belting over a succession of sophisticated laughs. Ruth Gordon and Garson Kanin have fashioned their amusing screenplay around the age-old battle of the sexes.

Setup has Spencer Tracy as an assistant d.a., married to femme attorney Katharine Hepburn. He believes no woman has the right to take shots at another femme. Hepburn believes a woman has the same right to invole the unwritten law as a man. They do courtroom battle over their theories whe Tracy is assigned to prosecute Judy Holliday.

This is the sixth Metro teaming of Tracy and Hepburn, and their approach to marital relations around their own hearth is delightfully saucy. A better realization on type than Holliday's portrayal of dumb Brooklyn femme doesn't seem possible.
☐ 1950: Nomination: Best Story & Screenplay

■ ADDAMS FAMILY, THE

1991, 99 MINS, US ◇ Ⓥ ☉
Dir Barry Sonnenfeld *Prod* Scott Rudin *Scr* Caroline Thompson, Larry Wilson *Ph* Owen Roizman *Ed* Dede Allen, Jim Miller *Mus* Marc Shaiman *Art Dir* Richard MacDonald
● Anjelica Huston, Raul Julia, Christopher Lloyd, Dan Hedaya, Elizabeth Wilson, Christina Ricci (Paramount)

Despite inspired casting and nifty visual trappings, the eagerly awaited *Addams Family* figures as a major disappointment. First-time director Barry Sonnenfeld never really gets past the skeletal plot, which plays like a collection of sitcom one-liners augmented by feature-film special effects. Script is one visual joke or pun after another based on the decidedly different family Charles Addams created in his New Yorker cartoons. The ABC TV series ran from 1964 to 1966.

The performers work gamely, but how many times are we expected to laugh at Morticia (Anjelica Huston) speaking wistfully about torture or Gomez (Raul Julia) imploring the disembodied digits Thing to 'lend a hand'?

The disjointed plot turns on the long-missing Uncle Fester and an attempt by the family lawyer (Dan Hedaya) to cash in on Fester's absence – and gain access to Gomez's hidden

fortune – by passing off the son of a loan-sharking client (Elizabeth Wilson) as Fester. After becoming acclimated to the ooky-kooky-spooky clan, the son (Christopher Lloyd) grows increasingly fond of them, prompting his conspirators to engage in drastic tactics.

The only moment that lives up to the film's potential involves tots Wednesday (Christina Ricci) and Pugsley (Jimmy Workman) enacting a scene from *Hamlet* for the school talent show. Huston is properly ethereal as Morticia, and Julia makes a swashbuckling Gomez, though neither can do much with the roles. Ricci is a perfect, somber Wednesday.
☐ 1991: Nomination: Best Costume Design

■ ADJUSTER, THE

1991, 102 MINS, CANADA ◇ Ⓥ ☉
Dir Atom Egoyan *Prod* Camelia Frieberg, Atom Egoyan *Scr* Atom Egoyan *Ph* Paul Sarossy *Ed* Susan Shipton *Mus* Mychael Danna *Art Dir* Linda Del Rosario, Richard Paris
● Elias Koteas, Arsine Khanjian, Maury Chaykin, Gabrielle Rose, Jennifer Dale, David Hemblen (Alliance/Ego)

In an escalating quest for eccentricity, Atom Egoyan's analysis of voyeurism is becoming profoundly shallow. Trying to streamline his radical and visionary *Family Viewing*, his follow-up pic *Speaking Parts* xeroxed the theme and polished the images but lost its edge in the process. Ditto for *The Adjuster*, with its cast of superbly photographed, eclectic characters who take an aimless walk on the wild side.

Noah (Elias Koteas), an insurance adjuster, is a wedded philanderer who exploits the vulnerability of female clients who've lost their homes to fires. His mate Hera (played by Egoyan's mate, Arsine Khanjian) is a film censor who secretly videotapes porn flicks for her sister Sete (Rose Sarkisyan), a matron with betwixt desires.

These frigid spouses rent their model home to a couple (Maury Chaykin, Gabrielle Rose) who stiffly stage their sexual fantasies in absurd and eventually violent acts. Their characters have potential that the script never develops.

At no point does the viewer ever gain in-depth knowledge of any character in the film. Visuals are gorgeous.

■ ADMIRABLE CRICHTON, THE

(US: Paradise Lagoon)

1957, 93 MINS, UK ◇
Dir Lewis Gilbert *Prod* Ian Dalrymple *Scr* Vernon Harris, Lewis Gilbert *Ph* Wilkie Cooper *Ed* Peter Hunt *Mus* Douglas Gamley *Art Dir* William Kellner
● Kenneth More, Diane Cilento, Cecil Parker, Sally Ann Howes, Martita Hunt, Jack Watling (Modern Screen Play)

Staged many times since its original production in London in 1902, and filmed in the silent days [1919] as *Male and Female*, this [J.M. Barrie] story of a butler who becomes master on a desert island is a sound starrer for Kenneth More.

A peer of one of England's stately homes takes his three daughters off on a yachting cruise with a few friends and domestic staff. They are shipwrecked and marooned on an uncharted island, and dig themselves in awaiting rescue. Crichton (More), the impeccable butler, is obliged to take complete control, because of the inefficiency of the other castaways. He now gives, not takes orders, and establishes himself as benevolent dictator.

Although More lacks the accepted stature of an English butler, his personality makes a more human and sympathetic figure of the servant who has a firmer sense of snob values than his master. Cecil Parker, alternately genial and pompous as the father, is perhaps more in keeping with the period.

■ ADVENTURE

1945, 130 MINS, US

Dir Victor Fleming *Prod* Sam Zimbalist *Scr* Frederick
Hazlitt Brennan, Vincent Lawrence *Ph* Joseph Ruttenberg
Ed Frank Sullivan *Mus* Herbert Stothart *Art Dir* Cedric
Gibbons, Urie McCleary
● Clark Gable, Greer Garson, Joan Blondell, Thomas
Mitchell, Tom Tully, Richard Haydn (M-G-M)

Clark Gable is bos'n mate on a Merchant
Marine vessel, and as tough as the toughest
sailor on board. Handy with his dukes, he has
a femme in every port. That is until he meets
Greer Garson, the librarian, who finally decides that the venturesome traits displayed by
Gable are just what she has been missing in
life. So, it's a hurried wedding, a honeymoon
in Reno. Then the romance collapses on the
pair. He decides the sea is still for him and
she decides on a divorce. The payoff is trite.

Film shows a new Gable. He has many of
the old mannerisms, but director Victor
Fleming [from a novel by Clyde Brion Davis],
makes him overly boisterous and stubborn, a
seafaring man who would toss aside his new
bride of a few days like she was another girl
in port.

Garson dominates every scene even when
being browbeaten by the obstinate mate. She
effects the transition from the prim, stand
offish office gal into a life-loving femme who
refuses to let her man get away.

Joan Blondell as her girl friend, who likes
Gable from the start, and even better after a
drinking session, seems almost a reborn actress in this role. Thomas Mitchell, who is the
God-fearing sailor and particular pal of
Gable, has a powerful characterization, a
does it up brown.

■ ADVENTURE FOR TWO
See: The Demi-Paradise

■ ADVENTURE OF SHERLOCK HOLMES'
SMARTER BROTHER, THE

1975, 91 MINS, UK ◇ ⑰

Dir Gene Wilder *Prod* Richard A. Roth *Scr* Gene
Wilder *Ph* Gerry Fisher *Ed* Jim Clark *Mus* John
Morris *Art Dir* Terence Marsh
● Gene Wilder, Madeline Kahn, Marty Feldman, Dom
DeLuise, Leo McKern, Roy Kinnear (20th-Century Fox)

Gene Wilder joins Mel Brooks in that elusive
pantheon of madcap humor, by virtue of
Wilder's script, title characterization and directorial debut, all of which are outstanding.

Wilder's script sends the famous Holmes
(played by Douglas Wilmer) and Dr Watson
(Thorley Walters) ostensibly out of England,
in order to fool Prof Moriarty (Leo McKern).
Latter has a plot going with Dom DeLuise,
the most unlikely blackmailing opera freak of
the season, to obtain some official state papers stolen from nobleman John Le Mesurier.

Holmes' strategy is to use his younger
brother, played by Wilder, as a decoy, back-
stopped by Feldman, a policeman blessed with
a photographic memory. Together, this fearless duo fumbles its way to ultimate success.

■ ADVENTURERS, THE

1970, 171 MINS, US ◇ ⑰

Dir Lewis Gilbert *Prod* Lewis Gilbert *Scr* Michael
Hastings, Lewis Gilbert *Ph* Claude Renoir *Ed* Anne
Coates *Mus* Antonio Carlos Jobim *Art Dir* Tony
Masters
● Bekim Fehmiu, Charles Aznavour, Alan Badel,
Candice Bergen, Thommy Berggren, Ernest Borgnine
(Paramount)

The Adventurers is a classic monument to bad
taste. Film is marked by profligate and
squandered production opulence; inferior,
imitative and curiously old-hat direction; banal, ludicrous dialog; sub-standard, lifeless

and embarrassing acting; cornball music; indulgent, gratuitous and boring violence; and
luridly non-erotic sex.

Harold Robbins' guess-who novel about the
jet set and South American politics was as
commercial as it was trashy; film version may
be fairly said to make the novel look better.

Story depicts the life of a South American
playboy who, if one were to swallow the specious sociology, was a victim of childhood
traumas which crystalized revolutionary violence and brutal rape.

On the romantic front there is Candice
Bergen, about the only principal to salvage
anything from the film, playing a fabulously
wealthy girl who marries the hero, but loses
their baby in a swing accident, becomes barren, and eventually turns lesbian.

■ ADVENTURES AT RUGBY
See: Tom Brown's Schooldays

■ ADVENTURES IN BABYSITTING
(UK: A Night on the Town)

1987, 99 MINS, US ◇ ⑰ ⊙

Dir Chris Columbus *Prod* Debra Hill, Lynda Obst
Scr David Simkins *Ph* Rick Waite *Ed* Fredric
Steinkamp, William Steinkamp *Mus* Michael Kamen
Art Dir Todd Hallowell
● Elisabeth Shue, Maia Brewton, Keith Coogan,
Anthony Rapp, Vincent D'Onofrio, Penelope Ann Miller
(Touchstone)

Ferris Bueller meets *Risky Business* in this teen-
dream set in (where else?) the suburbs of
Chicago. Chris Columbus weighs in adequately in his directorial debut, thanks to a
fresh, solid lead performance from Elisabeth
Shue. Yet the film can never rise above the
leaden script.

Chris Parker (Shue) takes an assignment
babysitting for two kids, the 15-year-old Brad
(Keith Coogan), who has a crush on her, and
Sara (Maia Brewton), a little brat who idolizes comicbook hero Thor. Trouble starts
when Chris gets a call from her best friend
Brenda (Penelope Ann Miller), who had decided to run away from home but had thought
better of it upon reaching the bus station in
downtown Chicago.

Chris heads down to the city with Brad, his
best friend Daryl (Anthony Rapp) and Sara in
tow and, in short order, blows out a tire, realizes she's left her purse back in the 'burbs,
gets a tow from a one-armed man who drives
by his house to find his wife cheating on him,
sneaks into the car that's being hotwired by
professional car thief Joe Gipp (Calvin
Levels), and winds up in the headquarters of
a national car-theft ring.

The only party not guilty of overacting is
Levels, who gives a sweetly controlled performance in his bit as the young thief with a conscience.

■ ADVENTURES OF BARON
MUNCHAUSEN, THE

1989, 125 MINS, UK/W. GERMANY ◇ ⑰ ⊙

Dir Terry Gilliam *Prod* Thomas Schuhly *Scr* Charles
McKeown, Terry Gilliam *Ph* Giuseppe Rotunno
Ed Peter Hollywood *Mus* Michael Kamen
Art Dir Dante Ferretti
● John Neville, Eric Idle, Jonathan Pryce, Oliver Reed,
Sting, Robin Williams (Prominent/Laura)

A fitting final installment in Terry Gilliam's
trilogy begun with *Time Bandits* and continued
with *Brazil*, *The Adventures of Baron Munchausen*
shares many of those films' strengths and
weaknesses, but doesn't possess the visionary
qualities of the latter.

The film offers a continual feast for the
eyes, and not enough for the funnybone or
the heart. Set in Europe in the 18th century,
tale begins with a city under intense siege by

the Turks. An elderly gent who purports to be
the Baron begins relating the true story of
how he caused he war.

With this, Gilliam takes the viewer into the
exquisite palace of the sultan, whose ferocity
is aroused when he loses a bet to the visiting
baron (John Neville). With the help of his variously and superhumanly gifted gang of four,
which consists of the fastest runner in the
world, a dwarf who can exhale with hurricane
force, an expert sharpshooter and an immeasurably strong black man, the Baron makes
off with the sultan's entire treasure, but his
city is left to suffer the consequences.

Promising to save the city from the renewed
attack, the Baron escapes in a gigantic hot-air
balloon fashioned out of ladies' underwear,
and goes in search of his four comrades. The
journey takes the unlikely pair to some unlikely places where they meet some unlikely
people.

☐ 1989: Nominations: Best Art Direction,
Costume Design, Makeup, Visual Effects

■ ADVENTURES OF BARRY MCKENZIE, THE

1972, 117 MINS, AUSTRALIA ◇

Dir Bruce Beresford *Prod* Phillip Adams *Scr* Bruce
Beresford, Barry Humphries *Ph* Don McAlpine
Ed John Scott *Mus* Peter Best *Art Dir* John Stoddart
● Barry Crocker, Barry Humphries, Paul Bertram, Dennis
Price, Avice Landon, Peter Cook (Longford)

Satirist Barry Humphries has put his talents
to a film, as coauthor and costar. The result is
what one would expect if the Marx Brothers
were put into an Aussie-brand *Carry On* pic.
It's based on a comic strip [*The Wonderful
World of Barry McKenzie*], written by
Humphries, around a very Aussie character in
London known as Bazza.

Barry Crocker plays title role of the gauche
young Aussie visiting Britain for the first
time. His turns of phrases are witty and original, often with bawdy twinge, and although
much is in the Australian vernacular (frequently invented by Humphries), few are
likely to miss the drift of the remarks.

■ ADVENTURES OF BUCKAROO BANZAI
ACROSS THE 8TH DIMENSION, THE

1984, 103 MINS, US ◇ ⑰ ⊙

Dir W.D. Richter *Prod* Neil Canton, W.D. Richter
Scr Earl Mac Rauch *Ph* Fred J. Koenekamp
Ed Richard Marks, George Bowers *Mus* Michael
Boddicker *Art Dir* J. Michael Riva
● Peter Weller, John Lithgow, Ellen Barkin, Jeff
Goldblum, Christopher Lloyd, Rosalind Cash (Sherwood)

The Adventures of Buckaroo Banzai plays more
like an experimental film than a Hollywood
production aimed at a mass audience. It violates every rule of storytelling and narrative
structure in creating a self-contained world of
its own.

First-time director W.D. Richter and writer
Earl Mac Rauch have created a comic book
world chock full of references, images, pseudo
scientific ideas and plain mumbo jumbo.

Buried within all this Banzai trivia is an indecipherable plot involving a modern band of
Robin Hoods who go to battle with enemy
aliens released accidentally from the eighth
dimension as a result of Buckaroo's experiments with particle physics .

Buckaroo is a world-class neurosurgeon,
physicist, race car driver and, with his band of
merry pranksters, the Hong Kong Cavaliers,
a rock 'n' roll star.

As the great one (Buckaroo), Peter Weller
presents a moving target that is tough to hit.
Also very funny is Jeff Goldblum, coming as if
from another dimension as every mother's
Jewish son. Ellen Barkin does a turn as
Buckaroo's mysterious girlfriend and looks
great but is another emotionless character.

ADVENTURES OF DON JUAN
(UK: The New Adventures of Don Juan)

1949, 110 MINS, US ◇ ⊙
Dir Vincent Sherman   Prod Jerry Wald   Scr George
Oppenheimer, Harry Kurnitz   Ph Elwood Bredell
Ed Alan Crosland Jr   Mus Max Steiner   Art Dir Edward
Carrere
● Errol Flynn, Viveca Lindfors, Robert Douglas,
Raymond Burr, Alan Hale, Ann Rutherford (Warner)

The loves and escapades of the fabulous Don
Juan are particularly adapted to the screen
abilities of Errol Flynn and he gives them a
flair that pays off strongly.

Plot depicts Don Juan adventuring in
England. Opening has him escaping an angry
husband, only to become immediately involved again with another femme. This time
his wooing ruins a state-arranged wedding
and he's shipped off to Spain to face his angry
monarch. The queen assigns him to post of
instructor in the royal fencing academy, he
discovers a plot against her majesty, instigated by a conniving prime minister. Viveca
Lindfors co-stars as the queen and she brings
a compelling beauty to the role

Top action is reached in the deadly duel between Flynn and Robert Douglas, the crooked
prime minister, climaxing with a long leap
down a huge flight of castle stairs.
□ 1949: Best Color Costume Design.
□ Nomination: Best Color Art Direction

ADVENTURES OF FORD FAIRLANE, THE

1990, 104 MINS, US ◇ ⊙ ⊙
Dir Renny Harlin   Prod Joel Silver, Steve Perry
Scr Daniel Waters, James Cappe, David Arnott
Ph Oliver Wood   Ed Michael Tronick   Mus Yello
Art Dir John Vallone
● Andrew Dice Clay, Wayne Newton, Priscilla Presley,
Morris Day, Lauren Holly, Robert Englund
(20th Century-Fox/Silver)

Surprisingly funny and expectedly rude, this
first starring vehicle by vilified standup comic
Andrew Dice Clay has a decidedly lowbrow
humor that is a sort of modern equivalent of
that of the Three Stooges.

Clay plays Ford Fairlane, a private eye specializing in cases involving rock acts (hence
his overused nickname, 'the rock & roll detective'). He gets drawn into a murder mystery
linked to a shock-radio deejay (Gilbert
Gottfried, in a hilarious cameo), and a sleazy
record executive (Wayne Newton) and his ex-
wife (Priscilla Presley).

With its heavy rock bent and the direction
of Renny Harlin (Die Hard 2), much of the
film resembles a musicvideo.

Aside from his appeal to rednecks and high-
school boys overly impressed by certain four-
letter words, Clay's chain-smoking goombah
in many ways self-parodies the macho ethic
that prize rock 'n' roll, fast cars and cheap
bimbos above all else.

The film's most significant find, undoubtedly, is Lauren Holly who brings a lot of flash
and charisma to a difficult role as Fairlane's
longing girl Friday. Also, Robert Englund
(aka Freddy Krueger) plays a sadistic killer,
sans makeup.

ADVENTURES OF HUCK FINN, THE

1993, 108 MINS, US ◇ ⊙ ⊙
Dir Stephen Sommers   Prod Laurence Mark
Scr Stephen Sommers   Ph Janusz Kaminski   Ed Bob
Ducsay   Mus Bill Conti   Art Dir Richard Sherman
● Elijah Wood, Courtney B. Vance, Robbie Coltrane,
Jason Robards, Ron Perlman, Dana Ivey (Walt Disney)

Disney's remake of Mark Twain's classic The
Adventures of Huckleberry Finn is a timely, literate and handsome film. However, the acting
of the two leads fails to provide the electrifying and stirring mood that the tale deserves.

Elijah Wood stars as the roguish Huck

Finn, living with the Widow Douglas (Dana
Ivey). The film improves considerably once
Huck encounters Jim (Courtney B. Vance),
the runaway slave whose goal is to escape to
the North and buy his family's freedom. The
two drifters strike up a unique friendship as
they start their fateful journey down the
Mississippi.

Scripter-director Sommers centers his narrative on the interracial friendship, providing
a thorough examination of a morally complex
bond. His direction, however, is uneven; the
first half-hour is oddly flat and not very engaging. But helmer's work improves as the
film progresses.

Fortunately, the two central roles are surrounded by a marvelous ensemble of supporting actors: the brilliant Jason Robards and
Robbie Coltrane as the King and the Duke,
respectively, Ron Perlman as the nasty Pap
Finn, Ivey as the Widow Douglas and Laura
Bundy as the precocious Susan Wilks.

Despite its faults, Huck Finn is superior to
Michael Curtiz's 1960 or J. Lee Thompson's
1974 efforts.

ADVENTURES OF HUCKLEBERRY FINN, THE

1960, 90 MINS, US ◇ ⊙
Dir Michael Curtiz   Prod Samuel Goldwyn Jr
Scr James Lee   Ph Ted McCord   Ed Frederic Steinkamp
Mus Jerome Moross   Art Dir George W. Davis, McClure
Capps
● Tony Randall, Eddie Hodges, Archie Moore, Patty
McCormack, Neville Brand, Mickey Shaughnessy
(M-G-M)

Mark Twain's Huckleberry Finn is all boy.
Eddie Hodges' Huck isn't. Therein lurks the
basic reason this production of the Twain
classic is not all it could, and should, be.

There is something artificial and self-conscious about young Hodges' all-important
portrayal of Huck, a lack of actor-character
chemistry for which he's certainly not wholly
responsible. An equal share of the rap must
be shouldered by director Michael Curtiz, not
only for the youthful star's shortcomings in
the role but for a general slack, a disturbing
shortage of vitality noticeable at several key
junctures.

James Lee's screenplay simplifies Twain's
episodic tale, erasing some of the more complex developments and relationships, presumably for the benefit of the young audience.
Some of the more sinister, frightening aspects of the story have been forgotten.

On the brighter side of the ledger, there
are some stimulating performances and the
handsome physical production itself. An extremely colorful and experienced cast has
been assembled. These include Tony Randall,
whose work as the roguish 'King' is a delightful balance of whimsy and threat. And Archie
Moore, the light heavyweight champion of
the world, who brings the story its only moments of real warmth and tenderness.

ADVENTURES OF MARCO POLO, THE

1938, 100 MINS, US
Dir Archie Mayo   Prod Samuel Goldwyn   Scr Robert E.
Sherwood   Ph Rudolph Mate, Archie Stout   Ed Fred
Allen   Mus Hugo Friedhofer   Art Dir Richard Day
● Gary Cooper, Sigrid Gurie, Basil Rathbone, George
Barbier, Binnie Barnes, Ernest Truex (Goldwyn)

A glamorous figure in history, which places
him in the 13th century as the first European
to visit the Orient, Marco Polo has been portrayed in as many different guises as imagination permits; as traveler, adventurer,
merchant, diplomat. He probably was all of
these and a first-class liar besides. Robert E.
Sherwood, who penned the screenscript [from
a story by N.A. Pogson], conceives him also as

an ardent lover and politician. Gary Cooper
fits the character to the apex of his six feet
two.

The plot is strictly meller, starting with
Ahmed (Basil Rathbone) as a conniving
prime minister to the Chinese ruler, Kublai
Kahn (George Barbier). Schemer has his eye
the throne and a desire for the dynastic
princess for his queen. Into such a vortex of
beauty and villainy come Marco Polo and his
business agent.

Marco Polo is admitted to the court and
there glimpses the beautiful princess, who is
much taken with his six feet two and easy
manner of love-making behind the Chinese
fountain.

It is all played on the dead level by a fine
cast. Rathbone is an excellent plotter, and
Sigrid Gurie, a Norwegian actress who makes
her American film debut in the picture, possesses beauty of a kind to start civil war in
any country.

ADVENTURES OF MARK TWAIN, THE

1944, 130 MINS, US
Dir Irving Rapper   Prod Jesse L. Lasky   Scr Alan LeMay,
Harry Chandlee   Ph Sol Polito   Ed Ralph Dawson
Mus Max Steiner   Art Dir John Hughes
● Fredric March, Alexis Smith, Donald Crisp, Alan Hale,
C. Aubrey Smith, John Carradine (Warner)

So rich and full was the life of Mark Twain,
born Sam Clemens, that it requires two
hours-plus to tell the full tale [adapted from
Twain's works, and Harold M. Sherman's play
Mark Twain, by Alan LeMay and Sherman]. It
is a film that has its measure of symbolism:
linking the humorist's lifetime of 75 years to
appearances of Halley's Comet. The astronomical display was visible when Sam
Clemens was born in Hannibal, Mo, on the
banks of the Mississippi, and 75 years later,
when the Chancellor of Oxford extols the
great American writer, at a time when the
famed university is also paying honor to
Rudyard Kipling with an honorary doctorate
of literature, it again makes its astral appearance.

In between Clemens has adventured as a
river boatman, journeyman reporter, and
western goldrusher, only to find sudden fame
with his saga of the jumping frogs. Soon follow renown and fortune as Tom Sawyer, Huck
Finn and the rest of his 'funny books' capture
the hearts and the minds of all America, only
to be dissipated in abortive attempts with an
automatic printing press, extravagant publishing ventures and the like.
□ 1944: Nominations: Best B&W Art
Direction, Scoring of a Dramatic Picture,
Special Effects

ADVENTURES OF ROBIN HOOD, THE

1938, 104 MINS, US ◇ ⊙ ⊙
Dir Michael Curtiz, William Keighley   Prod Henry Blanke
Scr Norman Reilly Raine, Seton I. Miller   Ph Tony
Gaudio, Sol Polito, W. Howard Greene   Ed Ralph
Dawson   Mus Erich Wolfgang Korngold   Art Dir Carl
Jules Weyl
● Errol Flynn, Olivia de Havilland, Basil Rathbone,
Claude Rains, Patric Knowles, Eugene Pallette (Warner)

Warners revives the legend with Errol Flynn
in the role in which Douglas Fairbanks Sr
scored his first big success in 1922. It is cinematic pageantry at its best, a highly imaginative telling of folklore in all the hues of
Technicolor.

Film is done in the grand manner of silent-
day spectacles with sweep and breadth of action, swordplay and hand-to-hand battles
between Norman and Saxon barons.
Superlative on the production side.

Played with intensity by an excellent company of actors, an illusion of fairy-story quality is retained throughout. Michael Curtiz

7

and William Keighley are credited as co-directors, the former having picked up the story soon after its filming started when Keighley was incapacitated by illness. There is skillful blending of their joint work.

Flynn makes the heroic Robin a somewhat less agile savior of the poor than Fairbanks portrayed him, but the Warner version emphasizes the romance. Teamed with Olivia de Havilland as Marian, Flynn is an ardent suitor and a gallant courtier. There are some convincing histrionics by Basil Rathbone, Claude Rains, Patric Knowles, Eugene Palette, Alan Hale and Melville Cooper. Lighter moments are furnished by Una O'Connor and Herbert Mundin.
□ 1938: Best Interior Decoration (Carl Jules Weyl), Original Score, Editing.
□ Nomination: Best Picture

- -

■ ADVENTURES OF SADIE, THE
See: Our Girl Friday

- -

■ ADVENTURES OF SHERLOCK HOLMES, THE

1939, 71 MINS, US 🔊 ☉
Dir Alfred Werker   *Prod* Gene Markey   *Scr* Edwin Blum, William Drake   *Ph* Leon Shamroy   *Ed* Robert Bischoff   *Mus* Cyril J. Mockridge (dir.)   *Art Dir* Richard Day, Hans Peters
● Basil Rathbone, Nigel Bruce, Ida Lupino, Alan Marshal, E.E. Clive, George Zucco (20th Century-Fox)

Choice of Basil Rathbone as Sherlock was a wise one. Nigel Bruce as Doctor Watson is equally expert. With the two key characters thus capably handled, the film has the additional asset of being well conceived and grippingly presented.

Plenty of ingenuity is concentrated into two concurrent mysteries with the impossible clues not made too absurd or too obvious for mystery devotees. The 'elementary, my dear Watson' type of dialog is soft-pedalled for more modern phrases or understandable patter.

George Zucco offers a splendid characterization as the arch-criminal and Ida Lupino is highly competent as the sole romantic figure in the mystery fable.

- -

■ ADVENTURES OF THE ROCKETEER, THE
See: Rocketeer

- -

■ ADVENTURES OF TOM SAWYER, THE

1938, 93 MINS, US ◇ 🔊
Dir Norman Taurog   *Prod* David O. Selznick   *Scr* John V.A. Weaver   *Ph* James Wong Howe, Wilfrid M. Cline   *Ed* Hal C. Kern, Margaret Clancey   *Mus* Lou Forbes   *Art Dir* Lyle Wheeler, William Cameron Menzies, Casey Roberts
● Tommy Kelly, Jackie Moran, Ann Gillis, May Robson, Walter Brennan, Victor Jory (Selznick/United Artists)

Adventures of Tom Sawyer is in Technicolor and contains visual beauty and appeal in addition to a faithful and nearly literal adaptation of the Mark Twain story.

The story of the boy in an isolated Missouri community of the 1880s, who made fence-painting an enviable art, who attended his own funeral services, who was the cynosure of all eyes in the witness chair at an exciting murder trial, who teased and plagued his elders and melted in tears at the slightest kindness, is imperishable.

Casting of the picture was reported a laborious job, in the course of which hundreds of boys were tested before Tommy Kelly, from the Bronx, NY, was selected for the role of Tom. His early scenes show self-consciousness but in the final sequences when he is being pursued by Injun Joe, Kelly performs like a veteran.

Walter Brennan is a standout among the adult players. He is the village drunkard, Muff Potter, accused of the graveyard murder.

May Robson loses no opportunities as Aunt Polly, whose life by turn is celestial and hellish depending upon the vagaries of Tom's vivid imagination.

Injun Joe is played by Victor Jory with all the fiendish villainy in the part.
□ 1938: Nomination: Art Direction

- -

■ ADVISE AND CONSENT

1962, 140 MINS, US
Dir Otto Preminger   *Prod* Otto Preminger   *Scr* Wendell Mayes   *Ph* Sam Leavitt   *Ed* Louis Loeffler   *Mus* Jerry Fielding   *Art Dir* Lyle R. Wheeler
● Henry Fonda, Charles Laughton, Don Murray, Walter Pidgeon, Gene Tierney, Peter Lawford (Columbia)

Allen Drury's big-selling novel has also served as a stage play. There are recognizable projections of character assassination, McCarthy-like demagoguery and use of the two hard-to-answer smears of this ill-natured generation: 'Are you now or were you once a homosexual and/or a communist?'

As interpreted by producer-director Otto Preminger and scripter Wendell Mayes, *Advise and Consent* is intermittently well dialogued and too talky, and, strangely, arrested in its development and illogical.

Preminger has endowed his production with wholly capable performers. Henry Fonda as the Secretary of State nominee, Charles Laughton as a Southern-smooth rebellious Solon, Don Murray as the focal point of the homo-suicidal scandal an Walter Pidgeon as a Majority leader fighting in best stentorian tradition in Fonda's behalf all register firmly. The characterizations come through with fine clarity.

Disturbing is lack of sufficiently clear motivation for the nub of the action. Why are Pidgeon and Laughton so pro and con about confirmation of the Presidential appointee? And isn't the Murray character too strong to kill himself?

The settings are powerfully like real. A Senate hearing room, the Senate itself, a party house in immediate Washington and varying apartments plus a place in DC suburbia all have the look of genuineness.

- -

■ AFFAIRS OF SUSAN, THE

1945, 110 MINS, US
Dir William A. Seiter   *Prod* Hal B. Wallis   *Scr* Thomas Monroe, Laszlo Gorog, Richard Flournoy   *Ph* David Abel   *Ed* Eda Warren   *Mus* Frederick Hollander   *Art Dir* Hans Dreier, Franz Bachelin
● Joan Fontaine, George Brent, Dennis O'Keefe, Don DeFore, Walter Abel, Rita Johnson (Paramount)

In this tale [from an original story by Thomas Monroe and Laszlo Gorog] about the four loves of Susan Darell (Joan Fontaine), producer Hal B. Wallis has invested the picture with considerable production values, but making the story and action the thing.

Fontaine, as Susan, legit actress just back from a USO Camp tour, accepts Walter Abel's proposal of marriage. He soon learns that there have been three men in her life previously.

Abel tosses a bachelor dinner party for the three, the ex-husband and stage producer, a young lumber millionaire, and the ardent author. They recite how they figured in Susan's life, with most of flashback sequences devoted to her contact with producer George Brent, her lone marriage.

Fontaine's sparkle in this first comedienne role is impressive. She swings easily from plain Jane to the seasoned actress type, then to the glamorous, and finally to the intellectual. Top male contribution is Brent, as the producer. He's a fine combination of the

hardboiled showman and admiring husband.
□ 1945: Nomination: Best Original Story

- -

■ AFFAIR TO REMEMBER, AN

1957, 115 MINS, US ◇ 🔊 ☉
Dir Leo McCarey   *Prod* Jerry Wald   *Scr* Delmer Daves, Leo McCarey   *Ph* Milton Krasner   *Ed* James B. Clark   *Mus* Hugo Friedhofer, Harry Warren   *Art Dir* Lyle R. Wheeler, Jack Martin Smith
● Cary Grant, Deborah Kerr, Richard Denning, Neva Patterson, Cathleen Nesbitt (20th Century-Fox)

Adding comedy lines, music, color and CinemaScope, Jerry Wald and Leo McCarey turn this remake of the 1939 *Love Affair* into a winning film that is alternately funny and tenderly sentimental. *An Affair to Remember*, using plenty of attractive settings (on and off the USS *Constitution*), is still primarily a film about two people; and since those two happen to be Cary Grant and Deborah Kerr the bitter-sweet romance sparkles and crackles with high spirits.

Story has Grant and Kerr fall in love aboard ship, though both are engaged to other people. They decide to meet in six months atop the Empire State Building. Meanwhile, Grant, a faintly notorious bachelor, is to change his life in a more useful direction. He shows up for the rendezvous, but she is struck by a car on her way to the meeting and may never win again.

McCarey, who with Delmer Daves wrote the screenplay, has done a fine job, and has gotten the most out of his players' talents. Both are experts in romantic comedy, sophisticated comedy. Both are able to get a laugh by waving a hand or raising an eyebrow. The Grant-Kerr romance is never maudlin, not even at the end.
□ 1957: Nominations: Best Cinematography, Costume Design, Score of a Dramatic Picture, Song ('An Affair to Remember'),

- -

■ AFRAID OF THE DARK

1992, 91 MINS, UK/FRANCE ◇ 🔊 ☉
Dir Mark Peploe   *Prod* Simon Bosanquet   *Scr* Mark Peploe   *Ph* Bruno de Keyzer   *Ed* Scott Thomas   *Mus* Richard Hartley   *Art Dir* Caroline Amies
● James Fox, Fanny Ardant, Paul McGann, Clare Holman, Robert Stephens, Susan Wooldridge (Telescope/Ariane/Cine Cinq)

Bernardo Bertolucci scripter Mark Peploe makes an ambitious bow behind the lens with *Afraid of the Dark*, a tricky mix of slasher movie and psychodrama that's strong on tease but weak on final delivery.

Double-headed plot centers on an 11-year-old (Ben Keyworth), whose dad (James Fox) is a cop and mother (Fanny Ardant) is blind. With a sicko terrorizing their west London nabe, kid is concerned for the safety of mom's blind friend (Clare Holman). Worse, he reckons the razor-man is someone he knows – the local window cleaner, locksmith or photog (Paul McGann), who has a sideline in nudie portraits.

At exact halfway point, Peploe springs his main surprise, and rest of pic has trouble building up a matching head of steam. But for pure technique (and Hitchcock/Michael Powell homework), Peploe can't be faulted.

As the scarily introverted boy, young Keyworth is on the money throughout. Holman handles her key role with style and shading, well matched by McGann. Fox is surprisingly flat as the moppet's dad, and Ardant (who only seems to be there because of French co-prod coin) makes a linguistically shaky British bow in a smallish part.

- -

■ AFRICAN FURY
See: Cry, the Beloved Country

- -

■ AFRICAN QUEEN, THE

1951, 104 MINS, UK ◇ ⓥ ⊙
Dir John Huston   *Prod* S.P. Eagle [= Sam Spiegel]
Scr James Agee, John Huston   *Ph* Jack Cardiff
Ed Ralph Kemplen   *Mus* Allan Gray   *Art Dir* Wilfrid Shingleton
● Humphrey Bogart, Katharine Hepburn, Robert Morley, Peter Bull, Theodore Bikel, Walter Gotell
(Horizon/Romulus)

This story of adventure and romance, experienced by a couple in Africa just as World War I got underway, is an engrossing motion picture. Just offbeat enough in story, locale and star teaming of Humphrey Bogart and Katharine Hepburn to stimulate the imagination. It is a picture with an unassuming warmth and naturalness.

The independent production unit took stars and cameras to Africa to film C.S. Forester's novel, *African Queen*, against its actual background. Performance-wise, Bogart has never been seen to better advantage. Nor has he ever had a more knowing, talented film partner than Hepburn.

The plot concerns a man and woman, completely incongruous as to coupling, who are thrown together when the war news comes to German East Africa in 1914. The man, a sloven gin-swilling, ne'er-do-well pilot of a steam-driven river launch, teams with the angular, old-maid sister of a dead English missionary to contribute a little to the cause of the Empire.

The impossible deed they plan is taking the little, decrepit 30-foot launch known as *African Queen* down uncharted rivers to a large Central Africa lake and then use the small boat as a torpedo to sink a German gunboat that is preventing invasion by British forces.

John Huston's scripting and direction, and the playing, leaven the story telling with a lot of good humor. Unfoldment has a leisurense that goes with the characters and situations.
□ 1951: Best Actor (Humphrey Bogart).
□ Nominations: Best Director, Actress (Katharine Hepburn), Screenplay

■ AFRICA – TEXAS STYLE

1967, 110 MINS, US ◇ ⓥ
Dir Andrew Marton   *Prod* Andrew Marton   *Scr* Andy White   *Ph* Paul Beeson   *Ed* Henry Richardson
Mus Malcolm Arnold   *Art Dir* Maurice Fowler
● Hugh O'Brian, John Mills, Nigel Green, Tom Nardini, Adrienne Corri (Paramount/Ivan Tors)

Africa – Texas Style is a slick and exceptionally well-turned-out piece of adventure picture-making, its title the only weight of heaviness about it.

Shot entirely in Kenya, director Andrew Marton, scripter Andy White and cameraman Paul Beeson have thoroughly caught feeling of Africa. They make effective use of the terrain as an atmospheric setting and thousands of animals of all descriptions to lend authenticity.

Story twirls about the subject of game ranching, the domestication and breeding of wild animal life as a potentially huge source of meat and as a means of preserving many of Africa's rapidly vanishing species of wild beasts.

Premise is given punch via its human story of rancher John Mills importing Texas cowboys Hugh O'Brian and his Navajo pal Tom Nardini to rope and corral as many animals as they can ride down.

■ AFTER HOURS

1985, 97 MINS, US ◇ ⓥ ⊙
Dir Martin Scorsese   *Prod* Amy Robinson, Griffin Dunne, Robert F. Colesberry   *Scr* Joseph Minton   *Ph* Michael Ballhaus   *Ed* Thelma Schoonmaker   *Mus* Howard Shore
Art Dir Jeffrey Townsend

● Griffin Dunne, Rosanna Arquette, Verna Bloom, Thomas Chong, Linda Fiorentino, Teri Garr
(Geffen/Double Play)

The cinema of paranoia and persecution reaches an apogee in *After Hours*, a nightmarish black comedy from Martin Scorsese. Anxiety-ridden picture would have been pretty funny if it didn't play like a confirmation of everyone's worst fears about contemporary urban life.

A description of one rough night in the life of a mild-mannered New York computer programmer, film is structured like a 'Pilgrim's Progress' through the anarchic, ever-treachous streets of SoHo. Every corner represents turn for the worse, and by the end of the night, he's got to wonder, like Kafka's K, if he might not actually be guilty of something.

It all starts innocently enough, as Griffin Dunne gets a come-on from Rosanna Arquette and ends up visiting he in the loft of avant-garde sculptress Linda Fiorentino. Both girls turn out to be too weird for Dunne, but he can't get home for lack of cash, so he veers from one stranger to another in search of the most mundane salvation and finds nothing but trouble.

This was Scorsese's first fictional film in a decade without Robert De Niro in the leading part, and Dunne, who doubled as co-producer, plays a mostly reactive role, permitting easy identification of oneself in his place. Supporting roles are filled by uniformly vibrant and interesting thesps.

■ AFTER THE FOX

1966, 102 MINS, UK/ITALY ◇ ⓥ
Dir Vittorio De Sica   *Prod* John Bryan   *Scr* Neil Simon, Cesare Zavattini   *Ph* Leonida Barboni   *Ed* Russell Lloyd
Mus Burt Bacharach   *Art Dir* Mario Garbugha
● Peter Sellers, Britt Ekland, Lidia Brazzi, Paola Stoppa, Victor Mature, Martin Balsam (Delagate/Nancy)

Peter Sellers is in nimble, lively form in this whacky comedy which, though sometimes strained, has a good comic idea and gives the star plenty of scope for his usual range of impersonations.

Neil Simon's screenplay is uneven but naturally has good quota of wit, and Vittorio De Sica's direction plays throughout for laughs. The Fox is a quickwitted crook who nevertheless manages to find himself in the cooler seven times in nine years. But he's equally adroit at getting out. This time he makes the break (a) because he's worried about his sister who, he has a hunch, is getting into bad habits as a film starlet, and (b) to arrange for the smuggling into Rome of the loot from a $3 million Cairo bullion robbery. He hits on the idea of pretending to make a film on an Italian beach and conning the local villagers and the police into landing the gold ashore as part of the 'film script'.

The filming parody is better in promise than when start of shooting is actually being made, but even these sequences are good for plenty of yocks. Much of this is created by Victor Mature, roped into the film within the film as an aging, corseted film star fighting the wrinkles and still living in the past.

■ AFTER THE THIN MAN

1936, 107 MINS, US ⓥ
Dir W.S. Van Dyke   *Prod* Hunt Stromberg   *Scr* Frances Goodrich, Albert Hackett   *Ph* Oliver T. Marsh
Ed Robert J. Kern   *Mus* Herbert Stothart, Edward Ward
Art Dir Cedric Gibbons, Harry McAfee
● William Powell, Myrna Loy, James Stewart, Elissa Landi, Joseph Calleia, Jessie Ralph (M-G-M)

First thing everyone will want to know about this one is whether it is as good as *The Thin Man*, and the answer is that it is – and it isn't. It has the same stars, William Powell and Myrna Loy; the same style of breezy direction by W.S. Van Dyke; almost as many sparkling

lines of dialog and amusing situations; but it hasn't, and probably couldn't have, the same freshness and originality of its predecessor.

The same author, Dashiell Hammett, wrote it, and the same screen writers, Frances Goodrich and Albert Hackett, did the adaptation. It's the 'same' all the way through, and while that's a guarantee of a certain general excellence, it's the reason why it does not shine so brightly.

Powell as the amateur detective, with Loy tagging along and getting herself tangled up in the plot, eventually gets his man. The two leading players seem to have a swell time throughout. They do a bedroom scene which is packed with laughs, but which is topped by a subsequent sequence when, having slept through an entire day, they have their breakfast in the evening and appear unable, or unwilling, to adjust themselves to the passing of time.
□ 1936: Nomination: Best Screenplay

■ AGAINST ALL ODDS

1984, 128 MINS, US ◇ ⓥ ⊙
Dir Taylor Hackford   *Prod* Taylor Hackford, William S. Gilmore   *Scr* Eric Hughes   *Ph* Donald Thorin
Ed Fredric Steinkamp, William Steinkamp   *Mus* Michel Colombier   *Art Dir* Richard James Lawrence
● Rachel Ward, Jeff Bridges, James Woods, Alex Karras, Jane Greer, Richard Widmark (Columbia)

If not for a somewhat murky and misanthropic ending, *Against All Odds* would stand as a well-engineered second-try at 1947's *Out of the Past*.

Jeff Bridges is a fading pro footballer with shady connections to James Woods, a small-time LA bookie-hood who has been keeping house with Rachel Ward until she stabbed him and got away.

Jane Greer, who played Ward's role in the earlier version of the Daniel Mainwaring yarn, is now Ward's mean mother who owns the team Bridges is cut from. Greer is allied with suave, sinister Richard Widmark, lawyer in a rapacious real-estate deal who will turn out to be more than suspected at first.

The action ranges all the way to remote Mexican areas whose scenic moods are captured nicely by cinematographer Donald Thorin, heating up the #2 love affair between Bridges and Ward. All the performances are firstrate.
□ 1984: Nomination: Best Song ('Against All Odds (Take a Look at Me Now)')

■ AGATHA

1979, 98 MINS, UK ◇ ⓥ
Dir Michael Apted   *Prod* Jarvis Astaire, Gavrik Losey
Scr Kathleen Tynan, Arthur Hopcraft   *Ph* Vittorio Storaro   *Ed* Jim Clark   *Mus* Johnny Mandel   *Art Dir* Shirley Russell
● Dustin Hoffman, Vanessa Redgrave, Timothy Dalton, Helen Morse, Celia Gregory, Paul Brooke (Warner/First Artists)

Billed as 'an imaginary solution to an authentic mystery', Kathleen Tynan's original story fills in the gaps of Agatha Christie's well-publicized disappearance in 1926.

Christie, portrayed by Vanessa Redgrave in superlative fashion, is confront with the breakdown of her marriage to war hero Timothy Dalton, who is prepared to marry his secretary (Celia Gregory). She flees to a remote health spa, where she sets in motion a unique form of revenge, while thousands scour the British countryside for some sign of her.

Enter Dustin Hoffman as a celebrated American journalist. He, too, joins the search, at first with the idea of a story, and then pursuing more romantic notions.

Director Michael Apted has perfectly recaptured the mood post-World War I Britain, and the film is gorgeously photographed by Italian cinematographer Vittorio Storaro.

Agatha packs a surprise twist that the real Agatha Christie might have envied.

☐ 1979: Nomination: Best Costume Design

. . . .

■ AGENT 8¾

See: *Hot Enough for June*

. . . .

■ AGE OF CONSENT

1932, 80 MINS, US

Dir Gregory La Cava   *Scr* Sarah Y. Mason, Francis Cockrell   *Ph* J. Roy Hunt   *Ed* Jack Kitchin
● Dorothy Wilson, Richard Cromwell, Eric Linden, Arline Judge, John Halliday (Radio)

Picture marks the first release of Dorothy Wilson, the stenographer in the Radio coast studio offices who was skyrocketed from her typewriter into semi-stardom.

Wilson turns out to be a highly interesting young type, suggesting in appearance a flapper Norma Shearer. The part of a college co-ed does not call for any histrionic fireworks, but the newcomer reveals a remarkable aptitude for natural acting.

Story is a sexy tale [based on the play *Cross Roads* by Martin Flavin, adapted by H. N. Swanson], dealing in often sprightly manner with the adolescent amours of a co-ed campus and its environs, this angle being insidiously exploited under cover of being a sympathetic study of the love problems of the young.

Cast is made up of young people, with just the leavening in the professor character, deftly handled as usual by John Halliday. Central male characters are played by Richard Cromwell, excellent choice as the young hero, and Eric Linden, once more a philandering student high-flyer.

. . . .

■ AGE OF CONSENT

1969, 103 MINS, AUSTRALIA ◇ ▼

Dir Michael Powell   *Prod* Michael Powell, James Mason   *Scr* Peter Yeldham   *Ph* Hannes Staudinger   *Ed* Anthony Buckley   *Mus* Stanley Myers   *Art Dir* Dennis Gentle
● James Mason, Helen Mirren, Jack MacGowran, Neva Carr-Glyn, Antonia Katsaros, Frank Thring (Nautilus)

Bradley Morahan (James Mason) is a famous Australian painter, paying a lot of alimony and about to return to his homeland.

He proceeds to the Great Barrier Reef to settle in a broken-down shack on a dream island, close to the mainland. The only other inhabitants are a gin-sodden old hag, her granddaughter Cora (Helen Mirren) and Isabel Marley (Antonia Katsaros), a man-hungry spinster living on annuity, but also rearing chickens and growing vegetables.

The film [from a novel by Norman Lindsay] has plenty of corn, is sometimes too slow, repetitious and badly edited, almost as if scenes had been deleted. Yet the picture has immense charm and the actual photography (particularly underwater scenes) and superb scenery make it a good travelog ad for the Great Barrier Reef area where most of it was filmed.

. . . .

■ AGNES OF GOD

1985, 98 MINS, US ◇ ▼ ⊙

Dir Norman Jewison   *Prod* Patrick Palmer, Norman Jewison   *Scr* John Pielmeier   *Ph* Sven Nykvist   *Ed* Antony Gibbs   *Mus* Georges Delerue   *Art Dir* Ken Adam
● Jane Fonda, Anne Bancroft, Meg Tilly, Anne Pitoniak, Winston Rekert, Gratien Gelinas (Columbia-Delphi IV)

John Pielmeier penned the screenplay from his own 1982 play about a young nun who is found to have given birth and then strangled the baby at an isolated convent. A psychiatrist, played by Jane Fonda, is appointed by the court to determine whether not the young woman (Meg Tilly) is fit to stand trial, and is

assured that the seemingly innocent, naive girl has no recollection of the child or conception.

In her aggressive quest for the facts in the case, Fonda goes head to head with Mother Superior Anne Bancroft, a cagey, very hip woman of God whose past as a wife and mother gives her a strong knowledge of the real world values represented by Fonda.

Fonda's relentless interrogating, mannered chain-smoking and enforced two dimensionality cause her to become tiresome very early on. She remains a brittle cliche of a modern professional woman.

Bancroft gives a generally highly engaging performance as a religious woman too knowledgeable to be one-upped by even the craftiest layman.

Tilly is angelically beautiful as the troubled youngster and brings a convincing innocence and sincerity to the role that would be hard to match.

☐ 1985: Nominations: Best Actress (Anne Bancroft), Supp. Actress (Meg Tilly), Original Score

. . . .

■ AGONY AND THE ECSTASY, THE

1965, 136 MINS, US ◇ ▼ ⊙

Dir Carol Reed   *Prod* Carol Reed   *Scr* Philip Dunne   *Ph* Leon Shamroy   *Ed* Samuel E. Beetley   *Mus* Alex North, Franco Potenza   *Art Dir* John DeCuir
● Charlton Heston, Rex Harrison, Diane Cilento, Harry Andrews, Alberto Lupo, Adolfo Celi (International Classics/20th Century-Fox)

Against a backdrop of political-religious upheaval during the Italian Renaissance, *The Agony and the Ecstasy* focuses on the personal conflict between sculptor-painter Michelangelo and his patron, Pope Julius II.

Scripter Philip Dunne has zeroed in on a four-year span during which the painter labored on the ceiling frescoes for the Sistine Chapel. The potent seeds in Dunne's excellent treatment [of the novel by Irving Stone] are the artistic arrogance of Michelangelo and equally stubborn mind of the soldier Pontiff Julius.

Rex Harrison is outstanding as the Pope, from the moment of his striking entrance as a hooded soldier leading the suppression of a pocket of revolt, to his later scenes as an urbane, yet sensitive, pragmatic ruler of a worldly kingdom.

Charlton Heston's Michelangelo is, in its own way, also outstanding. Combination of austere garb, thinned face, short hair and beard, plus underplaying in early scenes, effectively submerge the Heston image fostered by his earlier epix.

Assisting Harrison's verbal whiplashes are the grandiose engineering plans of the architect Bramante, then engaged in building the new basilica of St Peter. Harry Andrews excels in the role, while his protege, the painter Raphael, played by Thomas Milian, projects very well as Heston's possible replacement.

☐ 1965: Nominations: Best Color Cinematography, Color Costume Design, Color Art Direction, Original Music Score, Sound

. . . .

■ AIR AMERICA

1990, 112 MINS, US ◇ ▼ ⊙

Dir Roger Spottiswoode   *Prod* Daniel Melnick   *Scr* John Eskow, Richard Rush   *Ph* Roger Deakins   *Ed* John Bloom, Lois Freeman-Fox   *Mus* Charles Gross   *Art Dir* Allan Cameron
● Mel Gibson, Robert Downey Jr, Nancy Travis, Ken Jenkins, David Marshall Grant, Lane Smith (Carolco)

Spectacular action sequences and engaging perfs by Mel Gibson and Robert Downey Jr make this big-budgeter entertaining and provocative.

It's probably news to most even at this late date that the CIA, through its proprietary Air

America, was using drug money to finance the war in Southeast Asia and condoning the refining and exportation of heroin both to GIs in that part of the world and to the American public. Air America became known as 'a dope airline', as Christopher Robbins' 1979 source book puts it, and the filmmakers don't shrink from showing Gibson knowingly flying opium and cynically justifying it as essential to the US war effort.

Starting off as a reckless radio station helicopter pilot in a wild stunt sequence on an LA freeway in 1969, Downey is recruited by the CIA to perform his hair-raising flying feats for Uncle Sam in Laos, where oxymoronic military intelligence officer David Marshall Grant insists, 'We're not actually here.'

With his reported $35 million budget and a vast army of tech assistants to help carry out the stunt flying and crashes on the atmospheric Thailand locations, director Roger Spottiswoode does an efficient job in marshaling his forces and walking the thin line required to keep a black comedy from becoming gruesome or flippant.

. . . .

■ AIR FORCE

1943, 124 MINS, US ▼

Dir Howard Hawks   *Prod* Hal B. Wallis   *Scr* Dudley Nichols   *Ph* James Wong Howe   *Ed* George Amy   *Mus* Franz Waxman   *Art Dir* John Hughes
● John Ridgely, Gig Young, Arthur Kennedy, Harry Carey, Charles Drake, John Garfield (Warner)

Air Force is the saga of a Flying Fortress (the *Mary Ann*, a Boeing B-17). It is gripping, informative, entertaining, thrilling. It is a patriotic heart-throb in celluloid without preaching; it is inspirational without being phoney in it emotions.

Perhaps the best known cast component is John Garfield and it's the more effective that the principals are not as well known. John Ridgely is Capt Quincannon and Gig Young his co-pilot, both capital. Arthur Kennedy plays the bombardier; Charles Drake gives new and usually not suspected importance to the navigator's role in a Flying Fortress. Harry Carey gives a corking performance as the veteran crew chief, a career sgt from way back.

Ray Montgomery is the asst radio operator, and the surly Sgt Winocki, aerial gunner, is excellently played by John Garfield. Having flunked out as a flying officer, Garfield looks forward to three weeks hence, when his enlistment is over, but of course the Pearl Harbor debacle regenerates him into a vindictive American who stays on indef.

☐ 1943: Best Editing.
☐ Nominations: Best Original Screenplay, B&W Cinematography, Special Effects

. . . .

■ AIR MAIL

1932, 85 MINS, US

Dir John Ford   *Prod* Carl Laemmle Jr   *Scr* Dale Van Every, Frank W. Wead   *Ph* Karl Freund
● Pat O'Brien, Ralph Bellamy, Russell Hopton, Slim Summerville, Gloria Stuart, Lilian Bond (Universal)

Picture is a fund of interesting atmosphere about the air mail service. Radio exchanges are coming in and going out all the time, couched in technical language such as 'Visibility zero, ceiling zero. Caution to all planes.' It's interesting enough, but in essence the producer has dramatized the air mail service first and slipped in a human story as a second thought.

Duke Talbot (Pat O'Brien) is a great flyer and the bravest of the brave, in the air or on the ground. But he's a vainglorious show-off for one thing and a double-crossing lover. His disreputable affair with the wife of one of his service mates earns him the enmity of Mike Miller (Ralph Bellamy), in charge of the Desert Station post in the heart of the Rocky

Mountains. When the betrayed husband is killed during a flight through a violent storm, Duke declines to take his mail on to the next stage, in order to elope with the wife, now free. Instead he allows Mike to take the trip, although Mike has eye trouble that makes the journey especially hazardous.

The stunt stuff is breathtaking. There are long sequences of Duke surveying the terrain from a plane, vast stretches of jagged mountains involving hair-raising stunt flying, apparently within scant feet of peaks and rugged cliffs.

Slim Summerville turns in a capable performance in a comedy relief role while O'Brien and Bellamy give strong, simple handling to the main roles. Gloria Stuart is a pale heroine in a pale part. Lilian Bond does the more spirited playing in an unsympathetic role.

• •

■ AIRPLANE!

1980, 88 MINS, US ◇ ⑫ ⊙
Dir Jim Abrahams, David Zucker, Jerry Zucker   *Prod* Jon Davison   *Scr* Jim Abrahams, David Zucker, Jerry Zucker   *Ph* Joseph Biroc   *Ed* Patrick Kennedy   *Mus* Elmer Bernstein   *Art Dir* Ward Preston
● Robert Hays, Julie Hagerty, Lloyd Bridges, Peter Graves, Leslie Nielsen, Robert Stack (Paramount)

Airplane! is what they used to call a laff-riot. Made by team which turned out *Kentucky Fried Movie*, this spoof of disaster features beats any other film for sheer number of comic gags.

Writer-directors leave no cliche unturned as they lay waste to the *Airport*-style disaster cycle, among other targets. From the clever *Jaws* take-off opening to the final, irreverent title card, laughs come thick and fast.

Plot has former pilot Robert Hays, now terrified of flying due to wartime malfeasance, boarding an LA-to-Chicago flight in pursuit of ex-girlfriend stewardess Julie Hagerty.

When flight personnel, including sexually-deviant pilot Peter Graves and co-pilot Kareem Abdul-Jabbar, contract food poisoning on board, Hays is called upon to land the craft safely, an effort not made easier by fact that air controller Lloyd Bridges is completely crazed.

• •

■ AIRPLANE II THE SEQUEL

1982, 85 MINS, US ◇ ⑫ ⊙
Dir Ken Finkleman   *Prod* Howard W. Koch   *Scr* Ken Finkleman   *Ph* Joseph Biroc   *Ed* Dennis Virkler   *Mus* Elmer Bernstein   *Art Dir* William Sandell
● Robert Hays, Julie Hagerty, Lloyd Bridges, Peter Graves, William Shatner, Chad Everett (Paramount)

It can't be said that *Airplane II* is no better or worse than its predecessor. It is far worse, but might seem funnier had there been no original.

In the first *Airplane*, Jim Abrahams, David Zucker and Jerry Zucker had a fresh satiric crack at that hoary old genre, the airborne disaster film. But they wisely chose not to tackle a sequel, leaving incoming writer-director Ken Finkleman a tough task for his feature debut.

Robert Hays is still solid as the fearful pilot destined to take the controls. Ditto his daffy girlfriend Julie Hagerty. But instead of their hilariously earnest efforts the first time around, they seem (perhaps subconsciously) too aware what they're doing is supposed to be funny.

Peter Graves remains amusing as the captain with a fondness for naughty talk with young boys. Among those with nothing much to do are Raymond Burr, Sonny Bono, Chuck Connors, John Dehner, Rip Torn and Chad Everett. Among those with too much to do is William Shatner.

• •

■ AIRPORT

1970, 137 MINS, US ◇ ⑫ ⊙
Dir George Seaton   *Prod* Ross Hunter   *Scr* George Seaton   *Ph* Ernest Laszlo   *Ed* Stuart Gilmore   *Mus* Alfred Newman   *Art Dir* Alexander Golitzen, Preston Ames
● Burt Lancaster, Dean Martin, Jean Seberg, Jacqueline Bisset, George Kennedy, Helen Hayes (Universal)

Based on the novel by Arthur Hailey, over-produced by Ross Hunter with a cast of stars as long as a jet runway, and adapted and directed by George Seaton in a glossy, slick style, *Airport* is a handsome, often dramatically involving $10 million epitaph to a by-gone brand of filmmaking.

However, the ultimate dramatic situation of a passenger-loaded jet liner with a psychopathic bomber aboard that has to be brought into a blizzard-swept airport with runway blocked by a snow-stalled plane actually does not create suspense because the audience knows how it's going to end.

As the cigar chomping, bull boss of the maintenance men, George Kennedy gives a strong portrayal. But here again there's not a moment of plot doubt that he is going to get that stuck plane cleared off the runway in time for the emergency landing.
□ 1970: Best Supp. Actress (Helen Hayes).
□ Nominations: Best Picture, Supp Actress (Maureen Stapleton), Screenplay, Cinematography, Costume Design, Art Direction, Editing, Original Score, Sound

• •

■ AIRPORT '80 - THE CONCORDE

See: The Concorde - Airport '79

• •

■ AIRPORT 1975

1974, 106 MINS, US ◇ ⑫
Dir Jack Smight   *Prod* William Frye   *Scr* Don Ingalls   *Ph* Philip Lathrop   *Ed* J. Terry Williams   *Mus* John Cacavas   *Art Dir* George C. Webb
● Charlton Heston, Karen Black, George Kennedy, Efrem Zimbalist Jr, Susan Clark, Gloria Swanson (Universal)

Airport 1975 gathers its specimens into a 747 jetliner which collides mid-air with a private plane, precipitating a complicated rescue effort. Charlton Heston's formula characterization is, quite literally, Messiah-exmachina.

Don Ingalls is credited with the scripture, 'inspired' (as the crawl says) by Ross Hunter's 1970 pic which, in turn, came from Arthur Hailey's novel. Jack Smight's direction has the refreshing pace of a filmmaker who knows his plot can crash unless he hurries.

The redundant script massaging of the 747's elaborate backup controls, safety features and all those other yum-yum goodies that airlines keep yacking about would suggest that some of the dialog was written by Boeing.

• •

■ AIRPORT '77

(Aka: Airport III)

1977, 113 MINS, US ◇ ⑫
Dir Jerry Jameson   *Prod* William Frye   *Scr* Michael Scheff, David Spector   *Ph* Philip Lathrop   *Ed* J. Terry Williams, Robert Watts   *Mus* John Cacavas   *Art Dir* George C. Webb
● Jack Lemmon, Lee Grant, Brenda Vaccaro, Joseph Cotten, Olivia de Havilland, James Stewart (Universal)

Charlton Heston either busy elsewhere or exhausted from earthquakes, World War II and previous aerial disasters, Jack Lemmon assumed the Noah lead in *Airport '77*. This time around, a giant private jet gets hijacked and crashes off the Florida coast.

The story's formula banality is credible most of the time and there's some good actual US Navy search and rescue procedure interjected in the plot.

The story peg here [by H.A.L. Craig and Charles Kuenstle] has James Stewart, billionaire who has converted his home to museum status, loading his private plane with priceless paintings and a broader quality of people for a junket to the estate. However, Lemmon's copilot Robert Foxworth has joined with Monte Markham and Michael Pataki to hijack the plane for the artwork.
□ 1977: Nominations: Best Costume Design, Art Direction

• •

■ AIRPORT THE CONCORDE

See: The Concorde - Airport '79

• •

■ AIRPORT III

See: Airport '77

• •

■ AKENFIELD

1975, 95 MINS, UK ◇ ⑫
Dir Peter Hall   *Prod* Peter Hall, Rex Pyke   *Scr* Ronald Blythe   *Ph* Ivan Strasberg   *Mus* Michael Tippett   *Art Dir* Ian Whittaker, Roger Christian
● Garrow Shand, Peggy Cole, Barbara Tilney, Lyn Brooks, Ida Page, Ted Dedman (Angle Films)

Adapted from Ronald Blythe's social study of a Suffolk village, this is the story of three generations of farm laboring, intercutting flashbacks with present day to demonstrate that the more things change, the more they remain the same. It is funny and touching and seldom less than engrossing.

A virtue is that Hall has not idealized the subject. Throughout there's a strong current of melancholy, of dreams crushed and human potential stunted. Though it's not a despairing film, one is apt to feel that Suffolk's a lovely place to visit – only.

Ivan Strasberg's color photography, using only natural light (even indoors), is one of the conspicuous delights. His composition of the rolling English countryside is often lyrical, sometimes magical.

• •

■ ALADDIN

1992, 90 MINS, US ◇ ⑫ ⊙
Dir John Musker, Ron Clements   *Prod* John Musker, Ron Clements   *Scr* Ron Clements, John Musker, Ted Elliott, Terry Rossio   *Ed* H. Lee Peterson   *Mus* Alan Menken   *Art Dir* R.S. Vander Wende (Walt Disney)

Floridly beautiful, shamelessly derivative and infused with an irreverent, sophisticated comic flair thanks to Robin Williams' vocal calisthenics, *Aladdin* represents the ultimate synthesis of filmmaking and marketing, extracting winning elements from Disney's last two animated hits (*The Little Mermaid* and *Beauty and the Beast*) as well as more venerable sources, particularly the 1940 *Thief of Bagdad*.

Lyricist Tim Rice filled in seamlessly on three of the six songs after Howard Ashman's death, and while Alan Menken's score may not be as instantly hummable as *Beauty*'s, it's still impressive, with two show-stoppingly elaborate numbers.

Aladdin (voiced by Scott Weinger, sung by Brad Kane) is a thief and a street urchin who stumbles across the defiant and anachronistically liberated Princess Jasmine (Linda Larkin/Lea Salonga), who flees the palace to escape a law dictating that she must marry a prince.

The bad guy, functional if not one of the great Disney villains, is the Sultan's adviser Jafar (Jonathan Freeman), a sorcerer who recruits Aladdin to help claim the magic lamp from a huge cave hidden in the desert. The narrative moves somewhat unevenly before the kid uncorks William at which point things kick into another level.
□ 1992: Best Original Score, Song ('A Whole New World').

□ Nominations: Best Song ('Friends Like Me'), Sound, Sound Effects Editing

....

■ ALAMO, THE

1960, 192 MINS, US ◇ ⊛ ⊙
Dir John Wayne, [John Ford] *Prod* John Wayne
Scr James Edward Grant *Ph* William H. Clothier
Ed Stuart Gilmore *Mus* Dimitri Tiomkin *Art Dir* Alfred Ybarra
● John Wayne, Richard Widmark, Laurence Harvey, Frankie Avalon, Richard Boone, Linda Cristal (Batjac)

The Alamo, which was shot in 91 days at a stated cost of $12 million, has a good measure of mass appeal in its 192 minutes. But to get it, producer-director-star John Wayne has loaded the telling of the tale with happy homilies on American virtues and patriotic platitudes under life-and-death fire which smack of yesteryear theatricalism rather than the realism of modern battle drama.

Obviously Wayne and James Edward Grant, who penned the original screenplay, had an entertainment, not a history lesson, in mind. But in their zeal to reproduce a colorful, homespun account of what went on in the course of those 13 remarkable days in 1836, they have somehow shrouded some of the fantastic facts of the original with some of the frivolous fancies of their re-creation.

In spite of the painstaking attempts to explore the characters of the picture's three principal heroes (Bowie, Crockett, Travis), there is an absence of emotional feeling, of a sense of participation. It is almost as if the writer is willing to settle for the popular conception of familiar heroes such as Davy Crockett and Jim Bowie as sufficient explanation of their presence and activities.

With the rousing battle sequence at the climax (for which a goodly share of credit must go to second unit director Cliff Lyons) the picture really commands rapt attention.

It is as actor that Wayne functions under his own direction in his least successful capacity. Generally playing with one expression on his face, he seems at times to be acting like a man with $12 million on his conscience. Both Widmark and Harvey suffer minor lapses in their performances but there is vigor and color in them. Younger players Frankie Avalon and Patrick Wayne show spirit.
□ 1960: Best Sound (Samuel Goldwyn Studio Sound Dept, Todd A-O Sound Dept).
□ Nominations: Best Picture, Supp. Actor (Chill Wills), Color Cinematography, Editing, Score of a Dramatic Picture, Song ('The Green Leaves of Summer')

....

■ ALAMO BAY

1985, 98 MINS, US ◇ ⊛ ⊙
Dir Louis Malle *Prod* Louis Malle, Vincent Malle
Scr Alice Arlen *Ph* Curtis Clark *Ed* James Bruce
Mus Ry Cooder *Art Dir* Trevor Williams
● Amy Madigan, Ed Harris, Ho Nguyen, Donald Moffat, Truyen V. Tran, Rudy Young (Tri-Star/Delphi III)

Alamo Bay is a failed piece of social consciousness. The peripatetic Louis Malle hasn't managed to shed any meaningful light on his current subject, that of the conflict between refugee Vietnamese and local fisherfolk around Galveston Bay, Texas, circa 1979–81.

Malle dared to place an exceedingly unsympathetic character at the center of his drama. Here it is Ed Harris, a bruising, philandering, unreflective lout who resents the intrusion of Vietnamese into his community and final resorts to the easiest method of dealing with them, i.e. brutal, illegal violence.

Scene-setting is devoted to the native whites and newcomer Asians trying to fish the same waters, with the whites becoming increasingly irritated as the Vietnamese, in their view, horn in on their traditional territory, and work for lower wages to boot.

Mixed in with this is a re-ignition of a romance between Harris and Amy Madigan, latter being the daughter of controversial fish factory operat Donald Moffat and now at odds politically with her former boy friend.

On the other side of the fence is new arrival Ho Nguyen, who at first wears a permanent, subservient smile in hopes of ingratiating himself, but later refuses to be intimidated along with the rest of his people.

....

■ ALBERT, R.N.

(US: Break for Freedom)

1953, 88 MINS, UK
Dir Lewis Gilbert *Prod* Daniel M. Angel *Scr* Vernon Harris, Guy Morgan *Ph* Jack Asher *Ed* Charles Hasse
Mus Malcolm Arnold *Art Dir* Bernard Robinson
● Anthony Steel, Jack Warner, Robert Beatty, William Sylvester, Guy Middleton, Anton Diffring (Eros)

The setting is a German camp for Allied naval officers, the action taking place late in 1944. The camp is regarded by its German masters as escape-proof and admittedly various attempts to breakout have been frustrated by alert prison guards. That is until one of the internees hits on the idea of making a dummy to cover up for an absentee. The result is 'Albert, R.N.' with a papier mache head and a wire-framed body.

Camp atmosphere is effective. There is plenty of talk about women but it is an all-male cast. The main problem is the battle against monotony and for liberty.

A solid all-round cast admirably fits into the plot [from the play by Guy Morgan and Edwar Sammis]. Anthony Steel handsomely suggests the young artist responsible for the creation of 'Albert' and Jack Warner is reliably cast as the senior British officer who maintains discipline with understanding in the camp. Frederick Valk is a sympathetic camp commandant, but Anton Diffring suggests the typical ruthless Nazi type.

....

■ AL CAPONE

1959, 105 MINS, US ⊛
Dir Richard Wilson *Prod* John Burrows, Leonard Ackerman *Scr* Malvin Wald, Henry F. Greenberg
Ph Lucien Ballard *Ed* Walter Hannemann *Mus* David Raksin *Art Dir* Hilyard Brown
● Rod Steiger, Fay Spain, James Gregory, Martin Balsam, Nehemiah Persoff, Murvyn Vye (Allied Artists)

A tough, ruthless and generally unsentimental account of the most notorious gangster of the prohibition-repeal era, *Al Capone* is also a very well-made picture. There isn't much 'motivation' given for Capone, at least not in the usual sense. But the screenplay does supply reasons and they are more logical than the usual once-over-lightly on the warped youth bit.

Capone, played by Rod Steiger, is shown as an amoral personality with a native genius for leadership and organization. He became rich and famous in a way that seemed to him dandy. Nobody was more genuinely surprised than Capone when the revulsion his acts caused finally overwhelmed him.

The story picks up when Steiger is brought to Chicago as a low-grade torpedo by a fellow countryman (Nehemiah Persoff) to act as bouncer in his gambling establishment. Capone begins his rise when he murders the local political boss (Joe DeSantis), and eventually takes over Persoff's territory, on the latter's retirement. He teams with Bugs Moran and Dion O'Banion, to divide Chicago into territories.

Steiger's performance is mostly free of obvious technique, getting inside the character both physically and emotionally. Fay Spain has a role, that of the romantic attachment of Capone's life, that is probably more distracting than helpful. But she plays well. James Gregory as the honest cop, Martin Balsam as

the dishonest reporter and Persoff as Capone's mentor, give skillful performances.

....

■ ALEXANDER'S RAGTIME BAND

1938, 105 MINS, US
Dir Henry King *Prod* Harry Joe Brown (assoc.)
Scr Kathryn Scola, Lamar Trotti *Ph* Peverell Marley
Ed Barbara McLean *Mus* Alfred Newman (dir.)
Art Dir Bernard Herzbrun, Boris Leven
● Tyrone Power, Alice Faye, Don Ameche, Ethel Merman, Jack Haley, Jean Hersholt (20th Century-Fox)

Irving Berlin's *Alexander's Ragtime Band* is a grand filmusical which stirs and thrills, a medley of more than 30 pieces, selected from some 600 which Berlin has composed.

Although the story opens back in 1911, the narrative moves swiftly through the years. None of the characters ages a single grey hair in 25 years.

Richard Sherman conceived the story idea with a central figure, a San Francisco bandmaster who adopts the name of Alexander. It is strictly fiction with only slight similarity to the Berlin biog. The screenplay is a fine piece of work in its subtle and logical inclusions of the Berlin ballads. Henry King directs with humor and sentiment, letting loose with an occasional broadside of mass movement.

Berlin supervised the musical angles and, in addition, tossed off three new numbers, 'Now It Can Be told', 'My Walking Stick' and 'Marching Along with Time'.

In the foreground are Tyrone Power, as Alexander; Alice Faye; and Don Ameche, who carries most of the story with an occasional song number of his own. Cast is heavy with featured names. Although Ethel Merman is a late entry into the proceedings, she sings and acts excellently. Jack Haley shows advantageously in comedy.
□ 1938: Best Score (Alfred Newman).
□ Nominations: Best Picture, Original Story (Irving Berlin), Art Direction, Editing, Song ('Now It Can Be Told')

....

■ ALEXANDER THE GREAT

1956, 143 MINS, US ◇ ⊛
Dir Robert Rossen *Prod* Robert Rossen *Scr* Robert Rossen *Ph* Robert Krasker *Ed* Ralph Kemplen
Mus Mario Nascimbene *Art Dir* Andre Andrejew
● Richard Burton, Fredric March, Claire Bloom, Danielle Darrieux, Harry Andrews, Stanley Baker (Rossen/United Artists)

It took Alexander the Great some 10 years to conquer the known world back in the fourth century B.C. It seems to take Robert Rossen almost as long to recreate on film this slice of history. Despite the length, however, he has fashioned a spectacle tremendous size.

Written, produced and directed by Rossen, the presentation is neither niggardly in the coin lavished on its physical makeup nor in the outlay for the talented international cast that enacts the historical saga of a man who believed both that he was a god and in his destiny to unite the world.

Rossen is not always able to hold interest in his story and action, resulting in some long, dull stretches.

Nor do the players have much chance to be more than puppets against the giant sweep of the spectacle. There are a number of single scenes that give the individual characters a chance to grow.

Alexander's romance with Barsine (Claire Bloom) is more implied than realized, but she does have some fine, expressive moments.

....

■ ALEX AND THE GYPSY

1976, 99 MINS, US ◇
Dir John Korty *Prod* Richard Shepherd *Scr* Lawrence B. Marcus *Ph* Bill Butler *Ed* Donn Cambern
Mus Henry Mancini

● Jack Lemmon, Genevieve Bujold, James Woods, Gino Ardito, Robert Emhardt, Joseph X. Flaherty (20th Century-Fox)

Alex and the Gypsy is a cynical, distasteful film, full of grubby characters and situations.

Jack Lemmon stars as a burned-out tank-town bailbondsman still hung up on the gypsy girl (Genevieve Bujold) who long ago jilted him, but now needs his professional help. John Korty's direction brings out the pervasive and repulsive nihilism in the story and its people.

Lawrence B. Marcus has adapted Stanley Elkin's novella, *The Bailbondsman*, into a caterwauling and strident script lacking empathy, interest, humanity and punch. When Bujold is arrested for assault on her lover, Lemmon grudgingly (and partly sadistically) bails her out, knowing that they must be in close contact if he is to get his money back. They scream a lot, reminisce a lot, cavort about the countryside a lot.

■ ALEX IN WONDERLAND

1970, 110 MINS, US ◇

Dir Paul Mazursky *Prod* Larry Tucker *Scr* Paul Mazursky *Ph* Laszlo Kovacs *Ed* Stuart H. Pappe *Mus* Tom O'Horgan *Art Dir* Pato Guzman
● Donald Sutherland, Ellen Burstyn, Meg Mazursky, Glenna Sergent, Viola Spolin, Federico Fellini (M-G-M)

This fictional account of the personal and professional travails of a hotshot film director, played by Donald Sutherland, is partly admirable, partly realized, but also partly dull and somewhat deja vu to boot.

Sutherland is brought to a big studio after what must be presumed to be the sort of flop d'estime that has 'uncovered' many a real-life counterpart. With wife, played superbly by Ellen Burstyn, and children, Meg Mazursky and Glenna Sergent, Sutherland attempts to retain his integrity amid the trappings of fame and too-expensive Beverly Hills living accommodations.

Shortly into the film, however, Sutherland's character becomes as secondary as the various vignettes become all-too-overpowering. Perhaps Sutherland's man never had much to begin with.

■ ALFIE

1966, 114 MINS, UK ◇

Dir Lewis Gilbert *Prod* Lewis Gilbert *Scr* Bill Naughton *Ph* Otto Heller *Ed* Thelma Connell *Mus* Sonny Rollins *Art Dir* Peter Mullins
● Michael Caine, Shelley Winters, Millicent Martin, Julia Foster, Jane Asher, Shirley Anne Field (Sheldrake)

Alfie pulls few punches. With Michael Caine giving a powerfully strong performance as the woman-mad anti-hero, and with dialog and situations that are humorous, tangy, raw and, ultimately, often moving, the film may well shock. But behind its alley-cat philosophy, there's some shrewd sense, some pointed barbs and a sharp moral.

One of the biggest chances that the film takes is in its frequent use of the direct speech approach to the audience. This does not always come off in the picture as well as it used to do with Groucho in the old Marx Bros films. But the device served well enough in Bill Naughton's play, and does here.

Story concerns a glib, cynical young Cockney whose passion in life is chasing dames of all shape sizes, and dispositions, providing they are accommodating. The film traces the promiscuous path of this energetic young amoralist as he flits from one to the other without finding much lasting pleasure. In fact, he finishes up as a somewhat jaded, cutprice Lothario, disillusioned but still on the chase.

Caine brings persuasiveness, and a sardonic, thoroughly shabby and humorous charm to the role. The two best performances

among the women come from Julia Foster, becomingly wistful throughout, and Vivien Merchant as the married woman who suffers an abortion.
□ 1966: Nominations: Best Picture, Actor (Michael Caine), Supp. Actress (Vivien Merchant), Screenplay, Song ('Alfie')

■ ALFRED THE GREAT

1969, 122 MINS, UK ◇ ⓥ

Dir Clive Donner *Prod* Bernard Smith, James R. Webb *Scr* Ken Taylor, James R. Webb *Ph* Alex Thomson *Ed* Fergus McDonell *Mus* Raymond Leppard *Art Dir* Michael Stringer
● David Hemmings, Michael York, Prunella Ransome, Colin Blakely, Julian Glover, Ian McKellen (M-G-M)

Idea was to show that Alfred, Prince of Wessex, who became the first and only British King to be called 'Great', was not just a guy who burned the cakes.

He was the man who wanted to be a priest and only became a warrior against his will. He 'invented' the British Navy. He raised the standards of education and brought new laws to his subjects. But most of these facts have got lost in heavy-handed script.

Result is a film which hasn't the power or the passion to be a lavish historic film saga. Hints of the man's personality are given but they are sandwiched between two or three well staged hand-to-hand battles between Alfred's troops and the marauding Danes.

David Hemmings plays the title role with intelligence, and does his best to suggest the inner complexities of the man, but he is under age for the role and rarely matches the stature of the man he is portraying.

■ ALGIERS

1938, 93 MINS, US ⓥ

Dir John Cromwell *Prod* Walter Wanger *Scr* John Howard Lawson, James M. Cain *Ph* James Wong Howe *Ed* Otho Lovering, William Reynolds *Mus* Vincent Scott, Mohammed Igorbouchen *Art Dir* Alexander Toluboff
● Charles Boyer, Hedy Lamarr, Sigrid Gurie, Joseph Calleia, Gene Lockhart, Alan Haleei (Wanger/United Artists)

Charles Boyer creates an interesting portrait of a continental gangster, jewel thief and tough guy in *Algiers*. Other meritorious aspects include John Cromwell's direction and the first appearance in an American-made film of Hedy Lamarr, the alluring natatorial star of the much-censored *Ecstasy*.

Film is a remake of *Pepe le Moko* (1937), a French picture directed by Julien Duvivier in which Jean Gabin starred. Wanger purchased the world rights, retired the prints from the domestic field, and assigned John Howard Lawson to write the English adaptation.

Boyer is a Parisian youth who is hunted by police and finally located in the native section of Algiers. So long as he stays within the prescribed area and lives and moves among the natives, without attempting escape to the European section, he is allowed his liberty. Police informants report his whereabouts; an inspector of detectives is his confidante; yet he dares not show himself outside.

At this juncture Boyer meets Lamarr, a beautiful Parisian girl who falls madly in love with him. She cannot remain in the restricted section; to possess her he must escape and return to Paris.

In performances by a fine cast, Lamarr comes next to Boyer in a photo finish. On the side of the unrelenting police is Joseph Calleia, as the inspector. Gene Lockhart is a stand-out as one of the informers.
□ 1938: Nominations: Best Actor (Charles Boyer), Supp. Actor (Gene Lockhart), Cinematography, Art Direction

■ ALIBI

1929, 90 MINS, US

Dir Roland West *Prod* Roland West *Scr* Roland West, C. Gardner Sullivan *Ph* Ray June *Mus* Hugo Riesenfeld
● Chester Morris, Harry Stubbs, Mae Busch, Eleanor Griffith, Irma Harrison, Regis Toomey (United Artists/Roland West)

Jolt-packed crook melodrama in dialog. Lots of reliable excitement, de luxe production values and general audience satisfaction.

From the human interest standpoint picture belongs to Chester Morris, virile stage juvenile. In this picture he is a cruel, cold-blooded gangster.

Alibi starts out to give the cops the losing end of an expository tract on brutality. It winds up by hinting that the gendarmes have to be tough. Morris impersonates a clever young rodent with the instincts of a Chinese brigand. Picture is dedicated to the proposition that the man with a gun is a dirty name to start with.

There are loose ends and desultory passages in *Alibi*, but in general it has tempo and is punched with some gripping sequences. Police atmosphere and detail have realism and the ring of authenticity.

Roland West is the only entirely independent producer releasing through United Artists. He can sleep in peace in the security that his investment is safe and his picture there.
□ 1928/29: Nominations: Best Picture, Actor (Chester Morris)

■ ALICE

1990, 106 MINS, US ◇ ⓥ

Dir Woody Allen *Prod* Robert Greenhut *Scr* Woody Allen *Ph* Carlo Di Palma *Ed* Susan E. Morse *Art Dir* Santo Loquasto
● Mia Farrow, Joe Mantegna, Alec Baldwin, Blythe Danner, Judy Davis, William Hurt (Orion)

If *Stardust Memories* was Woody Allen's $8^1/_2$ and *Radio Days* his *Amarcord*, then *Alice* is his *Juliet of the Spirits*. It's a subtler, gentler retelling of Federico Fellini's tale of a pampered but unappreciated housewife who learns to shed her illusions by giving in to her fantasies.

In quick, hilarious strokes, Allen introduces Alice (Mia Farrow), who's been married 16 years to ultra-successful businessman William Hurt. Though her deepest daily concerns are gossip, decorators, fitness trainers, Bergdorf Goodman and pedicures, she feels a kinship with Mother Theresa.

But sudden fantasies about a divorced father (Joe Mantegna) at her kids' school and a trip to an unorthodox herbalist-acupuncturist (Keye Luke) set off a chain of sexual, mystical, frequently comic events.

Performances are strong all around, with a succession of top actors making the most of their brief turns. Alec Baldwin is Farrow's first love, who turns up in a surprising way; Bernadette Peters does some of her best film work in about two minute on screen; Luke is the gruff-voiced, chain-smoking healer; and Gwen Verdon and Blythe Danner are Farrow's mom and sister, respectively. But the center of the pic is Farrow, who's funny and touching.
□ 1990: Nomination: Best Original Screenplay

■ ALICE ADAMS

1935, 95 MINS, US ⓥ ⊙

Dir George Stevens *Prod* Pandro S. Berman *Scr* Dorothy Yost, Mortimer Offner, Jane Murfin *Ph* Robert De Grasse *Ed* Jane Loring *Mus* Max Steiner
● Katharine Hepburn, Fred MacMurray, Fred Stone, Evelyn Venable, Frank Albertson, Ann Shoemaker (RKO)

Translating Booth Tarkington's sometimes poignant and pathetic 1921 novel of the pretending, wistful Alice, whose economic background almost proves too much of a hurdle to surmount, must have been a yeoman task. That George Stevens' direction captures the wistfulness of Katharine Hepburn's superb histrionism, and yet has not sacrificed audience values at the altar of too much drabness and prosaic realism, is an achievement of no small order.

The star's own performance is uncompromising and unvacillating. If she's a silly little ninny in her pretenses and simple pretexes, she is permitted to run almost berserk on the petty inanities of small-town aspirations.

Ann Shoemaker, as the ambitious but firm and understanding mother, is effective contrast to Fred Stone's cinematic debut performance as the thankful-for-small-favors head of the Adams household.

Likewise, good taste in Evelyn Venable's rich girl's aspirant for Fred McMurray, principal juve, is shown in not toughening up the role unnecessarily.

☐ 1935: Nominations: Best Picture, Actress (Katharine Hepburn)

• • • • • • • • • • • • • • • • • • • •

■ ALICE DOESN'T LIVE HERE ANYMORE

1974, 112 MINS, US ◇ ⓥ ⊙
Dir Martin Scorsese *Prod* David Susskind, Audrey Maas *Scr* Robert Getchell *Ph* Kent L. Wakeford *Ed* Marcia Lucas *Mus* Richard LaSalle *Art Dir* Toby Carr Rafelson
● Ellen Burstyn, Kris Kristofferson, Billy Green Bush, Diane Ladd, Lelia Goldoni, Harvey Keitel (Warner)

Alice Doesn't Live Here Anymore takes a group of wellcast film players and largely wastes them on a smaller-than-life film – one of those 'little people' dramas that make one despise little people.

Script establishes Ellen Burstyn as the lovingly slovenly wife of Billy Green Bush, who gets killed near their New Mexico tract home. Burstyn decides to return to her long-ago Monterey origins.

Burstyn's young fatherless child is played to excruciating repulsiveness by Alfred Lutter. The pair wander westward through the story. Burstyn resumes her singing career as a saloon entertainer, then a waitress, as assorted minor characters come and go.

Eventually, just over an hour into the proceedings enter Kris Kristofferson. The last half of the film is, indeed, a picture; but as a whole it's a distended bore.

☐ 1974: Best Actress (Ellen Burstyn).
☐ Nominations: Best Supp. Actress (Diane Ladd), Original Screenplay

• • • • • • • • • • • • • • • • • • • •

■ ALICE IN WONDERLAND

1951, 74 MINS, US ◇ ⓥ ⊙
Dir Clyde Geronimi, Hamilton Luske, Wilfred Jackson *Prod* Ben Sharpsteen (sup.) *Scr* Winston Hibler, Bill Peet, Joe Rinaldi, Bill Cottrell, Joe Grant, Del Connell, Ted Sears, Erdman Penner, Milt Banta, Dick Kelsey, Dick Huemer, Tom Oreb, John Walbridge *Ed* Lloyd Richardson *Mus* Oliver Wallace (Walt Disney)

Walt Disney has gone a long way towards tightening the leisurely, haphazard adventure of Alice in the wonderland of her imagination. He has dropped some characters and sequences in the interest of a better picture, but the deletions are not missed.

The Mad Hatter, the March Hare, the Caterpillar, the Cheshire Cat, Tweedle Dee and Tweedle Dum, the White Rabbit, the Walrus and the Carpenter, the Queen of Hearts and other remembered characters are enchantingly projected as Alice strolls through her dream world to the accompaniment of ballads and musical nonsense.

Young Kathryn Beaumont enchants as the voice of Alice, Ed Wynn (Mad Hatter), Jerry Colonna (March Hare), Richard Haydn (Caterpillar, a particular standout in his smoke-ring alphabet scene with Alice), Sterling Holloway (Cheshire Cat), Bill Thompson (White Rabbit), Pat O'Malley (Tweedle Twins) and Verna Felton (Queen of Hearts) are among those whose tonal tricks help sell the pen-and-ink people.

☐ 1951: Nomination: Scoring of a Musical Picture

• • • • • • • • • • • • • • • • • • • •

■ ALICE'S ADVENTURES IN WONDERLAND

1972, 96 MINS, UK ◇ ⓥ
Dir William Sterling *Prod* Derek Horne *Scr* William Sterling *Ph* Geoffrey Unsworth *Ed* Peter Weatherley *Mus* John Barry *Art Dir* Michael Stringer
● Fiona Fullerton, Michael Crawford, Ralph Richardson, Flora Robson, Peter Sellers, Robert Helpmann (Fox-Rank)

Alice's Adventures in Wonderland, from the Lewis Carroll classic, is a major disappointment. Superior stylistic settings and often terrific process effects are largely wasted by the limp, lifeless pacing of adapter-director William Sterling.

The secret of family-film conception is providing interest to all age groups. Some such films forget teenagers and adults in favor of catering strictly to moppets. This film largely forgets all audience segments in favor of static tableaux and one-two-three-kick direction, and even the John Barry-Don Black score of 16 tunes is confined to key largo.

Fiona Fullerton is a pleasantly bland Alice as are all other players. The film just lies there, and dies there, for 96 minutes.

• • • • • • • • • • • • • • • • • • • •

■ ALICE'S RESTAURANT

1969, 111 MINS, US ◇ ⓥ
Dir Arthur Penn *Prod* Hillard Elkins, Joe Manduke *Scr* Venable Herndon, Arthur Penn *Ph* Michael Nebbia *Ed* Dede Allen *Mus* Arlo Guthrie *Art Dir* Warren Clymer
● Arlo Guthrie, Pat Quinn, James Broderick, Michael McClanathan, Geoff Outlaw, Tina Chen (United Artists/Florin)

Alice's Restaurant is the phantasmagorial account of the misadventures of a young folk singer in his brushes with the law and his draft board. Based on folk singer Arlo Guthrie's 18 minute, 20 second hit recording, 'Alice's Restaurant Massacree', in which he limned some of his real-life experiences, the whole is a rather weird collection of episodes losely strung together.

There are occasional flashes of wry humor and some rib-tickling sequences. But they are all too few.

The opening sequences particularly are too wispily-contrived to rivet full attention, their sole purpose seemingly to introduce Arlo as a very odd fellow indeed. Plotline is virtually nil.

Some of the acting is very good, but Arlo's performance is of the uncertain type and he appears to be living in a world of his own.

☐ 1969: Nomination: Best Director

• • • • • • • • • • • • • • • • • • • •

■ ALIEN

1979, 124 MINS, US ◇ ⓥ ⊙
Dir Ridley Scott *Prod* Gordon Carroll, David Giler, Walter Hill *Scr* Dan O'Bannon *Ph* Derek Vanlint *Ed* Terry Rawlings *Mus* Jerry Goldsmith *Art Dir* Michael Seymour
● Tom Skerritt, Sigourney Weaver, Veronica Cartwright, Harry Dean Stanton, John Hurt, Ian Holm (20th Century-Fox/Brandywine)

Plainly put, *Alien* is an old-fashioned scary movie set in a highly realistic sci-fi future, made all the more believable by expert technical craftsmanship[from a story by Dan O'Bannon and Ronald Shusett]. [Plot has several parallels with the 1958 lowbudgeter *It! The Terror from Beyond Space*.]

Director Ridley Scott, cameraman Derek Vanlint and composer Jerry Goldsmith propel the emotions relentlessly from one visual surprise – and horror – to the next.

There is very little involvement with the characters themselves.

Alien initially presents a mundane commercial spacecraft with crew members bitching and moaning about wages and conditions.

The tedium is shared by captain Tom Skerritt, his aide Sigourney Weaver and the rest of the crew, played by a generally good cast in cardboard roles.

Eventually, it is Weaver who gets the biggest chance and she carries it off well.

☐ 1979: Best Visual Effects.
☐ Nomination: Best Art Direction

• • • • • • • • • • • • • • • • • • • •

■ ALIEN NATION

1988, 94 MINS, US ◇ ⓥ ⊙
Dir Graham Baker *Prod* Gale Anne Hurd, Richard Kobritz *Scr* Rockne S. O'Bannon *Ph* Adam Greenberg *Ed* Kent Beyda, Don Brochu *Mus* Curt Sobel *Art Dir* Jack T. Collis
● James Caan, Mandy Patinkin, Terence Stamp, Kevin Major Howard, Leslie Bevins, Peter Jason (20th Century-Fox)

Solid performances by leads James Caan and his humanoid buddy-cop partner Mandy Patinkin move this production beyond special effects, clever alien makeup and car chases.

A whole culture of aliens, called 'newcomers', land in the Mojave desert in the 1990s and are allowed refuge by the US government as if they were Salvadorans or Vietnamese Boat People. Some are good, decent upstanding citizen types, others are just the opposite. They find America a land of ideological confusion. Americans speak of equality yet aren't consistent when it comes to acting on those beliefs.

Pic is handled by British director Graham Baker on a slightly more serious than comic book level. There's a lot of violence and noise in this futuristic adaptation of a drug pusher story, but also a compelling human-humanoid drama. Pic doesn't quite sustain a heart-pounding, eerie tone throughout.

• • • • • • • • • • • • • • • • • • • •

■ ALIENS

1986, 137 MINS, US ◇ ⓥ ⊙
Dir James Cameron *Prod* Gale Anne Hurd *Scr* James Cameron *Ph* Adrian Biddle *Ed* Ray Lovejoy *Mus* James Horner *Art Dir* Peter Lamont
● Sigourney Weaver, Carrie Henn, Michael Biehn, Lance Henriksen, Paul Reiser, Jenette Goldstein (20th Century-Fox/Brandywine)

Aliens proves a very worthy followup to Ridley Scott's 1979 sci-fi shocker, *Alien*. James Cameron's vault into the big time after scoring with the exploitation actioner *The Terminator* makes up for lack of surprise with sheer volume of thrills and chills – emphasis is decidedly on the plural aspect of the title.

Cameron [working from a story by him, David Giler and Walter Hill] picks up the thread 57 years later, when Sigourney Weaver and her cat (who have been in hibernation) are rescued by a deep space salvage team. The authorities ask her to accompany a team of marines back to the planet to investigate why all contact with the colony has suddenly been lost. Group sent this time consists of a bunch of tough grunts with a sour attitude about having been sent on such a dippy mission.

Weaver finds one human survivor – a cute, tough, terrified little girl played by Carrie Henn – on the planet.

The odds against the crew are, in a word, monstrous, and unsurprisingly, its members are dispatched one by one until it once again comes down to a battle royal between Weaver and one last monster.

A

Although film accomplishes everything it aims to do, overall impression is of a film made by an expert craftsman, while Scott clearly had something of an artist in him.

Weaver does a smashing job as Ripley. Henn is very appealing as the little girl and Jenette Goldstein makes a striking impression as a body-building recruit who is tougher than all of the guys in the outfit.

[A 1992 video release, with the handle *Special Edition*, featured an extra 17 mins of footage.]

□ 1986: Best Visual Effects, Sound Effects Editing.

□ Nominations: Best Actress (Sigourney Weaver), Art Direction, Editing, Original Music Score, Sound

• •

■ **ALIEN³**

1992, 115 MINS, US ◇ ⑫ ⊙

Dir David Fincher   *Prod* Gordon Carroll, David Giler, Walter Hill   *Scr* David Giler, Walter Hill, Larry Ferguson   *Ph* Alex Thomson   *Ed* Terry Rawlings   *Mus* Elliot Goldenthal   *Art Dir* Norman Reynolds
● Sigourney Weaver, Charles S. Dutton, Charles Dance, Paul McGann, Brian Glover, Ralph Brown (20th Century-Fox/Brandywine)

The shape-shifting *Alien* trilogy reverts back to the form of the first film in this third close encounter, a muddled effort offering little more than visual splendor to recommend it.

The action picks up in the opening credits where *Aliens* left off, as Ripley's hibernation pod crash-lands on a grim, all-male penal colony planet. It seems an alien egg was still on the shuttle (how is anybody's guess). In any event, Ripley (Weaver) finds herself stranded on a planet with a bunch of converted convicts who've embraced religion, led by Charles S. Dutton. The colony's kindly doctor (Charles Dance), with whom Ripley shares another kind of close encounter, suspects something is wrong.

Musicvideo director David Fincher doesn't reveal much finesse with actors in his big-screen debut, and the screenplay [based on a story by Vincent Ward, who was originally to have directed] proves fraught with lapses in reason, motivation and logic. Weaver's character is so encumbered with baggage that she can't really showcase the qualities (particularly evident in the second film) that made the audience empathize with her.

□ 1992: Nomination: Best Visual Effects

• •

■ **ALIVE**

1993, 127 MINS, US ◇ ⑫ ⊙

Dir Frank Marshall   *Prod* Robert Watts, Kathleen Kennedy   *Scr* John Patrick Shanley   *Ph* Peter James   *Ed* Michael Kahn, William Goldenberg   *Mus* James Newton Howard   *Art Dir* Norman Reynolds
● Ethan Hawke, Vincent Spano, Josh Hamilton, Bruce Ramsay, John Haymes Newton, David Kriegel (Touchstone/Paramount)

Producer-turned-director Frank Marshall and producer-partner-spouse Kathleen Kennedy have chosen the true story (already told by 1976 Par release *Survive!*) of a 1970s plane crash in which the survivors, a rugby team, held on for more than two months in the sub-freezing Andes largely by eating the corpses of the victims.

Marshall and writer John Patrick Shanley [adapting Piers Paul Read's book] deal with the topic seriously, exploring the survivors' desperation as well as their reluctance, down to an ethical debate prior to the initial meal, to engage in cannibalism.

It doesn't help that character personalities generally aren't distinct enough to keep track of who's who throughout the story, leaving the audience to empathize only generally. Heightening the problem is a strong resemblance among actors, including leads Ethan Hawke and Josh Hamilton.

For all its action elements, *Alive* also puts on some rather pretentious airs, among them a musical coda of *Ave Maria* and bookending an uncredited John Malkovich as one of the survivors, 20 years later.

• •

■ **ALL ABOUT EVE**

1950, 138 MINS, US ⑫ ⊙

Dir Joseph L. Mankiewicz   *Prod* Darryl F. Zanuck   *Scr* Joseph L. Mankiewicz   *Ph* Milton Krasner   *Ed* Barbara McLean   *Mus* Alfred Newman   *Art Dir* Lyle Wheeler, George Davis
● Bette Davis, Anne Baxter, George Sanders, Celeste Holm, Gary Merrill, Thelma Ritter (20th Century-Fox)

Anne Baxter, in the title role, is the radiant newcomer who has attained the thespic heights. And as she mounts the podium to receive the supreme accolade, the intimates who figured in her breathless success story project their own vignettes on what made this hammy glammy run.

Baxter plays a starry-eyed wouldbe actress who, by extraordinary design, finally meets Bette Davis, her histrionic idol (through the kind offices of Celeste Holm). She is taken into the household, machinates an under-study chore – and in return is ruthless in her pitch for both the beau and the husband of the two women who most befriended her.

The basic story is garnished with exceedingly well-cast performances wherein Davis does not spare herself, makeup-wise, in the aging star assignment. Baxter gives the proper shading to her cool and calculating approach in the process of ingratiation and ultimate opportunities.

Backgrounding are Gregory Ratoff, as the producer, and George Sanders as the debonair, machiavellian dramatic critic who knows the angles – plus.

It is obvious author-director Joe Mankiewicz knew what and how he wanted his cast to say and interpret.

□ 1950: Best Picture, Director, Supp. Actor (George Sanders), Screenplay, Sound Recording, B&W Costume Design.

□ Nominations: Best Actress (Anne Baxter, Bette Davis), Supp. Actress (Celeste Holm), B&W Cinematography, Art Direction, Editing, Original Music Score

• •

■ **ALLAN QUATERMAIN AND THE LOST CITY OF GOLD**

1987, 99 MINS, US ◇ ⑫

Dir Gary Nelson, Newt Arnold   *Prod* Menahem Golan, Yoram Globus   *Scr* Gene Quintano   *Ph* Alex Phillips, Frederick Elmes   *Ed* Alain Jakubowicz   *Mus* Michael Linn, [Jerry Goldsmith]   *Art Dir* Trevor Williams, Leslie Dilley
● Richard Chamberlain, Sharon Stone, James Earl Jones, Henry Silva, Robert Donner, Aileen Marson (Cannon)

Pic is a remake of Harry Alan Towers' 1977 film *King Solomon's Treasure*, which starred John Colicos as H. Rider Haggard's adventure hero Allan Quatermain (from the book by that name).

Embarrassing screenplay jettisons Haggard's enduring fantasy and myth-making in favor of a back-of-the-envelope plotline and anachronistic jokes about Cleveland. Quatermain (Richard Chamberlain) receives a gold piece from a dying man that inspires him to trek to East Africa in search of his brother Robeson (Martin Rabbett). Joining him are his archeologist girlfriend (Sharon Stone) and African warrior (James Earl Jones), a comic relief mystic (Robert Donner camping it up) and five expendable bearers.

After considerable filler, they find the lost race of Phoenicians, ruled by bland beauty contest queen Nyleptha (Aileen Marson).

A poor followup to the same producers' 1985 *King Solomon's Mines*, film relies frequently on

a very phony gimmick of a spear-proof tunic and story completely runs out of gas once the heroes arrive at their destination.

• •

■ **ALL FALL DOWN**

1962, 111 MINS, US

Dir John Frankenheimer   *Prod* John Houseman   *Scr* William Inge   *Ph* Lionel Lindon   *Ed* Fredric Steinkamp   *Mus* Alex North   *Art Dir* George W. Davis, Preston Ames
● Eva Marie Saint, Warren Beatty, Karl Malden, Angela Lansbury, Brandon de Wilde (M-G-M)

Within John Houseman's production of *All Fall Down* there are some truly memorable passages – moments and scenes of great pith, poignance, truth and sensitivity. How disheartening it is, then, that the sum total is an artfully produced, cinematically rich, historically noteworthy, dramatically uneven near-miss.

A 16-year-old boy (Brandon de Wilde) who idolizes his emotionally unstable older brother (Warren Beatty) is the pivotal figure in William Inge's screenplay based on James Leo Herlihy's novel. The important issue is that the adolescent matures into a decent young man. But his path to maturity is threatened by his adulation for this brother, a selfish, irrational free spirit who survives on odd jobs and loose women. When the older boy proceeds to destroy a young spinster (Eva Marie Saint) whom de Wilde adores in a hopeless, adolescent fashion, the latter has his moment of reckoning.

Angela Lansbury and Karl Malden, as the tragicomic elders, create indelible, dimensional and deeply affecting people.

• •

■ **ALL I DESIRE**

1953, 79 MINS, US

Dir Douglas Sirk   *Prod* Ross Hunter   *Scr* James Gunn, Robert Blees   *Ph* Carl Guthrie   *Ed* Milton Carruth   *Mus* Joseph Gershenson   *Art Dir* Bernard Herzbrun, Alexander Golitzen
● Barbara Stanwyck, Richard Carlson, Lyle Bettger, Marcia Henderson, Maureen O'Sullivan, Lori Nelson (Universal)

Plot [from the novel *Stopover* by Carol Brink, adapted by Gina Kaus] concerns the return of a mother to the family she ran away from 10 years previously for a fling at the stage. Homecoming is to see her daughter in the high school graduation play, but, secretly, the mother hopes for a reconciliation. Things are moving to this end, until the smalltown lothario, who had figured in her previous flight, tries to renew the affair.

The Ross Hunter production and Douglas Sirk's direction pull all stops to make the picture a 79-minute excursion into sentimentality. With help of Barbara Stanwyck's performance, the soap-operish tear-jerking is palatable. Richard Carlson plays the stiff-necked husband character straight to make it acceptable. Lyle Bettger is sadly misused as the former lover. Maureen O'Sullivan does what she can with the role of a school teacher hopelessly in love with Carlson.

• •

■ **ALLIGATOR**

1980, 94 MINS, US ◇ ⑫

Dir Lewis Teague   *Prod* Brandon Chase   *Scr* John Sayles   *Ph* Joseph Mangine   *Ed* Larry Bock, Ronald Medico   *Mus* Craig Hundley   *Art Dir* Michael Erler
● Robert Forster, Robin Riker, Michael Gazzo, Dean Jagger, Henry Silva, Jack Carter (Group 1)

Alligator is bloody and boisterous, featuring the only man-eating monster in memory named Ramone.

First seen, Ramone is a little baby alligator on a reptile farm in Florida, soon to be bought as a pet and taken to Missouri by sweet little Marisa. Bud dad gets mad and dumps Ramone down the toilet.

Fast forward 12 years and Marisa (Robin Riker) has grown up to be a world-famous herpatologist, while down below in the sewer Ramone has grown up unnoticed to be a 36-foot, one-ton, mean-tempered alligator.

Ramone developed his size and personality eating dead dogs thrown into the sewer by a chemical company experimenting on them in search of growth-inducing hormones. Ultimately tired of dog meat, the alligator starts to eat sewer workers and pet-store owners and policemen and finally a newspaper reporter.

Dumb as it is, director Lewis Teague brings some plusses to the pic. Robert Forster, as a detective, and Riker are amiable leads, never taking the film too seriously. Tech credits are cheap but serviceable. Exploitation fans will be glad to see Sue Lyon and Angel Tompkins, cameoed as news reporters.

●●●●●●●●●●●●●●●●●●●●●●●●●●●●●

■ ALLIGATOR EYES

1990, 101 MINS, US ◇ ⦾

Dir John Feldman   *Prod* John Feldman, Ken Schwenker
Scr John Feldman   *Ph* Todd Crockett   *Ed* Cynthia Rogers   *Mus* Sheila Silver
● Annabelle Larsen, Roger Kabler, Allen McCullough, Mary McLain, John Mackay (Laughing Man)

With this low-budget feature, first-time writer-director John Feldman creates some unusually strong characters and situations out of what could have been a routine road movie.

Pauline (Annabelle Larsen) is hitchhiking alone when picked up by a trio of friends from New York who take her along for the ride, not knowing at first that she's blind. Robbie (Roger Kabler) is a wise-cracking type on the rebound after a failed relationship. He immediately latches on to the pretty Pauline, and sleeps with her. Marjorie (Mary McLain) is recently divorced and trying to renew a relationship with former boyfriend Lance (Allen McCullough). The trio originally planned a vacation in North Carolina, but find that Pauline is directing their movements.

It's only when it attempts to become a thriller in the final reel that *Alligator Eyes* starts to falter; all the mythic details brought into the film prepare the way for something more intriguing as a resolution.

●●●●●●●●●●●●●●●●●●●●●●●●●●●●●

■ ALL MY SONS

1948, 98 MINS, US

Dir Irving Reis   *Prod* Chester Erskine   *Scr* Chester Erskine   *Ph* Russell Metty   *Ed* Ralph Dawson   *Mus* Leith Stevens   *Art Dir* Bernard Herzbrun, Hilyard Brown
● Edward G. Robinson, Burt Lancaster, Mady Christians, Howard Duff, Louisa Horton, Arlene Francis (Universal)

All My Sons comes to the screen with a potent impact. Whatever message may have been in the stage presentation may be resolved to the more fundamental one of man's duty to man, and gains strength by that switch. It's a serious, thoughtful study, loaded with dramatic dynamite.

Chester Erskine's approach to the Arthur Miller play benefits from the broader movement permitted by the screen. It's an ace scripting and production job that carefully measures every value to be found in the plot.

Script makes the point that we all are our brothers' keepers with a responsibility that can't be shunted aside for purely personal desires. Rather than hammering point over, it is gradually brought out in telling of a man who, in a desire for success, becomes responsible for the death of 21 fliers during the war.

Edward G. Robinson gives an effective performance as the small-town manufacturer who sends defective parts to the Army Air Forces. It's a humanized study that rates

among his best and lends the thought behind the film much strength. Burt Lancaster, as his war-embittered son, shades the assignment with just the right amount of intensity. His love and belief in his dad, whom he must betray to right the wrong done, cloaks the role with that human touch that marks all of the characters.

●●●●●●●●●●●●●●●●●●●●●●●●●●●●●

■ ALL NEAT IN BLACK STOCKINGS

1969, 106 MINS, UK ◇

Dir Christopher Morahan   *Prod* Leon Clore   *Scr* Jane Gaskell, Hugh Whitemore   *Ph* Larry Pizer   *Ed* Misha Norland   *Mus* Robert Cornford   *Art Dir* David Brockhurst
● Victor Henry, Susan George, Jack Shepherd, Clare Kelly, Anna Cropper (Warner)

A trite story taken from a Jane Gaskell novel, it suggests that it was aimed directly at the socalled woman's market.

Victor Henry plays an exuberant young window-cleaner with a lack of responsibility and a roving eye for the birds. Falling for a suburban chick that he picks up in a local tavern, he realizes that this is 'the real thing'. But he's thwarted by her over-possessive widowed mother.

Eventually his buddy, a young layabout with whom Henry shares everything, even chicks, gets the girl pregnant at a wild party, but is unaware of it.

There's not much to be done with such an anecdote, but brighten it up with smart dialog and standout performances. This one gets neither. Aforementioned Henry brings some humor and guts to the anti-hero's role and Jack Shepherd, as his mate, is laconic and personable.

●●●●●●●●●●●●●●●●●●●●●●●●●●●●●

■ ALL NIGHT LONG

1981, 88 MINS, US ◇

Dir Jean-Claude Tramont   *Prod* Leonard Goldberg, Jerry Weintraub   *Scr* W.D. Richter   *Ph* Philip Lathrop   *Ed* Marion Rothman   *Mus* Ira Newborn   *Art Dir* Peter Jamison
● Gene Hackman, Barbra Streisand, Diane Ladd, Dennis Quaid, Annie Girardot, William Daniels (Universal)

A weary premise and a hackeneyed theme are given some wry, offbeat twists in *All Night Long*. Film has the distinction of being one of the few – if not the only – Barbra Streisand starrers which was not designed as a vehicle for her.

Plot the same old middle-age-blues song, with Hackman chucking his dreary job, wife and lifestyle in favor of a younger woman and new reputation as a goofy carefree iconoclast. Familiar targets, such as uptight career businessmen, frivolous middle-class society ladies and sterile suburbia are knocked with easy precision.

With just one French feature, *Focal Point*, behind him, director Jean-Claude Tramont makes a good American debut here. Even though he has lived-and-on in the US for years, he lends an appealingly different eye to the Southern California lifestyle.

Hackman brings even more to his role than might have been apparent in the script. Playing a clearly subordinate role which she took over from Lisa Eichhorn shortly after lensing began, Streisand is more subdued than usual and effective as such.

●●●●●●●●●●●●●●●●●●●●●●●●●●●●●

■ ALL OF ME

1984, 93 MINS, US ◇ ⦿ ⦾

Dir Carl Reiner   *Prod* Stephen Friedman   *Scr* Phil Alden Robinson   *Ph* Richard H. Kline   *Ed* Bud Molin   *Mus* Patrick Williams   *Art Dir* Edward Carfagno
● Steve Martin, Lily Tomlin, Victoria Tennant, Madolyn Smith, Richard Libertini, Dana Elcar (Kings Road)

All of Me plays more like an old-fashioned screwball comedy than a contempo film, its premise of a woman dying and her soul inhabiting half of another person's body in the same vein as *Here Comes Mr Jordan*. When he is not arranging divorce settlements for rich husbands, Roger Cobb (Steve Martin) is a jazz guitarist. Martin's troubles really start on his 38th birthday when he inherits the soul of departing heiress and first-rank crank Edwina Cutwater (Lily Tomlin). Circumstances under which this occurs, assisted by guru Prahka Lasa (Richard Libertini), are patently ridiculous, but acceptable because of the charm of the characters.

Screenwriter Phil Alden Robinson [working from Ed Davis' novel *Me Two*, adapted by Henry Olek] has created enough interesting situations for the Martin-Tomlin mismatch. Urinating, shaving and making love take on new proportions when a man and woman are trying to do it in the same body.

For all its clowning, *All of Me* makes some good points about taking chances and doing what you want in life. Tomlin undergoes a transformation from a crabby sheltered poor little rich girl to a compassionate woman. It's a measure of her performance that even as a sourpuss she's irresistible.

●●●●●●●●●●●●●●●●●●●●●●●●●●●●●

■ ALL QUIET ON THE WESTERN FRONT

1930, 152 MINS, US ⦿ ⦿

Dir Lewis Milestone   *Prod* Carl Laemmle Jr
Scr Maxwell Anderson, Del Andrews, George Abbott   *Ph* Arthur Edeson, Karl Freund, Tony Gaudio   *Ed* Edgar Adams, Milton Carruth   *Mus* David Broekman   *Art Dir* Charles D. Hall, William R. Schmidt
● Lew Ayres, Louis Wolheim, John Wray, Raymond Griffith, Slim Summerville, Russell Gleason (Universal)

A harrowing, gruesome, morbid tale of war, compelling in its realism, bigness and repulsiveness.

Driving men and boys to their certain finish before murderous machine guns, dodging all kinds of missiles from the air, living with rats, starving while fighting, forgetting country and home, just becoming a fighting machine – that's the story and picture.

The story carries a group of German school boys, enthused by their professor's plea for fealty to country, from their training days through warfare to their deaths. In performance one might say it's due to Lewis Milestone's direction and let it go at that. But there are standout performances, even in bits. *All Quiet on the Western Front* [from the novel by Erich Maria Remarque] cost Universal $1.2 million.
□ 1929/30: Best Picture, Director.
□ Nominations: Best Writing, Cinematography (Arthur Edeson)

●●●●●●●●●●●●●●●●●●●●●●●●●●●●●

■ ALL THAT HEAVEN ALLOWS

1955, 89 MINS, US ◇

Dir Douglas Sirk   *Prod* Ross Hunter   *Scr* Peg Fenwick   *Ph* Russell Metty   *Ed* Frank Gross   *Mus* Frank Skinner   *Art Dir* Alexander Golitzen, Eric Orbom
● Jane Wyman, Rock Hudson, Agnes Moorehead, Conrad Nagel, Virginia Grey, Gloria Talbott (Universal)

Although this story of a long-suffering woman who, at 40 or so, finds romance with a man between 10 and 15 years her junior, is hardly designed to ignite prairie fires, scripter Peg Fenwick nevertheless has managed to turn the Edna L. and Harry Lee story into a slightly offbeat yarn with some interesting overtones that accent the social prejudices of a small town.

Jane Wyman is appealing and properly long-suffering. The script makes her into a rather weak character and it's difficult, aft a while, to rouse much sympathy for her plight.

Hudson is handsome and somewhat wooden. Laconic of speech, and imbued with an angel's patience and understanding, it's at times hard to understand his passion for the widow, what with pretty girls just spoiling for his attention.

Standout performance is delivered by a young newcomer, Gloria Talbott, playing Wyman's teenage daughter.

● ●

■ ALL THAT JAZZ

1979, 123 MINS, US ◇ ⓥ ⊙
Dir Bob Fosse *Prod* Robert Alan Aurthur *Scr* Bob Fosse, Robert Alan Aurthur *Ph* Giuseppe Rotunno *Ed* Alan Heim *Mus* Ralph Burns *Art Dir* Philip Rosenberg
● Roy Scheider, Jessica Lange, Ann Reinking, Cliff Gorman, John Lithgow, Erzebet Foldi (20th Century-Fox/Columbia)

All That Jazz is a self-important, egomaniacal, wonderfully choreographed, often compelling film which portrays the energetic life, and preoccupation with death, of a director-choreographer who ultimately suffers a heart attack.

The picture, reportedly based heavily on aspects of the real life of its director, Bob Fosse, deals with the director-choreographer Joe Gideon's career and his involvements with women.

Roy Scheider gives a superb performance as Gideon, creating a character filled with nervous energy. Running from project to project, the film portrays Gideon completing work on one film while working simultaneously on another project.

The film's major flaw lies in its lack of real explanation of what, beyond ego, really motivates Gideon.
☐ 1979: Best Art Direction, Adapted Score, Editing, Costume Design.
☐ Nominations: Best Picture, Director, Actor (Roy Scheider), Original Screenplay, Cinematography

● ●

■ ALL THAT MONEY CAN BUY

See: The Devil and Daniel Webster

● ●

■ ALL THE BROTHERS WERE VALIANT

1953, 94 MINS, US ◇ ⓥ
Dir Richard Thorpe *Prod* Pandro S. Berman *Scr* Harry Brown *Ph* George Folsey *Ed* Ferris Webster *Mus* Miklos Rozsa *Art Dir* Cedric Gibbons, Randall Duell
● Robert Taylor, Stewart Granger, Ann Blyth, Betta St John, Keenan Wynn, James Whitmore (M-G-M)

Special effects are used to advantage to spotlight the high romance of adventuring on the bounding main. Film's big moments include the excitement stirred up by the dangers of 19th century whaling and the climactic mass battle with mutineers aboard sailing vessel.

Directorial vigor of Richard Thorpe helps picture through its faltering spots. The latter come from shallow character development in the script [from a novel by Ben Ames Williams] and a rambling story line. Stars Robert Taylor, Stewart Granger and Ann Blyth are competent but the people they portray haven't enough depth or reality to come robustly alive.

Taylor and Granger are brothers in a seafaring family. When Granger, the elder, disappears on a whaling voyage, Taylor takes over his ship and, with his bride (Blyth) sails off to find him. At a South Seas stopover he finds Granger who goes for his brother's bride and incites a mutiny aboard ship, which he wants to use to recover a fortune in pearls he had found during his disappearance.
☐ 1953: Nomination: Best Color Cinematography

● ●

■ ALL THE FINE YOUNG CANNIBALS

1960, 112 MINS, US ◇
Dir Michael Anderson *Prod* Pandro S. Berman *Scr* Robert Thom *Ph* William H. Daniels *Ed* John McSweeney *Mus* Jeff Alexander *Art Dir* George W. Davis, Edward Carfagno
● Robert Wagner, Natalie Wood, Susan Kohner, George Hamilton, Pearl Bailey (M-G-M)

The handsome production surrounds a ludicrous *Modern Romances* sort of screenplay which was suggested by Rosamond Marshall's novel *The Bixby Girls*. Under scrutiny is the accelerated world of troubled youth where a one-night stand invariably results in pregnancy, fame or attempted suicide.

More specifically, the scenario explores the affairs of two young couples (Natalie Wood-George Hamilton and Robert Wagner-Susan Kohner) who eventually learn to live with the fact they share a mutual tax-deduction in the form of a bouncing babe who bounced out of the pre-marital union of one-half of each partnership (Wagner and Wood).

Director Michael Anderson attempts to establish and link the individual personalities of the central foursome by flashing rapidly to and fro from family to family. The technique backfires in that, by attempting to take in too much too swiftly, it leaves the audience out of focus on all four individual sets of motivations.

Wood is very pleasant to behold, even though a pained expression is about all she is required to project here. Kohner is not very convincing in her efforts to appear alternately gay, bored and distressed. Even less at ease are Wagner and Hamilton in a pair of incredibly unmasculine roles. Best emoting is done by Pearl Bailey, but even she can barely cope with a preposterous role of a celebrated blues singer who dies of a broken heart when jilted by 'that man who played horn for her.'

● ●

■ ALL THE KING'S MEN

1949, 109 MINS, US ⓥ ⊙
Dir Robert Rossen *Prod* Robert Rossen *Scr* Robert Rossen *Ph* Burnett Guffey *Ed* Al Clark, Robert Parrish *Mus* Louis Gruenberg *Art Dir* Sturges Carne
● Broderick Crawford, John Derek, Joanne Dru, John Ireland, Mercedes McCambridge, Shepperd Strudwick (Columbia)

The rise and fall of a backwoods political messiah, and the mark he left on the American scene, is given graphic celluloid treatment in *All the King's Men*.

Robert Rossen has produced and directed from his own script, based upon the Pulitzer Prize novel by Robert Penn Warren.

As a great man using the opinionless, follow-the-leader instinct of the more common voter, Broderick Crawford does a standout performance.

The story is told through the eyes of John Ireland, newspaperman. He becomes a devotee pursuing the Crawford career from small-time into bigtime.

Joanne Dru appears to advantage as a friend of Ireland's, but the most compelling of the femme players is Mercedes McCambridge, the mistress to the great man.
☐ 1949: Best Picture, Actor (Broderick Crawford), Supporting Actress (Mercedes McCambridge
☐ Nominations: Best Director, Supporting Actor (John Ireland), Screenplay, Editing

● ●

■ ... ALL THE MARBLES

(UK: *The California Dolls*)

1981, 113 MINS, US ◇ ⓥ
Dir Robert Aldrich *Prod* William Aldrich *Scr* Mel Frohman *Ph* Joseph Biroc *Ed* Irving C. Rosenblum, Richard Lane *Mus* Frank DeVol *Art Dir* Carl Anderson
● Peter Falk, Vicki Frederick, Laurene Landon, Burt Young, Tracy Reed, Richard Jaeckel (M-G-M/Aldrich)

By any measure *Marbles* is a major disappointment, given the deft casting of Peter Falk as a seedy, selfish and demanding manager of a couple of tag-team women wrestlers (Vicki Frederick and Laurene Landon).

The lead trio does get solid help from Burt Young as a crooked promoter and John Hancock as the decent manager of the opposing team consisting of Tracy Reed and Ursaline Bryant-Young.

For some odd reason, however, director Robert Aldrich and writer Mel Frohman have chosen to portray women's wrestling as a serious sport, aiming for another *Rocky*-like climb from obscurity to triumph. It never works for a minute. Except for a busted lip occasionally and a bruise or two, Frederick and Landon are always sprightly, pretty and ready for the road again after each bout.

Though Aldrich sometimes hints of hanky-panky and collusion among the teams, he generally insists that each match is won or lost on ability alone, building the 'California Dolls' up to a legitimate contest for the championship in Reno.

● ●

■ ALL THE PRESIDENT'S MEN

1976, 138 MINS, US ◇ ⓥ ⊙
Dir Alan J. Pakula *Prod* Walter Coblenz *Scr* William Goldman *Ph* Gordon Willis *Ed* Robert L. Wolfe *Mus* David Shire *Art Dir* George Jenkins
● Dustin Hoffman, Robert Redford, Jack Warden, Martin Balsam, Hal Holbrook, Jason Robards (Warner/Wildwood)

Some ingenious direction by Alan J. Pakula and scripting by William Goldman remove much of the inherent dramatic lethargy in any story of reporters running down a story.

Thus, *All the President's Men*, from the Bob Woodward and Carl Bernstein book about their experiences uncovering the Watergate coverup for *The Washington Post*, emerges close to being an American *Z*. Robert Redford and especially Dustin Hoffman excel in their starring roles.

Besides the stars, many of the featured players contribute mightily. As Deep Throat, the official who assisted the reporters in filtering out the facts, Hal Holbrook is outstanding; this actor, herein in near-total shadow, is as compelling as he is in virtually every role played.

Jason Robards, as *Post* exec editor Ben Bradlee, provides an excellent characterization, backed up strongly by Jack Warden and Martin Balsam as senior editors.
☐ 1976: Best Supporting Actor (Jason Robards), Adapted Screenplay, Art Direction, Sound.
☐ Nominations: Best Picture, Director, Supp. Actress (Jane Alexander), Editing

● ●

■ ALL THE RIGHT MOVES

1983, 91 MINS, US ◇ ⓥ ⊙
Dir Michael Chapman *Prod* Stephen Deutsch *Scr* Michael Kane *Ph* Jan De Bont *Ed* David Garfield *Mus* David Campbell *Art Dir* Mary Ann Biddle
● Tom Cruise, Craig T. Nelson, Lea Thompson, Charles Cioffi, Paul Carafotes, Christopher Penn (20th Century-Fox)

A smash directorial debut by well-known cinematographer Michael Chapman, *All the Right Moves* crackles with authenticity. The story is centered on characters fighting to get out of a dying Pennsylvania mill town to make a better life for themselves.

In a nice twist on expectations, the driven include Tom Cruise's girlfriend, sharply played by newcomer Lea Thompson, whose own aspirations take the frill out of the coed image, and the hard-nosed high school coach, superbly portray by Craig T. Nelson, who wants the big time as much as Cruise, his star safety.

Another welcome surprise is the touching relationship between high school senior Cruise and his father. For once, here's a pop in a redneck town who treats his son like a human being, and Charles Cioffi, however brief his screentime, conveys a durable dignity.

■ ALL THE WAY
See: The Joker is Wild

■ ALL THIS AND HEAVEN TOO

1940, 140 MINS, US ◇ ⓥ
Dir Anatole Litvak *Prod* Hal B. Wallis, David Lewis
Scr Casey Robinson *Ph* Ernest Haller *Ed* Warren Low
Mus Max Steiner *Art Dir* Carl Jules Weyl
● Bette Davis, Charles Boyer, Jeffrey Lynn, Barbara O'Neil, Virginia Weidler, Helen Westley (Warner)

Heaven is film theatre at its best. In the two starring roles are Bette Davis, as the young French governess, Henriette Deluzy-Desportes, and Charles Boyer, projecting one of his best performances as Duc de Praslin. The tragedy of their love affair, which resulted in the murder of the Duchesse de Praslin (Barbara O'Neil), the suicide of the Duc and the subsequent glimpse of some happiness for Henriette in her marriage to the American theological student, Henry Martyn Field (Jeffrey Lynn), is strong fare, involving delicate psychological shadings and understandings.

Casey Robinson in the scripting captures the quaintness of the manners and customs of Paris in 1848, and succeeds admirably in retaining both spirit and characters of Rachel Field's novel, despite much deletion of material. Anatole Litvak's direction is outstanding. Film throughout bears the mark of earnest and expert workmanship in all departments.

There are unusually effective performances of four youthful players as the de Praslin children. Every progressive step in the story is built around these youngsters, a bit of plot unfolding that takes the film far from conventional grooves. The children' roles are played with fine emotional results by Virginia Weidler, June Lockhart, Ann Todd and Richard Nichols.

As for Davis, she is off the screen during the briefest interludes. In her scenes with Boyer, she retains an outward composure which only intensifies her real feelings, never completely expressed. It is acting so restrained that a single overdrawn passage or expression would shatter the illusion.
□ 1940: Nominations: Best Picture, Supp. Actress (Barbara O'Neil), B&W Cinematography

---

■ ALL THROUGH THE NIGHT

1942, 107 MINS, US ⓥ
Dir Vincent Sherman *Prod* Hal B. Wallis (exec.)
Scr Leonard Spigelgass, Edwin Gilbert *Ph* Sid Hickox
Ed Rudi Fehr *Mus* Adolph Deutsch *Art Dir* Max Parker
● Humphrey Bogart, Conrad Veidt, Kaaren Verne, Jane Darwell, Frank McHugh, Peter Lorre (Warner)

Gripping espionage meller highlights three bad boys, with Humphrey Bogart this time working on the side of the law, order and liberty in trying to clean up a nest of Nazi spies and fifth-columnists. Two other toughies are sinister, soft-spoken Pete Lorre and immaculate, iron-fist-in-velvet-glove Nazi agent Conrad Veldt, both first rate. Locale is New York City.

Bogart, as retired mobster turned bigtime gambler, is easy to take. Protected against background of Nazi beatings and murders, US gangsters look like Sunday School kids fighting over marbles. Chase and gunbattle in Central Park, scraps in the warehouse district, the mystery girl in distress, emphasis on danger to American institutions from foreign

conspirators add up to elementary but sure-fire audience appeal.

Casting is a big asset, with Jane Darwell as Bogart's mother, Frank McHugh, Judith Anderson and William Demarest prominent. Kaaren Verne, femme lead, fills the bill nicely and pleasantly warbles two songs in a nitery sequence.

■ ALMOST AN ANGEL

1990, 95 MINS, US ◇ ⓥ ⊙
Dir John Cornell *Prod* John Cornell *Scr* Paul Hogan
Ph Russell Boyd *Ed* David Stiven *Mus* Maurice Jarre
Art Dir Henry Bumstead
● Paul Hogan, Elias Koteas, Linda Kozlowski, Charlton Heston, Doreen Lang, Joe Dallesandro (Paramount/Ironbark)

Almost an Angel is simply a no-effort vanity project with only Paul Hogan's easygoing charm to fill the space between the sprocket holes.

Instead of stretching his acting muscles, Hogan assigns himself the comfortable role of an electronics expert/cracksman just released from prison who turns into an inveterate do-gooder. In between bank heists, he instinctively saves a guy from a traffic accident and is himself run down.

Hospital scene has him dreaming of (or actually) floating to the clouds where uncredited guest star Charlton Heston as God reads him the riot act. He sends Hogan back to Earth for a second chance as an angel of mercy on probation.

Trekking to the small town of Fillmore, California, he sets about being kind to people. Chief recipients of his largesse are Elias Koteas, a bitter young man suffering from a terminal illness confining him to a wheelchair, and his self-sacrificing sister, Hogan's real-life wife and inevitable co-star Linda Kozlowski.

Koteas is affecting as the cripple with a chip on his shoulder. Kozlowski, styled plain with dark hair, is wasted as the mildest of romantic interests.

■ ALMOST PERFECT AFFAIR, AN

1979, 93 MINS, US ◇ ⓥ
Dir Michael Ritchie *Prod* Terry Carr *Scr* Walter Bernstein, Don Peterson *Ph* Henri Decae *Ed* Richard A. Harris *Mus* Georges Delerue *Art Dir* Willy Holt
● Keith Carradine, Monica Vitti, Raf Vallone, Christian De Sica, Dick Anthony Williams (Paramount)

The emotions director Michael Ritchie is parlaying in this slim fable, which revolve around tender egos and unlimited ambition, are universal. But the details are so specific, and so grounded in film industry reality, that the larger implications may be lost.

Keith Carradine is a young filmmaker, who wraps up two years of devotion to a film about executed murderer Gary Gilmore, *Choice of Ending*, by sinking all his remaining funds into a trip to Cannes. His film is seized at French customs until the censor can see it, an unlikely possibility until Monica Vitti intercedes on his behalf.

Carradine mirrors lotsa nouveau helmers adrift in their initial dealings with industry salesmanship.

Focus is the intriguing relationship between Vitti and Carradine, which starts out as a one-nighter, and turns into a brief, but ill-fated romance.

■ ALONG CAME JONES

1945, 90 MINS, US
Dir Stuart Heisler *Prod* Gary Cooper *Scr* Nunnally Johnson *Ph* Milton Krasner *Ed* Thomas Neff
Mus Arthur Lange *Art Dir* Wiard B. Ihnen
● Gary Cooper, Loretta Young, William Demarest, Dan Duryea, Frank Sully, Russell Simpson (International)

For his first independent production, Gary Cooper turned out a better-than-average western [from the novel by Alan LeMay]. Cooper is not only the producer but also the star, along with Loretta Young. Without Cooper and Young *Jones* would be just another horse opera.

Cooper plays a mild-mannered cowpoke who drifts into a small town with his sidekick (William Demarest), thus precipitating a situation in which he's mistaken for a notorious road agent. Cooper, actually, can't even handle a gun, but the inevitable result finds him the unwitting and indirect cause of the holdupman's slaying. And, of course, he gets the latter's girl (Young).

Cooper plays his usually languid self impressively, while Young is decorative and photographed well. Demarest is in for some comedy relief, of which there is too little, while Dan Duryea is properly menacing as the killer.

■ ALONG THE GREAT DIVIDE

1951, 88 MINS, US ⓥ
Dir Raoul Walsh *Prod* Anthony Veiller *Scr* Walter Doniger, Lewis Meltzer *Ph* Sid Hickox *Ed* Thomas Reilly *Mus* David Buttolph *Art Dir* Edward Carrere
● Kirk Douglas, Virginia Mayo, John Agar, Walter Brennan, Ray Teal, Hugh Sanders (Warner)

In his first western, Kirk Douglas is a US marshall, interested only in enforcing the letter of the law. Plot [from a story by Walter Doniger] is concerned with Douglas bringing in a prisoner charged with rustling and murder, and the efforts of a cattle baron to take justice in his own hands.

The prisoner (Walter Brennan) has been rescued from a lynching when Douglas and his two deputies stumble onto the necktie party being arranged by Morris Ankrum, who has accused Brennan of killing his son.

The law group, by now having Brennan's daughter (Virginia Mayo) in the party, flees across a desert from Ankrum's men, is attacked and deputy John Agar is killed. Douglas manages to capture Ankrum's other son (James Anderson) as hostage, a the dry, thirsty desert trek continues.

Douglas tries hard with his characterization and would have brought it off successfully had the scripting stuck to straight western action and not gone off in mental maneuverings. Mayo's character has several good scenes but mostly misses. Her dialect isn't consistent.

■ ALTERED STATES

1980, 102 MINS, US ◇ ⓥ ⊙
Dir Ken Russell *Prod* Howard Gottfried *Scr* Sidney Aaron [= Paddy Chayefsky] *Ph* Jordan Cronenweth
Ed Eric Jenkins *Mus* John Corigliano *Art Dir* Richard McDonald
● William Hurt, Blair Brown, Bob Balaban, Charles Haid, Drew Barrymore (Warner)

Altered States is an exciting combo science fiction-horror film [from the novel by Paddy Chayefsky]. Direction by Ken Russell has energy to spare, with appropriate match-up of his baroque visual style to special effects intensive material.

Producers weathered stormy pre-production problems, including the ankling of director Arthur Penn late in 1978, departure soon after of special effects wiz John Dykstra, and transfer of project from Columbia to Warners as proposed budget grew to $15 million.

Tall tale concerns a young psychophysiologist, Edward Jessup (William Hurt), working in New York and later at Harvard on dangerous experiments involving human consciousness.

Using himself as the subject, Jessup makes use of a sensory deprivation tank to hallucinate back to the event of his birth and beyond, regressing into primitive stages of human evolution.

Shattering use of Dolby stereo effects conspires with the images to give the viewer a vicarious LSD-type experience sans drugs. Hurt's feature film debut is arresting, especially during the grueling climactic sequence.
□ 1980: Nomination: Best Original Score, Sound

• •

■ **ALVAREZ KELLY**

1966, 110 MINS, US ◇ ⊛
Dir Edward Dmytryk   *Prod* Sol C. Siegel   *Scr* Franklin Coen, Elliott Arnold   *Ph* Joseph MacDonald   *Ed* Harold F. Kress   *Mus* John Green   *Art Dir* Walter M. Simonds
● William Holden, Richard Widmark, Janice Rule, Patrick O'Neal, Victoria Shaw, Roger C. Carmel (Columbia)

Based on a true US Civil War incident, *Alvarez Kelly* concerns successful cattle grab engineered by Southern forces and executed under the noses of Northern troops. Outdoor action sequences, including an exciting stampede, enliven a tame script routinely directed and performed erratically.

Franklin Coen and Elliott Arnold scripted Coen's story, which pits Mexican-Irish William Holden (hence, the title) against Confederate officer Richard Widmark, eyeing Holden's cattle as food for a starving South.

A lot of double-crossing takes place, with Victoria Shaw, mistress of a captured mansion, causing Holden's kidnapping by Widmark, who forces the former to teach his troops how to handle cattle. Janice Rule, Widmark's faithful sweetie, gives up her marriage hopes, and Holden helps her escape to NY with Scottish sea captain Roger C. Carmel. Patrick O'Neal is the Northern officer who is depicted in unsympathetic hues.

Director Edward Dmytryk has achieved uneven response from his players, in part due to scripting which overdevelops some characters and situations, and underdevelops others.

• •

■ **ALVIN PURPLE**

1973, 97 MINS, AUSTRALIA ◇ ⊛
Dir Tim Burstall   *Prod* Tim Burstall   *Scr* Alan Hopgood   *Ph* Robin Copping   *Ed* Edward McQueen Mason   *Mus* Brian Cadd   *Art Dir* Leslie Binns
● Graeme Blundell, George Whaley, Penne Hackforth-Jones, Elli Maclure, Jacki Weaver, Jenny Hagen (Hexagon)

Alvin Purple is a young man whom women find irresistible. At 16 he flees from schoolgirls right into the clutches of his school teacher's wife. At 21, still running from the opposite sex, Alvin becomes a waterbed salesman and discovers it isn't only the water-bed a bored housewife, body-painting fanatic, kinky woman, and a drag queen are after. Exhausted and bewildered by these multiple activities Alvin confesses to his girl friend Tina (with whom his relationship is utterly platonic) he is unable to resist sex.

This comedy, made in Melbourne with local actors, is beautifully scripted by Aussie playwright Alan Hopgood with double entendres and situations abounding. Pace is slick and the pic never sags.

In the title role Graeme Blundell gives a thoroughly convincing performance.

• •

■ **ALWAYS**

1985, 105 MINS, US ◇ ⊛ ⊙
Dir Henry Jaglom   *Prod* Henry Jaglom   *Scr* Henry Jaglom   *Ph* Hanania Baer   *Mus* Miles Kreuger (consult.)
● Patrice Townsend, Henry Jaglom, Joanna Frank, Alan Rachins, Melissa Leo, Jonathan Kaufer (Jagtown)

Always is writer-director-producer Henry Jaglom's confessional comedy about his

divorce from actress Patrice Townsend. The two star, more or less, as themselves, and are joined by two other couples who are, respectively, near the beginning and toward the middle of the marriage process for an alternately awkward, painful, loving and farcical July Fourth weekend. Pic's subject matter is at once highly personal and utterly universal.

Jaglom frames the proceedings with ruminations directed straight at the viewer, then jumps into a telling of how Townsend showed up one night at Jaglom's home to sign the divorce papers and ended up staying on for a weekend of emotional confrontations, recriminations, joyful reminiscences and partial reconciliation.

In French farce style, two unexpected flings take place, but mainly, picture is wall-to-wall talk about what went wrong between Jaglom and Townsend, about emotional happiness and lack of same, about sexual matters, and many related topics.

• •

■ **ALWAYS**

1989, 121 MINS, US ◇ ⊛ ⊙
Dir Steven Spielberg   *Prod* Steven Spielberg, Frank Marshall, Kathleen Kennedy   *Scr* Jerry Belson   *Ph* Mikael Salomon   *Ed* Michael Kahn   *Mus* John Williams   *Art Dir* James Bissell
● Richard Dreyfuss, Holly Hunter, Brad Johnson, John Goodman, Audrey Hepburn, Keith David (Universal/United Artists/Amblin)

Always is a relatively small scale, engagingly casual, somewhat silly, but always entertaining fantasy.

Richard Dreyfuss charmingly inherits the lead role of a pilot returned from the dead in this remake of the 1943 Spencer Tracy pic *Guy Named Joe* set among fire-fighters in national parks.

Steven Spielberg's transposition of the fondly remembered original to the spectacularly burning Montana forests – incorporating footage shot during the devastating 1988 fires at Yellowstone National Park – is a valid equivalent, for the most part, especially since his action sequences using old World War II-era planes are far more thrilling than those of *Guy Named Joe*.

Holly Hunter's dispatcher and semi-skilled aspiring pilot, lacking the womanly grace Irene Dunne brought to the part, comes off as gawky and ditzy in the early parts of *Always*. Bereavement seems to visibly mature the actress, whose emotional struggle between the memory of Dreyfuss and new love Brad Johnson becomes spirited and gripping.

• •

■ **AMADEUS**

1984, 158 MINS, US ◇ ⊛ ⊙
Dir Milos Forman   *Prod* Saul Zaentz   *Scr* Peter Shaffer   *Ph* Miroslav Ondricek   *Ed* Nena Danevic, Michael Chandler   *Mus* John Strauss (co-ord.)   *Art Dir* Patrizia Von Brandenstein
● F. Murray Abraham, Tom Hulce, Elizabeth Berridge, Simon Callow, Roy Dotrice, Christine Ebersole (Zaentz)

On a production level and as an evocation of a time and place, *Amadeus* is loaded with pleasures, the greatest of which derive from the on-location filming in Prague, the most 18th-century of all European cities.

With great material and themes to work with, and such top talent involved, film nevertheless arrives as a disappointment. Although Peter Shaffer adapted his own outstanding play for the screen, the stature and power the work possessed onstage have been noticeably diminished, and Milos Forman's handling is perhaps too naturalistic for what was conceived as a highly stylized piece.

Amadeus is Shaffer's fictionalized account, based on well-informed speculation, of the relationship between Viennese court composer Antonio Salieri and Wolfgang Amadeus

Mozart, during the 10 final years of the latter's life. It is a caustic study of the collision between mediocrity and genius, it is based on the provocative premise that the manipulative Salieri may have intentionally caused Mozart's death in 1791.

Shaffer has drawn Salieri as a character of Mephistophelian proportions, a man who needs to drag Mozart down in order to cope with his awareness of his own shortcomings.

Fueling the fire of Salieri's fury is Mozart's offensive personality. In opposition to the idealized, romanticized 19th-century view of the composer, the character is an outlandish vulgarian. As played by Tom Hulce, Mozart emerges as the John McEnroe of classical music.
□ 1984: Best Picture, Director, Actor (F. Murray Abraham), Adapted Screenplay, Art Direction, Sound, Costume Design, Make-Up.
□ Nominations: Best Actor (Tom Hulce), Cinematography, Editing

• •

■ **AMAZING DR. CLITTERHOUSE, THE**

1938, 87 MINS, US ◇
Dir Anatole Litvak   *Prod* Robert Lord   *Scr* John Wexley, John Huston   *Ph* Tony Gaudio   *Ed* Warren Low   *Mus* Max Steiner   *Art Dir* Carl Jules Weyl
● Edward G. Robinson, Claire Trevor, Humphrey Bogart, Allen Jenkins, Donald Crisp, Gale Page (Warner)

The Amazing Dr Clitterhouse was successful on the London stage and mildly so in New York.

The producers have retained the basic idea from the play [by Barre Lyndon] – that of a veteran physician whose study of the physiological effects of crime on its habitues takes him on a series of ventures with a skilled gang of crooks. This thread has been followed even to the deliberate poisoning of the gangster chief by the doctor when he learns of a hoodlum's blackmailing scheme.

But in many respects it is an outright gangster film with the medico's study of criminals as the excuse for carefully diagraming the gang's operations. In addition, the feature inculcates a bit of the sherlocking theme and modified romance. Claire Trevor, the ace fence for the thieves, is the sole romance that enters the doctor's life.

Edward G. Robinson, in the role of the criminal medico, is at his best. Humphrey Bogart's interpretation of the gangster chief, whose jealousy of Clitterhouse eventually builds to the blackmail scheme, is topflight.

• •

■ **AMAZING GRACE AND CHUCK**
(Aka: Silent Voice)

1987, 115 MINS, US ◇ ⊛ ⊙
Dir Mike Newell   *Prod* David Field   *Scr* David Field   *Ph* Robert Elswit   *Ed* Peter Hollywood   *Mus* Elmer Bernstein   *Art Dir* Dena Roth
● Jamie Lee Curtis, Alex English, Gregory Peck, William L. Petersen, Joshua Zuehlke (Tri-Star/Rastar/Turnstar)

Amazing Grace and Chuck is destined to go down in history as the camp classic of the anti-nuke genre. As amazingly bad as it is audacious, film will live forever in the hearts of connoisseurs of Hollywood's most memorably outrageous moments.

Little League baseball pitcher Chuck Murdock, having been shown a Minuteman missile under the Montana prairie, announces, 'I can't play because of nuclear weapons.' Who should read a news report of the incident but Boston Celtics star Amazing Grace Smith (played by Denver Nuggets great Alex English), who promptly gives up his $1 million-per-year salary to join Chuck in protest of nukes. In no time, hundreds of athletes on both sides of the Iron Curtain are refusing to play until the ultimate weapon is eliminated.

When it looks as though the upcoming baseball season will have to be cancelled the

President of the United States (an impressive Gregory Peck) summons young Chuck to the White House to drum some sense into him.

■ AMAZON

1992, 91 MINS, FINLAND/US ◇ ⓥ
Dir Mika Kaurismaki *Prod* Mika Kaurismaki, Pentti Kouri *Scr* Mika Kaurismaki, Richard Reitinger *Ph* Timo Salminen *Ed* Michael Chandler *Mus* Nana Vasconcelos *Art Dir* Tony de Castro
● Kari Vaananen, Robert Davi, Rae Dawn Chong, Minna, Aili Sovio, Rui Polanah (Villealfa/Noema)

Shot in CinemaScope with an international B-movie cast playing foreigners at the ends of their ropes in the Brazilian jungle, *Amazon* plays like a dualer that might have been made in the 1960s by Sam Fuller or Gordon Douglas starring Burt Reynolds or Stuart Whitman.

Opening with the nearly surreal sight of a Finnish man and his two daughters attempting to travel on the hellish Trans-Amazonian Highway to the accompaniment of some noirish narration, pic briefly flashes back to explain that banker Kari Vaananen has fled Finland with the girls upon his wife's accidental death.

But, lo and behold, they run out of gas, as does, in an amusing scene, their would-be saviour, a bitter American bush pilot named Dan (Robert Davi). A mercenary and treasure hunter of the old school, Dan speaks of searching for gold using a debilitated bulldozer he's found, and eventually Kari joins him in his quest.

Visually film is always stimulating but storytelling is wildly uneven, and director Mika Kaurismaki has an uncertain command of pic's tone. Acting is okay.

■ AMAZON WOMEN ON THE MOON

1987, 85 MINS, US ◇ ⓥ ⊙
Dir Joe Dante, Carl Gottlieb, Peter Horton, John Landis *Prod* Robert K. Weiss *Scr* Michael Barrie, Jim Malholland *Ph* Daniel Pearl *Ed* Bert Lovitt, Marshall Harvey, Malcolm Campbell *Art Dir* Alex Hajdu
● Rosanna Arquette, Ralph Bellamy, Carrie Fisher, Griffin Dunne, Steve Guttenberg, Russ Meyer (Universal)

Amazon Women on the Moon is irreverent, vulgar and silly and has some hilarious moments and some real groaners too. John Landis & Co have found some 1980s things to satirize – like yuppies, the vidcassette biz, dating, condoms – done up in a way that's not particularly shocking anymore.

Besides Landis, directors Joe Dante, Carl Gottlieb, Peter Horton and Robert K. Weiss take turns doing sketches – Weiss' *Amazon Women on the Moon* 1950s parody of bad sci-fi pics being the one that was stretched piecemeal throughout the film in a semi-successful attempt to hold this anthology together as one comedic work.

Eighteen other segs fill up the pic's 85 minutes, some mercifully short like Weiss' *Silly Pate* while Landis' *Hospital* is one of those slow-building, totally zany bits where the chuckles grow as the situation gets more ridiculous and you wish there was more.

■ AMBUSHERS, THE

1968, 101 MINS, US ◇ ⓥ ⊙
Dir Henry Levin *Prod* Irving Allen *Scr* Herbert Baker *Ph* Burnett Guffey *Ed* Harold F. Kress *Mus* Hugo Montenegro
● Dean Martin, Senta Berger, Janice Rule, James Gregory, Albert Salmi, Kurt Kasznar (Columbia/Meadway-Claude)

This third Matt Helm pic starts out with silly double entendre, then shifts for last half to tedious plot resolution. While production values remain strong, acting, writing and direction are pedestrian.

Plot is simple: US flying sauceress Janice Rule is kidnapped by despicable beast Albert Salmi; James Gregory sends Dean Martin to find out why; Senta Berger reps another foreign government (lucky place, too); Kurt Kasznar is a funny bad guy – a Mexican beer baron; assorted heavies get their desserts.

Although visual aspects – the Oleg Cassini wardrobe and overall fashion supervision – are very good, pic at same time has that slapdash quickie look.

■ AMERICA AMERICA

(UK: The Anatolian Smile)

1963, 177 MINS, US
Dir Elia Kazan *Prod* Elia Kazan *Scr* Elia Kazan *Ph* Haskell Wexler *Ed* Dede Allen *Mus* Manos Hadjidakis *Art Dir* Gene Callahan
● Stathis Giallelis, Frank Wolf, Harry Davis, Linda Marsh, Paul Mann, Lou Antonio (Warner)

Elia Kazan gives a penetrating, thorough and profoundly affecting account of the hardships endured and surmounted at the turn of the century by a young Greek lad in attempting to fulfill his cherished dream – getting to America from the old country.

Kazan's film stems from his book of the same title which evidently was inspired by tales of the experiences of his own ancestors that sifted down through the family grapevine. The picture begins with the young Greek hero witnessing Turkish oppression of Greek and Armenian minorities, circa 1896. It follows him to Constantinople, to which he has been sent by his family with its entire fortune to pave his way. He finally arrives in the promised land – America – where, as a lowly shoeshine boy, he painstakingly earns and saves the money that will bring the other members of his large family across the sea.

The acting is incredibly good. In the all-important focal role of the young man with the dream, Stathis Giallelis, an unknown, makes a striking screen debut. Virtually everyone is memorable, perhaps the three most vivid are Linda Marsh as the plain and unassuming maiden to whom the hero is treacherously betrothed, Paul Mann as her sybaritic, self-indulgent father and Lou Antonio as a thoroughly detestable crook.
□ 1963: Best B&W Art Direction.
□ Nominations: Best Picture, Director, Original Story & Screenplay

■ AMERICAN FLYERS

1985, 114 MINS, US ◇ ⓥ ⊙
Dir John Badham *Prod* Gareth Wigan, Paula Weinstein *Scr* Steve Tesich *Ph* Don Peterman *Ed* Frank Morriss *Mus* Lee Ritenour, Greg Mathieson *Art Dir* Lawrence G. Paull
● Kevin Costner, David Grant, Rae Dawn Chong, Alexandra Paul, Janice Rule, Luca Bercovici (Warner)

Story of two brothers who untangle their mixed emotions as they compete in a grueling bicycle race, *American Flyers* is most entertaining when it rolls along unencumbered by big statements. Unfortunately, overblown production just pumps hot air in too many directions and comes up limp.

Basic conflict between under-achiever David (David Grant) and older brother Marcus (Kevin Costner), a fierce competitor and no-nonsense sports doctor, is crammed into a hotbed of family problems including a career-woman mother (Janice Rule) who emotionally abandoned her dying husband.

If this isn't enough, one of the boys is destined for the same fate as the father. So, with the shadow of death hanging over them, the brothers set off for Colorado for 'the toughest bicycle race in America.'

Combativeness between brothers yields to camaraderie, but true nature of their conflict is difficult to get a handle on.

Performances are adequate considering that over-production makes the characters seem larger than life without being lifelike.

■ AMERICAN FRIENDS

1991, 95 MINS, UK ◇ ⓥ ⊙
Dir Tristan Powell *Prod* Patrick Cassavetti, Steve Abbott *Scr* Michael Palin, Tristram Powell *Ph* Philip Bonham-Carter *Ed* George Akers *Mus* Georges Delerue *Art Dir* Andrew McAlpine
● Michael Palin, Connie Booth, Trini Alvarado, Alfred Molina, David Calder (Millenium/Mayday)

Easy on the eyes and on the emotions, *American Friends* is a slim vignette about two Yank women who fall for a reserved Oxford don.

Pic opens in the 1860s at a stuffy Oxford college where bachelor classics don Francis Ashby (Michael Palin) is setting off for a walking vacation in Switzerland. Atop the Alps, he meets two Americans, Caroline (Connie Booth) and her doe-eyed ward, Elinor (Trini Alvarado). Emotions are stirred, and Elinor gets the first kiss.

Back in Oxford, Ashby is one of two candidates lined up to take over as college president when the current one dies. Ashby rival Oliver Syme (Alfred Molina) has hyperactive hormones, so if Ashby can stay respectably celibate, the job's virtually his. Enter, en route to Philadelphia, the two Yanks – and much trouble for Ashby.

There's a lot going on beneath the surface, but not much of it reaches the screen. Lack of dramatic tension can be blamed, in part, on the ex-Monty Python trouper's performance. Although yarn is based on an actual event discovered in his great-grandfather Edward's travel diaries, Palin is too lightweight for such a key role. His crusty, middle-aged bachelor doesn't ring true. Thesping otherwise is crisp and reliable.

■ AMERICAN GIGOLO

1980, 117 MINS, US ◇ ⓥ ⊙
Dir Paul Schrader *Prod* Jerry Bruckheimer *Scr* Paul Schrader *Ph* John Bailey *Ed* Richard Halsey *Mus* Giorgio Moroder *Art Dir* Fernando Scarfiotti
● Richard Gere, Lauren Hutton, Hector Elizondo, Nina Van Pallandt, Bill Duke, Brian Davies (Paramount)

A hot subject, cool style and overly contrived plotting don't all mesh in *American Gigolo*. Paul Schrader's third outing as a director is betrayed by a curious, uncharacteristic evasiveness at its core.

Things begin to go awry, both for Richard Gere and the picture, when senator's wife Lauren Hutton begins taking more than a passing interest in her man-for-hire and when a kinky sex murder is laid at his door. Gere's character has been portrayed with such moral and emotional ambivalence, which makes caring about his predicament and ultimate fate difficult.

As with several of Schrader's other scripts, this one charts the course of a loner, a solo driver navigating in a sea of sharks ready to eat him alive. Rarely offscreen, Gere is notably convincing in look and manner. Very lowkeyed, Hutton is not quite up to the difficult part of a woman-with-everything who throws it all over for her questionable lover.

■ AMERICAN GRAFFITI

1973, 109 MINS, US ◇ ⓥ ⊙
Dir George Lucas *Prod* Francis Coppola, Gary Kurtz *Scr* George Lucas, Gloria Katz, Willard Huyck *Ph* Haskell Wexler *Ed* Verna Fields, Marcia Lucas *Mus* Karin Green (sup.) *Art Dir* Dennis Clark
● Richard Dreyfuss, Ron Howard, Paul Le Mat, Charles Martin Smith, Cindy Williams, Candy Clark (Universal)

Set in 1962 but reflecting the culmination of the 1950s, the film is a most vivid recall of teenage attitudes and mores, told with outstanding empathy and compassion through an exceptionally talented cast.

Design consultant Al Locatelli, art director Dennis Clark and set director Douglas Freeman have brilliantly reconstructed the fabric and texture of the time, while Walter Murch's outstanding sound collage – an unending stream of early rock platter hits – complements in the aural department.

Against this chrome and neon backdrop is told the story of one long summer night in the lives of four school chums: Richard Dreyfuss, on his last night before leaving for an eastern college; Ron Howard, less willing to depart the presence of Cindy Williams; Charles Martin Smith, a bespectacled fumbler whose misadventures with pubescent swinger Candy Clark are as touching as they are hilarious; and Paul Le Mat, 22 years old on a birth certificate but still strutting as he did four years earlier.

□ 1973: Nominations: Best Picture, Director, Supp. Actress (Candy Clark), Original Screenplay, Editing

••••••••••••••••••••••••••••••

■ AMERICAN GUERRILLA IN THE PHILIPPINES, AN

(UK: I Shall Return)

1950, 104 MINS, US ◇

Dir Fritz Lang   *Prod* Lamar Trotti   *Scr* Lamar Trotti   *Ph* Harry Jackson   *Ed* Robert Simpson   *Mus* Cyril J. Mockridge   *Art Dir* Lyle Wheeler, J. Russell Spencer
● Tyrone Power, Micheline Presle, Tom Ewell, Bob Patton, Jack Elam, Robert Barrat (20th Century-Fox)

20th-Fox has made an interesting, if somewhat long, film version of Ira Wolfert's *American Guerrilla in the Philippines*. A story of the Second World War in the Pacific, from the spring of 1942 up to General MacArthur's return to the islands, is neatly staged.

The Philippine locales supply a lush tropical dressing to brighten the heroics of a small band of Americans and natives who fight the US cause against the invading Japs. Tyrone Power and Tom Ewell, escape into the jungle after the sinking of their P-T boat. They join the natives to fight guerrilla fashion against the Japs.

Footage has some good, male humor mixed in with the derrin-do, and Fritz Lang's direction develops a strong sense of expectancy and suspense in the story-telling.

••••••••••••••••••••••••••••••

■ AMERICAN HEART

1992, 113 MINS, US ◇ ⊚ ⊙

Dir Martin Bell   *Prod* Rosilyn Heller, Jeff Bridges   *Scr* Peter Silverman   *Ph* James Bagdonas   *Ed* Nancy Baker   *Mus* James Newton Howard   *Art Dir* Joel Schiller
● Jeff Bridges, Edward Furlong, Lucinda Jenney, Don Harvey, Tracey Kapinsky, Maggie Welsh (Avenue/Asis-Heller)

A long-in-the-works labor of love for all concerned, first fictional feature from Martin Bell is rooted in an elemental story about an irresponsible, ex-con father and his teenage son, who is so ignored he must fend for himself on the streets. Around the edges are a host of observations about the sorry state of urban America, and grafted on is a bit of crime melodrama that provides some conventional chase and shoot-'em-up action.

Released from prison on a work furlough program, Jack Keely (Jeff Bridges) reunites in Seattle with his 14-year-old son Nick (Edward Furlong), who has been staying with his aunt in the country. Bright, resourceful Nick is discouraged from signing up at school and increasingly hangs around with other dispossessed kids. Jack has trouble assuming the responsibilities of fatherhood, preferring to spend time with his g.f. (Lucinda Jenney).

Peter Silverman's screenplay (based on a

story by himself, director Bell and associate producer Mary Ellen Mark, a photographer who is also Bell's wife) offers many honest, reality-grappling scenes, but it could have used a dash of reality-heightening poetry to lift the pic out of the ordinary.

••••••••••••••••••••••••••••••

■ AMERICAN IN PARIS, AN

1951, 113 MINS, US ◇ ⊚ ⊙

Dir Vincente Minnelli   *Prod* Arthur Freed   *Scr* Alan Jay Lerner   *Ph* Alfred Gilks, John Alton   *Ed* Adrienne Fazan   *Mus* Johnny Green, Saul Chaplin (dirs.)   *Art Dir* Cedric Gibbons, Preston Ames
● Gene Kelly, Leslie Caron, Oscar Levant, Georges Guetary, Nina Foch, Eugene Borden (M-G-M)

An American in Paris is one of the most imaginative musical confections turned out by Hollywood, spotlighting Gene Kelly, Oscar Levant, Nina Foch, and a pair of bright newcomers (Leslie Caron and Georges Guetary) against a cavalcade of George and Ira Gershwin's music.

Kelly is the picture's top star and rates every inch of his billing. His diversified dancing is great as ever and his thesping is standout. But he reveals new talents in this one with his choreography. There's a lengthy ballet to the film's title song for the finale, which is a masterpiece of design, lighting, costumes and color photography. It's a unique blending of classical and modern dance with vaudestyle tapping.

Carron is a beauteous, lissome number with an attractively pert personality and plenty of s.a. She scores neatly with her thesping, particularly in the appealing love scenes with Kelly, and displays standout dancing ability. Guetary demonstrates a socko musicomedy tenor and okay acting talents. He's cast neatly as the older man whom Caron almost marries out of gratitude.

Story is sprightly yarn about an American GI (Kelly) who stayed on in Paris after the war to further his art study. Foch, as a wealthy American playgal, 'discovers' his art talents and takes him on as her protege to add him to her retinue of lovers. Kelly accepts the idea warily but then meets and falls for Caron.

Gershwin's music gets boffo treatment throughout. While some 10 songs get special handling, true Gershwin fans will recognize strains of most of his other tunes in the background score

□ 1951: Best Picture, Story & Screenplay, Color Cinematography, Color Art Direction, Score for a Musical Picture, Color Costume Design.

□ Nominations: Director, Editing

••••••••••••••••••••••••••••••

■ AMERICANIZATION OF EMILY, THE

1964, 115 MINS, US ⊚

Dir Arthur Hiller   *Prod* Martin Ransohoff   *Scr* Paddy Chayefsky   *Ph* Philip Lathrop   *Ed* Tom McAdoo   *Mus* Johnny Mandel   *Art Dir* George W. Davis, Hans Peters, Elliot Scott
● James Garner, Julie Andrews, Melvyn Douglas, James Coburn, Joyce Grenfell, Edward Binns (M-G-M)

Emily, with Julie Andrews in title role as an English motor pool driver in World War II, takes place immediately before the Normandy invasion. Most of the action unspools in London where Garner, a lieutenant commander who makes avowed cowardice his career, is 'dog robber' to Melvyn Douglas, an erratic admiral and one of the heads of the oncoming onslaught on the French coast.

Most of Garner's duties consist of rounding up delicacies and services, impossible to get, for his boss, until the admiral orders him to make a film showing activities of navy demolition on their landing at Omaha Beach.

Basic idea builds around the admiral being beset with an obsession to have the first man killed on Omaha Beach a sailor, to show the navy can have no peer in the service, and the script takes it from there.

Pic [based on the novel by William Bradford Huie] is primarily interesting for the romance between Andrews and Garner, the former struggling against being Americanized through her contact with the outgoing and freewheeling Garner.

Garner generally delivers a satisfactory performance. Douglas plays his admiral strictly for laughs. James Coburn as a navy officer is outstanding particularly for his comedy scenes. Joyce Grenfell as femme star's mother and Keenan Wynn, a salty old salt, likewise handle their roles well.

□ 1964: Nominations: Best B&W Cinematography, B&W Art Direction

••••••••••••••••••••••••••••••

■ AMERICAN ME

1992, 125 MINS, US ◇ ⊚

Dir Edward James Olmos   *Prod* Sean Daniel, Robert M. Young, Edward James Olmos   *Scr* Floyd Mutrux, Desmond Nakano   *Ph* Reynaldo Villalobos   *Ed* Arthur R. Coburn, Richard Candib   *Mus* Dennis Lambert, Claude Gaudette   *Art Dir* Joe Aubel
● Edward James Olmos, William Forsythe, Pepe Serna, Danny De La Paz, Evelina Fernandez, Cary-Hiroyuki Tagawa (Universal/YOY)

The criminal life is portrayed with all the glamour of a mugshot in *American Me*, a powerful indictment of the cycle of violence bred by the prisons and street culture. Project has been gestating since 1973, when Floyd Mutrux wrote the script. Al Pacino was once slated to star.

In a punchy prologue, the central figure of Santana (played as an adult by Edward James Olmos) is shown to be, literally, a child of the Pachuco riots of 1943. Pushed along by some incantatory, poetic narration, pic jumps to 1959, when the 16-year-old Santana forms a gang with his buddies Mundo (Pepe Serno) and J.D. (William Forsythe).

Long section detailing life at Folsom State Prison (where the company shot for three weeks) is as fascinating as it is disturbing. Film sketches racial divisions within the pen, the rise of the so-called Mexican Mafia, how drugs are smuggled inside, the scams that can make life there safer and how men inside control things outside. Olmos makes for a mesmerizing, implacable Santana, one of the least romanticized film gangsters since Paul Muni's Scarface.

••••••••••••••••••••••••••••••

■ AMERICAN NINJA

1985, 95 MINS, US ◇ ⊚ ⊙

Dir Sam Firstenberg   *Prod* Menahem Golan, Yoram Globus   *Scr* Paul de Mielche   *Ph* Hanania Baer   *Ed* Michael J. Duthie   *Mus* Michael Linn   *Art Dir* Adrian Gorton
● Michael Dudikoff, Steve James, Judie Aronson, Guich Koock, John Fujioka, Don Stewart (Cannon)

Michael Dudikoff is the titular hero, a sullen GI named Joe who arrives at US Army base Fort Sonora with a chip on his shoulder. He quickly alienates everyone except the pretty daughter of the commanding officer, Patricia Hickock (Judie Aronson), by singlehandedly saving her from the deadly ninjas working for corrupt arms dealer Ortega (Don Stewart).

Director Sam Firstenberg stages the numerous action scenes well, but engenders little interest in the non-story [by Avi Kleinberger and Gideon Amir].

Dudikoff comes off awkwardly as a new James Dean clone who's been pumping iron. Most winning performance is turned in by Steve James, Joe's sole pal on the base.

••••••••••••••••••••••••••••••

AMERICAN NINJA 2 THE CONFRONTATION

1987, 89 MINS, US ◇ ⓥ ⊙
Dir Sam Firstenberg   *Prod* Menahem Golan, Yoram Globus   *Scr* Gary Conway, James Booth   *Ph* Gideon Porath   *Ed* Michael J. Duthie   *Mus* George S. Clinton   *Art Dir* Holger Gross
● Michael Dudikoff, Steve James, Larry Poindexter, Gary Conway, Jeff Weston, Michelle Botes (Golan-Globus)

This time out, after *American Ninja* (1985) and *Avenging Force* (1986), globetrotting army hardbodies Michael Dudikoff and Steve James arrive on a small Caribbean island to investigate the disappearance of four US Marines. It turns out that a local drug kingpin is kidnaping soldiers and others to turn them into genetically reengineered ninja assassins who will do his bidding worldwide.

All this merely provides an excuse for an ample number of martial arts showdowns between the heroes and the black-robed baddies who swarm from all directions only to be dispatched in tidy fashion by the good guys.

Script by actors Gary Conway (who plays the narcotics overlord) and James Booth trades heavily upon the notion of Americans' inherent mental and physical superiority to native warriors, who are a dime a dozen, but in such a comic way that the viewer can laugh with it rather than at it.

Pic was lensed in South Africa, and is extremely picturesque despite the modest means.

....

AMERICAN NINJA 3 BLOOD HUNT

1989, 90 MINS, US ◇ ⓥ ⊙
Dir Cedric Sundstrom   *Prod* Harry Alan Towers   *Scr* Cedric Sundstrom   *Ph* George Bartels   *Ed* Michael J. Duthie   *Mus* George S. Clinton   *Art Dir* Ruth Strimling
● David Bradley, Steve James, Marjoe Gortner, Michele Chan, Yehuda Efroni, Calvin Yung (Breton)

With karate expert David Bradley replacing Michael Dudikoff in the leading role, series continues with a rehash of the enjoyable second entry, as top international martial arts combatants gather on a tropical isle for a tournament.

As before, the island plays host to an evil entrepreneur (Marjoe Gortner), who is on the verge of perfecting a virus that will become the ultimate terrorist weapon. Ridiculously, he is looking for the perfect specimen on whom to test the germ, and finds him in the hunky Bradley, who is prepared for a 'designer death.'

For his part, Bradley is determined to rescue his Japanese master, whom he believes has been kidnapped by the baddies. This provokes him and his fearless partners into an assault on the fortress-like laboratory.

Even for this level of by-the-numbers action filmmaking, Cedric Sundstrom's script is incredibly lame, and his staging of chopsocky violence is little better. Cheap-looking pic was produced in South Africa.

....

AMERICAN ROMANCE, AN

1944, 151 MINS, US ◇
Dir King Vidor   *Prod* King Vidor   *Scr* Herbert Delmas, William Ludwig   *Ph* Harold Rosson   *Ed* Conrad A. Nervig   *Mus* Louis Gruenberg   *Art Dir* Cedric Gibbons, Urie McCleary
● Brian Donlevy, Ann Richards, Walter Abel, John Qualen, Horace McNally (M-G-M)

One of Metro's greatest efforts (claimed to be two years in the making and cost over $3 million), this film is Brian Donlevy's baby from opening to closing, as the Czech immigrant who runs the gamut from poverty to become a wealthy industrialist.

King Vidor's story, coupled with his forthright direction and the excellent acting, are

assets that add up to a winning total. The one fault with *Romance* is that it is much too long in the telling.

Yarn takes more than an hour to get down to business. During that hour, true, Vidor lays the setting for the rest of the film, showing how Donlevy, who is held up at Ellis Island on landing in America because he did not own the equivalent of $25 in US money, overcomes this proverty by hard work in the Mesabi iron ore pits of Minnesota, and meets the girl whom he is to marry (Ann Richards).

Photographed in beautiful Technicolor, this romantic drama is notable for the documented montage shots of the intricate mining and shipping of iron ore; the making of steel in the huge mills of the midwest; films showing the way autos are made; and the excellent details of airplane-making.

....

AMERICAN SUCCESS
See: The American Success Company
....

AMERICAN SUCCESS COMPANY, THE
(Aka: American Success; Success)

1979, 94 MINS, US/W. GERMANY ◇
Dir William Richert   *Prod* Daniel H. Blatt, Edgar J. Scherrick   *Scr* William Richert, Larry Cohen   *Ph* Anthony Richmond   *Ed* Ralph E. Winters   *Mus* Maurice Jarre   *Art Dir* Rolf Zehetbauer
● Jeff Bridges, Belinda Bauer, Ned Beatty, Bianca Jagger, Steven Keats, John Glover (Columbia/Geria)

Although almost everything that happens on screen is done with considerable style and a morbid sense of humor, lack of overall point ultimately sinks the picture.

Jeff Bridges here plays the mild-mannered son-in-law of international credit card tycoon Ned Beatty. Called a loser by his boss and under the thumb of gorgeous wife Belinda Bauer, youth decides to turn the tables on them by assuming the guise of a gansterish tough-guy, then commencing to push them around to get his way.

Undeniable is William Richert's visual flair and sometimes startling sense of the absurd.

Billed as 'A William Richert-Larry Cohen Film', pic was to have been helmed by Cohen, writer of the original story, and was known during production as *The Ringer*.

[Pic was later released in re-edited versions as *American Success* and *Success*.]
....

AMERICAN TAIL, AN

1986, 80 MINS, US ◇ ⓥ ⊙
Dir Don Bluth   *Prod* Don Bluth, John Pomeroy, Gary Goldman   *Scr* Judy Freudberg, Tony Geiss   *Mus* James Horner (Amblin)

The film endeavors to tell the story of Russian immigrants, who happen in this case to be mice of the Mousekewitz clan, and their flight in the late 1800s to the United States, where, Papa Mousekewitz insists, 'There are no cats.'

Cartoons with ambitions even this noble are as rare as Steven Spielberg films that lose money, but every character and every situation presented herein have been seen a thousand times before.

The mouse-vs-cat stand-off is as old as animation itself, Dom DeLuise's friendly feline is uncomfortably close to the Cowardly Lion in concept, a little bug smacks directly of Jiminy Cricket, and assorted villains are straight out of Dickens by way of Damon Runyon.
□ 1986: Nomination: Best Song ('Somewhere Out There')
....

AMERICAN TAIL: FIEVEL GOES WEST, AN

1991, 74 MINS, US ◇ ⓥ ⊙
Dir Phil Nibbelink, Simon Wells   *Prod* Steven Spielberg, Robert Watts   *Scr* Flint Dille   *Ed* Nick Fletcher   *Mus* James Horner   *Art Dir* Neil Ross (Amblin)

Complete with legendary James Stewart voicing broken-down lawdog Wylie Burp, *An American Tail: Fievel Goes West* is an amiable sequel to the 1986 animated smash featuring the Russian immigrant mouse.

The story picks up the plucky Fievel an family living in grim, turn-of-the-century Bronx, menaced by omnipresent cats. The expansive shift to the Old West is welcome, as is the slowing of the pace to accommodate the relaxed, drawling and almost comatose personality of Fievel's hero/mentor Wylie Burp.

Fievel Goes West cleverly draws on the oft-expressed thought that the mythic West was largely an immigrant's wide-eyed dream of what America should be, in opposition to hellish big-city reality and the old country left behind.

Phillip Glasser's sweet rendition of the mouse's voice is a major asset, as are the voice parts of Dom DeLuise, as Fievel's scene-stealing companion, a scaredy-cat who turns brave; John Cleese, as the unctuously villainous Cat R. Waul; and Amy Irving, as the brassy saloon entertainer Miss Kitty. There isn't much of a plot to speak of.

....

AMERICAN TRAGEDY, AN

1931, 96 MINS, US
Dir Josef von Sternberg   *Scr* Samuel Hoffenstein   *Ph* Lee Garmes   *Art Dir* Hans Dreier
● Phillips Holmes, Sylvia Sidney, Frances Dee, Irving Pichel, Frederick Burton, Claire McDowell (Paramount)

An American Tragedy unreels as an ordinary program effort with an unhappy ending. Its relations to the book [by Theodore Dreiser] upon which it is based are decidedly strained. As Von Sternberg has seen fit to present it this celluloid structure is slow, heavy and not always interesting drama.

There is not a performance in the cast of any real interest. Histrionic honors belong to the elegantly voiced Irving Pichel, a veteran of the legit stage and one of the original founders of The Theatre Guild, as the district attorney.

The film spends a third or more of its 96 minutes on the trial. It's a big and theatrically good atmospheric scene, but has the handicap of involving neither of the girls as Roberta (for whose murder Clyde is convicted) is already dead, with Sondra escaping through the influence of a wealthy father. So the entire burden is on Phillips Holmes, as the floundering victim, which he is incapable of upholding for the camera.

On the sympathetic end Sylvia Sidney as the trusting Roberta, which she mainly accomplishes by means of a wistful smile. Frances Dee, as Sondra, merely registers as the Hollywood conception of a debutante and is not important, except as the brusque motivation for Clyde's reversal of his relations with Roberta and his longing to become of the younger social set of the small town.

It's questionable if even the admirers of this author's work condone the evident publicity complex he had developed, so it shouldn't be a matter of inflamed indignation by the minority in defense of the writer over the picture as an illustrated interpretation of the novel. Dreiser complained that the script first prepared by Sergei Eisenstein, to have directed, was entirely satisfactory. This, however was not the treatment finally used, with Von Sternberg replacing the Russian in the directorial chair.
....

AMERICAN WEREWOLF IN LONDON, AN

1981, 97 MINS, US ◇ ⓥ ⊙
Dir John Landis   *Prod* George Folsey Jr   *Scr* John Landis   *Ph* Robert Paynter   *Ed* Malcolm Campbell   *Mus* Elmer Bernstein   *Art Dir* Leslie Dilley
● David Naughton, Jenny Agutter, Griffin Dunne, John Woodvine, Brian Glover, Frank Oz (Universal/Lycanthrope)

A clever mixture of comedy and horror which succeeds in being both funny and scary, *An American Werewolf in London* possesses an overriding eagerness to please that prevents it from becoming off-putting, and special effects freaks get more than their money's worth.

Bumming around Europe, two American students (David Naughton and Griffin Dunne) seek refuge from the nasty North England elements in the Slaughtered Lamb pub. Natives there are uncommonly hostile, to the point of forcing the lads out into the night despite indications that there's trouble in these parts.

In short order, they're attacked by a fierce beast and, after the good-natured humor of this prelude, audience is instantly sobered up when Dunne is killed and Naughton is heavily gashed and gored.

Recovering in a London Hospital and, later, in the flat of amorous nurse Jenny Agutter, Naughton experiences some disturbing and visually outrageous nightmares and is visited by the 'Undead' Dunne, who urge his friend to commit suicide or turn into a werewolf with the next full moon.

Naughton ignores the advice and, sure enough, undergoes a complete transformation on camera, a highlight in which talents of special make-up effects designer Rick Baker are shown in full flower.
□ 1981: Best Make-Up

● ●

■ **AMITYVILLE HORROR, THE**

1979, 117 MINS, US ◇ ⑰ ⊙
Dir Stuart Rosenberg   *Prod* Ronald Saland, Elliot Geisinger   *Scr* Sandor Stern   *Ph* Fred J. Koenekamp   *Ed* Robert Brown   *Mus* Lalo Schifrin   *Art Dir* Kim Swados
● James Brolin, Margot Kidder, Rod Steiger, Don Stroud, Natasha Ryan (American International)

Taken from the Jay Anson tome, Sandor Stern's script deals faithfully with the supposedly true (but since challenged) story of the Lutz family who move into a home in Amityville, NY, at a knocked-down price because of its bloody history. The Lutz' fled 28 days later in terror.

Stepfather James Brolin, mother Margot Kidder and moppets Natasha Ryan, Meeno Peluce and K.C. Martel sympathetically play the happy innocent family and director Stuart Rosenberg – ably aided by efex specialists William Cruse and Delwyn Rheaume – have the house all ready for them.

Flies swarm where they shouldn't; pipes and walls ooze ick; doors fly open; and priests and psychic sensitives cringe and flee in panic. It's definitely a house that audience will enjoy visiting, especially if unfamiliar with the ending.
□ 1979: Nomination: Best Original Score

● ●

■ **AMITYVILLE II THE POSSESSION**

1982, 104 MINS, US ◇ ⑰ ⊙
Dir Damiano Damiani   *Prod* Ira N. Smith, Stephen R. Greenwald   *Scr* Tommy Lee Wallace   *Ph* Franco DiGiacomo   *Ed* Sam O'Steen   *Mus* Lalo Schifrin   *Art Dir* Pierluigi Basile
● Burt Young, Rutanya Alda, James Olson, Jack Magner, Diane Franklin, Andrew Prine (Orion/De Laurentiis)

It is never quite explained in the context of the film whether this is a prequel, sequel or entirely new version of the Amityville story. No matter. We still have the same house of horrors about to be occupied by a family who, as usual, never think to leave the house once it starts taking on a personality of its own.

Of course, this is not the typical American family. Burt Young, who gives new meaning to the word one-dimensional in his portrait of the father, loves beating the daylights out of

his wife and kids. Jack Magner, a screen newcomer saddled with the plum (?) role of the troubled oldest son, begins finding his sister sexually attractive. And Rutanya Alda, who does a lot of screaming as the spineless mother, spends a lot of time praying her problem will go away.

There are actually two films meandering in this mess – one a second-rate horror flick about a family in peril, and another that is a slight variation on the demon-possessed *Exorcist* theme.

● ●

■ **AMOROUS ADVENTURES OF MOLL FLANDERS, THE**

1965, 123 MINS, UK ◇
Dir Terence Young   *Prod* Marcel Hellman   *Scr* Denis Cannan, Roland Kibbee   *Ph* Ted Moore   *Ed* Frederick Wilson   *Mus* John Addison   *Art Dir* Syd Cain
● Kim Novak, Richard Johnson, Angela Lansbury, George Sanders, Leo McKern, Vittorio De Sica (Paramount)

Moll Flanders – the amorous adventures of – is a sprawling, brawling, gaudy, bawdy, tongue-in-cheek comedy that seeks to caricaturize an 18th-century London wench's desire to be a gentlewoman and her varying exploits thereof. Starring Kim Novak in title role, it has sex and color, slapstick and lusty, busty characterization, action which is sometimes very funny and, again, equally unfunny.

The foreword slyly states: 'Any similarity between this film and any other film is purely coincidental.' However that may be, it was a natural that the success scored by *Tom Jones* should be followed by a femme counterpart in this adaptation of Daniel Defoe's novel.

Director Terence Young seems constantly to keep in mind the comic potentialities of his subject and his helming is always broad, leavened with old-fashioned sight gags. The screenplay follows Moll as she goes to London, to seek her goal through a variety of affairs and marriages which culminate in a ceremony with a highwayman whom she mistook to be a wealthy landowner.

Richard Johnson (whom Novak wed after pic ended) gives colorful and romantic enactment to the highwayman character. George Sanders' portrayal of a rich banker wed to Moll is robust and comical. Leo McKern, as Johnson's outlaw henchman, also scores a comedy hit.

● ●

■ **AMOROUS PRAWN, THE**

1962, 89 MINS, UK
Dir Anthony Kimmins   *Prod* Leslie Gilliat   *Scr* Anthony Kimmins, Nicholas Phipps   *Ph* Wilkie Cooper   *Ed* Thelma Connell   *Mus* John Barry   *Art Dir* Albert Witherick
● Ian Carmichael, Joan Greenwood, Cecil Parker, Dennis Price, Robert Beatty, Liz Fraser (British Lion)

Anthony Kimmins' comedy, *The Amorous Prawn*, chalked up well over 1,000 performances on the stage. Now, directed by the author, it shapes up as non-demanding light entertainment, cheerfully put over by a reliable cast of popular British thesps.

General Fitzadam (Cecil Parker) is on the eve of retirement but is a bit short of cash. His wife hits on the idea of converting his military headquarters in Scotland into a guest house. The general's army staff is brought into the scheme.

Two major complications develop. One is the sudden, unexpected return of the general which, at first, calls for a considerable amount of repetitious camouflage by the conspirators. The second is when an unexpected guest turns up who is revealed as the Minister of State for War.

Parker produces one of his typical, bumbly performances, but Joan Greenwood, as his wife, is not so peppily in character as she

normally is in this sort of drawing room farce. Ian Carmichael does a shrewd job as the wily corporal who becomes maitre d'hotel in the scheme while Liz Fraser and Bridget Armstrong provide some pulchritude.

● ●

■ **AMOS & ANDREW**

1993, 94 MINS, US ◇ ⑰ ⊙
Dir E. Max Frye   *Prod* Gary Goetzman   *Scr* E. Max Frye   *Ph* Walt Lloyd   *Ed* Jane Kurson   *Mus* Richard Gibbs   *Art Dir* Patricia Norris
● Nicolas Cage, Samuel L. Jackson, Dabney Coleman, Michael Lerner, Margaret Colin, Brad Dourif (Castle Rock)

A one-joke sketch that doesn't work as a feature, *Amos & Andrew* raises the question: 'How did this film ever get made?' Debuting director E. Max Frye, who penned Jonathan Demme's wildly uneven *Something Wild*, attempts a satire of contemporary racism that employs strictly stereotyped characters and typecast actors.

Pulitzer Prize-winning African-American writer, Andrew Sterling (played unsympathetically by Samuel L. Jackson), buys a summer home on exclusive Watauga Island, Mass. Neighbors Michael Lerner and Margaret Colin think Jackson is a burglar because he's black. They summon Dabney Coleman (who's running for political office) and somehow deduce that Jackson is holding hostages.

To cover up the police gaffe, Coleman cajoles recently arrested car thief Nicolas Cage into breaking into Jackson's house to hold him hostage in exchange for being allowed to quietly leave town after letting Jackson go on cue.

Scenes like the police opening fire on Jackson at his home play like a dead-serious documentary and even slapstick gags fall flat. Film is technically competent but runs out of gas so fast it's tough to evaluate editing and atmosphere. For people who arrive late, the whole farrago is summarized in trivial terms in an out-theme rap song by Sir Mix-Alot.

● ●

■ **ANASTASIA**

1956, 105 MINS, US ◇ ⑰ ⊙
Dir Anatole Litvak   *Prod* Buddy Adler   *Scr* Arthur Laurents   *Ph* Jack Hildyard   *Ed* Bert Bates   *Mus* Alfred Newman   *Art Dir* Andrei Andrejew, Bill Andrews
● Ingrid Bergman, Yul Brynner, Helen Hayes, Akim Tamiroff, Martita Hunt, Felix Aylmer (20th Century-Fox)

The legit hit *Anastasia* has been made into a wonderfully moving and entertaining motion picture from start to finish, and the major credit inevitably must go to Ingrid Bergman who turns in a great performance.

Yet the picture is by no means all Bergman. Yul Brynner as General Bounine, the tough Russian exile, etches a strong and convincing portrait that stands up perfectly to Bergman's Anastasia, and Helen Hayes has great dignity as the Empress.

Story basically is the one from the French play of Marcelle Maurette adapted by Guy Bolton. Brynner and a group of conspirators are working in Paris to produce an Anastasia who might help them collect the £1 million deposited in England by the Czar's family. Brynner keeps the destitute Bergman from suicide, then grooms her to play Anastasia's part.

Bergman bears an amazing resemblance to the Czar's youngest daughter who was supposed to have been killed by the Reds in 1918. Desperate to forget the past, Bergman first resists, then begins to recover her regal bearing – and her memories.

Director Anatole Litvak and producer Buddy Adler imbue the story with realistic settings.
□ 1956: Best Actress (Ingrid Bergman).
□ Nomination: Best Scoring of a Dramatic Picture

● ●

■ ANATOLIAN SMILE, THE

See: America America

....

■ ANATOMY OF A MURDER

1959, 160 MINS, US 🅥 ⊙
Dir Otto Preminger   *Prod* Otto Preminger   *Scr* Wendell Mayes   *Ph* Sam Leavitt   *Ed* Louis R. Loeffler   *Mus* Duke Ellington   *Art Dir* Boris Leven
● James Stewart, Lee Remick, Ben Gazzara, Arthur O'Connell, Eve Arden, Kathryn Grant (Columbia/Carlyle)

Director Otto Preminger got his film on the screen for preview only 21 days after the final shooting on Michigan location. This dispatch may be one reason why *Anatomy* is over-long.

Wendell Mayes' screenplay otherwise is a large reason for the film's general excellence. In swift, brief strokes it introduces a large number of diverse characters and sets them in motion. An army lieutenant (Ben Gazzara) has killed a tavern operator whom he suspects of attempting to rape his wife (Lee Remick). James Stewart, former district attorney and now a privately-practicing attorney in a small Michigan city, is engaged for the defense.

Mayes' screenplay, from the book by the Michigan judge who uses the nom de plume Robert Traver, differs in some respects from the novel. Partly through casting, there is considerable doubt about the real innocence of Gazzara and Remick. This handsome young couple astray of the law are far from admirable.

Preminger purposely creates situations that flicker with uncertainty, that may be evaluated in different ways. Motives are mixed and dubious, and, therefore, sustain interest.

Balancing the fascinating nastiness of the younger players, there is the warmth and intelligence of Stewart and Arthur O'Connell. O'Connell, a bright, but booze-prone Irishman of great charm, is his ally. Joseph N. Welch, Boston attorney, is tremendous as the trial judge. George C. Scott, as the prosecution attorney, has the suave menace of a small-time Torquemada.
☐ 1959: Nominations: Best Picture, Actor (James Stewart), Supp. Actor (Arthur O'Connell, George C. Scott), Screenplay, B&W Cinematography, Editing

....

■ ANCHORS AWEIGH

1945, 138 MINS, US ◇ 🅥 ⊙
Dir George Sidney   *Prod* Joe Pasternak   *Scr* Isabel Lennart   *Ph* Robert Planck, Charles Boyle   *Ed* Adrienne Fazan   *Mus* George Stoll   *Art Dir* Cedric Gibbons, Randall Duell
● Frank Sinatra, Kathryn Grayson, Gene Kelly, Jose Iturbi, Dean Stockwell, Sharon McManus (M-G-M)

Anchors Aweigh is solid musical fare. The production numbers are zingy; the songs are extremely listenable; the color treatment outstanding.

Two of the potent entertainment factors are the tunes and Gene Kelly's hoofing. Jule Styne and Sammy Cahn cleffed five new numbers, three of which are given the Frank Sinatra treatment for boff results.

In the dance department Kelly sells top terping. There is a clever Tom and Jerry sequence combining Kelly's live action with a cartoon fairy story. Kelly also combines three Spanish tunes into another sock number executed with little Sharon McManus. His third is a class tango.

Kathryn Grayson, one of the three co-stars, figures importantly in the score with her vocaling. Jose Iturbi plays and conducts *Donkey Serenade*, Piano Concerto and *Hungarian Rhapsody No. 2* for additional potent musical factor.

Sinatra and Kelly are sailors on liberty. They come to Hollywood. Sinatra is a shy Brooklynite who's being instructed in the art of pickups by Kelly, the traditional gob with a gal in every port.

☐ 1945: Best Score for a Musical Picture.
☐ Nominations: Best Actor (Gene Kelly), Color Cinematography, Song ('I Fall in Love Too Easily')

....

■ AND BABY MAKES THREE

1949, 83 MINS, US
Dir Henry Levin   *Prod* Robert Lord   *Scr* Lou Breslow, Joseph Hoffman   *Ph* Burnett Guffey   *Ed* Viola Lawrence   *Mus* George Duning
● Robert Young, Barbara Hale, Robert Hutton, Janis Carter, Billie Burke (Columbia/Santana)

Fun starts confusingly but mood warms up as footage unfolds and plot line becomes clear. Robert Young has been divorced by Barbara Hale after being caught in a compromising spot. It's a hurry-up Reno untying and Hale is ready to do a quick re-bound marriage when she faints on the way to the altar. Pregnancy is the diagnosis. This upsets wedding plans with Robert Hutton and complications also develop when Young announces he'll fight for partial custody.

Young is his usual able self in taking care of his part of the footage. Hale delights as the wouldbe mother. Henry Levin's direction gets good movement into the script and comedy touches are neatly devised.

....

■ ANDERSON TAPES, THE

1971, 98 MINS, US ◇ 🅥 ⊙
Dir Sidney Lumet   *Prod* Robert M. Weitman   *Scr* Frank R. Pierson   *Ph* Arthur J. Ornitz   *Ed* Joanne Burke   *Mus* Quincy Jones   *Art Dir* Benjamin J. Kasazkow
● Sean Connery, Dyan Cannon, Martin Balsam, Alan King, Ralph Meeker, Christopher Walken (Columbia)

Sean Connery plays an ex-con who schemes to burglarize an entire apartment house on Manhattan's plush upper East Side. With backing from a new breed of organized mobster, led by Alan King, Connery recruits a band of diverse helpmates ranging from a homosexual antique dealer (Martin Balsam) to a fellow ex-con just released after 40 years in prison (Stan Gottlieb).

Overriding the machinations of the plot are the Anderson tapes themselves. Lawrence Sanders' novel was composed of snippets of surreptitious recordings compiled by local police, FBI agents, private investigators, treasury spies, etc., all snooping on the activities for various reasons, and all unable to piece together what they're overhearing.

Scripter Frank Pierson with director Sidney Lumet has injected broadly comic aspects and the laughs work without reducing suspense.

Essentially miscast but trying mightily to keep his accent under control, Connery's presence is strong. As a high priced mistress, frigid until Connery melts her, Dyan Cannon has little to do but look appetizing.

With the flashiest role, Martin Balsam swishes off with the honors, although gay activists will take umbrage at the abundance of conventional fag jokes.

....

■ AND GOD CREATED WOMAN

1988, 94 MINS, US ◇ 🅥 ⊙
Dir Roger Vadim   *Prod* George C. Braunstein, Ron Hamady   *Scr* R.J. Stewart   *Ph* Stephen M. Katz   *Ed* Suzanne Petit   *Mus* Thomas Chase, Steve Rucker   *Art Dir* Victor Kempster
● Rebecca DeMornay, Vincent Spano, Frank Langella, Donovan Leitch, Judith Chapman (Crow/Vestron)

A remake in name only of his first feature, made 32 years earlier, Roger Vadim's new film is considerably more legitimate dramatically than one might expect.

Vadim tells a modestly involving tale about how a woman with two strikes against her gives herself a shot at life through a combination of sex, imagination, energy and plenty of scheming.

Attention-grabbing opening has inmate Rebecca DeMornay escaping from prison and hitching a ride in a limo belonging to New Mexico gubernatorial candidate Frank Langella, only to be deposited right back where she came from.

In the picture's hottest scene, she then gets it on with carpenter Vincent Spano and wins early parole by convincing this earnest young single father to marry her. DeMornay lays a major surprise on her husband when she announces that their marriage contract does not include sex.

DeMornay throws herself deeply into the part as a life-long loser determined to win at all costs. Spano's macho exterior is nicely modified as the story progresses with considerable emotional shading, and Langella is just right as the politico who is most intrigued by DeMornay but knows he could get burned by her.

....

■ ... AND JUSTICE FOR ALL

1979, 120 MINS, US ◇ 🅥 ⊙
Dir Norman Jewison   *Prod* Norman Jewison, Patrick Palmer   *Scr* Valerie Curtin, Barry Levinson   *Ph* Victor J. Kemper   *Ed* John F. Burnett   *Mus* Dave Grusin   *Art Dir* Richard MacDonald
● Al Pacino, Jack Warden, John Forsythe, Lee Strasberg, Christine Lahti, Jeffrey Tambor (Columbia)

...And Justice for All is a film that attempts to alternate between comedy and drama, handling neither one incompetently, but also not excelling at either task.

Centering on the impossible circumstances a sensitive lawyer encounters whe dealing with the complexities and corruption of the American judicial system, pic is another good vehicle for Al Pacino.

Pic begins on a serious note with Pacino, jailed for contempt of court, witnessing jailers and inmates terrify a transvestite being locked up for robbery.

Mood quickly changes to comedy with Pacino going off to the scene of a car accident to aid an overemotional client.

The story most explored, that of John Forsythe's judge accused of brutally raping a young girl, is compelling but never fully fleshed out to satisfaction.
☐ 1979: Nominations: Best Actor (Al Pacino), Original Screenplay

....

■ ANDROCLES AND THE LION

1952, 98 MINS, US 🅥
Dir Chester Erskine   *Prod* Gabriel Pascal   *Scr* Chester Erskine, Ken Englund   *Ph* Harry Stradling   *Ed* Roland Cross   *Mus* Frederick Hollander
● Jean Simmons, Alan Young, Victor Mature, Robert Newton, Maurice Evans, Elsa Lanchester (RKO)

Bernard Shaw's satirical comedy on Romans and Christians provides the basis for a fair film offering. Picture is a curious mixture of basic comedy and Shavian wit. The romance between the Christian girl and the Roman captain is the most effective part of the film, differing from the original play.

The first filming of a Shaw play in Hollywood, the presentation has the confined feeling of having been made indoors. There's an amusing superficiality to some of the sequences involving the decadent Roman court, its customs and reactions, with real wit in the Shaw dialog.

Director Chester Erskine's strongest guidance is evidenced in the scenes with Jean Simmons and Victor Mature as the Christian girl and the Roman captain.

The familiar story deals with Androcles' love of animals, a feeling that saves the Greek tailor when he frees a lion from a thorn and later meets that lion in the Roman arena.

....

ANDROID

1982, 80 MINS, US ◇ ⑰ ⊙
Dir Aaron Lipstadt   *Prod* Mary Ann Fisher   *Scr* James
Reigle, Don Opper   *Ph* Tim Suhrstedt   *Ed* R.J. Kizer,
Andy Horvitch   *Mus* Don Preston   *Art Dir* K.C. Scheibel,
Wayne Springfield
● Klaus Kinski, Brie Howard, Norbert Weisser, Crofton
Hardester, Kendra Kirchner, Don Opper (New World)

Obsessed researcher Klaus Kinski inhabits a
remote space station in the year 2036 with his
android assistant, Max 404, played by co-
writer Don Opper. Doctor is on the verge of
perfecting his masterpiece, a perfect robot
who happens to be a beautiful blonde, and
who will render Max obsolete.

Onto the craft from a prison ship come
three escaped convicts with no precise plans
but with dangerous personalities. One way or
another, they intend to make their way back
to Earth, where a revolt by androids proved of
sufficient magnitude to make them illegal.

Although there are the obligatory fight
scenes and nudity, film works mainly due to
the unusual interaction between the all-too-
human Max robot and those around him.

Most pics of this ilk offer nothing but cardboard characters, so it's commendable that
not only Max but the three fugitives come
across with strong personalities. Kinski has
relatively little do, but is nevertheless plausible as a Dr Frankenstein type.

ANDROMEDA STRAIN, THE

1971, 127 MINS, US ◇ ⑰ ⊙
Dir Robert Wise   *Prod* Robert Wise   *Scr* Nelson
Gidding   *Ph* Richard H. Kline   *Ed* Stuart Gilmore, John
W. Holmes   *Mus* Gil Melle   *Art Dir* Boris Leven
● Arthur Hill, David Wayne, James Olson, Kate Reid,
Paula Kelly, George Mitchell (Universal)

The Andromeda Strain is a high-budget 'science-
fact' melodrama, marked by superb production, an excellent score, an intriguing story
premise and an exciting conclusion. But
Nelson Gidding's adaptation of the Michael
Crichton novel is too literal and talky.

In four acts representing days, a team of
civilian medics attempt to find and isolate an
unknown phenomenon which has killed most
of a desert town near the place where a space
satellite has fallen to earth. Arthur Hill,
David Wayne, James Olson and Kate Reid
are the specialists racing against time.

In the first half hour, the plot puzzle and
eerie mood are well established, and in the final half hour there is a dramatically exciting
climax with massive self-destruction machinery. The middle hour, however, drags proceedings numbingly. The four scientists
repeatedly get into long-winded discussions.
There are times when one wants to shout at
the players to get on with it.

The glacial internal plot evolution is not at
all relieved by the performances. Hill is dull;
Wayne is dull; Olson caroms from another
dull character to a petulant kid; and Reid's
unexplained-until-later epilepsy condition
does not generate much interest. Mitchell
and nurse Paula Kelly are most refreshing
changes of pace.
□ 1971: Nominations: Best Art Direction,
Editing

AND SOON THE DARKNESS

1970, 100 MINS, UK ◇ ⑰
Dir Robert Fuest   *Prod* Albert Fennell, Brian Clemens
Scr Brian Clemens, Terry Nation   *Ph* Ian Wilson
Ed Ann Chegwidden   *Mus* Laurie Johnson
● Pamela Franklin, Michele Dotrice, Sandor Eles, John
Nettleton, Clare Kelly, Hanna-Maria Pravda (Associated
British)

Story concerns two young British girls pedalling through a dull, flat, deserted part of
France on vacation. One's a pert miss
(Michele Dotrice), her chum is a more down-
to-earth girl (Pamela Franklin), worried by
her chum's desire to sunbathe, ogle the local
lads and generally throw a spanner wrench
into the timetable of the holiday.

After a tiff the two separate. Franklin,
lonely and remorseful, returns to find
Dotrice. But she is missing. The film mainly
concerns the trouble Franklin gets into while
trying to solve the problem of what happened
to her friend.

French atmosphere is conveyed excellently
and helps reward the doom-laden gloom but
overall there's a leering, sinister feeling
about this piece which is repellent.

AND THEN THERE WERE NONE

1945, 97 MINS, US ⑰
Dir Rene Clair   *Prod* Harry M. Popkin   *Scr* Dudley
Nichols   *Ph* Lucien Andriot   *Ed* Harvey Manger
Mus Mario Castelnuovo-Tedesco
● Barry Fitzgerald, Walter Huston, Louis Hayward,
Roland Young, June Duprez, C. Aubrey Smith (20th
Century-Fox)

This screen version of Agatha Christie's
[novel and stage play *Ten Little Niggers*] is a
dull whodunit. The Christie mag yarn [serial-
ized in the *Saturday Evening Post*] was a fair
mystery story and a Broadway hit as a stage
adaptation, called *10 Little Indians*, but the
film version adds no laurels to the original.

Plot concerns itself with 10 assorted characters, each with a bad spot in his past, who are
marooned on a lonely island off the English
coast. Like the nursery rhyme, the number is
decimated by sudden death until only two
leave the island alive. Victims are mysteriously gathered in the spot by a mad judge
who fancies himself as a dispenser of justice.

Picture rarely rises to moments of suspense
and despite the killings it gives the appearance of nothing ever happening as directed by
Rene Clair.

Barry Fitzgerald is only fair. Walter
Huston, Louis Hayward, Roland Young, June
Duprez, C. Aubrey Smith and others appear
equally out of place. Production is first venture by Harry M. Popkin, burlesque and film
theater operator.

ANGEL

1937, 98 MINS, US ⊙
Dir Ernst Lubitsch   *Prod* Ernst Lubitsch   *Scr* Samson
Raphaelson, Guy Bolton, Russell Medcraft   *Ph* Charles
Lang   *Ed* William Shea   *Mus* Boris Morros (dir.)
Art Dir Hans Dreier, Robert Usher
● Marlene Dietrich, Herbert Marshall, Melvyn Douglas,
Edward Everett Horton, Herbert Mundin, Ernest Cossart
(Paramount)

Angel is a rich Hollywood dish that copies foreign recipes. It is Ernst Lubitsch, with
Continental delight, tackling a plot to his liking [from a play by Melchior Lengyel] in a far
more serious manner than is his custom.

Angel is a drama more than it is comedy,
laugh lines being restricted almost to servants, who include Edward Everett Horton,
Ernest Cossart and Herbert Mundin. Cossart
gets the biggest chance to make good. He is a
particularly engaging butler in the swank
household of a British diplomat.

Lubitsch has used a comparatively small
cast, keeping the action almost entirely to
three people, Marlene Dietrich, Herbert
Marshall and Melvyn Douglas.

The story seriously portrays a girl of the old
world who loves her husband and home, yet
must graze around in strange pastures.
Authors seek to accentuate that a woman can
love two men at the same time. It also sets
out to prove that a husband is willing to recognize this on evidence and take chances on
the consequences.

Dietrich is glamour in double dress. This
time she is wearing eyelashes you could hang
your hat on and every now and then the star
flicks 'em as though a dust storm was getting
in her way. Marshall is excellent as the duped
husband. The usual, smooth performance is
obtained from Douglas as the persistent
lover.

ANGEL

1982, 90 MINS, IRELAND ◇ ⑰ ⊙
Dir Neil Jordan   *Prod* Barry Blackmore   *Scr* Neil Jordan
Ph Chris Menges   *Ed* Pat Duffner   *Mus* Paddy Meegan
Art Dir John Lucas
● Stephen Rea, Alan Devlin, Veronica Quilligan, Peter
Caffrey, Honor Heffernan, Ray McAnally (MPCI)

Angel carries knockout power. A story of retribution set against the troubles in Northern
Ireland which are kept way in the background, it's an impressive pic debut for director-scripter Neil Jordan.

A saxophonist with a traveling band unwittingly observes the murder of the band's
manager (involved in extortion payoffs) and
that of a deaf and dumb girl witness. The musician, vigorously played by Stephen Rea, is
obsessed to hunt down the murderers and
does so, becoming a murderer himself several
times over.

Played out with a minimum of violence, despite its theme, *Angel* contrasts the sweetness
of dance music and the dark side of daily life.
The acting is strong.

Camerawork by Chris Menges (the only
non-Irish native involved in the production) is
striking as are other credits.

ANGEL AT MY TABLE, AN

1990, 156 MINS, NEW ZEALAND/AUSTRALIA ◇ ⑰ ⊙
Dir Jane Campion   *Prod* Bridget Ikin   *Scr* Laura Jones
Ph Stuart Dryburgh   *Ed* Veronica Haussler   *Mus* Don
McGlashan   *Art Dir* Grant Major
● Kerry Fox, Alexia Keogh, Karen Fergusson, Melina
Bernecker, Glynis Angell, William Brandt (Hibiscus)

Jane Campion comes up with a touching and
memorable biography of New Zealand author
Janet Frame, originally made as a three-part
TV miniseries (each part 52 minutes). In the
1950s, Frame spent eight years in a mental
home undergoing shock treatment for
wrongly diagnosed schizophrenia.

Part one, *To the Island*, deals with the
writer's childhood in a rural community in
the country's South Island. Tragedy strikes
early when Janet's beloved older sister,
Myrtle (Melina Bernecker), drowns in a
swimming accident. As a teen (Karen
Fergusson), Janet undergoes a painful puberty and becomes exceptionally shy.

In part two, *An Angel at My Table*, Janet
(Kerry Fox) goes to university but is unable
to cope with practical teaching. Further
tragedy enters her life when her younger sister and best friend, Isabel (Glynis Angell),
also drowns. She spends the next eight years
in shock treatment.

With her first novel also published, Janet,
in part three (*The Envoy from Mirror City*), travels on a literary grant to London and then
Spain. She rents a room in a fishing village
and has her first (and only?) love affair with a
young poet (William Brandt).

A potentially painful and harrowing film is
imbued with gentle humor and great compassion, which makes every character come
vividly alive. Campion constructs the film in a
series of short, sometimes elliptical scenes.

ANGEL FACE

1953, 91 MINS, US
Dir Otto Preminger   *Prod* Otto Preminger   *Scr* Frank
Nugent, Oscar Millard   *Ph* Harry Stradling   *Ed* Frederic
Knudtson   *Mus* Dimitri Tiomkin   *Art Dir* Albert S.
D'Agostino, Carroll Clark

● Robert Mitchum, Jean Simmons, Mona Freeman, Herbert Marshall, Leon Ames, Barbara O'Neil (RKO)

Jean Simmons portrays the title role of a young lady behind whose beautiful face is a diseased mind that plots to murder her wealthy stepmother (Barbara O'Neil). Drawn into this scheme, although innocently, is Robert Mitchum, an ambulance driver who attends the stepmother when Simmons' first murder attempt backfires. Attracted to Mitchum, she gets him a chauffeur job with the family.

Mitchum and Simmons make a goo team, both delivering the demands of the script [from a story by Chester Erskine] and Preminger's direction ably. Co-starred are Mona Freeman, the girl Mitchum casts off for Simmons, and Herbert Marshall, but neither has much to do in the footage.

■ ANGEL HEART

1987, 113 MINS, US ◇ ❤ ⊙
Dir Alan Parker *Prod* Alan Marshall, Elliott Kastner *Scr* Alan Parker *Ph* Michael Seresin *Ed* Gerry Hambling *Mus* Trevor Jones *Art Dir* Brian Morris
● Mickey Rourke, Robert De Niro, Lisa Bonet, Charlotte Rampling (Carolco/Winkast-Union)

Even if it may be a specious work at its core, *Angel Heart* still proves a mightily absorbing mystery, a highly exotic telling of a small-time detective's descent into hell, with Faustian theme, heavy bloodletting and pervasive grimness.

Based on William Hjortsberg's novel *Falling Angel*, Alan Parker's screenplay, set in 1955, has seedy Gotham gumshoe Mickey Rourke engaged by mysterious businessman Robert De Niro to locate a certain Johnny Favorite, a big band singer from the pre-war days who, De Niro says, failed to live up to the terms of a contract.

Rourke as Harry Angel, quickly discovers that Favorite, a war casualty and reportedly a vegetable, was removed years earlier from the nursing home where he was supposedly under care, and follows his leads to New Orleans, and particularly the jazz and voodoo elements within its black community.

Rourke is a commanding lead, putting everyone around him (except De Niro) on edge. Charlotte Rampling is in very briefly as an elegant fortune teller, while Lisa Bonet's striking looks are rather undercut by her Valley Girl accent, not terribly convincing for a poor black girl from bayou country.

Controversial lovemaking scene between Rourke and Bonet becomes rather rough but, probably more to the point, involves torrents of blood leaking down on them from the ceiling, all of this being intercut with glimpses of voodoo rituals.

■ ANGEL OF VENGEANCE
See: Ms. 45

■ ANGELS AND THE PIRATES
See: Angels in the Outfield

■ ANGELS IN THE OUTFIELD
(UK: Angels and Pirates)

1951, 99 MINS, US
Dir Clarence Brown *Prod* Clarence Brown *Scr* Dorothy Kingsley, George Wells *Ph* Paul C. Vogel *Ed* Robert J. Kern *Mus* Daniele Amfitheatrof
● Paul Douglas, Janet Leigh, Keenan Wynn, Donna Corcoran, Lewis Stone, Spring Byington (M-G-M)

Clarence Brown has carved a tremendously satisfying filmization from a script [based on a story by Richard Conlin] that, from every evidence, could have gone completely haywire if handled clumsily, dealing as it does with fantasy. Religious angle also presented a

delicate situation, but Brown has handled it all masterfully.

Pivotal character is Paul Douglas, who plays one of the most tyrannical, blasphemous managers in the history of baseball. His team is in seventh place and is headed into the sub-basement when somebody unknown to Douglas intercedes with the Angel Gabriel. A voice tells Douglas to look for a miracle in the third inning of a crucial game.

Janet Leigh's paper, the *Pittsburgh Messenger*, prints her interview with a little orphan girl who swears she has seen angels standing alongside the men of Douglas' team, helping them win. Douglas, accidentally conked by a line drive, admits to the press that the angels are helping him. This brings on an investigation into his sanity by the baseball commissioner.

Douglas is perfect as the brawler reformed by a little girl's prayers. Leigh foils cleverly. Donna Corcoran plays the orphan.

■ ANGELS ONE FIVE

1952, 97 MINS, UK
Dir George More O'Ferrall *Prod* John W. Gossage, Derek Twist *Scr* Derek Twist *Ph* Christopher Challis *Ed* Daniel Birt *Mus* John Wooldridge (arr.) *Art Dir* Fred Pusey
● Jack Hawkins, Michael Denison, Dulcie Gray, Andrew Osborn, Cyril Raymond, John Gregson (Templar/Associated British)

Action of *Angels One Five* takes place during the period described by Winston Churchill as 'Britain's finest hour', when a handful of fighter pilots (the few against the many) stemmed the air invasion by Nazi war planes.

Breaking away from the more conventional treatment, the script [from a story by Pelham Groom] watches the progress of the battle, not from the actual combats, but from the messages received by and emanating from the operational control room.

Competent acting is followed by whole cast. Jack Hawkins and Michael Denison are the two big shots of the base and their sharp discipline is tempered by a generous measure of understanding. Dulcie Gray has little more to do than appear sympathetic as the wife of the harassed control room chief.

■ ANGELS OVER BROADWAY

1940, 78 MINS, US ❤ ⊙
Dir Ben Hecht, Lee Garmes *Prod* Ben Hecht, Douglas Fairbanks Jr *Scr* Ben Hecht *Ph* Lee Garmes *Ed* Gene Havlick *Mus* George Antheil *Art Dir* Lionel Banks
● Douglas Fairbanks Jr, Rita Hayworth, Thomas Mitchell, John Qualen, George Watts (Columbia)

Angels over Broadway is a synthetic tale of Broadway nightlife and the characters that roam around Times Square. Aside from Thomas Mitchell, as a screwball playwright who sees a story in every individual, and who delights in plotting a finish there's nothing much in the Hechtian tale. Picture stutters and sputters too often to carefully etch human beings, with result that it develops into an over-dramatic stage play transformed to celluloid.

Writer-director-producer Ben Hecht gets little movement in the unwinding, and depends too much on stage technique in trying to put over his points. An embezzler (John Qualen) is saved from committing suicide by the zany playwright (Mitchell) who proceeds to try and help the former out of his jam and give him a new lease on life. Douglas Fairbanks Jr is a slick youth who shills for a big poker game, and sets his sights for Qualen who he assumes is a rural hick. There's much byplay between the trio and a girl who moves in (Rita Hayworth) before plan is worked out to recoup the coin in the come-on game.

Characters are all over-drawn, with

Mitchell providing many sharp cracks on the philosophy of life and living. Mitchell does much to hold together the minor interest retained in the running. Fairbanks fails to get much sympathy or attention as the wise young Broadwayite who knows all the angles. Hayworth is passable as the girl, while Qualen is bewildered enough as the prospective suicide.
☐ 1940: Nomination: Best Original Screenplay

■ ANGEL STREET
See: Gaslight

■ ANGELS WITH DIRTY FACES

1938, 97 MINS, US ❤ ⊙
Dir Michael Curtiz *Prod* [Sam Bischoff] *Scr* John Wexley, Warren Duff *Ph* Sol Polito *Ed* Owen Marks *Mus* Max Steiner *Art Dir* Robert Haas
● James Cagney, Pat O'Brien, Humphrey Bogart, Ann Sheridan, George Bancroft, Billy Halop (Warner)

Another typical *Dead End* kids picture, but with the single exception that it has James Cagney and Pat O'Brien to bolster the dramatic interest.

Cagney is the tenderloin toughie who's the idol of the gutter-bred youngsters because of his criminal exploits and cocky belligerence. O'Brien is the priest who was a boyhood chum of Cagney's and who seeks to retrieve the neighborhood kids from trying to emulate their gangster hero. There's a singular ending for the story which has Cagney pretending to turn yellow as he goes to the electric chair so he'll kill the kids' unhealthy adoration. It is a novel twist to a commonplace story [by Rowland Brown], but it's thoroughly hokey.

The screenplay contains many effective cinematic touches. However, in at least one instance the same set is used for two supposedly different locales.

Cagney and O'Brien form an irresistible team. Their personalities and acting styles offer both a blend and an eloquent contrast. Cagney has a swagger and an aw-go-to-hell pugnacity, while O'Brien gives an eminently credible performance of the mild-mannered, two-fisted, compassionate priest. The *Dead End* kids are as rambunctious as usual.
☐ 1938: Nominations: Best Director, Actor (James Cagney), Original Story

■ ANGRY HILLS, THE

1959, 105 MINS, UK
Dir Robert Aldrich *Prod* Raymond Stross *Scr* A.I. Bezzerides *Ph* Stephen Dade *Ed* Peter Tanner *Mus* Richard Rodney Bennett
● Robert Mitchum, Elisabeth Mueller, Stanley Baker, Gia Scala, Theodore Bikel, Donald Wolfit (M-G-M)

The Angry Hills, set in Greece, is a rather confused yarn but has the merit of good direction by Robert Aldrich and some very competent performances.

Robert Mitchum plays an American war correspondent who is hunted by Gestapo chief Stanley Baker and fifth columnist Theodore Bikel when he arrives in Athens as Greece is about to fall to the Nazis. Baker and Bikel want Mitchum because he has a list of 16 Greek underground leaders which he is conveying to British intelligence in London. He is helped by Gia Scala and also by Elisabeth Mueller, both of whom fall in love with Mitchum.

Both Baker and Mitchum give very sound performances. Mueller brings a radiant charm to the part of the widow. A.I. Bezzerides' screenplay [from Leon Uris' book] falters towards the end when the love complications arise but he tells the story briskly and well.

■ ANGRY SILENCE, THE

1960, 95 MINS, UK
Dir Guy Green   *Prod* Richard Attenborough, Bryan Forbes   *Scr* Bryan Forbes   *Ph* Arthur Ibbetson
Ed Anthony Harvey   *Mus* Malcolm Arnold
● Richard Attenborough, Pier Angeli, Michael Craig, Bernard Lee, Alfred Burke, Penelope Horner (Beaver)

The Angry Silence details the impact of industrial unrest on individuals, told with passion, integrity and guts, but without false theatrical gimmicks. Apart from the message, there is a solid core of entertainment produced by taut writing, deft direction and topnotch acting.

Plot concerns a worker in a factory where there has been no trouble until a political troublemaker moves in. Insidiously he stirs up unrest, makes one of the workers his catspaw, creates a wildcat strike and then quietly moves on to spread his poison in other factories. The main victim of the strike is played by Richard Attenborough who, because he refuses to be pushed around, is sent to Coventry (shunned by his workmates) and is beaten up, and his family intimidated.

Original story by Richard Gregson and Michael Craig has been skilfully written for the screen by Bryan Forbes. Perhaps the end is slightly contrived, but Guy Green has directed with quiet skill, leaving the film to speak for itself.

Attenborough, as the quiet little man who just wants to be left alone to grapple with his home problems, has done nothing better on the screen for a long time. That goes, too, for Pier Angeli as his wife. Here she is a creature of flesh and blood, unhappily involved in a problem that she cannot understand. Michael Craig, as Attenborough's best friend, is also in his best form.
☐ 1960: Nomination: Best Original Screenplay

■ ANIMAL CRACKERS

1930, 97 MINS, US
Dir Victor Heerman   *Scr* Morrie Ryskind   *Ph* George Folsey
● Groucho Marx, Harpo Marx, Chico Marx, Zeppo Marx, Lillian Roth, Margaret Dumont (Paramount)

First give Paramount extreme credit for reproducing *Animal Crackers* intact from the stage [musical written by George S. Kaufman, Morrie Ryskind, Harry Ruby and Bert Kalmar], without too much of the songs and musical numbers.

Among the Marx boys there is no preference. Groucho shines; Harpo remains a pantomimic clown who ranks with the highest; Chico adds an unusual comedy sense to his dialog as well as business and piano playing; and Zeppo, if in on a split, is lucky.

Lillian Roth may have been cast here to work out a contract. She can't hurt because the Marxes are there, but if Roth is in for any other reason it doesn't appear. She sings one song in the ingenue role. That song is useless. Opposite is Hal Thompson, a juve who doesn't prove it here.

■ ANIMAL FARM

1954, 72 MINS, UK
Dir John Halas, Joy Batchelor, (animation) John Reed
Prod John Halas, Joy Batchelor   *Scr* John Halas, Joy Batchelor, Lothar Wolff, Borden Mace, Philip Stapp
Ph S.G. Griffiths   *Mus* Matyas Seiber (Halas & Batchelor)

Human greed, selfishness and conniving are lampooned in *Animal Farm* with the pigs behaving in a pig-like manner and the head pig, named Napoleon, corrupting and perverting an honest revolt against evil social conditions into a new tyranny as bad as, and remarkably similar to, the old regime. In short, this cartoon feature [from the novel by George Orwell] is a sermon against all that is bestial

in politics and rotten in the human will to live in luxury at the expense of slaves.

Made in Britain, the cartoon is vividly realized pictorially. The musical score, the narration, the sound effects and the editing all are of impressive imaginative quality.

■ ANNA AND THE KING OF SIAM

1946, 128 MINS, US ◇ ▽
Dir John Cromwell   *Prod* Louis D. Lighton   *Scr* Talbot Jennings, Sally Benson   *Ph* Arthur Miller   *Ed* Harmon Jones   *Mus* Bernard Herrmann   *Art Dir* Lyle R. Wheeler, William Darling
● Irene Dunne, Rex Harrison, Linda Darnell, Lee J. Cobb, Gale Sondergaard (20th Century-Fox)

Socko adult drama. *Anna and the King of Siam* is a rather faithful screen adaptation of Margaret Landon's biography, intelligently handled to spellbind despite its long footage.

Anna tells a straightforward narrative, bringing in the natural humor, suspense and other dramatic values of the story of an English widow who finds herself confronted with the many problems of educating the children and some of the wives of the King of Siam. The monarch, himself, needs some education, and Anna sees that he gets it.

Script builds fascinating adult interest without ever implying that relationship between teacher and pupil goes beyond the friendship stag

Irene Dunne does a superb enactment of Anna, the woman who influenced Siamese history by being teacher and confidante to a kingly barbarian. Rex Harrison shines particularly in his American film debut. It's a sustained characterization of the King of Siam that makes the role real. Linda Darnell, third star, has little more than a bit as one of the king's wives, who incurs his displeasure and is burned at the stake. She does well.
☐ 1946: Best B&W Cinematography, B&W Interior Decoration (Lyle R. Wheeler, William Darling).
Nominations: Best Supp. Actress (Gale Sondergaard), Screenplay, Scoring of a Dramatic Picture

■ ANNA CHRISTIE

1923, 87 MINS, US ⊗
Dir John Griffith Wray   *Prod* Thomas H. Ince
Scr Bradley King   *Ph* Henry Sharp
● Blanche Sweet, William Russell, George F. Marion, Eugenie Besserer (Ince/Associated First National)

Anna Christie is a picture that is as different to the regular runs of screen productions as the Eugene O'Neill plays are to the majority of hits and near-hits that come to the spoken stage.

There is one mistake John Griffith Wray makes in the direction. In the usual picture fashion he tries to force his leading woman to overshadow the character role. Blanche Sweet isn't the Anna Christie Pauline Lord was on the stage, but George Marion is Chris and as such he so far overshadows the leading woman that the director is undoubtedly forced to take the extremes he does to keep her in the eye of the audience. But that is not good direction.

William Russell makes Matt Burke a convincing sort of a brute Irish coal passer on a steam tramp and puts over his role with a wallop, and likewise Eugenie Besserer handles Marthy, so that in all Sweet is the only weak spot of the cast of four.

■ ANNA CHRISTIE

1930, 86 MINS, US ▽
Dir Clarence Brown   *Scr* Frances Marion   *Ph* William Daniels   *Ed* Hugh Wynn   *Mus* [uncredited]
Art Dir Cedric Gibbons

● Greta Garbo, George F. Marion, Marie Dressler, Charles Bickford (M-G-M)

In all departments a wow picture. Comparison is inevitable with the silent version made by Thomas Ince eight years earlier with Blanche Sweet and William Russell. In both instances Hollywood closely follows the Eugene O'Neill play.

Infinite care in developing each sequence, just the proper emphasis on characterizations and a part that exactly fits Greta Garbo put *Anna Christie* safely in the realm of the superlative.

'Garbo talks' is, beyond quarrel, an event. La Garbo's accent is nicely edged with a Norse 'yah', but once the ear gets the pitch it's okay.

George Marion, in the original Ince production, again plays the old sentiment-hungry seagoing father. Charles Bickford as the Irish sailor of massive muscles and primitive ideals is magnificent. Perhaps the greatest surprise is Marie Dressler, who steps out of her usual straight slapstick to stamp herself an actress.
☐ 1929/30: Nominations: Best Director, Actress (Greta Garbo), Cinematogrpahy

■ ANNA KARENINA

1935, 95 MINS, US ▽
Dir Clarence Brown   *Prod* David O. Selznick
Scr Clemence Dane, Salka Viertel, S.N. Behrman
Ph William Daniels   *Ed* Robert J. Kern   *Mus* Herbert Stothart   *Art Dir* Cedric Gibbons
● Greta Garbo, Fredric March, Freddie Bartholomew, Basil Rathbone, Maureen O'Sullivan, May Robson (M-G-M)

Greta Garbo starred in this story once before in 1927. Silent film was titled *Love* and John Gilbert had the role now handled by Fredric March. March handles his assignment firmly and with understanding and the film in toto is a more honest and sincere rendition of the Tolstoy classic than the silent.

Garbo, too, seems to have grown since 1927. There is no flaw to be found in her rendition of the love-wracked Russian girl, Anna.

Trimmed to its essentials the story is an extremely simple one: a married woman, hating her cold, unloving, hypocritical husband, falls in love with a young officer of the guards. Love sweeps everything from under her. Her husband won't give her a divorce. She gives up everything she has in life, including her baby, to go to her lover.

Casting throughout is excellent, although just a trifle annoying. There is a distinct clash of accents which might have been avoided. Reginald Denny, Basil Rathbone and Reginald Owen speak Oxfordese English, as opposed to Garbo's Stockholmese.

■ ANNA KARENINA

1948, 139 MINS, UK ▽
Dir Julien Duvivier   *Prod* Alexander Korda   *Scr* Jean Anouilh, Guy Morgan, Julien Duvivier   *Ph* Henri Alekan   *Ed* Russell Lloyd   *Mus* Constant Lambert   *Art Dir* Andre Andrejeff
● Vivien Leigh, Ralph Richardson, Kieron Moore, Hugh Dempster (London)

Fine as this fourth production of Tolstoy's novel is (Fox 1915, Metro 1927 and 1935), it misses greatness and has tedious stretches.

It would appear that far too much attention was paid to the sets and the artistic structure at the expense of the players. It would have been wise for Korda and Duvivier to realize that the story, for screen purposes, is frankly Victorian melodrama, and that there was always the danger of reducing the characters to puppets.

It speaks volumes for Leigh and Richardson that they are able to disentangle themselves from their overwhelming surroundings and become credibly human. Leigh dominates the picture, as she rightly should with her beauty, charm and skill. It isn't her fault that eyes remain dry and hearts unwrung when she moves to inevitable tragedy, as the neglected wife and discarded lover.

Richardson's portrayal of the priggish, unlikeable husband is masterly yet uneven. Sometimes he gives the impression of a Chinese philosopher with accent and staccato phrase. Incidentally, the multiplicity of pronunciations of 'Karenina' by various people is a trifle distracting.

■ ANNE OF THE INDIES

1951, 81 MINS, US ◇

Dir Jacques Tourneur   *Prod* George Jessel   *Scr* Philip Dunne, Arthur Caesar   *Ph* Harry Jackson   *Ed* Robert Fritch   *Mus* Franz Waxman   *Art Dir* Lyle Wheeler, Albert Hogsett
● Jean Peters, Louis Jourdan, Debra Paget, Herbert Marshall, Thomas Gomez, James Robertson Justice (20th Century-Fox)

As the femme pirate who sailed the Caribbean seas as the dreaded Captain Providence, Jean Peters outdoes the best Ruth Roland tradition and looks good while doing it. There's nothing ludicrous about her performance in the type of action usually handed to males.

The film plays along at an imaginative pace under Jacques Tourneur's direction. Sea battles are expertly staged to make the most of such actionful moments.

Plot [from a story by Herbert Ravenal Sass] finds Louis Jourdan, a French naval officer whose ship and wife are being held by the British, volunteering to capture Captain Providence. He manages to get aboard her pirate vessel, takes advantage of a natural attraction that springs up to trick her with a phoney treasure map, thus leading her into a British ambush. However, Anne escapes the trap and takes her vengance by kidnapping the wife, played by Debra Paget.

Jourdan supplies a good hero and Thomas Gomez a colorful Blackbeard. Herbert Marshall, as rum-sodden doctor aboard the pirate ship, James Robertson Justice, buccaneer first-mate, and the lineup of cut-throat characters all come over excellently.

■ ANNE OF THE THOUSAND DAYS

1970, 145 MINS, UK ◇ ⑫

Dir Charles Jarrott   *Prod* Hal B. Wallis   *Scr* Bridget Boland, John Hale   *Ph* Arthur Ibbetson   *Ed* Richard Marden   *Mus* Georges Delerue   *Art Dir* Maurice Carter, Lionel Couch
● Richard Burton, Genevieve Bujold, Irene Papas, Anthony Quayle, John Colicos, Michael Horden (Universal)

With Richard Burton as Henry VIII and Genevieve Bujold in the title role of Anne Boleyn, *Anne of the Thousand Days* is a stunning-acted, sumptuous, grand-scale widescreen drama of the royal bed chamber and political intrigues that created the Church of England.

Although Burton's portrayal is sensitive, vivid and arresting, it is still basically an unsympathetic role.

The screenplay, as adapted by Richard Sokolove, based on Maxwell Anderson's stage play, bristles with sharp epigrammatic dialog.

In his first feature film, TV director Charles Jarrot frames his Renaissance pageant handsomely and handles the skilled cast to achieve an effective uniform period style. However, there is a basically stagey pace to the drama that makes it more static and less cinematic than it might have been.
□ 1969: Best Costume Design.
□ Nominations: Best Picture, Actor (Richard Burton), Actress (Genevieve Bujold), Supp.

Actor (Anthony Quayle), Screenplay, Cinematography, Art Direction, Original Score, Sound

■ ANNIE

1982, 128 MINS, US ◇ ⑫ ⊙

Dir John Huston   *Prod* Ray Stark   *Scr* Carol Sobieski   *Ph* Richard Moore   *Ed* Margaret Booth, Michael A. Stevenson   *Mus* Ralph Burns (arr.)   *Art Dir* Dale Hennesy
● Albert Finney, Carol Burnett, Aileen Quinn, Ann Reinking, Bernadette Peters, Tim Curry (Columbia)

Many people said John Huston was an odd choice to direct *Annie* and he proves them right. In an effort to be more 'realistic' *Annie* winds up exposing just how weak a story it had to start with [stage play book by Thomas Meehan], not helped here by the music [songs by Charles Strouse and Martin Charnin]. Aside from the memorable 'Tomorrow' the show's songs weren't all that much in the first place and four new tunes penned for the $35 million film aren't any better.

In the title role, little Aileen Quinn acquits herself quite well. Carol Burnett gets most of what chuckles there are as the drunken Miss Hannigan who runs the orphanage.

Albert Finney is best of the bunch as Daddy Warbucks, but it's really not a test for his talents. Edward Herrman is acceptable as FDR, a part he has down pat. As the villainous phony parents, Bernadette Peters and Tim Curry add little.
□ 1982: Nominations: Best Art Direction, Original Song Score

■ ANNIE GET YOUR GUN

1950, 107 MINS, US ◇

Dir George Sidney   *Prod* Arthur Freed   *Scr* Sidney Sheldon   *Ph* Charles Rosher   *Ed* James E. Newcom   *Mus* Adolph Deutsch, Roger Edens (dirs.)
● Betty Hutton, Howard Keel, Louis Calhern, J. Carrol Naish, Edward Arnold, Keenan Wynn (M-G-M)

Annie Get Your Gun is socko musical entertainment on film, just as it was on the Broadway stage [in 1946]. In many respects, the film version gets the nod over the legit piece; at least there is enough pro and con to reprise that great novelty number, 'Anything You Can Do'.

Ten of the *Annie* Irving Berlin hits are used and two are reprised.

Briefly, Annie is a backwoods gal, a deadshot who is taken into a wildwest show, soon supplants the show's male marksman, goes on to become a star and then wins her man by losing a shooting match.

Annie is Wild West, shooting, Indians, daredevil-riding and action, never slowing a minute as put together for the screen by producer Arthur Freed and director George Sidney. They will find it hard to top.
□ 1950: Best Score for a Musical Picture.
□ Nominations: Best Color Cinematography, Color Art Direction, Editing

■ ANNIE HALL

1977, 93 MINS, US ◇ ⑫ ⊙

Dir Woody Allen   *Prod* Charles H. Joffe   *Scr* Woody Allen, Marshall Brickman   *Ph* Gordon Willis   *Ed* Ralph Rosenblum   *Art Dir* Mel Bourne
● Woody Allen, Diane Keaton, Tony Roberts, Carol Kane, Paul Simon, Colleen Dewhurst (United Artists)

Woody Allen's four romantic comedies with Diane Keaton strike a chord of believability that makes them nearly the 1970s equivalent of the Tracy-Hepburn films. *Annie Hall*, is by far the best, a touching and hilarious three-dimensional love story.

The gags fly by in almost non-stop profusion, but there is an undercurrent of sadness and pain reflecting a maturation of style.

Allen tells Keaton in the film that he has 'a very pessimistic view of life,' and it's true.

The script is loosely structured, virtually a two-character running conversation between Allen and Keaton as they meet, fall in love, quarrel, and break up. Meanwhile, he continues his career as a moderately successful TV-nightclub comic and she develops a budding career as a singer.
□ 1977: Best Picture, Director, Actress (Diane Keaton), Original Screenplay.
□ Nomination: Best Actor (Woody Allen)

■ ANNIVERSARY, THE

1968, 95 MINS, UK ◇ ⑫ ⊙

Dir Roy Ward Baker   *Prod* Jimmy Sangster   *Scr* Jimmy Sangster   *Ph* Harry Waxman   *Ed* Peter Wetherley   *Mus* Philip Martell
● Bette Davis, Sheila Hancock, Jack Hedley, James Cossins, Elaine Taylor, Christian Roberts (Hammer)

Derived from Bill McIllwraith's legit original, this was turned into a vehicle for the extravagant tantrums of Bette Davis, in her most ghoulish mood. This, together with its modish black-comedy lines and bold situation, is its chief asset.

Because it skates near the bone of family relationships, it rouses plenty of understanding yocks, but the exaggeration of the concept doesn't wear as well on film as it did on stage. It is a highly theatrical piece, and needs remoteness, rather than closeups, for its bitter characterizations not to come across as caricature.

Davis gets her teeth into the role of the ultra-possessive ma and hurls it out with splendid panache and flamboyance, but some might find her outsize portrayal too stark to carry the conviction. She bosses it over a family of three sons, all of whom are in an advanced stage of spinelessness.

The action, which little attempt has been made to transfer into the wider visual terms of a feature pic, takes place on the anniversary of Davis' husband's death, and the family gathers to do him honor.

■ ANOTHER COUNTRY

1984, 90 MINS, UK ◇ ⑫ ⊙

Dir Marek Kanievska   *Prod* Alan Marshall   *Scr* Julian Mitchell   *Ph* Peter Biziou   *Ed* Gerry Hambling   *Mus* Michael Storey   *Art Dir* Brian Morris
● Rupert Everett, Colin Firth, Michael Jenn, Robert Addie, Rupert Wainwright, Anna Massey (Goldcrest)

Julian Mitchell's adaptation of his successful West End play *Another Country* is an absorbing tale about life in a British public (i.e. private) boarding school in the 1930s. Story is supposedly based on the early friendship of Guy Burgess and Donald MacLean who, in the 1950s, spied for the USSR while working for the British government but defected to Moscow before they could be arrested.

Mitchell's contention is that the homosexuality of Burgess, called Bennett here, made him as much an outsider in the claustrophobic atmosphere of the British uppercrust as did MacLean's (Judd's) Marxism.

Film is marvelously acted down the line, with Rupert Everett standout as the tormented Bennett.

■ ANOTHER 48 HRS.

1990, 95 MINS, US ◇ ⑫ ⊙

Dir Walter Hill   *Prod* Lawrence Gordon   *Scr* John Fasano, Jeb Stuart, Larry Gross   *Ph* Matthew F. Leonetti   *Ed* Freeman Davies, Carmel Davies, Donn Aron   *Mus* James Horner   *Art Dir* Joseph C. Nemec III
● Eddie Murphy, Nick Nolte, Brion James, Kevin Tighe, Ed O'Ross, David Anthony Marshall (Paramount/Eddie Murphy)

A

Pic's really misnamed, since it's not *Another 48 HRS.* but the same *48HRS.*, the 1982 mismatched buddy action pic.

Director Walter Hill, reprising those chores, knows the terrain and tills it with all the familiar elements: bawdy humor, cannon-loud gunplay, hissable bad guys and plenty of action.

Eddie Murphy and Nick Nolte manage to recapture some of their initial chemistry, but for the most part the film is curiously flat – in part due to a jumped plot that's so quickly tied up at the end it seems everyone was in a hurry to get their checks and get out of town.

The plot even hinges on the first film, as two hit men are dispatched to kill Murphy, one the brother of the lead baddie offed in *48HRS*. Nolte, meanwhile, has spent the past four years chasing a faceless drug kingpin called the Iceman, who paid for the hit on Murphy. He's been thwarted at every turn, however, leading Murphy to suspect corruption within the police department.

Hill and his trio of screenwriters choose the stale and predictable route at almost every turn, the plot being strictly a slender means of allowing Murphy and Nolte to strut their stuff.

. . . .

■ ANOTHER MAN ANOTHER CHANCE

1977, 132 MINS, FRANCE ◇ ⓥ

Dir Claude Lelouch   *Prod* Alexandre Mnouchkine
Scr Claude Lelouch   *Ph* Jacques Lefrancois, Stanley Cortez   *Ed* Georges Klotz   *Mus* Francis Lai
Art Dir Robert Clatworthy
● James Caan, Genevieve Bujold, Francis Huster, Susan Tyrrell, Jennifer Warren (Films 13/Ariane/Artistes Associes)

A sort of valentine to the American western film with James Caan and Genevieve Bujold for the he-she interest. It's a Frenchman's perspective on the US.

It begins with a passage in steerage to America by Bujold and her boyfriend (Francis Huster), a photographer, in the 1870s.

James Caan meanwhile has been paralleled to Bujold's life and out west they pass each other often and finally meet. He is a Yank veterinarian, happy in his work.

Caan and Bujold finally fall in love. There are some simple observations of life in the west but not imitative of the general oater. They are at ease and inventive in their roles of headstrong, piquant woman settler and he as a relaxed charmer. Caan has warm failings as when he emerges a worse shot than his eight-year-old son.

It has good production dress and is spoken in French, when the French are on, and English in America when the Yanks are on.

. . . .

■ ANOTHER TIME, ANOTHER PLACE

1983, 101 MINS, UK ◇ ⓥ ⊙

Dir Michael Radford   *Prod* Simon Perry   *Scr* Michael Radford   *Ph* Roger Deakins   *Ed* Tom Priestley
Mus John McLeod   *Art Dir* Hayden Pearce
● Phyllis Logan, Giovanni Mauriello, Gian Luca Favilla, Claudio Rosini, Paul Young, Gregor Fisher (Umbrella)

It's not often that a British film is realized with as much creative integrity as *Another Time, Another Place*. The plot springs from the cultural difference between the inhabitants of a bleak Scottish agricultural village and a trio of Italians confined to the community during the World War II. One Italian in particular, the passionate Neopolitan Luigi (Giovanni Mauriello) mesmerizes Janie (Phyllis Logan) by seeming to offer an alternative to an emotionally cold marriage and a laborious penny-pinching life. The rest of the Scottish community remain suspicious of the strangers in their midst.

The developing relationship is narrated with a light and humorous touch, even though both parties are drawn to each other out of desperation.

Central to the film's effectiveness is the performance of Logan as the girl entranced. Eyes and gestures capture the initial longing followed by the remorse that follows surrender.

The film's impact derives also from representations of daily life and a landscape that changes with the seasons.

. . . .

■ ANOTHER WOMAN

1988, 84 MINS, US ◇ ⓥ ⊙

Dir Woody Allen   *Prod* Robert Greenhut   *Scr* Woody Allen   *Ph* Sven Nykvist   *Ed* Susan E. Morse
Art Dir Santo Loquasto
● Gena Rowlands, Mia Farrow, Ian Holm, Blythe Danner, Gene Hackman, Martha Plimpton (Rollins/Joffe)

Woody Allen once again explores the human condition via the inner turmoil of gifted New Yorkers.

Story deals with a very successful, often idolized character who discovers around the time of her 50th birthday that she has made many mistakes, but people have been more or less too deferential to confront her.

Gena Rowlands plays Marion Post, head of a graduate philosophy department, married to a doctor. She takes an apartment downtown in which to write a book, and begins overhearing analysis sessions from the psychiatrist's office next door. At first she's annoyed, then gets hooked as patient (Mia Farrow) tells of her unsettling conviction that her marriage has begun to disintegrate.

Soon, she's reliving some of the turning points in her life, through dreams, flashbacks and chance encounters with family and friends. Throughout, she's haunted by the memory of a man (Gene Hackman) who once loved her passionately.

Film that emerges is brave, in many ways fascinating, and in all respects of a caliber rarely seen.

. . . .

■ ANOTHER YOU

1991, 94 MINS, US ◇ ⓥ ⊙

Dir Maurice Phillips   *Prod* Ziggy Steinberg   *Scr* Ziggy Steinberg   *Ph* Victor J. Kemper   *Ed* Dennis M. Hill
Mus Charles Gross   *Art Dir* Dennis Washington
● Richard Pryor, Gene Wilder, Mercedes Ruehl, Stephen Lang, Vanessa Williams, Phil Rubenstein (Tri-Star)

Gene Wilder's frantic routines can't compensate for Richard Pryor's sadly depleted energy in *Another You*, and producer Ziggy Steinberg's feeble script is given slapdash direction by the man who replaced Peter Bogdanovich on what is billed a 'film by Maurice Phillips' (the best joke in the film).

The setup isn't without promise, as the 'mentally challenged' Wilder is released from a sanitarium into the dubious care of Hollywood street hustler Pryor, who's been ordered to do community service as a condition of his parole.

Some amiable, if predictable, gags about Wilder's readjustment to the sleazy outside world give way all too quickly to tiresome plot mechanics as Stephen Lang and Mercedes Ruehl maneuver to use the gullible Wilder to impersonate a missing brewery heir.

The depressing mood is worsened by the murky color scheme of production designer Dennis Washington and lenser Victor J. Kemper, who somehow manage to make Wilder's BevHills manse look almost as unattractive as Hollywood Boulevard.

. . . .

■ ANTHONY ADVERSE

1936, 139 MINS, US ◇ ⓥ

Dir Mervyn LeRoy   *Prod* Henry Blanke   *Scr* Sheridan Gibney   *Ph* Tony Gaudio   *Ed* Ralph Dawson
Mus Erich Wolfgang Korngold   *Art Dir* Anton Grot
● Fredric March, Olivia de Havilland, Edmund Gwenn, Claude Rains, Anita Louise, Louise Hayward (Warner)

In transmuting the Hervey Allen bestseller to the screen the producers were faced with the unusual problem of too much material. They have maneuvered a straightforward and comparatively logical story. It's a bit choppy and it's a bit long-winded, but it is a direct line and easy to follow.

Writer Sheridan Gibney managed to hew a straight course through the 1,200 pages of Allen's writing by concentrating on his titular character and avoiding the danger of skirting off and away. Thus he clips off the entire last portion of the book, for instance, and plenty of juicy matter in between.

Fredric March as Adverse is an ace choice, playing the role to the hilt. Much less theatrical than he occasionally becomes, March is convincing through a varied series of moods and portrayals.

Olivia de Havilland has, perhaps, the next important role as Adverse's wife, Angela. She handles it acceptably, especially in the emotional scenes. In the opera sequences she uncovers a lovely singing voice. In the supporting cast, Edmund Gwenn makes the past of John Bonyweather stand out. Claude Rains does a splendid job as Don Luis.

Pleasant, rather than exciting, is Eric Wolfang Korngold's musical accompaniment.
□ 1936: Best Supp. Actress (Gale Sondergaard), Cinematography, Score, Editing
□ Nominations: Best Picture, Art Direction, Assistant Director (William Cannon)

. . . .

■ ANTONY AND CLEOPATRA

1972, 160 MINS, UK ◇ ⓥ

Dir Charlton Heston   *Prod* Peter Snell   *Scr* Charlton Heston   *Ph* Rafael Pacheco   *Ed* Eric Boyd-Perkins
Mus John Scott   *Art Dir* Maurice Pelling
● Charlton Heston, Hildegard Neil, Eric Porter, John Castle, Fernando Rey, Freddie Jones (Snell)

Charlton Heston, whose ardor for Shakespeare goes back to his 16mm film college days in Chicago, has herein come up with a very creditable retelling of the Bard's Antony & Cleopatra passion. It is impressively mounted and well played, and though lengthy it sustains well.

The finished film is a neat balance of closeup portraiture and panoramic action; the big battle sequences on land and sea are impressive achievements, and the Spanish location landscape provides a stunning backdrop.

Heston's adaptation, for the most part, succeeds in avoiding the sort of character simplification that would have produced a picture simply for the eye. Hildegard Neil proves one of Cleo's more convincing screen incarnations.

Heston himself as Antony very often succeeds in capturing the nobility of the character. The real handicap is borne by John Castle as Octavius Caesar. It's one of those monochromatic, steadily dour parts that doesn't leave the actor much room.

. . . .

■ ANYTHING CAN HAPPEN

1952, 107 MINS, US

Dir George Seaton   *Prod* William Perlberg   *Scr* George Seaton, George Oppenheimer   *Ph* Daniel L. Fapp
Ed Alma Macrorie   *Mus* Victor Young
● Jose Ferrer, Kim Hunter, Kurt Kasznar, Eugenie Leontovich, Oscar Karlweis, Nick Dennis (Paramount)

Anything Can Happen, based on the bestselling book by George and Helen Papashvily detailing their own real-life adventures, is a heartwarming comedy, engagingly acted, slickly produced and directed.

Film concerns a loveable group of Near Eastern immigrants and their devotion for the new homeland in America. It shows Jose Ferrer's arrival in the new, strange country, his

29

struggles with the English language, his shy courting of an American (Kim Hunter), and his eventual ownership of California orange grove on which he is privileged to pay US taxes.

Ferrer proves his versatility with a restrained, believable performance. Hunter is always convincing as the seemingly unattainable American whose friendliness and interest in the 'foreigner' turn to real love.

. . . .

■ **ANYTHING GOES**

1935, 90 MINS, US
Dir Lewis Milestone   *Prod* Benjamin Glazer   *Scr* [uncredited]   *Ph* Karl Struss   *Ed* Eda Warren
● Bing Crosby, Ethel Merman, Charlie Ruggles, Ida Lupino, Grace Bradley, Arthur Treacher (Paramount)

Cole Porter's lyrics, which were the essence and chief asset of the original [1934] stage *Anything Goes*, have been replaced by plot motion in this adaptation. Of the Porter poetical sleight-of-hand which listened so well on Broadway for a couple of seasons, only 'I Get a Kick Out of You' and 'You're the Top' are used. The title song is in also, but just for thematic and strictly instrumental use. There are four new numbers, of which 'My Heart and I, ' 'Sailor Beware' and 'Moonburn' are the most likely.

Ethel Merman comes from the original cast and her job in the picture equals her job in the stage version, which means aces. But Charlie Ruggles as the gag gangster is miscast. His delivery is too vigorous for the sap character, and the role calls for low comeding, which is out of Ruggles' line.

With the story opening in a cabaret and finishing in a production scene, with most of the bulk in between taking place on a big ocean liner, the production is lavish, and logical most of the time. Only in the closing flash does it go beyond credibility. This occurs on the 'dock' at Southampton, upon the boat landing on the other side.

Crosby is fine singing 'Sailor Beware' alone. And he's also there when it comes to getting his quota of laughs.

. . . .

■ **ANYTHING GOES**

1956, 106 MINS, US ◇
Dir Robert Lewis   *Prod* Robert Emmett Dolan   *Scr* Sidney Sheldon   *Ph* John F. Warren   *Ed* Frank Bracht   *Mus* Cole Porter
● Bing Crosby, Donald O'Connor, Zizi Jeanmaire, Mitzi Gaynor, Phil Harris, Kurt Kasznar (Paramount)

Paramount's sock musical package borrows the title and songs from that yesteryear stage hit, *Anything Goes*. Male topliners Bing Crosby and Donald O'Connor go together as though born to give the zip to what scripter Sidney Sheldon has concocted.

While there are Cole Porter songs and the legit handle is still carried, that's about all that remains of what went on behind the footlights, and there's scant resemblance to Paramount's 1936 film version, in which Crosby also starred with Ethel Merman.

Choice of the two femme stars, Zizi Jeanmaire and Mitzi Gaynor, both leggy and appealing, is a click factor.

Script provides Crosby with plenty of those sotto voce, throwaway cracks he and his fans dote on. Plot, simply, has Crosby and O'Connor agreeing to do a B'way musical together after European vacations. Abroad, each signs a femme star and the remainder concerns fitting the gals in with previous plans.

Jeanmaire has two ballets that are clicks. Gaynor belts the title tune staged by Ernie Platt to score solidly in her solo showcasing.

. . . .

■ **ANY WEDNESDAY**
(UK: Bachelor Girl Apartment)

1966, 109 MINS, US ◇ ⊽

A

Dir Robert Ellis Miller   *Prod* Julius J. Epstein   *Scr* Julius J. Epstein   *Ph* Harold Lipstein   *Ed* Stefan Arnsten   *Mus* George Duning   *Art Dir* Al Sweeney
● Jane Fonda, Jason Robards, Dean Jones, Rosemary Murphy, Ann Prentiss, Jack Fletcher (Warner)

Based on Muriel Resnik's popular legiter, *Any Wednesday* emerges in screen translation as an outstanding sophisticated comedy about marital infidelity. Adaptation and production by Julius J. Epstein is very strong, enhanced by solid direction and excellent performances.

Epstein's zesty adaptation wisely distributes the comedy emphasis among all four principals – Jason Robards, the once-a-week philanderer; Jane Fonda, his two-year Wednesday date; Dean Jones, whose arrival rocks Robards' dreamboat; and Rosemary Murphy, recreating in superior fashion her original Broadway role as Robards' wife.

Interactions between principals are uniformly strong, both in dialog and acting as well as in very effective use of split-screen effects.

Fonda comes across quite well as the girl who can't make up her mind, although she has a tendency to overplay certain bits in what might be called an exaggerated Doris Day manner. Jones impresses as a likeable comedy performer whose underlying dramatic ability gets a good showcasing here. Robards is outstanding as the likeable lecher who winds up losing both his mistress and his wife.

. . . .

■ **ANY WHICH WAY YOU CAN**

1980, 116 MINS, US ◇ ⊽ ⊙
Dir Buddy Van Horn   *Prod* Fritz Manes   *Scr* Stanford Sherman   *Ph* David Worth   *Ed* Ferris Webster, Ron Spang   *Mus* Snuff Garrett (sup.)   *Art Dir* William J. Creber
● Clint Eastwood, Sondra Locke, Ruth Gordon, William Smith, Harry Guardino, Geoffrey Lewis (Warner)

Any Which Way You Can is a benign continuation of *Every Which Way But Loose*.

Clint Eastwood, Sondra Locke, Geoffrey Lewis, Ruth Gordon and numerous supporting players all repeat their characterizations from the first outing to similar effect. Main difference is that individuals this time seem almost forgiving, loving and considerate.

Eastwood's Philo Beddoe swears off his lucrative sideline career, better to settle down with Ma Gordon, a significantly tamed Locke and orangutan chum Clyde. However, the mob makes him an offer he can't refuse to battle he-man William Smith, and the two, despite having become good pals, end up in an epic brawl.

Original ape from *Loose* was not available to Eastwood here, but substitute performs heroically.

. . . .

■ **ANZIO**
(UK: The Battle for Anzio)

1968, 117 MINS, ITALY ◇ ⊽
Dir Edward Dmytryk   *Prod* Dino De Laurentiis   *Scr* Harry A.L. Craig   *Ph* Giuseppe Rotunno   *Ed* Alberto Gallitti, Peter Taylor   *Mus* Riz Ortolani   *Art Dir* Luigi Scaccianoce
● Robert Mitchum, Peter Falk, Robert Ryan, Arthur Kennedy, Earl Holliman, Mark Damon (Columbia)

Anzio, based on the World War II campaign in Italy, suffers from flat writing, stock performances, uninspired direction and dull pacing. Produced by Dino De Laurentiis, film would seem to be a largescale war epic, but it really is a pale tale of a small group of men trapped behind German lines. Robert Mitchum stars in a cast that is far better in potential than in reality.

Two US generals (Arthur Kennedy and Robert Ryan) play a cautious and a headline-hungry type, respectively. But from the moment the film begins, it is apparent that the overall pace is going to limp.

Mitchum's character, a wiseguy newspaper reporter, plays off against the brass, whom he puts down, and his seven army cohorts, who put him down for not getting involved. Only Earl Holliman has any significant life.

Peter Falk overacts an overwritten part of a rough-guy-with-heart-of-tin. He and Mitchum discuss some basic philosophical points, one of several forced injections of 'meaning' which not only fail to elevate the story but actually depress it further into banality.

. . . .

■ **APACHE**

1954, 86 MINS, US ◇ ⊽
Dir Robert Aldrich   *Prod* Harold Hecht   *Scr* James R. Webb   *Ph* Ernest Laszlo   *Ed* Alan Crosland Jr   *Mus* David Raksin   *Art Dir* Nicolai Remisoff
● Burt Lancaster, Jean Peters, John McIntire, Charles Bronson, John Dehner, Paul Guilfoyle (United Artists)

This initial Hecht – Lancaster release through United Artists is a rugged action saga in best Burt Lancaster style of muscle-flexing. Production is based on history, re-telling story of a diehard Apache who waged one-man war against United States a thereafter became a tribal legend. While its roots are historic, the James R. Webb screenplay from Paul I. Wellman's novel, *Bronco Apache*, gives it good old outdoor action punch true to western film tradition.

Main plot switch is viewing Indian from sympathetic angle, even though his knife, arrows, bullets often find their marks among white soldiers.

Lancaster and Jean Peters play their Indian roles understandingly without usual screen stereotyping.

Robert Aldrich, making second start as feature film director, handles cast and action well, waste movement being eliminated and only essentials to best storytelling retained, as attested by comparatively short running time.

. . . .

■ **APARTMENT, THE**

1960, 124 MINS, US ◇ ⊽ ⊙
Dir Billy Wilder   *Prod* Billy Wilder   *Scr* Billy Wilder, I.A.L. Diamond   *Ph* Joseph LaShelle   *Ed* Daniel Mandell   *Mus* Adolph Deutsch   *Art Dir* Alexandre Trauner
● Jack Lemmon, Shirley MacLaine, Fred MacMurray, Ray Walston, Edie Adams, Jack Kruschen (Mirisch/United Artists)

Billy Wilder furnishes *The Apartment* with a one-hook plot that comes out high in comedy, wide in warmth and long in running time. As with *Some Like It Hot*, the broad handling is of more consequence than the package.

The story is simple. Lemmon is a lonely insurance clerk with a convenient, if somewhat antiquated, apartment which has become the rendezvous point for five of his bosses and their amours. In return, he's promoted from the 19th floor office pool to a 27th floor wood-paneled office complete with key to the executive washroom. When he falls in love with Shirley MacLaine, an elevator girl who's playing Juliet to top executive Fred MacMurray's Romeo, he turns in his washroom key.

The screenplay fills every scene with touches that spring only from talented, imaginative filmmakers. But where their *Some Like It Hot* kept you guessing right up to fade-out, *Apartment* reveals its hand early in the game. Second half of the picture is loosely constructed and tends to lag.

Apartment is all Lemmon, with a strong twist of MacLaine. The actor uses comedy as it should be used, to evoke a rainbow of emotions. He's lost in a cool world, this lonely bachelor, and he is not so much the shnook as the well-meaning, ambitious young man who lets good be the ultimate victor. MacLaine, in pixie hairdo, is a prize that's consistent with the fight being waged for her affections. Her ability to play it broad where it should be broad, subtle where it must be subtle, enables the actress to effect reality and yet do much more.

□ 1960: Best Picture, Director, Original Story & Screenplay, B&W Art Direction, Editing.

□ Nominations: Best Actor (Jack Lemmon), Actress (Shirley MacLaine), Supp. Actor (Jack Kruschen), B&W Cinematography, Sound

. . . .

■ APARTMENT ZERO

1989, 124 MINS, UK ◇ ▽ ⓦ
Dir Martin Donovan   *Prod* Martin Donovan, David Koepp   *Scr* Martin Donovan, David Koepp   *Ph* Miguel Rodriguez   *Ed* Conrad M. Gonzalez   *Mus* Elia Cmiral   *Art Dir* Miguel Angel Lumaldo
● Colin Firth, Hart Bochner, Dora Bryan, Liz Smith, Fabrizio Bentivoglio (Summit)

Apartment Zero emerges as a genuinely creepy, disturbing and gripping psychological piece.

Story's fundamental opposition is between Colin Firth, the nervously repressed, emotionally constipated British cinephile, and Hart Bochner, a charming, loose, Yankee rascal whom Firth takes into his lovely flat as a boarder when finances demand it.

Periodically, there are reports of serial murders taking place throughout Buenos Aires, and suggestions that mercenary foreigners who came to Argentina in the employ of the Death Squads may still be active. Suspicion grows that the enigmatic Bochner may not be what he claims.

Both actors are excellent, with Firth expressing and transcending the irritating emotional constriction of a non-participant in life, and Bochner displaying hitherto unrevealed talent portraying a profoundly split personality.

. . . .

■ APOCALYPSE NOW

1979, 139 MINS, US ◇ ▽ ⓦ
Dir Francis Coppola   *Prod* Francis Coppola   *Scr* John Milius, Francis Coppola   *Ph* Vittorio Storaro   *Ed* Barry Malkin   *Mus* Carmine Coppola   *Art Dir* Dean Tavoularis, Angelo Graham
● Marlon Brando, Martin Sheen, Robert Duvall, Frederic Forrest, Dennis Hopper, Harrison Ford (United Artists)

Apocalypse Now, alternately a brilliant and bizarre $40 million war epic, Coppola's vision of Hell-on-Earth hews closely to Joseph Conrad's novella, *Heart of Darkness* and therein lies the film's principal commercial defect.

It's the first film to directly excoriate US involvement in the Indochina war. Coppola virtually creates World War III onscreen. There are no models or miniatures, no tank work, nor process screens for the airborne sequences.

Coppola narrows his focus on the members of a patrol boat crew entrusted with taking Intelligence assassin Martin Sheen on a hazardous mission upriver into Cambodia to track down Marlon Brando, an officer whose methods and motives have become 'unsound', as he leads an army of tribesmen on random genocide missions.

Apocalypse Now is emblazoned with firsts: a 70mm version without credits, a director putting himself personally on the hook for the film's $18 million cost overrun, and then obtaining rights to the pic in perpetuity, and a revolutionary sound system that adds immeasurably to the film's impact.

□ 1979: Best Cinematography, Sound.

□ Nominations: Best Picture, Director, Supp. Actor (Robert Duvall), Screenplay, Art Direction, Editing

. . . .

■ APPLAUSE

1929, 80 MINS, US ⓦ
Dir Rouben Mamoulian   *Prod* Monta Bell   *Scr* Garret Fort   *Ph* George Folsey

● Helen Morgan, Joan Peers, Fuller Mellish Jr, Jack Cameron, Henry Wadsworth, Dorothy Cumming (Paramount)

This is the real old burlesque, in its background, people and atmosphere. So was Beth Brown's book, and Garret Fort has adapted with sufficient fidelity to hold together the odd story that makes an odd picture.

Helen Morgan is Kitty Darling, a fading star of burlesque, aging on the stage as her daughter, born in a dressing room, grows up.

Joan Peers comes to the front toward the finish as the daughter, April. Earlier and in the convent scenes she's done an odd picture.

Hitch Nelson as done by Fuller Mellish Jr is the pic, Kitty's husband who tries to make the daughter. A turkey burlesque chiseler with the women stuff on the side, and always bullyragging his woman. A good performance every minute by Mellish. Henry Wadsworth is the juve, opposite Peers.

The picture was made at Paramount's Long Island studio.

. . . .

■ APPLEGATES, THE
See: Meet the Applegates

. . . .

■ APPOINTMENT, THE

1969, 100 MINS, US ◇ ⓦ
Dir Sidney Lumet   *Prod* Martin Poll   *Scr* James Salter   *Ph* Carlo Di Palma   *Ed* Thelma Connell   *Mus* John Barry, Don Walker   *Art Dir* Piero Gherardi
● Omar Sharif, Anouk Aimee, Lotte Lenya, Fausto Tozzi, Ennio Balbo (M-G-M/Marpol)

A flimsy love story which never really catches fire emerges from an Antonio Leonviola original which James Salter has shaped for the screen in this disappointing Sidney Lumet effort.

Omar Sharif plays a Roman lawyer who falls for a colleague's fiancee, a mannequin played by Anouk Aimee, and eventually marries her, undeterred by his pal's fear that she's secretly a high-priced call girl. Soon, however, suspicion begins to gnaw and he begins to tail his spouse.

Flat writing and an over-rigid performance by Sharif in a crucial role, which at times skirts the laughable, seriously flaw what might otherwise have been an intriguing love tale cum suspenser.

Instead, the love affair is never convincingly established from the start, and with the exception of a largely wasted contribution by Aimee the film drags along to its mellerish windup.

. . . .

■ APPOINTMENT FOR LOVE

1941, 88 MINS, US
Dir William A. Seiter   *Prod* Bruce Manning   *Scr* Bruce Manning, Felix Jackson   *Ph* Joseph Valentine   *Ed* Ted Kent   *Mus* Frank Skinner
● Charles Boyer, Margaret Sullavan, Rita Johnson, Eugene Pallette, Ruth Terry, Cecil Kellaway (Universal)

Appointment for Love is a neatly constructed piece of bright entertainment. Producer Bruce Manning, who also collaborated on the script with Felix Jackson [from an original by Ladislas Bus-Fekete], points up the romantic adventure while injecting numerous refreshing episodes to the oft-told tale of newlywed problems.

Charles Boyer, a successful playwright, suave with the femmes, falls in love with Margaret Sullavan, seriously immersed in the practice of medicine and with very novel and unusual ideas about marriage and continuance of separate careers. Sullavan takes a separate apartment in the same building with Boyer, explaining this unusual procedure in difference in time schedules of their work.

Situation created upsets Boyer, with con-

flict between the pair raging in merriest mood, including setups for jealousies on both sides.

William Seiter paces the direction with an expert hand, deftly timing the smacko laugh lines and situations for brightest effect Boyer handles his assignment with utmost assurance. Sullavan provides both charm and ability to her role of the serious medic who finally turns romantic.

□ 1941: Nomination: Best Sound

. . . .

■ APPOINTMENT WITH DANGER

1951, 90 MINS, US
Dir Lewis Allen   *Prod* Robert Fellows   *Scr* Richard Breen, Warren Duff   *Ph* John F. Seitz   *Ed* LeRoy Stone   *Art Dir* Victor Young
● Alan Ladd, Phyllis Calvert, Paul Stewart, Jan Sterling, Jack Webb, Henry Morgan (Paramount)

Exploits of the Postal Inspection Service furnish Alan Ladd with a good cops-and-robbers actioner. Film deals with government detectives tracking down the killers of a fellow postal inspector and preventing a million-dollar mail robbery. Ladd is right at home as the tightlipped, tough inspector assigned to the case. There is a neat contrasting byplay in the nun character done by Phyllis Calvert as costar, which adds an offbeat note to the meller plot.

While investigating the murder of an inspector, Ladd comes across a plot to loot the mails of a large cash shipment during transfer from one railway station to another. He sets himself up as a cop who can be bribed by demanding money from the gang on threat of spilling the robbery plans.

Calvert's character figures importantly as she is the only witness who can tie the gang to the original murder. Paul Stewart dominates the crooks, with capable assists on menace from Jack Webb, Stacy Harris and Henry Morgan. Jan Sterling supplies the s.a. on the wrong side of the law as Stewart's moll.

. . . .

■ APPRENTICESHIP OF DUDDY KRAVITZ, THE

1974, 120 MINS, CANADA ◇ ⓦ
Dir Ted Kotcheff   *Prod* John Kemeny   *Scr* Mordecai Richler   *Ph* Brian West   *Ed* Thom Noble   *Mus* Stanley Myers (sup.)   *Art Dir* Anne Pritchard
● Richard Dreyfuss, Micheline Lanctot, Jack Warden, Randy Quaid, Joseph Wiseman, Denholm Elliott (International Cinemedia/Center/CFDC)

Director Ted Kotcheff has taken Mordecai Richler's novel by the scruff of the neck and worked a zesty but somewhat muted nostalgic look at a nervy Jewish kid on the make in the 1940s [adaptation by Lionel Chetwynd].

On screen, *Duddy Kravitz* remains as it was when first published in 1959 to outraged cries from Jewish groups across North America and more particularly from Montreal where it is authentically set. That is an at-times bitter, satiric portrayal of a 19-year-old who gets his money, women and power by emulating the richest of those around him, selling everyone, closest friends included, out.

Kravitz, played by a continually-grinning, scratching, nervous-making yet vulnerable Richard Dreyfuss, comes across effectively and with force.

□ 1974: Nomination: Best Adapted Screenplay

. . . .

■ APRIL FOOLS, THE

1969, 95 MINS, US ◇ ⓦ
Dir Stuart Rosenberg   *Prod* Gordon Carroll   *Scr* Hal Dresner   *Ph* Michel Hugo   *Ed* Bob Wyman   *Mus* Marvin Hamlisch   *Art Dir* Richard Sylbert
● Jack Lemmon, Catherine Deneuve, Peter Lawford, Jack Weston, Myrna Loy, Charles Boyer (Cinema Center/Jalem)

Jack Lemmon is both funny and touching as the mild-mannered stockbroker, tied to a nothing of a wife. Given a big promotion by his boss (Peter Lawford), he meets the latter's wife (Catherine Deneuve) at a stultifying cocktail party. She's bored and he doesn't know her real identity but they depart for a night of self-discovery.

In addition to Lemmon, comedians Jack Weston (as his lawyer) and Harvey Korman (as a drinking companion they encounter in the commuter train's drinking car) provide their own brand of laughs and the contrasting styles of the three actors gives the plot most of its action.

Things slow down to a mere simmer, by contrast, in the romantic segments although Deneuve, in her first American film, is worth just looking at.

••••••••••••••••••••••••••••••

■ **ARAB, THE**

1924, 75 MINS, US ⊗

Dir Rex Ingram   *Scr* Rex Ingram   *Ph* John F. Seitz
Ed Grant Whytock
● Ramon Novarro, Alice Terry, Maxudian, Jerrold Robertshaw, Jean De Limur (Metro-Goldwyn)

This is the finest sheik film of them all. *The Arab* is a compliment to the screen, a verification of the sterling repute of director Rex Ingram.

As a sheik Ramon Novarro is the acme. Surrounded as he is by genuine men of the desert – for the scenes were shot in Algiers and the mobs are all natives in their natural environments – he seems as bona fide as the Arabs themselves.

Alice Terry as the wistful, frightened, assailed little Christian whose winsomeness and piety, even though they are foreign and even hostile to all that this thieving, concubinous rogue stands for, makes the presentation plausible, romantic and attractive.

The 'happy ending' is wisely left open – it is asking too much for her to dismiss the handsome noble Moslem who has saved her and her white family and flock, given up his indigenous rascalities for her and fallen in love with her.

••••••••••••••••••••••••••••••

■ **ARABELLA**

1969, 88 MINS, ITALY ◇

Dir Mauro Bolognini   *Prod* Maleno Malenotti
Scr Adriano Baracco   *Ph* Ennio Guarnieri   *Ed* Eraldo Da Roma   *Mus* Ennio Morricone   *Art Dir* Alberto Boccianti
● Virna Lisi, James Fox, Margaret Rutherford, Terry-Thomas, Paola Borboni, Giancarlo Giannini (Universal/ Malenotti)

Arabella, Italian-produced with an English and Italian cast, is a series of episodes none too adroitly woven together which focus on the larcenous activities of Virna Lisi as she tries to help her Italian princess-grandma (Margaret Rutherford) pay taxes dating back to 1895. There are bright flashes of comedy, and as many long sequences of contrived and amateurish action, which add up to a mildly amusing film.

One of the more humorous aspects of feature is Terry-Thomas, portraying three different characters in as many sequences, involving Lisi in her scramble to latch onto a bundle.

The production, benefitting by lush sets and costumes of the Italian 1928 period, is overly-burdened with a script not sufficiently developed and attempting comedy that frequently does not jell.

••••••••••••••••••••••••••••••

■ **ARABESQUE**

1966, 107 MINS, US/UK ◇ ⊙

Dir Stanley Donen   *Prod* Stanley Donen   *Scr* Julian Mitchell, Stanley Price, Pierre Marton [= Peter Stone]

Ph Christopher Challis   *Ed* Frederick Wilson
Mus Henry Mancini   *Art Dir* Reece Pemberton
● Gregory Peck, Sophia Loren, Alan Badel, Kieron Moore, Carl Duering, John Merivale (Universal/Donen)

Arabesque packs the names of Gregory Peck and Sophia Loren and a foreign intrigue theme, but doesn't always progress on a true entertainment course. Fault lies in a shadowy plotline and confusing characters, particularly in the miscasting of Peck in a cute role.

Based on the Gordon Cotler novel, *The Cipher*, script projects Peck as American exchange professor of ancient languages at Oxford drawn into a vortex of hazardous endeavor. He is called upon to decipher a secret message written in hieroglyphics, a document and its translation sought by several different factions from the Middle East. He is assisted by the paradoxical character played by Loren, as an Arab sexpot who seems to be on everyone's side. There are chases, murders and attempted assassinations to whet the appetite, as well as misuses of comedy.

Peck tries valiantly with a role unsuited to him and Loren displays her usual lush and plush presence. If her part is an enigma to Peck, it is to the spectator, too.

Menace is provided by Alan Badel and Kieron Moore, both trying to latch onto contents of the cipher and out to dispose of Peck.

••••••••••••••••••••••••••••••

■ **ARACHNOPHOBIA**

1990, 109 MINS, US ◇ ⊙ ⊙

Dir Frank Marshall   *Prod* Kathleen Kennedy, Richard Vane   *Scr* Don Jakoby, Wesley Strick   *Ph* Mikael Salomon   *Ed* Michael Kahn   *Mus* Trevor Jones
Art Dir James Bissell
● Jeff Daniels, Harley Jane Kozak, John Goodman, Julian Sands, Stuart Pankin, Brian McNamara (Tangled Web/Amblin)

Arachnophobia expertly blends horror and tongue-in cheek comedy in the tale of a small California coastal town overrun by Venezuelan killer spiders. Frank Marshall's sophisticated feature directing debut never indulges in ultimate gross-out effects and carefully chooses both its victims and its means of depicting their dispatch.

Beginning like an *Indiana Jones* film with an 18-minute prolog of British entomologist Julian Sands' expedition in the Venezuelan jungle, *Arachnophobia* cleverly follows the route of a prehistoric male spider hitching a ride to California and escaping to the farm of newly arrived town doctor Jeff Daniels.

The droll John Goodman has a relatively small part as the town's magnificently slobby and incompetent exterminator. Daniels is the one with the arachnophobia, which, like James Stewart's trauma in Hitchcock's *Vertigo*, must be agonizingly overcome in the spectacular climax.

Marshall has the directorial confidence to allow scripters (working from a story by Don Jakoby and Al Williams) plenty of screen time to develop characters more fully than usual in a horror film. With a variety of versatile spider performers including live South American tarantulas and more than 40 mechanical creatures devised by Chris Walas, Marshall is able to do just about anything he wants in terms of creepy-crawly effects.

••••••••••••••••••••••••••••••

■ **ARCH OF TRIUMPH**

1948, 120 MINS, US ⊙

Dir Lewis Milestone   *Prod* David Lewis   *Scr* Lewis Milestone, Harry Brown   *Ph* Russell Metty   *Ed* Duncan Mansfield   *Mus* Louis Gruenberg   *Art Dir* William Cameron Menzies
● Charles Boyer, Ingrid Bergman, Charles Laughton, Louis Calhern, Michael Romanoff, Ruth Warrick (Enterprise)

The Erich Maria Remarque novel, by very suggestion of authorship and the Lewis

Milestone association, conjures up analogy to the now classic *All Quiet*, the post-First World War film, also from a Remarque work. The analogy ends there because the character of both differs strikingly. Current entry is a frank romantic item, laid in a setting of Paris intrigue just before open war with the western allies broke out.

The surcharged atmosphere of pre-Polish aggression and its repercussions in the City of Light that suddenly grows into blackout is a dramatic background for the Boyer-Bergman romance. The very atmosphere of the boulevards, from the Eternal Light underneath the Arc de Triomphe to the gaiety of the Sheherezade and kindred boites 'on the hill' (Montmartre) make for surefire appeal.

Charles Laughton is rather wasted as a Nazi menace, obviously the victim of the cutting room shears, as was Ruth Warrick, the American dilettante. There is no question but that over $1 million of this film's cost never shows on the screen. It's reported to have hit near the $4 million negative cost.

••••••••••••••••••••••••••••••

■ **ARIA**

1987, 98 MINS, US/UK ◇ ⊙ ⊙

Dir Nicolas Roeg, Charles Sturridge, Jean-Luc Godard, Julien Temple, Bruce Beresford, Robert Altman, Franc Roddam, Ken Russell, Derek Jarman, Bill Bryden
Prod Don Boyd   *Ph* Harvey Harrison, Gale Tattersall, Carolyn Champeti, Oliver Stapleton, Dante Spinotti, Pierre Mignot, Frederick Elmes, Micke Southon, Gabriel Beristain   *Ed* Tony Lawson, Matthew Longfellow, Jean-Luc Godard, Neil Abrahamson, Marie-Therese Boiche, Robert Altman, Rick Elgood, Michael Bradsell, Peter Cartwright, Mike Cragg
● Theresa Russell, Nicola Swain, Buck Henry, Julie Hagerty, Tilda Swinton, John Hurt (RVP/Virgin)

Aria, a string of selections from 10 operas illustrated by 10 directors, is a film that could not have happened without the advent of music videos.

Producer Don Boyd, who orchestrated the project, instructed the directors not to depict what was happening to the characters in the operas but to create something new out of the emotion and content expressed in the music. The arias were the starting point.

Result is both exhilaratingly successful and distractingly fragmented. Individual segments are stunning but they come in such speedy succession that overall it is not a fully satisfying film experience.

Selections also represent a variety of film-making styles from Bruce Beresford's rather pedestrian working of a love theme from Korngold's *Die tote Stadt* to Ken Russell's characteristically excessive treatment of an idea distilled from Puccini's *Turandot*.

Structurally, the most ambitious of the selections is Jean-Luc Godard's working of Lully's *Armide* which he transposes to a body building gym where two naked women try to attract the attention of the men.

The most striking clash of images is achieved by Franc Roddam who moves Wagner's *Tristan und Isolde* to Las Vegas. As the lush strains of the music blare, the neon sea of the casinos has never looked more strange.

••••••••••••••••••••••••••••••

■ **ARISTOCATS, THE**

1970, 78 MINS, US ◇

Dir Wolfgang Reitherman   *Prod* Walt Disney, Wolfgang Reitherman, Winston Hibler   *Scr* Larry Clemmons
Ed Tom Acosta   *Mus* George Bruns (Walt Disney)

The Aristocats is a good animated feature from Walt Disney Studios, an original period comedy with drama about a feline family rescued from the plans of an evil butler who would prefer his mistress not to leave her fortune to the cats.

Helped immeasurably by the voices of Phil Harris, Eva Gabor, Sterling Holloway,

Scatman Crothers and others, plus some outstanding animation, songs, sentiment, some excellent dialog and even a touch of psychedelia.

Harris, who gave *Jungle Book* a lot of its punch, is even more prominent here as the voice of an alley cat who rescues Gabor and her three kittens. Gabor's voice and related animation are excellent, ditto that for two hound dogs, Pat Buttram and George Lindsey.

The technical details of the $4 million cartoon are marvelous to behold.

● ●

■ **ARIZONA DREAM**

1992, 142 MINS, FRANCE ◇ ⓥ ⊙
Dir Emir Kusturica   *Prod* Claudie Ossard   *Scr* David Atkins, Emir Kusturica   *Ph* Vilko Filac   *Ed* Andrija Zafranovic   *Mus* Goran Bregovic   *Art Dir* Miljen Kljakovic
● Johnny Depp, Jerry Lewis, Faye Dunaway, Lili Taylor, Vincent Gallo, Paulina Porizkova (Constellation/UGC/Hachette Premiere)

Despite gorgeous, sometimes surreal visuals and the valiant efforts of an interesting cast, Emir Kusturica's *Arizona Dream* is heavy going. Award-winning Sarajevo-born helmer's first English-lingo pic tackles dreams and flight only to alternately soar and crash.

Johnny Depp anchors the overlong pic as an unambitious 23-year-old fish and game warden summoned from Manhattan to Arizona. Depp's uncle (Jerry Lewis) is about to take a bride three decades his junior (Paulina Porizkova) and wants Depp to be his best man and stay on to work at his Cadillac dealership.

Depp finds himself torn between seductive, half-mad widow Faye Dunaway and Dunaway's equally unstable stepdaughter, heiress Lili Taylor. Vincent Gallo plays a womanizing aspiring actor who sells cars between auditions.

Kusturica grafts his sometimes unwieldy Europe-inflected concerns onto brash American landscapes with mixed results. Much is made of dreams that, either spoken of at length or illustrated, are offered in lieu of character development.

Impeccably lensed in Alaska, New York and Douglas, Ariz, pic remains stuck in an awkward netherworld between slapstick and pathos.

● ●

■ **ARMED AND DANGEROUS**

1986, 88 MINS, US ◇ ⓥ ⊙
Dir Mark L. Lester   *Prod* Brian Grazer, James Keach
Scr Harold Ramis, Peter Torokvei   *Ph* Fred Schuler
Ed Michael Hill, Daniel Hanley, George Pedugo
Mus Bill Meyers   *Art Dir* David L. Snyder
● John Candy, Eugene Levy, Robert Loggia, Kenneth McMillan, Meg Ryan, Brion James (Columbia)

Armed and Dangerous is a broad farce slightly elevated by the presence of John Candy and Eugene Levy.

Story [by Brian Grazer, Harold Ramis and James Keach] functions as little more than a fashion show for Candy. The piece de resistance is Candy in a blue tuxedo with a ruffled shirt that makes his enormous bulk look like a wrapped Christmas present.

Candy plays one of LA's finest until he's wrongfully kicked off the force for corruption. He winds up at Guard Dog Security where he teams with shyster lawyer Levy on a new career. Company, it turns out, is under the thumb of the mob headed by union honcho Robert Loggia.

It's all pretty basic stuff delivered with a minimum of imagination.

● ●

■ **ARMS AND THE GIRL**
See: Red Salute

● ●

■ **ARMY OF DARKNESS**
EVIL DEAD 3

1993, 95 MINS, US ◇ ⓥ ⊙
Dir Sam Raimi   *Prod* Robert Tapert   *Scr* Ivan Raimi, Sam Raimi   *Ph* Bill Pope   *Ed* Bob Muraski, R.O.C. Sandstorm   *Mus* Joe Lo Duca, Danny Elfman
Art Dir Anthony Trembay
● Bruce Campbell, Embeth Davidtz, Marcus Gilbert, Ian Abercrombie, Richard Grove, Michael Earl Reid (De Laurentiis/Renaissance)

Blending almost nonstop violence with humorous parody, Sam Raimi's latest excursion into horror-kitsch seems more like an irreverent *A Connecticut Yankee in King Arthur's Court*. The Yank, however, is equipped with a chainsaw for an arm and a '73 Oldsmobile instead of a steed.

Whisked from his country cottage by some evil force, Bruce Campbell and his car are plunked down in the midst of an Arthurian war, where Campbell is posthaste thrown into chains. He fights his way to freedom and ingratiates himself with Arthur.

The only way for him to get back to California is by retrieving a sacred book. On his quest he runs across various obstacles, including the evil dead (who turn the maiden he's sweet on into a witch). Wizardry and special effects abound.

In the version shown at Spain's Sitges, the hero miscalculates the time he wants to travel ahead in space and arrives at the end of the 21st century only to see a planet in ruins. This ending will be changed and the pic will lose 10 minutes for its US release.

● ●

■ **AROUND THE WORLD IN EIGHTY DAYS**

1956, 175 MINS, US ◇ ⓥ ⊙
Dir Michael Anderson   *Prod* Michael Todd   *Scr* S.J. Perelman, John Farrow, James Poe   *Ph* Lionel Lindon
Ed Gene Ruggiero, Paul Weatherwax   *Mus* Victor Young
Art Dir James Sullivan, Ken Adam
● David Niven, Cantinflas, Robert Newton, Shirley MacLaine, Charles Boyer, Ronald Colman (Todd)

This is a long picture – two hours and 55 minutes plus intermission. Little time has been wasted and the story races on as Phileas Fogg and company proceed from London to Paris, thence via balloon to Spain and the bullfights; from there to Marseilles and India, where Fogg and Passepartout rescue beautiful Shirley MacLaine from death on a funeral pyre; to Hong Kong, Japan, San Francisco, across the country by train to New York (notwithstanding an Indian attack) and thence back to England.

Todd-AO system here, for the first time, is properly used and fills the screen with wondrous effects. Images are extraordinarily sharp and depth of focus is striking in many scenes.

David Niven, as Fogg, is the perfect stereotype of the unruffled English gentleman and quite intentionally, a caricature of 19th-century British propriety. Matching him is Mexican star Cantinflas (Mario Moreno) as Passepartout. Robert Newton in the role of Mr Fix, the detective who trails Fogg whom he suspects of having robbed the Bank of London, is broad comic all the way through, and MacLaine is appealing as the princess.

There's rarely been a picture that can boast of so many star names in bit parts. Just to name a few in the more important roles: John Carradine as the pompous Col. Proctor; Finlay Currie, Ronald Squires, Basil Sydney, A.E. Matthews and Trevor Howard as members of the Reform Club who bet against Fog Robert Morley as the stodgy governor of the Bank of England; Cedric Hardwicke as a colonial militarist; Red Skelton, as a drunk; Marlene Dietrich and George Raft. There are many others, including Frank Sinatra in a flash shot as a piano player. Jose Greco, early in the footage, wows with a heel fandango.

Pic's sound is extraordinarily vivid and effective and a major asset. Saul Bass' final titles are a tribute to the kind of taste and imagination, the ingenuity and the splendor that mark this entire Todd production. It's all on the screen, every penny of the $5–6 million that went into the making.
☐ 1956: Best Picture, Adapted Screenplay, Color Cinematography, Scoring of a Dramatic Picture, Editing.
☐ Nominations: Best Director, Color Costume Design, Color Art Direction

● ●

■ **ARRANGEMENT, THE**

1969, 125 MINS, US ◇ ⓥ
Dir Elia Kazan   *Prod* Elia Kazan   *Scr* Elia Kazan
Ph Robert Surtees   *Ed* Stefan Arnsten   *Mus* David Amram   *Art Dir* Gene Callahan
● Kirk Douglas, Faye Dunaway, Deborah Kerr, Richard Boone, Hume Cronyn, Dianne Hull (Warner/Athena)

The Arrangement is a one-man production show; consequently, one man is responsible for a confused, overly-contrived and over-length film peopled with a set of characters about whom the spectator couldn't care less. In a four-way plunge, Elia Kazan produced and directed from his own screenplay based upon his own 1967 novel.

Three principals in a story focusing on a man's problems and bafflements are Kirk Douglas, Deborah Kerr and Faye Dunaway.

The talents of cast are taxed but they almost rise above their assignments. Douglas plays a successful Los Angeles advertising man, apparently a wizard account exec, wed to Kerr, a long-suffering wife who tries tounderstand her husband's obsession for Dunaway, with whom he's been carrying on a tumultous affair.

● ●

■ **ARROWHEAD**

1953, 105 MINS, US ◇ ⓥ ⊙
Dir Charles Marquis Warren   *Prod* Nat Holt
Scr Charles Marquis Warren   *Ph* Ray Rennahan
Ed Frank Bracht   *Mus* Paul Sawtell   *Art Dir* Hal Pereira, Al Roelofs
● Charlton Heston, Jack Palance, Katy Jurado, Brian Keith, Mary Sinclair, Milburn Stone (Paramount)

The southwest frontier is the setting for this good outdoor actioner. Plot is laid in Texas during 1878 in and around Fort Clark, historical old cavalry post, and Nat Holt films his production on the actual sites described in W.R. Burnett's novel, *Adobe Walls*.

Principals involved are Charlton Heston, army scout and bitter enemy of the Apaches, particularly Jack Palance, a chief's son who has aroused the braves and is leading them on the warpath. Katy Jurado, as a Mexican-Apache attracted to Heston but spying on him, gives the story s.a. touches, while Mary Sinclair furnishes a more ladylike part as an army widow also interested in the scout.

Conflict gets underway early as Heston, raised among the Apaches as a child, warns a stubborn cavalry officer that only treachery can result from his efforts to make peace with the Indians. Heston's point is made when the cavalry is ambushed and the officer slain. The new commander also refuses to believe the scout, by now fired for his views, and it's not until he saves them from further treachery that he is allowed to lead the soldiers in the kind of combat that can whip the redskins.

Charles Marquis Warren's direction and screenplay are forthright in dealing with the masculine action and lift the plentiful mass clash sequences.

● ●

■ **ARROWSMITH**

1931, 108 MINS, US ⓥ
Dir John Ford   *Prod* Samuel Goldwyn   *Scr* Sidney Howard   *Ph* Ray June   *Ed* Hugh Bennett   *Mus* Alfred Newman   *Art Dir* Richard Day

● Ronald Colman, Helen Hayes, Richard Bennett, A.E. Anson, Beulah Bondi, Myrna Loy (Goldwyn/United Artists)

That portion of the citizenry which has read the Sinclair Lewis novel will probably be in sympathy with the filmization. Those who haven't will not be prone to deem this macabre tale entertainment. Both factions will find it hard to believe Ronald Colman in the title role.

The responsible factors include complete elimination of the novel's expose phase as regards the medical profession; unusual length; a tendency on the part of the director, John Ford, to too often disregard or overlook tempo; and an unhappy ending. But above all these things is the inability of Coleman, a romantic juvenile, to convince as the intense scientist.

Helen Hayes, as the nurse who becomes the promising physician's wife is wholly delightful and gives an enlightening and natural performance. She is mostly responsible for the interest in the early reels. Richard Bennett, as Sondelius, a Swedish scientist, opens up impressively in the picture but eventually seems to pale. Along with Hayes, A.E. Anson is the most genuine figure in the film, although Claude King also makes a small part stand out.

□ 1931/32: Nominations: Best Picture, Adaptation, Cinematography, Art Direction

■ ARSENE LUPIN

1932, 64 MINS, US

Dir Jack Conway   *Prod* [uncredited]   *Scr* Carey Wilson, Bayard Veiller, Lenore Coffee   *Ph* Oliver T. Marsh   *Ed* Hugh Wynn   *Mus* [uncredited]   *Art Dir* Cedric Gibbons

● John Barrymore, Lionel Barrymore, Karen Morley, John Miljan, Tully Marshall, Henry Armetta (M-G-M)

First screen appearance of John and Lionel Barrymore together and their fine acting lifts the production to a high artistic level.

But the action often is allowed to lapse for dangerously long intervals while the two Barrymores elaborate their interpretation of the super-thief (John) and the dogged detective (Lionel).

A neat angle of this film version [of the French play by Maurice Le Blanc and Francis de Croisset] is the fact that the audience never sees Lupin in the act of larceny itself. This literary scheme is maintained until the last episode, when the elaborate plot to steal the Mona Lisa from the Louvre is worked out in detail and in sight, a fitting climax and a well-paced and balanced sequence.

Story has a touch of discreet but sophisticated spice in the love affair between Lupin and Sonia, the girl released from prison on parole and forced to aid the police in the pursuit. Femme lead is played Karen Morley with a beautiful balance of reticence and occasional emphasis.

■ ARSENE LUPIN RETURNS

1938, 81 MINS, US

Dir George Fitzmaurice   *Prod* John W. Considine Jr   *Scr* James Kevin McGuinness, Howard Emmett Rogers, George Harmon Coxe   *Ph* George Folsey   *Ed* Ben Lewis   *Mus* Franz Waxman   *Art Dir* Cedric Gibbons, Stan Rogers, Edwin B. Willis

● Melvyn Douglas, Virginia Bruce, Warren William, John Halliday, Nat Pendleton, Monty Woolley (M-G-M)

Supposedly killed by the police long ago, the gendarme mystifier, Lupin, a character created (and used before in films) by Maurice Leblanc is found by the writers of this original to have merely retired and gone legit. He is played by Melvyn Douglas whose two associates, Nat Pendleton and E.E. Clive, a couple of mugs, help him in his pseudo-crime re-entry.

Whole thing is deftly handled by director and cutter, the pace fast enough to always hold the viewer, and there's enough comedy to liv nearly every situation.

The beginning of the story concerns the FBI's casting out of Warren William, a publicity hog who becomes of no use to the government because he's known everywhere. He goes into private practice and gets an insurance company protective job watching a $250,000 jewel on transport from America to France. Only after the boat docks on the other side, does Lupin begin figuring. Last half becomes very much cops-and-robber.

■ ARSENIC AND OLD LACE

1944, 118 MINS, US

Dir Frank Capra   *Prod* Frank Capra   *Scr* Julius J. Epstein, Philip G. Epstein   *Ph* Sol Polito   *Ed* Daniel Mandell   *Mus* Max Steiner   *Art Dir* Max Parker

● Cary Grant, Priscilla Lane, Raymond Massey, Jack Carson, Peter Lorre, Edward Everett Horton (Warner)

Despite the fact that picture runs 118 minutes, Frank Capra has expanded on the original play [by Joseph Kesselring] to a sufficient extent to maintain a steady, consistent pace. With what he has crammed into the running time, film doesn't seem that long. The majority of the action is confined to one set, that of the home of the two amiably nutty aunts who believe it's kind to poison people they come in contact with and their non-violently insane brother who thinks he's Teddy Roosevelt.

Cary Grant and Priscilla Lane are paired romantically. They open the picture getting married but are delayed in their honeymoon when Grant finds his two screwy aunts have been bumping off people in their house, burying them in the cellar and even holding thoughtful funeral ceremonies for them. The laughs that surround his efforts to get John Alexander, the 'Teddy Roosevelt' of the picture, committed to an institution; troubles that come up when a maniacal long-lost brother shows up after a world tour of various murders with a phoney doctor, and other plot elements make for diversion of a very agreeable character.

■ ARTHUR

1981, 117 MINS, US ◇ ⓥ ⊙

Dir Steve Gordon   *Prod* Robert Greenhut   *Scr* Steve Gordon   *Ph* Fred Schules   *Ed* Susan E. Morse   *Mus* Burt Bacharach   *Art Dir* Stephen Hendrickson

● Dudley Moore, Liza Minnelli, John Gielgud, Geraldine Fitzgerald, Jill Eikenberry, Stephen Elliott (Orion)

Arthur is a sparkling entertainment which attempts, with a large measure of success, to resurrect the amusingly artificial conventions of 1930s screwball romantic comedies. Dudley Moore is back in top-'*10*' form as a layabout drunken playboy who finds himself falling in love with working-class girl Liza Minnelli just as he's being forced into an arranged marriage with a society WASP.

Central dilemma, which dates back to Buster Keaton at least, has wastrel Moore faced with the choice of marrying white bread heiress Jill Eikenberry or being cut off by his father from $750 million. After much procrastination, he finally agrees to the union but situation is complicated when, in a vintage (meet cute), he protects shoplifter Minnelli from the authorities and finds himself genuinely falling for someone for the first time in his padded life.

As Moore's eternally supportive but irrepressibly sarcastic valet, John Gielgud gives a priceless performance. Minnelli fills the bill in a less showbizzy and smaller part than usual, but pic's core is really the wonderful relationship between Moore and Gielgud.

□ 1981: Best Supp. Actor (John Gielgud), Song ('Best That You Can Do').

□ Nominations: Best Actor (Dudley Moore), Original Screenplay

■ ARTHUR 2
ON THE ROCKS

1988, 113 MINS, US ◇ ⓥ ⊙

Dir Bud Yorkin   *Prod* Robert Shapiro   *Scr* Andy Breckman   *Ph* Stephen H. Burum   *Ed* Michael Kahn   *Mus* Burt Bacharach   *Art Dir* Gene Callahan

● Dudley Moore, Liza Minnelli, Geraldine Fitzgerald, Paul Benedict, John Gielgud, Cynthia Sikes (Warner)

Arthur 2 is not as classy a farce as the original, but still manages to be an amusing romp.

Five years into their marriage and living the enviable Park Avenue lifestyle with the kind of digs photographed by Architectural Digest wife Linda (Liza Minnelli) finds she's unable to conceive and goes about adopting a baby.

While Minnelli is gung ho to expand the fold, Arthur's ex-girlfriend's father (Stephen Elliott) seeks to break it apart. Vindictive over having his love-struck daughter stood up at the altar by Arthur last time around, he works up a legal trick to take away the wastrel's $750 million fortune and force him to marry his daughter after all.

Though not critical to the pleasures of watching Moore in one of his best screen roles, it does undermine his performance when he has lesser personalities to tease. Minnelli loses some of her working class sassiness as the downtown-gone-uptown-gone-downtown wife trying to put her house in order, though credit is due her for carrying plot's best scenes.

■ ARTICLE 99

1992, 100 MINS, US ◇ ⓥ ⊙

Dir Howard Deutch   *Prod* Michael Gruskoff, Michael I. Levy   *Scr* Ron Cutler   *Ph* Richard Bowen   *Ed* Richard Halsey   *Mus* Danny Elfman   *Art Dir* Virginia L. Randolph

● Ray Liotta, Kiefer Sutherland, Forest Whitaker, Lea Thompson, Kathy Baker, Eli Wallach (Orion/Gruskoff-Levy)

With didactic intent behind a rabble-rousing story, filmmakers admirably draw attention to the scandalous condition of health care at the nation's Veterans' Administration hospitals while aiming for the seriocomic tone of *MASH*, *Catch-22* and *The Hospital*. Title refers to a fictional and apparently functioning regulation at the V.A. that withholds full medical benefits from vets if they can't prove their ailments are specifically related to military service.

Set almost entirely within a zoolike V.A. facility in Kansas City, screenplay presents a villainous bureaucracy ruled by hospital director John Mahoney. Opposing him are the irreverent but dedicated can-do doctors led by surgeon Ray Liotta.

Liotta and fellow medics Forest Whitaker, John C. McGinley and Lea Thompson naturally give newcomer Kiefer Sutherland a hard time, accusing him of having his sights set on a cushy private practice after a short stint in the trenches. Little by little, Sutherland's eyes are opened to the crazy methods his colleagues need to employ to do any good, and to the value of their work.

Kathy Baker enlivens every scene she's in as a warm-blooded shrink who gets right to the point when Liotta shows an interest in her. Lenser Richard Bowen has given the film a rough, verite look.

■ ARTISTS AND MODELS

1937, 95 MINS, US

Dir Raoul Walsh   *Prod* Lewis E. Gensler   *Scr* Walter DeLeon, Francis Martin   *Ph* Victor Milner   *Ed* Ellsworth Hoagland

● Jack Benny, Ida Lupino, Richard Arlen, Gail Patrick, Ben Blue, Judy Canova (Paramount)

Artists and Models holds enough variety, comedy, color, spec, flash, dash and novelty for a couple of pictures. It's so replete with a cavalcade of radio, nitery, vaudeville and revuesque ingredients that it's much to the credit of all concerned that this madcap musical [story by Sig Herzig and Gene Thackrey, adapted by Eve Greene and Harlan Ware] shapes up as well as it does.

There are a couple of misguided sequences, one of which is that 'Public Melody Number One' sequence, done in a frankly Harlem setting, with Louis Armstrong tooting his trumpet against a pseudo-musical gangster idea. While Martha Raye is under cork, this intermingling of the races isn't wise, especially as she lets herself go into the extremest manifestations of Harlemania torso-twisting and gyrations.

Jack Benny, Ida Lupino, Richard Arlen and Gail Patrick are chiefly responsible for holding the film together. This is Benny's first solo starrer and it's also a departure for him in that he's assigned the major romantic interest.

Benny is cast as the advertising agency head. Arlen is his biggest (and practically only) account. Lupino is a professional model who, because she's a p.m., is at first snubbed by Arlen for a ritzy ad campaign. Lupino hies to Miami posing as a socialite, in order to impress that being a pro model isn't a liability.
□ 1937: Nomination: Best Song ('Whispers in the Dark')

■ **ARTISTS AND MODELS**

1955, 108 MINS, US ◇ ⓥ
Dir Frank Tashlin   *Prod* Hal Wallis   *Scr* Frank Tashlin, Hal Kanter, Herbert Baker   *Ph* Daniel L. Fapp
Ed Warren Low   *Mus* Walter Scharf
● Dean Martin, Jerry Lewis, Shirley MacLaine, Dorothy Malone, Eddie Mayehoff, Anita Ekberg (Paramount)

Comedic diversion in the Martin and Lewis manner has been put together in this overdone, slaphappy melange of gags and gals. Six writers [three scripters, plus adaptation by Don McGuire from a play by Michael Davidson and Norman Lessing] figure in the production and, while giving the comics a story line to follow, also worked in everything but the proverbial kitchen sink.

Co-starring with the comedy team are Shirley MacLaine and Dorothy Malone. The former tackles her role of model with a bridling cuteness but has a figure to take the viewer's mind off her facial expression. Ditto Dorothy Malone, her artist roommate.

Dean Martin is an artist and Jerry Lewis is a would-be writer of kiddie stories, both starving in NY.

■ **ART OF LOVE, THE**

1965, 99 MINS, US ◇
Dir Norman Jewison   *Prod* Ross Hunter   *Scr* Carl Reiner
Ph Russell Metty   *Ed* Milton Carruth   *Mus* Cy Coleman
Art Dir Alexander Golitzen, George Webb
● James Garner, Dick Van Dyke, Elke Sommer, Angie Dickinson, Ethel Merman, Carl Reiner (Universal/Cherokee)

Ross Hunter's pic starts out as pure film satire aimed only at light, bright comedy entertainment. With the addition of a wide variety of often zesty elements it grows into a garbled mixture of coquettish comedy that has side-splitting moments, some unusually fine character performances, but so much of everything it never once settles down to a consistent point of view.

Story [by Richard Alan Simmons and William Sackheim] is of would-be American artist Dick Van Dyke who gives up to return the rich fiancee in America who is paying his bills – and those of his roommate would-be author James Garner. Garner is so devastated at the loss of his meal ticket, he tries everything to keep Van Dyke in Paris, including a mock suicide that unwittingly backfires into

what looks like the real thing. When Van Dyke reappears, he has to go into hiding because Garner has found a dead painter sells better than a live one.

Writer Carl Reiner and director Norman Jewison go aground by allowing too many bits to fill their pot. The picture looks like one that kept changing as each member of the company suggested some new cute bit.

■ **ASHANTI**

1979, 117 MINS, SWITZERLAND ◇ ⓥ
Dir Richard Fleischer   *Prod* Georges-Alain Vuille
Scr Stephen Geller   *Ph* Aldo Tonti   *Mus* Michael Melvoin   *Art Dir* Aurelio Crugnola
● Michael Caine, Peter Ustinov, Beverly Johnson, Omar Sharif, Rex Harrison, Willliam Holden (Columbia)

A polished but lacklustre adventure entertainment.

Michael Caine and Beverly Johnson are World Health Organization medics on a visit to an African tribe when the lady becomes a prize catch of Arabian slave trader Peter Ustinov. Caine's retrieval odyssey thereafter is variously aided by Rex Harrison as an ambiguous go-between, William Holden as a mercenary helicopter pilot, and Indian actor Kabir Bedi as a Bedouin with his own score to settle with Ustinov. All acquit with professional grace but unremarkable impact.

No help to the film's grip on interest is director Richard Fleischer's minuet pacing. He seems to have come under the spell of those Saharan sand dunes so lavishly and lengthily dwelled on as Caine and Bedi pick up Ustinov's trail.

■ **ASH WEDNESDAY**

1973, 99 MINS, US ◇ ⓥ
Dir Larry Peerce   *Prod* Dominick Dunne   *Scr* Jean-Claude Tramont   *Ph* Ennio Guarnieri   *Ed* Marion Rothman   *Mus* Maurice Jarre   *Art Dir* Philip Abramson
● Elizabeth Taylor, Henry Fonda, Helmut Berger, Keith Baxter, Maurice Teynac, Margaret Blye (Sagittarius/Paramount)

Ash Wednesday is a jolting tearjerker about middle-age marital trauma, compounded by the superficial and spiritual uplift of cosmetic surgery. Elizabeth Taylor stars as the fiftyish wife of Henry Fonda, and Helmut Berger is featured as her brief Italian resort affair after the beautification process has restored her surface charm.

Script is essentially a three-act play, about evenly divided over the film's 99 minutes. Act 1 is a gruesome, overdone series of ugly surgical scenes. Act 2 introduces Taylor to a new world of uncertain poise, while Act 3 precipitates the powerful, neatly restrained dissolution of her marriage to Fonda.

Taylor, fashionably gowned and bejewelled carries the film almost single-handedly. Fonda is excellent in his climatic appearance, an usually superb casting idea.

■ **ASK A POLICEMAN**

1939, 83 MINS, UK
Dir Marcel Varnel   *Scr* Marriott Edgar, Val Guest
Ph Derick Williams
● Will Hay, Graham Moffatt, Moore Marriott, Glennis Lorimer, Peter Gawthorne, Charles Oliver (Gainsborough)

Bits of *Dr Syn* (1937), with George Arliss, and *The Ghost Train* (1931) blend happily with amusing dialog and situations [story by Sidney Gilliatt] usually associated with Will Hay and his two stooges, the fat boy and old man.

A villa police station becomes the center of interest when it's discovered there's been no crime there for over 10 years. The sergeant (Hay) in command of two subordinates (Graham Moffatt, Moore Marriott), hearing

they're likely to be transferred or fired because of lack of 'business', plans to frame one or two cases.

Planting a keg of brandy on the beach, to stage a smuggler's racket, they discover another, real contraband keg. From then on it's a wild chase between the three witnits and a band headed by the local squire (Charles Oliver) which is carrying on a lucrative haul.

■ **ASPEN EXTREME**

1993, 117 MINS, US ◇ ⓥ ⊙
Dir Patrick Hasburgh   *Prod* Leonard Goldberg
Scr Patrick Hasburgh   *Ph* Steven Fierberg, Robert Primes   *Ed* Steven Kemper   *Mus* Michael Convertino
Art Dir Roger Cain
● Paul Gross, Peter Berg, Finola Hughes, Teri Polo, William Russ, Trevor Eve (Hollywood Pictures)

Poor scripting kills *Aspen Extreme*, an initially mild romance about finding one's self that eventually turns unconvincingly melodramatic.

Canadian hunk Paul Gross toplines as Ford assembly line auto worker who heads from Detroit to Aspen and a new life. He drags along reluctant buddy Peter Berg, who works at a dinky local ski area.

Gross becomes the hottest thing on the slopes and eventually a gigolo for jetsetter Finola Hughes. Berg also gets a girlfriend, Tina (stunning starlet Nicollette Scorsese), but after she's given a mysterious buildup the character suddenly disappears from the film without explanation.

Femme lead goes to lovely Teri Polo as a local d.j. who is the grudging Good Samaritan taking care of our heroes when they get into trouble.

Along the way there's some attractively lensed hotdogging footage of skiers doing dangerous stunts as well as exciting scenes of a fall into a watery crevasse and an avalanche.

■ **ASPHALT JUNGLE, THE**

1950, 112 MINS, US ⓥ ⊙
Dir John Huston   *Prod* Arthur Hornblow Jr   *Scr* Ben Maddow, John Huston   *Ph* Harold Rosson   *Ed* George Boemler   *Mus* Miklos Rozsa   *Art Dir* Cedric Gibbons, Randall Duell
● Sterling Hayden, Louis Calhern, Sam Jaffe, James Whitmore, Jean Hagen, Marilyn Monroe (M-G-M)

The Asphalt Jungle is a study in crime, hard-hitting in its expose of the underworld. Ironic realism is striven for and achieved in the writing, production and direction. An audience will quite easily pull for the crooks in their execution of the million-dollar jewelry theft around which the plot is built.

W.R. Burnett's lusty novel about criminal types, from the cheap hood to the mastermind, provided the punchy basis for the script. The actual heist is a suspenseful piece of filming as is the following police chase and gradual disintegration of the gang.

Sterling Hayden and Louis Calhern star as contrasting criminals, the former a mean, bitter hood who dreams of restoring an old Kentucky horse farm, and Calhern a crooked attorney who needs money to continue sating his desire for curvy blondes and high living.
□ 1950: Nominations: Best Director, Supp. Actor (Sam Jaffe), Screenplay, B&W Cinematography

■ **ASSASSINATION BUREAU, THE**

1969, 106 MINS, UK ◇
Dir Basil Dearden   *Prod* Michael Relph, Basil Dearden
Scr Michael Relph   *Ph* Geoffrey Unsworth   *Ed* Teddy Darvas   *Mus* Ron Grainer   *Art Dir* Michael Relph
● Oliver Reed, Diana Rigg, Telly Savalas, Curt Jurgens, Annabella Incontrera, Warren Mitchell (Paramount)

That dry, wry humor that flavors such British films as *Kind Hearts and Coronets* is apparent to a degree in *The Assassination Bureau*. Fused with the capable talents of Michael Relph and Basil Dearden picture emerges as a somewhat unusual and clever comedy after an over-leisurely opening.

Plotline, based on an idea from Jack London and Robert Fish's book, *The Assassination Bureau Limited*, is escapist fare throughout.

As a comedy thriller, film stands high, if the spectator isn't too meticulous about expository details, particulary the whys and wherefores of a determined young femme reporter (Diana Rigg) who decides that a strange outbreak of highly professional, apparently motiveless killings, must be the work of a single organization.

Entire cast play their respective roles broadly and each gives a good account of himself. Curt Jurgens as a German general, also a Bureau member, and Annabella Incontrera, as the wife of the Italian member of the bureau, are outstanding.

．．．．．．．．．．．．．．．．．．．．．．．．．．．．

■ ASSASSINATION OF TROTSKY, THE

1972, 105 MINS, FRANCE/ITALY ◇ ⑨
Dir Joseph Losey   *Prod* Norman Priggen, Joseph Losey
Scr Nicholas Mosley, Masolino D'Amico   *Ph* Pasqualino De Santis   *Ed* Reginald Beck   *Mus* Egisto Macchi
Art Dir Richard Macdonald
● Richard Burton, Alain Delon, Romy Schneider, Valentina Cortese, Luigi Vannucchi, Giorgio Albertazzi (Cinettel/CIAC/De Laurentiis)

The last days (1940) in the life of the Russian revolutionary figure, Leon Trotsky, are traced in this fairly cryptic film.

Intended as a sort of political thriller, the film remains cloudy vis-a-vis the Stalin menace though it works up dread, and the foreshadowed (pickaxe, skull-shattering) death. But there is too much forced symbolism, diffuse characterization and a sort of schematic feel sans enough interplay of people, historical perspective, or new insights into this political or psychological murder.

Richard Burton sometimes catches a cantankerous and surface aspect of the aging revolutionary, once almost as popular as Lenin in Russia.

The film rarely transcends a sort of banal look at the murder. It has little to say about political hatred and fanaticism.

．．．．．．．．．．．．．．．．．．．．．．．．．．．．

■ ASSASSIN OF THE TSAR

1992, 104 MINS, UK/USSR ◇ ⑨
Dir Karen Shakhnazarov   *Prod* Christopher Gawor, Erik Vaisberg, Anthony Sloman   *Scr* Alexander Borodyansky, Karen Shakhnazarov   *Ph* Nikolai Nemolyaev
Ed Anthony Sloman, Lidia Milioti   *Mus* John Altman, Vladimir Shut   *Art Dir* Ludmila Kusakova
● Malcolm McDowell, Oleg Yankovsky, Armen Dzhigarkhanian, Yuri Sherstnyov (Spectator/Mosfilm)

Part historical drama, part psycho suspenser, *Assassin of the Tsar* doesn't score clean hits on all its targets, but has powerful playing by topper Malcolm McDowell and excellent all-round production values.

Pic kicks off with a tinted re-creation of Tsar Alexander II's assassination in 1881. It's the first of a series of delusions told to doctors by Timofeyev (Malcolm McDowell), a schizo in a present-day Moscow hospital who thinks he singlehandedly wiped out the Russian royals.

Timofeyev thinks he was Yakov Yurovsky, in charge of icing Tsar Nicholas II and his family in 1918. Despite Timofeyev's claim that he's cured, new medico Smirnov (Oleg Yankovsky) reckons there's still a ghost to be exorcised. Smirnov becomes obsessed with discovering the truth of the assassination and even taking on the role of Nicholas II in Timofeyev's fantasies.

Climax comes when the haggard Smirnov visits Sverdlovsk (site of the 1918 slayings) and joins minds with Timofeyev to relive the actual assassination.

White-haired and craggy-faced as the wily loony, and dead-eyed as the secret police nobody, McDowell's totally believable in both roles. Soviet superstar Yankovsky is restricted in an underwritten part as the medico/tsar, but gives solid support. Other roles are mainly bits.

Pic was lensed in Moscow and Leningrad in two language versions, virtually identical shot-for-shot.

．．．．．．．．．．．．．．．．．．．．．．．．．．．．

■ ASSAULT OF THE KILLER BIMBOS

1988, 81 MINS, US ◇ ⑨ ⊙
Dir Anita Rosenberg   *Prod* David DeCoteau, John Schouweiler   *Scr* Ted Nicolaou   *Ph* Thomas Calloway
Ed Barry Zetlin   *Mus* Fred Lapides, Marc Ellis
Art Dir Royce Mathew
● Christina Whitaker, Elizabeth Kaitan, Tammara Souza, Nick Cassavetes, Griffin O'Neal, Jamie Bozian (Titan)

Assault of the Killer Bimbos is the kind of engagingly dumb, slyly hip pic that is tailor-made for cult enjoyment. First-timer Anita Rosenberg has fashioned an under-$1 million pic [from a story by her, Patti Astor and Ted Nicolaou] that dips and sways with its own kind of bimbotic integrity.

Chief bimbos are played by Christina Whitaker and Elizabeth Kaitan as go-go dancers in a dead-end nightclub who are mistakenly taken for murderers after their boss gets bumped off by hoods. On the 1am to Mexico, they pick up a willing hostage – truckstop waitress Tammara Souza – and three cartoonish surf bums played by Jamie Bozian and moviebiz brats Nick Cassavetes and Griffin O'Neal.

Road adventures, which include a high-speed chase on the desert highway complete with a flying police car stunt, end in a low-rent Tijuana motel. Head bimbo Whitaker has the kind of unshakeable cool that makes her look like she's cruising Ocean Avenue even while driving a getaway car out of a truckstop.

．．．．．．．．．．．．．．．．．．．．．．．．．．．．

■ ASSAULT ON A QUEEN

1966, 106 MINS, US ◇ ⑨
Dir Jack Donohue   *Prod* William Goetz   *Scr* Rod Serling   *Ph* William H. Daniels   *Ed* Archie Marshek
Mus Duke Ellington   *Art Dir* Paul Groesse
● Frank Sinatra, Virna Lisi, Anthony Franciosa, Richard Conte, Alf Kjellin, Errol John (Seven Arts/Sinatra)

Producer William Goetz has supervised a remarkable job of making plausible the admittedly wild-eyed adventures of an odd assortment of moral derelicts who salvage a submarine with the intent of robbing the *Queen Mary* (hence the title) [based on the novel by Jack Finney].

Virna Lisi, Anthony Franciosa and Alf Kjellin, on the hunt for a sunken treasure ship off the Bahamas, hire Frank Sinatra and his partner, Errol John, who run a fishing boat business, to help them find the treasure. Sinatra, instead, finds a small sunken German submarine. Kjellin, a former German U-boat commander, talks the group into salvaging it and holding up the *Queen Mary*.

Only Kjellin is able to create a well-rounded character and is outstanding as the apparently bland German, holding in control his diabolic intent. Sinatra and Lisi are very good in roles that make few demands on their acting ability. John, while efficient in the tenser moments, seems inhibited in scenes where he must wax sentimental over his rehabilitation by Sinatra.

．．．．．．．．．．．．．．．．．．．．．．．．．．．．

■ ASSAULT ON PRECINCT 13

1976, 91 MINS, US ◇ ⑨
Dir John Carpenter   *Prod* J.S. Kaplan   *Scr* John Carpenter   *Ph* Douglas Knapp   *Ed* John T. Chance [= John Carpenter]   *Mus* John Carpenter   *Art Dir* Tommy Vallance
● Austin Stoker, Darwin Joston, Laurie Zimmer, Martin West, Tony Burton, Kim Richards (CKK)

Novelty of a gang swearing a blood oath to destroy a precinct station and all inside is sufficiently compelling for the gory-minded to assure acceptance.

Gang is motivated by a man who kills one of their members for the murder of his small daughter and takes refuge in the Los Angeles station so distraught he cannot explain. Assault closely follows his arrival, and it's a war.

Precinct station is within hours of closing to move to new quarters, which explains why only a single cop and a policewoman remains to hold down the fort, abetted by two prisoners who are temporarily incarcerated on their way to Death Row in Salinas.

John Carpenter's direction of his screenplay, after a pokey opening half, is responsible for realistic movement.

．．．．．．．．．．．．．．．．．．．．．．．．．．．．

■ ASSIGNMENT, THE

1977, 97 MINS, SWEDEN ◇ ⑨
Dir Mats Arehn   *Prod* Ingemar Ejve   *Scr* Lars Magnus Jansson, Ingemar Ejve, Mats Arehn   *Ph* Lennart Carlsson
Ed Ingemar Ejve
● Thomas Hellberg, Christopher Plummer, Carolyn Seymour, Fernando Rey, Per Oscarsson, Walter Gotell (Nordisk/Svensk/SFI)

Story based on an early novel by Per Wahloo about a young Swedish diplomat sent to a violence-torn Latin American state as mediator. From the moment of his arrival, it is clear that everybody distrusts him and most want him killed.

The mediator played as a man of civil courage in spite of obvious fear by Thomas Hellberg, asserts his authority, what little he has, over such warring parties as a police captain, the local Mr Big and the Liberation Front leader, a village doctor and others. Carolyn Seymour as the mediator's secretary supplies a coolly sensual presence.

Film, fortunately, preaches no moral, but in its mix of solid little chills and thrills, it features both tender compassion, rage against injustice and a lot of subdued humor.

．．．．．．．．．．．．．．．．．．．．．．．．．．．．

■ ASYLUM

1972, 88 MINS, UK ◇ ⑨ ⊙
Dir Roy Ward Baker   *Prod* Max J. Rosenberg, Milton Subotsky   *Scr* Robert Bloch   *Ph* Denys Coop   *Ed* Peter Tanner   *Mus* Douglas Gamley   *Art Dir* Tony Curtis
● Peter Cushing, Britt Ekland, Herbert Lom, Patrick Magee, Sylvia Syms, Barbara Parkins (Amicus)

Herewith a dependable programmer off the Amicus belt line. It's a trim little chiller, with a moderate quota of blood and mayhem, polished performances and smooth direction. It also boasts some imaginative props – like the decapitated limbs, etc., Sylvia Syms metaphysically killing her murderer and errant husband, Richard Todd, and his sweetie Barbara Parkins.

The plot is essentially about a young shrink's (Robert Powell) voyage of discovery in an insane asylum where he hopes to become a staffer. He arrives to find that the bossman has himself become confined as a homicidal nut case. His successor (Patrick Magee), by way of putting the young doc to the test, has him interview several psychos.

Very few of the key thesps remain robust and vertical by the windup, for which scripter Robert Bloch comes up with an effective trick ending.

．．．．．．．．．．．．．．．．．．．．．．．．．．．．

A

■ AS YOU DESIRE ME

1932, 70 MINS, US ⑦
Dir George Fitzmaurice *Scr* Gene Markey *Ph* William Daniels *Ed* George Hiveley
● Greta Garbo, Melvyn Douglas, Erich von Stroheim, Owen Moore, Hedda Hopper, Rafaela Ottiano (M-G-M)

A romantic problem play interestingly played by the fascinating Greta Garbo, treated in a manner of high drama. The original [play by Luigi Pirandello] hasn't been broadly hoked in the manner that Metro has so often followed.

Story has to do with an Italian countess, victim of the Austrian invasion and violence from drunken soldiers and driven into a mental fog which has blotted out her past. She is recognized 10 years later in her wanderings as a music-hall singer by the painter who had do her portrait as a bride, and by him brought back to her grief-stricken husband.

But she cannot recall the past and is never entirely received by the people of her former life, with the exception of the portrait painter, who sees with the eyes of faith.

Garbo's performance is always absorbing, vivid in its acting and compelling in appeal. Melvyn Douglas is a rather lukewarm actor in a stencil husband role, impeccably played but unexciting. Owen Moore grabs the acting honors among the men with his jaunty handling of a minor part, while Erich von Stroheim fails signally to make himself the man you love to hate by revealing an accent of blended Yorkville and Ninth Avenue.

■ AT CLOSE RANGE

1986, 111 MINS, US ◇ ⑦ ⊙
Dir James Foley *Prod* Elliott Lewitt, Don Guest
Scr Nicholas Kazan *Ph* Juan Ruiz-Anchia *Ed* Howard Smith *Mus* Patrick Leonard *Art Dir* Peter Jamison
● Sean Penn, Christopher Walken, Mary Stuart Masterson, Christopher Penn, Millie Perkins, Candy Clark (Hemdale)

A downbeat tale [by Elliott Lewitt and Nicholas Kazan] of brutal family relations, James Foley's *At Close Range* is a very tough picture. Violent without being vicarious, this true story is set in a small Pennsylvania town in 1978. Story introduces young Brad (Sean Penn) as just another rather tough kid with an eye for a new girl (the charming Mary Stuart Masterson) and fiercely protective of his brother (Christopher Penn).

Along comes Brad's father (Christopher Walken) who has reputation as a criminal. Intrigued by his seemingly exciting parent, Brad Jr is encouraged to form his own gang to carry out more modest heists.

General audiences will respond to the very strong performances of the two leads, especially Walken in one of his best roles.

■ ATLANTIC CITY

1980, 104 MINS, CANADA/FRANCE/US ◇ ⑦ ⊙
Dir Louis Malle *Prod* Denis Heroux, Gabriel Boustani
Scr John Guare *Ph* Richard Ciupka *Ed* Suzanne Baron
Mus Michel Legrand
● Burt Lancaster, Susan Sarandon, Michel Piccoli, Kate Reid, Robert Joy, Hollis MacLaren (Selta/Kfouri/Cine Neighbour/FR3/SDICC)

Film is blessed with a spare, intriguing script by Yank John Guare, which always skirts impending cliches and predictability by finding unusual facets in his characters and their actions.

The film is well limned by Burt Lancaster as a smalltime mythomaniacal, aging mafia hood, Susan Sarandon as an ambitious young woman, Kate Reid as a fading moll and Robert Joy and Hollis MacLaren as Sarandon's husband and young sister.

Atlantic City is also a character as director Louis Malle adroitly uses decrepit old and new

facades; New Jersey voted to allow gambling at this resort which had boasted gangsters, prohibition capers and big show attractions.
□ 1981: Nominations: Best Picture, Director, Actor (Burt Lancaster), Actress (Susan Sarandon), Original Screenplay,

■ ATLANTIS, THE LOST CONTINENT

1961, 91 MINS, US ◇ ⑦
Dir George Pal *Prod* George Pal *Scr* Daniel Mainwaring *Ph* Harold E. Wellman *Ed* Ben Lewis
Mus Russell Garcia *Art Dir* George W. Davis, William Ferrari
● Anthony Hall, Joyce Taylor, Frank De Kova, John Dall (M-G-M)

After establishing legendary significance via an arresting prolog in which the basis for age-old suspicion of the existence of a lost continental cultural link in the middle of the Atlantic is discussed, scenarist Daniel Mainwaring promptly proceed to ignore the more compelling possibilities of the hypothesis in favor of erecting a tired, shopworn melodrama out of Gerald Hargreaves's play.

There is an astonishing similarity to the stevereevesian spectacles. An 'ordeal by fire and water' ritual conducted in a great, crowded stadium seems almost a replica of gladiatorial combat in the Colosseum. When Atlantis is burning to a cinder at the climax, one can almost hear Nero fiddling. Even Russ Garcia's score has that pompous, martial Roman air about it. And at least several of the mob spectacle scenes have been lifted from Roman screen spectacles of the past (the 1951 version of *Quo Vadis* looks like the source). The acting is routine.

■ AT LONG LAST LOVE

1975, 118 MINS, US ◇
Dir Peter Bogdanovich *Prod* Peter Bogdanovich
Scr Peter Bogdanovich *Ph* Laszlo Kovacs *Ed* Douglas Robertson *Mus* Artie Butler, Lionel Newman (sup.)
Art Dir Gene Allen
● Burt Reynolds, Cybill Shepherd, Madeline Kahn, Duilio Del Prete, Eileen Brennan, John Hillerman (20th Century-Fox/Copa De Oro)

At Long Last Love, Peter Bogdanovich's experiment with a mostly-singing 1930s upper-class romance, is a disappointing and embarrassing waste of talent.

Utilizing 16 Cole Porter songs, many of them not heard for years and all of them reple with additional lyrics hardly ever used, writer-producer-director Bogdanovich tries to float a bubble of gaiety involving three couples: bored playboy Reynolds with rent-hungry deb Cybill Shepherd; Broadway star Madeline Kahn and immigrant gambler Duilio Del Prete; and Eileen Brennan (Shepherd's maid) and John Hillerman (Reynold's urbane valet). The customary plot crises and romantic complications, recognized and adored by vintage film buffs, eventually resolve themselves.

The principals sang their numbers while being filmed, with orchestrations dubbed in later, in an attempt to eliminate the lifelessness of post-sync when it is done poorly. On the basis of this experiment, pre-recording can rest its case.

■ AT PLAY IN THE FIELDS OF THE LORD

1991, 187 MINS, US ◇ ⑦ ⊙
Dir Hector Babenco *Prod* Saul Zaentz *Scr* Jean-Claude Carriere, Hector Babenco *Ph* Lauro Escorel
Ed William Anderson *Mus* Zbigniew Preisner
Art Dir Clovis Bueno
● Tom Berenger, Aidan Quinn, Kathy Bates, John Lithgow, Daryl Hannah, Tom Waits (Zaentz)

At Play in the Fields of the Lord is how half-breed Cheyenne mercenary Lewis Moon describes

his location to missionaries before he parachutes into the Amazon jungle to seek his essence among a tribe called the Niaruna. Tale that follows – a challenging, cerebral and beautifully controlled take on Peter Matthiessens revered 1965 novel – amounts to a cry of warning against interference with a delicate ecological and cultural balance.

Central to this telling are two men: a callous, brooding jungle rat (Tom Berenger) and his nemesis (Aidan Quinn), a dedicated Evangelical worker. One is in the Brazilian jungle town of Mae de Deus to bring Christianity to the Indians; the other is there to bomb them out of their habitat so the Brazilian government can seize their land. Each subverts his own mission, only to find that his presence among the natives can bring them only ill.

Film has a bracing story that hews remarkably close to the novel. Action is a bit stiff and pedantic at first as it stakes out its philosophical turf but then softens and blooms.

Among the first-rate ensemble cast are Kathy Bates as Quinn's shrill, hysterically repressed wife; John Lithgow as a briskly buffoonish fellow missionary; Daryl Hannah as Lithgow's sweetly blank and dogmatic wife; and Tom Waits in his best showcase ever as Moon's sidekick and soul of self-mocking depravity.

Pic was shot over a harrowing six months in the remote jungle town of Belem, Brazil. Lauro Escorel's cinematography is spellbinding.

■ ATTACK

1956, 107 MINS, US ◇ ⑦
Dir Robert Aldrich *Prod* Robert Aldrich *Scr* James Poe
Ph Joseph Biroc *Ed* Michael Luciano *Mus* Frank DeVol
Art Dir William Glasgow
● Jack Palance, Eddie Albert, Lee Marvin, Robert Strauss, Richard Jaeckel, Buddy Ebsen (Associates & Aldrich)

Attack presents a cowardly officer who's murdered by his men. Entire film [from the play *Fragile Fox* by Norman Brooks] is treated with a hard realism that pays off in gutsy entertainment. It's a grim, extremely tough account of an infantry company during the Battle of the Bulge in World War II, brightly projected by the fine characterizations contributed by the cast.

Eddie Albert is the cowardly captain who's too yellow to back the actions attempted by his lieutenants (Jack Palance and William Smithers). Disastrous missions follow each other until Palance threatens to kill Albert if he fails on the next one.

Pic gains realism through depicting army brass and GIs as humans with different reactions to the reality of combat. Palance stands out in his portrayal of the gaunt, enraged lieutenant. Albert makes an unpleasant character quite real and understandable. Scoring exceptionally strong is Lee Marvin, the opportunistic colonel who keeps the coward command because he will be useful after the war in politics.

■ ATTACK OF THE 50 FOOT WOMAN

1958, 65 MINS, US ⑦ ⊙
Dir Nathan Hertz *Prod* Bernard Woolner *Scr* Mark Hanna *Ph* Jacques R. Marquette *Ed* Edward Mann
Mus Ronald Stein *Art Dir* [uncredited]
● Allison Hayes, William Hudson, Yvette Vickers, Roy Gordon, George Douglas, Ken Terrell (Allied Artists)

Attack of the 50 Foot Woman shapes up as a minor offering for the scifi trade where demands aren't too great.

The production is the story of a femme who overnight grows into a murderous giantess, out to get husband who's cheating with another woman. Growth was caused by ray burns suffered when she's seized by huge monster, who lands in the desert near home in a satellite from outer space. Breaking the chains used to restrain her in her luxurious mansion, she makes her way to a tavern where spouse is with his lady love and literally squeezes him to death before the sheriff kills her with a riot gun.

Allison Hayes takes title role as a mentally-disturbed woman who has been in a sanitarium, William Hudson is the husband and Yvette Vickers his girl friend, all good enough in their respective characters.

■ ATTACK OF THE KILLER TOMATOES

1979, 87 MINS, US ◇ ⑲

Dir John De Bello *Prod* Steve Peace, John De Bello *Scr* Costa Dillon, Steve Peace, John De Bello *Ph* John K. Culley *Ed* John De Bello *Mus* Gordon Goodwin, Paul Sundfor
● David Miller, George Wilson, Sharon Taylor, Jack Riley (Four Square)

Attack of the Killer Tomatoes, a low-budget indie production made by a group of young San Diego filmmakers, isn't even worthy of sarcasm. Plot, if it can be called that, concerns sudden growth spurt of tomatoes and their rampage.

Only saving grace is the satire pic's opening titles, a clever lampoon of theatre trailers and advertising pitches, including a mid-credit title card that boasts, 'This space for rent'. There's also a tongue-in-cheek parody of disaster pic music, sung in a deep basso voice, but that's over in about two minutes. Thereafter it's all downhill, rapidly.

■ AT THE CIRCUS

1939, 86 MINS, US ⑲

Dir Edward Buzzell *Prod* Mervyn LeRoy *Scr* Irving Brecher *Ph* Leonard M. Smith *Ed* William H. Terhune *Mus* Franz Waxman (dir.) *Art Dir* Cedric Gibbons, Stan Rogers
● Groucho Marx, Chico Marx, Harpo Marx, Margaret Dumont, Florence Rice, Eve Arden (M-G-M)

The Marx Bros. revert to the rousing physical comedy and staccato gag dialog of their earlier pictures in *At the Circus*.

Story is slight but unimportant. Kenny Baker, owner of a circus, is harrassed by pursuing James Burke, who wants to foreclose the mortgage he holds on the outfit. When Baker's bankroll is stolen, Chico and Harpo call in Groucho to straighten out the difficulties. Groucho winds up by selling the circus for one performance to Margaret Dumont, Baker's rich aunt and Newport social leader.

Chico does his pianolog in circus car, while Harpo's turn for a harp solo is set up in the menagerie with a production and choral background. A colored kid band and adult chorus (from Hollywood company of *Swing Mikado*) are used here.

■ AT THE EARTH'S CORE

1976, 89 MINS, UK ◇ ⑲

Dir Kevin Connor *Prod* John Dark *Scr* Milton Subotsky *Ph* Alan Hume *Ed* John Ireland, Barry Peters *Mus* Mike Vickers *Art Dir* Maurice Carter
● Doug McClure, Peter Cushing, Caroline Munro, Cy Grant, Godfrey James, Sean Lynch (Amicus)

At the Earth's Core, from the Edgar Rice Burroughs novel, is an okay fantasy adventure film. Made in England, it's a fast-paced, slightly tongue-in-cheek tale about stalwart hero Doug McClure's battles with underground monsters. There's old-fashioned rooting interest in the outlandish exploits of McClure and his doddering old professor sidekick, Peter Cushing, who goes through the entire ordeal carrying his umbrella.

Pic takes place in the Victorian Era, charmingly evoked at the beginning when The Iron Mole, McClure and Cushing's experimental earth-boring contraption, embarks on a test mission. The machine goes awry, and they wind up in the land of Pellucidar, becoming slaves to a race of bird-like creatures. McClure falls in love with Caroline Munro, another captive.

Director Kevin Connor keeps the right balance of humor and straightforward adventure in the story, never making the fatal mistake of condescending to his plot or his audience.

■ AUDREY ROSE

1977, 112 MINS, US ◇ ⑲

Dir Robert Wise *Prod* Joe Wizan, Frank De Felitta *Scr* Frank De Felitta *Ph* Victor J. Kemper *Ed* Carl Kress *Mus* Michael Small *Art Dir* Harry Horner
● Marsha Mason, Anthony Hopkins, John Beck, Susan Swift, Norman Lloyd, John Hillerman (United Artists)

Frank De Felitta's novel and screenplay of reincarnation comes to the screen fully realized in all creative aspects.

Film takes upper middle-class couple Marsha Mason and John Beck into a nightmare of torment when daughter Susan Swift begins acting strangely. Anthony Hopkins simultaneously menaces as the outsider who has a mysterious influence on the child.

The script does a good job in interpolating the necessary philosophical and metaphysical explanations of reincarnation without being overly didactic or tediously expository.

Herein, city streets, courtrooms, schools and other mundane locations familiar to audiences are the setting for the plot making the ethereal aspects even more subtly powerful.

■ AUNTIE MAME

1958, 143 MINS, US ◇ ⑲ ⊙

Dir Morton DaCosta *Prod* [uncredited] *Scr* Betty Comden, Adolph Green *Ph* Harry Stradling Sr *Ed* William Ziegler *Mus* Bronislau Kaper *Art Dir* Malcolm Bert
● Rosalind Russell, Forrest Tucker, Coral Browne, Fred Clark, Roger Smith, Joanna Barnes (Warner)

Auntie Mame is a faithfully funny recording of the hit play, changed only in some small details. Rosalind Russell recreates the title role for the film. Betty Comden and Adolph Green did the screenplay, based on the play by Jerome Lawrence an Robert E. Lee, which in turn was taken from the novel of Patrick Dennis. Russell plays the character described in the dialog as a 'loving woman – odd, but loving'. She is a high class – or, at least rich – Bohemian. She mixes Greek Orthodox bishops with Gertrude Stein-type females, for her own amusement, directing this chorus of mixed voices with a cigarette holder loaded with gems as phony as most of her guests. 'Life is a banquet' is her philosophy. Even when the stock market crash wipes her out, the depression that follows fails to depress her for long.

Russell scores because her native intelligence augments her sharp comedy sense. She can spike a line and drive it in, but she can also carry off the scenes of mother love and romance with her nephew and her husband.

As in the legit version, Peggy Cass is a comedy standout as the helpless Agnes Gooch. Coral Browne, as the alcoholic actress who is Mame's best friend, and Fred Clark, as the baffled banker assigned to trustee Mame's nephew, are also strong comedy supports. Forrest Tucker makes a human figure of his Southern millionaire but gets a great deal of fun out of it, too.

☐ 1958: Nominations: Best Picture, Actress (Rosalind Russell), Supp. Actress (Peggy Cass), Color Cinematography, Art Direction, Editing

■ AUNT JULIA AND THE SCRIPTWRITER

See: Tune in Tomorrow

■ AUTHOR! AUTHOR!

1982, 110 MINS, US ◇ ⑲

Dir Arthur Hiller *Prod* Irwin Winkler *Scr* Israel Horovitz *Ph* Victor J. Kemper *Ed* William Reynolds *Mus* Dave Grusin *Art Dir* Gene Rudolf
● Al Pacino, Dyan Cannon, Tuesday Weld, Alan King, Bob Dishy, Bob Elliott (20th Century-Fox)

Author! Author! is rather a mess, but a quite amiable one. This *Kramer vs Kramer* multiplied by five kids by no means approaches its full comic or emotional potential, but Israel Horovitz's marvelous screenplay and Al Pacino's warm performance provide constant pleasure.

Pacino plays a New York playwright who's attempting to get his first play in two years off the ground. Tale runs the course of the comedy's preparation, from initial director change to casting, rehearsals, rewrites and, finally, opening night.

Heart of the film, however, lies in Pacino's domestic life. His wife (Tuesday Weld) leaves him for another man, stranding kids of their own as well as from her previous three marriages.

Pacino takes it hard, but is momentarily soothed by the friendly attentions of Hollywood star Dyan Cannon, making the Broadway plunge for the first time in the leading role of the play.

■ AVALANCHE

1978, 91 MINS, US ◇ ⑲

Dir Corey Allen *Prod* Roger Corman *Scr* Claude Pola, Corey Allen *Ph* Pierre-William Glenn *Ed* Stuart Schoolnik, Larry Bock *Mus* William Kraft *Art Dir* Phillip Thomas
● Rock Hudson, Mia Farrow, Robert Forster, Jeanette Nolan, Rick Moses, Steve Franken (New World)

Rock Hudson and Mia Farrow head the cast of characters gathered at a ski lodge beneath an uneasy cornice of snow. They warned Hudson not to build the lodge on this particular spot, but he went ahead with the same stubbornness that cost him the wife he still loves.

Farrow, that's the ex-wife, is on hand for the grand opening and quickly beds down with Robert Forster, the naturalist photographer who keeps complaining about the trees Hudson is cutting down. Hudson, in turn, is having a steam-room fling with his secretary.

Eventually, the whole mountain top comes down on the crowd of skaters, skiers and sledders. Using a lot of archive footage of an actual massive avalanche, director Corey Allen and crew have done a very good job of creating realistic scenes. Unfortunately, much of the archive footage is badly scratched so some of the big boulders look like they're sliding down on wires.

Overall, the performances are fine.

■ AVALON

1990, 126 MINS, US ◇ ⑲ ⊙

Dir Barry Levinson *Prod* Mark Johnson, Barry Levinson *Scr* Barry Levinson *Ph* Allen Daviau *Ed* Stu Linder *Mus* Randy Newman *Art Dir* Norman Reynolds
● Leo Fuchs, Eve Gordon, Lou Jacobi, Armin Mueller-Stahl, Elizabeth Perkins, Joan Plowright (Tri-Star/Baltimore)

Dealing with an extended Jewish family headed by brothers who left Europe in the early 20th century, *Avalon* seeks to recapture both a period (the post-World War II era, as television became king) and the essence of family life, with all its feuding, pettiness and tumult.

Still, beyond the beautiful photography,

spotless classic cars and slavishly detailed sets, the film lacks focus or a real reason for being. The patriarch of the central nuclear family is Sam Krichinsky (Armin Mueller-Stahl), who arrives wide-eyed in the US on the Fourth of July. His reminiscences to his grandchildren introduce us to the extended clan.

Son Jules (Aidan Quinn) changes his name and goes into business selling TV sets. Jules marries and has his own son (Elijah Wood), who becomes close to Sam, while Jules' wife (Elizabeth Perkins) chafes under the intrusiveness of his mother (Joan Plowright).

After meandering through the family life for nearly two hours, Levinson rushes to what proves a moving conclusion, one that seeks to connect all that proceeded it on some higher level.

☐ 1990: Nominations: Best Original Screenplay, Cinematography, Original Score, Costume Design

■ AVANTI!

1972, 143 MINS, US ◇ ⓦ
Dir Billy Wilder *Prod* Billy Wilder *Scr* Billy Wilder, I.A.L. Diamond *Ph* Luigi Kuveiller *Ed* Ralph E. Winters *Mus* Carlo Rustichelli (arr.) *Art Dir* Ferdinando Scarfiotti
● Jack Lemmon, Juliet Mills, Clive Revill, Edward Andrews, Gianfranco Barra, Franco Angrisano (Phalanx/Jalem)

Billy Wilder has taken the Samuel Taylor Broadway play and given it his own peculiar treatment. In casting Jack Lemmon as an American corporation executive come to Italy to claim the body of his father, killed when he drove his car off a high cliff he has the perfect foil for the building situations, marking the fifth time pair have teamed up in a picture.

Scripted by Wilder and I.A.L. Diamond, two basic themes are nicely blended to lend motivation. There is the sort-of romance between Lemmon and Juliet Mills and the endless Italian governmental red tape which cues all the action.

Basic situation takes form as Lemmon discovers another person also met her death in the tragic accident, his father's longtime English mistress with whom he's been carrying on a clandestine love affair for past 12 years. He meets a chubby English dumpling (Mills) whom he learns is the daughter of the lady in question also heading to claim her mother's body.

Lemmon displays his usual aptitude in a frantic role, here a hardboiled American exec who is gradually drawn into the aura in which his father had found himself. Mills, who is said to have put on 25 pounds for character, which demands chubbiness, is a happy choice, endowing part with warmth and understanding.

■ AWAKENING, THE

1980, 102 MINS, UK ◇ ⓦ ⊙
Dir Mike Newell *Prod* Robert Solo, Andrew Scheinman *Scr* Allan Scott, Chris Bryant, Clive Exton *Ph* Jack Cardiff *Ed* Terry Rawlings *Mus* Claude Bolling *Art Dir* Michael Stringer
● Charlton Heston, Susannah York, Jill Townsend, Stephanie Zimbalist, Patrick Drury (Orion)

It seems that there was once a certain Egyptian Queen Kara whose father, following the custom of the day, induced her into an incestuous relationship. In revenge, Kara killed him and proceeded to have slaughtered everyone in the land who had even spoken with the late pharaoh. Dead at 18, the evil queen was buried, amidst the usual riches, in an isolated tomb bearing a 'do not disturb' sign.

Story [based on the novel *The Jewel of the Seven Stars* by Bram Stoker] possesses a strange fascination for archeologist Charlton Heston, who finally penetrates the chamber centuries later. Kara's nasty spirit transforms neatly to Heston's baby daughter.

It's hokum through and through. Veteran lenser Jack Cardiff contributes a highly professional sheen but first-time feature director Mike Newell exhibits a jumpy, disjointed style.

■ AWAKENINGS

1990, 121 MINS, US ◇ ⓦ ⊙
Dir Penny Marshall *Prod* Walter F. Parkes, Lawrence Lasker *Scr* Steven Zillian *Ph* Miroslav Ondricek *Ed* Jerry Greenberg, Battle Davis *Mus* Randy Newman *Art Dir* Anton Furst
● Robin Williams, Robert De Niro, Julie Kavner, Ruth Nelson, John Heard, Penelope Ann Miller (Columbia)

Robin Williams joins Robert De Niro in enacting the story of neurologist Oliver Sacks, who in 1966 encountered a group of statue-like paralytics in a Bronx hospital and insisted something could be done for them. Sacks/Sayer (Williams) discovers the were stricken with encephalitis, which claimed many victims in the 1920s.

Sayer wins permission to test L-DOPA, a new drug then being used to combat Parkinson's disease, and is able to 'awaken' Leonard Lowe (De Niro), frozen since contracting the sleeping sickness 30 years before. But the miracle cure proves temporary.

Rendered broadly and brightly accessible in the hands of director Penny Marshall and screenwriter Steven Zillian, who adapted Sacks' book, *Awakenings* dwells predictably on the picture's upbeat themes: the miracle of health taken for granted, and the joy and meaning in life's simple things.

Enacting the shy, fidgety doctor, Williams extends the extraordinary dramatic gifts he displayed in *Dead Poets Society*. Sympathy and tenderness shine from his bright blue eyes. De Niro, far more effective here than in his portrayal of an illiterate man in *Stanley & Iris*, has this visceral, demanding role by the tail.
☐ 1990: Nominations: Best Picture, Actor (Robert De Niro), Adapted Screenplay

■ AWFUL TRUTH, THE

1937, 90 MINS, US ⊙
Dir Leo McCarey *Prod* Leo McCarey *Scr* Vina Delmar *Ph* Joseph Walker
● Irene Dunne, Cary Grant, Ralph Bellamy, Robert Allen, Cecil Cunningham, Alexander D'Arcy (Columbia)

Vina Delmar accomplishes a slick job of hauling up to date the basic good yarn in Arthur Richman's Broadway success of 15 years earlier.

Pairs of leads are married. When Cary Grant isn't satisfied with simple, innocent explanation of where and how Irene Dunne spent the night away from home while he – faithful fellow – was feigning a trip to Florida and playing poker with pals around the corner, the couple obtain a divorce.

The divorcee starts tagging around with an ardent oil-rich Oklahoman (Ralph Bellamy), who furnishes not only a good performance, but spikes up the film with a lot of spontaneous comedy as a simple, rustic soul accustomed to staying always within the shadow of his mother's trailing skirts. Meanwhile, Grant has started looping around with an heiress.

The windup is accomplished with a maximum of fun, with the wife almost resorting to kidnapping the man to get him back. Direction is first-water in effectiveness, and the timing Leo McCarey plotted for the fast comedy lines flawless.
☐ 1937: Best Director.
☐ Nominations: Best Picture, Actress (Irene Dunne), Supp. Actor (Ralph Bellamy), Screenplay

B*b*

■ BABE, THE

1992, 113 MINS, US ◇ ⓦ ⊙
Dir Arthur Hiller *Prod* John Fusco *Scr* John Fusco *Ph* Haskell Wexler *Ed* Robert C. Jones *Mus* Elmer Bernstein *Art Dir* James D. Vance
● John Goodman, Kelly McGillis, Trini Alvarado, Bruce Boxleitner, Peter Donat, James Cromwell (Universal/Waterhorse)

Despite Haxell Wexler's alluring lensing, this thinly dramatized, overly episodic Babe Ruth biopic resembles a telepic that has lost its way onto the big screen.

Lovable TV star-erstwhile movie character actor John Goodman plays one of America' most endearing folk heroes. Though heavier with a bigger torso and thicker legs than the Bambino's incongruously spindly pins, Goodman otherwise has been made up into a remarkable likeness of the real Babe. Goodman has an exuberant, bumptious charm ideally suited to the overgrown child he's playing.

Starting in his Dickensian childhood when he's abandoned into the care of boys school in Baltimore, pic touchingly shows how the fat, unloved boy (Andy Voils) blossoms into an athletic marvel under the tutelage of a kindly Brother (James Cromwell). But it skips too quickly over Ruth's turbulent adolescent years. The rage and feelings of neglect that fueled Ruth's ambition aren't explored adequately.

Pic is so infatuated with the Babe, warts and all, that it fails to bring to life the feelings of his first wife (Trini Alvarado). His satisfying second marriage to a practical-minded showgirl (saucy Kelly McGillis) brings out a new strain of maturity in Ruth, but it's hardly big-league pic material.

■ BABES IN ARMS

1939, 93 MINS, US ⓦ ⊙
Dir Busby Berkeley *Prod* Arthur Freed *Scr* Jack MacGowan, Kay Van Riper *Ph* Ray June *Ed* Frank Sullivan *Mus* Georgie Stoll (dir.) *Art Dir* Cedric Gibbons, Merrill Pye
● Mickey Rooney, Judy Garland, Charles Winninger, Guy Kibbee, June Preisser (M-G-M)

Film version of the Rodgers and Hart [1937] musical has been considerably embellished in its transfer to the screen. Basic idea is there, and two songs are retained. Otherwise, it's a greatly enhanced piece of entertainment, with Mickey Rooney having a field day parading his versatile talents.

He sings, dances, gives out with a series of imitations including Eddie Leonard, Clark Gable, Lionel Barrymore, President Roosevelt.

With Judy Garland he sings 'Good Morning', a new tune by Nacio Herb Brown and producer Arthur Freed; he pounds the ivories; he directs a kid show to provide impersonations, and a dinner table sequence, with mixup of decision on the silverware, is an old routine but his technique and timing make for grand fun.

Direction by Busby Berkeley is enthusiastic and at a fast clip throughout.
☐ 1939: Nominations: Best Actor (Mickey Rooney), Score

■ BABES IN TOYLAND

1934, 79 MINS, US ⓦ ⊙
Dir Charles Rogers, Gus Meins *Prod* Hal Roach *Scr* Nick Grinde, Frank Butler *Ph* Art Lloyd, Francis Corby *Ed* William Terhune, Bert Jordan

● Stan Laurel, Oliver Hardy, Charlotte Henry, Felix Knight, Henry Brandon, Marie Wilson (Roach/M-G-M)

Babes in Toyland is far away from the Victor Herbert original operetta. The arithmetic song and 'March of the Toys' are the only outstanding survivors of Herbert's score, and these are merely background. Two other lesser numbers are used. Of the original book there is no trace at all.

This is not a musical brought to the screen. It is a fairy story in technique and treatment, but a gorgeous fairy tale which gives everything to Laurel and Hardy and to which, in return, they give the happiest best.

The story is simple. Tom-Tom loves Bo-Peep, who is one of the numerous progeny of the Old Woman who lived in a shoe. Barnaby, a miser, holds the mortgage. Bo-Peep must marry him or else. Hardy promises to redeem the mortgage, but he and Laurel get fired from the toy shop when they make 100 soldiers six feet tall instead of 600 each a foot high. For this they are punished, but Bo-Peep begs them off, promising Barnaby she will marry him. Barnaby really is married to Laurel in bride's dress. He frames Tom, who is exiled to Bogeyland, whither Bo-Peep follows him. The comedians follow and help them to effect their escape. This brings a smashing climax with the soldiers marching to the strains of 'March of the Toys'.

A Mother Goose characters are woven into the plot, not to mention the Three Little Pigs, but it's Laurel and Hardy's picture. While they are on the story zips along, but the mistake has not been made of asking them to fill the stage continuously.

■ BABES ON BROADWAY

1942, 121 MINS, US ◇ ⑰ ⊙
Dir Busby Berkeley   *Prod* Arthur Freed   *Scr* Fred Finklehoffe, Elaine Ryan   *Ph* Lester White   *Ed* Fredrick Y. Smith   *Mus* Georgie Stoll (dir.), Roger Edens (adapt.)   *Art Dir* Cedric Gibbons, Malcolm Brown
● Mickey Rooney, Judy Garland, Richard Quine, Fay Bainter (M-G-M)

If all the energy used by Mickey Rooney in making *Babes on Broadway* could be assembled in one place, there would be enough to sustain a flying fortress in the stratosphere from Hollywood to New York and return, non-stop. And there might be so left over. Teamed with Judy Garland in a filmusical which is very similar to their previous efforts, Rooney is as fresh as the proverbial daisy at the end of two hours of strenuous theatrical calisthenics. He dances, sings, acts and does imitations dozens of them.

There isn't time to catch one's breath from the opening moment to the closing fadeout of Rooney and Garland giving their all in one of those Metro production numbers, where the stage, the scenery, the actors and some of the audience are doing a gigantic revolution around the camera. In between, there is related a story [by Fred Finklehoffe] about young performers battling for their 'chance' on Broadway.

Busby Berkeley directs this sort of thing about as well as anybody. But both Rooney and Garland are fast outgrowing this type of presentation, which depends entirely on the ah's and oh's that spring from watching precocious children.

□ 1942: Nomination: Best Song ('How About You')

■ BABY BOOM

1987, 103 MINS, US ◇ ⑰ ⊙
Dir Charles Shyer   *Prod* Nancy Meyers   *Scr* Nancy Meyers, Charles Shyer   *Ph* William A. Fraker   *Ed* Lynzee Klingman   *Mus* Bill Conti   *Art Dir* Jeffrey Howard
● Diane Keaton, Harold Ramis, Sam Wanamaker, James Spader, Pat Hingle, Sam Shepard (United Artists)

A transparent and one-dimensional parable about a power-devouring female careerist and the unwanted bundle of joy that turns her obsessive fast-track life in Gotham upside down. Constructed almost entirely upon facile and familiar media cliches about 'parenting' and the super-yuppie set, *Baby Boom* has the superficiality of a project inspired by a lame New York magazine cover story and sketched out on a cocktail napkin at Spago's.

J.C. Wiatt (Diane Keaton) is a dressed-for-success management consultant whose steamroller ambition has earned this workaholic the proudly flaunted nickname, 'Tiger Lady'. She lives in trendy high-rise splendor with bland investment banker Steven Buchner (Harold Ramis), to whom she reluctantly allows a four-minute slot for lovemaking before returning to late-night paperwork.

Suddenly, J.C. learns that a cousin has died together with her husband in an accident in England. J.C. is intrigued to learn that she's inherited something from this misfortune but, to her considerable shock, this turns out to be a precious apple-cheeked 12-month old girl, Elizabeth (Kristina and Michelle Kennedy).

Baby Boom tries to be a lot funnier than it actually is, and handsome production design and cinematography do little to compensate for its annoying over-reliance on cornball action montages and a dreadfully saccharine soudtrack score.

■ BABY DOLL

1956, 114 MINS, US ⑰
Dir Elia Kazan   *Prod* Elia Kazan   *Scr* Tennessee Williams   *Ph* Boris Kaufman   *Ed* Gene Milford   *Mus* Kenyon Hopkins   *Art Dir* Richard Sylbert, Paul Sylbert
● Karl Malden, Carroll Baker, Eli Wallach, Mildred Dunnock, Lonny Chapman (Newtown)

Except for moments of humor that are strictly inherent in the character of the principals, *Baby Doll* plays off against a sleazy, dirty, depressing Southern background. Over it hangs a feeling of decay, expertly nurtured by director Elia Kazan.

Baby Doll is based on a 1941 Tennessee Williams story, dramatized on Broadway in 1955 as *27 Wagons Full of Cotton*.

Story briefly has Carroll Baker, an immature teenager, married to middle-aged Karl Malden who runs a cotton gin. When their on-credit furniture is carted away, Malden sets fire to the Syndicate cotton gin in town. Suspecting Malden, Eli Wallach – owner of the gin – carts his cotton to Malden's gin for processing but then proceeds to seduce Baker who signs a note confessing that Malden committed the arson. Malden, who has promised not to touch his young wife until one year after their marriage finds Baker and Wallach together in the house and goes berserk with jealousy.

Baker's performance captures all the animal charm, the naivete, the vanity, contempt and rising passion of Baby Doll.

Wallach as the vengeful Vacarro plays it to the hilt. Malden is cast to perfection and turns in a sock performance.

□ 1956: Nominations: Best Actress (Carroll Baker), Supp. Actress (Mildred Dunnock), Adapted Screenplay, B&W Cinematography

■ BABY FACE NELSON

1957, 85 MINS, US ⑰
Dir Don Siegel   *Prod* Al Zimbalist   *Scr* Irving Shulman, Daniel Mainwaring   *Ph* Hal Mohr   *Ed* Leon Barsha   *Mus* Van Alexander   *Art Dir* David Milton
● Mickey Rooney, Carolyn Jones, Cedric Hardwicke, Leo Gordon, Anthony Caruso, Jack Elam (Fryman-ZS/United Artists)

Nelson was a member of the notorious Dillinger gang that scourged the midwest

circa 1933. The script [from a story by Robert Adler] makes him a ruthless, trigger-happy, coldblooded killer.

The versatile Mickey Rooney is not particularly convincing as the pint-sized Nelson. He snarls, boils with hatred and is unrepentant. But he merely seems to be going through the motions and his performance never matches the acting found in gangster classics.

More impressive is Carolyn Jones' portrayal of Rooney's loyal moll. She's a plain jane who's attracted to him by some strange affection. But with the FBI closing in on the wounded Rooney, it is she who kills him when he admits he would even shoot down small boys.

■ BABY, IT'S YOU

1983, 105 MINS, US ◇ ⑰ ⊙
Dir John Sayles   *Prod* Griffin Dunne, Amy Robinson   *Scr* John Sayles   *Ph* Michael Ballhaus   *Ed* Sonya Polonsky   *Art Dir* Jeffrey Townsend
● Rosanna Arquette, Vincent Spano, Joanna Merlin, Jack Davidson, Nick Ferrari, Dolores Messina (Double Play)

Despite some strong thematic material and a vibrant central performance, *Baby, It's You* remains an essentially unfulfilled romantic drama. John Sayles' third directorial outing, penned from a story by coproducer Amy Robinson, improves as it moves along from 1966 to a slightly later time frame, but can't recoup from the ultimately unbelievable pairing of leading characters.

Film has an elegantly dressed Italian street kid with the mysterious name of Sheik pursue, win, lose and, at length, haunt the emotional life of a bright, ambitious and terribly attractive high school drama student, Jill.

When the pair split at the time of her prom, after an affectionate but still chaste courtship, the two travel radically different roads from Trenton, NJ, she to school and encroaching hippiedom, and he to Miami to follow his dream of being Frank Sinatra.

In spite of being a character which could have used more fleshing out in the writing, it's Rosanna Arquette who makes *Baby, It's You* persistently watchable. Resembling something of a more voluptous cross between Nastassja Kinski and Audrey Hepburn, to whom her character is compared in the film, Arquette's exceedingly alive performance shows great potential. As the Sinatra idolator, Vincent Spano, with his hair greased back and clothes beautifully pressed, looks just like the poor man's idea of elegance he's supposed to embody. He does a good turn, but unavoidably suffers from miscasting of his character opposite Arquette's.

■ BABYLON

1980, 95 MINS, UK ◇ ⑰
Dir Franco Rosso   *Prod* Gavrik Losey   *Scr* Martin Stellman, Franco Rosso   *Ph* Chris Menges   *Ed* Thomas Schwalm   *Mus* Denis Bovell, Aswad   *Art Dir* Brian Savegar
● Brinsley Forde, Karl Howman, Trevor Laird (Diversity Music/NFFC/Chrysalis/Lee Electric)

Like the reggae music that pulses through it, *Babylon* is rich, rough and real. And like the streetlife of the young black Londoners it portrays, it's threatening, touching, violent and funny. This one seems to explode in the gut with a powerful mix of pain and pleasure.

The screenplay was originally commissioned as a BBC-TV play. Subsequent rewrites, while triumphantly upgrading it to the level of big-screen fare, have at the same time sharpened rather than softened that controversial angle.

Brinsley Forde plays the dreadlocked fellow whose problems at the outset are no more than everyday irritants.

By the end, however, he's lost his job; been chased; beaten by police; discovered his precious sound equipment has been ripped to pieces at the group's backstreet base by nearby white residents; and he's plunged a screwdriver into the stomach of the man he knows is responsible.

······························

■ BABY MAKER, THE

1970, 109 MINS, US ◇ 📼

Dir James Bridges *Prod* Richard Goldstone *Scr* James Bridges *Ph* Charles Rosher Jr *Ed* Walter Thompson *Mus* Fred Karlin *Art Dir* Mort Rabinowitz

● Barbara Hershey, Collin Wilcox-Horne, Sam Groom, Scott Glenn, Jeannie Berlin, Lili Valenty (National General/Wise)

The Baby Maker is an offbeat story of a childless couple who hire a young girl to conceive by the husband.

Director James Bridges' story is stronger than his direction of players, though the physical staging is admirable.

Collin Wilcox-Horne and Sam Groom are a barren couple, who hire Barbara Hershey to bear his child. This in turn shatters the girl's relationship with Scott Glenn, both of whom are from the love generation. Development of an emotional relationship between Hershey and Groom is more than implicit.

Wilcox-Horne is excellent in a multifaceted performance: sometimes warm and loving, occasionally on the verge of jealousy, but always sincere in her character's motivations and reactions. Hers is the film's best performance.

Glenn comes over well as the frustrated but likeable lover. His role is important if subsidiary, and he handles it very well. -

☐ 1970: Nomination: Best Original Song Score

······························

■ BABY OF MACON, THE

1993, 122 MINS, NETHERLANDS/FRANCE ◇ 📼

Dir Peter Greenaway *Prod* Kees Kasander *Scr* Peter Greenaway *Ph* Sacha Vierny *Ed* Chris Wyatt *Art Dir* Ben Van Os, Jan Roelfs

● Julia Ormond, Ralph Fiennes, Philip Stone, Jonathan Lacey, Don Henderson, Jeff Nuttall (Allarts/UGC)

Peter Greenaway's *The Baby of Macon* is all fluff and no filling. Visually sumptuous and laden with religious refs and Brechtian devices, this elaborate but overlong film-of-a-play about the birth of a 17th-century miracle-child and his short-lived period of grace plays like a tired rerun of the director's previous extravaganzas.

Entire film takes place in a single giant set that includes audience and performers, gathered for an elaborate theatrical masque to celebrate fertility – the community is plagued by barrenness, seen as God's punishment for letting the local cathedral fall into disrepair.

The miracle-child quickly becomes an icon for the region's barren mothers, and one of its sisters (Julia Ormond) uses the window of opportunity to claim to be its rightful mother. The fact she's still a virgin doesn't cramp her style.

While Greenaway's previous movies have been a cornucopia of challenging ideas and intellectual jeux, this one quickly starts going round in circles once the board has been laid out. Still, as a master of the ornate Greenaway is firing on all cylinders.

······························

■ BABY
SECRET OF THE LOST LEGEND

1985, 95 MINS, US ◇ 📼

Dir B.W.L. Norton *Prod* Jonathan T. Taplin *Scr* Clifford Green, Ellen Green *Ph* John Alcott *Ed* Howard Smith, David Bretherton *Mus* Jerry Goldsmith *Art Dir* Raymond G. Storey

● William Katt, Sean Young, Patrick McGoohan, Julian Fellowes, Kyalo Mativo, Hugh Quarshie (Touchstone)

A huggable prehistoric hatchling is discovered by a young American couple in an African rain forest. Story has an engaging performance from William Katt, who plays the sportswriter husband of paleontologist Sean Young. Latter, whose maternal and scientific instincts propel events, is rather bland.

Evil foil is Patrick McGoohan as a rival, ruthless paleontologist who enlists the aid of a rapacious revolutionary army to capture Baby's towering brontosaurus mama, after overzealous soldier gun down the 70-or-so-foot tall papa.

Katt and Young risk their lives to save the baby, who stretches 10 feet, has a kind of *E.T.* winsomeness, and once even hops like a shaggy family pooch in between the covers of Katt and Young.

Dinosaur movements derive from both cable and from operators who were inside the gargantuan structures.

······························

■ BABY THE RAIN MUST FALL

1965, 93 MINS, US 📼 ⊙

Dir Robert Mulligan *Prod* Alan J. Pakula *Scr* Horton Foote *Ph* Ernest Laszlo *Ed* Aaron Stell *Mus* Elmer Bernstein *Art Dir* Roland Anderson

● Lee Remick, Steve McQueen, Don Murray, Paul Fix, Josephine Hutchinson, Ruth White (Park Place/Solar)

Chief assets of Pakula-Mulligan's *Baby the Rain Must Fall* [from Horton Foote's play *The Traveling Lady*] are outstanding performances by its stars and an emotional punch that lingers. Steve McQueen is exactly right as irresponsible rockabilly singer, Lee Remick portrays his wife sensitively, and newcomer Kimberly Block is charming and unaffected as their six-year-old daughter.

McQueen, raised by dictatorial spinster (Georgia Simmons) who disapproves of his singing in road-houses, is troubleprone rebel. When story opens he is free on parole for a stabbing, and is joined by Remick and Block, wife and daughter he had kept secret.

Remick is vividly alive in spontaneous-appearing scenes with daughter. But director Robert Mulligan apparently was so determined to avoid soap-opera cliches that he did not permit actress to register negative emotion beyond look of distraught unhappiness even though sad events should have allowed room for tears.

Other cast members are adequate, but roles suffer from editorial cuts (confirmed by director) that leave sub-plots dangling.

······························

■ BACHELOR AND THE BOBBY-SOXER, THE

1947, 94 MINS, US 📼 ⊙

Dir Irving Reis *Prod* Dore Schary *Scr* Sidney Sheldon *Ph* Robert de Grasse, Nicholas Musuraca *Ed* Frederick Knudson *Mus* Leigh Harline *Art Dir* Albert S. D'Agostino, Carroll Clark

● Cary Grant, Myrna Loy, Shirley Temple, Rudy Vallee (RKO)

The Bachelor and the Bobby-Soxer poses a plot easily adapted to fluffy situations. Tossed together are a lady judge, a playboy artist and an impressionable teenager. Grant, the artist, has already had a brush with the judge, Myrna Loy, so when the judge's kid sister, Shirley Temple, is found in the artist's apartment late at night, he's in plenty of trouble. Court psychiatrist proposes that, rather than make Grant a martyr in Temple's eyes, he be assigned to escort her around until she gets over her crush.

Chuckles get heartier and heartier as adult Grant plays at being a juvenile at basketball games, school picnics, etc. It's done with slapstick touch that pays off. Romance switch with Loy going for Grant is an obvious development but well done.

☐ 1947: Best Original Screenplay

······························

■ BACHELOR FLAT

1961, 92 MINS, US ◇

Dir Frank Tashlin *Prod* Jack Cummings *Scr* Frank Tashlin, Budd Grossman *Ph* Daniel L. Fapp *Ed* Hugh S. Fowler *Mus* John Williams *Art Dir* Jack Martin Smith, Leland Fuller

● Tuesday Weld, Richard Beymer, Terry-Thomas, Celeste Holm, Francesca Bellini, Howard McNear (20th Century-Fox)

Carry on Archaeologist might be an apt sub-title for this frivolous, farcical concoction about a British bone specialist (dinosaur variety) who is irresistibly attractive to the predatory modern American female.

Frank Tashlin directed from his own screenplay, written with Budd Grossman, who wrote the play. Terry-Thomas is the archaeology professor situated in California, where he is on the verge of wedlock with a roving fashion designer (Celeste Holm) who is abroad on business as the nuptial date aproaches. T-T's path to the altar is complicated by: (1) the unscheduled advent of Tuesday Weld, who is Holm's daughter, unbeknownst to the prof; (2) regular invasions of his bachelor quarters by campus cuties; (3) the irresponsible advice of cynical student-neighbor Richard Beymer, who has a crush on Tuesday; (4) the single-ness-of-purpose of Beymer's dachshund, a typical bona-Fido determined to bury the professor's prize possession – a rare dinosaur bone.

Except for Terry-Thomas, whose comic intuition and creativity is responsible for most of the merriment, it is the supporting cast, rather than the principals, that comes through on the comedy end. Neither Weld nor Beymer seems comfortably at home in farce, the strain often shows through. Holm, a formidable light comedienne, is stuck regrettably in a rather bland role. Francesca Bellini, a well-constructed ballerina, shows a flair for comedy as an oversexed lush equipped with an instant martini kit an disposition to match.

The dachshund, incidentally, is an accomplished low comedienne.

······························

■ BACHELOR GIRL APARTMENT
See: Any Wednesday

······························

■ BACHELOR MOTHER

1939, 80 MINS, US 📼 ⊙

Dir Garson Kanin *Prod* Buddy De Sylva *Scr* Norman Krasna *Ph* Robert de Grasse *Ed* Henry Berman, Robert Wise *Mus* Roy Webb *Art Dir* Van Nest Polglase, Carroll Clark

● Ginger Rogers, David Niven, Charles Coburn, Frank Albertson, E.E. Clive (RKO)

Story [by Felix Jackson] itself is a rather ordinary Cinderella yarn, gaining substance and strength through adroit direction, excellently tempoed lines and situations, and topnotch cast performances.

Ginger Rogers blossoms forth as a most competent comedienne. David Niven delivers strongly as the romantic interest.

Picking up a baby on the steps of a foundling home, Rogers finds her excuses inadequate and she's tabbed as the unwed mother of the child. Girl easily adopts maternal love for the baby, finding the home's intervention with her boss saves her job in the department store.

Niven, playboy son of the department store owner, becomes curiously interested in the foundling, and gradually generates romantic inclination toward Rogers.

Garson Kanin's direction keeps up a breezy and steady pace.

☐ 1939: Nomination: Best Original Story (Felix Jackson)

······························

B

■ BACHELOR OF HEARTS

1958, 94 MINS, UK ◇
Dir Wolf Rilla   *Prod* Vivian A. Cox   *Scr* Leslie Bricusse,
Frederic Raphael   *Ph* Geoffrey Unsworth   *Ed* Eric Boyd-
Perkins   *Mus* Hubert Clifford   *Art Dir* Edward Carrick
● Hardy Kruger, Sylvia Syms, Ronald Lewis, Miles
Malleson, Eric Barker, Barbara Steele (Independent
Artists)

Bachelor of Hearts is a switch on *A Yank at
Oxford*, and might have been more simply titled *A German at Cambridge*. It is a facetious,
rather embarrassing glimpse of life at
Cambridge University. Since the screenplay
was written by two ex-Cambridge students it
must be assumed to be authentic. In which
case, some rather adolescent malarkey appears to go on at the university.

The thin yarn has Hardy Kruger as a
German student on an exchange scholarship
system. At first treated with suspicion, he
proves himself a good fellow, passes his exams and falls in love. But the story is only an
excuse for some predictable situations and
jokes. This might have been acceptable had
there been more wit, but the wisecracks most
depend on the young German's inability to
understand the English idiom or the traditional behaviour at the university.

Kruger, who made a big impression with his
first British pic, *The One That Got Away*, is less
happy in this comedy. But has a pleasant personality to make his slight love affair with
Sylvia Syms acceptable.

■ BACHELOR PARTY, THE

1957, 92 MINS, US ▾
Dir Delbert Mann   *Prod* Harold Hecht   *Scr* Paddy
Chayefsky   *Ph* Joseph LaShelle   *Ed* William B. Murphy
Mus Paul Madeira   *Art Dir* Ted Haworth
● Don Murray, E.G. Marshall, Jack Warden, Philip
Abbott, Carolyn Jones, Patricia Smith (United
Artists/Norma)

The title tips that the comedy will come from
the international institution of giving the
groom-to-be his last fling as a single man.
The script [from Paddy Chayefsky's own TV
play] gets it all in – the drinking dinner, the
stag movies, the pub-crawling, the visit to a
strip show, and finally, the calling on a professional lady. Each sequence is vividly etched.

Cast, mostly from television and stage, is
headed by Don Murray. He's good as the
bookkeeper husband of Patricia Smith, who is
expecting a child. As he becomes a reluctant
member of the bachelor party, the round of
tawdry revelry is seen through his eyes, and
revealing viewing it is, even involving him
temporarily with a sexpot Greenwich Village
character, played with great vitality by
Carolyn Jones.

Philip Abbott scores as the frightened
groom-to-be, his manly abilities as yet untried.
The sequences wherein he makes an abortive
attempt to go through with the introduction
to sex arranged by the boys with Barbara
Ames is a standout. Jack Warden shows up
well as the office bachelor who masterminds
the party for Abbott, as does Larry Blyden,
married man who early departs the festivities.
□ 1957: Nomination: Best Supp. Actress
(Carolyn Jones)

■ BACHELOR PARTY

1984, 106 MINS, US ◇ ▾ ⊙
Dir Neal Israel   *Prod* Ron Moler, Bob Israel   *Scr* Neal
Israel, Pat Proft   *Ph* Hal Trussell   *Ed* Tom Walls
Mus Robert Folk   *Art Dir* Kevin Colin, Martin Price
● Tom Hanks, Tawny Kitaen, Adrian Zmed, George
Grizzard, Barbara Stuart, Robert Prescott (Aspect
Ratio/Twin Continental)

Bachelor Party is too contrived to capture the
craziness it strains for and ultimately becomes offensive rather than funny.

Filled with cartoon caricatures instead of
people, picture is built around a prenuptial
celebration that seems to bring the worst out
in people. Against the objections of her parents, Rick (Tom Hanks) is marrying Debbie
(Tawny Kitaen) and Rick's friends decide to
throw a bash for their departing pal.

While the film offers predictable shenanigans, such as a donkey snorting cocaine and
an attempted suicide with an electric razor,
main reason to see the pic is for Hanks' performance. Recalling a younger Bill Murray,
he's all over the place, practically spilling off
the screen with an over-abundance of energy.

Unfortunately the writers [working from a
story by producer Bob Israel] surround Hanks
with a bunch of run-of-the mill friends who
act as if they have never seen a woman before. Sexual attitudes throughout have
scarcely gotten out of grade school. Kitaen is
the one woman who gets slightly better treatment, but even her role amounts to little
more than looking good (which she does) and
smiling.

■ BACKDRAFT

1991, 135 MINS, US ◇ ▾ ⊙
Dir Ron Howard   *Prod* Richard B. Lewis, Pen Densham,
John Watson   *Scr* Gregory Widen   *Ph* Michael
Salomon   *Ed* Daniel Hanley, Michael Hill   *Mus* Hans
Zimmer   *Art Dir* Albert Brenner
● Kurt Russell, William Baldwin, Robert De Niro, Donald
Sutherland, Jennifer Jason Leigh, Scott Glenn (Universal/
Imagine)

Director Ron Howard torches off more
thrilling scenes in *Backdraft* than any Saturday
matinee serial ever dared. Visually, pic often
is exhilarating, but it's shapeless and dragged
down by corny, melodramatic characters and
situations.

Ex-fireman Gregory Widen's script about
Chicago smokeaters begins with a scene of
the two central characters as boys in 1971.
This provides shorthand for later formulaic
conflicts between fire-fighting brothers Kurt
Russell and William Baldwin.

Baldwin is ambivalent about fire-fighting as
a result of a childhood experience. His older
brother, the charismatic Russell, is a hard-
boiled sort, even more recklessly heroic than
the father.

Widen uncertainly blends these tiresome
family quarrels with a suspense plot involving
fire department investigator Robert De
Niro's search for a mysterious arsonist. His
intense obsessive characterization is a major
plus for the film but isn't given enough screen
time.

Though De Niro is portrayed as the
Sherlock Holmes of arson investigators, script
has him and Baldwin led to the truth by the
airheaded assistant (Jennifer Jason Leigh) of
a corrupt local alderman (J.T. Walsh) and by
an institutionalized pyromaniac played by
Donald Sutherland with his customary glee.

The spectacular fire scenes are done with
terrifying believability (usually with the actors in the same shot as the fire effects) and a
kind of sci-fi grandeur.
□ 1991: Nominations: Best Sound, Sound
Effects Editing, Visual Effects

■ BACK IN THE USSR

1992, 89 MINS, US ◇
Dir Deran Sarafian   *Prod* Lindsay Smith, Ilmar Taska
Scr Lindsay Smith   *Ph* Yuri Neyman   *Ed* Ian Crafford
Mus Les Hooper   *Art Dir* Vladimir Philippov
● Frank Whaley, Natalya Negoda, Roman Polanski,
Andrew Divof, Dey Young, Brian Blessed (Largo)

Back in the USSR is an amateurish adventure
about the Russian underworld shot entirely in
Moscow. This attempt to capitalize on pere-
stroika stumbles over a weak script, wooden
acting and inferior tech credits.

Story, by Lindsay Smith, founder of the
American/Soviet Film Initiative, and Russian
producer Ilmar Taska, involves vacationing
young American Frank Whaley, whose
amorous pursuits lead him into a cops-and-
robbers escapade featuring a parade of loathsome characters. Russian actress Natalya
Negoda is the love interest, and Roman
Polanski plays the chief villain. In an obvious
attempt at humor, nightclub owner Polanski
is shown in one scene relishing nubile maidens on stage.

■ BACK ROADS

1981, 94 MINS, US ◇ ▾
Dir Martin Ritt   *Prod* Ronald Shedlo   *Scr* Gary DeVore
Ph John A. Alonzo   *Ed* Sidney Levin   *Mus* Henry
Mancini   *Art Dir* Walter Scott Herndon
● Sally Field, Tommy Lee Jones, Michael Gazzo, M.
Emmet Walsh (Warner)

Plot focuses on Southern hooker Sally Field
who meets down-on-his-luck-boxer Tommy
Lee Jones in the course of a working night.
Jones can't pay for his fun but is intrigued by
the spunky Field – so much so that he
punches out a policeman about to bust her.

Forced to move out of her temporary abode,
Field spends the night at Jones' meager surroundings and sneaks out the next morning to
take a look at the little boy she gave up for
adoption some years ago. After the adoptive
mother threatens to call the police if she persists trying to make contact, Field returns to
Jones (who just lost his car-washing job) and
the pair decide to leave Alabama for the
promising California shores. Thrust of the film
is their adventures hitchhiking along the road.

Although both stars rise above script contrivances, they are somehow never an affecting romantic pair. All of their shared troubles
would seem to make a great love story but
they never share enough really intimate moments to carry it off.

■ BACK STREET

1932, 86 MINS, US
Dir John M. Stahl   *Prod* Carl Laemmle Jr.   *Scr* Gladys
Lehman, Lynn Starling   *Ph* Karl Freund   *Ed* Milton
Carruth   *Art Dir* Charles D. Hall
● Irene Dunne, John Boles, June Clyde, George Meeker,
ZaSu Pitts, Shirley Grey (Universal)

Just as Fannie Hurst's bestseller must have
fired the imagination of readers, this saga of
Ray Schmidt who lives in a shadowy 'back
street', and technically meretricious relationship with Walter Saxel, leaps off the screen
and smacks the viewer about the gray matter
and under the heart.

The sympathy for Schmidt is naturally, humanly and wallopingly developed, even unto
Irene Dunne's superb characterization winning her audience away from a slightly unconventional start where she is shown
hob-nobbing gaily, but harmlessly, with the
travelling salesmen in the Over-the-Rhine
beer gardens of Cincinnati.

Her ready acquiescence to every demand of
her lover (John Boles) despite his own imminent marriage, 'for family reasons', is as natural in its artlessness as having a cup of coffee,
and yet it is packed with human interest.

Dunne is excellent as Schmidt. She is the
personification of 'a real woman'. Boles, too,
is very effective, deftly highlighting the somewhat selfish man who makes heavy demands
of his mistress, and yet withal genuinely in
love with the No. 2 woman in his life.

■ BACK STREET

1941, 89 MINS, US
Dir Robert Stevenson   *Prod* Bruce Manning   *Scr* Bruce
Manning, Felix Jackson   *Ph* William Daniels   *Ed* Ted
Kent   *Mus* Frank Skinner

● Charles Boyer, Margaret Sullavan, Richard Carlson (Universal)

Second picturization of Fannie Hurst's novel – first turned out in 1932 with John Boles and Irene Dunne under direction of John Stahl – retains all of the tear-jerking qualities of the author's original work.

Universal has provided a class A production background on which to weave a straightforward and logical drama of a woman's love and devotion for one man over a span of years – and her complete willingness to remain in the shadowy alleys of his life. Generating strong sympathy for the plight of a woman unable to enjoy the security of marriage, picture carries hefty dramatic punch.

Margaret Sullavan delivers a strong and sympathetic characterization as the most willing victim of love and devotion. Charles Boyer provides a deft and restrained portrayal of the man willing to share his time and affections between wife and mistress. Richard Carlson is seen briefly to advantage as the boyhood sweetheart who rises to become an automotive tycoon and just misses marrying the gir.

■ BACK TO BATAAN

1945, 95 MINS, US ▼ ⊙
Dir Edward Dmytryk   *Prod* Robert Fellows (exec.)
Scr Ben Barzman, Richard H. Landau   *Ph* Nicholas Musuraca   *Ed* Marston Fay   *Mus* Roy Webb
Art Dir Albert S. D'Agostino, Ralph Berger
● John Wayne, Anthony Quinn, Beulah Bondi, Fely Franquelli, Richard Loo, Philip Ahn (RKO)

Events are based on fact, according to foreword, and clips of several US fighting men released from Jap prison camps with the return of MacArthur's army are used both at beginning and end. Plot [from a story by Aeneas MacKenzie and William Gordon] spans time from fall of Bataan and Corregidor to the Yank landings on Leyte, and depicts adventures of John Wayne as a colonel leading Filipino patriots in undercover sabotage against the 'islands' temporary conquerors.

Love interest is given over to Anthony Quinn, portraying the descendant of the Filipino hero, Bonifacio, and Fely Franquelli, Manila contact for the band of heroes. Quinn does a particularly outstanding job, as does Franquelli. Wayne makes a stalwart leader for the guerrillas, commendably underplaying the role for best results.

■ BACK TO THE FUTURE

1985, 116 MINS, US ◇ ▼ ⊙
Dir Robert Zemeckis   *Prod* Bob Gale, Neil Canton
Scr Robert Zemeckis, Bob Gale   *Ph* Dean Cundey
Ed Arthur Schmidt, Harry Keramidas   *Mus* Alan Silvestri
Art Dir Lawrence G. Paull
● Michael J. Fox, Christopher Lloyd, Crispin Glover, Lea Thompson, Claudia Wells, Thomas F. Wilson (Amblin)

The central winning elements in the scenario are twofold; hurtling the audience back to 1955, which allows for lots of comparative, pop culture humor, and delivering a 1985 teenager (Michael J. Fox) at the doorstep of his future parents when they were 17-year-old kids. That encounter is a delicious premise, especially when the young hero's mother-to-be develops the hots for her future son and his future father is a bumbling wimp.

Film is also sharply anchored by zestful by-play between Fox's Arthurian knight figure and Christopher Lloyd's Merlin-like, crazed scientist. The latter has mounted a nuclear-powered time machine in a spaced-out DeLorean car, which spirits the bedazed Fox 30 years back in time to the same little town in which he grew up.

In the film's opening sequences, the father (wonderfully played by Crispin Glover) is an unctuous nitwit, and the mother (Lea

Thompson) a plump, boozey, turtle-necked frau.

Performances by the earnest Fox, the lunatic Lloy the deceptively passionate Lea Thompson, and, particularly, the bumbling-to-confident Glover, who runs away with the picture, merrily keep the ship sailing.
☐ 1985: Best Sound Effects Editing.
☐ Nominations: Best Original Screenplay, Sound, Song ('Power of Love')

■ BACK TO THE FUTURE PART II

1989, 107 MINS, US ◇ ▼ ⊙
Dir Robert Zemeckis   *Prod* Bob Gale, Neil Canton
Scr Bob Gale   *Ph* Dean Cundey   *Ed* Arthur Schmidt, Harry Keramidas   *Mus* Alan Silvestri   *Art Dir* Rick Carter
● Michael J. Fox, Christopher Lloyd, Lea Thompson, Thomas F. Wilson, Harry Waters Jr, Elizabeth Shue (Amblin/Universal)

The energy and heart which Robert Zemeckis and strong-writing partner Bob Gale (who takes solo screenplay credit this time) poured into the ingenious story of part one is diverted into narrative mechanics and camera wizardry in *Future II*.

The story starts exactly where the original left off, with Michael J. Fox's Marty McFly and Christopher Lloyd's visionary inventor Dr Emmett Brown taking off in their flying DeLorean time machine for 2015 on an urgent mission to save Fox's children from a terrible fate.

Future II finds the McFly family living in shabby lower-middle class digs in a world that isn't so much Orwellian as a gaudier and tackier projection of the present day.

What matters to Fox is that his son has become a wimp, just like his father was in the 1955 segment of the original film.

Then, in a curious narrative lapse, Fox picks up a sports almanac which, if taken back to the past, will enable him to get rich by gambling on future events. But villainous Biff (Thomas F. Wilson) absconds with it in the time machine to give it to his 1955 self, and the chase begins.

Zemeckis' fascination with having characters interact at different ages of their lives hurts the film visually, and strains credibility past the breaking point, by forcing him to rely on some very cheesy makeup designs.
☐ 1989: Nomination: Best Visual Effects

■ BACK TO THE FUTURE PART III

1990, 118 MINS, US ◇ ▼ ⊙
Dir Robert Zemeckis   *Prod* Bob Gale, Neil Canton
Scr Bob Gale   *Ph* Dean Cundey   *Ed* Arthur Schmidt, Harry Keramidas   *Mus* Alan Silvestri   *Art Dir* Rick Carter
● Michael J. Fox, Christopher Lloyd, Mary Steenburgen, Thomas F. Wilson, Lea Thompson, Elisabeth Shue (Amblin)

Back to the Future Part III recovers the style and wit and grandiose fantasy elements in the original. The simplicity of plot, and the wide expansiveness of its use of space, are a refreshing change from the convoluted, visually cramped and cluttered second part.

Michael J. Fox's Marty McFly in his time-travelling DeLorean finds himself in the midst of a band of charging Indians in John Ford country, Monument Valley 1885. His mission is to bring back Doc (Christopher Lloyd) before he is shot in the back by Thomas F. Wilson's hilariously unhinged Buford 'Mad Dog' Tannen, an ancestor of McFly's 20th century nemesis Biff Tannen.

Fox steps into the background of the story and lets Lloyd have the chance to play the romantic lead for a change. Doc's offbeat romance with Mary Steenburgen's Clara Clayton, a spinster schoolmarm who shares his passion for Jules Verne, is funny, touching

and exhilarating. Their ultimate journey through time gives the plot trajectory an unexpected and entirely satisfying resolution.

The fun of this meta-Western is partly the recognition of elements familiar from genre classics: the dance from *My Darling Clementine*, the sobering-up concoction from *El Dorado*, the costume from *Fistful of Dollars*. Fox reexperiences all this, literally flying through the screen (at an incongruous Monument Valley drive-in) into every Western fan's dream of being a character in a 'real' Western.

■ BAD

1977, 105 MINS, US ◇ ▼
Dir Jed Johnson   *Prod* Jeff Tornberg   *Scr* Pat Hackett, George Abagnalo   *Ph* Allan Metzger   *Ed* Franca Silvi, David McKenna   *Mus* Mike Bloomfield   *Art Dir* Eugene Rudolph
● Carroll Baker, Perry King, Susan Tyrrell, Stefania Cassini, Cyrinda Foxe, Mary Boylan (New World)

Watching Andy Warhol's *Bad*, is a compellingly revolting experience. This is among the blackest of black comedies, featuring Carroll Baker as a Queens housewife who supplements her home electrolysis business by arranging for young girls to do repulsive errands for clients – killing dogs, retarded babies, etc. Don't see it after eating.

Pat Hackett and George Abagnalo wrote the script which, on a professional level, is a good piece of craftsmanship. Jed Johnson, who has edited prior Warhol pix, handles the direction in top fashion.

Baker plays a suburban Ma Barker, cherishing her TV commercial middle-class materialistic standards, while thinking nothing about her gruesome sideline. Susan Tyrrell is Baker's slovenly and abandoned daughter-in-law, complete with sniveling infant. Baker's crew of hit-persons is mainly a gaggle of slatternly young street maidens who carry out their assignments with truly frightening aplomb.

■ BAD AND THE BEAUTIFUL, THE

1952, 116 MINS, US ▼ ⊙
Dir Vincente Minnelli   *Prod* John Houseman
Scr Charles Schnee   *Ph* Robert Surtees   *Ed* Conrad A. Nervig   *Mus* David Raksin   *Art Dir* Cedric Gibbons, Edward Carfagno
● Kirk Douglas, Lana Turner, Walter Pidgeon, Dick Powell, Barry Sullivan, Gloria Grahame (M-G-M)

Contemporary Hollywood, including composites of the characters that make the town the glamour capital it is, is the setting for *The Bad and the Beautiful*.

It is the story of a first-class heel, a ruthless, driving individual whose insistent push changes a number of lives to the end that all have benefited in some way from his multiple double-crosses, despite the personal sorrow or loss experienced. The screenplay of the George Bradshaw story is exceptionally well-written.

Kirk Douglas scores as the ruthless individual out to prove he is the best when it comes to making pictures. Swung along with him is Lana Turner, the drunken, inferiority-complexed daughter of a former screen great; Dick Powell, the self-satisfied southern professor-writer who is pulled into the Hollywood mill; and Barry Sullivan, who, as an embryo director, gets Douglas his first chance and is double-crossed for the helping hand.
☐ 1952: Best Supp. Actress (Gloria Grahame), Screenplay, B&W Cinematography, B&W Art Direction, B&W Costume Design.
☐ Nomination: Best Actor (Kirk Douglas)

■ BAD BEHAVIOUR

1993, 100 MINS, UK ◇ ▼
Dir Les Blair   *Prod* Sarah Curtis   *Scr* [uncredited]

Ph Witold Stok   *Ed* Martin Walsh   *Mus* John Altman
Art Dir Jim Grant
● Stephen Rea, Sinead Cusack, Philip Jackson, Clare Higgins, Phil Daniels, Saira Todd (Channel 4/Parallax)

Stephen Rea heads a strong cast, crisply directed, in *Bad Behaviour*, a delightful comedy of manners set among a group of north Londoners.

Rea plays a district planning officer and amateur cartoonist, whose wife Ellie (Sinead Cusack) is quietly going through a midlife crisis. In strides Ellie's greaseball ex-husband (Philip Jackson), who's operating real estate scams. Things get real complicated when Jackson tries to rip off Rea et al. for some rebuilding work, a job done by identical twins (both played by Phil Daniels) to whom Jackson already owes money.

Working, in the style of Mike Leigh, from an improvised script, helmer Les Blair juggles his small cast with great dexterity, drawing tight playing down the line with no feel of treading water. The pic is a character, not knockabout, comedy, but this is a group of mild eccentrics you want to follow to the end.

■ **BAD BLOOD**

1982, 105 MINS, UK/NEW ZEALAND ◇ ⓥ
Dir Mike Newell   *Prod* Andrew Brown   *Scr* Andrew Brown   *Ph* Gary Hansen   *Ed* Peter Hollywood   *Mus* Richard Hartley   *Art Dir* Kai Hawkins
● Jack Thompson, Carol Burns, Dennis Lill, Donna Akersten, Martyn Sanderson, Marshall Napier (Southern)

Story revolves around Stan (Jack Thompson) and Dorothy Graham (Carol Burns), gun-happy dairy farmers who by 1941 have become ostracized from their neighbors in the isolated, close-knit New Zealand town of Kowhiterangi, mainly due to their own paranoia.

A gunpoint confrontation with two neighbors forces until now patient constable Ted Best (Dennis Lill) to confiscate Thompson's rifle, backed by a trio of fellow officers. When the gendarmes invade Thompson's farmhouse, his last refuge from a world of his own making, the inevitable violence ensues. Thompson then flees into the bush, and more will die before an amateurish manhunt reaches its inevitable conclusion.

Direction by Mike Newell stands out for conveying more meaning with pictures than words, though the film [from the book *Manhunt: The Story of Stanley Graham* by Howard Willis] stumbles somewhat through the narrative until the carnage begins.

Thompson turns in an okay performance, and he's clearly better in the early scenes when his character is still a semi-rational being. The actor seems stretched thin once his mainspring snaps.

■ **BAD BOYS**

1983, 123 MINS, US ◇ ⓥ ⊙
Dir Richard Rosenthal   *Prod* Robert Solo   *Scr* Richard Dilello   *Ph* Bruce Surtees, Donald Thorin   *Ed* Antony Gibbs   *Mus* Bill Conti   *Art Dir* J. Michael Riva
● Sean Penn, Reni Santoni, Esai Morales, Eric Gurry, Jim Moody, Ally Sheedy (EMI)

Bad Boys is a troubling and often riveting drama about juvenile delinquency. Director Richard Rosenthal does a topnotch job of bringing to life the seedy, hopeless environment of a jail for juvenile offenders and has gotten some terribly convincing performances from his young cast, notably topliner Sean Penn.

From the first scene where 16-year-old tough guy Penn breaks the window of a car and steals a woman's purse, it's clear this is not going to be the picture of youth most people are used to.

Penn's only safety is in the love of girlfriend Ally Sheedy, the one person who has ever

seemingly seen the softer side of his nature.

It is in jail that the film really takes off, pitting Penn against the abuses of his fellow inmates and the inherent hopelessness of his situation.

Penn is nothing short of terrific in the key role, which, given a minimal amount of dialog, calls for him to rely primarily on his emotional and physical abilities.

■ **BAD COMPANY**

1972, 91 MINS, US ◇ ⓥ
Dir Robert Benton   *Prod* Stanley R. Jaffe   *Scr* David Newman, Robert Benton   *Ph* Gordon Willis   *Ed* Ralph Rosenblum, Ron Kalish   *Mus* Harvey Schmidt   *Art Dir* Paul Sylbert
● Jeff Bridges, Barry Brown, Jim Davis, David Huddleston, John Savage, Jerry Houser (Jaffilms/Paramount)

Bad Company is an excellent film which combines wry humor and gritty action with indepth characterizations of two youths on the lam in the Civil War west. The production is generally sensitive in its treatment, though pockmarked with some incongruous 'fun-and-poetic' type violence unworthy of the otherwise quality story-telling. Robert Benton, who co-wrote the fine original script, makes a noteworthy directorial debut.

It's an intriguing story of the maturing-under-fire of Barry Brown, a midwest draft dodger but otherwise of 'good' stock, who gradually develops the educated, pragmatic survival instinct necessary in the old west. In this he is influenced primarily by Jeff Bridges, a more primitive con-artist character who knows the ropes of street-fighting and finagling.

Among the many highlights of the film is an outstanding performance by Brown.

■ **BAD DAY AT BLACK ROCK**

1954, 81 MINS, US ◇ ⓥ ⊙
Dir John Sturges   *Prod* Dore Schary   *Scr* Millard Kaufman, Don McGuire   *Ph* William C. Mellor   *Ed* Newell P. Kimlin   *Mus* Andre Previn
● Spencer Tracy, Robert Ryan, Anne Francis, Dean Jagger, Walter Brennan, John Ericson (M-G-M)

Considerable excitement is whipped up in this suspense drama, and fans who go for tight action will find it entirely satisfactory. Besides telling a yarn of tense suspense, the picture is concerned with a social message on civic complacency.

Basis for the smoothly valued production is a story by Howard Breslin, adapted by Don McGuire. To the tiny town of Black Rock, one hot summer day in 1945, comes Spencer Tracy, war veteran with a crippled left arm. He wants to find a Japanese farmer and give to him the medal won by his son in an action that left the latter dead and Tracy crippled. Tracy is greeted with an odd hostility and his own life is endangered when he puts together the reason for the cold, menacing treatment.

Film is paced to draw suspense tight and keep expectancy mounting as the plot crosses the point where Tracy could have left without personal danger and plunges him into deadly menace when he becomes the hunted.

There's not a bad performance from any member of the cast, each socking their characters for full value.

☐ 1955: Nominations: Best Director, Actor (Spencer Tracy), Screenplay

■ **BAD GIRL**

1931, 90 MINS, US
Dir Frank Borzage   *Scr* Edwin Burke   *Ph* Chester Lyons   *Ed* Margaret Clancy
● Sally Eilers, James Dunn, Minna Gombell, William Pawley, Frank Darien (Fox)

Story tells of two kids (Sally Eilers and James Dunn) who meet on a Coney Island boat, delve into marriage after a night in his boarding house room and Dorothy (Eilers) is consequently kicked out of a parentless home by her brother. Then Eddie (Dun gives up his dream of a radio shop of his own to furnish a new flat for his wife with the added complication of the baby which she has kept a secret from her inarticulate husband.

After which there is the misunderstanding of both thinking the other doesn't want the child, which is not brought out as strongly here as in the stage version [based on the novel by Vina Delmar]. Minna Gombell figures as the widowed girl friend of Dorothy and a constant source of annoyance to Eddie as his wife advisor.

As a whole *Bad Girl* classes as a workmanlike job, with Dunn's scene with the doctor as its strong point.

☐ 1931/32: Best Director, Adaptation.
☐ Nomination: Best Picture

■ **BAD GUYS**

1986, 86 MINS, US ◇ ⓥ
Dir Joel Silberg   *Prod* John D. Backe, Myron A. Hyman   *Scr* Brady W. Setwater, Joe Gillis   *Ph* Hanania Baer   *Ed* Peter Parasheles, Christopher Holmes   *Mus* William Goldstein   *Art Dir* Ivo Cristante
● Adam Baldwin, Mike Jolly, Michelle Nicastro, Ruth Buzzi, James Booth, Dutch Mann (Tomorrow)

Bad Guys is a poorly-scripted, would-be comedy attempting to cash in on the popularity of wrestling. Merest pretext of a story has young cops Adam Baldwin and Mike Jolly suspended from the LA police after a brawl with bikers in a bar owned by Dutch Mann (who pointlessly keeps cropping up in the film as their nemesis). After tasteless footage detailing their odd jobs (including a leering stint as male strippers), they turn their wrestling avocation into a fulltume job under the tutelage of pretty reporter-turned-manager Michelle Nicastro.

Quickly discovering that the dirty practitioners are the stars in wrestling's firmament, the heroes don masks and become the Boston Bad Guys, tutored in illegal moves by Gene LeBell and his wife (Ruth Buzzi).

Burdened with hoary, unfunny dialog, director Joel Silberg directs in frantic, comic strip fashion, having the lines exclaimed as if they were displayed in balloons above the actors' heads. Topliner Baldwin is unrecognizable here with blond-dyed hair. He doesn't have the body weight to be convincing as a wrestler. Costar Jolly is bland while Nicastro looks out of place in a role better suited to a comedienne in the Cyndi Lauper style.

■ **BAD INFLUENCE**

1990, 99 MINS, US ◇ ⓥ ⊙
Dir Curtis Hanson   *Prod* Steve Tisch   *Scr* David Koepp   *Ph* Robert Elswitt   *Ed* Bonnie Koehler   *Mus* Trevor Jones   *Art Dir* Ron Foreman
● Rob Lowe, James Spader, Lisa Zane, Christian Clemenson, Kathlene Wilhoite, Tony Maggio (Epic/Sarlui-Diamant/PRO)

Bad Influence proves a reasonably taut, suspenseful thriller that provides its share of twists before straying into silliness. Rob Lowe doesn't really project enough menace or charisma to pull off his role as Alex, a baby-faced psycho who slowly leads Michael (James Spader) through a liberating fantasy that ultimately turns into a yuppie nightmare.

Director and writer seem to draw their inspiration most closely from Alfred Hitchcock's *Strangers on a Train* – a chance meeting between a regular guy and an outwardly normal stranger whose hidden darkness ultimately leads to fatal complications.

Foremost, however, the film is about

Michael's seduction by Alex's free-wheeling attitude, only to find that the rewards don't come cheap.

Spader delivers a terrific performance, and some of the scenes have tremendous impact, especially when – via video – he discovers the depth of Alex's depravity, as fantasy turns into fatal distraction.

Director Curtis Hanson and writer David Koepp create a continued sense of tension and invest many scenes with much-needed humor.

••••••••••••••••••••••••••••••••

■ BADLANDERS, THE

1958, 85 MINS, US ◇ ⓥ

Dir Delmer Daves *Prod* Aaron Rosenberg *Scr* Richard Collins *Ph* John F. Seitz *Ed* William H. Webb, James Baiotto *Art Dir* William A. Horning, Daniel B. Cathcart
● Alan Ladd, Ernest Borgnine, Katy Jurado, Claire Kelly, Nehemiah Persoff, Kent Smith (M-G-M)

It is possible to make an adult western without making it a psychological western. Aaron Rosenberg proves the point with his production of *The Badlanders*, a truly original frontier drama, a suspense melodrama on one level and a huge horselaugh on another, with each element playing off on the other.

The heroes of the screenplay, based on a novel by W.R. Burnett [*The Asphalt Jungle*], are two ex-cons, released from the Nevada Territorial Prison, circa 1900, with little but revenge and larceny in their hearts. It is the plan of one of them (Alan Ladd) to do nothing less than rob a gold mine, and he enlists the other (Ernest Borgnine) in support. The problem, of course, is formidable. They must blast the ore – half a ton of it from a spot right next to a mine full of workmen, then get the huge load away from under the noses (and shotguns) of the legal owners.

Delmer Daves' direction has a facility of throwing a laugh into the midst of a suspense buildup, relieving an heightening it with flashes of humor.

Ladd is not required over-heroic, physically. His strength is emotional, and with casual grace and a way with an ironic line, he creates an effective contrast to Borgnine. Katy Jurado is handsomely colorful and alternatively touching as a Mexican girl. Claire Kelly, who makes her major bow in this picture, is a stunning redhead but she is not yet a strong enough actress to hold her own with this trio.

••••••••••••••••••••••••••••••••

■ BADLANDS

1973, 95 MINS, US ◇ ⓥ ⊙

Dir Terrence Malick *Prod* Terrence Malick *Scr* Terrence Malick *Ph* Brian Probyn, Tak Fujimoto, Stevan Larner *Ed* Robert Estrin, William Weber *Mus* George Tipton *Art Dir* Jack Fisk, Ed Richardson
● Martin Sheen, Sissy Spacek, Warren Oates, Alan Vint, Ramon Bieri, Gary Littlejohn (Pressman-Williams)

Badlands is a uniquely American fairy tale, a romantic account set in the late 1950s of a 15-year-old girl's journey into violence and out of love with a 25-year-old South Dakota garbageman turned thrill killer. Pic is told through the girl's eyes as she narrates in dumb *Teen Romance* style the saga of her hero, a James Dean carbon, who kills her father and whisks her away on a flight into myth that ends in the badlands of Montana.

Written, produced and directed by Terrence Malick, pic is his first feature and it's an impressive debut.

The killer-lead, played with cunning and charm by Martin Sheen, is a perverse Horatio Alger, a culturally-deprived American boy weaned on James Dean pix who works at his rebel image and achieves success, i.e. notoriety, capture, fame and death.

His girl (Sissy Spacek) is one of those mid-teen catatonics whose life is defined in terms of Hollywood gossip and visions of white

knights. Together they litter their escape route with the dead.

••••••••••••••••••••••••••••••••

■ BAD LIEUTENANT

1992, 96 MINS, US ◇ ⓥ ⊙

Dir Abel Ferrara *Prod* Edward R. Pressman, Mary Kane *Scr* Zoe Lund, Abel Ferrara *Ed* Anthony Redman *Mus* Joe Delia *Art Dir* Charlie Lagola
● Harvey Keitel, Frankie Thorn, Zoe Lund, Anthony Ruggiero, Victoria Bastel, Robin Burrows (Pressman)

Abel Ferrara's uncompromising *Bad Lieutenant* is a harrowing journey observing a corrupt NY cop sink into the depths, with an extraordinary and uninhibited perf by Harvey Keitel in the title role. Screenplay by Zoe Lund, who made her screen debut billed as Zoe Tamerlis in Ferrara's *Ms. 45*, ambitiously takes on taboo issues in looking at a degraded subculture in an era of faithlessness and despair.

Foul-mouthed cop Keitel is almost constant sniffing, smoking or injecting drugs he's stolen from police busts while also indulging in alcohol and time-outs for sex. Turning point for him is being assigned to the case of a gang-raped nun. He's a lapsed Catholic who makes light of the event, but when nun Frankie Thorn (in an unadorned, affecting performance) forgives her assailants Keitel faces a religious crisis of conscience.

Elsewhere, Keitel lets it all hang out in a nude Christ-like pose, and spends the final reel in howls of despair as he hallucinates the presence of Christ in a church.

••••••••••••••••••••••••••••••••

■ BAD NEWS BEARS, THE

1976, 102 MINS, US ◇ ⓥ ⊙

Dir Michael Ritchie *Prod* Stanley R. Jaffe *Scr* Bill Lancaster *Ph* John A. Alonzo *Ed* Richard A. Harris *Mus* Jerry Fielding *Art Dir* Polly Platt
● Walter Matthau, Tatum O'Neal, Vic Morrow, Joyce Van Patten, Ben Piazza, Jackie Earle Haley (Paramount)

The Bad News Bears is an extremely funny adult-child comedy film. Walter Matthau stars to perfection as a bumbling baseball coach in the sharp production about the foibles and follies of little-league athletics. Tatum O'Neal also stars as Matthau's ace pitcher.

Michael Ritchie's film has the correct balance of warmth and empathy to make the gentle social commentary very effective.

Premise finds activist politico Ben Piazza having won a class action suit to admit some underprivileged kids to an otherwise upwardly-mobile WASP suburban little league schedule. Piazza recruits Matthau, a one-time minor leaguer now cleaning swimming pools to coach the slapdash outfit. O'Neal and Jackie Earle Haley reluctantly join their juvenile peers to spark the team to a second place win.

••••••••••••••••••••••••••••••••

■ BAD NEWS BEARS GO TO JAPAN, THE

1978, 91 MINS, US ◇ ⓥ ⊙

Dir John Berry *Prod* Michael Ritchie *Scr* Bill Lancaster *Ph* Gene Polito, Kozo Okazaki *Ed* Richard A. Harris *Mus* Paul Chihara *Art Dir* Walter Scott Herndon
● Tony Curtis, Jackie Earle Haley, Tomisaburo Wakayama, Hatsune Ishihara, George Wyner, Lonny Chapman (Paramount)

The dangers inherent in sequel-making are clearly apparent in *The Bad News Bears Go to Japan*, third in the series of junior baseball antics that began with the smash *Bad News Bears* in 1976. Producer Michael Ritchie (who directed the first installment) and writer-creator Bill Lancaster encore with *Japan* resulting in a more vigorous film than the sodden *Bad News Bears in Breaking Training* [1977].

In keeping with tradition, the boys are taken in by yet another hustler (following in the steps of Walter Matthau and William

Devane), this time Tony Curtis as a Hollywood agent out for big bucks via promoting a game between the Bears and the Japanese all-star Little Leaguers.

Formula is strictly standard, with Curtis inviting the enmity of the kids, with exception of moppet Scoody Thornton, to be reformed before the final game which, of course, the Bears win. Japanese locations at least add a different look, and there is much joking about language a cultural customs, humor that went out of style with *Sayonara*.

••••••••••••••••••••••••••••••••

■ BAD SEED, THE

1956, 127 MINS, US ⓥ ⊙

Dir Mervyn LeRoy *Prod* Mervyn LeRoy *Scr* John Lee Mahin *Ph* Hal Rosson *Ed* Warren Low *Mus* Alex North
● Nancy Kelly, Patty McCormack, Henry Jones, Eileen Heckart, Evelyn Varden, William Hopper (Warner)

This melodrama about a child with an inbred talent for homicide is pretty unpleasant stuff on its own. Taken from Maxwell Anderson's stage play, adapted from William March's novel, the film remains more of the theatre than of the motion picture field. Nonetheless, it is well done within that qualification.

With the possible exception of the Production Code-conscious ending, the screenplay varies little from the Anderson legit piece. Some of the casting is from the stage success, too, with young Patty McCormack as the innocent-looking murderess, and Nancy Kelly as her distraught mother. Both are outstanding.

Scoring also is William Hopper, the father who never sees through the evil of his little girl.

It is the story of woman who discovers that her daughter, a sweet, innocent-faced child, is a killer. Director Mervyn LeRoy mounts sequences with shocking horror as it is brought out the girl deliberately murdered a schoolmate because she wanted the penmanship medal he had won.

☐ 1956: Nominations: Best Actress (Nancy Kelly), Supp. Actress (Eileen Heckart, Patty McCormack), B&W Cinematography

••••••••••••••••••••••••••••••••

■ BAD TIMING

1980, 123 MINS, UK ◇ ⓥ ⊙

Dir Nicolas Roeg *Prod* Jeremy Thomas *Scr* Yale Udoff *Ph* Anthony Richmond *Ed* Tony Lawson *Mus* Richard Hartley *Art Dir* David Brockhurst
● Art Garfunkel, Theresa Russell, Harvey Keitel, Denholm Elliott, Daniel Massey, Dana Gillespie (Recorded Picture/Rank)

Technically flashy, and teeming with degenerate chic, this downbeat tale of two destructively selfish lovers is unrelieved by its tacked-on thriller ending, and deals purely in despair.

Every scene is shot with at least one eye and one ear to the editing table: results are generally masterful but at times obtrusively pretentious. Director Nicolas Roeg's visual sense remains a peculiar talent.

Yale Udoff's screenplay plots the often brutal love affair exhaustively in terms of what the parties do to each other, but seldom why – beyond the fact that he is the possessive type and she isn't.

Most milestones are missing along the presumably tortuous psychological route by which Art Garfunkel's jealousy reaches such a pitch of hatred that he ravishes the girl's (Theresa Russell) drugged and senseless body instead of calling an ambulance. Alienation sets in early.

••••••••••••••••••••••••••••••••

■ BALCONY, THE

1963, 84 MINS, US ⓥ ⊙

Dir Joseph Strick *Prod* Ben Maddow, Joseph Strick *Scr* Ben Maddow *Ph* George Folsey *Ed* Chester W. Schaeffer

● Shelley Winters, Peter Falk, Lee Grant, Peter Brocco, Jeff Corey, Ruby Dee (Walter Reade-Sterling/Allen Hodgdon)

With Jean Genet's apparent approval, Joe Strick and Ben Maddow have eliminated the play's obscene language (though it's still plenty rough) and clarified some of its obscurations. The result is a tough, vivid and dispassionate fantasy.

This is never an easy film to watch, but also it is never boring or pretentious, and often it is acidly funny. Most of the action of the film, localed in an unnamed city in the throes of a bloody revolution, takes place in a highly special kind of brothel, equipped like a movie studio with sets, costumes, rear projection devices etc, which permit the patrons to enact their darkest fantasies (they can also pay with credit cards).

Presiding over the macabre revels is Shelley Winters, the madame who designs the illusions and is all the more ominous for her complete, almost tender detachment. The peace of the brothel is shattered with the arrival of the police chief, Peter Falk, the madame's occasional lover who is fighting a last ditch stand outside to destroy the revolution.

Strick and Maddow have provided this fantastic film with its own reality. It is never capricious nor purposefully obscure, proceeding always with a recognizable logic. It is full of chilling detail and knife-sharp scenes, as when the police chief harangues the populace via radio from the brothel, speaking a furious jargon of nonsensical political and TV commercial cliches.

The performances are excellent, beginning with those of Winters, Falk and Lee Grant, and including the entire supporting cast.
□ 1963: Nomination: B&W Cinematography

■ **BALLAD OF CABLE HOGUE, THE**

1970, 121 MINS, US ◇ ⑫ ⊙
Dir Sam Peckinpah   *Prod* Sam Peckinpah   *Scr* John Crawford, Edmund Penney   *Ph* Lucien Ballard
Ed Frank Santillo, Lou Lombardo   *Mus* Jerry Goldsmith
Art Dir Leroy Coleman
● Jason Robards, Stella Stevens, David Warner, Strother Martin, Slim Pickens, L.Q. Jones (Warner)

The Ballad of Cable Hogue is a Damon Runyonesque oater comedy from Sam Peckinpah.

Jason Robards is the title character, a charming desert rat; Stella Stevens is the cow-town harlot with the heart of gold; and David Warner is a preacher of sorts.

Robards is a grizzled prospector left to die in the desert wastes by Strother Martin and L.Q. Jones, two bumbling villains. Robards instead finds water where nobody ever had, and prospers as a rest-stop owner on a stage route owned by R. Armstrong, where Slim Pickens and Max Evans are the carriage drivers. Stevens becomes Robards' big romance, but exits for Frisco on her gold-digging hunt. Characterizations are fully developed.

■ **BALLAD OF THE SAD CAFE, THE**

1991, 100 MINS, US/UK ◇ ⑫
Dir Simon Callow   *Prod* Ismail Merchant   *Scr* Michael Hirst   *Ph* Walter Lassally   *Ed* Andrew Marcus
Mus Richard Robbins   *Art Dir* Bruno Santini
● Vanessa Redgrave, Keith Carradine, Cork Hubbert, Rod Steiger, Austin Pendleton, Beth Dixon (Merchant-Ivory/Film Four)

Simon Callow makes an assured feature directing debut adapting Carson McCullers' novella *The Ballad of the Sad Cafe*, a demanding, abstract fable.

Amelia (Vanessa Redgrave) is a violent, mannishly styled woman who threw out her husband (Keith Carradine) on their wedding night and has become a legendary figure in her little Southern town in the 1930s. With cropped hair and unglamorous makeup, Redgrave throws herself into the role with uncensored force.

Carradine, who replaced Sam Shepard, brings a naturalism to his embittered role as the ex-con and spurned spouse.

Catalyst in the piece is the fantasy character of Cousin Lymon (Cork Hubbert), a hunchbacked dwarf who pops up out of nowhere claiming to be Redgrave's cousin. He gets Redgrave to convert her general store into a cafe, serving the moonshine she prepares at her still. Carradine shows up midway through the pic fresh out of the state pen. He's out to avenge himself against Redgrave.

Film climaxes memorably in a bare-knuckles boxing match staged at the cafe between Carradine and Redgrave to settle their differences once and for all.

Redgrave's body English, strange accent and physical outbursts are a triumph of pure acting. Carradine's more natural approach helps bring pic closer to reality. An intense supporting performance by Rod Steiger also provides exposition as the town preacher.

■ **BALL OF FIRE**

1941, 110 MINS, US ⑫ ⊙
Dir Howard Hawks   *Prod* Samuel Goldwyn
Scr Charles Brackett, Billy Wilder   *Ph* Gregg Toland
Ed Daniel Mandell   *Mus* Alfred Newman   *Art Dir* Perry Ferguson
● Gary Cooper, Barbara Stanwyck, Oscar Homolka, Dana Andrews, Dan Duryea, Henry Travers (RKO/Samuel Goldwyn)

A simple gag is hardly enough on which to string 110 minutes of film. And that's all – one funny situation – that Samuel Goldwyn's director and writers have to support *Ball of Fire*. It's sufficient, however, to provide quite a few chuckles.

Gag on which the whole thing is based [from an original story by Billy Wilder and Thomas Monroe] is Gary Cooper's professorial efforts to write a learned piece on slang for an encyclopedia. He needs, for research purposes, someone who's hep to the last syllable of the lingo and brings into a sanctum, where he and seven colleagues are working on the encyclopedia, a burlesque stripper (Barbara Stanwyck). She upsets and excites the eight old men in the expected manner. Much of the dialog is rapid-fire slang, plenty labored, but frequently good for laughs.

Casting is meticulously perfect to make every character a caricature of itself. Cooper is in the familiar 'Mr Smith-John Doe' role of the brainy guy who's not quite hep to his surroundings until near the end, when he wises up in time to snatch victory from the smart boys. Stanwyck is likewise in a familiar part that she can play for maximum results.
□ 1941: Nominations: Best Actress (Barbara Stanwyck), Original Story, Scoring of a Dramatic Picture, Sound

■ **BALTIMORE BULLET, THE**

1980, 103 MINS, US ◇ ⑫
Dir Robert Ellis Miller   *Prod* John F. Brascia   *Scr* John F. Brascia, Vincent O'Neill   *Ph* James A. Crabe   *Ed* Jerry Brady   *Mus* Johnny Mandel   *Art Dir* Herman Blumenthal
● James Coburn, Omar Sharif, Bruce Boxleitner, Ronee Blakely, Jack O'Halloran, Calvin Lockhart (Avco Embassy)

James Coburn and Bruce Boxleitner limn a kind of father-son pool hustling team who make their living traveling through the country taking advantage of local would-be billiard sharks. They do occasionally enter tournaments, one of which will enable Coburn to reunite with his arch nemesis Omar Sharif.

Coburn and Boxleitner work well together although the former looks and speaks more like someone sipping champagne aboard a yacht than a journeyman dashing through an endlessly array of hick towns. Ronee Blakely is picked up by the pair along the way for moral support and fulfills the limited duties asked of her.

Problem here is script. Situations are just too inane to take seriously and not funny enough to be laughed at.

■ **BAMBI**

1942, 70 MINS, US ◇ ⑫ ⊙
Dir David D. Hand   *Prod* Walt Disney   *Scr* Larry Morey
Mus Frank Churchill, Edward Plumb (Walt Disney)

Bambi is gem-like in its reflection of the color and movement of sylvan plant and animal life. The transcription of nature in its moments of turbulence and peace heightens the brilliance of the canvas. The story [by Felix Salten] is full of tenderness and the characters tickle the heart.

Thumper, the rabbit, steals the picture. His human attributes are amazing and the voice that is attached to him in the earlier sequences proves an admirable piece of casting. It's a regret that there wasn't much more of him in the picture.

In this story of Bambi, and his friends of the forest, the span of the central character is from birth to the period in which he reaches bull buckhood. The episodes in between show him learning to adapt himself to his surroundings and to outwit the biped with the gun, falling in love, entering parenthood and finally taking his place beside his proud and hoary father, prince of the forest. The dramatic highlights of Bambi's career include the death of his mother by gunshot (a scene of deep pathos), and his fight to the death with another buck over the doe, Faline.

The interplay of color and movement makes their sharpest impress on the sensibilities during the sequences depicting the advent and passing of the various seasons. The glow and texture of the Disney brush reach new heights, especially in the treatment of a summer thunderstorm and a raging snowstorm.
□ 1942: Nominations: Best Scoring of a Dramatic Picture, Song ('Love Is a Song'), Sound

■ **BANANAS**

1971, 82 MINS, US ◇ ⑫ ⊙
Dir Woody Allen   *Prod* Jack Rollins, Charles H. Joffe
Scr Woody Allen, Mickey Rose   *Ph* Andrew M. Costikyan   *Ed* Ron Kalish   *Mus* Marvin Hamlisch
● Woody Allen, Louise Lasser, Carlos Montalban, Natividad Abascal, Jacobo Morales, Miguel Suarez (United Artists)

Bananas is chockfull of sight gags, one-liners and swiftly executed unnecessary excursions into vulgarity whose humor for the most part can't make up for content.

Woody Allen, as bumbling New Yorker working for an automation film, is rejected by his activist sweetheart Louise Lasser who is involved in revolutions, particularly in fictional San Marcos where dictator Carlos Montalban has seized control. Allen, disconsolate, bids farewell to parents Charlotte Rae and Stanley Ackerman while they are performing medical operation. Landing in San Marcos, he is feted by Montalban, who is setting him up as pigeon to be erased supposedly by revolutionary Jacobo Morales' men.

Allen and Mickey Rose have written some funny stuff, and Allen, both as director and actor, knows what to do with it. Scenes between Lasser and comedian have wonderfully fresh, incisive touch. Montalban's dictator is properly arrogant. Morales performs with assurance right up to the point when drunk with power, he proclaims Swedish the national language.

■ BANDIT OF SHERWOOD FOREST, THE

1946, 85 MINS, US ◇

Dir George Sherman, Henry Levin   *Prod* Leonard S. Picker, Clifford Sanforth   *Scr* Wilfrid H. Pettitt, Melvin Levy   *Ph* Tony Gaudio, William Snyder, George B. Meehan Jr   *Ed* Richard Fanti   *Mus* Hugo Friedhofer   *Art Dir* Stephen Goosson, Rudolph Sternad
● Cornel Wilde, Anita Louise, Jill Esmond, Edgar Buchanan, George Macready, Henry Daniell (Columbia)

Technicolor spectacle of high adventure in Sherwood Forest. It's a costume western, in effect, offering the fictional escapades of the son of Robin Hood, a hard-riding, hard-loving hombre who uses his trusty bow and arrow to right injustice and tyranny back in the days of feudal England.

There is considerable ineptness in writing, production and direction but it still stands up as okay escapist film fare for the not-too-critical.

There is a concentration of chases and 'they-went-thata-way' flavor about the doings that hints at the western feature training of producers and directors.

Plot has the son of Robin Hood coming back to Sherwood Forest to save England's Magna Carta and young king from the cruel plotting of a wicked regent. With his long bow, sword and trusty horse, Wilde proves himself more than a match for the villain, saves the young king's life, the Magna Carta and wins true love and knighthood. Concocting the script, full of dialog cliches and ten-twent-thirt dramatics, were Wilfrid H. Pettitt and Melvin Levy, working from a story by Paul A. Castleton and Pettitt, based on the novel *Son of Robin Hood* by Castleton.

Wilde is properly swashbuckling as the hero, and probably had himself a time enacting the dare-and-do.

■ BAND OF ANGELS

1957, 125 MINS, US ◇

Dir Raoul Walsh   *Prod* Jerry Wald   *Scr* John Twist, Ivan Goff, Ben Roberts   *Ph* Lucien Ballard   *Ed* Folmar Blangsted   *Mus* Max Steiner   *Art Dir* Franz Bachelin
● Clark Gable, Yvonne De Carlo, Sidney Poitier, Efrem Zimbalist Jr, Patric Knowles, Carolle Drake (Warner)

Subject of miscegenation is explored and developed in this colorful production of the Old South. Raoul Walsh is in top form in direction of the screenplay derived from a Robert Penn Warren novel. Screenwriters have captured the mood and spirit of the Deep South narrative which deals with a young woman of quality discovering that her mother was a slave.

Sold on the auction block to a former slave-trader, unfoldment dwells on the pair's relations, both in New Orleans and later on a plantation up-river. Beautiful and realistic backgrounds are achieved through locationing in Louisiana.

Clark Gable's characterization is reminiscent of his Rhett Butler in *Gone with the Wind*, although there is obviously no paralleling of plot. As former slave-runner turned New Orleans gentleman, with bitter memories of his earlier days, he contributes a warm, decisive portrayal that carries tremendous authority.

Yvonne De Carlo is beautiful as the mulatto, who learns of her true status when she returns from a Cincinnati finishing school to attend her father's funeral. Sidney Poitier impresses as Gable's educated protege, whom slaver picked up as an infant in Africa and reared as his son.

■ BANDOLERO!

1968, 107 MINS, US ◇ ⓥ

Dir Andrew V. McLaglen   *Prod* Robert L. Jacks   *Scr* James Lee Barrett   *Ph* William H. Clothier   *Ed* Folmar Blangsted   *Mus* Jerry Goldsmith   *Art Dir* Jack Martin Smith, Alfred Sweeney Jr

● James Stewart, Dean Martin, Raquel Welch, George Kennedy, Andrew Prine, Will Geer (20th Century-Fox)

Bandolero! is a dull western meller. Though competently produced, film suffers from distended scripting, routine direction and overlength.

Basic story is the escape and capture of a gang of post-Civil War vagabonds. Dean Martin heads an outlaw group which includes Will Geer, Tom Heaton, Sean McClory and Clint Ritchie.

Pre-title bank heist, in which Raquel Welch's husband is killed, lands the group in George Kennedy's jail, awaiting hanging by itinerant executioner Guy Raymond. Stewart, Martin's older brother who always has rescued him from mistakes, takes Raymond's place in order to effect gang's escape. Having accomplished this, the upright Stewart then robs a bank. This opening action, well developed, takes 40 minutes.

Welch is got up to look like a Mexican Sophia Loren. Her makeup is distressingly false-looking, her accent moreso. Of Kennedy, she says at one point, 'hee ees a good mahn.'

■ BAND WAGON, THE

1953, 111 MINS, US ◇ ⓦ ⓥ ⊙

Dir Vincente Minnelli   *Prod* Arthur Freed   *Scr* Betty Comden, Adolph Green   *Ph* Harry Jackson   *Ed* Albert Akst   *Mus* Adolph Deutsch (dir.)   *Art Dir* Cedric Gibbons, Preston Ames, Oliver Smith
● Fred Astaire, Cyd Charisse, Oscar Levant, Nanette Fabray, Jack Buchanan, James Mitchell (M-G-M)

Plot is the one about a dancing film star whose pictures aren't selling. A couple of writing pals conceive a stage musical for him and the rest of the story is concerned with making the show a success after a flop tryout and weeks of rewriting and new starts.

Twelve songs [staged by Michael Kidd] from various Broadway musicals are either chirped or terped. Showing up as an imaginative highlight is 'Girl Hunt', the modern jazz ballet finale done to a turn by Fred Astaire and Cyd Charisse. A takeoff in dance on the Mickey Spillane type of private eye, number is a new cleffing for the picture by Howard Dietz and Arthur Schwartz, credited with all of the songs.

Astaire, as the film star, shows his ability with a song and dance character. Oscar Levant and Nanette Fabray make up the writing team. Fabray is given enough chance to display her talent from legit musicals, and her personality is caught by the cameras. Charisse is an eye-filling filly, especially when dancing. Levant is his usual phlegmatic self. Buchanan enacts the show's director and costar and is one of the picture's strongpoints with his comedy moments.

□ 1953: Nominations: Best Story & Screenplay, Color Costume Design, Scoring of a Musical Picture.

■ BANK BREAKER, THE
See: Kaleidoscope

■ BANK DETECTIVE, THE
See: The Bank Dick

■ BANK DICK, THE
(UK: The Bank Detective)

1940, 69 MINS, US ⓦ ⊙

Dir Edward Cline   *Prod* [uncredited]   *Scr* Mahatma Kane Jeeves [= W.C. Fields]   *Ph* Milton Krasner   *Ed* Arthur Hilton   *Mus* Charles Previn (dir.)   *Art Dir* Jack Otterson, Richard Riedel
● W.C. Fields, Cora Witherspoon, Una Merkel, Jessie Ralph, Franklin Pangborn, Grady Sutton (Universal)

Story is credited to Mahatma Kane Jeeves, Fields' own humorous nom de plume. It's a deliberate rack on which to hang the varied Fieldsian comedic routines, many of them repeats from previous pictures but with enough new material inserted to overcome the antique gags. A wild auto ride down the mountainside for the climax is an old formula dating back to the Mack Sennett days, but director Edward Cline [and 'collaborating director' Ralph Ceder] has refurbished the episode with new twists that made it a thrill-laugh dash of top proportions.

Fields is the town's foremost elbow bender who injects himself into any situation without invitation. The unexpected hero of a bank robbery, he is rewarded with the job of detective to guard against future holdups. He involves his prospective son-in-law as a temporary embezzler to buy wildcat mining stock, and then holds off the bank examiner via the Mickey Finn route. Repeat bank robbery again results in Fields' accepting hero honors, the reward and sudden riches from a film directing contract.

Several times, Fields reaches into satirical pantomime reminiscent of Charlie Chaplin's best efforts during his Mutual and Essanay days. Directorial guidance by Edward Cline (graduate of the Keystone Kop school) smacks over every gag line and situation to the fullest extent.

Fields has a field day in tabbing the various characters. His own screen name, he is careful to explain, is pronounced Soo-zay, and not Souse, as it appear from English pronunciation.

■ BANK HOLIDAY
(US: Three on a Weekend)

1938, 86 MINS, UK

Dir Carol Reed   *Scr* Rodney Ackland, Roger Burford   *Ph* Arthur Crabtree   *Ed* R.E. Dearing, Alfred Roome   *Mus* Louis Levy (dir.)   *Art Dir* Alex Vetchinsky
● John Lodge, Margaret Lockwood, Hugh Williams, Rene Ray, Linden Travers, Merle Tottenham (Gainsborough)

This is good entertainment. A young nurse, Catherine (Margaret Lockwood), has planned to spend an illicit weekend with a man to whom she cannot be married until their financial position improves. Her patient dies in childbirth and her pity for the forlorn husband changes her whole life.

In the hectic rush of London's termini, she joins her waiting lover. They reach the coast, only to find no rooms available; they spend the night on the beach, duly chaperoned by hundreds of others. The tragedy she has left behind mars her pleasure; she flees her lover and with the aid of the police saves the widower from suicide.

Interspersed [in the story by Hans Wilhelm and Rodney Ackland] are many rich characters: a cockney family with squabbling kids, two young soldiers on leave, entrants for a beauty prize - one trying to get over a jilt, another aping society and making all the judges. None is overdrawn and all are depicted with human interest.

■ BARABBAS

1962, 144 MINS, ITALY ◇ ⓦ

Dir Richard Fleischer   *Prod* Dino De Laurentiis   *Scr* Christopher Fry, Diego Fabbri, Ivo Perilli, Nigel Balchin   *Ph* Aldo Tonti   *Ed* Raymond Poulton   *Mus* Mario Nascimbene   *Art Dir* Mario Chiari
● Anthony Quinn, Silvana Mangano, Arthur Kennedy, Jack Palance, Vittorio Gassmann, Ernest Borgnine (Columbia)

Barabbas is technically a fine job of work, reflecting big thinking and infinite patience on the parts of producer Dino De Laurentiis and director Richard Fleischer. In Technirama 70 and shot in Technicolor it has one or two sequences which stand up to the chariot race highlight in *Ben-Hur*.

Set in Jerusalem 2, 000 years ago, the film [based on the novel by Par Lagerkvist] tells the story of Barabbas, thief and murderer, who was released from prison by the will of the people and replaced, in jail and on the Cross, by Jesus Christ. Barabbas' conscience plagues him. In a struggling, almost bovine manner he tries to find the truth about the new wave of faith that is sweeping the country.

Where the film hits the bell is in Fleischer's bold, dramatic handling of certain scenes, allied to some slick lensing by Aldo Tonti. The scenes in the Rome gladiatorial pit, sharply etched by Jack Palance as the the boy, have an urgent excitement, with Palance's sadism matched only by Quinn's bewildered concentration.

Individually, the performances are uneven. Quinn is firstclass in a role which could have become monotonous after his beefy approach to his scenes with a vital Katy Jurado following his release from jail. Palance plays the sadistic gladiator with a liplicking panache that tends to pinpoint the fact that the whole pic is a shade too violent, but certainly the thesp makes Torvald a vivid and urgent figure in the setup.

Silvana Mangano does an adequate job of work as Rachel, but the part never comes to life, nor does that of Ernest Borgnine as a Christian doing undercover work among the Romans.

■ BARBARELLA

1968, 98 MINS, FRANCE/ITALY ◇ ⑫ ⊙

Dir Roger Vadim *Prod* Dino De Laurentiis *Scr* Terry Southern, Roger Vadim, Claude Brule, Vittorio Bonicelli, Clement Biddle Wood, Brian Degas, Tudor Gates, Jean Claude Forest *Ph* Claude Renoir *Ed* Victoria Mercanton *Mus* Michel Magne, Charles Fox *Art Dir* Mario Garbuglia

● Jane Fonda, John Phillip Law, Anita Pallenberg, Milo O'Shea, David Hemmings, Marcel Marceau (Marianne/De Laurentiis)

Despite a certain amount of production dash and polish and a few silly-funny lines of dialog, *Barbarella* isn't very much of a film. Based on what has been called an adult comic strip [by Jean Claude Forest], the Dino De Laurentiis production flawed with a cast that is not particularly adept at comedy, a flat script, and direction which can't get this beached whale afloat.

Jane Fonda stars in the title role, and com across as an ice-cold, antiseptic, wide-eyed girl who just can't say no. Fonda's abilities are stretched to the breaking point along with her clothes.

In key supporting roles, John Phillip Law is inept as a simple angel while Anita Pallenberg, as the lesbian queen, fares better because of a well defined character.

Made at De Laurentiis' Rome studios, film can't really be called overproduced, considering the slapdash special effects, grainy process and poor calibre of the props, though put together on a massive scale so as to appear of spectacle proportions.

■ BARBARIAN AND THE GEISHA, THE

1958, 105 MINS, US ◇ ⑫

Dir John Huston *Prod* Eugene Frenke *Scr* Charles Grayson *Ph* Charles G. Clarke *Ed* Stuart Gilmore *Mus* Hugo Friedhofer *Art Dir* Lyle R. Wheeler, Jack Martin Smith

● John Wayne, Eiko Ando, Sam Jaffe, So Yamamura, Morita, Hiroshi Yamato (20th Century-Fox)

The Barbarian and the Geisha is an Oriental pageant of primitive beauty based on the 'true' story of the exploits of the first US consul to establish headquarters in Japan. The production is lavish but it is light in other departments.

Once opened to Christian missionaries, then closed, Japan was a Forbidden Kingdom to outsiders in 1856 when US Consul-General Townsend Harris (John Wayne) arrives off the port of Shimoda, where the screenplay, based on Ellis St Joseph's story, begins. Harris is under orders to open the door on the hermetically-sealed country, and, armed only with his own personality and accompanied only by his European translator (Sam Jaffe) he prepares to do so.

After initial harassing and setbacks, Wayne gains the confidence of the local noble (So Yamamura) who agrees to take him to the court of the Shogun to plead his case. Meantime, to make Wayne's isolation easier, Yamamura delivers a geisha (Eiko Ando) to the non-Nipponese barbarian.

The Barbarian and the Geisha (originally titled *The Townsend Harris Story*) is rich in atmosphere and in some stirringly-staged scenes, such as Wayne's arrival by ship at Shimoda, his presentation to the Shogun's court and an archery meet of medieval pomp. It is less exciting in its personal delineations. Huston uses a technique of having the Japanese speak Japanese throughout. The character played by Ando acts as the narrator behind some of this action, but this device is only partially successful.

■ BARBAROSA

1982, 90 MINS, US ◇ ⑫ ⊙

Dir Fred Schepisi *Prod* Paul N. Lazarus III *Scr* William D. Wittliff *Ph* Ian Baker *Ed* Don Zimmerman, David Ramirez *Mus* Bruce Smeaton *Art Dir* Michael Levesque, Leon Ericksen

● Willie Nelson, Gary Busey, Isela Vega, Gilbert Roland, Danny De La Paz, Alma Martinez (Universal/Associated)

Australian director Fred Schepisi does a careful job of bringing the western legend to light with endearing performances from actors Willie Nelson and Gary Busey.

Nelson limns the renowned title character, who in essence is nothing more than a 'sensitive' outlaw forever eluding the assassination attempts of his wife's over-protective family. Nelson visits his spouse and daughter (who live with the family) several times a year, but past events coupled with his yearning for freedom make it impossible to live a normal life.

Busey turns in a natural portrayal of the poor, goofy farm boy the outlaw takes under his wing. While it's an honorable performance, the Busey character and his growth into a soulful human being primarily serves to point up what a nice guy Nelson is.

■ BARBARY COAST

1935, 97 MINS, US ⑫ ⊙

Dir Howard Hawks *Prod* Samuel Goldwyn *Scr* Ben Hecht, Charles MacArthur *Ph* Ray June *Ed* Edward Curtiss *Mus* Alfred Newman (dir.) *Art Dir* Richard Day

● Miriam Hopkins, Edward G. Robinson, Joel McCrea, Walter Brennan, Frank Craven, Brian Donlevy (Goldwyn/United Artists)

Sam Goldwyn picked *Barbary Coast* as a title and called in Ben Hecht and Charles MacArthur to write a story to fit. Result is a picture that has all it takes to get along in thoroughbred company.

Atmosphere of the period has been richly caught, even if the girl's efforts to free herself from the gambling hall proprietor aren't so sincere.

Miriam Hopkins is introduced when she arrives in Frisco to meet the man she is going to marry, admittedly because he has struck it rich. When learning he has been killed over a gambling loss, she throws herself toward Edward G. Robinson, town's underworld

leader. Story makes Hopkins a partially unsympathetic character until she falls in love with a young prospector and finds herself tangled up through prior associations. It is mostly Hopkins' picture but Robinson and Joel McCrea are also strong.

Harry Carey plays the organizer of vigilantes and gives a good performance. Other standout small parts are by Walter Brennan and Frank Craven.

□ 1935: Nomination: Best Cinematography

■ BAREFOOT CONTESSA, THE

1954, 128 MINS, US ◇ ⑫

Dir Joseph L. Mankiewicz *Prod* Forrest E. Johnston *Scr* Joseph L. Mankiewicz *Ph* Jack Cardiff *Ed* William Hornbeck *Mus* Mario Nascimbene

● Humphrey Bogart, Ava Gardner, Edmond O'Brien, Marius Goring, Valentina Cortese, Rossano Brazzi (United Artists/Figaro)

Sharpness of the characters, the high-voltage dialog, the cynicism and wit and wisdom of the story, the spectacular combination of the immorally rich and the immorally sycophantic – these add up to a click feature from writer-director Joseph L. Mankiewicz.

Ava Gardner is the contessa of the title, 'discovered' in a second-rate flamenco nitery in Madrid. The trio of discoverers: Humphrey Bogart as a writer-director and determined member of Alcoholics' Anonymous; Edmond O'Brien, as a glib, nervous, perspiring combination of pressagent and (apparent) procurer; and Warren Stevens, the rich producer.

Gardner is ideal in her spot, looking every inch the femme magnetism around which all the action revolves. Bogart is splendid throughout, taking part quietly and with maximum effectiveness in the twists and turns of the intriguing story.

At times, Mankiewicz, the writer, seems over-generous in providing his characters with words.

Mankiewicz has been quoted as saying none of his characters is for real. This was in answer to suspicion that the moneybags producer might be an only slightly distorted mirroring of Howard Hughes.

□ 1954: Best Supp. Actor (Edmond O'Brien).
□ Nomination: Best Story & Screenplay

■ BAREFOOT IN THE PARK

1967, 104 MINS, US ◇ ⑫ ⊙

Dir Gene Saks *Prod* Hal B. Wallis *Scr* Neil Simon *Ph* Joseph LaShelle *Ed* William A. Lyon *Mus* Neal Hefti *Art Dir* Hal Pereira, Walter Tyler

● Robert Redford, Jane Fonda, Charles Boyer, Mildred Natwick, Herbert Edelman, Mabel Albertson (Paramount)

Barefoot in the Park is one howl of a picture. Adapted by Neil Simon from his legit smash, retaining Robert Redford and Mildred Natwick from the original cast, and adding Jane Fonda and Charles Boyer to round out the principals, this is a thoroughly entertaining comedy delight about young marriage. Director Gene Saks makes a sock debut.

Redford is outstanding, particularly adept in light comedy. Fonda is excellent, ditto Natwick, her mother. A genuine surprise casting is Boyer, the Bohemian who lives in the attic above the newlyweds' top-floor flat. With only one slight flagging pace – about 30 minutes from the end, when Redford and Fonda have their late-night squabble – pic moves along smartly.

□ 1967: Nomination: Best Supp. Actress (Mildred Natwick)

■ BARFLY

1987, 99 MINS, US ◇ ⑫ ⊙

Dir Barbet Schroeder *Prod* Barbet Schroeder *Scr* Charles Bukowski *Ph* Robby Muller *Ed* Eva Gardos *Art Dir* Bob Ziembicki

● Mickey Rourke, Faye Dunaway, Alice Krige, Jack Nance, J.C. Quinn, Frank Stallone (Coppola/Cannon)

Barfly is a lowlife fairytale, an ethereal serio-comedy about gutter existence from the pen of one who's been there, Charles Bukowski. First American fictional feature from Swiss-French director Barbet Schroeder is spiked with unexpected doses of humor, much of it due to Mickey Rourke' quirky, unpredictable, most engaging performance as the boozy hero.

Much as in a Bukowski short story, a bar is the center of the universe here. Populating the dive in a seedy section of Los Angeles are a floating assortment of winos and derelicts, of which one is the youngest and most volatile is Henry (Rourke), a self-styled poet of the bottle.

He meets a terribly attractive fellow alcoholic, Wanda (Faye Dunaway), who immediately takes him in and keeps him well plied with drink and sex, to the extent they are both interested in and capable of the latter.

Rourke's performance is the centerpiece of the film, and keeps it buoyantly alive throughout. Dunaway also is on the right wavelength as the 'distressed goddess' who grows dependent upon and loyal to the wildly unreliable Rourke.

BARKLEYS OF BROADWAY, THE

1949, 102 MINS, US ◇ ⓥ ☉
Dir Charles Walters   *Prod* Arthur Freed   *Scr* Betty Comden, Adolph Green   *Ph* Harry Stradling   *Ed* Albert Akst   *Mus* Lenny Hayton
● Fred Astaire, Ginger Rogers, Oscar Levant, Billie Burke, Gale Robbins (M-G-M)

With Fred Astaire and Ginger Rogers *The Barkleys of Broadway* is an ace dance fest, presenting them at their terpsichorean best against a production background that is Metro at its lushest. However, the songs are ordinary.

The screen's most complementary dance team glides through five dance numbers with the grace and apparent spontaneity that is their trademark when appearing together.

Sixth dance number is done solo by Astaire. It is the combination of special effects and Astaire hoofing in a dance with shoes that spellbinds into standout terping.

Plot is light, but ties together neatly in depicting a more or less standard story of a Broadway star team of man and wife who have a misunderstanding, separate and then get back together for the finale. Dialog is good and the cast is very competent.
☐ 1949: Nomination: Best Color Cinematography

BARQUERO

1970, 108 MINS, US ◇
Dir Gordon Douglas   *Prod* Aubrey Schenk, Hal Klein   *Scr* George Schenck   *Ph* Jerry Finnerman   *Ed* Charles Nelson   *Mus* Dominic Frontiere   *Art Dir* Allen E. Smith
● Lee Van Cleef, Forrest Tucker, Warren Oates, Kerwin Mathews, Mariette Hartley, Marie Gomez (United Artists)

Barquero is a taut, bloody-as-a-slaughterhouse western morality play with Lee Van Cleef as the fierce pioneering individualist against Warren Oates, the personifsion of evil dressed all in black.

Oates is the twitchy, sadistic leader o a band of mercenaries from the Mexican Revolution, who sweep through the countryside as merciless as the Four Horsemen of the Apocalypse.

Van Cleef is the barquero who has hand-built and operates a primitive ferry across a river. At one side of the water the first bare-boards beginnings of a town have sprung up in the center of which stands the steepled skeleton of a church. On the other side is the wilderness, hostile Indians and Mexico.

Oates plans to evacuate his men and loot on th barque and burn it behind him.

BARRETTS OF WIMPOLE STREET, THE

1934, 110 MINS, US ⓥ
Dir Sidney Franklin   *Prod* [Irving G. Thalberg]   *Scr* Claudine West, Ernest Vajda, Donald Ogden Stewart   *Ph* William Daniels   *Ed* Margaret Booth   *Mus* Herbert Stothart   *Art Dir* Cedric Gibbons, Harry McAfee, Edwin B. Willis
● Norma Shearer, Fredric March, Charles Laughton, Maureen O'Sullivan, Katharine Alexander, Una O'Connor (M-G-M)

The Barretts of Wimpole Street is an artistic cinematic translation of the Katherine Cornell stage success [by Rudolf Besier].

As a film it's slow. Very. The first hour is wandering, planting-the-plot stuff that has some difficulty cementing the interest, but in the final stretch it grips and holds. It's talky throughout – truly an actor's picture, with long speeches, verbose philosophical observations.

The romance between Elizabeth Barrett (Norma Shearer) and Robert Browning (Fredric March) is a beautiful exposition in its ethereal and physically rehabilitating effect on the ailing Barrett. The unnatural love of Papa Barrett is graphically depicted by Charles Laughton, as the psychopathic, hateful character whose twisted affections for his children especially daughter Elizabeth, almost proves her physical and spiritual undoing.

Not the least of the many good performances is the nifty chore turned in by Marion Clayton as the lisping Bella Hadley. Maureen O'Sullivan, Katharine Alexander, Una O'Connor (exceptional as the mincing Wilson, the maid) and Ralph Forbes all register in a long but not too involved cast which director Sidney Franklin has at all times kept well in hand and never permitted to become confusing.

The confining locale of London's Wimpole Street in 1845 limits the action to the interior of the Barretts' home, but the general persuasiveness of all the histrionics achieves much in offsetting the lack of physic action.

March's bravado style is well suited to the role of the ardent Browning, the poet. Shearer is at all times sincerely compelling in her role, even in the bedridden portions.
☐ 1934: Nominations: Best Picture, Actress (Norma Shearer)

BARRETTS OF WIMPOLE STREET, THE

1957, 104 MINS, US/UK ◇
Dir Sidney Franklin   *Prod* Sam Zimbalist   *Scr* John Dighton   *Ph* F.A. Young   *Ed* Frank Clarke   *Mus* Bronislau Kaper   *Art Dir* Alfred Junge
● Jennifer Jones, John Gielgud, Bill Travers, Virginia McKenna, Jean Anderson, Vernon Gray (M-G-M)

Lovers of the classics will find *The Barretts of Wimpole Street* a reliving of the romance between Elizabeth Barrett and Robert Browning as originally plotted in Rudolf Besier's play and in a 1934 screen version, also made by Metro.

Sidney Franklin, who directed the original screen version starring Norma Shearer and Fredric March, helms this production.

Jennifer Jones, while a surprisingly healthy-looking Elizabeth, plays the invalid literary figure with great skill. Bill Travers Browning, the vigorous, colorful poet who managed to court and win the delicate Elizabeth under the nose of her despotic father, is personable and competent enough.

John Gielgud, the father with an almost incestuous attachment for his daughter, repeats the role originally done by Charles Laughton with all the stern menace it requires. Virginia McKenna is lively and appealing as the younger sister, Henrietta,

secretly in love with Vernon Gray, good as Captain Surtees Cook.

BARRY LYNDON

1975, 184 MINS, UK ◇ ⓥ ⦿ ☉
Dir Stanley Kubrick   *Prod* Stanley Kubrick   *Scr* Stanley Kubrick   *Ph* John Alcott   *Ed* Tony Lawson   *Mus* Leonard Rosenman (sup.)   *Art Dir* Ken Adam
● Ryan O'Neal, Marisa Berenson, Patrick Magee, Hardy Kruger, Gay Hamilton, Leonard Rossiter (Warner)

Stanley Kubrick scripts and directs a most elegant and handsome adaptation of William Makepeace Thackeray's early 19th-century novel.

Ryan O'Neal's character evolves from a passive, likable Irish lad, enamored of cousin Gay Hamilton whose eyes are fixed on the pocketbook of British officer Leonard Rossiter. Conned into fleeing his home after a fake duel, O'Neal learns about life from a highwayman, a Prussian captor-benefactor and a spy. O'Neal emerges from these trials as a cynical manipulator of people.

The pile of victims eventually includes Marisa Berenson, whose means provide a possible avenue to O'Neal's security in a peerage. But up from the ashes comes a discarded stepson who brings down O'Neal.
☐ 1975: Best Cinematography, Art Direction, Costume Design, Adapted Scoring.
☐ Nominations: Best Picture, Director, Adapted Screenplay

BARTLEBY

1971, 78 MINS, UK ◇ ⓥ ☉
Dir Anthony Friedmann   *Prod* Rodney Carr-Smith   *Scr* Rodney Carr-Smith, Anthony Friedmann   *Ph* Ian Wilson   *Ed* John S. Smith   *Mus* Roger Webb   *Art Dir* Simon Holland
● Paul Scofield, John McEnery, Thorley Walters, Colin Jeavons, Raymond Mason, Charles Kinross (Pantheon)

It's understandable that Paul Scofield, an intelligent, choosey actor, should have been intrigued by this enigmatic, short film.

Bartleby is virtually a duel between Scofield and John McEnery, who plays a young audit clerk, a fallout from society. He is no rebel or rabble-raiser; just a guy who can't adjust himself to the demands of these times. He gets a job with Scofield who patiently employs him but is astounded at the young man's attitude. Very politely he insists that 'he prefers not do this or that'. Baffled, Scofield does everything possible to get through to the young man but is thwarted and eventually, irritated, fires him. But Bartleby prefers not to go.

This modestly-budgeted picture, from Herman Melville's story, is downbeat. But it is intriguing because of the two main performances. Scofield, who radiates thought and integrity in every speech movement and gesture is fine. McEnery underplays the incomprehensible, pitiful Bartleby with just the right note to engender sympathy but not ridicule.

The film is a riddle but it should intrigue any thoughtful filmgoer.

BARTON FINK

1991, 116 MINS, US ◇ ⓥ ☉
Dir Joel Coen   *Prod* Ethan Coen   *Scr* Ethan Coen, Joel Coen   *Ph* Roger Deakins   *Ed* Roderick Jaynes   *Mus* Carter Burwell   *Art Dir* Dennis Gassner
● John Turturro, John Goodman, Judy Davis, Michael Lerner, John Mahoney (20th Century-Fox/Circle)

Joel and Ethan Coen's hermetic tale of a 'genius' playwright's brief stint as a studio contract writer is a painstakingly miniaturist work that can be read any number of ways. This film will appeal to buffs at least as much as the brothers' last, *Miller's Crossing*.

Title character, played with a creepily growing sense of dread by John Turturro, is a gravely serious New York dramatist who scores a soaring triumph on Broadway in 1941 with a deep-dish think piece about the working class. In Hollywood he is assigned a Wallace Beery wrestling programmer and told to come up with something by the end of the week.

Checking into a huge, slightly frayed and weirdly underpopulated hotel, he becomes friendly with the hulking fellow bachelor next door, Charlie Meadows (John Goodman), an insurance salesman with a gift for gab. Working at home, Fink suffers from intense writer's block.

After a little more than an hour, the pic is thrown in a wholly unexpected direction. There is a shocking murder, the presence of a mysterious box in Fink's room, the revelation of another's character's sinister true identity, three more killings, a truly weird hotel fire and the humiliation of the writer after he believes he's finally turned out a fine script.

Scene after scene is filled with a ferocious strength and humor. Michael Lerner's performance as a Mayer-like studio overlord is sensational. Goodman is marvelous as the folksy neighbor, rolling his tongue around pages of wonderful dialog. Judy Davis nicely etches a woman who has a way with difficult writers, and John Mahoney turns up as a near dead ringer for William Faulkner in his Hollywood period.

☐ 1991: Nominations: Best Supp. Actor (Michael Lerner), Art Direction, Costuem Design

● ●

■ **BASIC INSTINCT**

1992, 127 MINS, US ◇ ⊛ ⊙
Dir Paul Verhoeven *Prod* Alan Marshall *Scr* Joe Eszterhas *Ph* Jan De Bont *Ed* Frank J. Urioste *Mus* Jerry Goldsmith *Art Dir* Terence Marsh
● Michael Douglas, Sharon Stone, George Dzundza, Jeanne Tripplehorn, Denis Arndt, Leilani Sarelle (Carolco/Canal Plus)

Basic Instinct is grade-A pulp fiction. This erotically charged thriller about the search for an ice-pick murderer in San Francisco rivets attention through its sleek style, attractive cast doing and thinking kinky things, and story, which is as weirdly implausible as it is intensely visceral.

Tale gets off to a slambang start when, at the peak of mutual sexual excitement, an unidentifiable blonde ties up her lover's hands and does him in. Back on the streets of San Francisco, detective Michael Douglas and partner George Dzundza head up the coast to quiz the dead man's g.f., the fabulously wealthy and sexy Sharon Stone who has published a novel in which an identical murder is depicted. The very tough and ice-cold Stone quickly begins tantalizing Douglas, who has recently gone cold turkey off cigarettes, booze, drugs and sex.

Stone bends Douglas so out of shape that, in the first torrid sex scene, he roughly assaults his former lover and police department shrink (Jeanne Tripplehorn). Stone remains the prime suspect all the way through the tale, which includes four more killings. The extensively intertwined sexual histories of Douglas, Stone and Tripplehorn, not to mention Stone's jealous female lover (Leilani Sarelle), throws suspicion all over the place.

Douglas scores with a game and gamey portrayal of an iconoclastic cop not afraid to go over the line professionally or personally. After a decade of marking time in schlockers, Stone has a career-making role here as a beautiful, smart manipulator who is always several steps ahead of everyone else.

[Pic's uncut version, distributed outside the US, ran 42 seconds longer than version reviewed.]

☐ 1992: Nominations: Best Editing, Original Score

B

● ●

■ **BASIL THE GREAT MOUSE DETECTIVE**
See: The Great Mouse Detective

● ●

■ **BASKET CASE**

1982, 90 MINS, US ◇ ⊛
Dir Frank Henenlotter *Prod* Edgar Levens *Scr* Frank Henenlotter *Ph* Bruce Torbet *Ed* Frank Henenlotter *Mus* Gus Russo
● Kevin Van Hentenryck, Terri Susan Smith, Beverly Bonner, Robert Vogel, Diana Browne, Lloyd Pace (levens-Henenlotter)

Basket Case is an ultra-cheap monster film created by neophyte filmmaker Frank Henenlotter with a tongue-in-cheek approach.

Picture concerns a young man Duane (Kevin Van Hentenryck) from Glens Falls in upstate New York, who comes to the B Apple and checks into a seedy 42nd St. hotel carrying a large wicker basket. A lengthy mid-film flashback reveals he is bent on revenge, carried out by his Siamese twin monstrous brother Belial (residing in the basket), killing off the three doctors who separated them surgically at age 10.

Acting styles vary (creating intentional camp humor), but the leads are fine: Van Hentenryck creating great sympathy as a neurotic youngster and girlfriend Terri Susan Smith (as a doctor's receptionist) emerging in a blonde wig as an ingratiating performer. Robert Vogel in the stock role of a harried hotel manager gets some big laughs by forcefully playing it straight.

Tech credits are a drawback, particularly the variable sound recording, grainy blowup from 16mm and shrill musical score.

● ●

■ **BASKET CASE 2**

1990, 89 MINS, US ◇ ⊛ ⊙
Dir Frank Henenlotter *Prod* Edgar levens *Scr* Frank Henenlotter *Ph* Robert M. Baldwin *Ed* Kevin Tent *Mus* Joe Renzetti *Art Dir* Michael Moran
● Kevin Van Hentenryck, Annie Ross, Kathryn Meisle, Heather Rattray, Matt Mitler, Ted Sorel (Shapiro-Glickenhaus)

Belated sequel to the 1982 cult horror film, *Basket Case 2* is a hilarious genre spoof. Here Frank Henenlotter's paying homage to Tod Browning's 1932 classic *Freaks*.

Annie Ross as Granny Ruth is a crusader for the rights of 'unique individuals' (i.e. freaks) and welcomes the Siamese twin brothers Kevin and Belial into her home in Staten Island. Weird menagerie of youngsters, mostly crazy variations on the Elephant Man by makeup whiz Gabe Bartalos, are treated very sympathetically at first, but as in Browning's film their potential for scaring the audience also is exploited.

Pic climaxes with Belial's ultraviolent attacks on foes of freaks, namely tabloid reporter Kathryn Meisle, her shutterbug assistant Matt Mitler and cop Ted Sorel. En route is one of the oddest scenes in recent horror pics, Belial making love to Eve, a similarly grotesque Siamese twin.

Casting coup is Annie Ross, the legendary jazz singer, who is a lot of fun as the demented granny who goads her freakish charges to fight back.

● ●

■ **BASKET CASE 3**
THE PROGENY

1992, 90 MINS, US ◇ ⊛
Dir Frank Henenlotter *Prod* Edgar levens *Scr* Frank Henenlotter, Robert Martin *Ph* Bob Paone *Ed* Greg Sheldon *Mus* Joe Renzetti *Art Dir* William Barclay
● Annie Ross, Kevin Van Hentenryck, Dan Biggers, Gil Roper, Tina Louise Hilbert, James O'Doherty (Shapiro Glickenhaus)

Pic opens with a lengthy dose of footage from *Basket Case 2*, detailing sex between the two

monsters Belial and Eve and the death of Eve's sister Susan. Part three begins with Eve's pregnancy.

Granny Ruth (jazz vocalist Annie Ross) takes Eve, papa-to-be Belial and a commune of unique individuals (i.e. monsters) to a small town in Georgia to stay with Uncle Hal (Dan Biggers), a doctor who will help with the mutant birth. Ross is reunited there with her grotesque monstrosity of a son (stand-up comic James O'Doherty), while Belial's 'normal' twin brother (series regular Kevin Van Hentenryck) gets a crush on the sheriff's pretty daughter (Tina Louise Hilbert).

Henenlotter's mix of wild over-acting, cartoon color scheme and heavy-handed message regarding tolerance is tough to take for the uninitiated. His fans will enjoy seeing the growing menagerie of creatures, including the cute/grotesque progeny.

Van Hentenryck acts way over the top, while Ross literally dominates the film with her intensity and gets to lead the monsters in a sing-a-long of the golden oldie *Personality*. Heroine Hilbert makes a good impression in a Jekyll & Hyde role. Creature effects are quite inventive.

● ●

■ **BAT, THE**

1926, 91 MINS, US ⊗ ⊛
Dir Roland West *Prod* Roland West *Scr* Roland West, George Marion Jr *Ph* Arthur Edeson *Art Dir* William Cameron Menzies
● Tullio Carminati, Jewel Carmen, Louise Fazenda, Emily Fitzroy, Arthur Houseman, Jack Pickford (West/United Artists)

This picture runs 91 minutes – a long time for anybody's film, but it is interesting every minute of the way. The story is that its maker, Roland West, paid heavy money for the film rights to this long-run legit show [by Mary Roberts Rinehart and Avery Hopwood].

The mystery concerns the death of a bank president, the theft of $200,000, the disappearance of the young cashier, and the mysterious criminal whose sign is the shadow of bat projected from the front of an electric flashlight. This mysterious criminal is behind a thousand suspicious actions but meantime, every member of the cast is suspected of having been the culprit.

An Italian actor named Tullio Carminati gives a performance as the detective that is one of the best things done by a newcomer to the screen. Everybody else is okay and Louise Fazenda draws her share of laughs with the hoke maid's part, while Eddie Gribbon is good for a giggle or so as the hick detective who knows not his intelligence from the lining of a coat pocket.

● ●

■ **BATAAN**

1943, 113 MINS, US ⊛
Dir Tay Garnett *Prod* Irving Starr *Scr* Robert D. Andrews *Ph* Sidney Wagner *Ed* George White *Mus* Bronislau Kaper
● Robert Taylor, George Murphy, Thomas Mitchell, Lloyd Nolan, Robert Walker, Desi Arnaz (M-G-M)

Bataan is a melodramatic re-enactment of the last ditch stand of an American patrol detailed to guard a road in the Philippines following the evacuation of Manila. Picture pulls no punches in displaying the realistically grim warfare.

There's a sufficient amount of jungle battle action and a couple of hand-to-hand skirmishes where bayonets are brought into play, but major portion of the extended running time is devoted to dramatic incidents revolving around the hastily-recruited patrol unit and their efforts to stave off the Jap's advance into the Bataan peninsula so that the main American and Philippine forces could dig in.

Robert Taylor gives a strong performance

as the commanding sergeant, but picture focuses attention on screen debut of Robert Walker, who smacks over an arresting portrayal as the sensitive and sympathetic young sailor who attaches himself to the outfit to get a crack at the Japs.

■ BATHING BEAUTY

1944, 102 MINS, US ◇ ▼

Dir George Sidney   *Prod* Jack Cummings   *Scr* Dorothy Kingsley, Allen Boretz, Frank Waldman   *Ph* Harry Stradling   *Ed* Blanche Sewell   *Mus* Johnny Green   *Art Dir* Cedric Gibbons, Stephen Goosson, Merrill Pye
● Red Skelton, Esther Williams, Basil Rathbone, Bill Goodwin, Ethel Smith, Jean Porter (M-G-M)

Bathing Beauty is produced in the lush, lavish, manner which is as familiar as the Metro trademark.

Esther Williams, who formerly appeared in *Andy Hardy* films and briefly in *A Guy Named Joe*, is pulled to stardom by her swimsuit straps. Dressed in either bathing togs or street finery, she is a pretty picture indeed. The former swimming champ displays her aquatic and acting abilities in the role of a collegienne who travels the rocky road of love with songwriter Red Skelton.

Skelton is his usual effervescent self, bouncing in and out of the script, getting in and out of scrapes with his girl, and the authorities at the college she attends. His two speciality numbers are especially funny: one, where he attends a ballet dancing class with the girls of the school, dressed in a short, fluffy, pink dress with dancing slippers, endeavoring to go through the motions, and being slapped around by the instructress; the other, which he did in vaude for years prior to landing in films, is his impression of a gal getting up in the morning, prettying herself and dressing.

Unlike musicals prior to this one, Metro has investe in beautiful sequences rather than cast. Water ballet costumes by Irene Sharaff, and the water ballet, produced under the supervision of John Murray Anderson, are memorable.

■ BATMAN

1966, 105 MINS, US ◇ ▼ ⊙

Dir Leslie H. Martinson   *Prod* William Dozier   *Scr* Lorenzo Semple Jr   *Ph* Howard Schwartz   *Ed* Harry Gerstad   *Mus* Nelson Riddle   *Art Dir* Jack Martin Smith, Serge Krizman
● Adam West, Burt Ward, Lee Merriwether, Cesar Romero, Burgess Meredith, Frank Gorshin (20th Century-Fox)

Batman is packed with action, clever sight gags, interesting complications and goes all out on bat with batmania: batplane, batboat, batcycle, etc. etc. Humor is stretched to the limit, color is comic-strip sharp and script retrieves every trick from the highly popular teleseries' oatbag, adding a few more sophisticated touches.

It's nearly impossible to attempt to relate plot. Suffice to say that it's Batman and Robin against his four arch-enemies, Catwoman, The Joker, The Penguin and The Riddler. Quartet have united and are out to take over the world. They elaborately plot the dynamic duo's death again and again but in every instance duo escape by the skin of their tights.

The acting is uniformly impressively improbable The intense innocent enthusiasm of Cesar Romero, Burgess Meredith and Frank Gorshin as the three criminals is balanced against the innocent calm of Adam West and Burt Ward, Batman and Robin respectively.

■ BATMAN

1989, 126 MINS, US ◇ ▼ ⊙

Dir Tim Burton   *Prod* Jon Peters, Peter Guber   *Scr* Sam

Hamm, Warren Skaaren   *Ph* Roger Pratt   *Ed* Ray Lovejoy   *Mus* Danny Elfman   *Art Dir* Anton Furst
● Michael Keaton, Jack Nicholson, Kim Basinger, Robert Wuhl, Pat Hingle, Billy Dee Williams (Guber-Peters/Warner)

Director Tim Burton effectively echoes the visual style of the original Bob Kane comics while conjuring up a nightmarish world of his own.

Going back to the source elements of the cartoon figure, who made his debut in 1939 for Detective (now DC) Comics, the Jon Peters-Peter Guber production [from a story by Sam Hamm] will appeal to purists who prefer their heroes as straight as Clint Eastwood.

In a striking departure from his usual amiable comic-style, Michael Keaton captures the haunt intensity of the character, and seems particularly lonely and obsessive without Robin around to share his exploits.

The gorgeous Kim Basinger takes the sidekick's place, in a determined bow to heterosexuality which nonetheless leaves Batman something less than enthusiastic.

It comes as no surprise that Jack Nicholson steals every scene in a sizable role as the hideously disfigured Joker. Nicholson embellishes fascinatingly baroque designs with his twisted features, lavish verbal pirouettes and inspired excursions into the outer limits of psychosis. It's a masterpiece of sinister comic acting.

What keeps the film arresting is the visual stylization. It was a shrewd choice for Burton to emulate the jarring angles and creepy lighting of film noir.
□ 1989: Best Art Direction

■ BATMAN RETURNS

1992, 126 MINS, US ◇ ▼ ⊙

Dir Tim Burton   *Prod* Denise Di Novi, Tim Burton   *Scr* Daniel Waters   *Ph* Stefan Czapsky   *Ed* Chris Lebenzon   *Mus* Danny Elfman   *Art Dir* Bo Welch
● Michael Keaton, Danny DeVito, Michelle Pfeiffer, Christopher Walken, Michael Gough, Cristi Conaway (Warner)

On all counts Warner Bros.' reported $80 million-plus *Batman Returns* is a monster. Follow-up has the same dark allure, but many non-fans of *Batman* will find this sequel superior in several respects. Batman's new foes, Penguin and Catwoman, are both fascinating creations, wonderfully played. Much of the film is massively inventive and spiked with fresh, perverse humor.

Interest gets cranked up high immediately by a prologue that illustrates the creation of the Penguin. Playing the infant's parents, Diane Salinger and a virtually unrecognizable Paul (Pee-wee Herman) Reubens dump the cradled tot into a freezing stream in a park. Like Moses, he survives.

Disrupting a civic Christmas celebration, the adult Penguin (Danny DeVito) announces that he wants some respect. Forming an alliance with tycoon Max Shreck (Christopher Walken), a specialist in industrial waste, Penguin decides to run for mayor.

Equally intriguing character of Catwoman evolves out of th demeaning treatment dished out by Shreck to his lovely, somewhat disheveled secretary Selina Kyle. Michelle Pfeiffer becomes a kitten with a whip who can very much hold her own with Batman. In one, Batman gets a literal licking from her.

Lensed seemingly entirely indoors or on covered sets, pic is a magnificently atmospheric elaboration on German Expressionist design principles. All the way down the line, behind-the-scenesters can take deep bows.

On the performance side, the deck is stacked entirely in favor of the villains. Briskly waddling, cawing his rude remarks and conveying decades' worth of resentment and bitterness, DeVito makes Penguin very

much his own. Endearingly klutzy initially as Selina, Pfeiffer, who replaced the pregnant Annette Bening in the role, looks amazing in her skintight, S&M-like leather skin. Wild-maned Walken has the right comic understatement and sang froid as Shreck, an in-joke on the German actor Max Schreck (1922's *Nosferatu*).

As in the first film, Michael Keaton is encased in a role as constricting as his super-hero costume, and while the actor's instincts seem right, the range he is allowed is distinctly limited.
□ 1992: Nominations: Best Make-up, Visual Effects

■ *BATTERIES NOT INCLUDED

1987, 106 MINS, US ◇ ▼ ⊙

Dir Matthew Robbins   *Prod* Ronald L. Schwary   *Scr* Matthew Robbins, Brad Bird, Brent Maddock, S.S. Wilson   *Ph* John McPherson   *Ed* Cynthia Scheider   *Mus* James Horner   *Art Dir* Ted Haworth
● Hume Cronyn, Jessica Tandy, Frank McRae, Elizabeth Pena, Michael Carmine, Dennis Boutsikaris (Universal/Amblin)

batteries not included could have used more imaginative juices to distinguish it from other, more enchanting Spielbergian pics where lovable mechanical things solve earthly human dilemmas. Still, it's suitable entertainment for kids.

Instead of the suburbs, Spielberg's usual haunt, scene here is in one of the crumbling neighborhoods of Manhattan where some tenants of an old and much beloved brownstone are being harassed to move out so a sleek office/residential complex can up in its place. The most stubborn of the holdouts is an irascible cafe owner (Hume Cronyn) and his senile wife (Jessica Tandy).

Before too long, Tandy is visited in the middle of the night by a couple of – that is, a male and female – miniature flying saucers which take their energy from the electrical outlets in the building and repair their parts with the tenants' metal appliances. They also become little angels, repairing all that the local hoods have broken on any number of their rampages.

Led by the Cronyn-Tandy team, pic [based on a story by Mick Garris] has a good mix of personalities, even if perhaps Elizabeth Pena as an unwed mother may raise some questions in children's minds their parents just as soon would not answer. Tech credits are terrific.

■ BATTLE BEYOND THE STARS

1980, 104 MINS, US ◇ ▼ ⊙

Dir Jimmy T. Murakami   *Prod* Ed Carlin   *Scr* John Sayles   *Ph* Daniel Lacambre   *Mus* James Horner   *Art Dir* John Zabrucky
● Richard Thomas, Robert Vaughn, George Peppard, John Saxon, Darlanne Fleugel, Sybil Danning (New World)

The fascination of watching how the defenseless cope with marauding barbarians is put to the test with New World's production of *Battle beyond the Stars*.

In unfolding its saga of how the peace-loving bunch on a small planet rebuffs a genetically deficient but vicious band of bad guys, *Battle* incorporates touches of an old-fashioned western, horror pics and even a touch of softcore.

Despite the expense involved, the pic appears not to take itself too seriously. Principal characterizations are skin deep. Dialog takes the form of relaxed banter with a minimum of homilies.

George Peppard has fun as a Scotch-tippling cowboy from earth who turns up as one of the mercenaries hired by the planet's earnest young soldier (Richard Thomas). John Saxon is hilarious as the chief bad guy.

■ BATTLE CRY

1955, 147 MINS, US ◇ ⓥ ⊙
Dir Raoul Walsh   *Scr* Leon M. Uris   *Ph* Sid Hickox
Ed William Zeigler   *Mus* Max Steiner   *Art Dir* John Beckman
● Van Heflin, Aldo Ray, Mona Freeman, Nancy Olson, Tab Hunter, Dorothy Malone (Warner)

Amatory, rather than military, action is the mainstay of this saga of the United States Marines. While overboard in length, this comes from the detailing of several sets of romantics, each interesting in itself, plus the necessary battle action to indicate the basis is rather grim warfare.

The latter is at a minimum, however, since Leon Uris' screen adaptation of his own novel is more concerned with the liberties and loves of the World War II Marines with whom he served, than with actual winning the fight in the Pacific. It is the story of a group of enlisted men and their officers in a communications battalion, taking them from civilian life, through training and then to New Zealand, from which base the outfit participates in Pacific action.

Of the romantic pairings, the most impression is made by Aldo Ray and Nancy Olson, not only because it occupies the main portion of the film's second half after the two other principal teamings have been completed, but also because of the grasp the two stars have on their characters.
□ 1955: Nomination: Best Scoring of a Dramatic Picture

■ BATTLE FOR ANZIO

See: *Anzio*

■ BATTLE FOR RUSSIA, THE

1943, 80 MINS, US
Dir Frank Capra   *Prod* Anatole Litvak   *Ed* William C. Hornbeck, William A. Lyon   *Mus* Dimitri Tiomkin
(US War Department)

In *The Battle for Russia*, Lt Col Frank Capra, of the Special Service Division, Army Service Forces, turns out by far the most notable in the series of *Why We Fight* army orientation pictures. Fifth of the series of seven documentaries, *Battle for Russia* is a powerful, yet simple, drama vividly depicting the greatest military achievement of all time.

As in the case of its predecessors, *Prelude to War*, *The Nazis Strike*, *Divide and Conquer* and *Battle of Britain*, *Russia* is a brilliant compilation of carefully edited footage culled, in the latter instance, from official Soviet sources and from newsreel and Signal Corps film, with a good part of the Russian material made available to the War Dept exclusively for this production.

Portraying the historical background of Russia from the time of Alexander Nevsky to the present, the film explains the reasons motivating the various conquests over Russia. Effective use of animated maps helps detail its enormous resources, raw materials, manpower, etc.

Keyed to Gen Douglas MacArthur's statement that: 'The scale and grandeur of the (Russian) effort mark it as the greatest military achievement in all history', this Capra-Litvak documentary is primarily the story of the titanic struggle up to the successful defense of Stalingrad.

■ BATTLE FOR THE PLANET OF THE APES

1973, 88 MINS, US ◇ ⓥ
Dir J. Lee Thompson   *Prod* Arthur P. Jacobs   *Scr* John William Corrington, Joyce Hooper Corrington
Ph Richard H. Kline   *Ed* Alan L. Jaggs, John C. Horger
Mus Leonard Rosenman   *Art Dir* Dale Hennesy
● Roddy McDowall, Claude Akins, Natalie Trundy, Severn Darden, Lew Ayres, John Huston (20th Century-Fox)

The fifth and last film of the series depicts the confrontation between the apes and the nuclear mutated humans inhabiting a large city destroyed in previous episode. Roddy McDowall encores as the ape's leader, having his own tribal strife with Claude Akins, a militant trouble-maker.

Considering the usual fate of sequels, it's not so much that this final effort [from a story by Paul Dehn] is limp, but that the previous four pix maintained for so long a good quality level.

McDowell and Natalie Trundy head the cast, in which Paul Williams plays a philosopher-type, and Austin Soker is a black counselor, most respected of the humans who are more or less captives of the apes. Severn Darden is leader of the mutated humans. Lew Ayr has a good bit, and John Huston appears in another pompous cameo as an aged philosopher of future generations who sets the flashback motif for the story.

■ BATTLEGROUND

1949, 118 MINS, US ⓥ
Dir William A. Wellman   *Prod* Dore Schary   *Scr* Robert Pirosh   *Ph* Paul C. Vogel   *Ed* John Dunning
Mus Lennie Hayton
● Van Johnson, John Hodiak, Ricardo Montalban, George Murphy, James Whitmore, Leon Ames (M-G-M)

Film deals with a segment of the Battle of the Bulge and is 'dedicated to the battered bastards of Bastogne', those heroic unyielding GIs who were reinspired to the ultimate victory by General McAuliffe's famous 'Nuts' reply to the Krauts when they sought to negotiate a peaceful surrender by the Americans.

Through sharp focus on a group of characters it exposes all the griping disappointments and foxhole dreams and aspirations of the battle-wearied foot soldier.

The cast performs in inspired manner. Murphy is the 35-year-old 'Pop' who is being discharged but finds himself a civilian in No Man's Land because Bastogne is surrounded. Johnson plays the carefree GI, and with great credibility. Other standouts include: John Hodiak a the newspaperman who enlisted; Montalban as the Mexican-American.
□ 1949: Best Screenplay & Story, B&W Cinematography.
□ Nominations: Best Picture, Director, Supp. Actor (James Whitmore), Editing

■ BATTLE HELL

See: *Yangtse Incident*

■ BATTLE OF BRITAIN

1969, 133 MINS, UK ◇ ⓥ ⊙
Dir Guy Hamilton   *Prod* Harry Saltzman, S. Benjamin Fisz   *Scr* James Kennaway, Wilfred Greatorex
Ph Freddie Young   *Mus* Ron Goodwin, William Walton
Art Dir Maurice Carter
● Laurence Olivier, Trevor Howard, Michael Caine, Ralph Richardson, Susannah York, Michael Redgrave
(United Artists)

Battle sequences in the air are splendidly conceived and sweepingly dramatic, though sometimes repetitious.

The $12 million-plus film strikes a happy medium between action and human interest. Stressed admirably are the strained headaches of the RAF top brass as they tackled the perilous problems. The battle fatigue, the difference of opinion on tactics, the shortage of planes and pilots, and the dreadful anxiety of time running out are all revealed.

Standouts among the stars are Laurence Olivier as Sir Hugh Dowding, Fighter Command's supremo, and Trevor Howard as the tight-lipped, dedicated Air Vice-Marshall Keith Park.

Some of the star names are woefully wasted, notably Michael Caine, Patrick Wymark and Kenneth More, all playing routine parts.

■ BATTLE OF MIDWAY

See: *Midway*

■ BATTLE OF THE BULGE

1965, 167 MINS, US ◇ ⓥ ⊙
Dir Ken Annakin   *Prod* Milton Sperling, Philip Yordan   *Scr* Milton Sperling, Philip Yordan, John Nelson   *Ph* Jack Hildyard   *Ed* Derek Parsons   *Mus* Benjamin Frankel
Art Dir Eugene Lourie
● Henry Fonda, Robert Shaw, Robert Ryan, Dana Andrews, George Montgomery, Ty Hardin (Cinerama)

Based on the pivotal action which precipitated the end of the Second World War in Europe, but otherwise fictionalized, *Battle of the Bulge* is a rousing, commercial battlefield action-drama of the emotions and activities of US and German force

Script pits hard-charging German tank commander Robert Shaw against a US military hierarchy topped by Robert Ryan, intelligence chief Dana Andrews, and latter's assistant (Henry Fonda) who is initially unpopular with the higher brass because he insists that the Germans are building towards a winter offensive.

Shaw is outstanding in a multifaceted role which demands he be a true war-lover, coolly rational under battle pressure and somewhat contemptuous of rear echelon chief Werner Peters.

On the US side script is flawed in the introduction of stock military types. Ken Annakin's direction and the adroit spacing of skirmishes minimize the script softness, exemplified by Fonda's character, whose solo sleuthing and tactical analysis strains credulity. Withal, Fonda is excellent.

■ BATTLE OF THE RIVER PLATE

(US: *Pursuit of the Graf Spee*)

1956, 119 MINS, UK ⓥ
Dir Michael Powell, Emeric Pressburger   *Prod* Michael Powell, Emeric Pressburger   *Scr* Michael Powell, Emeric Pressburger   *Ph* Christopher Challis   *Ed* Reginald Mills   *Mus* Brian Easdale   *Art Dir* Arthur Lawson, Hein Heckroth
● John Gregson, Anthony Quayle, Peter Finch, Ian Hunter, Jack Gwillim, Bernard Lee (Arcturus/Rank)

Defeat of the *Graf Spee* was the first major naval victory for Britain in the last big war. Apart from the strategy involved, it was also an exercise in subterfuge and diplomacy. All these points are neatly and simply brought out in the Michael Powell-Emeric Pressburger filmization.

What they have failed to do is to achieve any degree of characterization for the three naval commanders who led the British cruisers to victory against the Germans' more powerful pocket battleship. The only really sympathetic character emerging from the screenplay is the skipper of the enemy ship.

The battle sequences, in which the lightweight British cruisers close in on the *Graf Spee* and force the enemy to take shelter in Montevideo harbor are powerful, exciting and technically impressive. Story is given a neat twist by the diplomatic exchanges which take place while the *Graf Spee* is sheltering. The atmosphere in Montevideo is heightened by a series of on-the-spot dramatic broadcasts to the US, a device which is most effective.

The players are mostly secondary to the ships themselves. John Gregson, as the skipper of the *Exeter*; Anthony Quayle, commodore on the *Ajax*; Ian Hunter, captain on the *Ajax*; and Jack Gwillim on the *Achilles*, give forthright portrayals. Peter Finch gets the plum role as the German captain, who emerges as a warm, sincere and kindly person.

●●●●●●●●●●●●●●●●●●●●●●●●●●●●

■ BATTLE OF THE SEXES, THE

1914, 60 MINS, US ⊗

Dir D.W. Griffith *Scr* Daniel Carson Goodman, Gemit J. Lloyd, D.W. Griffith *Ph* Billy Bitzer *Ed* James E. Smith, Rose Smith

● Donald Crisp, Robert Harron, Lillian Gish, Mary Alden, Owen Moore, Fay Tincher (Reliance)

The story is a familiar but intimate tale vividly illustrated on the screen. Griffith keeps it alive every minute.

A family of four – father, mother, son and daughter – are living in an apartment house. To the same floor comes an adventuress, who is planted there to make a play for the husband (Donald Crisp). His general reputation is undisclosed, but it may be taken for granted that he is a wealthy chaser. The woman (Fay Tincher), after renting the apartment, goes to work on the head of the house in the opposite flat by leaving her door ajar and her skirt slightly lifted, as the husband starts out.

From this beginning the story pictures a mistress, a broken home, a heart-broken mother (Mary Alden) and two sad children (Robert Harron and Lillian Gish).

The acting hit of the film, far and away over anything else, is the wife, played by Alden. As a middleaged woman, called upon to pantomimically represent all the emotions, including an impulse toward insanity upon the discovery of her husband's unfaithfulness, Alden is superb. Crisp gives a competent performance, Gish is girlish and nice, Harron does exceedingly well as the son, and Owen Moore as the lover, in a somewhat slim part, plays it well.

The blot on the acting is Fay Tincher as Cleo, the adventuress.

●●●●●●●●●●●●●●●●●●●●●●●●●●●●

■ BATTLE OF THE VILLA FIORITA, THE

1965, 111 MINS, US ◇

Dir Delmer Daves *Prod* Delmer Daves *Scr* Delmer Daves *Ph* Oswald Morris *Ed* Bert Bates *Mus* Mischa Spoliansky *Art Dir* Carmen Dillon

● Maureen O'Hara, Rossano Brazzi, Richard Todd, Phyllis Calvert, Olivia Hussey, Maxine Audley (Warner)

The Battle of the Villa Fiorita is a beautifully-photographed and well-mounted Delmer Daves production which falls short artistically by switching gears.

Daves' script (from Rumer Godden's novel) propels Maureen O'Hara into affair with Italian composer Rossano Brazzi when latter attends English tunefest during one of hubby Richard Todd's frequent absences from home. The lovers hie to Italian villa and set up housekeeping before her divorce action jells.

At this point concept shifts to attempts by her kids (Martin Stephens and Elizabeth Dear) to break it up, joined later by Brazzi's moppet, Olivia Hussey. Idea is played for laffs, from juves' trek from England through hunger strikes, faked illness and other gambits.

O'Hara looks appropriately shook up but script does not permit much acting. Brazzi projects very well as lover, father and foil. Phyllis Calvert is on for seconds as gossipy English lady.

●●●●●●●●●●●●●●●●●●●●●●●●●●●●

■ BATTLETRUCK

(Aka: Warlords of the 21st Century)

1982, 91 MINS, US ◇ ⓥ

Dir Harley Cokliss *Prod* Lloyd Philips, Rob Whitehouse *Scr* Irving Austin, Harley Cokliss, John Beech *Ph* Chris Menges *Ed* Michael Horton *Mus* Kevin Peck *Art Dir* Gary Hansen

● Michael Beck, Annie McEnroe, James Wainwright, John Ratzenberger, Randolph Powell, Bruno Lawrence (New World)

Battletruck is a well-made and engaging action picture. This is a feature debut for director Harley Cokliss, who was second-unit director of *The Empire Strikes Back*. Working on a limited budget in New Zealand, Cokliss gets more performing subtleties from his characters than these films usually have.

Pic takes place after civilization has nearly collapsed after the 'oil wars' depletes most of the world's petroleum supplies. The big truck is the main weapon for an outlaw army commandered by Straker (James Wainwright), excellent as a cold-blooded killer. However, his daughter Corlie (Annie McEnroe), doesn't share his ideas of a great career.

She flees and is befriended by reclusive biker Hunter (Michael Beck) and a peaceful community headed by Rusty (John Ratzenberger). From then on, it's a matter of counting the battles between Straker's band and Hunter's troops.

●●●●●●●●●●●●●●●●●●●●●●●●●●●●

■ BAT 21

1988, 105 MINS, US ◇ ⓥ ⊙

Dir Peter Markle *Prod* David Fisher, Gary A. Neill, Michael Balson *Scr* William C. Anderson, George Gordon *Ph* Mark Irwin *Ed* Stephen E. Rivkin *Mus* Christopher Young *Art Dir* Vincent Cresciman

● Gene Hackman, Danny Glover, Jerry Reed, David Marshall Grant, Clayton Rohner, Erich Anderson (Tri-Star/Vision/Eagle)

BAT 21 represents the flip side of *Rambo*. The true story of an officer forced to parachute into enemy-infested jungle during the Vietnam War and survive on his own until a rescue can be attempted, this is a straightforward, surprisingly somber picture [from William C. Anderson's book] that sticks to the facts.

Produced independently on location in Sabah, Borneo, with the cooperation of the Malaysian military, this $10 million venture recounts the exceptional efforts of a reconnaisance flyer nicknamed Bird-Dog (Danny Glover) to keep tabs on the downed missile intelligence expert, Lt Col Iceal Hambleton (Gene Hackman) who has never before seen actual combat or come face-to-face with the enemy. Only Glover's personal initiative and daring gives Hackman any chance of escaping before the jungle is napalmed to smithereens. Several times, he comes within inches of being spotted by VC patrols.

Weight of the picture falls on Glover, who does most of the talking during their radio communications, squares off on occasion with his superior, nicely etched by Jerry Reed (also exec producer) and enjoys the benefit of being at the joystick for the snazzy flying scenes. Glover turns in a solid job but, as with Hackman, he remains one-dimensional.

Peter Markle's direction is dramatically sound and visually crisp, and Christopher Young's score is a plus.

●●●●●●●●●●●●●●●●●●●●●●●●●●●●

■ BAT WHISPERS, THE

1931, 82 MINS, US ⓥ ⊙

Dir Roland West *Prod* Roland West *Ph* Ray June (standard version), Robert H. Planck (65mm version) *Ed* James Smith *Mus* [uncredited] *Art Dir* Paul Roe Crawley

● Chester Morris, Una Merkel, Chance Ward, Richard Tucker, Wilson Benge, DeWitt Jennings (Art Cinema/United Artists)

Of the clutching hand school that the stage smash, *The Bat* [by Mary Roberts Rinehart and Avery Hopwood], was probably the real parent of, *The Bat Whispers*, in its talking version, is a good picture in the class division, for shivers and smiles.

The wide-screen [Magnifilm] film, United Artists' first, is somewhat grandiloquent. Bits of direction with the camera, particularly early on, are very engaging. The same effects

will come over in a lesser way on the standard size screen

Most of the comedy is by Maude Eburne, as the lady's maid. Some more is quietly injected by Spencer Chartres. It's not the noisy kind of ghostly slapstick so long associated with haunted house stories.

Chester Morris [as Detective Anderson] has little to do. It's some time before his appearance and shortly after that he's knocked out for another lapse. At the finale the audience is halted by a cry from the screen not to leave, and, as a sort of epilog, Morris reappears to request the audience not to divulge the identity of the Bat in the picture. Other cast players take care of their portions without distinction either way. Una Merkel is the girl, with William Bakewell opposite.

●●●●●●●●●●●●●●●●●●●●●●●●●●●●

■ BAXTER!

1973, 105 MINS, UK ◇

Dir Lionel Jeffries *Prod* Arthur Lewis *Scr* Reginald Rose *Ph* Geoffrey Unsworth *Ed* Teddy Darvas *Mus* Michael J. Lewis *Art Dir* Anthony Pratt

● Patricia Neal, Jean-Pierre Cassel, Britt Ekland, Lynn Carlin, Scott Jacoby, Sally Thomsett (Anglo-EMI/Group W/Hanna-Barbera)

Baxter! is a good tearjerker about a young boy with a psychosomatic speech defect plus a bad family problem. Well directed by Lionel Jeffries, the British-lensed drama [from the novel *The Boy Who Could Make Himself Disappear* by Kin Plat stars Patricia Neal as a speech therapist, Britt Ekland and Jean-Pierre Cassel as lovers who help Scott Jacoby in the title character role, and Lynn Carlin, as the boy's mother.

This is Jeffries' second feature directorial work (*The Railway Children* marked his bow), and he does a very fine job, aided by Geoffrey Unsworth's strong camerawork.

Neal's dancing voice and eyes are as magnificent as ever. Carlin is particularly excellent as the mother.

●●●●●●●●●●●●●●●●●●●●●●●●●●●●

■ BAY BOY

1984, 104 MINS, CANADA ◇ ⓥ

Dir Daniel Petrie *Prod* John Kemeny, Denis Heroux, Rene Cleitman *Scr* Daniel Petrie *Ph* Claude Agostini *Ed* Susan Shanks *Mus* Claude Bolling *Art Dir* Wolf Kroeger

● Liv Ullmann, Kiefer Sutherland, Alan Scarfe, Mathieu Carriere, Peter Donat, Isabelle Mejias (ICC)

Canadian-born director Daniel Petrie had long cherished making a film about his early days in Nova Scotia. *Bay Boy* is the realization of that dream, but it's far from the pot of gold at the end of his rainbow.

Setting is a coastal mining community circa 1937. Principals are a family of non-miners barely eking out an existence during the Depression. Kiefer Sutherland has the pivotal part of Donald Campbell, a teenager whose family envision his future with the clergy. He's more dubious about this path.

The family travails – father's precarious fortunes, brother's debilitating disease, mother's profound religious guilt, etc – are cut with humorous vignettes and insights. However, Donald witnesses the murder of an old Jewish couple by a local policeman.

●●●●●●●●●●●●●●●●●●●●●●●●●●●●

■ BEACHES

1988, 123 MINS, US ◇ ⓥ ⊙

Dir Garry Marshall *Prod* Bonnie Bruckheimer-Martell, Bettle Midler, Margaret Jennings South, *Scr* Mary Agnes Donoghue *Ph* Dante Spinotti *Ed* Richard Halsey *Mus* Georges Delerue *Art Dir* Albert Brenner

● Bette Midler, Barbara Hershey, John Heard, Spalding Gray, Lainie Kazan, James Read (Touchstone/Silver Screen Partners IV/South-All Girl)

Story of this engaging tearjerker [from the novel by Iris Rainer Dart] is one of a profound friendship, from childhood to beyond the grave, between two wildly mismatched women, a lower-class Jew (Bette Midler) from the Bronx whose every breath is showbiz, and a San Francisco blueblood (Barbara Hershey) destined for a pampered but troubled life. Men, marriages and career vicissitudes come and go, but their bond ultimately cuts through it all.

Midler's strutting, egotistical, self-aware character gets off any number of zingers, but all in the context of a vulnerable woman who seems to accept, finally, that certain things in life, notably happiness in romance and family are probably unreachable for her.

By way of contrast, Hershey plays her more emotionally untouchable part with an almost severe gravity. Hillary seems to have no real center, which in Hershey's interpretation could be part of the point, as nothing really works out for this woman who has everything, looks, intelligence, money – going for her.
□ 1988: Nomination: Best Art Direction

● ●

■ **BEACH PARTY**

1963, 104 MINS, US ◇ ⊛
Dir William Asher *Prod* James H. Nicholson, Lou Rusoff *Scr* Lou Rusoff *Ph* Kay Norton *Ed* Homer Powell *Mus* Les Baxter
● Robert Cummings, Dorothy Malone, Frankie Avalon, Annette Funicello, Harvey Lembeck, Jody McCrea (American International)

Beach Party is a bouncy bit of lightweight fluff, attractively cast, beautifully set (Malibu Beach), and scored throughout with a big twist beat. It has a kind of direct, simple-minded cheeriness.

The comparatively elderly Robert Cumming toplines the cast (with Dorothy Malone) and provides the picture with what real comic substance it has. Plot is pegged on a study of teenage sex habits undertaken by anthropologist Cummings on the beach at Malibu.

As the square professor, Cummings shows himself to be an able farceur and notably at ease in surroundings which might embarrass a less professional star. Malone is along just for the ride in a small role as the prof's long-suffering secretary. It's a waste of her talent.

What plot complications there are centre around the romantic problems of a group of young surfers, principally Frankie Avalon and Annette Funicello, each of whom undertakes a campaign to make the other jealous – he with buxom Eva Six, she with the erudite professor. Story is padded out with some lovely surf-riding sequences and a whole string of Les Baxter songs.

● ●

■ **BEACH RED**

1967, 105 MINS, US ◇
Dir Cornel Wilde *Prod* Cornel Wilde *Scr* Clint Johnston, Donald A. Peters, Jefferson Pascal *Ph* Cecil R. Cooney *Ed* Frank P. Keller *Mus* Elbey Vid, Antonio Buenaventura *Art Dir* Francisco Balangue
● Cornel Wilde, Rip Torn, Burr DeBenning, Patrick Wolfe, Jean Wallace, Jaime Sanchez (United Artists)

In contrast to many professedly anti-war films, *Beach Red* is indisputably sincere in its war is hell message. Except for brief reveries of civilian life, the film focuses entirely on a single dreary campaign by an American unit out to take a Japanese-held island in the Pacific.

Notably absent are the usual stereotypes: the tough-talking sarge with the heart of gold, the frightened kid who becomes a man in combat, etc. The trouble with the screenplay, adapted from Peter Bowman's 1945 novel, is that little is substituted for these wisely-avoided cliches. The central characters

are spokesmen for differing points of view, not real, full-bodied people. The acting quality suffers as a result.

The captain (Cornel Wilde) loves his wife and hates war. The sergeant (Rip Torn) derives sadistic pleasure from the war. An 18-year-old minister's son (Patrick Wolfe) remembers his girl back home and inarticulately echoes the captain's pacificism. His Southern sidekick (Burr DeBenning) is a hearty illiterate for whom the armed forces is a haven.
□ 1967: Nomination: Best Editing

● ●

■ **BEAST, THE**

1988, 109 MINS, US ◇ ⊛
Dir Kevin Reynolds *Prod* John Fiedler *Scr* William Mastrosimone *Ph* Douglas Milsome *Ed* Peter Boyle *Mus* Mark Isham *Art Dir* Kuli Sander
● George Dzundza, Jason Patric, Steven Bauer, Stephen Baldwin, Don Harvey, Kabir Bedi (A & M)

A harrowing, tightly focused war film that becomes a moving, near-Biblical allegory, *The Beast* represents a stellar achievement for all involved. Based on William Mastrosimone's play *Nanawatai*, pic explores a single fictional incident set in 1981, the second year of the Russian occupation of Afghanistan.

A Russian tank gets trapped in a no-exit valley after its brutal decimation of a nearby Afghan village, and the surviving villagers, who've discovered a weapon capable of destroying a tank, decide to track it down for revenge.

'The Beast' is the tank, a formidably efficient war machine that becomes the center of the pic. Among its crew are Daskal (George Dzundza), a vicious, paranoid commander capable of killing his own crewmen, and Koverchenko (Jason Patric), a conscience-stricken former philosophy student. The Afghans, who see the war in religious terms, include a young man (Steven Bauer) struggling to attain a leadership role.

Performances, many of them repeated from the stage version, are remarkably evocative, particularly from the Afghans, who speak in subtitled dialect (the Russians speak English). Patric gives a resonant portrayal of the questioning Russian.

From pic's harrowing opening scene to its beautiful, meditative final stroke, director Kevin Reynolds (*Fandango*) displays remarkably mature and effective storytelling skills. Photography of Israeli desert locales is striking.

● ●

■ **BEAST FROM 20,000 FATHOMS, THE**

1953, 80 MINS, US ⊛ ⊙
Dir Eugene Lourie *Prod* Hal Chester, Jack Dietz *Scr* Lou Morheim, Fred Freiberger *Ph* Jack Russell *Ed* Bernard W. Burton *Mus* David Buttolph *Art Dir* [uncredited]
● Paul Christian, Paula Raymond, Cecil Kellaway, Kenneth Tobey, Donald Woods, Lee Van Cleef (Warner)

Producers have created a prehistoric monster that makes Kong seem like a chimpanzee. It's a gigantic amphibious beast that towers above some of New York's highest buildings. The sight of the beast stalking through Gotham's downtown streets is awesome. Special credit should go to Ray Harryhausen for the socko technical effects.

An experimental atomic blast in the Arctic region results in the 'unfreezing' of the strange prehistoric reptile of the dinosaur family. Scientist Tom Nesbitt (Paul Christian) report of the beast is attributed to hallucination resulting from Arctic exposure.

After several unsuccessful atttempts, Nesbitt enlists the aid of Prof Thurgood Elson (Cecil Kellaway) and his pretty assistant Lee Hunter (Paula Raymond). Elson is killed by the monster while exploring an undersea canyon in a diving bell 150 miles from New

York. The beast finally turns up in Manhattan.

Christian is firstrate as the determined scientist and Kellaway scores as the doubting professor. Raymond appears too stiff and unconvincing as the professor's assistant and Christian's romantic vis-a-vis. Screenplay [suggested by the *Saturday Evening Post* story *The Fog Horn* by Ray Bradbury] has a documentary flavor, whic Jack Russell's camera captures expertly.

● ●

■ **BEASTMASTER, THE**

1982, 118 MINS, US ◇ ⊛ ⊙
Dir Don Coscarelli *Prod* Paul Pepperman, Sylvio Tabet *Scr* Don Coscarelli, Paul Pepperman *Ph* John Alcott *Ed* Roy Watts *Mus* Lee Holdridge *Art Dir* Conrad E. Angone
● Marc Singer, Tanya Roberts, Rip Torn, John Amos, Josh Milrad, Rod Loomis (M-G-M/United Artists)

When *The Beastmaster* begins, it is very hard to tell what it is all about. An hour later, it is very hard to care what it is all about. Another hour later, it is very hard to remember what it was all about. From the early confusion, in which it seems that a cow gives birth to a baby boy, Marc Singer emerges as Dar.

Singer's destiny is to go after the villains led by Rip Torn to revenge the destruction of the village. Along the way he teams up with two ferrets, an eagle, a panther, Tanya Roberts and John Amos and other assorted creatures of equal acting ability. Much of the time they are involved in rescuing each other from rather non-interesting situations [adapted from Andre Norton's novel].

● ●

■ **BEASTMASTER 2**
THROUGH THE PORTAL OF TIME

1991, 107 MINS, US ◇ ⊛ ⊙
Dir Sylvio Tabet *Prod* Sylvio Tabet *Scr* R.J. Robertson, Jim Wynorski, Sylvio Tabet, Ken Hauser, Doug Miles *Ph* Ronn Schmidt *Ed* Adam Bernardi *Mus* Robert Folk *Art Dir* Allen Jones
● Marc Singer, Kari Wuhrer, Wings Hauser, Sarah Douglas, Charles Young (Republic/Films 21)

Despite this low-budget sequel's silly dialog and cheesy special effects, *Beastmaster 2* is a mildly engaging tongue-in-cheek fantasy about mythical characters traveling through a time warp to battle it out in the mean streets of contempo LA. Like its 1982 predecessor, pic should do well on homevid following a modest theatrical run.

Blond, lithely muscular Marc Singer returns in his loinclothed title role as a sort of violent St. Francis figure accompanied by a tiger, an eagle and two ferrets who help him out of scrapes with the evil rulers of his desert abode. Singer maintains a winning simplicity despite all the sword-and-sorcery hokum.

The dandy bad guy is laser-wielding Wings Hauser who turns out to be Singer's long-lost brother, and a half-human creature (John Fifer) gives Singer the unpleasant task of saving the land from destruction by committing fratricide.

Goofball script is rife with contemporary slang, even in the mythical kingdom. Hauser's voluptuous witch-companion (Sarah Douglas) has visited LA through the time warp. Ronn Schmidt's lensing is suitably noirish.

● ●

■ **BEAST WITH FIVE FINGERS, THE**

1946, 90 MINS, US ⊛
Dir Robert Florey *Prod* William Jacobs *Scr* Curt Siodmak *Ph* Wesley Anderson *Ed* Frank Magee *Mus* Max Steiner *Art Dir* Stanley Fleischer
● Robert Alda, Andrea King, Peter Lorre, Victor Francen (Warner)

The Beast with Five Fingers is a weird, Grand Guignol-ish conconction that puts the

B

customers strictly on their own. Till the last gasp, when J. Carrol Naish winks into the lens and gives out with a crack that 'it could happen', it gives more credit for intelligence than the average thriller.

Victor Francen, as a semi-invalid concert pianist, lives in a gloomy villa in northern Italy. His companions are his secretary, Peter Lorre; his nurse, Andrea King; a composer friend, Robert Alda, and his attorney, David Hoffman.

A good deal of the plot is projected through Lorre's eyes, without any explanation of the switches from straight narration to scenes registered by Lorre's deranged mind. Best and most gruesome parts of the picture are when Lorre is alone with his vivid imagination. He chases a ghoulish hand around the library several times, catching it finally and hammering it down in a bloodcurdling scene reminiscent in mood of *The Cabinet of Dr Caligari*. Stil it pursues him, escaping at last from the burning coals into which he has thrown it.

. . . .

■ BEAST WITHIN, THE

1982, 90 MINS, US ◇ ▣
Dir Philippe Mora *Prod* Harvey Bernhard, Gabriel Katzka *Scr* Tom Holland *Ph* Jack L. Richards *Ed* Robert Brown, Bert Lovitt *Mus* Les Baxter *Art Dir* David M. Haber
● Ronny Cox, Bibi Besch, Paul Clemens, Don Gordon, R.G. Armstrong, Kitty Moffat (M-G-M/United Artists)

Honeymooning, Ronny Cox and Bibi Besch get their car stuck in the woods and while he goes for help, she gets raped by something with hairy legs. Fastforward 17 years to find them parents of that most dreaded of monsters – a teenager. [Film is based on the novel by Edward Levy.]

The teenager (Paul Clemens) is bad sick, and reluctantly Mom and Dad go back to the Mississippi town where she was raped to see if there could be any connection between his illness and the hairy legs. Feeling better young Clemens follows and starts to chomp people.

There does come a time when Clemens has to get out of his body and get on with being a bigtime monster. Thanks to Thomas R. Burman's make-up effects, this sequence actually creates chills as the boy's head bubbles and bursts and his skin pops and stretches.

. . . .

■ BEAT THE DEVIL

1953, 100 MINS, UK/ITALY ▣ ⊙
Dir John Huston *Scr* John Huston, Anthony Veiller, Peter Viertel, Truman Capote *Ph* Oswald Morris *Ed* Ralph Kemplen *Mus* Franco Mannino *Art Dir* Wilfrid Shingleton
● Humphrey Bogart, Jennifer Jones, Gina Lollobrigida, Robert Morley, Peter Lorre, Edward Underdown (Romulus/Santana)

In an easy sort of way, the story [from a novel by James Helvick] describes the adventures of a bunch of uranium exploiteers who want to get hold of some valuable land in Africa. While they're waiting for a passage from Italy, their go-between (Humphrey Bogart) becomes involved with a young couple, played by Jennifer Jones and Edward Underdown. The way in which they get done out of their property, and the potential millions that go with it, provides the background for all the action.

All the exteriors were lensed on location in Italy, with fine matching work at Shepperton Studios. There are carefully timed laughs in the script as well as intended comedy situations that misfire. The best gag is derived from Bogart's interview with an Arab bigwig who provides a slow boat to Africa in exchange for a promised introduction to Rita Hayworth.

Under John Huston's stylish direction a fine acting standard is maintained by a front-

ranking cast. Bogart's virile performance is handsomely matched by Jones' pert and vivacious study of the wife of the Englishman who pretends to status and riches which neither has enjoyed.

Gina Lollobrigida gives a provocative portrayal as Bogart's wife while Edward Underdown stands out the Englishman.

. . . .

■ BEAU BRUMMELL

1924, 120 MINS, US ⊗ ▣
Dir Harry Beaumont *Scr* Dorothy Farnum *Ph* David Abel
● John Barrymore, Mary Astor, Willard Louis, Irene Rich, Alec B. Francis, Carmel Myers (Warner)

This has John Barrymore at the head of a cast that holds some strong picture names. The direction is not what it might have been, and the casting is also somewhat faulty. Irene Rich as the Duchess of York would have undoubtedly made a much better Lady Margery than Mary Astor, who played it. Although Astor is seen to advantage from the standpoint of beauty, she does not display any great histrionic ability.

Willard Louis as George, Prince of Wales, is one of the real outstanding figures. He walks away with practically every scene in which he appears.

Carmel Myers as a vamp is a modern vamp rather than one of the period in which the action is laid. Alec B. Francis as the servant to Beau Brummell makes a work of art of his role.

As to Barrymore, there are flashes in his characterization of the London dandy that are inspired, and there are other moments when he does not seem to get over at all.

. . . .

■ BEAU GESTE

1926, 129 MINS, US ⊗
Dir Herbert Brenon *Scr* Paul Schofield, John Russell, Herbert Brenon *Ph* J. Roy Hunt *Art Dir* Julian Boone Fleming
● Ronald Colman, Neil Hamilton, Ralph Forbes, Alice Joyce, Mary Brian, Noah Beery (Paramount)

Beau Geste is a 'man's' picture. The story revolves around three brothers and their love for each other. And a great looking trio – Ronald Colman, Neil Hamilton and Ralph Forbes. Beyond that the love interest is strictly secondary, practically nil.

The picture is all story. In fact, only one cast member seems to get above the scenario. This is Noah Beery as the bestial sergeant-major. A part that only comes along every so often, and Beery gives it the same prominence in which P.C. Wren, the author, conceived it. It's undoubtedly one of his best portrayals.

When all is said and done, Colman, in the title role, hasn't so very much to do. Hamilton equals him for footage and Forbes exceeds him. Forbes, in his first picture, impresses all the way. Hamilton also gives a sincere performance. But there can be no question that Beery is the outstanding figure of the picture.

. . . .

■ BEAU GESTE

1939, 114 MINS, US ▣ ⊙
Dir William A. Wellman *Prod* William A. Wellman *Scr* Robert Carson *Ph* Theodor Sparkuhl, Archie Stout *Ed* Thomas Scott *Mus* Alfred Newman *Art Dir* Hans Dreier, Robert Odell
● Gary Cooper, Ray Milland, Robert Preston, Brian Donlevy, Susan Hayward, J. Carrol Naish (Paramount)

Beau Geste has been produced with vigorous realism and spectacular sweep. Director William Wellman has focused attention on the melodramatic and vividly gruesome aspects of the story, and skimmed lightly over

the episodes and motivation which highlighted Percival Christopher Wren's original novel.

Beau employs the flashback method in unfolding the adventures of three Geste brothers in the Foreign Legion. Audience interest is gained at the start with presentation of the mystery of the desert fort with relief patrol finding the entire garrison dead and dead soldiers propped up for battle in the parapets. Confused by the weirdness of the situation, the head of the patrol pitches camp in the nearby oasis. Suddenly the fort is enveloped in flames and destroyed.

Gary Cooper is okay in the title spot. Ray Milland and Robert Preston work hard and competently to get over their respective characterizations. Trio are overshadowed, however, by the vivid Brian Donlevy as the savagely brutal sergeant of the Legion.
☐ 1939: Nominations: Best Supp. Actor (Brian Donlevy), Art Direction

. . . .

■ BEAU GESTE

1966, 105 MINS, US ◇ ▣
Dir Douglas Heyes *Prod* Walter Seltzer *Scr* Douglas Heyes *Ph* Bud Thackery *Ed* Russell F. Schoengarth *Mus* Hans J. Salter *Art Dir* Alexander Golitzen, Henry Bumstead
● Guy Stockwell, Doug McClure, Leslie Nielsen, Telly Savalas, David Mauro, Robert Wolders (Universal)

Third time out for one of the most memorable silent films still packs hardy entertainment. The production is an expertly-made translation of Percival Christopher Wren's novel of the French Foreign Legion in a lonely Sahara outpost, distinguished by good acting, fine photographic values and fast direction. Guy Stockwell delineates the title role.

Plot has been slightly changed. Beau and his brother, John, are now Americans instead of English, and the third brother, Digby, has been eliminated. While still a story of brother love under fire, this facet has been somewhat subordinated for a script focusing on the savagery of the sergeant, a dominant point previously but accentuated even more in this version. Basic storyline has been little altered, Beau having joined the Legion after shouldering the blame for a crime he did not commit to save another from disgrace.

Topnotch performances are contributed right down the line. Stockwell handles himself creditably and convincingly.

. . . .

■ BEAUTIFUL BLONDE FROM BASHFUL BEND, THE

1949, 76 MINS, US ◇ ▣
Dir Preston Sturges *Prod* Preston Sturges *Scr* Preston Sturges *Ph* Harry Jackson *Ed* Robert Fritch *Mus* Cyril Mockridge *Art Dir* Lyle Wheeler, George W. Davis
● Betty Grable, Cesar Romero, Rudy Vallee, Olga San Juan, Sterling Holloway, Hugh Herbert (20th Century-Fox)

Blonde is basically a rather silly western farce, loosely concocted. Producer-director-writer Preston Sturges plays his script [based on a story by Earl Felton] with frantic slapstick, stressing raw, bawdy comedy rather than genuine humor, to get the laughs. The pacing is erratic, as is the film editing.

Betty Grable is the chief asset as a western dancehall gal who knows how to handle a gun – and gets into trouble because of it. The boy friend is Cesar Romero. It's the latter that starts the trouble. Grable is out to kill him for two-timing but, in a dark room, shoots a judge in the posterior by mistake.

Cast goes about its business okay in answering Sturges' demands for burlesquing of the characters and occasionall makes the coarse humor pay off.

. . . .

■ BEAUTIFUL DREAMERS

1990, 105 MINS, CANADA ◇ ▽
Dir John Kent Harrison   *Prod* Michael Maclear, Martin Walters   *Scr* John Kent Harrison   *Ph* Francois Protat
Ed Ron Wisman   *Mus* Laurence Shragge
Art Dir Seamus Flannery
● Colm Feore, Rip Torn, Wendel Meldrum, Sheila McCarthy, Colin Fox (Cinexus/Famous Players)

A first pic by John Dent Harrison, *Beautiful Dreamers* is full of good intentions, but only some of them are realized. Pic centers on free-thinker Walt Whitman's actual visit to London, Ontario, in 1880, bringing fresh winds to the city's ment asylum and churning up most of the church and civic elite.

Much is made of the friendship between the older, white-bearded Whitman and the asylum's young superintendent, forcefully played by Canadian actor Colm Feore, who resists then traditionally harsh methods of treating the mentally ill.

Rip Torn plays Whitman large as a legend rather than on a human scale, but his grand actorly characterization bores quickly. Standout is Wendel Meldrum, a radiant beauty with classy acting skills to boot, who as the superintendent's wife is jealous of the time her husband spends with Whitman. Sheila McCarthy makes a powerful wordless cameo appearance as a married patient driven to the point of mad despair by overwork.

....

■ BEAUTY AND THE BEAST

1991, 85 MINS, US ◇ ▽
Dir Gary Trousdale, Kirk Wise   *Prod* Don Hahn
Scr Linda Woolverton   *Ed* John Carnochan   *Mus* Alan Menken   *Art Dir* Brian McEntee (Walt Disney)

A lovely film that ranks with the best of Disney's animated classics, *Beauty and the Beast* is a tale freshly retold. Darker-hued than the usual animated feature, with a predominant brownish-gray color scheme balanced by Belle's blue dress and radiant features, *Beauty* [from the classic French fairy tale] engages the emotions with an unabashed sincerity that manages to avoid the pitfalls of triteness and corn.

The character of Belle, magnificently voiced by Paige O'Hara, is a brainy young woman scorned as a bookworm by her townsfolk and kidnaped by the Beast. She finds her initial aversion overcome by a growing appreciation of his inner beauty and sensitivity. While the usually soft-spoken Robby Benson might seem an odd choice for the voice of the Beast, his booming bass voice in the early sections and the increasingly boyish timbre of his voice in the later parts perfectly capture the character's complexity.

Howard Ashman and Alan Menken's songs are witty, charming, richly orchestrated and smoothly integrated into the plot. The first-rate animation staff bring a strikingly three-dimensional look to the film, augmented in some spots by Jim Hillin's state-of-the-art computer graphics images.
□ 1991: Best Song ('Beauty and the Beast'), Original Score.
□ Nominations: Best Picture, Song ('Belle', 'Be Our Guest'), Sound

....

■ BEAUTY JUNGLE, THE

(US: (US: Contest Girl))

1964, 114 MINS, UK ◇
Dir Val Guest   *Prod* Val Guest   *Scr* Robert Muller, Val Guest   *Ph* Arthur Grant   *Ed* Bill Lenny   *Mus* Laurie Johnson   *Art Dir* Maurice Carter
● Ian Hendry, Janette Scott, Ronald Fraser, Edmund Purdom, Tommy Trinder, Francis Matthews (Rank)

There's some lively, if not over subtle, comedy in this yarn of a girl who gains quick rewards as a beauty queen, but finds the going full of disillusionment and pitfalls.

Screenplay tends to soft pedal the problems involved and the writers (Val Guest and an observant journalist-author Robert Muller, who studied the beauty queen scene) seem reluctant to come out with their views on whether such contests are degrading or even dangerous to comely damsels who take them too seriously, or whether they are just a harmless giggle.

Story concerns a pretty stenographer (Janette Scott) who is joshed by a local newspaper columnist into entering a seaside pier contest. She wins and he takes over and builds her up into a regular contestant at such junkets who progresses steadily around the familiar circuit and gets into the big time league of big money, overblown publicity, commercialism and spurious glitter that's the magnet.

Ian Hendry, as the poor man's Svengali, is brisk and credible while Ronald Fraser, as his lenser buddy, also turns in a ripe performance.

....

■ BECKET

1964, 148 MINS, US ◇ ▽ ⊙
Dir Peter Glenville   *Prod* Hal Wallis   *Scr* Edward Anhalt   *Ph* Geoffrey Unsworth   *Ed* Anne V. Coates
Mus Laurence Rosenthal   *Art Dir* John Bryan, Maurice Carter
● Richard Burton, Peter O'Toole, John Gielgud, Donald Wolfit, Martita Hunt, Pamela Brown (Paramount)

Made in Shepperton Studios in the UK, this is a very fine, perhaps great, motion picture. It is costume drama but not routine, invigorated by story substance, personality clash, bright dialog and religious interest. Not least among its virtues is the pace of the narrative in the astute handing of Peter Glenville, with his advantage of having also mounted the stage play from which the film is derived.

The screenplay owes much to Jean Anouilh's orginal stage script. The modern psychology of Anouilh lends fascination to these 12th century shenanigans by investing them with special motivational insights rare in costume drama. The basic story is, of course, historic, the murder on 29 December 1170 in the cathedral of Canterbury of its archbishop, Becket, by barons from the entourage of Henry II, greatgrandson of William the Conqueror. For fictional purposes, Becket and the King had been old roustabouts together, much as, later in English history, Henry V and Falstaff were.

In the title role, Richard Burton gives a generally convincing and resourceful performance. The transition from the cold, calculating Saxon courtier of a Norman king into a duty-obsessed sincere churchman is not easily managed. Burton does manage.

As Henry II, Peter O'Toole emerges as the fatter role, and the more colorful. The king is an unhappy monarch who has known little affection in life. His only satisfying companionship has been provided by the Saxon Becket. Hating-loving, miserably lonely when deserted by his friend, O'Toole makes of the king a tormented, many-sided baffled, believable human being.
□ 1964: Best Adapted Screenplay.
□ Nominations: Best Picture, Director, Actor (Richard Burton, Peter O'Toole), Supp. Actor (John Gielgud), Color Cinematography, Color Costume Design, Color Art Direction, Editing, Original Music Score, Sound

....

■ BECKY SHARP

1935, 84 MINS, US ◇ ▽
Dir Rouben Mamoulian   *Prod* Kenneth Macgowan
Scr Francis Edward Faragoh   *Ph* Ray Rennahan
Ed Archie Marshek   *Mus* Roy Webb   *Art Dir* Robert Edmond Jones, Wiard B. Ihnen
● Miriam Hopkins, Cedric Hardwicke, Nigel Bruce, Frances Dee, Alan Mowbray, G.P. Huntley Jr (Pioneer/RKO)

The first full-length talker in highly improved Technicolor, cinematographically it's a tribute to the new process and to Robert Edmond Jones' beautiful splashes of multi-tone visual values. The pastel shades of the interior properties, the faithfu reproduction even of the femmes' makeup, the gay carnival splashes of color such as that in the Brussels waltz-quadrille scene (climaxed by Napoleon's Waterloo return) impress optically, but the story falls flat dramatically and the dialog is likewise fraught with too much discordant stridency of tone.

Miriam Hopkins at times fairly shrieks her way through the footage [based on Thackeray's *Vanity Fair* and the play by Langdon Mitchell]. She's basically handicapped by a negative characterization. As the calculating Becky, her role of a temptress is neither lurid nor winsome. It's a wishy-washy compromise of a gamin who annexes a sextet of masculine conquests, with the character not sufficiently definite to impress her as a great siren.

With the exceptions of G.P. Huntley Jr, Nigel Bruce and Cedric Hardwicke, none of the support is particularly distinguished nor has it much opportunity for distinction.
□ 1935: Nomination: Best Actress (Miriam Hopkins)

....

■ BECOMING COLETTE

1992, 97 MINS, US/GERMANY ◇ ▽ ⊙
Dir Danny Huston   *Prod* Heinz J. Bibo, Peer J. Oppenheimer   *Scr* Ruth Graham, Burt Weinshanker
Ph Wolfgang Treu   *Ed* Peter Taylor, Roberto Silvi
Mus John Scott   *Art Dir* Jan Schlubach, Serge Douy
● Klaus Maria Brandauer, Mathilda May, Virginia Madsen, Paul Rhys, John van Dreelan, Jean Pierre Aumont (Bibo/BC/Arianes)

Not even Klaus Maria Brandauer's twinkly eyed, scene-stealing turn is enough to enliven *Becoming Colette*, a lumbering period drama based on the early life of novelist Sidonie Gabrielle Colette. Danny Huston's sophomore feature (after *Mr. North*) is lovely to look at but dramatically inert.

Episodic script is structured as an extended flashback, with Colette (Mathilda May) recalling her salad days after spotting her ex-husband (Brandauer) in the audience during one of her avant-garde theater performances.

Back in a small French town in the early 1890s, her financially pressed father allowed her marriage to Henri Gauthier-Villars, a rakish publisher who swept her away to Paris. Until she split from him in 1904, he forced her to write erotic novels published under her pseudonym. She began writing as Colette in 1916.

Playing like a truncated feature version of an epic miniseries, pic sporadically spices up its rote recapitulation of facts with the sort of high-gloss, softcore steaminess that used to be Radley Metzger's stock-in-trade. A nude love scene with Colette and a music-hall performer (Virginia Madsen, the director's wife) suddenly becomes three-part harmony when Brandauer joins in.

Pic was handsomely lensed in Berlin (mostly interiors at CCC Studios) and Bordeaux. Unfortunately, the scenes set in the famed Moulin Rouge only serve to remind audiences of a much better pic by the director's father.

....

■ BED & BREAKFAST

1992, 98 MINS, US ◇ ▽ ⊙
Dir Robert Ellis Miller   *Prod* Jack Schwartzman
Scr Cindy Myers   *Ph* Peter Sova   *Ed* John F. Burnett
Mus David Shire   *Art Dir* Suzanne Cavedon
● Roger Moore, Talia Shire, Colleen Dewhurst, Nina Siemaszko, Ford Rainey, Jamie Walters (Hemdale)

Set on the breathtaking coast of Maine, *Bed & Breakfast* is an old-fashioned family melodrama about a charming stranger who descends on a household of squabbling women.

Claire (Talia Shire), the young widow of a Kennedy-like senator, runs bed-and-breakfast owned by Ruth, her feisty mother-in-law (Colleen Dewhurst). The generational rift between the anxiety-ridden, repressed Shire and her rebellious adolescent daughter (Nina Siemaszko) occupies most of the narrative.

The depressingly stagnant tribe begins to change when the body of a mysterious stranger (Roger Moore), a con man pretending to have amnesia, washes ashore. Naming him Adam, the women hire him as a handyman.

The film's conflicts are usually staged a confrontations between two characters. It could have been fun to watch the always tanned and glamorous Moore in the midst of three bickering women, all attracted to him. But the film uses melodramatically conceived characters and situations.

Helmer Robert Ellis Miller, director of the deliciously bright comedy *Reuben, Reuben*, has not done himself proud here. He handles the film gently, showing too much respect for the slight material. Still, this is the kind of small, intimate picture actors relish.

....

■ BEDAZZLED

1967, 104 MINS, UK ◇ ⑰ ⊙
Dir Stanley Donen   *Prod* Stanley Donen   *Scr* Peter Cook, Dudley Moore   *Ph* Austin Dempster   *Ed* Richard Marden   *Mus* Dudley Moore   *Art Dir* Terence Knight
● Peter Cook, Dudley Moore, Eleanor Bron, Raquel Welch, Robert Russell, Barry Humphries (20th Century-Fox)

Bedazzled is smartly-styled and typical of certain types of high British comedy. It's a fantasy of a London short-order cook madly in love with a waitress, who is offered seven wishes by the Devil in return for his soul.

Stanley Donen production is pretty much the work of two of its three stars, Peter Cook and Dudley Moore. Pair scripted from Cook's original story, and Moore also composed music score. Eleanor Bron is third star, plus Raquel Welch, whose brief appearance is equalled only by her scant attire.

Mephistophelean overtones are inserted in this modern-day Faust legend tacked onto Moore, who would give his soul to possess Margaret, the waitress (Bron). Cook (Mephistopheles), parading under the mundane name of George Spiggot, appears mysteriously in Moore's flat as he flubs a suicide attempt and grants all of the cook's wishes.

....

■ BEDFORD INCIDENT, THE

1965, 102 MINS, US ◇ ⑰
Dir James B. Harris   *Prod* James B. Harris, Richard Widmark   *Scr* James Poe   *Ph* Gilbert Taylor   *Ed* John Jympson   *Mus* Gerard Schurmann   *Art Dir* Arthur Lawson, Lionel Couch
● Richard Widmark, Sidney Poitier, James MacArthur, Martin Balsam, Wally Cox, Eric Portman (Bedford/Columbia)

The Bedford Incident is an excellent contemporary sea drama based on a little-known but day-to-day reality of the Cold War, the monitoring of Russian submarine activity by US Navy destroyers. The production, made at England's Shepperton Studios, has salty scripting and solid performances, including one of the finest in Widmark's career.

James Poe's adaptation of the Mark Rascovich novel depicts the 'hunt-to-exhaustion' tactic in anti-submarine warfare, whereby a sub contact is pursued until one side or the other either gives up or eludes.

Widmark stars as the skipper of the USS *Bedford*, a modern destroyer, equipped with tactical nuclear weapons, on patrol in the North Atlantic. Widmark's skipper is that

rare breed whom the crew not only follows, but worships. The character of this sea dog is drawn out by the helicopter arrival of Sidney Poitier, as a wise-guy magazine writer, and Martin Balsam, a Reserve medic back on active duty.

Poitier does an excellent job in both the light and serious aspects of his role, and manages to leave a personal stamp on his scenes.

....

■ BEDKNOBS AND BROOMSTICKS

1971, 117 MINS, US ◇ ⑰ ⊙
Dir Robert Stevenson   *Prod* Bill Walsh   *Scr* Bill Walsh, Don DaGradi   *Ph* Frank Phillips   *Ed* Cotton Warburton   *Mus* Irwin Kostal (sup.)   *Art Dir* John B. Mansbridge, Peter Ellenshaw
● Angela Lansbury, David Tomlinson, Roddy McDowall, Sam Jaffe, John Ericson, Bruce Forsyth (Walt Disney)

The magic of Walt Disney lingers magnificently on in *Bedknobs and Broomsticks*.

The setting is a quaint olde-worlde English seaside village during the earlier days of World War II. Three Cockney kids (Roy Snart, Ian Weighill and Cindy O'Callaghan) are evacuated there and are as appalled by the dullness of it all as they are with the eccentricities and rules of Angela Lansbury with whom they are billetted. Then they discover she is studying witchcraft by correspondence course with the idea of using it against the Germans should they invade. Life takes on a rosier hue. They learn to perform all sorts of magic, fly to London on a bedstead and spend a joyous time in the never-never land [songs by Richard M. and Robert B. Sherman].

It is when the film [based on the book by Mary Norton] dives deeply into the realms of fantasy that it is most enjoyable. The trip with the principals on the bedstead through the underwater kingdom of the fishes and animated football match between jungle animals with a superimposed David Tomlinson refereeing are not only sheer delights but technical masterpieces.

☐ 1971: Best Special Visual Effects.
☐ Nominations: Best Costume Design, Art Direction, Original Song Score, Song ('The Age of Not Believing')

....

■ BEDROOM WINDOW, THE

1986, 112 MINS, US ◇ ⑰ ⊙
Dir Curtis Hanson   *Prod* Martha Schumacher
Scr Curtis Hanson   *Ph* Gil Taylor   *Ed* Scott Conrad   *Mus* Michael Shrieve, Patrick Gleeson   *Art Dir* Ron Foreman
● Steve Guttenberg, Elizabeth McGovern, Isabelle Huppert, Paul Shenar, Wallace Shawn, Carl Lumbly (De Laurentiis)

Cast against type, Steve Guttenberg plays a malleable young executive carrying on an affair with his boss' wife, the sexy Sylvia (Isabelle Huppert). During a tryst at Guttenberg's apartment one night after a party, Huppert, looking out his bedroom window, sees a girl (Elizabeth McGovern) being assaulted outside.

Guttenberg ultimately becomes a suspect in the rash of rape and murder cases, forcing him in the Hitchcock tradition to begin his own investigation in trying to prove who the real killer is.

Curtis Hanson's screenplay [from the novel *The Witnesses* by Anne Holden] involves several ingenious plot twists. Huppert carries the first half of the film, replaced by McGovern in importance in the final reels and both actresses are alluring and mysterious in keeping the piece suspenseful. Unfortunately, a lot of coincidences and just plain stupid actions by Guttenberg are relied upon to keep the pot boiling.

....

■ BED SITTING ROOM, THE

1970, 90 MINS, UK ◇ ⑰
Dir Richard Lester   *Prod* Oscar Lewenstein, Richard Lester   *Scr* John Antrobus, Charles Wood   *Ph* David Watkin   *Ed* John Victor Smith   *Mus* Ken Thorne   *Art Dir* Assheton Gordon
● Rita Tushingham, Ralph Richardson, Peter Cook, Dudley Moore, Spike Milligan, Michael Hordern (United Artists)

A play by Spike Milligan and John Antrobus serves as an ideal springboard for an offbeat anti-war film by Richard Lester which, miraculously, manages to convey its grim message with humor.

Sketch-like pic catches glimpses and comments of the 20-odd survivors of a London shredded by an A-bomb as they dig out of their holes to try and cope with the grey new world before they, too, become animals.

In the manner of vaude blackouts, they soon meld into a general mosaic of stiff-upper-lip acceptance of new conditions, some fizzlers but others very amusing.

Ralph Richardson is superb in a relatively brief stint as the diehard traditionalist who eventually 'becomes' the title's bed-sitting room, but all in a carefully-chosen roster of British character thesps who contribute stellar bits in almost impossibly difficult roles.

....

■ BEDTIME STORY

1941, 83 MINS, US
Dir Alexander Hall   *Prod* B.P. Schulberg   *Scr* Richard Flournoy   *Ph* Joseph Walker   *Ed* Viola Lawrence   *Mus* Werner Heymann   *Art Dir* Lionel Banks, Cary Odell
● Fredric March, Loretta Young, Robert Benchley, Allyn Joslyn, Eve Arden, Helen Westley (Columbia)

Picture is a combo of slick scripting, fast-paced direction and excellent performances. Richard Flournoy provides plenty of laugh embellishment to the original story by Horace Jackson and Grant Garrett; director Alexander Hall keeps his foot on the speed throttle from start to finish; and Fredric March teams with Loretta Young for a pair of topnotch performances in the starring spots.

Despite the light and fluffy tale unreeled, maximum entertainment is provided in the breezy exposition of the marital problems of producer-playwright March and his star-wife Young. After seven years of marriage and struggle, pair are top successes in their respective endeavors.

The wife desires to retire to their farm in Connecticut, while the energetic March hatches a new play in which he wants Young to star. Both Young and the audience keep intrigued by the inventive devices concocted by the playwright in trying to swing his wife into the new play.

....

■ BEDTIME STORY

1964, 99 MINS, US ◇ ⑰
Dir Ralph Levy   *Prod* Stanley Shapiro   *Scr* Stanley Shapiro, Paul Henning   *Ph* Clifford Stine   *Ed* Milton Garruth   *Mus* Hans J. Salter   *Art Dir* Alexander Golitzen, Robert Clatworthy
● Marlon Brando, David Niven, Shirley Jones, Dody Goodman, Aram Stephan, Marie Windsor (Universal)

Bedtime Story will divert the less discriminating, although there are times when even such major league performers as Marlon Brando and David Niven have to strain to sustain the overall meager romantic comedy material.

Some of the lines snap and crackle, and several of the situations (done with slapstick overtones) in which Brando and Niven find themselves involved as conmen in competition on the French Riviera broadly funny.

The screenplay has Niven as a bigtime operator and Brando a relatively petty practitioner of the confidence art who comes to challenge the 'king of the mountain' in his own background. The mercenary contest centers around 'American soap queen' Shirley Jones, who turns out to be merely the penniless winner of a soap queen contest.

Brando wins the girl, but he loses the histrionic contest to Niven, whose effortless flair for sophisticated comedy is not matched by his co-star.

■ **BEETHOVEN**

1992, 88 MINS, US ◇ ⓥ ☉
Dir Brian Levant *Prod* Joe Medjuck, Michael C. Gross
Scr Edmond Dantes, Amy Holden Jones *Ph* Victor J. Kemper *Ed* Sheldon Kahn, William D. Gordean
Mus Randy Edelman *Art Dir* Alex Tavoularis
● Charles Grodin, Bonnie Hunt, Dean Jones, Nicholle Tom, Christopher Castile, Sarah Rose Karr (Universal)

Six-year-olds and animal rights activists should warm up to the titular big slobbering dog, his perfect family and the experimentation ring that brings them together, and the pic rallies at the end to prevent chaperoning adults from feeling their time was completely wasted.

The real star is a 185-pound St Bernard. Stolen as a puppy, he stumbles into the Newton family's life. They are a demographically perfect group, with an uptight dad (Charles Grodin) who reluctantly agrees to adopt the beast.

Beethoven grows and, as only movie dogs can, manages to help the kids' lives in various creative ways, even as he mangles the house and antagonizes Dad. Ultimately, Grodin is forced into action when the dog becomes the victim of an animal-theft ring led by an oily vet (Dean Jones), leading to a resolution so predictable that even the youngest of tots can feel smug in having guessed it.

Director Brian Levant cut his teeth directing sitcoms before turning to features with *Problem Child 2*, and the influence shows, particularly in the cartoonish perfs he gets from villains.

■ **BEETLEJUICE**

1988, 92 MINS, US ◇ ⓥ ☉
Dir Tim Burton *Prod* Michael Bender, Larry Wilson, Richard Hashimoto *Scr* Michael McDowell, Warren Skaaren *Ph* Thomas Ackerman *Ed* Jane Kurson
Mus Danny Elfman *Art Dir* Bo Welch
● Alec Baldwin, Geena Davis, Michael Keaton, Jeffrey Jones, Winona Ryder, Sylvia Sidney (Geffen)

Beetlejuice springs to life when the raucous and repulsive Betelgeuse (Michael Keaton) rises from his moribund state to wreak havoc on fellow spooks and mortal enemies.

Geena Davis and Alec Baldwin are a couple of affectionate New Englanders who live in a big barn of a house that they lovingly are restoring. But they crash over a covered bridge and drown – consigned to an afterlife that keeps them stuck at home forever invisible to anyone not similarly situated.

No sooner is their funeral over when their beloved house is sold to a rich New York financier (Jeffrey Jones) and his wife, the affected artiste (Catherine O'Hara).

Help comes via a cryptically written book for the newly deceased that takes Davis and Baldwin into the afterlife – kind of a comical holding cell for people who died of unnatural causes like themselves – but better yet, from this freak of a character named Betelgeuse that lives in the graveyard that's part of the miniature table-top town that Baldwin built.

In the script [from a story by Michael McDowell and Larry Wilson], things above ground aren't nearly as inventive as they are below. Luckily, Keaton pops up from his grave to liven things up when the antics pitting the good ghosts against the intruders become a trite cat & mouse game.

☐ 1988: Best Make-Up

B

■ **BEFORE WINTER COMES**

1969, 107 MINS, UK ◇
Dir J. Lee Thompson *Prod* Robert Emmett Ginns
Scr Andrew Sinclair *Ph* Gil Taylor *Ed* Willy Kemplen
Mus Ron Grainer *Art Dir* John Blezard
● David Niven, Topol, Anna Karina, John Hurt, Anthony Quayle, Ori Levy (Columbia/Windward)

An unevenly-scripted, confusingly-directed drama about the treatment of displaced persons in Austria immediately following VE Day. *Before Winter Comes* is a modestly-budgeted British drama about conflict between military authority and humanist concepts in the peacetime army.

David Niven turns in his usual competent professional job as a major assigned to run a camp for displaced persons during the spring of 1945. Topol is the multilingual magician from among the DPs whom Niven chooses to assist him in deciding who should be turned over to American and who to Russian authorities.

To its basic military story [from short story *The Interpreter* by Frederick L. Keefe] film tries to add a *Zorba the Greek* aspect, with Topol representing an earthy life-force counter to Niven's harsh rigidity.

Nothing dims Topol's impact. He exudes a romantic masculinity not without sexual charm at the same time that he shows a formidable comedic timing and grace.

■ **BEGGAR'S OPERA, THE**

1953, 94 MINS, UK ◇ ⓥ
Dir Peter Brook *Prod* Herbert Wilcox, Laurence Olivier
Scr Dennis Cannan, Christopher Fry *Ph* Guy Green
Ed Reginald Beck *Mus* Arthur Bliss *Art Dir* William C. Andrews
● Laurence Olivier, Stanley Holloway, George Devine, Hugh Griffith, Athene Syler, Dorothy Tutin (British Lion)

A bold experiment which does not come off, *The Beggar's Opera* is an example of the uneasy partnership between screen and opera.

Herber Wilcox, who promoted the production, cast his net over a wide field for new and promising talent. Peter Brook was recruited from legit to direct his first motion picture. Denis Cannan, the noted playwright, authored the screenplay and additional dialog and lyrics were penned by Christopher Fry. Most important of all was the casting of Laurence Olivier in his first singing role.

At constant intervals events are brought to a standstill by the John Gay lyrics and, attractive though they a in their own right, they do not merge too happily in the film.

Brook brings an obviously arty approach to his direction, resorting to a surplus of subdued lights. He is at his best in handling the big crowd scenes. The sequence in which Macheath is being driven from Newgate Gaol to the gallows is boldly and imaginatively presented.

Apart from Olivier and Stanley Holloway, the singing voices of the cast are dubbed by leading British vocalists and the contrast is clear and distinct. Olivier's light baritone, pleasant enough in its own way, is no match for the other voices. This apart, his performance is as robust and as lively as could be expected.

Holloway as Lockit, the jailer, is a polished singer as well as being a first-class thesper and his is one of the best individual contributions to the pic. Arthur Bliss' score is outstanding.

■ **BEGINNING OR THE END, THE**

1947, 110 MINS, US
Dir Norman Taurog *Prod* Samuel Marx *Scr* Frank Wead *Ph* Ray June *Ed* George Boemler
Mus Daniele Amfitheatrof *Art Dir* Cedric Gibbons, Hans Peters
● Brian Donlevy, Robert Walker, Tom Drake, Audrey Totter, Hume Cronyn, Beverly Tyler (M-G-M)

The Beginning or the End tells its portentous tale in broad strokes of masterful scripting and production. Picture tees off with a pseudo news clip, showing the burying of a time capsule, not to be opened until A.D. 2446. In the time capsule is placed a motion picture film which records *The Beginning or the End*. Thereafter is unfolded the nearly two-hour picture.

It brings an appreciation of how science and big business were mobilized by America to achieve the Atomic Bomb even though President Roosevelt was told it would cost a billion dollars and possibly two billion; the mobilization of big business and stout young scientists to work with their more experienced elders; the rallying around Dr. J. Robert Oppenheimer (who Hume Cronyn expertly impersonates); the questioning by young Tom Drake whether he was doing the right thing.

Brian Donlevy is capital as Gen Groves, eclipsed only by Godfrey Tearle's extraordinary personation of President Roosevelt.

It's to the sum credit of everybody concerned that the documentary values are sufficiently there without becoming static.

■ **BEGUILED, THE**

1971, 105 MINS, US ◇ ⓥ ☉
Dir Don Siegel *Prod* Don Siegel *Scr* John B. Sherry, Grimes Grice *Ph* Bruce Surtees *Ed* Carl Pingitore
Mus Lalo Schifrin *Art Dir* Ted Haworth
● Clint Eastwood, Geraldine Page, Elizabeth Hartman, Jo Ann Harris, Darleen Carr, Mae Mercer (Malpaso/Universal)

Marking a distinct change of pace for both director Don Siegel and star Clint Eastwood, *The Beguiled* doesn't come off, and cues laughter in all the wrong places.

Eastwood eschews his usual action character to portray a wounded Union soldi recuperating within the confines of a small school for southern girls run by Geraldine Page. His presence cues a series of diverse sexual frustrations, and his wily handling of the ladies, spark jealousies of meller proportions.

Pic is essentially black comedy, but treatment is consistently heavy-handed. Script [from novel by Thomas Cullinan] resorts to tired symbolism, including that chestnut that equates southern womanhood with incestuous dreams under the Spanish moss.

Eastwood is not called upon to do much emoting; that is left in spades to the ladies. Page, per usual, runs away with the honors, whether girlishly remembering her erotic relationship with her brother or grimly sawing off Eastwood's leg in a sequence that would be nauseating if it weren't so funny.

■ **BEHIND THE GREEN DOOR**

1972, 72 MINS, US ◇ ⓥ
Dir Jim Mitchell, Art Mitchell *Prod* Jim Mitchell, Art Mitchell *Scr* Jim Mitchell *Ph* Jon Fontana *Ed* Jon Fontana
● Marilyn Chambers, George S. McDonald, Johnny Keyes, Ben Davidson (Mitchell Brothers)

Football fans attracted to the hardcore debut of Oakland Raider pro Ben Davidson should flag him for boxoffice clipping. His fully-clothed cameo appearance is hardly worth the time. But sports fans won't go away entirely disappointed, since ex-middleweight boxing champ Johnny Keyes is also featured – and he goes all the way.

Marilyn Chambers makes her hardcore debut in *Behind the Green Door*. Unlike the crones who used to populate pornos, Chambers may be remembered as the fresh-faced 'innocent' in *Together* [1971, directed by Sean S. Cunningham]. In that one, she was bare a lot, but never went all the way. In this, she does everything, quite realistically. Unfortunately, she never has enough to say to judge whether she qualifies as an actress.

Filmmakers lavished $50,000 on this feature, their biggest budget to date.

....

■ **BEHIND THE RISING SUN**

1943, 86 MINS, US ⓥ

Dir Edward Dmytryk   *Scr* Emnett Lavery   *Ph* Russell Metty   *Ed* Joseph Noriega   *Mus* Roy Webb
● Margo, Tom Neal, J. Carrol Naish, Robert Ryan, Gloria Holden (RKO)

Screenplay is from factual information contained in book by James R. Young, International News Service correspondent in Tokyo for several years prior to the war's outbreak at Pearl Harbor. Although foreword points out that the characters are imaginary, facts woven into the dramatics are real. Result is a good drama of inside info on Jap indoctrination and thinking.

Story is an intimate affair of a Jap family of the upper class; and the impress of the conquests in Asia and war against the United States on both father and son. Father is influential newspaper publisher (J. Carrol Naish), while son is Cornell-educated Tom Neal. When latter arrives from America after completing college education and figures to embark on career as an engineer with Don Douglas, there are family objections for a time. But when Neal further falls in love with lower-caste Jap girl (Margo) marriage is impossible.

....

■ **BEHOLD A PALE HORSE**

1964, 119 MINS, US ⓥ

Dir Fred Zinnemann   *Prod* Fred Zinnemann   *Scr* J.P. Miller   *Ph* Jean Badal   *Ed* Walter Thompson   *Mus* Maurice Jarre   *Art Dir* Alexandre Trauner
● Gregory Peck, Anthony Quinn, Omar Sharif, Raymond Pellegrin, Paola Stoppa, Mildred Dunnock (Columbia)

Pale Horse [from the novel *Killing a Mouse on Sunday* by Emeric Pressburger] is rooted in the Spanish Civil War, using introductory newsreel footage and the fighting to set the background for a story that happens 20 years later and essentially concerns a Spanish guerrilla (Gregory Peck) who continues to live the war alone. He is thrown again into the fray in a personal attack against a vain and arrogant police captain (Anthony Quinn) who has vowed his death.

The one-man fight against a corrupt and powerful adversary is an obvious losing battle, but the guerrilla's last stand, he knows, can be his most effective.

Peck is a worn-out, untidy broken man who once again surges with force and energy in a characterization that ranks among the better in his long career. There also is an excellent performance from Quinn, who is coarse, crude and worldly as the arrogant police chief but shows his own insecurity beneath a physically courageous false front. Omar Sharif shows a warm, sensitive side in this film, playing the role of a young priest torn between obligations of personal morality and the official laws of government.

....

■ **BEING THERE**

1979, 130 MINS, US ◇ ⓥ ⊙

Dir Hal Ashby   *Prod* Andrew Braunsberg   *Scr* Jerzy Kosinski   *Ph* Caleb Deschanel   *Ed* Don Zimmerman   *Mus* John Mandel   *Art Dir* Michael Haller
● Peter Sellers, Shirley MacLaine, Melvyn Douglas, Jack Warden, Richard Basehart (United Artists/Lorimar)

Being There is a highly unusual and an unusually fine film. A faithful but nonetheless imaginative adaptation of Jerzy Kosinski's quirky comic novel, pic marks a significant achievement for director Hal Ashby and

represents Peter Sellers' most smashing work since the mid-1960s.

Kosinski's story is a quietly outrageous fable which takes Sellers from his position as a childlike, unblinking naif who can't read or write to that of a valued advisor to an industrial giant and ultimately to the brink of a presidential nomination.

Tale possesses political, religious and consumer society undertones, but by no means is an overly symbolic affair trying to impress with its deep meanings.

Sellers' performance stands as the centerpiece of the film, and it's a beauty. Shirley MacLaine is subtle and winning, retaining her dignity despite several precarious opportunities to lose it. If such is possible in a picture dominated by Sellers, Melvyn Douglas almost steals the film with his spectacular performance as the dying financial titan.
□ 1979: Best Supp. Actor (Melvyn Douglas).
□ Nomination: Best Actor (Peter Sellers)

....

■ **BELL, BOOK AND CANDLE**

1958, 106 MINS, US ◇ ⓥ ⊙

Dir Richard Quine   *Prod* Julian Blaustein   *Scr* Daniel Taradash   *Ph* James Wong Howe   *Ed* Charles Nelson   *Mus* George Duning   *Art Dir* Cary Odell
● James Stewart, Kim Novak, Jack Lemmon, Ernie Kovacs, Hermione Gingold, Elsa Lanchester (Phoenix/Columbia)

Richard Quine's direction gets everything possible out of the screenplay and the cast. But with Kim Novak the central figure, the picture lacks the spontaneity and sparkle written in by playwright John Van Druten.

The offbeat story is concerned with witches and warlocks (male gender of the broomstick set) operating against today's world of skepticism and realism. James Stewart is the straight man thrust by chance into a group of people, headed by Novak, where incantations, spells and sorcery are accepted as realities as commonplace as processed foods. Novak literally weaves a spell on Stewart to make him fall in love with her.

There are some wonderfully weird proceedings here, including Elsa Lanchester and Hermione Gingold as rival witches, and Jack Lemmon as a clean-cut, bongo-beating warlock.

The hazard of the story is that there is really only one joke. This was sustained in the play by Van Druten's witty dialog. It is undercut in the picture by the fact that the backgrounds are too often as weird as the situations.
□ 1958: Nominations: Best Costume Design, Art Direction

....

■ **BELLE OF NEW YORK, THE**

1952, 82 MINS, US ◇ ⓥ

Dir Charles Walters   *Prod* Arthur Freed   *Scr* Robert O'Brien, Irving Elinson   *Ph* Robert Planck   *Ed* Albert Akst   *Mus* Harry Warren   *Art Dir* Cedric Gibbons, Jack Martin Smith
● Fred Astaire, Vera-Ellen, Marjorie Main, Keenan Wynn, Alice Pearce, Clinton Sundberg (M-G-M)

A film musical usually can get by with the lightest plot if the dance numbers and tunes are sock, but *Belle* has an even lighter plot than usual, and the numbers are just ordinary. It's all done pleasantly but not of a quality that rates more than passing interest.

Score contains nine songs, most of which are given some eye appeal in production staging, although not elaborately. Most pleasing is Vera-Ellen's 'Naughty But Nice', which she sings and dances to fit a story situation.

Script has Astaire as an early-New York playboy who falls for a Bowery mission worker (Vera-Ellen) and changes his ways, even getting employment to prove he is worthy of her pure, honest affection. Tunes and production numbers are hung on that framework.

....

■ **BELLE OF THE NINETIES**

1934, 75 MINS, US

Dir Leo McCarey   *Prod* William LeBaron   *Scr* Mae West   *Ph* Karl Struss   *Ed* LeRoy Stone   *Art Dir* Hans Dreier, Bernard Herzbrun
● Mae West, Roger Pryor, John Mack Brown, Katherine DeMille, John Miljan (Paramount)

Mae West's opera, *Belle of the Nineties*, is as ten-twent-thirt as its mauve decade time and locale. The melodramatics are put on a bit thick, including the arch-villain who is an arch-renegade, a would-be murderer, a welcher, an arsonist and everything else in the book of ye good old-time mellers.

The original songs by Sam Coslow and Arthur Johnston are 'My Old Flame', 'American Beauty' and 'Troubled Waters'. Duke Ellington's nifty jazzique is a natural for the Westian song delivery.

Just like she makes stooges of almost anybody assigned to bandy talk with her, West dittoes with her principal support, including Roger Pryor, the fave vis-a-vis, John Mack Brown as the good time Charlie, and John Miljan, a villyun of darkest mien. Katherine DeMille as the spurned gambler's sweetheart looks better and suggests better opportunities than the prima facie script accords her.

....

■ **BELLES OF ST. TRINIAN'S, THE**

1954, 91 MINS, UK ⓥ

Dir Frank Launder   *Prod* Frank Launder, Sidney Gilliat   *Scr* Frank Launder, Sidney Gilliat, Val Valentine   *Ph* Stanley Pavey   *Ed* Thelma Connell   *Mus* Malcolm Arnold   *Art Dir* Joseph Bato
● Alastair Sim, Joyce Grenfell, George Cole, Hermione Baddeley, Betty Ann Davies, Renee Houston (British Lion/London)

Inspired by Ronald Searle's British cartoons about the little horrors of a girls' school, *The Belles of St. Trinian's* makes an excellent start but never lives up to the promise of the opening reel.

By way of a story, Frank Launder and Sidney Gilliat have concocted an involved yarn about a plot to steal the favorite horse in a big race which is foiled by the girls in the fourth form after a battle royal with the sixth form.

Unrestrained direction by Launder is matched by the lively and energetic performances by most of the cast. As both the headmistress and her bookmaker brother, Alastair Sim rarely reaches comedy heights. Joyce Grenfell, however, as a police spy posing as a games teacher, is good for plenty of laughs. Best individual contribution is by George Cole, playing a wide-shouldered wiseguy, who acts as selling agent for the homemade gin brewed in the school lab, and also as go-between for the girls and the local bookie.

....

■ **BELL FOR ADANO, A**

1945, 103 MINS, US

Dir Henry King   *Prod* Louis D. Lighton, Lamar Trotti   *Scr* Lamar Trotti, Norman Reilly Raine   *Ph* Joseph La Shelle   *Ed* Barbara McLean   *Mus* Alfred Newman   *Art Dir* Lyle R. Wheeler, Mark-Lee Kirk
● Gene Tierney, John Hodiak, William Bendix, Richard Conte (20th Century-Fox)

John Hersey's story of an American major's administration of a town in Sicily, and his attempts to return it to its peaceful prewar status, has not been tampered with or elaborated upon. The film begins quietly to set the simple keynote, has some very beautiful, inspired moments, and finishes off with several scenes of emotional brilliance.

John Hodiak, in the difficult role of Major Joppolo, presents the right hardboiled type of civil affairs officer, determined to bring spiritual rebirth (through the return of its cityhall bell) to the community. Gene Tierney, too, as the blonde fisherman's daughter, has a certain quiet grace without always bringing sufficient poignancy to the role.

William Bendix, as the major's orderly, plays the part in subdued fashion for the most convincing portrayal of the three leads, rising superbly to his one big scene at the end. Here Bendix goes roaring drunk at learning that the major is to be displaced.

Henry King's direction caps the story's mood superbly, because of his ability to instill the thought of movement frequently where no action actually exists.

● ●

■ **BELL JAR, THE**

1979, 107 MINS, US ◇ ▼

Dir Larry Peerce   *Prod* Jerrold Brandt Jr   *Scr* Marjorie Kellogg   *Ph* Gerald Hirschfeld   *Ed* Marvin Wallowitz   *Mus* Gerald Fried   *Art Dir* John Robert Lloyd
● Marilyn Hassett, Julie Harris, Anne Jackson, Barbara Barrie, Donna Mitchell, Robert Klein (Avco Embassy)

The Bell Jar, based on the late poet Sylvia Plath's autobiographical novel, evokes neither understanding nor sympathy for the plight of its heroine, Esther Greenwood, the epitome of a straight-A, golden-girl-overachiever, who is mentally 'coming apart at the seams.'

As played by Marilyn Hassett, Esther emerges as a selfish, morbid little prig. She eventually confesses to hating her mother, admirably played by Julie Harris, presumably because her mother refuses to wallow in the details of her father's death with her.

Marjorie Kellogg's screenplay seems fairly faithful to the novel's spirit. Larry Peerce's direction provides a sense of headachey dullness 15 minutes into the film.

Donald Brooks' costumes are the perfect evocation of 1950s style, the film's time period, and the color of Gerald Hirschfeld's camera is almost too pretty.

● ●

■ **BELLS ARE RINGING**

1960, 126 MINS, US ◇ ▼ ⊙

Dir Vincente Minnelli   *Prod* Arthur Freed   *Scr* Betty Comden, Adolph Green   *Ph* Milton Krasner   *Ed* Adrienne Fazan   *Mus* Andre Previn (adapt.)   *Art Dir* George W. Davis, Preston Ames
● Judy Holliday, Dean Martin, Fred Clark, Eddie Foy, Jean Stapleton, Frank Gorshin (M-G-M)

Better Broadway musicals than *Bells Are Ringing* have come to Hollywood, but few have been translated to the screen so effectively. *Bells* is ideally suited to the intimacy of the film medium. Where it might have a tendency in several passages to become dwarfed on a big stage, it's always bigger than life onscreen, which actually is a desirable factor in broad, free-wheeling comedy such as this.

The Betty Comden-Adolph Green screenplay, based on their [1956] book musical, is not by any means the sturdiest facet of the picture, but it's a pleasant yarn from which several rather inspired musical numbers spring. 'Just in Time' and 'The Party's Over' are delivered smoothly by Dean Martin and Judy Holliday. The latter's outstanding turn, however, occurs near the end of the picture, when she demonstrates her verve and versatility on the amusing 'I'm Goin' Back' (Where I Can Be Me, at the Bonjour Tristesse Brassiere Factory).

Martin has a chance to get in some solid licks on the alcoholically-inspired 'Do It Yourself' and in a traffic-stopping, crowd elbowing street sequence labelled 'Hello'. A real show-stopper is a production number with symphonic overtones presided over dynamically by Eddie Foy.

Vincente Minnelli's graceful, imaginative direction puts spirit and snap into the musical sequences, warmth and humor into the straight passages, and manages to knit it all together without any traces of awkwardness

in transition, a frequent stumbling block in filmusicals. Jule Styne's bright score has been vibrantly adapted and conducted by Andre Previn.

Holliday, as might be expected, steals show with a performance of remarkable variety and gusto as a girl who takes her switchboard and humanity seriously, Martin is excellent as her writer friend, displaying more animation than customary.

□ 1960: Nomination: Best Scoring of a Dramatic Picture

● ●

■ **BELLS GO DOWN, THE**

1943, 86 MINS, UK

Dir Basil Dearden   *Prod* Michael Balcon   *Scr* Roger MacDougall   *Ph* Ernest Palmer   *Ed* Sidney Cole, Mary Habberfield   *Mus* Roy Douglas   *Art Dir* Michael Relph
● Tommy Trinder, James Mason, Mervyn Johns, Philippa Hiatt, Finlay Currie, Beatrice Varley (Ealing)

Like *Fires Were Started* this film depicts the activities of life in the London Auxiliary Fire Service. But the first one out was more legitimate in that it was portrayed by actual members of the service.

Viewed as a mere low comedy, *The Bells Go Down* [from the book by Stephen Black] ambles along amiably. There is a running commentary patterned on the lines of those made familiar by Quentin Reynolds, and the fire scenes alternate with the wisecracking of Tommy Trinder, which are often without provocation. Thrillingly effective conflagration scenes deserve a large share of the honors.

Trinder enacts a lovable East Side young man whose mother runs a fish-and-chip shop, and who owns a racing greyhound that never wins until his comrades have gone broke backing the pooch.

The supporting cast is very well chosen, with Mervyn Johns offering a scintillating portrayal. James Mason, as a fireman, scores as usual; Beatrice Varley, as Trinder's mother, and fully a score of others can be set down as efficient support. Direction, production and photography are praiseworthy.

● ●

■ **BELLS OF ST. MARY'S, THE**

1945, 126 MINS, US ▼ ⊙

Dir Leo McCarey   *Prod* Leo McCarey   *Scr* Dudley Nichols   *Ph* George Barnes   *Ed* Henry Marker   *Mus* Robert Emmett Dolan   *Art Dir* William Flannery
● Bing Crosby, Ingrid Bergman, Henry Travers, Ruth Donnelly, Rhys Williams, Una O'Connor (RKO/Rainbow)

The Bells of St. Mary's is warmly sentimental, has a simple story leavened with many laughs and bears comparison with *Going My Way*. Leo McCarey, who demonstrated his ability to combine wholesome sentiment into a potent attraction with *Going My Way*, duplicates that ability as producer-director on this one.

Bing Crosby's Father O'Malley is the same priest character seen in *Way*, and *Bells* tells of his new assignment as parish priest at the parochial school, St Mary's.

Story tells of how he aids the nuns' prayers for a new school building with a more practical application of guidance; steers a young girl through an unhappy domestic situation, and brings the parents together again. It's all done with the natural ease that is Crosby's trademark.

Ingrid Bergman again demonstrates her versatility as the sister in charge. Her clashes with Crosby – all good-mannered – over proper methods of educating children, her venture into athletics, and coaching of a youngster to return a good left hook instead of the other cheek, are moments that will have an audience alternately laughing and sniffling.

□ 1945: Best Sound Recording.
□ Nominations: Best Picture, Director, Actor

(Bing Crosby), Actress (Ingrid Bergman), Editing, Scoring of a Dramatic Picture, Song ('Aren't You Glad You're You')

● ●

■ **BELLY OF AN ARCHITECT, THE**

1987, 118 MINS, UK ◇ ▼

Dir Peter Greenaway   *Prod* Colin Callender, Walter Donohue   *Scr* Peter Greenaway   *Ph* Sacha Vierny   *Ed* John Wilson   *Mus* Wim Mertens, Glenn Branca   *Art Dir* Luciana Vedovelli
● Brian Dennehy, Chloe Webb, Lambert Wilson, Sergio Fantoni (Callender/Film Four/British Screen)

The Belly of an Architect is a visual treat, almost an homage to the style of Rome's architecture, lensed with skill and packed with esoteric nuances, but doubts about the story and the skill of the acting linger.

The belly in question is the stomach of a US architect, played by a suitably paunchy Brian Dennehy, who arrives in Rome with his fickle wife to set up an exhibition celebrating French architect Boullee. He becomes convinced he is being slowly poisoned by his wife (Chloe Webb) who is having an affair with a rival Italian architect (Lambert Wilson).

Dennehy, usually spotted in Yank actioners, makes an admirable effort as the troubled architect, but the rest of the cast – mostly European – turn in generally poor efforts. Webb as his wife looks okay, but her voice (apt in *Sid and Nancy*) just seems irritating, while Wilson as the rival architect/lover is little more than a clotheshorse.

● ●

■ **BEN**

1972, 83 MINS, US ◇ ▼

Dir Phil Karlson   *Prod* Mort Briskin   *Scr* Gilbert A. Raiston   *Ph* Russell Metty   *Ed* Harry Gerstad   *Mus* Walter Scharf   *Art Dir* Rolland M. Brooks
● Lee Harcourt Montgomery, Joseph Campanella, Arthur O'Connell, Rosemary Murphy, Meredith Baxter, Kaz Garas (Cinerama/Crosby)

Willard has a tension-packed sequel in *Ben*, which takes up minutes after Willard, the man who trained rats, was killed off by his rodents in original entry. Ben, the rat heavy of the other, plays title role here.

Chief protagonist is a young boy played by Lee Harcourt Montgomery, who befriends Ben. Latter's army of rats obey his orders, and they create a reign of terror as they indulge in a wave of killing.

Moppet plays his part to perfection and Phil Karlson's direction is responsible for mounting moments of excitement, well handled by cast headed by Joseph Campanella as a police lieutenant in charge of crisis and Meredith Baxter, Ben's sister.

□ 1972: Nomination: Best Song ('Ben')

● ●

■ **BEND OF THE RIVER**
(UK: Where the River Bends)

1952, 91 MINS, US ◇ ▼

Dir Anthony Mann   *Prod* Aaron Rosenberg   *Scr* Borden Chase   *Ph* Irving Glassberg   *Ed* Russell Schoengarth   *Mus* Hans J. Salter   *Art Dir* Bernard Herzbrun, Nathan Juran
● James Stewart, Arthur Kennedy, Julie Adams, Rock Hudson, Lori Nelson, Jay C. Flippen (Universal)

Basic plot line is a simple affair, as lifted from Bill Gulick's novel, *Bend of the Snake*. It deals with a band of settlers who make a long, wagon train trek into Oregon to claim the country from the wilderness and the hardships of such pioneering.

James Stewart is the wagon train guide, leading the settlers into Oregon. He rescues Arthur Kennedy, a former Missouri raider, from a hanging and the latter joins the party for the trek to Portland, where group boards a river steamer for a journey into the back country. The summer passes and promised

B

supplies that are to carry the settlers through the winter do not arrive. Stewart returns to Portland, finds the town gold-mad and the supplies held up for more money.

Stewart's handling of his role has punch. Kennedy socks his likeable heavy role. Julie Adams fulfills romantic demands of her top femme role, and Rock Hudson pleasantly projects the part of a young gambler who joins the settlers.

■ **BENEATH THE PLANET OF THE APES**

1970, 95 MINS, US ◇ ⦿ ⊙
Dir Ted Post *Prod* Arthur P. Jacobs *Scr* Paul Dehn *Ph* Milton Krasner *Ed* Marion Rothman *Mus* Leonard Rosenman *Art Dir* Jack Martin
● James Franciscus, Kim Hunter, Maurice Evans, Linda Harrison, Charlton Heston, Victor Buono (20th Century-Fox)

This sequel to the 1968 smash, *Planet of the Apes*, is hokey and slapdash. The story and Ted Post's direction fall far short of the original.

Film utilizes closing sequence of the original – where Charlton Heston and the silent Linda Harrison ride into an unknown country on the supposedly unknown planet, only to find the Head of the Statue of Liberty buried in the sand. Heston's curtain cry of anguish now is followed by new footage, as he and Harrison wander the vast wasteland, in which Heston suddenly disappears.

James Franciscus is yet another space explorer who crash-lands, centuries out of time. Dialog, acting and direction are substandard.

Heston appears in some new footage, and Franciscus looks just like a twin brother by this time, in face and in voice.

■ **BENEATH THE 12-MILE REEF**

1953, 102 MINS, US ◇ ⦿
Dir Robert D. Webb *Prod* Robert Bassler *Scr* A.I. Bezzerides *Ph* Edward Cronjager *Ed* William Reynolds *Mus* Bernard Herrmann *Art Dir* Lyle R. Wheeler, George Patrick
● Robert Wagner, Terry Moore, Gilbert Roland, J. Carrol Naish, Richard Boone, Peter Graves (20th Century-Fox)

Set among the sponge-diving Greek colony at Tarpon Springs, Fla, the squeeze-lensing gives punch in the display of underwater wonders, the seascapes and the brilliant, beautiful sunrises and sunsets of the Florida Gulf coast.

In handling the young cast, Robert D. Webb's direction is less effective, particularly in the case of Robert Wagner and Terry Moore. Both are likable, so the shallowness of their performances is no serious handicap to the entertainment. Thesping quality is maintained by the more experienced casters. Scoring resoundingly is Gilbert Roland, colorful Greek diver and father of Wagner. Angela Clarke also clicks as the wife and mother.

The plot takes on two lines of conflict – the age-old battle between man and the sea, the more personal rivalry between the diving Greeks of Tarpon Springs and the hook-spongers of the shallow Key West waters.

Romance gets in its licks when the daring Gilbert ventures into Key West waters controlled by Boone and the young Wagner meets conch-girl Moore. It's an instant attraction between the pair and their romance builds to a runaway marriage after Gilbert is killed diving at the dangerous 12-mile reef. Wagner then becomes the man of the family, proving his right to the title by diving where his father met his death, fighting off an octopus and beating Graves in an underwater battle.
□ 1953: Nomination: Best Color Cinematography

■ **BENEATH THE VALLEY OF THE ULTRA VIXENS**

1979, 93 MINS, US ◇ ⦿ ⊙
Dir Russ Meyer *Prod* Russ Meyer *Scr* R. Hyde [= Roger Ebert], B. Callum [= Russ Meyer] *Ph* Russ Meyer *Ed* Russ Meyer *Mus* William Tasker *Art Dir* Michele Levesque
● Francesca 'Kitten' Natividad, Anne Marie, Ken Kerr, June Mack, Lola Langusta (RM International)

For the fanciers of pneumatic pulchritude, Russ Meyer is back with *Beneath the Valley of the Ultra Vixens* which as the onscreen narrator says 'is a very simple story', presumably for very simple people.

Briefly, the strand of plot concern Lavonia (Francesca 'Kitten' Natividad), whose only fault is 'enthusiasm' and her unsatisfactory sex relationship with her man Lamar (Ken Kerr). In the course of curing Lamar so that he will straighten up and satisfy, Lavonia has a hot time with everybody in town.

This is the umpteenth in Meyer's vixen series. But are they satire, as Meyer would have one believe, or fantasy, or both? If anything, they are funny and though a bit too long, Meyer, who does everything (directs, edits, photographs and produces), keeps the action fast and furious.

■ **BEN-HUR**

1959, 212 MINS, US ◇ ⦿ ⊙
Dir William Wyler, [Andrew Marton, Richard Thorpe] *Prod* Sam Zimbalist *Scr* Karl Tunberg *Ph* Robert L. Surtees *Ed* Ralph E. Winters, John D. Dunning *Mus* Miklos Rozsa *Art Dir* William Horning, Edward Carfagno
● Charlton Heston, Jack Hawkins, Stephen Boyd, Haya Harareet, Hugh Griffith, Sam Jaffe (M-G-M)

The $15 million *Ben-Hur* is a majestic achievement, representing a superb blending of the motion picture arts by master craftsmen.

The big difference between Ben-Hur and other spectacles, biblical or otherwise, is its sincere concern for human beings. They're not just pawns reciting flowery dialog to fill gaps between the action. This has been accomplished without sacrificing the impact of the spectacle elements.

The famous chariot race between Ben-Hur, the Prince of Judea, and Messala, the Roman tribune – directed by Andrew Marton and Yakima Canutt – represents some 40 minutes of the most hair-raising excitement ever witnessed.

Wisely, however, the film does not depend wholly on sheer spectacle. The family relationship between Ben-Hur and his mother Miriam and his sister Tirzah; his touching romance with Esther, the former slave; his admiration of the Roman consul, Quintus Arrius, whom he rescues after a sea battle; his association with the Arab horseowner, Sheik Ilderim; and his struggle with Messala, the boyhood friend who becomes his mortal enemy, make moving scenes. And overshadowing these personal conflicts is the deeply religious theme involving the birth and crucifixion of Christ.

Karl Tunberg receives sole screen credit, although such heavyweight writers as Maxwell Anderson, S.N. Behrman, Gore Vidal and Christopher Fry also worked on the film. Fry, a respected British poet-playwright, was present on the set throughout the production in Rome.

Charlton Heston is excellent as the brawny yet kindly Ben-Hur who survives the life of a galley slave to seek revenge of his enemy Messala. Haya Harareet, an Israeli actress making her first appearance in an American film is sensitive and revealing as Esther. Jack Hawkins, as Quintus Arrius, the Roman consul who adopts Ben-Hur, adds another fine depiction to his career. Stephen Boyd, as Ben-Hur's enemy Messala, is not the standard villain, but succeeds in giving understanding to this position in his dedication to the Roman Empire.

The film took 10 months to complete at Rome's Cinecitta Studios. The 300 sets are one of the highlights of the film, particularly the massive arena for the chariot sequence. The musical score by Miklos Rozsa also contributes to the overall excellence of the giant project.

Ben-Hur is a fitting climax to Zimbalist's career as a producer. He died of a heart attack in Rome when the film was near completion.
□ 1959: Best Picture, Director, Actor (Charlton Heston), Supp. Actor (Hugh Griffith), Color Cinematography, Color Art Direction, Sound, Scoring of a Dramatic Picture, Editing, Special Effects, Color Costume Design.
□ Nomination: Best Adapted Screenplay

■ **BEN-HUR**
A TALE OF THE CHRIST

1925, 128 MINS, US ◇ ⊗ ⦿ ⊙
Dir Fred Niblo *Prod* Louis B. Mayer, Irving Thalberg *Scr* Bess Meredyth, Carey Wilson, June Mathis, Katherine Hilliker, H.H. Caldwell *Ph* Rene Guissart, Percy Hilburn, Karl Struss, Clyde De Vinna *Ed* Lloyd Nosler *Art Dir* Cedric Gibbons, Horace Jackson, Arnold Gillespie
● Ramon Novarro, Francis X. Bushman, May McAvoy, Betty Bronson, Carmel Myers (M-G-M)

Ben Hur is a picture that rises above spectacle, even though it is spectacle. On the screen it isn't the chariot race or the great battle scenes between the fleet of Rome and the pirate galleys of Golthar. It is the tremendous heart throbs that one experiences leading to those scenes that make them great.

It is the story of the oppression of the Jews, the birth of the Saviour, the progression of the Christus to the time of his crucifixion, the enslavement of the race from which Jesus himself sprang, and the tremendous love tale of the bond slave and a prince of Jerusalem that holds an audience spell bound.

As to individual performance: first the Mary of Betty Bronson. It is without doubt the most tremendous individual score that any actress has ever made, with but a single scene with a couple of close-ups. And in the color scenes she appears simply superb.

Then as to Ramon Novarro: anyone who sees him in this picture will have to admit that he is without doubt a man's man and 100 per cent of that. Francis X. Bushman does a comeback in the role of the heavy (Messala) that makes him stand alone.

As to the women, following Bronson, May McAvoy in blonde tresses as Esther deserves a full measure of credit for her performance. While Claire McDowell, as the mother of Hur, and Kathleen Key, as his sister, both score tremendously. Carmel Myers, as the vamp Iras, looks a million dollars' worth of woman and it is hard to understand how Ben-Hur could finally resist her.

■ **BENJI**

1974, 85 MINS, US ◇ ⦿
Dir Joe Camp *Prod* Joe Camp *Scr* Joe Camp *Ph* Don Reddy *Ed* Leon Smith *Mus* Euel Box *Art Dir* Harland Wright
● Patsy Garrett, Allen Fiuzat, Cynthia Smith, Peter Breck, Edgar Buchanan (Mulberry Square)

Benji is a dog's picture from first to last. From the moment he pokes his head through a broken door in a deserted house where he has his pad until he's adopted by the family whose two children he saves from kidnappers, interest rests squarel on the head of this pooch, of uncertain parentage.

One of the wonders of the production, told simply and with no pretense of grandiose

61

style, is the manner in which Benji – real name Benji – performs. In this case, it isn't a dog performing, but a dog acting, just as humans act.

Much of the footage is shot from about 18 inches above the ground, upward from Benji's point of view, and innovation is fascinating.
□ 1974: Nomination: Best Song ('I Feel Love')
• •

■ BENNY & JOON

1993, 98 MINS, US ◇ ⓥ ⊙
Dir Jeremiah Chechik   *Prod* Susan Arnold, Donna Roth   *Scr* Barry Berman   *Ph* John Schwartzman   *Ed* Carol Littleton   *Mus* Rachel Portman   *Art Dir* Neil Spisak
● Johnny Depp, Mary Stuart Masterson, Aidan Quinn, Julianne Moore, Oliver Platt, C.C.H. Pounder (M-G-M)

Johnny Depp and Mary Stuart Masterson render such startling performances in the romantic fable *Benny & Joon* they almost overcome being in a not particularly well-written or directed film [from a story by Barry Berman and Lesley McNeil].

Masterson stars as Joon, the mentally ill sister of Benny (Aidan Quinn), an auto mechanic who takes care of her. The quick-witted Joon spends her days at home, painting with passion.

This frail equilibrium is shattered when Sam (Depp), a modern-day clown in the mold of Chaplin and Keaton, shows up and changes the rules of the game. Quinn continues to worry, but he is also freer to pursue affairs of the heart with the charming Ruthie (Julianne Moore).

The pic's strength lies more in the nuances of the relationships than in the smooth flow of an episodic narrative. The love story is superficially placed in a frame that revolves around suspense over whether Benny will institutionalize Joon. In mood and theme, film bears some resemblance to *David and Lisa*, Frank Perry's 1963 sleeper.

As a fairy-tale clown, Depp is playing a variation on Edward Scissorhands, a misunderstood eccentric par excellence. Both Depp and Masterson, whose screen chemistry sparkles, excel in embodying the spirits of magic.
• •

■ BENNY GOODMAN STORY, THE

1955, 116 MINS, US ◇ ⓥ
Dir Valentine Davies   *Prod* Aaron Rosenberg   *Scr* Valentine Davies   *Ph* William Daniels   *Ed* Russell Schoengarth   *Mus* Henry Mancini
● Steve Allen, Donna Reed, Berta Gersten, Herbert Anderson, Robert F. Simon (Universal)

The Benny Goodman Story is of the same stripe as Universal's previously socko bandleader saga, *The Glenn Miller Story*. Both have bespectacled bandleaders with titles, both are Aaron Rosenberg productions.

If the romantics of the script and Steve Allen and Donna Reed's interpretations lack a bit, they are sufficiently glossed over because the major canvas is the saga of the Chicago youth with the licorice stick and his dedication to the cause of a new exciting tempo, later interpreted as 'swing'.

The unfolding is uncompromising on several fronts. The closeups on the very poor Jewish family and Goodman's humble environments are not glossed over. In the same idiom there is no fanfare about the interracial mixing, socially or professionally.
• •

■ BEQUEST TO THE NATION

(US: The Nelson Affair)

1973, 115 MINS, UK ◇
Dir James Cellan Jones   *Prod* Hal B. Wallis   *Scr* Terence Rattigan   *Ph* Gerry Fisher   *Ed* Anne V. Coates   *Mus* Michel Legrand   *Art Dir* Carmen Dillon
● Glenda Jackson, Peter Finch, Michael Jayston, Anthony Quayle, Margaret Leighton, Dominic Guard (Universal)

This is a deliberate, though stylish and genteel, de-glamorizing of the affair between Lord Nelson and Lady Hamilton which scandalized England. Production is based on Terence Rattigan's adaptation of his own play, and never completely escapes its legit origins.

The plot introduces Peter Finch's Nelson just returned from a successful thwarting of Napoleon's maritime maneuvers, as executed by Andre Maranne as French Admiral Villeneuve. Begging several months' leave, Nelson repairs to his adored mistress (Glenda Jackson), who like him, is showing signs of less-than-graceful aging. Increasingly embittered by their status as social pariahs and pressed by his superiors to return to sea, Nelson engages in a series of harangues with his love, who finally urges his return to sea.

The story-as-is permits Jackson to display a variety of her dramatic abilities. Finch is slightly less effective as Nelson, though he manages to project the complex facets of character.
• •

■ BERKELEY SQUARE

1933, 87 MINS, US
Dir Frank Lloyd   *Prod* Jesse L. Lasky   *Scr* Sonya Levien, John L. Balderston   *Ph* Ernest Palmer   *Mus* Louis De Francesco (dir.)   *Art Dir* William Darling
● Leslie Howard, Heather Angel, Valerie Taylor, Irene Browne, Alan Mowbray, Juliette Compton (Fox)

Berkeley Square is an imaginative, beautiful and well-handled production.

The atmosphere of Berkeley Square, London, is resurrected almost perfectly, as it is today, and presumably as it was in the 18th century. There's a devotion to detail and atmospherics that is almost painfully exacting.

Leslie Howard in the same role he played on the stage (he produced the stage play [by John L. Balderston] himself) is as near perfection as can be hoped for in screen characterization. The rest of the cast is more than adequate.

Story of *Berkeley Square* is still another variation on Mark Twain's *A Connecticut Yankee in King Arthur's Court*. Where Twain used the idea of flashing a character into another century for fun. However, Balderston takes the thing very seriously. Balderston's character, Peter Standish (Howard) moves back into a spot used by one of his forefathers and falls in love with a gal of that period. It's a new kind of love story.

Heather Angel, as the girl, turns in a splendid performance.
□ 1932/33: Nomination: Best Actor (Leslie Howard)
• •

■ BERLIN EXPRESS

1948, 86 MINS, US ⓥ ⊙
Dir Jacques Tourneur   *Prod* Bert Granet   *Scr* Harold Medford   *Ph* Lucien Ballard   *Ed* Sherman Todd   *Mus* Frederick Hollander   *Art Dir* Albert S. D'Agostino, Alfred Herman
● Merle Oberon, Robert Ryan, Charles Korvin, Paul Lukas, Robert Coote, Reinhold Schunzel (RKO)

Most striking feature of this production is its extraordinary background of war-ravaged Germany. With a documentary eye, this film etches a powerfully grim picture of life amidst the shambles. It makes awesome and exciting cinema.

Chief defect of the screenplay [based on a story by Curt Siodmak] is its failure to break away from the formula of anti-Nazi films. The Nazis, now underground, are still the heavies but it's difficult to get excited about such a group of ragged hoodlums. Their motivation in the pic, moreover, is never explained satisfactorily as they set about kidnapping a prominent German democrat, played by Paul Lukas.

Starting out on the Paris-to-Berlin express to an Allied conference on the unification of Germany, Lukas gets waylaid in Frankfurt despite an over-elaborate scheme of guarding him. Symbolizing the Big Four powers, other passengers on the train include an American (Robert Ryan), a Frenchwoman (Merle Oberon), an Englishman (Robert Coote), and a Russian (Roman Toporow) plus a dubious character of unknown nationality (Charles Korvin).

Ryan establishes himself as a firstrate actor in this film, demonstrating conclusively that his brilliant performance in *Crossfire* was no one-shot affair.
• •

■ BEST FRIENDS

1982, 116 MINS, US ◇ ⓥ ⊙
Dir Norman Jewison   *Prod* Norman Jewison   *Scr* Valerie Curtin, Barry Levinson   *Ph* Jordan Cronenweth   *Ed* Don Zimmerman   *Mus* Michel Legrand   *Art Dir* Joe Russo
● Burt Reynolds, Goldie Hawn, Jessica Tandy, Barnard Hughes, Audra Lindley, Keenan Wynn (Warner)

Best Friends is probably not the light romantic comedy audiences expect from a Burt Reynolds-Goldie Hawn screen pairing but is nevertheless a very engaging film. Addressing the problems two writers in a professional and personal relationship encounter when they decide to get married, almost all of the picture's funny moments are underscored by the more serious issues they face from themselves, their families and society as a 'married couple'.

Both stars are tremendously aided by an intelligent screenplay from Valerie Curtin and Barry Levinson, who are said to have based at least part of this work on their own relationship. They leave Hawn and Reynolds more than enough room to inject their own nuances.

Director Norman Jewison does a capable job of moving things along and a nice balance between comedy and drama.
□ 1982: Nomination: Best Original Song ('How Do You Keep the Music Playing')
• •

■ BEST LITTLE WHOREHOUSE IN TEXAS, THE

1982, 114 MINS, US ◇ ⓥ ⊙
Dir Colin Higgins   *Prod* Thomas L. Miller, Edward K. Milkis, Robert L. Boyett   *Scr* Larry L. King, Peter Masterson, Colin Higgins   *Ph* William A. Fraker   *Ed* Pembroke J. Herring, David Bretherton, Jack Hofstra, Nicholas Eliopoulos   *Mus* Patrick Williams   *Art Dir* Robert F. Boyle
● Burt Reynolds, Dolly Parton, Dom DeLuise, Charles Durning, Jim Nabors, Robert Mandan (Universal-RKO)

The Best Little Whorehouse in Texas is just about everything it's meant to be – a couple of diverting hours in the dark. Rollicking, good-natured, a bit spicy and with just enough heart to avoid seeming totally synthetic, the $26 million adaptation of the 1978 Broadway hit [play by Larry L. King and Peter Masterson] ideally teams powerhouse stars Burt Reynolds and Dolly Parton.

Nifty prolog sketches how the title establishment is a regular Texas institution. Modest abode is currently under the proprietorship of Miss Mona, a super lady played by Parton with all her accustomed humor, warmth and knockout charm. Local Sheriff Reynolds is her b.f. of long standing, a down-home boy technically corrupt because he protects the illegal goings-on.

But nothing is sacred to media crusader Dom DeLuise, an outrageously self-serving muckraker who 'exposes' the bawdyhouse on his glitzy, song-and-dance TV news show and will stop at nothing to shut the place down.
□ 1982: Nomination: Best Supp. Actor (Charles Durning)
• •

■ BEST MAN, THE

1964, 102 MINS, US ⊙

Dir Franklin J. Schaffner *Prod* Stuart Millar, Lawrence Turman *Scr* Gore Vidal *Ph* Haskell Wexler *Ed* Robert E. Swink *Mus* Mort Lindsey *Art Dir* Lyle R. Wheeler

● Henry Fonda, Cliff Robertson, Edie Adams, Margaret Leighton, Shelley Berman, Lee Tracy (United Artists)

Gore Vidal's provocative drama of political infighting on the national level has been skillfully converted to film. Although not an especially fresh or profound piece of work, it is certainly a worthwhile, lucid and engaging dramatization of a behind-the-scenes party power struggle that accompanies a contest for presidential nomination.

Vidal's straightforward, sharply-drawn scenario describes the bitter struggle for a party's presidential nomination between an ambitious self-righteous character assassin (many will see him as a Nixon-McCarthy composite) and a scrupulous intellectual (of Stevensonian essence) who, ultimately faced with a choice of resorting to his opponent's smear tactics or bowing out of the race gracefully, decides he'd rather be right than president – leading to a somewhat pat and convenient conclusive development.

Between these two antagonists, portrayed with conviction and sensitivity by Cliff Robertson and Henry Fonda respectively, stands the imposing figure of the mortally ill but still politically virile expresident, a character likely to be associated with Harry S. Truman. Lee Tracy repeats his Broadway characterization in the role and just about steals the show with his expressive, colorful portrayal.
□ 1964: Nomination: Best Supp. Actor (Lee Tracy)

■ BEST OF ENEMIES, THE

1961, 104 MINS, UK/ITALY ◇

Dir Guy Hamilton *Prod* Dino De Laurentiis *Scr* Jack Pulman, Incrocci Agenore, Furio Scarpelli, Suso Cecchi D'Amico *Ph* Giuseppe Rotunno *Ed* Bert Bates *Mus* Nino Rota

● David Niven, Alberto Sordi, Michael Wilding, Amedeo Nazzari, Harry Andrews, David Opatoshu (Columbia)

The Best of Enemies produced by Italy's Dino De Laurentiis for Columbia, is a splendidly warm, wryly witty and amusing hybrid. Written by one Englishman and three Italians, it is directed by an Englishman (Guy Hamilton), has an Anglo-Italian star cast, with a few exceptions (one being American David Opatoshu), and an Anglo-Italian crew. It was shot mainly in Israel, with some location and studio work in Italy. Israelites were used as extras. Some Abyssinians were imported to play Abyssinian and two trained gazelles were recruited in Frankfurt, Germany.

It's a wartime comedy, with a gently serious undertone for those who seek it. Locale is the Ethiopian desert in 1941. David Niven, a British major, and his pilot RAF officer Michael Wilding, crash on a reconnaissance trip. They are captured by an Italian patrol, led by an Italian officer (Alberto Sordi). He releases them on condition that they let his patrol move freely to a nearby fort. Back in base, Niven is ordered to attack the fort and does so reluctantly. From then on it's an hilarious, cat-and-mouse game, with captor and captive alternating as the fortunes of war sway. The serious undertone? That war is crazy.

The screenplay is peppered with brisk jokes and unexpected offbeat situations which keep the proceedings light and easy. Hamilton has directed with a sure touch which brings out the characteristics of the two opposed nations admirably. Niven, debonair, nonchalant and skilfully underplaying, is matched excellently by Sordi, playing his first English-speaking role.

■ BEST SELLER

(Aka: Hard Cover)

1987, 110 MINS, US ◇ ⓥ ⊙

Dir John Flynn *Prod* Carter De Haven *Scr* Larry Cohen *Ph* Fred Murphy *Ed* David Rosenbloom *Mus* Jay Ferguson *Art Dir* Gene Rudolf

● James Woods, Brian Dennehy, Victoria Tennant, Allison Balson, Paul Shenar, George Coe (Hemdale)

Best Seller combines the sinister appeal of James Woods at his cold-blooded best with the gruffly lovable persona of Brian Dennehy as a literary cop; on the level of detective thriller, it's a real page-turner.

Dennehy is Dennis Meechum, cop who writes a book based on a famous unsolved case, during which he was wounded and three other policemen were killed. Seventeen years after the incident, he is a lonely burn-out case who lives at home with his meek teenage daughter (Allison Balson), trying to crank out another book.

Into the picture comes mystery man Woods, full of unctuous charm and foreboding stares. He presents himself as Cleve, a former hit man who worked for a pillar of LA society who, Cleve claims, ordered murders on everyone from business associates to tax auditors.

The body of the film has Cleve bringing Meechum around the country, providing different details in his story in an attempt to prove its authenticity, while Meechum takes it all down a book.

Director John Flynn keeps things moving through action scenes but is at his best during the psychological cat-and-mouse games in which the two leads find out about one another. While the conclusion is pat, pic is ultimately carried by the lead performances.

■ BEST SHOT

See: Hoosiers

■ BEST THINGS IN LIFE ARE FREE, THE

1956, 104 MINS, US ◇

Dir Michael Curtiz *Prod* Henry Ephron *Scr* William Bowers, Phoebe Ephron *Ph* Leon Shamroy *Ed* Dorothy Spencer *Mus* Lionel Newman

● Gordon MacRae, Dan Dailey, Sheree North, Ernest Borgnine, Tommy Noonan, Murvyn Vye (20th Century-Fox)

In *The Best Things in Life Are Free*, producer Henry Ephron and director Michael Curtiz went on the reasonably sound theory that, in telling the story of Tin Pan Alley's fabulous team of Buddy DeSylva, Lew Brown and Ray Henderson, all that was necessary to fill the widescreen with a huge potpourri of their works.

Considering that John O'Hara wrote the story, this CinemaScope tinter leaves a few things to wish for in that department. It catches little of the Jazz Age feeling, exce in its costumes and the frantic shimmy and Black Bottom numbers, and the songwriting trio barely come to life as real people.

It's a sparkling string of hits that's presented with all the nostalgic attention they deserve. Performances are top calibre, from Gordon MacRae's and Dan Dailey's pleasant crooning, to Ernest Borgnine's clowning and Sheree North's agile terp routines.

There are no fewer than 20 numbers in this opus. Outstanding are the big production numbers – 'Birth of the Blues' and 'Black Bottom' – choreographed by Rod Alexander. North, who has trouble with her diction in the speaking parts, is standout in the dance numbers.
□ 1956: Nomination: Best Scoring of a Musical Picture

■ BEST YEARS OF OUR LIVES, THE

1946, 163 MINS, US ⓥ ⊙

Dir William Wyler *Prod* Samuel Goldwyn *Scr* Robert E. Sherwood *Ph* Gregg Toland *Ed* Daniel Mandell *Mus* Hugo Friedhofer *Art Dir* Perry Ferguson, George Jenkins

● Fredric March, Myrna Loy, Dana Andrews, Teresa Wright, Harold Russell, Cathy O'Donnell (RKO/Goldwyn)

This is the postwar saga [based on a screen treatment by MacKinley Kantor, later published as *Glory for Me*] of the soda jerk who became an army officer; the banker who was mustered out as the sergeant; and a seaman who came back to glory minus both hands.

Inspired casting has newcomer Harold Russell, a real-life amputee, pacing the seasoned trouper, and Fredric March, for personal histrionic triumphs. But all the other performances are equally good. Myrna Loy is the small town bank veepee's beauteous wife. Teresa Wright plays their daughter, who goes for the already-married Dana Andrews with full knowledge of his wife (Virginia Mayo, who does a capital job as the cheating looker). Both femmes in this triangle, along with Andrews, do their stuff convincingly.

Cathy O'Donnell does her sincerely-in-love chore with the same simplicity as Harold Russell, the $200-a-month war-pensioned hero, who, since he has lost his hands in combat, spurns O'Donnell because he never wants to be a burden. That scene, as he skillfully manages the wedding ring, is but one of several memorable highspots.

The pace of the picture is a bit leisurely. Almost a full hour is required to set the mood and the motivation, but never does it pall. Not a line or scene is spurious. The people live; they are not mere shadow etchings on a silver sheet.
□ 1946: Best Picture, Director, Actor (Fredric March), Supp. Actor (Harold Russell), Screenplay, Scoring of a Dramatic Picture, Editing, Special Award (Harold Russell).
□ Nomination: Best Sound

■ BETHUNE THE MAKING OF A HERO

1990, 115 MINS, CANADA/CHINA/FRANCE ◇ ⓥ

Dir Phillip Borsos *Prod* Pieter Kroonenburg, Nicolas Clermont *Scr* Ted Allan *Ph* Mike Molloy, Raoul Coutard *Ed* Yves Langlois, Angelo Corrao *Mus* Alan Reeves

● Donald Sutherland, Helen Mirren, Helen Shaver, Harrison Liu, Anouk Aimee, Ronald Pickup (Filmline/August 1st/Parmentier/Belstar)

This C$18 million political saga is a thorough documenting of the life of Canadian doctor Norman Bethune, a hero in China for his medical input during the long march in Mao Tse-tung's revolution.

The film belongs to Donald Sutherland, who delivers a stunning performance as the complex and controversial surgeon. Harrison Liu delivers a fine performance as Bethune's protege, Dr Fong, but Helen Shaver (as a missionary in China) and Helen Mirren (as Bethune's wife) pale beside Sutherland.

Bethune was at once a boozing womanizer, a loving husband, a revolutionary surgeon and an ardently committed anti-fascist. He made a slew of enemies among colleagues and government officials before he declared himself a 'red' and headed first to Spain and then to China (the latter of which provides magnificent scenery in the film).

After several years of financial problems from both coprod partners (China and Canada), it's a relief that the film is better than expected and a disappointment that it is not as good as hoped.

B

■ BETRAYAL

1983, 95 MINS, UK ◇ ⓥ

Dir David Jones   *Prod* Sam Spiegel   *Scr* Harold Pinter
Ph Mike Fash   *Ed* John Bloom   *Mus* Dominic
Muldowney   *Art Dir* Eileen Diss
● Jeremy Irons, Ben Kingsley, Patricia Hodge (Horizon)

As it was onstage in 1978, *Betrayal* is an absorbing, quietly amusing chamber drama for those attuned to Harold Pinter's way with words.

In laying out his study of a rather conventional menage-a-trois among two male best friends and the wife of one of them, Pinter's gambit was to present it in reverse chronological order. Tale thus starts in the present and gradually steps backwards over the course of nine years.

Kingsley comes across best, as the film only springs fully to life when he's onscreen. Irons also seems very much at home with the required style. As the fulcrum of the tale, Patricia Hodge knows her way around dialog but pales somewhat in the presence of the two men and lacks allure.

☐ 1983: Nomination: Best Adapted Screenplay

■ BETRAYED

1988, 127 MINS, US ◇ ⓥ ⊙

Dir Constantin Costa-Gavras   *Prod* Irwin Winkler
Scr Joe Eszterhas   *Ph* Patrick Blossier   *Ed* Joele Van
Effenterre   *Mus* Bill Conti   *Art Dir* Patrizia Von
Brandenstein
● Debra Winger, Tom Berenger, John Heard, Betsy
Blair, John Mahoney, Ted Levine (United Artists)

Betrayed is a political thriller that is more political than thrilling but never less than absorbing due to the combustible subject matter, that of the white supremacist movement.

Clearly inspired by the murder of Denver radio talk show host Alan Berg, opening scene has abrasive Chicago broadcaster Richard Libertini followed home and gunned down by assailants who identify themselves only by spraying the letters 'ZOG' on the victim's car.

Cut to the endless wheat fields of the rural Midwest, where Debra Winger has come up from Texas as a 'combine girl'. Local farmer Tom Berenger quickly takes a shine to the new gal in town, while she responds to the warmth of his family life. Winger soon hops back to Chicago to brief her superiors at the FBI on her progress in infiltrating the group suspected of perpetrating Libertini's murder.

Like Ingrid Bergman in *Notorious*, Winger is pushed even further in her masquerade by her chief government contact (John Heard) who from all appearances is in love with her himself.

Berenger proves forceful and properly unpredictable in his vulnerable macho role, and entire cast is nicely low-keyed.

■ BETSY, THE

1978, 125 MINS, US ◇ ⓥ

Dir Daniel Petrie   *Prod* Robert R. Weston   *Scr* William
Bast, Walter Bernstein   *Ph* Mario Tosi   *Ed* Rita Roland
Mus John Barry   *Art Dir* Herman A. Blumenthal
● Laurence Olivier, Robert Duvall, Katharine Ross,
Tommy Lee Jones, Jane Alexander, Lesley-Ann Down
(Allied Artists/Robbins)

It's a backhanded criticism, but there's something too classy about this version of the Harold Robbins novel. It's too tame. And too solemn.

To be blunt, where's the raunch? This should be *Peyton Place* with plenty of flesh. Don't entice audiences with the name of an author associated with a long list of best-selling seamy novels and then deliver a 125-minute film you wouldn't be embarrassed to bring your mother to.

The script has four main interests: cars, sex, money and power It's an American movie. Laurence Olivier is retired auto tycoon Loren Hardeman Sr, founder of Bethlehem Motor Co, now interested in manufacturing a revolutionary car – one too efficient, too practical and too benevolent for American industry. It is to be called the Betsy, after his great-granddaughter.

Through a series of flashbacks, Olivier ages from 40 to 90. Complete with midwest accent, he's on target, maybe too much so. Ditto for Robert Duvall as his grandson and current president of the auto company, Jane Alexander as Duvall's wife and Katharine Ross as Olivier's daughter-in-law and lover.

Tommy Lee Jones as a dare-devil race driver hired by Olivier to build the dream car plays his role with a mixture of edginess and off-handedness – a combination of Burt Reynolds and Harvey Keitel. His style – it's got a sense of humor and a campy quality to it – seems more to the point. It's almost trashy. (Now that's Harold Robbins.)

Lesley-Ann Down, as a jetsetting designer who becomes involved with both Jones and Duvall, adopts the same tone, as does Edward Herrmann, Duvall's right-hand man.

■ BETSY'S WEDDING

1990, 98 MINS, US ◇ ⓥ ⊙

Dir Alan Alda   *Prod* Martin Bregman, Louis A. Stroller
Scr Alan Alda   *Ph* Kelvin Pike   *Ed* Michael Polakow
Mus Bruce Broughton   *Art Dir* John Jay Moore
● Alan Alda, Madeline Kahn, Molly Ringwald, Ally
Sheedy, Anthony LaPaglia, Joe Pesci (Touchstone/Silver
Screen Partners IV)

From a bolt of ordinary cloth Alan Alda fashions a thoroughly engaging matrimonial romp in *Betsy's Wedding*. Most of the action comes from the clash of personalities and wills as unconventional daughter Betsy (Molly Ringwald) announces her plan to wed boyfriend Jake (Dylan Walsh), and everyone jumps into the act.

Overreaching dad (Alda) wants a big, wonderful Italian Jewish wedding, and plans accelerate into a one-upmanship contest when Jake's wealthy WASP parents try to take the rein. To finance the bash, Alda, a contractor, unwittingly throws in with some funny-money Italian business partners, as arranged by his double-dealing brother-in-law (Joe Pesci).

Setting a buoyant, anything-could-happen tone from the outset, Alda as director creates what he's striving for: a feeling of being caught up in the warm craziness of this family, as all its vivid characters push and tug to impose their will on the proceedings. His punchy, inpertinent script is equally good.

■ BETWEEN THE LINES

1977, 101 MINS, US ◇ ⓥ

Dir Joan Micklin Silver   *Prod* Raphael D. Silver
Scr Fred Barron   *Ph* Kenneth Van Sickle   *Ed* John
Carter   *Mus* Southside Johnny and the Asbury Jukes
Art Dir Stuart Wurtzel
● John Heard, Lindsay Crouse, Jeff Goldblum, Jill
Eikenberry, Bruno Kirby, Gwen Welles (Midwest/Silver)

A fresh and uncluttered look at what goes on behind the scenes at a grubby, underpaid but undaunted little newspaper.

Where it is strong is partially due to the excellently-written script, partially due to the overall firstrate acting by the entire cast.

It's a series of inter-relationships, professionally and romantically, between staff photographer Lindsay Crouse and top investigative reporter John Heard; reporter-cum-bookwriter Stephen Collins and staffer Gwen Welles; plus the story of underpaid and overworked rock music critic Jeff Goldblum, copyboy and would-be reporter Bruno Kirby and the other oddballs who work for the

newspaper, due to be taken over any day by a communications conglomerate.

■ BETWEEN TWO WORLDS

1944, 112 MINS, US

Dir Edward A. Blatt   *Prod* Mark Hellinger   *Scr* Daniel
Fuchs   *Ph* Carl Guthrie   *Ed* Rudi Fehr   *Mus* Erich
Wolfgang Korngold   *Art Dir* Hugh Reticker
● John Garfield, Paul Henreid, Sydney Greenstreet,
Eleanor Parker, Edmund Gwenn, George Tobias (Warner)

An artistic transcription of [Sutton Vane's] *Outward Bound*, the Broadway stage hit of 1925, this film was earlier brought to the screen by Warner Bros in 1930.

A 1944 opening has been provided here, the locale being an unidentified port in England from which a small assorted group of persons is preparing to sail for America. Unable to leave because his papers aren't in order is Paul Henreid, former pianist, who recently had fought with the Free French. As result he and his wife, played with much feeling by Eleanor Parker, take to the gaspipe, both wanting to die together. Meantime, in an air raid the bus carrying others to the evacuation ship are killed.

From here the action shifts to a mystery ship which, it finally becomes evident, is bound for the Great Beyond, with Henreid, Parker and the group which had been killed in the bomb raid. Brilliant dialog and excellent performances, as well as thoughtful, imaginative direction by Edward A. Blatt, neatly sustain the interest aboard ship on the long voyage. There is no place in the story for comedy relief.

On reaching High Olympus and judgement day, Sydney Greenstreet enters the scene as the examiner, taking his new arrivals one by one. His performance is outstanding, and the sequence, though quite lengthy, represents a productional, directional and acting triumph.

■ BEVERLY HILLS COP

1984, 105 MINS, US ◇ ⓥ ⊙

Dir Martin Brest   *Prod* Don Simpson, Jerry Bruckheimer
Scr Daniel Petrie Jr.   *Ph* Bruce Surtees   *Ed* Billy Weber,
Arthur Coburn   *Mus* Harold Faltermeyer
Art Dir Angelo Graham
● Eddie Murphy, Judge Reinhold, Lisa Eilbacher, John
Ashton, Ronny Cox, Steven Berkoff (Paramount)

Beverly Hills Cop is more cop show than comedy riot. Expectations that Eddie Murphy's street brand of rebelliousness would devastate staid and glittery Beverly Hills are not entirely met in a film that grows increasingly dramatic as Murphy's recalcitrant cop from Detroit runs down the killers of his best friend.

Film was originally tagged for Sylvester Stallone and the finished product still carries the melodramatic residue of a hard, violent property, pre-Murphy.

Strong assist come from a deceptively likable performance from Judge Reinhold as a naive Beverly Hills detective, from by-the-book chief Ronny Cox, and from the serpentine villainy of Steven Berkoff, who plays an art dealer involved in nefarious endeavors.

Best moments arrive early when Murphy, bouncy, determined and vengeful, arrives in Beverly Hills in what old Detroit friend turned Beverly Hills art dealer Lisa Eilbacher correctly calls his 'crappy blue Chevy Nova'.

☐ 1984: Nomination: Best Original Screenplay

■ BEVERLY HILLS COP II

1987, 102 MINS, US ◇ ⓥ ⊙

Dir Tony Scott   *Prod* Don Simpson, Jerry Bruckheimer
Scr Larry Ferguson, Warren Skaaren   *Ph* Jeffrey L.
Kimball   *Ed* Billy Weber, Chris Lebenson, Michael
Tronick   *Mus* Harold Faltermeyer   *Art Dir* Ken Davis

● Eddie Murphy, Judge Reinhold, Jurgen Prochnow, Ronny Cox, John Ashton, Brigitte Nielsen (Paramount/Murphy)

Beverly Hills Cop II is a noisy, numbing, unimaginative, heartless remake of the original film.

Getting Eddie Murphy back to Beverly Hills from his native Detroit turf is the critical wounding of police captain Ronny Cox by a group of rich baddies committing the 'Alphabet Crimes', a series of violent robberies at heavily guarded locations. Once again, he goads reluctant cops Judge Reinhold and John Ashton into straying from the straight and narrow, once again the group visits a strip joint that looks like a *Flashdance* spinoff, and finally shoot it out with the villains.

Criminal element is represented by enforcer Dean Stockwell, towering hitwoman Brigitte Nielsen, who looks like Max Headroom's sister, and kingpin Jurg Prochnow.

Murphy keeps things entertainingly afloat with his sassiness, raunchy one-liners, take-charge brazenness and innate irreverence. Murphy's a hoot in numerous scenes, but less so than on other occasions because of the frosty context for his shenanigans.
□ 1987: Nomination: Best Song ('Shakedown')

■ BEYOND A REASONABLE DOUBT

1956, 80 MINS, US
Dir Fritz Lang   *Prod* Bert Friedlob   *Scr* Douglas Morrow   *Ph* William Snyder   *Ed* Gene Fowler Jr   *Mus* Herschel Burke Gilbert   *Art Dir* Carroll Clark
● Dana Andrews, Joan Fontaine, Sidney Blackmer, Barbara Nichols, Philip Bourneuf, Shepperd Strudwick (RKO)

A trick ending wraps up the melodrama in *Beyond a Reasonable Doubt* but comes a little too late to revive interest in a tale that relies too often on pat contrivance rather than logical development. Fritz Lang's direction does what it can to inject suspense and interest but the melodrama never really jells.

Dana Andrews is a writer engaged to Joan Fontaine, daughter of newspaper publisher Sidney Blackmer. The latter talks Andrews into going along with his scheme for showing up the fallacy of circumstantial evidence that has given ambitious district attorney Philip Bourneuf a long string of convictions.

In brief, Blackmer plans to plant evidence that will get Andrews arrested, tried and convicted for the murder of a burlesque stripper, recently found dead without any clues to indicate the killer. Scheme works as planned, except at the crucial moment Blackmer gets himself killed.

Neither above-mentioned players nor others in the cast add much to make the events credible, seemingly performing with an almost casual air.

■ BEYOND REASONABLE DOUBT

1980, 127 MINS, NEW ZEALAND ◇ ⊚
Dir John Laing   *Prod* John Barnett   *Scr* David Yallop   *Ph* Alun Bollinger   *Ed* Michael Horton   *Mus* Dave Fraser   *Art Dir* Kai Hawkins
● David Hemmings, John Hargreaves, Martyn Sanderson, Grant Tilly, Diana Rowan, Ian Watkin (Endeavour)

For 10 years the New Zealand public lived with the murder mystery surrounding the deaths of Jeanette and Harvey Crewe. After an unprecendented two trials, Arthur Thomas was found guilty. He was pardoned late in 1979. The story had enough false trials and contradictions to interest Britain's investigative writer David Yallop, and his book, *Beyond Reasonable Doubt*, is credited with much of the final boost that led to Thomas' pardon.

Yallop has done a workmanlike job on the book's translation to screen, and if the aim was to persuade us that a tough cop, hellbent on a conviction, manipulated murder evidence even to the extent of planting a cartridge case at the scene of the crime to implicate Thomas, then it strikes a bullseye.

Roles have been sharply cast to have lookalikes doubling for the real-life protagonists. David Hemmings brings a chillingly vindictive venom to the role of the cop, no doubt an accurate portrayal in terms of the Yallop thesis. John Hargreaves is suitably bewildered as Thomas, the rather simple young farmer who can't believe it's happening to him.

The soundtrack is noisy, drowning the dialog at times. John Laing's direction is mostly straight down the middle.

■ BEYOND THE FOREST

1949, 95 MINS, US ⊚
Dir King Vidor   *Prod* Henry Blanke   *Scr* Lenore Coffee   *Ph* Robert Burks   *Ed* Rudi Fehr   *Mus* Max Steiner   *Art Dir* Robert Haas
● Bette Davis, Joseph Cotten, David Brian, Ruth Roman, Regis Toomey (Warner)

Beyond the Forest gives Bette Davis a chance to portray the neurotic femme she does so well. The character of Rosa Moline, a woman who yearns for broader vistas than those supplied by the Wisconsin mill town to which she is tied, furnishes plenty of bite for the Davis technique and she belts it across.

Character [from the novel by Stuart Engstrand] is a modern-day Madame Bovary, a woman who sets her traps for a rich man. Davis gets over the character of the black-hearted Rosa, expressing the part with a vitality and earnestness that gives it a stylized vividness.

Joseph Cotten is the small-town minded doctor married to Rosa. His chore as the doctor is quiet and effective and David Brian is colorful as the man on whom Rosa has set her sights. He and Davis make their scenes particularly red-blooded playing of illicit love.

King Vidor seldom falters in his direction.
□ 1949: Nomination: Best Scoring of a Dramatic Picture

■ BEYOND THE LIMIT
See: The Honorary Consul

■ BEYOND THE POSEIDON ADVENTURE

1979, 122 MINS, US ◇ ⊚
Dir Irwin Allen   *Prod* Irwin Allen   *Scr* Nelson Gidding   *Ph* Joseph Biroc   *Ed* Bill Brame   *Mus* Jerry Fielding   *Art Dir* Preston Ames
● Michael Caine, Sally Field, Telly Savalas, Peter Boyle, Jack Warden, Karl Malden (Warner)

Beyond the Poseidon Adventure comes off as a virtual remake of the 1972 original, without that film's mounting suspense and excitement. Recap of original premise, a luxury liner turned upside down by gigantic tidal wave, is accomplished in a few seconds.

New plot turn pits salvage tug operators Michael Caine, Karl Malden and Sally Field against evildoer Telly Savalas for looting rights to the big boat. Caine and company are after hard cash, while Savalas, posing as a medico, is searching out a cargo of valuable plutonium.

The only change in this group's struggle to reach the top (really, the bottom) of the boat is a set of different faces.

Because the outcome is so predictable, the defects in the script take on greater magnitude.

■ BEYOND THE VALLEY OF THE DOLLS

1970, 109 MINS, US ◇ ⊚
Dir Russ Meyer   *Prod* Russ Meyer   *Scr* Roger Ebert

Ph Fred J. Koenekamp   *Ed* Dann Cahn, Dick Wormel   *Mus* Stu Phillips   *Art Dir* Jack Martin Smith
● Dolly Read, Cynthia Myers, Marcia McBroom, John La Zar, Michael Blodgett, David Gurian (20th Century-Fox)

This trashy, gaudy, sound-stage vulgarity about low life among the high life is as funny as a burning orphanage.

Dolly Read, Cynthia Myers and Marcia McBroom head a busty cast as three pop singers who come to swinging Hollywood with manager David Gurian. Read has determined to pry some inheritance money from aunt Phyllis Davis, who runs with a super-groovy set, shepherded by John La Zar, a Shakespeare-spouting effete.

Michael Blodgett plays a film hero louse, Edy Williams a sex goddess, Erica Gavin the obligatory lesbian, and Duncan McLeod an unscrupulous lawyer. The sole good running gag involves Williams and Gurian; she's ready for sex any place except in bed.

■ B.F.'S DAUGHTER

1948, 107 MINS, US
Dir Robert Z. Leonard   *Prod* Edwin H. Knopf   *Scr* Luther Davis   *Ph* Joseph Ruttenberg   *Ed* George White   *Mus* Bronislau Kaper   *Art Dir* Cedric Gibbons, Daniel B. Cathcart
● Barbara Stanwyck, Van Heflin, Charles Coburn, Keenan Wynn, Richard Hart, Spring Byington (M-G-M)

The polished production supervision has been carefully handled to give it the expected Metro gloss, and performances are of top calibre. Script, however, makes an even more shallow exploration of the passing of a colorful era than did the John P. Marquand novel on which it is based. It's a boy meets girl story, backgrounded against the period from the early '30s into the war years. Barbara Stanwyck has been stunningly gowned and beautifully photographed.

Stanwyck and Van Heflin, as the two principal characters, wrap up the roles with smooth performances. Heflin gives an expressive interpretation as the poor, liberal college professor and lecturer who falls in love with and marries the daughter of an industrial giant.

Charles Coburn is his competent self as the industrialist. Richard Hart does well as the stuffy lawyer fiance who is tossed over for the poor prof. Keenan Wynn ably projects the opportunist newscaster.

■ BHOWANI JUNCTION

1956, 110 MINS, US ◇ ⊚
Dir George Cukor   *Prod* Pandro S. Berman   *Scr* Sonya Levien, Ivan Moffat   *Ph* Freddie Young   *Ed* Frank Clarke, George Boemler   *Mus* Miklos Rozsa   *Art Dir* Gene Allen, John Howell
● Ava Gardner, Stewart Granger, Bill Travers, Abraham Sofaer, Francis Matthews, Peter Illing (M-G-M)

To make *Bhowani Junction*, based on the John Masters novel, Metro went to Pakistan to shoot a film about India. The journey paid rich dividends, for the sense of realism in the film is one of the best things about it.

Bhowani Junction starring Ava Gardner as an Anglo-Indian, and Stewart Granger as a British colonel who falls in love with her, is a horse of many colors. Picture goes off in quite a few directions, ranging from romance and action to a half-hearted attempt to explain the Indians and a more serious effort to dramatize the social twilight into which the British withdrawal from India tossed a small group of people who were of mixed Indian and British blood.

Story has Gardner as the half-caste returning home to an India seething with discontent and boiling with riots prior to the departure of the British. At Bhowani Junction, a railroad center, she meets Granger who's been sent to command a security detail to guard the rail line against Communist saboteur

Gardner thinks she loves Bill Travers, the local rail superintendent, also an Anglo-Indian. She's soon torn between being European and Indian, kills a British lieutenant who's trying to rape her and is temporarily saved by the Communist boss (Peter Illing).

Director George Cukor, in staging his crowd scenes, achieves some magnificent effects and Freddie Young's lensing is firstrate. The milling, sweating, shouting crowds, egged on by Red agents, are almost frighteningly real and th screen comes alive with an abundance of movement.

. . . .

■ BIBLE, THE
IN THE BEGINNING . . .

1966, 174 MINS, US ◇ ⑩ ⊙
Dir John Huston *Prod* Dino De Laurentiis
Scr Christopher Fry *Ph* Giuseppe Rotunno *Ed* Ralph Kemplen *Mus* Toshiro Mayuzumi *Art Dir* Mario Chiari
● Michael Parks, Ulla Bergryd, Richard Harris, John Huston, Stephen Boyd, George C. Scott (De Laurentiis/20th Century-Fox)

The world's oldest story – the origins of Mankind, as told in the Book of Genesis – is put upon the screen by director John Huston and producer Dino De Laurentiis with consummate skill, taste and reverence.

Christopher Fry, who wrote the screenplay with the assistance of Biblical scholars and religious consultants, has fashioned a straightforward, sensitive and dramatic telling, through dialog and narration, of the first 22 chapters of Genesis.

A lavish, but always tasteful production – assaults and rewards the eye and ear with awe-inspiring realism.

Huston's rich voice functions in narration, and he also plays Noah with heart-warming humility, compassion and humor.

The seduction of Eve by the serpent, the latter well represented by a man reclining in a tree, cues a sudden shift of mood and pace. Richard Harris plays the jealous and remorseful Cain with a sure feeling, while Franco Nero's Abel conveys in very brief footage the image of a sensitive, obedient young man whose murder provoked a supreme outrage.

The 45-minute sequence devoted to Noah and the Flood is, in itself, a triumph in filmmaking. It plays dramatically and fluidly, and belies monumental logistics of production. Huston's Noah is, again, perfect casting.

Stephen Boyd then emerges as Nimrod, the proud king, whose egocentric monument became the Tower of Babel where the languages of his people suddenly were changed. The remainder of the film is devoted to Abraham, played with depth by George C. Scott. Ava Gardner is very good as the barren Sarah who, to give her husband a male heir, urges him to conceive with her servant, Zoe Sallis.
☐ 1966: Nomination: Best Original Music Score

. . . .

■ BIG

1988, 102 MINS, US ◇ ⑩ ⊙
Dir Penny Marshall *Prod* James L. Brooks, Robert Greenhut *Scr* Gary Ross, Anne Spielberg *Ph* Barry Sonnenfeld *Ed* Barry Malkin *Mus* Howard Shore *Art Dir* Santo Loquasto
● Tom Hanks, Elizabeth Perkins, John Heard, Jared Rushton, Robert Loggia, David Moscow (20th Century-Fox/Gracie)

A 13-year-old junior high kid Josh (David Moscow) is transformed into a 35-year-old's body (Tom Hanks) by a carnival wishing machine in this pic which unspools with enjoyable genuineness and ingenuity.

Immediate dilemma, since going back to school is not an option and his mom thinks

he's an intruder and doesn't buy into the explanation that he's changed into a man, is to escape to anonymous New York City and hide out in a seedy hotel.

Pretty soon, the viewer forgets that what's happening on screen has no basis in reality. The characters are having too much fun enjoying life away from responsibility, which begs the question why adults get so serious when there is fun to be had in almost any situation.

Hanks plays chopsticks on a walking piano at F.A.O. Schwarz with a man who turns out to be his boss (Robert Loggia) and as a result of this freespirited behavior is promoted way beyond his expectations, but it's what he does with all his newfound self-worth that propels this 'dramedy'.

Greatest growth comes from his involvement with coworker Elizabeth Perkins, though by no means is he the only one getting an education.
☐ 1988: Nominations: Best Actor (Tom Hanks), Original Screenplay

. . . .

■ BIG BAD MAMA

1974, 83 MINS, US ◇ ⑩
Dir Steve Carver *Prod* Roger Corman *Scr* William Norton, Frances Doel *Ph* Bruce Logan *Ed* Tina Hirsch *Mus* David Grisman *Art Dir* Peter Jamison
● Angie Dickinson, William Shatner, Tom Skerritt, Susan Sennett, Robbie Lee, Noble Willingham (New World)

The plotline is flimsy at best, opening circa 1932 with Angie Dickinson posturing as a hard-bitten mother, rum runner, bank robber, jewel thief, kidnapper and queen bee in the sack. Both producer Roger Corman and director Steve Carver make a feeble attempt at social import by having Mama and true-blue lover Tom Skerritt martyr themselves so that the children may live and spend their ill-got gains.

Carver's direction mostly consists of winks at the film buffs in the crowd, as he apes the wedding scene from *The Graduate* and swipes bank robbery and shootout scenes, as well as the bluegrass tempo from *Bonnie and Clyde*.

Big Bad Mama is mostly rehashed *Bonnie and Clyde*, with a bit more blood and Angie Dickinson taking off her clothes for sex scenes with the crooks in her life.

. . . .

■ BIG BRAWL, THE

1980, 95 MINS, US/HONG KONG ◇ ⑩
Dir Robert Clouse *Prod* Fred Weintraub, Terry Morse Jr *Scr* Robert Clouse *Ph* Robert Jessup *Ed* George Grenville *Mus* Lalo Schifrin *Art Dir* Joe Altadonna
● Jackie Chan, Jose Ferrer, Kristine De Bell, Mako, Rosalind Chao, Mary Ellen O'Neill (Warner/Golden Harvest)

Hong Kong martial arts star Jackie Chan makes an amiable American film debut in *The Big Brawl*, an amusing chopsocky actioner whose appeal is not limited to the usual audience for this genre. Key ingredient here is humor.

Story is set in Chicago, 1938, and filmed with engagingly artificial style that resembles vintage gangster pix. Epicene gangster lord Jose Ferrer runs his terrain with the aid of his foul-mouthed, cigar-chomping mother (Mary Ellen O'Neill).

Attempts to strong-arm a Chinese restaurateur run afoul when his son (Chan) gets into the act with chopsocky skills. Chan eventually is recruited by Ferrer to be his entrant into a Texas free for all (the 'big brawl' of the title).

Chan's physical prowess grows, leaving the flashiest stuff for the finale.

. . . .

■ BIG BROADCAST, THE

1932, 80 MINS, US
Dir Frank Tuttle *Scr* George Marion Jr *Ph* George Folsey

● Stuart Erwin, Bing Crosby, George Burns, Gracie Allen, Leila Hyams (Paramount)

It's an all-star show with a flock of the biggest air favorites. Bing Crosby, Burns and Allen, Kate Smith, Boswell Sisters, Arthur Tracy (The Street Singer), Donald Novis, and the Vincent Lopez and Cab Calloway orchestras are as varied a galaxy of radio favorites as they are ether-renowned.

Crosby and Burns and Allen alone went to the Coast to participate in the actual production, having lines and parts, with the rest shot in the east and cut in for their specialties. While disjointed in action, the cutting in of the variety interludes is skillfully accomplished.

The film is a credit to Crosby as a screen juve possibility, although he has a decidedly dizzy and uncertain role which makes him misbehave as no human being does. George Burns with his serious-miened straighting for the dumbdora-ish Gracie Allen are a sock interlude in themselves as the station manager and dumb stenog, although it evolves into more or less a specialty routine.

The chief fault with *Broadcast* is that it's not a feature film but a succession of talking shorts. The story is rather childish.

. . . .

■ BIG BROADCAST OF 1936, THE

1935, 97 MINS, US
Dir Norman Taurog *Prod* Benjamin Glazer *Scr* Walter DeLeon, Francis Martin, Ralph Spence *Ph* Leo Tover
● Jack Oakie, George Burns, Gracie Allen, Lyda Roberti, Bing Crosby, Ethel Merman (Paramount)

Big Broadcast of 1936 is a film broadcaster of plenty of names and considerable entertainment. It hasn't much story, but the lack won't bother much.

Names are in and out as fast and as often as a firefly's tail light. There just isn't time for a 'plot', and probably best that none was attempted. Jack Oakie, Burns and Allen, Lyda Roberti, Wendy Barrie, Henry Wadsworth, C. Henry Gordon and a few others carry on whatever yarn there is and they play it lightly, as required.

You have look quickly to see such names as Bing Crosby, Ethel Merman, Ray Noble's band, Amos 'n' Andy, Boland and Ruggles and Bill Robinson. These and other specialty turns are worked into the continuity via a crazy television gag.

Oakie is the slightly bankrupt operator of a small time station and doubles as the outlet's 'great lover'. Oakie does the spieling and his partner (Henry Wadsworth) the crooning. Burns and Allen come in with an ingenious and also nutty television contraption, invented by Gracie's uncle, which can pick up any event and also send. The plot flows in between frequent 'television' specialties, with the telebox the vital prop of the picture.
☐ 1935: Nomination: Best Dance Direction ('Elephant Number – It's the Animal in Me')

. . . .

■ BIG BROADCAST OF 1937, THE

1936, 100 MINS, US
Dir Mitchell Leisen *Prod* Lewis E. Gensler *Scr* Edwin Gelsey, Arthur Kober, Barry Trivers, Walter DeLeon, Francis Martin *Ph* Theodor Sparkuhl *Ed* Stuart Heisler *Art Dir* Hans Dreier, Robert Usher
● Jack Benny, George Burns, Gracie Allen, Martha Raye, Shirley Ross, Ray Milland (Paramount)

The third in the *Big Broadcast* series from Paramount, this one, with its large cast of radio, stage and screen talent, far outdistances the two that precede it.

There are enough comedians of one form or another in *Broadcast* to make a hit soley on the strength of the laughs: Jack Benny, Martha Raye, Bob Burns and Burns & Allen are the prominents poking at audience ribs.

Burns' best scenes are those in which he

B

bursts in on radio programs which are on the air, while lookin for conductor Leopold Stokowski. Raye is slow to get started but finishes strong. Towards the end she socks through with the 'Vote for Mr Rhythm' number.

Benny plays the manager of the radio studios. He is mostly having his troubles with everyo from Gracie Allen down. The latter clicks from the outset, getting in for the earlier laughs built around the rehearsal of a skit under cute circumstances.

Several well known New York niteries get their names into the footage through the director's manner of suggesting how Ray Milland and Shirley Ross make the town one night.

....

■ BIG BROADCAST OF 1938, THE

1938, 88 MINS, US

Dir Mitchell Leisen *Prod* Harlan Thompson *Scr* Walter DeLeon, Francis Martin, Ken Englund, Howard Lindsay, Russell Crouse *Ph* Harry Fischbeck *Ed* Eda Warren, Chandler House *Mus* Boris Morros *Art Dir* Hans Dreier, Ernst Fegte
● W.C. Fields, Martha Raye, Dorothy Lamour, Shirley Ross, Lynne Overman, Bob Hope (Paramount)

With the rejuvenated W.C. Fields at his inimitable best in a streamlined production which combines spectacle, melody and dance, *Big Broadcast of 1938* is pictorially original and alluring.

The outstanding moment of the film, however, is a contribution by Kirsten Flagstad, of the Metropolitan opera company, singing an aria from *Die Walkure*.

Surrounding Fields and the diva is a company of players who keep alive interest in a better than usual libretto and, at the same time, turn in a full quota of laughs and musical numbers. Martha Raye, Dorothy Lamour, Shirley Ross, Lynne Overman, Bob Hope, Ben Blue, Leif Erikson and Grace Bradley are clicks. Specialties also come from Tito Guizar and Patricia Wilder. Shep Fields and his orchestra appear in a cartoon novelty.

There are half a dozen good musical numbers by Ralph Rainger and Leo Robin. The smash production number is 'The Waltz Lives On', which is a fanciful bit of terp and song that carries the waltz strain through the past 100 years. Staged by LeRoy Prinz and featuring Shirley Ross and Bob Hope it is the high spot of Mitchell Leisen's direction.

Screenplay starting with Frederick Hazlitt Brennan's original story, has something to do with a transatlantic steamship race between two greyhounds of the deep, one of which is owned by Fields. Specialties are introduced as the entertainment supplied to the passengers.
□ 1938: Best Song ('Thanks for the Memory')

....

■ BIG BUS, THE

1976, 88 MINS, US ◇ ⦿

Dir James Frawley *Prod* Fred Freeman, Lawrence J. Cohen *Scr* Fred Freeman, Lawrence J. Cohen *Ph* Harry Stradling Jr *Ed* Edward Warschilka *Mus* David Shire *Art Dir* Joel Schiller
● Joseph Bologna, Stockard Channing, John Beck, Rene Auberjonois, Ned Beatty, Jose Ferrer (Paramount)

Heading the cast of this overkill spoof is Joseph Bologna, good as a down-and-out bus driver whose chance to make a comeback is the nuclear-powered behemoth designed by Stockard Channing and father Harold Gould.

The first half hour or so is devoted to preparations for boarding. Herein is presented also John Beck, assistant driver with only one hangup (he blacks out on the road); computerized control center; Larry Hagman, malpractice-wary doctor treating Gould for injuries from industrial sabotage efforts led by iron-lung-bound Jose Ferrer.

Next comes the parade of passengers, each with their own formula destiny.

Finally come the complications, too numerous to mention. Suffice it to say that no cliche is left unattached.

....

■ BIG BUSINESS

1988, 97 MINS, US ◇ ⦿ ⦿

Dir Jim Abrahams *Prod* Steve Tisch, Michael Peyser *Scr* Dori Pierson, Marc Rubel *Ph* Dean Cundey *Ed* Harry Keramidas *Mus* Lee Holdridge *Art Dir* William Sandell
● Bette Midler, Lily Tomlin, Fred Ward, Edward Herrmann, Michele Placido, Barry Primus (Touchstone/Silver Screen Partners III)

Big Business is a shrill, unattractive comedy which stars Bette Midler and Lily Tomlin, who play two sets of twins mixed up at birth. They have distinctly different comic styles, with the former's loud brashness generally dominating the latter's sly skittishness.

A mishap at a rural hospital pairs off the daughters of a hick couple with the sprigs of a major industrialist and his society wife. Jump to New York today, where dynamic Moramax Corp board chairman Sadie Shelton (Midler) is forced to tolerate her scatterbrained, sentimental sister Rose (Tomlin) while trying to push through the sale of a subsidiary firm in their birthplace of Jupiter Hollow.

To try to thwart the sale at a stockholders' meeting, another Sadie and Rose, of the Ratcliff clan, leave Jupiter Hollow for the big city. As soon as they arrive at the airport, the complications begin.

Of the four performances by the two leads, the one easiest to enjoy is Midler's as venal corporate boss Dressed to the nines and sporting a mincing but utterly determined walk, Midler tosses off her waspish one-liners with malevolent glee, stomping on everyone in her path.

There are moments of delight as well in her other characterization as a country bumpkin who has always yearned for the material pleasures of Babylon.

Tomlin has her moments, too, but her two sweetly flakey, nay-saying characters for a while seem so similar.

....

■ BIG CARNIVAL

See: Ace in the Hole

....

■ BIG CHILL, THE

1983, 103 MINS, US ◇ ⦿ ⦿

Dir Lawrence Kasdan *Prod* Michael Shamberg *Scr* Lawrence Kasdan, Barbara Benedek *Ph* John Bailey *Ed* Carol Littleton *Mus* John Williams *Art Dir* Ida Random
● Tom Berenger, Glenn Close, Jeff Goldblum, William Hurt, Kevin Kline, JoBeth Williams (Carson/Columbia)

The Bill Chill is an amusing, splendidly-acted but rather shallow look at what's happened to the generation formed by the 1960s.

Framework sees old college friends gathering on the Southeastern seaboard for the funeral of another old pal, who has committed suicide in the home of happily-married Glenn Close and Kevin Kline.

Others in attendance are: sharp-looking Tom Berenger, who has gained nationwide fame as a Tom Selleck-type private eye on TV; Jeff Goldblum, horny wiseacre who writes for *People* magazine; William Hurt, the Jake Barnes of the piece by virtue of having been strategically injured in Vietnam; Mary Kay Place, a successful career woman who just hasn't met the right man; and JoBeth Williams, whose older husband returns home to the two kids before the weekend has barely begun.

Also provocatively on hand is Meg Tilly, much younger girlfriend of the deceased who doesn't react with sufficient depth to the tragedy in the eyes of the older folk.

Except perhaps for Hurt, who still takes drugs heavily and is closest in personality to the dead man [played by Kevin Costner, but edited out of the finished film], characters are generally middle-of-the-roaders, and pic lacks a tough-minded spokesman who might bring them all up short for a moment.
□ 1983: Nominations: Best Picture, Supp. Actress (Glenn Close), Original Screenplay

....

■ BIG CLOCK, THE

1948, 95 MINS, US

Dir John Farrow *Prod* Richard Maibaum *Scr* Jonathan Latimer *Ph* John F. Seitz *Ed* Eda Warren, Gene Ruggiero *Mus* Victor Young *Art Dir* Hans Dreier, Roland Anderson, Albert Nozaki
● Ray Milland, Charles Laughton, Maureen O'Sullivan, George Macready, Elsa Lanchester, Dan Tobin (Paramount)

There are weaknesses lurking in this pic [based on the novel by Kenneth Fearing, adaptation by Harold Goldman], namely a too-patly tailored yarn and some spotty acting, but these matter little. The pace is so red-hot that there's no time or inclination, during the unfolding, to question coincident or misplaced mugging.

Laughton, in this instance, is cracking the whip as the topkick in a gigantic publishing house. Toiling under him is Ray Milland, editor of a crime mag, whose peculiar value is his ability to run down concealed felons and expose them in his sheet. Goaded by insane jealousy, Laughton kills his mistress and scurries for cover. It's at this point that story's peculiar twist shoves it into high.

Laughton is aware that he's been sighted by his unknown rival. As he sees it, there's only one way out, and that's to locate the sole witness and either buy him off or cancel him in some other way. Milland, of course, is hired for that job, and his desperate efforts are directed towards covering his own tracks while pinning the goods on the real murderer.

Milland turns in a workmanlike job, polished to groove to the unrelenting speed of the plot. Laughton, unfortunately, overplays his hand so that his tycoon-sans-heart takes on the quality of parodying the real article.

....

■ BIG COUNTRY, THE

1958, 166 MINS, US ◇ ⦿

Dir William Wyler *Prod* William Wyler, Gregory Peck *Scr* James R. Webb, Sy Bartlett, Robert Wilder *Ph* Franz F. Planer *Ed* Robert Swink, John Faure *Mus* Jerome Moross *Art Dir* Frank Hotaling
● Gregory Peck, Jean Simmons, Carroll Baker, Charlton Heston, Burl Ives, Charles Bickford (United Artists/ Anthony Worldwide)

The Big Country lives up to its title. The camera has captured a vast section of the southwest with such fidelity that the long stretches of dry country, in juxtaposition to tiny western settlements, and the giant canyon country in the arid area, have been recorded with almost three-dimensional effect.

Although the story – based on Donald Hamilton's novel, with Jessamyn West and Robert Wyler credited with the screen adaptation – is dwarfed by the scenic outpourings, *The Big Country* is nonetheless armed with a serviceable, adult western yarn.

Basically it concerns the feud between Major Henry Terrill (Charles Bickford) and Rufus Hannassey (Bur Ives), rugged individualists who covet the same watering area for their cattle. The water spot is open to both camps since it is the property of Julie Maragon (Jean Simmons) who has been willed the property by her grandfather.

Bickford is the 'have' rancher of the area, with a fine home, a large head of cattle, a beautiful daughter (Carroll Baker), and a full crew of ranch hands. Ives is the 'have not',

67

with a brood of unruly and uncouth sons, a bunch of shacks, and an army of 'white trash' relatives. Into the atmosphere of hate and vengeance comes Gregory Peck, a genteel eastern dude, to marry Baker. Peck arouses Baker's displeasure when he refuses to ride a wild horse and backs away from a fight with Charlton Heston, Bickford truculent foreman who's after Baker himself.

As the peace-loving easterner, Peck gives one of his better performances. Ives is top-notch as the rough but fair-minded Hannassey; Bickford is fine as the ruthless, unforgiving rancher. Chuck Connors a former professional baseball player, is especially convincing as Ives' uncouth son who attempts to rape Simmons. Jerome Moross' musical score is also on the plus side.

□ 1958: Best Supp. Actor (Burl Ives).
□ Nomination: Best Score of a Dramatic Picture

· ·

■ **BIG EASY, THE**

1986, 108 MINS, US ◇ ⊚ ⊙
Dir Jim McBride *Prod* Stephen Friedman *Scr* Dan Petrie Jr. *Ph* Afonso Beato *Ed* Mia Goldman *Mus* Brad Feidel *Art Dir* Jeannine Claudia Oppewall
● Dennis Quaid, Ellen Barkin, Ned Beatty, John Goodman, Ebb Roe Smith, Lisa Jane Persky (Kings Road)

Until conventional plot contrivances begin to spoil the fun, *The Big Easy* is a snappy, sassy battle of the sexes in the guise of a melodrama about police corruption.

Buildup is quite engaging. In the classic screwball comedy tradition of opposites irresistibly attracting, brash New Orleans homicide detective Dennis Quaid puts the make on Ellen Barkin, a northern import assigned by the d.a.'s office to investigate possible illegal activities in the department.

Not necessarily the likeliest of couples, Quaid and Barkin bring great energy and an offbeat wired quality to their roles. Quaid's character is always 'on', always performing for effect during most of the action, and actor's natural charm easily counterbalances character's overbearing tendencies. Barkin is sexy and convincing as the initially uptight target of Quaid's attentions.

Ned Beatty projects an appealing paternalism as the homicide chief, while top supporting turn comes from the Ridiculous Theater Co.'s Charles Ludlam as a very Tennessee Williams-ish defense attorney.

· ·

■ **BIG FISHERMAN, THE**

1959, 180 MINS, US ◇
Dir Frank Borzage *Prod* Rowland V. Lee *Scr* Howard Estabrook, Rowland V. Lee *Ph* Lee Garmes *Ed* Paul Weatherwax *Mus* Albert Hay Malotte *Art Dir* John De Cuir
● Howard Keel, Susan Kohner, John Saxon, Martha Hyer, Herbert Lom, Ray Stricklyn (Buena Vista)

The Big Fisherman is a pious but plodding account of the conversion to Christianity of Simon-Peter, the apostle called 'the fisher of men'. Its treatment is reverent but far from rousing.

There is plenty of opportunity for both spectacle and sex, and it is all the more curious, considering its big budget and leisurely production schedule, that both are almost absent. Although the climax of the film is in Herod's palace where Salome served the head of John the Baptist to the tyrant, this scene, laid in a sumptuous and impressively lavish banquet hall, is done almost entirely by shadows and is swiftly over. Salome, in fact, is not only never shown, she is never mentioned.

Although the title seems to make Simon-Peter the central character, the film [from the novel by Lloyd C. Douglas] is only incidentally about him. His part in the story is his influence on two young lovers, John Saxon as

an Arab prince and Susan Kohner as the daughter of Herod by an Arab princess. Saxon wants to succeed his father as chieftan of an Arab tribe and Kohner wants to kill her father for the unhappiness he has inflicted on her mother.

Kohnner and Saxon make a handsome young couple. But their problems seem trivial against the turbulent era. Howard Keel is handsomely picturesque as Simon-Peter, and shows he can hold his own as a straight actor. It is not his fault that there is no suggestion of the doughty strength identified with the chief apostle.

The 'Palestine' that is the film's setting was shot entirely on locations in the San Fernando Valley and the California desert. It seems entirely authentic.

· ·

■ **BIG FIX, THE**

1978, 108 MINS, US ◇ ⓥ
Dir Jeremy Paul Kagan *Prod* Carl Borack, Richard Dreyfuss *Scr* Roger L. Simon *Ph* Frank Stanley *Ed* Patrick Kennedy *Mus* Bill Conti *Art Dir* Robert F. Boyle
● Richard Dreyfuss, Susan Anspach, Bonnie Bedelia, John Lithgow, Ofelia Medina, F. Murray Abraham (Universal)

In *The Big Fix* Richard Dreyfuss delivers what is for him a particularly relaxed and confident performance as Moses Wine, the 1970s answer to Philip Marlowe, Lew Archer and Sam Spade.

Simply as a detective thriller, *The Bix Fix* has strong appeal. As a centerpiece it has a tough, cynical, intelligent detective – an independent man with a rathole for an apartment, a personal life in need of some investigating and a full supply of wisecracks.

Briefly, the film finds Dreyfuss employed by Susan Anspach, like Dreyfuss a former campus activist, gone straight as a campaign worker for a gubernatorial candidate. Someone is trying to sabotage the election by distributing leaflets linking the middle-of-the-road candidate with radical elements. Dreyfuss is a natural for the case because he knew people in the radical movement.

The trail leads through Los Angeles – from the Beverly Hills mansions and social clubs to the Mexican barrios. Jeremy Paul Kagan's direction is nicely paced, starting off slow with the development of Dreyfuss' character and then speeding up as the plot complications mount.

· ·

■ **BIGGER SPLASH, A**

1975, 105 MINS, UK ◇
Dir Jack Hazan *Scr* Jack Hazan, David Mingay *Ph* Jack Hazan *Ed* David Mingay *Mus* Patrick Gowers
● David Hockney, Peter Schlesinger, Celia Birtwell, Mo McDermott, Henry Geldzahler, Kasmin (Buzzy)

A Bigger Splash is a revealing last ripple of the so-called life style of 'Swinging London' invented mainly by journalists.

Jack Hazan uses painter David Hockney, his art dealer in the US and his fashion creator friend and the latter's wife. It has Hockney breaking with a boyfriend and not being able to work as his friends worry and his American dealer exhorts him. He finally does begin one on a swimming pool, which eventually has a man floating in it and the one who left him standing outside and staring.

Real people play themselves around a partly-fictionalized tale. Hockney was noted for his color and specialization in California subjects. The gay life around him is indicated with style and taste.

· ·

■ **BIGGER THAN LIFE**

1956, 95 MINS, US ◇
Dir Nicholas Ray *Prod* James Mason *Scr* Cyril Hume,

Richard Maibaum *Ph* Joe MacDonald *Ed* Louis Loeffler *Mus* David Raksin
● James Mason, Barbara Rush, Walter Matthau, Robert Simon, Christopher Olsen, Roland Winters (20th Century-Fox)

James Mason has picked a powerful subject for his first 20th-Fox production and delivers it with quite a bit of dramatic distinction in carrying out the supervisory duties and as the male lead. *Bigger Than Life* exposes the good and bad in cortisone.

A great deal of care is taken in the forceful, realistically drafted screenplay [based on a *New Yorker* article by Berton Rouche] to give both sides of the case, while at the same time telling a gripping, dramatic story of peopl that become very real under Nicholas Ray's wonder-working direction. The performances are standout, with Barbara Rush earning particular praise as Mason's wife.

Mason is exceptionally fine as the modestly-circumstanced grade school teacher who undergoes a series of experiments with cortisone in the hope he can be cured of a usually fatal disease. At first the experiments progress promisingly, but he begins to overdose himself and some startling personality changes occur.

Christopher Olsen scores with his tremendously effective study of Mason's young son.

· ·

■ **BIGGEST BUNDLE OF THEM ALL, THE**

1968, 105 MINS, US ◇
Dir Ken Annakin *Prod* Josef Shaftel *Scr* Sy Salkowitz *Ph* Piero Portalupi *Ed* Ralph Sheldon *Mus* Riz Ortolani *Art Dir* Arrigo Equini
● Vittorio De Sica, Raquel Welch, Robert Wagner, Godfrey Cambridge, Francesco Mule, Edward G. Robinson (M-G-M)

Title refers to the theft of $5 million in platinum ingots – by a gang composed of a deported Italian mobster and four amateurs.

Screenplay by Sy Salkowitz, from an original by the producer, is amusing, although never of the belly-laugh genre, and Ken Annakin's direction is imaginative enough to maintain a light mood. Yarn has a set of characters which fit nicely into the action.

What appeals most is the general ineptitude of the would-be criminals as they seek to rob the train beari the ingots. In need of $3,000 to buy proper equipment for the caper, all their plans go wrong.

Vittorio De Sica pumps plenty of heart and humor into his role of the erstwhile Chicago mobster who attends the funeral in Naples of a Chi comrade-in-arms and finds himself kidnapped by four strangers, headed by American Robert Wagner.

Wagner handles himself satisfactorily, and Raquel Welch is his voluptuous girl-friend, still playing bikini queen.

· ·

■ **BIG GIRLS DON'T CRY . . . THEY GET EVEN**
(UK: Stepkids)

1992, 102 MINS, US ◇ ⓥ
Dir Joan Micklin Silver *Prod* Laurie Perlman, Gerald T. Olson *Scr* Frank Mugavero *Ph* Theo Van de Sande *Ed* Janice Hampton *Mus* Patrick Williams *Art Dir* Victoria Paul
● Hillary Wolf, David Strathairn, Margaret Whitton, Griffin Dunne, Patricia Kalember, Adrienne Shelly (New Line)

This tale of a teenage girl overlooked by her parents never escapes its sitcom premise and finally gives in to an ending so hackneyed it practically defines the term. Even with the reasonably deft guidance of director Joan Micklin Silver, the film struggles under its heavy-handed screenplay, featuring a stilted narration by teen protagonist Hillary Wolf that's a mix of bad one-liners and romance-novel angst.

B

Wolf resides with her uncaring mother (Margaret Whitton), rich stepfather (David Strathairn) and three step-siblings, while her biological father (Griffin Dunne) is estranged from his kind second wife (Patricia Kalember) and shacked up with his pregnant, much younger New Age g.f. (Adrienne Shelly).

Muddle gets worse when Wolf flees to the woods with her stepbrother (Dan Futterman) to escape a family trip to Hawaii, with the rest of her extended family in hot pursuit.

Most of the kids prove annoyingly precocious, and even the generally appealing Wolf gets stuck with dialogue that clearly sounds written for her by a third party and not like the ruminations of a teenage girl.

· ·

■ **BIG HEART, THE**

See: Miracle on 34th Street

· ·

■ **BIG HEAT, THE**

1953, 89 MINS, US ⊛ ⊙
Dir Fritz Lang *Prod* Robert Arthur *Scr* Sydney Boehm
Ph Charles Lang *Ed* Charles Nelson *Mus* Daniele Amfitheatrof *Art Dir* Robert Peterson
● Glenn Ford, Gloria Grahame, Jocelyn Brando, Alexander Scourby, Lee Marvin, Jeanette Nolan (Columbia)

The picture starts with a tight, believable screenplay by Sydney Boehm, based on the William P. McGivern *SatEvePost* serial, and goes on from there through tense, forceful direction by Fritz Lang and topnotch trouping led by Glenn Ford.

It is the story of a cop, a homicide sergeant, who busts up the crime syndicate strangling his city and its administration. Because he prefers to do his job and collect his pay honestly, he finds the going tough. So tough that his wife is murdered by an auto bomb intended for him, his child is threatened with kidnapping, and he loses his police job because of pressure from higher ups.

Ford's portrayal of the homicide sergeant is honest and packs much wallop. Lang's direction builds taut suspense, throwing unexpected, and believable, thrills at the audience.

Gloria Grahame's character, that of a gangster's sweetie, is choice and she makes it a colorful, important part of the picture.

Alexander Scourby, the man who heads the corrupt syndicate; Lee Marvin, his chief lieutenant; and Jeanette Nolan, the widow of a crooked cop who blackmails the syndicate, turn in strong individual performances.

· ·

■ **BIG HOUSE, THE**

1930, 84 MINS, US
Dir George Hill *Scr* Frances Marion, Joe Farnham, Martin Flavin *Ph* Harold Wenstrom *Ed* Blanche Sewell *Art Dir* Cedric Gibbons, Frederic Hope
● Chester Morris, Wallace Beery, Lewis Stone, Robert Montgomery, Leila Hyams, Karl Dane (Cosmopolitan)

As Butch, Morgan and Kent, Wallace Beery, Chester Morris and Robert Montgomery are a great trio in 'the big house', where each is serving a stretch for homicide, forgery and manslaughter, respectively.

Prison life on the half-shell is plainly exposed. The big wallop is the prison revolt, resulting in several deaths and an expose of how the officials deal with foolhardy prisoners. The hand grenades, barrages, stench bombs, tractor attacks and other means to conquer rebellious prisoners, with variations in the dungeon, etc, are all graphically dovetailed into the tense story.

☐ 1929/30: Best Writing (Frances Marion), Sound.

☐ Nominations: Best Picture, Actor (Wallace Beery)

· ·

■ **BIG JAKE**

1971, 109 MINS, US ◇ ⊛
Dir George Sherman *Prod* Michael A. Wayne
Scr Harry Julian Fink, R.M. Fink *Ph* William H. Clothier
Ed Harry Gerstad *Mus* Elmer Bernstein *Art Dir* Carl Anderson
● John Wayne, Richard Boone, Maureen O'Hara, Patrick Wayne, Christopher Mitchum, Bruce Cabot (Batjac)

Big Jake is an extremely slick and commercial John Wayne starrer, this time as a long-gone husband out to rescue a grandson from kidnapper Richard Boone.

Harry Julian Fink and R.M. Fink's original story and script is well-structured and fleshed with solid dialog. It opens with a 10-person slaughter 13 minutes into the film. Maureen O'Hara, as a strong-willed woman whose husband (Wayne) has long since departed, sends for him to track down Boone's gang which has kidnapped grandson John Ethan Wayne (the star's own eight-year-old son). Sons Patrick Wayne and Christopher Mitchum mature, in a manner of speaking, when they team up with their father. Bruce Cabot's performance as an Indian scout is excellent.

There is gore spattered all over the screen. A Wayne film doesn't have to resort to such excess. Performances are totally professional. Wayne and Boone snarl extremely well at each other. Patrick Wayne handles his role with a fine cockiness. Mitchum is very good Bobby Vinton plays another son who has little footage.

· ·

■ **BIG JIM McLAIN**

1952, 90 MINS, US ◇ ⊛ ⊙
Dir Edward Ludwig *Prod* Robert Fellows *Scr* James Edward Grant, Richard English, Eric Taylor *Ph* Archie Stout *Ed* Jack Murray *Mus* Emil Newman *Art Dir* Alfred Ybarra
● John Wayne, Nancy Olson, James Arness, Alan Napier, Veda Ann Borg, Hans Conried (Wayne-Fellows/Warner)

Honolulu forms the setting for a story of the work to expose Communist activities. The picture was rushed into the market and bears evidence of that haste. Continuity is choppy, the script sketchy and lacking in clarity.

John Wayne and James Arness are crack investigators for the House Committee on Un-American Activities. When it is learned the Communists are threatening in the islands, the pair is dispatched there to get evidence against the Red cells that can be used for a documented public hearing.

The investigation is tedious and not too fruitful. During its course Wayne meets and falls for Nancy Olson, a secretary working for a suspected doctor (Gayne Whitman). He pursues Olson and the Commies, gradually making time on both counts.

· ·

■ **BIG KNIFE, THE**

1955, 111 MINS, US
Dir Robert Aldrich *Prod* Robert Aldrich *Scr* James Poe *Ph* Ernest Laszlo *Ed* Michael Luciano *Mus* Frank DeVol *Art Dir* William Glasgow
● Jack Palance, Ida Lupino, Wendell Corey, Shelley Winters, Jean Hagen, Rod Steiger (Associates & Aldrich)

Film is of the *Sunset Blvd.* and *A Star Is Born* genre, an inside Hollywood story. It's sometimes so brittle and brutal as to prove disturbing. It differs from the Clifford Odets stage play of 1949, when John Garfield starred.

Rod Steiger vividly interprets the Janus aspects of the studio head who knows when to con and cajole Jack Palance into a 14-year deal. He has no compunction about staging an 'accidental death' of one of those 'casting couch contractees' (Shelley Winters), foiled by his laconic and resourceful publicity director.

Wendell Corey is properly 'the cynical Celt', Steiger's resourceful hatchet-man in the clinches. Ida Lupino scores as the realistic wife who wants Palance to forget the Hollywood loot and return to his 'ideals'.

· ·

■ **BIG MAN, THE**

1990, 115 MINS, UK ◇ ⊛ ⊙
Dir David Leland *Prod* Stephen Wooley *Scr* Don MacPherson *Ph* Ian Wilson *Ed* George Akers *Mus* Ennio Morricone *Art Dir* Caroline Amies
● Liam Neeson, Joanne Whalley-Kilmer, Ian Bannen, Billy Connolly, Maurice Roeves, Hugh Grant (Palace/Miramax/BSB/British Screen)

Though unquestionably well-intentioned and determined not to pull any punches, *The Big Man* [from the book by William McIlvanney] has a depressing theme and ultra-violent conclusion.

The early scenes, set in a depressed Scottish village where an abandoned coal mine and mass unemployment reflect the aftermath of Britain's crippling miners' strike, look promising. Liam Neeson comes on strong as the unemployed Danny, who was imprisoned during the strike for hitting a policeman and now has a middle-class wife (Joanne Whalley-Kilmer) and two bright children to support.

His best friend, Frankie (an engaging 'straight' turn from Scottish comedian Billy Connolly), acts as a runner for Mason (Ian Bannen), a corrupt businessman who needs Danny to fight for him. Motives for the fight, a bare-knuckle affair with no rules, are obscure.

The fight, when it comes, is one of the most grueling ever caught on film. Top marks go to the makeup team, which provided the battered and bloodied faces for the actors.

· ·

■ **BIG MEAT EATER**

1982, 77 MINS, CANADA ◇ ⊛
Dir Chris Windsor *Prod* Laurence Keane *Scr* Phil Sarath, Laurence Keane *Ph* Doug MacKay *Ed* Laurence Keane, Chris Windsor, Lilla Pederson *Mus* J. Douglas Dodd
● George Dawson, Andrew Gillies, Big Miller, Stephen Dimopoulos, Georgina Hegedos (BDC Entertainment)

A delightfully unpretentious musical comedy which defies classification, although billed as a 'bizarre new wave comedy'.

The small town parable about progress owes something to both Canadian humorist Stephen Leacock and to Harold Lloyd. The principal figure is a cheery family butcher who has invented a new universal language and is a great booster for his hometown of Burquitlam.

From the massive, murderous heating engineer Abdulla, played effortlessly by an Albertan jazz singer, Big Miller, to the highly strung teenage whiz-kid Jan Wczinski, beautifully rendered by Christopher Reeve lookalike Andrew Gillies, the cast is put through its paces with grea style by debuting director Chris Windsor. Modest budget was $150,000.

· ·

■ **BIG NIGHT, THE**

1951, 70 MINS, US
Dir Joseph Losey *Prod* Philip A. Waxman *Scr* Joseph Losey, Stanley Ellin *Ph* Hal Mohr *Ed* Edward Mann *Mus* Lyn Murray *Art Dir* Nicholas Remisoff
● John Barrymore Jr, Preston Foster, Joan Lorring, Howard St. John, Dorothy Comingore, Philip Bourneuf (Waxman/United Artists)

John Barrymore Jr is the star of this story, ineptly scripted by Stanley Ellin and Joseph Losey from Ellin's novel, *Dreadful Summit*. Losey's direction pars the writing and the playing is in keeping.

Plot line that can be sorted out of the muddled script gets underway on Barrymore's 17th birthday. Just as he is ready to enjoy a birthday cake supplied by his father (Preston Foster), the latter is brutally caned, without resisting, by Howard St John, a disliked sports columnist. Barrymore, disturbed by the incident, later that night takes a pistol from his father's bar and goes looking for St John. Much footage, all lensed in such lowkey lighting as to be almost obscure is involved with the people he encounters and side adventures during a night of wandering.

Young Barrymore is called upon to suffer extensively during his mental travail. Joan Lorring, a girl he meets during the night; Foster, St John, Dorothy Comingore, Philip Bourneuf and the others in the cast provide no lift or interest.

••••••••••••••••••••••••••••

■ BIG PARADE, THE

1925, 150 MINS, US ⊗ ⓦ ⊙

Dir King Vidor *Scr* Laurence Stallings, Harry Behn, Joseph W. Farnham *Ph* John Arnold *Ed* Hugh Wynn *Mus* David Mendoza, William Axt *Art Dir* Cedric Gibbons, James Basevi

● John Gilbert, Renee Adoree, Hobart Bosworth, Claire McDowell, Claire Adams, Karl Dane (M-G-M)

King Vidor had a tough subject to deal with. He knew that he would have to show the horrors of war, and therefore worked his story out in such a manner that it has plenty of comedy relief and a love sequence.

John Gilbert's performance is a superb thing, while Renee Adoree, as the little French peasant, figuratively lives the role. The same may as well be said for Karl Dane and Tom O'Brien, for it is the excellent work of all these players and the manner in which Vidor has handled the that lift this production far above the ordinary.

Teamwork has made this picture. It makes 'em laugh, cry, and it thrills – plenty. Besides which the captions are an example and a lesson of how it should be done.

The continuity is replete with little things that ordinarily wouldn't draw attention. For example, while a company of infantry is advancing a German machine gun opens up and sprays the line. Four or five men drop and the middle private of the group becomes rooted to the ground in terror, with his knees trembling.

••••••••••••••••••••••••••••

■ BIG RED ONE, THE

1980, 111 MINS, US ◇ ⓦ ⊙

Dir Samuel Fuller *Prod* Gene Corman *Scr* Samuel Fuller *Ph* Adam Greenberg *Ed* David Bretherton, Morton Tubor *Mus* Dana Kaproff *Art Dir* Peter Jamison

● Lee Marvin, Mark Hamill, Robert Carradine, Bobby DiCicco, Stephane Audran, Kelly Ward (Lorimar)

The Big Red One was two years in the making and 35 years in Samuel Fuller's head. It's a terrific war yarn, a picture of palpable raw power which manages both intense intimacy and great scope at the same time.

The story of the First Infantry Division's exploits in North Africa and Europe between 1942–45, fast-paced pic attempts to tell entire story of the European land war through the eyes of five foot soldiers and pulls it off to a great degree.

Based on writer-director's own experiences as a GI, pic was announced as a John Wayne-starrer in the late 1950s and came close to realization on many other occasions, but only came together when producer Gene Corman found means to make it almost entirely in Israel.

Approach eschews usual sociological analysis used in many war pix. These men are there for one reason only, to survive the war.

••••••••••••••••••••••••••••

■ BIG SKY, THE

1952, 140 MINS, US ⓦ

Dir Howard Hawks *Prod* Howard Hawks *Scr* Dudley Nichols *Ph* Russell Harlan *Ed* Christian Nyby *Mus* Dimitri Tiomkin *Art Dir* Albert S. D'Agostino, Perry Ferguson

● Kirk Douglas, Dewey Martin, Elizabeth Threatt, Arthur Hunnicutt, Hank Worden, Jim Davis (Winchester/RKO)

Howard Hawks has spared nothing in the filming of A.B. Guthrie Jr's novel, *The Big Sky*, except the cutting shears. Pic is a gigantic outdoor epic, but its impact is dissipated by the marathon running time.

Kirk Douglas is cast as a Kentuc mountaineer. Story involves his joining a keelboat expedition up the Missouri river in the 1830s.

Story line centers on the 1,200-mile trek up the Missouri from St. Louis to the Blackfoot Indian tribe in the northwest. Expedition is headed by French fur trader, Jourdonnais, excellently played by Steven Geray. The long trip is filled with the usual obstacles, warring Indians, treacherous white men, nature's forces, etc.

Femme interest is supplied by newcomer Elizabeth Threatt, who plays the daughter of a Blackfoot chief being returned to her tribe by Geray.

☐ 1952: Nominations: Best Supp. Actor (Arthur Hunnicutt), B&W Cinematography

••••••••••••••••••••••••••••

■ BIG SLEEP, THE

1946, 113 MINS, US ⓦ ⊙

Dir Howard Hawks *Prod* Howard Hawks *Scr* William Faulkner, Leigh Brackett, Jules Furthman *Ph* Sid Hickox *Ed* Christian Nyby *Mus* Max Steiner *Art Dir* Carl Jules Weyl

● Humphrey Bogart, Lauren Bacall, John Ridgely, Martha Vickers, Dorothy Malone, Peggy Knudsen (Warner)

Brittle Chandler characters have been transferred to the screen with punch by Howard Hawks' production and direction, providing full load of rough, tense action most of the way.

Humphrey Bogart as Philip Marlowe and Lauren Bacall as Vivian, Marlowe's chief romantic interest, make a smooth team to get over the amatory play and action in the script. Hawks has given story a staccato pace in the development, using long stretches of dialogless action and then whipping in fast talk between characters. This helps to punch home high spots of suspense, particularly in latter half of picture.

Chandler plot deals with adventures of Bogart when he takes on a case for the eccentric Sternwood family. There are six deaths to please whodun fans, plenty of lusty action, both romantic and physical, as Bogart matches wits with dealers in sex literature, blackmail, gambling and murder. Before he closes his case he has dodged sudden death, been unmercifully beaten, threatened, fought off mad advances of one of the Sternwood females, and fallen in love with another.

Some good scenes are tossed to others in the cast. Dorothy Malone, a bookshop proprietress, has her big moment in a suggestive shot with sex implications as she goes on the make for Bogart.

••••••••••••••••••••••••••••

■ BIG SLEEP, THE

1978, 99 MINS, UK ◇ ⓦ ⊙

Dir Michael Winner *Prod* Elliott Kastner, Michael Winner *Scr* Michael Winner *Ph* Robert Paynter *Ed* Freddie Wilson *Mus* Jerry Fielding *Art Dir* Harry Pottle

● Robert Mitchum, Sarah Miles, Richard Boone, Candy Clark, Joan Collins, Edward Fox (United Artists)

Howard Hawks' lusty, if confusing, 1946 filming of Raymond Chandler's *The Big Sleep* takes on even more filmic history in light of

this remake which transplants from 1940s-California to 1970s-London. The move denatures the Chandler environment Robert Mitchum encores as he did in the 1975 *Farewell My Lovely* remake.

Mitchum is hired by wealthy cripple James Stewart to probe possible blackmail. This leads him into the tangled lives of the client's daughters – semi-nympho Candy Clark and the more mature Sarah Miles. Latter has a relationship with gambler Oliver Reed whose wife Diana Quick has disappeared. Edward Fox was once in love with Clark; he is killed by Simon Turner. Bookstore staff includes Joan Collins. Weak-willed Col Blakely is no match for hitman Richard Boone.

As for the police, the shift to London introduces John Mills, Richard Todd and James Donald. Back at the mansion, butler Harry Andrews acts officiously, while chauffeur Martin Potter dies in attempt to help Clark avoid implication in pornographer John Justin's murder; she has been posing for nude pix.

The production is handsome, but in the updating and relocation a lot has been lost. In particular, gone is the 1940s LA feel. Only Clark seems to project the requisite spoiled-rotten youthful spark. Nearly every other principal seems beyond the point of really caring.

••••••••••••••••••••••••••••

■ BIG STEAL, THE

1949, 78 MINS, US ⓦ ⊙

Dir Don Siegel *Prod* Jack J. Gross *Scr* Geoffrey Homes, Gerald Drayson Adams *Ph* Harry J. Wild *Ed* Samuel F. Beetley *Mus* Leigh Harline

● Robert Mitchum, Jane Greer, William Bendix, Patric Knowles, Ramon Novarro (RKO)

Steal was lensed on location in and around Mexico City. It gains added sight interest from this, as well as strengthened melodramatics. It takes a little time for an audience to sort out what all the shootin's about since the script dives immediately into its story without explanatory footage.

When it does become clear the interest is strong as director Don Siegel unfolds a good chase yarn. Dialog is often racy and saucy, sharpening Jane Greer's s.a. factors.

Footage is one long chase through Mexico. Robert Mitchum is chasing Patric Knowles and, in turn, is being chased by William Bendix. All are interested in a $300,000 army payroll, stolen fr Mitchum by Knowles.

There's a nifty performance by Ramon Novarro as the hep Mexican police officer.

••••••••••••••••••••••••••••

■ BIG STEAL, THE

1990, 100 MINS, AUSTRALIA ◇

Dir Nadia Tass *Prod* Nadia Tass, David Parker *Scr* David Parker *Ph* David Parker *Ed* Peter Carrodus *Art Dir* Paddy Reardon

● Ben Mendelsohn, Claudia Karvan, Steve Bisley, Marshall Napier, Tim Robertson (Cascade)

The third feature from husband-and-wife team Nadia Tass and David Parker has a low-key charm that's appealing, and a couple of riotously funny scenes.

Ben Mendelsohn is Danny, a shy 18-year-old who wants two things: to own a Jaguar and to date Joanna (Claudia Karvan). Danny's father (Marshall Napier in a rich comic performance) gives him a car for his birthday, but it's a 1963 Nissan Cedric the family has owned for years. Danny decides to trade this in for a 1973 Jag in time for his first date.

Trouble is that car dealer Gordon Farkas (Steve Bisley giving a splendidly sleazy performance) is a crook who's switched engines on Danny. He and his mates decide to hit back by lifting the engine from Farkas' Jag while he's having a drunken time at a sex club.

Teens here are incredibly unsophisticated compared to 18-year-olds in Hollywood teen comedies, and that's part of the film's charm. Mendelsohn and Karvan are quite sweet in their roles.

■ BIG STORE, THE

1941, 94 MINS, US Ⓦ
Dir Charles Riesner *Prod* Louis K. Sidney *Scr* Sid Kuller, Hal Fimberg, Ray Golden *Ph* Charles Lawton *Ed* Conrad A. Nervig *Mus* George Stoll
● Groucho Marx, Chico Marx, Harpo Marx, Tony Martin, Virginia Grey, Margaret Dumont (M-G-M)

A large department store serves as background for this display of familiar Marxian comedy, the final film appearance of Groucho, Chico and Harpo as a combo.

Groucho gets a job as bodyguard-detective for Tony Martin, co-owner of the store, when manager Douglass Dumbrille tries to get Martin out of the way. The freres Marx then proceed to romp through the store in their usual slaphappy manner, taking advantage of the numerous props available for comedy purposes. There's the ususal chase through the aisles at the finish which catches plenty of laughs with its speedy display of ribald Sennettian knockabout slapstick.

Martin is okay in the straight role, delivering his vocal assignments satisfactorily. Others in support include Margaret Dumont, who continues as femme foil for Groucho's amorous approaches.

Direction by Charles Riesner takes advantage of every opportunity for basic slapstick – the broader the better. Harp solo by Harpo, staged between mirrors to obtain unusual effects both musically and comedically, is most original.

■ BIG STREET, THE

1942, 88 MINS, US Ⓦ
Dir Irving Reis *Prod* Damon Runyon *Scr* Leonard Spigelgass *Ph* Russell Metty *Ed* William Hamilton *Mus* Roy Webb
● Henry Fonda, Lucille Ball, Agnes Moorehead, Barton MacLane, Eugene Pallette, Sam Levene (RKO)

Taken from a *Collier* mag story [*Little Pinks*] by Damon Runyon, this is a Cinderella-like fable of a Broadway cafe-singing golddigger who becomes more human long after a fall cripples her for life. Scripter Leonard Spigelgass makes the transition from the grasping, selfish little beauty to a bitter disillusioned girl entirely life-like albeit a prolonged affair. He's done a neat job of transferring the spirit of the piece to the screen, studding it with typical Runyon humor.

Lucille Ball, cast at first in an unsympathetic role, comes through with high laurels. Henry Fonda, as the mooning but intensely loyal Little Pinks, is at his best. Eugene Pallette is well teamed with Agnes Moorehead, the food-loving but realistic Violette whom he weds.

■ BIG TIME OPERATORS

See: *The Smallest Show on Earth*

■ BIG TOP PEE-WEE

1988, 86 MINS, US ◇ Ⓦ ⊙
Dir Randal Kleiser *Prod* Paul Reubens, Debra Hill *Scr* Paul Reubens, George McGrath *Ph* Steven Poster *Ed* Jeff Gourson *Mus* Danny Elfman *Art Dir* Stephen Marsh
● Pee-wee Herman [= Paul Reubens], Kris Kristofferson, Valeria Golino, Penelope Ann Miller, Susan Tyrrell, Terrence Mann (Paramount)

Big Top Pee-wee again demonstrates that Pee-wee Herman is one very strange screen per-

sonality; he previously scored with his 1985 feature debut, *Pee-wee's Big Adventure*.

Surrounded by animals as strange as himself, Herman pursues a career in agricultural extravagance with the help of his goggled talking pig Vincent (amusingly voiced by Wayne White). Together, they grow outsized vegetables and a hot dog tree while wanly romancing pretty Penelope Ann Miller.

A storm brings broken-down circus to Herman's farm, adding a menagerie of freakish animals and people to his already curious collection. Kris Kristofferson oversees the visitors and keeps them rallied with hearty circus sayings, along with explanations of how he came to marry his miniature wife (Susan Tyrrell) whom he carries around in his pocket.

Very little of this is interesting or amusing on paper, which must have been a real challenge to director Randal Kleiser, who ably keeps all the surrounding players in tune to whatever it is that Herman's up to at any given moment.

■ BIG TRAIL, THE

1930, 125 MINS, US Ⓦ
Dir Raoul Walsh *Scr* Jack Peabody, Marie Boyle, Florence Postal *Ph* Lucien Andriot, Don Anderson, Bill McDonald, Roger Sherman, Bobby Mack, Henry Pollack, (35mm version); Arthur Edeson, Dave Ragin, Sol Halprin, Curt Fetters, Max Cohn, Harry Smith, L. Kunkel, Harry Dave (Grandeur version) *Ed* Jack Dennis *Mus* Arthur Kay *Art Dir* Harold Miles, Fred Sersen
● John Wayne, Marguerite Churchill, El Brendel, Tully Marshall, Tyrone Power Sr, David Rollins (Fox)

A big screen effort [based on a story by Hal G. Evarts] and an elegantly directed job by Raoul Walsh. But the recurrence of the same things, interrupted now and then by a 'big scene', such as the river or cliff crossing, or El Brendel's dragged-in comedy with his mother-in-law, or the simple romance and the silly melodrama, commences to weary.

This leaves the historical portion, the Oregon trail, as the single interesting part.

Young John Wayne, wholly inexperienced, shows it, but also suggests he can be built up. He certainly has a great start as the lead role in a \$2 million production.

Marguerite Churchill is set much in the same key, with not a great deal to do. Hers is mostly a silent role through being continually in a scrap with her sweetheart (Wayne) and not speaking to him.

The widescreen Grandeur [process] seems to dim the photography; leaves ensemble scenes indistinct, except for figure or form.

■ BIG TROUBLE IN LITTLE CHINA

1986, 99 MINS, US ◇ Ⓦ ⊙
Dir John Carpenter *Prod* Larry J. Franco *Scr* Gary Goldman, David Z. Weinstein, W.D. Richter *Ph* Dean Cundey *Ed* Mark Warner, Steve Mirkovich, Edward A. Warschilka *Mus* John Carpenter *Art Dir* John J. Lloyd
● Kurt Russell, Kim Cattrall, Dennis Dun, James Hong, Victor Wong, Kate Burton (20th Century-Fox)

Story is promising, involving an ancient Chinese magician Lo Pan (James Hong) who controls an evil empire beneath San Francisco's Chinatown while he searches to find a green-eyed Chinese beauty to mate with and make him mortal.

Director John Carpenter seems to be trying to make an action-adventure along the lines of *Indiana Jones and the Temple of Doom*. The effect goes horribly awry.

Leading the cast is Kurt Russell who looks embarrassed, and should be, playing his CB philosophizing truck driver character as a cross between a swaggering John Wayne, adventurous Harrison Ford and wacky Bill Murray.

He's caught in Hong's supposedly ghostly underworld with restaurateur friend Wang Chi (Dennis Dun) while trying to rescue

Wang's green-eyed Chinese fiancee, Miao Yin (Suzee Pai), from Hong's lascivious clutches.

■ BIG WEDNESDAY

1978, 126 MINS, US ◇ Ⓦ ⊙
Dir John Milius *Prod* Buzz Feitshans *Scr* John Milius, Dennis Aaberg *Ph* Bruce Surtees *Ed* Robert L. Wolfe, Tim O'Meara *Mus* Basil Poledouris *Art Dir* Charles Rosen
● Jan-Michael Vincent, William Katt, Gary Busey, Patti D'Arbanville, Lee Purcell, Robert Englund (A-Team/Warner)

A rubber stamp wouldn't do for John Milius. So he took a sledgehammer and pounded Important all over *Big Wednesday*. This film about three Malibu surfers in the 1960s has been branded major statement and it's got Big Ideas about adolescence, friendship and the 1960s.

Big Wednesday has a character named Bear, a combination John Milius-Ernest Hemingway, played by Sam Melville. He is described this way: 'He knew where the waves came from and why'. Really.

But Melville is a secondary character. The film revolves around three friends, Jan-Michael Vincent, William Katt and Gary Busey. Each is a noted surfer with Vincent something of a legend. Their life is surfing, but man – not even boy – can not live by salt water alone. So they grow up, awkwardly.

The movie is divided into four movements with each section moving ahead a few years. It climaxes at the final segment, Big Wednesday, when the surf has swelled to unknown proportions and the three reunite as men to again conquer the ocean.

■ BILL & TED'S BOGUS JOURNEY

1991, 98 MINS, US ◇ Ⓦ ⊙
Dir Peter Hewitt *Prod* Scott Kroopf *Scr* Chris Matheson, Ed Solomon *Ph* Oliver Wood *Ed* David Finfer *Mus* David Newman *Art Dir* David L. Snyder
● Keanu Reeves, Alex Winter, William Sadler, Joss Ackland, Pam Grier, George Carlin (Interscope/Nelson)

In aptly named *Bill & Ted's Bogus Journey*, the characters of the dopey, sweet-spirited dudes from San Dimas, Calif, go undeveloped in a sequel that contrives another elaborate but non-excellent adventure. Same producing and writing team pumps much effort into production design and special effects, creating a few triumphant moments, but not enough to sustain pic's running time.

This time, evil robot versions of Bill and Ted (Alex Winter and Keanu Reeves) have been sent from the futur to kill the duo before their band, Wyld Stallyns, can win a local talent contest and inspire a Bill and Ted following that changes the world.

The 'evil us's,' as B&T call them, throw the good dudes off a cliff, but before the Grim Reaper can claim them, they get to try to beat him in a contest, and since they pick the games (Battleship, Clue, Twister), they win. His Royal Deathness (played by William Sadler in a takeoff on Ingmar Bergman's *The Seventh Seal*) is then at their service as they embark on an odyssey to try to overcome the evil robot dudes and win the battle of the bands.

These guileless airheads with the outrageous vocabulary are obviously a beloved creation, and filmmakers might have gotten more mileage if they'd rooted their adventure a bit more in reality.

■ BILL & TED'S EXCELLENT ADVENTURE

1989, 90 MINS, US ◇ Ⓦ ⊙
Dir Stephen Herek *Prod* Scott Kroopf, Michael S. Murphey, Joel Soisson *Scr* Chris Matheson, Ed Solomon *Ph* Timothy Suhrstedt *Ed* Larry Bock, Patrick Rand, Duwayne Dunham *Mus* David Newman *Art Dir* Roy

Forge Smith
● Keanu Reeves, Alex Winter, George Carlin, Terry Camilleri, Dan Shor (Nelson/Interscope)

Keanu Reeves (Ted) and Alex Winter (Bill) play San Dimas 'dudes' so close they seem wired together.

Preoccupied with plans for 'a most triumphant video' to launch their two-man rock band, The Wyld Stallyns, they're suddenly, as Bill put it, 'in danger of flunking most heinously' out of history.

George Carlin appears as a cosmic benefactor who offers them a chance to travel back through history and gather up the speakers they need for an awesome presentation.

Through brief, perilous stops here and there, they end up jamming Napoleon, Billy The Kid, Sigmund Freud, Socrates, Joan of Arc, Genghis Khan, Abraham Lincoln and Mozart into their time-traveling phone booth.

Each encounter is so brief and utterly cliched that history has little chance to contribute anything to this pic's two dimensions.

Reeves, with his beguilingly blank face and loose-limbed, happy-go-lucky physical vocabulary, and Winter, with his golden curls, gleefully good vibes and 'bodacious' vocabulary, propel this adventure as long as they can.

. . . .

■ BILLIE

1965, 86 MINS, US ◇ ▣

Dir Don Weis   Prod Don Weis   Scr Ronald Alexander
Ph John Russell   Ed Adrienne Fazan   Mus Dominic Frontiere   Art Dir Arthur Lonergan
● Patty Duke, Jim Backus, Jane Greer, Warren Berlinger, Billy De Wolfe, Charles Lane (Chrislaw/United Artists)

Patty Duke stars as *Billie*, the tomboy who complicates her family life before shedding athletic gear for maiden attire.

Ronald Alexander adapted his *Time Out for Ginger* legiter of the early 1950s, cutting some characters to focus on Duke, the younger daughter of understanding Jane Greer and bumbling Jim Backus who shines in field meets via a mental gimmick. Coach Charles Lane uses her to goad his less proficient males, including Warren Berlinger to whom the gal eventually reveals her secret and gives her heart.

Complications, pat and unreal, include a mayoralty battle between Backus and Billy De Wolfe, wasted herein as a heavy who exploits pop's platform in terms of barbs at Billie and older sister Susan Seafort Latter pair stand out, as does Berlinger.

Backus is good in his now-standard characterization, while Greer is radiant and charming. Duke has an infectious personality which comes across.

. . . .

■ BILLION DOLLAR BRAIN

1967, 111 MINS, UK ◇ ▣

Dir Ken Russell   Prod Harry Saltzman   Scr John McGrath   Ph Billy Williams   Ed Alan Osbiston
Mus Richard Rodney Bennett   Art Dir Bert Davey
● Michael Caine, Karl Malden, Francoise Dorleac, Oscar Homolka, Ed Begley (United Artists)

Plot takes too long to get moving, and when it does it is quite incredible and hard to follow. Harry Palmer (Michael Caine) is instructed by an electronic voice over the phone to take a package containing mysterious eggs to Finland, and meets up with a former American CIA man, Ed Newbigin (Karl Malden), whose life he has saved in the past.

Palmer, whose mission is known to his previous MI5 employers, pretends to join the organization, which turns out to be controlled by a crazy American General (Ed Begley) with a Senator McCarthy attitude re Commies and a determination to defeat them by fomenting revolution in satellite countries and attacking with his own private army.

It doesn't matter so much that the storyline offends belief – so do the Bond gambols – but it is deployed by director Ken Russell with such abrupt speed that it doesn't make immediate sense in its own frivolous terms.

Malden and Begley, always reliable, do what they can with roles conceived as stereotype of greed and fanaticism respectively, and Francoise Dorleac introduces a touch of glamor as an agent who might be working for anybody.

. . . .

■ BILL OF DIVORCEMENT, A

1932, 75 MINS, US

Dir George Cukor   Scr Howard Estabrook, Harry Wagstaff Gribble   Ph Sid Hickox   Ed Arthur Roberts
Mus Max Steiner   Art Dir Carroll Clark
● John Barrymore, Billie Burke, Katharine Hepburn, David Manners, Bramwell Fletcher (Radio)

Standout here is the smash impression made by Katharine Hepburn in her first picture assignment. She has a vital something that sets her apart from the picture galaxy.

The play [of the same name by Clemence Dane] has lost none of its tremendous grip in translation to celluloid. Ten years after its stage success, this peculiarly British version of the Ibsen *Ghosts* theme still has power to grip and hold.

John Barrymore distinguishes himself anew in the role of the unhappy Hilary, part far from his accustomed range. For Billie Burke, the role of the distracted wife holds out small promise of flourish and histrionic parade, but she looks miraculously fresh and young, giving much charm to the character of the secondary femme character. David Manners as the heroine's young sweetheart is another happy choice.

. . . .

■ BILL OF DIVORCEMENT, A

1940, 70 MINS, US

Dir John Farrow   Prod Lee Marcus   Scr Dalton Trumbo
Ph Nicholas Musuraca   Ed Harry Marker
● Maureen O'Hara, Adolphe Menjou, Fay Bainter, Herbert Marshall, May Whitty, C. Aubrey Smith (RKO)

Clemence Dane's play, originally turned out by RKO [in 1932], skyrocketed Katharine Hepburn into prominence and marquee lights. Maureen O'Hara, a capable Irish actress imported by Erich Pommer and Charles Laughton, essays the Hepburn role in this remake with utmost confidence and ability.

Story is of a woman's sacrifice of love, marriage, and an anticipated family in order to care for her demented father. Adolphe Menjou, escaping from an institution for the insane, returns to his English manor home on Xmas to find his wife has divorced him and is ready to remarry. His appearance upsets plans, including those of his young daughter (O'Hara) who is engaged to young Australian.

O'Hara takes fullest advantage of a meaty role which is attention-arresting and rich in acting opportunity. Menjou provides an excellent characterization of the father (previously handled by John Barrymore). Fay Bainter delive her usual warmful and sincere performance as the wife who falls in love with Herbert Marshall and gets a new start for happiness. May Whitty commands attention as the elderly Victorian aunt of the household.

Direction by John Farrow provides dramatic power in his handling of a delicate subject. Script by Dalton Trumbo is workmanlike, although here and there are found long dialog stretches that carry over from the stage technique of the original play.

. . . .

■ BILLY BATHGATE

1991, 106 MINS, US ◇ ▣ ⊙

Dir Robert Benton   Prod Arlene Donovan, Robert F. Colesberry   Scr Tom Stoppard   Ph Nestor Almendros

Ed Alan Heim, Robert Reitano, David Ray   Mus Mark Isham   Art Dir Patrizia Von Brandenstein
● Dustin Hoffman, Nicole Kidman, Loren Dean, Bruce Willis, Steven Hill, Stanley Tucci (Touchstone)

This refined, intelligent drama about thugs appeals considerably to the head but has little impact on the gut, which is not exactly how it should be with gangster films. Robert Benton's screen version of *Billy Bathgate*, E.L. Doctorow's 1988 bestseller about the last act of Dutch Shultz' life, is beautifully realized and a pleasure to watch, but its center is hard to locate.

Returning to the 1930s criminal milieu for the first time since *Bonnie and Clyde*, Benton has invested the picture with extensive class and storytelling smarts, and the $40 million-plus production bears no signs of the rumored troubles of its making.

Tom Stoppard's tight, neatly arcing screenplay kicks off powerfully with Schultz (Dustin Hoffman), arguably the king of the New York underworld in 1935, taking his once-trusted top enforcer (Bruce Willis) for a nocturnal tugboat ride, tying him up and planting his feet in cement.

Observing this showdown from close range is Billy (Loren Dean) a nervy kid who (as seen in an eventful 35-minute flashback) has worked his way up from the streets of the Bronx to become one of Dutch's valued flunkies. Dutch still may be prospering, but the Feds are moving in mercilessly.

All this is a backdrop to the personal drama that mainly concerns Billy earning a place in the gang and vowing to take care of the beautiful Drew Preston (Nicole Kidman), the dead enforcer's former girlfriend.

Despite Dean's alert, open performance, Billy remains an opaque witness to events that are unfolding over his head. Hoffman's performance also is problematic. There is a stiffness that sets his impersonation apart from his best contempo characterizations. Kidman comes on strongly, showing both girlish frivolousness and steely resolve in her portrait of the opportunistic Drew.

. . . .

■ BILLY BUDD

1962, 123 MINS, US/UK ▣

Dir Peter Ustinov   Prod Peter Ustinov   Scr Peter Ustinov, Robert Rossen   Ph Robert Krasker   Ed Jack Harris
Mus Anthony Hopkins   Art Dir Don Ashton
● Robert Ryan, Peter Ustinov, Melvyn Douglas, Terence Stamp, Ronald Lewis, David McCallum (Allied Artists)

Peter Ustinov's production of *Billy Budd* is a near miss, and Ustinov, alas, is the culprit. The ubiquitous Mr U is to be commended for spearheading the noble effort to translate Herman Melville's highly-regarded, thought-provoking last story the screen – a difficult task. But as director he is guilty of at least one major flaw of execution in which Ustinov, the actor is most prominently implicated.

Billy Budd is the allegorical tale of the clash of an incredibly good-hearted young foretopman and an inhumanly sadistic master-at-arms aboard a British fighting vessel in 1797, and the issue of moral justice vs. the wartime military code that arises when the former is condemned to hang for killing the latter, though recognized even by those who sit in judgment upon him as being spirituallly innocent.

The clash between Budd and his tormentor, Claggart – archtypes of good and evil – has been carried off well by Terence Stamp and Robert Ryan under Ustinov's guidance. Where Ustinov has slipped is in the development and delineation of the character he himself plays – the overly conscientious Captain Vere, whose judgment in favor of military over moral ramifications of the issue sends Budd to his death.

☐ 1962: Nomination: Best Supp. Actor (Terence Stamp)

. . . .

■ BILLY JACK

1971, 115 MINS, US ◇ ⓥ ☉
Dir T.C. Frank [= Tom Laughlin]   *Prod* Mary Rose Solti
Scr T.C. Frank, Teresa Christina [= Delores Taylor]
Ph Fred Koenekamp, John Stephens   *Ed* Larry Heath,
Marion Rothman   *Mus* Mundell Lowe
● Tom Laughlin, Delores Taylor, Clark Howat, Bert
Freed, Julie Webb, Ken Tobey (National Student)

Billy Jack appears to be a labor of love in
which the plight of the American Indian, are
pinpointed.

Produced by National Student Film Corp,
Warners bought picture outright. Leading
character is a half-breed named Billy Jack,
guardian of the Redman's rights and nemesis
of any white who may intrude on these rights.
He finds plenty of opportunity to assert himself, what with defending wild horses on the
Arizona reservation, wild kids, a school on the
reservation, and the actions of residents of a
neighboring town violently opposed both to
the school and Billy himself.

Screenplay attempts to encompass too
many story facets. Result is that the action
frequently drags and interest palls as some of
the young people in the school, many of them
white, spout their philosophy and question
the behavior of the whites.

Tom Laughlin, as the invincible defender, is
firstrate, handling himself effectively. So, too,
does Delores Taylor, a white woman who runs
the school. Clark Howat, as the sheriff who
understands the Indians' problems, is convincing.

■ BILLY JACK GOES TO WASHINGTON

1977, 155 MINS, US ◇
Dir T.C. Frank [= Tom Laughlin]   *Prod* Frank Capra Jr
Scr T.C. Frank, Teresa Christina [= Delores Taylor]
Ph Jack Marta   *Mus* Elmer Bernstein   *Art Dir* Hilyard
Brown
● Tom Laughlin, Delores Taylor, E.G. Marshall, Teresa
Laughlin, Sam Wanamaker, Lucie Arnaz (Taylor-Laughlin)

Billy Jack Goes to Washington, a remake of the
1939 Frank Capra classic *Mr Smith Goes to
Washington*, compensates for its lack of subtlety with an angry, attack on governmental
corruption.

The corruption of the Senate in the Capra
film is changed here to the issue of nuclear
plants.

In the old James Stewart role of the inno-
cent-turned-Senator, Tom Laughlin is fighting against the scheme of political boss Sam
Wanamaker and corrupt fellow Senator E.G.
Marshall to exploit a planned nuclear plant
for their financial gain.

Laughlin, identified with activist groups,
takes the same stand against the establishment Stewart did in the original.

By comparison with the brilliance of the
Capra version, the pic is much flatter and
largely devoid of performing or visual nuances.

■ BILLY LIAR

1963, 98 MINS, UK ⓥ
Dir John Schlesinger   *Prod* Joseph Janni   *Scr* Keith
Waterhouse, Willis Hall   *Ph* Denys Coop   *Ed* Roger
Cherrill   *Mus* Richard Rodney Bennett
● Tom Courtenay, Julie Christie, Wilfred Pickles, Mona
Washbourne, Finlay Currie, Rodney Bewes (Vic/Anglo-
Amalgamated)

Based on a West End hit play by Keith
Waterhouse (who wrote the novel) and Willis
Hall, *Billy Liar* is an imaginative, fascinating
film. It is perhaps unfair to label the film as
entirely realistic, since it moves into a world
of Walter Mitty-like fantasy, and that is its
only weakness. These scenes lack impact.

Billy Liar (Tom Courtenay) is a day-dreaming young man who leads an irresponsible life
as a funeral director's clerk. He fiddles the

petty cash, he is at war with his parents, he
has become involved with two young women
who share an engagement ring. Above all, he
is an incorrigible liar, dreaming dreams and,
whenever possible, retreating into an invented world where he is the dictator of an
imagined slice of Ruritania.

Courtenay who took over from Albert
Finney in the legit version of *Billy Liar*, has a
hefty part and is rarely off the screen. Of the
three girls with whom he is involved, Julie
Christie is the only one who really understands him. Christie turns in a glowing performance. Helen Fraser and Gwendolyn
Watts provide sharply contrasting performances as the other young women in Billy
Liar's complicated, muddled existence.

Mona Washbourne, as his dim mother,
Wilfred Pickles playing a hectoring, stupid father, and grandmother Ethel Griffies also
lend considerable color.

■ BILLY THE KID

1930, 95 MINS, US
Dir King Vidor   *Scr* Wanda Tuchock, Laurence Stallings,
Charles MacArthur   *Ph* Gordon Avil   *Ed* Hugh Wynn
Art Dir Cedric Gibbons
● John Mack Brown, Wallace Beery, Kay Johnson, Karl
Dane, Wyndham Standing, Russell Simpson (M-G-M)

Metro turned this one out on Realife – shooting with a 70mm camera [negative] after
which the result is reduced to 35mm for the
projectors on which a special lens supposedly
brings out all the condensed details on an enlarged screen. It spreads across the stage in
the same oblong shape as Fox's Grandeur
[process, used for *The Big Trail*, also 1930].
The panoramic exteriors all look good.
Director King Vidor evidently wanted to impress that fact early for the initial shot is an
imposing peek of what may be the Grand
Canyon.

Billy the Kid [from the book *The Saga of Billy
the Kid* by Walter Noble Burns] is replete with
gunfights and anti-climaxes. At least on two
occasions it looks as if the feature is finished
– but keeps right on going. There's little or
no love interest, albeit the script intimates
that the Kid would like to fall for best friend's
wife. That her fiance is shot on their wedding
day is the reason the Kid swears vengeance
upon one-half of the State of New Mexico and
they have to call in the cavalry to halt his ensuing feud with the Donovan mob.

■ BILLY TWO HATS

1974, 99 MINS, US ◇ ⓥ
Dir Ted Kotcheff   *Prod* Norman Jewison, Patrick Palmer
Scr Alan Sharp   *Ph* Brian West   *Mus* John Scott
Art Dir Tony Pratt
● Gregory Peck, Desi Arnaz Jr, Jack Warden, Sian
Barbara Allen, David Huddleston, John Pearce
(Algonquin)

This is a fresh, different oater (the first
filmed in Israel) that opens with violence and
contains some throughout but never lingers
lovingly on mayhem and gore.

A Scot and a young half-Indian (Billy Two
Hats, because his white father was an important man) commit a robbery with an unintended murder that nets them only $420.
They get away, but the far-off Scot is shot in
the leg with a buffalo gun. The lad makes a
rough stretcher and hauls him behind his
horse. They stop at the home of old rancher
with a young wife he'd bought for $100 in St.
Louis.

Gregory Peck, almost unrecognizable behind a broad Highland brogue and a bushy
beard, is splendid. Desi Arnaz Jr as the
'breed' treated with contempt by almost
everyone, is okay and shows promise.

■ BILOXI BLUES

1988, 106 MINS, US ◇ ⓥ ☉
Dir Mike Nichols   *Prod* Ray Stark   *Scr* Neil Simon
Ph Bill Butler   *Ed* Sam O'Steen   *Mus* Georges Delerue
Art Dir Paul Sylbert
● Matthew Broderick, Christopher Walken, Matt
Mulhern, Michael Dolan, Penelope Ann Miller, Markus
Flanagan (Rastar/Universal)

Biloxi Blues is an agreeable but hardly inspired film version of Neil Simon's second installment of his autobiographical trilogy,
which bowed during the 1984–85 season.
Even with high-powered talents Mike Nichols
and Matthew Broderick aboard, World War II
barracks comedy provokes just mild laughs
and smiles rather than the guffaws Simon's
work often elicits in the theater.

Film is narrated from an adult perspective
by Simon's alter ego, Eugene Morris Jerome
(Broderick), an aspiring writer called up for
service in the waning months of the war.

With 10 weeks of boot camp ahead of them,
it's not at all sure that Eugene and his cohorts will ever see action, but that doesn't
prevent basic training from being a living hell
relieved only by an excursion into town to
party and look for ladies.

Playing a character perched precisely on
the point between adolescence and manhood,
Broderick is enjoyable all the way.

Penelope Ann Miller is adorable as the girl
who inspires love at first sight in Eugene at a
dance, while the most intriguing performance
comes from Christopher Walken as the weird
sergeant.

■ BINGO LONG TRAVELING ALL-STARS AND MOTOR KINGS, THE

1976, 110 MINS, US ◇ ⓥ
Dir John Badham   *Prod* Rob Cohen   *Scr* Hal Barwood,
Matthew Robbins   *Ph* Bill Butler   *Ed* David Rawlins
Mus William Goldstein   *Art Dir* Lawrence G. Paull
● Billy Dee Williams, James Earl Jones, Richard Pryor,
Rico Dawson, Sam 'Birmingham' Brison, Jophery Brown
(Motown/Pan-Arts)

Billy Dee Williams and James Earl Jones are
superb as leaders of a barnstorming black
baseball team circa 1939. Based on a William
Brashler novel, the script is an adroit mix of
broad comedy and credible dramatic conflict.

Fed up with the hard-nosed ways of team
owner Ted Ross, Williams quits a team in the
old Negro (remember the film's period) baseball league. Shut out of the league, and not
yet admitted to mainstream sports, the slap-
happy crew discovers success by combining
top performance with farce.

But Ross's goons (Ken Force and Carl
Gordon) eventually get the upper hand.

Among the standout featured players is
Richard Pryor, shifting amusingly from
Cuban to Indian heritages as a way to break
the black barrier.

■ BIRD

1988, 161 MINS, US ◇ ⓥ ☉
Dir Clint Eastwood   *Prod* Clint Eastwood   *Scr* Joel
Oliansky   *Ph* Jack N. Green   *Ed* Joel Cox   *Mus* Lennie
Niehaus   *Art Dir* Edward C. Carfagno
● Forest Whitaker, Diane Venora, Michael Zelniker,
Samuel E. Wright, Keith David (Malpaso/Warner)

In taking on a biopic of late jazz great Charlie
Parker, Clint Eastwood has had to chart bold
new territory for himself as a director, and he
has pulled it off in most impressive fashion.

Sensitively acted, beautifully planned visually and dynamite musically, this is a dramatic telling of the troubled life of a
revolutionary artist.

That Parker (Forest Whitaker), who died in
1955 at 34, was the greatest sax man of them
all is virtually undisputed, but he also lived a
messy, complicated life, mixing drug addic-

tion and a multitude of women with an ongoing attempt at a home life with his wife Chan (Diane Venora) and their two children.

Joel Oliansky's big-framed script, originally written for Richard Pryor at Columbia some years earlier jumps around considerably at the beginning, skipping strikingly from Parker's Childhood to a suicide attempt in 1954, then to some other key incidents.

Naturally, the prolific artist's music provides the continuing thread for the film, and jazzman Lennie Niehaus does a sensational job in blending Bird's actual sax solos with fresh backups by contemporary musicians.

Whitaker makes an imposing, likable, very hip genius, with an especially memorable death scene. Venora is so riveting that her occasional long absences from the story are sorely missed. The one person who could really understand Bird is presented as a feisty woman of great character, awareness and strength.

☐ 1988: Best Sound

....

■ BIRDMAN OF ALCATRAZ

1962, 147 MINS, US ⑩ ⊙
Dir John Frankenheimer *Prod* Stuart Millar, Guy Trosper
Scr Guy Trosper *Ph* Burnett Guffey *Ed* Edward Mann
Mus Elmer Bernstein *Art Dir* Ferdie Carrere
● Burt Lancaster, Karl Malden, Thelma Ritter, Neville Brand, Telly Savalas, Edmond O'Brien (United Artists/Harold Hecht)

Birdman of Alcatraz is not really a prison picture in the traditional and accepted sense of the term. *Birdman* reverses the formula and brings a new breadth and depth to the form. In telling, with reasonable objectivity but understandably deep compassion the true story of Robert Stroud, it achieves a human dimension way beyond its predecessors.

Trosper's penetrating and affecting screenplay, based on the book by Thomas E. Gaddis, delicately and artfully sketches the 53-year imprisonment of the 72-year-old 'Birdman', Stroud, illustrating the highlights and lowlights of that terrible, yet miraculously ennobling span. The screenplay's, and the film's only real flaw is its dismissal of Stroud's background, leaving the audience to mull over psychological ramifications and expositional data by and large denied it.

Lancaster gives a superbly natural, unaffected performance – one in which nobility and indestrucibility can be seen cumulatively developing and shining from within through a weary exterior eroded by the deep scars of time and enforced privacy in a 'prison within a prison'. His running clash with the narrowminded and vengeful warden Shoemaker is a highlight of the film, consummating in a powerful scene depicting their opposing views on penology. Karl Malden is excellent as the warden.

Four distinguished top supporting performances light up the picture. They a those of Telly Savalas as a fellow inmate and birdkeeper, Thelma Ritter (in a change of pace from her customary characterization) as Stroud's mother (whose seemingly unselfish devotion to the cause of her son ultimately grows suspect), Neville Bran as an understanding guard, and Betty Field as the woman who married Stroud in prison, then reluctantly drifts away at his realistic request. Edmond O'Brien narrates and play the author.

☐ 1962: Nominations: Best Actor (Burt Lancaster), Supp. Actor (Telly Savalas), Supp. Actress (Thelma Ritter), B&W Cinematography

....

■ BIRD ON A WIRE

1990, 110 MINS, US ◇ ⑩ ⊙
Dir John Badham *Prod* Rob Cohen *Scr* David Seltzer, Louis Venosta, Eric Lerner *Ph* Robert Primes *Ed* Frank

Morriss, Dallas Puett *Mus* Hans Zimmer *Art Dir* Philip Harrison
● Mel Gibson, Goldie Hawn, David Carradine, Bill Duke, Joan Severance, Stephen Tobolowsky (Badham-Cohen/Interscope)

Frank Capra's *It Happened One Night* established the format, but John Badham is stuck with a terrible script on this 1990s version. Only the chemistry of Goldie Hawn and Mel Gibson makes the film watchable.

Gibson plays a shnook who's been hiding out for 15 years under an FBI witness relocation program. He gave testimony on a drug deal and the man he fingered (David Carradine) is just out of prison. Contrived and thoroughly unconvincing plot cog has Gibson discovered incognito by old flame Hawn at the Detroit gas station where he works just as Carradine and partner Duke catch up with him. Resulting shootout throws Hawn and Gibson together on the lam for the rest of the pic.

Rekindling of duo's romance is best thing about the repetitive chase format, set in numerous US locations but shot almost entirely in British Columbia. Main kudos goes to British designer Philip Harrison, who's allowed to run hog wild in a largescale climax set at a zoo exhibit depicting a Brazilian rain forest.

....

■ BIRDS, THE

1963, 120 MINS, US ◇ ⑩ ⊙
Dir Alfred Hitchcock *Prod* Alfred Hitchcock *Scr* Evan Hunter *Ph* Robert Burks *Ed* George Tomasini
Mus [none] *Art Dir* Robert Boyle
● Rod Taylor, Tippi Hedren, Jessica Tandy, Suzanne Pleshette, Veronica Cartwright, Charles McGraw (Universal)

Beneath all of this elaborate feather bedlam lies a Hitch cock-and-bull story that's essentially a fowl ball.

The premise is fascinating. The idea of billions of bird-brains refusing to eat crow any longer and adopting the hunt-and-peck system, with homo sapiens as their ornithological target, is fraught with potential. Cinematically, Hitchcock & Co have done a masterful job of meeting this formidable challenge. But dramatically, *The Birds* is little more than a shocker-for shock's-sake.

Evan Hunter's screenplay, from Daphne du Maurier's story, has it that a colony of our feathered 'friends' over California's Bodega Bay (it's never clear how far-reaching this avian mafia extends) suddenly decides, for no apparent reason, to swoop down en masse on the human population, beaks first. These bird raids are captivatingly bizarre and terrifying.

Where the scenario and picture slip is in the sphere of the human element. An unnecessary elaborate romantic plot has been cooked up and then left suspended. It involves a young bachelor attorney (Rod Taylor), his sister (Veronica Cartwright), their mother (Jessica Tandy), and a plucky, mysterious playgirl (Tippi Hedren) whose arrival from San Francisco with a pair of caged lovebirds for Taylor coincides with the outbreak of avian hostility.

Aside from the birds, the film belongs to Hedren, who makes an auspicious screen bow. She virtually has to carry the picture alone for the first 45-minute stretch, prior to the advent of the first wave of organized attackers from the sky.

Of the others, Tandy, a first-class actress, makes the most vivid impression. Taylor emotes with strength and attractiveness.

☐ 1963: Nomination: Best Special Effects

....

■ BIRDY

1984, 120 MINS, US ◇ ⑩ ⊙
Dir Alan Parker *Prod* Alan Marshall *Scr* Sandy

Kroopf, Jack Behr *Ph* Michael Seresin *Ed* Gerry Hambling *Mus* Peter Gabriel *Art Dir* Geoffrey Kirkland
● Matthew Modine, Nicolas Cage, John Harkins, Sandy Baron, Karen Young, George Buck (Tri-Star)

Belying the lightheartedness of its title, *Birdy* is a heavy adult drama about best friends and the after-effects of war, but it takes too long to live up to its ambitious premise.

Matthew Modine stars in the adaptation of William Wharton' novel as the title character who had been missing in action and now, psychologically ill and institutionalized, spends much of his time naked, curled up in bird-like positions and speaking to no one.

These posturings stem from a childhood affinity to birds which he shared to a significant degree with Nicolas Cage, who himself is banged up from the fighting, but is brought in to try to communicate with his boyhood pal.

Alan Parker's flashback direction ultimately serves to disjoint *Birdy*.

....

■ BIRTHDAY PARTY, THE

1968, 123 MINS, UK ◇ ⑩
Dir William Friedkin *Prod* Max Rosenberg, Milton Subotsky *Scr* Harold Pinter *Ph* Denys Coop *Ed* Tony Gibbs
● Robert Shaw, Patrick McGee, Dandy Nichols, Sydney Tafler (Continental/Palomar)

Harold Pinter's comedy of menace has been transfered to the screen as an intellectual exercise in verbal gymnastics. Its study of unreality at a dingy British seaside resort is geared for thoughtful interpretation by alert audiences.

Robert Shaw is the pivotal force in *The Birthday Party*. He is the frightened lost soul, put upon as humanity's non-conformist. It appears, and Shaw is least sure of all, that prior to vegetating the past year at Dandy Nichols' boarding-house he may have been a piano player and a deserting member of a criminal organization. Sydney Tafler and cohort Patrick McGee are the organization men sent to get Shaw.

On these bones, Pinter fleshes out his philosophy of the complex fictions people employ. The completed film is thus an elaboration of the images of reality.

Tafler milks the role for laughs on whatever intellectual level, and comes off quite well.

Director William Friedkin has obvious respect for Pinter's written word and left the film an observation on abstract ideas.

....

■ BIRTH OF A NATION, THE

1915, 187 MINS, US ⊗ ⑩ ⊙
Dir D.W. Griffith *Prod* D.W. Griffith, Harry E. Aitken
Scr D.W.Griffith, Frank E. Woods *Ph* Billy Bitzer
Ed James E. Smith *Mus* Joseph Carl Breil
● Henry B. Walthall, Miriam Cooper, Mae Marsh, Lillian Gish, Donald Crisp, Raoul Walsh (Epoch)

The Birth of a Nation is the main title David Wark Griffith gave to his version of Thomas Dixon's story of the South, *The Clansman*. It received its first New York public presentation in the Liberty theatre, New York, March 3. The daily newspaper reviewers pronounced it as the last word in picture making.

The story involves: the Camerons of the south and the Stonemans of the north and Silas Lynch, the mulatto Lieutenant-Governor; the opening and finish of the Civil War; the scenes attendant upon the assassination of Abraham Lincoln; the period of carpet-bagging days and union reconstruction following Lee's surrender; and the terrorizing of the southern whites by the newly freed blacks and the rise of the Ku Klux Klan. All these including some wonderfully well staged battle scenes taken at night are realistically, graphically and most superbly depicted by the camera.

Griffith took his time. Thousands of feet of celluloid were used and for some six months or so he and his co-directors worked day and night to shape the story into a thrilling, dramatic wordless play. The battle scenes are wonderfully conceived, the departure of the soldiers splendidly arranged, and the death of the famous martyred president deftly and ably handled. Henry Walthall makes a manly, straightforward character of the 'Little Colonel' and handles his big scenes most effectively. Mae Marsh as the pet sister does some remarkable work as the little girl who loves the south and loves her brother. Ralph Lewis is splendid as the leader of the House who helps Silas Lynch rise power. George Siegmann gets all there can be gotten out of the despicable character of Lynch. Walter Long makes Gus, the renegade negro, a hated, much despised type, his acting and makeup being complete.

The Birth of a Nation is said to have cost $300,000.

■ **BIRTH OF A NATION, THE**

1930, 108 MINS, US
Dir D.W. Griffith *Mus* Joseph Carl Breil (Griffith)

The original score, assembled by J.C. Breil, has been recorded for [this sound re-issue]. But though tuneful the music seems shallow in its tenderness and short of the sweeping spectacle that's the essence of this crossroads production. The print is surprisingly clear.

There is the blare of the Klan's trumpet as the horses and men gallop, and this ride remains a big thrill. There are also battle effects.

The picture startled the world in 1915 by showing in 12 reels. It has been shorn since in running time.

The film cost around $110,000 to make and Billy Bitzer's photography and Breil's score still stand out.

■ **BIRTH OF THE BLUES**

1941, 80 MINS, US
Dir Victor Schertzinger *Prod* Buddy DeSylva *Scr* Harry Tugend, Walter DeLeon *Ph* William Mellor *Ed* Paul Weatherwax *Mus* Robert Emmett Dolan (arr.)
● Bing Crosby, Mary Martin, Brian Donlevy, Carolyn Lee, Eddie 'Rochester' Anderson, J. Carrol Naish (Paramount)

Birth of the Blues has everything from melody to comedy, and for the show bunch it's just so much jive history in swingtime. A saga of Basin Street, New Orleans, cradle of the Dixieland jazz idiom, it projects its story with bounce and gusto; forthright in its allegiance to a then unorthodox jazz style; plus arresting romance, a plug-ugly cabaret meanace, and a wealth of cavalcade jazzapation.

Bing Crosby is the licorice-stick disciple who adheres to his premise that the colored man's levee music, at the foot of Basin Street, was bound to sweep the country.

Mary Martin is introduced in al fresco fashion, as is Brian Donlevy, a mean man on the horn from Memphis, just what the rest of the band has been waiting for – an ofay who can toot like a Satchmo.

When Crosby, as a kid, swings Paderewski and brings down the wrath of his musicianly father, it's solid stuff for the initiate. The jailhouse jam session with the Memphis horn man (Donlevy) in the clink is another directorial highlight.
□ 1941: Nomination: Best Scoring of a Musical Picture

■ **BISHOP'S WIFE, THE**

1947, 106 MINS, US ⍉ ⊙
Dir Henry Koster *Prod* Samuel Goldwyn *Scr* Robert E. Sherwood, Leonardo Bercovici *Ph* Gregg Toland *Ed* Monica Collingwood *Mus* Hugo Friedhofer *Art Dir* George Jenkins, Perry Ferguson

● Cary Grant, Loretta Young, David Niven, Monty Woolley, Gladys Cooper, Elsa Lanchester (RKO)

While a fantasy, there are no fantastic heavenly manifestations. There's a humanness about the characters, even the angel, that beguiles full attention. Henry Koster's sympathetic direction deftly gets over the warm humor supplied by the script, taken from Robert Nathan's novel of the same title.

Cary Grant is the angel of the piece and has never appeared to greater advantage. Role, with the exception of a minor miracle or two, is potently pointed to indicate character could have been flesh-and-blood person, a factor that embellishes sense of reality as the angel sets about answering the troubled prayers of Episcopalian bishop (David Niven).

Plot, essentially, deals with Grant's assignment to make people act like human being In great need of his help is Niven, a young bishop who has lost the common touch and marital happiness because of his dream of erecting a massive cathedral.

Loretta Young gives a moving performance as the wife whose life is touched by an angel without her knowledge of his heavenly origin. Niven's cleric character is played straight but his anxieties and jealousy loosen much of the warm humor gracing the plot.

Gregg Toland's camera work and the music score by Hugo Friedhofer, directed by Emil Newman, are ace credits among the many expert contributions.
□ 1947: Best Sound Recording.
□ Nominations: Best Picture, Director, Editing, Scoring of a Dramatic Picture

■ **BITCH, THE**

1979, 90 MINS, UK ◇ ⍉
Dir Gerry O'Hara *Prod* John Quested *Scr* Gerry O'Hara *Ph* Denis Lewiston *Art Dir* Malcolm Middleton
● Joan Collins, Michael Coby, Kenneth Haigh, Ian Hendry, Carolyn Seymour, Sue Lloyd (Brent Walker)

The Bitch offers more mock orgasm than plot as it oscillates between the disco floor and the sack – or the pool, shower, or wherever a couple can couple. Two Lesbos, at one point, are glimpsed pawing each other in a sauna.

Not to mince about the production, scripted and feverishly directed by Gerry O'Hara, is corny and coarse, but at least mercifully brief at 90 minutes.

Between all the sex and sybaritic palaver, there's some nuisance plotting involving Michael Coby as a debonair hustler in trouble with the mob.

Pic's ending, ostensibly ironic, only seems confusing as to who done what to whom. But for disco freaks, there's plenty of their kind of action. Joan Collins does her spoiled nympho rich girl turn with assurance.

■ **BITE THE BULLET**

1975, 131 MINS, US ◇ ⍉ ⊙
Dir Richard Brooks *Prod* Richard Brooks *Scr* Richard Brooks *Ph* Harry Stradling Jr *Ed* George Grenville *Mus* Alex North *Art Dir* Robert Boyle
● Gene Hackman, Candice Bergen, James Coburn, Ben Johnson, Ian Bannen, Jan-Michael Vincent (Columbia)

Bite the Bullet is an excellent, literate action drama probing the diverse motivations of participants in an endurance horse race. The contestants include Gene Hackman and James Coburn as ex-San Juan Hill Rough Riders; Candice Bergen as a former resident of Jean Willes frontier pleasure shanty, seeking money to help her imprisoned lover; vagabond Ben Johnson desperately wanting to 'be somebody' for a brief moment in life.

After a leisurely though intriguing buildup, the race begins, and during the daily ordeals of mountain, desert, rain, sun, cold and heat, the pressures and the secrets of the characters emerge plausibly and rationally.

Bergen's ulterior motivation in particular triggers a surprise, pre-climactic turn. Effective use of slow-motion in the final scene lends suspense to the outcome as the two surviving riders inch towards the ribbon.
□ 1975: Nominations: Best Original Song Score, Sound

■ **BITTER HARVEST**

1963, 96 MINS, UK ◇ ⍉ ⊙
Dir Peter Graham Scott *Prod* Albert Fennell *Scr* Ted Willis *Ph* Ernest Steward *Ed* Russell Lloyd *Mus* Laurie Johnson *Art Dir* Alex Vetchinsky
● Janet Munro, John Stride, Anne Cunningham, Alan Badel, William Lucas, Barbara Ferris (Independent Artists)

The story of the country innocent (Janet Munro) who gets caught up in the dizzy pitfalls of London nightlife is taken from a Patrick Hamilton novel, *Twenty Thousand Streets under the Sky*. Surprising thing is that scripter Ted Willis has not come up with any surprises or twist, and director Peter Graham Scott has been no help in this matter, either. Result is a conventional yarn.

Munro is given opportunities to portray innocence, gaiety, cupidity, depression, vanity, fear, cunning, tenderness, harshness, wonder and anger. All the emotions are fleeting but the star helps to mould them into a well-drawn picture of an innocent who learns quickly.

John Stride is solid, charming and resourceful as the infatuated bartender. Alan Badel makes a brief but telling contribution as a steely, unscrupulous theatre boss. There is also a beautifully underplayed performance by Anne Cunningham as a barmaid who has long been secretly in love with Stride.

■ **BITTER MOON**

1992, 139 MINS, FRANCE/UK ◇ ⍉ ⊙
Dir Roman Polanski *Prod* Roman Polanski *Scr* Roman Polanski, Gerard Brach, John Brownjohn, Jeff Gross *Ph* Tonino Delli Colli *Ed* Herve de Luze, Glenn Cunningham *Mus* Vangelis *Art Dir* Willy Holt, Gerard Viard
● Peter Coyote, Emmanuelle Seigner, Hugh Grant, Kristin Scott Thomas, Victor Bannerjee, Sophie Patel (RP/Burrill)

Four years after *Frantic*, Roman Polanski approaches rock bottom with *Bitter Moon*, a phony slice of *huis clos* drama between two couples aboard a Euro liner. Strong playing by topliner Peter Coyote can't compensate for a script [from Pascal Bruckner's novel *Lunes de fiel*] that's all over the map and a tone that veers from *outre* comedy to erotic game-playing.

Initial focus is on a couple of hoity-toity Brits (Hugh Grant, Kristin Scott Thomas) enjoying a seventh-anniversary Mediterranean cruise to Istanbul. Thing start to go awry when they help a distraught young femme, Mimi (Emmanuelle Seigner), who turns out to be the ship's glamorous cabaret act.

That night Grant is accosted by her American hubby (Peter Coyote), a wheelchair-bound misanthrope who lures the Englishman into a drinking session and insists on recounting his life story. Thereon, pic settles into a series of long flashbacks detailing Coyote-Seigner's tempestuous love life.

Despite its two-hour-plus length, pic holds a certain awful fascination as Polanski careens every which way with the material. Coyote gives a scenery-chewing performance as both the younger lovestruck scribe and the whisky-soaked cripple. Seigner, matured since her *Frantic* days, is eye-popping in the sex scenes, but the helmer's wife often sounds as if she's reading her dialogue off cue cards.

■ BITTER SWEET

1933, 76 MINS, UK ⦿

Dir Herbert Wilcox   *Prod* Herbert Wilcox   *Scr* Herbert Wilcox, Lydia Hayward, Monckton Hoffe   *Ph* F. A. Young   *Mus* Noel Coward   *Art Dir* L. P. Williams
● Anna Neagle, Fernand Gravet, Esme Percy, Clifford Heatherly, Ivy St Helier, Miles Mander (British & Dominions/United Artists)

Direction hampers Anna Neagle, a stunning blonde of compelling grace, but here restricted to an acting style. She is permitted no emotional range and her performance is flavorless except that she does manage to suggest that if she broke loose she might start something.

Fernand Gravet is young, dark and a vital type, a vigorous personality. Chief support role here doesn't bring out his engaging personality in full.

Clifford Heatherly does the Vienna cafe proprietor, Herr Schlick, contributing a splendidly flexible performance with a capital knack of legitimate comedy. Suggests something of the Charles Laughton technique in subtle villainy. Last of the quartet is Ivy St Helier, obviously French, who plays the soubrette role the hilt.

Continuity takes many liberties with the operetta script [by Noel Coward], usually without improving it. Story progress is jerky. Whole episode of the singer's second marriage is omitted, which is all right for economy of narrative though it does fog up the finish, which leaves the heroine rather indefinite. Love scenes are stretched out to great lengths.

Coward's score, hailed at the time of the stage presentation as brilliant, is a part of the picture and helps its class tone. The leads handle several numbers agreeably.

■ BITTER SWEET

1940, 92 MINS, US ◇ ⦿

Dir W.S. Van Dyke II   *Prod* Victor Saville   *Scr* Lesser Samuels   *Ph* Oliver T. Marsh, Allen Davey   *Ed* Harold F. Kress   *Mus* Noel Coward   *Art Dir* Cedric Gibbons, John S. Detlie
● Jeanette MacDonald, Nelson Eddy, George Sanders, Ian Hunter, Felix Bressart (M-G-M)

Bitter Sweet is a super-elaborate production providing a background for the fetching Noel Coward songs, in his highly successful operetta, delivered by Jeanette MacDonald and Nelson Eddy.

The story development receives minor attention. It is an obvious and static romance from the time music teacher Eddy elopes with his pupil (MacDonald); takes her to Vienna while he writes an operetta; and his tragic death just as his work is to be presented. The love scenes between the couple are staid and cold, neither providing any warmth to those proceedings which were a vital factor in the original play.

Both MacDonald and Eddy interpret Coward's numbers in excellent style. All the favorites of the operetta are here, including 'Zigeuner', 'Little Cafe', 'Tokay', and 'I'll See You Again'.

Final production number for background of MacDonald's rendition of 'Zigeuner', is most ingeniously contrived, having dancers in copper-brown and white costumes, with background in similar tones.

■ BITTER TEA OF GENERAL YEN, THE

1933, 87 MINS, US ◇ ⦿

Dir Frank Capra   *Prod* Frank Capra   *Scr* Edward Paramore   *Ph* Joseph Walker   *Ed* Edward Curtis   *Mus* W. Frank Harling
● Barbara Stanwyck, Nils Asther, Gavin Gordon, Toshia Mori, Walter Connolly, Richard Loo (Columbia)

This picture is a queer story [from a novel by Grace Zaring Stone] of a romance in China between a Chinese and a white woman. A young New England girl arrives in Shanghai to join her sweetheart missionary. They are to be married. China's unceasing civil wars are made the background of the girl's experiences from that point.

The Chinese war lord around whom the plot is built is a curious and rather questionable human composition of a poet, philosopher and bandit. He speaks rather fluent English and essays somewhat dainty American mannerisms, especially in manipulating a handkerchief. Nils Asther plays the role.

After the Chinese general goes on the make for the white girl the picture goes blah. That's before the film is even half way.

Barbara Stanwyck is the white girl. Pleasant enough and for the first half where she repulses the Chinaman gathers some audience sympathy. Subsequently, where the photography attempts to simulate that the girl, in her dreams, loves the Chinese, the role fails her. Besides which, as a New England missionary type, Stanwyck does not fit.

A fine actor from the legit, Walter Connolly takes the acting honors as the adventurous American financial advisor of General Yen. A kind of a tramp philosopher which Connolly does admirably.

■ BITTER VICTORY

1958, 97 MINS, FRANCE/US

Dir Nicholas Ray   *Prod* Paul Graetz   *Scr* Rene Hardy, Nicholas Ray, Gavin Lambert, Paul Gallico   *Ph* Michel Kelber   *Ed* Leonide Azar   *Mus* Maurice Le Roux   *Art Dir* Jean d'Eaubonne
● Richard Burton, Curt Jurgens, Ruth Roman, Raymond Pellegrin, Anthony Bushell, Christopher Lee (Transcontinental/Laffont)

Rene Hardy's novel has been translated for the screen into a literary, hard-hitting screenplay which almost always manages to overcome some of the incongruities of the original story line. This sets up a deadly struggle between two British Army officers during the Second World War African campaign.

Conflict between Capt Leith and Major Brand derives from fact that Leith knows of Brand's basic cowardice in action, and also from jealousy over Brand's wife, with whom Leith has had an affair. Returning from a dangerous mission in German-held Benghazi, Brand tries twice indirectly to bring about Leith's death, once by leaving him behind to guard two wounded Germans, again by deliberately letting a scorpion bite his rival.

Script is basically flawed by the unclearly delineated key character of the major – and Curt Jurgens' competent, straightforward performance is less successful because of it. Fine thesping by Richard Burton leads a series of top performances by other members of large cast.

■ BLACK ARROW, THE

1948, 76 MINS, US ⊗

Dir Gordon M. Douglas   *Prod* Edward Small   *Scr* Richard Schayer, David P. Sheppard, Thomas Seller   *Ph* Charles Lawton   *Ed* Jerome Thoms   *Mus* Paul Sawtell   *Art Dir* Stephen Goosson, A. Leslie Thomas
● Louis Hayward, Janet Blair, George Macready, Edgar Buchanan (Columbia)

Using Robert Louis Stevenson's *The Black Arrow* for the takeoff, Columbia has made an action-filled cloak-and-dagger romance. The picture is virtually a western of lethal combat, hard riding, intrigue and deep-dyed villainy – all in when-knighthood-was-in-flower terms. Maybe it isn't exactly art, but it is good entertainment.

The romantic angle has been accented heavily in the translation from Stevenson's dispassionate narrative. The red-blooded hero returns from the 30 Years War to learn that his uncle has murdered his father to seize the House of York and has had the neighboring Lord of the House of Lancaster executed for the crime. And he understandably tumbles hard for the nifty Lancaster daughter.

■ BLACKBEARD, THE PIRATE

1952, 98 MINS, US ◇ ⦿ ⊙

Dir Raoul Walsh   *Prod* Edmund Grainger   *Scr* Alan LeMay   *Ph* William E. Snyder   *Ed* Ralph Dawson   *Mus* Victor Young   *Art Dir* Albert S. D'Agostino, Jack Okey
● Robert Newton, Linda Darnell, William Bendix, Keith Andes, Torin Thatcher, Richard Egan (RKO)

Blackbeard, the Pirate is a rollicking swashbuckler stacked with high adventure, extensive swordplay and all the things big pirate pictures are made of.

Alan LeMay's scripting of the DeVallon Scott story gives a neat blending to the tongue-in-cheek and on-the-level ingredients.

It's the 17th century on the Spanish Main again. Torin Thatcher, a 'reformed' pirate, has been commissioned by the King of England to rid the seas of Robert ('Blackbeard') Newton. Keith Andes, a young sailor of fortune out to collect some reward money, allows himself to be shanghaied. Also going aboard, is Thatcher's adopted daughter (Linda Darnell). Once on board, the pair discover the captain has been murdered and 'Blackbeard' has taken over.

Newton turns in a memorable performance.

■ BLACK BELT JONES

1974, 85 MINS, US ◇ ⦿

Dir Robert Clouse   *Prod* Fred Weintraub, Paul Heller   *Scr* Oscar Williams   *Ph* Kent Wakeford   *Ed* Michael Kahn   *Mus* Luchi De Jesus, Dennis Coffy
● Jim Kelly, Gloria Hendry, Scatman Crothers, Alan Weeks, Eric Laneuville, Andre Phillipe (Warner)

Black Belt Jones reteams the *Enter the Dragon* producing team and director Robert Clouse, also Jim Kelly, this time heading the cast. The story strand pits a group of graceful black martial arts students against some cliche white gangsters, neither side taking things seriously.

Kelly, between the thousands of body blows given and taken, has time for Gloria Hendry, equally adept at physical jousting as providing a good romantic interest. She's the daughter of Scatman Crothers, whose karate studio is on land eyed for a building project by Malik Carter and his own crime superior (Andre Phillipe), a clumsy godfather-type.

The action sequences, coordinated by Robert Wall, are standard steps in the choreography martial arts.

■ BLACK BIRD, THE

1926, 76 MINS, US ⊗

Dir Tod Browning   *Scr* Tod Browning, Waldemar Young   *Ph* Percy Hilburn   *Ed* Errol Taggart   *Art Dir* Cedric Gibbons, Arnold Gillespie
● Lon Chaney, Renee Adoree, Owen Moore, Doris Lloyd (MGM)

In *The Black Bird* Lon Chaney plays a dual role, that of a crook and of his brother, a Limehouse missionary. Although the reverend fellow is crippled up plenty, the curse is taken off by one shot showing the crook throwing his arm and leg out joint and then assuming the role of the man whom the world thought to be his brother. That's the basis of the story, for the crook falls in love with a music hall performer, while a flashier crook from the West End also goes for the same girl.

It's a good melodrama, excellently produced. Chaney handles his two parts well and

B

Waldemar Young's scenario has been so constructed that the rather unique dual role is plausible at all times.

••••••••••••••••••••••••••••

■ **BLACK BIRD, THE**

1975, 98 MINS, US ◇ ⊚

Dir David Giler   *Prod* Saul David   *Scr* David Giler
Ph Phil Lathrop   *Ed* Margaret Booth, Walter Thompson,
Lou Lombardo   *Mus* Jerry Fielding   *Art Dir* Harry
Horner
● George Segal, Stephane Audran, Lionel Stander, Lee
Patrick, Elisha Cook Jr, Felix Silla (Columbia/ Rastar)

This satirical contemporary update of Dashiell Hammett's novel *The Maltese Falcon* emerges as fair whimsy.

Basis of the plot [from a story by Don M. Mankiewitz and Gordon Cotler] is that George Segal, as Sam Spade's son, has inherited the detective agency, still in its old location, but now a rundown black neighborhood. Lee Patrick, in a delightful recasting as Effie, the secretary, hangs in there, partly because she hasn't been paid in years, and despite an animosity towards Segal. The search for the elusive Maltese Falcon is reinstated, bringing in all sorts of mysterious characters.

The general tenor of the film shows a sentimental empathy for the original material with no heartless put-downs marring the work. There are lots of smiles, many chuckles, and a few strong laughs.

•••••••••••••••••••••••••••

■ **BLACKBOARD JUNGLE**

1955, 100 MINS, US ⊛ ⊚

Dir Richard Brooks   *Prod* Pandro S. Berman
Scr Richard Brooks   *Ph* Russell Harlan   *Ed* Ferris
Webster   *Mus* Charles Wolcott (adapt.)   *Art Dir* Cedric
Gibbons, Randall Duell
● Glenn Ford, Anne Francis, Louis Calhern, Vic Morrow,
Sidney Poitier, Margaret Hayes (M-G-M)

Director-scripter Richard Brooks, working from novel by Evan Hunter, has fashioned an angry picture that flares out in moral and physical rage at mental slovenliness, be it juvenile, mature, or in the pattern of society acceptance of things as they are because no one troubles to devise a better way.

The main issue is the juvenile bum who terrorizes schoolrooms and teachers.

The strong among the evil element, here represented by Vic Morrow, is already beyond any reform. The good, represented by Sidney Poitier, has had no stimulus to awaken his leadership abilities because he is a Negro. Glenn Ford, Morrow and Poitier are so real in their performances under the probing direction by Brooks that the picture alternatingly has the viewer pleading, indignant and frightened before the conclusion.

☐ 1955: Nominations: Best Screenplay, B&W Cinematography, B&W Art Direction, Editing

••••••••••••••••••••••••••••

■ **BLACK CAT, THE**

(UK: House of Doom)

1934, 65 MINS, US

Dir Edgar G. Ulmer   *Prod* Carl Laemmle Jr   *Scr* Peter
Ruric   *Ph* Jack Mescal   *Mus* Heinz Roemheld
Art Dir Charles D. Hall
● Boris Karloff, Bela Lugosi, David Manners, Julie
Bishop, Andy Devine, John Carradine (Universal)

Story is confused and confusing, and while with the aid of heavily-shadowed lighting and mausoleum-like architecture, a certain eeriness has been achieved, it's all a poor imitation of things seen before.

Boris Karloff occupies a spooky manor built over the ruins of a world war fort where 10,000 soldiers drenched the valley in blood in a terrible military defeat caused by Karloff's treachery. That is told but not shown. Bela Lugosi is a batty doctor just out

of a cruel jail in which he spent 15 years. Also due to Karloff's unworthy character.

Clash of the two eyebrow-squinting nuts involves an American bridal couple temporarily caught in the manor. It is the playful notion of nasty Karloff to make the bride Exhibit A in a devil cult of which he is the head, and it is the revenge of Lugosi to torture his enemy by skinning him alive.

Corpses standing upright in glass cases and operating table murders are other tricks which the story uses. Edgar Allan Poe's name is used for publicity purposes. All that is used is the title which belongs to a Poe short story.

Karloff and Lugosi are sufficiently sinister and convincingly demented.

••••••••••••••••••••••••••••

■ **BLACK CAULDRON, THE**

1985, 80 MINS, US ◇ ⊚

Dir Ted Berman, Richard Rich   *Prod* Joe Hale
Scr David Jonas, Vance Gerry, Ted Berman, Richard Rich,
Al Wilson, Roy Morita, Peter Young, Art Stevens, Joe
Hale, Rosemary Anne Sisson, Roy Edward Disney
Ed James Melton, Kim Koford, Armetta Jackson
Mus Elmer Bernstein (Walt Disney)

By any hard measure, the $25 million animated *Cauldron* is not very original. The characters, though cute and cuddly and sweet and mean and ugly and simply awful, don't really have much to do that would remain of interest to any but the youngest minds.

Storyline [based on *The Chronicles of Prydain* series by Lloyd Alexander] is fairly stock sword-and-sorcery, with a band of likable youngsters, animals and creatures forced to tackle an evil mob of monsters to keep them from using a magic cauldron to raise an army of the dead. No need to guess who wins. [Prolog is narrated by John Huston.]

•••••••••••••••••••••••••••

■ **BLACK CHRISTMAS**

1974, 93 MINS, CANADA ◇ ⊚

Dir Bob Clark   *Prod* Bob Clark, Gerry Arbeid   *Scr* Roy
Moore   *Ph* Reg Morris   *Ed* Stan Cole   *Mus* Carl Zittrer
Art Dir Karen Bromley
● Olivia Hussey, Keir Dullea, Margot Kidder, Andrea
Martin, John Saxon, Marian Waldman (August)

Black Christmas, a bloody, senseless kill-for-kicks feature, exploits unnecessary violence in a university sorority house operated by an implausibly alcoholic ex-hoofer. Its slow-paced, murky tale involves an obscene telephone caller who apparently delights in killing the girls off one by one, even the hapless housemother.

The plot has the usual abundant cliches: a drunken girl student, played by Margot Kidder, who goes to her death much too late in the film; a house-mother, who finds her hidden whiskey bottles after much swearing; a 'nice' girl, who finds herself pregnant much to the horror of her psycho piano student boyfriend; and stock dumb policemen.

Only Marian Waldman as the house-mother comes across with any life.

•••••••••••••••••••••••••••

■ **BLACK FURY**

1935, 94 MINS, US ⊛

Dir Michael Curtiz   *Prod* [Robert Lord]   *Scr* Abem
Finkel, Carl Erickson   *Ph* Byron Haskin   *Ed* Thomas
Richards   *Mus* Leo F. Forbstein (dir.)   *Art Dir* John
Hughes
● Paul Muni, Karen Morley, William Gargan, Barton
MacLane, John T. Qualen, J. Carrol Naish (Warner)

Pennsy coal-mining background is basically a masculine setting for intra-industry politics [from the story *Jan Volkanik* by M.A. Musmanno and play *Bohunk* by Henry R. Irving]. The fomenting anti-unionists who generate ill-will for benefit of ultimate strike-breaking maneuvers is the means for bringing in the strongarm coal mine police, the

scabs, etc. They become the abstract composite villain.

There are times when the footage is slow and Paul Muni's Polish brogue too thick but the main the general result is arresting. Muni is the fulcrum of the film but there are other fine performances. J. Carrol Naish is excellent as the strike fomenter. John Qualen's hunky-pal personation is a sympathetic characterization, parred by Sarah Haden in a slavey role, that of his wife. Barton MacLane's thankless assignment as the bullying head of the muscle bunch is sufficiently hateful to impress him.

••••••••••••••••••••••••••••

■ **BLACK HOLE, THE**

1979, 97 MINS, US ◇ ⊛ ⊚

Dir Gary Nelson   *Prod* Ron Miller   *Scr* Jeb Rosebrook,
Gerry Day   *Ph* Frank Phillips   *Ed* Gregg McLaughlin
Mus John Barry   *Art Dir* Peter Ellenshaw
● Maximilian Schell, Anthony Perkins, Robert Forster,
Joseph Bottoms, Yvette Mimieux, Ernest Borgnine (Walt
Disney)

The black hole itself gets short shrift in the screenplay, based on a story by Jeb Rosebrook, Bob Barbash and Richard Landau. Most of the pic is devoted to setting up the story of mad scientist Maximilian Schell, poised on the brink of his voyage to the unknown. An exploration ship staffed by Robert Forster, Anthony Perkins, Joseph Bottoms, Yvette Mimieux and Ernest Borgnine, stumbles on both Schell and the nearby black hole, with unpredictable results.

What ensues is sometimes talky but never dull. Director Gary Nelson's pacing and visual sense are right on target.

In typical Disney fashion, the most attractive and sympathetic characters are not human at all. George F. McGinnis has constructed a bevy of robots that establish a mechanical world all their own.

☐ 1979: Nominations: Best Cinematography, Visual Effects

•••••••••••••••••••••••••••

■ **BLACK JACK**

1979, 106 MINS, UK ◇

Dir Kenneth Loach   *Prod* Tony Garnett   *Scr* Kenneth
Loach   *Ph* Chris Menges   *Ed* Bill Shapter   *Mus* Bob
Pegg   *Art Dir* Martin Johnson
● Jean Franval, Stephen Hirst, Louise Cooper, Andrew
Bennett (Kestrel Films)

Basically an adventure yarn set in northern England in 1750, this collaboration of writer-director Kenneth Loach and producer Tony Garnett add first rate period recreation (more than could have been expected from the $1 million budget) to their already-established talents for sharp, telling realism.

Loach's screenplay, adapted from Leon Garfield's same-title novel, suffers from a meandering plotline, but that hardly matters as it is continuously engrossing, and enlivened with a wry wit.

After miraculously surviving a hanging, Black Jack, a gigantic Frenchman with few words of English, endearingly played by Jean Franval, takes along a young boy (Stephen Hirst) with him on his escape, to 'speak for him.' The main plot concerns a girl (Louise Cooper) they encounter by chance, whose irrational behavior has caused her wealthy parents to commit her to a privately run madhouse for fear of possible scandal.

•••••••••••••••••••••••••••

■ **BLACKMAIL**

1929, 88 MINS, UK ⊛ ⊚

Dir Alfred Hitchcock   *Prod* John Maxwell   *Scr* Alfred
Hitchcock, Ben W. Levy, Charles Bennett   *Ph* Jack Cox
Ed Emile de Ruelle   *Mus* Hubert Bath, Henry Stafford
(arr.)   *Art Dir* Wilfred C. Arnold, Norman Arnold
● Anny Ondra, Sara Allgood, Charles Paton, Donald
Calthrop, John Longden, Cyril Ritchard (British International)

Blackmail is most draggy. It has no speed or pace and very little suspense. Everything's open-face. It's a story [from the play by Charles Bennett] that has been told in different disguises – the story of a girl who kills a man trying to assault her.

The girl, Anny Ondra, leaves a very lively scene in one of the Lyons feederies after flirting with a stranger and airing her steady, a regular Scotland Yard dick, to join the other half of the flirtation. The other half lives near the cigar store of her father, and asks the girl upstairs to see his studio, he being an artist. She foolishly assents, and then follows the jam.

In performance the standout is Donald Calthrop as the rat crook. He looks it. Ondra is excellent as the girl.

Dialog is ordinary but sufficient. Camerawork rather well, especially on the British Museum [in the chase finale] and the eating house scenes. A bit of comedy here and there, but not enough to be called relief.

■ BLACK MARBLE, THE

1980, 112 MINS, US ◇ ⑲
Dir Harold Becker   *Prod* Frank Capra Jr   *Scr* Joseph Wambaugh   *Ph* Owen Roizman   *Ed* Maury Winetrobe   *Mus* Maurice Jarre   *Art Dir* Alfred Sweeney
● Robert Foxworth, Paula Prentiss, Harry Dean Stanton, Barbara Babcock, James Woods, Christopher Lloyd (Avco Embassy)

With *The Black Marble*, Joseph Wambaugh [adapting his own novel] at last comes close to presenting police as human, even humorous, beings, capable of balancing remorse, regret and romance without becoming total psychotics.

Transferred out of homicide after too much exposure to a string of child murders, Robert Foxworth is teamed on a burglary detail with Paula Prentiss. The crime is either terribly serious or impossibly trivial, depending on your love of animals. Barbara Babcock's show-dog is kidnapped and she proves superb in the role of a lonely, sex-starved woman with her whole life wrapped up in her schnauzer.

Director Harold Becker is at his best in maneuvering carefully through the minefields of animal worship.

Much of the credit for making the picture work goes to Harry Dean Stanton as the dognapper, driven to his dirty deed by debt.

■ BLACK NARCISSUS

1947, 100 MINS, UK ◇ ⑲ ⊙
Dir Michael Powell, Emeric Pressburger   *Prod* Michael Powell, Emeric Pressburger   *Scr* Michael Powell, Emeric Pressburger   *Ph* Jack Cardiff   *Ed* Reginald Mills   *Mus* Brian Easdale   *Art Dir* Alfred Junge
● Deborah Kerr, Sabu, David Farrar, Kathleen Byron, Flora Robson, Jean Simmons (Archers)

Cynics may dub this lavish production *Brief Encounter in the Himalayas* and not without reason. Stripped of most of its finery, the picture [based on the novel by Rumer Godden] resolves itself into the story of two sex-starved women and a man. And since the women are nuns, there can be no happy ending except perhaps in the spiritual sense.

At the invitation of an Indian ruler, five sisters of an Anglo-Catholic order open a school and hospital in a remote Himalayan village. They occupy an ancient palace, once known as 'The House of Women,' built on a ledge 6,000 feet in the air. The nuns find their task overwhelming and Deborah Kerr, as the sister in charge, has to call for help on the cynical British agent, David Farrar, in spit of her instinctive antagonism.

To add to their worries, a native girl in need of a few months cloistering is boarded with the nuns by Farrar. The peace of the convent is further disturbed when the young

general heir to the ruler enrolls as a pupil. Materially the work of the convent prospers, but Sister Kerr feels that spiritually most of the nuns are out of harmony. Her thoughts stray back to her girlhood sweetheart in Ireland. Another Sister is obviously thinking too much of Farrar and is taken to task.

Production has gained much through being in color. The production and camerawork atone for minor lapses in the story, Jack Cardiff's photography being outstanding.

The cast has been well chosen, but Kerr gets only occasional opportunities to reveal her talents.

Most effective acting comes from Kathleen Byron who has the picture's plum as the neurotic half-crazed Sister Ruth.
□ 1947: Best Color Cinematography, Color Art Direction

■ BLACK ORCHID, THE

1959, 94 MINS, US ⑲
Dir Martin Ritt   *Prod* Carlo Ponti, Marcello Girosi   *Scr* Joseph Stefano   *Ph* Robert Burks   *Ed* Howard Smith   *Mus* Alessandro Cicognini   *Art Dir* Hal Pereira, Roland Anderson
● Sophia Loren, Anthony Quinn, Mark Richman, Ina Balin, Virginia Vincent, Frank Puglia (Paramount)

Orchid has a flavor of *Marty*, a touch of *Wild Is the Wind*. The story threads and changing emotions are securely locked in through Martin Ritt's honest direction. Without pushing, he tells an intricately drawn story with a smooth, authoritative hand.

As the widower who falls in love with the pretty widow, Anthony Quinn is excellent, uniting charm with strength. Sophia Loren plays with notable feeling, convincingly portraying the mother, the widow and the bride.

The black orchid literally is a white rose – Rose Bianco – who is the late widow of a man she helped turn to crime to satisfy her own desires. Played by Loren, she mourns her husband and mourns what she has done when a widower (Quinn), with a daughter about to be married, comes along with a joyous manner and serious intentions.

The film technically is excellent, Robert Burks' photography standing out adeptly in black-and-white VistaVision. The musical score by Alessandro Cicognini aptly points up contrasts in the story.

■ BLACKOUT

See: *Contraband*

■ BLACK PIRATE, THE

1926, 88 MINS, US ◇ ⊗ ⑲
Dir Albert Parker   *Prod* Douglas Fairbanks   *Scr* Elton Thomas [= Douglas Fairbanks], Jack Cunningham   *Ph* Henry Sharp   *Ed* William Nolan   *Art Dir* Karl Oscar Borg
● Douglas Fairbanks, Billie Dove, Donald Crisp, Anders Randolf, Tempe Piggott, Sam De Grasse (Elton/United Artists)

Douglas Fairbanks' initial feature shot completely in color. It's as great a boost for the Technicolor process as for Fairbanks.

In the tale that it spins it's the weakest Fairbanks has ever had. It's simply a matter of scores of pirates in color and the Fairbanks curriculum of stunts.

Fairbanks is up and down the screen with his acrobatics, the punch being his taking of a merchant vessel singlehanded as a pirate. His best athletic bit is the manner in which he rips the sails by mounting to the cross arms, piercing the wide sail with his sword, grabbing the hilt and descending to the deck, his momentum retarded by the sword ripping the canvas as he comes down.

■ BLACK RAIN

1989, 126 MINS, US ◇ ⑲ ⊙
Dir Ridley Scott   *Prod* Stanley R. Jaffe, Sherry Lansing   *Scr* Craig Bolotin, Warren Lewis   *Ph* Jan DeBont   *Ed* Tom Rolf   *Mus* Hans Zimmer   *Art Dir* Norris Spencer
● Michael Douglas, Andy Garcia, Ken Takakura, Kate Capshaw, Yusaku Matsuda, John Spencer (Paramount)

Since this is a Ridley Scott film, *Black Rain* is about 90% atmosphere and 10% story. But what atmosphere! This gripping crime thriller about hardboiled NY cop Michael Douglas tracking a yakuza hood in Osaka, Japan, boasts magnificent lensing and powerfully baroque production design.

Douglas is utterly believable as a reckless and scummy homicide detective who takes kickbacks from drug dealers and resorts to the most brutal methods to capture escaped counterfeiter Yusaka Matsuda.

First collaring Matsuda after a shocking outbreak of violence in a NY restaurant, Douglas is sent with him to Osaka, where he promptly loses him to the yakuza and watches helplessly as his partner Andy Garcia is murdered. Coming into conflict with the Japanese police, Douglas turns to the criminal underground to help bring in his prey.

Script fascinatingly depicts the growing influence of Ken Takakura's higher concepts of honour and loyalty on Douglas, who in turn causes some of his expedient lack of morality to rub off on the Japanese police inspector.
□ 1989: Best Sound.
□ Nomination: Best Sound Effects Editing

■ BLACK RAINBOW

1990, 113 MINS, UK ◇ ⑲
Dir Mike Hodges   *Prod* John Quested, Geoffrey Helman   *Scr* Mike Hodges   *Ph* Gerry Fisher   *Ed* Malcolm Cooke   *Mus* John Scott   *Art Dir* Voytek
● Rosanna Arquette, Jason Robards, Tom Hulce, Mark Joy, Ron Rosenthal, John Bennes (Goldcrest)

This enjoyable supernatural thriller is set in the fundamentalist society of crumbling industrial towns where folks have a deep-rooted faith in the spiritualist movement. Pic opens with journalist Tom Hulce tracking down traveling clairvoyant Rosanna Arquette to fill in the background to a story he himself was involved in some years before.

During one act Arquette receives a message from a murdered man to pass on to his wife in the audience. Unfortunately he is not dead and his wife gets rather upset. Later that night the man is killed in his home.

Small-town reporter Hulce sets about uncovering the scoop, and follows Arquette and Jason Robards to their next town. There he gets drunk with Robards and sleeps with Arquette, but still doesn't believe her 'gift.' That night she predicts even more deaths, and again her vision comes true.

Arquette is excellent as the strange but seductive Martha. She has an ethereal quality combined with innate sexuality. Robards is in his element as the drunkard father. Hulce is intelligently restrained.

■ BLACK ROBE

1991, 100 MINS, CANADA/AUSTRALIA ◇ ⑲ ⊙
Dir Bruce Beresford   *Prod* Robert Lantos, Stephane Reichel, Sue Milliken   *Scr* Brian Moore   *Ph* Peter James   *Ed* Tim Wellburn   *Mus* Georges Delerue   *Art Dir* Herbert Pinter
● Lothaire Bluteau, Aden Young, Sandrine Holt, August Schellenberg, Tantoo Cardinal, Frank Wilson (Alliance/Samson)

First official co-production between Canada and Australia is a magnificently staged combination of top talents delivering a gripping and tragic story about a 17th-century Jesuit priest's expedition through remote areas of 'New France' (Quebec). Indian dialog is translated into English sub-titles.

Saga begins in 1634 at Fort Champlain, where newly arrived French Jesuit priest Lothaire Bluteau (whom the Indians call 'Black Robe' because of his austere garb), is assigned to a difficult a dangerous journey 1,500 miles north to the mission outpost of Ihonatiria. He's accompanied by a handful of friendly Algonquin Indians, led by the chief (August Schellenberg), his wife (Tantoo Cardinal), daughter (Sandrine Holt) and young son.

Also joining the party is Aden Young as a young French carpenter who develops a passionate relationship with the Algonquin girl. The travelers are captured, beaten and tortured. The priest arrives at his destination to find the priest in charge (Frank Wilson) dying and the local Indians decimated by a fever brought by the white men.

Director Bruce Beresford and writer Brian Moore [adapting his own novel] have made this intriguing yarn a small epic of endurance. The production has an austere beauty and thoughtful approach. Bluteau gives a moving performance in the central role, and Schellenberg is particularly notable as the friendly Chomina.

. . . .

■ BLACK ROSE, THE

1950, 120 MINS, UK ◇ ▼

Dir Henry Hathaway *Prod* Louis D. Lighton *Scr* Talbot Jennings *Ph* Jack Cardiff *Ed* Manuel del Campo *Mus* Richard Addinsell *Art Dir* Paul Sherriff, W. Andrews
● Tyrone Power, Orson Welles, Cecile Aubry, Jack Hawkins, Michael Rennie, Herbert Lom (20th Century-Fox)

Produced in England and North Africa with frozen currency, and with a supporting British cast, *Rose* is an adaptation of the Thomas B. Costain bestseller. It is 13th-century drama that seems hardly to have ignored a thing in its plotting.

Black Rose is the story of Saxon revolt against Norman domination, 200 years after the conquest. The central figure in the Saxon fight is Walter of Gurnie (Tyrone Power), the illegitimate son of a Saxon peer.

In a picture of warring, there is only the suggestion of battle. Perhaps one good scene, with some honest-to-goodness cinematic blood-letting, might have done something to increase the tempo of the picture.

Power is credible in the lead role, while Welles underplays effectively the part of Bayan.
□ 1950: Nomination: Best Color Costume Design

. . . .

■ BLACK STALLION, THE

1979, 118 MINS, US ◇ ▼ ⊙

Dir Carroll Ballard *Prod* Fred Roos, Tom Sternberg *Scr* Melissa Mathison, Jeanne Rosenberg, William D. Wittliff *Ph* Caleb Deschanel *Ed* Robert Dalva *Mus* Carmine Coppola, [Shirley Walker] *Art Dir* Aurelio Crugnola, Earl Preston
● Kelly Reno, Mickey Rooney, Teri Garr (United Artists)

The Black Stallion is a perfect gem. Based on Walter Farley's 1941 novel, Carroll Ballard's feature debut is rich in adventure, suspense and mythical elements and marks the prize-winning short-subjects director as a major talent. Ballard's camera eye and powers of sequence conceptualization are manifestly extraordinary.

Opening sees the American boy Alec on a ship with his amiable father. Also on board is 'the Black', stallion.

After both end up overboard, Alec and the horse find sanctuary on a deserted Mediterranean island, filmed on unusual Sardinian locations. Ensuing half hour, in which the two gradually make contact and establish rapport is pulled off completely without dialog, backed instead by Carmine Coppola's richly complementary score.

□ 1979: Nominations: Best Supp. Actor (Mickey Rooney), Editing

. . . .

■ BLACK STALLION RETURNS, THE

1983, 93 MINS, US ◇ ▼ ⊙

Dir Robert Dalva *Prod* Tom Sternberg, Fred Roos, Doug Claybourne *Scr* Richard Kletter, Jerome Kass *Ph* Carlo Di Palma, Caleb Deschanel *Ed* Paul Hirsch *Mus* Georges Delerue *Art Dir* Aurelio Crugnola
● Kelly Reno, Vincent Spano, Allen Garfield, Woody Strode, Ferdy Mayne, Teri Garr (Zoetrope)

The Black Stallion Returns is little more than a contrived, cornball story that most audiences will find to be an interminable bore. Much of the charm and innocence of the original are absent here as now young teen-hero Kelly Reno follows the unlikeliest of searches through the Sahara Desert for his devoted horse.

A band of supposed 'good guy' Moroccans steal the horse in order to bring him back to his real home in the deserts of nothern Africa (where he will run in a once-every-five-years horse race) much to the chagrin of the 'bad guy' Moroccans who represent a supposedly evil tribe.

Robert Dalva, who edited *The Black Stallion* serves as director here but doesn't manage to convincingly merge the feelings of fantasy and reality that made the first film so charming.

. . . .

■ BLACK SUNDAY

1977, 143 MINS, US ◇ ▼

Dir John Frankenheimer *Prod* Robert Evans *Scr* Ernest Lehman, Kenneth Ross, Ivan Moffat *Ph* John A. Alonzo *Ed* Tom Rolf *Mus* John Williams *Art Dir* Walter Tyler
● Robert Shaw, Bruce Dern, Marthe Keller, Fritz Weaver, Steven Keats, Bekim Fehmiu (Paramount)

John Frankenheimer's film of *Black Sunday* is an intelligent and meticulous depiction of an act of outlandish terrorism – the planned slaughter of the Super Bowl stadium audience.

Strong scripting and performances elevate Robert Evans' handsome production far above the crass exploitation level, which at least mitigates subject matter that can never be completely comfortable on the minds of an audience.

Thomas Harris' novel has been adapted into a well-plotted, well-executed countdown to potential mass disaster. The motivations of stars Robert Shaw, as an Israeli guerrilla, Black September activist Marthe Keller and mentally unbalanced pilot Bruce Dern are handled with unusual dramatic depth which displays the gray are of real life.

. . . .

■ BLACK SWAN, THE

1942, 83 MINS, US ◇

Dir Henry King *Prod* Robert Bassler *Scr* Ben Hecht, Seton I. Miller *Ph* Leon Shamroy *Ed* Barbara McLean *Mus* Alfred Newman *Art Dir* Richard Day, James Basevi
● Tyrone Power, Maureen O'Hara, Laird Cregar, Thomas Mitchell, George Sanders, Anthony Quinn (20th Century-Fox)

This is a lusty story [from a novel by Rafael Sabatini] of English buccaneers who plunder women and the Spanish Main with equal facility.

Some of the pirates reform, while the others meet their just deserts at sword's end and the gallows. Thus chief pirate Laird Cregar, playing Henry Morgan, winds up as the honest governor of Jamaica; his chief aide (Tyrone Power) likewise turns pure, even winning the love of Maureen O'Hara, whom he previously tries to compromise; Thomas Mitchell also winds up a reformed pirate, while such brutes as George Sanders and Anthony Quinn, as a one-eyed scourge of the sea, become dead pirates.

Some of the film's action stuff is of the cliff-hanger variety, but director Henry King keeps the fantasy pretty well in hand so that it doesn't become too ludicrous. He paces the story well with the dialog bright and peppery.
□ 1942: Best Color Cinematography

. . . .

■ BLACK WATCH, THE

1929, 91 MINS, US

Dir John Ford *Scr* John Stone, J.K. McGuinness *Ph* Joseph H. August *Ed* A. Troffey
● Victor McLaglen, Myrna Loy, David Rollins, Roy D'Arcy, Walter Long, Mitchell Lewis (Fox)

Story is loose jointed and far from well knit, the audience being asked to take plenty for granted.

Talbot Mundy's tale is that of the Scottish Captain King (Victor McLaglen), who is ordered to India to prevent a native uprising on the eve his regiment is leaving for France. He gets into a drunken brawl, during which he supposedly kills a fellow service man, the ruse being an escape among the pack of fanatics planning to overthrow British rule.

The natives worship a woman (Myrna Loy) as their goddess, who, in turn, succumbs to the brawn of King.

Just how King manages to get about a dozen British soldiers among the hordes, who, at a signal, throw off their robes to reveal khaki, is not explained.

Director John Ford's best work is the opening of a Scottish officers' dinner on the eve of war, with bagpipes wailing. Joseph August's camerawork is superb. McLaglen's performance is just normal. Loy sheds an attractive appearance under, at times, outstanding lighting, aide by long robes.

. . . .

■ BLACK WIDOW

1987, 103 MINS, US ◇ ▼ ⊙

Dir Bob Rafelson *Prod* Harold Schneider *Scr* Ronald Bass *Ph* Conrad L. Hall *Ed* John Bloom *Mus* Michael Small *Art Dir* Gene Callahan
● Debra Winger, Theresa Russell, Sami Frey, Dennis Hopper, Nicol Williamson, Diane Ladd (Mark/Americent/American Entertainment)

Lacking the snap and sharpness that might have made it a firstrate thriller, *Black Widow* instead plays as a moderately interesting tale of one woman's obsession for another's glamorous and criminal lifestyle.

Theresa Russell portrays an icy-hard, beautiful woman who, it quickly becomes clear, makes an exceptionally handsome living by marrying wealthy men, murdering them, then collecting the settlements from the wills.

Pattern would go unnoticed were it not for conscientious, disheveled Justice Dept agent Debra Winger, who thinks she smells a rat and begs permission to pursue the case.

Winger first takes off after her prey for purely professional reasons, but the most intriguing aspect of screenplay is the barely submerged sexual jealousy the overworked government employee feels for the sexy, utterly confident manipulator of sex and lives.

Winger and Russell are both talented and watchable young actresses, so the picture has a lot going for it thanks to their casting alone. At the same time, both play very tense, brittle women rather near the breaking point, so there is a nervousness and restraint in both performances that harnesses them slightly.

. . . .

■ BLACK WINDMILL, THE

1974, 106 MINS, UK ◇ ▼

Dir Don Siegel *Prod* Don Siegel *Scr* Leigh Vance *Ph* Ousama Rawi *Ed* Antony Gibbs *Mus* Roy Budd *Art Dir* Peter Murton
● Michael Caine, Donald Pleasence, Delphine Seyrig, Clive Revill, John Vernon, Joss Ackland (Universal)

Don Siegel's filmmaking takes a dip in *The Black Windmill*, a British espionage drama with Michael Caine as an agent whose son has been kidnapped by one of his own spy colleagues. All principal players are well cast, but the production fizzles in its final half-hour because the story premise gets clobbered by clumsy and ineffective resolution and execution.

Clive Egleton's novel, *Seven Days to a Killing*, has been adapted by Leigh Vance. Script sets Caine up well: his superior (Donald Pleasence) hates him anyway, so the kidnapping and later circumstantial evidence suggests Caine himself has arranged the snatch. Janet Suzman, estranged from Caine because of his work, returns to his side. John Vernon and Delphine Seyrig are key figures in the kidnap and concurrent entrapment of Caine.

■ **BLACULA**

1972, 92 MINS, US ◇ ▽ ⊙
Dir William Crain   *Prod* Joseph T. Naar   *Scr* Joan Torres, Raymond Koenig   *Ph* John Stevens   *Ed* Allan Jacobs   *Mus* Gene Page   *Art Dir* Walter Herndon
● William Marshall, Vonetta McGee, Denise Nicholas, Thalmus Rasulala, Gordon Pinsent, Charles McCauley (American International)

Count Dracula has a black counterpart. Following a prolog located in Transylvania (where else?), when Count Dracula places the vampire curse upon an African prince and condemns him to the realm of the undead, plot picks up in Los Angeles nearly two centuries later. A pair of interior decorators have purchased all the furnishings of Castle Dracula and shipped them to America, including the locked coffin in which Blacula is resting.

William Marshall portrays title role with a flourish and gets first rate support right down the line: Vonetta McGee, whom he believes to be his reincarnated wife; Thalmus Rasulala, a black doctor who hits upon mystery of the rash of murders in LA; and Gordon Pinsent, homicide lieutenant who learns the hard way that murders are the work of vampires.

■ **BLADE RUNNER**

1982, 114 MINS, US ◇ ▽ ⊙
Dir Ridley Scott   *Prod* Michael Deeley   *Scr* Hampton Fancher, David Peoples   *Ph* Jordan Cronenweth   *Ed* Terry Rawlings, Marsha Nakashima   *Mus* Vangelis   *Art Dir* Lawrence G. Paull
● Harrison Ford, Rutger Hauer, Sean Young, Edward James Olmos, M. Emmet Walsh, Daryl Hannah (Warner/Ladd)

Ridley Scott's reported $30 million picture is a stylistically dazzling film noir set 37 years hence in a brilliantly imagined Los Angeles marked by both technological wonders and horrendous squalor.

Basic premise taken from a novel [*Do Androids Dream of Electric Sheep*] by Philip K. Dick provides a strong dramatic hook – replicants, robots designed to supply 'Off World' slave labor, are outlawed on earth. But a few of them have infiltrated LA, and retired enforcer Harrison Ford is recruited to eliminate them before they can do any damage.

One of them, beautiful Sean Young, is an advanced model with implanted memories so 'real' that even she doesn't know she's a replicant until she's tested by Ford.

Unfortunately, Young disappears for long stretches at a time, and at others Ford merely sits morosely around his apartment staring at photographs, which slows up the action.

Dramatically, film is virtually taken over at the midway point by top replicant Rutger Hauer. After destroying his creator, the massive, albino-looking Hauer takes off after Ford, and the villain here is so intriguing and

charismatic that one almost comes to prefer him to the more stolid hero.

[In 1992 Scott's original cut, sans Ford's voiceover and final flying sequence, was released. This 117-min. version was billed on posters, but not on prints, as *The Director's Cut*.]
□ 1982: Nominations: Best Art Direction, Visual Effects

■ **BLAME IT ON RIO**

1984, 110 MINS, US ◇ ▽ ⊙
Dir Stanley Donen   *Prod* Stanley Donen   *Scr* Charlie Peters, Larry Gelbart   *Ph* Reynaldo Villalobos   *Ed* George Hively, Richard Marden   *Mus* Ken Wannberg, Oscar Castro Neves   *Art Dir* Marcos Flaksman
● Michael Caine, Joseph Bologna, Valerie Harper, Michelle Johnson, Jose Lewgoy, Demi Moore (Sherwood/20th Century-Fox)

Central premise of a secret romance between Michael Caine and the love-smitten daughter of his best friend (Joe Bologna) while the trio vacations together in torrid Rio may be adventurous comedy. Zany comedic conflict, however, is offputting, even times nasty, in this essentially dead-ahead comedy that sacrifices charm and a light touch for too much realism.

Newcomer Michelle Johnson comes off as callow and disagreeably spoiled in key role of buxom daughter lusting after dad's best buddy.

Caine and Bologna play colleagues in a Sao Paulo coffee company whose marriages are toppling – Bologna is getting a divorce and Caine's wife (Valerie Harper) tells Caine while couple is packing for Rio that she's splitting for Bahia in a separate vacation.

Director Stanley Donen gets sharp, comic performances from Caine and Bologna.

■ **BLAME IT ON THE BELLBOY**

1992, 77 MINS, UK/US ◇ ▽
Dir Mark Herman   *Prod* Jennie Howarth, Steve Abbott   *Scr* Mark Herman   *Ph* Andrew Dunn   *Ed* Michael Ellis   *Mus* Trevor Jones   *Art Dir* Gemma Jackson
● Dudley Moore, Bryan Brown, Richard Griffiths, Andreas Katsoulis, Patsy Kensit, Alison Steadman (Hollywood)

British farce meets the ghost of the *Carry On* series in *Blame It on the Bellboy*, a lightweight ensemble comedy in which ingenious plotting is let down by weak dialog and stop-go direction that largely squanders the talent involved.

Plot gets off to a promising start with three similarly named characters – Orton, Lawton and Horton – checking into a Venice hotel. Thanks to a bellboy who can't speak English, their mail gets mixed up. Realtor Dudley Moore gets a letter for hit man Bryan Brown, who gets a letter for blind-dater Richard Griffiths, who gets a letter for Moore.

Moore is soon wired up to a generator by local mobster Andreas Katsoulis; Brown thinks his target is lonely blind-dater Penelope Wilton; and Griffiths schmoozes with sexy Patsy Kensit, who's into a real estate scam rather than a roll in the hay.

Problem is first-time director-scripter Mark Herman couldn't decide to make a breakneck farce or goofy comedy. The Brit actors mostly phone in their performances.

■ **BLAZE**

1989, 108 MINS, US ◇ ▽ ⊙
Dir Ron Shelton   *Prod* Gil Friesen, Dale Pollock   *Scr* Ron Shelton   *Ph* Haskell Wexler   *Ed* Robert Leighton   *Mus* Bennie Wallace   *Art Dir* Armin Ganz
● Paul Newman, Lolita Davidovich, Jerry Hardin, Gailard Sartain, Jeffrey DeMunn (Touchstone/Silver Screen Partners IV)

A bawdy and audacious tale of politics and scandal, *Blaze* delivers a good love story and a brave and marvelous character turn by Paul Newman.

Newman plays Louisiana governor Earl K. Long in 1959-60 during his May-December romance with famed New Orleans stripper Blaze Starr (Lolita Davidovich).

'Ol' Earl', a self-decribed 'pro-gressive thinker', was a stump speaker extraordinaire, an advocate of black voting rights and a friend of the poor man. He was also, many believed, a tax evader, a drunk and a madman. Starr was a queen of tawdry New Orleans showbiz who'd come up from poverty in the Tennessee hills.

In Shelton's hands, their relationship, which churned up newspaper headlines and plagued Long's teetering career, is a great and comic love story.

Davidovich is impressive, taking the character from a clunky, overripe hillbilly teenager to a woman with her powers fully focused.
□ 1989: Nomination: Best Cinematography

■ **BLAZING SADDLES**

1974, 93 MINS, US ◇ ▽ ⊙
Dir Mel Brooks   *Prod* Michael Hertzberg   *Scr* Mel Brooks, Norman Steinberg, Andrew Bergman, Richard Pryor, Alan Uger   *Ph* Joseph Biroc   *Ed* John C. Howard, Danford Greene   *Mus* John Morris   *Art Dir* Peter Wooley
● Cleavon Little, Gene Wilder, Slim Pickens, David Huddleston, Mel Brooks, Madeline Kahn (Warner)

Blazing Saddles spoofs oldtime westerns with an avalanche of one-liners, vaudeville routines, campy shticks, sight gags, satiric imitations and comic anachronisms. Pic is essentially a raunchy, protracted version of a television comedy skit.

Although Cleavon Little and Gene Wilder head a uniformly competent cast, pic is handily stolen by Harvey Korman and Madeline Kahn. Kahn is simply terrific doing a Marlene Dietrich lampoon.

Rest of cast is fine, although Little's black sheriff doesn't blend too well with Brooks' Jewish-flavored comic style. Wilder is amusingly low-key in a relatively small role.
□ 1974: Nomination: Best Supp. Actress (Madeline Kahn), Editing, Song ('Blazing Saddles')

■ **BLEAK MOMENTS**

1972, 110 MINS, UK ◇
Dir Mike Leigh   *Prod* Les Blair   *Scr* Mike Leigh   *Ph* Bahram Manoochehri   *Ed* Les Blair   *Mus* Mike Bardwell   *Art Dir* Richard Rambant
● Anne Raitt, Sarah Stephenson, Eric Allan, Joolia Cappleman, Mike Bradwell, Liz Smith (Autumn/Memorial)

A film with downbeat themes of solitude, difficulties of communication, coping with a retarded 29-year-old sister, it has enough human insight sans mawkishness or undue sentimentality to make it wryly funny, with its recognition of human foibles that gives it an edge, charm and warmth, tempered with compassion.

Anne Raitt, a handsome, heavyset woman, works in an office with a candy-eating friend who dreams of a possible, but not probable, marriage. Raitt has a quiet suitor who turns out to be impotent. Their night out in a Chinese restaurant is a revealing setpiece. Raitt has rented her garage to a hippie who publishes an underground newspaper. As the hippie leaves, all revert to their original bleak but never depressing lives, which will go on unless something good or better comes along or they take a more affirmative stand.

■ **BLIND DATE**

1987, 93 MINS, US ◇ ▽ ⊙
Dir Blake Edwards   *Prod* Tony Adams   *Scr* Dale Launer

B

Ph Harry Stradling *Ed* Robert Pergament *Mus* Henry Mancini *Art Dir* Rodger Maus
● Kim Basinger, Bruce Willis, John Larroquette, William Daniels, Phil Hartman, Stepanie Faracy (Tri-Star)

Bruce Willis abandons his mugging TV personality in favor of playing an animated, amiable, hard-working, ambitious financial analyst in LA.

Stuck without a date for a company function, he reluctantly agrees to ask his brother's wife's cousin (Kim Basinger) to accompany him. His first impression: she's darling. His first mistake: he's not supposed to let her drink and ignores the advice. Two sips of champagne later, she's out of control.

Theme of pure mayhem works well because of chemistry between the main trio of actors, Willis, Basinger and her spurned ex-beau (John Larroquette).

Basinger is cool when sober and wacky when drunk. Her part is really secondary to Willis', who starts out a befuddled date with the manners of a gentleman and ends up not only befuddled, but crazy for the woman.

It's really the psychotic Larroquette who drives this romp. While Willis tries to control his date (or at least figure her out), Larroquette is hot on his tail trying to get her back. Their skirmishes are hilarious.

Pic is essentially a running string of gags with snippets of catchy dialog in-between.

■ **BLINDFOLD**

1966, 102 MINS, US ◇
Dir Philip Dunne *Prod* Marvin Schwartz *Scr* Philip Dunne, W.H. Menger *Ph* Joseph MacDonald *Ed* Ted J. Kent *Mus* Lalo Schifrin *Art Dir* Alexander Golitzen, Henry Bumstead
● Rock Hudson, Claudia Cardinale, Jack Warden, Guy Stockwell, Brad Dexter, Alejandro Rey (Universal/7 Pictures)

In their adaptation of Lucille Fletcher's novel, scripters have approached their task with sights set on combining romantic comedy with tome's adventurous elements. Director Philip Dunne follows through with this tenor in his visual exposition.

Hudson plays part of a famed NY psychologist treating a mentally-disturbed scientist sought by an international ring, who becomes involved in a plot to kidnap scientist from a top-secret hideout. Film takes its title from his being blindfolded whenever he is to visit his patient, held for self-protection by the government in a secluded spot in the swamp country of the South, where doctor is flown every night from NY.

Hudson offers one of his customary light portrayals, sometimes on the cloyingly coy side, and is in for more physical action than usual. Claudia Cardinale, as the chorus-girl sister of the scientist, displays plenty of appeal. Jack Warden, as an American general in charge of protecting the scientist and who hires Hudson to bring him out of his despondency, knows his way through a line and Guy Stockwell heads the ring.

■ **BLIND FURY**

1989, 85 MINS, US ◇ ⓥ ⊙
Dir Phillip Noyce *Prod* Daniel Grodnik, Tim Matheson *Scr* Charles Robert Carner *Ph* Don Burgess *Ed* David Simmons *Mus* J. Peter Robinson *Art Dir* Peter Murton
● Rutger Hauer, Brandon Call, Terrance O'Quinn, Lisa Blount, Meg Foster, Sho Kosugi (Tri-Star/Interscope)

Blind Fury is an action film with an amusing gimmick, toplining Rutger Hauer, as an apparently invincible blind Vietnam vet who wields a samurai sword with consummate skill.

Nick Parker (Hauer) is actually based on Zatoichi, the heroic blind samurai who starred in a couple of dozen popular actions films for Japanese company Daiei in the 1960s and early 1970s.

First problem for writer Charles Robert Carner [adapting a screen play by Ryozo Kasahara] is to find a way to Americanize such a character. This is solved by having Parker blinded and lost in action in Vietnam and then trained by friendly Vietnamese to use his other senses to survive.

Twenty years later, Parker is back in Miami to look up an old army buddy, Frank Deveraux (Terrance O'Quinn) who's in trouble with the mob in Reno. Parker's in time to prevent the Kidnapping of Billy (Brandon Call), Frank's son, but not to stop the murder of Frank's ex-wife, Lynn (Meg Foster, in for only one scene) by the vicious Slag, played by Randall 'Tex' Cobb.

The rest of the film is simply a series of fights and chases as Parker heads for Reno to reunite Billy with his father.

■ **BLIND TERROR**

See: See No Evil

■ **BLISS**

1985, 135 MINS, AUSTRALIA ◇ ⓥ ⊙
Dir Ray Lawrence *Prod* Anthony Buckley *Scr* Ray Lawrence, Peter Carey *Ph* Paul Murphy *Ed* Wayne Le Clos *Mus* Peter Best *Art Dir* Owen Paterson
● Barry Otto, Lynette Curran, Helen Jones, Miles Buchanan, Gia Carides, Tim Robertson (Window III/NSW Film Corp.)

Pic opens with the death of Harry Joy (Barry Otto), its central character. He runs an ad agency and leads an apparently happy life with wife and two children. A heart attack fells him during a family gathering, and he's dead for four minutes. When recovers, he believes he has entered Hell.

That's because everything seems to have changed. His loving wife (Lynette Curran) is having an open affair with his sleazy business partner (Jeff Truman); his son (Miles Buchanan) is a drug runner with ambitions to join the mafia; his daughter (Gia Carides) is an addict who gives her brother sexual favors to get free dope; and Harry discovers, too, that his biggest client manufactures products known to cause cancer. Faced with these unexpected upheavals, Harry goes a little mad.

The biggest flaw in *Bliss* is the way the novel has been adapted by its author, Peter Carey, and director Ray Lawrence. The best films of difficult books (and *Bliss* was a difficult book) have pared down the source material while keeping the spirit and intention of the original. Carey and Lawrence have left nothing out; the film teems with characters.

■ **BLISS OF MRS. BLOSSOM, THE**

1968, 93 MINS, UK ◇
Dir Joseph MacGrath *Prod* Josef Shaftel *Scr* Alec Coppel, Denis Norden *Ph* Geoffrey Unsworth *Ed* Ralph Sheldon *Mus* Riz Ortolani *Art Dir* Assheton Gorton
● Shirley MacLaine, Richard Attenborough, James Booth, Freddie Jones, William Rushton, Bob Monkhouse (Paramount)

The Bliss of Mrs Blossom is a silly, campy and sophisticated marital comedy, always amusing and often hilarious in impact. Shirley MacLaine stars as a wife with two husbands – Richard Attenborough, the legal and night-time spouse, and James Booth, who lives in the attic. Script covers the laugh spectrum from throwaway verbal and sight gags through broad comedy to satirical pokes at old-fashioned film romances.

MacLaine, bored but adoring wife, calls Attenborough, a noted brassiere manufacturer, for help when her sewing machine breaks down. Only plant worker available is the bumbling Booth, who is seduced by MacLaine. He refuses to leave the attic, and

MacLaine gets to liking the cozy arrangement. Gumshoes Freddie Jones and William Rushton pursue Booth's 'disappearance' over the course of many years.

Although basically a one-joke story, idea is fleshed out most satisfactorily so as to take undue attention away from the premise.

Performances are all very good, Attenborough's in particular.

■ **BLITHE SPIRIT**

1945, 96 MINS, UK ◇ ⓥ
Dir David Lean *Prod* Noel Coward *Scr* David Lean, Ronald Neame, Anthony Havelock-Allan *Ph* Ronald Neame *Ed* Jack Harris *Mus* Richard Addinsell *Art Dir* G. E. Calthrop, C.P. Norman
● Rex Harrison, Constance Cummings, Kay Hammond, Margaret Rutherford, Hugh Wakefield, Joyce Carey (Two Cities/Cineguild)

Inasmuch as this is largely a photographed copy of the stage play [by Noel Coward], the camerawork is outstandingly good and helps to put across the credibility of the ghost story more effectively than the flesh and blood performance does.

Acting honors go to Margaret Rutherford as Mme Arcati, a trance medium who makes you believe she's on the level. There is nothing ethereal about this 200-pounder. Her dynamic personality has all the slapdash of Fairbanks Sr in his prime.

Kay Hammond, dead Wife No 1, brings to the screen a faithful repetition of the performance she has been giving in the flesh for nearly four years. As a spoiled darling with murder in her heart for Wife No 2, she is as much a smiling menace as she is wistfully wraithlike.

As Ruth, the very much alive Wife No 2, Constance Cummings more than holds her own in an altogether capable cast – until her death in the automobile accident engineered by Elvira. As a ghost, Cummings is not at all convincing. As Charles Condomine, twice married novelist, Rex Harrison repeats his stage performance, which is so flawless as to merit some critics' charge of under-acting.
□ 1946: Best Special Effects

■ **BLOB, THE**

1958, 85 MINS, US ◇ ⓥ ⊙
Dir Irvin S. Yeaworth Jr *Prod* Jack H. Harris *Scr* Theodore Simonson, Kate Phillips *Ph* Thomas Spalding *Ed* Alfred Hillman *Mus* Jean Yeaworth *Art Dir* William Jersey, Karl Karlson
● Steve McQueen, Aneta Corseaut, Earl Rowe, Olin Howlin (Paramount/Tonylyn)

The initial production of Jack H. Harris, a regional distrib in the Philadelphia area, *The Blob* had a reported budget of $240, 000. Story, from an idea by Irvine H. Millgate, will tax the imagination of adult patrons.

A small Pennsylvania town has been plagued by teenage pranks. Hence, when highschoolers Steve McQueen and Aneta Corseaut report that a parasitic substance from outer space has eaten the local doctor and his nurse, no one will believe them. Especially when no bodies can be found.

Neither the acting nor direction is particularly creditable. McQueen, who's handed star billing, makes with the old college try while Corseaut also struggles valiantly as his girlfriend.

Star performers, however, are the camerawork of Thomas Spalding and Barton Sloane's special effects. Production values otherwise are geared to economy. Intriguing is the title number, written by Burt Bacharach and Mack David. It's sung offscreen by a harmony group as the credits unreel. Picture was lensed at the Valley Forge, Pa, studios.

■ BLOB, THE

1988, 92 MINS, US ◇ ⑰ ⊙
Dir Chuck Russell *Prod* Jack H. Harris, Elliott Kastner
Scr Chuck Russell, Frank Darabont *Ph* Mark Irwin
Ed Terry Stokes *Mus* Michael Hoenig *Art Dir* Craig
Stearns
● Shawnee Smith, Kevin Dillon, Donovan Leitch, Jeffrey
DeMunn, Candy Clark (Tri-Star)

A great B-movie with an A-pic budget, the
Blob is back with a vengeance. Updated [from
the 1958 original] with awesome, no-expense-
spared special effects and a feisty female
hero, horrific outing should prove thoroughly
satisfying for fans of the genre.

Starting life as an aggressive glueball that
creeps out of a fallen meteor and attacks a
vagrant in the woods, the malevolent plasma
grows to raging, ferocious proportions, gob-
bling unlucky locals and carrying their blood
and body parts along with it. Glutinous glut-
ton has only one weakness – ice – and that's
hard to come by in this warm, weather-
blighted ski town.

Director Chuck Russell (*A Nightmare on Elm
Street 3*) builds suspense slowly and carefully,
devoting 30 minutes to establishing apple-pie
normalcy before the first grisly strike.
Likewise, suspense in third-act crisis scenes is
pumped for all it's worth. Weakest moments
involve the creaky sci-fi explanation for Blob's
presence, which is part of a germ warfare experiment run amok.

Perfs by Devin Dillon as an outlaw kid who
ends up battling the Blob and Shawnee Smith
as a cheerleader who turns into a machine-
gun toting she-devil to save her town are adequate for the genre, with Dillon's the more
resonant.

■ BLONDE CRAZY

1931, 78 MINS, US ⑰ ⊙
Dir Roy Del Ruth *Scr* Kubec Glasmon, John Bright
Ph Sid Hickox *Ed* Ralph Dawson
● James Cagney, Joan Blondell, Louis Calhern, Noel
Francis, Guy Kibbee, Raymond Milland (Warner)

Wise remarks, a fresh guy and dame stuff.
Quick pace and a performance by James
Cagney typically Cagney. These give *Blonde
Crazy* a fast start and keep it going most of
the way. Finish is weak but not enough to kill
off the early impression.

Strictly a petty larceny guy is Cagney and
all the way to the finish, when stretched out
on a prison hospital cot, he hints he might go
straight. Original yarn gives Cagney plenty of
room for his customary fresh punk characterization.

Joan Blondell is Cagney's business partner
– and what a business – who loves him in
other ways besides biz but doesn't find that
out until her marriage to a comparative nice
boy proves a flop.

Everything depends on the dialog and playing both come through satisfactorily. Cagney
and Blondell make a natural pair. Louis
Calhern uses his long experience to good effect in a class cheater part.

■ BLONDE FIST

1991, 100 MINS, UK ◇ ⑰
Dir Frank Clarke *Prod* Joseph D'Morais, Christopher
Figg *Scr* Frank Clarke *Ph* Bruce McGowan *Ed* Brian
Peachey *Mus* Alan Gill *Art Dir* Colin Pocock
● Margi Clarke, Carroll Baker, Ken Hutchison, Sharon
Power, Angela Clarke, Lewis Bester (Blue Dolphin)

Margi Clarke packs a mean punch in *Blonde
Fist* as a scrappy Liverpudlian and devoted
mother who eventually wins in the boxing
ring and at home. In a gritty *Thelma & Louise*
meets *Rocky*, Clarke is a knockout and pic is
punchy, though the complex story drags.

After fleeing jail and ending up in New York,
Clarke befriends a fun-loving, aging ex-strip-
per (superbly played by Carroll Baker) who becomes her ally and 'manager' in the ring.

Fight scenes are dynamically choreographed,
beautifully shot and provide pic's most engaging footage. But there are too many characters
and scenarios for a tight film.

■ BLONDE SINNER
See: Yield to the Night

■ BLONDE VENUS

1932, 93 MINS, US ⑰
Dir Josef von Sternberg *Scr* S. K. Lauren, Jules Furthman
Ph Bert Glennon *Art Dir* Wiard Ihnen
● Marlene Dietrich, Herbert Marshall, Cary Grant,
Dickie Moore, Gene Morgan, Robert Emmett O'Connor
(Paramount)

A disappointer. Much of the blame is to be
laid at director Josef von Sternberg's
doorstep. In a desire to glamorously build up
Marlene Dietrich he sloughs almost every
other element that goes to round out a box
office production. He devotes two reels to her
flight from her husband and all the drab details that went with it, as she scrams from
Baltimore to Washington to Nashville to
Chattanooga to Savannah to New Orleans,
etc, etc. The police reports of her hunt sound
like a railroad timetable.

Then in a meteoric rise, with no details
whatsoever, she's suddenly again the queen of
the nite clubs, this time in Paris, where Cary
Grant (who had formerly maintained her)
once again meets up with her. In this and
previous nite club scenes, Dietrich sings two
numbers in that deep, throaty manner of
hers, one chorus being in French.

Herbert Marshall is sadly miscast as the ra-
dium-poisoned husband who needs funds so
badly for a European cure that his devoted
wife takes resource to financial succor from
such a remote source as influential politician
(Grant).

The 93 minutes, despite their episodic and
ofttimes ragged sequences, are much too
much considering the triteness of the basic
story, a theme of mother love of the German-
American cafe songstress whose child (well
played by Dickie Moore, in perhaps the only
convincing casting) is the sympathetic basis of
it all. Otherwise there's little sympathy for
any of the characters; neither the hapless husband, the faithless wife nor the other man.

■ BLONDIE OF THE FOLLIES

1932, 91 MINS, US
Dir Edmund Goulding *Scr* Frances Marion, Anita Loos
Ph George Barnes
● Marion Davies, Robert Montgomery, Billie Dove,
Jimmy Durante, James Gleason, ZaSu Pitts (M-G-M)

Jimmy Durante is rushed into a house party
scene for his first and only appearance after
the picture has gone 70 minutes. That's the
best evidence that this picture's big weakness
was analyzed by the producers. In the five
minutes that Durante is on, his Barrymore-
Garbo takeoff with Marion Davies easily becomes the bright spot on the picture.

The story is simply the rise of two New York
girls of the poor class to *Follies* girl status,
their temporary enjoyment of the luxurious
fancy living and then their return to normalcy.

Chief situation is love rivalry between the
two girl pals, with Blondie (Davies) finally
winning out.

Davies and Billie Dove are both real life
Follies grads, so their backstage conduct in
this picture probably is authentic. Of the two
Dove is more the showgirl type in looks and
manner. As usual, Davies is best in her few
comedy chances, but on the whole this try is
under par for her.

■ BLOOD AND SAND

1922, 110 MINS, US ⊗ ⑰ ⊙
Dir Fred Niblo *Prod* Jesse L. Lasky *Scr* June Mathis
Ph Alvin Wyckoff
● Rudolph Valentino, Lila Lee, Nita Naldi, George Field,
Walter Long (Paramount)

Rudolph Valentino's switch to a St Anthony
type comes as a shock. The essential moral
conflict of the bullfighter never gets to the
surface. He is just a bewildered simpleton,
which makes his gaudy clothes ridiculous.

The story [from the novel Vicente Blasco
Ibanez and the play by Tom Cushing] has
many picturesque elements but it is episodic
and scattered. It starts with the theme of a
humble shoemaker raised to eminence as a
national hero of the bull ring and an idol of
the people.

Soon the problem is changed to 'What will
be the fate of a man who lives by blood and
cruelty?' Then the conflict appears to be an
attack on the institution of the bull fight.

'Poor matador; poor beast, ' says the benign
philosopher, 'But the real bull is out there
(the crowd around the arena). There is the
beast with 10,000 heads'.

■ BLOOD AND SAND

1941, 123 MINS, US ◇ ⑰
Dir Rouben Mamoulian *Prod* Darryl F. Zanuck *Scr* Jo
Swerling *Ph* Ernest Palmer, Ray Rennahan *Ed* Robert
Bischoff *Mus* Alfred Newman *Art Dir* Richard Day,
Joseph C. Wright
● Tyrone Power, Linda Darnell, Rita Hayworth,
Nazimova, Anthony Quinn, John Carradine (20th
Century-Fox)

Blood and Sand [from the novel by Blasco
Vicente Ibanez] is associated in the memories
of theatre-goers as a hot and decidedly sexy
piece of merchandise, chiefly because of
Valentino's silent version two decades ago.
The revival follows the original as a straight
drama of the bullfight ring.

Especially effective are the bullfight arena
sequences, which disclose exceptional camera
angles and intercutting of shots of crowds at
arena in Mexico City with studio shots.

Tyrone Power is a peon kid in Seville, son of
a bullfighter killed in the ring, decidedly illiterate, and with a passion for bullfighting. He
has an adolescent love for Linda Darnell, and
finally runs off to Madrid with a bunch of his
pals. Ten years later, as minor league matador, he returns to Seville, marries Darnell
and goes on to become the most famous and
widely acclaimed matador of the time.
Surrounded by leeches, Power is continually
in debt, but happy with his wife until fascinated by sexy Rita Hayworth, socialite flame.

Power delivers a persuasive performance as
Ibanez's hero while Darnell is pretty and
naive as the young wife. Hayworth is excellent as the vamp and catches major attention
on a par with Nazimova, who gives a corking
performance as Power's mother.
□ 1941: Best Color Cinematography.
□ Nomination: Best Color Art Direction

■ BLOODBROTHERS

1978, 116 MINS, US ◇ ⑰
Dir Robert Mulligan *Prod* Stephen Friedman
Scr Walter Newman *Ph* Robert Surtees *Ed* Shelly
Kahn *Mus* Elmer Bernstein *Art Dir* Gene Callahan
● Paul Sorvino, Tony Lo Bianco, Richard Gere, Lelia
Goldoni, Yvonne Wilder, Kenneth McMillan (Warner)

Bloodbrothers is an ambitious, if uneven probe
into the disintegration of an Italian-American
family [from the novel by Richard Price].
Under Robert Mulligan's forceful direction,
sharply-drawn characters clash, scream and
argue, but fail to resolve any of their or the
film's conflicts.

B

Bloodbrothers delves into the steamy emotional mess known as the De Coco clan, headed by construction worker father Tony Lo Bianco, his brother Paul Sorvino, wife Lelia Goldoni, and sons Richard Gere and Michael Hershewe.

Although the focus of the film isn't clear until about half-way through, *Bloodbrothers* is concerned primarily with the plight of Gere, who is trying to make one of those crucial life decisions about whether he wants to join the men on the construction girders or opt for the job that gives him real pleasure, working with small children.

This pedestrian tale is placed against a background of vibrant machoism, with numerous scenes of boozing, whoring an fighting set in the Bronx.
□ 1978: Nomination: Best Adapted Screenplay

....

■ **BLOODFIST III**
FORCED TO FIGHT

1992, 88 MINS, US ◇ ⊛
Dir Oley Sassone *Prod* Roger Corman *Scr* Allison Burnett, Charles Mattera *Ph* Rick Bota *Ed* Eric L. Beason *Mus* Nigel Holton *Art Dir* James Shumaker
● Don Wilson, Richard Roundtree, Gregory McKinney, Rick Dean, Richard Paul, John Cardone (Concorde)

This prison story is the best screen vehicle to date for kick-boxing champ Don Wilson. He's a wrongly convicted guy in the state pen who continually has to prove himself against bigger and feistier convicts.

Under director Oley Sassone (a.k.a. Francis Sassone), who previously co-scripted the radically dissimilar Disney family film *Wild Hearts Can't Be Broken*, film is tightly constructed. Wilson befriends John Cardone, a nerdy prisoner shunned by the other inmates and is in turn taken under the wing of prison sage Richard Roundtree.

Racism is the key theme, as white and black cons are continually fighting, with 'half-breed' (half-Japanese) Wilson caught in the middle. Per genre tradition, when the baddies attack Wilson's best friends, star whips into action and cleans up the place. In a characteristic role, Roundtree is extremely sympathetic.

....

■ **BLOOD FOR DRACULA**

1974, 90 MINS, FRANCE/ITALY ◇ ⊛
Dir Paul Morrissey *Prod* Andrew Braunsberg *Scr* Paul Morrissey *Ph* Luigi Kueveillier *Ed* Ted Johnson *Mus* Claudio Gizzi
● Joe Dallesandro, Udo Kier, Vittorio De Sica, Maxime McKendry, Arno Juerging, Milena Vukotic (CC-Champion & 1/Ponti/Yanne/Rassam)

Dracula has about been Hammered to bits in his many British incarnations. Now Paul Morrissey takes a turn at the old bloodsucker, made in Italy in English [back-to-back with *Flesh for Frankenstein*] with a mixture of nationalities acting in it.

Morrissey long showed that his films, although more implicit in sex, drugs and characterizations, were really Hollywood films at the core.

Udo Kier is a youngish Dracula, in the 1930s. It seems he will die unless he gets virgin blood. So he has to leave his Transylvanian lair to go to Italy for that, since a Catholic country should have some.

Accepted by a supposedly rich family, who have four pretty daughters, Dracula gets his come-uppance.

....

■ **BLOOD FROM THE MUMMY'S TOMB**

1971, 94 MINS, UK ◇
Dir Seth Holt, [Michael Carreras] *Prod* Howard Brandy *Scr* Christopher Wicking *Ph* Arthur Grant *Ed* Peter Weatherley *Mus* Tristram Cary *Art Dir* Scott MacGregor

● Andrew Keir, Valerie Leon, James Villiers, Hugh Burden, George Coulouris, Mark Edwards (Hammer)

This polished and well-acted but rather tame Hammer horror entry revolves around an exploration group who discovered an ancient Egyptian tomb and brought relics, including the Princess Tera's mummy; home to England. The sacrilege is savagely avenged by Tera being reincarnated in the leader's beautiful daughter.

Valerie Leon has the dual role of the princess and the modern miss who brings a reign of terror to a quiet London suburb. Solid support comes from Andrew Keir, James Villiers, Hugh Burden, George Coulouris, Rosalie Crutchley and James Cossins who bring credence to the proceedings.

Director Seth Holt died suddenly a few days before shooting was completed and the lack of his guiding hand through post-production could explain, without justifying, certain vagaries and roughness.

....

■ **BLOODHOUNDS OF BROADWAY**

1989, 101 MINS, US ◇ ⊛ ⊙
Dir Howard Brookner *Prod* Howard Brookner *Scr* Howard Brookner, Colman DeKay *Ph* Elliot Davis *Ed* Camilla Toniolo *Mus* Jonathan Sheffner, Roma Baran *Art Dir* Linda Conaway-Parsloe
● Julie Hagerty, Randy Quaid, Madonna, Jennifer Grey, Rutger Hauer, Matt Dillon (American Playhouse)

Howard Brookner (who died after completing this first feature) and Colman DeKay interweave four of Damon Runyon's famous Broadway short stories [*The Bloodhound of Broadway*, *A Very Honorable Guy*, *Social Error* and *The Brain Goes Home*] about New Year's Eve on Broadway in 1928. It's a gangster's farce that falls somewhat short of true comic inspiration.

Strong character acting by an all-star cast enlivens this fluffy little piece about romance and gangsters during Prohibition.

There's Harriet Mackyle (Julie Hagerty), who delivered a fine performance as a rich society babe who's throwing the party and invites some local mobsters for added color.

Randy Quaid as Feet Samuels does a satisfying job as an honorable dimwit who's madly in love with a beautiful, diamond-hungry showgirl, Hortense Hathaway, very adeptly played by Madonna.

Matt Dillon gives a rather tepid performance as Regret, Broadway's lousiest horse player, especially in comparison with Jennifer Grey, who does a good job as Lovey Lou, an angel-faced showgirl in love with Regret.

....

■ **BLOOD IN BLOOD OUT**

1993, 174 MINS, US ◇ ⊛
Dir Taylor Hackford *Prod* Taylor Hackford, Jerry Gershwin *Scr* Jimmy Santiago Baca, Jeremy Iacone, Floyd Mutrux *Ph* Gabriel Beristain *Ed* Fredric Steinkamp, Karl F. Steinkamp *Mus* Bill Conti *Art Dir* Bruno Rubeo
● Damian Chapa, Jesse Borrego, Benjamin Bratt, Enrique Castillo, Victor Rivers, Delroy Lindo (Hollywood Pictures)

Producer-director Taylor Hackford clearly wants this to be a major cinematic exploration of the Latino experience, from its ponderous near-three-hour length to its more-than-occasional sermonizing. Unfortunately, disjointed storytelling and uneven performances undermine those aspirations.

With script help from poet and former convict Jimmy Santiago Baca, among others [from a story by Ross Thomas], Hackford – relying on a virtually unknown cast – has blended elements of *Boyz N the Hood* and *The Godfather*.

Starting in the early '70s, the plot centers

on three youths and follows them into their early 30s: Paco (Benjamin Bratt), a hot-tempered boxer; Cruz (Jesse Borrego), a gifted painter seemingly destined to escape the barrio; and Miklo (Damian Chapa), their half-white cousin who ultimately becomes the focus when he's drawn into an interracial turf war in San Quentin.

Blood In Blood Out (the title refers to the code of a prison gang) seems compelled to say something profound but too often stands on a soapbox to do it. Much of the story takes place in prison, unflinchingly exploring some of the same brutal themes touched on in Edward James Olmos' *American Me*.

....

■ **BLOODLINE**

1979, 116 MINS, US ◇ ⊛
Dir Terence Young *Prod* David V. Picker, Sidney Beckerman *Scr* Laird Koenig *Ph* Freddie Young *Ed* Bud Molin *Mus* Ennio Morricone *Art Dir* Ted Haworth
● Audrey Hepburn, Ben Gazzara, James Mason, Irene Papas, Romy Schneider, Omar Sharif (Paramount/Geria)

Even for the never-never land of high chic melodrama the film inhabits, the tale of a woman who, unprepared, inherits control of her father's vast pharmaceutical empire contains wild implausibilities.

Flashback reveals papa's medical genius in a Jewish Polish slum. Audience is then asked to swallow premise that, 40-odd years later, his family, making up the company's scheming board of directors, contains Italian and French upper-crusters as well as a member of the British Parliament.

This is Terence Young's first completed film since *The Klansman* five years earlier and he's clearly out of practice, as his performers range unevenly in tone from the comic (Omar Sharif, Irene Papas, Gert Frobe) to the merely drab (James Mason, Michelle Phillips, Maurice Ronet).

....

■ **BLOOD MONEY**
See: Requiem for a Heavyweight

....

■ **BLOOD MONEY**

1988, 90 MINS, UK/US ◇ ⊛ ⊙
Dir Jerry Schatzberg *Prod* Donald March *Scr* Robert Foster *Ph* Isidore Mankovsky *Ed* David Ray *Mus* Jan Hammer *Art Dir* Howard Barker
● Andy Garcia, Ellen Barkin, Morgan Freeman, Michael Lombard, Brad Sullivan (ITC)

Clinton and Nadine are the lead couple who muddle through a murder mystery tale linked to illicit Contra fundraising.

Andy Garcia is Clinton, a parrot smuggler who stumbles onto his brother's slaying and foils murderers' attempts to escape with backpack containing some audiocassettes.

Clinton also came away from the crime scene with a purse belonging to Nadine Powers (Ellen Barkin), a hooker on the run from the refuge of his brother's home. Lonely and confused, she is drawn reluctantly into Clinton's attempt to track down those responsible for the murders.

By the time the pair become lovers, one hardly cares and problem is compounded when the story becomes bewildering as everyone is transposed suddenly to Costa Rica for the denouement.

....

■ **BLOOD OATH**

1990, 105 MINS, AUSTRALIA ◇ ⊛ ⊙
Dir Stephen Wallace *Prod* Charles Waterstreet, Denis Whitburn, Brian Williams *Scr* Denis Whitburn, Brian Williams *Ph* Russell Boyd *Ed* Nicholas Beauman *Mus* David McHugh, Stewart D'Arrietta, Don Miller-Robinson *Art Dir* Bernard Hides

83

● Bryan Brown, George Takei, Terry O'Quinn, Toshi Shioya, John Bach, Deborah Unger (Village Roadshow/Blood Oath)

Blood Oath is a courtroom drama that raises questions about wartime crime and punishment. The drama, based on actual incidents, takes place on the Indonesian island of Ambon in late 1945.

Ambon, site of a Japanese POW camp for Australian prisoners, was under the command of aristocratic, Oxford-educated Vice-Admiral Baron Takahashi (George Takei). Bryan Brown plays Capt. Cooper, Aussie officer assigned to prosecute Takahashi and his men for war crimes. He finds his hands tied at every turn, mainly because an American 'observer' at the trial, Major Beckett (Terry O'Quinn), doesn't want Takahashi found guilty, figuring he'll be more useful in reconstructed postwar Japan.

At least half the film takes place in the courtroom, and director Stephen Wallace stages these surefire scenes with maximum tension. Brown brings sardonic humor and a wholly convincing feeling of frustration to the tenacious character of Cooper (based on the father of co-scripter/co-producer Brian A. Williams).

■ BLOOD OF HEROES, THE
See: The Salute of the Jugger

■ BLOOD ON MY HANDS
See: Kiss the Blood off My Hands

■ BLOOD ON THE SUN
1945, 98 MINS, US ⓥ ⊙
Dir Frank Lloyd   *Prod* William Cagney   *Scr* Lester Cole
Ph Theodor Sparkuhl   *Ed* Truman K. Wood, Walter Hanneman   *Mus* Miklos Rozsa   *Art Dir* Wiard B. Ihnen
● James Cagney, Sylvia Sidney, Wallace Ford, Robert Armstrong, John Emery, Rosemary De Camp (United Artists)

Cagney portrays an American editor of a Tokyo newspaper who dares to print the story of the world-conquest plan formulated by Jap militarists. Naturally, the fur flies when the sheet hits the street – the police confiscating the papers, the Jap secret police demanding a retraction from the publisher, and the editor threatening to walk out if the latter does so. Quickly, Cagney finds himself in the midst of a dual murder committed by the Japs upon a US newspaper pal and his wife, who were leaving Japan to bring to America the document describing the world-conquest plot in detail.

The stars of this picture are given plenty of opportunity to display their histrionics. Cagney is the same rough and tumble character he's always been, ready to tell the Jap bigshots off at the drop of a hat.

There are a couple of over-dramatic sequences, but they just add to the tension of whether they're going to get the envelope with the plot out of the country, or not.
□ 1945: Best B&W Interior Decoration (Wiard B. Ihnen)

■ BLOOD RED
1989, 91 MINS, US ◇ ⓥ
Dir Peter Masterson   *Prod* Judd Bernard, Patricia Casey   *Scr* Ron Cutler   *Ph* Toyomichi Kurita   *Ed* Randy Thornton   *Mus* Carmine Coppola   *Art Dir* Bruno Rubeo
● Eric Roberts, Giancarlo Giannini, Dennis Hopper, Burt Young, Carlin Glynn, Julia Roberts (Kettledrum)

Blood Red, a saga of oppressed Sicilian winegrowers in 19th century California, is an unsuccessful throwback to earlier forms of filmmaking. Project was announced in 1976 by producer Judd Bernard, filmed in 1986 and given a perfunctory regional release in summer 1989. It was the first-time screen teaming of siblings Eric and Julia Roberts.

A robust Giannini is patriarch of one of two families in Brandon, Calif., and soon is warring with robber baron railroad magnate Dennis Hopper (fitted with an unconvincing Scottish brogue here) determined to get his land for his railroad's right of way. Giannini's rebellious son (Roberts), is in love with the beautiful daughter (Lara Harris) of another winegrowing clan.

Roberts is more subdued than usual as the script fails to develop a three-dimensional character for him. His scenes with real-life sister Julia, cast as his sister, are intriguing because of the visual match. She doesn't get much chance to emote, but that nascent star quality already is evident.

■ BLOOD RELATIVES
1978, 100 MINS, FRANCE/CANADA ◇
Dir Claude Chabrol   *Prod* Denis Heroux, Eugene Lepecier   *Scr* Claude Chabrol, Sydney Banks   *Ph* Jean Rabier   *Ed* Yves Langlois   *Mus* Howard Blake
Art Dir Anne Pritchard
● Donald Sutherland, Stephane Audran, Micheline Lanctot, Aude Landry, Donald Pleasence, David Hemmings (Classic/Cinevideo/Filmel)

Made in Canada and based on a Yank police precinct novel of Ed McBain, film settles down as an inspector, played with a low profile and humanity by Donald Sutherland, probes a knife killing of a teenage girl and the wounding of another girl who was with her. At first it is felt to be the work of a psychotic but then segues into a middle-class family that might have been the crucible for the gory carryings-on.

French director Claude Chabrol has often used murder as a catalyst in his grim pics about upper-class French life. But here it is more psychosis, repression and jealousy than the more absorbing social patterns of his French work. It makes the pic somewhat ambivalent, for it is a sudden revelation of madness rather than having more depth in characterization and a harder edge focused on its police work.

Playing is generally good. Chabrol shows a narrative and atmospheric flair, ringing in some solid sidebar feel in Donald Pleasence's rendering of a middle-aged man who likes girls picked up as sex deviates and questioned, and David Hemmings as the older man falling for the victim.

■ BLOOD SIMPLE
1984, 97 MINS, US ◇ ⓥ ⊙
Dir Joel Coen   *Prod* Ethan Coen   *Scr* Joel Coen, Ethan Coen   *Ph* Barry Sonnenfeld   *Ed* Roderick Jaynes, Don Wiegmann   *Mus* Carter Burwell   *Art Dir* Jane Musky
● John Getz, Frances McDormand, Dan Hedaya, Samm-Art Williams, M. Emmet Walsh (River Road)

An inordinately good low-budget film noir thriller, *Blood Simple* is written, directed and produced by brothers Joel and Ethan Coen.

Aside from the subtle performances, usually lacking in a film of this size (around $1.5 million), the observant viewer will find a cornucopia of detail.

Dan Hedaya plays Marty, a brooding owner of a Texas bar. Hedaya hires a sleazy, onerous malcreant named Visser (played with appropriate malice by M. Emmet Walsh) to kill his wayward wife and her boyfriend Ray (John Getz).

Walsh takes a snapshot of the lovers asleep in bed, doctors the photo to make it appear he's fulfilled the contract, and meets Hedaya at the bar after hours to collect. Upon payment, Walsh pulls out the wife's gun and shoots Marty dead in the chest. But the victim has swapped the photo and put it in the office safe before his demise, making Walsh's perfect crime no so. Final confrontation between Walsh and the lovers is outright horrific.

Performances are top-notch all around, Walsh in particular conveying the villainy and scummy aspects of his character with convincing glee.

■ BLOODY MAMA
1970, 90 MINS, US ◇ ⓥ ⊙
Dir Roger Corman   *Prod* Roger Corman   *Scr* Robert Thorn   *Ph* John Alonzo   *Ed* Eve Newman   *Mus* Don Randi
● Shelley Winters, Pat Hingle, Don Stroud, Diane Varsi, Bruce Dern, Robert De Niro (American International)

The story of Kate (Ma) Barker, who with her four killer sons terrorized mountain country in the Depression era, *Bloody Mama* is a pseudo-biopic starring Shelley Winters in one of those all-over-the-screen performances which sometimes are labelled as bravura acting.

Film was made entirely on location in Arkansas, and manifests an apparently deliberate attempt at naturalistic filming.

Story is a loosely-connected string of macabre vignettes, with an emphasis on dramatic peaks but very little character development or motivation. Cast as ma's brood are Don Stroud as the psychotic, Robert Walden as the masochistic homosexual, Robert De Niro as the drug addict, and Clint Kimbrough as the quiet boy. Bruce Dern plays a sadist homosexual, mated with Walden, and Diane Varsi is Stroud's girl, a stray hooker.

The best performance in the film, and one of the most outstanding screen portrayals in many moons, is that of Pat Hingle, playing a wealthy businessman kidnapped for high ransom.

■ BLOSSOMS IN THE DUST
1941, 98 MINS, US ◇ ⓥ
Dir Mervyn LeRoy   *Prod* Mervyn LeRoy   *Scr* Anita Loos   *Ph* Karl Freund, M. Howard Greene   *Ed* George Boemler   *Mus* Herbert Stothart   *Art Dir* Cedric Gibbons, Urie McCleary
● Greer Garson, Walter Pidgeon, Felix Bressart, Marsha Hunt (M-G-M)

What Father Flanagan is to Boys Town in Nebraska, Edna Gladney was to an orphans' home in Texas operated entirely on a strong mother love instinct and the gracious donations of Texans. The home is the Texas Children's Home and Aid Society of Ft Worth. *Blossoms in the Dust* is a worthy production on which much care has been showered by Mervyn LeRoy and others, but the picture fails to impress as being big.

There are almost too many kids, with much attention paid to them. Result is sentimentally sugary flavor which also extends over the romantic portions of the film. There is no comedy relief.

Pidgeon is the Texan who marries Edna Gladney of Wisconsin and worships her. The baby born to them dies and subsequently Pidgeon passes away suddenly after they have done some charity work for poor kids and foundlings. From there on Garson takes up the placement of unfortunate children as a lifetime work and ultimately is instrumental in passing a law which eliminates from public record whether orphans were born illegitimately or not.

Playing Edna Gladney, Garson spans many years but does not appreciably age.
□ 1941: Best Color Interior Decoration.
□ Nominations: Best Picture, Actress (Greer Garson), Color Cinematography

■ **BLOW OUT**

1981, 107 MINS, US ◇ ▩ ⊙

Dir Brian De Palma   *Prod* George Litto   *Scr* Brian De Palma   *Ph* Vilmos Zsigmond   *Ed* Paul Hirsch   *Mus* Pino Donaggio   *Art Dir* Paul Sylbert
● John Travolta, Nancy Allen, John Lithgow, Dennis Franz, Peter Boyden, John Aquino (Filmways/Litto)

Writer-director Brian De Palma's *Blow Out* is a frequently exciting $18 million suspense thriller which suffers from a distracting emphasis upon homages to other motion pictures.

Travolta appears as a Philadelphia-based sound man working out of his studio on low-budget horror films. Film turns serious with plot of Travolta caught up in a murder and coverup scheme when the tire of a politician's car is blown out by a rifle shot at a bridge where he is recording sounds.

Saving a young woman (Nancy Allen) from drowning in the car, Travolta's fate becomes entwined with hers as he uses his professional expertise to unravel the murder mystery while both of them dodge the assassin (John Lithgow).

With attractive leads and a stylish flair for suspense, De Palma misses sustaining involvement by his distracting allusions to prior films (ranging broadly from *Blowup* to *Touch of Evil*).

Travolta scores with a combo of intensity and naturalism in the sympathetic lead role, but co-star Nancy Allen is stuck essaying a helpless loser instead of the romantic teammate favored by De Palma's avowed mentor, Alfred Hitchcock.

■ **BLOWUP**

1966, 110 MINS, UK ◇ ▩ ⊙

Dir Michelangelo Antonioni   *Prod* Carlo Ponti   *Scr* Michelangelo Antonioni, Tonino Guerra, Edward Bond   *Ph* Carlo Di Palma   *Ed* Frank Clarke   *Mus* Herbie Hancock   *Art Dir* Assheton Gorton
● David Hemmings, Vanessa Redgrave, Sarah Miles, Peter Bowles, Verushka, Jane Birkin (Bridge/M-G-M)

There may be some meaning, some commentary about life being a game, beyond what remains locked in the mind of film's creator, Italian director-writer Michelangelo Antonioni. But it is doubtful that the general public will get the 'message' of this film, [from a short story by Julio Cortazar]. As a commentary on a sordid, confused side of humanity in this modern age it's a bust.

Filmed in England and Antonioni's first English-speaking production, interesting use is made of London backgounds. There also is certain sustained interest at times as the audience presses hopefully to piece together the significance of the story (?).

Footage centers on a topflight London fashion photographer who learns of a murder through his secret lensing of a couple he sees embracing in a park. Through a series of blow-ups of the many exposures he snapped he finds indications of a murder, and visiting the park again discovers the body of the man whom he had been photographing.

David Hemmings makes an interesting impression as the bulber whose studio is invaded by various femmes, and Vanessa Redgrave, as the woman involved in the park, projects another vivid impression.
□ 1967: Nominations: Best Director, Original Story & Screenplay

■ **BLUE**

1968, 113 MINS, US ◇

Dir Silvio Narizzano   *Prod* Judd Bernard, Irwin Winkler   *Scr* Meade Roberts   *Ph* Stanley Cortez   *Art Dir* Hal Pereira Linder   *Mus* Manos Hadjidakis
● Terence Stamp, Joanna Pettet, Karl Malden, Ricardo Montalban, Anthony Costello, Joe De Santis (Paramount/Kettledrum)

Poor writing, dull performances and pretentious direction waste the rugged physical beauty of the location area. The $5 million-plus film is neither the intellectual drama it apparently was meant to be, nor even a reasonably satisfying programmer.

Terence Stamp stars in a title role which can't amount to more than 200 words, many of them dubbed, the rest in his British accent, incongruous to plot. Basic trouble with *Blue* is that there seems to have been an attempt to make a 'great' or 'definitive' film.

Setting is the uneasy border between Mexico and Texas, across which bandits Ricardo Montalban, and older brother Joe de Santis come for lootin raids. Stamp, raised by Montalban, is supposedly torn between loyalty to Montalban and his own (undefined) kin.

Allowing for the last-minute casting of Stamp, his performance is dull. He does not speak a word for 50 minutes (though he grunts a bit), and the first sentence is 'I'll do it,' betraying therein his native accent.

■ **BLUE ANGEL, THE**

1930, 99 MINS, GERMANY ▩ ⊙

Dir Josef von Sternberg   *Prod* Erich Pommer   *Scr* Robert Liebmann, Carl Zuckmayer, Karl Vollmoller   *Ph* Gunther Rittau, Hans Schneeberger   *Mus* Frederick Hollander   *Art Dir* Otto Hunte, Emil Hasler
● Emil Jannings, Marlene Dietrich, Kurt Gerron, Rosa Valetti, Hans Albers (UFA)

Splendid English version of a German original [released earlier the same year]. It's Emil Jannings' first talker with his name over the title and Marlene Dietrich's underneath.

It's a standout picture along typical UFA lines – meaning that the story [from the novel *Professor Unrath* by Heinrich Mann] is heavy, tends to drag and holds up more on the strength of the two principals than anything else.

Dietrich, as a cabaret girl of liberal morals with those Continental soubret costumes of much stocking, bare limb and garters, is an eyeful. She seems a bit timid as regards the dialog. This is not so when she sings. One tune carries a plaintive melody which has a tendency to linger, and Dietrich sings it better in English than in German.

Dietrich's final rendition of the main song astride a chair, as she tosses it with almost a sneer on her face at the low-brow mob in the sailors' dive, is something of a classic.

Emil Jannings gives a fine characterization of the circumspect school teacher who falls completely for the cabaret singer whom his students have been nightly sneaking away to see. He descends to become the pantomimic clown assistant of the magician-manager of the show, with the mimicking of a rooster as his comedy punch.

Josef von Sternberg, directing, stretches the picture beyond its limit but shows high judgment in handling the dialog.

■ **BLUE ANGEL, THE**

1959, 107 MINS, US ◇

Dir Edward Dmytryk   *Prod* Jack Cummings   *Scr* Nigel Balchin   *Ph* Leon Shamroy   *Ed* Jack W. Holmes   *Mus* Hugo Friedhofer   *Art Dir* Lyle R. Wheeler, Maurice Ransford
● Curt Jurgens, May Britt, Theodore Bikel, John Banner, Fabrizio Mioni (20th Century-Fox)

When UFA made *Der blaue Engel* it catapulted Emil Jannings, Marlene Dietrich, producer Erich Pommer and director Josef von Sternberg into international repute. Later that year (1930), Paramount dubbed an English version and 'Legs' Dietrich was on the road to Hollywood renown. This remake is not the rocket that the Jannings-Dietrich impact made but neither Germany's Curt Jurgens nor Sweden's May Britt need be ashamed of their performances.

Perhaps counting the most against them is the somewhat familiar plot motivation – the femme fatale and the destruction of the German professor who succumbs to her wiles. But the prime shortcoming is the decision to give this saga a post-midcentury topicality in 1950s West Germany.

Britt is an eyeful as the seductress. Her shoulder-length blonde hair; her saucy mien and manner; the Dietrichesque style of straddling the chairs, showing off her saucy gams, are eyefuls in every department. She handles two vocal reprises of Frederick Hollander's 'Falling in Love Again' and also projects the new thematic, 'Lola Lola' which Jay Livingston and Ray Evans fashioned for her.

Jurgens proves a flexible performer. He disguises his masculine attractiveness under an authentic German academician's mien, impersonating the unworldly schoolmaster with conviction.

Film was part-shot in Bavaria and the interiors in Hollywood. Support is authentic.

■ **BLUEBEARD**

1972, 123 MINS, US ◇ ▩

Dir Edward Dmytryk   *Prod* Alexander Salkind   *Scr* Ennio De Concini, Edward Dmytryk, Maria Pia Fusco   *Ph* Gabor Pogany   *Ed* Jean Ravel   *Mus* Ennio Morricone   *Art Dir* Tomas Vayer
● Richard Burton, Raquel Welch, Joey Heatherton, Virna Lisi, Nathalie Delon, Sybil Danning (Vulcano)

Bluebeard is high camp. Richard Burton portrays title role in a modernized version of the legendary character who had a way with women – doing them in – and in dignified tread saunters through a whole phantasmagoria of murders and a veritable shower of bare bosoms to a finale which shows why he was that way, poor guy.

Joey Heatherton is the principal protagonist, who discovers all his victims in a huge refrigerator-room and who, as a result of her discovery, is to be his next victim. To her, he relates in flashback form the fate of his other wives.

One of the most entertaining sequences focuses on Nathalie Delon, who after getting nowhere with Burton in bed prevails upon a prostitute (Sybil Danning) to instruct her in the art of seduction. Lesson ends with her learning the total ways of lesbianism and Burton drops a pointed chandelier on them.

■ **BLUEBEARD'S EIGHTH WIFE**

1938, 83 MINS, US

Dir Ernst Lubitsch   *Prod* Ernst Lubitsch   *Scr* Charles Brackett, Billy Wilder   *Ph* Leo Tover   *Ed* William Shea   *Mus* Frederick Hollander, Werner R. Heymann   *Art Dir* Hans Dreier, Robert Usher
● Claudette Colbert, Gary Cooper, Edward Everett Horton, David Niven, Elizabeth Patterson, Herman Bing (Paramount)

Par's talker remake of the Alfred Savoir farce [in the American version by Charlton Andrews], a thin piece basically, isn't given much more heft under the Lubitsch touch or with the celluloid trimmings. It's a light and sometimes bright entertainment, but gets a bit tiresome, despite its comparatively moderate running time.

Once the premise is established that Claudette Colbert wants to deflate the multimillionaire Gary Cooper, who buys his wives – seven of 'em prior to her – as he buys a fancy motor car, making pre-marriage settlements with them, etc, it then becomes an always obvious farce.

Atmosphere is rich and French. It starts on the Riviera and wanders over the European map, focusing finally in Paris. The Brackett-Wilder scripting is ofttimes bright but illogical and fragile.

Edward Everett Horton is more or less of a bit as her father and the rest are casual.

David Niven has a mild opportunity and Herman Bing, with his characteristic style, is another who makes his rather light chore stand up.

●●●●●●●●●●●●●●●●●●●●●●●●●●●●●●●●

■ **BLUE BIRD, THE**

1976, 100 MINS, US/USSR ◇ ⒲

Dir George Cukor *Prod* Paul Maslansky, Lee Savin, Paul Radnia *Scr* Hugh Whitemore, Alfred Hayes, Alexei Kapler *Ph* Freddie Young, Ionas Gritzus *Ed* Ernest Walter, Tatyana Shaprio, Stanford C. Allen *Mus* Irwin Kostal *Art Dir* Brian Wildsmith

● Elizabeth Taylor, Jane Fonda, Ava Gardner, Cicely Tyson, Robert Morley, Harry Andrews (20th Century-Fox)

Third film version of the Maurice Maeterlinck novel (after 1918 and 1939) takes spoiled peasant children Todd Lookinland (excellent, by the way) and Patsy Kensit on a dream trip from their humble abode through a fantasy world in search of the bluebird of happiness.

Elizabeth Taylor's four roles include the dominant (and dazzling) one as (a) Light; as mother (b) she's uncomfortable; as witch (c) she's fun to guess at; as maternal love (d) she's elegantly simple and believable.

Jane Fonda does Night, the princess of darkness, with a flair, while Ava Gardner is extremely effective as Luxury.

Nobody's going to laugh in ridicule at any of it (it's that good) but nobody's going to be strongly moved (it's that bad).

●●●●●●●●●●●●●●●●●●●●●●●●●●●●●●●●

■ **BLUE COLLAR**

1978, 110 MINS, US ◇ ⒲ ⊙

Dir Paul Schrader *Prod* Don Guest *Scr* Paul Schrader, Leonard Schrader *Ph* Bobby Byrne *Ed* Tom Rolf *Mus* Jack Nitzsche *Art Dir* Lawrence G. Paull

● Richard Pryor, Harvey Keitel, Yaphet Kotto, Ed Begley Jr, Harry Bellaver, George Memmoli (TAT)

Paul Schrader's directorial debut is an artistic triumph. Schrader has transformed a carefully researched original screenplay penned by him and his brother Leonard into a powerful, gritty, seamless profile of three automobile assembly line workers banging their heads against the monotony and corruption that is the factory system.

It is a picture about the monotony and routine of factory life that isn't monotonous, but *is* realistic. Regardless of where individual scenes are set – at the after-work tavern, at a bowling alley, at a worker's home, in the union headquarters, or in a Detroit street – the factory dominates every frame of this film.

The film's three stars – Richard Pryor, Harvey Keitel and Yaphet Kotto – all turn in outstanding and disciplined performances.

Plot centers around the three workers' attempts to confront and battle the reality of this system as Schrader views it. The three devise a plan to rob the union, which in the end turns into another helpless action.

●●●●●●●●●●●●●●●●●●●●●●●●●●●●●●●●

■ **BLUE DAHLIA, THE**

1946, 96 MINS, US

Dir George Marshall *Prod* John Houseman *Scr* Raymond Chandler *Ph* Lionel Lindon *Ed* Arthur Schmidt *Mus* Victor Young *Art Dir* Hans Dreier, Walter Tyler

● Alan Ladd, Veronica Lake, William Bendix, Howard da Silva, Doris Dowling (Paramount)

Playing a discharged naval flier returning home from the Pacific first to find his wife unfaithful, then to find her murdered and himself in hiding as the suspect, Alan Ladd does a bangup job. Performance has a warm appeal, while in his relentless track down of the real criminal, Ladd has a cold, steel-like quality that is potent. Fight scenes are stark and brutal, and tremendously effective.

Story gets off to a slow start, but settles to an even pace that never lets down in interest. Audience may guess the killer, as the story follows several alleys of suspects, but pic always has suspense, with sufficient variations in mood. Ladd is one of trio to return from the wars, others being William Bendix and Hugh Beaumont. Ladd's path crosses Veronica Lake's, latter being separated wife of a nightclub owner who is one of the killer-suspects. Scenes between Ladd and Lake are surprisingly sensitive, with an economy o dialog and emotion doubly appealing.

☐ 1946: Nomination: Best Original Screenplay

●●●●●●●●●●●●●●●●●●●●●●●●●●●●●●●●

■ **BLUE DENIM**

(UK: Blue Jeans)

1959, 89 MINS, US ◇

Dir Philip Dunne *Prod* Charles Brackett *Scr* Philip Dunne, Edith Sommer *Ph* Leo Tover *Ed* William Reynolds *Mus* Bernard Herrmann *Art Dir* Lyle R. Wheeler, Leland Fuller

● Carol Lynley, Brandon de Wilde, Macdonald Carey, Marsha Hunt, Warren Berlinger, Vaughn Taylor (20th Century-Fox)

Based on the Broadway stage play by James Leo Herlihy and William Noble, *Blue Denim* recounts, often movingly and intelligently, the torments of a pair of high school lovers who are about to become unwed parents. The desperation of these babes in the basement – a 15-year-old girl and a 16-year-old boy – is further highlighted by their inability to communicate with their parents.

The girl's father is a college professor determined to raise his only daughter to emulate his dead wife. The boy's father is a retired army officer given to reciting platitudes about the value of service life and unable to forget his moments of past glory.

The screenplay has been considerably watered down. The word 'abortion' is never mentioned although it is obvious what is taking place. Moreover, the ending deteriorates to cliche melodrama.

Carol Lynley repeats her stage role with the same eclat and sensitivity. As her young lover, Brandon de Wilde gives a moving performance as the confused 16-year-old learning the realities of sex. Warren Berlinger, also from the stage play, is fine as his wise-cracking buddy and confidante.

●●●●●●●●●●●●●●●●●●●●●●●●●●●●●●●●

■ **BLUE GARDENIA, THE**

1953, 90 MINS, US

Dir Fritz Lang *Prod* Alex Gottlieb *Scr* Charles Hoffman *Ph* Nicholas Musuraca *Ed* Edward Mann *Mus* Raoul Kraushaar *Art Dir* Daniel Hall

● Anne Baxter, Richard Conte, Ann Sothern, Raymond Burr, Jeff Donnell, Nat 'King' Cole (Warner)

A stock story and handling keep *The Blue Gardenia* from being anything more than a regulation mystery melodrama, from a yarn by Vera Caspary. Formula development has an occasional bright spot, mostly because Ann Sothern breathes some life into stock character and quips.

Anne Baxter is a telephone operator who believes she committed murder when she was drinking away the tears of a broken romance. Too much rum with Raymond Burr, a licentious artist, has blacked out her memory and when she reads a newspaper account of his violent death, she naturally thinks she did it while fighting for her honor. Richard Conte, all-powerful newspaper columnist, masterminds the disclosure of her identity strictly to get an exclusive, but falls in love with her and has to uncover the real killer.

Baxter and Conte do what they can but fight a losing battle with the script while Burr is a rather obvious wolf. Nat 'King' Cole is spotted to sing the title tune, written by Bob Russell and Lester Lee.

●●●●●●●●●●●●●●●●●●●●●●●●●●●●●●●●

■ **BLUE HAWAII**

1961, 103 MINS, US ◇ ⒲ ⊙

Dir Norman Taurog *Prod* Hal Wallis *Scr* Hal Kanter *Ph* Charles Lang Jr *Ed* Warren Low, Terry Morse *Mus* Joseph J. Lilley *Art Dir* Hal Pereira, Walter Tyler

● Elvis Presley, Joan Blackman, Nancy Walters, Roland Winters, Angela Lansbury, Howard McNear (Paramount)

Hal Kanter's breezy screenplay, from a story by Allan Weiss, is the slim, but convenient, foundation for a handsome, picture-postcard production crammed with typical South Seas musical hulaballoo. Plot casts Elvis Presley as the rebellious son of a pineapple tycoon who wants to make his own way in life, a project in which he succeeds after numerous romantic entanglements and misunderstandings.

Under Norman Taurog's broad direction, Presley, in essence, is playing himself. Romantic support is attractively dispatched by Joan Blackman and Nancy Walters. In a somewhat over-emphasized and incompletely-motivated role of an unhappy young tourist, pretty Jenny Maxwell emotes with youthful relish and spirit.

Musical numbers, about a dozen of them, are effectively staged by Charles O'Curran.

●●●●●●●●●●●●●●●●●●●●●●●●●●●●●●●●

■ **BLUE ICE**

1992, 104 MINS, UK ◇ ⒲ ⊙

Dir Russell Mulcahy *Prod* Martin Bregman, Michael Caine *Scr* Ron Hutchinson *Ph* Denis Crossan *Ed* Seth Flaum *Mus* Michael Kamen *Art Dir* Grant Hicks

● Michael Caine, Sean Young, Ian Holm, Alun Armstrong, Sam Kelly, Bob Hoskins (M & M)

Michael Caine re-dons spy-catcher duds in *Blue Ice*, a determinedly old-fashioned actioner that's terminally light on real thrills.

Caine is Harry Anders, a retired MI6 op who's whiling away his years running a London jazz bar. When a US ambassador's wife (Sean Young) literally bumps into him at a red light, he gets drawn back into espionage when she asks him to find a former b.f. (Todd Boyce) who supposedly holds old love letters.

The movie is a throwback to formula pics of the '60s, with transatlantic leads swanning around London tourist spots and an uncomplicated plot that has fewer twists than a cocktail spoon.

As the retired cockney spy who cooks a mean langoustine provencale [based on a character created by Ted Allbeury], Caine skirts close to an aging Harry Palmer. His settled, effortless performance carries the pic, but there's a lack of real electricity with Young.

Title refers to a chunk of ice falling off an airliner out of a clear blue sky and braining someone on the ground.

●●●●●●●●●●●●●●●●●●●●●●●●●●●●●●●●

■ **BLUE JEANS**

See: Blue Denim

●●●●●●●●●●●●●●●●●●●●●●●●●●●●●●●●

■ **BLUE LAGOON, THE**

1949, 103 MINS, UK ◇

Dir Frank Launder, Sidney Gilliat *Prod* Frank Launder, Sidney Gilliat *Scr* Frank Launder, John Baines, Michael Hogan *Ph* Geoffrey Unsworth, Arthur Ibbetson *Ed* Thelma Myers *Mus* Clifton Parker

● Jean Simmons, Donald Houston, Noel Purcell, James Hayter, Cyril Cusack (Individual)

Technicolor photography of a glorious South Sea setting provides appropriate romantic background for this picturization of Henry DeVere Stacpoole's novel.

There is very little plot to the film and the story of the two children, who are shipwrecked on a South Sea Island, is developed by a series of incidents rather than by a woven theme.

As the production relies for its appeal mainly on its eye-filling virtues, little demand has been made on the cast. Jean Simmons displays a sarong to advantage and Donald Houston has little more to do than show off his manly torso. Noel Purcell gives a warm study as the irascible old sailor shipwrecked with them.

. . . .

■ **BLUE LAGOON, THE**

1980, 102 MINS, US ◇ ⓥ ⊙
Dir Randal Kleiser   *Prod* Randal Kleiser   *Scr* Douglas Day Stewart   *Ph* Nestor Almendros   *Ed* Robert Gordon   *Mus* Basil Poledouris   *Art Dir* Jon Dowding
● Brooke Shields, Christopher Atkins, Leo McKern, William Daniels, Elva Josephson, Glenn Kohan (Columbia)

The Blue Lagoon is a beautifully mounted production, a low-keyed love story stressing the innocent eroticism of Brooke Shields and newcomer Christopher Atkins. This is the second adaptation of the 1903 novel by Henry DeVere Stacpoole about two shipwrecked children who grow from childhood in an isolated South Seas paradise.

Producer-director Randal Kleiser takes the pair through puberty and into parenthood with a charming candor that stresses natural, instinctive sexual development without leering at it.

Their romance is enhanced by Nestor Almendros' exquisite photography (and Basil Poledouris' score), as is the stunning beauty of the Fiji island where it was filmed.
□ 1980: Nomination: Best Cinematography

. . . .

■ **BLUE LAMP, THE**

1950, 82 MINS, UK ⓥ
Dir Basil Dearden   *Prod* Michael Balcon   *Scr* T.E.B. Clarke, Alexander Mackendrick   *Ph* Gordon Dines   *Ed* Peter Tanner   *Mus* Ernest Irving (dir.)   *Art Dir* Jim Morahan
● Jack Warner, Jimmy Hanley, Dirk Bogarde, Robert Flemyng, Bernard Lee, Peggy Evans (Ealing)

Dedicated to the British police force, the story [from an original treatment by Jan Read and Ted Willis] describes the post-war crime wave as seen through the eyes of the man on the beat. Clear-cut direction and interesting location shots of London back streets help the story along.

The crime-wave is spotlighted on two characters. At first they are smalltime crooks, but gradually become ambitious and go for the bigger stuff.

The all-round cast is topped by Jack Warner, who as always turns in a human, workmanlike performance. He takes the part of the constable and brings to that role the typical humor associated with the London copper. Jimmy Hanley plays a raw recruit to the police force with feeling, but the best performance comes from Dirk Bogarde who, with Patric Doonan, are the criminals.

. . . .

■ **BLUE MAX, THE**

1966, 154 MINS, UK ◇ ⓥ ⊙
Dir John Guillermin   *Prod* Christian Ferry   *Scr* David Pursall, Jack Seddon, Gerald Hanley   *Ph* Douglas Slocombe   *Ed* Max Benedict   *Mus* Jerry Goldsmith   *Art Dir* Wilfrid Shingleton
● George Peppard, James Mason, Ursula Andress, Jeremy Kemp, Karl Michael Vogler, Anton Diffring (20th Century-Fox)

The Blue Max is a World War I drama [from a novel by Jack D. Hunter] with some exciting aerial combat sequences helping to enliven a somewhat grounded, meller script in which no principal character engenders much sympathy.

A downbeat air prevails in the drama. The hero, a lowerclass climber played by George Peppard, is a heel; his adversary in the ranks of an air squadron, also for the free affections

of Ursula Andress, is also a negative character, played by Jeremy Kemp. James Mason, husband of Andress, is looking for a propaganda symbol, finds it in Peppard, and eventually causes the latter's death. Only Karl Michael Vogler, the squadron commander, evoke any sympathy as a gentleman.

Director John Guillermin, who derived the uniformly fine performances within the given plot frame, has at times an exciting visual sense. On the other hand, his technique in more intimate sequences becomes obvious a mechanical.

. . . .

■ **BLUE MURDER AT ST. TRINIANS**

1958, 86 MINS, UK ⓥ
Dir Frank Launder   *Prod* Frank Launder, Sidney Gilliat   *Scr* Gerald Gibbs, Val Valentine, Sidney Gilliat   *Ph* Gerald Gibbs   *Ed* Geoffrey Foot   *Mus* Malcolm Arnold   *Art Dir* Allan Harris
● Terry-Thomas, George Cole, Joyce Grenfell, Lionel Jeffries, Lisa Gastoni, Sabrina (British Lion)

The pic packs in quite a lot of yocks, but the humor is a bit obvious and the string of slapstick situations pinned on to a thin, yet complicated, story line does not add up to a very satisfactory comedy film.

There are all the obvious gags, with the 'awful schoolgirls' of Ronald Searle's cartoons behaving like little fiends. The school is without a headmistress and the army has been called in to keep order.

By cheating, the girls have won an Unesco essay contest with first prize a coach trip to Rome. The girls are anxious to go in order that one of them be married off to Prince Bruno of Italy. Further complications are caused by one of the girls' fathers pulling off a diamond robbery. To get him out of the country he poses as the headmistress of St. Trinians.

Trip enables Lionel Jeffries to pose as a woman, Joyce Grenfell to pose as an interpreter though actually a police woman, and Terry-Thomas to steal the film as a shady boss of a coach firm. The older girls of St. Trinians are easy on the eye but it seems stupid wasting Lisa Gastoni on this sort of tripe.

. . . .

■ **BLUES BROTHERS, THE**

1980, 133 MINS, US ◇ ⓥ ⊙
Dir John Landis   *Prod* Robert K. Weiss   *Scr* Dan Aykroyd, John Landis   *Ph* Stephen M. Katz   *Ed* George Folsey Jr   *Mus* Ira Newborn   *Art Dir* John J. Lloyd
● John Belushi, Dan Aykroyd, James Brown, Ray Charles, Carrie Fisher, Aretha Franklin (Universal)

If Universal had made it 35 years earlier, *The Blues Brothers* might have been called *Abbott & Costello in Soul Town*. Level of inspiration is about the same now as then, the humor as basic, the enjoyment as fleeting. But at $30 million, this is a whole new ball-game.

Enacting Jake and Elwood Blues roles created for their popular concert and recording act, John Belushi and Dan Aykroyd use the slenderest of stories – attempt to raise $5,000 for their childhood parish by putting their old band back together – as an excuse to wreak havoc on the entire city of Chicago and much of the Midwest.

Film's greatest pleasure comes from watching the likes of James Brown, Cab Calloway, Ray Charles and especially Aretha Franklin do their musical things.

Given all the chaos, director and, with Aykroyd, cowriter, John Landis manages to keep things reasonably controlled and in a straight line. Pic plays as a spirited tribute by white boys to black musical culture, which was inspiration for the Blues Brothers act in the first place.

. . . .

■ **BLUE SKIES**

1946, 104 MINS, US ◇
Dir Stuart Heisler   *Prod* Sol C. Siegel   *Scr* Arthur Sheekman   *Ph* Charles Lang   *Ed* LeRoy Stone   *Mus* Robert Emmett Dolan   *Art Dir* Hans Dreier, Hal Pereira
● Bing Crosby, Fred Astaire, Joan Caulfield, Billy De Wolfe, Olga San Juan, Frank Faylen (Paramount)

The cue sheet on *Blue Skies* lists 42 different Irving Berlin song items but some of it has been excised and the rest so skillfully arranged, orchestrated and presented that the nostalgic musical cavalcade doesn't pall. Fred Astaire's 'Puttin' on the Ritz' (originally written for Harry Richman) is the musical standout of the more than 30 items which have been retained.

The story of *Blue Skies* is of familiar pattern and rather sketchily hung together by Astaire. He's cast as a disk jockey stringing the cavalcade of Berliniana together by recounting the nostalgic episodes behind the success of the platters as they are miked.

Bing Crosby is the romantic winnah throughout. Joan Caulfield is partial to the nitery troubadour (Crosby) whose unusual flair for opening and closing niteries is a plot keynote. Astaire is the suave dancing star and she's in the line of one of his shows. Astaire's romantic interest carries her along but Crosby's crooning charms her.

Mark Sandrich, who with Berlin, Crosby and Astaire whipped up *Holiday Inn* was the key man in *Blue Skies* until his sudden death interrupted production plans for the pic. Then, too, there was the emergency substitution of Astaire for Paul Draper, but with it all this film emerges a winner in every respect.
□ 1946: Nominations: Best Scoring of a Dramatic Picture, Song ('You Keep Coming Back Like a Song')

. . . .

■ **BLUE STEEL**

1990, 102 MINS, US ◇ ⓥ ⊙
Dir Kathryn Bigelow   *Prod* Edward R. Pressman, Oliver Stone, Michael Rausch   *Scr* Kathryn Bigelow, Eric Red   *Ph* Amir Mokri   *Ed* Lee Percy   *Mus* Brad Fiedel   *Art Dir* Tony Corbett
● Jamie Lee Curtis, Ron Silver, Clancy Brown, Elizabeth Pena, Louise Fletcher, Philip Bosco (United Artists/Vestron/Lighting)

A taut, relentless thriller that hums with an electric current of outrage. Director and cowriter Kathryn Bigelow makes the most of her hook – the use of a female star (Jamie Lee Curtis) in a tough action pic – by stressing the character's vulnerability in remarkable early scenes.

As rookie cop Megan Turner, Curtis is hit with doubts and resistance from all corners, then suspended after she kills an armed robber (Tom Sizemore) her first night out and no gun is found at the scene. The psycho bystander who picked the gun up (Ron Silver) starts commiting serial murders with bullets he's carved her name onto, and Curtis, under deep suspicion, gets dragged back onto the force to help find him.

Curtis gives an eerily effective performance as Turner, getting across in palpable waves her shaky determination and inner steeliness.

Script is at its weakest where the villain (Silver) is concerned – his characterization as a schizophrenic nutso with violent religious hallucinations is a writeoff. Even so, pic lacks nothing for menace and suspense, and has a frightening, explosively violent second half.

. . . .

■ **BLUE THUNDER**

1983, 108 MINS, US ◇ ⓥ ⊙
Dir John Badham   *Prod* Gordon Carroll   *Scr* Dan O'Bannon, Don Jakoby   *Ph* John A. Alonzo   *Ed* Frank Morriss, Edward Abroms   *Mus* Arthur B. Rubinstein   *Art Dir* Sidney Z. Litwack

● Roy Scheider, Malcolm McDowell, Warren Oates, Candy Clark, Daniel Stern, Paul Roebling (Rastar/Columbia)

Blue Thunder is a ripsnorting live-action cartoon, utterly implausible but no less enjoyable for that.

Opening 15 minutes take vet LA police helicopter pilot Roy Scheider and rookie Daniel Stern on nocturnal rounds, which encompass apprehension of some liquor store hold-up men, a little voyeurism outside the window of a sexy babe and, more seriously, trying to help stem an assault on a female city councilwoman at her home.

Reprimanded by boss Warren Oates for the sex-show detour, Scheider is nevertheless invited to a demonstration of the Feds' latest creation, Blue Thunder, a top-secret anti-terrorist chopper loaded with artillery and all manner privacy invasion technology.

Craft has been brought to LA for possible use against subversives during the 1984 Olympic Games, and among those in charge of the program is cardboard villain Malcolm McDowell, with whom Scheider served in Vietnam. For sketchy reasons, they hated each other then and they hate each other now.

Although brief Vietnam flashbacks punctuate the film to 'explain' animosity between Scheider and McDowell, streamlined script has been shorn of almost all psychology and complexity, and it hardly matters.
☐ 1983: Nomination: Best Editing

■ **BLUE VEIL, THE**

1951, 113 MINS, US
Dir Curtis Bernhardt   *Prod* Jerry Wald, Norman Krasna   *Scr* Norman Corwin   *Ph* Franz Planer   *Ed* George J. Amy   *Mus* Franz Waxman   *Art Dir* Albert S. D'Agostino, Carroll Clark
● Jane Wyman, Charles Laughton, Joan Blondell, Richard Carlson, Agnes Moorehead, Don Taylor (Wald-Krasna/RKO)

Story [by Francois Campaux] is nothing more than a series of episodes strung together by the central character of a First World War war-widow who devotes her life to children after losing her only child. Footage opens with the child's death, a moving sequence, and carries Jane Wyman through a succession of jobs as a baby nurse until, old and wornout physically, she is given the lifetime job of caring for the offspring of one of her former charges.

Charles Laughton, as a portly, kindly corset manufacturer, is Wyman's first costar, in the initial episode.

Romance makes a bid for Wyman in her new job in the home of wealthy Agnes Moorehead, but she is unable to leave her charge to go off to foreign lands with Richard Carlson, a tutor who courts her.

Next is the episode in which she cares for Natalie Wood, daughter of fading musical actress Joan Blondell. This sequence is considerably enlivened by the pert vivacity of Blondell and her singing of two old tunes.

Wyman experiences real heartbreak at the end of eight years of caring for the abandoned son of Audrey Totter when the latter returns from England after the Second World War, with a stepfather, and claims the boy.

Curtis Bernhardt's direction handles the drama surely, if at times a bit measured, and never strives for dramatic tricks beyond the level of the simple, war story being told.
☐ 1951: Nominations: Best Actress (Jane Wyman), Supp. Actress (Joan Blondell)

■ **BLUE VELVET**

1986, 120 MINS, US ◇ ⑰ ⊙
Dir David Lynch   *Prod* Fred Caruso   *Scr* David Lynch   *Ph* Frederick Elmes   *Ed* Duwayne Dunham   *Mus* Angelo Badalamenti   *Art Dir* Patricia Norris
● Kyle MacLachlan, Isabella Rossellini, Dennis Hopper, Laura Dern, Hope Lange, Dean Stockwell (De Laurentiis)

Blue Velvet finds David Lynch back on familiar, strange, territory. Picture takes a disturbing and at times devastating look at the ugly underside of Middle American life.

The modest proportions of the film are just right for the writer-director's desire to investigate the inexplicable demons that drive people to deviate from expected norms of behavior and thought.

The setting, a small town called Lumberton, seems on the surface to be utterly conventional, placid, comforting and serene. The bland perfection is disrupted when a man collapses in Kyle MacLachlan's yard and is further upset when he discovers a disembodied human ear in an empty lot.

He begins investigating whose ear he might have found, and ends up spying on local roadhouse chanteuse and prostie Isabella Rossellini. Peeping through a closet keyhole, what he sees violent client Dennis Hopper do to sweet Laura Dern launches MacLachlan into another world, into an unfamiliar, dangerously provocative state of mind.

Rossellini, dressed in lingerie or less much of the time, throws herself into this mad role with complete abandon. Hopper creates a flabbergasting portrait of unrepentent, irredeemable evil.
☐ 1986: Nomination: Best Director

■ **BLUME IN LOVE**

1973, 115 MINS, US ◇ ⑰
Dir Paul Mazursky   *Prod* Paul Mazursky   *Scr* Paul Mazursky   *Ph* Bruce Surtees   *Ed* Donn Cambern   *Mus* Bill Conti   *Art Dir* Pato Guzman
● George Segal, Susan Anspach, Kris Kristofferson, Marsha Mason, Shelley Winters, Paul Mazursky (Warner)

Blume in Love is a technically well made, but dramatically distended comedy-drama starring George Segal as a man determined to win back the affections of Susan Anspach, the wife who divorced him for infidelity. Needless time-juggling flashback, indulgent writing, lazy structure, and intrusive and pretentious social commentary blunt some fine performances which occasionally inject life into the plot.

It takes Segal 115 minutes to win back Anspach's affections, the road being littered with relentless footage from Venice, Italy, and lots of cutesy sidebar micro-vignette which is lingeringly set up only for a fast cut from some limp gag line. There are a few good laughs, a handful of chuckles, several smiles, and a ton of songs, some by Kris Kristofferson who is starred as Anspach's dropout lover.

■ **BOARDWALK**

1979, 98 MINS, US ◇ ⑰
Dir Stephen Verona   *Prod* George Willoughby   *Scr* Stephen Verona, Leigh Chapman   *Ph* Billy Williams
● Ruth Gordon, Lee Strasberg, Janet Leigh, Joe Silver, Eddie Barth, Kim Delgado (Atlantic Releasing)

At times genuinely affecting, at others patently manipulative, *Boardwalk* is a small, well-wrought feature that centers on the efforts of an elderly Jewish couple to survive the barrenness and dangers of their decaying Brooklyn neighborhood.

But although there's a strong emotional core (and ample talent) to its portrait of the stubbornly 'youthful' eldsters (Lee Strasberg and Ruth Gordon), it's the film's chronicle of their mounting terrorization at the hands of a black youth gang that overrides its tone, shading the pic into a *Death Wish* finale.

Director and co-scripter Stephen Verona quickly establishes his focal family as a tightknit, mostly loving unit.

■ **BOB & CAROL & TED & ALICE**

1969, 104 MINS, US ◇ ⑰ ⊙
Dir Paul Mazursky   *Prod* Larry Tucker   *Scr* Paul Mazursky, Larry Tucker   *Ph* Charles E. Lang   *Ed* Stuart Pappe   *Mus* Quincy Jones   *Art Dir* Pato Guzman
● Natalie Wood, Robert Culp, Elliott Gould, Dyan Cannon, Horst Ebersberg, Lee Bergere (Columbia/Frankovich)

The story concerns a young documentary filmmaker (Robert Culp) and his wife (Natalie Wood) who visit an institute in Southern California which supposedly helps people expand their capacities for love and understanding. When our friends are back in their swank surroundings, chatting with friends, Elliott Gould and wife Dyan Cannon, the comedy begins and never lets up until the final scenes when the sociological effects of this pseudo-liberal thinking come into play.

The acting is superb. Cannon proves an expert comedienne. She and Gould practically steal the film, although admittedly they have the best lines. Wood and Culp give equally fine performances.

The film is almost flawless, presenting the issues in a pleasing, entertaining and thought-provoking manner.
☐ 1969: Nominations: Best Supp. Actor (Elliott Gould), Supp. Actress (Dyan Cannon), Original Story & Screenplay, Cinematography

■ **BOBBY DEERFIELD**

1977, 124 MINS, US ◇ ⑰
Dir Sydney Pollack   *Prod* Sydney Pollarck   *Scr* Alvin Sargent   *Ph* Henri Decae   *Ed* Fredric Steinkamp   *Mus* Dave Grusin   *Art Dir* Stephen Grimes
● Al Pacino, Marthe Keller, Anny Duperey, Walter McGinn, Romolo Valli, Stephan Meldegg (Columbia)

Bobby Deerfield is a brilliantly unusual love story, told in a European fashion which makes the Sydney Pollack film at first irritating, then intriguing, finally most rewarding and emotionally satisfying.

Stars Al Pacino and Marthe Keller are both excellent as shallow jet-set floaters who become whole persons in their romance. Foreign location footage is lavish.

Erich Maria Remarque's novel, *Heaven Has No Favorites*, served as the basis for screenplay. Pacino plays the title character, a Newark boy whose interest in car racing has propelled him into international celeb status where he'd rather forget his origins. Keller is a wealthy and elusive character, manic in her life style because of terminal illness.

■ **BOB ROBERTS**

1992, 105 MINS, US ◇ ⑰ ⊙
Dir Tim Robbins   *Prod* Forrest Murray   *Scr* Tim Robbins   *Ph* Jean Lepine   *Ed* Lisa Churgin   *Mus* David Robbins   *Art Dir* Richard Hoover
● Tim Robbins, Giancarlo Esposito, Ray Wise, Brian Murray, Gore Vidal, Rebecca Jenkins (Poly Gram/Working Title)

A sort of political *This Is Spinal Tap*, *Bob Roberts* is both a stimulating social satire and a depressing commentary on the devolution of the US political system. Caustic docudrama about a wealthy crypto-fascist folk singer who runs for Senate showcases the impressive multiple talents of Tim Robbins as director, writer, actor, singer and songwriter.

Roberts (Robbins) is a self-assured, highly successful singer who attempts to ride his popularity into public office. Castigated as yuppie scum by his detractors, he has secured his niche as an anti-1960s folk artist who blames the country's ills on liberals and the social programs of the Great Society. Roberts' aim is to unseat longtime Pennsylvania Sen. Brickley Paiste (Gore Vidal).

Entire film is framed as a British TV documentary being prepared on Roberts' campaign. Dogging Roberts' heels on the campaign trail is one Bugs Raplin (Giancarlo Esposito), a black journalist for an underground rag.

Robbins is spookily dead-on projecting the candidate's bland confidence and homogenized middle-American personality. He has cast a healthy number of w.k. thesps to enact cameos, mostly as cute, superficial and dumb TV newscasters. Largest of these roles goes Alan Rickman, ferociously good in a part that mainly has him heatedly denying major misdeeds.

....

■ BODIES, REST & MOTION

1993, 93 MINS, US ◇ ⓦ ⊙
Dir Michael Steinberg *Prod* Allan Mindel, Denise Shaw, Eric Stoltz *Scr* Roger Hedden *Ph* Bernd Heinl *Ed* Jay Cassidy *Mus* Michael Convertino *Art Dir* Stephen McCabe
● Phoebe Cates, Bridget Fonda, Tim Roth, Eric Stoltz (Fine Line/August)

Uncompelling but moderately engaging throughout due to its attractive cast and closeup look at contemporary spiritual ennui, *Bodies, Rest & Motion* is both flashy and laidback, eventful and static. Script feels as if it knows whereof it speaks.

Set in a sun-baked, fictional Arizona town called Enfield that is all malls and fast-food pit stops, the sharp-looking film looks at four young people coping with a malaise that seems neither easily diagnosable nor curable. Adapted by Roger Hedden from his own play, piece betrays its theatrical origins by taking place over one weekend mostly in a house shared by agitated, dissatisfied Tim Roth and his unfocused g.f., Bridget Fonda.

In the opening scene, Roth tells former g.f. Phoebe Cates, now Fonda's best friend, that they have decided to move to the 'city of the future' – Butte, Montana – and are packing up. However, Roth hits the road on his own, leaving the distraught Fonda alone with a pile of furniture and dope-smoking housepainter Eric Stoltz, and the new couple soon get it on.

Michael Steinberg, who makes his solo debut here after co-directing *The Waterdance*, is good with the actors, and the more intimate the scene, the more effectively it registers. However, many scenes don't really have much going on in them, resulting in a relatively low-impact experience.

....

■ BODY AND SOUL

1947, 101 MINS, US ⓦ ⊙
Dir Robert Rossen *Prod* Bob Roberts *Scr* Abraham Polonsky *Ph* James Wong Howe *Ed* Francis Lyon, Robert Parrish *Mus* Hugo Friedhofer *Art Dir* Nathan Juran
● John Garfield, Lilli Palmer, Anne Revere, Canada Lee, Hazel Brooks, William Conrad (United Artists/Enterprise)

Body and Soul has a somewhat familiar title and a likewise familiar narrative. It's the telling, however, that's different.

The story concerns a youngster with a punching flair who emerges from the amateurs to ride along the knockout trail to the middleweight championship. But to get himself a crack at the title he has to sell 50 per cent of himself to a bigtime gambler with a penchant for making and breaking champs at will.

There are a flock of loopholes in this story, but interest seldom lags. Some of the 'inside boxing' is authentic, but the 'inside gambling' is another story in itself, which this pic doesn't tell. John Garfield is convincing in the lead part, and the boxing scenes look the McCoy.

Poolhall and beer stube environments are effectively captured to indicate the sordidness that backgrounds the early careers of most boxers, who turn to the ring because of a proficiency with their fists on the streetcorner.

Lilli Palmer is miscast as Garfield's sweetheart and inspiration, especially with a continental accent that even the dialog can't properly clarify.
☐ 1947: Best Editing.
☐ Nominations: Best Actor (John Garfield), Original Screenplay

....

■ BODY DOUBLE

1984, 109 MINS, US ◇ ⓦ ⊙
Dir Brian De Palma *Prod* Brian De Palma *Scr* Robert J. Avrech, Brian De Palma *Ph* Stephen H. Burum *Ed* Jerry Greenberg, Bill Pankow *Mus* Pino Donaggio *Art Dir* Ida Random
● Craig Wasson, Gregg Henry, Melanie Griffith, Deborah Shelton, Guy Boyd, Dennis Franz (Columbia/Delphi Prods II)

Brian De Palma lets all his obsessions hang out in *Body Double*. A voyeur's delight and a feminist's nightmare, sexpenser features an outrageously far-fetched and flimsy plot.

The first half offers up virtually no storyline. Down-on-his-luck Hollywood actor Craig Wasson is befriended by fellow actor Gregg Henry, who invites him to housesit for him at a rich man's hilltop pad.

In a house across the way a beautiful woman enacts an elaborate striptease dance at the same hour every evening. Wasson digs the lady's act so much that he follows her the next day, when she is also pursued by a hideous-looking Indian.

Pivotal murder scene occurs at about the midpoint, and it's an offensive lulu, being performed with an enormous power drill. Remainder of the film sees Wasson getting involved in the porno film world as a way of solving the murder.

Thesping by Wasson, Henry and former Miss USA Deborah Shelton, as the lady across the hill, is serviceable, while Melanie Griffith, with punky dyed hair and teensy voice, is just right as a porno queen.

....

■ BODYGUARD, THE

1992, 129 MINS, US ◇ ⓦ ⊙
Dir Mick Jackson *Prod* Lawrence Kasdan, Jim Wilson, Kevin Costner *Scr* Lawrence Kasdan *Ph* Andrew Dunn *Ed* Richard A Harris, Donn Cambern *Mus* Alan Silvestri *Art Dir* Jeffrey Beecroft
● Kevin Costner, Whitney Houston, Gary Kemp, Bill Cobbs, Ralph Waite, Tomas Arana (Warner/Tig)

No wonder this Lawrence Kasdan script was on the shelf for more than a decade: in the custody of director Mick Jackson, it proves a jumbled mess with a few enjoyable moments but little continuity or flow.

Those shortcomings are puzzling since the pic's core is sheer simplicity: bodyguard-for-hire Frank Farmer (Kevin Costner), who fears becoming too attached to his clients, takes a job protecting actress-singer Rachel Marron (Whitney Houston) and ends up falling for her. Someone is trying to kill her, and it seems possible that one of the members of her entourage may be involved.

Blame it on the setting, but the collaboration of Kasdan and Jackson (the one-time BBC director who helmed *L.A. Story*) at times feels like a music video interrupted by a movie.

For all that, pic isn't without its pleasures, from Costner silently drubbing his charge's testy security chief (Mike Starr) to his bluntly deflating a predatory partygoer.

The chemistry between the leads stems more from their inherent appeal than anything the story develops. Houston makes a solid debut and looks glorious, snapping off saucy dialogue. Kasdan was inspired by Steve McQueen in *Bullitt* when he wrote the script in 1975, and Costner manages some of that quiet intensity.
☐ 1992: Nominations: Best Song ('I Have Nothing', 'Run to You')

....

■ BODY HEAT

1981, 113 MINS, US ◇ ⓦ ⊙
Dir Lawrence Kasdan *Prod* Fred T. Gallo *Scr* Lawrence Kasdan *Ph* Richard H. Cline *Ed* Carol Littleton *Mus* John Barry *Art Dir* Bill Kenney
● William Hurt, Kathleen Turner, Richard Crenna, Ted Danson, Mickey Rourke, J.A. Preston (Warner/Ladd)

Body Heat is an engrossing, mightily stylish meller in which sex and crime walk hand in hand down the path to tragedy, just like in the old days. Working in the imposing shadow of the late James M. Cain screenwriter Lawrence Kasdan makes an impressively confident directorial debut.

William Hurt is a spirited but struggling lawyer just getting by in a marginal Florida coast town whose persistent pursuit of sultry Kathleen Turner pays off in the way of a torrid affair, highly satisfying for both parties.

She's the young wife of loaded middle-aged businessman Richard Crenna, and it isn't long before the passion can't tolerate the limitations imposed. Just as in *Double Indemnity* it's the dame who hatches the murder plot, with the guy finally falling into line and coming up with the ingenious way to pull it off.

However familiar the elements, Kasdan has brought the drama alive by steeping it in humid, virtually oozing atmosphere. The heat of the title is palpably evident, both mundanely in the weather and in the irresistible attraction of the sexy leads.

Hurt successfully mixes both laconicism and innocence. In her film debut, Turner registers strongly as a hard gal with a past. Her deep-voiced delivery instantly recalls that of young Lauren Bacall without seeming like an imitation.

....

■ BODY OF EVIDENCE

1993, 99 MINS, US ◇ ⓦ ⊙
Dir Uli Edel *Prod* Dino De Laurentiis *Scr* Brad Mirman *Ph* Doug Milsome *Ed* Thom Noble *Mus* Graeme Revell *Art Dir* Victoria Paul
● Madonna, Willem Dafoe, Joe Mantegna, Anne Archer, Julianne Moore, Jurgen Prochnow (De Laurentiis)

A courtroom drama built around the charge that Madonna's body is a deadly weapon with which she 'fornicated' a man to death, this showcase for the singer-thesp as femme fatale is more silly than erotic.

The ever-self-inventing one plays the g.f. of a rich older man with a heart ailment who is found dead after a night in the sack with her. That he's left her $8 million and had cocaine in his system points the finger of guilt straight to the 'cokehead slut' – as the man's secretary (Anne Archer) calls her.

Defense attorney Willem Dafoe makes the unforgettable opening argument that, 'It's not a crime to be a great lay,' but soon discovers that Madonna isn't into old men exclusively. Dafoe just can't say no and the pair's several sex bouts are the film's main action set-pieces.

Trial begins a mere 20 minutes into the story, and most of the running time alternates between courtroom testimony – much of it racy – and Madonna-Dafoe face-offs.

Decked out in a short platinum blonde haircut and fancy clothes that rip easily, Madonna has little trouble passing as a predatory tramp whose credo would seem to be, 'I f—, therefore I am.' Dafoe holds his own manfully. Portland locations give the pic's exteriors an appealingly wet, cool feel.

....

■ BODY PARTS

1991, 88 MINS, US ◇ ⓦ ⊙
Dir Eric Red *Prod* Frank Mancuso Jr *Scr* Eric Red, Norman Snider *Ph* Theo Van de Sande *Ed* Anthony Redman *Mus* Loek Dikker *Art Dir* Bill Brodie
● Jeff Fahey, Lindsay Duncan, Kim Delaney, Brad Dourif, Zakes Mokae, Peter Murnik (Paramount)

What could have been a reasonably interesting thriller literally goes to pieces in last third, until the brain seems the most salient part missing. Pic was inspired by a novel [*Choice Cuts*, adapted by Patricia Herskovic and Joyce Taylor] by French authors Thomas Narcejac and Pierre Boileau, who wrote the novel that provided the basis for *Vertigo*. Hitchcock and others reportedly grappled with adapting this book.

Jeff Fahey plays a criminal psychologist who loses his arm in a car accident, only to have it replaced by a doctor (Lindsay Duncan) perfecting a new limb-grafting procedure. The psychologist is told that the new limb belonged to a serial killer, prompting him to wonder if the murderer's arm might be invading his own soul.

He even seeks out other donor recipients (Brad Dourif and Peter Murnik), who are initially unconcerned or unaware of any ill effects. Then, suddenly, the narrative hurriedly kicks into a slasher mode, replete with car chases, dismemberment and unintentional, if rather vulgar, hilarity.

• •

■ **BODY SNATCHER, THE**

1945, 70 MINS, US 🅥 ⊙
Dir Robert Wise *Prod* Val Lewton *Scr* Philip McDonald, Carlos Keith *Ph* Robert de Grasse *Ed* J.R. Whittredge *Mus* Roy Webb *Art Dir* Albert S. D'Agostino, Walter Keller
● Boris Karloff, Bela Lugosi, Henry Daniell, Edith Atwater, Russell Wade (RKO)

Based on a short story by Robert Louis Stevenson, and given tightly scripted adaptation, *Snatcher* seldom lacks interest. Yarn deals with the traffic on dead bodies by hansom cabbie Boris Karloff. Corpses are used for study purposes in a medic school mastered by Henry Daniell. Russell Wade, young assistant to Daniell, is caught in the web of the illicit dealings, with Edith Atwater playing the wife of Daniell. Bela Lugosi is seen briefly as a handyman at the med school.

Karloff portrays his sadistic role in characteristic style, but best performance comes from Daniell. Lugosi is more or less lost, probably on the cutting floor, since he is only in for two sequences.

Body Snatcher is located in Scotland over a century ago. Settings are inexpensive but sufficient for the needs. Production values, in general, however, aid materially in making this picture a winner.

• •

■ **BODY SNATCHERS**

1993, 87 MINS, US ◇ 🅥 ⊙
Dir Abel Ferrara *Prod* Robert H. Solo *Scr* Stuart Gordon, Dennis Paoli, Nicholas St John *Ph* Bojan Bazelli *Ed* Anthony Redman *Mus* Joe Delia *Art Dir* Peter Jamison
● Gabrielle Anwar, Terry Kinney, Billy Wirth, Meg Tilly, Forest Whitaker, Christine Elise (Warner)

The third screen version of Jack Finney's 1954 novel *The Body Snatchers* is a tremendously exciting thriller that compares favorably with Don Siegel's classic 1956 original.

Producer Robert Solo effectively remade the picture in 1978 and has carried over several innovations, notably the shrieking sound effects. Improvements include having a teenage heroine and setting the film [from a screen story by Raymond Cistheri and Larry Cohen] on an Alabama military base.

Gabrielle Anwar toplines in a star-building performance as teen Marty Malone, who has moved to an army base with her EPA biologist dad (Terry Kinney), stepmom (Meg Tilly) and younger brother (Reilly Murphy). She also narrates the tale.

Anwar is befriended by the punkette daughter (Christine Elise) of the base commander,

Gen. Platt (R. Lee Ermey). Unsettling events occur early: Anwar is accosted by a black man who warns her cryptically: 'They get you when you sleep.' Camp medical officer Forest Whitaker tells Kinney he's received many reports of delusional fixations in people afraid to sleep.

Kinney, a low-key type resembling Don Johnson, is on the money as the ambiguous father, while Billy Wirth exudes sex appeal as Anwar's b.f. and savior. Tilly is chilling.

Makeup effects eschew the genre's explicit gore, in favor of frightening tendrils snaking around the victims.

• •

■ **BOEING BOEING**

1965, 102 MINS, US ◇
Dir John Rich *Prod* Hal B. Wallis *Scr* Edward Anhalt *Ph* Lucien Ballard *Ed* Warren Low, Archie Marshek *Mus* Neal Hefti *Art Dir* Hal Pereira, Walter Tyler
● Tony Curtis, Jerry Lewis, Dany Saval, Christine Schmidtmer, Suzanna Leigh, Thelma Ritter (Paramount)

Boeing Boeing is an excellent modern comedy about two newshawks with a yen for airline hostesses. Firstrate performances and direction make the most of a very good script.

The fanciful dream of a dedicated bachelor is realized in this adaptation of a Marc Camoletti play in which Paris-based US newsman Tony Curtis has three airline gals on a string.

Director John Rich has done a topnotch job in overcoming what is essentially (except for a few Paris exteriors) a one-set, one-joke comedy. Curtis is excellent and neatly restrained as the harem keeper whose cozy scheme approaches collapse when advanced design Boeing aircraft (hence, the title) augur a disastrous overlap in femme availability.

Rich has also brought out a new dimension in Lewis, herein excellent in a solid comedy role as Curtis' professional rival who threatens to explode the plan.

The outstanding performance is delivered by Thelma Ritter, Curtis' harried housekeeper who makes the necessar domestic changes in photos, clothing and menu so that the next looker will continue to believe that she, alone, is mistress of the flat.

• •

■ **BOFORS GUN, THE**

1968, 105 MINS, UK ◇
Dir Jack Gold *Prod* Otto Plaschkes *Scr* John McGrath *Ph* Alan Hume *Ed* Anne V. Coates *Mus* Carl Davis *Art Dir* Terence Knight
● Nicol Williamson, Ian Holm, David Warner, Peter Vaughan, Richard O'Callaghan, Barry Jackson (Universal)

No question of the quality of this absorbing, though downbeat military pic set in a British barracks in Germany in the mid-1950s.

It has all the gripping fascination of a tussle between two wily, desperate young animals. Taut, icy direction and acting flawlessly tuned to what the writer [John McGrath, from his play *Events While Guarding the Bofors Gun*] has in mind bring a faultless realism.

Clash is between David Warner as an immature, indecisive one-striper and Nicol Williamson a half-crazy, embittered Irish rebel, alcoholic and self-tortured. Events sizzle powerfully on the night before Warner is due to go to England for an officers' course. Williamson is attached to Warner's guard and, with rebellion and anger rankling inside him, sets out to humiliate the NCO and wreck his prospects of promotion.

Williamson brings out the rebel's mood brilliantly, his features, speech and behavior veering alarmingly from good-humored cynicism to anger and viciousness. Warner is just as good as the weak young man.

• •

■ **BOHEMIAN GIRL, THE**

1936, 80 MINS, US 🅥 ⊙
Dir James W. Horne, Charles Rogers *Prod* Hal Roach *Scr* [uncredited] *Ph* Art Lloyd, Francis Corby *Ed* Bert Jordan, Louis McManus *Art Dir* Arthur I. Royce, William L. Stevens
● Stan Laurel, Oliver Hardy, Thelma Todd, Antonio Moreno, Jacqueline Wells, James Finlayson (M-G-M)

A comedy with little or no comedy. Laurel and Hardy are snatch-purses with an 18th-century band of roving gypsies. In retaliation for the flogging of a fellow-member (Antonio Moreno), caught red-handed in an attempted burglary, the gypsies steal the child of a nobleman and bring her up as one of their own. In the end the customary tell-tale medallion saves the peeress and restores her to her daddy.

There are no credits for screen adaptation. Responsibility is thrown back upon Michael Balfe who wrote the original opera in 1843 and should be permitted to rest in peace. He composed the score; original librettists also not credited – or blamed.

Chained to such a scenario, the picture has the additional liability of inept direction. Thelma Todd who goes through the motions of singing (a mere bit) with the voice track poorly synchronized to her lips, seems strangely unlike herself. (A good deal of her footage, fortunately for her rep, was cut out just prior to release.)

• •

■ **BOILING POINT**

1993, 90 MINS, US/FRANCE ◇ 🅥 ⊙
Dir James B. Harris *Prod* Marc Frydman, Leonardo de la Fuente *Scr* James B. Harris *Ph* King Baggot *Ed* Jerry Brady *Mus* Cory Lerios, John D'Andrea *Art Dir* Ron Foreman
● Wesley Snipes, Dennis Hopper, Lolita Davidovich, Viggo Mortensen, Dan Hedaya, Seymour Cassel (Hexagon)

Promoted as a hard-action film for Wesley Snipes fans, *Boiling Point* turns out to be an old-fashioned police procedural, low-key and bland in the extreme. Writer/director James B. Harris, in his zeal to re-create the mood and character acting of '40s film noir, seems to have forgotten about excitement and visual flair.

Snipes toplines as a US Treasury agent partnered with Dan Hedaya. The third T-man on their stakeout is killed by ruthless thug Viggo Mortensen, who gets away with partner Dennis Hopper before the feds can close in. Snipes is reassigned from LA to Newark. He holds out for one week's time to catch the killers; coincidentally Hopper is given a week to find the $50,000 he owes gangster Tony LoBianco.

Throughout the picture, Snipes keeps running into trouble, neither knowing one is methodically hunting the other. Because of terrific acting down to the smallest role, one's interest is maintained despite the minimalist direction and lack of story twists.

• •

■ **BOLERO**

1984, 104 MINS, US ◇ 🅥 ⊙
Dir John Derek *Prod* Bo Derek *Scr* John Derek *Ph* John Derek *Ed* John Derek *Mus* Peter Bernstein, Elmer Bernstein *Art Dir* Alan Roderick-Jones
● Bo Derek, George Kennedy, Andrea Occhipinti, Ana Obregon, Olivia D'Abo, Greg Bensen (Cannon/City)

Bolero is all about Bo Derek's determination to lose her virginity after graduating from an English boarding school. Accompanied by friend Ana Obregon and family retainer George Kennedy, Bo ventures first to Arabia where a sheik falls asleep her arms.

Still unviolated, Bo moves on to Spain where she meets handsome bullfighter Andrea Occhipinti. Ready for womanhood, Bo

B

utters the immortal lines: 'Do everything to me. Show me how I can do everything to you. Is there enough I can do for you so you can give ecstasy to me?'

Then the dog barks and the deed is done. But poor Bo no sooner has her initial introduction to amour than the new lover gets gored in a sensitive location, putting him out of commission.

. . . .

■ BONFIRE OF THE VANITIES, THE

1990, 125 MINS, US ◇ ⓦ ⊙
Dir Brian De Palma   *Prod* Brian De Palma   *Scr* Michael Cristofer   *Ph* Vilmos Zsigmond   *Ed* David Ray, Bill Pankow   *Mus* Dave Grusin   *Art Dir* Richard Sylbert
● Tom Hanks, Bruce Willis, Melanie Griffith, Kim Cattrall, Morgan Freeman, F. Murray Abraham (Warner)

Brian De Palma's take on Tom Wolfe's *The Bonfire of the Vanities* is a misfire of inanities. Wolfe's first novel boasted rich characters and teeming incident that proved highly alluring to filmmakers. Unfortunately, De Palma was not the man fo the job. It doesn't take long to turn off and tune out on this glitzy $45 million-plus dud.

Early sequences of marital discord between Wall Street maestro Sherman McCoy (Tom Hanks) and wife Judy (Kim Cattrall) possess a grating, uncertain quality, and film never manages to locate a consistent tone. McCoy is having an affair with Southern bombshell Maria Ruskin (Melanie Griffith), and clearly stands as a symbol for Success, 1980s style. Monkeywrench arrives in the form of an automobile mishap one night in deepest Bronx.

Seemingly threatened by two black youths, Maria backs Sherman's Mercedes into one of them, slightly injuring him. When the kid falls into a coma, the machinery of law, politics and journalism begins grinding. The rich man's status makes him an ideal scapegoat for multifarious social ills, as well for as the personal agendas of the city's most shameless operators, most prominently, Peter Fallow (Bruce Willis), a down-and-out alcoholic reporter who parlay the McCoy story into fame and fortune.

Unfortunately, the caricatures are so crude and the 'revelations' so unenlightening of the human condition, that the satire is about as socially incisive as a *Police Academy* entry.

. . . .

■ BONJOUR TRISTESSE

1958, 94 MINS, US ◇ ⓦ
Dir Otto Preminger   *Prod* Otto Preminger   *Scr* Arthur Laurents   *Ph* Georges Perinal   *Ed* Helga Cranston   *Mus* Georges Auric   *Art Dir* Roger Furse
● Deborah Kerr, David Niven, Jean Seberg, Mylene Demongeot, Geoffrey Horne, Juliette Greco (Columbia)

In transplanting Francoise Sagan's thin book to the screen, producer-director Otto Preminger basically has stayed with her first-person tale of the amours of a middle-aged, charming and wealthy Frenchman within both view and earshot of his daughter who, like the author at the time, is 17. It's hardly a matter of wonder that pere's free-living escapades should prove contagious, that the girl, too, should take a fling at same.

But it is not a Class A effort. Script deficiencies and awkward reading – some lines are spoken as though just that – have static results.

Detracting from the make-believe also is Jean Seberg's deportment. In her second cinematic try (her first was in Preminger's unfortunate *Saint Joan*), Seberg's Cecile is more suggestive of a high school senior back home than the frisky, knowing, close friend and daughter of a roue living it up in the sumptious French setting. She is, of course, a selfish and malicious character to start with.

David Niven is properly affable as the father who travels with a mistress and makes no attempt to disguise his pursuits. Deborah Kerr is a standout talent as the artist whom Niven proposes to marry and who speeds away to apparent suicide upon finding him in anoth illicit situation, but there are instances where she, too, has difficulty with the stiltedness of the dialog.

Mylene Demongeot fits in well as a silly, sunburned blonde; Geoffrey Horne rates adequate as playmate for Cecile; and Walter Chiari comes off as something of a cariacature of a rich South American.

. . . .

■ BONNIE AND CLYDE

1967, 111 MINS, US ◇ ⓦ ⊙
Dir Arthur Penn   *Prod* Warren Beatty   *Scr* David Newman, Robert Benton   *Ph* Burnett Guffey   *Ed* Dede Allen   *Mus* Charles Strouse   *Art Dir* Dean Tavoularis
● Warren Beatty, Faye Dunaway, Michael J. Pollard, Gene Hackman, Estelle Parsons, Denver Pyle (Warner/Seven Arts)

Warren Beatty's *Bonnie and Clyde* incongruously couples comedy with crime, in this biopic of Bonnie Parker and Clyde Barrow, a pair of Texas desperadoes who roamed and robbed the southwest and midwest during the bleak Depression days of the early 1930s.

Conceptually, the film leaves much to be desired, because killings and the backdrop of the Depression are scarcely material for a bundle of laughs. However, the film does have some standout interludes.

Scripters Newman and Benton have depicted these real-life characters as inept, bumbling, moronic types, and if this had been true they would have been erased in their first try. It's a picture with conflicting moods, racing from crime to comedy, and intermingling genuinely moving love scenes between Faye Dunaway as Bonnie and Beatty as Clyde.

This inconsistency of direction is the most obvious fault of *Bonnie and Clyde*, which has some good ingredients, although they are not meshed together well. Like the film itself, the performances are mostly erratic. Beatty is believable at times, but his characterization lacks any consistency. Dunaway is a knockout as Bonnie Parker, registers with deep sensitivity in the love scenes, and conveys believability to her role. Michael J. Pollard and Gene Hackman are more clowns than baddies as gang members; Estelle Parsons is good.

□ 1967: Best Supp. Actress (Estelle Parsons), Cinematography.
□ Nominations: Best Picture, Director, Actor (Warren Beatty), Actress (Faye Dunaway), Supp. Actor (Gene Hackman, Michael J. Pollard), Original Story & Screenplay, Costume Design

. . . .

■ BOOM

1968, 112 MINS, UK ◇
Dir Joseph Losey   *Prod* John Heyman, Norman Priggen   *Scr* Tennessee Williams   *Ph* Douglas Slocombe   *Ed* Reginald Beck   *Mus* John Barry   *Art Dir* Richard MacDonald
● Elizabeth Taylor, Richard Burton, Noel Coward, Joanna Shimkus, Michael Dunn, Romolo Valli (World Film Services/Moonlake/Universal)

The translation to film of Tennessee Williams's much-revised play, *The Milk Train Doesn't Stop Here Anymore*, has at least given more physical movement to the symbolic drama of not-so-dolce vita among the jaded rich. Joseph Losey directs stars Elizabeth Taylor, Richard Burton and Noel Coward in John Heyman's plush production.

Film is the uninteresting tale of a multimarried, aging shrew, played by Taylor. Coward, a neighboring swish from Capri, adds a good shot of life, unfortunately too early and too little.

Taylor's delineation of the lead role is off the mark; instead of an earthy dame, hypochondriac and hyperemotional, who has survived six wealthy husbands, she plays it like she has just lost the first, who would appear to have taken her away from a roadside truck stop job. The wealth is shown in too nouveau riche a manner. The gowns, jewels and sets only emphasize the point. Burton is far more believable as a freeloading poet working the Mediterranean circuit.

. . . .

■ BOOMERANG!

1947, 87 MINS, US
Dir Elia Kazan   *Prod* Louis de Rochemont   *Scr* Richard Murphy   *Ph* Norbert Brodine   *Ed* Harmon Jones   *Mus* David Buttolph   *Art Dir* Richard Day, Chester Gore
● Dana Andrews, Jane Wyatt, Lee J. Cobb, Arthur Kennedy, Karl Malden, Sam Levene (20th Century-Fox)

Boomerang! is gripping, real-life melodrama, told in semi-documentary style. Lensing was done on location at Stamford, Conn, the locale adding to realism. Based on a still unsolved murder case in Bridgeport, Conn, plot is backed up with stron cast.

Dana Andrews heads the convincing cast. His role is realistic and a top performance job. While carrying a fictional name as state's attorney, the role, in real life, has its counterpart in Homer Cummings, who went on from the state post the become Attorney-General of the United States. Case on which plot is based deals with murder of a Bridgeport priest and how the prosecuting attorney establishes the innocence of the law's only suspect.

All the leads have the stamp of authenticities. The dialog and situations further the factual technique. Lee J. Cobb shows up strongly as chief detective, harassed by press and politicians alike while trying to carry out his duties. Arthur Kennedy is great as the law's suspect.

□ 1947: Nomination: Best Screenplay

. . . .

■ BOOMERANG

1992, 118 MINS, US ◇ ⓦ ⊙
Dir Reginald Hudlin   *Prod* Brian Grazer   *Scr* Barry W. Blaustein, David Sheffield   *Ph* Woody Omens   *Ed* Earl Watson, John Carter, Michael Jablow   *Mus* Marcus Miller   *Art Dir* Jane Musky
● Eddie Murphy, Halle Berry, Robin Givens, David Alan Grier, Grace Jones, Eartha Kitt (Paramount)

In *Boomerang* Eddie Murphy straitjackets himself in an ill-fitting comedy vehicle that's desperately in need of a reality check.

For his 11th feature film, Murphy's credited with the high-concept story, developed by scripters as a cornball tale of comeuppance.

He's a marketing exec at a New York cosmetics firm that women find irresistible (all six female leads want to seduce him). After a merger with a French firm, his new departmental boss, Robin Givens, turns the tables on Murphy and treats him the way he's been treating women all his adult life.

Film works best when Murphy plays his strong suits, including a childlike innocence, flair for mimicry and self-deprecating humour. Unfortunately, his character's fat ego keeps hogging center stage. The fact that he's dominated during the middle reels by aggressive Givens doesn't make up for the blatant sexism of the script.

Only naturalistic character in a cast of caricatures is cute subordinate Halle Berry during the film's first half. Director Reginald Hudlin, making the big jump here from low budget *House Party* to major studio filmmaking, handles individual scenes well but misses the big picture.

. . . .

■ BOOST, THE

1988, 95 MINS, US ◇ ⓦ ⊙
Dir Harold Becker   *Prod* Daniel H. Blatt, Mel Howard   *Scr* Darryl Ponicsan   *Ph* Howard Atherton   *Ed* Maury

Winetrobe   *Mus* Stanley Myers   *Art Dir* Waldemar Kalinowski
● James Woods, Sean Young, John Kapelos, Steven Hill, Kelle Kerr, Amanda Blake (Hemdale)

Based on Benjamin Stein's book *Ludes*, well-wrought screenplay is a cautionary tale about a couple involved in a mutually destructive, coke-dominated lifestyle.

Young and very much in love, Lenny and Linda Brown (James Woods and Sean Young) are still struggling to make ends meet in New York City when Lenny, a born hustler with financial smarts, receives an extraordinary opportunity from businessman Steven Hill to make his fortune by moving to Los Angeles and selling tax shelters.

His expanding balloon is popped by word that Congress proposed to close the tax loopholes through which he and his clients are benefiting. Lenny suddenly finds himself deep in the hole financially, as well as hooked on the cocaine he started taking only as a 'boost' to get him through rough times.

For the film to work at all, the love story between Lenny and Linda must feel as overpowering as it is meant to, and Woods and Young put this over with miles to spare. Both actors are live wires, so the passion, care and commitment the characters have for one another is palpable at all times.

● ●

■ **BORDER, THE**

1982, 107 MINS, US ◇ ⓥ ⊙
Dir Tony Richardson   *Prod* Edgar Bronfman Jr
Scr Deric Washburn, Walon Green, David Freeman
Ph Ric Waite, Vilmos Zsigmond   *Ed* Robert K. Lambert   *Mus* Ry Cooder   *Art Dir* Toby Rafelson
● Jack Nicholson, Harvey Keitel, Valerie Perrine, Warren Oates, Elpidia Carrillo, Shannon Wilcox (Universal/RKO)

Despite Jack Nicholson's multi-leveled performance, *The Border* is a surprisingly uninvolving film. Story of the personal and professional pressures on border patrol guard Nicholson, caught between right and wrong on both fronts, becomes murky and disjointed under Tony Richardson's uninspired direction.

Nicholson etches a nice guy victimized by his surroundings instead of an eccentric. Living in depressed circumstances with whiney, materialistic wife Valerie Perrine, he is the quintessential poor working stiff.

Nicholson is then befriended by Harvey Keitel, husband of Perrine's bimbo girlfriend and a fellow guard. It is their job to make sure none of the Mexicans over the border get into the US a task to which the humane Nicholson is ill-suited.

This is particularly the case once Nicholson views the rampant corruption of his fellow workers. The situation escalates as the baby of a poor, beautiful Mexican girl is kidnapped for adoption and Nicholson has to decide whether to stand by or take action.

The picture was already in the can when Universal decided to go back and shoot a much more upbeat ending where Nicholson emerges as hero.

● ●

■ **BORDERLINE**

1980, 97 MINS, US ◇ ⓥ
Dir Gerrold Freedman   *Prod* Martin Starger   *Scr* Steve Kline, Gerrold Freedman   *Ph* Tak Fujimoto   *Ed* John Link   *Mus* Gil Melle   *Art Dir* Michael Levesque
● Charles Bronson, Bruno Kirby, Ed Harris, Karmin Murcelo, Michael Lerner (ITC)

This Charles Bronson vehicle tackles a serious subject – the profiteering in illicit Mexican immigration – with workmanlike dramatic skill and a notable preference for realism over hokum.

The film's big name is self-effacing almost to the point of elusiveness. As a long-serving,

compassionate border patrolman, Bronson is hunched and hated virtually throughout; his face is mostly masked by heavy shadow.

The professionally-honed, conventional plot pits him against a younger, ruthless racketeer who runs wetbacks across the border at an exploitative price on behalf of a US business corporation.

Newcomer Ed Harris is memorable as the frontline villain, displaying screen presence to match the star's and thus injecting a powerful sense of danger.

● ●

■ **BORN FREE**

1966, 95 MINS, UK ◇ ⓥ ⊙
Dir James Hill   *Prod* Sam Jaffe, Paul Radin   *Scr* Gerald L.C. Copley   *Ph* Kenneth Talbot   *Ed* Don Deacon   *Mus* John Barry
● Virginia McKenna, Bill Travers, Geoffrey Keen, Peter Lukoye, Omar Chambati, Bill Godden (Open Road/High Road)

Born Free is a heart-warming story of a British couple in Africa who, at the maturity of their pet lioness, educate the beast to survive in the bush.

It's an excellent adaptation of Joy Adamson's books (which were as much photos as text) with restraint, loving care, and solid emotional appeal that seldom becomes banal.

Gerald L. C. Copley has done a first rate adaptation of the true story of Joy Adamson, who with hubby George involuntarily domesticated several pet lions. They kept one, Elsa, until she was fully grown and then, to save her from government-ordered zoo captivity, trained her to survive as a wild animal. The apparently childless couple are portrayed in top form by real-life married couple Virginia McKenna and Bill Travers.

Geoffrey Keen is excellent as the friendly government commissioner who finally convinces them the lioness should be sent to a zoo or set free. Keen gives the role much depth via the humor engendered from his natural aversion to the lioness, balanced by his British reserve.
□ 1966: Best Song ('Born Free'), Original Score

● ●

■ **BORN IN FLAMES**

1983, 90 MINS, US ◇
Dir Lizzie Borden   *Prod* Lizzie Borden   *Scr* Lizzie Borden   *Ph* Ed Bowes, Al Santana, Phil O'Reilly   *Ed* Lizzie Borden   *Mus* The Bloods, The Red Crayolas, Ibis
● Honey, Jeanne Satterfield, Adele Bertel, Becky Johnson, Pat Murphy, Kathy Bigelow (Jerome Foundation)

Lizzie Borden's 16mm independent production, which took some two years to complete, appears to have all the advantages and the disadvantages of a home movie. It is impertinent, audacious, abounding in fresh ideas, considerably untraditional ideas. On the other hand, it is disjointed, with no real characters, preachy, the script unsufficiently developed and the acting often amateurish.

Situated in the near future after America has gone through a socialist revolution which has turned it into sort of one-party progressive democracy, the story deals with the condition of women in that new society, conditions that, in Borden's opinion, changed very little from those prevalent today.

Borden shows how the extremists are proven right, and how such a revolution should be prepared in future.

The film's main grace is its sense of humor, a rare quality indeed in a militant film. Nervously edited, it has an almost documentary touch in the use of the camera on real New York locations, and a powerful beat soundtrack.

● ●

■ **BORN ON THE FOURTH OF JULY**

1989, 144 MINS, US ◇ ⓥ ⊙
Dir Oliver Stone   *Prod* A. Kitman Ho   *Scr* Ron Kovic, Oliver Stone   *Ph* Robert Richardson   *Ed* David Brenner   *Mus* John Williams   *Art Dir* Bruno Rubeo
● Tom Cruise, Raymond J. Barry, Caroline Kava, Kyra Sedgwick, Willem Dafoe, Jerry Levine (Ixtlan/Universal)

Oliver Stone again shows America to itself in a way it won't forget. His collaboration with Vietnam veteran Ron Kovic to depict Kovic's odyssey from teenage true believer to wheelchair-bound soldier in a very different war results in a gripping, devastating and telling film about the Vietnam era.

Stone creates a portrait of a fiercely pure-hearted boy who loved his country and believed that to serve it and to be a man was to fight a war. It turned out to be Vietnam, and that's where the belief was shattered.

In 'Nam, things go terribly wrong – young Sgt Kovic accidentally kills a fellow marine in battle. His attempted confession is harshly denied him by a c.o. Later, he's shot in the foot, gets up for a gritty round of Sgt Rock grandstanding, and is hit again and paralyzed.

Stone drenches the picture in visceral reality, from the agonizing chaos of a field hospital to the dead stalemate of a Bronx veteran's hospital infested with rats, drugs and the humiliation of lying helplessly in one's own excrement.

The US Kovic left behind is unrecognizable, yet as he struggles uselessly to regain control of his body he remains steadfast in his ideas, shouting 'Love it or leave it!' at his peacenik brother (Josh Evans).

Tom Cruise, who takes Kovic from clean-cut eager teen to impassioned long-haired activist, is stunning. Dafoe, as a disabled vet hiding out in a Mexican beach town in a haze of mescal, whores and poker, gives a startling, razor-sharp performance.
□ 1989: Best Director, Editing.
□ Nominations: Best Picture, Actor (Tom Cruise), Adapted Screenplay, Cinematography, Original Score, Sound

● ●

■ **BORN TO DANCE**

1936, 105 MINS, US ⓥ
Dir Roy Del Ruth   *Prod* Jack Cummings   *Scr* Jack McGowan, Sid Silvers   *Ph* Ray June   *Ed* Blanche Sewell   *Mus* Alfred Newman (dir.), Roger Edens (arr.)   *Art Dir* Cedric Gibbons, Joseph Wright, Edwin B. Willis
● Eleanor Powell, James Stewart, Virginia Bruce, Una Merkel, Sid Silvers, Frances Langford (M-G-M)

Born to Dance is corking entertainment, more nearly approaching the revue type than most musical films, despite the presence of a 'book'. Cast is youthful, sight stuff is lavish, the specialties are meritorious, and as for songs, the picture is positively filthy with them. Cole Porter included at least two hits among the seven numbers delivered.

Eleanor Powell becomes a star in her second picture. She is given an opportunity to show that she's not just a good buck dancer, but an exceptionally versatile girl. As an actress she still has not arrived, as indicated in the few occasions when this plot calls for acting.

James Stewart's assignment calls for a shy youth. His singing and dancing are rather painful on their own, but he's surrounded by good people, and it's all done in a spirit of fun. Frances Langford has a running part, but her big responsibility is the singing build-up to Powell's finale dance and the pretentious production topper of the picture.

Buddy Ebsen has a couple of spots for his eccentric dancing and tackles the comedy, along with Sid Silvers, Una Merkel and Raymond Walburn.

It's a combination navy-backstage story [by Jack McGowan, Sid Silvers and B.G.

DeSylva], with the sailors, as usual, looking for their old girlfriends while on leave in the big town, and the understudy follows the rules by stepping into the indisposed star's part at the last moment
□ 1934: Nominations: Best Song ('I've Got You under My Skin'), Dance Direction ('Swingin' the Jinx')

● ●

■ BORN YESTERDAY

1950, 102 MINS, US ♥ ☉
Dir George Cukor   *Prod* S. Sylvan Simon   *Scr* Albert Mannheimer   *Ph* Joseph Walker   *Ed* Charles Nelson   *Mus* Frederick Hollander
● Broderick Crawford, Judy Holliday, William Holden, Howard St John, Frank Otto, Larry Oliver (Columbia)

The bright, biting comedy of the Garson Kanin legit hit adapts easily to film.

Judy Holliday repeats her legit success here as femme star of the film version. Almost alone, she makes *Born Yesterday*.

Holliday delights as she tosses off the mala-props that so aptly fit the character. Even though considerable amount of the dialog is unintelligible, its sound and her artful delivery smite the risibilities. William Holden is quietly effective as the newspaperman hired to coach her in social graces so she will better fit in with her junkman's ambitious plans.

Broderick Crawford, as the selfmade dealer in junk, comes off much less successfully. The actual and implied sympathy is missing, leaving it just a loud-shouting, boorish person.
□ 1950: Best Actress (Judy Holliday).
□ Nominations: Best Picture, Director, Screenplay, B&W Costume Design

● ●

■ BORN YESTERDAY

1993, 101 MINS, US ◇ ♥ ☉
Dir Luis Mandoki   *Prod* D. Constantine Conte   *Scr* Douglas McGrath   *Ph* Lajos Koltai   *Ed* Lesley Walker   *Mus* George Fenton   *Art Dir* Lawrence G. Paull
● Melanie Griffith, John Goodman, Don Johnson, Edward Herrmann, Max Perlich, Fred Dalton Thompson (Hollywood Pictures)

Updated remake of the Pygmalion-like *Born Yesterday* arrives with a credible modern resonance. The basic dynamics of the original Garson Kanin play have stood the test of time thanks to some clever contemporary tweaking. However, the verdict on the makeover is not all good news. The attractive cast, individually strong, fails to coalesce as an ensemble. There's also a problem in creating a uniform tone for the yarn of a real estate speculator and his socially awkward girlfriend who invade the power elite of Washington, DC.

Harry Brock (John Goodman), a scrap metal czar in the original, hies to DC when the evaporation of defense contracts near his super mall threaten to undo his empire. In tow is Billie Dawn (Melanie Griffith), a former showgirl with more moxie than college knowledge.

Harry asks lobbyist Ed Devery (Edward Herrmann) to 'smarten her up'. To that end he hires local reporter Paul Verrall (Don Johnson) to provide the Professor Higgins treatment and, in short order, she wises up and the sparks, romantic and otherwise, begin to fly.

Screenwriter Douglas McGrath expands his source material with the latest twists on power brokering. However, he also imbues the story with a glib, sitcom breeziness that favors cuteness over content. Griffith provides her own credible spin on Billie Dawn. The film also gives Johnson an opportunity for some effective light comic work.

● ●

■ BOSTONIANS, THE

1984, 120 MINS, UK ◇ ♥ ☉
Dir James Ivory   *Prod* Ismail Merchant   *Scr* Ruth Prawer

Jhabvala   *Ph* Walter Lassally   *Ed* Katherine Wenning, Mark Potter   *Mus* Richard Robbins   *Art Dir* Leo Austin
● Christopher Reeve, Vanessa Redgrave, Madeleine Potter, Jessica Tandy, Nancy Marchand, Wesley Addy (Merchant Ivory)

Like the Merchant-Ivory-Jhabvala team's 1979 *The Europeans*, this is a classy adaptation of a Henry James novel.

From the film's opening sequence at a women's meeting in late 19th-century Boston, the dice are loaded against the feminist cause. The young Verena Tarrant offers an impassioned exposition of woman's sufferings only after being 'touched' by the hands of her faith-healer father.

The emotional weight of the pic is carried by the relationship that evolves between Veren (Madeleine Potter) and Olive Chancellor (Vanessa Redgrave). Latter is a mature spinster who attempts to secure her charge to the cause with a promise that she will never marry.

Central obstacle to Olive's ambition is Basil Ransome, a persuasive lawyer from the south.

The film is ultimately convincing because of the central performance by newcomer Madeleine Potter as Verena who conveys all the dilemmas of a naive but strong-minded girl caught between her attachment to the cause and her longing for love.
□ 1984: Nominations: Best Actress (Vanessa Redgrave), Costume Design

● ●

■ BOSTON STRANGLER, THE

1968, 116 MINS, US ◇ ♥
Dir Richard Fleischer   *Prod* Robert Fryer   *Scr* Edward Anhalt   *Ph* Richard H. Kline   *Ed* Marion Rothman   *Mus* [none]   *Art Dir* Jack Martin Smith, Richard Day
● Tony Curtis, Henry Fonda, George Kennedy, Mike Kellin, Murray Hamilton (20th Century-Fox)

The Boston Strangler, based on Gerold Frank's book, emerges as a triumph of taste and restraint with a telling, low-key semi-documentary style. Adaptation is topnotch not only in structure but also in the incisive, spare dialog which defines neatly over 100 speaking parts.

Among other things it makes a very strong, but implicit, comment on police sleuthing. The screenplay suggests the irony that instinctive police methods remain the rounding up of pitiable segments of society which do harm only to themselves. As told here, police got onto the prime suspect only via the fluke of an elevator ride.

Action cross-cuts between police work and off-screen depictions of the earlier murders.

Henry Fonda's performance as rep of Massachusetts Attorney-General is excellent, from his initial dislike of the task assigned through a quiet, dogged determination to break down Tony Curtis' mental barriers.

● ●

■ BOTTOM OF THE BOTTLE, THE

1956, 88 MINS, US ◇
Dir Henry Hathaway   *Prod* Buddy Adler   *Scr* Sydney Boehm   *Ph* Lee Garmes   *Ed* David Bretherton   *Mus* Leigh Harline   *Art Dir* Lyle R. Wheeler, Maurice Ransford
● Van Johnson, Joseph Cotten, Ruth Roman, Jack Carson, Margaret Hayes, Bruce Bennett (20th Century-Fox)

An escaped convict's desperate efforts to reach his wife and three children in Mexico add up to 88 minutes of melodrama in *The Bottom of the Bottle*, based on the Georges Simenon novel.

The screenplay has an emotional field day as it touch on the Cain and Abel relationship between brothers Van Johnson and Joseph Cotten. Former, the con who's on the lam, turns to his kin to speed his flight across the border. But Cotten, a successful lawyer-rancher who's built a flourishing practice in southern Arizona, fears for his reputation.

The rancher fraternity, also comprising Jack Carson, his wife Margaret Hayes, Jim Davis and Margaret Lindsay, among others, has a penchant for one party after another and the liquor flows freely. Johnson, whose yen for alcohol was indirectly responsible for his prison stretch, again becomes a victim of the bottle.

Director Henry Hathaway, an old hand at spreading mellers on a broad CinemaScope canvas, accents the action and suspense at the right moments. Although some of the plot may tax the imagination, it's to Cotten's credit that he makes his own role relatively believable under the circumstances. Good support is provided by a long list of other players.

● ●

■ BOULEVARD NIGHTS

1979, 102 MINS, US ◇ ♥
Dir Michael Pressman   *Prod* Bill Benenson   *Scr* Desmond Nakano   *Ph* John Bailey   *Ed* Richard Halsey   *Mus* Lalo Schifrin   *Art Dir* Jackson DeGovia
● Richard Yniguez, Danny De La Paz, Marta du Bois, James Victor (Warner)

The film fails to carve out a separate identity of its own, rehashing a familiar story about inter-family conflicts.

The decision to film *Boulevard Nights* on location in the barrios, using a largely Hispanic cast, is admirable, but does not automatically provide a raison d'etre for the pic.

Authenticity is the key here, and director Michael Pressman has accurately captured the sense of despair in this community.

Richard Yniguez plays a graduate of the VGV gang, who still maintains his ties with the group. Yniguez' g.f. (Marta du Bois) has dreams of upward social mobility, but is unable to shake him loose from his ties to the machismo competition of 'hopping' hydraulic car lifts. Meanwhile his brother, Danny De La Paz, becomes heavily involved in a gang war, until a pat dramatic crisis wraps up the film in a depressing and inconclusive fashion.

● ●

■ BOUND FOR GLORY

1976, 147 MINS, US ◇ ♥ ☉
Dir Hal Ashby   *Prod* Robert F. Blumofe, Harold Leventhal   *Scr* Robert Getchell   *Ph* Haskell Wexler   *Ed* Robert Jones, Pembroke J. Herring   *Mus* Leonard Rosenman   *Art Dir* Michael Haller
● David Carradine, Ronny Cox, Melinda Dillon, Gail Strickland, John Lehne, Ji-Tu Cumbuka (United Artists)

Bound for Glory is outstanding biographical cinema, not only of the late Woody Guthrie but also of the 1930s Depression era which served to disillusion, inspire and radicalize him and millions of other Americans.

The plot [based on Guthrie's autobiography] advances smoothly and sensitively through about six major phases of Guthrie's earlier life: the natural tragedy of the southwest dust bowl; Guthrie's transit to California; his exposure to the horrors in the migrant worker valleys; his initial radio career; his political activism, finally his decision to strike out for large urban areas where his songs and experience might add some momentum to change.

Leonard Rosenman's selection of many Guthrie songs makes for discreet but effective underscoring.
□ 1976: Best Cinematography, Original Song Score.
□ Nominations: Best Picture, Adapted Screenplay, Costume Design, Editing

● ●

■ BOUNTY, THE

1984, 130 MINS, US ◇ ♥ ☉
Dir Roger Donaldson   *Prod* Bernard Williams   *Scr* Robert Bolt   *Ph* Arthur Ibbetson   *Ed* Tony Lawson   *Mus* Vangelis   *Art Dir* John Graysmark

● Mel Gibson, Anthony Hopkins, Laurence Olivier, Edward Fox, Daniel Day-Lewis, Bernard Hill (De Laurentiis)

The Bounty is an intelligent, firstrate, revisionist telling of the famous tale of Fletcher Christian's mutiny against Captain Bligh. The $20 million-plus film is particularly distinguished by a sensational, and startlingly human, performance by Anthony Hopkins as Bligh, heretofore one of history's most one-dimensional villains.

Present third version of the yarn was initiated by director David Lean, who brought Robert Bolt aboard to write the entire *Bounty* saga [based on the book *Captain Bligh and Mr Christian* by Richard Hough]. Lean eventually moved on, and Dino De Laurentiis paid for the construction of a replica ship.

This is a remake with a reason, that being the exoneration and rehabilitation of the reputation of William Bligh. A British Naval court-martial, which serves to frame Bolt's dramatization, ultimately absolved Bligh of blame for the mutiny, and he went on to enjoy a distinguished career.

The mutiny itself is here presented as a chaotic mess, with Christian nearly delirious. Bligh's subsequent 4,000-mile voyage to safety in an open boat is depicted as the amazing, arduous achievement that it was.

Tailor-made physically to fit the mold of old-style heroes, Mel Gibson gets across Christian's melancholy and torn motivations in excellent fashion.

■ BOWERY, THE

1933, 92 MINS, US
Dir Raoul Walsh   *Prod* Darryl F. Zanuck   *Scr* Howard Estabrook, James Gleason   *Ph* Barney McGill   *Ed* Allen McNeil   *Mus* Alfred Newman (dir.)   *Art Dir* Richard Day
● Wallace Beery, George Raft, Jackie Cooper, Fay Wray, Pert Kelton, George Walsh (20th Century)

Two old Bowery characters, Steve Brodie and Chuck Connors, have been dramatized to a point where the only thing that's recognizable from the record books about them are the jump from Brooklyn Bridge and Bowery lingo respectively.

This script [from the novel by Michael L. Simmons and Bessie Roth Solomon] makes them rivals for mass leadership on the old street, but the important point is that as rewritten the two practically legendary characters make good entertainment.

The Connors-Brodie honest rivalry over everything, from gals to fighting ability, giving the tale a Flagg-Quirt glow, is the story. Brodie (George Raft) gets the girl. But he takes a licking from Connors (Wallace Beery) in their private finish fight on river barge. The fight is an exciting interlude, and it comes in handy where it's placed – under the finale. Previously, in the extremely well-staged Brodie bridge leap, the picture has reached its peak. It then stumbles until the fight arrives, bu the latter brings home the bacon.

Beery is doing *The Champ* all over again to a great extent, with Jackie Cooper again as his foil. The Cooper kid, obviously outgrowing the baby type, is still a trouper and sends in another gem performance Raft, much improved, is an okay choice as Brodie. The other meat parts are carried by Fay Wray, who plays straight to the boys, and Pert Kelton, who sings and dances as a Bowery soubrette in Connors' joint.

■ BOXCAR BERTHA

1972, 88 MINS, US ◇ ⊙ ☉
Dir Martin Scorsese   *Prod* Roger Corman   *Scr* Joyce H. Corrington, John William Corrington   *Ph* John Stephens   *Ed* Buzz Feitshans   *Mus* Gib Guilbeau, Thad Maxwell

● Barbara Hershey, David Carradine, Barry Primus, Bernie Casey, John Carradine (American International)

Whatever its intentions, *Boxcar Bertha* is not much more than an excuse to slaughter a lot of people. Barbara Hershey stars in title role as a Depression wanderer. The Roger Corman production, shot on an austere budget in Arkansas area, is routinely directed by Martin Scorsese.

Joyce H. Corrington and John William Corrington adapted *Sister of the Road*, an autobiog by Boxcar Bertha Thompson. Hershey is introduced as a rural girl whose father dies in an unsafe airplane. She is upset, naturally, and suddenly begins a life of vagrancy.

Performances are dull. Whatever sociological, political or dramatic motivations may once have existed in the story have been ruthlessly stripped from the plot, leaving all characters bereft of empathy or sympathy. There's hardly a pretense toward justifying the carnage.

■ BOXING HELENA

1993, 107 MINS, US ◇ ⊙ ☉
Dir Jennifer Chambers Lynch   *Prod* Carl Mazzocone, Phillipe Caland   *Scr* Jennifer Chambers Lynch   *Ph* Frank Byers   *Ed* David Finfer   *Mus* Graeme Revell   *Art Dir* Paul Huggins
● Julian Sands, Sherilyn Fenn, Bill Paxton, Kurtwood Smith, Betsy Clark, Nicolette Scorsese (Main Line/Caland)

Feature debut of 24-year-old writer-director Jennifer Lynch (daughter of David) offers up Julian Sands as a top surgeon who has had a one-night stand with stunning neighbor Sherilyn Fenn and now can't get the voluptuous sexpot out of his mind.

Bitchy, condescending and cruel, Fenn tells Sands in a hundred different ways to get lost, until a horrible accident deprives her of her legs and places her forever in the sick doctor's hands.

Remainder of the warped story plays on the notion of whether one person can force another to love him through cumulative dependence, time and the force of his own love. Fenn remains defiantly belligerent even through Sands' unnecessary removal of her arms. The numerous sex scenes are good and steamy.

It's probably just as well that last-minute dropouts Kim Basinger or Madonna didn't take the title role, as the presence of a star lurking powerlessly on the little platform no doubt would have been distracting and more laughable than it now, on occasion, is. But the thesps give it all the overheated conviction they can muster.

■ BOY, DID I GET A WRONG NUMBER!

1966, 98 MINS, US ◇ ⊙
Dir George Marshall   *Prod* Edward Small   *Scr* Burt Styler, Albert E. Lewin, George Kennett   *Ph* Lionel Lindon   *Ed* Grant Whytlock   *Mus* Richard LaSalle, 'By' Dunham   *Art Dir* Frank Sylos
● Bob Hope, Elke Sommer, Phyllis Diller, Cesare Danova, Marjorie Lord, Kelly Thordsen (United Artists)

Bob Hope enters the realm of near-bedroom farce as he finds a near-unclad film star on his hands in a lake cottage and his ever-loving spouse continually appearing on the scene. If the action sometimes seems to get out of hand it really doesn't matter, for Phyllis Diller is there too, to help him hide the delectable Elke Sommer from the missus.

Hope plays his role straight for the most part, making the most of the situation. George Marshall's direction sparks events in proper perspective, wisely allowing his characters to go their separate ways in their own particular styles. Sommer, who knows her way through a comedy scene either with or without clothes, elects the latter state for most of her thesping, raimented mostly in a shirt. Diller is immense as the nosy domestic re-

sponsible for the majority of the funny lines that abound throughout the fast unfoldment.

■ BOY FRIEND, THE

1971, 108 MINS, UK ◇ ⊙ ☉
Dir Ken Russell   *Prod* Ken Russell   *Scr* Ken Russell   *Ph* David Watkin   *Ed* Michael Bradsell   *Mus* Peter Maxwell Davies (arr.)   *Art Dir* Tony Walton
● Twiggy, Christopher Gable, Max Adrian, Bryan Pringle, Murray Melvin, Glenda Jackson (M-G-M)

If for nothing else – but film has more – Ken Russell's screen translation of *The Boy Friend* is a beautiful vehicle for Twiggy, a clever young performer. It is delightful entertainment, novel and engaging.

Russell, who also directed and scripted the Sandy Wilson musical, has adopted a play within a play concept for the telling. Film might be a glorification of the Busby Berkeley manner of production. Russell has expanded the play into a kaleidoscope of the dance director's techniques during his heyday.

Narrative revolves around the personal lives of a group of repertory players who stage an English provincial production of *The Boy Friend*, and a film director strives to catch the performance.

Twiggy plays the unsophisticated young assistant stage manager – also errand and jack-of-all-trades girl – suddenly thrust into top role when the star injures her ankle. (Glenda Jackson unbilled, cameos as the injured 'star'.)

Twiggy acquits herself charmingly and professionally. There's an unspoiled charm about her, and she weaves a spell of her own both with her singing and dancing.

□ 1971: Nomination: Best Adapted Score

■ BOY ON A DOLPHIN

1957, 103 MINS, US ◇ ⊙
Dir Jean Negulesco   *Prod* Samuel G. Engel   *Scr* Ivan Moffat, Dwight Taylor   *Ph* Milton Krasner   *Ed* William Mace   *Mus* Hugo Friedhofer   *Art Dir* Lyle R. Wheeler, Jack Martin Smith
● Alan Ladd, Sophia Loren, Clifton Webb, Jorge Mistral, Laurence Naismith, Alexis Minotis (20th Century-Fox)

Shot in Greece's Aegean Sea and environs, with the interiors filmed in Rome's Cinecitta Studios, *Boy on a Dolphin* [from the novel by David Divine] develops into a 'chase' that is a pleasant blend of archaeological research, quasi-cloak & dagger stuff, and earthy, primitive acquisitiveness.

Alan Ladd is the archaeologist who has been engaged on several occasions in besting Clifton Webb's passion for antiquities. He has been invariably successful in restoring them to their rightful owners. The 'boy', in the same idiom, is historic Greek property. Sophia Loren's hunger for a home, the greed of an expatriate, alcohol-sotted British medico (Laurence Naismith) and the trickery of her Albanian lover (Jorge Mistral, a strong face in a chameleon role) conspire to thwart the American archaeologist and collaborate with the aesthetic, wealthy Webb in spiriting the ancient treasure from Greek waters.

Director Jean Negulesco has not overextended any of the values, playing it in the right tempo for the locale and likewise playing down the neo-melodramatics. Ladd is the all-American boy archaeologist; Webb the suave dastard (because of his dollars); Loren a lustily appealing native Greek girl whose endowments fall automatically into character.

□ 1957: Nomination: Best Scoring of a Dramatic Picture

■ BOYS FROM BRAZIL, THE

1978, 123 MINS, US ◇ ⊙ ☉
Dir Franklin J. Schaffner   *Prod* Martin Richards, Stanley O'Toole   *Scr* Heywood Gould   *Ph* Henri Decae

Ed Robert E. Swink   *Mus* Jerry Goldsmith   *Art Dir* Gil Parrondo
● Gregory Peck, Laurence Olivier, James Mason, Lilli Palmer, Uta Hagen, Denholm Elliott (Producer Circle/20th Century-Fox)

With two excellent antagonists in Gregory Peck and Laurence Olivier, *The Boys from Brazil* presents a gripping, suspenseful drama for nearly all of its two hours – then lets go at the end and falls into a heap.

In a fine shift from his usual roles, Peck plays the evil Josef Mengele, a real-life character who murdered thousands of Jews, including many children, carrying out bizarre genetic experiments at Auschwitz in Poland. Olivier, slipping completely into the role of an elderly Jewis gentleman, is the Nazi hunter who brings him to bay.

With the aid of James Mason, Peck is out to assassinate 94 fathers around the world. In a brief but lively part, Steven Guttenberg discovers the plot and tips Olivier, who sets out to find how the killings fit together. His search turns up three identical lads, all played menacingly by Jeremy Black, who are more than triplets.

What they are and whence they came are plausibly developed in Heywood Gould's script [from Iva Levin's novel] and director Franklin J. Schaffner builds the threatening menace well.
□ 1978: Nominations: Best Actor (Laurence Olivier), Editing, Original Score

■ **BOYS FROM SYRACUSE, THE**

1940, 73 MINS, US
Dir A. Edward Sutherland   *Prod* Jules Levey
Scr Leonard Spigelgass, Charles Grayson   *Ph* Joseph Valentine   *Ed* Milton Carruth
● Allan Jones, Joe Penner, Martha Raye, Rosemary Lane, Charles Butterworth, Irene Hervey (Mayfair/Universal)

Writers Leonard Spigelgass and Charles Grayson have transformed the legiter – which George Abbott authored in collaboration with Richard Rodgers and Lorenz Hart (with a plot copped from Bill Shakespeare's *Comedy of Errors*) – from a satire to plain burlesque.

Martha Raye and Joe Penner are particularly outstanding in the comedy leads. Penner, away from the stereotyped 'wanna buy a duck?' characterization, makes a droll slave. Raye, provided with the swell Rodgers and Hart tunes, gets good opportunity to use her pipes as well as exhibit her broad comedy style. Charles Butterworth and Eric Blore, in lesser roles, turn in plenty of additional laughs, while Allan Jones capably acts and warbles his way through the top characterization.

Four of the tunes have been retained and two new ones have been provided by R&H to sub for three that were dropped. 'Who Are You?', romantic ballad sung by Jones, is one of the new ones, and 'The Greeks Had No Word for It', a specialty for Martha Raye, is the other. Both are equal to the originals.

Writers have done everything possible to further the basically ludicrous idea of the stage show, in which all sorts of modernisms surround the toga-clad populace of ancient Greece. It gives plenty of opportunity for gags, and none is missed, even to the checkered chariot, with a meter. Stone 'newspapers' announce that 'Ephesus Blitzkriegs Syracuse,' while the gladiators' union pickets and a voice strangely like that of Winchell's gives gossip on station EBC.

Tale concerns twin brothers and their twin slaves. One brother and one slave are parted from the other brother and his slave as babies. One brother becomes ruler of Ephesus and conqueror of Syracuse, town in which he doesn't know he was born. The other son comes to Ephesus, also, in search of his father. Neither twin knows the other exists and

the resultant mixup of identity makes plenty of base for laughs.
□ 1940: Nominations: Best B&W Art Direction, Special Effects

■ **BOYS IN COMPANY C, THE**

1978, 125 MINS, US ◇ ⊛ ⊙
Dir Sidney J. Furie   *Prod* Andre Morgan   *Scr* Rick Natkin, Sidney J. Furie   *Ph* Godfrey A. Godar
Ed Michael Berman, Frank J. Urioste, Alan Pattillo, James Benson   *Mus* Jaime Mendoza-Nava   *Art Dir* Robert Lang
● Stan Shaw, Andrew Stevens, James Canning, Michael Lembeck, Craig Wasson, Scott Hylands (Golden Harvest)

The Boys in Company C is a spotty but okay popcorn trade drama about five young Marines and how their lives were changed by duty in the Vietnam war. Laden with barracks dialog and played at the enlisted man's level, the Raymond Chow production, directed well by Sidney J. Furie, features strong performances by some very fine actors.

Not that *The Boys in Company C* is anywhere near a definitive film about the Vietnam debacle. No geopolitics or other cosmic matters intrude; instead, it's a deliberate action programmer (shot in the Philippines).

Stan Shaw heads the cast as a dope pusher who sees Vietnam as a major new connection, until he matures into a natural leader. Andrew Stevens, son of Stella Stevens, is a Southern athlete who turns junkie in action. James Canning is an aspiring writer who records the bewildering and unnatural warfare.

■ **BOYS IN THE BAND, THE**

1970, 117 MINS, US ◇ ⊛ ⊙
Dir William Friedkin   *Prod* Mart Crowley   *Scr* Mart Crowley   *Ph* Arthur J. Ornitz   *Ed* Jerry Greenburg
Art Dir John Robert Lloyd
● Kenneth Nelson, Frederick Combs, Leonard Frey, Cliff Gorman, Reuben Greene, Robert La Tourneaux (Leo/Cinema Center)

Boys in the Band drags. But despite its often tedious postulations of homosexual case histories instead of realistic dialog, and the stagey posturing of the actors, the too literately faithful adaptation of Mart Crowley's off-Broadway swish-set piece has bitchy, back-biting humor, fascinating character studies, melodrama and, most of all, perverse interest.

As queen and host of the gay birthday party that is the film's only setting, Kenneth Nelson tells straight Peter White, it's like watching an accident, one is horrified and repulsed, but can't take his eyes away.

Crowley takes the fault for the self-indulgent dialog with prolonged speeches.

■ **BOYS NEXT DOOR, THE**

1985, 88 MINS, US ◇ ⊛ ⊙
Dir Penelope Spheeris   *Prod* Keith Rubinstein, Sandy Howard   *Scr* Glen Morgan, James Wong   *Ph* Arthur Albert   *Ed* Andy Horvitch   *Mus* George S. Clinton
Art Dir John Tarnoff
● Maxwell Caulfield, Charlie Sheen, Christopher McDonald, Hank Garrett, Patti D'Arbanville, Paul C. Dancer (New World/Republic Entertainment)

A before-credits sequence of *The Boys Next Door* helps explain the motives for making the film. Stills are shown of notorious figures in the US who, for no apparent reason, have gone on killing sprees. One commentator suggests young criminals are so brutalized by their own upbringing that they can't see other people as human beings.

Unfortunately the film itself doesn't live up to the expectations. Even if intentions are worthy, it emerges glib and uninvolving.

Two alienated and disturbed 18-year-olds,

Roy Alston (Maxwell Caulfield) and Bo Richards (Charlie Sheen), graduate from a small high school in California. Before taking up factory jobs, they decide to have a weekend in LA in which 'anything goes'.

An eruption of violence begins with the brutal beating of a gas station attendant. It ends with one boy shooting the other as the police close in on the pair in a shopping mall. In between there are beatings and killings of a homosexual, a young couple and a woman.

With conventional clean-cut good looks, Caulfield and Sheen clearly resemble the title, but they fail to adequately project the 'angry stuff' within.

■ **BOYS' NIGHT OUT**

1962, 113 MINS, US
Dir Michael Gordon   *Prod* Martin Ransohoff   *Scr* Ira Wallach   *Ph* Arthur E. Arling   *Ed* Tom McAdoo
Mus Frank DeVol   *Art Dir* George W. Davis, Hans Peters
● Kim Novak, James Garner, Tony Randall, Howard Duff, Janet Blair, Anne Jeffreys (M-G-M)

In *Boys' Night Out*, four grown men, genus Americus Suburbicus, rent a town pad on the co-op plan for the express purpose of sharing, one by one, an illicit evening per week with a voluptuous and accommodating blonde. Red-blooded male audience will be astonished to discover that boy one does nothing but gab, boy two nothing but putter, boy three nothing but eat, and that boy four ups and marries the girl.

Since the element of story surprise, so vital in humour, is completely absent in the Ira Wallach screenplay, adapted by Marion Hargrove from a story by Arne Sultan and Marvin Worth, the audience is forced to seek comedy rewards in isolated doses – individual gags and situations.

Kim Novak slinks and purrs through the role of the object of all this extra-marital monkeyshine, an upstanding young post-grad sociology student who is secretly compiling data for a thesis on *Adolescent Sexual Fantasies in the Adult Suburban Male*. James Garner seems comfortable in the part of the number one son-of-a-gun who wins her heart. Tony Randall and Howard Morris (television funnyman in his screen bow) walk off with comedy honors.

■ **BOYS TOWN**

1938, 96 MINS, US ⊛ ⊙
Dir Norman Taurog   *Prod* John W. Considine Jr
Scr John Meehan, Dore Schary   *Ph* Sidney Wagner
Ed John Veron   *Mus* Edward Ward
● Spencer Tracy, Mickey Rooney, Henry Hull, Leslie Fenton, Gene Reynolds, Bobs Watson (M-G-M)

The story of Father Flanagan's struggle to make a successful boy's home and then an entire community near Omaha, Neb, is the motivating theme throughout. Producers shrewdly have not made it entirely a paean of praise for Boys Town, but rather a realistic portrayal of Father Flanagan's untiring efforts to make something of wayward youngsters who otherwise might wind up in the electric chair.

With Spencer Tracy and Mickey Rooney as the priest and the incorrigible lad, in tailor-made roles, *Boys Town* is a tear-jerker of the first water. Yet it has equal distribution of humorous and bitter moments. Rooney virtually takes the production away from the capable and veteran Tracy, though not appearing until feature is half-finished.

Rooney is the toughie whose repartee is as laughable as his cocky walk and mannerisms. Slow curbing of his desires as he bucks Boys Town customs and rules is a transition of character that is logically worked out. Tracy, showing necessary restraint, makes his portrayal of Flanagan sincere and human. It is not the first time he has played the role of a priest on the screen.

Henry Hull, the money-supplying pawnbroker who makes possible the boys home, builds this comparatively minor role into an impressive assignment.

☐ 1938: Best Actor (Spencer Tracy), Original Story (Eleanore Griffin, Dore Schary).

☐ Nominations: Best Picture, Director, Screenplay

....

■ BOY TEN FEET TALL, A
See: Sammy Going South

....

■ BOY WHO STOLE A MILLION, THE

1961, 81 MINS, UK
Dir Charles Crichton   *Prod* George H. Brown   *Scr* John Eldridge, Charles Crichton   *Ph* Douglas Slocombe   *Ed* Peter Bezencenet   *Mus* Tristram Cary   *Art Dir* Maurice Carter
● Virgilio Texera, Maurice Reyna, Marianne Benet, Harold Kasket, Curt Christian, Bill Nagy (British Lion-Bryanston)

It's difficult to go wrong with the combo of an appealing kid, the inevitable pooch and a chase in which the youngster's up against the world. This one is marred by some slightly uneasy dubbing and an occasional lapse into slapstick when only light comedy was needed, but overall it's a warm little piece.

Though a British film, it was mainly shot in locations in Valencia, Spain. The yarn concerns a likeable youngster who lives with his widowed father and works as a bank messenger. He finds that his taxi-driver father needs money to get his cab out of hock and decides to borrow some from the bank. His haul, however, turns out to be a million pesetas (roughly $28,000) and that sets the city on its ears. At the drop of a peseta he is being chased by half the thugs in Valencia, the police and his father.

Young Maurice Reyna, making his screen debut, goes through the motions of thesping admirably. Harold Kasket is breezily effective as the friend of the kid's father, who is rather glumly played by Virgilio Texera.

....

■ BOY WITH GREEN HAIR, THE

1948, 82 MINS, US ◇ ▽
Dir Joseph Losey   *Prod* Stephen Ames   *Scr* Ben Barzman, Alfred Lewis Levitt   *Ph* George Barnes   *Ed* Frank Doyle   *Mus* Leigh Harline   *Art Dir* Albert S. D'Agostino, Ralph Berger
● Pat O'Brien, Robert Ryan, Barbara Hale, Dean Stockwell, Richard Lyon (RKO)

RKO has turned out an absorbing, sensitive story of tolerance and child understanding in *The Boy with Green Hair*.

Story is that of a war orphan, shifted around from one relative to another, who finally finds haven and security with a waiter in a small town. Then, one morning, he wakes to find his hair has turned green – and the world turns topsy-turvey about him. Other kids jeer at him; adults are perturbed; even the kindly milkman turns against him when accused of bringing it about through his product.

Film was made by Dore Schary for RKO before Howard Hughes gained control of the studio, and in its small way was one of the things that caused Schary to step out of the RKO setup. Pic had been completed, but Hughes ordered re-edited and the tolerance theme taken out, on Hughes' general theory that films should entertain only and eschew social significance. Studio found that pic couldn't be re-edited, although it's reported to be toned down somewhat.

Through this parable about the unconscious cruelty of people to what is different, and the need of tolerance, runs another theme, that of anti-war preachment. When the boy meets

children from war-orphan posters in a dream scene in the woods, and returns to annoy the townsfolk with the message that war is very bad – his green hair has thus acquired a meaning, to preach pacifism – the film hits a well-intentioned but false note.

....

■ BOYZ N THE HOOD

1991, 111 MINS, US ◇ ▽ ⊙
Dir John Singleton   *Prod* Steve Nicolaides   *Scr* John Singleton   *Ph* Charles Mills   *Ed* Bruce Cannon   *Mus* Stanley Clarke   *Art Dir* Bruce Bellamy
● Larry Fishburne, Ice Cube, Cuba Gooding Jr, Nia Long, Morris Chestnut, Tyra Ferrell (New Deal)

Boyz N The Hood is an absorbing, smartly made dramatic encyclopedia of problems and ethics in the black community, 1991. An impressive debut by 23-year-old John Singleton, sincere pic is ultra socially responsible, sometimes to the point of playing like a laundry list of difficulties faced specifically by the urban black community.

Tale principally looks at the lives of three boys in south-central LA, beginning in '84 and then jumping, after a half-hour, to the present, when the realities of violence hit the teens.

Tre Styles (Cuba Gooding Jr) is a bright but rather sullen and insolent kid who moves to his father's home when his mother decides he needs a man's discipline. Dad, whose first name is Furious (Larry Fishburne), is a walking lesson in how to live the right way. Tre's best friend is Ricky (Morris Chestnut), who wants to be a football player, and they hang out with the latter's half-brother, Doughboy (Ice Cube), a rough-houser with a generally bad attitude.

Singleton constantly and effectively lays in the constant irritants and reminders of violence in the 'hood – the jets and choppers flying overhead, the ever-present dense smog, the random, easily-provoked fights, the day-and-night wailing of police sirens, the nearby gunshots.

Lively dialog embraces everything from Furious' righteous sermons to Doughboy's rough, sexist diatribes. Director's skill clearly extends to handling actors, as leading players all do fine jobs of conveying various states of intensity. Produced for $6 million, pic is simple from a technical p.o.v.

☐ 1991: Nominations: Best Director, Original Screenplay

....

■ BRAINDEAD

1992, 101 MINS, NEW ZEALAND ◇ ▽ ⊙
Dir Peter Jackson   *Prod* Jim Booth   *Scr* Peter Jackson, Stephen Sinclair, Frances Walsh   *Ph* Murray Milne   *Ed* Jamie Selkirk   *Mus* Peter Dasent   *Art Dir* Kenneth Leonard-Jones
● Timothy Balme, Diana Penalver, Elizabeth Moody, Ian Watkin, Brenda Kendall, Stuart Devenie (WingNut)

Kiwi gore specialist Peter Jackson goes for broke with an orgy of bad taste and splatter humor. Set in 1957, the standard zombie plot is played for laughs with a nerdy hero (Timothy Balme) whose domineering Mum (Elizabeth Moody) is bitten by a rare carnivorous monkey while spying on her son and his Spanish g.f. (Diana Penalver) at the Wellington Zoo.

Mum goes rabid fast and attacks a nurse, who also becomes a zombie. The poor son locks the creatures in the cellar and tries to pacify them with liberal doses of a tranquilizer administered by a giant hypo.

Comic highlights include Balme trying to pacify the zombie baby in a public park (horrified moms look on as he beats the creature into submission), and Balme literally re-entering his mother's womb in a gore-spattered end. Technically, this is Jackson's best pic to date, with state-of-the-art creature and gore effects.

....

■ BRAIN DONORS

1992, 79 MINS, US ◇ ▽ ⊙
Dir Dennis Dugan   *Prod* Gil Netter, James D. Brubaker   *Scr* Pat Proft   *Ph* David M. Walsh   *Ed* Malcolm Campbell   *Mus* Ira Newborn   *Art Dir* William J. Cassidy
● John Turturro, Bob Nelson, Mel Smith, Nancy Marchand, John Savident, George De La Pena (Paramount/Zucker)

The title *Brain Donors* sounds like a horror film and for those expecting a comedy, it is. Patterned after *A Night at the Opera*, *Brain Donors* badly wants to be a latter-day Marx Bros pic. 'Badly' is the key word.

John Turturro is Roland T. Flakfizer – a Groucho-esque, ambulance-chasing attorney out to fleece a well-heeled and well-fed widow (Nancy Marchand). Bob Nelson and Mel Smith are his equally zany aides-de-camp, the former a clear Harpo derivative and the latter a British cabbie who at least never tries to play the piano.

Hoping to land a $500,000-a-year job heading the widow's ballet company, Flakfizer and his cohorts end up at odds with a snooty attorney (John Savident) and stuck-up dancer (George De La Pena) while championing the cause of two young lovers.

Director Dennis Dugan's first feature, *Problem Child*, was a curious box office success, and so he finds himself laboring on another broad farce, again with numbingly flat results.

....

■ BRAINSTORM

1983, 106 MINS, US ◇ ▽ ⊙
Dir Douglas Trumbull   *Prod* Douglas Trumbull   *Scr* Robert Stitzel, Philip Frank Messina   *Ph* Richard Yuricich   *Ed* Edward Warschilka, Freeman Davies   *Mus* James Horner   *Art Dir* John Vallone
● Christopher Walken, Natalie Wood, Louise Fletcher, Cliff Robertson, Jordan Christopher, Joe Dorsey (M-G-M/JF Prod.)

Shaken and embattled during its completion phase, and carrying the memory of Natalie Wood's death, *Brainstorm* is a high-tech $18 million movie dependent on the visualization of a fascinating idea.

Producer-director Douglas Trumbull's effects wizardry – and the concept behind it – is the movie. The fetching idea [story by Bruce Joel Rubin] is a brain-wave device that gives characters the power to record and experience the physical, emotional and intellectual sensations of another human being.

On the downside, majority players, including stars Christopher Walken and Wood as a married couple in a research environment, seem merely along for the ride. The film's acting surprise is Louise Fletcher, whose flinty, career scientist is a strong flavorful, workaholic portrait.

The film offers irrefutable evidence that Natalie Wood's drowning (in November 1981) did not cause the filmmakers to drastically re-write or re-shoot scenes. Her work appears intact and, reportedly, only one scene had to be changed (with actor Joe Dorsey replacing Wood in a scene with Walken).

Cliff Robertson earnestly plays the compromising head of a vast research complex that employs colleagues Walken and Fletcher. Predictably, a government bogeyman is trying to gum up pure science for the sake of national security.

....

■ BRAINWAVES

1983, 81 MINS, US ◇ ▽
Dir Ulli Lommel   *Prod* Ulli Lommel   *Scr* Ulli Lommel, Buz Alexander, Suzanna Love   *Ph* Jon Kranhouse, Ulli Lommel   *Ed* Richard Brummer   *Mus* Robert O. Ragland   *Art Dir* Stephen E. Graff
● Keir Dullea, Suzanna Love, Vera Miles, Percy Rodrigues, Tony Curtis, Paul Willson (CinAmerica)

Brainwaves is a briskly-told, engaging psychological thriller dealing with the sci-fi concept of transferring thought processes and memories electronically between different people.

Suzanna Love toplines as Kaylie Bedford, a young San Francisco housewife who suffers a severe brain trauma (leaving her in a coma-like trance) in an auto accident. Her husband, Julian (Keir Dullea), and mother (Vera Miles) agree to an experimental medical procedure, unaware that it has not yet been tested on humans.

Designed to transfer corrective patterns by computer from a donor brain to the victim's damaged brain areas, process goes awry when the donor turns out to be a murdered girl (Corinne Alphen). Kaylie is physically and mentally rehabilitated, but plagued with traumatic first-person memories of the murder. Worse yet, the murderer is now after her.

Well-edited by Richard Brummer, picture zips along with admirable verisimilitude.

••••••••••••••••••••••••••••

■ BRAMBLE BUSH, THE

1960, 93 MINS, US ◇
Dir Daniel Petrie   *Prod* Milton Sperling   *Scr* Milton Sperling, Philip Yordan   *Ph* Lucien Ballard   *Ed* Folmar Blangsted   *Mus* Leonard Rosenman   *Art Dir* John S. Poplin
● Richard Burton, Barbara Rush, Jack Carson, Angie Dickinson, James Dunn, Tom Drake (Warner)

So-called mercy killing is the subject of *The Bramble Bush*, but the principals have such a brisk sex life that the subject rather gets lost in the bedclothes.

The screenplay, from a novel by Charles Mergendahl, presents the doctor who performs the mercy killing as a sympathetic character. Setting of the film is one of those New England towns that seem to be a hotbed (sic) of sex. Richard Burton is a young doctor who returns to his home town to care for his best friend, Tom Drake who is dying of Hodgkin's disease. Burton has a brief affair with Drake's wife, Barbara Rush, who becomes pregnant.

Burton has left his home partly because his father, a doctor before him, committed suicide long before the action of the picture opens, on discovering his wife (Burton's mother) was having an affair with James Dunn. Other complications include nurse Angie Dickinson's unrequited torch for Burton.

Burton is intense and intelligent as the doctor, although he is miscast as a New Englander of laconic cast. Rush delivers a strong and sensitive performance. Dickinson's warmth overcomes some script deficiencies, and Dunn is interesting in a role not completely realized. Drake is excellent.

Art director John S. Poplin is expert at creating the New England atmosphere (out of what looks, on close inspection, to be local California coastline).

••••••••••••••••••••••••••••

■ BRANDED

1950, 50 MINS, US ◇ Ⓥ ⊙
Dir Rudolph Maté   *Prod* Mel Epstein   *Scr* Sydney Boehm, Cyril Hume   *Ph* Charles B. Lang Jr   *Ed* Doane Harrison   *Mus* Roy Webb   *Art Dir* Hans Dreier, Roland Anderson
● Alan Ladd, Mona Freeman, Charles Bickford, Robert Keith, Joseph Calleia, Peter Hansen (Paramount)

Branded is a pleasing western that has a bit more plot and appeal than the average.

Rudolph Maté, photographer-turned-director, demonstrates he has not lost his hand at his former art. He and cameraman Charles B. Lang Jr must be given a score for at least part of *Branded's* appeal on basis of the Technicolor scenic work along the Rio Grande.

Yarn [from a novel by Evan Evans] finds Alan Ladd a no-good who figures on stealing the fortune of a cattle family by making like he the long-lost son who was kidnapped at five. He doesn't figure, however, on falling for his 'sister' and getting right fond of mom and pop. Ladd's inability to indicate successfully a transition from scoundrel to a kid with a 24-karat heart makes the story at times harder to digest than it should be.

••••••••••••••••••••••••••••

■ BRANNIGAN

1975, 111 MINS, UK ◇ Ⓥ
Dir Douglas Hickox   *Prod* Jules Levy, Arthur Gardner   *Scr* Christopher Trumbo, Michael Butler, William P. McGivern, Michael Butler   *Ph* Gerry Fisher   *Ed* Malcolm Cooke   *Mus* Dominic Frontiere   *Art Dir* Ted Marshall
● John Wayne, Richard Attenborough, Judy Geeson, Mel Ferrer, John Vernon, Daniel Pilon (United Artists)

Okay John Wayne actioner, as a contemporary cop in London tracking down Chicago fugitive John Vernon, whose lawyer Mel Ferrer has concocted a bewildering escape cover. Richard Attenborough plays well against Wayne as an urbane Scotland Yard detective.

Judy Geeson, as Wayne's policewoman escort, and Daniel Pilon, as a hired gun carrying Vernon's contract on Wayne's life, round out the principal players. Car chases, booby traps, etc round out the formula plot turns.

••••••••••••••••••••••••••••

■ BRASS TARGET

1978, 111 MINS, US ◇ Ⓥ ⊙
Dir John Hough   *Prod* Arthur Lewis   *Scr* Alvin Boretz   *Ph* Tony Imi   *Ed* David Lane   *Mus* Laurence Rosenthal   *Art Dir* Rolf Zehetbauer
● Sophia Loren, John Cassavetes, George Kennedy, Robert Vaughn, Patrick McGoohan, Max Von Sydow (M-G-M)

Brass Target, like *The Eagle has Landed*, speculates on what might have happened to an historical figure in World War II had a given set of circumstances taken place.

This time, instead of Winston Churchill getting bumped off, it's General George Patton's turn. Writer Alvin Boretz has turned Frederick Nolan's speculative novel, *The Algonquin Project*, into a seemingly true-to-life revelation of how Patton actually died, not in a car accident, but at the hands of a clever paid assassin.

Robert Vaughn, Edward Herrman and Ed Bishop play three officers in occupied Germany who concoct a plan to steal the Third Reich's gold stores with the help of OSS head Patrick McGoohan.

Patton, as played by George Kennedy, gets into a snit when the Russian Allies taunt him about the theft, and personally supervises the investigation, joined by OSS vet John Cassavetes. Gradually, just about every cast member is eliminated by one side or the other, until only Cassavetes, assassin Max Von Sydow, and mutual lover Sophia Loren remain for the predictable finale.

Hough manages to interject some excitement into the action scenes, but these com few and far between. A generally competent cast is hamstrung by the material at hand.

••••••••••••••••••••••••••••

■ BRAVE BULLS, THE

1951, 106 MINS, US
Dir Robert Rossen   *Prod* Robert Rossen   *Scr* John Bright   *Ph* Floyd Crosby, James Wong Howe   *Ed* Henry Batista, Philip Cook   *Art Dir* Cary Odell
● Mel Ferrer, Miroslava, Anthony Quinn, Eugene Iglesias, Jose Torvay (Columbia)

Columbia has a distinctive, offbeat picture in this treatment of Tom Lea's bestseller novel. There's nothing routine in the way it has been filmed, producer-director Robert Rossen apparently preferring to sacrifice some commercial values in favor o an adult handling of the story of a Mexican matador and life and death in the bull arena.

The bullfight sequences have a shocker quality that will repel while fascinating. Script deals with a matador who rose to the fleeting status of public idol from a peasant beginning. At the top of his popularity he encounters mental confusion and fear because he doubts his real ability and believes his success comes from the mentoring of his manager-friend.

Rossen's direction and the camera work by Floyd Crosby and James Wong Howe are alive with the real flavor of Mexico, its bright, hard lights and shadows. Mel Ferrer seems the perfect choice to portray the very human matador. He has practically all of the footage and story emphasis, and dominates every bit of it.

••••••••••••••••••••••••••••

■ BRAVE ONE, THE

1956, 100 MINS, US ◇ Ⓥ
Dir Irving Rapper   *Prod* Maurice King, Frank King   *Scr* Harry Franklin, Merrill G. White   *Ph* Jack Cardiff   *Ed* Merrill G. White   *Mus* Victor Young
● Michel Ray, Rodolfo Hoyos, Elsa Cardenas, Carlos Navarro, Joi Lansing, Fermin Rivera (RKO)

A kid's love for his pet themes this sentimentally moving story of a small Mexican boy who raises a fighting bull. Told against some magnificent CinemaScope photography of the below-the-border setting, it's a picture of overall appeal.

The sensitive script was taken from a Robert Rich [pseudonym for blacklisted writer Dalton Trumbo] story based on an actual bullring incident that occurred in the Plaza de Toros in Barcelona in 1936 when a bull of much bravery and heart was pardoned to his young master.

Plot is the touching account of a young Mexican farm boy who raises a pet bull, only to have it taken away from him when the ranch owner is accidentally killed and the stock sold off. The bull is shipped to the Plaza de Mexico to face Fermin Rivera, matador playing himself.

There's some near schmaltz, along with the sensitivity, in the screenplay, but because of the warm, tender aspects, the touches of human comedy and the exciting bullring finale, most viewers won't find the tendency to oversentimentality objectionable. Irving Rapper's direction is sure-handed in the assorted aspects of the plot.

••••••••••••••••••••••••••••

■ BRAZIL

1944, 91 MINS, US
Dir Joseph Santley   *Prod* Robert North   *Scr* Frank Gill Jr, Laura Kerr   *Ph* Jack Marta   *Ed* Fred Allen   *Mus* Ary Barroso   *Art Dir* Russell Kimball
● Tito Guizar, Virginia Bruce, Robert Livingston, Henry Da Silva, Edward Everett Horton, Roy Rogers (Republic)

With Ary Barroso, Latin-American composer who did the lilting 'Brazil' song-dance number, contributing bulk of music, this is in the groove for all who like south-of-border music.

Unlike too many films with Latin-American locales, this has a plot [by Richard English] that adds up. Virginia Bruce, as author of *Why Marry a Latin?*, is in Rio to get material for a book on Brazil. She's hardly given a warm welcome because of that book. Otherwise, her stay in Brazil is okay because not recognized by natives. That is until she bumps into Tito Guizar. On learning she authored *Why Marry a Latin?* he decides to give her an object lesson, and prove that Latins aren't such lousy lovers. Of course, in trying to prove his point, Guizar falls in love with her.

Joseph Santley's direction is topflight throughout while Robert North has given the

picture elaborate production backgrounding. Special camera crew went to Brazil for background shots, most important being the Rio carnival scenes.
☐ 1944: Nominations: Best Scoring of a Musical Picture, Sound, Song ('Rio de Janeiro')

. . . .

■ **BRAZIL**

1985, 142 MINS, UK ◇ ⑰ ⊙
Dir Terry Gilliam   *Prod* Arnon Milchan   *Scr* Terry Gilliam, Tom Stoppard, Charles McKeown   *Ph* Roger Pratt   *Ed* Julian Doyle   *Mus* Michael Kamen   *Art Dir* Norman Garwood
● Jonathan Pryce, Robert De Niro, Michael Palin, Kim Greist, Katherine Helmond, Ian Holm (Embassy)

Brazil offers a chillingly hilarious vision of the near-future, set 'somewhere in the 20th Century.'

Director Terry Gilliam reportedly wanted to call the film *1984½*. As in Orwell's classic, society is monitored by an insidious, tentacular ministry, and the film's protagonist, a diligent but unambitious civil servant, Sam Lowry – played with vibrant comic imagination by Jonathan Pryce – becomes a victim of his own romantic delusions, and is crushed by a system he had never before thought of questioning.

He sees himself as a winged super-hero, part-Icarus, part-Siegfried, soaring lyrically through the clouds to the tune of 'Brazil', the old Xavier Cugat favorite, which as the film's ironic musical leitmotif, recurs in numerous mock variations.

Robert De Niro shows delightful comic flair in a small, but succulent characterization of a proletariat superhero, who disposes of some obnoxious rival repairmen in a disgustingly original manner, but meets a most bizarre end in the film's nightmare climax.

Gilliam has assembled a brilliant supporting cast of character actors, notably Ian Holm, as the edgy, paranoid ministry department chief hopelessly dependent on Pryce to untie bureaucratic knots.
☐ 1985: Nominations: Best Original Screenplay, Art Direction

. . . .

■ **BREAKDANCE**
See: *Breakin'*

. . . .

■ **BREAKDANCE 2**
ELECTRIC BOOGALOO
See: *Breakin' 2*

. . . .

■ **BREAKER MORANT**

1980, 106 MINS, AUSTRALIA ◇ ⑰ ⊙
Dir Bruce Beresford   *Prod* Matt Carroll   *Scr* Bruce Beresford, Jonathon Hardy, David Stevens   *Ph* Don McAlpine   *Ed* William Anderson   *Mus* Phil Cunneen (arr.)   *Art Dir* David Copping
● Edward Woodward, Jack Thompson, John Waters, Bryan Brown, Charles Tingwell, Lewis Fitz-Gerald (South Australian Film)

Harry 'The Breaker' Morant (Edward Woodward) was an Englishman who went to Australia in the last century. When Britain and the Boers squared off against each other in South Africa, he and a number of other Australians volunteered and were absorbed into the non-regular army contingent.

The nature of the war made prisoner-taking a difficult business logistically, and while the film [from a play by Kenneth Ross] in no way tries to justify the killing of them, it does make clear that the Establishment's blind-eye can become very quickly healed.

As an example to others, Morant and two other Australians, Handcock (Bryan Brown) and Witton (Lewis Fitz-Gerald) were tried by court martial. Morant and Handcock were convicted and sentenced to death by firing-squad.

The execution sequence as handled by Bruce Beresford and the two actors is profoundly affecting. Beresford then turns his audience into an unwitting jury; as a sheer exercise in manipulation, it approaches the masterful and is extremely effective.
☐ 1980: Nomination: Best Adapted Screenplay

. . . .

■ **BREAKFAST AT TIFFANY'S**

1961, 115 MINS, US ◇ ⑰ ⊙
Dir Blake Edwards   *Prod* Martin Jurow, Richard Shepherd   *Scr* George Axelrod   *Ph* Franz F. Planer   *Ed* Howard Smith   *Mus* Henry Mancini   *Art Dir* Hal Pereira, Roland Anderson
● Audrey Hepburn, George Peppard, Patricia Neal, Buddy Ebsen, Martin Balsam, Mickey Rooney (Paramount)

Out of the elusive, but curiously intoxicating Truman Capote fiction, scenarist George Axelrod has developed a surprisingly moving film, touched up into a stunningly visual motion picture. Capote buffs may find some of Axelrod's fanciful alteration a bit too precocious, pat and glossy for comfort, but enough of the original's charm and vigor has been retained.

What makes *Tiffany's* an appealing tale is its heroine, Holly Golightly, a charming, wild and amoral 'free spirit' with a latent romantic streak. Axelrod's once-over-go-lightly erases the amorality and bloats the romanticism, but retains the essential spirit ('a phony, but a real phony') of the character, and, in the exciting person of Audrey Hepburn, she comes vividly to life on the screen.

Hepburn's expressive, 'top banana in the shock department' portrayal is complemented by the reserved, capable work of George Peppard as the young writer whose love ultimately (in the film, not the book) enables the heroine to come to realistic terms with herself.

Excellent featured characterizations are contributed by Martin Balsam as a Hollywood agent, Buddy Ebsen as Hepburn's deserted husband, and Patricia Neal as Peppard's wealthy 'sponsor'. Mickey Rooney as a much-harassed upstairs Japanese photographer adds an unnecessarily incongruous note to the proceedings.

The film is a sleek, artistic piece of craftsmanship, particularly notable for Franz F. Planer's haunting photography and Henry Mancini's memorably moody score. The latter's 'Moon River', with lyrics by Johnny Mercer, is an enchanting tune.
☐ 1961: Best Song ('Moon River'), Scoring of a Dramatic Picture.
☐ Nominations: Best Actress (Audrey Hepburn), Adapted Screenplay, Color Art DIrection

. . . .

■ **BREAKFAST CLUB, THE**

1985, 97 MINS, US ◇ ⑰ ⊙
Dir John Hughes   *Prod* Ned Tanen, John Hughes   *Scr* John Hughes   *Ph* Thomas Del Ruth   *Ed* Dede Allen   *Mus* Keith Forsey   *Art Dir* John W. Corso
● Emilio Estevez, Judd Nelson, Molly Ringwald, Anthony Michael Hall, Ally Sheedy, Paul Gleason (A&M/Universal)

In typical Shermer High in Chicago, a cross-section of five students – the jock, Miss Popularity, the ruffian, the nerd and Miss Weirdo – are thrown together under adverse circumstances and cast aside all discord and unite under the sudden insight that none would be such a despicable little twit if mom or dad or both weren't so rotten. The querulous quintet are actually being forced to *spend the entire day at school on Saturday* for some previous infraction of the rules.

Coming together as strangers, none of the group initially likes thuggish loudmouth Judd

Nelson, who taunts pretty Molly Ringwald, torments dorkish Anthony Michael Hall and challenges champ athlete Emilio Estevez while the odd lady, Ally Sheedy, looks on from a different space.

When the causes of the Decline of Western Civilization are finally writ, Hollywood will surely have to answer why it turned one of man's most significant art forms over to the self-gratification of high-schoolers. Or does director John Hughes really believe, as he writes here, that 'when you grow up, your heart dies.' It may. But not unless the brain has already started to rot with films like this.

. . . .

■ **BREAKFAST FOR TWO**

1937, 67 MINS, US
Dir Alfred Santell   *Prod* Edward Kaufman   *Scr* Charles Kaufman, Paul Yawitz, Viola Brothers Shore, David Garth   *Ph* Roy Hunt   *Ed* George Hively   *Art Dir* Van Nest Polglase, Al Herman
● Barbara Stanwyck, Herbert Marshall, Glenda Farrell, Eric Blore, Frank M. Thomas, Donald Meek (Kaufman/RKO)

Breakfast for Two is loaded with a wide assortment of larynx and midriff ticklers, with Barbara Stanwyck and Herbert Marshall turning in slick performances. About the only time that the zany pace bogs down is toward the end when the action overstrains itself with an awkwardly contrived mess of house-wrecking and pie-tossing.

Barrage of screwy situations [story by David Garth] take their cue from the efforts of a rich dame (Stanwyck) to straighten out a tippling waster (Marshall) a make him realize his motives as the inheriting head of a steamship line. Also to land him as her husband. With such expert farceurs as Eric Blore and Glenda Farrell piling in to help keep things boiling, the plot gravitates from sly humor to fantastic goofiness.

. . . .

■ **BREAK FOR FREEDOM**
See: *Albert, R.N.*

. . . .

■ **BREAKHEART PASS**

1976, 95 MINS, US ◇ ⑰ ⊙
Dir Tom Gries   *Prod* Jerry Gershwin   *Scr* Alistair MacLean   *Ph* Lucien Ballard   *Ed* Byron (Buzz) Brandt   *Mus* Jerry Goldsmith   *Art Dir* Johannes Larsen
● Charles Bronson, Ben Johnson, Jill Ireland, Richard Crenna, Charles Durning, Ed Lauter (United Artists)

Production has Charles Bronson as a government undercover agent who trips up a gang of gun runners, and a marvellous old steam train as setting for most of the plot.

Working from a lean Alistair MacLean script (based on his own novel), director Tom Gries forges a brisk and polished cinematic tale in which the mysteries pile up as old No. 9 steams with troops and medical supplies to an army post gripped by a killer epidemic.

Even before embarkation, a couple of officers go missing. The along the journey, telegraphic contact is lost, bodies hurtle out of the train into gorges, and the train's rear section containing the relief troops becomes detached.

Seasoned support in stock turns is furnished by Ben Johnson as a crooked marshal, and Ed Lauter as an honest army colonel.

. . . .

■ **BREAKIN'**
(UK: *Breakdance*)

1984, 87 MINS, US ◇ ⑰ ⊙
Dir Joel Silberg   *Prod* Allen DeBevoise, David Zito   *Scr* Charles Parker, Allen DeBevoise, Gerald Scaife   *Ph* Hannania Baer   *Ed* Mark Helfrich   *Mus* Gary Remal, Michael Boyd   *Art Dir* Ivo G. Crisante
● Lucinda Dickey, Adolfo Quinones, Michael Chambers, Ben Lokey, Christopher McDonald, Phineas Newborn III (Golan-Globus)

Breakin' is the first feature film entirely devoted to the breakdancing craze.

On a plot level, concoction is too derivative of *Flashdance* for its own good, as the premise once again is untrained, but highly skilled and imaginative, street dancers versus the stuffy, inflexible dance establishment.

Filmmakers have also played it safe in focusing the action on a nice, middle-class white girl (Lucinda Dickey), whereas breakdancing is almost exclusively the domain of blacks and Latinos.

Aside from these fainthearted choices, however, film is quite satisfactory and breezily entertaining on its own terms.

■ BREAKIN' 2
ELECTRIC BOOGALOO

1984, 94 MINS, US ◇ ⓥ ⊙
Dir Sam Firstenberg *Prod* Menahem Golan, Yoram Globus *Scr* Jan Ventura, Julie Reichert *Ph* Hanania Baer *Ed* Marcus Manton *Mus* Mike Linn *Art Dir* Joseph T. Garrity
● Lucinda Dickey, Adolfo Quinones, Michael Chambers, Susie Bono, Harry Caesar, Jo de Winter (Cannon)

Breakin' 2 is a comic book of a film, and, as in a cartoon, kids can get away with anything to have a good time.

As a phenomenon, the hip-hop, breakdancing, sidewalk graffiti and rap music culture lends itself well to a comic book approac and to his credit director Sam Firstenberg doesn't try to interject too much reality into the picture.

This time around Ozone (Adolfo 'Shabba-Doo' Quinones) and Turbo (Michael 'Boogaloo Shrimp' Chambers) have turned their street dancing talents to teaching other disadvantaged youths at a rundown community club they've dubbed Miracles.

When a developer (Peter MacLean) and a corrupt politician (Ken Olfson) try to put up a shopping center where the community center stands, the kids decide to put on a show to raise the necessary $200,000.

■ BREAKING AWAY

1979, 100 MINS, US ◇ ⓥ ⊙
Dir Peter Yates *Prod* Peter Yates *Scr* Steve Tesich *Ph* Matthew F. Leonetti *Ed* Cynthia Scheider *Mus* Patrick Williams *Art Dir* Patrizia Von Brandenstein
● Dennis Christopher, Dennis Quaid, Daniel Stern, Jackie Earle Haley, Barbara Barrie, Robyn Douglass (20th Century-Fox)

Though its plot wins no points for originality, *Breaking Away* is a thoroughly delightful light comedy, lifted by fine performances from Dennis Christopher and Paul Dooley. The story is nothing more than a triumph for the underdog through sports, this time cycle racing.

Christopher, Dennis Quaid, Daniel Stern and Jackie Earle Haley are four recent high-school graduates with no particular educational ambitions, yet stuck in a small college town – and a fairly snooty college at that. But Christopher is a heck of a bike rider and such an adulator of Italian champions that he pretends to be Italian himself, even at home.

Pretending to be an Italian exchange student, Christopher meets pretty coed Robyn Douglass (an able film debut for her) and this ultimately brings the boys into conflict with the big men on campus that must finally be resolved in a big bike race.

The relationship among the four youths is warm and funny, yet full of different kinds of conflict Quaid is very good as the ex-quarterback facing a life with no more cheers; Haley is good as a sawed-off romantic; and Stern is superb as a gangly, wise-cracking mediator.

Though pic sometimes seems padded with too much cycle footage, the climax is exciting, even though predictable.

□ 1979: Best Original Screenplay.
□ Nominations: Best Picture, Director, Supp. Actress (Barbara Barrie), Adapted Score

■ BREAKING GLASS

1980, 104 MINS, UK ◇ ⓥ
Dir Brian Gibson *Prod* Davina Belling, Clive Parsons *Scr* Brian Gibson *Ph* Stephen Goldblatt *Ed* Michael Bradsell *Mus* Tony Visconti (dir.) *Art Dir* Evan Hercules
● Phil Daniels, Hazel O'Connor, Jon Finch, Jonathan Pryce (Allied Stars/Film & General)

Breaking Glass presents a cynical, off-the-peg view of the post-punk record business.

Cast opposite Hazel O'Connor, who's seen initially as a two-bit teenage performer playing a handful of her own numbers around lousy London gigs, is Phil Daniels, a hustling would-be manager who teams with O'Connor.

Ensuing success undermines the pair's tentative romantic partnership and, with the arrival on the scene of Jon Finch as an overly smooth-mannered producer, their professional interdependence as well.

Relentlessly fast-paced, the yarn relates to reality in much the same way as a fashion photo – that is, it works as an image-conscious reflection of a time and milieu, but does not purport to portray life as it really is.

■ BREAKING IN

1989, 91 MINS, US ◇ ⓥ ⊙
Dir Bill Forsyth *Prod* Harry Gittes *Scr* John Sayles *Ph* Michael Coulter *Ed* Michael Ellis *Mus* Michael Gibbs *Art Dir* Adrienne Atkinson
● Burt Reynolds, Casey Siemaszlo, Sheila Kelley, Lorraine Toussant, Albert Salmi, Harry Carey (Act III/Goldwyn)

Burt Reynolds plays Ernie Mullins, a 61-year-old, graying, professional burglar with a gammy leg and the beginning of a pot belly, in this charming buddy-caper movie.

He teams up with young Mike Lefebb (Casey Siemaszko), a garage hand who likes to break into houses to raid the fridge and read the mail, when they both hit the same place one night. They become partners, with the oldtimer teaching the youngster the tricks of the trade.

What follows is a gentle comedy, filled with incisive observation, which builds to a wry conclusion which won't set well with action fans.

Reynolds plays the old-timer with a relaxed charm that's wholly delightful. Siemaszko is fine, too, as the initially nervous and ultimately relaxed and confide young criminal. Sheila Kelley is fun as a prostie who favors colored condoms and likes to be known as an actress.

■ BREAKING THE SOUND BARRIER

See: The Sound Barrier

See: The Sound Barrier

■ BREAKOUT

1975, 96 MINS, US ◇ ⓥ ⊙
Dir Tom Gries *Prod* Robert Chartoff, Irwin Winkler *Scr* Howard B. Kreitsek, Marc Norman, Elliott Baker *Ph* Lucien Ballard *Ed* Bud Isaacs *Mus* Jerry Goldsmith *Art Dir* Alfred Sweeney Jr
● Charles Bronson, Robert Duvall, Jill Ireland, John Huston, Randy Quaid, Sheree North (Persky-Bright/Vista)

Breakout is a cheap exploitation pic with Charles Bronson as a carefree aviator who rescues Robert Duvall from the Mexican prison frameup engineered by his father-in-law, John Huston. Jill Ireland, Duvall's wife, wants him back badly.

The spitball plot [from the novel *The Second Jailbreak* by Warren Hinckle, William Turner and Eliot Asinof] is the sort of thing Columbia made before Frank Capra. Director

Tom Gries and the entire cast perform as though they all had better things to do.

■ BREATHLESS

1983, 100 MINS, US ⓥ ⓥ ⊙
Dir Jim McBride *Prod* Martin Erlichman *Scr* L.M. Kit Carson, Jim McBride *Ph* Richard H. Kline *Ed* Robert Estrin *Mus* Jack Nitzsche *Art Dir* Richard Sylbert
● Richard Gere, Valerie Kaprisky, Art Metrano, John P. Ryan, William Tepper, Robert Dunn (Orion/Miko)

More than a little guts was required to remake such a certified film classic as Jean-Luc Godard's *Breathless*, and the generation of film critics that had their lives changed by the 1959 film will easily be able to argue on behalf of the artistic superiority of the original. But the comparison remains virtually irrelevant to youthful audiences, who should find this update a suitably jazzy, sexy, entertainment.

On his way back from Las Vegas in a stolen car, Richard Gere accidentally mortally wounds a cop, then heads for the LA apartment of French UCLA student Valerie Kaprisky, with whom he's had just a brief fling but whom he is also convinced he loves.

A real romantic who dreams of escaping down to Mexico with his inamorata, Gere behaves as if he's oblivious to the heat closing in on him after the cop dies.

Gere's status as a sex star is certainly reaffirmed here, and not only does he appear with his shirt off through much of the pic, but he does som full-frontal scenes. Fresh and attractive, Kaprisky also does numerous scenes semi-clad or less.

■ BREED APART, A

1984, 101 MINS, US ◇ ⓥ
Dir Philippe Mora *Prod* John Daly, Derek Gibson *Scr* Paul Wheeler *Ph* Geoffrey Stephenson *Ed* Chris Lebenzon *Mus* Maurice Gibb *Art Dir* Bill Barclay
● Rutger Hauer, Powers Boothe, Kathleen Turner, Donald Pleasence, John Dennis Johnston, Brion James (Hemdale/Sagittarius)

The visual splendors of North Carolina deserve top billing in *A Breed Apart*. The tale of romance and chicanery in the backwoods simply lacks reason, dramatic tension or emotional involvement.

The core of the story centers on an obsessive bird egg collector's passion to secure specimens of a newly discovered breed of bald eagle. As the bird is protected by law, he has to hire a noted climber (Powers Boothe) to illegally pilfer the shells. However, apart from the physical danger of reaching their lofty peak, he must contend with their protector, a reclusive mystery man (Rutger Hauer) who inhabits a secluded island.

Also figuring into the story is the unstated emotional bond between Hauer and the storekeeper, played by Kathleen Turner, and her son who worships his independent ways.

■ BREEZY

1973, 106 MINS, US ◇
Dir Clint Eastwood *Prod* Robert Daley *Scr* Jo Heims *Ph* Frank Stanley *Ed* Ferris Webster *Mus* Michel Legrand *Art Dir* Alexander Golitzen
● William Holden, Kay Lenz, Roger C. Carmel, Mari Dusay, Joan Hotchkis, Jamie Smith Jackson (Malpaso/Universal)

Clint Eastwood's third directorial effort is an okay contemporary drama about middle-aged William Holden falling for teenage Kay Lenz. Associate producer Jo Heims' script works the problem over with perhaps too much ironic, wry or broad humor for solid impact.

Story has divorced Holden, embittered at women (sequence with Joan Hotchkis is a dramatic highlight), falling for Lenz, a persistent overly precocious teenage drifter in the Hollywood Hills. Roger C. Carmel and wife Shelley Morris provide sounding boards for Holden's misgivings, before and after Holden begins having sex with Lenz.

The script doesn't help Eastwood out: too much laugh/smile/chuckle sitcom patter and situation make the film more like a TV feature than a gripping and certainly relevant sudser.

....

■ BREWSTER MCCLOUD

1970, 104 MINS, US ◇ ⑩

Dir Robert Altman   *Prod* Lou Alder   *Scr* Doran William Cannon   *Ph* Lamar Boren, Jordan Cronenweth   *Ed* Louis Lombardo   *Mus* Gene Page   *Art Dir* George W. Davis, Preston Ames
● Bud Cort, Sally Kellerman, Michael Murphy, William Windom, Shelley Duvall, Rene Auberjonois (M-G-M/ Lion's Gate)

Brewster McCloud spares practically nothing in contemporary society. Literate original screenplay is a sardonic fairy tale for the times, extremely well cast and directed.

Bud Cort heads the cast as a young boy, hiding in the depths of Houston's mammoth Astrodome where he is building wings. He is, or is not, in reality a bird in human form.

His guardian angel is Sally Kellerman, always in the right spot to foil some nefarious person about to take advantage of Cort. Trouble is her protection involves a series of unexplained murders.

Michael Murphy is the sleuth brought in from Frisco to help oldfashioned gumshoe G. Wood.

Kellerman, gets sensational results from her part. She can project more ladylike sensuality and emotion in a look than most actresses can in an hour.

....

■ BREWSTER'S MILLIONS

1945, 79 MINS, US ⑩

Dir Allan Dwan   *Prod* Edward Small   *Scr* Siegfried Herzig, Charles Rogers, Wilkie Mahoney   *Ph* Charles Lawton   *Ed* Grant Whytock, Richard Heermance   *Mus* Hugo Friedhofer   *Art Dir* Joseph Sternad
● Dennis O'Keefe, Helen Walker, Eddie 'Rochester' Anderson, June Havoc, Gail Patrick, Mischa Auer (Small/United Artists)

Play [by Winchell Smith and Byron Ongley based on the novel by George Barr McCutcheon], first produced in 1907, remains somewhat dated despite efforts to refurbish background in this screen adaptation through introduction of wartime atmosphere.

The young, handsome soldier returns home to a swell girl waiting to marry him. He finds he's inherited 8 million bucks. Now here's the problem – he's got to spend $1 million in two months, or lose the entire estate. Even with the help of a flop musical, a bankrupt banker, the stock market, the racetrack and a spending society gal he has trouble. *Millions* is a broad farce, of course, and gets over as such.

□ 1945: Nomination: Best Scoring of a Dramatic Picture

....

■ BREWSTER'S MILLIONS

1985, 97 MINS, US ◇ ⑩ ⊙

Dir Walter Hill   *Prod* Lawrence Gordon, Joel Silver   *Scr* Herschel Weingrod, Timothy Harris   *Ph* Ric Waite   *Ed* Freeman Davies, Michel Ripps   *Mus* Ry Cooder   *Art Dir* John Vallone
● Richard Pryor, John Candy, Lonette McKee, Stephen Collins, Jerry Orbach, Pat Hingle (Universal)

It's hard to believe a comedy starring Richard Pryor and John Candy is no funnier than this one is, but director Walter Hill has overwhelmed the intricate genius of each with constant background action, crowd confusions and other endless distractions.

All the frenetic motion, unfortunately, never disguises the fact that the writers haven't done much of distinction with the familiar story [a 1902 novel by George Barr McCutcheon] that has been produced in many forms, dating back to a 1906 stage version. [Previous film versions were in 1914, 1921, 1935, 1945 and 1961.]

In one incarnation or another, the yarn always involves somebody who stands to inherit a huge fortune, but first must squander a small one over a short time. In order to enjoy the fantasy, the audience must be given good reason to root for the hero.

Though Pryor plays it likeably enough, he never seems particularly deserving of the fun, excitement and brief luxury he falls into in having to spend $3 million in 30 days, much less the $300 million inheritance he stands to receive if he succeeds.

....

■ BRIDE, THE

1985, 118 MINS, US ◇ ⑩ ⊙

Dir Franc Roddam   *Prod* Victor Drai   *Scr* Lloyd Fonvielle   *Ph* Stephen H. Burum   *Ed* Michael Ellis   *Mus* Maurice Jarre   *Art Dir* Michael Seymour
● Sting, Jennifer Beals, Anthony Higgins, Clancy Brown, David Rappaport, Geraldine Page (Columbia-Delphi III/Colgems)

Production departs from the host of other *Frankensteins* in its bright visual look, its lush Maurice Jarre score, its view of women, its younger characters, and its romantic scope.

Pic opens with a jolting laboratory sequence, when Sting as Baron Frankenstein brings to life the gauze-wrapped Jennifer Beals as the doctor's original monster creation looks on with frothing agitation.

In opting to tone down the horror aspect of the genre, producer Victor Drai and his team have created another kind of monster: a *Frankenstein* movie that's not scary.

While there is deliberate humor at times, most of it successfully produced by a lilting dwarf character who steals the movie (David Rappaport), the intention of the filmmaker is not camp. That's both the pic's virtue and, at the conclusion, its downfall.

....

■ BRIDE CAME C.O.D., THE

1941, 94 MINS, US ⑩

Dir William Keighley   *Prod* Hal B. Wallis (exec.)   *Scr* Julius J. Epstein, Philip G. Epstein   *Ph* Ernest Haller   *Ed* Thomas Richards   *Mus* Max Steiner   *Art Dir* Ted Smith
● James Cagney, Bette Davis, Stuart Erwin, Jack Carson, Eugene Pallette, George Tobias (Warner)

Bette Davis is teamed with James Cagney in a broad farce that combines spontaneous gaiety and infectious humor. It's a hefty package of laugh entertainment [from the story by Kenneth Earl and M.M. Musselman].

In handing Davis a comedy assignment Warners go all out in also making her the victim of continual physical and mental violence. She's dirtied up in a mine; acquires three doses of cacti needles in periodic falls; and even exposes her posterior as target for welldirected shots from Cagney's improvised slingshot.

Cagney is the owner of a plane about to be repossessed by the finance company. Davis is an oil heiress about to marry orchestra leader Jack Carson. Radio gossiper Stuart Erwin prevails on the pair to elope via pla to Las Vegas – and naturally Cagney's ship is chartered.

Cagney grooves in a familiar role as the aggressive and two-fisted battler – manhandling the girl periodically for maximum results. Davis clicks strongly as the oil heiress, displaying a flair for comedy.

....

■ BRIDE FOR SALE

1949, 87 MINS, US

Dir William D. Russell   *Prod* Jack H. Skirball   *Scr* Bruce Manning, Islin Auster   *Ph* Joseph Valentine   *Ed* Frederic Knudtson   *Mus* Frederick Hollander
● Claudette Colbert, Robert Young, George Brent, Max Baer, Gus Schilling (RKO/Crest)

Bride for Sale is a lot of escapist nonsense that manages to be generally amusing, and sometimes hilariously so. Screwball angles are played up for laughs, the pacing is good and the playing enjoyable, making it entirely acceptable for light entertainment.

Kingpinning the slapstick are Claudette Colbert, Robert Young and George Brent. Colbert does glib work as a tax expert for the accounting firm conducted by Brent. She figures to find the perfect husband, with suitable bankroll, by casing the returns the firm makes out. Brent wants to keep her on the job so enlists aid of Young to make like an eligible male, and woo the maiden.

On that basis of fun, William D. Russell's direction marches the plot and the players along a broad path of antics.

....

■ BRIDE OF FRANKENSTEIN, THE

1935, 73 MINS, US ⑩ ⊙

Dir James Whale   *Prod* Carl Laemmle Jr   *Scr* William Hurlbut, John L. Balderston   *Ph* John Mescall   *Ed* Ted Kent   *Mus* Franz Waxman   *Art Dir* Charles D. Hall
● Boris Karloff, Colin Clive, Elsa Lanchester, Valerie Hobson, Ernest Thesiger, O.P. Heggie (Universal)

In the previous Frankenstein film's finale the monster was burned in a huge fire. Here it's started off with the same fire scene, except that in a few moments he is revealed to have bored through the earth to a subterranean stream, which saved him from death. From there on, of course, it's a romp.

Perhaps a bit too much time is taken up by the monster and too little by the woman created to be his bride. Frankenstein, the monster's creator, is this time sorry and tries to crawl out but Dr Pretorious forces him to go into more life manufacturing, having conceived the idea of a woman to act as the monster's playmate. The woman is finally evolved, but she's just as horrified at him as everyone else.

Karloff manages to invest the character with some subtleties of emotion that are surprisingly real and touching. Especially is this true in the scene where he meets a blind man who, not knowing that he's talking to a monster, makes a friend of him.

Runner-up position from an acting standpoint goes to Ernest Thesiger as Dr Pretorious, a diabolic characterization if ever there was one. Elsa Lanchester handles two assignments, being first in a preamble as author Mary Shelley and then the created woman. In latter assignment she impresses quite highly, although in both spots she has very little to do.

□ 1935: Nomination: Best Sound

....

■ BRIDE OF RE-ANIMATOR

1991, 97 MINS, US ◇ ⑩ ⊙

Dir Brian Yuzna   *Prod* Brian Yuzna   *Scr* Woody Keith, Rick Fry   *Ph* Rick Fichter   *Ed* Peter Teschner   *Mus* Richard Band   *Art Dir* Philip J.C. Duffin
● Jeffrey Combs, Bruce Abbott, Claude Earl Jones, Fabiana Udenio, David Gale, Kathleen Kinmont (Wildstreet)

Fans of Stuart Gordon's 1985 *Re-Animator* will probably dig this campy gorefest sequel directed by the original's producer, Brian Yuzna.

Jeffrey Combs returns in top form as H.P. Lovecraft's dotty scientist Herbert West, this time [in a story by Yuzna, Woody Keith and Rick Fry] intent on joining the trendy club of

B

would-be Dr Frankensteins creating a female monster (a la *Frankenhooker*, *Steel & Lace*, *Eve of Destruction*).

Reluctantly assisting Combs again is fellow doctor Bruce Abbott, whose beautiful new Italian girlfriend Fabiana Udenio can't shake his grieving attachment to his true love Megan, who was killed in the first film. When Combs tells him that he's going to build his femme creation around Megan's preserved heart, Abbott joins the grisly experiment.

The over-the-top acting that Gordon encouraged in *Re-Animator* is continued here with Combs particularly adept at the darkly comic throwaway line. Overabundance of gore (an even more explicit unrated version will be made available in vidstores) will turn off mainstream viewers, however. Tall actress Kathleen Kinmont is a good choice for the monster, with her stitched together, see-through torso.

● ● ● ● ● ● ● ● ● ● ● ● ● ● ● ● ● ● ●

■ BRIDE WORE BOOTS, THE

1946, 85 MINS, US
Dir Irving Pichel   *Prod* Seton I. Miller   *Scr* Dwight Mitchell Wiley   *Ph* Stuart Thompson   *Ed* Ellsworth Hoagland   *Mus* Frederick Hollander   *Art Dir* Hans Dreier, John Meehan
● Barbara Stanwyck, Robert Cummings, Diana Lynn, Patric Knowles, Robert Benchley, Natalie Wood (Paramount)

The Bride Wore Boots is never as funny as its makers intended. It is only in the final 10 minutes or so when the story casts off all restraint and goes slapstick with a vengeance that comedy rates a genuinely hearty response.

Barbara Stanwyck and Robert Cummings are seen as married couple with divided interests. Stanwyck loves horses, in fact operates a breeding farm. Cummings is an author and hates horses. The wife hates the stuffy Civil War relics wished off on her husband by adoring Confederate Dames societies.

Star trio, which has Diana Lynn as a young southern vamp, make frantic efforts to put the material over, but often fail. Patric Knowles has a thankless spot as near-rival for Stanwyck's attention. Peggy Wood and Robert Benchley team for more adult chuckles and Willie Best is good as Cummings' handy-man. Natalie Wood and Gregory Muradian are seen as the obnoxious offspring of the married couple.

● ● ● ● ● ● ● ● ● ● ● ● ● ● ● ● ● ● ●

■ BRIDGE AT REMAGEN, THE

1969, 116 MINS, US ◇ ⓥ
Dir John Guillermin   *Prod* David L. Wolper   *Scr* Richard Yates, William Roberts   *Ph* Stanley Cortez   *Ed* William Cartwright   *Mus* Elmer Bernstein   *Art Dir* Alfred Sweeney
● George Segal, Robert Vaughn, Ben Gazzara, Bradford Dillman, E.G. Marshall, Peter Van Eyck (United Artists)

The taking of a bridge provides the basis for an actionful World War II melodrama. This time out it's the Ludendorff Bridge over the Rhine in the Remagen area, scene of desperate fighting for its control by both American and German forces.

Certain confusion in plot content exists, as it never appears overly clear the exact purpose of American and Nazi military thinking.

Against this background chief interest rests in the performance of George Segal, a hard-boiled American platoon leader, as he and his men attempt to accomplish the orders of their high command.

Director John Guillermin succeeds in realistic movement as he attempts to overcome deficiencies of script and generally manages strong characterizations from his cast.

● ● ● ● ● ● ● ● ● ● ● ● ● ● ● ● ● ● ●

■ BRIDGE ON THE RIVER KWAI, THE

1957, 161 MINS, UK ◇ ⓥ ⊙
Dir David Lean   *Prod* Sam Spiegel   *Scr* Pierre Boulle, [Carl Foreman, Michael Wilson, Calder Willingham]   *Ph* Jack Hildyard   *Ed* Peter Taylor   *Mus* Malcolm Arnold   *Art Dir* Donald M. Ashton
● William Holden, Alec Guinness, Jack Hawkins, Sessue Hayakawa, Geoffrey Horne, James Donald (Horizon)

The Bridge on the River Kwai is a gripping drama, expertly put together and handled with skill in all departments. From a technical standpoint, it reflects the care and competence that went into the $3 million-plus venture, filmed against the exotic background of the steaming jungles and mountains of Ceylon [repping Burma]. A story of the futility of war in general [adapted, uncredited, by Carl Foreman, Michael Wilson and Calder Willingham from the novel by Pierre Boulle], the underlying message is never permitted to impede.

Story is 'masculine'. It's about three men, William Holden, Alec Guinness and Sessue Hayakawa. Latter is the commandant of a Japanese prison camp in which Holden, a Yank sailor posing as a commander, is a prisoner. Guinness is a British colonel who commands a new group of prisoners. He's a strict rules-of-war man who clashes immediately with Hayakawa over the latter's insistence that officers as well as men must work on the railroad bridge being built over the River Kwai.

Guinness wins and then proceeds to guide his men in building a superb bridge to prove the mettle of British soldiers under any conditions. Holden, meanwhile, escapes to safety but is talked into leading Jack Hawkins and British commandos back to the bridge to blow it up.

There are notable performances from the key characters, but the film is unquestionably Guinness'. He etches an unforgettable portrait of the typical British army officer, strict, didactic and serene in his adherence to the book. It's a performance of tremendous power and dignity. Hayakawa, once a star in American silents and long absent from the screen, also is solidly impressive as the Japanese officer, limning him as an admixture of cruelty and correctness.

[In 1992 a letterboxed video reissue of the film featured a revised script credit, to Michael Wilson and Carl Foreman.]
☐ 1957: Best Picture, Director, Actor (Alec Guinness), Adapted Screenplay, Cinematography, Score, Editing.
☐ Nomination: Best Supp. Actor (Sessue Hayakawa)

● ● ● ● ● ● ● ● ● ● ● ● ● ● ● ● ● ● ●

■ BRIDGES AT TOKO-RI, THE

1955, 102 MINS, US ◇ ⓥ ⊙
Dir Mark Robson   *Prod* William Perlberg, George Seaton   *Scr* Valentine Davies   *Ph* Loyal Griggs   *Ed* Alma Macrorie   *Mus* Lyn Murray   *Art Dir* Hal Pereira, Henry Bumstead
● William Holden, Grace Kelly, Fredric March, Mickey Rooney, Robert Strauss, Charles McGraw (Paramount)

James A. Michener's hard-hitting novel of the Korean conflict finds slick translation in this topflight war spectacle.

In taking advantage of the navy's resources, aboard an aircraft carrier off the coast of Korea and through the use of planes and equipment, Mark Robson in his taut direction catches the spirit of the navy and what it stood for in the Korean War, never losing sight, however, of the personalized story of a Navy combat flier.

Narrative drives toward the climactic bombing by US fliers of the five bridges at Toko-Ri, which span a strategic pass in Korea's interior. Here the story of William Holden, a reserve officer recalled to service, unfolds. A fine flier, he is taken under the wing of the admiral, played by Frederic March, who understands his gripe of having been forced to leave his wife and children to return to the Navy.

Practically every principal performance is a standout. Holden lends conviction to his character, and March delivers a sock portrayal of the admiral, who is drawn to Holden beause he reminds him of his two sons lost in war. As Holden's wife who brings their two daughters to Tokyo so they may be near the flier, Grace Kelly is warmly sympathetic.
☐ 1955: Best Special Effects.
☐ Nomination: Best Editing

● ● ● ● ● ● ● ● ● ● ● ● ● ● ● ● ● ● ●

■ BRIDGE TOO FAR, A

1977, 175 MINS, UK ◇ ⓥ ⊙
Dir Richard Attenborough   *Prod* Joseph E. Levine, Richard P. Levine   *Scr* William Goldman   *Ph* Geoffrey Unsworth   *Ed* Anthony Gibbs   *Mus* John Addison   *Art Dir* Terry Marsh
● Dirk Bogarde, James Caan, Michael Caine, Sean Connery, Edward Fox, Elliott Gould (United Artists)

Futility and frustration are the overriding emotional elements in *A Bridge Too Far*, Joseph E. Levine's sprawling Second World War production [from the novel by Cornelius Ryan] about a 1944 military operation botched by both Allied and German troops.

Film opens with some vintage black and white newsreel footage in original frame ratio, setting up the falls. 1944, attempt to expedite the end of the Second World War by an enormous paratroop operation involving a series of bridges leading to Germany. The first part of the film introduces senior officers Dirk Bogarde, Sean Connery, Gene Hackman, Michael Caine, Anthony Hopkins and Edward Fox as the plans are outlined.

Later, as operations begin, periodic appearances are made by cocky Robert Redford, wise-cracking Elliott Gould, stolid Ryan O'Neal and James Caan. On the other side of hostilities, Hardy Kruger and Maximilian Schell and Wolfgang Priess represent different levels of German military thinking about, and reaction to, the offbeat Allied strategy. In the middle Laurence Olivier and Liv Ullmann are two Dutch residents who attend to the wounded.

● ● ● ● ● ● ● ● ● ● ● ● ● ● ● ● ● ● ●

■ BRIEF ENCOUNTER

1945, 83 MINS, UK ⓥ
Dir David Lean   *Prod* Anthony Havelock-Allan   *Scr* Noel Coward, David Lean, Ronald Neame   *Ph* Robert Krasker   *Ed* Jack Harris   *Mus* Rachmaninov   *Art Dir* L.P. Williams
● Celia Johnson, Trevor Howard, Stanley Holloway, Joyce Carey, Cyril Raymond, Valentine Dyall (Cineguild/Rank)

Based on his playlet, *Still Life* from *Tonight at 8.30*, *Brief Encounter* does more for Noel Coward's reputation as a skilled film producer than *In Which We Serve*. His use of express trains thundering through a village station coupled with frantic, last-minute dashes for local trains is only one of the clever touches masking the inherent static quality of the drama.

Celia Johnson as the small-town mother whose brief encounter with a doctor, encumbered with a wife and kids, plunges her into a love affair from which she struggles vainly to escape, is terrific. Co-starred with her, Trevor Howard, as the doctor, gives a performance calculated to win the sympathy of femmes of all ages. As for the dumb husband whose idea of marital happiness is summed up in his parrot-like iteration, 'Have it your own way, my dear', Cyril Raymond manages to invest the stodgy character with a lovable quality.
☐ 1946: Nominations: Best Director, Actress (Celia Johnson), Screenplay

● ● ● ● ● ● ● ● ● ● ● ● ● ● ● ● ● ● ●

B

■ BRIGADOON

1954, 108 MINS, US ◇ ⓥ ⊙
Dir Vincente Minnelli *Prod* Arthur Freed *Scr* Alan Jay
Lerner *Ph* Joseph Ruttenberg *Ed* Albert Akst
Mus Johnny Green (dir.) *Art Dir* Cedric Gibbons,
Preston Ames
● Gene Kelly, Van Johnson, Cyd Charisse, Elaine
Stewart, Barry Jones, Hugh Laing (M-G-M)

In transferring *Brigadoon*, a click as a [1947]
Broadway musical play, to the screen, Metro
has medium success. It's a fairly entertaining
tunefilm of mixed appeal.

Among the more noteworthy points are the
score, as directed by Johnny Green, and the
stage-type settings that represent the plot's
Highland locale. The latter are striking, even
though they are the major contribution to the
feeling that this is a filmed stage show, rather
than a motion picture musical.

Less noteworthy is the choreography by
Gene Kelly, who also plays the lead male role,
and his singing of the Alan Jay Lerner-
Frederick Loewe songs.

The Lerner musical play tells of two New
Yorkers who become lost while hunting in
Scotland and happen on Brigadoon on the
one day that it is visible every 100 years.
Besides, a wedding is to take place and Kelly
and Van Johnson, the modern-day males, join
in the fun. Particularly Kelly, who falls for
Cyd Charisse hard enough to be willing to
join his sweetheart in the long ago.
□ 1954: Nomination: Best Color Costume
Design, Color Art Direction, Sound

■ BRIGHAM YOUNG

1940, 112 MINS, US
Dir Henry Hathaway *Prod* Kenneth Macgowan
Scr Lamar Trotti *Ph* Arthur Miller *Ed* Robert Bischoff
Mus Alfred Newman *Art Dir* William Darling, Maurice
Ransford
● Tyrone Power, Linda Darnell, Dean Jagger, Brian
Donlevy, Jane Darwell, John Carradine (20th Century-
Fox)

Taking the favorable factual aspects of the
trek of Mormons to the west, and combining
them with well-concocted fictional ingredients, picture emerges as an epic filmization
of early American history.

There's dramatic power in the persecution
of the Mormons in their settlement at
Nauvoo, Illinois; the conviction and murder of
Joseph Smith; and the resultant decision of
Brigham Young to lead his flock across the
plains to their eventual home on the shores of
Salt Lake. Adversity hits the entourage at
every turn, but, despite recalcitrants in the
ranks, Young commands attention with a
most dominating personality which is most
vividly depicted.

Through it all runs a minor romance between Tyrone Power and Linda Darnell; and
a more important impress of man and wife on
the parts of Young (Dean Jagger) and his
first and favorite spouse, Mary Ann (Mary
Astor). Latter is decidedly sympathetic and
carries prominent appeal as standing solidly
behind the leader through adversity.

Jagger brings to the character of the
Mormon leader a personable humaness and
sympathy. Astor turns in one of the finest
performances of her career. Power and
Darnell are overshadowed by the above twain.

■ BRIGHT ANGEL

1990, 94 MINS, US ◇ ⓥ
Dir Michael Fields *Prod* Paige Simpson, Robert
MacLean *Scr* Richard Ford *Ph* Elliott Davis
Ed Melody London, Clement Barclay *Mus* Christopher
Young *Art Dir* Marcia Hinds Johnson
● Dermot Mulroney, Lili Taylor, Sam Shepard, Valerie
Perrine, Sheila McCarthy, Burt Young (Hemdale-
Northwood/Bright Angel)

Bright Angel is one of those films that breathe
freshness and life into familiar genres.
Basically a road movie about a pair of young
lovers who become involved in crime, Michael
Fields' first feature as a director boasts a full
cast-list of near-perfect performances. The
intelligent and spare screenplay is by Richard
Ford, who based it on two of his short stories
[*Children* and *Great Falls*].

The setting is Montana, 'where the Great
Plains begin'. George Russell (Dermot
Mulroney), 18, lives with his parents (Sam
Shepard and Valerie Perrine) who separate
violently when his father finds his mother
with another man. George is attracted to
Lucy (Lili Taylor), who has spent an afternoon in a motel with the father of his best
friend, an Indian. She needs to get to the
Wyoming town where her brother's in prison,
and George offers to drive her.

Much of the film is taken up with the relationship between the naive and good-hearted
George and the old-beyond-her-years Lucy as
they journey to their destination, and with
the characters they become involved with.

Fields and Ford deal with a familiar genre
here, but they avoid cliches: no sex scenes
(but a great deal of sexual tension); no shootouts (but an agonizing sequence of suspense);
no neat ending.

■ BRIGHT LIGHTS, BIG CITY

1988, 110 MINS, US ◇ ⓥ ⊙
Dir James Bridges *Prod* Mark Rosenberg, Sydney
Pollack *Scr* Jay McInerney *Ph* Gordon Willis
Ed John Bloom, George Berndt *Mus* Donald Fagen, Rob
Mounsey *Art Dir* Santo Loquasto
● Michael J. Fox, Kiefer Sutherland, Phoebe Cates,
Swoosie Kurtz, Frances Sternhagen, Tracy Pollan (United
Artists/Mirage)

This novel-cum-feature film (from Jay
McInerney's book) is a distinctly morose and
maudlin journey through one man's destructive period of personal loss.

Opening scene establishes Michael J. Fox as
a lonesome barfly with a cocaine habit in the
Big Apple. First reason given is that his wife
(Phoebe Cates) has dumped him to pursue
modeling in Paris. It's later learned that he's
also grieving over the death of his mother
(Dianne Wiest) a year earlier.

Fox is cast here as Jamie, a would-be writer
marking time as a fact checker for literary giant *Gotham* magazine. Jamie quickly slides so
badly that he's fired during a scene with editorial chief, Frances Sternhagen – an exchange that points up the benefit of placing
the youthful Fox in situations with seasoned
veterans.

Jason Robards' appearance as a drunken
fiction writer is all too familiar and a brief encounter with the fascinating William Hickey
and a pittance of time with Wiest round out
these cameos.

■ BRIGHTON BEACH MEMOIRS

1986, 108 MINS, US ◇ ⓥ ⊙
Dir Gene Saks *Prod* Ray Stark *Scr* Neil Simon
Ph John Bailey *Ed* Carol Littleton *Mus* Michael Small
Art Dir Stuart Wurtzel
● Blythe Danner, Bob Dishy, Brian Dillinger, Stacey
Glick, Judith Ivey, Lisa Waltz (Rastar)

The first of Neil Simon's semi-autobiographical trilogy, *Brighton Beach* bowed in Los
Angeles in late 1982 and opened in New York
in March, 1983.

Set in 1937 in a lower-middle class section
of Brooklyn, story details assorted life crises
of members of the Jerome family, hard-working moral Jews whose problems are all taken
to heart by Mama Kate, played by Blythe
Danner.

Despite the assurance of verbal reprisals,
all family members are expected to speak

their minds and share their difficulties (there
can be no secrets anyway, since nothing can
escape Mama's notice). Emotions are fully
felt, responsibilities accepted and decisions
taken, not avoided.

Performances are skilled all the way
through.

■ BRIGHTON ROCK
(US: *Young Scarface*)

1948, 92 MINS, UK
Dir John Boulting *Prod* Roy Boulting *Scr* Graham
Greene, Terence Rattigan *Ph* Harry Waxman *Ed* Peter
Graham Scott *Mus* Hans May *Art Dir* John Howell
● Richard Attenborough, Hermione Baddeley, William
Hartnell, Carol Marsh, Harcourt Williams, Nigel Stock
(Boulting Brothers)

British producers are competing with each
other in rushing mobster yarns to the screen.
This tends to prove that Britain can turn out
a gangster picture as brutal as any Hollywood
had devised.

With Graham Greene and Terence
Rattigan responsible for the screenplay
[based on Greene's own novel], something
more exciting might reasonably have been
expected. Some of blame goes to director
John Boulting whose tempo is much too
leisurely for this type of picture.

Story is laid in pre-war seaside resort
Brighton, where two razor-slashing race
gangs are feuding.

It is difficult to believe that any gang which
included William Hartnell could be led by
Richard Attenborough. Hartnell is so much
more the gangster type than Attenborough
that it is obvious that an exchange of parts
would have made the film more credible.

Acting honors are collared by that seasoned
actress, Hermione Baddeley. She steals every
scene in which she appears, making Ida, the
concert artist, a sympathetic character. Carol
Marsh (formerly Norma Simpson) plays the
waitress and gangster's wife with modesty.

■ BRINGING UP BABY

1938, 102 MINS, US ⓥ ⊙
Dir Howard Hawks *Prod* Howard Hawks *Scr* Dudley
Nichols, Hagar Wilde *Ph* Russell Metty *Ed* George
Hively *Mus* Roy Webb (dir.)
● Katharine Hepburn, Cary Grant, Charlie Ruggles,
Barry Fitzgerald, May Robson, Walter Catlett (RKO)

This harum-scarum farce comedy, Katharine
Hepburn's first of the type, is constructed for
maximum of laughs. Opposite her is Cary
Grant, who is perfectly at home as a farceur
after his work in *The Awful Truth* (1937).

Wacky developments [story by Hagar
Wilde] include pursuit of an heiress after a
zoology professor who expects to wed his
femme assistant in the museum on the same
day he plans to complete a giant brontosaurus; a pet leopard, 'Nissa', who makes a
playmate of 'Asta', a redoubtable Scots terrier; a wealthy woman who may endow the
prof's museum with $1 million; an escaped
wild leopard from the circus; a stupid town
constable; a forgetful ex-big game hunter; a
scientifically-minded brain specialist; and a
tippling gardener.

Hepburn is invigorating as the madcap deb.
Grant, who thinks more of recovering the
priceless missing bone for his uncompleted
brontosaurus than his impending wedding
and the companionship of the playful heiress,
performs his role to the hilt. Charlie Ruggles,
as the former African game hunter, does wonders with a minor characterization brought in
late in the picture.

Chief shortcoming is that too much time is
consumed with the jail sequence. Prime reason for it, of course, is that it gives Hepburn a
chance to imitate a gunmoll.

■ BRING ME THE HEAD OF ALFREDO GARCIA

1974, 112 MINS, US ◇ Ⓦ

Dir Sam Peckinpah *Prod* Martin Baum *Scr* Gordon Dawson, Sam Peckinpah *Ph* Alex Phillips *Ed* Garth Craven, Robbe Roberts, Sergio Ortega, Dennis E. Dolan *Mus* Jerry Fielding *Art Dir* Agustin Ituarte
● Warren Oates, Isela Vega, Gig Young, Robert Webber, Helmut Dantine, Kris Kristofferson (Optimus/Estudios Churubusco)

Bring Me the Head of Alfredo Garcia is turgid melodrama [from a story by Frank Kowalski and Sam Peckinpah] at its worst.

Warren Oates stars as an expatriate American piano bar musician making a stab for riches in Mexico by finding the never-seen title character sought by an outraged Mexican father. Naturally the search brings unhappiness, and, being a Peckinpah film, lots and lots of people get killed along the way, as well as audience interest.

The title derives from the command of wealthy Emilio Fernandez to find the father of his unwed daughter's child. Gig Young, Helmut Dantine and Robert Webber are the private detectives engaged. They meet Oates whose girl (Isela Vega) had been intimate with the stud. He is dead so Oates and Vega head off to steal the guy's head from a grave.

■ BRITANNIA HOSPITAL

1982, 115 MINS, UK ◇ Ⓦ

Dir Lindsay Anderson *Prod* Davina Belling, Clive Parsons *Scr* David Sherwin *Ph* Mike Fash *Ed* Michael Ellis *Mus* Alan Price *Art Dir* Norris Spencer
● Leonard Rossiter, Graham Crowden, Malcolm McDowell, Joan Plowright, Jill Bennett, Marsha Hunt (EMI/General)

Britannia Hospital is a witty, unsparing expose of British manners and mores.

The film revolves around a strike at a hospital where a royal personage is expected. This gives rise to union complaints about privileges showered on monied notables when the National Health system was supposed to make medicine equally available for all.

Medics' own misuse of National Health funds is pilloried in no uncertain style. A mad doctor experiments, from funds meant for socialized medicine to create Frankenstein-type creatures.

A zealous reporter with a small video camera sneaks in to tape the mad doctor's creature-building only to end up as the head of the Frankenstein figure.

Through it all, the hospital director tries to cope with typical British phlegm, assured by a Scotland Yard top cop that crowds and unions will be kept in check.

Malcolm McDowell is rightly overacting as the reporter who loses his head. Leonard Rossiter copes staunchly as the beset hospital director. Marsha Hunt, Jill Bennett and Joan Plowright do fine cameo work as nurse, doctor and the union head.

■ BROADCAST NEWS

1987, 131 MINS, US ◇ Ⓦ ⊙

Dir James L. Brooks *Prod* James L. Brooks *Scr* James L. Brooks *Ph* Michael Ballhaus *Ed* Richard Marks *Mus* Bill Conti *Art Dir* Charles Rosen
● William Hurt, Albert Brooks, Holly Hunter, Robert Prosky, Lois Chiles, Jack Nicholson (Gracie/20th Century-Fox)

Enormously entertaining *Broadcast News* is an inside look at the personal and professional lives of three TV journlists.

Brooks gently punctures the self-importance of his characters with a sly satrical edge. When veteran reporter Aaron Altman (Albert Brooks) and hard-nosed producer Jane Craig (Holly Hunter) go to the jungles of Central America to report on the revolution, the results are too humorous and self-serving to take seriously.

Where Craig and Altman are seasoned professionals with great talent, Tom Grunick (William Hurt) is a slick ex-sportscaster who knows how to turn on the charm and seduce an audience. But is it news, his colleagues wonder.

Tom loves himself and loves Jane. In short it's a case of scrambled emotions among people who heretofore have substituted work for pleasure.

Hunter is simply superb barking out orders from a mouth contorted with who-knows-what emotions. As the neurotic but brilliant reporter, Brooks gives an insightful performance while communicating his character's guardedness and anguish. As the hardest of the characters to read, Hurt does a good job keeping up the mystery so one never knows when he's sincere or faking, and maybe he doesn't either.
□ 1987: Nominations: Best Picture, Actor (William Hurt), Actress (Holly Hunter), Supp. Actor (Albert Brooks), Original Screenplay, Cinematography, Editing

■ BROADWAY

1942, 89 MINS, US

Dir William A. Seiter *Prod* Bruce Manning *Scr* Felix Jackson, John Bright *Ph* George Barnes *Ed* Ted Kent *Mus* Charles Previn
● George Raft, Pat O'Brien, Broderick Crawford, Janet Blair, Anne Gwynne, Marjorie Rambeau (Universal)

Universal's modernized presentation of *Broadway* retains the thrilling tenseness and dramatic suspense of both the original Philip Dunning-George Abbott play and the first film version turned out by Universal in 1929.

As modernized, *Broadway* could easily be the autobiography of George Raft – and this impression is carried through the unreeling via the medium of a prolog deftly contrived. Picture opens with Raft airlining to New York with companion-bodyguard-shadow, Mack Gray, for a short visit between pictures. Wandering onto Broadway, alone, he stops at a cellar being remodelled into a bowling alley. Looking around, he starts reminiscing to the old night-watchman about the heyday of the spot as a cabaret during the lush prohibition era – when Raft got his start as a hoofer in the place.

In addition to swift dramatic pace, provided both in script and direction, picture is studded with a group of excellent performances. Raft justifies his casting for the lead, and clicks solidly. Sharing honors with him is Pat O'Brien.

■ BROADWAY DANNY ROSE

1984, 86 MINS, US Ⓦ ⊙

Dir Woody Allen *Prod* Robert Greenhut *Scr* Woody Allen *Ph* Gordon Willis *Ed* Susan E. Morse *Mus* Dick Hyman *Art Dir* Mel Bourne
● Woody Allen, Mia Farrow, Nick Apollo Forte, Milton Berle, Sandy Baron, Corbett Monica (Orion)

Broadway Danny Rose is a delectable diversion which allows Woody Allen to present a reasonably humane, and amusing gentle character study without sacrificing himself to overly commercial concerns.

Allen's perfect as a small-time, good-hearted Broadway talent agent, giving his all for a roster of hopeless clients.

Agent's career is fondly recalled here by a group of Catskill comics (all played by themselves) sitting around over coffee, focusing mainly on Allen's attempt revive the career of an aging, overweight, boozing lounge singer, beautifully played by Nick Apollo Forte.

One of Forte's many problems that Allen must deal with is a floozy of a girlfriend. And it's truly one of the picture's early delights that this sunglassed bimbo is actually on screen for several minutes before most of the audience catches on that she's Mia Farrow.

Through Forte and Farrow, Allen becomes the target of a couple of hit men.
□ 1984: Nominations: Best Director, Original Screenplay

■ BROADWAY MELODY, THE

1929, 104 MINS, US ◇ Ⓦ ⊙

Dir Harry Beaumont *Scr* Edmund Goulding, James Gleason, Norman Houston *Ph* John Arnold *Mus* Herb Nacio Brown, Arthur Freed *Art Dir* Cedric Gibbons
● Anita Page, Bessie Love, Charles King, Jed Prouty, Kenneth Thomson, Edward Dillon (M-G-M)

Broadway Melody, the first screen musical, tells of a vaudeville sister team coming in from the middle west, with the older girl engaged to a song-and-dance boy in a Broadway revue. Latter goes for the kid sister, now grown up, who starts playing with one of the show's backers to stand off the boy and spare the blow to her sister, despite that she, too, is in love with her prospective brother-in-law.

In between are the troubles of the femme team making the revue grade.

Both girls, Bessie Love as the elder sister and Anita Page as the youngster, are great in their respective climaxes, especially Love. Charlie King looks as good as he plays and plants comed lines as they should be delivered. Other cast support is up to the mark with the exception of Kenneth Thomson, as the chaser, who plays too slow and doesn't convince.

Excellent bits of sound workmanship are that of camera and mike following Page and the heavy along the dance floor to pick up their conversation as they glide.
□ 1928/29: Best Picture
□ Nominations: Best Director, Actress (Bessie Love)

■ BROADWAY MELODY OF 1936

1935, 102 MINS, US Ⓦ ⊙

Dir Roy Del Ruth *Prod* John W. Considine Jr *Scr* Jack McGowan, Sid Silvers, Harry Conn *Ph* Charles Rosher *Ed* Blanche Sewell *Mus* Alfred Newman (dir.), Roger Edens (arr.) *Art Dir* Cedric Gibbons, Merrill Pye, Edwin B. Willis
● Jack Benny, Eleanor Powell, Robert Taylor, Una Merkel, Sid Silvers, Buddy Ebsen (M-G-M)

Everything revolves about Eleanor Powell, Robert Taylor and June Knight, the menace. She's the Park Avenue bankroll ($60,000) for the forthcoming musical comedy [dance direction by Dave Gould]. Columnist Jack Benny had been building up a phoney French comedienne, and so when Taylor fails to recognize his adolescent sweetheart from Albany she (Powell) essays an accent, bizarre make-up and goals everybody with her personality and her stepping as the pseudo-French star.

Story [by Moss Hart] is a curious hodge-podge of fantasy, realism and just hokum musical comedy. When the Ebsens (Vilma and Buddy) are doing their 'Sing Before Breakfast', it's quite Rene Clair-ish in the whimsical mating of the tempo with the attic time-stepping In other spots it goes Busby Berkeley with overhead ballet shots, or the sequence in what looks like the Rainbow Room at Radio City.

Songs are all good. 'Broadway Rhythm', sung by Frances Langford and with dance specialties by Powell, Nick Long Jr, Knight and the Ebsens, is a corking creation.
□ 1935: Best Dance Direction ('I've Got a Feeling You're Fooling')
□ Nominations: Best Picture, Original Story

■ BROADWAY MELODY OF 1938

1937, 115 MINS, US 🔊 ⊙
Dir Roy Del Ruth   *Prod* Jack Cummings   *Scr* Jack McGowan   *Ph* William Daniels   *Ed* Blanche Sewell   *Mus* George Stoll (dir.)
● Robert Taylor, Eleanor Powell, George Murphy, Binnie Barnes, Judy Garland, Sophie Tucker (M-G-M)

Much better than its predecessor of 1936, and not far behind the original 1929 *Broadway Melody*.

No use getting into the details until Sophie Tucker and Judy Garland are disposed of. Former is somewhere past 40, but when she walks on the screen something happens. Then she steps back and pushes Garland, still in her teens, into the camera foreground. Young Garland gives them 'Everybody sing', with a letter to the homefolks.

Each does numbers solo later on. Judy sings a plaint to Clark Gable's photograph which is close to great screen acting. Then, to top it off, Soph does 'Your Broadway and My Broadway', with lyrics which bring in the great names of the past generation.

Most of the rest is just filler-in-between the Tucker and the Garland numbers. There is a lot of plot [by Jack McGowan and Sid Silvers] about a racehorse which is owned by Eleanor Powell, and a Broadway musical show which Robert Taylor is trying to produce on a short bankroll.

Buddy Ebsen handles some first-class comedy bits on his own in addition to his eccentric dancing.

Music and lyrics by Nacio Herb Brown and Arthur Freed are first rate.

■ BROADWAY MELODY OF 1940

1940, 102 MINS, US 🔊 ⊙
Dir Norman Taurog   *Prod* Jack Cummings   *Scr* Leon Gordon, George Oppenheimer   *Ph* Oliver T. Marsh, Joseph Ruttenberg   *Ed* Blanche Sewell   *Mus* Alfred Newman (dir.), Roger Edens (arr.)   *Art Dir* Cedric Gibbons, John S. Detlie
● Fred Astaire, Eleanor Powell, George Murphy, Frank Morgan, Ian Hunter, Florence Rice (M-G-M)

Long on its display of corking dance routines and numbers by Fred Astaire, Eleanor Powell and George Murphy, mounted against elaborate production backgrounds, *Broadway Melody of 1940* slides through as moderately satisfying entertainment.

The story [by Jack McGowan and Dore Schary] is a typical backstage yarn. Astaire and Murphy are an ambitious team of hoofers working in a dance hall for coffee and cakes. Mistake in names shoots Murphy instead of Astaire into the lead of a Broadway musical opposite the star (Eleanor Powell). Murphy hits the bottle for the opening night, Astaire taking his place to protect his former partner.

This is the first teaming of Astaire and Powell in a filmusical. The result is as to be expected, both presenting several new and applause-generating numbers. But the numbers are too many and too extended for general purposes. This is particularly true of the finale, a super-lavish production background in which Astaire and Powell dance tap and whirl for six minutes. It's not sufficient to maintain interest for that length of time.

Murphy gains attention with a top performance as the hoofer-partner of Astaire. Latter is adequate in the role of the dance expert who goes to town when he starts stepping out with his new routines. Powell is an eyeful in her dances, and okay for the story sequences. Frank Morgan provides plenty of laughs in characterization of the musical show producer, while Ian Hunter is his partner who really stages the shows.

■ BROADWAY RHYTHM

1944, 115 MINS, US ◇
Dir Roy Del Ruth   *Prod* Jack Cummings   *Scr* Dorothy Kingsley, Harry Clork   *Ph* Leonard Smith   *Ed* Albert Akst   *Mus* Johnny Green (dir.)   *Art Dir* Cedric Gibbons, Jack Martin Smith
● George Murphy, Ginny Simms, Charles Winninger, Gloria DeHaven, Lena Horne (M-G-M)

Broadway Rhythm is a typical backstage filmusical wheeled out in the usual Metro elaborate and colorful style. Displaying group of toprank specialties and names among the entertainers, the fragile and hodge-podge yarn [based on the 1939 Kern-Hammerstein musical *Very Warm for May*] stops periodically while the guest stars appear.

Story follows run-of-mill formula for a backstager. George Murphy is a top musical comedy producer readying his next show for Broadway. Ginny Simms, Hollywood film star, hits town for a whirl at the stage after being stymied on new contract in films. Charles Winninger, veteran song-and-dance man, is Murphy's dad, while Gloria DeHaven is the young sister with stage ambitions.

Tommy Dorsey and his orchestra provide the musical backgrounds, and are spotlighted for opening number to get picture away to a good start and one other number later. Lena Horne socks over two songs – the Gershwins' 'Somebody Loves Me', and 'Brazilian Boogie', by Hugh Martin and Ralph Blane – and both are smartly presented for maximum effect.

■ BROADWAY TO HOLLYWOOD

1933, 88 MINS, US
Dir Willard Mack   *Prod* Harry Rapf   *Scr* Willard Mack, Edgar Allan Woolf   *Ph* William Daniels, Norbert Brodine   *Mus* William Axt (arr.)   *Art Dir* Stanford Rogers
● Alice Brady, Frank Morgan, Madge Evans, Russell Hardie, Jackie Cooper, Mickey Rooney (M-G-M)

Little from Metro's costly *March of Time* Technicolor musical has actually been resuscitated, although Metro's now historic and costly floppo venture inspired this combined effort by Harry Rapf, Willard Mack and Edgar Allan Woolf to retrieve something from the celluloid wreckage.

Patently it was primed to trace the hoofing variety Hacketts from their Tony Pastor's days until the third-generation success of grandson Ted Hackett III as a film juvenile star. Dovetailed in is all the array of venerable variety talent which Metro assembled for its *March of Time* production four years earlier.

It's all Alice Brady and Frank Morgan's picture in sterling characterizations as the original hoofing Hacketts of Tony Pastor's time and down through the years into the third generation. Madge Evans and Russell Hardie (Ted Hackett Jr) sustain the sub-romance interest.

The third generation has Jackie Cooper as Ted III as a child, and Eddie Quillan playing the matured Ted III when he becomes an overnight Hollywood click.

Cast names which are also included are dragged in by the heels, strictly for ballyhoo value. Among 'em are Jimmy Durante, whose brief appearance in a studio ante-room, as a would-be film aspirant, is strictly a one-to-fill; Fay Templeton and May Robson in the resurrected Technicolor stuff; Una Merkel in an anonymous bit merely shown flirting with the stage actor.

■ BROKEN ARROW

1950, 92 MINS, US ◇ 🔊
Dir Delmer Daves   *Prod* Julian Blaustein   *Scr* Michael Blankfort   *Ph* Ernest Palmer   *Ed* J. Watson Webb Jr   *Mus* Hugo Friedhofer
● James Stewart, Jeff Chandler, Debra Paget, Basil Ruysdael, Will Geer, Joyce MacKenzie (20th Century-Fox)

Broken Arrow is a western with a little different twist – the story of the attempt of whites and Apaches to learn to live together in the Arizona of 1870. Essentially it's an appealing, sentimental Indian romance, with plenty of action.

Pic has a quality of naive charm that peculiarly fits. There are colorful Indian tribal ceremonies that ring true.

Story [from a novel by Elliott Arnold] concerns a far-sighted young frontiersman (James Stewart) who, tired of the mutual killings of whites and redskins, boldly plans a visit to the feared Apache leader Cochise (Jeff Chandler) to propose a truce. Meeting not only succeeds, but Stewart falls in love with an Indian maiden (Debra Paget). Both truce and troth are impeded by treacher on the part of whites and Indians.

☐ 1950: Nominations: Best Supp. Actor (Jeff Chandler), Screenplay, Color Cinematography

■ BROKEN BLOSSOMS
OR THE YELLOW MAN AND THE GIRL

1919, 107 MINS, US ⊗ 🔊 ⊙
Dir D.W. Griffith   *Prod* D.W. Griffith   *Scr* D.W. Griffith   *Ph* Billy Bitzer, Herdrik Sartor, Karl Brown   *Ed* James E. Smith, Rose Smith   *Mus* Louis Gottschalk, D.W. Griffith   *Art Dir* Charles E. Baker
● Lillian Gish, Donald Crisp, Richard Barthelmess, Edward Peil, Arthur Howard, George Beranger (Artcraft)

Although the picture consumes only 90 minutes, it somehow seems draggy, for the reason that everything other than the scenes with the three principals seems extraneous and tends to clog the progression of the tale.

Broken Blossoms is adapted from a story by Thomas Burke entitled *The Chink and the Child*. The footage allotted the titles is a point to be commended, ample time being allowed to read them slowly and digest their meaning.

The story is a drama of pathos, culminating in tragedy. A pure-minded young Chinaman, reared in the beautiful teachings of Buddha, journeys to London with the altruistic idea of civilizing the white race.

In London there resides in his vicinity a brutish prize-fighter who beats his child into helplessness and she crawls away, half dead, falling insensible into the shop of the Mongolian. With perhaps a whiff of the lilied pipe still in his brain, he finds her on the floor, carries her to his living room above and watches over her with a love so pure as to be wholly unnatural and inconsistent.

Lillian Gish as the girl, shrinking, self-effacing, timid, fearful and wistful, has never before done anything so fine. Donald Crisp is the brutal father, as great a triumph of histrionic artistry as that registered by Gish.

Yet not one whit behind these two masterful portrayals is that of Richard Barthelmess as the young Chinaman, idealized, necessarily, in the matter of facial attractiveness, yet visualizing to the full the gentle delicacy of the idyllic Oriental youth.

■ BROKEN LANCE

1954, 96 MINS, US ◇ 🔊
Dir Edward Dmytryk   *Prod* Sol C. Siegel   *Scr* Richard Murphy   *Ph* Joe MacDonald   *Ed* Dorothy Spencer   *Mus* Leigh Harline
● Spencer Tracy, Robert Wagner, Jean Peters, Richard Widmark, Katy Jurado, Hugh O'Brian (20th Century-Fox)

Broken Lance is topnotch western drama. Seems too bad so much of the story [by Philip Yordan] is told via an unnecessary flashback. However, there is enough force in the trouping and direction to sustain mood and interest. This is particularly true of Spencer Tracy's performance, since he has the difficult task of making alive a character already dead when the picture opens.

Film starts with Robert Wagner's release from an Arizona prison after serving a three-year sentence. The enmity that lies between him and his three half-brothers (Richard Widmark, Hugh O'Brian and Earl Holliman) is quickly established.

The scene shifts from this strong early sequence, taking place in the office of the governor (E.G. Marshall), where they all try to get him to leave the state, to the once proud family ranch, now decayed from neglect. There Wagner recalls the events that led to his imprisonment.

Within the flashback Tracy is shown as a domineering cattle baron, who rules his four sons and vast empire ruthlessly by his own laws. However, time is running out for him as civilization advances, and he takes the law into his own hands once too often in destroying mining property and injuring miners.
□ 1954: Best Motion Picture Story.
□ Nomination: Best Supp. Actress (Katy Jurado)

■ BRONCO BILLY

1980, 119 MINS, US ◇ ⑩ ⊙
Dir Clint Eastwood   *Prod* Dennis E. Hackin, Neal Dobrofsky   *Scr* Dennis E. Hackin   *Ph* David Worth   *Ed* Ferris Webster, Joel Cox   *Mus* Snuff Garrett (sup.)   *Art Dir* Gene Lourie
● Clint Eastwood, Sondra Locke, Scatman Crothers, Bill McKinney, Sam Bottoms, Geoffrey Lewis (Warner)

In the title role, Clint Eastwood plays an ex-NJ shoe salesman who has trained himself to live out a fantasy as a sharpshooting, knife-throwing, stunt-riding cowboy. There's no place to practice it except as the leader of a run-down Wild West show touring tank towns and county fairs. The others in the troupe are also definitive losers of varying talents.

Along the same highways, however, comes Sondra Locke, an arrogant spoiled heiress, and Geoffrey Lewis, delightful as the idiotic husband she has just married. Fed up with Locke's mistreatment, Lewis abandons her without a dime and she winds up – quite reluctantly – as Eastwood's helper.

Bronco Billy is a caricature of many of the strong heroes whom Eastwood has played in other pics and he's obviously having a wonderful time with the satire.

■ BRONCO BULLFROG

1970, 86 MINS, UK ◇
Dir Barney Platts-Mills   *Prod* Andrew St John   *Scr* Barney Platts-Mills   *Ph* Adam Barker-Mill   *Ed* Jonathan Gili   *Mus* Howard Werth, Tony Connor, Keith Gemmell, Trevor Williams
● Del Walker, Anne Gooding, Sam Shepherd, Roy Haywood, Freda Shepherd, Dick Philpott (British Lion)

Producer Andrew St John and director-writer Barney Platts-Mills assembled a bunch of East End amateurs and, with a thin storyline and dialog that seems mainly improvised, let them loose in 'their own scene'. Made for only $48,000, film is a praiseworthy attempt to show the drab environment of an area and to indicate how boredom in that environment can drive youngsters into being layabouts, petty thieves, etc and how such trapped youngsters can develop into more hardened criminals.

Through the film is woven an inarticulate, but frequently touching Romeo and Juliet theme, about two minors who run away from home because there is nowhere to go and nothing to do.

It would be pointless to comment on the non-existent acting, there is behavior, instead.

■ BROOD, THE

1979, 91 MINS, CANADA ◇ ⑩ ⊙
Dir David Cronenberg   *Prod* Claude Heroux   *Scr* David Cronenberg   *Ph* Mark Irwin   *Ed* Alan Collins   *Mus* Howard Shore   *Art Dir* Carol Spier
● Oliver Reed, Samantha Eggar, Art Hindle, Cindy Hinds (New World)

A horror entry which casts children in the role of malevolent little monsters, *The Brood* is an extremely well made, if essentially unpleasant, shocker.

Cronenberg's helming is skillful enough to command attention even through his script's needlessly long stretches of dialog.

Action is relatively plodding stuff, with young parent Art Hindle trying to keep his daughter away from mother Samantha Eggar, who's supposedly in psychotherapy at the posh forested retreat of analyst Oliver Reed. Action is spiked with the mysterious murders of Eggar's parents.

Reed registers forcefully as the egotistical doctor and Eggar is appropriately flipped out but, unfortunately, most of the running time is spent with Hindle center stage and the actor is just too morose to enlist much sympathy, despite his plight.

■ BROTHER FROM ANOTHER PLANET, THE

1984, 104 MINS, US ◇ ⑩
Dir John Sayles   *Prod* Peggy Rajski, Maggie Renzi   *Scr* John Sayles   *Ph* Ernest R. Dickerson   *Ed* John Sayles   *Mus* Mason Daring   *Art Dir* Steve Lineweaver
● Joe Morton, Darryl Edwards, Steve James, Leonard Jackson, Bill Cobbs, Maggie Renzi (A-Train)

John Sayles takes a turn toward offbeat fantasy in *The Brother from Another Planet*, a vastly amusing but progressively erratic look at the Harlem adventures of an alien, a black E.T.

Brother begins with a tall, mute, young black fellow seeming to be dumped unceremoniously in New York harbor. Within minutes, he makes his way to Harlem, where his unusual, but not truly bizarre, behavior raises some cackles but in most respects blends into the neighborhood.

Pic is essentially a series of behavioral vignettes, and many of them are genuinely delightful and inventive. Once the Brother discovers the Harlem drug scene, however, tale takes rather unpleasant and, ultimately, confusing turn.

■ BROTHERHOOD, THE

1968, 96 MINS, US ◇ ⑩ ⊙
Dir Martin Ritt   *Prod* Kirk Douglas   *Scr* Lewis John Carlino   *Ph* Boris Kaufman   *Ed* Frank Bracht   *Mus* Lalo Schifrin   *Art Dir* Tambi Larsen
● Kirk Douglas, Alex Cord, Irene Papas, Luther Adler, Susan Strasberg, Murray Hamilton (Paramount/Bryna)

Mafia-themed story pits Kirk Douglas, as a middle-aged New Jersey syndicate chief, against Alex Cord, his ambitious younger brother not as attuned to the curious, but rigidly-structured old underworld code.

Martin Ritt's topnotch direction of an excellent cast maximizes the tragedy inherent in original screenplay.

Goading Douglas to progress are syndicate partners Luther Adler, Murray Hamilton, Val Avery and Alan Hewitt, repping in dialog and acting the commingling of Irish gangsters and Jewish gangsters with Sicilian-Italian gangsters.

Cord is excellent as the product of an environment which has smoothed out not only the rough edges of immigrant assimilation into the US, but also the surface emotions, noble and ignoble, which marked earlier generations. Urbane, cold, ambitious, unfeeling – Cord's character is chilling.

Since a prolog telegraphs some tragic cli-

max, there is not much suspense in the usual sense of the word.

■ BROTHERLY LOVE

See: Country Dance

■ BROTHERS

1977, 105 MINS, US ◇
Dir Arthur Barron   *Prod* Edward Lewis, Mildred Lewis   *Scr* Edward Lewis, Mildred Lewis   *Ph* John Morrill   *Ed* William Dornisch   *Mus* Taj Mahal   *Art Dir* Vince Cresciman
● Bernie Casey, Vonetta McGee, Ron O'Neal, Renny Roker, Stu Gilliam, John Lehne (Soho)

Most favorably judged, *Brothers* is an excellent dramatization of a contemporary dispute from one angry viewpoint. It's also a cheapshot, racist picture.

Though labeled 'fiction', pic only makes barest effort to differ from the true story San Quentin inmate George Jackson, whose younger brother Jonathan and a judge were killed during a wild shoot out at the Marin County Courthouse.

Jackson himself was later killed in prison and black activist Angela Davis was arrested – and acquitted – of charges of helping to plan the break out.

As seen by scripters Edward and Mildred Lewis, American prisons are torture chambers for blacks forced into them by white society. Once behind bars, blacks are dehumanized by guards (all white) and other white prisoners.

■ BROTHERS IN LAW

1957, 94 MINS, UK ⑩
Dir Roy Boulting   *Prod* John Boulting   *Scr* Frank Harvey, Jeffrey Dell, Roy Boulting   *Ph* Max Greene   *Ed* Anthony Harvey   *Mus* Benjamin Frankel   *Art Dir* Albert Witherick
● Richard Attenborough, Ian Carmichael, Terry-Thomas, Jill Adams, Miles Malleson, Eric Barker (Tudor/British Lion)

The three stars in *Private's Progress* are reunited in this Roy Boulting comedy. This time it's making fun of the law, doing full justice to a laugh-loaded script.

The witty and lighthearted yarn [from the novel by Henry Cecil] traces the experiences of a young lawyer from the day of his graduation until he achieves his first legal victory.

The raw legal recruit is Ian Carmichael, who through the good offices of his roommate and fellow attorney, is accepted as a pupil barrister Miles Malleson, a distinguished but absent-minded Queen's Counsel. Within a few minutes of his appointment he accompanies his senior to the High Court, and is left to plead the case without even knowing which side he's on. This unhappy start to his career affects Carmichael's confidence. He gets his chance from Terry-Thomas, a seasoned swindler with 17 appearances at the Criminal Court to his credit – and gets his first practical lesson in how to beat the law.

■ BROTHERS KARAMAZOV, THE

1958, 149 MINS, US ◇ ⑩
Dir Richard Brooks   *Prod* Pandro S. Berman   *Scr* Richard Brooks   *Ph* John Alton   *Ed* John Dunning   *Mus* Bronislau Kaper   *Art Dir* William A. Horning, Paul Groesse
● Yul Brynner, Maria Schell, Claire Bloom, Lee J. Cobb, Richard Basehart, William Shatner (M-G-M/Avon)

Bold handling of crude unbridled passion, of violently conflicting ideas, and of earthy humor makes up *The Brothers Karamazov*. Sex and Salvation are the twin obsessions of the brothers and father, and they are the two themes that are hammered relentlessly home by Richard Brooks, who directs his own screenplay.

Brooks wrote his screenplay from an adaptation by Julius J. and Philip G. Epstein of the Dostoievsky novel. Lee J. Cobb is the father of the Karamazov brothers, a lecherous ol buffoon who taunts, tantalizes and frustrates his sons into violence, despair and apathy. Yul Brynner is the handsome, cruel, profligate army officer, a combination of adult power and childish pleasure. He is in conflict with his father partly because they both lust after the same woman, Maria Schell as Grushenka.

Richard Basehart is in revolt because of his intellectual coldness, a rigidity brought on by revulsion at the open and untrammeled sexuality of the old rogue. The third son William Shatner, has chosen his way of survival in contest with his father; he has retreated into the church as a monk. The explosion that these figures ignite comes when Brynn imagines Schell has gone to his father in preference to him.

Brynner succeeds in making his Dmitri a hero despite the fact that every facet of his character is against it. Schell, in her American motion picture debut, illumines her role, seemingly able to suggest innocence and depravity with the same sweet face. Claire Bloom, as the alabaster beauty who saves Brynner from debtors' prison, is very moving particularly in the court scene as her facade cracks from within, rent by bitterness and despair. It is Lee J. Cobb, however, who walks – or rather gallops – away with the picture. The part is gargantuan and it is not a bit too big for the actor.

The Metrocolor used by Brooks and cameraman John Alton is rich in purples, reds and blues.

□ 1958: Nomination: Best Supp. Actor (Lee J. Cobb)

. . . .

■ BROTHER SUN SISTER MOON

1973, 121 MINS, ITALY/ UK ◇ ⓥ

Dir Franco Zeffirelli   *Prod* Luciano Perugia   *Scr* Suso Cecchi D'Amico, Kenneth Ross, Lina Wertmuller, Franco Zeffirelli   *Ph* Ennio Guarnieri   *Ed* Reginald Hills, John Rushton   *Mus* Donovan   *Art Dir* Lorenzo Mongiardino
● Graham Faulkner, Judi Bowker, Alec Guinness, Leigh Lawson, Kenneth Cranham, Michael Feast (Euro International/Vic)

Brother Sun, Sister Moon is a delicate, handsome quasi-fictional biography of one of the great saints of the Catholic Church, Francis of Assisi. Franco Zeffirelli has utilized a style of simple elegance, befitting both the period and the subject.

Graham Faulkner makes an important film debut as Francis of Assisi. Judi Bowker, cast as a young girl who eventually sheds her materialistic existence for religious poverty, is stunningly beautiful, projecting the very essence of innocence.

Evidently edited from original form, the film utilizes flashback to establish briefly Faulkner's early life as a spoiled wastrel, indulged by parents Valentina Cortese and Lee Montague until a rude spiritual awakening in the fevers of wartime pestilence.

Faulkner's character evolution slowly recruits to the humble life of his friends. The illwill of older characters against the growing band of mystics is portrayed with strength.

□ 1973: Nomination: Best Art Direction

. . . .

■ BROWNING VERSION, THE

1951, 90 MINS, UK ⓥ

Dir Anthony Asquith   *Prod* Teddy Baird   *Scr* Terence Rattigan   *Ph* Desmond Dickinson   *Ed* John D. Guthridge   *Art Dir* Carmen Dillon
● Michael Redgrave, Jean Kent, Nigel Patrick, Wilfrid Hyde-White, Brian Smith, Bill Travers (Javelin)

Terence Rattigan's play, which had a big success in the West End in 1948, has been faithfully translated to the screen. The celluloid version is crammed with emotional incidents and has two noteworthy tear-jerker scenes.

The background of the story is an English public school with the action spanning barely 48 hours. It is the last day of term, and Andrew Crocker-Harris, an austere disciplinarian, is retiring because of ill health without a pension. The events leading up to the final, powerful valedictory address make up a plot which is rich in incident and human understanding.

The role of the retiring master is not an easy one, but a prize in the right hands. Michael Redgrave fills it with distinction. Almost matching this performance is the role of his wife, played with a mixture of callousness and coyness by Jean Kent.

Nigel Patrick, in a less bombastic part than usual, chalks up another personal success as the science master who becomes ashamed of the intrigue he has had with Kent. Wilfrid Hyde-White is as smooth as ever as the headmaster.

. . . .

■ BRUBAKER

1980, 130 MINS, US ◇ ⓥ ⊙

Dir Stuart Rosenberg   *Prod* Ron Silverman   *Scr* W.D. Richter   *Ph* Bruno Nuytten   *Ed* Robert Brown   *Mus* Lalo Schifrin   *Art Dir* J. Michael Riva
● Robert Redford, Yaphet Kotto, Jane Alexander, Murray Hamilton, David Keith, Morgan Freeman (20th Century-Fox)

Even with a sharp cast topped by the star power of Robert Redford, it's hard to imagine a broad audience wanting to share the two hours of agony in this one.

For the squeamish, the first half hour is rough going, indeed, as Redford is inducted into a small state prison, isolated in the farmlands near a hamlet.

Joining the ranks, Redford discovers one horror after another. The prison administration is in corrupt cahoots with townspeople, leasing prisoners as slave labor; brutal trustee administer the discipline to fellow convicts, gaining good time for killing some off; minimally decent food and privileges must be bought for cash, with wormy gruel going to those who can't afford it.

□ 1980: Nomination: Best Original Screenplay

. . . .

■ BRUTE FORCE

1947, 94 MINS, US

Dir Jules Dassin   *Prod* Mark Hellinger   *Scr* Richard Brooks   *Ph* William Daniels   *Ed* Edward Curtiss   *Mus* Miklos Rozsa   *Art Dir* Bernard Herzbrun, John F. DeCuir
● Burt Lancaster, Hume Cronyn, Charles Bickford, Yvonne De Carlo, Ann Blyth, Howard Duff (Hellinger/Universal)

A closeup on prison life and prison methods, *Brute Force* is a showmanly mixture of gangster melodramatics, sociological exposition, and sex [from a story by Robert Patterson]. The s.a. elements are plausible and realistic, well within the bounds, but always pointing up the femme fatale. Thus Yvonne De Carlo, Ann Blyth, Ella Raines and Anita Colby are the women on the 'outside' whose machinations, wiles or charms accounted for their men being on the 'inside'.

Burt Lancaster, Charles Bickford, Sam Levene, Howard Duff, Art Smith and Jeff Corey, along with Hume Cronyn as the machinating prison captain (later warden), are the 'inside' cast.

Each of the more prominent criminals has a saga. The flashback technique shows how bookkeeper Whit Bissell embezzled $3,000 to give his ambitious wife (Raines) that mink

coat; how soldier Duff got jammed with the Military Police because of his love for his Italian bride (De Carlo) and through the snivelling skullduggery of her fascistic father; how the sympathetic Lancaster is in love with the invalided Blyth.

Bristling, biting dialog by Richard Brooks paints broad cameos as each character takes shape under existing prison life. Bickford is the wise and patient prison paper editor whose trusty (Levene), has greater freedom in getting 'stories' for the sheet. Cronyn is diligently hateful as the arrogant, brutal captain, with his system of stoolpigeons and bludgeoning methods.

The aspect of an audience rooting for the prisoners plotting a jailbreak is given a sharp turnabout, at the proper time, to point up that brute force by prisoners is as wrong as the brute force exercised by their keepers.

. . . .

■ BUCCANEER, THE

1958, 121 MINS, US ◇ ⓥ ⊙

Dir Anthony Quinn   *Prod* Henry Wilcoxon   *Scr* Jesse L. Lasky Jr, Bernice Mosk   *Ph* Loyal Griggs   *Ed* Archie Marshek   *Mus* Elmer Bernstein   *Art Dir* Hal Pereira, Walter H. Tyler, Albert Nozako
● Yul Brynner, Charlton Heston, Claire Bloom, Charles Boyer, Inger Stevens, E.G. Marshall (Paramount)

Romance is effectively brought in the Cecil B. DeMille-supervised production that focuses on the colorful historical character of Jean Lafitte. On the deficit side is a wordy script that lacks any large degree of excitement. It marks the debut for Anthony Quinn as director.

Continuity-wise, *Buccaneer* is a scrambled affair in the early reels. Open to question, also, are the story angles in the screenplay which derives from a previous *Buccaneer* scenario put out by DeMille in 1938 and, in turn, from an adaptation of the original book, *Lafitte the Pirate*, by Lyle Saxon.

It's the War of 1812 against Britain and the battle area in New Orleans. The action takes place on land except for the sinking of one ship, which is curiously underplayed, by a renegade buccaneer. Highpoint is the land battle between Andrew Jackson's forces and the British, with Jackson aided by Lafitte's personnel and ammunition. The British, like so many toy soldiers, go down in defeat as Lafitte rules the mast.

Yul Brynner is masterly as the pirate. Charlton Heston is a hard, firm Andrew Jackson, who, while mounted on horse, sees the wisdom of making a deal with the pirate Lafitte. Claire Bloom is a fiery creation who alternately hates and loves Lafitte; Charles Boyer is light as Lafitte's aide, and Inger Stevens is properly attractive as Lafitte's true love and daughter of the governor.

□ 1958: Nomination: Best Costume Design

. . . .

■ BUCHANAN RIDES ALONE

1958, 89 MINS, US ◇

Dir Budd Boetticher   *Prod* Harry Joe Brown   *Scr* Charles Lang   *Ph* Lucien Ballard   *Ed* Al Clark   *Mus* [uncredited]   *Art Dir* Robert Boyle
● Randolph Scott, Craig Stevens, Barry Kelley, Peter Whitney, Manuel Rojas, L.Q. Jones (Columbia)

Buchanan Rides Alone is one of those workhorses of saddle opera. Turned out on a relatively modest budget, still it is an honest picture, made with skill and craftsmanship.

Well-paced screenplay, based on a novel [*The Name's Buchanan*] by Jonas Ward, has Randolph Scott as a man more or less innocently involved in the problems of a frontier western border town, as he is passing through to his home in Texas from making his stake in Mexico. He befriends a young Mexican (Manuel Rojas), who kills the town bully. Scott is thrown in jail with Rojas and both are threatened with lynching.

The plotting is tricky, with the local First Family divided among itself by greed and lust for power. Scott plays one member off against another, until the final blow-off.

Scott gives an understated performance, taciturnity relieved by humour and warmth. Craig Stevens is intriguing as a man of mystery; L.Q. Jones is picturesque as an offbeat gunman, and Rojas handles his role with finesse.

....

■ BUDDY BUDDY

1982, 96 MINS, US ◇ ⑰

Dir Billy Wilder *Prod* Jay Weston *Scr* Billy Wilder, I.A.L. Diamond *Ph* Harry Stradling Jr *Ed* Argyle Nelson *Mus* Lalo Schifrin *Art Dir* Daniel A. Lomino
● Jack Lemmon, Walter Matthau, Paula Prentiss, Klaus Kinski, Dana Elcar, Miles Chapin (M-G-M)

The script, based on the [1973] French Jacques Brel-Lino Ventura starrer *L'em-merdeur*, directed by Edouard Molinaro and written by Francis Veber, is one of the rare Wilder projects not initiated by the director himself, and a certain lack of care and even thought permeate the effort, from script to casting to execution.

Abandoned by wife Paula Prentiss, Jack Lemmon is a nebbishy failure who checks into a Riverside hotel to end it all. In the next room is Walter Matthau, a stone-faced grouch and heartless hit man who's preparing to knock off a squealer.

The two men's paths quickly cross and, despite Matthau's claim that 'I'm nobody's friend,' he allows himself to become involved in Lemmon's plight, saving him from suicide attempts and actually driving him to the nearby sex clinic where Prentiss is attempting to achieve the ultimate orgasm under the guidance of oddball therapist Klaus Kinski.

Talented thesps Prentiss and Kinski bear the brunt of hopeless miscasting. Lalo Schifrin's dippy score sounds as if it were concocted in a few minutes for a sitcom pilot.

....

■ BUDDY HOLLY STORY, THE

1978, 113 MINS, US ◇ ⑰ ⊙

Dir Steve Rash *Prod* Fred Bauer *Scr* Robert Gittler *Ph* Stevan Larner *Ed* David Blewitt *Mus* Joe Renzetti *Art Dir* Joel Schiller
● Gary Busey, Don Stroud, Charles Martin Smith, Bill Jordan, Maria Richwine, Conrad Janis (Innovisions/ECA)

The Buddy Holly Story smacks of realism in almost every respect, from the dramaturgy involving Holly and his back-up band, The Crickets, to the verisimilitude of the musical numbers. Latter were recorded live, using 24 tracks, and there was no studio rerecording. It was a gamble that pays off in full, and the Holly repertoire (an extensive one) gives the pic its underlying structure.

Gary Busey not only imparts the driven, perfectionist side of Holly's character, but his vocal work is excellent, as is his instrumentation.

Robert Gittler's screenplay [from a story by Alan Swyer] takes Holly from his early days in Lubbock, Texas, where he churns out be-bop for the roller rink crowd, through his disastrous recording career (he punches out a Nashville producer), and up through national recognition on the heels of his big hit, 'That'll Be the Day'.

Along the way, director Steve Rash zeroes in on the growing conflict between Busey, drummer Don Stroud and bassist Charles Martin Smith, and the love relationship of Busey and Maria Richwine as his Puerto Rican bride. All principals register strongly.
□ 1978: Best Adapted Score.
□ Nominations: Best Actor (Gary Busey), Sound

....

■ BUFFALO BILL AND THE INDIANS OR SITTING BULL'S HISTORY LESSON

1976, 123 MINS, US ◇ ⑰

Dir Robert Altman *Prod* Robert Altman *Scr* Alan Rudolph, Robert Altman *Ph* Paul Lohmann *Ed* Peter Appleton, Dennis Hill *Mus* Richard Baskin
Art Dir Tony Masters
● Paul Newman, Joel Grey, Kevin McCarthy, Harvey Keitel, Allan Nicholls, Geraldine Chaplin (De Laurentiis/Lion's Gate)

It appears that the idea here is to expose and debunk the Buffalo Bill legend, revealing it for the promotional distortion which, in some ways, it most certainly has to have been. Project was shot completely in Alberta.

Film [based on the play *Indians* by Arthur Kopit] shows Paul Newman bumbling through the challenge of living up to a legend created by Burt Lancaster, regularly popping up with bartender Bert Remsen in scenes of verbal recall. Joel Grey is Newman's current showman partner, while Kevin McCarthy grinds out the press agent claptrap.

The serious plot note is the determination of Sitting Bull (played very well in total silence by Frank Kaquitts) and interpreter Will Sampson not to debase history through cheap carny melodrama.

....

■ BUFFY THE VAMPIRE SLAYER

1992, 86 MINS, US ◇ ⑰ ⊙

Dir Fran Rubel Kuzui *Prod* Kaz Kuzui, Howard Rosenman *Scr* Joss Whedon *Ph* James Hayman *Ed* Camilla Toniolo, Jill Savitt *Mus* Carter Burwell *Art Dir* Lawrence Miller
● Kristy Swanson, Donald Sutherland, Paul Reubens, Rutger Hauer, Luke Perry, Michele Abrams (20th Century Fox/Sandollar/Kuzui)

Buffy the Vampire Slayer is a bloodless comic resurrection of the undead that goes serious just when it should get wild and woolly. The marginal buoyancy of the opening reels quickly disappears from this threadbare (reportedly only $7 million) production, more effective as a sendup of Valley girls than as a clever take on bloodsuckers.

Blonde, bouncy Buffy (Kristy Swanson) is lead cheerleader and Miss Popular in the senior class at Hemery High. A dirty old man in a long overcoat (Donald Sutherland) turns up to inform Buffy that she is a female vampire slayer, and she passes her trial by fire with flying colors when she subdues two marauding cretins.

When it becomes apparent that L.A. is under threat of a serious vampire invasion led by king Rutger Hauer and cackling henchman Paul Reubens, Buffy dives into an Olympian workout regimen to sharpen her skills with a stake. After biting a few teens and menacing Buffy and her would-be b.f. (Luke Perry), the vampires crash a high school dance in a limp rehash of the big set-piece in *Carrie*.

Swanson has a robust, athletic sexiness that will keep boy viewers happy, while the amiable Perry, in his first screen appearance since hitting with *Beverly Hills, 90210*, will make this a must-see for many adolescent girls.

Director Fran Rubel Kuzui, whose previous credit was the so-so indie *Tokyo Pop*, keeps her camera subjects very close to the lens and aims to accomplish no more than one piece of action per shot.

....

■ BUG

1975, 99 MINS, US ◇ ⑰

Dir Jeannot Szwarc *Prod* William Castle *Scr* William Castle, Thomas Page *Ph* Michael Hugo *Ed* Allan Jacobs *Mus* Charles Fox *Art Dir* Jack Martin Smith
● Bradford Dillman, Joanna Miles, Richard Gilliland, Jamie Smith Jackson, Alan Fudge, Jesse Vint (Paramount)

Bug concerns some mutated cockroaches liberated by an earthquake from the earth's

core. Adapted from Thomas Page's book, *The Hephaestus Plague*, it starts off well with an earthquake in a farmland town, after which mysterious fires begin breaking out. The bugs, being from underground areas, are hot and eat carbon.

Bradford Dillman, an animal scientist, gets intrigued with them, so much so that, after wife Miles is incinerated in a bug attack, he becomes a recluse with the creatures and communicates with them. At the same time Dillman goes into seclusion, so does the film; its last half is largely static, and the film never revives much interest.

....

■ BUGSY

1991, 135 MINS, US ◇ ⑰ ⊙

Dir Barry Levinson *Prod* Mark Johnson, Barry Levinson, Warren Beatty *Scr* James Toback *Ph* Allen Daviau *Ed* Stu Linder *Mus* Ennio Morricone *Art Dir* Dennis Gassner
● Warren Beatty, Annette Bening, Harvey Keitel, Ben Kingsley, Elliott Gould, Joe Mantegna (Tri-Star/Mulholland/Baltimore)

A melancholy and intimate gangster saga about a romantic dreamer with fatal flaws, *Bugsy* emerges as a smooth, safe portrait of a volatile, dangerous character. An absorbing narrative flow and a parade of colorful underworld characters view for screen time with an unsatisfactory central romance.

Handsome pic about the inventor of Las Vegas tells how Benjamin Siegel (Warren Beatty) was sent to LA to take over the West Coast rackets but stayed to become one of the legendary Hollywood characters of the 1940s.

Siegel is a terrific subject for a film, but only part of the story comes across in this intelligently conceived drama. In James Toback's writing and Beatty's gutsy playing, Bugsy bursts out as a fully realized, psychologically complex character endowed with very human strengths and weaknesses. Unfortunately, his great love and female counterpart, Virginia Hill (Annette Bening), remains a one-dimensional and annoying stick figure, throwing great sections of the film out of whack.

Director Barry Levinson treats this punchy, emotionally eruptive story in fluid, almost dreamy fashion, rather like a sordid fairy tale. Although ethnically wrong and lacking a street-tough attitude, Beatty gives a dynamic performance, his most vital and surprising in a long time.

Among the standouts in the impressive supporting cast are Harvey Keitel as a feisty, appealing Mickey Cohen; Ben Kingsley as the impeccably businesslike Meyer Lansky; and director Richard Sarafian as the pathetic Jack Dragna; Elliott Gould effectively underplays the weak squealer Harry Greenberg. Joe Mantegna is oddly cast as George Raft.
□ 1991: Best Art Direction, Costume Design.
□ Nominations: Best Picture, Director, Actor (Warren Beatty), Supp. Actor (Harvey Keitel, Ben Kingsley), Original Screenplay, Cinematography, Original Score

....

■ BUGSY MALONE

1976, 93 MINS, UK ◇ ⑰ ⊙

Dir Alan Parker *Prod* Alan Marshall *Scr* Alan Parker *Ph* Michael Seresin, Peter Biziou *Ed* Gerry Hambling *Mus* Dave Garland (dir.) *Art Dir* Geoffrey Kirkland
● Scott Baio, Jodie Foster, Florrie Dugger, John Cassisi, Martin Lev, Paul Murphy (Goodtimes)

Set in 1929 Gotham, pic is a compendium of gangster/Prohibition pic situations and cliches, played tongue-in-cheek by a splendid cast of juves, a veritable casting treasure trove.

Jodie Foster is outstanding as a moll, but so are Scott Baio as Bugsy, John Cassisi as Fat Sam, Florrie Dugger as Blousey, Martin Lev as Dandy Dan, Paul Murphy and Albin Jenkins as, respectively, Leroy and Fizzy. Plus many others.

Writer-director Alan Parker deserves much of the credit for concept and execution, with Paul Williams sharing the spotlight on the strength of his songs (music and lyrics), all pleasantly reminiscent and tinkly.

In short, it's a brave, fun and winning pic which is nearly – but regrettably not quite – a triumph.

☐ 1976: Nomination: Best Adapted Score

. . . .

■ BUILD MY GALLOWS HIGH
See: Out of the Past

. . . .

■ BULLDOG DRUMMOND

1929, 80 MINS, US ⊛

Dir F. Richard Jones   *Prod* Samuel Goldwyn
Scr Sidney Howard   *Ph* George S. Barnes, Gregg Toland
Ed Frank Lawrence, Viola Lawrence   *Mus* [uncredited]
Art Dir William Cameron Menzies
● Ronald Colman, Claude Allister, Joan Bennett, Lilyan Tashman, Lawrence Grant, Montagu Love (Goldwyn)

Entertaining picture of the highly charged thriller meller kind, mostly because of the likable performance of Ronald Colman in his first screamer. As a picture it's intense, with the suspense often and sharply broken into for a laugh by a fop Englishman of the common stage type.

Adapted from the English stage play, many scenes are on the screen that could not have been set upon a stage. Bulldog Drummond is an idler looking for excitement. He gets it by saving the grandfather of a strange young woman from an insane asylum's crooks.

Play appears to have been pretty faithfully followed. Samuel Goldwyn gives the story a good production in all ways, with F. Richard Jones expertly handling the direction.

Lilyan Tashman is the she-devil. She takes her whisky straight. Lawrence Grant plays the fiendish doctor and well enough. Joan Bennett, the new lead, is oke on the looks side. She seems held down here, probably through inexperience.

☐ 1929/30: Nomination: Best Art Direction

. . . .

■ BULL DURHAM

1988, 108 MINS, US ◇ ⊛ ⊙

Dir Ron Shelton   *Prod* Thom Mount, Mark Burg
Scr Ron Shelton   *Ph* Bobby Byrne   *Ed* Robert Leighton, Adam Weiss   *Mus* Michael Convertino   *Art Dir* Armin Ganz
● Kevin Costner, Susan Sarandon, Tim Robbins, Trey Wilson, Robert Wuhl, Jenny Robertson (Mount/Orion)

Bull Durham is a fanciful and funny bush league sports story where the only foul ball is its overuse of locker-room dialog. Kevin Costner is the quintessential American male who loves romance, but loves baseball even more.

The Durham Bull of North Carolina dream of getting called up to be 'in the show' as they endure another season of riding town to town on the team bus and suffering the dubious distinction of being one of the losingest clubs in Carolina league history.

Sent over from another 'A' farm team to instruct, insult and inspire the Bulls' bullet-fast pitcher Ebby Calvin 'Nuke' Laloosh (Tim Robbins) is embittered veteran catcher Crash David (Kevin Costner). His job is to get the cocky kid's arm on target by game time.

Costner is a natural as the dyed-in-the-wool ballplayer. His best lines are when he's philosophizing, like on being an All-American male who hates anything by Susan Sontag.

Susan Sarandon is never believable as a community college English lit teacher who, at the start of every season, latches on to the most promising rookie – in this case Robbins.

☐ 1988: Nomination: Best Original Screenplay

. . . .

■ BULLETS OR BALLOTS

1936, 68 MINS, US ⊛

Dir William Keighley   *Prod* [Lou Edelman]   *Scr* Seton I. Miller   *Ph* Hal Mohr   *Ed* Jack Killifer   *Mus* Leo F. Forbstein (dir.)   *Art Dir* Carl Jules Weyl
● Edward G. Robinson, Joan Blondell, Humphrey Bogart, Barton MacLane, Frank McHugh, Joseph Keen (Warner/Frank McHugh)

This is a fast, smooth-working action picture. Story formula is along usual lines, with news events liberally sprinkled throughout. Martin Mooney, a New York reporter who got himself some front-page attention with a series of racketeering yarns in his newspaper, [is credited with co-writing the screen story with Seton I. Miller].

Edward G. Robinson bows out on his Warner contract in this picture with one of his most virile he-man characterizations. He's Johnny Blake, a tough but honest dick, duplicating the methods and mannerisms of an actual NY dick. Al Kruger (Barton MacLane), obviously based on Dutch Schultz, is the racketeer king who has everything beautifully organized.

Director William Keighley keeps the picture moving and real at all times. MacLane is tops, with the role neatly paralleled by the work of Humphrey Bogart as a first aid and a convicing menace. Joan Blondell is dragged in by the heels as a sort of minor romance note for Robinson, but not too emphasized.

. . . .

■ BULLFIGHTER AND THE LADY

1951, 87 MINS, US ⊛ ⊙

Dir Budd Boetticher   *Prod* John Wayne   *Scr* James Edward Grant   *Ph* Jack Draper   *Ed* Richard L. Van Enger   *Mus* Victor Young   *Art Dir* Alfred Ybarra
● Robert Stack, Joy Page, Gilbert Roland, Virginia Grey, John Hubbard, Katy Jurado (Republic)

Producer John Wayne and associate producer-director Budd Boetticher evidence a fondness for the Mexican scene through care in which they bring it accurately to the screen. Use of Robert Stack as an American vacationing below the border brings the plot and development closer to the Stateside audience and gives an understanding insight into the art of bullfighting and why it is the favorite Mexican pastime.

Stack falls in love with Joy Page's high-born Mexican girl. To impress her, he induces Gilbert Roland's matador idol to instruct him in the use of the cape and sword. Stack begins to feel the urge and thrill of the art but, in a careless, showoff moment, he causes Roland's death when the latter tries to save him. To atone, Stack fights another bull in honor of his friend.

The story [by Boetticher and Ray Nazarro] comes off much better in the viewing than in the telling as Boetticher keeps it punching at all times. A particular standout is Roland. Without overplaying, he gives his matador character color and vigor, bravery without bravado, and dignity.

☐ 1951: Nomination: Best Motion Picture Story

. . . .

■ BULLITT

1968, 113 MINS, US ◇ ⊛ ⊙

Dir Peter Yates   *Prod* Philip D'Antoni   *Scr* Alan R. Trustman, Harry Kleiner   *Ph* William A. Fraker   *Ed* Frank P. Keller   *Mus* Lalo Schifrin   *Art Dir* Albert Brenner
● Steve McQueen, Robert Vaughn, Jacqueline Bisset, Don Gordon, Robert Duvall, Simon Oakland (Warner/Seven Arts)

Conflict between police sleuthing and political expediency is the essence of *Bullitt*, an extremely well-made crime melodrama filmed in Frisco. Steve McQueen delivers a very strong performance as a detective seeking a man whom Robert Vaughn, ambitious politico, would exploit for selfish motives. Good scripting and excellent direction by Peter Yates maintain deliberately low-key but mounting suspense.

Arrival in Frisco of a Chi hood cues assignment of McQueen, plus assistants Don Gordon and Carol Reindel, to protect his life until headline-hunting Vaughn produces him dramatically before a senate crime committee. Hood's death, at the hands of Paul Genge, provokes the primary dramatic conflict: Vaughn wants a live witness, while McQueen is interested in apprehending the killer.

Simon Oakland, McQueen's superior, lets him pursue the case independently, while Vaughn, with aid from another senior detective, Norman Fell, is after independent sleuth's scalp.

☐ 1968: Best Editing.
☐ Nomination: Best Sound

. . . .

■ BUNNY LAKE IS MISSING

1965, 107 MINS, UK ⊛

Dir Otto Preminger   *Prod* Otto Preminger   *Scr* John Mortimer, Penelope Mortimer   *Ph* Denys Coop   *Ed* Peter Thornton   *Mus* Paul Glass   *Art Dir* Don Ashton
● Carol Lynley, Keir Dullea, Laurence Olivier, Noel Coward, Martita Hunt, Anna Massey (Columbia/Wheel)

Bunny Lake is about the only thing missing from Otto Preminger's exercise in suspense and the viewer is kept in uncertainty about her for most of the film. What Preminger has achieved is an entertaining, fast-paced exercise in the exploration of a sick mind. Evelyn Piper's 1957 novel dealt entirely with the unpredictable actions of a mother searching for her child (real or imaginary) who had disappeared. To this plot skeleton Preminger has added an equally important character whose predictable actions provide the search's principal obstacles.

Carrying much of the film on her shoulders, Carol Lynley, as the mother shoved into a state of near hysteria almost from the beginning, is outstanding.

Keir Dullea, as her brother, most effective in earlier scenes where he conveys the natural, if easily-aroused, anger of a devoted brother.

Laurence Olivier's police inspector, is played in the manner of a psychiatrist. While nothing more than a routine role, Olivier does give it dignity and purpose and makes it a calm and restful contrast to the highly-strung emoting of Dullea and Lynley.

. . . .

■ BUONA SERA, MRS. CAMPBELL

1968, 111 MINS, ITALY ◇

Dir Melvin Frank   *Prod* Melvin Frank   *Scr* Melvin Frank, Shelden Keller, Dennis Norden   *Ph* Gabor Pogany   *Ed* William Butler   *Mus* Riz Ortolani   *Art Dir* Arrigo Equini
● Gina Lollobrigida, Shelley Winters, Phil Silvers, Peter Lawford, Telly Savalas, Janet Margolin (United Artists/Connaught)

Buona Sera, Mrs. Campbell is a very entertaining comedy with solid, personal, human values. Story is about an Italian woman who has conned three American bed partners from World War II into support of her and an illegitimate daughter for more than 20 years.

Gina Lollobrigida, Shelley Winters, Phil Silvers, Peter Lawford, Telly Savalas and Lee Grant head an excellent cast.

Story is economically laid forth: Lollobrigida has fooled her neighbors into believing daughter Janet Margol was by a deceased US Air Force pilot. However, a reunion of the airmen, in the town where they were based, precipitates a potential crisis, since, in truth, the real father could have been Silvers, Lawford or Savalas.

Performances are strong: Lollobrigida, no comedy actress, is one here. Winters and Grant are great; Silvers and all the others are just right.

• •

■ 'BURBS, THE

1989, 103 MINS, US ◇ ⓥ ⊙
Dir Joe Dante   *Prod* Larry Brezner, Michael Finnell
Scr Dana Olsen   *Ph* Robert Stevens   *Ed* Marshall Harvey   *Mus* Jerry Goldsmith   *Art Dir* James Spencer
● Tom Hanks, Bruce Dern, Carrie Fisher, Rick Ducommun, Corey Feldman, Henry Gibson (Imagine/Universal)

Director Joe Dante funnels his decidedly cracked view of suburban life through dark humour in *The 'Burbs.* The action never strays beyond the cozy confines of the nightmarish block everyman Ray (Tom Hanks) inhabits along with an uproarious assemblage of wacky neighbors.

Poor Ray has a week off and just wants to spend it quietly at home with his wife Carol (Carrie Fisher). Instead, he's drawn into an increasingly elaborate sleuthing game involving the mysterious Klopeks, who reside in a 'Munsters'-esque house rife with indications of foul play.

Ray's more familiar neighbors are equally bizarre: the corpulent Art (Rick Ducommun), convinced the Klopeks are performing satanic sacrifices; Rumsfield (Bruce Dern), a shell-shocked ex-GI; Walter (Gale Gordon), who delights in letting his dog relieve himself on Rumsfield's lawn; and Ricky (Corey Feldman) a teenager who sees all the strange goings-on as viewing fodder for parties with his friends.

Hanks does a fine impersonation of a regular guy on the verge of a nervous breakdown, while Dern adds another memorable psychotic to his resume. The big breakthroughs, however, are Ducommun, superb in a role that would have well-suited John Candy; and Wendy Schaal as Dern's airhead wife.

• •

■ BURGLAR, THE

1957, 90 MINS, US
Dir Paul Wendkos   *Prod* Louis W. Kellman   *Scr* David Goodis   *Ph* Don Malkames   *Ed* Paul Wendkos
Mus Sol Kaplan   *Art Dir* Jim Leonard
● Dan Duryea, Jayne Mansfield, Martha Vickers, Peter Capell, Mickey Shaughnessy, Wendell Phillips (Kellman)

Dan Duryea, Jayne Mansfield and Martha Vickers manage to overcome handicaps posed by David Goodis' scripting and Paul Wendkos' direction to rate an okay for performance. The same can't be said for other casters, most of whom are permitted to overact to the point of oldtime scenery-chewing, especially radio's Peter Capell in his role as a member of Duryea's burglar gang.

Novel opening is a newsreel-type prolog, in which Duryea spots a necklace he wants. Plot then moves into the story, goes through the heist of the jewels from the mansion of a Philadelphia spiritualist, followed by the gang's holing-up in a battered old house while the police look for clues and set law-enforcement machinery into work.

Basic story idea, taken from Goodis' novel of the same title, is okay, but suspense and action are by-passed and sloughed while the assorted characters go into long soliloquizing about how they got into their various predicaments.

Don Malkames' lensing pays attention to highspots of the Philadelphia-Atlantic City locales while helping story mood.

• •

■ BURKE AND WILLS

1985, 140 MINS, AUSTRALIA ◇ ⓥ ⊙
Dir Graeme Clifford   *Prod* Graeme Clifford
Scr Michael Thomas   *Ph* Russell Boyd   *Ed* Tim Wellburn
Mus Peter Sculthorpe   *Art Dir* Ross Major
● Jack Thompson, Nigel Havers, Greta Scacchi, Matthew Fargher, Ralph Cotterill, Drew Forsythe (Hoyts Edgley)

Big in scope, and emotionally stimulating, this Australian pic about the doomed 1860 expedition of explorers Burke and Wills to cross the continent and back, is satisfying entertainment despite its length and seemingly downbeat subject.

That the story emerges quite differently on film is very much to the credit of director Graeme Clifford and screenwriter Michael Thomas, two expatriate Australians.

Russell Boyd's superior cinematography, on the locations originally traversed by the explorers, is quite ravishing. Clifford shrewdly inserts flashbacks into the desert material evoking scenes of Wills at home in England and Burke's dalliance with a comely opera singer.

Jack Thompson, with full beard, is an imposing Burke, a fiery-tempered Irishman whose determination to succeed clouds his judgment. This is one of Thompson's best performances. British actor Nigel Havers is excellent as the scientist, Wills, stubbornly following his friend into the unknown while barely concealing his fears for the outcome.

• •

■ BURNING SECRET

1989, 106 MINS, UK/US/W. GERMANY ◇ ⓥ ⊙
Dir Andrew Birkin   *Prod* Norma Heyman, Eberhard Junkersdorf, Carol Lynn Greene   *Scr* Andrew Birkin
Ph Ernest Day   *Ed* Paul Green   *Mus* Hans Zimmer
Art Dir Bernd Lepel
● Faye Dunaway, Klaus Maria Brandauer, David Eberts, Ian Richardson (NFH/CLG/BA)

Burning Secret is the intriguing story of a mother's near-adultery as seen through the impressionable eyes of her 12-year-old son, coupled with the elegant setting of post-World War I Austria in winter.

First-time director Andrew Birkin (brother of France-based actress Jane Birkin) has adapted a Stefan Zweig short story [*Brennendes Geheimnis*] set in 1919 and previously filmed in Germany in 1933 by Robert Siodmak. Drama has some of the same elements found in Zweig's more famous story, *Letter from an Unknown Woman.*

The woman is Sonya (Faye Dunaway), elegant wife of a stuffy diplomat (Ian Richardson) far older than she. When their young son, who suffers severely from asthma, is sent for treatment at a sanitorium in the mountains, the mother accompanies him.

On the first morning, the son meets Baron Alexander Maria von Hauenschild (Klaus Maria Bradenauer), a charming veteran of the war. Sonya is quite willing to seize the opportunity of a passionate love affair which is only constrained by the constant presence of her innocent, inquisitive son.

Although the material is a little slight, the drama works thanks to the flawless performances. Dunaway is coolly stylish and yet passionate. Brandauer brings a touch of menace to his charming character. Young David Eberts (son of former Goldcrest exec Jake Eberts) is a find as the trusting youngster. The production was filmed entirely in Czechoslovakia, on location in Prague (doubling for Vienna) and Marienbad.

• •

■ BUS RILEY'S BACK IN TOWN

1965, 93 MINS, US ◇
Dir Harvey Hart   *Prod* Elliott Kastner   *Scr* Walter Gage
Ph Russell Metty   *Ed* Folmar Blangsted   *Mus* Richard Markowitz   *Art Dir* Alexander Golitzen, Frank Arrigo

● Ann-Margret, Michael Parks, Janet Margolin, Brad Dexter, Jocelyn Brando, Larry Storch (Universal)

Where to pinpoint the blame for this well-intended major feature's failure is difficult. Certainly some of it must be allotted to former TV-director Harvey Hart's inexperience with the bigger-screen medium, and his lack of control over several of the thespians involved, but the erratic, chopped-up screenplay is also a major fault. Originally announced as the work of William Inge, screen credit is now given to Walter Gage, evidently a pseudonym for the several studio writers who had a go at it. Bits of Inge remain.

The story centers on the title character, played by newcomer Michael Parks. He tends to rely overmuch on 'method' methods – the tightly-constricted gesture, the stammer, the withdrawn, hunched-shoulder, hooded-eye type of acting that is rarely effective on the wide screen. Fortunately, Parks responds to the interplay provided by a bona fide talent. His scenes with Janet Margolin are his best, those with Ann-Margret, his poorest.

A simple plot – young ex-servicem seeking an identity and faced with the problem of succumbing to the wiles of bad girl (Ann-Margret) or meeting responsibility head on (with implied support of good girl).

• •

■ BUS STOP

1956, 96 MINS, US ◇ ⓥ ⊙
Dir Joshua Logan   *Prod* Buddy Adler   *Scr* George Axelrod   *Ph* Milton Krasner   *Ed* William Reynolds
Mus Alfred Newman, Cyril Mockridge, Ken Darby
● Marilyn Monroe, Don Murray, Arthur O'Connell, Betty Field, Eileen Heckart, Hope Lange (20th Century-Fox)

William Inge's rowdy play about a cowboy and a lady (sic) gets a raucous screen treatment. Both the scripter and director, George Axelrod and Joshua Logan respectively, were brought from the legit field to get the Inge comedy on film and, with a few minor exceptions, bring the chore off resoundingly.

New face Don Murray is the exuberant young cowhand who comes to the city to win some rodeo money and learn about women.

Marilyn Monroe fans will find her s.a. not so positive, but still potent, in her *Bus Stop* character, but this goes with the type of well-used saloon singer and would-be actress she portrays. Monroe comes off acceptably, even though failing to maintain any kind of consistency in the Southern accent.

Murr is a 21-year-old Montana rancher who comes to Phoenix for the rodeo, meets and kisses his first girl and literally kidnaps her. The girl, a 'chantoosie' in a cheap restaurant patronized by rodeo performers, is reluctant about marriage, but by the time Murray ropes her, shouts at her, and gets beat up for her, she gives in, both because love has set in, as well as physical exhaustion.

Arthur O'Connell milks everything from his spot as Murray's friend and watchdog and Betty Field clicks big as the amorous operator of the roadside bus stop.

☐ 1956: Nomination: Best Supp. Actor (Don Murray)

• •

■ BUSTER

1988, 103 MINS, UK ◇ ⓥ ⊙
Dir David Green   *Prod* Norma Heyman   *Scr* David Shindler   *Ph* Tony Imi   *Ed* Lesley Walker   *Mus* Anne Dudley   *Art Dir* Simon Holland
● Phil Collins, Julie Walters, Larry Lamb, Stephanie Lawrence, Ellen Beaven, Michael Attwell (NFH/Movie Group/Hemdale)

Buster is part romantic comedy, part crime thriller and part moral tale, but more importantly it features a charismatic big screen bow by popster Phil Collins in the title role.

Pic opens in London of 1963 with self-proclaimed smalltime 'lucky thief' Collins and

Julie Walters blissfully happy. Collins gets involved in a scheme to rob a Royal Mail train of £2.6 million, and when the gang pulls off the raid, hailed as The Great Train Robbery, they find themselves regarded as folk heroes.

Collins, wife Walters and daughter Ellen Beaven go into hiding, but police pressure mounts and the family is forced to go on the run to Switzerland and finally Acapulco. In Mexico, the Collins-Walters marriage is stretched.

Buster can't seem to make up its mind what sort of film it is. It plays as a romantic comedy to begin with, then switches to a caper pic before ending with domestic drama. Helmer David Green directs all aspects well, adding nice insights into the characters, especially when in Mexico, but there is an overall feeling that the pic is slightly disjointed.
☐ 1988: Nomination: Best Song ('Two Hearts')

■ BUSTER AND BILLIE

1974, 98 MINS, US ◇ ⓥ
Dir Daniel Petrie   *Prod* Ron Silverman   *Scr* Ron Turbeville   *Ph* Mario Tosi   *Ed* Michael Kahn   *Mus* Al De Lory
● Jan-Michael Vincent, Joan Goodfellow, Pamela Sue Martin, Clifton James, Robert Englund, Jessie Lee Fulton (Columbia)

Nostalgia gets another workout in *Buster and Billie*. Screenplay, conventionally directed by Daniel Petrie, has a good deal of charm and veristic detail until its romantic tale crashes in a last-reel melee of unmotivated violence.

On the surface pic is just 1948 Georgia graffiti. Jan-Michael Vincent and Pamela Sue Martin are the town sweethearts, petting heavily in his truck but delaying further action until their imminent wedding day. Meanwhile, the stags all get theirs from Joan Goodfellow, a rather dumpy blonde from the other side of the tracks.

Feeling more frustrated than usual, Vincent also pays the glumly obliging Goodfellow a visit one night, the finds himself falling in love with her.

The slim plot raises psychological questions that could have been profitably explored.

■ BUSTING

1974, 91 MINS, US ◇ ⓥ
Dir Peter Hyams   *Prod* Irwin Winkler, Robert Chartoff   *Scr* Peter Hyams   *Ph* Earl Rath   *Ed* James Mitchell   *Mus* Billy Goldenberg   *Art Dir* [uncredited]
● Elliott Gould, Robert Blake, Allen Garfield, Antonio Fargas, Sid Haig, Michael Lerner (United Artists)

Elliott Gould and Robert Blake star as vagrant vice squad detectives, the kind who in real life set law and order back decades. Production is confused, compromised and clumsy.

The plot eventually gets around to blaming nearly every criminal activity in town on Allen Garfield, cast as a local crime lord. Garfield, as ever an outstanding performer, brings dignity and a sense of being totally together to the part.

Atop the script problems is overlaid some embarrassingly forced direction by debuting Peter Hyams, a former TV newsman. In particular the crutch of an incessant slowly tracking camera, as though a pile of debris looks any different (or better) from assorted angles. There are a couple of well-staged vehicle chases which for a few minutes divert attention from the story.

■ BUSTIN' LOOSE

1981, 94 MINS, US ◇ ⓥ ⊙
Dir Oz Scott   *Prod* Richard Pryor, Michael S. Glick   *Scr* Roger L. Simon   *Ph* Dennis Dalzell   *Ed* David

Holden   *Mus* Mark Davis   *Art Dir* Charles R. Davis, John Corso
● Richard Pryor, Cicely Tyson, Robert Christian, Alphonso Alexander, Janet Wong (Universal)

Bustin' Loose is obviously a personal project for Pryor, who produced and wrote the story, which has admirable ambitions but is also the film's greatest weakness.

Still, Pryor is an infectious comedian and a master of body language, keeping the picture on the move with sheer energy. He's a bungling burglar but good mechanic whose parole officer (Robert Christian) forces him to go to the aid of Cicely Tyson, the director of a school for emotionally disturbed children about to close for lack of money.

She wants to flee Philly with eight of the kids and get to her family farm near Seattle. There's a bit of the *African Queen* to this journey as the prissy, prim and dominant Tyson and vulgar, unkempt Pryor find their initial hostility turning to romance.

On the way, it's the constant breakdowns of the bus, the impatience with the kids and other obstacles – including a hilarious encounter with the Ku Klux Klan – that feed Pryor his material and he makes the most of it.

This is a feature debut for Broadway director Oz Scott and he handles the chore comfortably.

■ BUTCH AND SUNDANCE THE EARLY DAYS

1979, 110 MINS, US ◇ ⓥ ⊙
Dir Richard Lester   *Prod* Gabriel Katzka, Steven Bach   *Scr* Allan Burns   *Ph* Laszlo Kovacs   *Ed* Antony Gibbs, George Trirogoff   *Mus* Patrick Williams   *Art Dir* Brian Eatwell
● William Katt, Tom Berenger, Brian Dennehy, Peter Weller, Jeff Corey, Jill Eikenberry (20th Century-Fox/Pantheon)

This prequel doesn't match its progenitor in either casting or style. Without Paul Newman or Robert Redford in the title roles, it doesn't matter whether *Butch* dwells on the pair's infancy or senility – there's no star chemistry. Tom Berenger and William Katt acquit themselves admirably, but they simply can't compete with the ghosts of two superstars.

Butch is standard sagebrush material, with few of the comic misadventures that characterized the original. There are some patented Richard Lester hijinks in the first half-hour of the prequel, but these peter out surprisingly soon.
☐ 1979: Nomination: Best Costume Design

■ BUTCH CASSIDY AND THE SUNDANCE KID

1969, 112 MINS, US ◇ ⓥ ⊙
Dir George Roy Hill   *Prod* John Foreman   *Scr* William Goldman   *Ph* Conrad Hall   *Ed* John C. Howard, Richard C. Meyer   *Mus* Burt Bacharach   *Art Dir* Jack Martin Smith, Philip Jefferies
● Paul Newman, Robert Redford, Katharine Ross, Strother Martin, Jeff Corey, Cloris Leachman (20th Century-Fox/Campanile)

Lighthearted treatment of a purportedly-true story of the two badmen who made Wyoming outlaw history, film emerges a near-comedy of errors.

Newman plays Butch, one of the most deadly outlaws of the West whose gang variously was known as The Wild Bunch and Hole-in-the-Wall Gang. Robert Redford portrays the Kid, wizard with a gun.

Butch is an affable, almost gay, individual who can turn on the power when he wishes but usually is a sociable, talkative sort of cuss; Redford, silent, menacing in the power of his fabled guns, displays no evidence of the evil temper which gained him his reputation.

Together, they make a fine team, accompanied by frequent banter.

Narrative starts in Wyoming where Butch and his gang are involved in various train holdups and pursuits by posses after bank robberies.

This leads to Butch and the Kid trying their luck in Bolivia.
☐ 1969: Best Original Story & Screenplay, Cinematography, Song ('Raindrops Keep Fallin' on My Head'), Original Score.
☐ Nominations: Best Picture, Director, Sound

■ BUTCHER'S WIFE, THE

1991, 104 MINS, US ◇ ⓥ ⊙ ⊙
Dir Terry Hughes   *Prod* Wallis Nicita, Lauren Lloyd   *Scr* Ezra Litwak, Marjorie Schwartz   *Ph* Frank Tidy   *Ed* Donn Cambern   *Mus* Michael Gore   *Art Dir* Charles Rosen
● Demi Moore, Jeff Daniels, George Dzundza, Mary Steenburgen, Frances McDormand, Margaret Colin (Paramount)

A gentle romantic comedy with a distinct 1940s flavor, *The Butcher's Wife* is blessed with a fine cast working from a storybook plot. The unpretentious and simple film has a 'make 'em weep like they used to' quality. Its belief in modern-day magic (in a sense similar to *Moonstruck*) softens an inherent predictability dictating that all loose ends be resolved to everyone's satisfaction in 100 minutes.

Demi Moore plays a country clairvoyant whose visions of romance are answered the surprising form of a New York butcher (George Dzundza) whom she marries immediately, returning with him to his neighborhood. Her visions immediately start to touch all those who cross her path, in the process increasingly nettling the local psychologist (Jeff Daniels), whose patients seem to need him far less as they bathe in the comfort of Moore's future gazing.

Those who encounter Moore include the shrink's girlfriend (Margaret Colin), a dowdy patient (Mary Steenburgen) with aspirations to sing the blues, and lesbian friend (Frances McDormand), who's told romance waits just around the corner.

Helmer Terry Hughes, a TV director, and first-time screenwriters bring a fresh, uncynical eye to familiar terrain. Pic's only real revelation is Steenburgen, not for her considerable acting skills, but for her fine voice in a trio of bluesy ballads.

■ BUTLEY

1974, 129 MINS, UK/US/CANADA ◇
Dir Harold Pinter   *Prod* Ely Landau   *Scr* Simon Gray   *Ph* Gerry Fisher   *Ed* Malcolm Cooke   *Art Dir* Carmen Dillon
● Alan Bates, Jessica Tandy, Richard O'Callaghan, Susan Engel, Michael Byrne, Georgina Hale (American Express/Landau)

Alan Bates' stage triumph in Simon Gray's *Butley* has been superbly recreated on the screen, with the added excellence of Harold Pinter's topnotch film directorial debut. It reunites both Richard O'Callaghan and Michael Byrne from the original London production.

The plot basically is one horrendous day in the life of an embittered teacher, who loses his estranged wife to a lesser professional colleague, his lover to another man, and his sense of superiority over a female associate whose lifelong book project has been accepted for publication while his lies unfinished.

Jessica Tandy, a middle-aged teacher who doesn't seem to understand her modern students, is excellent in projection of both a dedicated instructor and a skilled academic politician.

BUTTERCUP CHAIN, THE

1970, 95 MINS, UK ◇
Dir Robert Ellis Miller   *Prod* John Whitney, Philip
Waddilove   *Scr* Peter Draper   *Ph* Douglas Slocombe
Ed Thelma Conneli   *Mus* Richard Rodney Bennett
Art Dir Wilfrid Shingleton
● Hywel Bennett, Leigh Taylor-Young, Jane Asher, Sven-
Bertil Taube, Clive Revill, Roy Dotrice (Columbia)

The story's somewhat contrived and over glib.
Even superficial. But it is directed and written with sympathy and tact and acted by a
small cast that could hardly be bettered.

Film, based on Janice Elliott's graceful
novel, concerns four individualistic young
people who develop as intense friendship
among themselves which, during one frenzied
summer, strays into dangerous ground obviously aimed for tragedy.

Hywel Bennett is the catalyst, a brooding,
withdrawn young man who inevitably sets
things in motion. His cousin, a disturbed wary
young woman, from whom he's inseparable is
Jane Asher.

Leigh Taylor-Young has a radiant personality which gives life to all her scenes. Asher is
a shade less effective in a more complicated
role.

BUTTERFIELD 8

1960, 109 MINS, US ◇ ⑰ ⊙
Dir Daniel Mann   *Prod* Pandro S. Berman   *Scr* Charles
Schnee, John Michael Hayes   *Ph* Joseph Ruttenberg,
Charles Harten   *Ed* Ralph E. Winters   *Mus* Bronislau
Kaper   *Art Dir* George W. Davis, Urie McCleary
● Elizabeth Taylor, Laurence Harvey, Eddie Fisher, Dina
Merrill, Mildred Dunnock, Betty Field (M-G-M/Afton-
Linebrook)

Alterations made on John O'Hara's 1935
novel by the scenarists (among other things,
they have updated it from the Prohibition
era, spectacularized the ending and refined
some of the dialog) have given *Butterfield 8* the
form and pace it needs, but the story itself remains a weak one, the behavior and motivations of its characters no more tangible than
in the original work.

Under director Daniel Mann's guidance it
is an extremely sexy and intimate film, but
the intimacy is only skin deep, the sex only a
dominating behavior pattern.

It is the tragic tale of a young woman
(Elizabeth Taylor) tormented by the contradictory impulses of flesh and conscience.

Victim of traumatic childhood experiences,
a fatherless youth, a mother's refusal to face
facts and, most of all, her own moral irresponsibility, she drifts from one illicit affair to
another until passion suddenly blossoms into
love on a six-day sex spree with Laurence
Harvey, who's got the sort of 'problems' (loving, devoted wife, oodles of money via marriage, soft, respectable job) non-neurotic men
might envy.

The picture's major asset is Taylor. It is a
torrid, stinging portrayal with one or two brilliantly executed passages within. Harvey
seems ill-at-ease and has a tendency to exaggerate facial reactions. Eddie Fisher, as
Taylor's long-time friend and father image,
cannot unbend and get any warmth into the
role. Dina Merrill's portrayal of the society
wife is without animation or depth. But there
is better work from Mildred Dunnock as
Taylor's mother and Susan Oliver as Fisher's
impatient girl friend.
☐ 1960: Best Actress (Elizabeth Taylor).
☐ Nomination: Best Color Cinematography

BUTTERFLIES ARE FREE

1972, 109 MINS, US ◇ ⑰
Dir Milton Katselas   *Prod* Mike Frankovich   *Scr* Leonard
Gershe   *Ph* Charles B. Lang   *Ed* David Blewitt
Mus Bob Alcivar   *Art Dir* Robert Clatworthy

● Goldie Hawn, Edward Albert, Eileen Heckart, Michael
Glasser, Mike Warren (Columbia)

Although the setting has been changed from
New York to San Francisco for no apparent
reason, Leonard Gershe's screen adaptation
of his successful Broadway play, is an excellent example of how to switch from one
medium to another.

Several other carryovers – Eileen Heckart
and director Milton Katselas – from the stage
production were also brilliant moves. In the
move a slight change of emphasis has resulted, moving the center of attention from
the blind boy, handsomely played by Edward
Albert to the girl (Goldie Hawn). What
comes over with great strength is Gershe's intimate tale of the interrelationships of three
individuals, all of whom gain from their contacts with each other.

Hawn, funny and touching, is a delight
throughout and Heckart gets a film role that
enables her to display versatility.
☐ 1972: Best Supp. Actress (Eileen Heckart).
☐ Nominations: Best Cinematography, Sound

BUTTERFLY

1981, 107 MINS, US ◇ ⑰ ⊙
Dir Matt Cimber   *Prod* Matt Cimber   *Scr* John Goff,
Matt Cimber   *Ph* Eddy Van Der Enden   *Mus* Ennio
Morricone   *Art Dir* Dave De Carlo
● Stacy Keach, Pia Zadora, Orson Welles, Lois
Nettleton, James Franciscus, Stuart Whitman (Riklis/
Par-Par)

Pia Zadora plays Kady, a nymphet who's been
searching for her father in the Nevada silver
mines. She tracks him down at an abandoned
mine where he (Stacy Keach) is serving as a
guard.

The headstrong young woman brings out
incestuous desires in her God-fearing father.
Eventually, his inner passions overcome his
honest instincts. In an effort to keep Kady
close to him, he agrees to work the almost depleted mine and cash in the remaining ore.

For Kady, the act is motivated by revenge.
The mineowner's son got her pregnant and
refused to marry her. However, the son re-
considers his cowardice and agrees to marry.

Keach plays his role without shadings and
this self-righteousness is difficult to swallow
even with the picture's old-fashioned underpinnings. Zadora, in her screen debut, has
most of the picture's best moments and registers well with her little girl looks and Lolita
sensuality.

Orson Welles as a corrupt judge provides
the film with a few comic but misplaced moments. The final courtroom session sinks into
a farce better suited to a comedy of manners
on stage. Transferring novelist James M.
Cain's narrative and eroticism proves too
great a task for the filmmakers and the picture remains a series of partially realized
sketches.

The film, however, does not betray its modest budget. Made for $2 million, *Butterfly* has
the look of a studio production of three to
four times its cost.

BWANA DEVIL

1952, 79 MINS, US ◇
Dir Arch Oboler   *Prod* Arch Oboler   *Scr* Arch Oboler
Ph Joseph F. Biroc   *Ed* John Hoffman   *Mus* Gordon
Jenkins
● Robert Stack, Barbara Britton, Nigel Bruce, Ramsay
Hill, Paul McVey (Oboler/United Artists)

This novelty feature boasts of being the first
full-length film in Natural Vision 3-D.
Although adding backsides to usually flat actors and depth to landscapes, the 3-D technique still needs further technical advances.

Without the paper-framed, polaroid glasses
Natural Vision looks like a ghost television
picture. While watching 3-D, viewers are con-

stantly forced to refocus their vision as the focus of the film changes, resulting in a tiring
eye workout.

The Oboler production is full of tricks devised to show off the process, rather than to
tell the screen story effectively. The much-
ballyhooed point of a lion seemingly leaping
out of the screen into the auditorium comes
off very mildly. The single gasper is the
throwing of a spear by a native, which has the
illusion of coming right into the audience.

With banal dialog, stilted sequences and
impossibly-directed players, Oboler tells a
story, based on fact, of how two lions halt the
building of a railroad in British East Africa.

BYE BYE BIRDIE

1963, 120 MINS, US ◇ ⑰ ⊙
Dir George Sidney   *Prod* Fred Kohlmar   *Scr* Irving
Brecher   *Ph* Joseph Biroc   *Ed* Charles Nelson
Mus Johnny Green (sup.)   *Art Dir* Paul Groesse
● Janet Leigh, Dick Van Dyke, Ann-Margret, Maureen
Stapleton, Bobby Rydell, Jesse Pearson (Columbia)

Credit George Sidney with directing one of
the better fun and frolic tune packages. The
adaptation of the successful [1960] legit musical comedy clearly called for lots of visuals,
rather than just dialog and straight story-
telling. Additionally, there's apparently more
emphasis on the dance (interesting choreography by Onna White) – more so perhaps
than in the original.

Strikingly important in *Bye Bye Birdie* is
Ann-Margret. Singer, hoofer and cutie-pie, all
wrapped up into one, she has the magnetism
of early-vintage Judy Garland.

Story is the wacky thing about an Elvis
Presley type (Jesse Pearson) who's subject to
immediate army call. Goes by the name of
Conrad Birdie and he swoons the girls no
end, what with all that guitar and hip-notism.
Songwriter Dick Van Dyke, trying to make
time with Janet Leigh, while his mother,
Maureen Stapleton, interferes, also is engaged in having Presley-type appeal on the
Ed Sullivan TV show while doing his farewell
song in Sweet Apple, Iowa. Sullivan is on
view, playing the part of Ed Sullivan with remarkable authenticity.

There's lots of talent involved. The songs as
penned by Charles Strouse and Lee Adams,
fit in nicely. Van Dyke displays a showbiz
knowhow far more extensive than his television outings communicate. Leigh is called
upon to play it straight, and does so attractively. Stapleton is a comedienne of the first
order. Young songster Rydell gets the right
kind of chance to warble. Ann-Margret, to repeat, is a wow.
☐ 1963: Nominations: Best Adapted Score,
Sound

BYE BYE BRAVERMAN

1968, 94 MINS, US ◇
Dir Sidney Lumet   *Prod* Sidney Lumet   *Scr* Herbert
Sargent   *Ph* Boris Kaufman   *Ed* Gerald Greenberg
Mus Peter Matz   *Art Dir* Ben Kasazkow
● George Segal, Jack Warden, Joseph Wiseman,
Sorrell Booke, Phyllis Newman, Jessica Walter (Warner/
Seven Arts)

Bye Bye Braverman is a curious mixture of tasty
and tasteless jokes, all at the expense of
Jewish people. Pic describes, in padded vignette and travelog transition, the hypocritical mourning of a deceased man by four
alleged friends.

Herbert Sargent has taken the 'dark comedy' approach; were it black comedy, or
straight comedy, it might have worked better.
As it is, the curious and erratic use of Jewish
ruggedness of spirit and the native non-sequitur humor makes for a plot stew which will
offend the sensibilities of many, and titillate
the prejudices of others.

George Segal, Jack Warden, Joseph Wiseman and Sorrell Booke are the mourners of never-seen Braverman. Jessica Walter, the less-than-bereaved widow, has the yen for Segal (married to Zohra Lampert).

If the film meant to portray the four principals as basically clod characters, with some good points, it missed. If the idea was to portray them as basically good, with human frailties, insufficient depth was given along these lines, too.

....

■ **BY HOOK OR BY CROOK**
See: I Dood It

....

■ **BY LOVE POSSESSED**

1961, 115 MINS, US ◇ ⓥ
Dir John Sturges   *Prod* Walter Mirisch   *Scr* John Dennis
Ph Russell Metty   *Ed* Ferris Webster   *Mus* Elmer
Bernstein   *Art Dir* Malcolm Brown
● Lana Turner, Efrem Zimbalist Jr, Jason Robards,
George Hamilton, Susan Kohner, Barbara Bel Geddes
(United Artists/Mirisch)

James Gould Couzzen's thoughtful novel has been reduced to a complex soap opera. In barest outline, the screenplay seems much like the source material: a look into the lives of a half-dozen socially prominent, well-to-do citizens in a small eastern town.

The focal point is a successful lawyer (Efrem Zimbalist Jr) who, in the course of several climactic days, finds that his perfectly ordered life is, in reality, as full of self deception and chaos as the lives of some of his less stable friends. The latter include his law partner (Jason Robards) who, after a crippling accident, refuses the love-pity of his wife (Lana Turner) who subsequently turns to double scotches and solace with Zimbalist.

Further complications involve Zimbalist's inability to understand his son (George Hamilton) who seeks release with the town hussy, who charges the boy with rape.

Turner looks beautiful in a great wardrobe, but can only suggest the ironic, gutsy dame the character might have been. Zimbalist spends most of his time looking thoughtful while chomping on his pipe, and Robards just limps and looks pained. Scoring nicely is Yvonne Craig as the town trollop who persists in talking about herself in the third person.

....

■ **BY THE SWORD**

1992, 91 MINS, US ◇ ⓥ ⊙
Dir Jeremy Paul Kagan   *Prod* Peter E. Strauss, Marlon
Staggs   *Scr* John McDonald, James Donadio   *Ph* Arthur
Albert   *Ed* David Holden   *Mus* Bill Conti
● F. Murray Abraham, Eric Roberts, Mia Sara, Chris
Rydell, Elaine Kagan, Brett Cullen (Movie Group/Foil-
Film)

Little-explored world of competitive fencing is the setting for this dramatic crowd pleaser in which F. Murray Abraham delivers a riveting performance as a complex killer, ex-con, lover, janitor and swordsman.

Pic begins in flashback, where his surreal nightmares are haunted by the trainer he skewered 20 years earlier. The dead man's son (Eric Roberts) is now an undefeated, cold-hearted champ running a fencing academy, where most of the picture takes place.

Well-choreographed fencing scenes between Roberts' promising students are kept to a minimum and used as a backdrop for the mounting tension between Roberts and his dad's murderer.

....

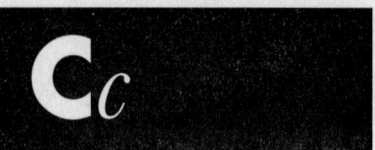

■ **CABARET**

1972, 124 MINS, US ◇ ⓥ ⊙
Dir Bob Fosse   *Prod* Cy Feuer   *Scr* Jay Presson Allen,
Hugh Wheeler   *Ph* Geoffrey Unsworth   *Ed* David
Bretherton   *Mus* Ralph Burns (dir.)   *Art Dir* Rolf
Zehetbauer, Jurgen Kiebach
● Liza Minnelli, Michael York, Helmut Griem, Marisa
Berenson, Fritz Wepper, Joel Grey (AA-ABC)

The film version of [the 1966 John Kander-Fred Ebb Broadway musical] *Cabaret* is most unusual: it is literate, bawdy, sophisticated, sensual, cynical, heart-warming, and disturbingly thought-provoking. Liza Minnelli heads a strong cast. Bob Fosse's generally excellent direction recreates the milieu of Germany some 40 years ago.

The adaptation of the stage book is expertly accomplished. The basic material derives from Christopher Isherwood's Berlin stories, and a 1951 dramatic play by John Van Druten, filmed in 1955, *I Am a Camera*.

The screenplay, which never seems to talk down to an audience while at the same time making its candid points with tasteful emphasis, returns the story to a variety of settings. The sleazy cabaret remains a major recurring set.

The choice of Minnelli for the part of Sally Bowles was indeed daring. Good-hearted, quasi-sophisticated amorality and hedonism are not precisely Minnelli's professional bag, and within many scenes she seems to carom from golly-gee-whiz-down-home rusticity to something closer to the mark.

□ 1972: Best Director, Actress (Liza Minnelli), Supp. Actor (Joel Grey), Cinematography, Art Direction, Sound, Adapted Scoring, Editing.
□ Nominations: Best Picture, Adapted Screenplay

....

■ **CABIN IN THE COTTON**

1932, 76 MINS, US
Dir Michael Curtiz   *Prod* Jack L. Warner   *Scr* Paul
Green   *Ph* Barney McGill   *Ed* George Amy
● Richard Barthelmess, Dorothy Jordan, Bette Davis,
Henry B. Walthall, Berton Churchill (First National)

Picture proves that a book that attracts a good deal of attention isn't necessarily screen material. Conflict is the feud between a southern cotton planter (landowner) and tenant farmer (here described as 'peckerwoods'). It's the industrial capital vs labor wrangle in another setting, and not a particularly fascinating one at that.

Picture is not well done and it presents Richard Barthelmess in another lukewarm role, a role which he plays without vigor. Nub of the drama is that Marvin Blake (Barthelmess) belongs to the underdog tenant farmer class, but is befriended by the planter and finds himself between two fires – torn by loyalty to his class and an obligation to his enemy who also is his benefactor. Also Marvin falls in love with the planter's daughter.

Bette Davis is the naughty-naughty planter's daughter. Dorothy Jordan, as a humble farm girl, is just a shadow. Indeed, most of the people are puppet-like, including the Barthelmess character.

....

■ **CABIN IN THE SKY**

1943, 98 MINS, US ⓥ ⊙
Dir Vincente Minnelli   *Prod* Arthur Freed   *Scr* Joseph
Schrank   *Ph* Sidney Wagner   *Ed* Harold F. Cress
Mus Vernon Duke, Harold Arlen

● Ethel Waters, Eddie 'Rochester' Anderson, Lena
Horne, Louis Armstrong, Rex Ingram (M-G-M)

The picture version of *Cabin in the Sky* is little changed from the original stage show. It still tells of Little Joe Jackson's weakness for dice, likker and the seductive Georgia Brown, of his mortal wound in a barroom brawl, and of his six-month period of grace obtained by his eternally-devoted wife, Petunia. It still shows the contest between Lucifer Jr and the General for Little Joe's soul.

In the legit version *Cabin* seemed constantly to be constricted by the limitations of the stage. But difficulty has not been solved in the present film adaptation. The yarn still appears weighed down by unimaginative conception, the few changes in the screen medium merely filling out the story, without expanding or developing its fantasy. In only one of two moments, such as the stairway to heaven finale, is there any apparent effort to utilize the facilities of the camera. There are far too many closeups, particularly in the vocal numbers.

Ethel Waters remains the one transcendant asset of the film *Cabin*, just as she was in the original. Her sincerity, compassion, personal warmth and dramatic skill, plus her unique talent as a singer make her performance as Petunia an overpowering accomplishment.
□ 1943: Nomination: Best Song ('Happiness Is a Thing Called Joe')

....

■ **CACTUS FLOWER**

1969, 103 MINS, US ◇ ⓥ ⊙
Dir Gene Saks   *Prod* Mike Frankovich   *Scr* I.A.L.
Diamond   *Ph* Charles E. Lang   *Ed* Maury Winetrobe
Mus Quincy Jones   *Art Dir* Robert Clatworthy
● Walter Matthau, Ingrid Bergman, Goldie Hawn, Jack
Weston, Rick Lenz, Vito Scotti (Columbia)

Cactus Flower drags, which is probably the worst thing that can be said of a light comedy. It's due to sloppy direction by Gene Saks and the miscasting of Walter Matthau opposite Ingrid Bergman.

The plot [from the play by Abe Burrows, based on a French play by Barillet & Gredy] is minimal and the lines are somewhat stilted and hollow, but if the direction were tighter and the mood kept light and airy it might have worked.

Matthau is cast as a dentist ready to marry his young mistre who enlists the aid of his stuffy but organized secretary. This too, might have worked had they found a suitable foil for him. Bergman, more believable in her role as the nurse, is too reserved and sophisticated opposite Matthau.

There are some laughs and Goldie Hawn, as the Greenwich Village kook with whom Matthau contemplates marriage, makes a credible screen debut.
□ 1969: Best Supp. Actress (Goldie Hawn)

....

■ **CADDIE**

1976, 107 MINS, AUSTRALIA ◇ ⓥ
Dir Donald Crombie   *Prod* Tony Buckley   *Scr* Joan Long
Ph Peter James   *Ed* Tim Wellburn   *Mus* Patrick Flynn
Art Dir Owen Williams
● Helen Morse, Takis Emmanuel, Jack Thompson, Jacki
Weaver, Melissa Jaffer, Ron Blanchard (Buckley)

Caddie is based on the autobiography of a Sydney barmaid who, abandoned by her husband, struggled through the Depression to bring up two children. It is a sensitively-told story of one woman's fight – not a militant, but rather one of the masses; an unsung heroine.

Helen Morse, in the title role, maintains a wonderful dignity that is typical of the character's social class and aspirations. She never slips, and her scenes with the children are natural, especially at the fade out when despite a crushing personal disappointment, she rallies as soon as they appear.

But it is in her scenes with Takis Emmanuel that Caddie's story takes on fire. Emmanuel, a Greek actor imported for the production, registers power immediately his face hits the screen.

••••••••••••••••••••••••••••••

■ CADDY, THE

1953, 95 MINS, US ♥

Dir Norman Taurog *Prod* Paul Jones *Scr* Edmund L. Hartmann, Danny Arnold, Ken Englund *Ph* Daniel L. Fapp *Ed* Warren Low *Mus* Joseph J. Lilley (dir.) *Art Dir* Hal Pereira, Franz Bachelin
● Dean Martin, Jerry Lewis, Donna Reed, Barbara Bates, Joseph Calleia, Fred Clark (Paramount/York)

Dean Martin and Jerry Lewis dig a lot of divots among the fairways of *The Caddy*. It's an amusing romp [from a story by Danny Arnold] that, while not always parring previous M & L successes, comes close enough.

Production tells how a couple of San Francisco boys, both liking golf, team for tournament play. Since Lewis can't stand the strain of competition, he's the caddy-manager for Martin. Early successes swell Martin's head and he tries to break from Lewis. Their quarrel during a big match at Pebble Beach turns on a riot that ends with their plunge into showbiz when golf kicks them out.

Emphasis is on warm humor with heart. The comics have two femme stars as curvy contrasts for their antics. Donna Reed plays a rich society gal who sets her cap for Martin and gets him, even if Lewis's ineptness does mix up the romance for awhile. Barbara Bates, as Martin's sister, is Lewis' sweetie.

Cut into the footage are some actual mob scenes of crowds around the NY Paramount Theatre when M & L were appearing there for a stage date.
□ 1953: Nomination: Best Song ('That's Amore')

••••••••••••••••••••••••••••••

■ CADDYSHACK

1980, 90 MINS, US ♦ ♥ ⊙

Dir Harold Ramis *Prod* Douglas Kenney *Scr* Brian Doyle-Murray, Harold Ramis, Douglas Kenney *Ph* Steven Larner *Ed* William Carruth *Mus* Johnny Mandel *Art Dir* Stan Jolley
● Chevy Chase, Rodney Dangerfield, Bill Murray, Michael O'Keefe, Ted Knight, Cindy Morgan (Orion/Peters)

In its unabashed bid for the mammoth audience which responded to the anti-establishment outrageousness of *National Lampoon's Animal House*, this vaguely likable, too-tame comedy falls short of the mark.

This time, the thinly plotted shenanigans unfold against the manicured lawns and posh backdrop of a restricted country club, generally pitting the free-living youthful caddies against the uptight gentry who employ them.

Stock characters include Chevy Chase as resident golf-pro; club prexy and jurist Ted Knight; and Rodney Dangerfield as the perfectly cast and very funny personification of anti-social, nouveau riche grossness.

Beyond Chase, prime lure is Bill Murray as a foul-habited, semi-moronic groundskeeper, constantly aroused by the older femme golfers.

••••••••••••••••••••••••••••••

■ CADILLAC MAN

1990, 97 MINS, US ♦ ♥ ⊙

Dir Roger Donaldson *Prod* Charles Roven, Roger Donaldson *Scr* Ken Friedman *Ph* David Gribble *Ed* Richard Francis-Bruce *Mus* J. Peter Robinson *Art Dir* Gene Rudolf
● Robin Williams, Tim Robbins, Pamela Reed, Annabella Sciorra, Zack Norman, Lori Petty (Donaldson-Roven/Cavallo)

Denied an opportunity to showcase his deft rapid-fire comic skills, Robin Williams pro-

duces few laughs amid wreckage of the screenplay and poorly paced direction. Only Tim Robbins gets out alive as a crazed, simple-minded, cuckolded husband who ultimately makes hostages of the womanizing Joey (Williams) and everyone else in the car dealership where he works, suspecting correctly that his wife (Annabella Sciorra) having an affair.

Williams lapses in and out of a what seems to be a New York-Italian street accent. Aside from being a smart aleck, however, he's rarely funny and shows little depth until the predictable ending. Some minor pleasures can be found in smaller roles drawn from the N.Y. street scene, especially Lauren Tom as a pushy and abusive waitress in a neighbourhood dim sum restaurant.

••••••••••••••••••••••••••••••

■ CAESAR AND CLEOPATRA

1946, 135 MINS, UK ♦ ♥

Dir Gabriel Pascal *Prod* Gabriel Pascal *Scr* George Bernard Shaw *Ph* Freddie Young, Robert Krasker, Jack Hildyard, Jack Cardiff *Mus* Georges Auric *Art Dir* Oliver Messel, John Bryan
● Vivien Leigh, Claude Rains, Stewart Granger, Flora Robson, Francis L. Sullivan, Cecil Parker (Eagle Lion)

Caesar and Cleopatra is a disappointment. In spite of its prodigal magnificence, indeed because of its production values, such vague story interest as it has is hopelessly swamped.

Claude Rains' Caesar – thanks to Shaw and Gabriel Pascal, director – is accurately and succinctly pinpointed by Vivien Leigh as Cleopatra when she calls him 'a nice old gentleman'. As for her portrayal of the Queen of Queens – again the responsibility of author and director – Rains calls the turn when he tells her with justifiable incredulity she is not Queen of Egypt, but a queen of the gypsies.

Sketchy references to an earlier visit of a young Roman 'with strong, round, gleaming arms' elicit his identification by Caesar as being Marc Antony. Apart from this vague, soft-pedal reference to the possibility of her knowing what passion means, Leigh's Cleopatra is as lacking in sex consciousness as the boy actor (Anthony Harvey) who plays the part of her brother, Ptolemy, whose throne she seizes.

Seemingly just to make things more irritating there appears halfway through the pic Stewart Granger as Apollodorus, a Sicilian with flashing eyes, dazzling white teeth and a torso of burnished bronze. But nix on anything like that, says Shaw. So Cleopatra passes Granger up as if he were a dirty deuce – instead of being what he so obviously, so vibrantly is, a grand chunk of three-quarters nude male s.a.

In a cast of more than 100 of Britain's finest stage actors individual performances of bits are all flawless. And make no mistake about it, the prodigality of this $6 million spectacle makes Griffith and DeMille and Von Stroheim look like niggards.
□ 1946: Nomination: Best Color Art Direction

••••••••••••••••••••••••••••••

■ CAGED

1950, 96 MINS, US

Dir John Cromwell *Prod* Jerry Wald *Scr* Virginia Kellogg, Bernard C. Schoenfeld *Ph* Carl Guthrie *Ed* Owen Marks *Mus* Max Steiner *Art Dir* Charles H. Clarke
● Eleanor Parker, Agnes Moorehead, Ellen Corby, Hope Emerson, Jan Sterling, Jane Darwell (Warner)

Caged makes a stab at objective reporting of life in a women's prison. A grim, unrelieved study of cause and effect, it adds up to very drab entertainment, unleavened with any measure of escapism.

Plot provides Eleanor Parker with what is known as a meaty femme role, completely

deglamourized. There are other strong portrayals among the predominantly femme cast, and the most colorful is the sadistic prison matron socked over by Hope Emerson.

Script is based on actual prison life incidents. Motivation on which it is hung is the downward path taken by a first offender after she rubs up against the assorted characters who people a prison. In that respect, story's finish is realistic, stating clearly that Parker will soon be back with her old cellmates.
□ 1950: Nominations: Best Actress (Eleanor Parker), Supp. Actress (Hope Emerson), Story & Screenplay

••••••••••••••••••••••••••••••

■ CAHILL, UNITED STATES MARSHAL

1973, 103 MINS, US ♦ ♥ ⊙

Dir Andrew V. McLaglen *Prod* Michael Wayne *Scr* Harry Julian Fink, Rita M. Fink *Ph* Joseph Biroc *Ed* Robert L. Simpson *Mus* Elmer Bernstein *Art Dir* Walter Simonds
● John Wayne, Gary Grimes, George Kennedy, Neville Brand, Clay O'Brien, Marie Windsor (Batjac/Warner)

John Wayne combines the problems of fatherhood with his activities as a lawman in *Cahill, United States Marshal* to give different motivation from the usual western theme.

Crux of the strained relationship between Wayne and his two young sons is his continued absence tracking down criminals, which leads to the boys, 17 and 12, becoming involved in a bank robbery and murder.

Script, based on a story by Barney Slater, opens strongly with Wayne catching up to a band of outlaws and shooting it out with them. When he returns to town he finds the bank has been robbed, sheriff and deputy murdered and four new prisoners in jail, including his elder son. Boys have been lured into crime by smooth-talking outlaw George Kennedy.

Wayne carries out characterization realistically and gets firm support right down the line. Kennedy is menacing.

••••••••••••••••••••••••••••••

■ CAINE MUTINY, THE

1954, 123 MINS, US ♦ ♥ ⊙

Dir Edward Dmytryk *Prod* Stanley Kramer *Scr* Stanley Roberts, Michael Blankfort *Ph* Franz Planer *Ed* William A. Lyon, Henry Batista *Mus* Max Steiner *Art Dir* Rudolph Sternad
● Humphrey Bogart, Jose Ferrer, Van Johnson, Fred MacMurray, Robert Francis, May Wynn (Columbia)

The Caine Mutiny is highly recommendable motion picture drama, told on the screen as forcefully as it was in the Herman Wouk best-selling novel. The intelligently adapted screenplay retains all the essence of the novel.

The Caine Mutiny is the story of a war-weary destroyer-minesweeper and its personnel, over which presides – by the book – Captain Queeg, a man beginning to crack from the strain of playing hero over the years while he hides deep his inferiority complex. L Tom Keefer is the first to spot the crack in Queeg's armor and he needles Maryk and the other officers into seeing it, too.

Little incidents of faulty command build until, during a raging typhoon when the tired ship is in extreme danger of foundering Maryk relieves the captain, using Navy Article 184, which permits the executive officer taking over under certain emergency conditions, to do so.

Scene after scene in the picture during the hour and one-half buildup to the court martial stand out, either for high action, drama or the beauty and grace of ships making their way proudly through the seas.
□ 1954: Nominations: Best Picture, Actor (Humphrey Bogart), Supp. Actor (Tom Tully), Screenplay, Editing, Scoring of a Dramatic Picture, Sound

••••••••••••••••••••••••••••••

■ CAIRO ROAD

1950, 88 MINS, UK ◇ Ⓥ
Dir David Macdonald   *Prod* Aubrey Baring   *Scr* Robert Westerby   *Ph* Oswald Morris   *Ed* Peter Taylor   *Mus* Robert Gill, Na'im al-Basri   *Art Dir* Duncan Sutherland
● Eric Portman, Laurence Harvey, Maria Mauban, Camelia, Karel Stepanek, John Gregson (ABPC/Mayflower)

Cairo Road is a so-so thriller dealing with dope smugglers. Action moves slowly in the first half and much of the story is veiled so as to obscure the plot. However, it winds up with a meaty climax. Action takes place in Cairo, Port Said and along the Suez.

Principal characters are the chief of the Anti-Narcotic Bureau, suavely played by Eric Portman, and his impetuous assistant (Laurence Harvey). Police are investigating a murder which leads them to the trail of hashish peddlers. Capture of the two major criminals is the climax.

Apart from the principals, the most distinctive performance comes from Harold Lang, who plays a smuggler. New Egyptian star Camelia is a looker, but is given little chance in a small part. The only other femme role is played by Maria Mauban as the sweet and understanding wife of Harvey.

■ CALAMITY JANE

1953, 100 MINS, US ◇ ⊙
Dir David Butler   *Prod* William Jacobs   *Scr* James O'Hanlon   *Ph* Wilfrid M. Cline   *Ed* Irene Morra   *Mus* Ray Heindorf (dir.)   *Art Dir* John Beckman
● Doris Day, Howard Keel, Allyn McLerie, Philip Carey, Dick Wesson, Paul Harvey (Warner)

Giving such Wild West characters as Calamity Jane and Wild Bill Hickok a workout in a tuned-in western doubtless had strong possibilities but Warners comes close to missing the stagecoach. Colorful settings and costumes add the entry some sparkle but the 'book' is lacking in originality and the players simply are uneasy.

Compensating factor is the total of 11 songs (music by Sammy Fain, lyrics by Paul Francis Webster) which gives the production some entertainment wallop. [Musical numbers staged and directed by Jack Donohue.]

Doris Day works very, very hard at being Calamity and is hardly realistic at all. She'd register fine as a country girl in calico or a cutie from the chorus line but strain shows through in her essaying of the hard and dynamic Calamity character. Howard Keel handles the Bill Hickok assignment with listless amiability.

While flavorful, a number of the *Calamity* songs suggest other scores of other years. As a matter of fact, the entire film seems a little familiar, having some ingredients in common with *Annie Get Your Gun* and *Oklahoma!*. The dialog throughout is commonplace.
□ 1953: Best Song ('Secret Love').
□ Nominations: Best Scoring of a Musical Picture, Sound

■ CALIFORNIA DOLLS, THE

See: . . . All the Marbles

■ CALIFORNIA MAN

See: Encino Man

■ CALIFORNIA SPLIT

1974, 108 MINS, US ◇ Ⓥ
Dir Robert Altman   *Prod* Robert Altman, Joseph Walsh   *Scr* Joseph Walsh   *Ph* Paul Lohmann   *Ed* Lou Lombardo   *Mus* Phyllis Shotwell   *Art Dir* Leon Ericksen
● George Segal, Elliott Gould, Ann Prentiss, Gwen Welles, Edward Walsh, Joseph Walsh (Columbia)

California Split is an aimless, strung-out series of vignettes starring George Segal and Elliott Gould as compulsive gamblers. The film is technically and physically handsome, all the more so for being mostly location work, but lacks a cohesion and reinforced sense of story direction.

The pic is well cast – Segal and Gould contrast well, while Ann Prentiss and Gwen Welles play happy hookers to good effect. Bert Remsen, an Altman stock player, herein does a drag number. Edward Walsh (the writer's father) is very good as a mean poker adversary, and the writer himself has a good scene as Segal's loan shark.

■ CALIFORNIA SUITE

1978, 103 MINS, US ◇ Ⓥ ⊙
Dir Herbert Ross   *Prod* Ray Stark   *Scr* Neil Simon   *Ph* David M. Walsh   *Ed* Michael A. Stevenson, Margaret Booth   *Mus* Claude Bolling   *Art Dir* Albert Brenner
● Alan Alda, Michael Caine, Bill Cosby, Jane Fonda, Walter Matthau, Elaine May (Columbia)

Neil Simon and Herbert Ross have gambled in radically altering the successful format of *California Suite* as it appeared on stage. Instead of four separate playlets, there is now one semi-cohesive narrative revolving around visitors to the Beverly Hills Hotel.

Alan Alda and Jane Fonda portray a divorced couple wrangling over possession of their child, while Michael Caine and Maggie Smith play a showbiz couple with varying sexual tastes holed up at the Bev-Hills prior to the Academy Awards. Walter Matthau has to explain his unwitting infidelity to spouse Elaine May in a third segment, and Richard Pryor and Bill Cosby, accompanied by their wives (Gloria Gifford and Sheila Frazier), manage to turn a vacation into a series of disastrous mishaps.

Ross and Simon have set up as counterpoint to the more tragicomic episodes (those involved Alda and Fonda, and Caine and Smith) some farcical moments around Matthau and blitzed floozy Denise Galik, along with the Pryor-Cosby shenanigans. The technique is less than successful, veering from poignant emotionalism to broad slapstick in sudden shifts.

Fonda demonstrates yet another aspect of her amazing range, although her brittle quips with Alda seem very stage-bound. Smith and Caine interplay wonderfully, as do Pryor and Cosby. The latter duo get the worst break, however, as their seg is chopped up, spread around and generally given short shrift.
□ 1978: Best Supp. Actress (Maggie Smith).
□ Nominations: Best Adapted Screenplay, Art Direction

■ CALIGULA

1979, 150 MINS, ITALY/US ◇ Ⓥ ⊙
Dir Tinto Brass   *Prod* Bob Guccione, Franco Rossellini   *Scr* [uncredited]   *Ph* Silvano Ippoliti   *Ed* Nino Baragli   *Mus* Paul Clemente   *Art Dir* Danilo Donati
● Malcolm McDowell, Teresa Ann Savoy, Helen Mirren, Peter O'Toole, John Gielgud (Penthouse/Felix)

With the biggest investment ever in porn to play with, Tinto Brass in a creative fit of paranoic obsession, sifts through the pages of first century Rome under syphilitic Tiberius and epileptic Caligula to demonstrate the unlimited baseness of the human condition [from a story by Gore Vidal].

Such established names as John Gielgud and Peter O'Toole will have to be seen to be believed. Malcolm McDowell as the sick and/or insane emperor runs the gamut of cardboard emotions from grand guign to hapless pathos.

Paid off to yield final cut and end two years of film freeze litigation, Brass gets a kind of ambiguous director credit ('scenes directed by'). He filmed everything on screen; though some reports mention added porno inserts during the post-Brass completion period. (A 210-minute version was clandestinely screened at Cannes earlier in the year.)

■ CALL ME BWANA

1963, 93 MINS, UK ◇
Dir Gordon Douglas   *Prod* Harry Saltzman, Albert R. Broccoli   *Scr* Nate Monaster, Johanna Harwood   *Ph* Ted Moore   *Ed* Peter Hunt   *Mus* Monty Norman
● Bob Hope, Anita Ekberg, Edie Adams, Lionel Jeffries, Percy Herbert (Eon)

Bob Hope's gags are tossed off in his usual slick fashion. And a great number of them are slyly but pointedly directed at Anita Ekberg's stimulating sculpture. The visual situations and incidents need spacing out a little more but they invariably crop up just in time to disguise the occasional repetition of plot.

Hope has built up a phoney reputation as an intrepid explorer of the jungles of Darkest Africa, by writing successful books based on old, secret diaries of his uncle. Actually, the nearest the timid character has ever been to Africa is to visit his aunt in Cape Cod. When an American moon-probe capsule is lost in the jungle and it's necessary to locate it before foreign powers get their thieving mitts on it, Hope is detailed for the task because of his supposed expert knowledge of the locale.

Overall, there's enough fun to keep this bubbling along merrily. There is Hope going through bravery tests to escape the native tribe, getting mixed up with a rogue elephant, a lion in his tub, having his pants repaired by Ekberg while he's wearing 'em (and with the poisoned needle from his suicide kit), and eventually becoming airborne in the moon-capsule.

Though most of the responsibility falls on Hope and his personality, Edie Adams gives a pleasantly unobtrusive performance and La Ekberg, though an unlikely Mata Hari, is a sound and decorative foil for Hope. Only the most fastidious carper will protest that the jungle often reeks of Pinewood Studio.

■ CALL ME GENIUS

See: The Rebel

■ CALL ME MADAM

1953, 114 MINS, US ◇
Dir Walter Lang   *Prod* Sol C. Siegel   *Scr* Arthur Sheekman   *Ph* Leon Shamroy   *Ed* Robert Simpson   *Mus* Alfred Newman (dir.)   *Art Dir* Lyle R. Wheeler, John De Cuir
● Ethel Merman, Donald O'Connor, Vera-Ellen, George Sanders, Billy De Wolfe, Helmut Dantine (20th Century-Fox)

A [1950] hit musical on Broadway, *Call Me Madam* scored a run of close to two years in Gotham with Ethel Merman, as Ambassador Sally Adams, the fabulous Femme diplomat, representing the US in the mythical Grand Duchy of Lichtenburg. Merman still reigns in the cinematic version.

In key spots, George Sanders is the tiny country's foreign department chief, and Donald O'Connor is the US press attache, Billy De Wolfe is the American charge d'affaires, Vera-Ellen plays the princess and Helmut Dantine is on hand as the prince who's spurned by the princess in favor of the American press rep.

Madam offers an ingratiating book loosely fashioned after the career of Perle Mesta, former US Minister to Luxembourg. Added plusses are via the widened scope and richness of the production, lush mountains and extra trimmings for the delightful Irving Berlin score. Also, there's the fresh, inventive choreography staged by Robert Alton, with

C

O'Connor and Vera-Ellen as a terping combo of top calibre.

The screenplay, from the Howard Lindsay-Russel Crouse book, is imaginative and whimsical. Merman is at her robust best with a tune. At the opening, she give 'Hostess with the Mostest on the Ball' a powerhouse delivery and it's a cinch to provoke heavy mitting. Her 'You're Just in Love' duet with O'Connor also is standout.

☐ 1953: Best Scoring of a Musical Picture.
☐ Nomination: Best Color Costume Design

....

■ CALL NORTHSIDE 777

1948, 111 MINS, US

Dir Henry Hathaway   *Prod* Otto Lang   *Scr* Jerome Cady, Jay Dratler   *Ph* Joe MacDonald   *Ed* J. Watson Webb Jr   *Mus* Alfred Newman   *Art Dir* Lyle R. Wheeler, Mark-Lee Kirk

● James Stewart, Richard Conte, Lee J. Cobb, Helen Walker, Betty Garde (20th Century-Fox)

Call Northside 777 has all the separate ingredients for a sock film but registers only with a mild impact due to a lack of integration. Among the film's principal drawbacks is James Stewart's jarring and unpersuasive performance in the key role. As a Chicago reporter who's assigned to dig up a human-interest angle out of an 11-year-old murder case, Stewart shuttles between a phoney cynicism and a sob-sister sentimentalism into a recognizable newspaperman.

Henry Hathaway's directing marks a retreat from the documentary form. Instead of consistent realism, he lapses into a hybrid technique with plenty of hokey melodramatic tones.

Based on a celebrated miscarriage of justice in 1932, when two innocent men were sentenced to 9 years apiece for killing a cop, the screenplay [based on articles by James P. McGuire, adaptation by Leonard Hoffman and Quentin Reynolds] constructs a serviceable plot on the factual groundwork. Film, however, tends to wander aimlessly in an over-sized running time.

Title is derived from a personal ad placed in the *Chicago Times-Herald* by the mother of one of the prisoners offering a $5,000 reward for information leading to the release of her son. Answering the ad, Stewart uses it as a peg for a series of human interest stories about the case. Initially skeptical, he's progressively drawn to a belief in the man's innocence. Richard Conte gives an intensely sincere performance as the young Polish-American who is railroaded to jail.

....

■ CALL OF THE WILD

1935, 89 MINS, US

Dir William Wellman   *Prod* William Goetz, Raymond Griffith   *Scr* Gene Fowler, Leonard Praskins   *Ph* Charles Rosher   *Ed* Hanoon Fritch   *Mus* Alfred Newman   *Art Dir* Richard Day, Alexander Golitzen

● Clark Gable, Loretta Young, Jack Oakie, Frank Conroy, Reginald Owen, Sidney Toler (20th Century/United Artists)

The lion-hearted dog that was Jack London's creation as the leading character of *Call of the Wild* emerges now as a stooge for a rather conventional pair of human love birds. Changes have made the canine classic hardly recognizable, but they have not done any damage.

The big and exceptionally wild St Bernard, known as Buck, is not entirely submerged, since such of his feats as the haul of a 1,000-pound load over the snow and his mating with a femme wolf are included, but he has been decidedly picture-house broken.

Clark Gable strong-and-silents himself expertly and Loretta Young, in the opposite corner of the revised love affair, is lovely and competent. But Jack Oakie has the laughs, and they land him on top.

It's a story of treachery, hardship, violence and unrequited love in Alaska, so anything that does away with sadness for a momentary giggle is highly welcome. Gable and Oakie's rescue of Young, whose husband has apparently lost his way and perished; their finding of the gold mine; their encounter with the villainous Reginald Owen; the return of Young's husband, lending a bitter-sweet finish to the romance, are the highlights of the story's human element.

This is the second trip for the London novel to the screen. Pathe made it silent in 1923.

....

■ CALL OF THE WILD, THE

1973, 100 MINS, UK/FRANCE/W. GERMANY/ITALY/NORWAY/SPAIN ◇ ⑰

Dir Ken Annakin   *Prod* Harry Alan Towers   *Scr* Peter Welbeck, Win Wells, Peter Yeldham   *Ph* John Cabrera   *Ed* Thelma Connell   *Mus* Carlo Rustichelli   *Art Dir* Knut Solberg

● Charlton Heston, Raimund Harmsdorf, Michele Mercier, George Eastman, Sancho Gracia, Maria Rohm (Towers of London)

Jack London's thrilling, often-filmed tale trails a couple of roughnecks, John and Pete, on their gold-digging, mail-hopping, and booze-deal fortune hunts in Alaska's snow-bound wilderness. Time and again, they are outsmarted and outroughed by an assorted pack of rivals.

Director Ken Annakin picked a few good actors (Charlton Heston and Italo-western hero George Eastman) and some others capable of no more than looking their parts (Raimund Harmsdorf, Michele Mercier). But everybody appear to play merely along action lines on his own and create a vacuum around him.

Thus lacking the density of London's original, the picture falls to pieces with all that frozen gore, dog fights, sled chases, saloon brawls and other knock-down melodramatics.

....

■ CAMELOT

1967, 179 MINS, US ◇ ⑰ ⊙

Dir Joshua Logan   *Prod* Jack L. Warner   *Scr* Alan Jay Lerner   *Ph* Richard H. Kline   *Ed* Folmar Blangsted   *Mus* Alfred Newman (dir.)   *Art Dir* John Truscott

● Richard Harris, Vanessa Redgrave, Franco Nero, David Hemmings, Lionel Jeffries, Estelle Winwood (Warner/Seven Arts)

On the sumptuous face of it, *Camelot* qualifies as one of Hollywood's alltime great screen musicals. While most big musicals have fine production, dazzling costumes and all that, what gives *Camelot* special value is a central dramatic conflict that throbs with human anguish and compassion.

Camelot never need resort to the more obvious kind of added action. The focus is kept on the three mentally-tortured people, the cuckolded king, the cheating queen, the confused knight.

All of this is against the often exquisite sets and costumes of John Truscott, the creative use of research that is constantly visible. The fine camera work of Richard H. Kline, the clever screenplay by Alan Jay Lerner, the singular appropriateness to time and place of the Frederick Loewe score as lovingly managed by Alfred Newman are all major contributions.

Joshua Logan rates extraordinary tribute for the performances he elicits from Richard Harris as King Arthur, Vanessa Redgrave as Guinevere, and Franco Nero as the knight whose idealism succumbs to passion.

☐ 1967: Best Art Direction, Adapted Scoring, Costume Design.
☐ Nominations: Best Cinematography, Sound

....

■ CAMILLE

1921, 90 MINS, US ⊗

Dir Ray C. Smallwood   *Prod* Nazimova   *Scr* June Mathis   *Ph* Rudolph Bergquist   *Art Dir* Natacha Rambova

● Nazimova, Rudolph Valentino, Arthur Hoyt, Zeffie Tilbury, Edward Connelly, Patsy Ruth Miller (Nazimova/Metro)

This production of Nazimova in *Camille* proves to be a modernized version of the story of *The Lady with the Camellias*, which fact is welcome for the major part, but not so felicitous as the concluding parts are reached. For, wonder of wonders, the director has entirely omitted the scene of Armand at the bedside of his beloved as she breathes her last. Perhaps this big moment was eliminated in the thought the picture fans, if unable to witness a happy ending, wanted one as happy as possible under the circumstances. Nothing could be further from the fact.

Nazimova totally immerses her own distinct personality into that of the famed heroine. Instead of the sinuous, clinging Nazimova, she appears an actress almost new-born for the part.

The surrounding company is excellent. Second to the star is the Armand of Rudolph Valentino. There are many opportunities for obtrusiveness in the role, but he keeps it correct to the minutest detail.

....

■ CAMILLE

1927, 96 MINS, US ⊗

Dir Fred Niblo   *Scr* Fred De Gresac, Olga Printzlau, Chandler Sprague, George Marion Jr.   *Ph* Oliver T. Marsh

● Norma Talmadge, Gilbert Roland, Lilyan Tashman, Maurice Costello, Harvey Clark, Alec B. Francis (Talmadge/First National)

Fred Niblo and Norma Talmadge have dedicated a pretty love story [from the novel by the younger Alexandre Dumas] to the screen that lacks the punch to make it a standout. Dramatic intensity only twice arises to make an audience forget it is watching a picture. This is when Armand returns to his suburban cottage to find Camille has left him, and when he next meets her in a gambling parlor escorted by her first financial amour, the Baron.

For some reason Niblo omitted the traditional sympathy that goes with Camille's death or a pull on the heart strings where she gives up Armand at the instigation of his father. For a demi-mondaine supposedly in the throes of the first and only real love of her life, Talmadge gives in much too easily as Niblo has screened it.

And through it all Talmadge looks beautiful. Never better, besides giving a sterling performance. Opposite Talmadge is Gilbert Roland. Other than Talmadge and Roland, no one shines except Harvey Clark.

....

■ CAMILLE

1937, 108 MINS, US ⑰

Dir George Cukor   *Prod* David Lewis   *Scr* Zoe Akins, Frances Marion, James Hilton   *Ph* William Daniels, Karl Freund   *Ed* Margaret Booth   *Mus* Herbert Stothart   *Art Dir* Cedric Gibbons, Fredric Hope

● Greta Garbo, Robert Taylor, Lionel Barrymore, Elizabeth Allan, Jessie Ralph, Henry Daniell (M-G-M)

George Cukor directs this famous play [by Alexandre Dumas] with rare skill. Interior settings, costumes and exteriors are lavish and beautiful. The film shows the great care which went into its preparation and making.

Robert Taylor plays with surprising assurance and ease. He never seems to be striving for a point. He speaks with a moderately modulated voice, never hurriedly, and in all the familiar Armand scenes, such as the first meeting, the parting from his mistress, the accusation the gambling hall and, finally, the death chamber sequence, Taylor holds up his end of the story with distinction.

Garbo's impersonation of Marguerite Gautier is one of her best portraits. She wears striking clothes, white usually, and while she looks older than the ardent young Armand, the disparity does not mitigate against the illusion.

The two principals play the love scenes for full worth. There is much talk of their affection for each other, but Cukor, with wisdom, shows a minimum of embrace footage.

Of the support players, Henry Daniell, as Baron de Varville, turns in a performance of unusual interest. He is the menace in the background, the lover whom Camille deserts for Armand and the one to whom she returns. Daniell is suave and properly elegant without being too obvious.

☐ 1937: Nomination: Best Actress (Greta Garbo)

■ CAMPBELL'S KINGDOM

1957, 100 MINS, UK ◇
Dir Ralph Thomas   *Prod* Betty E. Box   *Scr* Robin Estridge   *Ph* Ernest Steward   *Ed* Frederick Wilson   *Mus* Clifton Parker   *Art Dir* Maurice Carter
● Dirk Bogarde, Stanley Baker, Michael Craig, Barbara Murray, James Robertson Justice, Athene Seyler (Rank)

Campbell's Kingdom is virtually a British western. It is a straightforward, virile, action-packed yarn with ample excitement and mounting drama.

Story is a simple clash between a stiff-lipped hero and a glowering villain. When Dirk Bogarde with only six months to live, arrives in the township of Come Lucky in the Rockies to take up his grandfather's inheritance, a whole train of skulduggery is unleashed. Said inheritance is Campbell's Kingdom, a valley which has been a problem child for some years. The old man obstinately insisted that it held oil. The local inhabitants invested their money in his idea. Meanwhile ruthless contractor Stanley Baker wants to flood the valley as part of a new hydro-electric scheme involving building of a new dam with inferior cement.

The plot unfolds slowly but gathers tremendous momentum, with the dam crashing a great thrill. The alleged Rockies were lensed brilliantly in Cortina by Ernest Steward. Director Ralph Thomas wisely resists the temptation to allow his characters to indulge in personal rough stuff. Film keeps fairly close to the novel [by Hammond Innes].

■ CAMP ON BLOOD ISLAND, THE

1958, 82 MINS, UK
Dir Val Guest   *Prod* Anthony Hinds   *Scr* Jon Manchip White, Val Guest   *Ph* Jack Asher   *Ed* Bill Lenny, James Needs   *Mus* Gerard Schurmann   *Art Dir* John Stoll
● Carl Mohner, Andre Morell, Edward Underdown, Michael Goodliffe, Barbara Shelley, Michael Gwynn (Hammer)

The yarn, based on a real-life incident, takes place in a Japanese prisoner-of-war camp, ruled over by a sadistic commandant who has sworn to massacre all the British prisoners should Japan lose the war. The British officers learn on a secret radio that the war has ended but, somewhat implausibly, they manage to keep the secret from the Nips until the end of the film.

There are as many holes in the film as there are in a fishing net. Yet it holds the attention mainly because of the frightful realization that such things did actually happen in the war. The dialog and situations have been devised on the very simple premise that all Japs are rats.

■ CAN-CAN

1960, 134 MINS, US ◇ ⓥ ☉
Dir Walter Lang   *Prod* Jack Cummings   *Scr* Dorothy Kingsley, Charles Lederer   *Ph* William H. Daniels   *Ed* Robert Simpson   *Mus* Nelson Riddle (arr.)   *Art Dir* Lyle Wheeler, Jack Martin Smith
● Frank Sinatra, Shirley MacLaine, Maurice Chevalier, Louis Jourdan, Juliet Prowse, Marcel Dalio (20th Century-Fox)

Can-Can [based on the musical by Abe Burrows] is a serviceable musical. The more discriminating will find it wanting. It's Las Vegas, 1960; not Montmartre, 1896. The production somehow conveys the feeling that Clan members Frank Sinatra and Shirley MacLaine will soon be joined by other members of the group for another 'summit' meeting.

MacLaine is bouncy, outgoing, scintillating, vivacious and appealing – but French she ain't. Sinatra is, well, Sinatra, complete with the ring-a-ding-ding vocabulary of the insiders. The juxtaposition of Sinatra and MacLaine on the one hand, and authentic Parisians Maurice Chevalier and Louis Jourdan on the other, is jarring.

As the proprietor of a cafe that pays off the gendarme so that the imbibers can witness the illegal dance, MacLaine has the opportunity to indulge in uninhibited and brash clowning and frenzied dancing. Sinatra is her wisecracking playboy-lawyer who aptly handles her legal and private affairs. Both Chevalier and Jourdan, who clicked so strongly in *Gigi*, are wasted in thankless roles as corruptible and incorruptible judges, respectively.

The musical score has been enhanced with three Cole Porter songs that were not in the original Broadway musical – 'Let's Do It', 'Just One of Those Things' and 'You Do Something to Me.' The best tune from the original, as sung by Sinatra, is still 'C'est Magnifique.'

The dance numbers, for the most part, are the highlights of the film, particularly MacLaine's Apache dance. The famous 'Adam and Eve' ballet falls somewhat flat, although it does show off to good advantage Marc Wilder and Juliet Prowse. The can-can is fun, but about as lewd and lascivious as a Maypole dance.

☐ 1960: Nominations: Best Color Costume Design, Scoring of a Musical Picture

■ CANDIDATE, THE

1972, 109 MINS, US ◇ ⓥ ☉
Dir Michael Ritchie   *Prod* Walter Coblenz   *Scr* Jeremy Larner   *Ph* Victor J. Kemper   *Ed* Richard A. Harris, Robert Estrin   *Mus* John Rubinstein   *Art Dir* Gene Callahan
● Robert Redford, Peter Boyle, Don Porter, Allen Garfield, Karen Carlson, Melvyn Douglas (Warner)

The Candidate is an excellent drama starring Robert Redford as a naive liberal political novice who wises up fast. Walter Coblenz produced the zesty, gritty film, directed and paced superbly by Michael Ritchie. Peter Boyle and Allen Garfield are tops as campaign supervisors.

The well-structured and developed screenplay takes Redford from a rural legal assistance vocation through the temptations and tortures of mass-merchandising politics, to an upset victory over longtime Californian Senator Don Porter. Redford's superior acting talents, which not-often-enough are tapped by the scripts he decides to do, are nearly all on display herein in a virtuoso peformance.

Intercutting of some actual political banquet footage is excellent, and the entire film often seems like a documentary special in the best sense of the word.

☐ 1972: Best Original Story & Screenplay.
☐ Nomination: Best Sound

■ CANDY

1968, 123 MINS, US/ITALY/FRANCE ◇
Dir Christian Marquand   *Prod* Robert Haggiog   *Scr* Buck Henry   *Ph* Giuseppe Rotunno   *Ed* Frank Santillo, Giancarlo Cappelli   *Mus* Dave Grusin   *Art Dir* Dean Tavoularis
● Charles Aznavour, Marlon Brando, Richard Burton, James Burton, John Huston, Ewa Aulin (Selmur/Dear)

Candy is a mixed bag of goodies. Based on a novel [by Terry Southern and Mason Hoffenberg] which was a successful satire on pornographic stories, film is at times hilarious, delightfully outrageous, silly, flat, and routine. Director Christian Marquand utilizes a Buck Henry adaptation, a very fine comedy sexpot newcomer (Ewa Aulin) and a strong cast of cameo stars and character thesps.

Candy tells of the unbelievably naive and innocent sexpot heroine, whose adventures were setup for the de rigeur sexual incidents found in most pornography.

The continuing characters are excellent. Aulin's performance in the title role is a delight. John Astin plays both her square father and lecherous uncle, and he is terrific. Elsa Martinelli also is excellent as Aunt Livia.

In retrospect, a prime flaw in *Candy* is the over-exposition of the vignettes. Nearly every episode suffers from the temptation to get one or two more gags out of the material before cutting.

Richard Burton, first cameo star, comes across as the most effective. Ringo Starr, as the Mexican gardener, is very good.

■ CANDYMAN

1992, 93 MINS, US ◇ ⓥ ☉
Dir Bernard Rose   *Prod* Steve Golin, Sigurjon Sighvatsson, Alan Poul   *Scr* Bernard Rose   *Ph* Anthony B. Richmond   *Ed* Dan Rae   *Mus* Philip Glass   *Art Dir* Jane Ann Stewart
● Virginia Madsen, Tony Todd, Xander Berkeley, Kasi Lemmons, Vanessa Williams, DeJuan Guy (Propaganda)

Candyman is an uppper-register horror item that delivers the requisite shocks and gore but doesn't cheat or cop out.

Doctoral candidate Helen Lyle (Virginia Madsen) is studying neighborhood legends and learns that Candyman, the educated, talented son of a slave, had his hand cut off and was put to death by throwing him to a swarm of bees in revenge for impregnating a young upper-class woman.

Lyle's investigation leads her to the site of the century-old outrage, Cabrini Green, in crime-ridden housing projects in Chicago. Supposedly, Candyman (Tony Todd) has committed 21 murders thus far, and it doesn't take long for Lyle to discover his gruesome lair in the projects.

Working from a story [*The Forbidden*] originally set in Liverpool by horror meister Clive Barker, Brit helmer Bernard Rose provides plenty of jolts, both bogus and actual, along the way. Threat of Candyman bursting out from behind mirrors is ever-present, and his evisceration technique with his hook is particularly gruesome. Performances are unusually credible for this sort of fare.

■ CAN HEIRONYMUS MERKIN EVER FORGET MERCY HUMPPE AND FIND TRUE HAPPINESS?

1969, 117 MINS, UK ◇
Dir Anthony Newley   *Prod* Anthony Newley   *Scr* Herman Raucher, Anthony Newley   *Ph* Otto Heller   *Ed* Bernard Gribble   *Mus* Anthony Newley   *Art Dir* William Constable
● Anthony Newley, Joan Collins, Milton Berle, George Jessel, Connie Kreski, Bruce Forsyth (Universal/Taralex)

This film is the work of Anthony Newley, who not only produced and directed from the script on which he collabed with Herman

C

Raucher, and wrote the music, but stars as well in the title role.

Newley plays an introspective film singing idol who re-lives his part-real, part-illusionary past in a movie within a movie, drawing on strange characters to people this past as well as lovelies who line up in wild expectancy as Heironymus plucks them one by one.

Milton Berle in the fetching character-name of Good Time Eddie Filth is his agent who lures him into his career of concupiscence, and George Jessel as The Presence, perhaps an advance angel of death, occasionally emerges out of the blue before disappearing again to spout shaggy jokes as pointless parables.

Married to Polyester Poontang (Joan Collins), Heironymus cannot forget Mercy Humppe, the beautiful innocent so deliciously cavorted by Connie Kreski, one-time Playboy bunny.

. . . .

■ **CANNERY ROW**

1982, 120 MINS, US ◇ Ⓥ
Dir David S. Ward *Prod* Michael Phillips *Scr* David S. Ward *Ph* Sven Nykvist *Ed* David Bretherton *Mus* Jack Nitzsche *Art Dir* Richard MacDonald
● Nick Nolte, Debra Winger, Audra Lindley, Frank McRae, M. Emmet Walsh, Tom Mahoney ((M-G-M/United Artists)

Maybe Raquel Welch will have the last laugh after all. *Cannery Row*, pic from which she was ignominiously dismissed, gets somewhat better as it lurches along from vignette to vignette, but this long-in-the-works adaptation of John Steinbeck's waterfront tomes [*Cannery Row* and *Sweet Thursday*] displays more appreciation for the values inherent in the material than it does ability to breathe life into it.

Highly anecdotal in nature and tied together by some personable, literary narration by John Huston, 1940s tale centers mostly upon the sketchy activities of a self-employed marine biologist named Doc (Nick Nolte), who lives at ocean's edge, consorts with floozies, counts local bums as his best friends and conceals a troubled past behind his handsome physique.

Across the way stands the neighborhood bordello, into which comes mixed-up drifter girl Suzy (Debra Winger), who has eyes for Doc but little knowledge of how to pursue him or improve her lot in life. The two sort of get together and break up numerous times.

Nolte seems ideally cast as Doc and has no trouble carrying the film, but is nevertheless hampered by incomplete nature of the part as written. Winger's winning personality and great cracking voice carry her through here, but she relies unduly on a few pat mannerisms.

. . . .

■ **CANNONBALL**
(UK: Carquake)

1976, 93 MINS, US/HONG KONG ◇ Ⓥ
Dir Paul Bartel *Prod* Samuel W. Gelfman *Scr* Paul Bartel, Donald C. Simpson *Ph* Tak Fujimoto *Ed* Morton Tubor *Mus* David A. Axelrod *Art Dir* Michel Levesque
● David Carradine, Bill McKinney, Veronica Hamel, Gerrit Graham, Robert Carradine, Martin Scorsese (New World/Shaws)

Cannoball will please those who won't rest until they see every car in creation destroyed and aflame.

The sophisticated story line puts David Carradine, Bill McKinney and various other drivers and characters in autos in Los Angeles and promises $100,000 to the first to arrive in New York. Surely, goodness, mercy and high octane will triumph over villainy with lead in their guns, if not in their gas.

That's not to say *Cannonball* has no appeal beyond the crash crowd. It's full of handy highway hints, like what to do when someone

steals your jack and then blasts your back tire apart with a pistol.

Best of all, though, is Carradine's inspirational automotive fortitude. When frustrated, he spins in circles, kicks his wheels, mutters oaths – just like the average weekend driver.

. . . .

■ **CANNONBALL RUN, THE**

1981, 93 MINS, US ◇ Ⓥ ⊙
Dir Hal Needham *Prod* Albert S. Ruddy *Scr* Brock Yates *Ph* Michael Butler *Ed* Donna Cambern, William D. Gordean *Mus* Snuff Garrett (sup.) *Art Dir* Carol Wenger
● Burt Reynolds, Roger Moore, Farrah Fawcett, Dom DeLuise, Dean Martin, Sammy Davis Jr (20th Century-Fox)

Full of terribly inside showbiz jokes and populated by what could be called Burt and Hal's Rat Pack, film takes place in that redneck never-never land where most of the guys are beer-guzzling good ole boys and all the gals are fabulously built tootsies.

Cross-country race of the title comes off as almost entirely incidental to the star turns. Overall effect is akin to watching the troupe take a vacation.

Reynolds doesn't even lay a finger on Farrah Fawcett, settling instead for a nice chat in the back of his speedy ambulance. Tuxedoed Roger Moore drives around in his Aston-Martin and tries to convince everyone he's really Roger Moore and not one Seymour Goldfarb. Oriental driver Jackie Chan distracts (and almost kills) himself by putting on a videotape of *Behind the Green Door*, one way to stay awake on a coast-to-coast trip. Partner Michael Hui plays it straight.

. . . .

■ **CANNONBALL RUN II**

1984, 108 MINS, US ◇ Ⓥ ⊙
Dir Hal Needham *Prod* Albert S. Ruddy, Harvey Miller *Scr* Hal Needham, Albert S. Ruddy, Harvey Miller *Ph* Nick McLean *Ed* William Gordean, Carl Kress *Mus* Al Capps *Art Dir* Thomas E. Azzari
● Burt Reynolds, Dom DeLuise, Dean Martin, Sammy Davis Jr, Telly Savalas, Shirley MacLaine (Golden Harvest/Warner)

This film is so inept that the best actor in the pic is Jilly Rizzo. But he has a great advantage: he's on screen five seconds and he doesn't have to talk.

Sequel to the all-star, 1981 hit *The Cannonball Run*, which was in turn an embellishment of Roger Corman's *Cannonball* (1976), plays as if former colleagues – producer Albert Ruddy, director Hal Needham and stars Burt Reynolds, Dom DeLuise, Dean Martin and Sammy Davis Jr – don't even have to make an effort any more. It's the ole boy network kind of filmmaking, joined this time by Frank Sinatra (playing himself) and Shirley MacLaine, in terms not endearing.

Again, a bunch of crazies, in a disparate collection of cars, are engaged in racing across the country to collect a lot of money. Action on the road, as encounters with most of the supporting players resemble nothing more than day work for majority of the cast, is limited to dusty, desert highway scenes (filmed in Arizona). To depict the later momentum of the race, filmmakers engaged Ralph Bakshi to show the race's progress in animation.

Execution is uninspired, laughs are hard to find, and the script is also difficult to locate. Reynold's high-pitched laugh is wearing thin.

. . . .

■ **CAN SHE BAKE A CHERRY PIE?**

1983, 90 MINS, US ◇ Ⓥ
Dir Henry Jaglom *Prod* M.H. Simonson *Scr* Henry Jaglom *Ph* Bob Fiore *Mus* Karen Black
● Karen Black, Michael Emil, Michael Margotta, Frances Fisher, Martin Frydberg (Jagfilm)

Henry Jaglom follows his *Sitting Ducks* [1981] with a similar opus. This is once again a talky comedy, in which the scripter-director puts his characters in a number of sitcom situations, feeds them the opening lines of their scenes and lets them embroider the rest on their own.

Starting from the basic premise that human beings suffer from their inability to communicate with their fellow men, Jaglom builds up a romance of sorts between a fresh divorcee who is still not emotionally rid of her husband, and a man who has been living on his own for some years.

Characters are built very much around the personality of the two main actors, Karen Black giving a beautiful performance, humorous, edgy, nervous and implying deep fears and pains hidden barely under the surface, and Michael Emil brings back many of the peculiarities of his part in *Sitting Ducks*.

. . . .

■ **CANTERBURY TALE, A**

1944, 124 MINS, UK Ⓥ
Dir Michael Powell, Emeric Pressburger *Prod* Michael Powell, Emeric Pressburger *Scr* Michael Powell, Emeric Pressburger *Ph* Erwin Hillier *Ed* John Seabourne *Mus* Allan Gray *Art Dir* Alfred Junge
● Eric Portman, Sheila Sim, Dennis Price, John Sweet, Charles Hawtrey, Freda Jackson (Archers)

Sincerity and simplicity shine through every foot of this oversized modern version of the Chaucer epic tale. Here is rare beauty.

Without belittling the highly imaginative genius inspiring the two directors, Michael Powell and Emeric Pressburger, first honors go to Erwin Hillier, whose camerawork is superb. Nothing more effective by way of a time transition shot has been conceived than the way he carries his audience through nine centuries in a few seconds. Beginning with a close-up of a hooded falcon on the wrist of an ancient Canterbury pilgrim (400 years before Columbus discovered America), he follows the graceful bird as it soars aloft on speedy wings. When it becomes a mere speck, it turns and comes gliding back. On coming nearer, it is seen to be a Spitfire.

Sheila Sim is the sole femme in the story. As a London shop girl, turned farmeret for the duration, she turns in a polished performance. Although giving the American GI all the best of it, there is an equally well-drawn characterization, the British tank sergeant, done so well by Dennis Price. For him the cathedral works a miracle.

Star of the film, Eric Portman, gives a splendid restrained performance as a small-town justice of the peace. Four miracles occur in this story, one to each of the four principal characters.

. . . .

■ **CANTERVILLE GHOST, THE**

1944, 95 MINS, US ◇
Dir Jules Dassin *Prod* Arthur L. Field *Scr* Edwin Harvey Blum *Ph* Robert Planck *Ed* Chester W. Schaeffer *Mus* George Bassman *Art Dir* Cedric Gibbons, Edward Carfagno
● Charles Laughton, Robert Young, Margaret O'Brien, Peter Lawford, Una O'Connor, Mike Mazurki (M-G-M)

The Canterville Ghost is entertaining comedy-drama, with the accent on comedy despite the mystery-chiller emphasis in the title. Tight scripting, nimble direction and excellent casting are about equally responsible for the satisfactory result

Margaret O'Brien and Charles Laughton come through with topnotch performances, with the clever moppet a solid smash and topping everything. One of her outstanding bits is in a jitterbug terping number with an American soldier and her sedately demure dancing with Robert Young. Her solemn, dignified interpretation as the youthful Lady

Jessica de Canterville, head of one of the great English landowning families, is terrific. Yarn [from the Oscar Wilde short story] is about a 300-year-old ghost (Laughton), once walled up alive in the castle by his father because he proved a coward on the field of battle, who is looking for a kinsman to perform an act of bravery his name so that he can be freed from his miserable existence.

● ●

■ CAN'T STOP THE MUSIC

1980, 118 MINS, US ◇ ⓥ
Dir Nancy Walker   *Prod* Allan Carr, Jacques Morali, Henri Belolo   *Scr* Bronte Woodard, Allan Carr   *Ph* Bill Butler   *Ed* John F. Burnett   *Mus* Jacques Morali   *Art Dir* Harold Michelson
● Valerie Perrine, Steve Guttenberg, June Havoc, Barbara Rush, Leigh Taylor-Young, The Village People (AFD/Allan Carr)

Writers have recreated the old 'I know, we'll put on a show' gimmick to hinge their story on. Valerie Perrine plays the ex-model with a heart of gold. Her room-mate is an aspiring pop composer (Steve Guttenberg) whom she helps.

She recruits various friends (The Village People) to sing on a demo tape she's going to present to ex-lover and president of Marrakesh Records.

Among the standout sequences is the 'Y.M.C.A.' number, replete with a chorus line of young males side-diving just like in an Esther Williams aquastravaganza in the 1950s.

Director Nancy Walker clearly had trouble with the non-actors in the cast. The Village People, along with ex-Olympic decathlon champion Bruce Jenner, have a long way to go in the acting stakes.

● ●

■ CAPE FEAR

1962, 105 MINS, US ⓥ ⊙
Dir J. Lee Thompson   *Prod* Sy Bartlett   *Scr* James R. Webb   *Ph* Samuel Leavitt   *Ed* George Tomasini   *Mus* Bernard Herrmann   *Art Dir* Alexander Golitzen, Robert Boyle
● Gregory Peck, Robert Mitchum, Polly Bergen, Lori Martin, Martin Balsam, Telly Savalas (Universal/Melville-Talbot)

As a forthright exercise in cumulative terror *Cape Fear* is a competent and visually polished entry.

Taken from John D. MacDonald's magazine-serialized novel, *The Executioners*, the screenplay deals with the scheme of a sadistic ex-convict (Robert Mitchum) to gain revenge against a smalltown Georgia lawyer (Gregory Peck), his wife and daughter. Peck, it seems, had testified against him eight years earlier for the savage assault on a woman in a parking lot.

Mitchum's menacing omnipresence causes the family much mental anguish. Their pet dog is poisoned, the daughter has a harrowing encounter with the degenerate, and there is the culminating terror in Georgia swampland.

What ails Mitchum obviously requires violent sexual expression – the women he takes have to be clobbered as well as violated. But in the undiluted flow of evil, there is nothing in the script or J. Lee Thompson's direction which might provide audiences with some insight into Mitchum's behavior.

Peck, displaying his typical guarded self, is effective, if perhaps less distraught over the prospect of personal disaster than his character might warrant. Granting the shallowness of his motivation, Mitchum has no trouble being utterly hateful. Wearing a Panama fedora and chomping a cocky cigar, the menace of his visage has the hiss of a poised snake. Polly Bergen, breaking an eight-year screen absence, turns in a sympathetic job as Peck's wife.

● ●

■ CAPE FEAR

1991, 128 MINS, US ◇ ⓥ ⊙
Dir Martin Scorsese   *Prod* Barbara De Fina   *Scr* Wesley Strick   *Ph* Freddie Francis   *Ed* Thelma Schoonmaker   *Mus* Elmer Bernstein (adapt.)   *Art Dir* Henry Bumstead
● Robert De Niro, Nick Nolte, Jessica Lange, Juliette Lewis, Joe Don Baker, Illeana Douglas (Universal/Amblin)

Cape Fear is a smart and stylish remake of the 1962 suspenser. Sharply written adaptation follows the basic plot of J. Lee Thompson's solid black & white 1962 Universal release, which featured Robert Mitchum as a white trash ex-con who return from prison to torment the prosecuting attorney (Gregory Peck) who sent him up.

Changes, however, enrich and blacken the material, making the characters squirm physically, morally and sexually. Instead of being a 'normal' upstanding Southern family, the Bowdens (Nick Nolte, Jessica Lange and 15-year-old daughter Juliette Lewis) are troubled by father's history of infidelity and daughter's difficulties with both parents.

Enter Robert De Niro's Max Cady, a psychopath whose body is covered with a mural of threatening, religiously oriented tattoos, including the scales of 'truth' and 'justice' hanging off either side of a cross. Penned up for 14 years, Cady begins by just annoying the family, but soon launches his campaign of terror by killing the family dog and brutalizing a boozy young law clerk (Illeana Douglas) whom Nolte has been seeing.

In maximum souped-up style, director Martin Scorsese slams through the mandatory plot mechanics with powerful short scenes, dynamic in-your-face dollies and cranes and machine-gun editing. Director and his collaborators really cut to the quick in the disturbing sexual component, mainly between Cady and the teen.

De Niro's Cady is a memorable nasty right up there with Travis Bickle and Jake La Motta, a sickie utterly determined in his righteous cause. Nolte copes admirably with a difficult role written as somewhat unsympathetic. Lange's role plays as rather subsidiary to the others. Lewis is excellent as the troubled, tempted teen, and tale begins and ends with brief narration from her p.o.v. Robert Mitchum, Gregory Peck and Martin Balsam, all of whom appeared in the '62 version, pop up here in astutely judged roles. Bernard Herrmann's original score is adapted and rearranged by Elmer Bernstein.

□ 1991: Nominations: Best Actor (Robert De Niro), Supp. Actress (Juliette Lewis)

● ●

■ CAPONE

1975, 101 MINS, US ◇
Dir Steve Carver   *Prod* Roger Corman   *Scr* Howard Browne   *Ph* Vilis Lapenieks   *Ed* Richard Meyer   *Mus* David Grisman   *Art Dir* Ward Preston
● Ben Gazzara, Susan Blakely, Harry Guardino, John Cassavetes, Sylvester Stallone, Peter Maloney (20th-Century Fox)

Capone, a somewhat crude, violent and deja vu actioner, focusses on Ben Gazzara as Capone, showing his brutish, casual arrogance in a climb from neighborhood punk to a Chi rackets kingpin, then his decline via an income tax rap (arranged, it claimed by his own aide, Frank Nitti, very well played by Sylvester Stallone).

Susan Blakely again shows her sensual sparkle as a slumming rich chick taken to Capone; while John Cassavetes has a good cameo as the NY hood who discovers Capone's potential.

Gazzara has evidently gone to great lengths to attempt a full characterization of Capone, but it's hard to shoehorn developed drama between machine gun bullets.

● ●

■ CAPRICE

1967, 97 MINS, US ⓥ
Dir Frank Tashlin   *Prod* Aaron Rosenburg, Martin Melcher   *Scr* Jay Jayson, Frank Tashlin   *Ph* Leon Shamroy   *Ed* Robert Simpson   *Mus* Frank DeVol   *Art Dir* Jack Martin Smith, William Creber
● Doris Day, Richard Harris, Ray Walston, Jack Kruschen, Edward Mulhare, Michael J. Pollard (20th Century-Fox)

Caprice is one of those occasional pictures about which it can be said fairly that it could have been better than it is. A timely and inventive plot – industrial espionage – is never fully developed in either writing, acting or direction.

Doris Day and Richard Harris are double-crossing double agents working, variously, for US cosmetics king Jack Kruschen, British counterpart Edward Mulhare, or Interpol.

Ray Walston plays Kruschen's inventive genius, although it turns out that Lilia Skala, Walston's mother-in-law in Switzerland, is the creative brain.

Elements of comedy, murder, satire and psychology are blended uncertainly in the never-boiling pot.

● ●

■ CAPRICORN ONE

1978, 127 MINS, US ◇ ⓥ ⊙
Dir Peter Hyams   *Prod* Paul N. Lazarus III   *Scr* Peter Hyams   *Ph* Bill Butler   *Ed* James Mitchell   *Mus* Jerry Goldsmith   *Art Dir* Albert Brenner
● Elliott Gould, James Brolin, Brenda Vaccaro, Sam Waterston, O.J. Simpson, Hal Holbrook (Associated General)

Capricorn One begins with a workable, if cynical cinematic premise: the first manned space flight to Mars was a hoax and the American public was fooled through Hollywood gimmickry into believing that the phony landing happened. But after establishing the concept, Peter Hyams' script asks another audience – the one in the theatre – to accept something far more illogical, the uncovering of the hoax by reporter Elliott Gould.

The astronaut trio of James Brolin, Sam Waterston and O.J. Simpson together add up to nothing; there's no group chemistry. Still, scattershot casting means once in a while you hit and in the final scene Gould and Telly Savalas are teamed. The duo is a bullseye. Savalas, in a delightful cameo as a crop duster hired to help rescue Brolin in the desert and uncover the plot, is a marvelous complement to Gould.

Hal Holbrook plays the mission commander who calls off the Mars shot and engineers the dupe. His character must change from sincere – he believes he's doing the right thing by fooling the public – to menacing. In general, it is a script of conveniences.

● ●

■ CAPTAIN BLOOD

1935, 119 MINS, US ⓥ ⊙
Dir Michael Curtiz   *Scr* Casey Robinson   *Ph* Hal Mohr   *Ed* George Amy   *Mus* Erich Wolfgang Korngold   *Art Dir* Anton Grot
● Errol Flynn, Olivia de Havilland, Basil Rathbone, Lionel Atwill, Ross Alexander, Guy Kibbee (Cosmopolitan/Warner)

Captain Blood, from the Rafael Sabatini novel, is a big picture. It's a spectacle which will establish both Errol Flynn and Olivia de Havilland. Director Michael Curtiz hasn't spared the horses. It's a lavish, swashbuckling saga of the Spanish main.

The engaging Flynn is the titular Peter Blood, erstwhile physician, later sold into West Indian slavery, to emerge thereafter as a peer among Caribbean pirates, Capt Blood, only later to be pardoned, his crew of runaway slaves likewise granted their freedom, and sworn into the King's navy.

C

Flynn impresses favorably from the start. One lives with him in the unfairness of a tyrant King Charles which causes him and his fellow Englishmen to be sold into slavery. One suffers with their travail; the audience roots with them in their ultimately fruitless plot for escape from the island. And then he is catapulted into leadership of a pirate ship.

De Havilland, who came to attention in Warner's *A Midsummer Night's Dream*, is romantically beauteous as the unsympathetic plantation owner's (later governor's) niece. This supplies a modicum of romantic interest, although all too paltry. It's one of the prime shortcomings of the production. Lionel Atwill is sufficiently hateful as the uncle. Basil Rathbone is an effective co-pirate captain (French brigands, this time), he and Flynn engaging in an arresting duel in the course of events.

☐ 1935: Nominations: Best Picture, Sound

■ CAPTAIN FROM CASTILE

1947, 140 MINS, US ◇
Dir Henry King *Prod* Lamar Trotti *Scr* Lamar Trotti *Ph* Charles Clarke, Arthur E. Arling *Ed* Barbara McLean *Mus* Alfred Newman *Art Dir* Richard Day, James Basen
● Tyrone Power, Jean Peters, Cesar Romero, Lee J. Cobb, Antonio Moreno (20th Century-Fox)

Based on Samuel Shellaberger's 1945 bestselling historical novel, the cinema adaptation hews closely to the structure of the book, capturing the vast sweep of its story and adding to it an eye-stunning Technicolor dimension. The coin poured into this production, reported to be around $4.5 million, is visible in every inch of the footage.

For this plume-and-sabre epic of 16th-century Spanish imperial conquerors, producer and production thinker have assembled a group of thespers who are cleanly tailored for the various parts. Led by Tyrone Power, who's rarely been shown to better advantage, the roster is buttressed by Cesar Romero, in a stirringly virile protrait of Cortez; Lee J Cobb, as a fortune hunter; John Sutton, as a velvety villain, and newcomer Jean Peters, a buxom, appealing wench for the romantic byplay.

From one viewpoint, this picture is constructed like a self-contained double feature. In the first half, the locale is Spain during the Inquisition, with Power and his family unjustly persecuted for heresy. Escaping from Spain, Power finds himself during the second half in Mexico as a recruit in Cortez's expedition of plunder against the Aztec empire ruled by Montezuma.

There are, however several soft spots in the story that interfere with credibility. There is, for instance, the fact that Power narrowly escapes death no less than three times under the most extreme circumstance Sutton, likewise, cheats death two times despite his being stabbed through the heart with a foot of steel one time and near-strangled the next.

☐ 1947: Nomination: Best Scoring of a Dramatic Picture

■ CAPTAIN HORATIO HORNBLOWER R.N.

1951, 116 MINS, UK ◇
Dir Raoul Walsh *Prod* [uncredited] *Scr* Ivan Goff, Ben Roberts, Aeneas Mackenzie *Ph* Guy Green *Ed* Jack Harris *Mus* Robert Farnon *Art Dir* Tom Morahan
● Gregory Peck, Virginia Mayo, Robert Beatty, Dennis O'Dea, James Robertson Justice, Stanley Baker (Warner)

The exploits of one of Britain's greatest fictional naval adventurers have been filmed by Warner with spectacular success. *Captain Horatio Hornblower* has been brought to the screen as effervescent entertainment with action all the way.

Three C.S. Forester stories provide the basis for the pic, and the author, in preparing his own adaptation, has selected the best material. It is an incisive study of a man who is dispassionate, aloof and remote, yet often capable of finer feelings.

In his interpretation of the title role, Gregory Peck stands out as a skilled artist, capturing the spirit of the character and atmosphere of the period. Whether as the ruthless captain ordering a flogging as a face-saving act for a junior officer or tenderly nursing Virginia Mayo through yellow fever, he never fails to reflect the Forester character.

The film is divided into two halves. In the opening, Hornblower (Peck) is commanding the frigate *Lydia* throught the Pacific waters to fulfill a British mission to provide arms to enemies of Spain. On his return to England, he participates in an exiting adventure against Napoleon's fleet, eventually becoming a national hero. The major action sequences have been lensed with great skill.

■ CAPTAIN KRONOS – VAMPIRE HUNTER

1974, 91 MINS, UK ◇
Dir Brian Clemens *Prod* Albert Fennell, Brian Clemens *Scr* Brian Clemens *Ph* Ian Wilson *Ed* James Needs *Mus* Laurie Johnson *Art Dir* Robert Jones
● Horst Janson, John Carson, Shane Briant, Caroline Munro, John Cater, Ian Hendry (Hammer)

Captain Kronos – Vampire Hunter, as played by Horst Janson, is a prototype blond Germanic, superstud caped like an operetta leading man. Accompanied by faithful friend John Cater, playing a hunchback professor, Kronos solves a vampire mystery with a lot of swash and buckle.

Story is unusual in that the vampire, who turns out to be an elderly woman (her ladyship in the castle, halfway up the next hill), sucks blood to get a youthful appearance. Being a new horror character, Kronos naturally has a groupie in tow (Caroline Munro) who caters to his earthier needs between random jousts with bad guys and bad vampires.

Ian Hendry has one scene as a heavy, got up like an aging leather gang leader solely for the purpose of Kronos showing off his swordsmanship.

■ CAPTAIN NEWMAN, M.D.

1963, 126 MINS, US ◇
Dir David Miller *Prod* Robert Arthur *Scr* Richard L. Breen, Henry Ephron *Ph* Russell Metty *Ed* Alma Macrorie *Mus* Frank Skinner *Art Dir* Alexander Golitzen, Alfred Sweeney
● Gregory Peck, Tony Curtis, Angie Dickinson, Eddie Albert, Bobby Darin, Robert Duvall (Universal)

Captain Newman, M.D. oscillates between scenes of great dramatic impact and somewhat strained and contrived comedy of the heartwarming variety.

Leo Rosten's novel is the source of the hot-and-cold scenario. Hero of the story is Capt. Newman (Gregory Peck), chief of the neuropsychiatric ward of a wartime (1944) army hospital who places his medical obligations above military duty. Newman's treatment of three cases is illustrated. One involves a decorated corporal (Bobby Darin) who believes himself a coward for having deserted a buddy in a burning aircraft. Another concerns a colonel (Eddie Albert) who has gone berserk with a sense of guilt at having sent so many men to their deaths in aerial combat. The third (Robert Duvall) feels shame over having hidden alone in a cellar for over a year in Nazi-occupied territory.

In between all of this, Newman gets his kicks in a romance with his nurse (Angie Dickinson) and by observing the antics of his number one orderly (Tony Curtis), a glib, resourceful operator from Jersey City with a streak of Bergen County larceny.

Peck's portrayal of the title figure is characteristically restrained and intelligent. Curtis has some good moments, but essentially he is the pivotal figure in the film's secondary comic shenanigans. Dickinson is sweet, sometimes too darned sweet, as the nurse.

☐ 1963: Nominations: Best Supp. Actor (Bobby Darin), Adapted Screenplay, Sound

■ CAPTAINS COURAGEOUS

1937, 115 MINS, US ◎ ⊙
Dir Victor Fleming *Prod* Louis D. Lighton *Scr* John Lee Mahin, Marc Connolly, Dale Van Every *Ph* Harold Rosson *Ed* Elmo Vernon *Mus* Franz Waxman
● Spencer Tracy, Freddie Bartholomew, Lionel Barrymore, Melvyn Douglas, Charley Grapewin, Mickey Rooney (M-G-M)

Taking this Rudyard Kipling story, written when he visited America some years earlier, the producers have made the central character of the spoiled child younger than he was in the book, and for the purposes of the screen have indulged in other slight, unimportant alterations. Spencer Tracy is a Portuguese fisherman with an accent and a flair for singing songs of the briny. Lionel Barrymore is the happy-go-lucky but stern captain of a fishing schooner while Bartholomew, of course, is the boy.

The Kipling yarn, built around a wealthy, motherless brat who accidentally lands with a cod-fishing fleet, and undergoes regeneration during an enforced three months' piscatorial quest, has been given splendid production, performance, photography and dramatic composition.

Young Bartholomew plays the spoiled kid, only son of wealthy father, who falls off a liner bound for Europe and is picked up by Tracy, the fisherman to whom the recalcitrant boy finally becomes deeply attached. Bartholomew's transition from a brat to a lovable child is done with convincing strokes.

His performance is matched by Tracy, who also doesn't seem right doing an accent and singing songs, but he, too, later gets under the skin of the character. Barrymore is himself, as usual. As the father of the boy, Melvyn Douglas gives a smooth, unctuous performance. One of the fishermen is deftly portrayed by John Carradine.

☐ 1937: Best Actor (Spencer Tracy).
☐ Nominations: Best Picture, Screenplay, Editing

■ CAPTAINS OF THE CLOUDS

1942, 113 MINS, US ◇
Dir Michael Curtiz *Prod* Hal B. Wallis (exec.) *Scr* Arthur T. Horman, Richard Macaulay, Norman Reilly Raine *Ph* Sol Polito, Wilfrid M. Cline, Elmer Dyer, Charles Marshall, Winton C. Hoch *Ed* George Amy *Mus* Max Steiner *Art Dir* Ted Smith
● James Cagney, Dennis Morgan, Brenda Marshall, Alan Hale, George Tobias, Reginald Gardiner (Warner)

Story splits into two sections – first half depicts the adventurous and rowdy experiences of a group of freelance bush flyers of northern Canada who pilot supplies to the settlers and prospectors along the lakes and rivers of the northland – and second portion outlines their adventures as members of the Royal Canadian Air Force training schools.

Cast is of topnotch calibre throughout. James Cagney holds attention throughout as the nervy, adventurous and happy-go-lucky flying expert. It's a spotlight performance for Cagney in every foot of film.

Screenplay [from a story by Arthur T. Horman and Roland Gillett] is a fine admixture of vigorous adventure with narrative insight of pilot training procedure across the border. Michael Curtiz directs with a positive straight-line objective of pointing up the sweeping drama.

CAPTIVE

1986, 95 MINS, UK/FRANCE ◇ ⑩
Dir Paul Mayersberg *Prod* Don Boyd *Scr* Paul Mayersberg *Ph* Mike Southon *Ed* Marie-Therese Boiche *Mus* The Edge, Michael Berkeley *Art Dir* George Djurkovic
● Irina Brook, Oliver Reed, Xavier Deluc, Corinne Decla, Hiro Arai, Nic Reding (Virgin/World Audio)

The kidnapping of a beautiful rich young girl, not for money, nor for sex, but just for the joy of doing it is the theme intricately developed by Paul Mayersberg in *Captive*.

A trio of kidnapers – a French boy, a Japanese boy and an Englis girl – imprison a rich girl. She's drugged, handcuffed, blindfolded and gagged before being locked up in a chest for the night. As the action proceeds it becomes evident the object of the mission is a brainwashing exercise, to mold the girl to their mode of life. Gradually, they succeed.

Irina Brook (daughter of Peter Brook) is a handsome boy with a firm young body, and willing to show it off. Fortunately, she's also a competent actress in the difficult role of the captive. Oliver Reed gives a commanding performance as the girl's father.

CAPTIVE CITY, THE

1952, 91 MINS, US
Dir Robert Wise *Prod* Theron Warth *Scr* Karl Kamb, Alvin Josephy Jr *Ph* Lee Garmes *Ed* Ralph Swink *Mus* Jerome Moross *Art Dir* Maurice Zuberano
● John Forsythe, Joan Camden, Harold J. Kennedy, Marjorie Crossland, Victor Sutherland, Ray Teal (Aspen/United Artists)

The Captive City is a tense, absorbing drama [from a screen story by Alvin M. Josephy Jr] of a small town editor's fight against corruption. It has a documentary quality that rings with authenticity. Based on facts uncovered by probes of the Senate Crime Investigation Committee, it contains a cleverly interwoven epilog by Senator Estes Kefauver, who headed the latter group.

John Forsythe and Harold J. Kennedy, as former GI buddies, are co-owners of a newspaper in a city called Kennington. Then a local private detective, working on an apparently harmless divorce case, discovers the existence of a big-time gambling syndicate operating with the knowledge of the city fathers, the local police and the respectable elements of the community.

Forsythe succeeds in uncovering the whole mess. However, he is powerless to do anything.

CAPTIVE HEART, THE

1946, 108 MINS, UK
Dir Basil Dearden *Prod* Michael Balcon *Scr* Angus MacPhail, Guy Morgan *Ph* Douglas Slocombe *Ed* Charles Hasse *Mus* Alan Rawsthorne *Art Dir* Michael Relph
● Michael Redgrave, Rachel Kempson, Mervyn Johns, Jack Warner, Basil Radford, Gordon Jackson (Ealing)

Second only to the unrelieved grim reality of life as it was lived in Stalags, the outstanding merit of *The Captive Heart* is the number of superlatively good performances turned in. To Michael Balcon as producer must go chief credit for the newsreel fidelity of the prison camp sequences.

Michael Redgrave, as a Czech, educated in England and fleeing from the Gestapo, takes on the identity of a dead English army officer and is jailed in a Stalag with British soldiers. He escapes lynching only to find himself marked down for a visit to a Nazi gas chamber.

Even when he convinces the British of the truth of his story, and after he has won freedom through repatriation, he's up against the task of squaring himself with the wife of the dead man whose identity he has assumed. The fact that this final sequence holds one's attention says something for the writing, acting, and directing.

CAPTIVE IN THE LAND, A

1991, 96 MINS, FRANCE/US/USSR ◇ ⑩
Dir John Berry *Prod* Malcolm Stuart, John Berry *Scr* Lee Gold *Ph* Pierre William Glenn *Ed* Georges Klotz *Mus* Bill Conti *Art Dir* Yuri Konstantinov
● Sam Waterston, Alexander Potapov (Gloria/Gorky Studios/Soviet American)

A Captive in the Land is a ruggedly effective allegorical survival tale. Shot on forbidding Arctic wastelands as well as in Russian studios, pic plays as a potent two-character piece about strangers forced to battle nature together, with the element of continued misunderstanding and mistrust between the US and USSR as a subtext.

Striking opening sequence (with one of the last title jobs by the late Maurice Binder, a long-time friend of the director) economically presents the crash a Soviet military plane in the polar region and the follow-up rescue jump by an American (Sam Waterston). As the days wear on, no saviors appear and Waterston and the survivor (Alexander Potapov) have no choice but to settle in for the long haul.

The two men set out on an arduous journey, with Waterston pulling and rowing Potapov across ice, snow and water in search of possible civilization.

Production might have been an arduous one for many filmmakers, but for a director of 73 it is notable. Berry, who has worked mostly overseas since being blacklisted, elicits fine performances from the leads. Implicit in the personal/political exchanges is the notion that, while the American may think he's much freer than the disabled man he rescues, he's actually just as stuck as the Russian.

CAPTURE, THE

1950, 91 MINS, US
Dir John Sturges *Prod* Niven Busch *Scr* Niven Busch *Ph* Edward Cronjager *Ed* George Amy *Mus* Daniele Amfitheatrof
● Lew Ayres, Teresa Wright, Victor Jory, Jacqueline White (RKO/Showtime)

The Capture is an offbeat drama, with psychological overtones, that plays off against the raw and rugged background of Mexican locales.

Picture kicks off with a wallop, depicting a desperate chase that, storywise, sets up the plot's final Lew Ayres is fleeing the Mexican rurales, wanted on a charge of murder. He holes up in a priest's cabin and begins to disclose his story. A year before he had killed a fugitive, wanted for a robbery. The possibility of the man's innocence haunted him, and Ayres sought out the widow. They fall in love, are married, but his guilty conscience makes full happiness impossible.

Ayres and Teresa Wright are very capable in the lead characters, adding to the general realism given the story because of the locales used.

One of the interesting touches to the film is the incidental native music hauntingly spotted with the appearance of a blind guitar player.

CARAVAGGIO

1986, 89 MINS, UK ◇ ⑩
Dir Derek Jarman *Prod* Sarah Radclyffe *Scr* Derek Jarman *Ph* Gabriel Beristain *Ed* George Akers *Mus* Simon Fisher Turner *Art Dir* Christopher Hobbs
● Nigel Terry, Sean Bean, Garry Cooper, Spencer Leigh, Tilda Swinton, Michael Gough (BFI)

Derek Jarman's *Caravaggio* triumphantly rises above its financial restrictions and proves, once again, that less can be a lot more.

Pic is an imagined biopic of one of the last Renaissance painters, Michelangelo Merisi da Caravaggio (1571–1610), but the inspiration seems to be Italian film director Pier Paolo Pasolini, since both artists came from poor backgrounds and used beautiful young men from the slums in their work. Both also became involved in scandal and violence.

Jarman's film, in classical tradition, is told in flashback as the artist lies dying in poverty. Story takes a backseat, however, since much of the joy of the film is to be found in the way Jarman and his team recreate the look and color of the original paintings. But film lacks a certain warmth and emotional depth.

CARAVANS

1978, 127 MINS, US/IRAN ◇ ⑩
Dir James Fargo *Prod* Elmo Williams *Scr* Nancy Voyles Crawford, Thomas A. McMahon, Lorraine Williams *Ph* Douglas Slocombe *Ed* Richard Marden *Mus* Mike Batt *Art Dir* Ted Tester, Peter Williams, Peter James
● Anthony Quinn, Michael Sarrazin, Jennifer O'Neill, Christopher Lee, Joseph Cotten, Behrooz Vosoughi (Ibex/FIDCI)

The main trouble with this tale of 1948 Persia isn't the Iranians, it's Hollywood. Almost every fake moment in the film, and there are lots of them, has the touch of Hollywood laid on with a heavy coating. Fortunately for the average viewer, the scenic scope of the film, based on James Michener's epic story, and shot entirely on locations in Iran, is so sweeping that the tale that is told is almost palatable. But barely.

Briefly, the film deals with the search of a minor American consular employee (Michael Sarrazin) for an American woman (Jennifer O'Neill) who has married an Iranian colonel (Behrooz Vosoughi) but deserted him for a Kochi chieftain (Anthony Quinn) and has disappeared. Sarrazin finds her in short order. That's when the real trouble begins. She won't go back and he won't go back without her and off everyone goes into the desert.

Sarrazin, Quinn and O'Neill carry most of the story. The other non-Persians – Christopher Lee, Barry Sullivan, Jeremy Kemp and Joseph Cotten – are seen so briefly they may have done their roles over a long weekend. Histrionically, only Quinn is believable, followed closely by Vosoughi.

□ 1978: Nomination: Best Costume Design

CARAVAN TO VACCARES

1974, 98 MINS, UK/FRANCE ◇ ⑩
Dir Geoffrey Reeve *Prod* Geoffrey Reeve, Richard Morris-Adams *Scr* Paul Wheeler *Ph* John Cabrera, David Bevan, Ted Deason *Mus* Stanley Myers *Art Dir* Frank White
● Charlotte Rampling, David Birney, Michel Lonsdale, Marcel Bozuffi, Michael Bryant, Manitas de Plata (Reeve/Prodis)

There's good, reliable stuff in this Alistair MacLean action-adventure item, colorfully location-set in Southern France's Camargue area and well acted by a carefully chosen Franco-British cast.

Plot basics involve the attempt to smuggle an East European scientist out of France and into the US, attempt which is hampered by repeated harassment and kidnappings by a scrupleless rival gang bent on gleaning the fugitive's secrets for resale to the highest bidder.

Principally involved are a footloose young American (David Birney), hired by a French Duke (Michel Lonsdale) to whisk the scientist onto a US-bound plane, and a pretty young British photographer (Charlotte Rampling)

C

who gets involved when she hitches a ride with Birney.

••••••••••••••••••••••••••••••••

■ CARBON COPY

1981, 92 MINS, US ◇ ⓥ ⊙
Dir Michael Schultz   *Prod* Carter De Haven, Stanley Shapiro   *Scr* Stanley Shapiro   *Ph* Fred Koenekamp   *Ed* Marion Segal   *Mus* Bill Conti   *Art Dir* Ted Haworth
● George Segal, Susan Saint James, Denzel Washington, Jack Warden, Paul Winfield, Dick Martin (Hemdale/RKO)

Carbon Copy is a comedy which attempts to deal with racial issues much in the way that *Watermelon Man* did. This time the story is rooted in reality. *Carbon Copy* has business executive George Segal faced with the arrival of a long-lost and heretofore unknown son whom he describes as 'Hickory Bronze.'

Segal attempts to pass off son Denzel Washington as a social experiment in his all-white suburb, but paternal instincts force him to reveal the truth to his straight-laced wife Susan Saint James. Abruptly, he loses his job, credit cards and Saint James throws him out of the house.

Suddenly, without allies, Segal is forced to accept the lot of the racial minorities. Cut off from his money and powerful contacts, he accepts manual labor jobs and begins to experiment and appreciate the lot of his son. The Segal character, a Jew, could hide behind a name, but his son can't adopt a new color.

Segal is particularly effective as he begins to realize just how complacent he is under his liberal values.

Carbon Copy is admittedly a fairy tale, just as the Capra films of the 1930s were. However, director Michael Schultz maintains a convincing balance between the film's broad humor and its genuinely poignant moments.

••••••••••••••••••••••••••••••••

■ CARD, THE
(US: The Promoter)

1952, 91 MINS, UK ⓥ
Dir Ronald Neame   *Prod* John Bryan   *Scr* Eric Ambler   *Ph* Oswald Morris   *Ed* Clive Donner   *Mus* William Alwyn   *Art Dir* T. Hopwell Ash
● Alec Guinness, Petula Clark, Glynis Johns, Valerie Hobson, Edward Chapman, Gibb McLaughlin (British Film Makers/Rank)

The principal character in Arnold Bennett's novel *The Card*, depicting the progression of a washer-woman's son from poverty to wealth, from humble beginnings to the top of the civic tree, provides a made-to-measure part for Alec Guinness in a capital performance.

Set in the Potteries, without any attempt to glamorize the grimy, smoky, slum-ridden district, Eric Ambler's script keeps the focus entirely on Guinness.

The rise of the young lad is depicted in all its stages, from his dishonest beginning, when he alters examination results to ensure a place in high school. And from there he gradually makes his name in the world, advancing from a humble lawyer's clerk to rent collector and to big business as head and founder of a loan club.

□ 1952: Nomination: Best Sound

••••••••••••••••••••••••••••••••

■ CARDINAL, THE

1963, 175 MINS, US ◇ ⓥ ⊙
Dir Otto Preminger   *Prod* Otto Preminger   *Scr* Robert Dozier   *Ph* Leon Shamroy   *Ed* Louis R. Loeffler   *Mus* Jerome Moross   *Art Dir* Lyle Wheeler
● Tom Tryon, Carol Lynley, Romy Schneider, John Huston, Raf Vallone, John Saxon (Columbia)

Otto Preminger's *The Cardinal* is a long motion picture but for most of the way it is superlative drama, emotionally stirring, intellectually stimulating and scenically magnificent.

Like the Henry Morton Robinson novel that it lives up to more in spirit than plot-wise, it is a skillful, fascinating blend of fact and fiction. The story concerns the development of a Rome-educated American priest who has aspirations of clerical high office. However, he experiences shattering doubt of his ability to be a good priest and, indeed, if he ever had a true 'call', having from his earliest memory been destined, according to his parents, for the priesthood.

Without faulting scenarist Robert Dozier, *The Cardinal* is Preminger's picture for it moves on such a vast canvas – Rome, Boston and environs, New York (dockside scene only), Georgia, Vienna and back to Rome – with all the richly pictorial ritual of the ordination of a priest, the consecration of a Bishop, later a Cardinal, and the vast public excitement in St Peter's Square for the election of a Pope.

Preminger also selected his cast wisely. Tom Tryon, who has the title role, plays it very well indeed, although there are shadings to the character which do not surface as might be desired. Romy Schneider is captivating as the Viennese girl who cannot disguise her feelings toward Tryon. Carol Lynley is effective as his troubled sister and also in a subsequent role as the latter's illegitimate daughter.

There are, however, two who steal the picture as far as acting goes. They are John Huston and Raf Vallone. Both play the roles of cardinals on distinctive, captivating levels.

□ 1963: Nominations: Best Director, Supp. Actor (John Huston), Color Cinematography, Color Costume Design, Color Art Direction, Editing

••••••••••••••••••••••••••••••••

■ CAREER

1959, 105 MINS, US
Dir Joseph Anthony   *Prod* Hal B. Wallis   *Scr* James Lee   *Ph* Joseph LaShelle   *Ed* Warren Low   *Mus* Franz Waxman   *Art Dir* Hal Pereira, Walter Tyler
● Dean Martin, Anthony Franciosa, Shirley MacLaine, Carolyn Jones, Joan Blackman, Robert Middleton (Paramount)

This feature is so limited in production scope as to suggest the possibility that the producer was out to save money the hard way – that is, stinting on the pictorial values. But a closer look is reassuring, for it genuinely appears that Hal Wallis in placing on the screen James Lee's off-Broadway play of the same name, and director Joseph Anthony were bent on preserving the intimacy of the original.

It's a show business story done in honest-to-goodness fashion. It centers on the ambition-driven but nonetheless agreeable aspiring actor. Whether he's maladjusted husband or insignificant waiter he's where he is because, in his free time, he's out to become a star and his other roles in life are unimportant.

It's a serious theme, to be sure, but somewhere there must have been opportunity to get a little lighthearted. A couple of Lee's story angles hardly seem to fit in, and this is no help in the secondary last-half that follows the attention-getting earlier episodes. Anthony Franciosa's call to the Korean war, with a brief glimpse of same, is not correctly integrated. Neither is the exposure of Dean Martin, as a smalltime director on the way up, as a onetime Communist because, as he puts it, 'I was ambitious.'

Otherwise, Franciosa and Martin, however sombre their parts, perform convincingly. Shirley MacLaine as a producer's free-wheeling daughter has some misfitting dialog an story situations to cope with but gets across all right, and Carolyn Jones plays it straight as an agent.

□ 1959: Nominations: Best B&W Cinematography, B&W Costume Design, B&W Art Direction

••••••••••••••••••••••••••••••••

■ CAREER OPPORTUNITIES
(Aka: One Wild Night)

1991, 85 MINS, US ◇ ⓥ ⊙
Dir Bryan Gordon   *Prod* John Hughes   *Scr* John Hughes   *Ph* Don McAlpine   *Ed* Glenn Farr, Peck Prior   *Mus* Thomas Newman   *Art Dir* Paul Sylbert
● Frank Whaley, Jennifer Connelly, Dermot Mulroney, Kieran Mulroney, Barry Corbin, John Candy (Universal/Hughes)

Writer-producer John Hughes' followup to *Home Alone* lacks the spit-polish and magic of the blockbuster but still has plenty of absorbing characters, smart, snappy dialog and delightful stretches of comic foolery.

Like *Home Alone*, story has a young man on his own to defend a fortress against bungling burglars, but in this case he's a 21-year-old trapped in a job he hates (night janitor at a discount store) and pitted against gun-toting hoods out to clean out, not clean up, the store.

Jim (Frank Whaley) is a ne'er-do-well fast talker and nonstop liar bounced from as many deadend jobs as his humble hometown of Munroe, Ill, has to offer. He's been given his last chance to succeed by his blue-collar father – or get kicked out of the house.

That's when he discovers he's not alone. Darkly voluptuous Josie (Jennifer Connelly), princess daughter of the town land baron, is locked in after falling asleep during a shoplifting spree.

Trapped together, the misfits discover each other and, in the type of scenes Hughes writes best, sort out their differences and common ground from their horrifying high school years. But the guntoting hoods (Dermot and Kieran Mulroney) show up and they must turn their specialties to more immediate escape.

••••••••••••••••••••••••••••••••

■ CAREFUL HE MIGHT HEAR YOU

1983, 116 MINS, AUSTRALIA ◇ ⓥ
Dir Carl Schultz   *Prod* Jill Robb   *Scr* Michael Jenkins   *Ph* John Seale   *Ed* Richard Francis-Bruce   *Mus* Ray Cook   *Art Dir* John Stoddart
● Wendy Hughes, Robyn Nevin, Nicholas Gledhill, John Hargreaves, Geraldine Turner, Isabelle Anderson (Syme)

A top quality production about the struggle between two sisters for custody of an eight-year-old boy, their nephew, *Careful He Might Hear You* is a completely involving emotional experience.

The Sumner Locke Elliott novel on which Michael Jenkins' excellent screenplay is based was, for many years, a project for Joshua Logan with, at one point, Elizabeth Taylor announced for the role of Vanessa Scott, the lonely frigid spinster whose causes all the trouble, and who is played, commandingly, here by Wendy Hughes.

Story is set in the Depression in Sydney. The boy, nicknamed 'PS' by everyone, is homeless after the death of his mother and the departure of his feckless father, Logan, for the goldfields. He's taken in by a loving but impoverished aunt and uncle (Robyn Nevin and Peter Whitford).

Their lives are disrupted, however, by the arrival of Vanessa, another sister, but from the moneyed side of the family. She wants custody of the child.

••••••••••••••••••••••••••••••••

■ CARETAKER, THE
(US: The Guest)

1964, 105 MINS, UK
Dir Clive Donner   *Prod* Michael Birkett   *Scr* Harold Pinter   *Ph* Nicolas Roeg   *Ed* Fergus McDonnell   *Mus* Ron Grainer   *Art Dir* Reece Pemberton
● Alan Bates, Donald Pleasence, Robert Shaw (Caretaker)

Harold Pinter adapted his own three-character play for the screen, but made little attempt to broaden the canvas and its stage origins are barely disguised.

This production of *The Caretaker*, was financed by 10 prominent showbiz personalities, each of whom has a $14,000 stake in it, while the author, producer, director and three stars are all on deferment. Among its backers were stars, film producers and legit impresarios, including Elizabeth Taylor, Richard Burton, Peter Sellers, Noel Coward, Harry Saltzman and Peter Bridge.

Instead of using a conventional studio, the unit took over a house in a northeast London suburb, and that provides an ideal, shabby setting for Pinter's offbeat theme. Basically, it's a one-set play, and that made it a tough assignment for director Clive Donner. His fluent treatment, however, makes the most of the macabre verbal exchanges, and overcomes many of the static handicaps of the subject.

The three characters are two brothers and a tramp. One of the brothers, a building worker, owns a house, but it is his brother who lives in it, though just in one room, cluttered with furniture from the remainder of the house. The tramp, homeless and unemployed, is invited to stay the night, and finds himself being tossed around like a shuttlecock, in favor with one brother, and out of favor with the other.

Donald Pleasence's standout performance as the tramp is the acting highlight, but he easily has the choicest role. Robert Shaw gives an intelligent study as the brother who offers the tramp shelter, while Alan Bates completes the stellar trio with another forceful portrayal.

• •

■ **CAREY TREATMENT, THE**

1972, 101 MINS, US ◇ ▼
Dir Blake Edwards   *Prod* William Belasco   *Scr* James P. Bonner   *Ph* Frank Stanley   *Ed* Ralph E. Winters   *Mus* Roy Budd   *Art Dir* Alfred Sweeney
● James Coburn, Jennifer O'Neill, Pat Hingle, Skye Aubrey, Elizabeth Allen, Dan O'Herlihy (M-G-M)

The Carey Treatment stars James Coburn as a swinger-type pathologist who single-handedly solves a murder case in order to free a medic colleague from a bum rap. Written, directed, timed, paced and cast like a feature-for-TV, the production is serviceable release.

Filmed partly in Boston under the title *A Case of Need*, from Jeffery Hudson's novel of that name, screenplay has Coburn arriving from California to join Dan O'Herlihy's medical staff, which includes James Hong, arrest for the alleged abortion-manslaughter of O'Herlihy's daughter (Melissa Torme-March). Coburn gets time off from immediate superior Regis Toomey and wanders through several sequences, played and edited in no particularly meaningful or suspenseful order, until unearthing the real culprits.

• •

■ **CARLTON-BROWNE OF THE F.O.**
(US: Man in a Cocked Hat)

1959, 87 MINS, UK ▼
Dir Jeffrey Dell, Roy Boulting   *Prod* John Boulting   *Scr* Jeffrey Dell, Roy Boulting   *Ph* Max Greene   *Ed* Anthony Harvey   *Mus* John Addison   *Art Dir* Albert Witherick
● Terry-Thomas, Peter Sellers, Luciana Paluzzi, Thorley Walters, Ian Bannen, Raymond Huntley (Boulting)

The F.O. in the title stands for Foreign Office and the film is a crazy peck at the indiscretions of foreign diplomacy. Much of the dialog is brilliantly witty. There are some excellent situations and some first-class prods at dignity. But the come tends to get out of hand and, at times, develops merely into a series of not totally relevant sketches.

The pic concerns the mishaps that happen to a Foreign Office junior official when an ex-colony of Britain's – Gaillardia – becomes news. Rich mineral deposits are indicated on the tiny island. Learning that other Great Powers are sniffing around the island, Carlton-Browne (Terry-Thomas) is dispatched to sort things out.

Peter Sellers plays the Gaillardian blackguard of a prime minister with relish. But the Sellers personality tends to throw the part off-balance.

Best of the major performances come from Raymond Huntley, as a pompous Foreign Office minister, and Ian Bannen, who, as the young king suddenly brought to the throne, brings a most engaging charm and humor to his role.

• •

■ **CARMEN JONES**

1954, 105 MINS, US ◇ ⊙
Dir Otto Preminger   *Prod* Otto Preminger   *Scr* Harry Kleiner   *Ph* Sam Leavitt   *Ed* Louis R. Loeffler   *Mus* Georges Bizet   *Art Dir* Edward L. Ilou
● Dorothy Dandridge, Harry Belafonte, Olga James, Pearl Bailey, Diahann Carroll, Roy Glenn (20th Century-Fox)

As a wartime [1943] legit offering *Carmen Jones* – the modernized, all-Negro version of [Georges Bizet's] opera *Carmen* – was a long-run hit both on Broadway and on the road. Otto Preminger has transferred it to the screen with taste and imagination in an opulent production.

The screenplay closely follows the lines of the stage libretto by Oscar Hammerstein II in which Carmen is a pleasure-loving southern gal who works in a Dixie parachute factory, where Joe (Jose) is a member of the army regiment on guard duty. She lures him away from Cindy Lou (Micaela) and he deserts with her. Eventually Carmen tires of him and takes up with Husky Miller (Escamillo) the fighter and Joe kills her when she refuses to return to him.

Preminger directs with a deft touch, blending the comedy and tragedy easily and building his scenes to some suspenseful heights. He gets fine performances from the cast toppers, notably Dorothy Dandridge, a sultry Carmen whose performance maintains the right hedonistic note throughout.
□ 1954: Nominations: Best Actress (Dorothy Dandridge), Scoring of a Musical Picture

• •

■ **CARNAL KNOWLEDGE**

1971, 97 MINS, US ◇ ▼ ⊙
Dir Mike Nichols   *Prod* Mike Nichols   *Scr* Jules Feiffer   *Ph* Giuseppe Rotunno   *Ed* Sam O'Steen   *Art Dir* Richard Sylbert
● Jack Nicholson, Art Garfunkel, Candice Bergen, Ann-Margret, Cynthia O'Neal, Rita Moreno (Avco Embassy)

Mike Nichols' *Carnal Knowledge* is a rather superficial and limited probe of American male sexual hypocrisies. Jules Feiffer's episodic story follows for over 20 years the diverse paths of Jack Nicholson and Art Garfunkel as each tries to match their sexual fantasies with an uncooperative reality.

First, Nicholson and Garfunkel are college roommates in the 1940s, where Candice Bergen is the object of attention. Garfunkel, the more sensitive, wins her heart over Nicholson, whose ability to betray close friends is neatly established.

Time jumps ahead about a decade to the late 1950s. Nicholson falls in his own way for Ann-Margret, a sexpot who really would like to get married and have kids. Nicholson still can't cope, and at the same time introduces Garfunkel – now a slightly bored suburban husband – to Cynthia O'Neal.

The final 13 minutes are set in the late 1960s. Garfunkel has gone mod, latching onto Carol Kane, a hippie nymphet, while Nicholson has been reduced to periodic visits to Rita Moreno, a for-hire playmate who helps him play out his fantasies.

The story pussyfoots round some underlying psychological and psychiatric hangups. Nicholson's compulsive stud character is the type that hates women. The film fails by avoiding confrontation with his character.
□ 1971: Nomination: Best Supp. Actress (Ann-Margret)

• •

■ **CARNOSAUR**

1993, 82 MINS, US ◇ ▼ ⊙
Dir Adam Simon   *Prod* Mike Elliott   *Scr* Adam Simon   *Ph* Keith Holland   *Ed* Richard Gentner   *Mus* Nigel Holton   *Art Dir* Aaron Osborne
● Diane Ladd, Raphael Sbarge, Jennifer Runyon, Harrison Page, Clint Howard (Concorde/New Horizons)

This contemporary dino tale harks back to '50s monster epics in style and sophistication. The ever-vigilant Roger Corman film factory is once again first in the marketplace with an exploitable sensation [two weeks prior to the release of *Jurassic Park*], predictably plotted with bargain-basement effects.

Somewhere in the Nevada desert, genetic scientist Dr Jane Tiptree (Diane Ladd) has cross-fertilized chicken eggs with T-Rex DNA. The result is a lethal little pecker that dines on the Southwest smorgasbord of truckers and military/industrial support staff.

The unwitting hero is 'Doc' Smith (Raphael Sbarge), a plant operations employee who hooks up with Thrush (Jennifer Runyon), a member of a commune of eco-freaks. They eventually wind up in the underground lab, where the full horror is revealed.

Ladd chews up the scenery as the mad doctor; writer/director Adam Simon keeps the action about a step or two ahead of the silliness.

• •

■ **CARNY**

1980, 105 MINS, US ◇ ▼
Dir Robert Kaylor   *Prod* Robbie Robertson   *Scr* Thomas Baum   *Ph* Harry Stradling Jr   *Ed* Stuart Pappe   *Mus* Alex North   *Art Dir* William J. Cassidy
● Gary Busey, Jodie Foster, Robbie Robertson, Elisha Cook, Meg Foster, Kenneth McMillan (United Artists)

Edgy tale [from a story by Phoebe and Robert Kaylor and Robbie Robertson] of three born outsiders living on a tightrope vividly recalls, both in style and content, the doom-laden films noirs of the late 1940s.

Gary Busey plays a slightly demented bozo in a cage who mercilessly taunts spectators trying to dump him into water by throwing baseballs. Busey hooks up with runaway Jodie Foster.

As the carny makes its way through the South, Foster is gradually assimilated into the band of outcasts and a three-way relationship develops.

Busey is tremendous. Foster, ostensibly playing her first 'adult' role, works wonders with a somewhat underwritten part.

Director Kaylor displays an unerring eye for atmosphere and detail.

• •

■ **CAROUSEL**

1956, 128 MINS, US ◇ ▼ ⊙
Dir Henry King   *Prod* Henry Ephron   *Scr* Phoebe Ephron, Henry Ephron   *Ph* Charles G. Clarke   *Ed* William Reynolds   *Mus* Alfred Newman (sup.)   *Art Dir* Lyle R. Wheeler, Jack Martin Smith
● Gordon MacRae, Shirley Jones, Cameron Mitchell, Barbara Ruick, Gene Lockhart, Susan Luckey (20th Century-Fox)

Carousel, presented by the Theatre Guild in April 1945, ran 890 performances at the Majestic Theatre. It here gets the supertreatment in 55mm CinemaScope. There are two production numbers in the picture that are close to classic. Add the staging of the famed

C

'Soliloquy', as sung by Gordon MacRae for strong impact. Musical numbers are all in extremely good taste. Reservations as to some scenes and a certain slowness in pace are minor.

The stars of *Carousel* remain Rodgers & Hammerstein. The cast is uniformly attractive, from MacRae as the shiftless ne'er-do-well Billy Bigelow, to pretty Shirley Jones as Julie.

Production number that precedes the gay clambake is a tribute to the ingenuity of choreographer Rod Alexander.

If this scene is great, the finale, when Julie's daughter, Louise (danced by Susan Luckey), does a number with handsome Jacques D'Amboise, is even more of a rocking production success.

Carousel keeps elements of drama, humor and sentiment but starts out with MacRae already dead and in heaven. His courtship and marriage are then told in flashback.

■ CARPETBAGGERS, THE

1964, 150 MINS, US ◇ ⊚

Dir Edward Dmytryk *Prod* Joseph E. Levine *Scr* John Michael Hayes *Ph* Joseph MacDonald *Ed* Frank Bracht *Mus* Elmer Bernstein *Art Dir* Hal Pereira, Walter Tyler

● George Peppard, Alan Ladd, Bob Cummings, Martha Hyer, Elizabeth Ashley, Carroll Baker (Paramount)

Joseph E. Levine's screen version of *The Carpetbaggers* is lusty, vulgar and gusty and, on one notable occasion, painfully brutal.

The story of a ruthless, emotionally unstable chemical-aircraft-film tycoon is told in vague, often lurching manner in the scenario out of Harold Robbins' tome. The career of the 'hero' – a heel in fact – is traced sketchily from the point at which he succeeds his just-deceased father (whom he detests) in business to the phase in which he manages to pull himself together emotionally after an unbroken string of brutally cold-blooded dealings, business and personal.

George Peppard growls and glowers his way through the pivotal role, wearing one basic expression – a surly, like-it-or-lump-it look – but there is an underlying animal magnetism to this performance. The late Alan Ladd limns with conviction one of the few appealing characters – the cowboy star who ultimately restores Peppard to his senses. Carroll Baker has the flashy role of a Harlowesque sexpot, and makes the most of it.

■ CARQUAKE
See: Cannonball

■ CARRIE

1952, 118 MINS, US ⊚ ⊙

Dir William Wyler *Prod* William Wyler *Scr* Ruth Goetz, Augustus Goetz *Ph* Victor Milner *Ed* Robert Swink *Mus* David Raksin *Art Dir* Hal Pereira, Roland Anderson

● Laurence Olivier, Jennifer Jones, Eddie Albert, Miriam Hopkins, Basil Ruysdael, Ray Teal (Paramount)

Theodore Dreiser's novel of another era, *Sister Carrie*, has been given a literal adaptation for films and the result is a sometimes mawkish, frequently dated drama. As just plain *Carrie*, with such stars as Jennifer Jones and Laurence Olivier, it is a somber, low-key entertainment.

Carrie is the turn-of-the-century story of the small-town girl who goes to Chicago to make good. It is the story of her meeting a traveling salesman and of how he becomes her 'bene-factor'. The big love of her life, however, is the manager of a swank restaurant whom she meets while living with the salesman.

Jones gives one of the bright performances of her career. For Olivier, it is a role that

gives him little opportunity for shading or dramatic intensity. Eddie Albert is excellent as the traveling salesman.

□ 1952: Nominations: Best B&W Costume Design, B&W Art Direction

■ CARRIE

1976, 97 MINS, US ◇ ⊚ ⊙

Dir Brian De Palma *Prod* Paul Monash *Scr* Lawrence D. Cohen *Ph* Mario Tosi *Ed* Paul Hirsch *Mus* Pino Donaggio *Art Dir* William Kenny, Jack Fisk

● Sissy Spacek, Piper Laurie, Amy Irving, William Katt, John Travolta, Nancy Allen (United Artists)

Carrie is a modest but effective shock-suspense drama about a pubescent girl, her evangelical mother and cruel schoolmates.

Stephen King's novel, adapted by Lawrence D. Cohen, combines in unusual fashion a lot of offbeat story angles. Sissy Spacek heads cast in title role of an ugly duckling type schoolgirl.

Nancy Allen and other classmates, who normally berate her anyway, really go to town on the girl, until gym teacher Betty Buckley comes to her rescue.

At home, Carrie's mother is a dried-up, abandoned wife-turned-religious freak, played superbly by Piper Laurie, which explains in part the girl's ignorance. At the same time, Carrie discovers that, with intense concentration, she can make physical objects move.

□ 1976: Nominations: Best Actress (Sissy Spacek), Supp. Actress (Piper Laurie)

■ CARRINGTON V.C.
(US: Court Martial)

1954, 105 MINS, UK ⊚

Dir Anthony Asquith *Prod* Teddy Baird *Scr* John Hunter *Ph* Desmond Dickinson *Ed* Ralph Kemplen *Art Dir* Wilfrid Shingleton

● David Niven, Margaret Leighton, Noelle Middleton, Laurence Naismith, Clive Morton, Mark Dignam (British Lion/Remus)

Carrington V.C. by Dorothy and Campbell Christie, made a definite impact on the West End scene as a subject of dramatic intensity. In its translation to the screen, the drama loses none of the basic qualities.

The plot focusses on the title character, a wartime hero who has the routine job of commanding an artillery battery in peacetime. It's so secret that he is constantly feuding with his regimental commander, is in serious financial difficulties and is harassed by a wife who is desperately clamoring for money.

The army authorities owe him a substantial sum on his expense account, but this cash is not forthcoming. And in a moment of crisis, he helps himself to army funds 'to advertise a grievance'. His commander orders courtmartial and the main incident of the pic is concerned with this trial.

David Niven gives one of his best performances in recent times as the accused V.C. Some of his courtroom exchanges are dramatic high-spots of the plot.

■ CARRY ON AGAIN, DOCTOR

1969, 89 MINS, UK ◇ ⊚

Dir Gerald Thomas *Prod* Peter Rogers *Scr* Talbot Rothwell *Ph* Ernest Steward *Ed* Alfred Roome *Mus* Eric Rogers *Art Dir* Jack Blezard

● Kenneth Williams, Sidney James, Charles Hawtrey, Joan Sims, Hattie Jacques, Jim Dale (Rank)

Carry On Again, Doctor returns to a well-tilled field, with bedpans, undressed patients, discussions about symptoms, from wind to bowels, being regular dialog fodder. This time the flimsy yarn is mainly geared around the discovery in the Beatific Islands by Jim Dale, an

accident-prone young doctor, of a serum which helps girth-control. Jealousy and Machiavellian plots to prevent him making a fortune out of the discovery leads to double-crossing, female impersonation and a lot of predictable hanky-panky.

In this film much of the patter is flat and vulgar without being over-funny. Some situations (such as when Dale 'blows' an electric contraption and turns the hospital into chaos) are very funny. But there aren't enough.

Jim Dale, as the comedy hero, Sid James an an alcoholic steward of a medical mission, Joan Sims, Hattie Jacques, Kenneth Williams and Charles Hawtrey all play the nonsense without tongue in cheek, giving it a lift. Barbara Windsor, a blonde, curvey cutie, is in for pulchritude.

Stock shots cover the arrival of characters at the mythical Beatific Islands. The rest is Pinewood studio. It stands out a mile, but does it matter?

■ CARRY ON CABBY

1963, 91 MINS, UK ⊚

Dir Gerald Thomas *Prod* Peter Rogers *Scr* Talbot Rothwell *Ph* Alan Hume *Ed* Archie Ludski *Mus* Eric Rogers

● Sidney James, Hattie Jacques, Kenneth Connor, Charles Hawtrey, Esma Cannon, Liz Fraser (Anglo Amalgamated)

The golden formula of the *Carry On* series is back with a bang with *Carry On Cabby*.

Not at first intended to be one of the series, the film has a rather stronger storyline than usual [from an idea by S.C. Green and R.M. Hills]. Also has a different screenplay writer, Talbot Rothwell.

Sidney James is the cabby-owner of a prosperous fleet of taxicabs, but his domestic life is edgy because his wife claims he spends too much time with his beloved cabs. She sets up a rival garage called Glamcabs and decks out some shapely young women in revealing uniforms as her drivers. James, still not knowing that his wife is behind the rival firm, sets out to sabotage her business.

Hattie Jacques extracts fun from the role of James' wife. Kenneth Connor, Esma Cannon, Charles Hawtrey, as an accident-prone nitwit, and Liz Fraser, as Sally the glamorous waitress-Mata Hari, are old students of the *Carry On* technique, and effortlessly milk the laughter. So, too, are some of the cameo players often used for one gag.

■ CARRY ON CAMPING

1969, 88 MINS, UK ◇ ⊚

Dir Gerald Thomas *Prod* Peter Rogers *Scr* Talbot Rothwell *Ph* Ernest Steward *Ed* Alfred Roome *Mus* Eric Rogers *Art Dir* Lionel Couch

● Sidney James, Kenneth Williams, Joan Sims, Charles Hawtrey, Terry Scott, Barbara Windsor (Rank)

While sticking to its well tried, profitable formula, latest *Carry On* suffers somewhat in comparison to some of its predecessors in that it lacks a storyline, however slim.

Sidney James and Bernard Bresslaw (who make a good nonsense team) plan a vacation at a nudist holiday camp at which, they hope, they will be able to break down the prim resistance of their girl friends (Joan Sims and Dilys Laye). Camp turns out not to be nudie paradise, after all.

Meanwhile, other campers are involved in their own problems, with Terry Scott lumbered with an overhearty wife (Betty Marsden) and Charles Hawtrey as a cuckoo in a nest.

A bunch of schoolgirl teenagers from the St Chayste Ladies' Seminary (typical of most of the dialog), chaperoned by prissy Kenneth Williams as the headmaster and Hattie Jacques as the formidable matron, descend on the camp to bring some sexy complications. They're a goodlooking bunch, with Barbara Windsor a literal standout as an exuberant sex-mad young trollop.

••••••••••••••••••••••••••••••••

■ **CARRY ON CLEO**

1964, 92 MINS, US ◇ ⊛
Dir Gerald Thomas   *Prod* Peter Rogers   *Scr* Talbot Rothwell   *Ph* Alan Hume   *Ed* Archie Ludski   *Mus* Eric Rogers   *Art Dir* Bert Davey
● Sidney James, Kenneth Williams, Kenneth Connor, Charles Hawtrey, Joan Sims, Amanda Barrie (Anglo Amalgamated)

Intended as a parody of the expensive *Cleopatra*, this entry from the *Carry On* stables relies on the bludgeon rather than the rapier, so isn't entirely successful in its purpose.

Accent in this frolic is less on situation than on dialog and so there is less action to hold the audience. Talbot Rothwell's dialog is unabashedly corny but this doesn't much matter. But it is also unusually bristling with plodding double entendres. Gags, both verbal and visual, suffer from repetition and few are as neat as Julius Caesar's woeful complaint, 'Infamy! Infamy! Everybody's got it in for me!'

The practised cast of Old Regulars are also, mainly, up to form, with Sidney James as Mark Anthony and Kenneth Connor as Hengist the Wheelmaker particularly prominent as they disport among the vestal virgins. Kenneth Williams has a few twittering moments as Caesar but again irritatingly overplays. Charles Hawtrey's main function is to look incongruous and carry the weight of some of the least subtle sex patter.

On the femme side, Joan Sims is a hearty gal as Caesar's wife, Sheila Hancock is a shrill one as Hengist's spouse. Best discovery is Amanda Barrie as the poor man's Cleopatra. Her takeoff of the Queen of the Nile gets nearer to the tongue-in-cheek sense of what filmmakers were aiming at than any of her more experienced colleagues.

••••••••••••••••••••••••••••••••

■ **CARRY ON COLUMBUS**

1992, 91 MINS, UK ◇ ⊛
Dir Gerald Thomas   *Prod* John Goldstone   *Scr* Dave Freeman, John Antrobus   *Ph* Alan Hume   *Ed* Chris Blunden   *Mus* John Du Prez   *Art Dir* Harry Pottle
● Jim Dale, Bernard Cribbins, Maureen Lipman, Peter Richardson, Alexei Sayle, Rik Mayall (Comedy House)

Carry on Columbus resuscitates the bawdy, vaude-like humor of the original low-budget series with nary a nod to changing fashions. *Columbus* is the 30th in the *Carry On* series that started in 1958 with *Sergeant* and halted 20 years later with *Emmannuelle*. Vet director Gerald Thomas returns for behind-the-camera chores.

Current item continues the tradition of grafting on new comic talent but, with the trunk team now dead or absent, company feel is distinctly lacking.

Script starts weakly with the Sultan of Turkey (Rik Mayall, unfunny) sending two spies to spy on Chris Columbus (Jim Dale), a mapmaker with dreams of finding a new sea route to the gold-rich Indies. Financed by the king and queen of Spain (Leslie Phillips, June Whitfield), Columbus sets sail with a motley crew and a map in Hebrew translated by a dumb mariner (Bernard Cribbins). Losing their way, they end up in the Americas, where the natives are streetwise Indians with Brooklyn accents.

Best material is in the final half-hour, with Yank standup comics Larry Miller as a cigarchewing chieftain and Charles Fleischer (voice of Roger Rabbit) as his sidekick.

Pic's £2.25 million budget is all on the screen in handsome costuming and authentically cheesy Pinewood sets.

••••••••••••••••••••••••••••••••

■ **CARRY ON, CONSTABLE**

1960, 86 MINS, UK ⊛
Dir Gerald Thomas   *Prod* Peter Rogers   *Scr* Norman Hudis   *Ph* Ted Scaife   *Ed* John Shirley   *Mus* Bruce Montgomery   *Art Dir* Carmen Dillon
● Sidney James, Kenneth Williams, Hattie Jacques, Eric Barker, Kenneth Connor, Shirley Eaton (Anglo Amalgamated)

This is simply an anthology of police gags and situations. Insofar as there is a storyline [from an idea by Brock Williams], this concerns a flu-stricken police station which is reinforced by four fledgling cops straight from the police school. Of course, in the end the hapless quartet distinguishes itself by rounding up, in improbable fashion, a bunch of crooks.

The producer has brought back most of the team of stalwarts that has been on parade in the three previous *Carry On* films Kenneth Connor, Kenneth Williams, Charles Hawtrey and Leslie Phillips are the four zany cops; Hattie Jacques and Joan Sims are two policewomen, and Shirley Eaton and Jill Adams provide the glamour and slight touch of romance.

Eric Barker is excellent as the inefficient inspector in charge of the station while Sidney James, a newcomer to the team, is in his usual first-class form as the sergeant who is annoyed with the recruits.

••••••••••••••••••••••••••••••••

■ **CARRY ON COWBOY**

1966, 94 MINS, UK ◇ ⊛
Dir Gerald Thomas   *Prod* Peter Rogers   *Scr* Talbot Rothwell   *Ph* Alan Hume   *Ed* Rod Keys   *Mus* Eric Rogers   *Art Dir* Bert Davey
● Sidney James, Kenneth Williams, Jim Dale, Charles Hawtrey, Joan Sims, Angela Douglas (Anglo Amalgamated)

This Wild West spoof might well be subtitled *How The West Was Lost*.

Story, though familiar nonsense, is less a string of irrelevant situations than usual, giving the team more opportunity for comedy thesping.

Stodge City is taken over by The Rumpo Kid (Sidney James), to the horror of Judge Burke (Kenneth Williams), who calls for a marshal to clean up Stodge City. By error a sanitary engineer (Jim Dale) gets sent to the trouble spot, arriving on the same coach as Annie Oakley (Angela Douglas), daughter of the sheriff who has been bumped off by The Rumpo Kid. The sanitary engineer disposes of The Rumpo Kid in a spoof of the *High Noon* long walk along a deserted street, in which the bogus marshal uses his knowledge of drains to good ingenious effect.

Though actually filmed on a common in Surrey the 'Wild West locations' are adequately authentic, and Alan Hume's color lensing gives an extra touch of class.

••••••••••••••••••••••••••••••••

■ **CARRY ON CRUISING**

1962, 89 MINS, UK ◇ ⊛
Dir Gerald Thomas   *Prod* Peter Rogers   *Scr* Norman Hudis   *Ph* Alan Hume   *Ed* John Shirley   *Mus* Bruce Montgomery, Douglas Gamley   *Art Dir* Carmen Dillon
● Sidney James, Kenneth Williams, Kenneth Connor, Liz Fraser, Dilys Laye, Lance Percival (Anglo Amalgamated)

Latest in the *Carry On* string of boxoffice click comedies. Main difference in this is that it is now launched in color. Maybe Norman Hudis, who has so skillfully scribed this run of comedy hits, should have a Sabbatical.

Sidney James is the veteran, highly improbable, skipper of a Mediterranean cruising vessel. He is inflicted with five hamheaded substitutes for well-tried key men in his regular complement. They are all over anxious to please and so everything goes disastrously wrong.

Jumping, familiarly, through their well-placed circus hoops are Sidney James (he glowers), Kenneth Williams (he plays archly), Kenneth Connor (he dithers), Liz Fraser (she flaunts a shapely figure) and Esma Cannon (she twitters). Lance Percival as the tyro ship's cook, has some bright moments while Jimmy Thompson, as a suave bartender, copes with little material. Dilys Laye, a comparative newcomer to this frenzied scene, works hard in some brittle comedy campaigns.

Direction by Gerald Thomas is boisterously effective. Major switch in this series is that the original story is by Eric Barker, a comedian who has appeared in a couple of the series.

••••••••••••••••••••••••••••••••

■ **CARRY ON DOCTOR**

1968, 95 MINS, UK ◇ ⊛
Dir Gerald Thomas   *Prod* Peter Rogers   *Scr* Talbot Rothwell   *Ph* Alan Hume   *Ed* Alfred Roome   *Mus* Eric Rogers
● Frankie Howerd, Sidney James, Kenneth Williams, Charles Hawtrey, Jim Dale, Barbara Windsor (Rank)

Usual unabashed mixture of double meanings, down-to-earth vulgarity, blue jokes about hypodermic syringes, etc., and slapstick situations. This time the Carry On team returns to hospital life for its farcical goings-on.

Inevitably, the gags and situations waver in comic impact but the general effect is artless yocks in which audience participation is carried to fullest extent, in that part of the fun is anticipating the verbal and physical jokes.

Added zest is given by the inclusion of Frankie Howerd as a quack 'mind-over-matter' doctor who becomes a reluctant patient. Howerd's brilliantly droll sense of comedy is given plenty of scope.

Among the grotesque patients are Sidney James, very funny as a cheerful malingerer; Bernar Bresslaw, Charles Hawtrey (more subdued than usual) and Peter Butterworth. The hospital staff is equally energetic and resourceful in providing simple-minded yocks, with Kenneth Williams as a supercilious chief physician.

••••••••••••••••••••••••••••••••

■ **CARRY ON EMMANNUELLE**

1978, 88 MINS, UK ◇ ⊛
Dir Gerald Thomas   *Prod* Peter Rogers   *Scr* Lance Peters   *Ph* Alan Hume   *Ed* Peter Boita   *Mus* Eric Rogers   *Art Dir* Jack Shampan
● Suzanne Danielle, Kenneth Williams, Kenneth Connor, Jack Douglas, Joan Sims, Peter Butterworth (Thirtieth)

Carry On series now has 30 releases over 20 years. Formula is low budgets, low laughs. Which sums up *Carry On Emmannuelle*.

Emmannuelle, English-style, is wife to the French ambassador. She sleeps with most of London, from key government officials to servants, until an immigrant doctor restores hubby's priapic power and all ends happily in the embassy bedroom.

Rude, rollicking fun, at a breathless pace, was the order of earlier *Carry On* days. This one is rude, certainly, but the relentless phallic innuendo is as labored as makers' determination to show nothing to worry the censor. Leaden comic timing compares poorly with TV sitcoms which pic otherwise resembles in production values.

••••••••••••••••••••••••••••••••

■ **CARRY ON ENGLAND**

1976, 89 MINS, UK ◇ ⊛
Dir Gerald Thomas   *Prod* Peter Rogers   *Scr* David Pursall, Jack Seddon   *Ph* Ernest Steward   *Ed* Richard Marden   *Mus* Max Harris   *Art Dir* Lionel Couch
● Kenneth Connor, Windsor Davies, Patrick Mower, Judy Geeson, Jack Douglas, Joan Sims (Rank)

Carry On England suffers from a particularly unfortunate hangup. It's not funny! Peter

Rogers and Gerald Thomas, the producer/director double act who have canned 28 of these low budgeters, have worked over what must be the dullest script of the series. (Talbot Rothwell, who wrote most of the earlier screenplays, has been dropped.)

Action takes place in a mixed anti-aircraft battery at the start of World War II. There follows 89 minutes of gags, knockabout situations and innuendo which fall as flat as Kenneth Connor, as a bungling captain, is constantly required to do in search of belly laughs.

The cast, especially Connor, Windsor Davies and Jack Douglas, work hard to induce some excitement into the flagging dialog, but labor for a lost cause.

Rogers still manages to bring the pix in for £200,000 ($330,000), a considerable achievement.

....

■ **CARRY ON JACK**
(US: Carry on Venus)

1964, 91 MINS, UK ◇ ▼
Dir Gerald Thomas *Prod* Peter Rogers *Scr* Talbot Rothwell *Ph* Alan Hume *Ed* Archie Ludski *Mus* Eric Rogers *Art Dir* Jack Shampan
● Bernard Cribbins, Juliet Mills, Charles Hawtrey, Kenneth Williams, Donald Houston, Percy Herbert (Anglo Amalgamated)

Latest of the *Carry On* gang's shenanigans is an energetic skit on *Mutiny on the Bounty*, even bringing in joshing of certain characters and scenes from the [1962] nautical opus. Only two of the 'resident' company – Charles Hawtrey and Kenneth Williams – are on parade. This one, however, has an added credit in its very okay costuming and art work.

Mood is set by an opening cameo showing the epic, 'Kiss Me, Hardy' incident, played with brief, witty aplomb by Jimmy Thompson and Anton Rodgers. From then on director Gerald Thomas steers his cast through a maze of mixups and misadventure.

The screenplay involves a serving wench taking the place aboard HMS Venus of a green midshipman who, with the local nitwit, is press-ganged on to the same ship; a flogging that misfires; an operation at sea; a hilarious walking the plank sequence; a phoney mutiny; and the finale, when the Venus, now commanded by the middy, the girl and the birdbrain, puts the Spanish Armad out of action.

Williams, playing the precious Captain Fearless, who hates the sea and violence, is in excellent form while Hawtrey plays his familiar nincompoop with ease. Bernard Cribbins, as the sorely tried middy, Donald Houston, as the bullying second in command, and Percy Herbert, as his aide, bring some virile body to the proceedings. Only sizeable femme role is played by Juliet Mills who doesn't seem very comfortable in the robust male surroundings.

....

■ **CARRY ON LOVING**

1970, 90 MINS, UK ◇ ▼
Dir Gerald Thomas *Prod* Peter Rogers *Scr* Talbot Rothwell *Ph* Ernest Steward *Ed* Alfred Roome *Mus* Eric Rogers *Art Dir* Lionel Couch
● Sidney James, Kenneth Williams, Charles Hawtrey, Joan Sims, Hattie Jacques, Terry Scott (Rank)

This time the nondescript 'plot' hovers around a phoney matrimonial agency run by the plausible Sidney James and Hattie Jacques, posing as happy man and wife. Their efforts to pair off their unlikely and varied clients lead to riotous misunderstandings, sexy situations, intrigues, double-crossing and a custard-pie finale which is rather too deliberately planned and directed to achieve full comedy effect.

The string of situations, heavily garnished with indigo jokes, are often crazily irrelevant yet somehow manage to fit in with a kind of crazy mad logic.

James (aptly descibed in the film as looking like a dissipated old walnut) gives his usual genial, raffish display. Neat running gag falls to Michael Grady and Valerie Shute as a lovesick young couple who have no dialogue but are seen throughout the film smooching in the most unlikely spots.

....

■ **CARRY ON NURSE**

1959, 86 MINS, UK ▼
Dir Gerald Thomas *Prod* Peter Rogers *Scr* Norman Hudis *Ph* Reginald Wyer *Ed* John Shirley *Mus* Bruce Montgomery *Art Dir* Alex Vetchinsky
● Kenneth Connor, Kenneth Williams, Charles Hawtrey, Leslie Phillips, Hattie Jacques, Shirley Eaton (Anglo Amalgamated)

Carry On Nurse does for hospitals what its predecessor [*Carry On, Sergeant*] did for military life. The yocks come thick and fast. The humor tends to be repetitious, flirting with sex and dealing with such typical hospital subjects as bedpans, enemas, preparing patients for operations and so on.

There is no story, as such. Scriptwriter Norman Hudis has merely dreamed up an anthology of hospital humor, involving a string of vaude situations and eccentric characters [based on idea by Patrick Cargill and Jack Beale]. Several of the performers who were in *Carry On, Sergeant* crop up again. Others are added, including a number of easy-on-the-eye girls.

In a long cast which involves every type of nurse, a gorgon-like matron and a mixed bag of eccentric patients it is only possible to pick out Hattie Jacques, as the matron; Wilfrid Hyde White, as a suave patient; Ann Firbank, Shirley Eaton, Susan Stephen and Diana Beaumont as pretty, efficient nurses; Joan Sims, as the blunderer; and Kenneth Connor, a pugilist-patient with a broken hand.

Reginald Wyer's photography helps this film, which cost only about $200,000 to make.

....

■ **CARRY ON REGARDLESS**

1961, 90 MINS, UK ▼
Dir Gerald Thomas *Prod* Peter Rogers *Scr* Norman Hudis *Ph* Alan Hume *Ed* John Shirley *Mus* Bruce Montgomery
● Sidney James, Kenneth Connor, Charles Hawtrey, Joan Sims, Kenneth Williams, Liz Fraser (Anglo Amalgamated)

Any serious criticism of *Carry on Regardless* is futile. The story, such as it is, has Sidney James running Helping Hand Ltd, an agency prepared to take on any sort of job any time. On his staff are most of the trained imbeciles of previous films.

Disaster winds up every job. Typical of these are scenes which involve Kenneth Williams in taking a chimp for a walk through London, Kenneth Connor baby-sitting (the baby turns out to be a married woman), and Charles Hawtrey deputizing for a pugilist with this weedy comedian getting the job of a nightclub bouncer. Joan Sims has to demonstrate a bubble bath, Liz Fraser finds herself modelling underwear. The good slapstick climax has the whole gang cleaning out a filthy, antiquated house.

Ingenuity of scriptwriter Norman Hudis is sometimes a bit strained, but he has come up with some sound comedy situations. Film also introduces Stanley Unwin, a TV and radio man who specializes in double talk.

....

■ **CARRY ON SCREAMING**

1966, 97 MINS, UK ◇ ▼
Dir Gerald Thomas *Prod* Peter Rogers *Scr* Talbot Rothwell *Ph* Alan Hume *Ed* Rod Keys *Mus* Eric Rogers
● Harry H. Corbett, Kenneth Williams, Fenella Fielding, Joan Sims, Charles Hawtrey, Jim Dale (Anglo Amalgamated)

This 12th in the successful *Carry On* series puts the skids under horror pix. Snag is that most horror films themselves teeter on parody and it is rather tough trying to burlesque a parody.

Abduction of a girl by a monster starts a trail of goofy adventures as henpecked Detective Sergeant Bung (Harry H. Corbett) and his bovine assistant (Peter Butterworth) try to unravel this, the latest crime of a series. Investigations lead to an eerie mansion, inhabited by a ghoulish doctor, who is dead but re-incarnated, his attractively sexy, evil sister, a sinister butler and a couple of kidnapping monsters. There the brother-and-sister team ply their grisly trade of abducting girls, petrifying them and then selling them as shop dummies.

Gerald Thomas' direction as usual is assured, though some of the gags and situations would be helped by speeding up via more ruthless trimming. Corbett and Fenella Fielding, both debuting with the *Carry On* team, give it added strength. Corbett mugs a great deal but the role demands it and Fielding as the grisly vamp glitters with an overdone seductiveness which is often funny.

....

■ **CARRY ON, SERGEANT**

1958, 85 MINS, UK ▼
Dir Gerald Thomas *Prod* Peter Rogers *Scr* Norman Hudis, John Antrobus *Ph* Peter Hennessy *Ed* Peter Boita *Mus* Bruce Montgomery *Art Dir* Alex Vetchinsky
● William Hartnell, Bob Monkhouse, Shirley Eaton, Eric Barker, Dora Bryan, Kenneth Connor (Anglo Amalgamated)

Carry On Sergeant is an army farce [from a story by R.F. Delderfield, *The Bull Boys*] exploiting practically every army gag, but while some of the writing is careless and there is no attempt to develop a reasonable story, it is by no mea sloppily produced.

William Hartnell is a training sergeant who is about to retire from the service and has one more chance to fulfill his life ambition, which is to train the champion troop of the intake. Moreover, he has a $140 bet on the outcome. He is handed a bunch of rookies which is believable only in farce. The barrack-room attorney, the young man in love, the hypochondriac malingerer, the man always out of step . . . in fact, the repertory company of trainees. There's the sergeant with the bark, the fussy officer.

Kenneth Connor steals most of the honors as the hypochondriac being chased by a love-starved army waitress, played characteristically by Dora Bryan. He has a shade too much to do, but never misses a trick. Bob Monkhouse, called up on his wedding day, Shirley Eaton as his frustrated wife who crops up in camp, Eric Barker as a fussy officer, William Hartnell as the gravelly-voiced sergeant and Bill Owen as his faithful corporal add their quota.

....

■ **CARRY ON SPYING**

1964, 87 MINS, UK
Dir Gerald Thomas *Prod* Peter Rogers *Scr* Talbot Rothwell, Sid Colin *Ph* Alan Hume *Ed* Archie Ludski *Mus* Eric Rogers *Art Dir* Alex Vetchinsky
● Kenneth Williams, Bernard Cribbins, Charles Hawtrey, Barbara Windsor, Eric Pohlmann, Eric Barker (Anglo Amalgamated)

The Society for Total Extinction of Non-Conforming Humans (STENCH for short) has grabbed a secret formula and the British Operational Security Headquarters (BOSH in brief) tackles the job of getting back Formula X and outwitting its arch enemy, Doctor Crow. Through shortage of personnel, the assignment is handed to Simkins (Kenneth Williams), an agent in charge of training new spies, and three of his pupils.

Best knockabout sequences take place on the Orient Express, in a Viennese restaurant, a murky quarter of the Casbah and in the Automatum Plant where the inept foursome nearly come to a sticky end, but are rescued by good luck and the intervention of a beautiful spy.

Kenneth Williams' brand of camp comedy, while very funny in smallish doses, can pall when he has a lengthy chore as here. But Bernard Cribbins brings some useful virility to his fatuous role, Charles Hawtrey contributes his now familiar performance as the guileless one and Barbara Windsor proves a well-upholstered and perky heroine as the girl spy with a photogenic memory.

. . . .

■ CARRY ON, TEACHER

1959, 86 MINS, UK ⓦ
Dir Gerald Thomas   *Prod* Peter Rogers   *Scr* Norman Hudis   *Ph* Reginald Wyer   *Ed* John Shirley   *Mus* Bruce Montgomery
● Ted Ray, Kenneth Connor, Kenneth Williams, Joan Sims, Charles Hawtrey, Hattie Jacques (Anglo Amalgamated)

Third entry in Peter Rogers' sock *Carry On* series combines virtually the same team to use the same yock-raising formula, this time in the scholastic field, and the laughs come readily. This time screenplay writer Norman Hudis has developed a slightly stronger story line and made the characters more credible.

Ted Ray in the acting headmaster of a school who, after 20 years, has set his heart on the headmastership of a new one in the country. Much depends on the report put in to the Ministry of Education by a visiting inspector and a child psychiatrist. Because they don't want the popular master to leave, the students decide to sabotage his chances and start a well-planned campaign of bad behavior to influence the visiting inspectors.

Some of the gags are telegraphed but the cheerful impudence with which they are dropped into the script is completely disarming.

Ray, playing straighter than most of his colleagues, gives a pleasant performance. There's Kenneth Connor giving a fine performance as a nervous science master; Kenneth Williams and Charles Hawtrey, as a couple of precious masters in charge of literature and music respectively; Hattie Jacques as the formidable mistress who wages war on the saboteurs; and Joan Sims in her usual inimitable form as a games mistress. Leslie Phillips is the psychiatrist and Rosalind Knight is the inspector.

. . . .

■ CARRY ON UP THE JUNGLE

1970, 90 MINS, UK ◇ ⓦ
Dir Gerald Thomas   *Prod* Peter Rogers   *Scr* Talbot Rothwell   *Ph* Ernest Steward   *Ed* Alfred Roome   *Mus* Eric Rogers   *Art Dir* Alex Vetchinsky
● Frankie Howerd, Sidney James, Charles Hawtrey, Joan Sims, Terry Scott, Kenneth Connor (Rank)

Brought in at Pinewood for around $440,000 (the jungle foliage which kept melting under the lights was the most expensive item) and with plenty stock animal shots, this one is a skit on safari in the jungle, with a parody of Tarzan thrown in for good measure.

It involves the characters plunging in and out of the wrong tents mainly in search of sex, a tribe of headhunting cannibals, another tribe of lush dames in search of men to carry on their mating industry, a sex-starved stray gorilla and sundry other Darkest Africa situations and gags.

The usual core of the *Carry On* cast is on parade but notable absentees are the supercil-ious Kenneth Williams, Hattie Jacques, Peter Butterworth and Jim Dale, and they are missed. Instead, producer Peter Rogers has brought in another notable favorite, Frankie Howerd. Latter, a fine comedian with characteristics of his own, does not jell as well in situation comedy as when he is a standup comedian.

Sidney James and Joan Sims, veterans of this series, are towers of strength and, among a bunch of nubile maidens, a comparative newcomer, Jacki Piper, rings a bell.

. . . .

■ CARRY ON . . . UP THE KHYBER OR THE BRITISH POSITION IN INDIA

1968, 87 MINS, UK ◇ ⓦ
Dir Gerald Thomas   *Prod* Peter Rogers   *Scr* Talbot Rothwell   *Ph* Ernest Steward   *Ed* Alfred Roome   *Mus* Eric Rogers   *Art Dir* Alex Vetchinsky
● Sidney James, Kenneth Williams, Charles Hawtrey, Roy Castle, Joan Sims, Bernard Bresslaw (Adder/Rank)

This one has a slightly stronger storyline than some of its predecessors, but still continues to rely primarily on low-comedy visual and verbal gag situations for its yocks.

Up the Khyber centers on the British occupation of India in Queen Victoria's day and the reputation of the British is rocked when the local rulers suspect that the dreaded Scottish Devils in Skirts, members of the intrepid Third Foot and Mouth Regiment, actually wear drawers under their kilts. Settling of this urgent question causes considerable hoohah in the shape of a local uprising engineered by the local Khasi of Kalibar.

There's a small touch of genius in the way the Pass, for instance, can be shot in North Wales to everybody's complete satisfaction. Main highlight in this film is its finale, where the tribal chiefs launch a full-scale attack on the government residence while the governor and his guests with unshaken poise nonchalantly continue dinner amid the turmoil.

Performance of Sidney James as Sir Sidney Ruff-Diamond, the bluff, vulgar British governor, is a gem, impeccably timed, wily and always in character.

. . . .

■ CARRY ON VENUS

See: Carry On Jack

. . . .

■ CARS THAT ATE PARIS, THE

1974, 91 MINS, AUSTRALIA ◇ ⓦ
Dir Peter Weir   *Prod* Jim McElroy, Howard McElroy   *Scr* Peter Weir, Keith Gow, Piers Daries   *Ph* John McLean   *Ed* Wayne LeClos   *Mus* Bruce Smeaton
● Terry Camilleri, John Meillon, Melissa Jaffa, Kevin Miles, Max Gillies, Peter Armstrong (Australian Film Development/Royce Smeal)

Paris is a tiny Australian township with a surprising number of car accidents on its outskirts. Involved in one is Arthur, whose brother, driving a caravan-towing car, is killed.

Gradually it becomes evident that the car accidents are planned affairs. As each one occurs the townspeople swoop like vultures on the cars and retrieve any personal effects for themselves, whilst the doctor carries out strange experiments of his own upon the victims.

Attempting to preserve an air of normality, the mayor orders a scheduled dance to take place, which becomes macabre when the doctor brings his patients along.

Much of the pic is brilliant, although it does not always seem certain of the direction it is taking. At first it seem satirical, then black comedy, degenerating into a thriller.

. . . .

■ CARVE HER NAME WITH PRIDE

1958, 119 MINS, UK ⓦ
Dir Lewis Gilbert   *Prod* Daniel M. Angel   *Scr* Vernon Harris, Lewis Gilbert   *Ph* John Wilcox   *Ed* John Shirley   *Mus* William Alwyn   *Art Dir* Bernard Robinson
● Virginia McKenna, Paul Scofield, Jack Warner, Denise Grey, Alain Saury, Maurice Ronet (Rank)

The film pays tribute to the real life exploits of Violette Szabo, a beautiful young woman who became a British cloak-and-dagger agent in France and won a posthumous George Cross after being tortured and executed in Ravensbruck Camp. Part of the pic's attraction is its lack of hysteria. It keeps resolutely to the facts [from a book by R.J. Minney] and refuses to allow the espionage and torture sequences to go past the bounds of credulity.

Virginia McKenna is topnotch. She runs the gamut of humor, charm and toughness. By skillful playing and equally skillful makeup, McKenna's ordeal is expertly revealed. Paul Schofield, as the officer collleague who falls in love with his gallant young comrade, and Alain Saury, as her young husband; Jack Warner and Denise Grey, as her stolid middle-aged parents; Bill Owen, a standout as McKenna's sergeant instructor, all contribute admirably to the thesping.

. . . .

■ CAR WASH

1976, 97 MINS, US ◇ ⓦ
Dir Michael Schultz   *Prod* Art Linson, Gary Stromberg   *Scr* Joe Schumacher   *Ph* Frank Stanley   *Ed* Christopher Holmes   *Mus* Norman Whitfield   *Art Dir* Robert Clatworthy
● Franklyn Ajaye, Sully Boyar, Richard Brestoff, George Carlin, Irwin Corey, Ivan Dixon (Universal)

Car Wash uses gritty humor to polish clean the souls of a lot of likeable street people.

The setting is Sully Boyar's downtown car wash, where the colorful ethnic crew contends as much with oddball customers as with themselves.

Perhap the best known of the players is Richard Pryor, shining it on as a fancy-dressed preacher, complete with flashy car and retinue that includes The Pointer Sisters. Pryor's license plate spells out 'tithe', a sure evocation of the real-life character he suggests.

Woven into the main proceedings is the lonely sidewalk vigil of a streetwalker, Lauren Jones, which, combined with Bill Duke's equally sensitive portrayal of a frightened black militant, keeps the film in fine balance of humanism.

. . . .

■ CASABLANCA

1942, 99 MINS, US ⓦ ⊙
Dir Michael Curtiz   *Prod* Hal B. Wallis   *Scr* Julius J. Epstein, Philip G. Epstein, Howard Koch, [Casey Robinson]   *Ph* Arthur Edeson   *Ed* Owen Marks   *Mus* Max Steiner   *Art Dir* Carl Jules Weyl
● Humphrey Bogart, Ingrid Bergman, Paul Henreid, Claude Rains, Conrad Veidt, Sydney Greenstreet (Warner)

Although the title and Humphrey Bogart's name convey the impression of high adventure rather than romance, there's plenty of the latter. Adventure is there, too, but it's more as exciting background to the Bogart-Ingrid Bergman heart department. Bogart, incidentally, as a tender lover (in addition to being a cold-as-ice nitery operator) is a novel characterization.

Casablanca is pictured as a superficially gay town to which flee the monied refugees from Axis terror. There they await visas to Lisbon and then transportation to the United States. The waits are frequently interminable while arrangements for papers are being made with corrupt Vichy officials and the wealthy help to allay their impatience with chemin-de-fer and other games at Rick's. Rick is Bogart, who has opened his fancy joint after being 'jilted' by Bergman in Paris.

Bergman turns up one evening with her husband (Paul Henreid) whom she thought was dead during the period of her romance with Bogart. Henreid is leader of the underground in Europe and it is vital that he get to America. Bogart has two visas that will do the trick and the choice is between going off himself with Bergman – their torch still aflame – or sending her off with Henreid, who can do so much for the United Nations cause.

Bogart, as might be expected, is more at ease as the bitter and cynical operator of a joint than as a lover, but handles both assignments with superb finesse. Bergman, in a torn-between-love-and-duty role lives up to her reputation as a fine actress. Henreid is well cast and does an excellent job too.

Superb is the lineup of lesser players. Some of the characterizations are a bit on the overdone side, but each is a memorable addition to the whole [adapted from the play *Everybody Comes to Rick's* by Murray Burnett and Joan Alison].

□ 1943: Best Picture, Director, Screenplay.
□ Nominations: Best Actor (Humphrey Bogart), Supp. Actor (Claude Rains), B&W Cinematography, Editing, Scoring of a Dramatic Picture

• •

■ **CASINO ROYALE**

1967, 131 MINS, UK ◇ ⑨ ☉
Dir John Huston, Ken Hughes, Val Guest, Robert Parrish, Joe McGrath   *Prod* Charles K. Feldman, Jerry Bresler   *Scr* Wolf Mankowitz, John Law, Michael Sayers   *Ph* Jack Hildyard   *Ed* Bill Lenny   *Mus* Burt Bacharach   *Art Dir* Michael Stringer
● Peter Sellers, Ursula Andress, David Niven, Orson Welles, Woody Allen, William Holden (Columbia/Famous Artists)

Wacky comedy extravaganza, *Casino Royale* is an attempt to spoof the pants off James Bond. The $12 million film is a conglomeration of frenzied situations, gags and special effects, lacking discipline and cohesion. Some of the situations are very funny, but many are too strained.

Based on Ian Fleming's novel, the story line defies sane description. Sufficient to say that the original James Bond (David Niven), now knighted and living in eccentric retirement, is persuaded back into the Secret Service to help cope with a disastrous situation.

Niven seems justifiably bewildered by the proceedings, but he has a neat delivery of throwaway lines and enters into the exuberant physical action with pleasant blandness. Peter Sellers has some amusing gags as the gambler, the chance of dressing up in various guises and a neat near-seduction scene with Ursula Andress.

□ 1967: Nomination: Best Song ('The Look of Love')

• •

■ **CASSANDRA CROSSING, THE**

1977, 126 MINS, US ◇ ⑨
Dir George P. Cosmatos   *Prod* Carlo Ponti   *Scr* Tom Mankiewicz, Robert Katz   *Ph* Ennio Guarnieri   *Ed* Francois Bonnot, Roberto Silvi   *Mus* Jerry Goldsmith   *Art Dir* Aurelio Crugnola
● Sophia Loren, Richard Harris, Ava Gardner, Burt Lancaster, Martin Sheen, Ingrid Thulin (Associated General)

The Cassandra Crossing is a tired, hokey and sometimes unintentionally funny disaster film in which a trainload of disease-exposed passengers lurch to their fate.

One is asked to accept the premise that a terrorist bomber, accidentally exposed to some awesome plague, spreads the disease aboard a European express train.

Mismatched leading players all play directly to the camera, for themselves only, without betraying a hint of belief in their script.

While Richard Harris, cast as a brilliant doctor, is active among those posturing leads on the train, Burt Lancaster and Ingrid Thulin hold down a command post where desperate efforts are made to isolate the train from the rest of civilization.

• •

■ **CASS TIMBERLANE**

1947, 119 MINS, US
Dir George Sidney   *Prod* Arthur Hornblow Jr   *Scr* Donald Ogden Stewart   *Ph* Robert Planck   *Ed* John Dunning   *Mus* Roy Webb   *Art Dir* Cedric Gibbons, Daniel B. Cathcart
● Spencer Tracy, Lana Turner, Zachary Scott, Tom Drake, Mary Astor, Albert Dekker (M-G-M)

Metro has accomplished a highly successful translation to the screen of Sinclair Lewis' bookstore boff [adapted by Donald Ogden Stewart and Sonya Levien]. Lana Turner is the surprise of the picture via her top performance thespically. In a role that allows her the gamut from tomboy to the pangs of childbirth and from being another man's woman to remorseful wife, she seldom fails to acquit herself creditably. Spencer Tracy, as a matter of fact, is made to look wooden by comparison.

What fault the picture has is its overlong running time. Director George Sidney is unable to hold the pace for two hours and the film lags in the midsection.

This is a love story all the way. Essentially, it's the tenderness of an older man – 41, not too old, of course – for a young girl. Tracy, respected small-town judge, pays tender court to Turner, who's strictly out of his class socially as well as chronologically, until he wins her. She adapts herself to local society and the new life until she thinks she can stand it no more and then is off with the husband's best-friend, Zachary Scott. Scott, of course, doesn't want her when he can have her.

Tracy's meeting and early courting of the gal is difficult to accept, but once that's passed the only misgiving is that the yarn telegraphs its punches so far ahead.

• •

■ **CAST A GIANT SHADOW**

1966, 144 MINS, US ◇ ⑨
Dir Melville Shavelson   *Prod* Melville Shavelson   *Scr* Melville Shavelson   *Ph* Aldo Tonti   *Ed* Bert Bates, Gene Ruggiero   *Mus* Elmer Bernstein   *Art Dir* Michael Stringer
● Kirk Douglas, Senta Berger, Angie Dickinson, Frank Sinatra, Yul Brynner, John Wayne (Mirisch/Llenroc)

Cast a Giant Shadow exemplifies the problems in contemporary film biography, particularly when the subject is less well known than the events which brought him honor. Some complete fiction and fuzzy composites melodramatize the career of an American Jew who assisted in the fight for the creation of the State of Israel [from the book by Ted Berkman].

Story concerns Col David ('Mickey') Marcus, West Point grad, NY lawyer and cop, and participant in many facets of World War II, who, the late 1940s, is recruited to volunteer military help in the establishment of Israel, at that time still a dream subject to United Nations equivocation, militant Arab threats and uncertain world support.

Kirk Douglas stars as Marcus in a very good portrayal of a likeable, adventurous soldier-of-fortune who cannot get used to domestic inactivity even when wife Angie Dickinson is sitting by the hearth.

Unfortunately for the overall impact of the film, it is found necessary to go into World War II flashbacks to establish the Marcus character. John Wayne, in one of three featured special appearances, is a composite of

every superior officer under whom Marcus served in those days.

• •

■ **CASTAWAY**

1987, 118 MINS, UK ◇ ⑨ ☉
Dir Nicolas Roeg   *Prod* Rick McCallum   *Scr* Allan Scott   *Ph* Harvey Harrison   *Ed* Tony Lawson   *Mus* Stanley Myers   *Art Dir* Andrew Sanders
● Oliver Reed, Amanda Donohoe, Georgina Hale, Frances Barber (Cannon/United British Artists)

Picture this: London is cold, wet and miserable. What else does a girl do but answer an ad from a man looking for a 'wife' to take to a tropical island for a year?

Newcomer Amanda Donohoe spends most of the pic displaying the absence of bikini marks on her body (palm trees always seem to obscure the vital parts of Oliver Reed as Gerald Kingsland), and she copes well with a character whose motives and methods for going to the tiny desert island remain dubious.

Castaway is based on two nonfiction books – Lucy Irvine's version, also called *Castaway*, and Gerald Kingsland's *The Islander* – and tries to tread a path between the two conflicting versions of their sojourn.

Reed gives the performance of his career as a sexually frustrated middle-aged man in search of sun and sex, and is admirably complemented by Donohoe as the determined but fickle object of his lust.

Photography is excellent (especially underwater scenes) but though *Castaway* is a great ad for the tropical Seychelles, it won't be remembered as a Nicolas Roeg classic.

• •

■ **CASTLE KEEP**

1969, 106 MINS, US ◇ ⑨
Dir Sydney Pollack   *Prod* Martin Ransohoff   *Scr* Daniel Taradash, David Rayfiel   *Ph* Henri Decae   *Ed* Malcolm Cooke   *Mus* Michael Legrand   *Art Dir* Rino Mondellini
● Burt Lancaster, Patrick O'Neal, Jean-Pierre Aumont, Peter Falk, Scott Wilson, Bruce Dern (Columbia)

Film carries fast and savage action once the actual battle sequences are reached, but it's strictly a conversational war in footage leading up to these moments. Apparent efforts to insert a fresh side of war by concentrating on some of its grim humor act more as a deterrent than a booster to interest. Screenplay is based on William Eastlake's novel *Castle Keep*.

Burt Lancaster is a realistic, one-eyed major who leads a group of eight war-weary infantrymen come to occupy a Belgian castle in 1944 in the Ardennes Forest, which becomes a haven away from war for the men, who get up to all manner of frolics.

Lancaster enacts one of his fast-talking roles with a glib, almost tongue-in-cheek approach, and gets good mileage out of it. Patrick O'Neal as an art-loving captain out to save the treasures of the castle does a good job, as do Jean-Pierre Aumont and Peter Falk.

• •

■ **CASTLE ON THE HUDSON**
(UK: *Years without Days*)

1940, 76 MINS, US
Dir Anatole Litvak   *Prod* Hal B. Wallis (exec.)
Scr Seton I. Miller, Brown Holmes, Courtney Terrett   *Ph* Arthur Edeson   *Ed* Thomas Richards   *Mus* Adolph Deutsch   *Art Dir* John Hughes
● John Garfield, Ann Sheridan, Pat O'Brien, Burgess Meredith, Jerome Cowan, Henry O'Neill (Warner)

This is another in the extended series of Warners features based on Warden Lewis E. Lawes' *20,000 Years in Sing Sing*. It's a routine prison melodrama.

John Garfield is a tough, smart-alec gangster who draws a 25–30 year stretch in Sing Sing for knocking over a jewelry store. While he combats the discipline inside the 'castle', his loyal girl friend (Ann Sheridan) tries to effect his release. She is seriously injured in an auto crackup, which gives the parole-minded and humane warden (Pat O'Brien) a chance to let Garfield loose on honor system to see the girl.

Nothing unusual about Anatole Litvak's direction, except that he keeps the yarn moving at a speedy pace. Garfield reads his lines with over-emphasis, and is grooved in a routine portrayal. O'Brien is okay as the warden, while Sheridan provides a strong characterization as the gangster's girl. Burgess Meredith is fine in the prison scenes, but is bumped off after piloting a daring break.

■ CASUAL SEX?

1988, 97 MINS, US ◇ ⑫ ⊙
Dir Genevieve Robert   *Prod* Ilona Herzberg
Scr Wendy Goldman, Judy Toll   *Ph* Rolf Kestermann
Ed [uncredited]   *Mus* Van Dyke Parks   *Art Dir* Randy Ser
● Lea Thompson, Victoria Jackson, Stephen Shellen, Jerry Levine, Andrew Dice Clay, Mary Gross (Jascat/Universal)

Scripters have moved the setting of their stage version from the loose environs of a Club Med-type playground to a health and fitness resort, the Oasis [and added a question mark at the end of the title]. Now it's Lea Thompson and Victoria Jackson huffing and puffing through exercises as the excuse to meet an athletic guy who they suppose will have equally healthy attitudes about sex in these precarious times.

They spend a lot of time talking about the joys and disappointments of sex and how much each of them – especially Thompson as the formerly promiscuous Stacy – misses the occasional romp in the sack. With the late 1980s sensibility, their sex conversations are peppered with the girls' finding their own identities in relationships with men outside the sex act. Is it mature? Yes. Is it funny? No.

Andrew Dice Clay stands out as the Italian palooka from Jersey with the thick New Yawk accent and equally unsophisticated approach to the opposite sex. Stephen Shellen and Jerry Levine, objects of desire for Thompson and Jackson respectively, are typecast as nice dumb jocks and Oasis exercise instructors.

All of the inventiveness on this subject comes through when the girls' imaginations take over and director Genevieve Robert makes more of these diversions than any other.

■ CASUALTIES OF WAR

1989, 113 MINS, US ◇ ⑫ ⊙
Dir Brian De Palma   *Prod* Art Linson, Fred Caruso
Scr David Rabe   *Ph* Stephen H. Burum   *Ed* Bill Pankow
Mus Ennio Morricone   *Art Dir* Wolf Kroeger
● Michael J. Fox, Sean Penn, Don Harvey, John C. Reilly, John Leguizamo, Thuy Thu Le (Columbia)

A powerful metaphor of the national shame that was America's orgy of destruction in Vietnam, Brian De Palma's film deals directly with the harrowing rape and murder of a Vietnamese woman by four GIs.

Journalist Daniel Lang's account of the actual 1966 atrocity first appeared in 1969 as a *New Yorker* article and was later reprinted in book form.

Screen newcomer Thuy Thu Le is the Vietnamese woman kidnapped by a reconnaissance patrol as what the deranged sergeant (Sean Penn) calls 'a little portable R&R to break up the boredom, keep up morale.' When the men are through using her sexually, they stab and shoot her to death, over the futile objections of the lone holdout, a 'cherry' private played by Michael J. Fox.

Casting Fox was a brilliant coup on De Palma's part, since he brings with him an image of all-American boyishness and eager-beaver conservatism. Fox's beautifully acted

cowardly passivity in the face of the unthinkable challenges and implicates the viewer to examine his own conscience on the subject of Vietnam.

Wolf Kroeger's production design turns the Thailand locations into a convincing evocation of Vietnam's Central Highlands in 1966.

■ CAT AND THE CANARY, THE

1939, 72 MINS, US ⑫
Dir Elliott Nugent   *Prod* Arthur Hornblow Jr   *Scr* Walter De Leon, Lynn Starling   *Ph* Charles Lang   *Ed* Archie Marshek   *Mus* Ernst Toch   *Art Dir* Hans Dreier, Robert Usher
● Bob Hope, Paulette Goddard, John Beal, Douglass Montgomery, Gale Sondergaard (Paramount)

In *Canary* Bob Hope carries a straight dramatic characterization, with comedy quips and situations dropping into the plot naturally to accentuate the laughs.

Paulette Goddard gets her first co-star billing, displaying confidence and assurance in her role as the heir to the eccentric millionaire's fortune.

To provide chills and thrills, prospective heirs to the fortune assemble at the bayou home of the deceased 10 years after his death. Will is read, leaving estate to Goddard, when spooky manipulations start from strange sources. There's the low key lighting, eerie music, and secret passages – all utilized to fullest extent to accentuate the chiller aspect of the piece. After three murders during the night, Hope solves the mystery – but only after Goddard has been placed in constant jeopardy.

Script [from the play by John Willard] is a well-knit and workmanlike job of writing.

■ CAT BALLOU

1965, 97 MINS, US ◇ ⑫
Dir Elliot Silverstein   *Prod* Harold Hecht   *Scr* Walter Newman, Frank R. Pierson   *Ph* Jack Marta   *Ed* Charles Nelson   *Mus* Frank DeVol   *Art Dir* Malcolm Brown
● Jane Fonda, Lee Marvin, Michael Callan, Dwayne Hickman, Nat 'King' Cole, Stubby Kaye (Columbia)

Cat Ballou spoofs the Old West, whose adherents take their likker neat, and emerges middlingly successful, sparked by an amusing way-out approach and some sparkling performances.

Cat is a girl – Jane Fonda – and she's a young lady (educated to be a schoolteacher) vendetta-minded in Wyoming of 1894 when town baddies murder her father for his ranch. She turns into a rootin', tootin', lovin' gun-lady, rounds up gang of devoted followers and stages a train holdup, getting away with a payroll fortune, and holes up in the old Hole in the Wall outlaw lair.

Script juggles the elements of the Roy Chanslor novel producing a set of characters who fit the mood patly. A novel device has Stubby Kaye and Nat 'King' Cole as wandering minstrels of the early west, telling the story of the goings-on via a flock of spirited and tuneful songs composed by Mack David and Jerry Livingston.

Fonda delivers a lively interpretation as Cat. Lee Marvin doubles in brass, playing the gunman who shoots down her father and the legendary Kid Shelleen, a terror with the gun, whom she earlier called in to protect her father. In latter character, Marvin is the standout of the picture.

☐ 1965: Best Actor (Lee Marvin).
☐ Nominations: Best Adapted Screenplay, Editing, Adapted Music Score, Song ('The Ballad of Cat Ballou')

■ CAT CHASER

1989, 90 MINS, US ◇ ⑫
Dir Abel Ferrara   *Prod* Peter Davis, William Panzer
Scr Elmore Leonard, Jim Borrelli, Alan Sharp

Ph Anthony Richmond   *Ed* Anthony Redman
Mus Chick Corea   *Art Dir* Dan Leigh
● Peter Weller, Kelly McGillis, Charles Durning, Frederic Forrest, Tomas Milian, Juan Fernandez (Vestron/Whiskers)

Cat Chaser is another example of how difficult it is to transform a sharp and racy novel into a classy movie. Despite a fine cast and atmospheric direction by Abel Ferrara, the pic [from the novel by Elmore Leonard] doesn't quite make the grade, though it certainly is worth a look.

Peter Weller plays Miami hotel owner George Moran who fought during the American intervention of Santo Domingo. Years later he is drawn back to try and find the woman who taunted him with the name *Cat Chaser*.

He instead is joined by Mary (Kelly McGillis). Ensuing affair convinces Mary that she must end her marriage. Unfortunately she is married to Tomas Milian, former head of the Santo Domingo secret police, who has other thoughts on the matter.

Weller is fine as the intelligent, self-contained hero, but best of all is McGillis, seemingly relishing the part of a sexually charged femme fatale. Charles Durning, as always, gives the pic a dose of class, and manages to make his manipulative killer vaguely charming. Frederic Forrest, however, blusters badly and thankfully comes to a sticky end halfway through.

■ CATCHFIRE

1991, 98 MINS, US ◇ ⑫ ⊙
Dir Alan Smithee [= Dennis Hopper]   *Prod* Dick Clark, Dan Paulson   *Scr* Rachel Kronstadt Mann, Ann Louise Bardach   *Ph* Ed Lachman   *Ed* David Rawlins
Mus Curt Sobel   *Art Dir* Ron Foreman
● Dennis Hopper, Jodie Foster, Dean Stockwell, Vincent Price, Fred Ward, Joe Pesci (Vestron/Precision)

A quirky comedy-thriller about a hitman who falls for his femme target, scrambled pic [story by Rachel Kronstadt Mann] has an LA artiste (Jodie Foster) accidentally witnessing a mob killing when her car breaks down one night. The cops (Fred Ward, Sy Richardson) want her to talk, and the hoods (Joe Pesci, Dean Stockwell, Vincent Price) want her dead. So she dons a blond wig and an alias and goes AWOL.

Meanwhile, Pesci hires a top-league hitman (Dennis Hopper) to do the job his own goons can't, and after months of tracking her around the States finally runs her aground in an ad agency.

Hopper 'kidnaps' his quarry, possesses her for himself, and the dynamic duo set of on a weird road-movie-to-nowhere, with the mob and the law in hot pursuit.

Somewhere in here is a dark, sassy picture, but final product is more like a jigsaw with half the pieces. Pic was lensed in LA, Seattle and Taos, NM, in summer 1988 under Hopper's direction and the title *Backtrack*. After postproduction squabbles (reportedly over Hopper's three-hour cut), he opted for the Director's Guild of America moniker 'Alan Smithee'.

Apart from Foster, who's strong, shrewd and sexy, thesping is vaudeville all the way. Pesci rants and raves, Stockwell shows a nice line in low-key comedy, Ward looks like he hasn't been shown the whole script, and Hopper has a go at Humphrey Bogart in shades.

■ CATCH ME A SPY

1971, 94 MINS, UK/FRANCE ◇ ⑫
Dir Dick Clement   *Prod* Steven Pallos, Pierre Braunberger
Scr Dick Clement, Ian La Frenais   *Ph* Christopher Challis
Ed John Bloom   *Mus* Claude Bolling   *Art Dir* Carmen Dillon

C

● Kirk Douglas, Marlene Jobert, Trevor Howard, Tom Courtenay, Patrick Mower, Bernadette Lafont (Ludgate/Pleiade/Capitole)

Catch Me a Spy is a straight-forward spy thriller. Gimmicks are out but the whole has been put over with tongue nicely in cheek and an impish sense of humor. The cast play their parts for all they are worth.

Kirk Douglas, a smuggler of literary works from Iron Curtain countries, is mistaken for a spy and gets involved in devious situations. Most are provided by Marlene Jobert who resides with a rakish British cabinet minister (Trevor Howard) and is games mistress at a boys' school. Tom Courtenay is the counterespionage officer who is helplessly inept.

It is all highly improbable and involved but thanks to lively performances and Dick Clement's sharp direction, interest is continually held. The whole is climaxed with an exciting speedboat chase.

....

■ **CATCH-22**

1970, 121 MINS, US ◇ ⑰ ⊙
Dir Mike Nichols *Prod* John Calley, Martin Ransohoff
Scr Buck Henry *Ph* David Watkin *Ed* Sam O'Steen
Mus [none] *Art Dir* Richard Sylbert
● Alan Arkin, Martin Balsam, Richard Benjamin, Arthur Garfunkel, Jack Gilford, Buck Henry (Paramount)

Catch-22 stumbles its way through distended burlesque, and contrived stylism to its ultimate root theme: antisocial nihilism.

Alan Arkin heads a large cast of familiar names, playing characters scooped from Joseph Heller's famed novel by adapter Buck Henry. Low, cheap comedy mingles nervously with slick, high-fashion technical polish in a slow-boiling stew of specious philosophy and superficial characterization.

A technical filmmaking brilliance plus a few effective low-comedy gags constitute the pic's assets. Its major liabilities are the script and the directorial concept.

Arkin is Capt Yossarian, the generally reactive character who perceives all the sham and hypocrisy around him; befuddled laundry officer Bob Newhart, elevated to bewildering status as a squadron leader; urbane operations officer Jack Gilford; hard-boiled sex-teasing nurse Paula Prentiss; and Norman Fell, as the good-ole-sarge type.

....

■ **CATCH US IF YOU CAN**

(US: Having a Wild Weekend)

1965, 91 MINS, UK/US
Dir John Boorman *Prod* David Deutsch *Scr* Peter Nichols *Ph* Manny Wynn *Ed* Gordon Pilkington
Art Dir Tony Woollard
● Dave Clark, Barbara Ferris, David Lodge, Robin Bailey, Yootha Joyce, David De Keyser (Anglo Amalgamated/Warner)

Apparently producer David Deutsch's idea was to try for the same success formula that made *A Hard Day's Night* more than just a film about a rock 'n' roll group. He hasn't been too successful in trying to turn the Dave Clark Five into actors but has, as cinematic insurance, packed enough action into his 'chase' film to keep older members of the audience from squirming.

Dinah (Barbara Ferris), a pretty blonde model, is bored with her career and talks Steve (Clark) into escaping with her for a few days. The other members of the quintet, and, shortly thereafter, the rest of the cast, follow in quick pursuit. Her manager (David Lodge) tells the press that she has been kidnapped.

The pair, after losing their car, are picked by a strange couple (Robin Bailey and Yootha Joyce) with whom the youngsters attend a costume ball before the chase resumes.

The musical five do eight tunes as back-ground music. Cameraman Manny Wynn, who did some beautiful work on *Girl with Green Eyes*, provides some fresh views of the English countryside. Editing and sound recording are poor.

....

■ **CAT FROM OUTER SPACE, THE**

1978, 103 MINS, US ◇ ⑰
Dir Norman Tokar *Prod* Ron Miller, Norman Tokar
Scr Ted Key *Ph* Charles F. Wheeler *Ed* Cotton Warburton *Mus* Lalo Schifrin *Art Dir* John B. Mansridge
● Ken Berry, Sandy Duncan, Harry Morgan, Roddy McDowall, McLean Stevenson, Jesse White (Walt Disney)

Cartoonist Ted Key turns to noodling over a spaceship commanded by a cat, forced to land on earth for emergency repairs. For help, the cat turns to a likeable physicist, Ken Berry, to help him get $120,000 in gold needed to repair his saucer in time to rendezvous with the space fleet.

Before long, Berry's girlfriend Sandy Duncan and buddy McLean Stevenson are in on the problem and planning to parlay the cat's extra-terrestrial powers into a series of winning bets with bookie Jesse White. B veterinarian Alan Young mistakenly puts pussy to sleep in the middle of the wagering.

The fun, as usual with Disney pix, comes in the believable sight gags provided along the way. Also as usual, it's a good cast of veterans and nothing to tax them beyond their abilities, all ably kept in pace by director Norman Tokar.

....

■ **CATHERINE THE GREAT**

See: The Rise of Catherine the Great

....

■ **CATHY'S CHILD**

1979, 89 MINS, AUSTRALIA ◇
Dir Donald Crombie *Prod* Pom Oliver, Errol Sullivan
Scr Ken Quinnell *Ph* Gary Hansen *Ed* Tim Wellburn
Art Dir Ross Major
● Michelle Fawdon, Alan Cassell, Bryan Brown, Harry Michael, Anna Hruby, Bob Hughes (CB Films)

Cathy's Child is based on a true story [and the book by Dick Wordley] in which a young Greek mother living in Sydney had her three-year-old daughter abducted by the child's father who returned to Greece with it. The incident was made into a cause celebre by one of the local afternoon newspapers whose reporters turned the spotlight on bureaucracy's mishandling of the situation.

Michelle Fawdon turns in a super performance as the young migrant mother. To her aid comes battered old pro journalist Wordley (Alan Cassell) who with the help of his tough young city editor forces the story onto the front page. Bryan Brown is standout as the embittered editor who some years before had been through a similar experience.

Production values are excellent for the budget of less than $800,000, with shooting on location in Greece and in the Sydney area. Pic has an undeniable aura of soap opera; but that is no put down in this case since director Donald Crombie and the players keep interest up even though it's clear there'll be a happy ending come fadeout.

....

■ **CAT ON A HOT TIN ROOF**

1958, 108 MINS, US ◇ ⑰ ⊙
Dir Richard Brooks *Prod* Lawrence Weingarten
Scr Richard Brooks, James Poe *Ph* William Daniels
Ed Ferris Webster *Art Dir* William A. Horning, Urie McCleary
● Elizabeth Taylor, Paul Newman, Burl Ives, Jack Carson, Judith Anderson, Madeleine Sherwood (M-G-M/Avon)

Cat on a Hot Tin Roof is an intense, important motion picture. By no means is this a watered-down version, though 'immature dependence' has replaced any hint of homosexuality. Motivations remain psychologically sound.

Cat, per Tennessee Williams, is set in the South, but the land is not as decadent as he has so often pictured it. The earth is fertile, the plantation is large and Big Daddy's wealth now amounts to $10 million. Burl Ives, playing Big Daddy, unknowingly is dying of cancer, and his first son (Jack Carson) is out for more than his share of the estate. He and his obnoxious wife (Madeleine Sherwood) make capital of the problems besetting Big Daddy's favorite son (Paul Newman) and his wife (Elizabeth Taylor), he being a drunk and she being childless. It's an often gruesome, often amusing battle.

Taylor has a major credit with her portrayal of Maggie. The frustrations and desires, both as a person and a woman, the warmth and understanding she molds, the loveliness that is more than a well-turned nose – all these are part of a well-accented, perceptive interpretation.

Newman plays cynical underacting against high developed action. His command of the articulate, sensitive sequences is unmistakable, and the way he mirrors his feelings is basic to every scene. Ives, repeating his legit role, is a vibrant and convincing plantation king.

□ 1958: Nominations: Best Picture, Director, Actor (Paul Newman), Actress (Elizabeth Taylor), Adapted Screenplay, Color Cinematography

....

■ **CAT PEOPLE**

1942, 73 MINS, US ⑰
Dir Jacques Tourneur *Prod* Val Lewton *Scr* DeWitt Bodeen *Ph* Nicholas Musuraca *Ed* Mark Robson
Mus Roy Webb *Art Dir* Albert S. D'Agostino, Walter E. Keller
● Simone Simon, Kent Smith, Tom Conway, Jane Randolph, Jack Holt, Alan Napier (RKO)

This is a weird drama of thrill-chill caliber, with developments of surprises confined to psychology and mental reactions, rather than transformation to grotesque and marauding characters for visual impact on the audiences. Picture is well-made on moderate budget outlay.

Story is one of those it-might-happen dramas, if an old Serbian legend be true. Fable has it that women descendants of a certain tribe, when projected into a jealous rage, change into panthers or other members of the cat family for attack, later reverting to human form.

Script, although hazy for the average audience in several instances, carries sufficient punch in the melodramatic sequences to hold it together in good style. Picture is first feature directed by Jacques Tourneur. He does a fine job with a most difficult assignment.

....

■ **CAT PEOPLE**

1982, 118 MINS, US ◇ ⑰ ⊙
Dir Paul Schrader *Prod* Charles Fries *Scr* Alan Ormsby *Ph* John Bailey *Ed* Bud Smith *Mus* Giorgio Moroder, David Bowie *Art Dir* Edward Richardson
● Nastassja Kinski, Malcolm McDowell, John Heard, Annette O'Toole, Ruby Dee, Ed Begley Jr (RKO-Universal)

Paul Schrader's reworking of the 1942 Val Lewton-Jacques Tourneur *Cat People* is a super-chic erotic horror story of mixed impact.

DeWitt Bodeen's original story held that there is a breed of people descended from ancient coupling of women with big cats, and that when one of their number engages in sex, he or she physically reverts to the animalistic state and must kill before becoming human again. It is therefore 'safe' to mate only with relatives.

Reunited in New Orleans with her long-lost brother Malcolm McDowell, Nastassja Kinski meets zoo curator John Heard, takes a job there and soon moves into his home.

At the same time, the Louisiana community is being terrorized by a big black panther. Having repressed her sexuality for a long time, Kinski finally gives in to the genuine love of Heard and condemns herself to repeat the pattern of her brother and ancestors.

Kinski was essential to the film as conceived, and she's endlessly watchable.

■ **CAT'S EYE**

1985, 93 MINS, US ◇ ⑰ ☉
Dir Lewis Teague   *Prod* Martha J. Schumacher
Scr Stephen King   *Ph* Jack Cardiff   *Ed* Scott Conrad
Mus Alan Silvestri   *Art Dir* Giorgio Postiglione
● Drew Barrymore, James Woods, Alan King, Kenneth McMillan, Robert James, Candy Clark (De Laurentiis)

The idea for this three-parter was hatched during Dino De Laurentiis' production of King's *Firestarter*, which also starred little Drew Barrymore. Asked to do another script for Barrymore, King sketched out an idea about a cat who protects a young girl from a threatening troll in her bedroom wall.

Unfortunately, that idea got tacked onto two other King short stories that De Laurentiis had film rights to, *Quitters, Inc.* and *The Ledge*, lighting the fuse for the ultimate bomb.

The three stories just don't connect and efforts to join them never work. However, an excellent roster of talent does try its best.

■ **CATTLE ANNIE AND LITTLE BRITCHES**

1981, 97 MINS, US ◇
Dir Lamont Johnson   *Prod* Rupert Hitzig, Alan King
Scr David Eyre, Robert Ward   *Ph* Larry Pizer
Ed William Haugse, Robbe Roberts   *Mus* Sanh Berti, Tom Slocum   *Art Dir* Stan Jolley
● Burt Lancaster, John Savage, Rod Steiger, Scott Glenn, Amanda Plummer, Diane Lane (Hemdale)

Cattle Annie and Little Britches is as cutesy and unmemorable as its title. Primary focus falls upon two teenaged girls, the gutsy and rather reckless Amanda Plummer and the more demure Diane Lane, who aspire to become what might be called outlaw groupies.

They get their chance when the Doolin-Dalton gang, headed up by an aging but still vigorous Burt Lancaster, rides into town, Plummer taking up with dashing John Savage and Lane coming under the fatherly wing of Lancaster himself.

The girls more or less get lost in the shuffle, however, during the central stretch of the film, which has Lancaster and his roaming bank robbers pursued by determined lawman Rod Steiger. Story's only potential resonance rests in the mutual respect-hate relationship between these two veterans of the range.

In fact, whole film [from the novel by Robert Ward] washes over the viewer, with no images or moments sticking in the mind. Effect is partially due to director Lamont Johnson's exceedingly distanced visual style.

■ **CAUGHT**

1949, 88 MINS, US ⑰
Dir Max Ophuls   *Prod* Wolfgang Reinhardt   *Scr* Arthur Laurents   *Ph* Lee Garmes   *Ed* Robert Parrish
Mus Frederick Hollander   *Art Dir* P. Frank Sylos
● James Mason, Barbara Bel Geddes, Robert Ryan, Ruth Brady, Curt Bois, Art Smith (Enterprise/M-G-M)

Caught is an out-and-out soap opera on film. The performances are topnotch and consistent. So is the direction and physical production dressing. Where film falls down is in the

rather ordinary story [from the novel *Wild Calendar* by Libbie Block] that doesn't take to the twists introduced in an effort to lift it above romantic pulp fiction.

It's the saga of the carhop who aspires to marry a millionaire. She goes to a charm school, becomes a model, and meets and marries her man. A life of riches isn't everything, so she gives it up, goes to work in the office of an East Side medico. They fall in love.

The millionaire is better developed than usual in this type story. He's a tall, dark man of many business interests, odd hours, playboy tendencies and a reluctance to wedlock. Robert Ryan plays him to the hilt.

The shopgirl as played by Barbara Bel Geddes is more rounded and without the empty-headedness such characters usually display. James Mason gives an impressive, underplayed characterization to a not too impressive role.

■ **CAVALCADE**

1933, 110 MINS, US
Dir Frank Lloyd   *Prod* [Winfield Sheehan]   *Scr* Reginald Berkeley, Sonya Levien   *Ph* Ernest Palmer   *Ed* Margaret Clancy   *Mus* Louis de Francesco (dir.)   *Art Dir* William S. Darling
● Clive Brook, Diana Wynyard, Herbert Mundin, Una O'Connor, Ursula Jeans, Beryl Mercer (Fox)

Noel Coward concocted the original stage pageant the film was made from. In that London production it was all Coward. In the filmization Coward steps somewhat into the background.

Very good performances by almost the entire cast, especially the acting job by Diana Wynyard. But above everything recurs the unison and tenseness created by W.R. Sheehan as producer, and Frank Lloyd as director.

Coward's pageant begins at the birth of the 20th century and the beginning of the Boer War. From that it swells along on through three decades, and up through the World War, and to today. Nothing of world importance is lost sight of, including the sinking of the *Titanic*. And through it all is a strong, wistful story of the growth of a family, and the clinging through years of a loving couple.

The first couple of reels, from an American standpoint, at least, seem slow. The establishment of Jane and Robert Marryot (Wynyard and Clive Brook) as the family who are to be watched through 30 years, is a bit slow of development. The first thrill comes at the sailing of the troop ship for Africa. [War scenes by William Cameron Menzies.]

Then, a half reel or so later, an interior of a London music hall, another big scene as the antiquated show is reproduced and then broken up by the audience and actors going wild with enthusiasm at the announcement the war is over. It's the second big scene in the picture, the biggest scene in the original London play, and so well done in the film that from that point on the audience is completely won.

□ 1932/33: Best Picture, Director, Interior Decoration (William S. Darling)
□ Nomination: Best Actress (Diana Wynyard)

■ **CB4**

1993, 86 MINS, US ◇ ⑰ ☉
Dir Tamra Davis   *Prod* Nelson George   *Scr* Chris Rock, Nelson George, Robert LoCash   *Ph* Karl Walter Lindenlaub   *Ed* Earl Watson   *Mus* John Barnes
Art Dir Nelson Coates
● Chris Rock, Allen Payne, Deezer D, Chris Elliott, Phil Hartman, Charlie Murphy (Universal)

Just as *Wayne's World* cashed in lampooning the addled heavy-metal set, this is a rap spoof attempt by another *Saturday Night Live* performer, Chris Rock.

It starts promisingly enough like a hip-hop version of *This Is Spinal Tap* with Ice-T and Ice Cube among the well-known rappers turning up in interview-style cameos. That tactic is soon abandoned, however, in favor of a long flashback about how the middle-class trio (Rock, Allen Payne and rapper Deezer D) passed themselves off as bad-ass types (CB stands for 'cell block') in order to tap into the rap audience, running afoul of the vicious club owner/drug dealer (Charlie Murphy, a dead ringer for younger brother Eddie) who served as their inspiration.

Tamra Davis, musicvideo director with the well-received feature debut *Guncrazy* on her resume, might have really had something here had she settled on any one of the many paths the movie starts down. [Screen story by Rock and producer Nelson George.]

■ **C.C. AND COMPANY**

1970, 94 MINS, US ◇ ⑰
Dir Seymour Robbie   *Prod* Allan Carr, Roger Smith
Scr Roger Smith   *Ph* Charles Wheeler   *Ed* Fred Chulack
Mus Lenny Stack
● Joe Namath, Ann-Margret, William Smith, Jennifer Billingsley, Don Chastain, Teda Bracci (Avco Embassy/Rogallan)

Joe Namath frolics with Ann-Margret against a sordid milieu of motorbikes and an uneasy riders' commune in *C.C. and Company*.

Namath and Ann-Margret encounter by chance on the road and he rescues her from a rape attempt by a few of his hippie gang. This leads to sex in the raw between him and her as consenting partners, and then, for Namath, some violent clashes with cult leader William Smith.

It's all put together ineffectually with one exception: Smith is impressive as the motorcyclists' guru; he's a big and handsome young guy who knows how to project. Ann-Margret is cute and Namath is clumsy.

■ **CEILING ZERO**

1936, 95 MINS, US
Dir Howard Hawks   *Prod* [Harry Joe Brown]   *Scr* Frank Wead   *Ph* Arthur Edeson   *Ed* William Holmes
Mus Leo F. Forbstein (dir.)   *Art Dir* John Hughes
● James Cagney, Pat O'Brien, June Travis, Stuart Erwin, Barton MacLane, Henry Wadsworth (Cosmopolitan/Warner)

All the punch of the original stage play [by Frank Wead] is intact in *Ceiling Zero*. The Broadway stage version, which Warner bankrolled for a moderate success, depended on its dialog and whatever excitement it could steam up through offstage effects. Picture replaces the effects with visible illustration and the difference is considerable and for the better.

James Cagney reverts to the *Public Enemy* days in that he meets violent death at the finish. Up to then, as a daring and not strictly rational flyer, he has been a devil with the ladies, a pilot who loses his license through irresponsible acts and a man who is indirectly to blame for the death of a close friend.

Perhaps 65 of the picture's 95 minutes unfold in the superintendent's office of a commercial air line. It's here that the exciting drama behind the business of peacetime flying is so graphically and compellingly painted.

Structure of the stage play is faithfully followed.

Stuart Erwin as the ill-fated Clarke turns in a trouping job that always equals Cagney and Pat O'Brien, and now and then even transcends theirs. He approaches his big stuff in a quiet manner, but when he gets there he's in. June Travis is a lovely looking girl for the heart interest.

■ CELIA

1989, 102 MINS, AUSTRALIA ◇ ⓦ
Dir Ann Turner   *Prod* Timothy White, Gordon Glenn
Scr Ann Turner   *Ph* Geoffrey Simpson   *Ed* Ken Sallows
Mus Chris Neal   *Art Dir* Peta Lawson
● Rebecca Smart, Nicholas Eadie, Maryanne Fahey,
Victoria Longley, William Zappa (Seon)

Celia starts out as a likeable family pic about the traumas of a sensitive 9-year-old girl growing up in a Melbourne suburb in the conservative late 1950s. It winds up as something quite different.

Celia, played by Rebecca Smart, is an only child; when she discovers her grandmother's body, it's the first of several traumas. Troubled by nightmares featuring monsters from a book read to her at school, Celia is delighted when newcomers, with three children, come to live next door; and finds Alice (Victoria Longley) far more sympathetic than her own mother.

Trouble is, Alice and her husband are active members of the Communist Party, and before long Celia is forbidden to see her new friends.

The child's other obsession is her pet rabbit. When a national plague of rabbits results in the Victoria state government calling for the handing over of all domestic bunnies, she blames her uncle, the local policeman, for enforcing the law, and when her beloved rabbit dies in Melbourne Zoo, she takes a surprisingly violent revenge.

Smart, on-screen throughout, is effective as the ultimately scary Celia, but the film's best performance comes from Victoria Longley as the warm-hearted neighbor.

■ CEMENT GARDEN, THE

1993, 105 MINS, GERMANY/UK/FRANCE ◇ ⓦ ⊙
Dir Andrew Birkin   *Prod* Bee Gilbert, Ene Vanaveski
Scr Andrew Birkin   *Ph* Stephen Blackman   *Ed* Toby
Tremlett   *Mus* Edward Shearmur   *Art Dir* Bernd Lepel
● Andrew Robertson, Charlotte Gainsbourg, Alice
Coulthard, Ned Birkin, Sinead Cusack, Hanns Zischler
(Neue Constantin/Laurentic/Torii)

Gallic star Charlotte Gainsbourg makes a striking English-lingo debut in *The Cement Garden*, a moody, dramatically uneven drama of sibling incest and teenage alienation from British writer Ian McEwan's 1978 first novel.

The movie is a family affair in more ways that one. Director Andrew Birkin (*Burning Secret*) is Gainsbourg's uncle and his son Ned plays Charlotte's youngest brother in the film.

Pic's setting is a lone house amid a concrete wasteland. When the family's stern father (Hanns Zischler) dies of a heart attack, mom (Sinead Cusack) buckles under the strain of rearing her four children and becomes bedridden. When she, too, dies, the elder kids secretly bury her body in a cement box in the cellar to avoid being taken into care.

Left to their own devices, the children start to give freer vent to their sexual confusion. The eldest, Julie (Gainsbourg), 16, plays with the incestuous infatuation of 15-year-old brother Jack (Andrew Robertson), as well as inviting round an elder boyfriend (Jochen Horst).

The pic lacks the straightforward dramatic smarts of Jack Clayton's 1967 *Our Mother's House*, also about moppets hiding their mom's death. Birkin focuses more on the blurred areas between genders, and the vulnerable world of puberty blues.

■ CEMETERY CLUB, THE

1993, 106 MINS, US ◇ ⓦ ⊙
Dir Bill Duke   *Prod* David Brown, Sophie Hurst, Bonnie
Palef   *Scr* Ivan Menchell   *Ph* Steven Poster   *Ed* John
Carter   *Mus* Elmer Bernstein   *Art Dir* Maher Ahmad
● Ellen Burstyn, Olympia Dukakis, Diane Ladd, Danny
Aiello, Lainie Kazan, Jeff Howell (Touchstone)

Scripter Ivan Menchell adapted his play about three close Pittsburgh friends (Ellen Burstyn, Olympia Dukakis and Diane Ladd) and their experiences with widowhood. It plays as a fairly accurate, if sketchy, assessment.

Still, the episodic, rambling quality lifts it above the sitcom level. Helmer Bill Duke, like many actors turned director, affords his players the space to flesh out the bony material.

The three actresses, particularly Burstyn, do their darnedest to ground their perfs in reality, even in the broader scenes. The interplay between Burstyn and romantic interest Danny Aiello is credible, if a bit unfocused. Lainie Kazan gets most of the over-the-top business.

■ CEREMONY, THE

1963, 106 MINS, US
Dir Laurence Harvey   *Prod* Laurence Harvey   *Scr* Ben
Barzman, Laurence Harvey   *Ph* Brian West   *Ed* Ralph
Kemplen   *Mus* Gerard Schurmann
● Laurence Harvey, Sarah Miles, Robert Walker, John
Ireland, Ross Martin, Lee Patterson (United Artists)

Ben Barzman's screenplay relates the dreary tale of a man (Laurence Harvey) about to be executed in a Tangier prison for a crime he did not commit, a murder that actually he'd tried to prevent but for which he is paying the supreme penalty as a kind of scapegoat. An elaborate escape scheme cooked up by his brother (Robert Walker) succeeds, but Harvey then discovers that little brother has been making time with his girl (Sarah Miles).

Concern is never aroused for any of the characters. The audience is thrust into the heart of the situation and never really allowed to get its bearings. The players are all snowed under by ill-defined, unappealing roles and lack of proper direction. *The Ceremony* is a depressingly dark film.

■ CERTAIN SMILE, A

1958, 105 MINS, US ◇
Dir Jean Negulesco   *Prod* Henry Ephron   *Scr* Frances
Goodrich, Albert Hackett   *Ph* Milton Krasner   *Ed* Louis
Loeffler   *Mus* Alfred Newman   *Art Dir* Lyle R. Wheeler,
John F. DeCuir
● Rossano Brazzi, Joan Fontaine, Bradford Dillman,
Christine Carere, Eduard Franz, Kathryn Givney (20th
Century-Fox)

In the second of Francoise Sagan's novels to be filmed, once again the principal character is a young and attractive girl, only this time the 'shocker' involves her week-long affair with an older man.

Only the very basic elements in the slim Sagan book have been retained in this glossy, emotional yarn. None of the moody disenchantment of the girl in the book comes through and of course the ending has been totally changed. In Sagan's original the heroine blithely continued her affairs both with regular boyfriend and older lover.

As a film *A Certain Smile* is well made, reasonably well acted and quite magnificently photographed. Having so strenuously toned down the amoral aspects of their story, producer and director apparently decided to go whole hog for the visual aspects. As a result, the film abounds with mouth-watering vistas of the French Riviera, which is photographed from every possible vantage point, providing an idyllic setting for the romantic goings-on between Rossano Brazzi and Christine Carere. Scenes in the Paris streets also come alive temptingly.

Carere is charming and petite, turning in a capable performance that's just a shade too much on the wholesome side. Boyfriend Bradford Dillman, also a newcomer, is good-looking in an unconventional way. He does well in a frustrating role. Brazzi is suavely

Continental as the middle-aged Don Juan, and wife Joan Fontaine suffers as required by script.
☐ 1958: Nominations: Best Costume Design, Art Direction, Song ('A Certain Smile')

■ CHAD HANNA

1940, 86 MINS, US ◇
Dir Henry King   *Prod* Nunnally Johnson   *Scr* Nunnally
Johnson   *Ph* Ernest Palmer, Ray Rennahan   *Ed* Barbara
McLean   *Mus* David Buttolph   *Art Dir* Richard Day
● Henry Fonda, Dorothy Lamour, Linda Darnell, Guy
Kibbee, Jane Darwell, John Carradine (20th Century-Fox)

Chad Hanna is descriptive of early 19th century Americana through the eyes of a roving wagon circus through upper New York state. It's from Walter D. Edmonds' *Saturday Evening Post* serial, *Red Wheels Rolling*.

Chad Hanna (Henry Fonda) is a semi-illiterate stable boy along the Erie canal in the Mohawk valley region. Enamoured of the gaudily-dressed circus rider (Dorothy Lamour), he joins the small one-ringer as a roustabout; and finds Linda Darnell along as a runaway from whip-wielding father. Chad marries Darnell, who has taken spot of chief equestrienne with the show, and in a brief reunion with Lamour realizes he is really in love with his wife.

Mixed in between in liberal sprinklings are the vicissitudes of the circus in wading through financial, opposition and other battles, including the death of the main attraction, a man-eating lion.

Both script and direction handle the yarn in leisurely and rather uneventful tempo.

■ CHAINED HEAT

1983, 95 MINS, US/W. GERMANY ◇ ⓦ ⊙
Dir Paul Nicolas   *Prod* Billy Fine   *Scr* Vincent Mongol,
Paul Nicolas   *Ph* Mac Ahlberg   *Ed* Nino di Marco
Mus Joseph Conlon   *Art Dir* Bob Ziembicki
● Linda Blair, John Vernon, Sybil Danning, Tamara
Dobson, Stella Stevens, Henry Silva
(Heat/TAT/Intercontinental)

Chained Heat is a silly, almost campy follow-up to producer Billy Fine's women's prison hit, *The Concrete Jungle*, that manages to pack in enough sex tease and violent action to satisfy undiscriminating action fans.

Linda Blair toplines as Carol, an innocent young girl serving an 18-month stretch in a California prison run by Warden Backman (John Vernon) and Captain Taylor (Stella Stevens), as corrupt a pair as the scripters can imagine. Real power in stir is shared by statuesque Ericka (Sybil Danning) and Duchess (Tamara Dobson), lording it over the white and black prison populations, respectively.

German director Paul Nicolas displays little feel for the prison genre, emphasizing archaic sex-for-voyeurs scenes.

■ CHAIN OF DESIRE

1993, 107 MINS, US ◇ ⓦ ⊙
Dir Temistocles Lopez   *Prod* Brian Cox   *Scr* Temistocles
Lopez   *Ph* Nancy Schreiber   *Ed* Suzanne Fenn
Mus Nathan Birnbaum   *Art Dir* Scott Chambliss
● Linda Fiorentino, Grace Zabriskie, Assumpta Serna,
Patrick Bauchau, Seymour Cassel, Malcolm McDowell
(Distant Horizon)

A modern *La Ronde* played out under the shadow of AIDS, *Chain of Desire* is an uneven but alluringly sexy melodrama that gets better as it goes along.

Set in contempo New York, mostly downtown, this version introduces a somewhat jaded bisexual perspective to the tale, but the characters remain vibrantly alive to life's possibilities, at least where the libido is concerned.

Opening has club chanteuse Linda Fiorentino repairing to the solitude of a church after breaking up with a b.f. She is approached by seductive building restorer Elias Koteas, with whom she begins a torrid affair.

Koteas' sexy wife, Angel Aviles, works as a maid for depraved millionaire Patrick Bauchau, who tries to get her into the bondage games in which he indulges with Grace Zabriskie. Latter has seen the passion disappear from her marriage to Malcolm McDowell, a TV commentator.

The situations and incidents become more complex and intense once the pic switches into gay and bi territory. It turns out McDowell prefers boys these days.

Straight and gay viewers of both genders will have plenty to feast their eyes upon here, and thesps deliver with relaxed, humorous, knowing performances.

....

■ CHAIRMAN, THE
(UK: The Most Dangerous Man in the World)

1969, 104 MINS, US ◇ ⊗
Dir J. Lee Thompson   *Prod* Mort Abrahams   *Scr* Ben Maddow   *Ph* John Wilcox   *Ed* Richard Best   *Mus* Jerry Goldsmith   *Art Dir* Peter Mullins
● Gregory Peck, Anne Heywood, Arthur Hill, Alan Dobie, Conrad Yama, Zienia Merton (20th Century-Fox)

A quality film, made at Pinewood Studios and on location in the Far East, introducing improbable mission wrapped up in such style it becomes engrossing.

Nobel Prize winning American scientist Gregory Peck, teaching at the University of London, receives a letter from his former instructor, Professor Soong Li (Keye Luke), telling him it would be impossible for Peck to visit Red China.

Since Peck has no intentions of visiting China, he is further mystified when the President urges him slip out of London and into the Chinese mainland.

Peck is finally convinced when shown food growing in formerly arid or snowcovered areas inside China.

Task of presenting the film [from a novel by Jay Richard Kennedy] on screen was stupendous, and it has been accomplished with imagination and taste. Peck performs well in a part far more demanding than appears on the surface, while Heywood is totally wasted in what is hardly more than a bit part.

....

■ CHALK GARDEN, THE

1964, 106 MINS, UK ◇ ⊗
Dir Ronald Neame   *Prod* Ross Hunter   *Scr* John Michael Hayes   *Ph* Arthur Ibbetson   *Ed* Jack Harris   *Mus* Malcolm Arnold   *Art Dir* Carmen Dillon
● Deborah Kerr, Hayley Mills, John Mills, Edith Evans, Elizabeth Sellars, Felix Aylmer (Rank/Quota Rentals)

The Chalk Garden makes no bones about its legit background. Enid Bagnold's drama had a healthy 17 months' run at the Haymarket in 1956 and producer and director have not done much to disguise the original.

Hayley Mills vigorously plays a 16-year-old girl, in some ways perceptive beyond her years. But audiences will feel that a well-applied hairbrush on her derriere could have swiftly ironed out some of the problems that beset her and the surrounding adults.

The child suffers from the feeling that she is not loved. Her mother has remarried and her grandmother is more obsessed with her arid garden. So the confused, unhappy girl grows up in a world of fantasy and lying. On to the scene comes a mystery woman as governess. Deborah Kerr's background turns out to be that of a woman straight from prison after a suspended sentence for bumping off her stepsister.

On paper, this sounds like a ripe old piece of Victoriana, but curiously it works, largely because of confident, smooth performances by all concerned.
□ 1964: Nomination: Best Supp. Actress (Edith Evans)

....

■ CHALLENGE, THE

1982, 112 MINS, US ◇ ⊗
Dir John Frankenheimer   *Prod* Lyle Poncher, Robert L. Posen, Ron Beckman   *Scr* Richard Maxwell, John Sayles   *Ph* Kozo Okazaki   *Ed* Jack Wheeler   *Mus* Jerry Goldsmith   *Art Dir* Yoshiyuki Ishida
● Scott Glenn, Toshiro Mifune, Donna Kei Lenz, Atsuo Nakamura, Calvin Young, Clyde Kusatsu (CBS Theatrical)

Heads seen being split or cut off in swift but bloody closeups, along with a lot of aesthetic juxtaposition of ancient Japanese manners and architecture versus modern ditto, are the main attractions of John Frankenheimer's *The Challenge*.

Pitted against each other are two brothers (Toshiro Mifune and Atsuo Nakamura) and two swords of the kind that certain Japanese even today believe to have a soul of their own. The good one wants both weapons back at his own home shrine where the true martial arts are trained daily by a minor Kimono-clad army, while the industrialist's army uses guns and breaks all the rules of gamesmanship.

Into all this is lured a young American boxing bum known only as Rick (Scott Glenn).

Mifune carries himself with eye-twinkling dignity as the good brother. Calvin Young is a true menace as the cool American-Japanese bodyguard and killer. Donna Kei Lenz as the object of Rick's love is not given much to prove herself as an actress. Glenn, with the long donkey face and occasional grin to match, may well prove to be just the star material Frankenheimer thinks he is.

....

■ CHAMP, THE

1931, 85 MINS, US ⊗
Dir King Vidor   *Scr* Frances Marion, Leonard Praskins, Wanda Tuchock   *Ph* Gordon Avil   *Ed* Hugh Wynn   *Art Dir* Cedric Gibbons
● Wallace Beery, Jackie Cooper, Irene Rich, Roscoe Ates, Edward Brophy, Hale Hamilton (M-G-M)

A good picture, almost entirely by virtue of an inspired performance by a boy, Jackie Cooper. There is none of the usual hammy quality of the average child actor in this kid.

What also makes *The Champ* a good talker is a studied, understanding adult piece of work by the costar, Wallace Beery, who had to step to keep up with Jackie, and a Frances Marion original story that isn't bad for a boxing story.

Beery plays a broken down ex-heavyweight champ. He's anchored in Tiajuana with his kid and a couple of training camp leeches, and training for a comeback between stews. When not stewing he's gambling and the comeback always seems more distant. He wins enough to buy the kid a race horse. Then he loses the horse in a crap game.

In the attempts of the Champ's former wife and the boy's mother to regain her son there is some menace, though Irene Rich as the mother and Hale Hamilton as her second husband are painted lily white by the script.
□ 1931/32: Best Actor (Wallace Beery), Original Story.
□ Nominations: Best Picture, Director

....

■ CHAMP, THE

1979, 121 MINS, US ◇ ⊗ ⊙
Dir Franco Zeffirelli   *Prod* Dyson Lovell   *Scr* Walter Newman   *Ph* Fred J. Koenekamp   *Ed* Michael J. Sheridan   *Mus* Dave Grusin   *Art Dir* Theoni V. Aldredge
● Jon Voight, Faye Dunaway, Ricky Schroder, Jack Warden, Strother Martin, Joan Blondell (United Artists/M-G-M)

Walter Newman's script adroitly updates Frances Marion's original scenario, placing down-and-out boxer Jon Voight as a horse handler in Florida, accompanied by sprig Ricky Schroder. An inveterate gambler and drinker, Voight doesn't hit the comeback trail until ex-wife Faye Dunaway, now a society matron, reappears to threaten his and Schroder's buddy-buddy relationship.

Even those unfamiliar with the 1931 pic will feel resonances in the current *Champ* and in this edition Schroder projects a comparable emotional range and depth.

Most debatable, and in some respects unsettling, aspects of the update concern the Voight-Dunaway characters and relationships.

But Voight, under Italian director Franco Zeffirelli, has adopted an accent and outlook that seems at odds with the setting, and seriously weakens the credibility of a relationship between him and the elegant Dunaway.
□ 1979: Nomination: Best Original Score

....

■ CHAMPION

1949, 90 MINS, US ⊗
Dir Mark Robson   *Prod* Stanley Kramer   *Scr* Carl Foreman   *Ph* Franz Planer   *Ed* Harry Gerstad   *Mus* Dimitri Tiomkin
● Kirk Douglas, Marilyn Maxwell, Arthur Kennedy, Paul Stewart, Ruth Roman (Screen Plays)

Adapted from a Ring Lardner short story of the same title, *Champion* is a stark, realistic study of the boxing rackets and the degeneracy of a prizefighter.

Fight scenes, under Franz Planer's camera, have realism and impact. Unrelenting pace is set by the opening sequence.

Cast, under Mark Robson's tight direction, is fine. Kirk Douglas is the boxer and he makes the character live. Second honors go jointly to Arthur Kennedy, the fighter's crippled brother, and Paul Stewart as the knowing manager.

Where the Lardner story made the boxer a no-good from the start, Foreman's screenplay casts him as an appealing Joe in the earlier reels. Already stuck with a persecution complex because of his boyhood poverty, it doesn't take long for him to become a real heel.
□ 1949: Best Editing.
□ Nominations: Best Actor (Kirk Douglas), Supp. Actor (Arthur Kennedy), Screenplay, B&W Cinematography, Scoring of a Dramatic Picture

....

■ CHAMPIONS
See: The Mighty Ducks

....

■ CHANCES ARE

1989, 108 MINS, US ◇ ⊗ ⊙
Dir Emile Ardolino   *Prod* Mike Lobell   *Scr* Perry Howze, Randy Howze   *Ph* William A. Fraker   *Ed* Harry Keramidas   *Mus* Maurice Jarre   *Art Dir* Dennis Washington
● Cybill Shepherd, Robert Downey Jr, Ryan O'Neal, Mary Stuart Masterson, Christopher McDonald, Josef Sommer (Tri-Star)

Here comes *Chances Are* and there goes Mr Jordan, no doubt in a huff. While this new pic hinges on the same cloud-carpeted conception of heaven as a way station for earthbound souls, the similarity ends there, and a potentially charming premise yields only a handful of chuckles.

The plot hangs on the death of Cybill Shepherd's husband, who flees heaven to be reincarnated before being 'inoculated' to prevent a return of past-life memory. He comes back 23 years later as Robert Downey Jr and stumbles into the life of Corinne (Shepherd), as well as that of her daughter Miranda (Mary Stuart Masterson) and former best friend Philip (Ryan O'Neal). Philip harbors a long-suffering adoration for Corinne, who has kept him at arm's length.

There's a nice scene when Alex (Downey) first comes to dinner and starts to remember his past life, but from then on the screenplay is patently predictable. Downey sparkles at times simply with his stunned expressions. Beyond that, the rest of the characters are at best absurd: Masterson throws herself at him instantaneously.

••••••••••••••••••••••••••••

■ **CHANG**

1927, 70 MINS, US ⊗ ◊ ⊙
Dir Merian C. Cooper, Ernest B. Schoedsack
Prod Merian C. Cooper, Ernest B. Schoedsack   *Ph* Ernest B. Schoedsack
● Kru, Chantui, Nah, Ladah, Bimbo (Paramount)

Even before going into details on *Chang* [Thai for 'elephant'], mention must be made of the camerawork, primarily the photography, fine under the conditions it must have been taken in and around, and the apparent danger the cameramen seemingly and continuously exposed them to.

Every kind of wild animal is here. Most of them come head on to the camera, many at close range. With the elephants, a camera or two must have been buried.

As a picture, however, and a wild animal film, the elephant portion is but its biggest incident. Towering above all else as an animal picture is a melodramatic story of native life in the jungle.

Chang is the first animal picture having a scenario and with just an immense jungle for the background. It carries more of a thrill than the other pictures of its sort, for there seems danger frequently and the ferocity of a tiger or leopard here and there is most realistic.
□ 1927/28: Nomination: Best Artistic Quality of Production

••••••••••••••••••••••••••••

■ **CHANGELING, THE**

1980, 107 MINS, CANADA ◊ ⓥ
Dir Peter Medak   *Prod* Joel B. Michaels, Garth H. Drabinsky   *Scr* William Gray, Diana Maddox   *Ph* John Coquillon   *Ed* Lou Lombardo, Lilla Pedersen   *Mus* Rick Wilkins   *Art Dir* Trevor Williams
● George C. Scott, Trish Van Devere, Melvyn Douglas, John Colicos, Jean Marsh, Barry Morse (Michaels-Drabinsky)

The Changeling is a superior haunted house thriller. The story [by Russell Hunter] centers on George C. Scott, a recently widowed music professor, who has moved to Seattle to forget his personal tragedy. His new residence is an old home owned by the local historic society. After moving in, the house begins to do strange things.

It turns out that the noisy spirit is a young sickly boy who was murdered at the turn of the century. The child's father could not collect an inheritance unless the boy reached the age of 21. After the murder a changeling was put in the boy's place. The changeling is still alive and the dead child wants to wreak his vengeance on him.

Scott and Melvyn Douglas (as a powerful industrialist) register the strongest performances with Trish Van Devere as coming off rather wooden.

••••••••••••••••••••••••••••

■ **CHANGE OF SEASONS, A**

1980, 102 MINS, US ◊ ⓥ
Dir Richard Lang, [Noel Black]   *Prod* Martin Ransohoff
Scr Erich Segal, Ronni Kern, Fred Segal   *Ph* Philip Lathrop   *Ed* Don Zimmerman   *Mus* Henry Mancini
Art Dir Bill Kenney
● Shirley MacLaine, Anthony Hopkins, Bo Derek, Mary Beth Hurt, Michael Brandon, Ed Winter (Film Finance/Ransohoff)

It would take the genius of an Ernst Lubitsch to do justice to the incredibly tangled relationships in *A Change of Seasons*, and director Richard Lang is no Lubitsch. The switching of couples seems arbitrary and mechanical, and more sour than amusing.

Shirley MacLaine emerges as the most sympathetic person in the film, the wife of college professor Anthony Hopkins, whose philandering with coed Bo Derek shatters the complacency of their marriage. MacLaine retaliates by taking a young lover (Michael Brandon) and they all head off on a Vermont skiing vacation together in a dubious demonstration of open-mindedness.

Derek and Hopkins romp in slow-motion in a hot tub but that's about all the sexual charge the film carries. Hopkins comes off as a totally self-centered boor who never engages audience sympathy.

••••••••••••••••••••••••••••

■ **CHAN IS MISSING**

1982, 80 MINS, US ⓥ
Dir Wayne Wang   *Prod* Wayne Wang   *Scr* Wayne Wang, Isaac Cronin, Terrel Seltzer   *Ph* Michael Chin   *Ed* Wayne Wang   *Mus* Robert Kikuchi
● Marc Hayashi, Wood Moy, Laureen Chew, Judy Nihei, Peter Wang (Wang)

Rather roughly lensed in b&w and 16mm tale traces the odyssey of two San Francisco Chinese taxi drivers as they search for an older partner who's vanished with their funds. As in Antonioni's *L'Avventura*, the object of their quest is never found, but suspense in this regard couldn't be further from the point.

Instead, Chan's relatives, local businessmen, politicos and citizens-at-large who are interviewed by the pair constitute a fascinating and often amusing gallery of portraits of contempo Chinese Americans.

Joe, the elder cabbie who serves as narrator, is like a solid working stiff of any race. His youthful cohort, Steve, seems to have fashioned his looks after Burt Reynolds, hiply speaks in a sort of black jive lingo and has little patience for the caution, moderation and discretion widely found in the older generations of Chinese immigrants.

Any filmmaker who can so thoroughly force the viewer to look at the world through his eyes possesses a talent to reckon with.

••••••••••••••••••••••••••••

■ **CHANT OF JIMMIE BLACKSMITH, THE**

1978, 122 MINS, AUSTRALIA ◊ ⓥ
Dir Fred Schepisi   *Prod* Fred Schepisi   *Scr* Fred Schepisi
Ph Ian Baker   *Ed* Brian Kavanaugh
● Tommy Lewis, Freddy Reynolds, Ray Barrett, Jack Thompson, Peter Carroll, Elizabeth Alexander (Filmhouse/Australia Party)

Fred Schepisi, for his second film, reveals a sure hand, a dynamic thrust in using a true turn-of-the-century happening [from a book by Thomas Keneally] to delve into the racism of the times against aborigines and the beginnings of governmental federation of its many regions.

The tale of a mulatto aborigine, raised by a Methodist minister, and torn between his people and his Christian teachings, has sweep and interesting insights into the loss of the aborigine culture and the life of man who does not belong to either culture anymore.

Tommy Lewis, a non-actor, is well utilized as Jimmie Blacksmith. He works for a white family who allow him to build a hut for his family. When there is no food and no pay, he and his uncle go to the house, where the men are absent. The refusal of food leads to a sudden explosion of all the smoldering resentments and they slaughter the wife, two teenage daughters, a schoolteacher living with them and a young boy.

The violence is instinctive, harrowing but

not exploited. It is masterfully handled by Schepisi. Jimmie and his brother leave the old uncle and the wife and child and go on the lam as a great manhunt begins.

••••••••••••••••••••••••••••

■ **CHAPLIN**

1992, 144 MINS, US ◊ ⓦ ⊙
Dir Richard Attenborough   *Prod* Richard Attenborough, Mario Kassar   *Scr* William Boyd, Bryan Forbes, William Goldman, [Tom Stoppard, Diana Hawkins]   *Ph* Sven Nykvist   *Ed* Anne V. Coates   *Mus* John Barry
Art Dir Stuart Craig
● Robert Downey Jr, Dan Ackroyd, Geraldine Chaplin, Kevin Dunn, Anthony Hopkins, Moira Kelly (Carolco/Canal Plus/RCS Video)

Like a stone skipping across the top of a deep, turbulent sea, *Chaplin* runs through the dramatic highs and lows in the life of the screen's foremost comic genius without stirring the water much.

Telling the entire story of Charles Chaplin's 88 years was probably a hopeless goal for a feature-length film, but Richard Attenborough's latest epic biopic [from Chaplin's *My Autobiography* and David Robinson's *Chaplin: His Life and Art*] does offer the saving grace of an uncanny, truly remarkable central performance by Robert Downey Jr and a number of lovely moments along the way.

Attenborough attempts to relate the whole of Chaplin's exceedingly eventful life – his impoverished London East End childhood, early success vaudeville, quick rise to the top in movies, troubles with wives, young girls and the law, banishment from the US, European exile and eventual return to Hollywood in triumph.

As time goes on, the story structure becomes a matter of connecting the historical dots. Douglas Fairbanks (Kevine Kline, perfect) and Mary Pickford are brought on, but not a word is said of United Artists; Chaplin offends J. Edgar Hoover at a dinner party, and the FBI chief hounds him forever after; wives and girls come and go.

In a novel casting stroke, Geraldine Chaplin strongly etches her own grandmother's maternal love and incipient madness. Dan Ackroyd as comedy king Mack Sennett; Moira Kelly as both Chaplin's first love and last, Oona O'Neil; Penelope Ann Miller as his first leading lady, Edna Purviance; Paul Rhys as brother Sydney; John Thaw as music hall impresario Fred Karno – all ring as true as actors can in this sort of enterprise.
□ Nominations: Best Actor (Robert Downey Jr), Original Score, Art Direction

••••••••••••••••••••••••••••

■ **CHAPMAN REPORT, THE**

1962, 125 MINS, US ◊
Dir George Cukor   *Prod* Richard D. Zanuck   *Scr* Wyatt Cooper, Don M. Mankiewicz   *Ph* Harold Lipstein
Ed Robert Simpson   *Mus* Leonard Rosenman
Art Dir Gene Allen
● Efrem Zimbalist Jr, Shelley Winters, Jane Fonda, Claire Bloom, Glynis Johns, Ray Danton (Warner)

The Chapman Report is a talky melodramatization of several abnormal patterns in the sexual behaviour of the upper middleclass American female. The scenario, from an adaptation by Grant Stuart and Gene Allen of Irving Wallace's novel, attempts the feat of dramatically threading together the stories of four sexually unstable women who become voluntary subjects for a scientific sex survey conducted by a noted psychologist and his staff.

One (Claire Bloom) is a hopeless nympho and alcoholic. Another (Jane Fonda) suffers from fears of frigidity. The third (Glynis Johns), a kind of comedy relief figure, is an intellectual who feels there may be more to

133

sex than she has realized in her smugly satisfied marital relationship. The last (Shelley Winters) enters into a clandestine extra-marital affair with an irresponsible little theatre director.

Johns does the best acting in the film, rising above the flimsiest of the four episodes with a spirited and infectious performance. Fonda seems miscast and is affected and unappealing in her role. Bloom suffers up a storm. Winters plays with conviction. The men are all two-dimensional pawns.

■ **CHAPTER TWO**

1979, 124 MINS, US ◇ ▽ ⊙
Dir Robert Moore   *Prod* Ray Stark   *Scr* Neil Simon
Ph David M. Walsh   *Ed* Michael A. Stevenson
Mus Marvin Hamlisch   *Art Dir* Gene Callahan
● James Caan, Marsha Mason, Joseph Bologna, Valerie Harper, Judy Farrell, Debra Mooney (Columbia)

Chapter Two represents Neil Simon at his big-screen best. Film version of his successful and loosely autobiographical play is tender, compassionate and gently humorous all at once. Marsha Mason's tremendous performance under Robert Moore's sensitive direction gives the pic another boost.

Simon, producer Ray Stark and Moore, in their third film collaboration, have dared to alter the entire focus of the legit version of *Chapter Two*, by subtly but inalterably concentrating on Jennie MacLaine, the actress being wooed by author Schneider, rather than Schneider himself.

Result is to downplay the unusual casting of James Caan as Schneider (the choice still pays off richly), and affords Mason the opportunity for her best-realized film work to date.
□ 1979: Nomination: Best Actress (Marsha Mason)

■ **CHARADE**

1963, 113 MINS, US ◇ ▽
Dir Stanley Donen   *Prod* Stanley Donen   *Scr* Peter Stone   *Ph* Charles Lang Jr   *Ed* James Clark
Mus Henry Mancini
● Cary Grant, Audrey Hepburn, Walter Matthau, James Coburn, Ned Glass, George Kennedy (Universal)

Basically a suspenser or chase film, *Charade* has several moments of violence but they are leavened with a generous helping of spoofery. Director Stanley Donen plays the taut tale against a colorful background of witty dialogue, humorous situations and scenic beauty.

While vacationing at a French Alps ski resort, Audrey Hepburn meets Cary Grant casually. Returning to Paris, she finds herself a widow, her husband having been murdered. Aware that her own life may be in danger, she appeals for help to the US Embassy. There she learns that former World War II associates of her husband, his accomplices in the theft of $250,000 in gold, believe that she knows the money's whereabouts. Walter Matthau, her informant, advises her, for her own safety, to find the money (property of the US government) and turn it over to him.

The two stars carry the film effortlessly, with the only acting competition coming from the versatile Matthau. James Coburn, Ned Glass and George Kennedy make an effective trio of villainous cutthroats. Kennedy's fight with Grant on a slippery rooftop is a real gasper.

Fast-paced, from the pre-title shot of a body tossed from a train to the finale under a theatre stage, *Charade* seldom falters (amazing, considering its almost two-hour running time). Repartee between the two stars is sometimes subtle, sometimes suggestive, sometimes satirical but always witty.
□ 1963: Nomination: Best Song ('Charade')

■ **CHARGE OF THE LIGHT BRIGADE, THE**

1936, 115 MINS, US ▽ ⊙
Dir Michael Curtiz   *Prod* [Sam Bischoff]   *Scr* Michel Jacoby, Rowland Leigh   *Ph* Sol Polito   *Ed* George Amy
Mus Max Steiner   *Art Dir* John Hughes
● Errol Flynn, Oliva de Havilland, Patric Knowles, Henry Stephenson, Donald Crisp, David Niven (Warner)

Warner has turned out a magnificent production in this story [by Michel Jacoby] based on Tennyson's immortal poem and historical facts. Foreword explains that history was consulted for background, but characters and development are fictionized.

Before the climactic sweeping drive of the cavalry there is the dramatic defense of the Chukoti garrison and the ruthless massacre of soldiers, wives and children after they have surrendered. The major who witnessed the slaughter is depicted as switching an order of the British high command. This results in the 600 cavalrymen riding into 'the valley of death' in the face of cannon fire and a force four or five times their number.

The tremendous sweep of this surging charge constitutes the feature's highlight. It has been skillfully done by means of close-ups, a traveling camera shot depicting the changing pace of the horses as column after column races towards the enemy, and via some truly extraordinary process shots.

The dual love affair, two brothers seeking the hand of the colonel's daughter, is nicely intertwined with the more adventurous moments of the story.

Errol Flynn lives up to the promise of previous film efforts as the youthful major who sacrifices all to avenge the slaughter of his comrades. Donald Crisp is strong in the character portrayal of the colonel.
□ 1936: Best Assistant Director (Jack Sullivan).
□ Nominations: Best Score, Sound

■ **CHARGE OF THE LIGHT BRIGADE, THE**

1968, 145 MINS, UK ◇
Dir Tony Richardson   *Prod* Neil Hartley   *Scr* Charles Wood   *Ph* David Watkin   *Ed* Kevin Brownlow, Hugh Raggett   *Mus* John Addison   *Art Dir* Edward Marshall, Julia Trevelyan Oman
● Trevor Howard, Vanessa Redgrave, John Gielgud, Harry Andrews, Jill Bennett, David Hemmings (United Artists/Woodfall)

Thanks mainly to Lord Tennyson's piece of durable doggerel millions of people have at least a sketchy idea of the historical incident, though director Tony Richardson's treatment is almost disdainfully indifferent to the actual physical charge.

He is more concerned with analysing the reasons behind one of the most notorious blunders in military history. He's also intent on attacking by ridicule the class war and bigotry of the British mid-19th-century regime, and the futility of the Crimean War as a whole.

Those fascinated by the class distinction, crass stupidity, muddled thinking and old school tie snobbishness then prevailing will find richness in the earthy screenplay.

Film starts leisurely, carefully building up to the atmosphere of the times. In fact, despite Richardson's frequently lively direction and the brisk, electric editing, the pace of the film is remarkably easygoing, building up in a vague story line to the crass Charge as a finale which comes almost as an anti-climax.

Apart from some masterly directorial touches Richardson has made clever use of animated sequences wittily drawn by Richard Williams, living caricatures based on broadsides and cartoons of the mid-Victorian period.

They are not only consistently amusing but also deftly link the action, explain the historical background and compress what would be unwieldy scenes into quick, understandable comment.

■ **CHARIOTS OF FIRE**

1981, 123 MINS, UK ◇ ▽ ⊙
Dir Hugh Hudson   *Prod* David Puttnam   *Scr* Colin Welland   *Ph* David Watkin   *Ed* Terry Rawlings
Mus Vangelis   *Art Dir* Roger Hall
● Ben Cross, Ian Charleson, Nigel Havers, Alice Krige, John Gielgud, Lindsay Anderson (Allied Stars/Enigma)

Chariots of Fire, which weaves the stories of two former British track aces who both won major events at the 1924 Paris Olympics, is about the will to win and why. It's also a winner for director Hugh Hudson in his theatrical bow after an apprenticeship in commercials.

The Colin Welland script has a lot to admire in the engrossing way it counterpoints the progress of its two sporting heroes, each driven by impulse that has little to do with mere fame per se and even less with national honor.

Ian Charleson and Ben Cross are both exemplary as the respective super-runners, Eric Liddell and Harold Abrahams, the first a Christian Scot who believes that by winning can he best honor the Lord; the latter an English Jew with chip on the shoulder for whom over-achieving is his ticket to acceptance in a prejudiced society.

What with two social outsiders hogging the glory for dear old Albion, the snobby establishment doesn't come off to raves.

Hudson's direction gets it all together with admirable assurance and narrative style. No arty tricks, no self-conscious posturing. His use of slow motion and freeze frames for the various racing sequences turns out to be a valid device for sharpening emotional intensity.
□ 1981: Best Picture, Original Screenplay, Score, Costume Design.
□ Nominations: Best Director, Supp. Actor (Ian Holm), Editing

■ **CHARLEY VARRICK**

1973, 111 MINS, US ◇ ▽
Dir Don Siegel   *Prod* Don Siegel   *Scr* Howard Rodman, Dean Riesner   *Ph* Michael Butler   *Ed* Frank Morriss
Mus Lalo Schifrin   *Art Dir* Fernando Carrere
● Walter Matthau, Joe Don Baker, Felicia Farr, Andy Robinson, John Vernon, Sheree North (Universal)

Charley Varrick is a sometimes-fuzzy melodrama but so well put together that it emerges a hardhitting actioner with a sock finale.

Based the John Reese novel, *The Looters*, narrative carries the unusual twist of Walter Matthau, a small-time bank robber, trying to return his heist of a smalltown New Mexico bank aftr later discovering his $750,000 take belongs to the Mafia and he wants none of it. He is opposed by a young companion who doesn't see eye-to-eye, and menaced by a Mafia hit-man who arrives on the scene.

Director Don Siegel overcomes deficiencies in part by his rugged handling of action and making handsome us of the Nevada landscape where pic was filmed and which provided stuntmen with a field day.

Matthau delivers strongly as a man who wants to limit his heisting to small banks because legal heat isn't so hot. Joe Don Baker scores solidly as Mafia man.

■ **CHARLIE BUBBLES**

1968, 89 MINS, UK ◇
Dir Albert Finney   *Prod* Michael Medwin   *Scr* Shelagh Delaney   *Ph* Peter Suschitzky   *Ed* Fergus McDonnell
Mus Misha Donat   *Art Dir* Edward Marshall

● Albert Finney, Colin Blakely, Billie Whitelaw, Liza Minnelli, Timothy Garland, Richard Pearson (Memorial)

Albert Finney stars as, and makes his directorial debut in, *Charlie Bubbles*. Comedy-drama concerns a materially successful man, fighting vainly the old ennui. Unfortunately, audiences also are bound to experience the same tedium, via underplaying and limp direction.

Finney's boredom is shown in biz relations, brief encounter with secretary Liza Minnelli, and disintegrating ties to his estranged wife (Billie Whitelaw) and alienated child (Timothy Garland).

This type screenplay which, essentially, is little more than exposition of a point made obvious in the first 10 minutes, requires direction which is dynamic both physically and artistically. Finney provides little of the required animation, thereby setting a plodding pace.

Among the cast, Whitelaw scores best. Minnelli gets a trifle cloying, but is okay. Colin Blakely, Finney's booze companion, has some bright moments, and Alan Lake as a pushy hitchhiker scores neatly.

■ **CHARLIE CHAN AT THE OPERA**

1936, 62 MINS, US ⑳ ⊙
Dir H. Bruce Humberstone *Prod* John Stone *Scr* Scott Darling, Charles S. Belden *Ph* Lucien Andriot *Ed* Alex Troffey *Mus* Samuel Kaylin (dir.)
● Warner Oland, Boris Karloff, Keye Luke, Charlotte Henry, Thomas Beck, Gregory Gaye (20th Century-Fox)

Chan's interminable saga gets a shot in the arm which effectively dispels any monotony. It is the creation of a co-feature role, with Boris Karloff to play it.

Being set in an opera house, the action [story by Bess Meredyth, based on the Earl Derr Biggers character] is more complicated than in previous Chan stories and serves as an additional befuddlement for the tyro sleuths in the audience. Backstage nooks and crannies furthermore provide the proper spook atmosphere for Karloff to flit around in. As a cross between a madman and an amnesia victim, Karloff plays a role right down his alley. And 20th doesn't let the audience forget who he is. In one place there's a remark to the effect 'Who do you think you are, Frankenstein?'

Supporting cast works well, with Margaret Irving as the diva who gets murdered, Nedda Harrigan as the menace, and William Demarest as a dumb cop, drawing the longest footage. [Film's opera, *Carnival*, was created by Oscar Levant, from a libretto by William Kernell.]

■ **CHARLIE CHAN AT TREASURE ISLAND**

1939, 72 MINS, US
Dir Norman Foster *Prod* Sol M. Wurtzel *Scr* John Larkin *Ph* Virgil Miller *Ed* Norman Colbert
● Sidney Toler, Cesar Romero, Pauline Moore, Sen Yung, Douglas Fowley (20th Century-Fox)

In this one, Charlie Chan bumps into a murder mystery involved with the psychic and astrological rackets, and proceeds to unravel the affair at a performance in a Treasure Island (San Francisco Fair) theatre.

Picture is rather slow in spots, but holds up generally to pace set by [some 25] previous Chan adventures to satisfy whodunit fans.

When fiction writer friend of Chan is suicide on Clipper plane bound for Frisco, Chan interests himself in uncovering the reasons. Trail leads him to Zodiac, a racketeering mystic, who holds clients in his power through threats of blackmail. Chan is assisted by Cesar Romero, operating illusionist theatre at the fair, and Douglas Fowley, reporter exposing rackets of the mystics and astrologists. Chan's No. 2 son, Sen Yung, does much to confuse things.

■ **CHARLIE CHAN CARRIES ON**

1931, 69 MINS, US
Dir Hamilton MacFadden *Scr* Philip Klein, Barry Connors *Ph* George Schneidermann *Ed* Al DeGaetano *Art Dir* Joe Wright
● Warner Oland, John Garrick, Marguerite Churchill, Warren Hymer, Marjorie White, George Brent (Fox)

This story of the Honolulu detective who solves a murder mystery that baffled Scotland Yard and Europe is well directed and aptly photographed. Cast shows smart selection.

What aids the film more than anything is that the mystery angle is kept paramount to the romance in it. This is between Marguerite Churchill and John Garrick, both personable. She is the granddaughter of the wealthy American found dead in a London hotel. Garrick is the companion of the old man. This romance is kept mild and gets its start only after the dead body is discovered by the police. While the romance ends before the mystery, both follow fast to a happy ending with a wisecrack.

The picture is full of wisecracks: the flippant pieces of philosophy spoken by Chan (Warner Oland) in almost doggerel English and the more funny lingo of Warren Hymer, as the Chicago racketeer.

■ **CHARLIE CHAN IN EGYPT**

1935, 72 MINS, US
Dir Louis King *Prod* Edward T. Lowe *Scr* Robert Ellis, Helen Logan *Ph* Daniel B. Clark
● Warner Oland, 'Pat' Paterson, Thomas Beck, Rita Hayworth, Stepin Fetchit, James Eagles (Fox)

Story framed around Earl Derr Biggers' Chinese crime snooper taking a flyer among the tombs of the Pharaohs and the outcome has all that it takes to satiate the general run of mystery addicts. *Charlie Chan in Egypt* combines a suavely sustained concept of drama and another surehand interpretation of the central role by Warner Oland.

Chan pops up just outside of Luxor shortly after a noted archaeologist has disappeared. From this mysterious incident stems the plot which, before reaching a denouement, accounts for two slayings and a near murder. Chan, whose mission it is to find out for a French museum why objects taken by the missing explorer have found their way into the open market instead of being shipped to France, uncovers the first murder with the aid of an X-ray machine. The body is located in a sarcophagus which is supposed to contain a mummy.

Obsessed with a dread of impending harm are the dead professor's daughter and son, 'Pat' Paterson and James Eagles.

Next to Oland's, the standout performance is that of Eagles, whose superstitious fears drive him to near insanity and are brought to an end by his sudden death by a mysterious source.

■ **CHARLIE CHAN IN LONDON**

1934, 79 MINS, US
Dir Eugene Forde *Prod* John Stone *Scr* Philip MacDonald *Ph* L. William O'Connell *Mus* Samuel Kaylin (dir.)
● Warner Oland, Drue Leyton, Douglas Walton, Alan Mowbray, Mona Barrie, Ray Milland (Fox)

As mystery stories go this is well above average. The most conspicuous item about *London* is that, although it is not by the creator of the Chan series, the tempo is so well imitated by scenarist Philip MacDonald it would pass for an original Earl Derr Biggers composition. For Warner Oland the Chan role now is second nature.

Most of the action takes place on luxurious interior sets of a wealthy country home in England. The story takes advantage of the

locale to inject a fox hunt, which adds color without being superfluous.

Just who committed the murder is not paid off in any detail until the last reel. While the cast is well chosen its members are so completely subjugated to Chan's importance that they impress collectively rather than as individual players.

■ **CHARLIE CHAN IN SHANGHAI**

1935, 70 MINS, US
Dir James Tinling *Prod* John Stone *Scr* Edward T. Lowe *Ph* Barney McGill
● Warner Oland, Irene Hervey, Jon Hall, Russell Hicks, Keye Luke, Halliwell Hobbes (Fox)

Charlie Chan is in Shanghai this time. Strange that the Chinese detective has never been set there before, but that oversight is patched up very nicely in this film. It's right in line with the eight previous Chan pictures.

Warner Oland, the merry Swede who has won himself an international rep as a Chinaman, still handles the Chan assignment with competence and ease. This time he's after a gang of dope smugglers in China. Keye Luke is cast as his son and gets in some nice laughs.

■ **CHARLIE CHAN ON BROADWAY**

1937, 68 MINS, US
Dir Eugene Forde *Prod* John Stone *Scr* Charles Belden, Jerry Cady *Ph* Harry Jackson *Ed* Al De Gaetano *Mus* Samuel Kaylin (dir.)
● Warner Oland, Keye Luke, Joan Marsh, J. Edward Bromberg, Douglas Fowley, Harold Huber (20th Century-Fox)

Entry in the Charlie Chan Chinese sleuth series provides an opportunity for the Oriental Sherlock to perform his deductions while a guest of the NY police force. Chan uncovers the killer of two people mixed up in the big city's mob.

Some of the plausible deductions lend more credulity than usual to this typical yarn. Art Arthur, Robert Ellis and Helen Logan combined forces on the original story.

Chan is again faithfully personated by Warner Oland, with just as much interest as ever being shown in his clever portrayal. Keye Luke again is the effervescent son, with the lad even better than before if only because he does more things in his usual enthusiastic style. Joan Marsh makes a pert, candid-camera freelancer among the dailies, though the slight love interest she shows for the columnist is blotted out at the close. Harold Huber's conception of a police inspector is crisp and characteristic if a little too brusque.

■ **CHARLIE CHAN'S CHANCE**

1932, 73 MINS, US
Dir John Blystone *Scr* Barry Connors, Philip Klein *Ph* Joseph August
● Warner Oland, Alexander Kirkland, H. B. Warner, Marian Nixon, Ralph Morgan, James Kirkwood (Fox)

Earl Derr Biggers' magazine and novel yarns on the subject provide the structure for this chapter, like the others. Biggers also provided the constant philosophical sayings which are delivered through the principal character as a means of sewing the action together and maintaining a regular pace. Chan (Warner Oland) rolls them off his proverbial knife – like 'Some heads, like hard nuts, much better if well cracked'.

In solving the new mystery, Chan has the help of Inspector Fife of Scotland Yard (H. B. Warner) and Inspector Flannery of New York (James Kirkwood). But as far as really helping they're just a couple of stooges.

Another British detective, who gets into the plot as a corpse, is murdered while working

135

on a case in New York. The path to solution is studded with countless false clues and the all-important erroneous arrest of the juve love-interest team (Marian Nixon and Alexander Kirkland). Tre people are killed on the way. One is Li Gung (Edward Piel Sr), the Chinese accessory to the criminal mastermind. James Todd's too youthful appearance in the heavy role accounts for the picture's chief note of implausibility.

．．．．．．．．．．．．．．．．．．．．．．．．．．．

■ CHARLOTTE'S WEB

1973, 93 MINS, US ◇ ⓥ ⊙

Dir Charles A. Nichols, Iwao Takamoto   *Prod* Joseph Barbera, William Hanna   *Scr* Earl Hamner Jr   *Ph* Roy Wade, Dick Brundell, Ralph Miglioro, Dennis Weaver, George Epperson   *Ed* Larry Cowan, Pat Foley   *Mus* Irwin Kostal (sup.)   *Art Dir* Bob Singer, Ray Aragon, Paul Julian

(Hanna-Barbera/Sagittarius)

Charlotte's Web is a saga of a little white porker named Wilbur – petrified with fear he's fated to become a slab of tender bacon – and Charlotte, the benevolent spider, who saves him from this fate through the magic weaving in her web. Based on the E.B. White children's classic, the Hanna-Barbera animated musical [with music by Richard M. and Robert B. Sherman] is heartwarming entertainment.

Described by the author as a tale of 'friendship and salvation, a story of miracles – the miracle of birth, the miracle of friendship, the miracle of death', the premise is adroitly and charmingly caught. Debbie Reynolds is heard as the voice of Charlotte, Henry Gibson as Wilbur, Paul Lynde as Templeton, the gluttenous, grouchy rat, and Agnes Moorehead is a stuttering and diligent goose. Rex Allen acts as narrator.

Animation is imaginative and clever and interest is sustained as tale builds to its climax.

．．．．．．．．．．．．．．．．．．．．．．．．．．．

■ CHARLY

1968, 103 MINS, US ◇ ⓥ ⊙

Dir Ralph Nelson   *Prod* Ralph Nelson   *Scr* Stirling Silliphant   *Ph* Arthur Ornitz   *Ed* Fredric Steinkamp   *Mus* Ravi Shankar   *Art Dir* Chas Rosen
● Cliff Robertson, Claire Bloom, Leon Janney, Lilia Skala, Dick Van Patton, Ed McNally (Selmur)

Charly boasts a most intriguing premise – a variation on the Pygmalion theme in which a mentally retarded adult 'grows up' as the result of a brain operation.

Recognizing that this idea [from the short story and novel *Flowers for Algernon* by Daniel Keyes] could be developed along several different lines, producer-director Ralph Nelson and screenwriter Stirling Silliphant try them all, with the result that *Charly* merges a peculiar combination of sentimental documentary, romance, science fiction and social drama.

Instead of frittering away time on an unmotivated romance, it would have been interesting if the reasons for this psychologically complicated affair were explored.

Considering the innumerable stumbling blocks, cast does well. Cliff Robertson seems to overdo the external manifestations of retardation, but he is excellent in the post-operative scenes. With more help from the script he could have been a movingly tragic figure.
☐ 1968: Best Actor (Cliff Robertson)

．．．．．．．．．．．．．．．．．．．．．．．．．．．

■ CHASE, THE

1946, 86 MINS, US ⓥ

Dir Arthur Ripley   *Prod* Seymour Nebenzal   *Scr* Philip Yordan   *Ph* Franz Planer   *Ed* Edward Mann   *Mus* Michel Michelet   *Art Dir* Robert Usher
● Robert Cummings, Michele Morgan, Peter Lorre, Steve Cochran (United Artists)

The Chase is a meller that's taut as sprung steel for 75 minutes of its running time then slackens limply into the commonplace. Yarn [from the novel *The Black Path of Fear* by Cornell Woolrich] concerns the attempt of a killer's wife and his chauffeur to make their getaway from his household and henchman.

Through a series of adroit directorial strokes, in the Hitchcock tradition, the pic's momentum is made to mount in a steady, ascending line. Terror stalks the pair in their flight to Havana then explodes with the shocking stillness of a gun with a silencer on it.

Robert Cummings handles himself nicely but, though he tops the cast, is over-shadowed by the dominating personality and looks of a newcomer, Steve Cochran who plays the killer. Cochran is handsome, suave, confident, and menacing in the manner of a Humphrey Bogart. Peter Lorre, in one of his best roles, comes through with a solid assist as the killer's aide-de-camp. Michele Morgan registers nicely, although she isn't given much to do besides modelling a few flashy gowns.

．．．．．．．．．．．．．．．．．．．．．．．．．．．

■ CHASE, THE

1966, 138 MINS, US ◇ ⓥ ⊙

Dir Arthur Penn   *Prod* Sam Spiegel   *Scr* Lillian Hellman   *Ph* Joseph LaShelle   *Ed* Gene Milford   *Mus* John Barry   *Art Dir* Richard Day
● Marlon Brando, Jane Fonda, Robert Redford, James Fox, E.G. Marshall, Angie Dickinson (Horizon/Columbia)

Only the framework of Horton Foote's novel (but little of his play, which preceded it) has been utilized by Lillian Hellman in her screenplay. The original plot centered on an escaped convict seeking revenge on the sheriff who had sent him up but Hellman makes them only two of the many characters with which she has populated her sociologically sick Texas town.

Through introduction of various other types she manages to provide most of the social grievances which trouble the world today.

Robert Redford, as the escaped convict whose impending return to his hometown gives many of its citizens the jitters, gives the film's best performance. Marlon Brando, in the comparatively small but important role of the sheriff, has obviously given much time and study to the part, but such detailed preparation as a carefully-delivered Texas accent means little when other cast members read their lines with a mixture regional accents.

Jane Fonda, as Redford's wife and the mistress of wealthy oilman James Fox, makes the most of the biggest female role.

．．．．．．．．．．．．．．．．．．．．．．．．．．．

■ CHASE A CROOKED SHADOW

1958, 92 MINS, UK

Dir Michael Anderson   *Prod* Douglas Fairbanks Jr.   *Scr* David D. Osborn, Charles Sinclair   *Ph* Erwin Hillier   *Ed* Gordon Pilkington   *Mus* Matyas Seiber   *Art Dir* Paul Sheriff
● Richard Todd, Anne Baxter, Herbert Lom, Alexander Knox, Faith Brook (Associated Dragon/Associated British)

Chase a Crooked Shadow is a glossy, well-directed drama which has its fair quota of absurdities which occasionally strain credulity to the limit. Nevertheless, there are enough twists and artfully planned kicks to keep most audiences guessing.

The yarn concerns Anne Baxter as an heiress who becomes a frightened lady when Richard Todd arrives at her Costa Brava hangout and claims to be her brother, who Baxter knows was killed in a car crash in South Africa a year before. What is the purpose of his visit? Is he a crook? A fortune hunter? Todd builds up so much evidence that even the local chief cop (Herbert Lom) is convinced that his story is true. There begins a nightmare of terror as she believes the plot

is to drive her insane and then murder her. Final twist is a sock climax.

Director Michael Anderson carefully builds up the suspense and at one time or other even the most case hardened patron will be wondering about motives and who is really double crossing who. There are also the advantages of the breathtaking Costa Brava scenery and a rousing racing car sequence. Anderson, an ex-cutter, has edited the film with Gordon Pilkington very ingeniously.

．．．．．．．．．．．．．．．．．．．．．．．．．．．

■ CHATO'S LAND

1972, 100 MINS, UK ◇ ⓥ

Dir Michael Winner   *Prod* Michael Winner   *Scr* Gerald Wilson   *Ph* Robert Paynter   *Ed* Freddie Wilson   *Mus* Jerry Fielding   *Art Dir* Manolo Mampaso
● Charles Bronson, Jack Palance, Richard Basehart, James Whitmore, Simon Oakland, Ralph Waite (Scimitar)

British producer-director Michael Winner in his second western takes a hard look at the early American West and comes up with a violence-drenched meller.

Writer Gerald Wilson, adopting and-then-there-were-none theme, plots an Apache half-breed relentlessly pursued by a ragtag white posse headed by an ex-Confederate officer after the Indian has killed a white sheriff. Charles Bronson portrays the Apache – Chato – and Jack Palance the posse leader.

Action too often slows during an overage of dialog between posse members and an apparent attempt to build characterization defeats its purpose as bickering among posse detracts from the real objective of story. Narrative is fleshed out when the Indian reverts to a savage vengeful warrior after a few members of posse rape his squaw and the roles of hunter and hunted are reversed.

．．．．．．．．．．．．．．．．．．．．．．．．．．．

■ CHATTAHOOCHEE

1989, 103 MINS, US ◇ ⓥ ⊙

Dir Mick Jackson   *Prod* Faye Schwab   *Scr* James Hicks   *Ph* Andrew Dunn   *Ed* Don Fairservice   *Mus* John Keane   *Art Dir* Patrick Tagliaferro
● Gary Oldman, Dennis Hopper, Frances McDormand, Pamela Reed, Ned Beatty, M. Emmet Walsh (Hemdale)

Gary Oldman's bravura performance as a victimized patient in a Deep South prison hospital for the criminally insane, circa 1950s, fails to cure the film of its manifold structural and stylistic ills. The tale allegedly is based on a true story of Chris Calhoun, who could not handle the 'expectations' of others when he returned from the Korean War to the Deep South as a 'certified hero'.

In an opening setup that's frenetically bizarre, Oldman goes berserk one morning, shooting up his small tropical town with a handgun. He is promptly packed off to Chattahoochee, a maximum security hospital for the criminally insane.

The 'hospital' is sort of a cross between the Turkish prison barracks of *Midnight Express*, the hard-time join in *Brubaker* and the good ole' prison farm of *Cool Hand Luke*. Similarities to those three excellent movies end there.

Thoughtless medical bureaucrat Ned Beatty turns aside all complaints of maltreatment. Oldman's bunkmates are maniac blithering idiots and worldly wise weirdos like Dennis Hopper and M. Emmet Walsh.

Oldman becomes a jailhouse lawyer, discovers the rule of habeas corpus, and with the help of his steadfast sister (Pamela Reed), eventually gets the governor to investigate.

．．．．．．．．．．．．．．．．．．．．．．．．．．．

■ CHE

1969, 96 MINS, US ◇ ⓥ

Dir Richard Fleischer   *Prod* Sy Bartlett   *Scr* Michael Wilson, Sy Bartlett   *Ph* Charles Wheeler   *Ed* Marion

C

Rothman   *Mus* Lalo Schifrin   *Art Dir* Jack Martin Smith, Arthur Lonergan
● Omar Sharif, Jack Palance, Cesare Danova, Robert Loggia, Woody Strode, Barbara Luna (20th Century-Fox)

Producer Sy Bartlett and director Richard Fleischer claimed to have made an 'impartial, objective' film about Fidel Castro's Cuban Revolution and of subsequent events in that country. But it's emphatically not true about their viewpoint of Ernesto Che Guevara himself: to them, he was an evil genius who tried to lead Castro down wrong paths, a man whose revolutionary zeal took violent turns which ignored social reality.

As presented, Castro, played smokehouse by Jack Palance, is innocent not only of winning the initial revolution, but also of the deeds afterwards which condemn him in many American eyes. It was Guevara, adequately portrayed by Omar Sharif, who planned the military strategy which resulted in the fall of Havana, who maintained discipline within the rebel forces and who conducted executions after Castro took over.

Pic has been made in a mock-documentary style which comes out poorly. Supposedly, 'real' people are being interviewed who are telling Che's story in flashback.

．．．．．．．．．．．．．．．．．．．．．．．．．．．

■ CHEAP DETECTIVE, THE

1978, 92 MINS, US ◇ ⊙
Dir Robert Moore   *Prod* Ray Stark   *Scr* Neil Simon
Ph John A. Alonzo   *Ed* Sidney Levin, Michael A. Stevenson   *Mus* Patrick Williams   *Art Dir* Robert Luthardt
● Peter Falk, Ann-Margret, Eileen Brennan, Sid Caesar, Stockard Channing, James Coco (Columbia)

The Cheap Detective, which might also be called *Son of Casablanca*, is a hilarious and loving takeoff on all 1940s Warner Bros private eye and foreign intrigue mellers.

The time is 1940, San Francisco, where clumsy gumshoe Peter Falk is accused of murdering his partner, whose wife Marsha Mason (in early Janet Leigh curls) has been Falk's mistress. Detective Vic Tayback and assistants regularly blunder into matters.

Madeline Kahn, with as many smart clothes changes as aliases, appears in Falk's office. She's in league with John Houseman (Sydney Greenstreet to the core), Paul Williams (Elisha Cook Jr was never like this) and Dom DeLuise (a fat Peter Lorre) in search of ancient treasure – a dozen diamond eggs.

Amidst the confusing threads of mystery, Falk is regularly affronted by the overly explicit descriptions of sexual torture inflicted on all the dames. But at fadeout he's got a lot more going for him than Bogart did in the final dissolve.

．．．．．．．．．．．．．．．．．．．．．．．．．．．

■ CHECKING OUT

1989, 93 MINS, US ◇ ⊛ ⊙
Dir David Leland   *Prod* Ben Myron   *Scr* Joe Eszterhas
Ph Ian Wilson   *Ed* Lee Percy   *Mus* Carter Burwell
Art Dir Barbara Ling
● Jeff Daniels, Melanie Mayron, Michael Tucker, Kathleen York, Allan Havey (HandMade/Warner)

A dreadfully unfunny one-joke black comedy about hypochondria and mortality, *Checking Out* depends almost entirely for suspense of Jeff Daniels' 'Why don't Italians have barbecues?' Sadly, some 90 minutes elapse before he finds out.

In the interim Daniels, as budget airline executive Ray Macklin, witnesses the death by coronary of his irreverent best buddy Allan Havey. This trauma triggers the onset of a hysterical, fetishistic hypochondria that propels him through a series of discombobulating misadventures.

Daniels lives in a tacky California suburb with wife Melanie Mayron and two kids. The blue-sky normalcy of his middle-class life-

style is clearly intended to set up a big soft target for satirical demolition. Potshots also are misfired at American big business funeral homes, medicine and sexual hypocrisy.

Seeds of a more interesting film are scattered here and there, especially in a dazzlingly photographed dream sequence that imagines heaven as a cloyingly hellish redneck cabana club in a desert oasis.

．．．．．．．．．．．．．．．．．．．．．．．．．．．

■ CHELSEA GIRLS, THE

1967, 210 MINS, US ◇
Dir Andy Warhol   *Prod* Andy Warhol
● Robert Olivio, Ondine, Mary Might, Nico, Ingrid Superstar, Mario Montez (Warhol)

The Chelsea Girls, perhaps the first Underground film to be accorded specifically non-Underground screenings, is a pointless, excruciatingly dull three-and-a-half hours spent in the company of Andy Warhol's friends. Warhol has attempted to counter all conventional methods of filmmaking, and the result is an anti-film or, more accurately, a non-film.

There is no plot-line. The single unifying device is that the film takes place in several rooms of a downtown hotel. Typical scenes include a blank-looking blonde trimming and combing her hair, a lesbian bullying her roommates, another lesbian talking endlessly on the phone, a homosexual eating an orange, a middle-aged homosexual and a girl competing for the attentions of a half-nude male, a girl on LSD confessing to a homosexual priest.

．．．．．．．．．．．．．．．．．．．．．．．．．．．

■ CHERRY, HARRY & RAQUEL!

1969, 71 MINS, US ◇
Dir Russ Meyer   *Prod* Russ Meyer   *Scr* Tom Wolfe, Russ Meyer   *Ph* Russ Meyer   *Ed* Russ Meyer, Richard Serly Brummer   *Mus* William Loose   *Art Dir* [uncredited]
● Larissa Ely, Linda Ashton, Charles Napier, Bert Santos, Franklin H. Bolger, Astrid Lillimor (Eve/Panamint)

Film focuses on the narcotics traffic on the Mexican border, where Charles Napier is a sheriff in the pay of the drug operator.

Linda Ashton plays Cherry, his girlfriend, and Larissa Ely portrays Raquel, who takes on all comers. When the two ladies of the title get tired of it all with men, they try some Lesbian clinches. Flashes of nudes intersperse the unreeling every minute or so. Mebbe they're symbolic, they have no connection with the story.

Meyer inserts plenty of violence in Harry's search for a Yaqui Indian who is leaving the gang for private enterprise. The Yaqui shoots it out with the sheriff in a bloody sequence, and kills a Mexican member of the gang in another bloody encounter after an exciting and suspenseful auto chase. Dialog is on the stag side. Cost was $90,000, up from Meyer's previous $70,000 budgets.

．．．．．．．．．．．．．．．．．．．．．．．．．．．

■ CHERRY 2000

1988, 93 MINS, US ◇ ⊛ ⊙
Dir Steve de Jarnatt   *Prod* Edward R. Pressman, Caldecot Chubb   *Scr* Michael Almereyda   *Ph* Jacques Haitkin
Ed Edward Abroms, Duwayne Dunham   *Mus* Basil Poledouris   *Art Dir* John J. Moore
● Melanie Griffith, David Andrews, Ben Johnson, Tim Thomerson, Harry Carey Jr, Pamela Gidley (ERP/Orion)

A tongue-in-cheek sci-fi action pic which owes a considerable debt to the *Mad Max* movies, *Cherry 2000*'s greatest asset is topbilled Melanie Griffith, who lifts the material whenever she's on screen.

Griffith plays E. Johnson, a tracker who lives at the edge of a desert known as The Zone. The year is 2017, and white-collar yuppie Sam Treatwell (David Andrews) seeks Johnson's help in replacing his beloved

Cherry 2000 (Pamela Gidley), a robot sex-object who suffered internal meltdown when Treadwell unwisely tried to make love to her in soapsuds.

For obscure reasons, replacement Cherry clones are stored far out in the Zone, which is ruled over by the psychotic Lester (Tim Thomerson) and his gang. Bulk of the film [story by executive producer Lloyd Fonvielle] consists of efforts of Johnson and Treadwell to avoid capture by Lester and reach the robot warehouse.

Along the way they meet Ben Johnson as a philosophical old-timer and Harry Carey Jr as a treacherous gas-station owner.

Technically, pic is quite lavish and the Nevada locations suitably rugged.

．．．．．．．．．．．．．．．．．．．．．．．．．．．

■ CHEYENNE AUTUMN

1964, 161 MINS, US ◇ ⊛
Dir John Ford   *Prod* Bernard Smith   *Scr* James R. Webb
Ph William Clothier   *Ed* Otho Lovering   *Mus* Alex North
Art Dir Richard Day
● Richard Widmark, Carroll Baker, James Stewart, Edward G. Robinson, Karl Malden, Sal Mineo (Warner)

Cheyenne Autumn is a rambling, episodic account of a reputedly little-known historic Cheyenne Indian migration 1,500 miles through almost unbelievable hardships and dangers to the tribe's home near the Yellowstone in Wyoming. Somewhere in the telling, the original premise of the Mari Sandoz novel is lost sight of in a wholesale insertion of extraneous incidents which bear little or no relation to the subject.

Action follows a small band of Cheyennes attempting to escape from their barren Oklahoma reservation to their own lush Wyoming lands, from which they were transported after having surrendered to the army in 1877. Originally more than 900, their number now has been decimated to 286 through starvation and lack of medical attention.

Richard Widmark in one of his hardboiled roles is persuasive as a cavalry captain sympathetic to the Indians, detailed to bring them back to the reservation and finally going to Washington to see the Secretary of the Interior in charge of Indian affairs. Gilbert Roland and Ricardo Montalban portray the historic Dull Knife and Little Wolf, leaders of the Cheyennes, and carry off their work with honors. Carroll Baker is somewhat lost as a Quaker schoolteacher who accompanied the Cheyennes because of her love for the children.

James Stewart as Wyatt Earp is in strictly for laughs, not for plot motivation, and Arthur Kennedy also is in briefly as Doc Holliday, neither having much to do. Karl Malden scores as a German captain of US cavalry; Dolores Del Rio plays an Indian woman with conviction; Edward G. Robinson does well by the Interior Secretary part and Patrick Wayne plays brash young lieutenant with feeling.
□ 1964: Nomination: Best Color Cinematography

．．．．．．．．．．．．．．．．．．．．．．．．．．．

■ CHEYENNE SOCIAL CLUB, THE

1970, 103 MINS, US ◇ ⊛
Dir Gene Kelly   *Prod* Gene Kelly   *Scr* James Lee Barrett
Ph William Clothier   *Ed* Adrienne Fazan   *Mus* Walter Scharf   *Art Dir* Gene Allen
● James Stewart, Henry Fonda, Shirley Jones, Sue Ane Langdon, Elaine Devry, Jackie Russell (National General)

James Stewart and Henry Fonda are longtime cowpoke buddies, and when the former finds he has inherited from his brother a business in Cheyenne, the latter follows. Turns out the business is the town's pleasure dome, inhabited by Sue Ane Langdon, Elaine Devry, Jackie Russell, Jackie Joseph and Sharon De Bord, under Shirley Jones' supervision. Each girl has her own doorbell signal, so Stewart never can talk to them for long without callers interrupting.

When Stewart learns the truth and plans to shutter the place, the whole male population turns against him, but Fonda works his way through the house, room by room.

The story is a flimsy, one-joke affair, and Gene Kelly's direction is too sluggish to make it perk at the fast pace required to sustain momentum.

■ CHICAGO, CHICAGO
See: Gaily, Gaily

■ CHICAGO JOE AND THE SHOWGIRL

1990, 103 MINS, UK ◇ ⑫ ⊙
Dir Bernard Rose   *Prod* Tim Bevan   *Scr* David Yallop
Ph Mike Southon   *Ed* Dan Rae   *Mus* Hans Zimmer, Shirley Walker   *Art Dir* Gemma Jackson
● Emily Lloyd, Kiefer Sutherland, Patsy Kensit, Keith Allen, Liz Fraser, Alexandra Pigg (PolyGram/Working Title)

Scripter David Yallop was inspired and intrigued by the sensational Hulten/Jones murder case of 1944, which became known as the 'Cleft Chin Murder Case' after the disappearance of a London taxi driver. It made household names of American serviceman Karl Hulten and British showgirl Elizabeth Maud Jones, beating war news to the headlines. Shame is Yallop was unable to ignite anything sensational in the finished product.

The trial, which resulted in the hanging of Hulten (the only execution a Yank by the British) and the reprieve of Jones, is passed up. Yallop instead focuses on duo's six-day London crime spree, beginning with theft of an army truck and a fur, and finishing with murder of the cabbie.

Problem is that Emily Lloyd totally fails to deliver the necessary allurement, and Kiefer Sutherland is weak in playing a weak character. End result is a pair of languid leads fumbling their way through a passionless picture.

Whole pic was shot on sets rather than locatio and despite Gemma Jackson's thoughtful designs, the overall look is cheap.

■ CHILD IS WAITING, A

1963, 104 MINS, US ⑫
Dir John Cassavetes   *Prod* Stanley Kramer   *Scr* Abby Mann   *Ph* Joseph LaShelle   *Ed* Gene Fowler
Mus Ernest Gold
● Burt Lancaster, Judy Garland, Gena Rowlands, Steven Hill, Bruce Ritchey (United Artists)

As in *Judgment at Nuremberg*, producer Stanley Kramer dips into productive source of live television drama and comes up with a poignant, provocative, revealing dramatization. Again it is writer Abby Mann whose original work spawns the effort. This time it is the subject of mentally retarded children.

The film focuses on one profoundly touching case, around which are woven heartrending and often shocking illustrations of behavior and activity in institutions for the mentally retarded as well as academic discussions of the role in society to be played by the afflicted, and society's responsibility to them. There is no hokiness in the dramatization.

Burt Lancaster delivers a firm, sincere, persuasive and unaffected performan as the professionally objective but understanding psychologist who heads the institution. Judy Garland gives a sympathetic portrayal of an overly involved teacher who comes to see the error of her obsession with the plight of one child.

That child, a deeply touching 'borderline case', is played superbly by young Bruce Ritchey, a professional actor who manages to fit believably into a youthful cast that con-

sists, for the most part, of actual retarded children who are patients of Pacific State Hospital in Pomona. As the lad's two troubled parents, Gena Rowlands (director John Cassavetes' wife) and Steven Hill pitch in with two exceptionally vivid and convincing performances.

■ CHILDREN, THE

1990, 115 MINS, UK/W. GERMANY ◇ ⑫
Dir Tony Palmer   *Prod* Andrew Montgomery, Paul Templeton   *Scr* Timberlake Wertenbaker   *Ph* Nic Knowland   *Ed* Tony Palmer   *Art Dir* Chris Bradley
● Ben Kingsley, Kim Novak, Siri Neal, Geraldine Chaplin, Joe Don Baker, Karen Black (Isolde/Arbo/Film Four)

Previously filmed in 1929 by Paramount as *The Marriage Playground*, Edith Wharton's 1928 novel *The Children* comes to the screen as a somewhat dated enterprise. Story of a middle-aged man's infatuation for a teenage girl unfolds at a snail's pace.

Ben Kingsley is Martin Boyne, a middle-aged engineer returning to Europe after years in Brazil. He hopes to marry Rose Sellars (Kim Novak, looking ageless), his lifelong love recently widowed and living in an Alpine village. On th voyage home, he meets a group of seven children, the oldest of which is the budding Judith (Siri Neal).

Martin lingers on in Venice with the children, who seem to fascinate him, but eventually heads for the hills and Rose. The children soon follow. The rest of the film depicts Martin's indecision and his gradual emotional shift away from the demanding Rose to the guileless, appealing Judith, who appears to encourage him.

Kingsley gives one of his most affecting performances as th confused protagonist, and young Siri Neal is a find as the child-woman.

■ CHILDREN OF A LESSER GOD

1986, 110 MINS, US ◇ ⑫ ⊙
Dir Randa Haines   *Prod* Burt Sugarman, Patrick Palmer   *Scr* Hesper Anderson, Mark Medoff   *Ph* John Seale   *Ed* Lisa Fruchtman   *Mus* Michael Convertino
Art Dir Gene Callahan
● William Hurt, Marlee Matlin, Piper Laurie, Philip Bosco, Alison Gompf, John F. Cleary (Paramount)

Children of a Lesser God is the kind of good intentioned material that often gets weighed down with sentimentality on the screen. Fortunately, the translation of Mark Medoff's Tony Award-winning [1980] play avoids many of those traps by focusing on a touching and universal love story between a deaf woman and a hearing man.

At the heart of the picture is the attraction between William Hurt and Marlee Matlin. Their need and feeling for each other is so palpable that it is almost impossible not to share the experience and recognize it in one's own life.

It's another seamless performance for Hurt. Matlin, who makes her professional acting debut here and is in real life hearing impaired, as is much of the cast, is simply fresh and alive with fine shadings of expression.
□ 1986: Best Actress (Marlee Matlin).
□ Nominations: Best Picture, Actor (William Hurt), Supp. Actress (Piper Laurie), Adapted Screenplay

■ CHILDREN OF THE CORN

1984, 93 MINS, US ◇ ⑫ ⊙
Dir Fritz Kiersch   *Prod* Donald P. Porchers, Terrence Kirby   *Scr* George Goldsmith   *Ph* Raoul Lomas
Ed Harry Keramidas   *Mus* Jonathan Elias   *Art Dir* Craig Stearns
● Peter Horton, Linda Hamilton, R.G. Armstrong, John Franklin, Courtney Gains, Robby Kiger (Gatlin/Angeles)

Children of the Corn presents a normal couple, played by Peter Horton and Linda Hamilton, thrust into supernatural occurrences while on a cross-country trip. Horton is a newly graduated doctor on his way to start his internship in Seattle. Somewhere in Nebraska the couple happen on the children of the corn, a band of vicious youngsters who have murdered the adults and established a religious community worshipping a mysterious deity of the corn fields.

Led by Isaac (John Franklin) an adolescent with an old man's demeanor, the band of outsiders displays a sinister attraction. Shrouded in pseudo-Christian mythology, the children are more appealing than the mundane reality of the adults.

Director Fritz Kiersch and/or author Stephen King seem to play both ends against the middle, neither accepting nor denying the supernatural occurrences.

Children of the Corn does have a few good scare scenes but special effects are surprisingly disappointing.

■ CHILDREN OF THE CORN II
THE FINAL SACRIFICE

1993, 92 MINS, US ◇ ⑫ ⊙
Dir David F. Price   *Prod* Scott A. Stone, David G. Stanley   *Scr* A.L. Katz, Gilbert Adler   *Ph* Levie Isaacks   *Ed* Barry Zetlin   *Mus* Daniel Licht   *Art Dir* Greg Melton
● Terence Knox, Paul Scherrer, Ryan Bollman, Christie Clark, Rosalind Allen, Ned Romero (Fifth Avenue)

Coming nine years after the original, this supernatural horror sequel is a competently made but uninspired effort. Gore fans should dig it.

Surviving kids are sent to live in a nearby town, including brooding Micah (Ryan Bollman), who's taken in by lovely innkeeper Rosalind Allen. A journalist (Terence Knox) is driving by when he sniffs out an exploitable story. He's traveling with uppity son Paul Scherrer, who has little affection for his old man.

Adults are again murdered in grisly fashion, some by supernatural forces (a few represented by nice visual effects reminiscent of *Wolfen*), some by the deranged kids led by Micah.

Lensing on North Carolina locations (subbing for Nebraska) is well done, with director David Price (son of industry vet Frank Price) keeping the picture chugging along even when the script becomes risible.

■ CHILDREN OF THE DAMNED

1964, 90 MINS, UK
Dir Anton M. Leader   *Prod* Lawrence P. Bachmann
Scr Jack Briley   *Ph* Davis Boulton   *Ed* Ernest Walter
Mus Ron Goodwin   *Art Dir* Elliot Scott
● Ian Hendry, Alan Badel, Barbara Ferris, Alfred Burke, Sheila Allen, Clive Powell (M-G-M)

Like most sequels *Children of the Damned* isn't nearly as good as its predecessor – Metro's 1960 *Village of the Damned*. What weakens this sequel is the fact that, unlike the original, it is burdened with a 'message'.

Jack Briley's screenplay broadens the scope to an international scale of what was originally a taut little sci-fi shocker. This time those strange, handsome parthenogenetic children with the genius IQs, destructive dispositions and raygun eyes are not mere invaders from the outer limits bent on occupying earth, but are actually premature samplings of man as he will be in, say, a million years. And they have arrived for a curious purpose – to be destroyed, presumably to enable the silly, warlike contemporary man to learn some sort of lesson.

There are one or two genuinely funny lines in Briley's scenario and they are inherited by the character of a geneticist played engagingly by Alan Badel. A few of Badel's scenes with Ian Hendry, who plays an idealistic psychologist, are the best in the picture. Otherwise it's tedious going, and Anton Leader's lethargic direction doesn't help any.

....

CHILDREN'S HOUR, THE
(UK: The Loudest Whisper)

1961, 109 MINS, US Ⓥ
Dir William Wyler *Prod* William Wyler *Scr* John Michael Hayes *Ph* Franz Planer *Ed* Robert Swink *Mus* Alex North *Art Dir* Fernando Carrere
● Audrey Hepburn, Shirley MacLaine, James Garner, Miriam Hopkins, Fay Bainter, Karen Balkin (Mirisch)

Lillian Hellman's study of the devastating effect of malicious slander and implied guilt comes to the screen for the second time in this crackling production of *The Children's Hour*. William Wyler, who directed the 1936 production (*These Three*), which veered away from the touchier, more sensational aspects of Hellman's Broadway play, this time has chosen to remain faithful to the original source.

Story deals with an irresponsible, neurotic child who spreads a slanderous rumor of a lesbian relationship between the two headmistresses of the private school for girls she attends.

Audrey Hepburn and Shirley MacLaine, in the leading roles, beautifully complement each other. Hepburn's soft sensitivity, marvelous projecting and emotional understatement result in a memorable portrayal. MacLaine's enactment is almost equally rich in depth and substance. James Garner is effective as Hepburn's betrothed, and Fay Bainter comes through with an outstanding portrayal of the impressionable grandmother who falls under the evil influence of the wicked child.
□ 1961: Nominations: Best Supp. Actress, (Fay Bainter), B&W Cinematography, B&W Costume Design, B&W Art Direction

....

CHILD'S PLAY

1972, 100 MINS, US ◇
Dir Sidney Lumet *Prod* David Merrick *Scr* Leon Prochnik *Ph* Gerald Hirschfeld *Ed* Edward Warschilka, Joanne Burke *Mus* Michael Small *Art Dir* Philip Rosenberg
● James Mason, Robert Preston, Beau Bridges, Ronald Weyand, Charles White, David Rounds (Paramount)

Child's Play, a taut and suspenseful drama of a Catholic boys' school, which won critical acclaim on Broadway, repeats in interest as a film production. Unfoldment often carries the aspects of a chiller as mysterious malevolent forces create a reign of terror and build to a powerful climax.

David Merrick gives the same meticulous care to script, written by Leon Prochnik in adapting the Robert Marasco original, and what emerges is compelling.

Situation revolves around deliberate violence as practised by some of the students on others, senseless incidents which cause fear and suspicion.

James Mason delivers a solid performance as a man whose hate of his fellow professor is exceeded, he says, only by Robert Preston's hate of him. Role is deeply dramatic, and Preston, in a different type of characterization, lends equal potency.

....

CHILD'S PLAY

1988, 87 MINS, US ◇ Ⓥ ⊙
Dir Tom Holland *Prod* David Kirschner *Scr* Don Mancini, John Lafia, Tom Holland *Ph* Bill Butler *Ed* Edward Warschilka, Roy E. Peterson *Mus* Joe Renzetti *Art Dir* Daniel A. Lomino

● Catherine Hicks, Chris Sarandon, Alex Vincent, Brad Dourif, Dinah Manoff, Tommy Swerdlow (United Artists)

Child's Play is a near-miss at providing horrific thrills in a tale [by Don Mancini] of a doll come to murderous life, told with a knowing tongue-in-cheek attitude. Fun withers in stretching the thin material to feature length.

Director Tom Holland summons impressive technical skill in charting the preposterous story of a nutcase (Brad Dourif) who climaxes a fatal shootout in a Chicago toystore with cop Chris Sarandon by chanting a voodoo incantation and passing his spirit into a cute red-headed doll.

Next plot device also is hard to swallow as nice mom Catherine Hicks makes a last-minute buy of the doll from a grubby street peddler for her cute son Alex Vincent. The possessed doll, named Chucky, kills Alex' babysitter Dinah Manoff and who else but Sarandon is the detective on the case. Violence and paranoia escalate.

Both Hicks and Sarandon commendably keep straight faces during these outlandish proceedings. Top technical contributions milk the doll gimmick for all it's worth.

....

CHILD'S PLAY 2

1990, 85 MINS, US ◇ Ⓥ ⊙
Dir John Lafia *Prod* David Kirschner *Scr* Don Mancini *Ph* Stefan Czapsky *Ed* Edward Warschilka *Mus* Graeme Revell *Art Dir* Ivo Cristante
● Alex Vincent, Jenny Agutter, Gerrit Graham, Christine Elize, Brad Dourif, Grace Zabriskie (Universal)

Child's Play 2 is another case of rehashing the few novel elements of an original to the point of utter numbness. The novelty of a smiling doll spouting expletives and crinkling his nose has long since worn off, so the filmmakers simply hammer away at walk-down-the-hallway cliches in an effort to provide the cheapest thrills.

Here, little Andy (Alex Vincent) has separated from his mother, temporarily institutionalized after the original ordeal. He is placed with two drab parents (Jen Agutter, Gerrit Graham) and a rebellious teen (Christine Elize), ultimately the only person to believe him.

With Chucky (again voiced by Brad Dourif) doing mischief, poor little Andy is blamed for every bad thing that occurs. It's less amusing note that Andy, this time, is practically the sole focus of Chucky's homicidal rage.

The puppet techniques are finely executed, but it's difficult after a while to take this three-foot-high version of the Terminator seriously. The adults are essentially pincushions, with about as much personality.

....

CHILD'S PLAY 3

1991, 89 MINS, US ◇ Ⓥ ⊙
Dir Jack Bender *Prod* Robert Latham Brown *Scr* Don Mancini *Ph* John R. Leonetti *Ed* Edward Warschilka, Edward A. Warschilka Jr, Scott Wallace *Mus* Cory Lerios, John D'Andrea *Art Dir* Richard Sawyer
● Justin Whalin, Perrey Reeves, Jeremy Sylvers, Travis Fine, Dean Jacobson, Brad Dourif (Universal)

Foul-mouthed killer doll Chucky returns in this noisy, mindless sequel. Young protagonist Andy is now a 16-year-old personified by handsome Justin Whalin. First reel prolog is devoted to venal businessman Peter Haskell starting up production on the Good Guy dolls eight years after the factory catastrophe limned in *Child's Play 2*.

First doll off the assembly line is Chucky, possessed by the spirit of dead murderer Brad Dourif (who again ably voices the creature's wisecracks). Chucky tracks Whalin to a military school, has himself mailed there and then becomes obsessed with transferring his spirit to a pint-sized black cadet (Jeremy Sylvers).

Fine doll effects and sporadic gore are par for the genre. Acting is good, with honors going to the original *Dirty Harry* nemesis, Andrew Robinson, amusing as the school's obsessive barber.

....

CHIMES AT MIDNIGHT

1966, 113 MINS, SPAIN/SWITZERLAND ◇ Ⓥ
Dir Orson Welles *Prod* Emiliano Piedra, Angel Escolano *Scr* Orson Welles *Ph* Edmond Richard *Ed* Fritz Mueller *Mus* Angelo Francesco Lavagnino *Art Dir* Jose Antonio de la Guerra, Mariano Erdoza
● Orson Welles, John Gielgud, Jeanne Moreau, Norman Rodway, Keith Baxter, Margaret Rutherford (Internacional Films Espanola/Alpine)

This Swiss-Spanish pic chronicles the story of Shakespeare's Falstaff. Taken from several plays, it details the last days of Falstaff's relationship with the Prince of Wales, the future King Henry V of England. A personal viewpoint, it mixes the grotesque, bawdy, comic and heroic, and does have a melancholy under its carousing and battles.

Orson Welles has tried to humanize Falstaff in dwelling on his intimations of old age that make him accept a buffoonish part in the young prince's life. He contrasts this with the sombre reflections of the real father (Henry IV) on whose uneasy head lies the new crown of England. The prince finally has to choose between an indulgent father figure, Falstaff, and the real adult father who means responsibility, dedication and adulthood.

Welles himself is gigantically bloated and full of swagger that yet shows glints of lonely pride and fear of rejection under a pompous exterior. John Gielgud, on the other hand, is sombre, suffering and stately as the King Henry IV trying to sort out of the problems of the court and his vassals in order to unite his nobles.

....

CHINA

1943, 78 MINS, US
Dir John Farrow *Prod* Richard Blumenthal *Scr* Frank Butler *Ph* Leo Tover *Ed* Eda Warren *Mus* Victor Young
● Loretta Young, Alan Ladd, William Bendix, Philip Ahn, Iris Wong, Sen Yung (Paramount)

Tale opens in an interior China town, with Jap planes attacking the spot and populace. Among quick evacuees is Alan Ladd, who's been trucking gasoline to the Jap armies out of Shanghai. William Bendix is his sidekick. Along the road, truck is stopped and Ladd is forced to take aboard group of Chinese femme university students in the charge of American instructress Loretta Young. Ladd is arrogant and unconcerned over the Jap atrocities against the Chinese, but wakes up when a Jap plane strafes his truck.

Frank Butler generates authenticity in the dramatic evolvement of his screenplay [from a play by Archibald Forbes], while director John Farrow neatly blends the human and melodramatic elements of the yarn. Interest is hypoed in the early reels with pickup of a Chinese baby by Bendix at the bombed town, and gradual breakdown of Ladd's attitude towards the youngster until the point where the latter is murdered by the Jap soldiers and Ladd is transformed into a battler for the Chinese cause.

....

CHINA BLUE
See: Crimes of Passion

....

CHINA DOLL

1958, 99 MINS, US
Dir Frank Borzage *Prod* Frank Borzage *Scr* Kitty Buhler *Ph* William Clothier *Ed* Jack Murray *Mus* Henry Vars *Art Dir* Howard Richmond

● Victor Mature, Li Li-hua, Ward Bond, Bob Mathias, Johnny Desmond, Danny Chang (Romina/United Artists)

About average in its war story telling, *China Doll* has a field day with the warmth and humor of a romance between a burly air corps captain and a fragile oriental beauty.

The script, from a story by James Benson Nablo and Thomas F. Kelly, often is highly interesting, often humorous and sometimes corny. It's a tale of China in 1943, at a time when the Japanese had cut off all supply lines and American airmen took to flying the hump. Smack in the middle is Victor Mature, a lonely lead who has dropped good books and bad women and has taken to the bottle. In one of his most alcoholic states, he unknowingly purchases a young Chinese girl as a housekeeper, and she ends up carrying his child, drawing his love and marrying him, in that order.

Mature displays his share of love, emotion and humor. Highlight of the picture is sumptuous femme Li Li-hua in the title role. Ward Bond is excellent as an understanding man of the cloth, and Danny Chang is fine as the barracks' boy.

■ **CHINA GATE**

1957, 96 MINS, US ⊚

Dir Samuel Fuller   *Prod* Samuel Fuller   *Scr* Samuel Fuller   *Ph* Joseph Biroc   *Ed* Gene Fowler Jr, Dean Harrison   *Mus* Victor Young, Max Steiner   *Art Dir* John Mansbridge
● Gene Barry, Angie Dickinson, Nat 'King' Cole, Lee Van Cleef, Warren Hsieh, Paul Dubov (Globe/20th Century-Fox)

China Gate is an over-long but sometimes exciting story of the battle between Vietnamese and Red Chinese, told through the efforts of a small band of French Legionnaires to reach and destroy a hidden Communist munitions dump.

Samuel Fuller gives his indie good production values, early use of Oriental war footage clips establishing an interesting story setting. The dominating character is a beautiful Eurasian woman, who leads the Legion demolition patrol to its objective through enemy territory. An added exploitation turn is the casting of Nat 'King' Cole in dual assignment of a straight role and warbling title song.

Gene Barry and Angie Dickinson top the cast: former an American in the Legion, in charge of dynamiting operations of the Red ammunition cache; latter the Eurasian who is trusted by the Communists but on the side of the patriots. Romantic conflict is realized through their having once been married.

Dickinson does yeoman service with her colorful role. Barry also handles himself well but part sometimes is negative. Cole as the only other American in Legion patrol shows he can act as well as sing.

■ **CHINA GIRL**

1942, 98 MINS, US

Dir Henry Hathaway   *Prod* Ben Hecht   *Scr* Ben Hecht   *Ph* Lee Garmes   *Ed* James B. Clark   *Mus* Hugo Friedhofer
● Gene Tierney, George Montgomery, Lynn Bari, Victor McLaglen (20th Century-Fox)

Ben Hecht is listed as producer and scripter of this original by Melville Crossman, which is usually Darryl Zanuck's nom de plume when screen-scripting.

Plot has George Montgomery, as an American newsreel cameraman in Mandalay, falling in love with an American-educated Chinese girl (Gene Tierney). There are the usual Jap intrigue and paid spies in persons of Lynn Bari and Victor McLaglen, who try to get Montgomery into their clutches to turn over to the Japs.

Only angle for audience attention is the setting of China under Jap rule and bombing prior to Pearl Harbor, with romance of minor interest due to inadequacies of the script and original yarn. Otherwise, it's regulation stuff that has been re-told many times.

■ **CHINA GIRL**

1987, 88 MINS, US ◇ ⓥ ⊙

Dir Abel Ferrara   *Prod* Michael Nozik   *Scr* Nicholas St. John   *Ph* Bojan Bazelli   *Ed* Anthony Redman   *Mus* Joe Delia   *Art Dir* Dan Leigh
● James Russo, Sari Chang, Richard Panebianco, David Caruso, Russell Wong, Joey Chin (Street Lite/Vestron)

China Girl is a masterfully directed, uncompromising drama and romance centering on gang rumbles (imaginary) between the neighboring Chinatown and Little Italy communities in New York City.

Screenplay hypothesizes an outbreak of a gang war when a Chinese restaurant opens in Italian territory. In the midst of the battling, a beautiful Chinese teenager (Sari Chang) falls in love with a pizza parlor gofer (Richard Panebianco). A la *West Side Story*, the adults oppose the relationship and, more to the point, the Mafia dons and Chinese elder gansters are in cahoots to maintain peace in their bordered territory.

Russell Wong (as handsome as a shirt ad model) and sidekick Joey Chin dominate their scenes as the young Chinese gang leaders. Title roler Sari Chang is called upon merely to be an idealized porcelain beauty and she fills the bill.

■ **CHINA 9 LIBERTY 37**

1978, 102 MINS, ITALY ◇

Dir Monte Hellman   *Prod* Gianni Bozzacchi, Valerio De Paolis, Monte Hellman   *Scr* Jerry Harvey, Douglas Venturelli, Ennio De Concini, Vicente Soriano   *Ph* Giuseppe Rotunno   *Ed* Cesare D'Amico   *Mus* Pino Donaggio   *Art Dir* Luciano Spadoni
● Fabio Testi, Warren Oates, Jenny Agutter, Sam Peckinpah, Isabel Mestres, Richard C. Adams (CEA)

An oater made in Spain with Italo backing and American and English thesps in the main roles. Though the director, Monte Hellman, is American, this is a strange western that eschews Italo pasta violence and camp, Hispano romantics or more robust Yan counterparts.

Fabio Testi is a gunman who runs off after having raped the wife of a gunslinger he was sent by railroad reps to kill. But she follows him and there is love, until railroad men are sent after the gunslinger and the husband reappears with his brothers.

Warren Oates is gruff as the husband, Jenny Agutter pliant as the torn wife who finally ends up again with her husband when the gunman will not kill him.

The old west looks a bit flat. One cameo scene is done by Sam Peckinpah, a writer selling the legend rather than the reality of the west and who offers his services to the woman in the gunfighters' life but is refused.

■ **CHINA SEAS**

1935, 87 MINS, US ⓥ

Dir Tay Garnett   *Prod* Irving G. Thalberg, Albert Lewin   *Scr* Jules Furthman, James Kevin McGuinness   *Ph* Ray June   *Ed* William Levanway   *Mus* Herbert Stothart
● Clark Gable, Jean Harlow, Wallace Beery, Rosalind Russell, Lewis Stone, Dudley Digges (M-G-M)

This is a story of love – sordid and otherwise – of piracy and violence and heroism on a passenger boat run from Shanghai to Singapore [from a novel by Crosbie Garstin]. Clark Gable is a valiant sea captain, Wallace Beery a villainous pirate boss, and Jean Harlow a blond trollop who motivates the romance and

most of the action. All do their jobs expertly.

Harlow is crossed in love when Gable, who has been her sweetheart in a sort of sparring partner but true-love affair, is tempted to return to English aristocracy. Temptation arrives in the form of the refined Rosalind Russell, a home town acquaintance. The social gap between Harlow and Russell touches off the fireworks.

Spurned by Gable, Harlow seeks to get hunk by slipping Beery the key to the ship's arsenal which makes it a cinch for the raiding pirates. But the raid fails, for Gable refuses to reveal the hiding place of a cargo of gold.

The pirate raid and its unsuccessful termination (for the pirates) is full of shooting, suspense and action. Add a running atmosphere of suspense through the picture, and there's plenty of excitement.

■ **CHINA SKY**

1945, 78 MINS, US ⓥ ⊙

Dir Ray Enright   *Prod* Maurice Geraghty   *Scr* Brenda Weisberg, Joseph Hoffman   *Ph* Nicholas Musuraca   *Ed* Gene Milford   *Mus* Roy Webb   *Art Dir* Albert S. D'Agostino, Ralph Berges
● Randolph Scott, Ruth Warrick, Ellen Drew, Anthony Quinn, Carol Thurston, Philip Ahn (RKO)

Pearl Buck's novel of the tenacity of Chinese guerrillas who harass the Japanese advance, and the American medico who runs the hospital in the key Chinese village, turns out far from the spectacular production it might have been. The guerrilla and fighting angle is played down, while stress is laid on interior sets and romantic conflict. As often happens, this lack of action wears the interest thin.

Scripters and director are so concerned with the triangle between Randolph Scott, as the American doctor, his devoted hospital co-worker (Ruth Warrick), and his wife (Ellen Drew) that they neglect the story's movement. There finally is a bangup battle at the end between Jap paratroopers and the guerrillas as a wounded Jap officer wangles info out to his forces, but it's too late.

Scott is routine as the hospital head while Warrick is superb, but her role of the doctor's assistant is not sufficient to carry the whole load.

■ **CHINA SYNDROME, THE**

1979, 122 MINS, US ◇ ⓥ ⊙

Dir James Bridges   *Prod* Michael Douglas   *Scr* Mike Gray, T.S. Cook, James Bridges   *Ph* James Crabe   *Ed* David Rawlins   *Art Dir* George Jenkins
● Jane Fonda, Jack Lemmon, Michael Douglas, Scott Brady, James Hampton, Peter Donat (Columbia)

The China Syndrome is a moderately compelling thriller about the potential perils of nuclear energy, whose major fault is an overweening sense of its own self-importance.

Jane Fonda limns a TV anchorwoman stuck in a 'happy news' rut, who hires freelance cameraman Michael Douglas for a series on energy that she hopes will break her into the world of hard news.

While filming at a nuclear energy plant, they witness a control room crisis involving supervisor Jack Lemmon, which is surreptitiously lensed by Douglas. The resulting footage becomes a political hot potato, as station manager Peter Donat buckles under pressure from power company exec Richard Herd.

It's not until the final half-hour of *China Syndrome* that its promise catches up to its punch, and the wind-up packs a solid wallop.
☐ 1979: Nominations: Best Actor (Jack Lemmon), Actress (Jane Fonda), Original Screenplay, Art Direction

C

■ **CHINATOWN**

1974, 130 MINS, US ◇ ▽ ⊙

Dir Roman Polanski   *Prod* Robert Evans   *Scr* Robert Towne   *Ph* John A. Alonzo   *Ed* Sam O'Steen   *Mus* Jerry Goldsmith   *Art Dir* Richard Sylbert, W. Stewart Campbell

● Jack Nicholson, Faye Dunaway, John Huston, Perry Lopez, John Hillerman, Diane Ladd (Paramount)

Chinatown is an outstanding picture. Robert Towne's complex but literate and orderly screenplay takes gumshoe Jack Nicholson on a murder manhunt all over the Los Angeles of the late 1930s, where Faye Dunaway is the wife of a dead city official.

Towne, director Roman Polanski and Nicholson have fashioned a sort of low-key Raymond Chandler hero who, with assistants Joe Mantell and Bruce Glover, specializes in matrimonial infidelities. When Diane Ladd, posing as Dunaway, commissions a job on Darrell Zwerling, the city's water commissioner, Nicholson becomes involved in a series of interlocking schemes.

He is in disfavor with the local police, hounded by goons (Roy Jenson and Polanski, in a bit role) in the employ of John Huston, and partially conned by Dunaway despite a romantic vibration between the two.

The many plot angles, including a very discreet development of incest, eventually converge in Chinatown for a climactic shootout which, at fadeout, will likely be papered over as a typical ghetto incident, the kind of event that respectable people never hear about. The phrase *Chinatown* is thus used in a cynical context and has meaning only after the film is over.

☐ 1974: Best Original Screenplay.
☐ Nominations: Best Picture, Director, Actor (Jack Nicholson), Actress (Faye Dunaway), Cinematography, Costume Design, Art Direction, Editing, Original Dramatic Score, Sound

■ **CHISUM**

1970, 110 MINS, US ◇ ▽

Dir Andrew V. McLaglen   *Prod* Andrew J. Fenady   *Scr* Andrew J. Fenady   *Ph* William H. Clothier   *Ed* Robert Simpson   *Mus* Dominic Frontiere   *Art Dir* Carl Anderson

● John Wayne, Forrest Tucker, Christopher George, Ben Johnson, Glenn Corbett, Andrew Prine (Batjac/Warner)

John Wayne plays a rugged character set down in New Mexico Territory, circa 1878, as King of the Pecos, its greatest landholder and biggest cattle owner. Andrew J. Fenady, who scripted, has taken the events of the bloody Lincoln County cattle war which ended in 1878 to background his story.

Forrest Tucker plays Lawrence Murphy, the ambitious, land-grabbing and power-hungry newcomer who was one of the principals of the infamous cattle war.

Basis of picture is his move in on Chisum, who didn't create his empire through any lack of fighting, and the cattleman's powerful resistance.

Wayne clothes his interpretation of the early West figure with vigor and warmth.

■ **CHITTY CHITTY BANG BANG**

1968, 156 MINS, UK ◇ ▽ ⊙

Dir Ken Hughes   *Prod* Albert R. Broccoli   *Scr* Roald Dahl, Ken Hughes, Richard Maibaum   *Ph* Christopher Challis   *Ed* John Shirley   *Mus* Irwin Kostal (sup.)   *Art Dir* Ken Adam

● Dick Van Dyke, Sally Ann Howes, Lionel Jeffries, Gert Frobe, Anna Quayle, Benny Hill (United/Warfield)

Chitty derives from (late) Ian Fleming's sole excursion into children's literature, a collection of stories about a fanciful Edwardian motor car. Dick Van Dyke is starred as the widowed, absent-minded, unsuccessful inventor whose children convince him to save the pioneer racing auto from destruction. Turned into a spanking and sleek vehicle by Van Dyke, car develops ability to float on water and fly.

Brought into the story by this point are Sally Ann Howes, daughter of a wealthy candy manufacturer (James Robertson Justice), and Lionel Jeffries, Van Dyke's father who likes to imagine that he's still in India fighting the natives.

Gert Frobe, the bullyish, temperamental, childlike prince of a middle European nation, proceeds to kidnap auto and its inventor. He gets wrong car and wrong man, Jeffries, with result that Van Dyke, Howes and the kids fly off to the principality on a rescue mission.

The $10 million film lacks warmth. No real feeling is generated between any two characters. As well as one star performer, from *Mary Poppins* have come all the musical talent – songwriters Richard M. and Robert B. Sherman and the choreographers. But there has been no desire to reprise the Edwardian music hall tradition, aspects of which so informed *Poppins*.

Howes goes through the romantic motions with Van Dyke and the maternal ones with the kids, but there is no real sentiment between players.

☐ 1968: Nomination: Best Song ('Chitty Chitty Bang Bang')

■ **CHOICES**

1981, 90 MINS, US ◇ ▽

Dir Silvio Narizzano   *Prod* Alicia Rivera Alon, Rami Alon   *Scr* Rami Alon   *Ph* Hanania Baer   *Mus* Sonny Gordon, Paul Carafotes   *Art Dir* Nancy Auburn

● Paul Carafotes, Victor French, Lelia Goldoni, Val Avery, Demi Moore (Oaktree)

Director Silvio Narizzano's first US film in 13 years is an engaging feature that confronts its young hero with an unwanted tag of a physical handicap.

Paul Carafotes appears to be an average high schooler whose world consists of football and music. His family attempts to nurture the latter aspect. However, Carafotes is partially deaf and a school medical examiner rules this precludes him from the football team.

Carafotes resents his sudden freak status and his seeming lack of choices. His helplessness manifests itself in his behavior as he adopts an 'I don't care' attitude and falls in with a tough gang.

Choices has all its sympathies in the right place and one can't help but warm to its message even if its manipulation often lacks subtlety. At times its moralistic views and approach give the picture the feel of a propaganda piece commissioned by a handicapped rights organization.

Writer-co-producer Rami Alon provides a functional script in his maiden screen effort which has a dash too much preachiness.

■ **CHOIRBOYS, THE**

1977, 119 MINS, US ◇ ▽

Dir Robert Aldrich   *Prod* Merv Adelson, Lee Rich   *Scr* Christopher Knopf   *Ph* Joseph Biroc   *Ed* Maury Winetrobe, William Martin, Irving Rosenblum   *Mus* Frank DeVol   *Art Dir* Bill Kenney

● Charles Durning, Louis Gossett Jr, Perry King, Clyde Kusatsu, Stephen Macht, Randy Quaid (Lorimar/Airone)

When Robert Aldrich's filmmaking is good, it's very, very good; and when it's bad it's awful. This cheap-looking ultra-raunchy alleged comedy about policemen leaves no stone unturned in its exploitation of vulgarity.

The story peg apparently is that, underneath the public image of callousness, which many urban police departments today exude, lies the real callousness – bigoted, sexist, unfeeling, alienated, etc.

The leading characters represent a formula cross section of people – old-style cop Charles Durning all the way down through minorities, troubled Vietnam veterans (again!), naive twerps, sexually kinky All-American Boy type, and a special mention of Tim McIntyre who is terrific in portrayal of a person audiences will come to hate.

■ **CHOPPER CHICKS IN ZOMBIETOWN**

1990, 89 MINS, US ◇ ▽

Dir Dan Hoskins   *Prod* Maria Snyder   *Scr* Dan Hoskins   *Ph* Tom Fraser   *Ed* W.O. Garrett   *Mus* Daniel May   *Art Dir* Timothy Baxter

● Jamie Rose, Catherine Carlen, Kristina Loggia, Lycia Naff, Vicki Frederick, Gretchen Palmer (Chelsea Partners)

Chopper Chicks in Zombietown is a surprisingly funny B-movie spoof with a feminist edge. Writer-director Dan Hoskins has a great deal of fun scrambling genres. It's a classic story of bikers invading a secluded town and rattling the suspicious populace.

At the same time, it's another classic story: the local mad scientist is killing off citizens, reviving them as zombie slaves, and generally making the town a miserable place to live. The bikers are leather-and-chain-wearing women.

Leader of the pack Rox (Catherine Carlen) is a hard-bitten (but not bad-looking) motorcycle mama who proudly proclaims herself 'a big, bad bulldyke'. Her gang, the Cycle Sluts, includes an ex-homecoming queen (Jamie Rose), an AWOL demolitions expert (Kristina Loggia) and a sex-crazed 'nymfomaniac' (Whitney Reis). The mad scientist is played by Don Calfa.

Hoskins isn't able to sustain the level of lunacy and several scenes suggest the Harleyriding actresses have been asked to vamp until a funny line comes along. Still, there is a lot to laugh about, and dialog that moviegoers will quote for days afterward. [Additional scenes directed by Rodney McDonald.]

■ **CHORUS LINE, A**

1985, 113 MINS, US ◇ ▽ ⊙

Dir Richard Attenborough   *Prod* Cy Feuer, Ernest Martin   *Scr* Arnold Schulman   *Ph* Ronnie Taylor   *Mus* Marvin Hamlisch   *Ed* John Bloom   *Art Dir* Patrizia Von Brandenstein

● Michael Douglas, Terrence Mann, Alyson Reed, Cameron English, Vicki Frederick, Audrey Landers (Embassy/PolyGram)

Director Richard Attenborough has not solved the problem of bringing the 1975 musical *A Chorus Line* to the screen, but he at least got it there after nearly a decade of diddling around by others.

There's a common wisdom, of course, that a stage show must be 'opened up' for the camera, but *Chorus* often seems static and confined, rarely venturing beyond the immediate. Attenborough merely films the stage show as best he could.

Nonetheless, the director and lenser Ronnie Taylor have done an excellent job working within the limitations, using every trick they could think of to keep the picture moving. More importantly, they have a fine cast, good music and a great, popular show to work with. So if all they did was get it on film, that's not so bad.

Michael Douglas is solid as the tough choreographer and Terrence Mann is good as his assistant. Alyson Reed also is sympathetic as Douglas' dancing ex-girlfriend.

Worth special note, too, are Cameron English as the troubled young gay, Vicki Frederick as the older hoofer and Audrey Landers, who romps delightfully through the 'T&A' number.

☐ 1985: Nominations: Best Editing, Song ('Surprise, Surprise'), Sound

■ CHORUS OF DISAPPROVAL, A

1989, 100 MINS, US ◇ ⑫
Dir Michael Winner   *Prod* Michael Winner
Scr Michael Winner, Alan Ayckbourn   *Ph* Alan Jones
Ed Chris Barnes   *Mus* John DuPrez   *Art Dir* Peter Young
● Jeremy Irons, Anthony Hopkins, Prunella Scales, Jenny
Seagrove, Sylvia Sims, Patsy Kensit (South Gate)

It's tricky trying to convert stage to screen,
and this is one play that suffers in translation.
As a movie, *A Chorus of Disapproval*, chugs
along when Alan Ayckbourn's play raced.

Jeremy Irons shines as Jones, a shy, rather
nervous widower who comes to work in the
small English seaside town of Scarborough.
He is lonely and, to meet people, he joins the
local amateur group, which is practicing *A
Beggar's Opera*.

The production is directed by Dafydd
Llewellyn (Anthony Hopkins) a scruffy solicitor whose only passion is the theatre and who
only really comes alive when he is directing a
new play.

Jones, without really trying, soon becomes a
small Lothario, his actions having hilarious
effects on the various members of the drama
group. Jones becomes involved with
Llewellyn's lonely wife, Hannah (Prunella
Scales), but she finds she is not alone in his
affections.

Pic is a fine, if uninspired, first screen adaptation of one of Great Britain's favorite playwrights.

■ CHOSEN, THE

See: Holocaust 2000

■ CHOSEN, THE

1981, 108 MINS, US ◇ ⑫
Dir Jeremy Paul Kagan   *Prod* Edie Landau, Ely Landau
Scr Edwin Gordon   *Ph* Arthur Ornitz   *Ed* David
Garfield   *Mus* Elmer Bernstein   *Art Dir* Stuart Wurtzel
● Maximilian Schell, Rod Steiger, Robby Benson, Barry
Miller (Landau)

The Chosen is a first-rate adaptation of Chaim
Potok's novel of friendship between two
young Jewish men of widely different religio-
cultural upbringings and their individual relationships with strong fathers.

Set in the latter years of World War II, the
story has the principles, cultural Jew Barry
Miller and orthodox Hassidic Jew Robby
Benson, meeting as opponents in a baseball
game. To Miller, a typical American kid,
Benson's Hassidic upbringing complete with
19th-century attire and long side-curls makes
him akin to a creature from outer space.

Yet the relationship grows and Miller is
asked to meet with Benson's legendary father,
an orthodox rabbi portrayed by Rod Steiger.
In full-bearded Hassidic tradition, Steiger
must approve of his son's non-sect friends.

Director Kagan and writer Gordon do wonders with the poignant material. Despite the
obvious ethnic slant this is a picture which
communicates universally.

Steiger gives an exceptional performance as
the somewhat tyranical but loving patriarch
whose primary concern is his son's welfare.
Maximilian Schell provides an interesting
contrast as a Jewish intellectual, reacting to
the Holocaust and he instills his son with
deep moral values.

■ CHRISTINE

1983, 110 MINS, US ◇ ⑫ ⊙
Dir John Carpenter   *Prod* Richard Kobritz   *Scr* Bill
Phillips   *Ph* Donald M. Morgan   *Ed* Marion Rothman
Mus John Carpenter, Alan Howarth   *Art Dir* Daniel
Lomino
● Keith Gordon, John Stockwell, Alexandra Paul, Robert
Prosky, Harry Dean Stanton, Christine Belford
(Columbia/Delphi)

Christine seems like a retread. This time it's a
fire-engine red, 1958 Plymouth Fury that's
possessed by the Devil, and this deja vu
premise [from the novel by Stephen King]
combined with the crazed vehicle format,
makes *Christine* appeal pretty shop-worn.

Title character's nasty personality is neatly
established in an assembly line prolog, which
leaves one man dead and another injured.
Jump to 1978 and Christine is a broken-down
junker. Nevertheless, she's the object of love
at first sight for misfit high school student
Keith Gordon, who purchases her despite objections from his parents and best friend, and
restores her to her 1950s glory.

Gordon also undergoes a transformation,
evolving from campus klutz to Mr Cool a ac-
quiring the foxiest girl in the school
(Alexandra Paul) in the process. But when
the couple begins making out at a drive-in
movie, Christine nearly knocks off Paul in a
fit of romantic jealousy.

Director John Carpenter's principle challenge was to create a real character of the
car, and in this he has succeeded admirably.
Flashy auto dominates everything, its jealousy
is effectively, and sometimes humorously,
conveyed, and some of the best sequences involve incidents in which the car miraculously
restores itself to pristine condition after having been banged up and even torched.

Technically, the film is outstanding, and
Carpenter's choice of lenses and widescreen
work is as astute as ever.

■ CHRISTMAS HOLIDAY

1944, 98 MINS, US
Dir Robert Siodmak   *Prod* Frank Shaw   *Scr* Herman J.
Mankiewicz   *Ph* Woody Bredell   *Ed* Ted Kent
Mus Hans J. Salter   *Art Dir* John B. Goodman, Robert
Clatworthy
● Deanna Durbin, Gene Kelly, Dean Harens, Gale
Sondergaard, Richard Whorf (Universal)

The story is Somerset Maugham's tale of a
boy who grew up emotionally during a holiday
in France (with the locale changed to New
Orleans) and the plot switched around. A
young army lieutenant, disappointed in love,
finds himself stranded in the southern city,
and meets up with another heartsick kid in a
sad-faced singer at a cheap nightclub. From
then on the story is told in flashbacks, as the
singer (Deanna Durbin) tells the lieutenant
of her brief happy marriage to a young ne'er-
do-well her husband's arrest for murder, and
his imprisonment for life.

As the nitery thrush, Durbin has two incidental songs, 'Spring Will Be a Little Late
This Year' (Frank Loesser) and the Irving
Berlin oldie, 'Always'. But otherwise the dramatic role is unrelieved except by a few
glimpses of a happy, smiling past.

■ CHRISTMAS IN JULY

1940, 67 MINS, US ⑫ ⊙
Dir Preston Sturges   *Prod* Paul Jones   *Scr* Preston
Sturges   *Ph* Victor Milner   *Ed* Ellsworth Hoagland
Mus Sigmund Krumgold (dir.)   *Art Dir* Hans Dreier, Earl
Hedrick
● Dick Powell, Ellen Drew, Raymond Walburn,
Alexander Carr, William Demarest, Ernest Truex
(Paramount)

This is the second combined writer-producer
effort of Preston Sturges following his initial
dual chore on *Great McGinty*. A mildly diverting programmer, *Christmas in July* lacks both
the overall spontaneity and entertainment
impress of Sturges' first picture.

Sturges' original script details the adventures of a young romantic pair living on the
East Side and hoping for the day when fortune will smile broadly enough for them to
get hitched. Boy is victim of office joke that
advises he won $25,000 in a slogan contest,

even though the jury is still fighting over the
winner. But he collects the check and proceeds to run up a heavy charge account before cashing the winnings, plays Santa Claus
to everyone on the block, including his sweetheart, and then is presented with the payoff
that it's a phoney.

Picture has its moments of comedy and interest, but these are interspersed too frequently by obvious and boresome episodes
that swing too much to the talkie side. There
are flashes of the by-play and incidental intimate touches displayed by Sturges in his first
picture, but not enough to bridge over the tedious episodes.

Dick Powell progresses as a straight lead
without benefit of vocalizing, providing a
dominating performance as the slogan award
victim.

■ CHRISTOPHER COLUMBUS

1949, 104 MINS, UK ◇
Dir David Macdonald   *Prod* A. Frank Bundy
Scr Muriel Box, Sydney Box, Cyril Roberts   *Ph* Stephen
Dale   *Ed* V. Sagovsky   *Mus* Arthur Bliss
Art Dir Maurice Carter
● Fredric March, Florence Eldridge, Francis L. Sullivan,
Linden Travers, Kathleen Ryan, Derek Bond
(Gainsborough/Rank)

Highly dramatized version of discovery of
America by Christopher Columbus, with lush
Technicolor to enhance opulent settings and
colorful backgrounds, turns out to be an uncertain piece of entertainment.

Almost half of the footage covers the period
before Columbus sets sail on his expedition,
dealing with his near-frustrated efforts to get
the backing of the Spanish throne. Picture really does not get under way until Columbus
sails in the *Santa Maria*. How mutiny is
averted and land finally sighted brings in
some action.

From then on the picture sketchily traces
the closing stages of Columbus' life, including
his return to Spain as a shackled prisoner and
a deathbed scene is which he has a vision of
the New World he has discovered. This ending, designed for American audiences, is
omitted from the British version.

In the role of Columbus, Fredric March inevitably dominates the story. Francis L.
Sullivan has a made-to-measure part as the
Court conspirator and Florence Eldridge is
adequately dignified as the Queen of Spain.

■ CHRISTOPHER COLUMBUS
THE DISCOVERY

1992, 120 MINS, US ◇ ⑫ ⊙ ⊙
Dir John Glen   *Prod* Ilya Salkind   *Scr* John Briley, Cary
Bates, Mario Puzo   *Ph* Alec Mills   *Ed* Matthew Glen
Mus Cliff Eidelman   *Art Dir* Gil Parrondo
● Marlon Brando, Tom Selleck, George Corraface,
Rachel Ward, Robert Davi, Catherine Zeta Jones (Salkind)

Director John Glen's take on the Genoese explorer adds up to perfectly serviceable commercial entertainment: there are a few
moments where Kirk Douglas or Charlton
Heston would have felt right at home.

Using his James Bond-honed sense of expediency, Glen tells the story [by Mario Puzo]
with broad strokes. Columbus is quickly established as a lusty, playful and self-assured
man-with-a-vision whose life, in time-honored
biopic tradition, is an uninterrupted series of
lively events.

Although script is certainly not devoid of
cliches and corniness, good dialogue far outweighs the bad. Leading man George
Corraface has the diction and charisma it
takes to carry off his role. He is immensely
likable – perhaps too much so for authenticity's sake.

Marlon Brando makes a grand Grand
Inquisitor. Tom Selleck's wry turn as King

Ferdinand is a pleasant surprise, although a wan Rachel Ward as Queen Isabella could use more backbone in her evangelical enthusiasm.

Pic concentrates more on Columbus than on the indigenous peoples he conquered, but does boast a better-than-comic-book sensitivity to the initially docile locals, eventually shown to have minds of their own. Production design, especially aboard ship, is convincing.

. . . .

■ CHUCK BERRY: HAIL! HAIL! ROCK 'N' ROLL!

1987, 120 MINS, US ◇ ⑫

Dir Taylor Hackford *Prod* Stephan Bennett *Ph* Oliver Stapleton *Ed* Lisa Day *Mus* Keith Richards (prod.)
● Chuck Berry, Eric Clapton, Robert Cray, Etta James, Julian Lennon, Keith Richards (Delilah)

'If you had tried to give rock 'n' roll another name, you might call it Chuck Berry, ' pronounces John Lennon in an old interview at the outset of Taylor Hackford's glowing two-hour love letter to the kingpin of rock 'n' roll.

Chuck Berry: Hail! Hail! Rock 'n' Roll! is a joyous docu that effortlessly weaves luminary rock interviews with performance footage mostly shot at Berry's 60th birthday bash concert at the Fox Theatre, St Louis.

Talking heads interviews with such rockers Phil and Don Everly, Jerry Lee Lewis, Bo Diddley, Little Richard, Keith Richards, Roy Orbison and Bruce Springsteen testify to the fact that Berry's influence is all-pervasive in rock. As a singer songwriter, guitarist, and bop-till-you-drop performer, Berry was real 'troubadour.'

Berry's ruminations cover everything from his love of cars, to breaking the color code, payola, his 40-year marriage, and how he chose to adapt his lyrics and subjects to cross over to white audiences.

. . . .

■ CHUMP AT OXFORD, A

1940, 63 MINS, US ⑫ ⊙

Dir Alfred Goulding *Prod* Hal Roach *Scr* Charles Rogers, Felix Adler, Harry Langdon *Ph* Art Lloyd *Ed* Bert Jordan *Mus* Marvin Hatley *Art Dir* Charles D. Hall
● Stan Laurel, Oliver Hardy, James Finlayson, Forrester Harvey, Peter Cushing, Sam Lufkin (Roach/United Artists)

Stan Laurel and Oliver Hardy's farce is mildly comical without offending. Time-worn gags clutter up the earlier footage and only when Laurel and Hardy, as new initiates into Oxford, actually move into the dean's home does the action speed up.

Early episodes have Laurel as a maid and Oliver Hardy as butler in a rich man's home. It looks as though it had been tacked on in order to make up footage. James Finlayson is the wealthy host in this episode but not given any cast credit.

A dinner party brings in all the familiar dress-tearing, pastry-flinging, corkpopping and shot-gun gags. Even that venerable nifty where the cop says 'you are liable to blow my brains out' and then exhibits the bullet-marked seat of his trousers is left in.

But once the comedians land in England they fare better. Outside of the lost-in-the-woods stunt and ghost-at-midnight routine, the gagging and all-round material brightens up.

. . . .

■ CIAO, FEDERICO!

1970, 60 MINS, US/ITALY ◇

Dir Gideon Bachmann *Prod* Victor Herbert *Scr* Gideon Bachmann *Ph* Gideon Bachmann, Harvey Felderbaum, Anton Haakma *Ed* Regine Heuser (Herbert)

Yank critic-filmmaker Gideon Bachmann, a longtime Rome resident, made this 16mm docu on Italian director Federico Fellini making *Satyricon*.

Pic's glue-like coverage of the sly, wry Fellini, and the latter's charm and interest shows him as chameleon-like figure. He rages, but with an underlying lack of true anger, and a seeming watching of his own actions. So he rarely reveals himself in words but may do so in actions, even if they appear often calculated.

Pic is as airy, unrevealing but picturesque as Fellini's symbolical, circusy pix and his tender choosing of grotesques and beauty to limn his own fantasy world on film.

. . . .

■ CIAO MANHATTAN

1973, 90 MINS, US ◇ ⑫ ⊙

Dir John Palmer, David Weisman *Prod* Robert Margouleff, David Weisman *Scr* John Palmer, David Weisman *Ph* John Palmer, Kjell Rostad *Ed* Robert Farren *Mus* Gino Piserchio
● Edie Sedgwick, Wesley Hayes, Isabel Jewell, Paul America, Geoffrey Briggs, Tom Flye (Court)

Ciao Manhattan is Edie Sedgwick's filmed swansong – she died of acute barbituate intoxication in 1971. Monotonous and nearly incomprehensible, *Ciao* consists chiefly of pieced-together short ends from two Sedgwick vehicles, one [in b&w] begun with great fanfare by undergrounder Chuck Wein [from a story by him and Genevieve Charbin] in 1967 when the Andy Warhol 'superstar' was at the peak of her celebrity, and the second started three years later in California by John Palmer and David Weisman, who evidently believed they could reconstruct the ruin.

In the last years of her life, says this intendedly anti-dope film, Sedgwick took up residence at the bottom of a tented Santa Barbara pool, narcissistically surrounded by giant blowups of herself. It is here that the film dwells, cruelly exploiting her dope and booze bloated visage, her siliconed breasts (for at least half the pic she is topless, so proud is she of these new ornaments) and most of the non-plot consists of her drug-zonked recollections of her halcyon days.

. . . .

■ CIMARRON

1931, 124 MINS, US ⑫

Dir Wesley Ruggles *Prod* William LeBaron *Scr* Howard Estabrook *Ph* Edward Cronjager *Ed* William Hamilton *Mus* Max Steiner *Art Dir* Max Ree
● Richard Dix, Irene Dunne, Estelle Taylor, Nance O'Neil, William Collier Jr, Roscoe Ates (Radio)

An elegant example of super film making, this spectacular western [from the novel by Edna Ferber] holds action, sentiment, sympathy, thrills and comedy.

Two outstanders in the playing, Richard Dix and Edna May Oliver, each surprisingly excellent, Dix with his straight character playing of a westerner and an Oklahoma pioneer who dies before his statue is unveiled in that state, while Oliver is nothing less than exquisite in her eccentric comedy role of a Colonial dame in the wilds.

Perhaps nothing will draw more attention than the skillful aging of the main role players, from 1889 to 1930, a period they pass through of over 40 years on the screen.

Wesley Ruggles' direction misses nothing in the elaborate scenes, as well as in the usual film making procedure.

Big production bits start with the land rush into Oklahoma in 1889, then the gospel meeting in a frontier gambling hall where Dix makes his biggest mark, an attempted bank robbery and the court room trial of Dixie Lee, the harlot.

The land rush starts the action, men on horses and in wagons racing to capture some part of the two million acres released by the government to the first comers after the boom of a cannon at noon.

Estelle Taylor as Dixie Lee somewhat fades Irene Dunne as Dix's young and old wife. Taylor's showings are few but she makes them impressive. Dunne does nicely enough in a role of a loving wife and mother, which does not permit her to be much else. What she later accomplishes a political way is suggested rather than acted. Roscoe Ates as a stuttering printer lands several laughs.

□ 1930/31: Best Picture, Adaptation, Interior Decoration (Max Ree).

□ Nominations: Director, Actor (Richard Dix), Actress (Irene Dunne), Cinematography

. . . .

■ CIMARRON

1960, 140 MINS, US ◇

Dir Anthony Mann *Prod* Edmund Grainger *Scr* Arnold Schulman *Ph* Robert L. Surtees *Ed* John Dunning *Mus* Franz Waxman *Art Dir* George W. Davis, Addison Hehr
● Glenn Ford, Maria Schell, Anne Baxter, Arthur O'Connell, Russ Tamblyn, Mercedes McCambridge (M-G-M)

Edna Ferber's novel of the first Oklahoma land rush (1889) shapes up in its second film translation as a good balance between rousing action and the marriage of Glenn Ford and Maria Schell as Yancey and Sabra Cravet.

There are many subtle shadings in Schell's performance as she transforms over period of 25 years from adoring, lovable bride to embittered, abandoned wife, successful newspaper publisher and bigoted mother-in-law when son Cim marries a childhood friend Indian girl. Latter and her mother were taken into the Cravet family by Yancey during the homestead run when the father was lynched by an Indian-hating scoundrel, played in grand bullboy style by Charles McGraw.

Ford emerges a strong and thoroughly likeable adventurer-idealist as the restless rover, Yancey, who is loving and devoted after his own fashion and spurns opportunity to become governor by helping to defraud Indians of their oil rights. Pic pulls no punches in pointing up the greed that discovery of black gold brought out in the rags-to-riches Oklahoma pioneers.

Cimarron starts off with a bang. Spectacle of thousands of land seekers lined up in Conestoga wagons, buck-boards and even a surrey with the fringe on top, straining to dash into the new territory at high noon on 22 April 1889, is masterfully handled by director Anthony Mann. This is grand-scale action in spades. Fortunately Arnold Schulman's adaptation doesn't let the performers down after the whirlwind start.

As was the case with *Oklahoma!*, *Cimarron* was photographed on location in Arizona. Producer Edmund Grainger, apparently being more concerned about pictorial composition than actual topography, has permitted mountains to show in backgrounds alien to Oklahoma.

□ 1960: Nominations: Best Art Direction, Sound

. . . .

■ CINCINNATI KID, THE

1965, 102 MINS, US ◇ ⑫ ⊙

Dir Norman Jewison *Prod* Martin Ransohoff *Scr* Ring Lardner Jr, Terry Southern *Ph* Philip H. Lathrop *Ed* Hal Ashby *Mus* Lalo Schifrin *Art Dir* George W. Davis, Edward Carfagno
● Steve McQueen, Edward G. Robinson, Ann-Margret, Karl Malden, Tuesday Weld, Joan Blondell (M-G-M)

The Cincinnati Kid is the fastmoving story of a burningly-ambitious young rambling-gambling man who challenges the king of stud poker to a showdown for the champ title of

143

The Man. Adapted from Richard Jessup's realistically-written novel, it emerges a tenseful examination of the gambling fraternity.

Martin Ransohoff has constructed a taut, well-turned-out production. In Steve McQueen he has the near-perfect delineator of the title role. Edward G. Robinson is at his best in some years as the aging, ruthless Lancey Howard, champ of the poker tables for more than 30 years and determined now to defend his title against a cocksure but dangerous opponent. The card duel between the pair is dramatically developed through gruelling action, building in intensity as the final and deciding hand is played.

Ring Lardner Jr and Terry Southern have translated the major elements of the book, changing, however, tome's St Louis locale to a more picturesque New Orleans background. They have added a key situation, too, to point up the game – Karl Malden, in part of Shooter, dealer for the game, is forced by another gambler holding his markers to slip cards to the Kid so he'll cinch his victory. The Kid senses what's going on and eases Malden from his post.

■ CINDERELLA

1950, 74 MINS, US ◇ ⑫ ⊙
Dir Wilfred Jackson, Hamilton Luske, Clyde Geronimi *Prod* Ben Sharpsteen (sup.) *Scr* William Peed, Ted Sears, Homer Brightman, Kenneth Anderson, Erdman Penner, Winston Hibler, Harry Reeves, Joe Rinaldi *Ed* Donald Halliday *Mus* Oliver Wallace, Paul Smith (Walt Disney)

Disney outfit makes entertainment capital out of the animal world with clever drawing-board personifications of a quartet of mice doing battle with an ornery cat. The cartoon, in fact, has far more success in projecting the lower animals than in it central character, Cinderella, who is on the colorless, doll-faced side, as is the Prince Charming.

The menace is supplied by the literally-drawn stepmother, who's a lineal descendant of the flint-hearted, evil-eyed witch in *Snow White*. More inventiveness is used in the characterization of Cinderella's two comically-ugly stepsisters, the king, his monocled major domo, and the aunty-like fairy princess.

The musical numbers woven into the fantasy are generally solid, with at least two or three likely hit tunes standing out in the half-dozen songs. Ilene Woods, as Cinderella's voice, uses a sweet soprano on 'Cinderella', 'So This Is Love', and 'A Dream Is a Wish Your Heart Makes', all three being firstrate.
□ 1950: Nominations: Best Scoring of a Musical Picture, Song ('Bibbidy-Bobbidy-Boo'), Sound

■ CINDERELLA LIBERTY

1973, 117 MINS, US ◇ ⑫
Dir Mark Rydell *Prod* Mark Rydell *Scr* Darryl Ponicsan *Ph* Vilmos Zsigmond *Ed* Donn Cambera, Patrick Kennedy *Mus* John Williams *Art Dir* Leon Ericksen
● James Caan, Marsha Mason, Kirk Calloway, Eli Wallach, Allyn Ann McLerie, Burt Young (20th Century-Fox)

Cinderella Liberty is an earthy but very touching story of a sailor's love for a prostitute. James Caan stars in an outstanding performance, and Marsha Mason, in her second picture, is equally superb.

The title comes direct from navy slang referring to enlisted men's ashore time cut off at midnight, the one here being Caan's temporary hospitalization and pending transfer to a new ship. In a most realistic bar setting, he meets Mason, who takes him home where the first of many surprises for Caan is the existence of a partially-black son (Kirk Calloway). The next surprise is Caan's infatuation, to the extent of busting in on her to eject another trick.

Eli Wallach's strong featured role is that of

Caan's long-ago boot camp drill instructor, whose harsh methods provoke a fight years later.
□ 1973: Nominations: Best Actress (Marsha Mason), Original Score, Song ('Nice to Be Around')

■ CINERAMA HOLIDAY

1955, 119 MINS, US ◇
Dir Robert Bendick, Philippe de Lacey *Prod* Louis de Rochemont *Scr* Otis Carney, Louis de Rochemont *Ph* Joseph Brun, Harry Squire *Ed* Jack Murray, Leo Zochling, Frederick Y. Smith *Mus* Morton Gould, Van Cleave (Stanley-Warner Cinerama)

The Fred Waller Cinerama process is seen in its second mounting. Much of the excitement [of the first, *This Is Cinerama,*] remains, although there is some feeling of repeating tried-and-true pictorial effects.

Right off, one thing stands out. Here is the greatest trailer for travel ever produced. There is a wisp of continuity in *Holiday*, unlike the predecessor film. Betty and John Marsh of Kansas City and Beatrice and Fred Troller of Zurich do an exchange student type of act, each pair of newlyweds visiting the other's hemisphere.

Since the second part of the show, after a 15-minute intermission, is largely made up of an extended visit to Paris, the impression grows into a conviction that the American couple really went places, did things and met people far beyond the arrangements for the Swiss pair.

■ CIRCUS WORLD

(UK: The Magnificent Showman)

1964, 135 MINS, US/SPAIN ◇ ⑫
Dir Henry Hathaway *Prod* Samuel Bronston *Scr* Ben Hecht, Julian Halevy, James Edward Grant *Ph* Jack Hildyard *Ed* Dorothy Spencer *Mus* Dimitri Tiomkin *Art Dir* John F. DeCuir
● John Wayne, Claudia Cardinale, Rita Hayworth, Lloyd Nolan, Richard Conte, John Smith (Bronston-Roma)

Samuel Bronston's made-in-Spain *Circus World* is a bigscreen wedding of spectacle and romance. The pace, as directed by Henry Hathaway, is unslackening.

A major value throughout is the photography of Jack Hildyard, working harmoniously wit Hathaway (after Frank Capra Sr. departed). A second unit directed by Richard Talmadge had Claude Renoir on camera.

Special effects are numerous, perhaps the most memorable being Alex Weldon's capsizing on cue of a 4,000-ton freighter, loaded with the American circus folk, gear and animals, at Barcelona dockside. Barcelona's opera house was planked over to simulate the Hansa Circus Theatre of Hamburg, circa 1910. The plaza at Chinchon, used for the bullfight scene in *Around the World in 80 Days*, may also be recognized. Negative cost was around $8.5 million.

The basic story, by Philip Yordan and Nicholas Ray, is about a runaway aerialist (Rita Hayworth) who returns to watch her daughter (Claudia Cardinale) rehearsing on the lot, like Madame X of long ago, but this time there is a happy reunion of all, the final scene being the performance given hours after a terrible fire in which mother and daughter costar in a two-act.

Hayworth looks very good and acts with warmth and authority. Cardinale, in her fifth English-language film, is ideal for the girl-bursting-into-womanhood. The relationship to foster father John Wayne is developed with a steady sense of the interplay of the stern he-man and the passionate-natured ward.

Wayne is the center-pole, the muscle, the virility and the incarnate courage of this often down but never out circus. The role has been tailored to his talents and personality, a rooting-tooting-shooting figure.

■ CISCO PIKE

1971, 94 MINS, US ◇
Dir Bill L. Norton *Prod* Gerald Ayres *Scr* Bill L. Norton *Ph* Vilis Lapenieks *Ed* Robert C. Jones *Mus* Bob Johnston (sup.) *Art Dir* Alfred Sweeney
● Gene Hackman, Karen Black, Kris Kristofferson, Harry Dean Stanton, Viva, Joy Bang (Columbia)

Kris Kristofferson in title role makes an excellent formal acting debut as a faded and drug-busted rock star forced by corrupt cop Gene Hackman into selling marijuana. Well-written and directed by Bill L. Norton, the handsome Gerald Ayres production sustains a good plot while providing proper amounts of environmental color.

The weakest plot angle is Hackman's motivation: not until the surprise climax is it made clear that he wants some extra money since police are underpaid. There's a lot more breadth in that angle that writer Norton fails to make viable.

Principal supporting players include Karen Black in another Karen Black role as Pike's amiable but confused girl; the totally delightful Viva; Harry Dean Stanton, excellent as Pike's old partner, pitiably wasted on hard drugs; and Joy Bang, Viva's cruising partner.

Kristofferson's screen presence is very strong. There's a look in his eyes – a combination of resignation, optimism and torture – that sticks in the memory long after the film has ended.

■ CITADEL, THE

1938, 112 MINS, UK ⑫
Dir King Vidor *Prod* Victor Saville *Scr* Ian Dalrymple, Frank Wead, Elizabeth Hill *Ph* Harry Stradling *Ed* Charles Frend *Mus* Louis Levy *Art Dir* Lazare Meerson, Alfred Junge
● Robert Donat, Rosalind Russell, Ralph Richardson, Rex Harrison, Emlyn Williams, Penelope Dudley Ward (M-G-M)

The Citadel is Metro's second British-made production. It's an effective drama based on A. J. Cronin's novel which generated quite a controversy in medical circles due to presentation of its subject matter. Major change for picture is a switch to a happy ending.

Story details the adventures of a young physician (Robert Donat) who starts out with high ideals and determination to help humanity. When Welsh miners object to his research to prevent tuberculosis in the community, he goes to London, gets in with a coterie of mulcting doctors who brush aside medical ethics in their chase for money. Snapped out of his new surroundings by a bungling operation on his best friend, the young physician discards the shams of money for his original ideals.

Donat gives a most seasoned performance. Rosalind Russell turns in a sympathetic portrayal of the young wife who struggles through at his side, and gets him back to his ideals after the London experiences.

Picture is studded with many brilliantly human and dramatic sequences. Success of Donat in reviving a stillborn baby in a worker's home is a real heart-puller; chiller is episode where entrapped miner's arm is amputated in cave-in; and vivid drama springs forth when Donat stands by while his best friend dies during bungled operation performed by the incompetent, social-climbing surgeon.
□ 1938: Nominations: Best Picture, Director, Actor (Robert Donat), Screenplay

■ CITIZEN KANE

1941, 120 MINS, US ⑫ ⊙
Dir Orson Welles *Prod* Orson Welles *Scr* Herman J. Mankiewicz, Orson Welles, [Joseph Cotten, John Houseman] *Ph* Gregg Toland *Ed* Robert Wise, [Mark Robson] *Mus* Bernard Herrmann *Art Dir* Van Nest Polglase, Perry Ferguson

C

● Orson Welles, Joseph Cotten, Ray Collins, Paul Stewart, Dorothy Comingore, Everett Sloane (RKO/Mercury)

Citizen Kane is a film which distinguishes every daring entertainment venture that is created by a workman who is master of the technique and mechanics of his medium. It is a two-hour show, filled to the last minute with brilliant incident, unreeled in method and effects that sparkle with originality and invention.

In the film's story of a multi-millionaire newspaper publisher, political aspirant and wielder of public opinion, there are incidents that may be interpreted as uncomplimentary to William Randolph Hearst. Protests against the film release were made by executives and employees in his organization.

Story is credited jointly to Herman J. Mankiewicz and Welles. The early, rebellious, youthful years of the powerful Kane are described by the family attorney, who neither understood nor had any deep affection for the young man. The thread is picked up by Kane's faithful business manager, then by his second wife, by his only earnest friend and finally by his butler. Pieced together, like a jigsaw puzzle, the parts and incidents omitted by earlier narrators are supplied by others.

When completed the authors' conception of Kane is a man who had every material advantage in life, but who lacked a feeling of human sympathy and tolerance. It is a story of spiritual failure. So intent is the effort to prove Kane a frustrate that no allowance is made to picture him as a human being. On this account he is not wholly real. Neither he nor his associates is blessed with the slightest sense of humor.

Welles portrays the chief character with surprising success, considering that the picture marks his debut as a film actor. His associates are selected from his Mercury Theatre's actors, few of whom had previous screen experience. Whatever else *Citizen Kane* may be, it is a refreshing cinematic novelty, and the general excellence of its acting is not the least of its assets.
□ 1941: Best Original Screenplay.
□ Nominations: Best Picture, Director, Actor (Orson Welles), B&W Cinematography, B&W Art Direction, Editing, Scoring of a Dramatic Picture, Sound

■ **CITIZENS BAND**

1977, 98 MINS, US ◇ ⓦ
Dir Jonathon Demme *Prod* Shep Fields *Scr* Paul Brickman *Ph* Jordon Cronenweth *Ed* John F. Link II *Mus* Bill Conti *Art Dir* Bill Malley
● Paul Le Mat, Candy Clark, Ann Wedgeworth, Bruce McGill, Marcia Rodd, Charles Napier (Fields)

Plot peg is the truck accident of philandering husband Charles Napier, who's got Ann Wedgeworth in Dallas and Marcia Rodd in Portland, both with homes and children.

While he is recovering at the hands of Alix Elias (whose charms are mobile), the two suspicious women arrive in a small town where Paul Le Mat and estranged brother Bruce McGill are both courting Candy Clark. Roberts Blossom is the boy's irascible widower-father. Linking all their lives is the CB radio, buzzing away like a verbal Muzak.

The CB dialog exemplifies the good-natured horsing around that marks those channels, at the same time the serious emergency traffic that often saves lives.

■ **CITY BENEATH THE SEA**
(UK: One Hour to Doomsday)

1953, 87 MINS, US ◇
Dir Budd Boetticher *Prod* Albert J. Cohen *Scr* Jack Harvey, Ramon Romero *Ph* Charles P. Boyle *Ed* Edward Curtiss *Mus* Joseph Gershenson (dir.) *Art Dir* Alexander Golitzen, Emrich Nicholson

● Robert Ryan, Mala Powers, Anthony Quinn, Suzan Ball, George Mathews, Karel Stepanek (Universal)

High romance of the pulp-fiction variety is niftily shaped in *City Beneath the Sea*. The film stages a thrilling underseas 'earthquake' as a capper to the derring-do yarn laid in the West Indies.

A couple of lusty, adventurous deep-sea divers, a sunken treasure, comely femmes and the earthquake are expertly mixed to provide chimerical film entertainment. The direction by Budd Boetticher is slanted to take the most advantage of the action, amatory and thrill situations in the story based on Harry E. Rieseberg's *Port Royal – The Ghost City Beneath the Sea*. Picture is not necessarily logical, but it tells its tale with a robust sense of humor.

The earthquake sequence is a real thriller. Scene is the historic sunken city of Port Royal, Jamaica, which went to the bottom of the Caribbean during a 1692 earthquake. Robert Ryan and Anthony Quinn team excellently as the daring divers, ever ready for the adventures offered by sunken treasure or shapely femmes. They come to Kingston, Jamaica, to dive for $1 million in gold bullion that went down with a freighter, without knowing their employer (Karel Stepanek) doesn't want the treasure found just yet.

Plot tangents boil along while Ryan woos Mala Powers, owner of a small, coastwise ship, and Quinn makes time with Suzan Ball, singer in a waterfront nitery.

■ **CITY GIRL, THE**

1984, 85 MINS, US ◇ ⓦ ⊙
Dir Martha Coolidge *Prod* Martha Coolidge *Scr* Judith Tompson, Leonard-John Gates *Ph* Daniel Hainey *Ed* Linda Leeds, Eva Gardos *Mus* Scott Wilk, Marc Levinthal *Art Dir* Ninkey Dalton
● Laura Harrington, Joe Mastroianni, Carole McGill, Peter Riegert, Jim Carrington, Lawrence Phillips (Moon)

Martha Coolidge's *The City Girl* reps a hardnosed, if frequently funny, look at a young woman's attempt to forge a career and self-esteem. It's a predecessor to same director's 1983 indie hit, *Valley Girl*.

Lead character of Anne is a young lady who, in an awfully serious way, is trying to get a foot up as a professional photographer. Joey, her sympathetic but very straight boyfriend, indulges her to a point but would rather have her fill the conventional woman's role, something it's obvious she won't do.

Most bracing aspect of Coolidge's treatment of the relatively plain material is her rigorously objective, unindulgent perspective.

In line with the director's approach, Laura Harrington, who plays Anne, does not sentimentalize her character.

■ **CITY HEAT**

1984, 97 MINS, US ◇ ⓦ ⊙
Dir Richard Benjamin *Prod* Fritz Manes *Scr* Sam O. Brown [= Blake Edwards], Joseph C. Stinson *Ph* Nick McLean *Ed* Jacqueline Cambas *Mus* Lennie Niehaus *Art Dir* Edward Carfagno
● Clint Eastwood, Burt Reynolds, Jane Alexander, Madeline Kahn, Rip Torn, Richard Roundtree (Malpaso/Deliverance/Warner)

City Heat is an amiable but decidedly lukewarm confection geared entirely around the two star turns.

Set in an unnamed city around the end of Prohibition, Clint Eastwood and Burt Reynolds were old pals in their early days as cops, but the former has taken a dim view of the latter's jump over to the private detective business, resulting in a certain tension between them.

Reynolds' partner, Richard Roundtree, gets bumped off in the early going, and Reynolds

spends the remainder of the picture attempting to play two mobster kingpins off one another.

Some of the repartee is relatively amusing, and the two stars, with tongues firmly in cheek, easily set the prevailing tone of low-keyed facetiousness.

■ **CITY LIGHTS**

1931, 87 MINS, US ⓦ
Dir Charles Chaplin *Prod* Charles Chaplin *Scr* Charles Chaplin *Ph* Roland Totheroh *Ed* Charles Chaplin *Mus* Charles Chaplin *Art Dir* Charles D. Hall
● Charles Chaplin, Virginia Cherrill, Harry Myers, Allan Garcia, Hank Mann, Florence Lee (United Artists)

It's not Chaplin's best picture, because the comedian has sacrificed speed to pathos, and plenty of it. This is principally the reason for the picture running some 1,500 or more feet beyond any previous film released by him. But the British comic is still the consummate pantomimist.

All through Chaplin schemes how to procure money for a blind flower girl (Virginia Cherrill).

Script is something of a fable in discovering the comic asleep in the lap of a statue when it is unveiled and then having him in and out of trouble through the means of a millionaire (Harry Myers), whom Chaplin prevents from a drunken suicide, and who thereafter only recognizes the comic when drunk.

It can be imagined how much stuff has been tossed away in getting this picture down to its present length, after spasmodically shooting on it over a period of 18 months or more. As previously, Chaplin mainly paints in broad strokes, with his most subtle maneuvering here being the sly turning of the sympathy away from the girl to himself as the picture draws to a close.

■ **CITY LIMITS**

1985, 85 MINS, US ◇ ⓦ
Dir Aaron Lipstadt *Prod* Rupert Harvey, Barry Opper *Scr* Don Opper *Ph* Timothy Suhrstedt *Ed* Robert Kizer *Mus* John Lurie *Art Dir* Cyd Smilie
● Darrell Larson, John Stockwell, Kim Cattrall, Rae Dawn Chong, Robby Benson, James Earl Jones (Sho/Videoform)

Elements of *City Limits* fit it into the category of the post-holocaust pic, but the historical disaster is a plague which has wiped out an older generation. The young survive in a condition of controlled anarchy and resist attempts to impose centralized government.

Most successful aspect of the film [based on a story by James Reigle and Aaron Lipstadt] is its depiction of a tribal lifestyle regulated according to rules learned from comic strips. Two gangs of bikers, the Clippers an the DAs, have divided up the city and live under a truce. Infractions of their pact are regulated with competitive jousting or acts of reciprocal revenge. The dead are cremated with their vehicles like Vikings in their boats. The two groups may unite against outside threats.

Less convincing is the portrayal, with allusions to Fritz Lang's classic *Metropolis*, of the totalitarian-inclined Sunya Corp., which attempts to take over the city with the initial cooperation of the DAs.

Film features an ace ensemble cast. Action scenes are well-executed and there's a vibrant score.

■ **CITY OF HOPE**

1991, 129 MINS, US ◇ ⓦ
Dir John Sayles *Prod* Sarah Green, Maggie Renzi *Scr* John Sayles *Ph* Robert Richardson *Ed* John Sayles *Mus* Mason Daring *Art Dir* Dan Bishop, Dianna Freas
● Vincent Spano, Joe Morton, Tony LoBianco, Anthony John Denison, Barbara Williams, John Sayles (Esperanza)

John Sayles' ambitious, wide-ranging study of corruption and community in a small Eastern city has as many parallel plots and characters as *Hill Street Blues*, while at the same time having a richness of theme and specificity of vision more common to serious cinema.

Picture hinges on the oppposite directions of two characters: Nick (Vincent Spano), disillusioned son of a well-connected builder, who has easy access to the system but only wants out of it, and Wynn (Joe Morton), a young black city councilman who's determined to work within the system.

Nick soon gets involved in a robbery to get money to pay off his gambling debts. Meanwhile he's starting a romance with an old high school classmate Angela (Barbara Williams), which draws the wrath of her maddog ex-husband and cop (Anthony John Denison). Then a racial crisis erupts when two black kids attack a white college teacher.

For much of the film, the restlessness of focus seems a liability. But when the camera stops long enough to put two characters together one-on-one, dialog and emotional connection emerge.

■ **CITY OF JOY**

1992, 134 MINS, UK/FRANCE ◇ ⓥ ⊙
Dir Roland Joffe *Prod* Jake Eberts *Scr* Mark Medoff *Ph* Peter Biziou *Ed* Gerry Hambling *Mus* Ennio Morricone *Art Dir* Roy Walker
● Patrick Swayze, Pauline Collins, Om Puri, Shabana Azmi, Art Malik, Ayesha Dharker (Lightmotive)

A picture divided against itself, *City of Joy* is half American-style gangster melodrama and half inspirational social consciousness. Impressively produced in Calcutta's teeming poverty-ridden streets and slums, Roland Joffe's noble attempt to portray the tenacity and strength of the human spirit comes off as curiously ineffectual due to predictable plotting and character evolution.

Inspired by selected stories in Dominique Lapierre's 1985 international bestseller, *City of Joy* a direct descendant of the *Casablanca* school, with a disenchanted, cynical Yank heading for exotic climes to both alleviate and exult in his ennui, and finally finding something in himself he thought had died or never existed.

Fleeing from the rigors of life as a surgeon in Houston, Patrick Swayze's Dr Max Lowe arrives in Calcutta with the vague idea of seeking enlightenment. Assaulted and robbed, Max is taken to the City of Joy Self-Help School and Dispensary, presided over by a beleaguered but selflessly saintly British woman (Pauline Collins). Max becomes cheerleader for the dispossessed people of City of Joy in their battle against the local mafia.

An admittedly chancy choice to play a jaded medic, Swayze gives it the old college try, but he doesn't have depth. Appealing as always, Collins has nothing but routine buttons to push as she uses all her wiles to win the doc over to her cause.

■ **CITY SLICKERS**

1991, 112 MINS, US ◇ ⓥ ⊙
Dir Ron Underwood *Prod* Irby Smith *Scr* Lowell Ganz, Babaloo Mandel *Ph* Dean Semler *Ed* O. Nicholas Brown *Mus* Marc Shaiman, Hummie Mann *Art Dir* Lawrence G. Paull
● Billy Crystal, Daniel Stern, Bruno Kirby, Patricia Wettig, Helen Slater, Jack Palance (Columbia/Castle Rock)

The setup is sheer simplicity, as Billy Crystal, coming to grips with the doldrums of midlife thanks to his 39th birthday, is convinced by his wife (Patricia Wettig) and two best friends (Daniel Stern, Bruno Kirby) to take off for two weeks on a ranch driving cattle across the west.

The childhood fantasy comes to life in a number of ways, perhaps foremost in the presence of gnarled trail boss Curly (Jack Palance), a figure always seemingly backlit in larger-than-life silhouettes.

The other cowboy wannabes include a father-and-son dentist team (Bill Henderson, Phill Lewis), fraternal ice-cream tycoons (David Paymer, Josh Mostel) and a beautiful woman (Bonnie Rayburn) who braved the trip on her own. A series of increasingly absurd events lead the central trio toward an ultimate challenge that turns the vacation into a journey of self-discovery.

Crystal gets plenty of chance to crack wise while he, Stern and Kirby engage in playful and not-so-playful banter – Stern coming off a recently (and publicly) failed marriage while the womanizing Kirby grapples with his own fear of fidelity. Director Ron Underwood (who made his feature debut on *Tremors*) generally keeps the herd moving at a fine pace.
□ 1991: Best Supp. Actor (Jack Palance)

■ **CITY STREETS**

1931, 83 MINS, US
Dir Rouben Mamoulian *Prod* E. Lloyd Sheldon *Scr* Oliver H.P. Garrett, Max Marcin *Ph* Lee Garmes *Mus* Sidney Cutner
● Gary Cooper, Sylvia Sidney, Paul Lukas, William Boyd, Guy Kibbee, Stanley Fields (Paramount)

Probably the first sophisticated treatment of a gangster picture. Story is the usual love-redeeming tale of two kids caught in a gangster vortex.

Picture is lifted from mediocrity through the intelligent acting and appeal of Sylvia Sidney. This legit girl makes her first screen appearance here as co-star with Gary Cooper. From a histrionic standpoint she's the whole works, and that's not detracting from the others who perform ably.

Gang chieftain is shown controlling everything from his henchmen's women to his sidekicks' lives. He doesn't control his own life, though, and a jealous girl sends him low when he tries to shelve her for Babe (Sidney).

Finale has Babe and her boy friend (Cooper) make the heights of dececency when they trick three badmen executioners, trailing them, into a long and speedy ride thru the great outdoors.

Camera angles are piled on thick. Most of the time these shots serve to slow up the film and confuse.

■ **CITY THAT NEVER SLEEPS**

1953, 90 MINS, US ⓥ
Dir John H. Auer *Prod* John H. Auer (assoc.) *Scr* Steve Fisher *Ph* John L. Russell Jr *Ed* Fred Allen *Mus* R. Dale Butts *Art Dir* James Sullivan
● Gig Young, Mala Powers, William Talman, Edward Arnold, Chill Wills, Marie Windsor (Republic)

Production and direction loses itself occasionally in stretching for mood and nuances, whereas a straightline cops-and-robbers action flavor would have been more appropriate. Same flaw is found in the Steve Fisher screen original.

Playing of the four cast toppers, Gig Young, a crazy, mixed-up cop; Mala Powers, a cheap saloon dancer; William Talman, a magician turned hood; and Edward Arnold, suave, crooked attorney, is adequate to script and directorial demands. Chill Wills, principal featured player, walks through the film without any definition, presumably being a character that represents the city of Chicago itself.

One night in life on the Chicago police force finds Young ready to blow his job and wife (Paula Raymond) to run away with Powers. He accepts an assignment from Arnold to take Talman over the state line in order to get money for the flight from reality.

John L. Russell's photography makes okay use of Chicago streets and buildings for the low-key, night-life effect required to back the melodrama.

■ **CIVILIZATION**

1916, 121 MINS, US ⊗ ⓥ
Dir Raymond B. West *Prod* Thomas H. Ince *Scr* C. Gardner Sulivan *Ph* Joseph August, Clyde de Vinna, Irvin Willat *Ed* Thomas H. Ince *Mus* Victor Schertzinger
● Howard Hickman, Enid Markey, Herschel Mayall, George Fisher, J. Frank Burke (Triangle/KayBee)

Master producer Thomas H. Ince was handicapped here by the limitations of C. Gardner Sulivan's scenario, designed as a strong protest against the horrors of war.

The entertainment opens showing a nation at peace, suddenly plunged headlong into war by its king (Herschel Mayall), due wholly to his selfish desire for conquest. He is dependent for success upon Count Ferdinand (Howard Hickman), who has invented a submarine calculated to destroy the enemy's fleet, thus ensuring victory. The count is in love with Katheryn, 'a woman of the people'. Katheryn (Enid Markey) belongs to a secret society, which is opposed to war. She takes him to one of the meetings and he becomes a convert.

When the count receives a wireless message to blow up an enemy vessel carrying innocent passengers, he refuses to obey orders and, as his own crew attacks him, sinks his own vessel and deliberately drowns himself and crew. His body is picked up and the king sends for his scientists to restore life in order to secure the secrets of the death-dealing submarine. But it is only the count's body with the soul of Christ who resolves to return to Earth to teach the message of Love not Hate.

There is very little opportunity to criticise Ince's magnificent effort, but Sulivan's captions are altogether too preachy. In his effort to project pathos he slops over into bathos.

■ **CLAN OF THE CAVE BEAR, THE**

1986, 98 MINS, US ◇ ⓥ ⊙
Dir Michael Chapman *Prod* Gerald I. Isenberg *Scr* John Sayles *Ph* Jan de Bont *Ed* Wendy Greene Bricmont *Mus* Alan Silvestri *Art Dir* Kelly Kimbal
● Daryl Hannah, Pamela Reed, James Remar, Thomas G. Waites, John Doolittle (PSO/Guber-Peters/Jozak/Decade/Jonesfilm)

The Clan of the Cave Bear is a dull, overly genteel rendition of Jean M. Auel's novel. Handsomely produced on rugged Canadian exteriors, this is the story of pre-history's first feminist.

Although set 35,000 years ago, pic could more or less have been set in any time, as it displays little of the anthropological ambition of *Quest for Fire* and is pitched to appeal to the same sensibilities that responded to *The Blue Lagoon*.

Little imagination is in evidence here. A primitive language has been invented for these early humans to speak (subtitles run throughout), but nothing in their customs, habits or attitudes proves very interesting. Daryl Hannah, at least, is a fetching and sympathetic center of attention, but emoting of the entire cast is limited to expressive grunting.
□ 1986: Nomination: Best Makeup

■ **CLARA'S HEART**

1988, 108 MINS, US ◇ ⓥ ⊙
Dir Robert Mulligan *Prod* Martin Elfand *Scr* Mark Medoff *Ph* Freddie Francis *Ed* Sidney Levin *Mus* Dave Grusin *Art Dir* Jeffrey Howard
● Whoopi Goldberg, Michael Ontkean, Kathleen Quinlan, Neil Patrick Harris, Spalding Gray, Beverly Todd (MTM/Warner)

Buoyed by a beautifully measured star turn by Whoopi Goldberg and a smashing screen debut for young Neil Patrick Harris, *Clara's Dream* is a powerful, unabashedly sentimental drama. Adaptation of Joseph Olshan's novel pays attention to the values of a well-wrought character study of a noble Jamaican servant (Goldberg) and the young rich kid (Harris) she guides through adolescent rites of passage.

Goldberg enters Harris' spoiled, uppercrust world in a family mansion outside Baltimore in a roundabout fashion: Harris' weepy mom (Kathleen Quinlan) is vacationing in Jamaica with hubbie (Michael Ontkean), tormented by the death of her infant daughter, when the hotel maid Clara (Goldberg) brings her back to life with doses folk wisdom.

Captured in lush autumnal hues by ace British lenser Freddie Francis, *Clara's Heart* is a beauty to behold, buttressed by a moving, wistful Dave Grusin score. Goldberg's control and strength, including an unwavering Jamaican accent, build cumulatively to deep emotional impact. Support roles are ably filled including the required callousness of Quinlan's and Ontkean's characters.

• •

■ CLASH BY NIGHT

1952, 105 MINS, US 🔊 ⊙
Dir Fritz Lang   *Prod* Harriet Parsons   *Scr* Alfred Hayes, David Dortort   *Ph* Nicholas Musuraca   *Ed* George J. Amy   *Mus* Roy Webb   *Art Dir* Albert S. D'Agostino, Carroll Clark
● Barbara Stanwyck, Paul Douglas, Robert Ryan, Marilyn Monroe, J. Carrol Naish, Keith Andes (Wald-Krasna/RKO)

Clifford Odets' *Clash by Night*, presented on Broadway over a decade earlier, reaches the screen in a rather aimless drama of lust and passion.

Clash captures much of the drabness of the seacoast fishing town, background of the pic, but only occasionally does the narrative's suggested intensity seep through. It is the story of a woman, buffeted by life's realities, who returns to her hometown after 10 years, only to find that the escapism she has sought is still beyond her reach. She marries a fisherman for security reasons, ultimately being forced to choose between two men.

Barbara Stanwyck plays the returning itinerant with her customary defiance and sullenness. It is one of her better performances. Robert Ryan plays the other man with grim brutality while Marilyn Monroe is reduced to what is tantamount to a bit role.

• •

■ CLASH OF THE TITANS

1981, 118 MINS, UK ◇ 🔊 ⊙
Dir Desmond Davis   *Prod* Charles H. Schneer, Ray Harryhausen   *Scr* Beverly Cross   *Ph* Ted Moore   *Ed* Timothy Gee   *Mus* Laurence Rosenthal   *Art Dir* Frank White
● Laurence Olivier, Harry Hamlin, Claire Bloom, Maggie Smith, Burgess Meredith, Ursula Andress (United Artists/M-G-M)

Clash of the Titans is an unbearable bore that will probably put to sleep the few adults stuck taking the kids to it. This mythical tale of Perseus, son of Zeus, and his quest for the 'fair' Andromeda, is mired in a slew of corny dialog and an endless array of flat, outdated special effects.

Watching acclaimed actors like Laurence Olivier, Maggie Smith and Claire Bloom wandering through the clouds in long white gowns as Greek gods is funny enough. But when they start to utter the stylized dialog about what they're going to do to the mortals on the earth below, one wants to look to the Gods for help. But obviously, that's impossible here.

Unfortunately, none of the creatures of

effects that famed expert Ray Harryhausen (who also co-produced) designed seem anything more than rehashes from B-pictures.

Desmond Davis directs with a tired hand, not helped much by the lackadaisical writing.

• •

■ CLASS

1983, 98 MINS, US ◇ 🔊 ⊙
Dir Lewis John Carlino   *Prod* Martin Ransohoff   *Scr* Jim Kouf, David Greenwalt   *Ph* Ric Waite   *Ed* Stuart Pappe, Dennis Dolan   *Mus* Elmer Bernstein   *Art Dir* Jack Poplin
● Rob Lowe, Jacqueline Bisset, Andrew McCarthy, Stuart Margolin, Cliff Robertson, John Cusack (Orion)

Class is anything but classy. About a brainy but virginal prep school student (Andrew McCarthy) who unwittingly begins an affair with his upper-class roommate's sexy mother (Jacqueline Bisset), film seems something like an unofficial remake of one of Bisset's first Hollywood efforts, the 1969 *The First Time*, in which she initiated the nerdy Wes Stern in the pleasures of the flesh. Throw in aspects of *The Graduate*, with the young fellow's best friend, instead of girlfriend, getting mad at the betrayal, and you get the idea.

McCarthy and Rob Lowe (as his roommate) carry most of the picture, and both acquit themselves reasonably well under the circumstances. Lewis John Carlino's direction is frequently awkward notably in the nudity-less sex scenes.

• •

■ CLASS ACTION

1991, 109 MINS, US ◇ 🔊 ⊙
Dir Michael Apted   *Prod* Ted Field, Scott Kroopf, Robert W. Cort,   *Scr* Carolyn Shelby, Christopher Ames, Samantha Shad   *Ph* Conrad Hall   *Ed* Ian Crafford   *Mus* James Horner   *Art Dir* Todd Hallowell
● Gene Hackman, Mary Elizabeth Mastrantonio, Colin Friels, Joanna Merlin, Larry Fishburne, Donald Moffat (20th Century-Fox/Interscope)

Winning performances by Gene Hackman and Mary Elizabeth Mastrantonio and potent direction by Michael Apted pump life into the sturdy courtroom drama formula once again.

Hackman plays Jed Ward, a veteran civil rights lawyer still dedicated to defending the underdog, though his record, both professional and personal, is not without blotches.

Mastrantonio is his daughter Maggie, a ruthlessly effective corporate advocate and ladder-climber, whose disdain for her father has more to do with his amorous indiscretions than his politics.

They wind up on opposite sides of a class action suit filed against an auto company by the maimed survivors of crashes in which the cars exploded on impact.

For the first half, much of the script is by the numbers, as characters deliver plodding dialog to lay out the situation, but things pick up. Viewer sympathy accumulates quickly for Hackman, the charismatic, if flawed, man of the people, but Mastrantonio carves out her own turf and hangs on to it, truly taking on the senior actor.

• •

■ CLASS OF '44

1973, 95 MINS, US ◇ 🔊
Dir Paul Bogart   *Prod* Paul Bogart   *Scr* Herman Raucher   *Ph* Andrew Laszlo   *Ed* Michael A. Hoey   *Mus* David Shire
● Gary Grimes, Jerry Houser, Oliver Conant, William Atherton, Sam Bottoms, Deborah Winters (Warner)

Class of '44 is an okay follow-up to *Summer of '42* [1971], taking the three juveniles of the first film through their early college years at the end of World War II. Paul Bogart's production and direction are slightly better than Herman Raucher's script, in which nostalgia pellets fall like hailstones on an essentially programmer plot.

Encoring in the lead roles are Gary Grimes, Jerry Houser and Oliver Conant, all introduced graduating from high school. Conant joins the Marines and virtually disappears from the plot, leaving Houser and Grimes to head for college. Deborah Winters is Grimes' campus sweetheart, and William Atherton is very good as a fraternity president supervising the hazing of pledges.

• •

■ CLASS OF MISS MACMICHAEL, THE

1978, 100 MINS, UK/US ◇ 🔊
Dir Silvio Narizzano   *Prod* Judd Bernard   *Scr* Judd Bernard   *Ph* Alex Thomason   *Ed* Max Benedict   *Mus* Stanley Myers
● Glenda Jackson, Oliver Reed, Michael Murphy, Rosalind Cash, John Standing, Phil Daniels (Kettledrum/ Brut)

This pic [from the book by Sandy Hutson] is about dippy doings at a special school for unruly teenagers whose next steps may be reformatories. Treading the usual characterizations and situations, film adds a more permissive tone in language and freewheeling sex of the students not to forget the harassed teachers and a scheming head master.

Though predictable, and the script serviceable for this of-treated theme, with direction average, it has Glenda Jackson adding her presence to the part of a dedicated teacher who eschews a second marriage to stay with her impossible charges.

Jackson's dedicated but world weary air gives an edge to her character as she is the rare teacher who gets through to her charges. Michael Murphy's nice guy playing, but with hints of stodginess, make his boyfriend of Jackson role acceptable.

Oliver Reed overcharges his role of the martinet, hypocritical, mean principal who uses a false front to visitors and a mailed fist at the school.

• •

■ CLASS OF 1984

1982, 96 MINS, CANADA ◇ 🔊 ⊙
Dir Mark L. Lester   *Prod* Arthur Kent   *Scr* Tom Holland, John Saxton, Mark L. Lester   *Ph* Albert Dank   *Ed* Howard Kunin   *Mus* Lalo Schifrin
● Perry King, Timothy Van Patten, Merrie Lynn Ross, Roddy McDowall, Al Waxman, Michael J. Fox (Guerrilla High)

Class of 1984 is pure exploitation with plenty of action and a manipulative plot [from a story by Tom Holland] designed to have audiences cheering on the blood.

The Canadian production is set at Abraham Lincoln High School in a large American city. Newcomer music teacher Perry King finds his views on education rapidly altered at the school: students are frisked for weapons, teachers carry guns and the hallways are monitored by guards and cameras.

The chief purveyors of terror are a gang led by Timothy Van Patten. They run a drug and prostitution ring and wield a heavy blow to anyone obstructing their activities.

King refuses to buckle to their strongarm tactics and finds his car first vandalized and later fire-bombed. Walking into a cocaine deal in the school bathroom, King takes Van Patten to the principal, but lack of evidence places the teacher's actions in question.

Performances are generally good with King in fine form as the hard pressed hero while Van Patten is effectively chilling as Stegman.

• •

■ CLASS OF 1999

1990, 98 MINS, US ◇ 🔊
Dir Mark L. Lester   *Prod* Mark L. Lester   *Scr* C. Courtney Joyner   *Ph* Mark Irwin   *Ed* Scott Conrad   *Mus* Michael Hoenig

● Bradley Gregg, Traci Lind, Malcolm McDowell, Stacy Keach, Pam Grier, John P. Ryan (Original/Lightning)

A followup to the 1982 pic *Class of 1984* this violent exploitation film is too pretentious for its own good. Director Mark L. Lester takes a cynical, fake-hip view of young people's future.

The inconsistent screenplay posits high-schoolers out of control. So-called free-fire zones have been set up in urban areas around the schools as no man's land, and are literally under the control of youth gangs.

Hamming it up as an albino megalomaniac, Stacy Keach is carrying out an experiment sending three androids reconverted from army surplus to serve as teachers at Kennedy H.S. in Seattle and whip the students into shape. Simultaneously, hero Bradley Gregg has been let out of jail and returned to class at Kennedy in an experimental furlough program.

John P. Ryan and Pam Grier are loads of fun as the androids, latter mocking her image when not only her breasts but inner works are revealed for the final reel through hokey make-up effects.

■ **CLASS OF NUKE 'EM HIGH**

1986, 81 MINS, US ◇ ⊛
Dir Richard W. Haines, Samuel Weil [= Lloyd Kaufman]
Prod Lloyd Kaufman, Michael Hertz *Scr* Richard W. Haines, Mark Rudmitsky, Lloyd Kaufman, Stuart Strotin
Ph Michael Mayers *Ed* Richard W. Haines
Mus Michael Lattanzi
● Janelle Brady, Gilbert Brenton, Robert Pritchard, R.L. Ryan (TNT/Troma)

Class of Nuke 'Em High is a misguided attempt to extract grossout humor from the very real concerns about nuclear power plants.

Students at Tromaville High School are exposed to nuclear waste from a nearby power plant. Attractive couple Chrissy (Janelle Brady) and Warren (Gilbert Brenton) are exposed to a mild dose of radiation in the form of tainted reefers.

First effect is to cause them to make love at a party. Next day, both go through temporary physical transformations (expanding stomachs and necks), with Chrissy emitting a small, lizardlike creature.

Level of violence is extreme with slapstick overtures that are intended to be funny.

■ **CLASS OF NUKE 'EM HIGH PART II SUBHUMANOID MELTDOWN**

1991, 95 MINS, US ◇ ⊛
Dir Eric Louzil *Prod* Michael Herz, Lloyd Kaufman
Scr Lloyd Kaufman, Eric Louzil, Carl Morano, Marcus Roling, Jeffrey W. Sass, Matt Unger, Andrew Osborne
Ph Ron Chapman *Ed* Gordon Grinberg *Mus* Bob Mithoff *Art Dir* [uncredited]
● Brick Bronsky, Lisa Gaye, Leesa Rowland, Michael Kurtz, Scott Resnick, Shelby Shepard (Troma)

This unwarranted sequel is an incoherent mess that plays more like a trailer than a feature. Director Eric Louzil demonstrates he has no feel for satire or comedy, absolute prerequisites for a Troma pic.

Beefcake star Brick Bronsky narrates a film-long flashback. He's writing for the campus paper at Tromaville Institute of Technology, a combination college/nuclear power plant. Mad scientist Prof. Holt (attractive Lisa Gaye) has created a race of drone subhumanoid workers, including beautiful Victoria (Leesa Rowland). Unfortunately, they are subject to an ailment that causes them to melt into green goo.

An unfunny running gag insists on the subhumanoids having mouths where their belly buttons should be. This is an excuse for plenty of topless footage of starlets, including porn star Trinity Loren.

Lead cast members have trouble reading lines and the dumb sound effects aren't very funny.

■ **CLAUDINE**

1974, 92 MINS, US ◇ ⊛
Dir John Berry *Prod* Hannah Weinstein *Scr* Tina Pine, Lester Pine *Ph* Gayne Rescher *Ed* Luis San Andres
Mus Curtis Mayfield *Art Dir* Ted Haworth
● Diahann Carroll, James Earl Jones, Lawrence Hinton-Jacobs, Tamu, David Kruger, Yvette Curtis (Third World)

Claudine is an outstanding film. A gritty, hearty, heartful and ruggedly tender story of contemporary urban black family life avoiding blaxploitation genre.

Here we have some too-real problems – Diahann Carroll as a 36-year-old mother of six trying to keep a family together without a man around; James Earl Jones as her garbage collector-boyfriend trapped in the immorality of the welfare system which encourages impropriety and discourages decency.

The affair between Carroll and Jones is further complicated by various real problems with her kids. Eldest son Lawrence Hinton-Jacobs is torn apart by maturing black pride; daughter Tamu is experiencing her first adult female impulses; son David Kruger is on the verge of teenage dropout status.
□ 1974: Nomination: Best Actress (Diahann Carroll)

■ **CLEAN AND SOBER**

1988, 124 MINS, US ◇ ⊛ ⊙
Dir Glenn Gordon Caron *Prod* Tony Ganz, Deborah Blum *Scr* Tod Carroll *Ph* Jan Kiesser *Ed* Richard Chew *Mus* Gabriel Yared *Art Dir* Joel Schiller
● Michael Keaton, Kathy Baker, Morgan Freeman, M. Emmet Walsh, Brian Benben, Claudia Christian (Warner)

Covering the first 30 days of attempted recovery by middle-class cocaine addict Michael Keaton, *Sober* is sobering indeed, perhaps too grim.

Keaton carries his heavy load well enough, on screen a vast majority of time as a hotshot real estate executive whose cocaine use has gotten him $92,000 into hock on embezzled company money and into bed with a young girl dying of an overdose.

On the run, Keaton decides to hide out in a recovery hospital, attracted more by its policies of strict confidentiality than any desire for rehabilitation. There, he falls under the strict supervision of ex-junkie Morgan Freeman, which will do him good, but also develops a romantic interest in fellow recovering addict Kathy Baker, who won't.

Sober chooses to focus on the couple's shared attraction for each other (and cocaine), and follows them to a predictable end.

■ **CLEOPATRA**

1934, 102 MINS, US ⊛
Dir Cecil B. DeMille *Prod* Cecil B. DeMille *Scr* Bartlett Cormack, Waldemar Young, Vincent Lawrence
Ph Victor Milner *Ed* Anne Bauchens *Mus* Rudolph Kopp
● Claudette Colbert, Warren William, Henry Wilcoxon, Gertrude Michael, Joseph Schildkraut, Ian Keith (Paramount)

Splendor and intimacy do not blend any more than the traditional oil and water. Each treads on the other's toes. Cecil B. DeMille adds nothing to his directorial rep in this one other than to again demonstrate his rare skill in the handling of mass action.

Another tribute ought to go to C. Aubrey Smith as a soldier in one of the few sincerely written bits. Claudette Colbert's best moment is the death of Cleo. The rest of the time she's a cross between a lady of the evening and a rough soubrette in a country

melodrama. It is not so much her fault as the shortcoming of the scenarists.

In an effort to avoid the blank verse of Shakespeare, from which this story derives, the dialog is made to become colloquial with disastrous results. When Cleopatra stabs a man hiding behind the drapings she explains to Caesar that the eavesdropper was plotting against her life or his. The imperial Julius then strides to the door, throws it open and commands a couple of guards to 'take it away', referring to the body. The blankest of blank verse would have been better. The entire dialog, save for a few moments, is of like calibre.

Warren William, as Caesar, and Henry Wilcoxon, as Antony, play in the drawing room style, and a not too select drawing room at that. Joseph Schildkraut is a fair Herod.
□ 1934: Best Cinematography.
□ Nominations: Best Picture, Editing, Sound, Assistant Director

■ **CLEOPATRA**

1963, 243 MINS, US ◇ ⊛ ⊙
Dir Joseph L. Mankiewicz *Prod* Walter Wanger
Scr Joseph L. Mankiewicz, Ranald MacDougall, Sidney Buchman *Ph* Leon Shamroy *Ed* Dorothy Spencer
Mus Alex North *Art Dir* John DeCuir
● Elizabeth Taylor, Richard Burton, Rex Harrison, Roddy McDowall, Martin Landau, Hume Cronyn (20th Century-Fox)

Cleopatra is not only a supercolossal eye-filler (the unprecedented budget shows in the physical opulence throughout), but it is also a remarkably literate cinematic recreation of an historic epoch.

Director and co-author Joseph L. Mankiewicz and producer Walter Wanger's most stunning achievement is that they have managed to tell a story of such scope and complexity in such comparatively brief terms. The film covers the 18 turbulent years leading to the foundation of the Roman Empire, from Cleopatra's first meeting with Julius Caesar until her death in defeat with Mark Antony. The result is a giant panorama, unequalled in the splendor of its spectacle scenes and, at the same time, surprisingly acute in its more personal story.

This is due not only to the quality and focus of the screenplay, but to the talents of the three leading players. In the title role, one of the most difficult ever written, Elizabeth Taylor is a woman of continuous fascination. Though not fully at ease as the child-queen of the film's first part, she grows as the story progresses to become the mature queen who matches the star's own voluptuous assurance.

Rex Harrison is superb as Caesar, shrewd, vain and wise, formed somewhat in the image of the G.B. Shaw conception, but also unexpectedly ruthless and ambitious. His are the film's most brilliant lines, and something is lost with his assassination, which closes the film's first half.

Richard Burton then comes to the fore in the second half. Oddly he does not seem the romantic figure expected and plot-implied, partly perhaps because as a lover he is visibly overweight. The role is of a man of military competence consumed by envy of Caesar's genius and exposed in the end as self-pitying and drunken by the demands of Cleopatra's needs for a man in a larger sense than boudoir. Ironically some of the weakest moments in the film are the love scenes between Liz and Dickie.

Happily, however, the film sweeps along with a very real sense of time and place, building to a climax that is one of inevitable, tragic relief. Responsible to no little extent is the quality of the 'big' scenes – Cleopatra's triumphant entry into Rome, a dazzling display of color and sound and ancient pageantry; the grandeur of Cleopatra's barge, sailing into Tarsus; the crucial Battle of Actium, recreated on a scale perhaps unmatched in any spectacle.

The long windup of the story has Cleopatra taking longer to die than Camille. That Fox may still excise more footage is likely, and the second half is the place to do it. [The film was cut by 21 minutes very early in its New York run. No scenes were eliminated in their entirety, but cuts were made to shorten scenes and bridges.]

The real star of *Cleopatra*, however, is Mankiewicz, who brought order out of what had been production chaos. As Caesar observes to Cleopatra, early on: 'You have a way of mixing politics and passion'. So does Mankiewicz.
□ 1963: Best Color Cinematography, Color Art Direction, Special Effects, Color Costume Design.
□ Nominations: Best Picture, Actor (Rex Harrison), Editing, Original Music Score

································

■ CLEOPATRA JONES

1973, 89 MINS, US ◇ ⓥ
Dir Jack Starrett   *Prod* William Tennant, Max Julien
Scr Max Julien, Sheldon Keller   *Ph* David Walsh
Ed Allan Jacobs   *Mus* J.J. Johnson, Carl Brandt, Brad Shapiro   *Art Dir* Peter Wooley
● Tamara Dobson, Bernie Casey, Brenda Sykes, Antonio Fargas, Bill McKinney, Shelley Winters (Warner)

Cleopatra Jones is a good programmer with the offbeat twist of having a sexy woman detective as the lead character. The script incorporates a slew of action set pieces, capably directed by Jack Starrett.

Tamara Dobson makes a smart starring debut, after fashion model and teleblurb work, as the title character, a sophisticated undercover agent working to stamp out the world drug trade. But a phony raid on lover Bernie Casey's ghetto halfway house, in which Dobson has a great interest, draws her home to unravel the plot.

Behind Casey's problems, and serving as Dobson's arch-enemy, is Shelley Winters, in a vulgar characterization as a lesbian gangleader. The line between offbeat cameo and repulsive casting is wider than a freeway, but Winters crosses it with felicity.

································

■ CLIFFHANGER

1993, 112 MINS, US ◇ ⓥ ⊙
Dir Renny Harlin   *Prod* Alan Marshall, Renny Harlin
Scr Michael France, Sylvester Stallone   *Ph* Alex Thomson
Ed Frank J. Urioste   *Mus* Trevor Jones   *Art Dir* John Vallone
● Sylvester Stallone, John Lithgow, Michael Rooker, Janine Turner, Rex Linn, Caroline Goodall (Carolco/Canal Plus/Pioneer)

Cliffhanger lives up to its title as a two-hour rollercoaster ride that never stops from first minute to last, a high-octane action suspenser with thrilling vertiginous footage. Director Renny Harlin keeps the adventure in this reputed $65 million production [from a screen story by Michael France, based on a premise by John Long] coming at an astonishing pace.

Nine-minute opening sequence is a heart-stopping stunner. Rocky Mountain Rescue pro Gabe Walker (Sylvester Stallone) has climbed up a needle peak to help rescue the girlfriend of his partner Hal Tucker (Michael Rooker). But the rescue goes awry.

When Gabe returns to Colorado a year later, he's unable to patch things up with his own g.f., Jessie (Janine Turner), and Hal still blames him for causing the accident.

In the next gasp-quality sequence, a private Treasury Dept. jet is hijacked by turncoat T-Man Travers (Rex Linn) and the nefarious Qualen (John Lithgow). But the three suitcases from the haul containing $100 million fall to the ground and the villains make a crash landing on a mountain. Enter Gabe and Hal, who arrive to rescue the group but are promptly captured and forced to lead them through the snowy, icy terrain to the loot.

What really puts this in a class of its own is the verisimilitude of the action. Despite credits to stunt and climbing doubles and the occasional process shot, there is no doubt that Stallone and other actors were really up on the sides of mountains. Although set in Colorado and partly filmed in Durango, most of the picture was lensed in Italy, both near Cortina D'Ampezzo in the Alps and in Rome. Tech contributions throughout are aces.

································

■ CLIVE OF INDIA

1935, 90 MINS, US
Dir Richard Boleslavski   *Scr* W.P. Lipscomb, R.J. Minney
Ph Peverell Marley   *Mus* Alfred Newman
● Ronald Colman, Loretta Young, Colin Clive, Francis Lister, C. Aubrey Smith, Cesar Romero (20th Century/United Artists)

The Black Hole of Calcutta, the battle elephants (with their gargantuan and murderous barbed armor), the famous hindustani monsoons and, of course, the basically courageous warrior, Robert Clive, and his rise from an obscure clerkship with the East India Company – all these elements of fictionized fact and glorified history are recreated here vividly for the screen.

After the first three-quarters of an hour or so, the film plot veers to the personal romantic troubles besetting Clive and Margaret Maskelyne (later Lady Clive), whom he periodically deserts or ignores whenever trouble in the Far East summons him.

Ronald Colman is an excellent Clive sans his familiar mustache. The powdered wigs of the day do their bit in maintaining romantic illusion. Perhaps Loretta Young's spanning of the years is achieved somewhat too idealistically, but changing of the hairdressing with each period authentically gets across the idea of gracefully growing old.

Performances are consistently fine, notably Mischa Auer as the tyrannical native ruler, and Cesar Romero as the ambitious but friendly-to-Britain rival maharajah who double-crosses Auer.

································

■ CLOCK, THE
(UK: Under the Clock)

1945, 90 MINS, US ⓥ
Dir Vincente Minnelli   *Prod* Arthur Freed   *Scr* Robert Nathan, Joseph Schrank   *Ph* George Folsey
Ed George White   *Mus* George Bassman
Art Dir Cedric Gibbons, William Ferrari
● Judy Garland, Robert Walker, James Gleason, Keenan Wynn, Marshall Thompson, Lucille Gleason (M-G-M)

Producer Arthur Freed and director Vincente Minnelli, the combination that scored so heavily with the Judy Garland musical, *Meet Me in St. Louis*, show their versatility in this picture which is straight drama sans any music. It's her first straight dramatic role. The entire story takes place in the 48 hours that Cpl Joe Allen (Walker) is on furlough in NY City.

Minnelli has the knack of getting deep meaning into little footage. For instance, the beanery scene where the jolly inebriate (Keenan Wynn) spouts about life and America. The entire sequence is probably four minutes long, but it is real meat.

Then there's a sequence after the boy and girl get hitched at City Hall. They're sitting in a self-service restaurant and Garland is weeping because of the unattractiveness of the entire ceremony. The camera keeps concentrated on a lone diner, an unbilled character who just sits there and chews away, staring at the embarrassed couple, but not uttering a word. It is memorable humor.

································

■ CLOCKWISE

1986, 97 MINS, UK ◇ ⓥ ⊙
Dir Christopher Morahan   *Prod* Michael Codron
Scr Michael Frayn   *Ph* John Coquillon   *Ed* Peter Boyle
Mus George Fenton   *Art Dir* Roger Murray-Leach
● John Cleese, Alison Steadman, Penelope Wilton, Stephen Moore, Joan Hickson, Sharon Maiden (Thorn EMI/Moment)

Clockwise is a somewhat uneven comic road film. John Cleese plays the headmaster of a secondary school whose main trait, obsessive timewatching, turns out to be a strategy to dam up the natural disarray of his personality.

Film's plot is triggered when Stimpson (Cleese) misses the train for a headmaster's conference over which he has been invited to preside. Immediately panic-struck, he seeks some other way to get to the meeting on time.

The best moments depict his gradually going to pieces as he struggles to complete his journey in the company of an abducted schoolgirl (Sharon Maiden) and former girlfriend (Penelope Wilton).

Clockwise would be a bore were it not for Cleese's comic ability, which derives from broad expressive gesticulations and expressions which mark the simple man still trying to control his world long after he has gone over the edge. Christopher Morahan's direction, in his first feature since the late 1960s, is adequate.

································

■ CLOCKWORK ORANGE, A

1971, 137 MINS, UK ◇ ⓥ
Dir Stanley Kubrick   *Prod* Stanley Kubrick   *Scr* Stanley Kubrick   *Ph* John Alcott   *Ed* Bill Butler   *Mus* Walter Carlos   *Art Dir* John Barry
● Malcolm McDowell, Patrick Magee, Michael Bates, Miriam Carlin, Adrienne Corri, Aubrey Morris (Warner)

A Clockwork Orange is a brilliant nightmare. Stanley Kubrick's film takes the heavy realities of the 'do-your-thing' and 'law-and-order' syndromes, runs them through a cinematic centrifuge, and spews forth the commingled comic horrors of a regulated society. The film employs outrageous vulgarity, stark brutality and some sophisticated comedy to make an opaque argument for the preservation of respect for man's free will – even to do wrong.

Kubrick's screenplay, based on the 1962 Anthony Burgess novel, postulates a society composed of amoral young hedonists, an older generation in retreat behind locked doors, and a political-police government no longer accountable to anyone or to any principles except expediency and tenure.

In this world where youthful gangs control the street by night and disperse by dawn, lives anti-hero and narrator Malcolm McDowell and his sidekicks – Warren Clarke, James Marcus, and Michael Tarn. They have an Orwellian argot not difficult to grasp. Their escapades include beatings, rape and a bizarre murder.

The resolution is ambiguous to say the least. Is McDowell at last the subdued 'Orange' that runs like 'Clockwork' or has human nature begun to heal itself?
□ 1971: Nominations: Best Picture, Director, Adapted Screenplay, Editing

································

■ CLOSE ENCOUNTERS OF THE THIRD KIND

1977, 135 MINS, US ◇ ⓥ ⊙
Dir Steven Spielberg   *Prod* Julia Phillips, Michael Phillips
Scr Steven Spielberg   *Ph* Vilmos Zsigmond, William A. Fraker, Douglas Slocombe, John Alonzo, Laszlo Kovacs
Ed Michael Kahn   *Mus* John Williams   *Art Dir* Joe Alves, Dan Lomino
● Richard Dreyfuss, Francois Truffaut, Teri Garr, Melinda Dillon, Cary Guffey, Bob Balaban (Columbia)

Close Encounters of the Third Kind is a daring film concept which in its special and technical effects has been superbly realized. Steven Spielberg's film climaxes with a confrontation with life forms from another world.

Story involves a series of UFO appearances witnessed by Richard Dreyfuss, Indiana power company technician, and Melinda Dillon and her son Cary Guffey. Concurrent with this plot line are the maneuverings of a seemingly international and secret team of military and scientific personnel.

But there's no denying that the climax is an absolute stunner, literate in plotting, dazzling in execution [special photographic effects by Douglas Trumbull] and almost reverent in tone.

[In 1980 film was replaced by a 132-minute version, re-edited and with extra material. On posters, but not on prints, this was subtitled *The Special Edition*].

☐ 1977: Best Cinematography, Special Achievment Award (sound effects editing).
☐ Nominations: Best Director, Best Supp. Actress (Melinda Dillon), Art Direction, Editing, Original Score, Sound, Special Visual Effects

■ CLOSE MY EYES

1991, 105 MINS, UK ◇ ⓥ
Dir Stephen Poliakoff   *Prod* Therese Pickard
Scr Stephen Poliakoff   *Ph* Witold Stok   *Ed* Michael Parkinson   *Mus* Michael Gibbs   *Art Dir* Luciana Arrighi
● Alan Rickman, Clive Owen, Saskia Reeves, Karl Johnson, Lesley Sharp, Kate Gartside (Film Four/Beambright)

Close My Eyes is a powerful British film about incest, with topflight performances and intense handling of the material by writer-director Stephen Poliakoff.

The early scenes somewhat awkwardly chart the relationship between Natalie (Saskia Reeves) and her younger brother Richard (Clive Owen) over a five-year period. They live in different British cities; one night, Richard stays in his sister's apartment and both sense a new feeling of intimacy between them, though nothing happens.

Five years later, Natalie is married to the wealthy Sinclair (Alan Rickman) and they live in a magnificent house beside the Thames. Natalie visits her brother in his apartment, and the hitherto unspoken passion between them erupts into a sexual encounter.

The central triangular relationship is supported by well-observed and biting scenes involving marginal characters, such as Richard's boss (Karl Johnson), who is quietly dying of AIDS, or the girl (Kate Garside) he picks up to try to get over his passion for Natalie.

Reeves and Owen give brave, strong, unstinting performances. Rickman has his best screen role to date as the pompous but kindly husband.

■ CLOSET LAND

1991, 89 MINS, US ◇ ⓥ
Dir Radha Bharadwaj   *Prod* Janet Meyers   *Scr* Radha Bharadwaj   *Ph* Bill Pope   *Ed* Lisa Churgin   *Mus* Philip Glass (sup.), Richard Einhorn   *Art Dir* Eiko Ishioka
● Madeleine Stowe, Alan Rickman (Imagine)

The highly theatrical *Closet Land*, imaginatively produced on a modest $2.5 million, addresses the horror of political torture. It's a harrowing, focused two-character piece by first-time director Radha Bharadwaj.

Entire thing takes place in a gleaming, stylish, high-tech chamber, with a man (Alan Rickman) trying to break the will of a woman (Madeleine Stowe). Despite the claustrophobic setup, a great deal occurs to hold one's interest.

Rickman as interrogator is no ordinary

brute but a complex, highly civilized man who displays a range of emotions and talents, including the ability to voice-act other people to confuse his blindfolded victim.

Stowe is a physically captivating victim with a fierce attachment to justice. Given a chance early on to escape, she stays and demands an apology. It's a costly error.

Story has Stowe, an author of children's books, dragged from her bed to face a servant of the government (Rickman) who accuses her of peddling subversive ideas to children in the guise of innocent stories. At issue is her work in progress, *Closet Land*, about a little girl whose mother leaves her locked in a closet.

Rickman deserves a great deal of notice for his powerfully controlled, multifaceted performance. Stowe displays some flash and backbone, but not enough to make this a truly engaging match.

■ CLOSE TO EDEN

See: A Stranger Among Us

■ CLOUDED YELLOW, THE

1950, 95 MINS, UK
Dir Ralph Thomas   *Prod* Betty E. Box   *Scr* Janet Green   *Ph* Geoffrey Unsworth   *Ed* Gordon Hales
● Jean Simmons, Trevor Howard, Sonia Dresdel, Kenneth More, Maxwell Reed (Carillon)

Although the plot breaks little new ground, the film grips consistently. Jean Simmons and Trevor Howard make a strong team.

Yarn describes the adventures of an ex-secret service agent who helps an innocent girl to escape from a murder charge. On the theory of setting a thief to catch a thief, Scotland Yard puts another secret agent on his tracks. There follows an exciting chase across England into the dockland area of Liverpool, where the hunted pair are hoping to board a ship for Mexico.

The build-up until the man-hunt begins is done with a nice mixture of humor, sentiment and drama. But once the chase is on, the suspense is sustained solidly.

■ CLUB, THE

1980, 99 MINS, AUSTRALIA ◇ ⓥ
Dir Bruce Beresford   *Prod* Matt Carroll   *Scr* David Williamson   *Ph* Don McAlpine   *Ed* William Anderson   *Mus* Mike Brady   *Art Dir* David Copping
● Jack Thompson, Graham Kennedy, Frank Wilson, Harold Hopkins, John Howard, Alan Cassell (South Australia Film/New South Wales Film)

Based on his play of the same name, David Williamson's screen adaptation opens out the action, but in so doing somehow manages to close down the characters. The plot has to do with a football club and the behind-the-scenes machinations: ruthless powerplays that make what takes place on the field seem relatively tame.

The game in this case is a local aberration, confined to the State of Victoria mostly, called Australian Rules. Actually the game itself plays a background role and director Bruce Beresford has shrewdly kept the thrust of his film in the hands of his main characters.

Williamson's plays have been described as life at the top of your lungs, and *The Club* is no exception; there are few quiet passages.

■ CLUB PARADISE

1986, 104 MINS, US ◇ ⓥ ⊙
Dir Harold Ramis   *Prod* Michael Shamberg   *Scr* Harold Ramis, Brian Doyle-Murray   *Ph* Peter Hannan   *Ed* Marion Rothman   *Mus* David Mansfield   *Art Dir* John Graysmark
● Robin Williams, Peter O'Toole, Rick Moranis, Jimmy Cliff, Twiggy, Adolph Caesar (Warner)

There are enough funny skits in *Club Paradise* to make for a good hour of SCTV, where most of the cast is from, but too few to keep this Club Med satire afloat for 104 minutes.

Screenplay by Harold Ramis (*Ghost Busters*) and Brian Doyle-Murray was originally written with Doyle-Murray's comedian brother, Bill Murray, in mind as the lead.

Murray reportedly was unavailable and Robin Williams was signed to head the cast as a disabled Chicago fireman who uses his insurance settlement to become partners with a reggae musician (Jimmy Cliff) in a seedy Caribbean club they hope to turn into a first-class resort.

Williams can be a terrific actor/comedian, but the spark isn't there. Somehow, Murray might have come up with cleverer ways of getting back at complaining guests (Andrea Martin, Steven Kampmann), nerdy, sex-crazed weaklings (Rick Moranis and Eugene Levy, respectively) and the other expected amalgam of folks.

■ CLUE

1985, 87 MINS, US ◇ ⓥ
Dir Jonathan Lynn   *Prod* Debra Hill   *Scr* Jonathan Lynn   *Ph* Victor J. Kemper   *Ed* David Bretherton, Richard Haines   *Mus* John Morris   *Art Dir* John Lloyd
● Eileen Brennan, Tim Curry, Madeline Kahn, Christopher Lloyd, Lesley Ann Warren, Colleen Camp (Paramount)

Clue is campy, high-styled escapism. In a short 87 minutes that just zip by, the well-known board game's one-dimensional card figures like Professor Plum and others become multi-dimensional personalities with enough wit, neuroses and motives intrigue even the most adept whodunnit solver. [Screen story by co-executive producer John Landis and director Jonathan Lynn.] Film is released with three endings.

Tim Curry plays the loquacious organizer of the evening's murder game, which takes place in a Gothic hilltop mansion in New England in 1954 during a storm (of course).

He sends six individuals a letter providing the incentive to attend dinner at the mansion and when each arrives, assigns them a pseudonym – Professor Plum, Mr Green, Mrs White and so on.

The unlikely assemblage of characters is mostly portrayed by well-known actors and comedians of which Lesley Ann Warren's Miss Scarlet, Martin Mull's Colonel Mustard and Eileen Brennan's Mrs Peacock performances stand out.

Terrific performances also are given by relative unknowns: Michael McKean as Mr Green and Colleen Camp as the French maid, Yvette.

■ CLUNY BROWN

1946, 100 MINS, US
Dir Ernst Lubitsch   *Prod* Ernst Lubitsch   *Scr* Samuel Hoffenstein, Elizabeth Reinhardt   *Ph* Joseph La Shelle   *Ed* Dorothy Spencer   *Mus* Cyril Mockridge   *Art Dir* Lyle R. Wheeler, J. Russell Spencer
● Jennifer Jones, Charles Boyer, Peter Lawford, Reginald Owen, C. Aubrey Smith (20th Century-Fox)

Apart from its whammo entertainment and box-office aspects *Cluny Brown* can be recorded as glamorizing the first of a clan. A lady plumber. And a looker, no less. The kind for whom stopped-up pipes are a pleasure.

Jennifer Jones is the girl, Charles Boyer her anti-Nazi refugee vis-a-vis, Ernst Lubitsch produced and directed. *Cluny* is in the best Lubitsch tradition of subtle, punchy comedy, and his two stars make the most of it. It is a satire on British manners, with bite and relish. The insipidity of a specific family is the mirror through which is reflected Margery Sharp's novel of British pre-war aristocracy and the middle class. None of it is treated seriously of course.

When Cluny isn't cleaning stopped-up pipe she's a maid in the home of the aforementioned aristocrats. The family's bowing acquaintance with world events is confined, for example, to the knowledge that an Austrian named Hitler had written a book, or something.

■ **COAL MINER'S DAUGHTER**

1980, 125 MINS, US ◇ ⊛
Dir Michael Apted *Prod* Bernard Schwartz *Scr* Tom Rickman *Ph* Ralf D. Bode *Ed* Arthur Schmidt *Mus* Owen Bradley *Art Dir* John W. Corso
● Sissy Spacek, Tommy Lee Jones, Beverly D'Angelo, Levon Helm, Phyllis Boyens, Ernest Tubb (Universal)

Coal Miner's Daughter is a thoughtful, endearing film charting the life of singer Loretta Lynn from the depths of poverty in rural Kentucky to her eventual rise to the title of 'queen of country music'. Thanks in large part to superb performances by Sissy Spacek and Tommy Lee Jones, film [based on Lynn's autobiography, with George Vescey] mostly avoids the sudsy atmosphere common to many showbiz tales.

There is seldom a slow moment in the picture, although towards the end short shrift is given to Spacek's bout with drugs, nervous breakdown, marriage troubles and death of her best friend, Beverly D'Angelo, as country singer Patsy Cline.

Both Spacek and D'Angelo deserve a special nod for doing all of their own singing with style and accuracy.
□ 1980: Best Actress (Sissy Spacek).
□ Nominations: Best Picture, Adapted Screenplay, Cinematography, Art Direction, Editing, Sound

■ **COBRA**

1986, 87 MINS, US ◇ ⊛ ⊙
Dir George Pan Cosmatos *Prod* Menahem Golan, Yoram Globus *Scr* Sylvester Stallone *Ph* Ric Waite *Ed* Don Zimmerman *Mus* Sylvester Levay *Art Dir* Bill Kenney
● Sylvester Stallone, Brigitte Nielsen, Reni Santoni, Andrew Robinson, Lee Garlington, John Herzfeld (Cannon)

Cobra is a sleek, extremely violent and exciting police thriller.

Sylvester Stallone is cast as unconventional cop Marion Cobretti, nickname Cobra, who with partner Gonzales (Reni Santoni) works the LA zombie squad, doing jobs no other cops will do. They're called in to track down a serial killer who's claimed 16 victims in a month. They protect the one surviving witness, a beautiful model (Brigitte Nielsen) and discover that the killer is actually a neo-fascist army of killers.

Director George Pan Cosmatos tightens the screws for a very fast ride. His low-key personality defined by his funny throwaway lines of dialog, Stallone's Cobra is a far more ingratiating character than his recent Rocky and Rambo guises.

■ **COBRA WOMAN**

1944, 70 MINS, US ◇
Dir Robert Siodmak *Prod* George Waggner *Scr* Gene Lewis, Richard Brooks *Ph* George Robinson, W. Howard Greene *Ed* Charles Maynard *Mus* Edward Ward *Art Dir* John B. Goodman, Alexander Golitzen
● Maria Montez, Jon Hall, Sabu, Lon Chaney (Universal)

Cobra Woman is a super-fantastic melodrama backgrounded on a mythical island that might exist somewhere in the Indian Ocean. Elaborately and colorfully mounted for constant eye-appeal, and with the starring trio of Maria Montez, Jon Hall and Sabu, picture unfolds at fast pace to concentrate on action features of the tale.

Plot combines jungle-island romance with melodramatic complications, temple rituals, chases and fights. Montez is kidnapped on eve of wedding to Hall and carried back to an island where her twin sister rules ruthlessly as high priestess and preys on religious superstitions of the natives to keep latter under control. Hall follows his betrothed to the forbidden island, accompanied by native boy (Sabu) to rescue Montez.

Montez is decidedly shapely as sarong-draped native girl and dazzlingly gowned as the high priestess. She handles the dual assignment very well. Hall and Sabu are typed in regular characterizations.

■ **COBWEB, THE**

1955, 122 MINS, US ◇ ⊙
Dir Vincente Minnelli *Prod* John Houseman *Scr* John Paxton, William Gibson *Ph* George Folsey *Ed* Harold F. Kress *Mus* Leonard Rosenman
● Richard Widmark, Lauren Bacall, Charles Boyer, Gloria Grahame, Lillian Gish, John Kerr (M-G-M)

The neuroses of the staff and patients in a psychiatric clinic serve for drama in this filmization of William Gibson's novel, *The Cobweb*.

The screenplay gives a wordy account of the controversy developed around the hanging of a new set of drapes in the clinic's library, and the reactions of staff and patients sometime make wonder if identities should not be reversed. Gloria Grahame, the neglected wife of Richard Widmark, top doc at the clinic, wants to select the drapes. Lillian Gish waspish old maid who directs the clinic's business affairs, wants to use cheap muslin to save money. Widmark wants John Kerr, young patient with a suicide complex, to design the drapes.

Screen newcomers Kerr and Susan Strasberg, fellow patient, are responsible for one of the few touching sequences in the film – the simple act of his looking after her on a trip to a film theater has a great deal of heart, an ingredient generally lacking in the footage.

■ **COCKTAIL**

1988, 104 MINS, US ◇ ⊛ ⊙
Dir Roger Donaldson *Prod* Ted Field, Robert W. Cort *Scr* Heywood Gould *Ph* Dean Semler *Ed* Neil Travis *Mus* J. Peter Robinson *Art Dir* Mel Bourne
● Tom Cruise, Bryan Brown, Elisabeth Shue, Lisa Banes, Laurence Luckinbill, Kelly Lynch (Touchstone/Interscope)

Heywood Gould's script, based upon his book inspired by some years as a New York bartender, contains nary a surprise, as Tom Cruise hits Manhattan after a hitch in the army and immediately catches on as the hottest thing the uptown girls have seen a saloon in years.

Under the tutelage of old pro Bryan Brown, Cruise learns every trick in the book, and the pair soon move to the club scene downtown, where Cruise becomes poetaster to the too-hip crowd in addition to taking his pick of trendy ladies.

In Jamaica, Brown goads his buddy into setting his sights on one of the many women with big bucks who patronize the resort, which gets Cruise into trouble with the girl he's becoming sweet on (Elisabeth Shue).

Under Roger Donaldson' impeccably slick direction, film continually plays on Cruise's attractiveness, as women make googoo eyes at him throughout as he does his juggling act with liquor bottles, serves up drinks like a disco dancer and charms his way through every situation.

■ **COCOANUTS, THE**

1929, 90 MINS, US ⊛
Dir Robert Florey, Joseph Santley *Prod* Walter Wanger *Scr* Morrie Ryskind *Ph* George Folsey *Ed* Barney Rogan *Mus* Frank Tours (dir)
● Groucho Marx, Harpo Marx, Chico Marx, Zeppo Marx, Mary Eaton, Oscar Shaw (Paramount)

Here is a musical talker, with the musical background, music, songs and girls, taken from the [1925] Broadway stage success [by George S. Kaufman and Morrie Ryskind] with the Marxes.

Cocoanuts is set in a Florida development hotel barren of guests. Groucho is the fast-thinking and talking boniface. A couple of slickers, girls, bathing beach, etc, some undressing but no s.a.

Groucho is always around and talking as he did in the stage show. Harpo does his work with craftsmanship. Chico has more of the comedy end than usually falls to this foil. Zeppo has to be straight here all of the while.

Only Irving Berlin song of merit is the theme number, 'When Our Dreams Come True', good enough musically but as trite in idea as the title suggests.

■ **COCOON**

1985, 117 MINS, US ◇ ⊛ ⊙
Dir Ron Howard *Prod* Richard D. Zanuck, David Brown, Lili Fini Zanuck *Scr* Tom Benedek *Ph* Don Peterman *Ed* Daniel Hanley, Michael J. Hill *Mus* James Horner *Art Dir* Jack T. Collis
● Don Ameche, Wilford Brimley, Hume Cronyn, Brian Dennehy, Jack Gilford, Steve Guttenberg (20th Century-Fox/Zanuck-Brown)

A fountain of youth fable [from a novel by David Saperstein] which imaginatively melds galaxy fantasy with the lives of aging mortals in a Florida retirement home, *Cocoon* weaves a mesmerizing tale.

Film inventively taps a wellspring of universal desire: health and youth, a parable set, in this case, among a pallid group of denizens shuffleboarding their twilight days away until a mysterious quartet of normal-looking visitors shows up on their Floridian shores. They are arrivals from another galaxy, led by friendly Brian Dennehy and attractive Tahnee Welch (Raquel's daughter, in her first US film). Another nearly-silent member of the party is a debuting Tyrone Power Jr.

Dennehy hires a young, out-of-pocket charter boat skipper (engagingly played by Steve Guttenberg) for a plan to scuba dive for what appear to be weird, gigantic oyster shells. Dennehy rents an abandoned estate with a big indoor pool and rests the big pods in the pool's bottom.

Effectively intercut with these scenes is the life of the tight circle of nearby retirees, three of whom, played by Don Ameche, Wilford Brimley and Hume Cronyn, one day discover the cocoon-like shells and after a frolic in the water are soon diving in like 18-year-olds.

The effect of rejuvenation on the gray people, the inevitable mania when the whole retirement hospital wants in on the public bath, and the effect of this on the plans of the visitors from outer space propel the feature toward a suspenseful, ironic conclusion.
□ 1985: Best Supp. Actor (Don Ameche), Visual Effects

■ **COCOON: THE RETURN**

1988, 116 MINS, US ◇ ⊛ ⊙
Dir Daniel Petrie *Prod* Richard D. Zanuck, David Brown, Lili Fini Zanuck *Scr* Stephen McPherson *Ph* Tak Fujimoto *Ed* Mark Roy Warner *Mus* James Horner *Art Dir* Lawrence G. Paull
● Don Ameche, Wilford Brimley, Hume Cronyn, Steve Guttenberg, Maureen Stapleton, Jessica Tandy (Zanuck-Brown/20th Century-Fox)

Not altogether charmless, *Cocoon: The Return* still is far less enjoyable a senior folks' fantasy than *Cocoon*. An overdose of bathos weighs down the sprightliness of the characters, resulting in a more maudlin than magic effort.

Quandary begins with the return to St Petersburg, Fla, of the plucky group lead by the twinkle-eyed Don Ameche for a four-day visit from the utopian extra-terrestrial world of Antarea. Upon being reunited with family and friends, each questions his own choice for leaving in the first place and, at the end of the picture, the rationale for either returning to space or remaining on terra firma.

Jack Gilford as irascible widower Bernie Lefkowitz and Steve Guttenberg as Jack, the glass-bottom boat tour guide cum shlocky seashell merchandise salesman, keep this overly sappy production afloat.

Ameche, Gwen Verdon and occasionally Hume Cronyn want to play funny and loose but are restrained by Daniel Petrie's direction, which too often is unfocused.

■ **CODE OF SILENCE**

1985, 101 MINS, US ◇ ⓥ ⊙
Dir Andrew Davis *Prod* Raymond Wagner
Scr Michael Butler, Dennis Shryack, Mike Gray
Ph Frank Tidy *Ed* Peter Parasheles, Christopher Holmes
Mus David Frank *Art Dir* Maher Ahmed
● Chuck Norris, Henry Silva, Bert Remsen, Molly Hagan, Joseph Guzaldo, Mike Genovese (Orion)

With 27 stuntmen and Chuck Norris in the credits, *Code of Silence* is a predictability cacophonous cops-and-crooks yarn [by Michael Butler and Dennis Shryack] that is actually quite good for the type.

The best thing about Norris is he never gets involved in all that romance stuff. Granted, there's a pretty girl (Molly Hagan) whose life is at stake, but Norris never does more than hold her hand, lend his brawny chest for her to cry on, and – finally in a fit of passion – kiss her on the forehead.

Norris plays a police sergeant leading a raid on a drug den, who arrives a step behind another gang which gets away with all the dope and money, leaving a bloody mess behind. This sets off a gang war between forces led by properly menacing Henry Silva on one side and less prominent Mike Genovese on the other.

■ **COFFY**

1973, 91 MINS, US ◇ ⓥ ⊙
Dir Jack Hill *Prod* Robert A. Papazian *Scr* Jack Hill
Ph Paul Lohmann *Ed* Charles McClelland *Mus* Roy Ayers *Art Dir* Perry Ferguson
● Pam Grier, Booker Bradshaw, Robert DoQui, William Elliott, Allan Arbus, Sid Haig (American International)

Coffy is the story of a black tart, vengeance-minded, who sets out to kill everyone she holds responsible for her 11-year-old sister losing her mind by the dope habit. She blasts her victims, most of them lured into sex, with a shotgun that never misses.

Jack Hill, who wrote and directs with an action-atuned hand, inserts plenty of realism in footage in which Pam Grier in title role ably acquits herself. She takes on her prey, including pushers, crooked cops and politicians, pimps gangsters et al, with a ferocity which builds into often-suspenseful sequence.

Grier, a statuesque actress with a body she doesn't hesitate to show, is strongly cast. Booker Bradshaw as a city politician and William Elliott as an honest cop score well.

■ **COLD HEAVEN**

1992, 105 MINS, US ◇ ⓥ ⊙
Dir Nicolas Roeg *Prod* Allan Scott, Jonathan D. Krane
Scr Allan Scott *Ph* Francis Kenny *Ed* Tony Lawson
Mus Stanley Myers *Art Dir* Steven Legler
● Theresa Russell, Mark Harmon, James Russo, Talia Shire, Will Patton (MCEG)

Infidelity has seldom offered as broad a canvas for torment and religious guilt as in Nicolas Roeg's *Cold Heaven*, a tortured study of love on the rocks that comes off like a jumbled bad dream.

Theresa Russell stars as the restless wife of an unsuspecting surgeon (Mark Harmon). She gets involved with another doctor (James Russo) and plans to break things off with her husband during a Mexican business trip. Before she can do the deed, however, he's killed in a horrifying but oddly convenient boating accident. Or is he? Back home, the distraught wife gets a mysterious note requesting her presence in the cliffside hamlet of Carmel, at the same hotel where her infidelity began.

Intention of Brian Moore's novel on which *Cold Heaven* is based was apparently to make the surgeon's pseudo-death a metaphor for the emotional effect of his wife's betrayal. But the connection is all buried in the film.

Russell, under husband Roeg's direction, does terrific work in her scene with a priest (Will Patton), but she and Harmon have a tough and thankless task in playing out this tormenting psychodrama.

■ **COLDITZ STORY, THE**

1955, 97 MINS, UK ⓥ
Dir Guy Hamilton *Prod* Ivan Foxwell *Scr* Guy Hamilton, Ivan Foxwell, William Douglas Home
Ph Gordon Dines *Ed* Peter Mayhew *Mus* Francis Chagrin *Art Dir* Alex Vetchinsky
● John Mills, Eric Portman, Christopher Rhodes, Lionel Jeffries, Bryan Forbes, Ian Carmichael (Foxwell/British Lion)

Easily one of the best prisoner-of-war yarns to come from any British studio, *The Colditz Story* is a taut real-life meller, based on the personal experiences of the author, Pat Reid.

Colditz Castle, in the heart of Saxony, was the fortress to which the German High Command sent officers who had attempted to escape from conventional prison camps. They regarded it as impregnable although they threatened the death penalty for anyone attempting to break out.

Film is loaded with meaty suspense situations and neatly leavened with good-natured humor to strike an excellent balance between the grim and the natural. The all-male cast keeps the yarn rolling at a lively pace.

Eric Portman turns in a distinguished performance as the British colonel.

■ **COLD ROOM, THE**

1984, 92 MINS, UK ◇ ⓥ
Dir James Dearden *Prod* Mark Forstater *Scr* James Dearden *Ph* Tony Pierce-Roberts *Ed* Mick Audley
Mus Michael Nyman *Art Dir* Tim Hutchinson
● George Segal, Amanda Pays, Renee Soutendijk, Warren Clarke, Anthony Higgins, Ursula Howells (Jethro)

The Cold Room, a modestly intriguing psychological thriller, marks the feature debut (after a couple of interesting shorts) of director James Dearden. It's a very confident first feature, intelligently directed and always interesting to look at.

Story centers around an attractive if sulky British teenager (Amanda Pays), who joins her father (George Segal) for a vacation in (of all places) East Berlin.

Spending time in her tiny room in an old-fashioned hotel, she gradually comes under the spell of another girl who lived in the same house during the war.

Segal is relaxed as the baffled father who can't get through to his daughter and fears she may be going insane. Pays is a find as the possessed girl, but Dutch actress Renee Soutendijk has almost nothing to do as Segal's girlfriend.

■ **COLD WIND IN AUGUST, A**

1961, 79 MINS, US
Dir Alexander Singer *Prod* Phillip Hazelton *Scr* Burton Wohl *Ph* Floyd Crosby *Ed* Jerry Young *Mus* Gerald Fried
● Lola Albright, Scott Marlowe, Herschel Bernardi, Joe De Santis, Clark Gordon, Janet Brandt (United Artists/ Troy)

No matter how well Vladimir Horowitz might play 'Chopsticks', it would still be 'Chopsticks'. By roughly the same token, all the exceptional ability that went into *A Cold Wind in August* is levelled to the common denominator of its subject – a short course in the seduction, care and feeding of a healthy 17-year-old boy by a nymphomaniacal 28-year-old stripper. This is a hormone opera of considerable quality.

Burton Wohl's screenplay, from his novel, plants the handsome super's son (Scott Marlowe) in the flashy upstairs apartment of a sultry body-goddess (Lola Albright) who is on a kind of annual three-month vacation in respectable anonymity from the questionable life she leads the other nine. Passion matures into love, but the romance goes ker-plop for the lad when he discovers she is not the madonna he naively believed her to be.

Director Alexander Singer has endowed his picture with a blunt and powerful realism. His actors seem perfectly at home in the NY environment.

Another factor in the film's visual impact is the extraordinarily active, inventive camerawork by Floyd Crosby. There is a strip scene (Albright as object) that rivals in sensuality any strip scene ever put on non-stag celluloid – darting images of undulating sections of Albright's partially exposed and admirable epidermis formation.

■ **COLLECTOR, THE**

1965, 117 MINS, US ◇ ⓥ ⊙
Dir William Wyler *Prod* William Wyler, Jud Kinberg, John Kohn *Scr* Stanley Mann, John Kohn *Ph* Robert L. Surtees, Robert Krasker *Ed* Robert Swink *Mus* Maurice Jarre *Art Dir* John Stoll
● Terence Stamp, Samantha Eggar, Maurice Dallimore, Mona Washbourne (Columbia)

William Wyler undertakes a vastly difficult assignment, and carries it off with rare artistry, in bringing to the screen a solid, suspenseful enactment of John Fowles' best-selling novel.

As a character study of two persons – an inferiority-ridden young Englishman with an uncontrollable sex obsession and the young woman he abducts and holds prisoner in the cellar of his secluded farmhouse – the feature is adroitly developed and bears the stamp of class.

Color photography frequently is stunning, always of high quality, picture opening on a visually beautiful note as the leading male character (Terence Stamp) is introduced as a butterfly collector. The screenplay expands on this premise; he broadens his collecting to girls. He falls in love with a young art student, and has an uncontrollable desire to force her to reciprocate his feelings.

Both Stamp and Samantha Eggar turn in remarkably restrained performances under Wyler's guiding dramatic helmsmanship. Stamp makes his character of an insignificant London bank clerk entirely believable and carefully shades his characterization.

□ 1965: Nominations: Best Director, Actress (Samantha Eggar), Adapted Screenplay

■ **COLOR OF MONEY, THE**

1986, 119 MINS, US ◇ ⓥ ⊙
Dir Martin Scorsese *Prod* Irving Axelrad, Barbara De Fina *Scr* Richard Price *Ph* Michael Ballhaus
Ed Thelma Schoonmaker *Mus* Robbie Robertson

Art Dir Boris Leven
● Paul Newman, Tom Cruise, Mary Elizabeth Mastrantonio, Helen Shaver, John Turturro, Bill Cobbs (Touchstone)

The Color of Money is another inside look at society's outsiders from director Martin Scorsese. This time out it's the subculture of professional pool hustlers that consumes the screen with a keenly observed and immaculately crafted vision of the raw side of life. Pic has a distinctive pulse of its own with exceptional performances by Paul Newman and Tom Cruise.

Based on a reworking of Walter Tevis' novel by scripter Richard Price, *The Color of Money* is a continuation of the 1961 film, *The Hustler*, 25 years later.

Back as Fast Eddie Felson, Paul Newman is a self-proclaimed 'student of human moves' – a hustler. When he happens on Vincent Lauria (Tom Cruise) in a nondescript midwest pool hall, Eddie's juices start flowing and the endless cycle starts again.

As Vincent's girlfriend Carmen, Mary Elizabeth Mastrantonio is working on her own short fuse and is learning how to use her main talent too – her sexuality. It's a hot and disturbing performance as her actions contradict her choirgirl good looks.
□ 1986: Best Actor (Paul Newman).
□ Nominations: Best Supp. Actress (Mary Elizabeth Mastrantonio), Adapted Screenplay, Art Direction

• •

■ COLOR PURPLE, THE

1985, 152 MINS, US ◇ ⓥ ⊙
Dir Steven Spielberg   *Prod* Steven Spielberg, Kathleen Kennedy, Frank Marshall,   *Scr* Menno Meyjes   *Ph* Allen Daviau   *Ed* Michael Kahn   *Mus* Quincy Jones   *Art Dir* J. Michael Riva
● Danny Glover, Whoopi Goldberg, Margaret Avery, Oprah Winfrey, Willard Pugh, Akosua Busia (Amblin/Warner)

There are some great scenes and great performances in *The Color Purple*, but it is not a great film. Steven Spielberg's turn at 'serious' filmmaking is marred in more than one place by overblown production that threatens to drown in its own emotions. But the characters created in Alice Walker's novel are so vivid that even this doesn't kill them off and there is still much to applaud (and cry about) here.

Walker' tale is the story of a black family's growth and flowering over a 40-year period in the south starting around 1909. At the center of everything is Celie, who as a young girl gives birth to two children and is then married into a life of virtual servitude to a man she can refer to only as Mr (Danny Glover).

Above all *The Color Purple* is a love story between Celie and her sister, Nettie, from whom she is separated at childhood, and, later in life, the blues singer Shug Avery.

Saving grace of the film are the performances. As the adult Celie debuting Whoopi Goldberg uses her expressive face and joyous smile to register the character's growth. Equally good is Glover who is a powerful screen presence.
□ 1985: Nominations: Best Picture, Actress (Whoopi Goldberg), Supp. Actress (Margaret Avery, Oprah Winfrey), Adapted Screenplay, Cinematography, Costume Design, Art Direction, Original Score, Song ('Miss Celie's Blues'), Make-Up

• •

■ COLORS

1988, 120 MINS, US ◇ ⓥ ⊙
Dir Dennis Hopper   *Prod* Robert H. Solo   *Scr* Michael Schiffer   *Ph* Haskell Wexler   *Ed* Robert Estrin   *Mus* Herbie Hancock   *Art Dir* Ron Foreman
● Sean Penn, Robert Duvall, Maria Conchita Alonso, Randy Brooks, Grand Bush (Orion)

Colors is a solidly crafted depiction of some current big-city horrors and succeeds largely because of the Robert Duvall-Sean Penn teaming as frontline cops. They're terrific together as members of the gang crime division of the LAPD.

Filmmakers alert the uninitiated right off that theirs is a tale [story by Michael Schiffer and Richard DiLello] of unequal odds, pointing out that 600 street gangs roam America's second-largest city while local and county police directly assigned to the problem number only 250.

Drawn into this fracas is officer Bob Hodges (Duvall), married, the father of three, who's inexplicably been forced back into the action. He's savvy about his dealings with punks in 'bozoland', as Hodges calls the streets, and is unhappy about getting greenhorn Danny McGavin (Penn) as his sidekick.

Latter is a highly strung and cocksure volunteer. He not only busts them with bravado but roughs 'em up out there.

Plot takes Duvall and Penn through investigation of the latest offing of a 'Blood' gang-member by the rival 'Crips' and shows the police frustrations in working the case against nearly insurmountable obstacles. While nicely avoiding the feel of a docu, film seems to effective capture the gang 'culture'.

• •

■ COLOSSUS OF NEW YORK, THE

1958, 70 MINS, US
Dir Eugene Lourie   *Prod* William Alland   *Scr* Thelma Schnee   *Ph* John F. Warren   *Ed* Floyd Knudtson   *Mus* Van Cleave   *Art Dir* Hal Pereira, John Goodman
● Ross Martin, Mala Powers, Charles Herbert, Otto Kruger, John Baragrey, Ed Wolff (Paramount)

The Willis Goldbeck story, screenplayed by Thelma Schnee, is pretty hokey fare. The piece de resistance is surgeon Otto Kruger's transplant of a dead man's brain into the body of a mechanical monster.

Brain, incidentally, is that of Kruger's scientist-son Ross Martin who died in an accident. His father felt that Martin's death shouldn't end his services to mankind – hence the transplantation. But lacking a soul, the mechanical man refuses to follow instructions and goes on a rampage until subdued by moppet Charles Herbert who is Martin's son.

The story, direction and performances are just about as mechanical as the monster.

Either economy or perhaps the studio musicians' strike may have accounted for the Van Cleave novel score, played solely by a piano. It proves a lotta mood can be generated by one instrument.

• •

■ COMA

1978, 113 MINS, US ◇ ⓥ ⊙
Dir Michael Crichton   *Prod* Martin Erlichman   *Scr* Michael Crichton   *Ph* Victor J. Kemper, Gerald Hirschfeld   *Ed* David Bretherton   *Mus* Jerry Goldsmith   *Art Dir* Albert Brenner
● Genevieve Bujold, Michael Douglas, Elizabeth Ashley, Rip Torn, Richard Widmark, Lois Chiles (M-G-M)

Coma is an extremely entertaining suspense drama in the Hitchcock tradition. Director-adapter Michael Crichton neatly builds mystery and empathy around star Genevieve Bujold, a doctor who grows to suspect her superiors of deliberate surgical error. Michael Douglas also stars as her disbelieving lover.

Robin Cook's novel is adapted by Crichton into a smartly-paced tale which combines traditional Hitchcock elements with contemporary personal relationships. Thus Bujold and Douglas wrestle in sub-plot with separate identity and mutual romantic problems while she becomes the innocent enmeshed in suspicious medical wrongdoing. When lifelong friend Lois Chiles goes into permanent coma during an otherwise routine operation, Bujold begins probing a series of similar incidents.

Arrayed against her are hospital superiors Richard Widmark and Rip Torn, and even Douglas himself. Lance Le Gault is a hired killer whom Bujold outwits to the relief of the entire audience.

Elizabeth Ashley is notable as the head of a dubious medical experimental centre where the comatose victims vegetate pending ghoulish, but all-too-plausible disposition.

• •

■ COMANCHEROS, THE

1961, 107 MINS, US ◇ ⓥ
Dir Michael Curtiz   *Prod* George Sherman   *Scr* James Edward Grant, Clair Huffaker   *Ph* William H. Clothier   *Ed* Louis Loeffler   *Mus* Elmer Bernstein   *Art Dir* Jack Martin Smith, Alfred Ybarra
● John Wayne, Stuart Whitman, Ina Balin, Nehemiah Persoff, Lee Marvin, Michael Ansara (20th Century-Fox)

The Comancheros is a big, brash, uninhibited action-western of the old school about as subtle as a right to the jaw.

The screenplay, based on the novel by Paul I. Wellman, is a kind of cloak-and-dagger yarn on horseback. It is set against the Texas of the mid-19th century, a troubled time prior to its statehood when the Comanches were on the warpath and renegade white men, or 'Comancheros', were aiding the Indian cause with fighting equipment. The film relates the story of a Texas Ranger (John Wayne) and an itinerant gambler (Stuart Whitman) who team up to detect and destroy the renegade, parasitic society.

Wayne is obviously comfortable in a role tailor-made to the specifications of his easy-going, square-shooting, tight-lipped but watch-out-when-I'm-mad screen personality. Lee Marvin makes a vivid impression in a brief, but colorful, role as a half-scalped, vile-tempered Comanchero agent.

Director Michael Curtiz was fortunate in having aboard some excellent stuntmen whose hard falls, leaps and maneuvers during the raid and battle sequences (directed by Cliff Lyons) are something to see.

Cameraman William H. Clothier's sweeping panoramic views of the Moab, Utah site are something to behold.

• •

■ COMANCHE STATION

1960, 74 MINS, US ◇
Dir Budd Boetticher   *Prod* Budd Boetticher   *Scr* Burt Kennedy   *Ph* Charles Lawton Jr   *Ed* Edwin Bryant   *Mus* Mischa Bakaleinikoff   *Art Dir* Carl Anderson
● Randolph Scott, Nancy Gates, Claude Akins, Skip Homeier, Richard Rust, Rand Brooks (Ranown/Columbia)

Comanche Station is by any standard a good picture. The screenplay by Burt Kennedy is true to western traditions and at the same time there is romance, although not a conventional love story, and criminal elements for suspense, mystery and excitement. Kennedy does not rely on casting for characterization. The dialog is sparse, but colourful, and humor is not neglected.

Randolph Scott plays one of those loners of the old West, who is bringing back to her husband a settler's wife (Nancy Gates) who has been captured by Comanches. Accompanying them are a trio of bad ones, Claude Akins, Skip Homeier and Richard Rust. Jeopardy is compounded from without by Comanches trailing the group.

All of this is resolved with neat, but not pat, solutions. The characters are vivid and Budd Boetticher's direction of his good cast keeps interest high. It is obvious that Gates' Indian captors have, as the saying goes, had their way with her. The issue is not dodged.

Scott gives a characteristically stolid but convincing performance. Gates is satisfactory as the story's focal point.

Charles Lawton Jr's camera catches some

superb exteriors (there are no interior scenes at all) on the rugged location, and creates some striking personal compositions.

■ **COME BACK CHARLESTON BLUE**

1972, 100 MINS, US ◇ ⓦ
Dir Mark Warren *Prod* Samuel Goldwyn Jr
Scr Bontche Schweig, Peggy Elliott *Ph* Dick Kratina
Ed Gerald Greenberg, George Bowers *Mus* Donny Hathaway *Art Dir* Robert Gundlach
● Godfrey Cambridge, Raymond St Jacques, Peter De Anda, Percy Rodrigues, Jonelle Allen, Maxwell Glanville (Warner/Goldwyn)

Come Back Charleston Blue is an okay followup [from the novel *The Heat's On* by Chester Himes] by producer Samuel Goldwyn Jr to his successful 1970 *Cotton Comes to Harlem*, again featuring Godfrey Cambridge and Raymond St Jacques as offbeat, comedic Harlem gumshoes.

Cambridge and St Jacques find themselves caught between fading black drug king and mobster Maxwell Glanville, and Peter De Anda, ostensibly a successful photographer out to rid Harlem of drugs, but in reality eyeing the area for himself.

De Anda creates the impression that a series of gangland deaths has been caused by the ghost of Charleston Blue, a Depression-era hood, long dead.

The film lacks punch. The gags just don't quite add up to solid laughs or excitement.

■ **COME BACK, LITTLE SHEBA**

1952, 95 MINS, US ⓦ ⊙
Dir Daniel Mann *Prod* Hal B. Wallis *Scr* Ketti Frings
Ph James Wong Howe *Ed* Warren Low *Mus* Franz Waxman *Art Dir* Hal Pereira, Henry Bumstead
● Burt Lancaster, Shirley Booth, Terry Moore, Richard Jaeckel, Philip Ober (Paramount)

The Broadway legit success, *Come Back, Little Sheba*, has become a potent piece of screen entertainment. The production is faithful to the William Inge play.

Shirley Booth has the remarkable gift of never appearing to be acting. Opposite her is Burt Lancaster, bringing an unsuspected talent to his role of the middle-aged, alcoholic husband.

The story interest centers on the somewhat dull, middle-aged and middle-class husband and wife portrayed by Lancaster and Booth. She is a frowzy talkative, earnestly pleasant woman continually living in the past, while he is a man almost beaten by life and a great thirst. Their stoogy, routine existence is brightened one day when a student boarder (Terry Moore) rents a room in their home.

Her cheery, comely presence gives the couple renewed interest, but also brings about the film's climactic punch when Lancaster's fondness for her is jolted by believing the girl is going too far in an affair with another student and amateur romeo (Richard Jaeckel).
□ 1952: Best Actress (Shirley Booth).
□ Nominations: Best Supp. Actress (Terry Moore), Editing

■ **COME BACK TO THE 5 & DIME JIMMY DEAN, JIMMY DEAN**

1982, 109 MINS, US ◇ ⓦ ⊙
Dir Robert Altman *Prod* Scott Bushnell *Scr* Ed Graczyk
Ph Pierre Mignot *Ed* Jason Rosenfield *Art Dir* David Cropman
● Sandy Dennis, Cher, Karen Black, Sudie Bond, Marta Heflin, Kathy Bates (Sandcastle 5)

Story is set in a small Texas town in 1975. Five women, who were part of a James Dean fan club, hold a 20th anniversary reunion, in the local Woolworth 5 and Dime. Sandy Dennis and Cher play characters who remained in the town and at the outset are anx-

ious about which of the old crowd will appear.

Robert Altman had previously directed the story on Broadway with the same cast. However, while the location remains the area of the store, the action is far from claustrophobic.

The action occurs on two levels with incidents of the reunion run parallel to events of 20 years earlier. Altman uses a wall-length mirror to effect the time changes.

The women arrive and each offers her memories of the earlier time. The recollections are at first, comical and innocent but eventually the characters reveal their most painful secrets. The material is told with great emotion and Altman gets wonderful performances from his female ensemble.

■ **COME BLOW YOUR HORN**

1963, 112 MINS, US ◇ ⓦ
Dir Bud Yorkin *Prod* Norman Lear, Bud Yorkin
Scr Norman Lear *Ph* William H. Daniels *Ed* Frank P. Keller *Mus* Nelson Riddle *Art Dir* Hal Pereira, Roland Anderson
● Frank Sinatra, Lee J. Cobb, Molly Picon, Barbara Rush, Jill St John, Tony Bill (Paramount)

Art it ain't, fun it is. That about sums up *Come Blow Your Horn*. Like its legit parent, the screen version of Neil Simon's Jewish-oriented family comedy is a superficial but diverting romp.

The simple yarn is concerned with two brothers' opposite extremities of bachelorhood, the older one (Frank Sinatra) ultimately passing into a more mature, responsible phase of life when he sees in his younger brother's (Tony Bill) sensual excesses the reflection of a ferocious personality no longer especially becoming or appealing to him. This is mighty good news to his long-suffering father, a wax fruit manufacturer from Yonkers for whom any unmarried man over 30 is a bum.

Sinatra's role is perfectly suited to his rakish image. It also affords him an opportunity to manifest his most consummate talent – that of singer. He warbles the lilting title tune.

But it's Lee J. Cobb who steals the show (albeit in the juiciest part) with what might be described as a 'bum'-bastic portrayal of the explosively irascible old man who is forever appearing at the front door of his son's apartment when more glamorous company is expected.

Tony Bill makes a fairly auspicious screen bow as the younger brother. Barbara Rush is attractive as the girl who eventually gets Sinatra, and Jill St John is flashy as a guilelessly accommodating sexpot.
□ 1963: Nomination: Best Color Art Direction

■ **COMEDIANS, THE**

1967, 156 MINS, US ◇
Dir Peter Glenville *Prod* Peter Glenville *Scr* Graham Greene *Ph* Henri Decae *Ed* Francoise Javet
Mus Laurence Rosenthal *Art Dir* Francois De Lamothe
● Richard Burton, Elizabeth Taylor, Alec Guinness, Peter Ustinov, Paul Ford, Lillian Gish (M-G-M)

The despair of people living under a despot may, indeed, be a sort of living death. Producer-director Peter Glenville's pic, scripted by Graham Greene [from his own novel], is a plodding, low-key, and eventually tedious melodrama.

Greene's screenplay rambles on through a seemingly interminable 156 minutes. Not the least of film's flaws is the role played by Elizabeth Taylor (wife of South American ambassador Peter Ustinov), who has a recurring, deteriorating affair with hotel-owner Richard Burton.

The very poorly-made story point is that Burton gradually, finds something to live for, in his eventual flight to join mountain rebels,

pitiably equipped and pitilessly portrayed. Alec Guinness is a society-type arms promoter who fakes a military background. In a climactic scene where he confesses the fraud to Burton, Guinness excels.

■ **COMEDY MAN, THE**

1964, 92 MINS, UK
Dir Alvin Rakoff *Prod* Jon Penington *Scr* Peter Yeldham *Ph* Ken Hodges *Mus* Bill McGuffie
Art Dir John Blezard
● Kenneth More, Cecil Parker, Dennis Price, Billie Whitelaw, Norman Rossington, Angela Douglas (British Lion)

Douglas Hayes' lightweight novel about the struggle of a stock actor who has just passed the dangerous 40s, without making the grade, hardly scratches new ground. But the authenticity and atmosphere are complete and this well made little film recreates that atmosphere splendidly on the screen. A well drawn performance by Kenneth More adds greatly to the entertainment value of the film.

Fired from a stock company in the sticks for being found with the leading lady, who happens to be the producer's wife, More comes to London for one more crack at making good in the big time. In the seedy atmosphere of theatrical digs, promiscuous affairs, doing the agents' rounds he suffers all the humiliations and disappointments. Eventually pride breaks down, he takes a job doing TV commercials as 'Mr Honeybreath', which brings him dough and recognition.

■ **COME FLY WITH ME**

1963, 107 MINS, US ◇
Dir Henry Levin *Prod* Anatole de Grunwald
Scr William Roberts *Ph* Oswald Morris *Ed* Frank Clarke *Mus* Lyn Murray *Art Dir* William Kellner
● Dolores Hart, Hugh O'Brian, Karl Boehm, Pamela Tiffin, Karl Malden, Lois Nettleton (M-G-M)

Sometimes one performance can save a picture and in *Come Fly with Me* it's an engaging and infectious one by Pamela Tiffin. The production has other things going for it like an attractive cast, slick pictorial values and smart, stylish directing by Henry Levin, but at the base of all this sheer sheen lies a frail, frivolous and featherweight storyline that, in trying to take itself too seriously, flies into dramatic air pockets and crosscurrents that threaten to send the entire aircraft in a tailspin.

Airline hostesses and their romantic pursuits provide the peg upon which William Roberts has constructed his erratic screenplay from a screen story he concocted out of Bernard Glemser's *Girl on a Wing*. The affairs of three hostesses are described.

One (Dolores Hart) is looking for a wealthy husband and thinks she's found the fellow in a young Continental baron (Karl Boehm). Another (Lois Nettleton) is a nice girl type who succeeds in winning the heart and hand of yon multi-millionaire Texas businessman (Karl Malden). The third (Tiffin), after a series of cockpitfalls and hotelroominations, decides that flying so high with some guy in the sky is her idea of something to do. The 'some guy' is first flight officer Hugh O'Brian.

Much of the film was shot in Paris and Vienna.

■ **COMES A HORSEMAN**

1978, 118 MINS, US ◇ ⓦ
Dir Alan J. Pakula *Prod* Gene Kirkwood, Dan Paulson
Scr Dennis Lynton Clark *Ph* Gordon Willis *Ed* Marion Rothman *Mus* Michael Small *Art Dir* George Jenkins
● James Caan, Jane Fonda, Jason Robards, George Grizzard, Richard Farnsworth, Jim Davis (United Artists/Chartoff-Winkler)

Alan Pakula's *Comes a Horseman* is so lethargic not even Jane Fonda, James Caan and Jason Robards can bring excitement to this artificially dramatic story of a stubborn rancher who won't surrender to the local land baron.

The real star of the film doesn't get billing. It's a stretch of verdant land in Colorado known as the Wet Mountain Valley. Gordon Willis photographs this location with so much love and awe that talk by oil explorers about ripping it up is both moving and repulsive

Robards' part is the most troublesome. He's the land baron who wants both Fonda and Caan to sell their parcels to complete his empire. Every one of Robards' lines is shaded by a black hat. He is Evil in the most convenient way.

Caan, also a independent rancher who recently returned from serving in World War II, teams up with Fonda after his partner is killed (presumably on orders from Robards). When Fonda realizes what an accomplished cowboy Caan is and how much she needs him their relationship warms.

The only really good part in the film is Richard Farnsworth's Dodger, Fonda's aging hand. He's an altogether sympathetic character, close to the land and one of the few who really understands Fonda.

☐ 1978: Nomination: Best Supp. Actress (Richard Farnsworth)

■ **COME SEE THE PARADISE**

1990, 138 MINS, US ◇ ⓥ ⊙
Dir Alan Parker *Prod* Robert F. Colesberry *Scr* Alan Parker *Ph* Michael Seresin *Ed* Gerry Hambling *Mus* Randy Edelman *Art Dir* Geoffrey Kirkland
● Dennis Quaid, Tamlyn Tomita, Sab Shimono, Shizuko Hoshi, Stan Egi, Ronald Yamamoto (20th Century-Fox)

In Alan Parker's richly mounted romantic saga of the Second World War relocation camps, the Asian-American cast is exemplary and Dennis Quaid has never been better.

Noble if overlong effort depicts the love affair between the Irish-American labor activist and a woman from a well-established Japanese family ripped from its Los Angeles roots.

Quaid plays Jack McGurn, a newcomer to LA in 1936 who gets a job as a projectionist in a Little Tokyo theater and falls in love with the boss' daughter (Tamlyn Tomita). After he's fired and forbidden to see her again, they elope to Seattle, where, unlike in California, it was legal for a Japanese-American and a Caucasian to marry.

In general, Parker avoids most of the complexities behind the internment in favor of a broad, sentimental tale that emphasizes emotions.

Quaid gives a wonderfully open and unaffected performance, putting across romance, charm and integrity without resorting to any of the gimmicks he's used in earlier films. Tomita is a lovely, if under-nuanced, actress, and Egi as her brother is particularly interesting among the large supporting cast.

■ **COME SEPTEMBER**

1961, 112 MINS, US ◇
Dir Robert Mulligan *Prod* Robert Arthur *Scr* Stanley Shapiro, Maurice Richlin *Ph* William Daniels *Ed* Russell F. Schoengarth *Mus* Hans J. Salter *Art Dir* Henry Bumstead
● Rock Hudson, Gina Lollobrigida, Sandra Dee, Bobby Darin, Walter Slezak, Brenda De Banzie (Universal)

A rich US businessman (Rock Hudson), who ordinarily spends only one month (September) annually at his Italian villa, abruptly puts in a July appearance to the dismay of his enterprising major domo (Walter Slezak) who has been converting the private abode into a very public hotel for 11 months out of every year.

Even in the film's lesser spans there are occasional kicks and spurts of high good humor, but too often, in manipulating the plot for the purposes of introducing incongruous comedy spectacles (Hudson chasing after La Lollo at the wheel of a battered chicken truck, or the latter, garbed in full wedding gown regalia, chasing after the former in an old jeep), the writers seem inclined to telegraph, repeat and pile it on.

Under director Robert Mulligan's generally keen command, Hudson comes through with an especially jovial performance. Gina Lollobrigida need just stand there to generate sparks, but here she abets her eye-to-eye appeal with plenty of comedy savvy. Slezak is excellent. His scenes with Hudson are the best in the picture.

Sandra Dee has the misfortune to be overshadowed in the glamor department by La Lollo, but the young actress is plenty decorative and capable in her own right. In his first cinematic exposure, Bobby Darin does a workmanlike job.

■ **COMFORT AND JOY**

1984, 90 MINS, UK ◇
Dir Bill Forsyth *Prod* Davina Belling, Clive Parsons *Scr* Bill Forsyth *Ph* Chris Menges *Ed* Michael Ellis *Mus* Mark Knopfler *Art Dir* Adrienne Atkinson
● Bill Paterson, Roberto Bernardi, Eleanor David, Clare Grogan, Patrick Malahide, Rikki Fulton (Kings Road)

In *Comfort and Joy* director-scripter Bill Forsyth again sets up a wacko scenario about zany, off-center characters.

But evincing much laughter over an unexpectedly funny couple living together, Forsyth abruptly switches into a more conventional plot.

Pic opens with a well-dressed kleptomaniac (Eleanor David) lifting goods at a department store, followed by a man (Bill Paterson). It turns out he's her lover and aware of her stealing. They return home, make love off camera and after a meal she announces she's leaving.

Depressed, he adopts a stiff upperlip attitude and goes to his job as an MOR radio station early morning deejay. He then becomes, innocently at first, a go-between as two warring Mafia families fight for territorial control of selling ice cream by van.

David and Paterson are terrific together and almost every line between them is a joy. From the point she departs with no explanation the pic flashes a sparky moment or two, but it doesn't reach the high spots again.

■ **COMFORT OF STRANGERS, THE**

1990, 107 MINS, ITALY/US ◇ ⓥ ⊙
Dir Paul Schrader *Prod* Angelo Rizzoli *Scr* Harold Pinter *Ph* Dante Spinotti *Ed* Bill Pankow *Mus* Angelo Badalamenti *Art Dir* Gianni Quaranta
● Christopher Walken, Rupert Everett, Natasha Richardson, Helen Mirren (Erre/Sovereign)

Neither the beguiling romance of Venice nor the undraped bodies of Natasha Richardson and Rupert Everett can disguise the hollowness of *The Comfort of Strangers*.

Mary (Richardson) and Colin (Everett) are an unmarried, liveapart couple living together. While both actors are paradigms of beauty, Harold Pinter's labored scenario [from the novel by Ian McEwan] would have us believe that all of Venice is transfixed by the heart-stopping magnificence of – Everett.

Among the many Venetian souls smitten by Everett's Apollonian magnetism is a man in an icecream suit, Robert (Christopher Walken), the grave, courtly son of an Italian diplomat. Unbeknownst to the English tourists, Walken has been photographing Everett obsessively since their arrival. The couple are easy prey for Walken's blandishments.

Undermined by the script, the actors are constantly upstaged by the timeless glories of Venice.

■ **COMING HOME**

1978, 126 MINS, US ◇ ⓥ ⊙
Dir Hal Ashby *Prod* Jerome Hellman *Scr* Waldo Salt, Robert C. Jones *Ph* Haskall Wexler *Ed* Don Zimmerman *Art Dir* Mike Haller
● Jane Fonda, Jon Voight, Bruce Dern, Robert Ginty, Penelope Milford, Robert Carradine (United Artists)

Coming Home is in general an excellent Hal Ashby film which illuminates the conflicting attitudes on the Vietnam debacle from the standpoint of three participants. Jerome Hellman's fine production has Jane Fonda in another memorable and moving performance; Jon Voight, back on the screen much more matured, assured and effective; Bruce Dern, continuing to forge new career dimension.

Nancy Dowd's story was adapted by Waldo Salt and former film editor Robert C. Jones into a home-front drama. Gung-ho Marine officer Dern goes to Vietnam while loyal wife Fonda decides to work in a veterans' hospital where she meets high-school classmate Voight, now an embittered cripple from the war. Their lives become transformed completely.

Fonda and Ashby have reined in any tendencies to be smug or pedantic. Instead, she provides a superb characterization. Voight's character evolves as he and Fonda become lovers. A sex scene between the two is a masterpiece of discreet romantic eroticism.

Dern's character is the trigger for certain major events, but there remains enough exposure for him to be convincing as a career soldier disillusioned by Vietnam. Among the large supporting cast are Penelope Milford, excellent as another hospital worker keeping an eye on brother Robert Carradine, very effective as a pitiful, freaked-out and ultimately suicidal case.

☐ 1978: Best Actor (Jon Voight), Actress (Jane Fonda), Original Screenplay.
☐ Nominations: Best Picture, Director, Supp. Actor (Bruce Dern), Supp. Actress (Penelope Milford), Editing

■ **COMING TO AMERICA**

1988, 116 MINS, US ◇ ⓥ ⊙
Dir John Landis *Prod* George Folsey Jr., Robert D. Wachs *Scr* David Sheffield, Barry W. Blaustein *Ph* Woody Omens *Ed* Malcolm Campbell, George Folsey Jr. *Mus* Nile Rodgers *Art Dir* Richard MacDonald
● Eddie Murphy, Arsenio Hall, John Amos, James Earl Jones, Shari Headley, Eriq LaSalle (Paramount)

Coming to America starts on a bathroom joke, quickly followed by a gag about private parts, then wanders in search of something equally original for Eddie Murphy to do for another couple of hours. It's a true test for loyal fans.

Murphy [credited with the original story] has no difficulty creating a pampered young prince of Zamunda who would like a chance to live a little real life and select his own bride instead of being forced into a royal marriage of convenience. Murphy even makes the prince sympathetic and genuine, complete to his stilted English. He and courtly sidekick Arsenio Hall venture to Queens to find a queen.

Longing for someone to love him for himself, Murphy discovers beautiful Shari Headley and goes to work mopping floors in father John Amos' hamburger emporium to be near her.

She, no surprise, already has a well-to-do, insufferable boyfriend (Eriq LaSalle) that dad is anxious for her to marry. How does a

janitor capture the heart of such a maiden?
☐ 1988: Nominations: Best Costume Design, Makeup

••

■ **COMMAND, THE**

1954, 94 MINS, US ◇

Dir David Butler *Prod* David Weisbart *Scr* Russell Hughes *Ph* Wilfrid M. Cline *Ed* Irene Morra *Mus* Dimitri Tiomkin
● Guy Madison, Joan Weldon, James Whitmore, Carl Benton Reid, Harvey Lembeck, Ray Teal (Warner)

The first feature western under the CinemaScope label, *The Command* has a fundamentally sound cavalry-versus-Indians plot and highly charged action footage.

The picture was actually lensed in what was originally known as Vistarama and later as WarnerScope. With Warners' subsequent tieup with 20th-Fox for CinemaScope, it was decided to send the film out with the latter label. In *Command*, picture clarity is lacking in many scenes except for center screen, but as attention is centered there the fuzziness around the edges is of little consequence.

Guy Madison turns in a thoroughly able job of the heroics under David Butler's direction. Latter handles the Russell Hughes screenplay [from a *Saturday Evening Post* novel by James Warner Bellah, as adapted by Samuel Fuller] expertly for action, particularly in the latter half when the film takes on more movement.

Madison is an army medical captain unexpectedly assuming command of a cavalry troop after its regular commander is killed. Story is concerned with how he improvises battle tactics to defeat attacking Indians, wins the respect of his men and saves a wagon train, as well as two companies of infantry.

••

■ **COMMAND DECISION**

1948, 111 MINS, US ⊚

Dir Sam Wood *Prod* Sidney Franklin *Scr* William R. Laidlaw, George Froeschel *Ph* Harold Rosson *Ed* Harold F. Kress *Mus* Miklos Rozsa *Art Dir* Cedric Gibbons, Urie McCleary
● Clark Gable, Walter Pidgeon, Van Johnson, Brian Donlevy, Charles Bickford, John Hodiak (M-G-M)

Command Decision is a literate war drama, presented with a class touch. It tells of the Second World War from the top level of heavy brass, but with a slant that makes the star-wearers human. There's no romance, and none is needed.

In transferring the Broadway legit hit [by William Wister Haines] to the screen, producer Sidney Franklin and director Sam Wood have made it a faithful version. It's still laid, principally, in the GHQ of a bomber command and little attempt is made to broaden that essential locale. Where it gets its added sweep is in the lucid music score (which bows only to the bomber's roar) and in the graphic lensing that gives the story a movement not possible on stage.

Clark Gable walks off with a picture in which everyone of the cast stands out. His is a believable delivery, interpreting the brigadier-general who must send his men out to almost certain death with an understanding that bespeaks his sympathy with the soldier – brass or dogface.

Walter Pidgeon is the real big brass – the trafficker with politicos, wheedling and conniving to keep his Air Force supplied with planes and men despite homefront cries against losses.

••

■ **COMMANDO**

1985, 88 MINS, US ◇ ⊚ ⊙

Dir Mark L. Lester *Prod* Joel Silver *Scr* Steven de Souza *Ph* Matthew F. Leonetti *Ed* Mark Goldblatt, John F. Link, Glenn Farr *Mus* James Horner *Art Dir* John Vallone

● Arnold Schwarzenegger, Rae Dawn Chong, Dan Hedaya, Vernon Wells, David Patrick Kelly, Alyssa Milano (Silver/20th Century-Fox)

In *Commando*, the fetching surprise is the glancing humor between the quixotic and larky Rae Dawn Chong and the straight-faced killing machine of Arnold Schwarzenegger. Chong lights up the film like a firefly, Schwarzenegger delivers a certain light touch of his own, the result is palatable action comics.

Director Mark L. Lester, compelled to deal with an absurd plot [by Joseph Loeb III, Matthew Weisman and Steven de Souza], is blessed by the decision to cast Chong, who enjoys an offbeat sexuality and an insouciance that is irristible.

Credit Lester with chiseling the quick, subtly romantic byplay between the two stars – unlikely mates thrown together in pursuit of a deadly Latin neo-dictator – and pulling off a terrific series of tracking shots during a riotous chase in a crowded galleria complex.

Heavies are vividly drawn in the cases of the obsessed Vernon Wells, the punk David Patrick Kelly, and sullen, ice-cold Bill Duke.

••

■ **COMMITMENTS, THE**

1991, 116 MINS, US/UK ◇ ⊚ ⊙

Dir Alan Parker *Prod* Roger Randall-Cutler, Lynda Myles *Scr* Dick Clement, Ian La Frenais, Roddy Doyle *Ph* Gale Tattersall *Ed* Gerry Hambling *Mus* G. Mark Roswell (sup.), Paul Bushnell (arr.) *Art Dir* Brian Morris
● Robert Arkins, Michael Aherne, Angeline Ball, Maria Doyle, Johnny Murphy, Andrew Strong (Beacon/First Film/Dirty Hands)

Director Alan Parker's story of a band of hardscrabble young Dubliners playing American '60s soul is fresh, well-executed and original.

Set in the working-class north side of contemporary Dublin, where the music scene is rich and teeming, film, based on the novel by Roddy Doyle, tells the story of 21-year-old entrepreneur Jimmy Rabbitte (Robert Arkins), who envisions bringing soul music to Dublin. He pieces together a 10-piece outfit with real musical potential from among his raw or semi-talented contemporaries.

Diverse group includes a messianic 45-year-old trumpeter, Joey (Johnny Murphy) who claims to have toured with the American greats, a stout and vulgar lead singer (played by 16-year-old Andrew Strong) with a voice like a diesel engine, and three scrappy and fetching femme backup singers who blossom into singing leads. Constant friction among players means Jimmy spends much of his energy trying to hold the band together long enough to land at least one paying gig and pay off the rogue from whom he's more or less stolen the equipment.

Parker and the casting directors initially auditioned more than 3,000 Dublin hopefuls. They wound up casting mostly musicians with no acting experience. Ensemble cast, which underwent five weeks of rehearsal, handles itself extremely well, particularly Arkins as Rabbitte and Murphy as the trumpeter.

Pictorially, the film is full of variety and unexpected pleasures, and the complex editing work by Gerry Hambling is marvelously accomplished.
☐ 1991: Nomination: Best Editing

••

■ **COMPANY BUSINESS**

1991, 98 MINS, US ◇ ⊚ ⊙

Dir Nicholas Meyer *Prod* Charles Jaffe *Scr* Nicholas Meyer *Ph* Gerry Fisher *Ed* Ronald Roose *Mus* Michael Kamen *Art Dir* Ken Adam
● Gene Hackman, Mikhail Baryshnikov, Kurtwood Smith, Terry O'Quinn, Daniel Von Bargen, Oleg Rudnick (M-G-M)

This muddled comedic-thriller, which asks what spies do after the Cold War, has a few amusing political references but the indecisive tone scuttles the film.

Gene Hackman plays a former CIA agent wasting his talent in industrial espionage. He's drafted by 'the company' to return a former Soviet mole (Mikhail Baryshnikov) to the Soviets – along with $2 million in Colombian drug booty.

The swap goes bad, however, sending the two former spies racing around Europe, with their embarrassed and somewhat bumbling bosses from the CIA (Kurtwood Smith) and KGB (Oleg Rudnick) in lukewarm pursuit.

Writer-director Nicholas Meyer also is all over the map with his direction and script, which begins as a thriller (complete with portentously brooding music by Michael Kamen) then shifts to a sort of screwy comedy.

••

■ **COMPANY OF STRANGERS, THE**

1990, 100 MINS, CANADA ◇ ⊚

Dir Cynthia Scott *Prod* David Wilson *Scr* Gloria Demers, Cynthia Scott, David Wilson, Sally Bochner *Ph* David de Volpi *Ed* David Wilson *Mus* Marie Bernard *Art Dir* Christiane Gagnon
● Alice Diabo, Constance Garneau, Winifred Holden, Cissy Meddings, Mary Meigs, Catherine Roche (NFBC)

The seventh in the National Film Board of Canada series where non-actors play themselves in a fictitious setting, *The Company of Strangers* features seven elderly women marooned in an abandoned country house near an idyllic lake after their bus breaks down. A safe quiet journey becomes an adventure in survival, and in their quest for food they rediscover the hunger of youth.

These seven perfect strangers and their younger bus driver (a lively Montreal jazz singer, Michelle Sweeney) become fast friends through lengthy conversations, many of which shot in real time. Pacing is slow and Hollywood-style action nonexistent. Entire story revolves around the women's lives, secrets, fears and joys.

The Mohawk woman (Alice Diabo) teaches them about fishing with pantyhose. A nun (Catherine Roche) in jeans manages to catch a pail full of frogs for dinner and is the self-appointed savior who walks 20 miles for help. Mary Meigs is an artist and lesbian who publishes books. Winnie Holden does great bird imitations. Constance Garneau seems to regret most of her 88 years. Beth Webber is an 80-year-old woman who looks 50 and never stops worrying about looking old. Cissy Meddings steals the show with her sense of humor and indifference to life's perils.

••

■ **COMPANY OF WOLVES, THE**

1984, 95 MINS, UK ◇ ⊚ ⊙

Dir Neil Jordan *Prod* Chris Brown, Stephen Woolley *Scr* Angela Carter, Neil Jordan *Ph* Bryan Loftus *Ed* Rodney Holland *Mus* George Fenton *Art Dir* Anton Furst
● Angela Lansbury, David Warner, Stephen Rea, Tusse Silberg, Sarah Patterson, Graham Crowden (Palace)

Admirably attempting an adult approach to traditional fairy tale material, *The Company of Wolves* nevertheless represents an uneasy marriage between old-fashioned storytelling and contemporary screen explicitness.

Virtually the entire film is the dream of the gravely beautiful adolescent Sarah Patterson. Within her dream are other dreams and stories told by others, all of which gives director Neil Jordan, who penned the screenplay with story originator Angela Carter, free imaginative rein, but which also gives the tale a less than propulsive narrative.

Anton Furst's elaborate forest settings, all created within studio-confines, are lovely. Jordan maneuvers well within them, even if

Bryan Loftus' lush lensing is sometimes so dark that a claustrophobic feeling sets in.

● ● ● ● ● ● ● ● ● ● ● ● ● ● ● ● ● ● ● ●

■ COMPETITION, THE

1980, 129 MINS, US ◇ ⓦ ⊙
Dir Joel Oliansky   *Prod* William Sackheim   *Scr* Joel Oliansky   *Ph* Richard H. Kline   *Ed* David Blewitt   *Mus* Lalo Schifrin   *Art Dir* Dale Hennesy
● Richard Dreyfuss, Amy Irving, Lee Remick, Sam Wanamaker, Ty Henderson, James B. Sikking (Columbia/Rastar)

The Competition is a disappointment. Writer-director Joel Oliansky's glibly cynical view of the performing world and his dreary character portraits are matched in clumsiness by his ugly visual style and lack of genuine feeling for music.

The film needed a conductor and composer of background music with a sensitivity to the classical field, but instead it has Lalo Schifrin.

Richard Dreyfuss, an aging piano wunderkind, is reunited at a San Francisco music competition with Amy Irving, a less driven but more gifted young woman he had impressed briefly at an earlier festival. She tries to rekindle their attraction, but Dreyfuss is too absorbed in his music at first to respond.

The film is tedious and predictable, curiously portraying music as a grim and joyless profession for these youngsters.
☐ 1980: Nominations: Best Editing, Song ('People Alone')

● ● ● ● ● ● ● ● ● ● ● ● ● ● ● ● ● ● ● ●

■ COMPROMISING POSITIONS

1985, 98 MINS, US ◇ ⓦ ⊙
Dir Frank Perry   *Prod* Frank Perry   *Scr* Susan Isaacs   *Ph* Barry Sonnenfeld   *Ed* Peter Frank   *Mus* Brad Fiedel   *Art Dir* Peter Larkin
● Susan Sarandon, Raul Julia, Edward Herrmann, Judith Ivey, Mary Beth Hurt, Joe Mantegna (Paramount)

Falling midway between a campy send-up of suburban wives soap operas and a legitimate thriller, *Compromising Positions*, from the 1978 novel by Susan Isaacs, emerges as a silly little whodunnit that's a mild embarrassment to all involved.

Unlikely material, about the murder of a philandering Long Island dentist, the reactions of his many mistresses, and the official and unofficial investigations into it, has hardly been approached with a straight face. The victim is a loathesome gold chain type, and most of his conquests are ladies who lunch with little redeeming social or intellectual value.

Intrigued and naively amazed that nearly everyone she knows h been involved with the late Dr Fleckstein, upper-middle-class housewife Susan Sarandon undertakes some amateur sleuthing with an eye toward reviving her old profession of newspaper reporter.

Action moves along snappily enough. Supporting players such as Judith Ivey and Josh Mostel contribute some tolerably amusing comedy turns, and Sarandon is, as always, highly watchable.

● ● ● ● ● ● ● ● ● ● ● ● ● ● ● ● ● ● ● ●

■ COMPULSION

1959, 103 MINS, US
Dir Richard Fleischer   *Prod* Richard D. Zanuck   *Scr* Richard Murphy   *Ph* William C. Mellor   *Ed* William Reynolds   *Mus* Lionel Newman
● Orson Welles, Dean Stockwell, Bradford Dillman, Diane Varsi, E.G. Marshall, Martin Milner (20th Century-Fox)

Compulsion, from Meyer Levin's novel, is almost a literal case study of the notorious Leopold-Loeb murder of Bobby Franks.

The two protagonists, here called Artie and Judd, both have highly neurotic, seething minds bent on destruction as twisted proof of their superiority. That the boys have a homosexual relationship is quite clear, though the subject is not overstressed. Both come from wealthy families that spoiled them.

As Artie Straus, the sneering, arrogant youth who can no longer distinguish between reality and his dreams, but who knows how to hide under the veneer of smooth politeness, Bradford Dillman turns in a superb performance. Opposite him, as Judd Steiner, Dean Stockwell plays an impressionable, sensitive youth, caught up in the spell of his strong-willed companion.

Director Richard Fleischer establishes the characters' from the terrifying opening shot when the two try to run down a drunk on the road to their appearance in court, where lawyer Orson Welles pleads for their life in the same idiom that Clarence Darrow used to save Nathan Leopold Jr and Richard Loeb from the Illinois gallows. The lines he speaks become part of the man himself, an almost classic oration against capital punishment.

As the girl who understands more than she knows, and who reaches out for Stockwell, Diane Varsi seems at times awkward. It's not an easy part, and she brings to it a tenseness that doesn't always register.

● ● ● ● ● ● ● ● ● ● ● ● ● ● ● ● ● ● ● ●

■ COMRADES
A LANTERNIST'S ACCOUNT OF THE TOLPUDDLE MARTYRS AND WHAT BECAME OF THEM

1987, 160 MINS, UK ◇ ⓦ
Dir Bill Douglas   *Prod* Simon Relph   *Scr* Bill Douglas   *Ph* Gale Tattersall   *Ed* Mick Audsley   *Mus* Hans Werner Henze, David Graham   *Art Dir* Michael Pickwood
● Robin Soans, William Gaminara, Stephen Bateman, Philip Davis, Jeremy Flynn, Keith Allen (Skreba/NFFC/Curzon/Film Four)

Bill Douglas has an eye for fresh detail, the rituals of rural life, and the dignity of countryfolk. Rarely before have the poverty, the pains and the pleasures, the oppressiveness of the work routine, even of the weather, been so well conveyed on film.

However, because so much time is spent on building up this rich tapestry of rural England in the 1830s, the focus is lost.

Eventually one pieces together that the Tolpuddle Martyrs, film's subject, were a small group of peasant craftsmen who dared to form a union and ask for higher wages. They were singled out for their subversion by the British authorities and transported to Australia. After a public outcry they were subsequently recalled to England.

Although there is a unique vision at work in *Comrades* it's a pity that more ruthlessness in scripting and editing was not exercised.

● ● ● ● ● ● ● ● ● ● ● ● ● ● ● ● ● ● ● ●

■ COMRADE X

1940, 87 MINS, US
Dir King Vidor   *Prod* Gottfried Reinhardt   *Scr* Ben Hecht, Charles Lederer   *Ph* Joseph Ruttenberg   *Ed* Harold F. Kress   *Mus* Bronislau Kaper   *Art Dir* Cedric Gibbons, Malcolm Brown
● Clark Gable, Hedy Lamarr, Oscar Homolka, Felix Bressart, Eve Arden, Natasha Lytess (M-G-M)

As title implies, action is laid in Russia, with Clark Gable, a love-'em-and-leave-'em, elbow-bending American reporter cutting a wide swath as a carefree Lothario and outwitter of the censors in coding stories through to the outside. Gable hits a hurdle in maintaining his secret when simple-minded Felix Bressart, hotel porter, threatens exposure of the reporter's true identity unless Gable gets Bressart's daughter out of the country immediately.

Seems the girl, although a rabid Communist, is slated to be liquidated by the Kremlin. Matter-of-fact agreement of the girl to the plan, with ritual of typical Russian marriage ceremony and her quick breakdown under Gable's embraces, sets the stage for a continual series of laugh situations before the pair finally get out of the country.

Picture [from a screen story by Walter Reisch] resembles Garbo's *Ninotchka* only in that it again directs well-aimed shafts of humor at Communist actions and preachments, for plenty of rousing humor.

Gable provides a strong characterization of the ever-resourceful American newspaperman. Hedy Lamarr is handed her strongest role and demonstrates she can be more than decorative by a good display of both deadpan comedy and romantic antics. Natasha Lytess shines as a Russian secretary. Hair-pulling battle between latter and Lamarr over Gable's affections is a honey.
☐ 1940: Nomination: Best Original Story

● ● ● ● ● ● ● ● ● ● ● ● ● ● ● ● ● ● ● ●

■ CONAN THE BARBARIAN

1982, 129 MINS, US ◇ ⓦ ⊙
Dir John Milius   *Prod* Buzz Feitshans, Raffaella De Laurentiis   *Scr* John Milius, Oliver Stone   *Ph* Duke Callaghan   *Ed* C. Timothy O'Meara, Fred Stafford   *Mus* Basil Poledouris   *Art Dir* Ron Cobb
● Arnold Schwarzenegger, James Earl Jones, Max von Sydow, Sandahl Bergman, Mako, Gerry Lopez (De Laurentiis)

The opening is promising enough as child Conan witnesses the brutal deaths of his father and mother at the whim of the evil Thulsa Doom (James Earl Jones). Conan Jr grows up as a slave who eventually has the good fortune of turning into Arnold Schwarzenegger.

It's the baddies' fatal flaw that they shove Conan into an arena to fight chosen competitors to the death. The guy naturally realizes he's pretty strong and decides to strike out on his own to see how far his muscles can take him.

In those days it was pretty far. On the road he meets up with a fellow drifter (Gerry Lopez), beautiful cohort and eventual lover Sandahl Bergman, needy king Max von Sydow and goofy wizard Mako.

Director John Milius does a nice job of setting up the initial story. There is a real anticipation as Schwarzenegger is unveiled as the barbarian and sets off on the road to independence. But for whatever reasons, the actor has a minimum of dialog and fails to convey much about the character through his actions.

This is compounded by the script by Milius and Oliver Stone, which is nothing more than a series of meaningless adventures and ambiguous references until the final expected confrontation with Jones.

● ● ● ● ● ● ● ● ● ● ● ● ● ● ● ● ● ● ● ●

■ CONAN THE DESTROYER

1984, 103 MINS, US ◇ ⓦ ⊙
Dir Richard Fleischer   *Prod* Raffaella De Laurentiis   *Scr* Stanley Mann   *Ph* Jack Cardiff   *Ed* Frank J. Urioste   *Mus* Basil Poledouris   *Art Dir* Pier Luigi Basile
● Arnold Schwarzenegger, Grace Jones, Wilt Chamberlain, Mako, Tracey Walter, Sarah Douglas (De Laurentiis/Pressman)

Conan the Destroyer is the ideal sword and sorcery picture. Plot [by Roy Thomas and Gerry Conway] is appropriately elemental. Conan is recruited by sexy queen Sarah Douglas to accompany teenage princess Olivia D'Abo to a distant castle, where lies a gem that will supposedly unleash many secret powers.

Unbeknownst to Conan, Douglas has instructed her henchman Wilt Chamberlain to kill the muscleman once the mission is accomplished, and to deliver D'Abo back home with her virginity intact so that she can be properly sacrificed. Along the way, group also picks up fiery warrioress Grace Jones.

As Conan, Arnold Schwarzenegger seems more animated and much funnier under Fleischer's direction than he did under John

Milius' in the original – he even has an amusing drunk scene. Jones just about runs off with the picture. Coming on like a full-fledged star from her very first scene, singer throws herself into her wild woman role with complete abandon.

. . . .

■ CONCORDE – AIRPORT '79, THE

(UK: Airport '80 – The Concorde; aka: Airport – The Concorde)

1979, 123 MINS, US ◇ ⊚ ⊙
Dir David Lowell Rich   *Prod* Jennings Lang   *Scr* Eric Roth   *Ph* Philip Lathrop   *Ed* Dorothy Spencer   *Mus* Lalo Schifrin   *Art Dir* Henry Bumstead
● Alain Delon, Susan Blakely, Robert Wagner, Sylvia Kristel, George Kennedy, Eddie Albert (Paramount)

Unintentional comedy still seems the *Airport* series' forte, although excellent special effects work, and some decent dramatics help *Concorde* take off.

This time out [story by Jennings Lang], the title entity is pursued by a dogged electronic missile, avoids an attack by a French fighter jet, barely makes a runway landing with no brakes, suffers a lost cargo door that rips open the bottom of the plane, manages a crash landing in an Alpine snow bank, and explodes just as its chic passengers disembark. That's all just part of a couple of days' work for pilots George Kennedy, Alain Delon and flight engineer David Warner.

Concorde does feature some better-than-average thesping from Delon, who survives the transition to American pix surprisingly well.

. . . .

■ CONDEMNED OF ALTONA, THE

1963, 112 MINS, ITALY
Dir Vittorio De Sica   *Prod* Carlo Ponti   *Scr* Abby Mann, Cesare Zavattini   *Ph* Roberto Gerardi   *Ed* Adriana Novelli   *Mus* Nino Rota   *Art Dir* Elvezio Frigerio
● Sophia Loren, Maximilian Schell, Fredric March, Robert Wagner, Francoise Prevost (Titanus)

Filmed on location in Hamburg, with interiors in Italy, this tale of post-war Germany, as symbolized by the members of one family, is undoubtedly anti-German. Where Jean-Paul Sartre's play was written from the point of view of a French writer, scripters Abby Mann and Cesare Zavattini have changed these observations to Italian orientation.

The title refers to the Gerlachs, a wealthy Hamburg shipbuilding family, and Altona, the Hamburg suburb in which they live. Director Vittorio De Sica spins the tale as a series of disclosures about the family and the resultant emotional effect on Johanna (Sophia Loren), the actress-wife of the younger son (Robert Wagner).

This throws the major dramatic responsibility on Loren, who creates a shudderingly magnificent protrait of a beautiful, intelligent woman just beginning to recover her dignity and self-respect from the shambles of her country's militaristic past, only to have them threatened by 'secrets' of her husband's family.

Striking flames is Maximilian Schell as Franz, the eldest son whose personal war guilt has kept him a self-imposed prisoner in the attic of the Gerlach manor for 15 years until, bordering on insanity, he is roused from his self-delusion by Johanna. Reported as dead by his family, even to Johanna, Franz' self-delusion has been supported by his family, particularly his tycoon father (Fredric March), whose own war guilt has been kept subservient to his indomitable will and industrial genius.

March, whose impending death from cancer brings the family together, creates Gerlach as much through visualization as through dialog. Wagner makes one weak member of a strong family a memorable character.

. . . .

■ CONDUCT UNBECOMING

1976, 107 MINS, UK ◇ ⊚
Dir Michael Anderson   *Prod* Michael Deeley, Barry Spikings   *Scr* Robert Enders   *Ph* Bob Huke   *Ed* John Glen   *Mus* Stanley Myers   *Art Dir* Ted Tester
● Michael York, Richard Attenborough, Trevor Howard, Stacy Keach, Christopher Plummer, Susannah York (Lion/Crown)

Based on a play by Barry England, this has all the ingredients of good, slightly old-fashioned courtroom drama transposed to 19th-century, British-dominated India to give it an added dimension.

Basically, action centers around a secret trial by his fellow officers of a young lieutenant accused of assaulting an officer's widow in a colonial outpost. In defending the accused, a new arrival slowly uncovers not only the real assaulter, but more especially the hypocrisy which rules and motivates the garrison officers' lives.

Acting is uniformly excellent. Michael York as the defender and James Faulkner as the defendant get top-notch backing. But, perhaps because of his seemingly offbeat casting as a British officer, it's Stacy Keach who surprises and steals acting honors.

. . . .

■ CONFESSIONS OF A NAZI SPY

1939, 110 MINS, US
Dir Anatole Litvak   *Prod* Robert Lord   *Scr* Milton Krims, John Wexley   *Ph* Sol Polito   *Ed* Owen Marks   *Mus* Max Steiner   *Art Dir* Carl Jules Weyl
● Edward G. Robinson, Francis Lederer, George Sanders, Paul Lukas, Lya Lys (Warner)

The story itself is told for maximum mass comprehension. Based on articles by Leon G. Turrou, former G-man, it is an adaptation of the spy trials of 1937 which resulted in the conviction of four persons.

Its thesis is that espionage directed from Berlin is tied up with the German-American Bunds, their rallies and summer camps and general parading around in uniforms. The German goal is destruction of democracy.

The cast numbers a fine collection of scarfaced Gestapo agents, guys with crew haircuts and assorted livid sneerers.

Edward G. Robinson comes in very late in the film. Paul Lukas carries through as the Bund leader who finally falls out with the Gestapo. The missing motivation, anti-Semitism, is the one thing not named and ticketed.

. . . .

■ CONFIDENTIAL AGENT

1945, 113 MINS, US
Dir Herman Shumlin   *Prod* Robert Buckner   *Scr* Robert Buckner   *Ph* James Wong Howe   *Ed* George Amy   *Mus* Franz Waxman   *Art Dir* Leo Kuter
● Charles Boyer, Lauren Bacall, Wanda Hendrix, Peter Lorre, Katina Paxinou, George Coulouris (Warner)

The story attempts to show how in 1937 the success of Franco adherents was to become the prelude to an even greater conflict. The yarn's development is inept, and the link of the romance with the basic story [from a novel by Graham Greene] is too pat, at the expense of the major story line.

Charles Boyer plays a Spanish concert musician who has given up his career to fight the fascists. He's detailed to go to England and outbid the Francoites for British coal. The coal can be the difference between victory and defeat. The plot specifically deals with the obstacles that confront him, including the British fascists, and secondary to this is the romance that evolves between a British coal tycoon's daughter and Boyer.

Boyer as usual, underplays to gain an effect as adequate as possible under the circumstances. Lauren Bacall suffers from a monot-

ony of voice and an uncertainty of performance. Her s.a., however, is still plenty evident.

. . . .

■ CONFIDENTIAL REPORT

(US: Mr Arkadin)

1955, 99 MINS, FRANCE/SPAIN ⊚ ⊙
Dir Orson Welles   *Prod* Louis Dolivet   *Scr* Orson Welles   *Ph* Jean Bourgoin   *Ed* Renzo Lucidi   *Mus* Paul Misraki   *Art Dir* Orson Welles
● Orson Welles, Michael Redgrave, Patricia Medina, Akim Tamiroff, Robert Arden, Paola Mori (Filmorsa)

Confidential Report is at once a fascinating (inevitably) and dismaying effort, frequently suggestive of self-parody; and indeed, in scenario and technique, it is an echo of *Kane* and that film's bravura style. Instead of newspaper tycoon Charles Foster Kane, here is Gregory Arkadin, shadow figure, arch-capitalist, graduate of a Polish 'white slave' ring, but whose latter-day power and riches are shrouded.

Instead of Kane's Xanadu, Arkadin has a castle in Spain. Instead of inanimate 'Rosebud,' there is a daughter (Welles' wife, Paola Mori), pretty, vital and overprotected.

The visual trickery in *Report*, albeit often irrelevant, is almost always fascinating just because it's a Welles orchestration, filling the screen with arresting oddment, with delicious detail with, in short, excitement.

Welles' story is a parable, and verbalized as such by Arkadin at one point. It concerns a scorpion and a frog, and the moral is that character is immutable and thus logical even when seemingly illogical.

Told in flashback, Arkadin is an amnesiac and hires a smalltime Yank smuggler to trace his past. His ulterior purpose is to turn up, and eradicate, old nefarious associates who conceivably might disclose the truth about him to his daughter. The American goes to work, and the murders follow.

Engaging meller it may be, but missing the incisive delineation that marked *Kane*. The melange of darting narrative simply gets the upper hand case of visual virtuosity overwhelming the Arkadin parable.

. . . .

■ CONNECTICUT YANKEE, A

1931, 93 MINS, US ⊚
Dir David Butler   *Scr* William Conselman   *Ph* Ernest Palmer   *Mus* Erno Rapee
● Will Rogers, William Farnum, Myrna Loy, Maureen O'Sullivan, Frank Albertson, Mitchell Harris (Fox)

The [Mark Twain] story was originally turned down by Doug Fairbanks, after which Fox made it with Harry Myers. It was released late in 1920. The staff working on this sound version must have run off the silent print plenty. William Conselman gets the credit for the modern adaptation, but there's no telling how many writers worked on the script. Neither the beginning nor the end is entirely satisfactory, especially the finish. But the main section is a dream, and there are more than sufficient laughs to compensate.

Opening has Will Rogers as a smalltown radio store proprietor, called to a mysterious house to install a battery. An armored figure falls over, knocks Rogers out and thence into the dream. The change back to the modern story and finish is decidedly weak.

Rogers' main cast support comes from William Farnum as King Arthur. Mitchell Harris as Merlin, the magician, and Brandon Hurst playing the menace. Myrna Loy does not do much with her femme heavy, while Maureen O'Sullivan has nothing much more than a bit. Frank Albertson, supplying the other half of the love interest, appears to be at a loss in not being able to chatter at his generally furious rate.

. . . .

CONNECTICUT YANKEE IN KING ARTHUR'S COURT, A
(UK: A Yankee in King Arthur's Court)

1949, 106 MINS, US ◇ 🎬 ⊙
Dir Tay Garnett   *Prod* Robert Fellows   *Scr* Edmund Beloin   *Ph* Ray Rennahan   *Ed* Archie Marshek   *Mus* Victor Young   *Art Dir* Hans Dreier, Roland Anderson
● Bing Crosby, Rhonda Fleming, Cedric Hardwicke, William Bendix, Henry Wilcoxon (Paramount)

Bing Crosby, songs and color make pleasant entertainment out of *A Connecticut Yankee in King Arthur's Court*. It's not high comedy and there's little swashbuckling but it is pleasant.

A footnote emphasizes that this latest version of Mark Twain's gentle tale of a Yankee blacksmith who's knocked on the head and awakes in King Arthur's court is adapted strictly from the book as written by the author.

A bit more vigor in the handling would have sharpened the pace. Film also falls down in some of the technical work, which doesn't help to carry out the illusion of the romantic days of 528.

Rhonda Fleming's vocals please and her physical charms as Alisande, King Arthur's niece, are expressive enough to illustrate why the Yankee would develop a yen for her.

CONQUEROR, THE

1956, 111 MINS, US ◇ 🎬
Dir Dick Powell   *Prod* Dick Powell   *Scr* Oscar Millard   *Ph* Joseph LaShelle, Leo Tover, Harry J. Wild, William Snyder   *Ed* Robert Ford, Kennie Marstella   *Mus* Victor Young   *Art Dir* Albert S. D'Agostino, Carroll Clark
● John Wayne, Susan Hayward, Pedro Armendariz, Agnes Moorehead, Thomas Gomez, William Conrad (RKO)

Just so there will be no misunderstanding about *The Conqueror*, a foreword baldly states that it is fiction, although with some basis in fact. With that warning out of the way, the viewer can sit back and thoroughly enjoy a huge, brawling, sex-and-sand actioner purporting to show how a 12th Century Mongol leader became known as Genghis Khan.

The marquee value of the John Wayne-Susan Hayward teaming more than offsets any incongruity of the casting, which has him as the Mongol leader and she as the Tartar princess he captures and forcibly takes as mate.

Co-starring with Wayne and Hayward is excellent Mexican actor, Pedro Armendariz, who makes believable his role of Wayne's blood-brother and is an important essential in the entertainment.

The s.a. pitch is in a harem dance choreographed by Robert Sidney, in which a covey of lookers give the appearance of being almost completely bare while gyrating to the Oriental strains of Victor Young's firstrate music.

CONQUEROR WORM, THE
See: Witchfinder General

CONQUEST
(UK: Marie Walewska)

1937, 115 MINS, US ◇
Dir Clarence Brown   *Prod* Bernard H. Hyman   *Scr* Samuel Hoffenstein, Salka Viertel, S.N. Behrman   *Ph* Karl Freund   *Ed* Tom Held   *Mus* Herbert Stothart
● Greta Garbo, Charles Boyer, Reginald Owen, Alan Marshall, Henry Stephenson, Leif Erickson (M-G-M)

Conquest is said to have cost $2.6 million. Visually, it bears the mark of extravagant effort.

With Greta Garbo and Charles Boyer teamed as co-stars, in the characters of Marie Walewska, Polish mistress, and Napoleon Bonaparte, lover and soldier, the film is a romantic mixture of fact and fiction. Intensely emotional in spots, it is a moving and satisfying entertainment [from a book by Waclaw Gasiorowski and dramatization by Helen Jerome].

Major credit goes to Clarence Brown for direction. The Walewska episode in itself is a thrilling romance. Dramatic events led to the meeting of the young Polish countess (she was 18 at the time) and Napoleon when the latter visited Warsaw at the height of his military successes. He was enraptured by her beauty and wooed her ardently. She joined him during his banishment to Elba.

Walewska role would seem to be a natural for Garbo. Part calls for intense feminine feeling, for coquetry and renunciation. It is not due to any shortcomings on her part, however, that the audience interest is more closely held by Boyer's Napoleon. Boyer plays the love scenes with brusque tenderness, and makes the character understood as a blazing individualist acting under reckless urges for power.
□ 1937: Nominations: Best Actor (Charles Boyer), Art Direction

CONQUEST OF SPACE

1955, 80 MINS, US ◇ 🎬
Dir Byron Haskin   *Prod* George Pal   *Scr* James O'Hanlon   *Ph* Lionel Lindon   *Ed* Everett Douglas   *Mus* Van Cleave   *Art Dir* Hal Pereira, Joseph MacMillan
● Walter Brooke, Eric Fleming, Mickey Shaughnessy, Phil Foster, William Redfield, William Hopper (Paramount)

When Byron Haskin's direction has a chance at action and thrills they come over well, but most of the time the pacing is slowed by the talky script fashioned from the adaptation of the Chesley Bonestell-Willy Ley book by Philip Yordan, Barre Lyndon and George Worthington Yates.

Plot time is the future, with the setting divided between a space station wheeling some 1,000 miles above earth and a flight from this floating base to the planet Mars. Best moments deal with a meteor hitting the space station and spilling everything before the wheel is righted, and the near crash of the rocket ship with a meteor on the trip to Mars.

The rocket ship is manned by a stereotype crew. There's Walter Brooke, the commanding officer who loses his screws because he figures God didn't want man jetting off to new planets; Eric Fleming, his son, who didn't want to make the trip anyway; Mickey Shaughnessy, tough old master sergeant, devoted to the c.o.; Phil Foster, a wise-cracking Brooklynite, and Benson Fong and Ross Martin, UN personnel. These and others in the cast are acceptable in undemanding roles. The real stars are the props and lensing.

CONQUEST OF THE PLANET OF THE APES

1972, 87 MINS, US ◇ 🎬
Dir J. Lee Thompson   *Prod* Arthur P. Jacobs   *Scr* Paul Dehn   *Ph* Bruce Surtees   *Mus* Tom Scott   *Art Dir* Philip Jefferies
● Roddy McDowall, Don Murray, Ricardo Montalban, Natalie Trundy, Hari Rhodes, Severn Darden (20th Century-Fox/Apjac)

The *Planet of the Apes* series takes an angry turn in the fourth entry, *Conquest of the Planet of the Apes*.

The story begins about 20 years in the future, after a world epidemic has destroyed all dogs. People first had turned to apes as pets, but because of their intelligence the apes have become servants under civil regulation of computer-age overseer Don Murray. Into this milieu comes traveling circus operator Ricardo Montalban who, at the end of the prior film, had concealed the nearly-human offspring of the murdered Roddy McDowall

and Kim Hunter. McDowall now has shifted to the role of his son.

In the new world, McDowall has to Uncle-Tom his way through the prevailing slave environment, until Murray's inexorable search for the long-missing ape-human child leads to Montalban's death under torture-grilling by Severn Darden. McDowall then organizes a bloody revolt which occupies the last third of the film.

CONRACK

1974, 107 MINS, US ◇ 🎬
Dir Martin Ritt   *Prod* Martin Ritt, Harriet Frank Jr   *Scr* Irving Ravetch, Harriet Frank Jr   *Ph* John Alonzo   *Ed* Frank Bracht   *Mus* John Williams   *Art Dir* Walter Scott Herndon
● Jon Voight, Paul Winfield, Madge Sinclair, Tina Andrews, Antonio Fargas, Hume Cronyn (20th Century-Fox)

Jon Voight stars as a young Southerner who treks off to an isolated South Carolina island in 1969 for a teaching post, only to find the black children there uniformly illiterate and/or retarded. Through a combination of love and pedagogical razzmatazz, he opens their eyes to the wonders of yoga, Beethoven, Babe Ruth, Ho Chi Minh, and Halloween.

Some may resent the inadvertent white-liberal condescension evident in the initially one-dimensional portrait of the deprived youngsters. Others may be momentarily confused by the lack of explicit data – time, place, personal factors behind the teacher's willingness to submerge obvious intellectual gifts in a backwoods community.

But few will totally resist the surefire appeal of this latest variation on Pygmalion mythology.

CONSENTING ADULTS

1992, 100 MINS, US ◇ 🎬 ⊙
Dir Alan J. Pakula   *Prod* Alan J. Pakula, David Permut   *Scr* Matthew Chapman   *Ph* Stephen Goldblatt   *Ed* Sam O'Steen   *Mus* Michael Small   *Art Dir* Carol Spier
● Kevin Kline, Mary Elizabeth Mastrantonio, Kevin Spacey, Rebecca Miller, Forest Whitaker, E.G. Marshall (Hollywood Pictures)

Psychotic neighbors are the latest riff on the urban paranoia theme. Most distinctive element here proves to be Kevin Spacey's over-the-top performance as the smarmy newcomer to the block, who ultimately lures his risk-aversive neighbor (Kevin Kline into a proposed wife-swap that leads to the baseball-bat murder of Spacey's wife as part of an elaborate insurance scam.

Kline's character ends up framed for the murder, forcing him to try to decipher the mystery and win back his own wife (Mary Elizabeth Mastrantonio), who has conveniently and rather inexplicably fled to Spacey.

Pic suffers from an absurdity level that somewhat undermines its chills as well as its few geniune laughs. Director Alan J. Pakula can't seem to decide whether this is a legitimate drama or conventional thriller – of the cheap scare variety.

Perhaps because of those narrative flaws, neither Kline nor Mastrantonio (reunited after *The January Man*) are particularly distinguished here.

Rebecca Miller oozes sex appeal, but the real stand-out is Spacey, who established his inordinate skill playing psychopaths with a disarming sense of humor back during TV's *Wiseguy*.

CONSTANCE

1984, 103 MINS, NEW ZEALAND ◇ 🎬
Dir Bruce Morrison   *Prod* Larry Parr   *Scr* Jonathan Hardy   *Ph* Kevin Hayward   *Ed* Philip Howe   *Mus* John Charles   *Art Dir* Ric Kifoed

● Donogh Rees, Shane Briant, Judie Douglass, Martin Vaughan, Donald MacDonald, Marc Wignall (Mirage)

Constance is a highly stylized film about a beautiful young woman living in Auckland in 1946 who dreams she is a Hollywood super-star.

Constance (Donogh Rees) is given to such contrived charades as dressing as Marlene Dietrich at parties a singing along to a recording of Dietrich's hit, 'Falling in Love Again.'

Rees' stiffness of manner may be director Bruce Morrison's idea of the artificiality of the concept as a whole.

Imported actor Shane Briant has the right air of handsome, predatory decadence as a visiting Hollywood still-photographer. There is an outburst of sexual violence during a photo session which is given the blurred-lens, freeze-frame, jump-cut treatment, and it makes an effective contrast to the film's otherwise sharply focused sedate pace.

● ●

■ CONSTANT HUSBAND, THE

1955, 88 MINS, UK ◇
Dir Sidney Gilliat   *Prod* Frank Launder, Sidney Gilliat
Scr Sidney Gilliat, Val Valentine   *Ph* Ted Scaife   *Ed* G.
Turney-Smith   *Mus* Malcolm Arnold   *Art Dir* Wilfrid
Shingleton
● Rex Harrison, Margaret Leighton, Kay Kendall, Cecil
Parker, Nicole Maurey, George Cole (London)

A frothy comedy, *The Constant Husband* is one of the brightest efforts from the Frank Launder and Sidney Gilliat partnership. The screenplay is light and amusing, and none of the sparkle has been lost in the translation to the screen.

The story could not be more slender. Rex Harrison, an amnesia victim, learns, to his horror, that he has seven wives to his credit. A bigamy charge follows, but rather than face seven eager ex-spouses, he pleas in favor of jail.

Harrison is thoroughly diverting as the amnesia victim. Margaret Leighton makes a belated appearance on the screen, but her impact is nonetheless notable. Kay Kendall, as the last of the seven wives gives a sparkling portrayal. Cecil Parker is typically buoyant and Nicole Maurey is sufficiently alluring as another of the ex-wives.

● ●

■ CONSTANT NYMPH, THE

1934, 85 MINS, UK
Dir Basil Dean   *Scr* Dorothy Farnum, Basil Dean,
Margaret Kennedy   *Ph* Mutz Greenbaum   *Mus* Eugene
Goosens, John Greenwood   *Art Dir* Alfred Junge
● Brian Aherne, Victoria Hopper, Peggy Blythe, Jane
Baxter, Lyn Harding, Mary Clare (Gaumont-British)

Story [by Margaret Kennedy] opens in the Austrian mountains where a slightly mad composer and his daughters, all half-sisters and all hoydens, live a carefree life of idyllic sweetness. There is a younger composer (Brian Aherne) and for him one of the girls (Victoria Hopper) conceives an undying passion.

He marries a respectability-minded English cousin (Leonora Corbett) and moves to London. Ultimately he realizes he should have waited for the girl to add a year or two to her age and married her instead of the older woman.

It is a soft, delicate, fragile, meandering yarn, beautifully directed by Basil Dean.

● ●

■ CONSTANT NYMPH, THE

1943, 106 MINS, US
Dir Edmund Goulding   *Prod* Henry Blanke   *Scr* Kathryn
Scola   *Ph* Tony Gaudio   *Ed* David Weisbert
Mus Erich Wolfgang Korngold

● Charles Boyer, Joan Fontaine, Alexis Smith, Charles Coburn, Peter Lorre, Joyce Reynolds (Warner)

This is the film version of the novel and play of same title [by Margaret Kennedy and Basil Dean]. Devoting plenty of footage to character delineations and incidental episodes, it results in a bumpy screen tale with interlay of both draggy and interesting sequences. Major portion of excess footage is on the front end, where 40 minutes is consumed in setting up detailed background for the final event, which is a love triangle, with Charles Boyer the focal point for conflict betwen teenager played by Joan Fontaine and the older Alexis smith. The stretch hits yawning periods.

This early portion serves to detail movement of Boyer, composer of promise but lacking the necessary fire to write his outstanding composition, from Brussels to home of his friend and mentor (Montagu Love) in Switzerland. Of the four daughters in the house, Fontaine is next to the youngest, with adolescent adoration for Boyer. When Love dies and girls' uncle (Charles Coburn) arrives from England with his own daughter (Smith), Boyer and latter embark on romance culminating in marriage.

Script covers plenty of ground and detail, but general tightening would have helped materially. There's a tang of the stage in the unfolding, which director Edmund Goulding found impossible to overcome with his careful and even-tempoed direction.

☐ 1943: Nomination: Best Actress (Joan Fontaine)

● ●

■ CONTEST GIRL

See: The Beauty Jungle

● ●

■ CONTINENTAL DIVIDE

1981, 103 MINS, US ◇
Dir Michael Apted   *Prod* Bob Larson   *Scr* Lawrence
Kasdan   *Ph* John Bailey   *Ed* Dennis Virkler
Mus Michael Small   *Art Dir* Peter Jamison
● John Belushi, Blair Brown, Allen Garfield, Carlin
Glynn, Tony Ganios, Val Avery (Universal/Amblin)

For a picture that you can't really believe for a second, *Continental Divide* still comes off as a reasonably engaging entertainment thanks to some lively performances and a liberal dose of laughs throughout the script.

John Belushi plays star columnist for the *Chicago Sun Times* who loves dishing the dirt about the latest doings down at city hall. When his stories on a certain corrupt alderman get too hot, Belushi is sent to the Rocky Mountains to track down a crazy bird lady known for her reclusiveness and particular hatred of nosey reporters.

At first, beauteous Blair Brown orders the interloper from her mountaintop retreat but, as his guide won't be back to fetch him for two weeks, they gradually learn to cope and finally, love together.

The problem is that these two just don't seem made for each other. When Tracy and Hepburn sparred for two hours in films like *Adam's Rib* and *Pat and Mike*, airing every possible reason they shouldn't get, or remain, together, the inevitability of their ultimate match-up was crystal clear.

Lawrence Kasdan displays a keen ability to write sparkling male-female repartee and al creates a believable context for Belushi's beat on the Windy City streets. Michael Apted's direction is solid.

● ●

■ CONTRABAND

(US: Blackout)

1940, 91 MINS, UK ⊙
Dir Michael Powell   *Prod* John Corfield   *Scr* Emeric
Pressburger, Michael Powell, Brock Williams   *Ph* Freddie

Young   *Ed* John Seabourne   *Mus* Richard Addinsell,
John Greenwood   *Art Dir* Alfred Junge
● Conrad Veidt, Valerie Hobson, Hay Petrie, Joss
Ambler, Raymond Lovell, Esmond Knight (British National)

As a dissertation on how to do nothing well, film anent Britain's naval blockade earns a niche all its own. Producers have lavished their brainchild with a wealth of detail that takes care of all except one thing – imagination.

This yarn of the economic war staged by the navy through its control of shipping veers from the sea to take a jaunt on espionage in London. Conrad Veidt as the Danish seaman is authentic to the point where it's questionable as to his ease as a lover in the smart company of Valerie Hobson. Her role is handled with aplomb. All of the rest reach for the same standard, particular attention going to Hay Petrie for his comedy work in a dual role.

● ●

■ CONVERSATION, THE

1974, 113 MINS, US ◇ ⓥ ⊙
Dir Francis Coppola   *Prod* Francis Coppola, Fred Roos
Scr Francis Coppola   *Ph* Bill Butler   *Ed* Walter Murch,
Richard Chew   *Mus* David Shire   *Art Dir* Dean
Tavoularis
● Gene Hackman, John Cazale, Allen Garfield, Frederic
Forrest, Cindy Williams, Harrison Ford (Paramount)

Francis Coppola's *The Conversation* stars Gene Hackman as a professional surveillance expert whose resurgent conscience involves him in murder and leads to self-destruction.

He is introduced in SF's Union Square at midday, teamed with John Cazale and Michael Higgins in tracking the movements and voices of Frederic Forrest and Cindy Williams. The cleaned-up sound tapes, along with photographs, are to be delivered to a mysterious businessman, played in an un-billed part by Robert Duvall. What appears to be a simple case of marital infidelity suddenly shifts to a possible murder plot.

A major artistic asset to the film – besides script, direction and the top performances – is supervising editor Walter Murch's sound collage and re-recording. Voices come in and out of aural focus in a superb tease.

☐ 1974: Nominations: Best Picture, Original Screenplay, Sound

● ●

■ CONVERSATION PIECE

1975, 120 MINS, ITALY/FRANCE ◇ ⓥ
Dir Luchino Visconti   *Scr* Luchino Visconti, Suso Cecchi
D'Amico   *Ph* Pasqualino De Santis   *Ed* Ruggero
Mastroianni   *Art Dir* Mario Garbuglia
● Burt Lancaster, Silvana Mangano, Helmut Berger,
Claudia Marsani, Dominique Sanda, Claudia Cardinale
(Rusconi/Gaumont)

Conversation Piece eschews the usually operatic, museum-like pix of Luchino Visconti for a touching tale of the generation gap and the loss of life-contact of an intellectual.

A prof (Burt Lancaster) is addicted to collecting 18th-century British paintings of families called Conversation Pieces. Into this comes a haughty, middleaged, but still beautiful Italian woman who wants to rent his upstairs apartment.

Lancaster is finally persuaded by her, her cute teenage daughter and her rich fiance. There is also the mother's lover, young German (Helmut Berger). The professor gets tangled up with the young people despite himself.

Visconti has kept this talky but rarely verbose pic in the two apartments with only an outside studio view of Rome. The assorted accents are justified and even the peppering of blue lingo Americanisms fit these jet setters. Lancaster is highly effective as the professor.

● ●

C

■ CONVOY

1978, 110 MINS, US ◇ ▼
Dir Sam Peckinpah   *Prod* Robert M. Sherman
Scr B.W.L. Norton   *Ph* Harry Stradling Jr   *Ed* Graeme
Clifford, John Wright, Garth Craven   *Mus* Chip Davis
Art Dir Fernando Carrere
● Kris Kristofferson, Ali MacGraw, Ernest Borgnine, Burt
Young, Madge Sinclair, Franklyn Ajaye (United Artists)

Sam Peckinpah's *Convoy* starts out as *Smokey and the Bandit*, segues into either *Moby Dick* or *Les Miserables*, and ends in the usual script confusion and disarray, the whole stew peppered with the vulgar excess of random truck crashes and miscellaneous destruction. Kris Kristofferson stars as a likeable roustabout who accidentally becomes a folk hero, while Ali MacGraw recycles about three formula reactions throughout her nothing part.

B.W.L. Norton gets writing credit using C.W. McCall's c&w poptune lyric as a basis. No matter. Peckinpah's films display common elements and clumsy analogies, overwhelmed with logistical fireworks and drunken changes of dramatic emphasis.

This time around, Kristofferson (who, miraculously, seems to survive these banalities) is a trucker whose longtime nemesis, speed-trap-blackmailer cop Ernest Borgnine, pursues him with a vengeance through what appears to be three states. Every few minutes there's some new roadblock to run, alternating with pithy comments on The Meaning Of It All. There's a whole lot of nothing going on here.

■ COOGAN'S BLUFF

1968, 93 MINS, US ◇ ▼ ⊙
Dir Don Siegel   *Prod* Don Siegel   *Scr* Herman Miller,
Dean Reisner, Howard Rodman   *Ph* Bud Thackery
Ed Sam E. Waxman   *Mus* Lalo Schifrin
Art Dir Alexander Golitzen, Robert C.MacKichan
● Clint Eastwood, Lee J. Cobb, Susan Clark, Tisha
Sterling, Don Stroud, Betty Field (Universal)

Story of the clash between sophisticated law enforcement and frontier-style simplistics, which is perhaps one of the major internal American problems. Clint Eastwood stars as a laconic, taciturn stranger, this time a deputy sheriff from Arizona in City.

Herman Miller's story establishes Eastwood as a cold, selfish desert lawman sent to NY to extradite hippie Don Stroud, whose Arizona offense is never mentioned. Lee J. Cobb, a city detective, tries to explain to Eastwood that things are done differently.

Susan Clark is very good as a probation officer who falls for Eastwood. Tisha Sterling does well as Stroud's hippie girl friend. Betty Field has an excellent scene as Stroud's mother, impact being second only to Cobb's terrific work.

■ COOKIE

1989, 93 MINS, US ◇ ▼ ⊙
Dir Susan Seidelman   *Prod* Laurence Mark   *Scr* Nora
Ephron, Alice Arlen   *Ph* Oliver Stapleton   *Ed* Andrew
Mondshein   *Mus* Thomas Newman   *Art Dir* Michael
Haller
● Peter Falk, Dianne Wiest, Emily Lloyd, Michael V.
Gazzo, Brenda Vaccaro, Adrian Pasdar
(Lorimar/Warner)

Half-baked, bland and flat as a vanilla wafer, *Cookie* rolls out the tired marriage of comedy and organized crime to produce a disorganized mess with little nutritional or comedic value.

The story gets set in motion, such as it is, when mobster Dino Capisco (Peter Falk) is released from prison after 13 years, rejoining his wife (Brenda Vaccaro), mistress (Dianne Wiest) and the headstrong daughter he had with the latter, played by Emily Lloyd.

Sadly, about the only thing Lloyd gets to do here is prove she can affect a New York accent and chew gum at the same time. Thrown together with Falk as his driver, the two fail to build any of the warmth or even grudging admiration they display in the final reel.

The film ultimately turns into an elaborate scheme by which Falk can get even with his treacherous former partner (played by Michael V. Gazzo), and the payoff is hardly worth the protracted build-up.

Only Wiest emerges in top form with her brassy portrayal of a weepy red-haired gun moll in the Lucille Ball mode.

■ COOK, THE THIEF, HIS WIFE AND HER LOVER, THE

1989, 126 MINS, NETHERLANDS/FRANCE ◇ ▼ ⊙
Dir Peter Greenaway   *Prod* Kees Kasander   *Scr* Peter
Greenaway   *Ph* Sacha Vierny   *Ed* John Wilson
Mus Michael Nyman   *Art Dir* Ben Van Os, Jan Roelfs
● Richard Bohringer, Michael Gambon, Helen Mirren,
Alan Howard, Tim Roth, Gary Olsen (Allarts
Cook/Erato/Films Inc)

Peter Greenaway's grim sense of humor and cheerful assault on all our sacred cows is evident in this new outing from the iconoclastic filmmaker.

Setting is a smart restaurant, La Hollandaise, where Richard, the chef (Richard Bohringer) prepares a lavish menu every night. Among his regular customers are Albert Spica (Michael Gambon), a loudmouthed, vulgar, violent gangster, who dines with his entourage of seedy yes-men, and his bored, beautiful wife, Georgina (Helen Mirren).

At another table each night sits Michael, a quiet, diffident man who's always reading books. He and Georgina make eye contact, and soon they're having a series of secret rendezvous. Eventually Albert discovers his wife's infidelity, and takes a typically violent revenge, triggering a more unusual retaliation from her.

Albert is one of the ugliest characters ever brought to the screen. Ignorant, over-bearing and violent, it's a gloriously rich performance by Gambon.

In contrast, Helen Mirren (in a role which was originally to have been played by Vanessa Redgrave) is all calm politeness and mute acceptance until her passion is aroused by the (far from handsome) Michael.

■ COOLEY HIGH

1975, 107 MINS, US ◇ ▼ ⊙
Dir Michael Schultz   *Prod* Steve Krantz   *Scr* Eric Monte
Ph Paul vom Brack   *Ed* Christopher Holmes
Mus Freddie Perren   *Art Dir* William B. Fosser
● Glynn Turman, Lawrence-Hilton Jacobs, Garrett
Morris, Cynthia Davies (American International)

Cooley High is pitched as a black *American Graffiti*, and the description is apt. Furthermore, you don't have to be black to enjoy it immensely. The Steve Krantz production is a heartening comedy-drama about urban Chicago high school youths, written by Eric Monte.

The story focusses mainly on two frisky students, Glynn Turman and Lawrence-Hilton Jacobs. Girl trouble (principally charming Cynthia Davies), school trouble (with empathetic teacher Garrett Morris), and law trouble (via involvement with toughs Sherman Smith and Norman Gibson) lead the pair through experiences which range from broadly comic to deathly serious. The plot is simply about a lot of believable people and of course that's the way it should be.

■ COOL HAND LUKE

1967, 126 MINS, US ◇ ▼ ⊙
Dir Stuart Rosenberg   *Prod* Gordon Carroll   *Scr* Donn
Pearce, Frank R. Pierson, [Hal Dresner]   *Ph* Conrad Hall
Ed Sam O'Steen   *Mus* Lalo Schifrin   *Art Dir* Cary Odell
● Paul Newman, George Kennedy, J.D. Cannon, Lou
Antonio, Robert Drivas, Jo Van Fleet (Warner)

Paul Newman is *Cool Hand Luke*, a loner role in a film that depicts the social structure of a Dixie chain gang. Versatile and competent cast maintains interest throughout rambling exposition to a downbeat climax.

Luke, obviously supposed to be set in the South, was shot near Stockton, California, where the desired flat land, occasionally broken by gentle rolls, makes for an effective physical backdrop. In this case, it is a chain-gang compound, ruled by some patronizing, sadistic guards, to which Newman will not conform.

Newman gives an excellent performance, assisted by a terrif supporting cast, including George Kennedy, outstanding as the unofficial leader of the cons who yields first place to Newman.

Strother Martin's camp chief is chilling, a firstrate characterization. His goon squad likewise delivers strong performances: Morgan Woodward, Luke Askew, Robert Donner, John McLiam, Charles Tyner. Clifton James, the burly building overseer, is appropriately warmer.

□ 1967: Best Supp. Actor (George Kennedy).
□ Nominations: Best Actor (Paul Newman), Adapted Screenplay, Original Music Score

■ COOL WORLD, THE

1963, 125 MINS, US ◇ ▼
Dir Shirley Clarke   *Scr* Shirley Clarke, Carl Lee
Ph Baird Bryant   *Ed* Shirley Clarke   *Mus* Mal Waldron
● Hampton Clayton, Yolanda Rodriguez, Carl Lee
(Wiseman)

The Cool World is the world of Harlem. Film deals generally with its physical and human aspects and also comment on the personal feel and outlook of its characters. Both elements are well blended to make this a telling look at Harlem and probably one of the least patronizing films ever made on Negro life in New York.

A sharp, restless, whiplike camera picks up a Black Muslim spouting hate against the white man and claiming supremacy. Then the Harlem streets and the people listening, or letting the fanatic words float by, come to life and out of the crowd is picked a young teenager, Duke, whose one desire seems to be to own a gun that would give him standing in his own gang. Film [from the novel by Warren Miller] alternates Duke's story with general scenes of Harlem life.

The natural thesping is by a mainly non-pro cast. But it is chiefly the virile, well observed direction of Shirley Clarke that keeps this long film engrossing and revealing most of the way. She creates a tenseness around the familiar characters by a knowing look at Harlem rhythms, gaiety, lurking desperation, boredom tempered with joviality, and the general oppressiveness of bad housing and employment conditions.

Sometimes the characters get a bit lost in the general schematics of the pic, which at times waters down its underlying irony. But, overall, Clarke has a firm hold on her characters and story.

■ COOL WORLD

1992, 102 MINS, US ◇ ▼ ⊙
Dir Ralph Bakshi   *Prod* Frank Mancuso Jr   *Scr* Michael
Grais, Mark Victor, [Larry Gross]   *Ph* John A. Alonzo
Ed Steve Mirkovich, Annamaria Szanto   *Mus* Mark
Isham   *Art Dir* Michael Corenblith
● Kim Basinger, Gabriel Byrne, Brad Pitt, Michele
Abrams, Deidre O'Connell, Carrie Hamilton (Paramount)

Style has seldom pummeled substance as severely as in *Cool World*, a combination funhouse ride/acid trip that will prove an ordeal for most visitors in the form of trial by animation. Director Ralph Bakshi has let his imagination run wild with almost brutal vigor, resulting in a guerrilla-like assault virtually unchecked by any traditional rules of storytelling.

Although comparisons have been made to *Who Framed Roger Rabbit* because of the live-action/animation mix, this more closely resembles Joe Dante's *Gremlins* in its reliance on exploding the conventions of Warner Bros. cartoons.

The comic-book premise hinges on parallel worlds – the real world and a sphere of animated characters, known as Cool World, which has also been captured by cartoonist Jack Deebs (Gabriel Byrne).

Pulling Deebs into the Cool World is curvaceous fantasy girl Holli Wood, a 'doodle' (i.e. cartoon) who dreams of becoming human by coupling with a flesh-and-blood male. The odd-character-out in the story is Frank Harris (Brad Pitt), a human top cop yanked into Cool World in the '40s.

Kim Basinger, who doesn't appear in the flesh until nearly an hour into the film, is one of the few actresses who could convincingly breathe life into Holli, a 36-18-36 bombshell in animated form seemingly pulled straight from the paintings of Frank Frazetta, whose art inspired Bakshi's little-seen fantasy feature *Fire and Ice*.

Because the characters are so undeveloped *Cool World* is a realm with precious little humor and zero pathos, to be admired only for its brilliant synthesis of live-action and animation, as well as the staggering creation of credible comic book sets around human actors.

．．．．．．．．．．．．．．．．．．．．．．．．．．．．．．

■ **CORNERED**

1945, 102 MINS, US ⓥ ⊙

Dir Edward Dmytryk   *Prod* Adrian Scott   *Scr* John Paxton   *Ph* Harry J. Wild   *Ed* Joseph Noriega   *Mus* Roy Webb   *Art Dir* Albert S. D'Agostino, Carroll Clark
● Dick Powell, Walter Slezak, Nina Vale, Micheline Cheirel, Morris Carnovsky, Luther Adler (RKO)

It's the story [by John Wexley] of the relentless post-war hunt of a Canadian flier for the collaborationist who was responsible for the death of his French bride. Directed and played strictly for suspense and thrills, search gets underway in France switches to Belgium, Switzerland and then Argentina, where most of the action takes place.

While all evidence points towards the death of the collaborationist, Dick Powell believes the man still alive. His search reveals hibernation of pro-Nazi in the Argentine, where they are waiting to rise again in the future, and the efforts of good Argentinians to smoke them out.

Cast has many suspects weaving in and out to conceal identity of the mysterious 'Marcel Jarnac' whom Powell seeks, and finale has a definite surprise in store for audiences. Edward Dmytryk's direction makes the most of the suspense and concealment, building a mood that never lets down.

．．．．．．．．．．．．．．．．．．．．．．．．．．．．．．

■ **CORN IS GREEN, THE**

1945, 114 MINS, US ⓥ

Dir Irving Rapper   *Prod* Jack Chertok   *Scr* Casey Robinson, Frank Cavett   *Ph* Sol Polito   *Ed* Frederick Richards   *Mus* Max Steiner   *Art Dir* Carl Jules Weyl
● Bette Davis, Nigel Bruce, John Dall, Joan Lorring, Mildred Dunnock (Warner)

The performances, not only of Bette Davis but of newcomers John Dall and Joan Lorring, together with those of Nigel Bruce and others, capture attention and admiration far and above that of the story itself, which is some-

what slow in the first half. Several sequences could have been edited more sharply. While the exteriors of the Welsh countryside are almost entirely dreary and depressing, they reflect the mood of the Emlyn Williams play and its locale.

Davis, doing the emotional and serious-minded school mistress of the story, whose sociological ideals spur her to untiring efforts in raising the IQ of lowly Welsh mining folk, is cast in the kind of role she does well. Dall, her protege, is much less an admirable character, though interest stays with him all the way.

The youthful Lorring is also a very intriguing type. As the trollop Bessie Watty, she is particularly socko in the final reel, when returning to the village with the news that she has borne Dall's illegitimate child.
☐ 1945: Nominations: Best Supp. Actor (John Dall), Supp. Actress (Joan Loring)

．．．．．．．．．．．．．．．．．．．．．．．．．．．．．．

■ **CORPSE GRINDERS, THE**

1971, 72 MINS, US ◇ ⓥ

Dir Ted V. Mikels   *Prod* Ted V. Mikels   *Scr* Arch Hall, Joseph L. Cranston   *Ph* Bill Anneman   *Ed* Ted V. Mikels   *Art Dir* John Robinson, Laura Young
● Sean Kenney, Monika Kelly, Sanford Mitchell, J. Byron Foster, Warren Ball, Ann Noble (Mikels)

The Corpse Grinders revolves around the grinding of stolen cadavers into canned cat food which turns a gentle pussy into a raging man-eater. Film carries enough blood to satisfy any cravings for this type of divertissement but it's a cheapie every respect.

Most of the chills are in the factory where bodies, supplied by a cemetery caretaker, are fed into a machine and the product comes out feline puree. Ted V. Mikels, who produced and directed, manages a few horror shots. Script builds as a young doctor and his nurse suspect that cat attacks are tied in with food which tests indicate might be human flesh.

Sean Kenney and Monika Kelly portray these two, and Sanford Mitchell and J. Byron Foster the diabolical food operators, all delivering pedestrian performances.

．．．．．．．．．．．．．．．．．．．．．．．．．．．．．．

■ **CORSICAN BROTHERS, THE**

1941, 111 MINS, US ⓥ

Dir Gregory Ratoff   *Prod* Edward Small   *Scr* George Bruce   *Ph* Harry Stradling   *Ed* Grant Whytock, William Claxton   *Mus* Dimitri Tiomkin   *Art Dir* Nicolai Remisoff
● Douglas Fairbanks Jr, Ruth Warrick, Akim Tamiroff, J. Carrol Naish, H.B. Warner, Henry Wilcoxon (Small/United Artists)

Dumas story of the *Corsican Brothers* is widely known. Born Siamese twins of Corsican aristocracy, the babies are separated immediately after birth by a miraculous operation, and saved from a vendetta attack that kills their parents and immediate relatives. One child goes to Paris for upbringing and education, while the other remains to be reared by a former family servant.

Twenty-one years later the twins (both portrayed by Douglas Fairbanks Jr) are reunited, introduced, and informed of the enemy of their forebears. Swearing to avenge the family murders, the two boys separate to confuse their enemy with widely separated attacks on his henchmen.

Title foreword warns audiences that this is an incredible tale – and then the picture proceeds on that basis. Script [from a free adaptation by George Bruce and Howard Estabrook] is well set up to display the action qualities, but rather studious on the dialog and story motivation. Gregory Ratoff's direction is okay.

．．．．．．．．．．．．．．．．．．．．．．．．．．．．．．

■ **COTTON CLUB, THE**

1984, 127 MINS, US ◇ ⓥ ⊙

Dir Francis Coppola   *Prod* Robert Evans   *Scr* William

Kennedy, Francis Coppola   *Ph* Stephen Goldblatt   *Ed* Barry Malkin, Robert Q. Lovett   *Mus* John Barry, Bob Wilber   *Art Dir* Richard Sylbert
● Richard Gere, Gregory Hines, Diane Lane, Lonette McKee, Bob Hoskins, Nicolas Cage (Zoetrope)

The Cotton Club certainly doesn't stint on ambition. Four stories [by William Kennedy, Francis Coppola, Mario Puzo, suggested by James Haskins' pictorial history *The Cotton Club*] thread through and intertwine in the $47 million picture. While the earlier Francis Coppola gangster efforts had a firm hand on the balance between plot elements and characters, *The Cotton Club* emerges as uneven and sometimes unfocused.

Focus is on Dixie Dwyer (Richard Gere), a cornet player in small Gotham club. As the film opens in 1928, Dixie interrupts a solo to push a patron out of the way of a gunman's bullet. The thankful target turns out to be nightclub owner Dutch Schultz (James Remar).

Another thread involves club tap star Sandman Williams (Gregory Hines) who partners with his brother Clay (Maurice Hines) and has his eyes and heart set on chorus girl Lila Rose Oliver (Lonette McKee).

Dramatically, Coppola and coscreenwriter William Kennedy, juggle a lot of balls the air. The parallel stories of Gere and Hines' professional rise prove more potent, thanks largely to a mixture of romance, music and gangland involvement. Hines and McKee generate real sparks in their relationship and latter adds an interesting dimension as a light-skinned singer trying to hide her racial origins.
☐ 1984: Nominations: Best Art Direction, Editing

．．．．．．．．．．．．．．．．．．．．．．．．．．．．．．

■ **COTTON COMES TO HARLEM**

1970, 97 MINS, US ◇

Dir Ossie Davis   *Prod* Samuel Goldwyn Jr   *Scr* Arnold Perl, Ossie Davis   *Ph* Gerald Hirschfeld   *Ed* John Carter   *Mus* Galt MacDermot   *Art Dir* Manuel Gerard
● Godfrey Cambridge, Raymond St Jacques, Calvin Lockhart, Judy Pace, Redd Foxx, John Anderson (United Artists)

Actor-director Ossie Davis makes his feature film debut with this slam-bang, all stops out, comedy-action film about expatriate writer Chester Himes' two Harlem detectives, Grave Digger Jones and Coffin Ed Johnson. Godfrey Cambridge and Raymond St Jacques are Himes' tough, rough, foul-mouthed but incorruptible policemen. Cambridge is the buffoon of the pair while St Jacques (whose performance is easily the best in the film) is the spokesman for the Negro community.

There's occasional evidence of abrupt shortening of explanatory scenes to crowd as much action as possible into the running time. Action there is, from the opening seduction of gullible Harlem 'good folks' by con artist-cum-preacher Calvin Lockhart, to the final denouement as to what really happened to that $87,000 stashed away in a bale of cotton.

Strong support is provided by nitery comedian Redd Foxx, John Anderson as the police chief, Emily Yancy as the widow of Lockhart's partner, J. D. Cannon as the white ex-con accomplice of Lockhart, and Equity president Frederick O'Neal as a numbers racket hoodlum.

．．．．．．．．．．．．．．．．．．．．．．．．．．．．．．

■ **COUCH TRIP, THE**

1988, 98 MINS, US ◇ ⓥ ⊙

Dir Michael Ritchie   *Prod* Lawrence Gordon   *Scr* Steven Kampmann, Will Porter, Sean Stein   *Ph* Donald E. Thorin   *Ed* Richard A. Harris   *Mus* Michel Colombier   *Art Dir* Jimmie Bly
● Dan Aykroyd, Walter Matthau, Charles Grodin, David Clennon, Donna Dixon, Richard Romanus (Orion)

C

The Couch Trip is a relatively low-key Dan Aykroyd vehicle that restores some of the comic actor's earlier charm simply by not trying too hard. Relying as much on character as shtick, Aykroyd is a likable everyman here out to right the minor indignities and injustices in the world.

As an obstreperous prisoner biding his time in a Cicero, Ill, loony bin, Aykroyd trades places with his attending shrink, Dr Baird (David Clennon), and moves to LA to fill in for radio therapist Dr Maitlin (Charles Grodin) who is having a mental breakdown of his own.

Screenplay [from the novel by Ken Kolb] doesn't break any new ground in suggesting there is a thin line between the certifiably crazy and certifiably sane, but it still manages some gentle jabs at the pretensions of the psychiatric profession.

As a mock priest and another fringe member of society, Walter Matthau is Aykroyd's soulmate, but the connection between the men is too thinly drawn to have much meaning. Donna Dixon, stunningly beautiful though she is, is impossible to swallow as a brilliant psychiatrist, particularly since her duties include signaling commercial breaks on radio and standing around posing.

■ COUNTDOWN

1968, 101 MINS, US ◇ ☜
Dir Robert Altman *Prod* William Conrad *Scr* Loring Mandel *Ph* William W. Spencer *Ed* Gene Milford *Mus* Leonard Rosenman *Art Dir* Jack Poplin
● James Caan, Joanna Moore, Robert Duvall, Barbara Baxley, Charles Aidman, Steve Ihnat (Warner/Seven Arts)

Countdown, a story about a US space shot to the moon, is a literate and generally excellent programmer. Strong script [based on a novel by Hank Searls], emphasizing human conflict, is well developed and neatly resolved on a note of suspense.

James Caan is a civilian scientist, chosen because of political implications, to replace military officer Robert Duvall as the moonshot man. Added to this conflict is that between Steve Ihnat, project boss, and Charles Aidman, flight surgeon, who carry on the struggle between safety of life considerations and those of beating the Russians.

Although the emphasis is on personal interactions, pic interpolates some stock footage plus specially-shot technical mock-up scenes.

■ COUNTERPOINT

1967, 105 MINS, US ◇
Dir Ralph Nelson *Prod* Dick Berg *Scr* James Lee, Joel Oliansky *Ph* Russel Metty *Ed* Howard G. Epstein *Mus* Bronislau Kaper *Art Dir* Alexander Golitzen, Carl Anderson
● Charlton Heston, Maximilian Schell, Kathryn Hays, Leslie Nielsen, Anton Diffring, Linden Chiles (Universal)

Counterpoint is the story of an American symphony orchestra – on a USO tour in Belgium – taken prisoner by the Germans during the Battle of the Bulge. Some of the incidents are contrived and characterizations of its two leads, as developed in trying to make them strong, are sometimes confusing. But in the main subject has been well handled.

Script, based upon Alan Sillitoe's novel, *The General*, packs suspense as fate of the martinet symph conductor and his 70 musicians at hand of the Germans, under order to execute every prisoner, remains uncertain.

Something new has been added here for a war film; parts of five major music works, recorded by Los Angeles Philharmonic Orchestra for the action, which should have particular appeal for music lovers.

■ COUNTESS FROM HONG KONG, A

1967, 120 MINS, UK ◇
Dir Charles Chaplin *Prod* Jerome Epstein *Scr* Charles Chaplin *Ph* Arthur Ibbetson *Ed* Gordon Hales *Mus* Charles Chaplin *Art Dir* Bob Cartwright
● Marlon Brando, Sophia Loren, Sydney Chaplin, Tippi Hedren, Patrick Cargill, Michael Medwin (Universal)

Charles Chaplin says the story was inspired by a trip he made to Shanghai in 1931 but, though the period has been updated, the style of his screenplay and direction are obstinately reminiscent of the 1930s.

Countess is what may be described as a romantic comedy. It has a nebulous plot, slim characterizations and all the trappings of an old-fashioned bedroom farce.

Sophia Loren, who radiates an abundance of charm, plays a Russian emigree countess who, after a night out on the town Hong Kong with Marlon Brando, stows away in his cabin with the intention of getting to New York. Although the story barely taxes her acting resources, Loren adds a quality to every scene in which she appears. She is stylish, classy and striking. Brando, on the other hand, appears ill at ease in what should have been a light comedy role.

Sydney Chaplin as Brando's cruising companion gives a thoroughly reliable performance, while Tippi Hedren, as Brando's wife, is superb in her few scene at the tail-end of the picture.

■ COUNT OF MONTE CRISTO, THE

1934, 113 MINS, US
Dir Rowland V. Lee *Prod* Edward Small *Scr* Philip Dunne, Dan Totheroh, Rowland V. Lee *Ph* Peverell Marley *Mus* Alfred Newman
● Robert Donat, Elissa Landi, Louis Calhern, Sidney Blackmer, Raymond Walburn, O. P. Heggie (Reliance/United Artists)

Monte Cristo is a near-perfect blend of thrilling action and grand dialog, both of which elements are inherent in Alexandre Dumas' original story.

Robert Donat is a fortunate selection for the lead. His intelligent handling of the many-sided top role hallmarks a sparkling piece of acting. Louis Calhern (De Villefort), Sidney Blackmer (Mondego) and Raymond Walburn (Danglars) are the three principal male supports in the extra large cast, and as the trio upon whom Cristo wreaks his vengeance they fill the order. Elissa Landi as Mercedes looks and acts the part, but the acting in this case isn't as important as the looks, and Landi has had tougher assignments.

■ COUNT OF MONTE CRISTO, THE

1976, 103 MINS, UK ◇ ☜
Dir David Greene *Prod* Norman Rosemart *Scr* Sidney Carroll *Ph* Aldo Tonti *Ed* Gene Milford *Mus* Allyn Ferguson *Art Dir* Walter Patriarca
● Richard Chamberlain, Tony Curtis, Trevor Howard, Louis Jourdan, Donald Pleasence, Kate Nelligan (ITC)

Richard Chamberlain is Edmond Dantes, the romantic young sailor railroaded to prison for 15 years. After his escape, aided by an old fellow prisoner, the story gets down to his obsessive revenge against the four money and/or power-hungry men who conspired against him.

All this is retailed in a most workmanlike fashion. Script and moral values appear respectful of the original text, and the Alexandre Dumas saga is performed with ample conviction and polish. But it's developed with more sincerity than interest or dramatic originality, and with no style of its own.

Chamberlain is appealing and reasonably persuasive as the hero robbed of both his best years and his betrothed, the latter played

touchingly in a promising feature bow by British-based Canadian Kate Nelligan.

■ COUNTRY

1984, 109 MINS, US ◇ ☜ ⊙
Dir Richard Pearce *Prod* William D. Wittliff, Jessica Lange *Scr* William D. Wittliff *Ph* David M. Walsh *Ed* Bill Yahraus *Mus* Charles Gross *Art Dir* Ron Hobbs
● Jessica Lange, Sam Shepard, Wilford Brimley, Matt Clark, Therese Graham, Levi L. Knebel (Touchstone)

Jessica Lange's pet project took a while to get produced, but it winds up firmly on the right track, with its basic theme of the classic struggle of the working man against the forces of government.

Screenplay recalls recent real-life events of how farmers have taken on loans with the government's blessing in order to expand and wind up faced with foreclosure when unable to keep up with the payments.

Lange is the focal point, essaying the mother of the family faced with losing the farm which had been in her lineage for some 100 years. The family, like 40% of the farmers in the area, is about to be victimized by get-tough government policies.

Almost overshadowed by Lange, is Sam Shepard the husband, though he gives a quietly effective portrayal of the husband dealt a humiliating blow to his pride when the farm is fingered for liquidation.
□ 1984: Nomination: Best Actress (Jessica Lange)

■ COUNTRY DANCE

(US: *Brotherly Love*)
1970, 112 MINS, UK ◇ ☜
Dir J. Lee Thompson *Prod* Robert Emmett Gianna *Scr* James Kennaway *Ph* Ted Moore *Ed* Willy Kemplen *Mus* John Addison *Art Dir* Maurice Fowler
● Peter O'Toole, Susannah York, Michael Craig, Harry Andrews, Cyril Cusack, Judy Cornwell (Windward/Keep)

Country Dance is a confusing love triangle film, focusing on a woman and the two men in her life, one her husband and the other her brother.

Interiors were lensed at Ardmore Studios, Ireland, and exteriors in Ireland's Wicklow County and Perthshire, Scotland. The James Kennaway screenplay is based upon both his play, *Country Dance*, and his novel *Household Ghosts*.

Limning the decline and fall of Sir Charles Ferguson (Peter O'Toole), last scion of a noble Scottish family, there is in this descent the distasteful subject of the brother's unhealthy love for his sister (Susannah York), who has left her husband (Michael Craig) to make her home with her brother on their family estate.

O'Toole's enactment of the character who cannot face the reality of either losing his sister or the destruction of his traditional way of life on his dwindling estate is whimsically constructed.

■ COUNTRY GIRL, THE

1954, 104 MINS, US ☜
Dir George Seaton *Prod* William Perlberg *Scr* George Seaton *Ph* John F. Warren *Ed* Ellsworth Hoagland *Mus* Victor Young *Art Dir* Hal Pereira, Roland Anderson
● Bing Crosby, Grace Kelly, William Holden, Anthony Ross, Gene Reynolds, Jacqueline Fontaine (Paramount)

An exceptionally well-performed essay on an alcoholic song man, with Bing Crosby carrying on a bottle romance, *Country Girl* is a show business story that has depth and movement.

Adapted from the 1950 Clifford Odets play of the same title, its key player, a quondam star induced into trying a painful comeback, is a weak, lying, excessive drinker. Grace Kelly is resolute to the hilt, conveying a certain feminine strength and courage that enable her to endure the hardships of being th boozer's wife. William Holden registers in sock style as the legit director determined that Crosby can stand up to the demands of the starring role in a new play.

Crosby pulls a masterly switch, immersing himself into the part with full effect. The film has four songs by Ira Gershwin and Harold Arlen. The bare NY theatre where the show within the show is rehearsed, the Boston house which is the scene of the play's break-in, the squalid tenement apartment where Kelly and Crosby are first found – these are realistically staged. Robert Alton's staging of the musical numbers is adequate.

□ 1954: Best Actress (Grace Kelly), Screenplay.
□ Nominations: Best Picture, Director, Actor (Bing Crosby), B&W Cinematography, B&W Art Direction

....

■ COURT JESTER, THE

1956, 101 MINS, US ◇ ▽ ☺
Dir Norman Panama, Melvin Frank *Prod* Norman Panama, Melvin Frank *Scr* Norman Panama, Melvin Frank *Ph* Ray June *Ed* Tom McAdoo *Mus* Victor Shoen (dir.) *Art Dir* Hal Pereira, Roland Anderson
● Danny Kaye, Glynis Johns, Basil Rathbone, Angela Lansbury, Cecil Parker, Mildred Natwick (Paramount/Dena)

Costumed swashbucklers undergo a happy spoofing in *The Court Jester* with Danny Kaye heading the fun-poking. Norman Panama and Melvin Frank drag in virtually every time-honored, and timeworn, medieval drama cliche for Kaye and cast to re-play for laughs via not-so-subtle treatment.

A major assist comes from the Sylvia Fine-Sammy Cahn songs, of which there are five all tuned to the Kaye talent. There's the quite mad 'Maladjusted Jester'; a lullaby, 'Loo-Loo-Loo I'll Take You Dreaming a ballad, 'My Heart Knows a Lovely Song'; the comedic 'They'll Never Outfox the Fox', and 'Life Could Not Better Be.'

Glynis Johns, fetched from England for the hoydenish Maid Jean role opposite Kaye, does exceedingly well. The same is true of Basil Rathbone, a many-seasoned chief heavy; Angela Lansbury, cutting a pretty picture as the Princess Gwendolyn; Cecil Parker, the not-so-bright King Roderick who has ousted the real royal family; and Mildred Natwick, the princess's evil-eyed maid.

....

■ COURT MARTIAL
See: Carrington V.C.

....

■ COURT-MARTIAL OF BILLY MITCHELL, THE
(UK: One Man Mutiny)

1955, 100 MINS, US ◇ ▽ ☺
Dir Otto Preminger *Prod* Milton Sperling *Scr* Milton Sperling, Emmett Lavery *Ph* Sam Leavitt *Ed* Folmar Blangsted *Mus* Dimitri Tiomkin *Art Dir* Malcolm Bert
● Gary Cooper, Charles Bickford, Ralph Bellamy, Rod Steiger, Elizabeth Montgomery, Fred Clark (United States/Warner)

Dealing with real-life events of 1925, the subject-matter spotlights something which is always present tense, namely, official rigidity, redtape and intellectual hardening of the arteries in the brains of aging bureaucrats.

The picture is a real kick in the shins for the cult of blind military obedience and the lesson which is laid on the line relates to Pearl Harbor. The picture shows Mitchell predicting the Japanese sneak attack on Pearl Harbor, and describing American vulnerability, all this 16 years before that catastrophic Sunday and in the presence of Douglas MacArthur.

The main trouping is by Gary Cooper,

Ralph Bellamy as a congressman counsel with yellow journalistic instincts, Charles Bickford, Fred Clark and Rod Steiger. All are standout in professionalism though this is a writer's, not an actor's, picture.

□ 1955: Nomination: Best Story & Screenplay

....

■ COURTNEY AFFAIR, THE
See: The Courtneys of Curzon Street

....

■ COURTNEYS OF CURZON STREET, THE
(US: The Courtney Affair)

1947, 120 MINS, UK ▽
Dir Herbert Wilcox *Prod* Herbert Wilcox *Scr* Nicholas Phipps *Ph* Max Greene *Ed* Flora Newton, Vera Campbell *Mus* Tony Collins *Art Dir* William C. Andrews
● Anna Neagle, Michael Wilding, Gladys Young, Coral Browne, Michael Medwin, Bernard Lee (British Lion)

Wilcox hasn't worried about any significant theme in this. He tells his four-generation story with smiles and tears, and obviously enjoys seeing two people in love.

Story runs from 1900 to 1945, Michael Wilding plays the soldier's son and heir of baronet. He is in love with his mother's maid (Anna Neagle). Ignoring his mother's warning that he is risking social ostracism, he flouts tradition and marries the girl. Climax to society's persecution comes at a snobbish function with Queen Victoria present to hear first performance of Tchaikovsky's *Symphonie Pathetique*. His wife, nervous, does not behave with conventional stoicism and has to listen to catty remarks about her lowly beginning.

From then on the story tells of the joys and sorrows of the Courtneys, ending in 1945 when their grandson brings home his girl who hopes his humble family won't object to her marrying into the aristocracy.

....

■ COURTSHIP OF ANDY HARDY, THE

1942, 94 MINS, US
Dir George B. Seitz *Scr* Agnes Christine Johnston *Ph* Lester White *Ed* Elmo Veron
● Lewis Stone, Mickey Rooney, Donna Reed, William Lundigan (M-G-M)

Picture is studded with laugh lines throughout, and displays general effervescing tempo for maximum reaction. Mickey Rooney – between adolescence and manhood – successfully balances the assignment in excellent style. His is a strong performance with accent on straight acting ability and without recourse to the mugging antics that he called on previously.

Story [from characters created by Aurania Rouverol] opens with Judge Hardy endeavoring to reconcile a couple with an adolescent daughter. He invokes the aid of Andy to date the girl and break her of a haughty complex and Andy's campaign is successful in this respect.

Donna Reed is the girl who is turned over to Andy for regeneration, and how he finally succeeds is neatly contrived in the screenplay, with substance in both lines and situations provided by the script.

....

■ COURTSHIP OF EDDIE'S FATHER, THE

1963, 118 MINS, US ◇ ▽
Dir Vincente Minnelli *Prod* Joe Pasternak *Scr* John Gay *Ph* Milton Krasner *Ed* Adrienne Fazan *Mus* George Stoll *Art Dir* George W. Davis, Urie McCleary
● Glenn Ford, Shirley Jones, Stella Stevens, Dina Merrill, Roberta Sherwood, Jerry Van Dyke (M-G-M)

The story of a dad and a lad and their divergent views on what constitutes desirable step-

motherhood, the production is richly mounted, wittily written and engagingly played by an expert, spirited and attractive cast.

In adapting the novel by Mark Toby, John Gay has penned an aware, clever and generally well-constructed scenario. Glenn Ford portrays a widower who, in rearing his precocious six-and-a-half-year-old son (Ronny Howard) must, in the course of his romantic pursuits, take into account the future maternal preferences of the boy, whose comic-book-eye-view of candidate wives is inclined to judge statistically on the basis of bustlines and eyesockets.

Ford creates a warm, likeable personality and is especially smooth in his reaction takes in scenes with his charge.

Never any question about Shirley Jones' credentials as the kind of woman any red-blooded American type would love to call mommy, bustline notwithstanding. Dina Merrill is an attractive loser. Stella Stevens comes on like gangbusters in her enactment of a brainy but inhibited doll from Montana. It's a sizzling comedy performance of a kook.

Vincente Minnelli's direction tends toward melodramatic heaviness in some of the early 'serious' going and some exaggeration in several comic passages, but overall he has managed well enough, coaxing some bright performances from his cast.

....

■ COUSINS

1989, 110 MINS, US ◇ ▽ ☺
Dir Joel Schumacher *Prod* William Allyn *Scr* Stephen Metcalfe *Ph* Ralf Bode *Ed* Robert Brown *Mus* Angelo Badalamenti *Art Dir* Mark S. Freeborn
● Ted Danson, Isabella Rossellini, Sean Young, William Petersen, Lloyd Bridges, Norma Aleandro (Paramount)

As derivative as it is, *Cousins* still is a hugely entertaining Americanized version of the French film *Cousin, cousine*, with nearly the same insouciant tone as the Jean-Charles Tacchella comedy of 1975. It's been spiced with a dash of 1980s social commentary and a dollop of Italian ethnic flavoring.

Isabella Rossellini and Ted Danson's sappy, overly sentimental series of rendezvous are well compensated by their relatives' caustic comments, irreverent asides and other antics the three weddings, one funeral and other functions all attend during the course of the picture.

Object of most of the ridicule is William Petersen, the unctuous BMW car salesman and Don Juan pretender who starts everything off in the opening wedding scene drooling at Danson's flamboyantly dressed wife (Sean Young).

It's obvious enough that Rossellini, the martyred Madonna type who knows of her husband's philandering, represents prudishness and purity as much as Young, dressed in outlandish high-fashion ruffles of red and black, represents the opposite.

What's most fun is to get everyone else's thoughts on the matter. There's Rossellini's wealthy mother Edie (Norma Aleandro), cranky old Aunt Sofia (Gina De Angelis) and Danson's son Mitchell (Keith Coogan), who has a penchant for videotaping family gatherings.

Best of all is Lloyd Bridges, Danson's irascible, sporting uncle, who has as much pep in his step and gleam in his eye for Aleandro as the two main couples have combined.

....

■ COVERED WAGON, THE

1923, 119 MINS, US ⊗ ▽ ☺
Dir James Cruze *Scr* Jack Cunningham *Ph* Karl Brown *Ed* Dorothy Arzner *Mus* Hugo Riesenfeld
● J. Warren Kerrigan, Lois Wilson, Ernest Torrence, Charles Ogle, Alan Hale, Ethel Wales (Paramount)

The Covered Wagon was months in the making with its cost said to have been in the neighborhood of $800,000. It is the biggest thing since *Birth* made *The Birth of a Nation*.

Like *Birth* it is based on historic fact. Emerson Hough, who wrote *The Covered Wagon* for the *Saturday Evening Post*, chose for his subject those pioneers who left their farms and safe-guarded homes in the territory east of the Ohio and started in prairie schooners for the Pacific Coast in 1847, before the discovery that the California hills contained the glittering metal that was to be a tremendous lure in 1849.

This particular wagon train, whic has some 300 vehicles, starts for Oregon. Through it all a very pretty and simple love tale runs, as well as an element of intrigue, which together with the thrills that have been devised makes this production a real picture of pictures.

The big thrills are three. First and foremost is the fording of the Platte by the wagons of the train. Then there is the Indian attack with a corking battle staged and finally a prairie fire.

■ **COVER GIRL**

1944, 105 MINS, US ◇ ⓥ ⊙
Dir Charles Vidor *Prod* Arthur Schwartz *Scr* Virginia Van Upp *Ph* Rudolph Mate, Allen M. Davey *Ed* Viola Lawrence *Mus* Morris Stoloff (dir.) *Art Dir* Lionel Banks, Cary Odell
● Rita Hayworth, Gene Kelly, Lee Bowman, Phil Silvers, Otto Kruger, Eve Arden (Columbia)

Arthur Schwartz, in his initial film producer spot after years of experience with stage musicals, deftly injects surefire showmanship into the picture, neatly blending the talents of the players with an inspired script by Virginia Van Upp [story by Erwin Gelsey, adaptation by Marion Parsonnet and Paul Gangelin], fine and consistently-paced direction by Charles Vidor, and taking full advantage of the technical contributions.

Plot is neatly concocted to get over idea of sudden rise to theatrical fame of Rita Hayworth as result of winning a Cover Girl contest. Gene Kelly, operating the modest Brooklyn nightspot where he stages the floorshows, is in love with Hayworth, a dancer. Latter wins the contest to give the room immediate fame with the upper-crust customers from Manhattan.

Otto Kruger, responsible for her prominence, figures she should be lifted out of the lowly nightspot to a Broadway show. Result is break between the girl and Kelly when latter stubbornly blows off steam.

Dance sequences spotlighting the terping abilities of Hayworth and Kelly are expertly staged. Kelly devised his own routines for the picture. Score by Jerome Kern and Ira Gershwin, comprising seven tunes, is of high caliber.

□ 1944: Best Score for a Musical Picture.
□ Nominations: Best Color Cinematography, Color Art Direction, Song ('Long Ago and Far Away'), Sound

■ **COWBOYS, THE**

1972, 128 MINS, US ◇ ⓥ
Dir Mark Rydell *Prod* Mark Rydell *Scr* Irving Ravech, Harriet Frank Jr, William Dale Jennings *Ph* Robert Surtees *Ed* Robert Swink, Neil Travis *Mus* John Williams *Art Dir* Philip Jefferies
● John Wayne, Roscoe Lee Browne, Bruce Dern, Colleen Dewhurst, Sarah Cunningham, Allyn Ann McLerie (Warner)

The Cowboys stars John Wayne as a tough cattleman forced to use some green teenagers to get the beef to market. Handsome, placid and pastoral, the film is a family-type entry, produced and directed by Mark Rydell.

Rustler Bruce Dern fight with Wayne and eventually shoots him dead. This foul deed gives the boys enough courage to plot

vengeance under the leadership of Roscoe Lee Browne, an urbane black wagon-train cook who previously had exchanged some pithy comments with Wayne and the kids.

The story [from a novel by William Dale Jennings] is long and episodic, and its gentle treatment makes the length something of a hindrance to maximum enjoyment. Cast includes Colleen Dewhurst in an effective cameo as a travelling bordello madam.

■ **CRACKERS**

1984, 92 MINS, US ◇ ⓥ ⊙
Dir Louis Malle *Prod* Edward Lewis, Robert Cortes *Scr* Jeffrey Fiskin *Ph* Laszlo Kovacs *Ed* Susanne Baron *Mus* Paul Chihara *Art Dir* John J. Lloyd
● Donald Sutherland, Jack Warden, Sean Penn, Wallace Shawn, Larry Riley, Trinidad Silva (Universal)

A mild little caper comedy with plenty of sociological overtones, *Crackers* comes as a letdown from director Louis Malle. With a flimsy plot that is perhaps rightly treated in a throwaway manner, film basically consists of a wide assortment of character riffs which are offbeat enough to provide moderate moment-to-moment amusement but don't create a great deal of comic impact.

As in dozens of tenement-set plays from *Street Scene* on, virtually all the action takes place within or very near the central setting, in this case a pawnshop owned by shameless profiteer Jack Warden. His buddy, Donald Sutherland, is out of work, and all but a few of the other characters make up a rainbow microcosm of today's unemployed.

■ **CRACK IN THE MIRROR**

1960, 97 MINS, US
Dir Richard Fleischer *Prod* Darryl F. Zanuck *Scr* Mark Canfield *Ph* William C. Mellor *Ed* Roger Dwyre *Mus* Maurice Jarre *Art Dir* Jean d'Eaubonne
● Orson Welles, Juliette Greco, Bradford Dillman, Alexander Knox, Catherine Lacy, William Lucas (DFZ/20th Century-Fox)

The screenplay, based on a novel by Marcel Haedrich, tells two parallel stories, both age-old triangle situations in which a not-so-young woman throws over her elderly lover for a much younger man. The first situation involves three working class people and the second, three members of the Paris haute monde. The stories come together when the working class dame and her young paramour are brought to trial for the murder of the older man.

By casting Orson Welles as both the tyrannical old construction worker who is murdered and as the cuckolded lawyer, Juliette Greco as the mistress in both situations and Bradford Dillman as the young laborer and the young lawyer in-a-hurry, producer and director have obviously intended to make some pertinent statements about guilt and the ironies of justice.

This irony, however, is telegraphed early in the film when the audience first is let in on the fact that the two stories are essentially the same. Another problem is that about halfway through, film's focal point switches from the working class triangle to the problems of the upperclass trio, with the result that audience interest and emotional involvement are put to a severe test.

Welles is fine as the drunken old slob and close to superb as the elderly lawyer. Dillman is also good as the two young men, both equally opportunistic. However, it's Greco who comes off best – whether it's because of performance or the projection of a unique cinema personality, is hard to say. She's all-girl.

Produced entirely in Paris, picture has a thoroughly French look and sound.

■ **CRACK IN THE WORLD**

1965, 96 MINS, US ◇
Dir Andrew Marton *Prod* Bernard Glasser, Lester A. Sansom *Scr* Jon Manchip White, Julian Halevy *Ph* Manuel Berenguer *Ed* Derek Parsons *Mus* John Douglas *Art Dir* Eugene Lourie
● Dana Andrews, Janette Scott, Kieron Moore, Alexander Knox, Peter Damon, Gary Lasdun (Paramount)

Crack in the World, distinguished principally by some startling special effects, imaginatively focuses on an ill-fated experiment to tap the unlimited energy residing within the earth's core which nearly blows up the world.

Produced in Spain for Philip Yordan's Security Pictures, the Paramount release carries a more legitimate premise [story by Jon Manchip White] than the regular science-fiction entry, strictly fictional in tone and context. Here is an entirely logical scientific operation, of drilling through the earth's crust to reach the molten mass called magma, which, brought to the surface under controlled conditions, could give the world all the energy it would ever want.

Dana Andrews plays part of the scientist charge of the operation, dying with fast cancer, and Kieron Moore his assistant who believes his superior's plan will end in the disaster which eventuates, both handling their roles okay. Janette Scott is Andrews' scientist-wife, actually in love with Moore, a rather thankless role which she sparks as much as possible.

■ **CRASH OF SILENCE, THE**
See: *Mandy*

■ **CRAWLING EYE, THE**
See: *The Trollenberg Terror*

■ **CRAZY MAMA**

1975, 82 MINS, US ◇ ⓥ
Dir Jonathan Demme *Prod* Julie Corman *Scr* Robert Thom *Ph* Bruce Logan *Ed* Allan Holzman, Lewis Teague *Mus* Marshall Lieb (co-ord.) *Art Dir* Peter Jamison
● Cloris Leachman, Stuart Whitman, Ann Sothern, Tisha Sterling, Jim Backus, Donn Most (New World)

Spanning nearly three decades, Cloris Leachman stars as she starts in Jerusalem, Ark, 1932, when lawmen kill papa (Clint Kimbrough), making mother Ann Sothern a widow. They jump the 60-acres farm, next are in Long Beach, Calif, circa 1958, where the pair are evicted from their beauty salon for back rent, and Leachman has a pretty, pregnant teenage daughter (Linda Pure) with a boy friend (Donn Most). The three femmes, upset, steal cars and shoot their way across the US.

Next the sextet robs a motorcycle race box-office, then a bank heist, shooting all the way.

This *Bonnie and Clyde*-style, sadistic, sordid unveiling of wasted lives ends in 1959, with Leachman, her daughter and her studs running a Miami Beach snack bar. With go performances from familiar players, *Crazy Mama* appears a waste of top talent in a mindless life of crime.

■ **CRAZY PEOPLE**

1990, 90 MINS, US ◇ ⓥ ⊙
Dir Tony Bill *Prod* Tom Barad *Scr* Mitch Markowitz *Ph* Victor J. Kemper *Ed* Mia Goldman *Mus* Cliff Eidelman *Art Dir* John J. Lloyd
● Dudley Moore, Daryl Hannah, Paul Reiser, Mercedes Ruehl, J.T. Walsh, David Paymer (Paramount)

Crazy People combines a hilarious dissection of advertising with a warm view of so-called insanity. Pic had a rocky production history as two weeks into lensing John Malkovich was replaced by Dudley Moore, and screen-writer Mitch Markowitz ceded his directing chair to Tony Bill. Finished film is a credit to all hands.

Moore toplines as a burnt-out ad man working with fast-talking Paul Reiser (perfect as a type commonplace in business) for a tyranical boss, J.T. Walsh. Under deadline pressure, he turns in campaigns that attempt an honest approach.

This raises more than eyebrows, but when Moore hands in 'Most of our passengers get there alive' to promote United Air Lines, the film jumpcuts emphatically to Bennington Sanitarium, his new home.

Director Bill envisions this looney bin as an idyllic retreat, with a natural, warm and beautiful Daryl Hannah as Moore's nutty playmate there. The visual mismatch (she towers over the diminutive star) pays off.

Markowitz's ingenious twists overcome the gag-driven nature of the film. Moore's oddball ads accidentally get printed and create a consumer rush. Walsh hires Moore back and soon the inmates are virtually running the asylum.

● ●

■ **CREATURE FROM THE BLACK LAGOON**

1954, 79 MINS, US ⓦ ⊙
Dir Jack Arnold *Prod* William Alland *Scr* Harry Essex, Arthur Ross *Ph* William E. Snyder *Ed* Ted J. Kent *Mus* Joseph Gershenson
● Richard Carlson, Julie Adams, Richard Denning, Antonio Moreno, Nestor Paiva, Whit Bissell (Universal)

This 3-D hackle-raiser reverts to the prehistoric. After the discovery of a web-fingered skeleton hand in the Amazon region, a scientific expedition heads into the steaming tropics to hunt more fossils. In the back-washes of the Amazon they come across a still living Gill Man, half-fish, half-human.

The 3-D lensing adds to the eerie effects of the underwater footage, as well as to the monster's several appearances on land. The below-water scraps between skin divers and the prehistoric thing are thrilling and will pop goose pimples on the susceptible fan, as will the closeup scenes of the scaly, gilled creature. Jack Arnold's direction does a firstrate job of developing chills and suspense, and James C. Havens rates a good credit for his direction of the underwater sequences.

Richard Carlson and Julie Adams co-star in the William Alland production and carry off the thriller very well. As befitting the Amazonian setting, Adams appears mostly in brief shorts or swim suits.

● ●

■ **CREEPING UNKNOWN, THE**
See: The Quatermass Experiment

● ●

■ **CREEPSHOW**

1982, 129 MINS, US ◇ ⓦ ⊙
Dir George A. Romero *Prod* Richard P. Rubinstein *Scr* Stephen King *Ph* Michael Gornick *Ed* Pasquale Buba, Paul Hirsch, Michael Spolan, George A. Romero *Mus* John Harrison *Art Dir* Cletus Anderson
● Hal Holbrook, Adrienne Barbeau, Fritz Weaver, Leslie Nielsen, Carrie Nye, E.G. Marshall (Laurel)

George Romero, collaborating with writer Stephen King, again proves his adeptness at combining thrills with tongue-in-cheek humor. He links five tales with animated bridges in the style of the comics.

The gimmick is used with reserve and the segments work fine on their own merits. The first *Father's Day*, is a shaggy dog tale of a despised patriarch who returns from the grave to collect his holiday cake.

In *The Lonesome Death of Jordy Verrill*, author King takes on the title role. He's a dull hillbilly who sees dollar signs when a meteor falls on his property. However, his fate is to turn into a plant.

In *Something to Tide You Over*, Leslie Nielsen plans a slow watery death for his wife and her lover. This is followed by *The Crate*, about a malevolent creature in a box from an Arctic expedition and the program finishes off with *They're Creeping Up on You*, in which millionaire E.G. Marshall is literally bugged to death by his phobia of insects.

● ●

■ **CREEPSHOW 2**

1987, 89 MINS, US ◇ ⓦ ⊙
Dir Michael Gornick *Prod* David Ball *Scr* George A. Romero *Ph* Dick Hart, Tom Hurwitz *Ed* Peter Weatherly *Mus* Les Reed, Rick Wakemen *Art Dir* Bruce Miller
● Lois Chiles, George Kennedy, Dorothy Lamour, Tom Savini, Domenick John (Laurel)

Tied together with some humdrum animated sequences, three vignettes on offer obviously were produced on the absolute cheap, and are deficient in imagination and scare quotient.

Whatever interest some might have in seeing George Kennedy and Dorothy Lamour is undercut by their roles as helpless vicms of a smalltown robbery and double murder in the first tale, *Old Chief Wood'nhead*, a lifeless and listless yarn about a storefront Indian who comes to life to avenge the crimes.

The Raft concerns four goodtime teens trapped on a platform in the middle of a small lake, then eaten alive by what looks like tarpaulin covered with black goo.

The Hitchhiker is a painfully protracted telling of how rich gal Lois Chiles hits and runs from a hitchhiker on the highway at night and is then haunted by the bloodied but far-from-dead fellow.

● ●

■ **CRIME AND PUNISHMENT**

1935, 85 MINS, US
Dir Josef von Sternberg *Prod* B.P. Schulberg *Scr* S.K. Lauren, Joseph Anthony *Ph* Lucien Ballard *Mus* Arthur Honegger *Art Dir* Stephen Goosson
● Edward Arnold, Peter Lorre, Marian Marsh, Tala Birell, Elisabeth Risdon, Douglass Dumbrille (Columbia)

The murder of the miserly pawnbroker (Mrs Patrick Campbell in a ruthless, unsympathetic characterization) is the premeditated crime by Peter Lorre. Edward Arnold's old-fashioned police methods, combined with psychological auto-suggestion and ultimate self-destruction, is the reincarnation of the punishment. Both contribute capital performances.

Sometimes the situations get out of hand and even Sternberg's directorial and camera genius can't cope with them. Usually it's a script deficiency [from the novel by Dostoievsky] when that occurs.

One is permitted to become a bit too conscious of the incongruity of a Bible-totin' harlot, an ingenue of a prostie with a Dietrichesque physiognomy and hair-dress. When that realization comes, the audience starts thinking of the past Sternberg and Dietrich pictures. That's when the too pretty Marian Marsh, as the St Petersburg streetwalker, doesn't assist in the romance chores she's been endowed to sustain.

● ●

■ **CRIME IN THE STREETS**

1956, 91 MINS, US
Dir Don Siegel *Prod* Vincent M. Fennelly *Scr* Reginald Rose *Ph* Sam Leavitt *Ed* Richard C. Meyer *Mus* Franz Waxman *Art Dir* Serge Krizman
● James Whitmore, John Cassavetes, Sal Mineo, Mark Rydell, Virginia Gregg, Peter Votrian (Lindbrook/Allied Artists)

Crime in the Streets, in its jump from a TV origin, sets out to be a gutsy melodrama about slum area delinquents and, within the framework of Reginald Rose's highly contrived

story, succeeds in making its shock points under Don Siegel's pat directorial handling.

Plot poses the pitch that the young bums shown here need love and understanding to offset their squalid surroundings. However, as characterized by story and acting, it's likely they would be just as unpleasant and unwholesome in any setting.

John Cassavetes is the bitter, unlovable young tough who leads the street rat pack. When an adult (Malcolm Atterbury) slaps the young bum across the mouth for getting too uppity, the juve hood plots murder. Only two of the gang (Sal Mineo and Mark Rydell, latter repeating from TV) go along with the scheme to kill Atterbury.

James Whitmore heads the cast as a settlement worker who does little more than observe and offer unheeded counsel.

● ●

■ **CRIMES AND MISDEMEANORS**

1989, 104 MINS, US ◇ ⓦ ⊙
Dir Woody Allen *Prod* Robert Greenhut *Scr* Woody Allen *Ph* Sven Nykvist *Ed* Susan E. Morse *Art Dir* Santo Loquasto
● Martin Landau, Woody Allen, Mia Farrow, Alan Alda, Anjelica Huston, Sam Waterston (Rollins/Joffe)

Woody Allen ambitiously mixes his two favoured strains of cinema, melodrama and comedy, with mixed results in *Crimes and Misdemeanours*.

Two loosely linked stories here concern eye doctor Martin Landau and documentary director Allen, each facing moral dilemmas. The structural and stylistic conceit is that when Landau is onscreen, the film is dead serious, even solemn, while Allen's own appearance onscreen signals hilarious satire and priceless one-liners.

Landau's problem is simple: his mistress (Anjelica Huston, shrill in an underwritten role) threatens to go to his wife (Claire Bloom) and reveal all, including Landau's previous embezzlement activities. At wit's end, he seeks the assistance of his ne'er-do-well brother (Jerry Orbach), who orders up a hitman from out of town to waste Huston.

Meanwhile, Allen, unhappily married to Joanna Gleason, has fallen in love with TV documentary producer Mia Farrow, whom he meets while directing a TV docu profiling his enemy and brother-in-law, (Alan Alda). Alda is perfect casting as a successful TV comedy producer, whose pompous attitude and easy romantic victories with women (including Farrow) exasperate Allen. Though portrayed as filled with sour grapes and envy, Allen's plight is basically sympathetic.
☐ 1989: Nomination: Best Director, Supp. Actor (Martin Landau), Original Screenplay

● ●

■ **CRIMES OF PASSION**
(Aka: China Blue)

1984, 101 MINS, US ◇ ⓦ ⊙
Dir Ken Russell *Prod* Barry Sandler *Scr* Barry Sandler *Ph* Dick Bush *Ed* Brian Tagg *Mus* Rick Wakeman *Art Dir* Steve Marsh
● Kathleen Turner, Anthony Perkins, John Laughlin, Annie Potts, Bruce Davison (New World)

The evocative Kathleen Turner thuds into a wall of inanity in this dismally written, Ken Russell-directed serio-comic examination of sexual morality among American savages.

Painfully pretentious screenplay deflects the usual Russell outrageousness and traps the four principals (all other roles are momentary) into the most superficial of characterizations.

Turner leads two lives. By day she is Joanna, a compulsively laboring sportswear designer. She is divorced and, according to her employer, frigid. But by night she is, under a blond-banged wig, China Blue, the hottest $50 a trick hooker in the local combat zone.

Anthony Perkins' past also goes undetailed. So he has to lean on 'psycho'-somatic credentials to portray a glib, sweaty, presumably ministerial, homicidal wacko who would like to be China Blue if only he had the right hormones.

Whatever the intention, and despite the technical efficiency, *Crimes of Passion* falls between the cracks. The fault line here is quite identifiable – it's in the screenplay.

[A 106-minute version was released theatrically in Europe and on video in the US.]

■ CRIMES OF THE FUTURE

1970, 63 MINS, CANADA ◇
Dir David Cronenberg   *Prod* David Cronenberg
Scr David Cronenberg   *Ph* David Cronenberg
Ed David Cronenberg
● Ronald Mlodzik, Jon Lidolt, Tania Zolty, Paul Mulholland, Jack Messinger, Iain Ewing (Emergent)

Made on a $20,000 budget, David Cronenberg's second feature film, *Crimes of the Future*, bears a strong similarity to his first outing, *Stereo*, produced the year before.

Cronenberg's obsession for such matters as bodily mutation and grotesque growths, aberrant medical experiments, massive plagues and futuristic architecture are all here in a convoluted look at a future gone perverse.

The world's entire female population has evidently been wiped out, and the male population has turned to various, and disappointingly tame, alternative sexual fixations. Prime symptom of the illness is Rouge's Foam, a substance which leaks from bodily orifices and is sexually exciting in its initial stage, but deadly later on.

As he moves through the bleak but architecturally striking settings, the main character Tripod begins to take on the dimensions of an Edgar Allan Poe hero, a doomed figure traversing a devastated landscape.

■ CRIMES OF THE HEART

1986, 105 MINS, US ◇ Ⓥ ⊙
Dir Bruce Beresford   *Prod* Freddie Fields   *Scr* Beth Henley   *Ph* Dante Spinotti   *Ed* Anne Goursaud
Mus Georges Delerue   *Art Dir* Ken Adam
● Diane Keaton, Jessica Lange, Sissy Spacek, Sam Shepard, Tess Harper, Hurd Hatfield (Fields/Sugarman/De Laurentiis)

Thoughtfully cast, superbly acted and masterfully written and directed, *Crimes of the Heart* is a winner. Diane Keaton, Jessica Lange and Sissy Spacek are a delight in their roles as southern sisters attempting to come to grips with the world, themselves and the past.

Based on Beth Henley's 1980 play, Lenny (Keaton) is the eldest of three sisters and the only one still living in the large North Carolina home of their youth. It is Lenny's birthday, a day marked by youngest sister Babe (Spacek) jailing for shooting her husband and the arrival of middle sister Meg (Lange), visiting from LA where she pursues a singing career.

Far from being downbeat, the interplay between Keaton's nervously frantic Lenny, Spacek's unpredictable Babe and Lange as the hard-living Meg is as funny as it is riveting.

Bruce Beresford's direction within the house is graceful, effortlessly following the action from room to room. Sam Shepard notches a strong performance in the relatively small part of Doc, and Tess Harper shows her ability as a comic actress in the role of neighbor/relative Chick.

□ 1986: Nominations: Best Actress (Sissy Spacek), Supp. Actress (Tess Harper), Adapted Screenplay

■ CRIMINAL CODE, THE

1931, 97 MINS, US Ⓥ
Dir Howard Hawks   *Prod* Harry Cohn   *Scr* Seton I.

Miller, Fred Niblo Jr   *Ph* Ted Tetzlaff, James Wong Howe   *Ed* Edward Curtiss   *Mus* [uncredited]
Art Dir [Edward Jewell]
● Walter Huston, Phillips Holmes, Constance Cummings, Mary Doran, DeWitt Jennings, Boris Karloff (Columbia)

A prison picture but an excellent interpretation of the play of the same name [by Martin Flavin]. Howard Hawks' direction makes everything count, while Walter Huston here probably turns in his best modern characterization to date as a district attorney with a daughter who becomes warden of a prison. The love theme is taken care of by the girl and a young prisoner whom Huston has previously sent away for manslaughter while knowing a smart defense could have saved him.

The transposition from stage to screen has taken the proverbial liberties in dissolving the tragedy of the play into a happy ending.

Plenty of action all the way, in and out of the prison yard, with the performances of Huston. Phillips Holmes, and Boris Karloff always holding it together. Karloff is from the stage cast.

□ 1930/31: Nomination: Best Adaptation

■ CRIMINAL LAW

1988, 117 MINS, US ◇ Ⓥ ⊙
Dir Martin Campbell   *Prod* Robert Maclean, Hilary Heath   *Scr* Mark Kasdan   *Ph* Philip Meheux
Ed Christopher Wimble   *Mus* Jerry Goldsmith
Art Dir Curtis Schnell
● Gary Oldman, Kevin Bacon, Karen Young, Joe Don Baker, Tess Harper, Elizabeth Sheppard (Hemdale/Northwood)

A very good actor plays a good lawyer in a badly written and directed crime drama and loses the case for suspenseful filmmaking in *Criminal Law*.

Director Martin Campbell (BBC's *Edge of Darkness*) opens his feature with police in Boston (played by Montreal) discovering a mutilated rape victim in a rain-soaked tableau of blackish-blue gloom, a mood/color motif that's recycled throughout the movie. Action then fast-forwards to a courtroom where cocky lawyer Ben Chase, rendered with superb American accent and mannerisms by British Gary Oldman, pulls a sly trick out of his hat to demolish an eyewitness and free his wealthy, self-absorbed client Martin Thiel (Kevin Bacon).

No sooner is Bacon back on the streets, however, than the killer strikes again. Oldman realizes he's unleashed a monster, and is reminded of this constantly by two detectives (Joe Don Baker and Tess Harper). The stage is set for a clumsily plotted psychological cat-and-mouse game between Oldman and Bacon.

Although Bacon is convincing as the icy, deranged killer, his character's menace is undermined by the story's ill-defined pretensions as an essay on the American legal system and a herky-jerky continuity that's fatiguing instead of tingling.

■ CRIMSON KIMONO, THE

1959, 81 MINS, US
Dir Samuel Fuller   *Prod* Samuel Fuller   *Scr* Samuel Fuller   *Ph* Sam Leavitt   *Ed* Jerome Thoms   *Mus* Harry Sukman   *Art Dir* William E. Flannery, Robert Boyle
● Victoria Shaw, Glenn Corbett, James Shigeta, Anna Lee, Paul Dubov, Jaclynne Greene (Globe/Columbia)

In *The Crimson Kimono*, Samuel Fuller tries to wrap up a murder mystery with an interracial romance. The mystery melodrama part of the film gets lost during the complicated romance, and the racial tolerance plea is cheapened by its inclusion a film of otherwise straight action.

Fuller's story has Glenn Corbett and James Shigeta as officers of the LA Homicide Squad, buddies since they were fellow-soldiers in the Korean War. When they meet artist Victoria

Shaw, they're investigating murder. Corbett first falls in love with Shaw, then Shigeta succumbs.

The three principals bring credibility to their roles, not too easy during moments when belief is stretched considerably. Anna Lee, Paul Dubov, Jaclynne Green and Neyle Morrow are prominent in the supporting cast.

■ CRIMSON PIRATE, THE

1952, 104 MINS, UK/US ◇ Ⓥ ⊙
Dir Robert Siodmak   *Prod* [Harold Hecht]   *Scr* Roland Kibbee   *Ph* Otto Heller   *Ed* Jack Harris   *Mus* William Alwyn   *Art Dir* Paul Sheriff, Ken Adam
● Burt Lancaster, Eva Bartok, Nick Cravat, Torin Thatcher, James Hayter, Margot Grahame (Norma/Warner)

Swashbucking sea fables get a good-natured spoofing in *The Crimson Pirate*, with Burt Lancaster providing the muscles and dash for the takeoff.

The screen story is cloaked with a sense of humor as it pictures Lancaster, the famed Crimson Pirate, plying his trade on the high seas. Opening finds the pirates capturing a 30-gun galleon by trickery and then scheming to sell its cargo of cannon to rebels trying to shake off the shackles of the King of Spain. The buccaneers also plan to then reveal the rebel group's whereabouts to the crown for more gold, but there are a girl and such complications as an awakening to right and wrong.

Lancaster and his deaf-mute pal (Nick Cravat) sock the acrobatics required of hero and partner to a fare-thee-well under Robert Siodmak's direction.

■ CRISIS

1950, 95 MINS, US
Dir Richard Brooks   *Prod* Arthur Freed   *Scr* Richard Brooks   *Ph* Ray June   *Ed* Robert J. Kern   *Mus* Miklos Rozsa   *Art Dir* Cedric Gibbons, Preston Ames
● Cary Grant, Jose Ferrer, Paula Raymond, Signe Hasso, Ramon Novarro, Gilbert Roland (M-G-M)

Dictatorship versus the right of man to freedom is the theme, and the script [from a story by George Tabori] and direction by Richard Brooks lets it get up on the soapbox too frequently.

Footage kicks off with Cary Grant, a brain surgeon, and his wife (Paula Raymond) vacationing in a revolution-ridden Latin country. The doctor and his wife are kidnapped by the presidente's troops and taken to the besieged capital. There Grant finds the dictator-president suffering from a brain tumor and he is ordered to operate.

Meantime, revolutionaries, led by Gilbert Roland, exert pressure to have the president (Jose Ferrer) die under the knife.

Roland is very good. So is Ramon Novarro, the dictator's colonel.

■ CRISS CROSS

1949, 87 MINS, US Ⓥ
Dir Robert Siodmak   *Prod* Michael Kraike   *Scr* Daniel Fuchs   *Ph* Franz Planer   *Ed* Ted J. Kent   *Mus* Miklos Rozsa   *Art Dir* Bernard Herzbrun, Boris Leven
● Burt Lancaster, Yvonne De Carlo, Dan Duryea, Stephen McNally, Richard Long (Universal)

Utilizing liberal flashbacks, the film [from the novel by Don Tracy] unreels the relentless, unswerving devotion of Burt Lancaster for his divorced wife (Yvonne De Carlo). Basically he's an honest guy in contrast to the shaky character of his ex-spouse, who has become the moll of bigtime crook Dan Duryea.

Caught in a rendezvous with his old flame by Duryea, Lancaster fends off the jealousy of his rival by suggesting the group pull off an armored car holdup. As the driver of the payroll truck, he'll secretly work with the crooks.

Under Robert Siodmak's knowing direction, the flashbacks blend into a cohesive unit and are never confusing or draggy. His staging of the holdup scene is a masterful job.

Lancaster's role is a made-to-order part of a two-fisted square-shooter who gets fouled up in a jam through no fault of his own.

● ●

■ CRISS CROSS

1992, 100 MINS, US ◇ ⦿

Dir Chris Menges   *Prod* Anthea Sylbert   *Scr* Scott Sommer   *Ph* Ivan Strasburg   *Ed* Tony Lawson   *Mus* Trevor Jones   *Art Dir* Crispian Sallis
● Goldie Hawn, Arliss Howard, James Gannon, David Arnott, Keith Carradine, J.C. Quinn (M-G-M/Hawn-Sylbert)

Told from the perspective of a 12-year-old boy, this earnest, languid drama [from a novella by Scott Sommer] might have worked if it weren't so painfully obvious and slow.

Set at the time of the 1969 moon landing, *Criss Cross* deals with a boy, Chris (David Arnott), who's lost his moral compass, living with his mom (Goldie Hawn) in a run-down Key West hotel. Hawn's a waitress who turns stripper to pay the rent, while Dad (Keith Carradine, in a brief cameo) split three years earlier.

Almost an hour in, the story finally stumbles into a plot as Chris discovers he's been transporting hidden cocaine from a fisherman to one of the locals. He decides to try and score some cash on his own to help his mother find a respectable job.

Cinematographer-turned-director Chris Menges, who made his directing debut with the 1988 *A World Apart*, has a good eye for trappings of the Key West lifestyle but doesn't bring any life to the story or characters. Pic doesn't display much of Hawn except off-screen sessions with a physical trainer, evident thanks to the skimpy Key West attire and a striptease number.

● ●

■ CRITTERS

1986, 86 MINS, US ◇ ⦿ ⊙

Dir Stephen Herek   *Prod* Rupert Harvey   *Scr* Stephen Herek, Domonic Muir, Don Opper   *Ph* Tom Suhrstedt   *Ed* Larry Bock   *Mus* David Newman   *Art Dir* Gregg Fonseca
● Dee Wallace, M. Emmet Walsh, Billy Green Bush, Scott Grimes, Nadine Van Der Velde, Terrence Mann (New Line/Sho/Smart Egg)

Critters resemble oversize hairballs and roll like tumbleweeds when prodded into action, the perfect menace for this irritatingly insipid and lightweight film which unfolds with plodding predictability and leaves few cliches unturned.

Within minutes of film's start, a small band of voracious Krites (a.k.a. Critters) easily escape from a 'maximum security asteroid' and are whizzing toward Kansas with two crack bounty hunters in pursuit.

Establish the sleepy life of farmer (yes) Brown and his wife Helen, as credibly performed by Billy Green Bush and Dee Wallace as can be expected with such material, rambunctious son Brad and sexually budding daughter April. There's also M. Emmet Walsh as the familiar smalltown sheriff.

Co-writers Domonic Muir [who penned the original story] and Stephen Herek, latter doubling as film's director, manage to deflate what little suspense is created by subtitling the Critters' chatter. The final result is neither scary nor humorous

● ●

■ CRITTERS 2
THE MAIN COURSE

1988, 87 MINS, US ◇ ⦿ ⊙

Dir Mick Garris   *Prod* Barry Opper   *Scr* D.T. Twohy,

Mick Garris   *Ph* Russell Carpenter   *Ed* Charles Bornstein   *Mus* Nicholas Pike   *Art Dir* Philip Dean Foreman
● Scott Grimes, Liane Curtis, Don Opper, Barry Corbin, Tom Hodges (New Line/Sho/Smart Egg)

All concerned are back in small Grovers Bend, where Krites terrorized residents just two years earlier. Tipoff that they've returned is appearance of dozens and dozens of large eggs with colorful patterns on them.

Outer space bounty hunters Ug and Lee (Terrence Mann and Roxanne Kernohan), as well as Charlie (Don Opper), are dispatched to planet Earth to complete their earlier attempt to obliterate the nasty little killers.

Coincidentally, young Brad Brown (Scott Grimes) comes to visit his Nana (Herta Ware) and gets blamed again by some townfolk for arrival of the critters, which are now hatching and eating at a furious pace.

Film perfectly weaves together the gruesome behaviour of these bloodthirsty creatures and the comic asides that keep things gliding along.

● ●

■ CROCODILE DUNDEE

1986, 102 MINS, AUSTRALIA ◇ ⦿ ⊙

Dir Peter Faiman   *Prod* John Cornell   *Scr* Paul Hogan, Ken Shadie, John Cornell   *Ph* Russell Boyd   *Ed* David Stiven   *Mus* Peter Best   *Art Dir* Graham Walker
● Paul Hogan, Linda Kozlowski, John Meillon, Mark Blum, Michael Lombard, David Gulpilil (Rimfire)

As the title character, Paul Hogan limns a laconic if rather dim crocodile hunter who achieves some notoriety after surviving an attack by a giant croc. New York reporter Linda Kozlowski journeys to the Northern Territory to cover the story.

Plot bogs down somewhat as Hogan and Kozlowski trudge through the outback. However, proceedings are intermittently enlivened by John Meillon who is slyly humorous as Dundee's manager and partner in a safari tour business.

Rather implausibly, Kozlowski persuades Hogan to return to Gotham with her. Here he is initiated into the delights of the Big Apple.

Director Peter Faiman, essaying his first theatrical venture after an impressive career in Australian TV, directing Hogan's shows among others, has problems with the pacing and a script [from a story by Hogan] that has its flat, dull spots.

Hogan is comfortable enough playing the wry, irreverent, amiable Aussie that seems close to his own persona, and teams well with Kozlowski, who radiates lots of charm, style and spunk.

[Quotation marks were put around the word *Crocodile* by distributor Paramount on release outside Australia and seven minutes cut from the running time.]
□ 1986: Nomination: Best Original Screenplay

● ●

■ 'CROCODILE' DUNDEE II

1988, 111 MINS, US ◇ ⦿ ⊙

Dir John Cornell   *Prod* John Cornell, Jane Scott   *Scr* Paul Hogan, Brett Hogan   *Ph* Russell Boyd   *Ed* David Stiven   *Mus* Peter Best   *Art Dir* Lawrence Eastwood
● Paul Hogan, Linda Kozlowski, Charles Dutton, Hechter Ubarry, John Meillon, Juan Fernandez (Rimfire/Paramount)

'Crocodile' Dundee II is a disappointing follow-up to the disarmingly charming first feature with Aussie star Paul Hogan. Sequel is too slow to constitute an adventure and has too few laughs to be a comedy.

Story unfolds with Hogan making passable attempt to find gainful employment at just about the time Linda Kozlowski's ex-lover is

killed in Colombia for taking photos of a cocaine king as he shoots one of his runners. The nefarious Rico (Hechter Ubarry is much too cute for this role) learns the photos were sent to Kozlowski and in a flash he sets up an operation in a Long Island fortress with a handful of stereotypical Latino henchmen to get the incriminating evidence back. Hogan has the photos, which means Rico has Kozlowski kidnaped.

Using outback strategy, that is, getting the punks to yelp like a pack of wild dogs, Hogan gains entrance and frees his woman. Kozlowski basically does little but wait at the sidelines as Hogan flies into action.

● ●

■ CROMWELL

1970, 139 MINS, UK ◇ ⦿ ⊙

Dir Ken Hughes   *Prod* Irving Allen   *Scr* Ken Hughes   *Ph* Geoffrey Unsworth   *Ed* Bill Lenny   *Mus* Frank Cordell   *Art Dir* John Stoll
● Richard Harris, Alec Guinness, Robert Morley, Dorothy Tutin, Frank Finlay, Timothy Dalton (Allen/Columbia)

The nub of director Ken Hughes' $9 million film (from his own screenplay, with Ronald Harwood as 'script consultant') is the confrontation of the two complex leading characters, Oliver Cromwell and King Charles I. Richard Harris and Alec Guinness, respectively, give powerhouse performances.

Harris plays the idealistic, dedicated Cromwell with cold eyes, tortured, rasping voice and an inflexible spirit. He is the man who regarded Jehovah as his main ally and was determined at all costs to rescue the England he loved from the corruption of a weak, greedy court and to set up a Parliament that would be truly democratic, speaking for the people and not be the puppets of the King.

The battle scenes (shot in Spain and using the Spanish Army) at Nazeby and Edgehill are excitingly drawn.
□ 1970: Best Costume Design.
□ Nomination: Best Original Score

● ●

■ CROSS CREEK

1983, 122 MINS, US ◇ ⦿

Dir Martin Ritt   *Prod* Robert B. Radnitz   *Scr* Dalene Young   *Ph* John A. Alonzo   *Ed* Sidney Levin   *Mus* Leonard Rosenman   *Art Dir* Walter Scott Herndon
● Mary Steenburgen, Rip Torn, Peter Coyote, Dana Hill, Alfre Woodard, Joanna Miles (Thorn-EMI)

Cross Creek, based on the memoirs of *The Yearling* author Marjorie Kinnan Rawlings, offers a sanitized vision of her early struggle to publish a novel and the Florida backwoods which inspired her prose.

It's an uncompelling, yet warm tale which lightly skips over the woman's travails by illustrating a series of vignettes of rural humanity. The overall effect trivializes a life and provides little insight into the artistic process.

Story opens in 1928 with Rawlings (Mary Steenburgen) deciding to leave the security of a marriage to a wealthy New Yorker for the uncertainty of life in a remote region of Florida.

The drama, what little exists in the film, centers on Rawlings' inability to sell her work until she begins writing about the events of the Florida swamp folk.

Remainder of the film focuses on Rawlings' relationship with local hotelier Norton Baskin (Peter Coyote), the recovery of her land and the warm relationship between the author and her young black housekeeper.
□ 1983: Nominations: Best Supp. Actor (Rip Torn), Supp. Actress (Alfre Woodard), Costume Design, Original Score

● ●

■ CROSSFIRE

1947, 84 MINS, US Ⓦ ⊙
Dir Edward Dmytryk   *Prod* Adrian Scott   *Scr* John Paxton   *Ph* J. Roy Hunt   *Ed* Harry Gerstad   *Mus* Roy Webb   *Art Dir* Albert S. D'Agostino, Alfred Herman
● Robert Young, Robert Mitchum, Robert Ryan, Gloria Grahame, Paul Kelly, Sam Levene (RKO)

Crossfire is a frank spotlight on anti-Semitism. Producer Dore Schary, in association with Adrian Scott, has pulled no punches. There is no skirting such relative fol-de-rol as inter-marriage or clubs that exclude Jews. Here is a hard-hitting film [based on Richard Brooks' novel, *The Brick Foxhole*] whose whodunit aspects are fundamentally incidental to the overall thesis of bigotry and race prejudice.

There are three Roberts (Young, Mitchum and Ryan) all giving capital performances. Young is unusual as the detective captain; Mitchum is the 'right' sort of cynical GI; and Ryan a commanding personality, in this instance the bigoted soldier-killer, whose sneers and leers about Sam Levene and his tribe are all too obvious.

The pic opens with the fatal slugfest in Levene's apartment, when his hospitality is abused and Ryan kills him. Director Edward Dmytryk has drawn gripping portraitures. The flashback technique is effective as it shades and colors the sundry attitudes of the heavy, as seen or recalled by the rest of the cast.
☐ 1947: Nominations: Best Picture, Director, Supp. Actor (Robert Ryan), Supp. Actress (Gloria Grahame), Screenplay

■ CROSSING DELANCEY

1988, 97 MINS, US ◇ Ⓦ ⊙
Dir Joan Micklin Silver   *Prod* Michael Nozik   *Scr* Susan Sandler   *Ph* Theo Van de Sande   *Ed* Rick Shaine   *Mus* Paul Chihara   *Art Dir* Dan Leigh
● Amy Irving, Reizl Bozyk, Peter Riegert, Jeroen Krabbe, Sylvia Miles, Suzzy Roche (Warner)

In an unexpectedly enjoyable way, *Crossing Delancey* addresses one of the great societal issues of our day – the dilemma of how the 30-ish, attractive, successful, intelligent and unmarried female finds a mate she can be happy with.

Off-off-Broadway fans may remember the title from playwright Susan Sandler's semi-autobiographical 1985 comedy about how her loving, old-worldly and slightly overbearing Lower East Side NY Jewish grandmother engages the services of a matchmaker to find her a suitable marriage partner.

Amy Irving is the dutiful granddaughter who works in a pretentious Manhattan bookstore by day, keeps her own apartment and always finds time to make frequent visits to her precious Bubbie (Yiddish actress Reizl Bozyk).

Matchmaker (Sylvia Miles) brings Irving together with an unlikely candidate, pickle maker Sam Posner (Peter Riegert). The major set-ups focus on Irving's torn affections between the rakish, smooth-talking charm of pulp novelist Anton Maes (Jeroen Krabbe), who gives good readings on rainy days at the bookstore, and earnest, straight-forward, vulnerable Riegert, who unabashedly holds his heart in his hand for her. To the credit of most of the actors, the sentimentality doesn't sink the story.

■ CROSS OF IRON

1977, 130 MINS, UK/W. GERMANY ◇ Ⓦ
Dir Sam Peckinpah   *Prod* Wolf C. Hartwig   *Scr* Julius J. Epstein, Herbert Asmodi   *Ph* John Coquillon   *Ed* Tony Lawson, Mike Ellis, Herbert Taschner   *Mus* Ernest Gold   *Art Dir* Ted Haworth, Brian Ackland Snow
● James Coburn, Maximilian Schell, James Mason, David Warner, Klaus Lowitsch, Roger Fritz (EMI/Rapid/Terra)

Cross of Iron more than anything else affirms director Sam Peckinpah's prowess as an action filmmaker of graphic mayhem.

Told from the German viewpoint as the Wehrmacht's cream were being clobbered on the Russian front circa 1943, the production [from the book by Willi Heinrich] is well but conventionally cast, technically impressive, but ultimately violence-fixated.

The film efficiently employs James Coburn, Maximilian Schell, James Mason and David Warner as frontline Germans. Coburn plays a platoon sergeant of style, ability and soul, contemptuous of the military and sick of the war.

Cross of Iron's overwhelming image is not disillusion, even less war's absurdity, but the war itself.

■ CROSSPLOT

1969, 97 MINS, UK ◇
Dir Alvin Rakoff   *Prod* Robert S. Blake   *Scr* Leigh Vance, John Kruse   *Ph* Brendan J. Stafford   *Ed* Bert Rule   *Mus* Stanley Black   *Art Dir* Ivan King
● Roger Moore, Martha Hyer, Claudie Lange, Alexis Kanner, Francis Matthews, Bernard Lee (United Artists/Tribune)

A thriller with a few good jokes, red herrings, a few quick genuine thrills, chases, and some mystery. It doesn't jell because the mystery is too cloudy. Motivation of most characters is indecisive and some are badly undeveloped.

Roger Moore plays a debonair ad exec with a flair for his job and a roving eye for the chicks. When a flash, swinging campaign is okayed by a client, he has little time to find the girl around whom it will centre. His only clue is a portrait with her name on it.

His problem sparks off a search for the girl, a mysterious Hungarian, which lands him up to his neck in a bewildering political ploy involving Marchers of Peace members and some anarchists.

Some bright thesps keep the often puzzling events moving deftly and breezily. Moore is not wholly convincing as a man of action.

■ CROSSROADS

1942, 82 MINS, US
Dir Jack Conway   *Prod* Edwin Knopf   *Scr* Guy Trosper   *Ph* Joseph Ruttenberg   *Ed* George Boemler   *Mus* Bronislau Kaper
● William Powell, Hedy Lamarr, Claire Trevor, Basil Rathbone, Felix Bressart, H.B. Warner (M-G-M)

This is a Grade A whodunit, with a superlative cast. The novel story line, which would do credit to an Alfred Hitchcock thriller, has the added potency of Hedy Lamarr and William Powell.

A prominent member of France's Foreign Office, William Powell, is accused of having been a thief prior to a train accident in which he suffered a fractured skull and amnesia. Not remembering anything about his past, and since having married the beauteous Hedy Lamarr, Powell has a blackmailer arrested.

During the trial he first learns of his alleged criminal activities under another name, but at the last minute Basil Rathbone steps in as a witness and 'proves' that it's a case of mistaken identity; that the criminal Powell was supposed to have been had actually died in Africa. Once freed, Powell is then harassed by Rathbone, who says that Powell was, actually, his accomplice in the murder 13 years previously of a bank messenger and the robbery of 2 million francs.

It's good, escapist drama, without a hint of the war despite its Parisian locale, circa 1935, and evidences excellent casting and good direction. The script likewise well turned out, though better pace would have put the film in the smash class. Its only fault is a perceptible slowness at times, although the running time is a reasonable 82 minutes, caused by a plenitude of talk.

■ CROSSROADS

1986, 96 MINS, US ◇ Ⓦ ⊙
Dir Walter Hill   *Prod* Mark Carliner   *Scr* John Fusco   *Ph* John Bailey   *Ed* Freeman Davies   *Mus* Ry Cooder   *Art Dir* Jack T. Collis
● Ralph Macchio, Joe Seneca, Jami Gertz, Joe Morton, Robert Judd, Steve Vai (Carliner/Columbia-Delphi IV)

Penned partly on the basis of actual experiences he had as a teenager touring the South as a musician, John Fusco's screenplay makes ample use of the legend of the late bluesman Robert Johnson, who left behind a tiny but potent legacy.

Ralph Macchio, a classical guitar student at Juilliard, discovers an old travelling and playing companion of Johnson's in a New York hospital. Hoping to make his reputation by finding and recording Johnson's alleged 'unknown 30th song', Macchio springs old Joe Seneca from the facility, and the unlikely pair hit the road for Mississippi Delta country.

Seneca acquits himself very nicely, while director Walter Hill pulls off the expected professional mob, but he pushes so hard for pace that he skates right over the opportunities for thought that the subject calls for.

■ CROWD, THE

1928, 98 MINS, US Ⓦ
Dir King Vidor   *Scr* John V.A. Weaver, King Vidor, Harry Behn, Joe Farnham   *Ph* Henry Sharp   *Ed* Hugh Wynn   *Art Dir* Cedric Gibbons, A. Arnold Gillespie
● Eleanor Boardman, James Murray, Bert Roach, Daniel G. Tomlinson, Dell Henderson, Lucy Beaumont (M-G-M)

A drab actionless story of ungodly length and apparently telling nothing. The longness of the picture suggests it was designed for a Metro special, but on what, only its authors, John V.A. Weaver and King Vidor, must know. Superficially it reels off as an analytical insight into the life, worries and struggles of two young, ordinary people, who marry and become parents.

The husband is a plodder and dreamer, achieving nothing but two children and an $8 raise of salary in five years. For this he seems in constant reprimand from his wife and her family. Casting aside his permanent desk job through mental strain over the death by a truck of his little daughter, the young husband tries other jobs in vain, until his wife, disgusted, finally slaps him in the face and walks out.

James Murray is the young husband and catches the spirit at times, more in looks than anything else. Both he and Eleanor Boardman have the opportunity for a big scene when seeing their child trampled by a moving truck while walking toward their home. Both parents muff the chance by a mile.
☐ 1927/28: Nominations: Best Director, Artistic Quality of Production

■ CROWD ROARS, THE

1932, 84 MINS, US
Dir Howard Hawks   *Scr* Howard Hawks, Seton I. Miller, Kubec Glasmon, John Bright   *Ph* Sid Hickox   *Ed* John Stumar, Thomas Pratt   *Mus* Leo Forbstein (dir.)   *Art Dir* Jack Okey
● James Cagney, Joan Blondell, Ann Dvorak, Eric Linden, Guy Kibbee, Frank McHugh (Warner)

All auto-race pictures lead to Indianapolis, and there is no deviation from that schedule here.

Script doesn't unfold unusual acting opportunities for any of the principals. In this instance James Cagney's a front rank pilot who likes his grog and is mixed up with a girl by the time he revisits the old home town after achieving sport-page fame. The kid brother (Eric Linden) has caught the racing bug, too, and this provides the complication which has its source in the feminine angle.

Cagney, having added the brother to his crew, can't reconcile himself to having the kid on too friendly terms with the girl with whom he's been living (Ann Dvorak). To retaliate she sics her girlfriend (Joan Blondell), also of the same stripe, onto the brother, with this latter situation developing into a romance which splits the brothers.

Howard Hawks has received valiant service from his cameramen. The director doesn't seem to have taken his own story too seriously, and the picture is cut so that it just about holds the continuity together, always with the hint that it's anxious to get back to the track.

....

■ **CROWD ROARS, THE**

1938, 87 MINS, US

Dir Richard Thorpe *Prod* Sam Zimbalist *Scr* Thomas Lennon, George Bruce, George Oppenheimer *Ph* John Seitz *Mus* Edward Ward
● Robert Taylor, Edward Arnold, Frank Morgan, Maureen O'Sullivan, William Gargan, Lionel Stander (M-G-M)

The manly art of self-defense, otherwise known as the cauliflower industry, alias prize-fighting, is a rough-and-tumble racket operated by big time gamblers with small time ethics, according to the film, *The Crowd Roars* in which Robert Taylor leads with his left hand. It's exciting melodrama with plenty of ring action, some plausible romance and several corking good characterizations.

There are moments early in the film when it appears that George Bruce, the author, intends to dwell on the angle of mob psychology. He steers away from any depth in the treatment of his theme, however, and holds to a plot about a choir boy who becomes a contender for the light heavyweight championship.

Frank Morgan creates something interesting out of the role of the pug's father, a drunkard and braggart. Edward Arnold is the conventional bookmaker and fight manager, who works successfully on the theory that the smartest gamblers are the biggest suckers. Heart interest is centred in a love affair between Taylor and Maureen O'Sullivan.

....

■ **CRUEL SEA, THE**

1953, 120 MINS, UK 📺

Dir Charles Frend *Prod* Leslie Norman *Scr* Eric Ambler *Ph* Gordon Dines *Ed* Peter Tanner *Mus* Alan Rawsthorne *Art Dir* Jim Morahan
● Jack Hawkins, Donald Sinden, John Stratton, Denholm Elliott, Stanley Baker, Virginia McKenna (Ealing)

Ealing breaks from its traditional light comedies to offer a serious, authentic reconstruction of the battle of the Atlantic, based on Nicholas Monsarrat's bestseller. Production, despite its overall running time, emerges as a picture of dramatic intensity.

Much of the original novel's action has been telescoped and quite a few major incidents have been omitted. As the commentator explains, the heroes are the men, the heroines are the ships, and the villain is the cruel sea.

These three elements are put into focus via the activities of a corvette which puts to sea with only one experienced officer – the captain – aboard. The others are the normal wartime recruits from civilian life, including a freelance journalist, lawyer, bank clerk and second-hand car salesman. Their first operational duties land them into a storm, but subsequently they encounter enemy activity and are harassed by U-boats.

Notable thesping comes from Jack Hawkins, who plays the captain with requisite

authority. Surrounding cast is well matched, with sterling work contributed by Donald Sinden, John Stratton, Denholm Elliot and Stanley Baker at the head of a handpicked cast. Charles Frend directs with a sure touch.
□ 1953: Nomination: Best Screenplay

....

■ **CRUISING**

1980, 106 MINS, US ◇ 📺

Dir William Friedkin *Prod* Jerry Weintraub *Scr* William Friedkin *Ph* James Contner *Ed* Bud Smith *Mus* Jack Nitzsche *Art Dir* Bruce Weintraub
● Al Pacino, Paul Sorvino, Karen Allen, Richard Cox, Don Scardino (Lorimar)

In *Cruising* writer-director William Friedkin explores the S&M life of New York City. Like any approach to the bizarre, it is fascinating for about 15 minutes.

In many respects, *Cruising* [from the novel by Gerald Walker] resembles the worst of the 'hippie' films of the 1960s.

Taking away the kissing, caressing and a few bloody killings, Friedkin has no story, though picture pretends to be a murder mystery combined with a study of Al Pacino's psychological degradation.

Pacino is an innocent young cop chosen to go undercover in search of a killer. He ultimately zeroes in on the culprit but by now is almost as far around the bend as his prey. But that's not saying much more than the old maxim: 'he who lies down with dogs gets up with fleas.'

....

■ **CRUSADES, THE**

1935, 124 MINS, US

Dir Cecil B. DeMille *Prod* Cecil B. DeMille *Scr* Harold Lamb, Dudley Nichols, Waldemar Young *Ph* Victor Milner *Ed* Anne Bauchens *Mus* Rudolph Kopp
● Loretta Young, Henry Wilcoxon, Ian Keith, C. Aubrey Smith, Katherine DeMille, Joseph Schildkraut (Paramount)

Probably only Cecil B. DeMille could make a picture like *The Crusades* – and get away with it. It's long, and the story is not up to some of his previous films, but the production has sweep and spectacle.

DeMille patently intended his puppets to be subjugated by the generally transcendental theme of this holy war on the infidels. The loose footage at times defeats that. There is no great surge of human sympathy for the ecclesiastic offensive. Only the pious wandering hermit (capably done by C. Aubrey Smith) stands out as the sole symbol of the faith in the invasion of Acre and Jerusalem. Richard-the-Lion-Hearted frankly accepts the call to arms for selfish reasons – the only out he has to sidestep the state marriage to the French king's sister (Loretta Young).

Henry Wilcoxon plays Richard. Full weight of *The Crusades* falls on his performance. For sheer versatility, ranging from horsemanship to boudoir, there are few players who could have done as well.
□ 1935: Nomination: Best Cinematography

....

■ **CRUSH, THE**

1993, 89 MINS, US ◇ 📺 ⊙

Dir Alan Shapiro *Prod* James G. Robinson *Scr* Alan Shapiro *Ph* Bruce Surtees *Ed* Ian Crafford *Mus* Graeme Revell *Art Dir* Michael Bolton
● Cary Elwes, Alicia Silverstone, Jennifer Rubin, Amber Benson, Kurtwood Smith, Gwynyth Walsh (Morgan Creek)

The Crush is a by-the-numbers thriller longer on suspense than brains.

Cary Elwes plays a writer who moves into the guest house of a wealthy couple and befriends their beautiful, precocious 14-year-old daughter, Darian (Alicia Silverstone), who starts out cute and coquettish and ends up

reminiscent of a similarly named youth from *The Omen*.

Nick (Elwes) gives in to a momentary indiscretion and kisses the girl, then watches her grow gradually more obsessed, until she starts venting her wrath on him, a co-worker (Jennifer Rubin) and a teenage friend who may know too much.

Writer-director Alan Shapiro (making his feature debut after directing several movies for the Disney Channel) goes for the usual overwrought ending.

Elwes has a certain boyish charm as Nick but is so relentlessly dense he doesn't engender much sympathy. Silverstone brings the right mix of little-girl pouting and budding sensuality to a role that is, finally, a caricature.

....

■ **CRY-BABY**

1990, 85 MINS, US ◇ 📺 ⊙

Dir John Waters *Prod* Rachel Talalay *Scr* John Waters *Ph* David Insley *Ed* Janice Hampton *Mus* Patrick Williams *Art Dir* Vincent Peranio
● Johnny Depp, Amy Locane, Susan Tyrrell, Polly Bergen, Iggy Pop, Ricki Lake (Imagine)

John Waters' mischievous satire of the teen exploitation genre is entertaining as a rude joyride through another era, full of great clothes and hairdos.

Set on Waters' Baltimore turf, *Cry-Baby* returns to the nascent days of rock 'n' roll when teens were king, where the cleancut 'squares' are pitted against the hoodlum 'drapes'. Cry-Baby (Johnny Depp), a handsome delinquent with a perpetual tear in his eye (in memory of his criminal parents who died in the electric chair), takes the bait from a pony-tailed blonde from the well-bred set (Amy Locane).

Once it's clear the plot is just a raucous rebel without a cause with a handful of inspired elements clipped to a wornout *Romeo and Juliet* storyline, a lot of the foolery begins to wear thin. There's so much commotion in the pic, with its 11 full-fledged dance numbers and elaborate production values, that one can't help but catch on that a story's missing.

Depp is great as the delinquent juve, delivering the melodramatic lines with straight-faced conviction and putting some Elvis-like snap and wiggle into his moves.

....

■ **CRY DANGER**

1951, 79 MINS, US 📺

Dir Robert Parrish *Prod* Sam Wiesenthal, W.R. Frank *Scr* William Bowers *Ph* Joseph F. Biroc *Ed* Bernard W. Burton *Mus* Emil Newman, Paul Dunlap *Art Dir* Richard Day
● Dick Powell, Rhonda Fleming, Richard Erdman, William Conrad, Regis Toomey, Jean Porter (Olympic)

All the ingredients for a suspenseful melodrama are contained in *Cry Danger*. Plot [from a story by Jerome Cady] opens with Dick Powell returning after five years in prison, having been pardoned from a life sentence when new evidence turns up that clears him of a robbery rap. Evidence was manufactured by a crippled Marine vet (Richard Erdman) who figures Powell will be grateful enough to cut up some of the $100,000 loot he is supposed to have hidden.

Powell sees the pardon as an opportunity to bring the guilty parties to justice and free a friend still in prison. Scene of all the plot movement is the poorer section of Los Angeles, where Powell and Erdman have holed up in a crummy trailer camp to be near Rhonda Fleming, wife of the friend still in prison.

Robert Parrish, erstwhile film editor, makes a strong directorial bow.

....

CRY FREEDOM

1987, 157 MINS, US ◇ ⓥ ⊙

Dir Richard Attenborough *Prod* Richard Attenborough
Scr John Briley *Ph* Ronnie Taylor *Ed* Lesley Walker
Mus George Fenton, Jonas Gwangwa *Art Dir* Stuart
Craig
● Kevin Kline, Penelope Wilton, Denzel Washington,
Kevin McNally, John Thaw, Timothy West (Marble
Arch/Universal)

Cry Freedom personifies the struggle of South
Africa's black population against apartheid in
the evolving friendship of martyred black activist Stephen Biko and liberal white newspaper editor Donald Woods. It derives its
impact less from epic scope than from the
wrenching immediacy of its subject matter
and the moral heroism of its appealingly
played, idealistic protagonists.

John Briley's screenplay is based on two
books by Woods, who could publish them only
by escaping South Africa (where he was under virtual house arrest as a 'banned' person)
with his family in harrowing fashion. This
produces the singular flaw of *Cry Freedom* – an
overemphasis in the film's final hour on the
Woods family's escape to exile in England.

Film opens in 1975 with a pitiless dawn raid
by bulldozers and armed police on an illegal
shantytown of black squatters. Stephen Biko is
at first an offscreen presence, revered by blacks
as a charismatic advocate of racial self-worth
and self-determination, but distrusted by whites
– including liberals like Woods – as a dangerous
reverse racist whose condemnation of white
society carries an implicit threat of violence

Realizing he needs to form an alliance with
the liberals he so dislikes, Biko (Denzel
Washington) arranges to meet Woods (Kevin
Kline), an invitation that dedicated new-
shound cannot afford to turn down.

Kline's familiar low-key screen presence
serves him well in his portrayal of the strong-
willed but even-tempered journalist.
Washington does a remarkable job of transforming himself into the articulte and mesmerizing black nationalist leader, whose
refusal to keep silent led to his death in police custody and a subsequent coverup.
□ 1987: Nomination: Best Original Score,
Song ('Cry Freedom')

CRY HAVOC

1943, 96 MINS, US

Dir Richard Thorpe *Prod* Edwin Knopf *Scr* Paul
Osborn *Ph* Karl Freund *Ed* Ralph E. Winters
Mus Daniele Amfitheatrof
● Margaret Sullavan, Ann Sothern, Joan Blondell, Fay
Bainter, Marsha Hunt, Ella Raines (M-G-M)

Plot sets up all-femme cast tossed into a
bomb shelter at Bataan, with nine girls
rounded up from evacuation of Manila to
function as volunteers at an outland field hospital. Each of the nine are from various fields
of endeavor, including waitress Ann Sothern,
and former burlesque performer Joan
Blondell. Girls are assigned auxiliary spots
around the camp, but practically all of the
footage centers in the bomb shelter for
lengthy dialog and mental reactions of the individuals as the going gets tougher.

Best thing about the film is the capable cast
tossed in for group of generally fine performances, despite the inadequacies of the plot
in both suspense and movement. Sullavan delivers strong portrayal of the army nurse, with
Sothern and Blondell clicking solidly in respective roles.

Richard Thorpe is restricted on direction to
following too stagey a script [from the play by
Allan R. Kenward, first presented at a small
Hollywood theatre and then in New York under the new title *Proof thro' the Night*], with no
chance of generating more than nominal suspense at points where it should reach peaks.

CRYING GAME, THE

1992, 113 MINS, UK ◇ ⓥ ⊙

Dir Neil Jordan *Prod* Stephen Woolley *Scr* Neil
Jordan *Ph* Ian Wilson *Ed* Kant Pan *Mus* Anne
Dudley *Art Dir* Jim Clay
● Stephen Rea, Miranda Richardson, Forest Whitaker,
Jaye Davidson, Adrian Dunbar, Jim Broadbent
(Palace/Channel 4)

An astonishingly good and daring film that
richly develops several intertwined thematic
lines, *The Crying Game* takes giant risks that
are stunningly rewarded. Irish director Neil
Jordan's seventh film is also his best to date.

The IRA's kidnapping in Northern Ireland
of British soldier Jody (Forest Whitaker)
serves as the jumping off point for a fearlessly
penetrating examination of politics, race, sexuality and human nature.

First 40-minute act concerns Whitaker's
country house incarceration by a small band
of terrorists led by Maguire (Adrian Dunbar)
and the sexy Jude (Miranda Richardson).
They leave him mostly under the guard of
Fergus (Jordan stalwart Stephen Rea), who
develops an intense rapport with Jody.

Fergus later escapes to London, where he
finds Jody's great love, Dil (Jaye Davidson),
working in a beauty salon. Dil entices Fergus
into a relationship that will test just how far
he's willing to go for love.

Acting is uniformly superior. Whitaker's
simply terrific, and the Yank thesp has seemingly mastered a very specific British working-class accent. Rea is intriguingly
handsome-homely, decisive-passive, gentle-vi-
olent. Newcomer Davidson is almost impossibly right as the beautiful, mysterious Dil,
while Richardson is equal parts fire and ice as
the most resilient IRA member.
□ 1992: Best Original Screenplay.
□ Nominations: Best Picture, Director, Actor
(Stephen Rea), Supp. Actor (Jaye Davidson),
Editing

CRY IN THE DARK, A
(Australia: Evil Angels)

1988, 121 MINS, US ◇ ⓥ ⊙

Dir Fred Schepisi *Prod* Verity Lambert *Scr* Robert
Caswell, Fred Schepisi *Ph* Ian Baker *Ed* Jill Bilcock
Mus Bruce Smeaton *Art Dir* Wendy Dickson, George
Liddle
● Meryl Streep, Sam Neill, Bruce Myles, Charles
Tingwell, Nick Tate, Lewis Fitz-gerald (Cannon)

One of the oddest and most illogical murder
cases of modern times is recounted in intimate, incredible detail in the classy, disturbing drama *A Cry in the Dark* [from John
Bryson's Book *Evil Angels*].

The saga of Lindy Chamberlain's harassment, trial and imprisonment for having allegedly murdered her baby daughter, when
there was literally no evidence against her,
was the biggest news story in Australia of the
1980s.

In 1980, the Chamberlains visit the monumental Ayers Rock in the outback. With the
baby put to sleep in a tent, the family begins
enjoying a nighttime barbeque when a cry is
heard. Checking the tent, Lindy briefly
glimpses a dingo slipping out of it and then,
to her horror, finds Azaria missing from her
bed.

No trace of the infant is found, and the conclusion appears to be that the dingo made off
with her. Astonishingly, however, sentiment
begins to grow throughout the country to the
effect that Lindy killed her daughter. From
there, the press can't let the story die. Lindy
is charged with murder and Michael named
as accessory after the fact.

If one didn't know who Meryl Streep is, one
could easily guess Lindy was played by a fine,
unknown Australian actress. Sam Neill, who
here looks remarkably like the real Michael
Chamberlain, well conveys the tentative

strengths and very real weaknesses of a man
thrust into an unimaginable situation.
□ 1988: Nomination: Best Actress (Meryl
Streep)

CRY OF THE CITY

1948, 96 MINS, US

Dir Robert Siodmak *Prod* Sol C. Siegel *Scr* Richard
Murphy *Ph* Lloyd Ahern *Ed* Harmon Jones
Mus Alfred Newman *Art Dir* Lyle R. Wheeler, Albert
Hogsett
● Victor Mature, Richard Conte, Fred Clark, Shelley
Winters, Debra Paget, Hope Emerson (20th Century-Fox)

The hard-hitting suspense of the chase formula is given topnotch presentation in *Cry of
the City*. It's an exciting motion picture, credibly put together to wring out every bit of
strong action and tension inherent in such a
plot. Robert Siodmak's penchant for shaping
melodramatic excitement that gets through
to an audience is realistically carried out in
this one.

The telling screenplay by Richard Murphy,
based on a novel, *The Chair for Martin Rome* by
Henry Edward Helset, presents Victor
Mature as a police lieutenant in homicide
and Richard Conte as a cop-killer – antagonists, although both sprung from New York's
Italian sector.

Shelley Winters sparks small assignment of
a girl who drives the killer through the New
York streets while an unlicensed doctor works
desperately to patch up his wounds.

CRY, THE BELOVED COUNTRY
(US: African Fury)

1952, 103 MINS, UK ⓥ

Dir Zoltan Korda *Prod* Zoltan Korda *Scr* Alan Paton
Ph Robert Krasker *Ed* David Eady *Mus* R. Gallois-
Montbrun *Art Dir* Wilfrid Shingleton
● Canada Lee, Charles Carson, Sidney Poitier, Joyce
Carey, Geoffrey Keen, Michael Goodliffe (London/British
Lion)

Alan Paton's best-selling novel which was
made into a Broadway musical *Lost in the Stars*
[1949], has been turned into an absorbing
pic. Filmed in its native South African locale,
and in London, the pic emerges as a very
moving film, full of simplicity and charm.

The picture is a strong social document in
its study of the perplexed conditions of a submerged native population ruled by the whites
in South Africa.

More particularly, *Cry* is the story of a simple, native Negro country preacher (Canada
Lee), who goes to the big city of Johannes-
burg to seek a missing sister and wayward
son, and who finds both in the crime-ridden,
slum elements of the city.

Lee's performance, restrained and underplayed, is a rich, heartwarming portrayal,
dominating the film. Sidney Poitier is manly
and striking as a young Negro preacher.

CUBA

1979, 122 MINS, US ◇ ⓥ

Dir Richard Lester *Prod* Arlene Sellers *Scr* Charles
Wood *Ph* David Watkin *Ed* John Victor Smith
Mus Patrick Williams *Art Dir* Shirley Russell
● Sean Connery, Brooke Adams, Jack Weston, Chris
Sarandon, Denholm Elliott, Martin Balsam (United Artists)

Cuba is a hollow, pointless non-drama.
Cynical and evasive about politics, pic displays uniformly unsympathetic characters enacting a vague plot amidst a splendid
re-creation of Havana at the very end of the
Batista regime.

Basic *Two Weeks in Another Town* situation
has had all conventional melodrama calculatedly drained from it. Revolution is closing in
on the upper-crust-types who serve as story
focus, and Brooke Adams is torn between two

men, but treatment deliberately goes against the grain of sentiments normally encountered in such potent dramatic set-ups.

Given the worthless, motley crew seen to populate Havana – including gross American profiteer Jack Weston and cynical gentleman Denholm Elliott – political outlook would seem to be that things couldn't get much worse, and maybe Castro will be a little bit better.

• •

■ **CUJO**

1983, 91 MINS, US ◇ ⓥ ⊙
Dir Lewis Teague   *Prod* Daniel H. Blatt, Robert Singer   *Scr* Don Carlos Dunaway, Lauren Currier   *Ph* Jan De Bont   *Ed* Neil Travis   *Mus* Charles Bernstein   *Art Dir* Guy Comtois
● Dee Wallace, Danny Pintauro, Daniel Hugh-Kelly, Christopher Stone, Ed Lauter, Kaiulani Lee (Taft/Warner)

Although well-made, this screen adaptation of Stephen King's *Cujo* emerges as a dull, uneventful entry in the horror genre. Novel about a mad dog on the rampage occupies a low place in the King canon, which is understandable if the film's stupefying predictability is an accurate reflection of the book.

Opening sequence has a lovable looking St. Bernard bitten on the nose by a bat, whereupon audience is introduced to the Trentons, a family of young parents and a son which is disintegrating, mostly thanks to Dee Wallace's sideline affair with a local worker. Story basically marks time until, at least halfway through, the dog begins attacking Maine seacoast locals (pic was shot in Northern California).

Except for the appealing kid played by Danny Pintauro, the characters are of little interest.

• •

■ **CUL-DE-SAC**

1966, 111 MINS, UK ⓥ
Dir Roman Polanski   *Prod* Gene Gutowski   *Scr* Roman Polanski, Gerard Brach   *Ph* Gilbert Taylor   *Ed* Alastair McIntyre   *Mus* Krzysztof Komeda   *Art Dir* Voytek Roman
● Donald Pleasence, Francoise Dorleac, Lionel Stander, Jack McGowran, William Franklyn, Jacqueline Bisset (Compton)

As a study in kinky insanity, *Cul-de-Sac* creates a tingling atmosphere. This sags riskily at times when the director unturns the screws and does not keep control of his frequently introduced comedy.

Film was shot on location in and around lonely castle on remote Holy Island off the northeast coast of Britain. Gill Taylor's camera bleakly catches the loneliness and sinister background that sparks the happenings.

Donald Pleasence, with steel-rimmed glasses and head completely shaven, is an obvious neurotic. A retired businessman, he is living like a hermit with his young, bored and flirtatious French wife (Francoise Dorleac), who is blatantly contemptuous of him. Suddenly, two wounded gangsters on the run descend upon them. From then on it's a battle of nerves, a cat-and-mouse psychological tightrope walk, as an uneasy truce develops between Pleasence and Stander, while the latter waits to be rescued by the boss of his gang, who never shows.

Pleasence pours some exaggerated but distinctive thesping into his pathetic role while Lionel Stander, obviously more flamboyant, blends nicely with him, turning in a far more subtle performance of latent brutality, mixed with surface geniality, than the screenplay may have promised.

• •

■ **CULPEPPER CATTLE CO., THE**

1972, 92 MINS, US ◇ ⓥ
Dir Dick Richards   *Prod* Paul A. Helmick   *Scr* Eric Bercovici, Gregory Prentiss   *Ph* Lawrence Edward

Williams, Ralph Woolsey   *Ed* John F. Burnett   *Mus* Tom Scott, Jerry Goldsmith   *Art Dir* Jack Martin Smith, Carl Anderson
● Gary Grimes, Billy 'Green' Bush, Luke Askew, Bo Hopkins, Geoffrey Lewis, Wayne Sutherlin (20th Century-Fox)

The Culpepper Cattle Co. is an unsuccessful attempt to mount a poetic and stylistic ballet of death in the environment of a period western. Gary Grimes is featured as a teenager who matures in the course of a hard, violent and bloody cattle drive.

Director Dick Richards' story has been scripted into a pallid, stilted plot, where the characters mutter and grunt empty aphorisms. Clearly, we have here one of those 'important-statement-on-the-human-condition' rationalizations for a gruesome series of blood-lettings.

Billy 'Green' Bush plays Culpepper, hardbitten range boss who takes on Grimes, whose likeable, easy-going and natural manner come across as the only effective performance. Everyone else is saddled with limp dialog and unrestrained posturing. Lots of people are killed.

• •

■ **CURLY SUE**

1991, 101 MINS, US ◇ ⓥ ⊙
Dir John Hughes   *Prod* John Hughes   *Scr* John Hughes   *Ph* Jeffrey Kimball   *Ed* Peck Prior, Harvey Rosenstock   *Mus* Georges Delerue   *Art Dir* Doug Kraner
● James Belushi, Kelly Lynch, Alisan Porter, John Getz, Fred Dalton Thompson, Cameron Thor (Warner)

This predictable crowd-pleaser is at heart a two-hanky affair, a mix of childish gags and shameless melodrama.

Pic clearly aspires to Capraesque sentimentality: a drifting con man (James Belushi) and his adopted nine-year-old daughter (Alisan Porter) scam a corporate attorney (Kelly Lynch) and gradually win her heart, much to the chagrin of her snotty boyfriend (John Getz).

Writer-helmer-producer John Hughes strikes an uneasy balance between slapstick and sappiness, far too frequent relying on Porter's mugging and Georges Delerue's drippingly sentimental score.

Lynch gives an impressive performance that proves to be the film's high point. Belushi is less convincing as the protective dad, while Porter is in the tear-evoking-tots tradition.

• •

■ **CURSE OF FRANKENSTEIN, THE**

1957, 82 MINS, UK ◇ ⓥ
Dir Terence Fisher   *Prod* Anthony Hinds   *Scr* Jimmy Sangster   *Ph* Jack Asher   *Ed* James Needs   *Mus* Leonard Salzedo   *Art Dir* Ted Marshall
● Peter Cushing, Christopher Lee, Hazel Court, Robert Urquhart, Valerie Gaunt, Melvyn Hayes (Hammer)

This British version of the [Mary Shelley] classic shocker emphasizes not so much the uncontrollable blood lust of the created monster as the clinical details whereby the crazy scientist accumulates the odd organs with which to assemble the creature.

Story is unfolded to a priest while the infamous Baron Frankenstein is awaiting execution for multiple murders he vainly protests have been committed by his manmade monster. In the flashback he is seen as a young boy avid for scientific research and sharing with his tutor his determination to build up a human being through chemical hocus-pocus and graveyard snatchings. When their abominable purpose has been achieved, the tutor breaks off the unholy alliance.

Peter Cushing gets every inch of drama from the leading role, making almost believable the ambitious urge and diabolical accomplishment. Melvyn Hayes as the child skilfully conveys the ruthless self-possession of the embryo man.

• •

■ **CURSE OF THE CAT PEOPLE, THE**

1944, 70 MINS, US ⓥ ⊙
Dir Gunther von Fritsch, Robert Wise   *Prod* Val Lewton   *Scr* DeWitt Bodeen   *Ph* Nicholas Musaraca   *Ed* J.R. Whittredge   *Mus* Roy Webb   *Art Dir* Albert S. D'Agostino, Walter E. Keller
● Simone Simon, Kent Smith, Jane Randolph, Ann Carter, Elizabeth Russell (RKO)

Made as sequel to the profitable *Cat People*, this is highly disappointing because it fails to measure up as a horrific opus. Even though having the same principals as in the original chiller, this is an impossible lightweight. Chief trouble seems to be the over-supply of palaver and concern about a cute, but annoying child.

Two directors worked on *Curse of the Cat People*, suggesting production headaches. Pair has turned out a strange cinema stew that is apt to make audiences laugh at the wrong scenes. Many episodes are unbelievably bad, with hardly anything happening in the first three reels.

Plot has the offspring of the first wife of a naval architect (Kent Smith) apparently suffering from the same supernatural beliefs that brought the death of the child's mother. Yarn tries to show the child living in a dream world and imagining she is playing with her mother (Simone Simon). Youngster's visit to a supposedly haunted house where a half-crazed character actress (Julia Dean) lives with her daughter (Elizabeth Russell) builds into the slight horrific angle of film, resulting in the best episodes in the production.

• •

■ **CURSE OF THE MUMMY'S TOMB, THE**

1964, 80 MINS, UK ◇
Dir Michael Carreras   *Prod* Michael Carreras   *Scr* Henry Younger   *Ph* Otto Heller   *Ed* Eric Boyd Perkins   *Mus* Carlo Martelli   *Art Dir* Bernard Robinson
● Terence Morgan, Fred Clark, Ronald Howard, Jeanne Roland, George Pastell, John Paul (Hammer)

It needs a crystal ball to sort out the reasons for some of the contrived goings on in this modest and rather slapdash horror pic. But it doesn't need a soothsayer to guess, early, the identity of the heavy.

Plot hinges around the discovery of ancient tomb in the Egyptian desert, with a curse on anybody who opens it. Leader of the expedition intends giving the archaeological discoveries to the Egyptian government for its National Museum. But the expedition's smooth backer, a slick talking American showman, sees it as a coast-to-coast peepshow.

Murder and mayhem begins its gory trail and the motivation comes from a plausible stranger (Terence Morgan) who turns out to be a murderous descendant of the ancient Egyptian dynasty.

Morgan performs smoothly enough as the villain but is too patently up to no good from the start. Ronald Howard, Jack Gwillim and George Pastell are among those who provide sound support but the liveliest performance comes from Fred Clark.

• •

■ **CURSE OF THE PINK PANTHER**

1983, 109 MINS, UK ◇ ⓥ
Dir Blake Edwards   *Prod* Blake Edwards, Tony Adams   *Scr* Blake Edwards, Geoffrey Edwards   *Ph* Dick Bush   *Ed* Ralph E. Winters, Bob Hathaway, Alan Jones   *Mus* Henry Mancini   *Art Dir* Peter Mullins
● Ted Wass, David Niven, Robert Wagner, Herbert Lom, Capucine, Roger Moore (Titan/Edwards/United Artists)

The eighth in the hit comedy series, *Curse of the Pink Panther* resembles a set of gems mounted in a tarnished setting. Abetted by screen newcomer Ted Wass' flair for physical comedy, filmmaker Blake Edwards has created genuinely funny sight gags but the film's rickety, old-hat story values waste them.

Lensed simultaneously with *Trail of the Pink Panther*, *Curse* boasts all-new footage but virtually repeats the prior release's storyline. Instead of a newshen tracking down the missing Inspector Clouseau, this time Interpol's Huxley 600 computer (an uppity machine named Aldous) is secretly programmed by Clouseau's boss (Herbert Lom) to select the world's worst detective to search for his unwanted employee.

NY cop Clifton Sleigh (Ted Wass) is the bumbling man for the job, simultaneously trying to discover who has stolen (again) the Pink Panther diamond. As with *Trail*, format has him encountering and interviewing characters from earlier films in the series.

Guest stars David Niven (in his final film appearance), Robert Wagner and Capucine have little to do, while pert British blonde Leslie Ash is briefly impressive as a lethally-kicking martial arts partner for Wass.

■ CURSE OF THE WEREWOLF, THE

1961, 91 MINS, UK ◇ ⓥ

Dir Terence Fisher   *Prod* Anthony Hinds   *Scr* John Elder [= Anthony Hinds]   *Ph* Arthur Grant   *Ed* James Needs, Alfred Cox   *Mus* Benjamin Frankel   *Art Dir* Bernard Robinson

● Clifford Evans, Oliver Reed, Yvonne Romain, Catherine Feller, Anthony Dawson, Warren Mitchell (Hammer)

The screenplay, based on the novel *The Werewolf of Paris* by Guy Endore, dwells at extraordinary length, even for a horror picture, on expository background – on the vile heritage responsible for the genesis of the story's monster. But it is a credit to all concerned that this lengthy prolog sustains equal, if not greater, interest than the film's principal story which involves the personal plight of the wolfman himself.

Especially convincing characters are created by Oliver Reed as the compassionate werewolf, Clifford Evans, Anthony Dawson, Richard Wordsworth and Martin Matthews. And there is a restrained portrayal of the budding lycanthrope as a lad by young Justin Walters.

■ CUSTER OF THE WEST

1968, 143 MINS, US/SPAIN ◇

Dir Robert Siodmak   *Prod* Louis Dolivet, Philip Yordan   *Scr* Bernard Gordon, Julian Halevy   *Ph* Cecilio Paniagua   *Ed* Maurice Rootes   *Mus* Bernardo Segall   *Art Dir* Jean-Pierre D'Eaubonne, Eugene Lourie, Julio Molina

● Robert Shaw, Mary Ure, Jeffrey Hunter, Ty Hardin, Charles Stanlaker, Robert Hall (Cinerama/Security)

Capable, audience-involving adventure on the visual level which doesn't rise to the epic stature but is content to resume the 'facts' about the Seventh Cavalry without taking a coherent attitude to them.

The arid, rock Spanish vistas stand in okay for old Indian territory – especially for those not overly familiar with them.

At the end of the Civil War, Custer is assigned to tame the Cheyenne, whose rights under government treaty are being whittled away by white depredations. He is first content with his commission, and carries out his orders with zest and zeal. Conscience is represented by one of his junior officers, who looks mighty anxious about the moral probity of this constant onslaught on the Indians.

Robert Shaw gives Custer a simple forthrightness and dash that is effective, despite its naive context. Other thesp support is adequate within its straightforward idiom, with Jeffrey Hunter and Ty Hardin contrasting neatly as the troubled and dedicated junior officers respectively, Mary Ure as Custer's nebulous wife, and Robert Ryan guesting as the deserting gold-hungry soldier with a forceful cameo.

■ CUT ABOVE, A

See: Gross Anatomy

■ CUTTER AND BONE

See: Cutter's Way

■ CUTTER'S WAY

(Aka: Cutter and Bone)

1981, 105 MINS, US ◇ ⓥ ⊙

Dir Ivan Passer   *Prod* Paul R. Gurian   *Scr* Jeffrey Alan Fiskin   *Ph* Jorden Cronenweth   *Ed* Carline Ferriol   *Mus* Jack Nitzsche   *Art Dir* Josan Russo

● Jeff Bridges, John Heard, Lisa Eichhorn, Ann Dusenberry, Stephen Elliot, Nina Van Pallandt (United Artists)

Cutter's Way [from the novel by Newton Thornburg] suffers from a terminal case of creative indecision. With any number of initially intriguing plot lines, director Ivan Passer and scripter Jeffrey Alan Fiskin never come close to shedding light on what, if anything, this picture is really about. Jeff Bridges, John Heard and Lisa Eichhorn all deliver exceptionally fine topline performances, but their efforts seem wasted in such a weak vehicle.

Bridges limns a pretty beach boy type take to supporting himself through the kindness of rich matrons. His best friend is Heard, a wildly bitter yet fiercely adventurous alcoholic who lost his leg in Vietnam. Heard is married to Eichhorn, who's also taken to the bottle but, unlike the other two is aware that her personal world is crumbling.

Unfortunately, the trio is framed in an obtuse murder mystery concerning Bridges' witnessing an older man with sunglasses dumping the dead body of a teenage girl. Bridges thinks he spots the suspect, a powerful oil corporation head, in a civic parade he attends with Heard. Film then alternately gets mired in attempts to blackmail the oilman, Heard's increasing craziness, Bridges' inability to make a commitment, Eichhorn's love of both men, and a revelation of the unfortunate past of friend Arthur Rosenberg that is supposed to be related to the murder.

■ CUTTING EDGE, THE

1992, 101 MINS, US ◇ ⓥ

Dir Paul M. Glaser   *Prod* Ted Field, Karen Murphy, Robert W. Cort   *Scr* Tony Gilroy   *Ph* Elliot Davis   *Ed* Michael E. Polakow   *Mus* Patrick Williams   *Art Dir* David Gropman

● D. B. Sweeney, Moira Kelly, Roy Dotrice, Terry O'Quinn, Dwier Brown (Interscope)

The Cutting Edge it isn't, but this neatly formulaic romantic comedy has a sharp enough combination of teen-oriented elements and style. Pic pits frosty-tempered ice queen Kate Mosely (Moira Kelly) against brash, competitive Doug Dorsey (D.B. Sweeney), a former star of the US Olympic hockey team who approaches figure skating with great misgivings.

Doug's rough-hewn relatives view figure skating as a sport for sissies, plus he must contend with Moira's tendency to chew up and spit out would-be partners. But Doug rallies to the challenge, and the pic proceeds with this combustible young pair firing off verbal assaults at each other as they dig in to train, sweat and go for the Olympic gold.

Sport's close physical contact provides some *Dirty Dancing*-style titillation, with interest heightened by the watchable actors. Director Paul Michael Glaser opts for an impressionistic, adrenaline-pumped style in the sporting segs. Filmmakers use a skate-mounted Pogo Cam to get the point of view down where the blades meet the ice and the frost flies.

■ CYNARA

1932, 78 MINS, US

Dir King Vidor   *Prod* Samuel Goldwyn   *Scr* Frances Marion, Lynn Starling   *Ph* Ray June   *Ed* Hugh Bennett   *Art Dir* Richard Day

● Ronald Colman, Kay Francis, Phyllis Barry, Henry Stephenson, Viva Tattersall (Goldwyn/United Artists)

Stage play [by H. M. Harwood and Robert Gore-Brown] has been put on the screen with beautiful balance of directness and simplicity. Treatment leans heavily to the British ideal of maintaining a calm and mannered surface that only sharpens the suggestion of emotional tumult beneath. Ordinarily the device weakens a tale but here the play makes its point in spite of it, largely because it has to do with gallant and likable people – Ronald Colman's very human husband, Kay Francis' glamorous wife, and the eager young London shop girl who stumbled into being the other woman without very well knowing what she was doing, and afterward paying bitterly for her wayward impulse.

Story really is a romantic tragedy built out of a minor bit of philandering.

The coroner's inquest sequence is a model of brevity in dialog, conveying a maximum of dramatic effect with the utmost economy of words and practically no action at all. Tenseness of the passage is strangely conveyed by the very terseness and immobility of the actors.

The family friend is played by Henry Stephenson, who had the same role in the stage play and came within a narrow margin of stealing the honors. Here he is excellent. A newcomer to the screen is Phyllis Barry, an English girl from musical comedy. This story doesn't bring out her best points. For one thing she looks and acts a good deal too refined for the role. Chances are she was cast for the satisfying picture she makes in a bathing suit.

■ CYRANO DE BERGERAC

1950, 112 MINS, US ⓥ ⊙

Dir Michael Gordon   *Prod* Stanley Kramer   *Scr* Carl Foreman   *Ph* Franz Planer   *Ed* Harry Gerstad   *Mus* Dimitri Tiomkin

● Jose Ferrer, Mala Powers, William Prince, Morris Carnovsky, Lloyd Corrigan (United Artists)

More stage play than motion picture, Carl Foreman's screenplay is wisely concerned with letting the Brian Hooker words speak for themselves.

Interpreting the rhyme and prose of the play is Jose Ferrer. It comes to the screen as an outstanding achievement in histrionics, quick with humor and sadness.

The *Cyrano* plot needs little reprising. A man, made a clown by a great peninsular of a nose, supplies the love words so that another, more handsome of profile, may woo the girl to whom he has lost his heart.

Michael Gordon's direction doesn't always fulfill the romantic, tragic, comedic and action possibilities, but permits a number of players to account for solid moments in a story that, essentially, belongs to one performer, Ferrer.

□ 1950: Best Actor (Jose Ferrer)

Dd

■ DA

1988, 102 MINS, US ◇ Ⓥ ⊙
Dir Matt Clark   *Prod* Julie Corman   *Scr* Hugh Leonard
Ph Alar Kivilo   *Ed* Nancy Nuttal Beyda   *Mus* Elmer
Bernstein   *Art Dir* Frank Hallinan-Flood
● Barnard Hughes , Martin Sheen , William Hickey ,
Karl Hayden , Doreen Hepburn , Hugh O'Connor (Dallas)

This adaptation of Hugh Leonard's autobiographical play and book, *Home before Night*
about an Irish-American playwright's journey
of self-discovery from New York to his father's funeral in the Old Sod casts a beguiling
spell, thanks to the playful richness of its language and the finely knit acting of Martin
Sheen, Barnard Hughes and their supporting
cast.

The linchpin of the affecting story is provided by Leonard's dramaturgic sleight of
hand in presenting Charlie's (Sheen) dead father, Da (Hughes), and mother (Doreen
Hepburn) as living, breathing temporal characters animated by the successful playwright's grief-catalyzed imagination.

Sheen's performance is distinguished by its
subtlety, as he's swept up in the conflicting
emotions that attend his wry encounters with
his stubborn adolescent self (very capably
rendered by Karl Hayden), his domineering
mother and, most indelibly, the hard-headed,
lyrically aphoristic gardener whose failings as
an adoptive father the mature playwright
must reconcile with his own hard-earned
knowledge of human fallibility.

■ DAD

1989, 117 MINS, US ◇ Ⓥ ⊙
Dir Gary David Goldberg   *Prod* Joseph Stern, Gary
David Goldberg   *Scr* Gary David Goldberg   *Ph* Jan
Kiesser   *Ed* Eric Sears   *Mus* James Horner
Art Dir Jack DeGovia
● Jack Lemmon , Ted Danson , Olympia Dukakis , Kathy
Baker , Kevin Spacey , Ethan Hawke (Amblin/Universal)

Pic represents a promising feature directorial
debut for TV producer Gary David Goldberg.
There's certainly much that's funny, warm
and endearing about *Dad*, which, based on
William Wharton's novel, deals with the familiar theme of a grown child resolving his
sense of duty toward an ageing parent.

Unfortunately, prolonged tilling of that
emotional terrain and seemingly endless ver-
balization of feelings diminish most of what's
good about the film.

Ted Danson has the pivotal role of Jack
Lemmon's somewhat estranged son, who returns from his sheltered world of Wall Street
opulence to find his parents failing and infirm. Danson moves in with his parents to
ease their final days, in the process finding
new meaning in his relationship with his own
college-age son (Ethan Hawke).

There's some repartee nicely delivered by
the principals, including Kathy Baker and
Kevin Spacey as Danson's sister and brother-
in-law.
□ 1989: Nomination: Best Makeup

■ DADDY LONG LEGS

1931, 80 MINS, US
Dir Alfred Santell   *Scr* Sonya Levien, S.N. Behrman
Ph Lucien Andriot   *Ed* Ralph Dietrich   *Mus* Hugo
Friedhofer
● Janet Gaynor , Warner Baxter , Una Merkel , John
Arledge , Claude Gillingwater Sr. , Sheila Manners (Fox)

Nearly everybody either knows or imagines
the story of *Daddy Long Legs*. Mary Pickford
and Marshall Neilan, back in 1919, made a
silent hit of it for First National. Fox, in remaking the picture into a talker, has repeated.

Janet Gaynor is the orphanage drudge who
suddenly rebels against the harshness of the
matron. She is unceremoniously adopted by a
bachelor who is also a trustee of the orphanage. She falls in love with this man, who has
sent her to college unawares to her.

Aft the kids depart from sight another
funny group come in to keep the humorous
end of the story up. These are Una Merkel
and John Arledge as brother and sister. He's
in love with July Abbott (Gaynor) and his sister is her roommate at college.

Santell's direction is good enough throughout but never better than in the first part
where the kids run rampant with precocious
talk and action. The orphanage scenes are
helped by the presence of Elizabeth Patterson
as the dyspeptic matron. Warner Baxter as
the millionaire is an appealer here to women
on a big scale.

■ DADDY LONG LEGS

1955, 126 MINS, US ◇ Ⓥ ⊙
Dir Jean Negulesco   *Prod* Samuel G. Engel   *Scr* Phoebe
Ephron, Henry Ephron   *Ph* Leon Shamroy   *Ed* William
Reynolds   *Mus* Alfred Newman (sup.)   *Art Dir* Lyle
Wheeler, John DeCuir
● Fred Astaire , Leslie Caron , Terry Moore , Thelma
Ritter , Fred Clark , Charlotte Austin (20th Century-Fox)

Mary Pickford was the American sweetheart
of an actress who suffered the orphanage
hardships when First National made *Daddy
Long Legs* in 1919. With Leslie Caron and
Fred Astaire in the leads, the property [Jean
Webster's novel] was completely rewritten
and fashioned into an appealing musical
[words and music by Johnny Mercer; ballet
music by Alex North].

Astaire was a good choice and works well as
the undisciplined and friendly moneybags
who develops a wanna-get-married crush on
the girl he sends through college, this despite
the acknowledged difference in age. And he's
still the agile hoofer, although the choreography he and David Robel blue-printed doesn't
require too robust a workout. Caron is beguiling all the way.

Thelma Ritter and Fred Clark, as social and
business aides to Astaire, team up for laughs
– the Phoebe and Harry Ephron screenplay
has some crackling dialog.
□ 1955: Nominations: Best Color Art
Direction, Scoring of a Musical Picture, Song
('Something's Gotta Give')

■ DADDY'S DYIN' . . . WHO'S GOT THE WILL?

1990, 95 MINS, US ◇ Ⓥ ⊙
Dir Jack Fisk   *Prod* Sigurjon Sighvatsson, Steve Golin,
Monty Montgomery   *Scr* Del Shores   *Ph* Paul Elliott
Ed Edward Warschilka Jr   *Mus* David McHugh
Art Dir Michelle Minch
● Beau Bridges, Beverly D'Angelo, Tess Harper, Judge
Reinhold, Amy Wright, Keith Carradine (Propaganda)

Del Shores' hit play about squabbling Texas
siblings is brought to the screen with
panache. Shores' script presents a bittersweet
family reunion, as three sisters and a brother
who don't like each other convene in tiny
Loakie, Texas, to find out who got what in the
will.

Since dotty dad, who hasn't quite slipped
away yet, can't remember where he put it,
they're stuck together while they ransack the
rambling old farmhouse looking for it.

Amy Wright as the pious, mothering sister
who became a preacher's wife, Tess Harper
as the salty-tongued single gal who wound up

taking care of dad, and Molly McClure as
righteous Mama Wheelis are all excellent.

Beau Bridges has an uncanny bead on
blind, dumb cruelty as Orville, the boorish
younger brother, an obstinate redneck
garbage collector who keeps his hefty wife
Marlene (Patrika Darbo) pinned under his
meaty thumb with constant put-downs.
Beverly D'Angelo steals scenes as the spoiled,
scattered little runaround sister who's
brought home a beatific California hippie-
musician (Judge Reinhold) as the latest in a
long line of consorts.

■ DAISY KENYON

1947, 100 MINS, US
Dir Otto Preminger   *Prod* Otto Preminger   *Scr* David
Hertz   *Ph* Leon Shamroy   *Ed* Louis Loeffler   *Mus* David
Raksin
● Joan Crawford, Dana Andrews, Henry Fonda, Ruth
Warrick, Martha Stewart, Peggy Ann Garner (20th
Century-Fox)

Triangle, in which Dana Andrews and Henry
Fonda fight it out for the love of Joan
Crawford, is basically a shallow lending-
library affair [based on the novel by Elizabeth
Janeway], but it's made to seem important by
the magnetic trio's slick-smart backgrounds –
plus, of course, excellent direction, sophisticated dialog, solid supporting cast and other
flashy production values.

Crawford, a fashion illustrator living in a
glamorized Greenwich Village walkup, plays
Andrews' reluctant mistress. He's a wealthy,
ruthless attorney who refuses to give up his
wife (Ruth Warrick) and two kids (Peggy Ann
Garner and Connie Marshall) to make an
honest woman of Crawford (in the title role).
Fonda, an ex-soldier but somewhat less of a
he-man than Andrews, comes along and talks
her into marrying him and going to live in a
Cape Cod hideaway. But Andrews doesn't
give up that easily.

There are some torrid love scenes, a violent
sequence in which Crawford musses up
Andrews when he tries to break up her marriage, and the several scenes in which the
three get together for 'civilized discussions' of
their affairs. Charles LeMaire's wardrobe for
Crawford, Warrick and Martha Stewart, playing Crawford's girl friend, are knockouts.

Title role is a thesping plum, with the audience never knowing which guy Daisy is going
to wind up with, and Crawford really makes
the most of it.

■ DAISY MILLER

1974, 90 MINS, US ◇ Ⓥ
Dir Peter Bogdanovich   *Prod* Peter Bogdanovich
Scr Frederic Raphael   *Ph* Alberto Spagnoli   *Ed* Verna
Fields   *Art Dir* Ferdinando Scarfiotti
● Cybill Shepherd, Barry Brown, Cloris Leachman,
Mildred Natwick, Eileen Brennan, Duilio Del Prete
(Paramount)

Daisy Miller is a dud. Cybill Shepherd is miscast in the title role. Frederic Raphael's adaptation of the Henry James story doesn't play.
The period production by Peter Bogdanovich
is handsome. But his direction and concept
seem uncertain and fumbled. Supporting performances by Mildred Natwick, Eileen
Brennan and Cloris Leachman are, respectively, excellent, outstanding, and good.

The story has Shepherd flirting all over
Europe, shocking the mannered society there
as well as Barry Brown, very good as a captivated young man with a fondness for her. But
his aunt (Natwick) quietly disapproves, her
mother (Leachman) nervously tolerates it,
while a Rome socialite (Brennan) is vocally
offended. All form (much of it bad), no substance.
□ 1974: Nomination: Best Costume Design

■ DAMAGE

1992, 112 MINS, FRANCE/UK ◇ ⑰ ⊙
Dir Louis Malle   *Prod* Louis Malle   *Scr* David Hare
Ph Peter Biziov   *Ed* John Bloom   *Mus* Zbigniew Preisner
Art Dir Brian Morris
● Jeremy Irons, Miranda Richardson, Rupert Graves, Ian
Bannen, Leslie Caron, Peter Stormare
(Skreba/NEF/Canal Plus)

A complex look at an illicit affair that ends in
disaster for all concerned, *Damage* is a cold,
brittle film about raging, traumatic emotions.
Unjustly famous before its release for its
hardly extraordinary erotic content, this
veddy British-feeling drama from vet French
director Louis Malle proves both compelling
and borderline risible, wrenching and yet
emotionally pinched.

Jeremy Irons plays Stephen Fleming, a
graying, very proper figure in the Tory establishment who has married into money and
lives a carefully groomed and organized existence. His wife, Ingrid (Miranda Richardson),
may be more intelligent than he; and son
Martyn (Rupert Graves), has just embarked
upon a promising journalism career.

At a boring political cocktail party, Stephen
exchanges significant eye contact with his
son's striking g.f., Anna Barton (Juliette
Binoche), and destiny is written. At their next
encounter Stephen is in Anna's pants in
record time.

Irons' character becomes more loathsome
as he goes along, but thesp's is an expertly
calibrated performance. Richardson puts
frightening force behind her rage when all
hell finally breaks loose.
□ 1992: Nomination: Best Supp. Actress
(Miranda Richardson)

■ DAM BUSTERS, THE

1955, 125 MINS, UK
Dir Michael Anderson   *Prod* Robert Clark, W.A.
Whitaker   *Scr* R.C. Sherriff   *Ph* Erwin Hillier
Ed Richard Best   *Mus* Eric Coates, Leighton Lucas
Art Dir Robert Jones
● Richard Todd, Michael Redgrave, Ursula Jeans, Derek
Farr, Patrick Barr, John Fraser (Associated British)

As a record of a British operational triumph
during the last war, *The Dam Busters* [adapted
from Paul Brickhill's *Enemy Coast Ahead*] is a
small slice of history, told with painstaking
attention to detail and overflowing with the
British quality of understatement.

This is the story of the successful raid on
the Ruhr dams, when a small fleet of British
bombers, using a new type of explosive, successfully breached the water supplies, which
fed the Ruhr factories and caused desolation
and havoc to the German war machine.

For more than 90 minutes, the film is devoted to the planning and preparation, and
very absorbing material this proves to be. The
reconstruction of the raid and the pounding
of the dams is done with graphic realism. The
aerial photography is one of the major technical credits.

The production is a personal triumph for
Michael Anderson. Michael Redgrave, partic-
ularly, gives a vividly human portrayal of Dr
Barnes Wallis the scientist while Richard
Todd makes a distinguished showing as Guy
Gibson the RAF commander.
□ 1955: Nomination: Best Special Effects

■ DAMES

1934, 90 MINS, US ⑰
Dir Ray Enright, Busby Berkeley   *Scr* Delmer Daves
Ph Sid Hickox, George Barnes   *Ed* Harold McLernon
Art Dir Robert Haas, Willy Pogany
● Joan Blondell, Dick Powell, Ruby Keeler, ZaSu Pitts,
Guy Kibbee, Hugh Herbert (Warner)

Heavier on the comedy but lighter on the
story than WB's predecessors. There are five

song numbers and all amazingly well done.
Busby Berkeley pyramids attention in spectacular manner, at times making 'em wide-
eyed with his choreographic mating of
rhythmic formations with the camera.

Three sets of songwriters fashioned a corking score. Al Dubin and Harry Warren have
the cream of the crop with the title song, 'I
Only Have Eyes for You', and 'The Girl at the
Ironing Board'. Mort Dixon and Allie Wrubel
are responsible for 'Try and See It My Way',
and Irving Kahal and Sammy Fain (latter a
personable youth who plays himself in a songwriter's bit) contributed 'When You Were a
Smile on Your Mother's Lips'.

'I Only Have Eyes for You' one of the two
most spectacular numbers with the entire
chorus in Benda masks of Ruby Keeler.
'Dames' is the spectacular topper-offer with
the girls in opera length black tights and
white blouses.

Ruby Keeler and Dick Powell again are the
romantic interest, and again he is the ambitious songwriter who has just written a surefire musical comedy hit that's only begging
for a backer, and again Keeler is the sympathetic and romantic inspiration. Joan Blondell
is prominent in a decorously subdued but otherwise flip chorine who perpetrates a mild
'shake' on Guy Kibbee.

■ DAMIEN
OMEN II

1978, 109 MINS, US ◇ ⑰ ⊙
Dir Don Taylor   *Prod* Harvey Bernhard   *Scr* Stanley
Mann, Michael Hodges   *Ph* Bill Butler   *Ed* Robert Brown
Jr   *Mus* Jerry Goldsmith   *Art Dir* Philip M. Jeffries, Fred
Harpman
● William Holden, Lee Grant, Jonathan Scott-Taylor,
Robert Foxworth, Lew Ayres, Sylvia Sidney (20th Century-
Fox)

Alas, Little Orphan Damien, lucky enough to
be taken in by a rich uncle after bumping off
his first pair of foster parents, can't resist
killing the second set, too, along with assorted friends of the family. Damien is obviously wearing out his welcome.

Damien is 13 and has a double personality
problem, being both an anti-Christ and a
rather obnoxious teenager. Stoically played
by Jonathan Scott-Taylor, Damien has apparently been behaving himself for the past
seven years, since his uncle (William Holden)
and aunt (Lee Grant) suspect nothing and
love him very much as does his cousin (Lucas
Donat).

Only cranky old Aunt Marion (Sylvia
Sidney) knows something is wrong with the
boy, but a raven gets rid of her. Then a pesky
reporter (Elizabeth Shepherd) shows up. So
the raven pecks her eyes out and she stumbles in front of a truck.

One day, Damien's platoon sergeant at the
military school suggests he reads the *Book of
Revelations* and find out why he's special. He
soon gets the knack of killing people himself,
with spectacular touches that top the decapitations of his tender years. [Screen story by
Harvey Bernhard, based on characters created by David Seltzer.]

■ DAMNATION ALLEY

1977, 95 MINS, US ◇ ⑰
Dir Jack Smight   *Prod* Jerome M. Zeitman, Paul
Maslansky   *Scr* Alan Sharp, Lukas Heller   *Ph* Harry
Stradling Jr   *Ed* Frank J. Urioste   *Mus* Jerry Goldsmith
Art Dir Preston Ames
● Jan-Michael Vincent, George Peppard, Dominique
Sanda, Paul Winfield, Jackie Earle Haley, Kip Niven
(20th Century-Fox)

Damnation Alley is dull, stirred only occasionally by prods of special effects that only seem
exciting compared to the dreariness that proceeded it. What's worse, it's dumb, depending

on its stereotyped characters to do the most
stupid things under the circumstances in order to keep the story moving.

Jan-Michael Vincent and George Peppard
are air force officers on duty in a desert missile bunker when World War III comes with a
lot of stock shots of mushroom explosions.

Skip forward a couple of years through titled explanations that most of the country
was destroyed and Earth tilted on its axis.
But Vincent and Peppard are still in the
desert with the other troops.

■ DAMNED, THE

(US: These Are the Damned)

1963, 87 MINS, UK
Dir Joseph Losey   *Prod* Anthony Hinds   *Scr* Evan Jones
Ph Arthur Grant   *Ed* Reginald Mills, James Needs
Mus James Bernard   *Art Dir* Bernard Robinson
● Macdonald Carey, Shirley Anne Field, Viveca
Lindfors, Alexander Knox, Oliver Reed, Walter Gotell
(Hammer/Swallow)

'What is a director's picture?' This one is.
Although the cast is excellent, no one character dominates the action or overshadows the
others. Joseph Losey's hand is so apparent
that the film's considerable effectiveness
must be accredited to him as must its few
faults and the fearsome message it conveys.

Much of the film's appeal is visual, although the dialog is a credit to the scripter
Evan Jones, [from H.L. Lawrence's novel *The
Children of Light*]. The only objection is in its
failure to take a stand.

Macdonald Carey, Shirley Anne Field,
Alexander Knox (particularly good), Viveca
Lindfors and Oliver Reed have principal roles
in the quasi-sci-fi story which centers on a
group of children being exposed to radiation
in preparation for the day predicted by Knox
when global nuclear warfare will destroy all
living things – except these few.

All the principals are excellent, with Reed
playing a Teddy boy and brother of Field although his interest in her is strongly incestuous.

■ DAMNED, THE

1969, 163 MINS, ITALY/W. GERMANY ◇ ⑰
Dir Luchino Visconti   *Prod* Alfred Levy, Ever Haggiag
Scr Nicola Badalucco, Enrico Medioli, Luchino Visconti
Ph Armando Nannuzzi, Pasquale De Santis
Mus Maurice Jarre   *Art Dir* Pasquale Romano
● Dirk Bogarde, Ingrid Thulin, Helmut Berger, Charlotte
Rampling, Florinda Bolkan, Rene Kolldehoff
(Pegaso/Praesidens)

Luchino Visconti pulls out all stops to detail
the progress of Nazism in the 1930s as seen
via one upperclass family. This has got to be
the most violent family since the Borgias.
Screaming, yelling, scheming, and conniving
over factory ownership is but part of it: they
murder each other with no hesitation to
achieve their ends, they have perverse sexual
hang-ups, they are dope-fiends, and, in film's
most spectacular sequence, a mother
amongst them sleeps with her son.

Although obviously based on the Krupp
family of steel magnates, the family in *The
Damned* could never really exist in quite this
way, and it seems clear that Visconti knows
that it serves as a microcosm of Germany in
the 1930s, a symbol of a country that began a
world war.

The acting is so much in an older tradition
that it becomes very hard to judge, but
Helmut Berger's progress from meek son to
matricidal Nazi is clearly a superior job.
Ingrid Thulin is able to handle the violent
emotions required for her role as Berger's
mother, although Dirk Bogarde is sometimes
uncomfortable as her lover.
□ 1969: Nominations: Best Original Story &
Screenplay

■ **DAMN THE DEFIANT!**
See: H.M.S. Defiant

....

■ **DAMN YANKEES**
(UK: What Lola Wants)

1958, 110 MINS, US ◇ ▼ ⊙
Dir George Abbott, Stanley Donen   *Prod* George
Abbott, Stanley Donen   *Scr* George Abbott   *Ph* Harold
Lipstein   *Ed* Frank Bracht   *Mus* Richard Adler, Jerry
Ross   *Art Dir* William Eckart, Jean Eckart, Stanley
Fleischer
● Tab Hunter, Gwen Verdon, Ray Walston, Russ Brown,
Shannon Bolin, Nathaniel Frey (Warner)

The *Damn Yankees* team, which ran the score
high for three seasons in Broadway's legit
ballpark, was reassembled to go to bat in this
sparkling film version. Sole 'newcomers' in
the trek from Broadway to Burbank are
Stanley Donen, who co-produced and co-directed, and Tab Hunter, who stars.

Story, based on the Faust legend and
Douglass Wallop's novel, *The Year the Yankees
Lost the Pennant*, revolves around a Washington Senator fan who would give his soul for a
long-ball hitter and a chance to beat the New
York Yankees. Given his chance by the devil
himself, the fan is wooshed into a 22-year-old
who proceeds to become the national hero of
the national pastime in the national capital,
thus giving the Senators a pennant and the
Yankees a bad name.

Gwen Verdon makes a sprightly 172-year-
old witch who has been sumptuously embodied to stalk Tab Hunter. Ray Walston, with
exaggerated widow's peak and devilish red ac-
cessories, makes a perfect comedy Satan.
Hunter [substituting for Broadway's Stephen
Douglass] is sympathetic as the young baseball great, confused by all that's happening to
him.

Still held in prominence is the Richard
Adler-Jerry Ross musical score – a tuneful,
storytelling assortment of gag songs and ballads. Top production goes to 'Two Lost Souls'
(a la 'Hernando's Hideaway' from same pair's
Pajama Game) and 'Shoeless Joe from
Hannibal, Mo.' 'You've Gotta Have Heart' remains a standout, with a seductive 'Whatever
Lola Wants' and a fast-moving 'Who's Got
the Pain', danced with choreographer Bob
Fosse, himself a fine hoofer.
□ 1958: Nomination: Best Scoring of a
Musical Picture

....

■ **DAMSEL IN DISTRESS, A**

1937, 100 MINS, US/UK ▼ ⊙
Dir George Stevens   *Prod* Pandro S. Berman   *Scr* P.G.
Wodehouse, Ernest Pagano, S.K. Lauren   *Ph* Joseph H.
August   *Ed* Henry Berman   *Mus* Victor Baravalle (dir.)
Art Dir Van Nest Polglase, Carroll Clark
● Fred Astaire, George Burns, Gracie Allen, Joan
Fontaine, Reginald Gardiner, Constance Collier (RKO)

With Burns & Allen co-starred with the
screen's No. 1 tapster, *A Damsel in Distress*
holds plenty – dancing, comedy, the usual
sumptuous investiture accorded by Pandro
Berman and RKO to any Astaire picture. And
those Gershwin songs.

It's a gay, frothy book [story by P.G.
Wodehouse], in a British background. Astaire
is cast as the juvenile who resents the
Lothario buildup endowed him by George
Burns as his hyper-dynamic p.a. Joan
Fontaine is the titular 'maiden in distress', an
ingenu of nobility which brings the setting to
a suburban London estate belonging to Lord
Marshmorton (capitally played by Montagu
Love).

Astaire and his vet terp aide, Hermes Pan,
have devised four corking dance routines
which director George Stevens has expertly
envisioned and mounted. The finale is a four-
minute 'drum dance', Astaire's solo.

Burns & Allen blend excellently, and their

comedy is a standout. Fontaine is passively
fair as the ingenue, nicely looking the role
but otherwise undistinguished.

Gershwin songs are dandy. 'Nice Work If
You Can Get It', 'A Foggy Day in London
Town', 'Things Are Looking Up' and 'Can't
Be Bothered Now' are the titles and all okay.
□ 1937: Best Dance Direction ('Fun House')

....

■ **DANCE OF THE VAMPIRES**
**PARDON ME, BUT YOUR TEETH ARE IN MY
NECK**
(US: The Fearless Vampire Killers)

1967, 107 MINS, UK ◇ ▼
Dir Roman Polanski   *Prod* Gene Gutowski   *Scr* Gerard
Brach, Roman Polanski   *Ph* Douglas Slocombe
Ed Alastair McIntyre   *Mus* Christopher Komeda
Art Dir Wilfrid Shingleton
● Roman Polanski, Jack MacGowran, Alfie Bass, Jessie
Robins, Sharon Tate, Ferdy Mayne (M-G-M/
Cadre/Filmways)

Dance of the Vampires is a spoof on the Dracula
theme. Roman Polanski is on a quadruple assignment. He produced, directed and collabed on story and screenplay with Gerard
Brach and costars. Brach and Polanski wrote
script in French and piece then was translated into English by Gillian and John Sutton.
[Version reviewed is 91-minute US one, cut
by Martin Ransohoff and disowned by
Polanski.]

Plotline (?) deals with an old professor and
his assistant who arrive at a Central Europe
inn dead of winter on a crusade to hunt down
and destroy the chilling mystery figures of
generations of legends, the dreaded vampires
who stalk Slovania.

Jack MacGowran cavorts as the nimble oldster and Polanski plays his somewhat-dimwit-
ted assistant, both up to the demands (?) of
their roles. Ferdy Mayne is the menacing
Dracula, and Sharon Tate, lady in question,
looks particularly nice in her bath. Alfie Bass,
the innkeeper; Iain Quarrier as the count's
effeminate son, who has some fangs all his
own; Terry Downes, the toothy hunchback
castle handyman (who might be Quasimodo
returned), and Jessie Robbins, innkeeper's
spouse, lend proper support.

....

■ **DANCES WITH WOLVES**

1990, 183 MINS, US/UK ◇ ▼ ⊙
Dir Kevin Costner   *Prod* Jim Wilson, Kevin Costner
Scr Michael Blake   *Ph* Dean Semler   *Ed* Neil Travis
Mus John Barry   *Art Dir* Jeffrey Beecroft
● Kevin Costner, Mary McDonnell, Graham Greene,
Rodney A. Grant, Floyd Red Crow Westerman, Tantoo
Cardinal (Tig/Majestic)

In his directorial debut, Kevin Costner brings
a rare degree of grace and feeling to this elegiac tale of a hero's adventure of discovery
among the Sioux Indians on the pristine
Dakota plains of the 1860s.

Costner stars as Lt John Dunbar, a Union
officer in the Civil War invited to choose his
own post after an act of heroism. Opting for
the farthest reaches of the frontier because
he 'wants to see it before it disappears', he
transplants himself from a weary and cynical
war culture to the windswept clarity of the
Dakota plains.

His only company as he passes the days are
his horse, a gangling wolf who keeps a nervous distance, and finally, a Sioux Indian who
tries to steal the horse and is frightened off
by Dunbar.

He discovers a culture so deeply refreshing
to his spirit, compared with the detritus he's
left behind, that, by the time the US Army
bothers to look for him, he has become a
Sioux and his name is Dances With Wolves.

Lensed on location in South Dakota over 17
weeks, pic is infused with the natural
grandeur of the plains and sky. Score by John

Barry makes a major contribution, varying
from the elegiac tone of the main theme to
the heart-racing primal rhythms of the buffalo and scalp dances.

From its three-hour length, which amazingly does not become tiresome, to its bold
use of subtitled Lakota language (the Sioux
tongue) for at least a third of the dialog, it's
clear the filmmakers were proceeding without regard for the rules.

Mary McDonnell is impressive as Stands
With A Fist, an emotionally traumatized
white woman adopted by the Sioux who helps
Dunbar communicate with them.
□ 1990: Best Picture, Director, Adapted
Screenplay, Cinematography, Sound,
Original Score, Editing
□ Nominations: Best Actor (Kevin Costner),
Supp. Actor (Grahame Greene), Supp.
Actress (Mary McDonnell), Art Direction,
Costume Design

....

■ **DANCE WITH A STRANGER**

1985, 101 MINS, UK ◇ ▼ ⊙
Dir Mike Newell   *Prod* Roger Randall-Cutler
Scr Shelagh Delaney   *Ph* Peter Hannan   *Ed* Mick
Audsley   *Mus* Richard Hartley   *Art Dir* Andrew Mollo
● Miranda Richardson, Rupert Everett, Ian Holm,
Matthew Carroll, Tom Chadbon, Jane Bertish (First
Picture/Goldcrest/NFFC)

Dance with a Stranger is a tale of dark passions
based on a true story of the London underworld during the 1950s.

Film charts the rocky course of the relationship between Ruth Ellis, a divorcee and pros-
titute-turned-nightclub manageress, and the
upper-class dropout David Blakeley. He's too
emotionally immature to care while she's too
infatuated to take the commonsense course
of ending the affair. Film ends with Ellis entering mythology as the last woman to be
hanged under British law, for her shooting of
Blakeley.

The script is densely packed with social and
psychological nuances. Audiences are left
largely to draw their own conclusions as to
what drew the seemingly ill-matched couple
together.

Miranda Richardson's performance as Ruth
Ellis is firstrate. With her rolling eyes and impulsive gestures, she captures the delicate nuances of an attractive girl who's both cool and
coquettish Major flaw is Rupert Everett's inability to convey more about David Blakeley
than that he's set to fail consistently in work
and life.

....

■ **DANCING CO-ED**

1939, 80 MINS, US
Dir S. Sylvan Simon   *Prod* Edgar Selwyn   *Scr* Albert
Mannheimer   *Ph* Alfred Gilks   *Ed* W. Donn Hayes
Mus Edward Ward, David Snell   *Art Dir* Cedric
Gibbons, Harry McAfee
● Lana Turner, Richard Carlson, Artie Shaw, Ann
Rutherford, Lee Bowman, Thurston Hall (M-G-M)

This light and amusing comedy-drama with
collegiate background is intended as a showcase in studio's efforts to build up Lana
Turner (which it neatly accomplishes).
Picture focuses attention on Richard Carlson
as a juvenile lead; Ann Rutherford as something more than adolescent romance for
Mickey Rooney in the *Judge Hardy* series; and
highlights a fine straight performance by
Leon Errol.

Story [by Albert Treynor] has its foundation
on a film press agent stunt. Roscoe Karns
launches nationwide contest to seek a dancing co-ed as lead in a forthcoming picture.
Turner is planted in a college to be ultimate
winner, and is accompanied to the school by
Karns' secretary (Rutherford). Carlson, reporter on school paper, in trying to uncover

D

plant, falls in love with Turner.

S. Sylvan Simon's direction is crisp, moving his story along at a good pace. Songs are chiefly confined to the Artie Shaw band's jive sessions, being his own arrangements of a flock of pops.

••••••••••••••••••••••••••••••••

■ **DANCING LADY**

1933, 90 MINS, US ▼ ⊙
Dir Robert Z. Leonard *Prod* David O. Selznick (exec.)
Scr Allen Rivkin, P. J. Wolfson *Ph* Oliver T. Marsh
Ed Margaret Booth *Mus* Louis Silvers (dir.)
Art Dir Merrill Pye
● Joan Crawford, Clark Gable, Franchot Tone, May Robson, Winnie Lightner, Fred Astaire (M-G-M)

Joan Crawford's Winter Garden chorine days stand her in good stead in *Dancing Lady*, to demonstrate her versatility as a song-and-dance artist. A formula backstage plot [from a novel by James Warner Bellah] misses nothing, not even the Cinderella rise to stage prominence, the Park Avenue playboy (Franchot Tone) who casually mentions running his yacht down to Tahiti and Cuba, and the taciturn stage producer (Clark Gable) who finally succumbs to the charms of the alumna of the burlecue emporium who hits the limelight in a raid on the theatre.

The travail of pre-opening rehearsals, the financial ramifications, the backstage choristers' opinions of the 'Duchess' (Crawford), because of Tone's obvious romantic interest, the angeling and finally the staging of the big numbers are of generally familiar pattern.

The dance numbers here are all well done by Sammy Lee and Eddie Prinz. Crawford works with Fred Astaire in 'Let's Go, Bavarian', both doing their terp stuff with commendable expertness, as a 'magic carpet' idea transplants them into a Tyrolean locale amidst a flock of frolicking Bavarians.

Art Jarrett and Nelson Eddy, from radio and the varieties, figure, like Astaire, in lending authenticity to some of the musical stuff. Ditto Bob Benchley, who behaves like a Broadway columnist would.

•••••••••••••••••••••••••••••••

■ **DANCIN' THRU THE DARK**

1990, 95 MINS, UK ◇ ▼
Dir Mike Ockrent *Prod* Andree Molyneux, Annie Russell
Scr Willy Russell *Ph* Philip Bonham-Carter *Ed* John Stothart *Mus* Willy Russell *Art Dir* Paul Joel
● Claire Hackett, Con O'Neill, Angela Clarke, Mark Womack, Julia Deakin, Simon O'Brien (BBC/Formost)

Shirley Valentine writer Willy Russell returns to his native Liverpool with a gritty low-budget comedy.

Pic started life as the play *Stags and Hens* in 1978 and retains many stagebound aspects, especially the male and female toilets where much of the action takes place. Most of the Liverpudlian cast have been in Russell plays before, while tyro helmer Ockrent directed the original West End and US stage versions of Russell's *Educating Rita*.

The strong femme role is Linda (Claire Hackett), who is out on the town with friends on the night before her wedding. Unfortunately her hubbie-to-be and his friends also end up at the same nightspot. Arriving back in Liverpool for a gig is now successful popster Peter (Con O'Neill), Linda's ex-boyfriend. His friends in the band can't believe the seedy side of Liverpool ('Like Beirut without the sun') and the bad news is they're signed to perform at that same nightspot.

Pic is an amusingly accurate look at Liverpool lifestyles amongst the young and aimless, and while the transition from humor to drama is a bit uncomfortable *Dancin' thru the Dark* is ultimately satisfying and enjoyable.

••••••••••••••••••••••••••••••••

■ **DANDY IN ASPIC, A**

1968, 107 MINS, UK ◇ ▼ ⊙
Dir Anthony Mann, [Laurence Harvey] *Prod* Anthony Mann *Scr* Derek Marlowe *Ph* Christopher Challis
Ed Thelma Connell *Mus* Quincy Jones, Ernie Sheldon
Art Dir Carmen Dillon, Patrick McLoughlin
● Laurence Harvey, Tom Courtenay, Mia Farrow, Harry Andrews, Peter Cook, Lionel Stander (Columbia)

A routine, poorly-titled espionage meller loaded with uninteresting, cardboard characters. Laurence Harvey, who finished pic after sudden death in Europe of producer-director Anthony Mann, and Tom Courtenay, both evidently working off pix commitments, are stiff and dull.

All-location lensing, in London and West Berlin, provides some documentary flavor as well as excuse for irrelevant plot setups, interestingly photographed.

Dandy was adapted by Derek Marlowe from his book. Harvey, it seems, is a double agent and everyone in British Intelligence, except Courtenay, knows about it.

All of which leaves an audience wondering what Mia Farrow had to do with the film. Good question. She looks like a combination of Twiggy and the archetypical Hollywood girl-next-door. Farrow's footage is limited and so, unfortunately, is her apparent acting range.

••••••••••••••••••••••••••••••••

■ **DANGEROUS LIAISONS**

1988, 120 MINS, US ◇ ▼ ⊙
Dir Stephen Frears *Prod* Norma Heyman, Hank Moonjean *Scr* Christopher Hampton *Ph* Philippe Rousselot *Ed* Mick Audsley *Mus* George Fenton
Art Dir Stuart Craig
● Glenn Close, John Malkovich, Michelle Pfeiffer, Swoosie Kurtz, Mildred Natwick, Uma Thurman (NFH/Lorimar)

A scandalous, often-censored literary sensation for two centuries and a highbrow international theatrical hit, *Les Liaisons Dangereuses* has been turned into a good but incompletely realized film.

This incisive study of sex as an arena for manipulative power games takes too long to catch fire and suffers from a deficient central performance.

Choderlos de Laclos' 1782 epistolary novel expertly chronicled the cunning, cold-blooded sexual calculations of the French pre-revolutionary upper class as represented by two of its idle, brilliant members, the Marquise de Merteuil and the Vicomte de Valmont. Former lovers, these two ideally matched players hatch schemes of deceit, revenge and debauchery.

The classic rake, Valmont (John Malkovich) at the outset is challenged by Merteuil (Glenn Close) to deflower a 16-year-old virgin, Cecile de Volanges (Uma Thurman), before Merteuil's former lover can go through with his marriage to the exquisite adolescent.

Valmont considers this too easy, however, and instead proposes to seduce Madame de Tourvel (Michelle Pfeiffer), a virtuous, highly moral married woman.

Glenn Close is admirably cast as the proud, malevolent Merteuil while the real problem is Malkovich's Valmont. This sly actor conveys the character's snaky, premeditated Don Juanism. But he lacks the devilish charm and seductiveness one senses Valmont would need carry off all his conquests.

□ 1988: Best Art Direction, Adapted Screenplay, Costume Design.

□ Nominations: Best Picture, Actress (Glenn Close), Supp. Actress (Michelle Pfeiffer), Score

••••••••••••••••••••••••••••••••

■ **DANGEROUS MOONLIGHT**

(US: *Suicide Squadron*)

1941, 90 MINS, UK ▼
Dir Brian Desmond Hurst *Prod* William Sistrom

Scr Terence Young *Ph* George Perinal *Mus* Richard Addinsell
● Anton Walbrook, Sally Gray, Derrick de Marney, Cecil Parker (RKO)

Terence Young's screenplay glosses a lot, dialog is okay, but plot is short on action apart from a zingy air battle in last few hundred feet. The same prosaic line is taken by Brian Desmond-Hurst in directing tale of a young Polish composer with the hands of a musician and the heart of a flyer. Piloting is slow and methodical, sans highlights.

Fighting a losing air battle when Nazis invade Poland, Stefan Radetzky (Anton Walbrook) is fixed for an escape to Roumania since fellow pilots deem his music-making of more use to their country. Prior to winging he meets Carole Peters (Sally Gray), a newsgirl from the US. When booked later for a fund-raising concert tour of America, the pair's paths cross again. This time they marry, but Walbrook is unable to repress the pilot urge.

Walbrook enacts with his customary underplaying, this time almost to a point of self-suffocation. Similarly, Gray is screened for glamor that palls after too much of such footage. She's a nifty looker, but over-poses. Effect is something like a series of screentests.

••••••••••••••••••••••••••••••••

■ **DANGEROUS WHEN WET**

1953, 95 MINS, US ◇ ▼ ⊙
Dir Charles Walters *Prod* George Wells *Scr* Dorothy Kingsley *Ph* Harold Rosson *Ed* John McSweeney Jr
Mus Georgie Stoll (dir.) *Art Dir* Cedric Gibbons, Jack Martin Smith
● Esther Williams, Fernando Lamas, Jack Carson, Charlotte Greenwood, Denise Darcel, Donna Corcoran (M-G-M)

A light mixture of tunes, comedy, water ballet and Esther Williams in a bathing suit are offered in *Dangerous When Wet*. Best of the musical stints is an underwater cartoon sequence [by Fred Quimby, William Hanna and Joseph Barbera] involving Williams and Tom and Jerry to a reprise of 'In My Wildest Dreams'.

Plot deals with a swimming family that falls in with Jack Carson, a salesman of a liquid vitamin, and decides to swim the English Channel en masse, so they can get enough money buy a prize bull for their Arkansas farm. Romance comes Williams' way in the person of Fernando Lamas, wealthy peddler of French champagne, when he rescues her after she has lost her bearings in a heavy Channel fog while practicing.

Williams becomes the costumes designed by Helen Rose and looks good in her water work. Also, she handles dialog easily in scenes with Lamas and Carson. Lamas charms his way through a role that, essentially, requires that type of emphasis. Carson is topnotch as the producer, a sort of travelling salesman with an interest in the farmer's daughter that gets nowhere. Instead, he gets Denise Darcel, a French entry in the Channel swim, and she's worth getting.

••••••••••••••••••••••••••••••••

■ **DANGER ROUTE**

1968, 92 MINS, UK ◇
Dir Seth Holt *Prod* Max J. Rosenberg, Milton Subotsky
Scr Meade Roberts *Ph* Harry Waxman *Ed* Oswald Hafenrichter *Mus* John Mayer *Art Dir* Bill Constable
● Richard Johnson, Carol Lynley, Barbara Bouchet, Sylvia Syms, Diana Dors, Harry Andrews (United Artists)

Another Secret Agent a la 007 – British operative authorized to kill. The agent here, however, is sent on missions where his assignment is to dispose of his victims, usually by breaking their necks.

Overly confused in unfoldment, production winds on a rather indefinite note, as though the character of Jonas Wilde, portrayed by Richard Johnson, is to be called in again by the British government to pull chestnuts out of the fire.

Script is too vague to be conclusive and footage abounds in such plot and counterplot that audience is uncertain as to actual happenings.

Story thread focuses on Johnson, assigned to kill a Soviet scientist who has defected to the West. He is to do away with him before the Americans, who have him in custody, can question him.

Johnson makes a good impression with his role of an ex-Marine Commando and a karate expert, and lends conviction to his hard-hitting character. Carol Lynley as his girlfriend is pretty, but distaff interest rests primarily on Barbara Bouchet, as another secret agent.

• •

■ **DANIEL AND THE DEVIL**
See: The Devil and Daniel Webster

• •

■ **DANIEL**

1983, 129 MINS, US ◇ ⊛
Dir Sidney Lumet   *Prod* Burtt Harris   *Scr* E.L. Doctorow
Ph Andrzej Bartkowiak   *Ed* Peter C. Frank
Art Dir Philip Rosenberg
● Timothy Hutton, Mandy Patinkin, Lindsay Crouse, Edward Asner, Ellen Barkin, Julie Bovasso (World Film Services)

Faithfully adapted by E.L. Doctorow from his own acclaimed novel, *The Book of Daniel* and directed by Sidney Lumet with his customary intensity, *Daniel* is nonetheless a curiously detached filmization of the highly charged book.

It's generally well acted and occasionally evokes the sense of tragedy surrounding the effect of Julius and Ethel Rosenberg's trial and eventual execution as Russian atomic spies.

Taking its form from the novel, the film flashes back and forth in time between 1967 – as Daniel Isaacson (Timothy Hutton) an aloof, uncommitted grad student is prodded by the near-suicide of his activist sister (Amanda Plummer) into probing the events behind his parents' execution – and the period of his parents' last years from the 1930s to 1953.

Most effective portions of the film are those chronicling the parents (Lindsay Crouse in a staggeringly subtle performance as Daniel's mother, Mandy Patinkin superb as his father).

• •

■ **DARK ANGEL, THE**

1935, 105 MINS, US
Dir Sidney Franklin   *Prod* Samuel Goldwyn   *Scr* Lillian Hellman, Mordaunt Shairp   *Ph* Gregg Toland
Ed Sherman Todd   *Mus* Alfred Newman
Art Dir Richard Day
● Fredric March, Merle Oberon, Herbert Marshall, Janet Beecher, John Halliday, Henrietta Crosman (Goldwyn/United Artists)

A sockeroo woman's picture. Has Fredric March, Merle Oberon and Herbert Marshall and a forthright sentimental romance, well directed by Sidney Franklin to sustain almost every element [from the play by Guy Bolton, a.k.a. R.B. Trevelyan].

Grown together from childhood, the war throws Kitty Vane (Oberon) to March as her natural romantic choice. Marshall and Oberon later berate themselves in mistaken belief they have sent March to his doom. Instead, after nursing in a German prison camp and later back in his native England, March turns up under a nom-de-plume, an author of best sellers for juveniles, but permanently blind and in constant mental dread of becoming a burden to his bride without benefit of clergy.

Oberon is a revelation as a reformed vamp. In simple hairdo and sans any great sartorial display, her emotional opportunities are fully

met upon every occasion. Marshall and March are superb as the war-torn, love-torn boyhood chums, mutually in love with Oberon. Both refuse to avail themselves of any opportunities to stretch the emotional tension.
☐ 1935: Best Interior Decoration (Richard Day).
☐ Nomination: Best Actress (Merle Oberon)

• •

■ **DARK AT THE TOP OF THE STAIRS, THE**

1960, 123 MINS, US ◇
Dir Delbert Mann   *Prod* Michael Garrison   *Scr* Harriet Frank Jr, Irving Ravetch   *Ph* Harry Stradling Sr
Ed Folmar Blangsted   *Mus* Max Steiner   *Art Dir* Leo K. Kuter
● Robert Preston, Dorothy McGuire, Eve Arden, Angela Lansbury, Shirley Knight, Lee Kinsolving (Warner)

The William Inge play on which the picture is based is a poignant study of an Oklahoma family torn by internal conflicts. Its relationships are barred with perception and penetration, and the problems of the parents, described in frank terms but handled in good taste, center on the bed and the activities which do, or more accurately, do not, take place in it.

The film is well cast and persuasively acted. Its chief cast value lies in Robert Preston, whose newly-won fame via *The Music Man* can be used to spur boxoffice for the WB picture. Easily detectable is the similarity in manner and speech between his Harold Hill of *The Music Man* and Robin Flood of *Dark*. Each is a high-powered salesman – one flamboyant, the other serious. But there's a strength and an independence that comes through.

Dorothy McGuire is tops as the mother caught between devotion to her children and the knowledge she must sever the cord. Eve Arden is convincing and highly effective as the sister, performing with spirit and proving she could have done even more with her big scene if given the chance. Angela Lansbury plays one of her better and more sympathetic roles as the woman who wants Robin, and she fills it well. Shirley Knight is fine as the daughter.
☐ 1960: Nomination: Best Supp. Actress (Shirley Knight)

• •

■ **DARK CITY**

1950, 97 MINS, US
Dir William Dieterle   *Prod* Hal B. Wallis   *Scr* John Meredyth Lucas, Larry Marcus, Leonardo Bercovici
Ph Victor Milner   *Ed* Warren Low   *Mus* Franz Waxman (dir.)   *Art Dir* Hans Dreier, Franz Bachelin
● Charlton Heston, Lizabeth Scott, Viveca Lindfors, Dean Jagger, Jack Webb, Ed Begley (Paramount)

Picture serves to introduce Charlton Heston, from legit, and his film debut is impressive. The script [from a story by Larry Marcus, adaptation by Ketti Frings] leans towards psychosis to make its character tick.

Heston has turned to gambling. He and two associates trim Don DeFore in a fixed card game. DeFore hangs himself. A crazy older brother starts stalking the gamblers, intent on giving them the same kind of death suffered by DeFore.

Heston takes off to Los Angeles to see DeFore's widow so that he may get a clue to the killer's appearance.

Lizabeth Scott, nitery chirp and in love with Heston, gives a fine portrayal of the character. Viveca Lindfors as the widow has decided worth. Dean Jagger registers strongly as a police captain.

• •

■ **DARK CRYSTAL, THE**

1983, 94 MINS, UK ◇ ⊛
Dir Jim Henson, Frank Oz   *Prod* Jim Henson, Gary Kurtz
Scr David Odell   *Ph* Oswald Morris   *Ed* Ralph Kemplen
Mus Trevor Jones   *Art Dir* Brian Froud, Harry Lange (ITC)

The Dark Crystal, besides being a dazzling technological and artistic achievement by a band of talented artists and performers, presents a dark side of *Muppet* creators Jim Henson and Frank Oz that could teach a lesson in morality to youngsters at the same time it is entertaining their parents.

While there is plenty of humor in the film, it is actually an allegory of the triumph of good over evil, of innocence over the wicked. This world is inhabited with monstrously evil Skeksis, who are temporarily in command of the world wherein only a handful of wise and virtuous creatures manage to stay alive.

Until, of course, Jen and Kira, a boy and girl gelfling, set out to defeat the Skeksis by replacing a shard that has been taken from the Dark Crystal, which awaits its return before Doomsday is due.

The creation of a small world of memorable characters is the main contribution of Henson a Oz. The outstanding character is the Aughra, an ancient one-eyed harridan of an oracle who somehow reminds one of a truly blowsy Shelley Winters.

• •

■ **DARK HALF, THE**

1993, 122 MINS, US ◇ ⊛ ⊙
Dir George A. Romero   *Prod* Declan Baldwin
Scr George A. Romero   *Ph* Tony Pierce-Roberts
Ed Pasquale Buba   *Mus* Christopher Young
Art Dir Cletus Anderson
● Timothy Hutton, Amy Madigan, Michael Rooker, Julie Harris, Robert Joy, Chelsea Field (Orion/Dark Half)

The writer's desk intriguingly becomes a gladiatorial arena for warring manifestations of the same personality in *The Dark Half*, George A. Romero's adaptation of Stephen King's 1989 bestseller, a classic Jekyll-and-Hyde story.

After a 1968-set prologue establishes Thad Beaumont as a precocious kid writer and a grotesque operation gives physical evidence of a twin in Thad's brain, story proper picks up in the current day, with Thad (Timothy Hutton) married to the solid, resourceful Liz (Amy Madigan). Under the pseudonym George Stark, he's authored four disreputable bestsellers.

When a grungy student discovers Thad's double life and demands money to keep silent, Thad literally buries 'George Stark.' But Stark begins manifesting his existence in places other than the bestseller list. The killings mount up.

Hutton's George Stark is a terrific contrast, a cowboy greaser in black who's all razor edges, cigarettes and booze. All performers register favorably, including Madigan, Michael Rooker as the cop reluctantly on the writer's case, and Julie Harris as an eccentric academic colleague.

• •

■ **DARKMAN**

1990, 95 MINS, US ◇ ⊛ ⊙
Dir Sam Raimi   *Prod* Robert Tapert   *Scr* Chuck Pfarrer, Sam Raimi, Ivan Raimi, Daniel Goldin, Joshua Goldin
Ph Bill Pope   *Ed* Bud Smith, Scott Smith, David Stiven
Mus Danny Elfman, Jonathan Sheffer   *Art Dir* Randy Ser
● Liam Neeson, Frances McDormand, Colin Friels, Larry Drake, Nelson Mashita, Jenny Agutter (Universal/Renaissance)

Despite occasional silliness, Sam Raimi's *Darkman* has more wit, pathos and visual flamboyance than is usual in contemporary shockers. Universal, studio that first brought the Phantom of the Opera to the screen, returns to its hallowed horror-film traditions with this tale of a hideously disfigured scientist (Liam Neeson) seeking revenge on LA mobsters.

Raimi's gripping story (unevenly scripted by the director and others) more closely echoes the 1941 Peter Lorre chiller *The Face behind the*

D

Mask in its nightmarish tale of a man whose burned face makes him a social pariah and brutal criminal.

Neeson, working on a holographic technique to synthetically re-create damaged skin and body parts, is the innocent victim of sadistic thug Larry Drake, who likes to snip people's fingers off with his cigar cutter. He orders his minions to dip Neeson's head into an acid vat before blowing up his lab.

Drake's expertly vicious and campy villain is after an incriminating document left in Neeson's lab by the scientist's lawyer/g.f. (Frances McDormand) who has caught a client, real estate developer Colin Friels, in corrupt practices.

Director Raimi, lenser Bill Pope and production designer Randy Ser conjure up a flamboyantly expressionistic world out of downtown LA's bizarre architectural mix of gleaming skyscrapers and decaying warehouses.

....

■ **DARK MIRROR, THE**

1946, 85 MINS, US Ⓥ
Dir Robert Siodmak   *Prod* Nunnally Johnson
Scr Nunnally Johnson   *Ph* Milton Krasner   *Ed* Ernest Nims   *Mus* Dimitri Tiomkin   *Art Dir* Duncan Cramer
● Olivia de Havilland, Lew Ayres, Thomas Mitchell, Richard Long, Charles Evans, Gary Owen
(Universal/Inter-John)

The Dark Mirror runs the full gamut of themes currently in vogue at the box office – from psychiatry to romance back again to the double identity gimmick and murder mystery. But, despite the individually potent ingredients, somehow the composite doesn't quite come off.

Opening with a promising gait, the pic [from a story by Vladimir Pozner] gets lost in a maze of psychological gadgets and speculation that slow it down. Olivia de Havilland, playing a twin role, carries the central load of the picture. She's cast simultaneously as a sweet, sympathetic girl and her vixenish, latently insane twin sister. A murder is committed and while one girl has been positively identified as coming out of the man's apartment on the night of the murder, the other establishes a fool-proof alibi.

Lew Ayres is cast in his familiar role as a medico – a specialist on identical twins. Slightly older looking and sporting a mustache, Ayres still retains much of his appealing boyish sincerity. But in the romantic clinches, Ayres is stiff and slightly embarrassed looking. Copping thespic honors, despite a relatively light part, Thomas Mitchell plays the baffled dick with a wry wit and assured bearing that carries belief.
☐ 1946: Nomination: Best Original Story

....

■ **DARK OBSESSION**
See: *Diamond Skulls*

....

■ **DARK OF THE SUN**
See: *The Mercenaries*

....

■ **DARK PASSAGE**

1947, 106 MINS, US Ⓥ ⊙
Dir Delmer Daves   *Prod* Jerry Wald   *Scr* Delmer Daves
Ph Sid Hickox   *Ed* David Weisbart   *Mus* Franz Waxman   *Art Dir* Charles H. Clarke
● Humphrey Bogart, Lauren Bacall, Bruce Bennett, Agnes Moorehead, Tom D'Andrea, Clifton Young
(Warner)

The film [from the novel by David Goodis] has a sharp, brutal opening, macabre touches throughout, and a thick, gruesome quality. What starts out as a thriller switches en route into a sagging, psychological drama, but recovers in time to give out with the satisfying

gory stuff. Lauren Bacall's charm and Humphrey Bogart's ruggedness count heavily in a strange treatment of a murder story, which if it doesn't withstand scrutiny, does sustain mood and interest.

Scripting is superior and dialog frequently crackles. Direction is smart, with suggestion of the impressionistic approach. What begins as an apparent imitation of the *Lady in the Lake* technique with the central figure speaking but not being visible to the audience, explains itself part way into the film in a clever fashion. Bogart isn't shown at the start because he's supposed to look like someone else. When a doctor has done a plastic surgery job on him to hide him from the police, and he looks the familiar Bogart, the point of his late appearance in the film is evident.

Pic is a story of a man imprisoned on circumstantial evidence for the murder of his wife, his escape from jail, and the efforts of a girl to help him, because her father similarly had suffered unjust imprisonment.

Bacall, in a simple, unglamorous pose at the start, even then has a pleasant appeal, that hypoes intensely as soon as the old, sultry makeup and sexy charm are turned on. Bogart is impressive in something of a lacklustre character for him. Agnes Moorehead is sufficiently vicious as the discarded femme who turns killer, giving the film some of its most vivid moments.

....

■ **DARK STAR**

1974, 83 MINS, US ◇ Ⓥ ⊙
Dir John Carpenter   *Prod* John Carpenter   *Scr* John Carpenter, Dan O'Bannon   *Ph* Douglas Knapp   *Ed* Dan O'Bannon   *Mus* John Carpenter   *Art Dir* Dan O'Bannon
● Brian Narelle, Andreijah Pahich, Carl Duniholm, Dan O'Bannon (Carpenter/Harris)

Dark Star is a limp parody of Stanley Kubrick's *2001: A Space Odyssey* that warrants attention only for some remarkably believable special effects achieved with very little money. [Pic began in 1970 as 45-minute USC Film School short. Final budget was $60,000.]

The screenplay cloisters four astronauts together on a lengthy extraterrestrial jaunt. To pass the time, the men joke, record their diaries on videotape, take sunlamp treatments, reminisce about their past earth lives and play with their alien mascot (an inflated beach ball with claws). Eventually their talking female computer misfires, the spaceship conks out and only one, an ex-surfer, manages to career back to earth on an improvised board.

The dim comedy consists of sophomoric notations and mistimed one-liners.

....

■ **DARK VICTORY**

1939, 105 MINS, US Ⓥ ⊙
Dir Edmund Goulding   *Prod* Hal B. Wallis (exec.)
Scr Casey Robinson   *Ph* Ernest Haller   *Ed* William Holmes   *Mus* Max Steiner   *Art Dir* Robert Haas
● Bette Davis, George Brent, Humphrey Bogart, Geraldine Fitzgerald, Ronald Reagan, Henry Travers
(Warner)

Intense drama, with undercurrent of tragedy ever present, *Dark Victory* is a nicely produced offering. It presents Bette Davis in a powerful and impressive role.

In play form [by George Emerson Brewer Jr and Bertram Bloch] Tallulah Bankhead was not able to overcome the morbid dramatics of the piece and *Dark Victory* had a brief Broadway run. Film rights were originally purchased by David Selznick, but he shelved production plans some weeks before picture was due to hit the production stages.

Story unfolds the tragic circumstances of Davis, gay heiress, afflicted with a malignant brain tumor. A delicate operation by special-

ist George Brent is temporarily successful, but when the girl finally accidentally discovers her true condition, she embarks on a wild whirl of parties. In love with Brent, Davis quickly marries the medic for a brief happiness on his Vermont farm.

Important is the uncovering of Geraldine Fitzgerald in her first effort, as Davis' confidential secretary. Seems rather unnecessary to toss away the ability of Humphrey Bogart, himself satisfactory, but role is extraneous.
☐ 1939: Nominations: Best Picture, Actress (Bette Davis)

....

■ **DARK WIND, THE**

1992, 109 MINS, US ◇ Ⓥ ⊙
Dir Errol Morris   *Prod* Patrick Markey   *Scr* Eric Bergren, Neal Jimenez, Mark Horowitz   *Ph* Stefan Czapsky
Ed Freeman Davies   *Mus* Michel Colombier
Art Dir Ted Bafaloukos
● Lou Diamond Phillips, Fred Ward, Gary Farmer, John Karlen, Lance Baker, Jane Loranger (Dark Wind/Northfork)

The Dark Wind is a good-looking version of Tony Hillerman's 1982 cult policier that goes for the same slow burn. Lou Diamond Phillips toplines strongly as the Navajo flatfoot.

Corkscrew plot, set on an Arizona reservation divided between Navajo and Hopi, warms up gradually with the discovery of a Navajo corpse with its palms and soles flayed. Then the cop, on tedious night watch by a disputed water-windmill, finds a crashed airplane with two dead coke smugglers on board.

Story fans out as the feds turn up. Phillips is warned off the case by his superior (Fred Ward), and the main smuggler's young widow (Jane Loranger) comes looking for justice. All the locals, including store owner John Karlen, act mighty suspicious.

Despite the fact that most of the action is purely police procedure, the combination of Phillips' mystical voiceovers, Michel Colombier's atmospheric score and Stefan Czapsky's striking lensing of the ruddy mesa landscape keeps the mood taut.

....

■ **DARLING**

1965, 128 MINS, UK Ⓥ ⊙
Dir John Schlesinger   *Prod* Joseph Janni   *Scr* Frederic Raphael   *Ph* Ken Higgins   *Ed* James Clark   *Mus* John Dankworth   *Art Dir* Ray Simm
● Julie Christie, Dirk Bogarde, Laurence Harvey, Roland Curran, Jose Villalonga, Basil Henson (Vic)

In many ways, this Joseph Janni production can be described as a British *Dolce Vita*. Its central character is a lovely, young, irresponsible and completely immoral girl, who can see little wrong in jumping in and out of bed with a complete lack of discrimination, and who goes on a shop-lifting expedition in one of London's more famous stores just for kicks.

While a fair slice of the credit must go to the three stars and to scripter Frederic Raphael, the lion's share is due to John Schlesinger, a documentary-trained director who skillfully uses that technique to give in-depth portraits to three principals.

Everyone calls Diana Scott (Julie Christie) 'darling'. She's that kind of girl – gay, good-looking, amusing company. She is married to a young, immature man, and once she has met the more sophisticated Robert (Dirk Bogarde) there is little doubt that the marriage will go on the rocks. He, too, is married, but leaves his family to set up house with her. But no sooner has she met Miles (Laurence Harvey) than she hops into bed with him.

Christie almost perfectly captures the character of the immoral Diana, and very rarely misses her target.
☐ 1965: Best Actress (Julie Christie), Original Story & Screenplay, B&W Costume Design.

☐ Nominations: Best Picture, Director

....

■ **DARLING LILI**

1970, 139 MINS, US ◇ ☯
Dir Blake Edwards   *Prod* Blake Edwards   *Scr* Blake
Edwards, William Peter Blatty   *Ph* Russell Harlan
Ed Peter Zinner   *Mus* Henry Mancini   *Art Dir* Fernando
Carrere
● Julie Andrews, Rock Hudson, Jeremy Kemp, Lance
Percival, Michael Witney, Jacques Marin (Paramount/
Geoffrey)

Darling Lili is a conglomerate. In its World
War I expanse, the Blake Edwards presentation has comedy, adventure melodrama, aerial dogfights, spectacular production
numbers, nostalgia, Julie Andrews and Rock
Hudson, lush trappings, lack of a decisive
hand, and smash moments. These elements
are juggled sometimes with eclat and a flair,
on other occasions abruptly and none too successfully.

Andrews is a German spy whose mission is
to ferret out war secrets. She latches onto a
relationship with Hudson, in role of a dashing
American air squadron commander, who
knows all.

Andrews' best moments are her singing sequences, in which she does full justice to five
numbers cleffed by Johnny Mercer and Henry
Mancini.

☐ 1970: Nomination: Best Costume Design,
Original Song Score, Song ('Whistling Away
the Dark')

....

■ **D.A.R.Y.L.**

1985, 99 MINS, US ◇ ☯ ☉
Dir Simon Wincer   *Prod* John Heyman   *Scr* David
Ambrose, Allan Scott, Jeffrey Ellis   *Ph* Frank Watts
Ed Adrian Carr   *Mus* Marvin Hamlisch   *Art Dir* Alan
Cassie
● Mary Beth Hurt, Michael McKean, Kathryn Walker,
Colleen Camp, Josef Sommer, Barret Oliver (Paramount)

Pic manages to get off to a strong start with a
scenic chase through a curving mountain
road as a chopper bears down on a racing car.
Just before crashing, the driver pushes out a
young boy who is rescued and taken into a
foster home by the Richardsons (Mary Beth
Hurt and Michael McKean). The Richardsons
later find that this strange young man is a robot.

After establishing a cozy domestic situation
the film takes off in a different direction
when his 'parents' come to take Daryl (Barret
Oliver) home. Home is a top security research facility where scientists Josef Sommer
and Kathryn Walker have given birth to
D.A.R.Y.L. Acronym stands for Data
Analyzing Robot Youth Lifeform and Daryl is
described as 'an experiment in artificial intelligence.'

Second half of the picture is the most far-
fetched and also the most fun as the young
robot gets to show off some of his powers.

....

■ **DATE WITH A LONELY GIRL, A**
See: *T.R. Baskin*

....

■ **DATE WITH DEATH, A**
See: *The High Bright Sun*

....

■ **DAUGHTERS OF DARKNESS**

1971, 87 MINS, US/FRANCE ◇ ☯
Dir Harry Kumel   *Prod* Paul Collet, Alain C. Guilleaume
Scr Pierre Drouot, Harry Kumel   *Ph* Edward Van Der
Enden   *Ed* Gust Verschueren, Denis Bonan
Mus Francois de Roubiax
● Delphine Seyrig, Daniele Ouimet, John Karlen,
Andrea Rau, Paul Esser, Fons Rademakers
(Gemini/Maya)

Delphine Seyrig's silver lame presence and
Harry Kumel's evocative direction make this
an above-par vampire tale. Updating the old
chestnut about the butch countess who remains forever young by drinking and bathing
in the blood of maidens, *Daughters of Darkness*
is so intentionally perverse that it often slips
into impure camp, but Kumel and Seyrig hold
interest by piling twists on every convention
of the vampire genre.

Spending their honeymoon at a mammoth
but deserted seaside resort hotel in Belgium,
newlyweds John Karlen and Daniele Ouimet
are marked by the countess (Seyrig) and her
lesbian 'secretary' (Andrea Rau). Karlen is
actually a sadistic mama's boy, but 'Mother'
(played by Dutch film director Fons
Rademakers) is an aging homosexual who's
been keeping him in London. When Karlen
vents his belt-wielding sexuality on his bride,
she seeks refuge with the countess.

Avoiding standard fang-in-the-neck fright,
Kumel keeps the gore limited to the two
death sequences, but there he goes all out.
Both are stunningly directed and edited.

....

■ **DAVE**

1993, 110 MINS, US ◇ ☯ ☉
Dir Ivan Reitman   *Prod* Lauren Shuler-Donner, Ivan
Reitman   *Scr* Gary Ross   *Ph* Adam Greenberg
Ed Sheldon Kahn   *Mus* James Newton Howard
Art Dir J. Michael Riva
● Kevin Kline, Sigourney Weaver, Frank Langella, Kevin
Dunn, Ving Rhames, Ben Kingsley (Warner/Northern
Lights)

Dave, the story of a run-of-the mill guy asked
to stand-in for a major leader who suddenly
falls ill, is a delightful, buoyant new take on
an old theme, deftly mixing political cynicism
with elements of *Mr Smith Goes to Washington*.

In this case, the office is President of the
United States, and Dave (Kevin Kline), a
sometime presidential-impersonator, gets
drafted by White House chief of staff Bob
Alexander (Frank Langella) and his communications director (Kevin Dunn), who want to
keep Dave in office long enough to engineer a
sort-of coup in which Alexander can take
over.

Just to be safe, they dispatch the Vice
President (Ben Kingsley, in a small but effective cameo) on a fool's errand to Africa. Dave
also thaws the icy relationship between the
President and First Lady (Sigourney Weaver),
providing a nifty romantic element.

Kline stands forth as the glue that holds it
all together, but he benefits from strong supporting performances all around such as Ving
Rhames' stony Secret Service agent, who
pulls off the film's most affecting moment.

....

■ **DAVID AND BATHSHEBA**

1951, 153 MINS, US ◇ ☯ ☉
Dir Henry King   *Prod* Darryl F. Zanuck   *Scr* Philip
Dunne   *Ph* Leon Shamroy   *Ed* Barbara McLean
Mus Alfred Newman   *Art Dir* Lyle Wheeler, George
Davis
● Gregory Peck, Susan Hayward, Raymond Massey,
Kieron Moore, James Robertson Justice, Jayne Meadows
(20th Century-Fox)

This is a big picture in every respect. The
reign of King David projects the Old
Testament in broad sweeps, depicting the
obligation of David (Gregory Peck) to his subjects while at the same time spotlighting his
frailties, namely his relationship with the
beauteous Bathsheba (Susan Hayward). He is
shown forsaking his first wife (of his harem)
for Bathsheba, and pin-pointed is the stoning
of an adultress for the same crime – her faithlessness while her husband was off to the
wars with the Ammonites.

Expert casting throughout focuses on each
characterization. Raymond Massey plays the

prophet Nathan, whom Jehovah sends to King
David to hold him up to judgment. The parable of David's atonement for his lechery and
treachery is capped by the 23rd Psalm which
he, in his poetic youth, had conjured along
with his other psalms.

Peck is a commanding personality as the
youth destined to rule Israel. He shades his
character expertly. His emotional reflexes
are not as static as the sultry Hayward in the
femme lead. Kieron Moore is earnest as the
Hittite whom David betrays because he covets his wife, Bathsheba. Massey, as the
prophet, is a dominant personality throughout.

☐ 1951: Nominations: Best Story &
Screenplay, Color Cinematography, Color
Costume Design, Color Art Direction,
Scoring of a Dramatic Picture

....

■ **DAVID AND LISA**

1963, 85 MINS, US ☉
Dir Frank Perry   *Prod* Paul M. Heller   *Scr* Eleanor Perry
Ph Leonard Hirschfield   *Ed* Irving Oshman   *Mus* Mark
Lawrence   *Art Dir* Paul M. Heller
● Keir Dullea, Janet Margolin, Howard Da Silva, Neva
Patterson, Clifton James (Continental)

Tact, taste, insight and forthrightness make
this one of the most incisive and original
films treating mental problems.

A young man is brought to a mental home
by his doting mother. He seems intelligent,
haughty and sophisticated. But he cannot
bear to be touched by anybody.

He is worshipped by a younger boy and becomes interested in the case of a schizophrenic girl called Lisa who talks backwards
in rhyme and takes herself for two girls. He
manages to get to her and both are aware of
each other's weak spots.

Film appears clinically observant and authentic and is refreshingly free of jargon and
pseudo-psycho dramatics. It does have a tendency to be too spare and make each scene a
point about psychotic behaviour or reactions
it by outsiders.

But there is no forced love affair or cliche
suspense aspects. Keir Dullea has the knife-
like, frigid presence that is right in his case of
bottled up feelings that have made him fear
death and any human emotion. And Janet
Margolin has the touching disorder and mute
need for help required for the part of the girl.

For a first film Frank Perry shows a concise
feel for making the telling points in each scene.
A tightly ordered script by Eleanor Perry also
helps. It was taken from a book by a practicing
psychiatrist [Theodore Isaac Rubin].

☐ 1963: Nominations: Best Director,
Adapted Screenplay

....

■ **DAVID COPPERFIELD**

1935, 129 MINS, US ☯ ☉
Dir George Cukor   *Prod* David O. Selznick
Scr Howard Estabrook, Hugh Walpole   *Ph* Oliver T.
Marsh   *Ed* Robert J. Kern   *Mus* Herbert Stothart
● W.C. Fields, Lionel Barrymore, Freddie Bartholomew,
Frank Lawton, Edna May Oliver, Roland Young
(M-G-M)

Charles Dickens did not write with the idea
of being dramatized. The strange charm of
his characters is more important than the fidelity of his characterizations. It was almost
an adventure to try to bring to the screen the
expansively optimistic Micawber, but he lives
again in W.C. Fields, who only once yields to
his penchant for horseplay. In the main he
makes Micawber as real as David. The same
may be said for Edna May Oliver, who does
low comedy in the high comedy manner and
shows flash of the underlying tenderness of
Aunt Betsey.

The adapters have not always been as successful. Now and then they linger too elabo-

rately in a scene and they put the play completely off the track in introducing the mechanically melodramatic shipwreck scene, which might easily have been left undone.

Lionel Barrymore, as Dan Peggotty, proves again that it is possible to wear chin whiskers and still not be a comic, and Herbert Mundin does well by the willing Barkis.

A fine performance is that of Freddie Bartholomew as the child David. He is acceptable in his more quiet moments, but in times of stress he seems to be spurred up to the situation, and with Basil Rathbone, the Murdstone, he raises the whipping scene to a high point. Rathbone is not as happily cast as the others. Frank Lawton is a believable grown David and Maureen O'Sullivan, Madge Evans and Elizabeth Allan, as the three chief women, all ra bows.

☐ 1935: Nominations: Best Picture, Editing, Assistant Director (Joseph Newman)

••••••••••••••••••••••••••••••

■ DAVID COPPERFIELD

1970, 118 MINS, UK ◇ ▽

Dir Delbert Mann   *Prod* Frederick Brugger   *Scr* Jack Pulman   *Ph* Ken Hodges   *Ed* Peter Boita   *Mus* Malcolm Arnold   *Art Dir* Alex Vetchinsky
● Robin Phillips, Susan Hampshire, Edith Evans, Michael Redgrave, Ralph Richardson, Laurence Olivier (Omnibus)

Director Delbert Mann and his scriptwriter, Jack Pulman, elected to tell this version of *David Copperfield* through the eyes of David as a young man. A very woebegone chap he is. Just returned from a self-imposed exile abroad he wanders up and down a deserted beach, pondering over the last few years of his life and what went so despairingly wrong with them.

The story is jerkily and bitterly related, mainly in flashbacks, but the constant return to the brooding, self-pitying Copperfield makes for a melancholy drag.

It also means that through constant flashbacks few of Dickens' wonderful array of characters get much opportunity to develop their roles.

Notably, Laurence Olivier, as the schoolmaster Creakle, and Richard Attenborough, as his cringing, one-legged assistant, Tungay. Their brilliant brief appearances light up the screen in about 60 seconds flat. Then they disappear.

••••••••••••••••••••••••••••••

■ DAWN OF THE DEAD

(UK: Zombies)

1979, 125 MINS, US ◇ ▽ ⊙

Dir George A. Romero   *Prod* Richard Rubinstein   *Scr* George A. Romero   *Ph* Michael Gornick   *Ed* George A. Romero, Kenneth Davidow   *Mus* The Goblins, Dario Argento
● Scott Reiniger, Ken Foree, David Emge, Gaylen Ross, Tom Savini (Laurel/Cuomo-Argento)

Dawn pummels the viewer with a series of ever-more-grisly events – decapitations, shootings, knifings, flesh tearings – that make Romero's special effects man, Tom Savini, the real 'star' of the film – the actors are as woodenly uninteresting as the characters they play. Romero's script is banal when not incoherent – those who haven't seen *Night of the Living Dead* may have some difficulty deciphering exactly what's going on at the outset of *Dawn*.

The plot isn't worth detailed description. Enough said those carnivorous corpses that stalked through *Night* return in sufficient numbers to threaten extinction of the entire US population.

Pic was shot for under $1.5 million in the Pittsburgh area, Romero's professional base. Michael Gornick's photography warrants a special nod.

••••••••••••••••••••••••••••••

■ DAWN PATROL, THE

1930, 90 MINS, US

Dir Howard Hawks   *Prod* Robert North   *Scr* Dan Totheroh, Seton I. Miller   *Ph* Ernest Haller   *Ed* Ray Curtiss   *Mus* Leo F. Forbstein   *Art Dir* Jack Okey
● Richard Barthelmess, Douglas Fairbanks Jr, Neil Hamilton, Gardner James, Clyde Cook (First National)

Dawn Patrol finds well-bred English gentlemen running up against the grim realities of war and always remaining true to the best Oxford traditions.

At the start, the air exploits are more talked about than revealed, but as the woman-less chronicle unfolds the fighting becomes more visual and less commented upon. Richard Barthelmess and Douglas Fairbanks Jr in one sequence raid the home ground of the Germans and spend 10 minutes dropping bombs and ploughing the helpless German air squadron with machine-gun fire.

This little mission of death and destruction is in the nature of a boyish lark because the Germans had taunted them on the quality of their aviatory. Neil Hamilton, the commanding officer, awaits their return fury.

Howard Hawks has handled his material intelligently. Camerawork is excellent throughout and the effects are vivid.

☐ 1930/31: Best Original Story

••••••••••••••••••••••••••••••

■ DAWN PATROL, THE

1938, 103 MINS, US ▽

Dir Edmund Goulding   *Prod* Hal B. Wallis (exec.)   *Scr* Seton I. Miller, Dan Totheroh   *Ph* Tony Gaudio   *Ed* Ralph Dawson   *Mus* Max Steiner   *Art Dir* John Hughes
● Errol Flynn, David Niven, Basil Rathbone, Donald Crisp, Melville Cooper, Barry Fitzgerald (Warner)

Dawn Patrol sparkles because of vigorous performances of the entire cast and Edmund Goulding's sharp direction. Story [by John Monk Saunders] is reminiscent of previous yarns about the flying service at the front during the World War. Yet it is different in that it stresses the unreasonableness of the 'brass hats' – the commanders seated miles from the front who dispatched the 59th Squadron to certain death in carrying out combat assignments.

Picture emphasizes the routine of the 'dawn patrol', as day after day new replacements, each time consisting of younger men, come up to take the place of those killed in action.

Director Goulding maintains an even pace, alternating the happier, drinking scenes in barracks with the ill-fated takeoffs at dawn and battle gyrations in the sky.

Errol Flynn is Courtney, squadron flight commander. It is a character made to order for him. Even where he deliberately gets his junior officer intoxicated to take his place on a daring single-handed exploit, he makes the action appear life-like.

David Niven makes the character of Flynn's great friend stand out. Basil Rathbone is superb as the aviator who suffers inwardly the loss of every man while he is forced to remain in command on the ground.

••••••••••••••••••••••••••••••

■ DAY AT THE RACES, A

1937, 100 MINS, US ◇ ▽ ⊙

Dir Sam Wood   *Prod* Max Siegel   *Scr* Robert Pirosh, George Seaton, George Oppenheimer   *Ph* Joseph Ruttenberg   *Ed* Frank Hull   *Mus* Bronislau Kaper, Walter Jurmann   *Art Dir* Cedric Gibbons, Stan Rogers
● Groucho Marx, Chico Marx, Harpo Marx, Allan Jones, Maureen O'Sullivan, Margaret Dumont (M-G-M)

Surefire film fun and up to the usual parity of the madcap Marxes, even though a bit hectic in striving for jolly moments and bright quips.

This is the picture which the late Irving Thalberg started and Max Siegel, Sam Harris' former legit production associate,

completed as his initial Hollywood chore at Metro.

Obviously painstaking is the racehorse code-book sequence, a deft switch on the money-changing bit; the long-distance telephoning between the horse doctor (Groucho) and the light-heavy; the midnight rendezvous business between Groucho and Esther Muir, including the paper-handing slapstickery; the orchestra pit hokum, which permits the standard virtuosity by Chico at the Steinway and Harpo at the harp, including a very funny breakaway piano.

Allan Jones and Maureen O'Sullivan sustain the romance and Jones gets his baritone opportunities during a water carnival which is cameraed in light brown sepia.

Esther Muir is a good foil, topped only by Margaret Dumont as the moneyed Mrs Upjohn, who is stuck on Groucho and stands for much of his romantic duplicity, even unto paying off the mortgage on the sanatorium owned by O'Sullivan.

☐ 1937: Nomination: Best Dance Direction ('All God's Children Got Rhythm')

••••••••••••••••••••••••••••••

■ DAYBREAK

1931, 73 MINS, US

Dir Jacques Feyder   *Scr* Ruth Cumming, Zelda Sears, Cyril Hume   *Ph* Merritt B. Gerstad
● Ramon Novarro, Helen Chandler, Jean Hersholt, C. Aubrey Smith, William Bakewell, Karen Morley (M-G-M)

Lack of action stands against *Daybreak*, that gets its title because the two principals stay out all night the first time they met. Both of them, Ramon Novarro and Helen Chandler, give a perfectly blah performance.

With the locale apparent in Vienna and its Imperial Guard, Novarro speaks with his Latin accent.

In the Imperial Guards you pay your honor debts like an officer and a gentleman, which is in cash or suicide. And when Novarro goes in hock to Jean Hersholt for 14,000 guilders, Navarro has to either pay off or bump off. He is about ready to bump when his uncle comes across with his last 14,000 to save the lad, who thereupon resigns his lieutenancy in the Guards and doubles up with the dame who has become Hersholt's mistress.

The picture dies all the way through the playing. Chandler starts wrong and never rights herself. Novarro tries the light juvenile style as the lieutenant but it flattens at every try.

••••••••••••••••••••••••••••••

■ DAY IN THE DEATH OF JOE EGG, A

1972, 108 MINS, UK ◇ ▽

Dir Peter Medak   *Prod* David Deutsch   *Scr* Peter Nichols   *Ph* Ken Hodges   *Ed* Ray Lovejoy   *Mus* Marcus Dods (dir.)   *Art Dir* Ted Tester
● Alan Bates, Janet Suzman, Peter Bowles, Sheila Gish, Joan Hickson, Murray Melvin (Domino)

A splendid adaptation by Peter Nichols from his play, simpatico direction by Peter Medak and stellar playing combine to make *A Day in the Death of Joe Egg* a superior black comedy-drama about a young couple trying to cope with a spastic child.

Lachrymal but unsentimentalized, the gut moral issue is euthanasia. The almost surreal narrative unfolds yo-yo style – from bitter or hilarious (or both) humor to emotional wrench and back again, repeatedly. Medak achieves this with seemingly unerring timing and balance.

Alan Bates and Janet Suzman as the couple who play games to survive their nightmare are firstrate in their sardonic despair. *Joe Egg* is less about their defective moppet than the struggle of their own connubial existence, the often foiled appetite for carnal contact, and their very sanity.

••••••••••••••••••••••••••••••

■ **DAY OF THE DEAD**

1985, 102 MINS, US ◇ 🅥 ⊙
Dir George A. Romero   *Prod* Richard P. Rubinstein
Scr George A. Romero   *Ph* Michael Gornick
Ed Pasquale Buba   *Mus* John Harrison   *Art Dir* Cletus
Anderson
● Lori Cardille, Terry Alexander, Joseph Pilato, Jarlath
Conroy, Antone DiLeo Jr, Richard Liberty (Laurel)

Day of the Dead is an unsatisfying part three in
George A. Romero's zombie saga.

Set in Florida (but filmed mainly in
Pennsylvania plus Fort Myers, Fla.), *Day* postulates that the living dead have now taken
over the world with only a handful of normal
humans still alive, outnumbered by about
400,000 to one. In a claustrophobic format
reminiscent of early 1950s science fiction
films, the human protagonists debate and
fight among themselves in an underground
missile silo while the common enemy masses
topside.

Representing the scientific community are
stalwart heroine Sarah (Lori Cardille), who is
working on long-range research to find a way
to reverse the process whereby dead humans
become unreasoning, cannibalistic zombies,
and loony Dr Logan (Richard Liberty), engaged in conditioning experiments on captured zombies to domesticate them.

The acting here is generally unimpressive
and in the case of Sarah's romantic partner,
Miguel (Antone DiLeo Jr), unintentionally
risible.

■ **DAY OF THE DOLPHIN, THE**

1973, 104 MINS, US ◇ 🅥 ⊙
Dir Mike Nichols   *Prod* Robert E. Relyea   *Scr* Buck
Henry   *Ph* William A. Fraker   *Ed* Sam O'Steen
Mus Georges Delerue   *Art Dir* Richard Sylbert
● George C. Scott, Trish Van Devere, Paul Sorvino,
Fritz Wearer, Jon Korkes, Edward Herrmann (Avco
Embassy)

Mike Nichols' film of *The Day of the Dolphin* is a
rare and regrettably uneven combination of
ideas and action. George C. Scott stars as a
marine scientist whose work with dolphins
faces corruption by his own sponsors. The
story climax strains belief, but Nichols is one
of a handful of directors who can get away
with occasional improbability.

Robert Merle's novel has been adapted into
a screenplay which commingles creative obsession, materialism, covert espionage and
overt skulduggery. This rich mixture eventually turns to lead, but while it works it is very
mind boggling.

Scott and wife Trish Van Devere are conducting advanced research into dolphins, under the sponsorship of a foundation where
Fritz Weaver is a senior executive. Paul
Sorvino, at first an apparent blackmailing
writer, emerges in time as a government
agent investigating Weaver's outfit. Scott's
scientific breakthrough – communicating verbally with the mammals – becomes the means
by which Weaver an associates would blow up
the yacht of the US President.

A major asset of the film is the magnificent
score by Georges Delerue.
☐ 1973: Nominations: Best Original Score,
Sound

■ **DAY OF THE JACKAL, THE**

1973, 141 MINS, UK/FRANCE ◇ 🅥 ⊙
Dir Fred Zinnemann   *Prod* John Woolf   *Scr* Kenneth
Ross   *Ph* Jean Tournier   *Ed* Ralph Kemplen
Mus Georges Delerue   *Art Dir* Willy Holt, Ernest Archer
● Edward Fox, Alan Badel, Tony Britton, Cyril Cusack,
Michel Lonsdale, Delphine Seyrig (Universal)

Fred Zinnemann's film of *The Day of the Jackal*
is a patient, studied and quasi-documentary
translation of Frederick Forsyth's big-selling
political suspense novel. Film appeals more to

the intellect than the brute senses as it traces
the detection of an assassin hired to kill
French President Charles de Gaulle.

The recruitment of Edward Fox as the assassin and his planning of the murder is a
sort of carrier frequency for the story. Around
this is the mobilization of French and other
national law enforcement agencies to discover and foil the plot. The final confluence of
the plot lines is somewhat brief and anti-climactic.

The major asset of the film is that it succeeds in maintaining interest and suspense
despite obvious viewer foreknowledge of the
outcome.

Fox does very well as the innocent-looking
youth who plans his stalk with meticulous
care.
☐ 1973: Nomination: Best Editing

■ **DAY OF THE LOCUST, THE**

1975, 144 MINS, US ◇ 🅥 ⊙
Dir John Schlesinger   *Prod* Jerome Hellman   *Scr* Waldo
Salt   *Ph* Conrad Hall   *Ed* Jim Clark   *Mus* John Barry
Art Dir Richard MacDonald
● Donald Sutherland, Karen Black, Burgess Meredith,
William Atherton, Geraldine Page, Richard A. Dysart
(Paramount)

Magnificent production, combined with excellent casting and direction, make *The Day of the
Locust* as fine a film (in a professional sense)
as the basic material lets it be. Nathanael
West's novel about losers on the Hollywood
fringe has lost little of its verisimilitude in
adaptation.

The Day of the Locust puts its focus on the
loser, the never-was and the never-will-be.
The story of destined failure features Karen
Black in a fine performance as an aspiring,
selfish would-be starlet, the daughter of broken down vaudevillian Burgess Meredith (a
brilliant characterization). Donald Sutherland, laboring under the most striking burden
of fuzzy writing, still evokes a good measure
of pity as the hick whose immature love for
Black is abused by her.

The principals are surrounded by a truly superb supporting cast: and the physical and
technical support is beyond belief.
☐ 1975: Nominations: Best Supp. Actor
(Burgess Meredith), Cinematography

■ **DAY OF THE TRIFFIDS, THE**

1963, 93 MINS, UK ◇ 🅥 ⊙
Dir Steve Sekely   *Prod* George Pitcher   *Scr* Philip
Yordan   *Ph* Ted Moore   *Ed* Spencer Reeve   *Mus* Ron
Goodwin
● Howard Keel, Kieron Moore, Janette Scott, Nicole
Maurey, Mervyn Johns (Allied Artists)

Basically, this is a vegetarian's version of *The
Birds*, a science-fiction-horror melodrama
about a vile people-eater of the plant kingdom
with a voracious appetite. Although riddled
with script inconsistencies and irregularities,
it is a more-than-adequate film of its genre.

John Wyndham's novel served as the source
for exec producer Philip Yordan's screenplay.
The proceedings begin with a spectacular display of celestial fireworks, a meteorite shower
that leaves the earth's population heir to two
maladies: blindness and the sinister company
of a fast-multiplying plant aptly called
Triffidus Celestus that looks like a Walt
Disney nightmare and sounds like a cauldron
of broccoli cooking in Margaret Hamilton's
witchin' kitchen.

Hero of the piece is Howard Keel as a Yank
seaman who, ironically spared the ordeal of
blindness by having had his ill optics bandaged during the meteorite invasion, makes
his way through a world haplessly engaged in
a universal game of blind man's buff while
under mortal threat of the carnivorous
chlorophyll. Ultimately a marine biologist

(Kieron Moore) stranded in a lighthouse with
his wife (Janette Scott) discovers the means
to dissolve and destroy the triffid.

The acting is generally capable. Steve
Sekely's otherwise able direction has a bothersome flaw in the contradictory manner in
which the triffids seem to approach and assault their victims.

■ **DAYS OF HEAVEN**

1978, 95 MINS, US ◇ 🅥 ⊙
Dir Terrence Malick   *Prod* Bert Schneider, Harold
Schneider   *Scr* Terrence Malick   *Ph* Nestor Almendros,
Haskell Wexler   *Ed* Billy Weber   *Mus* Ennio Morricone,
Leo Kottke   *Art Dir* Jack Fisk
● Richard Gere, Brooke Adams, Sam Shepard, Linda
Manz, Robert Wilke, Stuart Margolin (OP/Paramount)

Days of Heaven is a dramatically moving and
technically breathtaking American art film,
one of the great cinematic achievements of
the 1970s. Told through the eyes and words of
an innocent but wise teenage migrant worker
(Linda Manz), it traces a trio of nomads as
their lives intersect with a wealthy wheat
farmer.

The story opens in Chicago with Richard
Gere shoveling coal in a steel mill. After an
altercation with a foreman he's fired. He, his
sister (Manz) and girlfriend (Brooke Adams),
hit the road to find work in the fields, traveling as brother and sisters.

They find employment on a farm owned by
a young, wealthy Sam Shepard. Like the other
performances Shepard's is quiet – this isn't
from the tour de force school but it is a marvel nonetheless.

The trio become entangled with Shepard
when he falls in love with Adams and marries
her. Suddenly the threesome – once so poor
they travelled in freight cars like cattle – are
rich. And it seems that the days of heaven
have arrived. But with wealth, they learn, also
comes idleness. And with idleness boredom.

Told in 95 minutes, it is an efficient, meaningful story filled with some offbeat touches,
literary references and beautifully developed
characters.
☐ 1978: Best Cinematography.
☐ Nominations: Best Costume Design,
Original Score, Sound

■ **DAYS OF THUNDER**

1990, 107 MINS, US ◇ 🅥 ⊙
Dir Tony Scott   *Prod* Don Simpson, Jerry Bruckheimer
Scr Robert Towne   *Ph* Ward Russell   *Ed* Billy Weber,
Chris Lebenzon   *Mus* Hans Zimmer   *Art Dir* Benjamin
Fernandez, Thomas E. Sanders
● Tom Cruise, Robert Duvall, Nicole Kidman, Randy
Quaid, Michael Rooker, Cary Elwes (Paramount)

This expensive genre film about stock car racing has many of the elements that made the
same team's *Top Gun* a blockbuster, but the
producers recruited scripter Robert Towne to
make more out of the story [by Towne and
Tom Cruise] than junk food.

There's the cocky but insecure young challenger (Tom Cruise) breaking into the big
time, the hardened champion he's trying to
unseat (Michael Rooker), the grizzled manager who dispenses fatherly wisdom (Robert
Duvall), the crass promoter (Randy Quaid),
and the sexy lady from outside (Nicole
Kidman) who questions the point of it all.

Director Tony Scott plunges the viewer into
the maelstrom of stock car racing. A highly
effective blending of car-mounted camerawork and long lenses imparts documentary
credibility and impact.

Days of Thunder zigzags between exploiting
Cruise's likable grin and charming vulnerability and portraying him as an emotional
loser. It's an uncertain and unsatisfying mix.

The film's real glory is Duvall. His duplicitous, ruthless streak hovers just below the

D

surface, giving a sense of inner danger to the racing scenes in which he coaches the untrusting Cruise by radio from trackside.
□ 1990: Nomination: Best Sound

. . . .

■ DAYS OF WINE AND ROSES

1962, 116 MINS, US ⦿ ⊙
Dir Blake Edwards *Prod* Martin Manulis *Scr* J.P. Miller
Ph Philip Lathrop *Ed* Patrick McCormack *Mus* Henry Mancini *Art Dir* Joseph Wright
● Jack Lemmon, Lee Remick, Charles Bickford, Jack Klugman, Alan Hewitt, Tom Palmer (Warner)

Days of Wine and Roses hails from television's *Playhouse 90* series, and has been faithfully and painstakingly translated to the screen by two of the men responsible for the praised TV version – producer Martin Manulis and writer J. P. Miller.

Miller's gruelling drama illustrates how the unquenchable lure of alcohol can supersede even love, and how marital communication cannot exist in a house divided by one-sided boozing. The wife (Lee Remick), originally a non-drinker with yen for chocolates that is a tip-off of her vulnerability to the habit pattern, begins to drink when her husband (Jack Lemmon), a p.r. man and two-fisted belter whose career is floundering, is dismayed by a gap in their togetherness. Upshot is the disastrous compatibility of mutual alcoholism.

Lemmon gives a dynamic and chilling performance. Scenes of his collapse, particularly in the violent ward, are brutally realistic and terrifying. Remick, too, is effective, and there is solid featured work from Charles Bickford and Jack Klugman and a number of fine supporting performances.
□ 1962: Best Song ('Days of Wine and Roses').
□ Nominations: Best Actor (Jack Lemmon), Actress (Lee Remick), B&W Costume Design, B&W Art Direction

. . . .

■ DAY THE EARTH CAUGHT FIRE, THE

1961, 99 MINS, UK ⦿
Dir Val Guest *Prod* Val Guest *Scr* Wolf Mankowitz, Val Guest *Ph* Harry Waxman *Ed* Bill Lenny
Mus Stanley Black *Art Dir* Tony Masters
● Janet Munro, Leo McKern, Edward Judd, Bernard Braden, Michael Goodliffe, Peter Butterworth (British Lion/Pax)

Val Guest's production has a fascinating yarn, some very sound thesping and an authentic Fleet Street (newspaper) background.

By mischance, an American nuclear test at the South Pole is conducted on the same day as a Russian one at the North Pole. It first causes a sinister upheaval in the world's weather and then it is discovered that the globe has been jolted out of orbit and is racing towards the sun and annihilation. It's figured that four giant bombs exploded simultaneously might save the grave situation and the world's powers unite, for once, to help a possibly doomed civilization.

Drama of this situation is played out as a newspaper scoop. Picture was shot largely in the building of the *Daily Express*. Arthur Christiansen, ex-editor of the *Express*, acted as technical advisor as well as playing the editor.

Guest's direction is brisk and makes good use of newsreel sequences and special effects, designed by Les Bowie. Dialog is racy and slick without being too parochial for the layman.

The acting all round is effective. Edward Judd, making his first star appearance, clicks as the hero, the reporter who brings in the vital facts that make the story take shape. He shows rugged charm in his lightly romantic scenes with Janet Munro, who is pert and pleasant in the only considerable distaff role. Outstanding performance comes from Leo McKern, who is tops as a dependable gruff and understanding science reporter.

. . . .

■ DAY THE EARTH STOOD STILL, THE

1951, 92 MINS, US ⦿ ⊙
Dir Robert Wise *Prod* Julian Blaustein *Scr* Edmund H. North *Ph* Leo Tover *Ed* William Reynolds
Mus Bernard Herrmann *Art Dir* Lyle Wheeler, Addison Hehr
● Michael Rennie, Patricia Neal, Hugh Marlowe, Sam Jaffe, Billy Gray, Frances Bavier (20th Century-Fox)

Screenplay, based on a story by Harry Bates, tells of an invasion of the earth by a single spaceship from an unidentified planet in outer space. Ship has two occupants, an eight-foot robot, and an earth-like human. They have come to warn the earth's people that all other inhabited planets have banded together into a peaceful organization and that peace is being threatened by the wars of the earth-people. If that happens, the inter-planetary UN is prepared to blast the earth out of the universe.

Spaceship lands in Washington and the man, leaving the robot on guard, leaves to hide among the people, to discover for himself what they are like. His findings of constant bickerings and mistrust aren't too favorable for the earth's humans. Situation naturally creates fear throughout the world and the US brings out army tanks, howitzers, etc, to guard the ship and the robot, while a frantic search goes on for the man.

Cast, although secondary to the story, works well. Michael Rennie is fine as the man from space. Patricia Neal is attractive and competent as the widowed mother of the young boy whom he befriends and who is the first to know his secret.

. . . .

■ DEAD, THE

1987, 83 MINS, US ◇ ⦿ ⊙
Dir John Huston *Prod* Wieland Schulz-Keil *Scr* Tony Huston *Ph* Fred Murphy *Ed* Roberto Silvi *Mus* Alex North *Art Dir* Stephen Grimes
● Anjelica Huston, Donal McCann, Rachael Dowling, Cathleen Delany, Helena Carroll, Dan O'Herlihy (Vestron Zenith/Liffey)

A well-crafted miniature, this dramatization of the Joyce story directly addresses the theme of how the 'shades' from 'that other world' can still live in those who still walk the earth.

Opening hour is set exclusively in the warm Dublin town house of two spinster sisters, who every winter holiday season throw a festive party and dinner for their relatives and friends. Time is 1904.

By evening's end, the focus clearly has been placed upon the handsome couple of Gretta and Gabriel (Anjelica Huston and Donal McCann). Back at their hotel, Gabriel attempts some rare intimacy with his distracted wife, who throws him into deep melancholy by telling him a secret of a youthful love. Gabriel sets upon a profound discourse about the living and the dead to the visual accompaniment of snow falling on bleak Irish landscapes.

Brought in for the California shoot, the virtually all-Irish cast brings the story to life completely and believably, with Helena Carroll's big-hearted Aunt Kate and Donal Donnelly's drunken Freddy Malins being special delights. Huston proves fully up to the demands of her emotionally draining monolog, and McCann simply is ideal as the thoughtful husband.
□ 1987: Nominations: Best Adapted Screenplay, Costume Design

. . . .

■ DEAD AGAIN

1991, 111 MINS, US ◇ ⦿ ⊙
Dir Kenneth Branagh *Prod* Lindsay Doran, Charles H. Maguire *Scr* Scott Frank *Ph* Matthew F. Leonetti
Ed Peter E. Berger *Mus* Patrick Doyle *Art Dir* Tim Harvey

● Kenneth Branagh, Emma Thompson, Andy Garcia, Derek Jacobi, Robin Williams, Hanna Schygulla (Paramount/Mirage)

Director and star Kenneth Branagh brings the same zest and bravura style to this actors' romp of a mystery-thriller as he did to *Henry V*. Supernatural tale of murder, hypnosis and reincarnation involves a woman (Emma Thompson) wandering around in an amnesiac daze, tormented by memories of someone else's life.

Taken into the care of a cavalier private detective (Branagh) who finds himself mysteriously drawn to her, she reveals to a hypnotist (Derek Jacobi) her shockingly vivid memories of a glamorous life as a 1940s concert pianist married to a celebrated composer who was sentenced to death after he allegedly murdered her with a pair of scissors. Mystery is Thompson's true identity. Is the detective really her ex-husband, come back to life to kill her again?

Branagh illustrates the 1940s segs in giddily stylized black & white, with a tongue-in-cheek Wellesian theatricality, while the present-day action takes place in a pungently humanistic LA rife with bizarre characters.

Engaging film style is buoyed by an infectious sense of fun and punctuated by wild and woolly character turns. Robin Williams plays a psychiatrist who's gone off the deep end, and Andy Garcia is a seedy journalist with an accent seemingly wafting in from various ports.

Branagh and real-life spouse Thompson – each of whom plays dual roles in past and present – are excellent thesps, but they don't make a very seductive screen couple. Jacobi is a pure delight as the eccentric antiques deal and hypnotist.

. . . .

■ DEAD CALM

1989, 96 MINS, AUSTRALIA ◇ ⦿ ⊙
Dir Phillip Noyce *Prod* Terry Hayes, Doug Mitchell, George Miller *Scr* Terry Hayes *Ph* Dean Semler
Ed Richard Francis-Bruce *Mus* Graeme Revell
Art Dir Graham 'Grace' Walker
● Sam Neill, Nicole Kidman, Billy Zane (Kennedy Miller)

Though not always entirely credible, *Dead Calm* is a nail-biting suspense pic [from the novel by Charles Williams] handsomely produced and inventively directed.

It's basically a three-hander: a happily married couple John and Rae Ingram (Sam Neill and Nicole Kidman), have found peace alone on the Pacific on their well-equipped yacht after the trauma of the death of their baby son in a car accident when they're threatened by a vicious, unstable young killer, Hughie (Billy Zane).

They come to Hughie's aid initially, when he seeks help, but Ingram doesn't believe his story that the passengers and crew on the decrepit yacht he's abandoned all died from food poisoning. Leaving Hughie asleep, Ingram goes across to the delapidated vessel to discover dead bodies in the bilges and a video tape indicating that a deranged Hughie killed them.

While he's away, Hughie awakens, overpowers Rae, and sets sail in the opposite direction, abandoning Ingram.

Throughout the film, Kidman is excellent. She gives the character of Rae real tenacity and energy. Neill is good, too, as a husband who spends most of the film unable to contact his wife, and Yank newcomer Zane is suitably manic and evil as the deranged Hughie.

. . . .

■ DEAD END

1937, 90 MINS, US ⦿ ⊙
Dir William Wyler *Prod* Samuel Goldwyn *Scr* Lillian Hellman *Ph* Greg Toland *Ed* Daniel Mandell
Mus Alfred Newman (dir.) *Art Dir* Richard Day

● Sylvia Sidney, Joel McCrea, Humphrey Bogart, Wendy Barrie, Claire Trevor, Allen Jenkins (Goldwyn/United Artists)

Producer Samuel Goldwyn has made a near-literal film translation of Sidney Kingsley's play *Dead End*, the New York stage success. The Kingsley theme is that tenements breed gangsters, and no one does anything about it. The play whammed the ide across the footlights; the picture says and does everything the play said and did, and stops right there.

All the action is limited merely to a larger background setting of the river front in the East 50s (NY) than the Belasco theatre cou contain. Only material plot change is to heroize the character of Dave, the student architect (Joel McCrea).

Performances are uniformly fine, topped by the acting of the boy players from the New York production who seem better in the film becau they do not crowd their lines so fast.

Sylvia Sidney is excellent. Her sister-and-brother scenes with the wild Tommy (Billy Halop) are tender, moving and tragic. McCrea do a fine bit in a scene with Wendy Barrie, the keptive in the fashionable apartment, when he turns down her proposition. The Barrie role is indefinite in outline, due to censoring.

Humphrey Bogart looks the part of Baby Face Martin and plays with complete understanding of the character. Claire Trevor is Francey, the street walker. In this instance also censorship has stripped the role of the shocking features which made it stand out in the play.
□ 1937: Nominations: Best Picture, Supp. Actress (Claire Trevor), Cinematography, Art Direction

■ **DEADFALL**

1968, 120 MINS, UK ◇
Dir Bryan Forbes   *Prod* Paul Monash   *Scr* Bryan Forbes   *Ph* Gerry Turpin   *Ed* John Jympson   *Mus* John Barry   *Art Dir* Ray Simm
● Michael Caine, Giovanna Ralli, Eric Portman, Nanette Newman, David Buck, Carlos Pierre (Salamander)

An apparent attempt to pull off an Alfred Hitchcock suspenser, with added Freudian schleps, *Deadfall* falls dead as little more than ponderous, tedious trivia. Adapted from Desmond Cory's novel, the talky, convoluted writing is hurt by hyped-u cinematics.

Michael Caine is introduced in a sanitorium as a cured alcoholic; Giovanna Ralli lures him to the home she shares with husband Eric Portman, who plays a homosexual, a point hammered home incessantly by dialog, plus the presence of Carlos Pierre, a pretty-boy-for-hire. The three principals join in a jewel heist, a 23-minute sequence which brings a halting pace to a complete stop. The 'real' story is Caine's love for Ralli, complicated by the presence of Portman.

Composer John Barry appears as a symphony conductor in that 23-minute sequence of cross-cuts between guitarist Renata Tarrago, and Caine-Portman at work stealing somebody's loot.

■ **DEAD HEAT ON A MERRY-GO-ROUND**

1966, 107 MINS, US ◇ ⊛
Dir Bernard Girard   *Prod* Carter DeHaven   *Scr* Bernard Girard   *Ph* Lionel Lindon   *Ed* William Lyon   *Mus* Stu Phillips   *Art Dir* Walter M. Simonds
● James Coburn, Camilla Sparv, Aldo Ray, Nina Wayne, Robert Webber, Rose Marie (Columbia)

The idea and the premise of *Dead Heat on a Merry-Go-Round* is okay but it doesn't jell, and the title, a deliberate attempt to be cute, is meaningless. What leads up to the comedy-melodrama O. Henry finale most likely was very funny in the producers' minds, but much of the action is so fragmentary and episodic

that there is not sufficient exposition and the treatment goes overboard in striving for effect.

James Coburn, who charms his way out of a prison into a parole via an affaire with a femme psychologist (a nice trick if you know how to do it), has in mind the burglary of a bank at LA International Airport. Date set for the heist coincides with arrival of the Russian premier, when security will engage full attention of all arms of the law.

Coburn plays a rather sardonic character who is capable of meeting every situation successfully and with what is given him comes through with a deft performance.

Camilla Sparv, whom he weds and is an innocent accomplice, rivals him in interest, displaying a fresh note which communicates engagingly.

■ **DEADLIER THAN THE MALE**

1967, 98 MINS, UK ◇
Dir Ralph Thomas   *Prod* Betty E. Box   *Scr* Jimmy Sangster, David Osborn, Liz Charles-Williams   *Ph* Ernest Steward   *Ed* Alfred Roome   *Mus* Malcolm Lockyer   *Art Dir* Alex Vetchinsky
● Richard Johnson, Elke Sommer, Sylva Koscina, Nigel Green, Suzanna Leigh, Steve Carlson (Universal/Rank)

There is no doubt that *Deadlier than the Male* is loaded with colorful and exciting production values. Opinion thereafter is likely to divide, however, for the film will strike some as okay dual-bill escapism, and others as overly raw and single entendre. Sadism, sex and attempted sophistication mark this Bulldog Drummond pic.

David Osborn, Liz Charles-Williams and Jimmy Sangster scripted the latter's original story, in which Elke Sommer and Sylva Koscina are two cohorts of Nigel Green in his industrial deal-making.

Green's modus operandi is simple: intervene in major deals and promise consummation, then kill off all opposition and collect the promised fee. Scripters had a major task in making explicit murder appear as nonchalant as taking tea, and they rarely achieve the goal.

■ **DEADLINE U.S.A.**

1952, 87 MINS, US
Dir Richard Brooks   *Prod* Sol C. Siegel   *Scr* Richard Brooks   *Ph* Milton Krasner   *Ed* William B. Murphy   *Mus* Cyril J. Mockridge   *Art Dir* Lyle Wheeler, George Patrick
● Humphrey Bogart, Ethel Barrymore, Kim Hunter, Ed Begley, Warren Stevens, Paul Stewart (20th Century-Fox)

Humphrey Bogart is the traditionally intrepid big-city, big-sheet editor whose responsibility to his job, his corps of 1,500 fellow-workers on *The Day* (as this composite but mythical rag is called), and his moxie in locking horns with the No. 1 mobster, is chiefly sparked when one of his news staff gets beaten up by Martin Gabel's gang.

Complicating this is the projected sale of the paper by the founder-publisher's heirs. In midst of the imminence of job layoffs, Bogart proceeds to break the mob, stall the courts' approval of the sale, on his impassioned, informal plea in the surrogate's court that a newspaper, its functions, and its relation to its 300,000 faithful daily readers, is more than that of just another chattel. Much of the footage was shot in the NY *Daily News* pressrooms.

Bogart gives a convincing performance all the way, from his constantly harassed deadline existence, his personal romantic stalemate, and his guts in avenging the beating given his crime reporter.

■ **DEADLY AFFAIR, THE**

1967, 107 MINS, UK ◇ ⊛
Dir Sidney Lumet   *Prod* Sidney Lumet   *Scr* Paul Dehn   *Ph* Freddie Young   *Ed* Thelma Connell   *Mus* Quincy Jones   *Art Dir* John Howell
● James Mason, Simone Signoret, Maximilian Schell, Harriet Andersson, Lynn Redgrave, Harry Andrews (Columbia/Lumet)

The Deadly Affair is based on *Call for the Dead* by John le Carré. Shrewd and powerful development is given this tale of a British Home Office intelligence officer seeking to unravel the supposed suicide of a high Foreign Office diplomat

Mason is cast as an unromantic civil servant whose official problems are further complicated by his being wed to a compulsively sexual young woman who has many affairs. His is a thorough acting job as he conducts his investigation in which he delivers one of his best performances.

Harry Andrews, as a retired CIP inspector called in to assist the intelligence officer, gives a rugged portrayal of police methods in dealing with criminals, which in this instance is a buildup to learning the identity of a foreign spy responsible for the death of the diplomat.

■ **DEADLY BEES, THE**

1967, 123 MINS, UK ◇
Dir Freddie Francis   *Prod* Max J. Rosenberg, Milton Subotsky   *Scr* Robert Bloch, Anthony Marriott   *Ph* John Wilcox   *Ed* Oswald Hafenrichter   *Mus* Wilfred Josephs   *Art Dir* Bill Constable
● Suzanna Leigh, Frank Finlay, Guy Doleman, Catherine Finn, John Harvey, Michael Ripper (Paramount/Amicus)

The Deadly Bees is like *The Birds* only on a smaller scale. It boasts of uneven suspense, a plot long in unravelling and some gripping cinematic moments, provided by bees in deadly pursuit.

Suzanna Leigh has a mental breakdown from overwork and is sent to rest on a remote British island. The innkeeper (Guy Doleman) is a beekeeper. Leigh stumbles across the chic cottage of Frank Finlay, who also keeps bees.

A swarm of killer bees soon attack Doleman's wife, and suspense builds in a manner that viewer does not know which of the beekeepers is responsible for these bee-havings. Throughout, characters show little emotional involvement, except for Leigh, who has command of all she does.

■ **DEADLY COMPANIONS, THE**

1961, 90 MINS, US ◇ ⊛ ☉
Dir Sam Peckinpah   *Prod* Charles B. FitzSimons   *Scr* A.S. Fleischman   *Ph* William B. Clothier   *Ed* Stanley E. Rabjon   *Mus* Marlin Skiles
● Maureen O'Hara, Brian Keith, Steve Cochran, Chill Wills, Strother Martin (Pathe-America)

A.S. Fleischman's adaptation of his own novel is the dramatic tale of four characters who encounter their respective moments of truth in a ghost town smack dab in the heart of Apache country. One (Maureen O'Hara) is a dancehall woman heading for the ghost town to bury her son next to her late husband, thus erasing the stigma of her shady reputation. Another is Brian Keith, whose motivation is revenge against Chill Wills, an unstable galoot with whom he has an old score to settle. Fourth member of the odd party is Steve Cochran, a gunslinger with eyes for O'Hara.

Fleischman's screenplay is pretty far-fetched and relies heavily on coincidence but, for the most part, it plays. This thanks to superior emoting by the four principals and a auspicious debut as director by Sam Peckinpah, a fine TV helmsman.

Keith plays with customary reserve and

masculine authority a character refreshingly different from the usual impregnable western 'tall man'.

■ **DEADLY FRIEND**

1986, 99 MINS, US ◇ ⓥ ⊙
Dir Wes Craven   *Prod* Robert M. Sherwood   *Scr* Bruce Joel Rubin   *Ph* Philip Lathrop   *Ed* Michael Eliot   *Mus* Charles Bernstein   *Art Dir* Daniel Lomino
● Matthew Laborteaux, Kristy Swanson, Michael Sharrett, Anne Twomey, Anne Ramsey, Richard Marcus (Pan Arts/Layton)

Pic has enough gore, suspense and requisite number of shocks to keep most hearts pounding through to the closing credits.

Paul (Matthew Laborteaux) is a bit accelerated for his age, having built a semi-intelligent robot named BB.

One night, neighbour Richard Marcus goes a bit too far slapping his daughter (Kristy Swanson) around and she ends up having to be hospitalized. Just when the doctors determine she's brain-dead, Laborteaux steals her body and transplants BB's 'brain' into her gray matter. That's when the fun begins.

Viewers can just as easily scream as laugh through *Deadly Friend* watching the obviously made-up Swanson come back to life and walk around like a robot, crushing her enemies one by one.

■ **DEADLY IS THE FEMALE**

See: Gun Crazy

■ **DEADLY PURSUIT**

See: Shoot to Kill

■ **DEAD MEN DON'T WEAR PLAID**

1982, 89 MINS, US ⓥ ⊙
Dir Carl Reiner   *Prod* David V. Picker, William E. McEwen   *Scr* Carl Reiner, George Gipe, Steve Martin   *Ph* Michael Chapman   *Ed* Bud Molin   *Mus* Miklos Rozsa   *Art Dir* John DeCuir
● Steve Martin, Rachel Ward, Reni Santoni, Carl Reiner, George Gaynes, Frank McCarthy (Universal/Aspen)

Lensed in black-and-white and outfitted with a 'straight' mystery score by Miklos Rozsa and authentic 1940s costumes by Edith Head, this spoof of film noir detective yarns sees Steve Martin interacting with 18 Hollywood greats by way of intercutting of clips from some 17 old pictures.

Thus, when sultry Rachel Ward enters his seedy LA office to discuss her father's murder, $10-per-day sleuth Martin is able to call Bogart's Philip Marlowe for assistance on the case. And so it goes with such additional tough guys as Burt Lancaster, Kirk Douglas and Edward Arnold and such dames as Barbara Stanwyck, Ingrid Bergman, Veronica Lake, Bette Davis, Lana Turner and Joan Crawford.

Film is most engaging in its romantic sparring between Martin and his gorgeous client, Ward. Latter looks sensational in period garb and is not above such Martinesque gags as removing bullets from his wounds with her teeth or having her breasts 'rearranged' by the hardboiled detective.

Sporting dark hair and facetious confidence, Martin also looks spiffy in trenchcoat and hat. Only other roles of note see Carl Reiner essentially essaying Otto Preminger as a Nazi, and Reni Santoni as a zealous Peruvian offficer.

■ **DEAD OF NIGHT**

1945, 103 MINS, UK ⓥ
Dir Alberto Cavalcanti, Basil Dearden, Robert Hamer, Charles Crichton   *Prod* Michael Balcon   *Scr* John V.

Baines, Angus MacPhail, T.E.B. Clarke   *Ph* Jack Parker, H. Julius   *Ed* Charles Hasse   *Mus* Georges Auric   *Art Dir* Michael Relph
● Googie Withers, Michael Redgrave, Sally Ann Howes, Mervyn Johns, Roland Culver, Frederick Valk (Ealing)

Tightly-woven script [from stories by John V. Baines, Angus MacPhail, E.F. Benson and H.G. Wells] tells the story of a man who has foreknowledge of the future through his dreams. Summoned on business to a British estate, he's shocked to find that the place and people have all been in his dreams. When he tells his dream, one of the house-guests, a psychiatrist, scoffs at the story and attempts to find a scientific explanation for it all. Other guests, however, are more sympathetic and each then tells of a strange, similarly psychic situation in which he's been involved.

Producer Michael Balcon turned each individual episode over to a different director and, told via flashback, they're equally good. Best is the one featuring Redgrave as a ventriloquist whose dummy seemed imbued with a human brain and soul. Redgrave turns in a masterful piece of acting as he's driven to 'kill' the dummy.

■ **DEAD OF WINTER**

1987, 100 MINS, US ◇ ⓥ ⊙
Dir Arthur Penn   *Prod* John Bloomgarden, Marc Shmuger   *Scr* Marc Shmuger   *Ph* Jan Weincke   *Ed* Rich Shaine   *Mus* Richard Einhorn   *Art Dir* Bill Brodie
● Mary Steenburgen, Roddy McDowall, Jan Rubes, William Russ, Mark Malone, Ken Pogue (M-G-M)

Mary Steenburgen is first-rate as the struggling actress hired by an unusually accommodating casting director (Roddy McDowall) to audition as a double for an actress removed from a film-in-progress because of an alleged nervous breakdown.

She's taken to the isolated country estate of a psychiatrist-turned-producer during a violent snowstorm (hence the title *Dead of Winter*) where she undergoes a complete makeover until she – quite uncannily – resembles the stricken actress.

Little does she know she's become the patsy for a couple of blackmailers who have bumped off the other actress, as revealed in the very first scene of the film.

Suspense is built artfully around her gradual realization that she's trapped with a sly shrink and his obsequious factotum, McDowall, considerably more malevolent than he first appeared.

Steenburgen and McDowall are the adversaries to follow, even though it would seem more likely that the wheel-chair bound doctor (Jan Rubes) should be the one to watch. Rubes is simply not sinister enough to be the mastermind behind this scheme.

■ **DEAD POETS SOCIETY**

1989, 128 MINS, US ◇ ⓥ ⊙
Dir Peter Weir   *Prod* Steven Haft, Paul Junger Witt, Tony Thomas   *Scr* Tom Schulman   *Ph* John Seale   *Ed* William Anderson   *Mus* Maurice Jarre   *Art Dir* Wendy Stites
● Robin Williams, Robert Sean Leonard, Ethan Hawke, Josh Charles, Gale Hansen, Dylan Kussman (Touchstone/Silver Screen Partners IV)

Pic is not so much about Robin Williams, as unconventional English teacher John Keating at a hardline New England prep school, as it is about the youths he teaches and how the creative flames within them are kindled and then stamped out.

Director Peter Weir fills the screen with a fresh gang of compelling teenagers, led by Robert Sean Leonard as outgoing Neil Perry and balanced by Ethan Hawke as deeply withdrawn Todd Anderson.

Keating enters their rigidly traditional world and has them literally rip out the pages of their hidebound textbooks in favor of his inventive didactics on the spirit of poetry. Captivated by Keating's spirit, the influential Neil provokes his mates into reviving a secret club, the Dead Poets Society, that Keating led in his prep school days.

Meanwhile the gifted, medical-school-bound Todd begins to pursue acting, his true aspiration, against the strenuous objections of his domineering father (Kurtwood Smith).

Story sings whenever Williams is onscreen. Screen belongs just as often to Leonard, who as Neil has a quality of darting confidence mixed with hesitancy. Hawke, as the painfully shy Todd, gives a haunting performance.
□ 1989: Best Original Screenplay.
□ Nominations: Best Picture, Director, Actor (Robin Williams)

■ **DEAD RECKONING**

1947, 100 MINS, US ⓥ ⊙
Dir John Cromwell   *Prod* Sidney Biddell   *Scr* Oliver H.P. Garrett, Steve Fisher   *Ph* Leo Tover   *Ed* Gene Havlick   *Mus* Marlin Skiles   *Art Dir* Stephen Goosson, Rudolph Sternad
● Humphrey Bogart, Lizabeth Scott, Morris Carnovsky, William Prince, Charles Cane, Marvin Miller (Columbia)

Humphrey Bogart's typically tense performance raises this average whodunit quite a few notches. Film has good suspense and action, and some smart direction and photography.

Columbia borrowed Bogart from Warners to play the role of a tough ex-paratrooper captain returning home with a pal to be honored by the War Dept for their achievements. When the pal jumps the DC train, to go home instead, the perplexed captain follows to find himself enmeshed in gangland, murders and romance. His pal, he learns, had enlisted under an alias because he was convicted of a killing. Two days after said pal arrives home, he gets bumped off.

Determined to solve the mystery and avenge his friend, the captain digs into his pal's haunts. Script uses a flashback method for part of the telling, to add variety.

Bogart absorbs one's interest from the start as a tough, quick-thinking ex-skyjumper. Lizabeth Scott stumbles occasionally as a nitery singer, but on the whole gives a persuasive sirenish performance.

■ **DEAD RINGERS**

1988, 115 MINS, CANADA ◇ ⓥ ⊙
Dir David Cronenberg   *Prod* David Cronenberg, Marc Boyman   *Scr* David Cronenberg, Norman Snider   *Ph* Peter Suschitzky   *Ed* Ronald Sanders   *Mus* Howard Shore   *Art Dir* Carol Spier
● Jeremy Irons, Genevieve Bujold, Heidi Von Palleske, Barbara Gordon, Shirley Douglas, Stephen Lack (Mantle Clinic II)

Dead Ringers is about identical twin gynecologists, both expertly played by Jeremy Irons, whose intense bond is fatally sliced when they both fall in love with the same internationally known actress (Genevieve Bujold).

The doctors are renowned, interchangeably taking on the same patients and making public appearances, with no one guessing who's who. Yet one is outgoing, a smooth talker and a ladies man, and the other, more dependent and less sociable. Bujold chooses the shy twin and from that point, disintegration of the twins bond and their careers sets in.

Director David Cronenberg handles his usual fondness for gore in muted style; a brief scene has the shy twin dreaming of biting apart the skin joining Siamese twin and the final operation, though bloody, is not lingered over.

■ DEAD ZONE, THE

1983, 102 MINS, US ◇ ⑰ ⊡ ⊙
Dir David Cronenberg   *Prod* Debra Hill   *Scr* Jeffrey
Boam   *Ph* Mark Irwin   *Ed* Ronald Sanders
Mus Michael Kamen   *Art Dir* Carol Spier
● Christopher Walken, Brooke Adams, Tom Skerritt,
Herbert Lom, Anthony Zerbe, Martin Sheen (Dino De
Laurentiis)

Joining the half-dozen shock-oriented directors who have filmed novelist Stephen King's horror and suspense yarns, David Cronenberg turns *The Dead Zone* into an accomplished psychological thriller.

Focus is Johnny Smith, a shy schoolteacher who snaps out of a long coma with the questionable gift of second sight. Convincingly played by Christopher Walken, Johnny can see into anybody's past or future merely by grasping the person's hand. The 'dead zone' seems to refer to the brain damage that enables him to change the outcome of events he 'sees'.

His first premonition enables a nurse to save her daughter from a domestic conflagration. The news of the patient's ESP spreads quickly and he experiences some pretty horrible incident inside and outside his head.

A lot happens in the 102-minute suspenser. There's the girlfriend (Brooke Adams) Johnny loses to his near-fatal accident and regains for awhile. There's also a sheriff (Tom Skerritt) who desperately needs a psychic solution to crack a murder case, and the wealthy businessman (Anthony Zerbe) who hires Johnny to tutor his problem son (Simon Craig).

■ DEALERS

1989, 89 MINS, UK ◇ ⑰
Dir Colin Bucksey   *Prod* William P. Cartlidge
Scr Andrew MacLear   *Ph* Peter Sinclair   *Ed* Jon
Costelloe   *Mus* Richard Hartley   *Art Dir* Peter J.
Hampton
● Paul McGann, Rebecca DeMornay, Derrick
O'Connor, John Castle, Paul Guilfoyle, Rosalind Bennett
(Euston)

Dealers, though well produced, is a less than enthralling pic about a yuppie high-flyer and his glamorous mistress.

Paul McGann is a dollar dealer in a London bank, set for promotion when his superior suicides after a botched deal. To his chagrin, McGann's boss brings in an outsider over his head, beautiful Rebecca DeMornay, the latest whizkid in the banking business (and the boss' mistress to boot). Before long, though, McGann is romancing his rival and taking her home for a nightcap in his seaplane, which he parks near Tower Bridge.

Pic's most interesting character is Derrick O'Connor as a cockney dealer who's pink-slipped from the bank and sinks into a coke-snorting decline.

■ DEAR BRIGITTE

1965, 100 MINS, US ◇ ⑰
Dir Henry Koster   *Prod* Henry Koster   *Scr* Hal Kanter
Ph Lucien Ballard   *Ed* Marjorie Fowler   *Mus* George
Duning   *Art Dir* Jack Martin Smith, Malcolm Brown
● James Stewart, Fabian, Glynis Johns, Cindy Carol,
Billy Mumy, Brigitte Bardot (20th Century-Fox)

An entertaining comedy with something for everyone, *Dear Brigitte* shapes up as an excellent family pic.

Hal Kanter's screenplay, based on John Haase's novel *Erasmus with Freckles*, focuses on poet-professor Robert Leaf who's not only pro-humanities but very much anti-science. James Stewart is perfect in characterization of the idealistic voice in academic wilderness, as nuclear labs and computer setups encroach upon his domain of arts and letters at mythical modern university.

Complications arise when eight-year-old son Erasmus turns tone-deaf, then color-blind (hence unsuited for artistic career) but displays mathematical genius which indicates great scientific future. Kanter's yarn is lightweight, but a sufficiently strong fiber to support a string of varied and effective comedy situations, including Erasmus' puppy love for Brigitte Bardot to whom he secretly writes letters from Sausalito riverboat home.

In role of Stewart's wife, Glynis Johns is standout steadying influence on hubby, son Billy Mumy, teenage daughter Cindy Carol and latter's boyfriend Fabian.

■ DEATH BECOMES HER

1992, 103 MINS, US ◇ ⑰ ⊡ ⊙
Dir Robert Zemeckis   *Prod* Robert Zemeckis, Joan
Bradshaw   *Scr* Martin Donovan, David Koepp
Ph Dean Cundey   *Ed* Arthur Schmidt   *Mus* Alan
Silvestri   *Art Dir* Rick Carter
● Meryl Streep, Bruce Willis, Goldie Hawn, Isabella
Rossellini, Ian Ogilvy, Adam Storke (Universal)

Mordant, daring and way, way out there, *Death Becomes Her* is a very dark comedy yielding far more strange fascination than outright laughs. Robert Zemeckis' stretch of state-of-the-art special effects within a character-orientated context is a treat for somewhat specialized tastes.

Long-arc script describes the epic competition between vain actress Meryl Streep and troubled author Goldie Hawn, initially for the love of superstar plastic surgeon Bruce Willis, but, more important, for the secret to eternal life and youth. After an amusing proglogue, Zemeckis serves up his first amazing scene with the introduction, seven years later, of Hawn as an embittered fat slob. As everywhere else here, effects work is seamless and first-rate, with a clearly big-time budget (estimated at $40 million).

Another seven years pass, and Streep, now a washed-up mess, is living in sterile BevHills splendor with alcoholic Willis. Streep insists on attending a chic book party for Hawn, but is horrified to discover the 50-year-old writer looks like a health club ad.

Frantic to outdo her bitter enemy, Streep ends up at the fabulous mansion of Isabella Rossellini, a kinky beauty who turns out to be a high priestess of eternal life.

Streep does an acid sendup of aging beauty queens that will be relished by devotees of showbiz and its icons. Hawn plays very well with her co-star but is mostly limited to rabid vengeance. Willis is okay, but lacks the daft quality of Kevin Kline, original choice for the role. An uncredited Sydney Pollack is great fun as a BevHills doctor.
□ 1992: Best Visual Effects.

■ DEATH GAME

1977, 89 MINS, US ◇ ⑰
Dir Peter Traynor   *Prod* Larry Spiegel, Peter Traynor
Scr Anthony Overman   *Ph* David Worth   *Mus* Jimmie
Haskell
● Sondra Locke, Colleen Camp, Seymour Cassel, Beth
Brickell, Michael Kalmansohn, Ruth Warshawsky (Levitt-
Pickman)

Plot places the utmost strain on credibility. Two young lesbians (Sondra Locke and Colleen Camp) show up one thunderously rainy night at the plush, suburban home of a San Francisco business exec (Seymour Cassel), just turned 40.

After being allowed to use the telephone (they claim they're lost), pair admire the house appointments, seduce the man into a sexual threesome, and proceed to move in (the man's wife is away with the two children for the weekend).

All this, given some restraint, might have been packed into a passable feature. But director Peter Traynor opts for the obvious both in the acting and special effects. Cassel appears as hysterical as a middle-manager whose luncheon plans have gone askew. Locke and Camp scream and lick their lips a lot.

■ DEATH IN VENICE

1971, 130 MINS, ITALY ◇ ⑰
Dir Luchino Visconti   *Prod* Luchino Visconti   *Scr* Luchino
Visconti, Nicola Badalucco   *Ph* Pasquale de Santis
Mus Gustav Mahler   *Art Dir* Ferdinand Scarfiotti, Piero Tosi
● Dirk Bogarde, Bjorn Andresen, Silvana Mangano,
Marisa Berenson, Mark Burns (Warner)

Based on Thomas Mann's novella, *Death in Venice* could have been no easy task to translate to the screen. But Visconti and Dirk Bogarde clearly have a rapport and Bogarde gives a subtle and moving performance which fits beautifully into the atmospheric realism of [pre-World War I] Venice.

Bogarde plays a German composer and conductor (made up to look very like Gustav Mahler, whose music is used for the score) who visits Venice on vacation when on the verge of a mental and physical collapse. He is concerned with the violent accusations of his friend (Mark Burns) that he has dodged the issue of emotion until he is now no longer capable of feeling it.

He is fastidious and will not react to the uncouth behavior of the people he meets until, at his hotel, he sees a young boy with his family. The lad looks to Bogarde to be the most beautiful thing he has ever seen. He never seeks to contact the lad but follows him and watches him with a hunger which, thanks to Bogarde's performance, is clearly more intellectual and emotional than homosexual.

The story has its troubles. It attempts to show how innocence can cause problems of corruption and yet there is a pervading air over the film that is far from innocent.

Bogarde is both pathetic and compelling. Bjorn Andresen undoubtedly is a remarkably attractively-featured lad and gives a memorable performance. Silvana Mangano plays his mother with a haughty charm.
□ 1971: Nomination: Best Costume Design

■ DEATH OF A GUNFIGHTER

1969, 94 MINS, US ◇ ⑰
Dir Allen Smithee [= Robert Totten, Don Siegel]
Prod Richard E. Lyons   *Scr* Joseph Calvelli   *Ph* Andrew
Jackson   *Ed* Robert F. Shugrue   *Mus* Oliver Nelson
Art Dir Alexander Golitzen, Howard E. Johnson
● Richard Widmark, Lena Horne, John Saxon, Carroll
O'Connor, David Opatoshu, Kent Smith (Universal)

Story concerns an offbeat sort of gunman, a smalltown marshal with 12 killings to his credit. But now he is to be removed by a disgruntled city council. His efforts to remain in post end in a flashy finish.

Richard Widmark punches over title role and gives tone to the character who has always tried to run a clean town. Script from Lewis B. Patten's novel builds suspense as the council plans his departure but doesn't know how, other than to gun him down.

Widmark elicits certain sympathy for his actions in his hardboiled interpretation, and for co-star has Lena Horne, in role of a madam.

[Pic is first use on a feature film of official Directors Guild of America pseudonym 'Allen Smithee' for directors who want no credit. Don Siegel replaced Robert Totten, who was fired after 25 days.]

■ DEATH OF A SALESMAN

1951, 115 MINS, US ⑰
Dir Laslo Benedek   *Prod* Stanley Kramer   *Scr* Stanley
Roberts   *Ph* Franz P. Planer   *Ed* William Lyon
Mus Alex North   *Art Dir* Rudolph Sternad, Cary Odell

D

● Fredric March, Mildred Dunnock, Kevin McCarthy, Cameron Mitchell, Howard Smith, Royal Beal (Kramer/Columbia)

The vise-like grip with which *Death of a Salesman* held Broadway theatregoers for almost two years continues undiminished in Stanley Kramer's production of the film version. Arthur Miller's Pulitzer Prize-winner has been closely followed in the screen adaptation.

Salesman starkly reveals how Willy Loman's disillusionments catch up with him, his sons, his wife Linda; of how, after 34 years selling for the same house, he is finally fired, thus bringing about his complete mental collapse. During the period when his mental processes are breaking down, the film images Willy's memories of the past 20 years in illustrating how his desire for importance somehow became enmeshed in his confused dreams.

Fredric March, in the part created on the New York stage by Lee Cobb, gives perhaps the greatest performance of his career. Mildred Dunnock, in her original Broadway part, is superb as Willy's wife Linda. Kevin McCarthy, as Biff, is a film newcomer who entrenches himself strongly in the role performed on Broadway by Arthur Kennedy, Cameron Mitchell is an engaging 'Happy' Loman, the other brother, which he played on Broadway.

□ 1951: Nominations: Best Actor (Fredric March), Supp. Actor (Kevin McCarthy), Supp. Actress (Mildred Dunnock), B&W Cinematography, Scoring of a Dramatic Picture

■ DEATH ON THE NILE

1978, 140 MINS, UK ◇ ⓥ ⊙
Dir John Guillermin   *Prod* John Brabourne, Richard Goodwin   *Scr* Anthony Shaffer   *Ph* Jack Cardiff   *Ed* Malcolm Cooke   *Mus* Nino Rota   *Art Dir* Peter Murton
● Peter Ustinov, Jane Birkin, Lois Chiles, Bette Davis, Mia Farrow, Jon Finch (EMI)

Death on the Nile is a clever, witty, well-plotted, beautifully-produced and splendidly acted screen version of Agatha Christie's mystery. It's old-fashioned stylized entertainment with a big cast and lush locations. Peter Ustinov is the fourth actor to play Belgian sleuth Hercule Poirot.

Anthony Shaffer's adaptation doesn't have a hole. When Ustinov reveals the killer in the final drawing room scene it comes as a complete surprise. Every one of the dozen characters floating down the Nile is a suspect. Every one on board could have and might have murdered Lois Chiles, the arrogant millionairess who has stolen her best friend's fiance.

Shaffer has also created a number of purposely exaggerated characters to complement Ustinov. There's Angela Lansbury's tipsy portrayal of a romantic novelist; Bette Davis as a stuffy and overbearing Washington socialite and Maggie Smith as her bitter companion; Jack Warden as an hysterical Swiss physician; I.S. Johar in a marvelously offbeat performance as the manager of the ship on which the murders take place; David Niven as Poirot's sidekick Colonel Race; and Jon Finch as a Marxist spouting rebel.

But the star is Ustinov and the penetrating mind of his character, Hercule Poirot.
□ 1978: Best Costume Design

■ DEATH RACE 2000

1975, 78 MINS, US ◇ ⓥ
Dir Paul Bartel   *Prod* Roger Corman   *Scr* Robert Thom, Charles Griffith   *Ph* Tak Fujimoto   *Ed* Tina Hersch   *Mus* Paul Chihara   *Art Dir* Robinson Royce, B.B. Neel
● David Carradine, Simone Griffeth, Sylvester Stallone, Mary Woronov, Roberta Collins, Martin Kove (New World)

Roger Corman's quickie production deals with ultra-violent sport in a futuristic society, in this case an annual cross-country road race with drivers scoring points by running down pedestrians.

Script, from an Ib Melchior story, makes its satirical points economically, and director Paul Bartel keeps the film moving quickly. Almost all of the film takes place on the road, with carnage and crashes occurring like clockwork.

David Carradine, clad in a spooky black leather outfit, is the national champion driver, challenged by thug-like Sylvester Stallone and four other drivers, including Amazon-like Mary Woronov. While fending off Stallone's attacks, Carradine also has to deal with radicals trying to sabotage the race.

■ DEATHSPORT

1978, 83 MINS, US ◇ ⓥ
Dir Henry Suso, Allen Arkush   *Prod* Roger Corman   *Scr* Henry Suso, Donald Stewart   *Ph* Gary Graver   *Ed* Larry Bock   *Mus* Andrew Stein   *Art Dir* Sharon Compton
● David Carradine, Claudia Jennings, Richard Lynch, William Smithers, Will Walker, David McLean (New World)

Deathsport is Roger Corman's futuristic science fiction gladiator picture. And what is a futuristic science fiction gladiator picture? It's a film set 1,000 years into the future, post neutron wars, where the good warriors ride horses and wield see-through sabres fighting bad guys known as Statesmen who drive lethal motorcycles known as 'Death Machines'.

The good guys, Ranger Guides, are quiet, live by a code, make temporary unions and roam desert wastelands trying to avoid the cannibal mutants and those motorcycles, which are very noisy.

Statesmen have other plans. They have two ways of amusing themselves: beating up Ranger Guides – no easy task since Ranger Guides are superior warriors – and capturing female rangers, who they strip, lock up in dark room with metal chandeliers and then apply electricity and special effects. Nice guys.

David Carradine is the quiet good guy and the best thing that can be said about his acting and his part is that he doesn't say much. Claudia Jennings is his partner good guy, the one who gets to amuse the bad guy in the dark room. The best thing that can be said about her performance is that she gets to take off her clothes, twice.

■ DEATH TAKES A HOLIDAY

1934, 79 MINS, US
Dir Mitchell Leisen   *Scr* Maxwell Anderson, Gladys Lehman   *Ph* Charles Lang   *Art Dir* Hans Dreier, Ernst Fegte
● Fredric March, Evelyn Venable, Guy Standing, Katherine Alexander, Gail Patrick, Helen Westley (Paramount)

Because it has the word 'death' in it, Paramount tested the picture under another title, *Strange Holiday*, in California. Results showed that the original title meant the most at the box office.

Action of picture [from a play by Alberto Casella] is laid in and around a foreign estate, the grandeur of which at times is singularly Hollywoodian. Fredric March is on top, playing Death. Wanting to take a holiday from that role, he wishes himself on a duke and his guests for three days, with death meanwhile stopping throughout the world.

Though highly fantastic, the plot provides many interesting situations as Death in the disguise of a prince moves through a strata of love interest which must end after the three-day furlough.

March turns in a skillful performance, here playing a foreigner in an accent from which there is never a break or slip. He has opposite him for main heart interest Evelyn Venable, who screens well.

■ DEATHTRAP

1982, 115 MINS, US ◇ ⓥ
Dir Sidney Lumet   *Prod* Burtt Harris   *Scr* Jay Presson Allen   *Ph* Andrzej Bartkowiak   *Ed* John J. Fitzstephens   *Mus* Johnny Mandel   *Art Dir* Tony Walton
● Michael Caine, Christopher Reeve, Dyan Cannon, Irene Worth, Henry Jones, Joe Silver (Warner)

Sidney Lumet is no stranger to stage adaptations. Despite its intermittently amusing dialog, however, *Deathtrap* comes across as a minor entertainment, cleverness of which cannot conceal its essential artificiality when blown up on the big screen.

There are countless twists and turns in the plot of Ira Levin's 1978 play and the dramatic surprises are not necessarily easy to predict.

Michael Caine essays a writer who was once the Neil Simon of Broadway mystery writers but has now cranked out a quartet of clinkers. Into his lap falls the manuscript of a perfect suspenser penned by unknown Christopher Reeve. Desperate for a hit, Caine invites Reeve over one evening in the guise of potential collaborator, while in fact he intends to kill him and then present the work as a new effort of his own.

Actors turn in pro jobs in a technical sense, with Reeve skillfully walking the fine line of his pretty boy part. But actors' charm just doesn't balance out the distastefulness of their characters.

■ DEATH WATCH

1980, 128 MINS, FRANCE/W. GERMANY ◇ ⓥ ⊙
Dir Bertrand Tavernier   *Prod* Gabriel Boustani, Janine Rubeiz   *Scr* Bertrand Tavernier, David Rayfiel   *Ph* Pierre-William Glenn   *Ed* Armand Psenny, Michael Ellis   *Mus* Antoine Duhamel   *Art Dir* Tony Pratt
● Romy Schneider, Harvey Keitel, Harry Dean Stanton, Therese Liotard, Max von Sydow, Caroline Langrishe (Selta/Little Bear)

The story, shrewdly crafted by Bertrand Tavernier and American screenwriter David Rayfiel from a novel by David Compton [*The Unsleeping Eye*], is a throat-catcher. In a future society people die of old-age, science having almost completely banished disease.

A cunning TV producer, Vincent Ferriman, played with chillingly unctuous serenity by Harry Dean Stanton, hits on the idea of a program that would cover live the last days of an individual who has managed to contract a terminal illness.

Ferriman's proposed subject is Katherine Mortenhoe (finely played by Romy Schneider), whose fierce independence and sensitivity would seem to provide poignant fodder for the camera eye. But Katherine, after signing a contract, flees the city.

Death Watch is a compelling drama centered on the human implications of its fanciful premise, as well as a harsh indictment of the media's role in society.

■ DEATH WISH

1974, 92 MINS, US ◇ ⓥ ⊙
Dir Michael Winner   *Prod* Hal Landers, Bobby Roberts, Michael Winner   *Scr* Wendell Mayes   *Ph* Arthur J. Ornitz   *Ed* Bernard Gribble   *Mus* Herbie Hancock   *Art Dir* Robert Gundlach
● Charles Bronson, Hope Lange, Vincent Gardenia, Steven Keats, William Redfield, Stuart Margolin (Paramount/De Laurentiis)

Poisonous incitement to do-it-yourself law enforcement is the vulgar exploitation hook on which *Death Wish* is awkwardly hung. Charles

Bronson stars as a husband-turned-assassin after his wife is killed and daughter raped by muggers.

Adaptation of Brian Garfield's novel is functionally simplistic, which is precisely the intellectual level desired for straightout exploitation treatment. Hope Lange and daughter Kathleen Tolan are victims of assault, after which husband Bronson freaks out in vengeance.

Plot angles are mostly overwhelmed by the easier, conventional cutting to the action, in this case one killing about every 10 minutes.

....

■ DEATH WISH II

1982, 93 MINS, US ◇ ⓥ ⊙
Dir Michael Winner *Prod* Menahem Golan, Yoram Globus *Scr* David Engelbach *Ph* Richard H. Kline, Tom Del Ruth *Ed* Arnold Crust [= Michael Winner], Julian Semilian *Mus* Jimmy Page *Art Dir* William Hiney
● Charles Bronson, Jill Ireland, Vincent Gardenia, J.D. Cannon, Anthony Franciosa, Ben Frank (Cannon/City)

Director Michael Winner, who usually leaves nothing to the imagination (censors permitting), does it again with *Death Wish* revisited. Charles Bronson, as the avenging vigilante Paul Kersey, is turned loose this time on the creeps of Los Angeles and the results are every bit as revolting as in the original 1974 jackpot fantasy.

For openers, Bronson's Spanish cook is gangbanged and killed, and his catatonic daughter (still unrecovered from the first assault in Gotham) is raped yet again before winding up impaled on an iron railing pike as she tries to elude her savage captors.

What little performing style pic offers comes from Vincent Gardenia encoring from the original edition as a NY gumshoe who finally gets knocked off for his trouble coming to the aid of Bronson in an LA ravine.

....

■ DEATH WISH 3

1985, 90 MINS, US ◇ ⓥ ⊙
Dir Michael Winner *Prod* Menahem Golan, Yoram Globus *Scr* Michael Edmonds *Ph* John Stanier *Ed* Arnold Crust [= Michael Winner] *Mus* Jimmy Page *Art Dir* Peter Mullins
● Charles Bronson, Deborah Raffin, Ed Lauter, Martin Balsam, Gavan O'Herlihy, Kirk Taylor (Cannon)

Death Wish 3 adds significantly to the body count scored to date in this street-rampant series. Thrills, however, are way down due to script's failure to build motivation for Paul Kersey's latest killing spree.

Set in NY, but lensed mostly in London, pic's release was timed to capitalize on the controversy around subway vigilante Bernhard Goetz.

Attempts to justify the ensuing mass-murder are perfunctory. Film opens with the butchering of an old man who turns out to be an old mate of Kersey, but there's no suggestion that the relationship was intimate. Kersey's response, like Bronson's acting, is automaton-like. Mystery is why he came to New York in the first place without the tools of his brutal trade and has to make regular visits to the post office to accumulate firepower.

Michael Winner directs with customary tongue-in-cheek panache. There are occasional moments of wit as when apartment resident Bennett (Martin Balsam) wields his rusty machine gun.

....

■ DEATH WISH 4
THE CRACKDOWN

1987, 99 MINS, US ◇ ⓥ ⊙
Dir J. Lee Thompson *Prod* Pancho Kohner *Scr* Gail Morgan Hickman *Ph* Gideon Porath *Ed* Peter Lee Thompson *Mus* Paul McCallum, Valentine McCallum, John Bisharat *Art Dir* Whitney Brooke Wheeler

● Charles Bronson, Kay Lenz, John P. Ryan, Perry Lopez, George Dickerson, Soon-Teck Oh (Cannon)

It's a risky business getting close to Charles Bronson. His wife, daughter and friends have been blown away in the first three installments of *Death Wish*. Now the vigilante is back to revenge the death of his girlfriend's daughter.

What raises *Death Wish 4* above the usual blowout is a semi-engaging script and sure pacing by veteran action director J. Lee Thompson.

As architect turned crusader, Paul Kersey (Bronson) is a curious blend of soft-spoken family man and detached seeker of justice. When he turns up the heat he does so with a measured, methodical passion as if it were his true calling in life to measure out justice in his corner of the world.

Bronson's treatment of drug trafficking is akin to chopping off the weeds and thinking that they won't grow back. It's a good excuse for him to break out some heavy ammunition in pursuit of the two rival gangs who supposedly supply 90% of the cocaine in Los Angeles.

....

■ DECEIVED

1991, 103 MINS, US ◇ ⓥ ⊙
Dir Damian Harris *Prod* Michael Finnell, Wendy Dozoretz, Ellen Collett *Scr* Mary Agnes Donoghue, Derek Saunders, [= Bruce Joel Rubin] *Ph* Jack N. Green *Ed* Neil Travis *Mus* Thomas Newman *Art Dir* Andrew McAlpine
● Goldie Hawn, John Heard, Robin Bartlett, Ashley Peldon, Tom Irwin, Maia Filar (Touchstone)

Thrills, chills and a convincing perf by Goldie Hawn mark this stylishly absorbing thriller. Farfetched plot doesn't bear much scrutiny, but mesmerizing visual tone, macabre developments and sound entertainment value should sweep audiences along.

Hawn plays a New York art restoration expert who appears to be living a perfect life with her attractive career, cute kid (Ashley Peldon) and attentive, romantic husband (John Heard), who's also in the ancient art biz. But when a forgery's discovered at the museum, fingers are pointed at Heard. Then he's killed in a car accident, and a Social Security worker informs Hawn her husband wasn't whom he said he was – the real guy died years ago.

Pic segues ably into thriller territory as the undead husband (corpse buried was actually a charred hitchhiker) begins haunting his former home to try to recover a stolen Egyptian necklace he left behind. Meanwhile, Hawn has turned sleuth and is closing in on the disheartening truth about the con she married.

Their inevitable encounter packs the requisite scream value, and pic heightens into a chilling game of cat and mouse, climaxed by a horrifically successful pursuit sequence.

Director Damian Harris appears in full control of the medium, weaving in some effective Hitchcockian allusions and a couple of intentional good laughs.

....

■ DECEIVERS, THE

1988, 112 MINS, US ◇ ⓥ ⊙
Dir Nicholas Meyer *Prod* Ismail Merchant *Scr* Michael Hirst *Ph* Walter Lassally *Ed* Richard Trevor *Mus* John Scott *Art Dir* Ken Adam
● Pierce Brosnan, Saeed Jaffrey, Shashi Kapoor, Helena Michell, Keith Michell, David Robb (Merchant Ivory)

Sumptuously produced historical action adventure tale, set in pre-Raj India circa 1825, falls short of fully developing its most interesting theme – the struggle of the rational Western psyche with the supernatural seductions of the East.

Pierce Brosnan is William Savage, a 'resident collector' for the British East India Co., which blazed the trail for England's colonialization of the Indian subcontinent. A company patrol is mysteriously ambushed and murdered in the dead of night. When Brosnan discovers the bodies in a gruesome mass grave, the fearless, straight-arrow officer is outraged.

A rising company star who has married the commander's daughter (Helena Michell), he risks his career by setting out to prove the murders are part of a horrifying conspiracy by the Thuggees – a centuries-old, pan-Indian brotherhood of evildoers who worship Kali, the goddess of destruction.

Adapting John Masters' fact-derived novel, director Nicholas Meyer makes the most of an opportunity for homage to Alexander Korda adventure movies. As psychological drama, Meyer's effort to depict Brosnan's spiritual struggle with dark forces unleashed by Kali-worship is undermined by the actor's limited range and an elliptical screenplay which fails to exploit the complex possibilities inherent in the cross-cultural confrontation.

....

■ DECEPTION

1946, 111 MINS, US ⓥ
Dir Irving Rapper *Prod* Henry Blanke *Scr* John Collier, Joseph Than *Ph* Ernest Haller *Ed* Alan Crosland *Mus* Erich Wolfgang Korngold *Art Dir* Anton Grot
● Bette Davis, Paul Henreid, Claude Rains, John Abbot, Benson Fong (Warner)

Deception, a story of matrimonial lies that builds to a murder climax, gives Bette Davis a potent vehicle. Plot is backed with lavish production, strong playing of a story loaded with femme interest, and bright direction.

Davis plays to the hilt, using full dramatic talent. It's not all her show, though. Claude Rains as her elderly teacher and sponsor walks off with considerable portion of the picture in a fine display of acting ability. By contrast, Paul Henreid suffers although turning in a smooth performance in a role with not too much color.

Plot [from a play by Louis Verneuil] concerns deception practised by Davis to prevent husband Henreid from discovering that she had been the mistress of Rains before her marriag Henreid, refugee cellist, is a jealous man whose temperamental instability is reason for the wife's deception. Pickup to story comes with Rains' entrance and his mad jealousy over his desertion by his mistress. To him falls juicy plums in the form of dialog and situations that carry the story along.

Music importance is emphasized by Erich Wolfgang Korngold's score and staging of orchestral numbers by LeRoy Prinz. Korngold's original music and the Cello Concerto are outstanding highlights.

....

■ DECISION AT SUNDOWN

1957, 77 MINS, US ◇
Dir Budd Boetticher *Prod* Harry Joe Brown *Scr* Charles Lang Jr *Ph* Burnett Guffey *Ed* Al Clark *Mus* Heinz Roemheld *Art Dir* Robert Peterson
● Randolph Scott, John Carroll, Karen Steele, Valerie French, Noah Beery, Andrew Duggan (Columbia/Ranown)

Complex screenplay from Vernon L. Fluherty tale spans a single day in cow town of Sundown. Randolph Scott, a mysterious, revengeful gunman, rides into town. He's after unsavory local wheel John Carroll, who's slated to marry local belle Karen Steele on that day. Scott breaks up the wedding and is besieged with sidekick Noah Beery by Carroll's henchmen. Step by step, it develops that Carroll, in his none-too-scrupulous past, had stolen and later discarded Scott's wife (since dead); and that she hadn't been unwilling, a fact Scott cannot face.

D

Role is an offbeat one for Scott, but he carries off the gunman's frustrated rage very well. Carroll makes convincingly menacing heavy in the suave tradition. Steele, as his understandably confused fiancee, shows much promise of things to come.

DECISION BEFORE DAWN

1951, 119 MINS, US
Dir Anatole Litvak   *Prod* Anatole Litvak, Frank McCarthy   *Scr* Peter Viertel   *Ph* Franz Planer   *Ed* Dorothy Spencer   *Mus* Franz Waxman
● Richard Basehart, Gary Merrill, Oskar Werner, Hildegarde Neff, O.E. Hasse, Hans Christian Blech (20th Century-Fox)

Anatole Litvak gives this Second World War spy thriller a strong feeling of reality through a semi-documentary treatment, the use of mostly unknown faces, and by location lensing entirely in Germany, where the scars of the War still fit graphically into the story's 1945 period.

Story [from the novel *Call It Treason* by George Howe] really gets going when Oskar Werner, a sensitive Allied prisoner, volunteers to aid his captors by obtaining information behind the lines in his own country. He believes his actions will help, rather than betray, Germany. Werner's excursion is fraught with danger, and his playing and Litvak direction milk the situation of drama while drawing a rather clear picture of events within Germany at that stage of the war and of how the people were taking it.

Richard Basehart and Gary Merrill, latter the commander of the intelligence unit using prisoners of war, are excellent. Hildegarde Neff creates a fine portrait of a German woman made a victim of war, and Dominique Blanchar is equally good as a French girl aiding the Allies.
□ 1951: Nominations: Best Picture, Editing

DECKS RAN RED, THE

1958, 97 MINS, US
Dir Andrew Stone   *Prod* Andrew Stone, Virginia Stone   *Scr* Andrew Stone   *Ph* Meredith M. Nicholson   *Ed* Virginia Stone
● James Mason, Dorothy Dandridge, Broderick Crawford, Stuart Whitman, Katharine Bard (M-G-M)

The Decks Ran Red is a descriptive title for this story, presented as fact, of an attempted mutiny at sea. Before the mutineers have been beaten down, they have spilled enough blood to make the decks sticky, if not running, with gore.

The plot is a plan by Broderick Crawford and Stuart Whitman, crew members of a chartered freighter, to kill off other members of the crew, rig the ship to make it look like an abandoned derelict, and then bring it in as salvage. According to maritime law, it's said, they will get half the ship's value – $1 million – as prize money.

James Mason, who has been first officer on a trim Matson liner, is flown to Australia to take charge of this dingy vessel when its captain mysteriously dies. He quickly discovers he is in for trouble from a lacklustre and sullen crew, trouble that is compounded by taking aboard a native Maori cook and his wife, latter being Dorothy Dandridge.

The story is faintly incredible at times and there is a tendency to impose dialog on a scene when the action has already spoken for itself. But the picture moves swiftly and absorbingly.

DECLINE AND FALL

1968, 90 MINS, US
Dir John Krish   *Prod* Ivan Foxwell   *Scr* Ivan Foxwell, Alan Hackney, Hugh Whitemore   *Ph* Desmond Dickinson   *Ed* Archie Ludski   *Mus* Ron Goodwin   *Art Dir* John Barry
● Robin Phillips, Genevieve Page, Donald Wolfit, Colin Blakely, Patience Collier, Leo McKern (20th Century-Fox)

This humorous and elegantly-confectioned adaptation of Evelyn Waugh's first (1928) literary success makes for a witty bundle of entertainment for discriminating audiences in search of tongue-in-cheek entertainment.

Writer-producer Ivan Foxwell has opted for a lightweight, spoofy approach to the Waugh story, with the result that everything is played one stop further out than normal. Consequently, some of the story's absurdities become almost acceptable in the context.

Pace is sprightly as we follow Paul Pennyfeather, the schoolboy who becomes teacher, then foil for a dazzling white slaver, then jailbird until his final rebirth as, literally, a different man.

Robin Phillips, in his first pic role, is excellent as the scapegoat predestined to a bittersweet fate. Genevieve Page is as elegant and alluring as ever in another tailor-cast role as the source of most of Paul's troubles.

John Krish's direction helps underline the spoofish plot elements.

DECLINE OF WESTERN CIVILIZATION, THE

1981, 100 MINS, US
Dir Penelope Spheeris   *Prod* Penelope Spheeris   *Ph* Steve Conant   *Ed* Charles Mullin, Peter Wiehl (Spheeris)

A bracing, stimulating and technically superb close-up look at the LA punk scene, pic is pitched at a perfect distance to allow for simultaneous engagement in the music and spectacle, and for rueful contemplation of what it all might mean.

Artistic strategy here is to combine provocative performance footage with 'at home' interviews with punk group members and talks with club owners, managers, critics and hardcore fans.

Film constitutes a 100-minute total immersion in the indigenous California punk world.

While a few of the rockers come off as artificial poseurs, many more surprise through revealing articulation of whys and wherefores of their lifestyle, and what comes through most strongly is purity of their dedication to their music.

Given top-notch craftsmanship, it's hard to believe effort was made independently for $100,000, and well-nigh impossible to detect that 35mm print is a 16mm blowup.

DEEP, THE

1977, 124 MINS, US
Dir Peter Yates   *Prod* Peter Guber   *Scr* Peter Benchley, Tracy Keenan Wynn   *Ph* Christopher Challis   *Ed* Robert L. Wolfe, David Berlatsky   *Mus* John Barry   *Art Dir* Tony Masters
● Robert Shaw, Jacqueline Bisset, Nick Nolte, Louis Gossett, Eli Wallach, Robert Tessier (Columbia-EMI/Casablanca Filmworks)

The Deep is an efficient but rather colorless film based on the Peter Benchley novel about a perilous search for treasure in the waters off Bermuda.

Fully 40% of the film takes place underwater, and the actors and crew learned how to dive playing long scenes without dialog on the ocean floor. Director Peter Yates keeps up the tension in a low-key way – with a few shocker moments thrown in from time to time – and these scenes are more involving than the ones above the surface.

It's possible that inside this slick piece of engineering there is a genuinely mordant satire of human greed struggling to get out, but it never quite gets to the surface.
□ 1977: Nomination: Best Sound

DEEP COVER

1992, 112 MINS, US
Dir Bill Duke   *Prod* Pierre David, Henry Bean   *Scr* Michael Tolkin, Henry Bean   *Ph* Bojan Bazelli   *Ed* John Carter   *Mus* Michel Colombier   *Art Dir* Pam Warner
● Larry Fishburne, Jeff Goldblum, Victoria Dillard, Charles Martin Smith, Gregory Sierra, Clarence Williams III (David-Bean)

Convoluted and mostly unconvincing as a portrait of the drug underworld, *Deep Cover* [based on a story by Michael Tolkin] still carries some resonance due to its vivid portrait of societal decay and a heavyweight performance by Larry Fishburne

Tough, straight-arrow cop Fishburne is recruited by government drug-enforcement chief Charles Martin Smith to infiltrate the cartel of dealer Arthur Mendoza, who controls 40% of the LA cocaine market on behalf of his uncle, a powerful Latin American politician the US government would like to cut down to size.

Taking a grungy downtown room and hitting the streets, Fishburne begins working his way up as a small-time dealer. His network includes suburban attorney dealer Jeff Goldblum, his supplier, vicious Gregory Sierra, and art importer-money launderer Victoria Dillard. Climax gives Fishburne the opportunity to choose which side of the law he wants to live on.

Performances are mostly of the intense, threatening and streetwise variety. Low-budget lensing ace Bojan Bazelli gives numerous sequences a sharp stylized look, but key behind-the-scenes contribution is Michel Colombier's superbly moody, dissonant jazz/rock score.

DEEP END

1970, 90 MINS, W. GERMANY/US
Dir Jerzy Skolimowski   *Prod* Maran Film-COKG-Kettledrum   *Scr* Jerzy Skolimowski, Jerzy Gruza, B. Sulik   *Ph* Charly Steinberger   *Mus* Cat Ten
● Jane Asher, John Moulder-Brown, Karl Michael Vogler, Christopher Sandford, Diana Dors (Maran/COKG/Kettledrum)

Though its main locale is a rather seamy London public bath, director Jerzy Skolimowski has avoided tawdriness by a sympathy in, and awareness of, the excessive but essentially pure actions of his love-smitten boy whose good looks make him prey for all types of women who come for their public ablutions.

Film gives the British scene a twist due to Skolimowski's treatment of the tangled desires of a young boy whose need for love goes to a rather vulgar, but enticing fellow worker at the baths.

John Moulder-Brown has the deep voice of the time between puberty and manhood and the childish yet dedicated pursuit of his first deeply troubled reaction to a woman. Skolimowski keeps the film alive with quirky incidents.

DEEPSTAR SIX

1989, 100 MINS, US
Dir Sean S. Cunningham   *Prod* Sean S. Cunningham, Patrick Markey   *Scr* Lewis Abernathy, Geof Miller   *Ph* Mac Ahlberg   *Ed* David Handman   *Mus* Harry Manfredini   *Art Dir* John Reinhart
● Taurean Blacque, Nancy Everhard, Greg Evigan, Miguel Ferrer, Nia Peeples, Cindy Pickett (Carolco)

Director-producer Sean Cunningham molds this tale of a sea monster attacking an ocean-bottom research team [story by Lewis Abernathy].

Crew, while trying to create a level launch site for some ocean-floor navy missiles, blows up a cavern in which the creature has been dwelling for eons. Enraged, it attacks their craft, manages to get inside, and more or less picks them off one by one.

But effect is diluted by implausibility, as creature never seems real – more like a goof on a 1950s horror movie monster than a true threat.

Pic's cast is a grab-bag ensemble with no real center (toplined Taurean Blacque is killed early on). It eventually finds its emotional core in an affair between crewmen Greg Evigan and Nancy Everhard. A sharp performance by Miguel Ferrer as a punchy, smartmouthed crewmen is diluted when character goes campily berserk.

■ **DEEP THROAT**

1972, 73 MINS, US
Dir Jerry Gerard [= Gerard Damiano] *Prod* Lou Perry
Scr Jerry Gerard *Ph* Harry Flecks *Ed* Jerry Gerard
Art Dir Len Camp
● Linda Lovelace (Vanguard)

While *Deep Throat* doesn't quite live up to its reputation as the *Ben-Hur* of porno pix, it is a superior piece which stands a head above the competition.

Pic takes a tongue-in-cheek approach to conventional hetero hardcore, dishing out enough laughs with the main course to prove sexpo features need as much comic relief as suspenders.

Plot centers on a young lady disappointed because she fails to 'hear bells' during her repeated sex bouts with as many as 14 men at a time.

Pic's technical quality is above par, including sharp color photography and a satirical musical score which spoofs, among other things, Coca-Cola's 'It's the Real Thing' television commercial.

Performances are spirited, especially that of the femme lead, and writer-director-editor Jerry Gerard puts it all together with some style.

■ **DEER HUNTER, THE**

1978, 183 MINS, US
Dir Michael Cimino *Prod* Barry Spikings, Michael Deeley, Michael Cimino, *Scr* Deric Washburn
Ph Vilmos Zsigmond *Ed* Peter Zinner *Mus* Stanley Myers *Art Dir* Ron Hobbs, Kim Swados
● Robert De Niro, John Cazale, John Savage, Christopher Walken, Meryl Streep, George Dzundza (Universal/EMI)

Among the considerable achievements of Michael Cimino's *The Deer Hunter* is the fact that the film remains intense, powerful and fascinating for more than three hours.

The picture is a long, sprawling epic-type in many ways more novel than motion picture. It employs literary references stylistically, forecasting events which will happen in the film.

It is a brutal work. Robert De Niro, John Cazale, John Savage and Christopher Walken head cast as friends living in a small Pennsylvania town. They attend a Russian Orthodox wedding at the beginning of the film. Directly afterwards three of them go deer hunting and soon afterwards they are to serve in Vietnam.

While in Southeast Asia, the trio is reunited during a battle scene and later captured by the Vietcong. As POWs they are forced to play a form of Russian roulette.

Throughout the film various ceremonies and cultural rituals are explored, compared and juxtaposed – the wedding, the game and the deer hunt. It is up to the viewer to decide how these rituals fit together and it is a big comprehension demand.

Many will wish that the screenplay by Deric Washburn was a bit more straightforward. Still, the film is ambitious and it succeeds on a number of levels and it proves that Cimino is an important director.

□ 1978: Best Picture, Director, Supp. Actor (Christopher Walken), Sound, Editing
□ Nominations: Best Actor (Robert De Niro), Supp. Actress (Meryl Streep), Original Screenplay, Cinematography

■ **DEFECTOR, THE**

1966, 108 MINS, W. GERMANY/FRANCE
Dir Raoul Levy *Prod* Raoul Levy *Scr* Robert Guenette, Raoul Levy *Ph* Raoul Coutard, *Ed* Albert Jurgenson, Roger Dwyre *Mus* Serge Gainsbourg *Art Dir* Pierre Guffroy
● Montgomery Clift, Hardy Kruger, Macha Meril, Roddy McDowall, David Opatoshu, Christine Delaroche (PECF/Rhein-Main)

The last motion picture made by Montgomery Clift prior to his death, *Defector* provides a part that allows him to substitute action of body and mind for the immobility of facial expression that clouded this fine actor's performances during his last years. His taut, troubled face is perfect for the role of a scientist pushed into espionage by his own country and almost erased from it by enemy agents.

Levy and Robert Guenette's collaboration on an adaptation of Paul Thomas's *The Spy* has gone for 'suspense' at the sacrifice of logic. Just plain logical loopholes appear that may escape most viewers but will disturb some.

Most of the intellectual byplay is between Clift, as an American scientist, and Hardy Kruger, as the German-born Russian agent given the assignment of getting Clift to defect. The physical action comes from Clift's evasion of the security police and his attempt to escape from East Germany. Kruger makes an excellent contrast, in his cool behavior, to Clift's nervousness.

■ **DEFENCE OF THE REALM**

1985, 96 MINS, UK
Dir David Drury *Prod* Robin Douet, Lynda Myles
Scr Martin Stellman *Ph* Roger Deakins *Ed* Michael Bradsell *Mus* Richard Harvey *Art Dir* Roger Murray-Leach
● Gabriel Byrne, Greta Scacchi, Denholm Elliott, Ian Bannen, Fulton MacKay, Bill Paterson (Enigma/NFFC)

The state of the nation's press and the evil antics of its secret services in the nuclear age are combined in this fast-paced thriller.

Script unravels a relatively uncomplicated story of events following the near crash of a nuclear bomber on a American airforce base in the English countryside. A left-wing MP who gets wind of the event is framed as a Russian spy and forced to resign. His journalist friend is bumped off secretly shortly before publishing details of the incident.

The story centers on a younger hack who enjoys the triumph of cracking the link between parliamentarian Markham and a Russian agent, only to discover after the death of his friend that he has been set up by the secret services.

A female character, Nina Beckman (Greta Scacchi), is strangely marginal. By the time she enters center stage as Mullen's journalistic accomplice, her only function is to tie up a few loose ends.

Gabriel Byrne is somewhat one-dimensional as Mullen. He's a perfect foil, however, to the older journalist caught between friendship, the truth and his career. Denholm Elliott gives an extraordinary performance in that role.

■ **DEFENDING YOUR LIFE**

1991, 112 MINS, US
Dir Albert Brooks *Prod* Michael Grillo *Scr* Albert Brooks *Ph* Allen Daviau *Ed* David Finfer
Mus Michael Gore *Art Dir* Ida Random
● Albert Brooks, Meryl Streep, Rip Torn, Lee Grant, Buck Henry, Shirley MacLaine (Geffen)

Defending Your Life is an inventive and mild bit of whimsy from Albert Brooks. The former standup comedian has a little fun with the *Liliom* idea of being judged in a fanciful afterlife, but he doesn't carry his conceit nearly far enough.

Brooks plays his familiar role of a neurotic, warm-hearted, insecure, bull-headed, upper-middle class mensch who, in the opening reel, dies after crashing his showroom-fresh BMW smack into a bus. The unlucky fellow instantly finds himself being whisked off by tram to Judgment City, a white-bread sort of resort community in which a prosecutor and defender present scenes from the life of the deceased to two judges.

The victim is forced to watch particularly embarrassing moments from his life while listening to a torrent of vilification from the prosecutor (Lee Grant) and just a measure of defence from his cheerleader (Rip Torn). Lending all of this some meaning is Meryl Streep, the dream woman who would be the love of his life if only they weren't dead.

■ **DEFENSELESS**

1991, 104 MINS, US
Dir Martin Campbell *Prod* Renee Missel, David Bombyk
Scr James Hicks *Ph* Phil Meheux *Ed* Lou Lombardo, Chris Wimble *Mus* Curt Sobel *Art Dir* Curtis A. Schnell
● Barbara Hershey, Sam Shepard, Mary Beth Hurt, J.T. Walsh, Kellie Overbey, Sheree North (New Visions)

A murder mystery with a fine cast and wild and woolly story, *Defenseless* almost continuously wobbles across the line between the deliberately ambiguous and the irritatingly murky. Barbara Hershey portrays T.K. Katwuller, a Los Angeles attorney who, for psychological reasons that remain unexplored, has managed to make a rather spectacular mess of her life.

T.K. is drawn into a web of lies when she discovers that her lover and client, Steven Seldes (the reliably snaky J.T. Walsh), is married to her long-lost college room-mate Ellie (Mary Beth Hurt). Steven is later found murdered, and the script asks the audience to swallow the idea that T.K., although she is a material witness to the crime, would become defense attorney for Steven's wife, who has been accused in the case.

James Hicks' screenplay, from a story he wrote with Jeff Burkhart, at least gives the actors some strong, if sometimes goofy, emotions to play with, and they generally make the most of them. As a detective on the case, Sam Shepard quietly but intently gets across multiple motives.

New Zealand-born, British-trained director Martin Campbell pushes things a bit too hard at times but must be given credit for the consistent acting.

■ **DEFIANT ONES, THE**

1958, 97 MINS, US
Dir Stanley Kramer *Prod* Stanley Kramer *Scr* Nathan E. Douglas, Harold Jacob Smith *Ph* Sam Leavitt
Ed Frederic Knudtson *Mus* Ernest Gold
Art Dir Rudolph Sternad
● Tony Curtis, Sidney Poitier, Theodore Bikel, Charles McGraw, Cara Williams, Claude Akins (United Artists)

The theme of *The Defiant Ones* is that what keeps men apart is their lack of knowledge of one another. With that knowledge comes respect, and with respect comradeship and even love. This thesis is exercised in terms of a colored and a white man both convicts chained together as they make their break for freedom from a Southern prison gang.

The performances by Tony Curtis and

D

Sidney Poitier are virtually flawless. Poitier captures all of the moody violence of the convict, serving time because he assaulted a white man who had insulted him. It is a cunning, totally intelligent portrayal that rings powerfully true.

As 'Jocker' Jackson, the arrogant white man chained to a fellow convict whom he hates, Curtis delivers a true surprise performance. He starts off as a sneering, brutal character, willing to fight it out to-the-death with his equally stubborn companion. When, in the end, he sacrifices a dash for freedom to save Poitier, he has managed the transition with such skill that sympathy is completely with him.

Picture has other surprises, not the least of which is Kramer's sensitive and skilled direction, this being only his third try at calling the scenes. The scenes of Poitier and Curtis groping their way painfully out of a deep clay pit, their perilous journey down the river, as well as their clumsy attempt to break into a store and the subsequent near-lynch scene, become integral parts of the larger chase, for the posse is never far behind.
□ 1958: Best Original Story & Screenplay, B&W Cinematography.
□ Nominations: Best Picture, Director, Actor (Tony Curtis, Sidney Poitier), Supp. Actor (Theodore Bikel), Supp. Actress (Cara Williams), Editing

■ **DELINQUENTS, THE**

1989, 101 MINS, AUSTRALIA ◇ ⑲ ⊙
Dir Chris Thomson *Prod* Alex Cutler, Michael Wilcox
Scr Clayton Frohman, Mac Gudgeon *Ph* Andrew Lesnie
Ed John Scott *Mus* Miles Goodman *Art Dir* Laurence Eastwood
● Kylie Minogue, Charlie Schlatter, Angela Punch-McGregor, Bruno Lawrence, Desiree Smith, Todd Boyce (Village-Roadster/Silver Lining)

The story, set in the late 1950s, about the passionate love affair of a couple of teens, is trite stuff. Lola (Kylie Minogue) and Brownie (Charles Schlatter) live in the small town of Bundaberg in Queensland. She's still at school when they become lovers and she gets pregnant. The youngsters plan to elope, but are parted by Lola's alcoholic mother (Angela Punch-McGregor), who forces her daughter to have a backstreet abortion (offscreen).

Brownie goes to sea in despair. However, he happen to walk into a Melbourne bar one night and sees Lola, her hair bleached, sadder but wiser. Love blossoms again but, once more, the lovers are parted by the authorities.

The screenplay [from a novel by Criena Rohan] is repetitive and tame. There is no hint of genuine passion between the young lovers. Far more interesting characters are Mavis (Desiree Smith) and Lyle (Todd Boyce) who befriend Lola and Brownie. Their scenes have a warmth that's lacking in the central relationship.

Technically, pic is good, with great care taken to make the late 1950s setting as authentic as possible.

■ **DELIRIOUS**

1991, 96 MINS, US ◇ ⑲ ⊙
Dir Tom Mankiewicz *Prod* Lawrence J. Cohen, Fred Freeman, Doug Claybourne *Scr* Lawrence J. Cohen, Fred Freeman *Ph* Robert Stevens *Ed* William Gordean, Tina Hirsch *Mus* Cliff Eidelman
Art Dir Angelo Graham
● John Candy, Mariel Hemingway, Emma Samms, Raymond Burr, Robert Wagner, David Rasche (M-G-M/Star Partners III)

Delirious is a witless comedy about soap operas in which the estimable John Candy mugs uncomfortably through a desperately unfunny script with a plot as tediously convoluted as those it spoofs.

Candy, as the head writer of a show called *Beyond Our Dreams*, has an unrequited crush on the overripe star (Emma Samms), a clone of Joan Collins' Alexis character on *Dynasty*. Mooning over Samms, who plays a treacherous and sluttish character both on and off the set, Candy naturally overlooks the true girl of his dreams, aspiring actress Mariel Hemingway.

A bump on the head sends Candy into a *Twilight Zone* like reverie in which he finds himself trapped in the fictional small-town setting of his show and inhabiting the character of a Wall Street shark involved with both Samms and Hemingway.

Resemblances to the overly imitated *It's a Wonderful Life* abound in Ashford Falls, a combination of studio backlot and Southern California locations that looks more like the setting for a primetime soap than a daytimer. Lighting, by Robert Stevens, is in the emptily glitzy style of a wine commercial.

■ **DELIVERANCE**

1972, 109 MINS, US ◇ ⑲ ⊙
Dir John Boorman *Prod* John Boorman *Scr* James Dickey *Ph* Vilmos Zsigmond *Ed* Tom Priestley
Art Dir Fred Harpman
● Jon Voight, Burt Reynolds, Ned Beatty, Ronny Cox, Billy McKinney, James Dickey (Warner)

Deliverance can be considered a stark, uncompromising showdown between basic survival instincts against the character pretensions of a mannered and material society.
Unfortunately for John Boorman's heavy film of James Dickey's first novel, it can just as easily be argued as a virile, mountain country transposition of nihilistic, specious philosophising which exploits rather than explores its moments of violent drama.

Against the majestic setting of a river being dammed, Dickey's story takes four city men out for a last weekend trip down the river. Unexpected malevolence forces each to test his personal values in order to survive.

It is, however, in the fleshing out that the script fumbles, and with it the direction and acting. The unofficial group leader of the sailing trip is Burt Reynolds, a volatile, calculating, aggressive and offensive temper of fate.

Why the best friend Jon Voight would maintain an apparent longstanding relationship with Reynolds' character is an early plot chuck-hole.

What makes for a pervading uneasiness is the implication of the story: the strongest shall survive. The values of Reynolds' character are repulsive; Ronny Cox is a cardboard-cutout as an intellectual type; Ned Beatty is the easy-going, middle-class figurehead patronized by both the 'doers' and the 'thinkers' of the world; leaving Voight apparently as the one to lead them out of travail.

In the depiction of sudden, violent death, there is the rhapsodic wallowing in the deadly beauty of it all: protruding arrows, agonizing expiration, etc. It's the stuff of which slapdash oaters and crime programmers are made but the obvious ambitions of *Deliverance* are supposed to be on a higher plane.
□ 1972: Nominations: Best Picture, Director, Editing

■ **DELTA FORCE, THE**

1986, 129 MINS, US ◇ ⑲ ⊙
Dir Menahem Golan *Prod* Menahem Golan, Yoram Globus *Scr* James Bruner, Menahem Golan *Ph* David Gurfinkel *Ed* Alain Jakubowicz *Mus* Alan Silvestri
Art Dir Luciano Spadoni
● Chuck Norris, Lee Marvin, Martin Balsam, Joey Bishop, Robert Forster, Lainie Kazan (Cannon)

Directed with the throttle wide open, pic roots itself firmly in very fresh history, then proceeds to brashly rewrite it, thereby turning itself into an exercise in wish fulfilment for those who favor using force instead of diplomacy.

First hour is mostly devoted to what seems to be a quite accurate rendition of the 1985 TWA Athens hijacking.

From here, film is purest fantasy pitting the noble Yankees against the dirty, low-down Palestinians. In an attempt at 'make my day' immortality, Chuck Norris growls at one of them, 'Sleep tight, sucker,' before blowing him away, and gets a chance to make ample use of his martial arts skills.

■ **DELTA FORCE 2**
THE COLOMBIAN CONNECTION

1990, 105 MINS, US ◇ ⑲ ⊙
Dir Aaron Norris *Prod* Yoram Globus, Chrisopher Pearce *Scr* Lee Reynolds *Ph* Joao Fernandes
Ed Michael J. Duthie *Mus* Frederic Talgorn
● Chuck Norris, Billy Drago, Bobby Chavez, John R. Ryan, Richard Jaeckel, Mateo Gomez (Cannon)

Chuck Norris fans have all they could ask for with *Delta Force 2*. Norris and a dozen US marines fly into the South American drug capital San Carlos, destroy half the country's cocaine production, and rub out the land's untouchable drug czar, a cartharic blaze of exploding missiles and flying fists.

(During the filming, five people were killed in a May 15 1989, helicopter crash in the Philippines: pilot Jo Jo Imperial, stuntmen Geoffrey Brewer, Mike Graham and Gadi Danzig, and gaffer Don Marshall. Three others were injured.)

Production values are high with an endless stream of ammunition and extras. Lensing is pro, and score has a tropical flavor that stays pleasantly in the background.

Norris is a minimalist actor, rightly concentrating on the action. As the sadistic Coda, Billy Drago has a Medusa-like presence that produces shivers just from looking at him.

■ **DEMETRIUS AND THE GLADIATORS**

1954, 101 MINS, US ◇ ⑲ ⊙
Dir Delmer Daves *Prod* Frank Ross *Scr* Philip Dunne *Ph* Milton Krasner *Ed* Dorothy Spencer, Robert Fritch *Mus* Franz Waxman
● Victor Mature, Susan Hayward, Michael Rennie, Debra Paget, Anne Bancroft, Jay Robinson (20th-Century-Fox)

Demetrius and the Gladiators is 20th-Fox's answer and followup to its tremendously successful *The Robe*. While Lloyd C. Douglas's fine novel from which 20th-Fox and Frank Ross filmed *The Robe* springboards this followup, it is a completely new story.

In the compelling screen story, and under the equally compelling direction by Delmer Daves, *Demetrius* swings from *The Robe*'s mysterious, religious miracle theme of the crucifixion, to a story of the trial of a man's faith by the temptations of an attractive, amoral woman and a pagan Rome.

Victor Mature again scores with the character of the slave. A mighty man is he battling three huge tigers in the Roman arena to satisfy the mad urges of the crazy Emperor Caligula and the wicked Messalina, dueling to the death with five of Rome's best gladiators, or making love to the same wicked temptress who has temporarily caused him to forget his God.

With Mature easily winning top acting honors for his splendidly projected Demetrius, he is pressed by Susan Hayward as the evil Messalina, and Jay Robinson, repeating his mad, effeminate Caligula.

■ **DEMI-PARADISE, THE**
(US: Adventure for Two)

1943, 115 MINS, UK ⑲
Dir Anthony Asquith *Prod* Anatole de Grunwald
Scr Anatole de Grunwald *Ph* Bernard Knowles
Mus Nicholas Brodszky

● Laurence Olivier, Penelope Ward, Marjorie Fielding, Margaret Rutherford, Leslie Henson, Felix Aylmer (Two Cities)

Script consists of a wealth of character drawings with a thin web of a story about a young Russian engineer, the inventor of a new-type propellor for use on icebreakers. He arrives in England some months before the war, with humorous misconception the average native of Britain. He is bewildered by its conventions, smugness and capacity for muddling through. It takes him some time to know the people for what they really are, with their foibles, humors and idiosyncrasies. There is a slight love story with an English girl.

Laurence Olivier, replete with Russian accent, gives a dignified and serious performance full of sincerity and repose. Ablest support comes from Felix Aylmer, veteran stage actor, as a wealthy shipbuilder with a series of eccentricities that would excite risibility in a mummy.

■ **DEMON SEED**

1977, 94 MINS, US ◇ ⓥ ⊙
Dir Donald Cammell *Prod* Herb Jaffe *Scr* Ronald Jaffe, Roger O. Hirson *Ph* Bill Butler *Ed* Francisco Mazzola *Mus* Jerry Fielding *Art Dir* Edward C. Carfagno
● Julie Christie, Fritz Weaver, Gerrit Graham, Berry Kroeger, Lisa Lu, Larry J. Blake (M-G-M)

Demon Seed tells of the impregnation of a female by a master computer system which seeks to perpetuate itself in human form. Julie Christie stars as the electronic Eve, along with Fritz Weaver as her scientist husband.

Excellent performances and direction (Donald Cammell), from a most credible and literate screenplay [from a novel by Dean R. Koontz], make production an intriguing achievement in story-telling.

Christie and Weaver live adjacent to an advanced computer center. Their marriage is crumbling because of his commitment to a new machine, Proteus IV, designed to do almost everything but think.

The burden of the story falls on Christie and she does indeed make the film come off.

■ **DENNIS**

See: Dennis The Menace

■ **DENNIS THE MENACE**

(UK: *Dennis*)

1993, 94 MINS, US ◇ ⓥ
Dir Nick Castle *Prod* John Hughes, Richard Vane *Scr* John Hughes *Ph* Thomas Ackerman *Ed* Alan Heim *Mus* Jerry Goldsmith *Art Dir* James Bissell
● Walter Matthau, Mason Gamble, Joan Plowright, Christopher Lloyd, Lea Thompson, Robert Stanton (Warner)

Dennis the Menace isn't really appropriate for anyone over the age of 12. Very young children may find the numbskull, by-the-numbers gags here amusing, but teens will consider this kids' stuff and adults will be pained.

Producer-screenwriter John Hughes continues his march down the age-scale from adolescence to babyhood with the antics of five-year-old Dennis Mitchell, for more than 40 years the star of Hank Ketcham's comic strip, for four years of an early 1960s TV series and now of a syndicated animated series.

There's no plot per se, just one lame gag after another. Opening scene has little blond Dennis (Mason Gamble) casually torturing next-door neighbor Mr Wilson (Walter Matthau) in bed. Natch Dennis' parents (Lea Thompson and Robert Stanton) admonish their sprog to cool it, but soon he's back to his tricks.

In an attempt to introduce some notion of suspense, Hughes drags in a sinister-looking stranger named Switchblade Sam (Christopher Lloyd) who stalks the idyllic town for awhile before kidnapping the little tyke.

The one real pleasure for adults in the film comes from watching Matthau, who has reached deep into his bag of tricks to deliver a huge assortment of slow burns, simmering grimaces, delayed howls and intolerant glances. It's a performance worthy of a real Sunshine boy.

■ **DE SADE**

1969, 113 MINS, US/W. GERMANY ◇
Dir Cy Endfield *Prod* Samuel Z. Arkoff *Scr* Richard Matheson *Ph* Richard Angst *Ed* Max Benedict, Hermann Haller *Mus* Billy Strange *Art Dir* Juergen Kiebach
● Keir Dullea, Senta Berger, Lilli Palmer, Anna Massey, Sonja Ziemann, Uta Levka (American International/CCC/TransContinental)

Pseudo-biography of the young French whippersnapper whose name became a household word. The film transcends reality. Chronology is warped in a continuum of time, fantasy, madness, staged drama and historical incidents.

Dullea's idea of a good time is to dive into a pile of nude women with his pants on, spank a few bottoms, pour wine over everybody, and howl his head off.

De Sade's rather exotic tastes were aggravated by a family-arranged marriage to a very rich girl (Anna Massey) with whose sister (Senta Berger) Dullea is in love.

Lilli Palmer is the mother of both girls, struggling to uphold the family respectability in the midst of her son-in-law's now publicly known debauches. She imparts dignity, strength and, in the end, sympathy to what is written as an unsympathetic role.

■ **DESERT ATTACK**

See: Ice Cold in Alex

■ **DESERT BLOOM**

1986, 104 MINS, US ◇ ⓥ ⊙
Dir Eugene Corr *Prod* Michael Hausman *Scr* Eugene Corr *Ph* Reynaldo Villalobos *Ed* David Garfield, John Currin, Cari Coughlin *Mus* Brad Fiedel *Art Dir* Lawrence Miller
● Jon Voight, JoBeth Williams, Ellen Barkin, Allen Garfield, Annabeth Gish (Carson/Columbia Delphi IV)

Desert Bloom emerges a muted, intelligently observed story of a girl's growing pains in an emotionally deprived and politically warped environment.

Arid setting in question is Las Vegas, 1950, where Second World War vet Jon Voight runs a gas station and is stepfather to JoBeth Williams' three daughters, the oldest of whom is the 13-year-old Rose, played by Annabeth Gish.

Big events in the household are the arrival of the girls' Aunt Starr (Ellen Barkin), a glamorous showgirl type who will live with the family for the 42 days necessary to obtain a quickie divorce, and the impending atmospheric A-bomb test, for which the entire community is preparing a if it were the second coming.

Due to her good housewife role, Williams can do little but be overshadowed by Barkin, who delivers a wonderfully splashy turn as the unlucky but resilient sexpot. Gish is a find as Rose. Obviously bright and physically reminiscent of another actress of about the same age, Jennifer Connelly, she almost single-handedly lends the film its intelligent air and makes one root for Rose to survive her squalid upbringing.

■ **DESERT FOX, THE**

(UK: *Rommel – Desert Fox*)

1951, 88 MINS, US ⓥ
Dir Henry Hathaway *Prod* Nunnally Johnson *Scr* Nunnally Johnson *Ph* Norbert Brodine *Ed* James B. Clark *Mus* Daniele Amfitheatrof *Art Dir* Lyle Wheeler, Maurice Ransford
● James Mason, Cedric Hardwicke, Jessica Tandy, Luther Adler, Everett Sloane, Leo G. Carroll (20th Century-Fox)

The story of Field Marshal Erwin Rommel, as biographed by Brigadier Desmond Young, comes to the screen as an episodic documentary difficult to follow or understand. A controversial angle is posed by the sympathetic pitch made for Rommel by Young, and the whitewashing given a number of Nazi military leaders previously charged with being war criminals by the British.

Battle action in the film is very good, both that concocted in the studio and that snatched from actual war footage. Picture gets off to an unusually sock opening, depicting the November 1941 raid on Rommel's North African headquarters by British Commandos. This all takes place before the title and credits are flashed but the promise is not borne out for a solid war film after narration and episodic character study take over.

Performances are good, with James Mason's portrait of the Desert Fox extremely able within the shadowy confines of the script. His scenes with Jessica Tandy, playing Frau Rommel, have sound emotional value through the underplaying of both performers. Luther Adler's screaming, hysterical Hitler also is good, although confined to brief footage.

■ **DESERT HEARTS**

1985, 93 MINS, US ◇ ⓥ ⊙
Dir Donna Deitch *Prod* Donna Deitch *Scr* Natalie Cooper *Ph* Robert Elswit *Ed* Robert Estrin *Mus* Robert Estrin (sup.) *Art Dir* Jeannine Oppewall
● Helen Shaver, Patricia Charbonneau, Audra Lindley, Andra Akers, Dean Butler, Katie La Bourdette (Goldwyn/Desert Hearts)

The plot focuses on a guest at a Nevada ranch, Vivian Bell, an English Literature lecturer from New York, frozen stiff by middle class morality and inbred prejudices, and totally confused by the drastic step she is about to take at the age of 35. She is about to get divorced.

To make matters much worse for her, once on the ranch she catches the fancy of the owner's adoptive daughter, who starts making advances, first timidly and then in a pressing fashion, until the prim, respectable East Coast intellectual has to drop her armour and face her own latent homosexuality.

Since the story [from the novel *Desert of the Heart* by Jane Rule] is placed in the 1950s, it is clear that what, by today's standards, would have been an unconventional but by no means an exceptional case, becomes an act of defiance against the accepted rules of society.

Helen Shaver, playing the lead, does a most commendable job as a character who starts by being all tied up inside, and ends up by melting and opening up to emotions she couldn't even conceive before.

Patricia Charbonneau, as the avowed lesbian desperate for true affection in female companionship, tends to look too much like the spoiled brat who will have her own way.

■ **DESERT PATROL**

See: Sea of Sand

■ **DESERT RATS, THE**

1953, 88 MINS, US ⓥ
Dir Robert Wise *Prod* Robert L. Jacks *Scr* Richard Murphy *Ph* Lucien Ballard *Ed* Barbara McLean

Mus Leigh Harline   *Art Dir* Lyle R. Wheeler, Addison Hehr
● Richard Burton, Robert Newton, Robert Douglas, James Mason, Torin Thatcher, Chips Rafferty (20th Century-Fox)

Battle of Tobruk is fought in *The Desert Rats* as a followup, but not a sequel, to *The Desert Fox*, the 1951 Field Marshal Rommel feature. Picture is a rather impersonal account of warfare that lacks the controversial flavor of the Rommel treatment. War scenes are realistically staged under Robert Wise's direction, and a high spot in this action is a commando raid on a Nazi ammunition dump.

James Mason is back to repeat his Rommel characterization, but appears only in a few scenes to tie the Tobruk battle in with the Nazi plan of conquest that fell in the desert because of the stubbornness of men on the other side who fought back against terrific odds. Mason's work is good, and Richard Burton is excellent as the British captain in charge of the Australian troops that resist attacks on Tobruk. Robert Newton figures as the third star, playing a drunken old schoolteacher of Burton's, whose cowardice poses a problem for the young officer.
□ 1953: Nomination: Best Story & Screenplay

．．．．．．．．．．．．．．．．．．．．．．．．．

■ **DESERT SONG, THE**

1929, 125 MINS, US
Dir Roy Del Ruth   *Scr* Harvey Gates   *Ph* Bernard McGill   *Ed* Ralph Dawson
● John Boles, Carlotta King, Louise Fazenda, Johnny Arthur, Edward Martindale, Myrna Loy (Warner)

Taking another step forward in the talking field by doing an operetta, following the story in detail and getting in the entire musical score and compositions, Warner Brothers have a winner. The only departures are for those scenes narrated in dialog such as the riding of the Riffs and desert perspectives.

Story starts off rather slowly with the unfolding of the identity of the Red Shadow (John Boles) by himself to his two faithful followers, but straightens itself out after the picture has run for an hour. Through it all there is little of the romantic on the screen as the principal players were chosen more for their voices than for ability to act screen roles.

Boles and Carlotta King do exceptionally well on the screen and, though they may be more convincing on the stage, their conceptions of the film characters are sincere and not flavoring of saccharine. Johnny Arthur as Benny Kid is exceptional. Aided by Louise Fazenda, as Susan, he supplies the lighter moments. Picture cost nearly $600,000.

．．．．．．．．．．．．．．．．．．．．．．．．．

■ **DESERT SONG, THE**

1944, 90 MINS, US ◇
Dir Robert Florey   *Prod* Robert Florey   *Scr* Robert Buckner   *Ph* Bert Glennon   *Ed* Frank Magee   *Mus* Sigmund Romberg   *Art Dir* Charles Novi
● Dennis Morgan, Irene Manning, Bruce Cabot, Victor Francen, Lynn Overman (Warner)

In modernizing story, German agents and plans to construct new railroad in North Africa for terminus at Dakar provide motivation for Riff uprising and leadership by Dennis Morgan, an American piano player in Morocco nightspot, who's been fighting Franco in Spain prior to moving across the Mediterranean to Africa. Irene Manning is the new singer at the cafe, with mutual romance developing.

Riffs are rounded up by French officers to work on the railroad, with native Victor Francen, a tool of the Nazis, impressing the natives to work. But Morgan, as El Khobar, leader of the Riffs, circumvents the plans by periodic appearances on the desert and in Morocco to lead the natives in revolt against

the forced labor regulations. From there on it's series of chases across the desert sands, pitched battles, and wild adventure.

Despite modernization to provide film technique and movement to the operetta, basic entertainment qualities of *Desert Song* are retained to provide most diverting audience reaction at this time.

Morgan is neatly cast as the Red Rider, delivering both dramatic and vocal assignments in top style. Manning capably handles the girl spot as singer and actress.
□ 1944: Nomination: Best Color Art Direction

．．．．．．．．．．．．．．．．．．．．．．．．．

■ **DESERT SONG, THE**

1953, 110 MINS, US ◇
Dir Bruce Humberstone   *Prod* Rudi Fehr   *Scr* Roland Kibbee   *Ph* Robert Burks   *Ed* William Ziegler   *Mus* Ray Heindorf (dir.), Max Steiner (adapt.)   *Art Dir* Stanley Fleischer
● Kathryn Grayson, Gordon MacRae, Steve Cochran, Raymond Massey, Dick Wesson, Allyn McLerie (Warner)

After two times around as a film vehicle, once in 1929 and again in 1943, this venerable romantic musical has just about run out of entertainment vitamins. Both story and the songs are well-worn [from the 1926 musical play by Otto Harbach, Oscar Hammerstein II, Sigmund Romberg and Frank Mandel]. Latter wear their age with charm and are nicely delivered by Kathryn Grayson and Gordon MacRae, but aren't of sufficient impact to create much of a stir in this era. Listening best are the title number, 'The Riff Song' and 'One Alone', as well as added Jack Scholl-Serge Walter cleffing, 'Gay Parisienne', which Grayson uses as a special piece.

Making a pretty picture is Grayson, and she serves up her tunes well. MacRae is unbelievable as the mysterious Riff leader, but fares better on the songs. Steve Cochran also has a hard time making anything out of his French legionnaire role, a character who is bothered both by Grayson, the general's flighty daughter, and by the fact he can't capture the Riff hero who plays Robin Hood to the natives oppressed by Raymond Massey, a cruel sheik who is plotting to overthrow the French.

．．．．．．．．．．．．．．．．．．．．．．．．．

■ **DESIGN FOR LIVING**

1933, 90 MINS, US
Dir Ernst Lubitsch   *Prod* Ernst Lubitsch   *Scr* Ben Hecht   *Ph* Victor Milner   *Ed* Francis Marsh
● Fredric March, Gary Cooper, Miriam Hopkins, Edward Everett Horton, Franklin Pangborn, Isabel Jewell (Paramount)

Ben Hecht's screen treatment has transmuted Noel Coward's idea better than Coward's original play. It's a competent job in every respect. What matter it – or perhaps it does – if Hecht threw Coward's manuscript out the window and set about writing brand new play? The dialog is less lofty, less epigrammatic, less artificial. There's more reality.

Coward, of course, has contributed a basic premise that's arresting – a girl and two men all of whom are very fond of each other. Edward Everett Horton, as the patient mentor of the girl (or, as the dialog puts it, 'in other words, you never got to first base'), is built up here, as much by the script as his own personal histrionic dominance.

Miriam Hopkins' expert handling of the delicate premise which motivates the other three men is a consummate performance in every respect. She glosses over the dirt, but gets the punch over none the less. She confesses quite naively she is stumped – she likes both Tom and George (Fredric March and Gary Cooper).

Hecht patterns Cooper to a rugged chapeau and March to a more formal top-piece, and

Hopkins interprets her reactions in relation to wearing one type of hat or another with the shifting moods.

．．．．．．．．．．．．．．．．．．．．．．．．．

■ **DESIGNING WOMAN**

1957, 117 MINS, US ◇ ⓦ
Dir Vincente Minnelli   *Prod* Dore Schary   *Scr* George Wells   *Ph* John Alton   *Ed* Adrienne Fazan   *Mus* Andre Previn   *Art Dir* Cedric Gibbons
● Gregory Peck, Lauren Bacall, Dolores Gray, Sam Levene, Tom Helmore, Mickey Shaughnessy (M-G-M)

Dore Schary's last personal effort before exiting the Metro lot is a Runyonesque-type romp, based on a 'suggestion' by designer Helen Rose and deftly directed by Vincente Minnelli. It cleverly brings together the worlds of haute couture, sports (particularly boxing), show business, and the underworld.

Gregory Peck, a crusading sports writer, marries Lauren Bacall, a prominent fashion designer, and abandons his cluttered Greenwich Village apartment for her elegant East Side abode. Her friends are the chi chi set; his cronies are fellow sports scribes and Stillman Gym characters. The never-the-twain-shall-meet groups get together at their apartment when there's a conflict between his weekly poker game and a reading for a Broadway musical for which she is designing the costumes.

Bacall, turning to comedy, is excellent as the fashion designer confronted by the world of fisticuffs. Peck is fine as the confused sportswriter and Dolores Gray scores solidly as his ex-girl friend. Topnotch characterizations are also turned in by Sam Levene, as the *Front Page*-type sports editor, Tom Helmore as the producer, Jack Cole as a choreographer, Jesse White as a peddler of information, and Chuck Connors as a mobster.

．．．．．．．．．．．．．．．．．．．．．．．．．

■ **DESIRE**

1936, 95 MINS, US ◇ ⓦ
Dir Frank Borzage   *Prod* Ernst Lubitsch   *Scr* Edwin Justus Mayer, Waldemar Young, Samuel Hoffenstein   *Ph* Charles Lang   *Ed* William Shea   *Mus* Frederick Hollander   *Art Dir* Hans Dreier, Robert Usher
● Marlene Dietrich, Gary Cooper, John Halliday, William Frawley, Ernest Cossart (Paramount)

Desire is the first Marlene Dietrich and Gary Cooper picture since *Morocco* (1930). The two stars work unusually well as a pair.

The direction is subtle and inspired, with many smart little Lubitschian touches adding to the general appeal of the yarn [by Hans Szekely and R.A. Stemmle] and its plot. Dietrich plays a jewel thief who gains possession of a valuable string of pearls. About half the footage is concerned with the efforts of Dietrich and a confederate to retrieve the pearls from Cooper who unknowingly has become their custodian.

The love scenes are excellently handled and written. A very good sequence is framed for the meeting between Cooper and the bogus nobleman, her accomplice, while another occurs later when efforts are made to get the two stars out of their beds one morning. The hand of producer Ernst Lubitsch is apparent here and in many other portions of the smartly-piloted romantic comedy.

．．．．．．．．．．．．．．．．．．．．．．．．．

■ **DESIRE & HELL AT SUNSET MOTEL**

1992, 90 MINS, US ◇ ⓦ
Dir Alien Castle   *Prod* Donald P. Borchers   *Scr* Alien Castle   *Ph* Jamie Thompson   *Ed* James Gavin Bedford   *Mus* Alien Castle, Doug Walter   *Art Dir* Michael Clausen
● Sherilyn Fenn, Whip Hubley, David Hewlett, David Johansen, Paul Bartel (Heron/Image)

The visuals are all that stand out in this low-budget sex comedy noir set against the stylish 1950s motifs of the turquoise-and-sand

Sunset Motel. Debuting writer-director Alien Castle, striving for a tongue-in-cheek blend of *Niagara* and *Union City*, has produced a vague, immature scenario that's as glossy and empty as the LA it parodies.

Sherilyn Fenn stars as the knockout wife of toy salesman (Whip Hubley) who checks them into the Sunset Motel in 1950s Anaheim for a sale meeting while she tries to get him to take her to Disneyland. Monkey business in no time, with Fenn toying with an amorous guy (David Johansen) who's got some anti-American goods on her husband; Hubley hiring a beatnik criminal (David Hewlitt) to spy on his wife, and blackmail and mayhem ensuing in a badly jumbled plot that isn't worth sorting out.

Fenn, in a bombshell role and easily as photogenic as Madonna, finds a light sensual style pretty much her own, but Hubley generates no sparks as her husband.

■ DESIREE

1954, 110 MINS, US ⑩

Dir Henry Koster   *Prod* Julian Blaustein   *Scr* Daniel Taradash   *Ph* Milton Krasner   *Ed* William Reynolds   *Mus* Alex North   *Art Dir* Lyle Wheeler, Leland Fuller
● Marlon Brando, Jean Simmons, Merle Oberon, Michael Rennie, Cameron Mitchell, Elizabeth Sellars (20th Century-Fox)

There is a theory in Hollywood that nothing bogs down a historical film as easily as the facts of history. It is a maxim which 20th-Fox must have had very much in mind when it CinemaScoped Annemarie Selinko's best-selling novel, *Desiree*.

It tells the story of Desiree, daughter of a Marseilles silk merchant, who meets an impoverished general, Napoleon Bonaparte. They plan to marry. But Napoleon goes to Paris and there meets and weds the rich and influential Josephine. Desiree marries Bernadotte, one of France's most successful generals, who later splits with the emperor and becomes regent – and finally king – of Sweden.

As Napoleon, Brando draws a portrait of a man so sure of the righteousness of his cause that no sacrifice is too great in accomplishing his ends. His Napoleon is arrogant, scheming and temperamental, and yet oddly human in his failings.

Jean Simmons as Desiree is lovely, innocent and naive, as prescribed.

■ DESIRE ME

1947, 90 MINS, US

Dir [George Cukor, Mervyn LeRoy, Jack Conway]   *Prod* Arthur Hornblow Jr   *Scr* Marguerite Roberts, Zoe Akins   *Ph* Joseph Ruttenberg   *Ed* Joseph Dervin   *Mus* Herbert Stothart   *Art Dir* Cedric Gibbons, Urie McCleary
● Greer Garson, Robert Mitchum, Richard Hart, George Zucco, Morris Ankrum (M-G-M)

Against the technical excellence of mounting, a confused flashback plot [based on the novel, *Karl und Anna*, by Leonhard Frank] is unfolded. Offered is a story of a wife who, after long years of faithful waiting, succumbs to lonesomeness on the eve of her supposedly dead husband's return from war. The husband kills his rival in a struggle. Locale is a small fishing village on the coast of Normandy and catches interest with colorful settings and seascapes.

Flashbacks within flashbacks make plot hard to follow as the wife talks over her story – and what caused it – with a doctor. There is no director credit, picture having had several during its long camera career, so kudos for some topnotch atmospheric effects, a number of strong, emotional scenes and occasional suspense go uncredited. George Cukor started it and Mervyn LeRoy finished it, but

neither wants the credit apparently. Otherwise pace is slow and interest slack.

Greer Garson's role requires continual emotional stress that makes for a heavy job but she is capable. Robert Mitchum has too little footage as the husband but he makes every scene count. Richard Hart, the betrayer of the faithful wife, is permitted to overstress his designs where underplaying would have aided.

■ DESIRE UNDER THE ELMS

1958, 111 MINS, US ⑩ ⊙

Dir Delbert Mann   *Prod* Don Hartman   *Scr* Irwin Shaw   *Ph* Daniel L. Fapp   *Ed* George Boemler   *Mus* Elmer Bernstein   *Art Dir* Hal Pereira, J. McMillan Johnson
● Sophia Loren, Anthony Perkins, Burl Ives, Frank Overton, Pernell Roberts, Rebecca Welles (Paramount)

Despite all the plus factors, *Desire under the Elms* is not satisfactory entertainment. It is painfully slow in getting underway, the characters are never completely understandable or believable, and the ghastly plot climax (of infanticide) plays with disappointingly little force.

Eugene O'Neill's play has been given a reverent translation. But Irwin Shaw, who did the screenplay, has not improved the story. O'Neill wrote a modern version of a Greek tragedy, as raw and chilling as anything in *Oedipus* or *Medea*. He chose the craggy New England of 1840 and its flinty characters with care. The casting of Sophia Loren in the role of the young (third) wife of farmer Burl Ives is a key error because it injects an alien-to-the-scene element that dislocates the drama permanently.

The passion of greed and lust that takes place, in which Anthony Perkins and Loren embark on a semi-incestuous love affair that ends with Loren's having a child that Ives thinks his, has been handled with discretion. Too much, perhaps.

O'Neill saw it as men fighting the gods and losing. Shaw apparently sees it as men understood through modern psychology, still doomed and damned, but for different reasons.

Despite Loren's unsuitability for the play, she exposes a great variety of emotion and manages the scenes of tenderness with special value. Perkins' character is not as exciting or vivid as it should be. Ives is the best, a bull of a man, cold in emotion a hot in passion.

■ DESPAIR

1978, 119 MINS, W. GERMANY ◇ ⑩

Dir Rainer Werner Fassbinder   *Scr* Tom Stoppard   *Ph* Michael Ballhaus   *Ed* Juliane Lorrenz, Franz Walsch   *Mus* Peer Raben   *Art Dir* Rolf Zehetbauer
● Dirk Bogarde, Andrea Ferreol, Volker Spengler, Klaus Lowitsch (Bavaria Atelier/SFP/Geria)

Despite a witty, albeit theatrical, script by Tom Stoppard, prolific German director Rainer Werner Fassbinder does not quite bring off the spirited linguistic innovations, wit and penetrating insights of Vladimir Nabokov's novel; but it is a good try. This tale of an exiled Russian in Germany in the late 1920s, who is driven to a weird murder, emerges over-long.

Dirk Bogarde, using a generally satisfactory Russo accent, has a pulpy, dim-witted, sensual wife, played in campy period style by Andrea Ferreol. He runs a chocolate factory that is going on the rocks as the Depression hits the world.

He has strange delusions of seeing another replica of himself watching his carryings-on with his wife or even imagining himself dressed as a budding Nazi going in for macho sadistic sexual actions.

He insures himself and then, on a business

trip, meets a down-and-out whom, he thinks, looks just like him. He decides to use this man in a trumped-up action that may be a holdup, but is aimed at killing the man, passing him off as himself and collecting his insurance.

■ DESPERATE

1947, 73 MINS, US ⑩

Dir Anthony Mann   *Prod* Michel Kraike   *Scr* Harry Essex, Martin Rackin   *Ph* George E. Diskant   *Ed* Marston Fay   *Mus* Paul Sawtell   *Art Dir* Albert S. D'Agostino, Walter E. Keller
● Steve Brodie, Audrey Long, Raymond Burr, Jason Robards Sr (RKO)

Desperate is a ripsnorting gangster meller. Yarn is strictly one of those things, and not unfamiliar.

Steve Brodie, honest truckdriver, becomes involved innocently in a fur warehouse robbery and cop slaying. He's beaten up by the mobsters when they realize he tipped off the police. Brodie flees with his wife, fearing gangster vengeance since the mobster's brother is captured and charged with murder. From then on, picture becomes more or less a continuing flight of Brodie and his wife Audrey Long, both from the gendarmes and the gangsters.

Surprise ending gives film a lift. Anthony Mann's direction mainly stresses suspense, being done skillfully.

Brodie is okay as the honest truckman who gets into one jam after another. Long, as his wife, shapes up nicely; at times she resembles Ginger Rogers.

■ DESPERATE HOURS, THE

1955, 112 MINS, US ⑩ ⊙

Dir William Wyler   *Prod* William Wyler   *Scr* Joseph Hayes   *Ph* Lee Garmes   *Ed* Robert Swink   *Mus* Gail Kubik   *Art Dir* Hal Pereira, Joseph MacMillan Johnson
● Humphrey Bogart, Fredric March, Arthur Kennedy, Martha Scott, Dewey Martin, Gig Young (Paramount)

Desperate Hours is an expert adaptation by Joseph Hayes of his own novel about three escaped desperadoes who gunpoint their way to temporary refuge in the suburban Indianapolis home of a respectable middleclass family.

This is a first for VistaVision in black and white. Wise, too, for color might have rendered less effective the strong fact-like appearance of *Hours*.

Wyler worked with major-league performers. This is Humphrey Bogart in the type of role that cues comics to caricature takeoffs. Here he's at his best, a tough gunman capable of murder, snarling delight with the way his captives must abide by his orders, and wise in the ways of self-preservation strategy.

Fredric March is powerful as head of the family, never before cited for bravery but now bent on protecting his family from the three intruders.

■ DESPERATE HOURS

1990, 105 MINS, US ◇ ⑩ ⊙

Dir Michael Cimino   *Prod* Dino De Laurentiis, Michael Cimino   *Scr* Laurence Konner, Mark Rosenthal, Joseph Hayes   *Ph* Doug Milsome   *Ed* Peter Hunt   *Mus* David Mansfield   *Art Dir* Victoria Paul
● Mickey Rourke, Anthony Hopkins, Mimi Rogers, Lindsay Crouse, Kelly Lynch, David Morse (De Laurentiis)

Desperate Hours is a coldly mechanical and uninvolving remake of the 1955 Bogart pic *The Desperate Hours*, with Mickey Rourke as the hood terrorizing a suburban family.

Joseph Hayes' plot (first written as a novel, then as a [1955] play) is pure 1950s paranoia about three scruffy guys who invade the sanctity of the home, mocking a family's helplessness until Dad reasserts his control. Despite

D

being minimally updated with intensified blood and brutality on the part of the hoods and the authorities, *Desperate Hours* has no new insights to offer.

The clunky script doesn't permit any vestige of humanity to Rourke, who's portrayed as a simple psycho with a low flashpoint, viciously brutalizing his improbably gorgeous pro-bono lawyer (Kelly Lynch) even as she helps him escape from prison.

Anthony Hopkins, in the Fredric March role of the initially weak-seeming father, brings his formidable skills to the task of involving the audience in the family's terror, but he seems mismatched with his estranged wife Mimi Rogers and implausibly reckless in his defiance of Rourke.

In place of the original film's sheriff (Arthur Kennedy), who made it a priority to avoid endangering the lives of the hostages, the Cimino version has a demented FBI agent (Lindsay Crouse).

Doug Milsome contributes handsome lensing of the autumnal locations of the Colorado wilderness and suburban Salt Lake City (substituting for the Indianapolis setting of the original).

● ● ● ● ● ● ● ● ● ● ● ● ● ● ● ● ● ● ●

■ DESPERATELY SEEKING SUSAN

1985, 104 MINS, US ◇ ▼ ☉
Dir Susan Seidelman   *Prod* Sarah Pillsbury, Midge Sanford   *Scr* Leora Barish   *Ph* Edward Lachman   *Ed* Andrew Mondshein   *Mus* Thomas Newman   *Art Dir* Santo Loquasto
● Rosanna Arquette, Madonna, Aidan Quinn, Mark Blum, Robert Joy, Laurie Metcalf (Orion)

Rosanna Arquette does more than her share in the pivotal part of a bored Yuppie housewife who follows the personal ads, wondering about the identities behind a 'desperately seeking Susan' item that runs from time to time.

The ads are the way one boyfriend (Robert Joy) communicates with free-spirited Madonna between her street-life liaisons with other men, one of whom has been bumped off after stealing a pair of rare Egyptian earrings. Before his demise, Madonna has lifted the jewelry, thinking they are trinkets.

Drawn by curiosity to spy on Madonna, Arquette winds up with a bump on the head and a case of amnesia, complicated by the fact that Joy's pal Aidan Quinn thinks Arquette is Madonna and Arquette doesn't know she isn't.

All of this is cause for consistent smiling and a few outright laughs, without ever building to complete comedy. It's not clear either that director Susan Seidelman and writer Leora Barish ever intend for it to be funnier, so that can't be faulted.

● ● ● ● ● ● ● ● ● ● ● ● ● ● ● ● ● ● ●

■ DESPERATE REMEDIES

1993, 93 MINS, NEW ZEALAND ◇ ▼
Dir Stewart Main, Peter Wells   *Prod* James Wallace   *Scr* Stewart Main, Peter Wells   *Ph* Leon Narbey   *Ed* David Coulson   *Mus* Peter Scholes   *Art Dir* Michael Kane
● Jennifer Ward-Lealand, Kevin Smith, Lisa Chappell, Cliff Curtis, Michael Hurst, Kiri Mills (Wallace)

An extravagant, opulent and mostly enjoyable exercise in high camp (or low kitsch), this ambitious first feature from Stewart Main and Peter Wells has 'cult item' written all over it.

Set in the mythical colonial seaport of Hope some time during the 19th century where Dorothea (Jennifer Ward-Lealand), an elegantly beautiful draper who likes to dress entirely in scarlet, lives with her assistant, Anne (Lisa Chappell), and worries about her young sister, Rose (Kiri Mills), addicted to opium thanks to a liaison with the sinister Fraser (Cliff Curtis).

Dorothea hires a handsome, penniless immigrant, Lawrence (Kevin Smith), to seduce Rose away from Fraser; instead, Lawrence falls for Dorothea.

All this is played out against a background of extravagantly stylized sets, magnificently designed costumes, and deafening opera music by Verdi and Berlioz. The corn is high, but the film is lots of fun, probably primarily appealing to a gay crowd.

● ● ● ● ● ● ● ● ● ● ● ● ● ● ● ● ● ● ●

■ DESTRY RIDES AGAIN

1939, 90 MINS, US ▼ ☉
Dir George Marshall   *Prod* Joe Pasternak   *Scr* Felix Jackson, Gertrude Purcell, Henry Myers   *Ph* Hal Mohr   *Ed* Milton Carruth   *Mus* Frank Skinner   *Art Dir* Jack Otterson, Martin Obzina
● Marlene Dietrich, James Stewart, Charles Winninger, Mischa Auer, Brian Donlevy, Allen Jenkins (Universal)

Destry Rides Again is anything but a super-western. It's just plain, good entertainment [from an original story by Felix Jackson suggested by Max Brand's novel], primed with action and laughs and human sentiment.

Marlene Dietrich's work a the hardened, ever-scrapping ginmill entertainer serves pretty much as the teeterboard from which this picture flips itself from the level of the ordinary western into a class item.

This gangster fable with an early West background revolves for the most part around the rowdy, gaudy ginmill and dancehall which Brian Donlevy operates in the frontier town of Bottle Neck. With the aid of his No. 1 entertainer (Dietrich), Donlevy cuts a wide swath cheating the townsmen at cards and working a waterhole racket until he makes the mistake of appointing the town rumpot (Charles Winninger) the local sheriff.

● ● ● ● ● ● ● ● ● ● ● ● ● ● ● ● ● ● ●

■ DETECTIVE, THE

1968, 114 MINS, US ◇ ▼
Dir Gordon Douglas   *Prod* Aaron Rosenberg   *Scr* Abby Mann   *Ph* Joseph Biroc   *Ed* Robert Simpson   *Mus* Jerry Goldsmith   *Art Dir* Jack Martin Smith, William Creber
● Frank Sinatra, Lee Remick, Ralph Meeker, Jaqueline Bisset, Jack Klugman, Horace McMahon (20th Century-Fox)

Although extremely well cast, and fleshed out with some on-target dialog, Abby Mann's script is strictly potboiler material.

Homosexuality, police brutality, corruption in high places, and nymphomania are the peas in this literary shell game, which the admirable professional razzle-dazzle of direction, acting and, to an extent, editing, cannot sufficiently legitimize.

Jack Klugman and Frank Sinatra are the only honest cops portrayed. Ralph Meeker is on the take, Robert Duvall likes to bust 'queers,' and Al Freeman Jr decides in time that Nazi-style interrogation produces desired results.

Repeated plot digression – made bearable by the fact that it involves Lee Remick – explores Sinatra's unstable married life.

The promise of erudition in the first reel gives way to programmer superficiality about the two main themes. For one thing, homosexuality is depicted as rampant in either truck stops, or else cheaply elegant salons. Also, the plot is heavily weighted against the police.

● ● ● ● ● ● ● ● ● ● ● ● ● ● ● ● ● ● ●

■ DETECTIVE STORY

1951, 105 MINS, US ▼
Dir William Wyler   *Prod* William Wyler   *Scr* Philip Yordan, Robert Wyler   *Ph* Lee Garmes   *Ed* Robert Swink   *Art Dir* Hal Pereira, Earl Hedrick
● Kirk Douglas, Eleanor Parker, William Bendix, Lee Grant, Cathy O'Donnell, Joseph Wiseman (Paramount)

William Wyler has polished the legit hit by Pulitzer-prizewinner Sidney Kingsley into a cinematic gem. Scripters have stuck almost to the letter of the original play. Even the location seldom changes from Kingsley's single set, the realistic headquarters room of the detective squad.

Kirk Douglas is the tortured detective determined unswervingly to do his duty as he sees it. Hunting an illicit doctor who has been delivering illegitimate children, Douglas suddenly finds himself being virtually blackmailed by the medico. Douglas' wife, long before she married him, had occasion to use the charlatan's services – and the doctor hadn't forgotten.

Eleanor Parker plays the wife with a dignity and emotional depth that makes a dramatic highlight of the scene in which she is forced to reveal her past. The personal drama is played against a broad and entertaining mosaic of other drama, humor and young love in the busy squad room. Lee Grant repeats one of the memorable stage roles of recent years as a pathetic albeit amusing little Brooklynesque femme shoplifter. Another holdover from the legiter, Joseph Wiseman, is tops as a sneering, dope-filled larcenist.

The unfrocked physician was an abortionist in the original. Screen version has him actually delivering the illicit children.
☐ 1951: Nominations: Best Director, Actress (Eleanor Parker), Supp. Actress (Lee Grant), Screenplay

● ● ● ● ● ● ● ● ● ● ● ● ● ● ● ● ● ● ●

■ DETOUR

1945, 67 MINS, US ▼ ☉
Dir Edgar G. Ulmer   *Prod* Leon Fromkess   *Scr* Martin Goldsmith   *Ph* Benjamin H. Kline   *Ed* George McGuire   *Mus* Leo Ordody   *Art Dir* Edward C. Jewell
● Tom Neal, Ann Savage, Claudia Drake, Edmund MacDonald, Tim Ryan, Esther Howard (PRC)

Detour falls short of being a sleeper because of a flat ending and its low-budgeted production mountings. Uniformly good performances and some equally good direction and dialog keep the meller moving, however.

Theme is the buffeting that man gets from the fates. Story revolves around Tom Neal as a down-and-out young pianist hitchhiking his way to the Coast. Director Edgar G. Ulmer achieves some steadily-mounting suspense as the pianist becomes implicated in two murders, neither of which he's committed. So he begins hitchhiking his way back east. Story is told by Neal in flashback.

Neal, who's been kicking around for some time in these minor items, does well with a difficult role that rates him a break in something better. Ann Savage is convincing as a tough girl of the roads and gets off some rough lines.

Benjamin H. Kline contributes some outstanding camera work that helps the flashback routine come off well. Leo Ordody's score, revolving around some Chopin themes, aids in backing up the film's grim mood.

● ● ● ● ● ● ● ● ● ● ● ● ● ● ● ● ● ● ●

■ DETOUR

1993, 89 MINS, US ◇ ▼ ☉
Dir Wade Williams   *Prod* Wade Williams   *Scr* Roger Hull, Wade Williams   *Ph* Jeff Richardson   *Ed* Herbert L Strock   *Mus* Bill Crain
● Tom Neal Jr, Lea Lavish, Erin McGrane, Duke Howze, Susanna Foster, Brad Bittiker (Williams)

Fans of Edgar G. Ulmer's noir classic, *Detour*, are in for a disappointment: Wade Williams' low-budget remake features both laughable dialogue and inept acting. And despite vintage cars and flashing neon, the attempt to create a period look is only intermittently successful.

The plot, and even some of the dialogue, is straight out of the hard-boiled original. Like the 1945 film, the remake centers on the incredibly bad fortune of Al Roberts (Tom Neal

Jr, whose father played the same part in the first *Detour*).

The film flashes back to a New York club, where he accompanies the singer Sue Harvey (Erin McGrane). Roberts falls in love with her, but she leaves him behind to try her luck in Los Angeles.

The remake's only significant departure from the original is in devoting more time to the singer's character in L.A. Unfortunately, her scenes are among the film's weakest.

● ●

■ DEVIL AND DANIEL WEBSTER, THE
(UK: All That Money Can Buy; Daniel and the Devil)

1941, 100 MINS, US ▼ ⊙

Dir William Dieterle   *Prod* William Dieterle   *Scr* Dan Totheroh, Stephen Vincent Benet   *Ph* Joseph August   *Ed* Robert Wise   *Mus* Bernard Herrmann   *Art Dir* Van Nest Polglase

● Edward Arnold, Walter Huston, Jane Darwell, Simone Simon, Anne Shirley, John Qualen (RKO)

Material for the screenplay is taken from Stephen Vincent Benet's short story, an O. Henry prize-winner, and the author had a hand in the film version with Dan Totheroh.

The locale is New Hampshire, in 1840, a background of muddy roads, Currier Ives farm settings, and peopled with struggling American peasantry. The legend is about the rise, fall and regeneration of a young farmer, Jabez Stone, who is alleged to have sold his soul to the devil for a pittance of gold and seven years of good luck. It's a twist on the Faust theme, but Benet isn't Goethe.

James Craig plays the youth who discovers that crime doesn't pay. He is a quite capable young actor, of pleasing appearance. Anne Shirley is the wife, who gets all the worst of it, and Jane Darwell is the rock-bound New England mother.

Trouble for Dieterle (and the audience) starts when Walter Huston appears on the scene via double-exposure and whispers beguiling temptations into the ear of the young husband-farmer. That's when gold coins appear from strange places and the boy pays off the mortgage. From there to the finish it's mostly symbols and morality play.

[Pic was previewed under the title *Here Is a Man*.]

□ 1941: Best Scoring of a Dramatic Picture.

□ Nomination: Best Actor (Walter Huston)

● ●

■ DEVIL AND MISS JONES, THE

1941, 92 MINS, US ▼

Dir Sam Wood   *Prod* Frank Ross   *Scr* Norman Krasna   *Ph* Harry Stradling   *Ed* Sherman Todd

● Jean Arthur, Charles Coburn, Robert Cummings, Edmund Gwenn, S.Z. Sakall, Spring Byington (RKO)

In a foreword, audiences are informed that this is a fanciful and imaginative story, put on the record mainly for amusement purposes. *The Devil and Miss Jones* then unwinds a light and fluffy tale of the richest man in the world who loses his stern front through association with the employees of one of his enterprises – a department store.

Jean Arthur is the Miss Jones, a decidedly personable salesgirl who takes the elderly shoe clerk under her wing to guide him through the intricacies of store routine. Charles Coburn is the richest man who steps into the store job incognito to ferret out the leaders of a union organization.

Coburn's performance as the millionaire who gradually unbends stands out as a fine characterization. Arthur excellently grooves as the salesgirl, but Robert Cummings' characterization is over-sketched in the main as a union organiser. Sam Wood injects deft direction with human byplay to lift the script considerably.

□ 1941: Nominations: Best Supp. Actor (Charles Coburn), Original Screenplay

● ●

■ DEVIL AT 4 O'CLOCK, THE

1961, 125 MINS, US ◇ ▼ ⊙

Dir Mervyn LeRoy   *Prod* Fred Kohlmar   *Scr* Liam O'Brien   *Ph* Joseph Biroc   *Ed* Charles Nelson   *Mus* George Duning   *Art Dir* John Beckman

● Spencer Tracy, Frank Sinatra, Kerwin Mathews, Jean-Pierre Aumont, Gregoire Aslan, Barbara Luna (Columbia)

A small volcanic South Seas isle makes a colorful setting for this tale of heroism and sacrifice, but vying with interest in characterizations are the exceptional special effects of an island being blown to pieces.

Based on a novel by Max Catto plot is off the beaten path for an adventure yarn. Story is of a priest (Spencer Tracy) who with three convicts (Frank Sinatra, Gregoire Aslan, Bernie Hamilton) saves the lives of the children in a mountain-top leper hospital by leading them throug fire and lava flow to the coast and a waiting schooner after the volcano erupts and island is doomed to certain destruction.

Tracy delivers one of his more colorful portrayals in his hard-drinking cleric who has lost faith in his God, walloping over a character which sparks entire action of film. Sinatra's role, first-class but minor in comparison, is overshadowed in interest by Aslan, one of the convicts in a stealing part who lightens some of the more dramatic action. Third con, Hamilton also delivers solidly as the strong man who holds up a tottering wooden bridge over a deep gorge while the children and others from hospital cross to safety.

Special effects of Larry Butler and Willis Cook highlight the picture, filmed impressively by Joseph Biroc on the vivid island of Maui in the Hawaiian group.

● ●

■ DEVIL-DOLL, THE

1936, 70 MINS, US ▼

Dir Tod Browning   *Prod* Edward J. Mannix   *Scr* Garrett Fort, Guy Endore, Erich von Stroheim   *Ph* Leonard Smith   *Ed* Frederick Y. Smith   *Mus* Franz Waxman

● Lionel Barrmore, Maureen O'Sullivan, Frank Lawton, Robert Greig, Lucy Beaumont, Henry B. Walthall (M-G-M)

The premise [from the novel *Burn, Witch, Burn* by Abraham Merritt] is a scientist's discovery of a process by which all living things, including humans, can be reduced to one-sixth their normal size. The director, cameraman and art department make the most of it, but the writers' contribution is lacking in originality and seldom is equal to the idea in back of it.

Lionel Barrymore, as a framed convict named Lavond and later in the disguise of old Madam Mandelip, is a scientific Count of Monte Cristo who avenges his false imprisonment. His companion in a prison escape is the inventor of the atom-shrinking process. The inventor dies on the first night of freedom and Barrymore carries on the 'great work' with the man's crazy widow

Two of the big moments derive their power from camerawork, while the third is a remake by Tod Browning of the scene which highlighted his *Unholy Three* (1925). Once again the stolen jewels are concealed in a toy doll and the police inspect has them in his grasp without knowing it.

For Barrymore the leading part is a field day. Rafaela Ottiano, with a white streak in her hair and hobbling on a crutch, is convincing as the scientist's wacky widow. Capable ingenue that she is, Maureen O'Sullivan had no trouble as Barrymore's daughter, but Frank Lawton, her opposite in the romantic secondary theme, is much too British and refined for a cab driver assignment.

● ●

■ DEVIL DOLL

1964, 80 MINS, UK ▼

Dir Lindsay Shonteff   *Prod* Kenneth Rive, Richard Gordon, Lindsay Shonteff   *Scr* George Barclay, Lance Z.

Hargreaves   *Ph* Gerald Gibbs   *Ed* Ernest Bullingham   *Art Dir* Stan Shields

● Bryant Halliday, William Sylvester, Yvonne Romain, Karel Stepanek (Gala/Galaworld)

This slow-paced pic never comes up to its title in the way of shocks, thrills, scares, sex or other dividends for meller regulars. Filmed in England, its gimmick – a ventriloquial dummy's revenge on his manipulator – has been done before and better by Cavalcanti and Michael Redgrave in a real horror classic – *Dead of Night* – and *The Great Gabbo* of 1929.

American newspaperman William Sylvester, assigned to do a story of a hypnotist-ventriloquist suspected of being a fake, takes his girlfriend (Yvonne Romain), along but both are impressed by the act. The hypnotist (Bryant Halliday), invited to perform at a charity affair at the home of Romain's aunt, hypnotizes the girl and, without the others knowing it, leaves her in a trance.

Haliday plans to repeat, with the girl, an experiment he had done years previously in Berlin, transferring a human soul to the body of a dummy, which he will keep subservient and force it to carry out his demands. While Sylvester is tracking down the truth, Halliday's dummy, Hugo, takes matters into his own hands.

Sylvester gives an honest, realistic touch to the role of the newspaperman. Halliday, howeve burdened with a messy beard and one expression, the hypnotic stare, depends on his resonant voice to make the role credible.

● ●

■ DEVIL IN MISS JONES, THE

1973, 74 MINS, US ◇

Dir Gerard Damiano   *Prod* Gerard Damiano   *Scr* Gerard Damiano   *Ph* Harry Flecks   *Ed* Gerard Damiano   *Mus* Alden Shuman

● Georgina Spevlin, John Clemens, Harry Reams, Albert Gork [= Gerard Damiano], Rick Livermore, Sue Flaken (Marvin/Damiano)

With *The Devil in Miss Jones*, the hardcore porno feature approaches an 'art form'. For its genre, the pic is a sensation, marked by a technical polish that pales some Hollywood product and containing some of the most frenzied and erotic sex sequences in porno memory.

Written, directed and edited by Gerard Damiano, the man who dittoed on *Deep Throat* (under his Jerry Gerard pseudonym), this ambitious meller delivers in spades.

A thirtyish virgin, Justine Jones (Georgina Spevlin), commits suicide and is condemned to eternal damnation. Her suicide has been the only damnable act in a lonely, despairing life, and to make herself 'worthy' of the punishment meted out to her, Jones requests a little more time in which to experiment with and to be consumed by lust.

Georgina Spevlin lacks the specific sexpertise of Linda Lovelace and she's no conventional beauty. Male performers are familiar porno vets, with the exception of Damiano himself who appears, under the name of Albert Gork, in pic's hellish finale.

● ●

■ DEVIL IS A WOMAN, THE

1935, 76 MINS, US

Dir Josef von Sternberg   *Scr* John Dos Passon, Sam Winston   *Ph* Josef von Sternberg, Lucien Ballard   *Ed* Sam Winston   *Mus* Ralph Rainger, Andrea Setaro (arr.)   *Art Dir* Hans Dreier

● Marlene Dietrich, Cesar Romero, Lionel Atwill, Edward Everett Horton, Alison Skipworth, Don Alvarado (Paramount)

Josef von Sternberg both directed and photographed *The Devil Is a Woman*, working with a Pierre Louys classic *The Woman and the Puppet* which gives the reader a cross-section of a ruthless courtesan and not much else. While *Devil* is somewhat monotonous picture,

D

Sternberg has given it clever photography and background. Marlene Dietrich has done the rest in playing the Louys trollop, turning in a fine performance.

Story is told in a background of southern Spain during a fiesta, this permitting Sternberg some big mob scenes and color, plus music. It opens on la Dietrich of today as a gorgeously desirable woman who has caught the eye of a young visitor. He is about to stage a rendezvous with her when he meets an old friend (Atwill), who tells him of his sad experience with the same woman, most of the story then being told by flashback.

Edward Everett Horton is in on a couple of sequences at opening and near close, he and his political associates raising th only laughs that occur. *Caprice Espagnol*, vet classic, and other Spanish music is employed for melodic background in an effective manner.

．．．．．．．．．．．．．．．．．．．．．．．．．．．．．

■ DEVIL MAKES THREE, THE

1952, 89 MINS, US

Dir Andrew Marton   *Prod* Richard Goldstone   *Scr* Jerry Davis   *Ph* Vaclav Vich   *Ed* Ben Lewis   *Mus* Rudolph G. Kopp (dir.)
● Gene Kelly, Pier Angeli, Richard Rober, Richard Egan, Claus Clausen, Wilfried Seyferth (M-G-M)

Postwar Germany provides the background for an interesting chase thriller. Snow-covered Munich, Salzburg, Berchtesgaden and Hitler's bombed-out Adlerhorst are the plot settings.

Lawrence Bachmann's story, *Autobahn*, supplies the basis for the script. Story deals with an underground movement to revive the Nazi Party and how Counter-Intelligence, with the aid of Gene Kelly's Air Force captain, and Pier Angeli's German B-girl, put down the aspirations of one would-be fuehrer.

The chase thrills and suspense moments come across expertly under Andrew Marton's direction, but he is inclined to pace the film a bit too slowly in other spots. One of the top thriller sequences is the motorcycle race on a frozen lake, during which the villain is revealed.

．．．．．．．．．．．．．．．．．．．．．．．．．．．．．

■ DEVIL NEVER SLEEPS, THE

See: *Satan Never Sleeps*

．．．．．．．．．．．．．．．．．．．．．．．．．．．．．

■ DEVIL RIDES OUT, THE

(US: *The Devil's Bride*)

1968, 95 MINS, UK ◇

Dir Terence Fisher   *Prod* Anthony Nelson-Keys   *Scr* Richard Matheson   *Ph* Arthur Grant   *Ed* James Needs   *Mus* James Bernard   *Art Dir* Bernard Robinson
● Christopher Lee, Charles Gray, Nike Arrighi, Leon Greene, Patrick Mower, Sarah Lawson (Hammer)

Director Terence Fisher has a ball with this slice of black magic, based on the Dennis Wheatley novel. He has built up a suspenseful pic, with several tough highlights, and gets major effect by playing the subject dead straight and getting similar serious performances from his capable cast.

Christopher Lee is for once on the side of the goodies. As the Duc de Richleau, he and his buddy (Leon Greene) are intent on saving the soul of a young man (Patrick Mower) caught up in black magic and at the mercy of Charles Gray, chief apostle of the evil. Also involved is a mysterious young girl (Nike Arrighi), in the thrall of the black sin.

Lee plays the Duc with his usual authority and Gray turns out another of his bland, cold essays in villainy. The weakness lies in the fact that these two rarely confront each other.

Arrighi as a slightly hysterical lass, Mower and Greene are all adequate.

Fisher's direction makes one of the Satanic orgies a production highspot, aided by some frenzied choreography by David Toguri and apt mood music.

．．．．．．．．．．．．．．．．．．．．．．．．．．．．．

■ DEVILS, THE

1971, 109 MINS, UK ◇ ⓥ

Dir Ken Russell   *Prod* Robert H. Solo, Ken Russell   *Scr* Ken Russell   *Ph* David Watkin   *Ed* Michael Bradsell   *Mus* Peter Maxwell Davies   *Art Dir* Robert Cartwright
● Vanessa Redgrave, Oliver Reed, Dudley Sutton, Max Adrian, Gemma Jones, Murray Melvin (Warner)

Working from John Whiting's play of the same title, and Aldous Huxley's book, *The Devils of Loudun*, Ken Russell has taken some historical liberties in fashioning the story of Father Grandier (Oliver Reed), sensually liberated priest in 17th-century France whose ethics brought him into conflict with the political ambitions of Cardinal Richelieu and the Catholic Church, and whose virile presence and backstairs reputation cued the erotic fantasies of a humpbacked nun, Sister Jeanne (Vanessa Redgrave).

When this sister's lustful ravings begin to infect other nuns in her convent, the Church, through its military agent (Dudley Sutton), brings in an exorcist (Michael Gothard) to stage circus-like public purges of the naked, foulmouthed nuns which result in Grandier's conviction on heresy charges, his torture and burning at the stake.

As if the story alone weren't bizarre enough, Russell has spared nothing in hyping the historic events by stressing the grisly at th expense of dramatic unity.

Given Russell's frantic pacing, performances tend to get lost amid the savagery. Reed carries the film with an admirably restrained portrayal of the doomed priest. Redgrave, on screen only sporadically, is stunning as the salacious sister.

．．．．．．．．．．．．．．．．．．．．．．．．．．．．．

■ DEVIL'S BRIDE, THE

See: *The Devil Rides Out*

．．．．．．．．．．．．．．．．．．．．．．．．．．．．．

■ DEVIL'S DISCIPLE, THE

1959, 82 MINS, US/UK ◇

Dir Guy Hamilton   *Prod* Harold Hecht   *Scr* John Dighton, Roland Kibbee   *Ph* Jack Hildyard   *Ed* Alan Osbiston   *Mus* Richard Rodney Bennett
● Burt Lancaster, Kirk Douglas, Laurence Olivier, Jeanette Scott, Eva LeGallienne, Harry Andrews (Bryna/United Artists)

The Devil's Disciple by George Bernard Shaw is better than this film version would indicate to those unfamiliar with the stage original. The final third of the picture is superb Shawmanship, but the major portion preceding it is fumbling and unsatisfactory.

That all is not lost may be credited almost entirely to Laurence Olivier. His character, that of General 'Gentleman Johnny' Burgoyne, is a witty, mocking figure and mouthpiece for Shaw's wicked shafts into convention and history in this case the American Revolution.

The other two stars, Burt Lancaster and Kirk Douglas, fare less well. Lancaster is Anthony Anderson, the peace-spouting person who eventually becomes a fiery rebel. Douglas is Dick Dudgeon, self-proclaimed, shameless, cowardly scoundrel, who in turn displays the truest Christian attitudes.

Shaw's play is the ironic Irishman's version of how the British, bumbling and fumbling, lost the American colonies. The reason, says Shaw, is that due to the long British weekend someone at the War Office forgot to notify Lord North to join forces with General Burgoyne and pinch off the Colonials.

Directors were changed in mid-filming and there seems in the finished product to be a division of style. Guy Hamilton must bear the blame for the uncertain mood and pace.

．．．．．．．．．．．．．．．．．．．．．．．．．．．．．

■ DEVIL'S PLAYGROUND, THE

1976, 107 MINS, AUSTRALIA ◇ ⓥ

Dir Fred Schepisi   *Prod* Fred Schepisi   *Scr* Fred Schepisi   *Ph* Ian Baker   *Ed* Brian Kavanagh   *Mus* Bruce Smeaton
● Arthur Dignam, Nick Tate, Simon Burke, Charles McCallum, John Frawley, Jonathon Hardy (Film House)

The Devil's Playground is a Roman Catholic boys' boarding school where the pupils are seen at their everyday work, play and worship. Stressed are the problems of puberty in such a community, and the evils of succumbing to self-abuse; one boy for instance is chastised for taking off his bathers whilst under a shower.

The more sensitive boys take such things to heart, others merely shrug it off and go their own way. In one quarter it breeds a cell where boys indulge in homosexual, masochistic and sadistic practices while the teachers react in different ways.

Film, almost like a factual documentary at times, has obviously been made with great sincerity Lensing is fine, with some superb outdoor photography. The direction is always competent and most of the scenes involving the boys, organized and natural.

．．．．．．．．．．．．．．．．．．．．．．．．．．．．．

■ DEVIL WITHIN HER, THE

See: *I Don't Want to Be Born*

．．．．．．．．．．．．．．．．．．．．．．．．．．．．．

■ DEVOTION

1946, 108 MINS, US

Dir Curtis Bernhardt   *Prod* Robert Buckner   *Scr* Keith Winter   *Ph* Ernest Haller   *Ed* Rudi Fehr   *Mus* Erich Wolfgang Korngold   *Art Dir* Robert M. Haas
● Ida Lupino, Paul Henreid, Olivia de Havilland, Sydney Greenstreet, Arthur Kennedy, Nancy Coleman (Warner)

Individual performances are expert, with a few standouts, in miming the situations in the script by Keith Winter, but it fails to stir more than a modest response. Script, taken from an original story by Theodore Reeves, is not substantial, and dialog switches confusingly from the modern to the prose of the period.

Plot depicts the Brontes in the village of Haworth. Yorkshire, opening in the period just before they found fame as authors. Shown are the love triangle between Ida Lupino, as Emily; Olivia de Havilland, as Charlotte, and Paul Henreid, as the curate who aids the girls' father in the parish; the brief stay of Emily and Charlotte in Brussels, and latter's romance with a schoolteacher, Victor Francen.

Lupino and de Havilland are expert as the two older sisters, while Nancy Coleman as the younger Anne Bronte has her moments. Henreid's portrayal is excellent. Greenstreet is good as Thackeray, a role that is almost a bit. Arthur Kennedy's performance as the drunken poet-painter brother of the sisters is a standout.

．．．．．．．．．．．．．．．．．．．．．．．．．．．．．

■ DIAL M FOR MURDER

1954, 105 MINS, US ◇ ⓥ ⊙

Dir Alfred Hitchcock   *Prod* Alfred Hitchcock   *Scr* Frederick Knott   *Ph* Robert Burks   *Ed* Rudi Fehr   *Mus* Dimitri Tiomkin   *Art Dir* Edward Carrere
● Ray Milland, Grace Kelly, Robert Cummings, John Williams, Anthony Dawson, Patrick Allen (Warner)

The melodramatics in Frederick Knott's legit hit, *Dial M for Murder*, have been transferred to the screen virtually intact, but they are not as impressive on film. *Dial M* remains more of a filmed play than a motion picture, unfortunately revealed as a conversation piece about murder which talks up much more suspense than it actually delivers. The 3-D camera's probing eye also discloses that there's very little that's new in the Knott plotting.

197

Co-starring with Ray Milland are Grace Kelly, his wife and the intended murder victim, and Robert Cummings, her lover, who has a rather fruitless part in the resolution of the melodramatics.

Milland plots his wife's death, figuring on using Anthony Dawson for the actual killing while he has an alibi established elsewhere. The scheme goes awry.

There are a number of basic weaknesses in the setup that keep the picture from being a good suspense show for any but the most gullible. Via the performances and several suspens tricks expected of Hitchcock, the weaknesses are glossed over but not enough to rate the film a cinch winner.

· ·

■ **DIAMOND HEAD**

1962, 107 MINS, US ◇ ⑩ ⊙

Dir Guy Green   *Prod* Jerry Bresler   *Scr* Marguerite Roberts   *Ph* Sam Leavitt   *Ed* William A. Lyon   *Mus* John Williams   *Art Dir* Malcolm Brown
● Charlton Heston, Yvette Mimieux, George Chakiris, France Nuyen, James Darren (Columbia/Bresler)

Improbabilities and inconsistencies galore reside in Marguerite Roberts' heavyhanded screenplay, from Peter Gilman's novel, about a Hawaiian agricultural tycoon, or King Bwana of Pineappleville, hellbent on holding-that-bloodline. When the baron's (Charlton Heston) baby sister (Yvette Mimieux) defiantly announces her engagement to a full-blooded Hawaiian lad (James Darren), the battle lines are drawn.

Heston etches a swaggering portrait of the bullying bigot. Mimieux is spirited as the liberal-minded sister, Chakiris is glum and inexpressive as the half-breed medic who captures the fair sister's heart. He also seems to be the only doctor on the Islands. Nuyen is sweet as Heston's unlikely heartthrob. Darren, despite a rich tan, seems about as 100% Hawaiian as Paul Revere.

Guy Green's direction, at any rate, is high-spirited, and production ingredients are slickly eye-appealing. Sam Leavitt's photography is Eastman colorful and dramatically calculating and alert.

· ·

■ **DIAMONDS**

1975, 106 MINS, US/ISRAEL ◇ ⑩

Dir Menahem Golan   *Prod* Menahem Golan, Yoram Globus   *Scr* David Paulsen, Menahem Golan   *Ph* Adam Greenberg   *Ed* Dov Hoenig   *Mus* Roy Budd   *Art Dir* Kuli Sander
● Robert Shaw, Richard Roundtree, Barbara Hershey, Shelley Winters, Shai K. Ophir, Gadi Yageel (Avco Embassy/Golan-Globus)

The thin screenplay has Robert Shaw playing a jaded London aristocrat who turns diamond thief because of rivalry with his brother (also Shaw), a security expert who constructed the intricate vault in Israel where the rocks are stashed.

Along on the heist are Richard Roundtree and Barbara Hershey, but no one in the cast gets much chance to develop a characterization. Shelley Winters has an estraneous role of an American widow putting the make on Shaw.

Diamonds is almost exclusively concerned with the technique of thievery, and there are some enjoyable scenes showing how the vault is cracked, but audiences surely demand more from a heist pic these days.

· ·

■ **DIAMONDS ARE FOREVER**

1971, 119 MINS, UK ◇ ⑩ ⊙

Dir Guy Hamilton   *Prod* Albert R. Broccoli, Harry Saltzman   *Scr* Richard Maibaum, Tom Mankiewicz   *Ph* Ted Moore   *Ed* Bert Bates, John W. Holmes   *Mus* John Barry   *Art Dir* Ken Adam

● Sean Connery, Jill St John, Charles Gray, Lana Wood, Jimmy Dean, Bruce Cabot (United Artists)

James Bond still packs a lethal wallop in all his cavortings, still manages to surround himself with scantily-clad sexpots. Yet *Diamonds Are Forever* doesn't carry the same quality or flair as its many predecessors.

Sean Connery is back in the role as in five previous Bond entries, and he still has his own way both with broads and deeds. Jill St John is an agent for the smuggling ring in an attempt to smuggle a fortune in diamonds into the US, and Charles Gray the head of the organization with all the most advanced stages of nuclear energy at its disposal. Somewhere in the telling, diamonds are forgotten, never to be recalled, while Bond valiantly tries to save the world – one guesses.

The diamond caper takes Bond and his lovely companion to Las Vegas, where one of the funniest sequences in memory focuses on Bond trying to elude the police in downtown Vegas. Up-to-the-minute scientific gadget use is made again when Bond steals a moon machine at a simulated lunar testing-ground in a wild drive across the Nevada desert dunes.

☐ 1971: Nomination: Best Sound

· ·

■ **DIAMONDS FOR BREAKFAST**

1968, 102 MINS, UK ◇

Dir Christopher Morahan   *Prod* Carlo Ponti, Pierre Rouve   *Scr* N.F. Simpson, Pierre Rouve, Ronald Harwood   *Ph* Gerry Turpin   *Ed* Peter Tanner   *Mus* Norman Kaye   *Art Dir* Reece Pemberton
● Marcello Mastroianni, Rita Tushingham, Elaine Taylor, Maggie Blye, Francesca Tu, Warren Mitchell (Paramount)

Potentially amusing, light-comedy, crime idea is marred by uncertain steering by director Christopher Morahan, making his feature debut, and clashing styles of the three scripters. Comedy is never fully developed and Marcello Mastroianni, debuting in British pix, lacks his usual elegant confidence.

Mastroianni is a London boutique owner who, happening to be fourth in succession to the Throne of All the Russians, hits on the idea of lifting the Imperial Jewels which he figures belong to him anyway.

He rustles up a gang of eyeworthy and skilful young femme crooks, cons the authorities into letting his girls wear the rocks at a charity fashion show but then runs into trouble as things go wrong.

Mastroianni is clearly not happy with his role in which he's too often the stooge, but the gals around him are good fun.

Femme star Rita Tushingham plays a nutty, Liverpool-Irish safecracker, who eventually gets the hero, but the part's skimpily developed and it's hardly Tushingham's league.

· ·

■ **DIAMOND SKULLS**
(US: *Dark Obsession*)

1990, 87 MINS, UK ◇ ⑩

Dir Nick Broomfield   *Prod* Tim Bevan   *Scr* Tim Rose Price   *Ph* Michael Coulter   *Ed* Rodney Holland   *Mus* Hans Zimmer   *Art Dir* Jocelyn James
● Gabriel Byrne, Amanda Donohoe, Michael Hordern, Judy Parfitt, Douglas Hodge, Sadie Frost (Film Four/British Screen)

A stylish melodrama about sex and violence among the British aristocracy, *Diamond Skulls* never quite delivers the punches it promises.

Gabriel Byrne is Sir Hugo, an ex-guards officer, now in business. He has a lovely wife (the delectable Amanda Donohoe) of whom he's extremely jealous, suspecting her of having an affair with an Argentine business colleague.

One night, after a drunken dinner with his friends, Hugo is driving someone else's car when he hits a young woman, fatally injuring her. He and his friends leave her to die, though one of them, Jamie (Douglas Hodge), the car owner, wants to report the accident.

Jamie, who's having an affair with Hugo's sister Rebecca (Sadie Frost), threatens to spill the beans, and the friends are forced to silence him.

Donohoe gives another hot performance as the elegant Virginia whose name belies her actions. Veteran Michael Hordern is amusing as Hugo's titled father, though comedy actor Ian Carmichael is totally wasted as the family butler.

· ·

■ **DIARY OF A CHAMBERMAID**

1946, 86 MINS, US ⑩

Dir Jean Renoir   *Prod* Benedict Bogeaus, Burgess Meredith   *Scr* Burgess Meredith   *Ph* Lucien Andriot   *Ed* James Smith   *Art Dir* Eugene Lourie
● Paulette Goddard, Burgess Meredith, Hurd Hatfield, Francis Lederer, Judith Anderson (United Artists)

Diary is interesting from several angles, no less of which is its adaptation from the original French. The transition is certainly the most important factor in drawing a line on its entertainment values. This is an odd yarn, the type done so well by the French – and so falteringly by almost anyone else. *Diary* in its American form has not nearly the intrigue, nor the color, suggested by the original French version, but it has names and an interest all its own.

It is the yarn of a chambermaid who, tiring of her station in life, vows to achieve wealth whoever the man. The men in her life aren't too sharply defined, nor especially interesting. Nor is the murder of the aging captain by the valet, so he can get money to marry the chambermaid, committed with any degree of climactic excitement.

There is Paulette Goddard, as the chambermaid with a gold glint to her orbs; Burgess Meredith, a psychopathic, aging army captain; Hurd Hatfield, the sensitive consumptive whom the girl loves, and Francis Lederer, the glowering valet-murderer.

· ·

■ **DIARY OF A HIT MAN**

1992, 91 MINS, US ◇ ⑩ ⊙

Dir Roy London   *Prod* Amin Q. Chaudhri   *Scr* Kenneth Pressman   *Ph* Yuri Sokol   *Ed* Brian Smedley-Aston   *Mus* Michel Colombier   *Art Dir* Stephen Hendrickson
● Forest Whitaker, Sherilyn Fenn, Sharon Stone, Seymour Cassel, James Belushi, Lois Chiles (Continental/Vision)

An actors' piece invested with remarkable humanity by debuting director Roy London and a gifted cast, the modest $2.5 million *Diary of a Hit Man* transcends an unlikely scenario [expanded by Kenneth Pressman from his 45-minute play *Insider's Price*] to offer moments of cinema well worth savoring.

A hired killer (Forest Whitaker) is losing his taste for his work. He's hired to knock off the wife and child of a born-again commodities broker (Lewis Smith) who claims his wife's a drug addict and the infant is a crack baby and not his. The reluctant killer breaks professional-conduct rules by conversing with the victim (Sherilyn Fenn) – and discovers the broker lied. Long scene that follows is the central conceit of the piece: that a killer and his intended victim could save each other.

Fenn is a revelation in the substance and texture she brings to the role. Whitaker invests his beleaguered hitman with mesmerizing depth and unpolished reality, aided by abundant voiceover elucidating his thoughts.

London, a writer and acting coach whose pupils include Fenn and Sharon Stone (included in the cast as Fenn's tarty and obnoxious sister), demonstrates firm control of the medium and a knack for engaging flourishes.

· ·

DIARY OF A MAD HOUSEWIFE

1970, 85 MINS, US ◇ ⊛

Dir Frank Perry   *Prod* Frank Perry   *Scr* Eleanor Perry
Ph Gerald Hirschfeld   *Ed* Sidney Katz   *Art Dir* Peter
Dohanos
● Richard Benjamin, Frank Langella, Carrie Snodgress,
Lorraine Cullen, Frannie Michel, Lee Addoms
(Universal)

An engrossing story of the disintegration of a
modern loveless marriage, with Richard
Benjamin and Frank Langella effectively portraying the inadequacies of husband and
lover, respectively, and Carrie Snodgress, as a
frustrated, sensitive wife.

Story line [from a novel by Sue Kaufman]
has Snodgress reach the breaking point under
a marriage to Benjamin that has become
sated with his selfish material values. She
turns to Langella as an afternoon lover, only
to find him just as bad.

Benjamin, who is top-billed, is saddled with
the most unsympathetic role as a disenchanted, post-JFK idealist now determined to
rise in the middle-class flotsam, he is excellent
in maintaining a character so delineated that
one wants to throw something at the screen.
☐ 1970: Nomination: Best Actress (Carrie
Snodgress)

DIARY OF ANNE FRANK, THE

1959, 170 MINS, US ⊛ ⊙

Dir George Stevens   *Prod* George Stevens   *Scr* Frances
Goodrich, Albert Hackett   *Ph* William C. Mellor, Jack
Cardiff   *Ed* David Bretherton, Robert Swink, William
Mace   *Mus* Alfred Newman   *Art Dir* Lyle R. Wheeler,
George W. Davis
● Millie Perkins, Joseph Schildkraut, Shelley Winters,
Richard Beymer, Lou Jacobi, Diane Baker (20th Century-
Fox)

The Diary of Anne Frank, first published in its
original form, then made into a play by
Frances Goodrich and Albert Hackett, is a
film of often extraordinary quality. It manages, within the framework of a tense and
tragic situation, to convey the beauty of a
young and inquiring spirit that soars beyond
the cramped confinement of the Frank family's hideout in Nazi-occupied Amsterdam.

And yet, with all its technical perfection,
the inspired direction and the sensitivity with
which man of the scenes are handled, *Diary* is
simply too long. Everything possible is done
to keep the action moving within its narrow,
cluttered space, and a remarkable balance is
achieved between stark terror and comedy relief, yet there are moments when the film
lags and the dialog becomes forced. Unlike
the play, the picture leaves too little to the
imagination.

Millie Perkins plays Anne. It is her first film
role and she turns in a charming and captivating performance. Whether Perkins, a
model, is absolutely right for the part is open
to question. It's certainly difficult to accept
her as a 13-year-old, which was Anne's age at
the time the Franks went into hiding.

As father Otto Frank, Joseph Schildkraut
repeats his marvellous performance on the
stage. There is dignity and wisdom in this
man, a deep sadness too, and a love for Anne
that makes the scene of his return to the
hideout after the war a moment full of pain
and compassion.

As the Van Daan couple, Shelley Winters
and Lou Jacobi come up with vivid characterizations that score on all levels. As young
Peter Van Daan, Richard Beymer is touchingly sincere and perfectly matched with
Perkins, a boy who discovers in the girl the
depth he has been seeking in himself. Diane
Baker's sensitive face is pleasing in the comparatively small role of Margot Frank.
☐ 1959: Best Supp. Actress (Shelley
Winters), B&W Cinematography, B&W Art
Direction.

☐ Nominations: Best Picture, Director, Supp.
Actor (Ed Wynn), B&W Costume Design,
Scoring of a Dramatic Picture

DICK TRACY

1990, 103 MINS, US ◇ ⊛ ⊙

Dir Warren Beatty   *Prod* Warren Beatty   *Scr* Jim Cash,
Jack Epps Jr   *Ph* Vittorio Storaro   *Ed* Richard Marks
Mus Danny Elfman   *Art Dir* Richard Sylbert
● Warren Beatty, Charlie Korsmo, Glenne Headly,
Madonna, Al Pacino, Dustin Hoffman (Touchstone/Silver
Screen Partners IV)

Though it looks ravishing, Warren Beatty's
longtime pet project is a curiously remote,
uninvolving film. Beatty and his collaborators
have created a boldly stylized 1930s urban milieu that captures the comic strip's quirky,
angled mood, while dazzling the eye with
deep primary colors.

Beatty – ultra-stylish in yellow raincoat and
snap-brim hat, black suit, red tie and crisp
white shirts – is so cool he appears frozen.
Torn between Madonna's allure – she's cus-
tomed in black & white to look like a steamy
low-rent version of Josef von Sternberg's
Marlene Dietrich – and the more low-key
beauty and sweetness of Glenne Headly's redhead Tess Trueheart, Beatty simply sits there
and mopes, occasionally rousing himself into
bursts of action.

A large part of what fun there is in the pic
comes from the inventive character makeup
by John Caglione Jr and Doug Drexler, who
mostly succeed in the difficult task of creating
live-action cartoon figures. Dustin Hoffman
takes an eerie turn as Mumbles, R.G.
Armstrong is chilling as Pruneface, Paul
Sorvino hilariously disgusting as Lips,
William Forsythe spooky as Flattop.

Al Pacino, virtually runs away with the show
in a sizable role as Tracy's nemesis, the
Richard III-like hunchbacked villain Big Boy
Caprice. His manic energy lifts the overall
torpor.

Equally fine is young street urchin Charlie
Korsmo who, together with the lovely Headly,
gives the film a necessary counter-balance of
normality.
☐ 1990: Best Art Direction, Song ('Sooner or
Later'), Make-Up
☐ Nominations: Best Supp. Actor (Al
Pacino), Cinematography, Costume Design,
Sound

DICTATOR, THE

1935, 86 MINS, UK

Dir Victor Saville, Alfred Santell   *Prod* Ludovico Toeplitz
Scr Benn W. Levy   *Ph* Franz Planer   *Ed* Paul
Weatherwax   *Mus* Karol Rathaus   *Art Dir* Andre
Andrejev
● Clive Brook, Madeleine Carroll, Emlyn Williams,
Alfred Drayton, Nicholas Hannen, Helen Hays (Toeplitz)

This is one of the most lavish costume pictures that has come out of England. Supposed
to have cost $500,000. Sets and costumes give
the impression of tremendous royal wealth;
entire action takes place in gorgeous palaces;
one banquet scene, with ballet music, is as
good as anything ever seen on the screen.

Picture has other fine qualities, too. Clive
Brook does an authoriative bit of acting, and
imposes lots of femme appeal; Madeleine
Carroll is attractive; Emlyn Williams is a
splendid young debauchee and Helen Hays
(not the American actress) a tough old queen
mother. There is humor, particularly in the
earlier scenes.

Trouble is with the story [by Ludovico
Toeplitz]. It's a love tale of a beautiful queen
and an ambitious young man – not developed
in such a way as to be really dramatic.

Setting is 18th-century Danish royalty.
Opens after the royal wedding, and shows the
king (Williams) trying in vain to get into the

bedroom of the queen (Carroll), whom he
only met the day before. This, like the rest of
the first dozen or so sequences, is effective.
Then the king beats it to Hamburg to have a
good time. Struensee, a Hamburg doctor
(Brook), makes an impressive entry. He's
called to attend the king, incognito, who has
passed out after too much wine and women,
and he wins the young man's favor by bringing him back to life unceremoniously.

Struensee, taken to Denmark, becomes the
power behind the throne. In this he replaces
the Queen mother, who, with her courtiers,
sets out to get him.

DIE! DIE! MY DARLING!

See: Fanatic

DIE HARD

1988, 131 MINS, US ◇ ⊛ ⊙

Dir John McTiernan   *Prod* Lawrence Gordon, Joel Silver
Scr Jeb Stuart, Steven E. de Souza   *Ph* Jan De Bont
Ed Frank J. Urioste, John F. Link   *Mus* Michael Kamen
Art Dir Jackson De Govia
● Bruce Willis, Alan Rickman, Bonnie Bedelia,
Alexander Godunov, Reginald VelJohnson, Paul Gleason
(Gordon-Silver/20th Century-Fox)

Die Hard is as high tech, rock hard and souped
up as an action film can be, a suspenser
[based on the novel *Nothing Lasts Forever* by
Roderick Thorpe] pitting a lone wolf cop
against a group of terrorists that has taken
over a highrise office tower.

Bruce Willis plays John McClane, an overworked New York policeman who flies into
Los Angeles at Christmas to visit his two
daughters and estranged wife Holly (Bonnie
Bedelia).

Planning a rather different holiday agenda
are the terrorists led by Hans Gruber (Alan
Rickman). The dastardly dozen invade the
plush 30th floor offices of Nakatomi Corp
during its Christmas party, and hold the employees hostage as a computer whiz cracks a
code that will put the mainly German bad
boys in possession of $600 million in nego-
tiable bonds.

Slipping out of the party in the nick of time
with nothing but his handgun, Willis is the fly
in the ointment of the criminals' plans, picking off one, then two more of the scouts sent
on pest control missions.

Beefed up considerably for his role, Willis is
amiable enough in the opening stretch, but
overdoes the grimacing and heavy emoting
later on. The cooler and more humorous he is
the better. Rickman has a giddy good time
but sometimes goes over the top as the
henchman.
☐ 1988: Nominations: Best Editing, Sound,
Sound Effects Editing, Visual Effects

DIE HARD 2

1990, 124 MINS, US ◇ ⊛ ⊙

Dir Renny Harlin   *Prod* Laurence Gordon, Joel Silver,
Charles Gordon   *Scr* Steven E. de Souza, Doug
Richardson   *Ph* Oliver Wood   *Ed* Stuart Baird
Mus Michael Kamen   *Art Dir* John Vallone
● Bruce Willis, Bonnie Bedelia, William Atherton,
Franco Nero, William Sadler, Reginald VelJohnson
(Gordon/Silver)

Die Hard 2 lacks the inventivenes of the original but compensates with relentless action.
The film [based on the novel *58 Minutes* by
Walter Wager] works for the most part as
sheer entertainment, a full-color comic book
with shootouts, brutal fistfights and bloodletting aplenty.

Minding his own business, John McClane
(Bruce Willis) is in DC's Dulles Airport to
pick up wife Holly (Bonnie Bedelia) to spend
Christmas with her folks. They've reconciled
since the events in *Die Hard* and the Gotham

cop has joined the LAPD. Unlike most domestic flights, the story takes off immediately, as terrorists seize control of the airport to free a Manuel Noriegaesque foreign dictator (Franco Nero) being transported to the US.

Director Renny Harlin does a creditable job with such a daunting large-scale assignment. But Harlin lacks *Die Hard* director John McTiernan's vicelike grip on action and strays into areas that derail certain scenes, using slow-motion in early sequences and sapping their energy.

....

■ DIGGSTOWN
(UK: Midnight Sting)

1992, 97 MINS, US ◇ ⓥ ⊙
Dir Michael Ritchie   *Prod* Robert Schaffel   *Scr* Steven McKay   *Ph* Gerry Fisher   *Ed* Don Zimmerman *Mus* James Newton Howard   *Art Dir* Steve Hendrickson
● James Woods, Louis Gossett Jr, Bruce Dern, Oliver Platt, Heather Graham, Randall 'Tex' Cobb (M-G-M/Eclectic)

Blending elements of *Rocky* and *The Sting*, this crowd-teaser mixes it up with boxing, revenge and salty one-liners that should satisfy audiences.

James Woods demonstrates his trademark intensity along with a comic flair as a just-paroled hustler who sets up a big-money boxing match pitting his ringer 'Honey' Roy Palmer (Louis Gossett Jr) against any 10 men from the burg of Diggstown.

Like *The Sting*, the target is truly despicable, and few can fit that description more capably than Bruce Dern, whose character stole the town from its citizens and rubs out anyone who crosses him.

All the trademark flourishes are there, including a couple of murders for motivation, a beautiful woman (Heather Graham) of little narrative consequence, a tenuous relationship between Dern and his son (a suddenly quite grown-up Thomas Wilson Brown), and Woods' and Gossett's scam-gone-wrong history, leading to ample good-natured bickering.

The boxing sequences are compelling, and Gossett convincingly comes across as an aging brawler with a potent right cross.

....

■ DILLINGER

1973, 107 MINS, US ◇ ⓥ ⊙
Dir John Milius   *Prod* Buzz Feitshans   *Scr* John Milius *Ph* Jules Brenner   *Ed* Fred R. Feitshans Jr   *Mus* Barry DeVorzon   *Art Dir* Trevor Williams
● Warren Oates, Ben Johnson, Michelle Phillips, Cloris Leachman, Harry Dean Stanton, Richard Dreyfuss (American International)

The violent life and death of John Dillinger is graphically portrayed. With Warren Oates in title role, screenplay captures the various highlights of the killer's short-lived career as Public Enemy No.1.

Oates is a good physical choice for role of the bank robber and killer who blazed his way to notoriety during 13 months of 1933 and 1934. Less known to the public was Melvin Purvis, the FBI man responsible for Dillinger's death in a Chicago alley, but as delineated by Ben Johnson he is as forceful a figure.

Actually, the tenor of the film is the FBI huntdown of Dillinger; Johnson acts as off-screen commentator as well as enacting him on screen. Pace is sometimes reduced during events sandwiched in between actual gunfire sequences of Dillinger's career, but there can be no criticism of Milius' ability to keep such action sequences at top-heat.

Michelle Phillips, making her film bow after having been a member of The Mamas & The Papas singing group, scores heavily as Dillinger's girl friend.

....

■ DIM SUM
A LITTLE BIT OF HEART

1985, 85 MINS, US ◇ ⓥ ⊙
Dir Wayne Wang   *Prod* Tom Sternberg, Wayne Wang, Danny Yung   *Scr* Terrel Seltzer   *Ph* Michael Chin *Ed* Ralph Wikke   *Mus* Todd Boekelheide   *Art Dir* Danny Yung
● Laureen Chew, Kim Chew, Victor Wong, Ida F.O. Chung, Cora Miao, John Nishio (CIM)

Dim Sum offers up a few charming observations about cultural differences among assorted generations of Chinese Americans, but the dramatic situations are so underplayed as to be mostly ineffectual.

Taking a cue from countless earlier Asian family pictures that have dwelt upon the subject of family traditions and the responsibilities of children for their aging parents, director Wayne Wang and scripter Terrel Seltzer [working from an idea by them and Laureen Chew] have focused upon the relationship between a traditional Chinese woman in her 60s and her 30-ish daughter, who unlike her brother and sister, is not yet hitched.

A great deal of the sought-after humor stems from the 'So when are you gonna get married?' attitudes of family friends.

The authenticity of Wang's depiction of San Francisco's Chinese need not be questioned, but the attitudes expressed are predictable in the extreme and are invested with little sense of dramatic urgency.

....

■ DINER

1982, 110 MINS, US ◇ ⓥ ⊙
Dir Barry Levinson   *Prod* Jerry Weintraub   *Scr* Barry Levinson   *Ph* Peter Sova   *Ed* Stu Linder   *Mus* Bruce Brody, Ivan Kral   *Art Dir* Leon Harris
● Steve Guttenberg, Daniel Stern, Mickey Rourke, Kevin Bacon, Timothy Daly, Ellen Barkin (M-G-M/United Artists)

It's easy to tell that *Diner* was chiefly conceived and executed by a writer. In his directorial debut, Barry Levinson takes great pains to establish characters.

The year is 1959 and the diner is in Baltimore, although the action could tak place in any American city. Using the diner as the proverbial street corner hangout, Levinson centers on a close-knit group of guys in their early 20s and how their early adult lives are taking shape.

In this case there's lots to worry about. Among the characters is a young gambler just footsteps ahead of his loanshark; a thinking grad student whose pregnant career-wise girlfriend won't get married; a compulsive husband unhappy with his new wife; a handsome rich kid who gets drunk to escape his cold family; and a closet 'virgin' who won't marry his girlfriend until she can pass a football quiz.

Steve Guttenberg, Daniel Stern, Mickey Rourke, Kevin Bacon, Paul Reiser and Timothy Daly are terrific as the friends as are Ellen Barkin and Kathryn Dowling as the two females involved with different group members.

☐ 1982: Nomination: Best Original Screenplay

....

■ DINNER AT EIGHT

1933, 110 MINS, US ⓥ ⊙
Dir George Cukor   *Prod* David O. Selznick *Scr* Frances Marion, Herman J. Mankiewicz, Donald Ogden Stewart   *Ph* William Daniels   *Ed* Ben Lewis *Mus* William Axt   *Art Dir* Hobe Erwin, Fred Hope
● Marie Dressler, John Barrymore, Wallace Beery, Jean Harlow, Lionel Barrymore, Lee Tracy (M-G-M)

Play [by George S. Kaufman and Edna Ferber] was fine drama on the stage and has been translated to the screen in workmanlike manner, changes mostly being in the interest of condensation. For this reason the below stairs action among the servants has been deleted and the finish has been slightly changed to give a gag line to Marie Dressler, the latter being a first-rate device, handing the curtain to the principal two comedy characters – the ancient stage belle and the Jean Harlow role, who have been shrewdly emphasized in the film version.

The story grips from beginning to end with never-relaxing tension, its sombre moments relieved by lighter touches into a fascinating mosaic for nearly two hours. Play is a more searching document than *Grand Hotel* but not quite its equal in dramatic vividness.

Acting honors probably will go to Dressler and Harlow, the latter giving an astonishingly well-balanced treatment of Kitty, the canny little hussy who hooks a hard-bitten and unscrupulous millionaire and then makes him lay down and roll over.

Role of Carlotta doesn't find Dressler in her popular vein. It's a dressed-up part for one thing. But she handles this politer assignment with poise and aplomb.

John Barrymore's playing of the has-been picture star is a stark, uncompromising treatment of a pretty thorough-going blackguard and ingrate. Billie Burke is eminently suited for the role of a fluttering society matron immersed in social trivialities while tragedy stalks unknowing through her home. Wallace Beery is again at home as the millionaire vulgarian, made to order for his type.

....

■ DIPLOMATIC COURIER

1952, 98 MINS, US ⓥ
Dir Henry Hathaway   *Prod* Casey Robinson   *Scr* Casey Robinson, Liam O'Brien   *Ph* Lucien Ballard   *Ed* James B. Clark   *Mus* Sol Kaplan   *Art Dir* Lyle Wheeler, John DeCuir
● Tyrone Power, Patricia Neal, Hildegarde Neff, Stephen McNally, Karl Malden, James Millican (20th Century-Fox)

A topnotch espionage yarn based on Peter Cheyney's novel, *Sinister Errand*, the script has Tyrone Power playing a diplomatic courier who is used by the Counter Intelligence Division to uncover the whereabouts of a missing Soviet timetable for invasion of Yugoslavia.

Power, the State Department's top postman, is sent to Salzburg to pick up vital secret papers from James Millican. At the arranged meeting place in a railway station, Millican refuses contact and is later killed. Aware the Soviets did not get the papers, Power is assigned to trace Hildegarde Neff, a Soviet agent in belief she will have some clue to the mystery. Power is hampered in his work by Patricia Neal, seemingly a slightly nutty American tourist.

....

■ DIPLOMATIC IMMUNITY

1991, 95 MINS, US ◇ ⓥ
Dir Peter Maris   *Prod* Peter Maris   *Scr* Randall Frakes, Jim Trombetta, Richard Donn   *Ph* Gerald B. Wolfe *Ed* Jack Tucker   *Mus* John Massari   *Art Dir* Leigh Nicolai Moon
● Bruce Boxleitner, Billy Drago, Tom Breznahan, Christopher Neame, Fabiana Udenio, Meg Foster (Shuster)

Diplomatic Immunity is a superior B actioner. In his best feature since the minor classic *Viper*, filmmaker Peter Maris is blessed with a clever script and topnotch cast.

Bruce Boxleitner, fitting a mature role comfortably, toplines a Marine training sergeant who goes over the top when his beautiful young daughter (Sharon L. Kase) is raped and murdered by her foreign b.f. (Tom Breznahan). Breznahan and his evil henchman Christopher Neame are returned to their home turf, Paraguay, since both hold diplomatic passports.

Gung-ho leatherneck Boxleitner takes matters in his own hands and heads to Paraguay. His contact there is cynical Billy Drago, offering him arms and information. The picture gains momentum when Boxleitner teams up with Breznahan's dominatrix mistress, Fabiana Udenio, and later Drago to mount an assault on the villain's island fortress. Good stuntwork and frequent action scenes are a plus.
••••••••••••••••••••••••••••••••••

■ **DIRIGIBLE**

1931, 100 MINS, US
Dir Frank Capra *Scr* Frank B. Wead, Jo Swerling *Ph* Joseph Walker *Ed* Maurice Wright
● Jack Holt, Ralph Graves, Fay Wray, Hobart Bosworth, Roscoe Karns, Clarence Muse (Columbia)

The big scene is a crack-up of the dirigible in the air; more interesting even than the explosion of the dirigible in *Hell's Angels*. The remainder of *Dirigible* is unconvincing, before or after the crack-up, the latter occurring about midway.

After the crack-up comes the South Pole expedition by plane and dirigible, the latter to rescue the survivors. As Ralph Graves piloting the airplane to the pole is ready to return, the explorer aboard wants to drop an American flag to mark the spot. Graves says no, he will land and let the explorer do it in person. 'See that snow', says Graves, 'it's perfect for landing', and he lands, right on his neck with the others, while the plane burns. After that it's homeward bound, 6,000 miles away and getting there at the rate of seven miles daily. Trudging, starving, dying.

Of the actors Fay Wray looks the best, earnestly sincere as the wife of Graves' glory-seeking aviator. Graves early in the film is light enough to give the zest the story needs. Jack Holt is the dirigible's commander and pal of Graves.
••••••••••••••••••••••••••••••••••

■ **DIRTY DANCING**

1987, 97 MINS, US ◇ ⓥ ⊙
Dir Emile Ardolino *Prod* Linda Gottlieb *Scr* Eleanor Bergstein *Ph* Jeff Jur *Ed* Peter C. Frank *Mus* John Morris *Art Dir* Mark Haack
● Jennifer Grey, Patrick Swayze, Jerry Orbach, Cynthia Rhodes, Jack Weston, Jane Brucker (Vestron)

It's summer 1963 and college kids carry copies of *The Fountainhead* in their back pocket and condoms in their wallet. It's also a time for *Dirty Dancing* and in her 17th summer, at a Borscht Belt resort, Baby Houseman (Jennifer Grey) learns how to do it in this skin-deep but inoffensive teen-throb pic designed to titillate teenage girls.

A headstrong girl bucking for a career in Peace Corps, Baby gets an education in life and loses her innocence when she befriends a young dancer (Cynthia Rhodes) in need of an abortion. She also gets involved with the hotel's maverick dance instructor Johnny Castle (Patrick Swayze).

Good production values, some nice dance sequences and a likable performance by Grey make the film more than watchable, especially for those acquainted with the Jewish tribal mating rituals that go on in the Catskill Mountain resorts. Swayze's character is played too soft to be convincing.
□ 1987: Best Song ('I've Had the Time of My Life')
••••••••••••••••••••••••••••••••••

■ **DIRTY DINGUS MAGEE**

1970, 90 MINS, US ◇ ⓥ
Dir Burt Kennedy *Prod* Burt Kennedy *Scr* Tom and Frank Waldman *Ph* Harry Stradling Jr *Ed* William B. Gulick *Mus* Jeff Alexander *Art Dir* George W. Davis

● Frank Sinatra, George Kennedy, Anne Jackson, Lois Nettleton, Jack Elam, Michele Carey (M-G-M)

Dirty Dingus Magee emerges as a good period western comedy, covering the spectrum from satire through double entendre to low slapstick, starring Frank Sinatra and George Kennedy as double-crossing buddies.

Burt Kennedy produced and directed a script [from the novel *The Ballad of Dingus Magee* by David Markson] which is loaded with effective vignette, and a strong supporting cast.

Sinatra plays an ambiable roustabout, always eager but never quite able to satisfy the unending passions of Indian maiden Michele Carey. When old pal Kennedy shows up en route to California, Sinatra robs him, thus setting up the basic running plot line of multiple compound double cross. The gag subplots move along at a good pace.
••••••••••••••••••••••••••••••••••

■ **DIRTY DOZEN, THE**

1967, 149 MINS, UK ◇ ⓥ ⊙
Dir Robert Aldrich *Prod* Kenneth Hyman *Scr* Nunnally Johnson, Lukas Heller *Ph* Edward Scaife *Ed* Michael Luciano *Mus* Frank DeVol *Art Dir* W.E. Hutchinson
● Lee Marvin, Ernest Borgnine, Charles Bronson, Jim Brown, John Cassavetes, George Kennedy (M-G-M)

The Dirty Dozen is an exciting Second World War pre-D-Day drama about 12 condemned soldier-prisoners who are rehabilitated to serve with distinction. Lee Marvin heads a very strong, nearly all-male cast in an excellent performance.

E.M. Nathanson's novel was careful to disclaim any truth to the basic plot, for, if ever pressed, the US Army apparently can claim that no records exist on the subject. Still, Nathanson's book, as well as the very good screenplay, has a ring of authenticity to it.

Marvin delivers a top performance probably because he seems at his best in a role as a sardonic authoritarian. Herein, he is a major, handed the task of selecting 12 hardened, stockaded punks, training them for a guerrilla mission with just faintest hope of amnesty. Seeds of official conflict are sewn into plot: Marvin and Robert Ryan do not get along – but later they must.

John Cassavetes is firstrate as the tough Chicago hood who meets his match in Marvin. Charles Bronson stands out as a Polish-American who, once affixing his loyalty, does not shift under even physical brutality.
□ 1967: Best Sound Effects.
□ Nomination: Best Supp. Actor (John Cassavetes)
••••••••••••••••••••••••••••••••••

■ **DIRTY HARRY**

1971, 102 MINS, US ◇ ⓥ ⊙
Dir Don Siegel *Prod* Don Siegel *Scr* Harry Julian Fink, R.M. Fink, Dean Riesner, [John Milius] *Ph* Bruce Surtees *Ed* Carl Pingitore *Mus* Lalo Schifrin *Art Dir* Dale Hennesy
● Clint Eastwood, Harry Guardino, Reni Santoni, John Vernon, John Larch, Andy Robinson (Malpaso/Warner)

You could drive a truck through the plotholes in *Dirty Harry*, which wouldn't be so serious were the film not a specious, phony glorification of police and criminal brutality [from a story by Harry Julian Fink and R.M. Fink]. Clint Eastwood, in the title role, is a superhero whose antics become almost satire. Strip away the philosophical garbage and all that's left is a well-made but shallow running-and-jumping meller. Don Siegel produces handsomely and directs routinely.

Andy Robinson plays a mad sniper who attempts to hold up San Francisco for money to stop his random carnage. Mayor John Vernon is willing, police chief John Larch goes along, police lieutenant Harry Guardino unctuously follows the prevailing wind, and the work falls to supercop Eastwood.

Eastwood is dedicated – to his own violence. Perhaps his anger at Robinson is more at the delay in capturing him; after all, between bites on a hot dog, Eastwood foils a bank heist at midday, talks down a suicide jumper, and otherwise expedites assorted 'dirty work'. The character nearly drools, but Eastwood is far too inert for this bit of business.

There are several chase sequences – before the sadist-with-badge dispatches the sadist-without-badge. Thereupon, Eastwood flings his badge to the wind and walks away. At least Frisco is safe from his protection (but think of the rest of us).
••••••••••••••••••••••••••••••••••

■ **DIRTY MARY CRAZY LARRY**

1974, 93 MINS, US ◇ ⓥ
Dir John Hough *Prod* Norman T. Herman *Scr* Leigh Chapman, Antonio Santean *Ph* Mike Margulies *Ed* Chris Holmes *Mus* Jimmy Haskell
● Peter Fonda, Susan George, Adam Roarke, Vic Morrow, Ken Tobey, Roddy McDowall (Academy/20th Century-Fox)

Screenplay is from Richard Unekis' novel *The Chase*, but what little narrative or characterization shows up on screen could barely fill an abridged short story. Racing enthusiasts Peter Fonda and Adam Roarke steal $150,000 from a supermarket manager (Roddy McDowall, strangely unbilled) in order to purchase a competition sports car. Joined by sluttish Susan George, they career around rural California with the law (demonic Vic Morrow) in pursuit.

With more than a third of the footage devoted to spectacular chases and collisions deftly staged by stunt coordinator Al Wyatt, there's little time left to hint at the reasons for Fonda's increasingly unappetizing monomania.

Cast performs ably. Fonda is less wooden than usual.
••••••••••••••••••••••••••••••••••

■ **DISHONORED**

1931, 91 MINS, US ⓥ
Dir Josef von Sternberg *Scr* Daniel N. Rubin *Ph* Lee Garmes *Art Dir* [Hans Dreier]
● Marlene Dietrich, Victor McLaglen, Lew Cody, Gustav von Seyffertitz, Warner Oland, Barry Norton (Paramount)

A secret service story [from *X-27* by Josef von Sternberg]. The start of the film, when Gustav von Seyffertitz as the Austrian intelligence chief picks up Dietrich on the street to make her a prize spy, is extremely nice work. But Dietrich rises above her director in this picture, as much as Sternberg smothered her while making *Morocco*. Dietrich is dominant in *Dishonored*. It is she who forces interest.

Her love for the Russian rival spy (Victor McLaglen) is made quite evident at the finish. Barring some silly dialog saddled upon him a couple of times, McLaglen gets through okay. Seyffertitz, always dependable, is more so than usual.
••••••••••••••••••••••••••••••••••

■ **DISHONORED LADY**

1947, 86 MINS, US ◇ ⓥ
Dir Robert Stevenson *Prod* Jack Chertok *Scr* Edmund H. North *Ph* Lucien Andriot *Ed* James E. Newcom, John Foley *Mus* Carmen Dragon *Art Dir* Nicolai Remisoff
● Hedy Lamarr, Dennis O'Keefe, John Loder, Morris Carnovsky, William Lundigan, Margaret Hamilton (United Artists)

In this remake of the stage play [by Edward Sheldon and Margaret Ayer Barnes] Hedy Lamarr character is more psychological than immoral and the film approach lessens interest and clarity. Plot still gets in shadowy implications of character's promiscuous love life, mostly through dialog.

It tells of editor of fashionable femme mag

who's not getting the best out of life although apparently enjoying it. Mental desperation drives her to attempted suicide, a visit with a psychiatrist, and renunciation of old way of living. She meets a young doctor, falls in love and becomes involved in a murder.

Male co-stars are Dennis O'Keeefe and John Loder as the young doctor and an old love, respectively. O'Keefe character isn't always even and Loder's role is a bit too smooth. William Lundigan, Morris Carnovsky (psychiatrist), Paul Cavanagh (publisher) and Natalie Schafer are okay among other principals. Margaret Hamilton rates some chuckles in typical rooming housekeeper role.

. . . .

■ DISORDERLY ORDERLY, THE

1964, 89 MINS, US ◇ ⑪
Dir Frank Tashlin   *Prod* Paul Jones   *Scr* Frank Tashlin
Ph W. Wallace Kelley   *Ed* Arthur P. Schmidt, John Woodcock   *Mus* Joseph J. Lilley   *Art Dir* Hal Pereira, Tambi Larsen
● Jerry Lewis, Glenda Farrell, Everett Sloane, Karen Sharpe, Kathleen Freeman, Susan Oliver (Paramount)

The Disorderly Orderly is fast and madcappish, with Lewis again playing one of his malaprop characters that seem to suit his particular talents.

As the orderly, Lewis is himself almost a mental patient as he takes on all the symptoms of the individual patients in the plush sanitarium where he's employed. Ambitious to be a doctor, he flunked out in medical school because of this particular attribute. He's cured through some fancy script-figuring when Susan Oliver, one of the patients, offers him love and he discovers that he's really in love with Karen Sharpe, a nurse. Sandwiched within this premise is Lewis at work, at play, always in trouble.

Star is up to his usual comicking and Frank Tashlin's direction of his own screenplay [from a story by Norm Liebmann and Ed Haas] is fast and vigorous in maintaining a nutty mood. Sharpe is pert and cute, Oliver ably transforms from a would-be suicide to a sexpot, and Glenda Farrell, cast as head of the sanitarium, displays the talent which once made her a star.

. . . .

■ DISRAELI

1929, 90 MINS, US
Dir Alfred E. Green   *Scr* Julian Josephson   *Ph* Lee Garmes
● George Arliss, Joan Bennett, Florence Arliss, Anthony Bushell, David Torrence, Doris Lloyd (Warner)

Acting and characterization are a continuous delight, not to mention a plot that concerns the diplomatic imperatives of possessing the Suez Canal.

Disraeli without George Arliss is to shudder. The professional equipment of the central figure carries and dominates both plot and conversation [from the play by Louis N. Parker].

Warners have done it right. Production is unstinted, sedate, and colorful, in the style of 1874. Small bits as well as principal roles are equally meritorious. Florence Arliss, wife of the star, plays his wife in the picture and makes the family circle complete by attaching runner-up honors.

Doris Lloyd as a woman spy is interesting and plausible as she weaves her little net of intrigue. She proves the 'menace' to the plan to purchase the big ditch through Egypt.
□ 1929/30: Best Actor (George Arliss).
□ Nominations: Best Picture, Writing

. . . .

■ DISTANT VOICES, STILL LIVES

1988, 84 MINS, UK ◇ ⑪ ⊙
Dir Terence Davies   *Prod* Jennifer Howarth   *Scr* Terence Davies   *Ph* William Diver, Patrick Duval   *Ed* William Diver   *Art Dir* Miki van Zwanenberg

● Freda Dowie, Pete Postlethwaithe, Angela Walsh, Dean Williams, Lorraine Ashbourne (BFI/Film Four)

This is the first feature film of Liverpudlian Terence Davies, obviously autobiographical, dealing with a family called Davies and their lives during the 1940s and 1950s.

The film is divided into two parts: *Distant Voices* (45 mins) centers on the wedding of Eileen, eldest of the three Davies children, and the funeral of her father, events which spark memories of the past, including the frightening war years when the city was bombed frequently; *Still Lives* (39 mins) actually was filmed two years after the first part, with the same actors but with a substantially different crew. It's a seamless continuation which climaxes with the wedding of another of the clan, son Tony.

The film is full of singing, as the characters break into familiar songs at family gatherings or in the local pub. This isn't a film based on nostalgia, though; its very special qualities stem from the beautiful simplicity of direction, writing and playing, and the accuracy of the incidents depicted.

. . . .

■ DISTINGUISHED GENTLEMAN, THE

1992, 113 MINS, US ◇ ⑪ ⊙
Dir Jonathan Lynn   *Prod* Leonard Goldberg, Michael Peyser   *Scr* Marty Kaplan   *Ph* Gabriel Beristain
Ed Tony Lombardo, Barry B. Leirer   *Mus* Randy Edelman
Art Dir Leslie Dilley
● Eddie Murphy, Lane Smith, Sheryl Lee Ralph, Joe Don Baker, Victoria Rowell, Grant Shaud (Hollywood Pictures)

Mr Murphy goes to Washington in *The Distinguished Gentleman*, an uneven but occasionally quite funny political satire [from a screen story by Marty Kaplan and Jonathan Reynolds].

The movie starts with a very funny premise but doesn't sustain it once the action shifts to the nation's capital: what if a con man was swept into Washington by using the same name as a recently deceased congressman – playing on the notion most people don't know if their rep is dead or alive anyway.

The twist, of course, is that the biggest scams of all go on legally in Washington. However, Murphy's better nature takes over and prompts him to do the ethical thing.

The screenplay by Marty Kaplan (a former speechwriter for Walter Mondale) certainly has its fun with the depraved ins and outs of politics, even if there are no new wrinkles.

The transformation of Jeff Johnson (Eddie Murphy) into a caring sort is never convincing, other than his understandable desire to woo the niece (Victoria Rowell) of a principled rep (Charles S. Dutton).

Pic is an amalgam of past Murphy roles but most closely resembles *Trading Places*. Director Jonathan Lynn maintains a steady pace but can't avoid arid stretches.

. . . .

■ DIVIDED HEART, THE

1954, 89 MINS, UK
Dir Charles Crichton   *Prod* Michael Balcon   *Scr* Jack Whittingham, Richard Hughes   *Ph* Otto Heller   *Ed* Peter Bezencenet   *Mus* Georges Auric
● Cornell Borchers, Yvonne Mitchell, Armin Dahlen, Alexander Knox, Geoffrey Keen, Liam Redmond (Ealing)

A human story taken from real life, *The Divided Heart* fails to tug the emotional heartstrings and ends up as little more than a conventional if convincing meller. Film is based on an actual story featured in *Life* in which a blood mother claims her son, who had legally been adopted during the war by German parents.

The narrative is sincerely developed from the actual documentation of the case. It spotlights the dilemma of the American tribunal which has to decide whether the boy should remain with his foster parents or be sent to

his real mother. The circumstances are mainly depicted in flashback during the hearing by the American judges.

At no time does the script measure up to the real heartache of the actual incident and there is rarely more than a superficial approach to this postwar problem. The cast is more than adequate, however, and Cornell Borchers and Yvonne Mitchell give stirring performances as the two mothers involved in the dilemma.

. . . .

■ DIVIDING LINE, THE
See: The Lawless

. . . .

■ DIVINE MADNESS

1980, 94 MINS, US ◇ ⑪ ⊙
Dir Michael Ritchie   *Prod* Michael Ritchie   *Scr* Jerry Blatt, Bette Midler, Bruce Vilanch   *Ph* William A. Fraker, Bobby Byrne   *Ed* Glenn Farr   *Mus* Tony Berg, Randy Kerber (arr.)   *Art Dir* Albert Brenner
● Bette Midler, The Harlettes, Irving Sudrow (Ladd)

After years of honing her act in gay baths and on concert stages, Bette Midler in 1980 committed it to film in four days at the Pasadena, Calif, Civic Auditorium. 'Because this is the time capsule version of my show,' she tells the aud, 'I might as well do everything I know.' Well, she doesn't quite do everything but she does not stint on energy and showmanship.

The film has a more carefully designed and visually opulent look than most concert pix. Director Michael Ritchie and his supervising cameraman, William A. Fraker, employed a 30-man camera team to shoot more than one million feet of film.

Midler's monologs between songs, largely blue material familiar to devotees of her show, are uproariously funny and she delivers them with infectious physical panache.

As for her voice, Midler is no Streisand, but she has a solid personality to back up her songs, and her versatility is one of her strongest assets.

. . . .

■ DIVINE WOMAN, THE

1928, 95 MINS, US ⊗
Dir Victor Seastrom   *Scr* Dorothy Farnum, John Colton   *Ph* Oliver Marsh   *Ed* Conrad A. Nervig
● Greta Garbo, Lars Hanson, Lowell Sherman, Polly Moran, Dorothy Cumming, John Mack Brown (M-G-M)

No denying Greta Garbo. Her beauty is of a simple sort; nothing exotic or hectic – just a super-pretty blonde. And director Victor Seastrom knows just how to handle her.

In this instance [from Gladys Unger's play *Starlight*] she is a peasant girl from Brittany, and here and there the incidents suggest anecdotes of the life of Sarah Bernhardt, though this thread is not consistently followed. She comes to Paris to find fame as an actress. The man who brings her there is her mother's lover, played by Lowell Sherman in his best manner. She falls in love with Lucien, a private soldier, and gets him into all sorts of grief, including arrest as a deserter and prosecution for stealing a dress she admires.

The romance is a rough-and-tumble, cute and juvenile. Greta flirts charmingly, and Lars Hanson, whose features do not indicate Scandinavian origin, takes his love-making quite seriously, which gives a fine effect to her work.

. . . .

■ DIVORCE AMERICAN STYLE

1967, 109 MINS, US ◇ ⑪
Dir Bud Yorkin   *Prod* Norman Lear   *Scr* Norman Lear
Ph Conrad Hall   *Ed* Ferris Webster   *Mus* Dave Grusin
Art Dir Edward Stephenson
● Dick Van Dyke, Debbie Reynolds, Jason Robards, Jean Simmons, Van Johnson, Joe Flynn (Columbia)

D

Comedy and satire, not feverish melodrama, are the best weapons with which to harpoon social mores. An outstanding example is *Divorce American Style* [from a story by Robert Kaufman], which pokes incisive, sometimes chilling, fun at US marriage-divorce problems.

Amidst wow comedy situations, story depicts the break-up after 15 years of the Van Dyke-Debbie Reynolds marriage, followed by the economic tragedies exemplified by Jason Robards and Jean Simmons, caught in a vicious circle of alimony and remarriage problems.

Shelley Berman and Dick Gautier, two chummy lawyers, spotlight the occasional feeling by litigants that their personal problems are secondary to the games attorneys play.

☐ 1967: Nomination: Best Original Story & Screenplay

■ **DIVORCEE, THE**

1930, 80 MINS, US ⓦ

Dir Robert Z. Leonard *Scr* Nick Grinde, Zelda Sears, John Meehan *Ph* Norbert Brodine *Ed* Hugh Wynn
● Norma Shearer, Chester Morris, Conrad Nagel, Robert Montgomery, Florence Eldridge, Helene Millard (M-G-M)

In its adaptation of *Ex-Wife*, the spicy 1929 novel by Ursula Parrott, Metro has taken liberties. Refinement has taken the upper hand here, with only the necessary touch of sauciness to satisfy readers of the novel, which was first published anonymously and later, after thousands of copies were sold, under the author's name.

Metro has even changed the names of the characters as they were in the Parrott story, given it a totally foreign opening, skipped much of the material that made *Ex-Wife* an interesting yarn, missed entirely the spirit with which the heroine accepts the futility of her marriage, suddenly broken off, and for a surprise ending takes the action to Paris and patches everything up.

Norma Shearer is excellent as the ad writer who in the novel finally despairs of ever getting her husband back, but in the picture does and with a very effective, formula-like clinch for the close. Opposite Shearer is Chester Morris, who is actually cast as a newspaper man. You only know that because he says so once. Audience figuring out things for the finish will probably be fooled to find that Conrad Nagel, the other man, doesn't successfully step in for the final fade, but that's the way it's been done here, the novel notwithstanding.

Besides good performances by Shearer, Morris and Nagel, unusually fine work is contributed by Robert Montgomery, the husband's friend, who helps himself to the wife as he would to an extended cocktail.
☐ 1929/30: Best Actress (Norma Shearer).
☐ Nominations: Best Picture, Director, Writing (John Meehan)

■ **DIVORCE OF LADY X, THE**

1938, 92 MINS, UK ◇ ⓦ

Dir Tim Whelan *Prod* Alexander Korda *Scr* Ian Dalrymple, Arthur Wimperis, Lajos Biro *Ph* Harry Stradling *Ed* L.J.W. Stockviss, William Hornbeck *Mus* Miklos Rozsa *Art Dir* Lazare Meerson
● Merle Oberon, Laurence Olivier, Binnie Barnes, Ralph Richardson, Morton Selten, Gus McNaughton (London Films)

Alexander Korda's Technicolored comedy is rich, smart entertainment, a comedy built around several situations and a wrong-identity hoax.

Robert E. Sherwood's deft writing is apparent in the screenplay job he did along with Lajos Biro, author of the play [*Counsel's Opinion*] from which the pic was evolved.

Comedy lines have that Sherwood sting.

Merle Oberon attends a costume ball in a London hotel and after the manager can't persuade an annoyed young lawyer (Laurence Olivier) to part with some space in his suite, Oberon maneuvers in and wheedles him out of his bed.

Next day girl vamooses before chap can find out much about her; he's convinced she's married. On arrival at his office, he is plagued by a college classmate to get the latter a divorce. He claims his wife spent the night with an unknown man in the same hotel, after attending the same dance. Girl continues to interest the chap and when she knows the sort he believes her to be maintains the ruse.

Oberon impresses. Olivier does his role pretty well, retarded somewhat by an annoying bit of pouting business. Two key performances which sparkle are those of Ralph Richarson and Morton Selten.

■ **D.O.A.**

1950, 83 MINS, US ⓦ ⊙

Dir Rudolph Mate *Prod* Leo C. Popkin *Scr* Russell Rouse, Clarence Green *Ph* Ernest Laszlo *Ed* Arthur H. Nadel *Mus* Dimitri Tiomkin *Art Dir* Duncan Cramer
● Edmond O'Brien, Pamela Britton, Luther Adler, Beverly Campbell, Lyn Baggett, William Chang (United Artists)

D.O.A. poses the novel twist of having a man looking for his own murderer. That off-beat idea and a strong performance by Edmond O'Brien do a lot to hold it together. But script is difficult to follow and doesn't get into its real meat until about 35 minutes of footage have passed.

O'Brien is seen as a tax counselor who trips to San Francisco for a round of the fleshpots. During a visit of hot spots he is slipped deadly luminous poison in a drink, and he is told he only has a few days to live. He spends the next few days trying to find his murderer and why he had been made a victim.

Rudolph Mate's direction of the first portion of the story lingers too long over it, spreading the expectancy very thin, but when he does launch his suspense-building it comes over with a solid wallop.

■ **D.O.A.**

1988, 96 MINS, US ◇ ⓦ ⊙

Dir Rocky Morton, Annabel Jankel *Prod* Ian Sander, Laura Ziskin *Scr* Charles Edward Pogue *Ph* Yuri Neyman *Ed* Michael R. Miller *Mus* Chaz Jankel *Art Dir* Richard Amend
● Dennis Quaid, Meg Ryan, Charlotte Rampling, Daniel Stern, Jane Kaczmarek, Christopher Neame (Touchstone)

An excessively morbid and unsubtle second remake of the 1949 film noir classic, *D.O.A.* remains unbelievable and unappealing despite a barnstorming central performance by Dennis Quaid.

Scripter uses two central MacGuffins to get the pot boiling. First Quaid is an English prof who's unwilling to read his precocious student Nick Lang's (played by Rob Knepper) novel. Just as hard-drinking Quaid marks an A on the still unread manuscript, Nick falls to his death past Quaid's window, an apparent suicide.

Second, pic's structure (bookended with black-&-white sequences at the police station) and catalyst are from Russell Rouse and Clarence Green's 1949 screenplay for *D.O.A.* In the third reel Quaid is diagnosed as having ingested a luminous poison, with only one to two days left to live. The protagonist who has given up on life since publishing his last novel four years back now has an obsession to live for: find his own killer.

Convoluted trail of murder and suicide teams Quaid with Meg Ryan, as a pretty coed with a crush on him.

Hailing from music videos and TV's *Max Headroom*, married helmers Rocky Morton and Annabel Jankel overload their maiden feature with visual gimmickry: lots of tilted, or swivelling first-person camerawork plus moire-patterned lighting to create distortion. Acting, particularly by Quaid, Ryan and Knepper, is fine, but Charlotte Rampling is very unflatteringly styled and photographed.

■ **DOC**

1971, 95 MINS, US ◇

Dir Frank Perry *Prod* Frank Perry *Scr* Pete Hamill *Ph* Gerald Hirschfield *Ed* Alan Helm *Mus* Jimmy Webb *Art Dir* Gene Callahan
● Stacy Keach, Faye Dunaway, Harris Yulin, Mike Witney, Denver John Collins, Dan Greenburg (United Artists)

Frank Perry in *Doc* attempts to remove the encrustations of myth and fantasy over the rough-hewn facts and persons of Wyatt Earp, Doc Holliday, Kate Elder and Tombstone.

Stacy Keach, Faye Dunaway and Harris Yulin star in good performances which may shock the naive, outrage the super-patriotic, offend those who prefer the cliches of the American West, but satisfy the well-adjusted.

Perry takes care to explore the reality of the situations, to recreate an earthy environment, and then to depict acts and events which, in their own time and morality, made sense. In order to achieve this, the first reel is as delicate as a kick in the groin; once over that pain the rest of the story evolves smoothly.

Earp (Yulin) emerges as a shifty politician of flexible motivation, by today's cynical standards a model pragmatic man of public life. His relationship with Holliday (Keach) has undertones left to the imagination (when little else is). Dunaway shakes her fashion-model fragility to become a believable frontier woman.

■ **DOC HOLLYWOOD**

1991, 103 MINS, US ◇ ⓦ ⊙

Dir Michael Caton-Jones *Prod* Susan Solt, Deborah D. Johnson *Scr* Jeffrey Price, Peter S. Seaman, Daniel Pyne *Ph* Michael Chapman *Ed* Priscilla Nedd-Friendly *Mus* Carter Burwell *Art Dir* Lawrence Miller
● Michael J. Fox, Julie Warner, Barnard Hughes, Woody Harrelson, George Hamilton, Bridget Fonda (Warner)

Doc Hollywood represents an attempt to rekindle the homespun humor and warmth of 1930s and '40s paeans to small-town American life. This heaped serving of recycled Capracorn [from Neil B. Schulman's book *What?. . . Dead Again?*, adapted by Laurian Leggett] has no real taste of its own, but, in its mildness and predictability, offers the reassurance of a fast-food or motel chain.

Arrogant young big-city doctor Ben Stone (Michael J. Fox) is, as he puts it, 'waylaid in "Hee-Haw" hell' on his way through the South to LA and prospective riches as a plastic surgeon. Detained in Grady, SC, the quaintest li'l ol' town you ever did see, the impatient Ben is forced to perform 32 hours of community service at the local clinic for destroying the judge's white picket fence with his Porsche.

Treating the minor maladies of the charmingly eccentric locals, Ben can't help but become a bit hooked by town happenings and intrigue. But most of all he's taken with the unusually feisty and attractive ambulance driver Lou (Julie Warner), a young woman with a four-year-old daughter. When Ben delivers his first baby, he feels pangs of attachment for the town.

Fox gives an energetic, agreeable, performance. Newcomer Warner is also perfectly pleasant, if not too believable as a young lady from the deep South. Supporting cast is fine down the line, with George Hamilton putting in what amounts to a cameo as the head of a chic cosmetic surgery clinic.

●●●●●●●●●●●●●●●●●●●●●●●●●●●●●●●●●●●

■ DOCK BRIEF, THE
(US: Trial and Error)

1962, 88 MINS, UK

Dir James Hill *Prod* Dimitri De Grunwald *Scr* Pierre Rouve *Ph* Edward Scaife *Ed* Ann Chegwidden *Mus* Ron Grainer *Art Dir* Ray Simm
● Peter Sellers, Richard Attenborough, Beryl Reid, David Lodge, Tristram Jellinek (M-G-M)

This offbeat, arty film gets away to a good start with the stellar pull of Peter Sellers and Richard Attenborough. Originally a radio play by John Mortimer, it is a bold attempt to present something different and, on the whole, it's a fair try.

Sellers plays an aging, unsuccessful barrister who gets the chance of a lifetime when briefed to defend Attenborough, a mild birdseed merchant who has murdered his wife because he wanted peace. He is bored with her because of her raucous sense of humour. It is the last straw when she doesn't elope with their equally raucous and boisterous lodger. Sellers plans his campaign optimistically and is quite undaunted when Attenborough admits the crime and shows the flaws in all Sellers' defense arguments.

The screenplay is a literate job, with a deft mixture of comedy and pathos. Sellers has the opportunity of showing many moods and much of his work is good. Attenborough comes out of the acting duel rather better.

●●●●●●●●●●●●●●●●●●●●●●●●●●●●●●●●●●●

■ DOCKS OF NEW YORK, THE

1928, 80 MINS, US ⊗ Ⓥ

Dir Josef von Sternberg *Scr* Jules Furthman, Julian Johnson *Ph* Harold Rosson *Art Dir* Hans Dreier
● George Bancroft, Betty Compson, Baclanova, Clyde Cook, Mitchell Lewis, Gustav von Seyffertitz (Paramount)

The Docks of New York is not Josef von Sternberg's greatest. But it's a corking program picture, thanks to George Bancroft, a good story and Julian Johnson's titles.

Sternberg's direction is excellent, but it is in the casting that the picture falls short of special classification. Betty Compson as an elliptical-heeled frail, who is punch drunk from life and attempts suicide, only to be rescued by Bancroft, a roughneck stoker, fails to get underneath the characterization. In real life she would probably have four husbands in the rack and be chalking up for the fifth.

Bancroft as Bill Roberts, the husky, hard-drinking, two-fisted stoker, has a role that he can make roll over. Roberts, on his one night ashore, saves the girl, and in a spirit of bravado marries her in a waterfront dive operated by a crimp (Guy Oliver).

Next morning Roberts again is ready for sea. He is on his way to a ship when a crowd and the arrival of the police arouses his curiosity. He returns to find the girl about to be arrested for shooting the third engineer of the crew (Mitchell Lewis), who had entered her room and tried to force his attentions on her.

The scenario is adapted from the John Monk Saunders original, *The Dock Walloper*. Exquisite photography helps a lot. Foggy mystic water shots give the waterfront the same quality of *Street Angel*.

●●●●●●●●●●●●●●●●●●●●●●●●●●●●●●●●●●●

■ DOC SAVAGE
THE MAN OF BRONZE

1975, 100 MINS, US ◇ Ⓥ

Dir Michael Anderson *Prod* George Pal *Scr* George Pal, Joe Morhaim *Ph* Fred Koenekamp *Ed* Thomas McCarthy *Mus* Frank DeVol (adapt.) *Art Dir* Fred Harpman

● Ron Ely, Paul Gleason, Bill Lucking, Michael Miller, Eldon Quick, Darrell Zwerling (Warner)

Execrable acting, dopey action sequences, and clumsy attempts at camp humor mark George Pal's *Doc Savage* as the kind of kiddie film that gives the G rating a bad name. Set in the 1930s and based on the Kenneth Robeson comic strip character, it is below the level of the *Batman* 1960s TV series, which it seems to be emulating.

Ron Ely looks impressive as the blond muscleman superhero, but doesn't do much beyond flexing his muscles and flashing smiles at the group of cronies who join him on an expedition into the South American jungles to avenge his father's murder.

Only thesp who survives the script with any dignity is Pamela Hensley, playing a native girl in love with the stolid hero.

●●●●●●●●●●●●●●●●●●●●●●●●●●●●●●●●●●●

■ DOCTOR, THE

1991, 125 MINS, US ◇ Ⓥ ⊙

Dir Runda Haines *Prod* Laura Ziskin *Scr* Robert Caswell *Ph* John Seale *Ed* Bruce Green, Lisa Fruchtman *Mus* Michael Convertino *Art Dir* Ken Adam

● William Hurt, Christine Lahti, Elizabeth Perkins, Mandy Patinkin, Adam Arkin, Charlie Korsmo (Touchstone)

The Doctor grapples powerfully with themes of mortality, compassion, social responsibility [from Ed Rosenbaum's book *A Taste of My Own Medicine*]. William Hurt's perf as an emotionally constricted heart and lung surgeon faced with his own medical crisis is all the more moving for its rigor and restraint.

Hurt espouses a philosophy of emotional distance, claiming that empathy interferes with technical demands made on a surgeon. He carries over the approach into his sterile family life in affluent Marin County, keeping wife Christine Lahti and son Charlie Korsmo at arm's length. His life is thrown into turmoil when he is diagnosed with throat cancer.

Director Randa Haines, who previously guided Hurt in *Children of a Lesser God*, first cast Warren Beatty in *The Doctor* before they parted over differences of interpretation. She is fortunate to have an icier actor such as Hurt in the role, because it's more of a stretch for him to evolve into a mensch.

Haines' intelligent direction is methodical in the best sense of the word, using documentary-like storytelling techniques with lenser John Seale to take the viewer through the doctor's journey of self-discovery in Ken Adam's chilling silver-blue hospital set.

Hurt's initial self-pity begins to evaporate when he enters the incandescent presence of fellow patient Elizabeth Perkins. Their platonic but intimate relationship becomes the film's emotional crux as Perkins (in a wondrously good performance) teaches Hurt what he failed to learn in med school about unconquerable pain and acceptance of death.

●●●●●●●●●●●●●●●●●●●●●●●●●●●●●●●●●●●

■ DOCTOR AT LARGE

1957, 104 MINS, UK ◇ Ⓥ

Dir Ralph Thomas *Prod* Betty E. Box *Scr* Nicholas Phipps *Ph* Ernest Steward *Ed* Frederick Wilson *Mus* Bruce Montgomery *Art Dir* Maurice Carter
● Dirk Bogarde, Muriel Pavlow, Donald Sinden, James Robertson Justice, Shirley Eaton, Michael Medwin (Rank)

This continues the adventures of the young medico who qualified in *Doctor in the House* and got his first appointment in *Doctor at Sea*. This time round he's on a job hunting spree and the film depicts his experiences and adventures while working for a mean provincial doctor and in a fashionable Park Lane practice.

The yarn develops with a blending of light comedy and a dash of sentiment, with punch comedy lines providing timely shots in the arm. They're welcome when they come, but they're too irregular.

Role of the young doctor again is played by Dirk Bogarde. The story opens at St Swithin's hospital where Bogarde hopes to achieve his vocational ambitions to practice surgery. But he falls foul of James Robertson Justice, who is the hospital's chief consultant. To gain experience (and pay the rent), he begins his job hunting trail.

Bogarde, of course, is the mainstay of the story, but Justice again emerges as the standout character, even though his role is reduced to more modest proportions.

●●●●●●●●●●●●●●●●●●●●●●●●●●●●●●●●●●●

■ DOCTOR AT SEA

1955, 93 MINS, UK ◇ Ⓥ

Dir Ralph Thomas *Prod* Betty E. Box *Scr* Nicholas Phipps, Jack Davies *Ph* Ernest Steward *Ed* Frederick Wilson *Mus* Bruce Montgomery
● Dirk Bogarde, Brigitte Bardot, Brenda De Banzie, James Robertson Justice, Maurice Denham, Michael Medwin (Rank)

As their first British venture in VistaVision, the Rank studios play safe with a sequel to *Doctor in the House*, but *Doctor at Sea* does not rise to the same laugh-provoking heights as its predecessor.

James Robertson Justice is a gruff ship's captain on whose freighter the young medico has his first appointment at sea. The ship is obliged to take on board the daughter of the chairman of the line and her friend, a pert and attractive cabaret chanteuse.

By far the most dominating performance of the cast is given by Justice. He towers above the others and is the focal point of every scene in which he appears. Dirk Bogarde plays the medico with a pleasing quiet restraint and Brigitte Bardot has an acting talent to match her charm.

●●●●●●●●●●●●●●●●●●●●●●●●●●●●●●●●●●●

■ DOCTOR DOLITTLE

1967, 152 MINS, US ◇ Ⓥ

Dir Richard Fleischer *Prod* Arthur P. Jacobs *Scr* Leslie Bricusse *Ph* Robert Surtees *Ed* Samuel E. Beetley, Marjorie Fowler *Mus* Lionel Newman, Alexander Courage (arr.) *Art Dir* Jack Martin Smith, Ed Graves
● Rex Harrison, Samantha Eggar, Anthony Newley, Richard Attenborough, Peter Bull, Muriel Landers (20th Century-Fox/Apjac)

Rex Harrison, physically, is not at all the rotund original from Hugh Lofting's stories; but histrionically, he's perfect. Gentle and loving with animals, patient and kind with obtuse and very young friends, he can become a veritable holocaust when confronted with cruel and uncomprehending adults who threaten his animal world.

Leslie Bricusse's adaptation retains the delightful aspects while taking considerable liberty with the plot. His music and lyrics, while containing no smash hits, are admirably suited to the scenario.

Outstanding, considering his brief appearance, is Richard Attenborough as Albert Blossom, the circus owner. He comes on so strong in his one song-and-dance bit that it's nearly a perfect example of why important cameo roles should be turned over to important talents.

Most of the $16 million budget evidently went into the production and it shows.

☐ 1967: Best Song ('Talk to the Animals'), Special Visual Effects.

☐ Nominations: Best Picture, Cinematography, Art Direction, Editing, Original Music Score, Adapted Music Score, Sound

●●●●●●●●●●●●●●●●●●●●●●●●●●●●●●●●●●●

■ DOCTOR EHRLICH'S MAGIC BULLET

1940, 103 MINS, US

Dir William Dieterle *Prod* Hal B. Wallis, Wolfgang Reinhardt *Scr* John Huston, Heinz Herald, Norman

D

Burnside *Ph* James Wong Howe *Ed* Warren Low *Mus* Max Steiner *Art Dir* Carl Jules Weyl
● Edward G. Robinson, Ruth Gordon, Otto Kruger, Donald Crisp, Maria Ouspenskaya, Albert Basserman (Warner)

Here is a splendid production, with much care and attention to detail. Historical biography is based on the life of Paul Ehrlich, famed bacteriologist, whose most noteworthy contribution to medical science was the search for, and eventual discovery of, 606, which proved to be a positive cure for syphilis.

The social disease is intelligently handled for effective presentation of its disastrous effects on humans prior to Ehrlich's discovery. Despite its straightforward presentation, there is nothing offensive in either action or dialog. Script, which necessitates care in combining the events of Ehrlich's career with scientific fact, is an excellently moulded screen biography.

Edward G. Robinson's portrayal of the famed Ehrlich is a distinguished performance. In tracing the scientist's accomplishments, story traces through a span of about 35 years. Robinson makes the gradual transition down the years in great style.

Ruth Gordon is a most sympathetic and understanding wife of a scientist absorbed in his work; Otto Kruger is excellent as Ehrlich's close friend and colleague; Donald Crisp is the health minister, and Albert Basserman is the noted scientist, Koch, who takes Ehrlich on his staff in the early part. Albert Basserman, well-known German actor, gets his first American role here.

■ **DOCTOR FAUSTUS**

1967, 92 MINS, UK ◇ ⊛
Dir Richard Burton, Nevill Coghill *Prod* Richard Burton, Richard McWhorter *Scr* Nevill Coghill *Ph* Gabor Pogany *Ed* John Shirley *Mus* Mario Nascimbene *Art Dir* John F. DeCuir
● Richard Burton, Elizabeth Taylor, Andreas Teuber, Ian Marter, Elizabeth O'Donovan, David McIntosh (Columbia)

An oddity that may have some archive appeal, for at least it records a performance by Burton [at Oxford University in 1966] that gives an insight into his prowess in classical roles. He is obviously captivated by Christopher Marlowe's 400-year-old verse, and speaks it with sonorous dignity and sense.

The story concerns the medieval doctor's attempt to master all human knowledge by selling his soul to the devil, who dangles before him such delights as nights with Elizabeth Taylor, who flits through the film in various undraped poses as the Helen of Troy siren promising a fate worse than death.

One surprise is the general adequacy of the Oxford amateurs, with a good performance in any terms from Andreas Teuber as Mephistopheles. But the impersonation of the seven deadly sins is hardly likely to send good men off the rail. Production was filmed in Rome.

■ **DOCTOR IN THE HOUSE**

1954, 92 MINS, UK ◇ ⊛
Dir Ralph Thomas *Prod* Betty E. Box *Scr* Nicholas Phipps *Ph* Ernest Steward *Ed* Gerald Thomas *Mus* Bruce Montgomery *Art Dir* Carmen Dillon
● Dirk Bogarde, Muriel Pavlow, Kenneth More, Donald Sinden, Kay Kendall, James Robertson Justice (Rank)

A topdraw British comedy, *Doctor in the House* is bright, diverting entertainment, intelligently scripted [from an adaptation of his own novel by Richard Gordon], and warmly played.

Background to the story is the medical school of a London hospital. Within 92 minutes, the film spans the five years in the life of a student group.

The new recruit to the school is Dirk Bogarde, who is taken under the protective wing of three old-timers who had all failed their preliminary exams. Kenneth More, Donald Sinden and Donald Houston make up a contrasted quartet who seem to have ideas on most subjects but not how to qualify as a medico.

Much of the comedy incident has been clearly contrived but it is nonetheless effective, particularly in the scenes featuring James Robertson Justice as a distinguished surgeon and More.

■ **DOCTOR'S DILEMMA, THE**

1959, 98 MINS, UK ◇
Dir Anthony Asquith *Prod* Anatole de Grunwald *Scr* Anatole de Grunwald *Ph* Robert Krasker *Ed* Gordon Hales *Mus* Joseph Kosma *Art Dir* Paul Sheriff
● Leslie Caron, Dirk Bogarde, Alastair Sim, Robert Morley, Felix Aylmer, Michael Gwynn (M-G-M/Comet)

George Bernard Shaw's stringent wit still shines in this film but, staged in 1903, his comments on Harley Street (London's medical row) and the doctoring profession have lost much of their impact. *Dilemma* remains, relentlessly, an easy-on-the-eye filmed version of an out-of-date play.

It concerns a young woman married to an artist who is a complete bounder – a sponger, a potential blackmailer and a man who can't resist other women. But she is blinded by hero-worship. He suffers from consumption, she pleads with a doctor to save his life. He thinks that he would do better to use his limited serum on a more worthwhile case.

Dirk Bogarde gives a stimulating performance as the selfish young artist and is particularly convincing in his final, highly theatrical death sequence. Leslie Caron is often moving in her blind belief in her man, but never suggests the strength necessary to fight the cynical doctors. These are played as caricatures.

■ **DOCTOR ZHIVAGO**

1965, 197 MINS, US ◇ ⊛ ⊙
Dir David Lean *Prod* Carlo Ponti *Scr* Robert Bolt *Ph* Freddie Young *Ed* Norman Savage *Mus* Maurice Jarre *Art Dir* John Box
● Omar Sharif, Julie Christie, Tom Courtenay, Geraldine Chaplin, Rod Steiger, Alec Guinness (M-G-M)

The sweep and scope of the Russian revolution, as reflected in the personalities of those who either adapted or were crushed, has been captured by David Lean in *Doctor Zhivago*, frequently with soaring dramatic intensity.

Some finely etched performances by an international cast illuminate the diverse characters from the novel for which Boris Pasternak won but did not accept the Nobel Prize. The Pasternak novel turns on an introspective medic-poet who essentially reacts to the people and events before, during and after the Bolshevik takeover.

At the center of a universe of nine basic characters is Omar Sharif as Zhivago, the sensitive man who strikes different people in different ways. To childhood sweetheart Geraldine Chaplin he is a devoted (if cheating) husband; to Julie Christie, with whom he is thrown together by war, he is a passionate lover; to Tom Courtenay, once an intellectual but later a heartless Red general, he's a symbol of the personal life which revolution has supposedly killed; to lecherous, political logroller Rod Steiger he's the epitome of 'rarefied selfishness'; and to halfbrother Alec Guinness, the cold secret police official, he's a man who must be saved from himself.

Sharif, largely through expressions of indignation, compassion and tenderness, makes the character very believable. Christie is out-

standing in a sensitive, yet earthy and full-blooded portrayal of a girl who is used and discarded by Steiger, then marries Courtenay only to lose him to his cause.

Lean has devoted as much care to physical values as he has to his players. The bitter cold of winter, the grime of Moscow, the lush countryside, the brutality of war, and the fool's paradise of the declining Czarist era are forcefully conveyed.
□ 1965: Best Adapted Screenplay, Color Cinematography, Color Art Direction, Original Musical Score, Color Costume Design.
□ Nominations: Best Picture, Director, Supp. Actor (Tom Courtenay), Editing, Sound

■ **DODGE CITY**

1939, 100 MINS, US ◇ ⊛ ⊙
Dir Michael Curtiz *Prod* [Robert Lord] *Scr* Robert Buckner *Ph* Sol Polito, Ray Rennahan *Ed* George Amy *Mus* Max Steiner *Art Dir* Ted Smith
● Errol Flynn, Olivia de Havilland, Ann Sheridan, Bruce Cabot, Frank McHugh, Alan Hale (Warner)

Dodge City is a lusty western, packed with action, including some of the dandiest melee stuff screened.

Falling in the cycle of pioneering and American frontier days, *Dodge City* (Kansas) is essentially a bad man-and-honest-sheriff saga. However Michael Curtiz's forceful direction lifts this into the big league division.

Errol Flynn is a soldier of fortune, which explains his clipped English-Irish brogue as a Texas cattleman, transplanted to this Kansas frontier. Olivia de Havilland is the romance interest, and Ann Sheridan the dancehall girl.

Cabot's gambling saloon effectively typifies all the wickedness of the lawlessness that was Dodge City, as the basic excuse for Flynn's ultimate taking over of the sheriff's post. The street fighting, licentiousness and the skullduggery having to do with cattle trading typify the lusty atmosphere that backgrounds this actioner.

■ **DODSWORTH**

1936, 90 MINS, US ⊛ ⊙
Dir William Wyler *Prod* Samuel Goldwyn *Scr* Sidney Howard *Ph* Ruldoph Mate *Ed* Danny Mandell *Mus* Alfred Newman *Art Dir* Richard Day
● Walter Huston, Ruth Chatterton, Paul Lukas, Mary Astor, David Niven, Gregory Gaye (Goldwyn/United Artists)

Dodsworth is a superb motion picture and a golden borealis over the producer's name.

Sidney Howard transposes his own stage play version of Sinclair Lewis' novel into a picture that uses the camera to open up the vista a little and enrich a basically fertile theme. Picture has a steady flow and an even dramatic wallop from zippy start to satisfying finish.

Dodsworth was Walter Huston on the stage and is logically and perfectly the same actor on the screen. This is the kind of a role stars dream about.

It is also obvious that this is Ruth Chatterton's fanciest opportunity on the screen in a long while. Fran Dodsworth is a silly, vain, selfish, shallow kitten and in the playing of Chatterton comes to life with vividness and humanity.

Mary Astor is the sympathetic other woman to whom Dodsworth ultimately turns. Her footage is limited. Her performance is varied and mature.

Three men cross the path of the age-fearing wife on her grand fling. First an Englishman played by David Niven. Then a suave continental played by Paul Lukas. Last a sincere and youthful Austrian played by George Gaye. Each of the lovers is a case of slick casting. Mother of the Austrian who finally strikes home with the pampered American woman is beautifully performed by Maria Ouspenskaya.

☐ 1936: Best Interior Decoration (Richard Day).
☐ Nominations: Best Picture, Director, Actor (Walter Huston), Supp. Actress (Maria Ouspenskaya), Screenplay, Sound

••••••••••••••••••••••••••••••

■ DOG DAY AFTERNOON

1975, 130 MINS, US ◇ ▼ ⊙
Dir Sidney Lumet *Prod* Martin Bregman, Martin Elfand *Scr* Frank Pierson *Ph* Victor J. Kemper *Ed* Dede Allen *Art Dir* Charles Bailey
● Al Pacino, John Cazale, Charles Durning, James Broderick, Chris Sarandon, Sully Boyar (Warner)

Dog Day Afternoon is an outstanding film. Based on a real life incident in NY it stars Al Pacino as the most unlikely bank robber ever to hit the screen.

The holdup was allegedly done for the purpose of financing a sex change operation for the male lover of one of the robbers. That incident is retained in the script, but it is just one of many key elements in a hilarious and moving story.

Pacino and laconic sidekick John Cazale take over the neighborhood bank branch managed by Sully Boyar. The malaprop heist gets the early laughs going, and then the film broadens and deepens as if re-enacting the Battle Of The Bulge.

The introduction of Pacino's lover (Chris Sarandon) is cleverly plotted, and comes as a surprise since Pacino's straight wife (Susan Peretz) has already appeared. The interactions between Pacino and other key characters are magnificently written, acted and directed.

The entire cast is excellent, top to bottom. *Dog Day Afternoon* is, in the whole as well as the parts, film-making at its best.
☐ 1975: Best Original Screenplay.
☐ Nominations: Best Picture, Director, Actor (Al Pacino), Supp. Actor (Chris Sarandon), Editing

••••••••••••••••••••••••••••••

■ DOGFIGHT

1991, 92 MINS, US ◇ ▼ ⊙
Dir Nancy Savoca *Prod* Peter Newman, Richard Guay *Scr* Bob Comfort *Ph* Bobby Bukowski *Ed* John Tintori *Mus* Mason Daring *Art Dir* Lester W. Cohen
● River Phoenix, Lili Taylor, Richard Panebianco, Anthony Clark, Mitchell Whitfield, Holly Near (Warner)

An inherently repellent subject has been given surprisingly benign treatment in *Dogfight*. Title refers to the central event of ex-Marine Bob Comfort's intermittently intriguing screenplay – a party to which a bunch of young servicemen bring the ugliest women they can find.

Full of obnoxious military attitude and macho bravado, Eddie Birdlace and his three buddies hit the streets of San Francisco on the portentous eve of Nov. 21, 1963, and separately scout for a 'dog' that might win the prize for most gruesome date. After a little trouble, Eddie (River Phoenix) manages to locate a candidate in young waitress Rose Fenney (Lili Taylor) and drags the unsuspecting young lady along to the nightclub.

The bringing together of a soldier headed for Vietnam and a future hippie on the night before President Kennedy's assassination represents a frightfully schematic screenwriting device. But Savoca underplays the character development to such an extent that the film has a muted, very modest impact. Shot mostly in Seattle, the dark looking film presents a strangely underpopulated San Francisco.

••••••••••••••••••••••••••••••

■ DOGS OF WAR, THE

1980, 122 MINS, UK ◇ ▼ ⊙
Dir John Irvin *Prod* Norman Jewison, Patrick Palmer *Scr* Gary DeVore, George Malko *Ph* Jack Cardiff

Ed Antony Gibbs *Mus* Geoffrey Burgon *Art Dir* Peter Mullins
● Christopher Walken, Tom Berenger, Colin Blakely, Hugh Millais, Paul Freeman, JoBeth Williams (United Artists)

The Dogs of War [from Frederick Forsyth's novel] is an intelligent and occasionally forceful treatment of a provocative but little-examined theme, that of mercenary warrior involvement in the overthrow of a corrupt black African dictatorship.

Script focuses almost exclusively on Christopher Walken, an 'irresponsible' American who is drawn to the mercenary's loner, adventurous life.

Film fails to really get at the heart of the whys and hows of mercenary life, and also rejects the idea of generating any sense of camaraderie among the men.

Details of life in a contempo African dictatorship country, from the bribery and censorship to the military strongarming and oppressive economic conditions, are effectively sketched. Pic displays the political realities without editorializing.

••••••••••••••••••••••••••••••

■ DOG SOLDIERS
See: Who'll Stop the Rain

••••••••••••••••••••••••••••••

■ $
(UK: The Heist)

1971, 120 MINS, US ◇ ▼ ⊙
Dir Richard Brooks *Prod* M.J. Francovich *Scr* Richard Brooks *Ph* Petrus Schloemp *Ed* George Grenville *Mus* Quincy Jones *Art Dir* Guy Sheppard
● Warren Beatty, Goldie Hawn, Gert Frobe, Robert Webber, Scott Brady, Arthur Brauss (Columbia)

Richard Brooks wrote and directed $ with a sardonic twist to a caper plot. Bank security expert Warren Beatty, aided by friendly hooker Goldie Hawn, steal $1.5 million from three Hamburg safety-deposit boxes used by assorted criminals. An exhausting chase sequence is the ultimate destination of the production which features some good authentic locales.

The key subordinate characters, Las Vegas skimming courier Robert Webber, corrupt US Army black marketeer Scott Brady, and European narcotics dealer Arthur Brauss, are on a dramatic parity with the principals and often overpower them. Hawn's trademark kookiness keeps getting in the way, and Beatty's low-key sensitivity can hardly survive.

This film is obviously what is sometimes called 'an entertainment'. Paradoxically, Brooks maybe is too serious a filmmaker for this sort of thing. He wants his characters to have depth and motivation, but the principle does not work well herein.

••••••••••••••••••••••••••••••

■ DOLL'S HOUSE, A

1973, 95 MINS, UK ◇ ▼
Dir Patrick Garland *Prod* Hillard Elkins *Scr* Christopher Hampton *Ph* Arthur Ibbetson *Ed* John Glen *Mus* John Barry *Art Dir* Elliott Scott
● Claire Bloom, Anthony Hopkins, Ralph Richardson, Denholm Elliott, Anna Massey, Edith Evans (Elkins/Freeward)

What is good here is largely what was good in the 1971 Broadway production from which pic directly derives. The latter was produced by Hillard Elkins, toplined his wife Claire Bloom, and was helmed and scripted by Patrick Garland and Christopher Hampton, respectively. All ditto for this film.

Package was assembled as though it were a legit production – two weeks of rehearsals preceded lensing, and scenes were shot in order.

Christopher Hampton's interpretation of

Henrick Ibsen's text successfully plays down the original's creakier verbal anachronisms but leaves its excellent construction intact. Film, as does play, unfolds grippingly, like a first-rate murder mystery with a cosmic consciousness.

Bloom is topnotch as the childlike and pampered wife of a stuffy bank manager. Bloom's portrayal beautifully captures Nora's initial coquettishness and her emergence as an independent woman of strength and character.

••••••••••••••••••••••••••••••

■ DOLL'S HOUSE, A

1973, 108 MINS, UK ◇ ▼
Dir Joseph Losey *Prod* Joseph Losey *Scr* David Mercer *Ph* Gerry Fisher *Ed* Reginald Beck *Mus* Michel Legrand *Art Dir* Eileen Diss
● Jane Fonda, David Warner, Trevor Howard, Delphine Seyrig, Edward Fox, Anna Wing (World)

The second version of the Henrik Ibsen classic to hit the screens in 1973, Joseph Losey's location-filmed (Norway) effort has the director's name plus that of Jane Fonda (playing the woman's lib pre-dating heroine, Nora) and a certain formal elegance to carry it.

Ironically, it is Fonda who appears miscast as the Ibsen heroine who dominates this Nordic drama, lacking as she does the vibrancy, depth and soul required to convey the transition of a fascinating character. The result, to all but Fonda die-hards, blurs the values of the film as a whole.

This is otherwise a rather striking if academic achievement: physically stunning, diligently acted, told in a linear style by a man who knows his cinema, unexcitingly effective here and there.

••••••••••••••••••••••••••••••

■ DOMINO KILLINGS, THE
See: The Domino Principle

••••••••••••••••••••••••••••••

■ DOMINO PRINCIPLE, THE
(UK: The Domino Killings)

1977, 97 MINS, US ◇ ▼
Dir Stanley Kramer *Prod* Stanley Kramer *Scr* Adam Kennedy *Ph* Fred Koenekamp, Ernest Laszlo *Ed* John F. Burnett *Mus* Billy Goldenberg *Art Dir* William J. Creber
● Gene Hackman, Candice Bergen, Richard Widmark, Mickey Rooney, Edward Albert, Eli Wallach (ITC/Associated General)

The Domino Principle is a weak and tedious potboiler starring Gene Hackman as a tool of mysterious international intrigue, and a barely recognizable Candice Bergen in a brief role as his perplexed wife. Stanley Kramer's film contains a lot of physical and logistical nonsense.

Adam Kennedy gets adaptation credit from his own novel. Hackman has been carefully spotted years earlier as an amoral and violent type, just the kind of guy that 'they' can use to assassinate selected public figures. We never know who 'they' are, but 'their' lower-level stooges include Richard Widmark, Eli Wallach and Edward Albert, each more or less archetypic organizational characters.

••••••••••••••••••••••••••••••

■ DON JUAN

1926, 100 MINS, US ▼ ⊙
Dir Alan Crosland *Scr* Bess Meredyth, Walter Anthony, Maude Fulton *Ph* Byron Haskin *Ed* Harold McCord *Mus* William Axt *Art Dir* Ben Carre
● John Barrymore, Mary Astor, Estelle Taylor, Warner Oland, Montagu Love, Myrna Loy (Warner)

Several outstanders in this splendidly written, directed and produced feature. Not alone does John Barrymore's superb playing become one of them, but his athletics, as well. A chase scene is a bear. It's of Don Juan carrying his Adriana away, followed by about a dozen swordsmen on horses, with Barrymore placing his charge in a tree, to return and knock off all of the riders, one by one or in twos.

The complete surprise is the performance of Estelle Taylor as Lucretia Borgia. Her Lucretia is a fine piece of work. She makes it sardonic in treatment, conveying precisely the woman Lucretia is presumed to have been. The other outstanding performance is that of Mary Astor's Adriana. Astor has but comparatively little action, but fills the part so thoroughly that she is a dominating figure. Warner Oland is Cesare, the savage brother, and he looks the role.

■ **DO NOT DISTURB**

1965, 102 MINS, US ◇
Dir Ralph Levy   *Prod* Aaron Rosenberg, Martin Melcher   *Scr* Milt Rosen, Richard Breen   *Ph* Leon Shamroy   *Ed* Robert Simpson   *Mus* Lionel Newman
● Doris Day, Rod Taylor, Hermione Baddeley, Sergio Fantoni, Reginald Gardiner, Maura McGiveney (20th Century-Fox)

Do Not Disturb is a light, entertaining comedy, set in England but filmed in Hollywood, with Doris Day teamed with a new screen hubby, Rod Taylor.

Milt Rosen and Richard Breen adapted a William Fairchild play, and Day and Taylor star as a Yank couple located in London, where hubby runs a woolen mill.

Stars play extremely well together, Day as the loving, but slightly wacky wife who grapples with English currency problems, rescues a pursued fox, and never quite gets the home in order, while Taylor is busy getting his factory into the black.

Their lives diverge when Maura McGiveney becomes too much of an assistant to Taylor, and sales chief Reginald Gardiner spells out the key for biz success: getting on the good side of Leon Askin, big wool buyer who throws swinging parties, meaning no wives.

Action cross cuts from Taylor's problem to Day, who becomes innocently entangled with Sergio Fantoni, antique dealer and a prototype Continental charmer.

■ **DONOVAN'S REEF**

1963, 104 MINS, US ◇ ▽ ⊙
Dir John Ford   *Prod* John Ford   *Scr* Frank Nugent, James Edward Grant   *Ph* William H. Clothier   *Ed* Otho Lovering   *Mus* Cyril Mockridge   *Art Dir* Hal Pereira, Eddie Imazu
● John Wayne, Lee Marvin, Jack Warden, Elizabeth Allen, Cesar Romero, Dorothy Lamour (Paramount/Ford)

Donovan's Reef, for a director of John Ford's stature, is a potboiler. Where Ford aficionados will squirm is during that occasional scene that reminds them this effort-less effort is the handiwork of the men who made *Stagecoach* and *The Informer*.

John Wayne, sailing along like a dreadnaught mothering a convoy of rowboats, conveys an exuberance to match the mayhem, moving from fracas to fracas, facing up to a gang of toughs or a belligerent Boston beauty with equal courage. The only demand made is on his muscles.

Lee Marvin, since their last excursion, has had his reins tightened by Ford. This is only a comic menace where once a malevolent terror smouldered. Jack Warden's role hints at earlier greater prominence, edited down to harmless support and irritating in its omissions.

Ford, best when he's faced with an unknown talent, brings out the ability of Elizabeth Allen, a darkling beauty. She's delightful as a Boston ice cube whose melting point is Wayne. Cesar Romero and Dorothy Lamour are the victims of acute scriptitis although

Dick Foran is briefly impressive as an Australian naval officer.

The visual beauty of Kauai, in northern Hawaii, is captured by William Clothier's photography. Frank Nugent (an old Ford hand) and James Edward Grant's script [from a story by Edmund Beloin] has more holes in it than Liberty Valance. They've created a paradisical setting, 'somewhere in the South Pacific', ruled by a native princess; governed by the French; protected by the Australian navy; 'run' by expatriate Americans; and peopled by a league of national types.

■ **DON Q, SON OF ZORRO**

1925, 110 MINS, US ◇ ⊗ ▽
Dir Donald Crisp   *Prod* Douglas Fairbanks   *Scr* Jack Cunningham   *Ph* Henry Sharp   *Ed* William Nolan   *Art Dir* Edward M. Langley
● Douglas Fairbanks, Mary Astor, Jack McDonald, Donald Crisp, Warner Oland, Jean Hersholt (Elton/United Artists)

Don Q gives Fairbanks a chance to play a double role, as the youthful Don Q and as Zorro, the father of the dashing young Californian who is completing his education in Spain. His adventures there form the basis of the picture. He becomes involved with royalty, is accused of the murder of a visiting archduke, feigns suicide, almost loses the girl, but in the end emerges triumphant.

Mary Astor plays opposite the star. She appears to beautiful advantage in the little that she has to do, while Donald Crisp as the heavy scores, although the supporting cast honors of the picture must be divided between Jean Hersholt and Warner Oland. Hersholt gets rather the better of it. His role isn't as strong as the one he had in *Greed*, but it shows him capable of intense characterization that registers heavily.

■ **DON'S PARTY**

1976, 90 MINS, AUSTRALIA ◇ ▽
Dir Bruce Beresford   *Prod* Philip Adams   *Scr* David Williamson   *Ph* Don McAlpine   *Ed* Bill Anderson   *Art Dir* Rhoisin Harrison
● Ray Barrett, Claire Binney, Pat Bishop, Graeme Blundell, Jeannie Drynan, John Gorton (Double Head)

The eponymous get-together takes place in Australia on Election Night, 1969. The 11 characters are all friends who, save two, have assembled to cheer in a Labor Party victory. The election day atmosphere is added to by a walk-on appearance by John Gorton as the prime minister of the day – which, indeed, he was.

The central characters in David Williamson's play may be grotesque, uncouth, drunken louts, but they do represent a streak in the Australian character that exists. Bringing them together at that particular time and place increases the claustrophobic effect they have on the others.

Don's Party is a vicious and unrelenting attack on suburbia and a harsh look at these who help populate it. The entire cast turn in superlative performances.

■ **DON'T BOTHER TO KNOCK**

1952, 76 MINS, US ▽
Dir Roy Ward Baker   *Prod* Julian Blaustein   *Scr* Daniel Taradash   *Ph* Lucien Ballard   *Ed* George A. Gittens   *Mus* Lionel Newman (dir.)   *Art Dir* Lyle Wheeler, Richard Irvine
● Richard Widmark, Marilyn Monroe, Anne Bancroft, Donna Corcoran, Jeanne Cagney, Elisha Cook Jr (20th Century-Fox)

Marilyn Monroe, co-starred with Richard Widmark, gives an excellent account of herself in a strictly dramatic role which com-

mands certain attention, but the story of a psycho baby-sitter lacks interest.

Femme star enters a NY hotel to take on a baby-sitting stint. Actually, she's newly released from a mental institution, sent there when her mind cracked after her fiance crashed in the Pacific and drowned. In Widmark, who glimpses her from his room across the court and comes calling with a bottle, she sees, in her dementia, the man she once loved.

Action progresses at a dull pace, and script by Daniel Taradash [from a novel by Charlotte Armstrong] tries to juggle too many elements.

Monroe's role seems an odd choice, and in this she's anything but glamorous, despite her donning a negligee. Widmark doesn't appear too happy with his role. Anne Bancroft, making her screen bow, scores brightly as a torch singer.

■ **DON'T BOTHER TO KNOCK**

1961, 88 MINS, UK ◇
Dir Cyril Frankel   *Prod* Richard Todd   *Scr* Denis Cannan, Frederick Gotfurt, Frederic Raphael   *Ph* Geoffrey Unsworth   *Ed* Anne V. Coates   *Mus* Elisabeth Lutyens   *Art Dir* Tony Masters
● Richard Todd, Nicole Maurey, Elke Sommer, June Thorburn, Judith Anderson, Eleanor Summerfield (Associated British/Haileywood)

Storyline has Richard Todd as an Edinburgh travel agent who goes off on a Continental business trip spree after quarreling with his fiancee (June Thorburn). He falls for a variety of charmers and hands out the key of his apartment to them with abandon. Having patched up his differences with his girl friend over the phone, he returns to Edinburgh and, of course, all the other feminine complications then arrive and take up residence.

Here is the basis of a spry bedroom farce, but the dialog [from a novel by Clifford Hanley] is heavy handed. And director Cyril Frankel has not been able to induce performances that disguise this sorry fact. Todd spends most of his time looking understandingly bewildered over the naive behavior of the character he is playing. Of the girls, Nicole Maurey is certainly the most attractive, June Thorburn the one who has to work hardest to make any effect and Elke Sommer the one who proves the biggest disappointment.

■ **DON'T LOOK BACK**

1967, 96 MINS, US ◇ ▽ ⊙
Dir D.A. Pennebaker   *Prod* Albert Grossman, John Court   *Ph* D.A. Pennebaker   *Ed* D.A. Pennebaker
(Leacock Pennebaker)

Don't Look Back is a cinema verite documentary by D. A. Pennebaker of Bob Dylan's spring 1965 concert tour of Britain. Pennebaker has fashioned a relentlessly honest, brilliantly edited documentary permeated with the troubador-poet's music.

During the month-long tour, Dylan was accompanied by Joan Baez, haunted by the rival reputation of Donovan, and badgered day and night by the press, teenie-boppers and hangers on. Pennebaker shot some 20 hours of film, and edited it chronologically to reveal a portrait that is not always flattering.

There is Dylan, faintly hostile, 'putting on' the press. In one classic scene he tells a *Time* magazine reporter exactly where *Time* and its readership are at, and if his outburst lacks tact, it seems to the point.

In one unique sequence Dylan's manager Albert Grossman and agent Tito Burns wheel, deal and bluff the BBC, playing them against Granada-TV to double the price for a Dylan appearance.

■ DON'T LOOK NOW

1973, 110 MINS, UK/ITALY ◇ ⓦ ⊙
Dir Nicolas Roeg   *Prod* Peter Katz   *Scr* Allan Scott,
Chris Bryant   *Ph* Anthony Richmond   *Ed* Graeme
Clifford   *Mus* Pino Donaggio   *Art Dir* Giovanni Soccol
● Julie Christie, Donald Sutherland, Hilary Mason, Clelia
Matania, Massimo Serato, Renato Scarpa
(Casey/Eldorado)

This British-Italian suspenser, in which the
horror gets to one almost subliminally, as in
Rosemary's Baby, is superior stuff. It can be
'read' on two levels: as simply a gripping tale
of mysterious goings-on in a wintertime
Venice or dealing with the supernatural and
the occult as related to the established patterns of life and society.

Story itself is concocted from a Daphne du
Maurier short story about a young British married couple who shortly after the accidental
death – or was it? – of their daughter get involved in some strange happenings in a wintry
Venice where the man is restoring a church.

A chance meeting in a restaurant with two
sisters, one of them blind and suggesting
she's 'seen' and spoken to the dead child, sets
things moving, with puzzling detail following
puzzling detail in a mosaic of mystery which
crescendos right up to a twist finale.

It's the fillips, visually introduced by director Nicolas Roeg in glimpses and flashes, that
make this much more than merely a well-
made psycho-horror thriller.

The performances are right on the button;
Donald Sutherland is (unusually) at his most
subdued, top effectiveness as the materialist
who ironically becomes the victim of his refusal to believe in the intangible; Julie
Christie does her best work in ages as his
wife; while a superbly-chosen cast of British
and Italian supporting players etch a number
of indelibly vivid portraits.

Editing too, is careful and painstaking (the
classically brilliant and erotic love-making
scene is merely one of several examples) and
plays a vital role in setting the film's mood.

■ DON'T LOSE YOUR HEAD

1967, 90 MINS, UK ◇
Dir Gerald Thomas   *Prod* Peter Rogers   *Scr* Talbot
Rothwell   *Ph* Alan Hume   *Ed* Rod Keys   *Mus* Eric
Rogers   *Art Dir* Lionel Couch
● Sidney James, Kenneth Williams, Jim Dale, Charles
Hawtrey, Peter Butterworth, Joan Sims (Rank)

Don't Lose Your Head is a wild parody of *Scarlet
Pimpernel* adventures in the *Carry On* mould.
The film is a crazy debauch of duelling, doublecrossing and disaster. The troupers jump
through their well-known hoops with agility.

Sidney James and Jim Dale are the two
bored English aristocrats who baffle
Robespierre and his chief of police (Citizen
Camembert – the Big Cheese) with their audacity. James, posing as 'The Black
Fingernail', turns up in a variety of disguises,
none of which attempts to hide his homely
features. He and Dale team up in sharp fashion. Kenneth Williams plays the police chief
in his usual shrill style, and Peter Butterworth, Joan Sims and Charles Hawtrey
valiantly cope with the passing nonsense in
their usual capable manner.

■ DON'T MAKE WAVES

1967, 100 MINS, US ◇
Dir Alexander Mackendrick   *Prod* John Calley, Martin
Ransohoff   *Scr* Ira Wallach, George Kirgo   *Ph* Philip H.
Lathrop   *Ed* Rita Roland, Thomas Stanford   *Mus* Vic
Mizzy   *Art Dir* George W. Davis, Edward Carfagno
● Tony Curtis, Claudia Cardinale, Robert Webber,
Joanna Barnes, Sharon Tate, Mort Sahl (M-G-M/
Filmways-Reynard)

Don't Make Waves is a mildly amusing film
which never gets off the ground in its intended purpose of wacky comedy. Based on
Ira Wallach's novel, *Muscle Beach*, film stars
Tony Curtis and Claudia Cardinale.

Script has a Southern California setting,
mixing romance, infidelity, beach antics and
sky diving with utter confusion as Curtis plays
a frantic young man and Cardinale a peppery
import with an accent.

Plot(?) gets underway as femme's car
causes Curtis' Volkswagen to plunge down a
hillside and burn, during which Curtis' pants
and all his worldly possessions also go up in
flames. Driving home with femme to look at
her insurance policy, Curtis finds himself involved in her romance with a swimming pool
operator, cheating on his wife.

■ DON'T PLAY US CHEAP

1973, 104 MINS, US ◇
Dir Melvin Van Peebles   *Prod* Melvin Van Peebles
Scr Melvin Van Peebles   *Ph* Bob Maxwell   *Ed* Melvin
Van Peebles   *Mus* Melvin Van Peebles
● Esther Rolle, Avon Long, Rhetta Hughes, George
'Ooppee' McCurn (Yeah)

Melvin Van Peebles' film of his play *Don't Play
Us Cheap* offers some terrific musical numbers
and an ebullient look at black culture.

Utilizing the same cast that he directed on
Broadway [in 1972], Van Peebles creates the
atmosphere of a house party in Harlem. His
fantasy premise of an imp and little devil
crashing the party to spoil it out of pure meanness allows the filmmaker's militant themes to
be expressed in humor and whimsy.

Fantasy elements climax with black comedy
of topliner Esther Rolle smashing the little
devil in the form of a cockroach with a rolled
up newspaper. Rolle is in great form as the
party hostess, ably supported by an ensemble
cast.

■ DON'T RAISE THE BRIDGE, LOWER THE RIVER

1968, 99 MINS, UK ◇ ⓦ
Dir Jerry Paris   *Prod* Walter Shenson   *Scr* Max Wilk
Ph Otto Heller   *Ed* Bill Lenny   *Mus* David Whitaker
Art Dir John Howell
● Jerry Lewis, Terry-Thomas, Jacqueline Pearce, Bernard
Cribbins, Patricia Routledge, Nicholas Parsons (Columbia)

Adapted by Max Wilk from his own novel,
Don't Raise the Bridge, Lower the River, is a
mildly diverting production, filmed at
Britain's Shepperton Studios, and starring
Jerry Lewis as a perennial dreamer. An initial
lack of clarity in plot premise, followed by
routine and not very exciting episodic treatment add up to a generally flat result.

Weaknesses are apparent at the very beginning: a series of disparate locations, after
which it finally is established that Lewis is an
eternal dreamer.

Subsequent to this revelation, story plods
along in a dramatic monotone, progressing,
but never building, towards an inevitable
happy ending, after 99 slow minutes.

Featured players Terry-Thomas as the typical promoter; Bernard Cribbins as a garage
mechanic who doubles as a steward on unscheduled airlines; and Patricia Routledge, a
man-hungry Girl Scout leader, are quite excellent in their appearances.

Lewis comes across as uncertain of whether
he is supposed to ham it up at times, play it
down at others.

■ DON'T TELL MOM THE BABYSITTER'S DEAD

1991, 105 MINS, US ◇ ⓦ ⊙
Dir Stephen Herek   *Prod* Robert Newmyer, Brian Reilly,
Jeffrey Silver   *Scr* Neil Landau, Tara Ison   *Ph* Tim
Suhrstedt   *Ed* Larry Bock   *Mus* David Newman, Bruce
Nazarian   *Art Dir* Stephen Marsh

● Christina Applegate, Joanna Cassidy, John Getz, Josh
Charles, Keith Coogan, David Duchovny (HBO/Outlaw)

Don't Tell Mom the Babysitter's Dead starts with
an enjoyable, if crude, black comedy situation
promised by the title, but then it turns into
an incredibly dumb teenage girl's fantasy of
making it in the business world.

Christina Applegate and her four siblings
(Keith Coogan, Robert Hy Gorman, Danielle
Harris, Christopher Pettiet) are left by their
ditzy vacationing mom (Concetta Tomei) in
their suburban LA home with a seemingly
sweet old lady babysitter (Eda Reiss Merin),
who turns out to be a 'deranged Mary
Poppins.'

Following the old lady's death from a heart
attack, Applegate has to earn money to support the kids so they won't have to ask mom
to come home from Australia. The leaden
script turns mind-numbingly silly. Applegate
improbably parlays a padded resume into a
high-paying job as administrative assistant to
glamorous LA garment industry exec Joanna
Cassidy.

Though she has promise, Applegate is misused in a part making her seem more airheaded than shrewd. Cassidy, whose mature
sexiness livens the film for a while, is gradually made to look more and more ridiculous
by the pic's clumsy director, Stephen Herek.

■ DOORS, THE

1991, 141 MINS, US ◇ ⓦ ⊙
Dir Oliver Stone   *Prod* Bill Graham, Sasha Harari, A.
Kitman Ho   *Scr* J. Randal Johnson, Oliver Stone
Ph Robert Richardson   *Ed* David Brenner, Joe Hutshing
Art Dir Barbara Ling
● Val Kilmer, Meg Ryan, Kevin Dillon, Kyle MacLachlan,
Frank Whaley, Kathleen Quinlan (Carolco/Imagine)

The Doors is another trip into 1960s hell from
Oliver Stone. This $40 million look at Jim
Morrison's short, wild ride through a rock
idol life is everything one expects from the
filmmaker – intense, overblown, riveting, humorless, evocative, self-important and impossible to ignore.

As rendered with considerable physical accuracy by Val Kilmer, Morrison is drunk
and/or stoned practically from beginning to
end, providing an acute case study of ruinous
excess. The singer's obsession with death and
mysticism is rooted, via a sepia-tinged prolog,
in a childhood experience in which he views
the aftermath of a traffic accident involving
some Indians.

Action proper begins in 1965, as Morrison
the would-be poet and pretentious UCLA student filmmaker hooks up with flower child
Pamela Courson (Meg Ryan) and launches a
band in Venice Cal, with John Densmore, Ray
Manzarek and Robby Krieger.

Outside of Morrison's abusive, drug-
drenched relationship with Courson, only two
of his innumerable sexual trysts are detailed
– one with the exotic Velvet Underground
star Nico, the other with the demonic Patricia
Kennealy (Kathleen Quinlan).

Kilmer is convincing in the lead role, although he never allows the viewer to share
any emotions. Morrison's own vocals have
been skillfully augmented by Kilmer in some
sequences.

The usually engaging Ryan brings little to a
vaguely conceived part, whereas Quinlan
commands the screen.

■ DOPPELGANGER

(US: Journey to the Far Side of the Sun)

1969, 100 MINS, UK ◇ ⓦ
Dir Robert Parrish   *Prod* Gerry Anderson, Sylvia
Anderson   *Scr* Gerry Anderson, Sylvia Anderson,
Donald James   *Ph* John Read   *Ed* Len Walter
Mus Barry Gray   *Art Dir* Bob Bell

D

● Roy Thinnes, Ian Hendry, Patrick Wymark, Lynn Loring, Loni von Friedl, Herbert Lom (Universal)

First feature production of British TV producers Gerry and Sylvia Anderson and based upon an original by them, *Journey* is a story of two astronauts' trek to a hitherto-undiscovered planet. Unfortunately, despite some of the finest and most imaginative special effects, and sharp production values, the film is so burdened with confusing elements that it frequently fails to make sense.

Narrative proceeds logically through the preparation and launching of the rocket. Astronauts take a pill to induce a three-week sleep during their flight. Thereafter the script falls to pieces in as many parts as their craft. How they return to earth remains a secret, and once back their story is doubted.

Actual star of this picture, uncredited, is the special effects expert who created the absorbing mechanics of the flight for the screen.

．．．．．．．．．．．．．．．．．．．．．．．．．．．．．．

■ DO THE RIGHT THING

1989, 120 MINS, US ◇ ▼ ⊙
Dir Spike Lee   *Prod* Spike Lee   *Scr* Spike Lee
Ph Ernest Dickerson   *Ed* Barry Alexander Brown
Mus Bill Lee   *Art Dir* Wynn Thomas
● Danny Aiello, Ossie Davis, Ruby Dee, Richard Edson, Giancarlo Esposito, Spike Lee (40 Acres & a Mule)

Spike Lee combines a forceful statement on race relations with solid entertainment values in *Do the Right Thing*.

Lee adopts the durable theatrical format of *Street Scene* as his launching point, painstakingly etching an ensemble of neighborhood characters on a Bedford Stuyvesant block in Brooklyn. Centrepiece is Danny Aiello's pizza parlor, which he runs with his sons John Turturro and Richard Edson, with Lee delivering takeout orders.

On the hottest day of the summer, a myriad of contemporary issues covering personal, social and economic matters are laid on the table in often shrill but sometimes funny confrontations. Ossie Davis is perfect casting as a sort of conciliator, a hobo nicknamed the Mayor who injects folk wisdom into the discussion.

Standing out in a uniformly solid cast are Ruby Dee, the Earth Mother of the microcosmic community; Aiello, Turturro and Edson as three quite different variations on an ethnic theme; Paul Benjamin, Frankie Faison and Robin Harris as the funny trio of kibitzers on the block, and Roger Guenveur Smith as he creates an unusual, poetic figure of a stammering simpleton (who sells photos of black leaders) in the midst of such confident figures.

☐ 1989: Nominations: Best Supp. Actor (Danny Aiello), Original Screenplay

．．．．．．．．．．．．．．．．．．．．．．．．．．．．．．

■ DOUBLE IMPACT

1991, 108 MINS, US ◇ ▼ ⊙
Dir Sheldon Lettich   *Prod* Ashok Amritraj, Jean-Claude Van Damme   *Scr* Sheldon Lettich, Jean-Claude Van Damme   *Ph* Richard Kline   *Ed* Mark Conte
Mus Arthur Kempel   *Art Dir* John Jay Moore
● Jean-Claude Van Damme, Geoffrey Lewis, Alan Scarfe, Alonna Shaw, Philip Chan, Cory Everson (Stone Group)

This double-dose of Jean-Claude Van Damme turns on a typically lame revenge plot while dragging out unimaginatively shot action sequences until no one will give a good Van Damme. The one-time karate champ nicknamed 'muscles from Brussels' apparently wanted to stretch his acting hamstring in this dual role as twins separated at six months.

Pic [from a story by Van Damme, Sheldon Lettich, Steve Meerson and Peter Krikes] starts off with the twins' parents being killed by an evil developer (Alan Scarfe). One grows up on the mean streets of Hong Kong, while the other was raised by a family friend (Geoffrey Lewis) and turns up 25 years later as a Los Angeles karate instructor. Lewis' character discovers the other twin is alive and takes his charge back to Hong Kong, reuniting the mismatched pair to reclaim their inheritance.

Van Damme uses two looks – glowering/nasty and friendly/bewildered – to differentiate the characters. It's disturbing that not a single Asian character exhibits any redeeming features. Equal opportunities are provided in the evil henchmen ranks, however, where female bodybuilder Cory Everson joins so-called 'Chinese Hercules' Bolo Yeung, a perennial martial arts bad guy who hasn't won a fight in one of these opuses dating back to *Enter the Dragon*.

．．．．．．．．．．．．．．．．．．．．．．．．．．．．．．

■ DOUBLE INDEMNITY

1944, 103 MINS, US ▼ ⊙
Dir Billy Wilder   *Prod* Joseph Sistrom   *Scr* Billy Wilder, Raymond Chandler   *Ph* John F. Seitz   *Ed* Doane Harrison   *Mus* Miklos Rozsa   *Art Dir* Hans Dreier, Hal Pereira
● Fred MacMurray, Barbara Stanwyck, Edward G. Robinson, Porter Hall, Jean Heather, Tom Powers (Paramount)

James M. Cain's novel *Double Indemnity*, apparently based on a sensational murder of the 1920s, is an absorbing melodrama in its Paramount adaptation. There are unmistakeable similarities between the pic and the famous Snyder-Gray murder wherein Albert Snyder was sash-weighted to death in 1927 in his Queens Village, NY, home by his wife, Ruth, and her lover, Judd Gray. Both the fictional and the real murders were for the slain men's insurance. Both were committed by the murdered men's wives and their amours.

The story's development revolves mainly around the characterizations of Fred MacMurray, Barbara Stanwyck and Edward G. Robinson, the first two as the lovers and Robinson as an insurance claims agent who balks the pair's 'perfect crime' from becoming just what they had intended it to appear – an accidental death from a moving train, for which there would have been a double indemnity.

Stanwyck plays the wife of an oilman, and when MacMurray, an insurance salesman, becomes her paramour, they sell to the husband, fraudulently, an accidental-death policy. They then kill him and place his body on the railway tracks.

It is a story told in flashback, film opening with MacMurray confessing voluntarily the entire setup into a dictaphone for use by the claims agent, from which the narrative then unfolds.

MacMurray has seldom given a better performance. It is somewhat different from his usually light roles, but is always plausible and played with considerable restraint. Stanwyck is not as attractive as normally with what is seemingly a blonde wig, but it's probably part of a makeup to emphasize the brassiness of the character. Robinson, as the infallible insurance executive quick to determine phoney claims, gives a strong performance, too.

☐ 1944: Nominations: Best Picture, Director, Actress (Barbara Stanwyck), Screenplay, B&W Cinematography, Score of a Dramatic Picture, Sound

．．．．．．．．．．．．．．．．．．．．．．．．．．．．．．

■ DOUBLE LIFE, A

1947, 103 MINS, US ▼
Dir George Cukor   *Prod* Michael Kanin   *Scr* Ruth Gordon, Garson Kanin   *Ph* Milton Krasner   *Ed* Robert Parrish   *Mus* Miklos Rozsa   *Art Dir* Harry Horner
● Ronald Colman, Signe Hasso, Edmond O'Brien, Shelley Winters, Ray Collins, Philip Loeb (Universal/Kanin)

Life is particularly distinguished for the manner in which the characters have been conceived and played. Each character rings true as the story goes into its play-within-a-play about actors and the theatre. There's murder, suspense, psychology, Shakespeare and romance all wrapped up into one polished package of class screen entertainment.

Plot poses an interesting premise – that an actor takes on some of the characteristics of the role he is playing if the run is long. In this instance Ronald Colman lives his roles without danger until he tackles *Othello*. Gradually, as the play goes into a second year, he is dominated more and more by the character he creates on the stage. It finally leads him to murder a chance acquaintance in the same manner in which Othello snuffs out the life of Desdemona each night on the stage.

Colman realizes on ever facet of the demanding part in a performance that is flawless. It's a histrionic gem of unusual versatility. Signe Hasso, his stage co-star and former wife, is a solid click, revealing a talent that has rarely been called upon in her other film roles. Her Desdemona is brilliant and her interpretation of the understanding ex-wife perfect.

☐ 1947: Best Actor (Ronald Colman), Score for a Dramatic Picture.
☐ Nominations: Best Director, Original Screenplay

．．．．．．．．．．．．．．．．．．．．．．．．．．．．．．

■ DOUBLE MAN, THE

1967, 105 MINS, UK ◇ ▼
Dir Franklin J. Schaffner   *Prod* Hal. E. Chester
Scr Frank Tarloff, Alfred Hayes   *Ph* Denys Coop
Ed Richard Best   *Mus* Ernie Freeman   *Art Dir* Arthur Lawson
● Yul Brynner, Britt Ekland, Clive Revill, Anton Diffring, David Bauer, Lloyd Nolan (Warner-Pathe/Albion)

Frank Tarloff and Alfred Hayes have tailored a solid screenplay from Henry Maxfield's novel, *Legacy of a Spy*, in which intelligence agent Dan Slater (Yul Brynner) is plunged into strange problems when he goes to the Austrian Alps to investigate the death of his son on a ski-slope. The police write it off as an accident. Brynner suspects murder.

The film builds up an intriguing sense of tension with the motives of various people rating suspicion, Brynner being tailed by obvious enemy agents and a big payoff when he is confronted with his double.

Clive Revill, an ex-agent pal of Brynner's, though not fully trusted by him, also turns in an interesting show as an honest but weak, indecisive character who rallies at the critical moment. Anton Diffring is a suave enemy scientist and David Bauer does excellent work as an agent detailed to bring Brynner back to Washington.

．．．．．．．．．．．．．．．．．．．．．．．．．．．．．．

■ DOUBLE THREAT

1992, 96 MINS, US ◇ ▼ ⊙
Dir David A. Prior   *Prod* Kimberley Casey   *Scr* David A. Prior   *Ph* Gerald B. Wolfe   *Ed* Tony Malanowski
Mus Christopher Farrell   *Art Dir* Linda Lewis
● Sally Kirkland, Andrew Stevens, Sherrie Rose, Chick Vennera, Gary Swanson, Anthony Franciosa (Winters)

Ingenious scripting and clever casting lift *Double Threat* above the commonplace in the erotic thriller genre.

Sally Kirkland is the tongue-in-cheek choice for the film's central role: a Hollywood star making her comeback in a melodrama whose producer, her ex-husband (Anthony Franciosa), demands that the film must be sexy. Kirkland amusingly takes a stand with her director (Chick Vennera): she's never had to do a nude scene and she's not starting now.

Solution is to hire a body double, lovely Sherrie Rose. Rub is that Kirkland's leading man and off-screen b.f., younger Andrew

209

Stevens, falls in love with Rose after making love to her before the cameras.

Filmmaker David A. Prior plants knowing in-jokes into his script but has the cast play everything straight, making for an entertaining package.

. . . .

■ DOVE, THE

1974, 105 MINS, UK ◇ ⑰

Dir Charles Jarrott *Prod* Gregory Peck *Scr* Peter Beagle, Adam Kennedy *Ph* Sven Nykvist *Ed* John Jympson *Mus* John Barry *Art Dir* Peter Lamont
● Joseph Bottoms, Deborah Raffin, John McLiam, Dabney Coleman, John Anderson, Colby Chester (EMI/Peck)

The Dove is based on the book by round-the-world solo sailor Robin Lee Graham [with Derek Gill]. Though basically a yarn about Graham's five-year solo trip around the world in a small sailboat, an odyssey which provides nautical chills and thrills (as well as breath-taking scenics) aplenty, pic is also a tale of character development as the hero finds himself (and manhood) enroute, plus an unpreachy thesis on ecology.

Pic really takes off when he meets the girl (played with gauche hesitation at first, but then with beauty and considerable charm by Deborah Raffin) who is to provide the driving force behind his trek and on into manhood and maturity. Their yes-no yes-no-yes affair is nicely handled.

Fiji to Australia, South Africa and Madagascar to Panama and the Galapagos Isles, are simply breathtaking.

. . . .

■ DOWN AND OUT IN BEVERLY HILLS

1986, 97 MINS, US ◇ ⑰ ⊙

Dir Paul Mazursky *Prod* Paul Mazursky *Scr* Paul Mazursky, Leon Capetanos *Ph* Donald McAlpine *Ed* Richard Halsey *Mus* Andy Summers *Art Dir* Pato Guzman
● Nick Nolte, Richard Dreyfuss, Bette Midler, Little Richard, Tracy Nelson, Elizabeth Pena (Touchstone)

Down and Out in Beverly Hills continues Paul Mazursky's love-hate relationship with the bourgeoisie and its institutions, especially marriage. It's a loving caricature of the nouveau riche (Beverly Hills variety) and although it is more of a comedy of manners than a well-developed story, there are enough yocks and bright moments to make it a thoroughly enjoyable outing.

Mazursky and co-writer Leon Capetanos have cleverly taken the basic premise of Jean Renoir's 1932 classic *Boudu Saved from Drowning* [from the play by Rene Fauchois] and used it as a looking glass for the foibles of the rich and bored.

Head of the household is the aptly named David Whiteman (Richard Dreyfuss). Bette Midler is the lady of the house with their near anorexic daughter Tracy Nelson and son Evan Richards.

In short it's a household of unhappy people and the fly (perhaps flea is more accurate) in the ointment is Nick Nolte as the bum Jerry Baskin. A disheveled and dirty street person, Jerry is an artist of sorts, a con artist. For the Whitemans he becomes their idealized bum, the family pet.

. . . .

■ DOWN BY LAW

1986, 106 MINS, US ⑰

Dir Jim Jarmusch *Prod* Jim Jarmusch *Scr* Jim Jarmusch *Ph* Robby Muller *Ed* Franck Kern *Mus* John Lurie *Art Dir* Roger Knight
● Tom Waits, John Lurie, Roberto Benigni, Nicoletta Braschi, Ellen Barkin (Black Snake/Grohenberger)

Zack (Tom Waits) is caught driving a car with a body in the trunk and Jack (John Lurie) is found by the cops in a hotel room with an unquestionably underage girl. Both men are framed. They wind up in the slammer, in the same cell. Third cell mate is Roberto (Roberto Benigni), who speaks fractured English but whose naive friendliness proves contagious.

After several funny scenes, the Italian proposes they escape, 'just like they do in American movies'. And so they do, out into the Louisiana swamps and eventually stumble on an isolated, unlikely diner where, surprise, surprise, the owner chef is a lonely Italian woman (Nicoletta Braschi) who immediately falls for Benigni.

The Jim Jarmusch penchant for off-the-wall characters and odd situations is very much in evidence. The black-and-white photography is a major plus, and so is John Lurie's score, with songs by Tom Waits. Both men are fine in their respective roles, but Benigni steals the film.

. . . .

■ DOWNHILL RACER

1969, 101 MINS, US/UK ◇ ⑰ ⊙

Dir Michael Ritchie *Prod* Richard Gregson *Scr* James Salter *Ph* Brian Probyn *Ed* Nick Archer, Richard Harris *Mus* Kenyon Hopkins *Art Dir* Ian Whittaker
● Robert Redford, Gene Hackman, Camilla Sparv, Karl Michael Vogler, Jim McMullan, Dabney Coleman (Paramount/Wildwood)

Downhill Racer is an intriguing film that balances skiing and the majesty of Alpine scenery with an absorbing story of hero Robert Redford, young American innocent abroad.

The picture was filmed in the Swiss, Austrian and French Alps. Screenplay [based on the novel *The Downhill Racers* by Oakley Hall] plunges into action when Colorado-born Redford, part of an American skiing team coached by tough Gene Hackman, asserts himself both with the personalities surrounding him and on the European slopes.

Redford contributes a sensitive, interesting portrayal. His interpretation is many-faceted and probing. Hackman's characterization is virile and thoroughly human.

Filming of the downhill course, made with camera attached to the skier's helmet, was properly nervewracking. And a heart-in-the-throat Olympic downhill race as a finale tops everything that has gone before.

. . . .

■ DOWN MEXICO WAY

1941, 72 MINS, US ⑰

Dir Joseph Santley *Prod* Harry Grey *Scr* Olive Cooper, Albert Duffy *Ph* Jack Marta *Ed* Howard O'Neill
● Gene Autry, Smiley Burnette, Fay McKenzie, Harold Huber (Republic)

After a pair of swindlers work over the small town of Sage City, Gene Autry discovers his townfolk have been bilked out of coin supposedly aimed for picture production. Accompanied by Smiley Burnette and reformed Mexican bad man (Harold Huber), Autry trails the crooks into Mexico, where the swindlers' confederates are repeating activities with a rich Mexican rancher as victim. From there on, it's up to Autry to uncover the machinations of the crooks, which he does with a rousing chase and gunfight for a finale.

Story carries along at a good pace, neatly intermingling action, romance and comedy. Autry carries his assignment as the hero in good style, singing several songs – including a couple of familiar pops – in usual fashion.

Picture carries ambitious production mounting in comparison to previous Autrys in the series; with climactic chase using an auto, horses and wildly careening motorcycles for variation.

. . . .

■ DOWN TO EARTH

1947, 100 MINS, US ◇ ⑰ ⊙

Dir Alexander Hall *Prod* Don Hartman *Scr* Don Hartman, Edwin Blum *Ph* Rudolph Mate *Ed* Viola Lawrence *Mus* George Duning, Heinz Roemheld, Mario Castelnuovo-Tedesco *Art Dir* Stephen Goosson, Rudolph Sternad
● Rita Hayworth, Larry Parks, Roland Culver, James Gleason, Edward Everett Horton, Marc Platt (Columbia)

Yarn is one of those tricky ideas that look so much better on paper than celluloid. It picks up the characters from Harry Segall's play, *Heaven Can Wait*, filmed by Columbia in 1941 as the tremendously successful *Here Comes Mr Jordan*, and puts them down in a new setting.

Producer Don Hartman has carried out his cute idea to the extent of using some of the same cast as *Jordan*. James Gleason is back as an agent and Edward Everett Horton is seen once again as the messenger who accompanies the spirit down to earth. Roland Culver subs for Claude Rains in the Jordan role, the guy who runs Heaven.

Rita Hayworth is pictured as Terpsichore, the Greek muse of the theatre. Looking down from Heaven she's unhappy over a Broadway musical about the nine muses, being done in jazz by producer Larry Parks. She makes a request to go down and help him so she can clean the show up. She lands in the star role and there's the usual falling-in-love with the vis-a-vis – in this case Parks.

Explanation necessary to get all this across takes interminable time and occasionally slows even the angels to a lazy walk. Making things worse is the fact that all the gags which should give the yarn a bit of pepper fall flat.

Definitely on the credit side are the fine tunes provided by Allan Roberts and Doris Fisher. Parks sings one tune. It's definitely a letdown. Hayworth does better in the vocal department and, of course is fine in the terp routines [staged by Jack Cole].

. . . .

■ DOWN TO THE SEA IN SHIPS

1949, 120 MINS, US ⑰

Dir Henry Hathaway *Prod* Louis D. Lighton *Scr* John Lee Mahin, Sy Bartlett *Ph* Joe MacDonald *Ed* Dorothy Spencer *Mus* Alfred Newman
● Richard Widmark, Lionel Barrymore, Dean Stockwell, Gene Lockhart, Cecil Kellaway (20th Century-Fox)

Down to the Sea in Ships is a lengthy saga of early whaling ships and the men who commanded them. It is told with emphasis on character study rather than action.

The first half is becalmed in a rather thorough development of the characters. In the last hour, picture really shakes out its sails and goes wing-and-winging before the wind.

The taking of a whale and the rendering of blubber to oil, the dangers of fog and the menace of a wreck on an iceberg is sturdy excitement that serves as a fitting climax to the story of an old whaler captain, his young grandson and of a young first mate.

Richard Widmark has a chance at a sympathetic role and proves himself versatile. Lionel Barrymore carries off the fat part of whaling captain with fewer of the usual Barrymore tricks. Despite his youth, Dean Stockwell is a skilled thespian who more than holds his own in scenes with the adults.

. . . .

■ DOWN WENT McGINTY

See: The Great McGinty

. . . .

■ DRACULA

1931, 64 MINS, US ⑰

Dir Tod Browning *Prod* Carl Laemmle Jr. *Scr* Garrett Fort, Dudley Murphy *Ph* Karl Freund *Ed* Milton Carruth *Art Dir* Charles D. Hall

D

● Bela Lugosi, Helen Chandler, Davis Manners, Dwight Frye, Edward Van Sloan, Herbert Bunston (Universal)

Treatment differs from both the stage version [by Deane and John Balderston] and the original novel [by Bram Stoker]. On the stage it was a thriller carried to such an extreme that it had a comedy punch by its very outre aspect. On the screen it comes out as a sublimated ghost story related with all surface seriousness and above all with a remarkably effective background of creepy atmosphere.

Early in the action is a barren rocky mountain pass, peopled only by a spectral coach driver and shrouded in a miasmic mist. Story proceeds thence into a tomb-like castle. In such surroundings the sinister figure of the human vampire, the living-dead Count Dracula who sustains life by drinking the blood of his victims, seems almost plausible.

It is difficult to think of anybody who could quite match the performance in the vampire part of Bela Lugosi, even to the faint flavor of foreign speech that fits so neatly. Helen Chandler is the blonde type for the clinging-vine heroine, and Herbert Bunston plays the scientist deadly straight, but with a faint suggestion of comedy that dovetails into the whole pattern.

■ DRACULA
(US: Horror of Dracula)

1958, 82 MINS, UK ◇ ⓦ
Dir Terence Fisher   Prod Anthony Hinds   Scr Jimmy Sangster   Ph Jack Asher   Ed James Needs, Bill Lenny   Mus James Bernard   Art Dir Bernard Robinson
● Peter Cushing, Christopher Lee, Melissa Stribling, Michael Gough, Carol Marsh, Miles Malleson (Hammer)

For those familiar with the original Dracula thriller, the screenplay has ably preserved the sanguinary aspects of the Bram Stoker novel. Here again we have Count Dracula sleeping in a coffin by day and plying his nefarious role of a blood-sucking vampire at night. Version has its usual quota of victims before his reign of terror is ended by a fearless doctor.

Both director Terence Fisher as well as the cast have taken a serious approach to the macabre theme that adds up to lotsa tension and suspense. Peter Cushing is impressive as the painstaking scientist-doctor who solves the mystery. Christopher Lee is thoroughly gruesome as Dracula, and Michael Gough is suitably skeptical as a bereaved relative who ultimately is persuaded to assist Cushing.

■ DRACULA

1979, 109 MINS, US ◇ ⓦ ⊙
Dir John Badham   Prod Walter Mirisch   Scr W.D. Richter   Ph Gilbert Taylor   Ed John Bloom   Mus John Williams   Art Dir Peter Murton
● Frank Langella, Laurence Olivier, Donald Pleasence, Kate Nelligan, Trevor Eve, Jan Francis (Universal)

With this lavish retelling of an oft-told tale, Dracula puts the male vamp back in vampire. Director John Badham and Frank Langella pull off a handsome, moody rendition, more romantic than menacing [based on a stage play by Hamilton Deane and John L. Balderston, from Bram Stoker's novel].

Langella is the key in coming up with one more interpretation of the vampire out of hundreds previously presented. More humanly seductive, he's terrific with the ladies and the men would like him well-enough if he weren't so good-looking and arrogant.

Film gets under way slowly, bringing the count to England where he's introduced to Donald Pleasence, his daughter Kate Nelligan, her fiance Trevor Eve and visiting friend Jan Francis. Finally, Francis is drained dry and the action starts to pick up.

■ DRACULA

1992, 123 MINS, US ◇ ⓦ ⊙
Dir Francis Coppola   Prod Francis Coppola, Fred Fuchs, Charles Mulvehill   Scr James V. Hart   Ph Michael Ballhaus   Ed Nicholas C. Smith, Glen Scantlebury, Anne Gorsaud   Mus Wojciech Kilar   Art Dir Thomas Sanders
● Gary Oldman, Winona Ryder, Anthony Hopkins, Keanu Reeves, Richard E. Grant, Cary Elwes (Columbia/American Zoetrope/Osiris)

Both the most extravagant screen telling of the oft-filmed story and the one most faithful to its literary scource, this rendition sets grand romantic goals for itself that aren't fulfilled emotionally, and it is gory without being at all scary.

James V. Hart sets epic parameters for his script with a prologue introducing Dracula's historical origins as Vlad the Impaler, a 15th century Romanian king who fought off Turkish invaders. As dramatically sketched here, the ruler's inamorata, Elisabeta, killed herself upon receiving false news of his death in battle, whereupon the monarch furiously renounced God and began his centuries-long devotion to evil.

In casting Winona Ryder as both Elisabeta and Mina Murray, the overarching story becomes Dracula's quest for recapturing his great love. Unfortunately, familiar plotting, Coppola's coldly magisterial style and Gary Oldman's plain appearance in the title role combine to prevent this strategy from working in more than theory.

Shot almost entirely on sound-stages, film has the feel of an old-fashioned, 1930s, studio-enclosed production made with the benefit of '90s technology. From the striking, blood-drenched prologue on, viewer is constantly made aware of cinema artifice in its grandest manifestations.

Oldman enacts Dracula with wit, sophistication and proper seriousness. However, the actor lacks the charisma that would put across Coppola's conception of a highly sexualized vampire.

Other performances range from a bit stiff (the young male contingent) to playfully energetic (Anthony Hopkins as Van Helsing) to compelling (Tom Waits as the insect-eating lunatic Renfield). Ryder has just the right combination of intelligence and enticing looks as Mina.
□ 1992: Best Sound Effects Editing, Costume Design, Make-up.
□ Nomination: Art Direction

■ DRACULA – PRINCE OF DARKNESS

1966, 90 MINS, UK ◇
Dir Terence Fisher   Prod Anthony Nelson-Keys   Scr John Sansom, Anthony Hinds   Ph Michael Reed   Ed Chris Barnes, James Needs   Mus James Bernard   Art Dir Bernard Robinson
● Christopher Lee, Barbara Shelley, Andrew Keir, Francis Matthews, Suzan Farmer, Charles Tingwell (Hammer/Seven Arts)

Four inquistive tourists are lured to Castle Dracula, met by a sinister butler and invited to dinner and to stay the night. The four treat this strange hospitality with incredibly bland acceptance. One of them (Charles Tingwell), wandering the castle at night, is killed and his blood used to reinfuse life into the Dracula ashes. Dracula then plunges his fangs into the neck of the corpse's wife, turning her into a vampire and the two are then arrayed against the other pair in the party.

This simple yarn [from an idea by John Elder (= Anthony Hinds)] is played reasonably straight and the main snag is that the thrills do not arise sufficiently smooth out of atmosphere. After a slowish start some climate of eeriness is evoked but more shadows, suspense and suggestion would have helped. Christopher Lee, an old hand at the horror

business, makes a latish appearance but dominates the film enough without dialog.

■ DRAGNET

1954, 89 MINS, US ◇ ⓦ
Dir Jack Webb   Prod Stanley Meyer   Scr Richard L. Breen   Ph Edward Colman   Ed Robert M. Leeds   Mus Walter Schumann
● Jack Webb, Ben Alexander, Richard Boone, Ann Robinson, Stacy Harris, Virginia Gregg (Warner/Mark VII)

In making the transition from radio-TV to the big screen and color, this is spotty in entertainment results. As on TV quite a bit is made of the long, tedious toil of thorough police methods. This can be kept in hand in a 30-minute period, but when that time is tripled the pace is bound to slow to a walk often.

Under Jack Webb's direction the film gets off on its melodramatic path with a brutal murder. Thereafter, the homicide and intelligence divisions of the LA Police Dept start a widespread hunt for evidence that will pin the killing on some redhot suspects.

Webb's direction of the screenplay is mostly a good job. He stages a four-man fight in which he and his police sidekick (Ben Alexander) are involved, rather poorly and it may invoke unwelcome laughs. Otherwise, when sticking to terse handling of facts, or in building honest emotion, such as in the splendidly-done drunk scene by Virginia Gregg, grieving widow of the murdered hood, he brings his show off satisfactorily.

■ DRAGNET

1987, 106 MINS, US ◇ ⓦ ⊙
Dir Tom Mankiewicz   Prod David Permut, Robert K. Weiss   Scr Dan Aykroyd, Alan Zweibel, Tom Mankiewicz   Ph Matthew F. Leonetti   Ed Richard Halsey, William Gordean   Mus Ira Newborn   Art Dir Robert F. Boyle
● Dan Aykroyd, Tom Hanks, Christopher Plummer, Harry Morgan, Alexandra Paul, Elizabeth Ashley (Universal/Applied Action)

Dragnet tries very hard to parody its 1950s TV series progenitor but winds up more innocuous than inventive. Dan Aykroyd as Jack Webb as Sgt. Joe Friday gives the role his best but confines of the ultra-straight cop make humor difficult to sustain. Unfettered by such limits, Tom Hanks becomes the pic's winning wildcard as Friday's zany sidekick, Pep Streebek.

Inevitably, Friday and Streebek must pursue a case. It is here that the pic starts unraveling rapidly – largely due to exaggerated caricatures that recall TV's Batman series and the feature film Superman outings. Christopher Plummer is the kinkiest of the lot as televangelist Reverend Whirley. He considers LA the 'current capital of depravity', heads up MAMA (Moral Advanced Movement of America) but secretly leads a cultist outfit called PAGANs (People Against Goodness And Normalcy).

Whirley is somehow allied with Police Commissioner Jane Kirkpatrick (Elizabeth Ashley) and is purportedly at odds with Bait sex magazine kingpin Jerry Caesar (Dabney Coleman). Friday and Streebek plunge into the bizarre goings-on by posing undercover as street freaks.

Script doesn't make enough of the opportunities for interplay that used to be a mainstay between Webb and Harry Morgan, who reprises the part here in a nice touch that finds him elevated to captain.

■ DRAGONSLAYER

1981, 108 MINS, UK ◇ ⓦ ⊙
Dir Matthew Robbins   Prod Hal Barwood   Scr Hal Barwood, Matthew Robbins   Ph Derek Vanlint   Ed Tony Lawson   Mus Alex North   Art Dir Elliot Scott

● Peter MacNicol, Caitlin Clarke, Ralph Richardson, John Hallam, Peter Eyre, Chloe Salaman (Paramount/Walt Disney)

A well intentioned fantasy with some wonderful special effects, *Dragonslayer* falls somewhat short on continuously intriguing adventure. Technically speaking, it is an expertly mounted period piece concerning a boy's attempt to slay a fire-breathing dragon in order to save an entire kingdom. However, the story line is often tedious and the major action sequences appear much too late in the picture.

Ralph Richardson limns the properly mysterious (and too seldom seen) sorcerer that members of a neighbouring kingdom seek as the only person who can slay the terrorizing dragon.

Early on Richardson's powers are put to the test by a representative of the king, who seems to kill the sorcerer. It is then up to his apprentice, newcomer Peter MacNicol, to fight the dragon with the magic at his disposal.

MacNicol has the proper look of innocence to be a little unnatural in his performance. Along the way he is given nice support by Caitlin Clarke as a spunky love interest.

The real stars (as expected) of this film are the fabulous special effects. Given the high failure rate, it's especially refreshing to see experts come up with the imaginative and effective devices.
□ 1981: Nomination: Best Visual Effects

....

■ DRAGON
THE BRUCE LEE STORY

1993, 121 MINS, US ◊ ⓥ ⊙
Dir Rob Cohen   *Prod* Raffaella De Laurentiis
Scr Edward Khmara, John Raffo, Rob Cohen   *Ph* David Eggby   *Ed* Peter Amundson   *Mus* Randy Edelman
Art Dir Robert Ziembicki
● Jason Scott Lee, Lauren Holly, Robert Wagner, Michael Learned, Nancy Kwan, Kay Tong Lim (Universal)

The meteoric, tragic life of martial arts star Bruce Lee forms the basis of *Dragon*, an unlikely pastiche of traditional biography, Hollywood saga and interracial romance.

The jumping off point of the biopic [from Linda Lee Cadwell's book *Bruce Lee: The Man Only I Knew*] finds the teenage Lee (the not-related Jason Scott Lee) as a young man in Hong Kong. Somewhat awkward socially, he transforms into a confident human dynamo when he's forced to fight.

Lee's physical prowess gets him into trouble with the authorities and he's sent to San Francisco for his own safety. Lee holds his own against campus bullies. But the situation propels him into a new career teaching students the art of self-defence. One, Linda Emery (Lauren Holly), becomes the love of his life despite her mother's fierce antipathy.

Director Rob Cohen, balancing disparate visual styles, keeps *Dragon* pretty straightforward. Lee's metaphoric demons, visualized as a towering, faceless samurai, avoid cuteness; and the potential hokum ranging from the spontaneous fights to the forays into 'inner strength' sidestep the high-toned silliness associated with the kung fu era. Overall it maintains a high technical sheen.

....

■ DRAGONWYCK

1946, 100 MINS, US
Dir Joseph L. Mankiewicz   *Prod* Darryl F. Zanuck
Scr Joseph L Mankiewicz   *Ph* Arthur Miller   *Ed* Dorothy Spencer   *Mus* Alfred Newman   *Art Dir* Lyle R. Wheeler, J. Russell Spencer
● Gene Tierney, Walter Huston, Vincent Price, Glenn Langan, Anne Revere, Jessica Tandy (20th Century-Fox)

Anya Seton's *Dragonwyck*, the bestseller, has been given a lucid, often-compelling transition to the screen. It's a psychological yarn, its mid-19th century American-feudal background being always brooding with never a break in its flow of morbidity. Yet, it is always interesting if somewhat too pointed at times in its fictional contrivance.

The screenplay concerns the feudal system passed down through the generations by the old-Dutch families on the Hudson. The story specifically concerns one Nicholas Van Ryn who exacts tribute from tenant farmers on his vast estate (the year is 1844). Van Ryn has a wife and daughter whom he dislikes, and his pet anathema is his failure to have a son to carry on the baronial tradition. When a distant relative is invited to be governess to the child, and he falls in love with her, he poisons his wife, thus leaving him free to marry the other girl.

Gene Tierney plays the governess and it is one of her most sympathetical roles. Tierney is photographed attractively, and paced well, too, in the direction, as are all the others.

....

■ DRAUGHTSMAN'S CONTRACT, THE

1982, 108 MINS, UK ◊ ⓥ ⊙
Dir Peter Greenaway   *Prod* David Payne   *Scr* Peter Greenaway   *Ph* Curtis Clark   *Ed* John Wilson
Mus Michael Nyman   *Art Dir* Bob Ringwood
● Anthony Higgins, Janet Suzman, Anne Louise Lambert, Hugh Fraser (BFI/Channel 4)

Though seemingly a comedy of manners taking place in the country home of a rich man, Herbert, there is an underlying viciousness of these rich denizens that foreshadows coming upheavals. It is the end of the 17th century.

Film has fine costumes, florid headpieces for men and lovely surroundings on the big estate. Well-lensed, with a fine limpid narration that switches from observation of this landed class to a sort of foreboding tale of murder.

Herbert is almost estranged from his wife and goes off for two weeks of carousing. His wife beseeches a known draughtsman and landscape painter, a guest, Neville, to stay and make 12 drawings of the estate to surprise her husband. He refuses but finally says yes if the contract includes daily sexual dalliance with Mrs Herbert. It is accepted.

The daughter, still without a child and oblivious to her husband and his effete ways, also begins to dally with the shrewd, talented Neville.

On the day Neville is to leave, Herbert is found dead in the moat. Suspicions are aimed at Neville for it is felt he may have somehow given clues to the murder in his drawings.

....

■ DR. CYCLOPS

1940, 75 MINS, US ◊ ⓥ ⊙
Dir Ernest B. Schoedsack   *Prod* Dale Van Every
Scr Tom Kilpatrick   *Ph* Henry Sharp, Winton C. Hoch
Ed Ellsworth Hoagland   *Mus* Ernst Toch, Gerard Carbonara, Albert Hay Malotte   *Art Dir* Hans Dreier, Earl Hedrick
● Albert Dekker, Janice Logan, Thomas Coley, Charles Halton, Victor Kilian, Frank Yaconelli (Paramount)

In detailing the discoveries of a madman scientist wherein he is able to reduce the size of men and animals to miniature pygmies, story and direction both fail to catch and hold interest. Achieved through continual use of process and trick photography, idea gets lost in a jumble and pancakes off for a dull effort.

Albert Dekker, researching in the jungles of South America, finds a rich radium deposit from which he can draw concentrated energy for experimental use. He has already used the power to reduce animals to minute size, when a pair of mining engineers (Thomas Coley and Victor Kilian) and two biologists (Janice Logan and Charles Halton) arrive and soon discover his secret. Dekker gets the quartet, together with native Frank Yaconelli, into the radium machine room and reduces the group down to beings of a foot tall. From there on, it's an unexciting adventure to escape the madman.
□ 1940: Nomination: Best Special Effects

....

■ DREAM LOVER

1986, 104 MINS, US ◊ ⓥ
Dir Alan J. Pakula   *Prod* Alan J. Pakula, Jon Boorstin
Scr Jon Boorstin   *Ph* Sven Nykvist   *Ed* Trudy Ship
Mus Michael Small   *Art Dir* George Jenkins
● Kristy McNichol, Ben Masters, Paul Shenar, Justin Deas, John McMartin, Gayle Hunnicutt (M-G-M)

With the advice of a Yale University Sleep Laboratory consultant, *Dream Lover* firmly sets itself among some rather fascinating scientific notions. Specifically, some dream doctors believe that, while 'asleep', part of the brain reacts to dreams as if they were really happening and sends signals to the muscles to take appropriate action.

Kristy McNichol is an average young lady living alone in a NY apartment. She becomes victim to an intruder (Joseph Culp) whom she stabs in the back.

Was the stabbing really necessary for self-defense or did it leap out of some subconscious fury connected to her domineering father (Paul Shenar) or unfaithful lover (Justin Deas)? Only her brain knows for sure. Limps to a conclusion with no real excitement.

....

■ DREAM OF KINGS, A

1969, 109 MINS, US ◊ ⓥ
Dir Daniel Mann   *Prod* Jules Schermer   *Scr* Harry Mark Petrakis, Ian Hunter   *Ph* Richard H. Kline   *Ed* Walter Hannemann, Ray Daniels   *Mus* Alex North
● Anthony Quinn, Irene Papas, Inger Stevens, Sam Levene, Val Avery (Schermer)

The adaptation of Harry Mark Petrakis' book about an epic Greek-American father, philanderer, and gambler whose dubious means of support is dispensing wisdom and wrestling instruction emerges as a warm, upbeat, artistically realized drama. It stars Anthony Quinn portraying super-mensch, the noble ethnic, and it is one of his most powerful and convincing performances.

In the Greek sector of Chicago, Quinn makes his hand-to-mouth living as a small time but honest gambler, since his counseling business in a walk-up dingy tenement building is considerably less than a living. His wife (Irene Papas), two girls and his fatally ill son (Radames Pera) exist on the widowed mother-in-law's life insurance.

The film captures the gritty visual feel of the Hellenic quarter of a large American city with the winter air redolent with feta and baking Greek bread.

....

■ DREAM OF PASSION, A

1978, 110 MINS, GREECE ◊ ⓥ
Dir Jules Dassin   *Prod* Jules Dassin   *Scr* Jules Dassin
Ph George Arvanitis   *Ed* George Klotz   *Mus* Iannis Markopoulos   *Art Dir* Dionysis Fotopoulos
● Melina Mercouri, Ellen Burstyn, Andreas Voutsinas, Despo Diamantidou, Dimitris Papamichael, Yannis Voglis (Brenfilm/Melina)

Two older women are caught up in a strange parallel. One, Melina Mercouri, is a film star who returns to her native Greece to do *Medea* on stage. The other, Ellen Burstyn, is an American living in Greece who has killed her three children 'just as Medea did' due to her husband's flaunting of her love and needs.

A misguided public relations idea, having Burstyn talk to Mercouri after seeing no one for a long time, backfires when photogs and press burst in. While Burstyn screams invectives, Mercouri feels cheapened, guilty and decides to take an interest in the case. She sees Burstyn again and gets her story.

Pic alternates two stories, as Mercouri's life and work are intertwined with her growing interest in Burstyn.

Burstyn is shattering as a religious, partially-educated woman caught up in a foreign land. At the end, Burstyn bursts into hysterical tears, which are intercut with Mercouri's dramatic finale in which she kills Medea's children in the play.

● ●

■ DREAMSCAPE

1984, 95 MINS, US ◇ ⑰ ☉
Dir Joseph Ruben   *Prod* Bruce Cohn Curtis   *Scr* David Loughery, Chuck Russell, Joseph Ruben   *Ph* Brian Tufano   *Ed* Richard Halsey   *Mus* Maurice Jarre
● Dennis Quaid, Max von Sydow, Christopher Plummer, Eddie Albert, Kate Capshaw, David Patrick Kelly (Zupnick-Curtis)

Film [from a screen story by David Loughery] centers on 'dreamlinking', the psychic projection of one person's consciousness into a sleeping person's subconscious, or his dreams. If that sounds far-fetched, it is.

Central character is played with gusto by Dennis Quaid as Alex Garland, a reluctant ex-psychic who hooks up with Dr Paul Novotny (Max von Sydow), who runs a dream research project at the local college that has an elaborate laboratory setup to study the phenomena.

There he meets Dr Jane de Vries (Kate Capshaw), Von Sydow's chief assistant who secretly lusts after Quaid, but only until he 'eavesdrops' on her erotic dream that involves Quaid. Enter Christopher Plummer as Bob Blair, a secretive and despicable government type who finances and oversees Von Sydow's research, but covertly plans to use its results for sinister ends.

● ●

■ DREAM TEAM, THE

1989, 113 MINS, US ◇ ⑰ ☉
Dir Howard Zieff   *Prod* Christopher W. Knight   *Scr* Jon Connolly, David Loucka   *Ph* Adam Holender   *Ed* C. Timothy O'Meara   *Mus* David McHugh   *Art Dir* Todd Hallowell
● Michael Keaton, Christopher Lloyd, Peter Boyle, Stephen Furst, Dennis Boutsikaris, Lorraine Bracco (Imagine/Universal)

The Dream Team is a hokey comedy that basically reduces mental illness to a grab bag of quirky schtick. Yet with a quartet of gifted comic actors having a field day playing loonies on the loose in Manhattan, much of that schtick is awfully funny.

In an attempt to give his patients a taste of the real world, New Jersey hospital doctor Dennis Boutsikaris decides to treat four of his charges to a day game at Yankee Statium.

Going along for the ride are the certified oddballs: Keaton, who seems to have his wits about him but periodically displays extreme delusions of grandeur, as well as a mean violent streak; Christopher Lloyd, a prissy fuss-budget who enjoys posing as a member of the hospital staff; Peter Boyle, a man with a heavy Jesus complex given to undressing at moments of intense spirituality; and Stephen Furst, an uncommunicative simpleton who speaks mainly in baseball jargon.

As soon as they hit the Big Apple, however, the good doctor is seriously injured after witnessing a killing, and the boys are left to their own devices.

Keaton is at his manic best, Lloyd prompts numerous guffaws with his impersonation of a self-serious tidiness freak, and Furst quietly impresses as the sickest and most helpless of the lot.

● ●

■ DREAM WIFE

1953, 99 MINS, US
Dir Sidney Sheldon   *Prod* Dore Schary   *Scr* Sidney Sheldon, Herbert Baker, Alfred Lewis Levitt   *Ph* Milton Krasner   *Ed* George White   *Mus* Conrad Salinger   *Art Dir* Cedric Gibbons, Daniel B. Cathcart
● Cary Grant, Deborah Kerr, Walter Pidgeon, Betta St John, Eduard Franz, Buddy Baer (M-G-M)

A battle-of-the-sexes theme is used for this fairly entertaining, highly contrived piece of screen nonsense.

Cary Grant, a man who wants a wife in the home, not in business, breaks with Deborah Kerr, State Dept official who is too busy with an oil crisis to have time for matrimony. Remembering a comely princess (Betta St John) whom he had met on a trip to Bukistan in the Middle East and the fact that she had been raised from birth in the art of pleasing man, Grant proposes via cable.

Because of the oil situation, the State Dept steps in and assigns Kerr to see that her ex-fiance sticks to protocol in his new courtship. The princess comes to the States, but the feminine craft of Kerr soon has St John figuring that emancipation is more fun than being a dream wife.

Able performers help to carry the script's silliness through the frenetics, but director Sidney Sheldon lets the action slop over into very broad slapstick too often. This loose handling reflects occasionally in the performances, most notably in Grant's. Dialog and situations have their chuckles, however.

● ●

■ DRESSED TO KILL

1980, 105 MINS, US ◇ ⑰ ☉
Dir Brian De Palma   *Prod* George Litto   *Scr* Brian De Palma   *Ph* Ralf Bode   *Ed* Jerry Greenberg   *Mus* Pino Donaggio   *Art Dir* Gary Weist
● Michael Caine, Angie Dickinson, Nancy Allen, Keith Gordon, Dennis Franz, David Margulies (Filmways)

Brian De Palma goes right for the audience jugular in *Dressed to Kill*, a stylish exercise in ersatz-Hitchcock suspense-terror. Despite some major structural weaknesses, the cannily manipulated combination of mystery, gore and kinky sex adds up to a slick commercial package.

The film begins with a steamy auto-erotic shower scene and segues to a session between Angie Dickinson and psychiatrist Michael Caine.

Matters begin in earnest when Dickinson enters an elevator and is razor-sliced to death. Enter high-priced hooker Nancy Allen who finds the body and is caught razor-in-hand with no alibi, smack into the arch Hitchcockian position of a circumstantially involved 'innocent' forced to clear herself by discovering the real murderer.

Instances of patent manipulation or cheating (and the film's stolen ending from *Carrie*) are generally more annoying in retrospect than while they're happening.

Dickinson, who has an abdominal stand-in for the steamier segments, is used exceptionally well as the sexually torn, quickly disposed-of heroine. Caine, until the film's internal logic breaks down, is excellent as the suave shrink.

● ●

■ DRESSER, THE

1983, 118 MINS, UK ◇ ⑰ ☉
Dir Peter Yates   *Prod* Peter Yates   *Scr* Ronald Harwood   *Ph* Kelvin Pike   *Ed* Ray Lovejoy   *Mus* James Horner   *Art Dir* Stephen Grimes
● Albert Finney, Tom Courtenay, Edward Fox, Zena Walker, Eileen Atkins, Michael Gough (Goldcrest/World Film Services)

Adapted by Ronald Harwood from his 1980 London comedy-drama, this is indisputably one of the best films ever made about theatre. It's funny, compassionate, compelling, and in its final moments pulls off an uncanny juxtaposition between the emotionally and physically crumbling Albert Finney and the character he's playing on stage for the 227th time, King Lear.

Finney portrays an aging, spoiled, grandiloquent actor-manager of a traditional English touring company whose dedication to his art creates chaos for those around him. The only character who can handle the old actor is his gofer-valet Norman, played with an amazing dexterity and energy by Tom Courtenay.

Director Peter Yates brings to the film, much of it shot at Pinewood, a strong visual sense of the British experience in wartime. And the whiff of greasepaint, particularly notable when aide Courtenay goads Finney into his makeup for Lear, lends the tawdry dressing room world of touring theatre its most physically felt detail.

Harwood is said to have based much of his story on his experiences with flamboyant actor-manager Donald Wolfit (1902–68) and his troupe.
☐ 1983: Nominations: Best Picture, Director, Actor (Albert Finney, Tom Courtenay), Adapted Screenplay

● ●

■ DREYFUS

1931, 80 MINS, UK
Dir F.W. Kraemer, Milton Rosmer   *Scr* Reginald Berkeley, Walter Mycroft   *Ph* W. Winterstein, J. Harvey Wheedon   *Ed* John Harlow
● Cedric Hardwicke, Beatrix Thomson, Charles Carson, George Merritt, Sam Livesey, Garry Marsh (British International/Sudfilm)

British International, in making the picture, is understood to have followed closely along the lines of the original film as made by Sudfilm for German consumption. The film has more movement than the average British film.

The Dreyfus case revolved around a framed-up charge against Captain Alfred Dreyfus of the French Army of treason. Treason had been committed and Dreyfus was charged, largely because he was the only Jew on the staff. After making the charge, the army had to hold up its case or lose face, so they trumped up the evidence against him.

What made it a world-famous matter, rather than a forgotten incident in French army life, was that Emile Zola, one of the greatest of French writers, took to the Dreyfus case and fought it in the courts. Despite having as counsel Georges Clemenceau, Zola lost, but the story had gotten worldwide attention. After about 15 years Dreyfus was fully vindicated.

The film is not over-acted. If anything it's a little under-acted in parts. Cecil Hardwicke as Dreyfus gives a fine performance; George Merritt as Zola is exceptional. Another striking performance is that of Charles Carson as Col. Picquart, who was also degraded because he found proof, after Dreyfus was sent to Devil's Island, pointing to the fact that Major Esterhazy was the criminal and not Dreyfus. Beatrix Thomson as the wife is only so-so, largely because she's not given much to do.

● ●

■ DRILLER KILLER, THE

1979, 90 MINS, US ◇ ⑰
Dir Abel Ferrara   *Prod* Rochelle Weisberg (exec.)   *Scr* Nicholas St John, Louis Mascolo   *Ph* Ken Kelsch   *Ed* Orlando Gallini, Bonnie Constant, Michael Constant, Jimmy Laine [= Abel Ferrara]   *Mus* Joseph Delia   *Art Dir* Louis Mascolo
● Jimmy Laine [= Abel Ferrara], Carolyn Marz, Baybi Day, Harry Schultz, Alan Wynroth, Maria Helhoski (Navaron)

This bit of gore was undoubtedly inspired by *The Texas Chain Saw Massacre*. It's hastily-shot and technically inept in every department operation.

An artist, living in a tenement near Union Square with two girlfriends who're not reluctant to turn to each other when his attentions are elsewhere, find it increasingly difficult to keep the wolf from the door. Things get worse. A punk rock band moves into the floor below him and the noise pushes him over the edge.

The most stupid thing about the film is why, when he turns into a murderer with an electric drill, he doesn't go downstairs and eliminate the band. No, he picks winos in doorways as his victims before turning to other targets – his girlfriends.

● ●

■ DRIVE, HE SAID

1971, 95 MINS, US ◇
Dir Jack Nicholson *Prod* Jack Nicholson, Steve Blauner, Bert Schneider *Scr* Jack Nicholson, Jeremy Larner
Ph Bill Butler *Ed* Pat Somerset, Donn Cambern, Christopher Holmes, Robert L. Wolfe *Mus* David Shire
Art Dir Harry Gittes
● William Tepper, Karen Black, Michael Margotta, Bruce Dern, Robert Towne, Henry Jaglom (BBS)

Director Jack Nicholson seems here to be making a sort of games-people-play charade which takes off on many of the would-be commitments of his characters.

William Tepper, as the central sports star character of the campus convolutions, reflects the changes and protest surrounding his simplistic existence.

His roommate (Michael Margotta), a Che-like student revolutionary, wants to destroy all for he feels the draft, life around him, the war, will destroy him. Margotta leads a gag raid on a basketball game with guerrilla-clad friends that puts them all in custody, but later they are freed. He beats the draft by playing mad in a raucous induction physical scene, but winds up going mad for real, trying to kill his roommate's woman, who he feels is simply a lech.

Karen Black is the sensual older woman, who sexually grapples with the basketball hero but finally resents being used and tries to claim a personality of her own.

Nicholson deftly illustrates the background cynicism of big time sports against the more obvious cynicism of college life.

● ●

■ DRIVER, THE

1978, 91 MINS, US ◇ ⊚
Dir Walter Hill *Prod* Lawrence Gordon *Scr* Walter Hill
Ph Philip Lathrop *Ed* Tina Hirsch, Robert K. Lambert
Mus Michael Small *Art Dir* Harry Horner
● Ryan O'Neal, Bruce Dern, Isabelle Adjani, Ronee Blakely, Matt Clark, Felice Orlandi (20th Century-Fox)

By the end of *The Driver*, you can almost smell rubber burning, there are so many screeching tires. This may be the first film where the star of the show isn't an actor or even a machine but a sound effect.

Ryan O'Neal plays a master getaway driver who does most of his talking with his accelerator toe. Bruce Dern, departing only slightly from his maniac roles, plays an obsessed detective out to nab O'Neal. Isabelle Adjani is another reticent character, a gambler hired as an alibi for O'Neal. Ronee Blakely, in a supporting role, portrays O'Neal's connection; she sets up the jobs.

There's not much more to the plot than that. O'Neal is a great driver and Dern is a detective. They're enemies and one of them is going to win the game.

Director Walter Hill and stunt coordinator Everett Creach have engineered a number of car chases and they are fabulous, if you like car chases.

Because of the quiet and mysterious mood of this picture, it has a pretentious quality to

it. Whenever someone does speak, the dialog seems precious, as if the last sentence of each speech were edited out.

● ●

■ DRIVING ME CRAZY
See: Dutch

● ●

■ DRIVING MISS DAISY

1989, 99 MINS, US ◇ ⊚ ⊙
Dir Bruce Beresford *Prod* Richard D. Zanuck
Scr Alfred Uhry *Ph* Peter James *Ed* Mark Warner
Mus Hans Zimmer *Art Dir* Bruno Rubeo
● Morgan Freeman, Jessica Tandy, Dan Aykroyd, Patti LuPone, Esther Rolle (Zanuck/Warner)

Driving Miss Daisy is a touching exploration of 25 years of change in Southern race relations (1948-73) as seen through the relationship of an elderly Jewish widow and her stalwart black chauffeur.

Bruce Beresford's sensitive direction complements Alfred Uhry's skillful adapation of his Pulitzer Prize-winning play.

Set in the relatively tolerant city of Atlanta, Daisy effortlessly evokes the changing periods on a limited budget.

Jessica Tandy's Daisy is a captious and lonely old stick, living a bleakly isolated widow's life in her empty old house, and her inability to keep from tyrannizing Morgan Freeman, housekeeper Esther Rolle, and other black helpers gives the film a current of bitter truth, making her gradual friendship with Freeman a hard-won achievement.

Freeman's Hoke is the essence of tact, with a quiet, philosophical acceptance of his role in life and a secret sense of amusement toward whites' behavior.

□ 1989: Best Picture, Actress (Jessica Tandy), Adapted Screenplay, Makeup.
□ Nominations: Best Actor (Morgan Freeman), Supp. Actor (Dan Aykroyd), Editing, Art Direction, Costume Design

● ●

■ DR. JEKYLL AND MR. HYDE

1932, 90 MINS, US ⊚ ⊙
Dir Rouben Mamoulian *Prod* Rouben Mamoulian
Scr Samuel Hoffenstein, Percy Heath *Ph* Karl Struss
● Fredric March, Miriam Hopkins, Rose Hobart, Holmes Herbert, Edgar Norton, Halliwell Hobbes (Paramount)

The fundamental story is that a brilliant scientist turns himself into an ogre who goes upon orgies of lust and murder in peaceful London, all in a misguided frenzy of scientific research, and after murdering a number of other people by extremely horrifying means, destroys himself. That was the length and breadth of the stage play [from the novel by Robert Louis Stevenson], and it served in that form for years.

The picture is infinitely better art – indeed, in many passages it is an astonishing fine bit of interpreting a classic, but as popular fare it loses in vital reaction.

Camera trick of changing a central figure from the handsome Fredric March into the bestial, ape-like monster Hyde, carries a terrific punch, but in each successive use of the device – and it is repeated four times – it weakens in hair-raising effort.

March does an outstanding bit of theatrical acting. His Hyde make-up is a triumph of realized nightmare. Other people in the cast matter little, except that Miriam Hopkins plays Ivy, the London soiled dove, with a capital sense of comedy and coquetry that contributes to the subsequent horror build-up.

Settings and lighting alone are worth seeing as models of atmospheric surroundings.
□ 1931/32: Best Actor (Fredric March).
□ Nominations: Best Adaptation, Cinematography

● ●

■ DR. JEKYLL AND MR. HYDE

1941, 127 MINS, US ⊚ ⊙
Dir Victor Fleming *Prod* Victor Saville *Scr* John Lee Mahin *Ph* Joseph Ruttenberg *Ed* Harold F. Kress
Mus Franz Waxman *Art Dir* Cedric Gibbons, Daniel B. Cathcart
● Spencer Tracy, Ingrid Bergman, Lana Turner, Ian Hunter, Donald Crisp, C. Aubrey Smith (M-G-M)

In the evident striving to make *Jekyll* a 'big' film, by elaborating the theme and introducing new characters and situations, some of the finer psychological points are dulled. John Lee Mahin's screenscript is over-length.

Nevertheless, it has its highly effective moments, and Spencer Tracy plays the dual roles with conviction. His transformations from the young physician, bent on biological and mental research as an escape from his own moral weaknesses, to the demoniac Mr Hyde are brought about with considerably less alterations in face and stature than audiences might expect.

Ingrid Bergman plays the enslaved victim of Hyde's debauches. In every scene in which the two appear, she is Tracy's equal as a strong screen personality.

The script is meagre on the very important phase of Jekyll's inner struggle to free himself from his deadly alter ego. Millions of Stevenson readers have long found excitement and thrill in the angle that Jekyll's predicament was self-conceived to hide criminal and vicious desires. Mahin emphasizes that misdirected scientific research was the cause of the good doctor's downfall.
□ 1941: Nominations: Best B&W Cinematography, Editing, Scoring of a Dramatic Picture

● ●

■ DR. JEKYLL AND SISTER HYDE

1971, 87 MINS, UK ◇ ⊚
Dir Roy Ward Baker *Prod* Albert Fennell, Brian Clemens
Scr Brian Clemens *Ph* Norman Warwick *Ed* James Needs *Mus* David Whitaker *Art Dir* Robert Jones
● Ralph Bates, Martine Beswick, Gerald Sim, Lewis Fiander, Dorothy Alison, Neil Wilson (Hammer)

Scripter Brian Clemens had the highly imaginative idea of letting Robert Louis Stevenson's 19th-century Dr Jekyll turn into a homicidal, glamorous Sister Hyde instead of the original hairy monster. He then pinned on him/her the responsibility for the Jack the Ripper murders.

Here, Jekyll, played by Ralph Bates, murders to remove organs needed for his experiments to prolong life and then gets his hormones wrong. Testing the drug he knocks himself out. Coming round he finds he likes himself as a glamor girl in the person of Martine Beswick and starts to get the best of both sexes when not killing. As male, he attracts the pure young miss living next door and as female fascinates her brother.

Director Roy Ward Baker has set a good pace, built tension nicely and played it straight so that all seems credible. He tops chills and gruesome murders with quite a lot of subtle fun. Bates and Beswick, strong, attractive personalities, bear a strange resemblance to each other making the transitions entirely believable.

● ●

■ DR. NO

1962, 110 MINS, UK ◇ ⊚ ⊙
Dir Terence Young *Prod* Harry Saltzman, Albert R. Broccoli *Scr* Richard Maibaum, Johanna Harwood, Berkely Mather *Ph* Ted Moore *Ed* Peter Hunt
Mus Monty Norman *Art Dir* Ken Adam
● Sean Connery, Ursula Andress, Joseph Wiseman, Jack Lord, Bernard Lee, Zena Marshall (United Artists/ Eon)

First screen adventure of Ian Fleming's hard-hitting, fearless, imperturbable, girl-loving

D

Secret Service Agent 007, James Bond, is an entertaining piece of tongue-in-cheek action hokum. Sean Connery excellently puts over a cool, fearless, on-the-ball, fictional Secret Service guy. Terence Young directs with a pace which only occasionally lags.

The hero is exposed to pretty (and sometimes treacherous) gals, a poison tarantula spider, a sinister crook, flame throwers, gunshot, bloodhounds, beating up, near drowning and plenty of other mayhem and malarkey, and comes through it all with good humour, resourcefulness and what have you.

Connery is sent to Jamaica to investigate the murder of a British confidential agent and his secretary. Since both murders happen within three or four minutes of the credit titles the pic gets away to an exhilarating start. He becomes involved with the activities of Dr. No, a sinister Chinese scientist (Joseph Wiseman) who from an island called Crab Key is using a nuclear laboratory to divert off course the rockets being propelled from Cape Canaveral.

Among the dames with whom Connery becomes involved are easy-on-the-eye Ursula Andress, who shares his perilous adventures on Crab Key, and spends most of her time in a bikini; Zena Marshall, as an Oriental charmer who nearly decoys him to doom via her boudoir; and Eunice Gayson, whom he picks up in a gambling club in London and who promises to be the biggest menace of the lot.

••••••••••••••••••••••••••••••••••••

■ DROP DEAD, DARLING

1966, 100 MINS, UK ◇
Dir Ken Hughes   *Prod* Ken Hughes   *Scr* Ken Hughes
Ph Denys Coop   *Ed* John Shirley   *Mus* Dennis Farnon
Art Dir Seamus Flannery
● Tony Curtis, Rosanna Schiaffino, Lionel Jeffries, Zsa Zsa Gabor, Nancy Kwan, Fenella Fielding (Paramount/Seven Arts)

Pic is a silly sex comedy, as amusing at times as it is tasteless, in which Tony Curtis plays a contemporary Bluebeard.

Producer-director Ken Hughes scripted, from a Hughes-Ronald Harwood story, in turn suggested by Richard Deming's *The Careful Man*. Curtis stars as a gold-digging spouse-killer, who meets his match in Rosanna Schiaffino, a femme counterpart.

Story attempts to make likeable a character who arranges the death of his femme guardian, her sailor suitor, later his first two wives and, unsuccessfully, Schiaffino, bride-widow of an a.k. who expires in honeymoon excitement.

Withal, Curtis does a very good job, plotting with Lionel Jeffries to do in Schiaffino. Latter is by no means without acting ability, either.

Script abounds in lecherous one-liners, ably put over by Anna Quayle, palpitating in the Marilyn Monroe manner as Curtis' guardian; Zsa Zsa Gabor, the non-stop gabber whom Curtis locks in a space vehicle at blast-off, and Fenella Fielding, the English heiress of robust appetites and bank accounts.

••••••••••••••••••••••••••••••••••••

■ DROP DEAD FRED

1991, 98 MINS, US/UK ◇ ⓥ ⊙
Dir Ate De Jong   *Prod* Paul Webster   *Scr* Carlos Davis, Anthony Fingleton   *Ph* Peter Deming   *Ed* Marshall Harvey   *Mus* Randy Edelman   *Art Dir* Joseph T. Garrity
● Phoebe Cates, Rik Mayall, Marsha Mason, Tim Matheson, Carrie Fisher, Keith Charles (Polygram/Working Title)

Oscillating between long arid stretches, inspired explosions of slapstick and disarming warmth, *Drop Dead Fred* [suggested by a story by Elizabeth Livingston] has an almost irresistible premise – kid's imaginary friend comes back to help the grown woman work out her problems – but it's probably too slow and mushy for kids and too sporadic in its rewards for adults.

Phoebe Cates stars as Elizabeth, a young wife who returns home to her domineering mother (Marsha Mason) after splitting up with her brazenly philandering husband (Tim Matheson). At home she discovers a music box that contains her long-forgotten imaginary friend, Drop Dead Fred (British comic Rik Mayall in a red Beethoven fright wig), who's been released to wreak havoc until she's having fun again.

Elizabeth then sets out to woo back her smarmy hubby, although it's patently obvious she'd be better off with nice if rather boring childhood friend, Mickey (Ron Eldard), who conveniently re-emerges.

Director Ate De Jong has captured the silliness of childhood with the hyperactive title character but too often drills jokes deep into the pavement, until even children will have long stopped laughing.

••••••••••••••••••••••••••••••••••••

■ DROWNING BY NUMBERS

1988, 118 MINS, UK/NETHERLANDS ◇ ⓥ ⊙
Dir Peter Greenaway   *Prod* Kees Kasander, Denis Wigman   *Scr* Peter Greenaway   *Ph* Sacha Vierny
Ed John Wilson   *Mus* Michael Nyman   *Art Dir* Ben Van Os, Jan Roelfs
● Bernard Hill, Joan Plowright, Juliet Stevenson, Joely Richardson, Jason Edwards, Bryan Pringle (Film Four/Elsevier Vendex/Allarts/VPRO TV Holland)

Drowning by Numbers deals with metaphorical game-playing of sex and death in the best traditions of black humor, all set in an idyllic English summer, and pays tribute to the games, landscape and especially a conspiracy of women.

Pic follows the darkly murderous acts of three women all named Cissie Colpitts (Joan Plowright, Juliet Stevenson and Joely Richardson) and their friend the local coroner Madgett (Bernard Hill) and his son Smut (Jason Edwards).

Pic opens with Plowright drowning her husband in a tin bath. The families and friends of the three murdered men suspect the three women of the killings and meet under a water tower.

When none of the three Colpitts women submit to Madgett's sexual advances he decides to admit his part in the murders. But his gameplaying instincts take the better of him, and he organizes a game of tug-of-war between the conspirators and the women.

As an aside Greenaway has placed the numbers 1-100 throughout the film (for example, 1 appears on a tree, 36 is on Joely Richardson's swimsuit) – yet another exercise in game-playing and a challenge for the viewer to spot all the numbers. The acting is uniformly excellent.

••••••••••••••••••••••••••••••••••••

■ DROWNING POOL, THE

1975, 108 MINS, US ◇ ⓥ
Dir Stuart Rosenberg   *Prod* Lawrence Torman, David Foster   *Scr* Tracey Keenan Wynn, Lorenzo Semple Jr, Walter Hill   *Ph* Gordon Willis   *Ed* John C. Howard   *Mus* Michael Small   *Art Dir* Paul Sylbert
● Paul Newman, Joanne Woodword, Anthony Franciosa, Murray Hamilton, Gail Strickland, Melanie Griffith (Coleytown/Warner)

Paul Newman again assumes the Lew Harper private eye role he first essayed in *Harper* (1966). *The Drowning Pool* [from Ross MacDonald's novel] is stylish, improbable, entertaining, superficial, well cast, and totally synthetic. Stuart Rosenberg's direction is functional and unexciting.

Newman is summoned by Joanne Woodward to her bayou home because of a blackmail letter to her husband Richard Derr alleging infidelity on her part; she's been unfaithful but the current rap is a bummer.

Lots of interesting characters begin appearing. Melanie Griffith, Woodward's sexpot jailbait daughter; Murray Hamilton, very good as an unscrupulous oil baron and Tony Franciosa, an old Woodward flame, now a police chief.

Title derives from an offbeat and exciting climactic sequence in an abandoned mental asylum hydro-therapy room where Hamilton has imprisoned his wife Gail Strickland and Newman to force disclosure of a black book which will explode lots of swampy intrigue.

••••••••••••••••••••••••••••••••••••

■ DR. PHIBES RISES AGAIN

1972, 88 MINS, UK ◇ ⓥ ⊙
Dir Robert Fuest   *Prod* Louis M. Heyward   *Scr* Robert Fuest, Robert Blees   *Ph* Alex Thomson   *Ed* Tristan Cones   *Mus* John Gale   *Art Dir* Brian Eatwell
● Vincent Price, Robert Quarry, Valli Kemp, Hugh Griffith, John Thaw, Keith Buckley (American International)

Dr Phibes, that bizarre evil genius of *The Abominable Dr. Phibes*, is back with all his old diabolic devilry for another excusion into musical camp fantasy.

Dr Phibes, who went into a state of suspended animation at close of *Abominable*, rises three years later to restore life to his wife who died many years before.

Quest for the necessary elixir hidden in an ancient chamber below a mountain once used by the pharaohs takes him to Egypt, where Robert Quarry is his rival in race for the re-incarnating drug. Phibes starts decimating Quarry's men who would prevent him from bringing his loved one back to life.

Vincent Price, as Phibes, delivers one of his priceless theatric performances, and Quarry is a properly ruthless rival who nearly matches Phibes in knowledge and cunning.

••••••••••••••••••••••••••••••••••••

■ DR. SOCRATES

1935, 74 MINS, US
Dir William Dieterle   *Scr* Robert Lord   *Ph* Tony Gaudio   *Ed* Ralph Dawson
● Paul Muni, Ann Dvorak, Barton MacLane, Raymond Brown, Ralph Remley, Robert Barrat (Warner)

Arriving at the tail end of the G-man and gangster cycle, *Dr Socrates* hasn't the vigor of some of its predecessors, but the constant and basic threat of violence is always present.

Plot [from a story by W.R. Burnett, adapted by Mary C. McCall Jr] departs from what is customary in the gangster school, in that it stars neither the gunman nor the officer of the law, but makes both subservient to a country doctor.

The chief gangster in this case is a Dillinger type of gent who terrorizes a section of the middle west. The young physician is adopted as the gang's medical man, and he takes a chance because he needs the money. But when the gang grabs his girl he goes on the offensive.

For Muni, *Socrates* is an easy role, calling for little or no emotional work. For an actor of his calibre the soft-spoken doc seems a minor effort. Ann Dvorak plays a hitchhiking girl who gets innocently tangled with the mobsters and brings romance to the small town sawbones.

••••••••••••••••••••••••••••••••••••

■ DR. STRANGELOVE OR: HOW I LEARNED TO STOP WORRYING AND LOVE THE BOMB

1964, 102 MINS, UK ⓥ ⊙
Dir Stanley Kubrick   *Prod* Stanley Kubrick   *Scr* Stanley Kubrick, Terry Southern, Peter George   *Ph* Gilbert Taylor   *Ed* Anthony Harvey   *Mus* Laurie Johnson   *Art Dir* Ken Adam
● Peter Sellers, George C. Scott, Sterling Hayden, Keenan Wynn, Slim Pickens, James Earl Jones (Columbia/Hawk)

215

Nothing would seen to be farther apart than nuclear war and comedy, yet Kubrick's caper eloquently tackles a *Fail Safe* subject with a light touch.

Screenplay based on the book *Red Alert* by Peter George is imaginative and contains many an offbeat touch. Some of the characters have a broad brush in their depiction, but this is the very nature of satire.

It all begins when a Strategic Air Command general on his own initiative orders bomb-carrying planes under his command to attack Russia. From here on it's a hectic, exciting series of events, alternating between the General who has started it all, the planes en route to the USSR, and the Pentagon's war room, where the Chief Executive is trying his best to head off the nuclear war.

It would seem no setting for comedy or satire, but the writers have accomplished this with biting, piercing dialogue and thorough characterizations. Peter Sellers is excellent, essaying a trio of roles – a British RAF captain assigned to the US base where it all begins, the President and the title character, Dr Strangelove, a German scientist aiding the US whose Nazi mannerisms overcome him.

George C. Scott as the fiery Pentagon general who seizes on the crisis as a means to argue for total annihilation of Russia offers a top performance, one of the best in the film. Odd as it may seem in this backdrop, he displays a fine comedy touch. Sterling Hayden is grimly realistic as the General who takes it on his own to send our nuclear bomb-carrying planes to attack Russia. He is a man who blames the Communists for fluoridation of water, and just about everything else.

☐ 1964: Nominations: Best Picture, Director, Actor (Peter Sellers), Adapted Screenplay

■ DR. TERROR'S HOUSE OF HORRORS

1965, 98 MINS, UK ◇ ⊛

Dir Freddie Francis *Prod* Milton Subotsky, Max J. Rosenberg *Scr* Milton Subotsky *Ph* Alan Hume *Ed* Thelma Connell *Mus* Elizabeth Lutyens, Tubby Hayes *Art Dir* Bill Constable

● Peter Cushing, Christopher Lee, Roy Castle, Donald Sutherland, Neil McCallum, Alan Freeman (Amicus)

Five short horror episodes, thinly linked, provide a usefully chilly package deal which will offer audiences several mild shudders and quite a lot of amusement. Even though occasional giggles set in, the cast, headed by experienced horror practitioners such as Peter Cushing, Michael Gough, Christopher Lee and Max Adrian, sensibly play it straight.

Five young men traveling on a routine train journey, meet up with the sixth passenger. He's a mysterious, bearded stranger (Cushing) who reveals himself as Dr Schreck. With the aid of a pack of Tarot cards, he foretells the grisly deaths in store for the quintet. The film emerges as a kind of Cinemagoers' Digest of how to come to a sticky end.

■ DRUGSTORE COWBOY

1989, 100 MINS, US ◇ ⊛ ⊙

Dir Gus Van Sant Jr *Prod* Nick Wechsler, Karen Murphy *Scr* Gus Van Sant Jr, Daniel Yost *Ph* Robert Yeoman *Ed* Curtiss Clayton *Mus* Elliot Goldenthal *Art Dir* David Brisbin

● Matt Dillon, Kelly Lynch, James Le Gros, Heather Graham, James Remar, Beah Richards (Avenue)

No previous drug-themed film has the honesty or originality of Gus Van Sant's drama *Drugstore Cowboy*. Pic addresses the fact that people take drugs because they *enjoy them*.

Set in Portland, Ore, in the early 1970s, *Drugstore Cowboy* tells of one self-confessed and completely unrepentant 'drug fiend' (his own description), Bob Hughes (Matt Dillon). He robs drugstores, not for money – for drugs.

Backed up by a 'crew' consisting of his wil-

lowy but tough wife Dianne (Kelly Lynch), his dimwitted but true-blue pal Rick (James Le Gros) and Le Gros' weepy, bumbling girlfriend, Nadine (Heather Graham), Dillon revels in his self-described life of crime.

Dillon's world begins to sour when Graham dies of an overdose. The incident so frightens him he vows to give up drugs entirely. Unfortunately, Lynch refuses to go along with him.

It's a novel conflict. Dillon is kicking the habit for personal reasons – he still likes drugs. He and Lynch still love each other, but for junkies, drugs make every romance a triangle.

Van Sant draws fine performances from his cast, particularly Lynch, who up to now has appeared as the obligatory Sexy Girl. This is her *acting* debut. He also gets one truly great performance from Dillon.

■ DRUM, THE
(US: Drums)

1938, 101 MINS, UK ◇ ⊛ ⊙

Dir Zoltan Korda *Prod* Alexander Korda *Scr* Lajos Biro, Arthur Wimperis, Patrick Kirwan, Hugh Gray *Ph* Georges Perinal, Osmond Borradaile *Ed* Henry Cornelius, William Hornbeck *Mus* John Greenwood, Miklos Rozsa *Art Dir* Vincent Korda, Ferdinand Bellan

● Sabu, Raymond Massey, Roger Livesey, Valerie Hobson, David Tree, Francis L. Sullivan (London)

Film is based on a story written specially for the screen by A.E.W. Mason. He supplies an excellent machine-made suspensive tale laid in India, with fine dialog.

Entire action is laid in the tribal territory of the northwest frontier of India. An elderly khan is anxious for British protection to ensure his throne for his son, Prince Axim (Sabu). Ruler's brother, Prince Ghul, is fanatically anti-British, kills the old man, and the plot involves the attempt to do away with the young prince.

Sabu, the 14-year-old Indian youth who came to attention in *Elephant Boy* (1937), lives up to the promise given in that film and conducts himself with requisite dignity. He now speaks very good English. Raymond Massey is sufficiently sinister as the throne usurper; Roger Livesey is excellent as the military commander.

■ DRUM

1976, 100 MINS, US ◇ ⊛

Dir Steve Carver *Prod* Ralph Serpe *Scr* Norman Wexler *Ph* Lucien Ballard *Ed* Carl Kress *Mus* Charlie Smalls *Art Dir* Stan Jolley

● Warren Oates, Isela Vega, Ken Norton, Pam Grier, Yaphet Kotto, John Colicos (De Laurentiis)

Drum is a grubby followup to *Mandingo* [1975] which invites its own derisive audience laughter. Ham acting like you wouldn't believe, coupled with non-direction by Steve Carver and a correspondence-school script by Norman Wexler, add up to cinematic trash.

There's slave-breeder Warren Oates who buys Ken Norton and Yaphet Kotto from bordello queen Isela Vega, who in reality is Norton's real mother though her lesbian lover-maid Paula Kelly raised the boy; Pam Grier goes along with the deal as Norton's girl and occasional wench to Oates, though Fiona Lewis, her eyes on Oates, has other plans.

Climax of the film is a slave revolt where lots of people get killed, including Royal Dano who manages to keep a straight face as a mean slaver.

■ DRUMS
See: The Drum

■ DRUMS ACROSS THE RIVER

1954, 77 MINS, US ◇

Dir Nathan Juran *Prod* Melville Tucker *Scr* John K. Butler, Lawrence Roman *Ph* Harold Lipstein *Ed* Virgil Vogel *Mus* Joseph Gershenson (dir.)

● Audie Murphy, Walter Brennan, Lyle Bettger, Lisa Gaye, Hugh O'Brian, Mara Corday (Universal)

Plenty of rough and ready action keeps this regulation western rolling over its course.

The script has Lyle Bettger trying to stir up trouble between the Utes and the whites for personal profit. He'd like to open up the Ute territory and its gold deposits, closed to the whites by treaty, on one hand and, on the other, he's scheming to rob the stage of a gold shipment and lay the blame at the doorstep of Audie Murphy and his dad (Walter Brennan).

■ DRUMS ALONG THE MOHAWK

1939, 100 MINS, US ◇ ⊛ ⊙

Dir John Ford *Prod* Darryl Zanuck *Scr* Lamar Trotti, Sonya Levien *Ph* Bert Glennon *Ed* Robert Simpson *Mus* Alfred Newman *Art Dir* Richard Day, Mark-Lee Kirk

● Claudette Colbert, Henry Fonda, Edna May Oliver, Arthur Shields, Ward Bond, John Carradine (20th Century-Fox)

Having great sweep and colorful backgrounding, with the photography unusually good, the picture is an outdoor spectacle which highly pleases the eye even if the story [from the novel by Walter D. Edmonds], on occasion, gets a bit slow and some incidents fail to excite.

While the backgrounding is beautiful, as photoged by Bert Glennon, it doesn't always look like the Mohawk Valley (upstate New York) region with wheat fields, evergreens, big birches, etc. as atmosphere.

The story deals with farming pioneers of the Mohawk Valley sector at the time of the Revolutionary war, with Indian terror and English intrigue, plus hardship, testing the stamina of the colonists. Romance of Henry Fonda and Claudette Colbert, who have married and are forging ahead to new frontiers, has pull.

☐ 1939: Nomination: Best Supp. Actress (Edna May Oliver)

■ DRY WHITE SEASON, A

1989, 97 MINS, US ◇ ⊛ ⊙

Dir Euzhan Palcy *Prod* Paula Weinstein *Scr* Colin Welland, Euzhan Palcy *Ph* Kelvin Pike, Pierre-William Glenn *Ed* Sam O'Steen, Glenn Cunningham *Mus* Dave Grusin *Art Dir* John Fenner

● Donald Sutherland, Winston Ntshona, Zakes Mokae, Jurgen Prochnow, Susan Sarandon, Marlon Brando (M-G-M)

A wrenching picture about South Africa that makes no expedient compromises with feel-good entertainment values, *A Dry White Season* displays riveting performances and visceral style.

Filmmaker Euzhan Palcy – who is black – never tempers her outrage, but the film [from the novel by Andre Brink] drives home the point that the story of South Africa is a story of two races that's unlikely to be resolved by either one alone.

Set in 1976, the film moves quickly to a searing sequence in which a demonstration by black schoolchildren of Soweto is broken up with gratuitous lethal force. Many are brutally beaten and arrested, including the son of Gordon Ngubene (Winston Ntshona), a gardener who works at the comfortable home of naive prep school teacher Ben du Toit (Donald Sutherland).

Du Toit is a basically decent man who cares enough to pay for the missing boy's schooling but not enough to question society's blatantly unjust status quo.

With mounting astonishment this community pillar comes to discover what he's always closed his eyes to: South African 'justice and law could be described as distant cousins – not on speaking terms.'

Those words are spoken by Ian McKenzie (Marlon Brando), rising with a world-weary magnificence to the role of a prominent human rights attorney whose idealism has been battered into resignation. Sarcasm is his only tactic, the moral high ground his only refuge as McKenzie proves Cpt Stolz (Jurgen Prochnow) a murderer, but loses his case before a judge who makes no effort to hide his disgraceful bias.

□ 1989: Nomination: Best Supp. Actor (Marlon Brando)

• •

■ DU BARRY WAS A LADY

1943, 96 MINS, US ◊ ⊗

Dir Roy Del Ruth   *Prod* Arthur Freed   *Scr* Irving Brecher, Wilkie Mahoney   *Ph* Karl Freund   *Ed* Blanche Sewell   *Mus* Georgie Stoll (dir.), Roger Edens (adapt.)   *Art Dir* Cedric Gibbons

● Red Skelton, Lucille Ball, Gene Kelly, Virginia O'Brien, Zero Mostel, 'Rags' Ragland (M-G-M)

In sapoloiing the script for celluloid, the studio has taken Red Skelton out of the men's room and put him in the coat room. Otherwise it follows the general outlines of the original 1939 Broadway show by Herbert Fields and B.G. DeSylva [with music and lyrics by Cole Porter]: the club caddy falls for the top warbler at the spot (Lucille Ball).

She pays no attention to him, being enamored of a broke songsmith (Gene Kelly), while she plays Douglas Dumbrille for his chips. Then Skelton wins a Derby pot and some attention from Ball, only to get a Mickey intended for Kelly mixed up with his own drink, which sends him into a dream sequence. He finds himself Louis XV and Ball his Du Barry.

With the weak plot and weaker dialog, Skelton has a tough time living up to his rep as a funnyman. Ball does a bit better, while Kelly, whose forte is terping, suffers from the histrionic and singing demands of his role and lack of opportunity to make with the feet. Virginia O'Brien is disappointing, too, except for the one tune she's given, 'Salome Was the Grandma of Them All,' in which she literally sparkles.

• •

■ DUCHESS AND THE DIRTWATER FOX, THE

1976, 104 MINS, US ◊ ⊗

Dir Melvin Frank   *Prod* Melvin Frank   *Scr* Melvin Frank, Barry Sandler, Jack Rose   *Ph* Joseph Biroc   *Ed* Frank Bracht, William Butler   *Mus* Charles Fox   *Art Dir* Trevor Williams, Robert Emmet Smith

● George Segal, Goldie Hawn, Roy Jenson, Thayer David, Pat Ast, Sid Gould (20th Century-Fox)

The Duchess and the Dirtwater Fox is a generally pleasant and amiable period western comedy starring George Segal as a fumbling gambler and Goldie Hawn as a singing-dancing frontier chick.

Pair get involved with Roy Jenson's robber gang, Thayer David's group of Mormons, a Jewish wedding, some good gags here, some forced humor there.

Barry Sandler's story has been scripted into sketches which tend to a predictably upbeat curtain. The Colorado scenery vies with the interactions of Hawn and Segal; the other players are more or less backdrop.

The stars work well together; Segal's comedy abilities seem in fullest flower when Mel Frank is directing, while Hawn's talents are showcased quite nicely.

• •

■ DUCK SOUP

1933, 70 MINS, US ⊗

Dir Leo McCarey   *Prod* [uncredited]   *Scr* Bert Kalmar,

Harry Ruby, Arthur Sheekman, Nat Perrin   *Ph* Henry Sharp   *Ed* [LeRoy Stone]   *Mus* [Arthur Johnston (adv.)]   *Art Dir* [Hans Dreier, Wiard B. Ihnen]

● Groucho Marx, Chico Marx, Harpo Marx, Zeppo Marx, Margaret Dumont, Louis Calhern (Paramount)

The laughs come often, too often sometimes, which has always been the case with Marx talkers, although in this instance more care appears to have been taken with the timing, since the step-on gags don't occur as frequently as in the past.

In place of the constant punning and dame chasing, *Duck Soup* has the Marxes madcapping through such bits as the old Schwartz Bros mirror routine, so well done in the hands of Groucho, Harpo and Chico that it gathers a new and hilarious comedy momentum all over again.

Story is a mythical kingdom burlesque that could easily have been written by a six-year-old with dust in his eyes, but it isn't so much the story as what goes with and on within it. Groucho is the prime minister. For his customary dowager-foil he has the high, wide and handsome Margaret Dumont, making it perfect for Groucho.

While Groucho soft pedals the verbal clowning for more physical effort this time the other boys also make a quick change. Chico and Harpo omit their musical specialties, which should make it much easier for the piano and harp numbers the next time, if needed. Zeppo is simply Zeppo.

Music and lyrics [by Bert Kalmar and Harry Ruby] through which much of the action is in rhyme and song, serve to carry the story along rather than to stand out on pop song merit on their own. Everything's in keeping with the tempo of the production.

• •

■ DUCK, YOU SUCKER

See: A Fistful of Dynamite

• •

■ DUDES

1987, 90 MINS, US ◊ ⊗ ⊙

Dir Penelope Spheeris   *Prod* Herb Jaffe   *Scr* J. Randal Johnson   *Ph* Robert Richardson   *Ed* Andy Horvitch   *Art Dir* Robert Ziembicki

● Jon Cryer, Daniel Roebuck, Flea, Lee Ving, Catherine Mary Stewart (Vista)

How can a film that brings punk rockers from Queens, cowboys, Indians and crazed homicidal villains together in Utah be taken seriously? The answer, of course, is that it can't.

Dudes tells the story of three punked-out New Yorkers – Milo, Grant and Biscuit – who set out for Hollywood in a Volkswagen and get attacked while camping out in Big Sky country. Milo is murdered by Missoula, leader of a wild-eyed gang that roams the west killing Mexicans. Grant and Biscuit vow to avenge Milo's death.

Even if one were inclined to overlook the derivative story line, *Dudes* still manages to throw itself from the saddle so many times it bruises the sensibilities. The humor, when intentional, is slapstick. The dialog is hopelessly adolescent, the music incredibly loud and the plot is dependent on a bizarre sequence of coincidences.

• •

■ DUEL

1971, 74 MINS, US ◊ ◊ ⊙

Dir Steven Spielberg   *Prod* George Eckstein   *Scr* Richard Matheson   *Ph* Jack A. Marta   *Ed* Frank Morriss   *Mus* Billy Goldenberg   *Art Dir* Robert S. Smith

● Dennis Weaver, Jacqueline Scott, Eddie Firestone, Lou Frizzell, Gene Dynarski, Lucille Benson (Universal)

In America, a man's car is his castle – a home away from home in which he is master of all he surveys. How well does this freeway monarch behave when his rolling fortress is

besieged by an apparently stronger force?

This is the problem the Universal made-for-tv film wrestles with. Dennis Weaver plays a salesman on his way to an appointment. He drives along a narrow highway located in a sparsely settled western locale. Along the way he passes an enormous oil tanker rig, and later he passes it again.

From then on the picture is all chase – with the trucker alternately playing dangerous games with Weaver and then actually seeming to want to kill him. A clear case of absolute power corrupting absolutely.

Neither Weaver nor the audience ever gets to see the face of the driver (indeed, he has no credit listing), beyond one view of his lower legs and feet and one of his hands waving Weaver on.

The story is adapted from a short tale [by Richard Matheson] in *Playboy* magazine. But it really plays much more like one of those old dramas in the Golden Age of Radio. For the most part, the production, although clearly not expensively mounted, keeps within the spirit of the teleplay and helps it roll. One intrusive note is the necessity for a good deal of inner dialog voiced over the action to indicate Weaver's feelings.

[Version reviewed is the original 74-minute telemovie networked by ABC as 'Movie of the Weekend' on November 13, 1971. The 90-minute theatrical version was released in Europe in 1973 and the US in 1983. Jacqueline Scott, as the wife, appears only in the latter version.]

• •

■ DUEL AT DIABLO

1966, 105 MINS, US ◊ ⊗

Dir Ralph Nelson   *Prod* Fred Engel, Ralph Nelson   *Scr* Marvin Alpert, Michel Grilikhes   *Ph* Charles F. Wheeler   *Ed* Fredric Steinkamp   *Mus* Neal Hefti   *Art Dir* Alfred Ybarra

● James Garner, Sidney Poitier, Bibi Andersson, Dennis Weaver, Bill Travers, William Redfield (United Artists)

Duel at Diablo packs enough fast action in its cavalry-Indians narrative to satisfy the most avid follower of this type of entertainment. Produced with knowhow, and directed with a flourish by Ralph Nelson, the feature is long on exciting and well-staged battle movement and carries a story that while having little novelty still stands to good effect.

Based on the Marvin Albert novel, *Apache Rising*, screenplay stars James Garner as a scout and Sidney Poitier as a former trooper who now makes his living breaking in horses for the service. Rivalling them in interest and importance, however, is Bill Travers, a cavalry lieutenant who heads the column of raw recruits to a distant fort and is attacked en route by the Apaches.

Garner is properly rugged and acquits himself handsomely, convincing as a plainsman who knows his Indians. Poitier tackles a new type of characterization here, far afield from anything he has essayed in the past. Travers in a strong character part is vigorous and appealing and endears himself with his light and human touch.

• •

■ DUEL IN THE SUN

1946, 134 MINS, US ◊ ⊗

Dir King Vidor   *Prod* David O. Selznick   *Scr* David O. Selznick   *Ph* Lee Garmes, Hal Rosson, Ray Rennahan   *Ed* Hal C. Kern   *Mus* Dimitri Tiomkin   *Art Dir* J. McMillan Johnson

● Jennifer Jones, Gregory Peck, Joseph Cotten, Lionel Barrymore, Lillian Gish, Walter Huston (Selznick)

The familiar western formula reaches its highest commercialization in *Duel in Sun*. It is raw, sex-laden, western pulp fiction, told in ten-twent-thirt style. The star lineup is impressive. Vastness of the western locale is splendidly displayed in color by mobile cameras. Footage is overwhelmingly expansive, too much so at times considering its length.

Single scenes that stand out include Jennifer Jones' peril in riding bareback on a runaway horse, filmed against the vast scope of the western scene; Gregory Peck's taming of a sex-maddened stallion; the tremendous sweep of hundreds of mounted horsemen riding to do battle with the invading railroad.

King Vidor's direction keeps the playing in step with production aims. He pitches the action to heights in the top moments and generally holds the overall mood desired. Sharing director credit on the mass sequences are Otto Brower and Reaves Eason.

Plot, suggested by a novel by Niven Busch, adapted by Oliver H. P. Garrett, concerns a half-breed girl who goes to the ranch of a Texas cattle baron to live after her father has killed her adulterous mother and lover. The baron's two sons fall for her but the unrestrained younger one captures her emotions. So strong is physical desire that he murders one man who wants to marry her and tries to kill the brother, shown in latter attempts to make the girl a lady.

Jones as the half-breed proves herself extremely capable in quieter sequences but is overly meller in others. Same is true of Peck as the virile younger Texan raised to love 'em and leave 'em. Contrasting is Joseph Cotten as the older son. Role in his hands is believable and never overdrawn.

□ 1946: Nominations: Best Actress (Jennifer Jones), Supp. Actress (Lillian Gish)

●●●●●●●●●●●●●●●●●●●●●●●●●●●

■ **DUELLISTS, THE**

1977, 95 MINS, UK ◇ ⑫ ⊙

Dir Ridley Scott   *Prod* David Puttnam   *Scr* Gerald Vaughan-Hughes   *Ph* Frank Tidy   *Ed* Pamela Power   *Art Dir* Bryan Graves

● Keith Carradine, Harvey Keitel, Cristina Raines, Edward Fox, Robert Stephens, Albert Finney (Enigma)

The Napoleonic Wars are behind this stubborn sword slashing and then pistols of two men whose personalities are caught up in their own personal vendetta within the epic European battles of the times.

Harvey Keitel is an almost obsessed dueller who is asked to appear before the general due to his duels, by Keith Carradine who practically volunteers for the job.

Keitel is jaunty and menancing and Carradine more determined and a bit troubled but also caught up in this strange need of one to prove honor and the other slaking a twisted nature.

It does not quite achieve a more lusty visual feel for the times and the strange relations of these two men to themselves and to the women in and out of their lives.

Fine thesps in smaller roles help with even Albert Finney in as the Napoleonic head of the Paris police.

●●●●●●●●●●●●●●●●●●●●●●●●●●●

■ **DUET FOR ONE**

1986, 107 MINS, US ◇ ⑫

Dir Andrei Konchalovsky   *Prod* Menahem Golan, Yoram Globus   *Scr* Tom Kempinski, Jeremy Lipp, Andrei Konchalovsky   *Ph* Alex Thomson   *Ed* Henry Richardson   *Mus* Michael Linn   *Art Dir* John Graysmark

● Julie Andrews, Alan Bates, Max Von Sydow, Rupert Everett, Margaret Courtenay, Cathryn Harrison (Cannon)

The story of a world-class violinist who contracts multiple sclerosis and is forced to abandon her career, as long as *Duet for One* [from the 1980 stage play by Tom Kempinski] stays personal and specific it is a moving portrait of a life in turmoil.

Initially the film is not really about illness but the relationship of an artist to her art. Film is full of lovely musical interludes, both in concert and practice, and Julie Andrews actually looks credible stroking her violin. At the same time Andrews approaches her predicament in a pragmatic, overly rational manner as she plans out her recording schedule and the remaining days of her career.

In addition to the suggestion of a story, first half of the film offers an array of eccentric characters swirling around Andrews' life. As the philandering husband, Bates is a complex and restless soul afraid to face his own failings, whose vulnerability and physical deterioration bring an added and welcome dimension to the film.

●●●●●●●●●●●●●●●●●●●●●●●●●●●

■ **DUFFY**

1968, 101 MINS, UK ◇

Dir Robert Parrish   *Prod* Martin Manulis   *Scr* Donald Cammell, Harry Joe Brown Jr   *Ph* Otto Heller   *Ed* Willie Kemplen   *Mus* Ernie Freeman   *Art Dir* Phillip Harrison

● James Coburn, James Mason, James Fox, Susannah York, John Alderton (Columbia)

Duffy is the story of two alienated sons stealing from their wealthy father. Weak writing and heavy-handed direction by Robert Parrish, eliciting only tepid performances, combine to snuff out much interest before the genuinely perky climax.

James Mason is a cold, calculating industrialist, loathed heartily by his sons, James Fox (who needs dad's money to pay for his hedonistic excesses) and John Alderton (who simply needs someone to rescue him from stupid blunders). Susannah York has some sort of affair going with Fox. Trio recruits drifter James Coburn to help with a money heist, designed to make them independently wealthy and also to embarrass Mason.

Fox's interpretation of his role is so swish (with costumes to match) that one wonders what attractions he holds for York. York in addition looks different in practically every setup. Only Alderton, who plays broadly to the pit, has what seems a definite concept of his part. Coburn tries awfully hard to be a hippie.

●●●●●●●●●●●●●●●●●●●●●●●●●●●

■ **DUKE WORE JEANS, THE**

1958, 90 MINS, UK

Dir Gerald Thomas   *Prod* Peter Rogers   *Scr* Norman Hudis   *Ph* Otto Heller   *Ed* Peter Boita   *Mus* Bruce Montgomery   *Art Dir* Harry White

● Tommy Steele, June Laverick, Michael Medwin, Alan Wheatley, Eric Pohlmann, Noel Hood (Insignia)

With his second film, *The Duke Wore Jeans*, Tommy Steele is lured into doing a certain amount of acting, and though no great shakes as a mummer, he emerges as a likeable personality with acting potentiality.

The lissom yarn [by Lionel Bart and Michael Pratt] has Steele playing a dual role. He is a young aristocrat who wants to evade wooing the princess of a wealthy South American oil-monarchy, as desired by his hard-up parents, mainly because he already is secretly married. When he meets a young, brash Cockney who is his exact double, he arranges for him to take his place.

Steele is happier when he takes over for the young peer than in the earlier stages. Opportunities are provided for him to sing several numbers of which 'It's All Happening,' 'Happy Guitar' and 'Thanks a Lot' are standouts. Most of the comedy is supplied via a suave performance by Michael Medwin, as a gentleman's gentleman.

●●●●●●●●●●●●●●●●●●●●●●●●●●●

■ **DUMBO**

1941, 64 MINS, US ◇ ⑫ ⊙

Dir Ben Sharpsteen   *Prod* Walt Disney   *Scr* Joe Grant, Dick Huemer   *Mus* Oliver Wallace, Frank Churchill   *Art Dir* Herb Ryman, Ken O'Connor, Terrell Stamp, Don Da Gradi, Al Zinnen, Ernest Nordli, Dick Kelsey, Charles Payzand (Walt Disney)

Walt Disney returns in *Dumbo* to the formula that accounted for his original success – simple animal characterization.

There's a pleasant little story, plenty of pathos mixed with the large doses of humor, a number of appealing new animal characters, lots of good music, and the usual Disney skillfulness in technique.

Defects are some decidedly slow spots and that the film is somewhat episodic in nature.

Story [from a book by Helen Aberson and Harold Pearl] points a nice moral, although not one that gets in the way. Dumbo is a little elephant who is jeered at because of his big ears. But he is shown how to make use of his ears, they enable him to fly, and his handicap thereby becomes his greatest asset.

Yarn is set to a circus background, complete with clowns, the big top and all the rest. There is also a neatly contrived comedy characterization of gossipy lady elephants, and the even more earthy humor of a typical Disney locomotive being spurred to speed by a goose from the car behind it.

□ 1941: Best Scoring of a Musical Picture.
□ Nomination: Best Song ('Baby Mine')

●●●●●●●●●●●●●●●●●●●●●●●●●●●

■ **DUNE**

1984, 140 MINS, US ◇ ⑫ ⊙

Dir David Lynch   *Prod* Raffaella De Laurentiis   *Scr* David Lynch   *Ph* Freddie Francis   *Ed* Antony Gibbs   *Mus* Toto, Marty Paich, Brian Eno   *Art Dir* Anthony Masters

● Francesca Annis, Brad Dourif, Kyle MacLachlan, Sian Phillips, Sting, Max von Sydow (De Laurentiis)

Dune is a huge, hollow, imaginative and cold sci-fi epic. Visually unique and teeming with incident, David Lynch's film holds the interest due to its abundant surface attractions but won't, of its own accord, create the sort of fanaticism which has made Frank Herbert's 1965 novel one of the all-time favorites in its genre.

Set in the year 10,991, *Dune* is the story of the coming to power of a warrior savior and how he leads the lowly inhabitants of the Dune planet to victory over an evil emperor and his minions.

Lynch's adaptation covers the entire span of the novel, but simply setting up the various worlds, characters, intrigues and forces at work requires more than a half-hour of expository screen time.

The anointed one, Paul Atreides, travels with his regal mother and father to the desert planet, where an all-powerful 'spice' is mined from beneath the sands despite the menace provided by enormous worms which gobble up harvesters in a single gulp.

The horrid Harkonnens conquer the city on Dune, but Paul and his mother escape to the desert. There Paul trains native warriors and achieves his full mystic powers.

Francesca Annis and Jurgen Prochnow make an outstandingly attractive royal couple, Sian Phillips has some mesmerizing moments as a powerful witch, Brad Dourif is effectively loony, and best of all is Kenneth McMillan, whose face is covered with grotesque growths and who floats around like the Blue Meanie come to life.

□ 1984: Nomination: Best Sound

●●●●●●●●●●●●●●●●●●●●●●●●●●●

■ **DUNKIRK**

1958, 135 MINS, UK

Dir Leslie Norman   *Prod* Michael Balcon   *Scr* David Divine, W.P. Lipscomb   *Ph* Paul Beeson   *Ed* Gordon Stone   *Mus* Malcolm Arnold   *Art Dir* Jim Morahan

● John Mills, Bernard Lee, Richard Attenborough, Robert Urquhart, Ray Jackson, Maxine Audley (Ealing)

Eighteen years after the event, Ealing Films tackled the mammoth task of committing Dunkirk to the screen. The story of a defeat which, miraculously, blossomed into ultimate victory because it stiffened Britain's resolve and solidarity, offered Michael Balcon and his team many challenging problems. *Dunkirk* is a splendid near-documentary which just fails to reach magnificence.

Director Leslie Norman planned his film [based on a novel by Elleston Trevor and also on a factual account] through the eyes of three men. John Mills, a spry Cockney corporal who with a few men becomes detached from his unit and leads them to the beaches without quite knowing what is happening. Bernard Lee, a newspaper correspondent who is suspicious of the red tape of the higher-ups. Richard Attenborough as a civilian having an easy time in a reserved occupation.

The film throughout is deliberately underplayed, with no false heroics and with dialog which has an almost clinical authenticity. On the whole, it is an absorbing rather than an emotion-stirring film.

••••••••••••••••••••••••••••••

■ DUST DEVIL
THE FINAL CUT

1993, 108 MINS, UK/US ◇ ⑰ ⊙
Dir Richard Stanley   *Prod* Joanne Sellar   *Scr* Richard Stanley   *Ph* Steven Chivers   *Ed* Derek Trigg, Paul Carlin   *Mus* Simon Boswell   *Art Dir* Joseph Bennett
● Robert Burke, Chelsea Field, Zakes Mokae, John Matshikiza, Rufus Swart, William Hootkins
(Palace/Miramax)

Overflowing with ideas, visual invention and genre references but saddled by a weak, unfocused script, *Dust Devil* is a brilliant mess. Mystical African-set slasher movie is the second feature of pop promo alum Richard Stanley.

The low-budget production was shot in late summer 1991 in Namibia, southern Africa, with Stanley delivering a 125-minute European cut in December. Stanley spent $45,000 of his own coin to reconstruct this version, [a compromise between his original and US coproducer Miramax's much shorter] US cut, American-dubbed and with a new voiceover.

The opening 45 minutes is a tour de force of elaborate cross-cutting and sustained tension as three characters compete for attention. First is a taciturn Yank (Robert Burke) hitching across country murdering and mutilating strangers and collecting their fingers in a box. Second is black cop Ben (Zakes Mokae), who turns to the witch-doctor owner of a desert drive-in (John Matshikiza) to solve the ghastly murders. Third is Wendy (Chelsea Field), a South African who walks out on her boring hubby (Rufus Swart) and drives north to Namibia on a journey to nowhere.

Story slides into focus halfway through, as the trio's destinies crisscross and it becomes clear Burke is trying to return to the spirit world but is trapped in the present, surviving by claiming human souls.

Final impression is of a film that's run amok with too many half-baked ideas, which might have cohered with a stronger script.

••••••••••••••••••••••••••••••

■ DUTCH
(UK/Australia: Driving Me Crazy)

1991, 105 MINS, US ◇ ⑰ ⊙
Dir Peter Faiman   *Prod* John Hughes, Richard Vane   *Scr* John Hughes   *Ph* Charles Minsky   *Ed* Paul Hirsch, Adam Bernardi   *Mus* Alan Silvestri   *Art Dir* Stan Jolley
● Ed O'Neill, Ethan Randall, JoBeth Williams, Christopher McDonald, Ari Meyers, E.G. Daily (20th Century-Fox)

In designing *Dutch*, writer-producer John Hughes lays in some oft-used parts, from the family holiday gathering to the travails of incompatible travelers. In this case, the focus is on Ed O'Neill as Dutch, a salt-of-the-earth guy who's volunteered to pick up his girl-friend's snotty kid, Doyle (Ethan Randall), at an elite boarding school and bring him home for Thanksgiving. Little does Dutch know what he's in for.

Full of rage over his mother's divorce from his callous but absurdly wealthy dad (Christopher McDonald), Doyle wants nothing to do with either his doting mom (JoBeth Williams) or her new boyfriend, and he spews his towering contempt at working-class Dutch.

The kid is so despicable that even Dutch soon loses his taste for the challenge. Therein lies the pic's weakness, as the boy's hateful behavior is so trying that this two-character journey – even with its attendant adventures with fireworks, hookers, tacky motels and homeless shelters – isn't all that enticing.

O'Neill is well cast as the tough and confident regular guy, but his comic gifts fall short of hilarious, and director Peter Faiman, helming his first project since *Crocodile Dundee*, never really sets a rollicking groove. Filmed in Georgia, Tennessee, rural Illinois and on LA soundstages, film draws texture and comedy from locations.

••••••••••••••••••••••••••••••

■ DUTCHMAN

1967, 55 MINS, UK
Dir Anthony Harvey   *Prod* Gene Persson   *Scr* Le Roi Jones   *Ph* Gerry Turpin   *Ed* Anthony Harvey   *Mus* John Barry   *Art Dir* Herbert Smith
● Shirley Knight, Al Freeman Jr (Persson)

Dutchman is a literal filming of Le Roi Jones' 1964 off-Broadway play, pitting a white slut against a middle-class Negro youth who is, in turn, seduced, disgraced and killed. Excellent direction and performances are enhanced by realistically grim production values.

Producer Gene Persson casts wife Shirley Knight and Al Freeman Jr as the leads, actually a re-teaming since both starred in his 1965 LA and Frisco legit mountings of the property.

Anthony Harvey makes his directorial debut after a long career as a film editor. It is a challenging debut, since there is no screenplay, only Jones' legit dialog, and the action is confined to a NY subway car, except for some second-unit lensing by Edward R. Brown. Withal, Harvey's work is impressive, in eliciting adroit performances, in camera setups, and in overall editing pace.

Knight, a red-neck Jezebel if there ever was one, is outstanding as she deliberately debases Freeman, dragging him down from insecure middle class status to that of an embittered, violent youth.

••••••••••••••••••••••••••••••

■ DYING YOUNG

1991, 105 MINS, US ◇ ⑰ ⊙
Dir Joel Schumacher   *Prod* Sally Field, Kevin McCormick   *Scr* Richard Friedenberg   *Ph* Juan Ruiz Anchia   *Ed* Robert Brown   *Mus* James Newton Howard   *Art Dir* Guy J. Comtois
● Julia Roberts, Campbell Scott, Vincent D'Onofrio, Colleen Dewhurst, David Selby, Ellen Burstyn (20th Century-Fox/Fogwood)

Julia's hot; *Dying Young* is lukewarm. In this rather thin and maudlin weeper Julia Roberts does little to extend her range in a performance that seems pieced together from aspects of previous roles.

Campbell Scott (*The Sheltering Sky*) plays Victor Geddes, an immensely wealthy young man who at 28 has been battling leukemia for 10 years. He places an ad for an attractive young lady to nurse him through the bouts of violent illness that accompany chemotherapy.

Enter Roberts as Hilary O'Neil, who in the interest of dramatic contrast is painted as a badly dressed, uneducated street-smart type from blue-collar Oakland. For the lonely, intellectual Victor, she's raw material to be shaped in his image – an irresistible draw.

Director Joel Schumacher (*Flatliners*) apparently doubting an audience will stick around just out of concern for Victor's illness, turns a rather shabbily exploitative camera on Roberts, whose legs seem to play the lead role in the first act. Much of the time pic operates on the level of a teaser sustained by the dangling question of Victor's unconsummated desire.

Roberts displays the usual combo of flintily self-sufficient and winningly vulnerable traits. Her portrayal of a working-class character is not exactly chameleon-like. Scott puts in a beguiling and technically polished turn as the desperately lonely sufferer.

Pic [from Marti Leimbach's novel] plays like a sentiment-soaked escapist fantasy for the bed-and-breakfast set.

••••••••••••••••••••••••••••••

■ EACH DAWN I DIE

1939, 92 MINS, US Ⓦ

Dir William Keighley   *Prod* David Lewis   *Scr* Norman
Reilly Raine, Warren Duff, Charles Perry   *Ph* Arthur
Edeson   *Ed* Thomas Richards   *Mus* Max Steiner
Art Dir Max Parker
● James Cagney, George Raft, Jane Bryan, George
Bancroft, Victor Jory (Warner)

Story structure [from a novel by Jerome
Odlum] is a bit thin in spots despite the best
efforts of director William Keighley, who isn't
always able to cover up. The loyalty theme
and seeming double-cross motive becomes too
involved just when the plot appears heading
for a clever climax.

Cagney is kept in typical toughie surroundings, framed by unscrupulous politicians because he has uncovered their crooked work
for his newspaper. Embittered by his inability
to win a pardon, Cagney is pictured as developing into a hardened prisoner. Then when
he helps an underworld big shot (George
Raft) go scot free in a daring courtroom
break, only to be double-crossed when the
big-timer thinks Raft has squealed, the reporter goes haywire.

Cagney fans will be pleasantly surprised at
his restrained, skillful performance. Raft is a
plausible, gripping underworld big-timer. He
rates the co-starring classification.

....

■ EAGLE HAS LANDED, THE

1977, 134 MINS, UK ◇ Ⓦ

Dir John Sturges   *Prod* Jack Wiener, David Niven Jr
Scr Tom Mankiewicz   *Ph* Tony Richmond   *Ed* Irene
Lamb   *Mus* Lalo Schifrin   *Art Dir* Peter Murton
● Michael Caine, Donald Sutherland, Robert Duvall,
Jenny Agutter, Donald Pleasence, Anthony Quayle
(ITC/Assoc. General)

In November 1943 Winston Churchill is due
to spend a weekend at a country house in
Norfolk – and the Germans propose to kidnap
him there. Under orders from Heinrich
Himmler (Donald Pleasence), purportedly
coming from Hitler himself, a Nazi colonel,
Robert Duvall, organizes the smuggling into
Britain of the English-hating Irishman
Donald Sutherland and the parachuting of a
16-man task force of Germans under the
command of another colonel (Michael
Caine).

The events take place in the small village of
Studley Constable.

Most performances [in this adaptation of
Jack Higgins' novel] are first rate with
Sutherland exuding great credibility as the
Irishman, and Caine thoroughly convincing
as the Nazi commander. Pleasence gives a
stand-out lifelike interpretation of
Himmler.

....

■ EAGLE'S WING

1979, 104 MINS, UK ◇ Ⓦ

Dir Anthony Harvey   *Prod* Ben Arbeid   *Scr* John Briley
Ph Billy Williams   *Ed* Lesley Walker   *Mus* Marc
Wilkinson   *Art Dir* Herbert Westbrook
● Martin Sheen, Sam Waterston, Harvey Keitel,
Stephane Audran, Caroline Langrishe, John Castle (Rank)

Claiming to evoke 'the West, the way it really
was, before the myths were born', British director Anthony Harvey's poised, loving linger
in the 1830s badlands of New Mexico is primarily a dawn art film – resolutely romantic, high
on production values, low on grit.

Ostensibly a tussle for possession of a
uniquely fleet white horse (poetically described
by the title), the distinctly allegorical plot [from
an original story by Michael Syson] pits Martin
Sheen as a city-bred, novice trapper against a
no-longer-so-young Indian brave, played with
remarkable success by Sam Waterston.

Sheen, wild-eyed and vulnerable, is good
casting and copes well with the central character's awkward soliloquizing. Harvey Keitel
is lowkey but impressive as Sheen's companion and mentor.

....

■ EARTH GIRLS ARE EASY

1988, 100 MINS, UK/US ◇ Ⓦ ⊙

Dir Julien Temple   *Prod* Tony Garnett   *Scr* Julie Brown,
Charlie Coffey, Terrence E. McNally   *Ph* Oliver Stapleton
Ed Richard Halsey   *Mus* Nile Rodgers, Chaz Jankel,
David Storrs   *Art Dir* Dennis Gassner
● Geena Davis, Jeff Goldblum, Julie Brown, Jim Carrey,
Damon Wayans, Michael McKean (Kestrel/Odyssey)

Earth Girls Are Easy is a dizzy, glitzy fish-out-
of-water farce about three horny aliens on the
make in LA.

Julie (Geena Davis), a gorgeous Valley Girl,
works as a manicurist in high-tech beauty salon
operated by Candy (Julie Brown) a Val-Queen
supreme who likes good times and good sex.

Meanwhile in outer space, three aliens who
look like tie-dyed werewolves are wandering
around our solar system going bonkers with
randiness. In keeping with the film's hot-pas-
tel, contempo-trash design motif, their spacecraft looks like the inside of a pinball
machine. When it lands in Julie's swimming
pool, the broken-hearted girl who's just broken off with her nogoodnik lover takes it for
an oversized hair dryer.

Julie brings this gruesome threesome to
Candy's beauty parlor for a complete
'makeover.' They emerge as three hairless
hunky dudes: the captain, Jeff Goldblum
and two flaked-out crewmen, Jim Carrey
and Damon Wayans. The two val-gals and
their alien 'dates' take off for a weekend of
LA nightlife, where the visitors' smooth
adaptation to Coast culture is intended by
director Julian Temple and his screenwriters to affectionately skewer Tinseltown
lifestyles.

....

■ EARTHQUAKE

1974, 122 MINS, US ◇ Ⓦ ⊙

Dir Mark Robson   *Prod* Mark Robson   *Scr* George Fox,
Mario Puzo   *Ph* Philip Lathrop   *Ed* Dorothy Spencer
Mus John Williams   *Art Dir* Alexander Golitzen, E.
Preston Ames
● Charlton Heston, Ava Gardner, George Kennedy,
Lorne Greene, Genevieve Bujold, Richard Roundtree
(Universal)

Mark Robson's *Earthquake* is an excellent dramatic exploitation extravaganza, combining
brilliant special effects with a multi-character
plot line which is surprisingly above average
for this type film. Large cast is headed by
Charlton Heston, who comes off better than
usual because he is not Superman, instead
just one of the gang.

Ava Gardner, ravishingly beautiful, plays
Heston's jealous wife, who also is the daugh-
ter of Lorne Greene, Heston's architect boss.
Gardner's fits of pique concern Genevieve
Bujold.

The film spends its first 53 minutes establishing most of the key plot situations, but
regularly teases with some foreshocks the big
quake. When that occurs, the first big special
effects sequence provides an excellent, unstinting panorama of destruction.

□ 1974: Best Sound, Special Visual Effects.
□ Nominations: Best Cinematography, Art
Direction, Editing

....

■ EASTER PARADE

1948, 102 MINS, US ◇ Ⓦ ⊙

Dir Charles Walters   *Prod* Arthur Freed   *Scr* Frances
Goodrich, Albert Hackett, Sidney Sheldon   *Ph* Harry
Stradling   *Ed* Albert Akst   *Mus* Johnny Green, Roger
Edens (dirs.)   *Art Dir* Cedric Gibbons, Jack Martin Smith
● July Garland, Fred Astaire, Peter Lawford, Ann Miller,
Jules Munshin (M-G-M)

Easter Parade is a musical with old and new
Irving Berlin tunes and standout dance numbers. The Berlin score includes 17 songs,
seven new and 10 from his extensive catalog.

The light story by Frances Goodrich and
Albert Hackett, scripted in conjunction with
Sidney Sheldon, makes a perfect backing for
the Berlin score and playing. Plot opens on
Easter 1911 and carries through to Easter
1912. It deals with splitup of Astaire and
Miller as partners and recruiting of Garland
by the dancer, who is determined to make her
outdraw his former hoofer.

Astaire's standout solo is the elaborate production piece 'Stepping Out with My Baby',
during which he does a slow-motion dance in
front of a large chorus terping in regular
time.

Highpoint of comedy is reached when
Astaire and Garland team for vocals and foot
work on 'A Couple of Swells'.
□ 1948: Best Score for a Musical Picture

....

■ EAST LYNNE

1931, 102 MINS, US

Dir Frank Lloyd   *Scr* Bradley King, Tom Barry   *Ph* John
Seitz   *Mus* Richard Fall   *Art Dir* Joseph Urban
● Ann Harding, Clive Brook, Conrad Nagel, Cecilia
Loftus, Beryl Mercer, O. P. Heggie (Fox)

An excellent piece of work in taking a legendary meller play and transposing it into a
screen drama of strength and charm.

The beauty of the cast is that they make the
characters believable. All are from the stage,
while the dialog is such that it avoids petty
pleasantries or overly dramatic orations. It
amounts to an outstanding performance by
Ann Harding, who is closely allied by Clive
Brook and Cecilia Loftus.

Second line of defense is in the able hands
of O.P. Heggie and Beryl Mercer. Heggie has
somewhat less to do, but impresses as the
girl's father.

Joseph Urban's settings are sumptuous and
tasteful, evidently having been given a free
hand in creating the interior of a big country
home. Besides which there is an elaborate
Viennese cafe interlude, as also a certain
amount of footage given over to the Franco-
Prussian war and the bombardment of Paris
by the latter forces. It's doubtful if Fox got
out with less than $800,000 in production
costs.

Frank Lloyd, who directed, has made everything count without lingering unnecessarily
over any one episode. His only hint of a false
note seems to be in the meeting of Isabel
(Harding) and her father in Paris, where she
pleads with him to seek permission from her
husband to see her child.
□ 1930/31: Nomination: Best Picture

....

■ EAST OF EDEN

1955, 114 MINS, US ◇ Ⓦ ⊙

Dir Elia Kazan   *Prod* Elia Kazan   *Scr* Paul Osborn
Ph Ted McCord   *Ed* Owen Marks   *Mus* Leonard
Rosenman   *Art Dir* James Basevi, Malcolm Bert
● Julie Harris, James Dean, Raymond Massey, Burl Ives,
Jo Van Fleet, Albert Dekker (Warner)

Powerfully somber dramatics have been captured from the pages of John Steinbeck's *East
of Eden* and put on film by Elia Kazan. It is a
tour de force for the director's penchant for
hard-hitting forays with life.

It is no credit to Kazan that James Dean
seems required to play his lead character as

though he were straight out of a Marlon Brando mold, although he has a basic appeal that manages to get through to the viewer despite the heavy burden of carboning another's acting style in voice and mannerisms.

Only the latter part of the Steinbeck novel is used in the screenplay, which picks up the principals in this Salinas Valley melodrama at the time the twin sons of a lettuce farmer are graduating in the 1917 class at high school.

Julie Harris gives her particular style to an effective portrayal of the girl.

☐ 1955: Best Supp. Actress (Jo Van Fleet). ☐ Nominations: Best Director, Actor (James Dean), Screenplay

■ EASY LIVING

1937, 88 MINS, US
Dir Mitchell Leisen   *Prod* Arthur Hornblow Jr
Scr Preston Sturges   *Ph* Ted Tetzlaff   *Ed* Doane Harrison
Mus Boris Morros (dir.)   *Art Dir* Hans Dreier, Ernst Fegte
● Jean Arthur, Edward Arnold, Ray Milland, Luis Alberni, Mary Nash, Franklin Pangborn (Paramount)

Slapstick farce, incredible and without rhyme or reason, is Paramount's contribution to the cycle of goofy pictures which started with *My Man Godfrey* (1936). This one is a poor imitation, lacking spontaneity and cleverness.

Screenplay by Preston Sturges [from a story by Vera Caspary] is a trivia of nonsense. Mitchell Leisen, who directs, tries to overcome the story faults with elaborate settings and Keystone gags.

Opening portrays Edward Arnold as a Wall Street speculative genius whose mad selling and buying has the street agog with his financial didoes. Conflict starts with an altercation between him and his wife over the purchase of a fur coat. Garment is tossed out of the window and strikes a young stenographer (Jean Arthur) on her way to work. In a jealous fit, Arnold insists the young woman retain the coat and whisks her to the milliner to buy a hat to match.

Meanwhile, the news spreads quickly that the big Wall Street man has a mistress, and Arthur, whose resources are measured in nickels, accepts an elaborate suite in the leading hotel. What she wants most is a cup of coffee, and she goes to the automat to get it. There she meets Ray Milland, son of the Wall Street wizard. He is a waiter in the joint.

Yarns of this sort are likely to get out of hand by introducing low slapstick comedy. When the food throwing ends there is nothing left for the players to do. All semblance of probability has vanished.

■ EASY RIDER

1969, 94 MINS, US ◇ ⓥ ⊙
Dir Dennis Hopper   *Prod* Peter Fonda   *Scr* Peter Fonda, Dennis Hopper, Terry Southern   *Ph* Laszlo Kovacs
Ed Donn Cambren   *Mus* The Byrds, The Band, Jimi Hendrix, Steppenwolf   *Art Dir* Jerry Kay
● Peter Fonda, Dennis Hopper, Jack Nicholson, Robert Walker Jr, Luana Anders, Phil Spector (Pando/Raybert)

Film deals with two dropouts on a long trip from Los Angeles to New Orleans' Mardi Gras, a search for freedom thwarted by that streak of ingrained, bigoted violence in the US and their own hangups.

Pic chronicles their trip that ends in tragedy. Their bikes whisk them through the good roads surrounded by all the stretches of land that have housed that mythic American creation of the western.

Script is literate and incisive and Hopper's direction is fluid, observant and catches the pictorial poetics with feeling.

Fonda exudes a groping moral force and Hopper is agitated, touching and responsive as the sidekick, hoping for that so-called freedom their stake should give them.

Jack Nicholson is excellent as an articulate alcoholic who fills in the smothered needs in a verbal way that the others feel but cannot express.

☐ 1969: Nominations: Best Supp. Actor (Jack Nicholson), Original Story & Screenplay

■ EAT A BOWL OF TEA

1989, 102 MINS, US ◇ ⓥ ⊙
Dir Wayne Wang   *Prod* Tom Sternberg   *Scr* Judith Rascoe   *Ph* Amir Mokri   *Ed* Richard Candib
Mus Mark Adler   *Art Dir* Bob Ziembicki
● Cora Miao, Russell Wong, Victor Wong, Lee Sau-kee, Eric Tsang (American Playhouse)

Wayne Wang returns to Chinatown with *Eat a Bowl of Tea*, and recaptures the relaxed humor and deep emotions of his earlier *Dim Sum* in the process.

Pic starts off with Wah Gay (Victor Wong), who runs a New York gambling club, deciding to send his soldier son Ben Loy (Russel Wong) to China to marry the daughter of his best friend. Fortunately, it's love at first sight between Ben and Mei Oi (Cora Miao), and they marry and return to the States.

Unfortunately, Ben finds the pressures of running a business so severe that his lovelife suffers. Basically, poor Ben is impotent, causing grief to his wife as well as to the couple's fathers, who eagerly want to become grandfathers.

Enter Ah Song (Eric Tsang), a cheerful, rascally gambler who becomes Mei's secret lover, and who succeeds in getting her pregnant. But when words gets out that Ben isn't the father, it's Wah Gay who tries to restore family honor by attacking Ah Song with a meat ax.

Typically, the aforementioned scene is played for laughs, and indeed is the comic high point of a generally charming and amusing film [from a novel by Louis Chu].

■ EATING

1990, 110 MINS, US ◇
Dir Henry Jaglom   *Prod* Judith Wolinsky   *Scr* Henry Jaglom   *Ph* Hanania Baer
● Lisa Richards, Mary Crosby, Gwen Welles, Nelly Alard, Frances Bergen, Daphna Kastner (International Rainbow)

The ladies who lunch – and munch, breakfast, binge, dine, diet, starve and sample – are delicious in *Eating*, but writer-director Henry Jaglom labors over the stove too long, harming a tasty souffle.

Convening a large collection of diverse friends to celebrate a three-tiered birthday party, Lisa Richards is observing her 40th, Mary Crosby her 30th, and Marlena Giovi her 50th. There's plenty of savvy conversation marking each passage, but mainly the birthday girls and their friends reveal how so much of their lives have been dominated by food, either as a substitute for affection or a form of self-destruction.

Richards, Crosby and Giovi are splendid, as is Frances Bergen as Richards' mother, ultimately shedding her own covers. At the other end of the age scale, Daphna Kastner is also captivating as Giovi's dominated daughter, plumping herself in defense. Gwen Welles stands out as a bitchy, back-biting bulemic.

■ EATING RAOUL

1982, 83 MINS, US ◇ ⓥ
Dir Paul Bartel   *Prod* Anne Kimmel   *Scr* Richard Blackburn, Paul Bartel   *Ph* Gary Thieltges   *Ed* Alan Toomayan   *Mus* Arlon Ober   *Art Dir* Robert Schulenberg
● Paul Bartel, Mary Woronov, Robert Beltram, Susan Salger, Ed Begley Jr, Buck Henry (Bartel)

All poor Paul and Mary Bland want in life is enough money to buy their own restaurant in Valencia, California and call it Paul and Mary's Country Kitchen. But they have little hope of raising the $20,000 they need to make their dreams come true.

To compound matters, the proper couple, who sleep in separate beds and find sex particularly dirty, live in a tacky Hollywood apartment building chock full of all kinds of crazies. When one of the 'low lifes' tries to rape Mary, Paul kills him by a blow to the head with a frying pan.

Alas, the victim had all kinds of money and both Paul and Mary soon realize they have a potential answer to their financial worries. They put an ad in a local sex publication and decide to lure new 'perverts' to their home. That way they can get the money for their restaurant and help clean up society in one sweeping stroke.

The appeal of Paul Bartel's tongue-in-cheek approach is that he manages to take his story to such a ridiculous extreme, remain genuinely funny and successfully tell his perverse story.

■ ECHO PARK

1985, 92 MINS, AUSTRIA/US ◇ ⓥ ⊙
Dir Robert Dornhelm   *Prod* Walter Shenson
Scr Michael Ventura   *Ph* Karl Kofler   *Ed* Ingrid Koller
Mus Paul Rickets   *Art Dir* Bernt Capra
● Susan Dey, Tom Hulce, Michael Bowen, Christopher Walker, Shirley Jo Finney, Heinrich Schweiger (Sascha-Wien)

Although lensed on location in the Echo Park section of Los Angeles, this is another of those quite successful views of the States made by talented European directors.

Wittily scripted and full of oddball twists from start to finish, *Echo Park* features three hapless people looking for the big break as they share an old-style duplex-apartment house in the rundown area of East Los Angeles.

May (Susan Dey) works as a waitress while dreaming of an acting career, but she also has to take care of her eight-year-old son Henry (Christopher Walker). Next door lives August (Michael Bowen), a bodybuilder from Austria who wants to become the second Arnold Schwarzenegger. May needs a tenant in her own flat to meet the payments, and this turns out to be the friendly pizza delivery boy, Jonathan (Tom Hulce), who reads books and writes poetry.

If all of this sounds vaguely like Nathaniel West's *Day of the Locust*, well, no matter. Austrian helmer Robert Dornhelm has a vision of his own. Played by Dey, May is a first-class performance in a role cut snugly to her talent. Ditto for Hulce and Bowen.

■ EDDIE AND THE CRUISERS

1983, 92 MINS, US ◇ ⓥ ⊙
Dir Martin Davidson   *Prod* Joseph Brooks, Robert K. Lifton   *Scr* Martin Davidson, Arlene Davidson   *Ph* Fred Murphy   *Ed* Priscilla Nedd   *Mus* John Cafferty
Art Dir Gary Weist
● Tom Berenger, Michael Pare, Joe Pantoliano, Matthew Laurance, Helen Schneider, Ellen Barkin (Aurora)

Eddie and the Cruisers is a mish-mash of a film, combining elements of the ongoing nostalgia for rock music of previous decades with an unworkable and laughable mystery plotline.

Eddie opens in strict *Citizen Kane* fashion as TV news mag reporter Maggie Foley (Ellen Barkin) is using old clips to pitch her investigative story on the early 1960s rock group Eddie and The Cruisers. Unit disbanded in 1964 with the suicide of its leader Eddie Wilson (Michael Pare).

She needs a news hook, and settles on the unlikely gimmick that Eddie (whose body was never found) is still alive and that a search for the missing tapes of his final, unreleased recording session will solve the mystery of his disappearance.

Foley interviews other surviving group members, including the lyricist-keyboard man Frank Ridgeway (Tom Berenger), who is prompted to remember (in frequent flashbacks) those glory days of 1962-63.

Under Martin Davidson's tedious direction (he also coscripted with his sister Arlene), *Eddie* only comes alive during the flashbacks when John Cafferty's songs provide a showcase for the magnetic screen presences of Pare and Helen Schneider. Real life rock singer Schneider is very sexy on screen, but her contemporary scenes are ruined by unplayable dialog.

· ·

■ EDDIE MACON'S RUN

1983, 95 MINS, US ◇ ⚙ ⊙
Dir Jeff Kanen *Prod* Louis A. Stroller *Scr* Jeff Kanen *Ph* James A. Contner *Ed* Jeff Kanen *Mus* Norton Buffalo *Art Dir* Bill Kenney
● Kirk Douglas, John Schneider, Lee Purcell, Leah Ayres, Lisa Dunsheath, Tom Noonan (Bregman)

Macon is an involving, enjoyable picture [based on a novel by James McLendon]. Most of the credit for that, however, goes to Kirk Douglas who brings interesting nuances to his part as the policeman in pursuit of John Schneider, and Lee Purcell as a bored but influential rich girl who gets more involved than she wants to in helping Schneider elude Douglas.

Schneider himself is okay and certainly brings more to his role than anything required of him on television. Without reaching towering dramatic heights, he nonetheless ably portrays the anguish of a young husband/father wrongly sent to prison and determined to escape to rejoin his family in Mexico.

With Schneider fleeing on foot for most of the picture, *Macon* has a tendency to drag in spots, especially in the beginning, but writer-director Jeff Kanen wisely keeps cutting back to Douglas in plotting his chase and figuring out the angles.

· ·

■ EDDY DUCHIN STORY, THE

1956, 123 MINS, US ◇ ⚙ ⊙
Dir George Sidney *Prod* Jerry Wald *Scr* Samuel Taylor *Ph* Harry Stradling *Ed* Viola Lawrence, Jack W. Ogilvie *Mus* Morris Stoloff
● Tyrone Power, Kim Novak, Victoria Shaw, James Whitmore, Rex Thompson (Columbia)

Jerry Wald's biopicturing of the career of '10 Magic Fingers' is not all the sorrow and woe that the story of Eddy Duchin might suggest. There's no escaping the fact that the pianist's first wife died shortly after childbirth. And that this was followed 12 years later by Duchin's own death, at the age of 41, as the result of leukemia.

But Samuel Taylor plays up humor and romance as well as the inherent hardship in his script [from a story by Leo Katcher] and George Sidney's direction, sensitive for the most part, sustains a high dramatic tone.

Key asset is Tyrone Power in the title role. He's personable and eager as he hits Gotham bent only on tapping out pop and pseudo-classical rhythms on the 88. He looks like he's genuinely thrilled with the splendors of New York and confident that his letter of introduction will land him a job with Leo Reisman's orchestra at the old Central Park Casino.

It's through the intervention of Kim Novak that the position in the band is his. The Novak-Power match builds tenderly.

Newcomer Victoria Shaw, Power's second wife, comes across with particular effectiveness, showing understanding of the role and executing it with proper feeling.
□ 1956: Nominations: Best Motion Picture Story, Color Cinematography, Scoring of a Musical Picture, Sound

· ·

■ EDGE OF DARKNESS

1943, 120 MINS, US
Dir Lewis Milestone *Prod* Henry Blanke *Scr* Robert Rossen *Ph* Sid Hickox *Ed* David Weisbart *Mus* Franz Waxman
● Errol Flynn, Ann Sheridan, Walter Huston, Judith Anderson, Helmut Dantine, Ruth Gordon (Warner)

In *Darkness*, as in *The Moon Is Down* the story treats with internal conditions and unrest, and, more important, the ruthlessness of the Nazis. The populace of Trollness in Norway seethes under the yoke of the Germans and finally erupts into a bloody revolt.

Best feature of this film is its cast. Errol Flynn and Ann Sheridan, as the stars, provide the proper romantic note, plus the necessary dash as the leaders of the Trollness underground. Both turn in some of their best film acting, yet some of the cast's lesser-knowns eclipse them in dramatic power. Notable in this respect are Morris Carnovsky, Ruth Gordon, Judith Anderson, Charles Dingle and Nancy Coleman.

Carnovsky, as an aged schoolmaster, is outstanding in a throat-catching scene when he pits his culture and kindliness against the brutish thinking of the Nazi commander, played by Helmut Dantine, who is guilty of most of the film's over-acting.

There's one other particularly outstanding scene – the meeting of the underground in the church under the guise of a religious service. Original in concept, it's emotion-gripping in execution.

· ·

■ EDGE OF THE CITY

1957, 85 MINS, US
Dir Martin Ritt *Prod* David Susskind *Scr* Robert Alan Aurthur *Ph* Joseph Brun *Ed* Sidney Meyers *Mus* Leonard Rosenman *Art Dir* Richard Sylbert
● John Cassavetes, Sidney Poitier, Jack Warden, Kathleen Maguire, Ruby Dee, Robert F. Simon (M-G-M)

The first film venture for producer David Susskind, writer Robert Alan Aurthur and director Martin Ritt is an auspicious bow. Trio, whose roots are in TV and legit, come up with a courageous, thought-provoking and exciting film.

Based on Aurthur's [1955] teleplay, *A Man Is Ten Feet Tall*, it marks a milestone in the screen presentation of an American Negro.

The peculiar aspect of *Edge* is that it is not a film dealing with the Negro problem. The protagonist is a guilt-ridden, psychologically mixed-up white youth, sensitively played by John Cassavetes. Plagued by the memory of his part in the accidental death of his brother and his inability to 'belong' either to his family or society, he AWOLs the army. He finds employment in a New York railroad yard where he immediately is befriended by a goodnatured, philosophical Negro lad (Sidney Poitier) and incurs the enmity of a vicious and tough hiring boss.

Filmed on location in New York, the film has a real-life flavor as it roams among New York's railroad yards and upper Manhattan's apartment house district.

· ·

■ EDISON, THE MAN

1940, 104 MINS, US ⚙
Dir Clarence Brown *Prod* John W. Considine Jr. *Scr* Talbot Jennings, Bradbury Foote *Ph* Harold Rosson *Ed* Fredrick Y. Smith *Mus* Herbert Stothart *Art Dir* Cedric Gibbons, John S. Detlie
● Spencer Tracy, Rita Johnson, Lynne Overman, Charles Coburn, Gene Lockhart, Henry Travers (M-G-M)

Edison, The Man is a sequel to *Young Tom Edison* (Mickey Rooney). The sequel takes up with Edison after he has gone to New York to pursue his vocation as an inventor.

Action opens on the Golden Jubilee of Light banquet held in 1929, at which the now aged Edison is guest of honor. As he is being eulogized for his contributions as an inventor, the story goes back to his early manhood, his heartaches, his ambitions, the romance that came into his life and the drama as well as lighter moments that figured in an amazing career. After Edison has brought forth the incandescent bulb after heroic struggles, followed by montage shots reviewing the achievements of the Wizard of Menlo Park, the action flashes back to the banquet.

Here, Spencer Tracy as an old, but benevolent Edison, makes his speech. It dwells largely on the march that science has made, emphasized by the fact that much that man has created for the benefit of mankind also possesses the ability to turn into monsters.

As a young man, Tracy progresses through the years in a forceful characterization of the noted inventor. Early portions are strong in romantic interest, but after Tracy has married the pretty Rita Johnson, two children being born, his home life is somewhat subjugated to the inventor's work in his laboratory, his financial troubles, the extreme loyalty of his workers, etc, although ostensibly he is a home-loving man.

Though going over his invention of the stock ticker, the phonograph and other things, the greatest stress [of the story by Hugo Butler and Dore Schary] is laid on the circumstances surrounding Edison's invention of the incandescent lamp. Dramatic interest is drawn largely from the months of toil and discouragement that precede the discovery of the light, topped by Edison's success in getting the franchise to illuminate New York by electricity. Scene when the dynamos go wild, like monsters out of control, is one of the highlights, and well done.
□ 1940: Nomination: Best Original Story

· ·

■ EDUCATING RITA

1983, 110 MINS, UK ◇ ⚙ ⊙
Dir Lewis Gilbert *Prod* Lewis Gilbert *Scr* Willy Russell *Ph* Frank Watts *Ed* Garth Craven *Mus* David Hentschel *Art Dir* Maurice Fowler
● Michael Caine, Julie Walters, Michael Williams, Maureen Lipman, Jeananne Crowley, Malcolm Douglas (Rank/Acorn)

Producer-director Lewis Gilbert has done a marvelous job of bringing the charming British play, *Educating Rita*, to the big screen. Aided greatly by an expert film adaptation by its playwright, Willy Russell, Gilbert has come up with an irresistible story about a lively, lower-class British woman hungering for an education and the rather, staid, degenerating English professor who reluctantly provides her with one.

Witty, down-to-earth, kind and loaded with common sense, Rita is the antithesis of the humorless, stuffy and stagnated academic world she so longs to infiltrate. Julie Walters injects her with just the right mix of comedy and pathos. Michael Caine is the sadly smart, alcoholic teacher who knows the fundamentals of English literature, but long ago lost the ability to enjoy life the way his uneducated pupil does.

The contradictions of the two characters are at the core of the picture, as Walters goes from dependent housewife to intelligent student and Caine begins to learn what it's like to feel again.
□ 1983: Nominations: Best Actor (Michael Caine), Actress (Julie Walters), Adapted Screenplay

· ·

■ EDWARD SCISSORHANDS

1990, 98 MINS, US ◇ ⚙ ⊙
Dir Tim Burton *Prod* Denise De Novi, Tim Burton *Scr* Caroline Thompson *Ph* Stefan Czapsky *Ed* Richard Halsey *Mus* Danny Elfman *Art Dir* Bo Welsh

● Johnny Depp, Winona Ryder, Dianne Wiest, Anthony Michael Hall, Alan Arkin, Kathy Baker (20th Century-Fox)

Director Tim Burton takes a character as wildly unlikely as a boy whose arms end in pruning shears, and makes him the center of a delightful and delicate comic fable.

Johnny Depp plays Edward, who lives in isolation in a gloomy mansion on the hill until a sunny Avon lady (Dianne Wiest) discovers him and takes him into her suburbia home and mothers him like a crippled bird. The creation of an inventor (Vincent Price) who died and left him unfinished, Edward sports an astonishing pair of hands – five-fingered, footlong blades that render him either lethal or extraordinarily skillful.

For the bevy of bored housewives in the pastel-colored nabe, gentle and exotic Edward becomes an instant celeb who amuses them by artistically pruning their hedges, their dogs and their coiffures.

But when he's wrongly accused in a burglary, his star falls and they turn on him. Meanwhile his wistful and impossible attraction to Kim (Winona Ryder), the Avon lady's teenage daughter, adds another level of tension.

Depp, former TV teen idol in his second starring screen role, gives a sensitive reading of Edward. With Ryder kept mostly in the background, Wiest's mother figure shares the screen with Depp, she's a smash. Also a hoot is Alan Arkin as her unexcitable husband, and Kathy Baker as a sex-starved vixen.
□ 1990: Nomination: Best Makeup

■ EDWARD II

1991, 90 MINS, UK ◇ ⓥ
Dir Derek Jarman   *Prod* Steve Clark-Hall, Antony Root   *Scr* Derek Jarman, Stephen McBride, Ken Butler   *Ph* Ian Wilson   *Ed* George Akers   *Mus* Simon Fisher Turner   *Art Dir* Christopher Hobbs
● Steven Waddington, Andrew Tiernan, Tilda Swinton, Nigel Terry, Kevin Collins, Dudley Sutton (Working Title/BBC/British Screen)

Derek Jarman comes up with a provocative and challenging adaptation of Christopher Marlowe's *Edward II*, a lengthy (about four hours onstage) bio of Britain's only acknowledged gay monarch, whose preference for his lover over his queen sparked conflict with his barons and, eventually, civil war.

Cutting the play to the bone, Jarman fashions the 16th century drama into a radical attack on antigay prejudices in contempo Brit society. Drama is staged in modern dress, with contemporary police/military uniforms for the forces of repression.

Queen Isabella, astringently played by Jarman regular Tilda Swinton, is cruelly treated in the film. Humiliated and rejected by her husband, she tries everything to win him back from his lover. The character finally turns into a raving monster who literally sucks the blood from her victims.

Jarman fails to make the film accessible to heterosexual male audiences. Pic seems to be provoking straight viewers while celebrating the play's homosexual theme.

■ EFFECT OF GAMMA RAYS ON MAN-IN-THE-MOON MARIGOLDS, THE

1972, 100 MINS, US ◇ ⓥ
Dir Paul Newman   *Prod* Paul Newman   *Scr* Alvin Sargent   *Ph* Adam Holender   *Ed* Evan Lottman   *Mus* Maurice Jarre   *Art Dir* Gene Callahan
● Joanne Woodward, Nell Potts, Roberta Wallach, Judith Lowry, Richard Venture, Estelle Omens (20th Century-Fox)

Producer-director Paul Newman has made his finest behind-the-camera film to date in the screen version of Paul Zindel's play. As the slovenly, introverted mother of two young girls, Joanne Woodward brilliantly projects the pitiable character.

Alvin Sargent's adaptation provides Woodward with a full complement of the despicable dimensions which make the focal character both a monster and an object of genuine pity.

Roberta Wallach is excellent as the elder daughter, Ruth, an epilepsy-prone, hardening creature almost destined to become her mother. As the younger girl, whose school experiments give the play its title, Nell Potts is equally impressive, with a sensitive screen presence most rare in young actresses.

Newman has gotten it all together here as a director, letting the story and the players unfold with simplicity, restraint and discernment.

■ EGG AND I, THE

1947, 108 MINS, US ⓥ ⊙
Dir Chester Erskine   *Prod* Chester Erskine, Fred F. Finklehoffe   *Scr* Chester Erskine, Fred F. Finklehoffe   *Ph* Milton Krasner   *Ed* Russell Schoengarth   *Mus* Frank Skinner   *Art Dir* Bernard Herzbrun
● Claudette Colbert, Fred MacMurray, Marjorie Main, Percy Kilbride, Louise Allbritton (Universal)

In this picturization of Betty MacDonald's best-selling book Chester Erskine and Fred Finklehoffe tamper very little with the load of amusing situations MacDonald gets herself into when her husband snaps her out of a Boston finishing school and takes her off to the modern-day frontier of the Pacific Northwest to embark on chicken farming.

Shortcoming is in an evenness of treatment – partially in the writing but more importantly in Erskine's direction – that fails to suck the drama out of the situations presented in the book. Even the supposedly big scene where a forest fire licks down at all that the chicken-raising couple have in the world – their home, barn and henhouses – fails to achieve suspense Claudette Colbert is appealing but not entirely believable as the city gal who accepts so willingly out of wifely love the rugged life husband Fred MacMurray lays out for her. MacMurray runs through his role in his routine, superficial fashion – which is unfortunately accentuated by the impassive manner of the telling of the story itself. Percy Kilbride and Marjorie Main, as the Kettles, the tobacco-road-like neighbors of Colbert and MacMurray, are literally tops as character players, accounting, by their feeling and understanding of their roles, for high points in the film every time they're on the screen.
□ 1947: Nomination: Best Supp. Actress (Marjorie Main)

■ EGYPTIAN, THE

1954, 140 MINS, US ◇ ⓥ
Dir Michael Curtiz   *Prod* Darryl F. Zanuck   *Scr* Casey Robinson, Philip Dunne   *Ph* Leon Shamroy   *Ed* Barbara McLean   *Mus* Alfred Newman, Bernard Herrmann   *Art Dir* Lyle Wheeler, George W. Davis
● Edmund Purdom, Jean Simmons, Victor Mature, Gene Tierney, Michael Wilding, Peter Ustinov (20th Century-Fox)

The decision to bring Mika Waltari's masterly scholarly-detailed [novel] The Egyptian to the screen must have taken a lot of courage, for this is a long way off the standard spectacle beat. The book tells a strange and unusual story laid against the exotic and yet harshly realistic background of the Egypt of 33 centuries ago, when there was a Pharaoh who believed in one god, and a physician who glimpsed a great truth and tried to live it.

Big coin – around $4.2 million – was splurged on bringing ancient Egypt to life again and the results justify the expense.

A big cast with good marquee appeal goes through its paces with obvious enjoyment. In the title part, Edmund Purdom etches a strong handsome profile. As the truth-seeking doctor who grows from weakness to the maturity of a new conviction, Purdom brings *The Egyptian* to life and makes him a man with whom the audience can easily identify and sympathize. Jean Simmons is lovely and warm as the tavern maid. Victor Mature as the robust Horemheb, the soldier who is to become ruler, is a strong asset to the cast.
□ 1954: Best Color Cinematography

■ EIGER SANCTION, THE

1975, 125 MINS, US ◇ ⓥ ⊙
Dir Clint Eastwood   *Prod* Robert Daley   *Scr* Hal Dresner, Warren B. Murphy, Rod Whitaker   *Ph* Frank Stanley   *Ed* Ferris Webster   *Mus* John Williams   *Art Dir* George Webb, Aurelio Crugnola
● Clint Eastwood, George Kennedy, Vonetta McGee, Jack Cassidy, Heidi Bruhl, Thayer David (Universal/Malpaso)

The Eiger Sanction, based on the novel by Trevanian, focuses on Clint Eastwood, a retired mountain climber and hired assassin, being recalled from retirement by head of a secret intelligence organization for another lethal assignment.

Pic takes its title from the leader's euphemism for assassination, to be carried out on Switzerland's Eiger Mountain during an international team's climb.

To condition himself for the ascent Eastwood flies to the Arizona ranch of George Kennedy, an old climbing friend, who puts him through his paces in the magnificent reaches of Monument Valley.

Eastwood, who also directs and according to studio did his own mountain climbing without doubles, manages fine suspense. His direction displays a knowledge that permits rugged action.

■ EIGHT MEN OUT

1988, 119 MINS, US ◇ ⓥ ⊙
Dir John Sayles   *Prod* Sarah Pillsbury, Midge Sanford   *Scr* John Sayles   *Ph* Robert Richardson   *Ed* John Tintori   *Mus* Mason Daring   *Art Dir* Nora Chavooshian
● John Cusack, Clifton James, David Strathairn, D.B. Sweeney, John Mahoney, Charlie Sheen (Orion)

Perhaps the saddest chapter in the annals of professional American sports is recounted in absorbing fashion in *Eight Men Out*.

Story tells of how the 1919 Chicago White Sox threw the World Series in cahoots with professional gamblers, in what became known as the Black Sox Scandal.

Based on Eliot Asinof's 1963 bestseller, John Sayles' densely packed screenplay lays out how eight players for the White Sox, who were considered shoo-ins to beat the Cincinnati Reds in the World Series, committed an unthinkable betrayal of the national pastime by conspiring to lose the Fall Classic.

The most compelling figures here are pitcher Eddie Cicotte (David Strathairn), a man nearing the end of his career who feels the twin needs to insure a financial future for his family and take revenge on his boss, and Buck Weaver (John Cusack), an innocent enthusiast who took no cash for the fix but, like the others, was forever banned from baseball.

■ 8 MILLION WAYS TO DIE

1986, 115 MINS, US ◇ ⓥ ⊙
Dir Hal Ashby   *Prod* Steve Roth   *Scr* Oliver Stone, David Lee Henry   *Ph* Stephen H. Burum   *Ed* Robert Lawrence, Stuart Pappe   *Mus* James Newton Howard   *Art Dir* Michael Haller
● Jeff Bridges, Rosanna Arquette, Alexandra Paul, Randy Brooks, Andy Garcia (PSO)

What could have been a better film delving into complexities of one tough-but-vulnerable alcoholic sheriff out to bust a cocaine ring, instead ends up an oddly-paced work that is sometimes a thriller and sometimes a love story, succeeding at neither.

A former LA Sheriff named Scudder (Jeff Bridges) comes close to death less than a handful of times while trying to dismantle a scummy Latino drug smuggler's empire and at the same time winning his girl (Rosanna Arquette).

Respected director Hal Ashby was reportedly fired from this picture before it was finished, which could explain its unevenness as he wasn't privy to what happened in the editing room.

In isolated scenes, the actors mannage to rise above it all to bring some nuances to their fairly stereo-typical roles. Arquette is best as the hooker with a heart, coyly playing off main squeeze Angel (Andy Garcia), the ultra chic cocaine dealer, until she goes over to Scudder's side.

■ 84 CHARING CROSS ROAD

1987, 97 MINS, US ◇ ⓥ ⊙
Dir David Jones   *Prod* Geoffrey Helman   *Scr* Hugh Whitemore   *Ph* Brian West   *Ed* Chris Wimble   *Mus* George Fenton   *Art Dir* Eileen Diss, Edward Pisoni
● Anne Bancroft, Anthony Hopkins, Judi Dench, Jean De Baer, Maurice Denham, Mercedes Ruehl (Brooksfilms)

An uncommonly and sweetly civilized adult romance between two transatlantic correspondents who never meet, *84 Charing Cross Road* is an appealing film on several counts, one of the most notable being Anne Bancroft's fantastic performance in the leading role.

Helene Hanff's slim volume of letters between herself and a dignified antiquarian bookseller in London [originally adapted for the stage by James Roose-Evans] is the basis of the film. They began in 1949 as formal requests by the New Yorker Hanff for old books over a 20-year period into a warm, loving exchange of missives and gifts between her and much of the staff of the bookshop of Marks & Co.

Built on a basis of mutually held taste, knowledge, interests and consideration, the bond between Hanff (Bancroft) and Frank Doel (Anthony Hopkins) becomes a form of pure love, which is why the film i so touching in spots.

Although well balanced between events on both sides of the pond, story suffers from an imbalance between the active, initiating Hanff, who occasionally addresses the camera directly, and the relatively passive, inexpressive Doel. At the end, the man's humor and high intelligence are described, but these traits are never revealed.

Anne Bancroft brings Helene Hanff alive in all her dimensions, in the process creating one of her most memorable characterizations.

■ 80,000 SUSPECTS

1963, 113 MINS, UK
Dir Val Guest   *Prod* Val Guest   *Scr* Val Guest   *Ph* Arthur Grant   *Ed* Bill Lenny   *Mus* Stanley Black   *Art Dir* Geoffrey Tozer
● Claire Bloom, Richard Johnson, Yolande Donlan, Cyril Cusack, Michael Goodliffe, Mervyn Johns (Rank)

Based on the novel [*The Pillars of Midnight*] by Elleston Trevor, the drama concerns a city supposedly gripped by an epidemic of smallpox. Director Val Guest chose the city of Bath and, with complete cooperation from local authorities, the film has a vital authenticity which gives a fine assist to the production.

The killer epidemic sparks intense activity by local health authorities as they try to trace potential smallpox carriers. It's a painstaking process, carefully reproduced by Guest.

Guest also plays up some human emotional angles. Dedicated doctor (Richard Johnson) is trying to keep together his marriage with an equally dedicated nurse (Claire Bloom).

Another medico (Michael Goodliffe) despairs of saving his own marriage to a nympho-dipso who has had an affair with Johnson, and eventually becomes a key figure in the search for the ultimate germ carrier.

The documentary and the fictional elements do not entirely jell. But Guest juggles adroitly enough with the problems to keep interest alert. The thesping is okay.

■ EL CID

1961, 180 MINS, US/SPAIN/ITALY ◇ ⓥ ⊙
Dir Anthony Mann   *Prod* Samuel Bronston   *Scr* Fredric M. Frank, Philip Yordan, [Ben Barzman]   *Ph* Robert Krasker   *Ed* Robert Lawrence   *Mus* Miklos Rozsa   *Art Dir* Veniero Colasanti, John Moore
● Charlton Heston, Sophia Loren, Raf Vallone, Gary Raymond, John Fraser, Genevieve Page (Bronston/Dear)

El Cid is a fast-action color-rich, corpse-strewn, battle picture. The Spanish scenery is magnificent, the costumes are vivid, the chain mail and Toledo steel gear impressive. Perhaps the 11th century of art directors Veniero Colasanti and John Moore exceeds reality, but only scholars will complain of that. Action rather than acting characterizes this film.

Yet the film creates respect for its sheer picturemaking skills. Director Anthony Mann, with assists from associate producer Michael Waszynski who worked closely with him, battle manager Yakima Canutt, and a vast number of technicians, have labored to create stunning panoramic images.

Of acting there is less to say after acknowledging that Charlton Heston's masculine personality ideally suits the title role. His powerful performance is the central arch of the narrative. Sophia Loren, as first his sweetheart and later his wife, has a relatively passive role.

Two actors in *King of Kings* who remained over in Spain to appear in *El Cid* ended up as bit actors. Hurd Hatfield is the court herald in a couple of scenes, Frank Thring is a most unconvincing Moorish emir with a shaved noggin who lolls about in a harem registering a kind of sulky impatience.

Italy's Raf Vallone is the other man who never has a chance with Chimene. After betraying El Cid he is spared and, at a later period, becomes a follower only to die, tortured, by the invading North African monster, Britain's Herbert Lom.

Most provocative performance among the supporting players is that of Genevieve Page, as the self-willed princess who protects the weakling brother (John Fraser) who becomes king after she, sweet sibling, has the older brother slain.
□ 1961: Nominations: Best Color Art Direction, Scoring of a Dramatic Picture, Song ('The Falcon and the Dove')

■ EL DORADO

1967, 126 MINS, US ◇ ⓥ ⊙
Dir Howard Hawks   *Prod* Howard Hawks   *Scr* Leigh Brackett   *Ph* Harold Rosson   *Ed* John Woodcock   *Mus* Nelson Riddle   *Art Dir* Hal Pereira, Carl Anderson
● John Wayne, Robert Mitchum, James Caan, Charlene Holt, Michele Carey, Ed Asner (Paramount)

Technical and artistic screen fads come and go, but nothing replaces a good story, well told. And Howard Hawks knows how to tell a good story. *El Dorado* [from the novel *The Stars in Their Courses* by Harry Brown] stars John Wayne and Robert Mitchum in an excellent oater drama, laced with adroit comedy and action relief, and set off by strong casting, superior direction and solid production.

Wayne, a hired gun, is dissuaded from working for land-grabber Ed Asner by Mitchum, a reformed gunslinger now a sharp-looking, disciplined sheriff.

■ ELECTRA GLIDE IN BLUE

1973, 106 MINS, US ◇ ⓥ ⊙
Dir James William Guercio   *Prod* James William Guercio, Rupert Hitzig   *Scr* Robert Boris, Michael Butler   *Ph* Conrad Hall   *Ed* Jim Benson, John F. Link II, Jerry Greenberg   *Mus* James William Guercio
● Robert Blake, Billy 'Green' Bush, Mitchell Ryan, Jeannine Riley, Elisha Cook, Royal Dano (United Artists)

Director-producer James William Guercio comes on tall in a first pic about a motorcycle cop in the US west, who is done in by the corruption, change and violence about him.

Guercio at one time played with the rock group of Frank Zappa and brings that balladlike, terse feel of rock to this extremely well-played and mounted pic.

Robert Blake is effective as a small motorcycle cop in Arizona who has a certain hard-headed dignity and feels he can help people and also wants to graduate to higher police echelons. He is a Viet vet without bitterness and expecting no condescension from anybody.

Billy 'Green' Bush as his slightly violent sidekick, Mitchell Ryan as a flamboyant, sadistic sheriff, Jeannine Riley as a disillusioned starlet all keep up with Blake's fine character composition.

Conrad Hall's extraordinary controlled hues are an asset to this look at the life of a motorized cop.

■ ELECTRIC HORSEMAN, THE

1979, 120 MINS, US ◇ ⓥ ⊙
Dir Sydney Pollack   *Prod* Ray Stark   *Scr* Robert Garland   *Ph* Owen Roizman   *Ed* Sheldon Kahn   *Mus* Dave Grusin   *Art Dir* Stephen Grimes
● Robert Redford, Jane Fonda, Valerie Perrine, John Saxon, Willie Nelson, Allan Arbus (Columbia)

The Electric Horseman is a moderately entertaining film, but no screen magic from Robert Redford and Jane Fonda. The pic is overlong, talky and diffused.

Even though Redford, as an ex-rodeo champ, and Fonda don't create the romantic sparks that might be expected, it's their dramatic professionalism that salvages *Horseman* and makes it a moving and effective film by the time the final credits roll by.

What *Electric Horseman* is peddling is the virtue of 'freedom', morally, economically and socially. Redford's attempt to liberate the prize-winning horse of the AMPCO conglomerate from an overabundance of steroids and pain-killing is presumably intended as an analogy for the way the American public is force-fed consumerism from today's corporate giants.
□ 1979: Nomination: Best Sound

■ ELECTRIC MAN, THE
See: *Man Made Monster*

■ ELENI

1985, 117 MINS, US ◇ ⓥ ⊙
Dir Peter Yates   *Prod* Nick Vanoff, Mark Pick, Nicholas Gage   *Scr* Steve Tesich   *Ph* Billy Williams   *Ed* Ray Lovejoy   *Mus* Bruce Smeaton   *Art Dir* Roy Walker
● Kate Nelligan, John Malkovich, Linda Hunt, Oliver Cotton, Ronald Pickup, Rosalie Crutchley (CBS)

Adapted from Nicholas Gage's best-selling book about his search for the truth about his mother, who was executed by the communists in Greece in the late 1940s, pic has the most noble of intentions, but comes off as flat, tedious and crudely biased.

Screenplay cuts back and forth between events separated by 30 years. The Gage figure (John Malkovich) is assigned to the *New York Times* Athens bureau, a base from which he can investigate the events surrounding his mother's death during the civil war. Eleni, Nick's mother (Kate Nelligan), was a peasant woman in the

E

tiny village of Lia. Portrayed as apolitical, she was forced from her home when the communists occupied the area in the fractious period following World War II, then courageously suffered countless other indignities until being convicted as a traitor in a mock trial.

The scenes involving Malkovich's extended search for the evil judge prove more successful than the period stuff, and the climactic scene of their confrontation is undeniably tense, by far the best in the film. It comes as much too little, too late.

Nelligan, Malkovich and Linda Hunt, superior performers all, have strong grips on their characters. Tech credits are fine, with the impoverished Greek village having been suitably recreated in Spain.

. . . .

■ ELEPHANT BOY

1937, 81 MINS, UK ⓦ

Dir Zoltan Korda, Robert Flaherty *Prod* Alexander Korda *Scr* John Collier, Akos Tolnay, Marcia De Silva *Ph* Osmond Borradaile *Ed* Charles Crichton *Mus* John Greenwood *Art Dir* Vincent Korda

● Sabu, Walter Hudd, Allan Jeayes, W.E. Holloway, Bruce Gordon, Wilfrid Hyde-White (London)

Elephant Boy is a legendary and rather fantastic tale built around the affection which grows up between a native Indian boy and his elephant, an animal which is tops as a hunter. It is a Rudyard Kipling story which reads better than it films, same as the Tarzan yarns, having nothing particularly exciting for the camera, nor any plot to speak of.

Kipling wrote the story under the title of *Toomai of the Elephants*. Toomai is the Indian lad whose great ambition is to be a hunter. Played by a native Indian named Sabu and he imparts to it as much charm and naivete as can be expected. Child has a pronounced native dialect which doesn't hurt, but many of the other characters are entirely too British to be convincing.

Walter Hudd, with the exception of a couple who appear only in brief scenes, is the only person cast as a white, he being the hunter commissioned by the government to round up much-needed pachyderms.

Aside from the footage used to emphasize the strong affection between the boy and his mammoth pal, the action concerns the routine job of rounding up men and animals for the big hunt, pitching of camp, killing by a tiger of one of the crew, and the rather accidental success of little Sabu in leading his trusty elephant to the big herd they're despairing of finding.

. . . .

■ ELEPHANT MAN, THE

1980, 125 MINS, US/UK ⓦ ⓞ

Dir David Lynch *Prod* Jonathan Sanger *Scr* Christopher DeVore, Eric Bergren, David Lynch *Ph* Freddie Francis *Ed* Anne V. Coates *Mus* John Morris *Art Dir* Stuart Craig, Bob Cartwright

● Anthony Hopkins, John Hurt, Anne Bancroft, John Gielgud, Wendy Hiller, Freddie Jones (Brooksfilms)

Director David Lynch has created an eerily compelling atmosphere in recounting a hideously deformed man's perilous life in Victorian England.

Screenplay was based on two books about the real-life Elephant Man, one [*The Elephant Man and Other Reminiscences*] written by his protector, Sir Frederick Treves, played in the film by Anthony Hopkins [and the other, *The Elephant Man: A Study in Human Dignity* by Ashley Montagu].

Hopkins is splendid in a subtly nuanced portrayal of a man torn between humanitarianism and qualms that his motives in introducing the Elephant Man to society are no better than those of the brutish carny. The center-piece of the film, however, is the virtuoso performance by the almost unrecognizable John Hurt.

Like Quasimodo in *The Hunchback of Notre Dame*, the Elephant Man gradually reveals suppressed depths of humanity.

Lynch commendably avoids summoning up feelings of disgust.

□ 1980: Nominations: Best Picture, Director, Actor (John Hurt), Adapted Screenplay, Costume Design, Art Direction, Editing, Original Score

. . . .

■ ELEPHANT WALK

1954, 102 MINS, US ◇ ⓦ

Dir William Dieterle *Prod* Irving Asher *Scr* John Lee Mahin *Ph* Loyal Griggs *Ed* George Tomasini *Mus* Franz Waxman

● Elizabeth Taylor, Dana Andrews, Peter Finch, Abraham Sofaer, Abner Biberman, Noel Drayton (Paramount)

The novelty of the Ceylon backgrounds and pictorial beauty are recommendable points in *Elephant Walk*, an otherwise leisurely-paced romantic drama.

Robert Standish's novel about life among the pekoe-planters rates a sprawling script and direction that lacks attention-holding pace from William Dieterle. Of interest is the fact that in some of the Ceylon-filmed longshots, Vivien Leigh is still seen, although not noticeably so. Illness forced the English star out of the picture after about a month of lensing, with Elizabeth Taylor replacing.

Elephants are the sympathetic heavies in this story of a bride who comes to Ceylon from England and finds her husband, the natives and the tea plantation still under the dominance of a dead man's memory. Added to this tradition worship is the always present threat that the pachyderms may eventually succeed in wrestling back from the white usurpers the trail they had used for centuries in coming down from the wilds to water. The plantation mansion had been built across the trail by the bridegroom's strong-willed late father, who had bowed to nothing, man or beast.

. . . .

■ 11 HARROWHOUSE

1974, 95 MINS, UK ◇ ⓦ

Dir Aram Avakian *Prod* Elliott Kastner *Scr* Jeffrey Bloom, Charles Grodin *Ph* Arthur Ibbetson *Ed* Anne V. Coates *Mus* Michael J. Lewis *Art Dir* Peter Mullins

● Charles Grodin, Candice Bergen, John Gielgud, Trevor Howard, James Mason, Helen Cherry (20th Century-Fox)

Charles Grodin stars in, adapted for the screen, and just about ruins *11 Harrowhouse*, a comedy-caper film about a theft of billions in diamonds. Cast as a low-key diamond salesman who wreaks vengeance on the diamond establishment, Grodin messes up the film with ineffective shy-guy acting, and clobbers it with catatonic voice-over that is supposed to be funny.

Gerald A. Browne wrote the novel. The main story, which takes a long time to get going, involves eccentric billionaire Trevor Howard commissioning Grodin and wealthy girl friend Candice Bergen to rob the diamond vaults presided over by dissatisfied James Mason, who is resentful of his pension treatment at the hands of John Gielgud.

Howard and Mason appear close to embarrassed in their roles.

. . . .

■ ELMER GANTRY

1960, 146 MINS, US ◇ ⓦ ⓞ

Dir Richard Brooks *Prod* Bernard Smith *Scr* Richard Brooks *Ph* John Alton *Ed* Marge Fowler *Mus* Andre Previn *Art Dir* Edward Carrere

● Burt Lancaster, Jean Simmons, Dean Jagger, Arthur Kennedy, Shirley Jones, Edward Andrews (United Artists)

In filming Sinclair Lewis' contentious 1927 study of a scandalous evangelist, *Elmer Gantry*,

Richard Brooks has framed a big story and bold religioso subject for the old-fashioned rectangular screen (aspect ratio 1.33:1).

Brooks honors the spirit of Lewis' cynical commentary on circus-type primitive exhortation with pictorial imagery that is always pungent. He also has written dialog that is frank and biting.

From the standpoint of technique this production plays like a symphony, with expertly ordered pianissimo and fortissimo story passages which build to a smashing crescendo in the cremation of Sister Sharon Falconer, an evangelist of questionable sincerity and propriety. The film ends roughly about the halfway mark in Gantry's life, whereas in the book he went on to become an influential Methodist minister, who married and raised a family but continued to indulge in the carnal pleasures he denounced vehemently from the pulpit.

Burt Lancaster pulls out virtually all the stops as Gantry to create a memorable characterization. He acts with such broad and eloquent flourish that a finely balanced, more subdued performance by Jean Simmons as Sister Sharon seems pale by comparison.

□ 1960: Best Actor (Burt Lancaster), Supp. Actress (Shirley Jones), Adapted Screenplay.
□ Nominations: Best Picture, Scoring of a Dramatic Picture

. . . .

■ EMBRYO

1976, 108 MINS, US ◇ ⓦ

Dir Ralph Nelson *Prod* Arnold H. Orgolini, Anita Doohan *Scr* Anita Doohan, Jack W. Thomas *Ph* Fred Koenekamp *Ed* John Martinelli *Mus* Gil Melle *Art Dir* Joe Alves

● Rock Hudson, Diane Ladd, Barbara Carrera, Roddy McDowall, Ann Schedeen, John Elerick (Cine Artists)

The story has doctor Rock Hudson grow a beautiful young woman (Barbara Carrera) in his laboratory from fetal beginnings. It's kind of a *Bride of Frankenstein* tale, cast in terms of scientific mumbo-jumbo, an effective blending of old and new plot elements.

Hudson plays with gentleness and restraint, and Carrera's pristine fashion-model beauty is perfect for the role, but there's little feeling of genuine passion or eroticism.

The script [from a story by Jack W. Thomas] is much stronger on plot than it is on character relationships. Suspense built up before Carrera's birth is dissipated in clumsy dramatic confrontations when she and Hudson set out in society.

Diane Ladd is wasted as Hudson's jealous housekeeper.

. . . .

■ EMERALD FOREST, THE

1985, 113 MINS, US ◇ ⓦ ⓞ

Dir John Boorman *Prod* John Boorman *Scr* Rospo Pallenberg *Ph* Philippe Rousselot *Ed* Ian Crafford *Mus* Junior Homrich, Brian Gascoigne *Art Dir* Simon Holland

● Powers Boothe, Meg Foster, Charley Boorman, Dira Pass, Rui Polonah, Claudio Moreno (Embassy)

Based on an uncredited true story about a Peruvian whose son disappeared in the jungles of Brazil, screenplay trades on numerous enduring myths and legends about the return to nature and growing up in the wild.

Powers Boothe, an American engineer and designer assigned to build an enormous dam in Brazil, loses his young son in the wilderness and, against seemingly hopeless odds, sets out to find him.

Ten years later, the two finally meet up under perilous circumstances. By this time, the son, played by the director's own sprog, Charley Boorman, has become well integrated into the ways of a friendly Indian tribe and has little desire to return to the outside world.

Once he has been exposed to the simple virtues of 'uncivilized' life, Boothe begins to have serious doubts about the nature of his work in the area.

Despite some lumps in the narrative and characterization and some occasionally awkward tension between the documentary realism enforced by the subject and the heavy stylization of the director's approach, film proves engrossing and visually fascinating.

....

■ **EMMA**

1932, 70 MINS, US
Dir Clarence Brown   *Scr* Leonard Praskins, Frances Marion, Zelda Sears   *Ph* Oliver Marsh   *Ed* William LeVanway
● Marie Dressler, Richard Cromwell, Jean Hersholt, Myrna Loy, John Miljan, Barbara Kent (M-G-M)

There are probably 20 actresses who would have fitted the role of the old servant who spent a lifetime with the Smith family, watching the children grow up and then turn against her in her old age. But there is only one Marie Dressler, a trouper with a genius for characters of comic surface but profound pathos.

The whole *Emma* affair is synthetic, in its comedy as well as in its sentiment the purest of hoke, sometimes skillfully wrought, but often far from clever in its manipulation. Dressler's acting alone gives it vitality. There are bits that drag sadly. Such a sequence is the old servant's departure for Niagara Falls on a long deferred vacation.

There is a courtroom scene that is the height of strong arm bathos and some of the passages toward the end are absurd in their determination to pull tears. Nothing but Dressler's astonishing ability to command conviction saves some of these sequences from going flat.

Jean Hersholt delivers a well-paced and nicely restrained performance as an absent minded inventor; Myrna Loy and Barbara Kent help to decorate the picture with grace; and Richard Cromwell gives just the right feeling of a loveable adolescent boy.
☐ 1931/32: Nomination: Best Actress (Marie Dressler)

....

■ **EMPEROR OF THE NORTH**

1973, 118 MINS, US ◇ ⓥ
Dir Robert Aldrich   *Prod* Stan Hough   *Scr* Christopher Knopf   *Ph* Joseph Biroc   *Ed* Michael Luciano
Mus Frank DeVol   *Art Dir* Jack Martin Smith
● Lee Marvin, Ernest Borgnine, Keith Carradine, Charles Tyner, Malcolm Atterbury, Simon Oakland (Inter-Hemisphere/20th Century-Fox)

Premise of a challenge by an easy going tramp to ride the freight train of a sadistic conductor reputed to kill non-paying passengers (as his hobo associates and train men lay bets on the outcome) is limited in scope.

The production takes its title from hobos crowning Lee Marvin 'Emperor' for riding Ernest Borgnine's train even a mile, something no other hobo has ever accomplished. While there is a wealth of violence under Robert Aldrich's forceful direction, the motivating idea is bogged down frequently with time out while Marvin expounds the philosophy and finer points of hobodom to a brash young kid (Keith Carradine).

Marvin scores again in one of his uncolorful but commanding characterizations. Borgnine's interpretation borders on a caricature of the heavies of the past. [Film was initially released as *The Emperor of the North Pole*.]

....

■ **EMPEROR WALTZ, THE**

1948, 106 MINS, US ◇
Dir Billy Wilder   *Prod* Charles Brackett   *Scr* Charles Brackett, Billy Wilder   *Ph* George Barnes   *Ed* Doane

Harrison   *Mus* Victor Young   *Art Dir* Hans Dreier, Franz Bacheli
● Bing Crosby, Joan Fontaine, Roland Culver, Richard Haydn, Sig Ruman (Paramount)

Film is a costumer laid 'in the days' (sic) of Emperor Franz Joseph, and is played to the hilt by Crosby, Joan Fontaine and their supporting cast. Picture has a free-and-easy air that perfectly matches the Crosby style of natural comedy. Co-star Joan Fontaine, better known for heavy, serious roles, demonstrates adaptability that fits neatly into the lighter demands and she definitely scores with charm and talent as the Crosby foil.

Multiple functions of Charles Brackett and Billy Wilder on *Waltz* have given film an infectious quality that surmounts the gorgeously apt trappings against which is projected the fable of an American travelling phonograph salesman and his dog who crash the court of the emperor.

There's plenty of pageantry in the staging of the title number, using the colorful swirling of richly costumed dancers in the palace ballroom as eye-filling backdrop. 'Friendly Mountains' has backdrop of processed Tyrol crags and valleys (actually Jasper National Park) filled with native yodelers and dancers.

....

■ **EMPIRE OF THE ANTS**

1977, 89 MINS, US ◇ ⓥ
Dir Bert I. Gordon   *Prod* Bert I. Gordon   *Scr* Jack Turley   *Ph* Reginald Morris   *Ed* Michael Luciano   *Mus* Dana Kaproff   *Art Dir* Charles Rosen
● Joan Collins, Robert Lansing, John David Carson, Albert Salmi, Jacqueline Scott, Pamela Shoop (American International)

The H.G. Wells-inspired exploitationer *Empire of the Ants*, is an above-average effort about ants that grow big after munching on radioactive waste, and terrorize a group headed by Joan Collins, Robert Lansing and John David Carson.

Periodic moments of good special effects are separated by reels of dramatic banality as players flounder in flimsy dialog and under sluggish direction.

Collins is a sharpie Florida real estate agent who takes a group of potential suckers on Lansing's boat to remote swampland. There the big ants attack.

....

■ **EMPIRE OF THE SUN**

1987, 152 MINS, US ◇ ⓥ ⊙
Dir Steven Spielberg   *Prod* Steven Spielberg, Kathleen Kennedy, Frank Marshall   *Scr* Tom Stoppard   *Ph* Allen Daviau   *Ed* Michael Kahn   *Mus* John Williams   *Art Dir* Norman Reynolds
● Christian Bale, John Malkovich, Miranda Richardson, Nigel Havers, Joe Pantoliano, Leslie Phillips (Amblin/Warner)

Story of an 11-year-old boy stranded in Japanese-occupied China during World War II is based on J.G. Ballard's autobiographical 1984 novel which marked the first non-science-fiction book by author. Both it and the film clearly are the work of sci-fi artists channelling their imaginations into a more traditional framework.

Leading the first troupe of Hollywood studio filmmakers ever into Shanghai, Steven Spielberg turns the grey metropolis into a sensational film set as he delineates the edginess and growing chaos leading up to Japan's entry into the city just after Pearl Harbor.

Jim (Christian Bale) is in every way a proper upper-class English lad but for the fact he has never seen England. Separated from his parents during the spectacularly staged evacuation of Shanghai, Jim hooks up with a pair of Amerian scavengers, with whom in due course he is rounded up and sent to a prison camp for the rest of the war.

It is there that Jim flourishes, expending his boundless energy on creative projects and pastimes that finally land him a privileged place among the entrepreneurially minded Americans.

John Malkovich's Basie, an opportunistic King Rat type, keeps threatening to become a fully developed character but never does. Other characters are complete blanks, which severely limits the emotional reverberation of the piece. No special use is made of the talents of Miranda Richardson, Nigel Havers, Joe Pantoliano and the others, so it is up to young English thesp Bale to engage the viewer's interest, which he does superbly.
☐ 1987: Nominations: Best Cinematography, Costume Design, Art Direction, Editing, Original Score, Sound

....

■ **EMPIRE STRIKES BACK, THE**

1980, 124 MINS, US ◇ ⓥ ⊙
Dir Irvin Kershner   *Prod* Gary Kurtz   *Scr* Leigh Brackett, Lawrence Kasdan   *Ph* Peter Suschitzky   *Ed* Paul Hirsch   *Mus* John Williams   *Art Dir* Norman Reynolds, Leslie Dilley, Harry Lange, Alan Tomkins
● Mark Hamill, Harrison Ford, Carrie Fisher, Billy Dee Williams, Frank Oz, Alec Guinness (20th Century-Fox/Lucasfilm)

The Empire Strikes Back is a worthy sequel to *Star Wars*, equal in both technical mastery and characterization, suffering only from the familiarity with the effects generated in the original and imitated too much by others.

From the first burst of John Williams' powerful score and the receding opening title crawl, we are back in pleasant surroundings and anxious for a good time.

This is exec producer George Lucas' world. Though he has turned over the director's chair and his typewriter [apart from providing the original story], there are no recognizable deviations from the path marked by Lucas and producer Gary Kurtz.

They're assisted again by good performances from Mark Hamill, Harrison Ford and Carrie Fisher. And even the ominous Darth Vader (David Prowse [voiced by James Earl Jones]) is fleshed with new – and surprising – motivations.

Among the new characters, Billy Dee Williams gets a good turn as a duplicitous but likeable villain-ally and Frank Oz is fascinating as sort of a guru for the Force.

Vader's admirals now look even more dressed like Japanese admirals of the fleet intercut with Hamill's scrambling fighter pilots who wouldn't look too out of place on any Marine base today.
☐ 1980: Best Sound, Special Achievement Award (visual effects).
☐ Nominations: Best Art Direction, Original Score

....

■ **ENCHANTED APRIL**

1991, 101 MINS, UK ◇ ⓥ ⊙
Dir Mike Newell   *Prod* Ann Scott   *Scr* Peter Barnes   *Ph* Rex Maidment   *Ed* Dick Allen   *Mus* Richard Rodney Bennett   *Art Dir* Malcolm Thornton
● Miranda Richardson, Joan Plowright, Josie Lawrence, Polly Walker, Michael Kitchen, Jim Broadbent (BBC)

A slim comedy of manners about Brits discovering their emotions in sunny Italy, *Enchanted April* doesn't spring many surprises. Strong cast's reliable playing is undercut by a script that dawdles over well-trod territory. Pic derives from British pubcaster BBC's Screen Two series.

Story centers on four women who rent a medieval dwelling in San Salvatore, Italy. For two of them (Miranda Richardson, Josie Lawrence), it's an excuse to get away from inattentive hubbies. Also on board are a waspish widow (Joan Plowright) and a society belle (Polly Walker).

Lawrence decides to invite her husband (Alfred Molina) over, and Richardson eventually fires off a letter to hers as well. Meanwhile, the house's British owner (Michael Kitchen), who'd already taken a shine to Richardson in Blighty, turns up one day.

Dialog-heavy script [from Elizabeth von Arnim's novel] is well turned but lacking in real conflict or development. All the actors give it their best shot, with Plowright spitting out bons mots with her usual aplomb and Molina brightening things up. Of the younger women, Walker is tops as the cool society vamp. Mike Newell's helming gets everything in the frame but rarely delivers more.
□ 1992: Nominations: Best Supp. Actress (Joan Plowright), Screenplay Adaptation, Costume Design

....

■ ENCHANTED COTTAGE, THE

1945, 91 MINS, US ⓥ ⊙
Dir John Cromwell *Prod* Harriet Parsons *Scr* DeWitt Bodeen, Herman J. Mankiewicz *Ph* Ted Tetzlaff *Ed* Joseph Noriega *Mus* Roy Webb *Art Dir* Albert S. D'Agostino, Carroll Clark
● Dorothy McGuire, Robert Young, Herbert Marshall, Mildred Natwick, Spring Byington, Hillary Brooke (RKO)

Sensitive love story of a returned war veteran with ugly facial disfigurements, and the homely slavey – both self-conscious of their handicaps – is sincerely told both in the script [based on the play by Arthur Wing Pinero] and outstanding direction of John Cromwell.

Brief prolog establishes Robert Young as the flyer who leases a cottage for his honeymoon, but is called to service on eve of his wedding. Two years later he returns to hide his war disfigurements from his family at the cottage, where Dorothy McGuire is hiding from people because of her ugliness. But the girl's tender attention to the flyer results in idyllic love, with each appearing beautiful to the other and pair sincerely believing that the cottage is enchanted and responsible for the transformations.

McGuire turns in an outstanding performance, with Young also sharing the limelight. Herbert Marshall is excellent, while Mildred Natwick scores as the housekeeper.
□ 1945: Nomination: Best Scoring of a Dramatic Picture

....

■ ENCINO MAN

(UK: California Man)

1992, 89 MINS, US ◇ ⓥ ⊙
Dir Les Mayfield *Prod* George Zaloom *Scr* Shawn Schepps *Ph* Robert Brinkmann *Ed* Eric Sears, Jonathan Siegal *Mus* J. Peter Robinson *Art Dir* James Allen
● Sean Astin, Brendan Fraser, Pauly Shore, Megan Ward, Robin Tunney, Michael DeLuise (Hollywood Pictures)

Encino Man is a mindless would-be comedy aimed at the younger set. Low-budget quickie is insulting even within its own no-effort parameters.

Incompetent screenplay [from a screen story by Shawn Schepps and producer George Zaloom] dawdles over the introductions, with well over a reel elapsing before Cro Magnon man Brendan Fraser unfreezes after turning up in a block of ice uncovered by Encino teen Sean Astin while digging a backyard swimming pool.

Pic's sci-fi pretense is immediately abandoned as Astin and buddy Pauly Shore contrive to pass off Fraser as a transfer student to Encino High. Only tension is that he wins the hearts of femmes, including Astin's dream girl Megan Ward.

Debuting feature director Les Mayfield exhibits low aptitude for comedy, resorting to prat-falls and food sloppiness for laughs. Film is nominally a vehicle for MTV comic Shore, who flunks out on screen with his tediously unfunny patter and smaller-than-life personality.

....

■ ENCORE

1951, 89 MINS, UK ⓥ
Dir Pat Jackson, Anthony Pelissier, Harold French *Prod* Antony Darnborough *Scr* T.E.B. Clarke, Arthur Macrae, Eric Ambler *Ph* Desmond Dickinson *Ed* Alfred Roome *Mus* Richard Addinsell *Art Dir* Maurice Carter
● Nigel Patrick, Roland Culver, Kay Walsh, Glynis Johns, Ronald Squire, Terence Morgan (Two Cities)

For the third time, a group of Somerset Maugham short stories have been collated to make a quality British film. *Quartet* (1948) was followed by *Trio* (1950). *Encore*, a co-production between Paramount and Rank, is also based on three of the writer's vignettes.

First of the stories is *The Ant and The Grasshopper* [directed by Pat Jackson, scripted by T.E.B. Clarke], in which Nigel Patrick is a ne'er-do-well who soaks his lawyer brother for cash until he lands a wealthy heiress. Acting of Patrick and Roland Culver, as his brother, sets a high standard.

Winter Cruise [Anthony Pelissier/Arthur Macrae] is another light piece, but of a contrasting type. Kay Walsh plays a middle-aged garrulous spinster who takes a trip by cargo boat to Jamaica, but whose non-stop chattering drives the captain and crew to distraction. Fine acting and a flawless script keeps the fun rolling in this.

The drama and tension of the series is provided by the third subject, *Gigolo and Gigolette* [Harold French/Eric Ambler]. This is a dramatic piece about a young vaud- eville artist whose specialty is diving from an 80-foot platform into a five-foot lake of flames. When the girl begins to feel that her husband is persisting with the act because of the money that goes with it, she loses her nerve. Glynis Johns makes a deep impression as the girl, and Terence Morgan aptly suggests the weak, scheming husband.

....

■ END, THE

1978, 100 MINS, US ◇ ⓥ ⊙
Dir Burt Reynolds *Prod* Lawrence Gordon *Scr* Jerry Belson *Ph* Bobby Byrne *Ed* Donn Cambern *Mus* Paul Williams *Art Dir* Jan Scott
● Burt Reynolds, Dom DeLuise, Sally Field, Strother Martin, David Steinberg, Joanne Woodward (United Artists)

The rather complete failure of Jerry Belson's script makes 'The End' of *The End* come none too soon. Star-director Burt Reynolds, as a medically-doomed sharpie, exercises and exorcises his fears while milking sympathy from everyone available. Production is a tasteless and overripe comedy that disintegrates very early into hysterical, undisciplined hamming.

For a few frames of the film, Reynolds' bearded face suggests that there was some effort to project a different image; to transform his familiar and likable charisma into something different, befitting the last days of a carefree, selfish person who has been informed of fatal illness.

There's little more to do than list the featured players: Dom DeLuise, absolutely dreadful; Sally Field, phoning in a kooky-pretty role; David Steinberg, an outtake that crept back into the print; Joanne Woodward, poorly utilized though adroitly cast.

....

■ ENDLESS LOVE

1981, 115 MINS, US ◇ ⓥ ⊙
Dir Franco Zeffirelli *Prod* Dyson Lovell *Scr* Judith Rascoe *Ph* David Watkin *Ed* Michael J. Sheridan *Mus* Jonathan Tunick *Art Dir* Ed Wittstein
● Brooke Shields, Martin Hewitt, Shirley Knight, Don Murray, Richard Kiley, Beatrice Straight (Polygram)

A Cotton-candy rendition of Scott Spencer's powerful novel, *Endless Love* is a manipulative tale of a doomed romance which careens repeatedly between the credible and the ridiculous.

With a nod to *Romeo and Juliet*, with which director Franco Zeffirelli enjoyed such success in 1968, plot concerns the scorching love affair between a 17-year-old boy, from a social-activist Chicago family, and a 15-year-old girl. Normally broad-minded, girl's father finally can't take it anymore when the boy more or less moves into his daughter's bedroom, and banishes him from the household for a month.

Since he's center stage most of the time, it's fortunate that newcomer Martin Hewitt registers so strongly. Zeffirelli has dressed and photographed his find almost in the style of some of his mentor Luchino Visconti's neo-realist heroes, with two-day beard growths and anachronistic Clark Gable undershirts.

Despite top billing, Brooke Shields disappears during entire center section of the film, which reduces extent to which film stands or falls by her work. One can never really tell what her responses to sex are because she's smiling all the time.
□ 1981: Nomination: Best Song ('Endless Love')

....

■ END OF INNOCENCE, THE

1990, 102 MINS, US ◇ ⓥ ⊙
Dir Dyan Cannon *Prod* Thom Tyson, Vince Cannon *Scr* Dyan Cannon *Ph* Alex Nepomniaschy *Ed* Bruce Cannon *Mus* Michael Convertino *Art Dir* Paul Eads
● Dyan Cannon, John Heard, George Coe, Lola Mason, Rebecca Schaeffer, Steve Meadows (Skouras)

A moralistic drama about a woman's struggle for self-determination, *The End of Innocence* is a well-intentioned vehicle for writer-director-star Dyan Cannon.

In its peppy opening, Cannon time-telescopes the childhood, adolescence (played by the late Rebecca Schaeffer) and young womanhood of Stephanie Lewis, a lovely if malleable only child of querulous middle-class Jewish parents.

Predictably enough, selfish struggling writer Michael (Steve Meadows), turns out to be not much different than the boorish cad who deflowered Stephanie on her prom night long ago.

A caring platonic male friend, lost in the narrative shuffle, tries to warn her off Michael to no avail. Drifting through life with no real career or focus, Stephanie (Cannon) deals with her deep unhappiness with junk food, mood pills and marijuana.

Cannon, looking remarkably good, has a field day dominating the film. But the auteur/star gets too carried away with a sense of mission here.

....

■ ENEMIES, A LOVE STORY

1989, 119 MINS, US ◇ ⓥ ⊙
Dir Paul Mazursky *Prod* Paul Mazursky *Scr* Roger L. Simon *Ph* Fred Murphy *Ed* Stuart Pappe *Mus* Maurice Jarre *Art Dir* Guzman
● Ron Silver, Anjelica Huston, Lena Olin, Margaret Sophie Stein, Alan King, Paul Mazursky (Morgan Creek)

Haunting, mordantly amusing, deliciously sexy, *Enemies, a Love Story* is Paul Mazursky's triumphant adapation of the Isaac Bashevis Singer novel about a Holocaust survivor who finds himself married to three women in 1949 New York.

Ron Silver is fascinatingly enigmatic in the lead role of Herman Broder. He's a quietly charming, somewhat withdrawn man whose cushy job as a ghostwriter for a very reformed rabbi (Alan King) gives him plenty of time to attend to his deliriously complicated love life.

The character simultaneously is married to a devoted but cloddish woman (Margaret Sophie Stein), is carrying on a passionate affair with a sultry married woman (Lena Olin), and also finds himself back in the arms of his long-vanished wife (Anjelica Huston), who was thought to be lost in the war.

Like Silver, the audience will find it difficult to prefer one of his three women over the others, since Stein, Olin, and Huston are equally captivating. Olin is sensational here as the doomed Masha, for whom lovemaking is the best assertion of life over the inevitability of self-destruction.

□ 1989: Nominations: Best Supp. Actress (Anjelica Huston, Lena Olin), Adapted Screenplay

. . . .

■ ENEMIES OF THE PUBLIC
See: The Public Enemy

. . . .

■ ENEMY FROM SPACE
See: Quatermass 2

. . . .

■ ENEMY MINE

1985, 108 MINS, US ◇ ⓦ ⊙
Dir Wolfgang Petersen *Prod* Stephen Friedman
Scr Edward Khmara *Ph* Tony Imi *Ed* Hannes Nikel
Mus Maurice Jarre *Art Dir* Rolf Zehetbauer
● Dennis Quaid, Louis Gossett Jr, Brion James, Richard Marcus, Carolyn McCormick, Bumper Robinson (Kings Road/20th Century-Fox)

Enemy MMine is a friendship story [by Barry Longyear] between two disparate personalities carried to extreme lengths. It may be a long way to go to a distant sun system to get to a familiar place, but the $33 million project is largely successful in establishing a satisfying bond.

Story is set up by a kind of videogame battle between the Earth forces and the war-ring Dracs from the distant planet of Dracon. Space pilot Willis Davidge (Dennis Quaid) goes down with a Drac ship and is the only survivor on a desolate planet. His initial response to the half-human, half-reptilian is inbred hatred, distrust and combativeness, all recognizable human triggers.

Hostility soon gives way to a common goal – survival. Davidge and the Drac (Louis Gossett Jr) peel away their outer layers and reveal two similar beings. It's an anthropomorphic view of life but touching nonetheless.

. . . .

■ ENEMY OF THE PEOPLE, AN

1978, 103 MINS, US ◇ ⓦ
Dir George Schaefer *Prod* George Schaefer
Scr Alexander Jacobs *Ph* Paul Lohman *Ed* Sheldon Kahn *Mus* Leonard Rosenman *Art Dir* Eugene Lourie
● Steve McQueen, Charles Durning, Bibi Andersson, Eric Christmas, Michael Cristofer, Richard Dysart (First Artists/Solar)

Transferring stage works to the screen has always been a procedure fraught with peril, and *An Enemy of the People* fails to avoid the obvious pitfalls.

The Henrik Ibsen drama, which was first performed in 1883, concerns a smalltown doctor who discovers that his village's new hot springs spa is contaminated by tannery waste. Over the objections of the town leaders (particularly his brother, the mayor), he attempts to publicize the scandal, only to be declared a social outcast, his family and career ruined.

Steve McQueen wanted to do the Ibsen work itself, and that was his undoing. While *Enemy of the People* has much relevance to current ecological dilemmas, the script, based on an Arthur Miller adaptation, isn't content to simply raise the issues. They are proclaimed in ringing tones, intensifying the preachiness of a work that is already condescending to its audience.

The imbalance wouldn't be so pronounced were Charles Durning not so magnificent in the role of the harshly realistic brother. Without an adequate presence to balance Durning's domination of the proceedings, *Enemy* founders in a sea of verbiage.

. . . .

■ ENFORCER, THE
(UK: Murder, Inc.)

1951, 86 MINS, US ⓦ
Dir Bretaigne Windust, [Raoul Walsh] *Prod* Milton Sperling *Scr* Martin Rackin *Ph* Robert Burks *Ed* Fred Allen *Mus* David Buttolph *Art Dir* Charles H. Clarke
● Humphrey Bogart, Zero Mostel, Ted De Corsia, Everett Sloane, Roy Roberts, King Donovan (United States/Warner)

The film plays fast and excitingly in dealing with Humphrey Bogart's efforts to bring the head of a gang of killers to justice. The script uses the flashback technique to get the story on film, but it is wisely used so as not to tip the ending and spoil suspense.

Footage kicks off with a brief prolog by Senator Estes Kefauver, crime investigation committee head, explaining necessity of bringing crooks to justice. Story starts with Bogart ready to crack a case on which he has worked four years; he has a witness who can pin a murder rap on the gang head. However, the witness, in fear, escapes and falls to his death. Seeking to find some other tiny clue in the bulk of evidence, Bogart reviews the material gathered over the long years, permitting flashbacks into the past, and finally picks a single twist that gives him his lead and sets up an exciting finale.

Bretaigne Windust's direction is thorough, never missing an opportunity to sharpen suspense values, and the tension builds constantly.

. . . .

■ ENFORCER, THE

1976, 96 MINS, US ◇ ⓦ ⊙
Dir James Fargo *Prod* Robert Daley *Scr* Stirling Silliphant, Dean Reisner *Ph* Charles W. Short
Ed Ferris Webster, Joel Cox *Mus* Jerry Fielding
Art Dir Allen E. Smith
● Clint Eastwood, Harry Guardino, Bradford Dillman, John Mitchum, DeVeren Bookwalter, Tyne Daly (Warner)

The bad guys in this third installment from Dirty Harry's life include not only the archly defined criminals (here, DeVeren Bookwalter and a group of post-Vietnam gun crazies), but also his police and political superiors – like Bradford Dillman, captain of detectives, and John Crawford, whose characterization of the mayor is one of the few highlights. Harry Guardino has the role of a weak-kneed detective.

Tyne Daly's casting as a femme cop injects some predictable, but enjoyable, male chauvinism sparks in dialog between her and Clint Eastwood.

The spitball script [from a story by Gail Morgan Hickman and S.W. Schurr] lurches along, stopping periodically for the blood-lettings and assorted running and jumping and chasing stuff.

. . . .

■ ENGLAND MADE ME

1973, 100 MINS, UK ◇ ⓦ
Dir Peter Duffell *Prod* Jack Levin *Scr* Peter Duffell, Desmond Cory *Ph* Ray Parslow *Ed* Malcolm Cooke
Mus John Scott *Art Dir* Tony Woollard
● Peter Finch, Michael York, Hildegard Neil, Michael Hordern, Joss Ackland, Tessa Wyatt (Atlantic)

England Made Me is the symbolic title for a tale of moral conflict set in prewar Germany, circa 1935. Based on an early Graham Greene novel, the film is also a well-observed evocation of time, place and mood, directed and co-authored by Peter Duffell with evident intelligence and sensitivity, if not optimum success.

Michael York plays an innocent idealist ultimately snuffed out by the intrigues and ruthlessness that marked Nazi Germany. The title is a reference to his character, his fairness and morality as shaped by a society where they were and are esteemed.

Superficially he runs afoul of rascally Peter Finch's great financial empire based in Germany, but his goodness is in wider conflict with the coarsened values of decadence and nihilism.

Finch plays the ruthless financier with competence and physical presence while Hildegard Neil scores well as York's dominating older sister and Finch's mistress.

. . . .

■ ENIGMA

1983, 101 MINS, UK/FRANCE ◇ ⓦ ⊙
Dir Jeannot Szwarc *Prod* Peter Shaw *Scr* John Briley
Ph Jean-Louis Picavet *Ed* Peter Weatherley *Mus* Marc Wilkinson, Douglas Gamley *Art Dir* Francois Comtat
● Martin Sheen, Brigitte Fossey, Sam Neill, Derek Jacobi, Michael Lonsdale, Frank Finlay (Archerwest/SFPC)

Enigma is a well-made but insufficiently exciting spy thriller which rather pleasingly emphasizes the emotional vulnerabilities of the pawns caught up in East-West intrigue.

Martin Sheen ably portrays an East German refugee who, after working as a Radio Free Europe-type broadcaster out of Paris, is recruited by the CIA to return to East Berlin. Assignment: steal a coded micro-processor, or scrambler, from the Russians before the KGB proceeds with the assassination of five Soviet dissidents in the West.

After neatly making his way to his destination. Sheen locates old flame Brigitte Fossey who, while resisting the idea of resuming their romance, sympathizes with his unexplained cause.

John Briley's screenplay [from the novel *Enigma Sacrifice* by Michael Barak] keeps everything coherent, not always easy with this sort of fare, and Jeannot Szwarc's direction is very handsome indeed.

. . . .

■ ENORMOUS CHANGES AT THE LAST MINUTE

1983, 110 MINS, US ◇ ⓦ ⊙
Dir Mirra Bank, Ellen Hovde, Muffie Meyer *Prod* Mirra Bank *Scr* John Sayles, Susan Rice *Ph* Tom McDonough *Ed* Mirra Bank, Ellen Hovde, Muffie Meyer
Mus Peter Link
● Ellen Barkin, Kevin Bacon, Maria Tucci, Lynn Milgrim, Sudie Bond, Ron McLarty (Ordinary Lives)

Enormous Changes at the Last Minute is an enormously uneven trilogy of modern urban woman's dilemma in the precarious area of relationships with men [from stories by Grace Paley].

Pic is first fictional feature for the three producer/directors, Mirra Bank, Ellen Hovde, and Muffie Meyer, all film editors. First vignette [directed by Hovde and Meyer] pits Virginia (Ellen Barkin) as a housewife with three kids who is newly deserted by her husband. Barkin succumbs to the advances of a former boyfriend (now married with kids), who is also the landlord's son.

In second entry, Faith (Lynn Milgrim) makes a trek to visit her artsy, literary parents in an old-age Jewish residence, to tell her father that she's separated from her husband Ricardo. This is the weakest and least successful section, failing to capture the potential intimacy and poignancy of the encounter. [Seg, by Bank and Hovde, was shot earliest, in 1978.]

Alexandra (Maria Tucci) is a middle-aged, divorced, social worker who has a ludicrous affair with frenetic cab driver/punk rocker Dennis (Kevin Bacon). When Alexandra becomes pregnant by Dennis she vehemently decides to go it alone and raise it herself. Dennis is hurt and confused by his forced exclusion from the event. [This seg directed by Bank.]

. . . .

E

ENTER ARSENE LUPIN

1944, 72 MINS, US
Dir Ford Beebe   *Prod* Ford Beebe   *Scr* Bertram
Millhauser   *Ph* Hal Mohr   *Ed* Saul A. Goodkind
Mus Milton Rosen   *Art Dir* John B. Goodman, Abraham
Grossman
● Charles Korvin, Ella Raines, J. Carrol Naish, George
Dolenz, Gale Sondergaard (Universal)

Enter Arsene Lupin a Universal cops-and-robbers saga, French style, is a slick enough combination of romance, action and suspense and offset phony, far-fetched plot.

Part of appeal is romantic team of Charles Korvin and Ella Raines in some torrid moments. Korvin isn't much of an actor, but he has the Continental ease of manner and attractive face to catch the femme trade. Also a draw is the flavorsome caricature of a stupid French detective which J. Carrol Naish, in a change of pace from gangster roles, plays very amusingly, even if he does milk the role.

Yarn concerns [Maurice LeBlanc's character] Lupin, renowned suave French thief, who robs a lady of her fabulous emerald on the Paris-Constantinople express. Pic is produced on good scale, with some rich interiors, to help illusion. Raines adds glamor and beauty to role of heiress, and Gale Sondergaard is menacing enough as one of sleek, murderous cousins.

ENTERTAINER, THE

1960, 96 MINS, UK
Dir Tony Richardson   *Prod* Henry Saltzman   *Scr* John
Osborne, Nigel Kneale   *Ph* Oswald Morris   *Ed* Alan
Osbiston   *Mus* John Addison
● Laurence Olivier, Brenda De Banzie, Joan Plowright,
Roger Livesey, Alan Bates, Albert Finney
(Woodfall/Bryanston)

There was a bit of a hassle over [the release of] *The Entertainer* what with arguments with the censor, the film having to be re-dubbed and cut from 104 to 96 minutes, and held over for three months before its West End showing. This version of John Osborne's play is raw, but vital stuff, which you'll either like or loathe.

The yarn is mainly a seedy character study of a broken-down, disillusioned vaude artiste with more optimism than talent, and of the various members of his family and their reactions to his problems. So it depends mainly on the thesping and the direction.

Tony Richardson, the director, makes several mistakes. But he has a sharp perception of camera angles, stimulates some good performances and, particularly, whips up an excellent atmosphere of a smallish British seaside resort.

Mainly, the interest is held by the acting and here there is a lot to praise, if some that may be condemned. The stage sequences in which the third-rate comedian, Archie Rice (Laurence Olivier), has to put over some tatty material in a broken down show, does not come over as effectively as it did on the stage. He is far happier in other sequences. The way he allows his sleazy facade to slip by a twist of the mouth, a throwaway line or a look in the eyes is quite brilliant.

Joan Plowright brings warmth and intelligence to the role of the loyal daughter while Roger Livesey, as Olivier's father, is sympathetic and completely believable. Brenda Da Banzie's role, as Olivier's wife, is at times irritating.
□ 1960: Nomination: Best Actor (Laurence Olivier)

ENTERTAINER, THE

1975, 105 MINS, US/AUSTRALIA ◇ ▼
Dir Donald Wrye   *Prod* Beryl Vertue, Marvin Hamlisch
Scr Elliott Baker   *Ph* James Crabe   *Mus* Marvin Hamlish
Art Dir Bob Mackichan

● Jack Lemmon, Ray Bolger, Sada Thompson, Tyne
Daly, Michael Cristofer, Annette O'Toole
(Stigwood/Persky-Bright)

This basically is the John Osborne play in which Laurence Olivier made such an impact. Setting is now America instead of England and period switched from Suez crisis days to 1944.

This time around it's Jack Lemmon as secondrate vaudevillian Archie Rice, desperately trying for laughs from nearly empty houses.

With debt problems, Archie meets Bambi Pasko, a young beauty with little talent but a rich father and starstruck mother. Archie persuades them to back a new show which will feature Bambi, whom he seduces, promising to marry.

Archie's father, Billy hears of the plan and he informs the Paskos Archie is already married; they immediately pull out of the new show, and when Billy realizes Archie will face prison, he agrees to return to the stage and saves the day.

Lemmon gives a fine performance as Archie, though is not so awful as he should be on stage.

ENTERTAINING MR SLOANE

1970, 94 MINS, UK ◇ ▼
Dir Douglas Hickox   *Prod* Douglas Kentis   *Scr* Clive
Exton   *Ph* Wolfgang Suschitzky   *Ed* John Trumper
Mus Georgie Fame   *Art Dir* Michael Seymour
● Beryl Reid, Peter McEnery, Harry Andrews, Alan
Webb (Canterbury)

The sacred cow of 'good taste' is in for a battering with *Entertaining Mr Sloane*, based on Joe Orton's play. *Sloane* blends morbid humor, an obsession with sex, and an underlying pathos and result is interest that is always held.

It's no detraction from the rest of the cast to say that it is firmly Beryl Reid's picture. She gives a superb study of a middle-aged, flabby, arch 'nymphette', hazily pining for a lost love.

Her brother (Harry Andrews) also falls for Sloane's superficial charm and makes him his chauffeur, clearly with more furtive and kinky motives.

Director Douglas Hickox, who does an astute job, though sometimes his direction meanders slightly, has opened up the play a little, though not at the expense of the claustrophobic atmosphere.

ENTER THE DRAGON

1973, 98 MINS, US/HONG KONG ◇ ▼ ☉
Dir Robert Clouse   *Prod* Fred Weintraub, Paul Heller,
Raymond Chow   *Scr* Michael Allin   *Ph* Gilbert Hubbs
Ed Kurt Hirschler, George Watters   *Mus* Lalo Schifrin
Art Dir James Wong Sun
● Bruce Lee, John Saxon, Jim Kelly, Shih Kien, Bob
Wall, Angela Mao (Warner/Concord)

Enter the Dragon marks the final appearance of Bruce Lee, who died suddenly in Hong Kong on July 20, 1973, only a few weeks after he completed the film.

Film is rich in the atmosphere of the Orient, where it was lensed in its entirety, and brims with frequent encounters in the violent arts. Lee plays a James Bond-type of super-secret agent, past-master in Oriental combat, who takes on the assignment of participating in brutal martial arts competition as a cover for investigating the suspected criminal activities of the man staging this annual tournament.

Lee socks over a performance seldom equalled in action. John Saxon, as an American expert drawn to the tournament, is surprisingly adept in his action scenes.

Robert Clouse's realistic direction results in constant fast play by all the principals.

ENTER THE NINJA

1982, 99 MINS, US ◇ ▼
Dir Menahem Golan   *Prod* Judd Bernard, Yoram Globus
Scr Dick Desmond   *Ph* David Gurfinkel   *Ed* Mark
Goldblatt, Michael Duthie   *Mus* W. Michael Lewis,
Laurin Rinder
● Franco Nero, Susan George, Sho Kosugi, Alex
Courtney, Will Hare, Christopher George (Cannon)

Enter the Ninja represents an unusual hybrid action film, an Italian Western-type story filmed as a contemporary Japanese martial arts action film in the Philippines. Results are pleasant though unspectacular.

After a misjudged opening consisting of a series of bloody one-on-one battles later revealed to be just a phony graduation exercise for American ninjitsu student Cole (Franco Nero), pic settles down to a simple landgrabbers story.

Cole arrives to help his old mercenary fighter buddy Landers (Alex Courtney) fight off various nasties out to steal away his plantation to exploit its oil rights. Landers's tough cookie wife (Susan George sporting a very sexy and giggly bra-less look) is on hand to help out.

Well-photographed pic is heavy on the chop-socky stuff, with baddie Venarius (Christopher George) hiring a real Japanese ninja (Sho Kosugi) to neutralize Cole.

ENTITY, THE

1982, 125 MINS, US ◇ ▼
Dir Sidney J. Furie   *Prod* Harold Schneider   *Scr* Frank
DeFelitta   *Ph* Stephen H. Burum   *Ed* Frank J. Urioste
Mus Charles Bernstein   *Art Dir* Charles Rosen
● Barbara Hershey, Ron Silver, David Lablosa, George
Coe, Margaret Blye, Jacqueline Brookes (Pelleport
Investors/20th Century-Fox)

Theoretically, at least, *The Entity* would have made a fine drama-docu. As is, a fascinating fact-based tale of the supernatural is reduced by cliches of narrative and characterization to routine exploitation fare.

Pic's disappointment rests with Sidney J. Furie's insipid direction and Frank DeFelitta's trite screen treatment, based on his own novel of the actual paranormal case history of a California woman who was 'violated' and otherwise terrorized over an extended period by an invisible something.

Aside from creditable acting by Barbara Hershey as the female in question and Ron Silver as a psychiatrist who presumes she's a victim of her own childhood-rooted hysteria, film's most inspired elements are the visual effects. These range from standard poltergeist effects to a climactic eruption by the 'entity'.

EQUINOX

1992, 115 MINS, US ◇ ▼ ☉
Dir Alan Rudolph   *Prod* David Blocker   *Scr* Alan
Rudolph   *Ph* Elliot Davis   *Ed* Michael Ruscio
Art Dir Steven Legler
● Matthew Modine, Lara Flynn Boyle, Tyra Ferrell,
Marisa Tomei, Kevin J. O'Connor, Lori Singer (SC
Entertainment)

Equinox is one of Alan Rudolph's patently personal ensemble pieces about criss-crossing destinies. More socially minded in its depiction of a decaying society some of the characters yearn to escape, film is full of ideas and evocative scenes.

Matthew Modine toplines in a double role. Henry is an awkward, nerdy chap who remarks, 'My whole life seems to be taking place without me in it,' while being induced to reignite a tentative romance with the lovely, painfully shy Beverly (Lara Flynn Boyle). Modine also appears as Freddy, a swaggering smalltime hood who is married to Sharon (Lori Singer) and works his way up in a gang controlled by Paris (Fred Ward).

At the film's heart is a touching little-people romance between Henry and Beverly. Modine and Boyle, both very attractive performers, are effectively dressed down for these roles, and Boyle, in particular, strongly registers the effort it takes for such a thin-skinned character to leap off the deep end into the emotional whirlpool.

. . . .

■ EQUUS

1977, 137 MINS, US ◇ ⑰ ⊙

Dir Sidney Lumet   *Prod* Lester Persky   *Scr* Peter Shaffer
Ph Oswald Morris   *Ed* John Victor-Smith   *Mus* Richard Rodney Bennett   *Art Dir* Tony Walton
● Richard Burton, Peter Firth, Colin Blakely, Joan Plowright, Harry Andrews, Eileen Atkins (United Artists)

Equus is an excellent example of film-as-theatre. Peter Shaffer's play, which he adapted for the screen, has become under Sidney Lumet's outstanding direction a moving confrontation between a crudely mystical Peter Firth and the psychiatrist (Richard Burton), who is trying to unravel the boy's mind.

The (screen) story is properly oriented to that of a suspense yarn: why did Firth blind Harry Andrews' horses? Judge Eileen Atkins wants Burton to find out. In the process, Burton discerns the boy's transference of extremely physical religious devotion to Jesus, to the spirit Equus as embodied in horses.

Jenny Agutter is excellent as the young girl whose plausible emotional attitudes trigger the boy's outrage at his personal deity.

□ 1977: Nominations: Best Actor (Richard Burton), Supp. Actor (Peter Firth), Adapted Screenplay

. . . .

■ ERASERHEAD

1977, 100 MINS, US ⑰

Dir David Lynch   *Prod* David Lynch   *Scr* David Lynch
Ph Fred Elms   *Ed* David Lynch   *Mus* Fats Waller
Art Dir David Lynch
● Jack Nance, Charlotte Stewart, Jeanne Bates, Allen Josephs, Judith Anna Roberts, Laurel Near (AFI/Lynch)

Eraserhead is a sickening bad-taste exercise made by David Lynch under the auspices of the American Film Institute.

Set, apparently, in some undefined apocalyptic future era, *Eraserhead* consists mostly of a man sitting in a room trying to figure out what to do with his horribly mutated child. Lynch keeps throwing in graphic close-ups of the piteous creature, and pulls out all gory stops in the unwatchable climax.

Like a lot of AFI efforts, the pic has good tech values (particularly the inventive sound mixing), but little substance or subtlety. The mind boggles to learn that Lynch labored on this pic for five years.

. . . .

■ ERIK THE VIKING

1989, 103 MINS, UK ◇ ⑰ ⊙

Dir Terry Jones   *Prod* John Goldstone   *Scr* Terry Jones
Ph Ian Wilson   *Ed* George Akers   *Mus* Neil Innes
Art Dir John Beard
● Tim Robbins, Gary Cady, Mickey Rooney, Eartha Kitt, Terry Jones, John Cleese (Prominent)

The idea of telling the story of a Viking warrior who thought there must be more to life than rape and pillage is an amusing one, and for the most part *Erik the Viking* is an enjoyable film.

Pic opens with Erik (Tim Robbins) falling in love with a girl just as he kills her. Spurred by her death he decides to try and bring the Age of Ragnarok – where men fight and kill – to an end.

He sets off with an unruly band of followers – including the local blacksmith who wants Ragnarok to continue as it helps his sword-making business – and is pursued by Halfdan the Black (John Cleese), the local warlord who quite enjoys Ragnarok and wants it to continue.

American Tim Robbins is fine as the softly spoken and sensitive Erik, and especially seems to enjoy himself in the battle scenes. The film's great strength, though, is the Viking crew, which is full of wonderful characters, such as Tim McInnerny's manic Sven the Berserk, heavily disguised Antony Sher's scheming Loki and best of all Freddie Jones' put-upon missionary.

. . . .

■ ESCAPE ARTIST, THE

1982, 93 MINS, US ◇ ⑰

Dir Caleb Deschanel   *Prod* Doug Claybourne, Buck Houghton   *Scr* Melissa Mathison, Stephen Zito
Ph Stephen H. Burum   *Ed* Arthur Schmidt   *Mus* Georges Delerue   *Art Dir* Dean Tavoularis
● Griffin O'Neal, Raul Julia, Teri Garr, Joan Hackett, Gabriel Dell, Jackie Coogan (Zoetrope)

The Escape Artist is a muted fable [from the novel by David Wagoner] about a gifted child in a never-never-land America. Treatment frequently pushes past the careful to the precious, and the quiet, odd tale never becomes more than mildly intriguing.

After brash but not arrogant youth Griffin O'Neal issues a challenge to the police department that he can break out of their jail in one hour, story flips into an hour-long flashback.

O'Neal imposes himself on his aunt and uncle, small-time vaudevillians, essayed by Joan Hackett and Gabriel Dell, and begins making trouble for himself and the entire Midwestern town by making off with the loot-filled wallet of the corrupt mayor's son, played as a real looney tune by Raul Julia.

It all ends with O'Neal royally turning the tables on Julia and mayor Desiderio (Desi) Arnaz.

In his film debut, O'Neal, who is Ryan's son and Tatum's brother, comes across as spry and able, but seems to come fully alive only in the confrontation scenes with Julia and in a nice flirtation with young waitress Elizabeth Daily.

. . . .

■ ESCAPE FROM ALCATRAZ

1979, 112 MINS, US ◇ ⑰ ⊙

Dir Don Siegel   *Prod* Don Siegel   *Scr* Richard Tuggle
Ph Bruce Surtees   *Ed* Ferris Webster   *Mus* Jerry Fielding
Art Dir Allen Smith
● Clint Eastwood, Patrick McGoohan, Fred Ward, Roberts Blossom, Bruce M. Fischer, Paul Benjamin (Paramount/Malpaso)

Considering that the escape itself from rock-bound Alcatraz prison consumes only the film's final half-hour, screenwriter Richard Tuggle [adapting the book by J. Campbell Bruce] and director Don Siegel provide a model of super-efficient filmmaking. From the moment Clint Eastwood walks onto The Rock, until the final title card explaining the three escapees were never heard from again, *Escape from Alcatraz* is relentless in establishing a mood and pace of unrelieved tension.

Pic's only fault may be an ambiguous ending, tied, of course, to the historical reality of the 1962 escape, only successful one in Alcatraz' 29-year history as America's most repressive penal institution.

Key counterpoint to Eastwood's character comes from Patrick McGoohan as the mega-lomaniacal warden.

. . . .

■ ESCAPE FROM NEW YORK

1981, 99 MINS, US ◇ ⑰ ⊙

Dir John Carpenter   *Prod* Larry France, Debra Hill
Scr John Carpenter, Nick Castle   *Ph* Dean Cundey
Ed Todd Ramsay   *Mus* John Carpenter, Alan Howarth
Art Dir Joe Alves
● Kurt Russell, Lee Van Cleef, Ernest Borgnine, Donald Pleasence, Isaac Hayes, Harry Dean Stanton (Avco Embassy/IFI/Goldcrest)

Although execution doesn't quite live up to the fabulous premise, *Escape from New York* is a solidly satisfying actioner. Impressively produced for $7 million, it reps director John Carpenter's biggest budget to date.

In the 1997 New York City neatly turned out (mostly in St Louis) by production designer Joe Alves, Manhattan is a walled, maximum security prison inhabited by millions of felons and loonies. The president of the US has the misfortune of crash landing on the island and being taken hostage by the crazies, who demand their release in exchange for the leader.

Into this cesspool is sent tough criminal Kurt Russell, who is charged with extricating the prexy within 24 hours.

Pic only falls a little short in not taking certain scenes to their dramatic limits. For instance, Russell is finally captured by Isaac Hayes and his cronies and thrown, like a doomed gladiator, into an arena with a hulking behemoth. Instead of milking the confrontation for all it's worth, Carpenter keeps cutting away to parallel events elsewhere.

Model and matte work, executed at New World's special effects studio in Venice, is obvious but imaginatively fun enough to get by.

. . . .

■ ESCAPE FROM THE PLANET OF THE APES

1971, 97 MINS, US ◇ ⑰ ⊙

Dir Don Taylor   *Prod* Arthur P. Jacobs   *Scr* Paul Dehn
Ph Joseph Biroc   *Ed* Marion Rothman   *Mus* Jerry Goldsmith   *Art Dir* Jack Martin Smith, William Creber
● Roddy McDowall, Kim Hunter, Bradford Dillman, Natalie Trundy, Eric Braeden, William Windom (20th Century-Fox)

Escape from the Planet of the Apes is an excellent film, almost as good as the original *Planet of the Apes*. Arthur Jacobs' production is marked by an outstanding script, using some of the original Pierre Boulle novel characters; excellent direction by Don Taylor; and superior performances from a cast headed by encoring Roddy McDowall and Kim Hunter.

In the previous film one will recall that the world seemed to be ending in nuclear holocaust. Something that trivial never stopped a good writer, so this film opens with Hunter, McDowall and Sal Mineo arriving on earth in a space vehicle.

After about half of the film's literate, suspenseful, delightful and thought-provoking 97 minutes, the story emphasis segues from broad comedic antics to a rather horrifying dilemma. Eric Braeden, scientific advisor to US President William Windom, suggests that, if indeed in our future apes would subdue humans, why not remove that distant threat by aborting the life of the child of McDowall and Hunter?

. . . .

■ ESCAPE ME NEVER

1935, 93 MINS, UK

Dir Paul Czinner   *Prod* Herbert Wilcox, Dallas Bower
Scr Margaret Kennedy, R.J. Cullen   *Ph* Georges Perinal, Sepp Allgeier   *Ed* Merrill G. White, David Lean
Mus William Walton   *Art Dir* Andre Andrejev, Wilfred Arnold
● Elisabeth Bergner, Hugh Sinclair, Irene Vanbrugh, Griffith Jones, Penelope Dudley-Ward, Lyn Harding (British & Dominions/United Artists)

Escape Me Never, produced as a play [by Margaret Kennedy] in London and New York with the same star, is a well-produced film transcription of a story of moods and morbidity.

Locale includes Venice, where the picture opens, the mountains, and finally London. At the outset Elisabeth Bergner is fashioned as an impish waif of immoral caste, who instantly becomes likable in spite of her character background. Further on, by degrees, she loses a part of this charm and becomes a helpless mother and wife who is figuratively kicked around by her musician husband.

Two brothers figure in the supporting cast, played by Hugh Sinclair and Griffith Jones. Story makes the brothers unreal to some extent, at the same time also stretching logic of actions of Bergner and the other girl (Penelope Dudley-Ward). Latter is unbelievably smitten with one brother, then with the other, and, though appealed to by Bergner, as the latter's wife, stolidly refuses to believe her second choice is married.

Some of the interiors tend to drabness, possibly to lend that touch to a depressing story. □ 1935: Nomination: Best Actress (Elisabeth Bergner)

. . . .

■ ESCAPE ME NEVER

1947, 101 MINS, US
Dir Peter Godfrey   *Prod* Henry Blanke   *Scr* Thames Williamson, Lenore Coffee   *Ph* Sol Polito   *Ed* Clarence Kolster   *Mus* Erich Wolfgang Korngold   *Art Dir* Carl Jules Weyl
● Errol Flynn, Ida Lupino, Eleanor Parker, Gig Young, Reginald Deny, Isobel Elsom (Warner)

Errol Flynn is given plenty of opportunity to flash the old charm but there's hardly a touch of the usual swashbuckling or boudoir romance activities in his role of a serious composer. Under the capable direction of Peter Godfrey, he turns in one of the best jobs of his career. Ida Lupino, although she's seldom been typed so much as Flynn, has a role here that she can really sink her teeth into and she demonstrates once more her versatility as a serious actress.

Story [from a novel and play by Margaret Kennedy] is cut sharply in half between light romance and heavy drama and therin lie its only fault of note.

Tale is imbued with much of the nostalgic flavor of pre-World War I Europe. It tees off in Venice where Gig Young, a struggling young composer, wants to marry the wealthy Eleanor Parker. Through a misunderstanding, however, her parents think Young is living with Lupino, a widowed waif with an infant son, and so rush Parker off to a resort in the Alps. Seems, though, that it's been Flynn, Young's happy-go-lucky brother, who took Lupino and child in off the streets. To set things right again, the two brothers, Miss Lupino and the moppet start off on foot through the Alps to find Parker and explain the mistake to her.

Chief production assist is lent by Erich Wolfgang Korngold's score, with both the ballet and theme music standout. Ballet sequences are tastefully staged by LeRoy Prinz and Milada Mladova sparkles in both terping and thesping as the prima ballerina.

. . . .

■ ESCAPE TO ATHENA

1979, 125 MINS, UK ◇ ⓥ
Dir George P. Cosmatos   *Prod* Jack Wiener
Scr Richard S. Lochte, Edward Anhalt   *Ph* Gil Taylor
Ed Ralph Kemplen   *Mus* Lalo Schifrin   *Art Dir* John Graysmark
● Roger Moore, Telly Savalas, David Niven, Claudia Cardinale, Richard Roundtree, Stefanie Powers (ITC/Grade)

Escape to Athena not only has the unabashed look of a cynical 'package' but also plays like one as well. It's a joke-up wartime action retread, feeble as to both humor and suspense, in which a group of Anglo-American prisoners of the Germans scramble to liberate (a) themselves and (b) some Greek art treasures.

Of those billed above the title, Roger Moore as the Nazi camp commander, Elliott Gould, David Niven, Sonny Bono, Stefanie Powers and Richard Roundtree as POWs (how's that for a motley bunch?), Telly Savalas as a Greek resistance leader, and Claudia Cardinale as a brothel madam, none has much scope to register with any dimension

and most are as implausible as the hammy action [based on a story by Richard S. Lochte and George P. Cosmatos].

. . . .

■ ESCAPE TO HAPPINESS
See: Intermezzo

. . . .

■ ESCAPE TO WITCH MOUNTAIN

1975, 97 MINS, US ◇ ⓥ ⊙
Dir John Hough   *Prod* Jerome Courtland   *Scr* Robert Malcolm Young   *Ph* Frank Phillips   *Ed* Robert Stafford
Mus Johnny Mandel   *Art Dir* John B. Mansbridge, Al Roelofs
● Eddie Albert, Ray Milland, Donald Pleasence, Kim Richards, Ike Eisenmann, Walter Barnes (Walt Disney)

The two leading protagonists are a young orphaned brother and sister who are psychic.

Based on a book by Alexander Key and directed with a light and sure hand by John Hough, script picks up the youngsters as they arrive at a children's home after the loss of their foster parents.

Their unusual powers, displayed early when they warn a man not to enter a car moments before it is demolished by a runaway truck, leads to an eccentric tycoon who craves a gifted clairvoyant who can make him omnipotent, arranging for their transfer to his palatial home where they are held prisoner.

Using their magical talents for an escape, they take up with a cranky oldtimer travelling in a motor home. Much of the action focuses on their efforts to elude the millionaire and his men who want the children returned.

Eddie Albert inserts just the proper type of crankiness as the camper-owner who gets entangled with them, and Ray Milland properly hams the multimillionaire. Donald Pleasence scores, too, as Milland's aide.

. . . .

■ ETERNITY

1990, 125 MINS, US ◇ ⓥ
Dir Steven Paul   *Scr* Jon Voight, Steven Paul, Dorothy Koster Paul   *Ph* John Lambert   *Ed* Christopher Greenbury, Peter Zinner, Michael Sheridan   *Mus* Michel Legrand   *Art Dir* Martin Zboril
● Jon Voight, Armand Assante, Eileen Davidson, Wilford Brimley, Kaye Ballard, Joey Villa (Paul)

Written in collaboration with director Steven Paul and his mother Dorothy Koster Paul, Jon Voight's vision of mankind's dilemma revolves around mystical notions of reincarnation. Opening reel is a medieval prolog in which Voight wars with his brother Armand Assante over a kingdom, resulting in the death of his beloved Eileen Davidson.

Voight wakes up and, in true *Wizard of Oz* style, recognizes all the people in his life as reincarnations of relatives and other folks from the dream. Assante is now a megalomaniacal, right-wing industrialist out to control the media, the US presidency, and to push a vast weapons project he believes will deter war.

Voight is a self-professed do-gooder, who opposes Assante's militaristic approach. Assante attempts to buy out Voight's show to silence him and then co-opts his girlfriend (Davidson again) by making her a TV star on his network.

Voight invests equal measures of naturalism and quirks in his messianic role which goes over the top occasionally. Davidson stands out in the supporting cast, possessing an unusual beauty reminiscent of Polish star Joanna Pacula.

. . . .

■ ETHAN FROME

1993, 99 MINS, US ◇ ⓥ ⊙
Dir John Madden   *Prod* Stan Wlodkowski   *Scr* Richard Nelson   *Ph* Bobby Bukowski   *Ed* Katherine Wenning
Mus Rachel Portman   *Art Dir* Andrew Jackness

● Liam Neeson, Patricia Arquette, Joan Allen, Tate Donovan, Katharine Houghton, Stephen Mendillo (American Playhouse)

An intimate tragedy of three stunted lives in rural New England, *Ethan Frome* is the quintessential American Playhouse movie: careful, literary, restrained, nicely acted and more than a bit dry.

Gary Cooper was ideally cast in WB's aborted 1940s effort to film Edith Wharton's pitiless short novel and Cooper comes instantly to mind upon seeing Liam Neeson as the once-promising young man who, as we see in flashback, took over his mother's farm upon her death and married the splintery woman, Zeena (Joan Allen), who nursed her during her fatal illness.

Zeena herself soon becomes a professional invalid. When she calls upon her destitute cousin Mattie Silver (Patricia Arquette) to help her at home, Ethan becomes enraptured by the young, spirited girl.

This stands as a genteel, polite adaptation of a caustic, surgically precise book. No visual equivalent for Wharton's literary carving was found for pic.

Still, Neeson makes a superb Ethan, a big man made small by his willingness to submit to the mean-spirited, manipulative Zeena. Arquette is an eminently suitable Mattie.

. . . .

■ E.T.
THE EXTRA-TERRESTRIAL

1982, 115 MINS, US ◇ ⓥ ⊙
Dir Steven Spielberg   *Prod* Steven Spielberg
Scr Melissa Mathison   *Ph* Allen Davlau   *Ed* Carol Littleton   *Mus* John Williams   *Art Dir* James D. Bissell
● Dee Wallace, Henry Thomas, Peter Coyote, Robert MacNaughton, Drew Barrymore, K.C. Martel (Universal)

E.T. may be the best Disney film Disney never made. Captivating, endearingly optimistic and magical at times, Steven Spielberg's fantasy is about a stranded alien from outer space protected by three kids until it can arrange for passage home.

E.T. is highly fortunate to be found by young Henry Thomas who, after some understandable initial fright, takes the 'goblin' in, first as a sort of pet and then as a friend he must guard against the more preying elements of human society. Over time, Thomas teaches E.T. how to talk and includes his older brother (Robert MacNaughton) and younger sister (Drew Barrymore) in on the secret.

Ultimately, of course, the official representatives of society locate E.T., which seems to occasion a rapid decline in its health until it appears to die.

As superlatively created by Carlo Rambaldi, the creature manages to project both a wondrous childlike quality and a sense of superior powers. It even gets to play a drunk scene, perhaps a first for screen aliens.

All performers fulfill the requirements, and Thomas is perfect in the lead, playing the childhood equivalent of Spielberg's everyman heroes of his previous pics.

□ 1982: Best Sound, Original Score, Sound, Sound Effects Editing, Visual Effects.
□ Nominations: Best Picture, Director, Original Screenplay, Cinematography, Editing

. . . .

■ EUREKA

1983, 129 MINS, UK ◇ ⓥ
Dir Nicolas Roeg   *Prod* Jeremy Thomas   *Scr* Paul Mayersberg   *Ph* Alex Thomson   *Ed* Tony Lawson
Mus Stanley Myers   *Art Dir* Michael Seymour
● Gene Hackman, Theresa Russell, Rutger Hauer, Jane Lapotaire, Ed Lauter, Mickey Rourke (JF Prods/Recorded Picture)

Even by his own standards, Nicolas Roeg's *Eureka* is an indulgent melodrama [based on a book by Marshall Houts] about the anticlimactic life of a greedy gold prospector after he has struck it rich.

Gene Hackman performs with predictable credit as the man whose jackpot fortune only leaves him bored, surly and suspicious of being ripped off, by one and all, family included.

Theresa Russell is the girl-woman daughter who rebelliously marries a putative gigolo (Rutger Hauer) whom paranoid papa psychs as a fortune hunter. Mother Jane Lapotaire, meanwhile, driven to the sauce by an uncaring husband, drifts through life in the tropics with sulky sarcasm.

Violent menace permeates pic, radiated by Joe Pesci as a Yiddish-speaking 'entrepreneur' who, foiled in his bid to buy a piece of Hackman's island in order to establish a casino, finally sends the hoods after Hackman, leading up to a gruesome pre-finale.

....

■ EUREKA STOCKADE

1949, 103 MINS, UK/AUSTRALIA

Dir Harry Watt   *Prod* Michael Balcon   *Scr* Harry Watt, Walter Greenwood   *Ph* George Heath   *Mus* John Greenwood
● Chips Rafferty, Gordon Jackson, Peter Finch, Jane Barrett, Jack Lambert, Peter Illing (Ealing)

Eureka Stockade is staged in the middle of the 19th century when the first gold strike in Australia leads to economic chaos in the colony. There are no men to till the land or sail the ships as they have all gone in search of gold. And there is also a large influx of foreigners, all of whom hope to find their fortune.

In an endeavor to save the nation's finances, vicious taxes are imposed on the diggers, and the men themselves are hounded by the police. The gold seekers seek to impose their will by mob law, but a leader arises.

If action alone could make a picture, this one would very nearly take full marks, for the entire emphasis is on movement, and the pitched battle comes as a climax to a series of big-scale scenes.

The main weakness of the production, which contributes in large measure to its failure to grip, is the low standard of acting.

....

■ EUROPEANS, THE

1979, 90 MINS, UK ◇ ⊛

Dir James Ivory   *Prod* Ismael Merchant   *Scr* Ruth Prawer Jhabvala   *Ph* Larry Pizer   *Ed* Jeremiah Rusconi   *Mus* Richard Robbins
● Lee Remick, Robin Ellis, Wesley Addy, Lisa Eichhorn, Tim Choate, Tim Woodward (Merchant-Ivory)

'The Europeans' are Americans who grew up in Europe in the mid-19th century. They come back to the US to visit rich cousins. Perhaps a bit down on their luck, the arrival leads to a mingling and interaction of cultures, that ends up with the more innocent Yankee outlooks holding their own with the worldly wiles of the European ways.

The European cousins are Lee Remick as a mid-30s baroness now estranged from her Austrian nobleman husband and her younger brother, a free-living portrait painter with bohemian attitudes.

Shot in the US, New England is a lovely backdrop with its languid, genteel ways and extraordinary houses that are a mixture of European and local influences.

Director James Ivory handles this roundelay [from the Henry James novel] with subtlety, delivering an engaging drama.

☐ 1979: Nomination: Best Costume Design

....

■ EVE

1962, 100 MINS, FRANCE/ITALY

Dir Joseph Losey   *Prod* Robert Hakim, Raymond Hakim   *Scr* Hugo Butler, Evan Jones   *Ph* Gianni Di Venanzo

Ed Reginald Beck, Franca Silvi   *Mus* Michel Legrand   *Art Dir* Richard MacDonald, Luigi Scaccianoce
● Jeanne Moreau, Stanley Baker, Virna Lisi, Giorgio Albertazzi, James Villiers, Lisa Gastoni (Paris/Interopa)

Made [from the novel by James Hadley Chase] by an American director in Italy using English, with French producers and French, British and Italo actors, this is a sleek, mannered look at an affair between a cold, almost psychotic, call girl and a writer, who is a fraught with overtones of masochism.

A blustering, self satisfied British writer, who has a bestseller and smash pic under his belt, has also amassed an Italian fiancee and lives in Venice and Rome. His film producer suspects him and, being in love with his fiancee, is having him investigated.

He has to come up with another story, and goes off to a posh secluded house on an isle near Venice. A broken rudder had let a boat in with an enigmatic, hard-looking French girl and an older man. They had broken into the house and she was calmly in the bathtub when the writer comes in. He wants to throw them out until he ogles the femme.

He throws out the older man who had paid off the girl in paintings for a night of love. The writer tries to get next to her but she knocks him cold with an ashtray. Thus starts an obsession.

Picture is reminiscent of pre-war Yank femme fatale films. But there is not enough character to give acceptance to the over-indulgence in Jeanne Moreau as the cold-hearted harlot. Moreau speaks good English but is hampered by the over-decorated, over-stylized vamp she is called on to play. Stanley Baker acquits himself acceptably as the climbing ex-coal miner, and others are adequate.

....

■ EVERGREEN

1934, 92 MINS, UK ⊛

Dir Victor Saville   *Prod* Michael Balcon   *Scr* Emlyn Williams, Marjorie Gaffney   *Ph* Glen MacWilliams   *Ed* Ian Dalrymple   *Mus* Harry Woods   *Art Dir* Alfred Junge, Peter Pride
● Jessie Matthews, Sonnie Hale, Betty Balfour, Barry Mackay, Ivor McLaren (Gaumont-British)

Jessie Matthews has the name part, which she created on the stage. The screen adaptation and dialog is, for picture purposes, a better story than the stage version. It is more definite and coherent. Benn Levy and Lorenz Hart wrote the original musical for C. B. Cochran.

In 1909 (this is the plot) Harriet Green is London's pet singing comedienne, making her farewell appearance at the old Tivoli prior to her marriage to a marquis. That night the father of her child, whom she believed to be dead, turns up and demands blackmail. She places the baby girl in the charge of a faithful maid and disappears.

Twenty-five years later the daughter seeks a job in the chorus and is recognized by the mother's old understudy, now the widow of an ancient lord. Daughter is foisted on the public as the original Harriet Green and starred in an elaborate musical. This gives scope for Edwardian and modern costuming and ample advantage is taken of the opportunities.

It is the astonishingly competent performances by the principals that is most impressive. They embrace, in addition to Matthews, Sonnie Hale and Ivor McLaren, Betty Balfour and Barry MacKay, all good.

....

■ EVERYBODY'S ALL-AMERICAN

(UK: When I Fall in Love)

1988, 127 MINS, US ◇ ⊛ ⊙

Dir Taylor Hackford   *Prod* Taylor Hackford, Laura Ziskin, Ian Sander   *Scr* Tom Rickman   *Ph* Stephen Goldblatt

Ed Don Zimmerman   *Mus* James Newton Howard   *Art Dir* Joe Alves
● Jessica Lange, Dennis Quaid, Timothy Hutton, John Goodman, Carl Lumbly, Ray Baker (New Visions)

Everybody's All-American [from a book by Frank DeFord] has its moments, and remains watchable due to its two attractive leads, but is too predictable and not nearly incisive enough.

The world of Baton Rouge in the mid-1950s was made for the likes of Gavin and Babs. Dashing, easy-going and likable, Gavin (Dennis Quaid) is the running back who leads his school to triumph in the Sugar Bowl. Gorgeous blond Southern belle Babs (Jessica Lange) represents everyone's dream girl but yearns only to become Mrs Gavin Grey.

The couple moves comfortably into the expected environs of suburbia, a steady flow of babies, sports-themed restaurant ownership and the like. However, the innocence of youth and the 1950s inevitably yield to the turmoil and doubt of the 1960s. The Greys get wiped out financially and then see Gavin's star fall as his playing career winds down, just as Babs belatedly starts coming into her own.

A viewer could do a lot worse than have to watch Lange and Quaid for two hours, and they definitely get far into their parts here. After just getting by posing as 21-year-olds, both age through the years convincingly.

....

■ EVERYBODY WINS

1990, 97 MINS, UK/US ◇ ⊛ ⊙

Dir Karel Reisz   *Prod* Jeremy Thomas, Ezra Swerdlow   *Scr* Arthur Miller   *Ph* Ian Baker   *Ed* John Bloom   *Mus* Mark Isham, Leon Redbone   *Art Dir* Peter Larkin
● Debra Winger, Nick Nolte, Will Patton, Judith Ivey, Jack Warden, Kathleen Wilhoite (Recorded Picture)

Everybody Wins is a very disappointing picture. Repping Arthur Miller's first feature film screenplay since *The Misfits* in 1961, the Karel Reisz-helmed film noir is obscure and artificial.

Overladen with pompous and frequently dated dialog, Miller's script (developed from his 1982 pair of one-act plays, *Two-Way Mirror*) is essentially a routine whodunit. Nick Nolte plays an investigator called in by seeming good Samaritan Debra Winger to get young Frank Military out of jail for a murder she claims he did not commit. Nolte doggedly pursues various leads, interviews odd people and discovers a web of corruption engulfing a small Connecticut town.

Winger as a schizo femme fatale copes uneasily with Miller's overblown dialog, which has her alternatively putting on airs to a bewildered Nolte or handing him non sequiturs. Not helping matters is the lack of chemistry between Nolte and Winger in their sex scenes.

....

■ EVERYTHING I HAVE IS YOURS

1952, 91 MINS, US ◇

Dir Robert Z. Leonard   *Prod* George Wells   *Scr* George Wells, Ruth Brooks Flippen   *Ph* William V. Skall   *Ed* Adrienne Fazan   *Mus* David Rose (dir.)
● Marge Champion, Gower Champion, Dennis O'Keefe, Monica Lewis, Dean Miller, Eduard Franz (M-G-M)

The talents of Marge and Gower Champion get a flashy showcasing. The star team is extremely likeable and almost generates enough verve and audience response to carry off even the sagging spots.

Marge Champion, particularly, continues to show promise as an ingenue who can get by even without a dance or song. Champion gives a very pleasing account of himself.

The plot finds the Champions opening to a smash hit on Broadway in an O'Keefe-produced show, only to discover that the gal's dizziness is caused by pregnancy. Forced to retire with only one night in the show, Marge Champion becomes a successful mother for the next few years while Champion continues in show business partnered with Monica Lewis.

● ●

■ **EVERYTHING YOU ALWAYS WANTED TO KNOW ABOUT SEX** BUT WERE AFRAID TO ASK**

1972, 87 MINS, US ◇ ⓥ ⊙
Dir Woody Allen   *Prod* Charles H. Joffe   *Scr* Woody Allen   *Ph* David M. Walsh   *Ed* James T. Heckart, Eric Albertson   *Mus* Mundell Lowe   *Art Dir* Dale Hennesy
● Woody Allen, John Carradine, Anthony Quayle, Tony Randall, Burt Reynolds, Gene Wilder (United Artists)

Borrowing only the title and some typically inane questions from Dr David Reuben's oft-ingenuous but widely read overview of sexual matters, Woody Allen writes his sixth screenplay and serves for the third time as his own director.

Pic is divided into seven segments – blackout sketches, really – that presumably are Allen's surrealistic answer to selected questions from the Reuben tome.

One of the episodes is a prolonged piece of nonsense involving a *2001*-inspired mission control centre that is engineering a bout of intercourse in a parked car. Idea of Allen as a reluctant sperm may sound funny on paper, but it plays like an adolescent jape.

Allen's gift is in the depiction of a contemporary intellectual schlump who cannot seem to make it with the chicks always tantalizingly out of reach. That persona could well have served him once more as the focus for a good bit of caustic comedy on today's sexual mores.

● ●

■ **EVERY TIME WE SAY GOODBYE**

1986, 95 MINS, US ◇ ⓥ ⊙
Dir Moshe Mizrahi   *Prod* Jacob Kotzky, Sharon Harel   *Scr* Moshe Mizrahi, Rachel Fabien, Leah Appet   *Ph* Giuseppe Lanci   *Ed* Mark Burns   *Mus* Philippe Sarde   *Art Dir* Micky Zahar
● Tom Hanks, Cristina Marsillach, Benedict Taylor, Anat Atzmen (Tri-Star)

Every Time We Say Goodbye is a tale of star-crossed lovers played out against a backdrop of Jerusalem in 1942. Tom Hanks is featured as an American pilot recovering from an injury who falls in love with a girl from a traditional Sephardic Jewish family (Cristina Marsillach).

The film is not devoid of humor. Early scenes when Hanks is accepted to dinner by the family as a friend and not yet a suitor are funny and believable. Culturally rich story is aided throughout by the pic's all-Israel shoot, nicely highlighting the different worlds these two lovers come from.

● ●

■ **EVERY WHICH WAY BUT LOOSE**

1978, 119 MINS, US ◇ ⓥ ⊙
Dir James Fargo   *Prod* Robert Daley   *Scr* Jeremy Joe Kronsberg   *Ph* Rexford Metz   *Ed* Ferris Webster, Joel Cox   *Mus* Snuff Garrett (sup.)   *Art Dir* Elayne Ceder
● Clint Eastwood, Sondra Locke, Geoffrey Lewis, Beverly D'Angelo, Ruth Gordon (Malpaso/Warner)

Screenplay has Clint Eastwood as a beer-guzzling, country music-loving truck driver who picks up spare change as a barroom brawler. When Sondra Locke, an elusive singer Eastwood meets at The Palomino Club, takes off for Colorado, Eastwood packs his pickup truck in pursuit.

Behind him are a motorcycle gang and an LA cop. Both have been victims of Eastwood's fists. They want revenge. Traveling with Eastwood is Geoffrey Lewis and Beverly D'Angelo, whom the two meet on the road.

There's also an orangutan. His name is Clyde. Eastwood won him a few years back in

a fight. He goes everywhere with Eastwood. He drinks beer, finds a one-night stand at a zoo in New Mexico and cheers on his friend.

For Eastwood fans, the essential elements are there. Lots of people get beat up, Eastwood walks tall and looks nasty, cars are crashed. James Fargo directs limply.

● ●

■ **EVIL, THE**

1978, 89 MINS, US ◇ ⓥ
Dir Gus Trikonis   *Prod* Ed Carlin   *Scr* Donald G. Thompson   *Ph* Mario Di Leo   *Ed* Jack Kirshner   *Mus* Johnny Harris   *Art Dir* Peter Jamison
● Richard Crenna, Joanna Pettet, Andrew Prine, Cassie Yates, Lynne Moddy, Victor Buono (Rangoon)

Any satanic-oriented film that actually has the nerve to display the Wicked One in the flesh can't be all bad, and in fact, *The Evil* is quite good.

Screenplay has psychologist Richard Crenna, accompanied by wife (also a medico) Joanna Pettet, picking up a lease on the proverbial haunted house, despite real estate agent Milton Selzer's recounting of the grisly horrors that took place there.

Crenna and Pettet are soon joined by college prof Andrew Prine with student companion Mary Louise Weller, and several of Crenna's patients. Just what they're all up to is never clearly delineated, but once the house (or something in it) begins to act up, it really doesn't matter.

Throughout, there is a spirit on the loose (resembling the White Tornado) in communication with Pettet, trying to warn her of the dangers ahead. But Crenna is a stubborn skeptic, only admitting his own helplessness in dealing with the situation when there is no other recourse.

This type of psychological insight is rare in suspensers, and is a credit to both Crenna, who delivers a strong performance, and director Gus Trikonis. Fulcrum of pic's success or failure comes in final scenes, when Crenna and Pettet confront the devil himself, played with sinister angelicism by Victor Buono.

● ●

■ **EVIL ANGELS**
See: *A Cry in the Dark*

● ●

■ **EVIL DEAD, THE**

1983, 85 MINS, US ◇ ⓥ
Dir Sam Raimi   *Prod* Robert Tapert   *Scr* Sam Raimi   *Ph* Tim Philo   *Ed* Edna Ruth Paul   *Mus* Joseph Lo Duca
● Bruce Campbell, Ellen Sandweiss, Betsy Baker, Hal Delrich, Sarah York (Renaissance)

The Evil Dead emerges as the ne plus ultra of low-budget gore and shock effects.

Story premise has five youngsters (in their 20s) holed up in a remote cabin where they discover a Book of the Dead. Archaeologist's tape recording reveals it having been found among the Khandarian ruins of a Sumerian civilization. Playing the taped incantations unwittingly summons up dormant demons living in the nearby forest, which possess the youngsters in succession until only Ash (Bruce Campbell) is left intact to fight for survival.

While injecting considerable black humor, neophyte Detroit-based writer-director Sam Raimi maintains suspense and a nightmarish mood in between the showy outbursts of special effects gore and graphic violence which are staples of modern horror pictures. Powerful camerawork suggests the lurking presence of the huge-scale demons in the forest.

Filmed in 1980 on Tennessee and Michigan locations for under $400,000, pic is a grainy blowup from 16mm. Cast is functional.

● ●

■ **EVIL DEAD II**

1987, 85 MINS, US ◇ ⓥ ⊙
Dir Sam Raimi   *Prod* Robert Tapert   *Scr* Sam Raimi, Scott Spiegel   *Ph* Peter Deming   *Ed* Kaye Davis   *Mus* Joseph Lo Duca   *Art Dir* Philip Duffin, Randy Bennett
● Bruce Campbell, Sarah Berry, Dan Hicks, Kassie Wesley, Theodore Raimi, Denise Bixler (Renaissance/De Laurentiis)

More an absurdist comedy than a horror film, *Evil Dead II* is a flashy good-natured display of special effects and scare tactics so extreme they can only be taken for laughs.

Action, and there's plenty, is centered around a remote cabin where Ash (Bruce Campbell) and girlfriend Linda (Denise Bixler) run into some unexpected influences. It isn't long before the forces of the Evil Dead have got ahold of Linda and her head winds up in a vise.

It seems Prof Knowby (John Peaks) has unleashed the spirits of the dead and they want to escape limbo by claiming possession of the living. They're a remarkably protean lot and take on all sorts of imaginative and grotesque forms almost instantaneously.

Story here is merely an excuse for director Sam Raimi to explore new ways to shock an audience and usually he keeps his sense of humor about it.

● ●

■ **EVIL OF FRANKENSTEIN, THE**

1964, 84 MINS, UK/US ◇ ⓥ ⊙
Dir Freddie Francis   *Prod* Anthony Hinds   *Scr* John Elder [= Anthony Hinds]   *Ph* John Wilcox   *Ed* James Needs   *Mus* Don Banks   *Art Dir* Don Mingaye
● Peter Cushing, Peter Woodthorpe, Duncan Lamont, Sandor Eles, Katy Wild, David Hutcheson (Hammer/Universal)

In this one Peter Cushing plays the baron with his usual seriousness, avoiding tongue-in-the-cheek, and he is the main prop in the proceedings.

This time Cushing returns to the castle which is his scientific playground and is bent on reviving and co-ordinating the brain of one of his homemade monsters. Earlier this character had escaped, but is found, conveniently preserved in a glacier. The baron has sundry other problems on his plate, notably a drunken, blackmailing hypnotist, a deaf and dumb beggar girl, the local Burgomaster and the police, but keeps a fairly stiff upper lip throughout.

● ●

■ **EVIL UNDER THE SUN**

1982, 102 MINS, UK ◇ ⓥ
Dir Guy Hamilton   *Prod* John Brabourne, Richard Goodwin   *Scr* Anthony Shaffer   *Ph* Christopher Challis   *Ed* Richard Marden   *Mus* Jack Larchbury (arr.)   *Art Dir* Elliot Scott
● Peter Ustinov, Jane Birkin, Colin Blakely, James Mason, Diana Rigg, Maggie Smith (EMI)

Director Guy Hamilton admits to hating Agatha Christie's writing style. He finds it overcrowded with characters and passe in general. Apart from cutting down the number of characters, Hamilton and scripter Anthony Shaffer have also had the audacity to switch things around in the inevitable denouement scene. Poirot points right away at the guilty party, while the true suspense is put into the how's and why's that follow.

But fun it is to follow this cast of English and US characters in their stay at the elegantly old-fashioned resort hotel on a remote Tyrrhenian island (shot in Mallorca, original novel took place in Cornwall), where a famous stage actress gives them all a good motive for doing her in.

Through it all, Peter Ustinov's Poirot paddles about, being demanding of staff (beeswax for his shoes) and cuisine and happy about himself.

233

Next to Ustinov, Maggie Smith shines as the hotel proprietress in love with the murdered woman's husband, played with quiet gusto by Denis Quilley. Diana Rigg as the stage star makes it believable in one short song-and-dance scene that she really is such a star.

■ **EXCALIBUR**

1981, 140 MINS, US ◇ ⓥ ⊙
Dir John Boorman   *Prod* John Boorman   *Scr* John Boorman, Rospo Pallenberg   *Ph* Alex Thomson   *Ed* John Merritt   *Mus* Trevor Jones   *Art Dir* Anthony Pratt
● Nigel Terry, Nicol Williamson, Nicholas Clay, Helen Mirren, Cheri Lunghi, Corin Redgrave (Orion)

Excalibur is exquisite, a near-perfect blend of action, romance, fantasy and philosophy, finely acted and beautifully filmed by director John Boorman and cinematographer Alex Thomson.

Not surprisingly, *Excalibur* is essentially the legend of King Arthur, embellished a bit by Boorman and coscripter Rospo Pallenberg, working from the Malory classic, *Morte d'Arthur*.

Filmed in timeless Irish locales, the film rests solidly on a feeling that this, indeed, must have been what life was like in the feudal ages, even as it resists bing pinned to any historical point and accepts magic and sorcery on faith.

Nicol Williamson stands out early as the wizard Merlin, at times a magician, flim-flam artist and philosopher, always interesting. The tangle of lust and betrayal that leads to Arthur's conception, the planting of Excalibur in the stone and Arthur's rise to Camelot after extracting it, is followed by restlessness and more dark deeds.

If *Excalibur* has a major fault, it's a somewhat extended sequence of the Knights of the Round Table in search of the Grail, seemingly ill-established and overdrawn.
☐ 1981: Nomination: Best Cinematography

■ **EXCESSIVE FORCE**

1993, 90 MINS, US ◇ ⓥ ⊙
Dir Jon Hess   *Prod* Thomas Ian Griffith, Erwin Stoff, Oscar L. Costo   *Scr* Thomas Ian Griffith   *Ph* Donald M. Morgan   *Ed* Alan Baumgarten   *Mus* Charles Bernstein   *Art Dir* Michael Z. Hanan
● Thomas Ian Griffith, Lance Henriksen, James Earl Jones, Charlotte Lewis, Tony Todd, Burt Young (New Line)

The best that can be said for this Chicago-shot, medium-budget opus: it certainly lives up to its title.

During the course of this otherwise unremarkable cops-and-killers melodrama, gang boss Burt Young expresses his displeasure by shoving a ballpoint pen into an underling's ear; another mobster crushes the legs of a captive cop with a baseball bat; and nominal hero Thomas Ian Griffith, playing a martial-arts-trained cop, breaks enough arms, dislocates enough shoulders and cracks enough heads to keep an emergency room staff gainfully employed for weeks.

Griffith and his two partners are marked for death by Young, who thinks one of the cops pilfered $3 million during a raid on a Young-financed drug deal. Griffith decides to launch a preemptive strike against Young's HQ. He gets surprising support from his superior (Lance Henriksen).

Griffith wrote and co-produced the pic, which he no doubt hoped would be his ticket to the major leagues of action stardom. Right now, though, he's strictly a minor-league heavy hitter – less graceful than Jean-Claude Van Damme, and not as personable as Steven Seagal.

■ **EXECUTIONER, THE**

1970, 111 MINS, UK ◇ ⓥ
Dir Sam Wanamaker   *Prod* Charles H. Schneer   *Scr* Jack Pulman   *Ph* Denys Coop   *Ed* R. Watts   *Mus* Ron Goodwin   *Art Dir* E. Marshall
● George Peppard, Joan Collins, Judy Geeson, Oscar Homolka, Charles Gray, Nigel Patrick (Schneer/Columbia)

George Peppard is a British undercover agent out to prove that a colleague is really a double agent.

Supposedly a triple-cross suspenser, film [from a story by Gordon McDonell] just lies there so that interest fades fast in the over-exposition and redundancy. Peppard is cast as an American-raised Briton whose latest spy caper has been aborted. Nigel Patrick and Charles Gray, Peppard's superiors, don't believe his charges that Keith Michell is a double agent.

Joan Collins appears occasionally as Michell's wife, and sometimes playmate of Peppard and also of George Baker. Judy Geeson appears even less frequently as Peppard's girl friend who helps him obtain secret information.

■ **EXECUTIVE ACTION**

1973, 91 MINS, US ◇ ⓥ ⊙
Dir David Miller   *Prod* Edward Lewis, Dan Bessie   *Scr* Dalton Trumbo   *Ph* Robert Steadman   *Ed* George Grenville, Irving Lerner   *Mus* Randy Edelman   *Art Dir* Kirk Axtell
● Burt Lancaster, Robert Ryan, Will Geer, Gilbert Green, John Anderson, Paul Carr (Lewis/Wakeford-Orloff)

The open lesion known as Watergate revealed a form of governmental-industrial syphilis, which in turn has made more plausible to millions the theory of an assassination conspiracy in 1963 against President John F. Kennedy. *Executive Action*, a part-fiction and documentary style film [from a story by Donald Freed and Mark Lane], dramatized with low key terror, is an emotional aftershock to the event.

Burt Lancaster, Robert Ryan and Will Geer star as informed men of industry and government service who concluded that JFK must be eliminated. Lancaster is the overall project officer. James MacColl, a remarkable look alike to Lee Harvey Oswald, depicts the alleged Oswald frameup. Oscar Oncidi plays Jack Ruby, Oswald's own assassin who, per this story, is wired into the plot.

■ **EXECUTIVE SUITE**

1954, 103 MINS, US ◇ ⓥ
Dir Robert Wise   *Prod* John Houseman   *Scr* Ernest Lehman   *Ph* George Folsey   *Ed* Ralph E. Winters   *Mus* [none]
● William Holden, June Allyson, Barbara Stanwyck, Fredric March, Walter Pidgeon, Shelley Winters (M-G-M)

This John Houseman production is a real pro job, of a calibre that doesn't come along too often. Cameron Hawley's novel, *Executive Suite*, was good reading, and Ernest Lehman has fashioned it into screen form as a dramatically interesting motion picture humanizing big business and its upper echelon personalities.

Eight scene-stealers vie for the star billing and each is fine, with some standing out over what amounts to standout performances by all concerned in the drama. Certainly Fredric March's characterization of the controller will be remembered among the really sock delineations. So will William Holden's portrayal of the idealistic, but practical, young executive.

Also effective as the other stars are Louis Calhern, cynical stockbroker who tries to turn misfortune to personal gain; Barbara Stanwyck, neurotic heiress; Walter Pidgeon, an executive never able to rise above a number two position; Paul Douglas, the hearty

sales executive; June Allyson, Holden's wife and Shelley Winters, Douglas's secretary and after-hour amour.

The drama is built on the efforts of the several vice-presidents to take over the top position, with most of the conflict in the film version centers on March, as he tries to seize power.
☐ 1954: Nominations: Best Supp. Actress (Nina Foch), B&W Cinematography, B&W Costume Design, B&W Art Direction

■ **EX-MRS. BRADFORD, THE**

1936, 80 MINS, US ⓥ ⊙
Dir Stephen Roberts   *Scr* Anthony Veiller   *Ph* J. Roy Hunt   *Ed* Arthur Roberts   *Mus* Roy Webb (dir.)
● William Powell, Jean Arthur, James Gleason, Eric Blore, Robert Armstrong (RKO)

Another sprightly entry for the school of smart comedy, detective mystery yarns, *The Ex-Mrs Bradford* has a neat combo of names – William Powell and Jean Arthur – backed up by excellent support.

Comparison with *The Thin Man* is natural. But the film is much better than a copy.

Teaming of Powell and Arthur, as doctor and divorced wife, is a happy one. Story [by James Edward Grant] brings the wife right back to the doorstep of the busy physician, where she 'moves in' and resumes where she left off annoying him with her interest in writing detective stories.

While the romance between the pair is slowly revived, the whole affair is treated with smart flippancy. Much the same attitude is taken towards the doctor's tumbling efforts to solve a series of killings that has the police baffled, until they attempt to pin them on him. Here, his wife's sharp wit and impertinence help.

■ **EXODUS**

1960, 212 MINS, US ◇ ⓥ ⊙
Dir Otto Preminger   *Prod* Otto Preminger   *Scr* Dalton Trumbo   *Ph* Sam Leavitt   *Ed* Louis R. Loeffler   *Mus* Ernest Gold   *Art Dir* Richard Day, Bill Hutchinson
● Paul Newman, Eva Marie Saint, Ralph Richardson, Peter Lawford, Lee J. Cobb, Sal Mineo (Carlyle/Alpha/United Artists)

Transposing Leon Uris' hefty novel to the screen was not an easy task. It is to the credit of director Otto Preminger and scenarist Dalton Trumbo that they have done as well as they have. One can, however, wish that they had been blessed with more dramatic incisiveness. (Estimated cost of pic was $3.5–4 million.)

The picture wanders frequently in attempting to bring into focus various political and personal aspirations that existed within the Jewish nationalist movement itself as well as in regards to Arab opposition to the partitioning of Palestine and the unhappy role that Great Britain played as custodian of the status quo while a young United Nations pondered the fate of a new nation.

One of the overwhelming moments is played aboard a rusty old freighter in which 611 Jews of all ages, from all over the face of Europe and spirited out of an internment camp on Cyprus under the nose of the British, attempt to sail to Palestine. The whole spirit that brought Israel into being is reflected in this particular sequence toward the end of the first part of the film. It's a real dramatic gem.

The romance that develops slowly between young, dedicated Hagana leader Paul Newman and Eva Marie Saint, as a widowed American who contributes her nursing abilities to Jewish refugees on Cyprus and later in Palestine, as Arabs attack the new settlers, is conventional. Technically Newman gives a sound performance, but he fails to give the role warmth. Saint has several good scenes and makes the most of them, as does Ralph Richardson, a sympathetic British general.

Lee J. Cobb gives his customary dependable, thoroughly professionl performance as a conservative elder Hagana community leader, father of Newman and brother of the fanatical violence advocate played by David Opatoshu. The brothers' silent meeting after years of separation through a barred slot in a prison door is great pictorial drama.

Sal Mineo as a loyal Irgun youngster, who has been brutalized by the Nazis, is excellent and John Derek stands out too as an Arab whose friendship for Newman and his family goes back to boyhood.

☐ 1960: Best Scoring of a Dramatic Picture
☐ Nominations: Best Supp. Actor (Sal Mineo), Color Cinematography

································

■ **EXORCIST, THE**

1973, 121 MINS, US ◇ ⊚ ⊙
Dir William Friedkin   *Prod* William Peter Blatty
Scr William Peter Blatty   *Ph* Owen Roizman, Billy Williams   *Ed* Jordan Leondopoulos, Evan Lottman, Norman Gay, Bud Smith   *Mus* Jack Nitzsche
Art Dir Bill Malley
● Ellen Burstyn, Max von Sydow, Lee J. Cobb, Kitty Winn, Jack MacGowran, Linda Blair (Hoya/Warner)

William Friedkin's film of William Peter Blatty's novel *The Exorcist* is an expert telling of a supernatural horror story. The well cast film makes credible in powerful laymen's terms the rare phenomenon of diabolic possession.

Blatty's story is based on a 1949 incident of documented possession, atop which came Friedkin's own investigations. The joint effort is cohesive and compelling, gripping both the senses and the intellect.

A compendium of production delays, some of puzzling origin (shooting alone occupied more than 10 months [of the 16-month period]), and rush to completion upped final costs to $8 million–$10 million.

Jesuit priest Max von Sydow is the leader of an archeological expedition. After unearthing some pagan hex symbol, several near fatal accidents occur. Thence to Georgetown, Maryland.

Ellen Burstyn, a divorced film actress, is on location with daughter Linda Blair, the latter becoming aware of some apparent inner spiritual friend whom she calls 'Captain Howdy', and their rented house now filled with strange sounds and movements. Finally, Jason Miller is a psychiatrist-Jesuit.

The lives of these three gradually converge as Blair's fits become genuinely vicious and destructive, provoking a shocking series of psychiatric tests. At length, Von Sydow, who has exorcised before, is sent to perform the rare rites. The climactic sequences assault the senses and the intellect with pure cinematic terror.

☐ 1973: Best Adapted Screenplay, Sound.
☐ Nominations: Best Picture, Director, Actress (Ellen Burstyn), Supp. Actor (Jason Miller), Supp. Actress (Linda Blair), Cinematography, Art Direction, Editing

································

■ **EXORCIST II**
THE HERETIC

1977, 117 MINS, US ◇ ⊚
Dir John Boorman   *Prod* John Boorman, Richard Lederer
Scr William Goodhart   *Ph* William A. Fraker   *Ed* Tom Priestley   *Mus* Ennio Morricone   *Art Dir* Richard Macdonald
● Linda Blair, Richard Burton, Louise Fletcher, Max Von Sydow, Kitty Winn, Paul Henreid (Warner)

Since any title containing Roman numerals invites comparison, the answer is: No, *Exorcist II* is not as good as *The Exorcist*. It isn't even close. Gone now is the simple clash between Good and Evil, replaced by some goofy transcendental spiritualism.

Linda Blair is back as Regan, four years older and still suffering the residual effects of her demonic possession. For the most part, however, she's cheerful and good, seemingly no more bothered by her lingering devil than a chronic zit that keeps popping out on prom night.

She is under the kindly care of psychiatrist Louise Fletcher and Kitty Winn, mom's secretary from the old days. Another self-doubting priest (Richard Burton) is assigned to investigate the death of the old exorcist (Max Von Sydow).

································

■ **EXORCIST III, THE**

1990, 110 MINS, US ◇ ⊚ ⊙
Dir William Peter Blatty   *Prod* Carter DeHaven
Scr William Peter Blatty   *Ph* Gerry Fisher   *Ed* Todd Ramsay   *Mus* Barry DeVorzon   *Art Dir* Leslie Dilley
● George C. Scott, Ed Flanders, Brad Dourif, Jason Miller, Nicol Williamson, Scott Wilson (Morgan Creek/20th Century-Fox)

Since *The Exorcist* was one of the most frightening films ever and *Exorcist II* one of the goofiest, chances favored *The Exorcist III* to fall somewhere in between, though not nearly far enough up the scale to rival the original.

The Devil and the Church have clashed in too many other pics since with increasingly ingenious ways to burst bodies, leaving director-writer William Peter Blatty [adapting his own novel, *Legion*] with all mood and no meat. Much too often, he lingers under flickering lights in dark corridors where nothing happens.

It's been 15 years since Father Karras battled the Devil for the little girl and ended up dead at the bottom of the stairway. Now his old policeman friend (George C. Scott) is confronted with a series of sacrilegious murders bearing the trademarks of a killer executed about the same time the priest died.

Anyway, there's a guy in chains over at the nuthouse who sometimes appears to Scott as Karras (Jason Miller) and sometimes as the executed killer (Brad Dourif), and it's all very confusing.

It would be downright incomprehensible, in fact, if Dourif didn't do such a dandy job in explaining things in a couple of long, madman monologs.

································

■ **EXPERIMENT IN TERROR**
(UK: The Grip of Fear)

1962, 123 MINS, US ⊚ ⊙
Dir Blake Edwards   *Prod* Blake Edwards   *Scr* Mildred Gordon, Gordon Gordon   *Ph* Philip Lathrop   *Ed* Patrick McCormack   *Mus* Henry Mancini   *Art Dir* Robert Peterson
● Glenn Ford, Lee Remick, Stefanie Powers, Roy Poole, Ned Glass, Anita Loo (Columbia)

Written by Mildred and Gordon Gordon from their book and *Ladies' Home Journal* serial *Operation Terror*. The film treatment embraces a number of unnecessary character bits that merely extend the plot and, despite their striking individual reaction, deter from the suspense buildup.

Edwards' particular interest seems to lie in the camera angles. He concentrates on overhead shots and unusual perspective merely for visual effect. Only in the climactic scenes, which take place in San Francisco's Candlestick Park during an actual baseball game of capacity attendance, does the overhead filming become fully valuable.

The 'experiment' is a terrifying episode in which a bank teller is forced by a psychopathic killer into embezzling $100,000 under threat of murder. She goes to the FBI.

Glenn Ford and Lee Remick play the FBI agent and bank teller, respectively. For Remick it is a handsome role played with nicely-modulated control and a natural feeling that is devoid of the extreme emotional tension often exposed in such characters. Ford has solidarity, but his role is merely that of a staunch agent doing his job well.

Picture was shot extensively in San Francisco, though story could be placed in any area. However, Philip Lathrop's camera took fine advantage of known Bay City landmarks, giving the film a nice visual style.

································

■ **EXPLORERS**

1985, 109 MINS, US ◇ ⊚ ⊙
Dir Joe Dante   *Prod* Edward S. Feldman, David Bombyk
Scr Eric Luke   *Ph* John Hora   *Ed* Tina Hirsch
Mus Jerry Goldsmith   *Art Dir* Robert F. Boyle
● Ethan Hawke, River Phoenix, Jason Presson, Amanda Peterson, Dick Miller, Robert Picardo (Paramount/Industrial Light & Magic)

Two young boys, a dreamer (Ethan Hawke) and a nerdy science genius type (River Phoenix), manage, through combining their talents and happening upon an unusual discovery, to fashion a homemade spacecraft.

In league with a lower-class misfit (Jason Presson) who falls in with them, the lads inventively use a leftover Tilt-A-Whirl as their basic chassis and elaborate upon their design with spare parts of all kinds.

Along with their extracurricular Advanced Shop work, opening hour is occupied with passable but far from original stuff devoted to bullies vs nerds, puppy love and schoolroom antics.

Throughout, director Joe Dante and writer Eric Luke load the proceedings with references to sci-fiers of an earlier day, such as *War of the Worlds, This Island Earth, Journey to the Center of the Earth* and many others, but this is nothing compared to what happens when the trio of youngsters finally take off into outer space and make contact with an alien race.

································

■ **EXPOSED**

1983, 100 MINS, US ◇ ⊚
Dir James Toback   *Prod* James Toback   *Scr* James Toback   *Ph* Henri Decae   *Ed* Robert Lawrence, Annie Charvein   *Mus* Georges Delerue   *Art Dir* Brian Eatwell
● Nastassja Kinski, Rudolf Nureyev, Harvey Keitel, Ian McShane, Bibi Andersson, Ron Randell (M-G-M/United Artists)

Intelligent and illogical, beautiful and erratic, *Exposed* is a provocative, jet-setter's visit to the worlds of high fashion and international terrorism.

After a prolog in which a foxy blonde is observed blowing up a Paris cafe, writer-director James Toback himself, as a college English teacher, breaks up romantically with one of his students (Nastassja Kinski).

Kinski returns to her home in Wisconsin and, in one of the film's most striking, and convincing, sequences, is attending an exhibition of photos featuring her when her eye is caught by Rudolf Nureyev.

After a bizarre, cat-and-mouse courtship, the inevitable big love scene arrives. As it happens, Nureyev is also a dedicated terrorist fighter with intensely personal motives, and when Kinski follows him to Paris, she naively becomes involved with the very forces Nureyev is intent upon wiping out. Kinski is delivered into the lair of Carlos-type terrorist Harvey Keitel, a provocateur dedicated to random violence.

Performers seem to have been chosen mostly for their physical attributes, and Kinski and Nureyev lead the way in ably fleshing out characters who are meant to remain mysterious.

································

■ **EXPRESSO BONGO**

1959, 111 MINS, UK ⊚
Dir Val Guest   *Prod* Val Guest   *Scr* Wolf Mankowitz
Ph John Wilcox   *Ed* Bill Lenny   *Mus* Monty Norman, Robert Farnon, Norrie Paramor, Bunny Lewis

● Laurence Harvey, Sylvia Syms, Yolande Donlan, Cliff Richard, Meier Tzelniker, Ambrosine Philpotts (British Lion/Britannia)

Soho, with its atmosphere of sleazy strip-peries, gaudy coffee bars and frenetic teenagers, is the setting for this amusing satire on how a little talent can be boosted overnight as the result of a successful disk and a click TV appearance. Wolf Mankowitz's story [from his own play] is slight and not particularly original, but it has pungency, wit and a sharp sense of observation.

Laurence Harvey is a cheap, opportunistic promoter, always on the lookout for an easy buck. In a Soho expresso bar, he picks up an amateur singer and bongo player, signs him up on a dubious contract and boosts him to what is now regarded as stardom.

Harvey gives a brashly amusing, offbeat per-formance as the smalltime operator while Sylvia Syms is cast as a stripper with aspira-tions towards stardom as a singer. Expresso Bongo is played by Cliff Richard, a wrong piece of casting. The songs are intended to spoof the whole business of pop crooning but they come over, in Richard's larynx, as completely feasi-ble entries into the pop market. Meier Tzelniker plays the part which he did so well on the stage. He's boss of a disk company and here's an excellent characterization – flamboy-ant, garrulous and only slightly exaggerated.

■ EXTERMINATOR, THE

1980, 101 MINS, US ◇ ⓥ ⊙
Dir James Glickenhaus   *Prod* Mark Buntzman
Scr James Glickenhaus   *Ph* Bob Baldwin   *Ed* Corky O'Hara   *Mus* Joe Renzetti
● Christopher George, Samantha Eggar, Robert Ginty, Steve James, Tony Di Benedetto (Interstar)

For his second pic, writer-director James Glickenhaus commits the major sin of shoot-ing an action film with little action. Contrived script instead opts for grotesque violence in a series of glum, distasteful scenes.

The Exterminator returns to New York City for a listlessly paced tale of Robert Ginty sud-denly deciding to avenge his war buddy, para-lyzed from an encounter with a youth gang. Absence of proper transition scenes and script's frequent reliance upon coincidence loses credibility for Ginty's actions early on.

Christopher George's walkthrough as a po-liceman is regrettable, while Samantha Eggar as both the buddy's doctor and George's girl-friend must have calculated that this travesty would never be released.

■ EXTERMINATOR 2

1984, 89 MINS, US ⓥ ⊙
Dir Mark Buntzman, William Sachs   *Prod* Mark Buntzman, William Sachs   *Scr* Mark Buntzman, William Sachs   *Ph* Bob Baldwin, Joseph Mangine   *Ed* Marcus Nanton, George Norris   *Mus* David Spear
Art Dir Mischa Petrow, Virginia Field
● Robert Ginty, Mario Van Peebles, Deborah Geffner, Frankie Faison, Scott Randolph, Reggie Rock Bythewood (Cannon)

Exterminator 2 is a silly and tiresome revenge actioner. Mark Buntzman, who produced the original, here wears (and shares with William Sachs) too many hats, ending up with a con-tradictory mishmash.

Reprising his title as Vietnam vet Johnny Eastland, an uncomfortable Robert Ginty is supposedly spurred into renewed vigilante ac-tion when his flashdancing girlfriend Caroline (Deborah Geffner) is murdered by all-pur-pose punks, led by a messianic leader ('I am the streets') X (Mario Van Peebles).

Eastland is teamed with an old mate from Vietnam, Be Gee (Frankie Faison), your friendly neighborhood black garbageman who eagerly endorses Eastland's murderous cleanup policy.

Generally, the sadistic element of the first film (which had Ginty ingeniously feeding bad guys to a meatgrinder, etc.) has been toned down. Geffner gets to show her nude body and dancing ability, while acting honors go to Van Peebles. Why it took such a huge crew (over 300 people are credited with be-hind-the-camera contributions) to make a B-picture is mighty strange.

■ EXTRAORDINARY SEAMAN, THE

1969, 79 MINS, US ◇
Dir John Frankenheimer   *Prod* Edward Lewis, John H. Cushingham   *Scr* Phillip Rock, Hal Dresner   *Ph* Lionel Linden   *Ed* Fredric Steinkamp   *Mus* Maurice Jarre
Art Dir George W. Davis, Edward Carfagno
● David Niven, Faye Dunaway, Alan Alda, Mickey Rooney, Jack Carter, Juan Hernandez (M-G-M)

The Extraordinary Seaman is strictly steerage cargo. A tepid story keel, not entirely – but al-most – devoid of amusement strength, has been ballasted with padding newsreel footage and other effect to yield an unstable comedy vessel. David Niven, Faye Dunaway, Alan Alda, Mickey Rooney and Jack Carter end up awash in the artistic debris.

Set in the Philippines where three US Navy men, in flight from the Japanese, discover an urbane Niven, as a Royal Navy officer, living in uncanny nattiness aboard a beached ship. Dunaway joins the crew as Niven sets sail for Australia.

To simulate the original environment, pic was shot in Baja, California, but what shows in the final cut could have been shot off Santa Barbara.

■ EXTREME PREJUDICE

1987, 104 MINS, US ◇ ⓥ ⊙
Dir Walter Hill   *Prod* Buzz Feitshans   *Scr* Deric Washburn, Harry Kleiner   *Ph* Matthew F. Leonetti
Ed Freeman Davis   *Mus* Jerry Goldsmith   *Art Dir* Albert Heschong
● Nick Nolte, Powers Boothe, Michael Ironside, Maria Conchita Alonso, Rip Torn, Clancy Brown (Carolco)

Extreme Prejudice is an amusing concoction that is frequently offbeat and at times compelling. Taut direction and editing prevail despite overstaged hyper-violence that is so gratu-itous to be farcical.

Story pivots on the adversarial relationship between small town Texas Ranger Nick Nolte and drug kingpin Powers Boothe. Originally childhood friends, they are now on opposite sides of the law and the US-Mexican border.

Presented as a severe and humorless straight arrow, Nolte's character is not easy to like but his acting nonetheless intrigues. Freewheeling and provocative, Boothe is the film's wild card as director Walter Hill signals right off that he's going to have some fun here.

Story proceeds through some interesting twists on the commando front while Nolte and Boothe try to reconcile their friendship and separate paths.

■ EXTREMITIES

1986, 90 MINS, US ◇ ⓥ ⊙
Dir Robert M. Young   *Prod* Burt Sugarman   *Scr* William Mastrosimone   *Ph* Curtis Clark   *Ed* Arthur Coburn
Mus J.A.C. Redford   *Art Dir* Chester Kaczenski
● Farrah Fawcett, James Russo, Diana Scarwid, Alfre Woodard (Atlantic)

Playwright William Mastrosimone adapted his 1982 off-Broadway work for the screen, but it seems to be director Robert M. Young who is responsible for virtually exploiting cin-ema's power to propel the viewer into the on-screen action.

Marjorie (Farrah Fawcett) is a museum em-ployee on her way home from work and a

workout. A ski-masked assailant imprisons and terrorizes her in her own car.

Marjorie manages to escape but the at-tacker knows her identity and address. Successive events document the trials of any woman in a similar predicament: essentially unsympathetic police and friends.

Finally, Marjorie's worst nightmare comes true. She is visited at her secluded home by the man who attacked her (James Russo).

Fawcett, who acquainted herself with the role of Marjorie on stage, following Susan Sarandon and Karen Allen, acts with a confi-dence and control not often seen in her screen work.

■ EYE FOR AN EYE, AN

1981, 106 MINS, US ◇ ⓥ
Dir Steve Carver   *Prod* Frank Capra Jr   *Scr* William Gray, James Bruner   *Ph* Roger Shearman   *Ed* Anthony Redman   *Mus* William Golstein   *Art Dir* Vance Lorenzini
● Chuck Norris, Christopher Lee, Richard Roundtree, Mako, Rosalind Chao, Maggie Cooper (Avco Embassy/Wescom)

An Eye for an Eye is an effective martial arts actioner vehicle for Chuck Norris.

Norris toplines as a San Francisco cop who quits the force and goes after revenge when his partner and partner's girlfriend are killed by drug traffickers. Aided by his former police boss Capt Stevens (Richard Roundtree), Norris evens the accounts and takes care of the drug ring.

Making solid atmospheric use of SF loca-tions, helmer Steve Carver segues from real-istic violence and tension to comic strip hokum in the form of a huge oriental villain (Toru Tanaka) whose menacing antics tip the audience that the film is all in fun.

Format has Norris, in traditional Western genre fashion, helped and jeckled by an old pro 'master' James Chan (Mako), whose wise-cracks provide comic relief.

■ EYE OF THE CAT

1969, 102 MINS, US ◇
Dir David Lowell Rich   *Prod* Bernard Schwartz, Phillip Hazelton   *Scr* Joseph Stefano   *Ph* Russell Metty, Ellsworth Fredricks   *Ed* J. Terry Williams   *Mus* Lalo Schifrin   *Art Dir* Alexander Golitzen, William D. DeCinces
● Michael Sarrazin, Gayle Hunnicutt, Eleanor Parker, Tim Henry, Laurence Naismith, Jennifer Leak (Universal)

Pic has a few good jolts, successful buildups, and good looking people, but stilted dialog and plot shot through with holes keep mys-tery at a minimum, suspense overdue. Despite San Francisco as backdrop, with North Beach and Sausalito tossed in for spice, film trips over its own cliches and errors.

Beautician Kassia (Gayle Hunnicutt), after witnessing emphysema attack of wealthy San Francisco matron Danny (Eleanor Parker), finds Danny's runaway favorite nephew Wylie (Michael Sarrazin).

Kassia plans to re-establish Wylie in the house and, after Aunt Danny changes her will in his favor, murder her and split the fortune.

David Lowell Rich's direction often mis-leads, but he does manage to get actors to speak bad lines with straight faces.

■ EYE OF THE DEVIL

1968, 89 MINS, UK
Dir J. Lee Thompson   *Prod* Martin Ransohoff, John Colley   *Scr* Robin Estridge, Dennis Murphy   *Ph* Erwin Hillier
Ed Ernest Walter   *Mus* Gary McFarland   *Art Dir* Elliot Scott
● Deborah Kerr, David Niven, Donald Pleasence, Edward Mulhare, Flora Robson, Sharon Tate (M-G-M/Filmways)

Originally titled *13*, film has a production history far more interesting than the final cut. From files, names of Julie Andrews and Kim Novak appear, latter forced out by an accident, after production started, and replaced by Deborah Kerr. Script-wise, *Day of the Arrow*, a Philip Loraine novel, went from Terry Southern (unbilled) to Robin Estridge, who shares screen credit with Dennis Murphy, engaged just before shooting.

The directorial montage includes Sidney J. Furie, Arthur Hiller and Michael Anderson, latter dropping out on medic's orders, with J. Lee Thompson taking over reins.

David Niven, a vineyard manor lord, is called back to his property because of another dry season. Kerr, against his wishes, follows with their children (Suky Appleby and Robert Duncan), latter acting mysteriously at start and finish. At the gloomy ancestral home, characters include Donald Pleasence, the local 'priest', butler Donald Bisset, Flora Robson, Niven's aunt who knows (and finally tells) what is going on, and Emlyn Williams, Niven's father.

Sharon Tate and David Hemmings loom as paper threats who speak deadpan dialog about the goings on. Kerr is our only touch with reality, and she tries to carry the pic, to little avail.

■ EYE OF THE NEEDLE

1981, 111 MINS, UK ◇ Ⓥ

Dir Richard Marquand *Prod* Stephen Friedman *Scr* Stanley Mann *Ph* Alan Hume *Ed* Sean Barton *Mus* Miklos Rozsa *Art Dir* Wilfrid Shingleton

● Donald Sutherland, Kate Nelligan, Ian Bannen, Christopher Cazenove, Philip Martin Brown (United Artists/Kings Road)

As a study of a ruthless, essentially unsympathetic killer, working for the wrong side, *Eye of the Needle* [from the 1978 best seller by Ken Follett] perhaps resembles *The Day of the Jackal*. Similarly, this tale of subtle intrigue and skilled maneuvers works rather better in print than on film.

Steely blue-eyed Donald Sutherland is introduced as a low-level British railway functionary in 1940. In prolog, Sutherland is shown murdering his friendly landlady when she discovers him working with a short-wave radio, and newlyweds Kate Nelligan and Christopher Cazenove suffer a horrible auto accident as they speed off on their honeymoon.

Cut to four years later, and Sutherland is soon revealed as perhaps Berlin's most reliable spy still working undetected within Britain. Armed with photos of a phony airbase in Eastern England, Sutherland makes his way to the aptly named Storm Island to rendezvous with a U-boat, waiting there to take him to Germany.

In the meantime, Nelligan and Cazenove have resettled on the bleak outpost of civilization. Formerly a dashing pilot, the latter has become a bitter paraplegic as a result of the accident, so his beauteous wife readily responds to the mysterious stranger when he temporarily lands in their household.

It's a good yarn, remindful of some of Alfred Hitchcock and Fritz Lang's wartime mellers as well as Michael Powell's 1939 tale of a World War I German agent in Scotland, *The Spy in Black*.

■ EYE OF THE TIGER

1986, 90 MINS, US ◇ Ⓥ

Dir Richard Sarafian *Prod* Tony Scotti *Scr* Michael Montgomery *Ph* Peter Collister *Ed* Greg Prange *Art Dir* Wayne Springfield

● Gary Busey, Yaphet Kotto, Seymour Cassel, Bert Remsen, William Smith (Scotti Bros)

Gary Busey is yet another lone vigilante out to avenge his wife's brutal murder in *Eye of the Tiger*. The pic opens with Buck Matthews' (Busey) release from prison. Matthews' hometown is being terrorized by a gang of motorcycle-riding drug peddlers, all of whom wear black with black helmets and ride in packs.

The motorcycle gang makes a visit to Matthews' house, killing his wife, beating him up and sending their daughter into a catatonic state. The rest of the film is about Matthews' one-man quest for vengeance, most of which is set to the pounding beat of rock music. The best character in the film is J.B. Deveraux (Yaphet Kotto), one of the sheriff's lackeys.

■ EYES OF LAURA MARS

1978, 104 MINS, US ◇ Ⓥ ⊙

Dir Irvin Kershner *Prod* Jon Peters *Scr* John Carpenter, David Zelag Goodman *Ph* Victor J. Kemper *Ed* Michael Kahn *Mus* Artie Kane *Art Dir* Gene Callahan

● Faye Dunaway, Tommy Lee Jones, Brad Dourif, Rene Auberjonois, Raul Julia, Rose Gregorio (Columbia)

Eyes of Laura Mars is a very stylish thriller [from a story by John Carpenter] in search of a better ending.

Faye Dunaway stars as a chic fashion photographer with mysterious and accurate premonitions about a series of murders. All of the victims are either friends or associates. Tommy Lee Jones, in an inspired bit of casting, plays a police lieutenant assigned to the case and an integral element in the mystery. Brad Dourif as Dunaway's driver, Rene Auberjonois as her trendy and obnoxious manager and Raul Julia as her ex-husband, add marvelous supporting performances.

Especially well handled are the screen realizations of Dunaway's premonitions. They look like a blurred videotape, as she explains to Jones at one point, a conception which works well on screen.

The relationships among the characters, Dunaway's portrayal of a chic and haggard photographer-artist and even the choice of Helmut Newton and Rebecca Blake's violent and stark photos as the work of the fictional Dunaway character are satisfying and engaging.

■ EYEWITNESS

(US: Sudden Terror)

1970, 95 MINS, UK ◇ Ⓥ

Dir John Hough *Prod* Irving Allen *Scr* Ronald Harwood *Ph* Ernest Robinson *Ed* Geoffrey Foot *Mus* Fairfield Parlor, Van Der Graff Generator

● Mark Lester, Lionel Jeffries, Susan George, Tony Bonner, Jeremy Kemp, Peter Vaughan (EMI)

Eyewitness has its groundroots in an often-used idea. Angle of a likeable kid with an imagination so vivid that unfeeling adults good-humoredly regard him as a chronic liar. Result is that when a crisis really arises no one fully believes him.

Young victim is Mark Lester and it's the hook on which is hung a fairly conventional crime chase yarn [from a novel by Mark Hebden] set on a Mediterranean island (it was shot in Malta) which has some exciting moments but lacks much of the tension that more astute and experienced directors than John Hough might have given it.

Adventure starts with the assassination of a visiting president. The moppet claims to have seen a policeman pull the fatal trigger. He has to avoid two cops and also convince his relatives that his story's on the level.

■ EYEWITNESS

(UK: The Janitor)

1981, 102 MINS, US ◇ Ⓥ ⊙

Dir Peter Yates *Prod* Peter Yates *Scr* Steve Tesich *Ph* Mathew F. Leonetti *Ed* Cynthia Scheider *Mus* Stanley Silverman *Art Dir* Philip Rosenberg

● William Hurt, Sigourney Weaver, Christopher Plummer, James Woods, Irene Worth, Morgan Freeman (20th Century-Fox)

Once an office-building janitor himself, writer Steve Tesich often wondered in the quiet of the night what evil deeds might be going on behind closed doors. Enter William Hurt on the night-shift discovering the murdered body of a mysterious Chinese businessman.

Tesich's other fantasy concerned a real-life infatuation with a lady reporter on CBS, wondering what she would be like and how far he would go to meet her. Hurt, too, has an obsession for newswoman Sigourney Weaver, so consuming he videotapes her every show to linger over.

When Weaver comes to his building to report on the murder, Hurt pretends to know something secret to prolong this unexpected encounter with his distant sweetheart. That in turn leads him into danger with assorted characters – Christopher Plummer in particular – who really do know something about the murder.

Weaver plays her part very well, but simply can't justify the character's actions, which ripple through the murder plot in several directions. Consequently, the story gets more and more strained before it's resolved.

■ FABULOUS BAKER BOYS, THE

1989, 113 MINS, US ◇ ⓥ ⊙
Dir Steve Kloves *Prod* Paula Weinstein, Mark Rosenberg
Scr Steve Kloves *Ph* Michael Ballhaus *Ed* William
Steinkamp *Mus* Dave Grusin *Art Dir* Jeffrey Townsend
● Jeff Bridges, Michelle Pfeiffer, Beau Bridges, Elie Raab,
Jennifer Tilly (Gladden/Mirage)

There's nothing startlingly original about this
smoothly made little romantic comedy of two
piano-playing brothers who find an attractive
young singer to give some much needed CPR
to their dying lounge act.

The first look at cynical, seen-it-all Jack
Baker (Jeff Bridges) and his bubbling, ever-
optimistic brother Frank (Beau Bridges) tells
us that's necessary to know about them.

When they're joined by sexy-surly singer
Susie Diamond (Michelle Pfeiffer), it's obvi-
ous exactly where the film is headed. Jack and
Susie are on a romantic collision course, with
Frank bound to be hurt by the explosion.

The fun part is seeing it all play out, thanks
to a standout cast and first-time director
Steve Kloves' skill in handling them.

The focus of all eyes is on Pfeiffer. The actress, who does all her own singing, is required to play a character whose vocal
abilities are good, but not so good as to make
a viewer wonder why she hasn't been signed
to a major label. Pfeiffer hits the nail right on
the head.

She also hits the spot in the film's certain-
to-be-remembered highlight – a version of
'Makin' Whoopee' that she sings while crawling all over a piano in a blazing red dress.
She's dynamite.

□ 1989: Nominations: Best Actress (Michelle
Pfeiffer), Editing, Original Score

■ FACE IN THE CROWD, A

1957, 125 MINS, US ⓥ
Dir Elia Kazan *Prod* Elia Kazan *Scr* Budd Schulberg
Ph Harry Stradling, Gayne Rescher *Ed* Gene Milford
Mus Tom Glazer *Art Dir* Richard Sylbert, Paul Sylbert
● Andy Griffith, Patricia Neal, Anthony Franciosa,
Walter Matthau, Lee Remick (Newtown/Warner)

Elia Kazan and Budd Schulberg, who teamed
to bring forth *On the Waterfront*, have another
provocative and hardhitting entry, based on
Schulberg's short story *The Arkansas Traveler*.
It's a devastating commentary on hero-worship and success cults in America.

Its basic story is somewhat similar to that of
The Great Man in that it exposes a beloved
television personality as an unmitigated heel.

Story plucks an ignorant guitar-playing hillbilly from an Arkansas jail and converts him
in a short space of time to America's most
popular and beloved television personality.
He is in private life an unsavory character, a
libertine and an opportunist with loyalty to
no one but himself. He enters the political
arena, becomes aligned with an 'isolationist'
senator, and pitches an extreme reactionary
philosophy.

Andy Griffith makes his film debut as
Lonesome Rhodes, the power-mad hillbilly.
As his vis-a-vis, Patricia Neal is the girl who
guides Griffith to fame and fortune. Anthony
Franciosa plays the unprincipled personal
manager, Walter Matthau a cynical writer.

■ FACE OF A STRANGER

See: The Promise

■ FACES

1968, 130 MINS, US
Dir John Cassavetes *Prod* Maurice McEndree *Scr* John
Cassavetes *Ph* Al Ruban *Ed* Maurice McEndree
Mus Jack Ackerman *Art Dir* Phedon Papamichael
● John Marley, Gena Rowlands, Lynn Carlin, Fred
Draper, Seymour Cassel (Maurice McEndree)

Faces is a long, long (at least an hour too long)
look at a 36-hour splitup in the 14-year marriage of a middle-class couple. At least John
Cassavetes, who also wrote the screenplay,
describes them as middle-class.

As the result of tensions, inhibitions created by years of trying to adjust, and temporary clashes of personality, John Marley and
his wife, played frigidly by Lynn Carlin, clash
and Marley leaves the house for the temporary emotional warmth of an attractive prostitute (Gena Rowlands).

Most of the running time of the film is devoted to a melange of observing the husband
and wife seeking emotional outlets outside
their home; the husband with the prostitute,
the wife in a discotheque.

The film uses two homes – that of the couple
and that of the prostitute – for most of the action. Rowlands and a few other members of the
cast are superior to their material but they're
unable to breathe life into an overblown opus.
□ 1968: Nominations: Best Supp. Actor
(Seymour Cassel), Supp. Actress (Lynn
Carlin), Original Story & Screenplay

■ FAHRENHEIT 451

1966, 113 MINS, UK ◇ ⓥ ⊙
Dir Francois Truffaut *Prod* Lewis M. Allen *Scr* Francois
Truffaut, Jean-Louis Richard *Ph* Nicolas Roeg *Ed* Thom
Nobie *Mus* Bernard Herrmann *Art Dir* Syd Cain
● Oskar Werner, Julie Christie, Cyril Cusack, Anton
Diffring, Jeremy Spenser, Bee Duffell (Anglo-Enterprise
Vineyard/Universal)

With a serious and even terrifying theme, this
excursion into science fiction has been
thoughtfully directed by Francois Truffaut
and there is adequate evidence of light
touches to bring welcome and needed relief
to a sombre and scarifying subject.

In author Ray Bradbury's glimpse into the
future, books are considered the opium of the
people. Their possession is a crime and the
state has a squad of firemen to destroy the illicit literature with flame throwers.
Fahrenheit 451, it is explained, is the temperature at which books are reduced to ashes.

The yarn develops just a handful of characters, emphasising the inevitable conflict between state and literate-minded citizens. One
of the principals is Montag (Oskar Werner)
an obedient and lawful fireman, who does his
book destroying job with efficiency and apparent enthusiasm, while his equally law-abiding
wife (Julie Christie) spends her days glued to
the mural TV screen.

A young probationary school teacher (also
played by Christie) whom Montag meets on
the monorail while on the way to the fire station, plants the first seeds of doubt in his
mind, and from then on he regularly steals
the odd book which he reads secretly.

Werner, in the difficult role of the once diffident and ambitious fireman who finally challenges authority, plays the part in low key style
which adds to the integrity of the character,
and Christie is standout in her dual roles.

Cyril Cusack plays the fire station captain
with horrifying dedication, and Anton
Diffring is effectively cast as a heavy who has
caught Montag in the book stealing act.

■ FAIL SAFE

1964, 112 MINS, US ⊙
Dir Sidney Lumet *Prod* Max E. Youngstein *Scr* Walter
Bernstein *Ph* Gerald Hirschfeld *Ed* Ralph Rosenblum
Mus [none] *Art Dir* Albert Brenner

● Henry Fonda, Walter Matthau, Frank Overton, Dan
O'Herlihy, Fritz Weaver, Larry Hagman (Columbia)

Fail Safe is a tense and suspenseful piece of
filmmaking dealing with the frightening implications of accidental nuclear warfare. It
faithfully translates on the screen the power
and seething drama of the Eugene Burdick-
Harvey Wheeler book, capturing the full
menace of the Strategic Air Command's fail-
safe device in respect to its possible malfunction, and paints a vivid canvas of an imaginary situation which conceivably could
arise.

An earlier Columbia release, *Dr Strangelove*
dealt with precisely the same situation: a US
plane loaded with hydrogen bombs is flying
toward Moscow and because of technical difficulties barring any communication it is impossible to recall the bomber before it can
drop its deadly cargo which unquestionably
will launch a world holocaust.

Identical basic premise and attendant situations between the two story properties led to
Columbia and others attached to the production of *Strangelove* to file a Federal Court suit
against the authors of *Fail Safe*, the book's
publishers and the production company –
ECA – which had announced it would film the
tome. Charge was made that *Safe* was plagia-
rized from book on which *Strangelove* was
based. Controversy was finally resolved when
Columbia took over the financing-distribution
of *Safe* and Max E. Youngstein, whose ECA
unit had planned its indie production before
dissolving, swung over as producer.

Fail Safe is a gripping narrative realistically
and almost frighteningly told as the US goes
all-out to halt the plane carrying the bombs,
even to the extent of trying to shoot it down
and advising the Russians of their peril and
urging them to destroy the plane. Particularly
dramatic are the sequences in which the president – tellingly portrayed by Henry Fonda –
talks with the Russian premier over the 'hot
wire'.

Fonda is the only big name in the cast,
which uniformly is topflight and socks over respective roles. Frank Overton, as the general
in charge of the SAC base in Omaha, home of
the fail-safe mechanism which fails to act
properly, is a particular standout; Dan
O'Herlihy, Edward Binns and Fritz Weaver
score as army officers; Walter Matthau as a
professor who urges that the US attack the
Soviets, and Larry Hagman as the president's
interpreter.

■ FALCON AND THE SNOWMAN, THE

1985, 131 MINS, US ◇ ⓥ ⊙
Dir John Schlesinger *Prod* Gabriel Katzka, John
Schlesinger *Scr* Steven Zaillian *Ph* Allen Daviau
Ed Richard Marden *Mus* Pat Metheny *Art Dir* James
D. Bissell
● Timothy Hutton, Sean Penn, David Suchet, Lori Singer,
Pat Hingle, Dorian Harewood (Hemdale)

All the way through *The Falcon and the
Snowman* director John Schlesinger and an exemplary cast grapple with a true story so
oddly motivated it would be easily dismissed
if fictional.

Working backwards from a 1977 espionage
trial, newspaperman Robert Lindsey wrote a
book examining how an idealistic 22-year-old
college dropout and a wacked-out drug
pusher carried off a successful scheme to sell
US secrets to the Soviets. With one working
with a mind confused by addled loyalties and
the other with a mind confused by chemicals,
it remains hard to fathom exactly what they
hoped to achieve or how they managed to
progress so far toward achieving it.

As the two lads, however, Timothy Hutton
and Sean Penn are superb. As the one who
comes into unexpected access to state secrets,
Hutton has the tougher job in making treason at all sympathetic while Penn is left with

the shallower part of the deteriorating druggie, to which he nonetheless adds necessary dimensions.

● ●

■ **FALLEN ANGEL**

1946, 97 MINS, US
Dir Otto Preminger   *Prod* Otto Preminger   *Scr* Harry Kleiner   *Ph* Joseph LaShelle   *Ed* Harry Reynolds   *Mus* David Raksin   *Art Dir* Lyle R. Wheeler, Leland Fuller
● Alice Faye, Dana Andrews, Linda Darnell, Charles Bickford, Anne Revere, Bruce Cabot (20th Century-Fox)

There are lapses in *Angel* from the story viewpoint and character development, but these are few and unlikely to militate against the film's over-all entertainment values. Pic deals with a trollop (Linda Darnell) who gets a flock of guys on the string, then gets bumped off. The yarn [from a novel by Marty Holland] revolves around which of her admirers committed the deed.

Linked to the plot is the story's basic romantic tie up between Alice Faye and Dana Andrews, the former as a respectable, wealthy small-town gal who is ripe for the takings, and Andrews is the guy who starts out to do the taking, even marrying her to do it, his idea being to get enough moola so he can cop the other gal.

This is Faye's first straight dramatic part and she handles herself well, generally, though her one dramatic scene could have gotten better direction. Andrews remains one of the better young dramatic actors in this film though his character is not always too clearly defined in the writing. Darnell looks the trollop part and plays it well.

● ●

■ **FALLEN IDOL, THE**

1948, 94 MINS, UK Ⓦ
Dir Carol Reed   *Prod* Carol Reed   *Scr* Graham Greene, Lesley Storm, William Templeton   *Ph* Georges Perinal   *Ed* Oswald Hafenrichter   *Mus* William Alwyn   *Art Dir* Vincent Korda, James Sawyer
● Ralph Richardson, Michele Morgan, Bobby Henrey, Sonia Dresdel, Jack Hawkins, Dora Bryan (London/20th Century-Fox)

A fine sensitive story, a brilliant child star and a polished cast, headed by Ralph Richardson and Michele Morgan, combine to make *The Fallen Idol* a satisfying piece of intelligent entertainment.

Based on a short story by Graham Greene, the script develops the triangle drama with powerful dramatic effect. Briefly, it's a story of the frustrated marriage of a butler, working at a foreign embassy in London, who's in love with an embassy typist. While the lovers are together, the wife, who has pretended to be in the country, comes in and after a hysterical row with her husband, accidentally falls and is killed.

Dominating the entire theme is young Felipe, son of the ambassador, who is left in the servants' care while the parents are away. The butler, Baines, and the boy are great friends, but Mrs Baines and Felipe are not. When a police investigation suggests that the wife might have been murdered, Felipe lies for all he is worth to defend the butler.

There's hardly a scene in the picture in which the kid, played by Bobby Henrey, doesn't appear and he comes through like a seasoned trouper. Setting the high standard for the acting is Ralph Richardson, whose masterly portrayal of the butler is a gratifying piece of work.
□ 1943: Nomination: Best Director, Screenplay

● ●

■ **FALLING DOWN**

1993, 115 MINS, US ◇ Ⓥ ⊙
Dir Joel Schumacher   *Prod* Arnold Kopelson, Herschel Weingrod, Timothy Harris   *Scr* Ebbe Roe Smith

Ph Andrej Bartkowiak   *Ed* Paul Hirsch   *Mus* Jame Newton Howard   *Art Dir* Barbara Ling
● Michael Douglas, Robert Duvall, Barbara Hershey, Rachel Ticotin, Tuesday Weld, Frederic Forrest (Warner)

This at first comes across like a mean-spirited black comedy and then snowballs into a reasonably powerful portrait of social alienation. The tone is unremittingly dour, however.

Seeking to journey 'home' to Venice from downtown Los Angeles, Michael Douglas abandons his car in bumper-to-bumper morning traffic and sets off on foot, venting his anger and frustration at all those he encounters.

A laid-off defense worker, estranged from his wife and child, with a borderline propensity for violence, he is a self-obsessed human powderkeg heading to a home no longer his while on the verge of going off.

The film provides Douglas with a real performer's showcase, and he delivers a strong, intense portrayal of a walking time bomb. Robert Duvall, as well, is at his congenial best as a henpecked burglary cop in his last day on the job.

The most notable supporting players are Rachel Ticotin as Duvall's former partner and Tuesday Weld in a remarkably unflattering turn as his skittish wife. Barbara Hershey is largely wasted as the protagonist's ex.

● ●

■ **FALLING FROM GRACE**

1992, 100 MINS, US ◇ Ⓥ
Dir John Mellencamp   *Prod* Harry Sandler   *Scr* Larry McMurtry   *Ph* Victor Hammer   *Ed* Dennis Virkler   *Art Dir* George Corsillo
● John Mellencamp, Kay Lenz, Mariel Hemingway, Claude Akins, Larry Crane, Deirdre O'Connell (Columbia/Little b)

Heartland rocker John Mellencamp, working from Larry McMurtry's fine script, turns his abiding interest in the heart of the common man into an absorbing, if occasionally murky, study of complex midwestern men and the women who put up with them. Mellencamp, debuting as both film director and star, plays exuberant, easygoing Bud Parks, a country music star who returns home with his California wife (Mariel Hemingway) to help celebrate the 80th birthday of his grandpa (Dub Taylor).

The family farm in tiny, fictional Doak City, Ind, is enduring a crisis in which a disease is killing chickens by the thousands. But more disturbing to Bud is the revelation that his old high school g.f. P.J. (Kay Lenz) is having an affair with Bud's randy, uncontrollable father (Claude Akins). Bud's odd reaction to the news is to take up with her himself. Straight-talking P.J. defines their liaison as just a frolic, but Bud confuses it for the real thing and lets his marriage fall apart.

Pic was shot in Mellencamp's hometown of Seymour, Ind, in the heart of the blighted farm belt. Best achievement is in the performances, with sharp work from the no-nonsense Lenz. Lensing is straight ahead and no-frills.

● ●

■ **FALLING IN LOVE**

1984, 107 MINS, US ◇ Ⓥ Ⓟ ⊙
Dir Ulu Grosbard   *Prod* Marvin Worth   *Scr* Michael Cristofer   *Ph* Peter Suschitzky   *Ed* Michael Kahn   *Mus* Dave Grusin   *Art Dir* Santo Loquasto
● Robert De Niro, Meryl Streep, Harvey Keitel, Jane Kaczmarek, George Martin, Dianne Wiest (Paramount)

Falling in Love is a polite little romance, the ambition and appeal of which are modestly slight. Dynamic starring duo of Robert De Niro and Meryl Streep keeps the film afloat most of the time.

Both De Niro, a construction engineer, and Streep, a graphic-designer, have marriages which, while not unhappy, have settled into the routine. Meeting in Manhattan and on

the commuter train to and from Westchester County, they are compelled to continue seeing one another, but are unsure where it's all headed. More quickly than Streep, De Niro decides he wants to have an affair, but she can't make up her mind.

De Niro is charming and, like Streep, plenty of fun to watch, but he is very contained here compared to his usual work.

● ●

■ **FALLING IN LOVE AGAIN**

1980, 103 MINS, US ◇ Ⓥ
Dir Steven Paul   *Prod* Steven Paul   *Scr* Steven Paul, Ted Allan, Susannah York   *Ph* Michael Mileham, Dick Bush, Wolfgang Suschitzky   *Ed* Bud Smith, Doug Jackson, Jacqueline Cambas   *Mus* Michel Legrand
● Elliott Gould, Susannah York, Michelle Pfeiffer, Kay Ballard, Robert Hackman, Steven Paul (OTA)

Elliott Gould is perfectly cast as Harry Lewis, a New Yorker entering middle age, suffering the usual crisis and recalling the good old days of his youth. On a cross-country trip by car with his family, Gould narrates flashbacks of his romance with Susannah York in the 1940s.

Lewis went after and married the beautiful, 'unattainable' rich girl. His hopes of career success did not materialize, with duo currently owning a clothing business.

Young actor-turned director Steven Paul shot *Falling in Love Again* in 1979 at age 20, but his feel for a past era and emphasis upon old-fashioned (but still effective) picture values bely his youthful status. Pic artfully captures the 1940s look and feel.

Michelle Pfeiffer makes a strong impression as York's younger self.

● ●

■ **FALL OF BABYLON, THE**

1919, 82 MINS, US ⊗
Dir D.W. Griffith   *Prod* D.W. Griffith   *Scr* D.W. Griffith   *Ph* Billy Bitzer
● Tully Marshall, Constance Talmadge, Elmer Clifton, Alfred Paget, Carl Stockdale, Seena Owen (Griffith)

The public wasn't entirely crazy about D.W. Griffith's massive production *Intolerance* when he presented it [in 1916]. At that time there was too much interest in the greatest drama of the time – the war – so D.W. laid *Intolerance* in mothballs. When he pulled it out of the camphor he decided to take the Babylonian story out of the big feature, shoot a few extra scenes to piece the story out and send it forth as *The Fall of Babylon*.

He opens with a tableau that is part stage and part screen, a special small screen to show New York, the modern Babylon, which, after a dissolve, brings the large screen and the opening scenes of the feature. After the first series of scenes there is a dance on stage by Kyra that outdoes anything that Gertrude Hoffman or Annette Kellerman ever tried.

The final scene of the first part is the beginning of the battle before the walls of Babylon.

The second part opens in one of the halls of Babylon and here there are 12 slave girls and Margaret Fritts, a soprano. A number here, entitled 'The Mountain Maid,' is very pretty and a dance by the girls also helps to fill the picture nicely. The scene is a fitting prelude to the revels that follow on the screen. Finally the fall of Babylon is accomplished and the love story that D.W. threads through the big battle scenes is brought to a fitting close with the lovers in a fond embrace.

The love story is not carried too much in the foreground any time in the feature, Griffith knowing full well that the tremendous scenes of the City of Babylon carry the feature along. Constance Talmadge is always on the job and one learns to look for her and to like her.

● ●

■ FALL OF THE HOUSE OF USHER, THE

See: House of Usher

■ FALL OF THE ROMAN EMPIRE, THE

1964, 185 MINS, US ◇ ⑲
Dir Anthony Mann   *Prod* Samuel Bronston   *Scr* Ben Barzman, Basilio Franchina, Philip Yordan   *Ph* Robert Krasker   *Ed* Robert Lawrence   *Mus* Dimitri Tiomkin   *Art Dir* Veniero Colasanti, John Moore
● Alec Guinness, Sophia Loren, Stephen Boyd, James Mason, Christopher Plummer, Omar Sharif (Bronston)

This made-in-Spain production is a giant-size, three-hour, sweeping pictorial entertainment. It probably tells all that most film fans will want to know about the glory, grandeur and greed of Rome.

The production reeks of expense – harness and hay for all those horses, arroz con pollo for all those Spanish extras, annuities for all those stars. Attention will focus upon the marblesque replica of downtown Rome in pagan days with temples, squares, forums, statuary, mosaic floors, columned chambers, luxury suites and a plunge for Caesar. If these sets cost a fortune they pay off in stunning camera angles.

The story gets under way speedily. Marcus Aurelius (Alec Guinness) has been campaigning for years in the bleak northern frontiers of Rome. He is dying and knows it, intends to disinherit his undependable son and neglects to do so. Stephen Boyd, a true-blue Tribune, will not claim the succession but instead supports the son, his old wrestling club chum Commodus. The entire subsequent plot swings on the failure of intention of the noble and just emperor to assure the continued peace and prosperity of Rome. In all of which the daughter, played attractively by Sophia Loren, is a desperately unhappy witness and victim.

There is much dialog about the factors which favor, and which oppose, good relations among peoples. The arrogance and cynicism in the Senate is part and parcel of the decline, as much as the vain and cruel Commodus, a man quick with the torch to homes, merciless in the ordering of wholesale crucifixions.

This anti-intellectual sadist is played with smiling malice by Christopher Plummer. He, Guinness and James Mason as a cultivated and honorable Roman minister to Marcus Aurelius pretty much wrap up the acting honors.
□ 1964: Nomination: Best Original Music Score

■ FALSE IDENTITY

1990, 92 MINS, US ◇ ⑲
Dir James Keach   *Prod* James Shavick   *Scr* Sandra Bailey   *Ph* Bernard Aurox   *Art Dir* Kevin Ryan
● Genevieve Bujold, Stacy Keach, Tobin Bell, Mike Champion, Veronica Cartwright (RKO)

This low-energy murder mystery, slow-moving and seamily produced, casts Stacy Keach as a man presumed dead who returns to his hometown after 17 years in prison. He tries to piece together his identity, but he's hampered by the fact that his face was carved up in a murder attempt. He also has a steel plate in his head.

Genevieve Bujold reprises her *Choose Me* assignment as a radio personality, but this time she's a terrier-like reporter who's gotten hold of a dirty bone involving the murder, some 20 years ago, of a local Vietnam vet.

Keach's role requires him to lurch around with a numbed brain in a project that has no discernible aspirations beyond its dubious entertainment value. Bujold, too, suffers some diminishment in these dim surroundings, although her performance surpasses the requirements.

■ FAME

1980, 134 MINS, US ◇ ⑲ ⊙
Dir Alan Parker   *Prod* David De Silva, Alan Marshall   *Scr* Christopher Gore   *Ph* Michael Seresin   *Ed* Gerry Hambling   *Mus* Michael Gore   *Art Dir* Geoffrey Kirkland
● Eddie Barth, Irene Cara, Paul McCrane, Laura Dean, Gene Anthony Ray, Anne Meara (M-G-M)

The idea behind Metro's *Fame* is that it is supposed to tell the story, via its actors, of New York's venerable High School of Performing Arts. In truth, the educational institution would have none of the project, so producers had to do with second best – the street outside the school.

Alan Parker has come up with an exposure for some of the most talented youngsters seen on screen in years. There isn't a bad performance in the lot.

The great strength of the film is in the school scenes – when it wanders away from the scholastic side as it does with increasing frequency as the overlong feature moves along, it loses dramatic intensity and slows the pace.

With all this talent, there are two individuals who are so outstanding that they dominate every scene they're in. Gene Anthony Ray, plays Leroy – a superb natural dancer, but resentful of anyone trying to help, especially a white. His continuing fight with English teacher Mrs Sherwood (Anne Meara) is the most believable plotline in the entire film.
□ 1980: Best Song ('Fame'), Original Score.
□ Nominations: Best Original Screenplay, Editing, Sound, Song ('Out Here on My Own')

■ FAME IS THE SPUR

1947, 116 MINS, UK
Dir Roy Boulting   *Prod* John Boulting   *Scr* Nigel Balchin   *Ph* Gunther Krampf   *Ed* Richard Best   *Mus* John Woodridge   *Art Dir* John Howell
● Michael Redgrave, Rosamund John, Bernard Miles, Carla Lehmann, Hugh Burden, Marjorie Fielding (Two Cities)

Few writers can give poverty such an air of adventure as Howard Spring, and in the Boulting Bros he found the right producer and director. It was not an easy matter to translate Spring's workmanlike novel of a self-made politician to the screen, but the Boultings have done this with praiseworthy conscientiousness.

Having wisely discarded the flashback, the Boultings begin in 1870 when Hamer Radshaw, a lad in a north country slum, dedicates his life to better the lot of his fellow workers. The sword his grandfather picked up at Peterloo (1819), when soldiers cut down workers crying for 'bread and liberty', becomes his talisman and symbol.

Attractive, he becomes a grand rabble-rouser. With his sword he can incite men to their own death, all for the 'cause', and as a Labour Member of Parliament he takes the line of least resistance, shedding old friends when necessary, making new ones if they can help, as long as it all leads to glory and power.

Michael Redgrave gives a grand performance as the earnest young idealist who becomes the vain selfish politician. It is a difficult part, but he makes it wholly credible.

■ FAMILY BUSINESS

1989, 115 MINS, US ◇ ⑲ ⊙
Dir Sidney Lumet   *Prod* Lawrence Gordon   *Scr* Vincent Patrick   *Ph* Andrzej Bartkowiak   *Ed* Andrew Mondshein   *Mus* Cy Coleman   *Art Dir* Robert Guerra
● Sean Connery, Dustin Hoffman, Matthew Broderick, Rosana DeSoto, Janet Carroll, Victoria Jackson (Regency/Gordon)

Sean Connery steals scenes as well as merchandise in an immensely charismatic turn in *Family Business*, a darkly comic tale about three generations brought together and torn apart by their common attraction to thievery.

Director Sidney Lumet has crafted a film with real pathos while writer Vincent Patrick (adapting his own novel) injects enough bawdy humor to create a delightful mixed bag spiced with almost a European sensibility.

The key, however, is Connery, who dives head-first into his part as amoral family patriarch Jessie.

He's an unabashed rogue well into his 60s who, when we meet him, must be bailed out of jail after savaging an off-duty cop in a bar fight. Connery cuts an irresistible figure to his sheltered Ivy League grandson (Matthew Broderick), who enlists the old man's aid to carry out a high-tech robbery.

Caught in the middle, literally and figuratively, is the boy's father (Dustin Hoffman), who once had the same relationship with his father and ended up doing hard time for it.

■ FAMILY LIFE

1972, 105 MINS, UK ◇
Dir Ken Loach   *Prod* Tony Garnett   *Scr* David Mercer   *Ph* Charles Stewart   *Ed* Roy Watts   *Mus* Marc Wilkinson   *Art Dir* William McCrow
● Sandy Ratcliff, Bill Dean, Grace Cave, Malcolm Tierney, Alan McNaughton, Michael Riddall (Kestrel)

Director Ken Loach has succeeded in creating a disturbing and provocative film about a girl sinking into schizophrenia. David Mercer's succinct screenplay [from his TV play *In Two Minds*], Loach's probing direction and the sensitive acting ward off the pitfalls of self-consciousness, didactics and schematics.

The parents, who have made firm middle-class lives for themselves, live on their prejudices and belief in the need for curing any rebelliousness in their children. One daughter has broken away but a younger one is still at home and unable to cut loose. When she gets pregnant there is parental outrage and a carefully planned abortion. But the girl loses job after job and her growing withdrawal from life has her parents seeking psychiatric help.

Sandy Ratcliff is effective as the weak but striving girl who is finally beaten by a system and misunderstanding. Originally a TV film, it has been effectively broadened without losing its intimacy. There are long talky scenes but they're revealing and effective.

■ FAMILY PLOT

1976, 120 MINS, US ◇ ⑲ ⊙
Dir Alfred Hitchcock   *Prod* [uncredited]   *Scr* Ernest Lehman   *Ph* Leonard J. South   *Ed* J. Terry Williams   *Mus* John Williams   *Art Dir* Henry Bumstead
● Karen Black, Bruce Dern, Barbara Harris, William Devane, Ed Lauter, Cathleen Nesbitt (Universal)

Family Plot is a dazzling achievement for Alfred Hitchcock masterfully controlling shifts from comedy to drama thoughout a highly complex plot. Witty screenplay, transplanting Victor Canning's British novel, *The Rainbird Pattern*, to a California setting, is a model of construction, and the cast is uniformly superb.

Bruce Dern and Barbara Harris are the couple who receive primary attention, a cabbie and a phony psychic trying to find the long-lost heir to the Rainbird fortune.

Dern is a more than slightly absurd figure, oddly appealing; Harris is sensational.

William Devane takes a high place in the roster of Hitchcockian rogues, while Karen Black, gives a deep resonance to her relationship with the mercurial Devane.

■ FAMILY PRAYERS

1993, 108 MINS, US ◇ ⓦ ⊙
Dir Scott Rosenfelt *Prod* Mark Levinson, Bonnie Sugar
Scr Steven Ginsberg *Ph* Jeff Jur *Ed* Susan Crutcher
Mus Steve Tyrell *Art Dir* Chester Kaczenski
● Joe Mantegna, Anne Archer, Tzvi Ratner-Stauber, Patti LuPone, Allen Garfield, Paul Reiser (Sugar)

Producer Scott Rosenfelt makes his feature directorial debut with *Family Prayers*, a modest, well-intentioned coming-of-age story full of heart, if not ingenuity.

Set in Los Angeles in 1969, tale depicts the effects of the Jacobs' family breakup on their son Andrew (Tzvi Ratner-Stauber), a sensitive adolescent who becomes a victim of his parents' fights and squabbles as his father, Martin (Joe Mantegna), a compulsive gambler, promises wife Rita (Anne Archer) he'll reform, but he breaks one vow after another. Andrew's main ambition is to keep his parents together at all costs.

Far behind in studies for his upcoming bar mitzvah, he is sent by cantor (Allen Garfield) to tutor (Paul Reiser), through whom he becomes aware of the 'outside' world, specifically Vietnam.

Steve Ginsberg's writing is personal and often heartfelt, but lacks subtlety. Good acting makes up for the unsatisfying tech credits.

■ FAMILY VIEWING

1987, 86 MINS, CANADA ◇
Dir Atom Egoyan *Prod* [uncredited] *Scr* Atom Egoyan
Ph Robert Macdonald *Ed* Atom Egoyan, Bruce Macdonald *Mus* Mychael Danna *Art Dir* Linda Del Rosario
● David Hemblen, Aidan Tierney, Gabrielle Rose, Arsinee Khanjian, Selma Keklikian (Ego)

He's something of a darling to the Canadian new wave cinema, but Atom Egoyan's second feature is particularly exasperating precisely because there are streaks of filmmaking talent visible through the pretentious murk of this disjointed story about a single-minded young man and his emotionally pulverized family life.

Egoyan's film stands shakily upon a glib foundation of familiar themes. These include ruptured familial communication in an impersonal urban society, the displacement of human feelings in an age of instant sensual gratification and the subsuming of modern life to the omnipresent value systems of the video tube.

At the center of all this is college graduate Van (Aidan Tierney), who lives in a high-rise co-op with his slightly kinky father Stan (David Hemblen) and dad's provocatively flirtatious mistress Sandra (Gabrielle Rose).

The devices of home movies (in which the family lives on in its happier nuclear past) and the tiresome use of b&w TV static patterns between scenes are clever mostly in the sophomoric sense. By the time Egoyan moves to bring this affair to a hopeful resolution the actors don't seem to care very much and neither should the audience.

■ FAMILY WAY, THE

1967, 114 MINS, UK ◇ ⓦ
Dir Roy Boulting *Prod* John Boulting *Scr* Bill Naughton
Ph Harry Waxman *Ed* Ernest Hosler *Mus* Paul McCartney *Art Dir* Alan Withy
● Hayley Mills, Avril Angers, John Comer, Hywel Bennett, John Mills, Wilfred Pickles (British Lion)

Based on Bill Naughton's warm-hearted play, *All in Good Time*, and adapted by Roy Boulting and Jeffrey Dell, film is the story of an innocent young couple who marry and are unable to consummate their marriage.

The youngsters (Hayley Mills and Hywel Bennett) marry and because of circumstances have to live with the lad's parents. Even the honeymoon is a disaster since a flyaway travel agent cheats them out of their package deal trip to the Continent.

Hayley Mills gets away from her Disney image as the young bride, even essaying an undressed scene. Bennett is excellent as the sensitive young bridegroom. But it is the older hands who keep the film floating on a wave of fun, sentiment and sympathy.

John Mills is firstclass in a character role as the bluff father who cannot understand his son and produces the lower working-class man's vulgarity without overdoing it. Avril Angers as the girl's acid mother and John Comer as her husband are equally effective, but the best performance comes from Marjorie Rhodes as John Mills' astute but understanding wife.

■ FAN, THE

1949, 79 MINS, US C
Dir Otto Preminger *Prod* Otto Preminger *Scr* Walter Reisch, Dorothy Parker, Ross Evans *Ph* Joseph LaShelle
Ed Louis Loeffler *Mus* Daniele Amfitheatrof
● Jeanne Crain, Madeleine Carroll, George Sanders, Richard Greene, Martita Hunt (20th Century-Fox)

Screen adaptation [from Oscar Wilde's *Lady Windermere's Fan*] is refreshing and neatly uses the flashback technique in telling the 19th-century narrative.

Yarn of the attractive mother who moves in English society so as to be near her married daughter is deftly told. It shows her trying to prevent the daughter from making the same elopement mistake that she herself made only to become one of the most notorious women in Europe.

Madeleine Carroll makes of the young, attractive mother a vivid personality, a woman sought by wealth and nobility in nearly every European capital. Only when pictured as an elderly woman (in postwar London) does she seem a bit unconvincing. George Sanders, as her ardent lover, contributes a believable characterization. Jeanne Crain, as Lady Windermere, achieves further acting laurels.

■ FAN, THE

1981, 95 MINS, US ◇ ⓦ ⊙
Dir Edward Bianchi *Prod* Robert Stigwood *Scr* Priscilla Chapman, John Hartwell *Ph* Dick Bush *Ed* Alan Helm
Mus Pino Donaggio *Art Dir* Santo Loquasto
● Lauren Bacall, James Garner, Maureen Stapleton, Michael Biehn, Hector Elizondo, Anna Maria Horsford (Paramount)

Lauren Bacall makes the film [from a novel by Bob Randall] work with a solid performance as a stage star pursued by a pyschotic fan whose adoration turns to hatred. To be sure, the part doesn't test the broadest range of Bacall's abilities, but she and director Edward Bianchi achieve the essential element: they make the audience care what happens to her.

In his first major feature, TV commercials veteran Michael Biehn contributes solidly toward the picture's believability, gradually transforming his character's fantasies into a deadly delusion. The more his performance is acceptable, the more perilous is Bacall's plight.

Maureen Stapleton is also necessarily sympathetic as Bacall's likable secretary who stands between Biehn and what he perceives as true romance, setting herself up as his first victim.

James Garner is given less to do as Bacall's ex-husband, whom she still loves. Mainly, he's limited to standing around for moral support.

■ FANATIC

(US: Die! Die! My Darling!)

1965, 97 MINS, UK ◇ ⓦ
Dir Silvio Narizzano *Scr* Richard Matheson *Ph* Arthur Ibbetson *Ed* James Needs *Mus* Wilfred Josephs

● Tallulah Bankhead, Stefanie Powers, Peter Vaughan, Maurice Kaufmann, Yootha Joyce, Donald Sutherland (Hammer)

Melodramatic script by Richard Matheson echoes with cliches from other stories set in sinister mansions in English countryside. But it provides Tallulah Bankhead with numerous chances to display virtuosity, from sweet-tongued menace to maniacal blood-lust, as religious-fanatic mother of Stefanie Powers' dead fiance.

Another standout in small cast is Peter Vaughan, ne'er-do-well major domo of manse, who has roving eye for Powers' trim figure and shapely legs, which are in sharp contrast to drabness of his housekeeper-wife, well-played by Yootha Joyce.

Story line has Powers, modern miss, paying courtesy call to former fiance's mother, only to be held prisoner while the mother tries to cleanse her soul so she will be fit to meet the son in the hereafter. Escape attempts are violently thwarted by Vaughan, Joyce and Donald Sutherland, who gives vivid portrayal of giant halfwit.

■ FANDANGO

1985, 91 MINS, US ◇ ⓦ
Dir Kevin Reynolds *Prod* Tim Zinnemann *Scr* Kevin Reynolds *Ph* Thomas Del Ruth *Ed* Arthur Schmidt, Stephen Semel *Mus* Alan Silvestri *Art Dir* Peter Landsdown Smith
● Kevin Costner, Judd Nelson, Sam Robards, Chuck Bush, Brian Cesak, Marvin J. McIntyre (Amblin/Warner)

Fandango emerges as a quite promising feature debut by writer-director Kevin Reynolds, with its feet squarely within the overused boys-coming-of-age genre but its heart betraying an appealingly anarchic, iconoclastic bent.

Pic is an elaboration upon *Proof*, a 22-minute picture Reynolds made at the USC Cinema School. Set in 1971, when the Vietnam War and the draft were still looming factors in students' lives, tale describes the final wild fling, or fandango, of five college roommates in Texas before splitting up to face the dreaded realities of the world at large.

Kevin Costner plays the ringleader, a reckless but knowing adventurer who has extended his college stay by three years. Judd Nelson is the outcast of the group by virtue of his involvement in ROTC, Sam Robards has drunkenly called off his wedding to Costner's former flame at the last moment, Chuck Bush is a hulking, silent giant given to reading Jean-Paul Sartre and Kahlil Gibran, while Brian Cesak remains a drunken package just along for the ride.

Despite the mildly rueful tone, pic's highlight is the comic mid-section dominated by hippie pilot and certifiable space cadet Marvin J. McIntyre. Costner, who previously starred in *Stacey's Knights* but was a cutting room floor casualty in both *The Big Chill* and *Frances*, is a dynamic presence at the film's center.

■ FANNY

1961, 133 MINS, US ◇ ⓦ
Dir Joshua Logan *Prod* Joshua Logan *Scr* Julius J. Epstein *Ph* Jack Cardiff *Ed* William H. Reynolds
Mus Harold Rome *Art Dir* Rino Mondellini
● Leslie Caron, Maurice Chevalier, Charles Boyer, Horst Buchholz, Salvatore Baccaloni, Lionel Jeffries (Warner)

Marcel Pagnol's enduring creation has a peculiar history. Center of a trilogy (*Marius*, *Fanny* and *Cesar*) penned around the early 1930s, it graduated from stage to screen in 1933 French film versions that, sans English titles, died after a week's exhibition in a New York theatre. Refurbished with titles and an additional 25 minutes in 1948, it became an unforgettable motion picture and an art house click. Earlier, in 1938, Metro produced a film (a Wallace Beery starrer titled *Port of the Seven Seas*) based on the Pagnol yarn. Then, of course, there was the Broadway musical version in 1956.

Although the deep sentiment in Pagnol's tale constantly threatens to lapse into maudlinity in this film, it never quite does. Pagnol's story, skillfully adapted out of the original Marseilles Trilogy and the legit book by S. N. Behrman and Joshua Logan, focuses upon four people: a thrifty waterfront bar operator (Charles Boyer); his son (Horst Buchholz), who has a yen to sail away to the 'isles beneath the wind'; a fishmonger's daughter (Leslie Caron) in love with the wanderlustful lad; and an aging, wealthy widower (Maurice Chevalier), whose great wish is to add '& Son' to the sign above his shop.

The contribution of cameraman Jack Cardiff is enormous, ranging from great, sweeping panoramic views of the port of Marseilles and the sea to tight, intimate shots of the faces of the principals. Caron employs that Gallic gamin quality to full advantage again, Buchholz does a nice job as Marius, but a couple of old pros named Boyer and Chevalier walk off with the picture.

☐ 1961: Nominations: Best Picture, Actor (Charles Boyer), Color Cinematography, Editing, Score of a Dramatic Picture

....

■ **FANNY BY GASLIGHT**
(US: Man of Evil)

1944, 108 MINS, UK ⓥ
Dir Anthony Asquith   *Prod* Edward Black   *Scr* Doreen Montgomery   *Ph* Arthur Crabtree   *Ed* R.E. Dearing   *Mus* Cedric Mallabey   *Art Dir* John Bryan
● Phyllis Calvert, James Mason, Wilfrid Lawson, Stewart Granger, Jean Kent, Nora Swinburne (Gainsborough)

Unfortunately, Anthony Asquith's direction is hurt by faulty film editing and irritatingly slow tempo. Although the script distorts the original story almost beyond recognition, there is still retained a lot of plot development in the house of ill-fame, which in the book is the main background. For all its being toned down from Michael Sadleir's frank treatment in the novel, the way the curvaceous femmes do their stuff in the underground joint hardly makes for best family trade.

As a matter of fact, the film would suffer little if all the bawdy-house sequences were removed. The main theme – the thorny path traveled by the true lovers because the man is 'well born' while the girl is an illegitimate child, foster-fathered by the bawdy housekeeper – would be preserved by the mid-Victorian pillorying they both receive.

With so many good performances, it is significant that Phyllis Calvert in the lead more than holds her own. She succeeds in portraying Fanny with girlish wistfulness and appeal.

....

■ **FANTASIA**

1940, 120 MINS, US ◇ ⓥ ⊙
Dir Ben Sharpsteen (sup.)   *Prod* Walt Disney   *Scr* Joe Grant, Dick Huemer   *Ed* Stephen Csillag   *Mus* Edward H. Plumb (dir.)   (Walt Disney)

In *Fantasia* Walt Disney enlists the assistance of Leopold Stokowski, the Philadelphia Symphony Orchestra, and Deems Taylor as screen commentator. The result of mixing all these ingredients, including his own unique approach to things theatrical, is a two-hour $2 million-plus variety show, which spans the formidable entertainment categories ranging from a Mickey Mouse escapade in the title role of Dukas' *The Sorcerer's Apprentice* to a very lovely musical and visual interpretation of Schubert's *Ave Maria*.

The first offering [directed by Samuel Armstrong] is a flight of sheer fancy on the part of the Disney illustrators. The Bach number, *Toccata and Fugue in D Minor*, is nine minutes of pictorial kaleidoscope, in the course of which various gay and bizarre representations of musical instruments are flashed in grotesque shapes across the screen.

The familiar Tchaikovsky *Nutcracker Suite* [directed by Armstrong] is the second offering, somewhat longer, as it runs 14 minutes. Pictorially, it is a series of charming ballets, the leading and supporting characters of which are flowers, fish and fairies that cavort in whimsical surroundings.

Comes Mickey next as the mischievous apprentice in the Dukas number [directed by James Algar], in the telling of which he becomes highly and humorously involved with a broomstick.

First part closes with Stravinsky's *Rite of Spring* [directed by Bill Roberts and Paul Satterfield], the most ambitious number on the program and a 20-minute gasp for breath. Here is visualized the birth of creation, the heavenly nebulae and the placement of the solar system in the universe.

Reserved for the second part are the Beethoven *Pastoral Symphony* and Ponchielli's *Dance of the Hours*. Former is a mythological allegory, employing Zeus and others on Mt Olympus. Hamilton Luske, Jim Handley and Ford Beebe supervised the execution which is one of the loveliest tales from the Disney plant. In contrast, the studio tackles the *Dance of the Hours* [directed by T. Hee and Norm Ferguson] in a facetious mood, burlesquing and satirizing the ballet traditions. Among the dancers are elephants, rhinos and ostriches.

Concluding film [directed by Wilfred Jackson] is a combination of Moussorgsky's *Night on Bald Mountain*, a terryifying exposition on evil, and the compensating *Ave Maria*, charmingly sung by Julietta Novis with appropriate decor.

☐ 1941: Special Awards (use of sound, creation of a new form of visualized music)

....

■ **FANTASTIC VOYAGE**

1966, 100 MINS, US ◇ ⓥ ⊙
Dir Richard Fleischer   *Prod* Saul David   *Scr* Harry Kleiner   *Ph* Ernest Laszlo   *Ed* William B. Murphy   *Mus* Leonard Rosenman   *Art Dir* Jack Martin Smith, Dale Hennesy
● Stephen Boyd, Raquel Welch, Edmond O'Brien, Donald Pleasence, Arthur O'Connell, Arthur Kennedy (20th Century-Fox)

Fantastic Voyage is just that. The lavish production, boasting some brilliant special effects and superior creative efforts, is an entertaining, enlightening excursion through inner space – the body of a man.

The original Otto Klement-Jay Lewis Bixby story, adapted by David Duncan, has been updated and fashioned into an intriguing yarn about five people who undergo miniaturization For injection into the bloodstream of a scientist.

Action cross cuts from lifesize medics to the shrunken quintet who encounter, and are endangered by, the miracles of life.

The competent cast is headed by Stephen Boyd, the US agent who has brought scientist Jean Del Val to America, only to have a last-ditch attempt on latter's life cause the blood clot which necessitates the weird journey to come. Boyd is assigned to join the expedition under the command of Donald Pleasence, a medical specialist in circulatory systems, thus qualifying him as navigator for William Redfield's sub.

Richard Fleischer's fine direction maintains a zesty pace. Ernest Laszlo's outstanding lensing brings out every lush facet in the superb production values. Over half of the $6.5 million cost went into the special values.

☐ 1966: Best Color Art Direction, Special Visual Effects
☐ Nominations: Best Color Cinematographer, Editing, Sound Effects

....

■ **FAR AND AWAY**

1992, 140 MINS, US ◇ ⓥ ⊙
Dir Ron Howard   *Prod* Brian Grazer, Ron Howard   *Scr* Bob Dolman   *Ph* Mikael Salomon   *Ed* Michael Hill, Daniel Hanley   *Mus* John Williams   *Art Dir* Jack T. Collis, Allan Cameron
● Tom Cruise, Nicole Kidman, Thomas Gibson, Robert Prosky, Barbara Babcock, Eileen Pollock (Universal/Imagine)

Old-fashioned is the word for *Far and Away*, a time-worn tale [by Bob Dolman and Ron Howard] of 19th-century immigrants making their way in the New World. Handsomely mounted and amiably performed, but leisurely and without much dramatic urgency, Howard's robust epic stars Tom Cruise and Nicole Kidman as class-crossed lovers who take nearly the entire picture to get together.

Pic is notable as the first narrative, non-effects-oriented Hollywood feature in more than two decades to have been shot on 65mm stock (with Panavision's new Super 70 equipment), and released in 70mm.

Cruise is Joseph, a tenant farmer in Western Ireland, circa 1892, who wants to kill his absentee landlord for torching the family home and, in effect, murdering his father.

In fact, just about every character here insists they are oppressed. Landlord's (Robert Prosky) pampered, spirited daughter Shannon (Kidman) is kept on the tightest of leashes by her mother (Barbara Babcock), and is constantly badgered by her darkly handsome suitor (Thomas Gibson). Joseph makes off with Shannon for the States, arriving in Boston (actually streets of Dublin nicely redressed). However, the land still beckons, and by the next year all the characters find themselves in the epochal Oklahoma land rush.

Cruise's physicality is forcibly in evidence, which will not be unwelcome to his many fans. Stripped down frequently, he is genuinely impressive in the fisticuff action of pic's midsection. Heavily garbed, Kidman has the requisite grit and defiant spirit in her eyes.

....

■ **FAR COUNTRY, THE**

1955, 96 MINS, US ◇ ⓥ
Dir Anthony Mann   *Prod* Aaron Rosenberg   *Scr* Borden Chase   *Ph* William Daniels   *Ed* Russell Schoengarth   *Mus* Joseph Gershenson (dir.)   *Art Dir* Bernard Herzbrun, Alexander Golitzen
● James Stewart, Ruth Roman, Corinne Calvet, Walter Brennan, John McIntire, Jay C. Flippen (Universal)

Rugged action is featured in *The Far Country* to go with its rugged outdoor scenery, and the results add up to film entertainment. Pic marks the fifth successful combination of James Stewart, as star, Aaron Rosenberg as producer, and Anthony Mann as director.

Cast and crew locationed around the Columbia Ice Fields and in Jasper Park to get the chilly atmosphere to go with a story of the far north, set back in the pioneer days [1896] when gold was luring adventurous souls to the snow country. The location areas in Canada provide the film with a good backstop for the Borden Chase outdoor action plot.

Stewart arrives in this setting driving a herd of cattle, which he and his partner (Walter Brennan) figure to unload at fancy prices in the gold-crazy country around Skagway and Dawson. The partners are in trouble almost immediately, because Skagway's self-styled law (John McIntire) tries to commandeer the herd before it can be driven to Dawson.

F

Stewart and Brennan are completely at home in this type of film and handle their characters with the expected ease. The distaff stars, saloon keeper Ruth Roman and Corinne Calvet, a gold fields girl who gets Stewart at the finale, add quite a bit to the entertainment values.

....

■ **FAREWELL, MY LOVELY**

See: Murder, My Sweet

....

■ **FAREWELL, MY LOVELY**

1975, 97 MINS, US ◇ ⓥ
Dir Dick Richards   *Prod* George Pappas, Jerry Bruckheimer   *Scr* David Zelag Goodman   *Ph* John A. Alonzo   *Ed* Walter Thompson, Joel Cox   *Mus* David Shire   *Art Dir* Dean Tavoularis
● Robert Mitchum, Charlotte Rampling, John Ireland, Sylvia Miles, Jack O'Halloran, Anthony Zerbe (EK-ITC)

Farewell, My Lovely is a lethargic, vaguely campy tribute to Hollywood's private eye mellers of the 1940s and to writer Raymond Chandler, whose Phillip Marlowe character has inspired a number of features.

Despite an impressive production and some firstrate performances, this third version fails to generate much suspense or excitement.

The plot has the cynical but humane Marlowe (Robert Mitchum) searching in seedy LA for the missing girl friend of an ex-con. After a number of false leads and predictable murders, Marlowe winds up on a gambling ship for the final confrontation, shoot-out and body count.

Mitchum, who might appear a natural for the Marlowe role, seems a bit adrift here, underplaying to the point of inertia. Remainder of cast makes effective use of smaller roles.
☐ 1975: Nomination: Best Supp. Actress (Sylvia Miles)

....

■ **FAREWELL TO ARMS, A**

1932, 90 MINS, US ⓥ ⊙
Dir Frank Borzage   *Prod* Frank Borzage   *Scr* Benjamin Glazer, Oliver H. P. Garrett   *Ph* Charles Lang   *Ed* Otho Lovering   *Art Dir* Hans Dreier, Roland Anderson
● Gary Cooper, Helen Hayes, Adolphe Menjou, Mary Phillips, Jack La Rue, Henry Armetta (Paramount)

A Farewell to Arms is a corking flicker [from the novel by Ernest Hemingway]. Director Frank Borzage skims over two hyper-delicate situations with deftness and ingenuity. He makes wholly palatable (and highly believable) the premise that a fleeting one hour's meeting behind the front with the resulting seduction (Gary Cooper and Helen Hayes) is the culmination of a love which, in another sphere, would have followed only a long span of courtship and flowers.

Equally acute is the hospital situation where she, as one of the nurses, violates every regulation and remains with the convalescent Cooper in his room.

All this builds up to the finale where Cooper deserts his regiment, to brave frontiers and sentinels to ultimately reach the woman.

Casting Hayes as Catherine Barkley was a natural. Cooper and Adolphe Menjou are aces in the two other major roles. Menjou's suave Italian Major Rinaldi becomes distinguished more through personal histrionics than the script's generosities. Cooper's sincerity as the enlisted American lieut attached to the Italian army, who abjures the dashing Rinaldi's penchant of patronizing joy palaces, once the romance sequences get under way, is consistently impressive in a none too easy assignment.
☐ 1932/33: Best Cinematography, Sound Recording.
☐ Nominations: Best Picture, Art Direction

....

■ **FAREWELL TO ARMS, A**

1957, 159 MINS, US ◇ ⓥ
Dir Charles Vidor   *Prod* David O. Selznick   *Scr* Ben Hecht   *Ph* Piero Portalupi, Oswald Morris   *Ed* James E. Newcom, Gerard J. Wilson, John M. Foley   *Mus* Mario Nascimbene   *Art Dir* Alfred Junge
● Rock Hudson, Jennifer Jones, Vittorio De Sica, Alberto Sordi, Kurt Kasznar, Mercedes McCambridge (20th Century-Fox)

New version of the Ernest Hemingway World War I story conveys some of the Hemingway spirit that speaks of the futility of war and a desperate love that grips two strangers in its midst. But sweep and frankness alone don't make a great picture; and *Farewell* suffers from an overdose of both.

Producer David O. Selznick and director Charles Vidor, shooting all of the film in Italy and a good part of it on location in the Dolomites, have concentrated heavily on nature and war. It's the more unfortunate that Ben Hecht's often mature dialog is also riddled with cliches, and that the relationship between Rock Hudson and Jennifer Jones never takes on real dimensions.

Story, briefly, has American Red Cross ambulance driver Hudson meeting up with nurse Jones and falling violently in love with her. When he's wounded on the front, he's brought back to the hospital, where she joins him. Their protracted affair ends when he's sent back to the front where he's caught up in the disastrous retreat from Caporetto.

Such a tragic story requires great performances to put it across. It gets only a few of them in this picture.

In the supporting roles, Selznick has cast a group of very good actors. Vittorio De Sica plays the cynical Major Rinaldi with dash, and in him the Hemingway spirit comes alive with full force.
☐ 1957: Nomination: Best Supp. Actor (Vittorio De Sica)

....

■ **FAREWELL TO THE KING**

1989, 117 MINS, US ◇ ⓥ ⊙
Dir John Milius   *Prod* Albert S. Ruddy, Andre Morgan   *Scr* John Milius   *Ph* Dean Semler   *Ed* John W. Wheeler, C. Timothy O'Meara, Anne V. Coates   *Mus* Basil Poledouris   *Art Dir* Gil Parrondo
● Nick Nolte, Nigel Havers, James Fox, Marilyn Tokuda, Frank McRae, Marius Weyers (Vestron)

The cliches are as thick as the foliage in *Farewell to the King*, John Milius' adaptation of a novel [*L'adieu au roi*] by French author-filmmaker Pierre Schoendoerffer. Pic recycles familiar situations and stock characters in an overlong actioner that never builds to a spiritual climax.

Two British army officers (Nigel Havers and Frank McRae) are parachuted into the Borneo jungle to rally the tribes against imminent Japanese invasion in the latter days of World War II. They come across a virile and fulfilled Nick Nolte, playing a freedom-loving white man who's anxious to protect his natives from the barbarities of civilization.

Nolte, however, needs no further prompting to fight when the Japanese slaughter his own family. Hitting the Rambo warpath, the ex-Yank sergeant (who deserted after General MacArthur's defeat at Corregidor) performs a ruthless clean-up operation.

Nolte, in a purely exterior performance, never rises to the nobility and tragic majesty the at-first skeptical British officers finally see in him. Havers is a sympathetic presence in an equally empty role. Other performers, including James Fox as Havers' commanding officer, are treated as trite thumbnail portraits.

....

■ **FAR FROM THE MADDING CROWD**

1967, 169 MINS, UK ◇ ⓥ ⊙
Dir John Schlesinger   *Prod* Joseph Janni   *Scr* Frederic Raphael   *Ph* Nicolas Roeg   *Ed* Malcolm Cooke   *Mus* Richard Rodney Bennett   *Art Dir* Richard MacDonald
● Julie Christie, Terence Stamp, Peter Finch, Alan Bates, Prunella Ransome, Fiona Walker (M-G-M)

Literary classics or semi-classics traditionally provide pitfalls in adaptation, and faithfulness can often prove a double-edged sword.

In this case, scripter Frederic Raphael has perhaps hewn too closely to Thomas Hardy's original. Thus he has allowed director John Schlesinger only occasional – and principally mechanical – chances to forge his own film.

It is the story of Bathsheba Everdene's multifaceted love for the three men in her life, Sergeant Troy, Gabriel Oak and Boldwood. Julie Christie, Peter Finch, Terence Stamp and Alan Bates are variedly handsome and have their many effective moments, but there is little they can ultimately and lastingly do to overcome the basic banality of their characters and, to a certain degree, their lines.

Christie has few real opportunities to branch out of her rather muted and pouty lead. Finch struggles manfully against his role as Boldwood, but never really defeats it by convincing one. Stamp is the cocky, sneering Sergeant to the part born, but there's nary a glint of anything more. Nor does Bates have more of a chance as the ever-reliable Oak.
☐ 1967: Nomination: Best Original Music Score

....

■ **FARMER'S DAUGHTER, THE**

1947, 90 MINS, US ⓥ
Dir H.C. Potter   *Prod* Dore Schary   *Scr* Allen Rivkin, Laura Kerr   *Ph* Milton Krasner   *Ed* Harry Marker   *Mus* Leigh Harline   *Art Dir* Albert S. D'Agostino, Feild Gray
● Loretta Young, Joseph Cotten, Ethel Barrymore, Charles Bickford, Harry Davenport, Lex Barker (RKO)

The Farmer's Daughter [based on a Finnish play by Juhni Tervataa] rolls irresistibly along in a light romantic comedy groove. One of the pic's chief assets is the political tilt given to the story line which, with its rapidly glossed over liberal democratic shibboleths, will give patrons a right-minded feeling in their hearts without disturbing their brain too much.

Loretta Young plays a Swedish country girl, complete with accent and rural garb who, upon coming to the big city, lands a second maid's job in the mansion of Joseph Cotten and his mother, Ethel Barrymore. Latter pair are well-intentioned leaders of the local political machine which is embroiled in a hot fight with the opposition over the election of a Congressman.

The country lass, being naive and frank as well as an eyeful for Cotten, openly voices her disapproval of the compromise candidate chosen by her employers and heckles him at the nominating rally.

Although politicking is used only as a once-lightly-over excuse for the romantic bickerings and final clinch, director H.C. Potter slips in a few satirical barbs against the sacrosanct political practice of blarney and buncombe.

Difficulty with the Swedish accent, which occasionally collapses into straight Americanese, is the only flaw in Young's performance.
☐ 1947: Best Actress (Loretta Young)
☐ Nomination: Best Supp. Actor (Charles Bickford)

....

■ **FARMER TAKES A WIFE, THE**

1935, 91 MINS, US ⓥ
Dir Victor Fleming   *Prod* Winfield R. Sheehan   *Scr* Edwin Burke   *Ed* Harold Schuster   *Mus* Oscar Bradley (dir.)

● Janet Gaynor, Henry Fonda, Charles Bickford, Slim Summerville, Andy Devine, Margaret Hamilton (Fox)

Too thin a plot trying to cover entirely too much area is a handicap to this screen adaptation of Walter Edmonds' novel *Rome Haul* [and the play by Frank B. Elser and Marc Connelly], of the Erie canal.

The plot proper is very simple. Molly (Janet Gaynor), cook on a canal boat, and bred in the belief that physical prowess is the only thing that counts and that all farmers are cravens, falls in love with Dan Harrow (Henry Fonda), who is driving a canal team to earn the money for the purchase of a farm.

Gaynor is given a part which permits her to get away from her sometimes too sweet assignments. She's a forthright young woman in this, and she plays the part extremely well. Fonda, as the farmer, is youthfully manly and shows nice personality, but he is made to dress as no York state farmer or canaler ever did. Charles Bickford, on the other hand, looks like the men who used to string along the Erie and the Champlain canals. Slim Summerville, out of his usual type of part, plays smoothly and with effect as a driver.

■ FARMER TAKES A WIFE, THE

1953, 80 MINS, US ◇ ▼

Dir Henry Levin   *Prod* Frank P. Rosenberg   *Scr* Walter Bullock, Sally Benson, Joseph Fields   *Ph* Arthur E. Arling   *Ed* Louis Loeffler   *Mus* Lionel Newman   *Art Dir* Lyle R. Wheeler, Addison Hehr
● Betty Grable, Dale Robertson, Thelma Ritter, John Carroll, Eddie Foy Jr (20th Century-Fox)

The Farmer Takes a Wife was first screened in 1935 as a straight drama, the same as it was on the stage, and it doesn't take smoothly to the injection of songs (by Harold Arlen-Dorothy Fields) and dances, probably because the tuning is unimpressive and the terp numbers are lacking in bounce.

The production tells the story of a farm boy who takes a job on the Erie Canal to save money for a farm, meets a barge cook, falls in love, and returns with her to the soil when the railroad puts the canal out of business. Henry Levin's direction hasn't much to work with in the screenplay [from the play by Frank B. Elser and Marc Connelly, based on the novel *Rome Haul* by Walter D. Edmonds] and he fails to add any punch that would keep up interest in the unfoldment.

Grable takes prettily to the Technicolor hues and the period costuming, latter being rather fancy for a canal boat cook. As the farmer turned boatman, Robertson is okay, but is out of his element in picture's musical requirements, light as they are. Carroll is asked to do little but bluster through his role of a rival boatman.

■ FAR NORTH

1988, 90 MINS, US ◇ ▼ ⊙

Dir Sam Shepard   *Prod* Carolyn Pfeiffer, Malcolm Harding   *Scr* Sam Shepard   *Ph* Robbie Greenberg   *Ed* Bill Yahraus   *Mus* The Red Clay Ramblers   *Art Dir* Peter Jamison
● Jessica Lange, Charles Durning, Tess Harper, Donald Moffat, Ann Wedgeworth, Patricia Arquette (Alive/Nelson)

In his film directing debut, Sam Shepard forsakes the fevered elliptical prose flights of his plays, for a straightforward approach of surprising flatness and sentimentality that never gets airborne in this conventional tale of a Minnesota farm family coming to terms with its past and present in a time of accelerating change.

Bertrum (Charles Durning), a veteran of two wars and the railroad, is thrown from a cart by his rebellious runaway horse, and lands in the hospital obsessed with exacting revenge from the nag. His citified, unmarried pregnant daughter Kate (Jessica Lange) flies out from New York to comfort the curmudgeon in his crisis.

In what's meant to be taken as a profound gesture of filial obeisance, Lange reluctantly agrees to assassinate the horse. This mystifies Lange's slightly dotty mom (Ann Wedgeworth) and outrages her fiery farm-bound sister Rita (Tess Harper).

Adding to the emotional fireworks in this world without men is the post-pubescent defiance of Harper's daughter Jilly (Patricia Arquette), who plays fast and loose with the local boys for amusement in this nowhere town.

This loving but fractious litle family is intended by Shepard to represent the dislocation of fundamental American values in the socially vertiginous 1980s.

■ FAST AND LOOSE

1930, 70 MINS, US

Dir Fred Newmeyer   *Scr* Doris Anderson, Jack Kirkland, Preston Sturges   *Ph* William Steiner
● Miriam Hopkins, Carole Lombard, Frank Morgan, Charles Starrett, Henry Wadsworth, Winifred Harris (Paramount)

A frothy bit of celluloid [from the play *The Best People* by Avery Hopwood and David Gray]. It is Miriam Hopkins' first picture. The stage artiste plays tick-tack-toe with the camera, sometimes winning, sometimes losing.

Cast principals are almost entirely from the stage, with Charles Starrett opposite Hopkins and Frank Morgan playing the financier father. Carole Lombard is the only name.

Hopkins is engaged to a theatric silly-ass and titled Englishman, while Henry Wadsworth is in love with an on-the-level chorus girl (Lombard). Hopkins seeks an out on her prospective marriage for a title and grasps her chance when accidentally meeting Charles Starrett. Later discovery that he's merely a garage mechanic enhances the romance for her, and it's a grand mixup when the entire family meets in a roadhouse raid.

The direction and the players hold the much-used script together.

■ FASTER, PUSSYCAT! KILL! KILL!

1966, 84 MINS, US ▼

Dir Russ Meyer   *Prod* Russ Meyer, Eve Meyer   *Scr* Jack Moran   *Ph* Walter Schenk   *Ed* Russ Meyer   *Mus* Paul Sawtell, Bert Shefter   *Art Dir* [uncredited]
● Tura Satana, Haji, Lori Williams, Susan Bernard, Stuart Lancaster, Paul Trinka (Eve)

Faster, Pussycat! Kill! Kill! is a somewhat sordid, quite sexy and very violent murder-kidnap-theft meller which includes elements of rape, lesbianism and sadism, clothed in faddish leather and boots and equipped with sports cars. Some good performances emerge from a one-note script via very good Russ Meyer direction and his outstanding editing. It was brought in at $44,000 and uses California desert exteriors throughout.

Jack Moran's story concerns a trio of bosomy swingers led by Tura Satana, her female lover Haji, and his ambiSEXtrous Lori Williams. Out for kicks, Satana does in Ray Barlow via explicit karate, then kidnaps latter's chick, a petite Susan Bernard. Greed takes them to crippled widower Stuart Lancaster's desert diggings, where he dominates his retarded, but muscular son, Dennis Busch, also Paul Trinka, a more sensitive offspring.

It is obvious that Meyer has a directorial talent which belongs in bigger and stronger films. His visual sense is outstanding, also his setups (executed by Walter Schenk's crisp camera). Meyer's editing has a zest and polish which, without being obvious post-production gimmickry, lends proper pace and emphasis. All he needs is stronger scripting and more adept performers.

■ FAST LADY, THE

1963, 95 MINS, UK ◇

Dir Ken Annakin   *Prod* Julian Wintle, Leslie Parkyn   *Scr* Jack Davies, Henry Blyth   *Ph* Reg Wyer   *Ed* Ralph Sheldon   *Mus* Norrie Paramor
● James Robertson Justice, Stanley Baxter, Leslie Phillips, Kathleen Harrison, Julie Christie, Eric Barker (Rank)

A thin idea is pumped up into a reasonably brisk, amusing situation comedy, which is helped by a cast of experienced farceurs. In dialog, the pic is short on wit but there is enough slapstick fun. Star of the film is an impressive vintage Bentley auto.

Film concerns the efforts of an obstinate, over patriotic and gauche young Scottish civil servant to learn to drive the Bentley sports car and thus ingratiate himself with the tycoon father of a girl for whom he has fallen. Much of the humor is of the prattfall variety but it provides predictable, easy yocks.

Mainly the comedy situations are short and often fairly unrelated. Most hilarious, thanks to a gem of a performance by Eric Barker, is the first driving test taken by the wouldbe driver (Stanley Baxter).

James Robertson Justice, as the gruff tycoon, who is not as tough as he makes out, has a custom-made part while Baxter, as the shy Scot, and Leslie Phillips, playing a typical role as a wolfish car salesman, are good.

Julie Christie looks cute, but lacks the experience to build up a frail role as the love interest.

■ FAST-WALKING

1982, 115 MINS, US ◇ ▼

Dir James B. Harris   *Prod* James B. Harris   *Scr* James B. Harris   *Ph* King Baggot   *Ed* Douglas Stewart   *Mus* Lalo Schifrin   *Art Dir* Richard Haman
● James Woods, Tim McIntire, Kay Lenz, Robert Hooks, M. Emmet Walsh, Timothy Agoglia Carey (Pickman)

A prison drama which focuses on guards rather than prisoners and which reeks of a sort of late-1960s, counter-culture existentialism, pic seems oddly out of time and place. Producer-director-writer James B. Harris, hasn't really pulled it all together into a meaningful finished work.

James Woods plays 'Fast-Walking' Miniver, a self-described redneck with little on his mind, who smokes dope even on his job as a prison guard. On the side he drums up business for small-time madam Susan Tyrrell. In due course, Woods becomes involved in two interconnecting plots brewing within the penitentiary walls. First, being engineered by his weird cousin Tim McIntire, involves the assassination of a newly-arrived Black militant (Robert Hooks), while the other is a competing scheme to spring Hooks.

He becomes at the same time implicated in McIntire's affairs when he takes up with his g.f. Kay Lenz, and in the blacks' plot by the promise of $50,000 once Hooks escapes. It's a dirty, no-good world, to be sure.

Woods is always interesting to watch, even if his character suffers most from not growing in the course of the drama. In a very strange part, McIntire again proves he's a commanding, offbeat actor, too little seen.

■ FATAL ATTRACTION

1987, 119 MINS, US ◇ ▼ ⊙

Dir Adrian Lyne   *Prod* Stanley R. Jaffe, Sherry Lansing   *Scr* James Dearden   *Ph* Howard Atherton   *Ed* Michael Kahn, Peter E. Berger   *Mus* Maurice Jarre   *Art Dir* Mel Bourne
● Michael Douglas, Glenn Close, Anne Archer, Fred Gwynne, Mike Nussbaum, Stuart Pankin (Paramount)

F

The screws are tightened expertly in this suspenseful meller about a flipped-out femme who makes life hell for the married man who scorns her.

New York attorney Michael Douglas is happily married to the gorgeous Anne Archer and has a lovely daughter, but succumbs to Glenn Close's provocative flirtations while his wife is out of town.

It appears that these two sophisticated adults are in it just for fun and sport, but when Close slits her wrists in despair over the end of the affair, Douglas knows he's taken on more of a burden than he bargained for.

Douglas, in a family man role, seems warmer and more sympathetic than before, and well conveys the evasiveness and anguish of his cornered character. Close throws herself into the physical abandon of the early reels with surprising relish, and become genuinely frightening when it comes clear she is capable of anything.

Unusual credit to James Dearden for his (very good) screenplay 'based on his original screenplay' stems from the fact that pic is based on Dearden's 45-minute film *Diversion*, which he wrote and directed in 1979.

[Pic's original preview version, in which Close commits suicide using a knife with Douglas' fingerprints on it, played theatrically in Japan and later on French TV, and was released on video in 1992.]

☐ 1987: Nominations: Best Picture, Director, Actress (Glenn Close), Supp. Actress (Anne Archer), Adapted Screenplay, Editing

■ **FAT CITY**

1972, 100 MINS, US ◇ ⓥ
Dir John Huston   *Prod* Ray Stark   *Scr* Leonard Gardner   *Ph* Conrad Hall   *Ed* Margaret Booth   *Mus* Marvin Hamlisch (sup.)   *Art Dir* Richard Sylbert
● Stacy Keach, Jeff Bridges, Susan Tyrrell, Candy Clark, Nicholas Colasanto, Art Aragon (Rastar/Columbia)

John Huston has a terse, sharp, downbeat but compassionate look at the underside of small-town American life in the west, actually in central California in the town of Stockton.

It is about boxing, about failures, about part-time agricultural workers, but really about those who, in defeat, still have meaning. The allusion stems from the old American dream of another chance, a reward for trying and for triumph in competition. Huston has been blessed by a brilliantly dialogued script by Leonard Gardner from his own much-praised [1970] novel.

Huston catches the feel of the community with a lean, no-nonsense economy, a hard-boiled but humanly alert feeling which raises the tale from a purely naturalistic lowlife depiction of the characters to make a statement on the life style of the drifters and those who accept a moderate place in the smalltown hierarchy.

☐ 1972: Nomination: Best Supp. Actress (Susan Tyrrell)

■ **FATE IS THE HUNTER**

1964, 106 MINS, US
Dir Ralph Nelson   *Prod* Aaron Rosenberg   *Scr* Harold Medford   *Ph* Milton Krasner   *Ed* Robert Simpson   *Mus* Jerry Goldsmith   *Art Dir* Jack Martin Smith, Hilyard Brown
● Glenn Ford, Nancy Kwan, Rod Taylor, Suzanne Pleshette, Jane Russell, Wally Cox (20th Century-Fox)

Fate Is the Hunter based upon the Ernest K. Gann book, is a realistically-produced picture, sparked by good acting right down the line. Its greatest asset is a stirring climax which brings the story line to a satisfactory conclusion, but the buildup, while meeting expository requirements, frequently plods due to lack of significant line and situations.

The production deals with the cause of a spectacular plane crash in which 53 people are killed. As the various elements are considered, then discarded, the investigation finally centers on the dead pilot, reported to have been drinking a few hours before the tragedy. With the Civil Aeronautics Board and the FBI already on the case, the airline's director of flight operations and old friend of the pilot pursues his own line of inquiry.

Glenn Ford as the operations director who was a war flyer with the dead pilot (Rod Taylor) underplays his character for good effect. Part isn't as outgoing as Ford generally undertakes, but is dramatically forceful. Taylor's role is more flamboyant and colorful, most of it in flashback sequences as the Harold Medford screenplay limns the character of the man and what made him tick.

Ralph Nelson's taut direction gets the most out of his script, the crash emerging as a thrilling experience and with suspense mounting in Ford's reenactment of the fatality. Under his helming, too, Nancy Kwan, as Taylor's fiancee, and Suzanne Pleshette, the stewardess, register nicely, and Jane Russell makes an appearance as herself playing a World War II army camp.

☐ 1964: Nomination: Best B&W Cinematography

■ **FATHER**

1990, 100 MINS, AUSTRALIA ◇ ⓥ
Dir John Power   *Prod* Damien Parer, Tony Cavanaugh, Graham Hartley   *Scr* Tony Cavanaugh, Graham Hartley   *Ph* Dan Burstall   *Ed* Kerry Regan   *Mus* Peter Best   *Art Dir* Phil Peters
● Max von Sydow, Carol Drinkwater, Julie Blake, Steve Jacobs, Tim Robertson (Barron/Latin Quarter)

Father is strikingly similar to Costa-Gavras' *Music Box*. The story unfolds in Melbourne where German-born Joe Mueller (Max von Sydow) has lived since the war. Since his wife's death, and his retirement, he's lived with his devoted daughter, Anne (Carol Drinkwater), son-in-law Bobby (Steve Jacobs) and two granddaughters.

Their peaceful lifestyle is disrupted by a television program in which an old woman, Iya Zetnick (Julia Blake) accuses Mueller of wartime atrocities. Mueller vigorously denies the charges, but winds up in an Australian court.

Writers introduced an extra element into the drama, however: a more general war guilt. Son-in-law is a Vietnam vet and admits that he knows all about making war against civilians. 'It's in all of us,' he says. Steve Jacobs gives an impressive performance.

Von Sydow is a tower of strength as the accused German who may, or may not, be guilty, while Blake is extremely touching as the accusing survivor of Nazi atrocities.

■ **FATHER BROWN**

1954, 91 MINS, UK ⓥ
Dir Robert Hamer   *Prod* Paul Finder Moss, Vivian A. Cox   *Scr* Thelma Schnee, Robert Hamer   *Ph* Harry Waxman   *Ed* Gordon Hales   *Mus* Georges Auric
● Alec Guinness, Joan Greenwood, Peter Finch, Cecil Parker, Bernard Lee, Sidney James (Columbia/Facet)

Father Brown is distinguished mainly by the excellent casting of Alec Guinness in the title role. The G.K. Chesterton stories were adapted by Thelma Schnee, who shares the credit with the director. Between them they've fashioned a warm-hearted narrative based on the exploits of the eccentric priest who sets out to outwit international crooks while the police forces of London and Paris are on his tail.

As the yarn opens Guinness decides that it would not be safe to entrust a priceless cross to Scotland Yard in its journey from London to Rome, and decides to transport it himself.

Needless to say he is outsmarted by an international thief with a reputation for stealing rare objets d'art.

This is, at all times, a gentle story, leisurely unfolded and always dominated by a masterly performance by Guinness. The near-sighted priest, who learns the secrets of unarmed combat from some of the tougher members of his flock, is admirably brought to life by Guinness. His performance, good though it is, does not overshadow a first-class thesping job by Peter Finch as the international thief who likes to collect the rare treasures he cannot afford.

■ **FATHER GOOSE**

1964, 115 MINS, US ◇ ⓥ
Dir Ralph Nelson   *Prod* Robert Arthur   *Scr* Peter Stone, Frank Tarloff   *Ph* Charles Lang Jr   *Ed* Ted J. Kent   *Mus* Cy Coleman   *Art Dir* Alexander Golitzen, Henry Bumstead
● Cary Grant, Leslie Caron, Trevor Howard, Jack Good, Sheryl Locke, Pip Sparke (Universal)

Cary Grant comes up with an about-face change of character in this World War II comedy [from a screen story by S. H. Barnett]. As a Japanese plane watcher on a deserted South Sea isle Grant plays an unshaven bum addicted to tippling and tattered attire, a long way from the suave figure he usually projects but affording him opportunity for nutty characterization. Leslie Caron and Trevor Howard are valuable assists to plottage which brings in a flock of refugee kids.

Under Ralph Nelson's shrewd helming the screenplay takes amusing form as Grant, who plies the South Seas in his own cruiser at the begining of the war, is pressed into service by Australian Navy Commander Howard to man a strategic watching station.

Into this harrassed existence comes further harrassment when Grant crosses 40 miles of open sea in an eight-foot dinghy to rescue another watcher, but ends up with Caron and seven young girls, marooned there when a pilot who was transporting them to safety from New Guinea was ordered to pick up survivors of a crashed bomber.

☐ 1964: Best Original Story & Screenplay.
☐ Nominations: Best Editing, Sound

■ **FATHERLAND**

1986, 110 MINS, UK/W. GERMANY ◇ ⓥ
Dir Ken Loach   *Prod* Raymond Day   *Scr* Trevor Griffiths   *Ph* Chris Menges   *Ed* Jonathan Morris   *Mus* Christian Kunert, Gerulf Pannach   *Art Dir* Martin Johnson
● Gerulf Pannach, Fabienne Babe, Sigfrit Steiner, Cristine Rose (Film Four/MK2/Clasart/Kestrel II)

Fatherland is a major film from Ken Loach. He has created an ambiguous yet penetrating work about two opposing cultures and the way they both manipulate and control artistic expression, and about the response of two generations to those cultures.

Focus of the drama is Klaus Dritteman, a dissident folk singer first silenced by the East Germans, then allowed to leave quietly. He is greeted in West Berlin with lavish treatment all round, but he is unhappy being treated as a commodity in the West and doesn't know if he can be creative in his new environment.

As usual with Loach, performers are not encouraged to 'act' in the expected emotive way, and everyone, notably singer Gerulf Pannach, who plays Klaus, is quietly thoughtful and low-key.

■ **FATHER OF THE BRIDE**

1950, 92 MINS, US ⓥ ⊙
Dir Vincente Minnelli   *Prod* Pandro S. Berman   *Scr* Frances Goodrich, Albert Hackett   *Ph* John Alton

Ed Ferris Webster   *Mus* Adolph Deutsch
● Spencer Tracy, Joan Bennett, Elizabeth Taylor, Don Taylor, Billie Burke, Russ Tamblyn (M-G-M)

Father of the Bride as a pic smites the risibilities just as hard as it did in book form [by Edward Streeter].

Screenplay provides director Vincente Minnelli with choice situations and dialog, sliced right from life and hoked just enough to bring out the comedy flavor. Opening shot is a daybreak scene among the debris created by a wedding reception. Weary, but relieved, Spencer Tracey recounts the sorry lot of a bride's father, emotionally and financially devastating, and gives a case history of the events leading up to his present state.

On the critical side: Minnelli could have timed many of the scenes so that laughs would not have stepped on dialog tag lines. Also he permits the wedding rehearsal sequence to play too long, lessening the comedic effect.
☐ 1950: Nominations: Best Picture, Actor (Spencer Tracy), Screenplay

· ·

■ **FATHER OF THE BRIDE**

1991, 105 MINS, US ◇ ⓦ ⊙
Dir Charles Shyer   *Prod* Nancy Meyers, Carol Baum, Howard Rosenman   *Scr* Frances Goodrich, Albert Hackett, Nancy Meyers, Charles Shyer   *Ph* John Lindley
Ed Richard Marks   *Mus* Alan Silvestri   *Art Dir* Sandy Veneziano
● Steve Martin, Diane Keaton, Kimberly Williams, Kieran Culkin, George Newbern, Martin Short (Touchstone)

Remake of the 1950 M-G-M pic with Spencer Tracy and Elizabeth Taylor bears little resemblance to the original. Modernized version [of novel by Edward Streeter] shaped by filmaking team Charles Shyer and Nancy Meyer (*Baby Boom*, *Private Benjamin*) gets by more on physical shtick than verbal sparkle.

Steve Martin plays the scion of a comfortable San Marino, Calif, family that goes a little nuts when he learns that his beloved 22-year-old daughter (Kimberly Williams) is engaged. Beset by separation anxiety, he can't find anything right about her perfectly appealing fiance (George Newbern) or the pricey wedding arrangements. He snoops around the home of the in-laws-to-be and watches *America's Most Wanted* in hopes of getting the goods on them.

Best stuff here comes strsight from Martin, such as his frenzied antics in the in-laws' house or his ridiculous Tom Jones imitation in front of a mirror in a too-tight tuxedo. A radiant Diane Keaton gives him first-rate support as the calm, sunny wife charged with the exhausting task of keeping up with him.

· ·

■ **FATHOM**

1967, 100 MINS, US ◇
Dir Leslie Martinson   *Prod* John Kohn   *Scr* Lorenzo Semple Jr   *Ph* Douglas Slocombe   *Ed* Max Benedict
Mus John Dankworth   *Art Dir* Maurice Carter
● Raquel Welch, Anthony Franciosa, Ronald Fraser, Greta Chi, Richard Briers, Tom Adams (20th Century-Fox)

Fathom, lensed on location in Spain to take full advantage of scenic backdrops, is a melange of melodramatic ingredients personalized by the lush presence of Raquel Welsh. Actress stars with Tony Franciosa in this production, highlighted by some exciting parachute scenes.

Script, based on the Larry Forrester novel, was obviously triggered by the real-life incident of an American H-bomb accidentally lost off the coast of Spain.

Welch's services, as a parachute jumper, are enlised to help recover what is described as an electronic device which will fire the bomb, now in the possession of certain evil forces, and which was not retrieved at the time the bomb itself was salvaged.

· ·

■ **FAT MAN AND LITTLE BOY**
(UK: *Shadow Makers*)

1989, 126 MINS, US ◇ ⓦ ⊙
Dir Roland Joffe   *Prod* Tony Garnett   *Scr* Bruce Robinson, Roland Joffe   *Ph* Vilmos Zsigmond
Ed Francoise Bonnot   *Mus* Ennio Morricone
Art Dir Gregg Fonseca
● Paul Newman, Dwight Schultz, Bonnie Bedelia, John Cusack, Laura Dern, Natasha Richardson (Light motive/Paramount)

The problems of this historical drama about the creation of the atom bomb are crystalized in its title. 'Fat Man' and 'Little Boy' were the nicknames given to the bombs dropped over Hiroshima and Nagasaki. These names aren't mentioned by any of the characters in the film, nor do the bombings figure in the action.

Film concentrates instead on Gen. Groves (Paul Newman), the man assigned to oversee the project, and J. Robert Oppenheimer (Dwight Schultz), the brilliant scientist with far-left-to- all-out-communist connections picked to lead it. This is all well and good, except that few dramatic sparks fly.

Newman has no trouble bringing the tough-talking 'can do' general to life. The trouble is the scriptwriters have no interest in exploring the man behind the mission.

This tends to tilt the dramatic balance toward Oppenheimer. The film falls short here, too, partially because of Schultz' lackluster performance, but primarily because the script fails to give a clue to what made this man tick.

· ·

■ **FAVOUR, THE WATCH, AND THE VERY BIG FISH, THE**

1992, 87 MINS, FRANCE/UK ◇ ⓦ ⊙
Dir Ben Lewin   *Prod* Michelle De Broca   *Scr* Ben Lewin
Ph Bernard Zitzermann   *Ed* John Grover   *Mus* Vladimir Cosma   *Art Dir* Carlos Conti
● Bob Hoskins, Jeff Goldblum, Natasha Richardson, Michel Blanc, Jacques Villeret, Angela Pleasence (Ariane/Fildebroc/Umbrella)

The only clumsy thing about *The Favour, the Watch, and the Very Big Fish* is its title. Surreal romantic farce about a Parisian photographer and a pianist who thinks he's Christ keeps the yocks coming and features tasty perfs from Bob Hoskins and Jeff Goldblum.

Story has Hoskins as a bespectacled lenser specializing in biblical tableaux. His boss (Michel Blanc) thinks he's a wimp, and his sister tortures him with inedible food. One day, an actor friend (Jean-Pierre Cassel) asks him a favor – to take his place in a dubbing session.

Pic in question turns out to be a porno movie. Following a marathon orgasm with fellow dubber Natasha Richardson, the two become chums. Hoskins, who's secretly fallen for Richardson, agrees to meet ex-b.f. Goldblum when he gets out of jail. Goldblum saves Hoskins' job when he agrees to pose as Christ on the Cross for a photo shoot. Problems start when he tries to perform miracles.

In his second feature (after the 1988 *Georgia*), Polish-born, Australian-raised helmer Ben Lewin shows a sharp eye for Euro-style loony-tune comedy. Though set in present-day Paris, pic has an almost fin-desiecle feel, thanks to picturesque locations, clever costuming and heightened playing by all the principals.

· ·

■ **FBI STORY, THE**

1959, 149 MINS, US ◇ ⓦ ⊙
Dir Mervyn LeRoy   *Prod* Mervyn LeRoy   *Scr* Richard L. Breen, John Twist   *Ph* Joseph Biroc   *Ed* Philip W. Anderson   *Mus* Max Steiner
● James Stewart, Vera Miles, Murray Hamilton, Larry Pennell, Nick Adams, Diane Jergens (Warner)

Mervyn LeRoy takes the factual material of Don Whitehead's best-selling *The FBI Story* and makes of it a tense, exciting film story told in human terms. The method used is to show the work of the FBI through the life of one of its agents (James Stewart), a familiar enough device, but correct and rewarding in this instance.

The fictional story used as a framework sounds conventional enough. Stewart and his wife (Vera Miles), are torn between his dedication to his job with the FBI and the fact that he could give his family a more rewarding life outside the bureau. But Stewart believes what J. Edgar Hoover tells his agents when he takes over the service, that its men must be imbued not only with the service of justice but the love of justice.

The dialog is exemplary, economical in words despite the film's length. Too, the story does not run out of plot. It plunges directly into a revelatory incident before the main titles, and one of the most suspenseful sequences, a fine chase through New York streets, is used for the final crisis.

Stewart gives a restrained performance, wry and intelligent, completely credible as the film covers a span of about 25 years to show both the fledgling agent and the older man. Miles, who plays particularly well with Stewart, synchronizes her more direct attack smoothly with his underplaying. Murray Hamilton is memorable as Stewart's fellow agent, felled by gangsters. Larry Pennell and Diane Jergens supply the young love interest believably.

· ·

■ **FEAR AND DESIRE**

1953, 68 MINS, US
Dir Stanley Kubrick   *Prod* Stanley Kubrick   *Scr* Howard O. Sackler   *Ph* Stanley Kubrick   *Ed* Stanley Kubrick
Mus Gerald Fried
● Frank Silvera, Kenneth Harp, Paul Mazursky, Steve Coit, Virginia Leith (Kubrick)

Fear and Desire is a literate, unhackneyed war drama, outstanding for its fresh camera treatment and poetic dialog.

Pic is work of Stanley Kubrick, who produced, directed, photographed and edited the film on a $100,000 shoestring budget. Film was written by 23-year-old poet Howard O. Sackler who has confected a blend of violence and philosophy, some of it half-baked, and some of it powerfully moving.

Story deals with four GIs stranded six miles behind enemy lines and what happens to their moral fibre as they try to escape. Kenneth Harp is a glib intellectual, grows weary with his own sophistication. Paul Mazursky, over-sensitive to violence, is a weakling who tries to befriend a captured enemy girl, Virginia Leith (a toothsome dish), shoots her, and then goes insane.

Steve Coit is a level-headed Southerner who also winds up confused about his values. Frank Silvera plays the one character who fulfills himself – a tough, brave primitive, who purposely draws the fire of the enemy on himself on a river raft, so that Harp and Coit can shoot an enemy general and escape in a captured plane.

Kubrick shot the entire film in the San Gabriel Mts and at a river at Bakersfield on the Coast, and he uses mists and tree leaves with telling effect.

Fear and Desire is definitely out of the potboiler class one would expect from a shoestring budget.

· ·

■ **FEAR CITY**

1984, 96 MINS, US ◇ ⓦ ⊙
Dir Abel Ferrara   *Prod* Bruce Cohn Curtis, Jerry Tokofsky
Scr Nicholas St John   *Ph* James Lemmo   *Ed* Jack Holmes, Anthony Redman   *Mus* Dick Halligan
Art Dir Cricket Rowland

F

● Tom Berenger, Billy Dee Williams, Jack Scalia, Melanie Griffith, Rossano Brazzi, Rae Dawn Chong (Zupnik/Curtis)

Fear City lives up to its title as a tough, nasty, big-league meller by throwing every element from the exploitation cookbook – gory violence, straight and gay sex, multiple murders, martial arts, raw-dialog, mobsters, drugs and gobs of female nudity – into the pot and letting them stew.

Pic is set in the fleshpot of mid-town Manhattan and is populated by strippers and the sleazy men who run their lives. Hovering above them are organized crime types on the one side and the cops on the other, and soon a third menace is introduced, that of a roving sicko who launches a systematic genocidal assault on the girls who work at the nude clubs.

Teeming plot has B-girl talent agent Tom Berenger trying to get things started again with old flame Melanie Griffith.

■ **FEAR IN THE NIGHT**

1947, 71 MINS, US ▼
Dir Maxwell Shane   *Prod* William H. Pine, William C. Thomas   *Scr* Maxwell Shane   *Ph* Jack Greenhalgh   *Ed* Howard Smith   *Mus* Rudy Schrager   *Art Dir* F. Paul Sylos
● Paul Kelly, DeForest Kelley, Ann Doran, Kay Scott, Robert Emmett Keane (Paramount)

Fear in the Night is a good psychological melodrama, unfolded at fast clip and will please the whodunit-and-how fans.

Maxwell Shane, who scripted from a William Irish [= Cornell Woolrich] story, [*Nightmare,*] also directed. It's his first directorial chore. He realizes on meller elements for full worth. Plot concerns young man who awakens one morning after dream that he has killed a man. Reality of dream is strengthened when he finds strange button and key in his pocket. He seeks aid from his detective brother-in-law.

Paul Kelly is a believable cop who aids DeForest Kelley solve nightmare riddle.

■ **FEAR IS THE KEY**

1973, 105 MINS, UK ◇ ▼ ⊙
Dir Michael Tuchner   *Prod* Alan Ladd Jr, Jay Kanter   *Scr* Robert Carrington   *Ph* Alex Thomson   *Ed* Ray Lovejoy   *Mus* Roy Budd   *Art Dir* Syd Cain, Maurice Carter
● Barry Newman, Suzy Kendall, John Vernon, Dolph Sweet, Ben Kingsley, Ray McAnally (KLK/Anglo-EMI)

Sustained interest and suspense mark *Fear Is the Key,* well-made action stuff [from the novel by Alistair MacLean] including the obligatory auto chase routine around the highways and byways of Louisiana where pic was shot.

Barry Newman and Suzy Kendall are top-featured, he as a deepsea salvage expert, she as an oil heiress and kidnap victim. When Newman's wife, brother and child are shot out of the sky while fetching a salvage cargo of priceless gems, he goes undercover in cahoots with the law to avenge the killings. An elaborate charade ensues wherein he feigns the murder of a cop and kidnap of Kendall from a courtroom, all designed to land him in the lair of the villains who are contriving to retrieve the gems from the aircraft on the floor of the Gulf of Mexico.

Michael Tuchner's direction, abetted by tight editing, unravels the yarn at a crisp clip. The auto pursuit sequence is superbly staged by stunt coordinator Carey Loftin and crew.

■ **FEARLESS VAMPIRE KILLERS, THE**
See: Dance of the Vampires

■ **FEAR NO EVIL**

1981, 99 MINS, US ◇ ▼
Dir Frank LaLoggia   *Prod* Frank LaLoggia, Charles LaLoggia   *Scr* Frank LaLoggia   *Ph* Fred Goodich   *Ed* Edna Ruth Paul   *Mus* Frank LaLoggia, David Spear
● Elizabeth Hoffman, Kathleen Rowe McAllen, Frank Birney, Stefan Arngrim, Daniel Eden (LaLoggia Productions)

Though the horror genre is sated with maniacs on the menace, *Fear No Evil* stands out. Spooky and surreal, the ultimately hopeful film has its basis in religious morality.

A rotten seed, born to horrified parents, grows into a menacing 17-year-old. He's a hopeless baddie consumed by the power to destroy. At Andrew/Lucifer's wicked island domain, he summons the undead and tangles with Margaret, an old woman with the power of God behind her.

Strong on atmospherics, thanks to slick lensing by Fred Goodich, *Fear No Evil* is a studious chiller that works best in scenes featuring Elizabeth Hoffman, who fairly glows with devotional fervour as Margaret.

At a cost of $1.5 million, *Fear No Evil* is an admirable first feature by writer-director Frank LaLoggia, 27, who also co-wrote the lush music. The former U of Miami drama student previously made three award-winning shorts and acted in three television pilots.

■ **FEAR STRIKES OUT**

1957, 100 MINS, US ▼ ⊙
Dir Robert Mulligan   *Prod* Alan J. Pakula   *Scr* Ted Berkman, Raphael Blau   *Ph* Haskell Boggs   *Ed* Aaron Stell   *Mus* Elmer Bernstein   *Art Dir* Hal Pereira, Hilyard Brown
● Anthony Perkins, Karl Malden, Norma Moore, Adam Williams, Perry Wilson, Peter J. Votrian (Paramount)

Baseball is only a means to an end in this highly effective dramatization of the tragic results that can come from a father pushing his son too hard towards a goal he, himself, was not able to achieve.

In trying to be the major leaguer his father had wanted to be, Jim Piersall so filled his life with pressure and tension that he went into a complete mental breakdown right after smashing a home run for the Boston Red Sox. Confined to the Westborough State Hospital under restraint, Piersall gradually started to respond to electro-shock treatments and was eventually restored. When the 1953 season opened for the Red Sox, Piersall was back in right field.

Anthony Perkins, in the young Piersall role, delivers a remarkably sustained performance of a sensitive young man, pushed too fast to the limits of his ability to cope with life's pressures. Karl Malden is splendid as the father who gets his own ambitions mixed up with love for his son.

■ **FEDORA**

1978, 110 MINS, W. GERMANY/FRANCE ◇ ▼ ⊙
Dir Billy Wilder   *Prod* Billy Wilder   *Scr* I.A.L. Diamond, Billy Wilder   *Ph* Gerry Fisher   *Ed* Stefan Arsten   *Mus* Miklos Rozsa   *Art Dir* Alexandre Trauner
● William Holden, Marthe Keller, Jose Ferrer, Hildegard Knef, Frances Sternhagen, Mario Adorf (Geria/Bavaria)

With *Fedora* based on a tale from Tom Tryon's bestseller, *Crowned Heads,* Billy Wilder goes serenely back to Hollywood treatment of itself as legend, illusion and dreams rather than reality.

In his more successful, acerbic look at an over-the-hill star, *Sunset Blvd.* [1950], the star was a real oldtimer, Gloria Swanson. Neither Marthe Keller, as the once great star Fedora, or Hildegard Knef as a crusty Polish countess and the star's keeper, have that allusive, self absorbed but camera-loving look that stars possessed, though they are good.

William Holden tells most of the tale, as he did in *Boulevard.* But here he is an indie producer down on his luck trying desperately to get a script to the amazingly still youthful star, at 67, Fedora, in a hideaway on a Greek island. It appears she is being held captive by a quack doctor, once famed for keeping personalities youthful, well mimed by Jose Ferrer.

Wilder's directorial flair, the fine production dress, Holden's solid presence and Michael York playing himself as a narcissistic actor and Henry Fonda, also as himself as head of the Academy who delivers a belated Oscar to Fedora, add some flavor to this bittersweet bow to the old star system.

■ **FEDS**

1988, 91 MINS, US ◇ ▼ ⊙
Dir Dan Goldberg   *Prod* Ilona Herzberg, Len Blum   *Scr* Len Blum, Dan Goldberg   *Ph* Timothy Suhrstedt   *Ed* Donn Cambern   *Mus* Randy Edelman   *Art Dir* Randy Ser
● Rebecca DeMornay, Mary Gross, Ken Marshall, Fred Dalton Thompson, Larry Cedar, Tony Longo (Warner)

Rebecca DeMornay and Mary Gross are FBI academy trainees in a buddy picture that plays more like a biddy picture. There isn't a fresh idea or a new one-liner in all of the script, an anthology of inert retreads from the *Police Academy* series and *Private Benjamin.*

DeMornay as the spunky athletic one and Gross as the uptight, studious one go up against the boys in pizza contests, chin-up exercises and constitutional law classes. They ultimately graduate at the end of the class but not before undergoing considerable humiliation.

Gross trying to stop some bank robbers by making a stick-'em-up gesture with her finger and later garbling her recitation of the Miranda rights to some poor extras cast in this film is groaner material. Dan Goldberg's direction is leaden.

■ **FELLOW TRAVELLER**

1990, 97 MINS, UK/US ◇ ▼
Dir Philip Saville   *Prod* Michael Wearing   *Scr* Michael Eaton   *Ph* John Kenway   *Ed* Greg Miller   *Mus* Colin Towns   *Art Dir* Gavin Davies
● Ron Silver, Hart Bochner, Imogen Stubbs, Daniel J. Travanti, Katherine Borowitz (BFI/BBC/HBO)

Fellow Traveller has the rare distinction of being a British film that actually looks international. Helmer Philip Saville shows a big-screen feel with the story of a blacklisted Hollywood screen-writer during the McCarthy era who is forced to Britain to find work.

Pic goes some way in covering the commie-bashing McCarthy Era 1950s, but eventually becomes rather simplistic when trying to debate the actual politics of the time.

Glossy opening is set beside a luxury swimming pool in Hollywood where film star Clifford Byrne (Hart Bochner) shoots himself. At the same time in London, his friend Asa Kaufman (Ron Silver) is escaping the McCarthyist witch-hunt and – illegally – looking for work.

A series of flashbacks shows that Bochner and Silver were best friends. In England Silver takes a false name, starts writing a TV series, *The Adventures of Robin Hood,* and searches for Bochner's English girlfriend (Imogen Stubbs), whom he has a brief affair with; he also mulls over politics with her leftie friends.

Silver is convincing as the cynical writer thrown into a strange English environment, and Hart Bochner looks the handsome leading man, replete with Errol Flynn mustache. Pic is excellent at re-creating the early heady days of independent TV in the UK.

FEMALE TROUBLE

1975, 95 MINS, US ◇ ⓥ
Dir John Waters   *Prod* John Waters   *Scr* John Waters
Ph John Waters   *Ed* Charles Roggero
● Divine, David Lochary, Mary Vivien Pearce, Mink Stole, Edith Massey, Cookie Mueller (Dreamland/New Line)

Female Trouble is the sordid tale of Dawn Davenport, who rises from high school hoyden to mistress of crime before frying in the electric chair. As she climbs the ladder of success, she is raped by a stranger, gives birth to an obnoxious child who later murders the father, marries a beautician whose mother she imprisons in a bird cage before cutting off her hand and opens a niteclub act during which she guns down members of the audience. A true original.

Repeating from *Pink Flamingos* in the stellar role is Divine, a mammoth 300-pound transvestite with a tinsel soul. Though Divine doesn't stoop to devouring dog excrement as at the *Flamingos* fade-out, he does everything else, from cavorting on a trampoline, to playing a rape scene opposite himself, and 'giving birth' on camera. Camp is too elegant a word to describe it all.

Sets, lighting, camerawork, editing and sound are all superior to their *Flamingos* counterparts and Waters makes the most of a reported $25,000 budget.

FERNGULLY
THE LAST RAINFOREST

1992, 76 MINS, US ◇ ⓥ ⊙
Dir Bill Kroyer   *Prod* Wayne Young, Peter Faiman
Scr Jim Cox   *Ed* Gillian Hutshing   *Mus* Alan Silvestri
Art Dir Susan Kroyer (FAI)

FernGully is a colorful, lively, extremely 'politically correct' animated feature pitting the elfin creatures of the wild against the rapacious monsters who would destroy their habitat. Drawn in brilliantly verdant colors immediately inviting the viewer into a special world, *FernGully* is certainly simple enough for any youngster to understand, yet is sufficiently hip around the edges to contain the sap.

For years, the evil spirit that once destroyed the forest has been locked up, but it is suddenly unleashed by an enormous, omnivorous machine that gobbles up vegetation and leaves waste in its relentless path. A workman on the machine, Zak, gets tossed into the jungle and is shrunk down, permitting a human to see things from the other POV.

Robin Williams asserts his unique personality and wacky humor amazingly well in an animated context as a crazed, brain-fried bat named Batty Koda. Cheech and Chong are reunited, at least vocally, as the raucous Beetle Boys; *Rocky Horror*'s Tim Curry essays the villainous Hexxus, liberated to destroy the forest.

These performers, in addition to such singers as Johnny Clegg, Sheena Easton and Elton John delivering original numbers written by a host of w.k. songsmiths, bring considerable pizzazz and variety to the tightly conceived picture, and provide regular distraction from the more insipid leads.

FERRIS BUELLER'S DAY OFF

1986, 103 MINS, US ◇ ⓥ ⊙
Dir John Hughes   *Prod* John Hughes, Tom Jacobson
Scr John Hughes   *Ph* Tak Fujimoto   *Ed* Paul Hirsch
Mus Ira Newborn   *Art Dir* John W. Corso
● Matthew Broderick, Alan Ruck, Mia Sara, Jeffrey Jones, Jennifer Grey, Cindy Pickett (Paramount)

Ferris Bueller exhibits John Hughes on an off day. Paucity of invention here lays bare the total absence of plot or involving situations.
In a nutshell, the thin premise demon-

strates the great lengths to which the irrepressible Ferris Bueller (Matthew Broderick) goes in order to hoodwink his parents and high school principal into thinking he's really sick when, in fact, all he wants to do is play hooky for a day.

Oddly, for a rich kid, Ferris doesn't have his own car, so he shanghais his best friend for the day, appropriates the vintage Ferrari of the buddy's father, spirits his girlfriend out of school and speeds off for downtown Chicago.

Broderick's essential likeability can't replace the loony anarchy of Hughes' previous leading man, Anthony Michael Hall. Alan Ruck can't do much with his underwritten second-banana role, and Mia Sara is fetching as Ferris' g.f.

Picture's one saving grace is the absolutely delicious comic performance of Jeffrey Jones as the high school principal.

FEVER PITCH

1985, 96 MINS, US ◇ ⓥ
Dir Richard Brooks   *Prod* Freddie Fields   *Scr* Richard Brooks   *Ph* William A. Fraker   *Ed* Jeff Jones
Mus Thomas Dolby   *Art Dir* Raymond G. Storey
● Ryan O'Neal, Catherine Hicks, Giancarlo Giannini, Bridgette Andersen, Chad Everett, John Saxon (M-G-M)

Weak script, poor acting and miscasting aside, it's the power of the subject that makes this an enjoyable ride. Writer/director Richard Brooks thoroughly researched the Territory of the compulsive gambler and captures the obsession with almost a documentary eye.

Unfortunately, plot is a totally unconvincing jumble and Ryan O'Neal as a sports reporter hooked on the gambling game is wooden and unsympathetic. Up to his ears in gambling debts, O'Neal just gets in deeper with loansharks and operators. He's already lost his wife due to gambling.

Most of the action takes place in Las Vegas where O'Neal wins and loses huge sums and gets involved with big-timer Giancarlo Giannini.

Rest of the cast is as stiff as the script. Catherine Hicks as a Vegas cocktail waitress and sometime call-girl goes through a few turns that don't quite fit.

FEW GOOD MEN, A

1992, 138 MINS, US ◇ ⓥ ⊙
Dir Rob Reiner   *Prod* David Brown, Rob Reiner, Andrew Scheinman   *Scr* Aaron Sorkin   *Ph* Robert Richardson
Ed Robert Leighton   *Mus* Marc Shaiman   *Art Dir* J. Michael Riva
● Tom Cruise, Jack Nicholson, Demi Moore, Kevin Bacon, Kiefer Sutherland, Kevin Pollak (Columbia/Castle Rock)

A Few Good Men is a big-time, mainstream Hollywood movie par excellence. Expert story construction and compelling thesping and direction make all the narrative elements pay off in this expose of peacetime military malfeasance laced with the story of a bright young lawyer's struggle to get out from under the imposing shadow of an illustrious father.

Adapting his own 1989 play, Aaron Sorkin has opened it up just enough to accommodate the requirements of the big screen and magnified the psychological father-son dilemma of the leading character.

Chosen to defend two young Marines charged with murder is Navy lawyer Lt. Kaffee (Tom Cruise), a hot dog who prefers baseball duds to military uniforms. Briefly alighting in Cuba to interview the base's commanding officer, Col. Nathan Jessep (Jack Nicholson), Kaffee is goaded to press further by the driven special counsel, Lt. Cdr. Joanne Galloway (Demi Moore).

Action ping-pongs back and forth between defense team strategy sessions, interroga-

tions of the two perpetrators, man-to-mans between Kaffee and the friendly but fiercely competitive skilled prosecuting attorney Capt. Ross (Kevin Bacon), and raging exchanges in which Joanne won't let Kaffee off the hook.

Director Rob Reiner hasn't missed a beat in extracting the most out the material and his actors. The showiest turn is reserved for Nicholson, and the crafty old pro makes more than the most of it. He's only got three major scenes, but they're all dynamite.

☐ Nominations: Best Picture, Supp. Actor (Jack Nicholson), Editing, Sound

FFOLKES
See: *North Sea Hijack*

F FOR FAKE

1975, 85 MINS, FRANCE/W. GERMANY/IRAN ◇
Dir Orson Welles, Francois Reichenbach   *Scr* [Orson Welles, Olga Palinkas]   *Ph* Christian Odasso, Gary Graver   *Ed* Marie-Sophie Dubus, Dominique Engerer
Mus Michel Legrand
● Orson Welles, Oja Kodar [= Olga Palinkas], Joseph Cotten, Francois Reichenbach (SACI/Astrophore/Janus)

Orson Welles has reworked the docu material of Francois Reichenbach on noted art forger Elmyr De Houry, made for TV about 1968, into an intriguing, enjoyable look at illusion in general and his own, Clifford Irving's and De Houry's dealing with it in particular.

He has deftly added himself to the affair as he is seen doing some magico stints and winkingly admitting he is a charlatan.

Welles also brings in his early fakery of becoming an actor in passing himself off as a New York thesp to the Abbey Theatre in Ireland at 16 and his Mars radio scare, also a fake, which, unlike Irving, did not lead him to prison but to Hollywood. There, according to Joseph Cotten, interviewed, he was thinking of making a fictional film on Howard Hughes which finally became *Citizen Kane*, loosely based on W.R. Hearst.

Welles shows his shrewd flair for visuals and montage even if he has shot only a part of the footage.

[Earlier title for pic was simply *?*, subtitled *about Fakes*.]

FIDDLER ON THE ROOF

1971, 180 MINS, US ◇ ⓥ ⊙
Dir Norman Jewison   *Prod* Norman Jewison
Scr Joseph Stein   *Ph* Oswald Morris   *Ed* Anthony Gibbs, Robert Lawrence   *Mus* John Williams (arr.)
Art Dir Michael Stringer, Robert Boyle
● Chaim Topol, Norman Crane, Leonard Frey, Molly Picon, Paul Mann, Rosalind Harris (United Artists/Mirisch)

Sentimental in a theatrical way, romantic in the oldfashioned way, nostalgic of immigration days, affirmative of human decency, loyalty, bravery and folk humor, here is the screen version of the long-running Hal Prince-Jerome Robbins stage musical smash.

Pictured is the Ukrainian village of pious and tradition-ruled Jews at the point the corrupt Czaristic regime was goading them to move out. A tight-lipped bigot, Vernon Dobtcheff drives into the village in his carriage with an escort of military horsemen and lays down to the reluctant constable (Louis Zorich) the obligatory political line, namely there must be a 'distractive' demonstration of the local peasants against 'those Christ-killers'.

Attention naturally falls on the Tevye. Norman Jewison chose the Israeli actor, Chaim Topol, who played the role on the London stage. An enormous man with sparkling (not melting) brown eyes, Topol has the necessary combination of bombast and compassion, vitality and doubts. His dialogs

F

with God (and/or the audience) are more cautious and less in the chutzpah style of, say, Zero Mostel. Topol sings passably, but 'If I Were a Rich Man' is too serious, losing the fun.

□ 1971: Best Cinematography, Sound, Adapted Score.
□ Nominations: Best Picture, Director, Actor (Chaim Topol), Supp. Actor (Leonard Frey), Art Direction

....

■ FIELD, THE

1990, 110 MINS, UK ◇ ⑰ ⊙
Dir Jim Sheridan   *Prod* Noel Pearson   *Scr* Jim Sheridan   *Ph* Jack Conroy   *Ed* J. Patrick Duffner   *Mus* Elmer Bernstein   *Art Dir* Frank Conway
● Richard Harris, John Hurt, Tom Berenger, Sean Bean, Frances Tomelty, Brenda Fricker (Granada)

Superb acting and austere visual beauty are offset by a somewhat overheated screenplay in this tragic tale [from the play by John B. Keane] about an indomitable Irish peasant's blood ties to the land.

Richard Harris is in the larger-than-life role of a patriarchal Irish tenant farmer with a ferocious temperament and blazing charisma. The time is the 1930s, when the memory of the great famine was fresh and feudal ways held sway in the Irish countryside.

For most of his life, Bull McCabe has farmed a field belonging to a wealthy widow (Frances Tomelty), who one day decides to sell the plot. Bull is outraged.

He holds in thrall his slow-witted son Tadgh (Sean Bean) and even slower-witted crony Bird O'Donnell (John Hurt). The suicide of another son during the famine still haunts Bull, and his wife Maggie (Brenda Fricker) has not spoken to him in the 20 years since.

'Who would insult me by bidding for my field?' he demands at the local pub. No one but an Irish-American from Boston (Tom Berenger), who has returned to his ancestral village with a plan to pave Bull's field for an access road to lucrative limestone deposits.

Harris gives a resonant, domineering performance as the prideful peasant, casting him as a pagan throwback who views God and nature as one. Incredibly disguised, Hurt is remarkable as the pathetic village idiot who lives for the reflected glory of the most fearsome man in town.
□ 1990: Nomination: Best Actor (Richard Harris)

....

■ FIELD OF DREAMS

1989, 106 MINS, US ◇ ⑰ ⊙
Dir Phil Alden Robinson   *Prod* Lawrence Gordon, Charles Gordon   *Scr* Phil Alden Robinson   *Ph* John Lindley   *Ed* Ian Crafford   *Mus* James Horner   *Art Dir* Dennis Gassner
● Kevin Costner, Amy Madigan, Gaby Hoffman, Ray Liotta, James Earl Jones, Burt Lancaster (Gordon/Universal)

Alternately affecting and affected, *Field of Dreams* is a fable about redemption and reconciliation that uses the mythos of baseball as an organizing metaphor.

Kevin Costner plays Ray Kinsella, a new-age farmer who has come to Iowa's cornfields with his college sweetheart (Amy Madigan).

In the fields one day Costner hears a celestial voice that cryptically advises: 'If you build it, he will come.' Once he convinces himself and his family that he's not going crazy, Costner sets out to sculpt a beautiful baseball diamond from his precious cornfield.

The whole town thinks the outsider has gone bonkers, but one night Costner's faith is rewarded: the spirit of Shoeless Joe Jackson, the most precipitously fallen of the disgraced World Series fixers, the 1919 Chicago White Sox, materializes on his ballfield.

Fully in the grip of supernatural forces, Costner leaves the farm on a cross-country pilgrimage to find the Boston home of America's best-known reclusive writer (James Earl Jones) – a cultural demigod depicted as a cross between J.D. Salinger and Bob Dylan.

Costner, Shoeless Joe, Jones and Burt Lancaster (a failed dead baseballer) are all haunted by regrets over failed relatonships, life-shattering mistakes and missed opportunities. All yearn for a collective second chance at inner peace. In spite of a script hobbled with cloying aphorisms and shameless sentimentality, *Field of Dreams* sustains a dreamy mood in which the idea of baseball is distilled to its purest essence: a game that stands for unsullied innocence in a cruel, imperfect world.
□ 1989: Nominations: Best Picture, Adapted Screenplay, Original Score

....

■ FIFTH AVENUE GIRL

1939, 82 MINS, US ⑰ ⊙
Dir Gregory LaCava   *Prod* Gregory LaCava   *Scr* Allan Scott   *Ph* Robert de Grasse   *Ed* William Hamilton, Robert Wise   *Mus* Robert Russell Bennett   *Art Dir* Van Nest Polglase, Perry Ferguson
● Ginger Rogers, Walter Connolly, Verree Teasdale, James Ellison, Tim Holt, Kathryn Adams (RKO)

Fifth Avenue Girl, is a cleverly devised comedy drama, expertly guided by Gregory LaCava. Story is basically of Cinderella pattern – always good. Millionaire Walter Connolly, shunned by his family on his birthday, meets Ginger Rogers in Central Park. After a night club celebration, he hires her to pose as a golddigger, and takes her to his Fifth Avenue mansion.

Sock laughs are supplied by situations and surprise dialog. Rogers, bewildered by her sudden catapult into a swank home, carries it all off with a blankness that accentuates her characterization. Connolly deftly handles the assignment of the prosperous manufacturer.

Production is distinctly a LaCava achievement. In motivation, its unfolding lies between the wacky *My Man Godfrey* and the more serious *Stage Door*.

....

■ 55 DAYS AT PEKING

1963, 150 MINS, US ◇ ⑰
Dir Nicholas Ray, [Andrew Marton, Guy Green]   *Prod* Samuel Bronston   *Scr* Philip Yordan, Bernard Gordon, Robert Hamer, [Ben Barzman]   *Ph* Jack Hildyard   *Ed* Robert Lawrence   *Mus* Dimitri Tiomkin   *Art Dir* Veniero Colasanti, John Moore
● Charlton Heston, Ava Gardner, David Niven, Flora Robson, John Ireland, Leo Genn (Bronston)

Producer Samuel Bronston shows characteristic lavishness in the pictorial scope, the vivid and realistic sets and extras by the thousands in his reproduction of the capital of Imperial China in 1900. The lensing was in Spain where the company built an entire city.

The screenplay presumably adheres to the historical basics in its description of the violent rebellion of the 'Boxers' against the major powers of the period – Great Britain, Russia, France, Germany, Italy, Japan, and the United States – because of their commercial exploitation of tradition-bound and unmodern (backward) China. These market-seeking nations have in their Peking outpost gallant fighting men who, although only a few hundred in number, withstand the merciless 55-day siege.

While Ray is identified as director, some of the battle scenes actually were directed by Andrew Marton. This came to be in a period when Ray was ill.

David Niven is the British embassy head who stubbornly refuses to surrender, risking the safety of all about him, including his wife

and two children. Both he and Charlton Heston perform with conviction, Heston as the American Marine major who commands the defense. Ava Gardner's role is not too well conceived. Hers is the part of the widow of a Russian bigshot who killed himself upon learning of his wife's infidelity with a Chinese official.

Lynne Sue Moon gives a poignant performance as an Oriental 12-year-old whose American father, an army captain, is killed in battle. Flora Robson appears strikingly authentic as the Dowager Empress Tzu Hsi whose sympathies lie with the outlaws.

Jack Hildyard's photography is excellent, particularly in getting on the big screen the savage attack scenes which take up the major part of the picture. Dimitri Tiomkin provides engaging music.
□ 1963: Nominations: Best Original Music Score, Song ('So Little Time')

....

■ 52 PICK-UP

1986, 114 MINS, US ◇ ⑰ ⊙
Dir John Frankenheimer   *Prod* Menahem Golan, Yoram Globus   *Scr* Elmore Leonard, John Steppling   *Ph* Jost Vacano   *Ed* Robert F. Shugrue   *Mus* Gary Chang   *Art Dir* Philip Harrison
● Roy Scheider, Ann-Margret, Vanity, John Glover, Robert Trebor, Kelly Preston (Cannon)

52 Pick-Up is a thriller without any thrills. Although director John Frankenheimer stuffs as much action as he can into the screen adaptation of Elmore Leonard's novel (previously filmed by Cannon in Israel in 1984 as *The Ambassador*), he can't hide the ridiculous plot and lifeless characters.

Roy Scheider is an all-American hero, married for 23 years to the still attractive Ann-Margret, who has worked his way up by his bootstraps and after many lean years now owns a successful business and a luxurious home in the Hollywood hills.

Caught in a blackmail scheme by an unlikely trio of porno operators who film him in bed with cute young Kelly Preston, Scheider balks at giving up his hard-earned wealth, but even more at being told what to do.

Chemistry between Scheider and Ann Margret is minimal and undermines the film's foundation. More lively are the three thugs who are fingering Scheider. Ring-leader John Glover gives the role such a decadently sinister turn that he's far more interesting and lively to watch than Scheider.

....

■ FIGHTING KENTUCKIAN, THE

1949, 109 MINS, US ⑰
Dir George Waggner   *Prod* John Wayne   *Scr* George Waggner   *Ph* Lee Garmes   *Ed* Richard L. Van Enger   *Mus* George Antheil
● John Wayne, Vera Ralston, Philip Dorn, Oliver Hardy, Marie Windsor, Hugo Haas (Republic)

Whether the story of two Kentucky riflemen coming to the aid of French refugees starts a bit incongruous, it all pans out as swift-moving melodrama. Pic also introduces Oliver Hardy, better known as the rotund half of the Laurel-Hardy slapstick team, as a tough albeit corpulent Kentucky backwoods fighter. That he registers speaks well for his natural thespian ability, mugging and all.

A little known bit of American history, that Congress granted four townships of land in Alabama to French officers of Napoleon's defeated armies and their families, forms the background for the story. That is until Wayne, one of the Kentucky troopers returning from final battle of the war of 1812, falls in love with Vera Ralston, daughter of French general Hugo Haas.

....

■ FIGURES IN A LANDSCAPE

1970, 95 MINS, UK ◇

Dir Joseph Losey   *Prod* John Kohn   *Scr* Robert Shaw
Ph Henri Alekan   *Ed* Reginald Beck   *Mus* Richard
Rodney Bennett   *Art Dir* Ted Tester
● Robert Shaw, Malcolm McDowell, Pamela Brown,
Henry Woolf, Christopher Malcolm (Cinema Center)

The plight of two prisoners escaping from a
relentless helicopter over '400 miles of hostile
terrain' is the armature around which this
yarn, which purposely never defines who the
prisoners or the forces chasing them are, is
spun.

MacConnachie, a 40-year-old 'coarse man
born to kill' and young Ansell, who supposedly is 'propelled by reason and perception'
have somewhere joined forces, are scrambling
over the wastelands, and are being pursued
by an acrobatic helicopter whose job it is to
spot them, and whose faceless pilot seems to
enjoy swooping down to give them a scare.

It is difficult to get into the characters, who
always remain as elusive as the country they
are traveling over is supposed to be.

■ FILE ON THELMA JORDON, THE

1950, 100 MINS, US

Dir Robert Siodmak   *Prod* Hal B. Wallis   *Scr* Ketti
Frings   *Ph* George Barnes   *Ed* Warren Low
Mus Victor Young   *Art Dir* Hans Dreier, Earl Hedrick
● Barbara Stanwyck, Wendell Corey, Paul Kelly, Joan
Tetzel, Stanley Ridges, Richard Rober (Paramount)

Thelma Jordon unfolds as an interesting,
femme-slanted melodrama, told with a lot of
restrained excitement.

Scripting [from a story by Marty Holland] is
very forthright, up to the contrived conclusion, and even that is carried off successfully
because of the sympathy developed for the
misguided and misused character played by
Wendell Corey.

Corey is seen as an assistant d.a., a husband
and father. One night, after a quarrel with
his wife Joan Tetzel, he is intrigued by the
Barbara Stanwyck character. It leads him to
further pursuit and a hot amour.

Stanwyck is pretending to be a poor cousin
to her rich aunt. When the latter is killed by a
house-breaker, Corey attempts to remove evidence which would point towards Stanwyck.
Despite this, she is charged with murder.

Robert Siodmak's direction pinpoints many
scenes of extreme tension.

■ FILOFAX

See: Taking Care of Business

■ FINAL ANALYSIS

1992, 124 MINS, US ◇ ⑰ ⊙

Dir Phil Joanou   *Prod* Charles Roven, Paul Junger Witt,
Tony Thomas   *Scr* Wesley Strick   *Ph* Jordan
Cronenweth   *Ed* Thom Noble   *Mus* George Fenton
Art Dir Dean Tavoularis
● Richard Gere, Kim Basinger, Uma Thurman, Eric
Roberts, Paul Guilfoyle, Keith David (Warner)

Final Analysis is a crackling good psychological
melodrama [from a screen story by Robert
Berger and Wesley Strick] in which star
power and slick surfaces are used to potent
advantage. Tantalizing double-crosses mount
right up to the eerie final scene.

In the course of treating a patient (Uma
Thurman), San Francisco psychiatrist
Richard Gere takes the unusual step of meet-
ing the young woman's older sister, who may
know more about certain events in
Thurman's past than the subject herself.

Sis turns out to be Kim Basinger, who has
no trouble overcoming his tenuous sense of
professional ethics about bedding a patient's
sibling. An aloof workaholic, Gere becomes
hopelessly ensnared in his secret affair with

Basinger, who in turn promises to find a way
out of her marriage. Sympathies ride with her
in a murder trial but with the trial's conclusion Basinger assumes the full dimensions of
a Warner Bros. bad girl that Joan Crawford
would have killed to play.

Greatest hurdle for some viewers may be
getting past the idea of Gere as a respected
psychiatrist, and the intellectual side of his
character is shortchanged. Similarly,
Basinger is mostly surface effect, but it's considerable here. Her wardrobe is stunning.

Physical production is one of the film's major stars, as lenser and production designer
have conspired to create a darkly shadowed,
outrageously attractive world that outdoes
even San Francisco's natural beauties.

■ FINAL CONFLICT, THE

1981, 108 MINS, US ◇ ⑰ ⊙

Dir Graham Baker   *Prod* Harvey Bernhard   *Scr* Andrew
Birkin   *Ph* Robert Paynter, Phil Meheux   *Ed* Alan
Strachan   *Mus* Jerry Goldsmith   *Art Dir* Herbert
Westbrook
● Sam Neill, Rossano Brazzi, Don Gordon, Lisa Harrow,
Mason Adams (20th Century-Fox)

The Final Conflict is the last chapter in the
Omen trilogy, which is too bad because this is
the funniest one yet.

This time Sam Neill plays Damien Thorn,
all grown up now after killing off two nice
families in the previous chapters. Fear of orphanage, of course, never worries Damien because his real father is the Devil, who only
wanted him to go to the best schools, get a
job and take over the world for evil.

And now he has, or almost. He's running
Thorn Industries and will soon be US
Ambassador to England when the fellow who
has the job sees a bad dog and goes back to
the office and blows his head off, the single
startling episode in the whole film.

Having memorized the Book of Hebron
from The Apocrypha, plus several dopy soliloquies in Andrew Birkin's script. Neill knows
the only obstacle to his plan is the baby born
when three stars conjoin overhead.

There's also the matter of the daggers. If
you remember the first two episodes, somebody or other, sometimes mom, sometimes
dad, sometimes a stranger, was always trying
to stab little Damien to death with the daggers.

This is the first feature for director Graham
Baker, a veteran of British TV commercials,
and it seems like he doesn't quite know what
to do when the daggers don't have a brand
name to hold toward the camera or the dialog
stretches beyond two sentences.

■ FINAL COUNTDOWN, THE

1980, 103 MINS, US ◇ ⑰ ⊙

Dir Don Taylor   *Prod* Peter Vincent Douglas   *Scr* David
Ambrose, Gerry Davis, Thomas Hunter, Peter Powell
Ph Victor J. Kemper   *Ed* Robert K. Lambert   *Mus* John
Scott   *Art Dir* Fernando Carrere
● Kirk Douglas, Martin Sheen, Katharine Ross, James
Farentino, Ron O'Neal, Charles Durning (Bryna/United
Artists)

As a documentary on the USS *Nimitz, The
Final Countdown* is wonderful. As entertainment, however, it has the feeling of a telepic
that strayed onto the big screen. The magnificent production values provided by setting
the film on the world's largest nuclear-powered aircraft carrier can't transcend the predictable cleverness of a plot that will seem
overly familiar to viewers raised on *Twilight
Zone* reruns.

The liberal sympathies typical of the work
of Kirk Douglas are evident in his characterization of the ship's commander as a man
whose sense of military honor will not allow

him to take the opportunity provided him by
a mysterious storm – his ship and crew find
themselves transported back in time to 6
December 1941, between Pearl Harbor and
the Japanese fleet heading to destroy the
American naval base and send the US into
World War II.

The philosophical issues raised by the film
hardly bear much examination, because the
patchwork screenplay by two pairs of writers
paints each character in too schematic a fashion. Martin Sheen has much more to work
with than Douglas, who seems uncharacteris-
tically subdued.

■ FINAL PROGRAMME, THE

(US: The Last Days of Man on Earth)

1973, 89 MINS, UK ◇ ⑰

Dir Robert Fuest   *Prod* Jon Goldstone, Sandy Lieberson
Scr Robert Fuest   *Ph* Norman Warwick   *Ed* Barrie Vince
Mus Paul Beaver, Bernard Krause   *Art Dir* Robert Fuest,
Philip Harrison
● Jon Finch, Jenny Runacre, Hugh Griffith, Patrick
Magee, Stirling Hayden, Julie Ege (Goodtimes/Gladiole)

Pic is a silly, pretentious pot-boiler, done in a
jazzed-up style which suggests Ken Russell on
an off day. Jon Finch is topcast as a rebellious
intellectual in a devastated world seeking a
new messiah. Pic alternates high-falutin' allegory with low-brow facetiousness, and the
film is a mishmash.

Robert Fuest, who directed, based the story
on Michael Moorcock's novel *The Final
Programme*. Whatever ideas Fuest is trying to
deal with, mostly in the pop cliche fashion of
run-of-the-mill scifi, are submerged by the relentlessly chic filming style.

The Finch character runs up against some of
England's most interesting supportng actors,
none of whom has much of a part, and when
the forlorn cast is coupled with the junk-
strewn landscape, pic could be taken as a sad
allegory of the British film industry. Among
the talents stranded here are Jenny Runacre,
Hugh Griffith, Patrick Magee, Harry Andrews,
Graham Crowden, and George Coulouris.
Sterling Hayden is in for a flash.

■ FINDERS KEEPERS

1966, 94 MINS, UK ◇ ⑰

Dir Sidney Hayers   *Prod* George H. Brown
Scr Michael Pertwee   *Ph* Alan Hume   *Ed* Tristam Cones
Mus The Shadows   *Art Dir* Jack Sheripan
● Cliff Richard, The Shadows, Robert Morley, Peggy
Mount, Viviane Ventura, Graham Stark (Interstate/United
Artists)

George H. Brown's storyline about a mini-
bomb dropped by accident from an American
plane over Spain and subsequent attempts by
various foreign 'spies' to locate it could have
had a good astringent and satirical tang. The
theme is not only largely frittered away but is
hardly suitable for a relaxed, easygoing musicomedy designed to showcase a pop group
such as Cliff Richard and The Shadows. Wit
gets lost, and incidents are held up, to make
room for inevitable song, dance and fiesta.

Richard and The Shadows hitchhike to a
hotel in Spain and find it deserted. The
dropped bomb has sent everybody scurrying
away. The lads, with the help of a local
charmer (Viviane Ventura), decide that it's in
their interests to find it and hand it over to
the US troops who have moved in on a similar
mission.

Michael Pertwee's screenplay does not
build up much urgency or suspense but provides opportunity for colorful fiesta, a gentle
romance between Richard and Ventura, some
verbal dueling between Robert Morley and
Graham Stark.

■ FINDERS KEEPERS

1984, 96 MINS, US ◇ ⊛
Dir Richard Lester   *Prod* Sandra Marsh, Terence Marsh
Scr Ronny Graham, Terence Marsh, Charles Dennis
Ph Brian West   *Ed* John Victor Smith   *Mus* Ken Thorne
Art Dir J. Dennis Washington
● Michael O'Keefe, Beverly D'Angelo, Louis Gossett Jr,
Ed Lauter, David Wayne, Brian Dennehy (CBS)

Director Richard Lester returns to his pell-mell trademark and the result is maddening. Interesting cast is wasted, with bright exception of Beverly D'Angelo.

Producers Sandra and Terence Marsh hang their frenetic tale of stolen money, chases and deceptions on several characters racing up and down a train en-route from California to Nebraska.

There's $5 million in a coffin in the baggage car, there's a sexy neurotic (D'Angelo, who steals the movie), a bumbling con man (toplined Michael O'Keefe), razor sharp con man (Louis Gossett Jr, on screen only briefly), a sweaty heavy (Ed Lauter), and a gregarious old train conductor (David Wayne). Its parts add up to pieces that artlessly lurch and hurtle around.

■ FINE AND DANDY

See: The West Point Story

■ FINE MADNESS, A

1966, 104 MINS, US ◇ ⊛
Dir Irvin Kershner   *Prod* Jerome Hellman   *Scr* Elliott
Baker   *Ph* Ted McCord   *Ed* William Ziegler   *Mus* John
Addison   *Art Dir* Jack Poplin
● Sean Connery, Joanne Woodward, Jean Seberg,
Patrick O'Neal, Colleen Dewhurst, Clive Revill (Pan
Arts/Warner)

A Fine Madness is offbeat, and downbeat, in many ways. Too heavyhanded to be comedy, yet too light to be called drama, the well-mounted production depicts a non-conformist poet-stud in an environment of much sex, some violence and modern headshrinking. Fine direction and some good characterizations enhance negative script outlook.

Sean Connery is a virile, headstrong poet, hung up in a dry spell of inspiration. He despises women in general, and to hammer home this point, all femme characters, except second wife Joanne Woodward, are shrews, battle-axes, or shallow broads.

Overdue back alimony cues an outburst, eventually leading Connery to psychiatric care, alternating with a running chase from the fuzz, and climaxed by a curiously ineffective brain lobotomy. A lot of sophisticated throwaway dialog is dispensed along with sight gags and slapstick.

Director Irvin Kershner has drawn effective performances from Connery, who makes a good comic kook in a switch from the somnambulism of his James Bond roles, and Woodward, almost unrecognizable in face and voice via a good characterization of the loud-mouthed, but loving, wife, done in the Judy Holliday style. Jean Seberg, bored wife of headshrinker Patrick O'Neal, is okay.

■ FINE MESS, A

1986, 88 MINS, US ◇ ⊛ ⊙
Dir Blake Edwards   *Prod* Tony Adams   *Scr* Blake
Edwards   *Ph* Harry Stradling   *Ed* John F. Burnett
Mus Henry Mancini   *Art Dir* Rodger Maus
● Ted Danson, Howie Mandel, Richard Mulligan, Stuart
Margolin, Maria Conchita Alonso, Paul Sorvino (BEE/
Columbia-Delphi V)

Blake Edward's obsession with the slapstick comedy genre has produced some all-time comedy classics and some best-forgotten clinkers. *A Fine Mess* belongs in the latter category.

Neither Ted Danson and Howie Mandel nor Richard Mulligan and Stuart Margolin offer audiences much affection, or are likely to receive much.

Danson plays a small-time actor who, during location filming at a racing stable, overhears two crooks (Mulligan and Margolin) as they dope a horse on the instructions of their boss (Paul Sorvino). Before long, Danson and his buddy Mandel are being chased all over LA by the incompetent villains, cueing in plenty of over-familiar car chases.

A Fine Mess is light on plot and instead concentrates on strenuous, familiar comedy routines. Trouble is, the principal players are all quite charmless.

■ FINE PAIR, A

1969, 88 MINS, ITALY/US ◇
Dir Francesco Maselli   *Prod* Leo L. Fuchs   *Scr* Francesco
Maselli, Luisa Montagnana, Larry Gelbart, Virgil C. Leone
Ph Alfio Contini   *Ed* Nicoletta Nardi   *Mus* Ennio
Morricone   *Art Dir* Luciano Puccino
● Rock Hudson, Claudia Cardinale, Tomas Milian, Leon
Askin, Ellen Corby, Walter Giller (Cinema Center)

A Fine Pair carries a promising original premise but film is so bogged down in contrived and confusing action that its impact is reduced to a minimum. Pic was lensed mostly in Italy. Script never rings true and Rock Hudson is called upon to enact an unconvincing character.

Film opens in NY, where Claudia Cardinale, a sexy 24-year-old who once knew Hudson when he visited her policeman-father in Italy 10 years before, arrives from her native country to enlist his assistance. She claims she's been involved with an international jewel thief and she wants Hudson's help in returning a fortune in jewels stolen from the winter villa of a rich American family in Austria.

Hudson plays his role in a grim manner and Cardinale is nice to look at even though difficult to understand.

■ FINIAN'S RAINBOW

1968, 145 MINS, US ◇ ⊛ ⊙
Dir Francis Coppola   *Prod* Joseph Landon   *Scr* E. Y.
Harburg, Fred Saidy   *Ph* Philip Lathrop   *Ed* Melvin
Shapiro   *Mus* Ray Heindorf, Ken Darby (sups.)
Art Dir Hilyard M. Brown
● Fred Astaire, Petula Clark, Tommy Steele, Don
Francks, Keenan Wynn, Barbara Hancock (Warner)

This translation of the 1947 legituner [music by Burton Lane, lyrics by E.Y. Harburg] is a light, pastoral fantasy with civil rights angles, underscored by comedy values.

Film opens leisurely with Fred Astaire and Petula Clark, his daughter, on a montage tour of the US. The stars come to rest in Rainbow Valley, just as the police henchmen of racist judge Keenan Wynn are about to foreclose on property owned by vagabond Don Francks.

Astaire bails out Francks, and latter's romance with Clark develops. Tommy Steele arrives as the leprechaun searching for gold which Astaire has stolen.

Overall, the $4 million film has an ethereal quality: it's a blend of real elements, such as love, greed, compassion, prejudice, and other aspects of human nature both noble and otherwise; yet it's also infused with mystical elements of magic, leprechauns, pixies and wishes that come true.

Clark, in her American film debut, has a winsome charm, which comes through despite a somewhat reactive role.
□ 1968: Nominations: Best Adapted Music Score, Sound

■ FIRE AND ICE

1983, 81 MINS, US ◇ ⊛ ⊙
Dir Ralph Bakshi   *Prod* Ralph Bakshi, Frank Frazetta
Scr Roy Thomas, Gerry Conway   *Ed* A. Davis Marshall
Mus William Kraft (PSO)

Ralph Bakshi's newest animation feature is interesting for two special reasons: (1) the production represents a clear design on Bakshi's part to capture a wider and younger audience and (2) the animation marks the film debut of America's leading exponent of heroic fantasy art, Frank Frazetta, who coproduced.

Known for his classic comic book and poster art, Frazetta works some of his famous illustrations into the film, such as his *Death Dealer* painting portraying an axe-wielding figure on horseback. Populating an Armageddon embellished with subhumans and flying dragonhawks are a blond hero, Larn; a sensuous-vulnerable dream girl in distress, Teegra; and an icy sorcerer and his willful mother, Lord Nekron and Juliana. Bakshi shot live actors first, to lay the foundation for the animation, in a process called Rotoscope.

■ FIRE BIRDS

(UK: Wings of the Apache)

1990, 85 MINS, US ◇ ⊛ ⊙
Dir David Green   *Prod* William Badalato   *Scr* Nick
Thiel, Paul F. Edwards   *Ph* Tony Imi   *Ed* Jon Poll,
Norman Buckley, Dennis O'Connor   *Mus* David
Newman   *Art Dir* Joseph T. Garrity
● Nicolas Cage, Tommy Lee Jones, Sean Young, Bert
Rhine, Bryan Kestner, Dale Dye (Touchstone/Nova)

Originally titled *Wings of the Apache* for the Apache assault helicopters prominently featured, *Fire Birds* resembles a morale booster project leftover from The Reagan era. A paean to Yankee air power, it shows the US Army as a take-charge outfit able to kick the butt of those South American drug cartel jerks.

Not surprisingly, given changing times and politics, *Fire Birds* has a tongue-in-cheek aspect. Camaraderie and rat-a-tat-tat dialog may have started out as fun a la Howard Hawks' classic *Only Angels Have Wings* but emerges at times as a satire of the genre.

Formula script, which inevitably recalls *Top Gun*, has Nicolas Cage training to use the army's Apache aircraft while vainly trying to rekindle a romance with old flame Sean Young. Tommy Lee Jones is dead-on as the taskmaster instructor who cornily singles out Cage for rough treatment. Film's main novelty is having Young also sent into combat instead of being the woman sitting on the sidelines.

■ FIRE DOWN BELOW

1957, 116 MINS, US ◇ ⊛
Dir Robert Parrish   *Prod* Irving Allen, Albert R. Broccoli
Scr Irwin Shaw   *Ph* Desmond Dickinson, Cyril Knowles
Ed Jack Slade   *Mus* Arthur Benjamin   *Art Dir* John Box
● Rita Hayworth, Robert Mitchum, Jack Lemmon,
Herbert Lom, Bernard Lee, Anthony Newley (Warwick/
Columbia)

Story [from a novel by Max Catto]: bad, bad girl (Rita Hayworth) meets youthful American, and finally agrees to marry him though warning him of her past – that of sort of a Mata Hari in Europe. Robert Mitchum, as Jack Lemmon's pal in a small fishing and smuggling boat operation, is vastly displeased with this development and tips off the Coast Guard on a smuggling trip so that Lemmon abandons the boat rather than be captured as a smuggler.

This lands him on a Greek freighter which crashes into a heavier ship in the fog. Lemmon is pinned down in the hold by a steel girder. Nearly all the second half of the film is centered on efforts to rescue him.

Hayworth is excellent as the comely femme who is always just one step ahead of the law. Lemmon (who takes a bow for composing the harmonica theme) shows plainly that he can handle a dramatic type role while Mitchum, as the tough man of the world, contributes one of his better portrayals.

■ **FIREFOX**

1982, 137 MINS, US ◇ ⊛ ⊙

Dir Clint Eastwood   *Prod* Clint Eastwood   *Scr* Alex Lasker, Wendell Wellman   *Ph* Bruce Surtees   *Ed* Ferris Webster, Ron Spang   *Mus* Maurice Jarre   *Art Dir* John Graysmark, Elayne Ceder

● Clint Eastwood, Freddie Jones, David Huffman, Warren Clarke, Ronald Lacey, Kenneth Colley (Warner)

Firefox is a burn-out. Lethargic, characterless and at least a half-hour too long, Cold War espionage saga [from the novel by Craig Thomas] about an American pilot smuggled into the USSR to steal an advanced fighter jet is a disappointment since it possessed the basic elements of a topflight, us vs them actioner.

It all sounded good on paper – Clint Eastwood, as a retired ace flyer, infiltrating the Russian Air Force to spirit away the supposedly top-secret Firefox, a plane capable of Mach 5 speed and equipped with a thought-controlled weapons system.

But Eastwood, who generally displays astuteness when controlling his own projects has inexplicably dropped the ball here. Despite the tense mission being depicted, there's no suspense, excitement or thrills to be had, and laxidaisical pacing gives viewer plenty of time to ponder the gaping implausibilities.

■ **FIRE OVER ENGLAND**

1937, 88 MINS, UK ⊛

Dir William K. Howard   *Prod* Erich Pommer   *Scr* Clemence Dane, Sergei Nolbandov   *Ph* James Wong Howe   *Ed* Jack Dennis   *Mus* Richard Addinsell   *Art Dir* Lazare Meerson

● Flora Robson, Raymond Massey, Leslie Banks, Laurence Olivier, Vivien Leigh, Lyn Harding (Pendennis London)

This is a handsomely mounted and forcefully dramatic glorification of Queen Bess. It holds a succession of brilliantly played scenes, a wealth of choice diction, pointed excerpts from English history and a series of impressive tableaux.

It projects Flora Robson in a conception of the British regent which holds the imagination. Her keen aptitude in dovetailing the strong and frail sides of Elizabeth's nature makes a solid keystone for the production.

Action ranges from cumbersomely dull to sharp, hardhitting flashes of excitement. Where director William K. Howard seems to get in his most telling dramatic effects are the sequences which build up to Laurence Olivier's undoing as an English spy and his subsequent escape, the queen's confronting of her coterie of exposed betrayers, and the burning of the Spanish armada.

Sprightly plied are the romantic passages. It's a two-cornered play for Olivier. First object of his deportment is his childhood sweetheart and lady-in-waiting to the queen, persuasively treated by Vivien Leigh. His other idyllic moments bring him in contact with the daughter of a Spanish nobleman. As the Spanish beauty Tamara Desni blends a compound of charm and sympathy.

■ **FIREPOWER**

1979, 104 MINS, UK ◇ ⊛

Dir Michael Winner   *Prod* Michael Winner   *Scr* Gerald Wilson   *Ph* Robert Paynter, Dick Kratina   *Ed* Arnold Crust [= Michael Winner], Max Benedict   *Mus* Gato Barbieri   *Art Dir* John Stoll, John Blezard

● Sophia Loren, James Coburn, O.J. Simpson, Eli Wallach, Anthony Franciosa, Vincent Gardenia (ITC)

Firepower is one of those international action thrillers designed to combine a top-name cast with lots of shooting and explosions so the story [by Bill Kerby and Michael Winner] can be followed regardless of whether you understand the language.

Though competent with chases and gunfire, producer-director Michael Winner handles the dialog scenes as if the most significant thing in the world were sunglasses.

Beautiful Sophia Loren believes her chemist husband was murdered at the order of Stegner (George Touliatos), a wealthy, seclusive industrialist. She persuades the Justice Department, who also wants Stegner, to put the pressure on mobster Eli Wallach to entice retired hitman James Coburn to get Stegner.

■ **FIRE SALE**

1977, 88 MINS, US ◇ ⊛

Dir Alan Arkin   *Prod* Marvin Worth   *Scr* Robert Klane   *Ph* Ralph Woolsey   *Ed* Richard Halsey   *Mus* Dave Grusin   *Art Dir* James H. Spencer

● Alan Arkin, Rob Reiner, Vincent Gardenia, Anjanette Comer, Kay Medford, Barbara Dana (20th Century-Fox)

Fire Sale, Alan Arkin's alleged comedy is a consummate sophomoric vulgarity. Marvin Worth's production matches in crippled creativity the physical infirmities on which most of the forced and strident humor is based. Arkin and Rob Reiner head the cast as two harried sons of Vincent Gardenia, himself the henpecked husband of Kay Medford.

Gardenia owns a dumpy department store, Reiner his cowed assistant after Arkin years earlier departed the family circle to become a failure as a basketball coach.

Sid Caesar is appropriately offensive as a Veterans' Hospital basket case coaxed by Gardenia into burning the store for insurance, thinking it's a World War II German installation.

■ **FIRESTARTER**

1984, 115 MINS, US ◇ ⊛ ⊙

Dir Mark L. Lester   *Prod* Frank Capra Jr   *Scr* Stanley Mann   *Ph* Giuseppe Ruzzolini   *Ed* David Rawlins   *Mus* Tangerine Dream   *Art Dir* Giorgio Postiglione

● David Keith, Drew Barrymore, George C. Scott, Martin Sheen, Heather Locklear, Art Carney (De Laurentiis)

Story of a nine-year-old girl who can enflame objects and people by power of her will balances human concern of a pursued and loving father and daughter (David Keith and Drew Barrymore) against a clandestine government agency that wants to use the girl's power for nefarious ends. Agency is headed by Martin Sheen, with Moses Gunn and George C. Scott as chilly support group.

Film marks the first major picture for director Mark L. Lester. But pic's stars are special effects team Mike Wood and Jeff Jarvis, whose pyrotechnics – flying fireballs, fire trenches, human balls of fire – create the film's impact.

Script by Stanley Mann is quite faithful to the Stephen King novel, but cinematically that loyalty is damaging. Picture's length can't sustain the material.

■ **FIRES WITHIN**

1991, 86 MINS, US ◇ ⊛ ⊙

Dir Gillian Armstrong   *Prod* Wallis Nicita, Lauren Lloyd   *Scr* Cynthia Cidre   *Ph* David Gribble   *Ed* Lou Lombardo, John Scott   *Mus* Maurice Jarre   *Art Dir* Robert Ziembicki

● Greta Scacchi, Jimmy Smits, Vincent D'Onofrio, Brit Hathaway, Luis Avalos, Bertila Damas (Pathe/M-G-M)

The timely, real-life situation involves an attractive emigre (Greta Scacchi) and her infant daughter (Brit Hathaway), among the 'raft people' who continue to flee Cuba via open ocean on makeshift, floating deathtraps – hoping for landfall in the Florida Keys. They're rescued by a seaman (Vincent D'Onofrio), with whom the woman forms a romantic relationship over the next eight years.

She left a husband behind in Cuba, Jimmy Smits as a writer imprisoned for criticizing the Castro regime. His sudden release and subsequent arrival in Miami as a hero creates a classic romantic triangle against the backdrop of Cuban emigre politics.

Director Gillian Armstrong's attempt to cover all the emotional and political ramifications of Cynthia Cidre's thoughtful tale is, for the most part, dramatically respectable. But it is a cold narrative that never lingers on any situation long enough to generate either suspense or romance.

Scacchi's woman-in-the-middle role is confused at worst, detached at best. Smits, as the husband, garners the film's appeal.

■ **FIRM, THE**

1993, 154 MINS, US ◇ ⊛ ⊙

Dir Sydney Pollack   *Prod* Scott Rudin, John Davis, Sydney Pollack   *Scr* David Rabe, Robert Towne, David Rayfiel   *Ph* John Seale   *Ed* William Steinkamp, Frederic Steinkamp   *Mus* Dave Grusin   *Art Dir* Richard Macdonald

● Tom Cruise, Jeanne Tripplehorn, Gene Hackman, Hal Holbrook, Ed Harris, Holly Hunter (Paramount/Mirage)

The Firm is a very smooth adaptation of John Grisham's giant 1991 bestseller. Tom Cruise's hotshot lawyer bent on toppling his corrupt bosses could be a brother to his *A Few Good Men* character. Readers are in for a few extra twists in the final third of the story, as director Sydney Pollack and his trio of screenwriters have added some dramatic and ethical complexity to this yarn.

Cruise portrays Mitch McDeere, a sought-after Harvard grad who shuns offers from big city law offices in favor of a small, lucrative Memphis concern that promotes itself as a family. Mitch's teacher wife Abby (Jeanne Tripplehorn) smells a rat from the outset, since the firm imposes unusually rigid codes of personal behavior, but Mitch jumps in with the enthusiasm of a puppy, working all hours, currying favor with the boss (Hal Holbrook) and lunching with mentor Avery Tolar (Gene Hackman).

After two of the firm's attorneys die in a mysterious boating accident, Mitch and Avery head to the Cayman Islands to investigate. Later, Mitch begins to suspect that the firm could be responsible for the deaths of four of its employees over the years.

Pollack has done an ultra-pro job in giving spit and polish to this star-driven, sure-fire commercial project. Close attention has been paid to story structure, the narrative is advanced in every sequence, and types of scenes are alternated carefully.

The more than 2½ hour length is a bit indulgent, but pic retains its grip. One couldn't imagine anyone better than Cruise at this sort of star turn, except Robert Redford 25 years ago. Tripplehorn gets to do a bit more than hold down the home front and expresses doubt and fury at Mitch's long hours. Hackman turns in another sterling perf as a top lawyer with unexpected depths of pain and remorse.

■ **FIRST A GIRL**

1935, 92 MINS, UK

Dir Victor Saville   *Prod* Michael Balcon   *Scr* Marjorie Gaffney   *Ph* Glen MacWilliams   *Ed* A. Barnes   *Art Dir* Oscar Werndorff

● Jessie Matthews, Sonnie Hale, Anna Lee, Griffith Jones, Alfred Drayton, Eddie Gray (Gaumont-British)

Jessie Matthews' admirers will love to see her rise from her humdrum niche in a dressmaking establishment to the giddy heights of thespian glory.

Though always longing for a stage career, her precipitous plunge comes about accidentally. She pals up with an aspiring Shakespearean actor, in reality a female impersonator. While sheltering her, he gets a wire giving him an unexpected date, which sudden loss of voice makes it impossible for him to accept. He coaches the bewildered girl and insists she take his place.

The variety hall is an awful dump. Billed, and trading, on the doubt concerning her sex, and carefully managed by her new partner, the act is a hit and she quickly makes a name.

The former wealthy customer, a 'princess' and her boyfriend become friendly with the couple, but suspect she is really a girl and trick her by stalling on a motor trip to the Riviera, forcing her to share a room at a wayside inn with the two men.

Sonnie Hale plays the impersonator and gives an air of sincerity to a rather dubious situation. The boyfriend (Griffith Jones) has charm and a quiet dignity. The starring role is a natural for Jessie Matthews, where her dancing is unobtrusively displayed.

●●●●●●●●●●●●●●●●●●●●●●●●●●●●●●

■ FIRST BLOOD

1982, 94 MINS, US ◇ ⓦ ⊙
Dir Ted Kotcheff   *Prod* Buzz Feitshans   *Scr* Michael Kozoll, William Sackheim, Sylvester Stallone   *Ph* Andrew Laszlo   *Ed* Thom Noble   *Mus* Jerry Goldsmith   *Art Dir* Stephane Reichel
● Sylvester Stallone, Richard Crenna, Brian Dennehy, David Caruso, Jack Starrett, Michael Talbot (Orion)

Sylvester Stallone plays a former Green Beret, a 'killing machine' who's so tough if there had been one more of him, the Viet Cong wouldn't have had a chance.

Arriving unshaven at the quiet community of Hope, he's greeted by sheriff Brian Dennehy, who does not invite him to join the local Lion's club. In fact, Dennehy won't even let him linger for a sandwich. This upsets the taciturn Stallone and he winds up at the slammer. Beating up the whole station house, he escapes into the woods.

Richard Crenna shows up, a Green Beret colonel who trained Stallone. They trap Stallone in a mine and blast the dickens out of it with a rocket. But our boy commandeers an army truck and machine gun and goes back to level Dennehy's quiet little town.

Director Ted Kotcheff has all sorts of trouble with this mess, aside from credibility. Supposedly, the real villain here is society itself, which invented a debacle like Vietnam and must now deal with its lingering tragedies. But *First Blood* cops out completely on that one, not even trying to find a solution to Stallone's problems.

●●●●●●●●●●●●●●●●●●●●●●●●●●●●●●

■ FIRST DEADLY SIN, THE

1980, 112 MINS, US ◇ ⓦ ⊙
Dir Brian Hutton   *Prod* George Pappas, Mark Shanker   *Scr* Mann Rubin   *Ph* Jack Priestley   *Ed* Eric Albertson   *Mus* Gordon Jenkins   *Art Dir* Woody Mackintosh
● Frank Sinatra, Faye Dunaway, Brenda Vaccaro, James Whitmore, David Dukes, Martin Gabel (Kastner/Artanis/Cinema 7)

Otherwise a fairly routine and turgid crime meller, *The First Deadly Sin* commands some interest as Frank Sinatra's first film in 10 years.

Pic presents audience with considerable barriers to involvement from the outset, as first few reels consist predominantly of a bloody operation, a violent murder, dialog conducted over mutilated bodies in an autopsy room and unappetizing hospital scenes.

Plot has Sinatra latching onto an apparent series of arbitrary murders.

Paralleling the crime-and-detection yarn, and slowing down the entire proceedings, are Sinatra's visits to wife Faye Dunaway, who's not recovering well from a kidney operation.

As for Sinatra, direct and not at all the wise guy, this amounts to a decent performance, even if the role might have called for a more desperate attitude.

●●●●●●●●●●●●●●●●●●●●●●●●●●●●●●

■ FIRST GREAT TRAIN ROBBERY, THE
(US: The Great Train Robbery)

1979, 110 MINS, UK ◇ ⓦ ⊙
Dir Michael Crichton   *Prod* John Foreman   *Scr* Michael Crichton   *Ph* Geoffrey Unsworth   *Ed* David Bretherton   *Mus* Jerry Goldsmith   *Art Dir* Maurice Carter
● Sean Connery, Donald Sutherland, Lesley-Anne Down, Wayne Sleep, Michael Elphick, Alan Webb (United Artists/De Laurentiis)

Based on fact, the story [from the novel by Michael Crichton] concerns the first recorded heist from a moving train. Suave arch-criminal Sean Connery enlists Donald Sutherland, Wayne Sleep, in a bid to lift a payroll of gold bars destined for the Crimea in 1855. A vital part, or rather series of parts, in the plan is played by Lesley-Anne Down as Connery's versatile yet reliable mistress.

The actual theft is ingenious. The film's highpoint comes when Connery clambers from car roof to car roof as the steam train speeds smokily under low bridges.

Crichton's films drag in dialog bouts, but triumph when action takes over.

Handling of the train sequences by cinematographer Geoffrey Unsworth is a lesson in the superior effectiveness of a well-placed camera over fancy tricks. A final caption dedicates the film to his memory, stating: 'His friends miss him.' So will his audiences.

●●●●●●●●●●●●●●●●●●●●●●●●●●●●●●

■ FIRST LOVE

1977, 91 MINS, US ◇ ⓦ
Dir Joan Darling   *Prod* Lawrence Turman, David Foster   *Scr* Jane Stanton Hitchcock, David Freeman   *Ph* Bobby Byrne   *Ed* Frank Morriss   *Mus* Joel Sill   *Art Dir* Robert Luthardt
● William Katt, Susan Dey, John Heard, Beverly D'Angelo, Robert Loggia, Tom Lacy (Paramount)

First Love is a sensitive and melancholy film about the impact of romance on college student William Katt when he falls for coed Susan Dey.

Harold Brodkey's *New Yorker* story, *Sentimental Education*, has been adapted into a script which takes Katt through the highs and lows of complicated young love.

But an unfortunate element in the story is the never-ending pall of doom that hangs over everything. From frame one the mood is a downer, which dampens the several nice bright moments of exuberance and telegraphs the coming climactic ambiguity. Katt is excellent. So is Dey, who has an appealing charisma of vivacious sensuality.

●●●●●●●●●●●●●●●●●●●●●●●●●●●●●●

■ FIRST MONDAY IN OCTOBER

1981, 96 MINS, US ◇ ⓦ ⊙
Dir Ronald Neame   *Prod* Paul Heller, Martha Scott   *Scr* Jerome Lawrence, Robert E. Lee   *Ph* Fred J. Koenekamp   *Ed* Peter E. Berger   *Mus* Ian Fraser   *Art Dir* Philip M. Jefferies
● Walter Matthau, Jill Clayburgh, Jan Sterling, Barnard Hughes, James Stephens, Joshua Bryant (Paramount)

Amiable talents of Walter Matthau and Jill Clayburgh make *First Monday in October* a mildly engaging talkfest in which all serious issues serve as window dressing for an almost-romantic comedy.

Rumpled and as likeable as ever, Matthau here portrays the court's 'great dissenter,' an individualistic civil libertarian a la the late William O. Douglas. In theory he greatly welcomes the appointment of a woman, but his hair stands on end when he learns that America's first female Supreme Court justice is the arch-conservative Clayburgh, 'the Mother Superior of Orange County.'

Decorum of the widow's installment into the men's club atmosphere of the court provokes smiles, if not big laughs, but it's all a prelude to the civilized sparks which fly when the two tangle over two major cases on the docket.

Scripters, working from their own popular play, have opted for the light treatment, with issues of the day merely providing a means for this odd couple to (sort of) get together.

●●●●●●●●●●●●●●●●●●●●●●●●●●●●●●

■ FIRST OF THE FEW, THE
(US: Spitfire)

1942, 118 MINS, UK ⓦ
Dir Leslie Howard   *Prod* Leslie Howard   *Scr* Anatole de Grunwald, Miles Malleson   *Ph* Jack Hildyard   *Ed* Douglas Myers   *Mus* William Walton   *Art Dir* Paul Sheriff
● Leslie Howard, David Niven, Rosamund John, Roland Culver, Anne Firth (British Aviation)

In interpreting the life of R.J. Mitchell, who designed the Spitfire plane, Leslie Howard's work ranks among his finest performances. And it is an epic picture.

Film portrays Mitchell's heartbreaking efforts to get his series of aircraft models accepted. His work was looked upon as too revolutionary, and the reluctance of Whitehall to sponsor anything new was most discouraging.

For big scenes there is the reproduction of a race for the Schneider Cup. For sweet domestic felicity there's Rosamund John as the wife of Mitchell. For a magnificent patriotic gesture there is Toni Edgar Bruce as Lady Houston, who contributed generously to the financing of the inventor. Finally (or should it be firstly?) there's Howard's young airman friend in the person of David Niven, as a lovable philanderer who shares the other's vicissitudes and glories.

●●●●●●●●●●●●●●●●●●●●●●●●●●●●●●

■ FIRST TIME, THE

1983, 95 MINS, US ◇ ⓦ
Dir Charlie Loventhal   *Prod* Sam Irvin   *Scr* Charlie Loventhal, Susan Weiser-Finley, William Franklin Finley   *Ph* Steve Fierberg   *Ed* Stanley Vogel   *Mus* Lanny Meyers   *Art Dir* Tom Surgal
● Tim Choate, Krista Errickson, Marshall Efron, Wendy Fulton, Raymond Patterson, Jane Badler (New Line/Goldmine)

The First Time is a mild but entertaining first feature by writer-director Charlie Loventhal and producer Sam Irvin, former assistants to Brian De Palma. Dealing fictionally with Loventhal's growing-up adventures while a student at formerly all-girls school Sarah Lawrence, the comedy owes much to De Palma's freewheeling satires made in the 1960s.

Charlie (Tim Choate) is an odd-man-out at college: unable to score with the pretty (but believably so) girls there while his black room-mate Ronald (Raymond Patterson) shows off and gives him tips.

While pursuing an unattainable dream girl Dana (Krista Errickson), Charlie links up with another lonely soul Wendy (Wendy Fulton), and ultimately loses his virginity with the inevitable older woman Karen (Jane Badler).

Choate is very sympathetic in the lead role, matched by the sex appeal of Errickson, naturalism of Fulton and comedy sex-bomb Wendie Jo Sperber.

●●●●●●●●●●●●●●●●●●●●●●●●●●●●●●

■ FISH CALLED WANDA, A

1988, 108 MINS, US ◇ ⑦ ⊙
Dir Charles Crichton *Prod* Michael Shamberg
Scr John Cleese *Ph* Alan Hume *Ed* John Jympson
Mus John Du Prez *Art Dir* Roger Murray-Leach
● John Cleese, Jamie Lee Curtis, Kevin Kline, Michael
Palin, Tom Georgeson, Maria Aitken (M-G-M/Prominent)

In *A Fish Called Wanda*, Monty Pythoners John
Cleese and Michael Palin get caught up in a
double-crossing crime caper with a mismatched and hilarious pair of scheming
Yanks, Jamie Lee Curtis and Kevin Kline.

Though it is less tasteless, irreverent and
satirical than the Python pics, film still is
wacky and occasionally outrageous in its own,
distinctly British way.

John Cleese is Archie Leach (Cary Grant's
real name) an uptight, respected barrister
who becomes unglued when Wanda (Jamie
Lee Curtis), the girlfriend of a crook he's defending, comes on to him for no apparent reason.

Curtis fakes it as an American law student
looking to learn about English law when really she just wants to get information out of
Cleese about some diamonds she's recently
heisted with his client George (Tom
Georgeson) and two others – her 'brother'
Otto (Kevin Kline), who's really no relation
and a stuttering animal rights freak Ken
(Michael Palin), the proud owner of a fish
tank and a fish named Wanda.

Cleese [scripting from a story by himself
and director Charles Crichton] takes an opportunity to poke fun at something ripe for
ridicule – this time, the love-hate rivalry between the Brits and the Yanks. It's funny
without being mean, since both sides gets
their due. Curtis steals the show with her
keen sense of comic timing and sneaky little
grins and asides. Palin has too limited a role.
□ 1988: Best Supp. Actor (Kevin Kline).
□ Nominations: Best Director, Original
Screenplay

■ FISHER KING, THE

1991, 137 MINS, US ◇ ⑦ ⊙
Dir Terry Gilliam *Prod* Debra Hill, Lynda Obst
Scr Richard LaGravenese *Ph* Roger Pratt *Ed* Lesley
Walker *Mus* George Fenton *Art Dir* Mel Bourne
● Robin Williams, Jeff Bridges, Amanda Plummer,
Mercedes Ruehl, Michael Jeter, Harry Shearer (Tri-Star)

The Fisher King has two actors at the top of
their form, and a compelling, well-directed
and well-produced story. First-time screenwriter Richard LaGravenese's lively, detailed
original script deftly delineates the top and
bottom rungs of human existence in
Manhattan. Jack Lucas (Jeff Bridges) is a callous, egotistical radio shock-jock who falls
apart after a caller he has blown off on the air
proceeds to blow away seven yuppies in a
trendy club. Just as he is about to end it all,
Jack is rescued by a goofy gang of derelicts
led by a maniac named Parry (Robin
Williams).

While recovering from his suicidal state,
Jack learns that Parry is obsessed with the
Holy Grail, as well as with a gawky young lady
Lydia (Amanda Plummer). Jack's earnest attempts to return Parry to normal life and set
him up with the elusive Lydia represent his
chance at personal redemption.

Film's first two hours zip by quickly and are
spiked with memorable scenes such as a
flight-of-fancy in which commuters waltz
through Grand Central. But the final 20 minutes unspool mechanically and interminably
as Jack implausibly follows through on the
mythological demands of the story.

Jeff Bridges gives what is undoubtedly his
strongest lead performance to date hitting
notes he's never tried before in conveying the
turmoil inside an arrogant man. Williams is
endlessly inventive as usual, Plummer is ter-

rific as the nerdy loner, and Mercedes Ruehl
sizzles as Jack's upfront companion, Anne.
□ 1991: Best Supp. Actress (Mercedes
Ruehl).
□ Nominations: Best Actor (Robin Williams),
Original Screenplay, Original Score, Art
Direction

■ F.I.S.T.

1978, 145 MINS, US ◇ ⑦ ⊙
Dir Norman Jewison *Prod* Norman Jewison *Scr* Joe
Eszterhas, Sylvester Stallone *Ph* Laszlo Kovacs
Ed Tony Gibbs, Graeme Clifford *Mus* Bill Conti
Art Dir Richard MacDonald
● Sylvester Stallone, Rod Steiger, Peter Boyle, Melinda
Dillon, David Huffman, Tony Lo Bianco (United Artists)

In its superb telling of how a humble but idealistic young man escalates to the corrupt
heights of unbridled power, *F.I.S.T.* is to the
labor movement in the United States what
All the King's Men was to an era in American
politics.

The first hour of the film presents the milieu of unorganized labor circa 1937, a time
when the phrase 'property rights' was as persistent (and often as shrill) a harangue as
'human rights' later became. Sylvester
Stallone and lifelong friend David Huffman
are among the workers in Henry Wilcoxon's
trucking company. They drift into organizing
drivers for local union rep Richard Herd,
whose assassination during a brawl triggered
by management goons drives Stallone into
league with Kevin Conway, a local hood.

The next act depicts the militant labor response of Stallone and Conway, highlighted
by a well-staged riot, after which the tentacles of mobsterism – Tony Lo Bianco personi-
fying them well – parallel the growth and
power of the truckers' union.

Action then cuts to the late 1950s, when
Stallone pushes international union leader
Peter Boyle out of office by some private
blackmail, only to run head-on into Rod
Steiger, crusading US senator.

■ FISTFUL OF DOLLARS

1964, 100 MINS, ITALY/W. GERMANY/SPAIN ◇ ⑦ ⊙
Dir Bob Robertson [= Sergio Leone] *Prod* Harry
Colombo [= Arrigo Colombo], George Papi [= Giorgio
Papi] *Scr* Bob Robertson, Duccio Tessari, Mark Lowell
Ph Jack Dalmas [= Massimo Dallamano] *Ed* Bob Quintle
[= Roberto Cinquini] *Mus* Dan Savio [= Ennio
Morricone] *Art Dir* Charles Simons [= Carlo Simi]
● Clint Eastwood, Marianne Koch, Johnny Wels [= Gian
Maria Volonte], Wolfgang Lukschy, Joe Edger [= Josef
Egger], Antonio Prieto (Jolly/Constantin/Ocean)

A cracker-jack western made in Italy and
Spain by a group of Italians and an international cast, this is a hard-hitting item, ably directed, splendidly lensed, neatly acted, which
has all the ingredients wanted by action fans
and then some.

Basically, it's about a loner, Joe (Clint
Eastwood), who arrives in a small
Southwestern settlement split by the rivalry
of two families. For money, he plays both
sides against the middle, eventually winning
his longstanding battle with the heavy. Tale
[by Toni Palombi, based on the 1961 Japanese
film *Yojimbo*] is well developed, and though
there is plenty of cliche, it's handled with an
all-stops-out style, vigorous use of widescreen
camera, effective juggling of closeups and
long shots.

Spanish landscapes pass well for
Southwestern areas bordering on Mexico as
do costumes and types chosen, be they
German, Italian, Spanish or 'original' Yanks.

Eastwood handles himself very well as the
stranger, shaping a character strong enough
to beg a sequel. Further plaudits go to title
animation by Luigi Lardani, which sets the
style of this film from the start. Also to music,

somewhat redundant but effective in the
western vein.

[Version reviewed was 100-minute Italian
one, with Eastwood dubbed by experienced
actor Enrico Maria Salerno. English version
was released in US and UK in 1967.]

■ FISTFUL OF DYNAMITE, A
(Aka: Duck, You Sucker)

1972, 139 MINS, ITALY ◇ ⑦ ⊙
Dir Sergio Leone *Prod* Fulvio Morsella *Scr* Luciano
Vincenzoni, Sergio Donati, Sergio Leone *Ph* Giuseppe
Ruzzolini *Ed* Nino Baragli *Mus* Ennio Morricone
Art Dir Andrea Crisanti
● Rod Steiger, James Coburn, Romolo Valli, Jean Michel
Antoine, Vivien Chandler, David Warbeck (Rafran/Euro
International)

Sergio Leone comes up with a tale [co-penned
with Sergio Donati] of the Mexican revolution. Rod Steiger plays a simple bandit who
wants to rob a bank in a Mexican town but instead gets mixed up in a revolution in which
he has no interest. He meets Coburn, a veritable storehouse of explosives on his person,
and together they become involved in the
peasants' revolt.

Leone occasionally inserts a light touch but
generally action which includes firing squads,
much shooting, a bridge which troops are
crossing blown up and a climaxing train collision are realistically portrayed. A paralleling
note is offered via flashbacks through Coburn
comparing some of his past experiences in
the Irish Rebellion to events at hand, but procedure sometimes is clumsy.

[Reviewed above as *Duck, You Sucker*. Film's
English-language title was changed soon after
to *A Fistful of Dynamite*.]

■ FITZWILLY

1967, 102 MINS, US
Dir Delbert Mann *Prod* Walter Mirisch *Scr* Isobel
Lennart *Ph* Joseph Biroc *Ed* Ralph Winters *Mus* John
Williams *Art Dir* Robert F. Boyle
● Dick Van Dyke, Barbara Feldon, Edith Evans, John
McGiver, Harry Townes, John Fiedler (United Artists)

An okay, but sluggish, comedy about a butler
who masterminds robberies. Potential in the
screenplay, the very good cast, and the handsome production, is not realized due To generally tame direction by Delbert Mann.

Isobel Lennart adapted Poyntz Tyler's novel
A Garden of Cucumbers, in which Dick Van Dyke
is the devoted butler to Edith Evans, one of
those lovable biddies who, in this case, is not
at all as wealthy as she thinks. Van Dyke and
crew keep planning heists in order to support
her fantasies, and philanthropies. Arrival of
new secretary Barbara Feldon upsets the
smooth-running machinery.

Results of the flat direction is a pic that, in
the main, draws smiles, not outright laughs,
until the department store panic scene,
staged in top fashion.

■ FIVE

1951, 93 MINS, US
Dir Arch Oboler *Prod* Arch Oboler *Scr* Arch Oboler
Ph Louis Clyde Stoumen *Ed* John Hoffman *Mus* Henry
Russell *Art Dir* Arch Oboler
● William Phipps, Susan Douglas, James Anderson,
Charles Lampkin, Earl Lee (Oboler/Columbia)

Intriguing in theme, but depressing in its assumption. *Five* ranks high in the class of out-
of-the-ordinary pix. It is the story of the last
five persons on earth, survivors of an atom
blast which turns thriving cities into ghost
towns.

Writer-producer-director Arch Oboler has
injected vivid imagination into the production, but draws a little too much on his radio
technique. Principal criticism lies in its

F

dearth of action. However, interest is sustained in suspenseful situations and convincing dialog.

Oboler has selected his characters with care. William Phipps and Susan Douglas are effective as the love interest, with James Anderson doing a commendable job as the heavy. Charles Lampkin is competent as the sole Negro in a minute white world, while Earl Lee makes the most of his role as a bank teller who because of his horror-stricken mind, believes he's on 'vacation' from his job.

■ FIVE BRANDED WOMEN

1960, 100 MINS, US

Dir Martin Ritt *Prod* Dino De Laurentiis *Scr* Ivo Perilli *Ph* Giuseppe Rotunno *Ed* Jerry Webb *Mus* Francesco Lavagnino *Art Dir* Mario Chiari

● Silvana Mangano, Vera Miles, Barbara Bel Geddes, Jeanne Moreau, Carla Gravina, Richard Basehart (Paramount/Laurentiis)

Dino De Laurentiis' *Five Branded Women* is a grim account of the Yugoslavian partisans' fight against the invading Nazi army during World War II. The film occasionally plots an overly familiar conflict, but it catches the fervency of the resistance movement.

The film's strength lies in Ritt's direction. If his story bogs down, he is quick to follow with a storm of action, gripping in tone and adventurous in concept. The horrors of war are hammered out with serious intentions by screenwriter Ivo Perilli, who adapted the film from an unpublished novel by Ugo Pirro.

He describes the partisans as savages, willing to execute their own members if necessary, because it is this savagery that ultimately will destroy the Nazis. Scene by scene, the Yugoslavs are depicted as cruel, inhuman fighters who are, in fact, less sympathetic than their German enemy.

The women are Silvana Mangano, Vera Miles, Barbara Bel Geddes, Jeanne Moreau and Carla Gravina. Not all the roles are long, but they are universally rewarding, and the five actresses successfully fashion contrasting personalities.

Van Heflin stars as a partisan leader in one of his better roles. Richard Basehart is excellent as a captured German officer. Steve Forrest is the German soldier whose lovemaking is responsible for the branding of the women, and he scores with an electrifying scene, shouting of his mutilation by the partisans.

■ 5 CARD STUD

1968, 101 MINS, US ◇ ⓥ

Dir Henry Hathaway *Prod* Hal B. Wallis *Scr* Marguerite Roberts *Ph* Daniel L. Fapp *Ed* Warren Low *Mus* Maurice Jarre *Art Dir* Walter Tyler

● Dean Martin, Robert Mitchum, Inger Stevens, Roddy McDowall, Katherine Justice, Yaphet Kotto (Paramount)

Dean Martin is cast as a frontier gambler and Robert Mitchum plays a frontier parson who woos his congregation with a fast six-shooter.

Script [from a novel by Ray Gaulden] pits them against one another in the unraveling of whodunit murders, but dramatic buildup suffers thru a premature disclosure of killer's identity and subsequent lessening of what should have been more potent impact.

Action follows the aftermath of a late night poker game when a stranger is caught cheating and is lynched by five angry players.

Martin injects certain amount of humor into his role and generally acquits himself strongly. Mitchum's character at times seems contrived but he handles himself well nevertheless. Inger Stevens, playing a gold-rush Delilah who mistresses a stable of lady 'barbers,' lends distaff interest, and Katherine Justice is a nice addition as a ranch girl in love with Martin.

■ FIVE CORNERS

1987, 92 MINS, UK ◇ ⓥ

Dir Tony Bill *Prod* Forrest Murray, Tony Bill *Scr* John Patrick Shanley *Ph* Fred Murphy *Ed* Andy Blumenthal *Mus* James Newton Howard *Art Dir* Adrianne Lobel

● Jodie Foster, Tim Robbins, Todd Graff, John Turturro, Elizabeth Berridge, Rose Gregorio (HandMade)

Five Corners starts out as an affectionate look back at a Bronx neighborhood circa 1964 and then about halfway through takes a darker turn into urban violence.

In his first produced script, Patrick Shanley clearly has drawn from his experience to create the variety of personalities and swirl of influences that make life in the boroughs of New York City so distinctive.

Before would-be freedom fighter in Mississippi Harry (Tim Robbins) goes off to save the world, there is business for him to take care of in the old neighborhood. Local no-goodnik Heinz (John Turturro) is out of jail and looking to renew his old battle with Harry and his old longing for Linda (Jodie Foster).

They are marvelously drawn parts and Robbins as the Irish working-class kid with a social conscience gets into the heart and soul of the character. Turturro is downright scary but also sympathetic as the schoolyard psychotic. Foster is serviceable, but a little out of her element as a tough Catholic kid.

■ FIVE DAYS ONE SUMMER

1982, 108 MINS, US ◇ ⓥ

Dir Fred Zinnemann *Prod* Fred Zinnemann *Scr* Michael Austin *Ph* Giuseppe Rotunno *Ed* Stuart Baird *Mus* Elmer Bernstein *Art Dir* Willy Holt

● Sean Connery, Betsy Brantley, Lambert Wilson, Jennifer Hilary, Isabel Dean, Anna Massey (Ladd/Warner)

An attempt at an intimate personal drama that just doesn't come off, *Five Days One Summer* is so slow that it seems more like *Five Summers One Day*. A tale of adultery, mountain climbing and death that is as dramatically placid as the Swiss landscape it inhabits, the $15 million production is Fred Zinnemann's first film since *Julia* [1977].

Seeming hale and hearty, Sean Connery plays a Scottish doctor off on an Alpine vacation in 1932 with a twentyish woman he introduces as his wife. He aims to introduce her to his great sport, mountain climbing.

Gradually, flashbacks reveal that the girl is not his wife at all, but his niece, that Connery has a wife back home and that young Kate has been not so secretly in love with Connery since she was a child.

Ultimately, it all comes down to whether or not the girl will stay or leave, and if Connery and/or the guide will survive their climb of one of the most difficult mountains in the vicinity.

■ FIVE EASY PIECES

1970, 96 MINS, US ◇ ⓥ ⊙

Dir Bob Rafelson *Prod* Bob Rafelson, Richard Wechsler *Scr* Adrien Joyce [= Carolyn Eastman] *Ph* Laszlo Kovacs *Ed* Christopher Holmes, Gerald Sheppard *Art Dir* Toby Rafelson

● Jack Nicholson, Karen Black, Lois Smith, Susan Anspach, Helena Kallianiotes, Sally Ann Struthers (Columbia/BBS)

Director Bob Rafelson has put together an absorbing, if nerve-wracking, film.

Despite its solid American roots, this pic is reminiscent of nothing so much as the French films of the 1940s and 1950s.

Jack Nicholson is first seen on the job as a Southern California oilrigger sporting a 'cracker' accent and consorting with three members of the same breed especially his dumb, sexy girlfriend Rayette (Karen Black).

It's clear from the beginning that he doesn't think he belongs in this environment. But only later, when he quits his job and goes back home to the State of Washington does it become clear that his hard hat and his accent were a masquerade.

The film's nervewracking quality is consistent with its content. Nicholson's performance is a remarkably varied and daring exploration of a complex character, equally convincing in its manic and sober aspects.

□ 1970: Nominations: Best Picture, Actor (Jack Nicholson), Supp. Actress (Karen Black), Story & Screenplay

■ FIVE FINGER EXERCISE

1962, 108 MINS, US

Dir Daniel Mann *Prod* Frederick Brisson *Scr* Frances Goodrich, Albert Hackett *Ph* Harry Stradling *Ed* William A. Lyon *Mus* Jerome Moross *Art Dir* Ross Bellah

● Rosalind Russell, Jack Hawkins, Maximilian Schell, Richard Beymer, Annette Gorman, Lana Wood (Columbia)

Frederick Brisson, who transplanted this 1958 London stage hit to Broadway in 1959, has transplanted it into the more taxing idiom of the screen. It appears that something has been misplaced in the translation, as adapted by Frances Goodrich and Albert Hackett, and directed by Daniel Mann.

For one thing, the trimming to 108 minutes apparently has taken its toll of both characterization and plot. Furthermore, although there are two solid performances by Rosalind Russell and Jack Hawkins, there are three equally weak ones by Maximilian Schell, Richard Beymer and Annette Gorman.

The title refers to the significance of five fingers operating in co-ordination to create harmonious music, as in a piano study for beginners. The thoroughly unco-ordinated 'five fingers' in this family melodrama, reset in California from the original England, are an uncultured, intolerant, self-made business-man-father (Hawkins), a culture-obsessed, pseudo-intellectual mother (Russell), a confused, educated, 'mama's boy' son (Beymer), an animated, high-spirited daughter (Gorman), and a young German refugee (Schell), who has been employed by the family as tutor, and yearns to become a permanent part of it.

■ 5 FINGERS

1952, 107 MINS, US ⓥ

Dir Joseph L. Mankiewicz *Prod* Otto Lang *Scr* Michael Wilson *Ph* Norbert Brodine *Ed* James B. Clark *Mus* Bernard Herrmann *Art Dir* Lyle Wheeler, George W. Davis

● James Mason, Danielle Darrieux, Michael Rennie, Walter Hampden, John Wengraf, Michael Pate (20th Century-Fox)

A good, if somewhat overlong, cloak-and-dagger thriller has been concocted from an actual World War II espionage case. Screenplay is based on the novel *Operation Cicero*, written by L.C. Moyzisch, Nazi agent in the espionage dealings with 'Cicero', the fabulous spy.

Mason portrays Ulysses Diello known to the Nazis as Cicero, a valet to the British Ambassador in Turkey. A cold, assured character, he decides to make himself a fortune by selling Allied war plans to the Germans. Cicero's operations are moving forward without a hitch until the British begin to suspect someone within the Embassy and turn Michael Rennie loose on a counter-espionage job.

The script runs to considerable dialog in the first portions. However, pace quickens and becomes sock suspense drama, tight and tingling, when the story gets down to cases. Actual locations in Berlin, Ankara, Turkey,

London and Istanbul were used for a documentary background effect.
□ 1952: Nominations: Best Director, Screenplay

. . . .

■ FIVE GRAVES TO CAIRO

1943, 96 MINS, US ◇ ⊛
Dir Billy Wilder   *Prod* Charles Brackett (assoc.)
Scr Charles Brackett, Billy Wilder   *Ph* John F. Seitz
Ed Doane Harrison   *Mus* Miklos Rozsa   *Art Dir* Hans Dreier, Ernst Fegte
● Franchot Tone, Anne Baxter, Erich von Stroheim, Peter van Eyck, Akim Tamiroff, Fortunio Bonanova (Paramount)

Idea of making Field Marshal Rommel's campaign into an exciting fable is by Lajos Biro, Hungarian writer, who did so many successful Ernst Lubitsch screen hits. It affords a vivid picture of Rommel, Erich von Stroheim doing a capital job. The characterization is tailor-made for him.

Surprisingly for such a dynamic, moving vehicle, there is a minimum of actual battle stuff. Director Billy Wilder handles the varied story elements, countless suspenseful moments and vivid portrayals in excellent fashion. In some instances the absence of spoken word or muffled sentences have been pointed up through skilful pantomime and action.

Basically *Five Graves* is the story of a British corporal (Franchot Tone) who impersonates a Nazi spy to gain military information from the Germans as they sweep towards Cairo.

Crackling dialog and fine scripting by director Wilder and Charles Brackett enhance the Biro original [play]. Camerawork of John Seitz is outstanding, as is the film editing by Doane Harrison. Use of sound effects, indicating superb recording, especially during the running gun fight, also is topflight.
□ 1943: Nominations: Best B&W Cinematography, B&W Art Direction, Editing

. . . .

■ FIVE HEARTBEATS, THE

1991, 122 MINS, US ◇ ⊛ ⊙
Dir Robert Townsend   *Prod* Loretha C. Jones
Scr Robert Townsend, Keenen Ivory Wayans   *Ph* Bill Dill
Ed John Carter   *Mus* Stanley Clarke   *Art Dir* Wynn Thomas
● Robert Townsend, Michael Wright, Leon, Harry J. Lennix, Tico Wells, Diahann Carroll (20th Century-Fox)

Convincing only in its sweet and dazzling musical sequences, this overly sincere effort otherwise misses its mark. Counteracting the negative black stereotyping he lampooned in his directorial debut, *Hollywood Shuffle*, Robert Townsend lays out a parade of positive role models in a clean, upbeat family-oriented entertainment that feels oddly square and unauthentic.

Story begins in 1965 when fictional group the Five Heartbeats begins to emerge among other black pop groups then combining harmonies and slick choreography. Film follows the bouncing ball through the paces of every mediocre musicbiz story ever told, from talent contest to record deal to shoestring radio support tour, racism, hit single, media blitz and superstardom.

Script renders characters in the big ensemble cast as little more than types, with a constantly shifting focus and no one to really follow, and Townsend's vision and direction are wildly schizophrenic, veering from tragic depths to manipulative, heart-tugging poignance.

Townsend seems most at home with the music, and there are scenes onstage in which the film really hits its stride.

. . . .

■ 5,000,000 YEARS TO EARTH

See: Quatermass and the Pit

. . . .

■ FIVE STAR FINAL

1931, 85 MINS, US
Dir Mervyn LeRoy   *Scr* Byron Morgan, Robert Lord
Ph Sol Polito   *Ed* Frank Ware   *Mus* Leo Forbstein (dir.)
Art Dir Jack Okey
● Edward G. Robinson, Marian Marsh, H.B. Warner, Anthony Bushell, George E. Stone, Boris Karloff (First National)

Playwright Louis Weitzenkorn's strong argument against the scandal type of tabloid newspaper makes a strong talker.

Edward G. Robinson means a lot to this entertainment. He represents the margin between Weitzenkorn's story on the stage and on the screen. The picture version had a head start with its unrestricted area foundation, but it needed someone like Robinson as the managing editor.

H.B. Warner and Frances Starr have a suicide scene that could have been botched very easily. But they play it. The experience in back of both stands up and gives its right age in this picture.

A bit of symbolism inserted in the picture is, for once, a help. The editor is given the habit of washing his hands often at the basin in his office. His first washing occurs during his introduction in a speak. Thereafter, as the job gets dirtier, he repeats the soap stunt more often. When Robinson finally washes his hands of the job, he does it with soap and water.

After the yellow tab, for circulation purposes, has caused two suicides by reviving a 20-year-old murder case, the picture starts to move speedily. The daughter of the unfortunate parents goes to the newspaper with a gun in her bag to ask 'Why did you kill my mother?'

Marian Marsh is as strong as the rest in the payoff scene. She stands with Georgie Stone, Warner, Starr and Robinson as punch members of the cast.
□ 1931/32: Nomination: Best Picture

. . . .

■ 5,000 FINGERS OF DR. T., THE

1953, 89 MINS, US ◇ ⊛ ⊙
Dir Roy Rowland   *Prod* Stanley Kramer   *Scr* Dr Seuss [= Ted Geisel], Allan Scott   *Ph* Franz Planer   *Ed* Al Clark
Mus Frederick Hollander   *Art Dir* Rudolph Sternad
● Peter Lind Hayes, Mary Healy, Hans Conried, Tommy Rettig (Columbia)

The mad humor of Dr Seuss (Ted Geisel) has been captured on film in this odd flight into chimerical fiction. Story and conception were shaped by Dr Seuss for the Stanley Kramer unit at Columbia, and he also contributed to the screenplay and did lyrics for the songs composed by Frederick Hollander. Results are sometimes fascinating, more often fantastic.

Of all the wild, weird happenings, the film's standout is the fantastically imaginative dungeon ballet – a mad creation.

Tommy Rettig is the kid who would rather be out playing with his baseball and dog than learning the scales under the tutelage of Hans Conried, the Dr Terwilliker who becomes the villain of the plot. Opening finds the youngster dreaming he is being pursued by strange creatures with butterfly nets in a land full of odd cylinders and mounds, eerie hues and fog.

This new land is a terrifying one, filled with a strong castle in which Dr T conducts a school of piano for the 500 boys he holds prisoner. In the dungeon, deep below the fortress, is a group of miserable creatures, grown green and moldy with age, who were imprisoned because they dared play instruments other than the piano.

Roy Rowland, an expert in the direction of kids, shows his skill in handling Rettig and does fairly well by most of the fantasy, although the material is such that it's hard to

keep the interest from lagging at times.
□ 1953: Nomination: Best Scoring of a Musical Picture

. . . .

■ FIXED BAYONETS

1951, 92 MINS, US ◇
Dir Samuel Fuller   *Prod* Jules Buck   *Scr* Samuel Fuller
Ph Lucien Ballard   *Ed* Nick De Maggio   *Mus* Roy Webb
Art Dir Lyle Wheeler, George Patrick
● Richard Basehart, Gene Evans, Michael O'Shea, Richard Hylton, Craig Hill, Skip Homeier (20th Century-Fox)

Story [suggested by a novel by John Brophy] revolves around a platoon left behind temporarily to fight a rearguard action for a retreating regiment in Korea.

The detail is supposed to be a hand-picked group of veterans. Yet among them is a corporal (Richard Basehart) who cannot bring himself to shoot an enemy soldier. How he shakes off this fixation and ultimately assumes command of the decimated platoon is an underlying theme that pervades the whole yarn.

Writer-director Samuel Fuller's platoon is a typical band of GIs. There's the sergeant (Gene Evans), a bearded vet of the last war who takes to his chores with a skill born of long experience. Sergeant Michael O'Shea is another hard-bitten '20-year man'. Privates include men of Italian, Polish and American Indian extraction, among others.

There's a wealth of suspense in the screenplay, for until the closing minutes filmgoers are unaware whether the platoon will succeed in its mission and rejoin the regiment.

. . . .

■ FIXER, THE

1968, 130 MINS, US ◇
Dir John Frankenheimer   *Prod* Edward Lewis
Scr Dalton Trumbo   *Ph* Marcel Grignon   *Ed* Henry Berman   *Mus* Maurice Jarre   *Art Dir* Bela Zeichan
● Alan Bates, Dirk Bogarde, Georgia Brown, Hugh Griffith, Elizabeth Hartman, Ian Holm (M-G-M)

Much of the unfoldment [of this adaptation of Bernard Malamud's novel] is in the filthy prison cell of its chief protagonist, a Jew accused of the murder of a young boy but never formally charged.

Czarist Russia at the turn of the century is the period and the locality is Kiev, where a handyman is caught up in the wave of anti-Semitism. In his long suffering that follows his refusal to confess to a crime he did not commit, his case becomes known to the world.

Basic character is enacted by Alan Bates in an indefinite delineation frequently baffling to the spectator. Victim of the Russian government's persecution of all Jews and its dedication to his conviction, he is subjected to every form of mental and physical punishment to make him confess.

But reaction to violence is not alone sufficient for a fine sustained performance and overall Bates suffers from the writing.

Dirk Bogarde is fairly persuasive as a government lawyer who tries to help Bates, but his character isn't well developed.

Scoring more satisfactorily, histrionically, is Elizabeth Hartman, as a young woman who tries to seduce Bates.
□ 1968: Nomination: Best Actor (Alan Bates)

. . . .

■ FLAME AND THE ARROW, THE

1950, 89 MINS, US ◇ ⊛ ⊙
Dir Jacques Tourneur   *Prod* Frank Ross, Harold Hecht
Scr Waldo Salt   *Ph* Ernest Haller   *Ed* Alan Crosland
Mus Max Steiner   *Art Dir* Edward Carrere
● Burt Lancaster, Virginia Mayo, Robert Douglas, Nick Cravat, Aline MacMahon, Frank Allenby (Warner/Norma-FR)

F

The Flame and the Arrow is a romantic costume drama geared to attract action audiences. Setting is medieval Italy with a Robin Hood plot of how injustice is put down under the daring leadership of a heroic mountaineer.

Burt Lancaster does the latter, portraying the Arrow of the title with just the right amount of dash.

Virginia Mayo is the niece of the hated ruler. She figures romantically with Lancaster in the byplay and also gives an assist to the rebellion of the mountain people against Hessian cruelty.

Jacques Tourneur does not overlook the development of any number of interesting characters. Best of these is Cravat, partner of Lancaster during latter's circus-vaude tumbling days before entering films.
□ 1950: Nominations: Best Color Cinematography, Scoring of a Dramatic Picture

. . . .

■ FLAME IN THE STREETS

1961, 93 MINS, UK ◇
Dir Roy Ward Baker   *Prod* Roy Ward Baker   *Scr* Ted Willis   *Ph* Christopher Challis   *Ed* Roger Cherrill   *Mus* Philip Green   *Art Dir* Alex Vetchinsky
● John Mills, Sylvia Syms, Brenda De Banzie, Earl Cameron, Johnny Sekka, Ann Lynn (Rank)

Story, which hasn't much dramatic bounce, concerns the dilemma of a staunch trade unionist who averts a threatened factory strike over a Negro foreman, swaying the staff by urging that the color of a man's skin is unimportant, only to find that his daughter has fallen in love with another colored man. How to reconcile his very different feelings over the two incidents is his problem.

John Mills makes a convincing figure as the father who has neglected his family because of his dedication to union work.

Brenda De Banzie, his wife, bitter and intolerant about colored people, has two telling scenes, one with her husband and one with her daughter. Sylvia Syms, the schoolmistress daughter who outrages her parents by her determination to marry a young Negro schoolteacher, contributes a neat performance in a role which is not developed fully.

Ann Lynn has a couple of neat cameos as a white girl married to the colored foreman, played with dignity and assurance by Earl Cameron. The Negro hero is Johnny Sekka, and he, too, has enough charm, dignity and good breeding to make it appear quite logical that Syms should fall in love with him.

The fact that *Flame in the Streets* is derived from a play *Hot Summer Night* is always obvious. However, by staging the film on Guy Fawkes' Night, the director is able to get his cameras out into well-filled streets for atmosphere. The street riot between the two factions is curiously anticlimactic, mainly because the film's appeal is largely the quietness of its direction and playing.

. . . .

■ FLAME OF NEW ORLEANS, THE

1941, 78 MINS, US
Dir Rene Clair   *Prod* Joe Pasternak   *Scr* Norman Krasna   *Ph* Rudolph Mate   *Ed* Frank Gross   *Mus* Charles Previn
● Marlene Dietrich, Bruce Cabot, Roland Young, Anne Revere, Mischa Auer (Universal)

This Marlene Dietrich starrer is a very thin and familiar tale of the romantic interludes of a lady of dubious reputation a century ago. Picture misses its apparent mark of being a smartly sophisticated farce by a considerable margin, winding up as a lightweight entry.

Dietrich arrives in New Orleans after a European tour, determined to grab off a wealthy admirer. Roland Young is an easy victim and proposes marriage, but Bruce Cabot, tough and roving ship captain, holds a strange fascination for her. Plot's a case of how long before she tosses over Young for Cabot.

Picture is Rene Clair's first in America. He works valiantly with the flimsy material, injecting many incidental by-plays that are amusing, but to meagre avail.

Dietrich provides a familiar performance as the questionable lady, shapely in appearance, but sparkles in a role calling for zest. Her attempts at coyness miss badly. Inclusion of a few songs fail to provide a lift to the proceedings.

. . . .

■ FLAME OF THE BARBARY COAST

1945, 91 MINS, US ⓥ
Dir Joseph Kane   *Prod* Joseph Kane   *Scr* Borden Chase   *Ph* Robert de Grasse   *Ed* Richard L. Van Enger   *Mus* Morton Scott   *Art Dir* Gano Chittenden
● John Wayne, Ann Dvorak, Joseph Schildkraut, William Frawley, Virginia Grey, Russell Hicks (Republic)

A Montana cattleman comes to scoff at the pre-earthquake Barbary Coast of San Francisco and stays to like it; a 'gentleman' gambler runs the most successful joint in the district until the guy from the tall grass decides to take over; and the gambler's singer-sweetheart is also the toast of the town's haut monde.

Through dialog, songs and music that's distinguished chiefly for the fact that it sounds like 1945 instead of 1906, the story winds a tortuous path until the earthquake breaks things up. But there is never any suspense in the piece, there is no juxtaposition of characters, no inner logic. One is conscious constantly of the dragging proceedings.

John Wayne handles imself very well in the role of the man from the plains. Ann Dvorak not only sings well but looks and acts the part of the nitery queen, Joseph Schildkraut as the gambler is socko.
□ 1945: Nominations: Best Scoring of a Dramatic Picture, Sound

. . . .

■ FLAME OVER INDIA
See: North West Frontier

. . . .

■ FLAMINGO KID, THE

1984, 100 MINS, US ◇ ⓥ ⊙
Dir Garry Marshall   *Prod* Michael Phillips   *Scr* Neal Marshall, Garry Marshall   *Ph* James A. Contner   *Ed* Priscilla Nedd   *Art Dir* Lawrence Miller
● Matt Dillon, Richard Crenna, Hector Elizondo, Jessica Walter, Molly McCarthy, Janet Jones (ABC/Mercury)

The Flamingo Kid, set in 1963, sports the amusing trappings connected with 18-year-old Matt Dillon working for a summer at the El Flamingo Beach Club in Far Rockaway, NY. At its heart, though, story has to do with the critical choices facing a youth of that age and how they will help determine the rest of one's life.

Taken out of his rundown Brooklyn neighborhood one day to play cards with friends at the club, Dillon ends up getting a job there parking cars. He is soon promoted to cabana boy, and also attracts the attention of blonde UCLA student Janet Jones, with whom he has a skin-deep summer fling, and her uncle Richard Crenna, a sharp-talking sports car dealer.

Dillon does a good job in his fullest, least narcissistic characterization to date.

. . . .

■ FLAMINGO ROAD

1949, 94 MINS, US ⓥ
Dir Michael Curtiz   *Prod* Jerry Wald   *Scr* Robert Wilder, Edmund H. North   *Ph* Ted McCord   *Ed* Folmar Blangsted   *Mus* Max Steiner   *Art Dir* Les Kuter
● Joan Crawford, Zachary Scott, Sydney Greenstreet, David Brian, Gertrude Michael, Gladys George (Warner)

Flamingo Road is a class vehicle for Joan Crawford, loaded with heartbreak, romance and stinging violence. Film is hooped together by a smart, well-meshed screenplay and reinforced by a strong cast and sound direction.

Yarn [from a play by Robert and Sally Wilder] swivels around a deadly antagonism between Crawford and Sydney Greenstreet, a sinister small-town sheriff with a ruthless appetite for power. Film rapidly gathers momentum after Crawford, stranded by a bankrupt sideshow company, falls in love with Zachary Scott, the sheriff's protege.

Crawford imparts convincing personality shadings ranging from strength to tenderness with a continuous and convincing style. As the heavy, Greenstreet delivers a suavely powerful performance that surmounts his overdrawn role.

. . . .

■ FLAMING STAR

1960, 92 MINS, US ◇ ⓥ
Dir Don Siegel   *Prod* David Weisbart   *Scr* Clair Huffaker, Nunnally Johnson   *Ph* Charles G. Clarke   *Ed* Hugh S. Fowler   *Mus* Cyril J. Mockridge   *Art Dir* Duncan Craimer, Walter M. Simonds
● Elvis Presley, Steve Forrest, Barbara Eden, Dolores Del Rio, John McIntire (20th Century-Fox)

Flaming Star has Indians-on-the-warpath for the youngsters, Elvis Presley for the teenagers and socio-psychological ramifications for adults who prefer a mild dose of sage in their sagebrushers. The plot – half-breed hopelessly involved in war between white man and Red man [from a novel by Clair Huffaker] – is disturbingly familiar and not altogether convincing, but the film is attractively mounted and consistently diverting.

Presley plays the half-breed, pivotal character in the conflict between a group of Texas settlers and the angry Kiowa tribe. Part of a heterogeneous family (full-blooded Indian mother, white father, half brother) resented and tormented by whites, taunted and haunted by Indian ties, Presley is buffeted to and fro between enemy camps by the prevailing winds of prejudice and pride.

The role is a demanding one for Presley. But he lacks the facial and thespic sensitivity and projection so desperately required here. The standouts are the veterans, Dolores Del Rio and John McIntire. Del Rio brings dignity and delicacy to the role of Presley's full-blooded Indian mother. McIntire adds nobility and compassion as the father of the doomed household. Steve Forrest is competent as the brother, Barbara Eden decorative as his girl.

Director Don Siegel has packed plenty of excitement into the picture, notably some realistically-staged fistfight, battle and chase passages. But there are a few equally unrealistic-looking scenes.

. . . .

■ FLASHBACK

1990, 108 MINS, US ◇ ⓥ ⊙
Dir Franco Amurri   *Prod* Marvin Worth   *Scr* David Loughery   *Ph* Stefan Czapsky   *Ed* C. Timothy O'Meara   *Mus* Barry Goldberg   *Art Dir* Vincent Cresciman
● Dennis Hopper, Kiefer Sutherland, Carol Kane, Paul Dooley, Cliff De Young, Richard Masur (Paramount)

Dennis Hopper does a delightful self-parody in *Flashback* as an Abbie Hoffman-like fugitive 'radical jester' brought to farcical justice in 1989 by uptight FBI agent Kiefer Sutherland. Unfortunately, the film's promising premise is dissipated by character cliches, mechanical plot twists and an uncertain grasp on political satire.

The fun part is the Rip Van Winkle story of

257

the gray-bearded Hopper, looking like he's been sleeping off a 20-year o.d., expounding on the political and sexual mores of the 1960s to Sutherland while en route to jail between San Francisco and the Pacific Northwest.

Scripter and director seem to be suffering from a serious case of cultural amnesia when it comes to remembering what was going on in the late 1960s.

When the pair find themselves back on the rundown commune in Oregon where Sutherland lived as a child, encountering dilapidated hippie Carol Kane dwelling among the portraits of martyred 1960s figures, the film taps briefly into the sadness of the time.

●●●●●●●●●●●●●●●●●●●●●●●●●

■ FLASHDANCE

1983, 96 MINS, US ◇ ⑫ ⊙
Dir Adrian Lyne   *Prod* Don Simpson, Jerry Bruckheimer
Scr Tom Hedley, Joe Eszterhas   *Ph* Don Peterman
Ed Bud Smith, Walt Mulconery   *Mus* Giorgio Moroder
Art Dir Charles Rosen
● Jennifer Beals, Michael Nouri, Lilia Skala, Sunny Johnson, Kyle T. Heffner, Belinda Bauer
(PolyGram/Paramount)

Watching *Flashdance* is pretty much looking at MTV for 96 minutes. Virtually plotless, exceedingly thin on characterization and sociologically laughable, pic at least lives up to its title by offering an anthology of extraordinarily flashy dance numbers.

Appealing newcomer Jennifer Beals plays an 18-year-old come to Pittsburgh to toil in a steel mill by day and work off steam at night by performing wild, improvised dances in a local bar (much of Beals' dancing was reportedly done by an uncredited double [Marine Jahan]).

What story there is [by Tom Hedley] sees Beals trying to get up the courage to audition for formal dance study and dealing with the advances of her daytime boss Michael Nouri who, to her fury, secretly intervenes to get her admitted to the school.

Female performances all come off as if the sole directorial command was, 'All right, girls, let's get physical!' Pic features better bodies and more crotch shots than *Personal Best*, and every effect is of the most vulgar and obvious variety.

□ 1983: Best Original Song ('Flashdance . . . What a Feeling')
□ Nominations: Best Cinematography, Editing, Original Song ('Maniac')

●●●●●●●●●●●●●●●●●●●●●●●●●

■ FLASH GORDON

1980, 110 MINS, UK ◇ ⑫ ⊙
Dir Mike Hodges   *Prod* Dino De Laurentiis   *Scr* Lorenzo Semple Jr   *Ph* Gil Taylor   *Ed* Malcolm Cooke
Mus Howard Blake, Queen   *Art Dir* Danilo Donati
● Sam J. Jones, Melody Anderson, Topol, Max Von Sydow, Ornella Muti, Brian Blessed (Universal/De Laurentiis)

The expensive new version of *Flash Gordon* is a lot more gaudy, and just as dumb, as the original series starring Buster Crabbe. Sam J. Jones in the title role has even less thespic range than Crabbe, but the badness of his performance is part of the fun of the film.

This film cost around $20 million, a hefty outlay of money for such frivolity.

The big differences between this film and the old serial are the lavish sets and costumes, and the colorful lensing by Gil Taylor, who also did *Star Wars*.

Jones, a former *Playgirl* nude centerfold whose only previous film role was the husband of Bo Derek in '*10*', lumbers vacantly through the part of Flash Gordon with the naivete, fearlessness, and dopey line readings familiar from the 1930s serials.

Film benefits greatly from the adroit performance of Max Von Sydow as Emperor Ming.

●●●●●●●●●●●●●●●●●●●●●●●●●

■ FLATLINERS

1990, 111 MINS, US ◇ ⑫ ⊙ ⊙
Dir Joel Schumacher   *Prod* Michael Douglas, Rick Bieber
Scr Peter Filardi   *Ph* Jan De Bont   *Ed* Robert Brown
Mus James Newton Howard   *Art Dir* Eugenio Zanetti
● Kiefer Sutherland, Julia Roberts, Kevin Bacon, William Baldwin, Oliver Platt, Kimberly Scott
(Stonebridge/Columbia)

Death, the ultimate rush, is the target experience for a group of daring young medical students who break on through to the other side – and live to tell about it. A cautionary tale that ends along fairly traditional horror-sci-fi lines, *Flatliners* is a strikingly original, often brilliantly visualized film from director Joel Schumacher and writer Peter Filardi.

Premise is that daring doctor-in-training Nelson (Kiefer Sutherland) decides to make his mark on medicine by stopping his heart and brain ('flatlining', as the lack of vital signs produces a flat line on the EKG and EEG monitors) and then having himself brought back by the gifted medical students he recruits to help him. Initially angry and reluctant, the others end up totally seduced, vying with each other for the chance to go next by offering to flatline the longest.

Problem is, as Nelson discovers, that the curtain of death, once penetrated, doesn't close behind you, and Nelson finds himself haunted by an aggressive demon from another world. Before he can bring himself to admit that his idea wasn't such a good one, all the others but one have gone over.

Sutherland, as always, registers real presence and pulls off a wildly demanding role, but the remarkably gifted Julia Roberts is the film's true grace note as the low-key, private and intensely focused Rachel.

□ 1990: Nomination: Best Sound Effects Editing

●●●●●●●●●●●●●●●●●●●●●●●●●

■ FLEET'S IN, THE

1942, 93 MINS, US
Dir Victor Schertzinger   *Prod* Paul Jones   *Scr* Walter DeLeon, Sid Silvers, Ralph Spence   *Ph* William Mellor
Ed Paul Weatherwax   *Mus* Victor Schertzinger
● Dorothy Lamour, William Holden, Eddie Bracken, Betty Hutton, Cass Daley, Leif Erickson (Paramount)

Paul Jones, the producer of this musical version of *Sailor Beware*, has surrounded Dorothy Lamour with a miscellaneous collection of talent, including two first-starters who click strongly; but while he has turned out something that generally pleases, it falls short of being a smash.

Holden handles himself well opposite Lamour as the sailor who falls for her while the battleship crew is on furlough in Frisco.

The quarrel is less with the story itself than the musical side. There are no production numbers but an overdose of vocalists, backed by the Dorsey band.

●●●●●●●●●●●●●●●●●●●●●●●●●

■ FLESH

1932, 95 MINS, US
Dir John Ford   *Scr* Leonard Praskins, Edgar Allan Woolf, Moss Hart   *Ph* Arthur Edeson   *Ed* William S. Gray
● Wallace Beery, Karen Morley, Ricardo Cortez, Jean Hersholt, John Miljan (M-G-M)

Wallace Beery plays a big-hearted, big-muscled, small-brained guy with lovable qualities, a sort of cross between Emil Jannings of *Variety* (1926) and the same Beery of *The Champ* (1931). Instead of being an acrobat or a punch drunk fighter, he's a wrestler. He goes chump for a faithless woman, according to pattern, and the finish is sad, only this time there's a suggestion of ultimate happiness to deaden the pain.

As an inside on the honorable profesh of grappling, the original yarn by Edmund Goulding takes huge Polikai (Beery) out of a

waiter's suit in a German beer garden to the wrassling championship of that country, and then to America where he has to play ball with the gamblers. He wins the world's title when he's supposed to lose.

Karen Morley is with him all through the climb as the double-crossing lady who loves her man on the side. Latter, and doing a perfect job of an 100% unsympathetic character, is Ricardo Cortez.

●●●●●●●●●●●●●●●●●●●●●●●●●

■ FLESH

1968, 105 MINS, US ◇
Dir Paul Morrissey   *Prod* Andy Warhol   *Scr* Paul Morrissey   *Ph* Paul Morrissey
● Joe Dallesandro, Geraldine Smith, John Christian, Maurice Bardell, Candy Darling, Patti D'Arbanville (Warhol)

Blithely, as if it were as natural a romantic yarn as would appear in a popular magazine, the synopsis of Andy Warhol's opus reads: 'The story of a young married couple and the efforts of the husband, Joe, to sell himself to earn money for his wife's girl friend's abortion.'

Paul Morrissey wrote, directed and lensed this hapless erotica freakout as Warhol was recuperating from gunshot wounds inflicted by Gloria Solanis. Morrisey's efforts, true to the master, are pedestrian in both form and content, but much worse is the technical amateurishness with camera and sound.

Half sentences are abundant. But it probably doesn't matter to any great extent since the wild sound recorded during the action bounces off the walls, rendering most interchanges between characters largely incoherent.

The principal character Joe concerns himself mainly with floating from one homosexual encounter to the next in order to make the required coin, sporting an abundance of frontal nudity. The anti-climax comes when Joe finds his wife in bed with her girlfriend.

●●●●●●●●●●●●●●●●●●●●●●●●●

■ FLESH + BLOOD

1985, 126 MINS, US ◇ ⑫
Dir Paul Verhoeven   *Prod* Gys Versluys   *Scr* Gerard Soeteman, Paul Verhoeven   *Ph* Jan de Bont   *Ed* Ine Schenkkan   *Mus* Basil Poledouris   *Art Dir* Felix Murcia
● Rutger Hauer, Jennifer Jason Leigh, Tom Burlinson, Jack Thompson, Susan Tyrrell, Ronald Lacey
(Orion/Riverside)

Flesh + Blood is a vivid and muscular, if less than fully startling, account of lust, savagery, revenge, betrayal and assorted other dark doings in the Middle Ages.

Drama opens with a successful siege on a castle by Lord Arnolfini (Fernando Hillbeck), who has recently been ousted from the premises. After promising them loot, Hillbeck goes back on his word and banishes the mercenaries who have helped him in his conquest.

Before long, warrior leader Martin (Rutger Hauer) and his ragtag band gets theirs back by nearly killing Hillbeck in an ambush and capturing lovely young Agnes (Jennifer Jason Leigh), the intended bride of Hillbeck's studious son Steven (Tom Burlinson).

Director Paul Verhoeven has told his tale in visceral, involving fashion and, for the amount of carnage that piles up, explicit gore is kept to a minimum.

Fine use is made of Belmonte Castle (on view in *El Cid*) and other Spanish locales.

●●●●●●●●●●●●●●●●●●●●●●●●●

■ FLESH AND FANTASY

1943, 92 MINS, US
Dir Julien Duvivier   *Prod* Charles Boyer, Julien Duvivier
Scr Ernest Pascal, Samuel Hoffenstein, Ellis St Joseph
Ph Paul Ivano, Stanley Cortez   *Ed* Arthur Hilton
Mus Alexandre Tansman

F

● Edward G. Robinson, Charles Boyer, Barbara Stanwyck, Betty Field, Robert Cummings, Thomas Mitchell (Universal)

This is a decidedly novel and unusual picture, displaying the impress on individuals of dreams, fortune-telling and other supernatural phenomena. Picture idea was contrived by Charles Boyer and Julien Duvivier and sold to Universal, with pair combining as producers, Duvivier also directing, and Boyer handling a major acting assignment.

Clubmen Robert Benchley and David Hoffman discuss dreams, predictions and the supernatural to provide necessary interweave of the three episodes on display.

First delves into romance of Betty Field, who's become calloused, bitter and defeated through ugly features. But on Mardi Gras night she is handed a beautiful face mask and romances with Robert Cummings and finally discovers truth in the moral: faith in yourself is the main thing.

Second episode presents Thomas Mitchell as a palmist at a socialite group, and after attorney Edward G. Robinson scoffs at the predictions, latter nevertheless submits to a reading, and becomes intrigued when he's told he will commit murder.

Boyer shares starring honors with Barbara Stanwyck in the final episode, which has the former upset by dream which predicts disaster to himself while performing as a circus high-wire artist.

■ FLESH AND THE DEVIL

1926, 91 MINS, US ⊗ ⓦ
Dir Clarence Brown   *Scr* Benjamin F. Glazer, Marian Ainslee   *Ph* William Daniels   *Ed* Lloyd Nosler
Art Dir Cedric Gibbons, Frederic Hope
● John Gilbert, Greta Garbo, Lars Hanson, Barbara Kent, William Orlamond (M-G-M)

This film [based on *The Undying Past* by Hermann Sudermann] is a battle between John Gilbert, starred, and Greta Garbo, featured, for honors. Gilbert has to keep moving to overshadow her, even though she has a most unsympathetic role.

The story is laid in a small German or Austrian town. Two boys have, as kids, sworn eternal friendship through a blood bond. They are both at military school when the picture opens. Back home there is a ball and Lee (Gilbert), the more sophisticated of the two, sees a girl that he admired at the station. He dances with her, but fails to learn her name. Her husband walks in on the picture and the youngster then knows for the first time that she is married. The husband strikes the boy, and it calls for a duel. The husband is killed. The military authorities 'advise' foreign service for five years for the youngster. Before going he asks his bloodbound friend to seek out the widow and console her.

After three years away, Leo discovers that she has wed the friend. Then a series of incidents occurs that almost brings on a duel between the friends.

A corking story, exceptionally acted and cleverly directed. A lot of glory to be distributed among all concerned.

■ FLESH FOR FRANKENSTEIN

1974, 95 MINS, FRANCE/ITALY ◇ ⓦ
Dir Paul Morrissey   *Prod* Andrew Braunsberg   *Scr* Paul Morrissey   *Ph* Luigi Kueveillier   *Ed* Ted Johnson
Mus Carlo Gizzi
● Joe Dallesandro, Udo Kier, Monique Van Vooren, Arno Juerging, Srdjan Zelenovic, Dalila Di Lazzaro (CC-Champion & 1/Ponti/Yanne/Rassam)

Paul Morrissey of the Andy Warhol stable made this pic back to back with *Blood for Dracula*, with an added gimmick of 3-D and more skillfully directed. Morrissey plays some

variations on the old Prometheus myth. He adds plenty of gore, with some dollops of sex.

Morrissey otherwise plays this for neat Gothic atmosphere in Frankenstein's castle where his nympho sister (Monique Van Vooren), also mother of his children, carries on with servants as the kids and Frankenstein (Udo Kier) look on.

Joe Dallesandro is a servant who suspects foul doings, especially when he sees the head of his friend on one of Frankenstein's monsters and breaks up things to find he may be a victim of the Baron's two children as he hangs helplessly by his hands.

■ FLESH GORDON

1974, 78 MINS, US ◇ ⓦ
Dir Howard Ziehm, Michael Benveniste   *Prod* Howard Ziehm, Bill Osco   *Scr* Michael Benveniste   *Ph* Howard Ziehm   *Mus* Ralph Ferraro   *Art Dir* Donald Harris
● Jason Williams, Suzanne Fields, Joseph Hudgins, John Hoyt, William Hunt (Graffiti)

Puerile is the word for this softcore spoof of the sci-fi serials of the 1930s which, for their time, had genuine merit as audience hairraisers. By attempting to combine sexplicity and low-level camp, pic emerges as an expensive-looking mish-mash of obvious double entendres, idiotic characterizations and dull situations. Only compensation is flash of bawdy humor.

Title character (Jason Williams) heads a group of earthlings out to defeat evil forces on the planet Porno, bent on flooding the universe with chaos-inducing sex rays. Porno is manned by sinister Emperor Wang (William Hunt). Flesh, his girl (Suzanne Fields) and sidekick (Joseph Hudgins) rocket to Porno and encounter various of the emperor's evil minions and a mildly entertaining series of monsters.

■ FLETCH

1985, 96 MINS, US ◇ ⓦ ⊙
Dir Michael Ritchie   *Prod* Alan Greisman, Peter Douglas   *Scr* Andrew Bergman   *Ph* Fred Schuler   *Ed* Richard A. Harris   *Mus* Harold Faltermeyer   *Art Dir* Boris Leven
● Chevy Chase, Dana Wheeler-Nicholson, Tim Matheson, Joe Don Baker, Richard Libertini, Geena Davis (Universal)

What propels this contempo LA yarn about a dissembling newspaper columnist on the trail of a nefarious con man (Tim Matheson) is the obvious and successful byplay between Chevy Chase's sly, glib persona and the satiric brushstrokes of director Michael Ritchie. Their teamwork turns an otherwise hairpinned, anecdotal plot into a breezy, peppy frolic and a tour de force for Chase.

Most supporting players have little to do, such as M. Emmet Walsh as an inane MD. The film is sparked by some hilarious moments, among them Chase as an unwitting surgeon in attendance at an autopsy conducted by a cackling pathologist and, in the script's funniest scene, Chase donning the guise of a legionnaire in a hall full of VFW stalwarts.

■ FLETCH LIVES

1989, 95 MINS, US ◇ ⓦ ⊙
Dir Michael Ritchie   *Prod* Alan Greisman, Peter Douglas   *Scr* Leon Capetanos   *Ph* John McPherson   *Ed* Richard A. Harris   *Mus* Harold Faltermeyer   *Art Dir* Cameron Birnie, Jimmie Bly, W. Steven Graham, Donald B. Woodruff
● Chevy Chase, Hal Holbrook, Julianne Phillips, Cleavon Little, R. Lee Ermey, Richard Libertini (Universal)

Chevy Chase is perfectly suited to playing a smirking, wisecracking, multiple-identified reporter in *Fletch Lives*.

Ridiculous and anecdotal plot that trans-

ports Chase from his beloved LA base to Louisiana's bayou country to take over his dead aunt's crumbling plantation works for the simple reason that Chase's sly, glib persona is in sync with Michael Ritchie's equally breezy direction.

From Gregory McDonald's popular novel, script works out an excessive and cliche-ridden portrait of a Southern, insular town. Dimwits abound as if inbreeding has been going on since the days of slavery.

The night Chase arrives, he beds the sexy executor/lawyer of his aunt's estate (Patricia Kalember as a convincing belle), who is then murdered while they're slumbering.

Chase tracks the murderer through some inane sequences as only he could do. Film's saving grace is its scathing satirical sketches of fictional televangelist preacher Jimmy Lee Farnsworth.

■ FLIGHT OF THE DOVES

1971, 101 MINS, US ◇
Dir Ralph Nelson   *Prod* Ralph Nelson   *Scr* Frank Gabrielson, Ralph Nelson   *Ph* Harry Waxman   *Ed* John Jympson   *Mus* Roy Budd   *Art Dir* Frank Arrigo
● Ron Moody, Jack Wild, Dorothy McGuire, Stanley Holloway, William Rushton, Dana (Columbia)

Ralph Nelson's film version of Walter Macken's story, *Flight of the Doves*, is a heartwarming, often funny, often suspenseful story of two runaway children, fleeing from a cruel stepfather (British) to their grandmother (Irish) who lives 'somewhere in Ireland'.

The screenplay, takes some liberties in casting. Dorothy McGuire is a delight as a brighteyed, most articulate grandmother, standing up to authority, both Irish and British, on behalf of the young runaways, but is much too young looking to make anyone believe that she could have a grandson as large as Jack Wild.

It allows Ron Moody to dominate the film from his first appearance. With almost as many character changes as Alec Guinness had in *Kind Hearts and Coronets*, Moody is so good at his diguises that the audience starts imagining that each new character who appears might be the irresponsible Moody. Ostensibly the villain, he's so captivating that no one really believes that he won't survive (even after seeing him plunged into a wild Irish sea).

As the uncle of Wild and Helen Raye, he's described as the eventual heir to money left by the children's grandfather should they die before he does.

■ FLIGHT OF THE INTRUDER

1991, 113 MINS, US ◇ ⓦ ⊙
Dir John Milius   *Prod* Mace Neufeld   *Scr* Robert Dillon, David Shaber, [John Milius]   *Ph* Fred J. Koenekamp   *Ed* C. Timothy O'Meara, Steve Mirkovich, Peck Prior   *Mus* Basil Poledouris   *Art Dir* Jack T. Collis
● Danny Glover, Willem Dafoe, Brad Johnson, Rosanna Arquette, Tom Sizemore, J. Kenneth Campbell (Paramount)

Flight of the Intruder is the most boring Vietnam War pic since *The Green Berets* (1968), but lacks the benefit of the latter's political outrageousness to spark a little interest and humor.

Set mostly aboard a giant aircraft carrier, yarn [from the novel by Stephen Coonts] unspools in 1972. Prevented from bombing Hanoi and other strategic spots while the Paris peace talks are in progress, fighter pilots are reduced to assaulting meaningless targets and facing the likelihood that the massive US war effort will have been in vain.

Nonetheless, officers have to keep discipline and morale up, a task that falls to Danny Glover, the tough-talking but humorous squadron leader.

Title refers to the A-6, a small, low-altitude bomber designed for quick in-and-out strikes. Ace of the outfit is Brad Johnson, who loses a bombardier in an elaborate credit sequence and is thereafter interested in 'payback'.

Opportunity presents itself with the arrival of a vet bombardier (Willem Dafoe) not averse to hijinks. Johnson and Dafoe cook up a scheme to devastate People's Resistance Park in downtown Hanoi, a.k.a. SAM City, where captured US artillery is on display.

Glover brings energy and glee to his reams of dialog. Dafoe puts a few cynical spins on his delivery, but his character pales next to his role in *Platoon*. Johnson, again playing a flier, is even more lackluster than in *Always*. Hawaiian locations, when viewed from the air, are too lushly recognizable to be an entirely credible Vietnam.

●●●●●●●●●●●●●●●●●●●●●●●●●●●●●●●●●●

■ FLIGHT OF THE NAVIGATOR

1986, 90 MINS, US ◇ ⊙ ⊙

Dir Randal Kleiser *Prod* Robby Wald, Dimitri Villard *Scr* Michael Burton, Matt MacManus *Ph* James Glennon *Ed* Jeff Gourson *Mus* Alan Silvestri *Art Dir* William J. Creber

● Joey Cramer, Veronica Cartwright, Cliff De Young, Sarah Jessica Parker, Matt Adler, Howard Hesseman (Walt Disney/PSO)

Instead of creating an eye-opening panorama, *Flight of the Navigator* looks through the small end of the telescope. Life on Earth is magnified but without an expansive vision.

Young David Freeman (Joey Cramer) vanishes from his Fort Lauderdale home only to return to the identical spot unchanged eight years later. When a sleek silver flying saucer turns up on the scene, NASA gets into the act and all roads lead to David. It seems his head has been filled with star charts and he's been serving as navigator for an exploratory ship from a distant planet.

Film finally gets on track when 12-year-old David is reunited with the spacecraft for a trip which ultimately will deposit him right back where he started. Along the way the journey is imaginative and fun but earth-bound, with a robotic flight commander (voiced by an uncredited Paul Reubens, a.k.a. Pee-wee Herman) who becomes fascinated with American pop culture.

As is often the problem with extraterrestrial adventures, all life forms are anthropomorphized with a selection of cute and cuddly creatures. There are some nifty special effects in the spacecraft sequences. Performances are all workmanlike, with Cramer doing a believable job.

●●●●●●●●●●●●●●●●●●●●●●●●●●●●●●●●●●

■ FLIGHT OF THE PHOENIX, THE

1965, 149 MINS, US ◇ ⊙ ⊙

Dir Robert Aldrich *Prod* Robert Aldrich *Scr* Lukas Heller *Ph* Joseph Biroc *Ed* Michael Luciano *Mus* Frank DeVol *Art Dir* William Glasgow

● James Stewart, Richard Attenborough, Peter Finch, Hardy Kruger, Ernest Borgnine, Ian Bannen (Associates & Aldrich/20th Century-Fox)

The Flight of the Phoenix is a grim, tenseful, realistic tale of a small group of men forced down on the North African desert and their desperate efforts to build a single-engine plane out of the wreckage of the twin job in which they crashed during a sandstorm. Robert Aldrich's filmic translation of the Elleston Trevor book is an often-fascinating and superlative piece of filmmaking highlighted by standout performances and touches that show producer-director at his best.

James Stewart, as the pilot of a desert oil company cargo-passenger plane who flies by the seat of his pants, is strongly cast in role and is strongly backed by entire cast. Each, seemingly hand-picked for the individual

parts, are every-day persons who might either be employees of an oil company or business visitors.

A young aircraft designer, who had been visiting his brother at the oil camp, comes up with the extraordinary idea that a make-shift plane might be fashioned to fly the survivors to safety. So work starts, and it is this endeavor in its various phases that makes the story.

□ 1965: Nominations: Best Supp. Actor (Ian Bannen), Editing

●●●●●●●●●●●●●●●●●●●●●●●●●●●●●●●●●●

■ FLIM-FLAM MAN, THE
(UK: One Born Every Minute)

1967, 104 MINS, US ◇ ⊙

Dir Irvin Kershner *Prod* Lawrence Turman *Scr* William Rose *Ph* Charles Lang *Ed* Robert Swink *Mus* Jerry Goldsmith *Art Dir* Jack Martin Smith

● George C. Scott, Sue Lyon, Michael Sarrazin, Harry Morgan, Jack Albertson, Alice Ghostley (20th Century-Fox)

An outstanding comedy starring George C. Scott as a Dixie drifter. Socko comedy-dramatic direction by Irvin Kershner makes the most of a very competent cast and a superior script. Michael Sarrazin, as Scott's fellow-traveler, makes an impressive feature film bow.

Guy Owen's novel, *The Ballad of the Flim-Flam Man*, has been adapted into a finely balanced screenplay which exploits inherent comedy situations while understating, appropriately, the loneliness of a rootless man. A series of flim-flams are pulled off only on people who seemingly deserve to be stiffed, thus minimizing any complaint that lawlessness is being made attractive.

●●●●●●●●●●●●●●●●●●●●●●●●●●●●●●●●●●

■ FLIPPER

1963, 87 MINS, US ◇ ⊙

Dir James B. Clark *Prod* Ivan Tors *Scr* Arthur Weiss *Ph* Lamar Bowen, Joseph Brun *Ed* Warren Adams *Mus* Henry Vars

● Chuck Connors, Luke Halpin, Connie Scott, Kathleen Maguire, Jane Rose, Joe Higgins (M-G-M)

Boy meets dolphin, boy loses dolphin, boy wins dolphin. Thus substituting gill for gal, producer Ivan Tors has fashioned a serviceable little family picture that to all intents and porpoises, should satisfy aquabrats everywhere.

Actually this little fish story, or Tors opera, amounts to a kind of bubbly variation on *Androcles and the Lion*. Arthur Weiss' screenplay, from a story by Ricou Browning and Jack Cowden, has a boy (Luke Halpin) rescuing an eight-foot dolphin from permanent residence in that big fish tank in the sky by removing a skin diver's spear from its torso and nursing it back to health in his dad's Florida Keys fish pen.

Chuck Connors limns the father firmly but agreeably, and young Halpin, in his screen bow, demonstrates keen acting instincts as the boy on a dolphin.

●●●●●●●●●●●●●●●●●●●●●●●●●●●●●●●●●●

■ FLIRTATION WALK

1934, 95 MINS, US

Dir Frank Borzage *Prod* Frank Borzage *Scr* Delmer Daves, Lou Edelman *Ph* Sol Polito, George Barnes *Ed* William Holmes *Art Dir* Jack Okey

● Dick Powell, Ruby Keeler, Pat O'Brien, Ross Alexander, John Eldredge (First National)

Flirtation Walk is bright and diverting entertainment in which the musical sequences [dance numbers directed by Bobby Connolly, music and lyrics by Allie Wrubel and Mort Dixon] are logically worked in, albeit with the usual Hollywood flair for exaggeration. Background of West Point allows the picture to possess some snappy drill and brass-button

stuff. Deft direction of Frank Borzage gives the production the tempo and zing that stamps it swell amusement.

Dick Powell, in his plebe year at the Point, plays the situations for excellent natural comedy. Ruby Keeler does not dance. She has a lot to do and does it with considerable assurance. Ross Alexander as Powell's roommate will be liked, a personable young man with a knack for light comedy and horseplay.

Laughs and drama of the story are derived from the interplay of officer-private class distinctions and military discipline. The quiet competence of John Eldredge's performance as the disappointed suitor rates a few merit stripes.

□ 1934: Nomination: Best Picture

●●●●●●●●●●●●●●●●●●●●●●●●●●●●●●●●●●

■ FLIRTING

1991, 96 MINS, AUSTRALIA ◇ ⊙ ⊙

Dir John Duigan *Prod* George Miller, Terry Hayes, Doug Mitchell *Scr* John Duigan *Ph* Geoff Burton *Ed* Robert Gibson *Art Dir* Roger Ford

● Noah Taylor, Thandie Newton, Nicole Kidman, Bartholomew Rose, Kiri Paramore, Kym Wilson (Kennedy Miller)

Miles ahead of the average teen film, *Flirting* is a most agreeable sequel to John Duigan's earlier pic *The Year My Voice Broke*. The new film doesn't pack the emotional wallop of the first, but it still charms. This depiction of well-to-do teens in sexually segregated schools also looks obliquely at latent racism at the time of the 'white Australia' policy. Events that led to the Vietnam War already were in motion.

Noah Taylor reprises his character of Danny Embling. It's 1965, and Danny's parents have sent him to a boys-only boarding school across the lake from a similar institution for girls. In the girls' school, a young Ugandan student suffers racial slurs. Thandiwe (Thandie Newton) and Danny meet and are attracted to each other.

Duigan handles this material with a great deal of humor and charm, demonstrating a sharp ear for contemporaneous teen dialog. A curiosity is Nicole Kidman's appearance as one of the girls' school students. *Flirting* was shot before she went to the States to appear in *Days of Thunder* [released in summer 1990].

●●●●●●●●●●●●●●●●●●●●●●●●●●●●●●●●●●

■ FLOWER DRUM SONG

1961, 133 MINS, US ◇ ⊙ ⊙

Dir Henry Koster *Prod* Ross Hunter *Scr* Joseph Fields *Ph* Russell Metty *Ed* Milton Carruth *Mus* Alfred Newman (sup.) *Art Dir* Alexander Golitzen, Joseph Wright

● Nancy Kwan, James Shigeta, Juanita Hall, Jack Soo, Miyoshi Umeki, Benson Fong (Universal)

Much of the fundamental charm, grace and novelty of Rodgers & Hammerstein's *Flower Drum Song* has been overwhelmed by the sheer opulence and glamour with which Ross Hunter has translated it to the screen. As a film, it emerges a curiously unaffecting, unstable and rather undistinguished experience.

The dominant issue in the screenplay, based on the novel by C. Y. Lee and adapted from the legit book by Joseph Fields and Oscar Hammerstein, is the clash of East-West romantic-marital customs as it affects four young people of Chinese descent living in San Francisco's Chinatown.

The four are Nancy Kwan, a gold-digging, husband-hungry nightclub dancer; Jack Soo, a kind of Chinese Nathan Detroit; James Shigeta, most eligible bachelor in Chinatown – the student prince of Grant Avenue; and Miyoshi Umeki, 'picture (or mail-order) bride' fresh (and illegally) off a slowboat from China and ticketed for nuptials with Soo.

As in most R&H enterprises, the meat is in the musical numbers. There are some bright

F

the musical numbers. There are some bright spots in this area but even here the effect isn't overpowering. Music supervisor-conductor Alfred Newman has fashioned some rousing orchestrations, with the assistance of Ken Darby. Dong Kingman's watercolored title paintings are a delight.

□ 1961: Nominations: Best Color Cinematography, Color Costume Design, Color Art Direction, Scoring of a Musical Picture, Sound

■ FLOWERS IN THE ATTIC

1987, 95 MINS, US ◇ ⓦ ⊙
Dir Jeffrey Bloom *Prod* Sy Levin, Thomas Fries
Scr Jeffrey Bloom *Ph* Frank Byers, Gil Hubbs
Ed Gregory F. Plotts *Mus* Christopher Young
Art Dir John Muto
● Louise Fletcher, Victoria Tennant, Kristy Swanson, Jeb Stuart Adams, Ben Ganger, Lindsay Parker (New World/Fries)

V. C. Andrews novel of incestuous relationships and confined childhood always has been a superb candidate for a film treatment, but director Jeffrey Bloom has taken this narrative and squeezed the life from it. Performances are as stiff and dreary as the attic these children are imprisoned in. The ridiculous ending (different from the book) was one of several shot.

After her husband's death, Corinne (Victoria Tennant) takes the family – teenagers Chris (Jeb Stuart Adams) and Cathy (Kristy Swanson) and pre-adolescent twins Carrie (Lindsay Parker) and Cory (Ben Ganger) – and becomes golddigger deluxe, moving back to her parents' house, intent on getting reinstated into her father's will.

Kids aren't crazy about the arrangement after meeting their sadistic, bible-toting, taskmaster grandmother (Louise Fletcher, doing a lot with this one-dimensional role) and getting locked into a guest room, where they are informed they must stay until their grandfather dies, so Tennant can win his affections.

Cathy and Chris' gradual mutual attraction has been excised and is only hinted at here. More problematic is the script, which attributes none of the qualities of teenagers to the teens and portrays the younger children as mindless drones.

■ FLY, THE

1958, 94 MINS, US ⓦ ⓦ ⊙
Dir Kurt Neumann *Prod* Kurt Neumann *Scr* James Clavell *Ph* Karl Struss *Ed* Merrill G. White *Mus* Paul Sawtell *Art Dir* Lyle R. Wheeler, Theobold Holsopple
● Al Hedison, Patricia Owens, Vincent Price, Herbert Marshall, Kathleen Freeman, Betty Lou Gerson (20th Century-Fox)

The Fly is a high-budget, beautifully and expensively mounted exploitation picture [derived from a story by George Langelaan]. Al Hedison plays a scientist who has invented a machine that reduces matter to disintegrated atoms and another machine that reassembles the atoms. He explains to his wife (Patricia Owens) that this will enable humans to travel – disintegrated – anywhere in the world at the speed of light. In experimenting on himself, however, a fly gets into the disintegration chamber with him.

When Hedison arrives in the integration chamber, he discovers some of his atoms have been scrambled with the fly's. Hedison has the head and 'arm' of a fly; the fly has the head and arm of the man – each, of course, in his own scale of size. The problem is to catch the fly and rescramble. But before this can happen, Hedison finds the predatory instincts of the insect taking over.

One strong factor of the picture is its unusual believability. It is told as a mystery suspense story, so that it has a compelling interest aside from its macabre effects. There is an appealing and poignant romance between Owens and Hedison, which adds to the reality of the story, although the flashback technique purposely robs the picture of any doubt about the outcome.

■ FLY, THE

1986, 100 MINS, US ◇ ⓦ ⊙
Dir David Cronenberg *Prod* Stuart Cornfeld
Scr Charles Edward Pogue, David Cronenberg *Ph* Mark Irwin *Ed* Ronald Sanders *Mus* Howard Shore
Art Dir Carol Spier
● Jeff Goldblum, Geena Davis, John Getz, Joy Booshel, Les Carlson (Brooksfilms)

David Cronenberg's remake of the 1958 horror classic *The Fly* is not for the squeamish. Casting Jeff Goldblum was a good choice as he brings a quirky, common touch to the spacey scientist role. Cronenberg gives him a nice girlfriend (Geena Davis), too.

But there's trouble in paradise. Goldblum's got a set of teleporters that he promises will 'change the world as we know it', and indeed, it changes his.

Even though the machinery is not yet perfected, Goldblum, in a moment of drunken jealousy, throws himself in the works. Unbeknownst to him a fly accompanies him on the journey and he starts to metamorphise.

Chris Walas' design for *The Fly* is never less than visually intriguing. Production design by Carol Spier, particularly for Goldblum's warehouse lab, is original and appropriate to the hothouse drama. Cronenberg contains the action well in a limited space with a small cast.

□ 1986: Best Make-Up

■ FLY II, THE

1989, 105 MINS, US ◇ ⓦ ⊙
Dir Chris Walas *Prod* Steven-Charles Jaffe *Scr* Mick Garris, Jim Wheat, Ken Wheat, Frank Darabont
Ph Robin Vidgeon *Ed* Sean Barton *Mus* Christopher Young *Art Dir* Michael S. Bolton
● Eric Stoltz, Daphne Zuniga, Lee Richardson, John Getz, Frank Turner, Ann-Marie Lee (Brooksfilm)

The Fly II is an expectedly gory and gooey but mostly plodding sequel to the 1986 hit that was a remake of the 1958 sci-fier that itself spawned two sequels.

After a shock opening in which the late man-fly's son is born within a horrible insect-like encasement, slickly produced pic [story by Mick Garris] generates some promise as little Martin Brundle is raised in laboratory conditions provided by scientific tycoon Anton Bartok (Lee Richardson).

Afflicted with a dramatically accelerated lifecycle, Martin quickly demonstrates genius, and by the age of five emerges fully grown in the person of Eric Stoltz. Martin becomes determined to perfect his father's teleportation machine, which Bartok controls, and also takes an interest in researcher Beth Logan (Daphne Zuniga).

Martin gradually becomes aware that Bartok's motives are far from benign, and simultaneously begins mutating into a hideous beast while retaining his human sensibility.

By the climax, the film more closely comes to resemble *Aliens* than the previous *Fly*, as the transformed Martin hides behind walls and in the ceiling before pouncing on Bartok's goons, spitting on them, chewing them up and spitting them out.

■ FLY BY NIGHT

1942, 74 MINS, US
Dir Robert Siodmak *Prod* Sol C. Siegel *Scr* Jay Drather, F. Hugh Herbert *Ph* John F. Seitz *Ed* Arthur Schmidt

● Nancy Kelly, Richard Carlson, Albert Basserman, Martin Kosleck (Paramount)

This is one of those sinister mellers, photographed in low light tones, with a generally implausible story populated with spies, secret weapons and nice young couples who get innocently mixed up in espionage. It's well done, but the maddeningly impossible plot [from an original story by Ben Roberts and Sidney Sheldon] sets it down as routine.

Nancy Kelly and Richard Carlson, as the innocents who get caught in the meshes of the spy ring, both give surprisingly good performances for roles of this type.

Carlson is a young physician into whose car climbs an inventor who has escaped from a sanitorium, where he has been held by the spies.

Robert Siodmak's direction varies from the slow pace of mystery thrillers to chase sequences, but never achieves full success at either end of the scale. That's largely due, however, to the unreal story.

■ FLYING DOWN TO RIO

1934, 88 MINS, US ⓦ ⊙
Dir Thornton Freeland *Prod* Merian C. Cooper, Louis Brock *Scr* Cyril Hume, H. W. Hanemann, Erwin Gelsey *Ph* J. Roy Hunt *Ed* Jack Kitchin *Mus* Max Steiner (dir.) *Art Dir* Van Nest Polglase, Carroll Clark
● Dolores Del Rio, Gene Raymond, Raul Roulien, Ginger Rogers, Fred Astaire, Blanche Friderici (RKO)

The main point of *Flying down to Rio* is the screen promise of Fred Astaire. He's distinctly likeable on the screen, the mike is kind to his voice and as a dancer he remains in a class by himself.

This picture makes its bid via numbers staged by Dave Gould to Vincent Youman melodies. But *Rio*'s story [by Louis Brock] lets it down. It's slow and lacks laughs to the point where average business seems its groove. From the time of the opening melody ('Music Makes Me' – and hot) to the next number, 'Carioca', almost three reels elapse and anybody can take a walk, come back and be that much ahead.

It takes all that time for Gene Raymond, as a band leader, to be enticed by Dolores Del Rio, as a South American belle, and frame her into a plane ride to Rio de Janeiro. This hop includes a faked overnight forced landing on a beach, strictly in the platonic manner. When they finally get off the sand and to Rio, Raymond finds his Brazilian pal is engaged to the girl, but the Latin member gives the damsel to him and takes a novel way out via a parachute dive at the finish. Meanwhile, the opening of a new hotel by the girl's father, for which Raymond's band has been engaged, is the premise for continuing the musical portion below the Equator.

□ 1934: Nomination: Best Song ('Carioca')

■ FLYING LEATHERNECKS

1951, 103 MINS, US ◇ ⓦ ⊙
Dir Nicholas Ray *Prod* Edmund Grainger *Scr* James Edward Grant *Ph* William E. Snyder *Ed* Sherman Todd *Mus* Roy Webb *Art Dir* Albert S. D'Agostino, James W. Sullivan
● John Wayne, Robert Ryan, Don Taylor, Janis Carter, Jay C. Flippen, William Harrigan (RKO)

Marquee pull of John Wayne and Robert Ryan in the action market has been teamed with a story of Marine fighter pilots.

Actual color footage of battle action in the Pacific has been smartly blended with studio shots to strike a note of realism.

James Edward Grant scripted the Kenneth Gamet story, which deals with a small squadron of flying leathernecks stationed in the Pacific and the frictions that develop between its commander (Wayne) and its executive officer (Ryan) when they are not busy fighting the war. Ryan is disappointed because he has not been recommended for command of the squadron but works with Wayne until latter's rigid discipline and impartiality build a bitter friction between them.

This purely masculine yarn sidetracks when Wayne goes on leave to the States for time with his wife (Janis Carter) and small son. These scenes are excellently done, both in playing, direction and writing, but do have the effect of ending the action. This starts in again, however, when Wayne is re-assigned to the Pacific.

● ●

■ FLYING TIGERS

1942, 96 MINS, US ⓥ ⊙
Dir David Miller   *Prod* Edmund Grainger   *Scr* Kenneth Gamet, Barry Trivers   *Ph* Jack Marta   *Ed* Ernest Nims   *Mus* Victor Young
● John Wayne, John Carroll, Anna Lee, Paul Kelly, Mae Clark, Gordon Jones (Republic)

Flying Tigers is based on exploits of American flyers in China who took up the cudgels against the Japs long before Pearl Harbor.

Aside from a foreword written by Generalissimo Chiang Kai-shek, paying tribute to the American Volunteer Group who 'have become the symbol of the invincible strength of the forces now upholding the cause of humanity and justice', there is nothing to distinguish this film from other conventional aviation yarns.

Handicapped primarily by a threadbare script, production also suffers from slow pacing while John Wayne, John Carroll, Anna Lee and Paul Kelly are barely adequate in the major acting assignments. Some of the scenes look repetitious, the same Jap flyers apparently being shot down and killed three or four times over.
□ 1942: Nominations: Best Scoring of a Dramatic Picture, Sound, Special Effects

● ●

■ FOG, THE

1980, 91 MINS, US ◇ ⓥ ⊙
Dir John Carpenter   *Prod* Debra Hill   *Scr* John Carpenter, Debra Hill   *Ph* Dean Cundey   *Ed* Tommy Lee Wallace, Charles Bornstein   *Mus* John Carpenter   *Art Dir* Tommy Lee Wallace
● Adrienne Barbeau, Hal Holbrook, Janet Leigh, Jamie Lee Curtis, John Houseman, Tommy Atkins (Avco Embassy)

John Carpenter is anything but subtle in his approach to shocker material. Premise is obvious from almost the first frame, as a grizzled John Houseman tells youngsters grouped around a campfire about a foggy curse that surrounds a coastal town where a horrible shipwreck took place 100 years ago.

Story exposition and setting are well-established before the opening titles are over, and *The Fog* proceeds to layer one fright atop another.

Adrienne Barbeau makes her film debut as the husky-voiced deejay of the town's sole radio station, perched atop a lighthouse from which the title phenomenon becomes increasingly apparent.

Thesping is okay in all departments although Janet Leigh isn't given much to do, nor is daughter Jamie Lee Curtis.

● ●

■ FOLIES BERGERE

1935, 83 MINS, US
Dir Roy Del Ruth   *Prod* William Goetz, Raymond Griffith   *Scr* Bess Meredyth, Hal Long   *Ph* Barney McGill   *Mus* Alfred Newman (dir.)
● Maurice Chevalier, Ann Sothern, Merle Oberon, Eric Blore, Ferdinand Munier, Walter Byron (20th Century/ United Artists)

Picture has nothing whatever to do with the

Folies Bergere of Paris, except that one of the characters is supposed to be the head comic of the show at the Paris music hall, and that allows for three musical numbers on the stage thereof. For plot and continuity purposes studio has taken an old continental farce, *The Red Cat* [by Rudolph Lothar and Hans Adler] and switched it about a bit.

Maurice Chevalier does excellent work. He handles the double assignment of Charlier, the Folies comic, and the Baron Cassini. Baron gets into a financial jam so Charlier is hired to impersonate him while he's off to London to dig up some coin. Baron has been having marital difficulties with his wife, too, and Charlier manages to fix up both the home work and the office work for the baron with happy fadeout all around.

Chevalier shows, perhaps for the first time in films, that he has range as an actor. Ann Sothern as Charlier's wife is pretty and effective. She sings and dances with Chevalier and makes a definite sock impression. Merle Oberon, as the baron's wife, on the other hand, gets a tough break.

Dance routines by Dave Gould are nifty.
□ 1935: Best Dance Direction ('Straw Hat')

● ●

■ FOLLOW THAT BIRD

1985, 88 MINS, US ◇ ⓥ ⊙
Dir Ken Kwapis   *Prod* Tony Garnett   *Scr* Tony Geiss, Judy Freudberg   *Ph* Curtis Clark   *Ed* Stan Warnow, Evan Landis   *Mus* Van Dyke Parks, Lennie Niehaus   *Art Dir* Carol Spier
● Caroll Spinney, Jim Henson, Frank Oz, Paul Bartel, Sandra Bernhard, John Candy (Warner)

Simple premise has the slightly goofy yellow, eight-foot fowl Big Bird taken away from Sesame Street by the officious Miss Finch so he can grow up among his own kind, a bird family named the Dodos, in Oceanview, Ill.

The Dodos are a bunch of loons, however, so B.B. begins the long trek back to New York on foot, while the Sesame Street gang mobilizes in assorted vehicles to find its dear friend.

En route, B.B. has a pleasant encounter with country singing truck driver Waylon Jennings, but a distinctly nasty one with the Sleaze Brothers (SCTV's Joe Flaherty and Dave Thomas), unscrupulous amusement parkoperators who abduct B.B. for their own nefarious purposes.

All turns out for the best, of course, and spicing things up along the way are Chevy Chase and Kermit The Frog as TV newscasters, Sandra Bernhard and Paul Bartel as the proprietors of a lowdown roadside diner, and John Candy as a motorcycle cop.

● ●

■ FOLLOW THAT CAMEL

1967, 95 MINS, UK ◇ ⓥ
Dir Gerald Thomas   *Prod* Peter Rogers   *Scr* Talbot Rothwell   *Ph* Alan Hume   *Ed* Alfred Roome   *Mus* Eric Rogers   *Art Dir* Alex Vetchinsky
● Phil Silvers, Jim Dale, Peter Butterworth, Charles Hawtrey, Kenneth Williams, Anita Harris (Rank)

Story line provides adequate excuse for a Carry On foray into the Foreign Legion territory, with a young hero (Jim Dale), accused of cheating at cricket, enlisting with his manservant to exculpate his disgrace. There he encounters Phil Silvers, as a sergeant who invents acts of heroism and is much decorated, Kenneth Williams as the German commanding officer, Charles Hawtrey, as his deft adjutant, and Joan Sims, as a much-cleavage siren.

They are involved in running skirmishes with an Arab chieftain, serving a master called Mustapha Leak, and the farrago climaxes in a hilarious battle at a desert fort, after a forced march through waterless wastes.

It all works with considerable bounce, with

elements of parody of *Beau Geste*-style movies for those alert to them. All the regular comics are on first-rate form.

● ●

■ FOLLOW THAT DREAM

1962, 109 MINS, US ◇ ⓥ
Dir Gordon M. Douglas   *Prod* David Weisbart   *Scr* Charles Lederer   *Ph* Leo Tover   *Ed* William B. Murphy   *Mus* Hans J. Salter   *Art Dir* Mal Bert
● Elvis Presley, Arthur O'Connell, Anne Helm, Joanne Moore, Jack Kruschen, Simon Oakland (United Artists)

Follow That Dream is a kind of second cinematic cousin to *Tammy* with Elvis Presley as the hinterland's answer to the supposed advantages of formal booklarnin'. Scenarist Charles Lederer has constructed several highly amusing scenes in tailoring Richard Powell's novel, *Pioneer, Go Home*, to fit the specifications of the screen. There are lags and lapses in the picture, to be sure, but, by Presley pix standards, it's above average.

Presley portrays what amounts to a cross between Li'l Abner and male counterpart of Tammy, a sort of number one son in a makeshift, itinerant brood of Real McCoy types who plant themselves on a strip of unclaimed Florida beach and proceed to play homesteaders whilst befuddled officials of city and state, welfare workers and thugs haplessly attempt to unsquat them from their profitable perch.

● ●

■ FOLLOW THE FLEET

1936, 110 MINS, US ⓥ
Dir Mark Sandrich   *Prod* Pandro S. Berman   *Scr* Dwight Taylor, Allan Scott   *Ph* David Abel   *Ed* Henry Berman   *Mus* Max Steiner (dir.)   *Art Dir* Van Nest Polglase, Carroll Clark
● Fred Astaire, Ginger Rogers, Randolph Scott, Harriet Hilliard, Astrid Allwyn, Betty Grable (RKO)

With Ginger Rogers again opposite, and the Irving Berlin music to dance to and sing, Astaire once more legs himself and his picture into the big-time entertainment class.

Imperfections in *Fleet* are confined to story. That's usual with musicals, stage or screen. This is a rather free adaptation of [Hubert Osborne's play] *Shore Leave*, a David Belasco oldie. Yet the story never detracts from the important element – the Astaire-Rogers musical efforts.

There are seven songs which is a bit too much – all by Irving Berlin, with 'Face the Music', a cross between 'Piccolino' and 'Lovely Day', easily the leader. The score on the whole is pleasant but save for 'Face the Music', the last number, not particularly distinguished.

Story is a double romance involving the starred duo and Harriet Hilliard-Randolph Scott. Yarn breaks them up and teams them again for the finish.

This is Hilliard's first picture. She's from radio, having sung mostly with the Ozzie Nelson band and chiefly on the Joe Penner programs. A blonde originally, she's in brunet wig in this film, presumably in deference to Rogers.

● ●

■ FOLLOW YOUR DREAMS

See: Independence Day

● ●

■ FOOL, THE

1991, 135 MINS, UK ⓥ
Dir Christine Edzard   *Prod* Richard Goodwin, Christine Edzard   *Scr* Christine Edzard, Olivier Stockman   *Ph* Robin Vidgeon   *Ed* Olivier Stockman   *Mus* Michel Sanvoisin
● Derek Jacobi, Cyril Cusack, Ruth Mitchell, Paul Brooke, Corin Redgrave, John McEnery (Sands/Film Four/British Screen/Tyler)

F

Three years after their marathon, *Little Dorrit*, husband-and-wife producers Richard Goodwin and Christine Edzard tread the same streets to lesser effect in *The Fool*.

In 1857, an obscure theater clerk (Derek Jacobi) engineers a financial scam to show up the monied classes. Problems start when, posing as the carefree Sir John, he's recognized by some theater folk, and he starts taking his alter ego too seriously.

Later scenes, with their *Wall Street* lingo and Jacobi's crisis of conscience, are an obvious allegory of the me-too 1980s. But they're a long time coming, and the thrill of the paper chase is lacking. Without a strong central yarn like Dickens' *Dorrit*, pic becomes a series of one-off routines by w.k. Brit thesps.

Helmer and co-scripter Edzard shows off her research and topnotch design with street characters based on interviews by 19th-century social journalist Henry Mayhew. They're fine on their own terms, right down to the dirt under their fingernails, but Edzard needs to make up her mind whether she's building a museum or making a movie.

· ·

■ FOOL FOR LOVE

1985, 106 MINS, US ◇ ⊛
Dir Robert Altman *Prod* Menahem Golan, Yoram Globus *Scr* Sam Shepard *Ph* Pierre Mignot *Ed* Luce Grunenwaldt *Mus* George Burt *Art Dir* Stephen Altman
● Sam Shepard, Kim Basinger, Harry Dean Stanton, Randy Quaid, Martha Crawford, Louise Egolf (Cannon)

Robert Altman directs a fine cast with all the authority and finesse a good play deserves, so it's too bad the play fooled them all. Sam Shepard's drama of intense, forbidden love in the modern West is made to seem like specious stuff filled with dramatic ideas left over from the 1950s.

Opening up the play, which was set entirely in a dingy motel room, Shepard and Altman have spread out the action all around a rundown motel complex on the edge of the desert.

Eddie, a rangy, handsome cowboy, returns after a long absence to try to get back with the sexy May, with whom he has a can't-live-with-or-without-her relationship. The two shout, argue, make up, make out, split up, pout, dance around each other and start up all over again, while an old drunk observer takes it all in. Finally, the arrival of another fellow to take May out prompts a nocturnal spilling of the beans about Eddie and May's taboo love affair.

Beginning with the impressive Shepard, cast is handpicked with care. As the saucy May, Kim Basinger alternately conjures up Marilyn Monroe in *The Misfits* and *Bus Stop* and Brigitte Bardot in *And God Created Woman*. Harry Dean Stanton is excellent as the washed-up cause of all the problems.

· ·

■ FOOLISH WIVES

1922, 180 MINS, US ⊗ ⊛ ⊙
Dir Erich von Stroheim *Scr* Erich von Stroheim *Ph* Ben Reynolds, William Daniels *Mus* Sigmund Romberg *Art Dir* E.E. Sheeley, Richard Day
● Erich von Stroheim, Rudolph Christians, Miss Du Pont, Maude George, Mae Busch, Louis K. Webb (Universal)

According to the Universal's press department, the picture cost $1,103,736.38; was 11 months and six days in filming; six months in assembling and editing; consumed 320,000 feet of negative, and employed as many as 15,000 extras for atmosphere.

Foolish Wives shows the cost – in the sets, beautiful backgrounds and massive interiors that carry a complete suggestion of the atmosphere of Monte Carlo, the locale of the story. And the sets, together with a thoroughly capable cast, are about all the picture has for all the heavy dough expended.

Obviously intended to be a sensational sex melodrama, *Foolish Wives* is at the same time frankly salacious.

Erich von Stroheim wrote the script, directed, and is the featured player. He's all over the lot every minute. His character is a Russian Captain of Hussars. The uniform may be Russian, but von Stroheim's general facial and physical appearance clearly suggests the typical Prussian military officer.

The story starts with a flirtation between the Count (Von Stroheim) and the American diplomat's wife, continues along with his obvious attempts to possess her, right under her husband's nose, and with the woman's evident liking for the count's attentions.

· ·

■ FOOLS OF FORTUNE

1990, 104 MINS, UK ◇ ⊛ ⊙
Dir Pat O'Connor *Prod* Sarah Radclyffe *Scr* Michael Hirst *Ph* Jerzy Zielinski *Ed* Michael Bradsell *Mus* Hans Zimmer *Art Dir* Jamie Leonard
● Mary Elizabeth Mastrantonio, Iain Glen, Julie Christie, Michael Kitchen, Sean T. McClory, Niamii Cusack (Polygram/Working Title)

Fools of Fortune is an historical saga written with lucidity and performed with sensitivity, but tending to melodrama.

The Irish war of independence is the starting point for the story [from the novel by William Trevor] of a family's destruction and the survival of an unlikely love. The Quinton family seem sheltered in their grand rural home until the British-employed soldiers, the Black and Tans, burn down the house. The only survivors of the massacre are Quinton's wife (Julie Christie), her son Willie (first, Sean T. McClory, and then as an adult, Iain Glen), and his maid (Niamii Cusack).

Willie becomes an introspective and withdrawn young man, while his mother becomes a manic depressive and chronic alcoholic, a role which Christie relishes in.

When Christie finally commits suicide, Willie is comforted by childhood playmate Marianne, who's grown into an exquisitely beautiful woman (Mary Elizabeth Mastrantonio). Result of this comfort is a child.

· ·

■ FOOTLIGHT PARADE

1933, 102 MINS, US ⊛ ⊙
Dir Lloyd Bacon, Busby Berkeley *Scr* Manuel Seff, James Seymour *Ph* George Barnes *Ed* George Amy *Art Dir* Anton Grot, Jack Okey
● James Cagney, Joan Blondell, Ruby Keeler, Dick Powell, Guy Kibbee, Ruth Donnelly (Warner)

Footlight Parade is not as good as *42nd Street* and *Gold Diggers* but the three socko numbers here eclipse some of the preceding Busby Berkeley staging for spectacle.

The first hour is a loose, disjointed plot to plant the Fanchon & Marco presentation production stuff. F&M isn't mentioned but that's the setting, with James Cagney as the unit stager who's being rooked by his partners.

As in *Gold Diggers*, where Ned Sparks puts on a Ziegfeld production with a $15,000 budget, similarly no picture house ever saw such tabs as Cagney gives 'em here. But that's cinematic license.

That water ballet, the hokum 'Honeymoon Hotel' and 'Shanghai Lil' are punchy and undeniable. They more than offset the lethargy of what has preceded and sweeps the spectator away.

Characters are formula. Ruby Keeler is again the mousey type who becomes a swell number, and Dick Powell again is the juve lead. Cagney is the dynamic stager of units and Joan Blondell is his overly efficient secretary who contributes an element of unrequited love while Cagney gets rid of one wife and falls for another phoney dame.

· ·

■ FOOTLIGHT SERENADE

1942, 81 MINS, US ⊛
Dir Gregory Ratoff *Prod* William Le Baron *Scr* Richard Ellis, Helen Logan, Lynn Starling *Ph* Lee Garmes *Ed* Robert Simpson *Mus* Lee Robin, Ralph Rainger
● John Payne, Betty Grable, Victor Mature, Jane Wyman, Phil Silvers, James Gleason (20th Century-Fox)

Footlight Serenade is a typical backstage number. New twist of minor importance has been provided for the boy-meets-girl-and-both-get-into-Broadway-show formula. Victor Mature is the champ, with the show built around him by producer James Gleason. His characterization is decidedly reminiscent of a heavyweight champ of the 1930s. Betty Grable gets a chorine job, while her fiance John Payne is projected into a line of candidates for stumble-bum for the champ in the show.

Although Mature successfully pictures the egoistic and swaggering fight champ for reverse angles, he's painted with lily-white duco for the finish.

Gregory Ratoff carries the direction at a good pace. With the backstage filmusical angles well culled, there was nothing new for the scripters to devise on their own.

· ·

■ FOOTLOOSE

1984, 107 MINS, US ◇ ⊛ ⊙
Dir Herbert Ross *Prod* Lewis J. Rachmil, Craig Zadan *Scr* Dean Pitchford *Ph* Ric Waite *Ed* Paul Hirsch *Mus* Miles Goodman (adapt.), Becky Shargo (sup.) *Art Dir* Ron Hobbs
● Kevin Bacon, Lori Singer, John Lithgow, Dianne Wiest, Christopher Penn, Sarah Jessica Parker (Paramount)

In addition to his usual directorial skill and considerable choreographic experience, Herb Ross brings to *Footloose* an adult sensibility often lacking in troubled-teen pics.

To be sure, from its toe-tapping titles onward, *Footloose* is mainly a youth-oriented rock picture, complete with big-screen reminders of what's hot today in music video. And there's usually a stereo in sight to explain where the music's coming from, even on the side of tractors. But by writing both the screenplay and contributing lyrics to nine of the film's songs, Dean Pitchford has come up with an integrated story line that works.

Essential to the result is young Kevin Bacon, superb in the lead part. Bacon really just wants to get along in the small town he's been forced to move to from Chicago. Sure to complicate his life, however, is pretty Lori Singer, a sexually and otherwise confused preacher's daughter.

☐ 1984: Nominations: Best Song ('Footloose', 'Let's Hear it for the Boy')

· ·

■ FOOTSTEPS IN THE DARK

1941, 96 MINS, US
Dir Lloyd Bacon *Scr* Lester Cole, John Wexley *Ph* Ernie Haller *Ed* Owen Marks *Mus* Frederick Hollander
● Errol Flynn, Brenda Marshall, Ralph Bellamy, Alan Hale, Lee Patrick, Lucile Watson (Warner/First National)

Errol Flynn becomes a detective book author and amateur Sherlock in *Footsteps in the Dark*, his first comedy in years. Not his best picture, this modest budgeter gives the star a chance to appear in a role different from his usual costume or military films. Lloyd Bacon's direction furnishes the film with plenty of suspense and hokey but socko absurdities.

Flynn is depicted as an investment banker, leading a double life as a writer under the nom-de-plume of F.X. Pettijohn. His search for story material takes him on nightly prowls which get him into hot water in his own home.

Flynn does well enough as the amateur Sherlock. It's a role that calls for much action, with the plot [from a play by Laslo

Fodor] centered about him in almost every scene. His portrayal indicates he could do better in future semi-comic roles, especially if given brighter material.

●●●●●●●●●●●●●●●●●●●●●●●●●●●●●●

■ **FOR A FEW DOLLARS MORE**

1966, 130 MINS, ITALY/SPAIN/W. GERMANY ◇ ⓥ
Dir Sergio Leone *Prod* [Sergio Leone], [Fulvio Morsella]
Scr Luciano Vincenzoni, Sergio Leone *Ph* Massimo Dallamano *Ed* Adriana Novelli, Eugenio Alabiso, Giorgio Ferralonga *Mus* Ennio Morricone
Art Dir Carlo Simi
● Clint Eastwood, Lee Van Cleef, Gian Maria Volonte, Mara Krup, Luigi Pistilli, Klaus Kinski
(PEA/Gonzales/Constantin)

A hard-hitting western with upper-case values out of the busy Italo stable, this is a top-notch action entry.

Story [by director Sergio Leone and Fulvio Morsella] deals with a race between two bounty killers (Clint Eastwood and Lee Van Cleef) for reward money riding on head of a bandit (Gian Maria Volonte). First separately, then via a somewhat shaky and untrusting allegiance, the pair manage to set the stage for the killing of the bandido, El Indio. In the finale, it turns out that Van Cleef's real reason for getting El Indio was not the coin involved.

Script generally manages to avoid the cliche pitfalls traditional to the western, and Luciano Vincenzoni's dialogue is literate and satisfying to the ear. But it's principally thanks to Leone's bigger-than-life style, which combines upfront action and closeup details with a hard-hitting pace, that this acquires its impactful dimension.

Eastwood is fine in a tailor-made role of the squint-eyed opportunist who plays his cards right. Van Cleef etches a neat picture of his partner-rival. Volonte makes a suitably villainous heavy (for an added fillip, script makes him a drug addict to boot).

Spanish countryside and Italo studio interiors combine for realistic southwestern effect. Ennio Morricone's music, without measuring up to his previous efforts in the oater belt, is nevertheless pleasing. Pic is somewhat overlong at 130 minutes.

[Version reviewed was Italian-language one. English-dubbed version was released in US in 1967 and UK in 1968.]

●●●●●●●●●●●●●●●●●●●●●●●●●●●●●●

■ **FORBIDDEN PLANET**

1956, 98 MINS, US ◇ ⓥ ⊙
Dir Fred McLeod Wilcox *Prod* Nicholas Nayfack
Scr Cyril Hume *Ph* George J. Folsey *Ed* Ferris Webster
Mus Louis Barron, Bebe Barron *Art Dir* Cedric Gibbons, Arthur Lonergan
● Walter Pidgeon, Anne Francis, Leslie Nielsen, Warren Stevens, Jack Kelly, Earl Holliman (M-G-M)

Imaginative gadgets galore, plus plenty of suspense and thrills, make the production a top offering in the space travel category. Best of all the gadgets is Robby, the Robot, and he's well-used for some comedy touches.

The conception of space cruisers, space planet terrain, the monstrous self-operating power plant, and of the terribly frightening spectre that threatens the human principals in the story are weird and wonderful.

With all the technical gadgetry on display and carrying the entertainment load, the players are more or less puppets with no great acting demands made. Leslie Nielsen, space cruiser commander, lands on Altair-4 to search for survivors from a previous flight. He finds Walter Pidgeon, super-scientist, and the latter's daughter (Anne Francis) who, with Robby, are the planet's only inhabitants.

Pidgeon, who has gained knowledge beyond usual human limits, wants the rescuers let be gone. Nielsen takes to Francis and she to him, so he determines to seek out the unseen menace.

Credited for the special effects that add the punch to the show are A. Arnold Gillespie, Warren Newcombe, Irving G. Ries and Joshua Meador.
□ 1956: Nomination: Best Special Effects

●●●●●●●●●●●●●●●●●●●●●●●●●●●●●●

■ **FORCE OF EVIL**

1948, 78 MINS, US ⓥ ⊙
Dir Abraham Polonsky *Prod* Bob Roberts
Scr Abraham Polonsky, Ira Wolfert *Ph* George Barnes
Ed Art Seid *Mus* David Raksin *Art Dir* Richard Day
● John Garfield, Beatrice Pearson, Thomas Gomez, Marie Windsor, Roy Roberts, Howland Chamberlin
(M-G-M/Enterprise)

Force of Evil fails to develop the excitement hinted at in the title. Makers apparently couldn't decide on the best way to present an expose of the numbers racket, winding up with neither fish nor fowl as far as hard-hitting racketeer meller is concerned. A poetic, almost allegorical, interpretation keeps intruding on the tougher elements of the plot. This factor adds no distinction and only makes the going tougher.

Garfield, as to be expected, comes through with a performance that gets everything out of the material furnished. Film also introduces Beatrice Pearson but she garners no great honors for herself.

Plot, based on Ira Wolfert's novel *Tucker's People*, deals with the racketeers who fatten off the little person's nickels and dimes that daily are played on the numbers game. It is not a lucid expose as filmed.

On the technical side, the production fares better than story-wise. The physical mounting is expertly valued; the New York locale shots give authenticity; and lensing by George Barnes, while a bit on the arty side, displays skilled craftsmanship.

●●●●●●●●●●●●●●●●●●●●●●●●●●●●●●

■ **FORCE 10 FROM NAVARONE**

1978, 118 MINS, UK ◇ ⓥ
Dir Guy Hamilton *Prod* Oliver A. Unger *Scr* Robin Chapman *Ph* Christopher Challis *Ed* Raymond Poulton
Mus Ron Goodwin *Art Dir* Geoffrey Drake
● Robert Shaw, Harrison Ford, Edward Fox, Barbara Bach, Franco Nero, Richard Kiel (American International)

This is not a sequel to the 1961 hit, *Guns of Navarone*, although *Force 10* opens with the bangup conclusion of the earlier exercise in World War II commando heroics.

Two survivors of the spiking of the guns, British Major Mallory (now played by Robert Shaw) and demolitions expert Miller (Edward Fox) provide the link that gives some purpose to the title [from the novel by Alistair MacLean; screen story by Carl Foreman].

Director Guy Hamilton manages over the course of almost two hours to keep his audience on edge. For a finale he has a double whammy destruction of a giant Yugoslav dam which sets loose forces of nature that crumble a seemingly indestructible bridge.

This next-to-last film appearance of Robert Shaw is not his glory farewell. He is very good in what he is called upon to do, but the role is not one that makes any particular demand upon an exceptionally talented person.

Harrison Ford does a creditable job as the American Colonel; Fox is excellent as the British demolitions expert; Carl Weathers gives a powerful performance as the unwanted black GI who proves himself in more ways than one. Barbara Bach, lone femme, does fine in a tragic, patriotic role as a Partisan. Franco Nero as a Nazi double agent who fools the Partisans is slickly nefarious.

●●●●●●●●●●●●●●●●●●●●●●●●●●●●●●

■ **FOREIGN AFFAIR, A**

1948, 113 MINS, US
Dir Billy Wilder *Prod* Charles Brackett *Scr* Charles Brackett, Billy Wilder, Richard Breen, Robert Harari

Ph Charles B. Lang Jr *Ed* Doane Harrison
Mus Frederick Hollander *Art Dir* Hans Dreier, Walter Tyler
● Jean Arthur, Marlene Dietrich, John Lund, Millard Mitchell, Peter Von Zerneck, Stanley Prager (Paramount)

A Foreign Affair is a witty satire developed around a Congressional investigation of GI morals in Germany. Much of the action is backgrounded against actual Berlin footage. The humor to which such a theme lends itself has been given a stinging bite, even though presented broadly to tickle the risibilities.

While subject is handled for comedy, Charles Brackett and Billy Wilder have managed to underlay the fun with an expose of human frailties and, to some extent, indicate a passive bitterness among the conquered in the occupied areas.

Jean Arthur is in a topflight characterization as a spinsterish congresswoman, who furnishes the distaff touch to an elemental girl-meets-boy angle in the story. The boy is John Lund, and Marlene Dietrich personifies the eternal siren as an opportunist German femme who furnishes Lund with off-duty diversion. Also, she gives the Dietrich s.a. treatment to three Frederick Hollander tunes, lyrics of which completely express the cynical undertones of the film.
□ 1948: Nominations: Best Screenplay, B&W Cinematography

●●●●●●●●●●●●●●●●●●●●●●●●●●●●●●

■ **FOREIGN BODY**

1986, 108 MINS, US/UK ◇ ⓥ
Dir Ronald Neame *Prod* Colin M. Brewer *Scr* Celine La Freniere *Ph* Ronnie Taylor *Ed* Andrew Nelson
Mus Ken Howard *Art Dir* Roy Stannard
● Victor Banerjee, Warren Mitchell, Geraldine McEwan, Denis Quilley, Amanda Donohoe, Trevor Howard (Neame/Brewer)

If *Foreign Body* [based on the novel by Roderick Mann] doesn't have quite the comic and narrative richness of Ronald Neame's Ealing Studios classics, this variation on the 'great impostor' plot device is still an unalloyed pleasure to watch.

Built solidly upon a fluid, comic virtuoso performance by Victor Banerjee, the picaresque fable of an impoverished refugee from Calcutta faking it as a doctor to London's upper crust [in 1975] makes some jaunty points about racism, gullibility and pluck.

Even though he's a deceiver, sincerity is a bedrock trait of the *Foreign Body* hero, Ram Das, and Banerjee is free to romp with bug-eyed zaniness through the improbable adventures of this Asian naif abroad.

●●●●●●●●●●●●●●●●●●●●●●●●●●●●●●

■ **FOREIGN CORRESPONDENT**

1940, 119 MINS, US ⓥ ⊙
Dir Alfred Hitchcock *Prod* Walter Wanger *Scr* Charles Bennett, Joan Harrison, James Hilton, Robert Benchley
Ph Rudolph Mate *Ed* Dorothy Spencer, Otho Lovering
Mus Alfred Newman *Art Dir* Alexander Golitzen
● Joel McCrea, Laraine Day, Herbert Marshall, George Sanders, Albert Basserman, Edmund Gwenn (Wanger/United Artists)

Story is essentially the old cops-and-robbers. But it has been set in a background of international political intrigue of the largest order. It has a war flavor, the events taking place immediately before and at the start of World War II; yet it can in no sense be called a war picture. Mystery and intrigue march in place.

Add to all this a cast carefully selected by director Alfred Hitchcock to the last, unimportant lackey. Joel McCrea neatly blends the self-confidence and naivete of the reporter-hero, while Laraine Day, virtually a fledgling in pictures, only in the most difficult sequences misses out as a top-grade dramatic player. Vet Herbert Marshall as the heavy,

F

George Sanders as McCrea's fellow-reporter, 72-year-old refugee Albert Basserman as a Dutch diplomat, Edmund Gwenn as a not-to-be-trusted bodyguard, Eduardo Ciannelli as the usual hissable villain, are all tops. Comic touch is provided by Robert Benchley and Eddie Conrad.

Story uncorks with the editor of a New York paper going nuts because his foreign correspondents cable nothing but rumor and speculation. He hits on the idea of sending one of his police reporters to dig factual material out of the Europe of August 1939. McCrea, who knows nothing of foreign affairs, immediately runs into the tallest story a reporter can imagine – a big-league peace organization, headed by Marshall, which is operating as nothing but a spy ring.

McCrea runs into the double-cross organization when it kidnaps an honest Dutch diplomat (Basserman) and assassinates his imposter to give the impression that he is dead. Assassination sequence in the rain on the broad steps of an Amsterdam building (set is a tremendous and excellent re-creation of a whole block in Amsterdam) is virtually a newsreel in its starkness.

☐ 1940: Nominations: Best Picture, Supp. Actor (Albert Basserman), Original Screenplay, B&W Cinematography, B&W Art Direction, Special Effects

. . . .

■ FOREVER AMBER

1947, 140 MINS, US ◇

Dir Otto Preminger *Prod* William Perlberg *Scr* Philip Dunne, Ring Lardner Jr *Ph* Leon Shamroy *Ed* Louis Loeffler *Mus* David Raksin *Art Dir* Lyle R. Wheeler
● Linda Darnell, Cornel Wilde, Richard Greene, George Sanders, Jessica Tandy, Anne Revere   (20th Century-Fox)

Here is a $4 million (and claimed to be more) picture that looks its cost. That goes even for the lost footage through mishap with Peggy Cummins, the original candidate until Linda Darnell replaced. And she does quite well.

The lusty yarn [from the novel by Kathleen Winsor] is treated for what it is. Darnell runs the gamut from romantic opportunist to prison degradation and up again to being the king's favorite and finally a discarded mistress, grateful that the royal equerry invites her to supper after Charles II gives her the brush-off.

In between there's a wealth of derring-do, 17th-century knavery and debauchery, the love of a good woman (Jane Ball), and the rest of a depraved court's atmosphere. It's solid escapology.

Darnell manages her chameleon Amber character very well. Her blonde beauty shows off well in Technicolor, and she is equally convincing when she is thrown in a pauper's gaol.

Cornel Wilde is the No. 1 juve, although Glenn Langan suggests he might have made an excellent choice for that role instead of a secondary swain. Richard Haydn plays his a.k. role well as the arrogant earl who Amber premeditatedly weds in order to gain a title. John Russell is convincing as the highwayman; Anne Revere is sufficiently despicable as a keeper of a thieves' den; Jessica Tandy does all right as Amber's maid; George Sanders turns a neat character when chiding Amber for thinking he could be played for a sucker in a supposedly compromising rendezvous.

☐ 1947: Nomination: Best Scoring of a Dramatic Picture

. . . .

■ FOREVER AND A DAY

1943, 104 MINS, US ⊛

Dir Rene Clair, Edmund Goulding, Cedric Hardwicke, Frank Lloyd, Victor Saville, Robert Stevenson, Herbert Wilcox *Scr* Charles Bennett, C.S. Forrester, Lawrence Hazard, Michael Hogan, W.P. Lipscomb, Alice Duer Miller, John Van Druten, Alan Campbell, Peter Godfrey, S.M. Herzig, Christopher Isherwood, Gene Lockhart,
R.C. Sherriff, Claudine West, Norman Corwin, Jack Hartfield, James Hilton, Emmet Lavery, Frederick Lonsdale, Donald Ogden Stewart, Keith Winter *Ph* Robert de Grasse, Lee Garmes, Russell Metty, Nicholas Musuraca   *Ed* Elmo J. Williams, George Crone *Mus* Anthony Collins
● Merle Oberon, Gladys Cooper, C. Aubrey Smith, Claude Rains, Anna Neagle, Ray Milland (RKO)

Forever and a Day is a sentimental romantic-adventure yarn, encompassing in cavalcade manner Britain's epochal struggles to retain the integrity of an empire and the freedom of its people in face of periodical threats of would-be world conquerors. Interwoven is the quaint history of a picturesque London mansion – its illustrious builder and his descendants – built during the Napoleonic period, that withstands the ravages of time and world-shattering conflict until the days of the Nazi blitz.

In a star-studded cast, including some 45 name players, a number of topnotchers are necessarily limited. However, a large proportion of the subordinate sequences have been handled $500,000 at RKO, which financed the production. This is exclusive of the players, who undertook the assignment on a gratis basis, some 21 writers and the seven accredited directors who also contributed their services.

Yarn revolves about the fusing of two families after a feud dating back to the early part of the 19th century when C. Aubrey Smith, as the robust, swashbuckling British admiral first built the house. Claude Rains, as the vindictive guardian of Anna Neagle, who runs away to marry one of the Smith tribe, does not impress as the menace.

. . . .

■ FOREVER IN LOVE

See: Pride of the Marines

. . . .

■ FOREVER YOUNG

1992, 102 MINS, US ◇ ⊛ ☉

Dir Steve Miner *Prod* Bruce Davey *Scr* Jeffrey Abrams *Ph* Russell Boyd *Ed* John Poll *Mus* Jerry Goldsmith *Art Dir* Gregg Fonseca
● Mel Gibson, Jamie Lee Curtis, Elijah Wood, Isabel Glasser, George Wendt, Joe Morton (Warner/Icon)

Warner Bros. has a big, rousing, old-fashioned romance on its hands, a perfect 'women's picture' alternative to action fare and kid-oriented sequels.

The action begins in 1939, as test pilot Daniel (Mel Gibson) can't bring himself to propose to Helen (Isabel Glasser), right up until the moment she walks in front of a speeding truck. Helen ends up in a coma, and the distraught Daniel volunteers for an experiment in which his best friend Harry (George Wendt) is to freeze him for a year in an early test of cryogenics.

Cut to 1992, when Daniel is thawed out by two mischievous 10-year-olds and moves in with one of the boys (Elijah Wood) and his single mom (Jamie Lee Curtis). With the Army in pursuit of their long-forgotten experiment gone awry, the film takes some clever and extremely satisfying turns.

The director manages to toe the line of melodrama without ever slipping over into camp, balancing those elements with humor and suspense to carry *Forever Young* if not over the moon, at least into the clouds.

. . . .

■ FOR LOVE OF IVY

1968, 101 MINS, US ◇ ⊛

Dir Daniel Mann *Prod* Edgar J. Scherick, Jay Weston *Scr* Robert Alan Aurthur *Ph* Joseph Coffey *Ed* Patricia Jaffe *Mus* Quincy Jones *Art Dir* Peter Dohanos
● Sidney Poitier, Abby Lincoln, Beau Bridges, Nan Martin, Lauri Peters, Carroll O'Connor (Palomar)

Ivy is at bottom an innocuous romantic comedy, not unlike those cranked out regularly in
the 1940s, without sufficiently high-powered drama, clever humor or moving romance to offer. What little force the pic has stems from Sidney Poitier's clear enjoyment of a role cut from Cary Grant cloth.

Simple storyline provided by Poitier is not rich in character motivation. He plays a lovable rogue who runs a (literally) floating crap game in the van of a truck, a gambling ploy that will probably strike even the most inveterate New York gamblers as doubtfully authentic.

Prodded by two teenagers into dating their late-20s maid (Abby Lincoln), who has threatened to abandon their household to the stupefying incompetence of their mother, he gradually falls in love.

Lincoln has a spirited freshness and supporting cast all performs diligently.

☐ 1968: Nomination: Best Song ('For the Love of Ivy')

. . . .

■ FOR LOVE OR MONEY

1963, 108 MINS, US ◇

Dir Michael Gordon *Prod* Robert Arthur *Scr* Larry Markes, Michael Morris *Ph* Clifford Stine *Ed* Alma Macrorie *Mus* Frank DeVol *Art Dir* Alexander Golitzen, Malcolm Brown
● Kirk Douglas, Mitzi Gaynor, Gig Young, Thelma Ritter, Julie Newmar, Leslie Parrish (Universal)

The glib, sharp scenario is seasoned with spicy spoofery of three worthy targets: motivational research, physical fitness and modern art – and the people who practice these fads and/or professions.

The wild plot has to do with a wealthy and eccentric widow's scheme to marry her three daughters off to the candidates of her choice, a goal for which she assigns her attorney the additional duties of matchmaker. All of this is engineered at a bright, effervescent clip by director Michael Gordon.

Kirk Douglas uncorks a flair for zany comedics as the pivotal figure in the proceedings. He plays the attorney-matchmaker who falls for the eldest daughter, a consumer research bug with Madison Avenue phraseology vivaciously played by Mitzi Gaynor. The other daughters are Julie Newmar, a delectable blonde amazon as the health addict, and Leslie Parrish, slightly miscast as the pretty beatnik. Even Thelma Ritter, as the screwball widow, gets the glamor treatment.

Gig Young delivers another of his amiable boozing wolf-playboy characterizations. William Bendix comes through nicely as a good-naturedly hapless Pinkerton.

. . . .

■ FOR ME AND MY GAL

1942, 104 MINS, US ⊛ ☉

Dir Busby Berkeley *Prod* Arthur Freed *Scr* Richard Sherman, Fred Finklehoffe, Sid Silvers *Ph* William Daniels *Ed* Ben Lewis *Mus* Georgie Stoll (dir.), Roger Edens (adapt.) *Art Dir* Cedric Gibbons, Gabriel Scognamillo
● Judy Garland, George Murphy, Gene Kelly, Marta Eggerth, Richard Quine, Keenan Wynn (M-G-M)

Story [by Howard Emmett Rogers] of vaudeville troupers before and during the First World War is obvious, naive and sentimental. It's also genuine and affectionate and lively.

Picture's title is taken from one of the song numbers, the oldie, 'For Me and My Gal.' The tune that brings Judy Garland and Gene Kelly together, first as vaudeville team and ultimately as a romance, it gets a sock presentation in a song-and-dance routine by them.

The picture's early scenes, as the vaudevillians tour the sticks and dream of some day playing the Palace, are colorful and convincing. Interpolated through them and the subsequent war sequences are numerous old faves, from 'Beautiful Doll' and 'You Wore a Tulip' to the World War I standbys, 'Over

There,' 'Long, Long Trail,' 'Oui, Oui, Marie' and so on.

Garland is a knockout as the warm-hearted young song-and-dance girl, selling a number of the songs persuasively and getting by neatly in the hoofing routines with Kelly. George Murphy is ingratiating as Garland's faithful but mute suitor, while Kelly gives a vividly drawn portrayal of the song-and-dance man and imperfect hero, practically another 'Pal Joey' character that he played so well on Broadway in the musical of that name.

....

■ FORMULA, THE

1980, 117 MINS, US ◇ ⑲

Dir John G. Avildsen *Prod* Steve Shagan *Scr* Steve Shagan *Ph* James Crabe *Ed* David Bretherton, John G. Avildsen, John Carter *Mus* Bill Conti
Art Dir Herman A. Blumenthal
● George C. Scott, Marthe Keller, Marlon Brando, John Gielgud, Beatrice Straight, Richard Lynch (M-G-M)

M-G-M refused to let director John Avildsen take his name off this picture. According to Avildsen, it was not his original cut, nor producer-writer Steve Shagan's cut, but sort of a combination of the two, plus a few snips and patches by M-G-M president David Begelman.

Given the combined efforts of 14 Oscar nominees and a solid bestseller [by Shagan] to start from, it's truly amazing that *The Formula* is such a clump of sludge, impossible to understand for at least an hour before it grinds to a halt.

Initial sequences solidly establish the closing hours of World War II when a German general (Richard Lynch) is entrusted with top secret documents to take to Switzerland in hopes the Nazis can use them to bargain for amnesty. But Lynch is captured by a US major (Robin Clarke) who recognizes what the secrets will be worth in the postwar world of commerce.

Cut forward 35 years and Clarke is a fresh corpse, murdered in his bed. George C. Scott is called in to investigate the murder of his old friend and before long establishes Clarke had some mysterious dealings with oil supertycoon Marlon Brando.

Appearing grotesquely fat and ridiculous, Brando apparently thinks he's making some visual comment on the nature of his character.
☐ 1980: Nomination: Best Cinematography

....

■ FOR PETE'S SAKE

1974, 90 MINS, US ◇ ⑲

Dir Peter Yates *Prod* Martin Erlichman, Stanley Shapiro
Scr Stanley Shapiro, Maurice Richlin *Ph* Laszlo Kovacs
Ed Frank Keller *Art Dir* Gene Callahan
● Barbra Streisand, Michael Sarrazin, Estelle Parsons, William Redfield, Molly Picon, Louis Zorich (Rastar/Columbia)

For Pete's Sake is a flaccid, relentlessly 'zany' comedy that in the 1960s might have been offered Doris Day.

Co-scripter and co-producer Stanley Shapiro, who penned those Doris Day-Rock Hudson comedies of yore, has tailormade this tale of a brash Brooklyn housewife (Barbra Streisand) married to a poor taxi driver (Michael Sarrazin) who yearns to return to school. Sarrazin is given inside info about a pending meat deal between the US and the Soviet Union which promises to zoom the price of pork bellies. (Pic's original title was *July Pork Bellies*.)

To get the $3,000 necessary to invest in pork belly futures on the stock exchange, Streisand secretly goes to a loan shark. When the Soviet deal is delayed and she can't pay up, her 'contract' is sold. Each contract sale increases the debt while allowing maximum opportunity for broad comedy schtik.

....

■ FORT APACHE

1948, 127 MINS, US ⑲ ⊙

Dir John Ford *Prod* Merian C. Cooper, John Ford
Scr Frank S. Nugent *Ph* Archie Stout *Ed* Jack Murray
Mus Richard Hageman *Art Dir* James Basevi
● John Wayne, Henry Fonda, Shirley Temple, John Agar, Pedro Armendariz, Victor McLaglen (Argosy/RKO)

Mass action, humorous byplay in the western cavalry outpost, deadly suspense, and romance are masterfully combined in this production [suggested by the story *Massacre* by James Warner Bellah]. Integrated with the tremendous action is a superb musical score by Richard Hageman, Score uses sound effects as tellingly as the music notes to point up the thrills. In particular, the massacre scene where the deadly drumming of the Indian ponies makes more potent the action that transpires.

Cast is as tremendous as the scope achieved by Ford's direction and, as a consequence, some of the roles are very short but all effective. Henry Fonda is the colonel, embittered because he has been assigned to the remote fort after a brilliant war record.

John Wayne makes a virile cavalry captain, wise in the way of the Indian. Shirley Temple, the colonel's daughter, perks her sequences in romance with John Agar, West Point graduate. Latter impresses. Pedro Armendariz is excellent as a sergeant. Making up a group of tough topkicks that are responsible for the film's humor are Victor McLaglen, Dick Foran and Jack Pennick.

....

■ FORT APACHE, THE BRONX

1981, 123 MINS, US ◇ ⑲ ⊙

Dir Daniel Petrie *Prod* Martin Richards, Tom Fiorello
Scr Heywood Gould *Ph* John Alcott *Ed* Rita Roland
Mus Jonathan Tunick *Art Dir* Ben Edwards
● Paul Newman, Edward Asner, Danny Aiello, Rachel Ticotin, Pam Grier, Ken Wahl (Time-Life) ·

Driving relentlessly to make points that are almost pointless. *Fort Apache, The Bronx* is a very patchy picture, strong on dialog and acting and exceedingly weak on story.

Even while shooting, *Apache* drew protests from neighborhood factions claiming it would show only the bad about the Bronx and ignore the good. Because of that, the pic starts with a tip-of-the-hat title card to the 'law abiding' citizens of the community. But that's the last to be seen of them.

Title is taken from the nickname for a real police station uptown, literally surrounded and often under siege from thieves, murderers, hookers, junkies, dealers.

One of the cops (Danny Aiello) is a murderer himself and even the heroes. (Paul Newman and Ken Wahl) aren't that all admirable in their feeble attempts to control crime in the streets, their abject cynicism about life in the station house and vacillation over whether to snitch on Aiello after they watch him kill a kid.

Typical of the problem director Daniel Petrie creates for himself, he introduces Pam Grier right away as a drug-crazed cop killer and brings her back a couple of more times for additional murders, effectively grizzly in detail. But she never says much and there's never an inkling of what motivates her, other than dope.

....

■ FOR THE BOYS

1991, 145 MINS, US ◇ ⑲ ⊙

Dir Mark Rydell *Prod* Bette Midler, Bonnie Bruckheimer
Scr Marshall Brickman, Neal Jimenez, Lindy Laub
Ph Stephen Goldblatt *Ed* Jerry Greenberg, Jere Huggins
Mus Dave Grusin *Art Dir* Assheton Gorton
● Bette Midler, James Caan, George Segal, Patrick O'Neal, Christopher Rydell, Arye Gross (20th Century-Fox/All Girl)

Fox's song-driven wartime showbiz meller *For the Boys* is a big, creaky balloon of a movie that lumbers along like a dirigible in a Thanksgiving parade, festooned with patriotic sentiment. Ambitious effort spans the 50-year relationship of two USO entertainers (Bette Midler and James Caan) whose song, dance and innuendo carries them through three wars. Allegedly a 'love story' between two difficult people who are each married to others, pic suffers from the couple's lack of electricity.

Story begins in the present day, when a dapper production assistant (Arye Gross) arrives by limo to pick up Dixie for a major awards show. Midler makes a shocker of an entrance; pic then dissolves to 1942, when she was a bubbly young mother called up to join the famous Eddie Sparks in a London wartime revue.

The picture doesn't move, it regroups: from Europe to North Africa, then to Korea, through the bloodbath of McCarthyism and finally to Vietnam. The details of costume and design are convincing, but the main idea isn't.

Midler steams through the outing with sass and charm, eking out laughs on her own merit whenever the script stumbles. But Caan, in a role that recalls his pallid backup to Barbra Streisand in *Funny Lady*, seems pinioned by the script and generally uncomfortable.
☐ 1991: Nomination: Best Actress (Bette Midler)

....

■ FORTRESS

1993, 89 MINS, AUSTRALIA/US ◇ ⑲ ⊙

Dir Stuart Gordon *Prod* John Davis, John Flock
Scr Steve Feinberg, Troy Neighbors, Terry Curtis Fox
Ph David Eggby *Ed* Timothy Wellburn *Mus* Frederic Talghorn *Art Dir* David Copping
● Christopher Lambert, Kurtwood Smith, Loryn Locklin, Lincoln Kilpatrick, Clifton Gonzales Gonzales, Jeffrey Combs (Village Roadshow/Davis)

Fortress is a grim, sometimes bloody, futuristic prison picture that has been well produced and directed within the limitations of a predictable, uninspired screenplay. Fans of director Stuart Gordon's early schlock efforts (*Re-Animator, From Beyond*) will be disappointed to find the helmer working with more conventional material.

Pic was shot with an Australian crew in the Warner Roadshow Movie World Studios in Queensland, and David Copping's production design of a privately run prison of the future built 30 stories underground is the star of the film.

Pic is set in the US after exploding population and depleted resources have resulted in a law against couples having more than one child. The Brennicks (Christopher Lambert and Loryn Locklin) lost their first baby, and now Locklin is pregnant a second time, a felony.

The couple are nabbed trying to cross into Mexico, and both wind up in the Fortress. Locklin manages to charm all-seeing prison director Kurtwood Smith, and uses every opportunity to plan her husband's escape.

Too much of the dialogue sounds as if it were written for Dennis Hopper. There are some moments of graphic bloodshed, but the general tone of the film is rather somber. Lambert is adequate in the lead, and Locklin is appealing.

....

■ FORTUNE, THE

1975, 88 MINS, US ◇

Dir Mike Nichols *Prod* Nichols, Don Devlin *Scr* Adrien Joyce [= Carol Eastman] *Ph* John A. Alonzo *Ed* Stu Linder *Mus* David Shire *Art Dir* Richard Sylbert
● Jack Nicholson, Warren Beatty, Stockard Channing, Florence Stanley, Scatman Crothers (Columbia)

The Fortune is an occasionally enjoyable comedy trifle, starring Jack Nicholson and Warren Beatty as bumbling kidnappers of heiress Stockard Channing, who is excellent in her first major screen role. Very classy 1920s production values often merit more attention than the plot.

Beatty elopes with Channing but, not yet free of a former wife, Nicholson actually marries her. Trio sets up housekeeping in Los Angeles, and after Channing is disinherited, the guys try to kill her. If lugging around a passed-out intoxicated girl in clumsy murder attempts does not offend sensibilities, then the alleged fun may be passable.

David Shire superbly recreates some old Joe Venuti-Eddi Lang jazz band arrangements.

■ FORTUNE COOKIE, THE
(UK: Meet Whiplash Willie)

1966, 125 MINS, US ◇ ⓦ ⊙
Dir Billy Wilder *Prod* Billy Wilder, I.A.L. Diamond *Ph* Joseph LaShelle *Ed* Daniel Mandell *Mus* Andre Previn *Art Dir* Robert Luthardt
● Jack Lemmon, Walter Matthau, Ron Rich, Cliff Osmond, Judi West, Lurene Tuttle (United Artists/Mirisch)

Producer-director-writer Billy Wilder presents in *The Fortune Cookie* another bittersweet comedy commentary on contemporary US mores. Generally amusing (often wildly so) but overlong, the pic is pegged on an insurance fraud in which Jack Lemmon and Walter Matthau are the conspirators.

Original screenplay is by Wilder, paired for seventh time with I.A.L. Diamond. Plot turns on the complications following TV cameraman Lemmon's accidental injury at the hands of grid star Ron Rich. Matthau, shyster lawyer and Lemmon's brother-in-law, sees fancy damages in the injury, and exwife Judi West smells money in a fake reunion with Lemmon.

Lemmon, confined perforce to sickroom immobility (bandages, wheelchair, etc) is saddled most of the time with the colorless image of a man vacillating with his conscience over the fraud, and its effect on Rich, whose playing has deteriorated from remorse.

Title derives from a scene where Lemmon breaks a fortune cookie, only to find inside Abraham Lincoln's famous aphorism about fooling all/some people all/some of the time.
□ 1966: Best Supp. Actor (Walter Matthau).
□ Nominations: Best Original Story & Screenplay, B&W Cinematography, B&W Art Direction

■ 48 HOURS
See: Went the Day Well?

■ 48HRS.

1982, 96 MINS, US ◇ ⓦ ⊙
Dir Walter Hill *Prod* Lawrence Gordon, Joel Silver *Scr* Roger Spottiswoode, Walter Hill, Larry Gross, Steven E. De Souza *Ph* Ric Waite *Ed* Freeman Davies, Mark Warner, Billy Weber *Mus* James Horner *Art Dir* John Vallone
● Nick Nolte, Eddie Murphy, Annette O'Toole, Frank McRae, James Remar, David Patrick Kelly (Paramount)

48HRS. is a very efficient action entertainment which serves as a showy motion picture debut for Eddie Murphy. Pairing of Nick Nolte as a rough-and-tumble San Francisco cop and Murphy as a small-time criminal sprung for two days to help track down former associates makes for a throwback to the buddy-buddy pics of the 1970s.

It's all pretty predictable stuff, but done with plenty of savvy and professionalism. Director Walter Hill has always worked within traditional action genres, but has generally applied an artier, more philosophical slant to them.

Speaking with a voice sanded by a constant supply of booze and cigarettes, Nolte lays on the gruff Wallace Beery stuff a little thick and is generally willing to play second fiddle to Murphy's more kinetic shtick, but registers strongly withal. For his part, Murphy has a lot to do and gets through it amusingly.

■ FORTY GUNS

1957, 76 MINS, US
Dir Samuel Fuller *Prod* Samuel Fuller *Scr* Samuel Fuller *Ph* Joseph Biroc *Ed* Gene Fowler Jr *Mus* Harry Sukman *Art Dir* John Mansbridge
● Barbara Stanwyck, Barry Sullivan, Dean Jagger, John Ericson, Gene Barry, Eve Brent (20th Century-Fox)

Samuel Fuller in triple capacity of producer-scripter-director has devised a solid piece of entertainment which has femme star Barbara Stanwyck playing a ruthless Arizona ranch owner, the boss of Cochise County. Into her realm rides Barry Sullivan and his two brothers, former an ex-gun slinger now working for the US Attorney General, his fame with a gun preceding him.

He's in Tombstone on official business, which means conflict with femme, who rules her domain, including the sheriff, with an iron hand. Further complications arise between the two, even as a romance develops, over Stanwyck's brother (John Ericson), a brawling, would-be killer.

Stanwyck socks over her role in experienced style and Sullivan is persuasive as the marshal who loses his 10-year record for non-killing by gunning down Ericson after latter has murdered his brother (Gene Barry).

■ 49TH PARALLEL
(US: The Invaders)

1941, 123 MINS, UK ⓦ ⊙
Dir Michael Powell *Prod* Michael Powell *Scr* Emeric Pressburger *Ph* Freddie Young *Ed* David Lean *Mus* Ralph Vaughan Williams *Art Dir* David Rawnsley
● Leslie Howard, Raymond Massey, Laurence Olivier, Anton Walbrook, Glynis Johns, Eric Portman (Ortus)

This is an important and effective propaganda film. Picture started in April 1940 and took 18 months to complete. The British Government invested over $100,000 in the venture.

The locales depict Canadian life from an Eskimo village to a Hutterite settlement in the Canadian wheatfields. Story is the strongest possible indictment against Nazism. Plot concerns six Nazi U-boat men whose craft is blown up in the Hudson Bay straits. They reach land and commit every sort of crime up to murder in their efforts to reach the neutral territory of the US. The script of Emeric Pressburger [from a scenario by him and Rodney Ackland] is direct and forceful.

The stars are Leslie Howard, with his comedy gifts at high tide; Laurence Olivier (a bit, but the best thing he has ever done); Raymond Massey (also a bit, but outstanding); and Anton Walbrook, as a dignified Hitlerite leader. Despite the heartbreaking difficulties encountered, such as the defection of Elizabeth Bergner after the picture was well on its way, Michael Powell, the director, has managed to maintain his stature among the top directors.
□ 1942: Best Original Story.
□ Nominations: Best Picture, Screenplay

■ FORTY POUNDS OF TROUBLE

1962, 106 MINS, US ◇
Dir Norman Jewison *Prod* Stan Margulies *Scr* Marion Hargrove *Ph* Joe MacDonald *Ed* Marjorie Fowler *Mus* Mort Lindsey *Art Dir* Alexander Golitzen, Robert Clatworthy
● Tony Curtis, Phil Silvers, Suzanne Pleshette, Claire Wilcox, Stubby Kaye, Larry Storch (Curtis/Universal)

Marion Hargrove's 'original' screenplay actually owes a little something to the Little Miss Marker-Sorrowful Jones school of screen comedy, but it's a precocious and likeable offspring. The troublesome 40-pounder of the title is moppet Claire Wilcox, who makes her screen debut as an orphaned youngster who gradually melts the heart of the businesslike, efficient manager of a Lake Tahoe, Nevada gambling resort (Tony Curtis).

In the course of her conquest, she also aids the cause of husband-hunting nitery canary Suzanne Pleshette, whose romance with Curtis is complicated by the latter's relationship with his ex-wife, to whom he refuses to pay alimony, a stubborn stance that places him in jeopardy every time he leaves his Nevada legal sanctuary and crosses the border to California.

Curtis dispatches his role with comic savvy. Pleshette, whose manner is reminiscent of Joan Bennett's, handles her romantic assignment with finesse. Little Miss Wilcox is an appealing youngster, although director Jewison (in his first screen assignment after TV credits) might have obtained even better results from her by striving for more spontaneous, less practiced, childish reactions.

Phil Silvers has some memorable moments as the owner of the gambling establishment, notably one sequence in which he grandly strides into his domain, gruffly urging his customers to 'play, play.'

■ 42ND STREET

1933, 89 MINS, US ⓦ ⊙
Dir Lloyd Bacon, Busby Berkeley *Scr* James Seymour, Rian James *Ph* Sol Polito *Ed* Thomas Pratt, Frank Ware *Art Dir* Jack Okey
● Warner Baxter, Bebe Daniels, George Brent, Ruby Keeler, Guy Kibbee, Ginger Rogers (Warner)

Everything about the production rings true. It's as authentic to the initiate as the novitiate.

There are good performances by Warner Baxter, as the neurotic showman who whips *Pretty Lady* into a hit musical comedy, and Bebe Daniels in a not particularly sympathetic assignment as the outmoded musical comedy ingenue whose unrequited association with a sap kiddie car manufacturer angels the production.

Una Merkel and Ginger Rogers, as a pair of dumb and not-so chorines, are types. George E. Stone, as the dance stager, is likewise a believable reflection of the type. Harry Akst is the piano rehearser, and Al Dubin and Harry Warren, who fashioned the film's song ditties, play themselves.

Ruby Keeler, as the unknown who comes through and registers a hit, is utterly convincing.

Not the least of the total belongs to the direction by Lloyd Bacon, who fashioned some novelties in presentation, with Busby Berkeley an excellent aide on the terp mountings. The same overhead style of camera angles, which Berkeley introduced in the Eddie Cantor pictures and elsewhere, are further advanced.
□ 1932/33: Nominations: Best Picture, Sound

■ FORTY THOUSAND HORSEMEN

1941, 100 MINS, AUSTRALIA ⓦ
Dir Charles Chauvel *Prod* Charles Chauvel *Scr* Elsa Chauvel *Ph* George Heath *Ed* Bill Shepherd *Mus* Lindley Evans, Willy Redstone, Alfred Hill *Art Dir* Eric Thompson, J. Alan Kenyon
● Grant Taylor, Betty Bryant, 'Chips' Rafferty, Pat Twohill, Harvey Adams, Eric Reiman (Chauvel)

With *Horsemen* Aussie production drops its diapers. The pic, made in cooperation with the Department of Defense, is a three years' dream of Charles Chauvel come true.

Pic portrays in sheer entertaining fashion the story [by Chauvel and E.V. Timms] of the Australian Light Horse, the famous regiment, in Palestine during World War I. Director Chauvel has with easy grace produced a telling action pic, yet carrying sufficient romance to fully satisfy the femme stubholders.

The acting is topnotch, with the honors going to Betty Bryant and 'Chips' Rafferty. The story is slight, telling the love of a French girl for an Aussie soldier. The action, however, is the highlight of the pic, with a corking charge sequence tempoing to a swift close. The camera work is high-class, editing deft, and the sets are tops.

■ **FOR WHOM THE BELL TOLLS**

1943, 166 MINS, US ◇

Dir Sam Wood   *Prod* Sam Wood   *Scr* Dudley Nichols   *Ph* Ray Rennahan   *Ed* Sherman Todd, John F. Link   *Mus* Victor Young   *Art Dir* Hans Dreier, Haldane Douglas
● Gary Cooper, Ingrid Bergman, Akim Tamiroff, Katina Paxinou, Arturo de Cordova, Vladimir Sokoloff (Paramount)

For Whom the Bell Tolls is one of the important pictures of all time although almost three hours of running time can overdo a good thing. Running sans intermission, the saga of Roberto and Maria (Gary Cooper and Ingrid Bergman) asks for too much concentrated attention on what is basically one dramatic episode, that of blasting a crucial bridge, in order to foil the Nationalists.

On a beautiful Technicolor canvas is projected an equally beautiful romance which, perhaps, lays a little too much emphasis on the amorous phase. It's one thing to punch up boy-meets-girl sequencing, but the nature of Ernest Hemingway's bestseller, of course, was predicated on a political aura resulting in the Spanish civil war.

Histrionically, *Bell Tolls* is a triumph for the four sub-featured players. Katina Paxinou, onetime foremost in her native Greek theatre, dominates everything by a shade. A masculine woman who, however, has known of love and beauty, despite her realistic self-abnegation that she is ugly, is standout in everything she does.

For the record *Bell* cost around $150,000 for the screen rights (Hemingway's book sales determined the overage on top of the basic $100,000 price) and the production cost was officially a few thousands under $3 million.
□ 1943: Best Supp. Actress (Katina Paxinou).
□ Nominations: Best Picture, Actor (Gary Cooper), Actress (Ingrid Bergman), Supp. Actor (Akim Tamiroff), Color Cinematography, Color Art Direction, Editing, Scoring of a Dramatic Picture

■ **FOR YOUR EYES ONLY**

1981, 127 MINS, UK ◇ ⑱ ⊙

Dir John Glen   *Prod* Albert R. Broccoli   *Scr* Richard Maibaum, Michael G. Wilson   *Ph* Alan Hume   *Ed* John Grover   *Mus* Bill Conti   *Art Dir* Peter Lamont
● Roger Moore, Carole Bouquet, Chaim Topol, Jill Bennett, Lois Maxwell, Lynn-Holly Johnson (United Artists/Eon)

For Your Eyes Only bears not the slightest resemblance to the Ian Fleming novel of the same title, but emerges as one of the most thoroughly enjoyable of the 12 Bond pix [to date] despite fact that many of the usual ingredients in the successful 007 formula are missing.

The film is probably the best-directed on all levels since *On Her Majesty's Secret Service*, as John Glen, moving into the director's chair after long service as second unit director and editor, displays a fine eye.

Story also benefits from presence of a truly sympathetic heroine, fetchingly portrayed by Carole Bouquet, who exhibits a humanity and

emotionalism not frequently found in this sort of pop adventure and who takes a long time (the entire picture, in fact) to jump into the sack with him.

M is gone, due to Bernard Lee's death; Bond doesn't make his first feminine conquest until halfway through the picture; there's no technology introduced by Q which saves the hero in the end; no looming supervillain dominates the drama; Bond bon mots are surprisingly sparse, and the fate of the whole world isn't even hanging in the balance at the climax.
□ 1981: Nomination: Best Song ('For Your Eyes Only')

■ **FOUL PLAY**

1978, 116 MINS, US ◇ ⑱ ⊙

Dir Colin Higgins   *Prod* Thomas L. Miller, Edward K. Milkis   *Scr* Colin Higgins   *Ph* David M. Walsh   *Ed* Pembroke J. Herring   *Mus* Charles Fox   *Art Dir* Alfred Sweeney
● Goldie Hawn, Chevy Chase, Burgess Meredith, Rachel Roberts, Eugene Roche, Dudley Moore (Paramount)

Foul Play revives a relatively dormant film genre – the crime-suspense-romantic comedy in which low-key leading players get involved with themselves while also caught up in monumental intrigue. The name missing from the credits is Alfred Hitchcock. Writer Colin Higgins makes a good directorial bow.

If you think you've been through the plot before, you have: Goldie Hawn, likable librarian, picks up undercover agent Bruce Solomon who passes her film evidence of how Rachel Roberts, Eugene Roche and other heavies are going to assassinate visiting Pope Pius XIII (played by SF socialite Cyril Magnin) at a performance of *The Mikado* in the Opera House. Chevy Chase, a detective, eventually believes Hawn's stories about attempts on her life. Car chases and theatre shootout climax the film's 116 minutes.

Entire cast comes off very well. In prominent support are Burgess Meredith as Hawn's landlord; Dudley Moore, a dedicated swinger who turns out to be the opera conductor; Marilyn Sokol, Hawn's girlfriend who carries anti-rapist tools in her handbag.
□ 1978: Nomination: Best Song ('Ready to Take a Chance Again')

■ **FOUNTAINHEAD, THE**

1949, 112 MINS, US ⑱

Dir King Vidor   *Prod* Henry Blanke   *Scr* Ayn Rand   *Ph* Robert Burks   *Ed* David Weisbart   *Mus* Max Steiner
● Gary Cooper, Patricia Neal, Raymond Massey, Kent Smith, Henry Hull, Robert Douglas (Warner)

Because the plot is completely devoted to hammering home the theme that man's personal integrity stands above all law, the picture develops a controversial element.

The garrulous script which Ayn Rand did from her novel calls for a great deal of posturing by the cast and King Vidor's direction permits much over-acting where underplaying might have helped develop a better emotional feeling and a truer sense of reality. Gary Cooper has an uneasy time in the miscasting as the plot's hero, an architect who is such an individualist that he dynamites a charity project when the builders alter his plans.

As Cooper's co-star, Patricia Neal makes a moody heroine, afraid of love or any other honest feeling. Raymond Massey is allowed to be too flamboyant as the publisher.

■ **FOUR DAUGHTERS**

1938, 90 MINS, US ⑱

Dir Michael Curtiz   *Prod* Benjamin Glazer   *Scr* Julius J. Epstein, Lenore Coffee   *Ph* Ernest Haller   *Ed* Ralph Dawson   *Mus* Max Steiner   *Art Dir* John Hughes

● Claude Rains, May Robson, Priscilla Lane, Lola Lane, Rosemary Lane, John Garfield (Warner)

Score one for Warners on this gentle drama from Fannie Hurst's novel, *Sister Act*. It's a beguiling film which reveals John Garfield as an interesting picture prospect. Formerly Jules Garfield, of Broadway's Group Theatre, the actor turns out to be much more forceful personality on the screen than he was on the stage.

This tale deals with the heart-throbs of the four talented daughters of a professor of music. It's a simple, gay and lovable small-town household. And as the various girls acquire beaux, the old man looks on with a twinkling eye, and kindly Aunt Etta bustles about to make the place homelike.

Michael Curtiz's direction is both affectionate and knowing. Claude Rains is irresistibly persuasive and attractive as the father. Priscilla Lane has the best part as the youngest sister. May Robson plays the aunt in proper mother-hen fashion. As the ill-starred newcomer, Garfield plays with such tight-lipped force that for a time he threatens to throw the picture out of focus by drawing too much interest.
□ 1938: Nominations: Best Picture, Director, Supp. Actor (John Garfield), Screenplay, Sound

■ **FOUR FEATHERS**

1929, 80 MINS, US ⊗

Dir Merian C. Cooper, Ernest B. Schoedsack   *Prod* Merian C. Cooper, Ernest B. Schoedsack   *Scr* Howard Estabrook, Hope Loring   *Mus* William Frederick Peters
● Richard Arlen, Fay Wray, Clive Brook, William Powell, Theodore von Eltz, Noah Beery (Paramount)

Four Feathers is a good picture. Merian C. Cooper and Ernest B. Schoedsack were the producers. They made *Chang*. It is no secret that *Feathers'* treatment was primarily photographic. The dramatics followed. Cooper and Schoedsack must also have been the directors of the story part, for no one else is credited. Nor is a photographer named.

Ever see a herd of hippo slide down a steep bank of a jungle watering place? Ever see a large family of baboons hop from limb to limb to escape a forest fire? Or a huge army of black savages dashing to battle on white camels? These three items are *Four Feathers*.

The white feather is the symbol of cowardice in the British army. The principal character and subsequent hero of A.W. Mason's novel receives four white feathers.

Tale is set late in the last century. *Four Feathers* is highly reminiscent of *Beau Geste*. Pictorially they are much the same.

Richard Arlen's performance is good most of the while, excellent at times. William Powell is next with the most to do and does it like Powell. Clive Brook is not handed his usual weighty part and isn't impressive because of that, while Theodore von Eltz, as the lesser of the four chums, has no opportunity to be more than satisfactory. Fay Wray only has to look good.

■ **FOUR FEATHERS, THE**

1939, 130 MINS, UK ◇ ⑱ ⊙

Dir Zoltan Korda   *Prod* Alexander Korda   *Scr* R.C. Sherriff, Lajos Biro, Arthur Wimperis   *Ph* Georges Perinal, Osmond Borradaile   *Ed* William Hornbeck, Henry Cornelius   *Mus* Miklos Rozsa   *Art Dir* Vincent Korda
● John Clements, Ralph Richardson, C. Aubrey Smith, June Duprez, Allen Jeayes, Jack Allen (London)

The Four Feathers has been filmed before, with the book [by A.E.W. Mason] from which it was adapted having enjoyed big world sale.

A young British officer resigns from his regiment the night before it embarks for an

F

Egyptian campaign. Three of his pals and his fiancee hand him white feathers, indicative of cowardice. The next day he disappears. Alone and unaided in Egypt, he goes through harrowing ordeals to gain his reinstatement in their eyes.

June Duprez, the fiancee, is the only woman in the cast. She postulates prettily and attractively, with little else to do. Rest of the cast is excellent, with C. Aubrey Smith, enacting a lovable, elderly bore. John Clements, the hero, is excellent.

Photography is excellent along with the direction by Zoltan Korda.

■ FOUR FOR TEXAS

1963, 124 MINS, US ◇ Ⓥ ⊙
Dir Robert Aldrich   *Prod* Robert Aldrich   *Scr* Teddi Sherman, Robert Aldrich   *Ph* Ernest Laszlo   *Ed* Michael Luciano   *Mus* Nelson Riddle   *Art Dir* William Glasgow
● Frank Sinatra, Dean Martin, Anita Ekberg, Ursula Andress, Charles Bronson, Victor Buono (Aldrich/Warner)

Four For Texas is a western too preoccupied with sex and romance to enthrall sagebrush-happy moppets and too unwilling to take itself seriously to sustain the attention of an adult. The screenplay [from a story by director-producer Robert Aldrich] is a choppy and haphazard dramatization of a feud between two soldiers of fortune (Frank Sinatra and Dean Martin) who ultimately have to join forces in vanquishing the threat of their mutual enemies, a treacherous banker (Victor Buono) and an irresponsible, incredibly hapless gunslinger (Charles Bronson).

Concern for the characters is never aroused by the screenplay, and the casual manner in which it is executed by the players under Aldrich's direction only compounds the problem.

Sinatra and Martin carry on in their accustomed manner, the latter getting most of what laughs their are. The film is loaded with distracting cleavage, thanks to the presence of Anita Ekberg and Ursula Andress. (Stacked up alongside Ekberg's stupendous proportions, even Mae West might seem anemic.) Buono, as the unappealing, dyspeptic and conniving banker, and Bronson as the gunman, make an impression.

Editing leaves something to be desired. At least one scene has been cut out that is still referred to in the dialog of a subsequent scene.

■ FOUR FRIGHTENED PEOPLE

1934, 95 MINS, US
Dir Cecil B. DeMille   *Prod* Cecil B. DeMille   *Scr* Bartlett Cormack, Lenore J. Coffee   *Ph* Karl Struss   *Ed* [Anne Bauchens]   *Mus* [Karl Hajos, Milton Roder, H. Rohenheld, John Leipold]
● Claudette Colbert, Herbert Marshall, Mary Boland, William Gargan, Leo Carrillo, Tetsu Komai (Paramount)

The adventures of the quartet who are lost in the Malayan jungle are episodic and disjointed, running the gamut from stark tragedy to unbelievable farce [from a novel by E. Arnot Robertson].

The four frightened people are thrown together by a bubonic plague outbreak on the Dutch coastal steamer which was carrying them from their respective ports of departure back to civilization. In self-preservation they shanghai a lifeboat and meet a half-caste guide who thinks he can safely trek them through the jungle to the sea.

The bombastic newspaper correspondent (William Gargan) talks like something out of Richard Harding Davis and never coincides with the post-*Front Page* conceptions of newspaperdom. Herbert Marshall is a chemist interested in Dutch plantation rubber, licked by life and a wife, who finds romance with the begoggled geography teacher from Chicago

(Claudette Colbert) who likewise asserts herself in the jungle. Mary Boland is the wife of a British official which accounts for her presence.

The DeMilleian bathtub penchant evidences itself even in the jungle when Colbert, sans cheaters and very Eve (when a playful chimpanzee steals her clothes), emerges with plenty of s.a. for both men.

An introductory title heralds that the film was actually shot in South Pacific locations.

■ FOUR HORSEMEN OF THE APOCALYPSE, THE

1921, 130 MINS, US ⊗
Dir Rex Ingram   *Scr* June Mathis   *Ph* John F. Seitz   *Ed* Grant Whytock   *Mus* Louis F. Gottschalk   *Art Dir* Joseph Calder, Amos Myers
● Rudolph Valentino, Alice Terry, Alan Hale, Nigel de Brulier, Jean Hersholt, Wallace Beery (Metro)

The magnitude of *The Four Horsemen* is staggering, and it is not hard to believe the statistics relative to the production. It is said to have cost approximately $800,000; director Rex Ingram had 14 assistants, each with a cameraman; more than 12,000 persons were used, and 125,000 tons of masonry and other material employed; $375,000 insurance was carried on the art works, furniture, etc, used in the picture, which was six months in the making.

Horror stalked grinningly bold through the book of Vicente Blasco Ibanez, the greatest of the World War I romances. Ingram has mercifully cloaked it with distance and delicacy of treatment. This is a characteristic of the director's handling of the entire subject. It is a production of many nuances, shadings so artistic and skillful as to intrigue the mind of the spectator.

■ FOUR HORSEMEN OF THE APOCALYPSE, THE

1962, 153 MINS, US ◇ Ⓥ
Dir Vincente Minnelli   *Prod* Julian Blaustein   *Scr* Robert Ardrey, John Gay   *Ph* Milton Krasner   *Ed* Adrienne Fazan, Ben Lewis   *Mus* Andre Previn   *Art Dir* George W. Davis, Urie McCleary, Elliot Scott
● Glenn Ford, Ingrid Thulin, Charles Boyer, Lee J. Cobb, Paul Henreid, Yvette Mimieux (M-G-M)

Although *The Four Horsemen of the Apocalypse* is a screen spectacle of dynamic artistic proportions, it gradually becomes a victim of dramatic anemia – a strapping hulk of cinematic muscle rendered invalid by a weak heart. Lamentably, the romantic nucleus of this tragic chronicle of a family divided and devoured by war fails in the adaptation to achieve a realistic and compassionate relationship between the lovers.

Director Minnelli and leads Glenn Ford and Ingrid Thulin must share responsibility with the writers for this fundamental weakness.

It is quite possible that Ford's characterization was plagued by the ghost of Valentino, whose enactment of the leading role in 1921 was his first screen triumph. There is, for instance, a tight eyeball shot of Ford's orbs reminiscent of Valentinography. At any rate, Ford's performance is without warmth, without passion, without magnetism. Warmth is also missing in the performance of Ingrid Thulin.

However, the film shines in other areas. Frank Santillo's montages contribute touches of art and explanation to a picture that is sometimes wobbly, choppy and incomplete in the area of exposition. The device of veiling black-and-white newsreel photography in a splash of hot, vivid color registers with great emotional effect, notably in passages utilizing the novel technique of quadruple image superimposition.

Another major assist is that of Andre

Previn, who has composed a tearing, soaring, emotionally affecting score to take up some of the slack in the love story.

■ FOUR IN THE MORNING

1966, 94 MINS, UK
Dir Anthony Simmons   *Prod* John Morris   *Scr* Anthony Simmons   *Ph* Larry Pizer   *Ed* Fergus McDonnell   *Mus* John Barry
● Ann Lynn, Brian Phelan, Judi Dench, Norman Rodway, Joe Melia (West One)

Writer-director Anthony Simmons shows two couples in crisis, tying them in with a gimmick, which works. There's an unidentified girl found in a river. Simmons gives the scene of the discovery and study of the drowned girl a metallic, sombre documentary flavor.

A seemingly rootless young man picks up a singer he knows after her work. At four in the morning they romp around the Thames' shores, steal a boat, leave it, almost touch each other emotionally but part still uncommitted. Hints of the instability of both are carefully and intelligently suggested.

The other couple is shown as a woman waiting for her husband, out on the town with a bachelor crony. The baby cries and exasperates her. The growing incompatibility of the couple is deftly outlined in bold, dramatic strokes.

Judi Dench has the right checked hysteria for her role of the wife with a disposition towards love that makes her poignant. Ann Lynn and Brian Phelan are also effective as the other couple with Joe Melia a pointed counterpoint to the married couple with his personal problems.

■ FOUR JUST MEN, THE
(US: The Secret Four)

1939, 85 MINS, UK ◇ Ⓥ
Dir Walter Forde   *Prod* Michael Balcon   *Scr* Angus MacPhail, Sergei Nolbandov, Roland Pertwee   *Ph* Ronald Neame   *Mus* Ernest Irving (dir.)   *Art Dir* Wilfrid Shingleton
● Hugh Sinclair, Griffith Jones, Francis L. Sullivan, Frank Lawton, Anna Lee, Alan Napier (Associated British)

A skilled and dramatic filmization of one of Edgar Wallace's best known novels. Murder, sabotage and international troublemaking form the basis of this exploit of the Four Just Men who, incognito, spend their lives breaking up dope rings and foiling plots of foreign agitators.

While incarcerated in a foreign prison, the youngest member of the quartet escapes execution by a few seconds, being rescued by two of the others disguised as higher officials. He has learned the name of an eastern conspirator; also that one of the members of parliament is responsible for a leakage of state secrets.

The casting is superb, Frank Lawton making a wistful and pathetic figure of the youngest patriot. Francis L. Sullivan as a French designer, playing one of his rare non-villainous roles, is his usual suave self as one of the four.

■ FOUR MUSKETEERS, THE
THE REVENGE OF MILADY

1975, 108 MINS, PANAMA/SPAIN ◇ Ⓥ
Dir Richard Lester   *Prod* Alexander Salkind   *Scr* George MacDonald Fraser   *Ph* David Watkin   *Ed* John Victor Smith   *Mus* Lalo Schifrin   *Art Dir* Brian Eatwell
● Oliver Reed, Raquel Welch, Richard Chamberlain, Michael York, Frank Finlay, Christopher Lee (20th Century-Fox)

The Four Musketeers continues the story of Oliver Reed, Richard Chamberlain, Frank

Finlay and Michael York as they joust with evil plotter Charlton Heston and evil seductress Faye Dunaway, defend fair lady queen Geraldine Chaplin, bypass imbecile King Jean Pierre Cassel, and eventually triumph over arch fiend Christopher Lee.

The same mixture of teenybopper naughtiness, acne spiciness, contrived tastelessness and derring don't as found in the earlier film (*The Three Musketeers*) are laid on with the same deft trowel herein. Perhaps the film is a triumph of controlled and deliberate mediocrity, but it still closer resembles a clumsy carbon of a bad satire on the original.
□ 1975: Nomination: Best Costume Design

• •

■ FOUR POSTER, THE

1953, 103 MINS, US
Dir Irving Reis   *Prod* Stanley Kramer   *Scr* Allan Scott
Ph Hal Mohr   *Ed* Henry Batista, Harry Gerstad
Mus Dimitri Tiomkin   *Art Dir* Rudolph Sternard, Carl Peterson
● Rex Harrison, Lilli Palmer (Kramer/Columbia)

The Four Poster as a pic is still limited to the same two characters of the play, with nary the suggestion of an interloper. Though the stars' performances are excellent, they are unable to salvage audience interest during the film's lesser moments. In fact, the major fault is the inability of the two characters to cope with the lack of incident.

With the four poster bed in the background as the common denominator of their marital relationship, pic traces the lives of a couple from the day the groom carries his bride across the threshold. From then on are detailed his struggles as a writer, the bride's faith in his ability, his success, their children, the son's death in World War I, the romantic escapades of the husband and wife, and finally their deaths.

Lilli Palmer imparts s.a. and natural beauty to the role of the wife.
□ 1953: Nomination: Best B&W Cinematography

• •

■ FOUR SEASONS, THE

1981, 107 MINS, US ◇ ⑩ ⊙
Dir Alan Alda   *Prod* Martin Bregman   *Scr* Alan Alda
Ph Victor J. Kemper   *Ed* Michael Economou
Mus Antonio Vivaldi   *Art Dir* Jack Collis
● Alan Alda, Carol Burnett, Len Cariou, Sandy Dennis, Rita Moreno, Jack Weston (Universal)

If *The Four Seasons* was never a play, it should have been, since it's based on the most stagey, dialog-bound original screenplay in memory. A lightweight, overly contrived examination of the relationship among three couples who vacation together four times over course of story, Alan Alda's feature directorial debut is middle-brow, middle-aged material.

Pic's structure is too strikingly similar to that of *Same Time Next Year* to ignore the fact that Alda starred in screen adaptation of that Broadway hit.

Tale is populated strictly with *Ordinary People*, but Alda's script doesn't begin to scratch the surface to discover what makes them tick and is particularly stingy in giving Carol Burnett and Rita Moreno anything to work with.

New England and Virgin Islands locations are fresh and well chosen, and Vivaldi background score helps lend a tony atmosphere to the proceedings.

• •

■ FOURTEEN HOURS

1951, 92 MINS, US
Dir Henry Hathaway   *Prod* Sol C. Siegel   *Scr* John
Paxton   *Ph* Joe MacDonald   *Ed* Dorothy Spencer
Mus Alfred Newman   *Art Dir* Lyle Wheeler, Leland Fuller

● Richard Basehart, Paul Douglas, Barbara Bel Geddes, Agnes Moorehead, Robert Keith, Grace Kelly (20th Century-Fox)

Suspense elements in a situation that has a would-be suicide swaying precariously on a high window ledge are fully realized in *Fourteen Hours*. Story [by Joel Sayre] is based on an actual suicide case in New York.

Paul Douglas is the traffic policeman who becomes a hero when his routine duties are interrupted one morning by the sight of Richard Basehart perched on a 14-storey high window ledge.

Tension reaches the screaming point often as Douglas and the others try to talk Basehart back into the building, while the citizens of New York make a Roman holiday of the event.

Douglas wallops his policeman role by sound underplaying. Basehart comes over solidly. Barbara Bel Geddes is his girlfriend, adding worth to the character. Agnes Moorehead scores as the selfish mother, and Robert Keith matches her excellence in his playing of the father.

A romance with a nice fresh touch is born in the chance meeting of Debra Paget and Jeffrey Hunter in the crowd. Grace Kelly, drawing a divorce property settlement in a nearby building, decides to make another try at marriage.
□ 1951: Nomination: Best B&W Art Direction

• •

■ 1492
CONQUEST OF PARADISE

1992, 150 MINS, UK/FRANCE/SPAIN ◇ ⑩ ⊙
Dir Ridley Scott   *Prod* Ridley Scott, Alain Goldman
Scr Roselyne Bosch   *Ph* Adrian Biddle   *Ed* William
Anderson, Francoise Bonnot   *Mus* Vangelis
Art Dir Norris Spencer
● Gerard Depardieu, Armand Assante, Sigourney Weaver, Loren Dean, Angela Molina, Fernando Rey (Percy Main/Legende/Cyrk)

All Ridley Scott's vaunted visuals can't transform *1492* from a lumbering, one-dimensional historical fresco into the complex, ambiguous character study that it strives to be.

French journalist and first-time screenwriter Roselyne Bosch offers up a humanistic pacifist driven by an enigmatic mix of motives to settle a new land. 'They are not savages, and neither will we be,' Columbus (Gerard Depardieu) announces to his crew.

A man allied with monks but disgusted by the Inquisition, he is able to charm the Spanish queen into sending him into the unknown. After a remarkably uneventful voyage spurred by one little inspirational speech to his nervous crew, Columbus reaches his promised 'earthly paradise'.

After his triumphant return home, a new, 17-ship expedition is launched. Minds dominated by military ambition, religious fervor and greed inevitably gain the upper hand and turn the lush tropical settlement into a living hell.

Scott takes slightly greater interest in the political dynamics informing the yarn. The Crown's treasurer (Armand Assante) plays out an ambiguous relationship with Columbus throughout all the latter's changing fortunes.

Sigourney Weaver briefly suggests a sexual susceptibility to Columbus behind the queen's approval of his grand scheme. But no one is allowed the opportunity to develop a character.

Depardieu's energy, passion and conviction are ideal for the role, but perhaps it remains beyond him at this point to act in English in depth.

• •

■ FOURTH PROTOCOL, THE

1987, 119 MINS, UK ◇ ⑩ ⊙
Dir John Mackenzie   *Prod* Timothy Burrill   *Scr* Frederick
Forsyth   *Ph* Phil Meheuy   *Ed* Graham Walker
Mus Lalo Schifrin   *Art Dir* Alan Cameron

● Michael Caine, Pierce Brosnan, Joanna Cassidy, Ned Beatty, Ray McAnally, Ian Richardson (Rank)

The Fourth Protocol is a decidedly contempo thriller, a tale of vying masterspies and a chase to head off a nuclear disaster. Its edge is a fine aura of realism.

Novelist Frederick Forsyth, who also was an executive producer, adapted the pic from his book.

The story is pretty straightforward. A ruthless KGB head plans to detonate a nuclear bomb close to a US airbase in England so the Brits blame the Yanks and the NATO alliance will collapse.

What follows is a good old-fashioned race against time as Caine tracks down his Russian alter ego Major Petrofsky (Pierce Brosnan) and after a hand-to-hand scuffle manages to defuse the bomb.

Michael Caine as a maverick counterespionage expert gives a thorough performance in a part that doesn't really stretch his abilities.

• •

■ FOURTH WAR, THE

1990, 91 MINS, US ◇ ⑩ ⊙
Dir John Frankenheimer   *Prod* Wolf Schmidt
Scr Stephen Peters, Kenneth Ross   *Ph* Gerry Fisher
Ed Robert F. Shugrue   *Mus* Bill Conti   *Art Dir* Alan
Manzer
● Roy Scheider, Jurgen Prochnow, Tim Reid, Lara Harris, Harry Dean Stanton, Dale Dye (Kodiak)

The Fourth War is a well-made Cold War thriller about private battling that might escalate out of control. Opening title sets the tale in November 1988 on the border of Czechoslovakia and East Germany.

Roy Scheider is well-cast as a hardline colonel who's caused nothing but trouble in his career and is now stationed at a post near the border by his general, Harry Dean Stanton. Scheider witnesses the murder of a fleeing defector through no man's land. He rightly blames the Soviet colonel (Jurgen Prochnow) for this dastardly deed and from this minor act of outrage ensues a man-to-man feud of Laurel & Hardy proportions.

Tightly directed by Frankenheimer with an eye for comic relief as well as tension maintenance, *The Fourth War* holds the fascination of eyeball-to-eyeball conflict.

Besides the two stars, Tim Reid is very effective as the man on the spot (his commanding officer is out of control), and Lara Harris is convincing as a duplicitous femme fatale.

• •

■ FOX, THE

1968, 110 MINS, US/CANADA ◇
Dir Mark Rydell   *Prod* Raymond Stross   *Scr* Lewis John
Carlino   *Ph* William Fraker   *Ed* Thomas Stanford
Mus Lalo Schifrin   *Art Dir* Charles Bailey
● Sandy Dennis, Keir Dullea, Anne Heywood, Glyn Morris (Warner/Seven Arts/Motion Pictures International)

D.H. Lawrence's lesbian-themed novella *The Fox* is turned into a beautifully photographed, dramatically uneven Canadian-made film.

Sandy Dennis and Anne Heywood are cast as lesbian lovers who have exiled themselves to a lonely farm. Arrival of Keir Dullea cues a disintegration of the femme relationship and eventual tragedy.

In early reels, Anne Heywood seems the dominant female. She is inwardly uneasy, perhaps afraid of eventual old age.

Dennis has the greater acting burden, and her performance is uneven. Her daffiness in early reels seems overdone, result of which is that her later remarks may draw unwanted smiles, even chuckles, from audiences.

Dullea plays his part with quiet determination to snare Heywood. Whether or not he suspects or comprehends the lesbian relationship is debatable, from script and actions.

First sexual encounter between him and Heywood is awkward – the gaspings, the clutching of turf, etc. A later romantic scene between the two gals, by contrast, is excellent.

☐ 1968: Nomination: Best Original Music Score

. . . .

■ FOXES

1980, 106 MINS, US ◇ ⓥ
Dir Adrian Lyne   *Prod* David Puttnam, Gerald Ayres
Scr Gerald Ayres   *Ph* Leon Bijou   *Ed* Jim Coblentz
Mus Giorgio Moroder   *Art Dir* Michael Levesque
● Jodie Foster, Scott Baio, Sally Kellerman, Randy Quaid, Marilyn Kagan, Cherie Currie
(Filmworks/Casablanca)

Foxes is an ambitious attempt to do a film relating to some of the not-so-acceptable realities among teenagers that ends up delivering far less than it is capable of.

Story of four teenage girls and their battles often becomes a depressing, one-sided and melodramatic treatise on American youth.

It soon becomes clear this is not the usual gaggle of girls portrayed as typical American teenagers. Cherie Currie is a stoned-out former hooker, Marilyn Kagan is an unhappy, overweight fat girl longing to shed her parents' protective shell, Kandice Stroh is a lying, confused flirt and Jodie Foster is a level-headed intellect.

Constant switching of action between the girls causes Stroh's character to be lost midway and Foster's identity to never fully be explored despite the fact she's the focal point.

. . . .

■ FOXES OF HARROW, THE

1947, 115 MINS, US
Dir John M. Stahl   *Prod* William A. Bacher   *Scr* Wanda Tuchock   *Ph* Joseph La Shelle   *Ed* James B. Clark
Mus Alfred Newman   *Art Dir* Lyle R. Wheeler, Maurice Ransford
● Rex Harrison, Maureen O'Hara, Richard Haydn, Victor McLaglen, Patricia Medina (20th Century-Fox)

The Foxes of Harrow is an elaborate filmization of Frank Yerby's novel. Invested with the polished direction of John M. Stahl, it builds into a powerful drama of an adventurer's rise to fame and fortune in New Orleans of the 19th century. Exciting story has strong production, vivid developments and helped along with excellent pace most of the time.

Technically, *Foxes* runs too long. It contains passages at the outset and near the end that appear superfluous. But because there are so many meaty scenes, even the more tedious ones overflow with nice performances.

Rex Harrison, the child born out of wedlock, rises to the heights in New Orleans business even though his first money is won gambling. Plot shows Harrison being put off a Mississippi steamboat for cheating at cards but being rescued from a sandbar by Victor McLaglen, captain of a pigboat. Harrison's audacity both at cards and with women catapult him to riches. His main ambition is to build another Harrow estate like his mother had known in Ireland. He finally persuades Maureen O'Hara, daughter of one of New Orleans' aristocrats, to become his wife.

Harrison is perfect as the suave gambler and O'Hara carries the highly dramatic scenes with surprising skill, but it seems a pity that she is not permitted to smile more often.

☐ 1947: Nomination: Best B&W Art Direction

. . . .

■ FOX MOVIETONE FOLLIES OF 1929

1929, 80 MINS, US ◇
Dir David Butler, Marcel Silver   *Ph* Charles Van Enger
● Sue Carol, David Rollins, Stepin Fetchit, Sharon Lynn, Warren Hymer (Fox)

Fox Movietone Follies is good entertainment all the way. The numbers, specialties and song and dance stuff come through very well. One bit done in Technicolor offers a variant from the black-and-white but achieves little itself.

'The Breakaway' and 'Walkin' with Susie' are the big numbers. Wisp of a story. A young Virginian sells his plantation and comes north to marry his sweetie. She is in the chorus of a new show and refuses to quit the theatre to settle down as a wife.

Chagrined by her refusal to chuck everything and go to the parson's, young man buys the controlling interest in the show and fires her. She refuses to quit and says he cannot fire her. 'Why not?' he demands. 'Because Equity won't let you,' she retorts. 'Who's he?' demands the hick.

Most of the action and the *Follies* part of the picture represents the opening night of the revue. Sue Carol takes first honors but needs dancing lessons. Warren Hymer makes a stage manager pretty rough, tough and nasty.

. . . .

■ FOXY BROWN

1974, 91 MINS, US ◇ ⓥ
Dir Jack Hill   *Prod* Buzz Feitshans   *Scr* Jack Hill
Ph Brick Marquard   *Ed* Chuck McClelland   *Mus* Willie Hutch   *Art Dir* Kirk Axtel
● Pam Grier, Antonio Fargas, Peter Brown, Terry Carter, Kathryn Loder, Harry Holcombe (American International)

Bosomy black starlet Pam Grier plays a gal whose dope-dealing brother (Antonio Fargas) rats on her undercover-narc boyfriend (Terry Carter), cuing latter's gangland murder on her doorstep. Not one to take romantic disappointment lightly, she sets her vengeful eye on the leaders of the local vice ring (Kathryn Loder and Peter Brown).

Before femme might makes right, Grier and callgirl Juanita Brown have a brawl in a lesbian bar, Fargas writhes to his gunned-down death, doxy Sally Ann Stroud has her throat slashed, two degenerate thugs who've raped Grier are burned to death, and Brown is castrated.

Even by the gutter-high standards of the genre, *Foxy Brown* is something of a mess. Jack Hill's screenplay has peculiar narrative gaps.

. . . .

■ FRANCES

1982, 140 MINS, US ◇ ⓥ ⊙
Dir Graeme Clifford   *Prod* Jonathan Sanger   *Scr* Eric Bergren, Christopher DeVore, Nicholas Kazan
Ph Laszlo Kovacs   *Ed* John Wright   *Mus* John Barry
Art Dir Richard Sylbert
● Jessica Lange, Kim Stanley, Sam Shepard, Bart Burns, Jeffrey DeMunn, Jordan Charney (EMI/Brooksfilms)

Rare to the memory is a film like *Frances* which runs 140 minutes and its star is on the screen 85% of the time in one intense scene after another. It's quite an accomplishment for Jessica Lange and it's too bad a better film didn't come of it.

Though her troubled life made headlines around the world, Frances Farmer is still much a mystery. What is agreed is that Farmer was a rebellious young girl in Seattle who first shocked the 1930s with a high-school essay questioning God, then outraged conservatives again a few years later with a visit to Moscow. The publicity, plus her talent, led to a successful Broadway and Hollywood career, followed by some kind of a breakdown and many years in mental institutions.

Resolving the doubts that haunt Farmer's life, the film presents her basically as a woman to be admired for standing behind her convictions regardless of the consequences.

As a directorial debut by editor Graeme Clifford, however, *Frances* tends to trivialize. It's hard to shake the persistent feeling that she brought a lot of woe on herself.

☐ 1982: Nominations: Best Actress (Jessica Lange), Supp. Actress (Kim Stanley)

. . . .

■ FRANKENHOOKER

1990, 90 MINS, US ◇ ⓥ ⊙
Dir Frank Henenlotter   *Prod* Edgar Ievins   *Scr* Robert Martin, Frank Henenlotter   *Ph* Robert M. Baldwin
Ed Kevin Tent   *Mus* Joe Renzetti
● James Lorinz, Patty Mullen, Charlotte Helmkamp, Shirley Stoler, Louise Lasser, Joseph Gonzalez (Shapiro Glickenhaus)

Frankenhooker is a grisly, grotesque horror comedy recommended only for the stout of heart and strong of stomach.

James Lorinz plays Jeffrey Franken, a New Jersey Gas & Electric worker who aspires to be a mad scientist. There isn't much left of his pretty girlfriend Elizabeth (Patty Mullen) after her fatal run-in with a remote-control lawn mower. But Franken has preserved her head in his garage laboratory. All he needs is a new body to make the package complete. Jeffrey drives across the river to Times Square to find streetwalkers more than willing to sell (or at least rent) their bodies.

Even by genre standards, *Frankenhooker* often is offensive in its repeated reliance on murdering, dismembering and humiliating women for laughs. Lorinz has some inspired moments of self-absorbed craziness as Jeffrey, and Mullen reveals a fine talent for physical comedy when Elizabeth returns as the lumbering, mind-blown Frankenhooker.

. . . .

■ FRANKENSTEIN

1931, 71 MINS, US ⓥ ⊙
Dir James Whale   *Prod* Carl Laemmle Jr.   *Scr* Garrett Fort, Francis Edwards Faragoh   *Ph* Arthur Edeson
Ed Maurice Pivar, Clarence Kolster   *Mus* [David Broekman]   *Art Dir* Charles D. Hall
● Colin Clive, Mae Clarke, John Boles, Boris Karloff, Edward Van Sloan, Dwight Frye (Universal)

Frankenstein looks like a *Dracula* plus, touching a new peak in horror plays and handled in production with supreme craftsmanship.

Picture [based on the compositon by John L. Balderston, from the play by Peggy Webling, based on the novel by Mary W. Shelley] starts with a wallop. Midnight funeral services are in progress on a blasted moor, with the figure of the scientist and his grotesque dwarf assistant hiding at the edge of the cemetery to steal the newly-buried body. Sequence climaxes with the gravedigger sending down the clumping earth upon newly-laid coffin. Shudder No.1.

Shudder No.2, hard on its heels is when Frankenstein cuts down his second dead subject from the gallows, presented with plenty of realism. The corpses are to be assembled into a semblance of a human body which Frankenstein seeks to galvanize into life, and to this end the story goes into his laboratory, extemporized in a gruesome mountain setting out of an abandoned mill.

Laboratory sequence detailing the creation of the monster patched up of human odds-and-ends is a smashing bit of theatrical effect, taking place during a violent mountain storm.

Playing is perfectly paced. Colin Clive, the cadaverous hero of *Journey's End* (1930), is a happy choice for the scientist driven by a frenzy for knowledge. He plays it with force, but innocent of ranting. Boris Karloff makes a memorable figure of the bizarre monster with its indescribably terrifying face of demoniacal calm.

. . . .

■ FRANKENSTEIN CREATED WOMAN

1967, 92 MINS, UK ◇ ⓥ
Dir Terence Fisher   *Prod* Anthony Nelson Keys
Scr John Elder [= Anthony Hinds]   *Ph* Arthur Grant

Ed James Needs *Mus* James Bernard *Art Dir* Don Mingaye
● Peter Cushing, Susan Denberg, Thorley Walters, Robert Morris, Peter Blythe, Barry Warren (Hammer/ Seven Arts)

In *Frankenstein Created Woman* the good doctor, as usual, played by Peter Cushing, doesn't really create woman, he just makes a few important changes in the design. Considering the result is beautiful blonde Susan Denberg, most film fans would like to see the doctor get a grant from the Ford Foundation, or even the CIA.

In this version, Frankenstein dabbles as much in transmigration of souls as actual patchwork surgery, capturing the psyche of an executed young man and instilling it in the body of a drowned young woman (Denberg). The girl, originally a disfigured, shy maiden, is rejuvenated as a beautiful femme whose touch proves tres fatale when the male soul uses the female body to wreak vengeance on the trio of young wastrels responsible for his execution (Peter Blythe, Barry Warren, Derek Fowlds).

....

■ FRANKENSTEIN MEETS THE WOLF MAN

1943, 72 MINS, US 🅥 ⊙
Dir Roy William Neill *Prod* George Waggner
Scr Curt Siodmak *Ph* George Robinson *Ed* Edward Curtiss *Mus* Hans J. Salter
● Lon Chaney, Ilona Massey, Patric Knowles, Lionel Atwill, Bela Lugosi, Maria Ouspenskaya (Universal)

In order to put the Wolf Man and the Monster through further film adventures, scripter Curt Siodmak has to resurrect the former from a tomb, and the Frankenstein creation from the ruins of the castle where he was purportedly killed. But he delivers a good job of fantastic writing to weave the necessary thriller ingredients into the piece, and finally brings the two legendary characters together for a battle climax.

Eerie atmosphere generates right at the start, when Lon Chaney, previously killed off with the werewolf stain on him, is disinterred and returns to life. After one transformation, he winds up in a hospital to gain the sympathetic attention of medico Patric Knowles, then seeks out gypsy Maria Ouspenskaya for relief, and she takes him to the continent and the village where Frankenstein held forth. This allows Chaney to discover and revive the monster, role handled by Bela Lugosi, and from there on it's a creepy affair in grand style.

....

■ FRANKENSTEIN MUST BE DESTROYED

1969, 97 MINS, UK ◇ 🅥
Dir Terence Fisher *Prod* Anthony Nelson Keys *Scr* Bert Batt *Ph* Arthur Grant *Ed* Gordon Hales *Mus* James Bernard *Art Dir* Bernard Robinson
● Peter Cushing, Veronica Carlson, Freddie Jones, Simon Ward, Thorley Walters, Maxine Audley (Hammer)

Frankenstein's (Peter Cushing) diabolical plan is, in the cause of science, to preserve the medical knowledge of a brilliant but insane surgeon. This he'll do by murdering the medico, removing his brain and inserting it in the body of a kidnapped man.

With the help of two young accomplices (a doctor, Simon Ward, and his girl friend, Veronica Carlson), drawn into the plot because Frankenstein is blackmailing them over a drug robbery offense, the mad scientist is hijacked from an asylum, operated on and the brains switched.

The film is a good-enough example of its low-key type, with artwork rather better than usual (less obvious backcloths, etc.), a minimum of artless dialog, good lensing by Arthur Grant and a solid all round cast.

....

■ FRANKENSTEIN UNBOUND

1990, 85 MINS, US ◇ 🅥 ⊙
Dir Roger Corman *Prod* Roger Corman, Thom Mount, Kabi Jaeger *Scr* Roger Corman, F.X. Feeney, Ed Neumeir *Ph* Armando Nannuzzi, Michael Scott *Ed* Jay Cassidy *Mus* Carl Davis *Art Dir* Enrico Tovaglieri
● John Hurt, Raul Julia, Bridget Fonda, Nick Brimble, Catherine Rabett, Catherine Corman (Mount)

Roger Corman's *Frankenstein Unbound* is a competent but uninspired riff on the venerable legend. For Corman, it's also a return trip to modern British sci-fi, adapting a Brian W. Aldiss novel.

John Hurt toplines as a mad scientist in New Los Angeles of 2031, trying to develop a laser weapon that causes objects to implode. Unfortunately, his experiments are causing time slips, violent dislocations including one that suddenly transports Hurt to Switzerland in 1817.

Hurt chances upon Dr Frankenstein in a local pub and he's soon visiting gothic folk Mary Godwin (soon to be Shelley), Lord Byron and Percy Shelley. Out on the rampage is Frankenstein's monster, killing people until his creator fabricates a mate for him.

While warring with Frankenstein and his monster, Hurt ultimately identifies with them, leading to an interesting, somber climax set in icy wastes as in Shelley's original novel.

Though some of the dialog is clutzy, acting is generally good with top honors to Raul Julia as a thoughtful Frankenstein. More single-minded is Hurt's sketchy role.

Bridget Fonda is attractive in the Mary Godwin role, overshadowed by British actress Catherine Rabett, who brings panache to the role of Frankenstein's fiancee, later resurrected as bride for the monster.

....

■ FRANKIE AND JOHNNY

1966, 87 MINS, US ◇ 🅥
Dir Frederick de Cordova *Prod* Edward Small
Scr Alex Gottlieb *Ph* Jacques Marquette *Ed* Grant Whytock *Mus* Fred Karger (dir.) *Art Dir* Walter Simonds
● Elvis Presley, Donna Douglas, Harry Morgan, Sue Ane Langdon, Nancy Kovack, Audrey Christie (Small/F&J)

Frankie and Johnny is Elvis all the way in a story built loosely around the classic folk song, coupled with a dozen or so tunes, pretty girls and Technicolor.

The screenplay from a Nat Perrin story has Elvis and Donna Douglas (in her first major film role) as entertainers on a Mississippi riverboat about 100 years ago. Elvis is Frankie, Donna is Johnny, and, like in the ageless song, they love each other. But Frankie gambles too much, losing all the time, until he finds a lucky redhead – Nellie Bly, natch – played by Nancy Kovack.

Elvis is Elvis. He sings and acts, apparently doing both with only slight effort. Presley does little hip swinging, no doubt in keeping with the period of the story, although he does get a chance to bounce out one number – 'Shout It Out' – with Dixieland accompaniment.

....

■ FRANKIE AND JOHNNY

1991, 118 MINS, US ◇ 🅥 ⊙
Dir Garry Marshall *Prod* Garry Marshall *Scr* Terrence McNally *Ph* Dante Spinotti *Ed* Battle Davis, Jacqueline Cambas *Mus* Marvin Hamlisch *Art Dir* Albert Brenner
● Al Pacino, Michelle Pfeiffer, Hector Elizondo, Nathan Lane, Kate Nellingan, Jane Morris (Paramount)

Frankie and Johnny is an all-star, high-gloss, feel-good romantic feature sitcom. Amiably written and performed but fearsomely predictable, this middle-of-the-road adaptation of Terrence McNally's off-Broadway hit [the

1987 *Frankie and Johnny in the Clair de Lune*] invites audiences to indulge in watching beautiful movie stars play lonely little people struggling to find love.

Al Pacino and Michelle Pfeiffer are cast in the roles originated onstage by Kathy Bates and F. Murray Abraham in the Manhattan Theater Club Workshop. *Pretty Woman* director Garry Marshall sprinkles a little of his Cinderella dust on this story of an ex-con who takes a job as a short-order chef in Manhattan and instantly falls for a hard-case waitress.

He is as persistent as she is resistant and, at one point during his efforts to woo Frankie, Johnny breaks down and takes a tumble with a brassy waitress (Kate Nelligan). But he is otherwise singleminded in his pursuit.

Like a warm, slobbering dog who can't leave people alone, Pacino's Johnny comes on real strong, and his pronounced neediness is too much at times. No one's going to believe that Pfeiffer hasn't had a date since Ronald Reagan was president, and no matter how hard she tries to look plain, there is no disguising that she just gets more beautiful all the time. But she gives a performance filled with many moods and numerous affecting moments.

....

■ FRANTIC

1988, 120 MINS, US ◇ 🅥 ⊙
Dir Roman Polanski *Prod* Thom Mount, Tim Hampton *Scr* Roman Polanski, Gerard Brach *Ph* Witold Sobocinski *Ed* Sam O'Steen *Mus* Ennio Morricone *Art Dir* Pierre Guffroy
● Harrison Ford, Emmanuelle Seigner, Betty Buckley, John Mahoney, Jimmie Ray Weeks (Mount/Warner)

Frantic is a thriller without much surprise, suspense or excitement. Drama about an American doctor's desperate search for his kidnapped wife through the demi-monde of Paris reveals director Roman Polanski's personality and enthusiasm only in brief humorous moments.

San Francisco medic Harrison Ford arrives in Paris with wife Betty Buckley to deliver a paper at a conference and, incidentally, to revisit the scene of their honeymoon 20 years before. While Ford is showering, Buckley disappears from the hotel room, thus setting off an urgent woman-hunt that takes the distraught husband to young Emmanuelle Seigner, a sleek, punky drugette and nightclubber who appears to be the only lead to the kidnappers.

The McGuffin, or object of everyone's pursuit, here is a miniature Statue of Liberty which contains an object that, predictably, could endanger the Free World. Action climax takes place alongside the small-scale replica of France's gift to New York Harbor.

Ford sweats a lot while conveying Polanski's view that anxiety is the natural state of the human condition. His latest discovery, Seigner, certainly is eye-catching and proves servicable in her part.

....

■ FRAUDS

1993, 92 MINS, AUSTRALIA/UK ◇ 🅥 ⊙
Dir Stephan Elliott *Prod* Andrena Finlay, Stuart Quin *Scr* Stephan Elliott *Ph* Geoff Burton *Ed* Frans Vandenburg *Mus* Guy Gross *Art Dir* Brian Thomson
● Phil Collins, Hugo Weaving, Josephine Byrnes, Peter Mochrie, Helen O'Connor, Rebel Russell (Live/J&M/Latent Image)

First-time director Stephan Elliott breaks a lot of the rules with his wayward first feature, *Frauds*, cheerfully mixing suspense with comic-strip comedy. Pic boasts a top-flight performance from Phil Collins as a con-man insurance investigator with a childlike sense of humor.

The home of a yuppie couple, Jonathan

(Hugo Weaving) and Beth (Josephine Byrnes), who like to play games, is burgled by a masked intruder; Beth shoots the stranger with an antique crossbow only to discover that he was a family friend.

Roland Copping (Collins) discovers that Jonathan was the burglar's accomplice and proceeds to play games with the couple, who are at first amused, then annoyed, and finally terrified by his strange, childish antics.

Elliott flings these disparate elements together with sublime confidence, driving the film along at a brisk pace and creating a strange and deliberately unreal world for his eccentric characters. He's aided by the clever production design of Brian Thomson and by Geoff Burton's sterling lensing.

....

■ FREAKS

1932, 61 MINS, US 🅿 ⊙

Dir Tod Browning *Prod* Tod Browning *Scr* Willis Goldbeck, Leon Gordon, Edgar Allan Woolf, Al Boasberg *Ph* Merritt B. Gerstad *Ed* Basil Wrangell *Art Dir* Cedric Gibbons
● Wallace Ford, Leila Hyams, Olga Baclanova, Roscoe Ates, Harry Earles, Daisy Earles (M-G-M)

Freaks is sumptuously produced, admirably directed, and no cost was spared. But Metro failed to realize that even with a different sort of offering the story still is important. Here it is not sufficiently strong to get and hold the interest, partly because interest cannot easily be gained for a too fantastic romance.

The plot outline is the love of a midget in a circus for a robust gymnast, her marriage with the idea of getting his fortune and putting him out of the way through poisoning and effecting a union with the strongman of the show.

The story [from *Spurs* by Tod Robbins] is laid in a European touring circus. It is only a one-ring affair, but it carries three times as many high-class freaks as the Ringling show ever trouped in one season, and the dressing tent is larger than the main top.

No effort is made to show the ring performance, most of the action occurring in the dressing tent and much of it while the show is closed. The midget leads are Harry and Daisy Earles. Earles builds on his fine performance in *The Unholy Three* (1930) but he fails in the stronger scenes, when he seeks to gain sympathy through his despair.

Daisy Earles is less successful as the midget rival to Olga Baclanova. She is a doll-like little woman who reads her lines with extreme care, but seldom succeeds in acting. Baclanova as the rather rowdy gymnast has several fine opportunities but at other times is handicapped by action too obvious and her cheerful effort to poison her tiny spouse carries no suggestion of menace. Harry Victor, as the strongman, is conventional and Wallace Ford and Leila Hyams, heading the cast, have little more than walk-through parts. The one sincere human note is Rose Dione in an unfortunately brief bit.

....

■ FREAKY FRIDAY

1976, 95 MINS, US ◇ 🅥 ⊙

Dir Gary Nelson *Prod* Ron Miller *Scr* Mary Rodgers *Ph* Charles F. Wheeler *Ed* Cotton Warburton *Mus* Johnny Mandel *Art Dir* John B. Mansbridge, Jack Senter
● Barbara Harris, Jodie Foster, John Astin, Patsy Kelly, Dick Van Patten, Ruth Buzzi (Walt Disney)

Freaky Friday is certainly one of the most offbeat films Walt Disney Productions has ever made, but it isn't one of the best. A promising concept – a quarreling mother and teenage daughter switch personalities for a day – has been bungled by a talky, repetitive screenplay and overbroad direction. Barbara Harris and

Jodie Foster salvage some scenes through sheer behavioral charm.

Mary Rodgers' screenplay, adapted from her 1972 book, touches more directly on modern social mores, particularly on women's lib issues, than is common for the studio. And pic has some eyebrow-raising Freudian undertones of the type which Disney pix usually avoid or suppress.

Foster is a normally unkempt and tomboyish prepubescent teen. She hates her mother (Harris) and worships her father (John Astin), a cardboard go-getter type. Both Harris and Foster reveal desires to escape their situations, and presto, they switch personalities while their bodies go about the usual daily routine.

The film's sexual undertones are mostly hidden beneath the continual barrage of sight gags, but they are there nonetheless. This is Disney's version of *Lolita*. Astin gets turned on when Harris starts calling him 'daddy,' and Foster gets furiously jealous when she encounters her father's curvaceous secretary. The film is a mine field of double meanings.

....

■ FREDDIE AS F.R.O.7.

1992, 90 MINS, UK ◇ 🅥 ⊙

Dir Jon Acevski *Prod* Norman Priggen, Jon Acevski *Scr* Jon Acevski, David Ashton *Ph* Rex Neville *Ed* Alex Rayment, Mick Manning *Mus* David Dundas, Rick Wentworth *Art Dir* Paul Shardlow
● (Hollywood Road)

A shake 'n' bake mixture of virtually every toon genre going, *Freddie As F.R.O.7.* makes up in energy what it lacks in originality.

Billing itself before the main titles as 'an amazing fantasy of a new kind,' pic delivers plenty of the former but short-changes on the latter. Yarn starts out as a Never Never Land fairy tale, segues rapidly to Disney-like anthropomorphism and finally launches into a mix of James Bonderie and *Star Wars*.

Plot kicks off with Freddie (voiced by Ben Kingsley) reminiscing about his origins as young Prince Frederic, turned into a frog by shape-shifting Aunt Messina (Billie Whitelaw) and saved from her cobra alter ego by kindly Nessie (Phyllis Logan), the Loch Ness monster. Growing up underwater, he later relocates to Paris as superagent F.R.O.7.

In place of a properly developed plot line, director Jon Acevski busies the screen with characters and incident, every now and then breaking into pleasant enough musical numbers that don't advance the action a jot.

....

■ FREDDY'S DEAD
THE FINAL NIGHTMARE

1991, 90 MINS, US ◇ 🅥 ⊙

Dir Rachel Talalay *Prod* Robert Shaye, Aron Warner *Scr* Michael DeLuca *Ph* Declan Quinn *Ed* Janice Hampton *Mus* Brian May *Art Dir* C.J. Strawn
● Robert Englund, Lisa Zane, Shon Greenblatt, Lezlie Deane, Ricky Dean Logan, Yaphet Kotto (New Line)

Sixth and final edition in the *Nightmare on Elm Street* feature series delivers enough violence, black humor and even a final reel in 3-D to hit paydirt with horror-starved audiences.

Tired nature of the original Wes Craven concept is acknowledged by a new plotline by debutante helmer Rachel Talalay, with vengeful, undead murderer Freddy Krueger (Robert Englund, again in fine form) supposedly having killed off all the local children and teens in a little Ohio town, now set 10 years in the future.

He's using a young amnesiac, John (Shon Greenblatt) to revitalize his powers and ultimately seeking his daughter (Lisa Zane), who works as a counsellor in a teen rehab shelter, in an effort to spread his vengeance to Elm Streets worldwide.

Most imaginative sequence deals with hear-

ing impaired teen Carlos (Ricky Dean Logan). Freddy tears out the kid's hearing aid and torments him silently. Less successful is the 15-minute 3-D capper. Projected using the old-fashioned anaglyphic (red & blue lenses) glasses, sequence's color is thereby distorted compared to modern polarized lens efforts.

Guest stars Roseanne Arnold and hubbie Tom Arnold (cast as a childless couple of the future) and Alice Cooper (typecast as Freddy's abusive stepfather) add little to the stew. Johnny Depp, featured in 1984 original, pops up briefly as a teen on TV.

....

■ FREEBIE AND THE BEAN

1974, 112 MINS, US ◇ 🅥 ⊙

Dir Richard Rush *Prod* Richard Rush *Scr* Robert Kaufman *Ph* Laszlo Kovacs *Ed* Fredric Steinkamp, Michael McLean *Mus* Dominic Frontiere *Art Dir* Hilyard Brown
● Alan Arkin, James Caan, Loretta Swit, Jack Kruschen, Mike Kellin, Valerie Harper (Warner)

Freebie and the Bean stars Alan Arkin and James Caan as two allegedly 'funny' lawless lawmen. Richard Rush's tasteless film, from a spitball script by Robert Kaufman, utilized lots of stunt and action crews disturbing the peace all over San Francisco.

The purported 'humor' between the two stars largely hinges on Caan's delivery of what are nothing more than repeated racist slurs on Arkin's character's Chicano ancestry. Arkin's performance adds even more concrete nuances to this characterization. What passes for a basic story line is something about their nabbing bigtime gangster Jack Kruschen, and between car chases and mindless destruction of cars and other things, the plot lurches forward.

....

■ FREEJACK

1992, 108 MINS, US ◇ 🅥 ⊙

Dir Geoff Murphy *Prod* Ronald Shusett, Stuart Oken *Scr* Steven Pressfield, Ronald Shusett, Dan Gilroy *Ph* Amir Mokri *Ed* Dennis Virkler *Mus* Trevor Jones *Art Dir* Joe Alves
● Emilio Estevez, Mick Jagger, Rene Russo, Anthony Hopkins, Jonathan Banks, Amanda Plummer (Morgan Creek)

Employing a nightmarish vision of the year 2009 solely as a backdrop for a banal action yarn [based on Robert Sheckley's novel *Immortality Inc.*], *Freejack* has a curious list of talent (Mick Jagger and Anthony Hopkins). The primary plot – about a racecar driver (Emilio Estevez) who's plucked from a fiery death in 1991 to become a host body for the consciousness of a dying rich man – feels as superfluous as it is strained next to the other depressing evils on display.

Director Geoff Murphy, seen as an up-and-coming talent after his US debut (*Young Guns II*) and two productions in his native New Zealand (*Utu*, *The Quiet Earth*), seems to have been either overwhelmed by the material or bored by it. Effect on the audience is a little of both.

The principal pursuers are equally one-dimensional, with Jagger as a body-snatching bounty hunter, and Jonathan Banks as the smarmy lieutenant of the business tycoon (Hopkins).

The most notable performance is that of Amanda Plummer as an abusive, gun-toting nun, providing a rare comic highlight.

....

■ FREE WILLY

1993, 111 MINS, US ◇ 🅥 ⊙

Dir Simon Wincer *Prod* Jennie Lew Tugend, Lauren Shuler-Donner *Scr* Keith A. Walker, Corey Blechman *Ph* Robbie Greenberg *Ed* O. Nicholas Brown *Mus* Basil Poledouris *Art Dir* Charles Rosen

273

F

● Jason James Richter, Lori Petty, Jayne Atkinson, August Schellenberg, Michael Madsen, Michael Ironside (Le Studio Canal Plus/Regency/Alcor)

Free Willy is an exhilarating drama of boy and nature that unabashedly pulls at the heart strings.

Jesse (Jason James Richter), an abandoned child in his umpteenth foster home, is running with a gang of outsiders who are into petty theft and random vandalism. But on one outing, he's nabbed at a Portland amusement park and winds up doing community service in lieu of juvenile detention.

The sullen Jesse soon becomes enthralled by Willy, a killer whale, who's the unwilling and unresponsive main attraction of the resident aquatic show. They are kindred souls.

Willy may at last be getting to apply himself to something practical but his new home life is by no means a slice of pristine Americana. His new folks (Jayne Atkinson, Michael Madsen) are unresolved about the decision to take him in and the boy's natural aversion to home life does little to make the transition easy.

Willy responds to to Jesse's commands after months of ignoring the park animal trainer (Lori Petty) and the knowing native supervisor (August Schellenberg). This attracts the park's evil owner (Michael Ironside), who sees an opportunity for a sell-out attraction. When that venture fails, the management decides the only way out is sabotage. Jesse gets wind of the danger and enlists his friends to do the right thing as the story hurtles to its exciting conclusion.

In director Simon Wincer's hands the process of caring and observation of the orca is handled to perfection. As Jesse, Richter is a welcome antidote to the scrubbed contemporary moppet stars. The adults have less meaty parts but Schellenberg and Madsen bring a dignity to what might have been predictable parts.

● ●

■ FRENCH CONNECTION, THE

1971, 104 MINS, US ◇ ⑰ ⊙
Dir William Friedkin   *Prod* Philip D'Antoni   *Scr* Ernest Tidyman   *Ph* Owen Roizman   *Ed* Jerry Greenberg   *Mus* Don Ellis   *Art Dir* Ben Kazaskow
● Gene Hackman, Fernando Rey, Roy Scheider, Tony LoBianco, Marcel Bozzuffi, Frederic De Pasquale (20th Century-Fox)

So many changes have been made in Robin Moore's taut, factual reprise of one of the biggest narcotics hauls in New York police history that only the skeleton remains, but Producer and screenwriter have added enough fictional flesh to provide director William Friedkin and his overall topnotch cast with plenty of material, and they make the most of it.

Gene Hackman and Roy Scheider are very believable as two hard-nosed narcotics officers who stumble onto what turned out to be the biggest narcotics haul to date. As suave and cool as the two cops are overworked, tired and mean, Fernando Rey is the French mastermind of the almost-perfect plan.

Friedkin includes a great elevated train-automobile chase sequence that becomes almost too tense to be enjoyable, especially for New Yorkers who are familiar with such activities.

Shot almost entirely in and around New York, Owen Roizman's fluid color camera explores most of Manhattan and much of Brooklyn without prettifying the backgrounds.
☐ 1971: Best Picture, Director, Actor (Gene Hackman), Adapted Screenplay, Editing.
☐ Nominations: Best Supp. Actor (Roy Scheider), Cinematography, Sound

● ●

■ FRENCH CONNECTION II

1975, 119 MINS, US ◇ ⑰ ⊙
Dir John Frankenheimer   *Prod* Robert L. Rosen
Scr Robert Dillon, Laurie Dillon, Alexander Jacobs

Ph Claude Renoir   *Ed* Tom Rolf   *Mus* Don Ellis
Art Dir Jacques Saulnier
● Gene Hackman, Fernando Rey, Bernard Fresson, Jean-Pierre Castaldi, Charles Millot, Cathleen Nesbitt (20th-Century Fox)

John Frankenheimer's *French Connection II* is both complementary to, yet distinctly different from, William Friedkin's *The French Connection*.

Gene Hackman as Popeye Doyle goes to Marseilles in search of heroin czar Fernando Rey (also encoring from the first pic). The assignment in reality is a setup (thereby implying that high-level law enforcement corruption still exists), and Hackman is duly kidnapped, drugged and left for dead by Rey.

Hackman's addiction and withdrawal sequences are terrifyingly real and make uncompromisingly clear the personal and social horror of drug abuse.

This plot turn is both intelligent and clever. Bernard Fresson is excellent as the French narc who must cope not only with his country's dope problem, but also Hackman's unruly presence.

Hackman's performance is another career highlight, ranging from cocky narc, Ugly American, helpless addict, humbled ego and relentless avenger.

● ●

■ FRENCH DRESSING

1964, 86 MINS, UK
Dir Ken Russell   *Prod* Kenneth Harper   *Scr* Peter Myers, Ronald Cass, Peter Brett   *Ph* Ken Higgins   *Ed* Jack Slade   *Mus* Georges Delerue   *Art Dir* Jack Stephens
● James Booth, Roy Kinnear, Marisa Mell, Alita Naughton, Bryan Pringle, Robert Robinson (Associated British)

It's a pity to see a promising comedy idea go busted through sheer lack of bright wit and irony. *French Dressing* is a light comedy which needed the satirical touch, but instead suffers from a flat, heavy treatment. This squelches many of the lighter, more promising moments.

Gormleigh-on-Sea is one of those British holiday resorts that suffer from acute dull-itis. A bright young deckchair attendant (James Booth) cons the local entertainments manager and the mayor into running a film festival. They persuade an ambitious young French actress to be the star of the proceedings which lead to some inevitable disasters and coy jokes such as a total washout at the opening of a new Nudist Beach and a riot at a premiere. Only quick thinking by the young American journalist girl friend of James Booth saves the situation.

Too much stodgy joking does not aid predictable slapstick situations. Quick cutting and speeding up of camerawork are not enough to disguise the fact that this is not a souffle but mainly an indigestible pancake.

● ●

■ FRENCH LIEUTENANT'S WOMAN, THE

1981, 127 MINS, UK ◇ ⑰ ⊙
Dir Karel Reisz   *Prod* Leon Clore   *Scr* Harold Pinter
Ph Freddie Francis   *Ed* John Bloom   *Mus* Carl Davis
Art Dir Assheton Gorton
● Meryl Streep, Jeremy Irons, David Warner, Leo McKern, Charlotte Mitchell, Hilton McRae (United Artists/Junipaer)

Diverse directing talents including Fred Zinnemann, Richard Lester and Mike Nichols all tried and failed to conquer the complicated narrative of John Fowles' epic romantic novel, *The French Lieutenant's Woman*.

Finally, it took director Karel Reisz and playwright Harold Pinter to develop an ingenious method to convey the essence of Fowles' book. The film retells the novel's story, set in 1867, of a strange young woman dishonored by her involvement with a French soldier and the English gentleman who finds her mystery

and sadness irresistible. Simultaneously, a parallel story of the affair between the two actors portraying the central roles in a film within-a-film unfolds on screen.

The effect of the two interwoven stories is at times irritating and confusing, but ultimately most affecting. This is due in large part to the strong performances of Meryl Streep as Sara Woodruff/Anna and Jeremy Irons as Charles Smithson/Mike.

The action flip-flops between the two tales, but favors the historic story. Reisz employs several lightning mixes to bridge the action, but more often abruptly moves from past to present.

The unconventional approach to Fowles' novel takes some getting used to but succeeds in conveying the complexity of the original in the final analysis.

Cameraman Freddie Francis deserves special mention for his painterly skill of recreating 19th-century Dorset and the contrasting sheen of the contemporary segments.

The casting of Meryl Streep as Sarah/Anna could not have been better. Sarah comes complete with unbridled passions and Anna is the cool, detached professional. There is never a false note in the sharply contrasting characters.
☐ 1981: Nominations: Best Actress (Meryl Streep), Adapted Screenplay, Costume Design, Art Direciton, Editing

● ●

■ FRENCH LINE, THE

1954, 102 MINS, US ◇ ⑰
Dir Lloyd Bacon   *Prod* Edmund Grainger   *Scr* Mary Loos, Richard Sale   *Ph* Harry J. Wild   *Ed* Robert Ford   *Mus* Constantin Bakaleinikoff
● Jane Russell, Gilbert Roland, Arthur Hunnicutt, Mary McCarty, Joyce Mackenzie, Paula Corday (RKO)

Except for a four-minute, censorably costumed dance by Jane Russell, this is a rather mild, gabby, fashion parade in 3-D.

The plot is the long-worked one about a rich girl who wants to be loved for herself and goes incognito as a working frail to find the right man. It's an okay basis for a musical if ingenuously handled, but there is little of the imaginative displayed in Lloyd Bacon's direction or in the screenplay by Mary Loos and Richard Sale [based on a story by Matty Kemp and Isabel Dawn]. Once in a while a snappy quip breaks through the long passages of verbiage that strain too hard to be smart talk. And in line with the film's principal concern, these snappy quips are bosom-conscious.

Russell is an eye-pleaser, and she can be a good musical comedy actress (*Gentlemen Prefer Blondes*) when given material and direction. Gilbert Roland's suave way with the ladies helps his character of the French lover who pursues oil-rich Russell for herself, not her millions.

● ●

■ FRENCHMAN'S CREEK

1945, 113 MINS, US ◇
Dir Mitchell Leisen   *Prod* Mitchell Leisen   *Scr* Talbot Jennings   *Ph* George Barnes   *Ed* Alma Macrorie   *Mus* Victor Young   *Art Dir* Hans Dreier, Ernst Fegte
● Joan Fontaine, Arturo de Cordova, Basil Rathbone, Nigel Bruce, Cecil Kellaway, Ralph Forbes (Paramount)

Frenchman's Creek is a 17th-century romance about the lady and the pirate, beautifully Technicolored and lavishly mounted. Film reputedly cost over $3 million to produce, Paramount's costliest investment [at the time].

The romantic pirate from France who invades the Cornish coast of England, hiding his frigate in what thus becomes known as Frenchman's Creek, plays his role with all the musical comedy bravado the part calls for.

The romance is supposedly forthright and played straight. Joan Fontaine seeks refuge in the Cornish castle to get away from a stupid husband (Ralph Forbes) and a ducal menace. The scoundrelly servant at the Cornish retreat is actually the pirate chief's hireling, and the romance between the two, is but one of a sequence of similar adventures.

The performances are sometimes unconsciously tongue-in-cheek, but withal come off well. Cecil Kellaway is particularly good as the servant.

The scripting [from the novel by Daphne du Maurier] at times borders on the ludicrous, especially when almost all the sympathetic figures wax near hysteria in their scoffing at the dangers which may beset them. Productionally it is ultra. And no minor assist is an excellent Victor Young score.

☐ 1945: Best Color Art Decoration

■ FRENCH VAMPIRE IN AMERICA
See: Innocent Blood

■ FRENZY

1972, 116 MINS, UK ◇ ⊛ ⊙
Dir Alfred Hitchcock *Prod* Alfred Hitchcock
Scr Anthony Shaffer *Ph* Gil Taylor *Ed* John Jympson
Mus Ron Goodwin *Art Dir* Syd Cain
● Jon Finch, Barry Foster, Barbara Leigh-Hunt, Anna Massey, Alec McCowen, Vivien Merchant (Universal)

Armed with a superior script by Anthony Shaffer, an excellent cast, and a top technical crew, Alfred Hitchcock fashions a firstrate melodrama about an innocent man hunted by Scotland Yard for a series of sex-strangulation murders.

Working from Arthur La Bern's novel, *Goodbye Piccadilly, Farewell Leicester Square*, Shaffer develops a finely-structured screenplay. Jon Finch heads the cast as something of a loser who becomes trapped by circumstantial evidence in the sordid murders of several women, including his former wife (Barbara Leigh-Hunt), and current girl-friend (Anna Massey). The audience knows early who the real culprit is – in this case, Finch's friend, Barry Foster – so the interest lies in hoping for the rescue of the hero. Hitchcock has used this basic dramatic situation before.

■ FRESHMAN, THE

1990, 102 MINS, US ◇ ⊛ ⊙
Dir Andrew Bergman *Prod* Mike Lobell *Scr* Andrew Bergman *Ph* William A. Fraker *Ed* Barry Malkin
Mus David Newman *Art Dir* Ken Adam
● Marlon Brando, Matthew Broderick, Bruno Kirby, Penelope Ann Miller, Paul Benedict, Maximilian Schell (Tri-Star)

Marlon Brando's sublime comedy performance elevates *The Freshman* from screwball comedy to a quirky niche in film history – among films that comment on cult movies.

Mario Puzo and Francis Coppola's *The Godfather* is director Andrew Bergman's starting point. Incoming NYU film student Matthew Broderick is exposed not only to that Paramount film (and its sequel) in pretentious prof Paul Benedict's classroom but meets up with a virtual doppelganger for Don Vito Corleone in the form of mobster Carmine Sabatini (Brando).

The ornate and intentionally screwy plotline has Brando making an irresistible offer to Broderick to work for him part-time as a delivery boy. Broderick's first assignment is transporting a huge (but real) lizard from the airport. Broderick quickly tumbles to the criminality of Brando and his nutty partner Maximilian Schell, but is unable to extricate himself.

Pic's weakest element is the recurring satire of film studies. Although Benedict is droll as an academic poseur, the mocking of film analysis is puerile and obvious.

Broderick is ably abetted by two previous

costars: Penelope Anne Miller (*Biloxi Blues*), winning as an offbeat form of mafia princess; and B.D. Wong (who popped up in *Family Business*) as Schell's goofy partner in culinary crime. Tech credits on the mixed New York and Toronto shoot are good, capturing the right amount of Greenwich Village ambience.

■ FREUD
(UK: *Freud – The Secret Passion*)

1962, 140 MINS, US
Dir John Huston *Prod* Wolfgang Reinhardt
Scr Charles Kaufman, Wolfgang Reinhardt *Ph* Douglas Slocombe *Ed* Ralph Kemplen *Mus* Jerry Goldsmith
Art Dir Stephen B. Grimes
● Montgomery Clift, Susannah York, Larry Parks, Susan Kohner, Eric Portman, David McCallum (Universal)

Intricate scenario by Charles Kaufman and producer Reinhardt, from the former's story, translates into dramatic, not biographical, terms the events of five key years (1885-90) in Freud's life, the years during which he formulated his principal theory – that sexual instinct is the basic one in the human personality – and led him to discover and describe the presence of sexual behavior even in infancy.

The drama revolves around Freud's (Montgomery Clift) treatment of a young patient (Susannah York) who has broken down mentally and physically upon the death of her father. In treating her, and relating her neuroses to his own, he is able not only to cure her, but to formulate the Oedipus Complex theory – the child's fixation on the parent of the opposite sex. This is the dramatic nucleus of the film.

The appropriately bewhiskered Clift delivers an intense, compassionate and convincing personification of Freud. York is vivid and true as his agitated patient, although the character is not always in sharp focus. Larry Parks etches a warm and appealing portrait of Freud's friend, colleague and associate. Susan Kohner is fine as Freud's understanding wife. Among the supporting players, Eric Portman stands out with a crisp, biting enactment of Freud's orthodox superior who reveals the contradictory nature of his inner personality only when he is dying.

☐ 1962: Nominations: Best Original Story & Screenplay, Original Music Score

■ FREUD – THE SECRET PASSION
See: Freud

■ FRIDAY FOSTER

1975, 89 MINS, US ◇ ⊛
Dir Arthur Marks *Prod* Arthur Marks *Scr* Orville Hampton *Ph* Harry May *Ed* Stanley Fragen
Mus Luchi De Jesus
● Pam Grier, Yaphet Kotto, Godfrey Cambridge, Thalmus Rosulala, Eartha Kitt, Jim Backus (American International)

Friday Foster, is based on a comic strip of the same name; Pam Grier is a fearless magazine fotog, sort of a female Clark Kent, who stumbles onto a St Valentine's Day-type massacre involving black millionaire Thalmus Rasulala and lots of political and underworld opponents mixed up on both sides.

There's a truly impressive credit sheet, including Yaphet Kotto as a cop, Godfrey Cambridge as a swishy criminal type, Eartha Kitt as an outrageously camp fashion designer, Seatman Crothers as a dirty-minded minister, Ted Lange as a sardonic pimp, and Jim Backus as the Mr Big who pulls the strings behind the action.

Grier has some steamy sex scenes and a lot of rugged action, though she isn't totally macho and radiates a lot of traditional feminine charm along the way.

■ FRIDAY THE THIRTEENTH

1933, 65 MINS, UK ◇
Dir Victor Saville *Scr* Emlyn Williams *Ph* Charles Van Enger *Ed* R. E. Dearing *Mus* Louis Levy (dir.)
Art Dir Alfred Junge, Alex Vetchinsky
● Sonnie Hale, Jessie Matthews, Edmund Gwenn, Max Miller, Emlyn Williams, Ralph Richardson (Gainsborough/Gaumont-British)

There's a good idea here and the execution is far from bad. It's a combination *Grand Hotel* and bus idea [story by C. H. Moresby-White and Sidney Gilliat] that's pretty well thought out.

Opens with a bus going down a London street in a rainstorm. A crash, two people are killed and several wounded. Then the clock goes back over the day of all the passengers that were in the bus, relating the incidents that got them there at the time. All unrelated, of course. But the bus crash fixes things up all around.

There's the chorus girl who's had a spat with her sweetie and, hurt, is en route to keep a date with the fresh guy who's been trying vainly to make her, up to then. There's the blackmailer who's just taken the last money from a poor boy with the threat of returning for more.

There's the henpecked husband, en route home late, after working overtime and not knowing that when he gets home he'll find his wife has run off with another man. There's a wise-cracking and rather sympathetic crook being baited by detectives. So on down the line and none of it boring.

Cast is exceptionally good. Jessie Matthews as the chorine, is best. Frank Lawton and Ursula Jeans don't come out too well, being over-directed and in unfortunate spots. Max Miller impresses nicely in a comedy bit and Ralph Richardson does well by a character bit. Gordon Harker repeats his comedy characterization that brought him attention in *Rome Express* and Edmund Gwenn and Mary Jerrold both do exceptionally well in character bits.

■ FRIDAY THE 13TH

1980, 95 MINS, US ◇ ⊛ ⊙
Dir Sean S. Cunningham *Prod* Sean S. Cunningham
Scr Victor Miller *Ph* Barry Abrams *Ed* Bill Freda
Mus Harry Manfredini *Art Dir* Virginia Field
● Betsy Palmer, Adrienne King, Harry Crosby, Laurie Bartram, Robbi Morgan (Cunningham)

Lowbudget in the worst sense – with no apparent talent or intelligence to offset its technical inadequacies – *Friday the 13th* has nothing to exploit but its title.

Another teenager-in-jeopardy entry, contrived to lure the profitable *Halloween* audience, this one is set at a crumbling New Jersey summer camp, shuttered for 20 years after a history of 'accidental' deaths and other spooky stuff, and about to be reopened for the summer.

Six would-be counselors arrive to get the place ready, then are progressively dispatched by knife, hatchet, spear and arrow.

Producer-director Sean S. Cunningham telegraphs the six murders too far ahead to keep anyone in even vague suspense, and without building a modicum of tension in between.

■ FRIDAY THE 13TH PART 2

1981, 87 MINS, US ◇ ⊛ ⊙
Dir Steve Miner *Prod* Steve Miner *Scr* Ron Kurz
Ph Peter Stein *Ed* Susan E. Cunningham *Mus* Harry Manfredini *Art Dir* Virginia Field
● Amy Steel, John Furey, Warrington Gillette, Adrienne King (Paramount)

Horror fans will probably delight in seeing yet another group of sexy, teen camp counselors gruesomely executed by yet another unknown (?)assailant, but the enthusiasm will dampen once they recognize too many of the same twists and turns used in the original.

When we last left Camp Crystal Lake one nubile counselor (Adrienne King) managed to survive the murderous spree of surprise villain Betsy Palmer who, it might be remembered, was killing all of the counselors as a symbolic revenge for her son drowning in camp years earlier.

Now five years have gone by and a new group of counselors (that seems to be the operating vocation here) have returned next door to the legendary camp. They know about the past violence and are even told of the legend of Palmer's son Jason, who supposedly lives on in the woods.

Producer-director Steve Miner doesn't move in and out of scenes with the flair of original producer-director Sean Cunningham nor is he able to create the same nauseatingly realistic murder situations (perhaps he's better off for the latter).

■ FRIDAY THE 13TH PART III

1982, 95 MINS, US ◇ ⓥ ⊙
Dir Steve Miner   *Prod* Frank Mancuso Jr   *Scr* Martin Kitrosser, Carol Watson   *Ph* Gerald Feil   *Ed* George Hively   *Mus* Harry Manfredini   *Art Dir* Robb Wilson King
● Dana Kimmell, Richard Brooker, Catherine Parks, Paul Kratka, Jeffrey Rogers, Tracie Savage (Paramount/Jason)

Friday the 13th was dreadful and took in more than $17 million. *Friday the 13th Part 2* was just as bad and took in more than $10 million. *Friday the 13th Part III* is terrible, too.

This time it's Dana Kimmell who leads the gang up to evil Lake Crystal for an outing. Crazy Jason is still there, though played this time by Richard Brooker instead of Warrington Gillette.

Kimmel has had some previous contact with Jason but doesn't quite remember it. All the kids are just about that bright, especially her boyfriend Paul Kratka. The most shocking scene in the film, in fact, is when Kratka gets his brains squeezed out; up until then, you would have sworn he didn't have any brains.

There are some dandy 3-D sequences, however, of a yo-yo going up and down and popcorn popping.

■ FRIDAY THE 13TH
THE FINAL CHAPTER

1984, 91 MINS, US ◇ ⓥ ⊙
Dir Joseph Zito   *Prod* Frank Mancuso Jr   *Scr* Barney Cohen, Daniel Loewenthal   *Ph* Joao Fernandes   *Ed* Joel Goodman   *Mus* Harry Manfredini   *Art Dir* Shelton H. Bishop III
● Crispin Glover, Kimberly Beck, Barbara Howard,, E. Erich Anderson, Corey Feldman, Alan Hayes (Paramount)

Opening line of film – 'I don't want to scare anyone, but Jason is still out there' – is fourth outing's only laugh, aside from unintended chuckle in the credit roll for First Aid. Everyone in sight of the lake gets it this time, except for a little boy with a fetish for masks who slaughters the crazed Jason and the boy's older sister (Corey Feldman and Kimberly Beck).

That leaves a dozen others who don't make it. More accurately, most are butchered after making it.

Of course, nobody is expected to take this stuff seriously. [Screen story by Bruce Hidemi Sakow.] Given, however, the consistent pro production value, the evisceration on parade is not campy. Implausibilities abound as Ever, and several *Friday the 13th* veteran players make brief appearances in an opening flashback compilation of old footage [from the three previous pics].

■ FRIDAY THE 13TH PART V
A NEW BEGINNING

1985, 92 MINS, US ◇ ⓥ ⊙
Dir Danny Steinmann   *Prod* Timothy Silver   *Scr* Martin Kitrosser, David Cohen, Danny Steinmann   *Ph* Stephen L. Posey   *Ed* Bruce Green   *Mus* Harry Manfredini   *Art Dir* Robert Howland
● John Shepard, Melanie Kinnaman, Shavar Ross, Richard Young, Carol Lacatell, Vernon Washington (Paramount)

The fifth *Friday the 13th* film reiterates a chronicle of butcherings with even less variation than its predecessors. Director Danny Steinmann (who made his theatrical debut with 1984's *Savage Streets*) does a lot with rain in this film and his conclusion is moderately well-orchestrated for maximum effect.

However, the film, which features a new Jason this time (but the same hockey mask), takes too long to set up its litany of eviscerations. For the record, the little boy who helped kill Jason in the last film is now a troubled teenager (John Shepard) hellbent on a crazed future of his own.

■ FRIDAY THE 13TH PART VI

See: Jason Lives

■ FRIDAY THE 13TH PART VII
THE NEW BLOOD

1988, 90 MINS, US ◇ ⓥ ⊙
Dir John Carl Buechler   *Prod* Iain Paterson   *Scr* Daryl Haney, Manuel Fidello   *Ph* Paul Elliott   *Ed* Barry Zetlin, Maureen O'Connell, Martin Jay Sadoff   *Mus* Harry Manfredini, Fred Mollin   *Art Dir* Richard Lawrence
● Jennifer Banko, John Otrin, Susan Blu, Lar Park Lincoln, Terry Kiser, Kevin Blair (Paramount)

After a prolog with scenes from earlier *Fridays*, routine screenplay introduces Tina (Lar Park Lincoln), a pretty young blonde who is under psychiatric care because flashbacks of her father's death won't go away. Her troubled mind's eye also sees tragedies before or just after they happen, and she can move objects without touching them.

On the advice of her less-than-dedicated shrink (Terry Kiser), Tina and her mother (Susan Blu), head up to Crystal Lake for a little on-site therapy. When a guilt-ridden Tina wishes her father back, she accidentally releases Jason from his watery grave. The rest is formula in both content and execution.

The still indestructible Jason (played by stunt coordinator Kane Hodder) has deteriorated so much that parts of his skeleton protrude from flesh and rags. He meets his match with the girl who cooks up her own storm with a willful stare. Although their duel offers original effects-laden thrills and stunts, it's too little and too late.

■ FRIDAY THE 13TH PART VIII
JASON TAKES MANHATTAN

1989, 100 MINS, US ◇ ⓥ ⊙
Dir Rob Hedden   *Prod* Randolph Cheveldave   *Scr* Rob Hedden   *Ph* Bryan England   *Ed* Steve Mirkovich   *Mus* Fred Mollin   *Art Dir* David Fischer
● Jensen Daggett, Scott Reeves, Peter Mark Richman, Barbara Bingham, V. C. Dupree, Kane Hodder (Horror/Paramount)

Paramount's latest cynical excursion into sadistic violence is lifted slightly above its generic mire by the stylish efforts of debuting director Rob Hedden.

The minimal variation this time in Hedden's script is to have most of the action take place on a cruise ship taking the Crystal Lake high school grads to Manhattan, where some humor naturally arises from the locals' indifference to the madman in their midst.

The film devotes its energies to recycling all the tried-and-true methods of dispatching

teens by stabbing, strangling, electrocuting, burning, head-smashing, slashing and spearing.

Jensen Daggett is a standout as the troubled young girl on whom Jason is fixated. V.C. Dupree has vibrant energy in his boxing scenes, Sharlene Martin has a fine time with the bitch role, and Martin Cummins is funny as a video freak who compulsively films the proceedings.

■ FRIEDA

1947, 97 MINS, UK ⓥ
Dir Basil Dearden   *Prod* Michael Balcon   *Scr* Ronald Millar, Angus MacPhail   *Ph* Gordon Dines   *Ed* Leslie Norman   *Mus* John Greenwood   *Art Dir* Jim Morahan
● Mai Zetterling, David Farrar, Glynis Johns, Flora Robson, Albert Lieven, Gladys Henson (Ealing)

The thoughtful play [by Ronald Millar] that scored a fair success on the London stage has been turned into a thoughtful picture.

Story begins in April 1945, in the bombed shell of a Polish Protestant church, when Robert (David Farrar), a British Officer, marries Frieda (Mai Zetterling), a Catholic German nurse who helped him escape. She loves him, but Robert is merely repaying a debt with a British passport and a trip to his home in a small English town.

Frieda gets a cool welcome. Only person to show any warmth is Robert's sister-in-law Judy (Glynis Johns), a war widow who loves Robert. Being the sixth year of the war, and the era of flying bombs, there is natural hostility among the townspeople. Peace comes, and gradually Frieda is accepted.

On the eve of the ceremony to ratify their marriage with the Roman Catholic Church brother Ricky (Albert Lieven) arrives dressed as a Polish Soldier. She soon discovers that beneath the uniform is a fanatical Nazi looking forward to the next war.

Political implications constantly intruding on this tragic love story, as they are doubtless intended to do hinder it from being poignant and moving. To play the name part, Zetterling was imported from Sweden. No pin up girl, and with a liking for the Veronica Lake hair-do, she has a strong personality but she's given a limited opportunuty to reveal her range.

■ FRIED GREEN TOMATOES

(UK: Fried Green Tomatoes at the Whistle Stop Cafe)

1991, 130 MINS, US ◇ ⓥ ⊙
Dir Jon Avnet   *Prod* Jon Avnet, Jordan Kerner   *Scr* Fanny Flagg, Jon Avnet   *Ph* Geoffrey Simpson   *Ed* Debra Neil   *Mus* Thomas Newman   *Art Dir* Barbara Ling
● Kathy Bates, Jessica Tandy, Mary Stuart Masterson, Mary-Louise Parker, Nick Searcy, Cicely Tyson (Universal/Act III)

Celebrating the crucial, sustaining friendships between two sets of modern-day and 1930s Southern femmes, pic [based on Fanny Flagg's novel *Fried Green Tomatoes at the Whistle Stop Cafe*] emerges as absorbing and life-affirming quality fare, but for a story celebrating fearlessness, it's remarkably cautious.

Kathy Bates plays a frumpy middle-aged Southern suburbanite, who finds inspiration in the tales spun by a feisty nursing-home resident (Jessica Tandy). These center on a gambling, brawling but good hearted rural Alabama girl (Mary Stuart Masterson), and how she almost got fingered for murder.

Seems the girl had developed a deep friendship with a demure, God-fearing young woman (Mary Louise Parker) who later on in life was having trouble with her abusive husband (Nick Searcy). Masterson helped her find the courage to run off with her baby and come to work as the cook at her Whistle Stop Cafe. When Searcy turns up missing

F

Masterson and her 'colored man' (Stan Shaw) are arrested on suspicion of murder.

Actual trial is merely a peg for a story that's mostly about the stalwart friendship between the two young femmes, isolated in a world of ham-handed, bigoted menfolk. Since the Masterson character is clearly in love with Parker, it's annoying that pic skates over the question of her sexuality.

Still, Tandy is at her sparkling best as the endearing old story-teller. Bates is also terrif in a funny and sympathetic turn. Director Jon Avnet, in his feature film debut, gets first-rate work from the featured performers.
□ 1991: Best Supp. Actress (Jessica Tandy).
□ Nomination: Best Adapted Screenplay

FRIED GREEN TOMATOES AT THE WHISTLE STOP CAFE
See: Fried Green Tomatoes

FRIENDLY PERSUASION

1956, 137 MINS, US ◇ ⓥ ⊙
Dir William Wyler Prod William Wyler Scr [Michael Wilson] Ph Ellsworth Fredricks Ed Robert Swink, Edward Biery Jr Mus Dimitri Tiomkin Art Dir Edward S. Haworth
● Gary Cooper, Dorothy McGuire, Anthony Perkins, Marjorie Main, Robert Middleton, Richard Eyer (Allied Artists)

While it is the simple story [from a novel by Jessamyn West] of a Quaker family in Indiana back in the 1860s, the footage contains just about everything in the way of comedy and drama, suspense and action.

Producer-director William Wyler had the project in mind for eight years and brought the property to Allied Artists from Paramount. Production cost was reportedly over $3 million. Film is without a screenplay credit.

After many warm, beguiling vignettes of family life, story works into its key dramatic point tying onto the Quaker feeling against bearing arms against a fellow man.

Role of the Quaker father, a man touched with gentle humor and inward strength, is glove-fit for Gary Cooper and he carries it off to an immense success. So does Dorothy McGuire in playing the mother of the family. Marjorie Main tops an extremely broad comedy episode involving Cooper's yen for a faster horse so he can beat a friend to church each Sunday, and three out-sized daughters who go on the make for Cooper's unworldly son (Anthony Perkins).

Figuring importantly in the way the picture plays is Dimitri Tiomkin's conducting of his own score.
□ 1956: Nominations: Best Picture, Director, Supp. Actor (Anthony Perkins), Adapted Screenplay [nominee unnamed, because of blacklist], Song ('Friendly Persuasion (Thee I Love)'), Sound

FRIENDS OF EDDIE COYLE, THE

1973, 100 MINS, US ◇ ⓥ
Dir Peter Yates Prod Paul Monash Scr Paul Monash Ph Victor J. Kemper Ed Patricia Lewis Jaffe Mus Dave Grusin Art Dir Gene Callahan
● Robert Mitchum, Peter Boyle, Richard Jordan, Steven Keats, Alex Rocco, Joe Santos (Paramount)

The Friends of Eddie Coyle is a very fine film about real people on the fringes of both crime and law enforcement. Shot in Boston, Paul Monash's top adaptation of a first novel by Mass asst attorney general George V. Higgins, stars Robert Mitchum and Peter Boyle as middle-aged, smalltime hoods.

Mitchum is very effective as an aging small-timer, complete with a most believable Boston-area accent (as are all the players), who retails in guns obtained from younger

hot-shot supplier Steven Keats. Boyle, ostensibly a bartender, is a conduit for murder contracts, criminal contacts, and, for weekly pay, tipoffs to Richard Jordan, terrific in a true 'Southie' evocation of a plainsclothes narc. Alex Rocco heads a bank heist gang which also includes Joe Santos.

The plot is electric with the endless, daily trading of favors and betrayals which are necessary for survival in this gray jungle.

FRIGHTENED CITY, THE

1961, 97 MINS, UK
Dir John Lemont Prod John Lemont, Leigh Vance Scr Leigh Vance Ph Desmond Dickinson Ed Bernard Gribble Mus Norrie Paramor Art Dir Maurice Carter
● Herbert Lom, John Gregson, Sean Connery, Alfred Marks, Yvonne Romain, Kenneth Griffiths (Anglo-Amalgamated/Zodiac)

The Frightened City is a conventional but brisk gangster yarn. Accent of the film is tough and hard-hitting and concerns intergang warfare plus the clash between the cops and the crooks, the cops, as a spokesman bitterly says, finding themselves hampered by outdated laws. 'We're trying to fight 20th-century crime with 19th-century legislation.'

Six main gangs are running the protection racket and a bent accountant hits on the idea of organizing the gangs into one all-powerful syndicate. All goes well for awhile but then the boss of the organization makes a successful play for a deal involving a $560,000 block of offices being built. One of the gangsters fights shy of this bigger game, backs out of the organization and re-forms his own gang. This sparks off gang warfare.

Herbert Lom plays the brains of the crooked organization with urbane villainy and equally reliable John Gregson makes a solid, confident job of the dedicated cop. Alfred Marks is cast offbeat as Lom's gangster lieutenant. Marks gives a rich, oily, sinister and yet often amusing portrayal of an ambitious thug who is prepared to turn killer to get his own way. Comparative newcomer, rugged Sean Connery makes a distinct impression as an Irish crook, with an eye for the ladies. Connery combines toughness, charm and Irish blarney.

FRIGHT NIGHT

1985, 105 MINS, US ◇ ⓥ ⊙
Dir Tom Holland Prod Herb Jaffe Scr Tom Holland Ph Jan Kiesser Ed Kent Beyda Mus Brad Fiedel Art Dir John De Cuir Jr
● Chris Sarandon, William Ragsdale, Amanda Bearse, Roddy McDowall, Stephen Geoffreys, Jonathan Stark (Columbia/Vistar)

Director Tom Holland keeps the picture wonderfully simple and entirely believable (once the existence of vampires is accepted, of course). In a quick 105 minutes, the film simply answers the question of what would probably happen if a charming, but deadly sinister, vampire moved in next door to a likable teenager given to watching horror films on the late show – and the only one the kid can turn to for help is a washed-up actor who hosts the show.

Chris Sarandon is terrific as the vampire, quite affable and debonair until his fingernails start to grow and his eyes get that glow. William Ragsdale superbly maintains due sympathy as a fairly typical youngster who can't get anybody to believe him about the odd new neighbor next door.

Roddy McDowall hams it up on the telly as the 'fearless vampire killer.' Naturally, when Ragsdale comes looking for help, McDowall is more than aware of his humanly limitations, becoming a consistently amusing, unwilling ally in invading Sarandon's lair.

FRIGHT NIGHT PART 2

1988, 101 MINS, US ◇ ⓥ ⊙
Dir Tommy Lee Wallace Prod Herb Jaffe, Mort Engelberg Scr Tim Metcalfe, Miguel Tejada-Flores, Tommy Lee Wallace Ph Mark Irwin Ed Jay Lash Cassidy Mus Brad Fiedel Art Dir Dean Tschetter
● Roddy McDowall, William Ragsdale, Traci Lin, Julie Carmen, Russell Clark, Brian Thompson (Vista)

Pic begins with scenes from 1985's original, and continues in the same vein. Though its camp humor and goopy effects are familiar, it's better than the average shlocker.

At the outset young Charley (William Ragsdale) has completed therapy and is cautiously certain he just imagined that vampire neighbor. Before long a quartet of sinister types has come to live in the old apartment where Charley's friend, TV horror host Peter Vincent (Roddy McDowall) resides and the mayhem starts all over again. This time, the vampires are led by a slinky femme fatale (Julie Carmen) and include an androgynous black, a leather-jacketed hood and a musclebound, silent type.

Helmer Tommy Lee Wallace brings freshness to the proceedings via inventive use of the wide screen and a ghoulish sense of humor. Special effects are very good.

FRISCO KID, THE

1979, 122 MINS, US ◇ ⓥ
Dir Robert Aldrich Prod Mace Neufeld Scr Michael Elias, Frank Shaw Ph Robert B. Hauser Ed Maury Winetrobe, Irving Rosenblum, Jack Horger Mus Frank DeVol Art Dir Terence Marsh
● Gene Wilder, Harrison Ford, Ramon Bieri, William Smith (Warner)

Director Robert Aldrich has always adroitly mixed comedic and dramatic aspects in his films, and Frisco Kid is no exception. For audiences expecting Mel Brooks belly-laughs amidst the Yiddishisms, however, there's bound to be disappointment.

As Avram Belinsky, Yeshiva flunky packed off to an American rendezvous with a leaderless 1850s San Francisco congregation, Gene Wilder has his best role in years. The manic gleam featured in early Wilder pix has now turned into a mature twinkle.

Excellent counterpoint is provided by Harrison Ford, as the cowboy, who proves the perfect foil for Wilder's gaffes.

Frisco Kid remains a series of set pieces, however, and not a cohesive film. For all his skills, Wilder is given too many solo shots. As is his practice, Aldrich has also inserted some action sequences that are jarring in their sadistic intensity.

FRITZ THE CAT

1972, 77 MINS, US ◇ ⓥ
Dir Ralph Bakshi Prod Steve Krantz Scr Ralph Bakshi Ed Renn Reynolds Mus Ed Bogas, Ray Shanklin (Krantz/Cinemation)

Fritz the Cat, X-rated cartoon feature based on the characters created by Robert Crumb, is an amusing, diverting, handsomely executed poke at youthful attitudes. Production follows the title character through a series of bawdy and playpen-political encounters. Excellent animation and montage shore up a plot which has a few howls, several chuckles and many smiles.

With an excellent vocal characterization by Skip Hinnant, Fritz lurches his amiable way through group sex encounters, police chases, black ghettos, motorcycle revolutionaries and assorted devastation of property. Rosetta Le Noire, John McCurry and Judy Engles vocalize the other characters, with as much success as Hinnant.

F

■ FROGS

1972, 90 MINS, US ◇ Ⓥ

Dir George McCowan *Prod* George Edwards, Peter Thomas *Scr* Robert Hutchison, Robert Blees *Ph* Mario Tosi *Ed* Fred R. Feitshans *Mus* Les Baxter
● Ray Milland, Sam Elliott, Joan Van Ark, Adam Roarke, Judy Pace, Lynn Borden (American International)

Frogs is a story [from an original by Robert Hutchison] of Nature striking back at man. Snakes, giant lizards, alligators, quicksand, frogs and toads, savage fish, granddad turtles.

Action takes place on a private island in the Deep South where great-grandfather Ray Milland has gathered his family at the ancestral mansion to celebrate his birthday and the Fourth of July. Instead of the usual joyousness a sense of strangeness pervades the air. Growing numbers of large frogs are beginning to appear, large lizards and strange crawling life are converging onto the estate, right up to the windows.

One by one different members of the family meet their tragic fate through violent attack. In each case it is a frightening finish.

Cast is generally firstclass and Milland's presence, though comparatively brief, is always commanding.

■ FROM HERE TO ETERNITY

1953, 118 MINS, US Ⓥ ⊙

Dir Fred Zinnemann *Prod* Buddy Adler *Scr* Daniel Taradash *Ph* Burnett Guffey *Ed* William Lyon *Mus* George Duning *Art Dir* Cary Odell
● Burt Lancaster, Montgomery Clift, Deborah Kerr, Donna Reed, Frank Sinatra, Ernest Borgnine (Columbia)

The James Jones bestseller is an outstanding motion picture in this smash screen adaptation. The bawdy vulgarity and the outhouse vocabulary, the pros and non-pros among its easy ladies, and the slambang indictment of army brass have not been emasculated in the transfer to the screen.

Burt Lancaster wallops the character of Top Sergeant Milton Warden, the professional soldier who wetnurses a weak, pompous commanding officer and the GIs under him. Montgomery Clift, with a reputation for sensitive, three-dimensional performances, adds another to his growing list as the independent GI who refuses to join the company boxing team, taking instead the 'treatment' dished out at the c.o.'s instructions. Frank Sinatra scores a decided hit as Angelo Maggio, a violent, likeable Italo-American GI.

Additional performance surprises are in the work turned in by Deborah Kerr, the nymphomaniac wife of the faithless c.o., and Donna Reed as a hostess (sic) in the New Congress Club, which furnished femme and other entertainment for relaxing soldiers.

The story opens in the summer of 1941 before Pearl Harbor with the setting Schofield Barracks, Honolulu, where much of the footage was taken. It deals with the transfer of Clift to the company under Philip Ober, the pompous, unfaithful husband of Kerr, who is interested only in getting a promotion to major, in his boxing team and extra-curricular affairs. When Clift refuses to join the boxing team, he is subjected to all the unpleasantness the idle GI mind can think up.

Eyes will moisten and throats will choke when Clift plays taps on an army bugle for his friend Sinatra after the latter dies from the brutality administered by Ernest Borgnine, the sadist sergeant in charge of the prison stockade.

☐ 1953: Best Picture, Director, Supp. Actor (Frank Sinatra), Supp. Actress (Donna Reed), Screenplay, B&W Cinematography, Sound Recording, Editing

☐ Nominations: Best Actor (Burt Lancaster, Montgomery Clift), Actress (Deborah Kerr), B&W Costume Design, Scoring of a Dramatic Picture

■ FROM NOON TILL THREE

1976, 98 MINS, US ◇ Ⓥ

Dir Frank D. Gilroy *Prod* Mike Frankovich *Scr* Frank D. Gilroy *Ph* Lucien Ballard *Ed* Maury Winetrobe *Mus* Elmer Bernstein *Art Dir* Robert Clatworthy
● Charles Bronson, Jill Ireland, Douglas V. Fowley, Stan Haze, Damon Douglas, Hector Morales (United Artists)

From Noon till Three is an offbeat and amiable, if uneven and structurally awkward, western comedy. Frank D. Gilroy scripted his novel and directed the good-looking production.

Film stars Charles Bronson as an amateur bank robber whose mistaken death supports a worldwide romantic legend, and Jill Ireland, beneficiary of the fantasy.

Bronson is a frontier drifter recruited into the bank robber gang headed by Douglas V. Fowley. En route, Bronson has a dream of a heist, later spoiled by an aware townsfolk. That's enough for him to stay behind at widow Ireland's prairie home when his horse goes lame.

He and the widow evolve from antagonism to the beginning of love, when news arrives that the Fowley gang is caught.

■ FROM RUSSIA WITH LOVE

1963, 110 MINS, UK ◇ Ⓥ ⊙

Dir Terence Young *Prod* Harry Saltzman, Albert R. Broccoli *Scr* Richard Maibaum, Johanna Harwood *Ph* Ted Moore *Ed* Peter Hunt *Mus* John Barry *Art Dir* Syd Cain
● Sean Connery, Daniela Bianchi, Pedro Armendariz, Lotte Lenya, Robert Shaw, Bernard Lee (Eon)

From Russia with Love is a preposterous, skillful slab of hardhitting, sexy hokum. After a slowish start, it is directed by Terence Young at zingy pace.

This one has to do with Sean Connery being detailed to go to Istanbul and lift a top secret Russian decoding machine from the embassy. British Intelligence senses that this may be a trap, but getting the machine is important. Connery can pull it off if he will help a young Russian cipher clerk (Daniela Bianchi) to escape to the West. She thinks she is working for her Russian government, but actually she is a pawn of Spectre, an international crime syndicate.

Bond has a glorious slap-up fight to the death with Robert Shaw, the killer detailed to bump him off. He is hounded by a helicopter as he runs across moorland clutching the decoding machine. He beats off his pursuers in a motor boat by setting fire to the sea. He referees a fight between two jealous gypsy girls just before the encampment is invaded by the crime gang.

Connery is well served by some crisp wisecracking dialog by Richard Maibaum. Robert Shaw is an impressive, icy, implacable killer and the late Pedro Armendariz weighs in with a formidable, yet lightly played, performance as the man who knows the sinister secrets of Istanbul.

The distaff side is less well served. Newcomer Daniela Bianchi is a good looking Italian girl with shapely legs and promising smile. Lotte Lenya has been lumbered with a part that doesn't fully come off. Disguised with an Eaton Crop and heavy pebble spectacles, she stands out as somebody up to no good from the first glimpse.

■ FROM THE TERRACE

1960, 144 MINS, US ◇ Ⓥ ⊙

Dir Mark Robson *Prod* Mark Robson *Scr* Ernest Lehman *Ph* Leo Tover *Ed* Dorothy Spencer *Mus* Elmer Bernstein *Art Dir* Lyle R. Wheeler, Maurice Ransford, Howard Richman
● Paul Newman, Joanne Woodward, Myrna Loy, Ina Balin, Leon Ames, Felix Aylmer (20th Century-Fox)

It's apparent that scripter Ernest Lehman faced a Herculean task in condensing John O'Hara's fat novel to the exigencies of the screen. On the assumption that Lehman followed the O'Hara story closely, the blame must be placed squarely on the novelist, for *From The Terrace* builds up to one big cliche.

The picture is the study of one man's pursuit of success and money. During his climb up the Wall Street ladder, he neglects his wife, sacrifices his integrity, and unrelentingly pursues his goal. But in keeping with American popular culture, he is overcome at end by the moment of truth.

Mark Robson's old-fashioned approach to the direction is no help. He has his characters speaking in sepulchral tones, particularly in the scenes between Paul Newman and Ina Balin, as if to give their conversations a world-shaking meaning. They seem to be reciting blank verse in a background of soft hearts-and-flowers music.

Woodward is excellent as the wife who married Newman despite the objections of her socially-prominent family. There is a strong indication that the marriage is based more on sexual attraction than on deeper love. Balin, a dark-haired beauty, makes a nice contrast to blonde Woodward. However, she plays her role with such a dedicated seriousness that it is difficult to believe.

■ FROM THIS DAY FORWARD

1946, 96 MINS, US

Dir John Berry *Prod* William L. Pereira *Scr* Hugo Butler *Ph* George Barnes *Ed* Frank Doyle *Mus* Leigh Harline *Art Dir* Albert S. D'Agostino, Alfred H. Herman
● Joan Fontaine, Mark Stevens, Rosemary DeCamp, Bobby Driscoll (RKO)

Story unfolds in flashback. This makes it sometimes difficult to follow as a whole, but there can be no quarrel with the merit of presentation and acting of the individual sequences. Plot deals with marriage of a young couple, fear for their security, the draft and the husband's return to establish himself again. Scenes show a soldier's mind as he goes through the redtape of government employment centers for the veteran.

Joan Fontaine and Mark Stevens are the young couple. Under John Berry's direction they make real the courtship, marriage and marital existence of the two young people.

Hugo Butler rates smart credit for his scripting job, working from adaptation by Garson Kanin, based on Thomas Bell's novel, *All Brides Are Beautiful*.

■ FRONT, THE

1976, 94 MINS, US ◇ Ⓥ ⊙

Dir Martin Ritt *Prod* Martin Ritt *Scr* Walter Bernstein *Ph* Michael Chapman *Ed* Sidney Levin *Mus* Dave Grusin *Art Dir* Charles Bailey
● Woody Allen, Zero Mostel, Herschel Bernardi, Michael Murphy, Andrea Marcovicci, Remak Ramsay (Columbia)

The Front is a disappointing drama about showbiz blacklisting. The offbeat casting of Woody Allen, as a perennial loser who lends his name and person to blacklisted writers, is far more showmanlike than successful.

Michael Murphy, very good as an Allen chum from high-school days, gets Allen to put his name on scripts for live TV producer Herschel Bernardi and story editor Andrea Marcovicci, latter becoming the target of Allen's emotions. Lloyd Gough and David Margulies also feed their scripts through Allen. This attracts the attention of Remak Ramsay, professional 'clearance consultant' to the network where Scott McKay is the liaison exec.

The real-life story of the blacklist in NY-based broadcasting is certainly not unfamiliar to several of the filmmakers here.

☐ 1976: Nomination: Best Original Screenplay

■ FRONT PAGE, THE

1931, 100 MINS, US ⊗

Dir Lewis Milestone   *Prod* Howard Hughes   *Scr* Bartlett Cormack, Charles Lederer   *Ph* Glen MacWilliams, Hal Mohr, Tony Gaudio   *Ed* W. Duncan Mansfield   *Art Dir* Richard Day

● Adolphe Menjou, Pat O'Brien, Mary Brian, Edward Everett Horton, Walter Catlett, George E. Stone (Caddo/United Artists)

A very entertaining picture. Action is here all of the time, even with and during the dialog. All of it is contained within a single setting, the press room at the court house. It's of newspaper men, waiting in the press room for a hanging the following morning at 7a.m. General tenor may be taken from one of the reporters asking the sheriff if he can't advance the hanging to 5a.m. so the story can make the first edition.

The star reporter for the *Post* is between love and a good story all the while. He has arranged for a wedding in New York, bought the tickets, but is obliged through the breaks and conniving of his managing editor to keep the girl and her mother waiting while he continues to be the reporter.

Lewis Milestone's big idea appears to have been to keep it moving, and he does. It's a panorama of blended action without fireworks.

A standout performance, one of three, is by Adolphe Menjou as the managing editor. He's the cold-blooded story man, knowing only news and believing nothing should ever get in its way. Next is Mae Clarke as Molly, a prostie who is the murderer's only sympathizer. The third is Pat O'Brien as the star reporter, who maintains the same even tempo of liveliness in his work and love making.

Ben Hecht and Charles MacArthur turned out a stage wallop that lasted a long while through George Kaufman's stage direction, but Bartlett Cormack's adaptation for the screen, with Milestone, improves the original.
□ 1930/31: Nominations: Best Picture, Director, Actor (Adolphe Menjou)

■ FRONT PAGE, THE

1974, 105 MINS, US ◇ ⊗ ⊙

Dir Billy Wilder   *Prod* Paul Monash   *Scr* Billy Wilder, I.A.L. Diamond   *Ph* Jordan S. Cronenweth   *Ed* Ralph E. Winters   *Mus* Billy May (adapt.)   *Art Dir* Henry Bumstead

● Jack Lemmon, Walter Matthau, Carol Burnett, Susan Sarandon, Vincent Gardenia, David Wayne (Universal)

The reteaming of Jack Lemmon and Walter Matthau, in a Billy Wilder remake of a famous 1920s period newspaper story, *The Front Page*, with a featured spot by Carol Burnett, sure looks good on paper. But that's about the only place it looks good. The production has the slick, machine-tooled look of certain assembly line automobiles that never quite seem to work smoothly.

The 1928 play by Ben Hecht and Charles MacArthur has, in this third screen version, been 'liberated' from old Production code restraints. The extent of the liberation appears to be in the tedious use of undeleted expletives.

The basic story takes place in a Chicago police press room on the eve of a politically-railroaded execution of a supposed radical who killed a cop in a scuffle.

Matthau and Lemmon again demonstrate their fine screen empathy.

■ FRONT PAGE WOMAN

1935, 80 MINS, US

Dir Michael Curtiz   *Prod* Samuel Bischoff   *Scr* Laird Doyle   *Ph* Tony Gaudio   *Ed* Terry Morse   *Mus* Heinz Roemheld

● Bette Davis, George Brent, June Martel, Dorothy Dare, Joseph Crehan, Winifred Shaw (Warner)

As the title indicates, this is a newspaper yarn and a completely screwy one. Lacks authenticity and is so far fetched it'll hand newsscribes around the country a constant run of ripples. But it's light and has some funny lines and situations [from a story by Richard Macauley, adapted by Roy Chanslor and Lillie Hayward].

George Brent and Bette Davis are working for opposition papers. They're in love but always trying to outdo each other on stories. They keep topping each other on one story or another for the entire length of the film and then clinch in a truce.

But there are some laughs. And there are grand performances by Davis, Brent, Winifred Shaw and Joseph Crehan. And nice bit work by Roscoe Karns, J. Farrell MacDonald, Addison Richards, Walter Walker, Dorothy Dare, June Martel and Mike Morita.

■ FUGITIVE, THE

1947, 99 MINS, US ◇ ⊗ ⊙

Dir John Ford   *Prod* John Ford, Merian C. Cooper   *Scr* Dudley Nichols   *Ph* Gabriel Figueroa   *Ed* Jack Murray   *Mus* Richard Hageman   *Art Dir* Alfred Ybarra

● Henry Fonda, Dolores Del Rio, Pedro Armendariz, J. Carrol Naish, Leo Carrillo, Robert Armstrong (Argosy/RKO)

Made in Mexico with Hollywood leads and native extras, *The Fugitive* tells how the government of one of the Mexican states, in a ruthless drive to stamp out religion, hunts down the last remaining priest, captures him by a cruel ruse and has him executed by a firing squad. The picture is rich in atmosphere and is sincerely done, but it is slow in spots and uneven in dramatic power.

According to the opening screen narration, *The Fugitive* is a true story, with Biblical overtones and with 'topical, timely and universal' qualities. It is apparently based on the efforts of the Mexican government 20-odd years ago to curtail the power of the Catholic church and control its priests. But it will probably be widely regarded as an attack on Communism.

Parts of the story [from Graham Greene's novel *The Labyrinthine Ways*, also published as *The Power and the Glory*] aren't clear. The government's drive against the church, for instance, isn't fully motivated. In addition, there is a character of an American bandit-murderer (Ward Bond) whose function isn't satisfactorily established, but who risks his life in helping the fleeing priest to reach temporary haven.

The Fugitive is handsomely photographed, with colorful village scenes and impressive landscapes. Henry Fonda is expressive in the subdued and somewhat static role of the priest. Dolores Del Rio is decorative and mutely impassioned as a devout victim of the law.

■ FUGITIVE KIND, THE

1960, 119 MINS, US ⊗

Dir Sidney Lumet   *Prod* Martin Jarow, Richard A. Shepherd   *Scr* Tennessee Williams, Meade Roberts   *Ph* Boris Kaufman   *Ed* Carl Lerner   *Mus* Kenyon Hopkins

● Marlon Brando, Anna Magnani, Joanne Woodward, Maureen Stapleton, Victor Jory, R.G. Armstrong (United Artists)

Another helping from Tennessee Williams' seemingly inexhaustible closet of mixed-up southern skeletons is exposed here with only occasional flashes of cinematic power.

The Fugitive Kind is not basically one of Williams' better works and, as directed by Sidney Lumet, it sputters more often than it sizzles. The combination of Marlon Brando and Anna Magnani fails to generate the electricity hoped for. Joanne Woodward, looking

like a battered fugitive from skid row, pops in and out of the story to provide a distasteful and often ludicrous extra dash of degeneracy.

The only fully rounded character is that of Lady Torrance portrayed by Magnani with a faded veneer of lustfulness. At least one can understand her frustration and loneliness, being married to a dying older man she doesn't love, and her bitterness toward fellow townsfolk, her father having died trying to save his wine garden set afire by vigilantes because he sold liquor to Negroes.

Brando's role as a disillusioned guitar-singer, who becomes involved, as hired hand and lover, with Lady in a small Mississippi town while trying to put aside the wild life he experienced in New Orleans hot spots, is less clearly defined. Brando is back to mumbling with marbles in his mouth too often.

Much of the picture was filmed on location in Milton, New York, and at the Gold Medal Studios in the Bronx. Boris Kaufman's photography is good.

■ FULL METAL JACKET

1987, 116 MINS, US ◇ ⊗ ⊙

Dir Stanley Kubrick   *Prod* Stanley Kubrick   *Scr* Stanley Kubrick, Michael Herr, Gustav Hasford   *Ph* Douglas Milsome   *Ed* Martin Hunter   *Mus* Abigail Mead [= Vivian Kubrick]   *Art Dir* Anton Furst

● Matthew Modine, Adam Baldwin, Vincent D'Onofrio, Lee Ermey, Dorian Harewood, Arliss Howard (Warner)

Stanley Kubrick's *Full Metal Jacket* is an intense, schematic, superbly made Vietnam War drama.

Like the source material, Gustav Hasford's ultra-violent novel *The Short-Timers*, Kubrick's picture is strikingly divided into two parts. First 44 minutes are set exclusively in a Marine Corps basic training camp, while remaining 72 minutes embrace events surrounding the 1968 Tet Offensive and skirmishing in the devastated city of Hue.

While it doesn't develop a particularly strong narrative line, script is loaded with vivid, outrageously vulgar military vernacular that contributes heavily to the film's power.

Performances by the all-male cast (save for a couple of Vietnamese hookers) are also exceptional. Surrounded on one side by humorously macho types such as Cowboy and Rafterman, Matthew Modine holds the center effectively by embodying both what it takes to survive in the war and a certain omniscience.
□ 1987: Nomination: Best Adapted Screenplay

■ FULL MOON IN BLUE WATER

1988, 94 MINS, US ◇ ⊗ ⊙

Dir Peter Masterson   *Prod* Lawrence Turman, David Foster, John Turman   *Scr* Bill Bozzone   *Ph* Fred Murphy   *Ed* Jill Savitt   *Mus* Phil Marshall

● Gene Hackman, Teri Garr, Burgess Meredith, Elias Koteas, Kevin Cooney, David Doty (Turman-Foster)

An interesting cast is stranded in this utterly ordinary film about a man who thinks he has nothing to live for being saved by the woman who loves him.

Story centers around Floyd (Gene Hackman), the proprietor of the Blue Water Grill, a run-down Texas Saloon. Floyd spends his time watching home movies of his wife Dorothy who disappeared the year before and is presumed dead.

The main people in his life are the wheelchair-bound general (Burgess Meredith); Jimmy (Elias Koteas), the mentally disturbed young man who looks after the general; and Louise (Teri Garr), a school bus driver who, inexplicably, carries a torch for Floyd. Main drive to the plot is a plan to cheat Floyd out of his property by not letting him know that land values are about to rise due to the construction of a bridge to the mainland.

Pic is very stagebound, with most of the action taking place at the Blue Water, and twists of the plot largely seem created to give the characters something to do. Cast does what they can with material, but principals are largely stuck with barely developed characters.

■ **FUNERAL IN BERLIN**

1967, 102 MINS, UK ◇ ⑲ ⊙
Dir Guy Hamilton   *Prod* Charles Kasher   *Scr* Evan Jones   *Ph* Otto Heller   *Ed* John Bloom   *Mus* Konrad Elfers   *Art Dir* Ken Adam
● Michael Caine, Paul Hubschmid, Oscar Homolka, Eva Renzi, Guy Doleman, Rachel Gurney (Paramount/Saltzman)

Funeral in Berlin is the second presentation of the exploits of Harry Palmer, the soft-sell sleuth, this time enmeshed in Berlin counter-espionage. Michael Caine encores in the role that made him a star. Excellent scripting, direction and performances, plus colorful and realistic production, add up to surprise-filled suspense, relieved adroitly by subtle irony. Len Deighton's novel has been adapted by Evan Jones to a taut, economical screenplay, just right for the semi-documentary feel.

Herein, amidst a clutch of running gags which never wear out their appeal, Caine is sent to East Berlin, where Communist spy chief Oscar Homolka is making the motions of trying to defect. Paul Hubschmid is the local British contact for Caine, and Eva Renzi pops up as an undercover agent for Israel, tracking down Nazis before statutes of limitation run out.

This being a well-developed suspenser, few people are as they seem, including prissy-pedantic Hugh Burden, a secret documents clerk in Doleman's British spy group.

■ **FUNHOUSE, THE**

1981, 96 MINS, US ◇ ⑲ ⊙
Dir Tobe Hooper   *Prod* Derek Power, Steven Bernhardt   *Scr* Larry Block   *Ph* Andrew Laszlo   *Ed* Jack Hofstra   *Mus* John Beal   *Art Dir* Morton Rabinowitz
● Elizabeth Berridge, Cooper Huckabee, Sylvia Miles, Largo Woodruff, William Finley, Kevin Conway (Universal)

The Funhouse is a spitty movie, full of great expectorations. That is, there's more drool on view than blood, which is a new twist for the horror genre.

Set-up is a variation on the old dark house premise, as four pot-smoking teens work up the nerve to spend the night in the spooky funhouse of a traveling carnival. After some hanky panky in the midst of goblins and skeletons, kids witness a carny Frankenstein being serviced by, then strangling, fortune teller Sylvia Miles, upon which malevolent barker Kevin Conway locks them in for a night of unanticipated chills and thrills.

For all the elegance of photography, pic has nothing in particular up its sleeves, and devotees of director Tobe Hooper's *The Texas Chain Saw Massacre* will be particularly disappointed with the almost total lack of shocks and mayhem.

■ **FUN IN ACAPULCO**

1963, 100 MINS, US ◇ ⑲
Dir Richard Thorpe   *Prod* Hal Wallis   *Scr* Allan Weiss   *Ph* Daniel L. Fapp   *Ed* Stanley E. Johnson   *Mus* Joseph J. Lilley   *Art Dir* Hal Pereira, Walter Tyler
● Elvis Presley, Ursula Andress, Elsa Cardenas, Paul Lukas, Alejandro Rey (Paramount)

Elvis Presley fans won't be disappointed – he sings serviceable songs and wiggles a bit to boot. However, Presley is deserving of better material than has been provided in this screenplay in which he portrays an ex-trapeze catcher who has lost his nerve after a fatal mishap.

Arriving in Acapulco, he hires on as an entertainer-life guard at a resort, in hopes the latter job may afford him the opportunity to dive off the high board and erase his fear of heights. A romantic entanglement leads to the moment of truth.

The other three-fourths of the central romantic quartet are Ursula Andress, Elsa Cardenas and Alejandro Rey, fine-looking specimens, all. Others of note in the cast are Paul Lukas as an ex-duke-turned-chef and young Larry Domasin as a business-minded urchin more or less adopted by Presley.

Richard Thorpe's direction keeps the routine story on the move, a strong asset since opportunity for developing characterization is virtually nil.

■ **FUNNY ABOUT LOVE**

1990, 101 MINS, US ◇ ⑲ ⊙
Dir Leonard Nimoy   *Prod* Jon Avnet, Jordan Kerner   *Scr* Norman Steinberg, David Frankel   *Ph* Fred Murphy   *Ed* Peter E. Berger   *Mus* Miles Goodman   *Art Dir* Stephen Storer
● Gene Wilder, Christine Lahti, Mary Stuart Masterson, Robert Prosky, Anne Jackson, Susan Ruttan (Paramount)

Funny about Love is a not-so-funny Gene Wilder vehicle. Tale of the biological clock regarding procreation is told from a male point of view here. However, Wilder's problems as a would-be-daddy aren't interesting or compelling.

Inability to conceive with wife Christine Lahti bogs the film down in almost clinical detail. Funniest bit has Wilder sticking ice cubes in his jockey shorts on doctor's advice to get his sperm temperature down.

Film takes an absurd turn in the third reel when Wilder's child bride of a mother (Anne Jackson) is killed by a falling stove (meant to be black humor). Pic hardly recovers from this failed bit of whimsy.

Co-star Mary Stuart Masterson doesn't enter the scene until a full hour has elapsed. Wilder meets her at a convention of beautiful sorority girls where he's guest speaker. Another whirlwind romance ensues, and Masterson is pregnant.

Wilder has his moments in a role that overdoes the crying jags and self-pity. Both Lahti and Masterson remain most appealing actresses in search of challenging roles, not provided here.

■ **FUNNY FACE**

1957, 103 MINS, US ◇ ⑲ ⊙
Dir Stanley Donen   *Prod* Roger Edens   *Scr* Leonard Gershe   *Ph* Ray June   *Ed* Frank Bracht   *Mus* Adolph Deutsch (adapt.)   *Art Dir* Hal Pereira, George W. Davis
● Audrey Hepburn, Fred Astaire, Kay Thompson, Michel Auclair, Robert Flemyng, Suzy Parker (Paramount)

While it wears the title and bears several of the songs, *Funny Face*'s relationship to the Broadway musical [of 1927] stops right there. With a different book and new, added tunes, this is a lightly diverting, modish, Parisian-located tintuner.

Originally slated for production at Metro, film moved to Paramount as a package so Audrey Hepburn could have the femme lead opposite Fred Astaire. This May-November pairing gives the production the benefits of Astaire's debonair style and terp accomplishments, and the sensitive acting talents of Hepburn.

Hepburn's plays a bookish introvert who is suddenly swept from her literary existence in a Greenwich Village shop to a heady, high fashion round of Paris when she's discovered by glamor photog Astaire.

Style runs rampant, with Hubert de Givenchy creating the Paris wardrobe worn by Hepburn as a model, while Edith Head takes care of things elsewhere. Tune-wise, there are six George and Ira Gershwin numbers from the stage musical and five from producer Roger Edens and scripter Leonard Gershe. All are either sung or used as backing for dance numbers, with director Stanley Donen handling the song staging while Astaire and Eugene Loring take care of the choreography.

□ 1957: Nominations: Best Original Story & Screenplay, Cinematography, Costume Design, Art Direction

■ **FUNNY FARM**

1988, 101 MINS, US ◇ ⑲
Dir George Roy Hill   *Prod* Robert I. Crawford   *Scr* Jeffrey Boam   *Ph* Miroslav Ondricek   *Ed* Alan Heim   *Mus* Elmer Bernstein   *Art Dir* Henry Bumstead
● Chevy Chase, Madolyn Smith, Kevin O'Morrison, Joseph Maher, Jack Gilpin, Brad Sullivan (Warner)

Chevy Chase tones down his goofy shtick, moves to the country with wife Madolyn Smith and has an occasional humorous encounter or two with the locals in *Funny Farm*. As pleasant yuppie comedies go, this is about par.

Chase is a sportswriter with ambitions as a novelist. The wife is a schoolteacher with no other apparent ambitions, except initially to make the clapboard home cozy with chintz and antiques from the local shop of nearby Redbud.

Along with the fact that Chase suffers from writer's block and then when he does manage to crank it out, his wife lets him know it's awful, none of the townsfolk are even friendly. This really goads him and he takes to the bottle.

Director George Roy Hill shows little distinction with this material [from Jay Cronley's book], but then again, the material here isn't very distinctive. Some of the setups work better than others, though most are of the sitcom variety.

■ **FUNNY GIRL**

1968, 145 MINS, US ◇ ⑲ ⊙
Dir William Wyler   *Prod* William Wyler, Ray Stark   *Scr* Isobel Lennart   *Ph* Harry Stradling   *Ed* Robert Swink   *Mus* Walter Scharf (sup.)   *Art Dir* Gene Callahan
● Barbra Streisand, Omar Sharif, Kay Medford, Anne Francis, Walter Pidgeon, Lee Allen (Columbia/Rastar)

Barbra Streisand in her Hollywood debut makes a marked impact. The saga of the tragi-comedienne Fanny Brice of the ungainly mien and manner, charmed by the suave card-sharp Nick Arnstein, is perhaps of familiar pattern, but it is to the credit of all concerned that it plays so convincingly.

Streisand's basic Grecian-profiled personality has not been photographically camouflaged.

The projection of Fanny Brice's rise from the pushcart-laden lower East Side to Ziegfeld stardom and a baronial Long Island estate is achieved in convincing broad strokes.

The durable Jule Styne-Bob Merrill songs, from the [1964] stage score, are given fuller enhancement under the flexibility of the cinematic sweep.

'People,' 'You Are Woman, I Am Man,' 'Don't Rain on my Parade,' 'I'm the Greatest Star' have been enhanced by the original Broadway songsmiths with 'Roller Skate Rag' a parody on 'The Swan' ballet and a title song, not part of the original score.

□ 1968: Best Actress (Barbra Streisand).
□ Nominations: Best Picture, Supp. Actress (Kay Medford), Cinematography, Editing, Scoring of a Musical Picture, Song ('Funny Girl'), Sound

■ FUNNY LADY

1975, 136 MINS, US ◇ ⍟ ⊙
Dir Herbert Ross *Prod* Ray Stark *Scr* Jay Presson
Allen, Arnold Schulman *Ph* James Wong Howe
Ed Marion Rothman *Mus* Peter Matz (arr.)
Art Dir George Jenkins
● Barbra Streisand, James Caan, Omar Sharif, Roddy
McDowall, Ben Vereen, Carole Wells (Rastar/Columbia)

Barbra Streisand was outstanding as the
younger Fanny Brice in *Funny Girl*, and in
Funny Lady she's even better. Ray Stark's extremely handsome period production also
stars James Caan in an excellent characterization of Billy Rose, the second major influence in Brice's personal life.

The story [by Arnold Schulman] picks up
Brice in 1930, an established Ziegfeld star in
a career lull as her mentor has trouble finding depression-era backing. Enter Rose, the
brash comer who learns some showmanship
savvy from her and marries her, after which
the two drift apart as public careers and personal attachments diverge.

The plot is partially fictionalized in its apparent main thrust of showing how Brice finally purged her first love, for gambler Nick
Arnstein (Omar Sharif), but in the process
lost Rose as well. Thereafter, she was prepared to go it alone, a perfect hook for
firstrate dramatic climax.

More than half a dozen older songs, on
which Billy Rose's name appears as one of the
authors, are used to good advantage. [Music
and lyrics of new songs are by John Kander
and Fred Ebb.]

The film cost about $8.5 million to which
Columbia contributed about $4.9 million and
the rest from one of those tax shelter consor-
tia.
□ 1975: Nominations: Best Cinematography,
Costume Design, Adapted Score, Song ('How
Lucky Can You Get'), Sound

■ FUNNY THING HAPPENED ON THE WAY TO THE FORUM, A

1966, 99 MINS, US ◇ ⍟ ⊙
Dir Richard Lester *Prod* Melvin Frank *Scr* Melvin
Frank, Michael Pertwee *Ph* Nicolas Roeg *Ed* John
Victor Smith *Mus* Ken Thorne (arr.) *Art Dir* Tony
Walton
● Zero Mostel, Phil Silvers, Buster Keaton, Jack Gilford,
Michael Crawford, Annette Andre (Quadrangle/United
Artists)

A Funny Thing Happened on the Way to the Forum
– after the [1962 Stephen Sondheim] stage
musicomedy of the same name – will probably
stand out as one of the few originals of two
repetition-weary genres, the film musical
comedy and the toga-cum-sandal 'epic'. Flip,
glib and sophisticated, yet rump-slappingly
bawdy and fast-paced, *Forum* is a capricious
look at the seamy underside of classical Rome
through a 20th-century hipster's shades.

Plot follows the efforts of a glib, con-man
slave, Pseudolus (Zero Mostel), to cheat, steal
or connive his freedom from a domineering
mistress, Domina (Patricia Jessel), and his
equally victimized master, the henpecked
Senex (Michael Hordern). Unwilling ally,
through blackmail, is the timorous toady
Hysterium (Jack Gilford), another household
slave.

Early instrument of Pseudolus' plot is the
callow Hero (Michael Crawford), who, smitten by one of the luscious courtesans peddled
by Lycus (Phil Silvers), local flesh supplier,
promises Mostel his freedom if he can finagle
the 'virgin's' purchase. Plot complications
multiply like the film's pratfalls, however, and
the winsome object of Hero's passion has already been sold to the egomaniacal Miles
(Leon Greene), a legion captain of legendary
ferocity, who thunders onto the scene to
claim the girl.

Interwoven through the plot is the presence

of Erronius (Buster Keaton) who, searching
for his lost children, unties the knotted situation.
□ 1966: Best Adapted Score

■ FUN WITH DICK AND JANE

1977, 95 MINS, US ◇ ⍟
Dir Ted Kotcheff *Prod* Peter Bart, Max Palevsky
Scr David Giler, Jerry Belson, Mordecai Richler *Ph* Fred
Koenekamp *Ed* Danford B. Greene *Mus* Ernest Gold
Art Dir James G. Hulsey
● George Segal, Jane Fonda, Ed McMahon, Dick
Gautier, Allan Miller, Hank Garcia (Columbia)

Fun with Dick and Jane is a great comedy idea
[from a story by Gerald Gaiser] largely shot
down by various bits of tastelessness, crudity
and nastiness. Stars George Segal and Jane
Fonda are an upper middle-class family which
turns to armed robbery when hubby loses his
aerospace job.

Fonda and Segal have all the basic comedy
essentials necessary to fulfill the minimum
demands of the story, and that seems to be
the problem: they seem to have gotten no
help from direction and/or writing in getting
off the ground.

Ed McMahon is terrific as Segal's employer
whose boozy bonhomie conceals the heart of a
true Watergater. Making this essentially
shallow and hypocritical character into a fascinating figure of corporate logrolling was a
major challenge.

■ FURIES, THE

1950, 109 MINS, US
Dir Anthony Mann *Prod* Hal Wallis *Scr* Charles
Schnee *Ph* Victor Milner *Ed* Archie Marshek
Mus Franz Waxman
● Barbara Stanwyck, Wendell Corey, Walter Huston,
Judith Anderson, Gilbert Roland (Paramount)

The Furies is a big-scale western drama, expertly put together by Hal Wallis. Story is the
familiar one about cattle barons and sprawling western empires.

Picture was the final assignment for Walter
Huston and to his role of cattle baron, ruler
of vast ranch acreage and the dwellers
thereon, he brought a colorful job that adds a
lot of punch.

Story [from the novel by Niven Busch] interest falls chiefly to Barbara Stanwyck,
strong-willed daughter of Huston who takes
the place of his son in guiding the cattle empire until the father marries a conniving
widow, craftily portrayed by Judith Anderson.
Stanwyck disfigures her stepmother in a fit of
rage. She swears to break the ranch, The
Furies, and her father when he spitefully
hangs Gilbert Roland, a Mexican friend
whose family has dwelt for ages on the ranch.

While the pacing keeps the plot moving at
climax-punctuated speed, it is the dialog that
has the sock to keep the attention intrigued
for adult viewers.

■ FURY

1936, 90 MINS, US ⍟
Dir Fritz Lang *Prod* Joseph L. Mankiewicz *Scr* Bartlett
Cormack, Fritz Lang *Ph* Joseph Ruttenberg *Ed* Frank
Sullivan *Mus* Franz Waxman *Art Dir* Cedric Gibbons,
William Horning
● Sylvia Sidney, Spencer Tracy, Walter Abel, Bruce
Cabot, Edward Ellis, Walter Brennan (M-G-M)

Punchy story [by Norman Krasna] has been
masterfully guided by the skillfull direction of
the Viennese Fritz Lang. It's his first in
America and represents the culmination of a
year and a half of waiting, while being carried
on the Metro payroll, until finally finding
something to his liking. It coincides also with
the debut efforts of Joseph L. Mankiewicz as
a Metro producer.

Spencer Tracy gives his top performance as
the upright young man until he's involved in
a kidnapping mess through mistaken identity.
Escaping a necktie lynching party, the jailhouse is burned down, despite the meagre
protective efforts of the constabulary, and
legally he is dead. But somehow he had managed to escape and he is intent on vengeance
on the 22 (including one woman who had
whirled the igniting torch into the kerosened
pyre at the jailhouse door), who are ultimately brought to trial.

Walter Abel, as the state attorney, virtually
walks away with the proceedings during the
courtroom scene. Sylvia Sidney, whose tender
love scenes in the early motivations are relatively passive, rises to the proper heights in
the dramatic testimony. Tracy is capital during the somewhat slowly pacing scenes until the pseudo-lynching; then he becomes the
dominating character in the scenes where he
hides out and permits the trial to proceed.
□ 1936: Nomination: Best Original Story

■ FURY, THE

1978, 117 MINS, US ◇ ⍟ ⊙
Dir Brian De Palma *Prod* Frank Yablans *Scr* John
Farris *Ph* Richard H. Kline *Ed* Paul Hirsch *Mus* John
Williams *Art Dir* Bill Malley
● Kirk Douglas, John Cassavetes, Carrie Snodgress,
Charles Durning, Amy Irving, Fiona Lewis (20th Century-
Fox)

The Fury features Kirk Douglas and John
Cassavetes as adversaries in an elaborate
game of mind control. Director Brian De
Palma is on more ground in moving the plot
pieces around effectively.

John Farris adapted his novel for the
screen. Most viewers will enjoy the razzle-
dazzle of the lengthy pursuit by Douglas of
son Andrew Stevens, kidnapped by
Cassavetes because of his mystical powers.
But apart from a few throwaway references to
government agencies and psychic phenomena, there is never, anywhere, a coherent exposition of what all the running and jumping
is about.

Strong cast also includes Carrie Snodgress
as a staffer in Charles Durning's research institute where Amy Irving (also blessed/cursed
with psychic powers) is being readied as a
substitute for Stevens. Seems that Stevens is
freaking out, despite the attentions and care
of Fiona Lewis, and he is targeted for elimination.

■ FUTURE COP

See: *Trancers*

■ FUTURE SCHLOCK

1984, 75 MINS, AUSTRALIA ◇
Dir Barry Peak, Chris Kiely *Prod* Barry Peak, Chris Kiely
Scr Barry Peak, Chris Kiely *Ph* Malcolm Richards
Ed Robert Martin, Ray Pond *Mus* John McCubbery,
Doug Sanders *Art Dir* John McWha
● Maryanne Fahey, Michael Bishop, Tracey Callander,
Tiriel Mora, Simon Thorpe, Peter Cox (Ultimate Show)

A chaotic, anarchic punk comedy, made on a
micro-budget, but with enough going for it to
reach its target audience, *Future Schlock* is a
mess, but fun.

Set in Melbourne in the 21st century, the
pic posits a post-civil war society in which the
middleclass suburbanites defeated the non-
conformists and then walled them up in a
huge ghetto. Action centers around a ghetto
watering hole, Alvin's, where the locals meet
to do their own thing. Leading lights are
Sarah (Maryanne Fahey) and Bear (Michael
Bishop) who do a brezzy nightclub act, often
directing hostility against suburbanites who
drop by on a slumming trip.

Film is a haphazard affair, with variable

performances, uneven writing, and rough sound.

....

■ **FUTUREWORLD**

1976, 107 MINS, US ◇ ⓥ
Dir Richard T. Heffron   *Prod* Paul Lazarus III, James T. Aubrey Jr   *Scr* Mayo Simon, George Schenck
Ph Howard Schwartz, Gene Polito   *Ed* James Mitchell
Mus Fred Karlin   *Art Dir* Trevor Williams
● Peter Fonda, Blythe Danner, Arthur Hill, Yul Brynner, Jim Antonio, John Ryan (American International)

Futureworld is a strong sequel to *Westworld* in which the rebuilt pleasure dome aims at world conquest by extending the robot technology to duplicating business and political figures.

Peter Fonda and Blythe Danner come across very well in their starring roles as investigative reporters on a junket to help promote the rebuilt and enlarged theme park.

The reporters are hosted by Arthur Hill, repping the theme park owners, and John Ryan, the chief scientist. Fonda and Danner eventually discover the world domination plot with the help of Stuart Margolin, one of the few non-robot technicians still employed.

Yul Brynner makes a cameo reappearance as the robot gunslinger so prominent in *Westworld*, a good bridging element between the two pix.

....

■ **FUZZ**

1972, 92 MINS, US ◇ ⓥ
Dir Richard A. Colla   *Prod* Jack Farren   *Scr* Evan Hunter   *Ph* Jacques Marquette   *Ed* Robert Kimble
Mus Dave Grusin   *Art Dir* Hilyard Brown
● Burt Reynolds, Jack Weston, Tom Skerritt, Yul Brynner, Raquel Welch, James McEachin (Filmways/Javelin)

Fuzz has an excellent screenplay by Evan Hunter, from his 87th Precinct series written under the name Ed McBain. The basic plot line is a search for a mysterious meticulous bomber, played by Yul Brynner, who keeps killing local officials. The search is conducted against a back-drop of an urban neighborhood police station where the cops are as humanized as those under arrest or suspicion.

The assorted people involved innocently or criminally with the police are neither patronized middle-class nor anointed low-life.

There is compassion in the treatment of all characters while at the same time their foibles are milked for both laughs and occasionally chilling reality.

Burt Reynolds is very good, Jack Weston and James McEachin are excellent, and Tom Skerritt is outstanding as the principal quartet of detectives.

....

■ **F/X**

(Aka: F/X - Murder by Illusion)

1986, 106 MINS, US ◇ ⓥ ⊙
Dir Robert Mandel   *Prod* Dodi Fayed, Jack Wiener
Scr Robert T. Megginson, Gregory Fleeman   *Ph* Miroslav Ondricek   *Ed* Terry Rawlings   *Mus* Bill Conti
Art Dir Mel Bourne
● Bryan Brown, Brian Dennehy, Diane Venora, Cliff De Young, Mason Adams, Jerry Orbach (Orion)

As contrived and plot-hole ridden as it is, *F/X* still works quite effectively as a crowd-pleasing popcorn picture. Basic premise here is so strong that it proves well-nigh indestructable, even in the face of numerous implausibilities, some silly dialogue and less-than-great casting in secondary roles.

Crackerjack film special-effects man Bryan Brown is recruited by the Justice Dept to stage a phony assassination of big-time mobster Jerry Orbach, who is ready to squeal. The authorities want the Mafia to think Orbach is dead. Brown is convinced to act the role of

hitman himself, but he finds himself a marked man, the target of both government goons and New York Police.

Last 80 minutes of film constitute a relentless, multi-faceted chase, as Brown must rely on his wits and resourseful talents as an F/X wizard to elude and, ultimately, hunt down the baddies who set him up. Old-style Irish cop Brian Dennehy so flagrantly disobeys the rule book in his pursuit of justice that he gets tossed off the force. But even this doesn't stop him.

Roles are one dimensional, but Brown and Dennehy possess sufficient personality and physical presence to fill them well. Special effects, stunts and special makeup are all they intended to be - top drawer.

....

■ **F/X2**

(Aka: FX2 – The Deadly Art of Illusion)

1991, 109 MINS, US ◇ ⓥ ⊙ ⊙
Dir Richard Franklin   *Prod* Jack Wiener, Dodi Fayed
Scr Bill Condon   *Ph* Victor J. Kemper   *Ed* Andrew London, Michael Tronick   *Mus* Lalo Schifrin, Michael Boddicker   *Art Dir* John Jay Moore
● Bryan Brown, Brian Dennehy, Rachel Ticotin, Joanna Gleason, Philip Bosco, Kevin J. O'Connor (Orion)

With all the ingenuity that went into toys and gadgetry in this five-years-removed sequel, it's a shame no one bothered to hook a brain up to the plot. Beyond the engaging leads, there's little here on the level that made 1986's *F/X* so entertaining, as the sequel throttles a stale police-corruption setup loaded with genre cliches.

Because the pic's basic conceit is so simple – a film effects man using his 'reel' skills to thwart dense public officials and criminals – the story actually gets off to a rather slow start, as the semiretired Rollie Tyler (Bryan Brown) is talked into participating in a police sting operation by his g.f.'s ex-husband (Tom Mason).

The operation goes haywire, the ex-husband is killed and Tyler starts looking into the intrigue behind it. In over his head, he recruits the help of Leo (Brian Dennehy), the cop he teamed with at the end of the first pic.

The lack of an interesting villain also hurts. Philip Bosco is more a comic foil than anything else, while other bad guys are merely shadowy mob types left on the film's fringe.

Dennehy remains one of the more effortlessly likable actors around, while Brown may be a little too self-assured this time in using his fantasy skills in life-or-death situations.

....

■ **GABLE AND LOMBARD**

1976, 131 MINS, US ◇ ⓥ
Dir Sidney J. Furie   *Prod* Harry Korshak   *Scr* Barry Sandler   *Ph* Jordan S. Cronenweth   *Ed* Argyle Nelson
Mus Michel Legrand   *Art Dir* Edward C. Carfagno
● James Brolin, Jill Clayburgh, Allen Garfield, Red Buttons, Melanie Mayron, Joanne Linville (Universal)

Gable and Lombard is a film with many major assets, not the least of which is the stunning and smashing performance of Jill Clayburgh as Carole Lombard. James Brolin manages excellently to project the necessary Clark Gable attributes while adding his own individuality to the characterization.

Sidney J. Furie's direction of handsome period production supplies zest as well as romance to the tragi-comedy aspects of the two stars' offscreen life together.

Barry Sandler's original screenplay conveys the excitement and fun of an era when everyone seemed to enjoy themselves in the profession of making pictures.

Gable and Lombard is candid without being prurient; delightful without being superficially glossy; heart-warming without being corny.

....

■ **GABRIEL OVER THE WHITE HOUSE**

1933, 83 MINS, US
Dir Gregory La Cava   *Prod* [Walter Wanger]   *Scr* Carey Wilson, Bertram Bloch   *Ph* Bert Glennon   *Ed* Basil Wrangell   *Mus* William Axt   *Art Dir* Cedric Gibbons
● Walter Huston, Karen Morley, Franchot Tone, Arthur Byron, Dickie Moore, C. Henry Gordon (M-G-M/Cosmopolitan)

A mess of political tripe superlatively hoked up into a picture of strong popular possibilities, Walter Wanger's first Metro production as a supervisor is a cleverly executed commercial release [from the anonymous novel of the same name].

A new President (Walter Huston), up to then a pretty practical politician, is dying after an automobile smash and is miraculously revived. Divine intervention stays the hand of the reaper and brings the President back to lead the nation and the world out of the trials of depression.

The resurrected President goes before Congress in a big scene, asks to be made a dictator to deal with the emergency, and when Congress refuses he declares martial law and takes control. While all these sprightly doings are in process the President's girl secretary (Karen Morley) and his young aide (Franchot Tone) fall in love.

Huston plays the part so persuasively that witnesses will be tricked into accepting its monstrous exaggerations. Tone, young newcomer for whom Metro has high hopes, and Morley, a satisfying player in almost any sort of an assignment, carry what amount to walk-on parts and make them look like leads.

....

■ **GAILY, GAILY**

(UK: Chicago, Chicago)

1969, 100 MINS, US ◇
Dir Norman Jewison   *Prod* Norman Jewison
Scr Abram S. Ginnes   *Ph* Richard Kline   *Ed* Ralph Winters   *Mus* Henry Mancini   *Art Dir* Robert Boyle
● Beau Bridges, Melina Mercouri, Brian Keith, George Kennedy, Hume Cronyn, Margot Kidder (Mirisch-Cartier)

Ben Hecht's pseudo-reminiscences of a cub reporter in 1910 Chicago emerges on the screen as a lushly staged, handsomely produced, largely unfunny comedy.

F

Director-producer Norman Jewison seemingly works on the comedic theory that nothing succeeds like excess. The very basic decision to play *Gaily, Gaily* broadly as possible, lay it on with a trowel, divorces the film from the realities of 1910 Chicago.

Based on Hecht's book *Gaily, Gaily* the situations and characters are unbelievable, and because they are, they are unfunny. The paradox is that Jewison sets the stage and Richard Kline photographs it with a lover's eye for the richness, earthiness, brawling vitality and raw meat of the era. The sets, costuming and resurrected locations in Chicago and Milwaukee are a glorious period pageant.

□ 1969: Nominations: Best Costume Design, Art Direction, Sound

••••••••••••••••••••••••••••••••••

■ **GALLIPOLI**

1981, 110 MINS, AUSTRALIA ◇ ⊛ ⊙
Dir Peter Weir   *Prod* Robert Stigwood, Patricia Lovell
Scr David Williamson   *Ph* Russell Boyd   *Ed* William Anderson   *Mus* Brian May   *Art Dir* Wendy Weir
● Mel Gibson, Mark Lee, Bill Kerr, Robert Grubb, Bill Hunter, David Argue (Associated R&R)

Against a backdrop broader than his previous outings, Weir has fashioned what is virtually an intimate epic [from his own screen story]. A very big picture by Aussie standards, the film is all the same a finely-considered story focussing closely on the relationship that builds between Frank (Mel Gibson) and Archy (Mark Lee), and how it is affected by events on the battlefield of Gallipoli.

Gallipoli is as much an essential part of the Australian ethos as, say The Alamo is to Texas: a military defeat that became rationalized over the years into a moral victory. In April 1915 a combined force of Australian and New Zealand troops numbering about 35,000 joined an Allied attempt to control the Dardanelles waterway by capturing Istanbul. Bungling by the generals allowed the Turks time to dig in and the landings devolved into stalemate, but not before much bitter fighting.

The Australian-New Zealand Army Corps in great part bore the brunt of the bitterest exchanges. Thus Peter Weir's *Gallipoli* tackles a legend in human terms and emerges as a highly entertaining drama on a number of levels, none of them inaccessible to anyone unfamiliar with the actual events.

••••••••••••••••••••••••••••••••••

■ **GAMBIT**

1966, 107 MINS, US ◇ ⊛
Dir Ronald Neame   *Prod* Leo L. Fuchs   *Scr* Jack Davies, Alvin Sargent   *Ph* Clifford Stine   *Ed* Alma Macrorie
Mus Maurice Jarre   *Art Dir* Alexander Golitzen, George C. Webb
● Shirley MacLaine, Michael Caine, Herbert Lom, Roger C. Carmel, Arnold Moss, John Abbott (Universal)

Shirley MacLaine and Michael Caine star in a firstrate suspense comedy, cleverly scripted, expertly directed and handsomely mounted.

Sidney Carroll's original story has been adapted into a zesty laugh-getter as MacLaine becomes Miss Malaprop in Caine's scheme to loot the art treasures of mid-East potentate Herbert Lom. An idealized swindle sequence lasting 27 minutes opens pic, after which the execution of the plan shifts all characterizations and sympathies.

Director Ronald Neame has obtained superior characterizations from all hands. MacLaine, playing a Eurasian gal, displays her deft comedy abilities after the opening segment, in which she is stone-faced and silent. Caine socks over a characterization which is at first tightlipped and cold, then turning warm with human and romantic frailty.

Lom is excellent as the potentate, so assured of his security devices that audience sympathy encourages the machinations of Caine and MacLaine.

□ 1966: Nominations: Best Color Costume Design, Color Art Direction, Sound

••••••••••••••••••••••••••••••••••

■ **GAMBLER, THE**

1974, 109 MINS, US ◇ ⊛ ⊙
Dir Karel Reisz   *Prod* Irwin Winkler, Robert Chartoff
Scr James Toback   *Ph* Victor J. Kemper   *Ed* Roger Spottiswoode   *Mus* Jerry Fielding   *Art Dir* Philip Rosenberg
● James Caan, Paul Sorvino, Lauren Hutton, Morris Carnovsky, Jacqueline Brookes, Burt Young (Paramount)

The Gambler is a compelling and effective film. James Caan is excellent and the featured players are superb. However, it is somewhat overlong in early exposition and has one climax too many.

James Toback's script commingles candor and compassion, without hostility or superficial sociology or patronizing.

After getting off to a good start, film slows down in some redundant and/or sluggishly paced exposition, at least understandable considering the calibre of players such as Paul Sorvino, Jacqueline Brookes, Morris Carnovsky (Caan's wealthy grandfather who declines to bail him out), Burt Young (a very cordial yet simultaneously merciless and brutal loan shark collection agent), whose roles provide full dimension and bitter irony to the story. The pace quickens towards the end.

Jerry Fielding's score, based on Mahler's Symphony No 1, is excellent, making the point that a contemporary urban drama can be underscored to great effect without tinny transistor radio source excerpts or mickey-mouse rock riffs.

••••••••••••••••••••••••••••••••••

■ **GAME IS OVER, THE**

1966, 95 MINS, FRANCE/ITALY ◇ ⊛
Dir Roger Vadim   *Scr* Jean Cau, Roger Vadim, Bernard Frechtman   *Ph* Claude Renoir   *Ed* Victoria Mercanton
Mus J.P. Bourtayre, Jean Bouchety   *Art Dir* Jean Andre
● Jane Fonda, Peter McEnery, Michel Piccoli, Tina Marquand, Jacques Monod (Marceau/Cocinor/Mega)

This melodrama is sleek and elegant if sometimes short on motivation. Updated version of an Emile Zola 19th-century novel [*La curee*] deals with a rich financier married to a very young woman (Jane Fonda). He also has a 22-year-old son (Peter McEnery). Love blossoms between this son and the young wife.

Director Roger Vadim has a glossy style that shows the aimless life of the bored wife and the drifting son that finally results in love only to be throttled by his weakness which ends in the woman's breakdown.

McEnery is effective as the weak son while Michel Piccoli does not have the right sort of role to be able to limn a strong and overpowering father figure to overcome love and desired freedom.

••••••••••••••••••••••••••••••••••

■ **GAME OF DEATH, A**

1945, 72 MINS, US
Dir Robert Wise   *Prod* Herman Schlom   *Scr* Norman Houston   *Ph* J. Roy Hunt   *Ed* J.R. Whittredge
Mus Paul Sawtell   *Art Dir* Albert S. D'Agostino, Lucius O. Croxton
● John Loder, Audrey Long, Edgar Barrier, Russell Wade, Jason Robards Sr, Russell Hicks (RKO)

A Game of Death is a remake of *The Most Dangerous Game*, filmed by RKO in 1932 from Richard Connell's short story. Despite implausibility, it has expert direction and some good acting to make it a juicy horror cantata.

Edgar Barrier portrays a big game hunter who has a maniacal desire to hunt humans instead. He appropriates an island, where he plots shipwrecks to bring in his human quarry.

After putting them up at the menage for several days, he scares them into the rushes,

then embarks on a manhunt with his bow and arrow. John Loder, hunter-novelist, is washed in from a wreck and soon penetrates the madman's scheme.

Loder and Barrier carry the picture with excellent portrayals of implausible roles, while Robert Wise directs in a tempo that sustains suspense.

••••••••••••••••••••••••••••••••••

■ **GAMES, THE**

1970, 97 MINS, UK ◇ ⊛
Dir Michael Winner   *Prod* Lester Linsk   *Scr* Erich Segal
Ph Robert Paynter   *Ed* Bernard Gribble   *Mus* Francis Lai
Art Dir Albert Witherick, Fred Carter, Roy Stannard
● Michael Crawford, Ryan O'Neal, Charles Aznavour, Jeremy Kemp, Elaine Taylor, Stanley Baker (20th Century-Fox)

Story turns on four runners from different nations who eventually compete in a climactic 26-mile marathon in the Rome Olympic Games.

Michael Crawford is the ex-milkman driven to prowess by Stanley Baker; Ryan O'Neal is a fun-loving American college kid – as only Hollywood can define and perpetuate this stereotype; Charles Aznavour is a Czech soldier, forced to return to running as a political pawn; and Athol Compton is the down-under Aborigine exploited by Jeremy Kemp.

Filmed in England, Italy, Austria, Czechoslovakia, Australia and Japan, the pic [from a novel by Hugh Atkinson] is long on production values and nothing else.

Technical adviser Gordon Pirie, a retired British track star and Olympics participant, did a creditable job in the exteriors.

Aznavour, Crawford and Jeremy Kemp come off best.

••••••••••••••••••••••••••••••••••

■ **GANDHI**

1982, 188 MINS, UK/USA/INDIA ◇ ⊛ ⊙
Dir Richard Attenborough   *Prod* Richard Attenborough, Rani Dube   *Scr* John Briley   *Ph* Billy Williams, Ronnie Taylor   *Ed* John Bloom   *Mus* Ravi Shankar, George Fenton   *Art Dir* Stuart Craig
● Ben Kingsley, Candice Bergen, Edward Fox, John Gielgud, Trevor Howard, John Mills (Columbia/IFI/Goldcrest/NFDC)

The canvas upon which the turmoil of India, through its harshly won independence in 1947 from British rule, is, as depicted by Richard Attenborough, bold, sweeping, brutal; tender, loving and inspiring. He has juggled the varied emotional thrusts with generally expert balance.

Attenborough and scenarist John Briley agreed to attempt to capture the 'spirit' of the man and his times, and in this they succeed admirably.

Ben Kingsley, the British (half-Indian) actor, who portrays the Mahatma from young manhood as a lawyer in South Africa, is a physically striking Gandhi and has captured nuances in speech and movement which make it seem as though he has stepped through black and white newsreels into the present Technicolor reincarnation.

From the time he first experiences apartheid in being unceremoniously booted off a train in South Africa after obtaining his law degree in London, Mohandas Karamchand Gandhi becomes a man with a mission – a peaceful mission to obtain dignity for every man, no matter his color, creed, nationality.

While the focus of the drama is naturally on the person of Kingsley who gives a masterfully balanced and magnetic portrayal of Gandhi, the unusually large cast, some with only walkthrough roles, responds nobly.

Calling for individual mention are Edward Fox as General Dyer; Candice Bergen as Margaret Bourke-White, Geraldine James as devoted disciple Mirabehn, John Gielgud as

Lord Irwin; Trevor Howard as Judge Broomfield; John Mills as The Viceroy; Rohini Hattangady as Mrs Gandhi; Roshan Seth as Nehru, and Athol Fugard as General Smuts.
□ 1982: Best Picture, Director, Actor (Ben Kingsley), Original Screenplay, Cinematography, Art Direction, Editing, Costume Design.
□ Nominations: Best Original Score, Sound, Makeup

. . . .

■ GANG'S ALL HERE, THE

1939, 75 MINS, UK
Dir Thornton Freeland   *Prod* Walter C. Mycroft, Jack Buchanan   *Scr* Ralph Spence   *Ph* Claude Friese-Greene   *Ed* E.B. Jarvis   *Art Dir* John Mead, Cedric Dawe
● Jack Buchanan, Googie Withers, Edward Everett Horton, Otto Kruger (Associated British)

Jack Buchanan plays a private detective for a large insurance company, and never takes anything seriously, even murder. He's ably partnered with Edward Everett Horton as his brother in the farcical by-play.

The story and its method of telling have in it innumerable surefire farcical ingredients, is played by a carefully selected cast and is competently produced.

Story opens with a banquet given in honor of John Forrest (Buchanan), who's retiring from his post as chief investigator for the Stamford Assurance Co. He intends to devote himself to the writing of detective novels. When he learns that his former firm's safe has been robbed of more than $1 million in jewels belonging to a foreign prince, he returns to the scent.

. . . .

■ GANG'S ALL HERE, THE

(UK: The Girls He Left Behind)

1943, 102 MINS, US ◇
Dir Busby Berkeley   *Prod* William LeBaron   *Scr* Walter Bullock   *Ph* Edward Cronjager   *Ed* Roy Curtiss   *Mus* Alfred Newman, Charles Henderson
● Alice Faye, Carmen Miranda, Charlotte Greenwood, Eugene Pallette, Edward Everett Horton, Phil Baker (20th Century-Fox)

A weak script is somewhat relegated by the flock of tuneful musical numbers that frequently punctuate the picture. Alice Faye has never been screened more fetchingly, and she still lilts a ballad for sock results. Carmen Miranda is given her fattest screen part to date, and she's a comedienne who can handle lines as well as put over her South American rhythm tunes. Phil Baker makes the most of invariably drab comedy lines, while Benny Goodman's orch is always prominently focused.

There's a supporting cast, notably Eugene Pallette, Charlotte Greenwood and Edward Everett Horton, that generally backs up the principals niftily in this yarn of a romantic tangle involving Faye, Sheila Ryan and James Ellison. Latter plays a wealthy doughboy who makes a pitch for Faye, a nitery chorine, though engaged to wealthy Ryan.

The Leo Robin-Harry Warren tunes include several potentially exploitable ones, namely 'A Journey to a Star', which Miss Faye reprises a couple of times.

Of the cast, Miranda is outstanding, and the way she kicks around the English lingo affords much of the film's comedy. Faye underplays as usual, but always clicko.
□ 1943: Nomination: Best Color Art Direction

. . . .

■ GANG WAR
See: Odd Man Out

. . . .

■ GARBO TALKS

1984, 103 MINS, US ◇ ⓥ
Dir Sidney Lumet   *Prod* Burtt Harris, Elliott Kastner   *Scr* Larry Grusin   *Ph* Andrzej Bartkowiak   *Ed* Andrew Mondshein   *Mus* Cy Coleman   *Art Dir* Philip Rosenberg
● Anne Bancroft, Ron Silver, Carrie Fisher, Catherine Hicks, Steven Hill, Hermione Gingold (United Artists)

Garbo Talks is a sweet and sour film clearly not for all tastes. Packed with New York in-jokes, not everyone will appreciate its aggressive charm. But beneath its cocky exterior, picture has a beat on some very human and universal truths.

Estelle Rolfe (Anne Bancroft) is a certifiable eccentric who has worshipped Garbo from afar since childhood, until the star has become woven into the fabric of her imagination. Her identification with Garbo has become a way for her to glamorize her day-to-day life.

Estelle is no ordinary housewife. Divorced from her husband (Steven Hill), she is continually arrested for defending any and all causes and fighting the everyday indignities of life in NY. If not for Bancroft's spirited performance, Estelle would deteriorate into a caricature.

. . . .

■ GARDEN, THE

1991, 90 MINS, UK ◇ ⓥ
Dir Derek Jarman   *Prod* James Mackay   *Scr* Derek Jarman   *Ph* Christopher Hughes   *Ed* Peter Cartwright   *Mus* Simon Fisher Turner   *Art Dir* Derek Brown, Christopher Hobbs
● Derek Jarman, Tilda Swinton, Johnny Mills, Kevin Collins, Pete Lee-Wilson, Roger Cook (Basilisk)

Derek Jarman's dense *The Garden* is a graphic look at homosexual discrimination laden with campy gestures, music and religious dream sequences. As in *Caravaggio* and *The Last of England*, Jarman forfeits the standard storyline for a panoply of images.

Michael Gough's gently resonant voiceover laments 'My friends went so silently', and the legacy of AIDS is alluded to powerfully. Jarman combines camera images and backdrops to juxtapose contempo England with the Passion of Christ.

A gay male couple are arrested and persecuted, culminating in an ugly tar-and-feathering session. Mary floats in and out. The gay couple wind up on the cross. Jesus walks under power lines near a nuclear plant.

Simon Fisher Turner's score is excellent, but often out of sync with the self-conscious, symbolic action on the screen.

. . . .

■ GARDEN OF ALLAH

1936, 80 MINS, US ◇ ⓥ
Dir Richard Boleslawski   *Prod* David O. Selznick   *Scr* W.P. Lipscomb, Lynn Riggs   *Ph* W. Howard Greene, Hal Rosson   *Ed* Hal C. Kern, Anson Stevenson   *Mus* Max Steiner
● Marlene Dietrich, Charles Boyer, Basil Rathbone, C. Aubrey Smith, Joseph Schildkraut, John Carradine (Selznick)

Garden of Allah, sumptuously and impressively mounted by David O. Selznick, impresses in color production but is a pretty dull affair. It is optically arresting and betimes emotionally gripping but, after a spell, the ecclesiastic significance of the Trappist monk whose earthly love cannot usurp his prior secular vows [from the book by Robert Hichens] peters out completely.

Marlene Dietrich and Charles Boyer are more than adequately competent in the leads, although sometimes slurring their lines. Basil Rathbone, C. Aubrey Smith, Tilly Losch (making her screen debut in a Bagdad cafe dancing sequence, and okay in what she does), Joseph Schildkraut (who almost steals the picture with his exaggerated oriental

ingratiations) and John Carradine as the sandseer leave nothing wanting.

The color is particularly flattering to Dietrich, who has also taken off a little weight. In the flowing capes to which she is so partial, the color camera has caught her at her photographic best.
□ 1936: Special Award (color cinematography).
□ Nominations: Best Score, Assistant Director (Eric G. Stacey)

. . . .

■ GARDENS OF STONE

1987, 111 MINS, US ◇ ⓥ ⊙
Dir Francis Coppola   *Prod* Michael I. Levy, Francis Coppola   *Scr* Ronald Bass   *Ph* Jordan Cronenweth   *Ed* Barry Malkin   *Mus* Carmine Coppola   *Art Dir* Dean Tavoularis
● James Caan, Anjelica Huston, James Earl Jones, D.B. Sweeney, Dean Stockwell, Mary Stuart Masterson (Tri-Star)

Gardens of Stone, Francis Coppola's muddled meditation on the Vietnam War, seems to take its name not so much from the Arlington Memorial Cemetery, where much of the action takes place, but from the stiffness of the characters it portrays.

Structured around the small details and formal rituals of military life, pic opens and closes with a funeral and in between is supposed to be the emotional stuff that makes an audience care about the death of a soldier. But there is a hollowness at the film's core.

As a two-time combat vet biding his time training young recruits for the Old Guard, the army's ceremonial unit at Fort Myer, Va, Clell Hazard (James Caan) knows the war is wrong but cannot oppose it. Rather than protest, he feels it is his responsibility to prepare the young soldiers as best he can, especially young Private Willow (D.B. Sweeney), the son of an old Korean war buddy.

Script, from Nicholas Proffitt's novel, attempts to create sympathetic soldiers whose first loyalty is to their brothers in arms. Indeed it is a world unto itself as Caan swaps tales of horrors and heroism with his buddy 'Goody' Nelson (James Earl Jones).

Most contrived of the relationships is Caan's affair with Anjelica Huston who plays a Washington Post reporter vehemently opposed to the war. Basically the supportive woman waiting in the wings, she also has enough stilted dialog to destroy her character.

. . . .

■ GAS, FOOD, LODGING

1992, 100 MINS, US ◇ ⓥ ⊙
Dir Allison Anders   *Prod* Daniel Hassid, Seth Willenson, William Ewart   *Scr* Allison Anders   *Ph* Dean Lent   *Ed* Tracy S. Granger   *Mus* J. Mascis   *Art Dir* Jane Ann Stewart
● Brooke Adams, Ione Skye, Fairuza Balk, James Brolin, Robert Knepper, David Lansbury (Cineville)

Gas, Food, Lodging is filled with the kind of personal, small-scale rewards indie filmmakers seem best at delivering. Lensed on location in Deming, NM, on a budget of about $1.3 million, Allison Anders' fresh and unfettered pic [from Richard Peck's novel *Don't Look and It Won't Hurt*] emerges distinctively as an example of a new cinema made by women and expressive of their lives.

Focus is on teenage Shade (Fairuza Balk) and her quest to find a man for her waitress mom, Nora (Brooke Adams), while sorting out her own romantic yearnings and dealing with her loose-living, surly-tempered older sister Trudi (Ione Skye).

Shade's self-conscious but eager to reach out; Trudi's sexually wounded and haunted by the specter of male abandonment; and Nora's keeping men at a distance while trying to set an example for her daughters that they're too young to appreciate. Rich, multi-level work is full of rueful humor, fresh turns and small, elegant surprises.

. . . .

■ **GASLIGHT**
(US: Angel Street)

1940, 80 MINS, UK
Dir Thorold Dickinson   *Prod* John Corfield   *Scr* A.R. Rawlinson, Bridget Boland   *Ph* Bernard Knowles, Cyril Knowles
● Anton Walbrook, Diana Wynyard, Cathleen Cordell, Robert Newton, Frank Pettingell, Jimmy Hanley (British National)

Patrick Hamilton's stageplay *Gaslight* had considerable London success as a legit vehicle. Excellent direction by Thorold Dickinson retains all the psychological drama of the original in presenting the tale of a woman being driven steadily mad.

In transferring story to the screen, scripters have embellished the action with an explanatory opening for the motive behind the events, and stretched it with one or two incidents which neither add nor detract.

Anton Walbrook's study of the half insane Paul Mallen, driven to further crime in a search of a handful of ruby stones, is an obnoxious type of characterization. He successfully avoids overplaying. Diana Wynyard brings a sympathy and understanding to her portrayal of the woman who, once married to Mallen, unwittingly stumbles on the secret of his early days, and is influenced by him that she is developing insanity.

. . . .

■ **GASLIGHT**
(UK: The Murder in Thornton Square)

1944, 114 MINS, US ⑳ ⊙
Dir George Cukor   *Prod* Arthur Hornblow Jr   *Scr* John Van Druten, Walter Reisch, John L. Balderston
Ph Joseph Ruttenberg   *Ed* Ralph E. Winters
Mus Bronislau Kaper   *Art Dir* Cedric Gibbons, William Ferrari
● Charles Boyer, Ingrid Bergman, Joseph Cotten, May Whitty, Angela Lansbury, Terry Moore (M-G-M)

Patrick Hamilton's London stage melodrama, is given an exciting screen treatment by Arthur Hornblow Jr's excellent production starring Charles Boyer, Ingrid Bergman and Joseph Cotten.

It is a faithful adaptation, conspicuously notable for fine performances of the stars and the screenplay by John van Druten, Walter Reisch and John L. Balderston. There are times when the screen treatment verges on a type of drama that must be linked to the period upon which the title is based, but this factor only serves to hypo the film's dramatic suspense where normally it might be construed as corny theatrics.

Gaslight is the story of a murderer who escaped detection for many years. He kills a famous opera singer for her jewels but is never able to uncover the baubles. Years later he marries the singer's niece so that he can continue his search for the gems in the late singer's home, which has been inherited by her niece and in which the newlyweds make their home.

Director George Cukor keeps the film at an even pace and is responsible for the film lacking the ten-twent-thirt element that was a factor in the stage play.
☐ 1944: Best Actress (Ingrid Bergman), B&W Art Decoration.
☐ Nominations: Best Picture, Actor (Charles Boyer), Supp. Actress (Angela Lansbury), Screenplay, B&W Cinematography

. . . .

■ **GAS-S-S-S**
OR IT BECAME NECESSARY TO DESTROY THE WORLD IN ORDER TO SAVE IT

1970, 79 MINS, US ◇ ⑳
Dir Roger Corman   *Prod* Roger Corman   *Scr* George

Armitage   *Ph* Ron Dexter   *Ed* George Van Noy
Mus Country Joe and the Fish
● Robert Corff, Elaine Giftos, Pat Patterson, George Armitage, Alex Wilson, Alan Braunstein (American International)

Ostensibly about the actions of the under-25s of the world, as displayed by a sample group in Texas, when an experimental gas kills off all those over that age, most of the screenplay is devoted to moving a group of six young people along the highways to a New Mexican commune where they've heard 'a brave new world' awaits them.

Obstacles appear in the form of automobile rustlers, headed by a character who calls himself Billy the Kid. After a night of rest, recuperation and rocking at a drive-in theatre, they encounter a gang of football players who try to force them to join the team (whose motto is loot, burn and rape), but they escape.

A brief idyll at the commune is threatened when the fascistic footballers lay siege, but they're converted just in time.

Robert Corff and Elaine Giftos, despite their top billing, devote most of their screen time smiling at and admiring each other's hair, which is almost of equal length.

. . . .

■ **GATHERING OF EAGLES, A**

1963, 115 MINS, US ◇ ⑳
Dir Delbert Mann   *Prod* Sy Bartlett   *Scr* Robert Pirosh
Ph Russell Harlan   *Ed* Russell F. Schoengarth   *Mus* Jerry Goldsmith   *Art Dir* Alexander Golitzen, Henry Bumstead
● Rock Hudson, Rod Taylor, Mary Peach, Barry Sullivan, Kevin McCarthy, Henry Silva (Universal)

Though scenarist Robert Pirosh and director Delbert Mann have been hemmed in by formula, within the narrow dramatic horizons of the story design they perform their tasks quite commendably. The familiar post-war air force situations are dramatized about as well as could be expected.

Eagles is a story of the men of the Strategic Air Command, more specifically that of a wing commander (Rock Hudson) whose dedication to the task of shaping up the somewhat negligent outfit to which he is newly assigned forces him, in the course of attempting to analyze and pinpoint what is ailing the unit, to make several unpleasant decisions that almost strain marital relations with his wife (Mary Peach) to the breaking point.

Hudson invests his role with the right blend of authority and warmth. Rod Taylor creates a colorful figure as the undesirably easy going vice-commander who shapes up when the chips are down. Peach, a British actress, manages to be appealing. Barry Sullivan capably handles the somewhat obvious role of a veteran base commander whose alcoholic intake gets him the heave-ho from Hudson.

. . . .

■ **GATOR**

1976, 115 MINS, US ◇ ⑳
Dir Burt Reynolds   *Prod* Jules Levy, Arthur Gardner
Scr William Norton   *Ph* William A. Fraker   *Ed* Harold F. Kress   *Mus* Charles Bernstein   *Art Dir* Kirk Axtell
● Burt Reynolds, Jack Weston, Lauren Hutton, Jerry Reed, Alice Ghostley, Dub Taylor (United Artists)

This follow-up to *White Lightning* never takes itself seriously, veering as it does through many incompatible dramatic and violent moods for nearly two hours.

William Norton's coloring books script picks up Burt Reynolds' Gator McKlusky character, now on parole from moonshining time. State governor Mike Douglas can't realize political ambitions until a notorious back-water county, run by crime czar Jerry Reed, gets cleaned up.

Enter Jack Weston as Dept of Justice undercover agent, who (somewhat unclearly) blackmails Reynolds into working against old pal Reed.

Reynolds clearly was shot down as a director by the story structure which also works to defeat much of the time even his screen charisma and credibility.

. . . .

■ **GAUCHO, THE**

1927, 102 MINS, US ◇ ⊗
Dir F. Richard Jones   *Prod* Douglas Fairbanks   *Scr* Lotta Woods, Elton Thomas [= Douglas Fairbanks]   *Ph* Tony Gaudio   *Ed* William Nolan   *Art Dir* Carl Oscar Borg
● Douglas Fairbanks, Lupe Velez, Gustav von Seyffertitz, Michael Vavitch, Nigel De Brulier, Mary Pickford (Elton/United Artists)

Doug Fairbanks is at it again. The story of *The Gaucho* is credited on the screen to Elton Thomas, but that person is none other than Doug. In doing so, however, he does not hog the picture, but permits a little Mexican girl, new to films, in on the racket.

This youngster, who got her first shot at screen work on the Roach lot, is Lupe Velez, and is not more than 16 or 17.

Though the first 30 minutes or so seem a little slow, the picture then settles down. Looks as though better than $500,000 has been expended, and the picture shows it.

To please the little mountain girl, the Gaucho has a house moved from its base by 100 horses to the town he has come to take because there is an abundance of gold there. The big punch is a stampede of cattle to save the day for the Gaucho. A tremendous herd sweeps the town, driving everything and everybody before it, with the Gaucho and his mob coming in and taking possession on the dust. A pip of a scene.

. . . .

■ **GAUNTLET, THE**

1977, 108 MINS, US ◇ ⊙
Dir Clint Eastwood   *Prod* Robert Daley   *Scr* Michael Butler, Dennis Shryack   *Ph* Rexford Metz   *Ed* Ferris Webster, Joel Cox   *Mus* Jerry Fielding   *Art Dir* Allen E. Smith
● Clint Eastwood, Sondra Locke, Pat Hingle, William Prince, Bill McKinney, Michael Cavanaugh (Warner/Malpaso)

In a major role reversal, Clint Eastwood stars in *The Gauntlet* as a person who might be on the receiving end of the violence epitomized in his famed Dirty Harry film series.

Eastwood, a flop cop sent to extradite hooker Sondra Locke, finds they are the targets of both the underworld and law enforcement elements tied to the mob.

William Prince is very good as a police commissioner with mob ties who selects Eastwood to bring Locke from Las Vegas as a key witness in a trial which could embarrass a lot of highly-placed people.

Plot provides a series of narrow escapes in van rides, motorcycle rides, train rides, car rides and climactic bus ride. Chuck Gaspar's special effects crew destroys a house, a helicopter and a cross-country bus as the film unfolds.

. . . .

■ **GAY CABALLERO, THE**

1940, 58 MINS, US
Dir Otto Brower   *Prod* Walter Morosco, Ralph Dietrich
Scr Albert Duffy, John Larkin, Walter Bullock   *Ph* Edward Cronjager   *Ed* Harry Reynolds   *Mus* Emil Newman
Art Dir Richard Day, Chester Cord
● Cesar Romero, Sheila Ryan, Robert Sterling, Chris-Pin Martin, Janet Beecher (20th Century-Fox)

The Cisco Kid [created by William Sydney Porter (O. Henry)] continues his Robin Hoodian adventures along the south-west border in a story which grooves along familiar lines of the series.

As usual, Cisco rides into the district with sidekick Chris-Pin Martin to find a grave marked with his name. Deciding to stick

285

around and find out what's going on, he discovers enough plot to step in to protect a pretty girl and her father from nefarious deeds.

Cesar Romero is in the familiar role of Cisco, never losing his composure in the darkest situations. Chris-Pin Martin continues as his Mexican stooge, while Sheila Ryan is the girl in this instance. Edmund MacDonald is the familiar moustached villain, aided by conniving skullduggery by Janet Beecher.

● ●

■ **GAY DIVORCE, THE**
See: The Gay Divorcee

● ●

■ **GAY DIVORCEE, THE**
(UK: The Gay Divorce)

1934, 107 MINS, US ⓥ ⊙
Dir Mark Sandrich   *Prod* Pandro S. Berman
Scr George Marion Jr, Dorothy Yost, Edward Kaufman   *Ph* David Abel   *Ed* William Hamilton   *Mus* Max Steiner (dir.)   *Art Dir* Van Nest Polglase, Carroll Clark
● Fred Astaire, Ginger Rogers, Alice Brady, Edward Everett Horton, Erik Rhodes, Eric Blore (RKO)

All through the picture there's charm, romance, gaiety and eclat. There's a dash of Continental spice in the situation of the professional male co-respondent who is to expedite Ginger Rogers' divorce.

The manner in which Fred Astaire taps himself into an individual click with 'Looking for a Needle in Haystack', a hoofing soliloquy in his London flat, while his man hands him his cravat, boutonniere and walking stick, is something which he alone elevates and socks over on individual artistry.

'The Continental', is the smash song and dance hit. Cole Porter's 'Night and Day', from the original [1932] show [*Gay Divorce*, book by Dwight Taylor], is alone retained and worthily so, especially as Astaire interprets it. After having done it for months on New York and London stages it's natural that its celluloid translation must be enhanced by much personable business and lyric mannerisms.

Rogers is also excellent, but the performances don't end there. Alice Brady and Edward Everett Horton, as the sub-team, are more than just good foils. Erik Rhodes and Eric Blore, both from legit, also impress in no small manner.

Mark Sandrich rates all sorts of bends on the direction. He's colored the story values with a flock of nifty business. His terp stager, Dave Gould, displays considerable imagination with the dance staging.
□ 1934: Best Song ('Continental').
□ Nominations: Best Picture, Art Direction, Score, Sound

● ●

■ **GAY MRS. TREXEL, THE**
See: Susan and God

● ●

■ **GAZEBO, THE**

1959, 102 MINS, US
Dir George Marshall   *Prod* Lawrence Weingarten
Scr George Wells   *Ph* Paul C. Vogel   *Ed* Adrienne Fazan   *Mus* Jeff Alexander   *Art Dir* George W. Davis, Paul Groesse
● Glenn Ford, Debbie Reynolds, Carl Reiner, John McGiver, Mabel Albertson, Doro Merande (Avon/ M-G-M)

Gazebo is based on the Alec Coppel play which starred Walter Slezak and Jayne Meadows on Broadway and Tom Ewell and Jan Sterling on the road. In its transfer to the screen, scripter George Wells has spiced the often far-fetched devices of the play with a number of his own delicacies, including a gregarious pigeon named Herman. Director George Marshall, achieving a frisky blend of suspense and tomfoolery, puts it all together with a bright, well-timed hand.

Glenn Ford plays a television writer who is married to a Broadway star (Debbie Reynolds). Several years earlier, Reynolds posed without proper attire, and now the possessor of said photographs is blackmailing Ford. Murder is his only out, Ford reasons, and he invites the blackmailer to his home and shoots him. He hides the body on the spot where a gazebo (summer house) is about to be positioned the following day.

The film is nearly all Ford, and he's up to every scene, earning both sympathy and laughs as he muddles through his farcical 'crime'. Reynolds is excellent, but her talents are beyond what her limited role requires. The part on Broadway was very minor and has not changed much. Carl Reiner, as the couple's district attorney friend, is good but also beyond the part.
□ 1959: Nomination: B&W Costume Design

● ●

■ **GEISHA BOY, THE**

1958, 95 MINS, US ◇ ⓥ
Dir Frank Tashlin   *Prod* Jerry Lewis   *Scr* Frank Tashlin   *Ph* Haskell Boggs   *Ed* Alma Macrorie   *Mus* Walter Scharf   *Art Dir* Hal Pereira, Tambi Larsen
● Jerry Lewis, Marie McDonald, Sessue Hayakawa, Barton MacLane, Suzanne Pleshette, Nobu McCarthy (Paramount)

The Geisha Boy is a good Jerry Lewis comedy, one that rips along with never a backward glance at shattered remnants of plot behind it. Frank Tashlin, who wrote and directed, loads in wild sight and sound gags, parodies and takeoffs that relieve Lewis of some comic burden and show him in his best light.

Tashlin's screenplay, from a story by Rudy Makoul, has Lewis as a very low man on the show business totem pole. He is a magician who 'can't even get a job on daytime television'. He and his rabbit, Harry, join a USO tour of the Orient, because they couldn't get a job anywhere else.

Lewis first tangles with the troupe's headliner (Marie McDonald) who serves the picture as a kind of young Margaret Dumont; then with the army brass, represented by Barton MacLane, and finally with the Japanese themselves. There is a romance between Lewis and a Japanese widow (Nobu McCarthy) whose young son (Robert Hirano) 'adopts' Lewis as his father.

Lewis is at his best when he eschews some of the stock physical mannerisms that were originally his trademarks. He is more appealing and much funnier when he is playing more or less straight, using his timing and more restrained reactions for fine comedy effect. He is also effective in the few serious moments.

● ●

■ **GENERAL, THE**

1927, 77 MINS, US ⊗ ⓥ ⊙
Dir Buster Keaton, Clyde Bruckman   *Prod* Joseph M. Schenck   *Scr* Buster Keaton, Clyde Bruckman, Al Boasberg, Charles Smith   *Ph* J. Devereaux Jennings, Bert Haines   *Ed* Sherman Kell   *Art Dir* Fred Gabourie
● Buster Keaton, Marien Mack, Glen Cavender, Jim Farley, Frederick Vroom, Charles Smith (Keaton/United Artists)

The General is far from fussy. Its principal comedy scene is built on that elementary bit, the chase, and you can't continue a fight for almost an hour and expect results. Especially is this so when the action is placed entirely in the hands of the star. It was his story, he directed, and he acted. The result is a flop.

The story is a burlesque of a Civil War meller. Buster Keaton has the role of a youthful engineer on the Watern and Atlantic RR, running through Georgia, when war is declared. He tries to enlist, but is turned down, as it is figured that he would be of greater value to the cause as an engineer. His girl,

however, won't believe this, and tells him not to see her again until he is in a uniform.

The girl is on a visit to her dad when 10 Union daredevils steal the train in the middle of Confederate territory and start off with it, intending to burn all bridges behind him, so that the line of communication and supplies for the enemy shall be cut. The girl is on the train, and Keaton, sore because his beloved engine has been stolen, gives chase in another locomotive.

There are some corking gags in the picture, but as they are all a part of the chase they are overshadowed.

● ●

■ **GENERAL DIED AT DAWN, THE**

1936, 98 MINS, US ⓥ
Dir Lewis Milestone   *Prod* William LeBaron   *Scr* Clifford Odets   *Ph* Victor Milner   *Mus* Werner Janssen   *Art Dir* Hans Dreier, Ernest Fegte
● Gary Cooper, Madeleine Carroll, Akim Tamiroff, Dudley Digges, Porter Hall, William Frawley (Paramount)

In Clifford Odets' first film attempt his hand is distinctly visible throughout. But without Gary Cooper and Madeleine Carroll to top an A-1 cast, all the splendid trouping, all the splendid imagery of direction, photography, music and general production might well have jelled into an artistic flop.

Story supplied by Charles G. Booth's novel is an old-fashioned piece of claptrap. It has to do with intrigue in the Far East, gun-runners, smugglers, and spies. Odets has left all that alone but has underlined Gary Cooper as the agent for the ammunition runners by making him engaged in the dangerous work not because of the adventure or money, but because he's trying to help the downtrodden Chinese rid themselves of a money-grubbing, rapacious Chinese war lord, General Yang (Akim Tamiroff).

Cooper, as the daredevil American, is at top form throughout; Madeleine Carroll as his vis-a-vis in a very difficult assignment, impresses. Two comparatively unknowns, Tamiroff and Porter Hall, turn in exceptionally strong performances. Hall, as a sniveling, broken-down villain, handles an unusual job beautifully; John O'Hara, the novelist, does a bit as a newspaperman, looking the part. Allegedly Odets, director Milestone and Sidney Skolsky, Hollywood columnist, are also in for a shot or two, but if so it's their secret which scene it is.
□ 1936: Nominations: Best Supp. Actor (Akim Tamiroff), Cinematography, Score

● ●

■ **GENEVIEVE**

1953, 86 MINS, UK ◇ ⓥ
Dir Henry Cornelius   *Prod* Henry Cornelius
Scr William Rose   *Ph* Christopher Challis   *Ed* Clive Donner   *Mus* Larry Adler   *Art Dir* Michael Stringer
● John Gregson, Dinah Sheridan, Kenneth More, Kay Kendall, Geoffrey Keen, Joyce Grenfell (Sirius)

The 'Genevieve' of the title is a vintage 1904 car which has been entered for the annual London-to-Brighton rally by its enthusiastic owner (John Gregson). His wife (Dinah Sheridan) hardly shares his enthusiasm but joins him on the run and there is constant good-natured bickering between them and their friendly rival (Kenneth More) and his girlfriend (Kay Kendall). But the rivalry becomes intense on the return journey, ending up with a wager as to which car will be first over Westminster Bridge.

First-rate direction by Henry Cornelius keeps the camera focused almost entirely on the four principals, and rarely has a starring foursome been so consistently good. Sheridan's sophisticated performance is a good contrast to Gregson's more sullen interpretation. More's exuberance is well-matched

G

by Kendall's effervescent portrayal.
☐ 1953: Nominations: Best Story &
Screenplay, Scoring of a Dramatic Picture

. . . .

■ GENGHIS KHAN

1965, 124 MINS, US ◇
Dir Henry Levin   *Prod* Irving Allen   *Scr* Clarke Reynolds,
Beverley Cross   *Ph* Geoffrey Unsworth   *Ed* Geoffrey
Foot   *Mus* Dusan Radic   *Art Dir* Maurice Carter
● Stephen Boyd, Omar Sharif, James Mason, Eli
Wallach, Francoise Dorleac, Telly Savalas (Allen/
CCC/Avala)

Genghis Khan is an introspective biopic about
the Mongol chief Temujin who unified Asia's
warring tribes in the Dark Ages. An international cast delivers okay performances in occasionally trite script which emphasizes
personal motivation rather than sweeping
pageantry.

The screenplay, from story by Berkely
Mather, hinges on continuing vendetta between tribal chieftain Stephen Boyd and
Omar Sharif, once enslaved by Boyd but escaping to forge an empire that threatened
western and eastern civilization some eight
centuries back.

Sharif does a near-excellent job in projecting with ease the zeal which propelled
Temujin from bondage to a political education in China, and finally to realizing at death
his dream of Mongol unity. Boyd is less successful as the brutish thorn in Sharif's side,
being overall too restrained for sustained
characterization despite flashes of earthiness.

Most unusual characterization is essayed by
James Mason, playing the neatly-contrasting
urbane imperial counsellor who mentors political savvy.

. . . .

■ GENTLEMAN JIM

1942, 104 MINS, US 🎬 ⊙
Dir Raoul Walsh   *Prod* Robert Buckner   *Scr* Vincent
Lawrence, Horace McCoy   *Ph* Sid Hickox   *Ed* Jack
Killifer   *Mus* Heinz Roemheld   *Art Dir* Ted Smith
● Errol Flynn, Alexis Smith, Jack Carson, Alan Hale,
John Loder, Ward Bond (Warner)

Warner Bros has managed to turn out a good
film based on the life of James J. Corbett. In
doing so, however, the scenarists have sacrificed a good deal of one of the best reputations the boxing game has ever known.

On celluloid, Corbett is a 'wise-guy', brash
character oozing with braggadocio. In real life
the heavyweight champ was a self-effacing,
quiet personality so distinctly apart from the
general run of mugg fighters of that day that
the 'gentleman' tag was a natural.

Errol Flynn is the screen Corbett and is a real-
life prototype only in the fact that Corbett was a
bank clerk in Frisco and that his father was a
bluff Irishman who operated a livery stable.

From there on, with the exception of some
of Corbett's fights, the film is pure fiction.
Corbett is shown as a young bachelor who,
because he got a prominent judge out of an
embarrassing jam at an illegal bareknuckle
fight, gets favored treatment at the bank
where he's employed; meets the beauteous
daughter of a millionaire miner and thus
gains entrance to Frisco's famed Olympic
club. At a party, according to the film,
Corbett and his friend, Jack Carson, are
tossed out of the Olympic when liquor makes
Carson's mouth and feet misbehave.

This is so far removed from fact that it's ludicrous. Corbett was a revered member of the
Olympic club to the very end.

All this fiction, plus the scenarists' depiction of Sullivan, after being kayoed by
Corbett, calling on the latter to wish him well
and present him with his championship belt,
take this picture out of the biographical class
and into fantasy.

■ GENTLEMAN'S AGREEMENT

1947, 118 MINS, US 🎬 ⊙
Dir Elia Kazan   *Prod* Darryl F. Zanuck   *Scr* Moss Hart
Ph Arthur Miller   *Ed* Harmon Jones   *Mus* Alfred
Newman   *Art Dir* Lyle R. Wheeler, Mark Lee Kirk
● Gregory Peck, Dorothy McGuire, John Garfield,
Celeste Holm, Anne Revere, Dean Stockwell (20th
Century-Fox)

Just as Laura Z. Hobson's original novel of
the writer (character), who poses as a Jew to
write a magazine series on anti-Semitism was
a milestone in modern fiction, the picture is
vital and stirring.

The basic elements of the Hobson work are
not only retained, but in some cases given
greater dimension and plausibility. The picture is memorable for numerous vivid, im-
pelling passages. For instance the breakfast
scene, when Green tries to explain anti-
Semitism to his innocent little son, stamps
the picture's urgent theme on the spectator's
mind virtually at once.

There are also disappointing or confusing
scenes. One is the party given by Kathy's sister which remains as unresolved on the
screen as in the book and as lacking in realistic atmosphere. In the same scene, the stupid
Connecticut dowagers seem exaggerated.
Celeste Holm, with some of the film's most
pungent lines, frequently reads them too fast
for intelligibility.

As Phil Green, the magazine writer,
Gregory Peck gives a fine performance. He is
quiet, almost gentle, progressively intense
and resolute, with just the right suggestion of
inner vitality and turbulence. Dorothy
McGuire too, is dramatically and emotionally
compelling as Kathy. The range from her
somewhat flippant opening scene to the searing final one with John Garfield is impressive.
Garfield is a natural in the part of Dave, giving it admirable strength and understated
eloquence.
☐ 1947: Best Picture, Director, Supp. Actress
(Celeste Holm).
☐ Nominations: Best Actor (Gregory Peck),
Actress (Dorothy McGuire), Supp. Actress
(Anne Revere), Screenplay, Editing

. . . .

■ GENTLEMEN PREFER BLONDES

1953, 91 MINS, US ◇ 🎬 ⊙
Dir Howard Hawks   *Prod* Sol C. Siegel   *Scr* Charles
Lederer   *Ph* Harry J. Wild   *Ed* Hugh S. Fowler
Mus Lionel Newman (dir.)   *Art Dir* Lyle R. Wheeler,
Joseph C. Wright
● Jane Russell, Marilyn Monroe, Charles Coburn, Elliott
Reid, Tommy Noonan, George Winslow (20th Century Fox)

An attractive screen tintuner has been fashioned from the musical stage hit, *Gentlemen
Prefer Blondes*. The Joseph Fields-Anita Loos
[1949] stage original has been modernized
but the general theme and principal characters are intact. Only three of the stage tunes
by Jule Styne and Leo Robin are used, but two
numbers were cleffed by Hoagy Carmichael
and Harold Adamson.

Together, the two femmes are the picture's
outstanding assets. Jane Russell is a standout
and handles the lines and songs with a comedy flair she has previously demonstrated.
Marilyn Monroe matches with a newly displayed ability to sex a song as well as point up
the eye values of a scene by her presence.

The big production number in the presentation is 'Diamonds Are a Girl's Best Friend',
flashily presented by Monroe and a male line
against a vivid red backdrop.

Monroe, a blonde who likes diamonds, and
Russell, a brunet who likes men, sail for Paris
and fun when Tommy Noonan, the blonde's
lovesick millionaire, is unable to make the
trip. Noonan's pop (Taylor Holmes), who
would like to bust up the son's attachment,
sends Elliott Reid, a private eye, along to
keep an eye on the girls.

Charles Coburn is in fine form as the diamond tycoon with an eye for dames. Reid and
Noonan carry off the romantic male spots
nicely. Little George Winslow's big voice in a
little body provides a comedy contrast to
Monroe's little girl voice in a big girl's body
for his two scenes with her.

. . . .

■ GEORGE WHITE'S 1935 SCANDALS

1935, 83 MINS, US
Dir George White   *Prod* George White   *Scr* Jack
Yellen, Patterson McNutt   *Ph* George Schneiderman
Ed [uncredited]   *Mus* Louis De Francesco (dir.)
Art Dir Gordon Wiles
● George White, Alice Faye, James Dunn, Ned Sparks,
Lyda Roberti, Eleanor Powell (Fox)

Once more George White presents himself in
his very own conception of a film *Scandals*, the
second of the series. Once more it is dull entertainment. Trouble is largely traceable directly to White.

From only one standpoint is the film worthy
top-screen entertainment and that is the
songs [by Jack Yellen, Cliff Friend, Joseph
Meyer, additional lyrics by Herb Magidson].
There are six, two of them real outstanders
from a tune standpoint, but all tops on lyrics.
Even these numbers, however, are wasted because of poor staging [by White].

Cast is big and studded with featured players, many of them wasted. Most of the work is
left to James Dunn and Alice Faye as the boy
and girl. They're in a small town show in
Georgia when White catches them. He brings
'em to New York and stars 'em immediately.
Then follows the usual back-stage filmusical
story. Inflated egos, pouting, quarrels, the
kids leave the show. Girl's aunt from down
Georgia way comes to catch the show, White
digs them up; they've learned their lesson; all
is well.

. . . .

■ GEORGE WHITE'S SCANDALS

1934, 79 MINS, US
Dir George White, Thornton Freeland, Harry Lachman
Prod Robert Kane   *Scr* Jack Yellen, George White
Ph Lee Garmes, George Schneiderman   *Ed* Paul
Weatherwax   *Mus* Louis De Francesco (dir.)
● George White, Rudy Vallee, Alice Faye, Jimmy
Durante, Dixie Dunbar, Adrienne Ames (Fox)

As the first musical talker turned out by an
important eastern legit revue producer, this
is an unintentional but flattering compliment
to Hollywood's own stagers of musicals.
George White contributes surprisingly little
in the way of technique or ideas. *Scandals* follows the regulation Hollywood pattern. He
not only borrows the backstage device, but
weighs his production down with a dressing-
room yarn that almost nullifies the picture's
few meritorious moments.

Alice Faye is pretty much on the spot, and
in an important part in her first picture. In
looks and performance she is a pleasant surprise. She sings adequately, for that's her
business. Rudy Vallee, a decidedly more versatile performer than the Vallee of a couple
of years earlier, also enjoys more complimen-
tary photography. The two make a pleasant
team of singing leads.

Jimmy Durante, carrying the secondary love
match with Dixie Dunbar, suffers from bad
material most of the time. When he has
something to work with, such as in his blackface number, he shines.

. . . .

■ GEORGE WHITE'S SCANDALS

1945, 95 MINS, US 🎬
Dir Felix E. Feist   *Prod* George White   *Scr* Hugh
Wedlock, Howard Snyder, Parke Levy, Howard J. Green
Ph Robert de Grasse   *Ed* Joseph Noriega   *Mus* Leigh
Harline (ballet)   *Art Dir* Albert S. D'Agostino, Ralph
Berges

287

● Joan Davis, Jack Haley, Martha Holliday, Philip Terry, Jane Greer (RKO)

The George White 'Scandals' legit musicals, Ziegfeld's 'Follies' and Earl Carroll's 'Vanities' date back to the Prohibition era and the current picture, produced by George White, also dates back in that it is reminiscent of the backstage musicals of the early talker days. Though there are a few moments that hit home, on the whole the picture is a drawn-out affair.

Joan Davis and Jack Haley, starred, yeomanly try to overcome the assignments handed them, as do others, but the net result is still very negative. One of the drawbacks is the padding to 95 minutes and the dreary routine concerned with planning a George White's 'Scandals' show, the auditioning, the picking of chorines, costuming, etc.

Story, a weak one, concerns two romances in connection with the staging of a 'Scandals', Davis and Haley being paired on the one side and specialty dancer Martha Holliday and Philip Terry on the other.

· ·

■ **GEORGY GIRL**

1966, 100 MINS, UK ▓ ⊙
Dir Silvio Narizzano   *Prod* Robert A. Goldston, Otto Plaschkes   *Scr* Margaret Forster, Peter Nichols   *Ph* Ken Higgins   *Ed* John Bloom   *Mus* Alexander Faris   *Art Dir* Tony Woollard
● James Mason, Alan Bates, Lynn Redgrave, Charlotte Rampling, Rachel Kempson, Bill Owen (Columbia)

The role of a gawky ungainly plain Jane [in this adaptation of the novel by Margaret Forster] is a natural for Lynn Redgrave's talents, and she frequently overwhelms her costars by sheer force of personality.

She's sharing a slovenly apartment with an attractive, brittle and promiscuous girl friend (Charlotte Rampling). And whenever a lover is being entertained in the communal bedroom, Redgrave takes herself off to the home of her parents' wealthy employer. Girl friend becomes pregnant, opts for marriage instead of another abortion, but when mother-to-be is in hospital, husband (Alan Bates) realizes he chose the wrong girl.

James Mason, as the wealthy employer, attempts to adopt a father figure in relations to the girl, but is actually nothing more than a conventional old roue.

Redgrave has a pushover of a part, and never misses a trick to get that extra yock, whether it's her first passionate encounter with Alan Bates or her fielding of Mason's amorous overtures.
□ 1966: Nominations: Best Actress (Lynn Redgrave), Supp. Actor (James Mason), B&W Cinematography, Song ('Georgy Girl')

· ·

■ **GERONIMO**

1962, 101 MINS, US ▓
Dir Arnold Laven   *Prod* Arnold Laven   *Scr* Pat Fielder   *Ph* Alex Phillips   *Ed* Marsh Hendry   *Mus* Hugo Friedhofer   *Art Dir* Roberto Silva
● Chuck Connors, Kamala Devi, Ross Martin, Pat Conway, Adam West (United Artists)

Time was when Indians on the warpath were known to claim a few scalps in their pursuits. Although Geronimo's band of idealistic warriors are acknowledged to be scalpers in Pat Fielder's screenplay, from the story she penned with producer Laven, there is no evidence of such menacing behaviour in this film. In fact, the Indians of Fielder's scenario are unbelievably henpecked, domesticated and generally wishy-washy – proud and arrogant in their war-making but meek enough to be bossed about by a frail, lone white woman in more intimate business.

The story describes the latter, leaner days of Geronimo's career, during which, denied humanitarian treatment by white supervisors

on the reservation, he escaped and fled with some 50 tribesmen to Mexico, where he waged a courageous 'war' against the US to focus attention on the principle of the issue – treatment of the Indian as a human being.

Chuck Connors gives the film a decided lift with an impressive portrayal in the title role.

The picture was filmed in Mexico, and is a fine physical production.

· ·

■ **GETAWAY, THE**

1972, 122 MINS, US ▓ ▓
Dir Sam Peckinpah   *Prod* David Foster, Mitchell Brower   *Scr* Walter Hill   *Ph* Lucien Ballard   *Ed* Roger Spottiswoode, Robert Wolfe   *Mus* Quincy Jones   *Art Dir* Ted Haworth, Angelo Graham
● Steve McQueen, Ali MacGraw, Ben Johnson, Sally Struthers, Al Lettieri, Slim Pickens (First Artists)

The Getaway has several things going for it: Sam Peckinpah's hard-action direction, this time largely channeled into material destruction, although fast-cut human bloodlettings occur frequently enough, and Steve McQueen and Ali MacGraw as stars.

Peckinpah's particular brand of storytelling comes through in the adaptation of the Jim Thompson novel. McQueen, denied parole despite four years of good behavior, gives in to crooked politico Ben Johnson's bank caper scheme in return for release from prison. MacGraw arranges and participates in the robbery plus the rambling escape which follows.

There is an overwritten secondary plot line involving Al Lettieri, so effective in projecting the greasy sadism of one of the robbery gang that his portion of the film eventually becomes vulgar overexposition.

· ·

■ **GET BACK**

1991, 90 MINS, UK ▓ ▓
Dir Richard Lester   *Prod* Philip Knatchbull, Henry Thomas   *Ph* Robert Paynter, Jordan Cronenweth   *Ed* John Victor Smith
● Paul McCartney (Allied Filmmakers/TDK/Front Page)

A stagebound record of Paul McCartney's 1990 world tour, *Get Back* is heavy on nostalgia and light on visual zap. Sans intro or background, pic kicks off on stage and stays there for 90 minutes. Filming took place in England, Holland, Brazil, Canada, Italy, Japan and the US, but individual locales are not identified. Audiences and songs blend into one big stage show.

Pic reunites the former Beatle with director Richard Lester, who helmed *A Hard Day's Night* and *Help!* There's none of those mid-1960s pics' groundbreaking elan here. By MTV standards, this is somewhere in a stone age. Lester mostly lets the powerful songs (half Beatles classics) speak for themselves, crosscutting between fans mouthing the lyrics and Macca & Co. on stage.

· ·

■ **GET CARTER**

1971, 111 MINS, UK ▓
Dir Mike Hodges   *Prod* Michael Klinger   *Scr* Mike Hodges   *Ph* Wolfgang Suschitzky   *Ed* John Trumper   *Mus* Roy Budd   *Art Dir* Assheton Gorton
● Michael Caine, Ian Hendry, Britt Ekland, John Osborne, Tony Beckley, George Sewell (M-G-M)

Get Carter is a superior crime action meller. Michael Caine stars as an English hood seeking vengeance for the murder of his brother. Mike Hodges' top-notch adaptation of a Ted Lewis novel not only maintains interest but conveys with rare artistry, restraint and clarity the many brutal, sordid and gamy plot turns.

Lewis' novel, *Jack's Return Home*, is adapted by Hodges into a fast-moving screenplay in which episodes of compounded criminal dou-

ble-crossing build gradually but steadily to a logical if ironic climax.

The curious death of Caine's brother triggers his departure from London, where he is a key torpedo for gangsters Terence Rigby and John Bindon, to his Newcastle home, where John Osborne (the playwright) appears the area crime boss. In tracking down his brother's murderer, Caine encounters the full spectrum of contemporary crime, including pornographic pix (in which his niece Petra Markham has been innocently compromised), drugs, high-stakes gambling, and vicious give-and-take retribution.

· ·

■ **GET OFF MY BACK**

See: Synanon

· ·

■ **GETTING IT ON**

1983, 96 MINS, US ▓ ▓ ⊙
Dir William Olsen   *Prod* Jan Thompson, William Olsen   *Scr* William Olsen   *Ph* Austin McKinney   *Ed* William Olsen   *Mus* Ricky Keller   *Art Dir* James Eric
● Martin Yost, Heather Kennedy, Jeff Edmond, Kathy Brickmeier, Mark Alan Ferri, Charles King Bibby (Comworld)

This North Carolina-lensed teenage comedy nimbly pumps new life into the overdone high school hijinks genre.

Filmmaker William Olsen targets our consumerist and video-obsessed culture for some ribbing in this story of high school freshman Alex Carson (Martin Yost), with a crush on the girl next door, Sally (Heather Kennedy). Devising a video software business to earn money, Alex borrows his startup capital from his very businesslike dad, and with the help of his cutup classmate Nicholas (Jeff Edmond) uses the video equipment to record hidden camera footage of Heather and other pretty girls.

When Nicholas is kicked out of school by mean principal White (Charles King Bibby), the heroes enlist the services of a friendly prostitute (Kim Saunders) to record footage of White in flagrante delicto.

What makes this material work is a fresh, enthusiastic cast, witty writing, and direction by Olsen that bears no hint of malice.

· ·

■ **GETTING IT RIGHT**

1989, 102 MINS, US ▓ ▓ ⊙
Dir Randal Kleiser   *Prod* Jonathan D. Krane, Randal Kleiser   *Scr* Elizabeth Jane Howard   *Ph* Clive Tickner   *Ed* Chris Kelly   *Mus* Colin Towns   *Art Dir* Caroline Amies
● Jessie Birdsall, Helena Bonham Carter, Peter Cook, Lynn Redgrave, Jane Horrocks, John Gielgud (MCEG)

Sweet love trimphs over hollow class consciousness in *Getting It Right*, a wonderful made-in-Britain sex comedy that celebrates romance in funny, quirky ways.

Maggie Thatcher's England, specifically London, is satirized here. Self-taught hairdresser Jesse Birdsall is a 31-year-old virgin still living at home but doing nothing about it. He suffers in silence, preferring instead to day-dream about girls. He gets yanked out one night to a trendy loft party along the Thames hosted by a socialite who dresses like a man in drag (Lynn Redgrave).

What ensues reminds one a bit of Griffin Dunne's predicament in *After Hours* except this is a much more complex adventure. It's filled with a cast of delightful English eccentrics. Redgrave, meanwhile, is determined to relieve the mystified Birdsall of his virginity.

Helena Bonham Carter is a terrific and surprisingly convincing bulimic tramp parading as an aristocrat. Director Randal Kleiser is in touch with his subjects and treats them well. The actors clearly know what they are speaking about and seem to enjoy every word of Elizabeth Jane Howard's clever, textured script [based on her own book].

• •

■ **GETTING OF WISDOM, THE**

1977, 100 MINS, AUSTRALIA ◇ ▽
Dir Bruce Beresford *Prod* Phillip Adams *Scr* Eleanor Witcombe *Ph* Don McAlpine *Ed* William Anderson *Mus* [uncredited] *Art Dir* John Stoddart
● Susannah Fowle, Barry Humphries, John Waters, Sheila Helpmann, Patricia Kennedy, Julia Blake (Southern Cross)

The Getting of Wisdom was a bold choice as the subject of a feature film. The novel by Henry Handel Richardson [pseudonym of Ethel Richardson] was published in 1910, 13 years after the action depicted and was so shocking at the time that the author's name was stricken from the records of the school in which she set the lightly-disguised autobiography.

It is the story of a young girl's trials and adjustment to life in a strict, Victorian boarding school. Laura (Susannah Fowle) is strongwilled and rebellious, which creates conflicts with her peers and her teachers. The only real soulmate she finds is a senior girl (Hilary Ryan), but her possessiveness drives a wedge in the relationship.

The plotline is episodic, charting the development of the lead character over the years between her arrival and her graduation.

• •

■ **GETTING STRAIGHT**

1970, 126 MINS, US ◇ ▽
Dir Richard Rush *Prod* Richard Rush *Scr* Robert Kaufman *Ph* Laszlo Kovacs *Ed* Maury Winetrobe *Mus* Ronald Stein *Art Dir* Sydney Z. Witwack
● Elliott Gould, Candice Bergen, Robert F. Lyons, Jeff Corey, Max Julien, Cecil Kellaway (Columbia)

Getting Straight is an outstanding film. It is a comprehensive, cynical, sympathetic, flip, touching and hilarious story of the middle generation [of the late 1960s] – those millions a bit too old for protest, a bit too young for repression.

The setting is a college campus where Elliott Gould is nearly through an education course. Bergen is his girl. Both represent the post-JFK/RFK generation, who perceive the tremendous flaws in organized civilization, but scorn the often-puerile methods used in protest.

The episodic story [updated from a novel by Ken Kolb] covers lots of ground as it permits the very large and extremely competent supporting cast to limn the attitudes of an entire population.

While the film is a parade of accurately-hewn postures, the root story never strays too far.

• •

■ **GHOST**

1990, 127 MINS, US ◇ ▽ ⊙
Dir Jerry Zucker *Prod* Lisa Weinstein *Scr* Bruce Joel Rubin *Ph* Adam Greenberg *Ed* Walter Murch *Mus* Maurice Jarre *Art Dir* Jane Musky
● Patrick Swayze, Demi Moore, Whoopi Goldberg, Tony Goldwyn, Rick Aviles, Vincent Schiavelli (Paramount/Koch)

An unlikely grab bag of styles that teeters, spiritlike, between life and death, this lightweight romantic fantasy delivers the elements a *Dirty Dancing* audience presumably hungers for.

Patrick Swayze and Demi Moore play Sam and Molly, a have-it-all Manhattan couple (he's a banker, she's an artist) who have just happily renovated their new Tribeca loft when he's shot and killed by a street thug. Unknown to her, he's walking around as a ghost, desperate to communicate with her

because she's still in danger. He stumbles upon a spirit-world medium (Whoopi Goldberg) and drags her in to help him as a money-laundering and murder plot unfolds around them.

As the first dramatic film directed by Jerry Zucker (who collaborated on *Airplane! Ruthless People* and *The Naked Gun* with David Zucker and Jim Abrahams), *Ghost* is an odd creation – at times nearly smothering in arty somberness, at others veering into good, wacky fun.

Two-hour-plus film really takes its time unfolding, and it's not until Goldberg is brought in that the first laughs do occur, but things do get wilder as Swayze explores his ghostly powers. Sporting a boyish haircut and her usual husky voice, Moore mostly has to spout tears and look vulnerable as she mourns Swayze and tries to avoid Goldberg, who she's convinced is a con artist.
□ 1990: Best Supp. Actress (Whoopi Goldberg), Original Screenplay.
□ Nominations: Best Picture, Editing, Original Score

• •

■ **GHOST AND MRS MUIR, THE**

1947, 103 MINS, US ▽ ⊙
Dir Joseph L. Mankiewicz *Prod* Fred Kohlmar *Scr* Philip Dunne *Ph* Charles Lang Jr *Ed* Dorothy Spencer *Mus* Bernard Herrmann *Art Dir* Richard Day, George Davis
● Gene Tierney, Rex Harrison, George Sanders, Edna Best, Natalie Wood, Robert Coote (20th Century-Fox)

This is the story of a girl who falls in love with a ghost – but not any ordinary spook. As that girl, Gene Tierney gives, what undoubtedly is her best performance to date. It's warmly human and the out-of-this-world romance pulls audience sympathy with an infectious tug that never slackens. In his role as the lusty, seafaring shade, Rex Harrison commands the strongest attention.

Philip Dunne's script lards the R. A. Dick novel with gusty humor and situations that belie the ghostly theme. Dialog makes full use of salty expressions to point up chuckles.

Plot, briefly, deals with young widow who leaves London at turn of century for a seaside cottage. The place is haunted by the ghost of its former owner, Capt Daniel Gregg. The salty shade seeks to frighten the widow away but she's stubborn and stays. When her income is wiped out, the shade dictates to her his life story; she sells it as successful novel.

George Sanders is in briefly, and effectively, as a married lothario who makes a play for the widow, much to Capt Gregg's discomfort. Edna Best shows brightly as the widow's maid-companion. Natalie Wood, as the young daughter, is good, as is Vanessa Brown who becomes the grownup Anna.
□ 1947: Nomination: Best B&W Cinematography

• •

■ **GHOST BUSTERS**

1984, 107 MINS, US ◇ ▽ ⊙
Dir Ivan Reitman *Prod* Ivan Reitman *Scr* Dan Aykroyd, Harold Ramis *Ph* Laszlo Kovacs *Ed* Sheldon Kahn, David Blewitt *Mus* Elmer Bernstein *Art Dir* John DeCuir
● Bill Murray, Dan Aykroyd, Sigourney Weaver, Harold Ramis, Rick Moranis, Annie Potts (Columbia/Delphi)

Ghost Busters is a lavishly produced ($32 million) but only intermittently impressive all-star comedy lampoon of supernatural horror films.

Originally conceived as a John Belushi – Dan Aykroyd vehicle called *Ghostsmashers* before Belushi's death in 1982, *Ghost Busters* under producer-director Ivan Reitman makes a fundamental error: featuring a set of top comics but having them often work alone.

A Manhattan apartment building inhabited by beautiful Dana Barrett (Sigourney

Weaver) and her nerd neighbor Louis Tully (Rick Moranis) becomes the gateway for demons from another dimension to invade the Earth.

To battle them come the Ghostbusters, a trio of scientists who have been kicked off campus and are now freelance ghost catchers for hire. Aykroyd is the gung-ho scientific type, Bill Murray is faking competency (he's had no higher education in parapsychology) and using the job to meet women, while Harold Ramis is the trio's technical expert.

Within the top-heavy cast, it's Murray's picture, as the popular comedian deadpans, ad libs and does an endearing array of physical schtick.
□ 1984: Nominations: Best Song ('Ghost Busters'), Visual Effects

• •

■ **GHOSTBUSTERS II**

1989, 102 MINS, US ◇ ▽ ⊙
Dir Ivan Reitman *Prod* Ivan Reitman *Scr* Harold Ramis, Dan Aykroyd *Ph* Michael Chapman *Ed* Sheldon Kahn, Donn Cambern *Mus* Randy Edelman *Art Dir* Bo Welch
● Bill Murray, Dan Aykroyd, Sigourney Weaver, Harold Ramis, Rick Moranis, Peter MacNicol (Columbia)

Ghostbusters II is babyboomer silliness. Kids will find the oozing slime and ghastly, ghostly apparitions to their liking and adults will enjoy the preposterously clever dialog.

In *II*, the foe is slime, a pinkish, oozing substance that has odd, selective powers – all of them (humorously) evil. Its origins have something to do with a bad imitation Rembrandt painting, the lecherous art historian with an indecipherable foreign accent who's restoring it (Peter MacNicol), and all the bad vibes generated by millions of cranky, stressed-out New Yorkers. The worse their attitude, the worse the slime problem, which is very bad indeed.

The Ghostbusters, naturally, are the only guys for the job.

Bill Murray gets the plum central role (or he forced it by seemingly adlibbing dozens of wisecracks) at the same time his character also manages to skip out on a lot of the dirty ghostbusting work, leaving it to his pals Dan Aykroyd, Harold Ramis and Ernie Hudson.

While they are zapping Slimer, the main nasty creature from the original film, Murray's time is spent wooing back Sigourney Weaver, now a single mother.

It may be a first time, but Weaver get to play a softie, a nice break for the actress and her admirers (even if shots with her cute imperiled baby are scene-stealers).

• •

■ **GHOST DAD**

1990, 84 MINS, US ◇ ▽ ⊙
Dir Sidney Poitier *Prod* Terry Nelson *Scr* Chris Reese, Brent Maddock, S.S. Wilson *Ph* Andrew Laszlo *Ed* Pembroke Herring *Mus* Henry Mancini *Art Dir* Henry Bumstead
● Bill Cosby, Kimberley Russell, Denise Nicholas, Ian Bannen, Christine Ebersole, Barry Corbin (SAH/Universal)

Cartoonish antics and ghostly special effects will entertain the kiddies but, like Bill Cosby's ghostly incarnation, this pic disappears when the lights come on.

Cosby plays a growly, funny, animated and lovable dad with lots of opportunities for physical, facial and vocal comedy. He dies and turns into a ghost 10 minutes into the picture; the story outlives him, but not by much.

Premise offers plenty of opportunity for optical illusions and gags, and they're abundant, but once the novelty of Cosby's plight wears off, it's the script that does the disappearing act. Overall thrust is that dad will learn it's more important to spend time with the kids (he's got only three days left before he'll be whisked off earth forever).

Sidney Poitier directs with vitality and punch, but when the script deserts him, things grow tedious.

••••••••••••••••••••••••••••

■ **GHOST GOES WEST, THE**

1935, 90 MINS, UK Ⓥ

Dir Rene Clair   *Prod* Alexander Korda   *Scr* Robert E. Sherwood   *Ph* Harold Rosson   *Ed* William Hornbeck, Harold Earle-Fischbacher, Henry Cornelius   *Mus* Mischa Spoliansky   *Art Dir* Vincent Korda
● Robert Donat, Jean Parker, Eugene Pallette, Elsa Lanchester, Ralph Bunker (London)

The first film in the English language directed by Rene Clair, ace French director, it shows that Clair still has full rein on his sense of humor and one of the screen's best from an artistic and intelligent standpoint.

Story is a bit different from his past (French) efforts. It has to do with an American who picks up a Scottish manse which has only one fault: it is ancient, it is famous, it has background, it has color – but it also has a ghost. Nevertheless, the American buys the castle and imports it to America stone by stone, ghost and all. In Florida he sets it up again, his daughter, by way of romance, falling for the penniless heir of the castle and ghost.

Robert Sherwood, in working up the story with Clair from a London *Punch* piece [by Eric Keown], has injected a number of hilarious sequences, and some splendid dialog. Robert Donat as the young heir and doubling as the ghost, Jean Parker as the girl, and Eugene Pallette as the father drain every possible bit of good out of their roles.

••••••••••••••••••••••••••••

■ **GHOSTS . . . OF THE CIVIL DEAD**

1988, 92 MINS, AUSTRALIA ◇ Ⓥ

Dir John Hillcoat   *Prod* Evan English   *Scr* Nick Cave, Gene Conkie, Evan English, John Hillcoat   *Ph* Paul Goldman   *Ed* Stewart Young   *Mus* Nick Cave   *Art Dir* Chris Kennedy
● Dave Field, Mike Bishop, Chris de Rose, Nick Cave, Vincent Gil, Bogdan Koca (Correctional Services/Outlaw Values)

The problem of overcrowded prisons and the fact that they often serve as breeding grounds for even tougher criminals, are the concerns of *Ghosts . . . of the Civil Dead*, an ambitious, confronting first feature from John Hillcoat, with ruggedly explicit language and violence.

Setting is a correctional institution of the near future (exterior of the facility was filmed in Nevada). Film traces the events leading up to a riot and 'lockdown'. Drama centers around the arrival of newcomer Dave Field, who discovers a nightmare world where drug-taking and gay sex are ignored by guards and where violence is the order of the day.

Cast includes rock performers Nick Cave, Chris de Rose and Dave Mason, a handful of pro actors (Vincent Gil, Bogdan Koca) and a large number of nonpros, some of them actual ex-cons. Production design is striking.

••••••••••••••••••••••••••••

■ **GHOST STORY**

1981, 110 MINS, US ◇ Ⓥ ⊙

Dir John Irvin   *Prod* Burt Weissbourd   *Scr* Lawrence D. Cohen   *Ph* Jack Cardiff   *Ed* Tom Rolf   *Mus* Philippe Sarde   *Art Dir* Norman Newberry
● Fred Astaire, Melvyn Douglas, Douglas Fairbanks Jr, John Houseman, Craig Wasson, Alice Krige (Universal)

Authors like Peter Straub can take an essentially familiar spook story and make it work as a novel because of the solitary hold on the reader and ample time to embroider the details. But it's a real challenge to put the novel on screen where hundreds can share the flaws.

Helped by solid casting, writer and director make a valiant effort but come up with iso-

lated and excellent moments separated by artful but ordinary stretches.

Even without reading Straub's novel, it's easy to guess early on that Fred Astaire, Melvyn Douglas, Douglas Fairbanks Jr and John Houseman share a dark secret that has prompted the appearance of Alice Krige in both bodily (sometimes very bodily) and ethereal forms. And whatever that secret is, they're going to pay for it.

Unfortunately, it then spins backward to an extremely long re-enactment of the events of long ago. By the time it gets back to the present to deal with the haunting menace, the mood is all wrong and the story riddled with questions that aren't answered.

••••••••••••••••••••••••••••

■ **GIANT**

1956, 198 MINS, US ◇ Ⓥ ⊙

Dir George Stevens   *Prod* George Stevens   *Scr* Fred Guiol, Ivan Moffat   *Ph* William C. Mellor   *Ed* William Hornbeck   *Mus* Dimitri Tiomkin   *Art Dir* Boris Leven
● Elizabeth Taylor, Rock Hudson, James Dean, Carroll Baker, Mercedes McCambridge, Sal Mineo (Warner)

Producers George Stevens and Henry Ginsberg spent freely to capture the mood of the Edna Ferber novel and the picture is fairly saturated with the feeling of the vastness and the mental narrowness, the wealth and the poverty, the pride and the prejudice that make up Texas.

Trio of Elizabeth Taylor, Rock Hudson and James Dean turns in excellent portrayals, with each character moulded in a strongly individual vein. Carroll Baker, in her first important part, proves herself a most competent actress.

Story starts when Hudson, as Bick Benedict, comes to Maryland and marries Taylor, a beautiful and strongwilled girl, who is transplanted from the gentle green of her state to the dusty gray of Texas in the early twenties. Jett, a ranchhand, played by James Dean, antagonistic to Hudson, finds oil on his little plot and realizes an ambition to become rich. At the start of World War II he convinces Hudson to allow oil drilling also on Hudson's ranch and the millions come flowing in. But money only intensifies Dean's bad characteristics.

Giant isn't preachy but it's a powerful indictment of the Texas superiority complex. In fact, the picture makes that point even stronger than it's in the book.

As the shiftless, envious, bitter ranchhand who hates society, Dean delivers an outstanding portrayal. It's a sock performance. Taylor turns in a surprisingly clever performance that registers up and down the line. Hudson achieves real stature.

☐ 1956: Best Director.
☐ Nominations: Best Picture, Actor (James Dean, Rock Hudson), Supp. Actress (Mercedes McCambridge), Adapted Screenplay, Color Costume Design, Color Art Direction, Editing, Scoring of a Dramatic Picture

••••••••••••••••••••••••••••

■ **G.I. BLUES**

1960, 115 MINS, US ◇ Ⓥ

Dir Norman Taurog   *Prod* Hal B. Wallis   *Scr* Edmund Beloin, Henry Garson   *Ph* Loyal Griggs   *Ed* Warren Low   *Mus* Joseph J. Lilley (arr.)   *Art Dir* Hal Pereira, Walter Tyler
● Elvis Presley, Juliet Prowse, Robert Ives, Leticia Roman, James Douglas, Sigrid Maier (Paramount)

About the creakiest 'book' in musicomedy annals has been revived by the scenarists as a framework within which Elvis Presley warbles 10 wobbly songs and co-star Juliet Prowse steps out in a pair of flashy dances.

Plot casts Presley as an all-American-boy tank-gunner stationed in Germany who woos supposedly icy-hearted Prowse for what starts

out as strictly mercenary reasons (if he spends the night with her, he wins a hunk of cash to help set up a nitery in the States). Needless to say, the ice melts and amor develops, only to dissolve when Miss Prowse learns of the heely scheme.

Responsibility for penning the 10 tunes is given no one on Paramount's credit sheet. Considering the quality of these compositions, such anonymity is understandable. Joseph J. Lilley is credited with scoring and conducting music for the film. It is not absolutely clear whether he had a hand in composing the pop selections, but it is doubtful. Presley sings them all as a slightly subdued pelvis.

Prowse is a firstrate dancer and has a pixie charm reminiscent of Leslie Caron. She deserves better roles than this.

••••••••••••••••••••••••••••

■ **GIDEON OF SCOTLAND YARD**

See: Gideon's Day

••••••••••••••••••••••••••••

■ **GIDEON'S DAY**

(US: Gideon of Scotland Yard)

1958, 91 MINS, UK ◇

Dir John Ford   *Prod* Michael Killanin   *Scr* T.E.B. Clarke   *Ph* Frederick A. Young   *Ed* Raymond Poulton   *Mus* Douglas Gamley   *Art Dir* Ken Adam
● Jack Hawkins, Dianne Foster, Anna Lee, Anna Massey, Cyril Cusack, Laurence Naismith (Columbia)

Screenwriter T.E.B. Clarke first earned applause for his police screenplay, *The Blue Lamp*. With his adaptation of J.J. Marric's novel, Clarke returns successfully to crime, with the spotlight on Scotland Yard.

This merely purports to be one busy day in the life of a CID chief inspector and it turns out to be quite a day. He accuses one of his sergeants of taking bribes. A pay snatch ties up with the killing of the sergeant in a hit-and-run car crash. A murder in Manchester has a maniac killer headed for London, and it all finishes up with a safe robbery which involves another slaying.

Jack Hawkins has played this type of role so often that he could probably do it blindfolded. And it is a tribute to him that he can hold the interest with such a run-of-the-mill character. He is also surrounded by some firstrate thesps who bring a touch of distinction to routine parts.

••••••••••••••••••••••••••••

■ **GIDGET**

1959, 95 MINS, US ◇ Ⓥ ⊙

Dir Paul Wendkos   *Prod* Lewis J. Rachmil   *Scr* Gabrielle Upton   *Ph* Burnett Guffey   *Ed* William A. Lyon   *Mus* Morris Stoloff (sup.)
● Sandra Dee, Cliff Roberston, James Darren, Arthur O'Connell, Mary La Roche, Jo Morrow (Columbia)

Sandra Dee is the 'gidget' of the title, being a young woman, so slight in stature she is tagged with a nickname which is a contraction of girl and midget. Dee is in that crucial period of growing up where she doesn't like boys very much but is beginning to realize they are going to play a big part in her life.

The screenplay, based on the novel by Frederick Kohner, is played mostly out-of-doors on the ocean front west of Los Angeles that constitutes the play grounds and mating grounds for the young of the area.

The simple plot is a contemporary restatement of the *Student Prince* theme. The surf bum who Dee falls in love with (James Darren), turns out to be the respectable son of a business acquaintance of her father.

Paul Wendkos' direction is ingenious in delineating the youthful characters, not so easy in presenting normal youngsters of no particular depth or variety. Direction could have been more fluid, however, particularly in the musical numbers.

Dee makes a pert and pretty heroine, and Cliff Robertson, as the only adult of the beach group, is acceptable. Darren is especially effective as the young man torn between the carefree life and the problems of growing up.

■ **GIG, THE**

1985, 92 MINS, US ◇ ⑨

Dir Frank D. Gilroy   *Prod* Norman I. Cohen   *Scr* Frank D. Gilroy   *Ph* Jeri Sopanen   *Ed* Rick Shaine   *Mus* Warren Vache

● Wayne Rogers, Cleavon Little, Andrew Duncan, Jerry Matz, Daniel Nalbach, Warren Vache (The Gig)

The Gig is a winning little film about a group of guys who try to fulfill their dream of being jazz players.

Wayne Rogers toplines as a New York businessman who has played Dixieland Jazz with his five pals for their own amusement once a week since 1970. He arranges a two-week pro engagement and talks the group into taking the step, the convincing argument being when their bass player George (Stan Lachow) drops out, promoting solidarity among the other five.

The replacement bassist, veteran player Marshall Wilson (Cleavon Little), causes friction in the group, because of his unfriendly personality and condescending attitude towards the budding amateurs.

Filmmaker Gilroy gets maximum comic mileage out of this contrast, while making good points concerning the snobbism and purist stance that pervades many jazz circles.

Aided by a very entertaining portrait of life at a Catskills resort, Rogers and Little make a solid team.

■ **GIGI**

1958, 116 MINS, US ◇ ⑨ ⊙

Dir Vincente Minnelli   *Prod* Arthur Freed   *Scr* Alan Jay Lerner   *Ph* Joseph Ruttenberg   *Ed* Adrienne Fazan   *Mus* Andre Previn (dir)   *Art Dir* Cecil Beaton

● Leslie Caron, Maurice Chevalier, Louis Jourdan, Hermione Gingold, Eva Gabor, Jacques Bergerac (M-G-M)

Gigi is a naughty but nice romp of the hyper-romantic naughty 90s of Paris-in-the-spring, in the Bois, in Maxim's and in the boudoir. Alan Jay Lerner's libretto is tailor-made for an inspired casting job for all principals, and Fritz Loewe's tunes (to Lerner's lyrics) vie with and suggest their memorable *My Fair Lady* score.

Gigi is a French variation, by novelist Colette, of the *Pygmalion* legend. As the character unfolds it is apparent that the hoydenish Gigi has a greater preoccupation with a wedding ring than casual, albeit super-charged romance.

The sophistication of Maurice Chevalier (who well nigh steals the picture), Isabel Jeans, Hermione Gingold and Eva Gabor are in contrast to the wholesomeness of the Leslie Caron-Louis Jourdan romance. Caron is completely captivating and convincing in the title role.

Produced in France, *Gigi* is steeped in authentic backgrounds from Maxim's to the Tuileries, from the Bois de Boulogne to the Palais de Glace which sets the scene for Gabor's philandering with Jacques Bergerac, her skating instructor, and establishes the pattern of playing musical boudoirs, which was par for the circa 1890s Paris course.

The performances are well nigh faultless. From Chevalier, as the sophisticated uncle, to John Abbott, his equally suave valet; from Gingold's understanding role as Gigi's grandma to Isabel Jeans, the worldly aunt who could tutor Gigi in the ways of demimondaine love; from Jourdan's eligibility as the swain to Bergerac's casual courting of

light ladies' loves. Caron's London experience in the stage version of Colette's cocotte (Audrey Hepburn did it in the US) stands her in excellent stead.
□ 1958: Best Picture, Director, Adapted Screenplay, Color Cinematography, Art Direction, Song ('Gigi'), Scoring of a Musical Picture, Editing, Costume Design

■ **GILDA**

1946, 110 MINS, US ⑨ ⊙

Dir Charles Vidor   *Prod* Virginia Van Upp   *Scr* Marion Parsonnet   *Ph* Rudolph Mate   *Ed* Charles Nelson   *Mus* Morris Stoloff, Marlin Skiles (dir.)   *Art Dir* Stephen Goosson, Van Nest Polglase

● Rita Hayworth, Glenn Ford, George Macready, Joseph Calleia, Steven Geray, Joe Sawyer (Columbia)

Practically all the s.a. habiliments of the femme fatale have been mustered for *Gilda*, and when things get trite and frequently far-fetched, somehow, at the drop of a shoulder strap, there is always Rita Hayworth to excite the filmgoer.

The story [by E. A. Ellington, adapted by Jo Eisinger] is a confusion of gambling, international intrigue and a triangle that links two gamblers and the wife of one of them. The setting is Buenos Aires. Sneaking in somehow is the subplot of a tungsten cartel operated by the husband, who also runs a swank gambling casino. A couple of Nazis are thrown in also.

Hayworth is photographed most beguilingly. The producers have created nothing subtle in the projection of her s.a., and that's probably been wise. Glenn Ford is the vis-a-vis, in his first picture part in several years.

There are a couple of songs ostensibly sung by Hayworth, and one of them, 'Put the Blame on Mame', piques the interest because of its intriguing, low-down quality.

Gilda is obviously an expensive production – and shows it. The direction is static, but that's more the fault of the writers.

■ **GIMME SHELTER**

1970, 90 MINS, US ◇

Dir David Maysles, Albert Maysles, Charlotte Zwerin   *Prod* Porter Bibb   *Ed* Ellen Gifford, Robert Farren, Joanne Burke, Kent McKinney, Mirra Bank, Susan Steinberg, Janet Laurentano (Maysles)

Maysles Brothers' 16mm documentary on 1969 Rolling Stones' US concert tour which culminated in violence and death at the Altamont Speedway in California.

What precedes the satanic finale is a riveting close-up look at the Stones in performance. Contrary to the popular image, lead singer Mick Jagger emerges in off-stage footage as a withdrawn, almost catatonic individual totally involved in his music and virtually immune to events occurring around him.

Onstage it's another matter, and *Gimme Shelter* captures that petulant omnisexuality that made many adults consider Jagger a threat to their daughters, sons and household pets alike. Pouting and bumping through such numbers as 'I Can't Get No Satisfaction,' he is seldom less than mesmerizing.

■ **GIRL CAN'T HELP IT, THE**

1956, 96 MINS, US ◇

Dir Frank Tashlin   *Prod* Frank Tashlin   *Scr* Frank Tashlin, Herbert Baker   *Ph* Leon Shamroy   *Ed* James B. Clark   *Mus* Lionel Newman

● Tom Ewell, Jayne Mansfield, Edmond O'Brien, Henry Jones, John Emery, Juanita Moore (20th Century-Fox)

The Girl Can't Help It is an hilarious comedy with a beat. On the surface, it appears that producer-director-scripter Frank Tashlin concentrated on creating fun for the juniors – a chore that he completes to a tee. However,

the suspicion lurks that he also poked some fun at the dance beat craze. There are so many sight gags and physical bits of business, including Jayne Mansfield and a couple of milk bottles, that males of any age will get the entertainment message.

Mansfield doesn't disappoint as the sexpot who just wants to be a successful wife and mother, not a glamor queen. She's physically equipped for the role, and also is competent in sparking considerable of the fun. Nature was so much more bountiful with her than with Marilyn Monroe that it seems Mansfield should have left MM with her voice. However, the vocal imitation could have been just another part of the fun-poking indulged in.

Edmond O'Brien, rarely seen in comedy, is completely delightful as the hammy ex-gangster who thinks his position demands that his girl be a star name. Tom Ewell scores mightily as the has-been agent who is haunted by the memory of Julie London, another girl he had pushed to reluctant stardom.

■ **GIRL CRAZY**

1943, 97 MINS, US ⑨ ⊙

Dir Norman Taurog, Busby Berkeley   *Prod* Arthur Freed   *Scr* Fred Finklehoffe   *Ph* William Daniels, Robert Plancke   *Ed* Albert Akst   *Mus* George Gershwin

● Mickey Rooney, Judy Garland, June Allyson, Nancy Walker, Gil Stratton, Rags Ragland (M-G-M)

This is the second film treatment of the 1930 stage click *Girl Crazy*, the first being an RKO 'B' starring Wheeler and Woolsey, with all of the crack tunes tossed out at that time except 'I Got Rhythm'.

Judy Garland is in the role originally played by Ginger Rogers on the stage, while Nancy Walker, new to the screen in *Best Foot Forward*, is in a semblance of Ethel Merman's part. But all the double entendre is tossed out with the locale switched from a dude ranch to a western university. It's to the latter that a NY newspaper publisher sends his playboy son (Mickey Rooney). Rooney puts the university on its financial feet and makes it coeducational. The girls he attracts are plenty and pretty.

The story thread is light, but enough to string together the George and Ira Gershwin songs, i.e., 'Embraceable You', 'Treat Me Rough', 'Bidin' My Time', 'Could You Use Me' and 'Not for Me'.

Garland is a nifty saleswoman of the numbers right down to the over-produced 'Rhythm' finale which was Busby Berkeley's special chore.

■ **GIRLFRIENDS**

1978, 86 MINS, US ◇ ⑨

Dir Claudia Weill   *Prod* Claudia Weill, Jan Sanders   *Scr* Vicki Polon   *Ph* Fred Murphy   *Ed* Suzanne Pettit   *Mus* Michael Small   *Art Dir* Patrizia von Brandenstein

● Melanie Mayron, Eli Wallach, Anita Skinner, Bob Balaban, Christopher Guest, Viveca Lindfors (Cyclops)

This is a warm, emotional and at times wise picture about friendship. It's documentary film-maker Claudia Weill's first feature, although there's no reason to apologetically pigeonhole this movie as a 'promising first feature'. It's the work of a technically skilled and assured director.

Melanie Mayron is outstanding as a photographer fresh out of college maturing under the strains of professional insecurity and loneliness.

Down the line Weill has extracted first-rate performances. Anita Skinner is Mayron's best friend and until she suddenly marries Christopher Guest, her room mate. Eli Wallach portrays a rabbi and almost paramor for whom Mayron sometimes photographs Bar Mitzvahs and weddings. Bob Balaban is Mayron's slightly off-center boy friend and

Viveca Lindfors is Beatrice, owner of a Greenwich Village gallery who believes in Mayron and gives her a big break.

Each performance is a little gem and so are the characters developed by Vicki Polon from a story by her and Weill. They look and act like people, which is a relief. There are no false touches of glamour.

■ **GIRL-GETTERS, THE**
See: The System

■ **GIRL HUNTERS, THE**

1963, 103 MINS, UK ▽
Dir Roy Rowland   *Prod* Robert Fellows   *Scr* Mickey Spillane, Roy Rowland, Robert Fellows   *Ph* Ken Talbot   *Ed* Sidney Stone   *Mus* Phil Green   *Art Dir* Tony Inglis
● Mickey Spillane, Shirley Eaton, Lloyd Nolan, Hy Gardner, Scott Peters (Fellane)

A slick and entertaining adventure meller, *The Girl Hunters* also debuts author Mickey Spillane portraying his rough 'n' tumble hero Mike Hammer for the first time on the screen. He turns in a credible job.

Plot finds the private eye in the gutter from seven years of boozing and fretting because he believes that he sent his secretary and best gal to her doom when he gave her an assignment to do. It develops, however, that she may still be alive and Hammer straightens out and goes in search of her 'just like the old days', as one of the characters comments.

Along the line he finds himself in a romantic entanglement with one of his prime info sources, played cooly and with seductive restraint by Shirley Eaton who spends much of her time in the film wearing just a bikini.

Scott Peters is police captain Pat Chambers. The actor puts plenty of bite into the role but sometimes tends to overplay his obvious distaste for his ex-chum.

As a federal agent who's also interested in the case which has the foreign intrigue element of the murder of a US Senator which is linked to an international Commie plot, Lloyd Nolan turns in a pro and reliable job.

Pic was lensed in London but considerable care is taken to preserve Gotham locales where the action takes place. Several fave watering spots around town like Al & Dicks and the Blue Ribbon have been faithfully reproduced by art director Tony Inglis.

■ **GIRL IN A SWING, THE**

1988, 117 MINS, US/UK ◇ ▽ ⊙
Dir Gordon Hessler   *Prod* Just Betzer, Benni Korzen   *Scr* Gordon Hessler   *Ph* Claus Loof   *Ed* Robert Gordon   *Mus* Carl Davis   *Art Dir* Rob Schilling
● Meg Tilly, Rupert Frazer, Nicholas Le Prevost, Elspet Gray, Lorna Heilbron, Helen Cherry (Panorama)

British writer-director Gordon Hessler has turned Richard Adams' 1980 psycho-chiller novel *The Girl in a Swing* into a smooth, fine-looking piece of romantic-erotic entertainment with many a fine Hitchcockian touch and a rather special star turn by Meg Tilly.

During their brief Florida honeymoon Karin's feelings of guilt and Alan's premonitions of disaster mount. They seek solace in their joy of sex. Karin also joins Alan in his hunt for ceramic treasures.

When she succeeds in finding, and buying for next to nothing, a third example of the porcelain rarity 'The Girl in the Swing', they are assured of instant wealth, and Karin tries to take Holy Communion from a vicar friend to make a clean break with the past.

Instead of absolution, Karin finds fear and guilt taking full possession of her, while Alan indulges her. It becomes more and more obvious that Karin must have killed the baby that came before the one she is now pregnant with.

The recurring theme of guilt, atonement and punishment is gently explored during the development of suspense.

■ **GIRL NAMED TAMIKO, A**

1962, 110 MINS, US ◇
Dir John Sturges   *Prod* Hal Wallis   *Scr* Edward Anhalt   *Ph* Charles Lang Jr   *Ed* Warren Low   *Mus* Elmer Bernstein   *Art Dir* Hal Pereira, Walter Tyler
● Laurence Harvey, France Nuyen, Martha Hyer, Gary Merrill, Michael Wilding, Miyoshi Umeki (Paramount)

This has its share of shortcomings; there's now and again a bit of fuzziness in character development and plot detail. But these may well be overlooked, for the story of emotional conflicts in modern-day Japan is a fairly arresting one.

Laurence Harvey's character is not one immediately easy to accept and this is one of the flaws. As Ivan Kalin, he's a Chinese-Russian photographer and looks, speaks and romances like a British matinee idol.

The girl of the title is France Nuyen, thoroughly enchanting as the librarian whose family adheres to the Japanese traditions while she breaks away to engage in the romance with Harvey. Martha Hyer, as an American girl, very much on the loose in flitting from man to man, handles the part fittingly.

Gary Merrill fits in as a brooding business man who cares and yearns for Hyer only to have her walk out on him. Michael Wilding is a British art dealer with a distaste for the devious measures taken by Harvey in order to get his much-wanted visa to go to the United States. Miyoshi Umeki is a cutie who does the co-habitat bit with Wilding. These two make for a colorful pair and their East-West mating game is rendered plausibly.

■ **GIRL ON A MOTORCYCLE, THE**
(Aka: Naked Under Leather)

1968, 91 MINS, UK/FRANCE ◇ ▽
Dir Jack Cardiff   *Prod* William Sassoon   *Scr* Ronald Duncan, Jack Cardiff   *Ph* Jack Cardiff, Rene Guissart   *Ed* Peter Musgrave   *Mus* Les Reed   *Art Dir* Russell Hagg, Jean D'Eaubonne
● Alain Delon, Marianne Faithfull, Roger Mutton, Marius Goring, Catherine Jourdan, Jean Leduc (Mid Atlantic/Ares)

A pretty young girl in a leather form-fitting getup covering her nudity rides a powerful motorcycle towards her lover after creeping out of her young husband's bed. Her ride is studded with flashbacks and even flash forwards and psychedelic inserts of torrid lovemaking. The ride gets a bit long and the film lacks a true erotic flair. But it is well lensed and has a shattering finale.

The motorcycle is a present from her lover and is supposed to be an erotic symbol. But treatment [of the 1963 novel *La motocyclette* by Andre Pieyre de Mandiargues] can rarely give the fiery dash to make this acceptable except in the girl's final mixing of metaphors as she literally makes love to the bike.

Marianne Faithfull appears a bit too showy and on the surface as the girl and uses facile facial expressions rather than being able to project the girl's feelings. Alain Delon is a sort of hedonistic young college don who does not believe in love in a romantic sense and is mad about motorcycles.

■ **GIRLS ABOUT TOWN**

1931, 80 MINS, US
Dir George Cukor   *Scr* Raymond Griffith, Brian Marlow   *Ph* Ernest Haller
● Kay Francis, Joel McCrea, Lilyan Tashman, Eugene Pallette, Alan Dinehart, Lucile Webster Gleason (Paramount)

There's an unwitting punch scene in this picture to draw laughter. It's where Kay Francis shows off her figure in undies while explaining she's through with the gold-digger racket and intends going straight because she's found love with a rich rube.

When Francis falls for a young-looking sucker from a hick town the burn is on. She's the dame with a twisted virtue. Only the boy friend would rather marry her than take her unawares even if she's willing.

There's some additional sentiment brought in between the elder of the two chumps, as played ingenuously by Eugene Pallette, and his middle-aged wife, as done by Lucile Gleason. He's a tightwad and practical joker from Lansing. With the help of Lilyan Tashman, who does the gold-digger role as natural as it can seem, the bird's wife works the old boy into a mad spree of jewelry buying.

■ **GIRLS! GIRLS! GIRLS!**

1962, 101 MINS, US ◇ ▽
Dir Norman Taurog   *Prod* Hal Wallis   *Scr* Edward Anhalt, Allan Weiss   *Ph* Loyal Griggs   *Ed* Warren Low   *Mus* Joseph J. Lilley   *Art Dir* Hal Pereira, Walter Tyler
● Elvis Presley, Stella Stevens, Jeremy Slate, Laurel Goodwin, Benson Fong (Paramount)

Girls! Girls! Girls! is just that – with Elvis Presley there as the main attraction. Hal Wallis' production puts the entertainer back into the non-dramatic, purely escapist light musical vein. The thin plot, scripted by Edward Anhalt and Allan Weiss from an original story by Weiss, has him the romantic interest of two girls. Hackneyed tale is of poor boy fisherman who meets rich girl who doesn't tell him she is rich but who, naturally, falls in love with him.

Weiss also penned story for the earlier *Blue Hawaii*, which Norman Taurog also directed for Wallis.

Most striking thing about the picture is the introduction of new Paramount pactee Laurel Goodwin, who makes an auspicious film bow. Youngster has the cute, home spun potential of a Doris Day.

Stella Stevens, however, is wasted in a standard role as a sultry torch singer who has given up ever really nailing the guy. She does her best but, aside from singing three songs (her first singing in a film) in a style suitable for the character, there just isn't enough for her to do.

■ **GIRLS HE LEFT BEHIND, THE**
See: The Gang's All Here

■ **GIRL WITH GREEN EYES**

1964, 91 MINS, UK ▽
Dir Desmond Davis   *Prod* Oscar Lewenstein   *Scr* Edna O'Brien   *Ph* Manny Wynn   *Ed* Brian Smedley-Aston   *Mus* John Addison   *Art Dir* Edward Marshall
● Peter Finch, Rita Tushingham, Lynn Redgrave, Marie Kean, Julian Glover, T.P. McKenna (United Artists/Woodfall)

This first film by Desmond Davis, who was a cameraman with Tony Richardson on *Loneliness of the Long Distance Runner* and *Saturday Night, Sunday Morning*, has the smell of success. Davis is imaginative, prepared to take chances and has the sympathy to draw perceptive performances from his cast.

Story [from the novel, *The Lonely Girl*, by Edna O'Brien] is set in Dublin where two shopgirls share a room. One (Rita Tushingham) is a quiet, withdrawn girl in the painful throes of awakening. The other (Lynn Redgrave) is a vivacious, gabby, good-natured colleen with a roving eye for the boys. But when the two girls casually meet a quiet, middle-aged writer (Peter Finch), the friendship that starts up is, naturally, between Tushingham and Finch.

Finch does a standout job as the tolerant writer who, despite occasional lapses into impatience, develops a fine understanding of the problems of the girl. Tushingham is often moving, sometimes spritely and always interesting to watch in her puzzled shyness. Redgrave makes an ebullient wench.

●●●●●●●●●●●●●●●●●●●●●●●●●●●●●●●●●●●●●●

■ **GIRLY**

See: Mumsy, Nanny, Sonny & Girly

●●●●●●●●●●●●●●●●●●●●●●●●●●●●●●●●●●●●●●

■ **GIRO CITY**

(US: And Nothing But the Truth)

1982, 102 MINS, UK ◇ ▼
Dir Karl Francis   *Prod* Sophie Balhetchet, David Payne
Scr Karl Francis   *Ph* Curtis Clark   *Ed* Neil Thomson
Mus Alun Francis   *Art Dir* Jamie Leonard
● Glenda Jackson, Jon Finch, Kenneth Colley, James Donnelly, Emrys James, Karen Archer (Silvercalm)

Giro City is a British thriller which examines political corruption and media attitudes to the rot on its doorstep. Story involves a documentary filmmaker and a reporter who work for a successful TV magazine programme, and their attempts to cover two controversial news stories.

In breaking new ground, the film (shot on Super-16) has to make up in freshness and conviction for the superficiality with which some of the many issues raised are treated. But a hard-hitting and emotional core is provided by the story of a family in South Wales who, alone but for the TV crew, take on the local council in their determination to stay on their land.

Glenda Jackson and Jon Finch as filmmaker and journalist are depicted as people for whom work covers up a hollow emotional core. Their pursuit of the corrupt councillor is determined and thrilling.

●●●●●●●●●●●●●●●●●●●●●●●●●●●●●●●●●●●●●●

■ **GIVE A GIRL A BREAK**

1953, 81 MINS, US ◇ ▼
Dir Stanley Donen   *Prod* Jack Cummings   *Scr* Albert Hackett, Frances Goodrich   *Ph* William Mellor
Ed Adrienne Fazan   *Mus* Andre Previn, Saul Chaplin (dir.)   *Art Dir* Cedric Gibbons, Paul Groesse
● Marge Champion, Gower Champion, Debbie Reynolds, Helen Wood, Bob Fosse, Kurt Kasznar (M-G-M)

The talents of a group of youthful performers are showcased in this routine tintuner, a passably pleasant, although uninspired, piece of entertainment. Five tunes were cleffed by Burton Lane and Ira Gershwin, while the sixth, a straight terp piece, was done by Andre Previn and Saul Chaplin.

In addition to the Champions, the other youthful talent consists of Debbie Reynolds, Helen Wood and Bob Fosse. The quintet works hard at its chores and manages to brighten proceedings in spots, although the material in the screenplay, from a story by Vera Caspary, is too lightweight to give much drive. Stanley Donen's direction falters, also, contributing to the draggy pace.

Plot twist revolves around Champion, Reynolds and Wood competing for the lead in a show being directed by Gower Champion after its femme star (Donna Martell) walks out. This showbiz background is ample excuse to work in the songs and dances and there is a certain amount of suspense over which girl will land the role.

●●●●●●●●●●●●●●●●●●●●●●●●●●●●●●●●●●●●●●

■ **GIVE MY REGARDS TO BROADWAY**

1948, 89 MINS, US ◇
Dir Lloyd Bacon   *Prod* Walter Morosco   *Scr* Samuel Hoffenstein, Elizabeth Reinhardt   *Ph* Harry Jackson
Ed William Reynolds   *Art Dir* Lyle R. Wheeler, J. Russell Spencer

● Dan Dailey, Charles Winninger, Nancy Guild, Fay Bainter, Charlie Ruggles, Barbara Lawrence (20th Century-Fox)

Despite the mental images of lush production numbers that might be conjured up by the title, *Broadway* has none of that. Instead, it's a simple story about an old vaude family that lives in the hope that the Palace two-a-day will some time be revived. Film has plenty of showbiz nostalgia. Title song, cleffed by George M. Cohan, runs through the film as its theme.

Although he's backed by a fine supporting cast that might otherwise steal his thunder, Dan Dailey has a personal field day. He gets a full chance to demonstrate his amazing versatility.

In addition to Dailey, who's standout as the son, the cast is excellent under the leisurely directorial touch of Lloyd Bacon. Winninger does one of his neatest characterizations as the oldtimer who refuses to toss in the sponge, and Bainter is fine as his understanding spouse.

●●●●●●●●●●●●●●●●●●●●●●●●●●●●●●●●●●●●●●

■ **GIVE US THIS DAY**

(US: Salt to the Devil)

1949, 120 MINS, UK
Dir Edward Dmytryk   *Prod* Rod Geiger, Nat A. Bronsten
Scr Ben Barzman   *Ph* C. Pennington Richards   *Ed* John Guthridge   *Mus* Benjamin Frankel
● Sam Wanamaker, Lea Padovani, Kathleen Ryan, Bonar Colleano (Plantagenet)

The moving simplicity of the Pietro Di Donato novel, *Christ in Concrete*, has been brought to the screen with rare sincerity. It is two hours of genuine human drama, which makes no concession to convention.

This is one of the few occasions in which British studios have embarked on a production with a New York setting. The expert hand of Edward Dmytryk's direction ensures faithful atmosphere.

Dmytryk presents the story of Geremio, an Italian bricklayer who works in Brooklyn. It is his wife's ambition to have a home of their own, and carefully they save for the down-payment. But the Depression overtakes them. Then comes Geremio's opportunity to work as a foreman on a job which he knows to be unsafe and which culminates in tragedy.

Sam Wanamaker has never been better, investing the part with warmth and emotion.

●●●●●●●●●●●●●●●●●●●●●●●●●●●●●●●●●●●●●●

■ **GLADIATOR**

1992, 98 MINS, US ◇ ▼ ⊙
Dir Rowdy Harrington   *Prod* Frank Price, Steve Roth
Scr Lyle Kessler, Robert Mark Kamen   *Ph* Tak Fujimoto
Ed Peter Zinner, Harry B. Miller III   *Mus* Brad Fiedel
Art Dir Gregg Fonseca
● Cuba Gooding Jr, James Marshall, Robert Loggia, Ossie Davis, Brian Dennehy, John Heard (Columbia/Price)

Gladiator is an exercise in audience manipulation, an interracial buddy movie. It's as if the producers called in their writers and said, 'Give us a boxing picture with some of that *Barton Fink* feeling.' Result is a formulaic attempt at an underdog saga that worked far better in the 1930s and 1940s.

Problem is that the filmmakers' bait-and-switch strategies are transparent. Cuba Gooding Jr (*Boyz N the Hood*) receives top billing, but the film is relentlessly centered around his white pal, James Marshall (*Twin Peaks*). Early reels exploit the racial tensions in a Chicago high school en route to a predictable revelation that both sets of youngsters have a common enemy, the white businessman (Brian Dennehy) who stages their illegal boxing matches.

Marshall, cast as the new kid in school, is sullen and far too low key through much of the picture. Director Rowdy Harrington, who

poured on the trash in *Road House*, aims for a grittier feel this time, with dull results. Gooding is sympathetic and a convincing pugilist.

●●●●●●●●●●●●●●●●●●●●●●●●●●●●●●●●●●●●●●

■ **GLASS BOTTOM BOAT, THE**

1966, 110 MINS, US ◇ ▼
Dir Frank Tashlin   *Prod* Martin Melcher, Everett Freeman
Scr Everett Freeman   *Ph* Leon Shamroy   *Ed* John McSweeney   *Mus* Frank DeVol   *Art Dir* George W. Davis, Edward Carfagno
● Doris Day, Rod Taylor, Arthur Godfrey, John McGiver, Paul Lynde, Edward Andrews (M-G-M)

Doris Day enters the world of rocketry and espionage in *The Glass Bottom Boat*, an expensively-mounted production given frequently to sight gags and frenzied comedy performances.

Star plays a conscientious public relations staffer in a space laboratory where Rod Taylor, the engineering genius heading the facility, has invented a device both the US government and the Soviets want. He falls for her and to keep her always by his side invents the idea of having her write a very definitive biography of him. She becomes a spy suspect because she has a dog named Vladimir, which she's always calling on the telephone so its ringing will give her pet exercise when she isn't there, and because she follows a standing order that every bit of paper should be burned.

Arthur Godfrey scores strongly as her father, operator of a glass-bottom sightseeing boat at Catalina. Taylor lends his usual masculine presence effectively, both as the inventor and romantic vis-a-vis.

●●●●●●●●●●●●●●●●●●●●●●●●●●●●●●●●●●●●●●

■ **GLASS KEY, THE**

1935, 77 MINS, US
Dir Frank Tuttle   *Prod* E. Lloyd Sheldon   *Scr* Kathryn Scola, Kubec Glasmon, Harry Ruskin   *Ph* Henry Sharp
Ed Hugh Bennett
● George Raft, Edward Arnold, Claire Dodd, Ray Milland, Rosalind Keith, Guinn Williams (Paramount)

This is a tale [from the story by Dashiell Hammett] of politics which involves murder, gangsterism and rocky romances. As murder mystery material, the story provides interesting plot situations. Performances by Raft and others are excellent, the direction is skilled and the dialog job leaves little to be desired, but too much has gone into the narrative that is up the alley of inconsistency.

It is a little unreasonable to expect that a daughter would dangerously turn against her father because of accusations that he murdered the man she loved, the son of a senator from whom the father was expecting patronage. It is equally implausible to expect that the politician would dig his own grave by shielding the senator.

Three romances are knitted into the murder mystery, but, in the main, the romantic aspects of the picture don't impress.

Raft gives a fine performance, as does Edward Arnold, playing the aspiring politician. Senator isn't much in the hands of Charles Richman, nor do Claire Dodd, Rosalind Keith or Ray Milland register any too well.

●●●●●●●●●●●●●●●●●●●●●●●●●●●●●●●●●●●●●●

■ **GLASS KEY, THE**

1942, 85 MINS, US ▼
Dir Stuart Heisler   *Prod* B.G. DeSylva (exec.)
Scr Jonathan Latimer   *Ph* Theodor Sparkuhl   *Ed* Archie Marshek   *Mus* Victor Young   *Art Dir* Hans Dreier, Haldane Douglas
● Brian Donlevy, Veronica Lake, Alan Ladd, Bonita Granville, William Bendix, Joseph Calleia (Paramount)

Parading a murder mystery amidst background of politics, gambling czars, romance and lusty action, this revised version of Dashiell Hammett's novel – originally made in 1935 – is a good picture of its type.

Brian Donlevy is the political boss, a role similar to that he handled in *Great McGinty*. Alan Ladd is his assistant and confidant. Veronica Lake is the vacillating daughter of the gubernatorial candidate who first makes a play for Donlevy but winds up in the arms of Ladd, while Joseph Calleia has the gambling house concessions around the city. Mixed well, the result is an entertaining whodunit with sufficient political and racketeer angles to make it good entertainment for general audiences.

Donlevy makes the most of his role of the political leader who fought his way up from the other side of the tracks.

· ·

■ GLASS MENAGERIE, THE

1950, 106 MINS, US

Dir Irving Rapper   *Prod* Jerry Wald, Charles K. Feldman
Scr Tennessee Williams, Peter Berneis   *Ph* Robert Burks
Ed David Weisbart   *Mus* Max Steiner
● Jane Wyman, Kirk Douglas, Gertrude Lawrence, Arthur Kennedy (Warner)

Spotting Jane Wyman as crippled Laura, Arthur Kennedy as her compassionate brother, Gertrude Lawrence as their frowzy mother and Kirk Douglas as the Gentleman Caller who unwittingly changes their lives, for better or worse, is a casting scoop.

Familiar plot [from Tennessee Williams' play] about the aging southern belle who holds her brood together in a St Louis tenement, only to lose her son when he decides he can take her nagging no longer, unreels engrossingly. Most remarkable is the subtle restraint employed to register Laura's awakening to the fact that life isn't a bust just because you've got a bum gam.

Kennedy, Wyman and Lawrence fight it out for thesp honors, and it would appear to be a draw.

· ·

■ GLASS MENAGERIE, THE

1987, 130 MINS, US ◇ ⓥ ⊙

Dir Paul Newman   *Prod* Burtt Harris   *Scr* [uncredited]
Ph Michael Ballhaus   *Ed* David Ray   *Mus* Henry Mancini   *Art Dir* Tony Walton
● Joanne Woodward, John Malkovich, Karen Allen, James Naughton (Cineplex Odeon)

Paul Newman's adaptation of *The Glass Menagerie* is a reverent record of Tennessee William's 1954 dream play, and one watches with a kind of distant dreaminess rather than an intense emotional involvement. It's a play of stunning language and brilliant performances creating living nightmares well defined by Newman's direction.

In this dreamscape Amanda (Joanne Woodward) is the center of a universe of her own making and her children are satellites. But she is every overbearing mother more than a specific character, and she and her children are drawn in broad strokes and dark colors that keep them at a distance and contain their emotional impact.

Newman has heightened this impression by framing the action at the beginning and the end with Tom (John Malkovich) returning years later to look back at the wreck of his life. Smack in the middle of Depression America, he, too, is any man who longs to escape the banality of his life and demands of his mother.

But the greater victim n this world is his crippled sister Laura (Karen Allen) who is doomed to live in perpetual waiting for a gentleman caller who will never come, and whose life is worthless because of it.

Woodward is a constantly moving center of nervous neurotic energy with her active hands and darting eyes always seeming to be reaching out for something to grab on to.

· ·

■ GLASS MOUNTAIN, THE

1949, 97 MINS, UK

Dir Henry Cass   *Prod* George Minter   *Scr* Joseph Janni, John Hunter, Henry Case   *Ph* William McLeod   *Ed* Lister Laurence   *Mus* Vivian Lambelet, Nino Rota, Elizabeth Anthony
● Dulcie Gray, Michael Denison, Valentina Cortese, Tito Gobbi, Sebastian Shaw (Victoria)

The Glass Mountain has a theme inspired by a legend of the mountains in the Dolomites.

The romantic legend of thwarted love captivates an airman who is rescued in the Italian mountain district during the war. But on his return home to his wife, obsessed with writing an operatic piece on the theme, he cannot forget the girl he left behind.

Throughout, the story emphasis is placed on the frankly sentimental, but when the plot breaks away from its narrow limitations and gets out among the snow and the mountains it becomes alive and moving.

Dulcie Gray and Michael Denison, husband and wife in real life, have little difficulty in interpreting that role convincingly on the screen, but the standout performance comes from Valentina Cortese, who possesses a refreshing charm, and an ability to act.

· ·

■ GLASS SLIPPER, THE

1955, 93 MINS, US ◇ ⓥ

Dir Charles Walters   *Prod* Edwin H. Knopf   *Scr* Helen Deutsch   *Ph* Arthur E. Arling   *Ed* Ferris Webster
Mus Bronislau Kaper
● Leslie Caron, Michael Wilding, Keenan Wynn, Estelle Winwood, Elsa Lanchester, Barry Jones (M-G-M)

Without making too strong a comparison with *Lili*, a previous click turned out by the principals connected with this offering, it is probable the makers figured on approaching the previous film's success. While *Slipper* has charm and a somewhat similar ugly duckling-love triumphant plot, it has neither the tremendous heart impact of *Lili* nor sufficient freshness of theme.

Leslie Caron, as drab and dirty as any scullery maid could have ever been, is the Cinderella who rides to the castle on her dreams, magically whisked into an enchantingly gowned, diademed princess fit for the prince played by Michael Wilding. Wilding does not seem happily cast in his character, nor does it get over to the viewer.

Where *Slipper* makes its best points is in the Bronislau Kaper score and in the ballets.

· ·

■ GLASS WEB, THE

1953, 81 MINS, US

Dir Jack Arnold   *Prod* Albert J. Cohen   *Scr* Robert Blees, Leonard Lee   *Ed* Ted J. Kent   *Mus* Joseph Gershenson   *Art Dir* Bernard Herzbrun, Eric Orbom
● Edward G. Robinson, John Forsythe, Kathleen Hughes, Marcia Henderson, Richard Denning, Hugh Sanders (Universal)

Albert J. Cohen's production is concerned with a TV crime show. A good cast, headed by Edward G. Robinson, a satisfactory murder-mystery script [based on a novel by Max Simon Ehrlich] and nicely valued direction by Jack Arnold make for an okay unfoldment of the melodramatics.

Robinson, frustrated researcher, and John Forsythe, writer, are responsible for the *Crime of the Week* program being televised each week. Both are being taken for money by Kathleen Hughes, TV actress, who is blackmailing Forsythe because of his summer dalliance with her while his wife was away, and bleeding Robinson on the strength of his infatuation for her.

The blonde blackmailer is killed and her death becomes the subject of a show, with her estranged husband apparently the patsy.

Robinson gives an excellent account of the frustrated researcher who feels his true worth isn't appreciated, and Forsythe comes over well as the writer. Hughes turns on the obvious s.a. for her hard-boiled role and brings it off neatly.

· ·

■ GLEAMING THE CUBE

1988, 105 MINS, US ◇ ⓥ ⊙

Dir Graeme Clifford   *Prod* Lawrence Turman
Scr Michael Tolkin   *Ph* Reed Smoot   *Ed* John Wright
Mus Jay Ferguson   *Art Dir* John Muto
● Christian Slater, Steven Bauer, Min Luong, Art Chudabala, Le Tuan, Richard Herd (Gladden)

A skateboarding-obsessed suburban kid (Christian Slater) goes about solving – exploitation style – the death of his adopted Vietnamese brother (Art Chudabala), who Slater knows in his heart was too smart to commit suicide.

Slater skateboards all over Little Saigon, going in and out of minimalls skillfully enough to elude Vietnamese hoods on his trail while conducting some Chuck Norris-inspired sleuthing.

Slater, who sounds as if he is trying to imitate Jack Nicholson, is the only character who has a shading of personality. His skateboarding buddies are funny, considering one needs a glossary to translate their dialog, while the Vietnamese are mostly sleazy cardboard figures. The police are inept and the mastermind villain (Richard Herd) seems to be right out of the Method acting school.

· ·

■ GLENGARRY GLEN ROSS

1992, 100 MINS, US ◇ ⓥ ⊙

Dir James Foley   *Prod* Jerry Tokofsky, Stanley R. Zupnick
Scr David Mamet   *Ph* Juan-Ruiz Anchia   *Ed* Howard Smith   *Mus* James Newton Howard   *Art Dir* Jane Musky
● Al Pacino, Jack Lemmon, Alec Baldwin, Ed Harris, Alan Arkin, Kevin Spacey (New Line/Zupnick-Curtis)

The theatrical roots show rather clearly in *Glengarry Glen Ross*. A superb cast acts out one of David Mamet's major works but it doesn't quite all come together here as it did onstage.

After runs in London and Chicago, Mamet's savage look at a group of slimy small-time real estate salesmen opened on Broadway in 1984. In adapting his short two-act, two-set, seven-character piece, Mamet has moved the action around a bit but the play's basic contours remain very much in place.

Harsh story examines the underhanded, eventually criminal activities of the salesmen as they compete to outdo each other in hustling dubious properties to phone clients.

Most in danger of getting the axe is the oldest employee, Shelley Leverne (Jack Lemmon). In the high-powered sales world personified by Blake (Alex Baldwin), the terrorist from the head office, there's clearly no place for a dinosaur like Shelley.

Also in jeopardy and strategizing in different ways are George (Alan Arkin) and Dave (Ed Harris). In contrast to all these drones is Ricky Roma (Al Pacino), a hotshot salesman who seems to know every trick in the book and how to play them.

Piece remains gripping in a way, but not in as captivating or edifying a way as it did onstage. Reasons for this have to do with the rhythms of the acting, the camera's magnification of artificial devices and director James Foley's mite fancy approach to stagebound material.

□ 1992: Nomination: Best Supp. Actor (Al Pacino)

· ·

■ GLENN MILLER STORY, THE

1954, 115 MINS, US ◇ ⓥ ⊙

Dir Anthony Mann   *Prod* Aaron Rosenberg
Scr Valentine Davies, Oscar Brodney   *Ph* William

Daniels   Ed Russell Schoengarth   Mus Joseph Gershenson (dir.), Henry Mancini (adapt.)
Art Dir Bernard Herzbrun, Alexand Golitzen
● James Stewart, June Allyson, Charles Drake, George Tobias, Henry Morgan, Barton MacLane (Universal)

Sentiment and swing feature in this biopic treatment on the life of the late Glenn Miller. The Miller music, heard in some 20 tunes throughout the production, is still driving, rhythmic swing at its best.

The Aaron Rosenberg supervision makes excellent use of the music to counterpoint a tenderly projected love story, feelingly played by James Stewart and June Allyson. The two stars, who clicked previously as a man-wife team in *The Stratton Story*, have an affinity for this type of thing.

The first 70 minutes of the picture is given over to Miller's search for a sound in music arrangement that would be his trademark and live after him. Remaining 45 minutes covers the rocketing Miller fame, his enlistment when World War II starts and the service band's playing for overseas troops.

To match the topflight performances of Stewart and Allyson, the picture has some strong thesping by featured and supporting players, as well as guest star appearances. Henry Morgan stands out as Chummy MacGregor. Charles Drake is good as Don Haynes, the band's manager.
□ 1954: Best Sound Recording.
□ Nominations: Best Story & Screenplay, Scoring of a Musical Picture

■ GLEN OR GLENDA

1953, 65 MINS, US ⊚
Dir Edward D. Wood Jr   Prod George G. Weiss
Scr Edward D. Wood Jr   Ph William C. Thompson
Ed Bud Schelling
● Bela Lugosi, Daniel Davis [= Edward D. Wood Jr], 'Tommy' Haynes, Lyle Talbot, Dolores Fuller, Timothy Farrell (Screen Classics)

Glen or Glenda is an exploitation film dealing with transvestism and sex-change.

Told mainly in semi-documentary fashion, story unfolds as two case histories related by a psychiatrist. main story concerns Glen (Daniel Davis), a man who secretly dresses in women's clothes, much to the dismay of his fiancee Barbara (Dolores Fuller). Other story briefly deals with Alan ('Tommy' Haynes), identified as a 'pseudohermaphrodite', who is changed into Ann by a sex-change operation (presented tastefully without the explicit shock visuals common to such case study pics).

Though opening credits warn of film's *stark realism*, director Edward Wood's use of stock footage, cheap sets, perfunctory visuals and recited-lecture dialog gives the picture a phony quality. What distinguishes it from other low-budget efforts are the occasional mad flights of fancy.

Most involve a weird scientist, delightfully played by Bela Lugosi in eye-popping fashion. Also out of the ordinary is a suggestive (but far from pornographic) sequence of women writhing in their sexy undies, laden with bondage overtones, as well as a surrealist nightmare scene.

■ GLORIA

1980, 123 MINS, US ◇ ⊚ ⊙
Dir John Cassavetes   Prod Sam Shaw   Scr John Cassavetes   Ph Fred Schuler   Ed George C. Villasenor
Mus Bill Conti
● Gena Rowlands, John Adames, Buck Henry, Julie Carmen, Lupe Guarnica (Columbia)

Gloria is a glorious broad perhaps pushing 40. She has been in prison but now has her nestegg and just wants to be let alone with her cat, friends and a fairly economically carefree life. But the way things happen, she

has to put her neck out again, and for a precocious kid, half Puerto Rican, whom she has inadvertently pledged to help.

Director-actor John Cassavetes eases up on his unusually probing, darting camera and closeups studying human problems and disarray. Here instead he stands back and churns out a chase film that pits Gloria and the kid against the powerful Mafia no less.

Gena Rowlands is excellent as the tired woman who decides to take her chances for the boy. The kid is a right blend of understanding and childish tantrums.
□ 1980: Nomination: Best Actress (Gena Rowlands)

■ GLORY

1989, 122 MINS, US ◇ ⊚ ⊙
Dir Edward Zwick   Prod Freddie Fields   Scr Kevin Jarre
Ph Freddie Francis   Ed Steven Rosenblum   Mus James Horner   Art Dir Norman Garwood
● Matthew Broderick, Denzel Washington, Cary Elwes, Morgan Freeman, Cliff DeYoung, Jane Alexander (Tri-Star)

A stirring and long overdue tribute to the black soldiers who fought for the Union cause in the Civil War, *Glory* has the sweep and magnificence of a Tolstoy battle tale or a John Ford saga of American history.

Glory tells the story of the 54th Regiment of Massachusetts Volunteer Infantry, the first black fighting unit raised in the North during the Civil War. As the war went on, 186,107 blacks fought for the Union and 37,300 of them died.

Matthew Broderick's starring role as Col. Shaw, the callow youth from an abolitionist family who proved his mettle in training and leading his black soldiers, is perfectly judged.

Broderick's boyishness becomes a key element of the drama, as the film shows him confiding his inadequacies in letters home to his mother (the unbilled Jane Alexander) and struggling to assert leadership of his often recalcitrant men.

The rage caused by ill treatment is searingly incarnated in a great performance by Denzel Washington, as an unbroken runaway slave whose combative relationship with Broderick provides the dramatic heart of the film.
□ 1989: Best Supp. Actor (Denzel Washington), Cinematography.
□ Nominations: Best Editing, Art Direction, Sound

■ GLORY GUYS, THE

1965, 111 MINS, US ◇ ⊚
Dir Arnold Laven   Prod Arnold Laven, Arthur Gardner, Jules Levy   Scr Sam Peckinpah   Ph James Wong Howe
Ed Melvin Shapiro, Ernst R. Rolf   Mus Riz Ortolani
● Tom Tryon, Harve Presnell, Senta Berger, James Caan, Andrew Duggan, Slim Pickens (United Artists)

The Glory Guys is an entertaining US Cavalry-Indian conflict, sparked by an opportunist army general who sacrifices dedicated soldiers to his ambition. Brawling fisticuffs, comedy and romantic triangle mark a slightly forced plot until an exciting climax.

Adaptation by Sam Peckinpah of Hoffman Birney's novel, *The Dice of God*, finds Andrew Duggan very effective as a general again in responsible command despite prior goofs.

Senta Berger is an adequate but voluptuous frontier woman with an unspecified past, who provides romantic interest as Tryon and Presnell vie for her favors. Jeanne Cooper is good as Duggan's vicious and perfectly-matched wife who never fails to insult Berger.

Although Tryon is somewhat wooden and Presnell too refined for a frontier scout, director Arnold Laven has drawn some fine performances from supporting names. Slim Pickens brings a new life to the gruff humor and

paternalism of a cliche role as non-com. James Caan makes a sharp impression as the stubborn recruit in an amusing running battle with shavetail Peter Breck.

■ G-MEN

1935, 84 MINS, US ⊚
Dir William Keighley   Prod Louis F. Edelman   Scr Seton I. Miller   Ph Sol Polito   Ed Jack Killifer   Art Dir John J. Hughes
● James Cagney, Margaret Lindsay, Ann Dvorak, Robert Armstrong, Barton MacLane, Lloyd Nolan (First National/Warner)

This is red hot off the front page. But beyond that it has nothing but a weak scenario [from a story by Gregory Rogers] along hackneyed lines.

Little Caesar, *Scarface* and *Public Enemy* were more than portrayals of gangster tactics: they were biographies of curious mentalities. In the new idea of glorifying the government gunners who wipe out the killers there is no chance for that kind of character development and build-up.

This time James Cagney is a government man, he's in love with his chief's sister and she's thumbs down on him until the final clinch. And his chief rides him constantly, only to give in at the end.

Sprinkled through and around that is just about every situation from the Dillinger-Baby Face Nelson etcetera saga. The Kansas City depot massacre is paralleled, the Dillinger escape from a Chicago apartment, the Wisconsin resort roundup, the bank holdups throughout Kansas-Missouri, et al.

The acting throughout is A-1, and that helps consistently. Beyond Cagney and Robert Armstrong, both at their best, there is Ann Dvorak, a moll who tips off the cops to the final capture. Margaret Lindsay is Armstrong's sister and Cagney's gal. An easy assignment, and she romps off with it.

■ GO-BETWEEN, THE

1971, 118 MINS, UK ◇ ⊚
Dir Joseph Losey   Prod John Heyman, Norman Priggen
Scr Harold Pinter   Ph Gerry Fisher   Ed Reginald Beck
Mus Michel Legrand   Art Dir Carmen Dillon
● Julie Christie, Alan Bates, Margaret Leighton, Michael Redgrave, Michael Gough, Edward Fox (M-G-M/EMI)

In its glimpse of the manners and mores of the British socialites at the beginning of the century, *The Go-Between* is both fascinating and charming. Joseph Losey's direction sets a pace in which incident and characterization take precedence over action.

The Harold Pinter screenplay, based on the L.P. Hartley novel, is, as one would naturally expect, literate and penetrating, yet there are certain obscurities in the treatment.

It is Michael Redgrave looking back at a definitive event of his boyhood, an experience which undoubtedly was largely responsible for his remaining unmarried. It is during the long hot summer in the lavish country home that the youngster becomes emotionally involved by acting as the contact (or go-between) between the daughter of the house – with whom he believes himself to be in love – and the tenant farmer, although the girl is already betrothed to a member of the aristocracy. And it is in that period that the boy gets his first inkling of what sex is all about.

Though Julie Christie and Alan Bates are starred as the girl and the farmer, it is the boy who has the pivotal role, and Dominic Guard, a screen newcomer, appears to play his part effortlessly, with an absence of precociousness.
□ 1971: Nomination: Best Supp. Actress (Margaret Leighton)

GODFATHER, THE

1972, 175 MINS, US ◇ ⓥ ⊙

Dir Francis Coppola   *Prod* Albert S. Ruddy   *Scr* Mario
Puzo, Francis Coppola   *Ph* Gordon Williams
Ed William Reynolds, Peter Zinner   *Mus* Nino Rota
Art Dir Dean Tavoularis
● Marlon Brando, Al Pacino, James Caan, Richard
Conte, Robert Duvall, Sterling Hayden (Paramount)

Paramount's film version of Mario Puzo's
sprawling gang-land novel has an outstanding
performance by Al Pacino and a strong characterization by Marlon Brando in the title
role. It also has excellent production values,
flashes of excitement, and a well-picked cast.

Puzo and director Francis Coppola are credited with the adaptation which best of all
gives some insight into the origins and heritage of that segment of the population
known off the screen (but not on it) as the
Mafia or Cosa Nostra.

In *The Godfather* we have the New York-New
Jersey world, ruled by five 'families', one of
them headed by Brando. This is a world
where emotional ties are strong, loyalties are
somewhat more flexible at times, and tempers are short. Brando does an admirable job
as the lord of his domain.

It is Pacino who makes the smash impression here. Initially seen as the son whom
Brando wanted to go more or less straight,
Pacino matures under trauma of an assassination attempt on Brando, his own double-
murder revenge for that on corrupt cop
Sterling Hayden and rival gangster Al
Lettieri, the counter-vengeance murder of his
Sicilian bride, and a series of other personnel
readjustments which att fadeout find him
king of his own mob.

Among the notable performances are Robert
Duvall as Hagen, the non-Italian number-two
man, Richard Conte as one of Brando's malev-
olent rivals and Diane Keaton as Pacino's early
sweetheart, later second wife.
□ 1972: Best Picture, Actor (Marlon
Brando), Adapted Screenplay.
□ Nominations: Best Director, Supp. Actor
(James Caan, Robert Duvall, Al Pacino),
Music [later declared ineligible], Costume
Design, Editing, Sound

GODFATHER PART II, THE

1974, 200 MINS, US ◇ ⓥ ⊙

Dir Francis Coppola   *Prod* Francis Coppola
Scr Francis Coppola, Mario Puzo   *Ph* Gordon Willis
Ed Peter Zinner, Barry Malkin, Richard Marks   *Mus* Nino
Rota, Carmine Coppola   *Art Dir* Dean Tavoularis
● Al Pacino, Robert Duvall, Diane Keaton, Robert De
Niro, John Cazale, James Caan (Paramount)

The Godfather Part II, far from being a spinoff
followup to its 1972 progenitor, is an excellent epochal drama in its own right providing
bookends in time to the earlier story. Al
Pacino again is outstanding as Michael
Corleone, successor to crime family leadership. The $15 million production cost about
two-and-a-half times the original.

The film's 200 minutes could be broken
down into two acts and 10 scenes. The scenes
alternate between Pacino's career in Nevada
gambling rackets from about 1958 and
Robert De Niro's early life in Sicily and New
York City. A natural break comes after 126
minutes when De Niro, involved with low
level thievery, brutally assassinates Gaston
Moschin the neighborhood crime boss with-
out a shred of conscience. It's the only shock-
ing brutality in the film.
□ 1974: Best Picture, Director, Supp. Actor
(Robert De Niro), Adapted Screenplay, Art
Direction, Original Score.
□ Nominations: Best Actor (Al Pacino),
Supp. Actor (Michael V. Gazzo, Lee
Strasberg), Supp. Actress (Talia Shire),
Costume Design

GODFATHER PART III, THE

1990, 161 MINS, US ◇ ⓥ ⊙

Dir Francis Coppola   *Prod* Francis Coppola   *Scr* Mario
Puzo, Francis Coppola   *Ph* Gordon Willis   *Ed* Barry
Malkin, Lisa Fruchtman   *Mus* Carmine Coppola, Nino
Rota   *Art Dir* Dean Tavoularis
● Al Pacino, Diane Keaton, Talia Shire, Andy Garcia,
Eli Wallach, Joe Mantegna (Zoetrope/Paramount)

The Godfather Part III matches its predecessors
in narrative intensity, epic scope, socio-political analysis, physical beauty and deep feeling
for its characters and milieu. In addition, the
$55 million-plus production is the most per-
sonal of the three for the director.

Like the original, Part III opens with a
lengthy festival celebration punctuated by
backroom dealings. It is 1979, and Michael
Corleone, having divested himself of his illegal operations, is being honored by the
Catholic Church for his abundant charitable
activities.

Hopeful of bringing his family closer together, Michael dotes on his daughter Mary
(Sofia Coppola), and understandably becomes
perturbed by her affair with cousin Vincent
(Andy Garcia), hot-headed, violence-prone illegitimate son of Michael's late brother
Sonny. Vincent has been unhappily working
for slumlord and old-style thug Joey Zasa (Joe
Mantegna), who has taken on Michael's less
savory holdings.

Bad blood between the ruthless Zasa and
the Corleone family mounts just as Michael
tries, with $600 million, to buy a controlling
interest in the European conglomerate
Immobiliare, a move that would cement his
business legitimacy and financial future.

After 80 minutes, the action switches to
Italy, where it remains for the duration.
Pacino and Eli Wallach's old dons can't help
begin scheming against one another. In one
of the most masterful examples of sustained
intercutting in cinema, the performance on
opening night of Pacino's son in *Cavalleria
Rusticana* serves as the backdrop for several
murderous missions.

For the third time out in his career role,
Pacino is magnificent. Garcia brings much-
needed youth and juice to the ballsy Vincent,
heir apparent to the Corleone tradition,
much as James Caan sparked the first film
and Robert De Niro invigorated the second.

Diane Keaton proves a welcome, if brief,
presence in warming the film, and Talia Shire
seems pleased with the opportunity to do
some dirty work at long last.

Film's main flaw, unavoidably, is Sofia
Coppola in the important, but not critical,
role of Michael's daughter. Unfortunate cast-
ing decision was made after original actress
Winona Ryder had to bow out at the start of
production.
□ 1990: Nominations: Best Picture, Director,
Supp. Actor (Andy Garcia), Cinematography,
Art Direction, Editing, Song ('Promise Me
You'll Remember')

GOD IS MY CO-PILOT

1945, 83 MINS, US

Dir Robert Florey   *Prod* Robert Buckner   *Scr* Peter
Milne, Abem Finkel   *Ph* Sid Hickox   *Ed* Folmer
Blangsted   *Mus* Franz Waxman   *Art Dir* John Hughes
● Dennis Morgan, Dane Clark, Raymond Massey, Alan
Hale, Andrea King (Warner)

Narrative uses flashback technique to condense life of Col Robert Lee Scott Jr, army
ace who gained fame with General
Chennault's Flying Tigers.

Air fight sequences bear an authentic
stamp, although studio-made and the thrills
are good drama. Title derives from Scott's realization that a pilot doesn't face danger
alone, and several of his real-life brushes with
death sustain the belief.

There has been considerable condensation

of Scott's story, taken from his best-selling
book of same title, and undoubtedly commercial license has pointed up some incidents for
better dramatic flavor. It's the story of a boy
born to fly and spans his days from the time
he first jumped off the barn with an umbrella,
through model planes, West Point, flying the
mail, instructing and his takeoff on a secret
mission to China after Pearl Harbor.

Condensation was evidently more in the
hands of the film editor than in the script.
Finished picture indicates there was considerable scissoring to hold footage to reasonable
length. Robert Florey's direction manages authenticity and obtains excellent performances
from the cast headed by Dennis Morgan.

GOD'S LITTLE ACRE

1958, 112 MINS, US ⓥ

Dir Anthony Mann   *Prod* Sidney Harmon   *Scr* Philip
Yordan   *Ph* Ernest Haller   *Ed* Richard C. Meyer
Mus Elmer Bernstein   *Art Dir* John S. Poplin Jr
● Robert Ryan, Aldo Ray, Tina Louise, Buddy Hackett,
Jack Lord, Fay Spain (United Artists)

Rousing, rollicking and ribald, *God's Little Acre*
is a rustic revel with the kick of a Georgia
mule. The production of Erskine Caldwell's
novel is adult, sensitive and intelligent.

The direct, bucolic humor is virtually intact,
and so is Caldwell's larger scheme, the morality play he told through the artless, sometimes disastrous behavior of his foolish and
lovable characters. A changed ending gives a
different meaning to the story, but the ending is sound, aesthetically and popularly.

The story remains that of a Georgia farmer
(Robert Ryan) who believes he can find gold
on his farm. In the book it was a gold mine; in
the picture it is buried treasure. Ryan has
spent years of his life digging for it, all his energies and those of his two sons (Jack Lord
and Vic Morrow) go into the search and the
dream it represents. The hunt leads everywhere on their farm except on the one acre
Ryan has set aside, in the olden way of
tithing, for God.

Ryan dominates the picture, as his character should. Aldo Ray, as his son-in-law, creates a moving characterization as the
husband torn between his wife, sensitively
played by Helen Westcott, and the voluptuous
barnyard Susannah, strikingly projected by
newcomer from legit Tina Louise.

GODS MUST BE CRAZY, THE

1981, 108 MINS, BOTSWANA ◇ ⓥ ⊙

Dir Jamie Uys   *Prod* Jamie Uys   *Scr* Jamie Uys
Ph Jamie Uys, Buster Reynolds, Robert Lewis   *Ed* Jamie
Uys   *Mus* John Boshoff
● Marius Weyers, Sandra Prinsloo, N!xau, Louw
Verwey, Michael Thys, Jamie Uys (CAT)

The Gods Must Be Crazy is a comic fable by one-
man-band South African filmmaker Jamie
Uys, who shot the picture in Botswana in
1979.

Uys' basic storyline has Xi (N!xau), a bushman who lives deep in the Kalahari desert,
setting off on a trek to destroy a Coca Cola
bottle which fell from a passing airplane and
by virtue of its strange usefulness as a utensil
(thought to be thrown by the gods from
heaven) has caused great dissension within
his tribe.

Xi plans to throw the unwanted artifact of
modern civilization off the edge of the world
and in his trek encounters modern people.

Film's main virtues are its striking,
widescreen visuals of unusual locations, and
the sheer educational value of its narration.

GODS MUST BE CRAZY II, THE

1989, 99 MINS, BOTSWANA/US ◇ ⓥ ⊙

Dir Jamie Uys   *Prod* Boet Troskie   *Scr* Jamie Uys

G

Ph Buster Reynolds   *Ed* Renee Engelbrecht, Ivan Hall
Mus Charles Fox
● N!xau, Lena Farugia, Hans Strydom, Eiros, Nadies, Erick Bowen (Troskie/Weintraub)

Jamie Uys has concocted a genial sequel to his 1981 international sleeper hit *The Gods Must Be Crazy* that is better than its progenitor in most respects.

His tongue-clicking Kalahari Bushman hero, again played by a real McCoy named N!xau, is once more unwittingly embroiled in the lunacies of civilization.

First plotline has N!xau's two adorable offspring getting innocently borne away on the trailer truck of a pair of unsuspecting ivory poachers. N!xau follows the tracks and comes across two other odd couples from the nutty outside world.

There is a New York femme lawyer (Lena Farugia), who is stranded in the middle of the Kalahari with a handsome, phlegmatic game warden (Hans Strydom) when their ultra-light plane is downed in a sudden storm.

Then there are two hapless mercenaries, an African and a Cuban, who keep taking one another prisoner in a series of table-turning pursuits through the brush.

Uys orchestrates a desert farce of criss-crossing destinies with more assured skill and charming sight-gags, marred only by facile penchant for speeded-up slapstick motion.

■ GODSPELL

1973, 103 MINS, US ◇

Dir David Greene   *Prod* Edgar Lansbury   *Scr* David Greene, John-Michael Tebelak   *Ph* Richard G. Heimann   *Ed* Alan Heim   *Mus* Stephen Schwartz   *Art Dir* Brian Eatwell
● Victor Garber, David Haskell, Jerry Sroka, Lynne Thigpen, Katie Hanley, Rubin Lamont (Columbia)

Godspell originated as a workshop production at off-off-Broadway's La Mama for a group of actor-graduates of Carnegie-Mellon Univ. Overall concept – a youth-slanted reworking of the gospel according to St Matthew – was that of director John-Michael Tebelak as part of a master's thesis.

Film follows original 1971 off-Broadway legit production closely but 'opens up' setting to include footage of virtually every New York City tourist landmark, graffiti and all.

Result is that original production's appealing aspects have remained intact – a strong Stephen Schwartz score and an infectious joie de vivre conveyed by an energetic, no-name cast. So also, unfortunately, have its flaws – a relentlessly simplistic approach to the New Testament interpreted in overbearing children's theatre-style mugging.

Story line merely consists of a series of ensemble interpretations of gospel parables as enunciated by a Christ figure (Victor Garber) in a superman sweatshirt and workman's overalls.

■ GOD'S WILL

1989, 100 MINS, US ◇ ⓦ

Dir Julia Cameron   *Prod* Julia Cameron, Pam Moore
Scr Julia Cameron   *Ph* William Nusbaum
Mus Christopher (Hambone) Cameron
● Marge Kotlisky, Daniel Region, Laura Margolis, Domenica Cameron-Scorsese, Linda Edmond (Power & Light)

Veteran Hollywood screen writer Julia Cameron moved home to Chicago to produce and direct her first feature, *God's Will*, and discovered first-hand one of a filmmaker's worst nightmares: the production soundtrack was stolen after shooting wrapped.

As a consequence, the scenes' delicate at best under normal low-budget conditions, simply don't play right.

A plus for the Cameron family is an outstanding debut by pre-teen daughter

Domenica Cameron-Scorsese (whose father is director Martin Scorsese).

Cameron's intent, obviously, was to create a lighthearted effort at family fun in which a divorced, self-centred show-business couple (Daniel Region and Laura Margolis) meet an untimely demise and wind up in heaven squabbling over what will happen now to their daughter.

The little girl has fallen into the custody of the couple's new spouses (Linda Edmond and Mitchell Canoff). Some ghostly haunting is therefore required to free Domenica into the hands of another couple preferred by the parents and the result is a romp.

■ GOING HOME

1971, 97 MINS, US ◇ ⊙

Dir Herbert B. Leonard   *Prod* Herbert B. Leonard
Scr Lawrence B. Marcus   *Ph* Fred Jackman
Ed Sigmund Neufeld Jr   *Mus* Bill Walker   *Art Dir* Peter Wooley
● Robert Mitchum, Brenda Vaccaro, Jan-Michael Vincent, Jason Bernard, Sally Kirkland, Josh Mostel (M-G-M)

Going Home is a most unusual and intruiging melodrama about a teenage boy's vengeance against his father for the long-ago killing of his mother. Robert Mitchum in an offbeat role gives an excellent performance as the crude but sensitive father. Jan-Michael Vincent is very effective as his son. Brenda Vaccaro, as Mitchum's sweetheart, makes a catalytic role into a memorable experience.

The script takes Vincent on a search from prison, where Mitchum was incarcerated, to the sleazy seashore environment where the paroled father is eking out a living. The boy's love-hate relationship with his father is developed neatly and often to a terrifying degree. Vaccaro, in the literal sense an innocent bystander who gets hurt for her trouble, fills in with human emotions the two men cannot express to each other.

As the undaunted but well worn-down Korean War hero 20 years later, fresh out of stir with a son who hates his guts, with a beer belly and a black future, Mitchum presents a characterization that combines a wide range of acting talents.

■ GOING MY WAY

1944, 126 MINS, US ⓦ ⊙

Dir Leo McCarey   *Prod* Leo McCarey   *Scr* Frank Butler, Frank Cavett   *Ph* Lionel Lindon   *Ed* LeRoy Stone
Mus Robert Emmett Dolan (dir)   *Art Dir* Hans Dreier, William Flannery
● Bing Crosby, Rise Stevens, Barry Fitzgerald, Gene Lockhart, Frank McHugh, James Brown (Paramount)

Bing Crosby gets a tailor-made role in *Going My Way*, and with major assistance from Barry Fitzgerald and Rise Stevens, clicks solidly to provide topnotch entertainment for wide audience appeal.

Picture is a warm, human drama studded liberally with bright episodes and excellent characterizations accentuated by fine direction of Leo McCarey [who wrote the original story]. Intimate scenes between Crosby and Fitzgerald dominate throughout, with both providing slick characterizations.

Crosby plays a young priest interested in athletics and music who's assigned as assistant to crusty Fitzgerald in an eastside church saddled with burdensome mortgage that might be foreclosed by grasping Gene Lockhart. Progressive youth and staid oldster clash continually, but Crosby gradually bends Fitzgerald to his way.

Major thread of gaiety runs through the proceedings, and McCarey has liberally sprinkled sparkling individual episodes along the way for cinch audience reaction. Rise Stevens comes on for the second half, introduced as a

Metropolitan Opera star and old friend of Crosby when both were interested in music.

Crosby's song numbers include three new tunes by Johnny Burke and James Van Heusen – 'Going My Way', 'Would You Like to Swing On a Star' and 'Day after Forever'.
□ 1944: Best Picture, Director, Actor (Bing Crosby), Supp. Actor (Barry Fitzgerald), Original Story, Screenplay, Song ('Swinging on a Star').
□ Nominations: Best Actor (Barry Fitzgerald), B&W Cinematography, Editing

■ GOIN' SOUTH

1978, 101 MINS, US ◇ ⓦ ⊙

Dir Jack Nicholson   *Prod* Harry Gittes, Harold Schneider
Scr John Herman Shaner, Al Ramus, Charles Shyer, Alan Mandel   *Ph* Nestor Almendros   *Ed* Richard Chew, John Fitzgerald Beck   *Mus* Van Dyke Parks, Perry Botkin Jr
Art Dir Toby Carr Rafelson
● Jack Nicholson, Mary Steenburgen, Christopher Lloyd, John Belushi, Veronica Cartwright, Danny DeVito (Paramount)

Jack Nicholson playing Gabby Hayes is interesting, even amusing at times, but Hayes was never a leading man, which *Goin' South* desperately needs.

Picture starts off promisingly enough with Nicholson as a hapless outlaw who makes it across the border but the posse cheats and comes across after him causing his horse to faint.

On his way to the gallows, Nicholson discovers an unordinary county ordinance that would allow him to go free if picked for marriage by a maiden lady in town. Up to now, *Goin' South* is still going strong. But here it stops as lovely young Mary Steenburgen steps out of the crowd and agrees to marry the bearded, dirty horse-thief.

Why she should do this is never satisfactorily established in the script carrying the names of four writers. Ostensibly, it's to get the manpower to help her mine her property for gold before the railroad takes over. But it never jells, as Nicholson continues to sputter and chomp, acting more like her grandfather than a handsome roue out to overcome her virginity.

■ GO INTO YOUR DANCE

1935, 92 MINS, US ⊙

Dir Archie Mayo   *Scr* Earl Baldwin, Bradford Ropes
Ph Tony Gaudio, Sol Polito   *Ed* Harold McLernon
● Al Jolson, Ruby Keeler, Glenda Farrell, Helen Morgan, Barton MacLane, Sharon Lynne (First National/Warner)

Go into Your Dance has much to recommend it as a lavishly produced, vigorously directed and agreeably entertaining musical picture. Besides everything else it has Al Jolson in top form, plus a nifty set of songs [by Al Dubin and Harry Warren].

Along with Jolson and for the first time his screen partner is the missus, Ruby Keeler. A sensible story setting, in which each is permitted to adhere to type, makes them a nice film couple.

Jolson plays the role of a talented star who has broken up many a hit show by going off on bats. The star is finally barred from the musical stage by the combined votes of Actors Equity and an association of producers.

With the help of his devoted sister and a dancing girl with whom he teams up, the banished star starts his comeback via the night-club field. The comeback is nearly interrupted by gangster bullets, but they miss the star and hit his girl partner.

Keeler is given plenty of footage for her dancing; perhaps more than any dancer, including Astaire, has been accorded in any one picture thus far. On the hoof she's a girl who can take good care of herself, and in the

histrionic moments she's carried along by Jolson's aggressive trouping.
☐ 1935: Nomination: Best Dance Direction ('Lady from Manhattan')

· ·

■ GOLD

1974, 118 MINS, UK ◇ ⓥ
Dir Peter Hunt   *Prod* Michael Klinger   *Scr* Wilbur Smith, Stanley Price   *Ph* Ousama Rawi   *Ed* John Glen   *Mus* Elmer Bernstein   *Art Dir* Alec Vetchinsky, Syd Cain
● Roger Moore, Susannah York, Ray Milland, Bradford Dillman, John Gielgud, Simon Sabela (Hemdale/Avton)

Power of a major physical disaster as theme for an exciting motion picture [based on Wilbur Smith's novel *Goldmine*] is evidenced in this British item, lensed entirely in the South Africa locale of its well-developed narrative. Punishing action is tempered by a modern love story.

Roger Moore plays a tough mine foreman unwittingly manipulated by an unscrupulous gang of financiers who want to flood the mine to raise the price of gold on the world market.

Particular attention has been given to the terrifying underground sequences, and tremendous realism is accomplished in an opening tragedy of men caught in the grip of a sudden flood and later in the climactic flooding.

Moore delivers in pat fashion and Susannah York is a love as the wife of the mine operator who is used by her husband in the web of deceit woven by an international syndicate whom he represents.
☐ 1974: Nomination: Best Song ('Wherever Love Takes Me')

· ·

■ GOLD DIGGERS OF 1933

1933, 94 MINS, US ⓥ ⊙
Dir Mervyn LeRoy, Busby Berkeley   *Prod* [uncredited]   *Scr* Erwin Gelsey, James Seymour, David Boehm, Ben Markson   *Ph* Sol Polito   *Ed* George Amy   *Mus* Leo f. Forbstein (dir.)   *Art Dir* Anton Grot
● Warren William, Joan Blondell, Aline MacMahon, Ruby Keeler, Dick Powell, Guy Kibbee (Warner)

Gold Diggers makes some sort of screen history in that it's the first of the 'second editions' of film musicals. In 1929 WB made *Gold Diggers of Broadway*. But the real feature of *Gold Diggers of 1933* are the numbers staged by Busby Berkeley.

The film's superiority to *42nd Street* lies in the greater romance interest with a multiplicity of amorous complications wherein Warren William and Joan Blondell, and Guy Kibbee and Aline MacMahon, are paired off as sub-interest to the Ruby Keeler-Dick Powell coupling. The subromances become mild menaces, for William and Kibbee are the Back Bay bluebloods who seek to quell the kid brother's (Powell) stage romance. Kibbee is the family attorney and William the elder brother. They both fall for show girls as well.

Adaptation from the Avery Hopwood-David Belasco-Ina Claire original is as liberal as was the 1929 version. At least, in 1933, they don't have Nick Lucas and Winnie Lightner warble numbers every other minute.

Once the numbers get going, nothing else matters. There are five impressive songs by Al Dubin and Harry Warren.

Some good trouping, especially where expert playing is necessary, to bolster the loose assignments, such as the difficult roles given William and Kibbee. Powell also overcomes the trite situation of the society blueblood with stage ambitions. For the rest, however, Keeler, Blondell and MacMahon are more or less faithful to their characters. Ned Sparks and Ginger Rogers also score.
☐ 1932/33: Nomination: Best Sound

· ·

■ GOLD DIGGERS OF 1935

1935, 95 MINS, US ⓥ ⊙
Dir Busby Berkeley   *Prod* [uncredited]   *Scr* Manuel Seff, Peter Milne   *Ph* George Barnes   *Ed* George Amy   *Mus* Leo F. Forbstein (dir.), Ray Heindorf (arr.)   *Art Dir* Anton Grot
● Dick Powell, Gloria Stuart, Adolphe Menjou, Glenda Farrell, Grant Mitchell, Alice Brady (Warner)

As in the previous *Diggers*, it's the spec that counts, and the story deficiencies are a bit more acute. Basically, the story [by Robert Lord and Peter Milne] lags for an hour before the fashionable charity show, which is the excuse for the spec, commences.

Dick Powell is the affable hotel clerk (no longer a songwriter) who falls for the stingy millionairess' daughter (Gloria Stuart). Frank McHugh, the scapegrace son, who's checked off three chorus-girl wives at the rate of $100,000 settlement to each, is the vis-a-vis of Dorothy Dare.

Adolphe Menjou does the best job as the irascible, chiseling entrepreneur, with Joe Cawthorn as comedy foil. Alice Brady is equally legit and effective in her skinflint assignment. Hugh Herbert's role of an eccentric snuffbox addict is rather hazy.

The Al Dubin-Harry Warren songs this time miss a bit. 'The Words Are In My Heart' is the waltz theme, reprised for the choreography with the baby grands – a highly effective ballet of the Steinways. 'Lullaby of Broadway' is the final musical elaboration. Latter number, led by Winifred Shaw, runs overboard in footage.
☐ 1935: Best Song ('Lullaby of Broadway').
☐ Nominations: Best Dance Direction ('Lullaby of Broadway', 'The Words Are in My Heart')

· ·

■ GOLD DIGGERS OF 1937

1936, 101 MINS, US
Dir Lloyd Bacon, Busby Berkeley   *Prod* [uncredited]   *Scr* Warren Duff   *Ph* Arthur Edeson   *Ed* Thomas Richards   *Mus* Leo F. Forbstein (dir.)   *Art Dir* Max Parker
● Dick Powell, Joan Blondell, Victor Moore, Glenda Farrell, Lee Dixon, Osgood Perkins (Warner)

Where some of the *Gold Digger* annuals from Warner have not been overburdened with heavy story material, the current musical opus gets moving with the advantage of a trim backstage yarn taken from *Mystery of Life*, the Broadway play by Richard Maibaum, Michael Wallach and George Haight.

Cast as a cocksure insurance salesman, Dick Powell breezes through the picture like he had been selling policies all his life. He has four outstanding songs, never overdoes them and breaks through with his ballads at the most opportune times.

Victor Moore enters the picture scene again back at his old trick of show thefting. In the role of the hypochondriac theatrical producer, he is the trouper of old and easily the comedy life of the party. Glenda Farrell, a typical gold-digging chorine in the story, works smoothly and for laughable results opposite the pompous show czar.

Joan Blondell, while not given her customary rowdy role, is effective as the chorine turned stenog. This spots her opposite Dick Powell again, with a modern-day romance deftly introduced and never permitted to go overboard.
☐ 1936: Nomination: Best Dance Direction ('Love and War')

· ·

■ GOLD DIGGERS OF BROADWAY

1929, 105 MINS, US ◇
Dir Roy del Ruth   *Scr* Robert Lord   *Mus* Al Dubin, Joe Burke
● Nancy Welford, Conway Tearle, Winnie Lightner, Ann Pennington, Lilyan Tashman, Nick Lucas (Warner)

Lots of color – Technicolor – lots of comedy, girls, songs, music, dancing, production in *Gold Diggers of Broadway*.

When they got through with [Avery Hopwood's play] *Gold Diggers*, Warners had only the title left. Around that they built another show, on and off stage.

Somebody tossed the picture into Winnie Lightner's lap. Mugging, talking, singing or slapsticking, she can do them all, and does in this picture. Nancy Welford does nicely enough what she has to do.

Next to Lightner in work is her comedy opposite, Albert Gran, as a grey-haired heavyweight lawyer, whom Winnie lands. Lilyan Tashman does an upstage show dame rather well. Helen Foster and William Bakewell are the kids in a very slim love thread.

In the rewritten *Gold Diggers* the love thing is only the alibi. The new story is hung onto it, with just enough of the digging to hold up the title. Well worked out, with plenty of speed all of the time, and color all of the while.

· ·

■ GOLDEN BRAID

1990, 91 MINS, AUSTRALIA ◇ ⓥ
Dir Paul Cox   *Prod* Paul Cox, Paul Ammitzboll, Santhana K. Naidu   *Scr* Paul Cox, Barry Dickins   *Ph* Nino Martinetti   *Ed* Russell Hurley   *Art Dir* Neil Angwin
● Chris Haywood, Gosia Dobrowolska, Paul Chubb, Norman Kaye, Marion Heathfield, Monica Maughan (AFC/Film Victoria)

Australia's most interesting auteur, Paul Cox, has often dealt with obsession in his work, and his protagonist here, Bernard (Chris Haywood) fits well and truly into this obsessive pattern. Of Central European extraction, Bernard lives alone among a world of clocks. For him, clocks represent in the passing of time, and he's also haunted by thoughts of aging and death.

Bernard is also, we discover, something of a womaniser, and at present is involved in an affair with Terese (Gosia Dobrowolska), wife of an unsuspecting Salvation Army major (Paul Chubb). The lovers enjoy a guilt-free relationship which cools only when Bernard is sidetracked by a new obsession: a braid of hair he discovers in a 100-year-old, supposedly Venetian, cabinet.

Though the mood of the film – loosely based on a Guy de Maupassant short story – is generally somber, it is leavened by the intensity of its love story. Dobrowolska, in a radiant performance, makes Terese a complex woman whose passion for the reclusive Bernard is seen in sharp contrast to her dying marriage.

· ·

■ GOLDEN CHILD, THE

1986, 93 MINS, US ◇ ⓥ ⊙
Dir Michael Ritchie   *Prod* Edward S. Feldman, Robert D. Wachs   *Scr* Dennis Feldman   *Ph* Donald E. Thorin   *Ed* Richard A. Harris   *Mus* Michel Colombier   *Art Dir* J. Michael Riva
● Eddie Murphy, Charles Dance, Charlotte Lewis, Victor Wong, J.L. Reate, Randall 'Tex' Cobb (Feldman/Meeker/Murphy)

A strange hybrid of Far Eastern mysticism, treacly sentimentality, diluted reworkings of Eddie Murphy's patented confrontation scenes across racial and cultural boundaries, and dragged-in ILM (Industrial Light & Magic) special effects monsters, film makes no sense on any level.

Concoction has Murphy as a social worker specializing in tracking down missing children who is recruited to rescue the virtually divine Golden Child. Eponymous character, a so-called perfect child with magical powers of good, has been kidnapped in an overblown opening sequence by an unmitigated villain portrayed by a bearded Charles Dance, who

G

wears a long leather coat like a Sergio Leone baddie.

Much nonsense ensues involving assorted bikers, chop-socky-happy Orientals and a serpentine sorceress.

⸱⸱⸱⸱⸱⸱⸱⸱⸱⸱⸱⸱⸱⸱⸱⸱⸱⸱⸱⸱⸱⸱⸱⸱⸱⸱⸱

◼ GOLDEN RENDEZVOUS

1977, 103 MINS, US ◇ Ⓥ
Dir Ashley Lazarus   *Prod* Andre Pieters   *Scr* Stanley Price   *Ph* Ken Higgins   *Ed* Ralph Kemplen
● Richard Harris, Ann Turkel, David Janssen, Burgess Meredith, John Vernon, Gordon Jackson (Film Trust/Okun/Golden Rendezvous)

Despite an overabundance of plot, deaths, and explosions, there's virtually nothing in this puddle of a mid-ocean thriller that wouldn't make a 12-year-old cringe in embarrassment.

Pic [adapted from an Alistair MacLean novel] tells the tale of the Caribbean Star, a combination cargo ship and floating casino, hijacked by mercenary John Vernon. Following the orders of an unknown mastermind, he and his men, with the aid of an atomic device, plan to exchange the captured passengers and bomb for the golden contents of a US Treasury ship.

And so it goes, albeit not as simply, until First Officer Richard Harris, accompanied by Ann Turkel and Gordon Jackson, step in to save the day.

⸱⸱⸱⸱⸱⸱⸱⸱⸱⸱⸱⸱⸱⸱⸱⸱⸱⸱⸱⸱⸱⸱⸱⸱⸱⸱⸱

◼ GOLDEN VOYAGE OF SINBAD, THE

1974, 105 MINS, UK ◇ Ⓥ ⊙
Dir Gordon Hessler   *Prod* Charles H. Schneer, Ray Harryhausen   *Scr* Brian Clemens   *Ph* Ted Moore   *Ed* Roy Watts   *Mus* Miklos Rozsa   *Art Dir* John Stoll
● John Phillip Law, Caroline Munro, Tom Baker, Douglas Wilmer, Martin Shaw, Gregoire Aslan (Columbia)

An Arabian Nightish saga told with some briskness and opulence for the childish eye, yet ultimately falling short of implied promise as an adventure spree.

As with producer Charles H. Schneer's *Jason and the Argonauts*, Ray Harryhausen encores as coproducer and special effects collaborator. Among his creations: an animated ship's figurehead, a grotesque centaur, a many-armed religious idol and swordplay adversary, and a couple of small bat-like creatures performing intelligence duty for the black artsy heavy of the piece. Good enough conjuring tricks to impress the kids.

Neither story nor running time are belabored under Gordon Hessler's capable direction. And the play-acting is up to snuff for this kind of throwback, in which John Phillip Law impersonates Sinbad with appealing understatement.

⸱⸱⸱⸱⸱⸱⸱⸱⸱⸱⸱⸱⸱⸱⸱⸱⸱⸱⸱⸱⸱⸱⸱⸱⸱⸱⸱

◼ GOLDFINGER

1964, 112 MINS, UK ◇ Ⓥ ⊙
Dir Guy Hamilton   *Prod* Harry Saltzman, Albert R. Broccoli   *Scr* Richard Maibaum, Paul Dehn   *Ph* Ted Moore   *Ed* Peter Hunt   *Mus* John Barry   *Art Dir* Ken Adam
● Sean Connery, Honor Blackman, Gert Frobe, Shirley Eaton, Tania Mallet, Harold Sakata (United Artists/Eon)

There's not the least sign of staleness in this third sample of the Bond 007 formula. Some liberties have been taken with Ian Fleming's original novel but without diluting its flavor. The mood is set before the credits show up, with Sean Connery making an arrogant pass at a chick and spying a thug creeping up from behind; he's reflected in the femme's eyeballs. So he heaves the heavy into bathful of water and connects it deftly to a handy supply of electricity.

Thereafter the plot gets its teeth into the real business, which is the duel between Bond and Goldfinger. The latter plans to plant an atomic bomb in Fort Knox and thus contaminate the US hoard of the yellow stuff so that it can't be touched, and thus increase tenfold the value of his own gold, earned by hard international smuggling.

Connery repeats his suave portrayal of the punch-packing Bond, who can find his way around the wine-list as easily as he can negotiate a dame. But, if backroom boys got star billing, it's deserved by Ken Adam, who has designed the production with a wealth of enticing invention. There's a ray-gun that cuts through any metal, and threatens to carve Bond down the middle. There's Goldfinger's automobile – cast in solid gold. And his farm is stocked with furniture that moves at the press of a button.

Honor Blackman makes a fine, sexy partner for Bond. As Pussy Galore, Goldfinger's pilot for his private plane, she does not take things lying down – she's a judo expert who throws Bond until the final k.o. when she's tumbled herself.

Gert Frobe, too, is near-perfect casting as the resourceful Goldfinger, an amoral tycoon who treats gold-cornering as a business like any other.
☐ 1964: Best Sound Effects

⸱⸱⸱⸱⸱⸱⸱⸱⸱⸱⸱⸱⸱⸱⸱⸱⸱⸱⸱⸱⸱⸱⸱⸱⸱⸱⸱

◼ GOLD OF THE SEVEN SAINTS

1961, 89 MINS, US
Dir Gordon M. Douglas   *Prod* Leonard Freeman   *Scr* Leigh Brackett, Leonard Freeman   *Ph* Joseph Biroc   *Ed* Folmar Blangsted   *Mus* Howard Jackson   *Art Dir* Stanley Fleischer
● Clint Walker, Roger Moore, Leticia Roman, Robert Middleton, Chill Wills, Gene Evans (Warner)

By gold-and-rod western standards this is no *Treasure of the Sierra Madre* by a long shot, but it's a darned good imitation-heir apparent, expertly written and colorfully enacted by a polished cast headed by Clint Walker and Roger Moore.

A strong screenplay is the firm foundation upon which the picture remains erect and engrossing until its disappointingly shaky conclusion. Working with a novel by Steve Frazee, the writers have penned some frisky dialog and constructed several gripping situations. Walker and Moore are cast as trapping partners who strike it rich and are chased persistently over the sprawling desert and through craggy hill country by several marauding parties who have one thing in common – total disdain for the golden rule.

Unlike *Treasure*, this film lays a golden egg through the unconvincing nature and transparent spirit of the climactic laughing jag, for the gold did not corrupt these heroes as it did the gentlemen of *Sierra Madre*.

Utilizing his customary heroically-reserved approach Walker does well by the role of anchor man. Moore, as his faithful but emotionally-unsettled Irish mate, gives a most colorfully compelling screen characterization.

⸱⸱⸱⸱⸱⸱⸱⸱⸱⸱⸱⸱⸱⸱⸱⸱⸱⸱⸱⸱⸱⸱⸱⸱⸱⸱⸱

◼ GOLD RUSH, THE

1925, 120 MINS, US ⊗ Ⓥ ⊙
Dir Charles Chaplin   *Prod* Charles Chaplin   *Scr* Charles Chaplin   *Ph* Rollie H. Totheroh   *Art Dir* Charles D. Hall
● Charles Chaplin, Mack Swain, Tom Murray, Georgia Hale (Chaplin)

The Gold Rush is a distinct triumph for Charlie Chaplin from both the artistic and commercial standpoints. Billed as a dramatic comedy, the story carries more of a plot than the rule with the star's former offerings.

Charlie is presented as a tramp prospector in the wilds of Alaska, garbed in his old familiar derby, cane, baggy pants and shoes. He seeks refuge from a raging Arctic storm in the cabin of Black Larson (Tom Murray), hunted outlaw, and is allowed to stay by the latter.

Big Jim McKay (Mack Swain), a husky prospector, discovers a huge vein of gold on his claim, but the storm uproots his tent and blows him to the hut of Larson. The latter objects to McKay's intrusion, and a struggle ensues between the two for possession of a rifle. Chaplin scores here with business in trying to keep out of line with the barrel of the gun. McKay finally subdues Larson and elects to stay till the storm subsides. But the blizzard continues for many days, and provisions give out.

The final scenes of Charlie and McKay journeying back to the States as multi-millionaires are unusual in that they show Chaplin out of his familiar attire. He is dressed in the height of fashion with evening dress and all the adornments.

Humor is the dominating force, with Chaplin reaching new heights as a comedian. Chaplin naturally carries practically the entire 10 reels of action and performs this task without difficulty.

⸱⸱⸱⸱⸱⸱⸱⸱⸱⸱⸱⸱⸱⸱⸱⸱⸱⸱⸱⸱⸱⸱⸱⸱⸱⸱⸱

◼ GOLD RUSH, THE

1942, 71 MINS, US Ⓥ
Dir Charles Chaplin   *Prod* Charles Chaplin   *Scr* Charles Chaplin   *Ph* Rollie Totheroh   *Ed* Reginald McGahann   *Mus* Charles Chaplin, Max Terr
● Charles Chaplin, Mack Swain, Georgia Hale, Tom Murray (United Artists)

With music and narrative dialog added, Charlie Chaplin's *The Gold Rush* [1925] stands the test of time. Chaplin's inimitable cane, derby, hobble and moustache of early days still retain solid comedy for both the younger generation and older folks.

Chaplin did a remarkable job in the editing, background, music and narrative for the new version of his greatest grosser. Original two hours of running time has been edited down to 71 minutes.

Result is a technical achievement in speeding up action of a silent picture to the requirements of sound, and still not making apparent the increased speed in projection.

All the episodes of *Gold Rush* are retained to provide strong comedy reaction of original, like the prospector's cabin marooned in the storm with Chaplin stewing the shoe when food runs out; Chaplin's own narrative is crisply delivered, and he refers to his screen character as 'The Little Fellow' throughout.
☐ 1942: Nominations: Best Scoring of a Dramatic Picture, Sound

⸱⸱⸱⸱⸱⸱⸱⸱⸱⸱⸱⸱⸱⸱⸱⸱⸱⸱⸱⸱⸱⸱⸱⸱⸱⸱⸱

◼ GOLDWYN FOLLIES, THE

1938, 113 MINS, US ◇ Ⓥ
Dir George Marshall   *Prod* Samuel Goldwyn   *Scr* Ben Hecht   *Ph* Gregg Toland   *Ed* Sherman Todd   *Mus* Alfred Newman (dir.)   *Art Dir* Richard Day
● Adolphe Menjou, Ritz Brothers, Zorina, Kenny Baker, Andrea Leeds, Ella Logan (Goldwyn/United Artists)

The astute Samuel Goldwyn has assembled top names from grand opera, class terpsichore, music, radio and films. The mixture, in the brilliant hues of Technicolor, turns out to be a lavish production in which certain individual performances and ensembles erase the memory of some dull moments. Four of the musical numbers were composed by the late George Gershwin, with lyrics by Ira Gershwin; Vernon Duke completed the score.

Filmusical is reported to have cost $2 million. It doesn't parade such extravagance on the screen, which probably is due to some heavy blue penciling en route. Not-withstanding, it is a hefty eyeful.

Start shows Adolphe Menjou much concerned that his productions have lost mass appeal – the common touch. Country girl (Andrea Leeds) tells him what's the matter, takes the job of studio censor and passes on the script and casting of the production in progress.

Meanwhile, Edgar Bergen and 'Charlie' wait in the outer office of the casting director and exchange quips on the world as they see it and some of the people in it. The Ritz Bros, owners of a traveling animal circus, drive in the studio gates intent on film careers. Phil Baker dashes from stage to wardrobe in an effort to keep pace with script changes of his part. Jerome Cowan directs the revised version, sequences of which introduce Helen Jepson in scenes from *La Traviata*, and Zorina dances with the American Ballet troupe. That's how all of them, except Kenny Baker, get in front of the camera.
☐ 1938: Nomination: Best Score

■ GONE TO EARTH
(US: The Wild Heart)

1950, 110 MINS, UK ◇
Dir Michael Powell, Emeric Pressburger   *Prod* David O. Selznick   *Scr* Michael Powell, Emeric Pressburger   *Ph* Christopher Challis   *Ed* Reginald Mills   *Mus* Brian Easdale   *Art Dir* Hein Heckroth
● Jennifer Jones, David Farrar, Cyril Cusack, Sybil Thorndike, Edward Chapman, Hugh Griffith (London/Vanguard)

Powell and Pressburger freely adapted the novel by Mary Webb which has English fox-hunting as its background.

Principal character, Jennifer Jones, lives with her father in the mountains. A simple girl, steeped in local mysticisms, when asked by her father if she will marry the first man to propose, she agrees. The first proposal is from the local parson, but after the wedding, she is induced to run away with the squire and is brought back home by her husband.

Primarily a simple yarn about simple people, it is without finesse, polish or sophistication. Dialog just about emerges from the monosyllabical state.

Jones makes the character of Hazel Woodus a pathetic, winsome creature. It is a genuine and at times glowing performance.

■ GONE WITH THE WIND

1939, 217 MINS, US ◇ ⊛ ⊙
Dir Victor Fleming, [George Cukor, Sam Wood, B. Reeves Eason]   *Prod* David O. Selznick   *Scr* Sidney Howard   *Ph* Ernest Haller, Ray Rennahan, Wilfrid M. Cline   *Ed* Hal C. Kern, James E. Newcom   *Mus* Max Steiner   *Art Dir* Lyle Wheeler, William Cameron Menzies
● Vivien Leigh, Clark Gable, Olivia de Havilland, Leslie Howard, Hattie McDaniel, Thomas Mitchell (Selznick)

After nearly a year of actual filming, editing and scoring, David O. Selznick's production of *Gone with the Wind*, from Margaret Mitchell's novel of the Civil War and reconstruction period, is one of the truly great films. The lavishness of its production, the consummate care and skill which went into its making, the assemblage of its fine cast and expert technical staff combine in a theatrical attraction completely justifying the princely investment of $3.9 million.

In the leading roles, the casting of which was the subject of national debate and conjecture for many months, are Clark Gable, as Rhett Butler; Vivien Leigh, who gives a brilliant performance as Scarlett O'Hara; Leslie Howard and Olivia de Havilland, as Ashley and Melanie.

In the desire apparently to leave nothing out, Selznick has left too much in.

As in the book, the most effective portions of the saga of the destroyed South deal with human incident against the background of the war between the states and the impact of honorable defeat to the Southern forces. Director Victor Fleming has caught a series of memorable views of plantation life and scenes and builds a strong case for a civilization of chivalry.

Among the players, Leigh's Scarlett com-

mands first commendation as a memorable performance, of wide versatility and effective earnestness. Gable's Rhett Butler is as close to Mitchell's conception as might be imagined. He gives a forceful impersonation.

On the heels of these two, Hattie McDaniel, as Mammy, comes closest with a bid for top position as a trouper. It is she who contributes the most moving scene in the film, her plea with Melanie that the latter should persuade Rhett to permit burial of his baby daughter.

Of the other principals, de Havilland does a standout as Melanie, and Howard is convincing as the weak-charactered Ashley.
☐ 1939: Best Picture, Director, Actress (Vivien Leigh), Supp. Actress (Hattie McDaniel), Screenplay, Color Cinematography, Art Direction, Editing, Special Awards (use of color design, and use of coordinated equipment)
☐ Nominations: Best Actor (Clark Gable), Supp. Actress (Olivia de Havilland), Original Score, Sound, Special Effects

■ GOODBYE CHARLIE

1964, 117 MINS, US ◇
Dir Vincente Minnelli   *Prod* David Weisbart   *Scr* Harry Kumitz   *Ph* Milton Krasner   *Ed* John W. Holmes   *Mus* Andre Previn   *Art Dir* Jack Martin Smith, Richard Day
● Tony Curtis, Debbie Reynolds, Pat Boone, Joanna Barnes, Ellen Burstyn, Walter Matthau (Venice/20th Century-Fox)

Even by delving into fantasy for its wildly implausible premise this picturization of George Axelrod's not-so-successful 1960 Broadway play doesn't come off as anything but the mildest type of entertainment.

A joint effort of Curtis' indie Venice banner and 20th-Fox, story framework of the David Weisbart production takes form when a hotshot Hollywood-writer Lothario named Charlie is thoroughly punctured by a gun-wielding Hungarian producer after catching him vis-a-vis with his wife, and writer is reincarnated as a luscious babe.

Debbie Reynolds takes on the task of creating an offbeat character as the reincarnated late-departed who combines the lecherous mind and mores of her former male self with a sexy exterior and newfound femininity while announcing to the world she is the writer's widow.

Tony Curtis plays another writer, victim's best friend who arrives from his Paris home to deliver the eulogy and finds himself saddled not only with a debt-plagued estate, as executor, but this reborn pal as well, now a blonde who decides to cash in on former affairs with filmdom wives and plays cozy with the producer who shot Charlie.

Pat Boone is an over-rich boy with a mother complex who falls for Debbie and wants to marry her, while Walter Matthau puts goulash in the producer role.

■ GOODBYE, COLUMBUS

1969, 104 MINS, US ◇ ⊛ ⊙
Dir Larry Peerce   *Prod* Stanley R. Jaffe   *Scr* Arnold Schulman   *Ph* Gerald Hirschfeld   *Ed* Ralph Rosenblum   *Mus* Charles Fox   *Art Dir* Manny Gerard
● Richard Benjamin, Ali MacGraw, Jack Klugman, Nan Martin, Michael Meyers, Lori Shelle (Paramount/Willow Tree)

This adaptation of Philip Roth's National Book Award-winning novella is sometimes a joy in striking a boisterous mood, and otherwise handling action.

Castwise the feature excels. Richard Benjamin as the boy, a librarian after serving in the army, and Ali MacGraw, making her screen bow as the daughter of wealthy and socially-conscious parents, offer fresh portrayals

seasoned with rich humor. Their romance develops swiftly after their meeting at a country-club pool.

As girl's hard-working father, Jack Klugman rates a big hand and there is a dramatic sequence between father and daughter at wedding of the son of the house which is both tender and memorable.

Several outstanding sequences, among them the gaiety of a Jewish wedding, and hilarious dinner-table action as Benjamin first meets the family.
☐ 1969: Nomination: Best Adapted Screenplay

■ GOODBYE GIRL, THE

1977, 110 MINS, US ◇ ⊛ ⊙
Dir Herbert Ross   *Prod* Ray Stark   *Scr* Neil Simon   *Ph* David M. Walsh   *Ed* Margaret Booth   *Mus* Dave Grusin   *Art Dir* Albert Brenner
● Richard Dreyfuss, Marsha Mason, Quinn Cummings, Paul Benedict, Barbara Rhoades, Theresa Merritt (M-G-M/Warner)

Richard Dreyfuss in offbeat romantic lead casting, and vibrant Marsha Mason head the cast as two lovers in spite of themselves.

Story peg finds Mason, once-divorced and now jilted, finding out that her ex-lover has sublet their NY pad to aspiring thesp Dreyfuss. Mason has two other problems: a precocious daughter, Quinn Cummings, and her own thirtyish age which will prevent a successful resumption of a dancing career necessary to make ends meet.

The Neil Simon script evolves a series of increasingly intimate and sensitive character encounters as the adults progress from mutual hostility to an enduring love.

Performances by Dreyfuss, Mason and Cummings are all great, and the many supporting bits are filled admirably.
☐ 1977: Best Actor (Richard Dreyfuss).
☐ Nominations: Best Picture, Actress (Marsha Mason), Supp. Actress (Quinn Cummings), Original Screenplay

■ GOODBYE, MR. CHIPS

1939, 110 MINS, UK ⊛ ⊙
Dir Sam Wood   *Prod* Victor Saville   *Scr* R.C. Sherriff, Claudine West, Eric Maschwitz   *Ph* Freddie Young   *Ed* Charles Frend   *Mus* Richard Addinsell   *Art Dir* Alfred Junge
● Robert Donat, Greer Garson, Terry Kilburn, John Mills, Paul Heinreid, Judith Furse (M-G-M)

A charming, quaintly sophisticated account [from the novel *Goodbye, Mr. Chips!* by James Hilton] of the life of a schoolteacher, highlighted by a remarkably fine Performance from Robert Donat.

Donat's range of character carries him from youth when he begins to teach at a boys school, through to his middle 30s, then to around the half-century mark, and finally into the slightly doddering age. The character he etches creates a bloodstream for the picture that keeps it intensely alive.

The romance of the schoolteacher and the girl he meets is adroitly and fascinatingly developed. Greer Garson is Katherine, who becomes Donat's wife, only to die all too soon, leaving the schoolmaster nothing but his desire to go forward, with his work and with the boys he tutors.
☐ 1939: Best Actor (Robert Donat).
☐ Nominations: Best Picture, Director, Actress (Greer Garson), Screenplay, Editing, Sound

■ GOODBYE, MR. CHIPS

1969, 151 MINS, UK ◇ ⊛ ⊙
Dir Herbert Ross   *Prod* Arthur P. Jacobs   *Scr* Terence Rattigan   *Ph* Oswald Morris   *Ed* Ralph Kemplen   *Mus* John Williams (sup.)   *Art Dir* Ken Adam

G

● Peter O'Toole, Petula Clark, Michael Redgrave, George Baker, Michael Bryant, Sian Phillips (M-G-M/Apjac)

Lightning seldom strikes in the same place twice, and Hollywood's record for remaking its classics is only slightly better. M-G-M's reproduction of *Goodbye, Mr. Chips* as a big-budget musical [music and lyrics by Leslie Bricusse] with Peter O'Toole and Petula Clark is a sumptuous near-miss that trips on its own overproduction.

The film tells the love story of an English public school master for his work and wife. The scholarly, somewhat prissy and martinetish teacher who frets that his students don't like him is a total departure from O'Toole's previous roles. But there is a curious lack of warmth and humor, a middle-aged bachelor crotchetiness in the opening sequences.

But as he transitions through his troubled love affair and unspectacular career, O'Toole creates a man of strength and dignity, whose tendency to appear ridiculous at times is endearing.
□ 1969: Nominations: Best Actor (Peter O'Toole), Adapted Music Score

● ●

■ **GOODBYE PEOPLE, THE**

1984, 104 MINS, US ◇ ▼ ⊙
Dir Herb Gardner *Prod* David V. Picker *Scr* Herb Gardner *Ph* John Lindley *Ed* Rick Shaine
Art Dir Tony Walton
● Judd Hirsch, Martin Balsam, Pamela Reed, Ron Silver, Michael Tucker, Gene Saks (Coney Island)

The Goodbye People marks stage author and director Herb Gardner's first foray into film direction. Based on his late 1960s stage flop of the same name, neither time nor the transferal of media has improved the story of three eccentric losers who band together in hopes of changing their luck.

Basically a one-set human comedy, the film centers on Arthur Korman (Judd Hirsch), a man in his 40s trapped in a job he cannot stand. To relieve the tension stemming from his inability to chuck working at a toy firm, he makes a daily early morning excursion to Coney Island to watch the sunrise. It is there he meets Max Silverman (Martin Balsam), the former owner of a boardwalk hot dog stand.

The uneasy alliance between the characters is treated in a glib fashion by Gardner.

● ●

■ **GOODBYE PORK PIE**

1981, 100 MINS, NEW ZEALAND ◇ ▼
Dir Geoff Murphy *Prod* Geoff Murphy, Nigel Hutchinson *Scr* Geoff Murphy *Ph* Alun Bollinger
Ed Michael Horton *Mus* John Charles (dir.) *Art Dir* Kai Hawkins
● Kelly Johnson, Tony Barry, Claire Oberman, Shirley Gruar, Bruno Lawrence, John Beach (Ama)

In *Goodbye Pork Pie*, *Easy Rider* meets the Keystone Kops. Following the classic road formula a car chase covers the length of the country and it is a major plus that the pace, fun and general mayhem are such that the pic does not get upstaged by the spectacular scenery.

In the breathing spells between, characters that might have been ciphers – the young punk on the run, the girl hitch-hiker and others whose paths intersect the speeding car – are given human dimensions.

Near the top of New Zealand's North Island Kelly Johnson steals a rental car and heads south, picking up a couple of passengers before he has gone very far. One is pursuing the wife who has walked out on him, and he persuades Johnson to extend what was to have been a short dash into a 1,000-mile marathon, taking in a car ferry crossing on the way.

Claire Oberman is a liberated blond whose frank confession that she is a virgin, given in the same breath with which she introduces herself, leads to a private $2 bet between the two men that this will be changed.

● ●

■ **GOOD COMPANIONS, THE**

1933, 110 MINS, UK
Dir Victor Saville *Prod* Angus McPhaill, Louis Levy, Ian Dalrymple, George Gunn *Scr* W. P. Lipscomb
Ph Bernard Knowles *Ed* Frederick Y. Smith
Art Dir Alfred Junge
● Jessie Matthews, Edmund Gwenn, John Gielgud, Mary Glynne, Percy Parsons, A. W. Baskcomb (Gaumont-British)

Picturization of the J. B. Priestley bestseller was difficult, the story texture being complex. Story [with songs by George Posford and Douglas Furber] deals with a concert party that goes from bankruptcy to fame and fortune, helped by the stray people who flit across the canvas, the schoolmaster who writes jazz, the fading damsel who finances the show from a thirst for adventure, the little chorus girl who rises to be a great star, and so on.

In comparison to the book, picture may seem sketchy, but the interest is held. Characterizations are outstanding. Edmund Gwenn, as the carpenter who is really the center of the story, does the best bit of work. Mary Glynne is very good as Miss Trant, suggesting the pathetic side of the character with real skill. Jessie Matthews is not as boisterous as usual as the chorus girl.

Max Miller, the music-hall man, contributes an outstanding sketch as a salesman. Victor Saville's direction is straight but sound.

● ●

■ **GOOD COMPANIONS, THE**

1957, 105 MINS, UK ◇
Dir J. Lee Thompson *Prod* Hamilton G. Inglis, J. Lee Thompson *Scr* T.J. Morrison, John Whiting, J.L. Hodson
Ph Gilbert Taylor *Ed* Gordon Pilkington *Mus* Laurie Johnson *Art Dir* Robert Jones
● Eric Portman, Celia Johnson, Hugh Griffith, Janette Scott, John Fraser, Rachel Roberts (Associated British)

J.B. Priestley's homely and colorful yarn of a thirdrate touring company makes a pedestrian musical. Much of the characterization and writing quality of the original is lost in the conventional screenplay. An old-fashioned story line, without surprise twists, is not aided by the moderate quality of the score.

Opening shows some promise. In three short cameos it depicts the way in which Eric Portman, Celia Johnson and John Fraser throw in their lot with the Dinky Doos concert party, who are out of funds and facing disbandment. Johnson provides the cash to keep them in business and the rest of the film describes their unhappy experiences playing No. 3 dates to empty houses, until Janette Scott, the youthful star of the company, and Fraser get their big West End chance.

Scott makes a refreshing and appealing showing as the concert party star with ambitions. Fraser also turns in a sincere performance as a composer-accompanist, but it's also hard to accept his music as so good the publishers would be competing for it. Joyce Grenfell makes a typical contribution as a wealthy admirer.

● ●

■ **GOOD EARTH, THE**

1937, 140 MINS, US ▼
Dir Sidney Franklin *Prod* Albert Lewin *Scr* Talbot Jennings, Tess Schlesinger, Claudine West *Ph* Karl Freund *Ed* Basil Wrangell *Mus* Herbert Stothart
● Paul Muni, Luise Rainer, Walter Connolly, Tillie Losch, Charley Grapewin, Jessie Ralph (M-G-M)

Transfer of the [Pearl S.] Buck novel from page to celluloid, with a stop-off via the stage [play by Owen and Donald Davis], is a tough adaptation job. The characters are 100% Chinese. In many scenes such occidentals as Paul Muni and Walter Connolly are mixed with genuine Orientals for direct conversational contact, and no harmful false note is struck. Luise Rainer's Viennese amidst this mumble-jumble of dialects is but slightly noticeable, and then only at the beginning.

The marriage of Wang and O-Lan, their raising of the family and care of their land, the drought, Wang's rise to wealth, his desertion of the farm and his taking of a second wife, his return to the farm and the earth are faithfully transcribed. There are some departures for brevity's sake and some additions, such as the locust plague, which is a helpful contribution rather than a distraction, but the members of the House of Wang are Pearl Buck's original creations without change in this reported $3 million production.

Muni as Wang, with a great makeup, is a splendid lead. Rainer has more difficulty, since her features are not so receptive to Oriental makeup. Yet a good actress overcomes these things, and Luise Rainer is an actress. Connolly as the semi-villainous and greedy uncle, takes the few laughs in a picture which is very sparing with its lightness. Tilly Losch, a dancer by profession, does little dancing, but plenty of good playing, as the second wife, and Charley Grapewin is splendid as the father of Wang.

The slightly tinted and brownish sepia hues, shading some of the farm sequences, give a magnificent effect.
□ 1937: Best Actress (Luise Rainer), Cinematography.
□ Nominations: Best Picture, Director, Editing

● ●

■ **GOOD FAIRY, THE**

1935, 98 MINS, US
Dir William Wyler *Prod* Henry Henigson *Scr* Preston Sturges *Ph* Norbert Brodine *Ed* Daniel Mandell
Art Dir Charles D. Hall
● Margaret Sullavan, Herbert Marshall, Frank Morgan, Reginald Owen, Alan Hale, Beulah Bondi (Universal)

Preston Sturges has translated Ferenc Molnar's dainty stage comedy for the screen, and has turned out a somewhat vociferous paraphrase. Slightly idealistic atmosphere of the original is missing, and in its place is substituted a style of comedy closely akin to slapstick.

A little too much time is given to the initial sequence in the asylum, which is not funny nor particularly convincing, serving only to give Alan Hale and Beulah Bondi their one opportunity. From the asylum action moves to the theatre where Lu (Margaret Sullavan) becomes an usher and her encounter, first with Reginald Owen and almost immediately with Frank Morgan, quickly puts the play into its stride. From there on it works to a farcical finish in which the burly waiter (Owen) removes her from the imagined lascivious attentions of her benefactor (Morgan).

Picture is fairly peppered with closeups which, delaying production, brought U and the director, William Wyler, to the mat. These closeups are so beautiful that they seem worthwhile even if a bit profuse.

Frank Morgan, as the benefactor, plays like an eccentric John Barrymore, but makes his points rapidly and surely. Reginald Owen, as a waiter, is an excellent foil and contributes some telling pantomime. Sullavan is uneasy in the asylum opening as she does not suggest the child. Later she performs more surely.

● ●

■ **GOODFELLAS**

1990, 146 MINS, US ◇ ▼ ⊙
Dir Martin Scorsese *Prod* Irwin Winkler *Scr* Nicholas Pileggi, Martin Scorsese *Ph* Michael Ballhaus
Ed Thelma Schoonmaker *Art Dir* Kristi Zea

● Robert De Niro, Ray Liotta, Joe Pesci, Lorraine Bracco, Paul Sorvino, Frank Sivero (Warner)

Simultaneously fascinating and repellent, *GoodFellas* is Martin Scorsese's colorful but dramatically unsatisfying inside look at Mafia life in 1955–80 New York City. Working from the non-fiction book *Wiseguy* by Nicholas Pileggi, Scorsese returns to the subject matter of his 1973 *Mean Streets* but from a more distanced, older, wiser and subtler perspective.

First half of the film, introing Ray Liotta, as an Irish-Italian kid, to the Mafia milieu, is wonderful. Scorsese's perfectly cast friezes of grotesque hoodlum types are caricatures in the best sense of the word. There's a giddy sense of exploring a forbidden world.

The second half, however, doesn't develop the dramatic conflicts between the character and the milieu that are hinted at earlier.

Liotta starts as a gofer for laconic neighborhood godfather Paul Sorvino, gradually coming under the tutelage of Robert De Niro, cast as a middle-aged Irish hood of considerable ruthlessness and repute. The skewed concept of loyalty involved is intertwined with an adolescent obsession with machismo, most memorably captured in Joe Pesci's short-statured, short-fused psycho.

One of the film's major flaws is that De Niro, with his menacing charm, always seems more interesting than Liotta, but he isn't given enough screen time to explore the relationship fully in his supporting role.
□ 1990: Best Supp. Actor (Joe Pesci).
□ Nominations: Best Picture, Director, Supp. Actress (Lorraine Bracco), Adapted Screenplay, Editing

■ GOOD MORNING, VIETNAM

1987, 120 MINS, US ◇ ⓥ ⊙
Dir Barry Levinson   *Prod* Mark Johnson, Larry Brezner   *Scr* Mitch Markowitz   *Ph* Peter Sova   *Ed* Stu Linder   *Mus* Alex North   *Art Dir* Roy Walker
● Robin Williams, Forest Whitaker, Tung Thanh Tran, Chintara Sukapatana, Bruno Kirby, J.T. Walsh (Touchstone)

After airman Adrian Cronauer (Robin Williams) blows into Saigon to be the morning man on armed forces radio, things are never the same. With a machine-gun delivery of irreverencies and a crazed gleam in his eye, Cronauer turns the staid military protocol on its ear.

On the air he's a rush of energy, perfectly mimicking everyone from Gomer Pyle to Richard Nixon as well as the working grunt in the battlefields, blasting verboten rock'n'roll over the airwaves while doing James Brown splits in the studio. From the start, the film bowls you over with excitement and for those who can latch on, it's a nonstop ride.

Although the film is set in Vietnam in 1965 the fighting seems to take a backseat to William's joking. Instead of the disk jockey being the eyes and ears of the events around him Williams is a totally self-contained character, and despite numerous topical references, his comedy turns in on itself rather than opening on the scene outside.

Bruno Kirby as Cronauer's uptight immediate superior has a few priceless comic moments of his own as he takes to the airwaves with an array of polka music.
□ 1987: Nomination: Best Actor (Robin Williams)

■ GOOD MOTHER, THE

1988, 103 MINS, US ◇ ⓥ ⊙
Dir Leonard Nimoy   *Prod* Arnold Glimcher   *Scr* Michael Bortman   *Ph* David Watkin   *Ed* Peter Berger   *Mus* Elmer Bernstein   *Art Dir* Stan Jolley
● Diane Keaton, Liam Neeson, Jason Robards, Ralph Bellamy, Teresa Wright, Asia Vieira (Touchstone)

The traumatic subject matter of a child custody fight is handled with restraint and intelligence in *The Good Mother*. Superbly acted by an imaginatively chosen cast, adaptation of Sue Miller's 1986 bestseller goes so far to avoid tear-jerking pathos the result may have come out a little drier than anticipated.

Well-judged script presents Anna Dunlap (Diane Keaton) as the recently divorced mother of Molly, an enthusiastic child of six. Living in the Boston area, working part-time in a lab and teaching piano, Anna is committed to her daughter above all else. Skittish and insecure where men are concerned, she nevertheless allows herself to be seduced by Leo (Liam Neeson), an iconoclastic, thoroughly charming Irish sculptor.

Shortly, the boom is lowered. Anna's cold ex-husband Brian (James Naughton), an attorney now remarried, slaps a custody suit on her, announcing that Molly has informed him that Leo in some way molested her sexually.

In the legal crunch, Brian and his attorney (Joe Morton) have the easier job to show, in this conservative era, that Anna's bohemian, live-in lifestyle, casual moral stance and negligent attitude toward her boyfriend's behavior with Molly [briefly allowing the curious child to touch his genitals] represent a clear danger to the child.

Despite the moderate dramatic reserve, which partly stems from director Leonard Nimoy's predominant use of medium-shots, this is compelling stuff, and the performances are uniformly first rate.

■ GOOD NEIGHBOR SAM

1964, 130 MINS, US ◇ ⓥ
Dir David Swift   *Prod* David Swift   *Scr* James Fritzell, Everett Greenbaum, David Swift   *Ph* Burnett Guffey   *Ed* Charles Nelson   *Mus* Frank DeVol   *Art Dir* Dale Hennesy
● Jack Lemmon, Romy Schneider, Edward G. Robinson, Dorothy Provine, Michael Connors, Neil Hamilton (Columbia)

Jack Lemmon's farcial flair finds amusing exposure in this situation comedy. Lemmon tops-bills star lineup in his usual competent and zany fashion but it is the Viennese Romy Schneider, making her first Hollywood-lensed feature, who shines the brightest.

Narrative [based on the novel by Jack Finney] jumps with crazy, mixed-up situations, Lemmon playing low man on the totem pole of a San Francisco advertising agency until he suggests a new approach built around the average man in a campaign for a dissatisfied client about to ankle agency. Suddenly, he is important business-wise. He also finds himself called upon to play the 'husband' to his nextdoor neighbour, who is divorced and must come up with a spouse if she is to meet the provisions of her grandfather's will in bequeathing her his $15 million estate.

Edward G. Robinson gets chuckles as the client, who demands a wholesome campaign and a wholesome man to conduct it.

■ GOOD, THE BAD AND THE UGLY, THE

1966, 161 MINS, ITALY ◇ ⓥ ⊙
Dir Sergio Leone   *Prod* Alberto Grimaldi   *Scr* Luciano Vincenzoni, Sergio Leone, Mickey Knox   *Ph* Tonino Delli Colli   *Ed* Nino Baragli, Eugenio Alabiso   *Mus* Ennio Morricone   *Art Dir* Carlo Simi
● Clint Eastwood, Eli Wallach, Lee Van Cleef, Aldo Giuffre, Mario Brega, Luigi Pistilli (PEA)

The third in the Clint Eastwood series of Italo westerns, *The Good, the Bad and the Ugly* is exactly that – a curious amalgam of the visually striking, the dramatically feeble and the offensively sadistic.

Story [by Incrocci Agenore, Furio Scarpelli, Luciano Vincenzoni and director Sergio Leone] concerns search for buried treasure by 'Good' Eastwood, 'Ugly' Eli Wallach and 'Bad' Lee Van Cleef (making his second appearance in an Eastwood western). Along the way they taunt and torture each other and also contribute a total of 20 dead bodies to the western landscape, reasonably well-faked by European exteriors. As befits his star status, Eastwood kills 10 of these; as befits his titular Goodness, his victims all draw first. Unlike the earlier Leone efforts, however, the violence here has little of the balletic, even erotic quality.

Leone's visual sense is as strong as ever, however, and his effective alternation of extreme closeups and long shots renders much of the pic graphically electric. Unfortunately, he allows several excursions into laughably sentimental characterization, and his three actors (especially Wallach) overplay to the point of absurdity.

Much of Tonino Delli Colli's photography is a knockout. Ennio Morricone's insistent music and Carlo Simi's baroque art direction further contribute to the pic's too-muchness.

■ GOOD WIFE, THE

1986, 92 MINS, AUSTRALIA ◇ ⓥ
Dir Ken Cameron   *Prod* Jan Sharp   *Scr* Peter Kenna   *Ph* James Bartle   *Ed* John Scott   *Mus* Cameron Allan   *Art Dir* Sally Campbell
● Rachel Ward, Bryan Brown, Sam Neill, Steven Vidler, Jennifer Claire, Bruce Barry (Laughing Kookaburra)

Ken Cameron's third feature, *The Good Wife* is a classy romantic drama set in the small Australian country town of Corrimandel in 1939. Rachel Ward toplines as the eponymous wife who's bored with her unexciting life in this rural backwater. She's married to a burly, well-intentioned logger (real-life hubby Bryan Brown) and spends her time cooking, cleaning and helping other women in childbirth; part of her problem is that she's childless herself.

Neville Gifford (Sam Neill) arrives in town. Marge becomes more and more obsessed with the handsome stranger, eventually openly chasing after him, bringing scandal and shame on herself and her uncomprehending spouse. Fine performances from Ward, Brown and Neill.

■ GOONIES, THE

1985, 111 MINS, US ◇ ⓥ ⊙
Dir Richard Donner   *Prod* Richard Donner, Harvey Bernhard   *Scr* Chris Columbus   *Ph* Nick McLean   *Ed* Michael Kahn   *Mus* Dave Grusin   *Art Dir* J. Michael Riva
● Sean Astin, Josh Brolin, Jeff Cohen, Corey Feldman, Kerri Green, Martha Plimpton (Amblin)

Territory is typical small town Steven Spielberg; this time set in a coastal community in Oregon. Story is told from the kids' point-of-view and takes a rather long time to be set in motion.

Brothers Mikey (Sean Astin) and Brand (Josh Brolin) are being forced to leave their home because land developers are foreclosing on their house to build a new country club. The boys are joined by compulsive eater Chuck (Jeff Cohen) and mumbling Mouth (Corey Feldman) for one final adventure together.

Searching through the attic holding museum pieces under the care of their curator father, the boys uncover a pirate treasure map. Sidetracked only temporarily by the nefarious Fratelli family (Robert Davi, Joe Pantoliano, Anne Ramsey), the boys begin their fairy tale treasure hunt.

The pirate One-Eyed Willie, it seems, was no one's fool; he left a deadly obstacle course to the treasure.

Linking the kids together is their identification as 'Goonies', residents of the boondocks.

G

Handle apparently imbues them with a mystical bond and idealized state of grace.

....

■ GORGEOUS HUSSY, THE

1936, 103 MINS, US ⊕

Dir Clarence Brown   *Prod* Joseph L. Mankiewicz
Scr Ainsworth Morgan, Stephen Morehouse Avery
Ph George Folsey   *Ed* Blanche Sewell   *Mus* Herbert Stothart   *Art Dir* Cedric Gibbons, William A. Horning, Edwin B. Willis
● Joan Crawford, Robert Taylor, Lionel Barrymore, Franchot Tone, Melvyn Douglas, James Stewart (M-G-M)

Picture is primarily Lionel Barrymore's, and not particularly because the character of Andrew Jackson he portrays calls for it. His tenderness towards his backwoods wife, his rough-and-ready fighting spirit in the campaign for presidency, his opening address to Congress, his sorrow over his wife's death and his bitter encounter with his cabinet – all are portrayed with acting acumen.

Joan Crawford figures in four love affairs, two of which are prominent in the picture and two of which result in marriage. Her first two sweethearts are Robert Taylor and Melvyn Douglas, and later James Stewart is spotted as a suitor. Last in the line is Franchot Tone, the cabinet member she is married to at the finish.

Title [from the novel by Samuel Hopkins Adams] obtains from the fact that the daughter of a tavern keeper (sneeringly called the Gorgeous Hussy) is the childhood friend of Andrew Jackson and his wife. When the latter dies, she promises to remain by Andy's side while he is President.

Crawford makes her debut in a costumer. Role naturally is more subdued and confining than generally associated with her. But she fills the role and the billing.

Douglas, as John Randolph, the state-righter Virginian Senator, clicks strongly. Tone contributes a smooth job as the war secretary who wins Crawford as his bride after her first husband is killed in action. Stewart isn't given many opportunities but makes something of them.

□ 1936: Nominations: Best Supp. Actress (Beulah Bondi), Cinematography

....

■ GORILLAS IN THE MIST
THE STORY OF DIAN FOSSEY

1988, 129 MINS, US ◇ ⊕ ⊙

Dir Michael Apted   *Prod* Arnold Glimcher, Terence Clegg   *Scr* Anna Hamilton Phelan   *Ph* John Seale   *Ed* Stuart Baird   *Mus* Maurice Jarre   *Art Dir* John Graysmark
● Sigourney Weaver, Bryan Brown, Julie Harris, John Omirah Miluwi, Iain Cuthbertson, Constantin Alexandrov (Universal/Warner)

The life story of the late anthropologist Dian Fossey posed considerable challenges to the filmmakers tackling it, and they have been met in admirable fashion in *Gorillas in the Mist* [from a screen story by Anna Hamilton Phelan and Tab Murphy based on Fossey's work and an article by Harold T.P. Hayes].

Fossey devoted nearly 20 years to observing, and trying to protect, the gorillas who live in a small area in the Virunga mountain range, which extends into Rwanda, where Fossey established her Karisoke Research Center. Thanks to National Geographic and films made by Bob Campbell, her work became internationally known, but she alienated a number of people, and was murdered in 1985. (Although her research assistant was convicted in absentia, many feel guilt lies elsewhere.)

After a while, just as Fossey began making unprecedented physical contact with these imposing animals, Sigourney Weaver seems to establish an exceptional familiarity and rapport with the jungle inhabitants. The intense bond

makes the later scenes relating to the gorilla slaughter by poachers all the more powerful.

Campbell, played by Bryan Brown, turns up unannounced to photograph her activities and, after initial resistance, Fossey not only welcomes his presence but takes the married man as her lover.

Weaver is utterly believable and riveting in the role. Her scenes with the apes are captivating. Brown lends a nice lilt to his sympathetic interloper. Lensed high in the mountains of Rwanda, the production looks impressive.

□ 1988: Nominations: Best Actress (Sigourney Weaver), Adapted Screenplay, Editing, Original Score, Sound

....

■ GORKY PARK

1983, 128 MINS, US ◇ ⊕ ⊙

Dir Michael Apted   *Prod* Gene Kirkwood, Howard W. Koch Jr   *Scr* Dennis Potter   *Ph* Ralf D. Bode   *Ed* Dennis Virkler   *Mus* James Horner   *Art Dir* Paul Sylbert
● William Hurt, Lee Marvin, Brian Dennehy, Ian Bannen, Joanna Pacula, Michael Elphick (Orion)

There's enough menace and romance in *Gorky Park* to appeal to many, especially those helped by the memory of Martin Cruz Smith's successful novel.

At the center, however, William Hurt is superb as a Moscow militia detective caught between his desires to be simply a good cop and the unfathomable motives of the secret Soviet government, all complicated by an unexpected love for Joanna Pacula.

Director Michael Apted sets Hurt up well with the discovery of three mutilated, faceless bodies in the city's Gorky Park, leading Hurt to suspect this is all the affair of the dangerous KGB and much to be avoided by plodding policemen such as himself.

Very quickly, Hurt's investigation brings him into contact with Lee Marvin, a wealthy American who enjoys high privilege in important Soviet circles, obviously not simply because he's a successful trader in sables.

Apted, cinematographer Ralf D. Bode and production designer Paul Sylbert do an excellent job in making Helsinki stand in for Moscow, where they were denied access for filming.

....

■ GO TELL THE SPARTANS

1978, 114 MINS, US ◇ ⊕ ⊙

Dir Ted Post   *Prod* Allan F. Bodoh, Mitchell Cannold   *Scr* Wendell Mayes   *Ph* Harry Stradling Jr   *Ed* Millie Moore   *Mus* Dick Halligan   *Art Dir* Jack Senter
● Burt Lancaster, Craig Wasson, Jonathan Goldsmith, Marc Singer, Joe Unger, Dennis Howard (Mar Vista/Spartan)

A good war film needs heroes. But Vietnam had no heroes in the eyes of most Americans. Even a reasonably well-made and well-acted earnest effort like *Go Tell The Spartans*, set in 1964 when the US involvement was limited to 'military advisors', can't overcome that disadvantage.

Based on Daniel Ford's novel, *Incident at Muc Wa*, Wendell Mayes' script follows a detachment of Americans and Vietnamese mercenaries as they occupy an outpost abandoned by the French a decade ago. Burt Lancaster is the commander of an advisory group at Penang who must order the raw detachment into the jungle. When the Vietcong move in on the soldiers, Lancaster arranges for their evacuation.

Lancaster leads a mostly untried cast, including Marc Singer as his assistant, Jonathan Goldsmith playing a burned-out veteran, Joe Unger as a naive over-zealous lieutenant on his first mission and Evan Kim as the tough leader of the Vietnam mercenaries. All turn in fine performances.

....

■ GOTHIC

1986, 90 MINS, UK ◇ ⊕ ⊙

Dir Ken Russell   *Prod* Penny Corke   *Scr* Stephen Volk   *Ph* Mike Southon   *Ed* Michael Bradsell   *Mus* Thomas Dolby   *Art Dir* Christopher Hobbs
● Gabriel Byrne, Julian Sands, Natasha Richardson, Myriam Cyr, Timothy Spall, Andreas Wisniewski (Virgin)

Ken Russell's films always have been very much an acquired taste, but with *Gothic* he is back to his theatrically extravagant self.

Set on a stormy June night in 1816 at the Villa Diodati in Switzerland, the drug-induced excesses of the poet Byron (Gabriel Byrne) and his four guests inspire both Mary Shelley to write *Frankenstein* and Dr Polidori *The Vampyre*, two gothic horrror classics.

As the group becomes more drug-soaked and terrified, the villa with its darkened passages, spiral staircases, shuttered rooms, and menacing candlelight, becomes a labyrinth of horror.

Ken Russell has made an unrelenting nightmare that is both uncomfortable and compulsive to watch. Gabriel Byrne and Natasha Richardson, as Mary Shelley, are powerful and hold the film together.

....

■ GO WEST

1940, 79 MINS, US ⊕

Dir Edward Buzzell   *Prod* Jack Cummings   *Scr* Irving Brecher   *Ph* Leonard Smith   *Ed* Blanche Sewell   *Mus* Georgie Stoll (dir.)   *Art Dir* Cedric Gibbons, Stan Rogers
● Groucho Marx, Harpo Marx, Chico Marx, John Carroll, Diana Lewis, Walter Woolf King (M-G-M)

The three Marx Bros ride a merry trail of laughs and broad burlesque in a speedy adventure through the sagebrush country. Story is only a slight framework on which to parade the generally nonsensical antics of the trio. Attracted to the wide open spaces by tales of gold lining the street, Chico, Harpo, and Groucho get involved in ownership of a deed to property wanted by the railroad for its western extension, and the action flashes through typical dance hall, rumbling stagecoach and desert waste episodes – with a wild train ride for a climax to outwit the villains.

Material provided by tightly knit script is topnotch while direction by Edward Buzzell smacks over the gags and comedy situations for maximum laughs. The Marxes secured pre-production audience reaction through tour of key picture houses trying out various sequences, which undoubtedly aided in tightening the action and dialog.

Groucho, Chico and Harpo handle their assignments with zestful enthusiasm. There's a bill-changing routine in Grand Central Station, wild melee and clowning in the rolling stagecoach, a comedy safe-cracking episode, and the train chase for a finish that winds up with the upper car structures dismantled by the silent Harpo to provide fuel for the engine. It's all ridiculous, but tuned for fun.

....

■ GRACE QUIGLEY

See: The Ultimate Solution of Grace Quigley

....

■ GRADUATE, THE

1967, 105 MINS, US ◇ ⊕ ⊙

Dir Mike Nichols   *Prod* Lawrence Turman   *Scr* Calder Willingham, Buck Henry   *Ph* Robert Surtees   *Ed* Sam O'Steen   *Mus* Dave Grusin   *Art Dir* Richard Sylbert
● Anne Bancroft, Dustin Hoffman, Katharine Ross, William Daniels, Murray Hamilton, Elizabeth Wilson (Embassy)

The Graduate is a delightful, satirical comedy-drama about a young man's seduction by an older woman, and the measure of maturity which he attains from the experience. Anne

Bancroft, Katharine Ross and Dustin Hoffman head a very competent cast.

An excellent screenplay, based on the Charles Webb novel, focuses on Hoffman, just out of college and wondering what it's all about. Predatory Bancroft, wife of Murray Hamilton, introduces Hoffman to mechanical sex, reaction to which evolves into true love with Ross, Bancroft's daughter.

In the 70 minutes which elapse from Hoffman's arrival home from school to the realization by Ross that he has had an affair with her mother, pic is loaded with hilarious comedy and, because of this, the intended commentary on materialistic society is most effective.

Only in the final 35 minutes, as Hoffman drives up and down the LA-Frisco route in pursuit of Ross, does film falter in pacing, result of which the switched-on cinematics become obvious, and therefore tiring.

☐ 1967: Best Director.
☐ Nominations: Best Picture, Actor (Dustin Hoffman), Actress (Anne Bancroft), Supp. Actress (Katharine Ross), Adapted Screenplay, Cinematography

．．．．．．．．．．．．．．．．．．．．．．．．．．．．．．

■ GRAFFITI BRIDGE

1990, 95 MINS, US ◇ ▼ ⊙
Dir Prince   *Prod* Arnold Stiefel, Randy Phillips
Scr Prince   *Ph* Bill Butler   *Ed* Rebecca Ross   *Mus* Prince
Art Dir Vance Lorenzini
● Prince, Ingrid Chavez, Morris Day, Jerome Benton, Mavis Staples, George Clinton (Warner/Paisley Park)

Reviving the characters from Prince's 1984 hit *Purple Rain*, including a reunited Morris Day and the Time, *Graffiti Bridge* is a $7.5 million indulgence that amounts to a half-baked retread of tired MTV imagery and childish themes.

Plot revolves around rivalry between the Kid (Prince) and Day for control of a club they co-own. Day wants to play the songs the people want to hear; the Kid wants to focus on the music he's hearing from a higher power. They duel it out in various musical showdowns.

Chief embarrassment is the spotlight on Ingrid Chavez, latest of Prince's femme discoveries, as the cooingly coy love child with a direct line to the Maker.

That Prince wrote and directed this homage to his own creative process is evident. Mostly this amounts to a cinematic sandbox in which the Mascaraed One can play, pose and change costumes, inviting most of his gang to join in.

．．．．．．．．．．．．．．．．．．．．．．．．．．．．．．

■ GRAND CANYON

1991, 134 MINS, US ◇ ▼ ⊙
Dir Lawrence Kasdan   *Prod* Lawrence Kasdan
Scr Lawrence Kasdan, Meg Kasdan   *Ph* Owen Roizman
Ed Carol Littleton   *Mus* James Newton Howard
Art Dir Bo Welch
● Danny Glover, Kevin Kline, Steve Martin, Mary McDonnell, Mary-Louise Parker, Alfre Woodard (20th Century-Fox)

Life in LA is the pits, according to scripters Lawrence and Meg Kasdan in *Grand Canyon*, their earnest, often moving but not totally successful film. Via its refreshing concentration on a black-white friendship (rare in non-action Hollywood pics), film explores contemporary racial tension and ambivalence.

Danny Glover (a tow-truck driver) and Kevin Kline (an immigration lawyer) come to a warm, if tentative, connection in their paradise-turned-hellhole, a city that still looks lustrous from the oddly smogless air but, up close, shows its 'gone to shit' as the film says of both LA and the country at large.

Glover is given a juicy role as the moral voice of a film mourning the loss of civility in

a society torn apart by the widening chasm – the Grand Canyon – between rich and poor. Kline, also very good in his more understated way, conveys the edgy uncertainty of a white liberal struggling to cope with life in a city whose police routinely terrorize angry black inhabitants.

Kline's also living on the moral edge by carrying on a half-hearted affair with his secretary, fresh young Mary-Louise Parker, who's driven to distraction by his lack of emotional involvement.

The Steve Martin character, who whines, 'Nobody in this town will admit that a producer is an artist,' is a wicked caricature of action pic maker Joel Silver. But the Kasdans' script vacillates uneasily between treating the character as a comic relief spouter of buzz words and a voice of genuine wisdom.

☐ 1991: Nomination: Best Original Screenplay

．．．．．．．．．．．．．．．．．．．．．．．．．．．．．．

■ GRAND HOTEL

1932, 105 MINS, US ▼ ⊙
Dir Edmund Goulding   *Scr* William A. Drake
Ph William Daniels   *Ed* Blanche Sewell
● Greta Garbo, John Barrymore, Joan Crawford, Wallace Beery, Lionel Barrymore, Jean Hersholt (M-G-M)

Better than just a good transcription of the Vicki Baum stage play. Story is many angled in characters and incidents. There is the romantic grip of the actress-nobleman lovers; there is the triumph of the underdog in the figure of Kringelein, the humble bookkeeper doomed to approaching death and determined to spend his remaining days in a splurge of luxury in the Grand Hotel; and there is the everlasting Cinderella element in the not-so-good stenographer who at last finds a friend and protector in the dying Kringelein.

First honors again go to Lionel Barrymore for an inspired performance as the soon-to-die bookkeeper. Greta Garbo gives the role of the dancer something of artificiality, risking a trace of acting swagger, sometimes stagey. Her clothes are ravishing in the well-known Garbo style.

John Barrymore is back where he belongs as the down-at-heel but glamorous baron, going about debonairly in a career of crime but with a heart of gold that will not stoop to small meanness.

There remains the stenographer Miss Flaemmchen, not the most fortunate casting for Joan Crawford, who is rather too capable a type to successfully play an unhappy plaything of fate.

Wallace Beery is at home in the part of the German industrialist, a grandiose but pathetic figure in his struggles with business rivals.

☐ 1931/32: Best Picture

．．．．．．．．．．．．．．．．．．．．．．．．．．．．．．

■ GRAND ISLE

1991, 112 MINS, US ◇ ▼ ⊙
Dir Mary Lambert   *Prod* Kelly McGillis, Carolyn Pfeiffer
Scr Hesper Anderson   *Ph* Toyomichi Kurita   *Ed* Tom Finan   *Mus* Elliot Goldenthal   *Art Dir* Michelle Minch
● Kelly McGillis, Jon DeVries, Adrian Pasdar, Ellen Burstyn, Glenne Headly, Julian Sands (Turner)

Reputation of Kate Chopin's novel *The Awakening* gains nothing from its screen adaptation. *Grand Isle* recreates the 1899 tale of a married woman's sexual and spiritual emancipation with a perplexing absence of drama, passion or skill. Kelly McGillis stars in and co-produced this languorous Louisiana period piece and, unfortunately, the lack of filmmaking experience at the top shows.

The McGillis character rebels against her comfortable married life after her bohemian instincts are awakened by an older artist friend (Ellen Burstyn) and the attentions of

an idle young man (Adrian Pasdar) who helps her overcome her fear of swimming in the ocean.

Script, commissioned from writer Hesper Anderson (*Children of a Lesser God*), offers prissy and unnatural dialog. Acting is obvious or wooden, and the Creole French accents are mismatched. Actors are lit and madeup to poor effect, and camerawork, aside from a lyrical opening, is remarkably awkward.

．．．．．．．．．．．．．．．．．．．．．．．．．．．．．．

■ GRAND PRIX

1966, 179 MINS, US ◇ ▼ ⊙
Dir John Frankenheimer   *Prod* Edward Lewis
Scr Robert Alan Aurthur, [William Hanley]   *Ph* Lionel Lindon   *Ed* Fredric Steinkamp, Henry Berman, Stewart Linder, Frank Santillo   *Mus* Maurice Jarre
Art Dir Richard Sylbert
● James Garner, Eva Marie Saint, Yves Montand, Toshiro Mifune, Brian Bedford, Jessica Walter (Douglas & Lewis/M-G-M)

The roar and whine of engines sending men and machines hurtling over the 10 top road and track courses of Europe, the US and Mexico – the Grand Prix circuits – are the prime motivating forces of this action-crammed adventure that director John Frankenheimer and producer Edward Lewis have interlarded with personal drama that is sometimes introspectively revealing, occasionally mundane, but generally a most serviceable framework.

Frankenheimer has shrewdly varied the length and the importance of the races that figure in the film and the overplay of running commentary on the various events, not always distinct above the roar of motors, imparts a documentary vitality. The director, moreover, frequently divides his outsized screen into sectional panels for a sort of montage interplay of reactions of the principals – a stream of consciousness commentary – that adroitly prevents the road running from overwhelming the personal drama.

There is a curious thing, however, about the exposition of the characters in this screenplay. Under cold examination they are stock characters. James Garner, American competitor in a field of Europeans, is somewhat taciturn, unencumbered by marital involvement. Yves Montand has a wife in name and forms a genuine attachment for American fashion writer Eva Marie Saint, a divorcee. Brian Bedford is the emotionally confused Britisher competing against the memory of his champion-driver brother and whose compulsion to be a champion almost wrecks his marriage to whilom American actress-model Jessica Walter.

☐ 1966: Best Sound, Editing, Sound Effects

．．．．．．．．．．．．．．．．．．．．．．．．．．．．．．

■ GRAND THEFT AUTO

1977, 89 MINS, US ◇ ▼
Dir Ron Howard   *Prod* Jon Davidson   *Scr* Ranse Howard, Ron Howard   *Ph* Gary Graver   *Ed* Joe Dante   *Mus* Peter Ivers   *Art Dir* Keith Michael
● Ron Howard, Nancy Morgan, Marion Ross, Pete Isacksen, Barry Cahill, Hoke Howell (New World)

Grand Theft Auto is a non-stop orgy of comic destructiveness.

Ron Howard has directed with a broad but amiable and well-disciplined touch in this screwball comedy about his elopement with heiress Nancy Morgan from LA to Las Vegas, with her father Barry Cahill and dozens of others in pursuit.

Howard never tries to hog the screen and lets his costars have plenty of funny moments. Morgan is pretty and charming as his spunky partner, and it's a nice touch that Howard lets her drive the getaway car, a gleaming black-and-tan Rolls-Royce.

Also along for the chase are Marion Ross as the angry mother of Morgan's oafish fiance, played amusingly straight by Paul Linke, and d.j. Don Steele, who broadcasts a cynical running commentary from a helicopter.

. . . .

■ GRAPES OF WRATH, THE

1940, 129 MINS, US ⑱ ⊙
Dir John Ford   *Prod* Darryl F. Zanuck   *Scr* Nunnally Johnson   *Ph* Gregg Toland   *Ed* Robert Simpson   *Mus* Alfred Newman (dir.)   *Art Dir* Richard Day, Mark-Lee Kirk
● Henry Fonda, Jane Darwell, John Carradine, Charley Grapewin, Dorris Bowdon, John Qualen (20th Century-Fox)

It took courage, a pile of money and John Ford to film the story of the dust bowl and the tribulations of its unhappy survivors, who sought refuge in inhospitable California. *The Grapes of Wrath*, adapted by Nunnally Johnson from John Steinbeck's best-seller, is an absorbing, tense melodrama, starkly realistic, and loaded with social and political fireworks. The film interprets the consequences of national disaster in terms of a family group – the Joads – who left their quarter-section to the wind and dust and started cross-country in an over-laden jalopy to the land of plenty.

It is not a pleasant story, and the pictured plight of the Joads, and hundreds of other dust bowl refugee families, during their frantic search for work in California, is a shocking visualization of a state of affairs demanding generous humanitarian attention. Neither book nor film gives any edge to citizens of California who are working diligently to alleviate suffering and conditions not of their origination. Steinbeck offers no suggestion. In this respect the film ends on a more hopeful note. Someway, somehow, Ma Joad declares 'the people' will solve the unemployment riddle.

It is all on the screen – everything except the unpalatable Steinbeck dialog, and such other portions of the book which good taste exclude. The characters are there, and under Ford's direction a group of actors makes them into living people, whose frustration catches at the heart and throat. There is humor, too, but the film as a whole scores as a gripping experience.

Henry Fonda does a swell job as Tom and John Carradine is excellent as Casey, the reformed preacher. Jane Darwell gives the family strength and leadership in the mother part. Charley Grapewin's grandpa is rich in humor and tragedy.
□ 1940: Best Director, Supp. Actress (Jane Darwell).
□ Nominations: Best Picture, Actor (Henry Fonda), Screenplay, Editing, Sound

. . . .

■ GRASSHOPPER, THE

1970, 96 MINS, US ◇ ⑱
Dir Jerry Paris   *Prod* Jerry Belson, Garry Marshall   *Scr* Jerry Belson, Garry Marshall   *Ph* Sam Leavitt   *Ed* Aaron Stell   *Mus* Billy Goldenberg   *Art Dir* Tambi Larsen
● Jacqueline Bisset, Jim Brown, Joseph Cotten, Corbett Monica, Ramon Bieri, Christopher Stone (National General)

The Grasshopper is the dark side of the Hollywood story, every schoolgirl's American Dream gone sour [from the novel *The Passing of Evil* by Mark McShane]. Jacqueline Bisset is the good-looking, well-built, lively chick, bored with a bankteller's job and the prospects of a middle-class husband, suburban home and kids, who is attracted by the tinsel of Las Vegas.

Attractive and busty enough to make the chorus, but neither talented nor ambitious enough to go beyond, she drifts into a bad marriage, being kept by a rich old man and then into outright hustling, having run the gamut by age 22.

Bisset is on camera for almost the entire film, kept carefully within her dramatic depth by Director Jerry Paris, with unexpected outbreaks of a kooky humor.

. . . .

■ GRASS IS GREENER, THE

1960, 105 MINS, US ◇ ⑱
Dir Stanley Donen   *Prod* Stanley Donen   *Scr* Hugh Williams, Margaret Williams   *Ph* Christopher Challis   *Ed* James Clark   *Mus* Douglas Gamley, Len Stevens (arrs.)   *Art Dir* Paul Sheriff
● Cary Grant, Deborah Kerr, Robert Mitchum, Jean Simmons, Moray Watson (Universal/Grandon)

Merry old England is the site of this not-always-so-merry comedy about a romantic clash between a British Earl-ionaire and an American oil-ionaire. The Hugh and Margaret Wilson screenplay, adapted from their London stage hit, slowly evolves into a talky and generally tedious romantic exercise, dropping the semi-satirical stance that brightens up the early going.

A romantic triangle develops among the Earl (Cary Grant), his wife (Deborah Kerr), and a 'rip-roaring Grade A romantic' American millionaire (Robert Mitchum) who wanders off-limits into milady's drawing room during a tour of the Earl's house and promptly and preposterously falls in love with her, she with him. Balance of the picture is concerned with Grant's efforts to woo his wife back to his side.

The uninspired screenplay has its staunchest ally in Grant, whose stiffest comedy competition comes not from his three costars but from Moray Watson, the butler.

There are some compelling views of the English countryside, and the incorporation of some of Noel Coward's memorable tunes gives matters a lift.

. . . .

■ GRAYEAGLE

1977, 104 MINS, US ◇ ⑱
Dir Charles B. Pierce   *Prod* Charles B. Pierce   *Scr* Charles B. Pierce   *Ph* Jim Roberson   *Ed* Jim Roberson   *Mus* Jaime Mendoza-Nava   *Art Dir* John Ball
● Ben Johnson, Iron Eyes Cody, Lana Wood, Jack Elam, Paul Fix, Alex Cord (American International)

Coupling handsome Montana vistas with Ben Johnson's sincere portrayal of a frontier trapper whose daughter (Lana Wood) is kidnapped by a young Cheyenne brave, *Grayeagle* has an aura of class that the dumb plot and weak characterizations belie.

Johnson's daughter is dragged across panoramic locations to the deathbed of Chief Running Wolf (Paul Fix), who turns out to be her real father. In hot pursuit are Johnson and Standing Bear (Iron Eyes Cody), a lifelong friend of Johnson's family.

As the plot advances – lethargically – it turns into a wild west soap opera. Girl meets kidnapper, falls in love with savage, finds comfort in discovering her true heritage. On screen the film looks okay, if crude.

. . . .

■ GRAY LADY DOWN

1978, 111 MINS, US ◇ ⑱
Dir David Greene   *Prod* Walter Mirisch   *Scr* James Whittaker, Howard Sackler   *Ph* Stevan Larner   *Ed* Robert Swink   *Mus* Jerry Fielding   *Art Dir* William Tuntke
● Charlton Heston, David Carradine, Stacy Keach, Ned Beatty, Stephen McHattie, Ronny Cox (Mirisch/Universal)

Charlton Heston is back in jeopardy. He's 60 miles off the coast of Connecticut stuck with 41 other sailors on the edge of an ocean canyon in a nuclear submarine, waiting for Stacy Keach to organize a rescue mission. If Keach doesn't hurry one of three disasters will soon happen: water pressure will crush

the sub's hull, oxygen will run out, or the boat will slip off the ledge.

David Carradine and Ned Beatty enter the scene after Heston and crew suffer a pair of double setbacks. First their surfacing vessel is rammed by a Norwegian freighter and plunges straight down. Then an earth tremor covers the sub's escape hatch.

Up to this point things are fairly routine [in a story based on the novel *Event 1000* by David Lavallee, adaptation by Frank P. Rosenberg]. Heston looks courageous; Ronny Cox, the second in command, freaks out; some crew members get sick, and a handful die; Heston's on-shore wife is informed of her husband's condition and adopts a visage of sadness; Keach, a very formal officer, promises Heston and crew that everything will be all right.

But the second disaster – the escape hatch burial – calls for special action. Enter Carradine, a subdued Navy captain and inventor of an experimental diving vessel known as the Snark, and his assistant, Beatty. They resemble a disaster movie's Laurel and Hardy. They're a nice twist.

. . . .

■ GREASE

1978, 110 MINS, US ◇ ⑱ ⊙
Dir Randal Kleiser   *Prod* Robert Stigwood, Allan Carr   *Scr* Bronte Woodard   *Ph* Bill Butler   *Ed* John F. Burnett   *Mus* Bill Oakes (sup.)   *Art Dir* Phil Jefferies
● John Travolta, Olivia Newton-John, Stockard Channing, Jeff Conaway, Eve Arden, Joan Blondell (Paramount)

Grease has got it, from the outstanding animated titles of John Wilson all the way through the rousing finale as John Travolta and Olivia Newton-John ride off into teenage happiness.

Allan Carr is credited with adapting the 1950s style legituner of Jim Jacobs and Warren Casey, which Bronte Woodard then fashioned into an excellent screenplay that moves smartly. Director Randal Kleiser and choreographer Patricia Birch stage the sequences with aplomb, providing as necessary the hoke, hand or heart appropriate to the specific moment.

Plot tracks the bumpy romantic road of Travolta and Newton-John, whose summer beach idyll sours when he feels he must revert to finger-snapping cool in the atmosphere of the high school they both wind up attending. Stockard Channing provides a nice contrast to Newton-John in a hard but really nice characterization. Jeff Conaway is very good as the type guy for whom Travolta is a natural leader.
□ 1978: Nomination: Best Song ('Hopelessly Devoted to You')

. . . .

■ GREASE 2

1982, 114 MINS, US ◇ ⑱ ⊙
Dir Patricia Birch   *Prod* Robert Stigwood, Allan Carr   *Scr* Ken Finkleman   *Ph* Frank Stanley   *Ed* John F. Burnett   *Mus* Louis St Louis (arr.)   *Art Dir* Gene Callahan
● Maxwell Caulfield, Michelle Pfeiffer, Adrian Zmed, Eve Arden, Connie Stevens, Tab Hunter (Paramount)

It's 1961 now at Rydell High, a becalmed, upbeat time when JFK's photo has replaced Ike's on the school wall. In fact, hardly anything is happening socially or musically.

It's not even a question of will boy get girl, but how. Gorgeous Michelle Pfeiffer plays the leader of the foxy Pink Ladies, whose members are only supposed to go out with greasers from the T-Birds gang. Maxwell Caulfield, fresh from England and complete with accent, is the new boy in school, and it's made clear to him that Pfeiffer is off limits until he proves himself as a leather-clad biker.

Where this film has a decided edge on its predecessor is in the staging and cutting of the musical sequences. Choreographer and director Patricia Birch has come up with some unusual settings (a bowling alley, a bomb shelter) for some of the scenes, and employs some sharp montage to give most of the songs and dances a fair amount of punch.

Pfeiffer is all anyone could ask for in the looks department, and she fills Olivia Newton-John's shoes and tight pants very well, thank you. Caulfield is a less certain choice.

....

■ GREASED LIGHTNING

1977, 96 MINS, US ◇ ⓥ
Dir Michael Schultz   *Prod* Hannah Weinstein
Scr Kenneth Vose, Lawrence DuKore, Melvin Van Peebles, Leon Capetanos   *Ph* George Bouillet   *Ed* Bob Wyman, Christopher Holmes, Randy Roberts   *Mus* Fred Karlin
Art Dir Jack Senter
● Richard Pryor, Beau Bridges, Pam Grier, Cleavon Little, Vincent Gardenia, Richie Havens (Third World)

Greased Lightning is a pleasant, loose and relaxed comedy starring Richard Pryor in an excellent characterization based on real-life racing driver Wendell Scott.

Beau Bridges plays a redneck driver who befriends Pryor's stolid efforts to break the color barrier in car racing. Pam Grier is smashingly decorous but wasted in a supportive wife role, while Cleavon Little is cast as Pryor's close friend.

Story covers about 25 years, from Pryor's release from Second World War Army service to championship race in 1971.

Another virtue of the film is its discreet conveyance of an important theme: In any large society, progress by any minority group is accomplished through particular individuals doing notable things.

....

■ GREAT AMERICAN BROADCAST, THE

1941, 90 MINS, US ◇ ⓥ
Dir Archie Mayo   *Prod* Kenneth Macgowan (assoc.)
Scr Don Ettlinger, Edwin Blum, Robert Ellis, Helen Logan   *Ph* Leon Shamroy, Peverell Marley   *Ed* Robert Simpson   *Mus* Alfred Newman (dir.)   *Art Dir* Richard Day, Albert Hogsett
● Alice Faye, Jack Oakie, John Payne, Cesar Romero, The Four Ink Spots, James Newill (20th Century-Fox)

The Great American Broadcast is light and breezy, a showmanly admixture of comedy, romance, drama and music woven around the extraordinary progress of radio broadcasting during the 1920s. Scripters fudge a few years in setting the year of the Dempsey-Willard heavyweight battle in Toledo. Original shots of the fight are utilized to accompany the radio account.

Picture has many attributes on the entertainment side despite its thin and sketchy story. Most prominent is the breezy and zestful performance of Jack Oakie, who works energetically throughout and holds audience attention every minute he is on the screen.

Story details the adventures of Oakie, John Payne, Faye and Cesar Romero as early pioneers in radio broadcasting. Oakie tinkers with a crystal set in his room, idea-minded Payne gets enthusiastic over wireless entertainment possibilities, Faye is radio's first singing star, and Romero supplies the early coin.

Direction by Archie Mayo carries the pace at good speed, and injects many surefire touches for laugh attention.

....

■ GREAT BALLS OF FIRE!

1989, 108 MINS, US ◇ ⓥ ⊙
Dir Jim McBride   *Prod* Adam Fields   *Scr* Jack Baran, Jim McBride   *Ph* Affonso Beato   *Ed* Lisa Day, Pembroke Herring, Bert Lovitt   *Mus* Jack Baran, Jim McBride
Art Dir David Nichols
● Dennis Quaid, Winona Ryder, Alec Baldwin, John Doe, Stephen Tobolowsky, Trey Wilson (Orion)

Rock 'n' roll and its legendary characters have always been a tempting subject for filmmakers, but rare is the non-documentary that adds anything to the music. *Great Balls of Fire!* is no exception. It's a thin, cartoonish treatment of the hellbent, musically energetic young Jerry Lee Lewis.

Full-bore performance by Dennis Quaid as the kinetic piano-pumper stops at surface level, and 108 minutes of his gum-cracking smirks and cock-a-doodle-doo dandyism are hard to take.

Pic focuses on the years 1956–59, when Lewis' career took off with the provocative hit 'Whole Lotta Shakin' Goin' On' and was nearly destroyed by his marriage to 13-year-old cousin, Myra Gayle Brown (Winona Ryder), which shocked British fans and cut short his first overseas tour.

Mixed up in the Memphis milieu are the presence of Elvis Presley, who preceded Lewis at Sun Studios; Jimmy Swaggart, Lewis' Bible-thumping cousin; and the heady, devilish allure of the jumpin' black juke joints from which Lewis lifts his best music.

Script is based on a book by Myra Lewis and is by-the-numbers, suffering from a lack of grace or metaphor and relying on cash and flash as character motivations.

....

■ GREAT CARUSO, THE

1951, 109 MINS, US ◇ ⓥ
Dir Richard Thorpe   *Prod* Joe Pasternak, Jesse L. Lasky
Scr Sonya Levien, William Ludwig   *Ph* Joseph Ruttenberg   *Ed* Gene Ruggiero   *Mus* Johnny Green (sup.)
Art Dir Cedric Gibbons, Gabriel Scognamillo
● Mario Lanza, Ann Blyth, Dorothy Kirsten, Jarmila Novotna, Richard Hageman, Carl Benton Reid (M-G-M)

This highly fictionalized, sentimental biog of the late, great Metropolitan Opera tenor, Enrico Caruso, handsomely mounted in Technicolor, has a lot of popular ingredients, including a boy-and-girl-vs-disapproving-parent romance, the draw of Caruso's rep, glamor of the Met, a host of surefire, familiar operatic arias, and the pull of Mario Lanza.

Otherwise, the film is a superficial pic, bearing little relationship to Caruso's actual story, which was a much more dramatic one than emerges here. There are strong omissions and some falsifications.

Story is a casual recital of part of Caruso's career, with a few, brief scenes of him as a young Neapolitan cafe singer, then his quick rise as tenor in Milan, London, and other European music capitals, and his triumphs at the NY Met. The film centers early on Caruso's romance with Dorothy Benjamin, his difficulty with her father and their happy marriage. It shows him in some of his Met successes and touches briefly on his breakdown and death.

Lanza is handsome, personable and has a brilliant voice. He's a lyric tenor, like Caruso; has his stocky build, his Italianate quality and some of his flair. Dorothy Kirsten, who plays a Met soprano befriending Caruso, is a good actress as well as a gifted singer.
□ 1951: Best Sound Recording.
□ Nominations: Best Color Costume Design, Scoring of a Musical Picture

....

■ GREAT CATHERINE

1968, 98 MINS, UK ◇
Dir Gordon Flemyng   *Prod* Jules Buck, Peter O'Toole
Scr Hugh Leonard   *Ph* Oswald Morris   *Ed* Anne V. Coates   *Mus* Dimitri Tiomkin   *Art Dir* John Bryan
● Peter O'Toole, Zero Mostel, Jeanne Moreau, Jack Hawkins, Akim Tamiroff, Kenneth Griffith (Warner/Seven Arts)

A foreword to this film, based on a George Bernard Shaw play, reads: 'Mr. Shaw stated that historical portraiture was not the motive of this story and the producers would like to

add that any similarity to any historical event will be nothing short of a miracle'.

Atmosphere it has, mammoth and impressive sets, Zero Mostel as a wildman like you've never seen, Peter O'Toole as a stuffy Englishman like you've never imagined, all wrapped around the amorous yearnings of Catherine of Russia.

This is a souped-up version of the Russian Empress' romantics, focused on her going on the make for a slightly-imbecilic English Light Dragoons captain. Jeanne Moreau essays Catherine with humor.

O'Toole, as the beaddled captain on his way to seek an audience with the Empress, and finding himself tossed on her bed by Mostel, in a mad-Russian character, lends credence through underplaying his role.

....

■ GREAT DICTATOR, THE

1940, 127 MINS, US ⓥ
Dir Charles Chaplin   *Prod* Charles Chaplin   *Scr* Charles Chaplin   *Ph* Karl Struss, Roland Totheroh   *Ed* Willard Nico   *Mus* Meredith Willson   *Art Dir* J. Russell Spencer
● Charles Chaplin, Paulette Goddard, Jack Oakie, Reginald Gardiner, Henry Daniell, Billy Gilbert (Chaplin/United Artists)

Chaplin makes no bones about his utter contempt for dictators like Hitler and Mussolini in his production of *The Great Dictator*. He takes time out to make fun about it, but the preachment is strong, notably in the six-minute speech at the finish.

Chaplin speaks throughout the film, but wherever convenient depends as much as he can on pantomime. His panto has always talked plenty.

Chaplin plays a dual role, that of a meek little Jewish barber in Tomania and the great little dictator of that country, billed as Hynkel. It's when he is playing the dictator that the comedian's voice raises the value of the comedy content of the picture to great heights. He does various bits as a Hitler spouting at the mouth in which he engages in a lot of double talk in what amounts to a pig-Latin version of the German tongue, with grunts thrown in here and there, plus a classical 'Democracy shtook'. On various occasions as Hitler he also speaks English. In these instances he talks with force, as contrasted by the mousey, half-scared way he speaks as the poor barber.

Somewhat of a shock is the complete transformation of the barber when he delivers the speech at the finish, a fiery and impassioned plea for freedom and democracy. It is a peculiar and somewhat disappointing climax with the picture ending on a serious rather than a comical note.

The vast majority of the action is built around Hynkel and the Jewish barber. Not so much is devoted to the dictator who is Napaloni (Mussolini). Jack Oakie plays the satirized Duce to the hilt and every minute with him is socko.

In making up the billing, Chaplin has displayed an unusually keen sense of humor. While Hynkel is the dictator of Tomania, Napaloni is the ruler of Bacteria. Tomania higher-ups include Garbitsch (Goebels) and Herring (Goering). These are played effectively by Henry Daniell and Billy Gilbert.
□ 1940: Nominations: Best Picture, Actor (Charles Chaplin), Supp. Actor (Jack Oakie), Original Screenplay, Original Score

....

■ GREAT ESCAPE, THE

1963, 169 MINS, US ◇ ⓥ ⊙
Dir John Sturges   *Prod* John Sturges   *Scr* James Clavell, W. R. Burnett   *Ph* Daniel Fapp   *Ed* Ferris Webster
Mus Elmer Bernstein   *Art Dir* Fernando Carrere
● Steve McQueen, James Garner, Richard Attenborough, Charles Bronson, Donald Pleasence, James Coburn (United Artists)

From Paul Brickhill's true story of a remarkable mass breakout by Allied POWs during World War II, producer-director John Sturges has fashioned a motion picture that entertains, captivates, thrills and stirs.

The film is an account of the bold, meticulous plotting that led to the escape of 76 prisoners from a Nazi detention camp, and subsequent developments that resulted in the demise of 50, recapture of a dozen.

Early scenes depict the formulation of the mass break design. These are played largely for laughs, at the occasional expense of reality, and there are times when authority seems so lenient that the inmates almost appear to be running the asylum.

There are some exceptional performances. The most provocative single impression is made by Steve McQueen as a dauntless Yank pilot whose 'pen'-manship record shows 18 blots, or escape attempts. James Garner is the compound's 'scrounger', a traditional type in the *Stalag 17* breed of war-prison film. Charles Bronson and James Coburn do solid work, although the latter's character is anything but clearly defined.

British thespians weigh in with some of the finest performances in the picture. Richard Attenborough is especially convincing in a stellar role, that of the man who devises the break. A moving portrayal of a prisoner losing his eyesight is given by Donald Pleasence. It is the film's most touching character.

Elmer Bernstein's rich, expressive score is consistently helpful. His martial, Prussianistic theme is particularly stirring and memorable.
☐ 1963: Nomination: Best Editing

....

■ **GREATEST, THE**

1977, 101 MINS, US ◇ ⊛
Dir Tom Gries *Prod* John Marshall *Scr* Ring Lardner, Jr *Ph* Harry Stradling Jr *Ed* Byron Brandt *Mus* Michael Masser *Art Dir* Bob Smith
● Muhammad Ali, Ernest Borgnine, John Marley, Lloyd Haynes, Robert Duvall, David Huddleston (Columbia)

Muhammad Ali is a natural performer. More to the point, starring in his own autobiopic, *The Greatest*, he brings to it an authority and a presence that lift John Marshall's production above some of the limitations inherent in any film bio.

The film gets off to a fine start with newcomer Phillip MacAllister playing the young Cassius Clay Jr displaying the engaging affrontery of a young talent so sure of himself that discretion in self-description knows no bounds.

Plot follows Ali from his early career through formal discipline, professional conflicts and the controversial refusal to be inducted in the US Army. En route is Ali's deliberate public baiting of Sonny Liston.

Intercut are actual sequences from Ali's major fights.

....

■ **GREATEST SHOW ON EARTH, THE**

1952, 151 MINS, US ◇ ⊛ ⊙
Dir Cecil B. DeMille *Prod* Cecil B. DeMille *Scr* Fredric M. Frank, Barre Lyndon, Theodore St John *Ph* George Barnes, Peverell Marley, Wallace Kelley *Ed* Anne Bauchens *Mus* Victor Young *Art Dir* Hal Pereira, Walter Tyler
● Betty Hutton, Cornel Wilde, Charlton Heston, Dorothy Lamour, Gloria Grahame, James Stewart (Paramount)

The Greatest Show on Earth is as apt a handle for Cecil B. DeMille's Technicolored version of the Ringling Bros.-Barnum & Bailey circus as it is for the sawdust extravaganza itself. This is the circus with more entertainment, more thrills, more spangles and as much Big Top atmosphere as RB-B&B itself can offer.

As has come to be expected from DeMille, the story line [by Frederic M. Frank,

Theodore St John and Frank Cavett] is not what could be termed subtle. Betty Hutton is pictured as the 'queen flyer' who has a yen for Charlton Heston, the circus manager. Lad has sawdust for blood, however. To strengthen the show and thus enable it to play out a full season, he imports another aerialist, the flamboyant and debonair Sebastian (Cornel Wilde). Latter promptly falls for her and she rifts with Heston. That's quickly exploited by elephant girl Gloria Grahame, who also finds Heston a pretty attractive guy.

James Stewart is woven into the pic as an extraneous but appealing plot element. He's pictured as a police-sought medico who never removes his clown makeup.
☐ 1952: Best Picture, Motion Picture Story.
☐ Nominations: Best Director, Color Costume Design, Editing

....

■ **GREATEST STORY EVER TOLD, THE**

1965, 225 MINS, US ◇ ⊛ ⊙
Dir George Stevens, [David Lean, Jean Negulesco] *Prod* George Stevens *Scr* George Stevens, James Lee Barrett *Ph* William C. Mellor, Loyal Griggs *Ed* Harold F. Kress, Argyle Nelson Jr, Frank O'Neill *Mus* Alfred Newman *Art Dir* Richard Day, William Creber
● Max Von Sydow, Dorothy McGuire, Robert Loggia, Claude Rains, Jose Ferrer, Charlton Heston (United Artists)

The prophets should speak with respect of this $20 million Biblical epic. *The Greatest Story Ever Told* is the word made manifest. Producer-director George Stevens has elected to stick to the straight, literal, orthodox, familiar facts of the four gospels. He has scorned plot gimmicks and scanted on characterization quirks. What Stevens puts on view, overall, is panoramic cinema, cannily created backgrounds, especially the stupendous buttes of Utah.

Stevens is not particularly original in his approach to the galaxy of talent, some 60 roles. Hollywood's fad for cameo bits by featured players may suffer some discredit in the light of the triviality of footage and impact by such players as Carroll Baker, Pat Boone, Richard Conte, Ina Balin, Frank De Kova, Victor Buono, Marian Seldes, Paul Stewart. John Wayne is ill-at-ease and a waste of name, many may feel, as the captain of the soldiers who escort the Redeemer to the cross. Claude Rains is standout in the opening sequence [directed by David Lean] as the dying ruler of Judea.

Quite properly Stevens has focused on the birth, ministry, execution and resurrection of the Son of God. In the casting of Jesus there is occasion for compliment. The performance of the Swedish actor, Max Von Sydow, and his English diction are ideal.

The Baptist (Charlton Heston) is the only out-and-out fanatic in the picture but this takes the form of roaring demands that Herod 'repent'. Herod, in the remarkably curbed performance of Jose Ferrer, is no worse than a cynical administrative stooge for the Romans.
☐ 1965: Nominations: Best Color Cinematography, Color Costume Design, Color Art Direction, Original Music Score, Visual Effects

....

■ **GREAT EXPECTATIONS**

1946, 110 MINS, UK ⊛
Dir David Lean *Prod* Ronald Neame *Scr* David Lean, Ronald Neame, Anthony Havelock-Allan *Ph* Guy Green *Ed* Jack Harris *Mus* Walter Goehr *Art Dir* John Bryan
● John Mills, Valerie Hobson, Francis L. Sullivan, Alec Guinness, Jean Simmons, Martita Hunt (Cineguild)

Only rabid Dickensians will find fault with the present adaptation, and paradoxically only lovers of Dickens will derive maximum pleasure from the film.

This adaptation tells how young Pip befriends an escaped convict, who, recaptured and transported to Australia, leaves Pip a fortune so he may become a gentleman with great expectations. Pip believes the unexpected fortune originated with the eccentric Miss Havisham at whose house he has met Estella the girl he loves.

To condense the novel into a two-hour picture meant sacrificing many minor characters. The period and people are vividly brought to life. But so particular have the producers been to avoid offending any Dickensian and every character is drawn so precise that many of them are puppets.

That's the great fault of the film. It is beautiful but lacks heart. It evokes admiration but no feeling.

With the exception of John Mills and Alec Guinness, only the secondary characters are entirely credible. Valerie Hobson, whose beauty is not captured by the camera, fails to bring Estella to life, and young Jean Simmons, who plays the role as a girl, is adequately heartless.
☐ 1947: Best B&W Cinematography, B&W Art Direction.
☐ Nominations: Best Picture, Director, Screenplay

....

■ **GREAT GABBO, THE**

1929, 91 MINS, US ◇ ⊛
Dir James Cruze *Prod* Henry D. Meyer, Nat Cordish *Scr* Ben Hecht, Hugh Herbert
● Erich von Stroheim, Betty Compson, Don Douglas, Margie Kane (Meyer-Cordish)

The story is simplicity itself. Just a pair of show people – one a lovely, considerate girl and the other a ventriloquist with a hyper-egotist complex. The expected break, followed by a rise from the grinds to the individual success of both. Then the too late realization of love by the dummy manipulator.

Erich von Stroheim, as the eccentric and arrogant performer who reveals a Pagliacci heart through the medium of Otto, the dummy, doubles the enhancement of a dominant screen personality with his lines. It is the voice, frenzied and then modulated to a pianissimo, that is one of the strongest threads, carrying the interest over sequences devoted to color and stage show that would be irrelevant gaps in productions less skillfully directed and enacted.

In part of the colored sequence the print is grainy and the characters blurred. But both of these conditions are too brief to be considered drawbacks.

....

■ **GREAT GATSBY, THE**

1949, 91 MINS, US ⊛
Dir Elliott Nugent *Prod* Richard Maibaum *Scr* Cyril Hume, Richard Maibaum *Ph* John F. Seitz *Ed* Ellsworth Hoagland *Mus* Robert Emmett Dolan *Art Dir* Hans Dreier, Roland Anderson
● Alan Ladd, Betty Field, Macdonald Carey, Ruth Hussey, Barry Sullivan, Shelley Winters (Paramount)

F. Scott Fitzgerald's story of the roaring '20s is peopled with shallow characters and the script [also from the play by Owen Davis] stresses the love story rather than the hi-jacking, bootlegging elements.

Gatsby is a fabulous bootlegger who has parlayed his relentless drive into fortune. When the stack of blue chips is large enough, he turns his attention to winning back a girl he lost years ago to a wealthy man.

Alan Ladd handles his characterization ably, making it as well-rounded as the yarn permits and fares better than other cast members in trying to make the surface characters come to life.

Elliott Nugent's direction skips along the

307

surface of the era depicted. The script doesn't give him much substance to work with.

■ **GREAT GATSBY, THE**

1974, 144 MINS, US ◇ ▼ ⊙
Dir Jack Clayton   *Prod* David Merrick   *Scr* Francis Coppola   *Ph* Douglas Slocombe   *Ed* Tom Priestley   *Mus* Nelson Riddle   *Art Dir* John Box
● Robert Redford, Mia Farrow, Bruce Dern, Karen Black, Scott Wilson, Sam Waterston (Paramount)

Paramount's third pass at *The Great Gatsby* is by far the most concerted attempt to probe the peculiar ethos of the Beautiful People of the 1920s. The fascinating physical beauty of the $6 million-plus film complements the utter shallowness of most principal characters from the F. Scott Fitzgerald novel.

Robert Redford is excellent in the title role, the mysterious gentleman of humble origins and bootlegging connections; Mia Farrow is his long-lost love, married unhappily but inextricably to brutish Bruce Dern, who has a side affair going along with restive working class wife Karen Black.

The Francis Coppola script and Jack Clayton's direction paint a savagely genteel portrait of an upper class generation that deserved in spades what it got circa 1929 and after.
□ 1974: Best Adapted Scoring, Costume Design

■ **GREAT McGINTY, THE**
(UK: Down Went McGinty)

1940, 81 MINS, US ▼ ⊙
Dir Preston Sturges   *Prod* Paul Jones   *Scr* Preston Sturges   *Ph* William C. Mellor   *Ed* Hugh Bennett   *Mus* Frederick Hollander   *Art Dir* Hans Dreier, Earl Hedrick
● Brian Donlevy, Muriel Angelus, Akim Tamiroff, Allyn Joslyn, William Demarest, Steffi Duna (Paramount)

The Great McGinty initiates Preston Sturges into the directing ranks, after a long stretch as a film scenarist. Piloting an original story and screenplay of his own concoction, Sturges displays plenty of ability in accentuating both the comedy and dramatic elements of his material, withal maintaining a consistent pace in the unreeling.

Sturges' story departs radically from accepted formula. His main character is a tough, rowdy and muscular individual who creates more interest than sympathy in his career as a prototype of many political rascals of the American scene.

Story is unfolded by flashback. Brian Donlevy is introduced as the toughened bartender of a dive in a Central American banana republic. He's a fugitive from justice, the same as the young bank clerk who absconded with funds in a weak moment. Across the bar Donlevy tells the latter his story – a life of crookedness where the first honest thing he attempted chased him from the country. When he first finds that illegal voting brings coin, he becomes a repeater, gets into favor of political boss (Akim Tamiroff) and gradually rises to positions of alderman, mayor and finally governor of the state.

Portrayal of Donlevy as the slightly-educated political apprentice who learns the ropes fast, and wields his fists at every opportunity, is excellent. Tamiroff clicks as the political boss, while Muriel Angelus provides a charming and warmful personality in the role of the politico's wife. Bill Demarest provides attention as a political stooge.
□ 1940: Best Original Screenplay

■ **GREAT MOMENT, THE**

1944, 83 MINS, US ▼
Dir Preston Sturges   *Prod* Preston Sturges   *Scr* Preston Sturges   *Ph* Victor Milner   *Ed* Stuart Gilmore

Mus Victor Young   *Art Dir* Hans Dreier, Ernst Fegte
● Joel McCrea, Betty Field, Harry Carey, William Demarest, Franklin Pangborn, Grady Sutton (Paramount)

Preston Sturges brings to the screen the compelling biography of Dr W.T.G. Morton, who in 1844 discovered anaesthesia. The film [from the book by Rene Fulop-Muller] is the story of the romance, the trials and the ultimate victory of a Boston dentist, who experimented until he finally hit upon a painless means of extracting teeth, then passed on his discovery to the world of medicine. Performances of Joel McCrea and Betty Field, as well as a solid supporting cast, are well in keeping with the dignity of the yarn.

McCrea gives an excellent portrayal in the role of the impoverished medical student, forced to forego the study of medicine in lieu of a dental career because of lack of funds. Field, as the wife who sometimes gets on his nerves because of her lack of understanding of what he is endeavoring to accomplish, proves again that she is an actress with loads of talent.

Supporting roles of Harry Carey, the doctor who gives McCrea a chance to prove that anaesthesia is suitable for surgical operations, and William Demarest, as the first patient of McCrea, are expertly handled by them.

■ **GREAT MOUSE DETECTIVE, THE**
(UK: Basil The Great Mouse Detective)

1986, 80 MINS, US ◇ ▼
Dir John Musker, Ron Clements, Dave Michener, Burny Mattinson   *Prod* Burny Mattinson   *Scr* TRon Clements, Burny Mattinson, Dave Michener, John Musker, Pete Young, Vance Gerry, Steve Hulett, Bruce M. Morris, Matthew O'Callaghan, Melvin Shaw   *Ph* Ed Austin, Roy M. Brewer Jr, James Melton   *Mus* Henry Mancini   *Art Dir* Guy Vasilovich
● (Walt Disney)

The animation is rich, the characters memorable and the story equally as entertaining for adults as for children.

Supersleuth Basil (voiced by Barrie Ingham) and bumbling partner Dawson (Val Bettin) are the Sherlock Holmes and Dr Watson of Victorian London's Mouse scene. Basil gets involved in a case where a master toymaker is kidnapped and the villain turns out to be none other than Basil's longtime adversary, the evil Prof. Ratigan (Vincent Price).

The story of the clever mouse detective determined to outwit Ratigan's plan to dethrone the Mouse Queen (Eve Brenner) lends itself to inventive gags, including the expected run-ins with a menacing oversized cat and a wonderfully creative scene where benign-looking toys seem to come alive to trap poor Basil and Dawson and foil their attempts to save the Empire.

Henry Mancini's scoring is adequate, but one wonders why there are only four songs and those written are not the kind children could, or would, learn to sing.

■ **GREAT MUPPET CAPER, THE**

1981, 95 MINS, UK ◇ ▼ ⊙
Dir Jim Henson   *Prod* David Lazar   *Scr* Tom Patchett, Jay Tarses, Jerry Juhl, Jack Rose   *Ph* Oswald Morris   *Ed* Ralph Kemplen   *Mus* Joe Raposo   *Art Dir* Harry Lange
● Charles Grodin, Diana Rigg, John Cleese, Robert Morley, Peter Ustinov, Jack Warden (Universal/AFD)

Muppet creator Jim Henson took over the directorial reins this second time out and, buttressed by a $14 million budget and top professionalism down the line in the production department, shows a sure hand in guiding his appealing stars through their paces.

Story hook has hapless reporters Kermit,

Fozzie Bear and The Great Gonzo literally plunked down in London Town to follow up on a major jewel robbery involving fashion world magnate Diana Rigg. Once there, Kermit mistakenly takes Miss Piggy for beautiful Lady Holiday and instantly falls in love with the rotund aspiring model.

At the same time, Rigg's sly brother Charles Grodin puts the make on Miss Piggy himself while also setting her up for arrest in the jewel robbery case.

As before, much of the dialog neatly walks the line between true wit and silly (and sometimes inside) jokes.

Grodin and Rigg are both fine, and cameo appearances are limited to nice turns by John Cleese, Robert Morley, Peter Ustinov and Jack Warden.
□ 1981: Nomination: Best Song ('The First Time It Happens')

■ **GREAT NORTHFIELD, MINNESOTA RAID, THE**

1972, 91 MINS, UK ▼
Dir Philip Kaufman   *Prod* Jennings Lang   *Scr* Philip Kaufman   *Ph* Bruce Surtees   *Ed* Douglas Stewart   *Mus* Dave Grusin   *Art Dir* Alexander Golitzen, George Webb
● Cliff Robertson, Robert Duvall, Luke Askew, R.G. Armstrong, Dana Elcar, Donald Moffat (Universal/Robertson & Associates)

The Great Northfield, Minnesota Raid – described as shedding 'new light' on Cole Younger and Jesse James – may be a valiant attempt but fails to come off.

Primarily, this is due to utter lack of sustained narrative, confused and inept writing, over-abundance of characters difficult for ready identification, often apparent indecision whether to make this drama or comedy and a mish-mash of irrelevant sequences.

Plottage bases its premise on the outlaws' decision to go from their native Missouri to Minnesota to rob what a newspaper ad claims to be the biggest bank west of the Mississippi. Cliff Robertson plays Cole and Robert Duvall is Jesse.

Perhaps Philip Kaufman, who directs and provides the screenplay, accurately attains historic accuracy in his recital of events leading up to the raid, and afterwards, but his treatment is such that characters throughout are dull fellows indeed, and picture itself is in kind.

■ **GREAT OUTDOORS, THE**

1988, 90 MINS, US ◇ ▼ ⊙
Dir Howard Deutch   *Prod* Arne L. Schmidt   *Scr* John Hughes   *Ph* Ric Waite   *Ed* Tom Rolf, William Gordean, Seth Flaum   *Mus* Thomas Newman   *Art Dir* John W. Corso
● Dan Aykroyd, John Candy, Stephanie Faracy, Annette Bening, Chris Young, Lucy Deakins (Universal/Hughes)

John Candy stars as a sweet, slightly dopey family man who wagoneers his happy brood up from Chicago for a big-pines getaway. No sooner do they unpack than obnoxious brother-in-law Dan Aykroyd and his maladjusted family blast in uninvited to spend the week. His pampered wife (Annette Bening) eggs him on, while his spooky kids (twins Hilary and Rebecca Gordon) never say a word.

Writer-executive producer John Hughes conjures up a romance between Candy's teenage son (Chris Young) and a local girl (Lucy Deakins), but that proves the film's biggest letdown. Last third of the film is a real mess, as filmmakers try to whip up a crisis that will unite the family, with the red-headed twins getting lost in a mineshaft during a wild rainstorm.

Despite all this, the Aykroyd-Candy pairing is charmed. Stephanie Faracy is excellent as

Candy's sweet, happy wife, and Bening is also savvy in her role. Pic teams director Howard Deutch with Hughes for the third time.

....

■ GREAT RACE, THE

1965, 157 MINS, US ◇ ▽

Dir Blake Edwards *Prod* Martin Jurow *Scr* Arthur Ross *Ph* Russell Harlan *Ed* Ralph E. Winters *Mus* Henry Mancini *Art Dir* Fernando Carrere
● Jack Lemmon, Tony Curtis, Natalie Wood, Peter Falk, Keenan Wynn, Arthur O'Connell (Warner)

The Great Race is a big, expensive, whopping, comedy extravaganza, long on slapstick and near-inspired tomfoolery whose tongue-in-cheek treatment liberally sprinkled with corn frequently garners belly laughs.

A certain nostalgic flavor is achieved, both in the 1908 period of an automobile race from New York to Paris and Blake Edwards' broad borrowing from *The Prisoner of Zenda* tale and an earlier Laurel and Hardy comedy for some of his heartiest action.

Characters carry an old-fashioned zest when it was the fashion to hiss the villain and cheer the hero. Slotting into this category, never has there been a villain so dastardly as Jack Lemmon nor a hero so whitely pure as Tony Curtis, rivals in the great race staged by an auto manufacturer to prove his car's worth.

Strongly abetting the two male principals is Natalie Wood as a militant suffragette who wants to be a reporter and sells a NY newspaper publisher on allowing her to enter the race and covering it for his sheet.

To carry on the overall spirit, Curtis always is garbed in snowy white, Lemmon in black, a gent whose every tone is a snarl, and whose laugh would put Woody Woodpecker to shame.

Lemmon plays it dirty throughout and for huge effect. Curtis underplays for equally comic effect. Wood comes through on a par with the two male stars.
□ 1965: Best Sound Effects.
□ Nominations: Best Color Cinematography, Editing, Sound, Song ('The Sweetheart Tree')

....

■ GREAT ROCK 'N' ROLL SWINDLE, THE

1980, 103 MINS, UK ◇ ▽

Dir Julian Temple *Prod* Jeremy Thomas, Don Boyd *Scr* Julian Temple *Ph* A. Barker-Mills *Ed* R. Bedford, M.D. Maslin, G. Swire *Mus* The Sex Pistols
● Malcolm McLaren, Johnny Rotten, Sid Vicious, Steve Jones, Paul Cook, Jess Conrad (Kendon/Matrix Best/Virgin)

The Great Rock 'n' Roll Swindle is the *Citizen Kane* of rock 'n' roll pictures. An incredibly sophisticated, stupefyingly multi-layered portrait of the 1970s phenomenon known as The Sex Pistols, unstintingly cynical pic casts a jaundiced eye at the entire pop culture scene and, if nothing else, represents the most imaginative use of a rock group in films since The Beatles debuted in *A Hard Day's Night*.

Pic, which stars and is narrated after a fashion by Pistols' manager Malcolm McLaren, begins with the basic premise that the campaign of shock tactics was premeditated.

A bubbling brew of devices and styles somehow mesh under firsttime helmer Julian Temple's wizardly direction to amplify McLaren's thesis on how to create a rock sensation in 10 easy lessons. Among his dicta are: Demonstrate To Record Companies The Enormous Potential Of A Band That Can't Play; Make It As Hard As Possible For The Press To See It; Insult Your Audiences As Much As Possible, and Cultivate Hatred.

....

■ GREAT SANTINI, THE

1980, 115 MINS, US ◇ ▽

Dir Lewis John Carlino *Prod* Charles A. Pratt *Scr* Lewis John Carlino *Ph* Ralph Woolsey *Ed* Houseley Stevenson *Mus* Elmer Bernstein *Art Dir* Jack Poplin

● Robert Duvall, Blythe Danner, Michael O'Keefe, Lisa Jane Persky, Julie Anne Haddock, Stan Shaw (Orion)

Robert Duvall gives an excellent portrayal of a semi-psychotic, softened with a warmer side. But Duvall has to fight for every inch of footage against the overwhelming performances by several others in the cast – and that's the strength of *The Great Santini*.

Title is a nickname Duvall picks up as the finest fighter pilot in the US Marines. But this isn't a war picture. Quite the contrary, it's the compellingly relevant story of a super-macho peacetime warrior with nobody to fight except himself and those who love him.

As the sensitive son who strives to meet all of his father's supermasculine standards, Michael O'Keefe is terrific and emerges as the major star of the picture.

Blythe Danner is also strong as the wife who suffers Duvall's excesses.
□ 1980: Nominations: Best Actor (Robert Duvall), Supp. Actor (Michael O'Keefe)

....

■ GREAT SCOUT & CATHOUSE THURSDAY, THE

1976, 102 MINS, US ◇ ▽

Dir Don Taylor *Prod* Jules Buck, David Korda *Scr* Richard Shapiro *Ph* Alex Phillips Jr *Ed* Sheldon Kahn *Mus* John Cameron *Art Dir* Jack Martin Smith
● Lee Marvin, Oliver Reed, Robert Culp, Elizabeth Ashley, Strother Martin, Kay Lenz (American International)

Richard Shapiro's up-and-down screenplay uses the plot about former partners in crime (here Lee Marvin and Indian sidekick Oliver Reed) going back to get revenge on the partner who cheated them and went respectable with the loot (Robert Culp).

In the mid-section, the May-December romance between Marvin's aging cowpoke and Kay Lenz' young prostie rouses some dramatic interest, coming through the general hokiness like rays of sunshine on a smoggy day. Marvin, to his credit, resists the strong temptation to mug it up, playing with an amusing attempt at dignity, and Lenz is a very appealing and spunky actress.

Reed's role is a hammy embarrassment, Culp seems uncomfortable as a strident politico and Sylvia Miles is wasted as a madam.

....

■ GREAT ST. TRINIAN'S TRAIN ROBBERY, THE

1966, 94 MINS, UK ◇ ▽

Dir Frank Launder, Sidney Gilliat *Prod* Leslie Gilliat *Scr* Frank Launder, Ivor Herbert *Ph* Kenneth Hodges *Ed* Geoffrey Foot *Mus* Malcolm Arnold *Art Dir* Albert Witherick
● Frankie Howerd, Reg Varney, Stratford Johns, Eric Barker, Dora Bryan, George Cole (British Lion)

Ronald Searle's little schoolgirl demons from St. Trinian's are berserk again on the screen in a yarn with a topical twist, the [1963] Great Train Robbery.

Having pulled off a $7 million train robbery, a hapless gang of crooks stash the loot in a deserted country mansion. But when they go back to collect they find the St. Trinian's school has taken over, and they are completely routed by the hockey sticks and rough stuff handed out by the little she-monsters. When the gang returns on parents' day for a second attempt at picking up the loot they run into further trouble and complications and eventually get involved in a great train chase which is quite the funniest part of the film, having a great deal in common with the old silent slapstick technique.

Among the many performances which contribute to the gaiety are those of Frankie Howerd as a crook posing as a French male hairdresser, Raymond Huntley as a Cabinet Minister with amorous eyes on the St.

Trinian's headmistress (Dora Bryan), Richard Wattis in one of his typical harassed civil servant roles and Peter Gilmore as his confrere. George Cole crops up again as Flash Harry, the school bookie.

....

■ GREAT TEXAS DYNAMITE CHASE, THE

1976, 90 MINS, US ◇ ▽

Dir Michael Pressman *Prod* David Irving *Scr* David Kirkpatrick *Ph* Jamie Anderson *Ed* Millie Moore *Mus* Craig Safan *Art Dir* Russel Smith
● Claudia Jennings, Jocelyn Jones, Johnny Crawford, Chris Pennock, Tara Strohmeier, Miles Watkins (Yasny Talking Pictures II)

The Great Texas Dynamite Chase is a well-made exploitation film which works on two levels, providing kicks for the ozoner crowd and tongue-in-cheek humor for the more sophisticated. The film had some initial playdates under the title *Dynamite Women*.

Claudia Jennings and Jocelyn Jones are stylish and attractive as a pair of brazen Texas bankrobbers. They stay firmly in character throughout as a loyal but very divergent criminal pair.

Jennings is a hardened prison escapee, while Jones goes on the road to avoid the boredom of being a smalltown bank teller. They use lots of dynamite along the way, but there's little bloodshed until the last part of the film, when the film's dominant spoof tone turns uncomfortably and unsuccessfully close to reality.

....

■ GREAT TRAIN ROBBERY, THE

See: The First Great Train Robbery

....

■ GREAT WALDO PEPPER, THE

1975, 108 MINS, US ◇ ▽ ⊙

Dir George Roy Hill *Prod* George Roy Hill *Scr* William Goldman *Ph* Robert Surtees *Ed* William Reynolds *Mus* Henry Mancini *Art Dir* Henry Bumstead
● Robert Redford, Bo Svenson, Bo Brundin, Susan Sarandon, Geoffrey Lewis, Edward Herrman (Universal)

The Great Waldo Pepper is an uneven and unsatisfying story of anachronistic, pitiable, but misplaced heroism. Robert Redford stars as an aerial ace, unable to cope with the segue from pioneer barnstorming to bigtime aviation.

George Roy Hill's original story was scripted by William Goldman into yet another stab at dramatizing the effect of inexorable social change on pioneers. In this case, Redford and Bo Svenson, two World War I airmen, scratch out a living, and feed their egos, via daring stunts in midwest fields. But Geoffrey Lewis has made the transition from cocky pilot to aviation official, and inventor Edward Herrmann unwittingly complements the shift through his technological advances.

The film stumbles towards its fuzzy climax.

....

■ GREAT WALL, A

(Aka: The Great Wall Is a Great Wall)

1986, 97 MINS, US ◇ ▽ ⊙

Dir Peter Wang *Prod* Shirley Sun *Scr* Peter Wang, Shirley Sun *Ph* Peter Stein, Robert Primes *Ed* Grahame Weinbren *Mus* David Liang, Ge Ganru *Art Dir* Wing Lee, Feng Yuan, Ming Ming Cheung
● Peter Wang, Sharon Iwai, Kelvin Han Yee, Li Qinqin, Wang Xiao (W&S/Nanhai)

A charming but unduly lightweight film, *A Great Wall* humorously accentuates the many cultural differences between the two giant nations of the US and China, but goes out of its way to avoid dealing with politics or any other issues of substance.

Peter Wang, who appeared in *Chan Is Missing*, himself portrays a San Francisco computer executive who takes advantage of the opening up of China to visit relatives there as well as to introduce his American-born wife and son to his native land.

Wang quickly sketches in his key players on both sides of the Pacific and deftly characterizes their differing lifestyles but he simply glosses over too many important issues for the film to be considered a true artistic success.

....

■ GREAT WALTZ, THE

1938, 107 MINS, US 🔟
Dir Julien Duvivier *Scr* Samuel Hoffenstein, Walter Reisch *Ph* Joseph Ruttenberg *Ed* Tom Held
Mus Dimitri Tiomkin (arr.)
● Luise Rainer, Fernand Gravet, Miliza Korjus, Hugh Herbert, Lionel Atwill, Curt Bois (M-G-M)

The Great Waltz is a field day for music lovers plus elegant entertainment. Producers were nearly two years on this film, but the extra effort shows in the nicety with which its many component parts fit together. It is Luise Rainer who makes the film.

While primarily a fanciful tale of Johann Strauss II's rise in the musical firmament [from an original story by Gottfried Reinhardt], entire plot has been constructed around his outstanding works.

The youthful Strauss (Fernand Gravet) is shown quitting his job in a Vienna banking house to carry on as a musician, first as a director of his own neighborhood orchestra playing his newest compositions, and then as a composer whose waltz tunes are recognized even in official court circles, something unheard of in those days.

Strauss marries the baker's daughter soon after he wins his first success. His part in the short-lived revolution serves to develop romance with the opera singer Carla Donner (Miliza Korjus). It is the sudden decision to fight for her mate, after months of self-sacrifice, that takes Mrs Strauss (Rainer) storming backstage after the successful premiere of his first opera.

Not cast in a thoroughly sympathetic role, operatic singer Korjus suffers at times from photographic angles and does not arouse as much excitement as obviously was intended [in her first American picture].

Besides Rainer's sterling portrayal of the adoring wife, Gravet does surprisingly well as the younger Strauss. Burden of romantic scenes rest on his shoulders and he comes through with elan. His singing measures up also.
☐ 1938: Best Cinematography
☐ Nominations: Best Supp. Actress (Miliza Korjus), Editing

....

■ GREAT WHITE HOPE, THE

1970, 102 MINS, US ◇ 🔟
Dir Martin Ritt *Prod* Lawrence Turman *Scr* Howard Sackler *Ph* Burnett Guffey *Ed* William Reynolds
Mus Lionel Newman *Art Dir* John DeCuir
● James Earl Jones, Jane Alexander, Lou Gilbert, Joel Fluellen, Chester Morris, Robert Webber (20th Century-Fox)

In its telling of the quasi-fictionalized public life of famed black heavyweight champ, circa 1910, Jack Johnson, the film's pacing and gritty cynicism resembles the best of the old Warner Bros Depression dramas; but in the distended playout of the fighter's tragic private life via involvement with a white woman, the picture sags.

However, a superior cast, headed by James Earl Jones encoring in his stage role, a colorful and earthy script, plus outstanding production, render film quite palatable.

Jones' re-creation of his stage role is an eye-riveting experience. The towering rages and unrestrained joys of which his character was capable are portrayed larger than life.
☐ 1970: Nominations: Best Actor (James Earl Jones), Actress (Jane Alexander)

....

■ GREAT ZIEGFELD, THE

1936, 170 MINS, US 🔟 ⊙
Dir Robert Z. Leonard *Prod* Hunt Stromberg
Scr William Anthony McGuire *Ph* Oliver T. Marsh, George Folsey, Ray June, Merritt B. Gerstad, Karl Freund *Ed* William S. Gray *Mus* Arthur Lange (dir.), Frank Skinner (arr.) *Art Dir* Cedric Gibbons, Merrill Pye
● William Powell, Myrna Loy, Luise Rainer, Frank Morgan, Fannie Brice, Virginia Bruce (M-G-M)

The Great Ziegfeld is the last gasp in filmusical entertainment. On its running time (10 minutes short of three hours), it is the record holder to date for length of a picture in the US. After two years, and a reported $1.5 million, Metro emerges with a picture whose sole shortcoming is its footage.

The production high mark of the numbers is 'Pretty Girl' as the first half finale. This nifty Irving Berlin tune becomes the fulcrum for one of Frank Skinner's best arrangements as Arthur Lange batons the crescendos into a mad, glittering pot-pourri of Saint-Saens and Gershwin, Strauss and Verdi, beautifully blended against the Berlinesque background.

Among riot of song and dance, Seymour Felix's dances and ensembles stand out for imagination and comprehensive execution.

William Powell's Zieggy is excellent. He endows the impersonation with all the qualities of a great entrepreneur and sentimentalist. Luise Rainer is tops of the femmes with her vivacious Anna Held. Myrna Loy's Billie Burke, perhaps with constant regard for a contemporaneous artiste, seems a bit under wraps. Frank Morgan almost pars Powell as the friendly enemy.

Fannie Brice is Fannie Brice; ditto Ray Bolger and Harriet Hoctor playing themselves. Character of Sampson is obviously the late Sam Kingston, long Zieggy's general manager who worried and fretted over the glorifier's extravagances. Reginald Owen's personation here is capital.
☐ 1936: Best Picture, Actress (Luise Rainer), Dance Direction ('A Pretty Girl Is Like a Melody')
☐ Nominations: Best Director, Original Story, Art Direction, Editing

....

■ GREED

1924, 114 MINS, US ◇ ⊗ 🔟
Dir Erich von Stroheim *Prod* Erich von Stroheim
Scr June Mathis, Erich von Stroheim *Ph* Ben F. Reynolds, William H. Daniels *Ed* Frank Hull, Joseph W. Farnham
Art Dir Cedric Gibbons, Richard Day
● Gibson Gowland, ZaSu Pitts, Jean Hersholt, Chester Conklin, Sylvia Ashton, Austin Jewell (Metro-Goldwyn)

Greed, the screen adaptation of the Frank Norris story, *McTeague*, was directed by Erich von Stroheim. He utilized two years and over $700,000 of Goldwyn and possibly some Metro money in its making.

Stroheim shot 130 reels in the two years. He finally cut it to 26 reels and told Metro-Goldwyn executives that was the best he could do. It was then taken into hand and cut to 10 reels.

McTeague, a worker in a gold mine, serves an apprenticeship with an itinerant dentist and in years after sets up an office in Market street, San Francisco. A chum brings in his cousin as a patient. McTeague falls in love with her, but, before Mac and she are married, the girl wins a $5,000 lottery prize.

Several years afterward, the chum, revengeful because of his failure to share in the spoils, tips off the Dentists' Society that Mac is practicing without a license. Mac then drifts from bad to worse. With a few drinks of whiskey under his belt he walks out on the money-grabbing wife. Months later he runs across her. She is working as a scrubwoman. He tries to compel her to give him money, later murdering her to secure it.

After the crime Mac makes his way to the

desert, in the direction of Death Valley. A posse starts after him from a small New Mexico town. In it is the former chum, still actuated by his greed for the $5,000.

The picture brings to light three great character performances by Gibson Gowland as McTeague, Jean Hersholt as the chum, and ZaSu Pitts as the wife. Chester Conklin is another who registers with a performance that is marked, although it is noticeable the part that Stroheim's direction plays in it.

....

■ GREEK TYCOON, THE

1978, 106 MINS, US ◇ 🔟
Dir J. Lee Thompson *Prod* Allen Klein, Ely Landau
Scr Mort Fine *Ph* Tony Richmond *Ed* Alan Strachan
Mus Stanley Myers *Art Dir* Michael Stringer
● Anthony Quinn, Jacqueline Bisset, Raf Vallone, Edward Albert, James Franciscus, Camilla Sparv (Abkco)

As a thinly disguised biopic of Aristotle Onassis and Jacqueline Kennedy Onassis – accent on thinly disguised – *The Greek Tycoon* has the conviction of its subject. It's a trashy, opulent, vulgar, racy $6.5 million picture. You've watched the headlines, now you can read the movie.

Mort Fine's script begins with Anthony Quinn as Theo Tomasis returning from a business trip. He greets his wife, wades through the guests at his island manor searching for his son and quickly spots Jackie Bisset with her husband Senator James Cassidy.

The story moves quickly onto Quinn's yacht. The Cassidys are persuaded to join the affair and while the senator is immersed in conversation with a former British prime minister, Quinn lays the seeds for his own affair.

Quinn is fabulous as Tomasis, a charming, wealthy, conniving and influential tycoon. Raf Vallone as Quinn's brother, James Franciscus as President Cassidy, Edward Albert as Quinn's son and the always reliable Charles Durning as Quinn's lawyer and later attorney general, all turn in good performances. As Liz Cassidy, Bisset capitalizes on her looks, but her accent seems off for the part and much of the acting is just posing.

....

■ GREEN BERETS, THE

1968, 141 MINS, US ◇ 🔟 ⊙
Dir John Wayne, Ray Kellogg *Prod* Michael Wayne
Scr James Lee Barrett *Ph* Winston C. Hoch *Ed* Otto Lovering *Mus* Miklos Rozsa *Art Dir* Walter M. Simonds
● John Wayne, David Janssen, Jim Hutton, Aldo Ray, Raymond St Jacques (Warner/Seven Arts/Batjac)

The Green Berets, based on Robin Moore's book about US Special Forces, sheds no light on the arguments pro and con US involvement in Vietnam. Cliche- cluttered plot structure and dialog, wooden performances by actors playing soldiers, pedestrian direction and lethargic editing dog this production. James Lee Barrett did the flat script, loaded with corn and cardboard.

John Wayne is a colonel sent to Vietnam, while David Janssen plays a hostile news- paper reporter who, from time-to-time, alters his thinking about the fighting.

Role is a shambles for Janssen, because it was a patent setup from the start, and nobody could buck the thankless, inarticulate development.

The interminable length permits about every hack character type to be introduced: Jim Hutton, the goofy kid who steals supplies; Aldo Ray, as 'good-old-Sarge' type; Raymond St. Jacques, the sensitive medic; Luke Askew, country-boy; Jason Evers, an all-American young officer type, and playing it like a toothpaste commercial; Mike Henry, beefy soldier who takes several enemy soldiers with him as he dies, and dies, and dies.

....

G

■ GREEN CARD

1990, 108 MINS, AUSTRALIA/FRANCE ◇ ⚥ ⊙
Dir Peter Weir   *Prod* Peter Weir   *Scr* Peter Weir   *Ph* Geoffrey Simpson   *Ed* William Anderson   *Mus* Hans Zimmer   *Art Dir* Wendy Stites
● Gerard Depardieu, Andie MacDowell, Bebe Neuwirth, Gregg Edelman, Robert Prosky, Jessie Keosian (Rio/UGC/DD/Serif/Green Card)

Although a thin premise endangers its credibility at times, *Green Card* is a genial, nicely played romance. Gerard Depardieu is winning in the tailor-made role of a French alien who pairs up with New Yorker Andie MacDowell in a marriage of convenience in order to remain legally in the United States.

An Australian-French co-production shot in Gotham and completed Down Under, modest pic is essentially a two-character piece and looks to have been made on a very low budget. Plot is an inversion of the 1930s screwball comedies in which a divorcing couple spend the entire running time getting back together.

Green Card begins with Depardieu and MacDowell, who have scarcely been introduced, getting married, then charts the tricky weekend the two temperamental opposites spend getting to know each other in a hurry when faced with a government probe of their relationship.

Elements that might look hokey on paper – he's a freewheeling bohemian, she's an uptight prude; he's a smoker and enthusiastic carnivore, she practically faints upon exposure to a cigarette or a piece of meat – go down easily because the two leads incorporate these attitudes believably into generally well-rounded characters.
☐ 1990: Nomination: Best Original Screenplay

■ GREEN DOLPHIN STREET

1947, 140 MINS, US ⚥
Dir Victor Saville   *Prod* Carey Wilson   *Scr* Samson Raphaelson   *Ph* George Folsey   *Ed* George White   *Mus* Bronislau Kaper   *Art Dir* Cedric Gibbons, Malcolm Brown
● Lana Turner, Van Heflin, Donna Reed, Richard Hart, Edmund Gwenn, Frank Morgan (M-G-M)

Metro throws the full weight of its moneybags into *Green Dolphin Street*. To salvage the $4 million or so that went into this epic [based on the novel by Elizabeth Goudge], it must primarily count on the eminent saleability of earthquakes, tidal waves and native uprisings. Its curiously unreal story offers no help.

Flaws in the novel, which verbiage may have made less perceptible, sore-thumb their way through the pic. There's the weak dramatic dodge, for one instance, of the wrong sister being married because she was mistakenly named by the suitor in a letter of proposal to her parents. And it's nothing but a hokey have-your-cake-and-eat-it device to confer happiness on the other by retiring her to a religious order.

Alternately localed in primitive New Zealand and one of the French channel isles (circa 1840), pic details how Lana Turner, mistaken for her sister Donna Reed, makes the perilous sea voyage to the Antipodes to marry a deserter from the British navy.

When Victor Saville's direction focuses on nature's vengeance on man's works, the handling is superb. The toppling of giant trees, the shuddering of splitting earth and, the sweep of a river rending everything in its path is simon-pure cinematography. Credit, too, the fetching grandeur of the New Zealand country.

Refusal by M-G-M's studio-ites to recognize the ravages of time and events on the human face hampers Turner in depicting her exacting and pivotal role. As the gentler of the sisters, Reed is bogged by the weight of the yarn. Patly performing in the early reels, she

fails to turn the hazardous trick of making her later conversion credible.
☐ 1947: Best Special Effects.
☐ Nomination: Best B&W Cinematography, Editing, Sound

■ GREEN FIRE

1954, 99 MINS, US ◇
Dir Andrew Marton   *Prod* Armand Deutsch   *Scr* Ivan Goff, Ben Roberts   *Ph* Paul Vogel   *Ed* Harold F. Kress   *Mus* Miklos Rozsa
● Stewart Granger, Grace Kelly, Paul Douglas, John Ericson, Murvyn Vye, Jose Torvay (M-G-M)

A good brand of action escapism is offered in *Green Fire*. Its story of emerald mining and romantic adventuring in South America is decorated with the names of Stewart Granger, Grace Kelly and Paul Douglas.

The location filming in Colombia ensured fresh scenic backgrounds under which to play the screen story. The script supplies believable dialog and reasonably credible situations, of which Andrew Marton's good direction takes full advantage, and the picture spins off at a fast 99 minutes.

The adventure end of the plot is served by the efforts of Granger to find emeralds in an old mountain mine; in the face of halfhearted opposition from his partner, Douglas; the more active interference of Murvyn Vye, a bandit, and the danger of the mining trade itself. Romance is served through the presence of Kelly, whose coffee plantation lies at the foot of the mountain on which Granger is mining, and the attraction that springs up between these two.

■ GREEN FOR DANGER

1946, 91 MINS, UK ⚥
Dir Sidney Gilliat   *Prod* Frank Launder, Sidney Gilliat   *Scr* Sidney Gilliat, Claud Curney   *Ph* Wilkie Cooper   *Ed* Thelma Myers   *Mus* William Alwyn   *Art Dir* Peter Prond
● Alastair Sim, Leo Genn, Trevor Howard, Sally Gray, Rosamund John, Judy Campbell (Individual)

This whodunit [from the novel by Christianna Brand] has the unusual setting of an emergency wartime hospital with the operating theatre as the scene of two apparently clueless murders. Wounded by a buzz-bomb, local postman is brought to hospital for a slight emergency operation, but dies under the anesthetic. Six people are present at the death – Leo Genn, Trevor Howard, Judy Campbell, Rosamund John, Sally Gray and Megs Jenkins. Judy Campbell finds evidence that the man was murdered and before she can inform the police she is stabbed to death.

Alastair Sim, unconventional detective from Scotland Yard, appears to enjoy the double murder case and has great fun annoying the suspects. He discovers each one had a motive, until an attempt on the life of Sally Gray reduces the number to four.

Gilliat and Launder, one-time masters of suspense, are losing their touch. The plot is too laboriously constructed, and the reason for the murders appears too incredible.

■ GREENGAGE SUMMER, THE
(US: Loss of Innocence)

1961, 100 MINS, UK ◇
Dir Lewis Gilbert   *Prod* Victor Saville   *Scr* Howard Koch   *Ph* Freddie Young   *Ed* Peter Hunt   *Mus* Richard Addinsell   *Art Dir* John Stoll
● Kenneth More, Danielle Darrieux, Susannah York, Jane Asher, Claude Nollier, Maurice Denham (Columbia)

Here's a stylish, warm romantic drama which gets away to a flying start in that it's set in the leisurely champagne country of France. Pic is always a delight to the eye apart from its other qualities.

The screenplay, based on Rumer Godden's novel, works up to a holding emotional pitch. Story concerns four English schoolchildren, the oldest (Susannah York) being just over 16. They are enroute to a holiday in France's champagne-and-greengage country when their mother is taken ill and is whisked off to hospital.

Alone and dispirited they arrive at the hotel which is run by Danielle Darrieux and managed by Claude Nollier. The children get a frigid reception but Kenneth More, a debonair, charming, mysterious Englishman insists that they stay. He's having an affair with Miss Darrieux and she cannot resist his whims. During the long summer the atmosphere thickens.

The early part of the film, when the relationship between More and the children is developing, is particularly charming and pleasantly staged. York progresses delightfully from the resentful, gawky schoolgirl to the young woman eager to live. She handles some tricky scenes (as when she gets drunk with champagne and when she is assaulted by an amorous scullery boy) with assurance.

More's scenes with the moppets are great as are his rather more astringent skirmishes with Darrieux. She plays the jealous, fading mistress on rather too much of one note, but with keen insight. And there is a subtly drawn relationship of hinted lesbianism between her and Nollier.

■ GREEN MANSIONS

1959, 104 MINS, US ◇
Dir Mel Ferrer   *Prod* Edmund Grainger   *Scr* Dorothy Kingsley   *Ph* Joseph Ruttenberg   *Ed* Ferris Webster   *Mus* Bronislau Kaper, Heitor Villa-Lobos
● Audrey Hepburn, Anthony Perkins, Lee J. Cobb, Sessue Hayakawa, Henry Silva, Nehemiah Persoff (M-G-M)

Filmization of W.H. Hudson's novel has been approached with reverence and taste but fantastic elements puzzle and annoy. Hudson wrote an allegory of eternal love in his story of Rima, the bird-girl, who is discovered in the Venezuelan jungles by the political refugee, Abel. In the screenplay, Rima (Audrey Hepburn), is a real girl, but one with unusual communion with the forest and its wild life.

She is found by Abel (Anthony Perkins) when he hides out with an Indian tribe after fleeing a political uprising in which his father had been killed. Rumors of gold in the neighborhood stir Perkins' imagination because he needs money to avenge his father's assassination.

Director Mel Ferrer and his cameraman had done some good location work in South America. It is skillfully utilized, by process and editing, with backlot work. But Ferrer has been less successful in getting his characters to come alive, or in getting his audience to care about them.

Hepburn is pretty as the strange young woman, but with no particular depth. Perkins seems rather frail for his role, despite a trial by ordeal given him by Henry Silva's tribe. Silva, on the other hand, gives an exciting performance, fatally damaging to Perkins, the hero, overshadowing him in their dramatic conflict.

■ GREEN PASTURES, THE

1936, 93 MINS, US ⚥
Dir Marc Connelly, William Keighley   *Prod* [Henry Blanke]   *Scr* Marc Connelly, [Sheridan Gibney]   *Ph* Hal Mohr   *Ed* George Amy   *Mus* [Erich Wolfgang Korngold]   *Art Dir* Allen Saalburg, Stanley Fleischer
● Rex Ingram, Oscar Polk, Eddie Anderson, Frank Wilson, Abraham Gleaves, Myrtle Anderson (Warner)

Green Pastures is a simple, enchanting, audience-captivating all-Negro cinematic fable.

The show [by Marc Connelly, suggested by Roark Bradford's novel *Ol' Man Adam an' His Chillun*] made history by touring the hinterland for three years after two years on Broadway.

Rex Ingram's glowing personality is a thoroughly satisfying and convincing Lawd. Ingram's is a yeoman protean contribution, as he also personates Adam and Hezdrel, his images re-created on earth.

The very essence of *Green Pastures* is the Sabbath school. It's the Harlem version of the Old Testament, as the pastor word-paints the mood of De Lawd from Genesis to Exodus and beyond.

Oscar Polk as Gabriel – whom De Lawd colloquially addresses as Gabe – is a human and humorous archangel who efficiently and matter-of-factly sees that De Lawed's will be done, and without the slightest hitches.

Punctuating all the Biblical background are mundane references to gay fishfries, ten cent seegars, generous fishing and plenty of milk-and-honey for the good folks, yet it's all in fine taste and with due regard to proportions and standards of all races and creeds.

Marc Connelly and William Keighley – the latter the more remarkable in view of his previous specialization in gangster mellers – rate most of the bends for their distinguished transition of the play to the screen.

Frank Wilson's Moses; George Reed's Mr Deshee; Edna M. Harris and Al Stokes as Zeba and Cain, a couple of hot potatoes, she a uke-strumming slut and he a fancy man; Ernest Whitman, impressive as the regally arrogant Pharaoh; plus the Hall Johnson choir, are among other stand-outs.

• •

■ GREEN YEARS, THE

1946, 127 MINS, US

Dir Victor Saville *Prod* Leon Gordon *Scr* Robert Ardrey, Sonya Levien *Ph* George Folsey *Ed* Robert J. Kern *Mus* Herbert Stothart *Art Dir* Cedric Gibbons, Hans Peters
● Charles Coburn, Tom Drake, Beverly Tyler, Hume Cronyn, Dean Stockwell, Jessica Tandy (M-G-M)

Metro, with the skill it has so often demonstrated in transforming a best-selling novel to a best-selling picture, turns the trick again with this filmization of A. J. Cronin's *The Green Years*.

Since this is essentially a yarn built on careful development of its various characters, a major contribution is in giving new stature and audience appeal to virtually every player in it. That's true all the way from vet Charles Coburn, who evidences his virtuosity in a new type role for him, to moppet Dean Stockwell and Beverly Tyler, both making their second screen appearances.

Ten-year-old Stockwell is the particularly bright spot in the well-turned cast. He gets real opportunity to demonstrate a sensitivity and true dramatic poignancy that definitely set him off from the usual studio moppets.

Young Stockwell plays an orphan boy in this Scottish-localed story of ambitious youth and amusing old age. The oldster, of course, is Coburn, as Dean's great-grandfather, a man of large heart and large desires for the native brew. While this not-so-venerable, but thoroughly enjoyable, citizen is getting himself into one minor scrape after another, the youth (later played by Tom Drake) goes through the process of growing up, going to school and falling in love.

The two principals are set against a household full of characters. Hume Cronyn wreaks every bit of tightfistedness and little man-meanness out of the role of head of the house that takes the small boy in. Tyler and Drake play the teenage romance.

□ 1946: Nomination: Best Supp. Actor (Charles Coburn), B&W Cinematography

• •

■ GREGORY'S GIRL

1982, 91 MINS, UK ◇ ⓥ ⊙

Dir Bill Forsyth *Prod* Davina Belling, Clive Parsons *Scr* Bill Forsyth *Ph* Michael Coulter *Ed* John Gow *Mus* Colin Tully *Art Dir* Adrienne Atkinson
● John Gordon Sinclair, Dee Hepburn, Jake D'Arcy, Clare Grogan, Robert Buchanan, William Greenlees (Lake/NFFC/Scottish TV)

Filmmaker Bill Forsyth, whose friendly, unmalicious approach recalls that of Rene Clair, is concerned with young students (in particular, a soccer team goalie, Gregory) seeking out the opposite sex. Much of the pic's peculiar fascination comes from tangential scenes, limning each character's odd obsession, be it food, girls, soccer, or just watching the traffic drive by.

Main narrative thread has Gregory becoming infatuated with the cute (and athletic) new girl on his soccer team, Dorothy (Dee Hepburn), while his schoolmates delightfully maneuver him into giving the out-going Susan (Clare Grogan) a tumble.

As Gregory, John Gordon Sinclair is adept at physical comedy. Hepburn is properly enigmatic as the object of his desire, with ensemble approach giving Greg's precocious 10-year-old sister played by Allison Forster a key femme role.

• •

■ GREMLINS

1984, 111 MINS, US ◇ ⓥ ⊙

Dir Joe Dante *Prod* Michael Finnell *Scr* Chris Columbus *Ph* John Hora *Ed* Tina Hirsch *Mus* Jerry Goldsmith *Art Dir* James H. Spencer
● Zach Galligan, Hoyt Axton, Frances Lee McCain, Phoebe Cates, Polly Holliday, Judge Reinhold (Amblin/Warner)

In what story there is, amiable Hoyt Axton comes across a mysterious creature in Chinatown and takes it home as a Christmas present for his likable teenage son, Zach Galligan. With the gift, he passes along a warning from the inscrutable Chinese that the creature must never get wet, be allowed into the sunshine or fed after midnight.

For a while, all is extremely precious as the little furry thing goes through an array of facial expressions and heart-warming attitudes.

Without giving away too much, suffice to say the creature spawns a townful of evil, snarling, drooling, maniacal killer-creatures who are bound to cause a lot of woe before their predictable downfall.

The humans are little more than dress-extras for the mechanics.

• •

■ GREMLINS 2
THE NEW BATCH

1990, 105 MINS, US ◇ ⓥ ⊙

Dir Joe Dante *Prod* Michael Finnell *Scr* Charlie Haas *Ph* John Hora *Ed* Kent Beyda *Mus* Jerry Goldsmith, Alexander Courage, Fred Steiner *Art Dir* James Spencer
● Zach Galligan, Phoebe Cates, John Glover, Robert Prosky, Robert Picardo, Christopher Lee (Amblin)

Joe Dante & Co. have concocted an hilarious sequel featuring equal parts creature slapstick for the small fry and satirical barbs for adults. Addition of Christopher Lee to the cast as a mad genetics engineering scientist is a perfect touch.

Film opens with a wrecking ball demolishing Keye Luke's old curiosity shop in downtown Manhattan to make way for another development project by megalomaniac Daniel Clamp, played with relish by John Glover.

The cuddly Mogwai creature Gizmo (wonderfully voiced by Howie Mandel) escapes but is immediately captured by twins Don & Dan Stanton as a research subject for Lee's science lab Splice of Life Inc. The lab is located in the new Clamp Center office building and, when Gizmo gets loose and exposed to water,

the first of hundreds of horrific gremlins are unleashed to wreak mayhem.

Gremlins 2 is sans starpower, but its creatures more than make up for the lack of marquee lure. As realized by Rick Baker, the innumerable creations are quite an eyeful.

• •

■ GREY FOX, THE

1982, 90 MINS, CANADA ◇ ⓥ ⊙

Dir Phillip Borsos *Prod* Peter O'Brian *Scr* John Hunter *Ph* Frank Tidy *Ed* Ray Hall *Mus* Michael Baker
● Richard Farnsworth, Jackie Burroughs, Wayne Robson, Ken Pogue, David Petersen, Timothy Webber (Mercury)

A graceful, stunningly-photographed bio of Bill Miner, a notorious train robber in Canada and the US at the turn of the century.

Director Phillip Borsos approaches his material – a stagecoach robber goes to jail for 30 years and is released into an unknown world where trains have started carrying the mail – as a kind of neo-western very much in sympathy with the bandit. Veteran Hollywood actor and western stunt man Richard Farnsworth was suggested for the role by Francis Coppola. His performance as the gentleman robber is one of the $3 million pic's strong points.

Until trapped by a Pinkerton detective, Miner lives a quiet life in a frontier town passing himself off as a gold-digger. Between train robberies, there is a delicately-handled love story with a cultured blue-stocking who makes a living as a photographer in the town.

• •

■ GREYFRIARS BOBBY

1961, 91 MINS, US ◇ ⓥ

Dir Don Chaffey *Prod* Walt Disney *Scr* Robert Westerby *Ph* Paul Beeson *Ed* Peter Tanner *Mus* Francis Chagrin *Art Dir* Michael Stringer
● Donald Crisp, Laurence Naismith, Alexander Mackenzie, Kay Walsh, Andrew Cruickshank, Gordon Jackson (Walt Disney)

Greyfriars Bobby sets out to melt the heart and does it skillfully. Central character is a little Skye terrier, and this engaging little animal is quite irresistible. He's a sort of Pollyanna Pooch. Story is a true one, set in and around Edinburgh some 100 years ago.

It tells of an old shepherd who died of old age, exposure and starvation, and was buried in the little Greyfriars Kirk in Edinburgh. From the day of the funeral Bobby resolutely refused to leave his beloved master. In the end he won over all the local burghers and was solemnly declared a Freeman of the City, handed a collar by the Lord Provost and adopted by the entire populace of Edinburgh. Yes, a true, if odd story, and there's a statue of Greyfriars Bobby in Edinburgh to prove it.

Patiently and brilliantly trained, Bobby wraps up the stellar honors for himself and the humans, knowing they don't stand a chance, wisely are content to play chorus. Nevertheless, there are some very effective pieces of thesping, largely by Scottish actors. Laurence Naismith gives a strong, likeable performance as the kindly eating-house owner who takes Bobby under his wing but, by standing up for a principle, brings the facts of the dog's case into court.

• •

■ GREYSTOKE
THE LEGEND OF TARZAN LORD OF THE APES

1984, 129 MINS, US/UK ◇ ⓥ ⊙

Dir Hugh Hudson *Prod* Hugh Hudson, Stanley S. Canter *Scr* P.H. Vazak [= Robert Towne], Michael Austin *Ph* John Alcott *Ed* Anne V. Coates *Mus* John Scott *Art Dir* Stuart Craig
● Ralph Richardson, Ian Holm, James Fox, Christopher Lambert, Andie MacDowell, Cheryl Campbell (Warner)

One of the main points of *Greystoke* is that the $33 million pic adheres much more closely to the original Edgar Rice Burroughs story than have the countless previous screen tellings of Tarzan stories.

While a little obligatory vine swinging is on view, this is principally the tale of the education of the seventh Earl of Greystoke, first by the family of apes which raises a stranded white child and eventually accepts him as its protector and leader, then by a Belgian explorer who teaches him language, and finally by the aristocracy of Britain, which attempts to make him one of their own. With the exception of the warm, slightly batty Ralph Richardson, nearly all the Englishmen on view are impossible, offensive snobs.

Christopher Lambert is a different sort of Tarzan. Tall, lean, firm but no muscleman, he moves with great agility and mimics the apes to fine effect.

Ian Holm is helpfully energetic as the enterprising Belgian, James Fox is the personification of stiff propriety, and Andie MacDowell [voiced by actress Glenn Close] smiles her way through as the eternally sympathetic Jane.

On a production level, film is a marvel, as fabulous Cameroon locations have been seamlessly blended with studio recreations of jungle settings.

□ 1984: Nominations: Best Supp. Actor (Ralph Richardson), Adapted Screenplay, Makeup

••••••••••••••••••••••••••••

■ **GRIFTERS, THE**

1990, 113 MINS, US ◇ ⑰ ⊙
Dir Stephen Frears   *Prod* Martin Scorsese, Robert A. Harris, Jim Painten   *Scr* Donald E. Westlake   *Ph* Oliver Stapleton   *Ed* Mick Audsley   *Mus* Elmer Bernstein   *Art Dir* Dennis Gassner
● John Cusack, Anjelica Huston, Annette Bening, Pat Hingle, J.T. Walsh, Charles Napier (Cineplex Odeon)

Jim Thompson's intriguing novel about the subculture of smalltime hustlers is fashioned into a curiously uneven movie in *The Grifters*.

John Cusack plays Roy Dillon, a Los Angeles con man whose salesman's job is a cover for his real vocation. Roy's mother, Lilly (Anjelica Huston), gave birth at the tender age of 14, then fashioned a lucrative career as a roving racetrack bag lady, putting down bets for the Baltimore mob.

Roy is ministered to by his sexy girlfriend Myra (Annette Bening), who lives by her wits and her tightly wrapped body. Meanwhile, the mob boss travels west to teach Lilly a painful lesson for skimming mob money at the track.

When Roy and Myra take a holiday in La Jolla, she reveals her true colors. Myra, is an expert at the 'big con', elaborate swindles geared to netting five- and six-figure scores. Myra correctly suspects Roy's little secret: a large horde of hidden cash accumulated from years of grifting.

Cusack underplays Roy, making him an unbelievable wiseguy, a colorless cipher too akin to the saps he loves to fleece.

□ 1990: Nominations: Best Director, Actress (Anjelica Huston), Supp. Actress (Annette Bening), Adapted Screenplay

••••••••••••••••••••••••••••

■ **GRIP OF FEAR, THE**

See: Experiment in Terror

••••••••••••••••••••••••••••

■ **GRISSOM GANG, THE**

1971, 127 MINS, US ◇ ⑰
Dir Robert Aldrich   *Prod* Robert Aldrich   *Scr* Leon Griffiths   *Ph* Joseph Biroc   *Ed* Michael Luciano, Frank J. Urioste   *Mus* Gerald Fried   *Art Dir* James Dowell Vance
● Kim Darby, Scott Wilson, Tony Musante, Irene Dailey, Robert Lansing, Connie Stevens (ABC/Associates & Aldrich)

The Grissom Gang offers no sympathy at all for the debased human beings it depicts. Rather, it denies their existence as people, treating them instead as the butts of a cruel joke.

The action takes place in Kansas City in 1931, and concerns the kidnapping of a young heiress by an unbelievably depraved gang presided over by venomous Ma Grissom (Irene Dailey) and her cretinous son (Scott Wilson). It begins in a wash of blood, opening the same vein throughout – and the key to its debasing approach is the laughter this mayhem often provokes.

Provided with a script [from a novel by James Hadley Chase] that offers absolutely no insight into the inner lives of its people, director Robert Aldrich takes matters a step further by directing his actors in performances that strain the bounds of credulity. Wilson and Kim Darby, as the kidnapped girl, make stabs at more than one dimension, but when they indulge in caricatures of feeling, as they often do, they cancel out the rest of their work. Dailey is the most persistent mugger, while Robert Lansing, in one of the few sympathetic roles, comes off best.

••••••••••••••••••••••••••••

■ **GROSS ANATOMY**
(UK: A Cut Above)

1989, 107 MINS, US ◇ ⑰ ⊙
Dir Thom Eberhardt   *Prod* Howard Rosenman, Debra Hill   *Scr* Ron Nyswaner, Mark Spragg   *Ph* Steve Yaconelli   *Ed* Bud Smith, Scott Smith   *Mus* David Newman   *Art Dir* William F. Matthews
● Matthew Modine, Daphne Zuniga, Christine Lahti, Todd Field, John Scott Clough, Alice Carter (Touchstone)

Gross Anatomy, a seriocomic look at the first year of medical school, should be required viewing for anyone with aspirations in that direction, but for all others, film is about as exciting as a pop quiz.

The film, trying to be another *Paper Chase*, follows Matthew Modine, as the 26-year-old son of a fisherman, and other students through their courses, with particular focus on the anatomy lab, in which he's teamed with four classmates to work on a cadaver. Dissecting group includes his too-serious, driven roommate Todd Field; married young mother Alice Carter; Modine's nemesis, the judgmental, ultrapreppy John Scott Clough; and hard-working Daphne Zuniga, who reluctantly provides love interest for Modine.

Gross offers some nice, unexpected details: the anatomy profs, and key figures of authority, just happen to be a woman and a black man, played by Christine Lahti and Zakes Mokae. Another plus is the film's convincing portrayal of med-school life.

However, the writers - working from a story by Mark Spragg, Howard Rosenman, Alan Jay Glueckman and Stanley Isaacs - could come up with nothing more than stick figures and repetitive, one-note problems. Biggest problem is Modine's character; though there's little on-screen evidence of his intelligence, he frequently is described as being so smart he can get by with minimum study. Lahti hasn't much to do but look stern, but she's good in her Big Scene near the end.

••••••••••••••••••••••••••••

■ **GROUNDHOG DAY**

1993, 103 MINS, US ◇ ⑰ ⊙
Dir Harold Ramis   *Prod* Trevor Albert, Harold Ramis   *Scr* Danny Rubin, Harold Ramis   *Ph* John Bailey   *Ed* Pembroke J. Herring   *Mus* George Fenton   *Art Dir* David Nichols
● Bill Murray, Andie MacDowell, Chris Elliott, Stephen Tobolowsky, Brian Doyle-Murray, Marita Geraghty (Columbia)

The premise of the romantic comedy *Groundhog Day* is essentially 'if you had to do it over again – and again – what would you do differently?' The film is inconsistent in tone and pace; fortunately the pay-off works, bringing some much needed warmth to the area.

Bill Murray, a cynical TV weatherman, finds himself stuck in a private, repetitious hell: Groundhog Day in Punxsatawney, Pa, where he has come for the annual festivities. The day begins, over and over, at 6 a.m., Sonny & Cher on the clock radio, and moves on almost invariably, as Murray undergoes every conceivable emotional permutation – from confusion to anger to cockiness to despair – finally thawing into a beneficent soul.

The situation [from an original story by Danny Rubin] is ripe with comic potential but script provides more chuckles than belly laughs. Some sequences are crisply paced and comically terse, some ramble and others just plain don't work.

Murray's weatherman is tailor-made for his smug screen persona, perhaps too much so. Of the supporting players, Stephen Tobolowsky is hilarious in a loose-limbed turn as Murray's cloying ex-schoolmate.

••••••••••••••••••••••••••••

■ **GROUNDSTAR CONSPIRACY, THE**

1972, 95 MINS, CANADA ◇ ⑰
Dir Lamont Johnson   *Prod* Trevor Wallace   *Scr* Matthew Howard   *Ph* Michael Reed   *Ed* Edward M. Abroms   *Mus* Paul Hoffert   *Art Dir* Cam Porteous
● George Peppard, Michael Sarrazin, Christine Belford, Cliff Potts, James Olson, Tim O'Connor (Universal/Roach)

George Peppard stars as a government agent trying to break up a spy ring. Spectacular locations around Vancouver, plus some excellent and offbeat music by Paul Hoffert, only partially compensate for a script that is as often routine as it is bewildering. Lamont Johnson's direction is one of his lesser efforts.

Matthew Howard adapted L. P. Davies' [novel] *The Alien* into a diffused whodunit. Michael Sarrazin is, or is not, a traitor who worked in a super-secret lab trying to break a computer code. The lab's destruction launches the story.

Hard by the facility is the summer house owned by Christine Belford who, before disappearing completely from the plot, plays an important role in Peppard's trackdown of Sarrazin. There is a lot of rough action and violence, compounded intrigue, and confusing shifts of focus.

••••••••••••••••••••••••••••

■ **GROUP, THE**

1966, 150 MINS, US ◇ ⑰
Dir Sidney Lumet   *Prod* Sidney Buchman   *Scr* Sidney Buchman   *Ph* Boris Kaufman   *Ed* Ralph Rosenbloom   *Mus* Charles Gross   *Art Dir* Gene Callahan
● Candice Bergen, Joan Hackett, Elizabeth Hartman, Shirley Knight, Joanna Pettet, Jessica Walter (Famous Artists/United Artists)

The principal problem Sidney Buchman had to face in adapting Mary McCarthy's very successful college classmates novel was to transfer its colorful characterizations and story-telling without overloading his script with the mass of novelistic detail. His script does not completely solve this.

There's little tampering with the original storyline but the filmscript concentrates on the story of Kay (Joanna Pettet), the first girl to be married and the one meeting the most tragic end. Throughout, she and Larry Hagman, as her philandering playwright husband, have the longest roles. However, if less important, the characters played by Joan Hackett and Jessica Walter, thanks to their performances, register as strongly as does Pettet. Hackett, particularly, is provided with a wide range of emotional changes.

Biggest letdown, and doubly so because her few scenes are so effective and played so well, is the part played by Candice Bergen. As Lakey, the ambisextrous leader of the Group (and the novel's most memorable character), her treatment in Buchman's script will puzzle the audience, as her few scenes at the beginning and at the end don't match with the billing she receives.

••

■ **GUADALCANAL DIARY**

1943, 90 MINS, US ⓥ
Dir Lewis Seiler   *Prod* Bryan Foy   *Scr* Lamar Trotti
Ph Charles Clarke   *Ed* Fred Allen   *Mus* David Buttolph
Art Dir James Basevi, Leland Fuller
● Preston Foster, Lloyd Nolan, William Bendix, Richard Conte, Anthony Quinn, Richard Jaekel (20th Century-Fox)

To anyone unfamiliar with the Richard Tregaskis book, the picture version may or may not be a faithful adaptation [by Jerry Cady] of the original. But it is without question a painstaking, dignified and, in general, eloquent expression of a heroic theme. It is at times a sobering film and at other times an exalting one. It is also an almost continuously entertaining one.

The diary form of the original book is utilized in the picture. Opening with a quiet scene aboard a transport on a Sunday afternoon, as the Marine Corps task force steams toward an as-yet undisclosed objective, the story is narrated by an off-screen voice, fading in and out of the action sequences.

All this is admirably free from bombast and chauvinistic boasting. Although the deeds of the men are heroic, the men themselves reveal no self-consciousness of heroism.

With minor exceptions, *Guadalcanal Diary* is skillfully produced. A few of the incidents seem synthetic and such scenes as the sinking of the Jap submarine are rather obviously faked, but in general both the action and the manner of its presentation are genuinely believable.

Of the cast, William Bendix stands out in a juicy comedy-straight part as a tough-soft taxi driver from Brooklyn, while Preston Foster and Lloyd Nolan give effective performances in the other principal leads.

••

■ **GUARDIAN, THE**

1990, 98 MINS, US ◇ ⓥ ⊙
Dir William Friedkin   *Prod* Joe Wizan   *Scr* Steven Volk, Dan Greenburg, William Friedkin   *Ph* John A. Alonzo
Ed Seth Flaum   *Mus* Jack Hues   *Art Dir* Gregg Fonseca
● Jenny Seagrove, Dwier Brown, Carey Lowell, Brad Hall, Miguel Ferrer, Natalia Nogulich (Universal)

Who knows what possessed director William Friedkin to straight-facedly tell this absurd 'tree bites man' tale, but it's an impulse he should have exorcised.

The scant plot [from Dan Greenburg's story *The Nanny*] involves an attractive yuppie couple (Dwier Brown, Carey Lowell) who hire a live-in nanny to take care of their infant son. The nanny (Jenny Seagrove) turns out to be some sort of evil spirit that sacrifices newborns to this big, anthropomorphic tree, a species apparently indigenous to the canyon areas of metropolitan Los Angeles.

Friedkin's first horror film since *The Exorcist*, *The Guardian* is more likely to make viewers think at best of the wan film adaptation of *Pet Sematary*, at worst of the talking trees in *The Wizard of Oz*. The design is so shoddy one half expects it to start talking and pitching apples.

Seagrove looks properly bewitching but never brings much menace or mystery to her role. Lowell, a former Bond girl, has the least to do as the confused wife.

••

■ **GUESS WHO'S COMING TO DINNER**

1967, 108 MINS, US ◇ ⓥ ⊙
Dir Stanley Kramer   *Prod* Stanley Kramer   *Scr* William Rose   *Ph* Sam Leavitt   *Ed* Robert C. Jones   *Mus* Frank DeVol   *Art Dir* Robert Clatworthy
● Spencer Tracy, Sidney Poitier, Katharine Hepburn,

Katharine Houghton, Cecil Kellaway, Beah Richards (Columbia)

Problem: how to tell an interracial love story in a literate, nonsensational and balanced way. Solution: make it a drama with comedy. *Guess Who's Coming to Dinner* is an outstanding Stanley Kramer production, superior in almost every imaginable way, which examines its subject matter with perception, depth, insight, humor and feeling.

Spencer Tracy, Sidney Poitier and Katharine Hepburn head a perfect cast. Script is properly motivated at all times; dialog is punchy, adroit and free of preaching; dramatic rhythm is superb.

The story covers 12 hours, from arrival in, and departure from, Frisco of Poitier and Katharine Houghton (Hepburn's niece, in a whammo screen debut). Tracy and Hepburn are her parents, of longtime liberal persuasion, faced with a true test of their beliefs: do they approve of their daughter marrying a Negro.

Between the lovers and two sets of parents, every possible interaction is explored admidst comedy angles which range from drawingroom sophistication to sight gag, from bitter cynicism to telling irony. Film must be seen to be believed.

Apart from the pic itself, there are several plus angles. This is the ninth teaming of Tracy and Hepburn, and the last, unfortunately; Tracy died shortly after principal photography was complete. Also, for Poitier, film marked a major step forward, not just in his proven acting ability, but in the opening-up of his script character.
□ 1967: Best Actress (Katharine Hepburn), Original Story & Screenplay.
□ Nominations: Best Picture, Director, Actor (Spencer Tracy), Supp. Actor (Cecil Kallaway), Supp. Actress (Beah RIchards), Art Direction, Editing, Adapted Score

••

■ **GUEST, THE**
See: *The Caretaker*

••

■ **GUIDE FOR THE MARRIED MAN, A**

1967, 89 MINS, US ◇ ⓥ
Dir Gene Kelly   *Prod* Frank McCarthy   *Scr* Frank Tarloff
Ph Joe MacDonald   *Ed* Dorothy Spencer   *Mus* John Williams   *Art Dir* Jack Martin Smith, William Glasgow
● Walter Matthau, Robert Morse, Inger Stevens, Sue Ane Langdon, Claire Kelly, Linda Harrison (20th Century-Fox)

Walter Matthau plays a married innocent, eager to stray under the tutelage of friend and neighbor Robert Morse. But this long-married hubby is so retarded in his Immorality (it takes him 12 years to get the seven-year-itch) that, between his natural reluctance and mentor Morse's suggestions (interlarded with warnings against hastiness), he needs the entire film to have his mind made up.

Guide [based on the book by Frank Tarloff] is packed with action, pulchritude, situations, and considerable (if not quite enough) laughs. Inger Stevens is beautiful as Matthau's wife, and so unbelievably perfect that it makes his reluctance most understandable.

Some of the guest talent have no more than one line (Jeffrey Hunter, Sam Jaffe), some are mimed (Wally Cox, Ben Blue) and others have several lines (Sid Caesar, Phil Silvers, Jack Benny, Hal March).

••

■ **GUILTY AS SIN**

1993, 104 MINS, US ◇ ⓥ ⊙
Dir Sidney Lumet   *Prod* Martin Ransohoff   *Scr* Larry Cohen   *Ph* Andrzej Bartkowiak   *Ed* Evan Lottman
Mus Howard Shore   *Art Dir* Philip Rosenberg
● Rebecca DeMornay, Don Johnson, Stephen Lang, Jack

Warden, Dana Ivey, Ron White (Hollywood Pictures)

It takes too long for the courtroom thriller *Guilty as Sin* to heat up and engage an audience. Despite some intruiging plot twists and a visceral windup, Sidney Lumet's study of a war of wills is of very limited interest.

Don Johnson is effectively cast as the literal ladykiller, who's just been accused of throwing his rich wife out of a highrise window. Like a stalker, he's become fixated on hotshot criminal lawyer Rebecca DeMornay and uses perverse psychology to get her to take his case.

Soon fearing for her very life when it becomes apparent that Johnson's killing spree is open-ended, DeMornay has detective Jack Warden gather evidence of Johnson's previous unsolved murders.

Johnson's upfront sexism and smug role reversal as a narcissistic gigolo generate comic relief and unintentional risibility in equal measure. DeMornay gets top billing but is saddled with a functional, reactive part.

Andrzej Bartkowiak's compositions and lighting add menace to the urban locations, lensed in Canada as a convincing double for Chicago settings.

••

■ **GUILTY BY SUSPICION**

1991, 105 MINS, US ◇ ⓥ ⊙
Dir Irwin Winkler   *Prod* Arnon Milchan, Alan C. Blomquist   *Scr* Irwin Winkler   *Ph* Michael Ballhaus
Ed Priscilla Nedd   *Mus* James Newton Howard
Art Dir Leslie Dilley
● Robert De Niro, Annette Bening, George Wendt, Patricia Wettig, Sam Wanamaker, Martin Scorsese (Warner)

First writing-directing effort by vet producer Irwin Winkler squarely lays out the professional, ethical and moral dilemmas engendered by the insidious political pressures brought to bear on filmmakers in the early 1950s. Robert De Niro is excellent as a top director brought down by reactionary paranoia. But the drama comes to life only fitfully.

De Niro portrays David Merrill, a director on a roll who lives only for his work. Arriving back in Hollywood in 1951 after a European sojourn, he soon finds the atmosphere changed. Charged by a colleague as having attended a couple of left-wing meetings years before, Merrill is asked by 20th Century-Fox boss Darryl F. Zanuck (Ben Piazza) to cooperate with the House Un-American Activities Committee before proceeding with his next big production.

After a disagreeable meeting with an attorney (Sam Wanamaker) and a HUAC rep, Merrill, refusing to cooperate, finds that the chill sets in almost immediately. He is yanked from the Fox film, listens to his agent demand back a $50,000 advance, looks to lose his house and hears his 10-year-old son doubting him. Worst of all, no one will return his calls.

Looking raffish and trim, De Niro perfectly conveys a charming, quiet confidence at the outset. During the extraordinary appearance before HUAC, he finally blossoms into a man of conviction and passion. The actor pulls off this last-minute transformation beautifully.

••

■ **GUMBALL RALLY, THE**

1976, 106 MINS, US ◇ ⓥ
Dir Chuck Bail   *Prod* Chuck Bail   *Scr* Leon Capetanos
Ph Richard C. Glouner   *Ed* Gordon Scott, Stuart H. Pappe, Maury Winetrobe   *Mus* Dominic Frontiere
Art Dir Walter Simonds
● Michael Sarrazin, Normann Burton, Gary Busey, John Durren, Susan Flannery, Harvey Jason (First Artists)

The Gumball Rally is a silly forced, one-note and strident comedy about a cross-country auto race by a bunch of formula-kooky characters. Former stunt coordinator Chuck Bail produced and directed but he didn't have

G

much of a plot.

Bail and Leon Capetanos concocted the story which the latter scripted. Dilettante businessman Michael Sarrazin and lifetime rival Tim McIntire are among a group of auto fanatics who periodically assemble for a cross-country race, sanctioned by nobody and psychotically opposed by policeman Normann Burton.

Latter's attempts to thwart the race are supposed to remind one of Wiley Coyote's snares for the Roadrunner; the animated capers remain the more effective.

. . . .

■ GUMSHOE

1971, 85 MINS, UK ◇ ▽

Dir Stephen Frears   *Prod* Michael Medwin   *Scr* Neville Smith   *Ph* Christopher Menges   *Ed* Charles Rees   *Mus* Andrew Lloyd Webber

● Albert Finney, Billie Whitelaw, Frank Finlay, Janice Rule, Carolyn Seymour, Fulton Mackay (Memorial)

Gumshoe is an affectionately nostalgic and amusing tribute to the movie-fiction private-eye genre of yesteryear.

Story's about a smalltime Liverpool nitery emcee and would-be comedian with a buff's passion for Bogie and Dashiell Hammett who gets involved in a gun- and drug-running caper. Though often twistful, the tale's not the thing but its telling, and this, thanks to screenplay and direction, is an almost constantly chucklesome homage to the vintage sleuthing era – as the hero acts out his Mittyish adventure in Bogieland – with more reverence than outright spoof, for a curious and effective amalgam.

Albert Finney is brilliant as the key figure with just the right dose of tightlipped panache or – to bridge a plot gap – soliloquizing by quoting chapter and verse from his favorite authors or, again, tipping his hat to them with a look or a gesture. He's ably backed by Billie Whitelaw, Frank Finlay, Janice Rule and especially Fulton Mackay as Straker, another would-be eye.

. . . .

■ GUMSHOE KID, THE

1990, 98 MINS, US ◇

Dir Joseph Manduke   *Prod* Joseph Manduke   *Scr* Victor Bardack   *Ph* Harvey Genkins   *Ed* Richard G. Haines   *Mus* Peter Matz   *Art Dir* Batia Grafka

● Jay Underwood, Tracy Scoggins, Vince Edwards, Arlene Golonka, Pamela Springstein, Gino Conforti (Argus)

The Gumshoe Kid, alternately titled *The Detective Kid*, is a charming little comedy that pays homage to the private eye genre.

Jay Underwood, performing with the self-assurance of a younger Tom Hanks, carries the picture as a guy obsessed with Bogart who gets a job in Vince Edwards' agency through the efforts of his mom, Arlene Golonka. Finally assigned to a field case in surveillance, he's thrown together with femme fatale Tracy Scoggins. The two of them are on the lam for the rest of the film after Scoggins' boyfriend is nabbed by persons unknown.

This is breezy, light entertainment. Helmer Joe Manduke maintains a lighthearted mood, giving both principal players a chance to let their hair down engagingly.

. . . .

■ GUN CRAZY

(Aka: Deadly Is the Female)

1950, 87 MINS, US ▽

Dir Joseph H. Lewis   *Prod* Maurice King, Frank King   *Scr* MacKinlay Kantor, Millard Kaufman   *Ph* Russell Harlan   *Ed* Harry Gerstad   *Mus* Victor Young   *Art Dir* Gordon Wiles

● Peggy Cummins, John Dall, Berry Kroeger, Morris Carnovsky, Anabel Shaw, Russ Tamblyn (Pioneer/United Artists)

MacKinlay Kantor's *Sat Eve Post* story, *Gun Crazy*, is a shoot-'em-up story of desperate love and crime.

After a slow beginning, it generates considerable excitement in telling a story of a young man, fascinated by guns, who turns criminal to keep the love of a girl with no scruples. It's not a pleasant story, nor is the telling, but John Dall builds some sympathy as the male. Opposite him is Peggy Cummins, a sideshow Annie Oakley without morals. She is not too convincing.

Because of so much establishing footage, the picture seems long. Latter half, however, races along under Joseph H. Lewis' direction, being a continual chase broken only by new holdup jobs pulled by Dall and Cummins.

Script points up the physical attraction between Dall and Cummins but, despite the emphasis, it is curiously cold and lacking in genuine emotions. Fault is in the writing and direction, both staying on the surface and never getting underneath the characters.

. . . .

■ GUNCRAZY

1992, 93 MINS, US ◇ ▽ ⊙

Dir Tamra Davis   *Prod* Zane W. Levitt, Diane Firestone   *Scr* Matthew Bright   *Ph* Lisa Rinzler   *Ed* Kevin Tent   *Mus* Ed Tomney   *Art Dir* Kevin Constant

● Drew Barrymore, James LeGros, Billy Drago, Joe Dallesandro, Michael Ironside, Ione Skye (Zeta)

A shoot-'em-up exploitationer with a few interesting ideas, *Guncrazy* lacks the exhilaration of a first-class lovers-on-the-run crime drama. After a promising beginning, competently made indie effort settles into a surprisingly somber mood.

Original screenplay contains echoes of Joseph H. Lewis' B classic, *Gun Crazy*, but script is not explicitly based on any recognizable antecedents, as characters and situations are thoroughly modern.

Drew Barrymore plays Anita, a ripe, lower-class 16-year-old who will willingly have sex with different boys because it's the only way she can feel liked. She also lets herself be bedded by her absent mother's b.f. (Joe Dallesandro), with whom she shares a miserable trailer.

For a class pen pal project, Anita starts corresponding with an imprisoned man, Howard (James LeGros). Helping spring Howard early by finding him a job, Anita welcomes him with feverish anticipation. Gun lust begins to get the better of them and, almost by accident, they begin killing.

Unfortunately, eliminating the sexual element from the pair's relationship saps the story of the thrill it might have had. Still, music video director Tamra Davis makes a credible debut in territory mined many times over.

. . . .

■ GUNFIGHT, A

1971, 89 MINS, US ◇ ▽

Dir Lamont Johnson   *Prod* A. Ronald Lubin, Harold Jack Bloom   *Scr* Harold Jack Bloom   *Ph* David M. Walsh   *Ed* Bill Mosher   *Mus* Laurence Rosenthal   *Art Dir* Tambi Larsen

● Kirk Douglas, Johnny Cash, Jane Alexander, Karen Black, Keith Carradine, Raf Vallone (Paramount)

A Gunfight is an offbeat western drama about two aging gunfighters who manipulate, and are manipulated by the blood lust of supposedly peaceful, average folks. Bankrolled by the Jicarilla Apache Tribe of American Indians, an investment-wealthy group making a first venture into pix, the handsome production stars Kirk Douglas and Johnny Cash. Lamont Johnson's very fine direction of the ruggedly sensitive script adds up to a fine depiction in discreet allegorical form of the darker sides of human nature.

Plot is essentially a three-acter. First the

stars meet, fence nervously but with good humor, and at Douglas' suggestion, they decide to turn the town's unofficial speculation on the results of a shoot-out confrontation into personal profit for the survivor.

Next, intercut with the objections of Jane Alexander, excellent as Douglas' wife, and Karen Black, very good as a saloon dame who takes to Cash, the pair plan the carnival duel, aided by Raf Vallone, a shop-keeper whose eyes long have been on Alexander. Finally, the event itself, with the survivor really no better off than the deceased, a fact recognized by the friends of both men.

. . . .

■ GUNFIGHT AT THE O.K. CORRAL

1957, 122 MINS, US ◇ ▽

Dir John Sturges   *Prod* Hal B. Wallis   *Scr* Leon Uris   *Ph* Charles B. Lang Jr   *Ed* Warren Low   *Mus* Dimitri Tiomkin   *Art Dir* Hal Pereira, Walter Tyler

● Burt Lancaster, Kirk Douglas, Rhonda Fleming, Jo Van Fleet, John Ireland, Lyle Bettger (Paramount)

Producer Hal Wallis has taken the historic meeting of Wyatt Earp, a celebrated lawman of the West, his brothers and Doc Holliday, with the Clanton gang in the O.K. Corral of Tombstone, Arizona, and fashioned an absorbing yarn [suggested by an article by George Scullin] in action leading up to the gory gunfight.

Burt Lancaster and Kirk Douglas enact the respective roles of Earp and Holliday, story opening in Fort Griffin, Texas, when the gun-handy Dodge City marshal saves the other from a lynch mob. Action moves then to the Kansas town, where Holliday, at first ordered to leave town but permitted to stay, helps Earp in gunning three badmen. When the marshal heeds the plea of one of his brothers, marshal of Tombstone, for aid in handling the dangerous Clanton gang, Holliday accompanies him.

Both stars are excellently cast in their respective characters. Rhonda Fleming is in briefly as a femme gambler whom Lancaster romances, beautifully effective, and Jo Van Fleet, as Holliday's constant travelling companion again demonstrates her ability in dramatic characterization.

☐ 1957: Nominations: Best Editing, Sound

. . . .

■ GUNFIGHTER, THE

1950, 84 MINS, US ▽ ⊙

Dir Henry King   *Prod* Nunnally Johnson   *Scr* William Bowers, William Sellers   *Ph* Arthur Miller   *Ed* Barbara McLean   *Mus* Alfred Newman   *Art Dir* Lyle Wheeler, Richard Irvine

● Gregory Peck, Helen Westcott, Millard Mitchell, Jean Parker, Karl Malden, Skip Homeier (20th Century-Fox)

The Gunfighter is a sock melodrama of the old west. There's never a sag or off moment in the footage as it goes about depicting a lightning draw artist, the fastest man with a gun in the old west, and what his special ability has done to his life.

Gregory Peck perfectly portrays the title role, a man doomed to live out his span killing to keep from being killed. He gives it great sympathy and a type of rugged individualism that makes it real. Peck is a man saddened by his talent, forced to stay on the run by all the young gunners seeking to make a reputation by shooting down the great man.

Despite all the tight melodrama, the picture [from a story by William Bowers and Andre de Toth] finds time for some leavening laughter.

☐ 1950: Nomination: Best Motion Picture Story

. . . .

■ GUNGA DIN

1939, 120 MINS, US ▽ ⊙

Dir George Stevens   *Prod* Pandro S. Berman   *Scr* Joel Sayre, Fred Guiol   *Ph* Joseph H. August   *Ed* Henry

Berman, John Lockert   Mus Alfred Newman
Art Dir Van Nest Polglase, Perry Ferguson
● Cary Grant, Victor McLaglen, Douglas Fairbanks Jr,
Sam Jaffe, Joan Fontaine, Montagu Love (RKO)

Aside from the feature's ability to tell a swiftly-paced, exciting yarn about British rule in India in the 1890s, it shows Cary Grant, Victor McLaglen and Douglas Fairbanks Jr as a trio of happy-go-lucky British army sergeants who typify the type of hard-bitten non-coms described by Rudyard Kipling in his famed poems *Barrack Room Ballads*.

Basis of Ben Hecht and Charles MacArthur's original story, from the barrack ballad, is the outbreak of the Thugs, cruel religious marauders, who revolted against English troops.

George Stevens employs superb change of pace, going from action to character closeups and then tossing in a romantic touch.

As Gunga Din, native water carrier, Sam Jaffe contributes possibly his best screen portrayal since *Lost Horizon*. Eduardo Ciannelli outdoes himself as ruthless native leader of India's Thugs.

■ **GUNG HO!**

1943, 88 MINS, US ▼
Dir Ray Enright   Prod Walter Wanger   Scr Lucien Hubbard, Joseph Hoffman   Ph Milton Krasner
Ed Milton Carruth   Mus Frank Skinner
● Randolph Scott, Grace McDonald, Noah Beery Jr, J. Carrol Naish, Robert Mitchum, Rod Cameron (Universal)

Randolph Scott has the lead in this story, adapted from what is said to be a factual account written by Lieut W.S. Le Francois, USMC.

Pertinently, it's the story of how, out of thousands of trainees, a picked group of Marines is slated for a special mission – the first raid on [the tiny Pacific] Makin Island. It's an at-times loosely written script. The 'boot training' preliminaries to the raid are just so much of a wait, but the actual attack has its compensating and exciting moments. Scott gives one of his usually fine heroic performances, while J. Carrol Naish is a tough lieutenant who, somehow, doesn't look the part. Noah Beery Jr and David Bruce play half-brothers in a heat ver the same blonde (Grace McDonald). Sam Levene, in a small role as a sergeant, is best of the support.

The direction has geared the pic for pace but some of that dialog is strictly for the younger element. The story has been needlessly glamorized, and it's here that it bogs down. It has a love yarn where one need not necessarily exist.

■ **GUNG HO**

1986, 111 MINS, US ◇ ▼ ⊙
Dir Ron Howard   Prod Tony Ganz, Deborah Blum
Scr Lowell Ganz, Babaloo Mandel   Ph Don Peterman
Ed Daniel Hanley, Michael Hill   Mus Thomas Newman
Art Dir James Schoppe
● Michael Keaton, Gedde Watanabe, George Wendt, Mimi Rogers, John Turturro, Soh Yamamura (Paramount)

Trying to save his town, auto worker Michael Keaton journeys abroad to plead with Japanese industrialists to re-open the plant in Hanleyville, Pa, that's been closed by foreign competition. Soon after, the Japanese invasion begins. From the first morning of calisthenics, it's clear the American workers will not adapt well to Japanese management.

Drawn from real life, the conflict between cultures is good for both a laugh and a sober thought along the way. Director Ron Howard has problems straddling the two, sometimes getting bogged down in the social significance.

Keaton can be funny as he puzzles the Japanese. Gedde Watanabe is excellent as the

young Japanese exec whose career is threatened by the lack of output by the Americans.

■ **GUN IN BETTY LOU'S HANDBAG, THE**

1992, 89 MINS, US ◇ ▼ ⊙
Dir Allan Moyle   Prod Scott Kroopf   Scr Grace Cary Bickley   Ph Charles Minsky   Ed Janice Hampton, Erica Huggins   Mus Richard Gibbs   Art Dir Michael Corenblith
● Penelope Ann Miller, Eric Thal, Alfre Woodard, Julianne Moore, Andy Romano, William Forsythe (Touchstone/Interscope)

The Gun in Betty Lou's Handbag is a clever premise that ends up being as bland as its put-upon title character.

Penelope Ann Miller has the title role as a mousy librarian who seizes on a found gun (used in the motelroom slaying of an FBI informant) to shake up her pristine image and become a femme fatale. Her girl-who-cries-wolf plot has one deadly drawback, however, in the form of the sadistic mobster Beaudeen (William Forsythe), who fears Betty Lou possesses evidence that could convict him.

The one area in which the film does excel is its occasionally sharp dialogue and supporting characters, with amusing moments from Alfre Woodard as a novice attorney, Julianne Moore as Betty Lou's hyperkinetic sister and Cathy Moriarty as a helpful hooker. In limited screen time, the reliable Forsythe also brings an uneasy sense of menace to his cajun-drawling heavy.

■ **GUNN**

1967, 94 MINS, US ◇
Dir Blake Edwards   Prod Owen Crump   Scr Blake Edwards, William Peter Blatty   Ph Philip Lathrop
Ed Peter Zinner   Mus Henry Mancini   Art Dir Fernando Carrere
● Craig Stevens, Laura Devon, Ed Asner, Albert Paulsen, Sherry Jackson, Helen Traubel (Paramount)

Blake Edwards has transplanted his three-season *Peter Gunn* NBC-TV series (which began in the 1959-60 season) to the screen in *Gunn*, a well-made, but a trifle longish, programmer.

Episodic scripting, as befits a murder suspense comedy, is combined with solid Owen Crump production supervision, Henry Mancini music, and a surprise ending.

There's a prolog murder of a top-dog gangster. Albert Paulsen, successor to the gangland throne, is the natural suspect. M. T. (Marion) Marshall, a seagoing madame, hires Craig Stevens to prove Paulsen guilty. Eventually, Paulsen forces Stevens to prove him innocent.

Popping up at intervals are Laura Devon, Gunn's occasional dame, Sherry Jackson, in a standout sexpot part, J. Pat O'Malley, excellent as a boozer informer who plays it like Alfred Hitchcock's old TV show intros, and skid-row topster Regis Toomey.

■ **GUNS AT BATASI**

1964, 102 MINS, UK ▼
Dir John Guillermin   Prod George H. Brown   Scr Robert Holles   Ph Douglas Slocombe   Ed Max Benedict
Mus John Addison   Art Dir Maurice Carter
● Richard Attenborough, Jack Hawkins, Flora Robson, John Leyton, Mia Farrow, Cecil Parker (20th Century-Fox)

Soldiering and politics don't mix, according to this well developed screenplay and story by Robert Holles [from his novel *The Siege of Battersea*, adapted by Leo Marks and Marshall Pugh, with additional material by C.M. Pennington-Richards] which dissects with a piercing personal touch the strict disciplinary attitudes that govern a true British soldier and makes him retain his own individual

pride in the face of political forces unappreciative of his principles.

Producer and director come up with a strong and frequently exciting piece of work, the story of a British battalion caught in the midst of the African struggle for independence.

Performances throughout are excellent. Richard Attenborough is tough, crisp and staunch as the sergeant, playing with as much starch as the character implies. Errol John has intense qualities of fanaticism as the lieutenant who seizes the government, and Jack Hawkins, in essentially a cameo spot, plays like the resigned warhorse he is meant to be.

■ **GUNS FOR SAN SEBASTIAN**

1968, 100 MINS, FRANCE/MEXICO/ITALY ◇
Dir Henri Verneuil   Prod Jacques Bar   Scr James R. Webb   Ph Armand Thirard   Ed Francoise Bonnot
Mus Ennio Morricone   Art Dir Robert Clavel
● Anthony Quinn, Anjanette Comer, Charles Bronson, Sam Jaffe, Silvia Pinal, Jaime Fernandez (M-G-M)

Anthony Quinn stars as an outcast, assumed to be a priest, in the Mexico of two centuries ago. The production, a plodding mix of religious–themed action and comedy-romance, has some good direction and battle scenes, but the very poor dubbing (in dramatic sense) is hard going.

Filmed entirely in Mexico, pic is a three-way coproduction of Mexican, French and Italian companies. Based on *A Wall for San Sebastian*, by William Barby Faherty, story concerns Quinn's influence on frightened mountain peasants, by which they become a cohesive town, instead of being terrorized by Charles Bronson, in league with Indian chief Jaime Fernandez.

Anjanette Comer plays a peasant gal, only one in town with slit skirts, by the way.

Sam Jaffe, as a priest who dies early and creates the situation whereby Quinn is assumed to be a cleric, is saddled with dubbed banalities. Of course, part of the fault is in the writing, acting and directing of the dubbing.

■ **GUNS OF DARKNESS**

1962, 102 MINS, UK
Dir Anthony Asquith   Prod Thomas Clyde   Scr John Mortimer   Ph Robert Krasker   Ed Frederick Wilson
Mus Benjamin Frankel   Art Dir John Howell
● Leslie Caron, David Niven, James Robertson Justice, David Opatoshu, Eleanor Summerfield, Ian Hunter (Cavalcade/Associated British)

Director Anthony Asquith is slightly off form with this one. An advocate of anti-violence, he pursues a theme that he has explored before, that violence is sometimes necessary to achieve peace. But the film does not stand up as a psychological study. And as a pure 'escape yarn', its moments of tension are only spasmodic.

John Mortimer's screenplay [from Francis Clifford's novel *Act of Mercy*] is not positive enough to enable Asquith to keep a firm grip on the proceedings. There are times when the film plods as laboriously as do the stars in their escape to the frontier. It opens in Tribulacion, capital of a South American republic, during a revolution. The president is deposed in a swift coup and, wounded, has to take off in a hurry.

David Niven, a rather boorish PRO with a British-owned plantation, elects to smuggle him across the border, for reasons which are not even clear to Niven himself. Tagging along is Niven's wife (Leslie Caron) with whom he is having an emotional upheaval.

Niven's charm seeps through his mask of boorishness but he manages skilfully to keep up an illusion of high voltage danger. David Opatoshu gives an excellent show as the disil-

G

lusioned, yet philosophical president. Caron, however, seems uncomfortable, with her role coming over as curiously colorless.

....

■ GUNS OF NAVARONE, THE

1961, 157 MINS, UK ◇ ⊛ ⊙
Dir J. Lee Thompson   *Prod* Cecil F. Ford   *Scr* Carl Foreman   *Ph* Oswald Morris, John Wilcox   *Ed* Alan Osbiston, Raymond Poulton, John Victor Smith, Oswald Hafenrichter   *Mus* Dimitri Tiomkin   *Art Dir* Geoffrey Drake
● Gregory Peck, David Niven, Anthony Quinn, Stanley Baker, Anthony Quayle, James Darren (Columbia/Open Road)

A real heap of coin ($6 million), labor, sweat, patience, tears, faith and enthusiasm went into the making of *The Guns of Navarone*. It faced the problem of a director-switch in midstream. But with a bunch of weighty stars, terrific special effects and several socko situations, [executive] producer Carl Foreman and director J. Lee Thompson sired a winner.

Story, adapted from Alistair MacLean's novel, is set in 1943. The Axis has virtually over-run Greece and its islands, except for Crete and the tiny island of Kheros. The only chance for the worn-out garrison of 2,000 men is evacuation by sea, through a channel which is impregnably guarded by a couple of huge, radar controlled guns on Navarone. A small bunch of saboteurs is detailed to spike these guns.

The saboteur gang consists of Anthony Quayle, Gregory Peck, David Niven, Stanley Baker, Anthony Quinn and James Darren. They all turn in worthwhile jobs. Of this sextet, Baker, playing a dour, war-sick expert with a knife, and Darren, as a baby-faced killer, get rather less opportunity than the others. Two women have been written into the story, Greek partisans played very well by Irene Papas and Gia Scala.

The cliff-scaling sequence, a scene when the saboteurs are rounded up by the enemy, a wonderfully directed and lensed storm segment and the final boffo climax are just a few of the nail-biting highlights.
□ 1961: Best Special Effects.
□ Nominations: Best Picture, Director, Adapted Screenplay, Editing, Score of a Dramatic Picture, Sound

....

■ GUNS OF THE MAGNIFICENT SEVEN

1969, 95 MINS, US ◇ ⊛
Dir Paul Wendkos   *Prod* Vincent M. Fennelly   *Scr* Herman Hoffman   *Ph* Antonio Macasoli   *Ed* Walter Hannemann   *Mus* Elmer Bernstein   *Art Dir* Jose Maria Tapiador
● George Kennedy, James Whitmore, Monte Markham, Bernie Casey, Joe Don Baker, Fernando Ray (United/Mirisch)

Guns of the Magnificent Seven is a handy follow-up to the 1960 original *Magnificent Seven* and *Return of the Seven*. It rises above a routine story line via rugged treatment and action builds to a blazing gunplay climax.

George Kennedy takes on role played by Yul Brynner in two previous films, the only remaining character of the original seven.

Filmed entirely in Spain, as was *Return*, director Paul Wendkos makes interesting use of backgrounds.

Period is Mexico in the late 1890s, the narrative setting an attempt by Kennedy and his men to rescue a patriot who is attempting to assist helpless and downtrodden peasants.

Cast is well-chosen and Kennedy is a good choice for the Brynner role.

....

■ GURU, THE

1969, 112 MINS, UK ◇
Dir James Ivory   *Prod* Ismail Merchant   *Scr* Ruth Prawer Jhabvala, James Ivory   *Ph* Subrata Mitra   *Ed* Prabhakar

Supare   *Mus* Ustad Vilayat Khan   *Art Dir* Bansi Chandragupta, Didi Contractor
● Michael York, Utpal Dutt, Madhur Jaffrey, Rita Tushingham, Aparna Sen (20th Century-Fox/Arcadia/Merchant-Ivory)

The Guru is a hazy study of how people can transfer their own ideas about the value or qualities of another person and in so doing miss what the person is all about. Script is never realized in concrete dramatic terms.

Michael York is cast as a young Englishman who comes to India to learn the secret of playing the sitar at the house of a master musician, Utpal Dutt. Dutt gives the film's outstanding performance, with just the right amount of annoying egotism and naive pomposity. He doesn't quite understand his guest and tries, without success, to teach him the 'mystic' significance of the complicated instrument and the Indian relationship between student and teacher or 'guru'.

At the same time that York comes into the musical household a wandering 'hippie', played by Rita Tushingham, talks her way into staying and learning from the master.

....

■ GUY NAMED JOE, A

1944, 120 MINS, US ⊛
Dir Victor Fleming   *Prod* Everett Riskin   *Scr* Dalton Trumbo   *Ph* George Folsey, Karl Freund   *Ed* Frederick Brennan   *Mus* Herbert Stothart
● Spencer Tracy, Irene Dunne, Van Johnson, Ward Bond, Lionel Barrymore, Esther Williams (M-G-M)

In taking a fling at the spirit world, Metro doesn't quite succeed in reaching the nebulous but manages to turn out an entertaining and excellently performed picture. Had the fantasy been interpreted wholly in terms of the sharp wit and dry humor which Spencer Tracy, as a ghostly visitor, only occasionally injects, instead of investing it with spiritual counselling, the film [from an original story by David Boehm and Chandler Sprague] might have attained smash proportions.

As it is, there hovers over too many scenes in the cloudy strata a fogginess that isn't made any more acceptable by the final solution. The latter only changes the mood of the film from one of light cockiness to the realm of metaphysics.

Tracy is cast as a squadron commander at an English base who's in a constant jam because of his foolhardy heroics.

Fulfilling a premonition felt by Dunne, he crashes on his last heroic stunt, proceeding to the land where all dead pilots go. There he meets up with The Boss, and is assigned to guide and instruct the new pilots in the earthly world who are making a bid for their wings. It's at this point that the serious overtones of the picture intrude themselves, with the offering of the matter-of-fact solution that 'life must go on for the living' too abruptly thrust into the story's continuity.
□ 1944: Nomination: Best Original Story

....

■ GUYS AND DOLLS

1955, 150 MINS, US ◇ ⊛ ⊙
Dir Joseph L. Mankiewicz   *Prod* Samuel Goldwyn   *Scr* Joseph L. Mankiewicz   *Ph* Harry Stradling   *Ed* Daniel Mandell   *Mus* Frank Loesser   *Art Dir* Oliver Smith, Joseph Wright, Howard Bristol
● Marlon Brando, Jean Simmons, Frank Sinatra, Vivian Blaine, Robert Keith, Stubby Kaye (M-G-M)

Guys and Dolls is a bangup filmusical in the topdrawer Goldwyn manner, including a resurrection of the Goldwyn Girls.

The casting is good all the way. Much interest will focus, of course, around Marlon Brando in the Robert Alda stage original and Jean Simmons as the Salvation Army sergeant (created by Isabel Bigley), and they deport themselves in inspired manner. They make believable the offbeat romance between

the gambler and the spirited servant of the gospel.

Vivian Blaine is capital in her original stage role. Frank Sinatra is an effective vis-a-vis in the Sam Levene original of Nathan Detroit and among the four they handle the burden of the score.

The action shifts from the Times Square street scenes to the Havana idyll, where Brando had taken the mission doll ('on a bet').
□ 1955: Nominations: Best Color Cinematography, Color Costume Design, Color Art Direction, Scoring of a Musical Picture

....

■ GYPSY

1962, 149 MINS, US ◇ ⊛ ⊙
Dir Mervyn LeRoy   *Prod* Mervyn LeRoy   *Scr* Leonard Spigelgass   *Ph* Harry Stradling Sr   *Ed* Philip W. Anderson   *Mus* Frank Perkins (sup.)   *Art Dir* John Beckman
● Rosalind Russell, Natalie Wood, Karl Malden, Paul Wallace, Ann Jilliann, Harvey Korman (Warner)

There is a wonderfully funny sequence involving three nails-hard strippers which comes when *Gypsy* has been unreeling about an hour. The sequence is thoroughly welcome and almost desperately needed to counteract a certain Jane One-Note implicit in the tale of a stage mother whose egotism become something of a bore despite the canny skills of director-producer Mervyn LeRoy to contrive it otherwise.

Rosalind Russell's performance as the smalltime brood-hen deserves commendation. It is cleverly managed all the way, with much help from the camera angles of Harry Stradling Sr.

Russell is less surprising than Karl Malden, as the mother's incredibly loyal lover who finally screams when he perceives that she cares for nobody and nothing except her own ego compulsions.

About Natalie Wood: it is not easy to credit her as a stripper but it is interesting to watch her, under LeRoy's guidance, go through the motions in a burlesque world that is prettied up in soft-focus and a kind of phony innocence. Any resemblance of the art of strip, and its setting, to reality is, in this film, purely fleeting.

There are some beguiling satirical touches in the re-creation of the hokey vaudeville routines starring 'Baby June' Havoc, well impersonated by Ann Jilliann, whose flight from the mother turns the latter's attention upon the previously neglected sister, Louise, the Gypsy Rose of later show biz. The film, of course, is based upon the autobiography of Gypsy Rose Lee and the [1959] musical comedy in which Ethel Merman starred.

More chronicle than musical, there are advantages still in some of the music (Jule Styne) and lyrics (Stephen Sondheim) and the choreography (Robert Tucker).
□ 1962: Nominations: Best Color Cinematography, Color Costume Design, Adpted Music Score

....

■ GYPSY GIRL

See: Sky West and Crooked

....

■ GYPSY MOTHS, THE

1969, 106 MINS, US ◇ ⊛
Dir John Frankenheimer   *Prod* Hal Landers, Bobby Roberts   *Scr* William Hanley   *Ph* Philip Lathrop   *Ed* Henry Berman   *Mus* Elmer Bernstein   *Art Dir* George W. Davis, Cary Odell
● Burt Lancaster, Deborah Kerr, Gene Hackman, Scott Wilson, Sheree North, Bonnie Bedelia (M-G-M)

The Gypsy Moths is the story of three barnstorming skydivers and subsequent events when they arrive in a small Kansas town to stage their exhibition. Pairing Burt Lancaster and Deborah Kerr, stars sometimes are lost in a narrative [from a novel by James Drought] that strives to be a tale of smouldering inner conflicts and pent-up emotions.

At best, aside from exciting sky-diving episodes, picture is a lack-lustre affair insofar as the character relationships are concerned. The stars do not appear particularly happy with their roles. Lancaster seldom speaking, Kerr not particularly well cast.

Lancaster delivers well enough considering what the script requires of him, and Kerr is mostly grim. Hackman and Wilson are forceful, both giving excellent accounts of themselves.

H*h*

■ HAIL THE CONQUERING HERO

1944, 101 MINS, US ▼

Dir Preston Sturges   *Prod* [uncredited]   *Scr* Preston Sturges   *Ph* John F. Seitz   *Ed* Stuart Gilmore   *Mus* Werner Heymann   *Art Dir* Hans Dreier, Haldane Douglas
● Eddie Bracken, Ella Raines, William Demarest, Bill Edwards, Raymond Walburn, Freddie Steele (Paramount)

The deft hand of Preston Sturges molded this film, further proof that he is one of the industry's best writer-directors. The numerous situations that lend themselves readily to comedy lines and business are taken advantage of by a cast that sparkles because of the swift pace they are put through.

Yarn finds Eddie Bracken, medically discharged from the Marines after only one month of service because of hay fever, befriended by six real Guadalcanal heroes. During the course of this friendship, Bracken is clothed in his old marine uniform, bodily taken back to his old home town, where he is welcomed as a hero.

Proof that a capable director can take an actor who is willing to listen and get a better-than-good performance out of him or her is amply displayed here. Sturges has a large cast of veterans supporting Bracken, and a former boxing champion, Freddie Steele, as Bugsy, one of the six marines. The vets all do a good job, but Steele's work is standout.
□ 1944: Nomination: Best Original Screenplay

■ HAIR

1979, 118 MINS, US ◇ ▼ ⊙

Dir Milos Forman   *Prod* Lester Persky, Michael Butler   *Scr* Michael Weller   *Ph* Miroslav Ondricek   *Ed* Lynzee Klingman   *Mus* Galt MacDermot   *Art Dir* Stuart Wurtzel
● John Savage, Treat Willilams, Beverly D'Angelo, Nicholas Ray, Annie Golden, Dorsey Wright (United Artists)

The storyline imposed on the original musical's book has large expository gaps. These are accentuated by director Milos Forman's determination to have free-form musical numbers evolve out of the tale of a draftee adopted by a bunch of New York hippies, who tune him into their uninhibited lifestyles.

John Savage plays the inductee, fascinated by the group he stumbles upon at a Central Park be-in, composed of Treat Williams, Annie Golden, Dorsey Wright and Don Dacus. They get him stoned, urge him on in his quest for debutante Beverly D'Angelo, and pursue him to his basic training camp in Nevada and a bittersweet finale.

The spirit and elan that captivated the Vietnam protest era are long gone, and what Forman tries to make up with splash and verve fails to evoke potent nostalgia.

■ HAIRSPRAY

1988, 90 MINS, US ◇ ▼ ⊙

Dir John Waters   *Prod* Rachal Talalay, Stanley F. Buchthal, John Waters   *Scr* John Waters   *Ph* David Insley   *Ed* Janice Hampton   *Mus* Bonnie Greenberg   *Art Dir* Vincent Peranio
● Sonny Bono, Ruth Brown, Divine, Colleen Fitzpatrick, Michael St Gerard, Debbie Harry (Buchthal/New Line Cinema)

John Waters' appreciation for the tacky side of life is in full flower in *Hairspray*, a slight but often highly amusing diversion about integration, big girls' fashions and music-mad teens in 1962 Baltimore.

Ricki Lake, chubette daughter of Divine and Jerry Stiller, overcomes all to become queen of an afternoon teenage dance show, much to the consternation of stuck-up blond Colleen Fitzpatrick, whose parents are Debbie Harry and Sonny Bono.

Divine spits out some choice bon mots while denigrating her daughter's pastime, but finally rejoicing in her success, takes Lake off for a pricelessly funny visit to Hefty Hideaway, where full-figure girls can shop to their hearts' content.

Divine, so big he wears a tent-like garment big enough for three ordinary mortals to sleep in, is in otherwise fine form in a dual role. Harry has little to do but act bitchy and sport increasingly towering wigs, while Pia Zadora is virtually unrecognizable as a beatnik chick. All the kids in the predominantly teenage cast are tirelessly enthusiastic.

■ HALF A SIXPENCE

1967, 148 MINS, UK ◇ ▼

Dir George Sidney   *Prod* Charles H. Schneer, George Sidney   *Scr* Beverley Cross   *Ph* Geoffrey Unsworth   *Ed* Bill Lewthwaite, Frank Santillo   *Mus* David Heneker   *Art Dir* Ted Haworth
● Tommy Steele, Julia Foster, Cyril Ritchard, Grover Dale, Elaine Taylor, Hilton Edwards (Paramount)

As with all good musicals, the story [from the stage musical adapted from H.G. Wells' novel *Kipps*] has a simple moral – that money can be a troublesome thing – and it is told in a straightforward narrative, without too much complication of character.

Thus Kipps is projected as a likable lad, temporarily aberrated by his coming into a fortune, and returning to the true common virtues when he loses it.

The cohesive force is certainly that of Tommy Steele, who takes hold of his part like a terrier and never lets go. His assurance is overwhelming, and he leads the terping with splendid vigor and elan.

Of course, the haunting title song and the ebullient 'Flash, Bang, Wallop!' remain the showstoppers, and David Heneker's score is a little short of socko tunes elsewhere.

■ HALF MOON STREET

1987, 90 MINS, UK/ US ◇ ▼ ⊙

Dir Bob Swaim   *Prod* Geoffrey Reeve   *Scr* Bob Swaim, Edward Behr   *Ph* Peter Hannan   *Ed* Richard Marden   *Mus* Richard Harvey   *Art Dir* Anthony Curtis
● Sigourney Weaver, Michael Caine, Patrick Kavanagh, Keith Buckley, Nadim Sawalha, Angus MacInnes (RKO/Pressman/Showtime – Movie Channel)

Half Moon Street is a half-baked excuse for a film that is redeemed not a whit by having Sigourney Weaver and Michael Caine in the starring roles. Script, based on Paul Theroux' thriller *Dr Slaughter*, has been rendered nonsensical and incoherent by screenwriters.

Weaver plays Dr Slaughter, a scholar at the Middle East Institute in London who turns to working as an escort to supplement her paltry income. She manages to avoid any emotional attachments with her clients until she arrives one rainy night to be the paid guest of Lord Bulbeck, played competently if uninvolvingly by Caine.

Caine is somehow mixed up with Arabs in a convoluted scheme and somehow Weaver becomes inextricably and unwittingly wound up in his dealings.

■ HALLELUJAH

1929, 109 MINS, US

Dir King Vidor   *Scr* Wanda Tuchock, Ransom Rideout   *Ph* Gordon Avil   *Ed* Hugh Wynn, Anson Stevenson   *Art Dir* Cedric Gibbons
● Daniel L. Haynes, Nina Mae McKinney, William Fountaine, Harry Gray, Fannie Belle DeKnight, Victoria Spivey (M-G-M)

In his herculean attempt to take comedy, romance and tragedy and blend them into a big, gripping, Negro talker, King Vidor has turned out an unusual picture from a theme that is almost as ancient as the sun. Vidor's strict adherence to realism is so effective at times it is stark and uncanny.

The story is a plain one, the characters not too many and no fancy long-drawn-out monickers and thus the average screen fan can follow its theme without the slightest difficulty. This is all a big feather in Vidor's hat.

Nina Mae McKinney as the dynamic, vivacious girl of the colored underworld, who lives by her wits and enmeshes the males by her personality, sex appeal and dancing feet, never had a day's work before a camera.

Daniel L. Haynes as Zeke, the principal male, is the big, rough, lazylike colored boy, happiest when he sings and who loves his women.

Victoria Spivey is the blues singer who does a pretty naturalistic bit of acting as the girl who loves and waits. William Fountaine becomes a dominant figure as the heavy, and acquits himself creditably. Fannie Belle DeKnight is the mother of the film, and what a mammy!

A characteristic figure is Harry Gray as the white bewhiskered parson and daddy of the Johnson family.

□ 1929/30: Nomination: Best Director

. . . .

■ HALLELUJAH, I'M A BUM!
(UK: Hallelujah, I'm a Tramp!)

1933, 83 MINS, US ℗
Dir Lewis Milestone   *Prod* Joseph M. Schenck   *Scr* S. N. Behrman, Ben Hecht   *Ph* Lucien Andriot   *Mus* Alfred Newman (dir.)   *Art Dir* Richard Day
● Al Jolson, Madge Evans, Frank Morgan, Harry Langdon, Chester Conklin (United Artists)

Almost Barrie-ish in its whimsy, the ethereal quality of the Ben Hecht-S. N. Behrman script foundation is its primary deficiency. Lorenz Hart, while solely credited for the lyrics to Richard Rodgers' music, probably merits as much authorship credit because his lyrical dialog constitutes the main burden of the proceedings.

The whole thing is an unconvincing mixture of the fictional and factional. Ultra-modern realism with the playboy mayor of the city of New York and his weakness for the Central Park Casino and a pretty femme in particular (Madge Evans) is blended with such unconvincing detail as non-existing Central Park's hobos of which Al Jolson is the unofficial mayor.

The rollicking fun of an uncertain but not too unsteady story structure collapses utterly when Evans, a victim of aphasia or amnesia, later figures as the romance interest opposite Jolson, until recovering her senses for the finale with the mayor (Frank Morgan).

The 'rhythmic dialog' and the Lewis Milestonian method of wedding the tempo'd music to the action has its moments. The laity will doubtlessly compare this to the Ernst Lubitsch technique in *Trouble in Paradise*.

This must have been one of the toughest pictures to shoot and undoubtedly the most trying for the rest of the cast who had to talk in rhyme and rhythm rather than their accustomed dramatic prose.

Jolson's selling of the title song and 'You Are Too Beautiful', the former reprised more often, of course leaves little wanting. 'Bum' is a pip of a number with its odd-rhythmed style and tempo. 'I'll Do It Again' and 'What Do You Want with Money' are other songs.

. . . .

■ HALLELUJAH, I'M A TRAMP!
See: Hallelujah, I'm a Bum!

. . . .

■ HALLELUJAH THE HILLS

1963, 88 MINS, US
Dir Adolfas Mekas   *Prod* David C. Stone   *Scr* Adolfas Mekas   *Ph* Ed Emshviller   *Ed* Adolfas Mekas
Mus Meyer Kupferman
● Peter H. Beard, Martin Greenbaum, Sheila Finn, Peggy Steffans (Vermont)

Formerly this offbeat NY filmmaking group mainly made dramas. But this zesty unusual romp twits its subject with knowing insight and also packs in some inside film buff gags and allusions.

There is not much of a story. It is mainly a joyous rush of images by a new director who has assimilated his classics and regular run of films. Two clean-cut, adventurous young American stalwarts vie for the hand of a beauteous young girl only to have her snapped up by a bearded character. Small town life and the seasons pass in review as the two men camp out and take their turns at wooing the girl or trying to cope with outdoor life in the snow and sun.

Writer-director-editor Adolfas Mekas displays a flair for visual revelation, gags and shenanigans that manage to keep this stimulating throughout. The intimations of noted pix culminates with a bow to D. W. Griffith in showing the great ice flow rescue of Lillian Gish by Richard Barthlemess in *Way Down East*.

Mekas assimilates rather than imitates. The actors are all fresh, and cavort with grace and a lack of self-consciousness. Camerawork is clear with editing sharp and the music a counterpoint help. There are glimpses and incisive satiric shafts against war, courting habits, youthful shyness and self absorption in this madcap, bright pic.

. . . .

■ HALLELUJAH TRAIL, THE

1965, 152 MINS, US ◇ ℗ ⊙
Dir John Sturges   *Prod* John Sturges   *Scr* John Gay   *Ph* Robert Surtees   *Ed* Ferris Webster   *Mus* Elmer Bernstein   *Art Dir* Cary Odell
● Burt Lancaster, Lee Remick, Jim Hutton, Pamela Tiffin, Donald Pleasance, Brian Keith (United Artists)

It all begins with the burgeoning city of Denver facing the worst threat of its existence – becoming bone dry in 10 days in the approaching winter of 1867. This awesome situation paves the way for one of the nuttiest cinematic mishmashes you ever saw, in which thirsty miners, a worried US Cavalry, a band of whiskey-mad Sioux, a crusading temperance group and a train of 40 wagons carrying 600 barrels of hard likker become so thoroughly involved that even the off-screen narrator has a hard time trying to keep track of them and their proper logistics.

Producer-director John Sturges has pulled every plug in spoofing practically every western situation known to the scripter, and the whole is beautifully packaged. Screenplay, from Bill Gulick's novel, approaches the situations straight.

The cavalry, coloneled by Burt Lancaster, is constantly threatened with breaching the articles of war and the Constitution itself by the demands of temperance leader Lee Remick. Sioux, leaving their reservation when they get wind of the approaching whiskey, can't be attacked by the cavalry because they carry certain signed government papers.

Performances, like situations, are played straight, and therein lies their beauty. Lancaster does a bangup job as the harassed cavalry colonel plagued with having to offer safe conduct to the whiskey train and to the temperance ladies.

One of the standouts in pic is Martin Landau, as Chief Walks-Stooped-Over, as deadpan as any Injun ever lived but socking over his comedy scenes mostly with his eyes.

■ HALLOWEEN

1978, 93 MINS, US ◇ ℗ ⊙
Dir John Carpenter   *Prod* Debra Hill   *Scr* John Carpenter, Debra Hill   *Ph* Dean Cundey   *Ed* Tomy Wallace, Charles Burnstein   *Mus* John Carpenter   *Art Dir* Tommy Wallace
● Donald Pleasence, Jamie Lee Curtis, Nancy Loomis, P.J. Soles, Charles Cyphers, Kyle Richards (Falcon)

After a promising opening, *Halloween* becomes just another maniac-on-the-loose suspenser. However, despite the prosaic plot, director John Carpenter has timed the film's gore so that the 93-minute item is packed with enough thrills.

The picture opens 15 years earlier, on Halloween night in a small midwestern town. A young boy spies his sister necking with her boyfriend. As they mount the steps for her bedroom he slips on his Halloween mask, pulls out a butcher knife and does some cutting.

For the rest of the thriller the Hitchcockian influence remains, but the plot ambles along to a predictable conclusion. It is now the present, also Halloween. Donald Pleasence, a psychiatrist who has been caring for the killer during the years, is on his way to the state hospital to make sure that the maniac is never freed.

Of course, the maniac escapes, returns to the scene of the original crime and searches for suitable victims, in this case a trio of babysitting friends.

. . . .

■ HALLOWEEN II

1981, 92 MINS, US ◇ ℗ ⊙
Dir Rick Rosenthal   *Prod* Debra Hill, John Carpenter   *Scr* John Carpenter, Debra Hill   *Ph* Dean Cundy   *Ed* Mark Goldblatt   *Mus* John Carpenter, Alan Howarth   *Art Dir* J. Michael Riva
● Jamie Lee Curtis, Donald Pleasence, Charles Cyphers, Dick Warlock, Lance Guest, Jeffrey Kramer (De Laurentiis)

This uninspired version amounts to lukewarm sloppy seconds in comparison to the original film that made director John Carpenter a hot property.

There are incredibly almost never any really terrific scares in 92 minutes – just multiple shots of violence and gore that are more gruesome than anything else.

Script commences with the finale from the original where concerned doctor Donald Pleasence shoots Jamie Lee Curtis' demented predator six times only to have him walk away and continue his killing spree. Young Curtis is rushed to the hospital for care where a whole set of young, nubile hospital staffers are primed as the next victims.

Meanwhile the zombie-like masked killer makes his way through the town, wandering in and out of houses slashing unsuspecting residents. So many people wander through the proceedings that it becomes difficult to care who is getting sliced or why.

. . . .

■ HALLOWEEN III SEASON OF THE WITCH

1982, 96 MINS, US ◇ ℗ ⊙
Dir Tommy Lee Wallace   *Prod* John Carpenter, Debra Hill   *Scr* Tommy Lee Wallace, [Nigel Kneale]   *Ph* Dean Cundey   *Ed* Millie Moore   *Mus* John Carpenter, Alan Howarth   *Art Dir* Peter Jamison
● Tom Atkins, Stacey Nelkin, Dan O'Herlihy, Ralph Strait, Michael Currie, Jadeen Barbor (De Laurentiis)

There's not much to say about *Halloween III* that hasn't already been said about either of the other two *Halloween* pics or a slew of imitators.

Interesting to note here is producer Debra Hill's earlier claim that this film would steer clear of gore and blood and instead go for the science fiction paranoia genre of *Invasion of the Body Snatchers*. Apparently, yanking someone's head off their shoulders, shoving fingers down a man's eyeballs or inserting a power drill in a woman's head don't qualify as particularly disgusting.

There is the tired old cliche of a crazed toy manufacturer (in this case he makes Halloween masks), the fearless couple out to figure what's 'really' going on, and plot holes big enough to shoot another film through. On the latter note, Nigel Kneale, credited screenwriter all through production, somehow managed to get his name removed from the credits.

. . . .

■ HALLOWEEN 4 THE RETURN OF MICHAEL MYERS

1988, 88 MINS, US ◇ ⍟

Dir Dwight H. Little *Prod* Paul Freeman *Scr* Alan B. McElroy *Ph* Peter Lyons Collister *Ed* Curtiss Clayton *Mus* Alan Howarth *Art Dir* Roger S. Crandall
● Donald Pleasence, Ellie Cornell, Danielle Harris, George P. Wilbur, Michael Pataki (Trancas)

Fourth entry in the *Halloween* horror series is a no-frills, workmanlike picture [story by Dhani Lipsius, Larry Rattner, Benjamin Ruffner and Alan B. McElroy].

Designed as a direct sequel to John Carpenter's 1978 hit, with no reference to the events chronicled in parts 2 and 3, pic resurrects monster Michael Myers (previously referred to mainly as The Shape), who escapes from a hospital to return home and wreak havoc, with the vague notion of getting to his niece (Danielle Harris).

His face scarred from an earliier altercation with the monster, Donald Pleasence reprises his role as Dr Loomis, now hell-bent on destroying the obviously unkillable Myers.

. . . .

■ HALLOWEEN 5

1989, 96 MINS, US ◇ ⍟ ⊙

Dir Dominique Othenin-Girard *Prod* Ramsey Thomas *Scr* Michael Jacobs, Dominique Othenin-Girard, Shem Bitterman *Ph* Robert Draper *Ed* Jerry Brady *Mus* Alan Howarth *Art Dir* Steven Lee, Chava Danielson
● Donald Pleasence, Dannielle Harris, Wendy Kaplan, Ellie Cornell, Donald L. Shanks, Jeffrey Landman (Magnum)

In its only novel twist, *Halloween 5* takes the liberty of setting up its sequel (albeit clumsily) at the film's end rather than 'killing' that pesky Michael Myers and then figuring out how to revive him after counting b.o. receipts. Otherwise, this is pretty stupid and boring fare.

The thread of a plot has the killer empathetically linked to his nine-year-old niece Jamie (Danielle Harris), who goes into a sort of epileptic seizure when she senses he's about to kill again. Meanwhile, the determine Dr Loomis (Donald Pleasence, getting a bit long in the tooth for this sort of duty) also seems to sense that Michael Myers is still alive and keeps badgering the little girl to help him end his scourge.

Director Dominique Othenin-Girard doesn't bring much to the action, with the exception of a protracted scene in which one of the dimwits in distress (Wendy Kaplan) harangues the killer in a car, thinking it's her boyfriend in Halloween garb.

Kaplan proves vivacious and fetching as the perky Tina even if the character is flaky. Harris is bright-eyed as the disturbingly beset Jamie.

. . . .

■ HALLS OF MONTEZUMA

1950, 113 MINS, US ◇ ⍟

Dir Lewis Milestone *Prod* Robert Bassler *Scr* Michael Blankfort *Ph* Winton C. Hoch *Ed* William Reynolds *Mus* Sol Kaplan
● Richard Widmark, Jack Palance, Robert Wagner, Karl Malden, Richard Hylton, Richard Boone (20th Century-Fox)

Halls of Montezuma is an account of Marine heroism during the fierce South Pacific fighting of the Second World War.

Rather than a presentation of mass battle, film deals intimately with a small group of Marines under the command of Richard Widmark and how it fulfills a mission to take Jap prisoners for questioning. Footage is long but there is no feeling of great length.

Opening shots feature flashbacks to acquaint the audience with the Marines as civilians and show their strengths and weaknesses.

Widmark is exceptionally good as an officer who masks his fear and encourages his men. Reginald Gardiner adds lightness as a Marine sergeant who scoffs at regulations. Karl Malden stands out as the pharmacist's mate.

. . . .

■ HAMBURGER HILL

1987, 110 MINS, US ◇ ⍟ ⊙

Dir John Irvin *Prod* Marcia Nasatir, Jim Carabatsos, Larry De Waay *Scr* Jim Carabatsos *Ph* Peter MacDonald *Ed* Peter Tanner *Mus* Philip Glass *Art Dir* Austen Spriggs
● Anthony Barrile, Michael Patrick Boatman, Don Cheadle, Michael Dolan, Don James, Dylan McDermott (RKO/Nasatir-Carabatsos/Interaccess)

Well-produced and directd with an eye to documentary-like realism and authenticity, pic centers upon a military undertaking of familiar futility during the Vietnam War. It follows a squad of 14 recruits from initial R&R through 10 days' worth of hell, as the men make 11 agonizing assaults on a heavily fortified hill.

First 40 minutes attempt to show the developing relationships among the guys, and screenwriter-coproducer Jim Carabatsos has been particularly attentive to delineating the tensions between the blacks and whites in the group.

More than an hour is devoted to the protected effort to scale the indistinguished piece of Vietnamese real estate of the title. As physically impressive as some of it is, the action also proves dispiriting and depressing, as the soldiers slide helplessly down the muddy slopes in the rain and are inevitably picked off by enemy gunfire.

Director John Irvin, who shot a documentary in Vietnam in 1969, the year the action takes place, makes fine use of the Philippines locations and the verisimilitude supplied by the production team.

. . . .

■ HAMLET

1948, 155 MINS, UK ⍟ ⊙

Dir Laurence Olivier *Prod* Laurence Olivier *Scr* William Shakespeare *Ph* Desmond Dickinson *Ed* Helga Cranston *Mus* William Walton *Art Dir* Roger Furse
● Laurence Olivier, Eileen Herlie, Basil Sydney, Jean Simmons, Norman Wooland, Felix Aylmer (Rank/Two Cities)

This is picture-making at its best. At a cost of $2 million it seems incredibly cheap compared with some of the ephemeral trash that is turned out.

Star-producer-director Laurence Olivier was the driving force behind the whole venture. Minor characters and a good deal of verse have been thrown overboard, and a four-and-a-quarter hour play becomes a two-and-a-half hour film.

Pundits may argue that Rosencrantz, Guildenstern and Fortinbras shouldn't have been sacrificed, and that many familiar gems are missing. They will argue about the bewildering crossing and intercrossing of motives. Scholars may complain that this isn't Hamlet as Shakespeare created him, but one that Olivier has made in his own image.

In his interpretation of Hamlet, Olivier thinks of him as nearly a great man, damned,

as most people are, by lack of resolution. He announces it in a spoken foreword as 'the tragedy of a man who couldn't make up his mind'.

Special praise is due Eileen Herlie for her playing of the queen. She has made the character really live. Her love for her son, the consciousness of evil-doing, her grief and agony, her death – made by Olivier to appear as sacrificing herself for Hamlet – make her a very memorable, pitiful figure. Jean Simmons as Ophelia brings to the role a sensitive, impressionable innocence, perhaps too childlike.

Basil Sydney repeats his stage success as the king, of whom ambition and lust have taken possession, and rises to his greatest height in his soliloquy trying to pray and seeing himself accursed like Cain.

☐ 1948: Best Picture, Actor (Laurence Olivier), B&W Art Direction, B&W Costume Design
☐ Nominations: Best Director, Supp. Actress (Jean Simmons), Scoring of a Dramatic Picture

. . . .

■ HAMLET

1990, 135 MINS, US ◇ ⍟ ⊙

Dir Franco Zeffirelli *Prod* Dyson Lovell *Scr* Christopher De Vore, Franco Zeffirelli *Ph* David Watkin *Ed* Richard Marden *Mus* Ennio Morricone *Art Dir* Dante Ferretti
● Mel Gibson, Glenn Close, Alan Bates, Paul Scofield, Ian Holm, Helena Bonham Carter (Warner/Nelson)

Mel Gibson's best moments come in the highly physical duelling scene that climaxes the Shakespeare play. Otherwise, Mel's Hamlet is blond and Franco Zeffirelli's *Hamlet* is bland.

By slicing the text virtually in half, and casting a matinee idol in the lead, the director clearly hoped to engage the masses. Unfortunately, this Hamlet seems no more modern or pertinent to contemporary concerns than any other on stage, screen or tube in recent decades. Nor does it possess the rugged freshness of Kenneth Branagh's *Henry V*.

Familiar story unfolds in and around a formidable fortress that is actually a combination of three ancient structures in the British Isles. Deeply aggrieved by the death of his father, Hamlet is commanded by his father to avenge his murder at the hands of his brother Claudius, who has since become king and married Hamlet's mother, Gertrude.

Performances all fall in a middle range between the competent and the lackluster. Gibson gets the dialog and soliloquies out decently, but rolls and bugs his eyes a lot. Best is probably Paul Scofield as the ghost, although Zeffirelli irritatingly cuts or pulls away from him midstream. Alan Bates is a solid Claudius. Glenn Close brings a juicy vigor to Gertrude.

☐ 1990: Nominations: Best Art Direction, Costume Design

. . . .

■ HAMMERSMITH IS OUT

1972, 108 MINS, US ◇ ⍟

Dir Peter Ustinov *Prod* Alex Lucas *Scr* Stanford Whitmore *Ph* Richard H. Kline *Ed* David Blewitt *Mus* Dominic Frontiere *Art Dir* Robert Benton
● Elizabeth Taylor, Richard Burton, Peter Ustinov, Beau Bridges, Leon Ames, George Raft (Crean)

What is, apparently, an exercise in spoofery on the part of Elizabeth Taylor, Richard Burton and the even more energetic Peter Ustinov, starts as a variation on the Faust legend but almost immediately turns into a belabored antic.

The somewhat sketchy screenplay is no more than a line on which the three principals hang their rarely inspired improvisations.

Burton, as the lunatic Hammersmith who flees the asylum with the connivance of male nurse Beau Bridges by promising him un-worldly riches, goes through the film with a single bored expression. Bridges is sleazy and repulsive and well deserving of his fate. Ustinov, as the asylum keeper, committed to recapturing Hammersmith, would be funnier if his lines, spoken with an unintelligible 'mad scientist' accent could be understood.

● ●

■ HAMMETT

1982, 94 MINS, US ◇ ⑩
Dir Wim Wenders *Prod* Fred Roos, Ronald Colby, Don Guest *Scr* Ross Thomas, Dennis O'Flaherty *Ph* Philip Lathrop, Joseph Biroc *Ed* Barry Malkin, Marc Laub, Robert Q. Lovett, Randy Roberts *Mus* John Barry *Art Dir* Dean Tavoularis, Eugene Lee
● Frederic Forrest, Peter Boyle, Marilu Henner, Roy Kinnear, Sylvia Sidney, Lydia Lei (Zoetrope)

Wim Wenders' problems with this, his first Hollywood film, are many and well known. Reportedly hired by producer Francis Coppola on the strength of his complicated murder opus, *The American Friend* [1977], Wenders' *Hammett* was early on dubbed a rough diamond.

Now, overpolished by too many script rewrites [credited adaptation by Thomas Pope, based on the book by Joe Gores], per-haps emasculated by massive footage scraps and belated re-shoots, project (all shot on in-teriors) emerges a rather suffocating film taking place in a rickety 'Chinatown'.

But *Chinatown* it is not. Film is a sort of homage to Dashiel Hammett. Based on a fic-tion by Joe Gores, it has Hammett far re-moved from his old private eye days and suffering from TB, eking out a precarious liv-ing with short stories penned for pulp detec-tive magazines.

Frederic Forrest looks like Hammett, talks like Humphrey Bogart and is acceptable. His old boss from the Pinkerton Private Eye Co is played with force by Peter Boyle.

A Chinese prostitute has disappeared and must be found for she might be dangerous to top monied interests. After several chases, killings and muggings, it emerges that the Chinese girl has some incriminating porn pic-tures of all the men who really run the town.

● ●

■ HAND, THE

1981, 104 MINS, US ◇ ⑩
Dir Oliver Stone *Prod* Edward R. Pressman *Scr* Oliver Stone *Ph* King Baggott *Ed* Richard Marks *Mus* James Horner *Art Dir* J. Michael Riva
● Michael Caine, Andrea Marcovicci, Viveca Lindfors, Bruce McGill, Mara Hobel, Annie McEnroe (Orion)

Director-scripter Oliver Stone takes on a premise – that of an autonomous appendage wreaking havoc on anyone crossing the hu-man it was previously attached to – that has in some form been effectively executed in many past pix.

Special visual effects consultant Carlo Rambaldi, who performed wonders on '*Alien*,' should probably share some of the blame for the ineffectiveness of the aforementioned vil-lain.

There is little relief to be found from the relationships in the script [from the book *The Lizard's Tail*]. Cartoonist Michael Caine evokes some sympathy after he loses his hand and particularly in scenes with daughter Mara Hobel, he spends most of his time sweating and grimacing into the camera lens. It's not a pretty sight.

James Horner has concocted an appropri-ately haunting score throughout.

● ●

■ HANDFUL OF DUST, A

1988, 118 MINS, UK ◇ ⑩
Dir Charles Sturridge *Prod* Derek Granger *Scr* Tim Sullivan, Derek Granger, Charles Sturridge *Ph* Peter Hannan *Ed* Peter Coulson *Mus* George Fenton *Art Dir* Eileen Diss
● James Wilby, Kristin Scott Thomas, Rupert Graves, Anjelica Huston, Alec Guinness, Judi Dench (LWT/Stagescreen)

A Handful of Dust is classy stuff based on an Evelyn Waugh novel, with a high production standard but an essentially empty story.

Kristin Scott Thomas as a lovely but fickle aristocrat is excellent, with an appealing fey manner. The virtual cameo appearances of Alec Guinness, Anjelica Huston and Judi Dench go some way to giving *Dust* a pedigree it might otherwise not be able to claim.

Set in Britain of the 1930s, at the beautiful country house Hetton Abbey, James Wilby and Scott Thomas and their young son seem content until the weekend visit of idle so-cialite Rupert Graves.

Scott Thomas slips into an affair with the penniless Graves while Wilby happily wan-ders his estate unaware he is being cuck-olded. When their son is killed in a freak riding accident, Scott Thomas tells her hus-band she wants a divorce.

When Wilby finds the divorce settlement would mean selling Hetton he promptly sets sail for South America in search of a lost Amazonian city with an eccentric explorer.

Technically, *A Handful of Dust* cannot be faulted. Where the film disappoints is the story, which though it ably highlights the vac-uous attitudes of the English upper classes, is essentially slight.

□ 1988: Nomination: Best Costume Design

● ●

■ HANDGUN

(US: Deep in the Heart)

1983, 101 MINS, UK ◇ ⑩
Dir Tony Garnett *Prod* Tony Garnett *Scr* Tony Garnett *Ph* Charles Stewart *Ed* William Shapter *Mus* Mike Post *Art Dir* Lilly Kilvert
● Karen Young, Clayton Day, Suzie Humphreys, Helena Humann, Ben Jones (Kestrel)

Handgun takes a subject which is the stuff of exploitation and steers it towards social com-mentary. The result is an intelligent analysis of the political and sexual values of male soci-ety in Texas.

Pic is cast in three chapters that follow the maturing of a pretty young girl who goes to the midwest to teach history after a protected Catholic upbringing in Boston. She's just too soft to counter the approaches of a macho at-torney who's obsessed with guns and hunting. It's only when he decides to have his own way with her that she realizes what she's up against.

Karen Young is sharp in her depiction of a nervy girl whose eyes are slowly opened. And Clayton Day plays all the subtleties of a de-cent chap who, nevertheless, has swallowed whole a value system that debases women and seeks to protect its integrity through vio-lent confrontation.

● ●

■ HANDMAID'S TALE, THE

1990, 109 MINS, US/W. GERMANY ◇ ⑩ ⊙
Dir Volker Schlondorff *Prod* Daniel Wilson *Scr* Harold Pinter *Ph* Igor Luther *Ed* David Ray *Mus* Ryuichi Sakamoto *Art Dir* Tom Walsh
● Natasha Richardson, Robert Duvall, Faye Dunaway, Aidan Quinn, Elizabeth McGovern, Victoria Tennant (Cinecom/Bioskop)

The Handmaid's Tale is a provocative protrait of a future totalitarian theocracy where women have lost all human rights. The adap-tation of Margaret Atwood's bestseller be-longs to that rare category of science fiction film dealing with dystopias.

Even rarer, *Handmaid's Tale* is sci-fi from a woman's point-of-view. Following a military coup, this future society called Gilead oper-ates under martial law in a perpetual state of warfare (a la *1984*), with Old Testament reli-gion the rule. The so-called sins of late 20th-century society, ranging from pollution to such activities as birth control and abortion are blamed by the authorities as causing God's plague of infertility, requiring drastic measures to preserve the race.

Natasha Richardson protrays a young mother who's rounded up by the authorities to serve as a breeder, or handmaid, assigned to the barren family of state security chief Robert Duvall and his wife Faye Dunaway. Her travails unfold in Harold Pinter's unchar-acteristically staight-forward screenplay rather mechanically.

Though helmer Volker Schlondorff suc-ceeds in painting the bleakness of this extrap-olated future, he fails to create a strong and persistent connection with the heroine's plight.

● ●

■ HANDS OF THE RIPPER

1971, 85 MINS, UK ◇ ⑩
Dir Peter Sasdy *Prod* Aida Young *Scr* L.W. Davidson *Ph* Kenneth Talbot *Ed* Christopher Barnes *Mus* Christopher Gunning *Art Dir* Roy Stannard
● Eric Porter, Angharad Rees, Jane Merrow, Keith Bell, Derek Godfrey, Dora Bryan (Hammer)

Hammer breaks away from its vampires and monster formula and gives a highly intriguing twist [from a story by Edward Spencer Shaw] to the Jack the Ripper murders which shook London back in the 1890s and have fascinated writers and filmmakers. Well-directed by Peter Sasdy, the tension is skillfully devel-oped. Murders are particularly gruesome and there are shocks that will have the most hard-ened filmgoer sitting up.

The suggestion is that Jack the Ripper, who murdered prostitutes, killed his wife to stop her denouncing him in front of their three-year-old daughter, and vanished, returning years later supernaturally to force her to murder most viciously.

It is a glossy, well-mounted production, ad-mirably performed by a first-rate cast. Angharad Rees makes the pretty killer en-tirely credible.

● ●

■ HAND THAT ROCKS THE CRADLE, THE

1992, 110 MINS, US ◇ ⑩ ⊙ ⊙
Dir Curtis Hanson *Prod* David Madden *Scr* Amanda Silver *Ph* Robert Elswit *Ed* John F. Link *Mus* Graeme Revell *Art Dir* Edward Pisoni
● Annabella Sciorra, Rebecca DeMornay, Matt McCoy, Ernie Hudson, Julianne Moore, Madeline Zima (Hollywood/Interscope)

The Hand That Rocks the Cradle is a low-key thriller that will make baby boomers double-check the references of any prospective nanny. First screenplay by Amanda Silver, who is the granddaughter of the late, great screenwriter Sidney Buchman, trades in the same devil woman theme that anchored *Fatal Attraction*, with the sanctity of the traditional family unit as the villain's target.

Pleasant existence of pregnant Seattle housewife Claire Bartel (Annabella Sciorra) is disrupted when her new gynecologist crosses the proper boundaries during an exam. With the encouragement of her hus-band Michael (Matt McCoy), Claire files charges, upon which the doctor commits sui-cide.

Medic's demise sends his pregnant wife into hysterics, causing her to lose her baby. Cut to six months later, and this woman (Rebecca DeMornay), who now calls herself Peyton, turns up to offer her services as nanny to the Bartels. They readily take her in, and the viewer knows the screw will soon begin turning.

Helmer has obtained taut, impressive per-formances, notably from cast women. A totally deglamorized Sciorra becomes unglued subtly and slowly, eliciting sympathy without begging for it. DeMornay, her Miss Congeniality exterior masking evil intent, is an ice queen viewers will enjoy watching get hers in the end.

. . . .

■ HANG 'EM HIGH

1968, 114 MINS, US ◇ ⦾ ⊙
Dir Ted Post   *Prod* Leonard Freeman   *Scr* Leonard Freeman, Mel Goldberg   *Ph* Leonard South, Richard Kines   *Mus* Dominic Frontiere
● Clint Eastwood, Inger Stevens, Ed Begley, Pat Hingle, Arlene Golonka, Ben Johnson (United Artists/Malpaso)

Hang 'em High comes across as a poor-made imitation of a poor Italian-made imitation of an American western. It stars Clint Eastwood as a man bent on vengeance and is an episodic, rambling tale which glorifies personal justice, and mocks orderly justice.

Eastwood is hanged (but not killed) by do it-yourself vigilantes, headed by Ed Begley; district judge Pat Hingle recruits Eastwood to be a deputy marshal, and part of the job is to round up those who wronged him. Inger Stevens drifts in and out as a forced romantic interest.

From then on, film drags along through at least a dozen killings and legal hangings, shown in meticulous, morbid detail. Plot makes Hingle practically psychotic in his pursuit of 'justice', and in the big hanging scene he fairly drools over the event.

Eastwood projects a likeable image, but the part is only a shade more developed over his Sergio Leone Italoaters. Begley goes way overboard in mugging the climactic shoot-out and hang-in.

. . . .

■ HANGFIRE

1991, 89 MINS, US ◇ ⦾
Dir Peter Maris   *Prod* Brad Krevoy, Steve Stabler   *Scr* Brian D. Jeffries   *Ph* Mark Norris   *Ed* Peter Maris   *Mus* Jim Price   *Art Dir* Stephen Greenberg
● Brad Davis, Kim Delaney, Jan-Michael Vincent, Ken Foree, George Kennedy, Yaphet Kotto (Krevoy-Stabler)

Hangfire is a tight little action thriller about a prison break that attempts to serve as a metaphor for the 1989-90 Middle East crisis, but strains credibility.

Character actor Lee de Broux, in a bravura performance, plays a serial killer/rapist who leads a prison escape in New Mexico. De Broux and his minions take over the town of Sonora and hold its fifty or so inhabitants prisoner. The National Guard is called in, led by gung-ho Jan-Michael Vincent.

Local sheriff Brad Davis and his Vietnam vet pal Ken Foree (who excels in Maris assignments such as *Viper*) are the secret weapons who manage to defeat de Broux and rescue Davis' wife (Kim Delaney) while the military proves largely ineffectual.

Rest of the cast, including Lyle Alzado and Lou Ferrigno for comic relief, is effective.

. . . .

■ HANGING TREE, THE

1959, 106 MINS, US ◇
Dir Delmer Daves   *Prod* Martin Jurow, Richard Shepherd   *Scr* Wendell Mayes, Halstead Welles   *Ph* Ted McCord   *Ed* Owen Marks   *Mus* Max Steiner
● Gary Cooper, Maria Schell, Karl Malden, Ben Piazza, George C. Scott, Karl Swenson (Warner)

Wendell Mayes and Halstead Welles did the screenplay from a long short story by Dorothy M. Johnson, who is a kind of western writers' western writer. Johnson's stories show the West as it was, a hard, cruel, lonely frontier, in which the humans were often stripped of the savagery of the country.

In essence, the story follows western classic form. Gary Cooper is the mysterious

stranger, a taciturn and quixotic man who drifts into a Montana gold-mining town. He quickly establishes himself as a man equally handy with a scalpel, a Colt and an inside straight, tender in his professional role as MD, and a paradoxically tough man when dealing with gamblers and con men.

His first action is to rescue young Ben Piazza from a lynch-minded mob and make him his bond-servant on threat of exposure. His second is to take on the recovery of Maria Schell, a Swiss immigrant, who is ill and blinded from exposure. Stirring in these complicated relationships is the character of Karl Malden, an evil and lascivious gold prospector, who wants Piazza's money and Schell's body, more or less in that order.

There are fine performances from a good cast, but the main contribution comes from the director. The natural splendor of the Washington location is thoroughly exploited in Technicolor, but Delmer Daves doesn't allow his characters to get lost in the forest or mountains.

☐ 1959: Nomination: Best Song ('The Hanging Tree')

. . . .

■ HANGIN' WITH THE HOMEBOYS

1991, 88 MINS, US ◇ ⦾ ⊙
Dir Joseph P. Vasquez   *Prod* Richard Brick   *Scr* Joseph P. Vasquez   *Ph* Anghel Decca   *Ed* Michael Schweitzer   *Mus* Joel Sill, David Chackler   *Art Dir* Isabel Bau Madden
● Doug E. Doug, Mario Joyner, John Leguizamo, Nestor Serrano, Kimberly Russell, Mary B. Ward (New Line)

Homeboys is a good example of what independents can bring to the party: a vibrant tale told at minimum cost (under $2 million), a focus on cultural minorities (ghetto blacks and Puerto Ricans) and access to the system for a talented minority director (Joseph P. Vasquez, who did *Street Story* and *The Bronx War*).

Ensemble piece follows the misadventures of four South Bronx youths from mid-morning Friday to Saturday dawn. It looks like it could be their last time together, as reality is bearing down.

Willie (Doug E. Doug) is a welfare sponger whose caseworker has run out of patience. Tom (Mario Joyner) is a would-be actor with a telemarketing gig. Johnny (John Leguizamo), a shy, serious Puerto Rican supermarket stocker, ignores his boss' encouragement to try for a Hispanic college scholarship. Vinnie (Nestor Serrano), a Puerto Rican who pretends to be an Italian stud, sleeps all day and funds his party life by cajoling money from young girlfriends.

With plenty of tensions among themselves, they mostly pick on one another and get high on perpetual motion as they bounce from cruising to party-crashing to bars, cafes, peepshows, a billiards hall and a disco. Film is infused with an aggressive and engaging street energy and plenty of humor.

. . . .

■ HANGMEN ALSO DIE!

1943, 131 MINS, US
Dir Fritz Lang   *Prod* Arnold Pressburger   *Scr* John Wexley, Bert Brecht, Fritz Lang   *Ph* James Wong Howe   *Ed* Gene Fowley Jr   *Mus* Hanns Eisler
● Brian Donlevy, Walter Brennan, Anna Lee, Gene Lockhart, Dennis O'Keefe (United Artists)

From a directorial standpoint this is a triumph for Fritz Lang, who succeeds with singular success in capturing the spirit of the Czech people in the face of the Nazi reign of terror.

UA sunk plenty of coin into the picture. Cameraman James Wong Howe, in particular, turns in a magnificent job.

The cast, topped by Brian Donlevy and Walter Brennan, is uniformly splendid, with the performances of Gene Lockhart, as a cow-

ering Quisling Czech, and Alexander Granach, as a shrewd, calculating and ruthless inspector of the Gestapo, being particularly outstanding. Story continuity is fine and absorbing throughout, but essentially it's the incisive terms of the message propounded that sets *Hangmen* apart and points up the fact that propaganda can be art.

Saga of the courageous spirit of the Czechs starts with the assassination of Heydrich, the hangman, by an appointed member of the underground (Donlevy), but the plans for his escape go awry and, due to the stringent curfew laws, he is forced to spend the night at the home of a professor and his daughter. In order to save her father, who is held as hostage along with several hundred others until the assassin will be given up, she goes to the Gestapo to reveal his identity, but realizes that the spirit of the Czech people has made of him a symbol of freedom and that the underground will protect him at all costs.

Both Donlevy and Brennan, as the professor, are excellent, the latter emerging in the film a figure of heroic proportions.
☐ 1943: Nomination: Best Scoring of a Dramatic Picture, Sound

. . . .

■ HANGOVER SQUARE

1945, 77 MINS, US
Dir John Brahm   *Prod* Robert Bassler   *Scr* Barre Lyndon   *Ph* Joseph La Shelle   *Ed* Harry Reynolds   *Mus* Bernard Herrmann   *Art Dir* Lyle R. Wheeler, Maurice Ransford
● Laird Cregar, Linda Darnell, George Sanders, Glenn Langan, Faye Marlowe, Alan Napier (20th Century-Fox)

Hangover Square is eerie murder melodrama of the London gaslight era – typical of Patrick Hamilton yarns, of which this is another. And it doesn't make any pretense at mystery. The madman-murderer is known from the first reel.

It is the story of a distinguished young composer-pianist with a Jekyll-Hyde personality. When he becomes over-wrought, he's a madman – and his lustful forages are always accompanied by a loss of memory during the periods during which he is murder-bent.

Laird Cregar as the madman-murderer shows markedly the physical decline, through dieting, said to have been a factor in [the actor's] death. Linda Darnell and George Sanders are co-stars, the former as the two-timing girl and Sanders as a Scotland Yard psychiatrist who provides the tell-tale clues responsible for the denouement.

Production is grade A, and so is the direction by John Brahm, with particular bows to the music score by Bernard Herrmann.

. . . .

■ HANKY PANKY

1982, 105 MINS, US ◇ ⦾ ⊙
Dir Sidney Poitier   *Prod* Martin Ransohoff   *Scr* Henry Rosenbaum, David Taylor   *Ph* Arthur Ornitz   *Ed* Harry Keller   *Mus* Tom Scott   *Art Dir* Ben Edwards
● Gene Wilder, Gilda Radner, Kathleen Quinlan, Richard Widmark, Robert Prosky, Josef Sommer (Columbia)

Hanky Panky is a limp romantic suspense comedy which manages to be neither romantic, suspenseful nor funny. What with Gene Wilder as a hapless Chicago architect caught up in a string of extraordinary coincidences involving government agents, a secret tape, and a big scene taking place at the Grand Canyon, pic appears to be an attempt to duplicate the classy thrills of *North by Northwest*.

Tale opens moodily with an unexplained suicide and then picks up Wilder, whose short cab ride with frantic Kathleen Quinlan plunges him into a web of intrigue obliging him to endure suspicion by the police for murder, beatings by agent Richard Widmark, and an attempt to kill him by a helicopter out in the desert.

He's an innocent, of course, but once he latches onto Gilda Radner, sister of the guy

H

who hanged himself in the opening scene, he's committed to seeing the escapade through.

Casting of Wilder and Radner strikes no sparks. Quinlan, a serious actress who deserves greater challenges than this, disappears in the early going.

●●●●●●●●●●●●●●●●●●●●●●●●●●●●●●●●●●●

■ HANNAH AND HER SISTERS

1986, 106 MINS, US ◇ ⓥ ⊙
Dir Woody Allen   *Prod* Robert Greenhut   *Scr* Woody Allen   *Ph* Carlo Di Palma   *Ed* Susan E. Morse   *Art Dir* Stuart Wurtzel
● Woody Allen, Michael Caine, Mia Farrow, Carrie Fisher, Barbara Hershey, Dianne Wiest (Orion)

Hannah and Her Sisters is one of Woody Allen's great films. Indeed, he makes nary a misstep from beginning to end in charting the amorous affiliations of three sisters and their men over a two-year period.

Its structure is a successful mixture of outright comedy, rueful meditation and sexual complications.

Pic begins at a Thanksgiving dinner, and ends at one two years later, with most of the characters going through mate changes in the interim.

Hannah, played by Mia Farrow, was formerly married to TV producer Woody Allen but is now happily wed to agent Michael Caine, who, in turn, secretly lusts for his wife's sexy sister, Barbara Hershey, the live-in mate of tormented painter Max von Sydow.

The third sister (Dianne Wiest) is by far the most neurotic of the bunch and, while waiting for her acting, singing or writing career to take off, runs a catering business with Carrie Fisher.

□ 1986: Best Supp. Actor (Michael Caine), Supp. Actress (Dianne Wiest), Original Screenplay.
□ Nominations: Best Picture, Director, Art Direction, Editing

●●●●●●●●●●●●●●●●●●●●●●●●●●●●●●●●●●●

■ HANNA'S WAR

1988, 158 MINS, US ◇ ⓥ ⊙
Dir Menahem Golan   *Prod* Menahem Golan, Yoram Globus   *Scr* Menahem Golan   *Ph* Elemer Ragalyi   *Ed* Alain Jakubowicz   *Mus* Dov Seltzer   *Art Dir* Tividar Bertaian
● Ellen Burstyn, Maruschka Detmers, Anthony Andrews, Donald Pleasence, David Warner, Vincenzo Ricotta (Cannon)

Hanna Senesh, a talented poet and a martyr who died in a Hungarian jail in 1944, before her 24th birthday, is a mythical figure in Israel, a symbol of gentle but determined heroism. In Menahem Golan's version, heroes and villains are easily distinguished, characters are respectfully observed and admired, or duly abhorred and discredited, and no time is spent dwelling on psychological niceties.

The straightforward script follows her steps from the point she decides, on graduating high school, to part with her family and leave antisemitic Hungary to go to Palestine for a new start. While there, she is drafted by the British for a special operation behind German lines in Eastern Europe and after a brief Yugoslav interlude, she crosses the border back into Hungary.

The rest is dedicated to the time she spent in Hungarian jail, the tortures she suffered, and her execution by the Hungarians without a trial.

Maruschka Detmers may not radiate the spiritual strength required by her role, but she is dedicated and often moving during the prison sequences. Donald Pleasence and David Warner each notch another villain to their credit. Topbilled Ellen Burstyn has at most a supporting part as Hanna's mother, and Anthony Andrews is a bit top-heavy as the British instructor who leads the expedition. Lensed in Hungary and Israel.

●●●●●●●●●●●●●●●●●●●●●●●●●●●●●●●●●●●

■ HANNIBAL BROOKS

1969, 101 MINS, UK ◇
Dir Michael Winner   *Prod* Michael Winner   *Scr* Dick Clement, Ian La Frenais   *Ph* Robert Paynter   *Ed* [uncredited]   *Mus* Francis Lai   *Art Dir* Jurgen Kiebach
● Oliver Reed, Michael J. Pollard, Karin Baal, Wolfgang Preiss, Helmut Lohner, Peter Karsten (United Artists/Scimitar)

A pleasant, tame tale about a British prisoner (Oliver Reed), assigned to nursemaid an elephant in a Munich Zoo. From here, it is a short jump into attempted escapes, with the elephant in tow, across some mountain passes (a la Hannibal, hence the title) into Switzerland.

The humorous vein which was evidently intended to be topmost throughout the film gets sidetracked by the excursion into action and there isn't a laugh in the second half of the film.

The British actor, playing a kindly, animal-loving and, for most of the film, pacifistic soldier carries the entire film on his admittedly broad shoulders but can't overcome the confused writing, or the even greater burden of a poor performance by costar Michael J. Pollard. The latter is simply dreadful as a cocky Yank prisoner.

Filmed almost entirely on location in Bavaria, the beautiful countryside is caught perfectly by Robert Paynter's color camera.

●●●●●●●●●●●●●●●●●●●●●●●●●●●●●●●●●●●

■ HANNIE CAULDER

1971, 85 MINS, UK/US ◇ ⓥ
Dir Burt Kennedy   *Prod* Patrick Curtis   *Scr* Z.X. Jones, [Burt Kennedy, David Haft]   *Ph* Edward Scaife   *Ed* Jim Connock   *Mus* Ken Thorne   *Art Dir* Jose Alguero
● Raquel Welch, Robert Culp, Ernest Borgnine, Strother Martin, Jack Elam, Diana Dors (Tigon/Curtwel)

Raquel Welch plays Hannie Caulder who, having been widowed and raped by the Clemens brothers, determines to avenge these wrongs. [Original story by Peter Cooper, based on characters created by Ian Quicke and Bob Richards.] With the aid of a bounty hunter she is soon showing that ladies shoot first and can be more deadly than the male.

The west may never have boasted so immaculate a markswoman but it seems highly unlikely that anyone is expected to take the film too seriously. Welch, with genteel modesty, makes the character for many rather ingratiating though others undoubtedly will find her plain ludicrous. All she has to wear after her farm has been set ablaze, while being raped by the drunken brothers, is a hastily-grabbed poncho. The avoidance of more than quick glimpses of a shapely thigh seems her main concern.

She is admirably supported by Ernest Borgnine as the meanest of the brothers and Robert Culp as the bounty hunter who befriends her. Christopher Lee, after his usual horror roles makes an unusual appearance as a sympathetic gunsmith.

●●●●●●●●●●●●●●●●●●●●●●●●●●●●●●●●●●●

■ HANOI HILTON

1987, 123 MINS, US ◇ ⓥ ⊙
Dir Lionel Chetwynd   *Prod* Menahem Golan, Yoram Globus   *Scr* Lionel Chetwynd   *Ph* Mark Irwin   *Ed* Penelope Shaw   *Mus* Jimmy Webb   *Art Dir* R. Clifford Searcy
● Michael Moriarty, Jeffrey Jones, Paul Le Mat, Stephen Davies, Lawrence Pressman, Aki Aleong (Cannon)

The Hanoi Hilton is a lame attempt by writer-director Lionel Chetwynd to tell the story of US prisoners in Hoa Lo Prison, in Hanoi during the Vietnam War. Pic is a slanted view of traditional prison camp sagas, injecting lots of hindsight and taking right-wing potshots that do a disservice to the very human drama of the subject.

Michael Moriarty heads a curiously bland cast. He's thrust into a position of authority when the ranking officer played by Lawrence Pressman is taken off to be tortured. Episodic structure introduces new prisoners as more pilots are shot down over a roughly 10-year span (including some comic relief such as one prisoner who says he fell off his ship accidentally and was captured).

Pic is desperately lacking side issues or subplots of interest with Chetwynd monotonously hammering away at the main issue of survival in the face of inhuman treatment.

●●●●●●●●●●●●●●●●●●●●●●●●●●●●●●●●●●●

■ HANOVER STREET

1979, 109 MINS, US ◇ ⓥ ⊙
Dir Peter Hyams   *Prod* Paul N. Lazarus III   *Scr* Peter Hyams   *Ph* David Watkin   *Ed* James Mitchell   *Mus* John Barry   *Art Dir* Philip Harrison
● Harrison Ford, Lesley-Anne Down, Christopher Plummer, Alec McCowen, Richard Masur, Patsy Kensit (Columbia)

Hanover Street is reasonably effective as a war film with a love story background. Unfortunately it's meant to be a love story set against a war background.

Drawing his inspiration from M-G-M's 1940 release, *Waterloo Bridge*, and other pix of that ilk, writer-director Peter Hyams has moved this tale of star-crossed lovers up to World War II England, where American flying ace David Halloran (Harrison Ford) and British hospital nurse Margaret Sellinger (Lesley-Anne Down) meet during an air raid, and fall hopelessly in love.

Only when Down takes a back seat, and Ford is thrown together with her cuckolded husband, Paul, a British secret service topper (Christopher Plummer), does *Hanover Street* manifest any vital life signs. The last third of the picture becomes a model of efficient war filmmaking.

Down again distinguishes herself in a role that doesn't seem up to her standards, while Ford back in the pilot's seat again projects an earnest, if dull, presence. Rest of the cast is under-utilized. John Barry has contributed a score that evokes Douglas Sirk's glossy tear-jerkers of the 1950s.

●●●●●●●●●●●●●●●●●●●●●●●●●●●●●●●●●●●

■ HANS CHRISTIAN ANDERSEN

1952, 112 MINS, US ◇ ⓥ ⊙
Dir Charles Vidor   *Prod* Samuel Goldwyn   *Scr* Moss Hart   *Ph* Harry Stradling   *Ed* Daniel Mandell   *Mus* Walter Scharf (dir.)   *Art Dir* Richard Day, Antoni Clare
● Danny Kaye, Farley Granger, Zizi Jeanmaire, Joey Walsh, Philip Tonge, Roland Petit (Goldwyn/RKO)

Hans Christian Andersen [based on a story by Myles Connolly] is a charming fairy tale about the Danish master of the childhood fantasy, done with the taste expected of a Samuel Goldwyn production.

Danny Kaye does a very fine job of the title role, sympathetically projecting the Andersen spirit and philosophy. No attempt at biography is made so the imaginative production has full rein in bringing in songs and ballet numbers to round out the Andersen fairy tales told by Kaye.

Socko is *The Little Mermaid* ballet, a spectacular display backed by the music of Franz Liszt, using six sets that range from a witch's underwater cave to a prince's castle. Roland Petit, who dances the prince in *Mermaid*, designed all the ballets.

On the song side, the picture has the top-notch talents of Frank Loesser contributing eight songs, all given first-rate vocal treatment by Kaye.

□ 19052: Nominations: Best Color Cinematography, Color Costume Design,

Color Art Direction, Scoring of a Musical Picture, Song ('Thumbelina')

....

■ HAPPENING, THE

1967, 101 MINS, US ◇

Dir Elliot Silverstein   *Prod* Jud Kinberg   *Scr* Frank R. Pierson, James D. Buchanan, Ronald Austin   *Ph* Philip Lathrop   *Ed* Philip W. Anderson   *Mus* Frank DeVol   *Art Dir* Richard Day
● Anthony Quinn, George Maharis, Michael Parks, Robert Walker, Martha Hyer, Faye Dunaway (Columbia/Horizon)

Intriguing offbeat item, *The Happening* attempts to blend various elements of kick-happy teeny-boppers, melodrama, pop culture, suburban tragedy, suspense, 'in' gags, 'black humor', Keystone Kops, 'beach party' pix, and alienation in the affluent society in a comedic potpourri, which, between expected laughs, seeks to offer satiric peeks at US life and values.

Well-tempered plotline [by James D. Buchanan and Ronald Austin], with several corkscrew twists, follows the weekend hegira of four ennui-laden but debauched Miami beachbums in search of some potent stimuli. They find it, albeit accidentally, by stumbling into an unlikely kidnapping.

What is bothersome about this tragi-farce is why it doesn't succeed, with all of the above and generally capable performers, going for it. George Maharis, playing a bull without horns, is spotty but fine, alternating swagger with weakness in his impersonation of a gigolo, while Michael Parks is less convincing but appropriately faceless as a blank-faced rich kid. Newcomer Faye Dunaway, though stunning to view and essaying her role with elan, is too womanly seductive for a teenybopper role.

....

■ HAPPIEST DAYS OF YOUR LIFE, THE

1950, 81 MINS, UK
Dir Frank Launder   *Prod* Frank Launder, Sidney Gilliat   *Scr* Frank Launder, John Dighton   *Ph* Stan Pavey   *Ed* Oswald Hafenrichter   *Mus* Mischa Spoliansky
● Alastair Sim, Margaret Rutherford, Joyce Grenfell, Richard Wattis, Edward Rigby, Muriel Aked (London)

Bright script and brisk direction conceal the stage origin. The story is given a wider canvas and isn't wanting in action. In fact, the pace never lets up and one hilarious farcical incident only ends to give place to another.

Setting of the film is a college for boys, to which, as a result of a slip at the Ministry of Education, a girl's school is evacuated. The story builds up to a boisterous climax in which the principals are trying to conceal the real situation from visitors to the college.

There is no shortage of laughs, but the joke is a little too protracted and wears thin before the end. It's an ideal vehicle for Alastair Sim as the harassed headmaster, while Margaret Rutherford admirably suggests the overpowering headmistress.

....

■ HAPPIEST MILLIONAIRE, THE

1967, 164 MINS, US ◇ Ⓥ
Dir Norman Tokar   *Prod* Bill Anderson (co-prod.)   *Scr* A.J. Carothers   *Ph* Edward Colman   *Ed* Cotton Warburton   *Mus* Jack Elliott (arr.)   *Art Dir* Carroll Clark, John B. Mansbridge
● Fred MacMurray, Tommy Steele, Greer Garson, Geraldine Page, Gladys Cooper, Hermione Baddeley (Walt Disney)

The Happiest Millionaire, last major live-action production of Walt Disney, is a family comedy, blending creative and technical elements, scripting, excellent casting, direction, scoring, choreography and handsome, plush production.

Fred MacMurray heads the cast, which in-cludes Britain's Tommy Steele in his US film debut as an Irish servant in 1916 Philadelphia. [Pic is from the play by Kyle Crichton, suggested by a book by Cordelia Drexel Biddle and Kyle Crichton.]

MacMurray, snug in an excellent characterization, is well teamed with Greer Garson as the Philadelphia parents. Lesley Ann Warren, introduced herein, plays the teenage daughter with charm and radiance.

□ 1967: Nomination: Best Costume Design

....

■ HAPPILY EVER AFTER

1990, 74 MINS, US ◇
Dir John Howley   *Prod* Lou Scheimer   *Scr* Robby London, Martha Moran   *Ph* Fred Ziegler   *Ed* Jeffrey C. Patch, Joe Gall   *Mus* Frank W. Becker   *Art Dir* John Grusd
● (Filmation)

An unauthorized sequel to the Walt Disney classic *Snow White*, *Happily Ever After* is a well-crafted but uninspired animated fantasy. Lou Scheimer's Filmation banner began work on the pic in 1986 simultaneously with another unauthorized sequel to a Disney masterpiece, *Pinocchio and the Emperor of the Night* (1987).

Action picks up here with the evil queen's brother Lord Maliss (drawn to resemble Basil Rathbone and voiced with gusto by Malcolm McDowell) in a vendetta to avenge sis' death by zonking Snow White and her handsome Prince. Snowy takes refuge in the seven dwarfs' cottage when the Prince is captured. The little fellows are away slaving in the mines, but their femme cousins, the seven dwarfelles, entertain Snowy with their fantastic control of natural phenomena.

Voice casting is pic's big plus. Irene Cara warbles a catchy, uptempo song 'Love Is the Reason' to bookend the film. Three other songs spotlight Ed Asner, Phyllis Diller and a very effective vocal from Tracey Ullman simulating a little girl's voice.

....

■ HAPPY BIRTHDAY, WANDA JUNE

1971, 105 MINS, US ◇
Dir Mark Robson   *Prod* Lester Goldsmith   *Scr* Kurt Vonnegut Jr.   *Ph* Fred Koenekamp   *Ed* Dorothy Spencer   *Art Dir* Boris Leven
● Rod Steiger, Susannah York, George Grizzard, Don Murray, William Hickey, Steven Paul (Filmakers/Sourdough/Red Lions)

Imagine Ulysses' long voyage home with nothing on board to read but the collected writings of Ernest Hemingway. That must have been in the mind of novelist-turned playwright-turned screenwriter Kurt Vonnegut Jr when he dreamed up the hero for *Happy Birthday, Wanda June*.

Rod Steiger shines as the self-deceiving ultra-masculine hero, returned from eight years in the Amazon jungle, to find that not only has his loving wife, a former pinheaded carhop (played brilliantly by Susannah York), become a levelheaded intellectual equal but has gone to his extreme opposite in seeking another soul mate.

She's trying to decide between a violin-playing doctor and practicing pacifist (George Grizzard) and a clumsy, eager vacuum-cleaner salesman (Don Murray). Only his son remembers him (resenting the non-observance of his supposedly dead father's birthday as a major catastrophe).

The treatment is too irreverent to be taken seriously for a moment, including Vonnegut's preachments.

....

■ HAPPY ENDING, THE

1969, 117 MINS, US ◇ Ⓥ
Dir Richard Brooks   *Prod* Richard Brooks   *Scr* Richard Brooks   *Ph* Conrad Hall   *Ed* George Grenville   *Mus* Michel Legrand
● Jean Simmons, John Forsythe, Lloyd Bridges, Teresa Wright, Dick Shawn, Nanette Fabray (United Artists/PaxFilms)

The American Dream, the affluent upper middleclass marriage, is a conjugal bed of nails peopled by bored-to-tears alcoholic wives and hard working, but less than faithful hubbies, according to producer-director-writer Richard Brooks. A well-developed and acted and potentially significant 'woman's movie' unfortunately drowns in Brooks' over indulgences and over-writing.

As Mrs America, class of '53, Jean Simmons fortifies herself with vodka and tranquilizers for her 16th wedding anniversary with tax lawyer John Forsythe.

As the still attractive but anxiously middle-aged and self-pitying matron who is financially secure but personally bankrupted, Simmons gives a moving, emotionally wringing performance. Forsythe has the patience of Job with his spoiled, high-strung wife. His is a basically dull, one-dimensional role.

□ 1969: Nominations: Best Actress (Jean Simmons), Song ('What Are You Doing the Rest of Your Life')

....

■ HAPPY NEW YEAR

1987, 85 MINS, US ◇ Ⓥ
Dir John G. Avildsen   *Prod* Jerry Weintraub   *Scr* Warren Lane [= Nancy Dowd]   *Ph* James Crabe   *Ed* Jane Kurson   *Mus* Bill Conti   *Art Dir* William J. Cassidy
● Peter Falk, Charles Durning, Wendy Hughes, Tom Courtenay, Joan Copeland, Tracy Brooks Swope (Columbia/Delphi IV)

Crime pays off in this unpretentious buddy picture about two middle-aged jewel thieves going for the big score in Palm Beach [based on Claude Lelouch's 1973 film *La bonne annee*]. Topliners Peter Falk and Charles Durning team with an easygoing charm.

Film is funniest and most engrossing in the first hour or so when Falk and Durning are casing the Palm Beach branch of Harry Winston, jewelers. This leads to a series of amusing encounters with the fey and smarmy jewelry store manager Edward Sanders (expertly rendered by Tom Courtenay), who from Falk's hardboiled honor-among-thieves perspective is a soulless money-grubber deserving the worst.

Along the way Falk meets and falls for a beautiful, high-toned antiques dealer, Carolyn Benedict (Wendy Hughes), who moves in a circle of insufferably smug and wealthy pseudo-sophisticates.

Although the film sags towards its resolution, director John G. Avildsen handles the story with a light touch, including a gentle soundtrack of pre-rock 'n' roll standards that would be at home in a Woody Allen film, and a cameo by Lelouch, who directed the original French film.

□ 1987: Nomination: Best Makeup

....

■ HARD CONTRACT

1969, 106 MINS, US ◇
Dir S. Lee Pogostin   *Prod* Marvin Schwartz   *Scr* S. Lee Pogostin   *Ph* Jack Hildyard   *Ed* Harry Gerstad   *Mus* Alex North   *Art Dir* Ed Graves
● James Coburn, Lee Remick, Lilli Palmer, Burgess Meredith, Patrick Magee, Sterling Hayden (20th Century-Fox)

The principle of the loner, the individual in the jungle of society, the solitary predator, is emphatically portrayed in this skillfully-mounted film about the killer-for-hire who agrees to a hard contract to eliminate three men in Europe.

James Coburn, as Cunningham, accepts the deal dished out by Burgess Meredith. Leaving the US for Torremelinos, he meets the self-indulgent jet-set quartet who bloom in the Spanish sun.

H

Leader of the group is Lee Remick, who finds herself in love with Coburn but not his profession.

Scenery of Spain and Belgium is in sharp focus, which isn't always true of story. A shift of values has been initiated, but no one has raised a signpost to tell where we're going.

Coburn and Remick, effective in their roles, allow characters to develop naturally.

•••••••••••••••••••••••••••••••••

■ HARDCORE
(UK: The Hardcore Life)

1979, 105 MINS, US ◇ ⦿ ☉
Dir Paul Schrader *Prod* Buzz Feitshans *Scr* Paul Schrader *Ph* Michael Chapman *Ed* Tom Rolf *Mus* Jack Nitzsche *Art Dir* Paul Sylbert
● George C. Scott, Peter Boyle, Season Hubley, Dick Sargent, Leonard Gaines, David Nichols (Columbia/A-Team)

George C. Scott, gives as fine a performance as he's ever done.

An unventuring Calvinist, Scott lives a contented small-town Michigan life until his daughter, Ilah Davis, disappears on a trip to LA. He hires seedy private-eye Peter Boyle who eventually finds her on film in a porno movie. Forced to watch, Scott's anguish at the sight bespeaks a clash of values still haunting the country.

For many, this will be the first up-close look at the world including nude-conversation encounters, massage parlors, bondage joints and the lowest degradation – 'snuff' films.

The easily shocked may want an exposé, or more a condemnation. The more sophisticated may grow tired of Scott's morality. But shocked, cynical or dissatisfied, nobody's going to be bored.

•••••••••••••••••••••••••••••••••

■ HARDCORE LIFE, THE
See: Hardcore

•••••••••••••••••••••••••••••••••

■ HARD DAY'S NIGHT, A

1964, 83 MINS, UK ⦿ ☉
Dir Richard Lester *Prod* Walter Shenson *Scr* Alun Owen *Ph* Gilbert Taylor *Ed* John Jympson *Mus* George Martin (dir) *Art Dir* Ray Simm
● John Lennon, Paul McCartney, George Harrison, Ringo Starr, Wilfrid Brambell, Norman Rossington (United Artists)

A Hard Day's Night is a wacky, offbeat piece of filming, charged with vitality, and inventiveness by director Dick Lester, slickly lensed and put over at a fair lick. No attempt has been paid to build the Beatles up as Oliviers; they are at their best when the pic has a misleading air of off-the-cuff spontaneity.

Running at 83 minutes, in black and white, it keeps Beatles within their ability. Alun Owen's screenplay merely attempts to portray an exaggerated 36 hours in the lives of the Beatles. But, though exaggerated, the thin story lines gives a shrewd idea of the pressure and difficulties under which they work and live.

Four set off by train to keep a live television date and, before taking off by helicopter for their next stint, they have some rum adventures. A skirmish with the police, mobbing by hysterical fans, then a press conference, riotous moments in a tavern, a jazz cellar, a gambling club and at TV rehearsals all work into the crazy tapestry and offer the Beatles a chance to display their sense of humor and approach to life.

To give the almost documentary storyline a boost scriptwriter Owen has introduced Paul's grandfather, a mischief making mixer with an eye on the main chance. Played by Wilfrid Brambell with sharp perception, his presence is a great buffer for the boys' throwaway sense of comedy.
□ 1964: Nominations: Best Story & Screenplay, Adapted Music Score

•••••••••••••••••••••••••••••••••

■ HARDER THEY FALL, THE

1956, 109 MINS, US ⦿
Dir Mark Robson *Prod* Philip Yordan *Scr* Philip Yordan *Ph* Burnett Guffey *Ed* Jerome Thoms *Mus* Hugo Friedhofer *Art Dir* William Flannery
● Humphrey Bogart, Rod Steiger, Jan Sterling, Mike Lane, Max Baer, Edward Andrews (Columbia)

Budd Schulberg's vehement novel about the fight racket is given a strong pictorial going-over in *The Harder They Fall*. It's main-event stuff.

The vicious racket within, the promoters and managers who exploit the pugs, tank divers on the take, the pressagent who builds the hoax about the phoney ring sensation – they're under scrutiny.

Story concerns a ruthless manager-gambler who imports a behemoth from South America, discovers he's a pugilistic cream puff, but gives him the buildup via fixed fights across the country.

Humphrey Bogart is the newspaper man who goes ethically awry when his paper folds. He's glib and persuasive in promoting the boxer, and finally reveals his courage when he breaks with the racket.

Rod Steiger rates hefty mitting as the crooked dealer in ring flesh. Jersey Joe Walcott is surprisingly effective in acting the part of a warm-hearted trainer. Jan Sterling fits in well as Bogart's wife; Mike Lane works well in striking a sympathetic chord as the musclebound captive of Steiger's who's too dumb to know his opponents are paid to fall.
□ 1956: Nomination: Best B&W Cinematography

•••••••••••••••••••••••••••••••••

■ HARD, FAST AND BEAUTIFUL

1951, 76 MINS, US
Dir Ida Lupino *Prod* Collier Young *Scr* Martha Wilkerson *Ph* Archie Stout *Ed* George O. Shrader, William Ziegler *Mus* Roy Webb *Art Dir* Albert S. D'Agostino, Jack Okey
● Claire Trevor, Sally Forrest, Carleton G. Young, Robert Clarke, Kenneth Patterson, Marcella Cisney (Filmakers)

A product of the indie Filmakers unit headed by Ida Lupino and Collier Young, film is an entertaining study of selfish mother love and amateur tennis.

Expose of 'expense' money and other coin-getting channels available to top amateur racket-wielders is not worked too hard. Emphasis is on 'mom-ism' and this story line is well exploited, without being overdone, in the topnotch script and through the authority and punch of Lupino's direction.

Claire Trevor socks over her character as the selfish mother of Sally Forrest. Forrest is strong as a promising tennis player whose mother pushes and shoves her into the championship in order to ride along and soak up some of the fame and glamour that goes with the top tennis brackets.

Tennis court footage is expertly interlaced with the story and, creditably, camera angles on the play are smartly set up and there is a minimum use of shots showing head-swinging spectators.

•••••••••••••••••••••••••••••••••

■ HARD FEELINGS

1982, 104 MINS, CANADA ◇
Dir Daryl Duke *Prod* Harold Greenberg *Scr* W.D. Richter, John Herzfeld *Ph* Harry Makin *Ed* Tony Lower *Mus* Mickey Erbe, Maribeth Solomon *Art Dir* Douglas Higgins
● Carl Marotte, Charlaine Woodward, Vincent Bufano, Grand Bush, Lisa Langlois, Michael Donaghue (Astral)

Hard Feelings is an admirable, if flawed, look at the perils of growing up. Directed by Daryl Duke, the script, based on a novel by Don Bredes, is certainly not lacking ambition. Set on Long Island in 1963, it concerns an aimless high school senior played by Carl Marotte.

Superficially, he's much like his classmates with scholastic, athletic (tennis) and social interests. The major difference in Marotte's life is he's been singled out by school bully Vincent Bufano as an object of persecution.

He's also confused about sex and in this area the intensity of his family situation reflects poorly on his attitude toward his girlfriend (Lisa Langlois). The story takes an abrupt turn when the combination of anxieties lead Marotte to run away.

Duke's film is a highly perplexing tale which is really more concerned with questions than in providing neat answers.

•••••••••••••••••••••••••••••••••

■ HARD PROMISES

1992, 95 MINS, US ◇ ⦿
Dir Martin Davidson *Prod* Cindy Chvatal, William Petersen *Scr* Jule Selbo *Ph* Andrzej Bartkowiak *Ed* Bonnie Koehler *Mus* Kenny Vance *Art Dir* Dan Leigh
● Sissy Spacek, William Petersen, Brian Kerwin, Mare Winningham, Jeff Perry, Peter MacNichol (Stone/High Horse)

William Petersen plays a footloose man who has largely absented himself from the lives of his wife (Sissy Spacek) and daughter (Olivia Burnette). He gets a wedding invitation to Spacek's marriage to Brian Kerwin, and hies back home to put a stop to it.

Early scenes make the film (shot in Austin, Texas) seem like a bucolic remake of *The Awful Truth*. He soon learns from her lawyer (Peter MacNichol) that they have been divorced in absentia. Remainder of the film revolves around Petersen trying to win Spacek back and the refusal of the couple-to-be to relegate Kerwin to the Ralph Bellamy role.

Spacek is in fine form as the ex-cheerleader who married the football captain but now wants to regain control of her life. The only problem is that most of the drama in her character's story has *already* taken place before the start of the film.

•••••••••••••••••••••••••••••••••

■ HARD TIMES
(UK: The Streetfighter)

1975, 92 MINS, US ◇ ⦿ ☉
Dir Walter Hill *Prod* Lawrence Gordon *Scr* Walter Hill, Bryan Gindorff, Bruce Hentsell *Ph* Philip Lathrop *Ed* Roger Spottiswoode *Mus* Barry De Vorzon *Art Dir* Trevor Williams
● Charles Bronson, James Coburn, Jill Ireland, Strother Martin, Maggie Blye, Michael McGuire (Columbia)

Hard Times stars Charles Bronson as a mysterious stranger whose fists make money for him and small-time gambler James Coburn in illegal slugging matches.

Coburn's character lacks substance; he's a likeable heel one minute, an unlikeable one the next. At fadeout, after Bronson has fought one last fight to save Coburn's hide, Bronson meanders out of the film.

Jill Ireland is excellent in a touching performance as a down-and-out girl who has a brief affair with Bronson. Strother Martin is also excellent as a dope addict and unlicensed medic who works with Coburn. Michael McGuire is strong as a bigtime gambler.

The production has a very handsome mid-1930s New Orleans period flavour but the cast can't lick the script.

•••••••••••••••••••••••••••••••••

■ HARD TO KILL

1990, 95 MINS, US ◇ ⦿ ☉
Dir Bruce Malmuth *Prod* Gary Adelson, Joel Simon, Bill Todmore Jr *Scr* Steven McKay *Ph* Matthew F. Leonetti *Ed* John F. Link *Mus* David Michael Frank *Art Dir* Robb Wilson King
● Steven Seagal, Kelly Le Brock, Bill Sadler, Frederick Coffin, Bonnie Burroughs, Branscombe Richmond (Warner)

The threadbare screenplay, which went into production as *Seven Year Storm*, uses a Rip van Winkle gimmick. As Mason Storm, cop Steven Seagal is nearly killed in the first reel after shooting surveillance film of corrupt politico Bill Sadler. His wife (Bonnie Burroughs) is murdered by Sadler's minions.

Cop buddy Frederick Coffin recognizes the danger and hides evidence of Seagal's last-minute recovery. Seven years later, under the tutelage of impossibly beautiful nurse (and real-life wife) Kelly Le Brock, Seagal comes out of his coma (sporting a laughable phony beard), uses Oriental methods of recovery and plots his revenge.

Sluggish direction by Bruce Malmuth doesn't help, but whenever Seagal is allowed to whip into action the film is a crowdpleaser. Unlike other loner prototypes, he goes beyond merely ruthless into the realm of sadistic, breaking opponents' limbs just for starters (as in a memorable fight here with latino heavy Branscombe Richmond). It ain't pretty, but it gets the action fans off.

■ **HARDWARE**

1990, 92 MINS, UK/US ◇ ⑫ ⊙
Dir Richard Stanley   *Prod* Joanne Sellar, Paul Trybits
Scr Richard Stanley   *Ph* Steven Chivers   *Ed* Derek Trigg
Mus Simon Boswell   *Art Dir* Joseph Bennett
● Dylan McDermott, Stacey Travis, John Lynch, William Hootkins, Iggy Pop, Mark Northover
(Palace/Millimeter/Wicked)

A cacophonic, nightmarish variation on the postapocalyptic cautionary genre, *Hardware* has the makings of a punk cult film.

After the nuclear holocaust, vast reaches of incinerated North America have been reduced to an infrared desert ravaged by guerrilla warfare and littered with cybernetic scrapheaps. Moses (Dylan McDermott) and Shades (John Lynch) are 'zone tripper' soldiers of fortune who scavenge the corpse-strewn, irradiated wasteland for techno-detritus to black market in the big city.

Moses, wasting away from radiation cancer, wants to return to his woman, Julie (Stacey Travis). She's a fiercely cynical techno-alchemist, fond of smoking packaged dope, who keeps a fortress workshop in a blasted downtown apartment block. Reunited in a frenzied sexual collision of pulse-pounding eroticism, the couple ponder their outer-limits relationship of love in the ruins.

Hardware veers loonily out of control and becomes a black comic exercise in F/X tour-de-force that's ceaselessly pushing itself over the top.

■ **HARD WAY, THE**

1991, 111 MINS, US ◇ ⑫ ⊙
Dir John Badham   *Prod* William Sackheim, Rob Cohen, Peter R. McIntosh   *Scr* Daniel Pyne, Lem Dobbs   *Ph* Don McAlpine, Robert Primes   *Ed* Frank Morriss, Tony Lombardo   *Mus* Arthur B. Rubinstein   *Art Dir* Philip Harrison
● Michael J. Fox, James Woods, Stephen Lang, Annabella Sciorra, LL Cool J, Penny Marshall
(Universal/Badham-Cohen)

Too bad there's more method in the acting than the script, as John Badham's tired action-comedy formula squanders its best moments during the film's first act and wastes the nifty pairing of James Woods and Michael J. Fox.

Fox is a popular star of action fluff, like *Smoking Gunn II*, who yearns for a leading role in a film 'without a Roman numeral in it'. Determined to play a tough street cop, he decides to research the role by partnering New York cop John Moss (Woods), who's involved in hunting a lunatic serial killer (Stephen Lang).

The film exhausts its best Hollywood in-jokes during the first 20 minutes, with a Penny Marshall cameo as Fox's agent and lots of lines about cappuccino, personal trainers and Mel Gibson.

After the initial meeting of Fox and Woods, however, the pic degenerates into a series of random melees that will bring the buddies together – and introduce a stale subplot that has the actor helping Moss woo his sort-of girlfriend (Annabella Sciorra) as an added bonus.

Woods is appropriately gruff and nasty as the cop, and his trademark intensity makes a broad target for Fox to play off.

■ **HAREM**

1985, 113 MINS, FRANCE ◇ ⑫
Dir Arthur Joffe   *Prod* Alain Sarde   *Scr* Arthur Joffe, Tom Rayfiel, Richard Prieur   *Ph* Pasqualino De Santis
Ed Dominique Martin   *Mus* Philippe Sarde
Art Dir Alexandre Trauner
● Nastassja Kinski, Ben Kingsley, Dennis Goldson, Zohra Segal, Michel Robin, Julette Simpson (Sara)

Harem is an album of gorgeous images, aligned to tell a story, but it's a poor excuse for a dramatic motion picture packaged for the international marketplace.

Despite an investment of $10 million, which afforded stars Ben Kingsley and Nastassja Kinski, producer has skimped on the essential – screenwriter. Instead he has disastrously allowed director Arthur Joffe, obviously not yet at ease with an elaborate full-length narrative, to develop his own original story idea.

Tale concerns a fabulously wealthy Arab prince who kidnaps a beautiful young New York girl and has her brought to his desert palace, where she joins his harem.

As played by Kingsley, the unscrupulous potentate turns out to be a hypersentive aesthete, trapped by tradition to maintain, for appearances' sake at least, a way of life he doesn't believe in.

The film is visually ravishing, often happily distracting the viewer from the emptiness of the script and the exasperating indigence of the main characters.

■ **HARLAN COUNTY, U.S.A.**

1976, 103 MINS, US ◇ ⑫
Dir Barbara Kopple   *Prod* Barbara Kopple
Scr Barbara Kopple   *Ph* Hart Perry, Kevin Keating, Phil Parmet, Flip McCarthy, Tom Hurwitz   *Ed* Nancy Baker, Mary Lampson, Lora Hays, Mirra Bank   *Mus* Merle Travis, David Morris, Nimrod Workman, Sarah Gunning, Hazel Dickens, Phyllis Boyens
● (Cabin Creek)

Harlan County, U.S.A. is in essence a straight-forward cinema verite documentary about a coal miners' strike in Kentucky. Director Barbara Kopple began the project in 1972 in Kentucky and was on hand to record the year-plus battle of coal miners at the Brookside Mine in Harlan to join the United Mine Workers.

There is much emphasis on the predictable elements which give the pic the impact of a carefully-plotted fiction feature.

Actual strike events are fleshed out with vintage film and stills of mining conditions over the years, of previous labor battles and of current living (and dying) conditions in the industry.

The stars of the film are the men and women of Harlan County, portrayed here not as patronized mountain folks but as human beings.
□ 1976: Best Feature Documentary

■ **HARLEM NIGHTS**

1989, 118 MINS, US ◇ ⑫ ⊙
Dir Eddie Murphy   *Prod* Robert D. Wachs, Mark Lipsky
Scr Eddie Murphy   *Ph* Woody Omens   *Ed* George

Bowers   *Mus* Herbie Hancock   *Art Dir* Lawrence G. Paull
● Eddie Murphy, Richard Pryor, Redd Foxx, Danny Aiello, Michael Lerner, Della Reese (Murphy)

This blatantly excessive directorial debut for Eddie Murphy is overdone, too rarely funny and, worst of all, boring.

The film features Richard Pryor as the sage Sugar Ray to Murphy's hot-tempered Quick, who risk losing their 1930s Harlem nightclub when a corpulent crime boss (Michael Lerner) sets his sights on it.

The pair hatches up a predictable scheme to turn the tables on the mobster, whose henchmen include a cold-hearted mistress (Jasmine Guy) and a crooked cop (Danny Aiello).

There's an obnoxious cameo by Murphy's chum Arsenio Hall that proves pointless and unnecessary, as well as a mean-spirited recurring gag involving the stuttering heavyweight champ (Stan Shaw).

But the film does have its moments, such as when Murphy dukes it out with Reese's growling club madam or beds the carnivorous Dominque (Guy).
□ 1989: Nomination: Best Costume Design

■ **HARLEY DAVIDSON & THE MARLBORO MAN**

1991, 93 MINS, US ◇ ⑫ ⊙
Dir Simon Wincer   *Prod* Jere Henshaw   *Scr* Don Michael Paul   *Ph* David Eggby   *Ed* Corky Ehlers
Mus Basil Poledouris   *Art Dir* Paul Peters
● Mickey Rourke, Don Johnson, Chelsea Field, Daniel Baldwin, Tom Sizemore, Vanessa Williams (M-G-M/Krisjair-Laredo)

A dopey, almost poignantly bad actioner about two legends-in-their-own-minds, who bungle their way through a bank robbery on behalf of a friend, stands out only for big stars Mickey Rourke and Don Johnson.

Set in the wild west of Burbank, Calif, in 1996, when gasoline has gone up to $3.50 a gallon and people are getting high on something called Crystal Drano – er, Crystal Dream – *Harley* has two rebellious drifters (Rourke and Johnson) blowing into town to check on an old friend who's in trouble because a bank wants to foreclose on his business, their old hangout, the Rock 'n' Roll Bar & Grill. The big-hearted boys go into action to rob the bank, but their stunt eventually winds up getting all their buddies killed.

Pic scores mainly in the second unit and stunt department, with hotly staged bike chases and an abundance of breaking glass, falling bodies and shoot-outs, and the production design is an asset.

■ **HARLOW**

1965, 107 MINS, US ⑫
Dir Alex Segal   *Prod* Lee Savin   *Scr* Karl Tunberg
Ph Jim Kilgore   *Mus* Al Ham, Nelson Riddle
Art Dir Duncan Cramer
● Carol Lynley, Efrem Zimbalist Jr, Ginger Rogers, Barry Sullivan, Hurd Hatfield, Celia Lovsky (Sargent)

This first-to-market biopic lensed in the quick-filming Electronovision process is peopled with a set of characters not altogether convincing and even the star part making small impression. Carol Lynley, as the tragic, platinum-tressed queen of the 1930s, who was a sex symbol of her time, tries valiantly but the outcome is not altogether a triumph.

The script follows the major points of the Harlow tradition although dramatic licenses are taken. The Paul Bern incident figures prominently, a dramatic hook utilized to mold the entire later character of the star. Hurd Hatfield in the role of the producer-writer who weds the sexy blonde and then commits suicide when he discovers he's impotent, delivers a sincere performance. Celia

H

Lovsky's is another honestly-offered delineation, as Maria Ouspenskaya, the veteran actress to whom Jean goes for dramatic instruction after she temporarily deserts her film career.

Technically, this third Electronovision production – preceded by *Hamlet* and *The TAMI Story* – and first to be shot under controlled conditions on a soundstage, still presents many problems. Photography continues to be a major difficulty, grainy and of general poor quality, and bad lighting heightens the effect of oldfashioned production. Filmed in eight days in the TV-type lensing process, picture very often looks it as action sketches the rise of the star until her untimely death while still a young woman. Alex Segal's direction is as good as the script and fast-filming process will permit.

■ **HARLOW**

1965, 125 MINS, US ◇ ⓥ
Dir Gordon Douglas   *Prod* Joseph E. Levine   *Scr* John Michael Hayes   *Ph* Joseph Ruttenberg   *Ed* Frank Bracht, Archie Marshek   *Mus* Neal Hefti   *Art Dir* Hal Pereira, Roland Anderson
● Carroll Baker, Martin Balsam, Red Buttons, Michael Connors, Angela Lansbury, Peter Lawford (Paramount/Levine)

Second biopic of Jean Harlow is handsomely mounted. As the ill-fated Jean Harlow, Carroll Baker is a fairly reasonable facsimile although she lacks the electric fire of the original.

Script by John Michael Hayes is based on the questionable (at least in Hollywood) biog by Irving Shulman, who wrote tome in collaboration with Arthur Landau, the star's first agent. The part of Landau is fashioned almost on a par with the star character herself in the opening reels, past the needs of the story which essentially focuses on girl's rise to become one of the hottest properties in films of that era.

Several real-life characters are thinly veiled while parts of star's mother and stepfather are importantly projected. Angela Lansbury undertakes role of Mama Jean with quiet conviction, and Raf Vallone in the Marino Bello-stepfather role, also lends a persuasive presence.

Martin Balsam, head of Harlow's studio (here called Majestic Pictures) who gives her her chance at stardom, is the thinly-veiled Louis B. Mayer.

■ **HAROLD AND MAUDE**

1971, 90 MINS, US ◇ ⓥ ⊙
Dir Hal Ashby   *Prod* Colin Higgins, Charles B. Mulvehill   *Scr* Colin Higgins   *Ph* John A. Alonzo   *Ed* William A. Sawyer, Edward Warschilka   *Mus* Cat Stevens   *Art Dir* Michael Haller
● Ruth Gordon, Bud Cort, Vivian Pickles, Cyril Cusack, Charles Tyner, Ellen Geer (Paramount)

Harold and Maude has all the fun and gaiety of a burning orphanage. Ruth Gordon heads the cast as an offensive eccentric who becomes a beacon in the life of a self-destructive rich boy, played by Bud Cort. Together they attend funerals and indulge in specious philosophizing.

Director Hal Ashby's second feature is marked by a few good gags, but marred by a greater preponderance of sophomoric, overdone and mocking humor.

Cort does well as the spoiled neurotic whose repeated suicide attempts barely ruffle the feathers of mother Vivian Pickles, whose urbane performance is outstanding. She solicits a computer dating service to provide three potential brides: Shari Summers and Judy Engles are frightened off by Cort's bizarre doings, but Ellen Geer is delightful as one who goes him one better.

One thing that can be said about Ashby – he begins the film in a gross and macabre manner, and never once deviates from the concept. That's style for you.

■ **HARPER**
(UK: *The Moving Target*)

1966, 121 MINS, US ◇ ⓥ ⊙
Dir Jack Smight   *Prod* Jerry Gershwin, Elliott Kastner   *Scr* William Goldman   *Ph* Conrad Hall   *Ed* Stefan Arnsten   *Mus* Johnny Mandel   *Art Dir* Alfred Sweeney
● Paul Newman, Lauren Bacall, Julie Harris, Arthur Hill, Janet Leigh, Pamela Tiffin (Warner)

Harper is a contemporary mystery-comedy with Paul Newman as a sardonic private eye involved in a missing person trackdown. Some excellent directorial touches and solid thesping are evident in the colorful and plush production. Abundance of comedy and sometimes extraneous emphasis on cameo characters make for a relaxed pace and imbalanced concept, resulting in overlength and telegraphing of climax.

Ross MacDonald's novel, *The Moving Target*, has Newman commissioned by Lauren Bacall to find her hubby (never seen until climax), although she has no love for either him or step-daughter Pamela Tiffin.

Complications include the spoiled Tiffin, casual companion of family pilot Robert Wagner, himself hung up on Julie Harris, a piano bar entertainer also a junkie. Shelley Winters is the aging actress failure who has known the missing man, and is married to Robert Webber, brains behind a wetback smuggling ring run by religious nut Strother Martin.

Director Jack Smight has inserted countless touches which illuminate each character to the highest degree. In this he complements William Goldman's sharp and often salty lingo. All principals acquit themselves admirably, including Newman, Bacall, Webber, and particularly Winters, who makes every second count as the once-aspiring film star now on the high-calorie sauce.

■ **HARRY & SON**

1984, 117 MINS, US ◇ ⓥ ⊙
Dir Paul Newman   *Prod* Paul Newman, Ronald L. Buck   *Scr* Paul Newman, Ronald L. Buck   *Ph* Donald McAlpine   *Ed* Dede Allen   *Mus* Henry Mancini   *Art Dir* Henry Bumstead
● Paul Newman, Robby Benson, Ellen Barkin, Wilford Brimley, Judith Ivey, Joanne Woodward (Orion)

Fuzzily conceived and indecisively executed, *Harry & Son* represents a deeply disappointing return to the director's chair for Paul Newman. Cowritten and coproduced by the star as well, pic [suggested by the novel *A Lost King* by Raymond DeCapite] never makes up its mind who or what it wants to be about and, to compound the problem, never finds a proper style in which to convey the tragicomic events that transpire.

Opening scenes are perhaps the strongest, as Newman gets fired from his job as a Florida construction worker due to an ailment which momentarily blinds him. He goads his son into expanding his horizons beyond polishing cars and pretending to be a young Hemingway.

As presented, Newman's character is in a position either to give up on life or make a fresh start, and perhaps film's overriding frustration is that he goes nowhere. Structurally, it's a mess.

■ **HARRY AND THE HENDERSONS**

1987, 110 MINS, US ◇ ⓥ ⊙
Dir William Dear   *Prod* Richard Vane, William Dear   *Scr* William Dear, William E. Martin, Ezra D. Rappaport   *Ph* Allen Daviau   *Ed* Donn Cambern   *Mus* Bruce Broughton   *Art Dir* James Bissell
● John Lithgow, Melinda Dillon, Margaret Langrick, Joshua Rudoy, Kevin Peter Hall, David Suchet (Universal/Amblin)

Harry and the Hendersons is proof that the folks at Amblin Entertainment, a.k.a. Steven Spielberg's production company, can't keep using the same *E.T.* formula for every kiddie pic. Here, they've taken Big Foot, put him in Chewbacca's leftover *Star Wars* costume and given him E.T.'s sweet disposition – resulting in a lobotomized hairy animal who is so wimpy, it's painful.

Film could be titled, *Big Foot Meets a Happy, Loving Suburban Family in the Woods Camping and Goes Home with Them to Become Docile When Bathed and Fed.*

The excitement and suspense of running into Big Foot, later named Harry (Kevin Peter Hall), is wrapped up in the first few minutes of the film when Dad (John Lithgow) runs over the beast in the family station-wagon and takes him home to Seattle.

Theirs is a typical Spielberg house in the 'burbs – decorated in yuppie coziness that's soon turned topsy-turvy when Harry revives and scares the living daylights out of the Hendersons.

Mom (Melinda Dillon) is genuinely good-natured, with a bratty son (Joshua Rudoy) and a very obedient teenage daughter (Margaret Langrick) to complement Dad's growing hysteria as Harry is sighted around town. Screenwriters milk it for all it's worth.
□ 1987: Best Makeup

■ **HARRY AND TONTO**

1974, 115 MINS, US ◇ ⓥ
Dir Paul Mazursky   *Prod* Paul Mazursky   *Scr* Paul Mazursky, Josh Greenfeld   *Ph* Michael Butler   *Ed* Richard Halsey   *Mus* Bill Conti   *Art Dir* Ted Haworth
● Art Carney, Ellen Burstyn, Chief Dan George, Geraldine Fitzgerald, Larry Hagman, Arthur Hunnicutt (20th Century-Fox)

Harry and Tonto stars Art Carney and a trained cat, respectively, in a pleasant film about an old man who rejuvenates himself on a cross-country trek. Script is a series of good human comedy vignettes, with the large supporting cast of many familiar names in virtual cameo roles.

Carney is excellent as an old NY widower, evicted by force from a building being torn down. The rupture in his life triggers an odyssey, with pet cat named Tonto, to LA, with family stopovers at the Jersey home of son Phil Bruns, then to Chicago where Ellen Burstyn remains a warm antagonist, finally to LA where Larry Hagman emerges as a failure in life. En route, Carney picks up young hitchhiker Melanie Mayron, eventually paired off with grandson Joshua Mostel.
□ 1974: Best Actor (Art Carney).
□ Nomination: Best Original Screenplay

■ **HARRY AND WALTER GO TO NEW YORK**

1976, 120 MINS, US ◇ ⓥ
Dir Mark Rydell   *Prod* Don Devlin, Harry Gittes   *Scr* John Byrum, Robert Kaufman   *Ph* Laszlo Kovacs   *Ed* Fredric Steinkamp, David Bretherton, Don Guidice   *Mus* David Shire   *Art Dir* Harry Horner
● James Caan, Elliott Gould, Michael Caine, Diane Keaton, Charles Durning, Lesley Ann Warren (Columbia)

Harry and Walter Go to New York is an alleged period comedy [from a story by Don Devlin and John Byrum] about two carnival types who get involved with a bigtime safecracker plus the femme leader of a radical movement. James Caan, Elliott Gould, Michael Caine and Diane Keaton are the respective stars in this two-hour embarrassment.

Busted for a carny ripoff, Caan and Gould are sent to prison where high-class, urbane

Caine is doing time for bank robbery, but living so well that Keaton, repping an underground paper, interviews Caine for a big expose.

The principals' paths intertwine through miles and miles of forced comedic footage, a climactic bank heist, plus all manner of running and jumping and screaming and hollering.

• •

■ HARRY IN YOUR POCKET

1973, 102 MINS, US ◇

Dir Bruce Geller   *Prod* Bruce Geller   *Scr* James David Buchanan, Ron Austin   *Ph* Fred Koenekamp   *Ed* Arthur L. Hilton   *Mus* Lalo Schifrin   *Art Dir* William Bates
● James Coburn, Michael Sarrazin, Trish Van Devere, Walter Pidgeon, Michael C. Gwynne, Tony Giorgio (United Artists)

Any earnest young man mulling a pickpocket career might pick up some valuable pointers in *Harry in Your Pocket*, story of a gang of slick dips. Producer-director Bruce Geller invades the underworld of cannons (master pick-pockets) with a fast expose of how they operate.

Well-paced and credible script poses the situation of a novice with his girlfriend joining a couple of smooth pros to learn the biz. James Coburn and Walter Pidgeon are the experts – Coburn the cannon and Pidgeon his cocaine-sniffing associate – and Michael Sarrazin and Trish Van Devere the apprentices. Presence of Van Devere leads to romantic complications and an underlying feud between Coburn and Sarrazin.

To assure authenticity, Geller hired Tony Giorgio, sleight-of-hand artist well versed in all the dip tricks, who worked both as technical advisor and appears as a detective.

Coburn delivers convincingly as he instructs his amateurs in the art of lifting wallets.

• •

■ HARVEY

1950, 103 MINS, US 🔞 ⊙

Dir Henry Koster   *Prod* John Beck   *Scr* Mary Chase, Oscar Brodney   *Ph* William Daniels   *Ed* Ralph Dawson   *Mus* Frank Skinner
● James Stewart, Josephine Hull, Peggy Dow, Charles Drake, Cecil Kellaway, Wallace Ford (Universal)

Harvey, Mary Chase's Pulitzer Prize play, loses little of its whimsical comedy charm in the screen translation.

Three of the principals, James Stewart, Josephine Hull and Jesse White, were seasoned in the wacky characters by playing them on stage.

The exploits of Elwood P. Dowd, a man who successfully escaped from trying reality when his invisible six-foot rabbit pal Harvey came into his life, continually spring chuckles, often hilarity, as the footage unfolds. Stewart would seem the perfect casting for the character so well does he convey the idea that escape from life into a pleasant half-world existence has many points in its favor. Josephine Hull, the slightly balmy aunt who wants to have Elwood committed, is immense, socking the comedy for every bit of its worth.
  □ 1950: Best Supp. Actress (Josephine Hull).
  □ Nomination: Best Actor (James Stewart)

• •

■ HARVEY GIRLS, THE

1946, 101 MINS, US ◇ 🔞 ⊙

Dir George Sidney   *Prod* Arthur Freed   *Scr* Edmund Beloin, Nathaniel Curtis, Harry Crane, James O'Hanlon, Samson Raphaelson, Kay Van Riper   *Ph* George Folsey   *Ed* Albert Akst   *Mus* Lennie Hayton (dir.)   *Art Dir* Cedric Gibbons, William Ferrari
● Judy Garland, John Hodiak, Ray Bolger, Angela Lansbury, Marjorie Main, Cyd Charisse (M-G-M)

The Harvey Girls [based on the novel by Samuel Hopkins Adams and the original story by Eleanore Griffin and William Rankin] is a curious blend of Technicolor wild-westernism, frontier town skullduggery and a troupe of Harvey restaurant waitresses who deport themselves in a manner that's a cross between a sorority and a Follies troupe.

John Hodiak is a curious casting in a musical of this nature. Judy Garland, however, makes much of it believable and most of it acceptable. Angela Lansbury is prominent as the Mae West of the casino, Hodiak's No. 1 flame until Garland, Virginia O'Brien and Cyd Charisse, appear on the scene.

There's the usual fol-de-rol such as hijacking all the good steaks; snakes in the Harvey gals' closets; incendiary tactics and the like.
  □ 1946: Best Song ('On the Atchison, Topeka and the Santa Fe').
  □ Nomination: Best Scoring of a Musical Picture

• •

■ HAS ANYBODY SEEN MY GAL

1952, 88 MINS, US ◇

Dir Douglas Sirk   *Prod* Ted Richmond   *Scr* Joseph Hoffman   *Ph* Clifford Stine   *Ed* Russell Schoengarth   *Mus* Joseph Gershenson (dir.)   *Art Dir* Bernard Herzbrun, Hilyard Brown
● Piper Laurie, Rock Hudson, Charles Coburn, Gigi Perreau, Lynn Bari, William Reynolds (Universal)

A rather solid piece of nostalgic entertainment is offered in this comedy-drama of the 1920s 'flapper' era [based on a story by Eleanor H. Porter]. While the younger Piper Laurie and Rock Hudson are starred over him, it is really Charles Coburn's vehicle.

He wallops the part of a rich old duffer who plans to leave his fortune to the family of a girl who had spurned his proposal of marriage years before.

Incognito, he travels to the small Vermont town where the family lives to find out what kind of people they are. Coburn arranges for the family to receive $100,000 from an 'unnamed' benefactor and sits back to observe the results.

Laurie and Hudson team well as the young lovers. She does things to a sweater that were not done during the time of the story, but otherwise the era is recreated rather faithfully.

• •

■ HASTY HEART, THE

1949, 102 MINS, US

Dir Vincent Sherman   *Prod* [uncredited]   *Scr* Ranald MacDougall   *Ph* Wilkie Cooper   *Ed* E.B. Jarvis   *Mus* Jack Beaver   *Art Dir* Terence Verity
● Ronald Reagan, Patricia Neal, Richard Todd, Anthony Nicholls, Howard Crawford, Ralph Michael (Warner)

The John Patrick play has grown in range of feeling on the screen, although the essentials of the legit staging have not been changed.Its background is the Second World War and the setting is an army hospital in Burma, in a ward where six assorted soldiers sweat out their injuries while awaiting shipment home.

Notable is the performance of Richard Todd in the role of the Scot who must die. Todd comes over with a performance that is star calibre in every facet.

Ronald Reagan plays the Yank with the exact amount of gusto such a character should have in a British outpost hospital. Patricia Neal gives feeling to her role as the nurse.

Vincent Sherman directed the production in England. Ranald MacDougall's scripting is wise to the humaneness that marked the play and the tremendous heart that backgrounds the telling.
  □ 1949: Nomination: Best Actor (Richard Todd)

• •

■ HATARI!

1962, 159 MINS, US ◇ 🔞 ⊙

Dir Howard Hawks   *Prod* Howard Hawks   *Scr* Leigh

Brackett   *Ph* Russell Harlan   *Ed* Stuart Gilmore   *Mus* Henry Mancini   *Art Dir* Hal Pereira, Carl Anderson
● John Wayne, Hardy Kruger, Elsa Martinelli, Gerard Blain, Red Buttons, Michele Girardon (Paramount)

Hatari! is an ambitious undertaking. Its cast is an international one, populated by players of many countries. Its wild animals do not come charging out of dusty stock footage studio libraries but have been photographed while beating around the bush of Tanganyika, East Africa. However, in this instance, the strapping physique of the film unhappily emphasizes the anemic condition of the story streaming within.

Leigh Brackett's screenplay, from an original story by Harry Kurnitz, describes at exhaustive length the methods by which a group of game catchers in Tanganyika go about catching wild animals for the zoo when not occupied at catching each other for the woo. Script lacks momentum. It never really advances toward a story goal.

John Wayne heads the colorful cast assembled for this zoological field trip. The vet star plays with his customary effortless (or so it seems) authority a role with which he is identified; the good-natured, but hard-drinking, hot-tempered, big Irishman who 'thinks women are trouble' in a man's world.

Germany's Hardy Kruger and French actor Gerard Blain manage, resourcefully, to pump what vigor they can muster into a pair of undernourished roles. Red Buttons and Elsa Martinelli emerge the histrionic stickouts, Buttons with a jovial portrayal of an excabbie who 'just pretends it's rush hour in Brooklyn' as he jockeys his vehicle through a pack of frightened giraffe, Martinelli as a sweet but spirited shutterbug and part time pachydermatologist.
  □ 1962: Nomination: Best Color Cinematography

• •

■ HATFUL OF RAIN, A

1957, 109 MINS, US

Dir Fred Zinnemann   *Prod* Buddy Adler   *Scr* Michael Vicente Gazzo, Alfred Hayes   *Ph* Joe MacDonald   *Ed* Dorothy Spencer   *Mus* Bernard Herrmann   *Art Dir* Lyle R. Wheeler, Leland Fuller
● Eva Marie Saint, Don Murray, Anthony Franciosa, Lloyd Nolan, Henry Silva, William Hickey (20th Century-Fox)

The first film dealing with dope addiction made with the prior approval of the industry's self-governing Production Code, *A Hatful of Rain* is more than a story of a junkie. It touches knowingly and sensitively on a family relationship. Michael V. Gazzo has converted his Broadway play into a provocative and engrossing film drama.

The people involved in this web of narcotics are basically decent human beings. The story revolves about their reactions when one of them turns out to be a junkie. As the pregnant wife of a narcotics addict, Eva Marie Saint handles the emotional peaks and tender moments with sensitive understanding. Don Murray scores, too, as the likeable junkie who desperately attempts to hide his secret from his wife and his obtusely devoted father.

The role of the brother who shares an apartment in a lower east side NY housing project with his dope-addicted relative and his wife is compellingly played by Anthony Franciosa, repeating his original stage assignment. Misunderstood and rejected by his father, Franciosa is moving as 'his brother's keeper' and sister-in-law's confidante. As the widowed father who left his sons in an orphanage at an early age, Lloyd Nolan turns in a topnotch portrayal. Henry Silva, also repeating his stage role, is convincingly unctuous and contemptible as the dope peddler.
  □ 1957: Nomination: Best Actor (Anthony Franciosa)

• •

■ HAUNTED HONEYMOON

1986, 82 MINS, US ◇ ⊛
Dir Gene Wilder   *Prod* Susan Ruskin   *Scr* Gene Wilder,
Terence Marsh   *Ph* Fred Schuler   *Ed* Christopher
Greenbury   *Mus* John Morris   *Art Dir* Terence Marsh
● Gene Wilder, Gilda Radner, Dom DeLuise, Jonathan
Pryce, Paul L. Smith, Peter Vaughan (Orion)

Gene Wilder is back in the rut of sending up
old film conventions in *Haunted Honeymoon*, a
mild farce. Title is a misnomer, since set-up
has radio actor Wilder taking his fiancee
Gilda Radner out to his family's gloomy country estate to meet the kinfolk just before tying the knot. Clan is presided over by the
tubby, genial Aunt Kate, played by Dom
DeLuise, who maintains that a werewolf is on
the loose in the vicinity.

In any event, Wilder is obliged to contend
with numerous assaults on his health, and
much of the blessedly brief running time is
devoted to frantic running among different
rooms in the mansion for reasons that occasionally prove faintly amusing but are singularly uncompelling. Pic provokes a few
chuckles along the way, but no guffaws.

....

■ HAUNTING, THE

1963, 112 MINS, US ⊛ ⊙
Dir Robert Wise   *Prod* Robert Wise   *Scr* Nelson
Gidding   *Ph* Davis Boulton   *Ed* Ernest Walter
Mus Humphrey Searle   *Art Dir* Elliot Scott
● Julie Harris, Claire Bloom, Richard Johnson, Russ
Tamblyn, Lois Maxwell, Fay Compton (M-G-M)

The artful cinematic strokes of director
Robert Wise and staff are not quite enough to
override the major shortcomings of Nelson
Gidding's screenplay from the Shirley Jackson
novel.

Gidding's scenario is opaque in spots, but
its cardinal flaw is one of failure to follow
through on its thematic motivation. After
elaborately setting the audience up in anticipation of drawing some scientific conclusions
about the psychic phenomena field, the film
completely dodges the issue in settling for a
half-hearted melodramatic climax.

The story has to do with the efforts of a
small psychic research team led by an anthropology professor (Richard Johnson) to study
the supernatural powers that seem to inhabit
a 90-year-old New England house with a reputation for evil. The group includes an unhappy spinster (Julie Harris) obsessed with
guilt feelings over the recent death of her
mother; a young woman (Claire Bloom) of
unnatural instincts (she has lesbian tendencies coupled with an extraordinary sense of
ESP); and a young man (Russ Tamblyn) who
is to inherit the house.

The acting is effective all around. The picture excels in the purely cinematic departments. Davis Boulton has employed his
camera with extraordinary dexterity in fashioning a visual excitement that keeps the picture alive with images of impending shock. As
photographed by Boulton, the house itself is a
monstrous personality, most decidedly the
star of the film. The pity is that all this production savvy has been squandered on a
screen yarn that cannot support such artistic
bulk.

....

■ HAVANA

1990, 145 MINS, US ◇ ⊛ ⊙
Dir Sydney Pollack   *Prod* Sydney Pollack   *Scr* Judith
Rascoe, David Rayfiel   *Ph* Owen Roizman   *Ed* Fredric
Steinkamp, William Steinkamp   *Mus* Dave Grusin
Art Dir Terence Marsh
● Robert Redford, Lena Olin, Alan Arkin, Tomas Milian,
Raul Julia, Mark Rydell (Mirage/Universal)

Much as the filmmakers would like to get
there, *Havana* remains a long way from
Casablanca. In their seventh outing over a 25-

year period, director Sydney Pollack and star
Robert Redford have lost their normally dependable quality touch as they slog through a
notably uncompelling $45 million-plus tale of
a gringo caught up in the Cuban revolution.

In a shipboard prolog, Redford's rogue gambler character, Jack Weil, strikes a few sparks
with Lena Olin's mysterious Bobby Duran
and agrees to smuggle into Havana a radio
that will help Castro spread his word in the
capital in the waning days of 1958.

Although the city is astir with rumors concerning the rebel leader's activities in the
mountains, it's still business as usual under
the Batista dictatorship.

Redford's eye for Olin leads him into dangerous political territory involving her
wealthy left-wing husband Arturo (played
suavely by an uncredited Raul Julia), a CIA
spook posing as a food critic, and various military toughs.

Unfortunately, the tentative romance between the two is never really credible. As
usual, Redford is cool, reserved and a bit bemused, while the striking Olin is mercurial
and intense. The combination doesn't take.

Judith Rascoe's original script was written
in the mid-1970s. As rewritten by David
Rayfiel, yarn is a mishmash of old-hat
Hollywood conventions, political pussyfooting
and loads of bad dialog.

☐ 1990: Nomination: Best Original Score

....

■ HAVING A WILD WEEKEND

See: See: Catch Us If You Can

....

■ HAWAII

1966, 186 MINS, US ◇ ⊛ ⊙
Dir George Roy Hill   *Prod* Walter Mirisch   *Scr* Dalton
Trumbo, Daniel Taradash   *Ph* Russell Harlan   *Ed* Stuart
Gilmore   *Mus* Elmer Bernstein   *Art Dir* Cary Odell
● Julie Andrews, Max von Sydow, Richard Harris,
Carroll O'Connor, Elizabeth Cole, Gene Hackman
(Mirisch)

Based on James A. Michener's novel, which
embraced centuries of history, *Hawaii* focuses
on a critical period – 1820-41 – when the islands began to be commercialized, corrupted
and converted to Western ways. Superior production, acting and direction give depth and
credibility to a personal tragedy, set against
the clash of two civilizations.

Filmed at sea off Norway, also in New
England, Hollywood, Hawaii and Tahiti, this
vast production reps an outlay of about $15
million, including $600,000 for film rights,
and seven years of work. Fred Zinnemann,
originally set to produce-direct, worked four
and a half years on it, after which Hill took
over.

Dalton Trumbo and original adapter Daniel
Taradash are both credited with the screenplay, which develops Max von Sydow's character from a young and over-zealous Protestant
missionary, through courtship of Julie
Andrews, to their religious work in Hawaii.
Richard Harris, an old beau, turns up occasionally at major plot turns.

Von Sydow's outstanding performance
makes his character comprehensible, if never
totally sympathetic. A less competent actor,
with less competent direction and scripting,
would have blown the part, and with that, the
film. Andrews is excellent in a demanding
dramatic role.

Hill's direction, solid in the intimate dramatic scenes, is as good in crowd shots which
rep the major external events.

☐ 1966: Nominations: Best Supp. Actress
(Jocelyn Lagarde), Color Cinematography,
Color Costume Design, Color Costume
Design, Original Music Score, Song ('My
Wishing Doll'), Sound, Visual Effects

....

■ HAWAIIANS, THE

(UK: Master of the Islands)

1970, 134 MINS, US ◇
Dir Tom Gries   *Prod* Walter Mirisch   *Scr* James R.
Webb   *Ph* Phil Lathrop, Lucien Ballard   *Ed* Ralph
Winters, Byron Brandt   *Mus* Henry Mancini
Art Dir Cary Odell
● Charlton Heston, Geraldine Chaplin, John Phillip Law,
Tina Chen, Alec McCowen, Mako (United Artists/Mirisch)

While James A. Michener's monumental
novel, *Hawaii*, contained enough material for
half a dozen films, the earlier version in 1966
used up most of the first half. This followup
film, devotes most of its time to the growth of
Hawaii in the present century and the huge
influx of other Orientals, particularly the
Chinese and Japanese, into the islands as
cheap labor.

Charlton Heston, as the American descendant of early settlers and the only man with
the vision and steadfastness to make the Hawaiian
Islands one of the garden spots of the world
(he's credited with introducing the pineapple
as a commercial crop), is less the larger-than-
life hero and more a stereotyped islander.

☐ 1970: Nomination: Best Costume Design

....

■ HAWKS

1988, 107 MINS, UK ◇ ⊛
Dir Robert Ellis Miller   *Prod* Steve Lanning, Keith Cavele
Scr Roy Clarke   *Ph* Doug Milsome   *Ed* Malcolm Cook
Mus Barry Gibb   *Art Dir* Peter Howitt
● Timothy Dalton, Anthony Edwards, Janet McTeer,
Camille Coduri, Connie Booth (Gibb/English/PRO)

This black comedy about terminal cancer patients escaping for one last fling stares death
in the face and laughs, but takes too long to
get to the punch line.

From the start, it's clear that director
Robert Ellis Miller is using the script about
men facing an early death to examine how
people deal with their fears and how they try
or fail to disguise it from others.

In this instance, terminal bone cancer pits
lawyer Bancroft (Timothy Dalton) and ex-
football pro Decker (Anthony Edwards) together in a team effort to thwart their disease
(and the ward nurses) with laughs, grit and a
last pilgrimage to a Dutch bordello.

Dalton goes a bit overboard as Bancroft, occasionally stretching believability. Edwards
plays it straight as the Yank jock, but brings
out the laconic ladies' man in his character despite being nonambulatory much of the time.

....

■ HEAD OVER HEELS

1979, 97 MINS, US ◇ ⊛
Dir Joan Micklin Silver   *Prod* Mark Metcalf   *Scr* Joan
Micklin Silver   *Ph* Bobby Byrne   *Ed* Cynthia Schneider
Mus Ken Lauber   *Art Dir* Peter Jamison
● John Heard, Mary Beth Hurt, Peter Riegert, Kenneth
McMillan, Gloria Grahame, Griffin Dunne (United
Artists/Triple Play)

Joan Micklin Silver's third directorial effort
possesses moderate charm and shows some of
the talent she's exhibited before, but ultimately emerges as somewhat thin and one-dimensional.

Based on Ann Beattie's novel *Chilly Scenes of
Winter*, Silver's screenplay has affable John
Heard reflecting back on his happy past with
Mary Beth Hurt from the wistful present.
Thrust of pic has him trying to win her back
from the clutches of king-sized jock Mark
Metcalf.

Ultimately, however, both characters rather
wear out their welcome, Heard becoming almost oppressively absolutist in his feelings
and Hurt seeming too confused and selfish to
be worth all the trouble. After all the difficulties and anxieties that have preceded it, resolution comes off as a bit pat and conventional.

....

■ HEAR MY SONG

1992, 113 MINS, UK ◇ ⊛ ⊙
Dir Peter Chelsom *Prod* Alison Owen *Scr* Peter
Chelsom, Adrian Dunbar *Ph* Sue Gibson *Ed* Martin
Walsh *Mus* John Altman *Art Dir* Caroline Hananna
● Ned Beatty, Adrian Dunbar, David McCallum, Tara
Fitzgerald, Shirley Ann Field, William Hootkins
(Limelight/Film Four/British Screen/Windmill Lane)

First feature from Peter Chelsom goes
straight for the heart with *Hear My Song*, an
unabashedly romantic fantasy about a concert
promoter (Adrian Dunbar), a seat-of-his-
pants operator who's this close to sealing a
relationship with his beautiful g.f. (Tara
Fitzgerald). The nightclub he's taken over in
an Irish neighborhood of Britain is ever on
the verge of collapse because of its unreliable
bottom-rung bookings.

Desperate for a hit, the promoter books a
Josef Locke lookalike (William Hootkins)
who's quite mad but seems to fill the billing as
'Mr X – Is He or Isn't He?' Legendary Irish
tenor Locke fled from public view at the height
of his popularity to avoid tax evasion charges.

Ned Beatty does much to stem the tide of
sentiment in a tough, grounded portrayal of
the real Locke, a man of substance and self-
awareness firmly entrenched in another life.
But by the final reels, it's become too much.
Dunbar carries off the lead role in winning
fashion, but the real discovery is likely to be
Fitzgerald, whose gamine charm is perfectly
introduced in this old-fashioned romance.

■ HEAR NO EVIL

1993, 97 MINS, US ◇ ⊛ ⊙
Dir Robert Greenwald *Prod* David Matalon *Scr* R.M.
Badat, Kathleen Rowell *Ph* Steven Shaw *Ed* Eva
Gardos *Mus* Graeme Revell *Art Dir* Bernt Capra
● Marlee Matlin, D.B. Sweeney, Martin Sheen, John C.
McGinley, Christina Carlisi, Greg Elan (20th Century-Fox)

A terminally dull would-be thriller, *Hear No
Evil* has a perfunctory story [by R.M. Badat
and Danny Rubin] with the gimmick of a deaf
damsel-in-distress grafted on uncertainly.
Oscar-winner Marlee Matlin's talents are
wasted.

Matlin plays a physical trainer in Portland
whose client (John C. McGinley) hides a rare
stolen coin in her beeper before being nabbed
by the cops.

McGinley's car blows up and corrupt cop
Martin Sheen starts harassing Matlin to retrieve the coin. McGinley's pal D.B. Sweeney
takes Matlin under his wing and the duo finally bring in the FBI to catch Sheen.

Director Robert Greenwald and his
scripters show little flair for suspense, nuance
or even elementary thrills. In the final reel
Matlin has a cat and mouse sequence trapped
in a mountain lodge with the killer, but unlike such effective films as *Wait Until Dark*,
her handicap (deafness) is not used as an
equalizer but instead merely increases her
jeopardy.

■ HEARTACHES

1981, 83 MINS, CANADA ◇ ⊛ ⊙
Dir Donald Shebib *Prod* Pieter Kroonenburg, David J.
Patterson, Jerry Ralbourn *Scr* Terence Heffernan
Ph Vic Sarin *Ed* Gerry Hambling, Peter Bolta
Mus Simon Michael Mastin
● Margot Kidder, Annie Potts, Robert Carradine,
Winston Rekert, George Touliatis (Rising Star)

Heartaches is a female buddy picture with actresses Margot Kidder and Annie Potts involved in a series of delightful misadventures
in love. Film, plagued by its own financial
heartaches, emerges unscathed from production delays and shut downs.

Potts is the wife of perennial juvenile
Robert Carradine who spends most of his
time racing cars and getting drunk. She splits

rather than face him with the hard fact that
he's not the father of the child she's carrying.

On her way to the big city for an abortion
Potts reluctantly teams up with Kidder.
Kidder in blond wig, tight pants, and outrageous jewelry looks the part of a kook. Her
foul-mouthed, man-hungry character is in
sharp contrast to Potts' relative innocence.

Cast is outstanding with Kidder giving full
performance. However, it is basically Potts'
film as the runaway wife who's tired of her
husband's immature attitude.

■ HEART BEAT

1979, 109 MINS, US ◇ ⊛
Dir John Byrum *Prod* Alan Greisman, Michael
Shamberg *Scr* John Byrum *Ph* Laszlo Kovacs *Ed* Eric
Jenkins *Mus* Jack Nitzsche *Art Dir* Jack Fisk
● Nick Nolte, Sissy Spacek, John Heard, Ray Sharkey,
Anne Dusenberry, Tony Bill (Orion)

Heart Beat never manages to expand its
loosely biographical tale of Jack Kerouac,
Neal and Carolyn Cassady beyond a very narrow scope.

Nick Nolte and Sissy Spacek, as the Cassadys
enmeshed in a love-hate relationship, are
standout in a film where performances dominate. Ditto Ray Sharkey, in a manic performance as a disguised Allen Ginsberg
character. John Heard struggles manfully with
the Kerouac character, but writer-director
John Byrum has given him few compass points
on which to base a reading.

Heat Beat fails to establish either a coherent
story line, or a definitive treatment of the
forces that shaped the literary and social explosion following publication of Kerouac's *On
the Road* in 1957.

■ HEARTBREAKERS

1984, 98 MINS, US ◇ ⊛
Dir Bobby Roth *Prod* Bob Weis, Bobby Roth
Scr Bobby Roth *Ph* Michael Ballhaus *Ed* John
Carnochan *Mus* Tangerine Dream
● Peter Coyote, Nick Mancuso, Carole Laure, Max Gail,
James Laurenson, Carol Wayne (Jethro)

Amusing and dramatic, sexy and insightful,
Heartbreakers is about contemporary relations
between the sexes and men's emotional lives.
Study of two male best friends in their mid-
30s who experience convulsions in their careers, romances and their own relationship
emerges as a potent portrait of modern
mores and neuroses.

Peter Coyote is superb, managing to maintain viewer sympathy even when his character
is unreasonable and wrong, and producing
genuine joy for him when his long artistic
struggle finally pays off.

Despite built-in limitations, Nick Mancuso
is appealing and holds his own, and admirably
registers his confusion and desperation in his
scenes with Carole Laure, fine as the insecure
but strong-minded art gallery assistant.

■ HEARTBREAK HOTEL

1988, 93 MINS, US ◇ ⊛ ⊙
Dir Chris Columbus *Prod* Linda Obst, Debra Hill
Scr Chris Columbus *Ph* Stephen Dobson *Ed* Raja
Gosnell *Mus* Georges Delerue *Art Dir* John Muto
● David Keith, Tuesday Weld, Charlie Schlatter, Angela
Goethais, Jacque Lynn Colton, Chris Mulkey (Touchstone)

Even Elvis never made a picture this bad.
Writer-director Chris Columbus' weakly conceived fantasy makes the ultimate mockery of
the late idol.

Charlie Schlatter plays a small-town teen
who kidnaps Elvis Presley after a 1972 concert appearance and brings him home to
cheer up his ditzy mom (Tuesday Weld),
who's been roughed up by her latest rotten
boyfriend (Chris Mulkey). Seems the only

thing that makes mom smile is memories of
Elvis, who apparently resembles dad.

Once he arrives out in Nowheresville, Elvis
(David Keith) offers some token resistence,
then settles right into the family for a few
days, soothing bedtime traumas for little sister and lonely mama alike. In the end, he flies
off in a big airplane after letting each member of the family know how swell they are and
that he'd stay if he could.

Columbus seems at a loss to decide what his
story's about or convey a consistent tone or
message. One minute he makes a monkey out
of Elvis, the next he takes a cornball stab at
making him a hero.

Weld's role is vacuous; she does what she
can with it. Keith is credible enough as Elvis
under the dismal circumstances. What passes
for rock 'n' roll in this pic is the sanitized
Disneyland variety.

■ HEARTBREAK KID, THE

1972, 104 MINS, US ◇ ⊛ ⊙
Dir Elaine May *Prod* Edgar J. Scherick *Scr* Neil Simon
Ph Owen Roizman *Ed* John Carter *Mus* Garry
Sherman *Art Dir* Richard Sylbert
● Charles Grodin, Cybill Shepherd, Jeannie Berlin,
Eddie Albert, Audra Lindley, William Prince (Palomar/
20th Century Fox)

The Heartbreak Kid is the bright, amusing saga
of a young NY bridegroom whose bride's
maddening idiosyncrasies freak him and he
leaves her at the end of a three-day Miami
honeymoon to pursue and wed another doll.
Scripted by Neil Simon from Bruce Jay
Friedman's *Esquire* mag story [*A Change of
Plan*], film has a sudden shut-off ending with
no climax whatever.

Elaine May's deft direction catches all the
possibilities of young romance and its tribulations in light strokes and cleverly accents
characterization of the various principals.
Most of the pace is as fast as Charles
Grodin's speeding to his Florida honeymoon,
and falling for a gorgeous blonde on the
beach the first day there.

Grodin is slick and able as the fast-talking
bridegroom whose patience is worn thin and
he's a natural for the charms of another.
□ 1972: Nominations: Best Supp. Actor
(Eddie Albert), Supp. Actress (Jeannie Berlin)

■ HEARTBREAK KID, THE

1993, 97 MINS, AUSTRALIA ◇ ⊛
Dir Michael Jenkins *Prod* Ben Gannon *Scr* Michael
Jenkins, Richard Barrett *Ph* Nino Martinetti *Ed* Peter
Carrodus *Mus* John Clifford White *Art Dir* Paddy
Reardon
● Claudia Karvan, Alex Dimitriades, Steve Bastoni, Nico
Lathouris, William McInnes, Doris Younane (View)

The Heartbreak Kid, which has no connection
with Elaine May's homonymous 1972 pic, is a
warm-hearted, liberating love story.

Set in the ethnically mixed suburbs of
Melbourne, pic establishes Claudia Karvan as
22-year-old Christina, a well-educated Greek-
Australian with wealthy parents. She's just
become engaged to the upwardly mobile
Dimitri (Steve Bastoni).

Embarking on a teaching career, Christina
has been assigned to work a rowdy high
school in a working class area. Spunky 17-
year-old Nick (Alex Dimitriades) makes it
clear that he has the hots for his teacher and
she, gradually, responds, eventually borrowing her girlfriend's apartment for secret afternoon trysts with her willing pupil.
Inevitably, the secret gets out.

Kid started life as a stage play, though you'd
never guess it, thanks to the skillful adaptation of playwright Richard Barrett and director Michael Jenkins, aided by fine work from
lenser Nino Martinetti.

H

■ HEARTBREAK RIDGE

1986, 130 MINS, US ◇ ⑰ ⊙
Dir Clint Eastwood   *Prod* Clint Eastwood   *Scr* James
Carabatsos   *Ph* Jack N. Green   *Ed* Joel Cox
Mus Lennie Niehaus   *Art Dir* Edward Carfagno
● Clint Eastwood, Marsha Mason, Everett McGill, Moses
Gunn, Eileen Heckart, Bo Svenson (Malpaso/Weston)

Heartbreak Ridge offers another vintage Clint
Eastwood performance. There are enough
mumbled half-liners in this contemporary
war pic to satisfy those die-hards eager to see
just how he portrays the consummate marine
veteran.

Eastwood is Gunnery Sergeant Tom
Highway – a man determined to teach some
of today's young leathernecks how to behave
like a few good men.

Eastwood's stern ways inevitably prevail as
his platoon is called up for emergency overseas combat. Guns are blazing as Clint's
cadre faces its first real action after hitting
the beaches. As film moves towards its jingoistic peak in these sequences, Eastwood's in-
subordinate bent culminates in a final conflict
with a modern major (Everett McGill).
☐ 1986: Nomination: Best Sound

■ HEARTBURN

1986, 108 MINS, US ◇ ⑰ ⊙
Dir Mike Nichols   *Prod* Mike Nichols, Robert Greenhut
Scr Nora Ephron   *Ph* Nestor Almendros   *Ed* Sam
O'Steen   *Mus* Carly Simon   *Art Dir* Tony Walton
● Meryl Streep, Jack Nicholson, Jeff Daniels, Maureen
Stapleton, Stockard Channing, Richard Masur
(Paramount)

Heartburn is a beautifully crafted film with
flawless performances and many splendid moments, yet the overall effect is a bit disappointing.

From the start Meryl Streep and Jack
Nicholson are never quite a couple. He's a
Washington political columnist and she's a
New York food writer. They meet at a wed-
ding and he overpowers her. Soon they're
having their own wedding.

Nora Ephron adapted her own novel for the
screen which in turn borrowed heavily from
her marriage with Watergate reporter Carl
Bernstein.

While the day-to-day details are drawn with
a striking clarity, Ephron's script never goes
much beyond the mannerisms of middle-class
life. Even with the sketchy background information, it's hard to tell what these people are
feeling or what they want.

Where the film does excel is in creating the
surface and texture of their life. Director
Mike Nichols knows the territory well enough
to throw in some subtle but biting satire and
Nicholson (who replaced Mandy Patinkin during production) and Streep fill in the canvas.

■ HEART CONDITION

1990, 95 MINS, US ◇ ⑰ ⊙
Dir James D. Parriott   *Prod* Steve Tisch   *Scr* James D.
Parriott   *Ph* Arthur Albert   *Ed* David Finfer
Mus Patrick Leonard   *Art Dir* John Muto
● Bob Hoskins, Denzel Washington, Chloe Webb, Roger
E. Mosley, Janet Dubois, Alan Rachins (New Line)

From what seems like a far-fetched premise –
a cop who gets a heart transplant ends up depending on his worst enemy's ticker – writer-
director James D. Parriott spins a most
engrossing and rewarding tale in an auspicious feature debut.

Bob Hoskins plays vice detective Moony, an
intense, crazy, racist slob who briefly has a
girl in his life – a hooker, Crystal (Chloe
Webb). She disappears and gets involved with
her black lawyer, Stone (Denzel Washington),
a handsome self-possessed smooth operator
who becomes the object of Moony's obsessive
rage.

Moony, who lives on greaseburgers and
booze, has a heart attack the same night
Stone is killed in a car crash. Thanks to expedient transplant surgery he ends up a 'blood
brother' to his enemy. To Moony's horror,
the sarcastic, clever Stone appears in ghost-
like form visible only to him, and becomes his
constant, unwanted companion.

Washington creates a most compelling
character in Stone, finding the rhythm of the
role with an assurance that never flags;
Hoskins is gutsy and amusing, exhibiting bug-
eyed discomfort when he's manicured and
barbered in a Stone-style transformation.

■ HEART IS A LONELY HUNTER, THE

1968, 122 MINS, US ◇ ⑰
Dir Robert Ellis Miller   *Prod* Thomas C. Ryan, Marc
Merson   *Scr* Thomas C. Ryan   *Ph* James Wong Howe
Ed John F. Burnett   *Mus* Dave Grusin   *Art Dir* LeRoy
Deane
● Alan Arkin, Sondra Locke, Laurinda Barrett, Stacy
Keach, Chuck McCann, Cicely Tyson (Warner)

Translating to the screen the delicate if specious tragedy of Carson McCullers' first novel
was clearly not an easy matter. Nor an entirely successful one, either. *The Heart is a
Lonely Hunter* emerges as a fragmented
episodic melodrama, with uneven dramatic
impact and formula pacing.

Alan Arkin's starring performance as a
deaf-and-mute loner is erratic and mannered,
but supporting cast generally is on target.

Story turns on Arkin and his influence on
the lives of others. Pivotal character is little
more than a prop, but, as rendered by Arkin,
a destructive one.

Arkin's performance is marred by twitching
mannerism. Result is slapstick at times,
bathos at others. Suffice it to say that when
the focus of attention returns to the main
character, the pic has a tendency to fall apart.

The motivations of other characters are defined in better fashion, although the credibility of most is doubtful. Actors have an uphill
fight, and to their personal credit they rise
above the material.
☐ 1968: Nominations: Best Actor (Alan
Arkin), Supp. Actress (Sondra Locke)

■ HEARTLAND

1980, 98 MINS, US ◇ ⑰
Dir Richard Pearce   *Prod* Annick Smith   *Scr* Beth Ferris
Ph Fred Murphy   *Ed* Bill Yahraus   *Mus* Charles Gross
Art Dir Carl Copeland
● Conchata Ferrell, Rip Torn, Lilia Skala, Barry Primus,
Megan Folson, Amy Wright (Wilderness Women's
Productions/Filmhaus)

Heartland is a film with heart about the tribulations of homesteading life in Wyoming circa
1910. The entire budget of $600,000 was
backed by the National Endowment for the
Humanities.

The ruggedness of ranch life is mainly
shown from the viewpoint of a hearty, strong
but never overbearing widow with a 10-year-
old child who goes to a ranch in an isolated
part of Wyoming to be the housekeeper for a
taciturn Scottish rancher.

The seasons are neatly etched by lenser
Fred Murphy and perceptive script, based on
the books of the real widow Elinore Randall
Stewart, is also an asset.

Richard Pearce, who made many docus and
some TV films, handles this simple tale with
a nice balance of regional feel and elemental
drama.

■ HEART LIKE A WHEEL

1983, 113 MINS, US ◇ ⑰ ⊙
Dir Jonathan Kaplan   *Prod* Charles Roven   *Scr* Ken
Friedman   *Ph* Tak Fujimoto   *Ed* O. Nicholas Brown

Mus Laurence Rosenthal   *Art Dir* James William Newport
● Bonnie Bedelia, Beau Bridges, Leo Rossi, Hoyt Axton,
Bill McKinney, Anthony Edwards (Aurora/20th Century-
Fox)

Heart Like A Wheel is a surprisingly fine biopic
of Shirley Muldowney, the first professional
female race car driver. What could have been
a routine good ol' gal success story has been
heightened into an emotionally involving, superbly made drama.

Winning prolog as pa Hoyt Axton letting
his little daughter take the wheel of his
speeding sedan, an indelible experience
which prefigures Shirley, by the mid-1950s,
winning drag races against the hottest rods in
town.

Happily married to her mechanic husband
Jack and with a young son, Shirley finds her
innate ability compelling her, by 1966, to enter her first pro race. Roadblocked at first by
astonished, and predictably sexist, officials,
Shirley proceeds to set the track record in her
qualifying run, and her career is underway.

But her husband ultimately can't take her
career-mindedness, and she's forced to set
out on her own.

Director Jonathan Kaplan has served a long
apprenticeship but nothing he has done before prepares one for his mature, accomplished work here.

■ HEART OF MIDNIGHT

1988, 101 MINS, US ◇ ⑰ ⊙
Dir Matthew Chapman   *Prod* Andrew Gaty
Scr Matthew Chapman   *Ph* Ray Rivas   *Ed* Penelope
Shaw   *Mus* Yanni   *Art Dir* Gene Rudolf
● Jennifer Jason Leigh, Peter Coyote, Gale Mayron, Sam
Schact, Denise Dommont, Frank Stallone (Goldwyn)

Heart of Midnight is a twisted little sado-
masochistic outing whose plot centers on
Carol Rivers (Jennifer Jason Leigh), a young
woman with psychological problems. When
her uncle Fletcher (Sam Schact) dies of AIDS,
she inherits property being transformed into
the 'Midnight' club.

Against the wishes of her mother Betty
(Brenda Vaccaro), Carol moves to the building, only to find a bizarre series of rooms upstairs. They suggest Fletcher was hosting sex
parties for people of various persuasions.

Carol is plunged into her own hell as a couple of workmen try to rape her. If the assault
wasn't problem enough, signs appear that
someone else is on the premises.

Events proceed to particularly sadistic circumstances, in which the reason for Carol's
years of torment and her relationship to her
late uncle also come to light.

Performances are strong all around, particularly by Leigh and Vaccaro.

■ HEART OF THE MATTER, THE

1953, 105 MINS, UK
Dir George More O'Ferrall   *Prod* Ian Dalrymple
Scr Ian Dalrymple   *Ph* Jack Hildyard   *Ed* Sidney Stone
Mus Edric Connor (adv.)   *Art Dir* Joseph Bato
● Trevor Howard, Elizabeth Allan, Maria Schell,
Denholm Elliott, Peter Finch, Gerard Oury (British
Lion/London)

The film is set in Sierra Leone during the last
war, where Trevor Howard, the assistant police commissioner, is not getting along too
well with his wife (Elizabeth Allan). He is
forced to borrow money from an unscrupulous blackmailer and made to send his wife
away on a vacation. During her absence, he
falls in love with a young widow (Maria
Schell), one of the survivors of a ship wrecked
by a German U-boat.

The story is told in painstaking and deliberate terms. Subject matter is Graham
Greene's favorite topic of Catholicism [from
his novel, adapted by Lesley Storm]. Stripped

of its deeper significance, the story is little more than the conventional triangle meller, but husband and wife are ardent Catholics, and divorce and remarriage cannot be contemplated.

There is considerable merit in the script and much of the dialog has adult appeal. But the conflict between love and religion never emerges with real conviction. The backgrounds filmed on location have an authentic look.

Howard plays his role with great intensity. The part of his wife is done in two contrasting keys by Allan, almost wildly hysterical, and subdued and restrained. The third member of the triangle is etched by Maria Schell with real tenderness.

....

■ HEARTS OF FIRE

1987, 95 MINS, US ◇ ⓥ ⊙
Dir Richard Marquand   *Prod* Richard Marquand, Jennifer Miller, Jennifer Alward   *Scr* Scott Richardson, Joe Eszterhas   *Ph* Alan Hume   *Ed* Sean Barton   *Mus* John Barry   *Art Dir* Kit Surrey, Barbara Dunphy
● Bob Dylan, Rupert Everett, Fiona, Julian Glover, Ian Drury, Richie Havens (Phoenix/Lorimar)

It is unfortunate that the last film of helmer Richard Marquand, who died shortly after completing it, should be *Hearts of Fire*. As an epitaph it leaves something to be desired, failing to fire on all cylinders despite a nimble performance by the enigmatic Bob Dylan typecast as a reclusive rock star.

Pic opens with would-be rock singer Molly McGuire (exuberantly played by Yank singer Fiona) meeting rock star Billy Parker (Dylan) and agreeing to hop over to England with him.

In Blighty she is spotted by British popster James Colt (Rupert Everett), who takes her under his wing – and into his bed – while a drunken Dylan flies home to the security of his chicken farm.

Fiona and Everett head off on tour together and, while Fiona agonizes about the real price of success and worries about which man she prefers, the inevitable climax of the gig in her hometown fast approaches.

Dylan performs well, though he looks a mite uncomfortable during the musical numbers. He certainly appears fitter than Everett whose voice is as wet and stilted as his performance.

....

■ HEARTS OF THE WEST
(UK: *Hollywood Cowboy*)

1975, 102 MINS, US ◇ ⓥ
Dir Howard Zieff   *Prod* Tony Bill   *Scr* Rob Thompson   *Ph* Mario Tosi   *Ed* Edward Wearschilka   *Mus* Ken Lauber   *Art Dir* Robert Luthardt
● Jeff Bridges, Andy Griffith, Donald Pleasence, Blythe Danner, Alan Arkin, Richard B. Schull (M-G-M)

Hearts of the West is a pleasant, amusing period comedy featuring Jeff Bridges in an excellent characterization as a cliche-quoting novice western pulp writer who discovers that his correspondence school is no more than a remote Nevada mailbox pickup operation, the swindle of Richard B. Shull and Anthony James. Escaping their robbery attempt, Bridges accidentally takes their cash stash into the desert wastes where he is rescued by an oater quickie film location unit.

The casting is very adroit, with all principals complementing in style and charisma. The structure of the film is notable in that it tells its story in the manner of films of the 1930s, while in turn keeping separate the ways in which they were then artistically conceived and executed.

....

■ HEARTS OF THE WORLD

1918, 117 MINS, US/UK ⊗ ⓥ
Dir D.W. Griffith   *Prod* D.W. Griffith   *Scr* Gaston de Tolignac [= D.W. Griffith], Translated into English by Capt Victor Marier, [= D.W. Griffith]   *Ph* Billy Bitzer   *Ed* James E. Smith, Rose Smith   *Mus* Carl Henfrit Santor Elinor
● Lillian Gish, Robert Harron, Dorothy Gish, George Fawcett, Erich von Stroheim, Noel Coward (Griffith/Artcraft)

In *Hearts of the World* D.W. Griffith makes his principal love story a fleshless skeleton upon which to hang a large number of brilliant war scenes, in an effort to show the horrors at close range – its effect upon the combatants and non-combatants alike.

Selected for his principals the son and daughter, respectively, of two American painters who made their homes in France. They fall in love and are betrothed. When war is declared the youth makes the heroic declaration that a country that is good enough to live in is worth fighting for, and joins the French army.

The picture opens with scenes showing the little French village in time of peace and then goes into a depiction of the struggle with the Germans for its possession.

Another role admirably planted, but which fails to develop to the full strength of its promise, is The Little Disturber. Dorothy Gish is the Disturber and her sister Lillian is the heroine. Both are excellent and wholly equal to the demands of their respective parts.

Robert Harron, as the young American is the outstanding artist of the picture.

....

■ HEAT

1972, 100 MINS, US ◇ ⓥ
Dir Paul Morrissey   *Prod* Andy Warhol   *Scr* Paul Morrissey, John Hollowell   *Ph* Paul Morrissey   *Ed* Lara Idel, Jed Johnson   *Mus* John Cale
● Sylvia Miles, Joe Dallesandro (Warhol)

Paul Morrissey, who made *Flesh* and *Trash* for the Andy Warhol Factory Group, always had a soft spot for the so-called Hollywood film. In fact, he often claimed he was making Hollywood films, albeit impregnated by new permissiveness, plus scenes of drugs, sexual freedom and his own kind of social observation.

This one, main centered in Hollywood, might be a sort of homage to Billy Wilder's *Sunset Blvd*. Sex is more implicit here, if tactful, and it is about an out-of-work young actor and an ex-star with daughter troubles and a turning point in her career.

Morrissey has given more fluidity than his other pix but relies mainly on actors in a series of well-meshed scenes as they play out the drama and comedy of a Hollywood that is sliding away.

....

■ HEAT AND DUST

1983, 133 MINS, UK ◇ ⓥ ⊙
Dir James Ivory   *Prod* Ismail Merchant   *Scr* Ruth Prawer Jhabvala   *Ph* Walter Lassally   *Ed* Humphrey Dixon   *Mus* Richard Robbins   *Art Dir* Wilfrid Shingleton
● Julie Christie, Christopher Cazenove, Greta Scacchi, Julian Glover, Susan Fleetwood, Shashi Kapoor (Merchant-Ivory)

Scripted from her own novel by Ruth Prawer Jhabvala, *Heat and Dust* intercuts the stories of two women and of India past and present. The device is sometimes irritating in its jumps but ultimately successful in conveying the essential immutability of India's mystic character and ambivalent appeal.

Julie Christie, as a distinctly modern Englishwoman researching and to some extent reliving the Indian past of a late great aunt, is the top name in a fine and well-

matched Anglo-Indian cast. But the principal impact, partly by virtue of role, is supplied by British newcomer Greta Scacchi. Portraying the great aunt as a young bride of scandalous behavior in colonial India, she creates an impressive study of classic underplayed well-bred English turmoil as her affections oscillate between loyal husband and an Indian potentate.

....

■ HEATHERS

1989, 102 MINS, US ◇ ⓥ ⊙
Dir Michael Lehmann   *Prod* Denise Di Novi   *Scr* Daniel Waters   *Ph* Francis Kenney   *Ed* Norman Hollyn   *Mus* David Newman   *Art Dir* Jon Hutman
● Winona Ryder, Christian Slater, Shannen Doherty, Lisanne Falk, Kim Walker, Penelope Milford (Cinemarque/New World)

Heathers is a super-smart black comedy about high school politics and teenage suicide that showcases a host of promising young talents.

Daniel Waters' enormously clever screenplay blazes a trail of originality through the dead wood of the teen-comedy genre by focusing on the *Heathers*, the four prettiest and most popular girls at Westerburg High, three of whom are named Heather.

Setting the tone for the group is founder and queen bitch Heather No. 1, who has a devastating put-down or comeback for every occasion and could freeze even a heat-seeking missile in its tracks with her icy stare.

Heathers No. 2 and 3 get off their own zingers once in a while, while the fourth nubile beauty, Veronica (Winona Ryder), goes along for the ride but seems to have a mind of her own. She also has eyes for a rebellious-looking school newcomer named J.D. (Christian Slater).

Goaded by the seductive J.D., Veronica half-heartedly goes along with an attempt to murder Heather No. 1, who has become irritating beyond endurance.

Winona Ryder is utterly fetching and winning as an intelligent but seriously divided young lady. Oozing an insinuating sarcasm reminiscent of Jack Nicholson, Christian Slater has what it takes to make J.D. both alluring and dangerous. The three Heathers (Shannen Doherty, Lisanne Falk and Kim Walker) look like they've spent their lives practicing putdowns.

....

■ HEAT'S ON, THE

1943, 79 MINS, US
Dir Gregory Ratoff   *Prod* Milton Carter   *Scr* Fitzroy Davis, George S. George, Fred Schiller   *Ph* Franz E. Planer   *Ed* Otto Meyer
● Mae West, Victor Moore, Lloyd Bridges, Mary Roche, Hazel Scott, Lester Allen (Columbia)

Picture opens on *Indiscretions*, a Broadway musical that's having trouble getting along, with Mae West singing 'I'm Just a Stranger in Town', done in the typical Westian manner, while for the close she is surrounded by a male chorus in 'Hello, Mi Amigo', which rates okay. 'There Goes That Guitar', used by the Xavier Cugat band as background for a Latinesque dance double, is also a part of the structure of this musical.

Story of *Heat's On*, with West as the actress-siren, her hips a-swinging in a familiar manner and arms akimbo for added familiar effect, plus the affected hard-boiled Westian diction, concerns the efforts of a legit producer, in love with his star, to wrest her from a rival producer after latter has been hood-winked into believing she's been blacklisted by a reform society.

West looks well but her technique somehow seems dated. William Gaxton does well as the legit producer who's soft for his glamorous star, while Alan Dinehart does okay as a rival prod.

....

■ HEATWAVE

1981, 93 MINS, AUSTRALIA ◇ ⱳ
Dir Phillip Noyce *Prod* Hillary Linstead, Ross Matthews
Scr Marc Rosenberg, Phillip Noyce *Ph* Vincent Monton
Ed John Scott *Mus* Cameron Allan *Art Dir* Ross Major
● Judy Davis, Richard Moir, Chris Haywood, Bill Hunter, John Gregg, Anna Jemison (Preston Crothers/M & L)

In his first feature film since the widely acclaimed *Newsfront* [1978] director Phillip Noyce projects Sydney as a cauldron in which hapless individuals are scalded by big business, organized crime, lawyers, police and journalists, working in an unholy alliance.

Noyce's chief protagonists are Richard Moir as a visionary young architect who has designed a $100 million residential complex, and Judy Davis as a radical activist in the forefront of the residents' resistance to its construction.

In part, pic takes on the trappings of the conventional mystery-thriller, pointing to a conspiracy involving the project's financial backer (Chris Haywood), his oily lawyer (John Gregg), Moir's boss (Bill Hunter), a journalist (John Meillon), and union official (Dennis Miller).

Davis, a formidable actress, wrestles with her ambiguous and enigmatic character, and does not quite jell. Moir, however, is a strong, sustaining force as the arrogant, moody, idealistic architect.

■ HEAVEN

1987, 80 MINS, US ◇ ⱳ ⊙
Dir Diane Keaton *Prod* Joe Kelly *Ph* Frederick Elmes, Joe Kelly *Ed* Paul Barnes *Mus* Howard Shore
Art Dir Barbara Ling
● (Perpetual/RVF)

Heaven represents an exercise in frivolous metaphysics, an engagingly light-hearted but ultimately light-headed inquiry into the nature of paradise. Diane Keaton's feature directorial debut is a small-scale, non-narrative work using trendily shot interviews, snazzy optical effects and loads of film clips and songs to illustrate fanciful notions of the hereafter.

Close to 100 individuals, all unknown except for boxing promoter Don King, are quizzed on such matters as, 'What is Heaven?' and 'How do you get to Heaven?'

Peppering all these speculations are often goofy clips from old films and TV shows. Excerpts, none of which is identified, range from extravagant depictions of the afterlife, Hollywood-style, to the hilarious expostulations of early broadcast ministers and evangelists.

■ HEAVEN CAN WAIT

1943, 112 MINS, US ◇ ⱳ ⊙
Dir Ernst Lubitsch *Prod* Ernst Lubitsch *Scr* Samson Raphaelson *Ph* Edward Cronjager *Ed* Dorothy Spencer *Mus* Alfred Newman *Art Dir* James Basevi, Leland Fuller
● Gene Tierney, Don Ameche, Charles Coburn, Marjorie Main, Laird Cregar, Louis Calhern (20th Century-Fox)

Provided with generous slices of comedy, skillfully handled by producer-director Ernst Lubitsch, this is for most of the 112 minutes a smooth, appealing and highly commercial production. Lubitsch has endowed it with light, amusing sophistication and heartwarming nostalgia. He has handled Don Ameche and Gene Tierney, in (for them) difficult characterizations, dexterously.

The Lazlo Bus-Fekete play [*Birthday*] covers the complete span of a man's life, from precocious infancy to in this case, the sprightly senility of a 70-year-old playboy. It opens with the deceased (Ameche) asking Satan for a passport to hell, which is not being issued unless the applicant can justify his right to it.

This is followed by a recital of real and fancied misdeeds from the time the sinner discovers that, in order to get girls, a boy must have plenty of beetles, through the smartly fashioned hilarious drunk scene with a French maid at the age of 15, to the thefting of his cousin's fiancee, whom he marries.

Charles Coburn as the fond grandfather who takes a hand in his favorite grandson's romantic and domestic problems, walks away with the early sequences in a terrific comedy performance.
□ 1943: Nominations: Best Picture, Director, Color Cinematography

■ HEAVEN CAN WAIT

1978, 100 MINS, US ◇ ⱳ ⊙
Dir Warren Beatty, Buck Henry *Prod* Warren Beatty
Scr Warren Beatty, Elaine May *Ph* William A. Fraker
Ed Robert C. Jones, Don Zimmerman *Mus* Dave Grusin
Art Dir Paul Sylbert
● Warren Beatty, Julie Christie, James Mason, Jack Warden, Charles Grodin, Dyan Cannon (Paramount)

Heaven Can Wait is an outstanding film. Harry Segall's fantasy comedy-drama play, made in 1941 by Columbia as *Here Comes Mr Jordan*, returns in an updated, slightly more macabre treatment.

Warren Beatty plays an aging football star, prematurely summoned to judgment after a traffic accident because celestial messenger (played by co-director Buck Henry) jumped the gun. This embarrasses James Mason into permitting Beatty to inhabit temporarily another body. The only available one is that of a wealthy industrialist whose death is plotted by floozy wife Dyan Cannon and Charles Grodin, the tycoon's nerd secretary.

Julie Christie falls for the rich guy, whose main ambition is to resume his football career in which coach Jack Warden plays an important part.

Script and direction are very strong, providing a rich mix of visual and verbal humor that is controlled and avoids the extremes of cheap vulgarity and overly esoteric whimsy.
□ 1978: Best Art Direction.
□ Nominations: Best Picture, Directors (Warren Beatty, Buck Henry), Actor (Warren Beatty), Supp. Actor (Jack Warden), Supp. Actress (Dyan Cannon), Adapted Screenplay, Cinematography, Original Score

■ HEAVEN HELP US

(UK: *Catholic Boys*)

1985, 104 MINS, US ◇ ⱳ ⊙
Dir Michael Dinner *Prod* Dan Wigutow, Mark Carliner
Scr Charles Purpura *Ph* Miroslav Ondricek
Ed Stephen A. Rotter *Mus* James Horner
Art Dir Michael Molly
● Donald Sutherland, John Heard, Andrew McCarthy, Mary Stuart Masterson, Kevin Dillon, Malcolm Danare (HBO/Silver Screen Partners)

Heaven Help Us focuses upon several Catholic school boys, three in particular, who get into an increasing amount of trouble with the presiding priests. Andrew McCarthy, a new arrival at St Basil's, instantly latches onto reigning outsider in his class, Malcolm Danare, a chubby egghead who is constantly picked on by school bully Kevin Dillon.

It's virtually inconceivable that the intelligent, sensible McCarthy or Danare would have anything to do with the likes of ne'er-do-well Dillon in real life, but Dillon intimidates them into something resembling friendship. Along with a couple of other large, silent boys, they receive their share of corporal punishment for relatively harmless offenses, wreak havoc during confession and communion and ultimately inspire some helpful changes to be made in the school hierarchy.

Very funny in spots and wonderfully evocative of Brooklyn, circa 1965, pic suffers somewhat by dividing its attention between outrageous pranks and realistic sketches of the Catholic school experience.

■ HEAVEN KNOWS, MR. ALLISON

1957, 107 MINS, US ◇ ⱳ
Dir John Huston *Prod* Buddy Adler, Eugene Frenke
Scr John Lee Mahin, John Huston *Ph* Oswald Morris
Ed Russell Lloyd *Mus* Georges Auric *Art Dir* Stephen Grimes
● Deborah Kerr, Robert Mitchum (20th Century-Fox)

Behind the misleading title is an intriguing yarn [from the novel by Charles Shaw] about two people on opposite ends of the social ladder, thrown together in a highly unusual situation. It's about a marine, marooned on a small Pacific atoll [Tobago] with a nun. They divide their time dodging Japs and trying to steer clear of their emotions.

The film, directed by John Huston with something less than outstanding imagination, but with a good measure of humor and bravado, holds out an early promise which it doesn't keep. The parallel is drawn between the nun and her vocation and the marine with his, both subject to strong discipline. But – apart from a few remarks – the character and motivations of Deborah Kerr remain shrouded in mystery and she reveals very little of herself.

The high spots of the film involve Robert Mitchum's exploits – and fantastic ones they are – in the midst of the occupying Japanese force when he raids its supply depot for food. These scenes are staged with noise, gusto and a good deal of suspense.
□ 1957: Nominations: Best Actress (Deborah Kerr), Adapted Screenplay

■ HEAVENS ABOVE!

1963, 118 MINS, UK ⱳ
Dir John Boulting *Prod* John Boulting, Roy Boulting
Scr Frank Harvey, John Boulting *Ph* Max Greene
Ed Teddy Farvas *Mus* Richard Rodney Bennett
● Peter Sellers, Bernard Miles, Eric Sykes, Irene Handl, Miriam Karlin, Isabel Jeans (British Lion/Romulus)

A measure of the merit of *Heavens Above!* is that its theme could have been just as acceptably used as a straight drama. But the Boulting Brothers effectively Employ their favorite weapon, the rapier of ridicule. The screenplay is full of choice jokes, but the humor is often uneven.

Story concerns the appointment, by a clerical error, of the Reverend John Smallwood (Peter Sellers) to the parish of Orbiston Parva, a prosperous neighborhood ruled by the Despard Family, makers of Tranquilax, the three-in-one restorative (Sedative! Stimulant! Laxative!). He's a quiet, down-to-earth chap who happens to believe in the scriptures and lives by them.

From the moment he gives his first sermon all hell breaks out, so to speak. He shocks the district by making a Negro trashman his warden and takes a bunch of disreputable evicted gypsies into the vicarage. Soon he makes his first convert, Lady Despard.

Within this framework there are some very amusing verbal and visual jokes, and both are largely aided by some deft acting. Sellers gives a guileful portrayal of genuine simplicity. Bernard Miles, as an acquisitive butler; Eric Sykes, Irene Handl, Miriam Karlin and Roy Kinnear (leader of the gypsies); and Isabel Jeans, a regal Lady Despard, all contribute heftily.

■ HEAVEN'S GATE

1980, 219 MINS, US ◇ ⱳ ⊙
Dir Michael Cimino *Prod* Joann Carelli *Scr* Michael Cimino *Ph* Vilmos Zsigmond *Ed* Tom Rolf, William Reynolds, Lisa Fruchtman, Gerald Greenberg

Mus David Mansfield   *Art Dir* Tambi Larsen
● Kris Kristofferson, Christopher Walken, Isabelle Huppert, Sam Waterston, John Hurt, Jeff Bridges (United Artists)

The first scenes of *Heaven's Gate* are so energetic and beautiful that anyone who knows the saga of the $35 million epic might begin to think it was going to be worth every penny. Unfortunately the balance of director Michael Cimino's film is so confusing, so overlong at three-and-a-half hours and so ponderous that it fails to work at almost every level.

What structure the film does have is based on the Johnson County wars which took place in the 1890s in Wyoming.

The story deals with a group of established cattlemen headed by Canton (Sam Waterston) who are convinced their herds are being looted by immigrant settlers. With the approval of the state, the operators of the large cattle ranches draw up a death list of 125 poor immigrants in Johnson County who are supposedly doing the 'rustling'. Kris Kristopherson plays the Federal marshall who turned against his class.

Cimino's attempts to draw a portrait of the plight of the immigrants in the west in that period are so impersonal that none of the victims ever get beyond pat stereotypes.

Cimino, who wrote the script himself, has simply not provided enough details for his story, leaving his audience guessing.
□ 1981: Nomination: Best Art Direction

....

■ HEAVY METAL

1981, 90 MINS, US ◇
Dir Gerald Potterton   *Prod* Ivan Reitman   *Scr* Dan Goldberg, Len Blum   *Ed* Janice Brown   *Mus* Elmer Bernstein   *Art Dir* Michael Gross (Reitman-Moyer)

This technically firstrate six-segment animated anthology is an amalgam of science fiction, sword and sorcery, hip humor, violence, sex and a smidgen of drugs.

The film, which draws its title and sensibility from the adult fantasy magazine of the same name, tends to frontload its virtues. Initial segments have a boisterous blend of dynamic graphics, intriguing plot premises and sly wit that unfortunately slide gradually downhill.

Courtesy of a vastly overlong, relatively unrousing 27-minute end-piece that may be the technical highpoint of the film, but lacks the punch and tightness of the earlier segments, the venture tends to run out of steam. Still, the net effect is an overridingly positive one.

....

■ HEAVY TRAFFIC

1973, 78 MINS, US ◇ Ⓥ
Dir Ralph Bakshi   *Prod* Steve Krantz   *Scr* Ralph Bakshi   *Ph* Ted C. Bemiller, Gregg Heschong   *Ed* Donald W. Ernst   *Mus* Ray Shanklin, Ed Bogas
(Film Creations/Krantz)

After their first x-rated animated feature, *Fritz the Cat*, producer Steve Krantz and writer-director Ralph Bakshi turn to 'human' creatures, combining animation and live action, a blatant example of hardcore pornography.

There's something to offend everyone in this melange of crudely conceived, amateurishly animated stuff. From the one extreme of a crude sexually-oriented attack on Christianity, it manages to take a crack at every type - from the Jewish mother to the Mafia.

There are heavyhanded attempts to ridicule Godfather-attuned Italian-Americans, homosexuals, the physically deformed, capitalists and labor, slum dwellers, the Church. Even M-G-M is made a victim by the use of an insertion of scenes from the Jean Harlow- Clark Gable *Red Dust*.

....

■ HEDDA

1975, 104 MINS, UK ◇ Ⓥ
Dir Trevor Nunn   *Prod* Robert Enders   *Scr* Trevor Nunn   *Ph* Douglas Slocombe   *Ed* Peter Tanner   *Mus* Laurie Johnson   *Art Dir* Ted Tester
● Glenda Jackson, Timothy West, Peter Eyre, Jennie Linden, Patrick Stewart, Constance Chapman (Brut)

Hedda is a gem, taking the Royal Shakespeare production of the Henrik Ibsen classic, complete with a fine cast headed by Glenda Jackson.

It's heady stuff, nearly every line to be relished, as one watches the destructively dominant Hedda torturing her friends and relations with rapier-sharp lines and stiletto-like glances.

So persuasively talented and self-assured a performer as Jackson is not everyone's cup of tea, but few should quibble with one of her best parts.
□ 1975: Nomination: Best Actress (Glenda Jackson)

....

■ HEIRESS, THE

1949, 115 MINS, US Ⓥ
Dir William Wyler   *Prod* William Wyler   *Scr* Ruth Goetz, Augustus Goetz   *Ph* Leo Tover   *Ed* William Hornbeck   *Mus* Aaron Copland   *Art Dir* John Meehan, Harry Horner
● Olivia de Havilland, Montgomery Clift, Ralph Richardson, Miriam Hopkins (Paramount)

The Heiress is a meticulous reproduction of the Victorian scene, so faithful to its mores that it is a museum piece.

William Wyler, in his producer-director role, has seen fit to cling exactly to the period portrayed in the Ruth and Augustus Goetz script, based on their stage play suggested by Henry James' novel *Washington Square*.

Olivia de Havilland, in the title role, is the homely daughter of a wealthy physician. A social shyness that cloaks the quick wit and puckishness has kept her suitorless despite a sizeable wealth that will be augmented when her father passes. Montgomery Clift is the first male to show her attention. The father sees through his courting, tries to break up a quick engagement.

Clift plays the difficult part of an ambiguous character who is more opportunist than crook in his fortune-hunting. Ralph Richardson is grand as the stern, strait-laced father.
□ 1949: Best Actress (Olivia de Havilland), B&W Art Direction, Scoring of a Dramatic Picture, B&W Costume Design.
□ Nominations: Best Picture, Director, Supp. Actor (Ralph Richardson), B&W Cinematography

....

■ HEIST, THE

See: $

....

■ HELEN OF TROY

1955, 118 MINS, US ◇
Dir Robert Wise   *Scr* John Twist, Hugh Gray   *Ph* Harry Stradling   *Ed* Thomas Reilly   *Mus* Max Steiner   *Art Dir* Edward Carrere
● Rossana Podesta, Jacques Sernas, Cedric Hardwicke, Stanley Baker, Niall MacGinnis, Robert Douglas (Warner)

The retelling of the Homeric legend, filmed in its entirety in Italy, makes lavish use of the CinemaScope screen.

WB and director Robert Wise piled on the extras in Greek and Trojan armies. Production values ride over shortcomings in John Twist and Hugh Gray's script and dialog. Like many tales of antiquity, the story is occasionally stilted.

As Helen and Paris, the love-smitten Trojan prince, Warners cast two unknowns – Rossana Podesta, an exquisite Italian beauty,

and Jacques Sernas, a brawny and handsome Frenchman. Visually both meet the demands of the roles. Their voices have been dubbed.

The story opens with Paris' journey to Sparta to effect a peace treaty between the Greeks and Troy. He falls in love with Helen not knowing she is the queen of Sparta. His peace mission fails, and in making his escape from Sparta, takes Helen with him. The 'abduction' unites the Greeks and sends them off on a war against Troy.

....

■ HELL AND HIGH WATER

1954, 103 MINS, US ◇
Dir Samuel Fuller   *Prod* Raymond A. Klune   *Scr* Jesse L. Lasky Jr, Samuel Fuller   *Ph* Joe MacDonald   *Ed* James B. Clark   *Mus* Alfred Newman   *Art Dir* Lyle R. Wheeler, Leland Fuller
● Richard Widmark, Bella Darvi, Victor Francen, Cameron Mitchell, Gene Evans, David Wayne (20th Century-Fox)

CinemaScope and rip-roaring adventure mate perfectly in *Hell and High Water*, a highly fanciful, but mighty entertaining action feature [from a story by David Hempstead].

As the male star, Richard Widmark takes easily to the rugged assignment, giving it the wallop needed. It is a further projection of the action-adventure type of hero he does quite often, and good. The picture introduces as a new star Polish-born, French-raised Bella Darvi and she creates an interesting impression in her debut.

Plot has to do with a group of individuals of many nationalities who band together to thwart a scheme to start a new world war with an atomic incident that will be blamed on the United States. These private heroes hire Widmark, a former naval submarine officer, to command an underwater trip to the Arctic, where scientists on the voyage will check reports that a Communist atomic arsenal is being built on an isolated island.
□ 1954: Nomination: Best Special Effects

....

■ HELL BENT

1918, 77 MINS, US ⊗
Dir John Ford   *Scr* John Ford, Harry Carey   *Ph* Ben Reynolds
● Harry Carey, Neva Gerber, Duke Lee, Joseph Harris (Universal)

Hell Bent was rediscovered at the Czech Film Archives. Current print is presently the only one of two complete films surviving from the director's 1917-19 beginning years at Universal Studios.

Hell Bent was Ford's 14th film and his ninth feature. Its leading player, Harry Carey was Ford's most frequent early star and collaborator. Here, Carey again plays his laconic Cheyenne Harry protagonist.

Harry rides into the town of Rawhide where in a long winded comic turn he strikes up a friendship with Cimmaron Bill (Duke Lee) and is then smitten by love for Bess (Neva Gerber), a 'good girl' forced by circumstances to work in a dance hall. B-plot mechanics take over as Harry tries to rid town of outlaws but is stymied when he learns Bess' weak-willed brother is member of gang led by Bean Ross (Joseph Harris).

Film is enlivened by some of Ford's special moments. As his relationship with Bess develops Harry awkwardly carries her home in the rain while in the next shot his abandoned pal wanders through the darkened saloon.

....

■ HELLBOUND
HELLRAISER II

1988, 96 MINS, UK/US ◇ Ⓥ ⊙
Dir Tony Randel   *Prod* Christopher Figg   *Scr* Peter Atkins   *Ph* Robin Vidgeon   *Mus* Christopher Young   *Art Dir* Mike Buchanan

● Clare Higgins, Ashley Laurence, Kenneth Cranham, Imogen Boorman, Sean Chapman, Doug Bradley (Film Futures)

Hellraiser II is a maggotty carnival of mayhem, mutation and dismemberment, awash in blood and recommended only for those who thrive on such junk.

Helmer Tony Randel returns to the off-the-wall tale of a psychotic psychiatrist's long struggle to get the better of something called the Lament Configuration, a kind of demonic, silver-filigreed Rubik's Cube whose solution opens the transdimensional doors into a parallel world of sinful pleasure and unspeakably hellish pain.

This fiendish shrink takes a special interest in a new patient, Kristy, whose family was massacred in appropriately gruesome fashion by box-sprung flesh-eating ghouls called Cenobites.

As Kristy and the shrink head toward the big showdown in Hades, the movie unfolds with a tableau of can-you-top-this gross-outs.

● ●

■ HELL DRIVERS

1957, 108 MINS, UK ⓦ

Dir Cy Endfield   *Prod* S. Benjamin Fisz   *Scr* John Kruse, Cy Endfield   *Ph* Geoffrey Unsworth   *Ed* John D. Guthridge   *Mus* Hubert Clifford   *Art Dir* Ernest Archer
● Stanley Baker, Herbert Lom, Peggy Cummins, Patrick McGoohan, Jill Ireland, Sean Connery (Aqua/Rank)

Hell Drivers is a slab of unabashed melodrama. The story [from a short story by John Kruse, adaptation by Cy Endfield], said to be based on a real one, has to do with the rivalries of a gang of haulage truck drivers, operating between gravel pits and a construction site.

Stanley Baker is an ex convict who gets a job as one of these drivers and immediately falls foul of Patrick McGoohan, the firm's ace driver. Baker discovers that McGoohan and William Hartnell, the manager, are running a racket. The drama comes to an uneasy head when Baker's lorry is doctored.

Endfield's direction is straightforward and conventional, but some of the speed sequences provide some tingling thrills. Acting is adequate, but uninspired. Baker gives a forceful performance of restrained strength and Herbert Lom has some neat moments as his Italian buddy. Patrick McGoohan gives an exaggerated study as the villain. Peggy Cummins, as a village vamp, fails to spark a tepid love interest.

● ●

■ HELLER IN PINK TIGHTS

1960, 100 MINS, US ◇ ⓦ

Dir George Cukor   *Prod* Carlo Ponti, Marcello Girosi   *Scr* Dudley Nichols, Walter Bernstein   *Ph* Harold Lipstein   *Ed* Howard Smith   *Mus* Daniele Amfitheatrof   *Art Dir* Hal Pereira, Eugene Allen
● Sophia Loren, Anthony Quinn, Eileen Heckart, Ramon Novarro, Margaret O'Brien, Steve Forrest (Paramount)

With *Heller In Pink Tights* director George Cukor puts tongue in cheek to turn an ordinary story into a gaudy, old-fashioned western satire with gleeful touches of melodrama.

Taken from a novel by Louis L'Amour, *Heller* follows The Great Healy Dramatic and Concert Co in two red wagons through the wilds of Wyoming. The traveling theatre is fighting for its survival, and Sophia Loren and Anthony Quinn put up a strong enough battle to make things interesting and amusing. It's when the film's plottage dissolves into pure western that it becomes somewhat commonplace.

Loren dons blonde tresses for the role of an actress who has a knack for getting into situations. She looks fine with golden head and turns in a respectable, most believable performance. Quinn, as head of the Healy company, adeptly projects as the he-man, yet properly building a tender, calm characterization.

Eileen Heckart just about steals the whole shootin' match as an actress who has given up a 'promising' career for her daughter's chances on stage. It's real comedy, and Heckart carries it off with polish. Steve Forrest makes a lovable villain, evil but never evil enough to lose his attraction. Margaret O'Brien is fine in a role that offers her more chances to be seen than heard; Edmund Love is very good as a 'Shakespearean' actor; and Ramon Novarro is aptly sinister as a well-heeled banker.

● ●

■ HELL IN KOREA

See: A Hill in Korea

● ●

■ HELL IN THE PACIFIC

1968, 103 MINS, US ◇ ⓦ

Dir John Boorman   *Prod* Reuben Bercovitch   *Scr* Alexander Jacobs, Eric Bercovici   *Ph* Conrad Hall   *Ed* Thomas Stanford   *Mus* Lalo Schifrin   *Art Dir* Anthony D.G. Pratt, Masao Yamazaki
● Lee Marvin, Toshiro Mifune (Selmur)

Tale of two warriors forced to co-exist. Lee Marvin and Toshiro Mifune comprise the entire cast of this World War II drama, directed with an uncertain hand by John Boorman.

Story [by Reuben Bercovitch] takes off with the discovery by Mifune that he no longer is alone on a desolate Pacific island. Pair stalk each other, then attempt to outwit each other, finally collaborate on survival in the form of a raft.

Mifune's unrestrained grunting and running about create an outdated caricature of an Oriental. Marvin has sardonic lines which resemble wisecracks, intended for on-lookers. The subtle humor which was meant to exist becomes overpowering.

Lalo Schifrin could not have served worse the purposes of the film. Phony suspense bits – snapping twigs, etc. – are punched to death through maladroit composing. Net effect of this is the impression that there have got to be 50 musicians lurking just off-camera.

Marvin's arresting screen presence requires appreciative surrounding characters, none of which are present, or meant to be.

Mifune gets few chances to project three-dimensional characterization.

● ●

■ HELL IS A CITY

1960, 98 MINS, UK

Dir Val Guest   *Prod* Michael Carreras   *Scr* Val Guest   *Ph* Arthur Grant   *Ed* John Dunsford   *Mus* Stanley Black   *Art Dir* Robert Jones
● Stanley Baker, John Crawford, Donald Pleasence, Maxine Audley, Billie Whitelaw, Joseph Tomelty (Hammer)

Hell Is a City is an absorbing film of a conventional cops and robbers yarn. Val Guest's taut screenplay [from a novel by Maurice Proctor], allied to his own deft direction, has resulted in a notable film in which the characters are all vividly alive, the action constantly gripping and the background of a provincial city put over with authenticity.

The film was shot largely in Manchester. Arthur Grant's camerawork has arrestingly caught the feel of the big city with its grey, sleazy backstreets, its saloons, the surrounding factory chimneys, the bleakness of the moors and the bustle of the city.

The yarn has Stanley Baker as a detective inspector who, married to a bored, unsympathetic wife (Maxine Audley) spends most of his time on his job. In this instance he is concerned with a dangerous escaped convict who, he suspects, will be returning to Manchester to pick up the stolen jewels that sent him to the cooler. When the girl clerk of the local bookie is attacked while on her way to the bank and then found murdered on the nearby

moors, Baker suspects that the crook and a small gang are the criminals. Doggedly he starts to track them down.

From the moment when the killer (John Crawford) makes his sudden surprise entrance and sets the wheels of the robbery in motion, suspense rarely lets up. The robbery itself is briskly pulled off, there is a firstrate scene on the moors when the police raid an illegal gathering of gamblers and some down-to-earth police station sequences, with Baker pulling no punches in his determination to get at the truth. Acting all round is admirable.

● ●

■ HELL IS FOR HEROES

1962, 90 MINS, US ⓦ ☉

Dir Donald Siegel   *Prod* Henry Blanke   *Scr* Robert Pirosh, Richard Carr   *Ph* Harold Lipstein   *Ed* Howard Smith   *Mus* Leonard Rosenman   *Art Dir* Hal Pereira, Howard Richmond
● Steve McQueen, Bobby Darin, Fess Parker, Harry Guardino, James Coburn, Bob Newhart (Paramount)

Producer Henry Blanke has framed and mounted a gripping, fast-paced, hard-hitting dramatic portrait of an interesting World War II battlefield incident. But there are occasional duds in the film's dramatic arsenal.

Recollections of an actual and tightly classified incident near the dragon's teeth of the Siegfried Line during the dark days of World War II inspired the story by Robert Pirosh, adapted into screenplay form by Richard Carr and Pirosh, creative activator of the film who bowed out as its producer along the way.

Pivotal character of the drama is a surly, rebellious, busted NCO (Steve McQueen) whose front-line courage, leadership and keen sense of improvisation in the course of a grim and seemingly hopeless campaign to hold off a large German force in the face of incredible odds backfires into a potential court martial rap for usurping authority.

McQueen plays the central role with hard-bitten businesslike reserve and an almost animal intensity, permitting just the right degree of humanity to project through a war-weary-and-wise veneer. Bobby Darin has a colorful role of a battlefield hoarder, which he portrays with relish. Harry Guardino is excellent as an uncertain sergeant. James Coburn fine as a practical corporal.

● ●

■ HELLO, DOLLY!

1969, 129 MINS, US ◇ ⓦ ⓥ ☉

Dir Gene Kelly   *Prod* Ernest Lehman   *Scr* Ernest Lehman   *Ph* Harry Stradling   *Ed* William Reynolds   *Mus* Lennie Hayton, Lionel Newman (arrs.)   *Art Dir* John DeCuir
● Barbra Streisand, Walter Matthau, Michael Crawford, Louis Armstrong, Marianne McAndrew, Tommy Tune (20th Century-Fox/Chenault)

Hello, Dolly! is an expensive, expansive, sometimes exaggerated, sentimental, nostalgic, wholesome, pictorially opulent $20 million filmusical [from the 1964 Broadway production, music and lyrics by Jerry Herman] with the charisma of Barbra Streisand in the title role.

Streisand is a unique performer, with that inborn vitality which marks great personalities. She brings her own special kind of authority. There is a certain inconsistency, or even confusion, in the speech pattern.

Walter Matthau is hard to accept at first, his dancing being the step-counting sort and his singing somewhat awkward. Nonetheless his experience cannot be discounted.

The film 'opens cute' with a long-held still of the 14th St replica. Immensely and imaginatively detailed it intrigues the eye and mind directly. When the still 'wipes' into live action, the film is off in a flurry of promise and introducing the times (1890) and the heroine (Dolly) en route to Yonkers.
□ 1969: Best Art Direction, Sound, Adapted Score for a Musical Picture.

☐ Nominations: Best Picture, Cinematography, Costume Design, Editing

....

■ HELLRAISER

1987, 90 MINS, UK ◇ ⓥ ⊙
Dir Clive Barker *Prod* Christopher Figg *Scr* Clive Barker *Ph* David Worley *Mus* Christopher Young *Art Dir* Jocelyn James
● Andrew Robinson, Clare Higgins, Ashley Laurence, Sean Chapman, Oliver Smith, Robert Hines (Film Futures)

Hellraiser is a well-paced sci-fi cum horror fantasy [from Clive Barker's own novel *The Hellbound Heart*].

Film concerns a dissipated adventurer who somewhere in the Orient buys a sort of magic music box which is capable of providing its owner hitherto undreamt of pains and pleasures, and which ultimately causes him to be torn to shreds in a temple which transforms itself into a torture chamber.

Back home, his brother has just moved into a rickety old house with his new wife or girlfriend; digs had formerly been the dwelling of the ill-fated adventurer. Latter returns, by rising through the floorboards, partly decomposed, seeking human flesh and blood which, when devoured, will enable him to regain his human form. Pic is well made, well acted, and the visual effects are generally handled with skill.

....

■ HELLRAISER III

1992, 92 MINS, US ◇ ⓥ ⊙
Dir Anthony Hickox *Prod* Lawrence Mortorff *Scr* Peter Atkins *Ph* Gerry Lively *Ed* Christopher Cibelli, James D.R. Hickox *Mus* Randy Miller, Christopher Young *Art Dir* Steve Hardie
● Terry Farrell, Doug Bradley, Paula Marshall, Kevin Bernhardt, Ken Carpenter, Peter Boynton (Fifth Avenue)

Hellraiser III is a highly commercial horror entry. Well-produced effort is an effective combination of imaginative special effects with the strangeness of author Clive Barker's original conception, on which the characters are based. Screen story is by Peter Atkins and Tony Randel.

The previous two *Hellraisers* were filmed in London; the latest was shot in North Carolina. All three films are set in New York.

Terry Farrell toplines as an attractive TV newswoman summoned by the ghost of British World War I Capt. Elliott Spencer, who's contacted her via her recurring nightmares about her dad who was killed in Vietnam combat before she was born.

Spencer's experiments with the supernatural had unleashed evil on the world in the race of the Cenobites, led by Pinhead, whose adventures were limned in the prior pics. Pinhead is back, with a strange little box that's key to sending him back to Hell.

Farrell is a strong heroine binding the film together, and British thesp Doug Bradley is a commanding presence as Pinhead, while also doubling sans makeup as the good guy captain.

....

■ HELL'S ANGELS

1930, 119 MINS, US ◇
Dir Howard Hughes *Scr* Joseph Moncure March, Howard Estabrook, Harry Behn *Ph* Tony Gaudio, Harry Perry, E.B Steene, Harry Zach, Dewey Wrigley, Elmer Dyer, Pliny Goodfriend, Alvin Wyckoff, Sam Landers, William Tuers, Glenn Kerschner, Donald Keyes, Roy Klaffki, Paul Ivano, Charles Boyle, Herman Schopp, L. Guy Wilky, John Silver, Edward Snyder, Ed Krull, Jack Greenhalgh, Henry Cronjager, Edward Cohen, Frank Breamer, Ernest Lazlo *Ed* Frank Lawrence, Douglas Biggs, Perry Hollingsworth *Mus* Hugo Riesenfeld *Art Dir* J. Boone Fleming, Carroll Clark
● Ben Lyon, James Hall, Jean Harlow, John Darrow, Lucien Prival, Frank Clarke (Caddo)

Howard Hughes' air film was advertised as

costing $4 million, which likely means $3 million – plenty.

It's no sappy, imbecilic tale. One of the brothers (Ben Lyon) is strictly a 'good-time Charlie' continuously on the make and humanly afraid to die; the girl (Jean Harlow) is no good in the sense that she has and will try anything with either brother, but only does so with Lyon. This is because Jimmy Hall has ideals, idolizes her and wants to make everything official.

The first half of the film builds up to a Zeppelin raid on London which runs two reels and is given a big screen. Second half's main display is an aerial dog fight in which at least 30, maybe 40, planes simultaneously start diving and zooming at each other.

Story actually opens in Munich with Lyon trying to date every femme in town. Highly seasoned portion of the second half comes with Lyon and Hall on a spree. Hall finds Harlow half soused and entwined with another officer in a barroom booth.

Hughes spent three years working on his pet. The story was remade three times. Originally it was silent, with Greta Nissen as the girl; then it was made once in sound and remade again after that. Air shots were taken silent with the sound dubbed in afterward.

James Whale is programmed as having staged the dialog and does that smartly. The one color sequence [a London ball] runs just about a reel and is not important.

☐ 1929/30: Nomination: Best Cinematography (Tony Gaudio, Harry Perry)

....

■ HELL'S HIGHWAY

1932, 62 MINS, US
Dir Rowland Brown *Prod* David O. Selznick *Scr* Samuel Ornitz, Robert Tasker, Rowland Brown *Ph* Edward Cronjager *Art Dir* Carroll Clark
● Richard Dix, Tom Brown, Louise Carter, Rochelle Hudson, C. Henry Gordon, Warner Richmond (Radio)

In *Hell's Highway* the entire action, with the exception of one scene, occurs in and around a prison camp in some southern state; the preponderance of the convict labor is negro. The convicts have been hired to work on a new road. The contractor tells his foreman that he bid 50% under his nearest competitor and to win a profit he must get twice as much work out of the convicts.

To force their efforts recourse is had to the lash and the sweatbox, the latter a structure of corrugated iron barely large enough to contain a man, and placed so that the metal absorbs the full force of the burning sun.

Richard Dix is one of the convicts. His brother (Tom Brown) is sent to the gang for having shot and wounded Dix's betrayer. Dix, who is planning an escape, has to prevent the kid from coming along.

The direction is remarkably good at most points. Some handsome scenic backgrounds are created during the hunt for the convicts.

The director is rather less successful in his effort to inject comedy. Once or twice a nance camp laborer is employed, once for a genuine if smutty laugh. Other humor is supposed to arise from the smug mouthings of the Hermit (Charles Middleton), a crazed religionist type.

Dix is wasted as the young convict, with Brown much more effective as the kid. Louise Carter is an almost total loss in her single scene, as is Rochelle Hudson. Clarence Muse, in a very small bit, strikes one of the few really human notes.

....

■ HELLZAPOPPIN'

1942, 92 MINS, US
Dir H.C. Potter *Prod* Jules Levey *Scr* Nat Perrin, Warren Wilson *Ph* Woody Bredell *Ed* Milton Carruth
● Ole Olsen, Chic Johnson, Martha Raye, Hugh Herbert, Mischa Auer, Elisha Cook Jr. (Universal/Mayfair)

There's the thinnest thread of a romantic

story, but it's incidental to Olsen and Johnson's [1938] stage formula for *Hellzapoppin'*.

The yarn itself can be summed up in a few words: the rich girl in love with the poor boy, who in turn doesn't want to cross his rich pal, favored by the girl's socially conscious parents. The poor boy stages a charity show for the girl, and his stagehand pals (O&J) think they can save him from the girl, by lousing it up.

One of the picture's saving graces is the originality of presentation of screwball comedy. The business of O&J talking from the screen to the comic projectionist (Shemp Howard) is one such detail; ditto the slide bit telling a kid in the audience, 'Stinky go home', with Jane Frazee and Robert Paige interrupting a duet until Stinky finally leaves.

Don Raye and Gene DePauf have contributed several nice songs for this film. There are some lavish production numbers. Jules Levey (Mayfair), producer, was obviously unstinting.

☐ 1942: Nomination: Best Song ('Pig Foote Pete')

....

■ HELP!

1965, 92 MINS, UK ◇ ⓥ ⊙
Dir Richard Lester *Prod* Walter Shenson *Scr* Marc Behm, Charles Wood *Ph* David Watkin *Ed* John Victor Smith *Mus* Ken Thorne (dir.) *Art Dir* Ray Simm
● John Lennon, Paul McCartney, Ringo Starr, George Harrison, Leo McKern, Eleanor Bron (Shenson/Subafilms)

The Beatles' second effort is peppered with bright gags and situations and throwaway nonsense. Richard Lester's direction is expectedly alert and the color lensing is a delight. But there are also some frantically contrived spots and sequences that flag badly. The simple good spirits that pervaded *A Hard Day's Night* are now often smothered as if everybody is desperately trying to outsmart themselves and be ultra-clever-clever. Nevertheless, *Help!* is a good, nimble romp with both giggles and belly-laughs.

Story [by Marc Behm] concerns the efforts of a gang of Eastern thugs, led by Leo McKern, to get hold of a sacrificial ring which has been sent to Ringo by a fan and which he is innocently wearing. Also after the ring is a nutty, powerdrunk scientist who sees the ring as a key to world domination. The Beatles are given a heck of a runaround which takes them from London to Stonehenge, the Alps and the Bahamas.

The Beatles prove more relaxed in front of the camera but they have still to prove themselves to be actors; as screen personalities they are good material and have a touch of the Marx Bros in their similarly irreverent flights of fantasy.

....

■ HEMINGWAY'S ADVENTURES OF A YOUNG MAN

1962, 145 MINS, US ◇
Dir Martin Ritt *Prod* Jerry Wald *Scr* A.E. Hotchner *Ph* Lee Garmes *Ed* Hugh S. Fowler *Mus* Franz Waxman *Art Dir* Jack Martin Smith, Paul Groesse
● Richard Beymer, Diane Baker, Paul Newman, Ricado Montalban, Dan Dailey, Arthur Kennedy (20th Century-Fox)

The formidable task of assembling the bits and pieces of Ernest Hemingway's autobiographical young hero, Nick Adams, and welding them into a single, substantial flesh-and-blood screen personality has nearly been accomplished in *Adventures of a Young Man*. But, while the film has been executed with concern, integrity and respect for the pen from which it flows, it has a disquieting tendency to oscillate between flashes of artistry and truth and interludes of mechanics and melodramatics.

Hotchner's scenario, gleaned from the prose of 10 of Hemingway's short stories, traced the path to maturity of Nick Adams. It follows him in his restless, searching pursuit of knowledge and worldly experience with which to build his character, advance his potential, shape his identity and prepare him for his destiny in the higher sphere to which he aspires.

There are a host of fine performances, and a few weak ones. Paul Newman, almost unrecognizable behind a masterfully grotesque yet realistic makeup mask by Ben Nye, re-creates the punchdrunk Battler character. It's a colorful and compassionate acting cameo.

Other important standouts are Ricardo Montalban as a perceptive Italian officer, Fred Clark as a slick but sympathetic burlesque promoter, Dan Dailey as a down-and-out advance man, Juano Hernandez as the Battler's devoted watchdog 'trainer', and Eli Wallach as a practical but kind Italian Army orderly. Probably the finest performance in the film is Arthur Kennedy's as Nick's peace-loving, recessive father. And Jessica Tandy is excellent as the fanatical, domineering mother who leads Kennedy to his self-destruction.

. . . .

■ HENNESSY

1975, 104 MINS, UK ◇ ⍟
Dir Don Sharp   *Prod* Peter Snell   *Scr* John Gay
Ph Ernest Steward   *Ed* Eric Boyd-Perkins   *Mus* John Scott   *Art Dir* Ray Simm
● Rod Steiger, Lee Remick, Richard Johnson, Trevor Howard, Eric Porter, Peter Egan (American International)

Good suspense drama starring Rod Steiger as a man planning to blow up the British Parliament in revenge for his family's accidental death in Belfast.

Richard Johnson, who wrote the intriguing original story, plays a Scotland Yard inspector, well-versed (and earlier wounded) in Irish tumult, working under Trevor Howard in the attempt to find Steiger, who has come to London with a plan to substitute himself for MP Hugh Moxey on 5 November and, triggering himself as a human bomb, destroy the British power structure.

Ironically, IRA leader Eric Porter, knowing that event would lead to more British, rather than less, in Northern Ireland, sets out to kill Steiger. Steiger does very well in the title role.

. . . .

■ HENRY & JUNE

1990, 136 MINS, US ◇ ⍟ ⊙
Dir Philip Kaufman   *Prod* Peter Kaufman   *Scr* Rose Kaufman, Philip Kaufman   *Ph* Philippe Rousselot
Ed Vivien Hillgrove, William S. Scharf, Dede Allen   *Art Dir* Guy-Claude Francois
● Fred Ward, Uma Thurman, Maria de Medeiros, Richard E. Grant, Kevin Spacey, Jean-Philippe Ecoffey (Universal/Walrus)

Henry & June, will be considered liberating by some and obscene by others. The lovemaking scenes in his previous film, *The Unbearable Lightness of Being* (1988), proved that director Philip Kaufman was perhaps the best director to handle the story of the long-secret, passionate affair between writers Henry Miller and Anais Nin in Paris in 1931–32.

Pic's title, also the title of the Nin book, is actually a misnomer. This is the story of Henry and Anais; June, playing a marginal role, is offscreen much of the time.

The film opens with Anais and their banker husband, Hugo, establishing themselves in Paris. It quickly becomes clear that, although fond of the rather stuffy Hugo, Anais, who keeps a secret diary, isn't telling him everything, and is eager to experience the kind of things she imagines in her erotic dreams. Miller's arrival is the catalyst.

Anais is also attracted to Miller's wife, June, who visits occasionally from America, and dreams of erotic experiences in which June assumes the male role.

In its depiction of Depression Paris and sexual candor, *Henry & June* succeeds. The central performances of Fred Ward, as the cynical, life-loving Miller, and Maria de Medeiros, as the beautiful, insatiable Anais, splendidly fulfill the director's vision.

Pic is less successful in gaining audience sympathy for these hedonists. Also, the character of June (Uma Thurman) is ill-defined.
□ 1990: Nomination: Best Cinematography
. . . .

■ HENRY VIII AND HIS SIX WIVES

1972, 125 MINS, UK ◇ ⍟
Dir Waris Hussein   *Prod* Roy Baird   *Scr* Ian Thorne
Ph Peter Suschitzky   *Ed* John Bloom   *Mus* David Munro
Art Dir Roy Stannard
● Keith Michell, Donald Pleasence, Charlotte Rampling, Jane Asher, Frances Cuka, Lynne Frederick (Anglo-EMI)

A beautifully crafted epic, *Henry VIII* is told in flashback form from the king's deathbed. Pic deals almost exclusively with Henry and his succession of wives, deliberately relegating historic events to backdrops, even though audiences are kept in touch at all times with what else was going on in the realm.

Thanks also to a fine, tight script and sensitive but firm direction, the king acquires many more dimensions than those usually credited him. Keith Michell gives an upper-case performance all the way, through a succession of equally very believable makeup transformations.

Somewhat over-stolid at times, and taking itself too seriously, it perhaps needs more amusing change-of-pace sequences such as the one which finds the king saddled, sight-unseen, with the ugly Anne of Cleves.

. . . .

■ HENRY V

1946, 127 MINS, UK ◇ ⍟
Dir Laurence Olivier   *Prod* Laurence Olivier
Scr Laurence Olivier, Arthur Dent   *Ph* Robert Krasker
Ed Reginald Beck   *Mus* William Walton   *Art Dir* Paul Sheriff
● Laurence Olivier, Robert Newton, Renee Asherson, Esmond Knight, Leo Genn, Felix Aylmer (Two Cities)

Production cost ran to about $2 million and every cent of it is evident on the screen. The color, the sets, the expanse and the imaginative quality of the filming are unexcelled. *Henry V* as a picture, however, requires that the spectator takes more with him into the theatre in the way of mental preparedness than mere curiosity.

Story is considerably simpler than the boys from Hollywood turn out. Henry's a British king, hardly more than a moppet, when, with the aid of a couple of clergymen, he cons himself into believing that he ought to muscle his way into France and stake his royal claim there on the basis of ancestry. So he loads some 30,000 men and their horses on the 15th-century version of LSTs and hies across the channel.

There are many interesting scenes and one really exciting one – the battle. With thousands of horses, knights in armor and longbowmen in colorful costumes, it's a Technicolor setup. Strong contrast is made between the overstuffed French warriors in armor so heavy they have to be lowered onto their horses with block and tackle, and the British, who won the battle with the longbow, used by men afoot and unhindered by iron pants.

Memorable for their deft humor and poignancy are both scenes in which Renee Asherson, as Princess Katharine, appears. Even Olivier is put well back into the No. 2 spot in the scene in which he woos her.

Treatment is interesting and adds much to the general effect. Picture opens with the camera panning over London and coming into the Old Globe theatre. Heralds' horns announce the opening of the play as the camera gets to the stage – and the show is on.

Acting, at the beginning, is in the stylized pattern of the 16th century and it doesn't get far away from that even when the camera is given full sweep after the Old Globe has been left behind. Sets throughout also give a feeling that you haven't left the theatre for while tri-dimensional close to the camera, they fade into purposely obvious painted scenics in the background.
□ 1946: Nominations: Best Picture, Actor (Laurence Olivier), Color Art Direction, Scoring of a Dramatic Picture
. . . .

■ HENRY V

1989, 137 MINS, UK ◇ ⍟ ⊙
Dir Kenneth Branagh   *Prod* Bruce Sharman
Scr Kenneth Branagh   *Ph* Kenneth MacMillan
Ed Michael Bradsell   *Mus* Patrick Doyle   *Art Dir* Tim Harvey
● Kenneth Branagh, Derek Jacobi, Brian Blessed, Ian Holm, Paul Scofield, Emma Thompson (Renaissance)

Henry V is a stirring, gritty and enjoyable pic which offers a plethora of fine performances from some of the U.K.'s brightest talents.

Laurence Olivier's *Henry V* (1944) was designed to rally the English with its glorious battle scenes and patriotic verse. Branagh's version is more realistic and tighter in scale, and is a contempo version of Shakespeare.

Pic opens with Derek Jacobi as the chorus wandering around a film studio setting the scene. Branagh (Henry V, King of England) prepares for an invasion of France to secure his legal claim to the French throne. Paul Scofield (the French king) sadly ponders his country's situation and is urged to enter in bloody battle by Michael Maloney (the Dauphin).

After many battles, Branagh's tired and bedraggled army prepares for the final conflict with the massive French forces. After wandering among his troops in disguise, Branagh makes an impassioned speech and his forces win.

One subplot has Emma Thompson (the French king's daughter Katherine) and her maid (Geraldine McEwan) playing at learning English. Branagh declares his love for Thompson after he has won the French throne.
□ 1989: Best Costume Design.
□ Nominations: Best Director, Actor (Kenneth Branagh)
. . . .

■ HENRY . . . PORTRAIT OF A SERIAL KILLER

1989, 83 MINS, US ◇ ⍟ ⊙
Dir John McNaughton   *Prod* John McNaughton, Lisa Dedmond, Steven A. Jones   *Scr* Richard Fire, John McNaughton   *Ph* Charlie Lieberman   *Ed* Elena Maganini   *Mus* John McNaughton, Ken Hale, Steven A. Jones   *Art Dir* Rick Paul
● Michael Rooker, Tom Towles, Tracy Arnold (Maljack)

Hard-driving, riveting pic is an unsentimental look at a sociopath as his bloody trail passes through Chicago. Film was finished in 1987.

From the opening shot of a woman's nude body lying in a ditch to the closing shot of a bloody suitcase, there isn't a wasted moment. Story follows Henry (Michael Rooker) while he rooms with his old prison buddy Otis (Tom Towles) and Otis' sister Becky (Tracy Arnold).

Henry has a philosophy about murder, which he shares with Otis. He constantly changes his methods so as not to leave a pattern for the police to follow. Somewhat nervous at first, Otis quickly joins in.

Film uses two strategies to keep audiences off balance. First is the use of violence, which starts off subtly but finally moves to a gory extreme. Early killings are shown in flashback, where we only see bodies as grotesque still lifes. The second tactic is the use of Becky to humanize Henry.

Low budget pic looks surprisingly good, capturing the gritty feel of the characters' lives. Thesping is solid.

....

■ HER ALIBI

1989, 94 MINS, US ◇ ☻ ⊙
Dir Bruce Beresford   *Prod* Keith Barish   *Scr* Charlie Peters   *Ph* Freddie Francis   *Ed* Anne Goursaud   *Mus* Georges Delerue   *Art Dir* Henry Bumstead
● Tom Selleck, Paulina Porizkova, William Daniels, James Farentino, Hurd Hatfield, Patrick Wayne (Warner)

He's a mystery writer, she's a mystery; and it's also a mystery how TV fodder like this manages to get the high-gloss, top-talent treatment at studios.

Bestselling writer Phil Blackwood (Tom Selleck), out of stories and under pressure for his next book, decides to rescue drop-dead beautiful Nina (Czech-born model Pauline Porizkova) from court custody as a murder suspect.

He gives her an alibi by telling the canny d.a. (rigorously played by James Farentino) that they're having an affair and were together during the time of the alleged murder.

To maintain the facade, Selleck has to take the aloof Rumanian beauty out to his lush country estate to live while he pecks away at his new novel – about her, naturally, and his feverishly imagined version of their relationship.

Porizkova has the disconcerting habit of hurling kitchen knives at the wall and otherwise inventing Selleck's demise. He soon begins to suspect she is a murderer.

Mix of sexual tension, physical danger and quirky black humour has a certain appealing buoyancy, but ultimately it's deflated by general lack of credibility.

....

■ HERBIE GOES TO MONTE CARLO

1977, 105 MINS, US ◇ ☻
Dir Vincent McEveety   *Prod* Ron Miller   *Scr* Arthur Alsberg, Don Neson   *Ph* Leonard J. South   *Ed* Cotton Warburton   *Mus* Frank DeVol   *Art Dir* John B. Mansbridge
● Dean Jones, Don Knotts, Julie Sommars, Jacques Marin, Roy Kinnear, Bernard Fox (Walt Disney)

Herbie, the spunky little Volks beetle with a mind of his own, gets romantic buildup when he becomes a Romeo on wheels infatuated with a flirty powder-blue Lancia named Giselle, as both participate in the annual Paris to Monte Carlo road rally. Herbie is reunited with his original owner and driver, Dean Jones, a former second-rate racer whom he once adopted and won a flock of races for in the US.

Together again, Jones finds once more he is at the mercy of Herbie, who time and again takes matters into his own hands for often slapstick and mirthful effect as they roar toward their destination.

Herbie performs in the qualifying races outside Paris where he falls hood over wheels in love with the smart Lancia, driven by Julie Sommars who takes Jones' eye as well.

....

■ HERBIE RIDES AGAIN

1974, 88 MINS, US ◇ ☻ ⊙
Dir Robert Stevenson   *Prod* Bill Walsh   *Scr* Bill Walsh   *Ph* Frank Phillips   *Ed* Cotton Warburton   *Mus* George Bruns   *Art Dir* John B. Mansbridge, Walter Tyler
● Helen Hayes, Ken Berry, Stefanie Powers, John McIntire, Keenan Wynn, Huntz Hall (Walt Disney)

Herbie Rides Again is Disney's sequel to *The Love Bug*, and a team encore for producer Bill Walsh and director Robert Stevenson. Walsh also scripted from a Gordon Buford story. It adds up, natch, to another fat plug for the Volkswagen 'bug' as the runaway (literally) titular star.

Keenan Wynn is a San Francisco construction tycoon hellbent on putting up the tallest skyscraper yet, but the plan is frustrated and ultimately foiled by sweet little old widow lady Helen Hayes. She owns the ramshackle Victorian firehouse that stands in Wynn's greedy way, and she won't budge.

Ken Berry, as Wynn's hayseed nephew lawyer from the midwest, is enlisted to pull off the trick, but instead succumbs to the charms of widow and miniskirted friend, Stefanie Powers.

....

■ HERCULES

1983, 98 MINS, ITALY ◇ ☻ ⊙
Dir Lewis Coates [= Luigi Cozzi]   *Prod* Menahem Golan, Yoram Globus   *Scr* Lewis Coates   *Ph* Alberto Spagnoli   *Ed* James Beshears   *Mus* Pino Donaggio   *Art Dir* M.A. Geleng
● Lou Ferrigno, Mirella D'Angelo, Sybil Danning, Ingrid Anderson, Brad Harris, Rossana Podesta (Golan-Globus)

Golan and Globus have corralled 'The Incredible Lou Ferrigno' to topline in a cheesy epic that could just about be titled *Hercules in Outer Space*. Since a lumpy space suit would cover Ferrigno's mighty physique from view, the all-powerful one travels through the universe wearing nothing but his gladiatorial briefs.

A lot of it takes place on the moon, as Zeus and wife and daughter Hera and Athena toy from above with the fate of mortals. It is Hercules's tasks to try to rescue the Princess Cassiopea from the clutches of her evil kidnappers, and given the changing times, the muscleman doesn't have to battle cardboard monsters, but hi-tech mechanical beasts made of metal and which emit deadly laser blasts from their jaws.

Ferrigno is perfectly affable, and physically (if not physiognomally) he more than lives up to his billing. Sybil Danning, Mirella D'Angelo and Ingrid Anderson comprise a fetching trio of femmes.

....

■ HERCULES RETURNS

1993, 80 MINS, AUSTRALIA ◇ ☻
Dir David Parker   *Prod* Philip Jaroslow   *Scr* Des Mangan   *Ph* David Connell   *Ed* Peter Carrodus   *Mus* Philip Judd   *Art Dir* Jon Dowding
● David Argue, Bruce Spence, Mary Coustas, Michael Carman, Brendon Suhr (Philm)

Hercules Returns follows in the footsteps of Woody Allen's *What's Up Tiger Lily?* by completely revamping and revoicing a bad old foreign film.

Melbourne-based comics Des Mangan and Sally Patience have adapted their live show, 'Double Take Meets Hercules,' with assistance from first-time director David Parker, who's better known as a screenwriter and cinematographer working in partnership with his wife, Nadia Tass. Parker has directed about 18 minutes of framing footage, but most of *Hercules Returns* consists of the revoiced film.

The framing material features film buff Brad McBain (David Argue), who refurbishes a rundown picture palace to show his favorite movies. But his manic projectionist, Sprocket (Bruce Spence), discovers at the last moment that the print has arrived in its Italo-language version, sans subtitles. McBain, Sprocket and publicist Lisa (Mary Coustas) frantically improvise a voiceover translation for the black-tie audience, and it's a hit.

The improvisation turns the original clinker

[Giorgio Capitani's 1965 *Ercole, Sansone, Maciste & Ursus: gli invincibili*] into a hilarious romp, with Hercules now a frustrated singer sent by Zeus to perform at the Pink Parthenon nightclub where he's offered the hand of the lovely Labia, daughter of the club's owners. She, however, prefers Testiculi and rejects Hercules.

Film has an endearing, slapdash feel to it.

....

■ HERE COMES MR. JORDAN

1941, 93 MINS, US ☻ ⊙
Dir Alexander Hall   *Prod* Everett Riskin   *Scr* Sidney Buchman, Seton I. Miller   *Ph* Joseph Walker   *Ed* Viola Lawrence   *Mus* Frederick Hollander
● Robert Montgomery, Evelyn Keyes, Claude Rains, Rita Johnson, Edward Everett Horton, James Gleason (Columbia)

Story [from Harry Segall's play *Heaven Can Wait*] humorously poses the theory of reincarnation of a personality and soul that has been snatched from its earthly body 50 years before the cosmic schedule. Robert Montgomery is an aggressive prizefighter, determined to be champ, with an airplane and saxophone as hobbies. Flying from training camp to New York, the plane crashes, and Montgomery is snatched by Heavenly messenger Edward Everett Horton from his earthly body, and taken to Heaven for celestial registration.

When it is found Montgomery's arrival is premature, and his earthly body has already been cremated to prevent replacement, it's up to registrar Claude Rains (Mr Jordan) to secure another body suitable to Montgomery. In this body, retaining his own soul, Montgomery falls in love with Evelyn Keyes, daughter of a duped financial agent. After wandering for weeks in search of another landing, under guidance of Rains, Montgomery lands permanently in the body of a contender for the boxing championship.

Montgomery's portrayal is a highlight in a group of excellent performances. Keyes displays plenty of charm. James Gleason scores as the fast-gabbing fight manager, who is bewildered by the proceedings. Direction by Alexander Hall sustains a fast pace throughout.

□ 1941: Best Original Story, Screenplay.
□ Nominations: Best Picture, Director, Actor (Robert Montgomery), Supp. Actor (James Gleason), B&W Cinematography

....

■ HERE COMES THE GROOM

1951, 113 MINS, US ☻ ⊙
Dir Frank Capra   *Prod* Frank Capra   *Scr* Virginia Van Upp, Liam O'Brien, Myles Connolly   *Ph* George Barnes   *Ed* Ellsworth Hoagland   *Mus* Joseph J. Lilley   *Art Dir* Hal Pereira, Earl Hedrick
● Bing Crosby, Jane Wyman, Alexis Smith, Franchot Tone, James Barton, Robert Keith (Paramount)

Paramount has a topnotch piece of comedy diversion in *Here Comes the Groom*. The incredibly swift 113 minutes are jampacked with the kind of fun that never lets up on the risibilities.

Robert Riskin and Liam O'Brien provided the merry yarn of a carefree newspaperman (Bing Crosby) who must marry within a week to be able to adopt two war orphans he has picked up during a lengthy Paris assignment. He hopes the bride will be Jane Wyman, but arrives back in Boston to find her tired of waiting and about to marry wealthy Franchot Tone. His problem is to break up the impending rebound marriage before the adoption deadline.

Crosby is at his casual best, nonchalantly tossing his quips for the most effect. Wyman is a wow as the girlfriend who makes him really work to win her. The two join on the Hit Parade tune 'In the Cool, Cool, Cool of the

Evening', by Johnny Mercer and Hoagy Carmichael, in a socko song-and-dance session.

☐ 1951: Best Song ('In the Cool, Cool, Cool of the Evening')

☐ Nomination: Best Motion Picture Story

....

■ HERE COMES THE NAVY

1934, 88 MINS, US

Dir Lloyd Bacon *Scr* Ben Markson, Earl Baldwin *Ph* Arthur Edeson *Ed* George Amy *Mus* Leo F. Forbstein (dir.) *Art Dir* Esdras Hartley
● James Cagney, Pat O'Brien, Gloria Stuart, Frank McHugh, Dorothy Tree, Robert Barrat (Warner)

Here Comes the Navy is a saga of the US fleet. It's light on story, and because of that it borders on being an elaborate newsreel, i.e. the inner workings of the gobs at maneuvers and navy life, from enlistment to war formations.

The James Cagney-Pat O'Brien feud throughout the footage reminds of the Quirt-Flagg school of masculine venom. Only here Gloria Stuart is O'Brien's sister and he wants Cagney to stay away from her.

Frank McHugh stooges for Cagney as his lone faithful pal, even after the gobs have given wise-guy Cagney a little dose of coventry, having steered clear of him because they think he's a wrong guy. Cagney is twice catapulted into heroic situations, the double parachute jump for the finale packing something of a kick.

☐ 1934: Nomination: Best Picture

....

■ HERE COME THE CO-EDS

1945, 85 MINS, US

Dir Jean Yarbrough *Prod* John Grant *Scr* Arthur T. Horman, John Grant *Ph* George Robinson *Ed* Arthur Hilton *Art Dir* John B. Goodman, Richard H. Riedel
● Bud Abbott, Lou Costello, Peggy Ryan, Martha O'Driscoll, Lon Chaney, Donald Cook (Universal)

Abbott and Costello are easily up to their high laugh standards in *Here Come the Co-Eds*. Pic is helped considerably by presence of Phil Spitalny's nifty all-girl 'Hour of Charm' orchestra and Peggy Ryan, who plays a typical college hepcat.

Co-Eds is smartly gagged, smoothly paced, and even the familiar routines are given new twists. The gags or bits cover the field from the face-slapping episodes, down through a comedy wrestling match, farcical basketball game, a mad scramble in a kitchen, to the payoff chase sequence.

Yarn shows a moss-covered, tradition-bound femme college that's stirred out of its lethargy by Abbott and Costello.

John Grant, originally from musical comedy, who's done scripts from the A&C team ever since they began to go places, does well by the comedy duo on the production end. He's also responsible for the screen story along with Arthur T. Horman [from a story by Edmund L. Hartmann]. Jean Yarbrough's direction is aces.

....

■ HER ENLISTED MAN

See: Red Salute

....

■ HERE WE GO ROUND THE MULBERRY BUSH

1968, 94 MINS, UK ◇

Dir Clive Donner *Prod* Clive Donner *Scr* Hunter Davies *Ph* Denis Leiston *Ed* Fergus McDonnell *Mus* Spencer Davis Group, Stevie Winwood, The Traffic
● Barry Evans, Judy Geeson, Angela Scoular, Sheila White, Adrienne Posta, Denholm Elliott (United Artists)

A lightfooted look at the teenagers with engaging performances from hitherto largely unknown youngsters, the film was made en-tirely on location in a new town near London. It has a nimble alertness to juve characteristics and a nice flair for comedy.

Story is based on a successful novel by journalist Hunter Davies. Its strength is the wit of characterization and it's pleasantly salted with lines about young sexual ambitions.

The hero is a final-year student at high school, absorbed with stalking gals but finding the hunt leaves him too often up a cul-de-sac.

Barry Evans wins both sympathy and laughs as the boy. Story is spliced with Mitty-type dream bits, which give additional bite to the gap between ideal and reality.

The girls are well chosen, with Angela Scoular scoring with fine comic precision as the uppercrust girl, Judy Geeson purveying easy charm as the final near-conquest, and Adrienne Posta and Sheila White making the most of their chances.

....

■ HER HUSBAND'S AFFAIRS

1947, 84 MINS, US

Dir S. Sylvan Simon *Scr* Ben Hecht, Charles Lederer *Ph* Charles Lawton Jr *Ed* Al Clark *Mus* George Dunning *Art Dir* Stephen Goossen, Carl Anderson
● Lucille Ball, Franchot Tone, Edward Everett Horton, Mikhail Rasumny, Gene Lockhart, Jonathan Hale (Columbia)

Her Husband's Affairs is well-premised fun that has a laugh a minute. As a comedy team, Lucille Ball and Franchot Tone excel. Tone is a slightly screwball advertising-slogan genius while Ball is his ever-loving wife who somehow always winds up with the credit for his spectacular stunts.

Director S. Sylvan Simon's pace is perfect and he welds zany situations into socko laughs. Motivation for much of the comedy comes from Tone's sponsorship of a screwball inventor and the products that he develops while searching for the perfect embalming fluid. Gentle fun is poked at advertising agencies and bigshot sponsors and public figures.

Mikhail Rasumny is the crazy inventor and wraps up the role for honors, Edward Everett Horton, Gene Lockhart, a business tycoon, Nana Bryant, his wife, and Jonathan Hale are among others who keep the laughs busy.

....

■ HERO

(UK/Australia: Accidental Hero)

1992, 116 MINS, US ◇ ⓥ ⊙

Dir Stephen Frears *Prod* Laura Ziskin *Scr* David Webb Peoples *Ph* Oliver Stapleton *Ed* Mick Audsley *Mus* George Fenton *Art Dir* Leslie McDonald
● Dustin Hoffman, Geena Davis, Andy Garcia, Joan Cusack, Kevin J. O'Connor, Maury Chaykin (Columbia)

Third-act heroics help but can't rescue filmmaker Stephen Frears' most concerted mainstream push. Muddled effort cleverly skewering media and societal fascination with heroes doesn't create compelling characters for its big-name leads.

The story centers on Bernie Laplante (Dustin Hoffman), a shiftless, small-time hood who stumbles on to a plane crash and ends up saving the people aboard. A TV reporter on the plane (Geena Davis) begins a search to find the unknown hero, dubbed 'the angel of Flight 104'.

Eventually, that titles falls to John Bubber (Andy Garcia), a homeless Vietnam veteran with movie-star looks under the dirt, who comes forward to claim the $1 million reward after giving Bernie a lift after the accident. Bubber is hailed as the next coming of Jesus and Gandhi, even as Bernie's fortunes continue to sour.

Written by David Webb Peoples (*Unforgiven*), *Hero* is peppered with occasional gems but has to sift through a lot of wreckage to find them. Lacking focus, pic jumps back and forth between Davis, probably pic's most marketable asset as the career-driven reporter attracted to her pseudo-saviour, and the self-centered Bernie, who's hard-pressed to explain his act of selfless heroism.

Unfortunately, action tilts too heavily toward Hoffman, who simply mucks it up, seemingly playing a bad version of Ratso Rizzo had he survived events in *Midnight Cowboy*.

....

■ HEROES

1977, 113 MINS, US ◇ ⓥ

Dir Jeremy Paul Kagan *Prod* David Foster, Lawrence Turman *Scr* James Carabatsos *Ph* Frank Stanley *Ed* Patrick Kennedy *Mus* Jack Nitzsche, Richard Hazard *Art Dir* Charles Rosen
● Henry Winkler, Sally Field, Harrison Ford, Val Avery, Olivia Cole, Hector Elias (Universal)

Heroes is a poorly-written melodrama about a troubled Vietnam veteran and a girl who helps him work out his problems. The multi-location production stars Henry Winkler, in a good though flawed performance, and Sally Field.

Plot peg is standard – boy and girl, running from separate problems, meet 'cute' and fall in love with some ups and downs enroute.

Speaking of the writing 'cutes', there's a plague in this screenplay, mainly in the Winkler character and the actor's performance. Since the character has a history of mental malaise, the kooky bits are many and just awful. See Winkler confound his doctor, Hector Elias. See him escape from the hospital. See him run and jump and streak and shout.

....

■ HEROES OF TELEMARK, THE

1965, 131 MINS, UK ◇ ⓥ

Dir Anthony Mann *Prod* S. Benjamin Fisz *Scr* Ivan Moffat, Ben Barzman *Ph* Robert Krasker *Ed* Bert Bates *Mus* Malcolm Arnold *Art Dir* Tony Masters
● Kirk Douglas, Richard Harris, Ulla Jacobsson, Michael Redgrave, Anton Diffring, Eric Porter (Benton/Rank)

Producer Benjamin Fisz and director Anthony Mann have made a $5.6 million motion picture that emerges as hefty, gripping and carefully made entertainment.

It's 1942 in Nazi-occupied Norway. The Germans are ahead of the Allies on atomic fission, as reports from the Norsk Hydro heavy water factory near Telemark reveal. It's the job of a tiny band of nine resistance workers to scotch the Nazi plans.

Kirk Douglas, as the scientist drawn unwillingly into the exploit, and Richard Harris, as the resistance leader, turn in powerhouse performances. They detest each other on sight (never satisfactorily explained) but learn to respect and grudgingly like each other during mutual danger. Ulla Jacobsson, as Douglas' ex-wife, also fighting for the resistance, has a sketchy role but plays it with charm and conviction.

Krasker's work over ice and snow-girt Norway is a joy. Craftily he used Helge Stoylen, a Norwegian ski coach, to help out on some lensing. Stoylen held a Panavision camera between his legs for some of the graceful and gripping ski shots.

....

■ HER WEDDING NIGHT

1930, 78 MINS, US

Dir Frank Tuttle *Scr* Henry Myers *Ph* Harry Fischbeck *Ed* Denis Drought
● Clara Bow, Ralph Forbes, Charles Ruggles, Skeets Gallagher (Paramount)

Smart showmanship. Combination of jaunty comedy of the spicy Avery Hopwood type, [based on his play, *Little Miss Bluebeard*] generous flavoring of spice in title and action, and a wealth of gay romance in hoke farcical setting.

Whole production is deftly handled. Settings and atmosphere beautifully manage to set off the gay tone of the whole affair. And the cast surrounding the Paramount redhead has been fitted to tailor-made roles with nicety. Clara Bow plays the racy heroine with a vigor that compensates for some of her shortcomings of voice and diction.

Plot doesn't matter except that Larry (Ralph Forbes), composer of sentimental songs, persuades his friend, Bob (Skeets Gallagher), to impersonate him to escape hero-worshipping flappers. Bob goes off on a romantic spree under his pal's name, inadvertently marrying Norma (Bow) before a rural Italian magistrate.

● ●

■ HE SAID, SHE SAID

1991, 115 MINS, US ◇ ▣ ⊙
Dir Ken Kwapis, Marisa Silver *Prod* Frank Mancuso Jr
Scr Brian Hohlfeld *Ph* Stephen H. Burum *Ed* Sidney
Levin, Rick Sparr *Mus* Miles Goodman
Art Dir Michael Corenblith
● Kevin Bacon, Elizabeth Perkins, Nathan Lane, Anthony
LaPaglia, Sharon Stone, Stanley Anderson (Paramount)

He Said, She Said is two awful films rolled into one. The potentially provocative idea of having a male and female director take separate but interlocking looks at the same love story fizzles here in the hokiest, most contrived telling imaginable. Co-directors Ken Kwapis and Marisa Silver, who got engaged during the production, have turned out segments that differ slightly in tone, pacing and lighting styles, but are equal in banality and obviousness.

Sitcom slickness of the enterprise is established at the outset, as TV news commentator team of Kevin Bacon and Elizabeth Perkins apparently breaks up on the air when she beans him with a coffee cup. Pushed along at a frantic, wearying pace, initial hour is devoted to mirthless jokes about the young hotshot's womanizing, fear of marriage and need to feel professionally superior.

Kwapis' high gloss garishness and antic staging contrasts with the slower, more subdued approach of Silver, who, in covering the same ground, underlines a sense of romance and optimism in Perkins' character to which the male has been oblivious.

What's shocking is how impersonal and unfelt the film is on both sides. On screen virtually throughout, Bacon and Perkins are unable to escape this collision. Supporting performances are uniformly broad and one-dimensional.

● ●

■ HESTER STREET

1975, 90 MINS, US ▣
Dir Joan Micklin Silver *Prod* Raphael D. Silver
Scr Joan Micklin Silver *Ph* Kenneth Van Sickle
Ed Katerine Wenning *Mus* William Bolcon
● Steven Keats, Carol Kane, Mel Howard, Dorrie
Kavanaugh (Midwest)

Hester Street deftly delves into Jewish emigration to the US just before the turn-of-the-century. Hester Street is a sort of mobile ghetto as Eastern European Jews pour in and go in for their Americanization before moving on to other NY boroughs or to further west US climes.

Adapted from Abraham Cahan's story *Yekl*, it concerns Jake who has gone in for Americanization.

He sends for his wife and son but their arrival first fills him with shame at their old world clodishness. However, the wife cannot keep up with her husband's ways as she goes another way towards becoming an American.

Joan Micklin Silver displays a sure hand for her first pic.

● ●

■ HE WAS HER MAN

1934, 70 MINS, US
Dir Lloyd Bacon *Scr* Robert Lord, Tom Buckingham,
Niven Busch *Ph* George Barnes *Ed* George Amy
Mus Leo F. Forbstein (dir.) *Art Dir* Anton Grot
● James Cagney, Joan Blondell, Victor Jory, Frank
Craven, Harold Huber, Russell Hopton (Warner)

With Joan Blondell and James Cagney lending apt cast personalities, director Lloyd Bacon has woven from an original story by Robert Lord a forthright narrative about two pieces of human flotsam.

Most of the action is set against the background of a Portuguese fishing village on the Pacific coast. Both Blondell and Cagney turn in deftly confected performances.

Plot gets its motivation from the efforts of a double-crossing cracksman (Cagney) to escape the penalty of gang law. In his flight from the torpedoes Cagney winds up in San Francisco. There he is spotted by an underworld tipoff (Frank Craven) and the word is passed on to the mob back east. Meanwhile he meets the girl (Blondell), who has just decided to call it quits with the wayfaring life she's been leading and accept a proposal of marriage from a Portuguese fisherman located 100 miles south of Frisco. Cagney elects to join the girl on her trip to the groom.

Cagney settles down in the village and the fisherman, capably played by Victor Jory, goes about making the marriage arrangements. In the interim the girl falls for Cagney and there's talk between them of going away together. Overnight Cagney becomes leery of getting himself entangled and unbeknown to her prepares to scram. From here the action starts building to a tense climax.

● ●

■ HE WHO RIDES A TIGER

1966, 103 MINS, UK ▣ ⊙
Dir Charles Crichton *Prod* David Newman *Scr* Trevor
Peacock *Ph* John Von Kotze *Ed* Jack Harris, John S.
Smith *Mus* Alexander Faris *Art Dir* Richard Harrison,
Seamus Flannery
● Tom Bell, Judi Dench, Paul Rogers, Kay Walsh, Ray
McAnally, Jeremy Spenser (British Lion)

Legal and financial hassles upset the smooth production of this crime meller, but it does not show on the screen. Story concerns a young, nerveless cat burglar (specialty: rocks from stately homes) with a split personality. Kind to children and animals, suave, good-mannered on the one hand. But this personable young guy is equally prone to violent outbursts of impatience and hot temper. Released from the cooler, he sets out on a string of profitable crimes, with Superintendent Taylor (Paul Rogers) breathing down his neck.

Trevor Peacock's screenplay is crisp, and even in the love scenes and with the kids does not teeter overmuch towards the sentimental. Tom Bell as the anti-hero is one of the crop of young actors who emerged around the Finney, Courtenay, Lynch, O'Toole era. He has an easy style and diamond-hard personality which put him among the leading runners in this field.

Judi Dench, in a somewhat indecisive part, again shows her very bright talent and Rogers is fine as the determined, disgruntled cop.

● ●

■ HEXED

1993, 90 MINS, US ◇ ▣
Dir Alan Spencer *Prod* Marc S. Fischer, Louis G.
Friedman *Scr* Alan Spencer *Ph* James Chressanthis
Ed Debra McDermott *Mus* Lance Rubin
Art Dir Brenton Swift
● Ayre Gross, Claudia Christian, Adrienne Shelly, Ray
Baker, R. Lee Ermey, Michael Knight (Price)

Some surefire slapstick footage is about all that's funny in the stillborn comedy *Hexed*.

Writer-director Alan Spencer's debut pic makes one long for the sophistication of *Police Academy* movies.

Hotel desk clerk Matthew (Arye Gross) is anxious to end his rut and pump some excitement into his life. Enter beautiful French model and cover girl Hexina (Claudia Christian). Gross and Christian have sex in scenes imitating *Fatal Attraction* and *Basic Instinct*, after which he finds out she's really a psychotic killer who's spent six years in a mental institution.

Gross is an able farceur but hard-pressed to make any of the increasingly silly plot twists believable. Christian's acting is way over the top, though she's well cast as the beautiful loon. Adrienne Shelly, familiar from Hal Hartley films, is appealing as Gross's co-worker and would-be girlfriend.

● ●

■ HICKEY AND BOGGS

1972, 111 MINS, US ◇ ▣
Dir Robert Culp *Prod* Fouad Said *Scr* Walter Hill
Ph Wilmer Butler *Ed* David Berlatsky *Mus* Ted Ashford
● Bill Cosby, Robert Culp, Rosalind Cash, Carmen, Louis
Moreno, Michael Moriarty (Film Guarantors/United Artists)

Title of this Bill Cosby-Robert Culp starrer might indicate comedy, but action pairs former stars of pop *I Spy* teleseries, making their first appearance together since they were down-at-the-heel private eyes operating just outside the law.

Culp makes his directorial bow and Fouad Said, who started in the industry as cameraman on *I Spy* series, debuts as a producer. Latter should have paid more attention to story line of the Walter Hill screenplay, which suffers through audience never being entirely certain as to the identity of some of the characters.

Dicks are employed to find a missing femme and become innocently involved in search for a $400,000 haul stolen from a Pittsburgh bank. Somehow, the femme is connected with missing loot but audience is never let in on secret.

● ●

■ HIDDEN, THE

1987, 96 MINS, US ◇ ▣ ⊙
Dir Jack Sholder *Prod* Robert Shaye, Gerald T. Olson,
Michael Meltzer *Scr* Bob Hunt *Ph* Jacques Haitkin
Ed Michael Knue *Mus* Michael Convertino *Art Dir* C.J.
Strawn, Mick Strawn
● Michael Nouri, Kyle MacLachlan, Ed O'Ross, Clu
Gulager, Claudia Christian, Clarence Felder (New
Line/Heron)

The Hidden is a well-constructed thriller, directed with swift assurance by Jack Sholder, brought down by an utterly conventional sci-fi ending.

Just as LA homicide detective Tom Beck (Michael Nouri) is prepared to close the books on a businessman who went on a crime spree, he's approached by taciturn FBI agent Lloyd Gallagher (Kyle MacLachlan) from Seattle, who's searching for the same man, Jack DeVries (Chris Mulkey).

Gallagher is unsatisfied when Beck informs him DeVries is about to die in an LA hospital, and the plot begins to unfold when the dying man forcefeeds a reptilian alien down the throat of a fellow patient. A few minutes later the mild-mannered accountant bolts out of bed, escapes the hospital, murders a record store clerk and heads on another crime spree. This leads to a series of calamitous, well-shot chase scenes in which Beck and Gallagher are trying to catch up with the possessed human before the alien goes mouth to mouth into another life form.

Nouri finally shakes off his *Flashdance* shadow by turning in the best performance of his career.

● ●

H

■ HIDDEN AGENDA

1990, 108 MINS, UK ◇ ⓥ ⊙
Dir Ken Loach   *Prod* Eric Fellner   *Scr* Jim Allen
Ph Clive Tickner   *Ed* Jonathan Morris   *Mus* Stewart
Copeland   *Art Dir* Martin Johnson
● Frances McDormand, Brian Cox, Brad Dourif, Mai
Zetterling, Bernard Archard, Maurice Roeves
(Hemdale/Initial)

Hidden Agenda is a hard-hitting attack on allegedly ruthless methods of the British police in Northern Ireland. Pic is set in 1982, and seems inspired by the notorious Stalker case. Stalker was a top-level British police officer sent to Northern Ireland to investigate the Royal Ulster Constabulary. His eventual highly critical report was hushed up, and he resigned and went public.

Brian Cox plays the Stalker-like Kerrigan, brought to Belfast to investigate the killings of an IRA sympathizer and an American lawyer (Brad Dourif in a tiny role). Kerrigan befriends Dourif's bereaved girlfriend (Frances McDormand, good in a Jane Fonda-type role). He quickly discovers the men were killed by members of the Royal Ulster Constabulary, and exposes a high-level coverup.

Jim Allen's provocative screenplay includes references to British secret service and their dirty tricks against the Heath and Wilson governments of the 1970s.

But though it attempts to make an acceptable theatrical entertainment out of a complex political saga, *Hidden Agenda* lacks bigscreen impact.

■ HIDDEN CITY

1988, 107 MINS, US ◇ ⓥ
Dir Stephen Poliakoff   *Prod* Irving Teitelbaum
Scr Stephen Poliakoff   *Ph* Witold Stok   *Ed* Peter Coulson
Mus Michael Storey   *Art Dir* Martin Johnson
● Charles Dance, Cassie Stuart, Bill Paterson, Richard E.
Grant, Alex Horton, Tusse Silberg (Hidden City)

First-time writer-director Stephen Poliakoff, an established legit playwright, tries very hard with *Hidden City*. Unfortunately he tries too hard, and the result is an overlong film with too many storylines and not enough good acting that rambles along with an air of self-importance.

Charles Dance plays a statistician whose well-ordered and smug life is shattered when he gets involved with Cassie Stuart, who is obsessed with finding a mysterious piece of film that appears to have been hidden by the government. The search for fragments of the lost film takes them into a maze of tunnels underneath London packed with official government archive film and discarded classified material, and into brushes with the police. At this point the action loses its way.

Dance is in good form as the sexy statistician, though he looks a bit bemused at some of the situations the storyline pushes him into. Stuart has an appealing waif-like quality, but her acting here amounts to looking intense, running about, and shouting 'quick, hurry up' to Dance a great deal.

■ HIDDEN ROOM, THE

See: Obsession (1949)

■ HIDE IN PLAIN SIGHT

1980, 92 MINS, US ◇ ⓥ
Dir James Caan   *Prod* Robert Christiansen, Rick
Rosenberg   *Scr* Spencer Eastman   *Ph* Paul Lohmann
Ed Fredric Steinkamp, William Steinkamp   *Mus* Leonard
Rosenman   *Art Dir* Pato Guzman
● James Caan, Jill Eikenberry, Danny Aiello, Robert
Viharo, Joe Grifasi, Barbra Rae (M-G-M)

Hide in Plain Sight has some of the makings of a good, honest film. It tells the true story of a

working man's fight against the system, features several poignant moments, and makes a number of political messages in an effective yet unobtrusive manner. But in his directorial debut, James Caan never musters the energy or emotion needed to break the unbearably slow, dismal tone.

Caan is wonderfully accurate as the factory worker who becomes an innocent victim of a new witness relocation program that gives a new identity to any person (and his family) who informs on organized crime. In this case, two-bit mobster Robert Viharo testifies against his cronies and the authorities relocate him, his wife (who happens to be Caan's former spouse), and her two children by Caan to another state.

The frustration of the almost hopeless search Caan attempts could have been excellent fodder for a gripping, human drama. Screenplay, based on a book by Leslie Waller, seems true to its subject but somehow fails to create enough dramatic sparks.

■ HIGH AND DRY

See: The 'Maggie'

■ HIGH AND THE MIGHTY, THE

1954, 147 MINS, US ◇
Dir William A. Wellman   *Scr* Ernest K. Gann
Ph Archie Stout, William Clothier   *Ed* Ralph Dawson
Mus Dimitri Tiomkin
● John Wayne, Claire Trevor, Laraine Day, Robert
Stack, Jan Sterling, Phil Harris (Warner/Wayne-Fellows)

Ernest K. Gann's gripping bestseller *The High and the Mighty* has been turned into an equally socko piece of screen entertainment. It is a class drama, blended with mass appeal into a well-rounded show.

The plot has to do with human reactions to danger as a troubled plane, carrying 22 persons, limps through stormy skies en route from Honolulu to San Francisco. Shortly after the takeoff, suspense sets in when the audience is tipped there's trouble, maybe death, aboard. Gradually the crew and then the passengers become aware of danger.

Virtually every member of the large cast delivers a discerning performance but the lineup is too long to give each the individual credit rated. Especially good are John Wayne, the older co-pilot under the younger pilot captain, Robert Stack, Wally Brown and William Campbell, crew members, and Doe Avedon, very fine as the stewardess.

The technical departments deliver outstandingly. The same can't be said for the score composed and conducted by Dimitri Tiomkin.

□ 1954: Best Score of a Dramatic Picture.
□ Nominations: Best Director, Supp. Actress
(Jan Sterling, Claire Trevor), Editing, Song
('The High and the Mighty')

■ HIGH ANXIETY

1977, 94 MINS, US ◇ ⓥ ⊙
Dir Mel Brooks   *Prod* Mel Brooks   *Scr* Mel Brooks, Ron
Clark, Rudy DeLuca, Barry Levinson   *Ph* Paul Lohmann
Ed John C. Howard   *Mus* John Morris   *Art Dir* Peter
Wooley
● Mel Brooks, Madeline Kahn, Cloris Leachman, Harvey
Korman, Ron Carey, Howard Morris (Crossbow/20th
Century-Fox)

High Anxiety is a straight Hitchcockian sendup – homage applies as well – with highs and lows ranging from a brilliant restaging of the shower scene in *Psycho* to childish bathroom humor.

Besides playing the role of a Harvard professor and psychiatrist with a fear of heights who takes over the Psycho-Neurotic Institute for the Very, Very Nervous, Mel Brooks dons the producer, director and cowriter caps.

Even more than the games he can play with the Hitchcock story, Brooks seems to enjoy toying with the technical references – the tight closeups, shots of hands and feet, stairway sequences and manipulation of the interaction between music and visuals. Nearly all of these gags, and none of them require the background of a buff, score.

■ HIGH BRIGHT SUN, THE

(US: McGuire, Go Home; aka: A Date with Death)

1965, 114 MINS, UK ◇ ⓥ
Dir Ralph Thomas   *Prod* Betty E. Box, Ralph Thomas
Scr Ian Stuart Black   *Ph* Ernest Steward   *Ed* Alfred
Roome   *Mus* Angelo Lavagnino
● Dirk Bogarde, George Chakiris, Susan Strasberg,
Denholm Elliott, Gregoire Aslan, Colin Campbell (Rank)

Betty E. Box and Ralph Thomas elected to make this film because they regarded it 'as a suspenseful drama which could be played against any background'. They certainly played safe. Though set in Cyprus during the 1957 troubles, this sits firmly on a fence and makes virtually no attempt to analyze the troubles, the causes or the attitudes of the cardboard characters.

Film comes out with the British looking at times rather silly and at others very dogged, the Cypriots clearly detesting the British occupation, the Turks shadowy almost to a point of non-existence and America, represented by Susan Strasberg, merely a bewildered intruder.

Strasberg, a dewy-eyed young American archeology student of Cypriot parentage, is visiting Cypriot friends who, unbeknown to her, are mixed up in the local terrorist racket. She gets to know more than is good for her and is torn between loyalty to the Cypriots and to the British, as represented by an intelligence major (Dirk Bogarde) whose job it is to keep alive the unhelpful young dame for whom he has fallen.

Strasberg brings intelligence and charm to a sketchy role while Bogarde has no trouble with a part as the major which scarcely strains his thesping ability.

■ HIGH HOPES

1988, 112 MINS, UK ◇ ⓥ
Dir Mike Leigh   *Prod* Victor Glynn, Simon Channing-
Williams   *Scr* Mike Leigh   *Ph* Roger Pratt   *Ed* John
Gregory   *Mus* Andrew Dixon   *Art Dir* Diana Charnley
● Philip Davis, Ruth Sheen, Edna Dore, Philip Jackson,
Heather Tobias, Lesley Manville (Portman/Film
Four/British Screen)

In the working-class London district of King's Cross, yuppies are moving into old houses, restoring them, and driving out the locals who've lived there for ages. Old Mrs Bender, a widow, lives in one house; her neighbors are the fearfully uppercrust Booth-Braines and they treat the old lady with ill-disguised contempt.

Mrs Bender's two children are an ill-assorted pair. Cyril, with long hair and beard, works as a courier, lives with his down-to-earth girlfriend Shirley, and despises the British establishment.

Daughter Valerie, on the other hand, is a would-be yuppie, married to a crass used-car dealer, and living in a garishly over-decorated home. She's completely self-centered and insensitive to her elderly mother's needs.

Around these characters, Leigh builds a slight story intended to be a microcosm of today's London.

■ HIGHLANDER

1986, 111 MINS, US ◇ ⓥ ⊙
Dir Russell Mulcahy   *Prod* Peter S. Davis, William N.
Panzer   *Scr* Gregory Widen, Peter Bellwood, Larry

Ferguson *Ph* Gerry Fisher *Ed* Peter Honess *Mus* Michael Kamen *Art Dir* Allan Cameron
● Christophe Lambert, Roxanne Hart, Clancy Brown, Sean Connery, Beatie Edney (20th Century-Fox)

Film starts out with a fantastic sword-fighting scene in the garage of Madison Square Garden and then jumps to a medieval battle between the clans set in 16th-century Scotland.

Adding to the confusion in time, director Russell Mulcahy can't seem to decide from one scene to the next whether he's making a sci-fi, thriller, horror, music video or romance – end result is a mishmash.

A visit by Sean Connery, playing a campy Obe Wan Kenobi-type character named Ramirez, teaches Connor MacLeod (Christophe Lambert) how to wield a sword like a warrior and understand his fate is to be immortal man who cannot have children, facing instead a life fending off other immortals like the evil Kurgan.

Lambert looks and acts a lot better in a tartan than as a nearly non-verbal antiques dealer. Clancy Brown never seems to frighten whether as the supposedly-terrifying Kurgan or as the shaven-headed punker.

■ HIGHLANDER II THE QUICKENING

1991, 96 MINS, US ◇ ⓥ ⊙
Dir Russell Mulcahy *Prod* Peter S. Davis, William Panzer *Scr* Peter Bellwood *Ph* Phil Meheux *Ed* Herbert C. de la Boullerie *Mus* Stewart Copeland *Art Dir* Roger Hall
● Christopher Lambert, Sean Connery, Virginia Madsen, Michael Ironside, John C. McGinley, Allan Rich (Davis-Panzer/El Khoury-Defait/Lam Bear)

Audiences unfamiliar with the first film will be hard put to follow the action [from a story by Brian Clemens] as it incoherently hops about in time and space.

Original topliners Christopher Lambert and Sean Connery are back (as is Aussie director Russell Mulcahy). Lambert plays immortal Connor MacLeod, who, despite his Scottish ancestry, hails from the planet Zeist. He and partner Ramirez (Connery) were banished to Earth for participating in a failed rebellion.

One storyline involves assassins led by Michael Ironside, and the other concentrates on the disappearing ozone layer. Connor joins with scientists to devise a sun shield projected into space. The shield is controlled by a large, untrustworthy (natch) corporation, which keeps the later renewal of the ozone layer a secret.

Lambert manages to decapitate the villains arrayed against him while teaming up with attractive environmental terrorist Virginia Madsen. Connery, sporting long white hair in a ponytail, occasionally appears wielding a broadsword.

Highlander II comes alive during the action scenes, including an unexplained but nail-biting segment in which deranged Ironside takes over a subway train and drives it at 400 mph, sending its terrified passengers crashing through windows.

Pic was lensed in Argentina on an apparently generous budget.

■ HIGH NOON

1952, 84 MINS, US ⓥ ⊙
Dir Fred Zinnemann *Prod* Stanley Kramer *Scr* Carl Foreman *Ph* Floyd Crosby *Ed* Harry Gerstad, Elmo Williams *Mus* Dimitri Tiomkin *Art Dir* Rudolph Sternad
● Gary Cooper, Grace Kelly, Thomas Mitchell, Lloyd Bridges, Katy Jurado, Otto Kruger (Kramer/United Artists)

A basic western formula has been combined with good characterization in *High Noon*, making it more of a western drama than the usual outdoor action feature.

The production does an excellent job of pre-senting a picture of a small western town and its people as they wait for a gun duel between the marshal and revenge-seeking killer, an event scheduled for high noon. The mood of the citizens, of Gary Cooper the marshal, and his bride (Grace Kelly), a Quaker who is against all violence, is aptly captured by Fred Zinnemann's direction and the graphic lensing of Floyd Crosby, which perfectly pictures the heat and dust of the sun-baked locale.

Script is based on John W. Cunningham's mag story, *The Tin Star*, and is rather derisive in what it has to say about citizens who are willing to accept law and order if they do not have to put personal effort into obtaining it.

Cooper does an unusually able job of portraying the marshal, ready to retire with his bride and then, for his own self-respect, called upon to perform one last chore as a lawman even though it is the duty of the town's citizens. Kelly fits the mental picture of a Quaker girl nicely, but the femme assignment that has color and s.a. is carried by Katy Jurado, as an ex-girl friend of the marshal.

Throughout the film is a hauntingly-presented ballad that tells the story of the coming gun duel, and is tellingly sung by Tex Ritter.

☐ 1952: Best Actor (Gary Cooper), Song ('High Noon'), Scoring of a Dramatic Picture, Editing.
☐ Nominations: Best Picture, Director, Screenplay

■ HIGH PLAINS DRIFTER

1973, 105 MINS, US ◇ ⓥ ⊙
Dir Clint Eastwood *Prod* Robert Daley *Scr* Ernest Tidyman *Ph* Bruce Surtees *Ed* Ferris Webster *Mus* Dee Barton *Art Dir* Henry Bumstead
● Clint Eastwood, Verna Bloom, Mariana Hill, Mitchell Ryan, Jack Ging, Stefan Gierasch (Malpaso/Universal)

High Plains Drifter is a nervously-humorous, self-conscious near satire on the prototype Clint Eastwood formula of the avenging mysterious stranger. Script has some raw violence for the kinks and some dumb humor for audience relief. Eastwood's second directorial effort is mechanically stylish.

Untidy patchwork script involves one of those towns with a collective guilt streak, having engineered the death-by-whipping of its honest marshal by some hoods who themselves were framed after getting out of hand. Into this setting rides Eastwood, emerging from heat waves (among other obvious evocations of films past) as a sort of archangel of retribution.

After establishing himself as a force to be reckoned with Eastwood is engaged by the town fathers to help them defend against the former local police who are being released from jail after their frame-up.

■ HIGH PRESSURE

1932, 72 MINS, US
Dir Mervyn LeRoy *Scr* Joseph Jackson *Ph* Robert Kurrle *Ed* Ralph Dawson *Mus* Leo Forbstein (dir.)
● William Powell, Evelyn Brent, George Sidney, Guy Kibbee, Evalyn Knapp, John Wray (Warner)

The phoney stock or 'wall paper' grift gets a pretty expert expose in this yarn [by S. J. Peters]. William Powell does a swell job as Gar Evans, a fast-talking and thinking promoter. He keeps his larceny just within the law, but it's when the racket is nearest the edge that the story becomes most interesting.

Powell is first found in a speak's backroom on the tail end of a five-day bender. He told his girl friend he was going out to the drug store for a dose of bicarbonate. The girl friend is interpreted by Evelyn Brent, who is called on to do little else than get mad at and make up with her racketeer sweetheart.

George Sidney teams with Powell in grab-bing the picture most of the way, Sidney for laughs and Powell for the action. Rest of the cast very good, with still more excellent casting of salesmen types in the 'boiler-room' sequence. Whoever framed this scene must have had experience, for it's perfect.

■ HIGH ROAD TO CHINA

1983, 120 MINS, US ◇ ⓥ ⊙
Dir Brian G. Hutton *Prod* Fred Weintraub *Scr* Sandra Weintraub Roland, S. Lee Pogostin *Ph* Ronnie Taylor *Ed* John Jympson *Mus* John Barry *Art Dir* Robert Laing
● Tom Selleck, Bess Armstrong, Jack Weston, Wilford Brimley, Robert Morley, Brian Blessed (Golden Harvest/Warner)

High Road to China is a lot of old-fashioned fun, revived for Tom Selleck after his TV schedule kept him from taking the Harrison Ford role in *Raiders of the Lost Ark*. Ford clearly got the better deal because *China* just isn't as tense and exciting.

But it has the same Saturday-matinee spirit, with director Brian G. Hutton nicely mixing a lot of action with a storyline [from a book by Jon Cleary] that never seems as absurd as it is, allowing the two hours to move by very quickly.

Selleck is perfect as a grizzled, boozing biplane pilot whom 1920s flapper Bess Armstrong is forced to hire to help her find her father before he's declared dead and her inheritance is stolen. Selleck and Armstrong make a cute couple, even though their bantering, slowly developing romance is deliberately predictable throughout.

■ HIGH SEASON

1987, 92 MINS, US ◇ ⓥ ⊙
Dir Clare Peploe *Prod* Clare Downs *Scr* Mark Peploe, Clare Peploe *Ph* Chris Menges *Ed* Gabriella Cristianti *Mus* Jason Osborn *Art Dir* Andrew McAlpine
● Jacqueline Bisset, James Fox, Irene Papas, Sebastian Shaw, Kenneth Branagh, Robert Stephens (Hemdale)

Someone should have told helmer Clare Peploe that shots of beautiful scenery do not a boffo film make, and since she co-wrote the screenplay (with Mark Peploe), she has to shoulder some of the blame for a weak and generally unfunny script.

High Season has a weaving plot with lead characters meandering in and out, but it pivots around Jacqueline Bisset as a photographer and the folk she meets up with in a tiny village in Rhodes. As well as poking fun at the tourists, also thrown in are subplots about a valuable Grecian urn, an elderly Russian spy – an art-historian friend of Bisset, with overtones of Anthony Blunt – and a rebellious Greek national.

Best of the cast are Kenneth Branagh and Lesley Manville as a seemingly archetypal English tourist couple. Irene Papas seems to enjoy herself overacting madly, while James Fox, as Bisset's estranged hubby, looks unsure about what sort of film he is appearing in.

■ HIGH SIERRA

1941, 100 MINS, US ⓥ ⊙
Dir Raoul Walsh *Prod* Hal B. Wallis (exec.), Mark Hellinger (assoc.) *Scr* John Huston, W.R. Burnett *Ph* Tony Gaudio *Ed* Jack Killifer *Mus* Adolph Deutsch *Art Dir* Ted Smith
● Humphrey Bogart, Ida Lupino, Arthur Kennedy, Joan Leslie, Alan Curtis, Henry Hull (Warner)

High Sierra is something of a throwback to the gangster pictures of the prohibition era; purely and simply an action story that's partially salvaged by the fine performances of Humphrey Bogart and Ida Lupino. They actually carry a film that is weighted down by too much extraneous story and production matter.

H

Throwback nature of the yarn is evident in the semi-glorification of Bogart's gangster character. Story depicts him as a country boy who went wrong with John Dillinger's mob, but still retaining a soft spot for green fields and trees, a crippled girl and a stray dog.

The screenplay [from a novel by W.R. Burnett] brings in too many side issues that clutter up the picture. There's no logical reason why the migrant family of Henry Travers and Elizabeth Risdon, with granddaughter Joan Leslie, was included, except as an effort to pad out the yarn in showing Bogart to be a nice guy at heart.

If anything, the film now suffers from slowness, Raoul Walsh's direction evidently being unable to overcome the screenplay plotting.

■ HIGH SOCIETY

1956, 107 MINS, US ◇ ⓥ ⊙
Dir Charles Walters   *Prod* Sol C. Siegel   *Scr* John Patrick   *Ph* Paul C. Vogel   *Ed* Ralph E. Winters   *Mus* Cole Porter   *Art Dir* Cedric Gibbons, Hans Peters
● Bing Crosby, Grace Kelly, Frank Sinatra, Celeste Holm, John Lund, Louis Armstrong (M-G-M)

Fortified with a strong Cole Porter score, film is a pleasant romp for cast toppers Bing Crosby, Grace Kelly and Frank Sinatra. Their impact is almost equally consistent. Although Sinatra has the top pop tune opportunities, the Groaner makes his specialties stand up and out on showmanship and delivery, and Kelly impresses as a femme lead.

The original Philip Barry play, *The Philadelphia Story*, holds up in its transmutation from the Main Line to a Newport jazz bash. Casting of Louis Armstrong for the jazz festivities was an inspired booking also.

The unfolding of the triangle almost assumes quadrangle proportions, when Sinatra (as the *Life*-mag-type feature writer), sent with Celeste Holm, almost moves in as a romantic vis-a-vis to the slightly spoiled and madcap Tracy Lord (Kelly).

Crosby is her first, now ex-husband, a hip character with song-smithing predilections, hence the Armstrong band booking on the local scene. Satchmo is utilized as a sort of pleasant play moderator, opening with 'High Society Calypso', which sets the al fresco mood of the picture.

Porter has whipped up a solid set of songs with which vocal pros like the male stars and Holm do plenty. Latter and Sinatra have a neat offbeat number with 'Who Wants to Be a Millionaire?' Crosby makes 'Now You Has Jazz' (aided by Armstrong) as his standout solo, although he is also effective with Kelly on 'True Love'. Crosby and Sinatra milk 'Well, Did You Evah?' in a sophisticated smoking room sequence.
☐ 1956: Nominations: Best Motion Picture Story [withdrawn from final ballot], Scoring of a Musical Picture, Song ('True Love')

■ HIGH SPIRITS

1988, 97 MINS, UK/US ◇ ⓥ ⊙
Dir Neil Jordan   *Prod* Stephen Woolley, David Saunders   *Scr* Neil Jordan   *Ph* Alex Thomson   *Ed* Michael Bradsell   *Mus* George Fenton   *Art Dir* Anton Furst
● Daryl Hannah, Peter O'Toole, Steve Guttenberg, Beverly D'Angelo, Liam Neeson, Ray McAnally (Vision/Palace)

High Spirits is a piece of supernatural Irish whimsy with a few appealing dark underpinnings, but it still rises and falls constantly on the basis of its moment-to-moment inspirations.

Elaborate physical production is set almost entirely at Castle Plunkett, a rundown Irish edifice that proprietor Peter O'Toole opens as a tourist hotel in order to meet the mortgage payments. With the American market in mind, O'Toole bills the place as a haunted

castle, to this end having his staff dress up like ghouls of various persuasions.

It comes as little surprise that the castle turns out to be actually haunted. Steve Guttenberg, who is not getting along with wife Beverly D'Angelo, comes to meet ghost Daryl Hannah, who was killed on the premises years ago on her wedding night by Liam Neeson, who takes a fancy to D'Angelo.

■ HIGH TIDE

1987, 104 MINS, AUSTRALIA ◇ ⓥ ⊙
Dir Gillian Armstrong   *Prod* Sandra Levy   *Scr* Laura Jones   *Ph* Russell Boyd   *Ed* Nicholas Beauman   *Mus* Mark Moffatt, Ricky Fataar   *Art Dir* Sally Campbell
● Judy Davis, Jan Adele, Claudia Karvan, Colin Friels, Frankie J. Holden, Monica Trapaga (FGH/SJL)

A powerful emotional, beautifully made film which will touch the hearts of all but the very cynical.

Setting is the small New South Wales coastal town of Eden where Judy Davis rents a cheap trailer by the sea while she awaits completion of the auto repairs. One night, when hopelessly drunk in the toilet block, she's helped by an adolescent girl (Claudia Karvan) who lives with her grandmother (Jan Adele) in another trailer.

Davis befriends the child; only when she meets the grandmother does she realize Karvan is her own daughter who she'd left years before in the aftermath of her husband's death.

Adele makes the grandmother, who still enjoys a sexual fling even though she has a regular lover, a wonderfully warm character. Karvan sharply etches the pain and insecurity hiding beneath the tough, tomboyish exterior of the child; and Judy Davis, always a consummate actress, provides great depth and subtlety, making her character come vividly alive.

■ HIGH WALL

1947, 98 MINS, US
Dir Curtis Bernhardt   *Prod* Robert Lord   *Scr* Sydney Boehm, Lester Cole   *Ph* Paul Vogel   *Ed* Conrad A. Nervig   *Mus* Bronislau Kaper   *Art Dir* Cedric Gibbons, Leonid Vasian
● Robert Taylor, Audrey Totter, Herbert Marshall , H.B. Warner, Warner Anderson (M-G-M)

High Wall [based on a play by Alan R. Clark and Bradbury Foote] garners a high score as a strong entry in the psycho-melodrama cycle. Unfolded credibly and with almost clinical attention for detail, film holds the interest and punches all the way.

Robert Lord has given the melodramatics fine production polish and able handling to spotlight best features in story of a man who believes he has murdered his wife during a mental blackout.

Robert Taylor is seen as a man believed homicidally insane, being treated at mental hospital pending trial for murder of his wife. His case seems hopeless until a femme doctor breaks down his reluctance to try treatment to penetrate details that occurred during the lapse of memory.

Taylor scores in his role, making it believable. Audrey Totter registers strongly as the doctor, displaying a marked degree of talent able to handle most any character. Herbert Marshall is another who clicks as the murderer who cloaks his sin behind the garb of a pious publisher of biblical tracts. H. B. Warner movingly creates a pathetic mental case.

■ HIGH, WIDE AND HANDSOME

1937, 110 MINS, US
Dir Rouben Mamoulian   *Prod* Arthur Hornblow Jr
Scr Oscar Hammerstein II   *Ph* Victor Milner, Theodore

Sparkuhl   *Ed* Archie Marshek   *Mus* Boris Morros (dir.)
Art Dir Hans Dreier, John Goodman
● Irene Dunne, Randolph Scott, Dorothy Lamour, Elizabeth Patterson, Raymond Walburn, Charles Bickford (Paramount)

Film shapes up as a $1.9 million western, although possessed of all the elements to have made it a saga of Pennsylvania oilwell pioneering. Something went wrong on scripting and production from what was, undoubtedly, an intriguing script on paper.

Film's title sounds like a musical or operetta, but it's more of a melodramatic romance, with six songs by Jerome Kern and Oscar Hammerstein II, latter also credited for the original story and the screenplay. Wherein lies the film's principal deficiency. It's a cross-section of Americana tinged with too much Hollywood hokum.

As a result, *High, Wide*, after teeing off vigorously, flounders as it progresses, and winds up in a melodramatic shambles of fisticuffs, villainy and skullduggery which smacks of the serial film school.

Irene Dunne is too coy as the daughter of a medicine-show owner and Randolph Scott too forthright as her romantic vis-a-vis. And the menacing by Charles Bickford, at the helm of his hired plug-uglies, with Alan Hale as the villainous banker, is very ten-twent-thirt. Dorothy Lamour is rather heavy eye-laden for the nitery gal who ultimately repays the Scott-Dunne combo for previous kindnesses.

Rouben Mamoulian's production is heavyhanded. While endowed with an elastic budget, save for the fighting scenes there's little that's spectacular or impressive about the result. The mob scenes are as much to the credit of the camera as to the direction.

■ HIGH WIND IN JAMAICA, A

1965, 104 MINS, UK ◇ ⓥ
Dir Alexander Mackendrick   *Prod* John Croydon   *Scr* Ronald Harwood, Dennis Cannan, Stanley Mann   *Ph* Douglas Slocombe   *Ed* Derek York   *Mus* Larry Adler   *Art Dir* John Howell, John Hoesli
● Anthony Quinn, James Coburn, Dennis Price, Gert Frobe, Lila Kedrova, Nigel Davenport (20th Century-Fox)

Anthony Quinn's penchant for grizzled characterization gets a colorful boost in this picturization of Richard Hughes' 1929 bestseller, which projects him as a Caribbean pirate. British production is a curious mixture of high melodrama and light overtones, the latter occasioned by presence of a flock of youngsters aboard a pirate ship.

Most of the action takes place at sea. Filmed on location around Jamaica, Alexander Mackendrick's direction keeps his movement alive within the somewhat limited confines of a schooner where Quinn, the Spanish pirate captain, is confronted with the disturbing question of what to do with seven children who unbeknownst to him have slipped from another ship he attacked and now are found in the hold of his own craft.

Quinn endows his role with a subdued humanness in which there is occasional humor. James Coburn, costarred with Quinn as his English mate, socks over character in which he combines humor with dramatic strength.

■ HILL, THE

1965, 125 MINS, UK ⓥ ⊙
Dir Sidney Lumet   *Prod* Kenneth Hyman   *Scr* Ray Rigby   *Ph* Oswald Morris   *Ed* Thelma Connell   *Mus* [none]   *Art Dir* Herbert Smith
● Sean Connery, Harry Andrews, Ian Bannen, Alfred Lynch, Ossie Davis, Michael Redgrave (M-G-M/Seven Arts)

Kenneth Hyman's production of *The Hill* is a tough, uncompromising look at the inside of a British military prison in the Middle East during the last war. It is a harsh, sadistic and brutal entertainment, superbly acted and made without any concessions to officialdom.

The 'hill' of the title is a man-made pile of sand up and down which the soldier-prisoners have to run with full kit, often until they are physically exhausted, as part of a punishment designed more to break a man's spirit rather than provide corrective treatment.

The screenplay [from a play by Ray Rigby and R.S. Allen] puts the spotlight on a new bunch of prisoners, one of whom (Sean Connery) is a 'busted' sergeant-major, and a natural target for the vindictive and sadistic treatment. Another is a Negro sent down for drinking three bottles of Scotch from the officers' mess.

One of the new intake collapses and dies, and that sparks off a mutiny, which is one of the most powerful and dramatic sequences of the pic.

Connery gives an intelligently restrained study, carefully avoiding forced histrionics. The juiciest role, however, is that of the prison regimental sergeant major, and Harry Andrews does a standout job.

● ●

■ HILL IN KOREA, A

(US: Hell in Korea)

1956, 81 MINS, UK

Dir Julian Amyes   *Prod* Ian Dalrymple   *Scr* Ian Dalrymple   *Ph* Freddie Francis   *Ed* Peter Hunt
Mus Malcolm Arnold
● George Baker, Harry Andrews, Stanley Baker, Michael Medwin, Ronald Lewis, Stephen Boyd (Wessex/British Lion)

Story is based on a book [by Max Catto] but records actual events.

It is little more than an incident, depicting the adventures of a small patrol sent to find out if a village is inhabited by the enemy.

There are no base camp sets, nor home scenes before the inducted boys join the army. All the action, humor and pathos centres on the mixed bunch from every walk of life, wisecracking, beefing and just plain scared, comprising one rookie officer, three regular soldiers, including one sergeant. The remainder are untried civilians.

With the subdued lighting used throughout most of the shots, owing to night marches, and the indistinguishable drab jungle outfit, anonymity swamps most of the characters. Only the closeups of their sweaty faces, and calling each other's names brings individuality to the actors.

All the cast has equal opportunities to score, George Baker as the conscientious officer, Harry Andrews as the tough sergeant and Ronald Lewis as the outsider, disliked by his buddies.

● ●

■ HILLS HAVE EYES, THE

1978, 89 MINS, US ◇ ⓥ ⊙

Dir Wes Craven   *Prod* Peter Locke   *Scr* Wes Craven
Ph Eric Sadrinen   *Ed* Wes Craven   *Mus* Don Peake
Art Dir Robert Burns
● Susan Lanier, Robert Houston, Virginia Vincent, Russ Grieve, Dee Wallace, Martin Speer (Blood Relations)

Wes Craven's blood-and-bone frightener about an all-American family at the mercy of cannibal mutants is a satisfying piece of pulp.

Reputedly based on genuine 17th-century Scottish cave-dwellers, these savages terrorize a strip of Californian desert in which the Carters are stranded by a snapped axle. Hollywood Movie-dog tradition is put to use in the forms of Beauty and the Beast, Carters' protective pets, which play their part in final outwitting of the marauders.

But there's plenty of death before then, survivors of the symbolic struggle being the teenagers on both sides, one dog and a baby, on whose future (in the world or in the pot) much of the rival hysterias have centered.

Gratifying aspects are Craven's businesslike plotting and pacy cutting, and a script which takes more trouble over the stock characters than it needs. There are plenty of laughs, in the dialog and in the story's disarming twists.

● ●

■ HILLS HAVE EYES PART II, THE

1985, 88 MINS, US/UK ◇ ⓥ ⊙

Dir Wes Craven   *Prod* Barry Cahn, Peter Locke
Scr Wes Craven   *Ph* David Lewis   *Ed* Richard Bracken
Mus Harry Manfredini
● Michael Berryman, Tamara Stafford, Kevin Blair, John Bloom, Janus Blythe (Castle Hill/Fancey/New Realm/VTC)

The Hills Have Eyes Part II is a lower case followup by Wes Craven to his 1977 cult horror pic.

Film concerns two grownup survivors of the earlier pic. Young Bobby Carter (Robert Houston) is plagued by nightmares of the desert massacre that he survived. He has invented a super formula of gasoline which his local moto-cross club is testing in an upcoming race. Ruby (Janus Blythe), a nice-gal survivor, is taking the bikers to the race, when they foolishly try a shortcut across the desert.

From then on, it's dull, formula terror pic cliches, with one attractive teenager after another picked off by the surviving cannibals.

Acting is on the level of a formula shocker, featuring a winsome Candice Bergen-lookalike, Tamara Stafford, as a blind girl.

● ●

■ HINDENBURG, THE

1975, 125 MINS, US ◇ ⓥ ⊙

Dir Robert Wise   *Prod* Robert Wise   *Scr* Nelson Gidding   *Ph* Robert Surtees   *Ed* Donn Cambern
Mus David Shire   *Art Dir* Edward Carfagno
● George C. Scott, Anne Bancroft, William Atherton, Roy Thinnes, Gig Young, Burgess Meredith (Universal/Filmakers)

Michael M. Mooney's non-fiction compendium of the facts and theories behind the German zeppelin's 1937 air disaster at NAS, Lakehurst, new Jersey, was earlier dramatized for the screen by Richard A. Levinson and William Link, and both receive a screen story credit.

George C. Scott stars as an air ace assigned as special security officer on the fatal Atlantic crossing.

The array of characters is dealt boringly from a well-thumbed deck: Anne Bancroft, eccentric German countess; Roy Thinnes, Scott's nasty partner; Gig Young, mysterious and nervous ad agency exec; Burgess Meredith and Rene Auberjonois, an improbable and dull effort at comedy relief as tourist-trapping card cheats; Robert Clary, also bombing in cardboard comedy relief, the list goes on. William Atherton emerges as the good-guy crewman saboteur who plans to blow up the ship. A battle of mental wits ensues between Scott, Thinnes and Atherton; it's as exciting as watching butter melt.
☐ 1975: Honorary Award (visual and sound effects).
☐ Nominations: Best Cinematography, Art Direction, Sound

● ●

■ HIRED HAND, THE

1971, 90 MINS, US ◇ ⓥ

Dir Peter Fonda   *Prod* William Hayward   *Scr* Alan Sharp   *Ph* Vilmos Zsigmond   *Ed* Frank Mazzola
Mus Bruce Langhorne   *Art Dir* Lawrence G. Paull
● Peter Fonda, Warren Oates, Verna Bloom, Robert Pratt, Severn Darden, Ann Doran (Pando)

The Hired Hand doesn't work very well. An offbeat western, starring and directed by Peter Fonda, the film has a disjointed story, a largely unsympathetic hero, and an obtrusive amount of cinematic gimmickry which ren-

ders inarticulate the confused story subtleties. Warren Oates appears as Fonda's loyal and more mature friend, while Verna Bloom is Fonda's abandoned wife.

The script discovers Fonda en route to California with Oates, a fellow-wanderer in the seven years since Fonda abandoned his wife. Robert Pratt, pair's younger companion, is brutally murdered by Severn Darden's henchmen in a frame-up; Fonda and Oates exact an appropriate revenge, then Fonda returns home with Oates.

Film evidently is trying to show a truer picture of early western life, as opposed to formula plotting; but when one is trying to buck an entrenched cliche, extreme care and artfulness are required to persuade those few not already convinced.

● ●

■ HIRELING, THE

1973, 95 MINS, UK ◇ ⓥ

Dir Alan Bridges   *Prod* Ben Arbeid   *Scr* Wolf Mankowitz   *Ph* Michael Reed   *Ed* Peter Weatherley
Mus Marc Wilkinson   *Art Dir* Natasha Kroll
● Robert Shaw, Sarah Miles, Peter Egan, Elizabeth Sellars, Caroline Mortimer, Patricia Lawrence (World)

Based on a novel by L.P. Hartley set in 1923, this heavily atmospheric, painstakingly accoutred and splendidly acted pic deals with the increasingly close relationship, on a conversational-companionship level at first, of a young widow (Sarah Miles) and the hired chauffeur (Robert Shaw) who drives her home after a spell in a clinic recovering from a nervous depression.

Temporarily, class barriers are down – or so he begins to believe. Shortly, however, as she recovers her equilibrium and social contacts, the barriers and demarcations return.

Item has quality written all over it, and patient viewers will savor its many plusses. Miles is splendid as the confused lady, Shaw fine as her momentarily blinded opposite.

● ●

■ HIS GIRL FRIDAY

1940, 92 MINS, US ⓥ

Dir Howard Hawks   *Prod* Howard Hawks   *Scr* Charles Lederer   *Ph* Joseph Walker   *Ed* Gene Havlick
Art Dir Lionel Banks
● Cary Grant, Rosalind Russell, Ralph Bellamy, Gene Lockhart, Helen Mack, John Qualen (Columbia)

No doubt aiming to dodge the stigma of having *His Girl Friday* termed a remake, Columbia blithely skips a pertinent point in the credits by merely stating 'From a play by Ben Hecht and Charles MacArthur.' It's inescapable, however, that this is the former legit and pic smash *The Front Page*. The trappings are different – even to the extent of making reporter Hildy Johnson a femme – but it is still *Front Page*.

Casting is excellent, with Cary Grant and Rosalind Russell in the top roles. Grant is the sophisticated, hard-boiled, smart-alec managing editor who was portrayed by Adolphe Menjou in the earlier version. A newly-injected part, required by the switch in sex of Hildy, is taken by Ralph Bellamy.

Principal action of the story still takes place in a courthouse pressroom. All of the trappings are there, including the crew of newshawks who continue their penny-ante poker through everything and the practice of the sheriff's crew on the gallows for an execution in the morning. With the wider vista given with the story, there is, in addition, the newspaper office.

Star-reporter Russell tells managing editor Grant, from whom she has just been divorced, that she is quitting his employ to marry another man. Grant neither wants to see her resign nor marry again, retaining hope of a rehitching. To prevent her escaping, he prevails upon her to cover one more story, that of a deluded radical charged with murder and whom the paper thinks is innocent. Escape of the convicted man, his virtual falling into Russell's lap as she sits alone in the press-room, and attempts by Grant and Russell to bottle up the story, are w.k., but still exciting.

■ **HIS MAJESTY O'KEEFE**

1953, 89 MINS, US ◇ ⑦
Dir Byron Haskin   *Prod* [Harold Hecht]   *Scr* Borden Chase, James Hill   *Ph* Otto Heller   *Ed* Manuel Del Campo   *Mus* Robert Farnon   *Art Dir* Ted Haworth, W. Simpson Robinson
● Burt Lancaster, Joan Rice, Andre Morell, Abraham Sofaer, Archie Savage, Benson Fong (Warner)

This swashbuckling South Seas adventure feature is ideally suited to Burt Lancaster's muscular heroics. The Fiji Islands location lensing is a plus factor for interest.

The island of Viti Levu in the South Pacific is the locale used. Lancaster is seen as a dare-devil Yankee sea captain, cast overboard off the island by a mutinous crew. Intrigued by the possibilities of making a fortune off the island's copra, he stays on to battle other traders, native idleness and superstition, becoming His Majesty O'Keefe with a beautiful Polynesian (Joan Rice) as queen.

The action emphasis of the screenplay, suggested by a novel by Lawrence Kingman and Gerald Green, provides Byron Haskin's direction innumerable opportunities for movement, so the film's pace is quick-tempoed. Rice is a sweet romantic foil for Lancaster's swashbuckling. Tessa Prendergast, as another island beauty, teases the eyes.

■ **HISTORY OF MR. POLLY, THE**

1949, 94 MINS, UK
Dir Anthony Pelissier   *Prod* John Mills   *Scr* Anthony Pelissier   *Ph* Desmond Dickinson   *Ed* John Seabourne   *Mus* William Alwyn
● John Mills, Sally Ann Howes, Finlay Currie, Betty Ann Davies, Edward Chapman, Megs Jenkins (Two Cities)

Faithful adherence to the original H. G. Wells story is one of the main virtues of *The History of Mr Polly* which is noted for its fine characterizations.

The story of Mr Polly is retold simply from the time of his father's death, his inheritance and marriage, subsequent failure as a shop-keeper and final happiness and freedom as a general handyman in a small country inn. Its success is a personal tribute to the sterling acting of John Mills.

Director Anthony Pelissier has put all the emphasis on the principal characters, and has extracted every ounce of human interest from the classic. Every part, right down to the smallest bit, has been selected with care and there is some notable work from an experienced cast.

■ **HISTORY OF THE WORLD – PART I**

1981, 92 MINS, US ◇ ⑦ ⊙
Dir Mel Brooks   *Prod* Mel Brooks   *Scr* Mel Brooks   *Ph* Woody Omens, Paul Wilson   *Ed* John Howard   *Mus* John Morris   *Art Dir* Harold Michelson, Stuart Craig
● Mel Brooks, Dom DeLuise, Madeline Kahn, Cloris Leachman, Gregory Hines, Sid Caesar (20th Century-Fox)

Boisterous cinematic vaudeville show is comprised of five distinct sections: the *2001* parody *Dawn of Man, The Stone Age,* featuring Brooks' acid comment on the role of the art critic, and a brief 'Old Testament' bit, which together run 10 minutes; *The Roman Empire,* the best-sustained and, at 43 minutes, longest episode; *The Spanish Inquisition,* a splashy nine-minute production number; *The French Revolution,* a rather feeble 24-minute sketch; and *Coming Attractions* which, with end credits, runs six minutes and at least punches up the

finale with the hilarious *Jews in Space* inter-galactic musical action number.

Although Monty Python's *Life of Brian* went well beyond Brooks in the blasphemy department, many of the pic's most successful gags poke holes in religious pieties. When Brooks as Moses comes down from the mountain, he's carrying three tablets. Frightened by a lightning blast, he drops one of them and quickly switches to 10 commandments instead of 15.

The one interlude which really brings down the house has Brooks working as a waiter at the Last Supper and asking the assembled group. 'Are you all together or is it separate checks?'

As the old ad line said, there's something here to offend everybody, particularly the devout of all persuasions and homosexuals.

■ **HIT!**

1973, 134 MINS, US ◇
Dir Sidney J. Furie   *Prod* Harry Korshak   *Scr* Alan R. Trustman, David M. Wolf   *Ph* John A. Alonso   *Ed* Argyle Nelson   *Mus* Lalo Schifrin
● Billy Dee Williams, Richard Pryor, Paul Hampton, Gwen Welles, Warren Kemmerling, Janet Brande (Paramount)

Too bad that so much of the script relies on illogical plotting and heavy-handed irony, because the basic idea is excellent and many of the details are richly conceived.

Billy Dee Williams plays a Federal operative whose daughter dies from drug overdose. Unable to get official action that would lead to capture of the key figures in a Marseilles drug syndicate, he launches his own vendetta against the 'murderers.'

The juxtaposition of grubby US pushers and users against the elegant refinement of the French suppliers is a labored echo of *The French Connection*'s opening. Once the exposition is out of the way, however, *Hit!* really scores with a number of sharp-edged secondary roles, a charismatic dimension to Williams' leading performance, some tautly edited and dramatically photographed action setpieces and some nifty comic business deftly handled by Furie. Production values are topnotch.

■ **HIT, THE**

1984, 97 MINS, UK ◇ ⑦ ⊙
Dir Stephen Frears   *Prod* Jeremy Thomas   *Scr* Peter Prince   *Ph* Mike Molloy   *Ed* Mick Audsley   *Mus* Paco De Lucia, Eric Clapton   *Art Dir* Andrew Sanders
● John Hurt, Tim Roth, Laura Del Sol, Terence Stamp, Bill Hunter, Fernando Rey (Central/Recorded Picture)

This astringent, sardonically funny thriller is only the second theatrical feature for director Stephen Frears since *Gumshoe* (1971). Frears and writer Peter Prince have taken a potentially familiar tale of a gangland betrayal and revenge and made something richly inventive and most entertaining.

Pic opens in London in 1972 as Willie Parker (Terence Stamp) fingers his fellow criminals. Ten years later, Parker is living an apparently carefree existence in the Spanish countryside when four toughs kidnap him and hand him over to an experienced hit man, Braddock (John Hurt) and his novice sidekick, Myron (Tim Roth), to deliver him to the boss in Paris. It's a journey on which things keep going wrong.

Most disconcerting for the hitmen is that Parker is so relaxed and philosophical about his fate. A stopoff at a secret apartment provides a further problem: the apartment is occupied by an Australian criminal, Harry (Bill Hunter) and his young Spanish mistress, Maggie (Laura Del Sol). Maggie is taken along as hostage.

Acting is marvelous. Best of all is Roth as a

cocky little hood, a bit puzzled as to what's going on and wanting to assert himself a little.

■ **HITCHER, THE**

1986, 97 MINS, US ◇ ⑦ ⊙
Dir Robert Harmon   *Prod* David Bombyk, Kip Ohman   *Scr* Eric Red   *Ph* John Seale   *Ed* Frank J. Urioste   *Mus* Mark Isham   *Art Dir* Dennis Gassner
● Rutger Hauer, C. Thomas Howell, Jennifer Jason Leigh, Jeffrey DeMunn (HBO/Silver Screen)

The Hitcher is a highly unimaginative slasher that keeps the tension going with a massacre about every 15 minutes.

Film proves mom's admonition not to pick up hitchhikers, especially if they're anything like John Ryder, a psychotic and diabolical killer played with a serene coldness by Rutger Hauer.

Along comes an innocent young man (C. Thomas Howell), who is falling asleep at the wheel and stops to pick Hauer up in the hopes that having a companion will keep him awake. What ensues for the rest of the film is a cat and mouse game where Hauer eliminates just about everyone Howell comes in contact with.

In addition to working with a script that has many holes, filmmakers didn't allow for one laugh in the entire 97 minutes.

■ **HITLER'S CHILDREN**

1943, 80 MINS, US ⑦
Dir Edward Dmytryk   *Prod* Edward A. Golden   *Scr* Emmett Lavey   *Ph* Russell Metty   *Ed* Joseph Noriega   *Mus* Roy Webb
● Tim Holt, Bonita Granville, Kent Smith, Otto Kruger, H.B. Warner, Lloyd Corrigan (RKO)

The philosophies of Nazism and the manner in which the youth of Germany was moulded to a militaristic order are forcefully brought to the screen in *Hitler's Children* [from the novel *Education for Death* by Gregor Zeimer].

Tim Holt essays the leading role of the German boy who grows up to become a Gestapo officer, but cannot grow away from the childhood love he had for a girl who suffers the tortures of the Nazis.

Holt gives an excellent performance and looks the part he plays. Opposite him, Bonita Granville likewise acquits herself very creditably. An outstanding job is done by H.B. Warner as a bishop, whose church service is broken up by Gestapo agents on the hunt for Granville, who has taken shelter there. The dialog given Warner proves very trenchant.

■ **HITLER**
THE LAST TEN DAYS

1973, 108 MINS, UK/ITALY ◇ ⑦
Dir Ennio De Concini   *Prod* Wolfgang Reinhardt   *Scr* Ennio De Concini, Maria Pia Fusco, Wolfgang Reinhardt, Ivan Moffat   *Ph* Ennio Guarnieri   *Ed* Kevin Connor   *Mus* Mischa Spoliansky   *Art Dir* Roy Walker
● Alec Guinness, Simon Ward, Adolfo Celi, Diane Cilento, Gabriele Ferzetti, Eric Porter (Reinhardt/West)

A major fault of the film is that there's no German feeling to it. The cast, with the exception of German actress Doris Kunstmann as Eva Braun, is made up of British and Italian actors. The film's interiors (and a few exteriors) were shot at Shepperton Studios, England.

What is good about the film is the treatment of Hitler by Alec Guinness, who gives perhaps the best portrayal yet of that bizarre figure. Even he, however, never conveys the fanaticism which Hitler certainly had and which he so powerfully conveyed to millions of susceptible German minds.

As the film [from Gerhard Boldt's *The Last Days of the Chancellery*] revolves almost entirely around him, other cast members have to work hard to make even a momentary impression. The talent most lost in the shuffle is Simon Ward.

Most outstanding, considering her brief appearance, is Diane Cilento as a test pilot who gets across the authentic if misguided obsessive devotion to Der Fuehrer of some Germans.

• •

■ **HITMAN, THE**

1991, 95 MINS, US ◇ ⓥ ⊙
Dir Aaron Norris   *Prod* Don Carmody   *Scr* Robert Geoffrian, Don Carmody   *Ph* Joao Fernandes   *Ed* Jacqueline Carmody   *Mus* Joel Derouin   *Art Dir* Douglas Higgins
● Chuck Norris, Michael Parks, Al Waxman, Alberta Watson, Salim Grant, Ken Pogue (Cannon)

Chuck Norris goes to Canada in this dreary, unconvincing action vehicle. *The Hitman* is short on action and adopts a film noir visual style that masks its limited production values. Feature is a comedown from their big-budget *Delta Force 2*.

Prolog has Norris and Michael Parks as cops on a stakeout, with Parks shooting Norris and leaving him for dead. Three years later Norris is in Seattle undercover as unsuspecting Italo gangster Al Waxman's No. 2 in command. Working for agent Ken Pogue, Norris' assignment is to get the two rival mobs, Waxman's and Marcel Sabourin's French heavies in Vancouver, to unite so that both can be nabbed. Fly in the ointment is a group of Iranian thugs led by Frank Ferrucci.

Norris is okay as a pretend heavy, but a very poor script violates many rules of the genre. Best thing about *Hitman* is some good stuntwork.

• •

■ **HIT PARADE OF 1943**

1943, 90 MINS, US
Dir Albert S. Rogell   *Prod* Albert J. Cohen   *Scr* Frank Gill Jr, Frances Hyland   *Ph* Jack Marta   *Ed* Thomas Richards   *Mus* Jule Styne, Harold Adamson
● John Carroll, Susan Hayward, Gail Patrick, Eve Arden, Dorothy Dandridge (Republic)

Here's a little musical which is 'little' only compared to some of the majors' past gargantuan efforts, but which actually blends a fetching set of songs, a wealth of variety talent, mostly colored, to a fair story.

The cast names aren't breath-taking as some of the others stabled in the major league studios, but from Al Cohen's production and Al Rogell's direction to the dance-staging and songsmithing it's a very satisfying confection indeed.

You may get captious with the idea of making a thieving songwriter your hero, which is what John Carroll personates, but thus is Susan Hayward, talented young tunesmith, thrown together with him. In fact, the characterization of Rick Farrell, who even continues to let Hayward ghost his songs, is never wholly palatable, but Carroll's personal charm glorifies the double-crossing, two-timing lothario of Lindy's into a model swain in time for the fadeout.

□ 1943: Nominations: Best Scoring of a Musical Picture, Song ('Change of Heart')

• •

■ **HIT THE DECK**

1955, 112 MINS, US ◇ ⓥ ⊙
Dir Roy Rowland   *Prod* Joe Pasternak   *Scr* Sonya Levien, William Ludwig   *Ph* George Folsey   *Ed* John McSweeney Jr   *Mus* Vincent Youmans
● Jane Powell, Tony Martin, Debbie Reynolds, Walter Pidgeon, Vic Damone, Ann Miller (M-G-M)

The emphasis of youth, in the person of a number of personable young players on the Metro contract list, has been put on this re-

make of the [1927] legit musical, *Hit the Deck*.

There's not much producer Joe Pasternak could do to refurbish the shopworn plot about three sailors on the loose, with three femmes on their mind, and the sundry complications that batter at the steadfast portals of Navy redtape and credibility. With the limitations, he has made it a pretty picture, replete with songs from the old footlight piece, complete with new lyrics and flashy production numbers.

The vintage musical takes on its best semblance to life when Debbie Reynolds and Russ Tamblyn are lending their enthusiasm, either alone or together, to the action.

• •

■ **HIT THE DUTCHMAN**

1992, 118 MINS, US/RUSSIA ◇ ⓥ
Dir Menahem Golan   *Prod* Menahem Golan   *Scr* Joseph Goldman   *Ph* Nicholas Von Sternberg   *Ed* Bob Ducsay   *Mus* Terry Plumeri   *Art Dir* Clark Hunter
● Bruce Nozick, Eddie Bowz, Will Kempe, Sally Kirkland, Matt Servitto, Christopher Bradley (Power/Start)

Fast-moving, splendidly trashy mobster yarn dishes up the genre goods with grindhouse glee. Pic is the top-rouble half of two back-to-backers lensed in Russia, with similar casts and crews and overlapping plots. Its sibling is *Mad Dog Coll*.

Bruce Nozick toplines as Arthur Fleggenheimer, a cocky 24-year-old Jewish con who's freed from West Hampton pen and straight-away slips off the straight and narrow. After literally biting the nose of Vince Coll (Christopher Bradley), he's introed to Legs Diamond (Will Kempe) by best friend Joey (Eddie Bowz) and soon starts sniffing around Legs' warbler g.f. Frances Ireland (Jennifer Miller). He also adopts the name Dutch Schultz.

Unlike *Coll*, pic isn't constrained by endless interiors and night scenes. Look is considerably bigger budget (though not enough to forge a convincing New York) and the wealth of characters and incidents easily fills up the running time. The large cast plays the dime novel script at full tilt.

• •

■ **H.M. PULHAM, ESQ.**

1941, 119 MINS, US
Dir King Vidor   *Prod* King Vidor   *Scr* King Vidor, Elizabeth Hill   *Ph* Ray June   *Ed* Harold F. Kress   *Mus* Bronislau Kaper
● Hedy Lamarr, Robert Young, Ruth Hussey, Charles Coburn, Van Heflin, Leif Erickson (M-G-M)

What will please the book-readers – and probably the non-readers as well – is the faithfulness with which King Vidor and Elizabeth Hill have transferred the John P. Marquand novel to the screen.

Major defect in the celluloid version is the casting of Hedy Lamarr in principal femme role. It's Lamarr's Viennese accent which is jarring, although her looks and acting otherwise are tops.

Pulham (Robert Young) is of the wool-dyed Boston Backbay, bred in its Brahmanism from the day he was born, when his father registered him for entrance in St Swithin's School 12 years hence. Coming back from the war, he succeeds in breaking away from his family to take a job in a New York agency, where he and fellow-copywriter Lamarr fall in love. She carries a torch for him for some 20 years.

But Lamarr is not of Boston and refuses to take to it or give up her career. Pulham, when his father dies, marries a family-approved gal (Ruth Hussey) and they live the conventional Hub humdrum until Pulham is called upon to write a biog of himself for a Harvard reunion and sits down to reminisce.

• •

■ **H.M.S. DEFIANT**
(US: Damn the Defiant!)

1962, 101 MINS, UK ◇ ⓥ
Dir Lewis Gilbert   *Prod* John Brabourne   *Scr* Nigel Kneale, Edmund H. North   *Ph* Christopher Challis   *Ed* Peter Hunt   *Mus* Clifton Parker   *Art Dir* Arthur Lawson
● Alec Guinness, Dirk Bogarde, Anthony Quayle, Tom Bell, Maurice Denham, Victor Maddern (Columbia)

H.M.S. Defiant is a strong naval drama about the days of the Napoleonic wars, enhanced by the strong appeal of Alec Guinness, Dirk Bogarde and Anthony Quayle.

Based on Frank Tilsley's novel, *Mutiny*, story is of the time of old press gangs. British navy conditions were appalling and it was the mutiny depicted in this pic which did much to give the British naval men a new deal. Guinness plays the skipper of the *Defiant* which, when it sets out to help tackle the Napoleonic fleet, is ruptured by a tussle for power between Guinness and his first lieutenant (Bogarde).

Guinness is a humane man, though a stern disciplinarian. Bogarde is a sadist, anxious to jockey Guinness out of position.

Below deck the crew, led by Quayle and Tom Bell, is plotting mutiny against the bad food, stinking living conditions and constant floggings ordered by Bogarde.

Guinness' role does not give this actor scope for his fullest ability. Bogarde's is the more showy portrayal. Quayle makes an impressive appearance as the leader of the rebels, determined and tough, but realizing that there is a right and a wrong way to stage a mutiny, like anything else.

• •

■ **HOBSON'S CHOICE**

1954, 107 MINS, UK ⓥ ⊙
Dir David Lean   *Prod* David Lean   *Scr* David Lean, Norman Spencer, Wynyard Browne   *Ph* Jack Hildyard   *Ed* Peter Taylor   *Mus* Malcolm Arnold   *Art Dir* Wilfrid Shingleton
● Charles Laughton, John Mills, Brenda de Banzie, Daphne Anderson, Prunella Scales, Richard Wattis (British Lion/London)

There is a wealth of charm, humor and fine characterization in David Lean's picture [of Harold Brighouse's play] made under the Korda banner. The period comedy, with a Lancashire setting, is essentially British in its makeup. Charles Laughton returned to his native country to star.

Laughton plays the widower Hobson, a shoemaker with three unmarried daughters, one of whom is regarded as being permanently on the shelf. After all, as he is always explaining to his cronies in the saloon, she is past it at 30. But the daughter will have none of it; she railroads one of her father's assistants into marriage.

Although Laughton richly overplays every major scene, his performance remains one of the film's highlights. Mills also makes a major contribution in his interpretation of the illiterate shoemaker's assistant who learns to assert himself. Brenda de Banzie captures top femme honors for her playing of the spirited daughter who triumphs over the ridicule of her father and sisters.

• •

■ **HOFFA**

1992, 140 MINS, US ◇ ⓥ ⊙
Dir Danny DeVito   *Prod* Edward R. Pressman, Danny DeVito, Caldecot Chubb   *Scr* David Mamet   *Ph* Stephen H. Burum   *Ed* Lynzee Klingman, Ronald Roose   *Mus* David Newman   *Art Dir* Ida Random
● Jack Nicholson, Danny DeVito, Armand Assante, J.T. Walsh, John C. Reilly, Frank Whaley (20th Century Fox)

Hoffa presents the controversial labor leader as public icon, a man of iron, granite and *co-jones* who bullies his way across the union and

H

political landscape of the mid-century all for the good of the working man. Unfortunately, this grimly ambitious biopic goes no deeper than that, offering hardly a trace of psychology, motivation or inner life.

First section consists almost entirely of Hoffa's harangues and agitations on behalf of the union. Jumping into the truck of fictitious everyman Bobby Ciaro (Danny DeVito) one night, Hoffa (Jack Nicholson) preaches the gospel of the Teamsters, expressing it with almost mathematical logic.

As soon as Hoffa achieves some stature, he is abducted by a few fellows whose native language is Italian. Hoffa continues his rise, mixing it up with company goons when he feels like it, finally ascending to the Teamster presidency. But mixed in with the roots of his success are the seeds of his downfall.

Intercut with the flow of historical action are scenes of the aging Hoffa and Ciaro waiting for unknown associates at a roadside cafe. Matter of Hoffa's fate is neatly wrapped up without being too specific.

Mainly because of Nicholson's galvanizing performance and scriptwriter David Mamet's peppery, confrontational dialogue, all this is not exactly dull, but it is very dry and uninvolving. DeVito's direction tends toward the over-busy, with plenty of crane shots and imaginative but fussy scene transitions.
□ 1992: Nominations: Best Cinematography, Make-up

■ **HOLCROFT COVENANT, THE**

1985, 112 MINS, UK ◇ ▽ ⊙
Dir John Frankenheimer   *Prod* Edie Landau, Ely Landau   *Scr* George Axelrod, Edward Anhalt, John Hopkins   *Ph* Gerry Fisher   *Ed* Ralph Sheldon   *Mus* Stanislas
Art Dir Peter Mullins
● Michael Caine, Anthony Andrews, Victoria Tennant, Lilli Palmer, Mario Adorf, Michael Lonsdale (Thorn EMI)

This muddled thriller is seemingly aimed at cinemagoers fearful of a fourth Reich. Various scripters have not created a clear narrative line out of Robert Ludlum's complex potboiler novel. Result is a muddled narrative deficient in thrills or plausiblity.

Film starts with the revelation to Noel Holcroft (Michael Caine) that his father, the financial wizard who kept Hitler's plans afloat, left a bequest valued at over $4 billion with which the son is to make amends for the evils of Hitler's Germany. His mother (Lilli Palmer) suspects that the money is designated for the building of a new Nazi empire.

Argument is supported by various deaths that happen around Holcroft. The character doesn't attempt to discover what is going on and his attractive escort Helden von Tiebolt (Victoria Tennant) has to keep on reminding him that their lives are in danger.

Caine, whose reputation was built acting wily Britishers in local thrillers, just doesn't convince as a naive New Yorker. (James Caan was originally to play the role.) Victoria Tennant plays her part of *femme fatale* as if she doesn't know which side she's on.

■ **HOLD BACK THE DAWN**

1941, 114 MINS, US
Dir Mitchell Leisen   *Prod* Arthur Hornblow   *Scr* Charles Brackett, Billy Wilder   *Ph* Leo Tover   *Ed* Doane Harrison   *Mus* Victor Young   *Art Dir* Hans Dreier, Robert Usher
● Charles Boyer, Olivia de Havilland, Paulette Goddard, Victor Francen, Walter Abel, Rosemary DeCamp
(Paramount)

While *Hold Back the Dawn* is basically another European refugee yarn, scenarists Charles Brackett and Billy Wilder exercised some ingenuity and imagination and Ketty Frings' original emerges as fine celluloidia.

Charles Boyer is cast similarly to his role in *Algiers* – a rogue of hypnotic charm over

women. A gigolo in Europe, he's washed up in Mexico by the war and the quota laws make his entry into the United States a dream at least eight years distant. Caught among numerous other Europeans likewise waiting for the bars to be let down, Boyer is rapidly going to seed in the Mexican town when he meets up with Paulette Goddard, his former partner in crime in Paris, Vienna, etc.

She crashed the US by marrying an American jockey, ditching him later, and, still in love with Boyer, she puts him wise to the simple gimmick for making the immigration authorities relax. This sets the trap for Olivia de Havilland, a romance-hungry school teacher escorting a flock of young boys on an excursion in Mexico over the 4 July holiday.

Mitchell Leisen's only visible mistake is a tendency of the film to drag in spots, but this might be unavoidable due to Boyer's slow delivery.
□ 1941: Nominations: Best Picture, Actress (Olivia de Havilland), Screenplay, B&W Cinematography, B&W Art Direction, Scoring of a Dramatic Picture

■ **HOLIDAY**

1938, 93 MINS, US ▽ ⊙
Dir George Cukor   *Prod* Everett Riskin   *Scr* Donald Ogden Stewart, Sidney Buchman   *Ph* Franz Planer
Ed Otto Meyer, Al Clark   *Mus* Morris Stoloff (dir.)
Art Dir Stephen Goosson, Lionel Banks
● Katharine Hepburn, Cary Grant, Doris Nolan, Lew Ayres, Edward Everett Horton, Henry Kolker (Columbia)

Philip Barry's play, *Holiday*, in film form was a smash hit in the Depression's depth in 1930. Futility of riches is the topic and Donald Ogden Stewart and Sidney Buchman, who wrote this version, have tossed in a few timely shots which bolster the Barry original. Changes and interpolations are few, however.

Katharine Hepburn is in her best form and type of role in *Holiday*. Her acting is delightful and shaded with fine feeling and understanding throughout. Cary Grant plays this one straight.

George Cukor brings out the best from all the players. Lew Ayres is the despondent younger brother in the wealthy family who seeks some relief from the monotony of riches by resorting to strong liquor. Comedy by Edward Everett Horton and Jean Dixon is good, and Henry Kolker's portrait of the father is splendid.
□ 1938: Nomination: Best Art Direction

■ **HOLIDAY INN**

1942, 100 MINS, US ▽ ⊙
Dir Mark Sandrich   *Prod* Mark Sandrich   *Scr* Claude Binyon   *Ph* David Abel   *Ed* Ellsworth Hoagland
Mus Irving Berlin, Robert Emmett Dolan (arr)
● Bing Crosby, Fred Astaire, Virginia Dale, Marjorie Reynolds, Walter Abel, Louise Beavers (Paramount)

Loaded with a wealth of songs, it's meaty, not too kaleidoscopic and yet closely knit for a compact 100 minutes of tiptop filmusical entertainment. The idea is a natural, and Irving Berlin has fashioned some peach songs to fit the highlight holidays.

Plot is a new slant on a backstage story. Bing Crosby is the crooner, Fred Astaire the hoofer, partnered with brunet and fickle Virginia Dale. Latter jilts Crosby for Astaire (who subsequently becomes No. 2 to a Texan millionaire) which thus leaves the frankly lazy Crosby to carry out his Holiday Inn idea on his own. The crooner has figured out there are some 15 holidays in the year and by operating a Connecticut roadhouse on those festive occasions only he can loaf the rest of the 340 days.

Thus are strung together these songs and ideas: 'White Christmas'; 'Let's Start the New Year Right'; 'Abraham', a modern spiri-

tual for Lincoln's Birthday holiday; 'Be Careful, It's My Heart' (St Valentine's Day); 'I Gotta Say I Love You, 'Cause I Can't Tell a Lie' (Washington's birthday); 'Easter Parade', of course; 'I'm Singing a Song of Freedom', wherein Crosby, attired as the Freedom Man (with a snatch of 'Any Bonds Today?') introduces himself as an American Troubadour.

Mark Sandrich's production and direction are more than half the success of the picture.
□ 1942: Best Song ('White Christmas').
□ Nominations: Best Original Story, Scoring of a Musical Picture

■ **HOLLYWOOD BOULEVARD**

1976, 83 MINS, US ◇ ⦿
Dir Joe Dante, Allan Arkush   *Prod* John Davison
Scr Patrick Hobby   *Ph* Jamie Anderson   *Ed* Amy Jones, Allan Arkush, Joe Dante   *Mus* Andrew Stein
Art Dir Jack DeWolfe
● Candice Rialson, Mary Woronov, Rita George, Jeffrey Kramer, Dick Miller, Richard Doran (New World)

Roger Corman's New World Pictures does as good a satire job on itself as anyone could in *Hollywood Boulevard*.

Writing credit goes to one Patrick Hobby, also the name of the plot's screenwriter, played by Jeffrey Kramer. Candice Rialson goes to Hollywood where agent Dick Miller sends her to low-budget Miracle Pictures' producer Richard Doran who turns out one a week, as director Paul Bartel combines high aspiration with low achievement.

It seems that Mary Woronov, queen of the B-hive, doesn't like the competition from Rialson, Rita George and Tara Strohmeier. A series of bizarre murders gradually eliminate the challengers. Intercut with the new material is a lot of older Corman footage.

■ **HOLLYWOOD CANTEEN**

1944, 124 MINS, US ▽
Dir Delmer Daves   *Prod* Alex Gottlieb   *Scr* Delmer Daves   *Ph* Bert Glennon   *Ed* Christian Nyby   *Mus* Ray Heindorf (adapt.)   *Art Dir* Leo Kuter
● Robert Hutton, Joan Leslie, Bette Davis, John Garfield, Sydney Greenstreet, Joan Crawford (Warner)

Author-director Delmer Daves scripted *Stage Door Canteen* for Sol Lesser in early 1943 and he parlayed himself into another smasheroo for Warners with *Hollywood Canteen*.

Robert Hutton and Joan Leslie emerge as the real stars of the filmusical. They carry the story and a human one it is, too. Hutton looks like the ideal GI Joe, back with a Purple Heart from the South Pacific, and his buddy (Dane Clark) looks the perfect Brooklynite.

Story has Hutton winding up not only meeting his dream-girl (Leslie) but is also the lucky winner as the millionth guest of the Hollywood Canteen. That entitles him to an Arabian Nights suite, car, gifts and his choice of actresses for his weekend date. Natch, it's Leslie. What's nice is that real-life Leslie plays herself with charm, poise and ease, and the plot is so glib one accepts the romance wholeheartedly.
□ 1944: Nominations: Best Scoring of a Musical Picture, Sound, Song ('Sweet Dreams Sweetheart')

■ **HOLLYWOOD CAVALCADE**

1939, 100 MINS, US ◇
Dir Irving Cummings   *Prod* Darryl F. Zanuck   *Scr* Ernest Pascal   *Ph* Allen M. Davey   *Ed* Walter Thompson
Mus Louis Silvers (dir)   *Art Dir* Richard Day, Wiard B. Ihnen
● Alice Faye, Don Ameche, Buster Keaton, Ben Turpin, Chester Conklin, Mary Forbes (20th Century-Fox)

Hollywood Cavalcade relates an interesting and sentimental story of film producing in California, beginning in the pie-throwing,

Keystone era of 1913, and winding up when Al Jolson sang from the screen in *The Jazz Singer*, and the silent picture days were ended.

Mack Sennett plays an important off-screen role in the film, principal novelty of which is the successful and amusing introduction of oldtime Sennett comedy routines and formula.

Scenes from the older films are projected in black and white, sometimes framed in colored borders.

As for the yarn itself, it relates the rise, fall and rise again of an enthusiastic young director, played by Don Ameche. He sees a promising understudy (Alice Faye) who is substituting for the leading woman. He persuades her to make the jump to Hollywood and the films.

■ HOLLYWOOD CHAINSAW HOOKERS

1988, 74 MINS, US ◊ ⓦ

Dir Fred Olen Ray   *Prod* Fred Olen Ray   *Scr* Fred Olen Ray, T.L. Lankford   *Ph* Scott Ressler   *Ed* William Shaffer   *Mus* Michael Perilstein   *Art Dir* Corey Kaplan

● Gunnar Hansen, Linnea Quigley, Jay Richardson, Michelle Bauer, Dawn Wildsmith (Savage Cinema)

Hollywood Chainsaw Hookers is a self-styled cult film that is entertaining for its intended fringe audience.

Private dick Jay Richardson is hired to find runaway teenage beauty Linnea Quigley, whose dad had been suspected of child abuse. He finds her stripping in a topless club; she slips him a mickey and he awakes to find himself in the midst of a blood cult ritual presided over by Gunnar Hansen (Leatherface in *The Texas Chain Saw Massacre*).

Spoof goes over the edge when cult is revealed to be worshipping the chainsaw, 'the cosmic link by which all things are united.' Pic's highpoint is an outrageous sequence when voluptuous Michelle Bauer, posing as a hooker, covers her Elvis wall poster with plastic as she strips to an Elvis soundalike record and then bloodily cuts up her customer with a chainsaw. Pic climaxes with a dueling chainsaws battle between Quigley and Bauer.

Richardson is okay as the private eye given to clutzy voiceover, but Hansen's line readings are flat.

■ HOLLYWOOD COWBOY

See: Hearts of the West

■ HOLLYWOOD HOTEL

1937, 100 MINS, US

Dir Busby Berkeley   *Prod* [uncredited]   *Scr* Jerry Wald, Maurice Leo, Richard Macauley   *Ph* Charles Rosher, George Barnes   *Ed* George Amy   *Mus* Ray Heindorf (arr.)   *Art Dir* Robert Haas

● Dick Powell, Rosemary Lane, Lola Lane, Ted Healy, Hugh Herbert, Glenda Farrell (Warner)

Hollywood Hotel is a smash musical entertainment, with a lively and amusing story and some popular song numbers. Warners has assembled an excellent cast, not the least interesting of whom is Louella O. Parsons, newspaper columnist, who makes an effective debut as an actress.

Production is elaborate, and Busby Berkeley's direction keeps the players going at top speed. Hollywood film studios and broadcasting are the basis of a farcical story which pokes fun at both the picture-making business and the radio industry. Story is by Jerry Wald and Maurice Leo, who have developed a satire which is original and humorous. Eight musical numbers are by Dick Whiting and Johnny Mercer, best of which are 'I'm Like a Fish out of Water' and 'Silhoueted in the Moonlight'.

Lane sisters, Rosemary and Lola, turn in

good performances, and Ted Healy and Hugh Herbert have some very funny material. Dick Powell's song numbers are first rate.

■ HOLLYWOOD HOT TUBS

1984, 102 MINS, US ◊ ⓦ

Dir Chuck Vincent   *Prod* Marke Borde   *Scr* Mark Borde, Craig McDonnell   *Ph* Larry Revene   *Ed* Michael Hoggan   *Mus* Joel Goldsmith   *Art Dir* Loma Lee Brookbank

● Donna McDaniel, Michael Andrew, Paul Gunning, Katt Shea, Edy Williams, Jewal Shepherd (Manson International)

A very good premise simply sinks in the Hollywood hot tub.

To save young Jeff from the slammer, his parents get him a job mixing plumbing with pleasure in the Hollywood hot tubs. Everything that can be done to, with, for, in or around hot water finds its way into a plot that goes from the quick and the dirty to the gothic. Each half-hour delivers a coupling in this not-too-funny comedy full of booze, broads and bubbles. The final party offers lookalikes of Burt Reynolds, Lauren Bacall and Bozo. Only the last is convincing.

The kids, at whom this pic is aimed, witness more sex than they enjoy. The most promising moments come with Jewal Shepard, who takes the valley girl far beyond its usual dips.

■ HOLLYWOOD HOT TUBS 2 EDUCATING CRYSTAL

1990, 100 MINS, US ◊ ⓦ

Dir Ken Raich   *Prod* Mark Borde, Ken Raich   *Scr* Brent V. Friedman   *Ph* Areni Milo   *Ed* Michael Hoggan   *Mus* John Lombardo, Bill Bodine   *Art Dir* Thomas Cost

● Jewel Shepard, Patrick Day, David Tiefen, Remy O'Neil, Bart Braverman, J.P. Bumstead (Alimar)

Beneath its come-on title, this sequel to Chuck Vincent's 1984 feature moves out of the exploitation film arena to a well-scripted comic look at west coast life styles.

The Crystal of the title, Jewel Shepard, encores as the bubbley, jiggly valley girl who heads for business school to learn how to run her mom Remy O'Neill's hot tubs/health spa establishment. Evil Bart Braverman (convincing with beard as a prince) is conspiring to take over the business, even planning to marry O'Neill to achieve his ends. Film is told from the point of view of handsome hero David Tiefen, who's working as a chauffeur to Braverman while writing a book about Shepard.

Under newcomer Ken Raich's direction, film works due to the quirky touches of Brent Frieman's screenplay. Previously wasted in purely decorative assignments, Shepard comes into her own here in a funny and sympathetic role. It's not quite *Educating Rita*, but the formula of gawky ingenue blossoming is a sure-fire one.

■ HOLLYWOOD OR BUST

1956, 94 MINS, US ◊ ⓦ

Dir Frank Tashlin   *Prod* Hal Wallis   *Scr* Erna Lazarus   *Ph* Daniel Fapp   *Ed* Howard Smith   *Mus* Walter Scharf (arr.)   *Art Dir* Hal Pereira, Henry Bumstead

● Dean Martin, Jerry Lewis, Anita Ekberg, Pat Crowley, Maxie Rosenbloom (Paramount)

Hollywood's in the label and does make a finale appearance, but most of this comedy caper takes place on a cross-country junket from New York, with way stops enroute, including Las Vegas.

Direction by Frank Tashlin scores enough comedy highspots to keep the pace fairly fast, even with the slow spots that his handling and the team's talent cannot overcome. One of the film's funniest bits comes before the ti-

tle with Dean Martin introducing Jerry Lewis as different types of movie-watchers. Lewis' encounter with a bull and making like a matador is another fun-filled sequence, as is his champagne binge in Vegas after hexing the gambling devices into a big payoff.

By way of making the latter part of the title legit, Anita Ekberg appears as guest star on whom Lewis has a crush. She doesn't have much more to do than to display what nature has wrought in the fjords of Sweden, so it's still a big part. Enroute west Martin and Lewis pick up Pat Crowley so that Martin will have someone to sing romantic songs to.

■ HOLLYWOOD REVUE

1929, 113 MINS, US ◊ ⊙

Dir Charles Reisner   *Prod* Harry Rapf   *Scr* Al Bonsberg, Robert Hopkins   *Ph* John Arnold, I.G. Reis, Maximilian Fabian   *Ed* William Gray   *Mus* Arthur Lange (arr.)   *Art Dir* Cedric Gibbons

● John Gilbert, Norma Shearer, Joan Crawford, Bessie Love, Marion Davies, Buster Keaton (M-G-M)

First shot following the list of credits is the original billboard: 16 girls sitting for raised letters spelling the title and reciting the opening lyric in unison. The opening number is terrific: a formation tap routine by the ensemble in black-and-white costume.

The staging of 'Singin' in the Rain' is a sweet dance melody delivered by Cliff Edwards and his uke under a side-screen tree as the water pours down into a stage-wide pool.

Individually no one stands out like Marie Dressler. Stage veteran has the one real comedy number of the picture in 'For I'm the Queen', and runs away with the femme trio, rounded out by Bessie Love and Polly Moran.

Trick camerawork is confined to Jack Benny taking Bessie Love out of his pocket, not as well done as might be supposed, and Charlie King's sudden diminutiveness after hearing Conrad Nagel sing 'You Were Meant for Me', and King's song in 'Broadway Melody' to Anita Page.

First of the [two] color sequences is John Gilbert and Norma Shearer's *Romeo and Juliet*, a modern version, with Lionel Barrymore briefly flashed directing. Both principals look great and play well, Gilbert appearing a bit nervous on the straight interpretation, but hopping to the slang phrasing.

Joan Crawford sings 'Gotta Feelin' for You', assisted by a male quartet, but doesn't do much with it.

It's a revue from gong to gong [in two acts, eight scenes and 18 numbers]. No semblance of a story, and considering cast nobody is going to care.

□ 1928/29: Nomination: Best Picture

■ HOLLYWOOD SHUFFLE

1987, 82 MINS, US ◊ ⓦ ⊙

Dir Robert Townsend   *Prod* Robert Townsend   *Scr* Robert Townsend, Keenen Ivory Wayans   *Ph* Peter Deming   *Ed* W.O. Garrett   *Mus* Patrice Rushen, Udi Harpaz   *Art Dir* Melba Katzman Farquhar

● Robert Townsend, Anne-Marie Johnson, Starletta Dupois, Helen Martin, Craigus R. Johnson, Domenick Irrera (Conquering Unicorn)

Brimming with imagination and energy, *Hollywood Shuffle* is the kind of shoestring effort more appealing in theory than execution. Produced, directed and co-written by actor Robert Townsend, pic is a freeform look at the trials and tribulations of black actors trying to make it in today's Hollywood. Scattershot humor misses as much as it hits.

At a cattle call for a blaxploitation pic to be made by a white production company, Townsend starts to feel guilty and questions if what he's doing is right after he gets the part. Scenes in the actor's subconscious are dramatized on screen.

Most amusing of these is a school for black actors, run by whites, of course, where the students are trained to shuffle, jive and generally fit the preconceived notion of what blacks are like. Another brilliantly conceived bit is *Sneakin' into the Movies*, a takeoff of the Siskel & Ebert film reviewing TV show.

Performances of the ensemble cast, many of whom play more than one role, are likeable but without much that sticks to the ribs. Production values are predictably crude given the film's $100,000 budget.

••••••••••••••••••••••••••••••••

■ **HOLOCAUST 2000**
(US: The Chosen)

1977, 102 MINS, ITALY/UK ◇ ⓥ
Dir Alberto De Martino   *Prod* Edmondo Amati
Scr Sergio Donati, Aldo De Martino, Michael Robson
Ph Enrico Menczer   *Ed* Vincenzo Tomassi   *Mus* Ennio Morricone   *Art Dir* Umberto Betacca
● Kirk Douglas, Agostina Belli, Simon Ward, Anthony Quayle, Virginia McKenna, Alexander Knox (Embassy/Aston)

Take the threat of nuclear disaster, the ecological deterioration of the earth, the terror of an all-powerful Antichrist; mix it with an international cast topped by Kirk Douglas, Agostina Belli and a number of convincing British actors like Simon Ward, Anthony Quayle, Alexander Knox and Virginia McKenna and shake well.

The conflict is between Robert Caine (Douglas), an idealist in the realm of nuclear power plants and his demon son Angelo (Ward) with tenebrous plans to push dad's project for fission power to wipe out human life. The supernatural pushes superficial arguments about nuclear power to the side and gives the spectator a sense of human helplessness to contend with such an evil and destructive force as the Antichrist.

As striking a beauty as Belli is catapulted into the conflict with only symbolic story roots in a Biblical-like finale and with a slow, pronounced accent for her lines. The dramatic picture-long father-son duel between Douglas with a mid-American accent and Ward with a British lilt keeps the plot in place right up to the inconclusive finale.

••••••••••••••••••••••••••••••••

■ **HOMBRE**

1967, 119 MINS, US ◇ ⓥ ⊙
Dir Martin Ritt   *Prod* Martin Ritt, Irving Ravetch
Scr Irving Ravetch, Harriet Frank Jr   *Ph* James Wong Howe   *Ed* Frank Bracht   *Mus* David Rose   *Art Dir* Jack Martin Smith, Robert E. Smith
● Paul Newman, Fredric March, Richard Boone, Diane Cilento, Cameron Mitchell, Martin Balsam (20th Century-Fox)

Hombre develops the theme that socially and morally disparate types are often thrown into uneasy, explosive alliance due to emergencies.

An unhurried, measured look at interacting human natures, caught up only for story purposes in a given situation, the characters speak truisms which, sometimes, are overdone platitudes.

Adapted from Elmore Leonard's novel, it tells the story of an Apache-raised white boy who becomes the natural leader of a group in its survival against a robber band headed by Richard Boone.

Paul Newman is excellent as the scorned (but only supposed) Apache. Fredric March, essaying an Indian agent who has embezzled food appropriations for his charges, also scores in a strong, unsympathetic – but eventually pathetic – role. Richard Boone is very powerful, yet admirably restrained as the heavy.

••••••••••••••••••••••••••••••••

■ **HOME ALONE**

1990, 102 MINS, US ◇ ⓥ ⊙
Dir Chris Columbus   *Prod* John Hughes   *Scr* John Hughes   *Ph* Julio Macat   *Ed* Raja Gosnell   *Mus* John Williams   *Art Dir* John Muto
● Macauley Culkin, Joe Pesci, Daniel Stern, Catherine O'Hara, John Heard, John Candy (20th Century-Fox)

The family of poor little dumped-upon Kevin (Macauley Culkin) has rushed off to catch their holiday plane and accidentally left him behind. Now they're in Paris, frantically trying to reach him, and he's home alone, where a storm has knocked out the telephones, the neighbors are away for the holiday and the houses on the street are being systematically cleaned out by a team of burglars.

Generally perceived by his family as a helpless, hopeless little geek, Kevin is at first delighted to be rid of them, gorging on forbidden pleasures like junk food and violent videos, but when the bandits (Joe Pesci, Daniel Stern) begin circling his house, he realizes he's on his own to defend the place.

Kevin proves he's not such a loser by defending the fort with wits and daring and by the time Mom (Catherine O'Hara) comes rushing back from Europe, everything's in order.

A firstrate production in which every element contributes to the overall smartly realized tone, pic boasts wonderful casting, with Culkin a delight as funny, resilient Kevin, and O'Hara bringing a snappy, zesty energy to the role of mom. Pesci is aces in the role of slippery housebreaker Harry, who does a Two Stooges routine with lanky side-kick Stern.
□ 1990: Nominations: Best Original Score, Song ('Somewhere in My Memory')

••••••••••••••••••••••••••••••••

■ **HOME ALONE 2 LOST IN NEW YORK**

1992, 120 MINS, US ◇ ⓥ ⊙
Dir Chris Columbus   *Prod* John Hughes   *Scr* John Hughes   *Ph* Julio Macat   *Ed* Raja Gosnell   *Mus* John Williams   *Art Dir* Sandy Veneziano
● Macauley Culkin, Joe Pesci, Daniel Stern, Catherine O'Hara, John Heard, Tim Curry (20th Century-Fox)

Some day scholars will devote courses to the monstrous box office allure of the original *Home Alone*, which, at the time, surprised even Fox. For a sequel the studio has simply remade the first movie, but with bigger pratfalls. Pic delivers on that level.

Once again, Kevin (Macauley Culkin), provoked by his older brother, finds himself in the doghouse just before a family vacation, this time accidentally boarding the wrong plane and ending up in New York while the McCallister brood jets off to Florida. Meanwhile, the inept thieves from the first movie, Harry (Joe Pesci) and Marv (Daniel Stern), have conveniently escaped from prison and caught a truck that arrives in New York about the same time Kevin does.

Using his dad's credit card, Kevin checks into a ritzy hotel, where he finds more adults to outwit, in this case a snooty concierge (Tim Curry) as well as the equally haughty staff. Ultimately, however, it's again Kevin versus the two bad guys, setting up elaborate traps at his uncle's being-remodeled home.

Under Chris Columbus' careful direction, the wide-eyed Culkin again shows his skill at being an Everykid – cutely precocious, yet still vulnerable to childish whims such as running up a whopping room-service tab on chocolate sundaes.

••••••••••••••••••••••••••••••••

■ **HOME AT SEVEN**
(US: Murder on Monday)

1952, 85 MINS, UK
Dir Ralph Richardson   *Prod* Maurice Cowan
Scr Anatole De Grunwald   *Ph* Jack Hildyard, Edward

Scaife   *Ed* Bert Bates   *Mus* Malcolm Arnold
Art Dir Vincent Korda, Frederick Pusey
● Ralph Richardson, Margaret Leighton, Jack Hawkins, Campbell Singer, Michael Shepley, Meriel Forbes (London/British Lion)

When [R.C. Sherriff's] *Home at Seven* was produced on the London stage in 1950, it proved to be one of the major successes of the legit season. Ralph Richardson repeats his starring role.

The production is notable for three 'firsts'. It was the first independent venture of Maurice Cowan; Richardson's first attempt at direction; and the first picture under the Alexander Korda banner to be produced under the speed-up technique of three weeks shooting schedule after extensive rehearsals.

The principal character, a bank clerk, loses a day in his life, and during the time he was an amnesia victim, the funds of his sports club are stolen and the steward is murdered. When the police starts its inquiries, he gives a false alibi, but that is soon exploded and he is convinced of his own guilt.

Richardson directs the piece with a straightforward competence.

••••••••••••••••••••••••••••••••

■ **HOME BEFORE DARK**

1958, 137 MINS, US
Dir Mervyn LeRoy   *Prod* Mervyn LeRoy   *Scr* Eileen Bassing, Robert Bassing   *Ph* Joseph F. Biroc   *Ed* Philip W. Anderson   *Mus* Franz Waxman   *Art Dir* John Beckman
● Jean Simmons, Dan O'Herlihy, Rhonda Fleming, Efrem Zimbalist Jr, Mabel Albertson, Steve Dunne (Warner)

Home before Dark should give the Kleenex a vigorous workout. Based on one woman's battle to regain her slipping sanity, it is a romantic melodrama of considerable power and imprint.

The screenplay, based on Eileen Bassing's novel of the same name, sometimes seems rather skimpy in its character motivation. It is also difficult at times to understand the mental tone of the mentally ill heroine (Jean Simmons). But while the tale is unfolding it is made so gripping that factual discrepancies are relatively unimportant.

Simmons is the wife of Dan O'Herlihy, who has ceased to love her before mental breakdown and has not changed his attitude on her recovery. Living in their home, to which she returns on her release from hospitalization, are her stepmother (Mabel Albertson) and her stepsister (Rhonda Fleming). They are masterful females who could drive anyone to the edge of madness.

Her only real ally in the house is a stranger (Efrem Zimbalist Jr), who is also an alien in the setting of the inbred New England college community. Zimbalist is the only Jewish member of the faculty, and ostensibly a protege of O'Herlihy's.

The whole picture is seen from Simmons' viewpoint, which means she is 'on' virtually the whole time. Her voice is a vibrant instrument, used with thoughtful articulation and placement, the only vital part of her at times.

Joseph Biroc's photography is suited to the grim New England atmosphere. It is winter, a depressingly gray winter, and the locations in Massachusetts give the picture the authentic feel.

••••••••••••••••••••••••••••••••

■ **HOMEBOY**

1988, 112 MINS, US ◇ ⓥ ⊙
Dir Michael Seresin   *Prod* Alan Marshall, Elliott Kastner   *Scr* Eddie Cook   *Ph* Gale Tattersall   *Ed* Ray Lovejoy   *Mus* Eric Clapton, Michael Kamen   *Art Dir* Brian Morris
● Mickey Rourke, Christopher Walken, Debra Feuer, Thomas Quinn, Kevin Conway, Anthony Alda (Redbury)

Actor Mickey Rourke's decade-old pet project about a battered, burnt-out smalltime boxer is a sort of *Raging Bull* without horns, wallowing dully in the cliches of movieland gutter romanticism.

Though nominally written by Eddie Cook [from a story by Mickey Rourke] and directed by Alan Parker's habitual lenser Michael Seresin in his helming debut, this in fact is all Rourke's show. He's refused himself nothing – except a good screenplay and direction.

Rourke's tale is a purported homage to a boxer he idolized in his youth when he himself trained to be a fighter. Here called Johnny Walker, Rourke's hero is just another inarticulate All-American lowlife. Adopting a neo-Neanderthal expression and cowboy duds, Rourke is first seen slouching into an Atlantic coastal town for a fight engagement.

His zombie-like condition doesn't prevent him from being befriended by Christopher Walken, who steals the show with a colorful portrayal of a narcissistic two-bit hoodlum. Walken tries to sucker Rourke into taking part in a jewelry shop hold-up he has long been dreaming of. But Rourke decides to go back into the ring for the love of a young fairground operator (Debra Feuer, the ex-Mrs Rourke), whose business is failing.

■ HOMECOMING

1948, 113 MINS, US ◇ ⑫ ⊙
Dir Mervyn LeRoy   *Prod* Sidney Franklin   *Scr* Paul Osborn   *Ph* Harold Rosson   *Ed* John Dunning   *Mus* Bronislau Kaper   *Art Dir* Cedric Gibbons, Randall Duell
● Clark Gable, Lana Turner, Anne Baxter, John Hodiak, Ray Collins, Gladys Cooper (M-G-M)

Performances are of top quality all down the line, with Gable and Turner pacing the playing. Story line makes a direct play for the tear ducts and has heart. These two factors overcome some patness in resolving plot's problems.

Gable portrays a successful surgeon, happily married, who joins the Army. Three years of patching up the wounded in close association with his nurse, Turner, gradually changes the man's character from smug successfulness to an awareness of his obligations to others.

Story, scripted by Paul Osborn from an original by Sidney Kingsley, is told in flashback and draws its title from the surgeon's return home after his great war love. The dialog and the characters are made real by the forceful playing. There is strong sympathy for the love between Gable and Turner, even though the doctor's wife, Anne Baxter, waits at home.

A considerable portion of the footage is devoted to detailing heroic work done by doctors and nurses under fire at the front, but film does not class as a war picture. Combat medical scenes add punch.

■ HOME FROM THE HILL

1960, 150 MINS, US ◇ ⑫ ⊙
Dir Vincente Minnelli   *Prod* Edmund Grainger   *Scr* Harriet Frank Jr, Irving Ravetch   *Ph* Milton Krasner   *Ed* Harold F. Kress   *Mus* Bronislau Kaper   *Art Dir* George W. Davis, Preston Ames
● Robert Mitchum, Eleanor Parker, George Peppard, George Hamilton, Everett Sloane, Luana Patten (M-G-M)

A full-blown melodrama, high-octane in situation and characters, *Home from the Hill* is like an over-taxed engine. The production throws a plot rod or two in its final moments, but when it is concluded the spectator is at least aware he has seen something.

Even though the screenplay, from William Humphrey's novel, is florid and complicated, in the customary Deep South literary manner, it does not neglect humor and the lighter touches. Vincente Minnelli's direction is rich and satisfying.

Illicit and illegitimate romance in two generations occupy the principals. Setting is Texas, a town of which Robert Mitchum is not only the richest citizen but the busiest stud. The latter characteristic has iced his marriage to Eleanor Parker since the birth of their now-grown son (George Hamilton). Mitchum has another son (George Peppard), born out of wedlock at about the same time as Hamilton. Hamilton has been so marked by his parents' relationship that when he falls in love with Luana Patten he lacks the courage to marry her.

Despite the intricacies, the story plays well, due to a fine cast and Minnelli's sure-handed direction.

Mitchum delivers his strongest performance in years, and Parker handles her end of the conflict well, too, although her role is less interesting. But it is Peppard, from the NY stage, who shines through.

■ HOME MOVIES

1979, 90 MINS, US ◇ ⑫ ⊙
Dir Brian De Palma   *Prod* Brian De Palma, Jack Temchin, Gil Adler   *Scr* Robert Harders, Gloria Norris, Kim Ambler, Dana Edelman, Stephen Le May, Charles Loventhal   *Ph* James L. Carter   *Ed* Corky Ohara   *Mus* Pino Donaggio   *Art Dir* Tom Surgal
● Kirk Douglas, Nancy Allen, Keith Gordon, Gerrit Graham, Vincent Gardenia (SLC)

Home Movies, resulted from Brian De Palma teaching students at Sarah Lawrence College, New York, how to make films by making one with them.

The story has Kirk Douglas running a cult called Star Therapy. He exhorts each pupil to 'put your name above the title' in life. Practicing what he preaches, he has his own life continuously filmed, with himself as director and star. The sessions, filmed with a mask reducing the frame, as if by Douglas' own 16mm camera crew, are recurrently hilarious.

Singling out one pupil as an example of 'an extra in his own life', Douglas spurs the boy – engagingly played by Keith Gordon – into an ego-quest which involves a successful pursuit of his elder brother's fiancee and some laughably inept attempts to film himself doing not-so-dramatic things like falling asleep.

■ HOMER AND EDDIE

1989, 99 MINS, US ◇ ⑫ ⊙
Dir Andrei Konchalovsky   *Prod* Moritz Borman, James Cady   *Scr* Patrick Cirillo   *Ph* Lajos Koltai   *Ed* Henry Richardson   *Mus* Edvard Artemyev   *Art Dir* Michel Levesque
● James Belushi, Whoopi Goldberg, Karen Black, John Waters, Beah Richards (Kings Road/Borman/Cady)

This road film about a mentally deficient dishwasher and a homicidal escaped cancer patient is a downer from beginning to end.

Homer, a mentally retarded dishwasher in Arizona, decides to hitchhike up to Oregon to see his father, who is dying of cancer. He meets up with wacky vagabond Eddie in an old jalopy, and soon they become pals.

On the road Eddie tries to enlighten Homer to the ways of the world. She takes him to a brothel and gets the money to pay for it by holding up a store. Her criminal activities increase, and she winds up shooting people while robbing their stores. The twosome argue about the existence of God. Meanwhile, Eddie tells Homer that the doctors have only given her a month to live.

It is hard to feel much sympathy for these two mental patients. The image of two underprivileged people in a cruel world is rather too pat to be convincing.

■ HOMETOWN USA

1979, 93 MINS, US ◇ ⑫
Dir Max Baer   *Prod* Roger Comrass, Jesse Vint   *Scr* Jesse Vint   *Ph* [uncredited]   *Ed* Frank Morriss   *Mus* Marshall Leib
● Gary Springer, David Wilson, Brian Kerwin, Pat Delaney, Julie Parsons, Sally Kirkland (Film Ventures)

In *Hometown USA* director Max Baer has drawn liberally from *American Graffiti*, but pic still contains generous amount of earthy wit that flows naturally from pic's characters and action.

Baer has obviously put some effort into establishing proper, circa 1957, atmosphere for story of adolescents fixated on hot rods, necking and cruising hometown boulevards all night.

Screenplay set pieces mostly deals with a meek, sexually naive teenager, Gary Springer, and his cronies, David Wilson and Brian Kerwin, who supposedly want to fix him up with a date, but who always seem to end up with the girls themselves.

Baer doesn't hesitate to satirise at kids whose story he's telling, adding an unexpected bit of depth to what is basically a piece of entertainment.

■ HOMEWARD BOUND
THE INCREDIBLE JOURNEY

1993, 84 MINS, US ◇ ⑫ ⊙
Dir Duwayne Dunham   *Prod* Franklin R. Levy, Jeffrey Chernov   *Scr* Caroline Thompson, Linda Woolverton   *Ph* Reed Smoot   *Ed* Jonathan P. Shaw   *Mus* Bruce Broughton   *Art Dir* Roger Cain
● Robert Hays, Kim Greist, Jean Smart, Benj Thall, Veronica Lauren, Kevin Chevalia (Walt Disney)

Leave it to the Disney marketing machine to dust off a venerable nature-adventure film like 1963's *The Incredible Journey* and wed it with *Look Who's Talking*, creating a sprightly little entertainment that applies animation principles to live-action by giving personalities to the movie's wayward dogs and cat through the clever use of the voices of Michael J. Fox, Sally Field and Don Ameche.

Although the story [from Sheila Burnford's book] also gets spruced up with some '90s twists, the plot still centers on three pets, left with a family friend, who try to cross the wilderness and make it back home, encountering menaces from bears to porcupines on the way.

The aging Shadow (a golden retriever voiced with stately dignity by Ameche) leads the way, followed by the upstart mutt Chance (Fox) and snooty feline Sassy (Field). For the most part the writers – Linda Woolverton (of *Beauty and the Beast*) and Caroline Thompson (*Edward Scissorhands*) – have done a splendid job capturing what animals seem to be thinking without making them cognizant of what humans are saying, except for the few words the pets recognize.

Duwayne Dunham, a veteran film editor making his [feature film] directing debut, keeps *Journey's* pace brisk. Pic is dedicated to producer Franklin R. Levy, who died during production.

■ HOMICIDE

1991, 100 MINS, US ◇ ⑫ ⊙
Dir David Mamet   *Prod* Michael Hausman, Edward R. Pressman   *Scr* David Mamet   *Ph* Roger Deakins   *Ed* Barbara Tulliver   *Mus* Aeric Jans   *Art Dir* Michael Merritt
● Joe Mantegna, William H. Macy, Natalija Nogulich, Ving Rhames, Rebecca Pidgeon (Pressman/Cinehaus)

David Mamet's first-rate writing and boldly idiosyncratic directing redeem this story of a toughened Jewish cop torn between two worlds. *Homicide* presents an urban hell in which stoic survivor Bobby Gold (Joe Mantegna) must negotiate through rotten politics, unpredictable violence and virulent racial tension just to get through a day of police work.

Gold sees a chance to regain his enthusiasm when he becomes a key player in a team effort to bring in a cop killer who's eluded the FBI. But he's callously reassigned to a routine investigation of an elderly Jewish woman shot down in her candy store in a black ghetto.

To the disgust of his cynical Irish partner (William H. Macy), Gold gets caught up in the family's claims that they are targets of a deep-rooted and violent anti-Semitic conspiracy. When his fellow cops need him to help bring down the killer, he's busy with initiation rites into his new sect.

Mamet's direction gives much of the film a bracing, refreshing tone as he works to express the shattering tensions of Gold's work.

Excellent work by Mantegna does much to enlist sympathies and interest. Macy is also strong as the flinty partner.

....

■ HONDO

1953, 84 MINS, US ◇
Dir John Farrow   *Scr* James Edward Grant   *Ph* Robert Burks, Archie Stout   *Ed* Ralph Dawson   *Mus* Emil Newman, Hugo Friedhofer   *Art Dir* Alfredo Ybarra
● John Wayne, Geraldine Page, Ward Bond, Michael Pate, James Arness, Rodolfo Acosta (Warner/Wayne-Fellows)

Hondo is an exciting offbeat western. The stereoscopic 3-D cameras and WarnerColor successfully capture the vast natural beauty of Camargo, Mexico, where the picture was filmed on location.

Hondo, like *Shane*, gives the western an aura of maturity. It depicts a conflict of interests rather than an individual battle of good versus evil. Vittorio, the Apache chief, is shown as a just leader, concerned about the problems of his people and bewildered by the white man's violations of treaties.

While the skirmishes and armed battles with the Indians are excitingly presented, the screenplay of Louis L'Amour's *Collier's* magazine story deals considerably with the relationship of individuals. John Wayne, as a civilian scout for the US Cavalry, arrives at the isolated ranch in Indian territory of Geraldine Page and her young son. Practically abandoned by her ne'er-do-well husband, she is forced to do the ranch chores by herself, a task with which Wayne assists.

Wayne accidentally comes across Page's husband and kills him in self-defense. While the romantic attachment between Wayne and Page grows, a conflict arises over the death of her husband.

Wayne scores as the silent-yet-outspoken Indian scout. Page, no glamor girl, gives a sensitive portrayal as the ranch wife.
☐ 1953: Nominations: Best Supp. Actress (Geraldine Page), Motion Picture Story (writer not eligible)

....

■ HONEY, I BLEW UP THE KID

1992, 89 MINS, US ◇ ⑫ ⊙
Dir Randal Kleiser   *Prod* Dawn Steel, Edward S. Feldman   *Scr* Thom Eberhardt, Peter Elbling, Garry Goodrow   *Ph* John Hora   *Ed* Michael A. Stevenson, Harry Hitner, Tina Hirsch   *Mus* Bruce Broughton   *Art Dir* Leslie Dilley
● Rick Moranis, Marcia Strassman, Robert Oliveri, Daniel Shalikar, Joshua Shalikar, Lloyd Bridges (Walt Disney)

Honey, I Blew Up the Kid is a diverting, well-crafted sequel to Disney's '89 hit *Honey I Shrunk the Kids*. Taking its cue from 1950s sci-fi pics and inverting the shrinking gags from the original, the sequel has wacky inventor Rick Moranis accidentally blowing up his two-year-old to huge proportions.

There's nothing genuinely menacing about the baby, though, and even his cartoonish would-be captor John Shea, who wants to make him a guinea pig for government exper-

iments, doesn't unduly darken the mood of this tongue-in-cheek yarn, smartly scripted from a story by Garry Goodrow.

Nor does *Kid* have the creepy feeling of the original. The sequel is a romp, escapism at its breeziest, smoothly engineered by director Randal Kleiser and a top-flight tech staff.

A lousy businessman, Moranis has made the mistake of selling his invention to a sinister company headed by Lloyd Bridges, whose huge warehouse includes such items as the Rosebud sled. Moranis and Shea are supposed to be co-directors of the project to develop a new version of his ray machine to enlarge objects for government use, but Moranis has been frozen out.

Initially growing into a 7-foot house-wrecker, Adam soon passes the 50-foot mark and eventually balloons into a blithe 112-foot behemoth stomping down the Las Vegas Strip like *The Amazing Colossal Man*. Joining Moranis' quest to rescue Adam and bring him back to normal is the kid's babysitter (Keri Russell).

....

■ HONEY, I SHRUNK THE KIDS

1989, 86 MINS, US ◇ ⑫ ⊙
Dir Joe Johnston   *Prod* Penney Finkelman Cox   *Scr* Ed Naha, Tom Schalman   *Ph* Hiro Narita   *Ed* Michael A. Stevenson   *Mus* James Horner   *Art Dir* Gregg Fonseca
● Rick Moranis, Matt Frewer, Marcia Strassman, Kristine Sutherland, Thomas Brown, Jared Rushton (Walt Disney)

Borrowing two good end elements from two 1950s sci-fi pics, *The Incredible Shrinking Man* and *Them!*, scripters pit two sets of unfriendly neighbor kids, mistakenly shrunk to only ¼-inch high, against what ordinarily would be benign backyard fixtures, both alive and inanimate.

Their misfortune was to get caught in the beam of ne'er-do-well inventor Wayne Szalinski's (Rick Moranis) molecule-reducing contraption while he's out giving a lecture to a group of skeptical scientists.

He sweeps them into the dustpan along with the other flotsam that goes out with the trash.

Now, they must make it back to the house among towering vegetation, homungous bugs and fierce water showers on a quest that would be nightmarish except that it seems mostly like a lot of fun.

Pic [story by Stuart Gordon, Brian Yuzna and Ed Naha] is in the best tradition of Disney and even better than that because it is not so juvenile that adults won't be thoroughly entertained.

....

■ HONEYMOON IN VEGAS

1992, 95 MINS, US ◇ ⑫ ⊙
Dir Andrew Bergman   *Prod* Mike Lobell   *Scr* Andrew Bergman   *Ph* William A. Fraker   *Ed* Barry Malkin   *Mus* David Newman   *Art Dir* William A. Elliott
● James Caan, Nicolas Cage, Sarah Jessica Parker, Pat Morita, Anne Bancroft, Peter Boyle (Castle Rock)

Writer-director Andrew Bergman has plenty of fun with the premise of *Honeymoon in Vegas*, an adult twist on Damon Runyon's *Little Miss Marker*. Sarah Jessica Parker is the saucy, sympathetic prize in a poker game between her divorce-detective fiance Nicolas Cage and sharkish Vegas gambler James Caan.

Schoolteacher Parker has coerced N.Y. shamus Cage into marrying her, and they take a honeymoon suite at Bally's Casino Resort during the midst of a convention of Elvis impersonators, whose presence provides hilarious running gags throughout.

In an enjoyably manic, self-kidding performance, Caan plays a thug who for a while shows an unexpectedly gentlemanly streak, putting the hapless Cage to shame. 'If I was a medieval knight, I woulda jostled for ya,' Caan tells Parker after winning a weekend

with her in his poker game with Cage.

Parker's natural, unforced charm and honest, strong-willed personality give the film a scintillating uncertainty after she begins taking Caan seriously. William A. Fraker's lensing is cheesy-looking, but the Hawaiian locations compensate in this airy light entertainment.

....

■ HONEYMOON KILLERS, THE

1969, 115 MINS, US ⑫ ⊙
Dir Leonard Kastle   *Prod* Warren Steibel   *Scr* Leonard Kastle   *Ph* Oliver Wood   *Ed* Stan Warnow
● Shirley Stoler, Tony LoBianco, Mary Higbee, Kip McArdle, Barbara Cason, Doris Roberts (A.I.P./Roxanne)

Made on a very low budget by a writer-director Leonard Kastle, *The Honeymoon Killers*, based on the Lonely Hearts murder case of the late 1940s, is made with care, authenticity and attention to detail.

The acting throughout the film never falters, each of the lonely heart victims presented as a fully rounded character.

Theme, presented with perhaps a shade too heavy an underlining is the desperate search for love in the US, the idea that no woman is complete without a man beside her.

Fernandez has disappeared from the lives of a score of women, after receiving their 'dowries', when he meets Martha, but it is only when she becomes intimately involved in his life, bringing her fantastic jealousy to bear on his new targets, that murder enters the picture. There are a few lapses, but the pic goes towards its harrowing climax without losing step.

....

■ HONEY POT, THE

1967, 150 MINS, UK ⑫
Dir Joseph L. Mankiewicz   *Prod* Joseph L. Mankiewicz, Charles K. Feldman   *Scr* Joseph L. Mankiewicz   *Ph* Gianni Di Venanzo   *Ed* David Bretherton   *Mus* John Addison   *Art Dir* John F. DeCuir
● Rex Harrison, Susan Hayward, Cliff Robertson, Capucine, Edie Adams, Maggie Smith (United Artists)

An elegant, sophisticated screen vehicle for more demanding tastes, previously billed as *Mr Fox of Venice* and *Anyone for Venice?* Vaguely drawing its inspiration from Ben Jonson's *Volpone*, film's updated plot centers around the fabulously rich Cecil Fox (Rex Harrison) who with the aid of a sometimes gigolo and secretary, William McFly (Cliff Robertson), plays a joke of sorts on three one-time mistresses by feigning grave illness and gauging their reactions as they come flocking to his bedside.

There is the wisecracking hypochondriac, Mrs Sheridan (Susan Hayward), who was Fox's first love, accompanied by the attractive nurse, Sarah Watkins (Maggie Smith). There's Princess Dominique, a glacially beautiful jetsetter played by Capucine. And there's the ebullient Merle McGill (Edie Adams), a Hollywood star without a care in the world – except for a massive debt to Uncle Sam.

The dialog is often a delight in its hark-back to the days when the turn of a phrase and the tongue-in-cheek were a staple of better Hollywood product. The playing is all of a superior character.

....

■ HONEYSUCKLE ROSE

1980, 119 MINS, US ◇ ⑫ ⊙
Dir Jerry Schatzberg   *Prod* Gene Taft   *Scr* Carol Sobieski, William D. Whitliff, John Binder   *Ph* Robby Muller   *Ed* Aram Avakian, Norman Gay, Mark Laub, Evan Lottman   *Mus* Willie Nelson, Richard Baskin   *Art Dir* Joel Schiller
● Willie Nelson, Dyan Cannon, Amy Irving, Slim Pickens, Joey Floyd, Charles Levin (Warner)

This is not a picture for anybody who doesn't like Willie Nelson. But the picture adroitly blends his musical performances with a gently dramatic acting job in an old-fashioned love story.

Picture catches Nelson at that point in his career around 1970 when his touring band was wildly popular in Texas and nearby regions, but he had yet to break out with the big hit that would make him nationally famous.

Dyan Cannon and Joey Floyd nicely set up Nelson's approaching conflict as the wife and son who wait affectionately at home for him to finish his periodic tours.

Slim Pickens is right on target as the guitar-picking sidekick. Amy Irving is near perfect as the woman who has adored Nelson since girlhood.

☐ 1980: Nomination: Best Song ('On the Road Again')

■ **HONKY TONK FREEWAY**

1981, 107 MINS, US ◇ ⓥ

Dir John Schlesinger   *Prod* Don Boyd, Howard W. Koch Jr   *Scr* Edward Clinton   *Ph* John Bailey   *Ed* Jim Clark   *Mus* George Martin   *Art Dir* Edwin O'Donovan
● Beau Bridges, Hume Cronyn, Beverly D'Angelo, William Devane, Teri Garr, Geraldine Page (Universal/AFD/EMI)

Veteran director John Schlesinger, who was responsible for such screen classics as *Midnight Cowboy* and *Sunday Bloody Sunday,* has concocted a kind of *Nashville on Wheels* here.

The thin story line of this $26 million film revolves around the residents of a small Florida town, Ticlaw, who are miffed that the new super duper freeway won't have an exit for tourists to stop off and spend their money in the area.

Ticlaw's Mayor William Devane tries to bribe some officials for the exit but is double-crossed early on. Major portion of the picture then switches to the collection of people who travel the freeway and eventually (through no fault of their own) wind up in Ticlaw.

Only Hume Cronyn and Jessica Tandy as an offbeat elderly couple, and Deborah Rush as a discontented nun, brighten up the trip along the road. Rest of the cast falls victim to Edward Clinton's meandering script and dismal sense of humor.

■ **HONKYTONK MAN**

1982, 122 MINS, US ◇ ⓥ ⊙

Dir Clint Eastwood   *Prod* Clint Eastwood   *Scr* Clancy Carlile   *Ph* Bruce Surtees   *Ed* Ferris Webster, Michael Kelly, Joel Cox   *Mus* Steve Dorff   *Art Dir* Edward Carfagno
● Clint Eastwood, Kyle Eastwood, John McIntire, Alexa Kenin, Verna Bloom, Matt Clark (Warner/Malpaso)

Honkytonk Man is one of those well-intentioned efforts that doesn't quite work. It seems that Clint Eastwood took great pains in telling this story of an aging, struggling country singer but he is done in by the predictability of the script [from Clancy Carlile's own novel] and his own limitations as a warbler.

It is initially funny to see a drunk Eastwood drive his spiffy car into the rural, Depression-era farm his sister and her burdened family live in. Though he is a breath of fresh air for them, especially his 14-year-old nephew, it soon becomes clear that he is more accurately an alcoholic on his last legs.

Eastwood does his best, though he never really manages to be fully convincing because of his own vocal limitations. His son, Kyle, who has limited acting experience, doesn't seem to know what to do with his key role of the emerging teenager.

■ **HONORARY CONSUL, THE**
(US: Beyond the Limit)

1984, 103 MINS, UK ◇ ⓥ ⊙

Dir John Mackenzie   *Prod* Norma Heyman   *Scr* Christopher Hampton   *Ph* Phil Meheux   *Ed* Stuart Baird   *Mus* Stanley Myers, Richard Harvey   *Art Dir* Allan Cameron
● Michael Caine, Richard Gere, Bob Hoskins, Elpidia Carrillo, Joaquim De Almeida, Geoffrey Palmer (World Film Services)

The Honorary Consul represents a weak attempt to adapt Graham Greene's 1973 novel for the screen. Strong talents on both sides of the camera haven't managed to breathe life into this intricate tale of emotional and political betrayal and result is a steady dose of tedium.

Greene's central character was one Eduardo Plarr, a half-Paraguayan, half-British doctor in provincial Argentina who quietly assists some revolutionaries in their attempt to kidnap the American ambassador and equally casually impregnates the very young native wife of the besotted honorary consul from Britain, Charley Fortnum. The rebels blunderingly capture Fortnum instead of the intended Yank, but detain and threaten to execute him anyway unless some of their comrades are released from prison.

First handicap is the casting of Richard Gere as the dispirited Englishman. Actor's accent only manages to stay on course when his lines consist of five words or less. Gere performs another of his seemingly obligatory post-shower nude scenes here, as well as a couple of in-the-buff sex scenes with Elpidia Carrillo, first seen in *The Border,* and acquits herself in decent fashion as a former prostie who opts for a life of leisure with the consul.

Acting honors easily fall to Michael Caine as the small-time, dipsomaniacal diplomat. Character in the book was in his 60s, but Caine proves an ideal choice. Bob Hoskins registers strongly as a heartless but engaging South American police chief.

Playwright Christopher Hampton's script faithfully follows the dramatic line of the Greene tale, but virtually eliminates the subtle religious, moral and political discussions which were really the substance of the work.

Using Mexican locales, director John Mackenzie and lenser Phil Meheux have evoked a good sense of place, but end result is on the dull side.

■ **HOODLUM PRIEST, THE**

1961, 100 MINS, US

Dir Irvin Kershner   *Prod* Don Murray, Walter Wood   *Scr* Don Deer [= Don Murray], Joseph Landon   *Ph* Haskell Wexler   *Ed* Maurice Wright   *Mus* Richard Markowitz   *Art Dir* Jack Poplin
● Don Murray, Larry Gates, Cindi Wood, Keir Dullea, Logan Ramsey (United Artists)

Biographically based on the offbeat activities of the Rev Charles Dismas Clark, a Jesuit priest in St Louis noted for his rehabilitation work with ex-cons, the screenplay pinpoints Clark's problems against the tragedy of a confused, but far from hopeless, youth who pays with his life for crimes of which he is not solely responsible. Along the way, the writers illustrate the necessity of meeting ex-cons on their own terms to urge them away from a life of crime, and even take a swipe at capital punishment, going right into the gas chamber to do so in the film's most powerful scene.

The picture, largely photographed in St Louis, is burdened with loose motivational ends and has a tendency to skip over key expository details. But it is a case of the whole justifying its parts. The moving parts are erratic, but the machine does its job.

Don Murray gives a vigorous, sincere performance in the title role. But the film's most moving portrayal is delivered by Keir Dullea

as the doomed lad. Larry Gates manages to be effective as an attorney whose motivations aren't quite clear.

■ **HOOK**

1991, 144 MINS, US ◇ ⓥ ⊙

Dir Steven Spielberg   *Prod* Kathleen Kennedy, Frank Marshall, Gerald R. Molen   *Scr* Jim V. Hart, Malia Scotch Marmo   *Ph* Dean Cundey   *Ed* Michael Kahn   *Mus* John Williams   *Art Dir* Norman Garwood
● Dustin Hoffman, Robin Williams, Julia Roberts, Bob Hoskins, Maggie Smith, Charlie Korsmo (Tri-Star/Amblin)

Hook feels as much like a massive amusement park ride as it does a film. Spirited, rambunctious, often messy and undisciplined, this determined attempt to recast the Peter Pan story in contempo terms [from a screen story by Jim V. Hart and Nick Castle, from J.M. Barrie's play and books] splashes every bit of its megabudget (between $60 million and $80 million) onto the screen.

Screenplay sends a modern, grown-up Peter, a man who has forgotten his youth, back to Neverland to rescue his children from the clutches of the ever-vengeful Captain Hook.

Setup is deftly done, sweeping the viewer right into the world of the Banning family. Peter (Robin Williams) is a workaholic corporate attorney. But he manages to tear himself away to take his wife Moira (Caroline Goodall) and children Jack (Charlie Korsmo) and Maggie (Amber Scott) to London to visit Granny Wendy (Maggie Smith).

Back in Blighty, Jack and Maggie are spirited away, courtesy of Captain James Hook. Mystified, Peter is visited by Tinkerbell (Julia Roberts) and, 36 minutes into the story, is transported to Neverland, where Hook (Dustin Hoffman) lords over a raucous Pirate Town from the deck of his enormous ship.

Sweet and likable through the first half-hour, pic becomes dominated by a vaudeville tone and in-jokes during the pirate section (Glenn Close turns up in a male disguise as a sailor victimized by Hook).

Despite the cascade of wondrous special effects, massive battles between the kids and pirates and face-offs between Pan and Hook, the film doesn't truly take flight. Jokiness gets the better of both Hoffman and Bob Hoskins, who plays the captain's loyal hand Smee. Williams inhabits the main role splendidly. But the standout supporting turns come from Smith, perfect as the aged Wendy, and Goodall.

☐ 1991: Nominations: Best Art Direction, Costume Design, Song ('When You're Alone'), Makeup, Visual Effects

■ **HOOPER**

1978, 99 MINS, US ◇ ⓥ ⊙

Dir Hal Needham   *Prod* Hank Moonjean   *Scr* Thomas Rickman, Bill Kerby   *Ph* Bobby Byrne   *Ed* Donn Cambern   *Mus* Bill Justis   *Art Dir* Hilyard Brown
● Burt Reynolds, Jan-Michael Vincent, Sally Field, Brian Keith, John Marley, James Best (Warner/Reynolds-Gordon)

Individually, the performances in this story of three generations of Hollywood stuntmen are a delight. And Hal Needham's direction and stunt staging are wonderfully crafted.

But it's the ensemble work of Burt Reynolds, Jan-Michael Vincent, Sally Field and Brian Keith, with an able assist from Robert Klein, which boosts an otherwise pedestrian story with lots of crashes and daredevil antics into a touching and likable piece.

Reynolds, in a further extension of his brash, off-handed wise guy screen persona, plays the world's greatest stuntman. He took over that position 20 years back from Brian Keith. His status is being challenged by newcomer Jan-Michael Vincent.

H

To cement a place in the stuntman's record books, Reynolds must perform one last stunt, in this case a 325-foot jump in a jet-powered car over a collapsed bridge. All this is to take place in a film, *The Spy Who Laughed At Danger*, some sort of a disaster James Bond type picture being directed by the deliciously obnoxious Klein.

Besides the final jump over the bridge, Needham and stunt coordinator Bobby Bass have arranged a smorgasbord of stunts – car crashes, barroom brawls, chariot races, helicopter jumps and motorcycle slides.

☐ 1978: Nomination: Best Sound

....

■ HOOSIERS
(UK: Best Shot)

1986, 114 MINS, US ◇ ⑨ ⊙
Dir David Anspaugh   *Prod* Carter De Haven, Angelo Pizzo   *Scr* Angelo Pizzo   *Ph* Fred Murphy   *Ed* C. Timothy O'Meara   *Mus* Jerry Goldsmith   *Art Dir* David Nichols
● Gene Hackman, Barbara Hershey, Dennis Hopper, Sheb Wooley, Fern Persons, Brad Boyle (Hemdale)

Hoosiers is an involving tale about the unlikely success of a smalltown Indiana high school basketball team that paradoxically proves both rousing and too conventional, centered around a fine performance by Gene Hackman as the coach.

During the opening reels, first-time feature director David Anspaugh paints a richly textured portrait of 1951 rural American life, both visually and through glimpses of the guarded reticence of the people. Dialog rings true, and the characters are neither sentimentalized nor caricatured. Tension is built nicely as the farmboys advance through the playoffs.

Pic belongs to Hackman, but Dennis Hopper gets another opportunity to put in a showy turn as a local misfit.

☐ 1986: Nominations: Best Supp. Actor (Dennis Hopper), Original Score

....

■ HOPE AND GLORY

1987, 113 MINS, UK ◇ ⑨ ⊙
Dir John Boorman   *Prod* John Boorman   *Scr* John Boorman   *Ph* Philippe Rousselot   *Ed* Ian Crafford   *Mus* Peter Martin   *Art Dir* Anthony Pratt
● Sarah Miles, David Hayman, Derrick O'Connor, Susan Wooldridge, Sammi Davis, Ian Bannen (Columbia)

Essentially a collection of sweetly autobiographical anecdotes of English family life during World War II.

Tale is narrated from an adult perspective by Billy, an exquisite-looking nine-year-old who finds great excitement in the details of warfare but also has the air of a detached observer and, therefore, possible future writer.

Best scenes are those with Billy centerstage, and particularly those showing the unthinking callousness kids can display in the face of others' misfortune and tragedy.

Then the Rohan family's home is destroyed, and mom Sarah Miles takes the kids out to grandpa's idyllic home by a river in the country, where the raging conflict becomes an afterthought.

Happily, young Sebastian Rice-Edwards is a marvelous camera subject and holds the center well as Bill. His younger sister, played by Geraldine Muir, is even cuter, as is Sara Langton as the girl whose mother is killed. The adults, however, come off rather less well, with Sarah Miles overdoing things and projecting little inner feeling and no one else making much of an impression.

☐ 1987: Nominations: Best Picture, Director, Original Screenplay, Cinematography, Art Direction

....

■ HOPSCOTCH

1980, 104 MINS, US ◇ ⑨ ⊙
Dir Ronald Neame   *Prod* Edie Landau, Ely Landau   *Scr* Brian Garfield, Bryan Forbes   *Ph* Arthur Ibbetson   *Ed* Carl Kress   *Mus* Ian Fraser   *Art Dir* William Creber
● Walter Matthau, Glenda Jackson, Ned Beatty, Sam Waterston, Herbert Lom (Avco Embassy)

Hopscotch is a high-spirited caper comedy which, unfortunately, reaches its peak too soon.

Grizzled as usual, Walter Matthau plays CIA agent whose independent ways are too much for his finicky, double-dealing boss (Ned Beatty). So Matthau is put in charge of the files.

But he never shows up for the new assignment, deciding instead to hide out and write a book that will embarrass not only the CIA but spies in every country, making himself a target for extinction from several directions.

Hiding out, Matthau takes up with Glenda Jackson. They are old flames and their initial moments together serve up the same good bantering chemistry of *House Calls*.

It's all for laughs as Matthau evades the hunters while dreaming up additional ways to make fools of them.

....

■ HORIZONS WEST

1952, 80 MINS, US ◇ ⑨
Dir Budd Boetticher   *Prod* Albert J. Cohen   *Scr* Louis Stevens   *Ph* Charles P. Boyle   *Ed* Ted J. Kent   *Mus* Joseph Gershenson   *Art Dir* Bernard Herzbrun, Robert Clatworthy
● Robert Ryan, Julie Adams, Rock Hudson, John McIntire, Raymond Burr, James Arness (Universal)

Plot is laid in the post-War Between the States period, opening with three Texans returning to their home state. Rock Hudson and James Arness welcome a resumption of ranching, but Robert Ryan's ambition is for a quick dollar. He turns his attention towards easy money and a desire to build a western empire.

From a rather slow start, it then becomes a session of pretentious, cliche-laden talk that even spurts of hardy action fail to enliven. Ryan does what he can with his character but beyond endowing it with a certain ruthless ruggedness can't make it believable enough to carry the tale.

Hudson turns in a sympathetic performance, and Arness is good as the brothers' soldiering buddy. Julie Adams makes a pretty picture as the widow with an eye for Ryan.

....

■ HORN BLOWS AT MIDNIGHT, THE

1945, 80 MINS, US
Dir Raoul Walsh   *Prod* Mark Hellinger   *Scr* Sam Hellman, James V, Kern   *Ph* Sid Hickox   *Ed* Irene Morra   *Mus* Franz Waxman   *Art Dir* Hugh Reticker, Clarence Steensen
● Jack Benny, Alexis Smith, Guy Kibbee, Margaret Dumont, Dolores Moran, Reginald Gardiner (Warner)

This one is a lightweight comedy that never seems able to make up its mind whether to be fantasy or broad slapstick. There are some good laughs but generally *The Horn Blows at Midnight* is not solid.

Jack Benny works hard for his laughs and some come through with a sock, but generally the chuckles are dragged in and overworked. Biggest howls are the scenes depicting Benny and others dangling from atop a 40-story building.

Benny plays third trumpet in a radio station orch. Falling asleep during reading of commercials, Benny dreams he's an angel in Heaven – and still playing third trumpet. The Big Chief, disgusted with conditions on the planet earth, dispatches Benny to earth to destroy it. The angel is to blow his special horn promptly at midnight, the blast to do away with the earth.

Heaven, as depicted, is certainly not a very soul-satisfying spot. It's portrayed as a satire on government and the many bureaus and sub-bureaus, etc.

....

■ HORROR OF DRACULA
See: Dracula (1958)

....

■ HORSE FEATHERS

1932, 70 MINS, US ◇ ⑨ ⊙
Dir Norman Z. McLeod   *Scr* Bert Kalmar, Harry Ruby, S. J. Perelman, Will B. Johnstone   *Ph* Ray June
● Groucho Marx, Chico Marx, Harpo Marx, Zeppo Marx, Thelma Todd, David Landau (Paramount)

The madcap Marxes, in one of their maddest screen frolics, the premise of Groucho Marx as the college prexy and his three aides and abettors putting Huxley College on the gridiron map promises much and delivers more.

Zeppo is his usual straight opposite Thelma Todd as the college widow. She's a luscious eyeful and swell foil for the Marxian boudoir manhandling, which is getting to be a trademarked comedy routine.

On the matter of formula, the harp and piano numbers were repeated against the Marxes' personal wishes but by exhibitor demands to the studio. The piano is oke, but the harp reprise of 'Everyone Says I Love You' (by Bert Kalmar and Harry Ruby) substantiates the boys' opinion that it tends to slow up the comedy.

The plot, such as it is, is motivated around gambler David Landau's planting of two pros on the Darwin team which meets Huxley. Groucho visits the speak where the Darwin ringers have been engaged and mistakes dogcatcher Harpo and bootlegging iceman Chico as gridiron material.

....

■ HORSEMEN, THE

1971, 108 MINS, US ◇ ⑨
Dir John Frankenheimer   *Prod* Edward Lewis   *Scr* Dalton Trumbo   *Ph* Claude Renoir   *Ed* Harold Kress   *Mus* Georges Delerue   *Art Dir* Pierre Thevenet
● Omar Sharif, Leigh Taylor-Young, Jack Palance, David De, Peter Jeffrey, Mohammed Shamsi (Columbia)

The Horsemen is a would-be epic stretched thin across Hollywood's 'profound peasant' tradition. It's a misfire, despite offbeat Afghanistan locations and some bizarre action sequences.

Omar Sharif, son of rural Afghanistan clan leader Jack Palance, is injured and humiliated (he thinks) in a brutal ritual soccer-type game played with the headless carcass of a calf. Returning home in company of his now treacherous servant (David De) and a wandering 'untouchable' out for his money (Leigh Taylor-Young), Sharif's leg is amputated below the knee in a remote mountain village. Back with his clan, Sharif forgives De and Taylor-Young for two attempts they made on his life and then trains hard to reestablish his honor and reputation as the greatest horseman in the area.

Dalton Trumbo's cliche script, based on the novel by Joseph Kessel, opts for the kind of mock-poetic dialog even Hugh Griffith might have trouble mouthing. Sharif, however, maintains his composure.

....

■ HORSE SOLDIERS, THE

1959, 120 MINS, US ◇ ⑨
Dir John Ford   *Prod* John Lee Mahin, Martin Rackin   *Scr* John Lee Mahin, Martin Rackin   *Ph* William Clothier   *Mus* David Buttolph
● John Wayne, William Holden, Constance Towers, Althea Gibson, Hoot Gibson, Anna Lee (Mirisch)

Give John Ford a company of brawny men, let

him train his cameras on the US cavalry and provide a script with plenty of action and he's off on the road to glory. In *The Horse Soldiers*, which involves a little-known incident in the Civil War, all these elements are present.

This is the story [from the novel by Harold Sinclair] of Colonel Benjamin Grierson who, in April of 1863, was ordered by General Grant to take three cavalry regiments and ride 300 miles into the heart of the Confederacy to destroy the rail link between Newton Station and Vicksburg and thus choke off supplies from Southern-held Vicksburg.

But with all of Ford's skill for staging battle scenes, and his superb eye for pictorial composition, the film is extremely uneven. The long shots of men on horses tend to become tedious and they considerably slow up the flow of the story. Also, the dramatic scenes involving John Wayne, William Holden and newcomer Constance Towers don't come off with much conviction.

William Clothier's photography is outstanding. Some of the scenes have the quality of paintings. As in all of the Ford films, the music has a fitting, masculine quality, being sung mostly by a male chorus.

．．．．．．．．．．．．．．．．．．．．．．．．．．．．．

■ HOSPITAL, THE

1971, 103 MINS, US ◇ ▽

Dir Arthur Hiller   *Prod* Howard Gottfried   *Scr* Paddy Chayefsky   *Ph* Victor J. Kemper   *Ed* Eric Albertson   *Mus* Morris Surdin   *Art Dir* Gene Rudolf

● George C. Scott, Diana Rigg, Barnard Hughes, Nancy Marchand, Stephen Elliott, Donald Harron (United Artists)

The Hospital is a civilian mis-*MASH*. George C. Scott stars as a NY medical center chief surgeon whose ruined personal life alternates with a daily routine of apparently inept, callous, bored, overworked and murdered staff members. Diana Rigg is the daughter of a deranged doctor-patient whose unmasking destroys most of author Paddy Chayefsky's basic premise.

In the plot's medico environment stands Scott, at 53 a washout as husband and father and on the verge of suicide. The heavily sprayed-on sociological angle is that hospitals today treat patients like baggage.

Rigg turns Scott on to the promise of a peaceful life in the western mountains; she is in the hospital because father Barnard Hughes, a gone-berserk Boston doctor, has been treated in bungled fashion by Richard Dysart, a medic whose eye is on the stock market more than his avowed profession.

The film is larded with vignettes strung on a series of mysterious murders: girl-chasing doctor Lenny Baker, internist Robert Anthony and nurse Angie Ortega.
□ 1971: Best Original Story & Screenplay.
□ Nomination: Best Actor (George C. Scott)

．．．．．．．．．．．．．．．．．．．．．．．．．．．．．

■ HOTEL

1967, 124 MINS, US ◇ ▽

Dir Richard Quine   *Prod* Wendell Mayes   *Scr* Wendell Mayes   *Ph* Charles Lang   *Ed* Sam O'Steen   *Mus* Johnny Keating   *Art Dir* Cary Odell

● Rod Taylor, Catherine Spaak, Karl Malden, Melvyn Douglas, Merle Oberon, Richard Conte (Warner)

Hotel is a very well made, handsomely produced drama about the guests and management of an old hostelry which must modernize or shutter. Uniformly strong performances, scripting and direction make for good pacing.

In an impressive debut as a film producer, Wendell Mayes has dressed the pic with lush settings and wardrobe, while not neglecting scripting chores in adapting Arthur Hailey's novel.

Merle Oberon, dripping in gems, registers well as the wife of Michael Rennie, whose hit-

and-run driving cues a blackmail attempt by house gumshoe Richard Conte. Catherine Spaak, in her US film debut, is charming and sexy as Kevin McCarthy's mistress who drifts to Rod Taylor. Karl Malden has a choice role of a key thief who is frustrated at many turns by double-crossing accomplices.

．．．．．．．．．．．．．．．．．．．．．．．．．．．．．

■ HOTEL BERLIN

1945, 98 MINS, US

Dir Peter Godfrey   *Prod* Louis F. Edelman   *Scr* Jo Pagano, Alvah Bessie   *Ph* Carl Guthrie   *Ed* Frank Magee   *Mus* Franz Waxman   *Art Dir* John Hughes

● Helmut Dantine, Andrea King, Raymond Massey, Faye Emerson, Peter Lorre, Alan Hale (Warner)

Grand Hotel in a 1945 Nazi setting, now known as *Hotel Berlin*, [both of them based on novels by Vicki Baum] is socko. The war's already lost – or, at least, there's that defeatist aura about Hotel Berlin – and the Nazi higherups are packing their loot for a South American getaway.

Producer Lou Edelman has guided his charges well. Productionally the lavishness is by suggestion rather than in reality. There are the periodic Allied air blitzes which chase everybody into the shelters, but otherwise it's a Grand Hotel in the lobby or on the sundry floors, but particularly in the apartments of a general (Raymond Massey), an informer (Faye Emerson), or a theatre darling (Andrea King).

There are many suspenseful touches right along. The footage is replete with arresting meller. Whether it's Dickie Tyler as the resourceful little bellboy of the underground, or the femme star who apparently first falls for Helmut Dantine (the escaped anti-Nazi) and later would turn him in, the situations are constantly intriguing.

．．．．．．．．．．．．．．．．．．．．．．．．．．．．．

■ HOTEL IMPERIAL

1927, 67 MINS, US ⊗

Dir Mauritz Stiller   *Prod* Erich Pommer   *Scr* Jules Furthman   *Ph* Bert Glennon

● Pola Negri, James Hall, George Siegmann (Paramount)

In direction and camerawork the picture [based on a play by Lajos Biro] stands out, but the story isn't one that is going to give anyone a great thrill. Mauritz Stiller and Erich Pommer have done their work well, and they have made Pola Negri look like a gorgeous beauty in some shots, and effectively handled her in others, such as her scenes with the Russian general, but to what avail are good direction and supervision, plus acting, when the story isn't there?

It has to do with the advance of Russian armies into Galicia after their defeat of the Austrians. The Hotel Imperial is located in one of the border towns of Austria-Hungary. Here a fleeing Austrian hussar seeks rest and is caught behind the lines of the enemy when they move into the town.

Negri, as the hotel slavey, shelters him and suggests that he act as the waiter to cover himself. The Russian general makes the hotel his headquarters and falls for the girl. The waiter, in turn, loves her also and she reciprocates his feeling.

A corking leading man is James Hall. He has an air that denotes that he is capable of real things in picture work. George Siegmann, as the Russian general, puts all that there should be into the heavy.

．．．．．．．．．．．．．．．．．．．．．．．．．．．．．

■ HOTEL NEW HAMPSHIRE, THE

1984, 110 MINS, US ◇ ▽ ⊙

Dir Tony Richardson   *Prod* Neil Hartley   *Scr* Tony Richardson   *Ph* David Watkin   *Ed* Robert K. Lambert   *Mus* Jacques Offenbach, Raymond Leppard

Art Dir Jocelyn Herbert

● Jodie Foster, Beau Bridges, Rob Lowe, Nastassja Kinski, Wilford Brimley, Dorsey Wright (Woodfall)

While it is decidedly not to all tastes, *The Hotel New Hampshire* is a fascinating, largely successful adaptation of John Irving's 1981 novel. Writer-director Tony Richardson has pulled off a remarkable stylistic tight-rope act, establishing a bizarre tone of morbid whimsicality at the outset and sustaining it throughout.

Tale concerns an eccentric New England family that, spurred on by an ever-searching father, establishes a new hotel in locale after locale and mutates in the process.

Among the unusual family members is Jodie Foster, who must endure a punishing gang rape and a prolonged fascination with the young man who did it; her brother, Rob Lowe, an impossibly good-looking fellow who takes on most of the women in the cast; their 'queer' brother Paul McCrane; and their little sister Jennie Dundas.

Also virtually part of the family by association, if not by blood, are black jock Dorsey Wright; voluptuous hotel waitress Anita Morris; and Nastassja Kinski, a girl so insecure that she hides most of the time inside an enormous bear suit.

．．．．．．．．．．．．．．．．．．．．．．．．．．．．．

■ HOTEL PARADISO

1966, 100 MINS, UK ◇

Dir Peter Glenville   *Prod* Peter Glenville   *Scr* Peter Glenville, Jean-Claude Carriere   *Ph* Henri Decae   *Ed* Anne V. Coates   *Mus* Laurence Rosen   *Art Dir* Francois de Lamothe

● Alec Guinness, Gina Lollobrigida, Robert Morley, Peggy Mount, Akim Tamiroff, Marie Bell (M-G-M)

Film version of Georges Feydeau's turn-of-the-century *L'hotel du libre echange* is a second generation production of Peter Glenville's legit revival of the French farceur in London.

Plot involves a complicated series of mishaps triggered by the 40-year-old 'itch' of M. Boniface, played with wearily glossy perfection by Alec Guinness, for the wife of his next-door neighbor, Henri Cot, assayed with appropriate bluster by Robert Morley. Miffed by her neglectful husband, Mme Cot, adequately acted by Gina Lollobrigida, succumbs to Boniface's suggestion that they rendezvous at the seedy Parisian assignation locale, Hotel Paradiso.

A concatenation of endless coincidences, laboriously contrived for the better part of the film, conspire to relegate the rendezvous to farce.

Main problem with the film is a bloodless script. Glenville, in an attempt to infuse theatrical brio into the play, only succeeds in over-stylizing it.

．．．．．．．．．．．．．．．．．．．．．．．．．．．．．

■ HOT ENOUGH FOR JUNE

(US: Agent 8¾)

1964, 98 MINS, UK ◇

Dir Ralph Thomas   *Prod* Betty E. Box   *Scr* Lukas Heller   *Ph* Ernest Steward   *Ed* Alfred Roome   *Mus* Angelo Lavagnino   *Art Dir* Syd Cain

● Dirk Bogarde, Sylva Koscina, Robert Morley, Leo McKern, Roger Delgado, John Le Mesurier (Rank)

A faster pace from director Ralph Thomas and a few more red herrings and surprise situations could have worked wonders in lifting this amiable enough spoof of espionage into a top league comedy-thriller.

June is by no means a skit on the Bond adventures. It is simply a genial leg-pull of some of the situations which, in tougher circumstances, Bond might easily be facing. Dirk Bogarde, who plays the hero with ingratiating efficiency, is an unsuccessful writer, content to live on national assistance. When the Labour Exchange unexpectedly sends him to take up a post as a trainee junior-executive in a glassworks, Bogarde finds the combination of a good salary and useful expenses irresistible. He is assigned to visit a Czech factory and bring back a written message which he guilelessly believes to be a simple commercial job. He does not know that he is now attached to the Espionage Department of the Foreign Office.

Most of the humor comes from witty prods at the expense of the Foreign Office and the Iron Curtain Party system. Robert Morley is superb as the boss of the department, with his old Etonian tie, benign plottings and general appearance of a well-poised walrus.

● ●

■ HOT MILLIONS

1968, 106 MINS, UK ◇

Dir Eric Till   *Prod* Mildred Freed Alberg   *Scr* Ira Wallach, Peter Ustinov   *Ph* Ken Higgins   *Ed* Richard Marden   *Mus* Laurie Johnson   *Art Dir* Bill Andrews
● Peter Ustinov, Maggie Smith, Karl Malden, Bob Newhart, Robert Morley, Cesar Romero (M-G-M)

Very good writing, excellent acting, zesty direction and pacing, and handsome production make this story of computer embezzlement a strong laugh-getter. Peter Ustinov, Maggie Smith and Karl Malden, plus Bob Newhart and cameos by Robert Morley and Cesar Romero, comprise the talented cast.

The screenplay gives motivated development to characters, all of whom hit the target. Ustinov, released from prison, decides that the modern embezzler must be a computer expert. Conning his way into the good graces of Malden, head of the British wing of an American industrial conglomerate, Ustinov eventually programs into the computer three phony companies, to which large checks are sent.

Complicating Ustinov's progress are Newhart, suspicious assistant to Malden, and Smith, who falls for Ustinov.

Ustinov makes as good an ensemble player as in his solo moments. Malden is excellent in a well-restrained, broad interpretation.
□ 1968: Nomination: Best Original Story & Screenplay

● ●

■ HOT ROCK, THE

(UK: How to Steal a Diamond in Four Uneasy Lessons)

1972, 105 MINS, US ◇ ⊚

Dir Peter Yates   *Prod* Hal Landers, Bobby Roberts   *Scr* William Goldman   *Ph* Ed Brown   *Ed* Frank P. Keller, Fred W. Berger   *Mus* Quincy Jones   *Art Dir* John Robert Lloyd
● Robert Redford, George Segal, Ron Leibman, Paul Sand, Zero Mostel, Moses Gunn (20th Century Fox)

With its mixture of suspense, satire and broad comedy, *The Hot Rock* emerges as an offbeat crime feature. Stars Robert Redford and George Segal head a quartet of thieves who usually miss the objective, here a famous diamond which inspired the title of the piece.

Peter Yates' direction and uniformly good cast partly overcome a William Goldman script [from Donald E. Westlake's novel] that has many exciting and funny bits, but lacks a clear, unifying thrust.

However, the plot involves four separate heists, and, given the deliberate exposition of the human frailty of the hoods, the sequential capers lose a lot of momentum, giving the film as a whole the look of a spliced-together multi-episode TV show.
□ 1972: Nomination: Best Editing

● ●

■ HOT SHOTS!

1991, 85 MINS, US ◇ ⊚ ⊙

Dir Jim Abrahams   *Prod* Bill Badalato   *Scr* Jim Abrahams, Pat Proft   *Ph* Bill Butler   *Ed* Jane Kurson, Eric Sears   *Mus* Sylvester LeVay   *Art Dir* William A. Elliot

● Charlie Sheen, Cary Elwes, Valeria Golino, Lloyd Bridges, Kevin Dunn, Kristy Swanson (20th Century Fox/PAP)

Jim Abrahams tries to tap the zany *Airplane!* vein with this *Top Gun* spoof but bats far too low a percentage with the usual rapid-fire assault of numbingly stupid gags. Pic bogs down in motion picture in-jokes, drawing liberally on *Top Gun* and *An Officer and a Gentleman*, while intercutting homages to scenes from *The Fabulous Baker Boys*, *9½ Weeks* and *Gone with the Wind*.

Charlie Sheen is the maverick pilot competing with self-obsessed Kent (Cary Elwes). One film spoof does provide the biggest belly laugh, quite literally, when Sheen begins erotically feeding Valeria Golino grapes and, in escalating passion, cooks breakfast on her sizzling stomach.

Most characters are gratingly cartoonish, especially Lloyd Bridges' way over-the-top tin-headed admiral.

● ●

■ HOT SHOTS! PART DEUX

1993, 89 MINS, US ◇ ⊚ ⊙

Dir Jim Abrahams   *Prod* Bill Badalato   *Scr* Jim Abrahams, Pat Proft   *Ph* John R. Leonetti   *Ed* Malcolm Campbell   *Mus* Basil Poledouris   *Art Dir* William A. Elliot
● Charlie Sheen, Lloyd Bridges, Valeria Golino, Richard Crenna, Brenda Bakke, Miguel Ferrer (20th Century-Fox)

This much better sequel is a clever spoof of *Rambo* and a dozen other movies that employs the usual scattershot *Airplane!* approach but boasts a higher shooting percentage than its forebear.

The latest raid uses the *Rambo* and *Missing in Action* series to pull the audience along, and finds time to throw in clever skewerings of numerous other films, among them *Apocalypse Now*, *Casablanca*, *Star Wars*, *The Wizard of Oz*, even *Lady and the Tramp*.

Charlie Sheen, with wild locks and a buffed-up physique, returns as Topper Harley, recruited by a former commander (Richard Crenna, a brilliant bit of casting due to his *Rambo* role) and a stunningly limber CIA agent (Brenda Bakke) to try to rescue US servicemen held prisoner after Desert Storm.

Valeria Golino also returns as Sheen's former love interest though Bakke, with her impossibly short dresses, serves as the primary ice cube-melting surface this time around.

Technically, pic doesn't cut corners just because it's a parody. If you haven't seen *The Crying Game*, don't read the closing credits.

● ●

■ HOT SPOT, THE

1990, 120 MINS, US ◇ ⊚ ⊙

Dir Dennis Hopper   *Prod* Paul Lewis, Deborah Capograsso   *Scr* Nona Tyson, Charles Williams   *Ph* Ueli Steiger   *Ed* Wende Pheiffer Mate   *Mus* Jack Nitzsche   *Art Dir* Cary White
● Don Johnson, Virginia Madsen, Jennifer Connelly, Charles Martin Smith, William Sadler, Barry Corbin (Orion)

Director Dennis Hopper just won't say no to kinky amorality, and that's all to the good in this twisting, languorous and very sexy thriller [based on Charles Williams' novel *Hell Hath No Fury*].

Hopper elicits a sharp, understated performance from *Miami Vice* star Don Johnson, who's neither a cop nor a good guy here. As the low-key, manipulative drifter Harry Madox, Johnson shakes things up in a godforsaken Texas town, where his job at a used car lot involves him with two restless women yearning to beat the heat.

Gloria Harper (Jennifer Connelly) is the sweetly stunning office girl; Dolly Harshaw (Virginia Madsen) is the irresistibly tempting boss' wife. This is the type of town, says Madsen, where there are 'only two things to

do', and one of them is watching TV. Johnson charts a sexual collision course with both women. But he has another agenda. Once he's insinuated himself into the town, Johnson aims to con the yokels.

Hopper clearly was impressed by what he learned from working with David Lynch on *Blue Velvet*. *The Hot Spot* seeps with atmosphere, unfolds at a deceptively relaxed pace, steadily accumulates noirish grit, then dizzily plunges into a Lynch-like plumbing of the dark passions and nasty secrets at the heart of Main Street, USA.

● ●

■ HOUDINI

1953, 105 MINS, US ◇ ⊚

Dir George Marshall   *Prod* George Pal   *Scr* Philip Yordan   *Ph* Ernest Laszlo   *Ed* George Tomasini   *Mus* Roy Webb   *Art Dir* Hal Pereira, Al Nozaki
● Tony Curtis, Janet Leigh, Torin Thatcher, Angela Clarke, Douglas Spencer, Sig Ruman (Paramount)

A typical screen biography, presenting a rather fanciful version of Houdini's life. Production does well by illusions and escapes on which Houdini won his fame, using these tricks to give substance to a plot that uses a backstage formula that follows pat lines. Under George Marshall's direction, story spins along nicely, with occasional emphasis on drama in several of escape sequences to keep interest up. Performances of two stars are likeable, although neither shows any aging in the time span that covers Houdini from 21 to death.

Screenplay, based on book by Harold Kellock, opens at the turn of the century to find Houdini performing as a 'wild man' and magician in Schultz' Dime Museum in New York. To this amusement spot comes a group of school girls, including Janet Leigh, and Houdini (Tony Curtis) is attracted to her. After an extremely brief courtship, they marry, try an act together, before she persuades him to take a job in a lock factory. Later, after winning a prize at a magicians' convention, Houdini and his bride go to Europe and he becomes a success with miracle escapes.

● ●

■ HOUND OF THE BASKERVILLES, THE

1939, 78 MINS, US ⊚ ⊙

Dir Sidney Lanfield   *Prod* Gene Markey   *Scr* Ernest Pascal   *Ph* Peverell Marley   *Ed* Robert Simpson   *Mus* Cyril J. Mockridge   *Art Dir* Richard Day, Hans Peters
● Richard Greene, Basil Rathbone, Nigel Bruce, Lionel Atwill, John Carradine, Wendy Barrie (20th Century-Fox)

The Hound of the Baskervilles retains all of the suspensefully dramatic ingredients of Conan Doyle's popular adventure of Sherlock Holmes. It's a startling mystery-chiller developed along logical lines without resorting to implausible situations and over-theatrics.

Doyle's tale of mystery surrounding the Baskerville castle is a familiar one. When Lionel Atwill learns that Richard Greene, heir to the estate, is marked for death, he calls in Basil Rathbone.

Rathbone gives a most effective characterization of Sherlock Holmes. Greene, in addition to playing the intended victim of the murderer, is the romantic interest opposite Wendy Barrie.

Chiller mood generated by the characters and story is heightened by effects secured from sequences in the medieval castle and the dreaded fogbound moors. Low key photography by Peverell Marley adds to suspense.

● ●

■ HOUND OF THE BASKERVILLES, THE

1959, 88 MINS, UK ◇ ⊚

Dir Terence Fisher   *Prod* Anthony Hinds   *Scr* Peter Bryan   *Ph* Jack Asher   *Ed* James Needs   *Mus* James Bernard   *Art Dir* Bernard Robinson

● Peter Cushing, Andre Morell, Christopher Lee, Marla Landi, Miles Malleson, David Oxley (Hammer)

This first Sherlock Holmes pic in color takes place in the desolate setting of Dartmoor. The private eye and his faithful stooge, Doctor Watson, are called in following the mysterious slaying of Sir Charles Baskerville. It's thought that his successor, Sir Henry, may meet the same fate.

It is difficult to fault the performance of Peter Cushing, who looks, talks and behaves in precisely the way approved by the Sherlock Holmes Society. Andre Morell is also a very good Watson – stolid, reliable and not as stupidly bovine as he is sometimes depicted. Christopher Lee has a fairly colorless role as the potential victim of the legendary hound, but he plays it competently. Miles Malleson contributes most of the rare humor with one of his first class studies, as a bumbling bishop.

Terence Fisher's direction captures the eeriness of the atmosphere. Some of the settings are a shade stagey but Jack Asher's lensing also helps to build up the dank gloom of the Dartmoor area.

■ **HOUNDS OF ZAROFF, THE**
See: The Most Dangerous Game

■ **HOUR OF GLORY**
See: The Small Back Room

■ **HOUR OF THE GUN**

1967, 101 MINS, US ◇ ⓥ
Dir John Sturges   *Prod* John Sturges   *Scr* Edward Anhalt   *Ph* Lucien Ballard   *Ed* Ferris Webster   *Mus* Jerry Goldsmith   *Art Dir* Alfred Ybarra
● James Garner, Jason Robards, Robert Ryan, Albert Salmi, Charles Aidman, Steve Ihnat (United Artists/Mirisch)

Edward Anhalt, using Douglas D. Martin's *Tombstone's Epitaph*, has fashioned a heavily-populated script which traces Wyatt Earp's moral decline from a lawman to one bent on personal revenge. Produced under earlier title of *The Law and Tombstone*, it continues the story of Earp after *Gunfight at the O.K. Corral.*

Unfortunately, for any filmmaker, probing too deeply into the character of folk heroes reveals them to be fallible human beings – which they are, of course – but to mass audiences, who create fantasies, such exposition is unsettling. Reality often makes for poor drama.

Jason Robards and James Garner play well together, the former supplying an adroit irony in that he, an admitted gambler as much outside the law as in, becomes more moral as Garner lapses into personal vendetta. Robert Ryan is a perfect heavy.

■ **HOUSE**

1986, 92 MINS, US ◇ ⓥ ☉
Dir Steve Miner   *Prod* Sean S. Cunningham   *Scr* Ethan Wiley   *Ph* Mac Ahlberg   *Ed* Michael N. Knue   *Mus* Harry Manfredini   *Art Dir* Gregg Fonseca
● William Katt, George Wendt, Richard Moll, Kay Lenz, Mary Stavin, Michael Ensign (New World)

Filmmakers Sean S. Cunningham and Steve Miner scored hits with several simple *Friday the 13th* films but tackle a more complex story here with embarrassing results. Cornball script [from a story by Fred Dekker] posits Roger Cobb (William Katt) as a successful horror novelist who moves into the spooky house where he was raised following the suicide of his aunt, as he writes a book based on his war experience in Vietnam.

Cobb immediately experiences odd happenings which play as hallucinations, but which the audience is supposed to believe are real.

His estranged TV actress wife Susan (Kay Lenz), shows up, apparently changes into a puffy monster and is killed by Cobb.

Though much of this nonsense is played tongue-in-cheek, an audience can hardly be expected to swallow the screenplay's arbitrary approach to Cobb's character. Compounding such credibility problems is a ludicrous sub-plot with Cobb's neighbor, a wolf-whistle beauty, Tanya (Mary Stavin).

Cast cannot be faulted, especially lead Katt. The monsters are fake and rubbery, better suited to a comedy than a film in search of scares.

■ **HOUSE II**
THE SECOND STORY

1987, 85 MINS, US ◇ ⓥ ☉
Dir Ethan Wiley   *Prod* Sean S. Cunningham   *Scr* Ethan Wiley   *Ph* Mac Ahlberg   *Ed* Marty Nicholson   *Mus* Harry Manfredini   *Art Dir* Gregg Fonseca
● Arye Gross, Jonathan Stark, Royal Dano, Bill Maher, John Ratzenberger, Amy Yasbeck (New World)

This house isn't worth a visit. What passes for a plot has Arye Gross move into the house in which his parents were murdered 25 years earlier. He hears about the existence of a skull filled with jewelry, supposedly buried with the body of one of his ancestors, so he and entrepreneur pal Jonathan Stark exhume the 170-year-old corpse, played by Royal Dano, unrecognizable under disfiguring makeup.

The oldtimer wants to have fun now that he's alive again, but an evil spirit wants that skull, and soon the trio are transported through the walls of the house into another world – a primeval jungle – to do battle.

Director Ethan Wiley is determined to be cute rather than scary. He intros some cuddly creatures – a baby pterodactyl, plus a critter who's a cross between a dog and a caterpillar – but they don't add anything to the pic's charm. Action scenes aren't very thrilling or suspenseful.

■ **HOUSEBOAT**

1958, 112 MINS, US ◇ ⓥ
Dir Melville Shavelson   *Prod* Jack Rose   *Scr* Melville Shavelson, Jack Rose   *Ph* Ray June   *Ed* Frank Bracht   *Mus* George Duning   *Art Dir* Hal Pereira, John Goodman
● Cary Grant, Sophia Loren, Martha Hyer, Harry Guardino, Eduardo Ciannelli, Mimi Gibson (Paramount/Scribe)

The voyage of *Houseboat* is to a nearly extinct era in motion pictures when screens and hearts bubbled over with the warmth of original family humor.

It's a perfect role for Cary Grant, who plays a government lawyer separated from his wife and who, upon her accidental death, is brought into contact with his three children, none of whom are very friendly toward him. Enter Sophia Loren, a full-blown lass with lovely knees who's been kept in tow by her father, a noted Italian symphony conductor and who takes the first chance to get away from it all. Grant, though he takes her for a tramp, hires her as a maid at seeing her ability to handle his children upon first meeting. Off goes everyone to the country, and through living together begin to understand and love each other. This, of course, also goes for the two adults (by now, he's noticed her knees).

Grant mixes concern with disconcern and says more with a head tilt than most residents of situation comedy are able to say with an entire script. Loren acts better in irate Italian than in emotional English, but she is believable and sometimes downright warm as the lover of Grant and his children.

Harry Guardino is outstanding as a fiery wolf who will take anything but a wife, and

Martha Hyer, as the rich 'other' woman, is beautiful and skillfully competent. As one might expect, the moppets steal the show.
□ 1958: Nominations: Best Original Story & Screenplay, Song ('Almost in Your Army')

■ **HOUSE BY THE RIVER**

1950, 88 MINS, US
Dir Fritz Lang   *Prod* Howard Welsch   *Scr* Mel Dinelli   *Ph* Edward Cronjager   *Ed* Arthur D. Hilton   *Mus* George Antheil   *Art Dir* Boris Leven
● Louis Hayward, Lee Bowman, Jane Wyatt, Dorothy Patrick, Ann Shoemaker, Jody Gilbert (Republic/Fidelity)

House by the River is a fair mystery which lacks sufficient plot twists and suspense.

As screenplayed from an A.P. Herbert novel, the film departs from the conventional whodunit in that the audience knows the identity of the murderer from the opening reel. Subsequent footage is chiefly a character study of the three principals.

Bulk of the action takes place in a gloomy mansion and a courtroom. Yarn revolves around a hack writer who strangles the maid when she rebuffs his advances. His brother, an accountant, realizes murder has been committed, but somehow lets his kin persuade him to assist in disposing of the body.

Role of the writer represents a meaty part for Louis Hayward who essays it with such gusto that he frequently overplays.

■ **HOUSE CALLS**

1978, 98 MINS, US ◇ ⓥ ☉
Dir Howard Zieff   *Prod* Alex Winitsky, Arlene Sellers   *Scr* Max Shulman, Julius J. Epstein, Alan Mandel, Charles Shyer   *Ph* David M. Walsh   *Ed* Edward Warschilka   *Mus* Henry Mancini   *Art Dir* Henry Bumstead
● Walter Matthau, Glenda Jackson, Art Carney, Richard Benjamin, Candice Azzara, Dick O'Neill (Universal)

Despite some horsepower casting, *House Calls* is overall a silly and uneven comedy about doctors which wants to be as macabre as, say, *Hospital*, and at the same time as innocuous as a TV sitcom. It manages to be neither.

Walter Matthau, engaging as a middle-aged lech, is one of four stars in the film, herein a newly-widowed medic out to make up for lost infidelity time; Glenda Jackson, divorced from a philanderer, seeks a faithful new mate; Art Carney is a near-senile hospital chief of staff whose mistakes are supposed to be funny but come off as really nasty; Richard Benjamin is a young doctor whose part is essentially to provide plot exposition.

The film is thus a middle-years comedy-romance vehicle [story by Max Shulman and Julius J. Epstein] for Matthau and Jackson, latter in her first made-in-Hollywood project and appearing none too comfortable either; the lightness of her *A Touch of Class* Oscar-winning performance is gone.

Carney also huffs and puffs his way uncomfortably through an unsympathetic part. Benjamin relaxes and Matthau seems mellow enough.

■ **HOUSEKEEPING**

1987, 116 MINS, US ◇ ⓥ
Dir Bill Forsyth   *Prod* Robert I. Colesberry   *Scr* Bill Forsyth   *Ph* Michael Coulter   *Ed* Michael Ellis   *Mus* Michael Gibbs   *Art Dir* Adrienne Atkinson
● Christine Lahti, Sara Walker, Andrea Burchill, Anne Pitoniak, Bill Smillie (Columbia)

Both enervating and exhilarating, *Housekeeping* is a very composed film about eccentric behavior. It is beautifully observed in many of its details, particularly in its very close examination of the relationship between sisters.

Based upon Marilynne Robinson's well-regarded novel, Forsyth's screenplay is structured around the impulsive arrivals and departures of characters fundamental to the lives of two sisters in Washington State after World War II. Men never enter the picture, as the girls successively live with their mother, grandmother, great-aunts and mother's sister in the splendid isolation of a small mountain town.

Six years after their abandonment, when the girls are on the brink of adolescence, into their lives steps their long-lost aunt Sylvie (Christine Lahti). Tale then becomes that of the proverbial crazy ladies in the old house on the edge of town, but played rigorously without sentimentality or cuteness.

Newcomers Sara Walker and Andrea Burchill are splendid as the girls, as they manage to suggest the lifelong and quite particular bond between the sisters as much through body language and looks as through dialog.

■ HOUSE OF BAMBOO

1955, 102 MINS, US ◇
Dir Samuel Fuller   *Prod* Buddy Adler   *Scr* Harry Kleiner, Samuel Fuller   *Ph* Joe MacDonald   *Ed* James B. Clark   *Mus* Leigh Harline   *Art Dir* Lyle Wheeler, Addison Hehr
● Robert Ryan, Robert Stack, Shirley Yamaguchi, Cameron Mitchell, Brad Dexter, Sessue Hayakawa (20th Century-Fox)

House of Bamboo is a regulation gangster story played against a modern-day Tokyo setting.

Novelty of scene and a warm, believable performance by Japanese star Shirley Yamaguchi are two of the better values in the production. Had story treatment and direction been on the same level of excellence, *House* would have been an allround good show.

Pictorially, the film is beautiful to see; the talk's mostly in the terse, tough idiom of yesteryear mob pix. While plot deals with some mighty tough characters who are trying to organize Tokyo along Chicago gangland lines, the violence introduced seems hardly necessary to the melodramatic points being made.

Robert Stack, required to overplay surliness by the direction, is an undercover agent out to get the murderer of a GI and break up the gang of renegade Yanks.

■ HOUSE OF CARDS

1968, 105 MINS, US ◇ Ⓥ
Dir John Guillermin   *Prod* Dick Berg   *Scr* James P. Bonner   *Ph* Alberto Pizzi   *Ed* Terry Williams   *Mus* Francis Lai   *Art Dir* Aurelio Crugnola
● George Peppard, Inger Stevens, Orson Welles, Keith Michell, William Job, Maxine Audley (Universal)

George Peppard is in breezy vigorous form as rescuer of a lady in distress in a thriller that has quite a measure of excitement and style, though the screenplay, based on Stanley Ellins' novel, has plenty of straggly ends. However, there are elements of a Hitchcockian thriller.

Story has Peppard as a Yank drifter in France who falls into the job of tutor to the young son of the widow of a French general killed in the Algerian war. He's installed in the de Villemont mansion and meets the curious and sinister de Villemont family.

Peppard offers a nice combo of exuberant cheek and muscle and Inger Stevens as the young widow keeps the romantic angle dangling tantalizingly. Orson Welles is not over used, but his flamboyance fits the role of a menacing conspirator effectively, and Keith Michell is suavely sinister.

Director John Guillermin makes the most of highspots but often cannot get the conversational and plot-laying bits off the ground.

■ HOUSE OF CARDS

1993, 107 MINS, US ◇
Dir Michael Lessac   *Prod* Dale Pollock, Lianne Halfon, Wolfgang Glattes   *Scr* Michael Lessac   *Ph* Victor Hammer   *Ed* Walter Murch   *Mus* James Horner   *Art Dir* Peter Larkin
● Kathleen Turner, Tommy Lee Jones, Asha Menina, Shiloh Strong, Esther Rolle, Park Overall (Penta)

Well made but narrowly one-note in its concerns, *House of Cards* plays like a top-of-the-line disease-of-the-week TV movie.

Drama [from a screen story by Michael Lessac and Robert Jay Litz] is triggered by the fatal plunge of an archeologist off a site in Mexico, leaving Ruth Matthews (Kathleen Turner) a widow. Returning to the US with her son and daughter, Ruth soon has to deal with the fact that little Sally (Asha Menina) is not talking any more.

Instead, Menina emits almost deafening, rhythmic shouts when anything seems amiss to her and begins to do weird things, such as building an extraordinary tower of cards in her room. Child psychiatrist Jake Beerlander (Tommy Lee Jones) wants to get his hands on this mysterious six-year-old, whom he believes exhibits classic autistic symptoms.

Ruth is an incompletely written character, and Turner does little to add to its depth or complexity. Menina makes a striking Sally, impressing with the sense of power and other-worldliness she throws off. Jones quietly underplays the shrink.

■ HOUSE OF DOOM
See: The Black Cat

■ HOUSE OF GAMES

1987, 102 MINS, US ◇ Ⓥ ☉
Dir David Mamet   *Prod* Michael Hausman   *Scr* David Memet   *Ph* Juan Ruiz Anchia   *Ed* Trudy Ship   *Mus* Alaric Jans   *Art Dir* Michael Merritt
● Lindsay Crouse, Joe Mantegna, Mike Nussbaum, Lilia Skala, J.T. Walsh (Filmhaus/Orion)

Writer David Mamet's first trip behind the camera as a director is entertaining good fun, an American film noir with Hitchcockian touches and a few dead bodies along the way. The action unfolds at a steady pace.

Any story that pairs a psychiatrist and a con man has possibilities. Here the famous Dr. Margaret Ford (Lindsay Crouse) finds her patients' lives more interesting than her own, and with the unwitting encouragement of her mentor (Lilia Skala), allows herself to be drawn into a nest of confidence sharks.

In the tense atmosphere of a smoky backroom cardtable, the irresistible heel Mike (Joe Mantegna) sets her up for a $6,000 drubbing. The good doctor gets out of that one by comic chance, but drawn to Mike and his dangerous life, she comes back the next night for more.

Mantegna is right on target as one of the screen's most likable baddies. His big con involves an elaborate setup to convince a conventioneer, picked up by partner Mike Nussbaum, to offer 'security' for a suitcase full of money found on the street. *House of Games* cleverly selects its cons, explains their workings, then twists them around again, all without boring or losing the viewer.

■ HOUSE OF ROTHSCHILD

1934, 94 MINS, US ◇
Dir Alfred Werker   *Scr* Nunnally Johnson   *Ph* Peverell Marley   *Mus* Alfred Newman
● George Arliss, Boris Karloff, Loretta Young, Robert Young, C. Aubrey Smith, Florence Arliss (Twentieth Century)

A fine picture on all counts in the acting, writing, and directing. It handles the delicate subject of anti-semitism with tact and restraint. The Rothschild family, through its intimate financial connection with the Napoleonic wars, affords a meaty story [based on the play by G.H. Westley].

George Arliss plays the father and founder of the family, Mayer Rothschild, and when the narrative skips 35 years he is also the son, Nathan, head of the London branch of the banking firm. Nathan's daughter is played by Loretta Young, who never looked better. She falls in love with an English gentile officer (Robert Young).

Nathan opposes the marriage, fearing his daughter will suffer indignities because of her race. Ultimately his opposition melts and the pair are last seen in the luxuriant colors of the Technicolor sequence, in which Rothschild is made an English baron at a regal investiture, which brings the picture to an opulent close.

The real Mrs Arliss plays her husband's make-believe wife. Her performance is very able and she is at all times an attractive matron. There are numerous minor performance of merit, including a sentimentalized Duke of Wellington handled by the astute C. Aubrey Smith.
□ 1934: Nomination: Best Picture

■ HOUSE OF STRANGERS

1949, 104 MINS, US Ⓥ
Dir Joseph L. Mankiewicz   *Prod* Sol C. Siegel   *Scr* Philip Yordan   *Ph* Milton Krasner   *Ed* Harmon Jones   *Mus* Daniele Amfitheatrof   *Art Dir* Lyle Wheeler, George W. Davis
● Edward G. Robinson, Susan Hayward, Richard Conte, Luther Adler, Paul Valentine, Efrem Zimbalist Jr (20th Century-Fox)

Despite a rather weak title, *House of Strangers* is a strong picture. Edward G. Robinson plays a New York eastside Italian banker who switches from barbering to money-lending when he discovers the high interest obtainable. Yarn [from Jerome Weidman's novel *I'll Never Go There Again*] deals with the hate of three of his sons for their father's unyielding nature and slave-driving tactics. The fourth son (Richard Conte), an attorney with headquarters at the bank, sticks by his father.

Care has been used to faithfully show the homelife of a typical Old World Italian family (in the US), while contrasting it with the younger generation.

Robinson is especially vivid when he realizes that the three sons have turned against him and when he seeks revenge through his fourth son. Conte is excellent, and Susan Hayward chips in with one of her standout performances as a society beaut.

■ HOUSE OF USHER
(UK: The Fall of the House of Usher)

1960, 79 MINS, US ◇ Ⓥ
Dir Roger Corman   *Prod* Roger Corman   *Scr* Richard Matheson   *Ph* Floyd Crosby   *Ed* Anthony Carras   *Mus* Les Baxter   *Art Dir* Daniel Haller
● Vincent Price, Mark Damon, Myrna Fahey, Harry Ellerbe (American International/Alta Vista)

It's not precisely the Edgar Allan Poe short story that emerges in *House of Usher*, but it's a reasonably diverting and handsomely mounted variation. In patronizingly romanticizing Poe's venerable prose, scenarist Richard Matheson has managed to preserve enough of the original's haunting flavor and spirit. The elaborations change the personalities of the three central characters, but not recklessly so.

In Poe's tale, the first-person hero is a friend of Roderick Usher, not his enemy and the romantic wooer of his doomed sister, the Lady Madeline. Matheson's version, however, accomplishes this alteration without ruining

357

the impact of the chilling climax, in which Madeline (Myrna Fahey), buried alive by her brother (Vincent Price) while under a cataleptic trance, breaks free from her living tomb.

Price is a fine fit as Usher, and Fahey successfully conveys the transition from helpless daintiness to insane vengeance. Hero Mark Damon has his better moments when the going gets gory and frenzied, but lacks the mature command required for the role. Harry Ellerbe is outstanding as an old family retainer.

The cobweb-ridden, fungus-infected, mist-pervaded atmosphere of cadaverous gloom has been photographed with great skill by Floyd Crosby and enhanced further by Ray Mercer's striking photographic effects and the vivid color, most notably during a woozy dream sequence.

....

■ HOUSE OF WAX

1953, 90 MINS, US ◇ ⓥ ⊙

Dir Andre de Toth *Prod* Bryan Foy *Scr* Crane Wilbur
Ph Bert Glennon, Peverell Marley *Ed* Rudi Fehr
Mus David Buttolph *Art Dir* Stanley Fleischer
● Vincent Price, Frank Lovejoy, Phyllis Kirk, Carolyn Jones, Paul Picerini, Charles Bronson (Warner)

This remake of Charles Belden's *Mystery of the Wax Museum* (1933) is given the full 3-D treatment in Crane Wilbur's screenplay [from a story by Charles Belden]. Andre de Toth's direction, while uneven, nonetheless gears it to the medium – chairs flying into the audience, cancan dancers pirouetting full into the camera, the barker's pingpong ball, as a pitchman's prop, likewise shooting out at the audience, the muscular menace springing as if from the theatre into the action. The stereophonic sound further assists in the illusion.

Warners employs the Gunzburg Bros' NaturalVision technique, first introduced in Arch Oboler's *Bwana Devil*. It achieves maximum results with the eerie chases, ghoulish shenanigans in the NY City morgue, the '14th St. Music Hall' (sic!) interior for the cancan, the police headquarters' flashbacks, and the like.

Casting is competent, Vincent Price is capital as the No. 1 menace. Frank Lovejoy is authoritative as the lieutenant. Phyllis Kirk is purty as the ingenue who looks fairly convincingly scared but not so in the scream department – she needs a good, shrill, piercing shrieker as voice standin. Paul Picerni is okay as the juvenile and Carolyn Jones makes her moments count as the flighty kid who gets bumped off. Charles Bronson is the No. 2 menace, as the deaf-mute, and Reggie Rymal, as the barker, is also standout.

....

■ HOUSE ON CARROLL STREET, THE

1988, 100 MINS, US ◇ ⓥ ⊙

Dir Peter Yates *Prod* Peter Yates, Robert F. Colesberry
Scr Walter Bernstein *Ph* Michael Ballhaus *Ed* Ray Lovejoy *Mus* Georges Delerue *Art Dir* Stuart Wurtzel
● Kelly McGillis, Jeff Daniels, Mandy Patinkin, Christopher Rhode, Jessica Tandy, Trey Wilson (Orion)

In this story of a sleuth trailing improbable characters involved in a ridiculous conspiracy, Kelly McGillis is the idealistic and hardly convincing political activist who in 1951 refuses to answer questions before a Senate hearing on her involvement in a controversial organization.

She takes a job reading to a crochety old blind lady (Jessica Tandy) whose row house garden is adjacent to another brownstone where there are mysterious goings-on. It just so happens the same senator (Mandy Patinkin) who grilled her about her political leanings is in the house shouting as an interpreter translates into German.

McGillis is intrigued. She collects about three clues and figures out Patinkin is smuggling Nazis in by having them take the names of dead Jews.

Jeff Daniels is Ned to McGillis' Nancy Drew. He is the FBI agent who manages to come in at exactly the right moments to save her from whatever perilous predicament she is in at the time – no matter how preposterous.

....

■ HOUSE ON HAUNTED HILL

1958, 75 MINS, US ⓥ ⊙

Dir William Castle *Prod* William Castle *Scr* Robb White *Ph* Carl E. Guthrie *Ed* Roy Livingston
Mus Von Dexter *Art Dir* David Milton
● Vincent Price, Carol Ohmart, Richard Long, Alan Marshal, Carolyn Craig, Elisha Cook Jr (Allied Artists)

The screenplay is the one about the group of people who promise to spend the night in a haunted house. In this case, it's for pure monetary gain. Vincent Price, owner of the house, is offering $10,000 to anyone who lasts out the night. There is a gimmick in the plot which explains the screams, ghosts, bubbling vats of lye and perambulating skeletons.

Haunted Hill is expertly put together. There is some good humor in the dialog which not only pays off well against the ghostly elements, but provides a release for laughter so it does not explode in the suspense sequences. The characters are interesting and not outlandish, so there is some basis of reality. Director William Castle keeps things moving at a healthy clip.

Robb White and Castle have a new gimmick called 'Emergo'. This device is an illuminated skeleton mounted on trolley wires, moving out from the side of the screen over the heads of the audience.

....

■ HOUSE ON 92ND STREET, THE

1945, 83 MINS, US

Dir Henry Hathaway *Prod* Louis de Rochemont
Scr Barre Lyndon, Charles G. Booth, John Monks Jr
Ph Norbert Brodine *Ed* Harmon Jones *Mus* David Buttolph *Art Dir* Lyle Wheeler, Lewis Creber
● William Eythe, Lloyd Nolan, Signe Hasso, Gene Lockhart, Leo G. Carroll, Mike Evans (20th Century-Fox)

Twentieth-Fox, employing somewhat the technique of *The March of Time* has parlayed the latter with facilities and files of the FBI in arriving at *The House on 92nd Street*. It doesn't matter much whether it's east or west 92nd – the result is an absorbing documentation that's frequently heavily-steeped melodrama.

House is comprised of prewar and wartime footage taken by the FBI, and it ties together revelations of the vast Nazi spy system in the United States. Woven into this factual data, along with what the foreword reveals is a thorough cooperation of the FBI in making the film, are the dramatic elements inserted by Hollywood in general and 20th-Fox in particular.

Lloyd Nolan is the FBI inspector in charge of ferreting out the espionage on a secret formula sought by the Nazis; William Eythe is the young German-American sent to Germany by US-located Nazis (and the FBI) to learn espionage and sabotage; Signe Hasso plays a key link to the Nazi system in this country.
□ 1945: Best Original Story (Charles G. Booth)

....

■ HOUSE ON TELEGRAPH HILL, THE

1951, 93 MINS, US

Dir Robert Wise *Prod* Robert Bassler *Scr* Elick Moll, Frank Partos *Ph* Lucien Ballard *Ed* Nick De Maggio *Mus* Sol Kaplan *Art Dir* Lyle Wheeler, John DeCuir
● Richard Basehart, Valentina Cortese, William Lundigan, Fay Baker, Steven Geray (20th Century-Fox)

This is a slow but interesting melodrama about a psychopathic killer, with San Francisco's quaint hill residential sections as background.

Yarn [from the novel *The Frightened Child* by Dana Lyon] starts a little unexpectedly in the femme concentration camp at Belsen under the Germans. This section is brief, but it's vivid enough to convey the brutalities sustained by Poles and other refugees under the Nazi terror. One Polish woman (Valentina Cortese) sustains herself with the thought that she must someday come out alive.

She gets to America, on a dead woman's identity papers, to find she's pseudo-mother to a boy, heir to a fortune, whose guardian (Richard Basehart) is scheming to acquire the inheritance. Basehart makes a play for Cortese, gets her to marry him, and then plots her death, as he's been plotting that of the child. Rest of film is taken up with his scheming and Cortese's efforts to escape him after she discovers his designs.

Sinister mood, and heightened tensions, are well sustained, and performances by Basehart and Cortese convey the drama convincingly. William Lundigan is okay as the attorney who befriends the woman.
□ 1951: Nomination: Best B&W Art Direction

....

■ HOUSE PARTY

1990, 100 MINS, US ◇ ⓥ ⊙

Dir Reginald Hudlin *Prod* Warrington Hudlin
Scr Reginald Hudlin *Ph* Peter Deming *Ed* Earl Watson *Mus* Marcus Miller *Art Dir* Bryan Jones
● Christopher Reid, Robin Harris, Christopher Martin, Martin Lawrence, Tisha Campbell, A.J. Johnson (New Line)

House Party captures contemporary black teen culture in a way that's fresh, commercial and very catchy. Filmmaking team of Reggie and Warrington Hudlin make a strikingly assured debut feature blending comedy, hip-hop music and dancing in a pic that moves to a kinetic, nonstop rhythm.

Rap duo Kid 'N' Play (Christopher Reid and Christopher Martin) play colleagues in rhyme, trying to get away with throwing a booming house party the night Play's parents are away and Kid is grounded by his Pop (Robin Harris) for getting in a fight at school.

En route to the party, Kid is pursued by the school thugs (rap trio Full Force), and all of them are pursued by the neighborhood cops. Then unwitting Kid becomes an object of desire for both of the young ladies Play is trying to impress (Tisha Campbell and A.J. Johnson).

Writer-director Reggie Hudlin, who expanded *House Party* from a short he made while a student at Harvard, injects pic with the cartoonish style and captivating rhythm of today's rap scene.

....

■ HOUSE PARTY 2

1991, 94 MINS, US ◇ ⓥ ⊙

Dir Doug McHenry, George Jackson *Prod* Doug McHenry, George Jackson *Scr* Rusty Cundieff, Daryl G. Nickens *Ph* Francis Kenny *Ed* Joel Goodman
Mus Vassal Benford *Art Dir* Michelle Minch
● Christopher Reid, Christopher Martin, Tisha Campbell, Iman, Martin Lawrence, D. Christopher Judge (New Line)

The crowd's the same, but the atmosphere's different in this disappointing followup to low-budget hit *House Party*. Absence of filmmakers Reggie and Warrington Hudlin, who've moved on to other things, is keenly felt in a film lacking the original's smarts and cinematic flair.

Debut directors Doug McHenry and George Jackson (*New Jack City* producers) trace the continuing misadventures of rap team Kid 'N' Play (Christopher Reid, Christopher Martin) as they tackle life after high school.

Kid has lost his father (the late Robin Harris) and plans on going to college, but Play is set on pursuing a record contract dangled by a shady promoter (fashion model Iman).

Unfortunately, pic relies heavily on vulgarities and no-brainer plot twists. Whoopi Goldberg cameos as a nightmarish college disciplinarian in a dream scene.

. . . .

■ **HOUSESITTER**

1992, 100 MINS, US ◇ ✇ ⊙
Dir Frank Oz *Prod* Brian Grazer *Scr* Mark Stein *Ph* John A. Alonzo *Ed* John Jympson *Mus* Miles Goodman *Art Dir* Ida Random
● Steve Martin, Goldie Hawn, Dana Delany, Julie Harris, Donald Moffat, Peter MacNicol (Universal/Imagine)

Housesitter, a tediously unfunny screwball comedy, is a career misstep for both Steve Martin and Goldie Hawn. Hawn is grating as the kind of giggly flake she played two decades ago on *Laugh-In*, and Martin is more obnoxious than endearing as the architect whose life she invades.

Martin's in love with wholesome Dana Delany, who lives in the quaint New England village of Dobbs Mill, but she deals him an emotional blow by refusing to marry him and move into the new architectural showcase he's built out in the countryside.

Enter Hawn. After they have a one-night stand, she tracks him to the empty house. She moves in, telling everyone in town that she's his new wife, and they believe her.

Frank Oz proves no wizard with his direction of this nonsense. John A. Alonzo's crisp, sunny lensing is about all that keeps the pic bearable to watch.

. . . .

■ **HOWARDS END**

1992, 140 MINS, UK ◇ ✇ ⊙
Dir James Ivory *Prod* Ismail Merchant *Scr* Ruth Prawer Jhabvala *Ph* Tony Pierce-Roberts *Ed* Andrew Marcus *Mus* Richard Robbins *Art Dir* Luciana Arrighi
● Anthony Hopkins, Vanessa Redgrave, Helena Bonham Carter, Emma Thompson, James Wilby, Sam West (Merchant Ivory)

E. M. Forster's *Howards End* makes a most compelling drama, perhaps the best film made during the 30-year partnership of Ismail Merchant and James Ivory. Longtime Merchant Ivory collaborator Ruth Prawer Jhabvala has distilled the 1910 novel into pungent, concise scenes that grab the viewer and maximize the impact of Forster's themes about class differences and the harm caused by repressing true feelings.

Aristocratic matriarch Ruth Wilcox (Vanessa Redgrave) on her deathbed scrawls a note bequeathing her beloved estate Howards End to a recent acquaintance, Margaret Schlegel (Emma Thompson). Redgrave's aristocratic husband Henry (Anthony Hopkins) and daughter Evie (real-life daughter Jemma Redgrave) hardly know Thompson and callously destroy the note to selfishly keep the estate in the family even though they don't live there anymore.

A crucial, initially cryptic, subplot involves insurance company clerk Leonard Bast (Sam West) and his wife Jacky (Nicola Duffett). After chance encounters, Schlegel's high-spirited sister Helen (Helena Bonham Carter) begins to look out for West's welfare, resulting in an impromptu tryst and pregnancy.

Hopkins can do no wrong in the acting department, portraying an uppercrust nasty with chilling understatement. In the film's largest role, Thompson is immensely sympathetic. Bonham Carter proves again that she's the best actress today at embodying the look and spirit of period roles. Vanessa Redgrave uses unusual phrasing to create an eerie presence in her successful casting

against type as the matriarch in failing health.
□ 1992: Best Actress (Emma Thompson), Adapted Screenplay, Art Direction.
□ Nominations: Best Picture, Director, Supp. Actress (Vanessa Redgrave), Cinematography, Original Score, Costume Design

. . . .

■ **HOWARD THE DUCK**

1986, 111 MINS, US ◇ ✇ ⊙
Dir Willard Huyck *Prod* Gloria Katz *Scr* Willard Huyck, Gloria Katz *Ph* Richard H. Kline *Ed* Michael Chandler, Sidney Wolinsky *Mus* John Barry *Art Dir* Peter Jamison
● Lea Thompson, Jeffrey Jones, Tim Robbins, Ed Gale, Chip Zein, Paul Guilfoyle (Lucasfilm)

Scripters have taken the cigar chompin', beer drinkin' comic book character [created by Steve Gerber] and turned him into a wide-eyed, cutesy, midget-sized extraterrestrial accidentally blown to Cleveland from a misdirected laser beam.

Howard encounters rock singer Beverly Switzler (Lea Thompson) after a few harrowing minutes on Earth and they become instant friends after he defends her from a couple of menacing punkers.

Pic then lapses into formulaic predictability with nearly an hour of frenetic chase scenes and technically perfect explosions from Industrial Light & Magic as Thompson and Tim Robbins try to thwart the authorities' attempts to capture the duck before he gets a chance to be beamed.

. . . .

■ **HOW GREEN WAS MY VALLEY**

1941, 120 MINS, US ✇ ⊙
Dir John Ford *Prod* Darryl F. Zanuck *Scr* Philip Dunne *Ph* Arthur Miller *Ed* James B. Clark *Mus* Alfred Newman *Art Dir* Richard Day, Nathan Juran
● Walter Pidgeon, Maureen O'Hara, Donald Crisp, Roddy McDowall, Barry Fitzgerald, Anna Lee (20th Century-Fox)

Based on a best-selling novel, this saga of Welsh coal-mining life is replete with much human interest, romance, conflict and almost every other human emotion. It's a warm, human story that Richard Llewellyn wrought basically, and the skillful John Ford camera-painting, from a fine scenario by Philip Dunne, needed only expert casting to round out the job.

Donald Crisp and Sara Allgood, as Pa and Ma Morgan, the heads of the Welsh mining family, are an inspired casting. Walter Pidgeon is excellent as the minister; Maureen O'Hara splendid as the object of his unrequited love, who marries the mineowner's son out of pique.

And, above all, there is Roddy McDowall. He's winsome, manly, and histrionically proficient in an upright, two-fisted manner.

The transition from book to screen also utilizes the first person singular narrative form, with graphic delineations of how green, indeed, was young Huw (pronounced Hugh) Morgan's valley as he recounts his life from childhood, unfolding the fullness of the Morgans' honest, God-fearing, industrial life span in the Welsh valley.
□ 1941: Best Picture, Director, Supp. Actor (Donald Crisp), B&W Cinematography, B&W Interior Decoration (Richard Day, Nathan Juran)
□ Nominations: Best Supp. Actress (Sara Allgood), Screenplay, Editing, Scoring of a Dramatic Picture, Sound

. . . .

■ **HOW I WON THE WAR**

1967, 109 MINS, UK ◇ ✇ ⊙
Dir Richard Lester *Prod* Richard Lester *Scr* Charles Wood *Ph* David Watkin *Ed* John Victor Smith *Mus* Ken Thorne *Art Dir* Philip Harrison, John Stoll

● Michael Crawford, John Lennon, Roy Kinnear, Lee Montague, Jack MacGowran, Michael Hordern (United Artists)

Patrick Ryan's novel has been adapted into a screenplay which, as directed by Richard Lester, substitutes motion for emotion, reeling for feeling, and crude slapstick for telling satire. Film opens at a superficial level of fast comedy, but never develops further.

Michael Crawford is top-featured as a gee-whiz British Army officer whose unthinking ineptitude kills off, one by one, all members of his unit. John Lennon, whose billing far exceeds his part, and contribution, plays one of the crew.

Episodic treatment cross-cuts between plot turns, and actual footage of Second World War battles, latter tinted in different hues.

. . . .

■ **HOWLING, THE**

1981, 91 MINS, CANADA ◇ ✇ ⊙
Dir Joe Dante *Prod* Daniel H. Blatt *Scr* John Sayles, Terence H. Winkless *Ph* John Hora *Ed* Mark Goldblatt, Joe Dante *Mus* Pino Donaggio *Art Dir* Robert A. Burns
● Dee Wallace, Patrick Macnee, Kevin McCarthy, John Carradine, Slim Pickens, Dennis Dugan (International/Avco Embassy)

Director Joe Dante's work reflects Alfred Hitchcock's insistence that terror and suspense work best when counterbalanced by a chuckle or two.

There are good one-liners throughout, some delivered straight-faced by Kevin McCarthy as an empty-headed TV news producer and Dick Miller as the colorful expert on werewolves. And in a picture like this. John Carradine and Slim Pickens only have to open their mouths to get a laugh from long-time appreciative fans.

But this is supposed to be a horror film, after all. And it definitely is in a good old-fashioned way, complete with a girl venturing out alone with a flashlight to investigate a weird noise. In large part the picture works because of the make-up effects created by Rob Bottin.

Wallace, who was exceptional as the lonely woman at the bar in *10*, turns in another solid performance in a much dumber role. As the anchorlady, she has set herself out as bait for psycho Robert Picardo, meeting him in a porno shop where he winds up shot to death by cops. Back at the TV station, Belinda Balaski and Dennis Dugan are still working on the Picardo story, picking up clues that lead them into a study of werewolves.

If the picture has a major problem, it is that Dante uses up his best effects midway through the picture, leaving him with little for the grand surprise that's supposed to come at the end.

. . . .

■ **HOWLING II**
YOUR SISTER IS A WEREWOLF
(UK: Howling II: Stirba – Werewolf Bitch)

1985, 90 MINS, US ◇ ✇ ⊙
Dir Philippe Mora *Prod* Steven Lane *Scr* Robert Sarno, Gary Brandner *Ph* Geoffrey Stephenson *Ed* Charles Bernstein *Mus* Steve Parsons *Art Dir* Karel Vacer
● Christopher Lee, Annie McEnroe, Reb Brown, Marsha A. Hunt, Sybil Danning, Ferdy Mayne (Hemdale/Granite)

Customers who expect a werewolf pic in the tradition of Joe Dante's invigorating *The Howling* are in for a disappointment; this is a generally lackluster horror item [based on the novel *Howling II* by Gary Brandner].

Tale opens with the funeral of a femme newsperson; in attendance is Christopher Lee as an expert on werewolves. He advises that the dead woman was such a creature, and is joined by her brother (Reb Brown) and colleague (Annie McEnroe) on a trip to Transylvania to destroy the werewolf queen (Sybil Danning), who is actually Lee's sister.

359

Despite fancy editing tricks and a few touches of grim humor, suspense is woefully lacking, as Danning is an unformidable villain (she looks as though she's stepped out of a soft-core sex pic) and the plot development is strictly by-the-numbers. Apart from a few moments shot in LA, pic was lensed in Czechoslovakia, but relatively little is made of the settings. Lee brings a tired authority to the role.

....

■ HOW THE WEST WAS WON

1962, 155 MINS, US ◇ ⓦ ⊙
Dir Henry Hathaway, John Ford, George Marshall *Prod* Bernard Smith *Scr* James R. Webb *Ph* William H. Daniels, Milton Krasner, Charles Lang Jr, Joseph LaShelle *Ed* Harold F. Kress *Mus* Alfred Newman *Art Dir* George W. Davis, William Ferrari, Addison Hehr
● James Stewart, Hendry Fonda, Gregory Peck, Debbie Reynolds, Richard Widmark, John Wayne (M-G-M/Cinerama)

It would be hard to imagine a subject which lends itself more strikingly to the wide-screen process than this yarn of the pioneers who opened the American West. It's a story [suggested by the series *How the West Was Won* in *Life* magazine] which naturally puts the spotlight on action and adventure, and the three directors between them have turned in some memorable sequences.

George Marshall, for example, has the credit for the buffalo stampede, started by the Indians when the railroad was moving out West. This magnificently directed sequence is as vivid As anything ever put on celluloid. Undoubtedly the highlight of Henry Hathaway's contribution is the chase of outlaws who attempt to hold up a train with a load of bullion. John Ford's directorial stint is limited to the Civil War sequences, and though that part does not contain such standout incident, there is the fullest evidence of his high professional Standards.

The storyline is developed around the Prescott family, as they start on their adventurous journey out west. Karl Malden and Agnes Moorehead are the parents, and with them are their two daughters, played by Debbie Reynolds and Carroll Baker. They start their journey out West down the Erie Canal, and when James Stewart, a fur trapper, comes on the scene, it's love at first sight for Baker.

Although they've headed in opposite directions, she eventually gets her man. After her parents lose their lives when their raft capsizes in the rapids – and that's another of the highly vivid sequences directed by Hathaway – Reynolds joins a wagon train to continue her journey and tries, in vain, to resist the charms of Gregory Peck, a professional gambler, who is first attracted to her when she's believed to have inherited a gold mine.

Peck gives a suave and polished gloss to his role of the gambler, and Stewart has some fine, if typical, moments in his scenes.

Richard Widmark makes a vital impression as the head man of the construction team building the railroad. John Wayne has a minor part as General Sherman, but he, too, makes the charactor stand out. Spencer Tracy is heard but not seen as the narrator.
□ 1963: Best Original Story & Screenplay, Sound, Editing.
□ Nominations: Best Picture, Color Cinematography, Color Costume Design, Color Art Direction, Original Music Score

....

■ HOW TO BE VERY, VERY POPULAR

1955, 89 MINS, US ◇
Dir Nunnally Johnson *Prod* Nunnally Johnson *Scr* Nunnally Johnson *Ph* Milton Krasner *Ed* Louis Loeffler *Mus* Cyril J. Mockridge *Art Dir* Lyle Wheeler, John DeCuir
● Betty Grable, Sheree North, Robert Cummings, Charles Coburn, Tommy Noonan, Fred Clark (20th Century-Fox)

The wild and wacky doings dreamed up by Nunnally Johnson are dressed up considerably in eye appeal by having Betty Grable and Sheree North running through most of the footage in costumes appropriate to their striptease profession.

Bearing only a fleeting resemblance to the 1933 stage play, *She Loves Me Not* (and a subsequent screen version) these caperings concern two strippers who can identify the bald-headed man who guns down ecdysiast Noel Toy right in the middle of her act in a San Francisco honkytonk. He promises the two dolls the same treatment if they don't get lost. They do, and after a bus ride along the coast take refuge in a fraternity dorm at a college.

....

■ HOW TO FILL A WILD BIKINI

See: *How to Stuff a Wild Bikini*

....

■ HOW TO GET AHEAD IN ADVERTISING

1989, 95 MINS, UK ◇ ⓦ ⊙
Dir Bruce Robinson *Prod* David Wimbury *Scr* Bruce Robinson *Ph* Peter Hannan *Ed* Alan Strachan *Mus* David Dundas, Rick Wentworth *Art Dir* Michael Pickwood
● Richard E. Grant, Rachel Ward, Richard Wilson, Jacqueline Tong, John Shrapnel, Susan Wooldridge (Handmade)

As a hotshot go-getter in the British equivalent of Madison Avenue, Richard E. Grant is having a problem coming up with an original campaign for a pimple cream and the pressure is on from the client and his boss (wonderfully droll Richard Wilson).

As dutiful wives do, Rachel Ward tries to assure him that something in his genius will come forward, but he's floundering.

When a small boil breaks out on his own neck, Grant realizes the stress has become too much and it's time to quit the business. It's too late. The boil begins to grow – and starts to talk, giving form to all that's vile and venal in his nature.

The picture would be genuinely hilarious were the subject matter not so overworked.

....

■ HOW TO MARRY A MILLIONAIRE

1953, 95 MINS, US ◇ ⓦ ⊙
Dir Jean Negulesco *Prod* Nunnally Johnson *Scr* Nunnally Johnson *Ph* Joe MacDonald *Ed* Louis Loeffler *Mus* Cyril Mockridge *Art Dir* Lyle R. Wheeler, Leland Fuller
● Betty Grable, Marilyn Monroe, Lauren Bacall, David Wayne, Rory Calhoun, Cameron Mitchell (20th Century-Fox)

The script draws for partial source material on two plays, Zoe Akins' *The Greeks Had a Word for It* and *Loco* by Dale Eunson and Katherine Albert. Nunnally Johnson has blended the legiter ingredients with his own material for snappy comedy effect.

The plot has three girls pooling physical and monetary resources for a millionaire man hunt and as the predatory sex game unfolds the chuckles are constant. Each winds up with a man. One is David Wayne, a fugitive from Uncle Sam's Internal Revenue agents whose apartment the girls have leased as a base for the chase. He gets Marilyn Monroe.

Another is Cameron Mitchell, a young tycoon who dresses like a lowly wage slave. He winds up with Lauren Bacall. Third is Rory Calhoun, a poor but honest forest ranger who gains Betty Grable as a fire-watching companion. None is what the femme trio expected to get when the hunt started.

Certain for audience favor is Monroe's blonde with astigmatism who goes through life bumping into things, including men, because she thinks glasses would detract. Also captivating is Grable's Loco, a friendly, cuddly blonde who turns situations to advantage until the great outdoors overwhelms her. As the brains of the trio, Bacall's Schatze is a wise-cracking, hard-shelled gal who gives up millions for love and gets both.

A real standout among the other players is William Powell as the elderly Texas rancher who woos, wins and then gives up Bacall.
□ 1953: Nomination: Best Color Costume Design

....

■ HOW TO MURDER YOUR WIFE

1965, 118 MINS, US ◇ ⓦ
Dir Richard Quine *Prod* George Axelrod *Scr* George Axelrod *Ph* Harry Stradling *Ed* David Wagner *Mus* Neal Hefti *Art Dir* Richard Sylbert
● Jack Lemmon, Virna Lisi, Terry-Thomas, Eddie Mayehoff, Claire Trevor, Sidney Blackmer (Murder/United Artists)

George Axelrod's plot deals with the antics of a bachelor cartoonist, played by Jack Lemmon, who has a policy of acting out the escapades of his newsprint sleuth hero to test their credibility before actually committing them to paper. So it is that, awakening one morning to find himself married to an Italian dish who had popped out of a cake at a party the night before and after trying to make a go of this unwanted wedlock, he simulates the 'murder' of said spouse one evening by dumping a dummy likeness of her into a building construction site.

When Lemmon's wife, played by Virna Lisi, spots the cartoonist's sketches of his 'crime' on his work table she panics and flees. The strip appears in the papers and, unable to explain his wife's whereabouts, Lemmon is arrested for murder and brought to trial.

All of this has moments of fine comic style but, overall, emerges as prefabricated as Lemmon's comic strip character. The comedian's efforts are considerable and consistent but finesse and desire aren't enough to overcome the fact that Axelrod's script doesn't make the most of its potentially antic situations.

....

■ HOW TO SAVE A MARRIAGE AND RUIN YOUR LIFE

1968, 102 MINS, US ◇
Dir Fielder Cook *Prod* Stanley Shapiro *Scr* Stanley Shapiro *Ph* Lee Garmes *Ed* Philip Anderson *Mus* Michel Legrand *Art Dir* Robert Clatworthy
● Dean Martin, Stella Stevens, Eli Wallach, Anne Jackson, Betty Field, Jack Albertson (Columbia)

How to Save a Marriage and Ruin Your Life is an amusing Stanley Shapiro comedy about divorce and marital infidelity. Made under the title *Band of Gold*, the lush production stars Dean Martin, Stella Stevens, Eli Wallach and Anne Jackson.

Plot complications derive from Wallach's longtime infidelity with Jackson, Katherine Bard demonstrating in her brief footage that Wallach's home life is nothing. Martin confuses Jackson with Stevens, latter assuming his romantic advances are legit, instead of the ruse which Martin intends.

Gag situations include a fake deceased wife, milked for more than it's worth. The situations play better than they can be described; on the other hand, none is especially hard-core hilarity.

....

■ HOW TO STEAL A DIAMOND IN FOUR UNEASY LESSONS

See: *The Hot Rock*

....

■ HOW TO STEAL A MILLION

1966, 127 MINS, US ◇ ⓦ
Dir William Wyler *Prod* Fred Kohlmar *Scr* Harry Kurnitz *Ph* Charles Lang *Ed* Robert Swink *Mus* John Williams *Art Dir* Alexandre Trauner

H

● Audrey Hepburn, Peter O'Toole, Eli Wallach, Hugh Griffith, Charles Boyer, Marcel Dalio (20th Century-Fox)

How to Steal a Million returns William Wyler to the enchanting province of the *Roman Holiday*. Lensed in Paris, advantageous use is made of the actual story locale to give unusual visual interest.

Plot centers on a fraud in the art world via forging 'masterpieces'. Based on a story by George Bradshaw, the script twirls around Audrey Hepburn, daughter of a distinguished French family whose father, Hugh Griffith, is a faker of genius. She has given up trying to reform him, continuing only to hope he won't get into too much trouble. Peter O'Toole is a private detective who specializes in solving crimes in the world of art, but whom femme thinks is a burglar after she discovers him in the family home in the middle of the night apparently trying to make off with a canvas.

Griffith is a particular standout as the elegant Parisian oddball with a compulsion to forge the greatest impressionistic painters.

■ HOW TO STUFF A WILD BIKINI
(UK: How to Fill a Wild Bikini)

1965, 90 MINS, US ◇ ▼
Dir William Asher *Prod* James H. Nicholson, Samuel Z Arkoff *Scr* William Asher, Leo Townsend *Ph* Floyd Crosby *Ed* Fred Feitshans, Eve Newman *Mus* Les Baxter
● Annette Funicello, Dwayne Hickman, Brian Donlevy, Harvey Lembeck, Buster Keaton, Mickey Rooney (American International)

American International's youth contender carries a catchy – if wayout – title, but is a lightweight affair lacking the breeziness and substance of earlier entries. Whole affair seems to have been given the once-over-lightly treatment.

Script by William Asher – who directs – and Leo Townsend is hit and miss, twirling around a mysterious redhead suddenly appearing to fill a bikini which has been floating in midair. Frankie Avalon, on duty in Tahiti with his Naval Reserve unit, enlists the services of Buster Keaton, a witch doctor, to determine whether his girlfriend back home – Annette Funicello – is being true to him. Then there's Mickey Rooney, a fast-talking pressagent, trying to promote a motorcycle race with femme stuffed in the wild bikini.

Funicello, usually with a bulk of the footage in these beach romps, obviously is enceinte here, and aside from a couple of songs she has little to do. Avalon, too, has little more than a bit.

■ HOW TO SUCCEED IN BUSINESS WITHOUT REALLY TRYING

1967, 121 MINS, US ◇ ▼ ⊙
Dir David Swift *Prod* David Swift *Scr* David Swift *Ph* Burnett Guffey *Ed* Ralph E. Winters, Allan Jacobs *Mus* Nelson Riddle (sup.) *Art Dir* Robert Boyle
● Robert Morse, Michele Lee, Rudy Vallee, Anthony Teague, Maureen Arthur, Sammy Smith (Mirisch)

An entertaining, straightforward filming of the [1961] legituner, featuring many thesps in their stage roles. David Swift's production is generally fast-moving in tracing the rags-to-riches rise of Robert Morse within Rudy Vallee's biz complex. Colorful production values maintain great eye appeal.

Swift, besides producing-directing (and appearing briefly as an elevator operator), adapted the legit book by Abe Burrows, Jack Weinstock and Willie Gilbert, based on Shepherd Mead's novel.

Most of Frank Loesser's literate melodies have been retained including 'I Believe in You', 'The Company Way', 'Been a Long Day', and 'Brotherhood of Man'.

Plot concerns windowwasher Morse who, by superior instinct for advancement and sur-vival, becomes a top exec in Vallee's company in a matter of days. He becomes so big that former well-wishers plot his downfall.

The pixie-like Morse is excellent, with both voice and facial expressions right on target all the time. Michele Lee shows the same uninhibited freshness and charm that made Doris Day a film star.

■ HUCKLEBERRY FINN

1931, 79 MINS, US
Dir Norman Taurog *Scr* Grover Jones, William Slavens McNutt *Ph* David Abel
● Jackie Coogan, Mitzi Green, Junior Durkin, Jackie Searl, Clara Blandick, Jane Darwell (Paramount)

It's the second Mark Twain story to be done by Paramount, first being *Tom Sawyer*. Same quartet that did *Sawyer* reunite in Jackie Coogan, Junior Durkin, Mitzi Green and Jackie Searl. The latter two only appear in a minor way at the beginning. That's after the first 1,000 feet or so when Searl, Green and the others practically disappear, a young adolescent (looking like sweet 16) taking up from there on. She's attractive, soft-voiced Charlotte V. Henry for whom Huck Finn changes his mind about women.

Durkin is excellent throughout, overshadowing Coogan, who in spots is permitted to appear and talk in a too adult manner. His early love scene assignments with Mitzi Green drag in an unnatural touch. But for Durkin's able and natural characterization all the way, this might have meant serious injury to the picture.

Norman Taurog's direction is balanced and smooth.

■ HUCKLEBERRY FINN

1939, 88 MINS, US ▼
Dir Richard Thorpe *Prod* Joseph L. Mankiewicz *Scr* Hugo Butler *Ph* John F. Seitz *Ed* Frank E. Hull *Mus* Jerome Moross *Art Dir* Cedric Gibbons, Randall Duell
● Mickey Rooney, Walter Connolly, William Frawley, Rex Ingram, Lynne Carver (M-G-M)

Picture is a fairly close adaptation of the original Mark Twain work, but has not been able to catch the rare and sparkling humor and general sincerity of the author's original. Furthermore, young Rooney seems too mature for his years.

Huckleberry Finn is naturally the dominating character in the story. Taken under the wings of Elizabeth Risdon and Clara Blandick for upbringing and an education, Mickey can't stand for school and dressing up. When his father appears to demand money from the sisters, Rooney disappears. Meeting Rex Ingram, an escaping slave, pair start down the river on a raft.

Many opportunities for comedy situations are missed.

Rex Ingram stands out boldly in support. He gives an honest and effective characterization of the runaway slave.

■ HUD

1963, 113 MINS, US ▼ ⊙
Dir Martin Ritt *Prod* Martin Ritt, Irving Ravetch *Scr* Irving Ravetch, Harriet Frank Jr *Ph* James Wong Howe *Ed* Frank Bracht *Mus* Elmer Bernstein *Art Dir* Hal Pereira, Tambi Larsen
● Paul Newman, Melvyn Douglas, Patricia Neal, Brandon de Wilde, Whit Bissell, Graham Denton (Paramount/Salem/Dover)

Hud is a near miss. Where it falls short of the mark is in its failure to filter its meaning and theme lucidly through its characters and story.

The screenplay, adapted from a novel by Larry McMurtry, tells a tale of the modern American West, of its evolution from the land of pioneer ethics, of simple human gratifications unmotivated by greed, to the rangy real estate of shallow, mercenary creatures who have inherited the rugged individualism of the early settlers, but not their souls, their morals or their principles.

The new westerner is Hud (Paul Newman), noxious son of old Homer Bannon (Melvyn Douglas), pioneer Texas Panhandler who detests his offspring with a passion that persists to his bitter end, after he has just witnessed the liquidation of his entire herd of cattle (hoof and mouth disease) and the attempt of his son to have him declared incompetent to run his ranch.

It is in the relationship of father and son that the film slips. It is never clear exactly why the old man harbors such a deep-rooted, irrevocable grudge against his lad.

But the picture has a number of elements of distinction and reward. The four leading performances are excellent. Newman creates a virile, pernicious figure as that ornery title critter. The characteristics of old age are marvelously captured and employed by Douglas. Another fine performance is by Brandon de Wilde as Newman's nephew. Patricia Neal comes through with a rich and powerful performance as the housekeeper assaulted by Newman.

□ 1963: Best Actress (Patricia Neal), Supp. Actor (Melvyn Douglas), B&W Cinematography.
□ Nominations: Best Director, Actor (Paul Newman), Adapted Screenplay, B&W Art Direction

■ HUDSON HAWK

1991, 95 MINS, US ◇ ▼ ⊙
Dir Michael Lehmann *Prod* Joel Silver *Scr* Steven E. de Souza, Daniel Waters *Ph* Dante Spinotti *Ed* Chris Lebenzon, Michael Tronick *Mus* Michael Kamen, Robert Kraft *Art Dir* Jack DeGovia
● Bruce Willis, Danny Aiello, Andie MacDowell, James Coburn, Richard E. Grant, Sandra Bernhard (Tri-Star/Silver/ABC Bone)

Ever wondered what a Three Stooges short would look like with a $40 million budget? Then meet *Hudson Hawk*, a relentlessly annoying clay duck that crash-lands in a sea of wretched excess and silliness. Those willing to check their brains at the door may find sparse amusement in pic's frenzied pace.

Bruce Willis plays just-released-from-prison cat burglar Hudson Hawk, who's immediately drawn into a plot to steal a bunch of Leonardo Da Vinci artifacts by, among others, a twisted billionaire couple (Richard E. Grant, Sandra Bernhard), a twisted CIA agent (James Coburn) and an agent for the Vatican (Andie MacDowell). Mostly, though, Hawk hangs with his pal Tommy (Danny Aiello), as the two croon old tunes to time their escapades.

Director Michael Lehmann, who made his feature debut with the deliciously subversive *Heathers*, simply seems overwhelmed by the scale and banality of the screenplay [from a story by Willis]. Very few of the scenes actually seem connected.

The film primarily gives Willis a chance to toss off poor man's *Moonlighting* one-liners in the midst of utter chaos. Grant, Bernhard and Coburn do produce a few bursts of scatological humor based on the sheer energy of their over-the-top performances.

■ HUE AND CRY

1947, 82 MINS, UK ▼
Dir Charles Crichton *Prod* Michael Balcon *Scr* T.E.B. Clarke *Ph* Douglas Slocombe *Ed* Charles Hasse *Mus* Georges Auric *Art Dir* Norman Arnold
● Alastair Sim, Valerie White, Jack Warner, Harry Fowler (Ealing)

Principal actor is ex-news vendor Harry Fowler, who has played various cockney parts on the screen, but who fails to make the main character credible. And everything depends on believing in him.

Story revolves around a gang of crooks who use a serial story in *The Trump*, a kids' weekly, as a means of communication. Joe Kirby, an imaginative youngster, spots this, and in spite of discouragement from his boss and an alleged detective, he perseveres, interests his pals, and brings off a great coup when boys of all ages flock to the bomb-ravaged wastes of dockland for a roundup of the criminals.

Director Charles Crichton has been conscientious, but queer camera angles and shadows can add little thrill when the original material lacks it.

••••••••••••••••••••••••••••••••••

■ **HUMAN COMEDY, THE**

1943, 119 MINS, US ⬤

Dir Clarence Brown   *Prod* Clarence Brown   *Scr* William Saroyan, Howard Estabrook   *Ph* Harry Stradling   *Ed* Conrad A. Nervig   *Mus* Herbert Stothart
● Mickey Rooney, Frank Morgan, Fay Bainter, Ray Collins, Van Johnson, Donna Reed (M-G-M)

William Saroyan's initial original screenplay is a brilliant sketch of the basic fundamentals of the American way of life, transferred to the screen with exceptional fidelity by director Clarence Brown and cast headed by Mickey Rooney.

Saroyan, after being promoted by Metro to write an original screenplay, reportedly wrote his script in 18 days. Studio heads acclaimed it a 'masterpiece', until advised that yarn would consume nearly four hours of running time, and then chilled on the tale.

Figuring the picture would never be produced by Metro, Saroyan returned to northern California and battled out a novel of the yarn. But Clarence Brown, assured he could obtain Mickey Rooney to handle the lead, as originally intended by the writer, decided to get front office approval to make a film version of the Saroyan tale.

Script is episodic, but this is easily overlooked in the entity of the production. Sorayan's original script was lengthy for current picture requirements, and even when it was in rough-cut form for initial sneak review ran about 170 minutes. Editing required that whole chunks and episodes be lifted out, and this was accomplished without detracting from the entertainment factors remaining.

Rooney is the major breadwinner of his little family following departure of his older brother (Van Johnson) into the army service. Rooney, displaying the strongest performance of his career under the Metro banner, shines brilliantly as the boy of Saroyan's tale.
□ 1943: Best Original Story.
□ Nominations: Best Picture, Director, Actor (Mickey Rooney), B&W Cinematography

••••••••••••••••••••••••••••••••••

■ **HUMAN DESIRE**

1954, 90 MINS, US ⬤

Dir Fritz Lang   *Prod* Lewis J. Rachmil   *Scr* Alfred Hayes   *Ph* Burnett Guffey   *Ed* William A. Lyon   *Mus* Daniele Amfitheatrof   *Art Dir* Robert Peterson
● Glenn Ford, Gloria Grahame, Broderick Crawford, Edgar Buchanan, Kathleen Case, Peggy Maley (Columbia)

The audience meets some wretched characters on the railroad in this adaptation of the Emile Zola novel, *The Human Beast*. A French picturization of the work was done earlier with heavy accent on psychological study of an alcohol-crazed killer.

Fritz Lang, director, goes overboard in his effort to create mood. Long focusing on locomotive speeding and twisting on the rails is neither entertaining nor essential to the plot.

At the outset the screenplay provides much

conversation about the fact that Glenn Ford, who's back on the job as an engineer, had been fighting the war in Korea. There's not much point to this, considering that Ford's background has little bearing on the yarn.

Broderick Crawford, Gloria Grahame and Ford make a brooding, sordid triangle, hopelessly involved. Crawford is utterly frustrated in his effort to please his wife (Grahame) and stay on an even keel with his heartless boss. Grahame is a miserable character, alternately denying and admitting she has given herself to other men. Ford dates Grahame and toys with the idea of murdering her husband.

••••••••••••••••••••••••••••••••••

■ **HUMAN FACTOR, THE**

1979, 115 MINS, UK ◇ ⬤

Dir Otto Preminger   *Prod* Otto Preminger   *Scr* Tom Stoppard   *Ph* Mike Molloy   *Ed* Richard Trevor   *Mus* Richard Logan, Gary Logan   *Art Dir* Ken Ryan
● Richard Attenborough, John Gielgud, Derek Jacobi, Robert Morley, Ann Todd, Nicol Williamson (M-G-M/Preminger)

Graham Greene's low-keyed, highly absorbing 1978 novel of an aging English double agent finding himself trapped into defecting to Moscow and leaving his family behind may have seemed like ideal material for Otto Preminger's style of dispassionate ambiguity, but helmer doesn't seem up to the occasion, bringing little atmosphere or feeling to the delicate ticks of the story.

Nicol Williamson limns the lead role of a Secret Service desk man who, due not to political commitment but loyalty to a friend from his days in Africa, discreetly passes occasional information to the East.

When a leak in his department is discovered and office partner Derek Jacobi, mistakenly identified as the culprit, is eliminated, Williamson feels the walls closing in on him.

••••••••••••••••••••••••••••••••••

■ **HUMAN JUNGLE, THE**

1954, 82 MINS, US

Dir Joseph M. Newman   *Prod* Hayes Goetz   *Scr* William Sackheim, Daniel Fuchs   *Ph* Ellis Carter   *Ed* Lester Sansom, Samuel Fields   *Mus* Hans Salter   *Art Dir* David Milton
● Gary Merrill, Jan Sterling, Paula Raymond, Emile Meyer, Regis Toomey, Chuck Connors (Allied Artists)

The Human Jungle is a sock big-city police story packed with sex as well as violence and excitement. The politics of a metropolitan police department backdrop an almost documentary narrative which has been imaginatively directed by Joseph M. Newman with punchy overtones.

Feature is marked by standout portrayals of a hand-picked cast who insert forceful realism into natural characterizations. Gary Merrill, a police captain who had passed his bar exams and is about to leave the force, is prevailed upon to head the notorious Heights district of the city, where conditions have reached the point that no one is safe. In his revitalization of his department and attempts to solve a murder he meets with opposition both from some of his own men and those above him, but finally cracks the case and whips the district into shape.

Merrill gives true meaning to his part and Jan Sterling belts over the role of a tough blonde who is used as an alibi by Chuck Connors, excellent in his characterizing of the murderer.

••••••••••••••••••••••••••••••••••

■ **HUMANOIDS FROM THE DEEP**

1980, 80 MINS, US ◇ ⬤

Dir Barbara Peeters   *Prod* Martin B. Cohen, Hunt Lowry   *Scr* Frederick James   *Ph* Daniele Lacambre   *Ed* Mark Goldblatt   *Mus* James Horner   *Art Dir* Michael Erler

● Doug McClure, Ann Turkel, Vic Morrow, Cindy Weintraub, Anthony Penya, Denise Galik (New World)

With *Humanoids from the Deep*, Roger Corman comes full circle back to his very first film as a producer, *Monster from the Ocean Floor* [1954]. Despite costing 100 times as much, new pic has similar premise and same raison d'etre, that of pocketing a profit from drive-in dates.

Tried-and-true formula of countless sci-fiers of the 1950s is revived as gruesome, amphibious creatures rise from the ocean to stalk and destroy terrified humans. General pattern here has monsters systematically killing the guys and raping the girls.

Given the nonsensical script and fact that considerable footage was added, editor Mark Goldblatt did a good job in making disparate elements at least hang together and play coherently. James Horner's score makes it seem that more is happening than actually takes place.

••••••••••••••••••••••••••••••••••

■ **HUMORESQUE**

1946, 123 MINS, US ⬤ ⊙

Dir Jean Negulesco   *Prod* Jerry Wald   *Scr* Clifford Odets, Zachary Gold   *Ph* Ernest Haller   *Ed* Rudi Fehr   *Mus* Franz Waxman (cond.)   *Art Dir* Hugh Reticker
● Joan Crawford, John Garfield, Oscar Levant, J. Carroll Naish, Joan Chandler, Tom D'Andrea (Warner)

Humoresque combines classical music and drama into a top quality motion picture. A score of unusual excellence gives freshness to standard classics and plays as important a part as Fannie Hurst's familiar story of a young violinist who rises to concert heights from the lower East Side of New York. Technically a remake (it was first produced in 1920) this version is virtually a new story, stripped of any racial connotations as was the case originally. Footage is long, running more than two hours, but does not drag because of the score potency and performance quality.

Integration of music and drama ties the two together so tightly there is never a separation. Some 23 classical numbers are included, plus a number of pop pieces used as background for cafe sequences.

Principal footage goes to John Garfield as the young violinist who, encouraged by his mother's interest, devotes his life to music. He turns in a distinguished, thoroughly believable performance. Adding to the effectiveness is the nigh-flawless fingering and bowing during the violin shots. Joan Crawford's role is an acting part, rather than a typical femme star assignment, and she makes the most of it.
□ 1946: Nomination: Best Scoring of a Dramatic Picture

••••••••••••••••••••••••••••••••••

■ **HUNCHBACK OF NOTRE DAME, THE**

1923, 135 MINS, US ⊗ ⬤ ⊙

Dir Wallace Worsley   *Scr* Edward T. Lowe, Perley Poore Sheehan   *Ph* Robert Newhard, Tony Kornman   *Art Dir* E.E. Sheeley, Sydney Ullman, Stephen Goosson
● Lon Chaney, Ernest Torrence, Patsy Ruth Miller, Norman Kerry, Kate Lester, Brandon Hurst (Universal Super-Jewel)

The programmed statistical recordings say this picture cost U over a million; that it called for tons of materials and hundreds of people, all sounding truthful enough (except the cost) after seeing it and the total achieved seems to have been a huge – mistake. *The Hunchback of Notre Dame* [from the novel by Victor Hugo] is a two-hour nightmare. It's murderous, hideous and repulsive.

Lon Chaney's performance as a performance entitles him to starring honors. His misshapened figure from the hump on his back to the deadeyed eye on his face cannot stand off his acting nor his acrobatics, nor his general work of excellence throughout this film. And, when the hunchbank dies, you see

Jehan (Brandon Hurst) stab him not once, but twice, and in the back or in the hump.

Knives were plentiful in the reign of Louis XI, 1482, in France. So were the tramps, with Clopin (Ernest Torrence) as King of the Bums making the misery stand out.

Patsy Ruth Miller is Esmeralda, a sweetly pretty girl carrying her troubles nicely enough for the heavy work thrust upon her and with the absence of heavy emoting. Norman Kerry is the gallant Phoebus and a lukewarm lover at times.

....

■ **HUNCHBACK OF NOTRE DAME, THE**

1939, 115 MINS, US ⚉ ⊙
Dir William Dieterle *Prod* Pandro S. Berman
Scr Sonya Levien *Ph* Joseph H. August *Ed* William
Hamilton, Robert Wise *Mus* Alfred Newman
Art Dir Van Nest Polglase, Al Herman
● Charles Laughton, Cedric Hardwicke, Maureen
O'Hara, Thomas Mitchell, Edmond O'Brien, Alan Marshal
(RKO)

Parading vivid and gruesome horror, with background of elaborate medieval pageantry and mob scenes, *Hunchback of Notre Dame* is a super thriller-chiller.

From a strictly critical viewpoint, picture has its shortcomings. The elaborate sets and wide production sweep overshadows to a great extent the detailed dramatic motivation of the Victor Hugo tale. While the background is impressive and eye-filling, it detracts many times from the story, especially in the first half.

Supporting cast is studded with topnotch performers for each role. Cedric Hardwicke is the villainous King's High Justice; Thomas Mitchell is the king of the beggars; Maureen O'Hara (excellent) is the gypsy girl who befriends the hunchback on the pillory and is saved by him later.

Production displays lavish outlay in costs for elaborate sets and thousands of extras for the mob scenes.
☐ 1939: Nominations: Best Score, Sound

....

■ **HUNCHBACK OF NOTRE DAME, THE**

1957, 103 MINS, US ⚉ ⚉
Dir Jean Delannoy *Prod* Robert Hakim, Raymond Hakim
Scr Jean Aurenche, Jacques Prevert *Ph* Michel Kelber
Ed Henri Taverna *Mus* Georges Auric *Art Dir* Rene
Renoux
● Gina Lollobrigida, Anthony Quinn, Jean Danet, Alain
Cuny, Maurice Sarfati, Danielle Dumont (Allied Artists)

This version of the Victor Hugo classic, although beautifully photographed and extravagantly produced, is ponderous, often dull and far overlength.

Gina Lollobrigida is co-starred with Anthony Quinn, who plays the Quasimodo role previously enacted by Lon Chaney and Charles Laughton. Producers seem more inclined to offer spectacle than concentrate on pointing up story line with any degree of freshness.

Lollobrigida appears to be somewhat miscast as a naive gypsy girl of 15th-century Paris, but occasionally displays flashes of spirit. Quinn, as the hunchbacked bellringer of Notre Dame who saves the gypsy girl from hanging and hides her within the sanctuary of the cathedral, where he becomes her devoted slave, gives a well-etched impression of the difficult role. His makeup is not as extreme as either of the two previous characterizations.

....

■ **HUNGER, THE**

1983, 97 MINS, US ⚉ ⚉
Dir Tony Scott *Prod* Richard A. Shepherd *Scr* Ivan
Davis, Michael Thomas *Ph* Stephen Goldblatt
Ed Pamela Power *Mus* Michel Rubini, Denny Jaeger
Art Dir Brian Morris

● Catherine Deneuve, David Bowie, Susan Sarandon,
Cliff De Young, Beth Ehlers, Dan Hedaya (Richard
Shepherd/M-G-M/United Artists)

Like so many other films from British commercials directors, *The Hunger* [from the novel by Whitley Strieber] is all visual and aural flash, although this modern vampire story looks so great, as do its three principal performers, and is so bizarre that it possesses a certain perverse appeal.

Opening sequence provides viewers with a pretty good idea of what's in store. Catherine Deneuve and David Bowie pick up a couple of punky rock 'n' rollers. Deneuve and Bowie commit a double murder in their elegantly appointed New York apartment, and the prevailing motif of sex mixed with bloody death is established.

Although Deneuve and Bowie privately vow to stay with one another forever, Bowie soon notices himself growing rapidly older and visits author-doctor Susan Sarandon, who is preoccupied with the problem of accelerated aging. Shunned by her, Bowie deteriorates quickly and Deneuve buries him in a box in her attic next to her previous lovers.

Distraught over her mistreatment of Bowie, Sarandon begins visiting Deneuve, and a provative highlight is their seduction and lovemaking scene.

In his feature debut, director Tony Scott, brother of Ridley, exhibits the same penchant for eleborate art direction, minimal, humorless dialog and shooting in smoky rooms.

....

■ **HUNTER, THE**

1980, 117 MINS, US ⚉ ⚉ ⊙
Dir Buzz Kulik *Prod* Mort Engelberg *Scr* Ted Leighton,
Peter Hyams *Ph* Fred J. Koenekamp *Ed* Robert Wolfe
Mus Michel Legrand *Art Dir* Ron Hobbs
● Steve McQueen, Eli Wallach, Kathryn Harrold, Ben
Johnson (Paramount/Rastar/Mort Engelberg)

Fact that the overlong pic is based on adventures of a modern-day bounty hunter may have hampered filmmakers' imagination, as attempt to render contradictions of real-life Ralph 'Papa' Thorson, who's into classical music and astrology as well as hauling in fugitives from justice, has made for an annoyingly unrealized and childish onscreen character.

Steve McQueen may have felt that the time had come to revise his persona a bit, but what's involved here is desecration. Given star's rep since *Bullitt* as a terrific driver, someone thought it might be cute to make him a lousy one here, but seeing him crash stupidly into car after car runs the gag into the ground. *The Hunter* [based on the book by Christopher Keane] is a western in disguise.

Only sequence which remotely delivers the goods has McQueen chasing a gun-toting maniac in Chicago. Pic's finale, which has star fainting when pregnant g.f. Kathryn Harrold gives birth, merely puts capper on overall misconception.

....

■ **HUNT FOR RED OCTOBER, THE**

1990, 137 MINS, US ⚉ ⚉ ⊙
Dir John McTiernan *Prod* Mace Neufeld *Scr* Larry
Ferguson, Donald Stewart, [John Milius] *Ph* Jan De Bont
Ed Dennis Virkler, John Wright *Mus* Basil Poledouris
Art Dir Terence Marsh
● Sean Connery, Alec Baldwin, Scott Glenn, Sam Neill,
James Earl Jones, Joss Ackland (Paramount)

The Hunt for Red October is a terrific adventure yarn. Tom Clancy's 1984 Cold War thriller has been thoughtfully adapted to reflect the mellowing in the US-Soviet relationship.

Sean Connery is splendid as the renegade Soviet nuclear sub captain pursued by CIA analyst Alec Baldwin and the fleets of both superpowers as he heads for the coast of Maine. The filmmakers have wisely opted to keep the story set in 1984 – 'shortly before Gorbachev came to power', as the opening title puts it.

Looking magnificent in his captain's uniform and white beard, Connery scores as the Lithuanian Marko Ramius, a coldblooded killer and a meditator on Hindu scripture.

Baldwin's intelligent and likable performance makes his Walter Mittyish character come alive. He's combating not only the bulk of the Soviet fleet but also the reflexive anti-Communist mentality of most pursuing on the US side – not including his wise and avuncular CIA superior James Earl Jones.

The Industrial Light & Magic special visual effects unit does yeoman work in staging the action with cliffhanger intensity.
☐ 1990: Best Sound Effects Editing.
☐ Nominations: Best Editing, Sound

....

■ **HUNTING PARTY, THE**

1971, 108 MINS, UK ◇ ⚉
Dir Don Medford *Prod* Lou Morheim *Scr* William
Norton, Gilbert Alexander, Lou Morheim *Ph* Cecilio
Paniagua *Ed* Tom Rolf *Mus* Riz Ortolani
Art Dir Enrique Alarcon
● Oliver Reed, Candice Bergen, Gene Hackman, Simon
Oakland, Mitchell Ryan, L.Q. Jones (United Artists)

It isn't as hard to believe that excellent actors Oliver Reed and Gene Hackman would accept roles like those they are given in *The Hunting Party* because they were undoubtedly well paid (indeed, overpaid, considering the performances they give). But to find such fine supporting players as Mitchell Ryan, Simon Oakland and Dean Selmier in this minor effort is really surprising.

Basically, Reed (who's illiterate) and his gang, kidnap a teacher (Candice Bergen) who turns out to be the wife of the local cattlebaron (Gene Hackman), who is out on a hunting party with some other millionaire friends. When he hears the news, Hackman starts a search for the gang, armed with new highpower rifles capable of killing from 800 yards. One by one the gang is picked off from a safe distance until the eventual showdown with only Hackman trailing Reed and Bergen (by now in love with the outlaw, of course) onto a desert.

Seldom has so much fake blood been splattered for so little reason.

....

■ **HURRICANE, THE**

1937, 110 MINS, US ⚉ ⊙
Dir John Ford *Prod* Samuel Goldwyn *Scr* Dudley
Nichols *Ph* Bert Glennon *Ed* Lloyd Nosler
Mus Alfred Newman (dir.) *Art Dir* Richard Day,
Alexander Golitzen
● Dorothy Lamour, Jon Hall, Mary Astor, C. Aubrey
Smith, Thomas Mitchell, Raymond Massey (Goldwyn)

Turned out on a broad canvas, *The Hurricane* is a scenically pretentious and colorful spectacle which has as its climax a hurricane sequence that is compellingly realistic. The authors of the novel, Charles Nordhoff and James Norman Hall, also wrote the story of *Mutiny on the Bounty*.

The force of the story [adapted by Oliver H.P. Garrett] does not stop with the hurricane triumph nor the brutality of prison officers, pictured as worse than ever accredited to Devil's Island. neither does it stop with the successful dramatic escape of the romantic lead (Jon Hall) amidst frightful odds. There is also a highly emotional love story woven around Hall and Dorothy Lamour, latter playing the native girl who marries him as the picture opens.

The big blow is reputed to cost $300,000. That's not unbelievable. It is understood the total cost of the picture ran to $1.75 million.

Performances are specially good from Hall down. A finely turned character is that of the governor, another Javert (*Les Miserables*), done capitally and forcefully by Raymond Massey.

☐ 1937: Best Sound Recording.
☐ Nomination: Best Score

••••••••••••••••••••••••••••

■ HURRICANE

1979, 119 MINS, US ◇ ⓦ
Dir Jan Troell   *Prod* Dino De Laurentiis   *Scr* Lorenzo
Semple Jr   *Ph* Sven Nykvist   *Ed* Sam O'Steen
Mus Nino Rota   *Art Dir* Danilo Donati
● Jason Robards, Mia Farrow, Max Von Sydow, Trevor
Howard, Dayton Ka'ne, Timothy Bottoms (Paramount/De
Laurentiis)

The storm blows fiercely but the love story
doesn't match its power in *Hurricane*. Dino De
Laurentiis' epic reportedly delivered with a
$22 million negative cost.

Charles Nordhoff and James Norman Hall's
novel, *The Hurricane*, was filmed relatively
faithfully in 1937 by John Ford.

The context and conflicts in the new production have been altered significantly. Script
sets the tale in Eastern Samoa, circa 1920,
with Jason Robards lording it over the natives
on behalf of the US navy. The female love interest is now a white woman, with Mia
Farrow sailing in from Boston to see her commander father, but gradually becoming involved with the young chieftain of a nearby
island (Dayton Ka'ne).

The hurricane itself, which runs 25 minutes
and was created entirely on location in Bora
Bora by a special effects team led by Glen
Robinson, who performed the same function
on the 1937 production, Aldo Puccini and Joe
Day, is impressive enough.

••••••••••••••••••••••••••••

■ HURRY SUNDOWN

1967, 146 MINS, US ◇
Dir Otto Preminger   *Prod* Otto Preminger   *Scr* Thomas
C. Ryan, Horton Foote   *Ph* Milton Krasner, Loyal Griggs
Ed Louis Loeffler, James D. Wells   *Mus* Hugo
Montenegro   *Art Dir* Gene Callahan
● Michael Caine, Jane Fonda, John Phillip Law,
Diahann Carroll, Faye Dunaway, Burgess Meredith
(Paramount/Sigma)

In *Hurry Sundown*, based on the novel [by K.B.
Gilden], producer-director Otto Preminger
has created an outstanding, tasteful but hard-
hitting, and handsomely-produced film about
racial conflict in Georgia circa 1945. Told with
a depth and frankness, the story develops its
theme in a welcome, straight-forward way that
is neither propaganda nor mere exploitation
material. Cast with many younger players, all
of whom deliver fine performances.

Michael Caine leads the stars, and delivers
an excellent performance as the white social
climber managing the Georgia land holdings
of wife Jane Fonda.

Two tracts block Caine's plans, those of distant relative John Phillip Law and Negro
Robert Hooks, both just-returned war vets.

••••••••••••••••••••••••••••

■ HUSBANDS
A COMEDY ABOUT LIFE, DEATH & FREEDOM

1970, 154 MINS, US ◇
Dir John Cassavetes   *Prod* Al Ruban, Sam Shaw
Scr John Cassavetes   *Ph* Victor Kemper   *Ed* Peter
Tanner
● Ben Gazzara, Peter Falk, John Cassavetes, Jenny
Runacre, Jenny Lee Wright, Noelle Kao (Columbia)

Appalled and horrified by the death of their
best friend, three middleclass, not-quite-mid-
dleaged family men explode and ricochet off
on a marathon New York-to-London binge.

Director-writer-actor John Cassavetes, Ben
Gazzara and Peter Falk are the 'husbands',
who, in the face of death, revert to drunken,
giggling, horseplaying adolescence, and, with
a stunningly-talented supporting cast, create
and improvise a memorably touching, human
and very funny film.

Fleeing from the beer foam and grime of a

lower New York bar in a sudden panicked
flight to London, Cassavetes, Falk and
Gazzara are three of the uncoolest married
men to ever go on the make.

In a superb cast, Jenny Runacre, a tall
lovely blonde English girl gives a touching
performance as Cassavetes' neurotic pick-up.

••••••••••••••••••••••••••••

■ HUSBANDS AND WIVES

1992, 107 MINS, US ◇ ⓦ ☉
Dir Woody Allen   *Prod* Robert Greenhut   *Scr* Woody
Allen   *Ph* Carlo Di Palma   *Ed* Susan E. Morse
Mus [various]   *Art Dir* Santo Loquasto
● Woody Allen, Blythe Danner, Judy Davis, Mia Farrow,
Juliette Lewis, Liam Neeson (Tri-Star)

Husbands and Wives is major Woody. This
sometimes comic drama stands with
Manhattan and *Hannah and Her Sisters* as a
richly satisfying ensemble piece about N.Y.
neurotics falling in and out of love.

Jarring opening scene gives a strong indication of things to come. Arriving to dine with
their best friends Allen and Mia Farrow, married couple Sydney Pollack and Judy Davis announce almost matter-of-factly that they're
separating. It quickly becomes apparent Allen
and Farrow have their own troubles. They've
never agreed upon having a child: she's for it,
he's not. College English instructor Allen
takes a special interest in a talented and
provocative student (Juliette Lewis) but
steers clear of sexual involvement.

Pollack takes up with knockout New Age
bimbo Lysette Anthony. Infuriated with how
quickly Pollack has replaced her, the intense
Davis goes out with Irish dreamboat Liam
Neeson. When Neeson goes for Davis in a big
way, Farrow becomes distraught, realizing
the depth of her own feelings for him.

Allen creates a full-bodied gallery of hard-
headed urbanites who more often than not
operate out of self-destructive impulses. This
is definitely his edgiest, rawest work in a good
while.

While his subjects have remained much the
same, Allen's style has undergone a radical
change here. Carlo Di Palma's lensing appears to be almost entirely hand-held, creating a look somewhere between early French
New Wave and cinema verite. Acting is of a
very high caliber across the board, but Davis,
in a very meaty part, is incandescent, revealing a whole new side to her onscreen personality.

☐ 1992: Nominations: Best Supp. Actress
(Judy Davis), Original Screenplay

••••••••••••••••••••••••••••

■ HUSH . . . HUSH, SWEET CHARLOTTE

1964, 134 MINS, US ⓦ
Dir Robert Aldrich   *Prod* Robert Aldrich   *Scr* Henry
Farrell, Lukas Heller   *Ph* Joseph Biroc   *Ed* Michael
Luciano   *Mus* Frank DeVol   *Art Dir* William Glasgow
● Bette Davis, Olivia de Havilland, Joseph Cotten, Agnes
Moorehead, Cecil Kellaway, Mary Astor (Associates &
Aldrich/20th Century-Fox)

Robert Aldrich's followup (but no relation) to
What Ever Happened to Baby Jane? is a shocker.
Bette Davis again stars, with Olivia de
Havilland returning to the screen in the role
which Joan Crawford started but due to con-
tinued illness had to abandon.

Davis lives in the reflection of a dreadful
past, the macabre murder and mutilation of
her married lover hanging over her as she frequently confuses the past with the present as
her mental balance is threatened. De
Havilland, as her cousin, lives very much for
the present – and future – as she attempts to
soothe and rationalize with the deeply emotional mistress of the house.

Based upon a story by Henry Farrell, who
also authored *Baby Jane*, screenplay by Farrell
and Lukas Heller (latter scripted *Jane*) opens
in 1927 in the Louisiana plantation house of

Davis' father, who warns a neighboring married man to break off all romantic relations
with his daughter. The main story swings to
the present, again in the mansion where
Davis lives alone with her memories which
threaten to destroy her.

Davis' portrayal is reminiscent of *Jane* in its
emotional overtones, in her style of characterization of the near-crazed former Southern
belle, aided by haggard makeup and outlandish attire. It is an outgoing performance,
and she plays it to the limit. De Havilland, on
the other hand, is far more restrained but
none the less effective dramatically in her offbeat role.

☐ 1964: Nominations: Best Supp. Actress
(Agnes Moorehead), B&W Cinematography,
B&W Costume Design, B&W Art Direction,
Editing, Original Music Score, Song ('Hush
. . . Hush, Sweet Charlotte')

••••••••••••••••••••••••••••

■ HUSSY

1980, 95 MINS, UK ◇ ⓦ
Dir Matthew Chapman   *Prod* Jeremy Watt
Scr Matthew Chapman   *Ph* Keith Goddard   *Ed* Bill
Blunden   *Mus* George Fenton   *Art Dir* Hazel Peiser
● Helen Mirren, John Shea, Jenny Runacre, Murray
Salem, Paul Angelis, Patti Boulaye (Kendon)

Somewhere in scripter-director Matthew
Chapman's first feature there's a valid love
story trying to get out. It stays buried for lack
of an objective eye – that of an experienced
producer, perhaps – to see the pitfalls of an
acceptably lightweight project that strives for
serious significance.

John Shea's performance as Helen Mirren's
lover, a transient American working as spotlight operator at the London stripjoint where
she hosts and hooks is mostly bland, but occasionally effective in hinting at a murkier past
than his guileless looks suggest. Mirren would
have come off better had she been directed towards a less ponderous conception of the role.

Neither lead is helped by dialog which badly
needed that ruthless impartial eye; as it is,
there are some leaden, even laughable, moments.

••••••••••••••••••••••••••••

■ HUSTLE

1975, 120 MINS, US ◇ ⓦ
Dir Robert Aldrich   *Prod* Robert Aldrich   *Scr* Steve
Shagan   *Ph* Joseph Biroc   *Ed* Michael Luciano
Mus Frank DeVol   *Art Dir* Hilyard Brown
● Burt Reynolds, Catherine Deneuve, Ben Johnson, Paul
Winfield, Eileen Brennan, Eddie Albert (Paramount/
RoBurt)

Robert Aldrich's sharp-looking film reunites
him with Burt Reynolds, starring here as a
hardening detective trying to short circuit the
solution of a femme teenager's dope suicide
because the trail may lead to Eddie Albert, a
noted lawyer with many uptown and downtown connections.

Reynolds is torn between his duty and his
personal attraction-resistance to mistress
Catherine Deneuve.

Ben Johnson and Eileen Brennan are the
parents of the dead girl, and Johnson on his
own doggedly tracks down clues which explode some darker family secrets with goading Reynolds into frantic coverup action.

The film's drawbacks are simply a lack of
some restraint, since otherwise all the elements are present for a sensational, hardhitting human story.

••••••••••••••••••••••••••••

■ HUSTLER, THE

1961, 134 MINS, US ⓦ ☉
Dir Robert Rossen   *Prod* Robert Rossen   *Scr* Robert
Rossen, Sidney Carroll   *Ph* Gene Shufton   *Ed* Dede
Allen   *Mus* Kenyon Hopkins   *Art Dir* Harry Horner,
Albert Brenner

● Paul Newman, Jackie Gleason, Piper Laurie, George C. Scott, Myron McCormick, Murray Hamilton (20th Century-Fox)

The Hustler belongs to that school of screen realism that allows impressive performances but defeats the basic goal of pure entertainment.

Film is peopled by a set of unpleasant characters set down against a backdrop of cheap pool halls and otherwise dingy surroundings. Chief protagonist is Paul Newman, a pool shark with a compulsion to be the best of the lot – not in tournament play but in beating Chicago's bigtime player (Jackie Gleason). Unfoldment of the screenplay, based on novel by Walter S. Tevis, is far overlength and despite the excellence of Newman's portrayal of the boozing pool hustler the sordid aspects of overall picture are strictly downbeat.

Newman is entirely believable in the means he takes to defeat Gleason, and latter socks over a dramatic role which, though comparatively brief, generates potency. In some respects, the quiet strength of his characterization overshadows Newman in their scenes together. Piper Laurie establishes herself solidly as a hard-drinking floosie who lives with Newman, and George C. Scott scores as a gambler who promotes Newman and teaches him the psychology of being a winner.
□ 1961: Best B&W Cinematography, B&W Art Direction.
□ Nominations: Best Picture, Director, Actor (Paul Newman), Actress (Piper Laurie), Supp. Actor (Jackie Gleason, George C. Scott [latter nom. refused]), Adapted Screenplay

● ● ● ● ● ● ● ● ● ● ● ● ● ● ● ● ● ● ● ●

I*i*

■ I ACCUSE!

1958, 99 MINS, UK
Dir Jose Ferrer   *Prod* Sam Zimbalist   *Scr* Gore Vidal
Ph Freddie A. Young   *Ed* Frank Clarke   *Mus* William Alwyn   *Art Dir* Elliot Scott
● Jose Ferrer, Anton Walbrook, Viveca Lindfors, Leo Genn, Emlyn Williams, David Farrar (M-G-M)

This version of the drama of the Dreyfus case, one of the greatest miscarriages of justice in history, makes strong, if plodding, entertainment.

The story concerns the plight of a Jewish staff officer of the French army who is unjustly accused of treason, found guilty through being framed to save the army's face, and condemned to life imprisonment on Devil's Island. Friends fighting to restore his tarnished honor force a re-trial.

Jose Ferrer takes on the heavy task of playing Dreyfus and of directing. His performance is a wily, impeccable one, but it comes from the intellect rather than the heart and rarely causes pity. He makes Dreyfus a staid, almost fanatical patriot. The action is throughout rather static, but the court scenes are pregnant with drama, thanks to a literate screenplay by Gore Vidal [from a book by Nicholas Halasz].

Anton Walbrook, the real culprit, gives a splendid performance – suave, debonair and fascinating. And equally impressive is Donald Wolfit as the army's top guy who claims that the honor of the French army is more important than the fate of one man.

● ● ● ● ● ● ● ● ● ● ● ● ● ● ● ● ● ● ● ●

■ I AM A FUGITIVE

See: I Am a Fugitive From a Chain Gang

● ● ● ● ● ● ● ● ● ● ● ● ● ● ● ● ● ● ● ●

■ I AM A FUGITIVE FROM A CHAIN GANG
(UK: I Am a Fugitive)

1932, 93 MINS, US ⓥ
Dir Mervyn LeRoy   *Prod* [Hal B. Wallis]   *Scr* Howard J. Green, Brown Holmes   *Ph* Sol Polito   *Ed* William Holmes   *Mus* Leo Forbstein (dir.)   *Art Dir* Jack Okey
● Paul Muni, Glenda Farrell, Helen Vinson, Noel Francis, Preston Foster, Allen Jenkins (Warner)

I Am a Fugitive from a Chain Gang is a picture with guts. It grips with its stark realism and packs lots of punch.

It's a sympathetic, unbiased cinematic transposition of the Robert E. Burns autobiography.

Paul Muni breaks away from the chain gang twice. In between he achieves success in his preferred field of engineering until a romantic angle prompts him voluntarily to surrender as the wanted fugitive, on the promise and belief he will be pardoned in 90 days. The prison board stalls that, despite influential appeals, leading into the second break away from the chain gang. The finale is stark in its realism.

Muni turns in a pip performance. Glenda Farrell and Helen Vinson, the only two femmes of any prominence, are oke in their parts. Hale Hamilton as an overly benign and saccharine rev, the brother of the escaped convict, is an especial click in the characterization.
□ 1932/33: Nominations: Best Picture, Actor (Paul Muni), Sound

● ● ● ● ● ● ● ● ● ● ● ● ● ● ● ● ● ● ● ●

■ I CAN GET IT FOR YOU WHOLESALE
(UK: This Is My Affair)

1951, 91 MINS, US
Dir Michael Gordon   *Prod* Sol C. Siegel   *Scr* Abraham

Polonsky   *Ph* Milton Krasner   *Ed* Robert Simpson   *Mus* Sol Kaplan   *Art Dir* Lyle Wheeler, John DeCuir
● Susan Hayward, Dan Dailey, George Sanders, Sam Jaffe, Randy Stuart, Marvin Kaplan (20th Century-Fox)

Background of New York's garment- manufacturing sector provides the setting for this adult drama [adapted by Vera Caspary from Jerome Weidman's novel].

Uniformly excellent trouping is turned in by the three stars, Susan Hayward, Dan Dailey and George Sanders. It's the setup of an ambitious woman who schemes her way to establish her own business, then almost throws over her partners for a love nest arrangement with a merchant prince who can make her a world-renowned costume designer.

Hayward is the ambitious femme. She partners with Dailey, a hot garment salesman, and Sam Jaffe, an experienced production man, and their business grows, but not fast enough to satisfy the girl. She meets and charms Sanders, merchant prince, who offers her fame if she can break with her partners. It's more than business with Dailey, who eyes Hayward romantically. This provides some conflict when she goes for Sanders.

● ● ● ● ● ● ● ● ● ● ● ● ● ● ● ● ● ● ● ●

■ ICE CASTLES

1978, 113 MINS, US ◇ ⓦ
Dir Donald Wrye   *Prod* John Kemeny   *Scr* Donald Wrye, Gary L. Bain   *Ph* Bill Butler   *Ed* Michael Kahn, Maury Winetrobe, Melvin Shapiro   *Mus* Marvin Hamlisch   *Art Dir* Joel Schiller
● Lynn-Holly Johnson, Robby Benson, Colleen Dewhurst, Tom Skerritt, Jennifer Warren, David Huffman (Columbia)

Ice Castles combines a touching love story with the excitement and intense pressure of Olympic competition skating.

Lynn-Holly Johnson portrays a farm girl from upstate Iowa who has the raw talent to be a great skater. Under the training and encouragement of local ice rink operator Colleen Dewhurst, she wins a regional competition, where she is spotted by Olympic coach Jennifer Warren.

Warren propels Johnson to instant stardom as a Cinderella figure who comes out of nowhere to win the hearts of the American people. All is progressing smoothly until Johnson has a freak accident, and is partially blinded. Robby Benson, who plays Johnson's boyfriend, and Tom Skerritt, her father, bring the teenager out of her shell, leading up to the inspiring ending.

Dewhurst, who appears all too infrequently in pix, excels in her role as the hard-bitten ex-skater trying not to live out her failed dreams through Johnson. Skerritt gives another outstanding perf as the overly-protective father who also realizes his failings. Johnson shows the potential of being an excellent actress, in addition to a top skater. She is consistently believable, even in the more maudlin moments.
□ 1979: Nomination: Best Song ('Through the Eyes of Love')

● ● ● ● ● ● ● ● ● ● ● ● ● ● ● ● ● ● ● ●

■ ICE COLD IN ALEX
(US: Desert Attack)

1958, 132 MINS, UK ⓥ
Dir J. Lee Thompson   *Prod* W.A. Whittaker   *Scr* T.J. Morrison, Christopher Landon   *Ph* Gilbert Taylor   *Ed* Richard Best   *Mus* Leighton Lucas   *Art Dir* Robert Jones
● John Mills, Sylvia Syms, Anthony Quayle, Harry Andrews, Diane Clare, Peter Arne (Associated British)

Based on a slight, real-life anecdote, pic [from Christopher Landon's novel] is the story of a handful of people who drive an ambulance through the mine-ridden, enemy-occupied desert after the collapse of Tobruk in 1942.

There are a nerve-strained officer who has taken to the bottle, his tough, reliable sergeant-major, a couple of nurses and a South African officer. Director J. Lee Thompson captures the stark, pitiless atmosphere of the desert superbly. The screenplay skillfully blends excitement, a hint of romance and a fearful sense of danger.

John Mills is the skipper, strained to the limit, who seeks solace in a few swift swigs. This is a credible, edgy performance. Anthony Quayle, as the South African, has a suspect accent but brings a plausible charm to the role. Harry Andrews is first-rate as the sergeant-major. Stripped of any glamor, Sylvia Syms fits snugly into the plot. Diane Clare, a newcomer, plays a frightened nurse who gets bumped off half way through the film.

••••••••••••••••••••••••••••••

■ ICE STATION ZEBRA

1968, 152 MINS, US ◇ ⑰ ⊙

Dir John Sturges *Prod* Martin Ransohoff *Scr* Douglas Heyes *Ph* Daniel L. Fapp *Ed* Ferris Webster *Mus* Michel Legrand *Art Dir* George W. Davis, Addison Hehr

● Rock Hudson, Ernest Borgnine, Patrick McGoohan, Jim Brown, Tony Bill, Lloyd Nolan (M-G-M/Filmways)

Action adventure film, in which US and Russian forces race to recover some compromising satellite photography from a remote Polar outpost. Alistair MacLean's novel adapted into a screen story [by Harry Julian Fink] is seeded with elements of intrigue, as Rock Hudson takes aboard a British secret agent, Patrick McGoohan; an expatriate, professional anti-Communist Russian, Ernest Borgnine; and an enigmatic Marine Corps captain, Jim Brown.

Action develops slowly, alternating with some excellent submarine interior footage, and good shots – of diving, surfacing and maneuvering under an ice field.

Film's biggest acting asset is McGoohan, who gives his scenes that elusive 'star' magnetism. He is a most accomplished actor with a three-dimensional presence all his own.

Hudson comes across quite well as a man of muted strength. Borgnine's characterization is a nicely restrained one. Brown, isolated by script to a suspicious personality, makes the most of it.

□ 1968: Nominations: Best Cinematography, Visual Effects

••••••••••••••••••••••••••••••

■ I CONFESS

1953, 95 MINS, US ⑰ ⊙

Dir Alfred Hitchcock *Prod* Alfred Hitchcock *Scr* George Tabori, William Archibald *Ph* Robert Burks *Ed* Rudi Fehr *Mus* Dimitri Tiomkin *Art Dir* Edward S. Haworth

● Montgomery Clift, Anne Baxter, Karl Malden, Brian Aherne, O.E. Hasse, Roger Dann (Warner)

An interesting plot premise holds out considerable promise for this Alfred Hitchcock production, but *I Confess* is short of the suspense one would expect. Hitchcock used the actual streets and buildings of picturesque Quebec to film the Paul Anthelme play on which the screenplay is based.

Intriguing story idea finds a priest facing trial for a murder he didn't commit, and refusing to clear himself even though the killer had confessed to him in the sanctity of the church. Quite a moral question is posed in the problem of just how sacred is a church confessional, particularly when it leaves a killer to roam free to kill again.

Chief exponents of the melodrama are Montgomery Clift, the priest, and Anne Baxter, a married woman who still believes she is in love with him, even though he ended their youthful romance and entered the church.

While Hitchcock short-changes on the expected round of suspense for which he is noted, he does bring out a number of topflight performances and gives the picture an interesting polish that is documentary at times. Clift's ability to project mood with restrained strength is a high spot of the film, and he is believable as the young priest. Physically, he doesn't have as mature an appearance as the role opposite Baxter calls for, but otherwise, his work is flawless.

••••••••••••••••••••••••••••••

■ I COVER THE WATERFRONT

1933, 72 MINS, US ⑰

Dir James Cruze *Prod* Edward Small *Scr* Wells Root, Jack Jevne *Ph* Ray June *Ed* Grant Whytock *Art Dir* Albert D'Agostino

● Claudette Colbert, Ben Lyon, Ernest Torrence, Hobart Cavanaugh, Maurice Black (United Artists)

Rather than an adaption of the Max Miller book, this is a homemade studio yarn carrying the original's title.

Around Ernest Torrence's Eli Kirk, a deep-sea skipper and smuggler who has few scruples, except those concerning his daughter, the scenarist has built a fable that manages to keep some of Miller's waterfront-reporting color alive, but much of it accomplished by the exaggeration route. Ben Lyon, as the reporter, is still another legman who calls his editor names on the phone and in the office, but holds his job anyway. For years he's been promising a sensational expose on Kirk's activities and finally he delivers. Kirk is caught while landing Chinamen inside shark skins.

Meanwhile Lyon and Claudette Colbert, Kirk's unsuspecting daughter, carry on a hot love affair, including a night at Lyon's apartment, with the customary breakfast in the a.m. Lyon originally intended to get Kirk through his daughter, but he falls in love, which is a cinch to see in advance, as is the finish.

••••••••••••••••••••••••••••••

■ IDEAL HUSBAND, AN

1947, 96 MINS, UK ◇ ⑰

Dir Alexander Korda *Prod* Alexander Korda *Scr* Lajos Biro *Ph* Georges Perinal *Ed* Oscar Hafenrichter *Mus* Arthur Benjamin *Art Dir* Vincent Korda

● Paulette Goddard, Michael Wilding, Hugh Williams, Diana Wynyard, C. Aubrey Smith, Glynis Johns (British Lion)

This version of the Oscar Wilde 1895 play is given handsome mounting by Alexander Korda. Yet he could do little more than put the play on the screen, stage asides and all.

Story relates how Hugh Williams, undersecretary of the foreign office and marked for a Cabinet post, in his youth profited by selling a Cabinet secret about the Suez Canal, thereby founding his fortune and his political career. Arrival of Paulette Goddard, an adventuress and old school friend of his wife complicates matters. She knows about Williams' misdeed and threatens him with exposure if he doesn't support a phony Argentine canal scheme in parliament.

At first he agrees, but his wife, Diana Wynyard, persuades him to refuse. It looks like the end of his career and marriage, until his best friend, Michael Wilding, takes a hand.

It seems a brave experiment to cast Goddard as the adventuress. But it doesn't quite come off. Not a solitary epigram is thrown off with spontaneity, and her loveliness in gorgeous costumes is inadequate compensation.

••••••••••••••••••••••••••••••

■ IDOLMAKER, THE

1980, 107 MINS, US ◇ ⑰ ⊙

Dir Taylor Hackford *Prod* Gene Kirkwood, Howard W Koch Jr *Scr* Edward Di Lorenzo *Ph* Adam Holender *Ed* Neil Travis *Mus* Jeff Barry *Art Dir* David L. Snyder

● Ray Sharkey, Paul Land, Olympia Dukakis, Peter Gallagher, Joe Pantoliano, Tovah Feldshuh (United Artists)

Though it's marred by an overly melodramatic and dubious finale, *The Idolmaker* is an unusually compelling film about the music business in the late 1950s and early 1960s. It shows how teen idols were created, promoted, and discarded by entrepreneurs cynically manipulating the adolescent audience. Ray Sharkey is superb in the title role.

Script is a roman-a-clef of the career of Bob Marcucci who, along with Dick Clark, guided Frankie Avalon to stardom and then created Fabian as Avalon's successor.

Viewers will have no trouble recognizing Paul Land as the Avalon figure or Peter Gallagher as Fabian.

All of the elements are shown in believable detail, though the payola and organized crime elements of the record industry are not indicated on the higher levels, an unfortunate omission.

••••••••••••••••••••••••••••••

■ I DON'T BUY KISSES ANYMORE

1992, 112 MINS, US ◇ ⑰

Dir Robert Marcarelli *Prod* Mitchel Matovich *Scr* Jonnie Lindsell *Ph* Michael Ferris *Ed* Joanne D'Antonio *Mus* Cobb Bussinger *Art Dir* Byrnadette di Santo

● Jason Alexander, Nia Peeples, Lainie Kazan, Lou Jacobi, Eileen Brennan, David Bowe (Web-Marc)

A middle-brow romantic comedy steeped in Jewish and Italian stereotype, *I Don't Buy Kisses Anymore*, a detailed portrait of a lifelong fatty who sweats and diets his way to a new life, is really quite inspiring. Less convincing is its broad, clumsy love story.

Jason Alexander plays Bernie, a lonely, chubby bachelor who slogs along under the thumb of his overbearing Jewish family and the shoestore he inherited from his dad. Then he meets peppy, ambitious aerobics nut Tress (Nia Peeples) at the bus stop and loses his heart. In no time he's joined her gym and is battering away at the extra 50 pounds on his stocky frame, while trying unsuccessfully to date her.

Set in a blue-collar Philly suburb that has dodged the winds of change, pic is buoyed by a warm, engaging chemistry between Peeples and Alexander. Cast is uneven, with Eileen Brennan charming as a candy store owner and Lainie Kazan and Lou Jacobi playing fully into unflattering ethnic stereotypes.

••••••••••••••••••••••••••••••

■ I DON'T WANT TO BE BORN
(US: The Devil Within Her)

1975, 90 MINS, UK ◇ ⑰

Dir Peter Sasdy *Scr* Stanley Price *Ph* Kenneth Talbot *Ed* Keith Palmer *Mus* Ron Grainer *Art Dir* Roy Stannard

● Joan Collins, Eileen Atkins, Donald Pleasence, Ralph Bates, Caroline Munro, Hilary Mason (Unicapital)

This is an exceedingly stylish thriller about a satanically possessed infant, Joan Collins' abnormally strong newborn son, who inflicts scratches on cribside visitors, and wreaks havoc on his room when no one is around.

After a succession of bizarre occurrences, including the mysterious death of the baby's nursemaid, a frantic Collins (looking and acting splendidly as the begrieved mother) and her Italian husband, nicely played by horror vet Ralph Bates, turn to doctor Donald Pleasence for the answers, then to Bates' nun sister (Eileen Atkins, in a striking performance).

Director Peter Sasdy, whose pacing is near-flawless, works as much below the surface as above it with great effect. There are plenty of shots of the sweetest baby imaginable, followed with shots of the violence it apparently perpetrated, showing only the terrified victims.

••••••••••••••••••••••••••••••

■ I DOOD IT
(UK: By Hook or By Crook)

1943, 102 MINS, US ⊛
Dir Vincente Minnelli   *Prod* Jack Cummings   *Scr* Sig
Herzig, Fred Saidy   *Ph* Ray June   *Ed* Robert J. Kern
Mus George Stoll (dir.)
● Red Skelton, Eleanor Powell, Lena Horne, Patricia
Dane, Richard Ainley, Sam Levene (M-G-M)

Metro has wrapped Red Skelton and Eleanor
Powell, among other names, around a popular
Skelton radio phrase that's used for the film's
title, and the net result is moderate entertainment.

I Dood It is by Metro's usual standards, not
one of its best musicals, but that's due mostly
to the screenplay. While the plot of a musical
can generally be accepted only as a cue for
the song-and-dance, the failing is particularly
apparent in *Dood It*. The yarn is too unbelievable, though the absurdities fashioned for
Skelton have their compensations in the actual performance.

Story is a retake of an old situation, dealing
with the love of a valet aide for a dancing
star. Skelton courts Powell from a distance, a
fashion plate through borrowing his customers' clothes. Then follows a series of situations that find him mixed up in a 'spite'
marriage with Powell, followed by his discovery and rout of a spy plot. It's all very hectic
and uncertain, but pretends to be nothing
more than a vehicle for the comic's fol-de-rol.

■ I DREAM OF JEANIE

1952, 90 MINS, US ◇
Dir Allan Dwan   *Prod* Allan Dwan   *Scr* Alan Le May
Ph Reggie Lanning   *Ed* Fred Allen   *Mus* Robert
Armbruster (adapt.)   *Art Dir* Frank Hotaling
● Ray Middleton, Bill Shirley, Muriel Lawrence, Eileen
Christy, Richard Simmons, Rex Allen (Republic)

A pseudo-biopic around the life and songs of
Stephen Foster gets a pretentious treatment.

Foster's folksy tune-smithing is featured in
21 of his cleffings that are used for the musical portions. Picture could have used a script
and performances to match the singing.

The formula plot shows young Foster as a
dreamer who makes nothing from his music
until his business-like brother takes over. An
unrequited love affair finally causes Foster to
run away but he is pursued by another femme
named Jeanie and when she catches up with
him he realizes she's the girl, and thus the title tune is born.

Bill Shirley plays Foster, tenoring 'Oh
Susanna', 'Old Dog Tray', 'Camptown Races'
and others. Eileen Christy is the vivacious
Jear.ie who gets Foster. Among her songs is 'I
See Her Still in My Dreams' with Shirley.

■ IF. . . .

1968, 110 MINS, UK ◇ ⊛ ⊙
Dir Lindsay Anderson   *Prod* Michael Medwin, Lindsay
Anderson   *Scr* David Sherwin   *Ph* Miroslav Ondricek
Ed David Gladwell   *Mus* Marc Wilkinson
Art Dir Jocelyn Herbert
● Malcolm McDowell, David Wood, Richard Warwick,
Christine Noonan, Robert Swann, Peter Jeffrey (Memorial)

Punchy, poetic pic that delves into the epic
theme of youthful revolt.

if. . . . is ostensibly about a rigid tradition-
ridden British private boarding school for
boys from 11 to 18. The film blocks out a series of incidents that lead to a small group rebelling with mortars, machine guns, gas
bombs and pistols. Film is divided into chapter headings as the boys arrive for a new
term.

The teachers, nurses, housemasters, etc.,
are all fairly typed characters but never descend to caricatures, which is true of the
many students.

There is a romantic dash during the early

part of the film in the growing insistence of
three rebel friends that all is not right in this
caste-ridden school. But there is never any
sentimentality, which makes the film's veering to a bloody revolt acceptable.

Film is a generalized tale of revolt. The violence is symbolical and reflects and comments
on it rather than sentimentalizing it or trying
to make it realistic.

■ IF I HAD A MILLION

1932, 85 MINS, US
Dir Ernst Lubitsch, Norman Taurog, Stephen Roberts,
Norman McLeod, James Cruze, William A. Seiter, H.
Bruce Humberstone   *Scr* Claude Binyon, Whitney Bolton,
Malcolm Stuart Boyl, John Bright, Sidney Buchman, Lester
Cole, Isabel Dawn, Boyce De Gaw, Robert Sparks, Oliver
H.P. Garrett, Harvey Gates, Grover Jones, Ernst Lubitsch,
Lawton Mackall, Joseph L. Mankiewicz, William Slavens
McNutt, Robert Sparks
● Gary Cooper, Charles Laughton, W. C. Fields, Charlie
Ruggles, George Raft, Jackie Oakie (Paramount)

The episodes depicting what certain individuals would do if they had $1 million are not
without their moments, some, of course, more
effective than others. With so many cooks concerned, this cinematic porridge [based on a
story by Robert D. Andrews] is naturally replete with a diversity of seasonings. Just who's
responsible for which sequence isn't disclosed,
although the scene with Charles Laughton giving his boss a lusty Bronx cheer, upon becoming one of the beneficiaries, is said to be 100%
Ernst Lubitsch in writing and direction.

George Raft's million is worthless because
he is a fourth-time offender for forgery, and
none believes his signature on the certified
check.

Similarly Gary Cooper, Jack Oakie and
Roscoe Karns as the triumvirate of marines
look at the million dollar check received by
Cooper, and also observe that it's April 1 on
the calendar, and that's that.

May Robson converts the old ladies' home
in which she's a 'guesst' into a clubhouse,
when her million arrives, and bakes pies for
Richard Bennett, who plays the eccentric millionaire who had hit upon the telephone directory potshot idea as a means for distributing his wealth.

Charlie Ruggles' sequence has about the
longest footage, while Laughton's Bronx
cheerio is the snappiest, and probably most
effective.

W. C. Fields and Alison Skipworth man a
vanguard of used flivvers as the means to attack the road hogs who endanger the other
motorists, by running them up the sidewalks
and into wrecks themselves.

■ IF IT'S TUESDAY, THIS MUST BE BELGIUM

1969, 99 MINS, US ◇
Dir Mel Stuart   *Prod* Stan Margulies   *Scr* David Shaw
Ph Vilis Lapenieks   *Ed* David Saxon   *Mus* Donovan
Art Dir Marc Frederix
● Suzanne Pleshette, Ian McShane, Mildred Natwick,
Murray Hamilton, Sandy Baron, Reva Rose (United Artists)

David Shaw's screenplay manages to cover
many of the European tour cliches. There are
some script anomalies that briefly puzzle, but
not to a degree that they detract from the fun.

Although the touring group is conducted by
a British guide (Ian McShane), supposedly
versed in all languages and emergencies, they
suddenly find themselves with a fluttery
femme type (Patricia Routledge). She's unexplained, unorthodox and delightful.

While Shaw's main storyline is based on the
adventures of a polyglot pack of Yank tourists,
trying to keep up with a hectic schedule, it is
padded with enough sidebar items to make it
a miniature *Grand Hotel* on wheels.

Besides the friction caused by the inconven-
iences enroute, there's personal friction be-

tween McShane and femme tourist Suzanne
Pleshette.

■ IF LOOKS COULD KILL
(UK: Teen Agent)

1991, 88 MINS, US ◇ ⊛ ⊙
Dir William Dear   *Prod* Craig Zadan   *Scr* Darren Star
Ph Doug Milsome   *Ed* John F. Link   *Mus* David Foster
Art Dir Guy J. Comtois
● Richard Grieco, Linda Hunt, Roger Rees, Robin
Bartlett, Gabrielle Anwar, Geraldine James (Warner)

Young TV star Richard Grieco barely survives
silly first film vehicle *If Looks Could Kill*, which
spoofs the James Bond formula in tiresome
fashion. One-joke script, based on Fred
Dekker's story, runs out of gas before the
halfway mark.

Grieco plays a high school student who's
headed for France with his French teacher
(Robin Bartlett) and class. Coincidentally, a
CIA spy with same name is booked on the
same plane, and rest of the film stems from
both villains and good guy spooks mistaking
young Grieco for a secret agent.

Nominal plot has Roger Rees as the megalomaniac chairman of the European Economic Community who plans to take over
Europe and issue gold coinage bearing his
own likeness.

Grieco puts up with the silliness, including
being clad only in his underpants during a
lengthy segment opposite femme fatale
Carole Davis. Linda Hunt has only intermittent success with the comic-strip role of Rees'
chief enforcer, a bullwhip-wielding heavy
named Ilsa Grunt. Heroine Gabrielle Anwar
as the vengeful daughter of Britain's late
great top spy (played in a miscast, no-impact
cameo by Roger Daltrey) looks too young on
screen. Best role goes to Bartlett.

■ IF YOU FEEL LIKE SINGING
See: *Summer Stock*

■ I KNOW WHERE I'M GOING!

1945, 91 MINS, UK ⊛
Dir Michael Powell, Emeric Pressburger   *Prod* Michael
Powell, Emeric Pressburger   *Scr* Michael Powell, Emeric
Pressburger   *Ph* Erwin Hillier   *Ed* John Seabourne
Mus Allan Gray   *Art Dir* Alfred Junge
● Wendy Hiller, Roger Livesey, Pamela Brown, Petula
Clark, Nancy Price, Finlay Currie (Archers)

I Know Where I'm Going! has all the values of a
documentary as a foundation for the tale of a
girl who is sure she knows where she is going
until she gets sidetracked – and likes it.

As the girl Wendy Hiller repeats her convincing portrayal of character development
which made *Pygmalion* a personal triumph for
her. Hard as nails in the opening sequences,
when she tells her father, a bank manager,
she is off to the Island of Mull to marry the
multi-millionaire boss of a great chemical
combine, she dismisses his objections to the
May-December misalliance by insisting her fiance is no older than her father – 'and you're
rather nice, daddy.'

It is only when a gale prevents her from
reaching the island and her waiting bride-
groom-to-be she finds heartless ambition to
marry money becoming less attractive, the
process of disillusionment aided and abetted
by her proximity to a young navy officer
(Roger Livesey) who begins by telling her
what he thinks of gold diggers generally, and
winds up by walloping her in the best-ap-
proved Cagney fashion.

■ I LIKE MONEY
See: *Mr Topaze*

■ I LIVE IN GROSVENOR SQUARE
(US: A Yank in London)

1945, 114 MINS, UK
Dir Herbert Wilcox *Prod* Herbert Wilcox *Scr* Nicholas Phipps, William D. Bayles *Ph* Otto Heller *Ed* Vera Campbell *Mus* Anthony Collins *Art Dir* William C. Andrews
● Anna Neagle, Dean Jagger, Rex Harrison, Robert Morley (Associated British)

Story by British newspaperman Maurice Cowan is based on the real-life events – that of the Air Corps crew sacrificing themselves to save inhabitants of an English village.

Anna Neagle gives a most convincing performance. Dean Jagger's love scenes, though a trifle long, are played with the subtlety one would expect in an American sergeant's diffidence towards a duke's grand-daughter. Rex Harrison as the major looks sure to impress American femmes in the service, even though the heroine jilts him.

Of the other players, Jane Darwell gives a lesson in how to play a bit part so it won't be forgotten. Herbert Wilcox's direction is perfect.

■ I'LL CRY TOMORROW

1955, 117 MINS, US ▼ ⊙
Dir Daniel Mann *Prod* Lawrence Weingarten *Scr* Helen Deutsch, Jay Richard Kennedy *Ph* Arthur E. Arling *Ed* Harold F. Kress *Mus* Alex North *Art Dir* Cedric Gibbons, Malcolm Brown
● Susan Hayward, Richard Conte, Eddie Albert, Jo Van Fleet, Don Taylor, Margo (M-G-M)

This pulls no punches in showing a rising star's fall into alcoholic degradation that plumbs Skid Row sewers before Alcoholics Anonymous provides the faith and guidance to help her up again. [The biopic is based on Lillian Roth's own book.]

No particular person or circumstance is blamed for Roth's downfall, but the viewers will be able to fasten on any one of several possible causes. The first is the stingingly cruel portrayal of the stage mother, played with great trouping skill by Jo Van Fleet, as she pushes her daughter towards the career she never had. The death of Roth's first love, effectively realized by Ray Danton, is a blow of fate and the start of the crackup.

Susan Hayward, along with the sock of her sustained character creation, reveals pleasant pipes and song-belting ability.
□ 1955: Best B&W Costume Design.
□ Nominations: Best Actress (Susan Hayward), B&W Cinematography, B&W Art Direction

■ ILLEGALLY YOURS

1988, 102 MINS, US ◇ ▼
Dir Peter Bogdanovich *Prod* Peter Bogdanovich *Scr* M.A. Stewart, Max Dickens *Ph* Dante Spinotti *Ed* Richard Fields *Mus* Phil Marshall *Art Dir* Jane Musky
● Rob Lowe, Colleen Camp, Kenneth Mars, Harry Carey Jr, Kim Myers (De Laurentiis/Crescent Moon)

Illegally Yours is an embarrassingly unfunny attempt at screwball comedy, marking a career nadir for producer-director Peter Bogdanovich and his miscast star Rob Lowe.

Hectic pre-credits sequence, loaded with telltale, expository voiceover by Lowe, crudely sets up an uninteresting story of a blackmailer's murder, witnessed by young Kim Myers and her friend L.B. Straten, in which innocent Colleen Camp is arrested as the fall guy. An audiotape recording of the murder is the item everyone is trying to get their hands on.

Lowe is cast, with unbecoming glasses throughout, as a college dropout trying to get his life in order back home in St Augustine, Fla. Between endless pratfalls Lowe finds himself on jury duty in Camp's case.

En route to sorting out the boring mystery of what became of the kidnaper's corpse, Lowe is thoroughly out of his element, even adopting a silly voice for a dumb drag scene. Camp is given little to do and no chemistry develops between the mismatched stars.

■ ILL MET BY MOONLIGHT
(US: Night Ambush)

1957, 104 MINS, UK ▼
Dir Michael Powell, Emeric Pressburger *Prod* Michael Powell, Emeric Pressburger *Scr* Michael Powell, Emeric Pressburger *Ph* Christopher Challis *Ed* Arthur Stevens *Mus* Mikis Theodorakis *Art Dir* Alex Vetchinsky
● Dirk Bogarde, Marius Goring, David Oxley, Cyril Cusack, Laurence Payne, Michael Gough (Rank/Archers)

Michael Powell and Emeric Pressburger take as their subject an operation in occupied Crete [from the book by W. Stanley Moss]. Two British officers, with the aid of local patriots, are given the job of kidnapping the German commander-in-chief and transporting him to Cairo.

The job of hijacking the general is accomplished with remarkable ease and luck. His car is ambushed and he's driven through endless road blocks to a mountain hideout. Then comes the tricky part. The general has to be led to the beachhead selected by the British navy for transportation to Egypt.

Dirk Bogarde turns in a smooth and satisfying performance as a British major, with David Oxley giving valuable aid as his No. 2 man. Marius Goring, as the general, is smugly confident that he'll be rescued by his own men and gallantly accepts the fact that he's been outwitted by a bunch of amateurs.

■ I'LL NEVER FORGET WHAT'S 'IS NAME

1967, 97 MINS, UK ◇
Dir Michael Winner *Prod* Michael Winner *Scr* Peter Draper *Ph* Otto Heller *Ed* Bernard Gribble *Mus* Francis Lai *Art Dir* Seamus Flannery
● Orson Welles, Oliver Reed, Carol White, Harry Andrews, Michael Hordern, Wendy Craig (Universal/Scimitar)

Story concerns a successful and resentful whizkid of the advertising game (Oliver Reed), who opts out to join a pal in running an esoteric literary magazine. Separated from his wife, he is a womanizer of perpetual appetite, taking one off to a lonely and disused railroad station and establishing a flightly relationship with a secretary (Carol White), who is prim at heart and takes it all seriously.

Thus the theme is the aridity of fashionable achievement, and the sour smell of success is hammered home by director Michael Winner with an insistence that destroys its own claims and closes with a final scene of stunning vulgarity.

Oliver Reed looks grim and disenchanted throughout, but hasn't the power to suggest that there's much talent going to waste.

In addition to Orson Welles, White registers as the girl torn between her virginal upbringing and her beckoning by Reed. The role is inconclusive, but she gives it the stamp of charm and unforced sweetness.

■ ILLUSTRATED MAN, THE

1969, 103 MINS, US ◇ ▼
Dir Jack Smight *Prod* Howard B. Kreitsek, Ted Mann *Scr* Howard B. Kreitsek *Ph* Philip Lathrop *Ed* Archie Marshek *Mus* Jerry Goldsmith *Art Dir* Joel Schiller
● Rod Steiger, Claire Bloom, Robert Drivas, Don Dubbins, Jason Evans (Warner/Seven Arts)

The Illustrated Man has going for it two major aspects: a derivative Ray Bradbury story and an obtuse, time-fragmented, humanistic, allegorical morality play.

Rod Steiger and Claire Bloom star in a story told in flashback and flash-forward, from a rural lakeside camp occupied for an afternoon and a night around Labor Day 1933 by wandering drifter Steiger and neighborhood boy Robert Drivas.

Steiger is gradually revealed to be almost totally covered with tattoos – he prefers the phrase 'skin illustrations' – each representing some sort of adventure. Plot selects three of those adventures.

The interpretations of the story are manifold. Steiger's character is apparently an eternal Adam, wandering through the ages and encountering challenges, the marks and memories of which are the tattoos.

■ I LOVE MELVIN

1953, 76 MINS, US ◇ ▼
Dir Don Weis *Prod* George Wells *Scr* George Wells, Ruth Brooks Flippen *Ph* Harold Rosson *Ed* Adrienne Fazan *Mus* George Stoll (dir.) *Art Dir* Cedric Gibbons, Jack Martin Smith, Eddie Imazu
● Donald O'Connor, Debbie Reynolds, Una Merkel, Richard Anderson, Jim Backus, Robert Taylor (M-G-M)

This is a lively, youthful musical comedy with a script, taken from a story by Laslo Vadney, that provides interesting substance to a fluffy affair.

Donald O'Connor and Debbie Reynolds are the youthful sparkplugs and both perform to advantage under Don Weis' direction. Bounciest number they do together is 'Where Did You Learn to Dance', an informal affair of charm. O'Connor does some skating terps to 'Life Has Its Funny Little Ups and Downs', with little Noreen Corcoran supplying the appealing vocal. The big production number is 'Saturday Afternoon before the Game', in which Reynolds plays the football and reveals every curve in a pigskin costume. The songs are by Josef Myrow and Mack Gordon.

Plot finds O'Connor a bulb-carrier for Jim Backus, *Look* photog. He falls in love with Reynolds, a chorus cutie, and gives her the impression he is a photographer. He launches a campaign of picture-taking with her as model and she, and her family, believe the gal will make the *Look* cover. O'Connor fakes a cover but the stunt backfires.

Una Merkel and Allyn Joslyn are very good as Reynolds' parents, as is little Corcoran as her kid sister. Richard Anderson is delightful as Reynolds' stuffed-shirt suitor, favored by Joslyn. Backus plays his photog role for sure chuckles. Robert Taylor makes a brief guest appearance. Robert Alton staged and directed the dances.

■ I LOVE YOU, ALICE B. TOKLAS!

1968, 92 MINS, US ◇ ▼
Dir Hy Averback *Prod* Charles Maguire *Scr* Paul Mazursky, Larry Tucker *Ph* Philip Lathrop *Ed* Robert C. Jones *Mus* Elmer Bernstein *Art Dir* Pato Guzman
● Peter Sellers, Jo Van Fleet, Leigh Taylor-Young, Joyce Van Patten, David Arkin, Herb Edelman (Warner/Seven Arts)

Film is not heavyhanded in its approach either to hippie life, or to what is considered 'normal' modes of behavior. Instead, there is a sympathetic look at the advantages and disadvantages of each.

Pic derives its prime value from an excellent screenplay. Story is relatively simple: Peter Sellers, an LA lawyer, turns on to hippie life as an escape from conformity and hypocrisy. Later, he finds out that human nature is independent of superficial environment, returns briefly to his former life, but winds up running away again.

Film blasts off into orbit via top-notch acting and direction. Sellers' performance – both in scenes which spotlight his character as well as ensemble sequences in which everyone is balanced nicely – is an outstanding blend of warmth, sensitivity, disillusion and optimism.

Jo Van Feet is simply brilliant as Sellers' mother, with Salem Ludwig also on target as his dad. Joyce Van Patten's performance as Sellers' pushy fiancee is delightful.

....

■ I LOVE YOU TO DEATH

1990, 96 MINS, US ◇ ⊗ ⊙
Dir Lawrence Kasden   *Prod* Jeffrey Lurie, Ron Moler, Patrick Wells,   *Scr* John Kostmayer   *Ph* Owen Roisman   *Ed* Anne V. Coates   *Mus* James Horner   *Art Dir* Lilly Kilvert
● Kevin Kline, Tracey Ullman, Joan Plowright, River Phoenix, William Hurt, Keanu Reeves (Chestnut Hill)

I Love You to Death is a stillborn attempt at black comedy.

Opening credits stress tale is based on a true story, but John Kostmayer's screenplay never makes events remotely interesting. Kevin Kline creates a stereotypical Italian restaurant owner who can't help cheating with scores of women on his frumpish wife, Tracey Ullman. Awkward script has Ullman discovering Kline in a tryst at a library and, after brief consultation with her Yugoslav mom Joan Plowright, resolving to kill him.

Harold and Maude it ain't. Film founders because the cast is out of control. Chief culprit is Hurt, as a hired space cadet hitman, who pulls faces embarrassingly here as a retarded hippie.

At the other extreme, the three British actresses are models of professionalism. Ullman unfortunately fades into the woodwork by steadfastly adopting a bland speech pattern and looking as homely as possible. Plowright is solid as her mom.

....

■ IMAGES

1972, 100 MINS, UK ◇
Dir Robert Altman   *Prod* Tommy Thompson   *Scr* Robert Altman   *Ph* Vilmos Zsigmond   *Ed* Graeme Clifford   *Mus* John Williams   *Art Dir* Leon Ericksen
● Susannah York, Rene Auberjonois, Marcel Bozzuffi, Hugh Millais, Cathryn Harrison (Lion's Gate/Hemdale)

Robert Altman made this interior drama about a woman going through hallucination and nearing madness in Ireland. Delving into effects of permissiveness on a hidebound, repressed nature, it also shows a probing insight into mental disorder.

Susannah York, writing a fairy tale for children about mysterious woods and a unicorn that acts as a counterpoint to her real life losing of touch with reality, imagines phone calls saying her husband is with another woman and when they go to their country house for the weekend two men in her life intrude as imaginary, or, in one case, real.

York has the intensity and innocence marked by strain as well as sensual underpinnings, and brings off the final denouement with restraint and potency.
□ 1972: Nomination: Best Original Score

....

■ I'M ALL RIGHT, JACK

1959, 105 MINS, UK ⊗
Dir John Boulting   *Prod* Roy Boulting   *Scr* Frank Harvey, John Boulting   *Ph* Max Greene   *Ed* Anthony Harvey   *Mus* Ken Hare
● Ian Carmichael, Peter Sellers, Terry-Thomas, Richard Attenborough, Dennis Price, Margaret Rutherford (British Lion/Boulting Brothers)

The Boulting Brothers' target [from the novel by Alan Hackney] is British factory life, trade unionism and the general possibility that everybody is working for one person – himself.

Ian Carmichael plays an ex-university type who wants to get an executive job in industry. Instead, he is given a job as a factory worker

by his uncle who wants him in as a stooge for a secret, dirty financial deal. Carmichael becomes the unwitting cause of a factory strike that swells to nationwide proportions. Gradually he begins to realize that he has been taken for a ride.

Carmichael slides smoothly through his performance, but it is Peter Sellers, as the chairman of the factory's union works committee, who makes the film. With a makeup that subtly suggests Hitler, he brings rare humor and an occasional touch of pathos to the role. Sellers' strength is that he does not deliberately play for laughs. He produces them from the situations and sharp dialog.

Dennis Price and Richard Attenborough as shady employers and Terry-Thomas as a bewildered personnel manager also provide rich roles.

....

■ I MARRIED A COMMUNIST

(UK: The Woman on Pier 13)

1949, 72 MINS, US
Dir Robert Stevenson   *Prod* Sid Rogell   *Scr* Charles Grayson, Robert Hardy Andrews   *Ph* Nicholas Musuraca   *Ed* Roland Gross   *Mus* Leigh Harline
● Laraine Day, Robert Ryan, John Agar, Thomas Gomez, Janis Carter (RKO)

As a straight action fare, *I Married a Communist* generates enough tension to satisfy the average customer. Despite its heavy sounding title, pic hews strictly to tried and true meller formula.

Screenplay uses the simple and slightly naive device of substituting Communist for gangsters in a typical underworld yarn.

Pic is so wary of introducing any political gab that at one point when Commie trade union tactics are touched upon, the soundtrack is dropped.

Robert Ryan plays an ex-comrade who turns up in San Francisco as vice-prexy of a shipping company and bigtime labor relations expert. In the midst of waterfront union negotiations, the Commie chieftain (Thomas Gomez) enters to remind Ryan that he can't quit the mob and had better follow the Party's directive to stir up labor trouble.

....

■ I MARRIED A MONSTER FROM OUTER SPACE

1958, 78 MINS, US ⊗
Dir Gene Fowler Jr   *Prod* Gene Fowler Jr   *Scr* Louis Vittes   *Ph* Haskell Boggs   *Ed* George Tomasini   *Art Dir* Hal Pereira, Henry Bumstead
● Tom Tryon, Gloria Talbott, Ken Lynch, John Eldridge, Alan Dexter, Jean Carson (Paramount)

Premise of the screenplay deals with a race of monsters from another galaxy who invade the earth and secretly take over the form of some of the male townspeople. Film opens with Gloria Talbott marrying Tom Tryon, unaware the man she loves is now one of these monsters.

After a year of tension she follows him one night and watches him change into his original form and enter a spaceship. Through her doctor, to whom she goes in her terror, enough normal people are recruited to successfully break up the invasion by an attack on spaceship.

Gene Fowler Jr's direction, while sometimes slow, latches onto mounting suspense as action moves to a climax. He gets the benefit of outstanding special photographic effects from John P. Fulton, which aid in maintaining interest.

....

■ I MARRIED A WITCH

1942, 82 MINS, US ⊗ ⊙
Dir Rene Clair   *Prod* Rene Clair   *Scr* Robert Pirosh, Marc Connelly   *Ph* Ted Tetzlaff   *Ed* Eda Warren   *Mus* Roy Webb

● Fredric March, Veronica Lake, Robert Benchley, Susan Hayward, Cecil Kellaway, Elizabeth Patterson (United Artists)

I Married a Witch, which deals with spirits, is a fantastic type of story that carries some interest on the novelty angles, if nothing else, but on the whole is generally tepid.

The story opens in 1690 in New England where a strait-laced Puritan condemns a sorcerer and his witch daughter who are burned at the stake. As a result, a curse is laid on the Puritan and any of his descendants, the action then jumping to the present when Fredric March, a descendant, is running for election as governor. He is in love with the daughter of a publisher backing him. The romance is upset and it appears that March is going to lose in consequence of the actions taken by two departed spirits.

Neither March nor Veronica Lake impresses very importantly, while Robert Benchley has not been well equipped with material designed to afford comic relief.
□ 1942: Nomination: Best Scoring of a Dramatic Picture

....

■ I'M DANCING AS FAST AS I CAN

1982, 106 MINS, US ◇ ⊗ ⊙
Dir Jack Hofsiss   *Prod* Edgar J. Scherick, Scott Rudin   *Scr* David Rabe   *Ph* Jan de Bont   *Ed* Michael Bradsell   *Mus* Stanley Silverman   *Art Dir* David Jenkins
● Jill Clayburgh, Nicol Williamson, Dianne Wiest, Joe Pesci, Geraldine Page, James Sutorius (Paramount)

Crucial inability of a film to get inside a character's head spells big trouble for *I'm Dancing As Fast As I Can*. Result here is that Jill Clayburgh's constantly center-stage character comes off as the 'pill-popping dingbat' she's called at one point, rather than as a fascinating lady with a major problem.

Based on Barbara Gordon's popular autobiographical tome, screenplay minutely charts Clayburgh's compulsive reliance on Valium, her disastrous effort to go cold turkey and her subsequent rehabilitation in an institution.

At the outset, Clayburgh is presented as a successful docu filmmaker for television. A little professional crisis presents itself. Pop goes a pill or two. A teeny tiff with b.f. Nicol Williamson. Down with another couple of blue tablets.

Only two members of the large supporting cast, Dianne Wiest and Geraldine Page, have any chance to develop their characters, and both do well.

....

■ IMITATION OF LIFE

1934, 116 MINS, US
Dir John M. Stahl   *Prod* Carl Laemmle Jr   *Scr* William Hurlburt   *Ph* Merritt Gerstad   *Ed* Philip Cahn, Maurice Wright   *Mus* Heinz Roemheld (dir.)   *Art Dir* Charles D. Hall
● Claudette Colbert, Warren William, Louise Beavers, Fredi Washington, Rochelle Hudson, Alan Hale (Universal)

Imitation of Life is a strong picture with an unusual plot. A young white widow (Claudette Colbert) with a baby girl goes into a business partnership with her colored maid (Louise Beavers) who also has a baby girl. In the passage of years a small business becomes a factory and they are wealthy. But neither the white woman nor the negress derive much joy. And because of their daughters.

Most arresting part of the picture and overshadowing the conventional romance between the late thirtyish white widow and Warren William is the tragedy of Aunt Delilah's girl born to a white skin and Negro blood. This subject is treated on the screen for the first time here. Girl is miserable being unable to adjust herself to the lot of her race and unable to take her place among the whites.

John M. Stahl directs this kind of thing very

well. He keeps the Fannie Hurst 'success story' brand of snobbishness under control and the film flows with mounting interest, if at moments a trifle slowly.

Picture is stolen by the Negress, Beavers, whose performance is masterly. This lady can troupe. She takes the whole scale of human emotions from joy to anguish and never sounds a false note.

☐ 1934: Nominations: Best Picture, Sound, Assistant Director

••••••••••••••••••••••••••••••

■ IMITATION OF LIFE

1959, 125 MINS, US ◇ ▽

Dir Douglas Sirk   *Prod* Ross Hunter   *Scr* Eleanore Griffin, Allan Scott   *Ph* Russell Metty   *Ed* Milton Carruth   *Mus* Frank Skinner   *Art Dir* Alexander Golitzen, Richard H. Riedel

● Lana Turner, John Gavin, Sandra Dee, Dan O'Herlihy, Robert Alda, Susan Kohner (Universal)

Imitation of Life is a remake of Fannie Hurst's novel of the early 1930s. Lana Turner is outstanding in the pivotal role played in Universal's 1934 version by Claudette Colbert. Scripters Eleanore Griffin and Allan Scott have transplanted her from the original pancake-and-flour business to the American stage.

While this device lends more scope, it also results in the overdone busy actress/neglected daughter conflict, and thus the secondary plot of a fair-skinned Negress passing as white becomes the film's primary force. The relationship of the young colored girl and her mother – played memorably by Susan Kohner and Juanita Moore – is sometimes overpowering, while the relationship of Turner and her daughter, Sandra Dee, comes to life only briefly when both are in love with same man, John Gavin.

Turner plays a character of changing moods, and her changes are remarkably effective, as she blends love and understanding, sincerity and ambition. The growth of maturity is reflected neatly in her distinguished portrayal. In smaller roles, both Robert Alda, as an opportunist agent, and Dan O'Herlihy, as a playwright, are excellent.

☐ 1959: Nominations: Best Supp. Actress (Juanita Moore, Susan Kohner)

••••••••••••••••••••••••••••••

■ IMMACULATE CONCEPTION

1992, 122 MINS, UK ◇ ▽ ⊙

Dir Jamil Dehlavi   *Prod* Jamil Dehlavi   *Scr* Jamil Dehlavi   *Ph* Nic Knowland   *Ed* Chris Barnes   *Mus* Richard Harvey   *Art Dir* Mike Porter

● James Wilby, Melissa Leo, Shabana Azmi, Zia Mohyeddin, James Cossins, Ronny Jhutti (Film Four/Dehlavi)

An ambitious culture-clash drama set in troubled 1988 Pakistan, *Immaculate Conception* tries to cover too many bases to score a solid hit.

James Wilby is Alistair, a wildlife conservationist based in Karachi with Jewish-American spouse Hannah (Melissa Leo), daughter of a powerful U.S. senator. Desperate to conceive a child, the couple visit a eunuch-run shrine reputed to have a cure for infertility. In fact, the eunuchs slip them the local version of a Mickey and get teenager Kamal (Ronny Jhutti) to do the business with a semi-comatose Hannah.

Final turn of the screw is Kamal spilling the beans about what really happened when Hannah's brother (Tim Choate) hotfoots it from the States with instructions from Daddy.

Franco-Pakistani helmer Jamil Dehlavi can't be faulted for ambition or political objectivity (pic is often scathing on Pakistan's faults). But without a stronger central dramatic line, pic perpetually shifts in and out of focus, to overall mild emotional effect. Weak dialogue in several crucial scenes is a further minus.

••••••••••••••••••••••••••••••

■ IMMEDIATE FAMILY

1989, 95 MINS, US ▽ ⊙

Dir Jonathan Kaplan   *Prod* Sarah Pillsbury, Midge Sanford   *Scr* Barbara Benedek   *Ph* John W. Lindley   *Ed* Jane Kurson   *Mus* Brad Fiedel   *Art Dir* Mark Freeborn

● Glenn Close, James Woods, Mary Stuart Masterson, Kevin Dillon, Linda Darlow, Jane Greer (Columbia/Sanford-Pillsbury)

Definitely no comedy, *Immediate Family* nonetheless explodes with bursts of laughter that lighten the heartbreak of a lot of nice people tormented by their own best intentions.

For Solomon and generations of juvenile judges since, there's no tougher case to call than competing claims for a baby. But Solomon's solution wouldn't work for *Family*, in which Glenn Close and Mary Stuart Masterson are each so deserving.

Granted, the plot requires no elaborate examination: after 11 years of marriage, James Woods and Glenn Close are still achingly childless. After no years of marriage, young Mary Stuart Masterson and boyfriend Kevin Dillon face impending parenthood under circumstances that could wreck their chances for a happier life later.

The solution, so obviously simple in a lawyer's office, is that Woods and Close will adopt Masterson's baby. But first the lawyer thinks everybody should get better acquainted.

Clever as she is, Close keeps her potentially cloying part understated; there's no need to hang a sign on her suffering. Young Masterson is simply superb, managing to first earn the audience's sympathy and then keep hold when some might be tempted to turn away.

••••••••••••••••••••••••••••••

■ IMMORTAL BATTALION

See: The Way Ahead

••••••••••••••••••••••••••••••

■ I'M NO ANGEL

1933, 87 MINS, US

Dir Wesley Ruggles   *Scr* Mae West   *Ph* Leo Tover   *Mus* Harvey Brooks

● Mae West, Cary Grant, Edward Arnold, Ralf Harolde, Russell Hopton, Gregory Ratoff (Paramount)

It's fairly obvious that the same plot mechanics and situations [from suggestions by Lowell Brentano] and a treatment by Harlan Thompson] without Mae West wouldn't be a motion picture at all. But that's no criticism. It's all West, plus a good directing job by Wesley Ruggles and first-rate studio production quality in all departments.

Laughs are all derived froom the West innuendos and the general good-natured bawdiness of the heroine, whose progress from a carnival mugg-taker to a deluxe millionaire-annexer is marked by a succession of gentlemen friends, mostly temporary and usually suckers.

When reaching affluence the carnival gal is serviced by four colored maids in an ultra-penthouse and garbed in the flashy manner of an Oriental potentate's pampered pet.

Every now and again West bursts into a song, generally just a chorus or a strain. They're of the Frankie and Johnny genre, but primarily she plays a lion tamer, not a songstress.

••••••••••••••••••••••••••••••

■ I, MOBSTER

(UK: The Mobster)

1958, 80 MINS, US ▽

Dir Roger Corman   *Prod* Edward L. Alperson, Roger Corman, Gene Corman   *Scr* Steve Fisher   *Ph* Floyd Crosby   *Ed* William B. Murphy   *Mus* Gerald Fried, Edward L. Alperson Jr   *Art Dir* Daniel Haller

● Steve Cochran, Lita Milan, Robert Strauss, Celia Lovsky, Lili St. Cyr (20th Century-Fox)

I, Mobster is a well-turned-out melodrama with Steve Cochran in title role delivering a slick characterization of the rise and fall of a mobsman.

Steve Fisher screenplay utilizes the flashback technique, opening with Cochran, who heads the national crime syndicate, invoking the Fifth Amendment as he appears before the Senate Rackets Committee in Washington. Narrative dips back to his youth, when he collected horse race bets for a local hoodlum, Robert Strauss; then spans his whole career in crime as he becomes involved in dope traffic, later his hard-hitting entry into strike-breaking and 'protection' of strike-breaking unions.

Under Roger Corman's knowhow direction action unfolds smoothly and swiftly. Through very creditable performances, Corman manages to capture the gangster feeling and in addition to Cochran outstanding portrayals are contributed by Lita Milan, as his sweetheart; Strauss, socking over his henchman role after Cochran rises above him; and Celia Lovsky, as Cochran's sorely tried mother.

••••••••••••••••••••••••••••••

■ IMPORTANCE OF BEING EARNEST, THE

1952, 95 MINS, UK ◇ ▽ ⊙

Dir Anthony Asquith   *Prod* Teddy Baird   *Scr* Anthony Asquith   *Ph* Desmond Dickinson   *Ed* John D. Guthridge   *Mus* Benjamin Frankel   *Art Dir* Carmen Dillon

● Michael Redgrave, Edith Evans, Michael Denison, Dorothy Tutin, Margaret Rutherford, Joan Greenwood (Javelin/Two Cities)

All the charm and glossy humor of Oscar Wilde's classic comedy emerges faithfully in this British production. Apart from a few minor cuts, director Anthony Asquith has taken few liberties with the original. His skilful direction extracts all the polish of Wilde's brilliant dialog.

Michael Redgrav brings a wealth of sincerity to the role of the earnest young man, without knowledge of his origin, whose invention of a fictitious brother leads to romantic complications. Michael Denison plays the debonair Algernon Moncrieff in a gay lighthearted style, and makes his characterization the pivot for much of the comedy.

The two romantic femme roles are adroitly played by Joan Greenwood and Dorothy Tutin.

••••••••••••••••••••••••••••••

■ IMPOSSIBLE OBJECT

1973, 110 MINS, FRANCE ◇

Dir John Frankenheimer   *Scr* Nicolas Mosley   *Ph* Claude Renoir   *Ed* Albert Jurgenson   *Mus* Michel Legrand   *Art Dir* Alexandre Trauner

● Alan Bates, Dominique Sanda, Evans Evans, Lea Massari, Michel Auclair, Laurence de Monaghan (Franco-London/Euro International)

John Frankenheimer spent over a year in Paris and then made this film for a local company, albeit mainly in English with passages between French people in French. It is a many-pronged affair in a tale of a writer whose inventions and real life may not always be extricable. It mixes romantic drama, situation comedy and insights into Americans or British abroad.

Alan Bates is a writer, living in a country home in France, outside Paris, with three sons and an American wife. He meets brooding but delicately sensual Dominique Sanda, who is married, in a museum and love blossoms. Film flits lightly over the affair, the writer's embroidery on it and sideline events that reflect on it until sudden swerve to tragedy.

Though pic segues from fantasy to implied realism, pic has an airy grace, fine playing down the line.

••••••••••••••••••••••••••••••

IMPOSTOR, THE

1944, 93 MINS, US

Dir Julien Duvivier *Prod* Julien Duvivier *Scr* Julien
Duvivier, Stephen Longstreet, Marc Connelly, Lynn
Starling *Ph* Paul Ivano *Ed* Paul Landres *Mus* Dimitri
Tiomkin *Art Dir* John B. Goodman, Eugene Lourie
● Jean Gabin, Richard Whorf, Ellen Drew, Peter Van
Eyck (Universal)

Fall of France in 1940, and subsequent formation of Free French units in Africa, forms basis for this adventure drama, which unfolds
tale of regeneration of a confirmed criminal
through comradeship in arms. Julien Duvivier
fails to generate pace fast enough to carry
picture along for more than moderate attention.

Story tells of how Jean Gabin is saved from
the guillotine, for murder, at Tours by Nazi
air bombing, heads south and assumes the
identity, papers and uniform of a dead French
soldier along the road. Joining group of
refugee soldiers who enlist in the Free French
forces, Gabin's army association gradually
transforms the criminal; he leads a small unit
overland for attack on Italian desert base and
is decorated for gallantry, under the name of
the dead man whose identity he assumed.

IMPROMPTU

1991, 109 MINS, US ◇ ⊛ ⊙

Dir James Lapine *Prod* Stuart Oken, Daniel A. Sherkow
Scr Sarah Kernochan *Ph* Bruno De Keyzer *Ed* Michael
Ellis *Mus* John Strauss (arr.) *Art Dir* Gerard Daoudal
● Judy Davis, Hugh Grant, Mandy Patinkin, Bernadette
Peters, Julian Sands, Emma Thompson (Sovereign)

Impromptu is a retelling of the oft-filmed
George Sand/Chopin story that's an entertaining comedy-drama. First-time director
James Lapine, who's had Broadway successes
(*Into the Woods*), makes the most of a terrific
ensemble. Bright playing, a bit broad at times
but fitting the material, is pic's strongest suit.

Aussie thesp Judy Davis plays Sand, the
strong-willed author who dresses mannishly,
smokes cheroots and gets a maddening crush
on composer Chopin (Hugh Grant at his most
foppish). Bulk of film is light-hearted, set at
the royal mansion of Emma Thompson and
Anton Rodgers, where Chopin, Liszt (Julian
Sands), artist Delacroix (Ralph Brown) and
an uninvited George Sand show up for vacation.

Film's tone turns a bit darker in later reels
as the duels and fights of the first half turn
more serious. Some abrupt editing and overly
contrived resolutions of plot threads keep the
finale from carrying much emotional force.

Directed by Lapine with a very long leash,
Davis is terrific. Bruno De Keyzer captures
lovely French locations in realistic terms, not
distracting from the protagonists.

IMPROPER CHANNELS

1981, 91 MINS, CANADA ◇ ⊛ ⊙

Dir Eric Till *Prod* Morrie Ruvinsky, Alfred Pariser
Scr Morrie Ruvinsky, Ian Sutherland, Adam Arkin
Ph Tony Richmond *Mus* Mickey Erbe, Maribeth Solomon
Art Dir Minkey Dalton, Charles Dunlop
● Alan Arkin, Mariette Hartley, Sarah Stevens, Monica
Parker, Harry Ditson (Paragon)

Alan Arkin puts his hapless schnook characterization to good use in *Improper Channels*. It's
a screwball comedy that starts slowly, shifts
into overdrive, peters out a bit halfway
through and then gets its second wind for a
fast-paced, down-with-the-computer finish.

He's an architect, separated from his writer
spouse (Mariette Hartley) and precocious
five-year-old daughter (Sarah Stevens). And
one thing leads to another; the daughter is injured slightly in his camper and when taken
to hospital she is thought to have been beaten
by her father.

A domineering social worker (Monica
Parker) has a computer expert call up all
available information on Arkin and the
daughter is bundled off by court order to an
orphanage. Arkin and Hartley attempt to get
her back.

Eric Till's direction is surefire most of the
time, though he's let down by a script that
wants to do too much. Pic was shot under the
title of *Proper Channels* and was changed for
reasons not explained.

IMPULSE

1984, 88 MINS, US ◇ ⊛ ⊙

Dir Graham Baker *Prod* Tim Zinnemann *Scr* Bart
Davis, Don Carlos Dunaway *Ph* Thomas Del Ruth
Ed David Holden *Mus* Paul Chihara *Art Dir* Jack T.
Collins
● Tim Matheson, Meg Tilly, Hume Cronyn, John Karlen,
Bill Paxton, Amy Stryker (ABC)

Impulse is an ugly little picture that would
play better as a comedy if it wasn't so mean-
spirited. Picture preys on the premise that
when people are allowed to act according to
their impulses, they will become violent, destructive and totally anti-social.

Wholesome young couple Meg Tilly and
Tim Matheson are literally called to Tilly's
hometown when her mother (Lorinne Vozoff)
blows her brains out while talking to her
daughter on the phone. The fact that she's
still alive is only the first of the implausible
happenings in Sutcliffe.

Nothing is quite what it seems in this town.
Upon their arrival Matheson and Tilly encounter a seething family feud between her
father (John Karlen) and her brother (Bill
Paxton). Kids set Tilly's car on fire while her
old friend (Amy Stryker) tells her it's not easy
having children.

Editing has no internal logic with the time
sequence totally jumbled. Performances are
adequate given the material, with Matheson
more convincing as a doctor than a mad-man.
Hume Cronyn as the old town doc who succumbs early to the mass mania is effective
though he has little to do. Tilly too is under-
utilized.

IMPULSE

1990, 108 MINS, US ◇ ⊛ ⊙

Dir Sondra Locke *Prod* Albert S. Ruddy, Andre Morgan
Scr John De Marco, Leigh Chapman *Ph* Dean Semler
Ed John W. Wheeler *Mus* Michel Colombier
Art Dir William A. Elliott
● Theresa Russell, Jeff Fahey, George Dzundza, Alan
Rosenberg, Shawn Elliott, Nicholas Mele (Ruddy-
Morgan/Warner)

Theresa Russell gives a solid performance in
Sondre Locke's well-directed film noir.
Russell is a beautiful undercover cop whose
life is going nowhere, hence the title: she
would like to break out of her rut and act on
impulse like one of the prostitute or druggie
personas she routinely adopts in her work.

Along with her sexist boss George Dzundza,
she's assigned to work with young assistant
d.a. Jeff Fahey to find missing witness Shawn
Elliott in an important gangster case. Elliott
has $900,000 stolen in a Colombian drug
deal, and there's only three weeks to find him
before Fahey begins the trial.

Russell and Fahey have some interesting
exchanges that expose their characters.
Sharpest writing comes in a scene of Fahey
and his partner Alan Rosenberg talking about
women and relationships in terms from real
estate.

Director Locke, in her second feature after
Ratboy, gets high marks for the visceral, swift
nature of her violent stagings. She also manages an impressively tactile sex scene that involves Russell and Fahey.

INADMISSIBLE EVIDENCE

1968, 94 MINS, UK

Dir Anthony Page *Prod* Ronald Kinnoch *Scr* John
Osborne *Ph* Kenneth Hodges *Ed* Derek York
Art Dir Seamus Flannery
● Nicol Williamson, Eleanor Fazan, Jill Bennett, Peter
Sallis, David Valla, Eileen Atkins (Woodfall)

As a play, the best thing about *Inadmissible
Evidence* was Nicol Williamson, who brought
to life the tormented, mediocre, bullying coward that John Osborne had conceived on paper. Same holds true for the screen version in
which same actor appears. There is value and
insight to the film. Yet much of it is opaque
and confusing.

Evidence remains primarily a play. It is
Osborne talking about a certain stage of civilization and various kinds of people it produces.

Williamson, as the lawyer who has achieved
a certain measure of material success, is flagrantly promiscuous, professionally mediocre
and personally a boor.

Williamson achieves the feat of making a
big man look fragile, of gaining sympathy for
boorish behavior and pitying insights of a
coward and scoundrel.

Picture is in black-and-white and it adds to
the bleakness of the portrait being presented.
Yet the same effect could have been achieved
had film been done in color.

IN A LONELY PLACE

1950, 92 MINS, US ⊛

Dir Nicholas Ray *Prod* Henry S. Kesler (assoc.)
Scr Andrew Solt *Ph* Burnett Guffey *Ed* Viola Lawrence
Mus George Antheil *Art Dir* Robert Peterson
● Humphrey Bogart, Gloria Grahame, Frank Lovejoy,
Robert Warwick, Jeff Donnell, Martha Stewart
(Columbia/Santana)

In *Lonely Place* Humphrey Bogart has a sympathetic role though cast as one always ready
to mix it with his dukes. He favors the underdog; in one instance he virtually has a veteran, brandy-soaking character actor (out of
work) on his very limited payroll.

As the screenplay scrivener who detests the
potboilers, Bogart finds himself innocently
suspected of a girl's slaying. Although continually kept under suspicion, he ignores the police attempt to trap him into a confession, at
the same time falling for a gal neighbor.

Director Nicholas Ray maintains nice suspense. Bogart is excellent. Gloria Grahame,
as his romance, also rates kudos. [Screenplay
is from a story by Dorothy B. Hughes,
adapted by Edmund H. North.]

IN BED WITH MADONNA

See: Truth or Dare: In Bed with Madonna

INCHON

1981, 140 MINS, S. KOREA/US ◇

Dir Terence Young *Prod* Mitsuharu Ishii *Scr* Robin
Moore, Laird Koenig *Ph* Bruce Surtees *Mus* Jerry
Goldsmith
● Laurence Olivier, Jacqueline Bisset, Ben Gazzara,
Toshiro Mifune, Richard Roundtree (One Way)

A major battle of the Korean war is given a
decidedly religious viewpoint via *Inchon*, a $46
million pic from One Way Prods, an org affili-
ated with the Rev Sun Myung Moon (who
gets screen credit as special advisor on
Korean matters).

Laurence Olivier plays Gen Douglas
MacArthur in this film that was four years in
the making and bills 50,000 extras.

Plot involves the general's orchestration of
the 1950 landing at the South Korean port of
Inchon by United Nations forces, with heavy

371

emphasis on divine guidance. Olivier is convincing in his role throughout most of the saga, the only member of the cast to achieve that status.

Screenplay [from a story by Robin Moore and Paul Savage] generally treats all others as one-dimensional buffoons, giving them lines that are unintentionally laughable. One reason is that all plot digressions are simply window dressing to the film's focus on the brutally invading North Koreans and the big-scale counterattack by the good guys. No speaking roles are given the Communists, for example.

....

■ **INCIDENT, THE**

1967, 99 MINS, US ◇ ⓥ ⊙
Dir Larry Peerce   *Prod* Monroe Sachson, Edward Meadow   *Scr* Nicholas E. Baehr   *Ph* Gerald Hirschfeld   *Ed* Armand Lebowitz   *Mus* Terry Knight   *Art Dir* Manny Gerard
● Tony Musante, Martin Sheen, Beau Bridges, Bob Bannard, Ed McMahon, Diana Van der Vlis (20th Century-Fox/Moned)

Strong casting, impressive direction and generally sharp writing (from an old TV script) make *The Incident* a very fine episodic drama about two toughs who intimidate passengers on a NY subway train.

Some overexposition and relaxed editing flag the pace, but, overall, the production is a candid indictment, in situation and in dialog, of alienation.

Baehr's screenplay spotlights Tony Musante and Martin Sheen, out-for-kicks pair, who terrorize 16 train riders. Latter include soldiers Beau Bridges and Bob Bannard, middle-class couple Ed McMahon and Diana Van der Vlis (with child), elderly marrieds Jack Gilford and Thelma Ritter. The two toughs lay bare the weaknesses in all characters.

....

■ **IN COLD BLOOD**

1967, 133 MINS, US ⓥ ⊙
Dir Richard Brooks   *Prod* Richard Brooks   *Scr* Richard Brooks   *Ph* Conrad Hall   *Ed* Peter Zinner   *Mus* Quincy Jones   *Art Dir* Robert Boyle
● Robert Blake, Scott Wilson, John Forsythe, Paul Stewart, Gerald S. O'Loughlin, Jeff Corey (Columbia)

In the skillful hands of adapter-director-producer Richard Brooks, Truman Capote's *In Cold Blood*, the non-fiction novel-like account about two Kansas killers, becomes on screen a probing, sensitive, tasteful, balanced and suspenseful documentary-drama.

Film has the look and sound of reality, in part from use of action locales in six states and non-pros as atmosphere players, the rest from Brooks' own filmmaking professionalism. Planned as a $3 million, 124-day pic, it came in for $2.2 million in 80 days.

Heading the competent cast are Robert Blake and Scott Wilson, bearing a striking resemblance to the now-dead Kansas drifters who, in the course of a burglary on 15 November, 1959, murdered four of a family. Almost six years later, after an exhausted appeal route, they were hanged. John Forsythe plays the chief investigator who broke the case.

Brooks' screenplay and direction are remarkable in that pic avoids so many pitfalls: it is not a crime meller, told either from the police or criminal viewpoint; it is not social tract against capital punishment; it is not cheap exploitation material; and it is not amateurish in technical execution, despite its realistic flavor.

□ 1967: Nominations: Best Director, Adapted Screenplay, Cinematography, Original Music Score

....

■ **IN COUNTRY**

1989, 120 MINS, US ◇ ⓥ ⊙
Dir Norman Jewison   *Prod* Norman Jewison, Richard Roth   *Scr* Frank Pierson, Cynthia Cidre   *Ph* Russell Boyd   *Ed* Anthony Gibbs, Lou Lombardo   *Mus* James Horner   *Art Dir* Jackson DeGovia
● Bruce Willis, Emily Lloyd, Joan Allen, Kevin Anderson, John Terry, Judith Ivey (Warner)

Norman Jewison usually is a commanding storyteller, but *In Country* is a film with two stories that fail to add up to something greater: a country girl's coming of age, and a troubled Vietnam veteran's coming to terms with his haunting memories of war [from the novel by Bobbie Ann Mason].

Emily Lloyd, in a sparky performance that seizes control of the movie, plays Samantha Hughes, a spirited, just-minted high school graduate from the small town of Hopewell, Ky. She lives in a ramshackle house with Bruce Willis, who turns in a likable but unremarkable interpretation of her moody uncle Emmett, a veteran who has suffered lasting emotional damage from his nightmarish tour of duty in 'Nam.

Lloyd's father, who also served 'in country,' was killed in combat before she was born. She likes the freedom of living with Willis, who permits Lloyd unsupervised liaisons with her callow basketball star boyfriend (Kevin Anderson). She's not especially close to her mother, Willis' sister, played deftly by Joan Allen.

Willis generates sympathy for his tormented character, but the one-dimensional script and his still limited range conspire to make Emmett a stolid caricature of the spirtually wounded veteran.

....

■ **INCREDIBLE JOURNEY, THE**

1963, 86 MINS, US ◇ ⓥ
Dir Fletcher Markle   *Prod* James Algar   *Scr* James Algar   *Ph* Kenneth Peach   *Ed* Norman Palmer   *Mus* Oliver Wallace
● Emile Genest, John Drainie, Tommy Tweed, Sandra Scott, Syme Jago, Marion Finlayson (Walt Disney)

Sheila Burnford's book of the same title has been given a vivid translation in *The Incredible Journey*, a live actioner exquisitely photographed in the Canadian outdoors.

A bull terrier, Siamese cat and Labrador retriever comprise the unlikely trio of pals who, farmed out to a friend of their owners, embark on the journey – over 200 miles of treacherous terrain. They encounter crisis after crisis in what is a remarkable, nay incredible, fight to survive all sorts of adversities in their trip all the way home.

Director Fletcher Markle, with the assist of an animal trainer, has gotten an abundance of child-appealing excitement on the screen. And he sees to it that the story is told simply and directly, what with the humans on view exchanging dialog in honest fashion and an offscreen commentary by Rex Allen. The astutely-guided animals steal the show.

....

■ **INCREDIBLE SARAH, THE**

1976, 105 MINS, UK ◇ ⓥ ⊙
Dir Richard Fleischer   *Prod* Helen M. Strauss   *Scr* Ruth Wolff   *Ph* Christopher Challis   *Ed* John Jympson   *Mus* Elmer Bernstein   *Art Dir* Elliot Scott
● Glenda Jackson, Daniel Massey, Yvonne Mitchell, Douglas Wilmer, David Langton, Simon Williams (Readers Digest)

Ruth Wolff's script, conceded in opening titles to be a 'free' interpretation of Sarah Bernhardt's early years, follows the famed actress from her early halting years on the French stage, then through an initial period of fame, notoriety and finally a youthful comeback of sorts at age 35. Glenda Jackson's versatile performance ranges from backstage,

intimate situations to several lengthy excerpts from Bernhardt vehicles.

This is the story of a theatrical personality, not your average housewife. The achievement here is that Jackson makes the character comprehensible and, in a qualified way, admirable, notwithstanding the clear evidence of a totally selfcentered nature.

Strong supporting cast includes Daniel Massey as a playwright friend, and Simon Williams as an early lover and father of Bernhardt's son.

□ 1976: Nominations: Best Costume Design, Art Direction

....

■ **INCREDIBLE SHRINKING MAN, THE**

1957, 81 MINS, US ⓥ ⊙
Dir Jack Arnold   *Prod* Albert Zugsmith   *Scr* Richard Matheson   *Ph* Ellis W. Carter   *Ed* Al Joseph   *Mus* Joseph Gershenson (sup.)   *Art Dir* Alexander Golitzen, Robert Clatworthy
● Grant Williams, Randy Stuart, April Kent, Paul Langton, Raymond Bailey, William Schallert (Universal)

Richard Matheson scripted from his novel and, while most science-fiction thrillers usually contrive a happy ending, there's no compromise here. Six-footer Grant Williams and his wife (Randy Stuart) run into a fog while boating. She's below, so is untouched, but Williams gets the full force. Soon after, he finds himself shrinking and doctors decide the radioactivity in the fog has reversed his growth processes.

Director Jack Arnold works up the chills for maximum effect by the time Williams is down to two inches and the family cat takes after him. Also harrowing are his adventures in the cellar with, to him, a giant spider, which he manages to kill using a straight pin as a lance.

The technical staff has done an outstanding job of the trick stuff. Optical effects by Roswell A. Hoffman and Everett H. Broussard make the shrinking visually effective.

....

■ **INCREDIBLE SHRINKING WOMAN, THE**

1981, 88 MINS, US ◇ ⓥ ⊙
Dir Joel Schumaker   *Prod* Hank Moonjean   *Scr* Jane Wagner   *Ph* Bruce Logan   *Ed* Jeff Gourson   *Mus* Suzanne Ciani   *Art Dir* Raymond A. Brandt
● Lily Tomlin, Charles Grodin, Ned Beatty, Henry Gibson, Maria Smith, Mark Blankfield (Universal)

Story of a contemporary housewife whose consistent use of chemically injected brand name foods, soap powders and aerosol-propelled products causes her to shrink to miniscule proportions is often strangely humorous with an underlying note of scathing social satire.

Director Joel Schumacher and writer-exec producer Jane Wagner have done a commendable job of creating a portrait of life in Anywhere USA where the tireless wife-mother (Lily Tomlin) must run a household, referee screaming kids and spruce up for her hard-working husband by the time evening rolls around.

Unfortunately, even Tomlin's talents begin to wear thin two-thirds into the film when she's kidnapped by baddies who want to use her to formulate a serum that will reduce the size of anyone in their way.

In supporting roles, ad exec hubby Charles Grodin (who perpetuates the very products that brought Tomlin to her unfortunate circumstance) and his boss Ned Beatty are first-rate. Problem is the premise just tires prematurely.

....

■ **INDECENT PROPOSAL**

1993, 117 MINS, US ◇ ⓥ ⊙
Dir Adrian Lyne   *Prod* Sherry Lansing   *Scr* Amy Holden Jones   *Ph* Howard Atherton   *Ed* Joe Hutshing   *Mus* John Barry   *Art Dir* Mel Bourne

● Robert Redford, Demi Moore, Woody Harrelson, Oliver Platt, Seymour Cassel, Billy Connolly (Paramount)

This is one of those high-concept pictures [from Jack Engelhard's novel] with a big windup and weak delivery. On paper, a film in which billionaire Robert Redford offers down-on-their-luck married couple Woody Harrelson and Demi Moore a cool million in exchange for one-night stand with Moore sounds surefire. Onscreen, the result has little sex, goes nowhere interesting or believable in the long second hour, and sports an idiotic conclusion that looks like Test Marketing Ending No. 6.

Director Adrian Lyne spends the first reel establishing college sweethearts Harrelson and Moore as really in love and still ripping each other's clothes off. But the recession has dented his architecture career and her real estate sales. Needing $50,000 to keep their house, they head for Vegas. When they hit bottom, fate appears in the guise of Redford.

Dressed impeccably and smiling nearly all the time, Redford glides through the action like a latter-day Gatsby, a man who has it all – except a woman to love. What emotional legitimacy the film does possess stems from Moore's performance, which is lively, heartfelt and believable until the script stops letting it. Tech credits are ultralush.

．．．．．．．．．．．．．．．．．．．．．．．．．．

■ **INDEPENDENCE DAY**
(Aka: Follow Your Dreams)

1983, 110 MINS, US ◇ ⊛

Dir Robert Mandel   *Prod* Daniel H. Blatt, Robert Singer
Scr Alice Hoffman   *Ph* Chuck Rosher   *Ed* Dennis
Virklor, Tina Hirsch   *Mus* Charles Bernstein
Art Dir Stewart Campbell
● Kathleen Quinlan, David Keith, Frances Sternhagen, Cliff DeYoung, Dianne Wiest, Josef Sommer (Warner)

Independence Day is an unpleasant dramatic study of young people in a small southwestern town facing family problems and the perennial career decision: to stay home or trek to the big city. Despite some yeoman acting by a talented cast of character actors, the predictable and contrived storyline proves intractable.

Alice Hoffman's unfocused screenplay centers upon two people in their 20s: Mary Ann Taylor (Kathleen Quinlan), a waitress in her dad's diner in the tiny south-western town and Jack Parker (David Keith), a gas station mechanic just home after an unsuccessful stay at engineering school.

While the duo's romance blossoms, Parker is coping with his suicidal sister Nancy (Dianne Wiest), her philandering, wife-beating husband Les (Cliff DeYoung) and his own brutish father (Noble Willingham).

Keith reinforces his image as a likable and forceful young performer while Quinlan demonstrates the ambivalence of love vs a career quite skillfully.

．．．．．．．．．．．．．．．．．．．．．．．．．．

■ **INDIANA JONES AND THE LAST CRUSADE**

1989, 127 MINS, US ◇ ⊛ ⊙

Dir Steven Spielberg   *Prod* Robert Watts   *Scr* Jeffrey
Boam   *Ph* Douglas Slocombe   *Ed* Michael Kahn
Mus John Williams   *Art Dir* Elliot Scott
● Harrison Ford, Sean Connery, Denholm Elliott, Alison Doody, John Rhys-Davies, River Phoenix
(Paramount/Lucasfilm)

More cerebral than the first two Indiana Jones films, and less schmaltzy than the second, this literate adventure should entertain and enlighten kids and adults alike.

The Harrison Ford-Sean Connery father-and-son team gives *Last Crusade* unexpected emotional depth, reminding us that real film magic is not in special effects.

Witty and laconic screenplay, based on a story by George Lucas and Menno Meyjes,

takes Ford and Connery on a quest for a prize bigger than the Lost Ark of the Covenant – the Holy Grail.

Connery is a medieval lit prof with strong religious convictions who has spent his life assembling clues to the grail's whereabouts. Father and more intrepid archaeologist son piece them together in an around-the-world adventure, leading to a touching and mystical finale. The love between father and son transcends even the quest for the Grail, which is guarded by a spectral 700-year-old knight beautifully played by Robert Eddison.

This film minimizes the formulaic love interest, giving newcomer Alison Doody an effectively sinuous but decidedly secondary role.
□ 1989: Best Sound Effects Editing.
□ Nomination: Best Original Score, Sound

．．．．．．．．．．．．．．．．．．．．．．．．．．

■ **INDIANA JONES AND THE TEMPLE OF DOOM**

1984, 118 MINS, US ◇ ⊛ ⊙

Dir Steven Spielberg   *Prod* Robert Watts   *Scr* Willard
Huyck, Gloria Katz   *Ph* Douglas Slocombe   *Ed* Michael
Kahn   *Mus* John Williams   *Art Dir* Elliot Scott
● Harrison Ford, Kate Capshaw, Ke Huy Quan, Amrish Puri, Roshan Seth, Philip Stone (Lucasfilm)

Steven Spielberg has packed even more thrills and chills into this followup than he did into the earlier pic, but to exhausting and numbing effect.

Prequel finds dapper Harrison Ford as Indiana Jones in a Shanghai nightclub in 1935, and title sequence, which features Kate Capshaw chirping Cole Porter's 'Anything Goes' looks like something out of Spielberg's *1941*.

Ford escapes from an enormous melee with the chanteuse and Oriental moppet Ke Huy Quan and they head by plane to the mountains of Asia where they are forced to jump out in an inflatable raft coming to rest in an impoverished Indian village.

Community's leader implores the ace archaeologist to retrieve a sacred, magical stone which has been stolen by malevolent neighbors.

Remainder of the yarn is set in labyrinth of horrors lorded over by a prepubescent maharajah, where untold dangers await the heroes.

What with John Williams' incessant score and the library full of sound effects, there isn't a quiet moment in the entire picture.

Ford seems effortlessly to have picked up where he left off when Indiana Jones was last heard from, although Capshaw, who looks fetching in native attire, has unfortunately been asked to react hysterically to everything that happens to her.
□ 1984: Best Visual Effects.
□ Nomination: Best Original Score

．．．．．．．．．．．．．．．．．．．．．．．．．．

■ **INDIAN FIGHTER, THE**

1955, 88 MINS, US ◇

Dir Andre de Toth   *Prod* William Schorr   *Scr* Frank
Davis, Ben Hecht   *Ph* Wilfrid M. Cline   *Ed* Richard
Cahoon   *Mus* Franz Waxman   *Art Dir* Wiard Ihnen
● Kirk Douglas, Elsa Martinelli, Walter Abel, Walter
Matthau, Diana Douglas, Eduard Franz (Bryna/United
Artists)

This frontier actioner, more derring-do than dramatic, spins off 88 minutes of entertainment that will satisfy the demands of the outdoor fan. Andre de Toth's direction reaches its high points in a refreshingly novel Indian attack on a frontier fort and in the death duel, Sioux-style, between Kirk Douglas and Harry Landers. Otherwise, footage is inclined to get monotonous at times.

Sex in the person of Elsa Martinelli, Italian actress introduced here, and the relationship of her Indian maid character with Douglas is a story factor and ballyhoo point.

Douglas dashes about as a grinning, virile

hero in the title role. His job here is to lead a wagon train through Indian country into Oregon but he gets sidetracked from duty in wooing Martinelli long enough for some crooks to stir up trouble over Indian gold.

．．．．．．．．．．．．．．．．．．．．．．．．．．

■ **INDIAN RUNNER, THE**

1991, 126 MINS, US ◇ ⊛ ⊙

Dir Sean Penn   *Prod* Don Phillips   *Scr* Sean Penn
Ph Anthony B. Richmond   *Ed* Jay Cassidy   *Mus* Jack
Nitzsche   *Art Dir* Michael Haller
● David Morse, Viggo Mortensen, Valeria Golino,
Patricia Arquette, Charles Bronson, Sandy Dennis (Mount)

A tortured examination of the disintegration of a Mid-western family, *The Indian Runner* is very much actors' cinema. Rambling, indulgent and joltingly raw at times, Sean Penn's first outing as a director takes a fair amount of patience to get through but has an integrity that intermittently serves it well.

Inspired by the Bruce Springsteen song 'Highway Patrolman,' overwrought piece looks at the muted tragedy of two brothers in the late 1960s. Joe (David Morse) is a small-town Nebraska cop who tries to welcome his brother Frank (Viggo Mortensen) back into the fold after the latter returns from a stint in Vietnam, but Frank immediately takes off.

Learning that Frank has been in prison, Joe goes to pick him up but Frank shacks up with a blonde sprite named Dorothy (Patricia Arquette). Along the way, traumas hit the family like clockwork.

All this takes more than two hours to get through because Penn, as writer and director, lets his scenes play out at great length. Actors, notably Morse and Mortensen, come off to decent advantage. Charles Bronson puts in a supporting interp of repressed hysteria as the father, while Sandy Dennis and Dennis Hopper are in briefly as the mother and a local bartender. Valeria Golino and Arquette are vital as the women in the brothers' lives.

．．．．．．．．．．．．．．．．．．．．．．．．．．

■ **INDIAN SUMMER**

1993, 97 MINS, US ◇ ⊛ ⊙

Dir Mike Binder   *Prod* Jeffrey Silver, Robert Newmyer
Scr Mike Binder   *Ph* Tom Sigel   *Ed* Adam Weiss
Mus Miles Goodman   *Art Dir* Craig Stearns
● Alan Arkin, Matt Craven, Diane Lane, Bill Paxton,
Elizabeth Perkins, Vincent Spano (Touchstone/Outlaw)

Awash in romantic nostalgia for childhoods spent in summer camps, *Indian Summer* is a sentimental, TV sitcom-like film. This *Big Chill* regrouping takes place in gorgeous Camp Tamakwa, the site of their 1972 summer.

The seven returning campers include the single and increasingly desperate Jennifer (Elizabeth Perkins), Matthew and Kelly (Vincent Spano and Julie Warner), whose marriage seems in trouble, insensitive 'macho' Jamie (Matt Craven) and his much younger g.f. Gwen (Kimberly Williams). Presiding over the group is Unca Lou (Alan Arkin), a benevolent patriarch who has devoted his entire life to the camp.

Drawing on his personal experience in Canada's Algonquin Provincial Park, where actual lensing was done, Binder has constructed a loose series of vignettes, some funnier than others. Fortunately, the highly accomplished ensemble keeps this confection tasty and enjoyable.

Of the entire cast, the three stand-out performers are Elizabeth Perkins and Bill Paxton in two showy roles and Diane Lane in a subtler and more difficult part.

．．．．．．．．．．．．．．．．．．．．．．．．．．

■ **INDISCREET**

1931, 93 MINS, US ⊛

Dir Leo McCarey   *Scr* DeSylva, Brown and Henderson
Ph Ray June, Gregg Toland   *Ed* Hal C. Kern

Art Dir Alfred Newman
● Gloria Swanson, Ben Lyon, Monroe Owsley, Barbara Kent, Arthur Lake, Maude Eburne (United Artists)

An original story of the musical comedy writing trio of DeSylva, Brown and Henderson, it is without music of moment or quantity. The three boys have fashioned a composite of a lot of other stories, giving it all an original slant. Direction, production and playing fit. As a comedy-drama it is more comedy than drama.

Story starts with s.a. and never stops. The menace is ever on the make, becoming engaged to a younger sister after being thrown down by the sister he had lived with.

Gloria Swanson has most of the laughs, through dialog mostly, but Arthur Lake, as a lovesick kid, gets his points over punchily. They are not as plentiful as Swanson's but they are more bangy and longer remembered. Ben Lyon plays the light minded but sincere author who falls for Jerry (Swanson) but won't listen about her past when she gets to the point of should a woman tell.

■ INDISCREET

1958, 100 MINS, US ◇ ⊛
Dir Stanley Donen   *Prod* Stanley Donen   *Scr* Norman Krasna   *Ph* Frederick A. Young   *Ed* Jack Harris   *Mus* Richard Rodney Bennett, Ken Jones   *Art Dir* Don Ashton
● Cary Grant, Ingrid Bergman, Cecil Parker, Phyllis Calvert, David Kossoff, Megs Jenkins (Grandon/Warner)

A beguiling love story delicately deranged by the complications of sophisticated comedy, *Indiscreet* is an expert film version of Norman Krasna's 1953 stage play, *Kind Sir*. Though tedious in its opening reels, the production warms up in direct relation to the heat of the love affair and, in the end, manages to fade out in a blaze of playful merriment.

As the successful actress who has yet to find love, Ingrid Bergman is alluring, most affectionate and highly amusing. Cary Grant makes a ripping gadabout, conniving and gracious, his performance sometimes hilarious and always smooth.

Moving from the New York of *Kind Sir*, the locale has been shipped to London where Bergman lives and wants to love. Grant, a rich American who holds a NATO post, lives there too (at least on weekends, commuting as he does from Paris) and he too wants to love. But the difference is he wants nothing of marriage and, to protect all concerned, advises Bergman on first meeting that he is a married man, separated and unable to obtain a divorce. Still she invites him to the ballet.

Cecil Parker, as the brother-in-law, becomes funnier as he becomes more unnerved, and Phyllis Calvert is excellent as the sister. Megs Jenkins turns in a fine performance as the maid, and David Kossoff, as the chauffeur, admirably grabs the high spot of hilarity with his pseudo-lover stroll-on.

■ INDISCRETION

See: *Indiscretion of an American Wife*

■ INDISCRETION OF AN AMERICAN WIFE

(UK: *Indiscretion*)

1954, 63 MINS, ITALY/US ⊛
Dir Vittorio De Sica   *Prod* Vittorio De Sica   *Scr* Cesare Zavattini, Luigi Chiarini, Giorgio Prosperi, Truman Capote   *Ph* G.R. Aldo   *Ed* Eraldo Da Rema, Jean Barker   *Mus* Alessandro Cicognini
● Jennifer Jones, Montgomery Clift, Gino Cervi, Richard Beymer (Columbia)

The plot of *Indiscretion of an American Wife* is told rather precisely in the title. It is an Italian-filmed feature, very consciously arty and foreign, but with the American star names of Jennifer Jones and Montgomery Clift.

The picture was directed by Vittorio De Sica from Cesare Zavattini's story, *Terminal Station*. The lensing was done in its entirety in the Stazione Termini in Rome, where the story of an American housewife saying farewell to her holiday lover takes place.

US distribution rights to the picture, held by Selznick Releasing Organization, were turned over to Columbia and the footage edited down considerably from its foreign release length [87 minutes]. In fact the trimming was so drastic Columbia ordered a musical prolog from SRO to pad out the footage, so *Indiscretion* got an eight-minute hitchhiker riding along.

As typical of foreign film pretentions, much use is made of bits and types flowing through the busy railway terminal to color and add movement to the picture. Outside of the agonizing moments of farewells between Jones, Philadelphia housewife returning to her safe hearth, and her younger holiday lover, Clift, the story's dramatic suspense pull is developed around the couple's arrest after being discovered in an extremely compromising embrace in a secluded spot.

The stars give the drama a real pro try and the professional standards of delivery are high, even though the character interpretations will not be liked by all.
□ 1954: Nomination: Best B&W Costume Design

■ I NEVER PROMISED YOU A ROSE GARDEN

1977, 96 MINS, US ◇ ⊛
Dir Anthony Page   *Prod* Terence F. Deane, Daniel H. Blatt, Michael Hausman   *Scr* Lewis John Carlino, Gavin Lambert   *Ph* Bruce Logan   *Ed* Garth Craven   *Mus* Paul Chihara   *Art Dir* Toby Rafelson
● Kathleen Quinlan, Bibi Andersson, Ben Piazza, Lorraine Gary, Darlene Craviotto, Reni Santoni (Imorh/New World)

Good intentions and sensationalism compete for viewer interest in this filmization of Joanne Greenberg's novel about the tentative recovery of a psychotic young woman. Unfortunately, both lose. Good intentions resolve into highminded tedium.

The pic's central problem is its structure. The girl (Kathleen Quinlan) is presented at the outset as a certifiable nutto teenager, being escorted by her parents (Lorraine Gary and Ben Piazza) to what appears to be a tastefully landscaped institution. An improved mental state is a certainty, otherwise there's no film.

Quinlan is an untypical young actress, who lends freshness and admirable reserve to a role that could have lapsed entirely into histrionic hysterics.
□ 1977: Nomination: Best Adapted Screenplay

■ I NEVER SANG FOR MY FATHER

1970, 92 MINS, US ◇ ⊛
Dir Gilbert Cates   *Prod* Gilbert Cates   *Scr* Robert Anderson   *Ph* Morris Hartzband   *Ed* Angelo Ross   *Mus* Al Gorgoni, Barry Mann   *Art Dir* Hank Aldrich
● Melvyn Douglas, Gene Hackman, Dorothy Stickney, Estelle Parsons, Elizabeth Hubbard, Lovelady Powell (Columbia/Jamel)

Film version of Robert Anderson's 1968 play is distended and lacking clear point of view. Mostly the story of a middle-aged man still strung up by a family umbilical cord, the film veers awkwardly into problems of the aged. However, the performances of father Melvyn Douglas, mother Dorothy Stickney, son Gene Hackman and daughter Estelle Parsons are superb.

Anderson's basic plot line involves the widower Hackman, still lashed to his parents through the verbal bonds of Douglas' cold-hearted feelings. Parsons as the daughter was luckier: she was banished for marrying a Jew, and was forced to make a new life.

Trouble is, given all this acting talent, the direction, writing and pacing are dreary.
□ 1970: Nominations: Best Actor (Melvyn Douglas), Supp. Actor (Gene Hackman), Adapted Screenplay

■ INFERNO

1953, 83 MINS, US ◇
Dir Roy Ward Baker   *Prod* William Bloom   *Scr* Francis Cockrell   *Ph* Lucien Ballard   *Ed* Robert Simpson   *Mus* Paul Sawtell
● Robert Ryan, Rhonda Fleming, William Lundigan, Larry Keating, Henry Hull, Carl Betz (20th Century-Fox)

Three-D and Technicolor are used effectively to make this suspense melodrama a fairly entertaining entry. Film, announced as 20th-Fox's first and only 3-D presentation, is a romantic triangle that springboards the plot of how a rich, spoiled man finds himself when left to die on the desert by his wife and her lover.

Playboy Carson (Robert Ryan) is left to die of thirst and a broken leg by Geraldine (Rhonda Fleming) and Duncan (William Lundigan) while on a prospecting trip. Driven by a desire to defeat their murder plot and get revenge, he finds resources within himself to conquer the burning heat, the bitter cold and other dangers of a laborious, painful crawling across sands and up and down canyons.

Major acting assists come from Henry Hull, old prospector; Larry Keating, Ryan's business manager; and Carl Betz and Robert Burton, officers directing the search. Roy Baker's direction accents the forceful drama capably. There are no obvious 3-D tricks in the excellent photography by Lucien Ballard.

■ INFORMER, THE

1935, 91 MINS, US ⊛ ⊙
Dir John Ford   *Prod* John Ford   *Scr* Dudley Nichols   *Ph* Joseph H. August   *Ed* George Hively   *Mus* Max Steiner   *Art Dir* Van Nest Polglase, Charles Kirk
● Victor McLaglen, Heather Angel, Preston Foster, Margot Grahame, Wallace Ford, Una O'Connor (RKO)

The Informer is forcefully and intelligently written, directed and acted. Story [by Liam O'Flaherty] deals with the Irish rebellion against British authority prior to 1922, when the Irish Free State's creation finally removed the hated symbols of British domination.

Amidst the rebellion-rife slums of Dublin a huge ox of a peasant, named Gypo Nolan (Victor McLaglen) loves Katie Fox (Margot Grahame) who picks up her room rent on the streets. Gypo reproaches her and is in turn taunted for his miserable poverty and inability to provide money. Stung by the girl's bitterness, Gypo, in fascinated horror at his own wickedness, deliberately turns informer on his best friend to obtain $100 reward. Irony of this deed is that Gypo is really a softie, having been court martialed and expelled from the Republican army for failing to carry out a political assassination.

What makes the picture powerful is the faithful characterization of McLaglen as guided and developed by the direction of John Ford. Gypo is a blundering, pathetic fool who is not basically vicious yet is guilty of a truly foul betrayal.

Wallace Ford, as the boy who is turned in, is smartly cast. Margot Grahame grabs some attention as the harlot. Preston Foster, a good actor, is the head of the Republican underground battalion.
□ 1935: Best Director, Actor (Victor McLaglen), Screenplay, Score.
□ Nominations: Best Picture, Editing

■ INFORMERS, THE
(US: Underworld Informers)

1963, 105 MINS, UK
Dir Ken Annakin *Prod* William McQuitty *Scr* Alun
Falconer *Ph* Reginald Wyer *Ed* Alfred Roome
Mus Clifton Parker
● Nigel Patrick, Frank Finlay, Derren Nesbitt, Colin
Blakely, Catharine Woodville, Maggie Whiting (Rank)

Here's a tough, hard-hitting, cops-and-robbers thriller set in London's underworld which, despite the story line, situations and characters occasionally tripping themselves up, crackles along at a brisk pace and has the smell of authenticity.

Douglas Warner's novel, *Death of a Snout*, has been turned into a slick screenplay. Central character is Chief Inspector Johnno (Nigel Patrick) a dedicated cop at Scotland Yard. He has many contacts in the underworld and the snouts, or informers, feed him with many a juicy lead to solving a crime. But Johnno's chief insists that personal contact with informers should be out. From now on, scientific methods must be used. But Johnno believes he is close to cracking the gang that has been pulling off some audacious banknote robberies and is sure that one of his most wily informants can put him on the trail. So he disobeys orders.

Patrick gives a suave, dominating performance in which, till the finale, he uses brain rather than brawn. Of the assorted villains, outstanding are Frank Finlay as the bossman and Derren Nesbitt, with an insidious study in oily menace, as the pimp who organizes the robberies.

■ IN GOD WE TRUST
OR: GIMME THAT PRIME TIME RELIGION

1980, 97 MINS, US ◇ ⒱
Dir Marty Feldman *Prod* Howard West, George
Shapiro *Scr* Marty Feldman *Ph* Charles
Correll *Ed* David Blewitt *Mus* John Morris
Art Dir Lawrence G. Paull
● Marty Feldman, Peter Boyle, Louise Lasser, Wilfrid
Hyde White, Richard Pryor, Andy Kaufman (Universal)

In God We Trust is a rare achievement – a comedy with no laughs.

This one has totally innocent monk Marty Feldman cast out into the mean and nasty world to raise some quick cash to keep his monastery in business. He ends up on Hollywood Blvd. Object of his search is outrageous TV evangelist Armageddon T. Thunderbird (Andy Kaufman) who puts off the meek man of God before taking him in as a partner, only to later turn against him when Feldman wins the ear of G.O.D. (Richard Pryor). At the same time, Feldman takes a tumble or two with gold-hearted prostie Mary (Louise Lasser).

Beneath all the strained attempts at humor, there's a germ of sweetness in Feldman's innocent led astray, but as a director he's unable to give it any play. Nor does he do any favors for the remainder of the cast. Technically, film is a near-shambles.

■ IN HARM'S WAY

1965, 165 MINS, US ⒱
Dir Otto Preminger *Prod* Otto Preminger *Scr* Wendell
Mayes *Ph* Loyal Griggs *Ed* George Tomasini, Hugh S.
Fowler *Mus* Jerry Goldsmith *Art Dir* Lyle Wheeler
● John Wayne, Kirk Douglas, Patricia Neal, Tom Tryon,
Paula Prentiss, Henry Fonda (Paramount)

John Wayne is in every sense the big gun of *In Harm's Way*. Without his commanding presence, chances are director-producer Otto Preminger probably could not have built the head of steam this film generates and sustains for two hours and 45 minutes.

Although the personal drama that unites and divides the lives of navy people caught up in this dramatization of US efforts to strike back within the year after the Pearl Harbor disaster doesn't win any prizes for creativity, Preminger uses it effectively to establish a bond between the characters and the audience. It's a full, lusty slice of life in a time of extreme stress that Wendell Mayes has fashioned from the novel by James Bassett.

Romantic coupling of Wayne and Patricia Neal, as a navy nurse, is the most natural stroke of man and woman casting in many a year. Neal brings to her role a beautifully proportioned, gutsy strength and sensitivity.

Through skillful blending of fact and fiction, Preminger provides, in the picture's action stretches, a highly suspenseful and, at times, shatteringly realistic account of an underdog US Navy task force boldly seeking out a Japanese group of ships. The sea battle sequences are filmmaking at its best.

There are some heroics that come out of a traditional mold and fall to Kirk Douglas to carry off as a hard-drinking exec officer, and buddy of Wayne, brooding the loss at Pearl Harbor of his double-timing wife. Henry Fonda, as the four-star boss of this navy show, moves in and out of the story, hitting the mark every time.

☐ 1965: Nomination: Best B&W
Cinematography

■ INHERIT THE WIND

1960, 126 MINS, US ⒱ ⊙
Dir Stanley Kramer *Prod* Stanley Kramer *Scr* Nathan
E. Douglas, Harold Jacob Smith *Ph* Ernest Laszlo
Ed Fredric Knudtson *Mus* Ernest Gold *Art Dir* Rudolph
Sternad
● Spencer Tracy, Fredric March, Gene Kelly, Florence
Eldridge, Harry Morgan, Philip Coolidge (United Artists)

This is a rousing and fascinating motion picture. Producer-director Stanley Kramer has held the action in tight check.

One suspects it needed a strong hand to restrain the forensics of Spencer Tracy and Fredric March as defense and prosecution attorneys in this drama inspired by the 1925 trial in Dayton, Tennessee, of a young high school teacher, John T. Scopes, for daring to teach Darwin's theory of evolution. Roles of Tracy and March equal Clarence Darrow and William Jennings Bryan who collided on evolution.

Tracy and March go at each other on the thespic plane as one might imagine Dempsey and Louis. March actually has the more colorful role as Matthew Harrison Brady (Bryan) because, with the aid of face-changing makeup, he creates a completely different character, whereas Tracy has to rely solely upon his power of illusion, a most persuasive power indeed.

The scenario, which broadens the scope of the play by Jerome Lawrence and Robert E. Lee, is a most commendable job. It is shot through with dialog that it florid, witty, penetrating, compassionate and sardonic. A good measure of the film's surface bite is contributed by Gene Kelly as a cynical Baltimore reporter (patterned after Henry L. Menken) whose paper comes to the aid of the younger teacher played by Dick York. Kelly demonstrates again that even without dancing shoes he knows his way on the screen.

☐ 1960: Nominations: Best Actor (Spencer
Tracy), Adapted Screenplay, B&W
Cinematography, Editing

■ IN-LAWS, THE

1979, 103 MINS, US ◇ ⒱
Dir Arthur Hiller *Prod* Arthur Hiller *Scr* Andrew
Bergman *Ph* David M. Walsh *Ed* Robert E. Swink
Mus John Morris *Art Dir* Pato Guzman
● Peter Falk, Alan Arkin, Richard Libertini, Nancy
Dussault, Arlene Golonka, Ed Begley Jr (Warner)

Peter Falk and Alan Arkin were the perfect choices to play an addled CIA agent and a Gotham dentist, respectively. Brought together by the impending marriage of their individual offspring (Michael Lembeck and Penny Peyser), they're quickly at one another's throats, as Falk lures Arkin into a neverending series of improbable adventures.

Script elements include stolen US treasury plates, underworld thugs, and a South American banana republic and its deranged leader.

Under Arthur Hiller's fast-paced and engaging direction, everything keeps moving quickly enough to stymie audience qualms about plotting, character developments and a rapidly-compressed time frame.

■ IN LIKE FLINT

1967, 115 MINS, US ◇ ⒱ ⊙
Dir Gordon M. Douglas *Prod* Saul David *Scr* Hal
Fimberg *Ph* William C. Daniels *Ed* Hugh S. Fowler
Mus Jerry Goldsmith *Art Dir* Jack Martin Smith, Dale
Hennesy
● James Coburn, Lee J. Cobb, Jean Hale, Andrew
Duggan, Anna Lee, Yvonne Craig (20th Century-Fox)

Girls, gimmicks, girls, gags, and more girls are the essential parameters of *In Like Flint*. With James Coburn encoring as the urbane master sleuth, also harried boss Lee J. Cobb, this pic turns on a femme plot to take over the world.

As for the story, the tongue is best put way out in the cheek. Anne Lee, ever a charming and gracious screen personality, is part of a triumvirate bent on seizing world power.

Lee's plot in this film comes a cropper when her male allies – corrupt General Steve Ihnat and cohorts, who have substituted an actor, Andrew Duggan, for the real US President, also played by Duggan – move in to snatch the ultimate prize.

While the dialog scenes tend to be a mite sluggish, pace picks up regularly with slam-bang action sequences.

■ IN LOVE AND WAR

1958, 107 MINS, US ◇
Dir Philip Dunne *Prod* Jerry Wald *Scr* Edward Anhalt
Ph Leo Tover *Ed* William Reynolds *Mus* Hugo
Friedhofer *Art Dir* Lyle R. Wheeler, George W. Davis
● Robert Wagner, Dana Wynter, Jeffrey Hunter, Hope
Lange, Bradford Dillman, Sheree North (20th Century-Fox)

In Love and War is a keen appraisal of the utility of love and the futility of war. Based on Anton Myrer's novel, *The Big War*, it is hard-hitting, both in action and dialog. The characterizations are built in San Francisco and the Monterey Peninsula, and the sequences are particularly effective. The Pacific war footage, however, tends to ramble and with little or no forward movement.

Story is of the changing ideals and growing maturity of three marines entrenched in the Second World War. At the start, Jeffrey Hunter is the patriot, Robert Wagner the coward and Bradford Dillman the intellectual who fights because he must. More than one of war, the tale is one of love, Wagner for Sheree North, Hunger for Hope Lange and Dillman, having discarded Dana Wynter, for France Nuyen.

High spots are numerous, and the seven stars – plus comic Mort Sahl in his first film role – are excellent. Sahl's Jewish marine role was written especially for him, and, from the sound of it, by him.

■ INNER CIRCLE, THE

1991, 134 MINS, US ◇ ⒱
Dir Andrei Konchalovsky *Prod* Claudio Bonivento
Scr Andrei Konchalovsky, Anatoli Usov *Ph* Ennio

Guarnieri   *Ed* Henry Richardson   *Mus* Eduard Artemiev
Art Dir Ezio Frigerio
● Tom Hulce, Lolita Davidovich, Bob Hoskins, Alexandre
Zbruev, Feodor Chaliapin Jr, Irina Kupchenko (Columbia)

The first Western film to shoot within the
Kremlin and KGB h.q., and Andrei
Konchalovsky's first Soviet-based pic in 12
years, this idiosyncratic look at the life of
Stalin's personal projectionist has numerous
points of interest but is too muddled and mis-
conceived.

Set in Moscow beginning in 1939 and based
on a true story, this odd tale focuses on Ivan
Sanshin (Tom Hulce), a groveling, pathetic
projectionist for the KGB who has a kind of
greatness thrust upon him when he is sum-
marily ordered to screen a film for the
supreme leader.

At home on Slaughterhouse Street, Ivan
and his bride (Lolita Davidovich) celebrate
their honeymoon evening as a Jewish family is
evicted from the building. Davidovich maintains an obsessive devotion to the family's orphan daughter. Ivan admits he loves Stalin
more that his wife, and has her give herself
on a train one night to a notoriously brutal
KGB head (Bob Hoskins).

Pic excels in glimpses of power at the top.
Several scenes take place in Stalin's personal
projection room, a salon of plush chairs and
ample food and drink where the air is
checked for possible poisoning. Ultimately,
however, the story proves unwieldy with
Konchlovsky unable to integrate the diverse
sides of the tale and give it a proper dramatic
arc.

Hulce's performance is typically enthusiastic, but the character is so thick-headed that
one tires of him after more than two hours.
Hoskins makes a sketchily conceived but utterly convincing thug.

■ INNERSPACE

1987, 120 MINS, US ◇ ⦿ ⊙
Dir Joe Dante   *Prod* Michael Finnell   *Scr* Jeffrey Boam,
Chip Proser   *Ph* Andrew Laszlo   *Ed* Kent Beyda
Mus Jerry Goldsmith   *Art Dir* James H. Spencer
● Dennis Quaid, Martin Short, Meg Ryan, Kevin
McCarthy, Fiona Lewis, Henry Gibson (Warner/Amblin)

Hot Dog Air Force flyer Dennis Quaid is prepared at the outset to be shrunken and pilot a
tiny craft through the bloodstream of a laboratory rabbit. Evildoers are on to the unprecedented experiment and the syringe bearing
the fearless voyager finally implants itself in
the behind of Martin Short, a hapless grocery
clerk.

Filmmakers' ingenuity [screen story by
Chip Proser] quickly begins asserting itself.
As Quaid travels through different parts of
the unsuspecting shnook's body and speaks to
him over his radio, Short believes he's going
crazy before finally accepting what's happened to him.

Quaid is engagingly reckless and gung-ho
as the pioneer into a new dimension, although he is physically constrained in his little capsule for most of the running time.
Short has infinitely more possibilities and
makes the most of them, coming into his own
as a screen personality as a mild-mannered
little guy who rises to an extraordinary situation. Meg Ryan is game as the spirited doll
both men hanker for, and supporting cast is
filled out with a good assortment of familiar
faces.
□ 1987: Best Visual Effects

■ INNOCENT BLOOD

(Australia: French Vampire in America)

1992, 112 MINS, US ◇ ⦿ ⊙
Dir John Landis   *Prod* Lee Rich, Leslie Belzberg
Scr Michael Wolk   *Ph* Mac Ahlberg   *Ed* Dale Beldin
Mus Ira Newborn   *Art Dir* Richard Sawyer

● Anne Parillaud, Robert Loggia, Anthony LaPaglia,
David Proval, Don Rickles, Chazz Palminteri (Warner)

Teens and genre fans should eat up John
Landis' latest mix of horror and camp comedy. They will 'ooh' at the various gross-out
scenes and nifty special effects, 'aah' at the
film's sensuality and Anne Parillaud's easy
nudity, and savor the numerous in-jokes and
horror references, from cameos by other
goremeister directors to clips from various
late-show staples.

Using a set-up (by first-time screenwriter
Michael Wolk) that can best be described as
Fright Night meets Landis' *The Blues Brothers*,
the director also benefits from a toothy performance by Robert Loggia as a mob boss
who, endowed with vampiric powers by the
mysterious Marie (Parillaud), goes on a rampage.

Marie ends up dining on several of Loggia's
henchmen as well. She normally kills her
'food' after draining it but doesn't get the
chance in Loggia's case, forcing her to team
up with a cop (Anthony LaPaglia) to stop
him.

Making her US film debut, Parillaud
(*Nikita*) struggles a bit with enunciation and a
quickly abandoned voiceover narration but
nonetheless has charisma to spare, oozing
sexuality, playfulness and menace all at once.
LaPaglia is likable and properly confused as
the cop, while much of the rest of the cast
provide a convincing gallery of *Godfather* rejects.

Cameos include sci-fi/horror guru Forrest J.
Ackerman, directors Frank Oz, Sam Raimi,
Tom Savini and Michael Ritchie, plus Don
Rickles as the mob boss's lawyer. Tech credits
are top-notch.

■ INNOCENT BYSTANDERS

1972, 111 MINS, UK ◇
Dir Peter Collinson   *Prod* George H. Brown   *Scr* James
Mitchell   *Ph* Brian Probyn   *Ed* Alan Pattillo   *Mus* John
Keating   *Art Dir* Maurice Carter
● Stanley Baker, Geraldine Chaplin, Donald Pleasence,
Dana Andrews, Sue Lloyd, Warren Mitchell (Sagittarius)

Innocent Bystanders is a violence-packed, often-
confusing but usually-interesting meller of secret agents on the prowl to track down and
capture a Russian scientist escaped from a
Siberian prison. Scene shifts from London to
N.Y., thence to Turkey, where major portion
of action unfolds against colorful location
backgrounds.

Stanley Baker is chief protagonist, once top
agent of Britain's hush-hush spy organization
but now regarded as slipped by his chief
(Donald Pleasence), who in a final assignment gives him a chance to redeem himself
on the scientist caper.

Never exactly explained is the reason for
the desperate hunt of the scientist. Script by
James Mitchell [from a novel by James
Munro] is sufficiently exciting, however, and
direction by Peter Collinson so realistic, that
interest never lags.

■ INNOCENT MAN, AN

1989, 113 MINS, US ◇ ⦿ ⊙
Dir Peter Yates   *Prod* Ted Field, Robert W. Cort
Scr Larry Brothers   *Ph* William A. Fraker   *Ed* Stephen
A. Rotter, William S. Scharf   *Mus* Howard Shore
Art Dir Stuart Wurtzel
● Tom Selleck, F. Murray Abraham, Laila Robins, David
Rasche, Richard Young (Touchstone/Silver Screen
Partners IV)

This collection of cliches accomplishes the almost unthinkable by bringing the prison
genre to a new low.

Nightmarishly structured, the film takes
half-hour before Tom Selleck's everyman,
Jimmie Rainwood, gets wrongfully framed by
two corrupt vice cops (David Rasche and

Richard Young). Then he spends more than
an hour in stir before he gets released to seek
vengeance on the duo in one of the more absurd finales in memory.

In between, Jimmie gets a lesson in prison
survival from the cell-wise Virgil (F. Murray
Abraham), learning to do the previously unthinkable to survive the hellish conditions.

■ INNOCENTS, THE

1961, 99 MINS, UK
Dir Jack Clayton   *Prod* Jack Clayton   *Scr* William
Archibald, Truman Capote   *Ph* Freddie Francis
Ed James Clark   *Mus* Georges Auric   *Art Dir* Wilfrid
Shingleton
● Deborah Kerr, Michael Redgrave, Peter Wyngarde,
Megs Jenkins, Martin Stephens, Pamela Franklin (20th
Century-Fox)

Based on Henry James' story *Turn of the Screw*
this catches an eerie, spine-chilling mood right
at the start and never lets up on its grim, evil
theme. Director Jack Clayton makes full use of
camera angles, sharp cutting, shadows, ghost
effects and a sinister soundtrack.

Deborah Kerr has a long, arduous role as a
governess in charge of two apparently angelic
little children in a huge country house.
Gradually she finds that they are not all that
they seem on the surface. Her determination
to save the two moppets' corrupted souls
leads up to a tragic, powerful climax.

Clayton's small but expert cast do full justice to their tasks, Kerr runs a wide gamut of
emotions in a difficult role in which she has to
start with an uncomplicated portrayal and
gradually find herself involved in strange, unnatural goings-on, during which she sometimes doubts her own sanity. Clayton has also
coaxed a couple of remarkable pieces of playing from the two youngsters, Martin Stephens
and Pamela Franklin, extraordinary blends of
innocence and sophistry.

■ INN OF THE SIXTH HAPPINESS, THE

1958, 160 MINS, UK ◇ ⦿
Dir Mark Robson   *Prod* Buddy Adler   *Scr* Isobel Lennart
Ph Freddie A. Young   *Ed* Ernest Walter   *Mus* Malcolm
Arnold   *Art Dir* John Box, Geoffrey Drake
● Ingrid Bergman, Curt Jurgens, Robert Donat, Ronald
Squire, Athene Seyler, Peter Chong (20th Century-Fox)

Based on Alan Burgess' novel *The Small
Woman* which, in turn, was based on the adventures of a real person, the film has Ingrid
Bergman as a rejected missionary in China,
who gets there determinedly under her own
steam. First met with hostility by the natives,
she gradually wins their love and esteem. She
falls in love with a Eurasian colonel, converts
a powerful mandarin to Christianity and becomes involved in the Chino-Japanese war.
Finally she guides 100 children to the safety
of a northern mission by leading them on an
arduous journey across the rugged mountains
and through enemy territory.

The inn in the film is run by Bergman and
an elderly missionary (Athene Seyler). Here
they dispense hospitality and Bible stories to
the muleteers in transit. Bergman's early
scenes as she strives to get to China and begins the urgent task of winning the confidence of the Chinese are brilliantly done with
humor and a sense of urgent dedication.

A standout performance comes from Robert
Donat as an astute yet benign mandarin. It
was Donat's swansong before his untimely
death and only rarely can signs of his physical
collapse be detected.

The film was shot in Wales and in the
Elstree studio, converted expertly into a
Chinese village. Mark Robson's direction
slickly catches both the sweep of the crowd
sequences and the more intimate ones.
□ 1958: Nomination: Best Director

■ IN OLD ARIZONA

1929, 94 MINS, US

Dir Irving Cummings, Raoul Walsh   *Scr* Tom Barry
Ph Arthur Edeson
● Warner Baxter, Edmund Lowe, Dorothy Burgess, J.
Farrell McDonald, Fred Warren (Fox)

It was said that Fox would never turn loose a
full-length talker until the studio was convinced the picture was right. *In Old Arizona*
that it's right is unquestioned at this time.
It's the first outdoor talker and a western,
with a climax twist to make the story stand
out from the usual hill and dale thesis. It's
outdoors, it talks and it has a great screen
performance by Warner Baxter. That it's long
and that it moves slowly is also true, but the
exterior sound revives the novelty angle
again.

Dorothy Burgess is cast as Tonia, a
Mexican vixen who plays the boys across the
boards and finally gets into a jam between the
Cisco Kid (Baxter) and the army sergeant
who is pursuing the bandit.

Raoul Walsh is given screen and program
credit for having co-directed this film, as he
actually started it and was intent on finishing
and playing the Cisco Kid in it. An unfortunate accident made this impossible, hence
Irving Cumming's assignment.
□ 1928/29: Best Actor (Warner Baxter).
□ Nominations: Best Picture, Director,
Writing, Cinematography

■ IN OLD CHICAGO

1938, 110 MINS, US

Dir Henry King   *Prod* Darryl Zanuck   *Scr* Lamar Trotti,
Sonya Levien   *Ph* Peverell Marley   *Ed* Barbara McLean
Mus Louis Silvers (dir.)   *Art Dir* William Darling, Rudolph
Sternad
● Tyrone Power, Alice Faye, Don Ameche, Alice Brady,
Andy Devine, Brian Donlevy (20th Century-Fox)

An elaborate and liberally budgeted entertainment, the pictorial climax is the Chicago
fire of 1871. This portion envisaging mob
panic, desperate efforts to stop the fire by dynamiting, etc, is highly effective.

It is historically cockeyed in the placement
of its main characters, and its story [by Niven
Busch] is mere rehash of corrupt political
mismanagement of a growing American city.
But as a film entertainment it is socko.

The O'Leary family plays the most important part in the story, even to the point where
one of the sons is projected as mayor of the
city at the time of the fire, and another is pictured as the dishonest political boss, saloonkeeper and villain.

First portion (80 minutes) carries the characters to the eve of the great fire. Scores of
elaborate scenes establish the primitive type
of architecture of the frame-built, rambling
town with its unpaved, muddy streets. Most of
the action is laid in gaudy saloons and beer
halls. Chicago is pictured as a dirty and corrupt city, a Sodom on the brink, ready for the
torch of annihilation. Second part contains
views of the holocaust, and a devastating series of actual and processed shots.

Alice Brady and Alice Faye give the outstanding performances. Brady is Mrs
O'Leary, an honest, hardworking laundress
with a pleasing Irish brogue. Tyrone Power as
the film's heavy is good in his romantic scenes
with Faye, who appears as a musical hall
singer. Latter is especially effective when
singing several musical numbers, tuned by
Mack Gordon and Harry Revel, of which 'In
Old Chicago' is the best. Don Ameche is a vehement political reformer and Brian Donlevy
plays a dive keeper and crooked politician.
□ 1937: Best Supp. Actress (Alice Brady),
Assistant Director (Robert Webb).
□ Nominations: Best Picture, Original Story,
Score, Sound

■ IN SEARCH OF GREGORY

1970, 90 MINS, UK/ITALY ◇

Dir Peter Wood   *Prod* Joseph Janni, Daniele Senatore
Scr Tonnio Guerra, Lucille Laks   *Ph* Otto Heller, Giorgio
Tonti   *Ed* John Bloom   *Mus* Ron Grainer   *Art Dir* Piero
Poletto
● Julie Christie, Michael Sarrazin, John Hurt, Paola
Pitagora, Roland Culver, Tony Selby (Vic/Vera)

A superbly-wrought gem about the romantic
illusions people, especially would-be lovers,
search for in one another, with Julie Christie
ideally cast as the seeker and Michael
Sarrazin as her fantasy.

Christie, the daughter of an incurably romantic and frequently married Swiss financier, played with charming elan by Adolfo
Celi, is living a life of quiet domesticity in
Rome when she is invited by papa to attend
his latest nuptial.

Her real attraction in Geneva is Celi's calculating description of his house guest from
San Francisco, a tall, handsome 'likeable maniac'. At the airport, she spots a giant poster
of Sarrazin, an auto-ball champion, and in her
imagination he becomes the physical embodiment of her romantic fantasies about
Gregory.

■ IN SEARCH OF THE CASTAWAYS

1962, 100 MINS, US ◇ ⑫ ⊙

Dir Robert Stevenson   *Prod* Walt Disney   *Scr* Lowell S.
Hawley   *Ph* Paul Beeson   *Ed* Gordon Stone
Mus William Alwyn   *Art Dir* Michael Stringer
● Maurice Chevalier, Hayley Mills, George Sanders,
Wilfrid Hyde White, Michael Anderson Jr, Wilfrid
Brambell (Walt Disney)

Castaways is a blend of every Disney trick,
combining adventure and humor. Jules
Verne's yarn concerns a French scientist who
finds a bottle containing a note which reveals
the whereabouts of Captain Grant who mysteriously disappeared two years before. The
Frenchman and the sea captain's two children persuade a wealthy shipping owner and
his son to set off for South America in search
of the missing man. The trail eventually leads
successfully to Australia and New Zealand.

The party survives giant condors, jaguars,
flood, lightning, crocodiles, an avalanche, an
earthquake, a huge waterspout, mutiny by
Grant's former quartermaster, imprisonment
by unfriendly Maoris and an erupting volcano.

Thesping is done throughout with a tongue
in the cheek exuberance which suggests that
Disney and director Robert Stevenson have
given the actors the go ahead to have fun. At
times it almost looks as if they are making up
the situations and dialog as they go along.

■ INSERTS

1975, 117 MINS, UK ◇ ⑫

Dir John Byrum   *Prod* Davina Belling, Clive Parons
Scr John Byrum   *Ph* Denys Cooper   *Ed* Mike Bradsell
Art Dir John Clark
● Richard Dreyfuss, Jessica Harper, Stephen Davis,
Veronica Cartwright, Bob Hoskins (United Artists)

Despite its British label, this is a thoroughly
Yank pic that dips into nostalgia and Hollywood 1930s themes. Richard Dreyfuss is all
coiled disdain as a once-great director reduced to stag pix.

Dreyfuss manages to add some unusual
touches to them as the moneyman walks in
with a lissome girl he is planning to marry
but whom he treats as a child.

The boss leaves the girl with Dreyfuss; the
girl wants to be in pictures and finally decides
to pose for inserts; they are caught by the
boss, who is not sure what happened but
takes off with the camera and material.

Jessica Harper scores as the shrewd innocent and Stephen Davies and Bob Hoskins are

right as the actor and boss respectively. But it
is all somewhat too surface despite allusions
to Hollywood 1930s types.

■ INSIDE DAISY CLOVER

1965, 128 MINS, US ◇ ⑫ ⊙

Dir Robert Mulligan   *Prod* Alan J. Pakula   *Scr* Gavin
Lambert   *Ph* Charles Lang   *Ed* Aaron Stell   *Mus* Andre
Previn   *Art Dir* Robert Clatworthy
● Natalie Wood, Christopher Plummer, Robert Redford,
Roddy McDowall, Ruth Gordon, Katharine Bard (Park
Place/Warner)

There will be those who may claim *Inside
Daisy Clover* is based upon the true-life story of
an actress who rose to shining blonde stardom. Alan J. Pakula and Robert Mulligan focus their sights upon a teenage beach gamin
who becomes a Hollywood star of the 1930s.
Covering a two-year period, the outcome is at
times disjointed and episodic as the title
character played by Natalie Wood emerges
more nebulous than definitive.

Femme star seems to be eternally searching for the meaning of her role; she is almost
inarticulate for long intervals and whoever is
in a scene with her generally engages in a
monolog since there is seldom dialog between
them. The Gavin Lambert screenplay, based
on his own novel, hop-skips through a brief
romance with a screen idol, her one-day marriage, desertion and divorce; a nervous breakdown after the death of her mother.

Probably the outstanding parts of pic are
two novel musical numbers [staged by
Herbert Ross], one in which the studio boss
introduces his new star in a specially-made
film shown at a party and second featuring
her after she's reached stardom.

Wood is better than her part. Her co-star is
Christopher Plummer, who gives polish and
some stiffness to the sadistic studio head
bound to build himself a star.
□ 1965: Nominations: Best Supp. Actress
(Ruth Gordon), Color Costume Design, Color
Art Direction

■ INSIDE MONKEY ZETTERLAND

1992, 92 MINS, US ◇ ⑫

Dir Jefery Levy   *Prod* Chuck Grieve, Tani Cohen
Scr Steven Antin, John Boskovich   *Ph* Christopher Taylor
Ed Lauren Zuckerman   *Mus* Rick Cox, Jeff Elmassian
Art Dir Jane Stewart
● Steven Antin, Katherine Helmond, Patricia Arquette,
Tate Donovan, Bo Hopkins, Sandra Bernhard (Coast
Entertainment)

A charming comedy about contempo L.A. life,
Inside Monkey Zetterland is infused with a sophisticated gay sensibility. Although pic is
populated by gay and lesbian characters, its
broad canvas, humanistic vision, magnetic
cast and inspired writing extend its appeal.

At the heart of scripter Steven Antin's poetic, loosely autobiographical comedy is the
complex, Oedipal relationship between aspiring writer Monkey Zetterland (Antin) and his
domineering Jewish mother (Katherine
Helmond), a TV soap star.

Dad Mike (Bo Hopkins) is not around
much, but Monkey is close to his brother
(Tate Donovan), a handsome hairdresser, and
even closer to his lesbian sister (Patricia
Arquette), who moves into his house during a
strain in her relationship with her lover (Sofia
Coppola).

Pic's best sequences depict collective gatherings (Thanksgiving dinner, evenings in
front of the TV) in which Monkey's friends
behave like one big, extended family, expanding the conventional meaning of family life.

In tone, the pic resembles Alan Rudolph's
best pics (*Welcome to L.A.*, *Choose Me*), and its
ironic view and whimsical absurdity contain
light and dark humour in equal measure.

Unfortunately, the film's last half-hour becomes too cute and TV-like in its artificial tempo. Pic also errs in deliberating on its least convincing subplot involving a terrorist act against a homophobic insurance company.

• •

■ INSIDE MOVES
THE GUYS FROM MAX'S BAR

1980, 113 MINS, US ◇ ⓥ ⊙

Dir Richard Donner *Prod* Mark M. Tanz, R.W. Goodwin *Scr* Valerie Curtin, Barry Levinson *Ph* Laszlo Kovacs *Ed* Frank Morriss *Mus* John Barry *Art Dir* Charles Rosen
● John Savage, David Morse, Diana Scarwid, Harold Russell, Amy Wright, Tony Burton (AFD/Goodmark)

Inoffensive and essentially compassionate, *Inside Moves* is also a highly conventional and predictable look at handicapped citizens trying to make it in everyday life.

Director Richard Donner focuses on the intermittently tense relationship between insecure, failed suicide John Savage and volatile David Morse.

Basic plot movement [from the novel by Todd Walton] has Savage, permanently hobbled after jumping off a building, gradually regaining confidence.

Performances can't be faulted, with Savage seeming truly disturbed at the start, only to slowly come to terms with himself. In his feature debut, Morse puts across the called-for ambition and later shallowness, and Diana Scarwid hits the right notes as a 'normal' young woman forced to confront her own limitations via the outwardly afflicted.

☐ 1980: Nomination: Best Supp. Actress (Diana Scarwid)

• •

■ INSIGNIFICANCE

1985, 108 MINS, UK ◇ ⓥ ⊙

Dir Nicolas Roeg *Prod* Jeremy Thomas *Scr* Terry Johnson *Ph* Peter Hannan *Ed* Tony Lawson *Mus* Stanley Myers *Art Dir* David Brockhurst
● Gary Busey, Tony Curtis, Michael Emil, Theresa Russell, Will Sampson (Zenith/Recorded Picture)

A comedy set in a New York hotel room over a sweaty night in 1953 might seem an odd assignment for such a serious and innovative director as Nicolas Roeg.

Story concerns four celebrated American figures of the 1950s who, for legal reasons are not specifically named. That's all to the good since pic dispenses with biographical detail to focus on the nature of celebrity in Cold War America.

Film was scripted by Terry Johnson from his stage play. Although legit text is not opened out in a traditional way, beautifully lensed views of the NY landscape and flashbacks give the film a sense of scale. When, towards the end of the film, the Elevator Attendant greets the dawn Cherokee-style, the hotel room has become a microcosm of the world outside.

Those on the lookout for philosophical reflections will find plenty to think about in the pic's meditations upon relativity and the coming together of time. *Insignificance* also works on a simpler level as a depiction of four people struggling against despair.

• •

■ IN SOCIETY

1944, 73 MINS, US

Dir Jean Yarbrough *Prod* Edmund L. Hartmann *Scr* John Grant, Edmund L. Hartmann, Hal Fimberg *Ph* Jerome Ash *Ed* Philip Cahn *Mus* Edgar Fairchild (dir.) *Art Dir* John B. Goodman, Eugene Lourie
● Bud Abbott, Lou Costello, Marion Hutton, Kirby Grant, Margaret Irving, Anne Gillis (Universal)

Basic idea of story [by Hugh Wedlock Jr and Howard Snyder] spots Abbott and Costello as two struggling, extra-dumb plumbers being

accidentally invited to a high society weekend soiree. Their exertions and blundering efforts to adjust themselves to new surroundings furnish the pegs on which many gags are strung. But even before reaching Hollywood's idea of effete society, a bunch of new and old comedy routines are dusted off and whipped across deftly.

Costello works in his old stride, while Abbott is more efficient, smooth-working than ever as straight in the laugh combo. Marion Hutton, a femme taxi driver, provides the slight romantic twist opposite the wealthy Kirby Grant. She's supposed to be Costello's sweetie, but that's strictly for laughs, Hutton being Betty Hutton's sis.

• •

■ INSPECTOR CLOUSEAU

1968, 105 MINS, UK ◇ ⓥ

Dir Bud Yorkin *Prod* Lewis J. Rachmil *Scr* Tom Waldman, Frank Waldman *Ph* Arthur Ibbetson *Ed* John Victor Smith *Mus* Ken Thorne *Art Dir* Michael Stringer
● Alan Arkin, Frank Finlay, Delia Boccardo, Patrick Cargill, Beryl Reid, Barry Foster (United Artists/Mirisch)

Inspector Clouseau, the gauche and Gallic gumshoe, gets a healthy revitalization via Alan Arkin in the title role and director Bud Yorkin.

Film is a lively, entertaining and episodic story of bank robbers. Good scripting, better acting and topnotch direction get the most out of the material.

Clouseau is assigned to Scotland Yard to help solve a major bank heist. Story develops to a simultaneous robbery of about a dozen Swiss banks, by a ring whose members wear face masks patterned after Clouseau.

Story develops in leisurely fashion, which could have worked to overall disadvantage were it not for the excellent work of Arkin and Yorkin which keeps plot adrenalin flowing. Instead, enough momentum is sustained to hold amused interest.

• •

■ INSPIRATION

1931, 73 MINS, US ⓥ ⊙

Dir Clarence Brown *Scr* Gene Markey *Ph* William Daniels *Ed* Conrad A. Nervig
● Greta Garbo, Robert Montgomery, Lewis Stone, Marjorie Rambeau, Judith Vosselli, Beryl Mercer (M-G-M)

Garbo has never looked nor played better than in this suitable assignment. Replete with heavy love stuff, she plays it easily and convincingly, even contributing a sparkling brief bit of light comedy, and often helping long passages of awkward dialog to sound almost real.

What happens to the free-wheeling Parisian artist's model and the nice boy from the country in this picture can happen to any other pair similarly situated. This model is introduced rather tritely as the town toast amongst the artistic set. She's the inspiration for the latest successful works of an artist, a sculptor, a composer and a writer, and even that flattery doesn't seem undue. The introduction is at a party in a home that looks like Roseland ballroom.

After the model completes the meeting the nice boy takes her home. They fall in love. Her past then becomes and remains the issue until the finish.

Robert Montgomery is an excellent nice boy. Lewis Stone and Marjorie Rambeau are also outstanding.

• •

■ INTERIORS

1978, 93 MINS, US ◇ ⓥ ⊙

Dir Woody Allen *Prod* Charles H. Joffe *Scr* Woody Allen *Ph* Gordon Willis *Ed* Ralph Rosenblum *Art Dir* Mel Bourne

● Kristin Griffith, Mary Beth Hurt, Richard Jordan, Diane Keaton, E.G. Marshall, Geraldine Page (United Artists)

Watching this picture a question keeps recurring: what would Woody Allen think of all this? Then you remember he wrote and directed it.

The film is populated by characters reacting to situations Allen has satirized so brilliantly in other pictures. Diane Keaton is a suffering poet married to Richard Jordan, a novelist overshadowed by Keaton's accomplishments and talents. Keaton has two sisters – Kristin Griffith, a television actress, and Mary Beth Hurt, the most gifted of the three, but the least directed.

What would be called the film's action – like Ingmar Bergman's pictures, the movement is interior, in the mind – revolves around the relationship among the sisters and their parents, E.G. Marshall and Geraldine Page.

Interiors also looks like a Bergman film. Characters are photographed against blank walls, Keaton's discussions with her analyst appear almost to be a confession into the camera. And the final third of *Interiors* was shot near the ocean in Long Island and looks like the Swedish island on which Bergman has photographed so many of his films.

Keaton's role is the most difficult, but her performance the least believable of the eight principals. Maureen Stapleton as the woman Marshall marries after divorcing Page, is the only character who reacts more from the heart than the head.

☐ 1978: Nominations: Best Director, Actress (Geraldine Page), Supp. Actress (Maureen Stapleton), Original Screenplay, Art Direction

• •

■ INTERLUDE

1968, 113 MINS, UK ◇ ⓥ

Dir Kevin Billington *Prod* David Deutsch *Scr* Lee Langley, Hugh Leonard *Ph* Gerry Fisher *Ed* Bert Bates *Mus* Georges Delerue *Art Dir* Tony Woollard
● Oskar Werner, Barbara Ferris, Virginia Maskell, Donald Sutherland, Nora Swinburne, John Cleese (Columbia/Domino)

Interlude is not just another *Brief Encounter* type of romantic drama; it is one of the best of its class. Oskar Werner and Barbara Ferris are the star-crossed, and star-billed, lovers in this handsome production, filmed in England.

All the excitement and ecstasy, as well as the bittersweet, foredoomed disenchantment of extra-marital romance are contained in the original screenplay. Strong writing, superior acting and firstrate direction make this a powerful, personal drama.

Werner plays a temperamental symphonic conductor who is interviewed by Ferris, a newspaper reporter, the story unfolding in flashback format. A tender, fragile atmosphere is established early, and sustained quite well.

Werner's performance is excellent, despite some wardrobe and makeup which occasionally fights the credibility of his character. Ferris is outstanding; to her goes the burden of commingling the love-hate, up-down, sweet-sour aspects of the affair, and she carries it superbly. Virginia Maskell's character, unlike the stock 'wife,' comes to life.

• •

■ INTERMEZZO
A LOVE STORY
(UK: *Escape to Happiness*)

1939, 70 MINS, US ⓥ ⊙

Dir Gregory Ratoff *Prod* David O. Selznick *Scr* George O'Neil *Ph* Gregg Toland *Ed* Hal C. Kern, Francis D. Lyon *Mus* Louis Forbes (dir.) *Art Dir* Lyle R. Wheeler
● Leslie Howard, Ingrid Bergman, Edna Best, John Halliday, Cecil Kellaway (Selznick)

Intermezzo is an American remake of a picture turned out three years earlier in Sweden which Gustav Molander directed, with Ingrid Bergman in the femme lead.

Story structure [based on original by Molander and Gosta Stevens] is a love triangle involving a famed concert violinist and a young girl pianist, but the romance lacks persuasiveness.

Leslie Howard, who functions as star and associate producer, is eclipsed by Bergman. Latter is beautiful, talented and convincing, providing an arresting performance and a warm personality that introduces a new stellar asset to Hollywood. She has charm, sincerity and an infectious vivaciousness.

Picture unwinds at a leisurely pace, without theatrics of too great intensity in the romantic passages.
□ 1939: Nomination: Best Score

■ INTERNAL AFFAIRS

1990, 117 MINS, US ◇ ⓦ ⊙
Dir Mike Figgis   *Prod* Frank Mancuso Jr   *Scr* Henry Bean   *Ph* John A. Alonzo   *Ed* Robert Estrin   *Mus* Mike Figgis, Anthony Marinelli, Brian Banks
Art Dir Waldemar Kalinowski
● Richard Gere, Andy Garcia, Nancy Travis, Laurie Metcalf, William Baldwin, Annabella Sciorra (Paramount)

The title is a clever double entendre, as Andy Garcia plays LAPD internal affairs division investigator Raymond Avila, pulled into a psychological game of chicken with quarry Dennis Peck (Richard Gere), a much-honored street cop who manipulates his position as easily as he does the people around him.

Played by Gere with a constant sense of menace, Peck preys on Raymond's insecurities by insinuating that he's bedded his wife (Nancy Travis) – increasingly neglected, ironically, as Raymond thrusts his all into the case.

While hardly new territory, director Mike Figgis wrings every ounce of tension from tyro writer Henry Bean's screenplay and, most impressively, elicits firstrate performances from top to bottom.

The look, too, immeasurably helps in creating a foreboding atmosphere. Figgis never lets the pace slow long enough to expose the story's thinness despite, in retrospect, a moderate amount of action.

■ INTERNATIONAL VELVET

1978, 125 MINS, UK ◇ ⓦ
Dir Bryan Forbes   *Prod* Bryan Forbes   *Scr* Bryan Forbes   *Ph* Tony Imi   *Ed* Timothy Gee   *Mus* Francis Lai
Art Dir Keith Wilson
● Tatum O'Neal, Christopher Plummer, Anthony Hopkins, Nanette Newman, Peter Barkworth, Dinsdale Landen (M-G-M)

International Velvet is an extremely fine film for (in the best sense) family audiences. Bryan Forbes wrote, produced and directed the sequel to *National Velvet* [1944] in such a way as to provide sentiment, excitement and dual-level drama that should ring true with its target audience. Tatum O'Neal heads a strong cast as an orphaned teenager whose attachment to a horse leads to her own adjustment and maturity.

In the new script, the original Velvet Brown is now nearing middle age as a childless divorcee though happy in a relationship with Christopher Plummer, an author who provides her much emotional support. It's Nanette Newman's good fortune to play the role, and she does so excellently.

All this is to the good while O'Neal evolves from a hostile alien orphan to a high degree of adolescent maturity. Anthony Hopkins is excellent as the equestrian team trainer whose dedication to the sport will give contemporary audiences a graceful exposition of what is going on.

■ INTERNS, THE

1962, 130 MINS, US ⓦ ⊙
Dir David Swift   *Prod* Robert Cohn   *Scr* Walter Newman, David Swift   *Ph* Russell L. Metty   *Ed* Al Clark, Jerome Thoms   *Mus* Leith Stevens   *Art Dir* Don Ament
● Michael Callan, Cliff Robertson, James MacArthur, Nick Adams, Telly Savalas, Stefanie Powers (Columbia)

In its apparent attempt to dramatize candidly and irreverently the process by which school-finished candidate medics manage to turn into regular doctors, the film somehow succeeds in depicting the average intern as some kind of a Hippocratic oaf. At times it comes perilously close to earning the nickname, *Carry On, Intern*.

The separate stories of five interns, four male and one female, are traced alternately in a sort of razzle-dazzle style by the screenplay from Richard Frede's novel. Three of the stories are predictable from the word go and the other two are thoroughly unbelievable.

As these personal stories unfold, a kind of cross-section of hospital life is transpiring in the background. Chief features are a rather gory childbirth sequence, a mercy killing incident and a wild party passage imitative of the one in *Breakfast at Tiffany's*, but hardly as appropriate or amusing. Support characters run to stereotype, i.e. the ugly, prim nurse who removes her spex, lets her hair down, gets stinko and becomes the hit of the party.

■ IN THE COOL OF THE DAY

1963, 91 MINS, US ◇
Dir Robert Stevens   *Prod* John Houseman   *Scr* Meade Roberts   *Ph* Peter Newbrook   *Ed* Thomas Stanford
Mus Francis Chagrin
● Peter Finch, Jane Fonda, Angela Lansbury, Constance Cummings, Arthur Hill, Alexander Knox (M-G-M)

John Houseman production was written for the screen from the novel by Susan Ertz. It concerns the romantic encounter that is briefly consummated during a mutual visit to Greece by an English book publisher (Peter Finch) who is taunted and tormented by a grudging, embittered, anti-social wife (Angela Lansbury), and a fragile American girl (Jane Fonda) who has been sheltered and protected to the point of absurdity by her adoring, but overly-finicky husband (Arthur Hill).

Most of this romantic schmaltz is set against some interesting Greek scenery such as the Parthenon and the Acropolis.

Peter Newbrook photographs ruins well, but is less effective with people. For example, he manages to disregard the dancers' legs in the course of a Grecian folk dance scene.

Lansbury gets off the best acting in the film as Finch's sour, scarfaced wife. She stirs up the only fun in the generally sour proceedings. Fonda, sporting a Cleopatra haircut, is all passion and intensity. When she loves, boy, she really loves. Finch wears one expression. It appears to be boredom, which is understandable.

■ IN THE FRENCH STYLE

1963, 104 MINS, US
Dir Robert Parrish   *Prod* Irwin Shaw, Robert Parrish
Scr Irwin Shaw   *Ph* Michel Kelber   *Ed* Renee Lichtig   *Mus* Joseph Kosma   *Art Dir* Rino Mondellini
● Jean Seberg, Stanley Baker, Addison Powell, James Leo Herlihy, Philippe Forquet, Claudine Auger (Shaw-Parrish)

Irwin Shaw and Robert Parrish have fashioned a sophisticated love story of Paris, of an American girl in love with the life not quite for her, in their indie based upon two of Shaw's stories, *In the French Style* and *A Year to Learn the Language*.

Jean Seberg stars as the 19-year-old Chicago girl, a would-be painter who dreams of conquering the capital of art, naive, ambitious, impressionable, who has her father's financial backing for one year to prove herself. She meets early romantic disillusionment, when she becomes involved with a young French engineering student whom she believes older than she.

Seberg brings life and brilliance to her portrayal, registering strongly both in the more dramatic and lighter moments. In Stanley Baker, the correspondent with whom she has a lingering affair, she has a firstrate costar who makes a good impression. Philippe Forquet, the youth, is brash and talented.

■ IN THE HEAT OF THE NIGHT

1967, 109 MINS, US ◇ ⓦ ⊙
Dir Norman Jewison   *Prod* Walter Mirisch   *Scr* Stirling Silliphant   *Ph* Haskell Wexler   *Ed* Hal Ashby
Mus Quincy Jones   *Art Dir* Paul Groesse
● Sidney Poitier, Rod Steiger, Warren Oates, Lee Grant, Scott Wilson, Larry Gates (Mirisch/United Artists)

An excellent Sidney Poitier performance, and an outstanding one by Rod Steiger, overcome some noteworthy flaws to make *In the Heat of the Night*, an absorbing contemporary murder drama, set in the deep, red-necked South. Norman Jewison directs, sometimes in pretentious fashion, an uneven script.

Stirling Silliphant's script, adapted from John Ball's novel *Heat*, is erratic, indulging in heavy-handed, sometimes needless plot diversion, uncertain character development, and a rapid-fire denouement.

Intriguing plot basis has Poitier as the detective, accidentally on a visit to his Mississippi hometown where a prominent industrialist is found murdered. Arrested initially on the assumption that a Negro, out late at night, must have done the deed, Poitier later is thrust, by his boss in Philadelphia, his own conscience, and a temporary anti-white emotional outburst, into uneasy collaboration with local sheriff Steiger.

Steiger's transformation from a diehard Dixie bigot to a man who learns to respect Poitier stands out in smooth comparison to the wandering solution of the murder.
□ 1967: Best Picture, Actor (Rod Steiger), Adapted Screenplay, Sound, Editing.
□ Nominations: Best Director, Sound Effects

■ IN THE LINE OF FIRE

1993, 128 MINS, US ◇ ⓦ ⊙
Dir Wolfgang Petersen   *Prod* Jeff Apple   *Scr* Jeff Maguire   *Ph* John Bailey   *Ed* Anne V. Coates
Mus Ennio Morricone   *Art Dir* Lilly Kilvert
● Clint Eastwood, John Malkovich, Rene Russo, Dylan McDermott, Gary Cole, Fred Dalton Thompson (Apple Rose/Columbia/Castle Rock)

In the Line of Fire is a proficiently made thriller pitting Clint Eastwood's vet Secret Service agent against John Malkovich's insidious would-be presidential assasin.

Frank Horrigan (Eastwood) has been haunted since November 22, 1963 by the possibility that he could have saved John F. Kennedy's life. As JFK's favorite Secret Service agent, Horrigan was with the president in Dallas, and was closest to him when the shot rang out.

It's this weakness that is manipulated by Mitch Leary (Malkovich), a professional assasin who makes no secret of his intention to kill the current president sometime before the election.

Horrigan wins an assignment to cover the chief of state while he tries to nail Leary, who calls to every so often to taunt him, and at the same time must endure the gibes of his colleagues, who consider him a 'borderline burnout with questionable social skills' and a 'dinosaur'.

What neophyte scripter Jeff Maguire's plot comes down to is the cat-and-mouse game between Horrigan and Leary, and the craftiness and strategies involved on both sides, while not exactly ingenious, are tantalizing enough to compel interest.

Director Wolfgang Petersen sends the story efficiently down its straight and narrow track, deftly engineering the battle of wills between two desperately committed men.

Eastwood splendidly gives Horrigan humor, grit and imagination. Malkovich provides a delicious villain, a true psychopath so sure of himself that he's willing to give his pursuer half a chance of catching him.

●●●●●●●●●●●●●●●●●●●●●●●●●●●

■ IN THE NAVY

1941, 85 MINS, US ▼ ⊙
Dir Arthur Lubin   *Prod* Alex Gottlieb (assoc.)
Scr Arthur T. Horman, John Grant   *Ph* Joseph Valentine
Ed Philip Cahn   *Mus* Charles Previn (dir.)   *Art Dir* Jack Otterson, Harold H. MacArthur
● Bud Abbott, Lou Costello, Dick Powell, Claire Dodd, Andrews Sisters, Dick Foran (Universal)

Abbott and Costello continue their zany and familiar antics in nautical garb ashore and aboard a battlewagon [in a story by Arthur T. Horman].

Dick Powell is a radio crooner fed up by continual pestering of fans. He disappears to join the navy in San Diego, where Abbott and Costello are gobs ashore. Claire Dodd discovers identity of Powell in her ambitions to get a newspaper job, and continually attempts to candid camera Powell for a sensational expose. She even gets aboard the battleship, which suddenly pulls out for Hawaii.

Costello is center of a dream sequence in which he becomes established in the captain's cabin, and gives orders to the bridge, that send the battleship in a wild ride through the harbor and other boats in the fleet.

Induction of Powell in this instance allows for broader use of songs than in *Buck Privates*. Powell delivers two tunes in effective style. Andrews Sisters handle three numbers in their usually capable, rhythmic fashion, all delivered with production backgrounds [musical numbers staged by Nick Castle].

●●●●●●●●●●●●●●●●●●●●●●●●●●●

■ IN THE SPIRIT

1990, 93 MINS, US ◇ ▼
Dir Sandra Seacot   *Prod* Julian Schlossberg
Scr Jeannie Berlin, Laurie Jones   *Ph* Dick Quinlan
Ed Brad Fuller   *Mus* Patrick Williams   *Art Dir* Michael C. Smith
● Elaine May, Marlo Thomas, Jeannie Berlin, Peter Falk, Melanie Griffith, Olympia Dukakis (Running River/Castle Hill)

Elaine May and Marlo Thomas make a memorable screen odd couple in *In the Spirit*. Kooky black comedy is an unusual case of big-name talent gathering with friends to make a low-budget pic freed of mainstream good taste and gloss.

Like Jules Feiffer's *Little Murders* (1971) New York is a nightmare, with May moving back to Gotham from Beverley Hills with her just-fired hubby Peter Falk. She's thrown together with ditzy mystic Thomas after hiring her to redecorate an apartment.

Almost as goofy as Thomas is Jeannie Berlin, a prostie neighbor (and real life daughter of May). Coscripter Berlin writes herself out of the picture after the second reel and *Spirit* spins off in a different direction. Thomas and May flee the city to hole up at Michael Emil's new age retreat in upstate NY, pursued by a murderer.

First-time director Sandra Seacat emphasizes slapstick but also female bonding as the gals on the lam reach beyond their wacky survivalist tactics to address feminist issues.

May is very funny, giving a lesson in rat-a-tat-tat delivery. Thomas proves a perfect foil.

●●●●●●●●●●●●●●●●●●●●●●●●●●●

■ IN THIS OUR LIFE

1942, 95 MINS, US ▼
Dir John Huston   *Prod* Hal B. Wallis (exec.)
Scr Howard Koch   *Ph* Ernest Haller   *Ed* William Holmes
Mus Max Steiner   *Art Dir* Robert Haas
● Bette Davis, Olivia de Havilland, George Brent, Dennis Morgan, Charles Coburn, Hattie McDaniel (Warner)

Story, adapted from the novel by Ellen Glasgow, displays the ruthless and selfish personality of Bette Davis and its impress on other members of her family. She lies, cheats and steals to gain her ends; and, when cornered, schemes her way out. As the yarn opens she woos and steals her sister's husband, eloping with him to Baltimore.

John Huston, in his second directorial assignment, provides deft delineations in the varied characters in the script. Davis is dramatically impressive in the lead but gets major assistance from Olivia de Havilland, George Brent, Dennis Morgan, Billie Burke and Hattie McDaniel.

Script succeeds in presenting the inner thoughts of the scheming girl, and carries along with slick dialog and situations. Strength is added in several dramatic spots by Huston's direction.

●●●●●●●●●●●●●●●●●●●●●●●●●●●

■ INTOLERANCE

1916, 209 MINS, US ⊗ ▼ ⊙
Dir D.W. Griffith   *Prod* D.W. Griffith   *Scr* D.W. Griffith
Ph Billy Bitzer, Karl Brown   *Ed* James E. Smith, Rose Smith   *Mus* Joseph Carl Breil
● Lillian Gish, Mae Marsh, Robert Harron, Miriam Cooper, Walter Long, Tully Marshall (Wark)

Intolerance reflects much credit to the wizard director, for it required no small amount of genuine art to consistently blend actors, horses, monkeys, geese, doves, acrobats and ballets into a composite presentation of a film classic.

It attempts to tell four distinct stories at the same time – more or less successfully accomplished by the aid of flashbacks, fade-outs and fade-ins. The four tales are designed to show that intolerance in various forms existed in all ages.

Three of the exemplifications are based upon historical fact, the fourth visualized by a modern melodrama that hits a powerful blow at the hypocrisy of certain forms of up-to-date philanthropy. The ancient periods depict mediaeval France in the reign of Charles IX, with the horrors of massacre perpetrated by Catherine de Medici; Jerusalem at the birth of the Christian era, with one or two historical episodes in the life of Christ, and a shadow suggestion of the Crucifixion.

The martial visualizations confined principally to the Babylonian period (about 500 B.C.), when Belshazzar's army was defeated by the Persians under the military direction of Cyrus. Words cannot do justice to the stupendousness of these battle scenes or feasts.

●●●●●●●●●●●●●●●●●●●●●●●●●●●

■ IN TOO DEEP

1990, 106 MINS, AUSTRALIA ◇
Dir Colin South, John Tatoulis   *Prod* Colin South, John Tatoulis   *Scr* Deborah Parsons   *Ph* Mark Gilfedder, Peter Zakharov   *Ed* Michael Collins, Nicolas Lee
Mus Tassos Ioannides   *Art Dir* Phil Chambers
● Hugo Race, Santha Press, Rebekah Elmaloglou, John Flaus (Media World)

This moody, erotic thriller from two first-time directors overcomes its slight narrative with its confident, bravura direction and cinematography.

Pic has the look and feel of a French film, in that atmosphere and sexual tension take pride of place over a slender plotline involving an affair between a femme jazz singer, Wendy (Santha Press), and Mack (Hugo Race) a knife-wielding young hood. Also in-

volved is Wendy's young sister, JoJo (Rebekah Elmaloglou), a 15-year-old who gets turned on by her sister's sexual activities.

Tale takes place in an Australian city (Melbourne) in the middle of summer; heat is a factor in every sense of the word. Characters perspire a lot, and no wonder, given the energy of the numerous sex scenes.

Race, an Aussie rock singer, gives Mark a sinister persona. Newcomer Press is a knockout. Elmaloglou is touching as the aroused teen whose attraction for her sister's dangerous boyfriend nearly ends in tragedy.

●●●●●●●●●●●●●●●●●●●●●●●●●●●

■ INTO THE NIGHT

1985, 115 MINS, US ◇ ▼ ⊙
Dir John Landis   *Prod* George Folsey Jr, Ron Koslow
Scr Ron Koslow   *Ph* Robert Paynter   *Ed* Malcolm Campbell   *Mus* Ira Newborn   *Art Dir* John Lloyd
● Jeff Goldblum, Michelle Pfeiffer, Richard Farnsworth, Irene Papas, Kathryn Harrold, Paul Mazursky (Universal)

Over in the suburbs dwells quiet aerospace engineer Jeff Goldblum whose job is going nowhere while his wife goes too far with another man. Mulling all this over in the middle of the night, Goldblum ambles aimlessly out to the airport where Michelle Pfeiffer has just arrived with six smuggled emeralds.

Apparently, Pfeiffer has performed this chore for one or more boyfriends and the promise of some cash, but she is hardly prepared for the four killers awaiting her arrival. Fleeing them, she leaps into Goldblum's car and from then on, it's just one misadventure and murder after another.

In pursuit of the jewels are a series of cameo-plus parts handled by Irene Papas, Roger Vadim, David Bowie and a band of Iranian zanies that includes director John Landis himself.

The film itself tries sometimes too hard for laughs and at other times strains for shock. Goldblum is nonetheless enjoyable as he constantly tries to figure out just what he's doing in all of this.

●●●●●●●●●●●●●●●●●●●●●●●●●●●

■ INTO THE SUN

1992, 100 MINS, US ◇ ▼ ⊙
Dir Fritz Kiersch   *Prod* Kevin M. Kallberg, Oliver G. Hess
Scr John Brancato, Michael Ferris   *Ph* Steve Grass
Ed Barry Zetlin   *Mus* Randy Miller   *Art Dir* Gary T. New
● Anthony Michael Hall, Michael Pare, Deborah Maria Moore, Terry Kiser, Brian Haley, Michael St Gerard (Trimark)

Top Gun meets *The Hard Way* in the oddball comedy-adventure *Into the Sun*. This time US pilot Michael Pare is assigned to show an action movie star (Anthony Michael Hall) how to portray the real thing. Pare is solid as the real McCoy and even gets to laugh and unbend a bit, compared to his usually stiff roles, as the twosome become friends.

Pic goes over the top when real-life skirmishes with unspecified Arab enemies in the Middle East break out, and Pare disobeys orders in taking the civilian into combat. Their derring-do, with Hall rising to the occasion, is fun if ridiculous. Pic is an important transition effort for Hall, whose comic timing is excellent.

Roger Moore's daughter Deborah (previously billed in *Bullseye!* as Deborah Barrymore) is pert and attractive but overly reserved as the romantic interest of both heroes. Reliable comedian Terry Kiser earns some big laughs as a fast-talking agent.

●●●●●●●●●●●●●●●●●●●●●●●●●●●

■ INTO THE WEST

1992, 102 MINS, UK/US ◇ ▼ ⊙
Dir Mike Newell   *Prod* Jonathan Cavendish, Tim Palmer
Scr Jim Sheridan, David Keating   *Ph* Tom Sigel

Ed Peter Boyle *Mus* Patrick Doyle *Art Dir* Jamie Leonard
● Gabriel Byrne, Ellen Barkin, Ciaran Fitzgerald, Ruaidhri Conroy, David Kelly (Majestic/FFI/Miramax/Newcom/Little Bird)

Into the West is a likable but modest pic about two Dublin moppets who take to the hills on a beautiful white stallion. Scripter Jim Sheridan, whose *My Left Foot* and *The Field* showed outsiders coping inspiringly with the real world, works with thinner material [a story by Michael Pearce] this time round.

Gabriel Byrne is Papa Reilly, a modern-day gypsy 'traveller' (hobo) who's finally settled in a grim, high-rise nabe of Dublin with his two kids, Tito (Ruaidhri Conroy) and Ossie (Ciaran Fitzgerald). His fanciful old father-in-law (David Kelly) captures the brats' imagination with elaborate fairy tales woven around a white horse he's brought back.

When the kids move the equine into their ramshackle apartment, the law moves in and sells it to a rich farmer. The kids promptly steal it back and set out for the 'wild' west of Ireland, fired by grandpa's stories and cowboy movies. Byrne, joined by fellow 'traveller' Kathleen (Ellen Barkin), sets out in hot pursuit, closely followed by the authorities.

A major asset throughout is Patrick Doyle's rich, Gaelic-flavoured scoring that carries the movie's emotional line and fairy tale atmosphere.

Byrne gives a credible, if low-key, rendering of the weak, illiterate father. Barkin downplays her looks and carries off an Irish accent with aplomb. The real stars are the two kids, notably Fitzgerald as the younger bro.

● ●

■ INTRUDER, THE

1953, 84 MINS, UK
Dir Guy Hamilton *Prod* Ivan Foxwell *Scr* Robin Maugham, John Hunter, Anthony Squire *Ph* Ted Scaife *Ed* Alan Osbiston *Mus* Francis Chagrin *Art Dir* Joseph Bato
● Jack Hawkins, Hugh Williams, Michael Medwin, George Cole, Dennis Price, Arthur Howard (British Lion)

The film [based on Robin Maugham's novel *Line on Ginger*] attempts to answer the question: what turns a wartime hero into a postwar thief? As the yarn opens, Jack Hawkins, a former colonel of the Tank regiment, returns to his home to find that a burglar has broken in. The intruder (Michael Medwin) turns out to be a former member of his regiment.

Through a misunderstanding, the thief believes that Hawkins has telephoned for the police and makes a dash for it over the garden wall. From there on, Hawkins is involved in a countrywide search, containing other members of the old regiment in the hopes of their leading him on the right track

As each former soldier is contacted, the film switches into a nostalgic flashback. There is the rich comedy scene of George Cole's first night in the officers' mess, with Nicholas Phipps doing some magnificent scene-stealing; there is a reminder, too, of Medwin's own heroism in saving the unit while under heavy fire, and that the suave Dennis Price, for all his peace-time arrogance, was a cowardly captain in action; and finally a highly diverting incident when Arthur Howard, a peace-time schoolmaster, is caught by the general while showing Dora Bryan the inside of a tank.

● ●

■ INTRUDER, THE

1962, 84 MINS, US ⓥ
Dir Roger Corman *Prod* Roger Corman *Scr* Charles Beaumont *Ph* Taylor Byars *Ed* Ronald Sinclair *Mus* Herman Stein
● William Shatner, Frank Maxwell, Beverley Lunsford, Robert Emhardt, Jeanne Cooper, Leo Gordon (Pathe America/Filmgroup)

Roger and Gene Corman's *The Intruder* comes

to grips with a controversial issue – integration, and those who would defy the law of the land – in an adult, intelligent and arresting manner.

Charles Beaumont's screenplay, from his novel, dramatizes the campaign instigated in a Southern US town by a slick, cocky, vain, unstable merchant of hate (from the so-called Patrick Henry Society in Washington) to urge the white residents to strike back against the law of integration. The man's primary incentive is actually personal ambition, but the mobs that at first rally round turn away in disgust when the true motives surface after a series of terrifying, reprehensible incidents.

William Shatner masterfully plays the bigot. Especially sharp, noteworthy support is contributed by Jeanne Cooper and Leo Gordon.

● ●

■ INVADERS, THE

See: 49th Parallel

● ●

■ INVADERS FROM MARS

1953, 78 MINS, US ◇ ⓥ ⊙
Dir William Cameron Menzies *Prod* Edward L. Alperson Jr (assoc.) *Scr* Richard Blake *Ph* John Seitz *Ed* Arthur Roberts *Mus* Raoul Kraushaar *Art Dir* William Cameron Menzies
● Helena Carter, Arthur Franz, Jimmy Hunt, Leif Erickson, Hillary Brooke, Morris Ankrum (20th Century-Fox)

Screenplay is pegged around a typical American family which resides in a small California town. Their existence is tranquil until the 12-year-old son (Jimmy Hunt) awakens in a thunderstorm to observe a Martian spaceship land on a nearby sandpit. His scientist-father (Leif Erickson) and mother (Hillary Brooke) investigate the scene, but return with a sinister demeanor that's in abrupt contrast to their usual cheerful attitudes. A city physician (Helena Carter) and astronomer (Arthur Franz) are convinced that an invader has landed and the country is in vital danger.

Imaginative yarn makes full use of astronomical and lab equipment as well as government atomic research installations as backgrounds to heighten the realism.

The cast turns in creditable portrayals under William Cameron Menzies' fine direction. Carter is coolly efficient as the femme doctor; Franz likewise is mentally adroit as the astronomer who alerts the army, while young Hunt impresses as the frightened lad.

● ●

■ INVADERS FROM MARS

1986, 100 MINS, US ◇ ⓥ ⊙
Dir Tobe Hooper *Prod* Menahem Golan, Yoram Globus *Scr* Dan O'Bannon, Don Jakoby *Ph* Daniel Pearl *Ed* Alain Jakubowicz *Mus* Christopher Young *Art Dir* Leslie Dilley
● Karen Black, Hunter Carson, Timothy Bottoms, Laraine Newman, James Karen, Louise Fletcher (Cannon)

Tobe Hooper's remake of *Invaders from Mars* is an embarrassing combination of kitsch and boredom. Inferior screenplay fails to bring in new ideas or provide interesting dialog.

First 45 minutes are interminably dull. Little David Gardner (Hunter Carson) sees a spaceship land one night and soon after his father George (Timothy Bottoms), biology teacher Mrs. McKeltch (Louise Fletcher) and even the police chief who investigates (Jimmy Hunt, who as a child played the lead role in the 1953 original) begin behaving out of normal character. Next day mom (Laraine Newman) is scarred and zombie-like as well.

David finally gets his school nurse Linda (Karen Black) to believe his tall tale and they whip into action to stop the invasion and spread of controlled people. Film finally

comes alive when David wanders into Martian subterranean tunnels.

Not helping is some subpar acting. Trick casting of Black, who's Carson's real-life mother, not as his fictional mom but rather his only friend, doesn't pay off. Best acting is by James Karen as a stereotyped gung-ho marine.

● ●

■ INVASION OF THE BODY SNATCHERS

1956, 80 MINS, US ⓥ ⊙
Dir Don Siegel *Prod* Walter Wanger *Scr* Daniel Mainwaring *Ph* Ellsworth Fredricks *Ed* Robert S. Eisen *Mus* Carmen Dragon *Art Dir* Ted Haworth
● Kevin McCarthy, Dana Wynter, Larry Gates, King Donovan, Carolyn Jones, Whit Bissell (Allied Artists)

This tense, offbeat piece of science-fiction is occasionally difficult to follow due to the strangeness of its scientific premise. Action nevertheless is increasingly exciting.

Plotwise, narrative opens on a strange hysteria that is spreading among the populace of a small California town. Townspeople appear as strangers to their relatives and friends, while retaining their outward appearances. Kevin McCarthy, a doctor, is confronted with solving these mysterious happenings, and helping him is Dana Wynter, with whom he's in love.

A weird form of plantlife has descended upon the town from the skies. Tiny, this ripens into great pods and opens, from each of which emerges a 'blank', the form of each man, woman and child in the town. During their sleep, the blank drains them of all but their impulse to survive.

Adapted from Jack Finney's *Collier's* serial, characterizations and situations are sharp. Don Siegel's taut direction is fast-paced generally, although in his efforts to spark the climax he permits McCarthy to overact in several sequences.

● ●

■ INVASION OF THE BODY SNATCHERS

1978, 115 MINS, US ◇ ⓥ ⊙
Dir Philip Kaufman *Prod* Robert H. Solo *Scr* W.D. Richter *Ph* Michael Chapman *Ed* Douglas Stewart *Mus* Denny Zeitlin *Art Dir* Charles Rosen
● Donald Sutherland, Brooke Adams, Leonard Nimoy, Veronica Cartwright, Jeff Goldblum, Kevin McCarthy (United Artists)

Invasion of the Body Snatchers validates the entire concept of remakes. This new version of Don Siegel's 1956 cult classic not only matches the original in horrific tone and effect, but exceeds it in both conception and execution.

W.D. Richter has updated and changed the locale of Jack Finney's serial story to contemporary San Francisco, where Donald Sutherland is a public health inspector, assisted by Brooke Adams. Following the blanketing of the city by spidery webs, Adams notices unusual and sudden changes in b.f. Art Hindle, who becomes emotionless and distant.

Similar transformations are happening all over the city, and while at first Sutherland doubts Adams' sanity, he is soon won over to her paranoia. He invokes the help of an est-type of psychiatrist played with wonderful shading by Leonard Nimoy.

Jeff Goldblum and Veronica Cartwright portray a couple who stumble on one of the blank pod bodies before Goldblum succumbs. As the legions of zombies grows, these four remain about the only humans left, and the latter part of *Body Snatchers* details with methodical ominousness their pursuit.

Sutherland has his best role since *Klute*. He gets excellent support from Adams, who projects a touching vulnerability.

Film buffs will have a delight in spotting Kevin McCarthy, who starred in the original version, picking up exactly where he left off at the first pic's finale.

•••••••••••••••••••••••••••••••••

■ INVASION QUARTET

1961, 87 MINS, UK
Dir Jay Lewis *Prod* Ronald Kinnoch *Scr* Jack Trevor Story, John Briley *Ph* Geoffrey Faithfull, Gerald Moss *Ed* Ernest Walter *Mus* Ron Goodwin *Art Dir* Elliot Scott
● Bill Travers, Spike Milligan, John Le Mesurier, Gregoire Aslan, Maurice Denham, Millicent Martin (M-G-M)

Invasion Quartet is a kind of *Guns of Navarone* for laughs. The screenplay, from a yarn spun by Norman Collins, has to do with a quartet of disabled limeys so anxious to return to active duty they sneak out of a Dover hospital, cross the Channel, and proceed to blow up a long-range cannon on the coast of France utilized by the Nazis to keep the residents of the English coastline in a constant state of shell-shock.

It would have been a better comedy had its creators been able to sustain the on-the-level realism that marks the film's first half-hour, before it lapses into out-and-out farce. Anyway, some of the farce is pretty funny farce, and director Jay Lewis extracts every ounce of fun the script provides.

•••••••••••••••••••••••••••••••••

■ INVASION U.S.A.

1952, 73 MINS, US
Dir Alfred E. Green *Prod* Albert Zugsmith, Robert Smith *Scr* Robert Smith *Ph* John L. Russell *Ed* W. Donn Hayes *Mus* Albert Glasser
● Gerald Mohr, Peggie Castle, Dan O'Herlihy, Robert Bice, Tom Kennedy, Wade Crosby (Columbia)

This production imaginatively poses the situation of a foreign power invading the US with atom bombs.

Plot, starting out in a Gotham bar, is picked up when voice of a TV broadcaster reports that Alaska has been invaded and taken over by a huge enemy air task force. Almost in minutes, further forces capture the state of Washington through use of atom bombs. Action then has the enemy blasting eastward, to destroy NY and invade Washington, DC, where a futile defense is being formulated in the Pentagon.

Human story is worked into this background through Gerald Mohr, a TV reporter, and others who are introduced in the bar. Peggie Castle is a debutante; Robert Bice a Frisco manufacturer whose return to his factory is marked by his murder by the enemy and Erik Blythe, an Arizona rancher.

Startling aspects of the screenplay [from a story by Robert Smith and Franz Spencer] are further parlayed through effective use of war footage secured from the various armed services and the Atomic Energy Commission.

•••••••••••••••••••••••••••••••••

■ INVASION U.S.A.

1985, 107 MINS, US ◇ ⊕ ⊙
Dir Joseph Zito *Prod* Menahem Golan, Yoram Globus *Scr* James Bruner, Chuck Norris *Ph* Joao Fernandes *Ed* Daniel Loewenthal, Scott Vickrey *Mus* Jay Chattaway *Art Dir* Ladislav Wilheim
● Chuck Norris, Richard Lynch, Melissa Prophet, Alexander Zale, Dehl Berti, Shane McCamey (Cannon)

A brainless plot would be almost forgiveable were it not for the perverse depiction of innocents butchered in *Invasion U.S.A.* Star Chuck Norris hits his nadir with this vicious-minded commodity [from a screen story by Aaron Norris and James Bruner].

An international hoard of ruthless mercenaries, led by foreign agents with Russian-sounding names like Rostov (Richard Lynch) and Nikko (Alexander Zale), invade the southeast US, turn neighbor against neighbor in selective slaughters, and are ultimately throttled by Norris' loner of a hero.

A picture like this needs a terrific crazie and Lynch, with solid classical training, is the only excuse to see the film. Melissa Prophet (associate producer on *The Cotton Club*) plays a callow, strident photojournalist in the year's least credible supporting performance in an exploitation film.

•••••••••••••••••••••••••••••••••

■ INVISIBLE MAN, THE

1933, 70 MINS, US ⊕ ⊙
Dir James Whale *Prod* Carl Laemmle Jr *Scr* R. C. Sherriff *Ph* Arthur Edeson *Ed* Ted Kent *Mus* [uncredited] *Art Dir* Charles D. Hall
● Claude Rains, Gloria Stuart, Henry Travers, William Harrigan, Una O'Connor, Holmes Herbert (Universal)

The strangest character yet created by the screen [from the novel by H.G. Wells] roams through *The Invisible Man*. Sometimes he is seen, dressed and bandaged up into a fantastic, eerie-looking figure, at other times he is moving through the action unseen.

As the invisible madman (Claude Rains) is moving around, the negative reflects the things he does, such as rocking in a chair, smoking a cigarette, carrying something, opening doors, or socking someone in the jaw with the impact felt rather than seen.

First reel evokes considerable comedy in sequences at a small country inn where the invisible one secures lodging and indulges in his first murder. The innkeeper and his wife (Forrester Harvey and Una O'Connor, respectively) are swell comedy types and make the most of the opportunity. O'Connor relies a lot on a very shrill scream.

At the outset it is learned that a young chemist has discovered a terrible formula, including a very dangerous one, that makes human flesh invisible. His interest was strictly scientific but the drug had the effect, after use, of turning him into a maniac. At about the time he starts the murders he is looking for the antidote to bring him back to a normal condition.

•••••••••••••••••••••••••••••••••

■ INVITATION TO THE DANCE

1956, 93 MINS, US ◇ ⊙
Dir Gene Kelly *Prod* Arthur Freed *Scr* Gene Kelly *Ph* Freddie Young, Joseph Ruttenberg *Ed* Raymond Poulton, Robert Watts, Adrienne Fazan *Mus* Andre Previn, Ibert, Rimsky-Korsakov
● Gene Kelly, Igor Youskevitch, Claire Sombert, Carol Haney, David Kasday, Tamara Toumanova (M-G-M)

Invitation to the Dance, a full-length dance feature, is a bold and imaginative experiment in film-making. Through the medium of the dance alone, producer Arthur Freed and director-choreographer-performer Gene Kelly tell three separate stories. There is no dialog. Just ballet music, colorful costumes, and skillful photography.

Kelly has assembled a crew of outstanding hoofers, including such experts as Tamara Toumanova, Claire Sombert, Carol Haney, Diana Adams, Igor Youskevitch, and Belita. Standout sequence is the middle entry, *Ring around the Rosy*. Using the children's song and game as the teeoff, the dance story to Andre Previn's music follows the career of a bracelet as it changes hands in the perennial game of love.

The opening number is similar to the Pagliacci theme as the clown (Kelly) is frustrated in his unrequited love for the beautiful ballerina (Sombert).

The final sequence is a combination of live action and animations, the cartoon sequences being provided by Fred Quimby, William Hanna and Joseph Barbera.

•••••••••••••••••••••••••••••••••

■ IN WHICH WE SERVE

1942, 113 MINS, UK ⊕
Dir Noel Coward, David Lean *Prod* Noel Coward *Scr* Noel Coward *Ph* Ronald Neame *Mus* Noel Coward *Art Dir* David Rawnsley
● Noel Coward, John Mills, Bernard Miles, Celia Johnson, Michael Wilding, Richard Attenborough (Two Cities)

No less than half a dozen credits for this film go to Noel Coward. And they're well earned. It is the story of a British destroyer, from its completion to its destruction at sea by the Germans. She is dive-bombed in the Battle of Crete, but the survivors carry on the fight. It is a grim tale sincerely picturized and splendidly acted throughout. Only one important factor calls for criticism. It is that all the details are too prolonged.

The author-producer-scriptwriter-composer and co-director gives a fine performance as the captain of the vessel, but acting honors also go to the entire company.

Stark realism is the keynote of the writing and depiction, with no glossing of the sacrifices constantly being made by the sailors. They are seen clinging to a rubber raft, with cut-ins of several of them thinking of their wives and families at home and then flashing back to them in the water. This effect is impressive to a degree.
☐ 1942: Special Award (outstanding production achievement by Noel Coward)
☐ 1943: Nominations: Best Picture, Original Screenplay

•••••••••••••••••••••••••••••••••

■ I OUGHT TO BE IN PICTURES

1982, 107 MINS, US ◇ ⊕
Dir Herbert Ross *Prod* Herbert Ross, Neil Simon *Scr* Neil Simon *Ph* David M. Walsh *Ed* Sidney Levin *Mus* Marvin Hamllisch *Art Dir* Albert Brenner
● Walter Matthau, Ann-Margret, Dinah Manoff, Lance Guest, Lewis Smith, Martin Ferrero (20th Century-Fox)

Neil Simon's *I Ought to Be in Pictures* is a moving family drama, peppered with the author's patented gag lines and notable for sock performances by Dinah Manoff and Walter Matthau.

Nimbly opened-out from the 1980 stage version by helmer Herbert Ross, film concerns a 19-year-old, spunky Brooklyn girl Libby (Dinah Manoff reprising her stage role), who hitchhikes to Los Angeles to break into films as an actress but more importantly see her dad who left her, a brother and mom for good 16 years earlier.

Dad is Herb Tucker (Walter Matthau), a once-successful feature and TV scripter now given over to gambling and drinking. Tucker's loyal g.f. Steffie (Ann-Margret) is supportive but has her own children to take care of.

Key factor in making this work is apt casting, with Manoff outstanding in avoiding direct sentimentality in the showy central role. For his part, Matthau makes a ne'er-do-well character immensely sympathetic in spite of his shortcomings.

•••••••••••••••••••••••••••••••••

■ IPCRESS FILE, THE

1965, 109 MINS, UK ◇ ⊕
Dir Sidney J. Furie *Prod* Harry Saltzman *Scr* Bill Canaway, James Doran *Ph* Otto Heller *Ed* Peter Hunt *Mus* John Barry *Art Dir* Ken Adam
● Michael Caine, Nigel Green, Guy Doleman, Sue Lloyd, Gordon Jackson, Aubrey Richards (Rank)

Harry Saltzman and Albert R. Broccoli, who produce the Bond razamatazz, diversify by bringing to the screen a kind of 'anti-Bond' spy in the character of Harry Palmer, based on Len Deighton's novel. The result is probably rather more true to the facts of intelligence life than the Bond world of fantasy.

Intelligence man Harry Palmer (Michael

Caine) is an undisciplined sergeant who is seconded to intelligence work and finds that it is more legwork and filling in forms than inspired hunches and glamorous adventure.

Present adventure concerns the steps taken to retrieve a missing boffin and involves the agent being captured by the enemy and subjected to acute brainwashing. Pic does not build up to the type of suspense usually demanded of such thrillers.

Sidney J. Furie's direction, allied with Otto Heller's camera, provides some striking effects. But sometimes he gets carried away into arty-crafty fields with low-angle shots and symbolism adding to the confusion of the screenplay.

Caine skillfully resists any temptation he may have had to pep up the proceedings. In fact, his consistent underplaying adds considerably to the pull of the picture.

••••••••••••••••••••••••••

■ **I REMEMBER MAMA**

1948, 137 MINS, US Ⓥ ⊙

Dir George Stevens *Prod* Harriet Parsons *Scr* DeWitt Bodeen *Ph* Nicholas Musuraca *Ed* Robert Swink *Mus* Roy Webb *Art Dir* Albert S. D'Agostino, Carroll Clark

● Irene Dunne, Barbara Bel Geddes, Oscar Homolka, Philip Dorn, Cedric Hardwicke, Edgar Bergen (RKO)

With *I Remember Mama*, RKO is spreading a layer of warm and deeply moving nostalgia. Based on the John van Druten legiter, [and the novel, *Mama's Bank Account*, by Kathryn Forbes] the film encompasses those same broad, human values which lifted the play into the smash hit class.

DeWitt Bodeen's screenplay is a faithful adaptation of the original, adding only an extra dimension of background depth and story detail. In extending the scope, however, it doesn't blunt the impact of the yarn. This reminiscence of growth in a San Francisco Norwegian family is related in a simple and genuine manner. It's frequently sentimental but never hokey.

Irene Dunne is the central pillar of this production. In holding down the most demanding role of her career, she earns new honors as an actress of outstanding versatility. Her Norwegian dialect sounds queer for the first couple of minutes but soon establishes itself solidly as a natural part of her lingo.

The rest of the cast also do yeoman's service in draping this pic with a flesh-and-blood reality. Oscar Homolka, repeating his stage role of the uncle, contributes a massive and memorable performance. As the youngster who matures into an authoress, Barbara Bel Geddes plays a 15-year-old schoolgirl in a tour de force. Her portrait of adolescence is sensitive, compelling and authentic.

□ 1948: Nominations: Best Actress (Irene Dunne), Supp. Actor (Oscar Homolka), Supp. Actress (Barbara Bel Geddes), B&W Cinematography

••••••••••••••••••••••••••

■ **IRENE**

1940, 104 MINS, US ◇ Ⓥ

Dir Herbert Wilcox *Prod* Herbert Wilcox *Scr* Alice Duer Miller *Ph* Russell Metty *Ed* Elmo Williams *Mus* Harry Tierney, Joseph McCarthy *Art Dir* L.P. Williams

● Anna Neagle, Ray Milland, Roland Young, Alan Marshal, May Robson, Billie Burke (Imperadio/RKO)

Back in 1919 – 20 a smash musical comedy and then in 1926 a hit First National film starring Colleen Moore, *Irene* emerges this time as dated celluloidia. It's old-fashioned from several angles, further handicapped by familiar story pattern.

Starring combination of Anna Neagle and Ray Milland cannot wholly carry this film over the hurdles. The negative factors are not so much in the acting as they are in Alice

Duer Miller's screenplay and Herbert Wilcox's direction, neither of which is ultra-1940. The screenplay and direction, too, closely follow the original film. In the Colleen Moore starrer a 1,000-foot segment of a grand ball was given over to a color sequence, quite revolutionary in those days, but reprised now it just makes the fore and after-parts in black and white look all the more ordinary in comparison.

Neagle, as the girl who steps from the tenements to a modeling job and then into society, gives a rather spotty performance. She's too broadly Irish, for one thing, and not flattered by the camera in the first 50 minutes for another. In the color sequences she shows up much better, her red hair being especially noticeable, and is okay in one feathery dance routine, and when singing 'Alice Blue Gown'. However, she doesn't give the part the comedy content Moore did, which makes the Hibernian dialect all the more unnecessary. 'Castle In Your Dreams', 'Gown' and the title song are still very worthy tunes, from the original score.

Roland Young, noted for his dry comedy, is merely dry in this picture as manager of Mme Lucy's. Two other performers wasted are Isabel Jewell and Doris Noland, Neagle's tenement house pals. Marsha Hunt hasn't much to do as the almost-jilted sweetie of Alan Marshal, while May Robson's role as the motherly but straitlaced Irish grandmother is overdone and unbelievable.

□ 1940: Nomination: Best Score

••••••••••••••••••••••••••

■ **IRISHMAN, THE**

1978, 108 MINS, AUSTRALIA ◇ Ⓥ

Dir Donald Crombie *Prod* Anthony Buckley *Scr* Donald Crombie *Ph* Peter James *Ed* Tim Wellburn *Mus* Charles Marawood *Art Dir* Owen Williams

● Michael Craig, Simon Burke, Robin Nevin, Lou Brown, Vincent Ball, Bryan Brown (Forest Home)

The north of Queensland in the 1920s must have been much like west Texas at the turn of the century if we can believe the movies. A hard land populated by hard men and women working hard in hard conditions. But times are a-changing, and whenever that happens there's usually a rugged but dogged individual who praises the candle and cries out against the light of progress. One such is Paddy Doolan, the eponymous migrated Celt.

Paddy the teamster, with his team of 20 giant Clydesdale draught horses crossing the great wide river, open the film and immediately create awe and admiration. They are such superb beasts that it is made that much easier to accept Paddy's stubbornness later when he refuses to see that his team is being superseded by the internal combustion engine.

His wife is sensible, yet acquiescent; his older son, Will, defiant; the youngest, and most sensitive – and ultimately therefore the most affected – is bewildered, but devotedly and hopelessly goes with Paddy. And his 'My father, right or wrong' feelings are inevitably eroded. In any event Paddy's recalcitrance demolishes the family, eventually destroys his self-esteem and ultimately himself.

The film has great moments of emotional triumph, and at times is unabashedly sentimental, but it never descends to mawkishness.

••••••••••••••••••••••••••

■ **IRMA LA DOUCE**

1963, 147 MINS, US ◇ Ⓥ ⊙

Dir Billy Wilder *Prod* Billy Wilder *Scr* Billy Wilder, I.A.L. Diamond *Ph* Joseph LaShelle *Ed* Daniel Mandell *Mus* Andre Previn *Art Dir* Alexander Trauner

● Jack Lemmon, Shirley MacLaine, Lou Jacobi, Bruce Yarnell, Herschel Bernardi, Hope Holiday (United Artists)

On the plus side of the *Irma* ledger, there are

scintillating performances by Jack Lemmon and Shirley MacLaine, a batch of jovial supporting portrayals, a striking physical production and a number of infectious comedy scenes.

But *Irma* also misses on several important counts, and the fact that it does illustrates the sizable problems inherent in an attempt to convert a legit musical into a tuneless motion picture farce. But what hurts the film the most is its length. Two hours and 27 minutes is an awfully long haul for a frivolous farce.

The hot-and-cold scenario, based on the play by Alexandre Breffort, traces the love affair of Irma (MacLaine), a proud and profitable practitioner of the oldest profession, and a young gendarme (Lemmon) who gets bounced off the force when he makes the mistake of taking his job seriously. Lemmon becomes number one mec, or pimp, on the block when he knocks his predecessor's block off, thereby inheriting Irma and the rights to her estate.

Lemmon plays his juicy role to the hilt, and there are moments when his performance brings to mind some of the great visual comedy of the classic silent film clowns. His portrayal of his British alter ego is a kind of cross between Jose Ferrer's characterization of Toulouse-Lautrec and Richard Haydn's caricature of an Englishman. MacLaine delivers a winning performance in the title role, and has never looked better. There's a whale of a comedy portrayal by Lou Jacobi as the versatile bistro boss-barkeep, Moustache.

□ 1963: Best Adapted Musical Score.
□ Nominations: Best Actress (Shirley MacLaine), Color Cinematography

••••••••••••••••••••••••••

■ **IRON & SILK**

1991, 90 MINS, US ◇ Ⓥ

Dir Shirley Sun *Prod* Shirley Sun *Scr* Mark Salzman, Shirley Sun *Ph* James Hayman *Ed* Geraldine Peroni, James Y. Kwei *Mus* Michael Gibbs *Art Dir* Calvin Tsao

● Mark Salzman, Pan Qingfu, Jeanette Lin Tsui, Vivian Wu, Sun Xudong, Zheng Guo (Sun)

A fascinating film version of Mark Salzman's book about his experiences in China, *Iron & Silk* is similar in many respects to Peter Wang's *A Great Wall*, also produced and co-written by Shirley Sun.

In his autobiographical account of his two years as an English teacher in China, Salzman co-wrote the screenplay and stars as himself, though the name is changed to Mark Franklin. Soon after arriving there, one of his Chinese students takes him to see a legendary *wushu* instructor named Teacher Pan, played by Salzman's actual teacher, Pan Qingfu.

His other instructor is Teacher Hei (Jeanette Lin Tsui), who gives Salzman lessons in manners and social customs, as well as in Chinese and tai chi. Salzman starts a relationship with a Chinese doctor named Ming (Vivian Wu).

The script reveals much about China, but some dialog is stilted. *Iron & Silk* was filmed in Hangzhou, a southern city with picturesque bridges and beautiful lakes. The day after wrapping filming, the military crushed the student movement in Tiananmen Square.

••••••••••••••••••••••••••

■ **IRON EAGLE**

1986, 119 MINS, US ◇ Ⓥ ⊙

Dir Sidney J. Furie *Prod* Ron Samuels, Joe Wizan *Scr* Kevin Elders, Sidney J. Furie *Ph* Adam Greenberg *Ed* George Grenville *Mus* Basil Poledouris *Art Dir* Robb Wilson King

● Louis Gossett Jr, Jason Gedrick, David Suchet, Tim Thomerson, Larry B. Scott, Caroline Lagerfelt (Tri-Star)

Iron Eagle is a crackerjack fighter-pilot picture focusing on a daring rescue of a hostage in a small Middle East country.

Young Jason Gedrick swings into action when word comes that pilot pop Tim Thomerson has been shot down for venturing too near the borders of the little nation defended by swarthy David Suchet, who almost twirls his moustache in anticipation of hanging the Yankee intruder.

At first Gedrick is hopeful that the US will respond officially, but the government waffles. Fortunately, dad has often taken Gedrick up in an F-16. Equally fortunate, all his high-school friends are Air Force kids, too. After faking the military computers into assigning two jets for their use, Gedrick persuades veteran combat pilot Louis Gossett Jr to lead the mission and off the pair go into the wild blue yonder.

Director Sidney J. Furie fills in the rest with breakneck action and some dandy dogfights. Much of the dialog is simply laughable.

■ **IRON EAGLE II**

1988, 105 MINS, CANADA/ISRAEL ◇ ⓥ ⊙
Dir Sidney J. Furie   *Prod* Jacob Kotzky, Sharon Herel, John Kemeny   *Scr* Kevin Elders, Sidney J. Furie
Ph Alain Dostie   *Ed* Rit Wallis   *Mus* Amin Bhatia
Art Dir Ariel Roshko
● Lou Gossett Jr, Mark Humphrey, Stuart Margolin, Alan Scarfe, Sharon H. Brandon, Maury Chaykin (Alliance)

Iron Eagle II nervily tries to update the formula [of the 1986 original]. Plot meanders and fails to really fire its engines until deep into the story.

Puppyfaced rock 'n' roll fighter pilots, including Tom Cruise-lookalike Mark Humphrey, accidentally stray into Soviet airspace and one gets shot down. The survivor, Cooper (Humphrey), starts nursing a big grudge against Soviets.

Next thing you know he's recruited for a secret mission led by Louis Gossett Jr (reprising his role as Chappy) who's been given a general's star as incentive to lead US and Soviet pilots on a joint mission to destroy a nuclear weapons base in an unnamed Mideast country that is a threat to them both.

The American team members are shown as prejudiced slobs given to pranks, insults and dirty tricks. To make things worse, Vardovsky (Alan Scarfe) was part of the squadron that gunned down Cooper's buddy, an also keeps a jealous eye on an alluring female Soviet pilot, Valeri Zuyeniko (Sharon H. Brandon), whom Cooper wastes no time strutting for.

Pic's chief weakness is that for much of the screentime, the 'joint mission' seems like just a weak premise to bring together both sides for lowbrow *Police Academy*-style antics and infighting. On the plus side, the goons slowly and grudgingly develop a bond and understanding that proves to be pic's crowning glory.

■ **IRON HORSE, THE**

1924, 130 MINS, US ⊗
Dir John Ford   *Prod* John Ford   *Scr* Charles Kenyon, John Russell, Charles Darnton   *Ph* George Schneiderman
Ed Hettie Gray Baker
● George O'Brien, Madge Bellamy, Charles Edward Hull, Cyril Chadwick, Fred Kohler, J. Farrell MacDonald (Fox)

The Iron Horse is the story of the winning of the West through the linking of the Atlantic and Pacific coasts by rail. It contains a powerful theme of historical value as the basis around which a romance has been woven that ties the leading characters to the history of the building of the first transcontinental railway.

There are comedy, tragedy and a love theme, Indians and soldiers, hordes of construction gangs, camp followers, both men and women, gamblers and dance hall girls,

shooting and riding, a tremendous cattle drive, the fording of a river by a herd of beeves.

John Ford, who directs, puts his story over on the screen with a lot of punch. His handling of the trio of ex-soldiers of the Civil War who as the three musketeers of America battled through the building of the great Union Pacific railroad is exceedingly clever. They lend a touch of comedy as did Ernest Torrence and Tully Marshall in *The Covered Wagon*.

Francis Powers, J. Farrell MacDonald and James Welch enact the roles and Ford touches them with just a bit of pathos in the end that makes them stand out as real humans and not as out-and-out buffoons just created for a laugh.

The love interest is carried on by George O'Brien and Madge Bellamy. O'Brien gives a corking performance as the youthful scout and lover and Bellamy shines as his beloved. Kohler's characterization is a piece of classic work.

■ **IRON MAZE**

1991, 104 MINS, US/JAPAN ◇ ⓥ
Dir Hiroaki Yoshida   *Prod* Ilona Herzberg, Hidenori Ueki
Scr Tim Metcalfe   *Ph* Morio Saegusa   *Ed* Bonnie Koehler   *Mus* Stanley Myers   *Art Dir* Toby Corbett
● Jeff Fahey, Bridget Fonda, Hiroaki Murakami, J.T. Walsh, Gabriel Damon, John Randolph (Trans-Tokyo)

A provocative notion has been tiresomely elaborated in *Iron Maze*, a contemporary retelling of the *Rashomon* story [from a screen story by Hiroaki Yoshida and Tim Metcalfe] in which misunderstandings between Japanese and Americans are meant to compound the tale's inherent mysteries and ambiguities.

Ryunosuke Akutagawa's 1927 short story *In the Grove* inspired Akira Kurosawa's celebrated 1950 drama *Rashomon*, which indicated there can be as many versions of a story or incident as there were witnesses to it. And so it is here, as Sugita (Hiroaki Murakami), the son of a Japanese billionaire, is critically wounded in an abandoned steel mill he has just bought in a depressed Pennsylvania town.

It appears to be an open-and-shut case, as longhaired biker Barry (Jeff Fahey) turns himself in to police chief Jack Ruhle (J.T. Walsh). In flashbacks, Sugita is shown arriving in the once thriving, Pittsburgh vicinity town, flaunting his Mercedes, trendy clothes and flashy blonde wife Chris (Bridget Fonda). Through the prisms afforded by Barry, Chris and, finally, Sugita himself, one is given different versions leading up to the bloody fight between the two men at the dilapidated mill.

Screenplay provides too little information about the subjects and delivers no good scenes between the moody Japanese businessman and his feisty gaijin wife, which leaves Murakami and Fonda striking attitudes rather than fleshing out characters.

■ **IRONWEED**

1987, 144 MINS, US ◇ ⓥ ⊙
Dir Hector Babenco   *Prod* Keith Barish, Marcia Nasatir
Scr William Kennedy   *Ph* Lauro Escorel   *Ed* Anne Goursaud   *Mus* John Morris   *Art Dir* Jeannine Oppewall
● Jack Nicholson, Meryl Streep, Carroll Baker, Michael O'Keefe, Diane Venora, Fred Gwynne (Taft/Barish/Tri-Star)

Unrelentingly bleak, *Ironweed* is a film without an audience and no reason for being except its own self-importance. It's an event picture without the event. Whatever joy or redemption William Kennedy offered in his Pulitzer prize-winning novel is nowhere to be found, surprising since he wrote the screenplay.

The story of Francis Phelan (Jack Nicholson) who returns to his native Albany in 1938 literally carrying a lifetime of ghosts with him

is loaded with elaborate expository passages trying to account for why an obviously intelligent individual has abandoned his family for a bum's life.

Phelan's movement around Albany is like a passage through the rings of hell, but instead of coming out at paradise, he's still the same old bum at the end.

Nicholson and Meryl Streep have approximately three scenes together and though they clearly have a great deal of affection for each other, they are beyond passion.

☐ 1987: Nominations: Best Actor (Jack Nicholson), Actress (Meryl Streep)

■ **IRRECONCILABLE DIFFERENCES**

1984, 114 MINS, US ◇ ⓥ ⊙
Dir Charles Shyer   *Prod* Alex Winitsky, Arlene Sellers
Scr Nancy Meyers, Charles Shyer   *Ph* William Fraker
Ed John Burnett   *Mus* Paul de Senneville   *Art Dir* Ida Random
● Ryan O'Neal, Shelley Long, Drew Barrymore, Sam Wanamaker, Allen Garfield, Sharon Stone (Hemdale)

Irreconcilable Differences begins strongly as a human comedy about a nine-year-old who decides to take legal action to divorce her parents. Unfortunately, this premise is soon jettisoned for a rather familiar tale of a marriage turned sour as shown step-by-step. Set in the world of Hollywood writers and filmmakers, the story is also more fun for the cognoscenti than the average filmgoer.

On the witness stand the seeds of her dissatisfaction emerge in the three principals' testimony. It is regrettably an uninspired and improbable device to tell the yarn. Not a great deal of perception emerges.

Ryan O'Neal and Shelley Long spark off a nice romantic chemistry but really need a better vehicle to show off their craft.

■ **ISADORA**
(US: The Loves of Isadora)

1969, 141 MINS, UK ◇ ⓥ
Dir Karel Reisz   *Prod* Robert Hakim, Raymond Hakim
Scr Melvyn Bragg, Clive Exton, Margaret Drabble
Ph Larry Pizer   *Ed* Tom Priestley   *Mus* Maurice Jarre
Art Dir Jocelyn Herbert
● Vanessa Redgrave, John Fraser, James Fox, Jason Robards, Ivan Tchenko, Bessie Love (Universal)

The tragic lifelong odyssey of Isadora Duncan, whose consistent non-conformity brought her as much public success as it did personal failure, is told with a remarkable degree of excellence.

The free-thinking aspects of Duncan's life (unabashed out-of-wedlock affairs and births, hedonism, political idealism, naivete, etc.), are emphasized in this sensitive, lucid, beautifully fashioned, and masterfully executed personal tragedy [based on *My Life* by Duncan and *Isadora Duncan – An Intimate Portrait* by Sewell Stokes].

Story unfolds as Duncan (Vanessa Redgrave) dictates memoirs to her secretary. Redgrave's performance in these scenes, with hollow eyes and a weathered face suggesting the inevitable ends of dissipation, plus her perfect projection of aging flamboyance, demands equality with Gloria Swanson's classic performance in *Sunset Blvd*. Where the film falters is its length and pacing.

☐ 1969: Nomination: Best Actress (Vanessa Redgrave)

■ **I SHALL RETURN**
See: An American Guerrilla in the Philippines

■ **I SHOT JESSE JAMES**

1949, 81 MINS, US ⓥ
Dir Samuel Fuller   *Prod* Charles K. Hittleman

Scr Samuel Fuller   *Ph* Ernest Miller   *Ed* Paul Landres
Mus Albert Glasser
● Preston Foster, Barbara Britton, John Ireland, Reed Hadley, J. Edward Bromberg (Screen Guild)

I Shot Jesse James is a character study of the man who felled the west's most famous outlaw with a coward's bullet. It's an interesting treatment that doesn't overlook necessary plot and action.

While Preston Foster and Barbara Britton carry star roles, it's John Ireland, as the notorious Bob Ford, who dominates the story.

Spiced in the plot footage are any number of forthright physical clashes, capably staged by Samuel Fuller's direction. Latter is not quite as adept in handling the character study motivation but the players carry off these angles with considerable ability.

Ireland's performance is clearly drawn and even manages a trace of sympathy. Britton fits well into the role of his beloved, who turns to Foster in the end. Foster is good as the prospector who turns marshal.

■ ISHTAR

1987, 107 MINS, US ◇ ⓥ ☉
Dir Elaine May   *Prod* Warren Beatty   *Scr* Elaine May
Ph Vittorio Storaro   *Ed* Stephen A. Rotter, William Reynolds, Richard Cirincione   *Mus* John Strauss (co-ord.)
Art Dir Paul Sylbert
● Warren Beatty, Dustin Hoffman, Isabelle Adjani, Charles Grodin, Jack Weston, Tess Harper (Columbia)

Here's how the story goes: Warren Beatty and Dustin Hoffman are struggling and mightily untalented songwriters-singers in New York. They hook up with talent agent Jack Weston (who delivers a fine character performance) and wind up getting booked into the Chez Casablanca in Morocco. Yes, there's the obvious parallels to the Hope-Crosby *Road* films.

Arrival in Africa finds Beatty-Hoffman stopping in the mythical kingdom of Ishtar, where swirl of events leads them into vortex of Middle East political turmoil, with Isabelle Adjani functioning as a left-wing rebel trying to overthrow the US-backed Emir of Ishtar.

Enter Charles Grodin, who upstages all involved via his savagely comical portrayal of a CIA agent. He provides the connecting link as a series of zigzag plot points unfold because of an important map.

Desert sequences provide some of the film's high points as Beatty and Hoffman finally develop some genuine rapport under adverse conditions. There are also a few hilarious scenes as vultures circle an exhausted Hoffman and later as he's thrust into role as a translator for gunrunners and their Arab buyers.

■ ISLAND, THE

1980, 114 MINS, US ◇ ⓥ ☉
Dir Michael Ritchie   *Prod* Richard D. Zanuck, David Brown   *Scr* Peter Benchley   *Ph* Henri Decae
Ed Richard A. Harris   *Mus* Ennio Morricone
Art Dir Dale Hennesy
● Michael Caine, David Warner, Angela Punch McGregor, Frank Middlemass, Don Henderson, Zakes Mokae (Universal/Zanuck-Brown)

This latest summertime tale from the water-obsessed pen of Peter Benchley gets off to a bristling start as a charter boat-load of boozy business types is ambushed by something or someone that leaves hatchets planted in their skulls and severed limbs scattered aboard.

Cut to British journalist Michael Caine, who persuades his editor that his latest Bermuda Triangle-type ship disappearance justifies his personal research.

But once the mystery is banally resolved – the island is inhabited by a tribe of buccaneers who've been inbreeding for 300 years

and prey on pleasure ships – the film degenerates to a violent chase melodrama.

Michael Ritchie's witty direction is abandoned in the violence, and periodic efforts to revive the built-in comedy fall flat.

■ ISLAND AT THE TOP OF THE WORLD, THE

1974, 95 MINS, US ◇ ⓥ
Dir Robert Stevenson   *Prod* Winston Hibler   *Scr* John Whedon   *Ph* Frank Phillips   *Ed* Robert Stafford
Mus Maurice Jarre   *Art Dir* Peter Ellenshaw
● David Hartman, Donald Sinden, Jacques Marin, Mako, David Gwillim, Agneta Eckemyr (Walt Disney)

Title pretty much describes pic's theme, carrying the story of four Polar explorers discovering a lost land inhabited by Vikings. Based on the novel [*The Lost Ones*] by Ian Cameron, script limns a rich Englishman in 1907 flying into the Arctic wilderness in search of his missing son.

Pic occasionally takes on the aspect of old-fashioned adventure, as the explorers find a mysterious valley warmed by volcanic heat in the midst of the Arctic wastes and a settlement of Norsemen who might be the descendants of Eric the Red's second expedition to Greenland in the 10th century.

Donald Sinden portrays the titled Englishman and Jacques Marin plays the French designer and captain of the balloon which figures so prominently in suspenseful action. All deliver realistic performances. An interesting newcomer is Agneta Eckemyr, cast as a Viking maid.

□ 1974: Nomination: Best Art Direction

■ ISLAND IN THE SKY

1953, 108 MINS, US
Dir William A. Wellman   *Prod* Robert Fellows
Scr Ernest K. Gann   *Ph* Archie Stout   *Ed* Ralph Dawson
Mus Emil Newman   *Art Dir* James Basevi
● John Wayne, Lloyd Nolan, Walter Abel, James Arness, Andy Devine (Warner/Wayne-Fellows)

An articulate drama of men and planes has been fashioned from Ernest K. Gann's novel. The Wayne-Fellows production was scripted with care by Gann for aviation aficionado William A. Wellman who gives it sock handling to make it a solid piece of drama revolving around an ATC plane crash in Arctic wastes.

The film moves back and forth very smoothly from the tight action at the crash site to the planning and execution of the search. It's a slick job by all concerned.

John Wayne is the ATC pilot downed with his crew, James Lydon, Hal Baylor, Sean McClory and Wally Cassell, in an uncharted section of Labrador. How he holds them together during five harrowing days before rescue comes on the sixth is grippingly told. Each of the players has a chance at a big scene and delivers strongly.

The snow-covered Donner Lake area near Truckee, Calif, subbed for the story's Labrador locale and provides a frosty, shivery dressing to the picture. Both the lensing by Archie Stout and the aerial photography by William Clothier are important factors in the drama and thrills. Title derives from the fancy that pilots are men apart, their spirits dwelling on islands in the sky.

■ ISLAND OF DR MOREAU, THE

1977, 98 MINS, US ◇ ⓥ
Dir Don Taylor   *Prod* John Temple-Smith, Skip Steloff
Scr John Herman Shaner, Al Ramrus   *Ph* Gerry Fisher
Ed Marion Rothman   *Mus* Laurence Rosenthal
Art Dir Philip Jefferies
● Burt Lancaster, Michael York, Nigel Davenport, Barbara Carrera, Richard Basehart, Nick Cravat (American International)

This $6 million adaptation of the H.G. Wells horror-fantasy tale, previously filmed in 1932 by Paramount as *Island of Lost Souls*, is a handsome, well-acted, and involving piece of cinematic storytelling, made in the Virgin Islands.

Burt Lancaster has the lead role of the renegade scientist who dabbles in forbidden eugenic experiments on a remote Pacific island, where Michael York is washed up in a shipwreck in the early days of the 20th century.

Wells showed an uncanny gift for prophecy in his imaginative tales, and the doctor's experiments on beasts and humans eerily foreshadowed the Nazis' use of humans as guinea pigs.

Lancaster, despite his ungodly ideas, is given some resonance as a man who thinks his demented work is for the betterment of the human race. York gives one of his best performances, and Barbara Carrera's enigmatic beauty is evocatively treated.

■ ISLAND OF LOST SOULS

1933, 72 MINS, US
Dir Erle C. Kenton   *Scr* Waldemar Young, Philip Wylie
Ph Karl Struss
● Charles Laughton, Bela Lugosi, Richard Arlen, Leila Hyams, Kathleen Burke, Arthur Hohl (Paramount)

With such actors as Charles Laughton, Richard Arlen and Bela Lugosi in the cast, *Souls* is provided with a mainstay.

While the action is not designed to appeal to other than the credulous, there are undoubtedly some horror sequences which are unrivaled. Those studies of a galaxy of Dr Moreau's 50-50 man and beast creations, as an example, will pique any type of mentality.

The tramp steamer in a fog, its decks laden with crates of wild animals consigned to Moreau's mysterious island, is good picturization.

Romance is essentially light, and with a story of this kind [by H. G. Wells] it should be. The extra billing given Kathleen Burke as Lota, the Panther Woman, is strictly for the marquee. Girl is too much like a girl to even suggest transformation from a beast.

■ ISLANDS IN THE STREAM

1977, 105 MINS, US ◇ ⓥ ☉
Dir Franklin J. Schaffner   *Prod* Peter Bart, Max Palevsky
Scr Denne Bart Petitclerc   *Ph* Fred Koenekamp
Ed Robert Swink   *Mus* Jerry Goldsmith   *Art Dir* William J. Creber
● George C. Scott, David Hemmings, Gilbert Roland, Susan Tyrrell, Richard Evans, Claire Bloom (Paramount)

While too introspective a story to be really compelling screen drama, Franklin J. Schaffner's film of *Islands in the Stream* is at least a proper valedictory to the era epitomized by author Ernest Hemingway. Hawaiian locations provide a superb physical backdrop (simulating The Bahamas, circa 1940) for the production.

George C. Scott's semi-Hemingway pivotal character lives on a remote island, to which travel his three sons by broken marriages, as the world moves into the globe-shrinking holocaust of World War II.

One can admire and follow the film without ever really getting enthusiastic about it, because of the way in which it has been written, acted and directed. There's a pervading sensitivity and restrained respect for the moral antiquity which is herein represented.

□ 1977: Nomination: Best Cinematography

■ ISLE OF THE DEAD

1945, 72 MINS, US ⓥ ☉
Dir Mark Robson   *Prod* Val Lewton   *Scr* Ardel Wray, Josef Mischel   *Ph* Jack Mackenzie   *Ed* Lyle Boyer

Mus Leigh Harline   *Art Dir* Albert S. D'Agostino, Walter Keller
● Boris Karloff, Ellen Drew, Marc Cramer, Alan Napier, Jason Robards (RKO)

Isle of the Dead is a slow conversation piece about plagues and vampires on an eerie Greek island. It's better handled and directed than most though thriller fans will still find its lack of action a drag. Even Boris Karloff fans will note the tired way he rambles through it all.

Yarn is a psychological drama of an assorted group of people gathered on the island, when a plague breaks out and death takes one of them. A doctor is sure only a south wind can blow away the plague; a superstitious native is as positive that one of the guests is a vampire, carrying the plague's spirit within her. A couple of murders help to decimate the group until only a couple are left when the plague runs its course.

Karloff, as a Greek general trying to keep the plague from reaching his troops, is more paternal than menacing. Ellen Drew lends poignancy as a misunderstood nurse, and she and Marc Cramer present an attractive romantic couple.

●●●●●●●●●●●●●●●●●●●●●●●●●●●●

■ IS PARIS BURNING?

1966, 185 MINS, US/FRANCE ◇ ▽
Dir Rene Clement   *Prod* Paul Graetz   *Scr* Gore Vidal, Francis Coppola, Marcel Moussy   *Ph* Marcel Grignon   *Ed* Robert Lawrence   *Mus* Maurice Jarre   *Art Dir* Willy Holt
● Jean-Paul Belmondo, Charles Boyer, Gert Frobe, Anthony Perkins, Simone Signoret, Orson Welles (Paramount/Seven Arts)

This French-made Yank-backed spectacle traces the uprising in Paris leading to the oncoming Allies changing their plans to invade the city rather than bypass it, as intended. Underlying dilemma faces the German commander, General Von Choltitz, who has been ordered to destroy Paris, if necessary or if it could not be held. The title is from Hitler's maniacal telephone demands to know if Paris was burning.

It is built on the premature uprising within the French resistance groups, and then the tensions as Paris is undermined with explosives and Von Choltitz hesitates as he realizes that Hitler is mad and that destruction of Paris will not help the German cause or the now hopeless Nazi war effort.

Gert Frobe has the pivotal part as Von Choltitz who is a career soldier and not above destroying Paris if a necessity. He plays it with proper despair and does not overdo the sentimental aspect of the man.

The street fighting is done with fervor and dynamism and little cameos gives an ironic, tender, dramatic, pathetic feel to the overall happening.
□ 1966: Nominations: Best B&W Cinematography, B&W Art Direction

●●●●●●●●●●●●●●●●●●●●●●●●●●●●

■ I START COUNTING

1970, 105 MINS, UK ◇ ▽
Dir David Greene   *Prod* David Greene   *Scr* Richard Harris   *Ph* Alex Thomson   *Ed* Kwith Palmer   *Mus* Basil Kirchin   *Art Dir* Arnold Chapkis
● Jenny Agutter, Bryan Marshall, Clare Sutcliffe, Simon Ward, Gregory Phillips, Lana Morris (United Artists)

Jenny Agutter plays a schoolgirl, adopted, who worships her elder 'brother' who, unwittingly, has become a father-figure in the household. A series of local sex crimes strikes a sinister note and from slender clues (neatly produced as red herrings) the girl suspects that her worshipped brother is the perpetrator.

Her friend (Clare Sutcliffe) is an extroverted little chippie, pert, provocative and pathetic in the way that she tries to kid

everybody that she's sexually experienced. Agutter, who tries to keep up with the fantasy, is the more believable but perhaps the less amusing character.

The two kids spend much time in the condemned house in which Agutter used to live. It's bang in the middle of woods which is the danger area operated by the sex-maniac.

●●●●●●●●●●●●●●●●●●●●●●●●●●●●

■ IT

1927, 64 MINS, US ⊗ ▽ ⊙
Dir Clarence Badger   *Prod* B.P. Schulberg   *Scr* Hope Loring, Louis D. Lighton, George Marion Jr., Elinor Glyn   *Ph* H. Kinley Martin   *Ed* E. Lloyd Sheldon
● Clara Bow, Antonio Moreno, William Austin, Jacqueline Gadsdon, Julia Swayne Gordon, Gary Cooper (Paramount)

It is one of those pretty little Cinderella stories where the poor shop girl marries the wealthy owner of the big department store in which she works. Elinor Glyn makes her debut as a picture actress.

But you can't get away from this Clara Bow girl. She certainly has that certain 'It' for which the picture is named, and she just runs away with the film.

Antonio Moreno looks just about old enough to fall for the Bow type of flapper, in fact, just a little too old and ready to fall. William Austin is immense and furnishes the greater part of the laughs.

It starts in a department store, where the father has just turned the business over to the son. His pal comes in to congratulate him and makes a tour of inspection with him. He is all het up over the Glyn story of 'It' in a magazine and starts looking for 'It' among the shop girls, ending up with being sure that he has found 'It' in Betty Lou (Bow).

●●●●●●●●●●●●●●●●●●●●●●●●●●●●

■ ITALIAN JOB, THE

1969, 100 MINS, UK ◇ ▽
Dir Peter Collinson   *Prod* Michael Deeley   *Scr* Troy Kennedy Martin   *Ph* Douglas Slocombe   *Ed* John Trumper   *Mus* Quincy Jones   *Art Dir* Disley Jones
● Michael Caine, Noel Coward, Benny Hill, Raf Vallone, Tony Beckley, Rossano Brazzi (Paramount/Oakhurst)

Michael Caine plays a minor crook who inherits from a dead pal (Rossano Brazzi) the idea and key plan of a heist for landing a haul of $4 million in gold ingots from a security van in Turin, Italy. Scheme involves an elaborate way of throwing the Turin traffic into a colossal, chaotic tangle on which the robbery and getaway depends.

The crime is bankrolled and masterminded by Noel Coward, a top criminal, from a London jail which he virtually controls with sybaratic authority. Caine's assembled gang of crooks seem a bumbling crowd, unfitted to take on the Mafia, which is naturally taking a menacing interest in the scheme.

The cast does its stuff to good effect. Coward, as the highly patriotic, business-like master crook, brings all his imperturbable sense of irony and comedy to his role.

●●●●●●●●●●●●●●●●●●●●●●●●●●●●

■ IT CAME FROM OUTER SPACE

1953, 80 MINS, US ▽
Dir Jack Arnold   *Prod* William Alland   *Scr* Harry Essex   *Ph* Clifford Stine   *Ed* Paul Weatherwax   *Mus* Joseph Gershenson (dir.)   *Art Dir* Bernard Herzbrun, Robert Boyle
● Richard Carlson, Barbara Rush, Charles Drake, Russell Johnson, Kathleen Hughes, Joseph Sawyer (Universal)

Picture has been smartly fashioned to take advantage of all the tricks of science-fiction and 3-D. Stereo process is not used as just an excuse to pelt an audience with flying objects and, with one exception, when missiles come out of the screen they are tied in logically with the story.

Direction by Jack Arnold whips up an air of suspense and there is considerable atmosphere of reality created, which stands up well enough if the logic of it all is not examined too closely. Some of the threat posed by the landing of visitors from space on earth is lessened when it is established the chance visitors intend no harm.

Otherwise, the Ray Bradbury story proves to be good science-fiction. Yarn opens with Richard Carlson, a scientist, and Barbara Rush, his school-teacher fiancee, observing the landing of a fiery object in the Arizona desert. At first believing it is a meteor, Carlson changes his opinion when he ventures into the crater. Strange things begin to happen in the community. Townspeople disappear and their likenesses are taken over by the space visitors.

Carlson is excellent as the scientist, and Rush makes an attractive partner. Charles Drake is good as the sheriff, and there are some excellent supporting performances.

●●●●●●●●●●●●●●●●●●●●●●●●●●●●

■ IT HAPPENED HERE

1964, 99 MINS, UK
Dir Kevin Brownlow, Andrew Mollo   *Prod* Kevin Brownlow, Andrew Mollo   *Scr* Kevin Brownlow, Andrew Mollo   *Ph* Peter Suschitzky, Kevin Brownlow   *Mus* Jack Beaver   *Art Dir* Andrew Mollo
● Pauline Murray, Sebastian Shaw, Nicolette Bernard, Bart Allison, Stella Kemball, Fiona Leland (Rath)

It Happened Here tells the story of what might have happened had England been occupied by the Germans. The action takes place in 1943. There's also a story line going through. It centres on the experience of an English nurse who, in order to help, joins the Fascist-controlled Immediate Organization. She soon finds out that her uniform alienates those around here. She eventually tries to help a wounded partisan. Her action is discovered and she's punished for associating with 'the other side'.

The film shows brutality on both sides. Its message is that Nazism leads to violence everywhere. Film poses the question: can Nazism only be wiped out by Nazi methods?

But despite all controversy, film reveals a tremendous task. Compliments galore should go to the two young men who created it: Kevin Brownlow and Andrew Mollo, the former a professional film editor, the latter assistant director to Tony Richardson who, incidentally, contributed the money to complete the film.

It Happened Here is a non-professional feature which began as an amateur project on 16mm and remained so until financing was secured six years (!) after production had started. The early material was then 'blown-up' and rest of the film was shot on standard 35mm. Most of the cast is nonprofessional. One is hardly aware of this. Film cost a mere $20,000.

●●●●●●●●●●●●●●●●●●●●●●●●●●●●

■ IT HAPPENED IN BROOKLYN

1947, 102 MINS, US ▽
Dir Richard Whorf   *Prod* Jack Cummings   *Scr* Isobel Lennart   *Ph* Robert Planck   *Ed* Blanche Sewell   *Mus* Johnny Green   *Art Dir* Cedric Gibbons, Leonid Vasian
● Frank Sinatra, Kathryn Grayson, Peter Lawford, Jimmy Durante, Gloria Grahame, Marcy McGuire (M-G-M)

Much of the lure will result from Frank Sinatra's presence in the cast. Guy's acquired the Bing Crosby knack of nonchalance, throwing away his gag lines with fine aplomb. He kids himself in a couple of hilarious sequences and does a takeoff on Jimmy Durante, with Durante aiding him, that's sockeroo.

Other stars also shine, although Durante has to struggle with some lines that don't do his particular brand of comedy too much good. Kathryn Grayson is beauteous and appealing as the love interest but the sound recording doesn't do her singing any good. Peter Lawford also makes out well and pulls a surprise with a jive rendition of a novelty tune 'Whose Baby Are You?'

Isobel Lennart's nicely-handled adaptation of an original story by John McGowan has Sinatra as a lonesome GI in London, thirsting for the Flatbush camaraderie. Before heading for home, he meets Lawford, young British nobleman whose longhair inclinations have made him a stuffed shirt, and tries to pull the Britisher out of his rut.

Back in Brooklyn, Sinatra returns to his old highschool to check with his draft board and meets Grayson, the music teacher, plus Durante, the school's oldtime janitor. Unable to find a room, he moves in with Durante, and begins falling in love with Grayson. Lawford appears on the scene and also immediately falls in love with Grayson.

Interspersed in the story are a group of six new tunes from the able pianos of Sammy Cahn and Jule Styne. Richard Whorf has directed the film with a light touch that gets the most out of the comedy situations. [Piano solos are played by Andre Previn.]

■ IT HAPPENED ONE NIGHT

1934, 105 MINS, US ⓦ ☉
Dir Frank Capra   *Prod* Frank Capra   *Scr* Robert Riskin
Ph Joseph Walker   *Ed* Gene Havlick   *Mus* Louis Silvers
(dir.)   *Art Dir* Stephen Goosson
● Clark Gable, Claudette Colbert, Walter Connolly, Roscoe Karns, Jameson Thomas, Alan Hale (Columbia)

The story [by Samuel Hopkins Adams] has that intangible quality of charm which arises from a smooth blending of the various ingredients. It starts off to be another long-distance bus story, but they get out of the bus before it palls.

Plot is a simple one. The headstrong but very charming daughter of a millionaire marries a suitor of whom her father does not approve. She quarrels with her father on the yacht off Miami, and the girl goes over the rail. She seeks to make her way to New York, with the old man raising the hue and cry. Clark Gable who has just been fired from his Florida correspondent's job, is on the same bus.

But the author would have been nowhere without the deft direction of Frank Capra and the spirited and good-humored acting of the stars and practically most of their support. Walter Connolly is the only other player to get much of a show, but there are a dozen with bit parts well played.

Claudette Colbert makes hers a very delightful assignment and Gable swings along at sustained speed. Both play as though they really liked their characters, and therein lies much of the charm.

□ 1934: Best Picture, Director, Actor (Clark Gable), Actress (Claudette Colbert), Adaptation

■ IT HAPPENED TOMORROW

1944, 84 MINS, US ⓦ
Dir Rene Clair   *Prod* Arnold Pressburger   *Scr* Dudley Nichols, Rene Clair   *Ph* Archie J. Stout   *Ed* Fred Pressburger   *Mus* Robert Stolz   *Art Dir* Erno Metzner
● Dick Powell, Linda Darnell, Jack Oakie, Edgar Kennedy, Edward Brophy, George Cleveland (United Artists)

It Happened Tomorrow poses a novel premise on which to spin a comedy-drama – what happens when a cub reporter gets a copy of tomorrow's newspaper. Results provide diverting escapist entertainment, with many sparkling moments and episodes along the line.

Although there are numerous broadly sketched sequences aimed for laugh reaction, picture carries undercurrent of Continental directing technique of Rene Clair. The welding is more than passably successful, but main credit for picture's status can be handed to script by Clair and Dudley Nichols [based on 'originals' by Lord Dunsany, Hugh Wedlock and Howard Snyder, and ideas of Lewis R. Foster]; it picks up every chance for a chuckle or laugh in both dialog and situation.

Dick Powell, cub on the sheet, is befriended by the rag's veteran librarian who, after death, hands the youth copies of the next day's paper for three successive days.

Interwoven is his meeting and quick romance with Linda Darnell, medium and niece of mindreader Jack Oakie.

□ 1944: Nominations: Best Scoring of a Dramatic Picture, Sound

■ I, THE JURY

1953, 87 MINS, US
Dir Harry Essex   *Prod* Victor Saville   *Scr* Harry Essex
Ph John Alton   *Ed* Frederick Y. Smith   *Mus* Franz Waxman   *Art Dir* Wiard Ihnen
● Biff Elliot, Preston Foster, Peggie Castle, Margaret Sheridan, Alan Reed, Elisha Cook Jr (United Artists/Parklane)

Harry Essex both directed and wrote from Mickey Spillane's novel of the same title. The suspense element is not too strong, but such ingredients as brutal mob strong boys, effete art collectors with criminal tendencies, sexy femmes with more basic tendencies, and a series of unsolved killings, are mixed together in satisfactory quantities. The raw sex that is a prime feature of Spillane's book characters is less forthright on film.

Hardboiled private eye Mike Hammer traces the killer of a friend, uncovers some unsavory rackets while doing so and then shoots down the killer at the finale. The stereo lensing by John Alton is good, and without obvious 3-D trickery. Depth treatment and the Franz Waxman score are good assists for meller mood.

Picture introduces Biff Elliot as the sadistic Hammer, a character with a big chip on his shoulder. Elliot does okay by the assignment, although seemingly a bit less mature than readers may picture the book private eye. Peggie Castle, a psychiatrist, is the chief sex lure and is excellent. Preston Foster is competent as the police captain. Margaret Sheridan shows up in firstrate style as Hammer's secretary.

■ I, THE JURY

1982, 109 MINS, US ◇ ⓥ
Dir Richard T. Heffron   *Prod* Robert Solo   *Scr* Larry Cohen   *Ph* Andrew Laszlo   *Ed* Garth Craven   *Mus* Bill Conti   *Art Dir* Robert Gundlach
● Armand Assante, Barbara Carrera, Laurene Landon, Alan King, Geoffrey Lewis, Paul Sorvino (American Cinema/Larco/Solofilm)

Almost 30 years after the first screen edition of Mickey Spillane's first Mike Hammer novel, the update of *I, the Jury* has all the updated violence, nudity, wit and style that was missing from the puritanical 1953 original.

By comparison, the souped-up remake is hard as nails, with Armand Assante plausibly macho and ruggedly sexy as the amoral private eye who avenges the murder of his old Vietnam war buddy.

Scripter Larry Cohen's plotting is swift, suitably enigmatic and well stocked with well-stacked and well-exposed babes, of which the prime specimen is Barbara Carrera in an arousingly arranged seduction scene with Assante.

Carrera is just one of numerous villains as

the operator of a not-to-be believed sex therapy clinic. The ultimate heavy in this tangled tale is proficiently portrayed by Barry Snider as a former CIA operative whose computerized exurban fortress is penetrated by Hammer in a penultimate sequence of rousing action.

■ IT HURTS ONLY WHEN I LAUGH
See: Only When I Laugh

■ IT LIVES AGAIN

1978, 91 MINS, US ◇ ⓥ
Dir Larry Cohen   *Prod* Larry Cohen   *Scr* Larry Cohen
Ph Fenton Hamilton   *Ed* Curt Burch, Louis Friedman, Carol O'Blath   *Mus* Bernard Herrmann, Laurie Johnson
● Frederic Forrest, Kathleen Lloyd, John P. Ryan, John Marley, Andrew Duggan, Eddie Constantine (Warner)

In his sequel to *It's Alive*, Larry Cohen aims squarely at the same audience, which should be attracted back for more of the murderous babies.

As in the original, producer-director-writer Cohen does not show a lot of the demonic infants nor explain what they really are. But whatever got into the blood of the first mom is now rampant through the country and they're aborning everywhere, threatening the survival of humanity.

Though this is all so much silliness, Cohen effectively uses a good cast topped by Frederic Forrest and Kathleen Lloyd to build up suspense for the slashing, growling attacks by the terrible tykes.

Since the babies are fairly defenseless except at close range, Cohen must go to ridiculous lengths to get his well-armed characters into vulnerable positions, wrapping up with a totally absurd police siege. When the kids are about to bite, though, it's good horror-house fun.

■ IT'S A GIFT

1935, 73 MINS, US ⓦ ☉
Dir Norman McLeod   *Prod* William LeBaron   *Scr* Jack Cunningham, Charles Bogle [= W.C. Fields], J.P. McEvoy   *Ph* Henry Sharp   *Art Dir* Hans Dreier, John B. Goodman
● W.C. Fields, Jean Rouverol, Julian Madison, Kathleen Howard, Tammany Young, Baby LeRoy (Paramount)

Practically a comedy monolog for W.C. Fields, with little help from a number of others. No plot, no suspense; rather coarse-grained in spots, but packing a load of belly laughs for people who like that sort of humor.

The plot is merely that Fields buys a California orange grove and drives the family out in the car. It's a bit of desert in between the other groves, but Fields is tipped off that it's vital to the building of a racetrack, so he gets $40,000 and a real grove.

Fields holds the screen about 80% of the time, which is just as well since no one else is given anything. Kathleen Howard acts the bossy wife with main strength.

■ IT'S ALIVE

1974, 90 MINS, US ◇ ⓥ
Dir Larry Cohen   *Prod* Larry Cohen   *Scr* Larry Cohen
Ph Fenton Hamilton   *Ed* Peter Honess   *Mus* Bernard Herrmann
● John Ryan, Sharon Farrell, Andrew Duggan, Guy Stockwell, James Dixon, Michael Ansara (Larco)

This stomach-churning little film is a 'Son of the Exorcist' horror pic about a monstrous newborn baby who goes on a murder rampage through LA before being blown to smithereens in a police ambush.

Bernard Herrmann's score, while not one of his most memorable, is highly effective in creating tension, but one wonders why an artist of his caliber lowered himself into such muck.

Script sidesteps an answer to what caused the aberration in the womb of Sharon Farrell. Hubby John Ryan feels vaguely guilty, and his earlier contemplation of an abortion is thrown back in his face.

The far-fetched rampage by the fleetingly-glimpsed infant gives director Larry Cohen the chance to shoot a few technically interesting scenes.

● ●

■ IT'S ALWAYS FAIR WEATHER

1955, 102 MINS, US ◇ ⚈ ⊙

Dir Gene Kelly, Stanley Donen   *Prod* Arthur Freed
Scr Betty Comden, Adolph Green   *Ph* Robert Bronner
Ed Adrienne Fazan   *Mus* Andre Previn   *Art Dir* Cedric
Gibbons, Arthur Lonergan
● Gene Kelly, Dan Dailey, Cyd Charisse, Dolores Gray,
Michael Kidd, David Burns (M-G-M)

As well as spoofing television, *It's Always Fair Weather* also takes on advertising agencies and TV commercials, and what emerges is a delightful musical satire.

Betty Comden and Adolph Green, vet scripters of both Broadway and film tuners, present Gene Kelly, Dan Dailey, and Michael Kidd as a trio of former GI buddies who meet 10 years after World War II. Somehow the warm friendship that existed during the war years has deteriorated into a sour reunion as different interests have driven the buddies apart.

Dolores Gray, as the temperamental, syrupy hostess, registers excellently in appearance, emoting and warbling. Kidd, better known as a choreographer, emerges as a seasoned musicomedy performer.

Kelly, Dailey and Kidd score in group routines and Kelly and Dailey have a field day in solo outings. Kelly's roller skating routine and Dailey's drunk act at a chi-chi party are standouts. Cyd Charisse has only one terp routine, but she carries it off to perfection.
□ 1955: Nominations: Best Story & Screenplay, Scoring of a Musical Picture,

● ●

■ IT'S A MAD MAD MAD MAD WORLD

1963, 190 MINS, US ◇ ⚈ ⊙

Dir Stanley Kramer   *Prod* Stanley Kramer   *Scr* William
Rose, Tania Rose   *Ph* Ernest Laszlo   *Ed* Fred Knudtson
Mus Ernest Gold   *Art Dir* Rudolph Sternad
● Spencer Tracy, Milton Berle, Sid Caesar, Mickey
Rooney, Ethel Merman, Phil Silvers (United Artists)

It's a mad, mad, mad, mad picture. Being a picture of extravagant proportions, even its few flaws are king-sized, but the plusses outweigh by far the minuses. It is a throwback to the wild, wacky and wondrous time of the silent screen comedy, a kind of Keystone Kop Kaper with modern conveniences.

The plot is disarmingly simple. A group of people are given a clue by a dying man (Jimmy Durante) as to the whereabouts of a huge sum of money he has stolen and buried. Unable to come to a compromise in apportionment of the anticipated loot, each sets out for the roughly specified site of the buried cash, breaking his back to beat the others there. All are unaware that they are under secret surveillance by state police authorities, who are allowing them simply to lead the way to the money.

Nothing is done in moderation in this picture. All the stops are out. Nobody goes around what they can go over, under, through or into. Yet, as noted, the film is not without its flaws and oversights. Too often it tries to throw a wild haymaker where a simple left jab would be more apt to locate the desired target. Certain pratfalls and sequences are unnecessarily overdone to the point where they begin to grow tedious and reduce the impact of the whole.

An array of top-ranking comics has been

rounded up by director Stanley Kramer, making this one of the most unorthodox and memorable casts on screen record. The comic competition is so keen that it is impossible to single out any one participant as outstanding.
□ 1963: Best Sound Effects.
□ Nominations: Best Color Cinematography, Editing, Original Music Score, Song ('It's a Mad Mad Mad Mad World'), Sound

● ●

■ IT'S A WONDERFUL LIFE

1946, 120 MINS, US ⚈ ⊙

Dir Frank Capra   *Prod* Frank Capra   *Scr* Frances
Goodrich, Albert Hackett, Frank Capra, Jo Swerling
Ph Joseph Walker, Joseph Biroc   *Ed* William Hornbeck
Mus Dimitri Tiomkin   *Art Dir* Jack Okey
● James Stewart, Donna Reed, Lionel Barrymore,
Thomas Mitchell, Henry Travers, Gloria Grahame (Liberty)

The tale [based on a story by Philip Van Doren Stern], flashbacked, essentially is simple. At 30 a small-town citizen feels he has reached the end of his rope, mentally, morally, financially. All his plans all his life have gone awry. Through no fault of own he faces disgrace. If the world isn't against him, at least it has averted its face. As he contemplates suicide, Heaven speeds a guardian angel, a pixyish fellow of sly humor, to teach the despondent most graphically how worthwhile his life has been and what treasures, largely intangible, he does possess.

The recounting of this life is just about flawless in its tender and natural treatment; only possible thin carping could be that the ending is slightly overlong and a shade too cloying for all tastes.

James Stewart's lead is braced by a full fanspread of shimmering support. In femme lead, Donna Reed reaches full-fledged stardom. As a Scrooge-like banker, Lionel Barrymore lends a lot of lustre. Thomas Mitchell especially is effective as lead's drunken uncle.
□ 1946: Nomination: Best Picture, Director, Actor (James Stewart), Editing, Sound

● ●

■ IT'S A WONDERFUL WORLD

1939, 84 MINS, US

Dir W.S Van Dyke   *Prod* Frank Davis   *Scr* Ben Hecht
Ph Oliver T. Marsh   *Ed* Harold F. Kress   *Mus* Edward
Ward   *Art Dir* Cedric Gibbons, Paul Groesse
● Claudette Colbert, James Stewart, Guy Kibbee,
Frances Drake, Nat Pendleton, Edgar Kennedy (M-G-M)

Metro saturates the screwball comedy type of picture with some pretty broad burlesque in *It's a Wonderful World*.

Claudette Colbert is a zany poetess in continual conflict and love with James Stewart. Story [an original by Ben Hecht and Herman J. Mankiewicz] is thinly laid foundation to provide the wacky and slapsticky situations and rapid-fire laugh dialog.

Stewart, a novice private detective, is assigned to watch millionaire Ernest Truex. Latter goes on a bender, and winds up convicted of a murder. Stewart is implicated, and escapes from the train en route to prison determined to solve the murder mystery and save his client. Kidnapping Colbert and requisitioning her car, Stewart runs through series of disguises – a Boy Scout leader, chauffeur, and actor.

W.S. Van Dyke presents the yarn with good humor and a let's-have-fun attitude.

● ●

■ IT SHOULD HAPPEN TO YOU

1954, 86 MINS, US ⚈ ⊙

Dir George Cukor   *Prod* Fred Kohlman   *Scr* Garson
Kanin   *Ph* Charles Lang   *Ed* Charles Nelson
Mus Frederick Hollander
● Judy Holliday, Peter Lawford, Jack Lemmon, Michael
O'Shea, Vaughn Taylor, Connie Gilchrist (Columbia)

Judy Holliday is reunited with director George Cukor and scripter Garson Kanin, a trio that clicked big with *Born Yesterday*, and the laugh range is from soft titters to loud guffaws as Cukor's smartly timed direction sends the players through hilarious situations. Plot is about a small town girl who comes to the big city to make a name for herself. Fresh angles belt the risibilities while dialog is adult, almost racy at times.

As the Gladys Glover of the plot, Holliday has a romp for herself, and she gets major assists in the comedy from Peter Lawford and Jack Lemmon, making his major screen bow.

Gladys has a different angle to flashing her name in the best places. With her meager savings she rents a signboard on Columbus Circle and has her name emblazoned thereon. This quest for fame sets off a lot of repercussions. She becomes a television celebrity and is pursued romantically by Lawford. Also in the amatory chase is Lemmon, who has a hard time keeping his romance with the new celebrity on even keel.
□ 1954: Nomination: Best B&W Costume Design

● ●

■ IT'S LOVE AGAIN

1936, 83 MINS, UK ⚈

Dir Victor Saville   *Prod* [uncredited]   *Scr* Marion Dix,
Lesser Samuels, Austin Melford   *Ph* Glen MacWilliams
Ed Al Barnes   *Mus* Louis Levy, Bretton Byrd
Art Dir Alfred Junge
● Jessie Matthews, Robert Young, Sonnie Hale, Ernest
Milton, Robb Wilton, Sara Allgood (Gaumont-British)

British-made picture has Jessie Matthews at her best. Matthews is the star, but the story [by Marion Dix] is based on rival columnists who invent people to make exclusive news.

Peter Carlton (Robert Young) invents a 'Mrs Smythe-Smythe', supposedly a tiger hunter from India, pursued by a maharajah. Matthews assumes the role of the non-existent 'Mrs Smythe-Smythe' to strut her stuff and possibly get an opening on the stage. She does, but gives up the impersonation when Carlton's rival senses her disguise and threatens to expose her unless she gives him the inside track on scoops.

Matthews does a variety of dances [arranged by Buddy Bradley], one a mock Indian number in a striking, if scanty, costume. There is a big production number, less impressive, perhaps, than Hollywood numbers, but as well devised and given an unusual staging. Here the costume is full tights with sequins. There is another pretty dance bit in a park and a near society dance in a restaurant set.

Matthews carries her part well and sings several songs [by Sam Coslow and Harry Woods], a couple of which are not in perfect synchrony. Young is a personable columnist and Sonnie Hale, as his idea man, is handicapped by a drunk assignment.

● ●

■ IT'S MY TURN

1980, 91 MINS, US ◇ ⚈ ⊙

Dir Claudia Weill   *Prod* Martin Elfland   *Scr* Eleanor
Bergstein   *Ph* Bill Butler   *Ed* Byron Brandt, Marjorie
Fowler, James Coblenz   *Mus* Patrick Williams
Art Dir Jack Delovia
● Jill Clayburgh, Michael Douglas, Charles Grodin,
Beverly Garland, Steven Hill, Daniel Stern (Columbia/
Rastar)

In her second feature, director Claudia Weill has managed to zero in on both the funny and tragic sides of falling in love while keeping the action moving and the story intact. If there is a tendency for the editing to be a bit choppy and the camera shots a tinge forced or unimaginative, Weill is a pro with actors.

Jill Clayburgh limns an offbeat but intellectually over-achieving mathematics professor residing with perpetually humorous building developer Charles Grodin in Chicago. She quickly finds herself in the arms of Michael Douglas during a trip to New York.

Probably the most endearing aspect here is the way action so easily moves from screwball to intellectual humour and then on to numerous emotionally touching moments.

· ·

■ IT STARTED IN NAPLES

1960, 100 MINS, US ◇ ▾
Dir Melville Shavelson *Prod* Jack Rose *Scr* Melville Shavelson, Jack Rose, Suso Cecchi D'Amico *Ph* Robert L. Surtees *Ed* Frank Bracht *Mus* Alessandro Cicognini, Carlo Savina *Art Dir* Hal Pereira, Roland Anderson
● Clark Gable, Sophia Loren, Vittorio De Sica, Marietto, Paolo Carlini, Claudio Ermelli (Paramount)

Within this charming pictorial study weaves a frothy, frank and irreverent comedy that stumbles, sputters and stammers when its stretches its one basic gag – American puritanism vs Italian moral abandon – too far, but partially restores its equilibrium with a parting shot of irony.

The screenplay, from a story by Michael Pertwee and Jack Davies, deposits Philadelphia lawyer Clark Gable in Naples to settle the estate of his brother, recently deceased via an auto accident. What Gable discovers is that his brother's extra-legal spouse also perished in the mishap, leaving their 10-year-old son (Marietto) in the care of the wife's sister (Sophia Loren). While debating (in and out of court and courtship) the relative merits of a Philadelphia and Neapolitan environment for the child, Gable and Loren fall in love.

Both the script and Melville Shavelson's direction try too hard to make the film up- roariously funny and risque. When the wit flows naturally, it is a delight; when it strains, it pains.

Gable and Loren are a surprisingly effective and compatible comedy pair. The latter, more voluptuous then ever, is naturally at home in her native surroundings and gives a vigorous and amusing performance, even tackling a couple of nightclub song-and-dance routines with gusto.

Vittorio De Sica is suave as Gable's roving-eyed, pulchritudinously-influenced Italian attorney. Young Marietto, as the orphaned waif who smokes ciggies, guzzles wine and ogles the babes, is occasionally the victim of director's apparent desire to overpower the spectator with overly cute postures and smart quips.
☐ 1960: Nomination: Best Color Art Direction

· ·

■ IT STARTED WITH EVE

1942, 90 MINS, US
Dir Henry Koster *Prod* Henry Koster, Joe Pasternak *Scr* Norman Krasna, Leo Townsend *Ph* Rudolph Mate *Ed* Bernard W. Burton *Mus* Hans J. Salter
● Deanna Durbin, Charles Laughton, Robert Cummings, Guy Kibbee (Universal)

Expertly tailored to the combined talents of Deanna Durbin and Charles Laughton. *It Started with Eve* is a neatly-devised romantic comedy drama. Story is one of those typical Cinderella tales, developed at a consistently fast pace, with plenty of spontaneous comedy exploding en route.

Laughton, crusty and cantankerous old millionaire, has the presses stopped, ready to toss his obit across the front pages. His son (Robert Cummings) suddenly arrives from a Mexican trip with his fiancee. Dying man insists on seeing the future wife, and when Cummings fails to locate her quickly, grabs a hatcheck girl (Durbin) as substitute. Miraculous recovery results from Durbin's visit, with Cummings getting into deep complications through necessity of continuing the duplicity – at the same time placating his fiancee.

Henry Koster gets the utmost out of Durbin's unsophisticated youthfulness, contrasting this effectively with the character performance of Laughton as the dictatorial tycoon for a slick piloting job.
☐ 1942: Nomination: Best Scoring of a Musical Picture

· ·

■ IT!
THE TERROR FROM BEYOND SPACE

1958, 68 MINS, US ▾
Dir Edward L. Cahn *Prod* Robert E. Kent *Scr* Jerome Bixby *Ph* Kenneth Peach Sr *Ed* Grant Whytock *Mus* Paul Sawtell, Bert Shefter *Art Dir* William Glasgow
● Marshall Thompson, Shawn Smith, Kim Spalding, Ann Doran, Richard Benedict, Ray Corrigan (Vogue)

'It' is a Martian by birth, a Frankenstein by instinct, and a copycat. The monster dies hard, brushing aside grenades, bullets, gas and an atomic pile, before snorting its last snort. It's old stuff, with only a slight twist.

Film starts some dozen years in the future [from 1958] with a disabled US rocketship on Mars. Only one of the 10 space travellers has survived, and a second rocketship has landed to drag him back to Earth where he is to face a courtmartial. The government is of the opinion the spaceman murdered his companions so he could hoard the food and stay alive until help arrived. But the accused swears the nine deaths came at the hands of a strange 'It'-type monster.

Most of the film is spent aboard the second rocketship on its way to Earth, and, to spice up the trip, the monster has stowed away. It kills with a swat of its grisly hand, then sucks all available liquids from its victims.

None of the performances is outstanding. Ray 'Crash' Corrigan makes a fetching monster. Technical credits are capable.

· ·

■ IVANHOE

1952, 107 MINS, UK ◇ ▾
Dir Richard Thorpe *Prod* Pandro S. Berman *Scr* Noel Langley, Aeneas MacKenzie *Ph* Freddie Young *Ed* Frank Clarke *Mus* Miklos Rozsa *Art Dir* Alfred Junge, Roger Furse
● Robert Taylor, Elizabeth Taylor, Joan Fontaine, George Sanders, Emlyn Williams, Robert Douglas (M-G-M)

Ivanhoe is a great romantic adventure, mounted extravagantly, crammed with action, and emerges as a spectacular feast.

Both the romance and the action are concentrated around Robert Taylor who, as Ivanhoe, is the courageous Saxon leader fighting for the liberation of King Richard from an Austrian prison and his restoration to the throne. Two women play an important part in his life. There is Rowena (Joan Fontaine), his father's ward, with whom he is in love; and Rebecca (Elizabeth Taylor), daughter of the Jew who raises the ransom money. She is in love with him.

Taylor sets the pace with a virile contribution which is matched by George Sanders as his principal adversary. Fontaine contributes to all the requisite charm and understanding as Rowena.
☐ 1952: Nominations: Best Picture, Color Cinematography, Scoring of a Dramatic Picture

· ·

■ I'VE HEARD THE MERMAIDS SINGING

1987, 81 MINS, CANADA ◇ ▾ ⊙
Dir Patricia Rozema *Prod* Patricia Rozema, Alexandra Raffe *Scr* Patricia Rozema *Ph* Douglas Koch *Ed* Patricia Rozema *Mus* Mark Korven *Art Dir* Valanne Ridgeway
● Sheila McCarthy, Paule Baillargeon, Ann-Marie McDonald, John Evans (Vos)

I've Heard The Mermaids Singing neatly blends film and video and comedy with serious undertones.

Plot centers on a klutzy and innocent temporary secretary (Sheila McCarthy) who is jobbed in at an art gallery run by an older femme, whom it is established quickly on takes a flagged fancy to her without the secretary cottoning on.

Living alone in cramped quarters, the secretary lives a fantasy life via deliberately grainy black-&-white scenes in which she flies through the air, walks on water and actually hears mermaids singing. Those sequences are soaringly portrayed with accompanying classical music [from Delibes' *Lakme*]. In other off-times, she observes daily life by taking photographs.

The secretary later discovers what appears to be the owner's own thrill-making canvases. Taking one of them, cleverly just a blaze of framed white light, the secretary hangs it in the gallery; it's heralded by the press, and the gallery owner attains fame. But the secretary is dejected because of the growing love affair between the two other women and rejection of her photos.

McCarthy, a waif-faced Canadian stage thesp in her first lead film role, gives a dynamic, strongly believable and constantly assured performance. She is ably assisted by Paule Baillargeon (the gallery owner).

· ·

■ IVORY HUNTER
See: Where No Vultures Fly

· ·

■ I WAKE UP SCREAMING

1942, 81 MINS, US ▾
Dir H. Bruce Humberstone *Prod* Milton Sperling *Scr* Dwight Taylor *Ph* Edward Cronjager *Ed* Robert Simpson *Mus* Cyril J. Mockridge (dir.) *Art Dir* Richard Day, Nathan Juran
● Betty Grable, Victor Mature, Carole Landis, Laird Cregar, William Gargan, Alan Mowbray (20th Century-Fox)

Most murder mysteries are B's regardless of budget, but this one is an exception to the rule. The director, H. Bruce Humberstone, has been equipped with a good script [from Steve Fisher's novel] and from his cast has obtained results that are all that may be asked in a murder meller with a romantic strain of more than ordinary strength.

Victor Mature plays in a tougher groove than usual. This time he's a sports promoter who is dogged by a detective who loses his girl (Carole Landis) when Mature takes her from obscurity and glamourizes her to the point where she wins a film contract. The murder of this girl then provides the premise for the remainder of the yarn. Betty Grable is enormously appealing here as the sister of the slain girl.

Dwight Taylor, who did the script, has dotted it with trenchant dialog. There isn't much comedy, but no more than the few laughs included are needed in this instance. Force of the melodramatic and romantic features of the yarn is sufficient.

· ·

■ I WALK ALONE

1948, 97 MINS, US
Dir Byron Haskin *Prod* Hal B. Wallis *Scr* Charles Schnee *Ph* Leo Tover *Ed* Arthur Schmidt *Mus* Victor Young *Art Dir* Hans Dreier, Franz Bachelin
● Burt Lancaster, Lizabeth Scott, Kirk Douglas, Wendell Corey, Kristine Miller, George Rigaud (Paramount)

I Walk Alone is tight, hard-boiled melodrama. A number of unusually tough sequences are spotted. One, in particular, is bloody beating handed out to Burt Lancaster by a trio of bruisers who spare no punches. Another is the dark-street stalking and gore-tinged death meted out to Wendell Corey.

There's a Rip Van Winkle angle to the plot wherein a gangster returns from 14 years in prison to find that his former cronies now wear the garb of respectability and are in such pseudo-legit rackets as used cars, night clubs, etc. Charles Schnee's screenplay, from the play *Beggars Are Coming to Town* by Theodore Reeves, makes much of the basic story's flavor, although letting dialog run away with a few scenes.

Lancaster belts over his assignment as the former jailbird who returns from prison to find the parade has passed him by and that old friends have given him the double-cross. Melodrama develops as Lancaster plots to muscle in on Kirk Douglas' nitery.

Lizabeth Scott holds up her end capably as co-star, making role of nitery singer who falls for Lancaster after a cross from Douglas, believable. Douglas is a standout as the hood turned respectable and fighting a losing battle to hold his kingdom together against Lancaster's assault.

• •

■ I WALKED WITH A ZOMBIE

1943, 69 MINS, US ⓥ ⊙

Dir Jacques Tourneur *Prod* Val Lewton *Scr* Curt Siodmak, Ardel Wray *Ph* J. Roy Hunt *Ed* Mark Robson *Mus* Roy Webb *Art Dir* Albert S. D'Agostino, Walter E. Keller
● Tom Conway, Frances Dee, James Ellison, Edith Barrett, Christine Gordon, James Bell (RKO)

I Walked with a Zombie fails to measure up to the horrific title. Film contains some terrifying passages, but is overcrowded with trite dialog and ponderous acting.

Scripters haven't particularly improved the Inez Wallace original [story], which hinges on the premise that West Indies voodoo priests actually can produce a 'zombie,' a live person unable to speak, hear or feel. Weird yarn has two half-brothers competing for the love of a girl, married to one of the pair, and their mother employing voodooism to turn the girl into a robot-like existence.

With few exceptions, cast walks through the picture almost as dazed as the zombies. James Ellison makes a loud but totally ineffective 'bad' brother. Frances Dee, as a comely nurse, tries to make sense in the inanimate proceedings. Tom Conway is terrifically British as the righteous brother, but inexcusably dull most of the time.

• •

■ I WALK THE LINE

1970, 96 MINS, US ◇ ⓥ

Dir John Frankenheimer *Prod* Harold D. Cohen *Scr* Alvin Sargent *Ph* David M. Walsh *Ed* Henry Berman *Mus* Johnny Cash *Art Dir* Albert Brenner
● Gregory Peck, Tuesday Weld, Estelle Parsons, Ralph Meeker, Lonny Chapman, Charles Durning (Columbia)

Like the Johnny Cash ballads that comprise its background scores and make an intangible emotional commentary on the story, *I Walk the Line* has an authentic, somber and gritty feel of life in the Tennessee back hills. Gregory Peck is the sheriff compromised by Tuesday Weld, moonshiner Ralph Meeker's nubile and sexually precocious daughter, and Estelle Parsons is Peck's desperate wife.

Each create thoroughly believable characters whose passions and individual codes are on a course of inevitable tragedy. Aesthetically, director John Frankenheimer has made a ownbeat folk ballad that rings true to its people and setting.

Weld is striking as the moonshiner's daughter, capturing just the right accent and qualities of late teenage sensuality, amorality and dumb innocence to make her a fatal attraction for an older married man.

• •

■ I WANT TO GO HOME

1989, 105 MINS, FRANCE ◇ ⓥ

Dir Alain Resnais *Prod* Marin Karmitz *Scr* Jules Feiffer *Ph* Charlie Van Damme *Ed* Albert Jurgenson *Mus* John Kander *Art Dir* Jacques Saulnier
● Adolph Green, Gerard Depardieu, Linda Lavin, Laura Benson, Micheline Presle, Geraldine Chaplin (MK2/Films A2/La Sept)

Jules Feiffer and Alain Resnais make strange bedfellows – the product of their union is this stillborn satiric comedy about an American cartoonist in Paris.

Central character is a cantankerous American cartoonist, played as a likable kvetch by songwriter and musical comedy veteran Adolph Green. He is making his first trip abroad, accompanied by Linda Lavin, to attend an exhibition of comic strip art in which his work figures.

Green's real reason is to see his neurotic daughter (Laura Benson), who's fled uncivilized Cleveland to enroll as a literature student at the Sorbonne. Mad about Flaubert, she has become starryeyed before her evasive professor Gerard Depardieu, who happens to be a comic book fan and one of Green's most ardent admirers.

Depardieu drags the flattered Green and Lavin to the posh country manor of his mother Micheline Presle, who indulges her son's obsessive Yank-collecting.

The performances are broad Broadway. Depardieu, in his first English-speaking part, knows how to charm with blithe timing but the role never grows beyond the cultural stereotype of the philandering Paris intellectual.

• •

■ I WANT TO LIVE!

1958, 120 MINS, US ⓥ

Dir Robert Wise *Prod* Walter Wanger *Scr* Nelson Gidding, Don M. Mankiewicz *Ph* Lionel Lindon *Ed* William Hornbeck *Mus* Johnny Mandel *Art Dir* Edward Haworth
● Susan Hayward, Simon Oakland, Virginia Vincent, Theodore Bikel, Wesley Lau, Philip Coolidge (United Artists/Figaro)

I Want to Live! is a drama dealing with the last years and the execution of Barbara Graham (Susan Hayward), who was convicted at one time or another of prostitution, perjury, forgery and murder. It is a damning indictment of capital punishment.

There is no attempt to gloss the character of Barbara Graham, only an effort to understand it through some fine irony and pathos. She had no hesitation about indulging in any form of crime or vice that promised excitement on her own, rather mean, terms. The screenplay is based on newspaper and magazine articles by San Francisco reporter Ed Montgomery, and on letters written by the woman herself. Its premise is that she was likely innocent of the vicious murder for which she was executed in the California gas chamber.

The final 30-40 minutes of the film are a purposely understated account of the mechanics involved in the state's legal destruction of life. The execution sequence is almost unbearable, mounting unswervingly in its intensity.

Hayward brings off this complex characterization. Simon Oakland, as Montgomery, who first crucified Barbara Graham in print and then attempted to undo what he had done, underplays his role with assurance.

☐ 1958: Best Actress (Susan Hayward).
☐ Nominations: Best Director, Adapted Screenplay, B&W Cinematography, Editing, Sound

• •

■ I WAS A COMMUNIST FOR THE F.B.I.

1951, 82 MINS, US

Dir Gordon Douglas *Prod* Bryan Foy *Scr* Crane Wilbur *Ph* Edwin B. DuPar *Ed* Folmar Blangsted

Art Dir Leo K. Kuter
● Frank Lovejoy, Dorothy Hart, Philip Carey, James Millican, Richard Webb, Konstantin Shayne (Warner)

From the real life experiences of Matt Cvetic [published in the *Saturday Evening Post* as *I Posed as a Communist for the F.B.I.*], scripter Crane Wilbur has fashioned an exciting film. Direction of Gordon Douglas plays up suspense and pace strongly, and the cast, headed by Frank Lovejoy in the title role, punches over the expose of the Communist menace.

Cvetic's story is that of a man who, for nine years, was a member of the Commie party so he could gather information for the FBI. His informer role was made all the harder because his patriotic brothers and young son hated him for the Red taint. Picture picks up the double life as Gerhardt Eisler comes to Pittsburgh to ready the Red cell for strike violence and racial hatred.

Excitement and suspense are set up in the many near-escapes from exposure that Lovejoy goes through before he completes his job by revealing Commies and their activities before the UnAmerican Activities Committee. There's a brief touch of romance, too, in the person of Dorothy Hart, a card-carrying schoolteacher who finally sees the light and is saved from Commie reprisal by Lovejoy.

• •

■ I WAS A MALE WAR BRIDE

(UK: You Can't Sleep Here)

1949, 105 MINS, US

Dir Howard Hawks *Prod* Sol C. Siegel *Scr* Charles Lederer, Leonard Spigelgass, Hagar Wilde *Ph* Norbert Brodine, Osmond Borrodaile *Ed* James B. Clark *Mus* Cyril J. Mockridge
● Cary Grant, Ann Sheridan, Marion Marshall, Randy Stuart, William Neff, Ken Tobey (20th Century-Fox)

Title describes the story perfectly. Cary Grant is a French army officer who, after the war, marries Ann Sheridan, playing a WAC officer. From then on it's a tale of Grant's attempts to get back to the US with his wife by joining a contingent of war brides.

Picture's chief failing, if it can be called that in view of the frothy components, is that the entire production crew, from scripters to director Howard Hawks and the cast, were apparently so intent on getting the maximum in yocks that they overlooked the necessary characterizations.

Story was filmed for the most part in Germany, until illness of the stars and several of the supporting players forced their return to Hollywood, where the remaining interiors were lensed. Illness, however, did not hamper the cast's cavortings.

• •

■ I WAS A SPY

1933, 90 MINS, UK ⓥ

Dir Victor Saville *Prod* Michael Balcon *Scr* W. P. Lipscomb, Ian Hay *Ph* Charles Van Enger *Ed* Frederick Y. Smith *Art Dir* Alfred Junge
● Madeleine Carroll, Conrad Veidt, Edmund Gwenn, Herbert Marshall, Donald Calthrop, Gerald du Maurier (Gaumont-British)

Story is based on the life of Martha Cnockhaert, a Belgian girl who was an Allied spy in the World War. A reproduction of the Belgian village, where most of the action takes place, is most realistic, and the German troops of occupation, headed by Kommandant Conrad Veidt, are fine. Their military equipment is remarkable.

The acting honors go to Madeleine Carroll as the fine-spirited young girl. Veidt as the head of the German troops looks his part; Edmund Gwenn makes a realistic burgomaster; and Herbert Marshall is a first-rate Herbert Marshall.

• •

I WAS A TEENAGE WEREWOLF

1957, 76 MINS, US 🔊

Dir Gene Fowler *Prod* Herman Cohen *Scr* Ralph Thornton *Ph* Joseph LaShelle *Ed* George Gittens *Mus* Paul Dunlap
● Michael Landon, Yvonne Lime, Whit Bissell, Tony Marshall, Dawn Richard, Barney Phillips (American International)

Only thing new about this combo teenager and science-fiction yarn is a psychiatrist's use of a problem teenager who comes to him for help using the youth for an experiment in regression, but it's handled well enough to meet the requirements of this type of film.

There are plenty of story points which are sloughed over in the screenplay, but good performances help overcome deficiencies. Final reels, when the lad turns into a hairy-headed monster with drooling fangs, are inclined to be played too heavily.

Michael Landon delivers a first-class characterization as the high school boy constantly in trouble, and has okay support right down the line. Yvonne Lime is pretty as his girl friend who asks him to go to the psychiatrist, and Whit Bissell handles doctor part capably, although some of his lines are pretty thick.

• •

I WAS HAPPY HERE

(US: Time Lost and Time Remembered)

1966, 91 MINS, UK ◇

Dir Desmond Davis *Prod* Roy Millichip *Scr* Edna O'Brien, Desmond Davis *Ph* Manny Wynn *Ed* Brian Smedley-Aston *Mus* John Addison *Art Dir* Tony Woollard
● Sarah Miles, Cyril Cusack, Julian Glover, Sean Caffrey, Marie Kean, Cardew Robinson (Partisan)

Sarah Miles plays a girl who escapes from an Irish village to London, believing that her fisherboy sweetheart will follow her. He doesn't and Miles, lonely and unhappy in the big city, falls into a disastrous marriage with a pompous, boorish young doctor. After a Christmas Eve row, she rushes back to the Irish village, but is disillusioned when she finds that though the village has not changed, she has.

The story is told largely in flashback but Davis has skillfully woven the girl's thoughts and the present happenings by swift switching which, occasionally, is confusing but mostly is sharp and pertinent.

Miles gives a most convincing performance, a slick combo of wistful charm but with the femme guile never far below the surface. But Julian Glover makes heavy weather of his role as the girl's insufferable husband.

Filmed entirely on location in County Clare, Ireland, and London, the contrast between the peaceful, lonely sea-coast village and the less peaceful but equally lonely bustling London is artfully wed.

• •

I WAS MONTY'S DOUBLE

1958, 100 MINS, UK 🔊

Dir John Guillermin *Prod* Maxwell Setton *Scr* Bryan Forbes *Ph* Basil Emmott *Ed* Max Benedict *Mus* John Addison *Art Dir* W.E. Hutchinson
● John Mills, Cecil Parker, M.E. Clifton James, Michael Hordern, Marius Goring, Vera Day (Associated British)

I Was Monty's Double tells about a great and important wartime hoax, almost incredible in its audacity. Clifton James, a smalltime stock actor serving as a junior officer in the Royal Army Pays Corps, bore a startling resemblance to General Montgomery. This was used in a daring scheme devised by Army Intelligence to persuade the Germans that the forthcoming Allies' invasion might well take place on the North African coast.

The deception proved so successful that the enemy moved several divisions to the North African coast, a move which helped the actual invasion tremendously. The film has several moments of real tension.

Plenty of news footage has been woven into the pic and it has been done with commendable ingenuity. Bryan Forbes' taut screenplay [based on James' book] is liberally spiced with humor. James plays both himself and Montgomery. Apart from his uncanny resemblance to Monty, James shows himself to be a resourceful actor in his own right.

• •

I WILL . . . I WILL . . . FOR NOW

1976, 107 MINS, US ◇ 🔊

Dir Norman Panama *Prod* George Barrie *Scr* Norman Panama, Albert E. Lewin *Ph* John A. Alonzo *Ed* Robert Lawrence *Mus* John Cameron *Art Dir* Fernando Carrere
● Elliott Gould, Diane Keaton, Paul Sorvino, Victoria Principal, Robert Alda, Warren Berlinger (Brut)

I Will . . . I Will . . . For Now is passable fluff. Elliott Gould and Diane Keaton (as unhappy marriage/divorce partners), their less-than-disinterested lawyer Paul Sorvino, and condominium sexpot Victoria Principal, star.

Story finds horny Gould jealous that divorced wife Keaton has a lover, but he doesn't know it's Sorvino. When Keaton's sister Candy Clark has a modern contract-type marriage, pair decide to try life again under that new form, drafted with an eye to self-destruction by Sorvino.

Principal and her distant husband Warren Berlinger supply the formula comedy when couples get rooms mixed up in chic sex clinic run by Robert Alda and Madge Sinclair.

• •

JABBERWOCKY

1977, 100 MINS, UK ◇ 🔊 ⊙

Dir Terry Gilliam *Prod* Sandy Lieberson *Scr* Terry Gilliam, Charles Alverson *Ph* Terry Bedford *Ed* Michael Bradsell *Mus* De Wolfe *Art Dir* Roy Smith
● Michael Palin, Harry H. Corbett, John Le Mesurier, Warren Mitchell, Max Wall, Deborah Fallender (Umbrella/White)

A Monty Python splinter faction bears responsibility for *Jabberwocky*, a medieval farce based on a Lewis Carroll poem. Film is long on jabber but short on yocks.

Ex-Pythonite Terry Gilliam directed and co-scripted. Michael Palin is well-cast as a bumpkin who threads his way through jousting knights, grubby peasants, 'drag' nuns, and damsels both fair and plump to become the inadvertent hero who slays the vile monster menacing Max Wall's cartoon kingdom. The monster, who doesn't appear till the final minutes, is a work of inspired dark imagination.

Film goes for gags instead of sustained satire, including several typically English lavatorial jokes and also some repulsively bloody ones.

Some of the slapstick works okay but at a very intermittent pace in a mish-mash scenario.

• •

JACARE

1942, 65 MINS, US

Dir Charles E. Ford *Prod* Jules Levey *Scr* Thomas Lennon *Mus* Miklos Rozsa
● Frank Buck, James M. Dannaldson, Miguel Rojinsky (Mayfair)

Produced in Brazil, excepting for studio scenes introducing Frank Buck, this typical 'bring-'em-back-alive' jungle thriller stacks up strongly in the Buck string of wild animal screen epics.

This Buck jungler is outstanding for the smooth way in which it unfolds an intelligent story, minus dull spots. Aside from the introductory trimmings, the picture is a series of adventures and struggles to capture denizens of the jungle.

Recital builds suspense as to what the Jacare really is, with climax sharply pointed up as a whole river-bank filled with them is revealed.

Charles E. Ford, former Universal newsreel editor, is credited on the film with directing. Ford died on the Coast after returning from the trip. Production is a credit to his skill at maintaining maximum interest. Buck employs his familiar clipped phrases in narrating the whole picture, and is okay in his brief initial appearance.

• •

JACK LONDON

1944, 92 MINS, US 🔊

Dir Alfred Santell *Prod* Samuel Bronston *Scr* Ernest Pascal *Ph* John W. Boyle *Ed* William Ziegler *Mus* Fred Rich
● Michael O'Shea, Susan Hayward, Osa Massen, Virginia Mayo (United Artists)

Samuel Bronston has brought to the screen one of the great men of American letters, Jack London, and if ever there was a blood-and-guts subject for Hollywood treatment, London has long seemed a natural. But the play's still the thing. *Jack London*, an adaptation of a book written by the author's wife, Charmian, has much of the writer-adventurer's life crammed into its 92 minutes, but somewhere along the line it has missed fire.

One of the main snags to *London* is the fact that one of the film's two most important characters – Charmian London, the author's wife – fails to appear until the film has consumed half its running time. Susan Hayward is starred in the role, as is Michael O'Shea in the title part, and for a starred performer to be absent for that length of time is dangerous scripting and directing, let alone producing.

O'Shea, comparative newcomer to Hollywood from the Broadway stage, is miscast in the title role. His physique, for one, is not what one might expect of a two-fisted Jack London, and a couple of the scenes in which he delivers kayo blows are too obviously staged. His performance generally is uncertain.

□ 1944: Nomination: Best Scoring of a Dramatic Picture

....

■ JACKNIFE

1989, 102 MINS, US ◇ ⚉ ⊙
Dir David Jones   *Prod* Robert Schaffel, Carol Baum
Scr Stephen Metcalfe   *Ph* Brian West   *Ed* John Bloom
Mus Bruce Broughton   *Art Dir* Edward Pisoni
● Robert De Niro, Ed Harris, Kathy Baker, Charles Dutton, Loudon Wainwright III (Kings Road/Sandollar-Schaffel)

Robert De Niro's tour de force turn as a feisty Vietnam vet fails to save *Jacknife*, a poorly scripted three-hander drama [from Stephen Metcalfe's play *Strange Snow*].

De Niro is Megs (alternately nicknamed Jacknife by his war buddy Bobby, who was killed in action), a burnout working as a Connecticut car repairman. He decides to get another war buddy, Dave (Ed Harris), to break out of his shell by forcing him to have a good time and remember those blocked-out adventures the trio had in 'Nam.

A romance eventually blossoms between Harris' high school teacher sister (Kathy Baker) and De Niro (with Harris opposing the alliance), leading to a prom night where she is the chaperone with De Niro her date; Harris violently disrupts the event.

Besides its romance of 'little people,' film's central treatment of the Vietnam hangover that hamstrings Harris' return to normal living proves to be flat and uninvolving.

De Niro is spectacular, bringing life to every scene he's in. Unfortunately, helmer David Jones, who had better luck with the Harold Pinter three-hander *Betrayal*, fails to generate much interest in the material.

....

■ JACKSON COUNTY JAIL

1976, 89 MINS, US ◇ ⚉
Dir Michael Miller   *Prod* Jeff Begun   *Scr* Donald
Stewart   *Ph* Bruce Logan   *Ed* Caroline Ferriol
Mus Loren Newkirk   *Art Dir* Michael McCloskey
● Yvette Mimieux, Tommy Lee Jones, Robert Carradine, Frederic Cook, Severn Darden, Howard Hesseman (New World)

Pic has a predictable, uncomplicated plot. A fashionable ad woman (Yvette Mimieux) leaves her career and her cheating lover behind in LA, destination New York. Along the way, she gets beaten up by juvenile hitchhikers (Robert Carradine is one of them) who steal her car, leaving her stranded in some ambiguous western town where she's promptly thrown in jail on phony charges and raped by a psychotic jailkeeper.

She kills the jailkeeper and is forced to go on the lam with a rowdy but caring inmate (Tommy Lee Jones), a radical country boy who steals 'because everyone is dishonest'.

The after-effects of the rape are handled with more care than usual, and Mimieux turns in a convincing, well-controlled performance.

....

■ JACK THE BEAR

1993, 98 MINS, US ◇ ⚉ ⊙
Dir Marshall Herskovitz   *Prod* Bruce Gilbert   *Scr* Steven
Zaillian   *Ph* Fred Murphy   *Ed* Steven Rosenblum
Mus James Horner   *Art Dir* Lilly Kilvert
● Danny DeVito, Robert J. Steinmiller Jr, Miko Hughes, Gary Sinise, Julia Louis-Dreyfus, Reese Witherspoon (American Filmworks/Lucky Dog)

Jack the Bear, a mostly likable first feature from *thirtysomething* co-creator Marshall Herskovitz, concerns a boy who discovers that monsters are to be found not only on television but also in real life. A clever portrayal of eccentric fatherhood by Danny DeVito and a socko performance from young Robert J. Steinmiller Jr. as the eponymous hero are major assets.

Based on Dan McCall's 1974 tome, and set in suburban Oakland in 1972, film mixes comedy and horror to make its points about latent evil.

Twelve-year-old Jack (Steinmiller) and his younger brother Dylan (Miko Hughes) have moved here with their oddball father, John Leary (DeVito), after the death of their mother (Andrea Marcovicci, glimpsed only in stylized flashbacks). Leary gets a gig as host of a latenight show that recycles old horror movies. But he drinks too much and is often on the brink of losing his job.

The real menace is saved for the final act, when deranged war vet Strick (Gary Sinise) kidnaps Dylan and then, like some monster from a real horror flick, comes after Jack.

....

■ JACOB'S LADDER

1990, 113 MINS, US ◇ ⚉ ⊙
Dir Adrian Lyne   *Prod* Alan Marshall   *Scr* Bruce Joel
Rubin   *Ph* Jeffrey L. Kimball   *Ed* Tom Rolf, Peter
Amundsun, B.J. Sears   *Mus* Maurice Jarre
Art Dir Brian Morris
● Tim Robbins, Elizabeth Pena, Danny Aiello, Matt Craven, Ving Rhames, Macaulay Culkin (Carolco)

Jacob's Ladder means to be a harrowing thriller about a Vietnam vet (Tim Robbins) bedeviled by strange visions, but the $40 million production is dull, unimaginative and pretentious.

Writer Bruce Joel Rubin (*Ghost*) telegraphs his plot developments and can't resist throwing in supernatural elements that prompt giggles at the most unfortunate moments. Right from the battlefield prolog in Vietnam, where members of Robbins' battalion act strangely and throw fits, it's clear that somebody messed with their brains.

Robbins, whose earnest and touching performance belongs in a better film, spends most of the story struggling to understand the 'demons' pursuing him back home in NY. Director Adrian Lyne adds nothing fresh visually or dramatically to previous film and TV depictions of troubled Viet vets' psyches.

Living in a dim, dingy apartment and working in a dronelike postal service job, Robbins was wrongly told by the army that he was discharged on psychological grounds. His very existence denied by the Veterans Administration, he thinks he's possessed, but eventually pieces together the truth with the help of his battalion buddies.

....

■ JAGGED EDGE

1985, 108 MINS, US ◇ ⚉ ⊙
Dir Richard Marquand   *Prod* Martin Ransohoff   *Scr* Joe
Eszterhas   *Ph* Matthew F. Leonetti   *Ed* Sean Barton,
Conrad Buff   *Mus* John Barry   *Art Dir* Gene Callahan
● Jeff Bridges, Glenn Close, Peter Coyote, Robert Loggia, Leigh Taylor-Young, John Dehner (Columbia)

A well-crafted, hardboiled mystery by Joe Eszterhas, with sharp performances by murder suspect Jeff Bridges and tough-but-smitten defense attorney Glenn Close.

The murder victim was a socialite and heiress. Her husband (Bridges), a very upwardly mobile San Francisco newspaper publisher, now owns his wife's fortune. Embittered by past experiences in criminal law, Close is pressed to defend Bridge, once he convinces her of his innocence. Then she falls in love with him. Triple-Oscar nominees Bridges and Close play a balancing act that is both glossy and psychologically interesting.

Courtroom drama, which is becoming increasingly hard to make on the big screen, consumes perhaps 30% of this film and, for the most part, the benchmarks are compelling.

Pic, in quick strokes, raises jagged questions about an imperfect justice system. Although the conflicting parameters of mother-lover-professional woman are becoming naggingly repetitive, the Close persona is a fully realized and dimensional one.
□ 1985: Nomination: Best Supp. Actor (Robert Loggia)

....

■ JAILHOUSE ROCK

1957, 96 MINS, US ⚉ ⊙
Dir Richard Thorpe   *Prod* Pandro S. Berman   *Scr* Guy
Trosper   *Ph* Robert Bronner   *Ed* Ralph E. Winters
Mus Jeff Alexander (sup.)   *Art Dir* William A. Horning,
Randall Duell
● Elvis Presley, Judy Tyler, Mickey Shaughnessy, Vaughn Taylor, Jennifer Holden, Dean Jones (M-G-M/Avon)

The production carries a contrived plot but under Richard Thorpe's deft direction unfolds smoothly. Director has been wise enough to allow Elvis Presley (in his third starrer) his own style, and build around him.

Narrative [from a story by Ned Young] intros Presley as a hot-tempered but affable youngster who goes to prison on a manslaughter rap after being involved in a bar-room fight. In stir he's cell-mated with Mickey Shaughnessy, who teaches him his dog-eat-dog philosophy, and also some singing tricks. Released, but now embittered and cynical, he claws his way to fame in the music world, riding alike over friend and foe, even Judy Tyler, a music exploitation agent who has helped in his discovery and is partnered with him in their own record company.

Singer is on for six songs, top being the title production number in a prison setting. Star receives good support, Tyler – killed in an auto accident [soon after film completed] – coming through nicely and Shaughnessy hard-hitting as the tough ex-con who becomes Presley's flunky after following youngster in release from prison.

....

■ JAKE SPEED

1986, 100 MINS, US ◇ ⚉ ⊙
Dir Andrew Lane   *Prod* Andrew Lane, Wayne Crawford,
William Fay   *Scr* Wayne Crawford, Andrew Lane
Ph Bryan Loftus   *Ed* Fred Stafford, Michael Ripps
Mus Mark Snow   *Art Dir* Norm Baron
● Wayne Crawford, Dennis Christopher, Karen Kopins, John Hurt, Leon Ames, Donna Pescow (New World)

Jake Speed is fun – a deliberately mindless adventure that keeps tongue firmly in cheek.

A family is worried about their daughter's disappearance in Paris. Pop wanders in, saying they ought to hire Jake Speed, a hero of paperback thrillers to find her. Pop gets sent to bed because he's obviously senile.

But daughter number two gets a note to meet Jake Speed at a seedy bar. She goes, meets Speed and his sidekick author Remo.

After a hilarious false start once in Africa (where the daughter has been sent to), the trio crashes the den of the international white slavers lorded over by a malicious and deliciously evil John Hurt.

Speed is well played by a heavy-lidded and

laconic Wayne Crawford who talks as an old-fashioned paperback hero would – in cliches.

● ●

■ JAMAICA INN

1939, 99 MINS, UK ⓥ
Dir Alfred Hitchcock   *Prod* Erich Pommer, Charles Laughton   *Scr* Sidney Gilliat, Joan Harrison, J.B. Priestley   *Ph* Harry Stradling, Bernard Knowles   *Ed* Robert Hamer   *Mus* Eric Fenby   *Art Dir* Tom Morahan
● Charles Laughton, Maureen O'Hara, Emlyn Williams, Robert Newton, Basil Radford, Mervyn Johns (Mayflower)

Superb direction, excellent casting, expressive playing and fine production offset an uneven screenplay to make *Jamaica Inn* a gripping version of the Daphne du Maurier novel. Since it's frankly a blood-'n'-thunder melodrama, the story makes no pretense at complete plausibility.

Yarn concerns a gang of smugglers and shipwreckers on the Cornish coast in the early 19th century and the district squire who is their undercover brains. Young naval officer joins the band to secure evidence against them and a young girl who comes from Ireland to stay with her aunt saves him from being hanged by the desperadoes.

Balance of the story is a development of the chase technique. Atmosphere of the seacoast and the moors is strikingly recreated and the action scenes have a headlong rush. Withal, there are frequent bits of brilliant camera treatment and injections of salty humor. It's a typical Alfred Hitchcock direction job.

Charles Laughton has a colorful, sinister part in the villainous squire with a strain of insanity. Maureen O'Hara is a looker and plays satisfactorily in the limited confines of the ingenue part.

● ●

■ JAMES BROTHERS, THE

See: The True Story of Jesse James

● ●

■ JANE EYRE

1944, 97 MINS, US ⓥ ⊙
Dir Robert Stevenson   *Prod* William Goetz   *Scr* Aldous Huxley, Robert Stevenson, John Houseman   *Ph* George Barnes   *Ed* Walter Thompson   *Mus* Bernard Herrmann   *Art Dir* William Pereira
● Orson Welles, Joan Fontaine, Margaret O'Brien, Peggy Ann Garner, Agnes Moorehead, Elizabeth Taylor (20th Century-Fox)

Charlotte Bronte's Victorian novel, *Jane Eyre*, reaches the screen in a drama that is as intense on celluloid as it is on the printed page. This picture has taken liberties with the novel that may be chalked off to cinematic expediency, but there is, nonetheless, a certain script articulation that closer heed to the book could possibly not have achieved.

Jane Eyre is the story of a girl who, after a childhood during which she was buffeted about in an orphanage, secures a position as governess to the ward of one Edward Rochester, sire of an English manor house called Thornfield. Jane Eyre eventually falls in love with him, and he with her. When their wedding is interrupted by a man who accuses Rochester of already being married, there is divulged the secret that Rochester has kept for many years.

Joan Fontaine and Orson Welles are excellent, though the latter is frequently inaudible in the slur of his lines. It is a large cast and one that acquits itself well. Notable in the support are Henry Daniell, as Brocklehurst, the cruel overseer of the orphanage; Margaret O'Brien, the ward of Rochester.

● ●

■ JANE EYRE

1971, 110 MINS, UK ◇ ⓥ
Dir Delbert Mann   *Prod* Frederick Brogger   *Scr* Jack Pulman   *Ph* Paul Beeson   *Ed* Peter Boita   *Mus* John Williams   *Art Dir* Alex Vetchinsky

● George C. Scott, Susannah York, Ian Bannen, Jack Hawkins, Nyree Dawn Porter, Rachel Kempson (Omnibus/Sagittarius)

Charlotte Bronte's tearjerker is put over stolidly and fails to touch and move the emotions as fluently as the 1943 version with Joan Fontaine and Orson Welles.

Delbert Mann's direction and Jack Pulman's screenplay both tend to play up incident rather than characters underlining that, despite its fame, Bronte's story is pretty much a novelletish theme.

Casting is by no means right. George C. Scott as Rochester tends to play the role rather like Patton on a well-deserved leave, and fails to bring out the smouldering romanticism, mixed with tyranny and selfishness, which characterized Rochester, though his first scene with Jane has a sharp, sardonic tang. Since Jane Eyre is constantly described as plain, and as Susannah York who plays the heroine, patently isn't plain, credibility is strained. York gives a pleasant but not wholly convincing portrayal.

● ●

■ JANITOR, THE

See: Eyewitness

● ●

■ JANUARY MAN, THE

1989, 97 MINS, US ◇ ⓥ ⊙
Dir Pat O'Connor   *Prod* Norman Jewison, Ezra Swerdlow   *Scr* John Patrick Shanley   *Ph* Jerzy Zielinski   *Ed* Lou Lombardo   *Mus* Marvin Hamlisch   *Art Dir* Philip Rosenberg
● Kevin Kline, Susan Sarandon, Mary Elizabeth Mastrantonio, Harvey Keitel, Danny Aiello, Rod Steiger (M-G-M)

Kevin Kline as an unorthodox but indispensable detective tracking a serial strangler infuses this improbable Gotham-set romantic policier with personality.

Kline is Nick Starkey, a disgraced cop who can't get along with the establishment but is summoned from exile to crack an unsolvable crime. Kline has been hung out to dry on dubious allegations of graft by his mean-spirited brother, Police Commissioner Frank Starkey (Harvey Keitel), and brutish Mayor Eamon Flynn (Rod Steiger).

Apparently he's also the only investigative genius in the entire NYPD, which Kline agrees to rejoin if he's allowed to cook dinner for Keitel's haughty, social climbing wife Christine (Susan Sarandon). Kline also strikes sexual sparks with the mayor's daughter Bernadette (Mary Elizabeth Mastrantonio) whose friend was murdered by the break-and-enter strangler.

There 's a false ending that does little to make up for the picture's dearth of dry-throat suspense. Steiger has some volcanic moments in this comeback turn, while the other supporting actors provide serviceable foils for Kline's quirky cop.

New York is so bereft of grit and character that it could be Toronto – which it often is, with the exception of the Times Square opening and pick-up shots.

● ●

■ JAPANESE WAR BRIDE

1952, 91 MINS, US
Dir King Vidor   *Prod* Joseph Bernhard, Anson Hall   *Scr* Catherine Turney   *Ph* Lionel Lindon   *Ed* Terry Morse   *Mus* Emil Newman, Arthur Lange   *Art Dir* Danny Hall
● Shirley Yamaguchi, Don Taylor, Cameron Mitchell, Marie Windsor, James Bell (Bernhard/20th Century-Fox)

Shirley Yamaguchi, Japanese film star, plays the title role and fits naturally into the story. Her restrained personality is ingratiating. Don Taylor is good as the Korean War veteran who marries her and brings her to Salinas, Cal, for a new life in an American farming community where public opinion is prejudiced.

The Catherine Turney script, based on a story by Anson Bond, brings the bride up against such pitfalls as reluctant acceptance by the groom's family, a jealous sister-in-law, anti-Jap feeling among some of the farmers and similar standard dramatic angles that go with plot. Story comes to its head when the sister-in-law spreads rumor that the child born to the couple was actually fathered by a neighboring Japanese farmer.

● ●

■ JASON AND THE ARGONAUTS

1963, 104 MINS, UK ◇ ⓥ ⊙
Dir Don Chaffey   *Prod* Charles H. Schneer   *Scr* Jan Read, Beverley Cross   *Ph* Wilkie Cooper   *Ed* Maurice Rootes   *Mus* Bernard Herrmann   *Art Dir* Geoffrey Drake
● Todd Armstrong, Nancy Kovack, Gary Raymond, Laurence Naismith, Niall MacGinnis, Douglas Wilmer (Columbia)

Jason and the Argonauts stems from the Greek mythological legend of Jason and his voyage at the helm of the Argo in search of the Golden Fleece. The $3 million film has a workable scenario and has been directed resourcefully and spiritedly by Don Chaffey, under whose leadership a colorful cast performs with zeal.

Among the spectacular mythological landscape and characters brought to life through the ingenuity of illusionist Ray Harryhausen are a remarkably lifelike mobile version of the colossal bronze god, Talos; fluttery personifications of the bat-winged Harpies; a miniature representation of the 'crashing rocks' through which Jason's vessel must cruise; a menacing version of the seven-headed Hydra; a batch of some astonishingly active skeletons who materialize out of the teeth of Hydra; and a yare replica of the Argo itself.

Handsome Todd Armstrong does a commendable job as Jason and Nancy Kovak is beautiful as his Medea.

● ●

■ JASON LIVES
FRIDAY THE 13TH PART VI

1986, 87 MINS, US ◇ ⓥ ⊙
Dir Tom McLoughlin   *Prod* Don Behrns   *Scr* Tom McLoughlin   *Ph* Jon Kranhouse   *Ed* Bruce Green   *Mus* Harry Manfredini   *Art Dir* Joseph T. Garrity
● Thom Mathews, Jennifer Cooke, David Kagen, Renee Jones, Kerry Noonan, Tom Fridley (Paramount/Terror)

Jason lives, but 18 other people die in this sixth entry in *Friday the 13th* series. Body count works out to an average of one corpse every 4.83 minutes.

Vivid and vigorous opening sequence has two dopey kids digging up the grave of the Masked One on a dark and stormy night to make sure he's dead. A bolt of lightning brings the insatiable killer back to life. Believing old Jason croaked for good in *Part V*, the powers-that-be in Crystal Lake refuse to believe Tommy (Thom Mathews) when he insists a new rampage has begun.

But the sheriff's pert teenage daughter (Jennifer Cooke) thinks Tommy's cute, so she gets him out of jail and they head back to the summer camp where it all began to try to head off Jason before he starts playing with all the little kids there.

Writer-director Tom McLoughlin, who made the scare entry *One Dark Night*, puts comic spin on some of the predictable material and turns in a reasonably slick performance under the circumstances.

● ●

■ JAWS

1975, 124 MINS, US ◇ ⓥ ⊙
Dir Steven Spielberg   *Prod* Richard D. Zanuck, David Brown   *Scr* Peter Benchley, Carl Gottlieb, [John Milius]   *Ph* Bill Butler   *Ed* Verna Fields   *Mus* John Williams   *Art Dir* Joseph Alves Jr

● Roy Scheider, Robert Shaw, Richard Dreyfuss, Lorraine Gary, Murray Hamilton, Carl Gottlieb (Universal)

Jaws, Peter Benchley's bestseller about a killer shark and a tourist beach town, is an $8 million film of consummate suspense, tension and terror. It stars Roy Scheider as the town's police chief torn between civic duty and the mercantile politics of resort tourism; Robert Shaw, absolutely magnificent as a coarse fisherman finally hired to locate the Great White Shark; and Richard Dreyfuss, in another excellent characterization as a likeable young scientist.

The fast-moving film engenders enormous suspense as the shark attacks a succession of people; the creature is not even seen for about 82 minutes, and a subjective camera technique makes his earlier forays excruciatingly terrifying all the more for the invisibility. The final hour of the film shifts from the town to a boat where the three stars track the shark, and vica versa.

The adroit casting extended through the ranks of supporting players, notably Lorraine Gary, very good as Scheider's wife, and Murray Hamilton, excellent as the town mayor.

John Williams' haunting score adds to the mood of impending horror. All other production credits are superior.
□ 1975: Best Sound, Original Score, Editing.
□ Nomination: Best Picture

••••••••••••••••••••••••••••••••

■ **JAWS 2**

1978, 117 MINS, US ◇ ⓥ ⊙
Dir Jeannot Szwarc *Prod* Richard D. Zanuck, David Brown *Scr* Carl Gottlieb, Howard Sackler *Ph* Michael Butler *Ed* Neil Travis *Mus* John Williams *Art Dir* Joe Alves
● Roy Scheider, Lorraine Gary, Murray Hamilton, Joseph Mascolo, Jeffrey Kramer, Collin Wilcox (Universal)

Despite a notable but effective change in story emphasis, *Jaws 2* is a worthy successor in horror, suspense and terror to its 1975 smash progenitor.

The Peter Benchley characters of offshore island police chief Roy Scheider, loyal spouse Lorraine Gary, temporizing mayor Murray Hamilton and Gee-whiz deputy Jeffrey Kramer are used as the adult pegs for the very good screenplay. The targets of terror, and the principal focus of audience empathy, are scores of happy teenagers.

So strong is the emphasis on adolescent adrenalin that *Jaws 2* might well be described as the most expensive film ($20 million) that American International Pictures never made.

Suffice to say that the story again pits Scheider's concern for safety against the indifference of the town elders as evidence mounts that there's another great white shark out there in the shallow waters. Evermore complicated teenage jeopardy leads to the climactic showdown with a buried cable.

••••••••••••••••••••••••••••••••

■ **JAWS III**

1983, 97 MINS, US ◇ ⓥ ⊙
Dir Joe Alves *Prod* Robert Hitzig *Scr* Richard Matheson, Carl Gottlieb *Ph* James A. Contner *Ed* Randy Roberts *Mus* Alan Parker *Art Dir* Woods Mackintosh
● Dennis Quaid, Bess Armstrong, Simon MacCorkindale, Louis Gossett Jr, John Putch, Lea Thompson (Universal/Landsburg)

The *Jaws* cycle has reached its nadir with this surprisingly tepid [Arrivision] 3-D version.

Gone are Roy Scheider, the summer resort of Amity, and even the ocean. They have been replaced by Florida's Sea World, a lagoon and an Undersea Kingdom that entraps a 35-foot Great White, and a group of young people who run the tourist sea park.

The picture [from a screen story by Guerdon Trueblood] includes two carry-over

characters from the first two *Jaws*, Scheider's now-grown sons, who are played by nominal star Dennis Quaid as the older brother turned machine engineer and kid brother John Putch.

Femme cast is headed by Bess Armstrong as an intrepid marine biologist who lives with Quaid.

Director Joe Alves, who was instrumental in the design of the first *Jaws* shark and was the unsung production hero in both the first two pictures, fails to linger long enough on the Great White.

••••••••••••••••••••••••••••••••

■ **JAWS
THE REVENGE**

1987, 100 MINS, US ◇ ⓥ ⊙
Dir Joseph Sargent *Prod* Joseph Sargent *Scr* Michael de Guzman *Ph* John McPherson *Ed* Michael Brown *Mus* Michael Small *Art Dir* John J. Lloyd
● Michael Caine, Lorraine Gary, Lance Guest, Mario Van Peebles, Karen Young, Judith Barsi (Universal)

Story for part four picks up after the Roy Scheider character of *Jaws* and *Jaws 2* has died of a heart attack. Lorraine Gary nicely reprises her role as the now-widowed Ellen Brody, living a peaceful life in the New England resort town of Amity. One of her sons, a deputy sheriff, is killed by a shark while out in the channel on a routine complaint.

Ellen heads down to the Bahamas to be with her other son, marine biologist Michael (Lance Guest), and his family (Karen Young makes the most out of the small role of Michael's wife), and tries to convince him to quit his job because she's sure 'it' is out to get the family.

Michael Caine is Ellen's delightfully irresponsible suitor, but doesn't get enough screen time to really develop the character. After the shark practically walks up the beach to get a bite out of the third generation Brody (Judith Barsi), Ellen goes after 'it' by herself.

Pacing leaves a lot to be desired and the moment-of-attack sequences, full of jagged cuts and a great deal of noise, more closely resemble the view from inside a washing machine.

••••••••••••••••••••••••••••••••

■ **JAZZ ON A SUMMER'S DAY**

1959, 78 MINS, US ◇ ⓥ
Dir Bert Stern *Ph* Bert Stern, Ray Phelan, Courtney Hafela *Ed* Aram Avakian *Mus* Hoagy Carmichael, Duke Ellington, Count Basie, Seymour Simons, Gerald Marks, Thelonious Monk, Chuck Berry
● (Raven)

Outstanding feature-length documentary centered around the Newport Jazz Festival. It's a document of the medium, spanning most of the jazz styles and including a rich selection of top performers and material. It's Americana, and a document of its time as well via observation of audiences and the life surrounding the Newport event, not least the neatly-integrated footage concerning the America Cup Yacht Races.

Structure of the film basically follows that of the two-day event around which it centers, with occasional digressions, over the jazz soundtrack, to other nearby scenes such as the cup races, children playing, wave and water effects, reflections, all neatly matched to mood of motif being played. Juxtaposition is sometimes humorous, sometimes ironic, at others merely illustrative, but always deft.

On-the-spot lensing under difficult lighting conditions, both daytime and night-time, is often incredibly good. Some unprecedented effects are achieved by cameramen Bert Stern, Ray Phelan, and Courtney Hafela (under Stern's imaginative and stylish guidance). Similar plaudits also for an outstanding (magnetic) sound recording job, all part of near-perfect teamwork on pic.

••••••••••••••••••••••••••••••••

■ **JAZZ SINGER, THE**

1927, 88 MINS, US ⓥ ⊙
Dir Alan Crosland *Scr* Al Cohn, Jack Jarmuth *Ph* Hal Mohr *Ed* Harold McCord
● Al Jolson, May McAvoy, Warner Oland, Eugenie Besserer, William Demarest, Otto Lederer (Warner)

Undoubtedly the best thing Vitaphone has ever put on the screen. The combination of the religious heart interest story [based on the play by Samson Raphaelson] and Jolson's singing 'Kol Nidre' in a synagog while his father is dying and two 'Mammy' lyrics as his mother stands in the wings of the theatre, and later as she sits in the first row, carries abundant power and appeal.

But *The Jazz Singer* minus Vitaphone [synchronized sound system] is something else again. There's really no love interest in the script, except between mother and son.

Al Jolson, when singing, is Jolson. There are six instances of this, each running from two to three minutes. When he's without that instrumental spur Jolson is camera-conscious. But as soon as he gets under cork the lens picks up that spark of individual personality solely identified with him. That much goes with or without Vitaphone.

The picture is all Jolson, although Alan Crosland, directing, has creditably dodged the hazard of over-emphasizing the star as well as refraining from laying it on too thick in the scenes between the mother and the boy. The film dovetails splendidly, which speaks well for those component parts of the technical staff. Cast support stands out in the persons of Eugenie Besserer, as the mother; Otto Lederer, as a friend of the family; and Warner Oland as the father.
□ 1927/28: Special Award (pioneer talking picture).
□ Nominations: Best Adapted Screenplay, Engineering Effects

••••••••••••••••••••••••••••••••

■ **JAZZ SINGER, THE**

1952, 106 MINS, US ◇
Dir Michael Curtiz *Prod* Louis F. Edelman *Scr* Frank Davis, Leonard Stern, Lewis Meltzer *Ph* Carl Guthrie *Ed* Alan Crosland Jr *Mus* Ray Heindorf (dir.) *Art Dir* Leo K. Kuter
● Danny Thomas, Peggy Lee, Mildred Dunnock, Eduard Franz, Tom Tully, Allyn Joslyn (Warner)

Warners' remake of Al Jolson's 1927 Vitaphone film hit is still sentimental, sometimes overly so. A drama with songs importantly spotted with beautiful Technicolor cloaking.

Peggy Lee, in her first feature film lead, sparks the song offerings in sock style, and is okay in the acting demands as a musical comedy-record star who loves and promotes the career of a cantor's son (Danny Thomas). Latter is excellent in a sentimental part, making the most of several genuine tearjerker sequences.

Eduard Franz is the cantor expecting his son to follow in his footsteps, but the updated plot has Thomas returning from two years in Korea with showbiz in mind. He breaks with his father, and goes to New York for a precarious career-launching with the help of Lee, already established.
□ 1952: Nomination: Best Scoring of a Musical Picture

••••••••••••••••••••••••••••••••

■ **JAZZ SINGER, THE**

1980, 115 MINS, US ◇ ⓥ ⊙
Dir Richard Fleischer, [Sidney J. Furie] *Prod* Jerry Leider *Scr* Herbert Baker *Ph* Isidore Mankofsky *Ed* Frank J. Urioste, Maury Winetrobe *Mus* Neil Diamond, Leonard Rosenman *Art Dir* Harry Horner
● Neil Diamond, Laurence Olivier, Lucie Arnaz, Catlin Adams, Paul Nicholas (AFD/Leider)

This third screen version of *The Jazz Singer* asks the same question as the 1927 Al Jolson

J

394

history maker and the 1952 Danny Thomas update – can a nice cantor's son break with family and tradition to make it as a popular entertainer? No one's going to get sweaty palms waiting for the answer, as Samson Raphaelson's venerable chestnut lacks urgency and plausible incidental detail.

Screenplay, credited to Herbert Baker, with adaptation by Stephen H. Foreman, follows general line of earlier incarnations. However, elimination of the mother character in favor of a traditional wife k.o.'s any attempt at a reprise of 'Mammy'.

Richard Fleischer took over midway through shooting, and the best that can be said for the direction is that there's no disruption of the by-the-numbers style.

. . . .

■ JENNIFER EIGHT

1992, 124 MINS, US ◇ ⑩ ⊙
Dir Bruce Robinson   *Prod* Gary Lucchesi, David Wimbury   *Scr* Bruce Robinson   *Ph* Conrad Hall
Ed Conrad Buff   *Mus* Christopher Young
Art Dir Richard Macdonald
● Andy Garcia, Uma Thurman, Lance Henriksen, Kathy Baker, Kevin Conway, John Malkovich (Paramount)

Jennifer Eight is an unusually intelligent and unexploitative thriller, notable for avoiding most standard suspense film contrivances.

British writer-director Bruce Robinson's script possesses all the elements for yet another product of the *Fatal Attraction-Basic Instinct* cookie cutter: a burned-out big-city homicide cop getting involved with a mysterious blonde, brutal attacks on women, gruff career cops who resent the probing maverick, an opportunity for female retribution and, in the bargain, a couple of unfortunate plot holes.

Andy Garcia toplines as a wreck of a detective who joins a small-town Northern California police force after crashing and burning in the LA fast lane. His sister (Kathy Baker) lives there with cop hubby (Lance Henriksen), and Garcia becomes latter's partner in the search for a woman whose hand is found – in a stunningly shot nocturnal opening sequence – at a dump.

With little evidence to go on, Garcia postulates that the killing is just the latest in a string of murders. Next target could be Uma Thurman, who's blind like the most recent victim and was the last person to 'see' her alive.

Lenser Conrad Hall quite possibly surpasses himself here with a virtuoso job highlighted by numerous sequences lit only by flashlights or other single light sources.

Best of all is Thurman, who very touchingly conveys the vulnerability of the blind femme without for a moment begging for audience sympathy.

. . . .

■ JENNIFER ON MY MIND

1971, 90 MINS, US ◇
Dir Noel Black   *Prod* Bernard Schwartz   *Scr* Erich Segal   *Ph* Andrew Laszlo   *Ed* Jack Wheeler
Mus Stephen J. Lawrence   *Art Dir* Ben Edwards
● Michael Brandon, Tippy Walker, Lou Gilbert, Steve Vinovich, Peter Bonerz, Renee Taylor (United Artists)

Jennifer on My Mind is a black comedy about an aimless wealthy Jewish youth who falls in love with a bored and impulsive upperclass suburban girl whom he meets in Venice. Story unravels through a series of flashbacks narrated by the youth, Marcus, speaking into a tape recorder as he attempts to cope with the fact that he has killed his love, Jennifer, when in response to her painful pleading, he reluctantly injected her with heroin.

Film, written by Erich Segal and directed by Noel Black, is sort of a cross between their respective previous features, *Love Story* and *Pretty Poison* with an added sprinkling of 'relevant' social commentary.

The delightfully ridiculous plot, mock-sentimental narration, absurd dialog, infectious syrupy music and intermittent idyllic interludes all parody *Love Story*. And yet, like *Pretty Poison*, this is a potpourri of disarming satire, black comedy and poignancy that creates a strangely haunting aura.

Michael Brandon, as Marcus, is charmingly boyish and natural. Tippy Walker, as Jennifer, comes across with a bitchy ethereal allure.

. . . .

■ JEOPARDY

1953, 68 MINS, US
Dir John Sturges   *Prod* Sol Baer Fielding   *Scr* Mel Dinelli   *Ph* Victor Milner   *Ed* Newell P. Kimlin
Mus Dimitri Tiomkin   *Art Dir* Cedric Gibbons, William Ferran
● Barbara Stanwyck, Barry Sullivan, Ralph Meeker, Lee Aaker (M-G-M)

The misadventures that befall a family of three vacationing at an isolated coast section of Lower California have been put together in an unpretentious, tightly-drawn suspense melodrama.

There's no waste motion or budget dollars in the presentation. Plot has a tendency to play itself out near the finale, but otherwise is expertly shaped in the screenplay from a story by Maurice Zimm.

Barbara Stanwyck, Barry Sullivan and their small son (Lee Asker) are vacationing at a deserted Mexican beach. An accident pins Sullivan's leg under a heavy piling that falls from a rotten jetty. Knowing the rising tide will cover him within four hours Stanwyck takes off in the family car to find either help or a rope strong enough to raise the piling. The mission is sidetracked when she comes across Ralph Meeker, a desperate escaped convict. He takes her prisoner and commandeers the car.

The performances by the four-member cast are very good, being expertly fitted to the change of mood from the happy, carefree start to the danger of the accident and the menace of the criminal. Scenes of Sullivan and young Aaker together bravely facing the peril of the tide while Stanwyck frantically seeks help are movingly done.

. . . .

■ JEREMIAH JOHNSON

1972, 110 MINS, US ◇ ⑩ ⊙
Dir Sydney Pollack   *Prod* Joe Wizan   *Scr* John Milius, Edward Anhalt   *Ph* Duke Callaghan   *Ed* Thomas Stanford   *Mus* John Rubinstein, Tim McIntire
Art Dir Ted Haworth
● Robert Redford, Will Geer, Stefan Gierasch, Delle Bolton, Josh Albee, Joaquin Martinez (Warner)

Jeremiah Johnson, based on Vardis Fisher's novel *Mountain Man* and a story, *Crow Killer*, by Raymond W. Thorp and Robert Bunker, is the sort of man of whom legends or sagas are made. Pic leans towards the latter as it meticulously, sans grandiloquence, lays out the life of a male dropout, circa 1825, who decides to live in the Rocky Mountains as a trapper.

Director Sydney Pollack has given a skilled, observant mounting as he carefully allows the man to grow in experience and knowhow.

Robert Redford, as Johnson, has a solid stamina, a fine feel for the speech of the time, giving an auto-didactic flair as he sometimes comments the actions. He begins to trade with the Indians and wins the esteem of a Crow nation chief to whom he gives a present, to find he must accept the chief's daughter in return.

The film has its own force and beauty and the only carp might lie in its not always clear exegesis of the humanistic spirit and freedom most of its characters are striving for.

. . . .

■ JEREMY

1973, 90 MINS, US ◇
Dir Arthur Barron   *Prod* Elliott Kastner   *Scr* Arthur Barron   *Ph* Paul Goldsmith   *Ed* Zina Voynow, Nina Feinberg   *Mus* Lee Holdridge, Joseph Brook
Art Dir Peter Bocour
● Robby Benson, Glynnis O'Connor, Len Bari, Leonard Cimino, Ned Wilson, Chris Bohn (Kenasset/United Artists)

Jeremy, played with adolescent rumpled and bumbling charm by Robby Benson, falls for a newcomer to his school, reserved but lovely little child-woman Glynnis O'Connor. Jeremy plays the cello, loves horses. The girl, Susan, studies classical dancing. Their idyll is shattered by her father deciding to leave New York and go back to Detroit.

Arthur Barron does not force things and handles this slight but glowing pic with insight. Jeremy's waiting outside her house in the morning and faking running into her and admitting it, their visit to horses' training, their first love, done with modesty and the right flair, and their final disarray and her leaving are executed touchingly.

. . . .

■ JERK, THE

1979, 104 MINS, US ◇ ⑩ ⊙
Dir Carl Reiner   *Prod* David V. Picker, William E. McEuen   *Scr* Steve Martin, Carl Gottlieb, Michael Elias   *Ph* Victor J. Kemper   *Ed* Bud Molin   *Mus* Jack Elliott
Art Dir Jack Collis
● Steve Martin, Bernadette Peters, Catlin Adams, Mabel King, Richard Ward (Universal/Aspen)

Pic is an artless, non-stop barrage of off-the-wall situations, funny and unfunny jokes, generally effective and sometimes hilarious sight gags and bawdy non sequiturs.

The premise of *The Jerk* can be found in one of Steve Martin's more famous routines. Upon receiving the stunning news that he's the adopted, not natural, son of black parents Martin leaves home with his dog to make his way in the world. Opening sequences with the family are among the best.

Martin's odyssey through contemporary America sees him taking odd jobs, such as a gas station attendant for proprietor Jackie Mason and as the driver of an amusement park train, and taking up with women.

But lunacy is never strayed from very far, as Martin strikes it rich as the inventor of a ridiculous nose support device for eyeglasses. Hilarity ebbs during his decline and fall.

. . . .

■ JERSEY GIRL

1992, 95 MINS, US ◇ ⑩ ⊙
Dir David Burton Morris   *Prod* David Madden, Nicole Seguin, Staffan Ahrenberg   *Scr* Gina Wendkos   *Ph* Ron Fortunato   *Ed* Norman Hollyn   *Mus* Misha Segal
Art Dir Lester Cohen
● Jami Gertz, Dylan McDermott, Sheryl Lee, Joseph Mazzello, Joseph Bologna, Aida Turturro (Electric/Interscope)

Jami Gertz gives a winning perf in *Jersey Girl*, an unoriginal variation on such Italo-Yank romances as *Moonstruck*.

Gertz is the prototypical young woman from New Jersey, living with her dad Joseph Bologna (who fears her becoming an old maid) and working in a day care center. She spends much of her time hanging out at the local Bendix Diner with her pals Aida Turturro, Molly Price and Star Jasper.

Script's main theme is that old standby: get out of your provincial rut and blossom. Instead of the *Working Girl* approach, Gertz takes a more old-fashioned route, trying to win some young hunk (Dylan McDermott) from Manhattan.

Very attractively lensed by Ron Fortunato, Gertz shows a big talent in her first top-billed film appearance. McDermott certainly looks the part but operates a notch lower. As tough-talking buddy Cookie, Price is a terrific scene-stealer.

••••••••••••••••••••••••

■ JERUSALEM FILE, THE

1972, 95 MINS, US ◇ ⑰
Dir John Flynn   *Prod* Ram Ben Efraim   *Scr* Troy Kennedy Martin   *Ph* Raoul Coutard, Brian Probyn   *Ed* Norman Wanstall   *Mus* John Scott   *Art Dir* Peter Williams
● Bruce Davison, Nicol Williamson, Daria Halprin, Donald Pleasence, Ian Hendry, Koya Yair Rubin (Sparta/Leisure)

This minor effort, shot entirely on location in Israel, particularly Jerusalem and Tel Aviv University, is almost as confused in its production as it is in its political message. The latter, presumably, is meant to be an example of university student idealists combating Establishment rules and regulations. What it comes off as, instead, is making an American student (albeit, a pretty stupid one) the deus ex machina for some wholesale slaughter of both Israeli students and their Arabian counterparts.

For students, indeed, this is a most inviting school where a girl student (Daria Halprin) can live openly with one of her instructors (Nicol Williamson). There's little academic work shown. Purportedly archaeology students, there are some fast shots of a small excavation and an even faster remark by Williamson to some 'interesting shards on the table'.

••••••••••••••••••••••••

■ JESSE JAMES

1939, 103 MINS, US ◇ ⑰ ⊙
Dir Henry King   *Prod* Nunnally Johnson (assoc.)
Scr Nunnally Johnson   *Ph* George Barnes, W. Howard Greene   *Ed* Barbara McLean   *Mus* Louis Silvers (dir.)
Art Dir William Darling, George Dudley
● Tyrone Power, Henry Fonda, Nancy Kelly, Randolph Scott, Brian Donlevy, John Carradine (20th Century-Fox)

Jesse James, notorious train and bank bandit of the late 19th century, and an important figure in the history of the midwest frontier, gets a drastic bleaching. Script by Nunnally Johnson is an excellent chore, nicely mixing human interest, dramatic suspense, romance and fine characterizations for swell entertainment.

Tyrone Power capably carries the title spot, but is pressed by Henry Fonda as his brother.

Story follows historical fact [assembled by Rosalind Schaeffer and Jo Frances James] close enough with allowance for dramatic license, hitting sidelights of James in his brushes with the law. Initial train holdup is vividly presented, with all other robberies left to imagination.

Picture starts with foreword on the ruthless manner in which railroads acquired farms for right-of-way through midwest.

••••••••••••••••••••••••

■ JESUS CHRIST SUPERSTAR

1973, 107 MINS, US ◇ ⑰ ⊙
Dir Norman Jewison   *Prod* Norman Jewison, Robert Stigwood   *Scr* Melvyn Bragg, Norman Jewison
Ph Douglas Slocombe   *Ed* Anthony Gibbs
Mus Andrew Lloyd Webber   *Art Dir* Richard MacDonald
● Ted Neeley, Carl Anderson, Yvonne Elliman, Barry Dennen, Bob Bingham, Joshua Mostel (Universal)

Norman Jewison's film version of the 1969 legit stage project in a paradoxical way is both very good and very disappointing at the same time. The abstract film concept veers from elegantly simple through forced metaphor to outright synthetic in dramatic impact.

The filming concept is that of a contemporary group of young players performing sequential production numbers in the barren desert, utitlizing sketchy props and costumes. No mob scenes a la DeMille, no heavy

production spectaculars, no familiar screen names in cameos. So far, so good. But then something happens as Carl Anderson (outstanding as Judas in the film's best performance) finds himself, in the midst of 'Damned for All Time' running away from tanks and ducking modern jet fighters. Suddenly it's *Catch 22*-time, which the very moving 'Last Supper' sequence can only counteract instead of contributing to a mounting dramatic impact.

Barry Dennen's Pontius Pilate is intrusively effective far beyond the pragmatic urbanity called for, Joshua Mostel's King Herod is less a dissolute sybarite tha a swishy, roly-poly cherub. Finally 'Superstar' blares forth with the shallow impact of an inferior imitation of Isaac Hayes.

□ 1973: Nomination: Best Adapted Score

••••••••••••••••••••••••

■ JET PILOT

1957, 112 MINS, US ◇
Dir Josef von Sternberg   *Prod* Jules Furthman   *Scr* Jules Furthman   *Ph* Winton C. Hoch   *Ed* Michael R. McAdam, Harry Marker, William M. Moore
Mus Bronislau Kaper   *Art Dir* Albert S. D'Agostino, Feild Gray
● John Wayne, Janet Leigh, Jay C. Flippen, Paul Fix, Richard Rober, Roland Winters (RKO)

Jet Pilot was made around 1950 and kept under wraps by indie film-maker Howard Hughes for unstated (but much speculated upon) reasons. Its story has a pretty, young girl as a Russian jet pilot who, on a spy mission, wings into a love match with an American airman in the United States.

Questionable is the casting of Janet Leigh. While John Wayne fits the part of a colonel in the Yank Air Force, the slick chick looks more at home in a bathing suit at Palm Springs than she does jockeying a Soviet MIG, and shooting down her own countrymen, in Russia. The incongruity would appear less glaring if *Pilot* were out to be a takeoff on secret agent stuff. But much of it is played straight.

Film opens at a US airbase in Alaska where Wayne is in charge. Leigh flies in, tells skeptic Wayne that she escaped from Russia, and is taken in tow by the colonel who gets the assignment of seeking information from her. Picture moves to Palmer Field and Palm Springs, love blossoms, marriage follows. Then it's discovered that Leigh is a spy.

••••••••••••••••••••••••

■ JEWEL OF THE NILE, THE

1985, 104 MINS, US ◇ ⑰ ⊙
Dir Lewis Teague   *Prod* Michael Douglas   *Scr* Mark Rosenthal, Lawrence Konner   *Ph* Jan De Bont
Ed Michael Ellis, Beter Boita   *Mus* Jack Nitzsche
Art Dir Richard Dawking, Gerry Knight
● Michael Douglas, Kathleen Turner, Danny DeVito, Spiros Focas, Avner Eisenberg, Paul David Magid (20th Century-Fox)

As a sequel to *Romancing the Stone*, the script of *The Jewel of the Nile* is missing the deft touch of the late Diane Thomas but Lewis Teague's direction matches the energy of the original.

Michael Douglas and Kathleen Turner again play off each other very well, but the story is much thinner. The main problem is the dialog, which retains some of the old spirit but too often relies on the trite.

Story picks up six months after *Stone's* happy ending and Douglas and Turner have begun to get on each other's nerves. She accepts an invitation from a sinister potentate (Spiros Focas) to accompany him and write a story about his pending ascendency as desert ruler.

Left behind, Douglas runs into the excitable Danny DeVito and they become unwilling allies, again in pursuit of a jewel.

••••••••••••••••••••••••

■ JEW SUSS

1934, 120 MINS, UK
Dir Lothar Mendes   *Prod* Michael Balcon   *Scr* A. R. Rawlinson   *Ph* Bernard Knowles   *Ed* Otto Ludwig
Mus Louis Levy (dir.)   *Art Dir* Alfred Junge
● Conrad Veidt, Frank Vosper, Cedric Hardwicke, Benita Hume, Gerald du Maurier, Pamela Ostrer (Gaumont-British)

It's a spectacle of no small proportions, the saga of Jew Josef Suss-Oppenheimer, who ruthlessly achieves the economic power which permits him, a truly sensitive alumnus of the ghetto, to mingle with the Wurttemberg ducal nobility.

In transmuting Lion Feuchtwanger's weighty book to the screen, director Lothar Mendes and his scriptists manifest much ingenuity and skill to paint in celluloid what the German author did in his powerful novel. They just miss in presenting the major story thread. There are too many loose skeins in the plot knitting. (Locale and period is 18th century Duchy of Wurttemberg, Germany.)

Jew Suss is all Conrad Veidt, a consummate screen artist whose histrionic skill pars the best on stage or screen. Frank Vosper as the rapacious duke is excellent. Likewise Cedric Hardwicke and Gerald du Maurier in character assignments, along with Paul Graetz as the homely philosophical Landauer and Pamela Ostrer as Naomi, Suss' daughter.

••••••••••••••••••••••••

■ JEZEBEL

1938, 100 MINS, US ⑰ ⊙
Dir William Wyler   *Prod* William Wyler   *Scr* Clements Ripley, Abem Finkel, John Huston   *Ph* Ernest Haller
Ed Warren Low   *Mus* Max Steiner   *Art Dir* Robert Haas
● Bette Davis, Henry Fonda, George Brent, Margaret Lindsay, Donald Crisp, Fay Bainter (Warner)

This just misses sock proportions. That's due to an anti-climactic development on the one hand, and a somewhat static character study of the Dixie vixen, on the other.

Against an 1852 New Orleans locale, when the dread yellow jack (yellow fever epidemic) broke out, the astute scriveners have fashioned a rather convincing study of the flower of Southern chivalry, honor and hospitality. Detracting is the fact that Bette Davis' 'Jezebel' suddenly metamorphoses into a figure of noble sacrifice and complete contriteness.

However, William Wyler's direction draws an engrossing cross-section of old southern manners and hospitality. It's undoubtedly faithful to a degree, and not without its charm. At times it's even completely captivating.

Henry Fonda and George Brent are the two whom Davis viciously pits against each other; and later, Richard Cromwell must likewise challenge the champ dueling Brent. Latter's conception of the southern gentleman who exaggeratedly arranges pistols-for-two, whether in tavern or drawing room, and with equal eclat and Dixie elan, is in keeping with what is the most virile characterization in the picture.

Particularly noteworthy is Max Steiner's expert musical score, which more than merely sets the moods.

□ 1938: Best Actress (Bette Davis), Supp. Actress (Fay Bainter).
□ Nominations: Best Picture, Cinematography, Score

••••••••••••••••••••••••

■ JFK

1991, 189 MINS, US ◇ ⑰ ⊙
Dir Oliver Stone   *Prod* A. Kitman Ho, Oliver Stone
Scr Oliver Stone, Zachary Sklar   *Ph* Robert Richardson
Ed Joe Hutshing, Pietro Scalia, Hank Corwin   *Mus* John Williams   *Art Dir* Victor Kempster
● Kevin Costner, Sissy Spacek, Joe Pesci, Tommy Lee Jones, Gary Oldman, Donald Sutherland (Warner/Ixtlan)

A rebuke to official history and a challenge to continue investigating the crime of the century, Oliver Stone's *JFK* is electric muckraking filmaking. This massive, never-boring political thriller, which most closely resembles Costa-Gavras' *Z* in style and impact, lays out just about every shred of evidence yet uncovered for the conspiracy theory surrounding the Nov. 22, 1963 assassination of President John F. Kennedy.

The Warren Report is treated as a cover-up, a myth against which the director, for lack of hard answers that never may be provided, is proposing a myth of his own.

Working in a complex, jumbled style that mixes widescreen archival footage, TV clips, black & white, slow motion, docu-drama recreations, time jumps, repeated actions from various view-points, still photos, the Zapruder film and any other technique at hand [with narration by Martin Sheen], Stone uses the sum of conspiracy theory points made by New Orleans d.a. Jim Garrison and others since to suggest as strongly as possible that Oswald was, as he claimed before he was killed, 'a patsy.'

[Script is based on the books *On the Trail of the Assassins* by Jim Garrison and *Crossfire: The Plot That Killed Kennedy* by Jim Marrs.]

Garrison (Kevin Costner) begins delving into a mysterious netherworld of right-wing, anti-Castro homosexuals populated by the bewigged David Ferrie (Joe Pesci), suave businessman Clay Shaw (Tommy Lee Jones) and unpredictable hustler Willie O'Keefe (Kevin Bacon). Garrison begins to suspect that the US government's military industrial complex initiated the killing.

Costner may not resemble the real Garrison much, and Stone no doubt slides over many of the attorney's flaws. But the actor, in a low-key but forceful performance, nicely conveys the requisite grit, curiosity and fearlessness. Sissy Spacek is stuck with almost nothing but nagging lines, complaining that his obsessive quest is driving them apart.

□ 1991: Best Cinematography, Editing.
□ Nominations: Best Picture, Director, Supp. Actor (Tommy Lee Jones), Adapted Screenplay, Original Score, Sound

....

■ JIM THORPE – ALL-AMERICAN

(UK: Man of Bronze)

1951, 107 MINS, US Ⓥ ⊙
Dir Michael Curtiz   *Prod* Everett Freeman   *Scr* Douglas Morrow, Everett Freeman   *Ph* Ernest Haller   *Ed* Folmar Blangsted   *Mus* Max Steiner
● Burt Lancaster, Charles Bickford, Steve Cochran, Phyllis Thaxter, Dick Wesson, Nestor Paiva (Warner)

One of the great stories in American sports history – the real-life yarn of Jim Thorpe, the Indian athlete – is compellingly told in *Jim Thorpe – All-American*. Only a few fictional liberties have been taken in telling of how Thorpe came off an Oklahoma reservation to establish himself as the greatest all-round athlete of modern times.

Pic re-creates a number of events from sports history. There is the sensational 13-13 tie between unbeaten gridiron Titans – Penn and Carlisle – in the duel in which Ashenbrunner of Penn stacked up against Thorpe of Carlisle. There are re-creations of the 1912 and 1924 Olympics (with an assist from stock shots). There are neatly directed sequences of Thorpe as a professional grid star, of his Herculean mastery of every track event in the book.

All these Burt Lancaster has helped capture in the spirit of the grim-visaged, moody Indian. Charles Bickford plays 'Pop' Warner, Thorpe's Carlisle mentor and friend, with restraint and credence. Phyllis Thaxter plays the white girl who became Thorpe's wife, only to divorce him when she could no longer tolerate the sullenness and despair that gripped

him following the death of their son and his subsequent athletic decline.

....

■ JINXED!

1982, 103 MINS, US ◇ Ⓥ
Dir Don Siegel   *Prod* Herb Jaffe   *Scr* Bert Blessing, David Newman   *Ph* Vilmos Zsigmond   *Ed* Doug Steward   *Mus* Bruce Roberts, Miles Goodman   *Art Dir* Ted Haworth
● Bette Midler, Ken Wahl, Rip Torn, Val Avery, Jack Elam, Benson Fong (M-G-M/United Artists/Jaffe)

They tried and tried to come up with a better title for *Jinxed!*, but somehow they kept returning to the only one that was fitting. The exclamation point emphasizes the totality of the disaster. Director Don Siegel's w.k. disillusionment with the project is fully understandable.

Idea seems to have been a darkly comic version of *The Postman Alway Rings Twice*, with perhaps a touch of *A Place in the Sun*.

Set in Loserville, USA, represented by Reno, tale presents casino dealer Ken Wahl as the hapless victim of seedy gambler Rip Torn. Once Torn sits down at his blackjack table, Wahl knows he'll soon be out of a job, such is the fantastic luck his tormentor enjoys. Torn also gives grief to his smalltime singer g.f. Bette Midler, who is sufficiently taken with Wahl's charms to rope him into a scheme, a la James M. Cain, to bump off her lover.

....

■ JOANNA

1969, 107 MINS, UK ◇
Dir Michael Sarne   *Prod* Michael S. Laughlin   *Scr* Michael Sarne   *Ph* Walter Lassally   *Ed* Norman Wanstall   *Mus* Rod McKuen   *Art Dir* Michael Wield
● Genevieve Waite, Christian Doermer, Calvin Lockhart, Donald Sutherland, Glenna Forster-Jones (20th Century-Fox/Laughlin)

White girl loves black boy, black girl loves white boy. A sometimes funny, often tearful tale of the deflowering of a scatterbrained English girl turned loose in wicked, wanton London. Director Michael Sarne's script contains too few hits and too many misses.

Genevieve Waite moves into London to study art. What she actually studies is male anatomy, mostly out of class.

Waite, with a most irritating voice, is pretty, all wide-eyed innocence even after she's introduced to London's la dolce vita by a Negro girl friend. Having devoted the best years of her life learning to put on eye makeup instead of the facts of life, it figures that Waite winds up pregnant but unwed. The knave who does her in is a Negro nightclub owner-hoodlum played well by Calvin Lockhart.

The film abounds with strange but colorful types, the most impressive being Donald Sutherland as a fatalistic young lord who's dying of leukemia. The best thing about *Joanna* is the superb color photography of Walter Lassally.

....

■ JOAN OF ARC

1948, 150 MINS, US ◇ Ⓥ ⊙
Dir Victor Fleming   *Prod* Walter Wanger   *Scr* Maxwell Anderson, Andrew Solt   *Ph* Joseph Valentine   *Ed* Frank Sullivan   *Mus* Hugo Friedhofer   *Art Dir* Richard Day
● Ingrid Bergman, Jose Ferrer, Ward Bond, Francis L. Sullivan, Cecil Kellaway (RKO/Sierra)

Joan of Arc [from the play, *Joan of Lorraine*, by Maxwell Anderson] is a big picture in every respect. It has size, color, pageantry, a bold, historic bas-relief. It has authority, conviction, an appeal to faith and a dedication to a cause that leaves little wanting. And then, of course, *Joan of Arc* has Ingrid Bergman and a dream supporting cast.

Fleming has done an exciting job in blending the symbolism, the medieval warfront heroics, and the basic dramatic elements into a generally well-sustained whole.

There are certain misfires and false keynotes which militate against the desired consistency, such as Jose Ferrer's tiptop impersonation of the Dauphin, later to become the King of France, who makes his characterization so much the complete nitwit that the audience may well wonder at the complete obeisance of Joan to this weakling sovereign, regardless of the fact he is a symbol of the realm. The churchly gradations are also script shortcomings.

The majesty of the earlier sequences is compelling almost all the way. When Joan edicts that 'our strength is in our faith', when she leads her army in the Battle of Orleans, when she is betrayed by the Burgundians in calumny with the English, when in the earlier scenes she wins the grudging alliance of the Governor of Vaucouleurs and the courtiers at Chinon, Bergman makes Joan a vivid albeit spiritual personality.

The color by Technicolor is magnificent. The production is lavish and looks every bit of its $4 million-plus.

□ 1948: Best Color Cinematography, Color Costume Design.
□ Nominations: Best Actress (Ingrid Bergman), Supp. Actor (Jose Ferrer), Color Art Direction, Editing, Scoring of a Dramatic Picture

....

■ JOE

1970, 107 MINS, US ◇ Ⓥ ⊙
Dir John G. Avildsen   *Prod* David Gil   *Scr* Norman Wexler   *Ph* John G. Avildsen   *Ed* George T. Norris
● Dennis Patrick, Peter Boyle, Susan Sarandon, Patrick McDermott, Audrey Caire, K. Callan (Cannon)

Joe deals with a NY ad agency exec (Dennis Patrick) who murders his daughter's junkie lover after the girl winds up in Bellevue suffering from an overdose of speed. Through a somewhat implausible coincidence, he is found out by a hardhat factory worker, the Joe of the title (Peter Boyle), who applauds his action as a blow struck for God and country.

The two begin a class-spanning relationship which brings them nervously together in the realization that the American dream has somehow turned sour for them.

Pretty, it's not. By concentrating on the extremist fringes of the various social elements involved, Norman Wexler's script makes audience identification well-nigh impossible and at the same time abstracts the questions in a way that gives the pic real importance.

□ 1970: Nomination: Best Original Story & Screenplay

....

■ JOE KIDD

1972, 87 MINS, US ◇ Ⓥ ⊙
Dir John Sturges   *Prod* Sidney Beckerman   *Scr* Elmore Leonard   *Ph* Bruce Surtees   *Ed* Ferris Webster   *Mus* Lalo Schifrin   *Art Dir* Alexander Golitzen, Henry Bumstead
● Clint Eastwood, Robert Duvall, John Saxon, Don Stroud, Stella Garcia, James Wainwright (Malpaso/Universal)

Not enough identity is given Clint Eastwood in a New Mexico land struggle in which no reason is apparent for his involvement, but John Sturges' direction is sufficiently compelling to keep guns popping and bodies falling.

Spectator is never entirely certain of Eastwood's status, apart from his owning a small spread and being hired to lead a party of gunmen to kill a rebellious Spanish-American who heads fight to save original Spanish land grants of his people. Elmore Leonard's script lacks proper motivation as

Eastwood throws in with the oldtimers whose land his temporary mployer is trying to take over.

Highlight of entire footage is when Eastwood and a few men run a railroad engine through the bar where some of the gunmen are holding forth and mow them down.

••••••••••••••••••••••••••••••

■ **JOE LOUIS STORY, THE**

1953, 88 MINS, US ⊗

Dir Robert Gordon *Prod* Sterling Silliphant *Scr* Robert Sylvester *Ph* Joseph Brun *Ed* David Kummins *Mus* George Bassman

● Coley Wallace, Paul Stewart, Hilda Simms, James Edwards, John Marley, Dots Johnson (United Artists)

The Joe Louis Story is a dramatic recap of the personal and ring history of the respected Negro American fighter. The film, acted out by a predominantly colored cast headed by Coley Wallace (as the champ), rates high on sincerity, is alternately touching, understanding and heartpoundingly exciting.

Coley Wallace is the spitting image of Joe, from his muscular body to the expressionless face that so unexpectedly breaks out into a broad, friendly grin. He carries off the ring scenes and does well against Hilda Simms who plays Mrs Louis.

Integration of real fight shots, from the early bouts to the pummeling Joe took from Schmeling, the triumphant return match and the tragic attempt in 1951 when the aging Louis came out of retirement to be 'murdered' by Rocky Marciano, is excellently handled and accounts for the picture's sock appeal.

Director Robert Gordon deserves kudos for keeping the action tight and dramatic, never losing sight that he is trying to humanize the story of an idol whom most people only knew in the glare of the arena. Sylvester's intelligent script helps a great deal in making Louis come alive as a slugger and as a colored boy with decent instincts but incompletely equipped to live up to everything that being a 'celebrity' implies.

••••••••••••••••••••••••••••••

■ **JOE MACBETH**

1955, 90 MINS, UK

Dir Ken Hughes *Prod* Mike Frankovich *Scr* Philip Yordan *Ph* Basil Emmott *Ed* Peter Rolfe Johnson *Mus* Trevor Duncan *Art Dir* Alan Harris

● Paul Douglas, Ruth Roman, Bonar Colleano, Gregoire Aslan, Sidney James, Harry Green (Columbia)

Joe Macbeth is far removed from the famous Shakespearean character, but there is an analogy between this modern gangster story and the Bard's classic play. Although made in Britain, the film has an American setting. It is expensively mounted, expertly staged and directed with a keen sense of tension.

The plot is basically a battle for supremacy, waged by Paul Douglas, in the title role, and egged on by his determined bride (Ruth Roman).

The lead role makes substantial demands on Douglas, but he emerges with honorable distinction. His characterization changes naturally from the confident henchman to the domineering and frightened bully. Roman has the looks and talent to give a genuine veneer to her performance as his wife.

••••••••••••••••••••••••••••••

■ **JOE VERSUS THE VOLCANO**

1990, 102 MINS, US ◇ ⊗ ⊙

Dir John Patrick Shanley *Prod* Teri Schwartz *Scr* John Patrick Shanley *Ph* Stephen Goldblatt *Ed* Richard Halsey *Mus* Georges Delerue *Art Dir* Bo Welch

● Tom Hanks, Meg Ryan, Lloyd Bridges, Robert Stack, Abe Vigoda, Ossie Davis (Amblin/Warner)

Joe Versus the Volcano is an overproduced, disappointing shaggy dog comedy: A nebbish is bamboozled by unscrupulous types to trade his meaningless existence for a grand adventure that's linked to a suicide pact.

Pic starts promisingly with Tom Hanks going to work in the ad department of the grungy American Panascope surgical supplies factory. Meg Ryan as DeDe (in the first of her three gimmicky roles) sports dark hair in an amusingly ditzy Carol Kane impression as his mousey coworker. As an in-joke, the real Carol Kane pops up also in black wig later in the film, uncredited.

Hanks is a hypochondriac and his doctor, guest star Robert Stack, diagnoses a 'brain cloud', giving the hapless guy only six months to live. Coincidentally, eccentric superconductors tycoon Lloyd Bridges pops in to offer Hanks to 'live like a king' for 20 days before heading for a remote Polynesian island to 'die like a man', i.e. jump into an active volcano to appease the fire god.

Hanks indulges himself in some rather unfunny solo bits. Ryan has fun in her three personas, but they're simply revue sketches.

••••••••••••••••••••••••••••••

■ **JOEY**

1985, 95 MINS, US ◇ ⊗

Dir Joseph Ellison *Prod* Joseph Ellison *Scr* Joseph Ellison *Ph* Oliver Wood *Ed* Christopher Andrews *Mus* Jim Roberge

● Neill Barry, James Quinn, Elisa Heinsohn, Linda Thorson, Ellen Hammill, Rickey Ellis (Rock 'n' Roll/Satori)

An intelligent, engaging pic about a youngster who's into the rock 'n' roll music of the 1950s.

Joey (Neill Barry), age 17, likes to play guitar the way his dad, Joe Sr (James Quinn) used to. In fact, Joe Sr was lead singer for a rock group, the Delsonics, before falling on hard times and taking to the bottle. Joey and his high school friends have formed a group of their own, and they win a successful audition to play backup to some of the original 1950s and 1960s groups due to appear in the Royal New York Doo-Wopp Show, to be held at Radio City. Show's creator and producer Frankie Lanz plays himself in the film.

Leads are excellent, with Barry a very personable hero, Elisa Heinsohn a charming heroine and Quinn managing to give Joey's has-been father genuine dimension.

••••••••••••••••••••••••••••••

■ **JOHN AND MARY**

1969, 92 MINS, US ◇ ⊗

Dir Peter Yates *Prod* Ben Kadish *Scr* John Mortimer *Ph* Gayne Rescher *Ed* Frank P. Keller *Mus* Quincy Jones *Art Dir* John Robert Lloyd

● Dustin Hoffman, Mia Farrow, Michael Tolan, Sunny Griffin, Stanley Beck, Tyne Daly (20th Century-Fox/Debrod)

John and Mary is a slight, indeed simple story that begins with sex and ends with love. The two title characters, played by Dustin Hoffman and Mia Farrow, do not even learn each other's name until the final frame.

The skeletal plot [from a novel by Mervyn Jones] has John meet Mary in one of those desperate, swinging singles establishments on New York's upper east side. They return to his apartment, have sex and the film opens with their awakening the next morning.

John is selfish and self-satisfied, but Hoffman projects a screen personality which insists that more is present than is getting through the camera's eye. Mary is much more attractive, feminine and alive. And Farrow enlarges the character sufficiently to make her worth caring about.

The entire charade is smoothly contrived.

••••••••••••••••••••••••••••••

■ **JOHN HUSTON & THE DUBLINERS**

1987, 60 MINS, US ◇

Dir Lilyan Sievernich *Prod* Lilyan Sievernich *Ph* Lisa Rinzler *Ed* Miroslav Janek *Mus* Alex North

● John Huston, Anjelica Huston, Tony Huston, Donal McCann, Rom Shaw (Liffen)

John Huston & The Dubliners is a perceptive documentary on legendary director John Huston and his working methods, shot on the set of his film *The Dead* (1987).

Documaker Lilyan Sievernich (whose husband Chris is an executive producer of *The Dead*) succeeds in revealing, by interviews with Huston, his cast and crew members, plus verite footage of scenes being filmed and rehearsed, how Huston gets exactly what he wants by gentle suggestions, cajoling and simply doing things till they come out right.

When Sievernich presses Huston with a leading question or threatens to become overly analytical towards his work, he smoothly scoffs at such notions and sets the discussion back on track in self-effacing fashion. As his film editor Roberto Silvi says: 'He's one of the last gentlemen in this industry.'

Docu give glimpses of some moving scenes from *The Dead*, including 78-year-old actress Cathleen Delany singing a song, coached by Irish tenor Frank Patterson, who's also in the cast.

••••••••••••••••••••••••••••••

■ **JOHNNY ALLEGRO**

1949, 80 MINS, US

Dir Ted Tetzlaff *Prod* Irving Starr *Scr* Karen DeWolf, Guy Endore *Ph* Joseph Biroc *Ed* Jerome Thomas *Mus* George Duning

● George Raft, Nina Foch, George Macready, Will Geer, Gloria Henry (Columbia)

Johnny Allegro is a typical George Raft melodrama. Plot rings in a twist or two to dress up the melodrama of an ex-gangster who is trying to go straight and who takes on a dangerous assignment from the government to help prove his good intentions. From the time Raft crosses paths with Nina Foch, wife of a big-time international agent, his fate is marked with danger.

Foch pleases in her assignment as a gal who is not all bad and only needs Raft to put her on the proper course. George Macready is the villainous husband, working with foreign powers to flood the country with counterfeit and disrupt the national economy.

••••••••••••••••••••••••••••••

■ **JOHNNY BELINDA**

1948, 101 MINS, US ⊗

Dir Jean Negulesco *Prod* Jerry Wald *Scr* Irmgard von Cube, Allen Vincent *Ph* Ted McCord *Ed* David Weisbart *Mus* Max Steiner *Art Dir* Robert M. Haas

● Jane Wyman, Lew Ayres, Charles Bickford, Agnes Moorehead, Stephen McNally, Jan Sterling (Warner)

Johnny Belinda is a story that easily could have become a display of scenery-chewing theatrics. It has its theatrics but they spring from a rather earnest development of story fundamentals, tastefully handled. Jean Negulesco's direction never overplays the heart-strings, yet keeps them constantly twanging, and evidences a sympathetic instinct that is reflected in the performance.

[In this adaptation of the stage play by Elmer Harris,] Jane Wyman portrays a mute slattern completely devoid of film glamour. It is a personal success; a socko demonstration that an artist can shape a mood and sway an audience through projected emotions without a spoken word.

Plot essentials cover a deaf-mute girl, dwelling with her father and resentful aunt on a barren farm in Nova Scotia. A village romeo rapes her. She has a baby and events move forward until the deaf-mute kills her ravisher when he tries to take the baby. She is tried for murder.

Charles Bickford walks off with the assignment of Belinda's father. His handling of the part of the dour Scot farmer registers strongly, pulling audience interest all the way.

J

□ 1948: Best Actress (Jane Wyman).
□ Nominations: Best Picture, Director, Actor (Lew Ayres), Supp. Actor (Charles Bickford), Supp. Actress (Agnes Moorehead), Screenplay, B&W Cinematogrpahy, B&W Art Direction, Editing, Score of a Dramatic Picture, Sound

························

■ JOHNNY COOL

1963, 103 MINS, US

Dir William Asher   *Prod* William Asher, Peter Lawford   *Scr* Joseph Landon   *Ph* Sam Leavitt   *Ed* Otto Ludwig   *Mus* Billy May
● Henry Silva, Elizabeth Montgomery, Marc Lawrence, Telly Savalas, Jim Backus, Sammy Davis Jr (Chrislaw)

Henry Silva, as a Sicilian-born assassin, is at home as the 'delivery boy of death' for deported underworld kingpin Marc Lawrence. While his escapades would probably fall apart if analyzed, he puts such driving force into them that the viewer becomes too involved to dispute his actions.

Elizabeth Montgomery, however, plays the emotionally and morally mixed-up heroine like a high-school drama teacher demonstrating to her class how to play a nymphomaniac – 10% sex, 90% self-consciousness.

Joseph Landon's script [from John McPartland's novel *The Kingdom of Johnny Cool*] has more holes in it than a Swiss cheese but he stuffs most of them with action and director William Asher cuts the action in thick slices. Plot centers on Silva doing a job for Lawrence which takes him from Sicily to Rome, then to NY, LA and Las Vegas before he's finished. When a doll comes into his life and gets worked over by some hoods, he adds revenge to his baser reasons for wiping out his assorted victims.

························

■ JOHNNY DANGEROUSLY

1984, 90 MINS, US ◇ ⓥ

Dir Amy Heckerling   *Prod* Michael Hertzberg   *Scr* Norman Steinberg, Bernie Kukoff, Harry Colomby, Jeff Harris   *Ph* David M. Walsh   *Ed* Pem Herring   *Mus* John Morris   *Art Dir* Joseph R. Jennings
● Michael Keaton, Joe Piscopo, Marilu Henner, Maureen Stapleton, Peter Boyle, Griffin Dunne (20th Century-Fox)

Opening with a zip, young Byron Thames gets this 1930s gangster sendup off solidly as the good-hearted, honest lad forced to take up crime to pay for the operations on his multi-ailing mum (Maureen Stapleton).

Stapleton is also well-cast in her cliched role, as are Peter Boyle as the good mobster Dundee and Joe Piscopo as the bad Vermin. Deliberately overworking the Cagney mannerisms, Michael Keaton is initially good too, in the title role, as is Griffin Dunne as Johnny's D.A. brother. Unfortunately, the material given all of them just gets worse and worse.

As a streetcorner pope extorting Keaton for cash, Dom DeLuise appears for only a few lines, none of them funny. It's Ray Walston's brief contribution that exemplifies the overall content of the film: as a blind news vendor, he gets hit in the head with a bundle of papers, restoring his sight. Then he gets hit again, turning him deaf. Hit a third time, he regains his hearing but loses his memory. Funny stuff.

························

■ JOHNNY GUITAR

1954, 111 MINS, US ◇ ⓥ ⊙

Dir Nicholas Ray   *Prod* Herbert J. Yates   *Scr* Philip Yordan   *Ph* Harry Stradling   *Ed* Richard L. Van Enger   *Mus* Victor Young   *Art Dir* James Sullivan
● Joan Crawford, Sterling Hayden, Mercedes McCambridge, Scott Brady, Ward Bond, Ernest Borgnine (Republic)

Joan Crawford, whose previous western was *Montana Moon* in 1930, has another try at the wide open spaces with *Johnny Guitar*. Like *Moon*, it proves the actress should leave saddles and levis to someone else and stick to city lights for a background.

The Roy Chanslor novel on which Philip Yordan based the screenplay provides this Republic release with a conventional oater basis. Scripter Yordan and director Nicholas Ray became so involved with character nuances and neuroses, that 'Johnny Guitar' never has enough chance to rear up in the saddle and ride at an acceptable outdoor pace.

Crawford plays Vienna, strong-willed owner of a plush gambling saloon standing alone in the wilderness of Arizona. She knows the railroad's coming through and she will build a whole new town and get rich. Opposing her is Mercedes McCambridge, bitter, frustrated leader of a nearby community.

Love, hate and violence, with little sympathy for the characters, is stirred up during the overlong film.

························

■ JOHNNY HANDSOME

1989, 95 MINS, US ◇ ⓥ ⊙

Dir Walter Hill   *Prod* Charles Roven   *Scr* Ken Friedman   *Ph* Matthew F. Leonetti   *Ed* Freeman Davies   *Mus* Ry Cooder   *Art Dir* Gene Rudolf
● Mickey Rourke, Ellen Barkin, Elizabeth McGovern, Morgan Freeman, Forest Whitaker, Scott Wilson (Carolco/Guber-Peters)

A promising idea is gunned down by sickening violence and a downbeat ending in *Johnny Handsome*, a Mickey Rourke vehicle.

At the outset, John Sedley (Rourke) is anything but handsome. Born with a cleft palate and badly disfigured face, he's struggled through life and wound up a petty criminal.

Johnny is sent to the pen where he comes to the attention of kindly Dr Resher (Forest Whitaker), a plastic surgeon who, after a series of painful ops, has Johnny looking like Mickey Rourke. Johnny is allowed out of prison each day to work on the docks, where he meets pretty accountant Elizabeth McGovern and a relationship blossoms.

But Johnny isn't content with his new circumstances: he wants revenge. He plots with his old gang members (who don't recognize him) to rob the dockyard payroll, meaning to double-cross them. It all leads to a grim, violent downer of an ending.

Rourke works hard at his character but fails to make Johnny the least bit sympathetic. Ellen Barkin creates one of the ugliest femme characters seen in recent films, while Lance Henriksen is typecast as yet another seedy hood.

························

■ JOHNNY IN THE CLOUDS

See: The Way to the Stars

························

■ JOHNNY O'CLOCK

1947, 95 MINS, US

Dir Robert Rossen   *Prod* Edward G. Nealis   *Scr* Robert Rossen   *Ph* Burnett Guffey   *Ed* Warren Low, Al Clark   *Mus* George Duning   *Art Dir* Stephen Goosson, Cary Odell
● Dick Powell, Evelyn Keyes, Lee J. Cobb, Ellen Drew, Nina Foch, Jeff Chandler (Columbia)

This is a smart whodunit, with attention to scripting, casting and camerawork lifting it above the average. Pic has action and suspense, and certain quick touches of humor to add flavor. Ace performances by Dick Powell, as a gambling house overseer, and Lee J. Cobb, as a police inspector, also up the rating.

Plot concerns Powell's operation as a junior partner in Thomas Gomez's gambling joint, and his allure for the ladies, especially Ellen Drew, the boss's wife. A cop tries to cut into the gambling racket and is murdered. The hatcheck girl, sweet on the cop, is also killed. When the checker's dancer sister (Evelyn Keyes) comes to find out what happened to the girl, she steps into a round of mystery centering about Powell.

Although the plot follows a familiar pattern, the characterizations are fresh and the performances good enough to overbalance. Dialog is terse and topical, avoiding the sentimental, phoney touch. Unusual camera angles come along now and then to heighten interest and momentarily arrest the eye. Strong teamplay by Robert Rossen, doubling as director-scripter, and Milton Holmes, original writer and associate producer, also aids in making this a smooth production.

························

■ JOHNNY SUEDE

1992, 95 MINS, US ◇ ⓥ ⊙

Dir Tom DiCillo   *Prod* Yoram Mandel, Ruth Waldburger   *Scr* Tom DiCillo   *Ph* Joe DeSalvo   *Ed* Geraldine Peroni   *Mus* Jim Farmer, Link Wray   *Art Dir* Patricia Woodbridge
● Brad Pitt, Calvin Levels, Alison Moir, Catherine Keener, Tina Louise, Nick Cave (Vega)

Taking place in an imaginary slum that could be on the outskirts of any east coast metropolis (pic was actually shot in New York), Tom DiCillo's gently ironic fantasy focuses on a dreamy young man who rejects reality and, after a pair of suede shoes is literally dropped on his head, adopts the name Johnny Suede and sets out to be a pop star, using the late Ricky Nelson as his model.

Johnny starts a tentative affair with pretty young Alison Moir, who lives nearby with an older, abusive photographer. His dream fades once she decides she prefers rough treatment. On the rebound, he reluctantly picks up a tutor of retarded children (Catherine Keener), and under her guidance he starts on the journey that will land him with both feet on the ground.

One-time cameraman (*Stranger Than Paradise, Variety*), DiCillo exploits pastel colors to advantage in order to flesh out Johnny's fantasy world. Brad Pitt, fresh from stealing scenes in *Thelma & Louise*, gives Johnny the right kind of innocent appeal, and the rest of the cast surround him with loving care.

························

■ JOHN PAUL JONES

1959, 126 MINS, US ◇

Dir John Farrow   *Prod* Samuel Bronston   *Scr* John Farrow, Jesse Lasky Jr   *Ph* Michel Kelber   *Ed* Eda Warren   *Mus* Max Steiner   *Art Dir* Franz Bachelin
● Robert Stack, Marisa Pavan, Charles Coburn, Erin O'Brien, Jean-Pierre Aumont, Bette Davis (Warner)

John Paul Jones has some spectacular sea action scenes and achieves some freshness in dealing with the Revolutionary War. But the Samuel Bronston production doesn't get much fire-power into its characters. They end, as they begin, as historical personages rather than human beings.

John Farrow's direction of such scenes as the battle of Jones' *Bon Homme Richard* with the British *Serapis* is fine, colorful and exciting. Perhaps because Jones himself was a man of action, the story gets stiff and awkward when it moves off the quarterdeck and into the drawing room.

The screenplay attempts to give the story contemporary significance by opening and closing with shots of the present US Navy, emphasizing the tradition Jones began almost single-handed. The interim picks up Jones as a Scottish boy who runs away to sea, becomes a sea captain, and winds up in the American colonies as they prepare for the War of Independence.

The historical figures tend to be stiff or unbelievable. Charles Coburn, as Benjamin Franklin, has a fussy charm, and Macdonald Carey, as Patrick Henry, is good. The brief appearance of Bette Davis as Catherine the Great of Russia is the cliche portrait of that vigorous empress, a woman bordering on nymphomania.

Robert Stack in the title role gives a robust portrayal. Marisa Pavan, as a titled Frenchwoman, is sweet but rather lifeless, while Jean-Pierre Aumont, as Louis XVI, seems a stronger monarch than the usual portrait of that doomed king.

■ JOKER IS WILD, THE
(Aka: All the Way)

1957, 126 MINS, US ◇
Dir Charles Vidor   *Prod* Samuel J. Briskin   *Scr* Oscar Saul   *Ph* Daniel L. Fapp   *Ed* Everett Douglas   *Mus* Walter Scharf
● Frank Sinatra, Mitzi Gaynor, Jeanne Crain, Eddie Albert, Beverly Garland, Jackie Coogan (Paramount)

The Joker is Wild purports to be the case history of a Prohibition era entertainer who lived through a savage attack by mobsters; loved and lost a pretty, rich girl; married a dancer whom he neglected; often was a self-pitying heel; hit the bottle and gambled all the time; and meanwhile gagged his way to being a heavy favorite in the club-date sweepstakes.

Frank Sinatra was first to carry the ball with this one, having bought Art Cohn's story of Joe E. Lewis in galley proof form and thereafter taking a key part in the packaging. Sinatra obviously couldn't be made to look like Lewis; and Lewis' style of delivery is unique. But these are minor reservations in light of the major job Sinatra does – alternately sympathetic and pathetic, funny and sad.

Eddie Albert plays Austin Mack, Lewis' longtime piano accompanist and intimate friend, with considerable feel. Jeanne Crain is touching and fits in fine as the wealthy gal who falls for Lewis (and he for her). The leggy, shapely, cutie-pie-faced Mitzi Gaynor is colorful as a chorus dancer who marries Lewis after Crain takes the powder.

Under Charles Vidor's direction, *Joker* plays out in well organized and smooth fashion. But it goes overboard on length.
□ 1957: Best Song ('All the Way')

■ JOKERS, THE

1967, 94 MINS, UK ◇
Dir Michael Winner   *Prod* Maurice Foster, Ben Arbeid   *Scr* Dick Clement, Ian La Frenais   *Ph* Kenneth Hodges   *Ed* Bernard Gribble   *Mus* Johnny Pearson   *Art Dir* John Blezard
● Michael Crawford, Oliver Reed, Harry Andrews, James Donald, Daniel Massey, Michael Hordern (Rank Gildor-Scimitar)

Pic has the supreme virtue of portraying young people as they are, without patronizing or exploiting them: restless, somewhat disenchanted, privately aware of their immaturity, and with a tendency to rush needlessly into action with a later psychological hangover in many cases.

Michael Crawford and Oliver Reed are two brothers, the former just expelled from still another college for a practical joke, the latter the author of that scheme. Together, they plan and execute a national outrage – theft of the Crown Jewels, with no intent to keep them, just to carry off the theft.

Sight gags and underplayed British throwaway gags are interleaved neatly with the growing suspense over whether the guys will succeed.

■ JOLSON SINGS AGAIN

1949, 96 MINS, US ◇ Ⓥ ⊙
Dir Henry Levin   *Prod* Sidney Buchman   *Scr* Sidney Buchman   *Ph* William Snyder   *Ed* William Lyon   *Mus* George Duning
● Larry Parks, Barbara Hale, William Demarest, Ludwig Donath, Bill Goodwin (Columbia)

It is only natural that the durability of Al Jolson, as the all-time No 1 performing personality in show business, would be matched by an equally rich real-life story. *Jolson Sings Again* proves that.

On a broad canvas is projected Jolson's wartime tours under Special Services, singing from the Aleutians to the Caribbean bases until he finally contracts the serious fever which laid him low in North Africa. Barbara Hale reenacts the nurse technician from Little Rock who is now Mrs Jolson.

Larry Parks, again playing Jolson, remains an uncannily faithful personator of the star.
□ 1949: Nominations: Best Story & Screenplay, Color Cinematography, Scoring of a Musical Picture

■ JOLSON STORY, THE

1946, 120 MINS, US ◇ Ⓥ ⊙
Dir Alfred E. Green   *Prod* Sidney Skolsky   *Scr* Stephen Longstreet   *Ph* Joseph Walker   *Ed* William Lyon   *Mus* Morris Stoloff (dir.)   *Art Dir* Stephen Goosson, Walter Holscher
● Larry Parks, Evelyn Keyes, William Demarest, Bill Goodwin, Ludwig Donath, Tamara Shayne (Columbia)

Jolson's singing proves the big excitement for this Technicolorful film biog of the great mammy-singer's career.

The Jolson Story emerges as an American success story in song. The yearning to sing to give generously of himself, cued by the still famed-in-showbiz catchphrase, 'You ain't heard nothin' yet'; the Sunday nights at the Winter Garden, the birth of the runway as Jolson got closer to his audience, the incidental whistling in between vocalizing – all these are recaptured for the screen.

But there's lots more on and off the screen. As Evelyn Keyes plays Ruby Keeler – only she's called Julie Benson – in meticulous manner, she helps carry the boy-girl saga.

But the real star of the production is that Jolson voice and that Jolson medley. It was good showmanship to cast this film with lesser people, particularly Larry Parks as the mammy kid. It's quite apparent how he must have studied the Jolson mannerisms in black-and-white because the vocal synchronization (with a plenitude of closeups) defies detection.
□ 1946: Best Sound Recording, Scoring for a Musical Picture.
□ Nominations: Best Actor (Larry Parks), Supp. Actor (William Demarest), Color Cinematography, Editing

■ JONATHAN LIVINGSTON SEAGULL

1973, 114 MINS, US ◇ Ⓥ
Dir Hall Bartlett   *Prod* Hall Bartlett   *Scr* Richard Bach, Hall Bartlett   *Ph* Jack Couffer   *Ed* Frank Keller   *Mus* Neil Diamond   *Art Dir* Boris Leven
● (Paramount)

Before the fact, nobody could have foretold the success of Richard Bach's book, *Jonathan Livingston Seagull*, and Hall Bartlett's $1.5 million film version poses the same question. The pastoral allegory, filmed with live birds and locations while some well-known players essay the vocal chores, is a combination of teenybopper psychedelics, facile moralizing, Pollyanna polemic, and superb nature photography.

Though not credited, per arrangement, the vocal cast draws on many fine players. James Franciscus dubs the title bird, a non-conformist who wants to dive for fish instead of foraging in garbage like gulls always do. A

puzzlement to his early girl friend, essayed by Kelly Harmon, and his parents (Dorothy McGuire and Richard Crenna), Jonathan is banished from the flock by elder Hal Holbrook. After cruising the world, he passes (via saturated color printing) to another level of existence.

Now there's nothing wrong with uplift, except that exhortations customarily are banal. That is, the end is nearly destroyed by the means.
□ 1973: Nominations: Best Cinematography, Editing

■ JOSEPH ANDREWS

1977, 103 MINS, UK ◇ Ⓥ
Dir Tony Richardson   *Prod* Neil Hartley   *Scr* Allan Scott, Chris Bryant   *Ph* David Watkin   *Ed* Thom Noble   *Mus* John Addison   *Art Dir* Michael Annals
● Ann-Margret, Peter Firth, Michael Hordern, Beryl Reid, Jim Dale, Natalie Ogle (Woodfall)

Joseph Andrews is a tired British period piece about leching and wenching amidst the high- and low-life of Henry Fielding's England. Tony Richardson's film is a ludicrous mix of underplayed bawdiness and sporadic vulgarity.

Large cast of otherwise British players is headed by Ann-Margret, sometimes appearing grotesque in her rendition of Lady Booby, the noblewoman-with-a-past with the hots for servant Peter Firth in title role.

Fielding's story of concealed identities and misplaced birth origins has of course been the inspiration for generations of successively updated farce. Herein, Richardson has attempted to pump up the project via the casting of some famed British thesps – John Gielgud, Peggy Ashcroft, Hugh Griffith among some 14 guest stars in cameos.

■ JOURNEY, THE

1959, 122 MINS, US ◇
Dir Anatole Litvak   *Prod* Anatole Litvak   *Scr* George Tabori   *Ph* Jack Hildyard   *Ed* Dorothy Spencer   *Mus* Georges Auric   *Art Dir* Werner Schlichting, Isabella Schlichting
● Yul Brynner, Deborah Kerr, Jason Robards, Robert Morley, E.G. Marshall, Kurt Kasznar (M-G-M/Alby)

The Journey is a relatively short one, geographically speaking. It leads from Budapest to the Austrian frontier, a distance of about 100 miles. A group of passengers, American, British, French, Israeli etc, is trapped at Budapest airport by the 1956 Hungarian uprising. The Red Army grounds the civilian planes, so this particular group has to take a bus to Vienna.

At the last checkpoint on the border the Russian commander is Yul Brynner. He delays the party, ostensibly to verify their passports and exit permits. His reasons are not clear. One seems to be his purely whimsical desire for western company. Another is his suspicion that one member of the party (Jason Robards) is one of the Hungarian rebel leaders.

What it eventually simmers down to is a political-sexual triangle, with Brynner jealous of Deborah Kerr's attachment to Robards. Litvak finds he can tell his story almost entirely through Kerr (the west) and Brynner (the east), so the subsidiary characters and their subplots suffer.

This neglect is justified, however, chiefly by the projection of Brynner's characterization. He is capricious, sentimental, cruel, eager for love and suspicious of attention. Kerr has the difficult assignment of being in love with one man, Robards, and yet unwillingly attracted to another, Brynner, who is the opposite of all she admires and loves. She is brilliant and moving as a woman alone in an unbearable situation. Jason Robards in his film bow, is excellent.

JOURNEY INTO FEAR

1943, 68 MINS, US 🔲 ⊙
Dir Norman Foster, [Orson Welles]   *Prod* Orson Welles
Scr Orson Welles, Joseph Cotten   *Ph* Karl Struss
Ed Mark Robson   *Mus* Roy Webb   *Art Dir* Albert S.
D'Agostini, Mark-Lee Kirk
● Joseph Cotten, Dolores Del Rio, Ruth Warrick, Orson
Welles, Agnes Moorehead, Everett Sloane (RKO/
Mercury)

In *Journey into Fear*, Orson Welles' third release for RKO, he handles only the production reins and takes one of the character
leads but leaves direction in the hands of
Norman Foster. Picture attempts to catch attention through series of dramatic peaks, but
misses that mark by a considerable margin,
being too stagey and talky.

Joseph Cotten is the pivotal character – an
American naval ordnance engineer returning
to the US from Istanbul.

Welles delivers an above-par characterization as the Turkish secret police chief. Cotten
is okay in the lead, despite the fact that the writers present him as a rather weakling hero
throughout.

Direction by Foster is deliberate and slow,
pausing too much on unimportant incidentals. Adaptation of Eric Ambler's novel was
prepared by Welles and Cotten, and there's
nothing new in technique or treatment.

JOURNEY OF HONOR

1992, 106 MINS, US/JAPAN ◇ 🔲 ⊙
Dir Gordon Hessler   *Prod* Sho Kosugi   *Scr* Nelson
Gidding   *Ph* John Connor   *Ed* Bill Butler   *Mus* John
Scott   *Art Dir* Adrian Gorton
● Sho Kosugi, David Essex, Kane Kosugi, Christopher
Lee, Toshiro Mifune, John Rhys-Davies (Sanyo/
Kosugi/Sho/Mayeda)

Brainchild of martial arts star Sho Kosugi,
film cleverly mixes various genres of swashbucklers into an entertaining package as
Kosugi gets to indulge in swordfights on
palace stairs reminiscent of vintage Errol
Flynn/Basil Rathbone screen encounters.

Kosugi casts himself as chief warrior for an
eastern kingdom lord (guest star Toshiro
Mifune). He helps win a 1600 battle conquering Japan's western kingdom and is sent by
Mifune to Spain in search of firearms.

On the trip is the lord's son (played by
Sho's real-life son Kane Kosugi). The
Japanese heroes must contend with a self-
serving Portuguese missionary (Norman
Lloyd), a quick-tempered Spanish aristocrat
(David Essex) and an Arab pirate (John Rhys-
Davies).

Derring-do is excitingly staged in
Yugoslavian and Japanese locations by vet
Yank director Gordon Hessler. Essex (star of
original London stage edition of *Evita*) is a
terrific dashing villain, and both Kosugis are
bona fide action heroes.

JOURNEY OF NATTY GANN, THE

1985, 105 MINS, US ◇ 🔲 ⊙
Dir Jeremy Paul Kagan   *Prod* Mike Lobell   *Scr* Jeanne
Rosenberg   *Ph* Dick Bush   *Ed* David Holden
Mus James Horner   *Art Dir* Paul Sylbert
● Meredith Salenger, John Cusack, Ray Wise, Scatman
Crothers, Barry Miller, Lainie Kazan (Walt Disney)

More a period piece of Americana than a
rousing adventure, *The Journey of Natty Gann* is
a generally diverting variation on a boy and
his dog: this time it's a girl and her wolf.

Set in the Depression in Chicago, story has
widower Saul Gann desperate to find employment to support himself and daughter Natty.
He's offered a job at the lumber camp out in
Washington State and reluctantly takes it,
promising to send for Natty as soon as he can.
He leaves her under the auspices of a floozie
hotel manager.

The girl runs away and remainder of pic is
her sojourn across America in search of her
dad. Along the way she rescues a wolf from its
captors, and he becomes her endearing traveling partner.

Director Jeremy Paul Kagan extracts an engaging performance from Meredith Salenger
as the heroine. Rest of the cast is fine, with
John Cusack as her begrudging but good
buddy and Barry Miller as the witty entrepre-
neurial leader of a hobo brat pack.
☐ 1985: Nomination: Best Costume Design

JOURNEY TOGETHER

1945, 95 MINS, UK 🔲
Dir [John Boulting]   *Scr* [Terence Rattigan]   *Ph* [Stanley
Sayer, Harry Waxman]   *Mus* Gordon Jacob
● Edward G. Robinson, Richard Attenborough, Jack
Watling, David Tomlinson, Ronald Squire, Bessie Love
(RAF)

The screen calls it 'a story dedicated to the
few who trained the many.' It's a convincing
tribute to the last war aces (Yanks as well as
British) and to grounded veterans of the
Battle of Britain who took the rawest of raw
material and made good airmen out of them.

The production was written, directed, photographed and produced by members of the
RAF [all uncredited], some of them vets of
the film biz, but all of them honest-to-God
fliers. Also the cast, with four exceptions, was
recruited from RAF personnel. Ronald Squire
and Reginald Beck, in minor roles, and
Edward G. Robinson and Bessie Love are the
four pros who figure in the cast.

Film covers a wide range of territory, from
the cloistered halls of Cambridge University
to Falcon Field in Arizona, from the
Canadian Navigation School to the blazing inferno of bomb-plastered Berlin. But it is the
aerial camerawork in *Journey Together* that sets
a new high. Most of final 15 minutes are shot
inside a bomber with a degree of great skill.

JOURNEY TO THE CENTER OF THE EARTH

1959, 132 MINS, US ◇ 🔲 ⊙
Dir Henry Levin   *Prod* Charles Brackett   *Scr* Charles
Brackett, Walter Reisch   *Ph* Leo Tover   *Ed* Stuart
Gilmore, Jack W. Holmes   *Mus* Bernard Herrmann
● Pat Boone, James Mason, Arlene Dahl, Diane Baker,
Peter Ronson, Thayer David (20th Century-Fox)

The Charles Brackett production takes a
tongue-in-cheek approach to the Jules Verne
story, but there are times when it is difficult
to determine whether the film-makers are
kidding or playing it straight. The actors neither take themselves nor the picture seriously, which is all on the plus side.

The story concerns an expedition, led by
James Mason, who plays a dedicated scientist,
to the center of the earth. Among those who
descend to the depths with Mason are Pat
Boone, one of his students; Arlene Dahl, the
widow of a Swedish geologist who steals
Mason's information and tries to beat him to
the 'underworld'; and Peter Ronson, an
Icelandic guide and jack-of-all-trades.

The descent is a treacherous one, filled with
all kinds of dangers – underground floods, unusual winds, excessive heat, devious paths.
Before reaching their goal, the intrepid explorers confront prehistoric monsters, a forest of mushrooms, a cavern of quartz crystals,
and a salt vortex.

Boone is given an opportunity to throw in a
couple of songs. Romance is not neglected.
Waiting at home in Edinburgh for Boone is
Diane Baker, Mason's niece. And it's obvious
that Mason and the widow Dahl will end up
in a clinch despite their constant bickering
during the expedition.
☐ 1959: Nominations: Best Color Art
Direction, Sound, Special Effects

JOURNEY TO THE FAR SIDE OF THE SUN
See: Doppelganger

JOY IN THE MORNING

1965, 101 MINS, US ◇
Dir Alex Segal   *Prod* Henry T. Weinstein   *Scr* Sally
Benson, Alfred Hayes, Norman Lessing   *Ph* Ellsworth
Fredericks   *Ed* Tom McCarthy   *Mus* Bernard Herrmann
Art Dir George W. Davis, Carl Anderson
● Richard Chamberlain, Yvette Mimieux, Arthur Kennedy,
Oscar Homolka, Joan Tetzel, Sidney Blackmer (M-G-M)

Undoubted appeal of the Betty Smith novel
fails to come through in any appreciable measure in its filmic translation, at best a lightweight entry.

Story is of a young couple's first year of
marriage at a small mid-western college in
late 1920s where groom is working his way
through law school. Weakness of picture lies
in the treatment. There is an absence of anything unusual happening and nothing is accomplished to overcome this lack through
strong buildup of characterization.

Richard Chamberlain seldom appears at
ease as the young husband-student who has
difficulty in making ends meet as he takes a
night watchman job to augment his day jobs,
leaving only scarce time for family life and
classes. Yvette Mimieux fares a little better,
as she babysits to help out, then leaves
Chamberlain when she finds she's pregnant
so he won't have additional worries. Arthur
Kennedy as the husband's father brings them
together again in a gruff role.

JUAREZ

1939, 125 MINS, US 🔲
Dir William Dieterle   *Prod* Hal B. Wallis (exec.)
Scr John Huston, Wolfgang Reinhardt, Aeneas Mackenzie
Ph Tony Gaudio   *Ed* Warren Low   *Mus* Erich Wolfgang
Korngold   *Art Dir* Anton Grot
● Paul Muni, Bette Davis, Brian Aherne, Claude Rains,
John Garfield, Donald Crisp (Warner)

To the list of distinguished characters whom
he has created in films, Paul Muni adds a portrait of Benito Pablo Juarez, Mexican patriot
and liberator. With the aid of Bette Davis, co-
starring in the tragic role of Carlota, and of
Brian Aherne giving an excellent performance as the ill-fated Maximilian, Muni
again commands attention.

Muni does not dominate in this film [based
in part on a play by Franz Werfel and novel
The Phantom Crown by Bertita Harding] emphasis constantly is on the figure of
Maximilian, the young Austrian prince who
was persuaded by Napoleon III of France to
proclaim himself and his wife, Carlota, rulers
of the Mexican people.

Juarez, native Indian, was the elected head
of the republic when the Hapsburg prince
took over under sponsorship of French troops.
Defeated by foreign invaders Juarez carried
on guerilla warfare for several years.

Aherne seldom has appeared to such advantage as in this picture. His desire for fair play,
his hopeless plea for Mexican unity and the
manner in which he accepts defeat and court
martial provide ample reasons for sympathy.
☐ 1939: Nomination: Best Supp. Actor (Brian
Aherne)

JUBAL

1956, 100 MINS, US ◇ 🔲 ⊙
Dir Delmer Daves   *Prod* William Fadiman   *Scr* Delmer
Daves, Russell S. Hughes   *Ph* Charles Lawton Jr   *Ed* Al
Clark   *Mus* David Raksin   *Art Dir* Carl Anderson
● Glenn Ford, Ernest Borgnine, Rod Steiger, Valerie
French, Felicia Farr, Charles Bronson (Columbia)

The strong point of this gripping dramatic
story set in pioneer Wyoming is a constantly
mounting suspense.

Delmer Daves' direction and the script from Paul I. Wellman's novel carefully build towards the explosion that's certain to come, taking time along the way to make sure that all characters are well-rounded and understandable. Capping all this emotional suspense is the backdrop of the Grand Teton country in Wyoming.

Glenn Ford, a drifting cowpoke, runs into trouble when he takes a job on the cattle ranch operated by Ernest Borgnine. Valerie French, the rancher's amoral wife, makes an open but abortive play for him and Rod Steiger, who doesn't like to see himself replaced in her extra-marital activities, plots to get even with his possible rival.

Oddly enough, much of the footage is free of actual physical violence, but the nerves are stretched so taut that it's almost a relief when it does come. Ford is effective in his underplaying of the cowpoke who wants to settle down. Borgnine is excellent as the rough but gentle man. Steiger spews evil venom as the cowhand who wants the ranch and the rancher's wife.

• •

■ **JUBILEE**

1978, 103 MINS, UK ◇ ⑰

Dir Derek Jarman   *Prod* Howard Malin, James Whaley
Scr Derek Jarman   *Ph* Peter Middleton   *Ed* Tom
Priestley, Nick Barnard   *Mus* Suzi Pinns, Brian Eno,
Adam and the Ants and others   *Art Dir* Christopher
Hobbs
● Jenny Runacre, Jordan, Little Nell, Linda Spurrier,
Toyah Wilcox, Ian Charleson (Megalovision)

Derek Jarman's *Jubilee* is one of the most original, bold, and exciting features to have come out of Britain in the 1970s.

The year is 1578. Queen Elizabeth I is transported by an angel into the future (roughly the present), where she has 'the shadow of the time' revealed to her.

Observing a renegade women's collective (a pyromaniac, a punk star, a nympho, a bent historian, etc), Her Majesty watches as the 'ladies' and their friends go about their picaresque misadventures – disrupting a cafe, a punk audition, a murder spree.

Through this process of disemboweling the present through the memory of the past and the anticipation of the future, Jarman unravels the nation's social history in a way that other features haven't even attempted.

At times, amidst the story's violence (there are two vicious killings), black humor, and loose fire hose energy, the film – like the characters – seems to career out of control.

Toyah Wilcox, as an over-the-edge firebug, gives the film's finest performance, Jenny Runacre, in a demanding dual role as Elizabeth I and the leader of the collective, is marvelous. And Orlando, as the world-owning impresario Borgia Ginz, steals every scene he's in.

• •

■ **JUDGE PRIEST**

1934, 80 MINS, US ⑰

Dir John Ford   *Prod* Sol M. Wurtzel   *Scr* Dudley
Nichols, Lamar Trotti   *Ph* George Schneiderman
Mus Cyril J. Mockridge
● Will Rogers, Henry B. Walthall, Tom Brown, Anita
Louise, Rochelle Hudson, Berton Churchill (Fox)

Difficult, beforehand, to reconcile the idea of Irvin Cobb's *Judge Priest* with Will Rogers. Cobb's long series of stories have suggested another type; portly, slightly pompous on occasion and somewhat lethargic in movement, and that isn't Will Rogers. But Rogers makes the old judge completely his own.

At best the story is thin: the love of his nephew for the girl whose father is not known. The father is in town, and when he slugs a man for jeering at her victim later gangs up on him with two of his pals. The father cuts his assailant and is put on trial. He refuses to make the explanation which would be his legal out anywhere in the south.

The judge's political rival demands that he surrender the bench, since his nephew is lawyer for the defense. Heartbroken at this aspersion of his integrity, the judge appoints a substitute. But that night the minister talks with him. By a ruse they persuade the pompous old prosecutor to reopen the case.

It's a play of strange reactions. In the court scenes a bit of comedy relief is the effort of one of the jurors to rid himself of the product of his cud chewing. Several of the scenes are punctured with a laugh when the well-aimed shot lands in the cuspidor. Most of the comedy, however, is contributed by Rogers and Stepin Fetchit, a natural foil to the Rogers character. Other efforts at local color through the use of Negroes are less effective.

• •

■ **JUDGMENT AT NUREMBERG**

1961, 190 MINS, US ⑰ ⊙

Dir Stanley Kramer   *Prod* Stanley Kramer   *Scr* Abby
Mann   *Ph* Ernest Laszlo   *Ed* Fred Knudtson
Mus Ernest Gold   *Art Dir* Rudolph Sternad
● Spencer Tracy, Burt Lancaster, Richard Widmark,
Marlene Dietrich, Maximilian Schell, Judy Garland
(United Artists)

At 190 minutes *Judgment at Nuremberg* is more than twice the size of the concise, stirring and rewarding production on television's *Playhouse 90* early in 1959. A faster tempo by producer-director Stanley Kramer and more trenchant script editing would have punched up picture.

Abby Mann's drama is set in Nuremberg in 1948, the time of the Nazi war crimes trials. It deals not with the trials of the more well-known Nazi leaders, but with members of the German judiciary who served under the Nazi regime.

The intense courtroom drama centers on two men: the presiding judge (Spencer Tracy) who must render a monumental decision, and the principal defendant (Burt Lancaster), at first a silent, brooding figure, but ultimately the one who rises to pinpoint the real issue and admit his guilt.

Where the stars enjoy greater latitude and length of characterization, such as in the cases of Tracy, Maximilian Schell and Richard Widmark (latter two as defense counsel and prosecutor, respectively), the element of personal identity does not interfere. But in the cases of those who are playing brief roles, such as Judy Garland and Montgomery Clift, the spectator has insufficient time to divorce actor from character.

Tracy delivers a performance of great intelligence and intuition. He creates a gentle, but towering, figure, compassionate but realistic, warm but objective. Schell repeats the role he originated, with electric effect, on the TV program, and again he brings to it a fierce vigor, sincerity and nationalistic pride. Widmark is effective as the prosecutor ultimately willing to compromise and soft-pedal his passion for stiff justice when the brass gives the political word.

Lancaster as the elderly, respected German scholar-jurist on trial for his however-unwilling participation in the Nazi legal machine never quite attains the cold, superior intensity that Paul Lukas brought to the part on TV. Marlene Dietrich is persuasive as the aristocratic widow of a German general hanged as a war criminal, but the character is really superfluous to the basic issue.

☐ 1961: Best Actor (Maximilian Schell), Adapted Screenplay.

☐ Nominations: Best Picture, Director, Actor (Spencer Tracy), Supp. Actor (Montgomery Clift), Supp. Actress (Judy Garland), B&W Cinematography, B&W Costume Design, B&W Art Direction, Editing

• •

■ **JUDGMENT IN BERLIN**

1988, 92 MINS, US ◇ ⑰ ⊙

Dir Leo Penn   *Prod* Joshua Sinclair, Ingrid Windisch
Scr Joshua Sinclair, Leo Penn   *Ph* Gabor Pogany
Ed Teddy Darvas   *Mus* Peter Goldfoot   *Art Dir* Jan
Schlubach, Peter Alteneder
● Martin Sheen, Sam Wanamaker, Max Gail, Jurgen
Heinrich, Harris Yulin, Sean Penn (Bibo/January)

Judgement in Berlin, about an atypical defection that occurred in West Berlin in the late 1970s, is a quality production made on a tight budget but with obvious care and commitment, avoiding didacticism.

An East German couple traveling with a child hijacked a Polish airliner headed for East Berlin, forcing the pilot to land at a West Berlin airport that serves as a US military installation. The big question is who has legal jurisdiction to prosecute the hijackers. It is decided that since they landed in US-occupied territory, a trial conducted by a US judge is the humane solution.

Though the film's action essentially evolves around a courtroom drama, we also get glimpses of the personal lives of the principal characters, including the trial judge (Martin Sheen), and the couple accused of the hijacking, effectively played by Heinz Honig and Jutta Speidel.

There is good work by all concerned, including Leo Penn's deft, understated direction and the serviceable screenplay, adapted from an actual account written by the story's real trial judge Herbert J. Stern.

Sean Penn (Leo's son) has a plum role as an airline passenger who decided to defect when the opportunity presented itself. His trial testimony provides the film's dramatic center

• •

■ **JUDITH**

1966, 105 MINS, US ◇ ⑰

Dir Daniel Mann   *Prod* Kurt Unger   *Scr* John Michael
Hayes   *Ph* John Wilcox   *Ed* Peter Taylor   *Mus* Sol
Kaplan   *Art Dir* Wilfrid Shingleton
● Sophia Loren, Peter Finch, Jack Hawkins, Hans
Verner, Zharira Charifai, Shraga Friedman (Paramount)

Israel in its birth pains back-drops this frequently-tenseful adventure tale realistically produced in its actual locale. The production combines a moving story with interesting, unfamiliar characters.

The screenplay, based on an original by Lawrence Durrell, is two-pronged: the story of Sophia Loren, as the Jewish ex-wife of a Nazi war criminal who betrayed her and sent her to Dachau, intent upon finding him and wreaking her own brand of vengeance, and the efforts of the Haganah, Israel's underground army, to capture him.

Under Daniel Mann's forceful direction, the two points are fused as femme finds herself obliged to throw in with the Israelis, who use her to track down the man they know is in the Middle East but do not know how to identify.

Loren is excellent. It is a colorful role for her, particularly in her recollections of the young son she thought murdered until the Nazi, finally captured, tells her he is still alive.

Peter Finch, as a kibbutz leader and one of the Haganah, registers effectively and creates an indelible impression of what Israeli leaders accomplished in setting up their own state.

Nicolas Roeg is credited with second unit direction and additional photography.

• •

■ **JUDITH OF BETHULIA**

1914, 62 MINS, US ⊗

Dir D.W. Griffith   *Scr* D.W. Griffith   *Ph* Billy Bitzer
Ed James E. Smith
● Blanche Sweet, Henry B. Walthall, Robert Harron,
Mae Marsh, Lillian Gish, Lionel Barrymore (Biograph)

Judith of Bethulia is in four-and-a-half reels, founded upon the biblical tale, with the captions probably culled from the poem of Thomas Bailey Aldrich.

In spite of the undoubtedly vast sum expended for architectural and other props to conform to the period in which the story is laid, Lawrence Marsden did not deem it necessary to recruit a cast of star players. He succeeded in utilizing the services of competent ones in the regular Biograph company. For the name part he selected Blanche Sweet; Henry Walthall for Holofernes; Robert Harron for Nathan; J. Jiquel Lanoe for the Chief Eunuch; Harry Carey for the Traitor, and so on.

There are two parts that stand out – Judith far beyond all the others, with Holofernes a safe second. Fine as is the acting of the principals, the chief thing to commend is the totally wonderful handling of the mobs and the seriousness with which each super performs his individual task.

....

■ JUGGERNAUT

1974, 109 MINS, UK ◇ ⓥ
Dir Richard Lester *Prod* Richard DeKoker *Scr* Richard DeKoker, Alan Plater *Ph* Gerry Fisher *Ed* Tony Gibbs *Mus* Ken Thorne *Art Dir* Terence Marsh
● Richard Harris, Omar Sharif, David Hemmings, Anthony Hopkins, Shirley Knight, Ian Holm (United Artists)

Juggernaut stars Richard Harris as an explosives demolition expert aboard Omar Sharif's luxury liner where several bombs have been planted.

The action aboard the ship, to which Harris, David Hemmings and other demolition team members have been flown, alternates with land drama, where shipline executive Ian Holm, detective Anthony Hopkins (whose wife Caroline Mortimer and children are aboard the vessel), and others, attempt to locate the phantom bomber who calls himself Juggernaut in a series of telephone calls demanding a huge ransom.

At sea, Shirley Knight wanders in and out of scenes as a romantic interest for Sharif, while Roy Kinnear comes off best of the whole cast as a compulsively cheerful social director.

....

■ JUGGLER, THE

1953, 84 MINS, US
Dir Edward Dmytryk *Prod* Stanley Kramer *Scr* Michael Blankfort *Ph* Roy Hunt *Ed* Aaron Stell *Mus* George Antheil *Art Dir* Rudolph Sternad
● Kirk Douglas, Milly Vitale, Paul Stewart, Joey Walsh, Alf Kjellin (Kramer/Columbia)

The Juggler deals with a man who has become a neurotic from his long imprisonment in Nazi concentration camps, and how he gradually comes to realize his illness and seek help from new-found friends. The story-telling [from the novel by Michael Blankfort] has one serious flaw. It fails to establish early the nature and cause of Kirk Douglas' illness and, as a result, his acts of violence have an adverse reaction, instead of gaining sympathy.

Once a famous European juggler, Douglas arrives with other DPs for refuge in Israel. While in a temporary camp, his strange actions arouse interest of the camp psychiatrist. Douglas denies any illness and runs away. In his flight across the country, he takes up with Joey Walsh, a young orphan, and together they head north for Nazareth where Douglas hopes to lose himself.

Douglas, under Edward Dmytryk's well-coordinated direction, does an excellent job of selling the erratic character of the juggler. Milly Vitale is very appealing as the girl Douglas meets on a kibbutz.

The camerawork of Roy Hunt flows freely over the Israel countryside, giving an authentic, almost documentary flavor to the story.

....

■ JUICE

1992, 96 MINS, US ◇ ⓥ ⊙
Dir Ernest R. Dickerson *Prod* David Heyman, Neal H. Moritz, Peter Frankfurt *Scr* Gerard Brown, Ernest R. Dickerson *Ph* Larry Banks *Ed* Sam Pollard, Brunilda Torres *Mus* Hank Shocklee & the Bomb Squad *Art Dir* Lester Cohen
● Omar Epps, Tupac Shakur, Jermaine Hopkins, Khalil Kain, Cindy Herron, Vincent Laresca (Paramount)

Spike Lee cinematographer Ernest R. Dickerson starts off the pic promisingly, introducing a well-played quartet of New York ghetto youths and exploring their lives and frustrations in what could almost be viewed as an inner-city *Breaking Away*. After a sudden, tragic robbery attempt, the film takes a peculiar turn into the thriller realm, as one of the teens (Tupac Shakur) – high on the 'juice' of having killed the grocery store clerk – begins menacing his one-time friends.

Dickerson and co-writer Gerard Brown exhibit a sharp ear for dialog and have some real finds in their largely unknown cast, particularly Omar Epps as Q, the most introspective and reasoned of the four friends. Shakur, of rap group Digital Underground, is also impressive.

There are several lurches in story logic, from the sudden agreement of the group's leader (Khalil Kain, giving a solid performance) to engage in the robbery, to Q's puzzling relationship with a somewhat older nurse (Cindy Herron).

....

■ JULIA

1977, 116 MINS, US ◇ ⓥ ⊙
Dir Fred Zinnemann *Prod* Richard Roth *Scr* Alvin Sargent *Ph* Douglas Slocombe *Ed* Walter Murch *Mus* Georges Delerue *Art Dir* Gene Callahan, Willy Holt, Carmen Dillon
● Jane Fonda, Vanessa Redgrave, Jason Robards, Maximilian Schell, Hal Holbrook, Rosemary Murphy (20th Century-Fox)

Fred Zinnemann's superbly sensitive film explores the anti-Nazi awakening in the 1930s of writer Lillian Hellman via persecution of a childhood friend, portrayed in excellent characterization by Vanessa Redgrave in title role. Richard Roth's production is handsome and tasteful.

Hellman's book *Pentimento* was the basis for literate screenplay. The warm and innocently-intimate childhood relationship between two girls serves as the solid foundation for later contrasting tragedy when their lives diverge.

The period environment, brilliantly recreated in production design, costuming and color processing, complements the topflight performances and direction.

Jane Fonda and Redgrave, neither one a shrinking violet in real life, are dynamite together on the screen.
□ 1977: Best Supp. Actor (Jason Robards), Supp. Actress (Vanessa Redgrave), Adapted Screenplay.
□ Nominations: Best Picture, Director, Actress (Jane Fonda), Supp. Actor (Maximilian Schell, Cinematography, Costume Design, Editing, Original Score

....

■ JULIA HAS TWO LOVERS

1990, 85 MINS, US ◇ ⓥ
Dir Bashar Shbib *Prod* Bashar Shbib *Scr* Daphna Kastner, Bashar Shbib *Ph* Stephen Reizes *Ed* Dan Foegelle, Bashar Shbib *Mus* Emilio Kauderer
● Daphna Kastner, David Duchoveny, David Charles, Tim Ray, Clare Bancroft, Martin Donovan (Oneira)

While this tale of romance on the telephone has an interesting story concept, the conversation itself drags on for too long, leading to the film's uneven and frequently too-slow pace.

Julia (Daphna Kastner), an attractive but somewhat frustrated woman, has lived with her lover Jack (David Charles) for two years. When he unexpectedly asks her to marry him, she stalls. As Jack leaves for work, Julia answers the phone and encounters an amicable young man, Daniel (capably played by David Duchoveny).

Julia soon finds herself drawn to Daniel, who apparently has dialed the wrong number. Neither of them wants to hang up. They spend the morning together following their daily routines, telling each other about themselves. Inevitably (and finally), she invites Daniel over for lunch. At this point (nearly two-thirds into the film), the story begins to take new twists, adding considerably more interest.

Production values are mediocre, with too many blurred images.

....

■ JULIA MISBEHAVES

1948, 99 MINS, US
Dir Jack Conway *Prod* Everett Riskin *Scr* William Ludwig, Harry Ruskin, Arthur Wimperis *Ph* Joseph Ruttenberg *Ed* John Dunning *Mus* Adolph Deutsch *Art Dir* Cedric Gibbons, Daniel B. Cathcart
● Greer Garson, Walter Pidgeon, Peter Lawford, Elizabeth Taylor, Cesar Romero (M-G-M)

All forms of comedy but the subtle are used to spring the laughs that come from the frenetic antics of a middle-aged couple, long separated but bent on trying romance again. It's gag and situation farcing that's as artful as a slap in the face.

Jack Conway's direction [of this film, based on Margery Sharp's novel, *The Nutmeg Tree*] is fast and vigorous in walloping over the comedy. Laughs are piled on top of each other, making a lot of the dialog unheard and unnecessary.

Garson is punched, doused, muddied and tossed in her unbending process. She wears tights, takes a bubble bath, sings and generally acquits herself like a lady out to prove she can be hoydenish when necessary. The other half of middleaged team, Walter Pidgeon gives away no honors. He's pitching all the time and skillfully injects just the right amount of underplaying to balance broader delivery of his partner in fun.

The fun starts when Garson, entertainer, receives an invitation to the wedding of her daughter. Not having seen the girl since she was a baby, the mother journeys to France for the wedding.

En route to France, Garson joins an acrobatic act, becomes involved with an elderly wolf, and generally has herself a time. Garson's song, spotlighted during her acro stint, is 'When You're Playing with Fire' and is delivered with unharmonious vocals, complete with gestures, for laughs.

....

■ JULIUS CAESAR

1953, 121 MINS, US ⓥ
Dir Joseph L. Mankiewicz *Prod* John Houseman *Scr* Joseph L. Mankiewicz *Ph* Joseph Ruttenberg *Ed* John Dunning *Mus* Miklos Rozsa *Art Dir* Cedric Gibbons, Edward Carfagno
● Marlon Brando, James Mason, John Gielgud, Louis Calhern, Greer Garson, Deborah Kerr (M-G-M)

To those normally allergic to Shakespeare, this will be a surprise – a tense, melodramatic story, clearly presented, and excellently acted by one of the finest casts assembled for a film. Presented in its traditional, classic form, there is no attempt to build up the spectacle or battle scenes to gain sweep. The black-&-white camera has been used effectively, the stylized settings simulate scope, and the costumes breathe authenticity.

Highlight of the film is the thesping. Every performance is a tour de force. Any fears about Marlon Brando appearing in Shakespeare are dispelled by his compelling portrayal as the revengeful Mark Antony. The entire famous funeral speech takes on a new light.

John Gielgud, as the 'lean and hungry' Cassius is superb. The English actor portrays the chief conspirator with sympathetic understanding. James Mason, as the noble, honorable Brutus, is equally excellent. As the close friend of Caesar, who joined the conspiracy out of noble motives, Mason is determined though ridden by guilt feelings. His falling out with Cassius at the Battle of Philippi and the scene with his wife, portrayed by Deborah Kerr, make for moving drama.

Louis Calhern's Caesar is another triumph. He plays the soldier-hero with proper restraint and feeling. Edmond O'Brien, though better known for his toughguy roles, is an effective Casca. The picture is so big that the two femme stars, Kerr and Greer Garson, are seen in gloried bits. However, both acquit themselves creditably.

□ 1953: Best B&W Art Direction.
□ Nominations: Best Picture, Actor (Marlon Brando), B&W Cinematography, Scoring a Dramatic Picture

••

■ **JULIUS CAESAR**

1970, 117 MINS, UK ◇ ⓥ ⊙
Dir Stuart Burge   *Prod* Peter Snell   *Scr* Robert Furnival
Ph Ken Higgins   *Ed* Eric Boyd Perkins   *Mus* Michael Lewis   *Art Dir* Julia Trevelyan Oman
● Charlton Heston, Jason Robards, John Gielgud, Richard Johnson, Robert Vaughn, Richard Chamberlain (Commonwealth United)

This stab at Shakespeare's *Julius Caesar*, a drama of political intrigue, corruption, ambition, envy, rhetoric and conspiratorial cunning, is disappointing.

Under Stuart Burge's firm direction the highspots are brought out effectively but the backgrounds and crowd sequences are stagey and lack the passion and abandon needed to project the star scenes.

Biggest disappointment is Jason Robards' Brutus. He rarely suggests 'the noblest Roman of them all' and his delivery of Shakespeare's verse is flat, uninspired and totally dull.

John Gielgud in the significant but smallish title role, is probably the one that comes nearest to true Shakespearian thesping.

Charlton Heston makes a praiseworthy stab at Mark Antony, giving the role a dominating power.

••

■ **JUMBO**

(Aka: Billy Rose's Jumbo)

1962, 123 MINS, US ◇ ⓥ ⊙
Dir Charles Walters   *Prod* Joe Pasternak, Martin Melcher
Scr Sidney Sheldon   *Ph* William H. Daniels   *Ed* Richard W. Farrell   *Art Dir* George W. Davis, Preston Ames
● Doris Day, Stephen Boyd, Jimmy Durante, Martha Raye, Dean Jagger (M-G-M)

One of the final productions ever seen in the old N.Y. Hippodrome, *Jumbo* was a dull book musical of the 1935 season, with a curious mid-Depression tie-in with Texaco Gas. The showmanship of Metro has turned the combo musical and circus into a great film entertainment.

Much of the Rodgers and Hart score for the 1935 legit version has been retained. 'Little Girl Blue', 'My Romance', and 'Most Beautiful Girl in the World' are given fullscale production. 'This Can't Be Love', from Rodgers and Hart's 1938 *Boys From Syracuse* and 'Why Can't I?' from their 1929 *Spring Is Here*, have been added.

Jimmy Durante is the circus-owner, with Doris Day as his daughter, and Martha Raye as his 14-year-awaiting fiancee. Durante plays the role as Durante.

Stephen Boyd, handsome, virile, excellent within the limits of his role, has star billing but his part is strictly in support of his lead-

ing lady. It's doubtful that singing is his own, but he handles his musical sequences well.

Sidney Sheldon's screenplay (he receives full credit although report has it that several scripters have had a go at it) retains only the basic circus-boy-meets-circus-girl format of Ben Hecht and Charles MacArthur's original book, with the ending the most important switch. Instead of the originally-conceived merger of the two circuses then the wedding of the boy and girl, Dean Jagger's villainy drives Boyd into leaving, with Jumbo rejoining Day, Durante and Martha Raye.

□ 1962: Nomination: Best Adapted Music Score

••

■ **JUMPIN' JACK FLASH**

1986, 100 MINS, US ◇ ⓥ ⊙
Dir Penny Marshall   *Prod* Lawrence Gordon, Joel Silver
Scr David H. Franzoni, J.W. Melville, Patricia Irving, Christopher Thompson   *Ph* Matthew F. Leonetti
Ed Mark Goldblatt   *Mus* Thomas Newman
Art Dir Robert Boyle
● Whoopi Goldberg, Jonathan Pryce, Jim Belushi, Carol Kane, Annie Potts, Peter Michael Goetz (Gordon/Silver)

Jumpin' Jack Flash is not a gas, it's a bore. A weak idea and muddled plot poorly executed not surprisingly results in a tedious film with only a few brief comic interludes from Whoopi Goldberg to redeem it.

Anyone who has been longing for a film in which an office worker talks dirty to a computer terminal should find *Jumpin' Jack Flash* just what they've been waiting for.

Goldberg is Terry Doolittle. Just when her life is looking most bleak along comes Jack (Jonathan Pryce). He's a British spy trapped somewhere behind the Iron Curtain who somehow, someway, taps into Goldberg's terminal and asks for help to escape.

Goldberg is plunged into a web of intrigue involving a sinister repairman (Jim Belushi) who conveniently disappears, a crippled diplomat (Roscoe Lee Browne) and another spy (Jeroen Krabbe) who winds up floating face down in the East River.

••

■ **JUNGLE BOOK**

1942, 108 MINS, US ◇ ⓥ ⊙
Dir Zoltan Korda   *Prod* Alexander Korda   *Scr* Laurence Stallings   *Ph* Lee Garmes, W. Howard Greene
Ed William Hornbeck   *Mus* Miklos Rozsa
Art Dir Vincent Korda
● Sabu, Joseph Calleia, John Qualen, Frank Puglia, Rosemary De Camp, Patricia O'Rourke (Korda)

On the same grand scale of pictorial elaborateness which characterized *Thief of Bagdad*, Alexander Korda brings again to the screen the diminutive East Indian player, Sabu, in a film version of Rudyard Kipling's *Jungle Book*.

Kipling's character, Mowgli, who strayed into the jungle as a child and was brought up by a she-wolf, is most likely to be confused by filmgoers with Tarzan. Laurence Stallings wrote the screenplay and some of the human-interest elements are slighted. Mowgli's return to the native village as a grown-up youth and his subsequent adventures in civilization are handled in neither a humorous nor dramatic manner. The saga of the boy who could converse with animals is related very seriously, whereas the theme might have been better entertainment if treated in a lighter vein.

□ 1942: Nominations: Best Color Cinematography, Color Art Direction, Scoring of a Dramatic Picture, Special Effects

••

■ **JUNGLE BOOK, THE**

1967, 78 MINS, US ◇ ⓥ ⊙
Dir Wolfgang Reitherman   *Prod* Walt Disney   *Scr* Larry Clemmons, Ralph Wright, Ken Anderson, Vance Gerry
Ed Tom Acosta, Norman Carlisle   *Mus* George Bruns
● (Walt Disney)

The Jungle Book, based on the Mowgli stories by Rudyard Kipling, was the last animated feature under Walt Disney's personal supervision before his death.

It was filmed at a declared cost of $4 million over a 42-month period. Full directorial credit is given to Wolfgang Reitherman, a 35-year Disney vet. Reitherman was one of several *Jungle* hands who worked on Disney's first animated feature, *Snow White and the Seven Dwarfs*.

Friendly panther, vocalized by Sebastian Cabot, discovers a baby boy in the jungle and deposits him for upbringing with a wolf family, John Abbott and Ben Wright. At aged 10, boy, looped by Clint Howard, is seen in need of shift to the human world, because man-hating tiger (George Sanders) has returned to the jungle.

Encounters along the way include a friendship with a devil-may-care bear, expertly cast with the voice of Phil Harris. The standout song goes to Harris, a rhythmic 'Bare Necessities' extolling the value of a simple life and credited to Terry Gilkyson.

Robert B. and Richard M. Sherman wrote five other songs, best of which is 'Wanna Be Like You', sung in free-wheeling fashion by Louis Prima, vocalizing the king of a monkey tribe.

□ 1967: Nomination: Best Song ('Bare Necessities')

••

■ **JUNGLE FEVER**

1991, 132 MINS, US ◇ ⓥ ⊙
Dir Spike Lee   *Prod* Spike Lee   *Scr* Spike Lee
Ph Ernest Dickerson   *Ed* Sam Pollard   *Mus* Stevie Wonder, Terence Clanchard   *Art Dir* Wynn Thomas
● Wesley Snipes, Annabella Sciorra, Spike Lee, Ossie Davis, Ruby Dee, John Turturro (Universal/40 Acres & a Mule)

The jungle is decidedly present but the fever is notably missing in Spike Lee's exploration of racial tensions in urban America. Lee tackles the subject of interracial romance from the unavoidable vantage point that, while things today are more open, they are also considerably more volatile and complex.

Little time is actually spent with the black man and white woman whose relationship is the core of the drama. Steering clear of conventional romantic scenes once the couple gets together, Lee instead uses the affair to detonate dozens of reactive sequences, showing how the blacks and Italians close to the principals deal with the developments.

Given the violent emotions triggered in others, it would have helped to see more of Flipper Purify (Wesley Snipes) and Angie Tucci's (Annabella Sciorra) feelings about each other as the surrounding fireworks go off.

Flipper is unceremoniously kicked out his Harlem apartment and forced to move back in with his father (Ossie Davis), an ultra-righteous ex-preacher, and kindly mother (Ruby Dee). Angie is brutally beaten by her father and sent packing to a girlfriend's.

Performances are all pointed and emotionally edgy. Film feels too long, but it ends powerfully, as the audience exits with the view that both the white and black communities are deeply troubled and have a very long way to go to resolve their differences.

••

■ **JUNGLE FIGHTERS**

See: The Long and the Short and the Tall

••

■ **JUNIOR BONNER**

1972, 100 MINS, US ◇ ⓥ
Dir Sam Peckinpah   *Prod* Joe Wizan   *Scr* Jeb Rosebrook   *Ph* Lucien Ballard   *Ed* Robert Wolfe, Frank Santillo   *Mus* Jerry Fielding   *Art Dir* Edward S. Haworth
● Steve McQueen, Robert Preston, Ida Lupino, Ben Johnson, Joe Don Baker, Barbara Leigh (ABC)

The latterday film genre of misunderstood-rodeo-drifter gets one of its best expositions in *Junior Bonner*. Steve McQueen stars handily in the title role.

Jeb Rosebrook's original screenplay, combined with uniformly adroit casting and sensitive direction, has the virtues of solid construction and economy of dialog. To be sure, the plot is somewhat biased in favor of the restless wanderings of McQueen, in that the alternatives are nearly caricature conformity; but overall there is a good balance.

Filmed in and around Prescott, Arizona, the film depicts the efforts of McQueen to look good in his hometown rodeo.

Director Sam Peckinpah's reputation for violence is herein exorcised in the rodeo and brawl sequences. Audiences which consider such rough-and-tumble as innocuous, vicarious ventilation will get their fill, though others may perceive a bit more.

....

■ JUNO AND THE PAYCOCK

1930, 95 MINS, UK

Dir Alfred Hitchcock   *Prod* John Maxwell   *Scr* Alfred Hitchcock, Alma Reville   *Ph* Jack Cox   *Ed* Emile de Ruelle   *Art Dir* Norman Arnold
● Sara Allgood, Edward Chapman, Maire O'Neil, Sydney Morgan, Kathleen O'Regan, John Laurie (British International)

Cast consists almost entirely of Irish players. Kathleen O'Regan succeeds only in looking awkward. Edward Chapman is by no means the Paycock of Arthur Sinclair's stage interpretation. He loses a lot of the humor and mugs too much. Sara Allgood is a flat Juno and Maire O'Neil introduces some of the gestures she used on the stage when playing Juno.

Three-quarters of the film is just photographed stage play [by Sean O'Casey] – excellently photographed, but slow in action. The rest moves fast, building up a swift climax of drab tragedy with the seduction of Mary (O'Regan), the shooting of Jerry (John Laurie), and the loss of the money due under the will. The end of the play has been dropped.

Irish atmosphere of the tenement life incidental to the country is well caught, director Alfred Hitchcock having a flair for sniping the real feeling of the submerged tenth.

....

■ JUPITER'S DARLING

1955, 93 MINS, US ◇ ⓥ ⊙

Dir George Sidney   *Prod* George Wells   *Scr* Dorothy Kingsley   *Ph* Paul C. Vogel, Charles Rosher   *Ed* Ralph E. Winters   *Mus* David Rose   *Art Dir* Cedric Gibbons, Urie McCleary
● Esther Williams, Howard Keel, Marge Champion, Gower Champion, George Sanders, Richard Haydn (M-G-M)

As a takeoff, with satirical treatment, on costume actioners, *Jupiter's Darling* is a fairly entertaining, although a hit-and-miss affair. It has Esther Williams in some outstanding swim numbers, and Howard Keel's robust singing.

Robert E. Sherwood's stage play, *Road to Rome*, dealing with Hannibal's invasion of Rome, served as the foundation for Dorothy Kingsley's screenplay.

The two water numbers given Williams stack up with her best. One is an imaginatively staged dream ballet. The other carries an essential part of the story, and its chase theme is developed into taut suspense drama as she flees through vast underwater reaches from pursuing barbarians seeking to recapture her for Keel's conquering Hannibal.

....

■ JURASSIC PARK

1993, 126 MINS, US ◇ ⓥ ⊙

Dir Steven Spielberg   *Prod* Kathleen Kennedy, Gerald R. Molen   *Scr* Michael Crichton, David Koepp   *Ph* Dean Cundey   *Ed* Michael Kahn   *Mus* John Williams   *Art Dir* Rick Carter
● Sam Neill, Laura Dern, Jeff Goldblum, Richard Attenborough, Bob Peck, Martin Ferrero (Universal/Amblin)

Steven Spielberg's scary and horrific thriller may be one-dimensional and even clunky in story and characterization, but definitely delivers where it counts, in excitement, suspense and the stupendous realization of giant reptiles.

The $60 million production (a bargain at the price) follows the general idea if not the letter of co-scripter Michael Crichton's 1990 bestseller.

Basis of this hi-tech, scientifically based, up-to-date version lies in the notion that dinosaurs can be biologically engineered using fossilized dino DNA. Having accomplished this in secret on an island off Costa Rica, zillionaire entrepreneur/tycoon John Hammond (Richard Attenborough) brings in a small group of experts to endorse his miracle, which is to be the world's most expensive zoo-cum-amusement park.

Arriving to inspect the menagerie are paleontologists Dr Alan Grant (Sam Neill) and Ellie Sattler (Laura Dern), as well as oddball mathematician Ian Malcolm (Jeff Goldblum), advocate of the Chaos Theory. Also along are Donald Gennaro (Martin Ferrero), a hard-nosed attorney repping the park's investors, and Hammond's two fresh-faced grandchildren, Lex (Ariana Richards) and Tim (Joseph Mazzello).

Introductory scenes are surprisingly perfunctory and Spielberg lets the dinosaurs out of the bag very early, showing some of them in full view after only 20 minutes. Still, none of these problems ends up mattering once the film clicks into high gear. When a storm strands two carloads of Hammond's guests in the middle of the park at night, a Tyrannosaurus Rex decides it's dinnertime. Events from here on frighteningly verify the mathematician's view of an unpredictable universe.

The monsters are far more convincing than the human characters. Neill's paleontologist comes off rather like a bland Indiana Jones, while Dern considerably overdoes the facial oohs and ahhs. The kids are basically along for the ride, while Jeff Goldblum, attired in all-black, helpfully fires off most of the wisecracks. As for Attenborough, agreeably back onscreen for the first time since 1979, his role has been significantly softened from the book.

....

■ JUST A GIGOLO

1978, 105 MINS, W. GERMANY ◇ ⓥ ⊙

Dir David Hemmings   *Prod* Rolf Thiele   *Scr* Joshua Sinclair, Ennio De Concini   *Ph* Charly Steinberger   *Ed* Susan Jaeger, Maxine Julius, Fred Srp   *Mus* Gunther Fischer   *Art Dir* Peter Rothe
● David Bowie, Sydne Rome, Kim Novak, David Hemmings, Maria Schell, Marlene Dietrich (Leguan)

Handsomely photographed in Berlin and directed with finesse by David Hemmings, David Bowie is a Prussian war vet back from the dead who drifts from one demeaning job to another and finally into employment as a gigolo.

The fascinating casting includes Marlene Dietrich and the return of Kim Novak. Sydne Rome is an appealing revelation.

Dietrich, so long away from the screen, is perforce hypnotic in what amounts to a cameo (she also touchingly croons the evergreen title song), in which she adds Bowie to her gigolo stable. Novak also makes a strong impression.

The film delivers a lot of bittersweet entertainment and is never less than engrossing. Period mood is a great strength, with an effective visual mixture of sepia and soft color tints, and a music track of period ballads and jolly ragtime tunes.

....

■ JUSTINE

1969, 117 MINS, US ◇ ⓥ

Dir George Cukor   *Prod* Pandro S. Berman   *Scr* Lawrence B. Marcus   *Ph* Leon Shamroy   *Ed* Rita Rowland   *Mus* Jerry Goldsmith   *Art Dir* Jack Martin Smith, William Crebee, Fred Harpman
● Anouk Aimee, Dirk Bogarde, John Vernon, Anna Karina, Philippe Noiret, Michael York (20th Century-Fox)

Difficulties and hazards involved in compressing four novels into a single film are self-revelatory. Based upon Lawrence Durrell's novel, *Justine* and three other volumes comprising author's *Alexandria Quartet*, the plottage is particularly difficult to follow.

While the story rivets on Anouk Aimee as the Egyptian Jewess, a prostitute wed to one of her country's most powerful financiers, there are such a multiplicity of elements and forms of love as to prove overly-burdensome for the screen.

As a further hurdle to easy comprehension, Aimee, a French actress, frequently cannot be understood.

Aimee is arresting in her delineation and frequently gives an exciting performance. Michael York, as the Englishman, shares male honors with Dirk Bogarde, playing a British diplomat, and John Vernon, the husband, who heads the Coptics' plans to save their own necks in Egypt.

....

■ JUST LIKE A WOMAN

1992, 106 MINS, UK ◇ ⓥ ⊙

Dir Christopher Monger   *Prod* Nick Evans   *Scr* Nick Evans   *Ph* Alan Hume   *Ed* Nicolas Gaster   *Mus* Michael Storey   *Art Dir* John Box
● Julie Walters, Adrian Pasdar, Paul Freeman, Gordon Kennedy, Ian Redford, Shelley Thompson (Rank/LWT/Zenith)

Except for Edward D. Wood's notorious *Glen or Glenda*, which wasn't intentionally amusing, *Just Like a Woman* is the funniest plea for tolerance of transvestites ever made.

Adrian Pasdar stars as a Yank financial whiz employed by a London investment firm. At first, he seems to have it all: a rewarding job, a wife, two children and all the lacy underwear a cross-dresser could want.

His world comes crashing down when his wife, finding some unfamiliar panties at home, figures her husband is unfaithful and kicks him out. Pasdar moves into a rooming-house operated by the somewhat older (and appreciably wiser) Julie Walters, cast as a divorcee longing for excitement.

Walters offers a tasty mix of sauciness and common sense in her best big-screen turn since *Educating Rita*. Pasdar is sympathetic and engaging in a tricky role, and he certainly looks androgynous enough for the basic gimmick [from Monica Jay's novel *Geraldine*] to work.

....

■ JUST LIKE IN THE MOVIES

1990, 90 MINS, US ◇

Dir Bram Towbin, Mark Halliday   *Prod* Alon Kasha   *Scr* Bram Towbin, Mark Halliday   *Ph* Peter Fernberger   *Ed* Jay Keuper   *Mus* John Hill   *Art Dir* Marek Dobrowolski
● Jay O. Sanders, Alan Ruck, Kathrine Borowitz, Michael Jeter, Alex Vincent (Alon Kasha)

The codirectors drew on their experience as cinematographers for a private investigator to fashion a screenplay that could be described as a seriocomic cross between *The Conversation* and *Kramer vs. Kramer*.

Jay O. Sanders is exceptionally good as Ryan Legrand, a New York investigator who specializes in matrimonial cases. Legrand takes a dead-serious, just-the-facts approach to gathering evidence of adultery, leaving most of the jokes to his free-spirited cinematographer, Dean (Alan Ruck).

Legrand has kept a tight leash on his emotions for far too long. So he joins a video dating service, and gets involved with a struggling actress, Tura (Katherine Borowitz). When Legrand ruins a weekend with her friends with his moody peevishness, she drifts away from him. Heartbroken, Legrand responds the only way he knows how – he begins a surveillance of her.

The biggest laughs come from incidental details and loony supporting characters; *Just Like in the Movies* makes the most of a limited budget.

• •

■ JUST ONE OF THE GUYS

1985, 100 MINS, US ◇ ⓥ ⊙

Dir Lisa Gottlieb   *Prod* Andrew Fogelson   *Scr* Dennis Feldman, Jeff Franklin   *Ph* John McPherson   *Ed* Lou Lombardo   *Mus* Tom Scott   *Art Dir* Paul Peters
● Joyce Hyser, Clayton Rohner, Billy Jacoby, William Zabka, Toni Hudson, Sherilyn Fenn (Summa/Triton)

Popular and tenacious high school girl passing herself off as a boy at a rival campus serves as a deceptive cover for this comedy that's really about what it's like to be an outsider in the rigid teenage caste system.

Joyce Hyser, affecting a lower register, a short haircut, and a subtle swagger, is not totally convincing as a boy because she's too pretty and too chic.

The scenario sets up the motivation for Hyser to act a boy when she becomes convinced that she lost a chance to win a summer intern job on the local daily newspaper because her journalism teacher considered her another pretty face instead of an intelligent writer.

But this feminist point is then abandoned when her new teacher makes it clear she lost the job because her contest entry was boring. You guessed it: she writes about what it's like to be a girl playing a boy in high school locker rooms, etc.

Key male part of quiet outsider whom Hyser brings to life is essayed by another film newcomer, Clayton Rohner, but Rohner looks too old to be a high school kid.

• •

■ J.W. COOP

1971, 112 MINS, US ◇

Dir Cliff Robertson   *Prod* Cliff Robertson   *Scr* Cliff Robertson   *Ph* Frank Stanley   *Ed* Alex Beaton
Mus Louie Shelton, Don Randi
● Cliff Robertson, Geraldine Page, Cristina Ferrare, R.C. Armstrong, John Crawford (Columbia)

J.W. Coop is an engaging yarn which follows the reorientation of a rodeo rider, who after spending 10 years in jail for passing a bum check and fighting with a sheriff, is released to discover he is in collision with a totally-unexpected present.

Cliff Robertson, who stars, produced, directed and scripted, has fashioned from all angles a strong, believable character study of a professional rider who finds he must not only adjust to radically altered American attitudes, but also to the rodeo circuit, which has taken on a big business air that is alien to him.

There are also startling social changes that Coop must cope with, including adjusting to a free-thinking, on-the-road woman who besides offering him no-strings companionship, attempts to turn him around by educating him to the reality of an altered society, the problems of pollution and humorously trying to turn him on to soybeans and other health foods.

Robertson's sensitive treatment and savvy direction has created a character at once heroic and tragic.

• •

■ KAFKA

1991, 98 MINS, US ◇ ⓥ ⊙

Dir Steven Soderbergh   *Prod* Stuart Cornfeld, Harry Benn   *Scr* Lem Dobbs   *Ph* Walt Lloyd   *Ed* Steven Soderbergh   *Mus* Cliff Martinez   *Art Dir* Gavin Bocquet, Tony Woollard
● Jeremy Irons, Theresa Russell, Joel Grey, Ian Holm, Jeroen Krabbe, Alec Guinness (Baltimore/Renn-Pricel)

Defiantly not a biopic, Steven Soderbergh's first outing since he burst on the scene with *sex, lies, and videotape* places the literary world's first alienated man in a sinister Prague, c. 1919, echoing author's fictional universe. But the story ultimately feels too conventional, and the portrait of the artist is too shallow to stand as a compelling or convincing evocation of a complex mind.

Penned more than 10 years earlier, Lem Dobbs' script tells of a mild-mannered insurance company clerk who, by night, writes strange stories for little-read magazines. Although somewhat antisocial, Kafka (never Franz) lives a relatively routine, orderly life.

Kafka (Jeremy Irons) is introduced to a group of anarchists by another co-worker (Theresa Russell), and although he rejects their overtures to him, Kafka is increasingly drawn into a maze of intrigue through an array of puzzling circumstances. Soon the femme co-worker disappears, and Kafka finds himself with a briefcase bomb on a secret mission to the dreaded Castle.

The villain of the piece is not named Dr Murnau (Ian Holm) for nothing. The old-world setting and exaggerated visual style readily recall German Expressionism. Although shot on the virtually unchanged streets of Prague, and despite some strong staging of individual scenes, *Kafka* is, finally, too normal. Ironically, Soderbergh scores his greatest visual coup when, 74 minutes in, he suddenly switches to color, a la *The Wizard of Oz*, upon Kafka's penetration of the castle.

Irons acts Kafka's bewilderment expertly but never truly seems like a pawn of society. Nice one-dimensional character turns are put in by the distinguished men in the cast, but Russell, with her untempered US accent, and flat readings, sticks out like a sore thumb.

• •

■ KALEIDOSCOPE

(Aka: The Bank Breakers)

1966, 102 MINS, UK/US ◇

Dir Jack Smight   *Prod* Elliott Kastner   *Scr* Robert Carrington, Jane-Howard Carrington   *Ph* Christopher Challis   *Ed* John Jympson   *Mus* Stanley Myers   *Art Dir* Maurice Carter
● Warren Beatty, Susannah York, Clive Revill, Eric Porter, Murray Melvin, George Sewell (Winkast/Warner)

Kaleidoscope is an entertaining comedy suspenser about an engaging sharpie who tampers with playing card designs so he can rack up big casino winnings. The production has some eyecatching mod clothing styles, inventive direction and other values which sustain the simple story line.

The original screenplay turns on the exploits of Warren Beatty as he etches hidden markings on cards, wins big at various Continental casinos and, via an affair with Susannah York, comes under o.o. of her dad, Scotland Yard inspector Clive Revill.

The relaxed progress of the story becomes, under Jack Smight's direction, more dynamic through his use of Christopher Challis' mobile camera. Subsidiary events and characterizations – York's dress shop, her

estrangement from Revill, latter's mechanical toy hobby, Eric Porter's deliberate viciousness, climactic card game, chase, etc – keep the pace moving.

• •

■ KANGAROO

1986, 108 MINS, AUSTRALIA ◇ ⓥ

Dir Tim Burstall   *Prod* Ross Dimsey   *Scr* Evan Jones   *Ph* Dan Burstall   *Ed* Edward McQueen-Mason   *Mus* Nathan Waks   *Art Dir* Tracy Watt
● Colin Friels, Judy Davis, John Walton, Julie Nihill, Hugh Keays-Byrne, Peter Hehir (Naked Country)

Kangaroo was written in 1922 by D.H. Lawrence after a brief visit to Australia. The resulting film is a serious, literary pic, handsomely produced and boasting a very strong cast of accomplished players.

Pic opens with a 10-minute prologue set in Cornwall, England, in 1916 and establishing the problems that Lawrence (Colin Friels) called Somers in the book and film, and his German born wife Harriet (Judy Davis) experienced during the war.

Setting then shifts to Sydney in 1922 as the couple arrive and settle into a suburban house next to Jack and Vicky Calcott. Jack is secretly involved with a society of returned soldiers, The Diggers; under the leadership of the wealthy and charming 'Kangaroo', they're training to fight an expected socialist revolution. Somers is courted both by socialist leader Struthers and by the dangerously charming 'Kangaroo', a sexually ambivalent fascist.

Given the source material, the film is full of dialog, but it's interesting, well-written dialog. Davis gives another outstanding performance as a very modern woman, abrasive and a bit cynical and world weary, yet passionate. Friels gives a tense, brooding performance, filled with charm.

• •

■ KANSAS CITY BOMBER

1972, 99 MINS, US ◇ ⓥ

Dir Jerrold Freedman   *Prod* Marty Elfand   *Scr* Thomas Rickman, Calvin Clements   *Ph* Fred Koenekamp   *Ed* David Berlatsky   *Mus* Don Ellis   *Art Dir* Joseph R. Jennings
● Raquel Welch, Kevin McCarthy, Helena Kallianiotes, Norman Alden, Jeanne Cooper, Jodie Foster (M-G-M)

Kansas City Bomber provides a gutsy, sensitive and comprehensive look at the barbaric world of the roller derby. Rugged, brawling action will more than satisfy those who enjoy that type of commercial carnage, while the script explores deftly the cynical manipulation of players and audiences.

Barry Sandler's original story, written for a university thesis, has been scripted into a well-structured screenplay, in which most dialog is appropriate to the environment.

Raquel Welch, who did a lot of her own skating, is most credible as the beauteous but tough star for whom team owner Kevin McCarthy has big plans. A fake grudge fight moves her from KC to Portland, where McCarthy is building his team for a profitable sale. At the same time, Welch is torn between her professional life and her two fatherless children.

• •

■ KANSAS CITY CONFIDENTIAL

(UK: The Secret Four)

1952, 98 MINS, US ⓥ

Dir Phil Karlson   *Prod* Edward Small   *Scr* George Bruce, Harry Essex   *Ph* George Diskant   *Ed* Buddy Small   *Mus* Paul Sawtell   *Art Dir* Edward L. Ilon
● John Payne, Coleen Gray, Preston Foster, Lee Van Cleef, Neville Brand, Jack Elam (Edward Small/United Artists)

A fast-moving, suspenseful entry for the action market [from a story by Harold R. Greene and Rowland Brown].

Mastermind of a holdup on a Kansas City bank is former police captain Preston Foster. Wearing a mask to conceal his identity, he rounds up three gunmen to pull the job. Heist is executed successfully but police seize ex-con John Payne as a prime suspect.

Cleared later, Payne hunts down the gang whom he suspects of framing him. It's a dangerous mission that leads to Guatemala.

With exception of the denouement, director Phil Karlson reins his cast in a grim atmosphere that develops momentum through succeeding reels.

Payne delivers an impressive portrayal of an unrelenting outsider who cracks the ring.

....

■ KARATE KID, THE

1984, 126 MINS, US ◇ ⓥ ⊙
Dir John G. Avildsen   *Prod* Jerry Weintraub   *Scr* Robert Mark Kamen   *Ph* James Crabe   *Ed* Bud Smith, Walt Mulconery, John G. Avildsen   *Mus* Bill Conti *Art Dir* William J. Cassidy
● Ralph Macchio, Noriyuki 'Pat' Morita, Elisabeth Shue, Martin Kove, Randee Heller, William Zabka (Columbia)

John G. Avildsen is back in the *Rocky* ring with *The Karate Kid*. More precisely, it is a *Rocky* for kids.

Daniel (Ralph Macchio) and his mother (Randee Heller) move from their home in New Jersey to Southern California. Daniel encounters the attacks of his schoolmates and he is well established as an underdog.

Enter Mr Miyagi (Noriyuki 'Pat' Morita), the mysterious maintenance man who takes Daniel under-wing. Daniel wants Miyagi to teach him how to defend himself, but the old man resists until Daniel learns that karate is a discipline of the heart and mind, of the spirit, not of vengeance and revenge.

Morita is simply terrific, bringing the appropriate authority and wisdom to the part.
□ 1984: Nomination: Best Supp. Actor (Noriyuki 'Pat' Morita)

....

■ KARATE KID PART II, THE

1986, 113 MINS, US ◇ ⓥ ⊙
Dir John G. Avildsen   *Prod* Jerry Weintraub   *Scr* Robert Mark Kamen   *Ph* James Crabe   *Ed* David Garfield, Jane Kurson, John G. Avildsen   *Mus* Bill Conti *Art Dir* William J. Cassidy
● Ralph Macchio, Noriyuki 'Pat' Morita, Nobu McCarthy, Danny Kamekona, Yuji Okumoto, Tamlyn Tomita (Columbia)

Film literally picks up where the 1984 one left off, with spunky teen Ralph Macchio winning a karate contest against no-good ruffians.

Informed that his father is gravely ill, Noriyuki 'Pat' Morita heads back to his native Okinawa, with Macchio in tow. His father, who soon dies, turns out to be the last of Morita's concerns.

Morita loved a young woman on the island but left in deference to her arranged marriage to Sato. Latter, also a karate expert, has never forgiven Morita for backing out of a fight which would have determined who got the girl. In addition, Sato's nephew takes an instant disliking to Macchio.

Script delivers any number of wise old Eastern homilies. Anyone over the age of 18 is liable to start fidgeting when Macchio dominates the action, but then viewers beyond that advanced age are irrelevant with this film.
□ 1986: Nomination: Best Song ('Glory of Love')

....

■ KARATE KID PART III, THE

1989, 111 MINS, US ◇ ⓥ ⊙
Dir John G. Avildsen   *Prod* Jerry Weintraub   *Scr* Robert Mark Kamen   *Ph* Stephen Yaconelli   *Ed* John Carter, John G. Avildsen   *Mus* Bill Conti   *Art Dir* William F. Matthews

● Ralph Macchio, Noriyuki 'Pat' Morita, Robyn Lively, Thomas Ian Griffith, Martin Kove, Sean Kanan (Columbia)

The makers of *The Karate Kid Part III* – also responsible for its successful predecessors – have either delivered or taken a few too many kicks to the head along the way, resulting in a particularly dimwitted film that will likely spell the death of the series.

The only remarkable things about it are that Ralph Macchio still looks young enough to play a 17-year-old, and that Noriyuki 'Pat' Morita can still milk some charm from his character by mumbling sage Miyagi-isms about things like life and tree roots, despite their utter inanity this time around.

Martin Kove reprises his role from the first pic as Kreese, the nasty karate master previously humbled by Miyagi (Morita) and still bitter from the experience.

This time, however, he has a patron – former Vietnam buddy Terry (Thomas Ian Griffith), who apparently has made millions dumping toxic chemicals yet has nothing better to do than devote his time to seeking vengeance against Miyagi and protege Daniel (Macchio) on Kreese's behalf.

....

■ KEEP, THE

1983, 96 MINS, UK/US ◇ ⓥ ⊙
Dir Michael Mann   *Prod* Gene Kirkwood, Howard W. Koch Jr   *Scr* Michael Mann   *Ph* Alex Thomson *Ed* Dov Hoenig   *Mus* Tangerine Dream   *Art Dir* John Box
● Scott Glenn, Alberta Watson, Jurgen Prochnow, Robert Prosky, Gabriel Byrne, Ian McKellen (Paramount)

Buried deep within *The Keep*'s mysterious exterior lies that chilling Hollywood question: how do these dogs get made?

After his promising debut with *The Thief*, this is writer-director Michael Mann's second feature [from a novel by F. Paul Wilson], testimony again to the one-step- forward, two-steps-back career theory.

Some Germans have arrived at a small Rumanian village, unaware and unafraid that the keep where they will be headquartered has an uneasy history. Their commander (Jurgen Prochnow) is a nice guy despite his job with the Wehrmacht and it's hardly his fault that his troops are gradually being eaten alive and blown apart by an unseen force that moves smokily through the keep.

Professorial Ian McKellen is brought from a concentration camp to help solve the mystery, and brings his imminently assaultable daughter (Alberta Watson). While she's being raped, the monster emerges from his fog and blows those bad guys apart, making a friend of her father.

Somewhere across the dark waters, all this commotion wakes up Scott Glenn, who sets out for the keep to make sure the monster doesn't use the professor to get out.

....

■ KEEP SMILING

1938, 91 MINS, UK
Dir Monty Banks   *Prod* Robert T. Kane   *Scr* William Conselman, Val Valentine, Rodney Ackland   *Ph* Mutz Greenbaum   *Ed* James B. Clark
● Gracie Fields, Roger Livesey, Mary Maguire, Peter Coke, Jack Donohue, Hay Petrie (20th Century-Fox)

Keep Smiling was carefully prepared with an eye to establishing the topflight British star Gracie Fields in the US. Results are meritorious, mainly due to preparation of the screenplay by William Conselman, Hollywood veteran, and direction by Monty Banks, which injects more of the American type of humor than has been present in earlier Fields starrers.

Film is good entertainment, a fast-moving filmusical with several songs delivered in crackerjack style by Fields. Story concerns show troupe headed by Fields which gets

stranded; beds in at farm of girl's grandfather; luckily acquires a bus for a tour; and winds up for a two-year engagement at a pavilion near Brighton.

Fields delivers three comedy numbers, a torch song, one swing tune that has possibilities of popularity with the bands, 'Swing Your Way to Happiness', and scores decisively in singing the religious choral, 'Jerusalem', in a small church setting.

Mary Maguire is only American player in cast, and is satisfactory as the dancing ingenue who provides the romantic interest. Mr Skip, the wirehair, is the canine who became rather famous as Astra in *The Thin Man*.

....

■ KELLY'S HEROES

1970, 148 MINS, US/YUGOSLAVIA ◇ ⓥ ⊙
Dir Brian G. Hutton   *Prod* Gabriel Katzka, Sidney Beckerman   *Scr* Troy Kennedy Martin   *Ph* Gabriel Figueroa   *Ed* John Jympson   *Mus* Lalo Schifrin *Art Dir* Jonathan Barry
● Clint Eastwood, Telly Savalas, Don Rickles, Carroll O'Connor, Donald Sutherland, Gavin MacLeod (M-G-M)

Clint Eastwood, Telly Savalas, Don Rickles and Donald Sutherland are among the stars cast as lovable roughnecks who decide to steal $16 million in gold bullion; it belongs to the Germans, so that's okay.

Nearly satirical in its overall effect, plot caroms between cliche dogface antics, detailed and gratuitous violence, caper melodramatics, and outrageous anachronism.

Eastwood stumbles onto knowledge of the gold stash from captured German officer David Hurst. Savalas, senior non-com in the platoon leisurely commanded by Hal Buckley, comes around to participating in the theft during a dull r&r period.

Eastwood's performance remains in his traditional low-key groove, thereby creating an adrenalin vacuum filled to the brim by the screen-dominating presence of Savalas and Sutherland.

....

■ KENTUCKIAN, THE

1955, 103 MINS, US ◇ ⓥ
Dir Burt Lancaster   *Prod* Harold Hecht   *Scr* A.B. Guthrie Jr   *Ph* Ernest Laszlo   *Ed* William B. Murphy *Mus* Bernard Herrmann
● Burt Lancaster, Dianne Foster, Diana Lynn, John McIntire, Walter Matthau, John Carradine (United Artists)

The rather simple story of a pioneer father, his son and their dream of new lands is the basis for this adventure-drama. The footage is long and often slow, with the really high spots of action rather scattered.

Burt Lancaster takes on the added chore of director for the production. He does a fairly competent first-job of handling most every one but himself.

Dianne Foster makes a strong impression as Hannah the bound girl who takes up with Lancaster and his young son (Donald MacDonald) after they use their riverboat passage money to pay off her indentures to a mean tavernkeeper. She, more than anyone else in the cast, adds something other than just a surface response to the story situations.

Diana Lynn is competent and attractive but, unfortunately, her role doesn't count for much in the overall drama. There's too much of ten-twent-thirt flamboyance to Walter Matthau's portrayal of the whip-cracking heavy.

....

■ KENTUCKY FRIED MOVIE, THE

1977, 90 MINS, US ◇ ⓥ
Dir John Landis   *Prod* Robert K. Weiss   *Scr* David Zucker, Jim Abrahams, Jerry Zuker   *Ph* Stephen M. Katz *Ed* George Folsey Jr   *Mus* Igo Kantor   *Art Dir* Rich Harvel

● Donald Sutherland, George Lazenby, Henry Gibson, Bill Bixby, Tony Dow (Kentucky Fried Theatre)

The Kentucky Fried Movie boasts excellent production values and some genuine wit, though a few of the sketches are tasteless.

Some of the appeal of this kind of material is purely juvenile – the dubious kick of hearing 'TV performers' use foul language and seeing them perform off-color activities – but there is also a more substantial undertone in using satire of TV and films as a means of satirizing American cultural values.

Though each viewer will have his favourites, the standout segs certainly include *Zinc Oxide*, a terrific physical comedy routine spoofing an educational film, and *Cleopatra Schwartz*, parody of a Pam Grier action film, but with a black Amazon woman married to a rabbi.

● ●

■ **KES**

1970, 112 MINS, UK ◇ ▼
Dir Ken Loach *Prod* Tony Garnett *Scr* Barry Hines, Ken Loach, Tony Garnett *Ph* Chris Menges *Ed* Roy Watts *Mus* John Cameron *Art Dir* William McCrow
● David Bradley, Freddie Fletcher, Lynne Perrie, Colin Welland, Brian Glover, Bob Bowes (Woodfall/Kestrel)

Based on a book by Barry Hines film tells of a lad brought up in a drab Yorkshire village. He's the product of a downbeat home with a permissive mum and a drunken, bullying brother. He goes to a school where the kids are also bullies and the teaching staff mainly a bunch of aggressive, unsympathetic, impatient robots. Then he finds a baby kestrel (a small falcon) on the moors. He determines to train the kestrel to fly and from then on he's a loner, obsessed by his new interest which gives him his first purpose in life.

Simply, the filmmakers have brought the background of the boy's life vividly into reality. They have surrounded him with local people (only one or two are minor actors) and turned the spotlight on this black side of British education and home life.

The young hero is brilliantly played by David Bradley, particularly in one memorable scene when an understanding master (Colin Welland) persuades him to tell the class about his kestrel and how he trains it.

Filmed entirely on location, *Kes* sometimes seems rough and ready but much of the moorland stuff is superb, and writing, editing and, above all, Ken Loach's direction are all done with dedicated affection.

● ●

■ **KEY, THE**

1934, 82 MINS, US
Dir Michael Curtiz *Scr* Laird Doyle *Ph* Ernest Haller *Ed* William Clemens, Thomas Richards *Art Dir* Robert Haas
● William Powell, Edna Best, Colin Clive, Hobart Cavanaugh, Halliwell Hobbes, Henry O'Neill (Warner)

Setting of *The Key*, adapted from the London stage play [by R. Gore-Browne and J. L. Hardy], is the Irish revolution of 1920. Recalled is that chapter of Anglo-Gaelic relations in which the marauding Black-and-Tan troops, the street-sniping patriots and the phantom-moving Michael Collins combined to make a gory, tumultuous time of it.

Only a minor part of the color and dynamic drama that these pages afford has been captured by the picture. But there is enough pulsing sweep to the background episodes to overcome the vapidity of a formula triangle – husband (Colin Clive), wife (Edna Best) and returned lover (William Powell) – to give the film an above-average rating.

Powell is starred, but the acting honors go to Clive. Fault doesn't lie with Powell. It's a role that's as wooden as the central plot itself. When the characterization calls for a debonair, glib fellow with a flair for getting himself out of femme complications, the

Powell personality clicks on all cylinders. Later, when the tale gives way to self-sacrificing, Powell becomes a puppet moving this way and that to the tug of the strings.

For Best it's a debut in American films. Hers is also a puppetlike part, giving her little chance to register anything but anguish. Next to Clive the standout bit of acting is delivered by J.M. Kerrigan who, as a noncombatant Irish, does the contacting between the revolutionists and the invading Black-and-Tans.

● ●

■ **KEY, THE**

1958, 134 MINS, UK ▼ ⊙
Dir Carol Reed *Prod* Carl Foreman *Scr* Carl Foreman *Ph* Oswald Morris *Ed* Bert Bates *Mus* Malcolm Arnold *Art Dir* Wilfrid Shingleton
● William Holden, Sophia Loren, Trevor Howard, Oscar Homolka, Kieron Moore, Bernard Lee (Open Road/ Columbia)

Based on Jan De Hartog's novel *Stella*, this is a wartime yarn, with William Holden and Trevor Howard as commanders of tugs engaged on convoy rescue duty in U-Boat Alley – the Western Approaches. This highly hazardous chore provides *The Key* with some standout thrills which alone make the pic great entertainment.

When Holden joins up with his old buddy Howard, he finds him sharing an apartment with a beautiful Swiss refugee, played with dignity and sensitive understanding by Sophia Loren. She identifies both these men with her dead fiance. When Howard is killed, Holden uses the spare key that Howard has given him to keep the apartment among tug men. Holden and Loren fall in love.

There are some outstanding scenes as, for instance, when Holden takes over command of his ship and indulges in crazy maneuvers to test its seaworthiness; a splendidly played tipsy scene between Howard and Holden; a fierce bombing and fire sequence at sea; and a tender moment when Holden and Loren fall in love.

● ●

■ **KEY LARGO**

1948, 100 MINS, US ▼ ⊙
Dir John Huston *Prod* Jerry Wald *Scr* Richard Brooks, John Huston *Ph* Karl Freund *Ed* Rudi Fehr *Mus* Max Steiner *Art Dir* Leo K. Kuter
● Humphrey Bogart, Edward G. Robinson, Lauren Bacall, Lionel Barrymore, Claire Trevor, Thomas Gomez (Warner)

A tense film thriller has been developed from Maxwell Anderson's play, *Key Largo*. Emphasis is on tension in the telling, and effective use of melodramatic mood has been used to point up the suspense.

There are overtones of soapboxing on a better world but this is never permitted to interfere with basic plot. Key West locale is an aid in stressing tension that carries through the plot. Atmosphere of the deadly, still heat of the Keys, the threat of a hurricane and the menace of merciless gangsters make the suspense seem real, and Huston's direction stresses the mood of anticipation.

Humphrey Bogart is seen as a veteran, stopping off at Key Largo to visit the family of a buddy killed in the war. He finds the rundown hotel taken over by a group of gangsters, who are waiting to exchange a load of counterfeit for real cash. Kept prisoners over a long day and night, during which a hurricane strikes, the best and the worst is brought out in the characters.

The excitement generated is quiet, seldom rambunctious or slambang, although there are moments of high action. The performances are of uniform excellence and go a long way towards establishing credibility of the events.

☐ 1948: Best Supp. Actress (Claire Trevor)

● ●

■ **KEYS OF THE KINGDOM, THE**

1945, 137 MINS, US ▼
Dir John M. Stahl *Prod* Joseph L. Mankiewicz *Scr* Joseph L. Mankiewicz, Nunnally Johnson *Ph* Arthur Miller *Ed* James B. Clark *Mus* Alfred Newman *Art Dir* James Basevi, William Darling
● Gregory Peck, Thomas Mitchell, Vincent Price, Roddy McDowall, Edmund Gwenn, Cedric Hardwicke (20th Century-Fox)

A cavalcade of a priest's life, played excellently by Gregory Peck, what transcends all the cinemaction is the impact of tolerance, service, faith and godliness.

Where the monsignor (Cedric Hardwicke) comes to out the aged, limping and poor father (Peck), he departs with humility and a new respect after he reads the good father's journal, first of unrequited love (in youth) and later in unselfish devotion, self-punishing denials and unswerving fealty to his mission as it covers more than a half century. The action (from A.J. Cronin's bestseller) starts in Scotland, shifts to China and thence back to the land of his birth.

There is a spell of prime-of-life accomplishment as he makes some headway in the far province of Chek Kow, even unto saving the life of the wealthy local mandarin's son and heir through emergency lancing of the boy's blood-poisoned arm. But comes civil war, and his mission on the beautiful Hill of the Green Jade happens to fall in direct line of fire between the authoritative army and the Chinese bandits.

☐ 1945: Nominations: Best Actor (Gregory Peck), B&W Cinematography, B&W Art Direction, Scoring of a Dramatic Picture

● ●

■ **KEY TO THE CITY**

1950, 100 MINS, US
Dir George Sidney *Prod* Z. Wayne Griffin *Scr* Robert Riley Crutcher *Ph* Harold Rosson *Ed* James E. Newcom *Mus* Bronislau Kaper
● Clark Gable, Loretta Young, Marilyn Maxwell, Frank Morgan, Raymond Burr (M-G-M)

Key to the City is a noisy, wise-cracking comedy. Dialog is flip and pseudo-sophisticated, proper for telling the plot of a quickie romance that is bred at a mayors' convention in San Francisco. Clark Gable is the honest mayor of a northern California city. Story brings Loretta Young, the equally honest mayor from New England, into antagonistic contact.

Together they strike sparks despite character opposites, become involved in unwelcome adventures that keep them in and out of jail, and find love on the fog-shrouded Telegraph Hill.

George Sidney's direction captures the noisy convention atmosphere and keys the entire movement in that vein. Raucousness was the best method of selling the yarn and keeping the laugh punchy.

● ●

■ **KHARTOUM**

1966, 134 MINS, UK ◇ ▼ ⊙
Dir Basil Dearden *Prod* Julian Blaustein *Scr* Robert Ardrey *Ph* Edward Scaife *Ed* Fergus McDonell *Mus* Frank Cordell *Art Dir* John Howell
● Charlton Heston, Laurence Olivier, Richard Johnson, Ralph Richardson, Alexander Knox, Johnny Sekka (United Artists)

Khartoum is an action-filled entertainment pic which contrasts personal nobility with political expediency. The colorful production builds in spectacular display, enhanced by Cinerama presentation, while Charlton Heston and Laurence Olivier propel towards inevitable tragedy the drama of two sincere opponents.

Filmed in Egypt and finished at England's Pinewood Studios, the historical drama depicts the events leading up to the savage death of General Charles Gordon, famed British soldier, as he sought to mobilize public opinion against the threat of a religious-political leader who would conquer the Arab world.

Heston delivers an accomplished performance as Gordon, looking like the 50-year-old trim soldier that Gordon was when picked to evacuate Khartoum of its Egyptian inhabitants.

Olivier, playing the Mahdi, is excellent in creating audience terror of a zealot who sincerely believes that a mass slaughter is Divine Will, while projecting respect and compassion for his equally-religious adversary.

Basil Dearden directs with a fine hand, while Yakima Canutt, second unit director given prominent screen credit, works simultaneously to create much big-screen razzledazzle action.
□ 1966: Nomination: Best Original Story & Screenplay

· ·

■ KICKBOXER

1989, 105 MINS, US ◇ ◈ ⊙
Dir Mark DiSalle, David Worth   *Prod* Mark DiSalle
Scr Glenn Bruce   *Ph* Jon Kranhouse   *Ed* Wayne
Wahram   *Mus* Paul Hertzog   *Art Dir* Shay Austin
● Jean-Claude Van Damme, Denis Alexio, Dennis Chan, Tong Po, Haskell Anderson, Rochelle Ashana (Kings Road)

Combine *Karate Kid* and *Rocky* with a bit more blood and gore, dull direction and a smattering of inept actors and you have *Kickboxer*.

Pic opens with Dennis Alexio (Eric Sloane) being crowned world kickboxing champion, watched by his younger brother Jean-Claude Van Damme. The duo head off to Thailand to take on the originators of kickboxing after being asked some inane questions by a journalist.

Alexio fights, and is crippled by top Thai fighter Tong Po, leaving Van Damme to swear revenge. He finds out the only way he can defeat Po is by learning Muay-Thai fighting and sets off to convince eccentric Dennis Chan (Xian Chow) to teach him.

Much of *Kickboxer* is macho nonsense full of cliche characters and risible dialog. There is no denying, though, that the fight scenes – choreographed by Van Damme – are well handled.

· ·

■ KID, THE

1921, 80 MINS, US ⊗ ◈
Dir Charles Chaplin, Chuck Reisner   *Prod* Charles
Chaplin   *Scr* Charles Chaplin   *Ph* Rollie Totheroh
● Charles Chaplin, Jackie Coogan, Edna Purviance, Carl Miller, Tom Wilson, Chuck Reisner (Chaplin/First National)

In this, Chaplin is less of the buffoon and more of the actor. But his comedy is all there and there is not a dull moment once the comedian comes into the picture, which is along about the middle of the first reel.

Introduced as 'a picture with a smile – perhaps a tear', it proves itself just that. For while it will move people to uproarious laughter and keep them in a state of uneasing delight, it also will touch their hearts and win sympathy, not only for the star, but for his leading woman, and little Jackie Coogan.

There are characteristic 'Chaplin touches'. A fine instance of imagination is where he dreams of Heaven. His slum alley is transformed into a bit of Paradise, with everybody – including his Nemesis, the cop, and a big bully who had wrecked a brick wall and bent a lamppost swinging at Charlie – turned into angels.

· ·

■ KID BROTHER, THE

1927, 83 MINS, US ⊗
Dir Ted Wilde   *Prod* Harold Lloyd   *Scr* John Grey, Tom
Crizer, Ted Wilde   *Ph* Walter Lundin

● Harold Lloyd, Jobyna Ralston, Walter James, Leo Willis, Olin Francis (Lloyd/Paramount)

Harold Lloyd has clicked again with *The Kid Brother*, about as gaggy a gag picture as he has ever done. It is just a series of gags, one following the other, some funny and others funnier.

Lloyd is somewhat different in the picture than he has been heretofore. In this case he is the youngest son of a family of three boys who live with their father, a widower.

His opening scene shows him performing this last task with the aid of a butter churn, an ingenious mechanical arrangement for the wringing out and hanging of the clothes with the aid of a kite which carries the clothes aloft as they come from the wringer.

When dad finds out that a medicine show has made a pitch and that the boy has given them a license, her orders the youngster to go down and close up the show. There are a couple of gags here that get over for howls, especially that of causing the amateur sheriff to disappear and his final hanging up against the back of the stage securely handcuffed.

Jobyna Ralston plays opposite Lloyd as the little medicine show girl and handles herself perfectly. Walter James as the comedian's father acquits himself with honors.

· ·

■ KID FOR TWO FARTHINGS, A

1955, 96 MINS, UK ◇ ◈
Dir Carol Reed   *Prod* Carol Reed   *Scr* Wolf Mankowitz
Ph Ted Scaife   *Ed* A.S. Bates   *Mus* Benjamin Frankel
Art Dir Wilfrid Shingleton
● Celia Johnson, Diana Dors, David Kossoff, Brenda De Banzie, Joe Robinson, Lou Jacobi (London)

Carol Reed has extracted a great deal of charm from Wolf Mankowitz's novel. This is not a conventional story, but a series of cameos set in the Jewish quarter of London and around the famed Petticoat Lane.

Some of the Petticoat Lane scenes were filmed on location, and the characters mainly are real enough.

Reed's direction is bold and authoritative. He uses color for the first time in his career with telling effect and, within the framework of the setting, has achieved all that could have been expected. David Kossoff gives a performance as the trouser-maker (with an unusual bent towards philosophy) that is a model of sincerity. Diana Dors plays her part as a blonde popsie with complete conviction. Celia Johnson is badly miscast as the boy's mother, and hardly ever comes to grips with the role.

· ·

■ KID FROM BROOKLYN, THE

1946, 114 MINS, US ◇ ◈ ⊙
Dir Norman Z. McLeod   *Prod* Samuel Goldwyn
Scr Don Hartman, Melville Shavelson   *Ph* Gregg Toland
Ed Daniel Mandell   *Mus* Louis Forbes (sup.), Carmen
Dragon (dir.)   *Art Dir* Perry Ferguson, Stewart Chaney,
McClure Capps
● Danny Kaye, Virginia Mayo, Vera-Ellen, Steve Cochran, Eve Arden, Lionel Stander (Goldwyn)

Based on the old Harold Lloyd starrer, *The Milky Way* (originally legit play by Lynn Root and Harry Clork), the film is aimed straight at the bellylaughs and emerges as a lush mixture of comedy, music and gals, highlighted by beautiful Technicolor and ultra-rich production mountings.

Danny Kaye is spotted in almost three-fourths of the picture's sequences, but the audience will be clamoring for more at the final fadeout. Zany comic clicks with his unique mugging, song stylizing and antics, but still packs in plenty of the wistful appeal.

With a top cast and screenplay to work with, director Norman Z. McLeod gets the most out of each situation. Story [from a screenplay by Grover Jones, Frank Butler and

Richard Connell] has Kaye as a mild-mannered milkman who gets involved with a prizefight gang when he accidentally knocks out the current middleweight champ. With the champ's publicity shot to pieces, his manager decides to capitalize on the situation by building Kaye into a contender and then cleaning up on the title bout.

Kaye's supporting cast does uniformly fine work, keeping their sights trained on the comedy throughout. Virginia Mayo, as the love interest, serves as a beautiful foil for Kaye's madcap antics and sings two ballads in acceptable fashion. Vera-Ellen gets in ably on the comedy and does some spectacular terpsichore in two equally spectacular production numbers.

· ·

■ KID GALAHAD

1937, 100 MINS, US ◈
Dir Michael Curtiz   *Prod* [uncredited]   *Scr* Seton I.
Miller   *Ph* Tony Gaudio   *Ed* George Amy   *Mus* Leo F.
Forbstein (dir.)   *Art Dir* Carl Jules Weyl
● Edward G. Robinson, Bette Davis, Humphrey Bogart, Wayne Morris, Jane Bryan, Harry Carey (Warner)

One of the oldest stories in pictures – the grooming of a heavyweight champion – has been done again with good results [from the *Saturday Evening Post* story by Francis Wallace].

The treatment is sophisticated and production deluxe. Also more than the usual amount of romance for a slugfest. This allows room for Bette Davis to moon over the clean kid from the farm, and for the fight manager's convent-bred sister to also fall in love with him.

But essentially it's the story of the kid's manager (Edward G. Robinson) who maneuvers to match the bellhop-pugilist (Wayne Morris) in order to pay off the grudge he holds for a felonious fellow-manager (Humphrey Bogart) whose methods are always on the muscle side.

Davis has two or three nice opportunities and as usual handles herself throughout with plenty of noodle work. She's been photographed for glittering results in a couple of the sequences by Tony Gaudio. Script adroitly avoids any line or allusion that could identify her as the mistress of Robinson, who, however, is constantly walking into her apartment with a proprietary air. Davis also sings one song in a night club sequence, voice seemingly being doubled.

Robinson and Bogart, both grim guys, make their rivalry entirely plausible. Both performers know how.

· ·

■ KID GALAHAD

1962, 95 MINS, US ◇ ◈
Dir Phil Karlson   *Prod* David Weisbart   *Scr* William Fay
Ph Burnett Guffey   *Ed* Stuart Gilmore   *Mus* Jeff
Alexander   *Art Dir* Cary Odell
● Elvis Presley, Gig Young, Lola Albright, Joan Blackman, Charles Bronson, Ned Glass (United Artists)

Two of the screen's most salable staples are united in *Kid Galahad*. One is Elvis Presley. The other is one of the most hackneyed yarns in the annals of cinema fiction – the one about the wholesome, greenhorn kid who wanders into training camp (be it Stillman's Gym or the Catskills), kayoes with one mighty right the hardest belter on the premises, gets an instant nickname and proceeds to score a string of victories en route to the inevitable big fight in which the fix is in.

Presley's acting resources are limited. It is, however, a surprisingly paunchy Presley in this film, and the added avoirdupois, unaided by camera, is not especially becoming. Elvis sings some half a dozen songs.

Gig Young labors through the trite, confusing part of the mixed-up proprietor of the upstate boxing stable. Pretty Joan Blackman overacts as Presley's girl. But there are two strong principal performers. One is Lola Albright as Young's unrequited torch-carrier, the other Charles Bronson as an understanding trainer.

Idyllwild, California, does not closely resemble the Catskill Mountain terrain of NY, locale of the story.

■ KID GLOVE KILLER

1942, 76 MINS, US
Dir Fred Zinnemann   *Prod* Jack Chertok   *Scr* Allen Rivkin, John C. Higgins   *Ph* Paul Vogel   *Ed* Ralph Winters   *Mus* David Snell
● Van Heflin, Marsha Hunt, Lee Bowman, Samuel S. Hinds (M-G-M)

Kid Glove Killer is one of those moderately-budgeted programmers that appear at long intervals to rise far above the level intended. Spotlight shines brightly on Van Heflin in the lead. His skillful timing and delivery of lines holds interest in many sequences that might easily have crumbled in less capable hands.

Story unfolds a compact and interesting drama of political corruption, and the experiences of a scientific criminologist in getting a test-tube solution to the murder of the mayor. Heflin is the expert of the police department, assisted by Marsha Hunt.

In addition to neatly devising entertaining dramatic content, story provides an interesting exposition of the inner workings of a scientific crime detecting laboratory; including functions of spectographs, microscopes, and chemicals.

Newcomer Fred Zinnemann deftly handles the various episodes for fine overall blending.

■ KID MILLIONS

1934, 90 MINS, US ◇ ▼
Dir Roy Del Ruth   *Prod* Samuel Goldwyn   *Scr* Arthur Sheekman, Nat Perrin, Nunnally Johnson   *Ph* Ray June   *Ed* Stuart Heisler   *Art Dir* Richard Day
● Eddie Cantor, Ann Sothern, Ethel Merman, George Murphy, Eve Sully, Jesse Block (Goldwyn/United Artists)

Another Samuel Goldwyn-Eddie Cantor musical comedy extravaganza and again strong entertainment. Follows more or less the comedy lines of all Cantor pictures. And with Cantor singing the same kind of songs.

For a final sequence an ice cream factory number in Technicolor is one of the finest jobs of tint-work yet turned out by the Kalmus lab, and the joint Seymour Felix-Willy Pogany handling of the colors, mass movements and girls creates a flaming crescendo for the production.

Cantor gives a lot of punch-lines to Eve Sully. Vaudeville comedienne makes a nice impression on her film debut. Jesse Block, her partner, gets plenty of neglect in the script, and so leaves little behind. Ethel Merman tops all her previous screen appearances. Warren Hymer is a strong asset, also.

Story works up to an Egyptian comedy sequence, with harem, mummy, torture chamber and underground wealth as elements.

■ KIDNAPPED

1960, 97 MINS, US ◇ ▼ ⊙
Dir Robert Stevenson   *Prod* Hugh Attwooll   *Scr* Robert Stevenson   *Ph* Paul Beeson   *Ed* Gordon Stone   *Mus* Cedric Thorpe Davie   *Art Dir* Carmen Dillon
● Peter Finch, James MacArthur, Bernard Lee, Niall MacGinnis, John Laurie, Peter O'Toole (Walt Disney)

Walt Disney's live-action feature is a faithful recreation of the Robert Louis Stevenson classic. The film itself is sluggish because its story line is not clear enough and for other reasons does not arouse any great anxiety or excitement in the spectator.

James MacArthur plays the young 18th-century Scottish boy cheated of his inheritance by a conniving uncle. The boy is kidnapped by a cruel shipsmaster for sale as an indentured servant in the Carolinas. He escapes through the aid of a dashing fellow Scotsman (Peter Finch).

From a story point of view, the screenplay is weak. It is never clear what the aim of the principals is, so there is not much for the spectator to pull for. Individual scenes play, but there is no mounting or cumulative effect.

Kidnapped was photographed on location in Scotland and at Pinewood, London. The locations pay off richly, with an authentic flavor. Perhaps too richly, with accents as thick as Scotch oatmeal.

Finch as the swashbuckling follower of the exiled Stuart kings is a tremendous aid to the production. MacArthur gives a sturdy performance, handicapped by little opportunity for flexibility of character.

■ KIDNAPPED

1972, 100 MINS, UK ◇ ▼
Dir Delbert Mann   *Prod* Frederick H. Brogger   *Scr* Jack Pulman   *Ph* Paul Beeson   *Ed* Peter Boita   *Mus* Roy Budd   *Art Dir* Alex Vetchinsky
● Michael Caine, Trevor Howard, Jack Hawkins, Donald Pleasence, Gordon Jackson, Vivien Heilbron (Omnibus)

Combination of Robert Louis Stevenson's *Kidnapped* and its lesser-known sequel *Catriona* results in an intriguing adventure piece set against that period in Scottish history when the English were trying to take over that country's rule.

The dying struggle between a few remaining clans who refuse to relinquish their sovereignty, and English King George who sends his redcoats into the Highlands to stamp out rebellion, is graphically depicted through the personalized story of one of the Stuarts. This overshadows the story of David Balfour, hero of *Kidnapped*, the 18th-century Scottish lad cheated of his inheritance by a conniving uncle, but pic loses nothing in the telling.

Michael Caine plays the swashbuckling character of Alan Breck, who embodies the spirit of the bloody but unbowed Highlanders. Delbert Mann's direction catches the proper flavor of the times.

Lawrence Douglas portrays David Balfour, who becomes a follower of Breck, a man with a price on his head, trying to escape to France after the bloodbath of Culloden in 1746.

■ KILLER ELITE, THE

1975, 122 MINS, US ◇ ▼ ⊙ ⊙
Dir Sam Peckinpah   *Prod* Martin Baum, Arthur Lewis   *Scr* Marc Norman, Stirling Silliphant   *Ph* Phil Lathrop   *Ed* Garth Craven, Tony De Zarroga, Monty Hellman   *Mus* Jerry Fielding   *Art Dir* Ted Haworth
● James Caan, Robert Duvall, Arthur Hill, Bo Hopkins, Mako, Gig Young (Exeter/Persky-Bright/United Artists)

The Killer Elite is an okay Sam Peckinpah actioner starring James Caan and Robert Duvall as two modern mercenaries who wind up stalking each other in a boringly complex double-cross plot [from the novel by Robert Rostand].

The initial Caan-Duvall camaraderie abruptly ends when Duvall switches sides to kill Helmut Dantine and disable Caan. Latter rehabilitates himself, with the help of nurse Katy Heflin (who could cure many a serious illness).

But CIA exec Tom Clancy's subcontract, to protect Asian political leader Mako and family from some other Asian killers who have also hired Duvall, brings Caan back into action. Street shootouts, car chases and a climactic facedown resolve many of the convoluted plot turns.

■ KILLER McCOY

1947, 103 MINS, US
Dir Roy Rowland   *Prod* Sam Zimbalist   *Scr* Frederick Hazlitt Brennan   *Ph* Joseph Ruttenberg   *Ed* Ralph E. Winters   *Mus* David Snell   *Art Dir* Cedric Gibbons, Eddie Imazu
● Mickey Rooney, Brian Donlevy, Ann Blyth, James Dunn, Tom Tully, Sam Levene (M-G-M)

Metro has concocted a fast action melodrama in *Killer McCoy* [based on the screenplay for their 1938 film, *The Crowd Roars*], to introduce Mickey Rooney to adult roles. Sentimental hoke is mixed with prize ring action but never gets too far out of hand.

Rooney makes much of his tailormade assignment in the title role. He's a tough kid who comes up to ring prominence after accidentally killing his friend, the ex-champ, who had started him on the road up. There's nothing that's very original with the story but scripting by Frederick Hazlitt Brennan has given it realistic dialog that pays off.

Plot develops from time Rooney and his sot of a father, James Dunn, become a song-and-dance team to pad out vaude tour being made by a lightweight champion. Through this association Rooney moves into the ring.

Highlights are 'Swanee River' soft-shoed by Rooney and Dunn; sweet, sentimental courting of Rooney and Ann Blyth; and the fistic finale that features plenty of rugged action.

Brian Donlevy gives strong touch to the gambler role and Blyth gets the most out of every scene. Dunn hokes up assignment as the drunken actor-father with just the right amount of overplaying to stress 'ham' character.

■ KILLERS, THE

1946, 103 MINS, US
Dir Robert Siodmak   *Prod* Mark Hellinger   *Scr* Anthony Veiller   *Ph* Woody Bredell   *Ed* Arthur Hillton   *Mus* Miklos Rozsa   *Art Dir* Jack Otterson, Martin Obzina
● Burt Lancaster, Ava Gardner, Edmond O'Brien, Albert Dekker, Sam Levene, William Conrad (Universal/Hellinger)

Taken from Ernest Hemingway's story of the same title, picture is a hard-hitting example of forthright melodrama in the best Hemingway style.

Performances without exception are top quality. It's a handpicked cast that troupes to the hilt to make it all believable. Film introduces Burt Lancaster from legit. He does a strong job, serving as the central character around whom the plot revolves. Edmond O'Brien, insurance investigator who probes Lancaster's murder, is another pivotal character who adds much to the film's acting polish. Ava Gardner is the bad girl of the piece.

Plot opens with Lancaster's murder in a small town. O'Brien takes it from there, trying to piece together events that will prove the murder of smalltown service station attendant has more significance than appears on the surface. Story has many flashbacks, told when O'Brien interviews characters in Lancaster's past, but it is all pieced together neatly for sustained drive and mood, finishing with expose of a colossal double-cross. Every character has its moment to shine and does.

Hellinger assured a music score that would heighten mood of this one by using Miklos Rozsa, and the score is an immeasurable aid in furthering suspense.

□ 1946: Nominations: Best Director, Screenplay, Editing, Scoring of a Dramatic Picture

■ KILLERS, THE

1964, 95 MINS, US ◇ ▼
Dir Don Siegel   *Prod* Don Siegel   *Scr* Gene L. Coon   *Ph* Richard L. Rawlings   *Ed* Richard Belding   *Mus* Johnny Williams   *Art Dir* Frank Arrigo, George Chan

● Lee Marvin, Angie Dickinson, John Cassavetes, Ronald Reagan, Clu Gulager, Claude Akins (Universal)

Spawned as the pilot (*Johnny North*) of Revue's projected series of two-hour films for television, but scratched when NBC balked at what was deemed an overdose of sex and brutality, this rehash of *The Killers* was redirected to theatrical exhibition, where it emerges a throwback to the period of crime and violence that monopolized the screen in the late 1930s and early 1940s.

Gene L. Coon's scenario is similar in basic structural respects, but different in character and plot specifics, to Mark Hellinger's 1946 vintage elaboration on Hemingway's concise short story. In this version, the 'hero' (John Cassavetes) is a racing car driver, which provides the background for some flashy track scenes. But Coon's screenplay is burdened with affected dialog and contrived plotwork. Virtually nothing of the original Hemingway remains.

Of the actors, Cassevetes and Clu Gulager come off best, the former arousing interest with his customary histrionic drive and intensity, the latter fashioning a colorful study in evil, a portrait of playful sadism. Lee Marvin has some impact as another distorted menace, approaching his role with the cold-blooded demeanor for which he is celebrated. Ronald Reagan fails to crash convincingly through his goodguy image in his portrayal of a ruthless crook.

● ●

■ KILLER'S KISS

1955, 67 MINS, US ⓥ

Dir Stanley Kubrick   *Prod* Stanley Kubrick, Morris Bousel
Scr Stanley Kubrick   *Ph* Stanley Kubrick   *Ed* Stanley Kubrick   *Mus* Gerald Fried
● Frank Silvera, Jamie Smith, Irene Kane, Jerry Jarret (Minotaur)

Ex-*Look* photographer Stanley Kubrick turned out *Killer's Kiss* on the proverbial shoestring. *Kiss* was more than a warm-up for Kubrick's talents, for not only did he co-produce but he directed, photographed and edited the venture from his own screenplay and original story.

Familiar plot of boy-meets-girl finds small-time fighter Jamie Smith striking up a romance with taxi dancer Irene Kane.

Kubrick's low-key lensing occasionally catches the flavor of the seamy side of Gotham life. His scenes of tawdry Broadway, gloomy tenements and grotesque brick-and-stone structures that make up Manhattan's downtown eastside loft district help offset the script's deficiencies.

● ●

■ KILLING, THE

1956, 84 MINS, US ⓥ ⊙

Dir Stanley Kubrick   *Prod* James B. Harris   *Scr* Stanley Kubrick, Jim Thompson   *Ph* Lucien Ballard   *Ed* Betty Steinberg   *Mus* Gerald Fried   *Art Dir* Ruth Sobotka
● Sterling Hayden, Coleen Gray, Marie Windsor, Elisha Cook, Vince Edwards, Jay C. Flipper (Harris-Kubrick)

This story of a $2 million race track holdup and steps leading up to the robbery, occasionally told in a documentary style which at first tends to be somewhat confusing, soon settles into a tense and suspenseful vein which carries through to an unexpected and ironic windup.

Sterling Hayden, an ex-con, masterminds the plan which includes five men. Stanley Kubrick's direction of his own script [from the novel *Clean Break* by Lionel White, dialogue by Jim Thompson] is tight and fast-paced, a quality Lucien Ballard's top photography matches to lend particular fluidity of movement.

Characters involved in the crime include Elisha Cook, a colorless little cashier at the track who is hopelessly in love with his glam-

orous, trampish wife, Marie Windsor; Ted De Corsia, a racketeering cop; Jay C. Flippen, a reformed drunk; and Joe Sawyer, track bartender.

Hayden socks over a restrained characterization, and Cook is a particular standout. Windsor is particularly good, as she digs the plan out of her husband and reveals it to her boyfriend.

● ●

■ KILLING DAD

1989, 93 MINS, UK ◇ ⓥ ⊙

Dir Michael Austin   *Prod* Iain Smith   *Scr* Michael Austin   *Ph* Gabriel Beristain   *Ed* Edward Marnier
Art Dir Adrienne Atkinson
● Denholm Elliott, Julie Walters, Richard E. Grant, Anna Massey, Laura del Sol (Scottish TV/British Screen)

First-time writer-director Michael Austin here proves he can direct; unfortunately his script is not up to par. The black humor he is trying for does not come off and he has to resort to slapstick to get the odd laugh.

Pic opens when Edith Berg (Anna Massey) receives a letter from her long-lost husband Nathy (Denholm Elliott) who left home 23 years ago claiming he was going to buy some cigarettes. He wants to come home, but the news doesn't please his son Alistair Berg (Richard E. Grant) who enjoys a peaceful existence with his mother.

He travels to Southend, on the coast, checks into the same faded hotel as his father with the plan to kill Elliott. What he finds is an unreformed character who gets drunk, lies and 'borrows' money and lives with Judith (Julie Walters).

The acting is all first-rate. Elliott has his drunk act down to a fine art, and gives his character an added sly and charming edge. Walters as the faded Judith is excellent, but for her the role is not particularly testing. Grant sports a wacky pudding bowl haircut in an attempt to get laughs, but his performance is gently menacing.

● ●

■ KILLING FIELDS, THE

1984, 141 MINS, UK ◇ ⓥ ⊙

Dir Roland Joffe   *Prod* David Puttnam   *Scr* Bruce Robinson   *Ph* Chris Menges   *Ed* Jim Clark   *Mus* Mike Oldfield   *Art Dir* Roy Walker
● Sam Waterston, Haing S. Ngor, John Malkovich, Julian Sands, Craig T. Nelson, Bill Patterson (Enigma/Goldcrest/IFI)

A story of perseverance and survival in hell on earth, *The Killing Fields* represents an admirable, if not entirely successful, attempt to bring alive to the world film audience the horror story that is the recent history of Cambodia.

Based on Pulitzer Prize-winning NY *Times* reporter Sydney Schanberg's 1980 article *The Death and Life of Dith Pran*, film is designed as a story of friendship, and it is on this level that it works least well. The intent and outward trappings are all impressively in place, but at its heart there's something missing.

Action begins in 1973, with Schanberg (Sam Waterston) arriving in Cambodia and being assisted in his reporting by Dith Pran (Haing S. Ngor), an educated, exceedingly loyal native.

Through a stupendous effort, and at great risk to his own existence, Dith Pran manages to save the lives of Schanberg and some colleagues after their capture by the victorious Khmer Rouge two years later.

Dith Pran is later transferred to a re-education camp in the Cambodian Year Zero. It is during the long camp and escape sequences, which are largely silent, that the film reaches its most gripping heights.

Because of the overall aesthetic, which does not go in for nuances of character, performances are basically functional. Fortunately, nonpro Haing S. Ngor is a naturally sympa-

thetic and camera-receptive man and he effectively carries the weight of the film's most important sequences.
□ 1984: Best Supp. Actor (Haing S. Ngor), Cinematography, Editing.
□ Nominations: Best Picture, Director, Actor (Sam Waterston), Adapted Screenplay

● ●

■ KILLING OF A CHINESE BOOKIE, THE

1976, 135 MINS, US ◇

Dir John Cassavetes   *Prod* Al Ruban   *Scr* John Cassavetes   *Ph* [uncredited]   *Ed* Tom Cornwell
Mus Bo Harwood   *Art Dir* Sam Shaw
● Ben Gazzara, Timothy Agoglia Carey, Azizi Johari, Meade Roberts, Seymour Cassel, Alice Friedland (Faces)

True to form, John Cassavetes challenges a Hollywood cliche: that technology is so advanced even the worst films usually look good. With ease, he proves that an awful film can look even worse.

As a LA strip-show operator, Ben Gazzara gets into hock to the mob, which asks him to erase the debt by knocking off an elderly Chinese bookie (Soto Joe Hugh) who accepts the bullet as if he's glad to get out of the picture.

In the process, Gazzara picks up a stomach wound of his own, which causes great pain initially, but is soon forgotten in the thrill of more aimless improvisation with girls and gangsters.

There's no cinematography credit, which suggests Cassavetes either added that hat to his writer-director wardrobe, or the real culprit left town ahead of the posse.

● ●

■ KILLING OF ANGEL STREET, THE

1981, 101 MINS, AUSTRALIA ◇ ⓥ

Dir Donald Crombie   *Prod* Anthony Buckley   *Scr* Evan Jones, Michael Craig, Cecil Holmes   *Ph* Peter James
Ed Tim Wellburn   *Mus* Brian May   *Art Dir* Lindsay Hewson
● Liz Alexander, John Hargreaves, Alexander Archdale, Reg Lye, Gordon McDougall (Forest Home/AFC)

Director Donald Crombie's fourth feature, like his best-known works, *Caddie* and *Cathy's Child*, boldly tackles an urban problem – rampant redevelopment by unscrupulous corporate manipulators. It is a powerful, hard-hitting and provocative story about corruption permeating the highest levels of society – the more so because it has a strong basis in fact.

The eponymous Angel Street consists of a row of old but charming terrace houses on the shores of Sydney Harbor, almost within spitting-distance of the famed bridge. An outwardly respectable development company, headed by a Knight of the Realm, wants to buy the homes, raze them, and erect high-rise apartments. Their methods of persuasion are far from subtle.

Then the crusty leader of the residents' action group B.C. Simmonds (Alexander Archdale), dies under suspicious circumstances. His daughter, Jessica (Liz Alexander), takes up the cudgels, aided by Communists union official, Elliot (John Hargreaves), with whom she has a brief, if improbable romantic interlude. Their opponents are not simply the developers. The film depicts an unholy alliance between big business and government.

● ●

■ KILLING OF SISTER GEORGE, THE

1968, 138 MINS, US ◇ ⓥ

Dir Robert Aldrich   *Prod* Robert Aldrich   *Scr* Lukas Heller   *Ph* Joseph Biroc   *Ed* Michael Luciano
Mus Gerald Fried   *Art Dir* William Glasgow
● Beryl Reid, Susannah York, Coral Browne, Ronald Fraser, Patricia Medina, Hugh Paddick (Palomar/Associates & Aldrich)

Frank Marcus' legiter, adapted by Lukas Heller, describes the erosion of a longtime lesbian affair between Beryl Reid – by day, the bleeding-heart heroine of a British TV sudser; by night, gin-guzzling dominant lover – and Susannah York.

Breakup is cued by decision to write Reid out of her key TV role, as executed with relish by Coral Browne, a broadcast exec who catches York's eye.

The basic thrust of the plot is the gradual development of a rapport and sympathy with Reid, in inverse ratio to the loss of respect for York.

Reid, for her part, carries it off superbly, from her pre-title nastiness to the pathetic freeze-frame-out, as she sits alone in a TV studio, contemplating her future career – that of a cartoon voice-over. Browne, with a role pitched at constant level, is excellent.

Director Robert Aldrich has achieved the look and feel of a made-in-Britain pic, although most of it was shot near downtown LA.

■ **KILL-OFF, THE**

1989, 95 MINS, US ◊ ⊕

Dir Maggie Greenwald   *Prod* Lydia Dean Pilcher
Scr Maggie Greenwald   *Ph* Declan Quinn   *Ed* James Y. Kwei   *Mus* Evan Lurie   *Art Dir* Pamela Woodbridge
● Loretta Gross, Andrew Lee Barrett, Jackson Sims, Steve Monroe, Cathy Haase (Filmworld)

The Kill-Off is a rigorous, well-acted adaptation of a hardboiled novel by Jim Thompson, with an unrelentingly grim view of human nature.

Loretta Gross gives a strong performance as Luane DeVore, an acid-tongued gossip-monger hated by almost everyone in her little community. She feigns a bedridden, feeble condition so that her husband (Steve Monroe), 20 years her junior, will take care of her hand and foot.

Things come to a head when folks decide to get rid of her, including Monroe, a slow-witted fellow whose new girlfriend (Cathy Haase) plots against his wife. Gross' death is followed by some bitter confrontations and a nihilistic finish.

Ensemble acting brings out the bitterness and hopelessness of a ragtag group of trapped characters. It's not a pretty picture, but helmer Maggie Greenwald keeps tight control of mood and tone.

■ **KIM**

1950, 112 MINS, US ◊ ⊕

Dir Victor Saville   *Prod* Leon Gordon   *Scr* Leon Gordon, Helen Deutsch, Richard Schayer   *Ph* William Skall   *Ed* George Boemler   *Mus* Andre Previn
Art Dir Cedric Gibbons, Hans Peters
● Errol Flynn, Dean Stockwell, Paul Lukas, Robert Douglas, Thomas Gomez, Cecil Kellaway (M-G-M)

Metro has quite a spectacle, but not much else, in this version of Rudyard Kipling's *Kim*. The story of youthful adventure in India comes to the screen as rambling, overlength, spotty entertainment.

Visual dressing helps somewhat to carry the episodic plot line and story does have its appealing moments, particularly when young Dean Stockwell is on screen – a young orphan who plays at being a native and encounters derrin-do adventures while aiding British intelligence ferret out a dastardly Czarist Russian plot to seize India.

Errol Flynn is the star, playing with flamboyant gusto the wily and amorous horse-trader who aids the government and Kim.

The lama sequences, in which Paul Lukas plays the holy man who advises young Kim, are much too long and slow.

■ **KINDERGARTEN COP**

1990, 110 MINS, US ◊ ⊕ ⊙

Dir Ivan Reitman   *Prod* Ivan Reitman, Brian Grazer
Scr Murray Salem, Herschel Weingrod, Timothy Harris   *Ph* Michael Chapman   *Ed* Sheldon Kahn, Wendy Bricmont   *Mus* Randy Edelman   *Art Dir* Bruno Rubeo
● Arnold Schwarzenegger, Penelope Ann Miller, Pamela Reed, Linda Hunt, Richard Tyson, Carroll Baker (Universal)

The polished comic vision that gave *Twins*, Arnold Schwarzenegger's comedy breakthrough, a storybook shine completely eludes director Ivan Reitman here. Result is a mishmash of violence, psycho-drama and lukewarm kiddie comedy [story by Murray Salem].

Schwarzenegger plays a stoic, unfriendly and ultra-dedicated LA cop obsessed with putting away a murderous drug dealer (Richard Tyson). He needs the testimony of Tyson's ex-wife, who's supposedly living in Oregon on piles of drug money she stole from Tyson. Plan is for Schwarzenegger's goofy gal-pal partner (Pamela Reed) to infiltrate the kindergarden as a teacher and figure out which kid is Tyson's, but when Reed gets a bad stomach flu Schwarzenegger has to report for the job.

It's supposed to be wildly funny to have this grim, musclebound control freak confronted with five-year-olds he can't intimidate, but it isn't. Schwarzenegger has to carry the pic alone; he never finds his focus.

Reed takes a good, feisty stab at holding up her corner of the pic, and Penelope Ann Miller is fittingly sweet and vulnerable as the single mother who romances Schwarzenegger.

■ **KIND HEARTS AND CORONETS**

1949, 106 MINS, UK ⊕ ⊙

Dir Robert Hamer   *Prod* Michael Balcon   *Scr* Robert Hamer, John Dighton   *Ph* Douglas Slocombe, Jeff Seaholme   *Ed* Peter Tanner   *Mus* Ernest Irving (dir.)
Art Dir William Kellner
● Dennis Price, Alec Guinness, Valerie Hobson, Joan Greenwood, Miles Malleson, Arthur Lowe (Ealing)

Story of the far-removed heir to the Dukedom of Chalfont who disposes of all the obstacles to his accession to the title and subsequently finds himself tried for a murder of which he is innocent may appear to be somewhat banal. But translation to a screen comedy has been effected with a mature wit.

Opening shot shows the arrival of the executioner at the prison announcing that this is his grand finale. Then the story is told in a constant flashback, recounting the methodical manner in which the one-time draper's boy works his way up to the dukedom. In this role Dennis Price is in top form, giving a quiet, dignified and polished portrayal. Greatest individual acting triumph, however, is scored by Alec Guinness who plays in turn all the members of the ancestral family.

■ **KIND OF LOVING, A**

1962, 112 MINS, UK ⊕

Dir John Schlesinger   *Prod* Joseph Janni   *Scr* Willis Hall, Keith Waterhouse   *Ph* Denys Coop   *Ed* Roger Cherrill   *Mus* Ron Grainer   *Art Dir* Ray Simm
● Alan Bates, June Ritchie, Thora Hird, James Bolam, Leonard Rossiter, Gwen Nelson (Anglo-Amalgamated)

The screenplay by Keith Waterhouse and Willis Hall [based on the novel by Stan Barstow] is set in a Lancashire industrial town and tells the bittersweet yarn of a young draftsman who is attracted by a typist in the same factory. It is a physical attraction which he cannot resist. She, on the other hand, has a deeper feeling for him.

The fumbling romance proceeds, often hurtfully, often poignantly. The inevitable happens. She becomes pregnant and he grudgingly marries her. It is obvious from the start that the union is purely physical and it is not helped by the nagging of her mother.

Schlesinger handles this film with a sharp documentary eye, but does not forget that he is unfolding a piece of fiction. The tremulous moment when the girl first gives in to the boy's physical craving, an opening wedding sequence, the desolate seashore when they go on honeymoon, the girl discussing birthcontrol hesitantly, a pub crawl, the tender scenes as the young lovers walk in the park. These and many other sequences are all handled with tact, shrewd observation and wit.

June Ritchie makes an appealing debut as the bewildered Lancashire lass. Alan Bates is a likeable hero who will hold most audience's sympathy despite his weaknesses. Photographed in many parts of Lancashire to represent a composite town, lenser Coop has skillfully caught the peculiar grey drabness of the area.

■ **KING & COUNTRY**

1964, 88 MINS, UK

Dir Joseph Losey   *Prod* Joseph Losey, Norman Priggen   *Scr* Evan Jones   *Ph* Denys Coop   *Ed* Reginald Mills   *Mus* Larry Adler   *Art Dir* Richard Macdonald
● Dirk Bogarde, Tom Courtenay, Leo McKern, Barry Foster, James Villiers, Peter Copley (BHE)

The story of Private Hamp, a deserter from the battle front in World War I, has already been told on radio, television and the stage, but undeterred by this exposure, director Joseph Losey has attacked the subject with confidence and vigor, and the result is a highly sensitive and emotional drama, enlivened by sterling performances and a sincere screenplay.

The action takes place behind the lines at Passchendaele, where Hamp, a volunteer at the outbreak of war, and the sole survivor of his company, decides one day to 'go for a walk'. In fact, he contemplates walking to his home in London, but after more than 24 hours on the road, he's picked up by the Military Police and sent back to his unit to face court-martial for desertion.

The job of defending the private goes to Dirk Bogarde, a typically arrogant officer who accepts the assignment because it is his duty to do so. But during his preliminary investigation, he responds to Hamp's beguiling simplicity and honesty, coming to the inevitable conclusion that he was not responsible for his actions.

Notwithstanding its technical excellence, the picture [based on a play by John Wilson and a novel by James Lansdale Hodson] is carried by the outstanding performances of its three stars. Tom Courtenay gives a compelling study of a simple minded soldier, unable to accept the fact that he has committed a heinous crime. Bogarde's portrayal of the defending officer is also distinguished by its sincerity. Completing the stellar trio, Leo McKern's study of the medical officer is faultless, and in his big scene he unerringly stands up to Bogarde's cross-examination.

■ **KING AND I, THE**

1956, 133 MINS, US ◊ ⊕ ⊙

Dir Walter Lang   *Prod* Charles Brackett   *Scr* Ernest Lehman   *Ph* Leon Shamroy   *Ed* Robert Simpson
Mus Alfred Newman (dir.)   *Art Dir* Lyle R. Wheeler, John DeCuir
● Deborah Kerr, Yul Brynner, Rita Moreno, Martin Benson, Terry Saunders, Rex Thompson (20th Century-Fox)

All the ingredients that made Rodgers & Hammerstein's [1951] *The King and I* a memorable stage experience have been faithfully transferred to the screen. The result is a pic-

K

torially exquisite, musically exciting, and dramatically satisfying motion picture.

With Deborah Kerr in the role originally created by Gertrude Lawrence, and Yul Brynner and Terry Saunders repeating their stage performances, the production has the talent to support the opulence of this truly blockbuster presentation. CinemaScope 55, originally introduced with R&H's *Carousel*, attains its full glory with *The King and I*.

As the Victorian Englishwoman who comes to Siam to teach Western manners and English to the royal household, Kerr gives one of her finest performances. She handles the role of Mrs Anna, with charm and understanding and, when necessary, the right sense of comedy.

As the brusque, petulant, awkwardly-kind despot confused by the conflicts of Far Eastern and Western cultures, Yul Brynner gives an effective, many-shaded reading.

Although unbilled, the singing voice of Kerr is Marni Nixon. It is ghosted so well that it is hard to believe that it is not Kerr.

The film suggests a stronger romantic feeling between Mrs Anna and the king than was presented in the legituner, but it is done with the utmost delicacy.

☐ 1956: Best Actor (Yul Brynner), Color Art Direction, Sound Recording, Scoring of a Musical Picture, Color Costume Design.
☐ Nominations: Best Picture, Director, Actress (Deborah Kerr), Color Cinematography, Color Art Direction

••••••••••••••••••••••••••••••

■ **KING CREOLE**

1958, 116 MINS, US ⓥ
Dir Michael Curtiz *Prod* Hal B. Wallis *Scr* Michael V. Gazzo, Herbert Baker *Ph* Russell Harlan *Ed* Warren Low *Mus* Walter Scharf (arr.) *Art Dir* Hal Pereira, J. McMillan Johnson
● Elvis Presley, Carolyn Jones, Walter Matthau, Dolores Hart, Dean Jagger, Vic Morrow (Paramount)

The picture is based on Harold Robbins' novel, *A Stone for Danny Fisher*, but the locale has been switched to New Orleans, to Bourbon Street and to an indigenous cafe called the King Creole. Elvis Presley is a high school youth who is prevented from graduation by his attempts to take care of his weak-willed father and the density of his school teachers. He gets involved in a minor theft but thereafter goes straight when given a chance to perform in Paul Stewart's Vieux Carre saloon. His brief fling at crime returns to haunt him when the local crime boss (Walter Matthau) decrees that Presley shall leave Stewart and come sing for him.

Essentially a musical, since Presley sings 13 new songs, including a title number, film runs a little long and the premise that Matthau would launch a minor crime wave just to get one performer for his club is a little shaky.

Presley shows himself to be a surprisingly sympathetic and believable actor on occasion. He also does some very pleasant, soft and melodious, singing. Carolyn Jones contributes a strong and bitter portrait of a good girl gone wrong, moving and pathetic.

••••••••••••••••••••••••••••••

■ **KING DAVID**

1985, 114 MINS, US ◇ ⓥ ⊙
Dir Bruce Beresford *Prod* Martin Elfand *Scr* Andrew Birkin, James Costigan *Ph* Donald McAlpine *Ed* William Anderson *Mus* Carl Davis *Art Dir* Ken Adam
● Richard Gere, Edward Woodward, Denis Quilley, Niall Buggy, Jack Klaff, Cherie Lunghi (Paramount)

King David is an intensely literal telling of familiar portions of the saga of Israel's first two rulers, more historical in approach than religious.

David moves from one monumental event to the next, trying to cover as much of the story

as possible. The result is to minimize each step and every complex relationship (and doubtlessly confuse many of those who haven't been to Sunday School for awhile).

Though the overall problems may not be of his making, Richard Gere is of little help in the title role. Granted, he could have been truly awful (which he isn't), but he doesn't seem comfortable, either.

Holding back, Gere rarely makes it felt why he loves Absalom so, or lusts after Bathsheba or tolerates Saul's persecution beyond the fact that it says so in the Bible (or in the script).

David really isn't as trifling as summary makes it seem. There's a lot of history here, brought to life with good period film work and performances are generally fine.

••••••••••••••••••••••••••••••

■ **KINGDOM OF THE SPIDERS**

1977, 94 MINS, US ◇ ⓥ
Dir John Cardos *Prod* Igo Canter, Jeffrey M. Sneller *Scr* Richard Robinson, Alan Caillou *Ph* John Morrill *Ed* Steve Zaillian, Igo Canter *Art Dir* Rusty Rosene
● William Shatner, Tiffany Bolling, Woody Strode, Lieux Dressler, Altovise Davis, David McLean (Dimension)

Though hardly original, *Kingdom of the Spiders* creates its creeps and scares with care, accomplishing exactly what it sets out to do. The filmmakers have done a job that will satisfy the audience.

On paper, the picture sounds like most of many predecessors: likable scientist William Shatner, helped by beautiful, but capable woman scientist, Tiffany Bolling, find something amiss among the tarantulas of Arizona.

This time it's not nuclear testing, but chemical insecticides that's causing the trouble. Their problem: stop the little beasties before they eat the world.

But Shatner and Bolling work well together on a believable script, adding an amusing mach-feminism clash along the way that's well done.

••••••••••••••••••••••••••••••

■ **KING IN NEW YORK, A**

1957, 105 MINS, UK ⓥ
Dir Charles Chaplin *Prod* Charles Chaplin *Scr* Charles Chaplin *Ph* Georges Perinal *Ed* Spencer Reeves *Mus* Charles Chaplin *Art Dir* Allan Harris
● Charles Chaplin, Dawn Addams, Oliver Johnston, Maxine Audley, Harry Green, Michael Chaplin (Archway)

Charles Chaplin's first British offering is a tepid disappointment. Tilting against American TV is fair game and while doing this Chaplin contributes some shrewd, funny observations on a vulnerable theme. But when he sets his sights on the problem of Communism and un-American activities, the jester's mask drops. He loses objectivity and stands revealed as an embittered man.

The story has Chaplin as the amiable, dethroned monarch of Estrovia. He survives a revolution and, with his ambassador, seeks New York sanctuary. He arrives to find that his prime minister has decamped with the treasury and the king is financially flat. His matrimonial status is also rocky.

Dawn Addams is a winning tele personality who charmingly tricks Chaplin into guesting on her show. Overnight, he becomes a TV star. He then befriends a politically-minded 10-year-old whose parents are on the mat for not squealing on friends who are suspect by the Un-American Activities Committee. As a result, Chaplin is himself arraigned before this committee.

The way in which Chaplin poses his political problems through the mouth of a child is both queasy and embarrassing. On the funny side, there are such good moments as when Chaplin is being fingerprinted while being enthusiastically interviewed on US as the land of the free. But, largely, the humor is half-hearted and jaded.

••••••••••••••••••••••••••••••

■ **KING KONG**

1933, 100 MINS, US ⓥ ⊙
Dir Ernest B. Schoedsack, Merian C. Cooper *Prod* Ernest B. Schoedsack, Merian C. Cooper *Scr* James Creelman, Ruth Rose, Merian C. Cooper *Ph* Edward Lindon, Vernon L. Walker, J. O. Taylor *Ed* Ted Cheeseman *Mus* Max Steiner *Art Dir* Carroll Clark, Al Herman
● Fay Wray, Robert Armstrong, Bruce Cabot, Frank Reicher, Sam Hardy, Noble Johnson (RKO)

Highly imaginative and super-goofy yarn is mostly about a 50-foot ape who goes for a five-foot blonde. According to the billing the story is 'from an idea conceived' by Merian C. Cooper and Edgar Wallace. For their 'idea' they will have to take a bend in the direction of the late Conan Doyle and his *Lost World*, which is the only picture to which *Kong* can be compared.

Kong is the better picture. It takes a couple of reels for *Kong* to be believed, and until then it doesn't grip. But after the audience becomes used to the machine-like movements and other mechanical flaws in the gigantic animals on view, and become accustomed to the phoney atmosphere, they may commence to feel the power.

Neither the story nor the cast gains more than secondary importance, and not even close. Technical aspects are always on top. The technicians' two big moments arrive in the island jungle, where Kong and other prehistoric creatures reign, and in New York where Kong goes on a bender.

Fay Wray is the blonde who's chased by Kong, grabbed twice, but finally saved. It's a film-long screaming session for her, too much for any actress and any audience. The light hair is a change for Wray. Robert Armstrong, as the explorer, and Bruce Cabot, as the blonde's other boy friend who doesn't make her scream, are the remaining principal characters and snowed under by the technical end.

A gripping and fitting musical score and some impressive sound effects rate with the scenery and mechanism in providing *Kong* with its technical excellence.

••••••••••••••••••••••••••••••

■ **KING KONG**

1976, 134 MINS, US ◇ ⓥ ⊙
Dir John Guillermin *Prod* Dino De Laurentiis *Scr* Lorenzo Semple Jr *Ph* Richard H. Kline *Ed* Ralph E. Winters *Mus* John Barry *Art Dir* Archie J. Bacon, David A. Constable, Robert Gundlach
● Jeff Bridges, Charles Grodin, Jessica Lange, John Rudolph, Rene Auberjonois, Julius Harris (Paramount)

Faithful in substantial degree not only to the letter but also the spirit of the 1933 classic for RKO, this $22 million-plus version neatly balances superb special effects with solid dramatic credibility.

In the original, documentary producer-promoter Robert Armstrong took aspiring actress Fay Wray on an expedition to a lost Pacific island. A gigantic humanoid gorilla was found, then brought back to civilization where he wasted part of NY searching for Wray.

In Lorenzo Semple's literate modernization, Charles Grodin is the promoter, this time a scheming oil company explorer.

Rick Baker is acknowledged for his 'special contributions' to the Kong character; this means that Baker did virtually all of the perfectly-matched and expertly-sized closeups, in which the beast's range of emotions emerges with telling effect.

☐ 1976: Honorary Award (visual effects)
☐ Nominations: Best Cinematography, Sound

••••••••••••••••••••••••••••••

■ **KING KONG LIVES**

1986, 105 MINS, US ◇ ⓥ ⊙
Dir John Guillermin *Prod* Martha Schumacher *Scr* Ronald Shusett, Steven Pressfield *Ph* Alec Mills

413

Ed Malcolm Cooke   *Mus* John Scott   *Art Dir* Peter Murton
● Peter Elliot, George Yiasomi, Brian Kerwin, Linda Hamilton, John Ashton (De Laurentiis)

Film leads off with the previous [1976] pic's closing footage. Advancing to the present, the giant ape is stunningly revealed to be breathing via life-support systems, with Linda Hamilton heading a surgical team preparing to give him an artificial heart.

Brian Kerwin enters from far-off Borneo, where he has stumbled on a female Kong. He delivers her to the Hamilton group so her blood can be used for the heart transplant operation.

In portraying an Indiana Jones-type figure Kerwin strains for plausibility and film swiftly begins to lose some early credibility. His tough jungle ways are unconvincingly transformed into sensitive concern for both animals.

Meantime, the proximity of the two Kongs prompts these primates to discover what comes naturally. This would prove to be the moment when director John Guillermin loses all control of the pic. Mindless chase then proceeds pell mell for the rest of the film, with the army in hot pursuit.

●●●●●●●●●●●●●●●●●●●●●●●●●●●●

■ **KING OF COMEDY, THE**

1983, 101 MINS, US ◇ ⊛ ⊙
Dir Martin Scorsese   *Prod* Arnon Milchan   *Scr* Paul D. Zimmerman   *Ph* Fred Schuler   *Ed* Thelma Schoonmaker   *Mus* Robbie Robertson   *Art Dir* Boris Leven
● Robert De Niro, Jerry Lewis, Diahnne Abbott, Sandra Bernhard, Shelley Hack, Tony Randall (20th Century-Fox)

The King of Comedy is a royal disappointment. To be sure, Robert De Niro turns in another virtuoso performance for Martin Scorsese, just as in their four previous efforts. But once again – and even more so – they come up with a character that it's hard to spend time with. Even worse, the characters – in fact, all the characters – stand for nothing.

De Niro plays a would-be stand-up comic, determined to start at the top by getting a gig on Jerry Lewis' popular talk show. Worse still, he has a sidekick, (Sandra Bernhard) who's even nuttier than he is, only slightly more likable because she's slightly more pathetic in her desperate fantasy love for Lewis.

When all else fails, the pair kidnap Lewis to get what they want: He a spot on the show, she a night of amour.

Diahnne Abbott is excellent as a girl embarrassingly drawn into De Niro's fantasy world.

●●●●●●●●●●●●●●●●●●●●●●●●●●●●

■ **KING OF JAZZ, THE**

1930, 98 MINS, US ◇ ⊛
Dir J. Murray Anderson   *Ph* Hal Mohr, Jerome Ash   *Ed* Robert Carlisle   *Mus* Ferde Grofe (dir.)   *Art Dir* Herman Rosse
● Paul Whiteman and His Band, John Boles, Laura La Plante, Jeanette Loff (Universal)

The King of Jazz as directed by J. Murray Anderson on his first talker attempt cost Universal $2 million in his inexperienced hands.

The millions who never heard the great Paul Whiteman band play George Gershwin's *Rhapsody in Blue* won't hear it here, either. Anderson sees fit to scramble it up with 'production'. It's all busted to pieces.

Nothing here counts excepting Whiteman, his band and the finale, 'The Melting Pot'. This is an elaborately produced number, in the same manner that Anderson or Ziegfeld would have put it on in a stage show.
□ 1929/30: Best Interior Decoration (Herman Rosse)

●●●●●●●●●●●●●●●●●●●●●●●●●●●●

■ **KING OF KINGS, THE**

1927, 155 MINS, US ◇ ⊗ ⊛
Dir Cecil B. DeMille   *Prod* Cecil B. DeMille   *Scr* Jeanie Macpherson   *Ph* Peverell Marley   *Ed* Anne Bauchens, Harold McLernon   *Art Dir* Mitchell Leisen, Anton Grot
● H.B. Warner, Dorothy Cumming, Ernest Torrence, Joseph Schildkraut, James Neill, Jacqueline Logan (DeMille/PDC)

Tremendous is *The King of Kings* – tremendous in its lesson, in the daring of its picturization for a commercial theatre and tremendous in its biggest scene, the Crucifixion of Christ.

Technicolor is employed in two sections of the 14 reels, at its commencement and near the finish.

In scenes such as the Last Supper, the seduction of Judas by the Romans to betray The Christ, the healing miracles, the driving out of the evil spirits from Mary or the carrying of the Cross by Jesus (one of the most excellent in execution after the Crucifixion of the picture), there is a naturalnes that is entrancing.

And the acting is no less. The Schildkrauts (father and son), after H.B. Warner, come first to attention, the father as Caiaphas, the High Priest of Israel, and the younger as Judas, the traitor. And again no less is Ernest Torrence as Peter, Robert Edeson as Matthew, and perhaps others likewise of the Twelve Disciples, whose desertion of Jesus is brought out pathetically, almost, while His reappearance amidst them after the resurrection is an inner thrill.

●●●●●●●●●●●●●●●●●●●●●●●●●●●●

■ **KING OF KINGS**

1961, 168 MINS, US/SPAIN ◇ ⊛
Dir Nicholas Ray, [Charles Walters]   *Prod* Samuel Bronston   *Scr* Philip Yordan, [George Kilpatrick, Ray Bradbury]   *Ph* Franz F. Planer, Milton Krasner, Manuel Berenguer, [George Folsey]   *Ed* Harold F. Kress, [Margaret Booth, Renee Lichtig]   *Mus* Miklos Rozsa   *Art Dir* Georges Wakhevitch
● Jeffrey Hunter, Hurd Hatfield, Ron Randell, Harry Guardino, Rip Torn, Frank Thring (M-G-M/Bronston)

King of Kings wisely substitutes characterizations for orgies. Director Nicholas Ray has brooded long and wisely upon the meaning of his meanings, has planted plenty of symbols along the path, yet avoided the banalities of religious calendar art.

The sweep of the story presents a panorama of the conquest of Judea and its persistent rebelliousness, against which the implication of Christ's preachments assume, to pagan Roman overlords, the reek of sedition. All of this is rich in melodrama, action, battle and clash. But author Philip Yordan astutely uses the bloodthirsty Jewish patriots, unable to think except in terms of violence, as telling counterpoint to the Messiah's love-one-another creed.

Jeffrey Hunter's blue orbs and auburn bob (wig, of course) are strikingly pictorial. The handling of the Sermon on the Mount which dominates the climax of the first part before intermission is wonderfully skillful in working masses of people into an alternation of faith and skepticism while cross-cutting personal movement among them of the Saviour and his disciples.

Irish actress Siobhan McKenna as the Virgin Mary infuses a sort of strength-through-passivity, infinitely sad yet never surprised. The 16-year-old Chicago schoolgirl, Brigid Bazlen, portrays Salome as a Biblical juvenile delinquent, who bellydances rather than jitterbugs.

The brutish, muscle-bound Barabbas of Harry Guardino makes a pretty good case that sedition frequently hurts only itself.

●●●●●●●●●●●●●●●●●●●●●●●●●●●●

■ **KING OF MARVIN GARDENS, THE**

1972, 103 MINS, US ◇
Dir Bob Rafelson   *Prod* Bob Rafelson   *Scr* Jacob Brackman   *Ph* Laszlo Kovacs   *Ed* John F. Link II

Art Dir Toby Carr Rafelson
● Jack Nicholson, Bruce Dern, Ellen Burstyn, Julia Anne Robinson, Scatman Crothers, Charles Lavine (BBS/Columbia)

Admirers of director Bob Rafelson's previous feature, *Five Easy Pieces*, will be stunned by the tedious pretensions of his newest effort.

Chief culprit is undoubtedly former film critic Jacob Brackman, who drafted the screenplay from a story contrived jointly with Rafelson. Tale centres on the relationship between two brothers – the older (Bruce Dern) a self-deceiving wheeler-dealer, flanked by two chippies (Ellen Burstyn and Julia Anne Robinson); the younger (Jack Nicholson) a self-effacing FM-radio monologist who allows himself to be seduced by his brother's bravura lifestyle.

Yet for all the artistic and intellectual shortcomings, there are sufficient moments of demonstrable talent that suggest what Rafelson could have achieved with better material. Both Dern and Burstyn go far toward filling in the many characterizational holes.

●●●●●●●●●●●●●●●●●●●●●●●●●●●●

■ **KING OF NEW YORK**

1990, 103 MINS, ITALY ◇ ⊛ ⊙
Dir Abel Ferrara   *Prod* Mary Kane   *Scr* Nicholas St John   *Ph* Bojan Bazelli   *Ed* Anthony Redman   *Mus* Joe Delia   *Art Dir* Alex Tavoularis
● Christopher Walken, David Caruso, Larry Fishburne, Victor Argo, Wesley Snipes, Janet Julian (Reteitalia/Scena/Caminito)

A violence-drenched fable of Gotham druglords, *King of New York* is unusual in being an all-American production fully financed by European sources (Italy in this case). It's the first bit that's unusual.

The screenplay coolly depicts Christopher Walken as a fresh-out-of-prison gangster who vows to take over Gotham's $1 billion-plus drug industry. With his mainly black henchmen he blows away leading Colombian, Italian and Chinese kingpins and soon sets up shop at the Plaza Hotel (protected by two beautiful femme bodyguards) as the King of New York.

Director Abel Ferrara has an ominous view of New York where deadly violence can erupt instantaneously. Also impressive are large-scale setpieces, including a climax shot in Times Square, as well as a balletic orgy of bloodletting (in which Walken's bodyguards are killed).

Complementing Walken's bravura turn are equally flamboyant performances by David Caruso as the young Irish cop out to destroy Walken, and Larry Fishburne as Walken's slightly crazy aide-de-camp.

●●●●●●●●●●●●●●●●●●●●●●●●●●●●

■ **KING OF THE HILL**

1993, 102 MINS, US ◇ ⊛
Dir Steven Soderbergh   *Prod* Albert Berger, Barbara Maltby, Ron Yerxa   *Scr* Steven Soderbergh   *Ph* Elliot Davis   *Ed* Steven Soderbergh   *Mus* Cliff Martinez   *Art Dir* Gary Frutkoff
● Jesse Bradford, Jeroen Krabbe, Lisa Eichhorn, Karen Allen, Spalding Gray, Elizabeth McGovern (Wildwood/Bona Fide)

King of the Hill has all the rich satisfactions of a fine novel, a marvelous comeback for writer-director Steven Soderbergh after his problematic sophomore effort *Kafka*.

Drawing upon A.E. Hotchner's 1972 book about his St Louis childhood, Soderbergh creates a vibrant picture of the Middle American social fabric while maintaining sharp focus on the changing fortunes of 12-year-old Aaron Kurlander (Jesse Bradford), and his disintegrating family, living in the seedy Empire Hotel in a working-class section.

While Mr Kurlander (Jeroen Krabbe) scrapes by, awaiting word of a good job,

Aaron excels at school and becomes involved with some of the down-and-outers at the hotel. Ella (Amber Benson) is a nervous, bespectacled, epileptic girl. Mr Mungo (Spalding Gray) is a formerly wealthy alcoholic who eases his pain with prostie Lydia (Elizabeth McGovern). The grungy bellboy (Joseph Chrest) keeps an eagle eye on everyone.

Down to the smallest roles, all the characters are indelibly drawn, a brilliant gallery of types from all social levels. But the film wouldn't work nearly so well without Bradford. His Aaron is an examplar of the limitless potential that can exist in children before they are damaged, limited or brought down.

· ·

■ KING OF THE KHYBER RIFLES

1953, 100 MINS, US ◇

Dir Henry King   *Prod* Frank P. Rosenberg   *Scr* Ivan Goff, Ben Roberts   *Ph* Leon Shamroy   *Ed* Barbara McLean   *Mus* Bernard Herrmann   *Art Dir* Lyle R. Wheeler, Maurice Ransford

● Tyrone Power, Terry Moore, Michael Rennie, John Justin, Guy Rolfe (20th Century-Fox)

Picture is laid in the India of 1857 when British colonial troops were having trouble with Afridi tribesmen. The plot opens with Tyrone Power, a half-caste English officer, being assigned to the Khyber Rifles, a native troop at a garrison headed by Michael Rennie, English general. For romance, Rennie has a daughter, Terry Moore, who is instantly attracted to Power despite British snobbery over his mixed blood.

From here on, the footage is taken up with developing the romance while the hero protects the heroine from native dangers and kidnap attempts by Guy Rolfe, leader of the Afridis and a foster brother of Power's.

The male heroics are played with a stiff-lipped, stout-fellowish Britishism perfectly appropriate to the characters. Power is a good hero, Moore attractively handles the heroine unabashedly pursuing her man. Rennie is excellent as the commanding general and Rolfe does another of his topnotch villains.

A rousing finale climaxes the story, based on the Talbot Mundy novel, and in between CinemaScope adds sweep and spectacle to the India settings, facsimiled by the terrain around California's Lone Pine area.

· ·

■ KING, QUEEN, KNAVE

1972, 92 MINS, W. GERMANY/US ◇

Dir Jerzy Skolimowski   *Prod* Lutz Hengst   *Scr* David Seltzer, David Shaw   *Ph* Charly Steinberger   *Ed* Mel Shapiro   *Mus* Stanley Myers   *Art Dir* Rolf Zehetbauer

● David Niven, Gina Lollobrigida, John Moulder Brown, Mario Adorf, Carl Fox-Duering, Christopher Sandford (Maran/Wolper)

Polski director Jerzy Skolimowski, working in Germany, brings off an intermittently funny black comedy on first love, avariciousness and, underneath, a subversive look at economic booms and human relations in the upper classes.

Based on Vladimir Nabokov's pithy novel, its obvious tricky word play, ironic nostalgia and interplay of love, are hard to duplicate on film. Skolimowski wisely concentrates on making it as visual as possible. It does not work, for the characters are not well blocked out and the humor is oblique, but present enough for some yoks.

A gauche young orphan is invited, by an uncle he has never seen, to Germany. The blundering boy likes his easygoing uncle, David Niven, but is smitten by his sexy aunt Gina Lollobrigida who first decides to seduce the boy and then have him kill her husband to inherit the fortune.

· ·

■ KING RALPH

1991, 97 MINS, US ◇

Dir David S. Ward   *Prod* Jack Brodsky   *Scr* David S. Ward   *Ph* Kenneth MacMillan   *Ed* John Jympson   *Mus* James Newton Howard   *Art Dir* Simon Holland

● John Goodman, Peter O'Toole, John Hurt, Camille Coduri, Richard Griffiths, Leslie Phillips (Universal/Mirage/Jbro)

Crowned with John Goodman's lovable loutishness and a regally droll performance by Peter O'Toole, *King Ralph* doesn't carry much weight in the story department, though the wispy premise is handled with a blend of sprightly comedy and sappy romance.

Britain's entire royal family dies in a pre-credit sequence, resulting in a boorish American nightclub entertainer – the product of a dalliance between a prince and the American's paternal grandmother – becoming king.

After that, it's a basic fish-out-of-water tale, with King Ralph (Goodman) adjusting to the perks and constraints of nobility, aided by a group of harried advisers including his mentor Willingham (O'Toole) and officious bureaucratic Phipps (Richard Griffiths).

John Hurt plays a British lord seeking to bring the new king down so his own family can regain the throne. He facilitates a liaison between the king and a buxom lower-class British girl (Camille Coduri) in order to force his resignation.

Lensing was done on UK locations and at London's Pinewood Studios.

· ·

■ KING RAT

1965, 134 MINS, US

Dir Bryan Forbes   *Prod* James Woolf   *Scr* Bryan Forbes   *Ph* Burnett Guffey   *Ed* Walter Thompson   *Mus* John Barry   *Art Dir* Robert Smith

● George Segal, Tom Courtenay, James Fox, Patrick O'Neal, Denholm Elliott, John Mills (Coleytown/Columbia)

Filmed near Hollywood but having the feel and casting of an overseas pic, *King Rat* is a grim, downbeat and often raw prison camp drama depicting the character destruction wrought by a smalltime sharpie on fellow inmates of a Japanese POW site in the final days of the Second World War pic has some fine characterizations and directions, backed by stark, realistic and therefore solid production values, which offset in part its overlength and some script softness.

George Segal does an excellent job as US Corporal King, the 'Rat', a con artist who manipulates the meagre goods and characters of other prisoners, most of whom have higher military rank. Director Bryan Forbes has sharply etched his main character.

Ditto for Tom Courtenay, the young British officer trying to perform provost-marshal duties in the behind-the-wire hierarchy topped by weary, but worldly and practical John Mills, effective in brief footage.

James Fox, another young British officer, registers solidly as he comes under Segal's influence and develops an affection for him.

□ 1965: Nominations: Best B&W Cinematography, B&W Art Direction

· ·

■ KING RICHARD AND THE CRUSADERS

1954, 113 MINS, US ◇

Dir David Butler   *Prod* Henry Blanke   *Scr* John Twist   *Ph* J. Peverall Marley   *Ed* Irene Morra   *Mus* Max Steiner

● Rex Harrison, Virginia Mayo, George Sanders, Laurence Harvey, Robert Douglas, Michael Pate (Warner)

The Talisman, Walter Scott's classic about the third crusade, gets the full spectacle treatment in this entry.

The Scott classic details the efforts of

Christian nations from Europe, marshalled under the leadership of England's King Richard, to gain the Holy Grail from the Mohammedans. In addition to the fighting wiles of the crafty Moslems, King Richard must contend with the sinister ambitions of some of his entourage and these rivalries almost doom the crusade.

David Butler's direction manages to keep a long show nearly always moving at a fast clip. Especially attractive to the action-minded will be the jousting sequences, either those showing training or those in deadly seriousness, and the bold battling is mostly concerned with combat between the forces of good and evil among the crusaders themselves. The script is especially good in its dialog, particularly that handed to Rex Harrison.

· ·

■ KINGS GO FORTH

1958, 109 MINS, US

Dir Delmer Daves   *Prod* Frank Ross   *Scr* Merle Miller   *Ph* Daniel L. Fapp   *Ed* William Murphy   *Mus* Elmer Bernstein   *Art Dir* Fernando Carrere

● Frank Sinatra, Tony Curtis, Natalie Wood, Leora Dana, Karl Swenson, Ann Codee (United Artists)

Frank Sinatra goes soldiering in this adaptation of Joe David Brown's novel, *Kings Go Forth*. It's a simple, rather straightforward action-romance, laid against the attractive background of the French Riviera and the Maritime Alps.

The race angle is played to the hilt. The girl, played by Natalie Wood – an American living in France – is of mixed blood, her mother being white and the (dead) father having been a Negro. This revelation is the key to Wood's romantic entanglements.

It's an odd war that is being fought in this picture. The men fight and die in the mountains during the week. On weekends, there are passes for visits to the Riviera. The year is late 1944, and while Allied armies push into and beyond Paris the American Seventh Army has the job of cleaning out pockets of German resistance in the south.

Among the replacements joining Sinatra's platoon is Curtis, a rich man's son, with charm to spare and an eye for all the angles. Sinatra meets Wood and falls in love with her. She in turn falls in love with Curtis.

Sinatra, the rough-tough soldier, creates sympathy by underplaying the role. Wood looks pretty, but that's just all. Curtis has experience acting the heel, and he does a repeat. He's best when acting the charm boy.

· ·

■ KINGS OF THE SUN

1963, 108 MINS, US ◇

Dir J. Lee Thompson   *Prod* Lewis J. Rachmil   *Scr* Elliott Arnold, James R. Webb   *Ph* Joseph MacDonald   *Ed* William Reynolds   *Mus* Elmer Bernstein   *Art Dir* Alfred Ybarra

● Yul Brynner, George Chakiris, Shirley Anne Field, Richard Basehart, Brad Dexter, Barry Morse (Mirisch)

The screenplay from a story by Elliott Arnold is a kind of southern western. It describes, in broad, vague, romantic strokes the flight of the Mayan people from their homeland after crushing military defeat, their establishment of a new home, and their successful defense of it against their former conquerors thanks to the aid of a friendly resident tribe that has been willing to share the region in which the Mayans have chosen to relocate.

In more intimate terms, it is the story of the young Mayan king (George Chakiris), the leader (Yul Brynner) of the not-so-savage tribe that comes to the ultimate defense of the Mayans, and a Mayan maiden (Shirley Anne Field).

Brynner easily steals the show with his sinewy authority, masculinity and cat-like grace. Chakiris is adequate, although he lacks the epic, heroic stature with which the role might have been filled. Field is an attractive pivot for the romantic story. Others of importance include Richard Basehart as a high priest and advisor who gives consistently lousy advice.

Direction by J. Lee Thompson has its lags and lapses, but he has mounted his spectacle handsomely and commandeered the all-important battle sequences with vigor and imagination. The picture was filmed entirely in Mexico: interiors in Mexico City and exteriors in the coastal area of Mazatlan and in Chichen Itza near Yucatan.

■ KING SOLOMON'S MINES

1937, 80 MINS, UK

Dir Robert Stevenson Prod Geoffrey Barkas
Scr Michael Hogan, Roland Pertwee, A.R. Rawlinson, Charles Bennett, Ralph Spence Ph Glen MacWilliams Ed Michael Gordon Mus Mischa Spoliansky Art Dir Alfred Junge
● Paul Robeson, Cedric Hardwicke, Roland Young, John Loder, Anna Lee, Makubalo Hlubi (Gaumont-British)

With all the dramatic moments of H. Rider Haggard's adventure yarn, and production values reaching high and spectacular standards, here is a slab of genuine adventure decked in finely done, realistic African settings and led off by grand acting from Cedric Hardwicke and Paul Robeson, whose rich voice is not neglected.

Entire action is laid in the African interior, and shifts from the veldt and the desert to a native kraal, where the tale is enlivened by spectacular sequences of native war councils, with a pitched battle between two tribes magnificently and thrillingly staged.

Climax carries the action into the long-lost mines, where untold diamond wealth is hoarded, closing with a terrifying eruption of a volcano.

Robeson is a fine, impressive figure as the native carrier proved to be a king, and puts on a proud dignity that his frequent lapses into rolling song cannot bring down. Hardwicke is excellent as a tough white hunter, and Roland Young puts in his lively vein of comedy to excellent effect. John Loder and Anna Lee are less effective on the romantic side.

■ KING SOLOMON'S MINES

1950, 102 MINS, US

Dir Compton Bennett, Andrew Marton Prod Sam Zimbalist Scr Helen Deutsch Ph Robert Surtees Ed Ralph E. Winters, Conrad A. Nervig Mus [native music] Art Dir Cedric Gibbons, Paul Groesse
● Stewart Granger, Deborah Kerr, Richard Carlson, Hugo Haas, Lowell Gilmore (M-G-M)

King Solomon's Mines has been filmed against an authentic African background, lending an extremely realistic air to the H. Rider Haggard classic novel of a dangerous safari and discovery of a legendary mine full of King Solomon's treasure.

The standout sequence is the animal stampede, minutes long, that roars across the screen to the terrifying noise of panic-driven hoofbeats. It's a boff thriller scene.

Cast-wise, the choice of players is perfect. Stewart Granger scores strongly as the African hunter who takes Deborah Kerr and her brother (Richard Carlson) on the dangerous search for her missing husband. Kerr is an excellent personification of an English lady tossed into the raw jungle life, and Carlson gets across as the third white member of the safari.

□ 1950: Best Color Cinematography, Editing.
□ Nomination: Best Picture

■ KING SOLOMON'S MINES

1985, 100 MINS, US

Dir J. Lee Thompson Prod Menahem Golan, Yoram Globus Scr Gene Quintano, James R. Silke Ph Alex Phillips Ed John Shirley Mus Jerry Goldsmith Art Dir Luciano Spadoni
● Richard Chamberlain, Sharon Stone, Herbert Lom, John Rhys-Davies, Ken Gampu, June Buthelezi (Cannon)

Cannon's remake of King Solomon's Mines treads heavily in the footsteps of that other great modern hero, Indiana Jones – too heavily.

Where Jones was deft and graceful in moving from crisis to crisis, King Solomon's Mines is often clumsy with logic, making the action hopelessly cartoonish. Once painted into the corner, scenes don't resolve so much as end before they spill into the next cliff-hanger.

It's an unrelenting pace with no variation that ultimately becomes tedious. Neither the camp humor or the romance between Richard Chamberlain as the African adventurer Allan Quatermain and heroine-in-distress Sharon Stone breaks the monotony of the action.

Script plays something like a child's maze with numerous deadends and detours on the way to the buried treasure.

■ KINGS ROW

1942, 127 MINS, US

Dir Sam Wood Prod Hal B. Wallis (exec.) Scr Casey Robinson Ph James Wong Howe Ed Ralph Dawson Mus Erich Wolfgang Korngold Art Dir William Cameron Menzies
● Ann Sheridan, Robert Cummings, Ronald Reagan, Betty Field, Charles Coburn, Claude Rains (Warner)

Kings Row, Henry Bellamann's widely-read novel of small-town life at the turn of the century, becomes an impressive and occasionally inspiring, though overlong picture under Sam Wood's eloquent direction. It is an atmospheric story, steadily engrossing and plausible.

In broad outline, it is the story of the town, Kings Row, as well as of several of its people. Yarn is in three distinct parts, opening with the childhood of the five leading characters. Narration then jumps 10 years, picking up the thread as the hero begins studying medicine under the tutelage of the stern, awesome local physician-recluse.

Concluding portion includes the hero's return from studying in Vienna, his beginnings as a pioneer psychiatrist, his treatment and saving of his boyhood friend, and his romance with a new resident of the town, a beauteous girl from Vienna.

Ann Sheridan seems too casual in the early sequences as the clear-eyed, wholesome girl from the slums. However, she rises admirably to the emotional demands of the later scenes.

Robert Cummings is not entirely able to redeem a slight stuffiness in the character of the hero.

□ 1942: Nominations: Best Picture, Director, B&W Cinematography

■ KISMET

1944, 100 MINS, US

Dir William Dieterle Prod Everett Riskin Scr John Meehan Ph Charles Rosher Ed Ben Lewis Mus Herbert Stothart Art Dir Cedric Gibbons, Daniel B. Cathcart
● Ronald Colman, Marlene Dietrich, James Craig, Edward Arnold, Florence Bates, Joy Ann Page (M-G-M)

The sheer mystic fantasy of Baghdad and its royal pomp and splendor [from Edward Knoblock's play] remain acceptable escapism. The fantasy under lavish Culver City and Natalie Kalmus (Technicolor) production auspices is beautifully investitured. Ronald Colman as the beggar-sometimes-prince,

Marlene Dietrich as the dancing girl with the gold-painted gams, Edward Arnold as the double-dealing Grand Vizier, James Craig as the Caliph-sometimes-turned-gardener's son, and Joy Ann Page as Colman's sheltered daughter are a convincing casting.

Colman, the king of beggars, is impressive as the phoney prince. He lends conviction to his role, so dominating the proceedings that he makes Legs Dietrich more or less of a stooge. However, she comes through in the highlight opportunity accorded her when she does her stuff for the Vizier and Colman. Dietrich's terp specialty and getup is out of the dream book, but boffo. Thereafter Kismet (fate) follows the beggar-prince's hopes.
□ 1944: Nominations: Best Color Cinematography, Color Art Direction, Sound, Scoring of a Dramatic Picture

■ KISMET

1955, 112 MINS, US

Dir Vincente Minnelli Prod Arthur Freed Scr Charles Lederer, Luther Davis Ph Joseph Ruttenberg Ed Adrienne Fazan Mus Robert Wright, George Forrest Art Dir Cedric Gibbons, Preston Ames
● Howard Keel, Ann Blyth, Dolores Gray, Vic Damone, Monty Woolley, Sebastian Cabot (M-G-M)

Opulent escapism is what Kismet has to sell. Howard Keel is the big entertainment factor and, in somewhat lesser degree, so is Dolores Gray. Without these two there would be very few minutes that could be counted as really good fun. Robust in voice and physique, Keel injects just the right amount of tongue-in-cheek into his role of Bagdad rogue.

The other two stars are Ann Blyth and Vic Damone. Vocally, as Keel's daughter, Blyth does the proper thing with 'Baubles, Bangles and Beads', 'And This Is My Beloved' and 'Stranger in Paradise'. So does Damone, as the young caliph who loves the poet's daughter. But otherwise their romantic pairing does not come off.

Founded on Edward Knoblock's Kismet, the Bagdad fable tells of how the supposedly magical powers of street poet Keel are commandered by the scheming wazir to advance his own power.

■ KISS, THE

1929, 62 MINS, US

Dir Jacques Feyder Scr Hans Kraly Ph William Daniels Ed Ben Lewis Art Dir Cedric Gibbons
● Greta Garbo, Conrad Nagel, Anders Randolf, Holmes Herbert, Lew Ayres, George Davis (M-G-M)

The Kiss is one of Greta Garbo's best, without stretching the elastic of kindness. Few actresses could weather the series of close-ups required of Garbo in this one.

In several of the sequences, especially the intro when Irene (Garbo) tells Andre (Conrad Nagel) of her love but the impossibility of securing consent for a parting from her husband, Nagel registers the manner of an interpreter.

Pierre, the juvenile admirer of Irene who does not know until the last few story feet of her real interest, is essayed superbly by Lew Ayres.

The title is introduced in the climax when Irene is found in the wild embrace of the lad. Anders Randolf does exceptionally fine playing as the infuriated husband returning unexpectedly.

Action [from a story by George M. Saville] is laid in France. During the trial the tedium of courtroom scenes is minimized by camera moving from short semi-closes on Nagel and the judge to almost a study in black presented by Garbo.

KISS, THE

1988, 101 MINS, US ◇ ⓥ ⊙
Dir Pen Densham *Prod* Pen Densham, John Watson
Scr Stephen Volk, Tom Ropelewski *Ph* Francois Protat
Ed Stan Cole *Mus* J. Peter Robinson *Art Dir* Roy Forge
Smith
● Nicholas Kilbertus, Joanna Pacula, Meredith Salenger,
Mimi Kuzyk, Priscilla Mouzakiotis (Tri-Star/Astral/Trilogy)

Kernel of a decent story [by Stephen Volk], of
an evil woman (Joanna Pacula) who passes on
her powers via a kiss, is never fleshed out in
the script. If the setups were hokier, they
might have been funny.

There's a chilling enough moment when
the first devastating kiss is bestowed on the
younger version of Pacula (Priscilla
Mouzakiotis), but when the action moves
back to present-day suburbia in the backyard
barbecue of the Hallorans who are celebrating daughter Amy's (Meredith Salenger) confirmation, whatever suspense is foretold
dissipates quickly.

There are few connectives to link the elements of the plot. To add to the goulash,
there's a shrieking little monster that attacks
Pacula's victims, howling winds, mysteriously
opened windows and other formula attempts
to prop up this weak effort. Of the cast, Mimi
Kuzyk is the one saving grace as the
Hallorans' neighbor Brenda.

KISS BEFORE DYING, A

1956, 94 MINS, US ◇
Dir Gerd Oswald *Prod* Robert L. Jacks *Scr* Lawrence
Roman *Ph* Lucien Ballard *Ed* George Gittens
Mus Lionel Newman
● Robert Wagner, Jeffrey Hunter, Joanne Woodward,
Virginia Leith, Mary Astor, George Macready (Crown/
United Artists)

This multiple-murder story is an offbeat sort
of film, with Robert Wagner portraying a calculating youth who intends to allow nothing
to stand in his way to money. The screenplay
is from a novel by Ira Levin. Gerd Oswald's
restrained direction suits the mood.

Wagner's troubles start in opening scene,
when he learns that his college sweetheart
(Joanne Woodward) is expecting a baby, a circumstance that means she'll be disinherited
by her wealthy father and his plans to latch
onto the family fortune ruined. He pushes
her to her death from the top of a building
where they've gone to get a wedding license,
and since no one knows they've been dating
(hard for the spectator to swallow), Wagner is
in the clear.

Wagner registers in killer role. Woodward
is particularly good as the pregnant girl, and
Virginia Leith acceptable as her sister. Jeffrey
Hunter is lost as a part-time university professor responsible for the final solution of the
crimes. Mary Astor and George Macready are
okay as Wagner's mother and the girls' father.

KISS BEFORE DYING, A

1991, 95 MINS, US ◇ ⓥ ⊙
Dir James Dearden *Prod* Robert Lawrence *Scr* James
Dearden *Ph* Mike Southon *Ed* Michael Bradsell
Mus Howard Shore *Art Dir* Jim Clay
● Matt Dillon, Sean Young, Max von Sydow, James
Russo, Diane Ladd, Martha Gehman (Initial)

Played with a satirical edge, this update on
the pulpy 1956 thriller about a murderous social climber might have been good for a chill
and a hoot, but played straight it's a real
clunker.

Based on Ira Levin's novel, director James
Dearden's script gives us a brooding,
wounded nobody (Matt Dillon) who grew up
next to the Pennsylvania railroad tracks, obsessed with the fortunes of the local industrial magnate (Max von Sydow) whose

Carlsson Copper cars rumble down the
tracks. At college he gets involved with the
magnate's daughter, Dory (Sean Young), but
throws her over (a ledge, that is) when he
learns she is pregnant.

He then moves to New York and gets involved with her twin, social worker Ellen
(Young again), passing himself off as her type
and eventually marrying her and getting a job
as right-hand man to von Sydow. The only
problem is Ellen's relentless interest in her
sister's unsolved murder.

Young, in a blandly uncommitted perf, connects not at all with Dillon's hunky young
beau, and the two of them seem a cardboard
couple, going through the paces of a false life.
Not even their explicit sex scenes add excitement.

KISSIN' COUSINS

1964, 96 MINS, US ◇ ⓥ
Dir Gene Nelson *Prod* Sam Katzman *Scr* Gerald
Drayson Adams, Gene Nelson *Ph* Ellis W. Carter
Ed Ben Lewis *Mus* Fred Karger (sup.) *Art Dir* George
W. Davis, Eddie Imazu
● Elvis Presley, Arthur O'Connell, Glenda Farrell, Jack
Albertson, Pam Austin, Yvonne Craig (M-G-M/Four Leaf)

This Elvis Presley concoction is a pretty
dreary effort. Gerald Drayson Adams came
up with a ripe story premise, but he and Gene
Nelson appear to have run dry of creative inspiration in trying to develop it. Yarn is concerned with the problem faced by the US
government in attempting to establish an
ICBM base on land owned by an obstinate
hillbilly clan. To solve the problem, the air
force sends in a lieutenant (Presley) who is
kin to the stubborn critters, among whom is
his lookalike cousin (Elvis in a blond wig, no
less).

Histrionically, Presley does as well as possible under the circumstances. He also sings
eight songs. Arthur O'Connell is excellent as
the patriarch of the mountain clan, but what
a mountainous waste of talent.

KISS ME DEADLY

1955, 105 MINS, US ⓥ
Dir Robert Aldrich *Prod* Robert Aldrich *Scr* A. I.
Bezzerides *Ph* Ernest Laszlo *Ed* Michael Luciano
Mus Frank DeVol *Art Dir* William Glasgow
● Ralph Meeker, Albert Dekker, Paul Stewart, Wesley
Addy, Maxine Cooper, Cloris Leachman (Parklane)

The ingredients that sell Mickey Spillane's
novels about Mike Hammer, the hardboiled
private eye, are thoroughly worked over in
this presentation built around the rock-and-
sock character. Ralph Meeker takes on the
Hammer character and as the surly, hit first,
ask questions later, shamus turns in a job
that is acceptable, even if he seems to go soft
in a few sequences.

From the time Hammer picks up a half-
naked blonde on a lonely highway he's in for
trouble. The girl is killed and he nearly so in
an arranged accident. This gets his curiosity
aroused and he sets about trying to unravel
the puzzle.

The trail leads to a series of amorous
dames, murder-minded plug-uglies and dangerous adventures that offer excitement but
have little clarity to let the viewer know
what's going on.

KISS ME GOODBYE

1982, 101 MINS, US ◇ ⓥ
Dir Robert Mulligan *Prod* Robert Mulligan *Scr* Charlie
Peters *Ph* Donald Peterman *Ed* Sheldon Kahn
Mus Ralph Burns *Art Dir* Philip M. Jefferies
● Sally Field, James Caan, Jeff Bridges, Paul Dooley,
Claire Trevor, Mildred Natwick
(Boardwalk/Sugarman/Barish/20th Century-Fox)

Essentially a mild, de-sexed remake of the
1977 Brazilian art house hit *Dona Flor and Her
Two Husbands*, tale begins with Sally Field
starting her life up again after the death,
three years earlier, of her talented theatrical
hubby (James Caan).

Field opens up her old apartment again
and, to the bewilderment of her snobbish
mother (Claire Trevor), has decided to marry
Egyptologist Jeff Bridges. Shortly before the
wedding, however, Caan's ghost decides to
join Field back in the apartment, making possible all sorts of 'zany' scenes such as having
Caan talk to his former wife while Bridges
tries to make love to her.

Almost all the alleged humor stems from
Field relating to Caan, whom no one else can
hear or see, while she tries to engage in
everyday activities.

Supporting performers are simply called
upon to register stock reactions to the same
joke, over and over again.

KISS ME KATE

1953, 109 MINS, US ◇ ⓥ ⊙
Dir George Sidney *Prod* Jack Cummings *Scr* Dorothy
Kingsley *Ph* Charles Rosher *Ed* Ralph E. Winters
Mus Andre Previn, Saul Chaplin (dir.) *Art Dir* Cedric
Gibbons, Urie McLeary
● Kathryn Grayson, Howard Keel, Ann Miller, Keenan
Wynn, Bobby Van, James Whitmore (M-G-M)

Kiss Me Kate is Shakespeare's *Taming of the
Shrew* done over in eminently satisfying fasion
via a collaboration of superior song, dance
and comedy talents. The pictorial effects
achieved with the 3-D lensing mean little in
added entertainment.

But the play's the thing, of course, and *Kate*
has it. Dorothy Kingsley's screenplay, from
the [1948] Samuel and Bella Spewack legiter,
was hep handling of a tricky assignment.
Under George Sidney's skilled direction, *Kate*
unfolds smoothly all the way as it goes back
and forth from the backstage story to the play
within the play and works in the numerous –
and brilliant – Cole Porter tunes.

Howard Keel is a dynamic male lead, in
complete command of the acting role and
registering superbly with the songs. Kathryn
Grayson is fiery and thoroughly engaging as
Kate, tamed by Keel in *Shrew* (play within
play) and succumbing to his charms backstage after much romantic maneuvering.

Only song not from the play prototype is
'From This Moment On' and it's an agreeable
newcomer, as delivered by Tommy Rall.

Keenan Wynn and James Whitmore play a
couple of hoods bent on collecting an IOU received in a floating crapgame. In a bit of delightful incongruity they segue into a song
and dance piece titled 'Brush Up Your
Shakespeare' that has hilarious effect.

Choreography (Hermes Pan) and musical
direction (Andre Previn and Saul Chaplin)
round out the list of important credits.
□ 1953: Nomination: Best Scoring of a
Dramatic Picture

KISS ME, STUPID

1964, 126 MINS, US ⓥ ⊙
Dir Billy Wilder *Prod* Billy Wilder *Scr* Billy Wilder,
I.A.L. Diamond *Ph* Joseph LaShelle *Ed* Daniel Mandell
Mus Andre Previn *Art Dir* Alexandre Trauner
● Dean Martin, Kim Novak, Ray Walston, Felicia Farr,
Cliff Osmond, Barbara Pepper (Lopert/Phalanx)

Kiss Me, Stupid is not likely to corrupt any sensible audience. But there is a cheapness and
more than a fair share of crudeness about the
humor of a contrived double adultery situation that a husband-wife combo stumble into.
In short, the Billy Wilder-I.A.L. Diamond
script – the credits say it was triggered by an
Italian play, *L'oradella fantasia* by Anna
Bonacci – calls for a generous seasoning of

Noel Coward but, unfortunately, it provides a dash of same only now and again.

Wilder, usually a director of considerable flair and inventiveness (if not always impeccable taste), has not been able this time out to rise above a basically vulgar, as well as creatively delinquent, screenplay, and he has got at best only plodding help from two of his principals, Dean Martin and Kim Novak.

The thespic mainstays are Ray Walston and Cliff Osmond, while Felicia Farr registers nicely as the former's attractive and sexually aggressive wife.

Wilder has directed with frontal assault rather than suggestive finesse the means by which Walston and Osmond, a pair of amateur songwriters in a Nevada waystop – called Climax – on the route from Las Vegas to California, contrive to bag girl-crazy star Martin and sell him on their ditties. Idea is to make Martin stay overnight in Walston's house, to get latter's wife out of the way by creating a domestic crisis and substitute as wife for a night of accommodation with the celebrity a floozy (Novak) from a tavern.

The score, which figures rather prominently as story motivation and is orchestrated appropriately under the baton of Andre Previn, carries the unusual credit of songs by Ira and George Gershwin. Introed are three unpublished melodies by the long deceased composer to which brother Ira has provied special lyrics.

....

■ **KISS OF DEATH**

1947, 98 MINS, US ⑬

Dir Henry Hathaway   *Prod* Fred Kohlmar   *Scr* Ben Hecht, Charles Lederer   *Ph* Norbert Brodine   *Ed* J. Watson Webb Jr   *Mus* David Buttolph   *Art Dir* Lyle R. Wheeler, Leland Fuller
● Victor Mature, Brian Donlevy, Coleen Gray, Richard Widmark, Karl Malden, Mildred Dunnock   (20th Century-Fox)

Kiss of Death [based on a story by Eleazar Lipsky] is given the same semi-documentary treatment that 20th-Fox used in its three fact dramas, *The House on 92nd Street, 13 Rue Madeleine* and *Boomerang!*.

Theme is of an ex-convict who sacrifices himself to gangster guns to save his wife and two small daughters. Henry Hathaway's real-life slant on direction brings the picture close to authentic tragedy.

Victor Mature, as the ex-convict, does some of his best work. Brian Donlevy and Coleen Gray also justify their star billing, Donlevy as the assistant district attorney who sends Mature to Sing Sing for a jewelry store robbery, and later makes use of him as a stool pigeon, Gray as the girl Mature marries after being paroled.

The acting sensation of the piece is Richard Widmark, as the dimwit, blood-lusty killer.

Plot hook of the script is the decision of Mature to turn stoolie when he learns that his wife has been driven to suicide by his pals, who had promised to care for her while he was in prison, and that his two children have been put in an orphanage. He fingers Widmark for a murder rap in return for parole, marries Gray and starts a new home for his children, only to live in terror when Widmark is acquitted and set at liberty.
□ 1947: Nominations: Best Supp. Actor (Richard Widmark), Original Story

....

■ **KISS OF THE SPIDER WOMAN**

1985, 119 MINS, US/BRAZIL ◇ ⑬ ⊙

Dir Hector Babenco   *Prod* David Weisman   *Scr* Leonard Schrader   *Ph* Radolfo Sanchez   *Ed* Mauro Alice   *Mus* John Neschling   *Art Dir* Clovis Bueno
● William Hurt, Raul Julia, Sonia Braga, Jose Lewgoy, Nuno Leal Maia, Antonio Petrim (SugarLoaf/HB Filmes)

Drama [based on the novel by Manuel Puig]

centers upon the relationship between cellmates in a South American prison. Molina, played by William Hurt, is an effeminate gay locked up for having molested a young boy, while Valentin, played by Raul Julia, is a professional journalist in for a long term due to his radical political activities under a fascist regime.

They have literally nothing in common except their societal victimization, but to pass the time Molina periodically entertains Valentin with accounts of old motion pictures.

Puig kicked his book off with a ravishing account of the 1940s horror pic *Cat People*, but director Hector Babenco and scenarist Leonard Schrader have opted to concentrate on two purely imaginary films to intertwine with the narrative.

Individual reactions to the work overall will depend to a great extent on feelings about Hurt's performance. Some will find him mesmerizing, others artificially lowkeyed. By contrast, Julia delivers a very strong, straight and believable performance as an activist who at first has little patience with Hurt's predilection for escapism, but finally meets him halfway.

After the raw street power of *Pixote*, Babenco has employed a slicker, more choreographed style here. Shot entirely in Sao Paulo, film boasts fine lensing.
□ 1985: Best Actor (William Hurt).
□ Nominations: Best Picture, Director, Adapted Screenplay

....

■ **KISS THE BLOOD OFF MY HANDS**
(UK: *Blood on My Hands*)

1948, 79 MINS, US

Dir Norman Foster   *Prod* Richard Vernon   *Scr* Leonardo Bercovici, Hugh Gray   *Ph* Russell Metty   *Ed* Milton Carruth   *Mus* Miklos Rozsa   *Art Dir* Bernard Herzbrun, Nathan Juran
● Joan Fontaine, Burt Lancaster, Robert Newton, Lewis L. Russell, Aminta Dyne, Jay Novello (Universal)

Kiss the Blood Off My Hands, adapted from Gerald Butler's novel of postwar violence and demoralization [by Ben Maddow and Walter Bernstein], is an intensely moody melodrama.

concerns an uprooted vet of the Second World War whose life is shattered after he accidentally kills a man in a London pub. Although based on a formula plot, this film is lifted out of the run-of-the-mill class through Norman Foster's superior direction, first-rate thesping and well-integrated production mountings.

Lancaster delivers a convincing and sympathetic portrayal of a tough hombre who can't beat the bad breaks. Fontaine performs with sensitivity and sincerity in a demanding role. As the heavy, Newton is properly oily and detestable.

....

■ **KISS THE BOYS GOODBYE**

1941, 83 MINS, US

Dir Victor Schertzinger   *Prod* William LeBaron   *Scr* Harry Tugend, Dwight Taylor   *Ph* Ted Tetzlaff   *Ed* Paul Weatherwax   *Mus* Victor Schertzinger
● Mary Martin, Don Ameche, Oscar Levant, Jerome Cowan, Raymond Walburn, Barbara Jo Allen (Paramount)

In converting Clare Boothe's satirical comedy to films, Paramount made some major revisions of the original, substituting a group of tuneful songs for the playwright's satirical barbs, and coming up with a light, humorous and breezy piece of entertainment.

Picture effectively showcases the acting and vocal talents of Mary Martin, who ably carries the full burden of the picture with a topnotch performance.

Boothe's play was a satire on the search for the Scarlett to portray the lead in *Gone with the Wind*. For picture purposes, the lead sought is a southern beauty for a Broadway

show to be produced by Jerome Cowan, angeled by Raymond Walburn and staged by Don Ameche. Publicity stunt sends Ameche and composer Oscar Levant on tour of the south.

Schertzinger most ably pilots the compact and laugh-studded script. Songs are deftly spotted, and numerous spontaneous Dixie cracks against the 'damn' Yankees catch attention and laughs.

Ameche grooves as the play director and romantic interest in a straight line without much enthusiasm. Levant is Levant – a dour composer without a smile but withal credited with discovering the abilities of Martin about the same time the audience does.

....

■ **KISS TOMORROW GOODBYE**

1950, 102 MINS, US ⑬ ⊙

Dir Gordon Douglas   *Prod* William Cagney   *Scr* Harry Brown   *Ph* Peverell Marley   *Ed* Truman K. Wood, Walter Hannemann   *Mus* Carmen Dragon   *Art Dir* Wiard Ihnen
● James Cagney, Barbara Payton, Helena Carter, Ward Bond, Luther Adler, Barton MacLane (Warner)

Yarn [from Horace McCoy's story of the same name] opens with the trial of an assorted bunch of heavies and then quickly segues into a flashback to tell how circumstances put them in the courtroom. Flashback kicks off with a jailbreak, and the pace doesn't slow down as it takes James Cagney through a series of murders, robberies and romantic episodes.

Character is tough, but Cagney gives it an occasional light touch. He starts displaying his wanton meanness immediately by ruthlessly killing his jailbreak partner, beating the latter's sister into romantic submission and staging a daring daylight robbery of a market.

Cagney has two femme stars to court. Barbara Payton impresses as the girl who first falls victim to his tough fascination. Helena Carter is very good as a bored rich girl.

....

■ **KITCHEN TOTO, THE**

1987, 95 MINS, UK ◇ ⑬ ⊙

Dir Harry Hook   *Prod* Ann Skinner   *Scr* Harry Hook   *Ph* Roger Deakins   *Ed* Tom Priestley   *Mus* John Keane   *Art Dir* Jamie Leonard
● Bob Peck, Phyllis Logan, Edwin Mahinda, Kirsten Hughes, Robert Urquhart, Edward Judd (British Screen/ Film Four/Skreba)

Pic unfolds in 1950 when the British were facing attacks from a Kikuyu terrorist group known as Mau Mau. Bob Peck plays a regional police officer in charge of a small force of native Africans who lives with his frustrated wife (Phyllis Logan) and son.

When Mau Mau murder a black priest who's condemned them from his pulpit, Peck agrees to take in the dead man's young son (Edwin Mahinda) as his 'kitchen toto', or houseboy.

Story unfolds from the perspective of this alert, intelligent youngster who's torn between his tribal feelings on the one hand and the loyalties he has both to his murdered father and to the British who, despite their unthinking and ingrained racism, have been kind to him.

Peck is solid as the cop, Logan suitably tight-lipped as his repressed wife, and young Edwin Mahinda excellent as the troubled, tragic hero, torn between two sides in an ugly conflict.

....

■ **KITTEN WITH A WHIP**

1964, 82 MINS, US

Dir Douglas Hayes   *Prod* Harry Keller   *Scr* Douglas Hayes   *Ph* Joseph Biroc   *Ed* Russell F. Schoengarth

K

Mus Joseph Gershenson (dir.)
● Ann-Margret, John Forsythe, Peter Brown, Patricia Barry, Richard Anderson, James Ward (Universal)

Contrived plot carries an unpleasant theme, and film's only apparent reason is to offer a number of sadistic characters in the hope that the overall effect will be shocking.

Script frames on a vicious femme juvenile hall escapee (Ann-Margret) who breaks into the home of a politically-ambitious family man, whose wife is out of town, and refuses to leave. She threatens him with scandal should he call the police; then calls in a couple of strong-arm associates who take over the house and keep owner a virtual prisoner. Action is burdened with frequent uncalled-for violence.

Ann-Margret plays the unsympathetic lead with a display of over-acting and John Forsythe fares little better as her victim. Peter Brown and James Ward are the slap-happy goons.

● ●

■ **KITTY**

1945, 103 MINS, US
Dir Mitchell Leisen   *Prod* Mitchell Leisen   *Scr* Darrell Ware, Karl Tunberg   *Ph* Daniel L. Fapp   *Ed* Alma Macrorie   *Mus* Victor Young   *Art Dir* Hans Dreier, Walter Tyler
● Paulette Goddard, Ray Milland, Patric Knowles, Reginald Owen, Cecil Kellaway (Paramount)

Plot [from a novel by Rosamond Marshall] tells of an 18th-century easy lady who rose from the London slums to high position in court society – a society that was no better than that from which she rose; it only dressed better.

The Kitty depicted in the film is a petty thief and beggar who gets a start towards a cleaner life after becoming a model for Gainsborough's portrait of a lady. The portrait and Kitty attract the attention of several society fops. One, an impoverished nobleman with few scruples, takes her into his home, gives her a fictional background and plots her marriage to a duke.

Paulette Goddard credibly depicts Kitty in the various phases of the slum girl's rise in station. Ray Milland has the more difficult task of keeping the unpleasant, foppish character of Sir Hugh Marcy, Kitty's beloved, consistent and does well by it. Reginald Owen and Cecil Kellaway deliver character gems. The first is the doddering Duke of Malmunster, who strives to keep his faded youth revived with port wine. The other is Gainsborough, the painter who discovers Kitty.

● ●

■ **KITTY AND THE BAGMAN**

1982, 95 MINS, AUSTRALIA ◇ ⦿
Dir Donald Crombie   *Prod* Anthony Buckley   *Scr* John Burney, Philip Cornford   *Ph* Dean Semler   *Mus* Brian May   *Art Dir* Owen Williams
● Liddy Clark, John Stanton, Val Lehman, Gerard Maguire, Collette Mann, Reg Evans (Forest Home)

Donald Crombie, best known for *Caddie* [1976], scores again with a light, frothy bag of entertainment set in Sydney during the naughty 1920s. Pic veers wildly from serious drama to a zany spoofing of the underworld genre.

Yarn revolves around two waterfront crime queens, their pimps and beaus and 'bagmen'. Latter are not the counterpart of Gotham's bag women, but rather corrupt police go-betweens who hover betwixt the law and the crooks. Kitty, wonderfully and zestfully portrayed by Liddy Clark, rises from an innocent young bride arriving at the end of World War I, to the owner of the 'Top Hat' a no-holds-barred niterie.

Story weaves in and out, punctuated by dockside brawls, hair-pulling fights between Kitty and her Irish competitor Big Lil Delaney, shoot-outs in the streets and car chases, most of them handled whimsically.

● ●

■ **KITTY FOYLE**
THE NATURAL HISTORY OF A WOMAN

1940, 105 MINS, US ⦿ ⊙
Dir Sam Wood   *Prod* David Hempstead   *Scr* Dalton Trumbo, Donald Ogden Stewart   *Ph* Robert de Grasse   *Ed* Henry Berman   *Mus* Roy Webb   *Art Dir* Van Nest Polglase, Mark-Lee Kirk
● Ginger Rogers, Dennis Morgan, James Craig, Eduardo Ciannelli, Ernest Cossart, Gladys Cooper (RKO)

This is a film translation of Christopher Morley's bestseller expounding the romantic life of a white-collar girl – her happiness and heartbreaks and final decision for lifelong happiness. Picture is unfolded in retrospect from the time the girl is forced to choose between two men – one whom she madly loves, but cannot offer marriage, and the other waiting at church.

This swings the story back to Philadelphia, at time she falls madly in love with scion of rich family on the other side of the tracks. Romance proceeds apace, with girl followed to New York and married. But boy's straight-laced family provides disillusionment, separation and finally divorce, with Kitty suffering double tragedy of her baby's death and re-marriage of husband in his own social set.

Despite its episodic, and at times, vaguely-defined motivation, picture on whole is a poignant and dramatic portraiture of a typical Cinderella girl's love story. Several good comedy sequences interline the footage, deftly written and directed.

Ginger Rogers provides a strong dramatic portrayal in the title role, aided by competent performances by Dennis Morgan and James Craig.
□ 1940: Best Actress (Ginger Rogers).
□ Nominations: Best Picture, Director, Screenplay, Sound

● ●

■ **KLANSMAN, THE**

1974, 112 MINS, US ◇ ⦿
Dir Terence Young   *Prod* William Alexander   *Scr* Millard Kaufman, Samuel Fuller   *Ph* Lloyd Ahern   *Ed* Gene Milford   *Mus* Dale O. Warren, Stu Gardner   *Art Dir* John S. Poplin
● Lee Marvin, Richard Burton, Cameron Mitchell, Lola Falana, Luciana Paluzzi, David Huddleston (Paramount)

The Klansman is a perfect example of screen trash that almost invites derision. Terence Young's miserable film stars Lee Marvin, as a Dixie sheriff with lots of unoriginal, cliche racial trouble on his hands, and Richard Burton as an unpopular landowner in a performance as phony as his southern accent. There's not a shred of quality, dignity, relevance or impact in this yahoo-oriented bunk [from a novel by William Bradford Huie].

The small town is a Ku Klux Klan hotbed, headed by mayor David Huddleston. When Linda Evans gets raped, the KKK, including Marvin's deputy (Cameron Mitchell), suspect Spence Wil-Dee, but take out their frustration on a friend of film-debuting O. J. Simpson.

● ●

■ **KLUTE**

1971, 114 MINS, US ◇ ⦿ ⊙
Dir Alan J. Pakula   *Prod* Alan J. Pakula, David Lange   *Scr* Andy Lewis, Dave Lewis   *Ph* Gordon Willis   *Ed* Carl Lerner   *Mus* Michael Small   *Art Dir* George Jenkins
● Jane Fonda, Donald Sutherland, Charles Cioffi, Roy Scheider, Dorothy Tristan, Rita Gam (Warner)

Despite a host of terminal flaws, *Klute* is notable for presenting Jane Fonda as a much-matured actress in a role which demands that she make interesting an emotionally-unstable professional prostitute. Produced handsomely in New York, but directed tediously by Alan J. Pakula, the film is a suspenser without much suspense. Donald Sutherland shares above-title billing in a line-throwing, third-banana trifle of a part.

The script concerns a mysterious disappearance in New York of out-of-towner Robert Milli. Sutherland, a family friend who is also a cop named Klute, tries to discover what happened. The only clue is Fonda, known to the police as a hooker.

It becomes obvious too early that Charles Cioffi, a family friend and business associate of the missing man, has a few kinky sex problems. The film's wanderings through the sordid side of urban life come across more as titilation than logical dramatic exposition.

The only rewarding element is Fonda's performance. At last, and by no means not too late, there is something great coming off the screen.
□ 1971: Best Actress (Jane Fonda).
□ Nomination: Best Original Story & Screenplay

● ●

■ **KNACK, THE
. . . AND HOW TO GET IT**

1965, 84 MINS, UK
Dir Richard Lester   *Prod* Oscar Lewenstein   *Scr* Charles Wood   *Ph* David Watkin   *Ed* Anthony Gibbs   *Mus* John Barry   *Art Dir* Assheton Gorton
● Rita Tushingham, Ray Brooks, Michael Crawford, Donal Donnelly, John Bluthal, Wensley Pithey (Woodfall)

There is, according to the theory expounded in *The Knack*, quite a knack in the art of making it successfully with girls. And that about sums up the plot [from the play by Ann Jellicoe] of this offbeat production.

The expert exponent of the knack is played by Ray Brooks, and the immediate target is Rita Tushingham, a young girl just up from the country and hopefully setting off in search of the YWCA. The other two characters are both young men being instructed how to acquire the knack from the master. As Michael Crawford plays a schoolteacher, it is a neat trick to cut into schoolroom lessons with the same dialog as that used by Brooks to his two friends.

The four performances are exceptionally good. Tushingham's wide-eyed innocence is just right, and she plays with her familiar charm. Brooks is superbly confident as the glamor boy with the knack, and Crawford and Donal Donnelly both hit the right mixture of eagerness and innocence.

● ●

■ **KNIGHTRIDERS**

1981, 145 MINS, US ◇ ⦿
Dir George A. Romero   *Prod* Richard P. Rubinstein   *Scr* George A. Romero   *Ph* Michael Gornick   *Ed* George A. Romero, Pasquale Buba   *Mus* Donald Rubinstein   *Art Dir* Cletus Anderson
● Ed Harris, Gary Lahti, Tom Savini, Brother Blue, Cynthia Adler (Laurel)

A potentially exciting concept – that of modern-day knights jousting on motorcycles – is all that's good with *Knightriders*. Otherwise, George A. Romero's homage to the Arthurian ideal falls flat in all departments.

Premise is that of an itinerant troupe devoted to ancient principles which pays its way staging Renaissance fairs featuring bloodless jousts. Opening reel or so features one such event in agreeable fashion, even as it plants seeds of dissent within the ranks.

But all Romero can come up with in the way of drama over the next two-plus hours is the spectacle of invidious, greedy big city promoters and agents preying upon the group, with the pure, idealistic King Arthur figure going off to sulk when several of his men are seduced by the notion of becoming media stars.

Both the film's look, with its medieval costumes and bucolic settings, and the long stretches of high-minded talk, most about how pressures to be co-opted into society must be resisted, lend proceedings the air of a stale hippie reverie.

Another liability is the sullen, essentially unsympathetic 'King' of Ed Harris, who is never allowed to project the magnetism or romance expected of such a dreamer.

. . . .

■ KNIGHTS OF THE ROUND TABLE

1953, 115 MINS, US/UK ◇ ▼ ⊙
Dir Richard Thorpe   *Prod* Pandro S. Berman   *Scr* Talbot Jennings, Jan Lustig, Noel Langley   *Ph* Freddie Young, Stephen Dade   *Ed* Frank Clarke   *Mus* Miklos Rozsa
Art Dir Alfred Dunge, Hans Peters
● Ava Gardner, Mel Ferrer, Anne Crawford, Stanley Baker, Gabriel Woolf, Felix Aylmer (M-G-M)

Metro's first-time-out via CinemaScope is a dynamic interpretation of Thomas Malory's classic *Morte d'Arthur*. The action is fierce as the gallant Lancelot fights for his king, and armies of lancers are pitted against each other in combat to the death. The story has dramatic movement – it could easily have come off stiltedly under less skillful handling – as the knight's love for his queen nearly causes the death of both.

The carefully developed script plus knowing direction by Richard Thorpe give the legendary tale credibility. It's storybook stuff – and must be accepted as such – but the astute staging results in a walloping package of entertainment for all except, perhaps, the blase.

Robert Taylor handles the Lancelot part with conviction; apparently he's right at home with derring-do heroics. Not apparently so at home is Ava Gardner. She gets by fair enough but the role of the lovely Guinevere calls for more projected warmth. Mel Ferrer does an excellent job of portraying the sincere and sympathetic King Arthur. Gabriel Woolf, as the knight in search of the Holy Grail, is standout.
□ 1953: Nominations: Best Color Art Direction, Sound

. . . .

■ KNIGHT WITHOUT ARMOUR

1937, 108 MINS, UK ▼
Dir Jacques Feyder   *Prod* Alexander Korda
Scr Frances Marion, Lajos Biro, Arthur Wimperis
Ph Harry Stradling   *Ed* Francis Lyon, William Hornbeck
Mus Miklos Rozsa   *Art Dir* Lazare Meerson
● Marlene Dietrich, Robert Donat, Irene Vanbrugh, Herbert Lomas, Austin Trevor, Basil Gill (London Films)

A labored effort to keep this picture neutral on the subject of the Russian Revolution finally completely overshadows the simple love story intertwining Marlene Dietrich and Robert Donat.

Film is not a standout because Frances Marion's screenplay, for one thing, has lost a great deal of James Hilton's characterization in the original novel and dispensed almost entirely with the economic and physical-privation angles leading up to the revolution. Result is that only those familiar with the pre-1917 Russia will understand what the shootin's all about.

Story reveals Donat as a young British secret service agent who becomes a Red to achieve his purpose. He's sent to Siberia just before the outbreak of the World War and returns after the revolution as an assistant commissar. He rescues Dietrich's countess from execution.

Performances on the whole are good, though Dietrich restricts herself to just looking glamorous in any setting or costume. Donat handles himself with restraint and capability. There's only one other important cast assignment, John Clements as a hypersensitive commissar.

. . . .

■ K-9

1989, 102 MINS, US ◇ ▼ ⊙
Dir Rod Daniel   *Prod* Lawrence Gordon, Charles Gordon
Scr Steven Siegel, Scott Myers   *Ph* Dean Semler
Ed Lois Freeman-Fox   *Mus* Miles Goodman
Art Dir George Costello
● James Belushi, Mel Harris, Kevin Tighe, Ed O'Neill, Jerry Lee, James Handy (Gordon/Universal)

The mismatched-buddy cop picture has literally and perhaps inevitably gone to the dogs, and the only notable thing about *K-9* is that it managed to dig up the idiotic premise first.

Since the black-white pairing in *48HRS.*, there have been numerous cop film teamings. *K-9* has all the trapping of its precedessors: a flimsy plot dealing with the cop (Belushi) trying to break a drug case, an unwanted partner (Jerry Lee, a gifted German shepherd) being foisted on him and a grudging respect that develops between the two during the course of a series of shootouts, brawls and sight gags.

There are a few amazing moments (the dog's rescue of Belushi in a bar). In between lingers lots of standard action-pic fare, plenty of toothless jokes and some down-right mangy dialog.

. . . .

■ KNOCK ON ANY DOOR

1949, 98 MINS, US ▼ ⊙
Dir Nicholas Ray   *Prod* Robert Lord   *Scr* Daniel Taradash, John Monks Jr   *Ph* Burnett Guffey   *Ed* Viola Lawrence   *Mus* George Antheil   *Art Dir* Robert Peterson
● Humphrey Bogart, John Derek, George Macready (Santana)

An eloquent document on juvenile delinquency, its cause and effect, has been fashioned from *Knock on Any Door*. John Derek is the bad boy of the picture. Story opens when the youth, arrested for the wanton killing of a cop, calls on lawyer Humphrey Bogart to defend him. Bogart, himself a slums product who rose above it, reluctantly takes the case after being convinced Derek, no matter how bad, is innocent.

Nicholas Ray's direction stresses the realism of the script taken from Willard Motley's novel of the same title, and gives the film a hard, taut pace that compels complete attention.

. . . .

■ KNUTE ROCKNE ALL AMERICAN

1940, 97 MINS, US ▼
Dir Lloyd Bacon   *Prod* Hal B. Wallis (exec.)   *Scr* Robert Buckner   *Ph* Tony Gaudio   *Ed* Ralph Dawson
Mus Ray Heindorf (arr.)   *Art Dir* Robert Haas
● Pat O'Brien, Gale Page, Ronald Reagan, Donald Crisp, Albert Basserman, John Qualen (Warner)

Highlights in the colorful life of Knute Rockne, one of the most prominent figures in the world of football, are woven into a biographical film drama [based on private papers of his wife and the University of Notre Dame] that carries both inspirational and dramatic appeal on a wide scale.

Picture is studded with familiar incidents in Rockne's life – the meeting with George Gipp, latter's brief grid glories and death from pneumonia, defeat by army after a long winning streak and the early morning reception of Rock on his return to South Bend, his decision to accept coaching as a life work in preference to chemical research, and his memorable 'go out and win this one for the Gipper' in an army game. Through it all runs the theme of Rockne's whole purpose in life – moulding boys under his care to become good Americans who are conscious of their responsibilities and opportunities.

Pat O'Brien delivers a fine characterization of the immortal Rockne, catching the spirit of the role with an understanding of the human qualities of the man. Donald Crisp turns in his usual capable performance as Father John

Callahan, head of Notre Dame. Four outstanding grid coaches, friends and contemporaries of Rockne – Howard Jones, Glenn 'Pop' Warner, Alonzo Stagg and William Spaulding – are brought in for brief appearances in one sequence.

. . . .

■ KOTCH

1971, 113 MINS, US ◇ ▼
Dir Jack Lemmon   *Prod* Richard Carter   *Scr* John Paxton   *Ph* Richard H. Kline   *Ed* Ralph E. Winters   *Mus* Marvin Hamlisch   *Art Dir* Jock Poplin
● Walter Matthau, Deborah Winters, Felicia Farr, Charles Aidman, Ellen Geer, Darrell Larson (ABC Pictures)

Kotch is a great film in several ways: Jack Lemmon's outstanding directorial debut; Walter Matthau's terrific performance as an unwanted elderly parent who befriends a pregnant teenager; John Paxton's superior adaptation of Katharine Topkins' novel and a topnotch supporting cast. This heart-warming, human comedy will leave audiences fully nourished, whereas they should be left a bit starved for more.

Paxton's script fully develops many interactions between Matthau and the other players. There's Charles Aidman, smash as his loving son, slightly embarrassed at Dad's apparent dotage; Felicia Farr, Aidman's wife who wants Pop out of the house; and Deborah Winters, as the couple's baby-sitter made pregnant by Darrell Larson, then shipped off in disgrace by her brother.

The film's somewhat too leisurely pace often sacrifices primary plot movement to brilliantly-filmed digression-vignette. Basically the story has Matthau and Winters sharing a desert house together. She learns a lot about life from him, and he has the opportunity to act as a loving father and friend.
□ 1971: Nominations: Best ACtor (Walter Matthau), Editing, Song ('Life Is What You Make It'), Sound

. . . .

■ KOYAANISQATSI

1982, 87 MINS, US ◇ ▼
Dir Godfrey Reggio   *Prod* Godfrey Reggio   *Scr* Ron Fricke, Godfrey Reggio, Michael Hoenig, Alton Walpole
Ph Ron Fricke   *Ed* Alton Walpole, Ron Fricke
Mus Philip Glass, Michael Hoenig
● (IRE)

Koyaanisqatsi is at first awe-inspiring with its sweeping aerial wilderness photography. It becomes depressing when the phone lines, factories, and nuke plants spring up. The pic then runs the risk of boring audiences with shot after glossy shot of man's commercial hack job on the land and his resulting misery.

The viewer is relentlessly bombarded with images reminiscent of the title's Hopi Indian meaning, 'crazy life', while Philip Glass' tantalizing but dirgelike score drones on.

A lion's share of the pic is a cynical display of decadence intending to edify and anger to action, but instead alienating with its one-sidedness. Simple message in Godfrey Reggio's direction seems to state that Americans are not much more than the cars they assemble and the hot dogs and Twinkies they package.

. . . .

■ KRAKATOA EAST OF JAVA

1969, 135 MINS, US ◇ ▼
Dir Bernard L. Kowalski   *Prod* William R. Forman
Scr Clifford Newton Gould, Bernard Gordon   *Ph* Manuel Berenguer   *Ed* Maurice Rootes, Warren Low, Walter Hanneman   *Mus* Frank DeVol   *Art Dir* Eugene Lourie
● Maximilian Schell, Diane Baker, Brian Keith, Barbara Werle, Sal Mineo, Rossano Brazzi (ABC/Cinerama)

Krakatoa plods through a search for a sunken treasure on a boat that contains a score of one-dimensional characters.

It is the late 19th century and somewhere in the Far East a boat is loading. An amiable captain, Maximilian Schell, is forced to take on convicts. He has a diver and balloonist to help him, his girl, who is searching for her son, and a mixed crew.

In the background is a rumbling and warning that a big volcano near where they are going, Krakatoa, may erupt again but the captain scoffs that it has been quiet for 200 years.

Director Bernard L. Kowalski, for his first pic, steers for simplicity and gives it a standard action feeling. More inventiveness and perhaps a sympathetic tongue-in-cheek approach could have given this the lift and charm that it lacks.

□ 1969: Nomination: Best Visual Effects

....

■ **KRAMER VS. KRAMER**

1979, 105 MINS, US ◇ ▣ ⊙

Dir Robert Benton   *Prod* Stanley R. Jaffe   *Scr* Robert Benton   *Ph* Nestor Almendros   *Ed* Jerry Greenberg   *Art Dir* Paul Sylbert

● Dustin Hoffman, Meryl Streep, Justin Henry, Jane Alexander, Howard Duff, JoBeth Williams (Columbia)

Kramer vs. Kramer is a perceptive, touching, intelligent film about one of the raw sores of contemporary America, the dissolution of the family unit. In refashioning Avery Corman's novel, director-scripter Robert Benton has used a highly effective technique of short, poignant scenes to bring home the message that no one escapes unscarred from the trauma of separation.

It is in the latter arena that *Kramer* takes place, as Meryl Streep breaks with up-and-coming ad exec Dustin Hoffman and tyke Justin Henry to find her own role in life. Hoffman is thus left with a six-year-old son and begins a process of 'parenting' that is both humorous and affecting. Three-quarters into the film, Streep comes to claim her first-born with the traditional mother's prerogative and a nasty court battle ensues.

□ 1979: Best Picture, Director, Actor (Dustin Hoffman), Supp. Actress (Meryl Streep), Adapted Screenplay.

□ Nominations: Best Supp. Actor (Justin Henry), Supp. Actress (Jane Alexander),Cinematography, Editing

....

■ **KRAYS, THE**

1990, 119 MINS, UK ◇ ▣ ⊙

Dir Peter Medak   *Prod* Dominic Anciano, Ray Burdis   *Scr* Philip Ridley   *Ph* Alex Thomson   *Ed* Martin Walsh   *Mus* Michael Kamen   *Art Dir* Michael Pickwood

● Billie Whitelaw, Tom Bell, Gary Kemp, Martin Kemp, Susan Fleetwood, Kate Hardie (Parkfield/Fugitive)

The Krays is a chilling, if somewhat monotonous, biopic charting the rise and fall of two prominent hoods in 1950-60s London, cockney lads whose psychosexual warping leads them into ultraviolence.

Screenwriter Philip Ridley deftly explores the cynical amorality of the us-vs-them lower-class milieu, and the destructive effect of smothering mom Billie Whitelaw (in a superb performance) on her sociopathic twins, while virtually ignoring the standard cops-and-robbers dramaturgy of gangster films.

As the Krays, the brothers Kemp, who both had considerable acting experience before beginning their rock careers in Spandau Ballet, are just right in their deadeyed portrayal of what a rival thug calls 'a pair of movie gangsters'. Indeed, they are among the most repellent gangsters to come along since Richard Widmark pushed an old lady in a wheelchair down the stairs in *Kiss of Death*.

Director Peter Medak, who knew the Krays when he was an a.d., works skilfully to conjure up a cold and eerie atmosphere.

....

■ **KREMLIN LETTER, THE**

1970, 118 MINS, US ◇

Dir John Huston   *Prod* Carter De Haven, Sam Wiesenthal   *Scr* John Huston, Gladys Hill   *Ph* Ted Scaife   *Ed* Russell Lloyd   *Mus* Robert Drasnin   *Art Dir* Ted Haworth

● Bibi Andersson, Richard Boone, Nigel Green, Dean Jagger, Max von Sydow, Orson Welles (20th Century-Fox)

An American official sends a letter about China to the Kremlin and it must be gotten back because of its explosiveness and lack of authorization. This is the nub of Noel Behn's novel.

The story in cinematic form is a conglomerate of scenes, each of which makes for valuable viewing, but with the piecing together another thing. Thus is this nastiness of the spy business graphically described. It is an engagingly photographed piece of business.

Max Von Sydow is a political strong man within the Russian regime. Ex-US Navy officer Patrick O'Neal has the job of salvaging the Kremlin Letter. But Russia, in the person of Richard Boone, also would like to retrieve the document. Participants include George Sanders, as a homo female impersonator in San Francisco. Orson Welles is a key Soviet man who is in New York to address the United Nations; Bibi Andersson is a prostitute married to agent Von Sydow.

....

■ **KRONOS**

1957, 78 MINS, US ▣ ⊙

Dir Kurt Neumann   *Prod* Kurt Neumann   *Scr* Lawrence Louis Goldman   *Ph* Karl Struss   *Ed* Jodie Copelan   *Mus* Paul Sawtell, Bert Shefter   *Art Dir* Theobold Holsopple

● Jeff Morrow, Barbara Lawrence, John Emery, George O'Hanlon, Morris Ankrum, Kenneth Alton (Regal)

Kronos is a well-made, moderate budget science-fictioner which boasts quality special effects that would do credit to a much higher-budgeted film.

Script [from a story by Irving Block] tells of the efforts of a people from outer space to capture Earth's energy. To do this, they send an accumulator to Earth, which is directed in its movement by the head of a great American lab, whose brain has been seized by a higher intelligence from space.

Feature takes its title from the accumulator a huge metal cube-shaped figure 100 feet high, after the mythological god of evil, and which nothing seemingly can destroy.

Jeff Morrow heads cast as a scientist who has charted the course of the asteroid which has transported the accumulator to Earth. John Emery is convincing as the lab head forced by the outer-space intelligence to direct the monster. Barbara Lawrence is in strictly for distaff interest, but pretty.

....

■ **KRULL**

1983, 117 MINS, US ◇ ▣ ⊙

Dir Peter Yates   *Prod* Ron Silverman   *Scr* Stanford Sherman   *Ph* Peter Suschitzky   *Ed* Ray Lovejoy   *Mus* James Horner   *Art Dir* Stephen Grimes

● Ken Marshall, Lysette Anthony, Freddie Jones, Francesca Annis, Alun Armstrong, David Battley (Columbia)

Although inoffensively designed only to please the senses and appeal to one's whimsical sense of adventure, *Krull* nevertheless comes off as a blatantly derivative hodgepodge of *Excalibur* meets *Star Wars*. Lavishly mounted at a reported cost of $27 million, the collection of action set pieces never jells into an absorbing narrative.

Plot is as old as the art of story-telling itself. Young Prince Colwyn (Ken Marshall) falls heir to a besieged kingdom, but must survive a Ulysses-scaled series of tests on the way to rescuing his beautiful bride from the clutches of the Beast, whose army of slayers imperils his journey every step of the way.

Crucial to Colwyn's quest is his recovery of the glaive, a razor-tipped, spinning boomerang which will enable him to combat the Beast. This fancy piece of magical jewelry holds the same importance as the Excalibur sword did for Arthur.

Professionalism of director Peter Yates, the large array of production and technical talents and, particularly, the mainly British actors keep things from becoming genuinely dull or laughable.

....

■ **K2**

1991, 111 MINS, UK/US ◇ ▣ ⊙

Dir Franc Roddam   *Prod* Jonathan Taplin, Marilyn Weiner, Tim Van Rellim   *Scr* Patrick Meyers, Scott Roberts   *Ph* Gabriel Beristain   *Ed* Sean Barton   *Mus* Hans Zimmer   *Art Dir* Andrew Sanders

● Michael Biehn, Matt Craven, Raymond J. Barry, Hiroshi Fujioka, Luca Bercovici, Patricia Charbonneau (Trans Pacific)

The buddy movie hits the Himalayas in Franc Roddam's *K2*, an entertaining enough mountain-climbing saga [from the 1983 one-act play by Patrick Meyers]. Script's lack of oxygen is offset by pic's slick packaging plus good on-screen bonding between leads Michael Biehn and Matt Craven.

Story rapidly sets up two main characters: yuppy, womanizing Seattle lawyer Biehn and gentler, married-with-child professor Craven. When a US climbing group funded by millionaire Raymond J. Barry loses two of its members in an Alaskan training session, Biehn and Craven take their place for the big one – an attempt on K2, the world's second highest peak and a w.k. engorger of climbers.

Both thesps perform far better than the script deserves, with Biehn cocksure but likable, and Craven serious but caring. Barry is solid as the aging sponsor and Luca Bercovici ditto as Biehn's nemesis.

There's no attempt at any mystical relationship between the characters and the mountain. Pic concentrates instead on sheer thrills and spills, with plenty of product placement.

....

■ **KUFFS**

1992, 101 MINS, US ◇ ▣ ⊙

Dir Bruce A. Evans   *Prod* Raynold Gideon   *Scr* Bruce A. Evans, Raynold Gideon   *Ph* Thomas Del Ruth   *Ed* Michael Faltermeyer   *Mus* Harold Faltermeyer   *Art Dir* Victoria Paul, Armin Ganz

● Christian Slater, Tony Goldwyn, Milla Jovovich, Bruce Boxleitner, Troy Evans, George de la Pena (De Laurentiis)

Christian Slater's energy fails to carry *Kuffs*, a mishmash cop comedy very reminiscent of several Eddie Murphy films. Film veers from ultra-violence to slapstick comedy in an arbitrary and irritating fashion.

Slater is the fish out of water this time, inheriting his murdered brother's police protection business. Plot hook makes good use of the San Francisco setting, where neighborhoods have relied on these private Patrol Specials since the 1850s.

Gimmick allows ne'er-do-well high school dropout Slater to become an instant cop and prove his mettle under fire. Avenging brother Bruce Boxleitner's death is an utterly conventional quest, but the few laughs along the way are the film's raison d'etre.

As Slater's unwilling partner, Tony Goldwyn demonstrates solid comic talents. Wearing a variety of goofy outfits, Leon Rippy makes a fun killer. Former ballet star George de la Pena is utterly convincing as the slick villain. Less fortunate is lovely Milla Jovovich, too young for the nothing part of Slater's g.f.

....

Ll

■ LA BAMBA

1987, 108 MINS, US ◇ ⓥ ⊙

Dir Luis Valdez   *Prod* Taylor Hackford, Bill Borden
Scr Luis Valdez   *Ph* Adam Greenberg   *Ed* Sheldon
Kahn, Don Brochu   *Mus* Carlos Santana, Miles
Goodman   *Art Dir* Vince Cresciman
● Lou Diamond Phillips, Esai Morales, Rosana De Soto,
Elizabeth Pena, Danielle von Zerneck, Joe Pantoliano
(New Visions)

There haven't been too many people who died
at age 17 who have warranted the biopic
treatment, but 1950s rock 'n' roller Ritchie
Valens proves a worthy exception in *La Bamba*.

Known primarily for his three top-10 tunes,
Come On Let's Go, *Donna* and the title cut,
Valens was killed – just eight months after
signing his first recording contract – in the
1959 private plane crash that also took the
lives of Buddy Holly and The Big Bopper, and
thus attained instant legendhood.

For anyone to achieve his dreams by 17 is
close to miraculous. It was even more so for
Valens who, less than two years before his
death, was a Mexican-American fruitpicker
named Ricardo Valenzuela living in a tent
with his family in Northern California.

La Bamba is engrossing throughout and
boasts numerous fine performances. In Lou
Diamond Phillips' sympathetic turn, Valens
comes across as a very fine young man, caring
for those important to him and not overawed
by his success. Rosana De Soto scores as his
tireless mother, and Elizabeth Pena has numerous dramatic moments as Bob's distraught mate.

....

■ LABYRINTH

1986, 101 MINS, US ◇ ⓥ ⊙

Dir Jim Henson   *Prod* Eric Rattray   *Scr* Terry Jones
Ph Alex Thomson   *Ed* John Grover   *Mus* Trevor Jones
Art Dir Elliot Scott
● David Bowie, Jennifer Connelly, Toby Froud, Shelley
Thompson, Christopher Malcolm, Natalie Finland
(Henson/Lucasfilm)

An array of bizarre creatures and David Bowie
can't save *Labyrinth* from being a crashing bore.
Characters created by Jim Henson and his
team become annoying rather than endearing.

What is even more disappointing is the failure of the film on a story level. Young Sarah
(Jennifer Connelly) embarks on an adventure
to recover her baby stepbrother from the
clutches of the Goblin King (David Bowie)
who has taken the child for some unknown
reason to his kingdom.

Story soon loses its way and never comes
close to archetypal myths and fears of great
fairy tales. Instead it's an unconvincing coming of age saga.

As the Goblin King, Bowie seems a fish out
of water – too serious to be campy, too dumb
to be serious.

....

■ LADY AND THE TRAMP

1955, 75 MINS, US ◇ ⓥ ⊙

Dir Hamilton Luske, Clyde Geronimi, Wilfred Jackson
Prod Walt Disney   *Scr* Erdman Penner, Joe Rinaldi,
Ralph Wright, Don DaGradi   *Ed* Don Halliday
Mus Oliver Wallace
● (Walt Disney)

A delight for the juveniles and lots of fun for
adults, *Lady and the Tramp* is the first animated feature in CinemaScope and the wider
canvas and extra detail work reportedly
meant an additional 30% in negative cost. It
was a sound investment.

This time out the producer turned to members of the canine world and each of these
hounds of Disneyville reflects astute drawing-
board knowhow and richly-humorous invention. The songs by Peggy Lee and Sonny
Burke figure importantly, too.

Characters of the title are a cutie-pie faced
and ultra-ladylike spaniel and the raffish
mutt from the other side of the tracks. In
'featured' roles are Trusty, the bloodhound
who's lost his sense of smell, and Jock, a
Scottie with a sense of thrift. Both have a
crush on Lady but her on-and-off romance
with Tramp finally leads to a mating of the
minds, etc, and a litter basket.

....

■ LADY BE GOOD

1941, 110 MINS, US ⓥ

Dir Norman Z. McLeod   *Prod* Arthur Freed   *Scr* Jack
McGowan, Kay Van Riper, Jock McClain   *Ph* George
Folsey, Oliver Marsh   *Ed* Frederick J. Smith
Mus Georgie Stoll (dir.)
● Eleanor Powell, Ann Sothern, Robert Young, Lionel
Barrymore, John Carroll, Red Skelton (M-G-M)

The plot bears no resemblance to the Guy
Bolton book of the original 1924 stage musical, which was one of the major springboards
for Fred and Adele Astaire. The songs in this
picture are likewise no relation to the click
Gershwin score.

There are flagrant examples in the film of
poor direction, unimaginative story-telling
and slipshod photography. The picture looks
as though director Norman Z. McLeod was
given a time allotment to fill, no matter how,
and he did.

While confused, the story pattern is familiar
– that of a crack songwriting team splitting up
and becoming individually unsuccessful until
resuming their partnership. In this instance
it's the case of ex-waitress Ann Sothern and
composer Robert Young, who click, marry and
then get divorced when Young goes high-hat
and social. Then they click and marry again –
and again she goes into the divorce courts,
which gives the audience a double-dose of
flashbacks out of the stories told Judge Lionel
Barrymore. It's a waste of Barrymore.
□ 1941: Best Song ('The Last Time I Saw
Paris')

....

■ LADYBUGS

1992, 90 MINS, US ◇ ⓥ ⊙

Dir Sidney J. Furie   *Prod* Albert S. Ruddy, Andre E.
Morgan   *Scr* Curtis Burch   *Ph* Dan Burstall   *Ed* John
W. Wheeler, Timothy N. Board   *Mus* Richard Gibbs
Art Dir Robb Wilson King
● Rodney Dangerfield, Jackee, Jonathan Brandis, Ilene
Graff, Vinessa Shaw, Tom Parks (Paramount/Ruddy &
Morgan)

A klutzy would-be comedy about a girls' soccer team, *Ladybugs* is sexist, homophobic and
woefully unfunny to boot. Paramount apparently thought it was ordering up another *Bad
News Bears*, but the garish *Ladybugs* has the
look of a third-rate TV movie.

As a salesman for a Colorado tycoon (Tom
Parks), Rodney Dangerfield is put in charge
of a soccer team. His bright idea for turning
them into winners is to have his fiancee's son
join the team in drag.

Jonathan Brandis, saddled with a most embarrassing role, is the horny teen who makes
minimal attempts to act like a girl but fools
everyone anyway. Most of the wisecracks
Dangerfield gets here wouldn't go over with a
drunken Vegas crowd.

....

■ LADY CAROLINE LAMB

1972, 122 MINS, UK/ITALY ◇ ⓥ

Dir Robert Bolt   *Prod* Fernando Ghia   *Scr* Robert Bolt
Ph Oswald Morris   *Ed* Norman Savage   *Mus* Richard
Rodney Bennett   *Art Dir* Carmen Dillon

● Sarah Miles, Jon Finch, Richard Chamberlain, John
Mills, Margaret Leighton, Pamela Brown (Anglo-EMI/
Pulsar/Vides)

If it's that relative rarity, a lushly, unabashedly romantic – yet tastefully executed
– tale that you relish, then *Lady Caroline Lamb*
is your likely cup of tea.

For his first stint behind the camera,
Robert Bolt comes up with a period piece
which rings a number of contemporary bells,
both emotional and intellectual. His tragic
heroine, a controversial free thinker of the
early British 1800s, has obvious parallels in
present-day femme emancipation.

Outlined, her story follows her headlong
flight into matrimony with the politically
promising Lamb, then into an equally breathless and unpondered but this time scandalous
affair with Byron, and on to her final climactic sacrifice on behalf of her husband's career.

Sarah Miles shines in a tailored role.
Similarly, Jon Finch, as her husband, lends
conviction to the film's most difficult part.

....

■ LADY CHATTERLEY'S LOVER

1981, 105 MINS, FRANCE/UK ◇ ⓥ ⊙

Dir Just Jaeckin   *Prod* Andre Djaoui, Christopher Pierce
Scr Just Jaeckin, Christopher Wicking   *Ph* Robert Fraisse
Ed Eunice Mountjoy   *Mus* Stanley Myers   *Art Dir* Anton
Furst
● Sylvia Kristel, Shane Briant, Nicholas Clay, Ann
Mitchell, Elizabeth Spriggs (Producteurs Associes/
Cannon)

This Franco-British production of *Lady
Chatterley's Lover* is a cop-out adaptation of
D.H. Lawrence's one time scandalous literary
hymn to human sexuality. It's coy and superficial, worth little as erotic fare and not considerably more as sentimental drama.

The sex scenes are all the more unmoving
because the surrounding story and characters
are inadequately realized. Lady Chatterley
(Sylvia Kristel) is the wife of an English aristocrat wounded in the World War I and totally
paralyzed from the waist down. Starved for
carnal affection, she becomes the lover of
Chatterley's gamekeeper and meets him daily
for long sessions of passionate lovemaking.

The love scenes are commonplace, summary, tritely lyrical and lacking in sensuality;
no more daring than equivalent scenes in any
other commercial product with a frank romantic angle.

Kristel is attractive but inexpressive as an
actress. Nicholas Clay lacks rawness and definition as her lower-class lover.

....

■ LADY EVE, THE

1941, 90 MINS, US ⓥ ⊙

Dir Preston Sturges   *Prod* Paul Jones   *Scr* Preston
Sturges   *Ph* Victor Milner   *Ed* Stuart Gilmore
Mus Sigmund Krumgold (dir.)   *Art Dir* Hans Dreier,
Ernst Fegte
● Henry Fonda, Barbara Stanwyck, Charles Coburn,
Eugene Pallette, William Demarest, Eric Blore (Paramount)

Third writer-director effort of Preston
Sturges [from a story by Monckton Hoffe] is
laugh entertainment of top proportions with
its combo of slick situations, spontaneous dialog and a few slapstick falls tossed in for good
measure.

Basically, story is the age-old tale of Eve
snagging Adam, but dressed up with continually infectious fun and good humor. Barbara
Stanwyck is girl-lure of trio of confidence operators. She's determined, quick-witted, resourceful and personable. Henry Fonda is a
serious young millionaire, somewhat sappy,
deadpan and slow-thinking, returning from a
year's snake-hunting expedition up the
Amazon. He's a cinch pushover for girl's advances on the boat – but pair fall in love,
while girl flags Charles Coburn's attempts to
coldeck the victim at cards.

Sturges provides numerous sparkling situations in his direction and keeps picture moving at a merry pace. Stanwyck is excellent in the comedienne portrayal, while Fonda carries his assignment in good fashion. Coburn is a finished actor as the con man.

□ 1941: Nomination: Best Original Story

■ **LADY FOR A DAY**

1933, 93 MINS, US Ⓥ

Dir Frank Capra   *Prod* Frank Capra   *Scr* Robert Riskin   *Ph* Joseph Walker   *Ed* Gene Havlick
● Warren William, May Robson, Guy Kibbee, Glenda Farrell, Ned Sparks, Jean Parker (Columbia)

Lady for a Day asks the spectator to believe in the improbable. It's Hans Christian Andersen stuff written by a hard-boiled journalist and transferred to the screen by trick-wise Hollywoodites. While not stinting a full measure of credit to director Frank Capra, it seems as if the spotlight of recognition ought to play rather strongly on scriptwriter Robert Riskin [adapting Damon Runyon's story *Madame La Gimp*].

On the performance end, May Robson dominates the first reel but is thereafter rather subordinated as the story gets into the comedy side-plots.

Actually in a well-balanced, smartly-directed cast like this it's hard to split the posies. Even in a small role as a nite-club hostess Glenda Farrell looks great. There are half a dozen bits, including a superbly ironic English butler that ought really to get a shoulder pat. Warren William is the superstitious gambler for whom Apple Annie is a good luck omen. It is he who stage manages the gigantic make-believe whereby the shoddy peddler of apples becomes a 'lady for a day', to preserve her finely-reared daughter's illusions that her mother is a society somebody.

□ 1932/33: Nominations: Best Picture, Director, Actress (May Robson), Adaptation

■ **LADY FROM SHANGHAI, THE**

1948, 86 MINS, US Ⓥ ◉

Dir Orson Welles   *Prod* Orson Welles   *Scr* Orson Welles   *Ph* Charles Lawton Jr   *Ed* Viola Lawrence   *Mus* Heinz Roemheld   *Art Dir* Stephen Goosson, Sturges Carne
● Rita Hayworth, Orson Welles, Everett Sloane, Ted De Corsia, Glenn Anders, Gus Schilling (Columbia)

Script is wordy and full of holes which need the plug of taut story telling and more forthright action. Rambling style used by Orson Welles has occasional flashes of imagination, particularly in the tricky backgrounds he uses to unfold the yarn, but effects, while good on their own, are distracting to the murder plot. Contributing to the stylized effect stressed by Welles is the photography, which features artful compositions entirely in keeping with the production mood.

Story [from the novel *Before I Die* by Sherwood King] tees off in New York where Welles, as a philosophical Irish seaman, joins the crew of a rich man's luxury yacht. Schooner's cruise and stops along the Mexican coast en route to San Francisco furnish varied and interesting backdrops. Welles' tries for effect reach their peak with the staging of climatic chase sequences in a Chinese theatre where performers are going through an Oriental drama, and in the mirror room of an amusement park's crazy house.

Welles has called on players for stylized performances. He uses an Irish brogue and others depict erratic characters with little reality. Hayworth isn't called on to do much more than look beautiful. Best break for players goes to Everett Sloane, and he gives a credible interpretation of the crippled criminal attorney.

■ **LADY HAMILTON**

See: That Hamilton Woman!

■ **LADYHAWKE**

1985, 124 MINS, US ◇ Ⓥ ◉

Dir Richard Donner   *Prod* Richard Donner, Lauren Schuler   *Scr* Edward Khmara, Michael Thomas, Tom Mankiewicz   *Ph* Vittorio Storaro   *Ed* Stuart Baird   *Mus* Andrew Powell   *Art Dir* Wolf Kroeger
● Matthew Broderick, Rutger Hauer, Michelle Pfeiffer, Leo McKern, John Wood, Ken Hutchison (Warner/20th Century-Fox)

LadyHawke is a very likeable, very well-made fairytale that insists on a wish for its lovers to live happily ever after.

Handsome Rutger Hauer is well-cast as the dark and moody knight who travels with a hawk by day. Lovely Michelle Pfeiffer is perfect as the enchanting beauty who appears by night, always in the vicinity of a vicious but protective wolf.

As readers of one or more variations of this legend will instantly recognize, Pfeiffer is the hawk and Hauer the wolf, each changing form as the sun rises and sets, former lovers cursed to never humanly share the clock together.

The spell was cast by an evil bishop (John Wood) when Pfeiffer spurned him for Hauer, who is now bent on revenge, with the help of young Matthew Broderick, the only one to ever escape Wood's deadly dungeon.

Though simple, the saga moves amidst beautiful surroundings (filmed in Italy), and is worthwhile for its extremely authentic look alone.

■ **LADY ICE**

1973, 93 MINS, US ◇ Ⓥ

Dir Tom Gries   *Prod* Harrison Starr   *Scr* Alan Trustman, Harold Clemens   *Ph* Lucien Ballard   *Ed* Robert Swink, William Sanda   *Mus* Perry Botkin Jr   *Art Dir* Joel Schiller
● Donald Sutherland, Jennifer O'Neill, Robert Duvall, Patrick Magee, Eric Braeden (Tomorrow)

Lady Ice comes off as a routine programmer, due for the most part to the listless performance of Donald Sutherland in the male lead. It is due to the superior work by Robert Duvall in a small role as a Dept of Justice officer and Jennifer O'Neill, as the gorgeous lady crook of the title, that the film comes off at all.

Shot on location for the most part, the handsomely-lensed actioner [from a story by Alan Trustman] pits jewel thieves against an insurance company private eye (Sutherland) in recovery of $3 million in ice from a Chicago holdup. O'Neill turns out to be the lady in charge of the caper. The rather thin plot is made up of numerous chases, a bit of violence and long, dull passages of Sutherland trying to make it with the lady criminal.

■ **LADY IN A CAGE**

1964, 94 MINS, US Ⓥ

Dir Walter Grauman   *Prod* Luther Davis   *Scr* Luther Davis   *Ph* Lee Garmes   *Ed* Leon Barsha   *Mus* Paul Glass   *Art Dir* Hal Pereira, Rudy Sternad
● Olivia de Havilland, Ann Sothern, Jeff Corey, James Caan, Jennifer Billingsley, Rafael Campos (Paramount)

There's not a single redeeming character or characteristic to producer Luther Davis' sensationalistically vulgar screenplay [based on a novel by Robert Durand]. It is haphazardly constructed, full of holes, sometimes pretentious and in bad taste.

Had the basic premise – of an invalid woman trapped in her private home elevator when the power is cut off – been developed simply, neatly and realistically, gripping dramatic entertainment might have ensued. But Davis has chosen to employ his premise as a means to expose all the negative aspects of the human animal. He has infested the caged woman's house with as scummy an assortment of characters as literary imagination might conceive.

Among those who greedily invade her abode are a delirious wino (Jeff Corey), a plump prostitute (Ann Sothern) and three vicious young hoodlums (James Caan, Jennifer Billingsley and Rafael Campos).

Olivia de Havilland plays the unfortunate woman in the elevator, and gives one of those ranting, raving, wild-eyed performances often thought of as Academy Award oriented. Actually, the role appears to require more emotional stamina than histrionic deftness. Caan, as the sadistic leader of the little rat-pack, appears to have been watching too many early Marlon Brando movies.

■ **LADY IN CEMENT**

1968, 93 MINS, US ◇ Ⓥ

Dir Gordon Douglas   *Prod* Aaron Rosenberg   *Scr* Marvin H. Albert, Jack Guss   *Ph* Joseph Biroc   *Ed* Robert Simpson   *Mus* Hugo Montenegro   *Art Dir* Leroy Deane
● Frank Sinatra, Raquel Welch, Richard Conte, Martin Gabel, Lainie Kazan, Joe E. Lewis (20th Century-Fox)

Lady in Cement, follow-up to *Tony Rome*, stars Frank Sinatra as a Miami private eye on the trail of people in whom there couldn't be less interest. Raquel Welch adds her limited, but beauteous contribution, and Dan Blocker is excellent as a sympathetic heavy.

Episodic script is from Marvin H. Albert's novel, in which Sinatra, while scuba-diving off his beat, discovers a nude looker anchored in cement on the floor of the bay. Blocker hires Sinatra to find his lost sweetie, who turns out to be the dead gal.

Welch, Martin Gabel and Steve Peck come under suspicion. Richard Conte is a local police detective, and Paul Henry appears as a vice squad officer, one of whose jobs involves working the streets in drag.

■ **LADY IN RED, THE**

1979, 93 MINS, US ◇ Ⓥ ◉

Dir Lewis Teague   *Prod* Julie Corman   *Scr* John Sayles   *Ph* Daniel Lacambre   *Ed* Larry Bock, Ron Medico, Lewis Teague   *Art Dir* Joe McAnelly
● Pamela Sue Martin, Robert Conrad, Louise Fletcher, Christopher Lloyd, Robert Hogan (New World)

Ostensibly a return to the gangster genre, *The Lady in Red* is in many ways a compendium of variations on the 'woman in jeopardy' format.

The lady of the title gamely struggles through life as a tyrannized daughter, mistreated lover, ill-paid working girl, prisoner in a women's ward, professional hooker and full-fledged gangster, among other roles.

With her sights vaguely set on Hollywood, farm girl Pamela Sue Martin heads first for Chicago, where one mishap after another lands her in prison, then in the employ of classy madam Louise Fletcher.

Lewis Teague, a former second-unit director, guides his large cast reasonably well through John Sayles' craftsmanlike script.

■ **LADY IN THE DARK**

1944, 100 MINS, US ◇

Dir Mitchell Leisen   *Prod* Mitchell Leisen   *Scr* Frances Goodrich, Albert Hackett   *Ph* Ray Rennahan   *Ed* Alma Macrorie   *Mus* Robert Emmett Dolan (dir.)   *Art Dir* Hans Dreier (sup.), Raoul Pene du Bois
● Ginger Rogers, Ray Milland, Jon Hall, Warner Baxter, Barry Sullivan, Mischa Auer (Paramount)

Produced on a lavish scale and in very fine taste against backgrounds of a glittering character with costuming that fills the eye, *Lady in the Dark* is at the outset a technically superior piece of craftsmanship. Paramount spent $185,000 on costuming, and total negative nick is reported at $2.8 million. It looks it.

Mitchell Leisen produced and also directed from a surefire script based on the [1941] Broadway stage hit by Moss Hart, with music by Kurt Weill and lyrics by Ira Gershwin. An additional song, 'Suddenly It's Spring', was written by Johnny Burke and James Van Heusen.

Ginger Rogers plays the editor of a fashion magazine who, realizing she's on the edge of a nervous breakdown, finally places herself in the hands of a psychoanalyst. She resists his ministrations but ultimately goes through with it all and finally finds herself, the wall she had built around herself and her emotions since childhood ultimately being broken down. The dream sessions are reflections of her disturbed mind.

Playing the ad manager for the society mag and the only man in her life who has sought to set himself up as Rogers' superior, irritating her all along the line, Ray Milland gives an excellent performance.
□ 1944: Nominations: Best Color Cinematography, Color Art Direction, Scoring of a Musical Picture

• •

■ LADY IN THE LAKE

1947, 103 MINS, US ⓥ
Dir Robert Montgomery   *Prod* George Haight
Scr Steve Fisher   *Ph* Paul C. Vogel   *Ed* Gene Ruggiero
Mus David Snell   *Art Dir* Cedric Gibbons, Preston Ames
● Robert Montgomery, Audrey Totter, Lloyd Nolan, Tom Tully, Leon Ames, Jayne Meadows (M-G-M)

Lady in the Lake institutes a novel method of telling the story, in which the camera itself is the protagonist, playing the lead role from the subjective viewpoint of star Robert Montgomery. Idea comes off excellently, transferring what otherwise would have been a fair whodunit into socko screen fare.

Montgomery starts telling the story in retrospect from a desk in his office, but when the picture dissolves into the action, the camera becomes Montgomery, presenting everything as it would have been seen through the star's eyes. Only time Montgomery is seen thereafter is when he's looking into a mirror or back at his desk for more bridging of the script.

Camera thus gets bashed by the villains, hits back in turn, smokes cigarettes, makes love and, in one of the most suspenseful sequences, drives a car in a hair-raising race that ends in a crash. Paul C. Vogel does a capital job with the lensing throughout, moving the camera to simulate the action of Montgomery's eyes as he walks up a flight of stairs, etc. Because it would be impossible under the circumstances to cut from Montgomery to another actor to whom he's talking, the rest of the cast was forced to learn much longer takes than usual.

Steve Fisher has wrapped up the Chandler novel into a tightly-knit and rapidly-paced screenplay. Montgomery plays private detective Philip Marlowe, who's dealt into a couple of murders when he tries to sell a story based on his experiences to a horror story mag. Audrey Totter, as the gal responsible for it all, is fine in both her tough-girl lines and as the love interest.

• •

■ LADY IN WHITE

1988, 112 MINS, US ◇ ⓥ ⊙
Dir Frank LaLoggia   *Prod* Andrew G. La Marca, Frank LaLoggia   *Scr* Frank LaLoggia   *Ph* Russell Carpenter
Ed Steve Mann   *Mus* Frank LaLoggia   *Art Dir* Richard K. Hummel
● Lukas Haas, Len Cariou, Alex Rocco, Katherine Helmond, Jason Presson, Renata Vanni (New Century/ Vista)

Lady in White is a superb supernatural horror film from independent filmmaker Frank LaLoggia who, with the help of cousin Charles LaLoggia, raised production money from 4,000 investors – many of whom live in and around the small town of Lyons in upstate New York that doubles for the fictional spooky Willowpoint Falls of the early 1960s.

At the center is big-eyed Lukas Haas, the youngest boy of a loving and earthy Italian family that is headed by his widowed dad, Angelo (Alex Rocco). On Halloween night, his school chums lock him in his classroom cloakroom where he is visited by those who wouldn't oridinarily be there – the ghost of a young girl about his age and a masked man searching for something in the heating grate. As the mystery unravels, it is revealed how they are connected.

LaLoggia manages to direct Haas equally well as a junior sleuth as he does the innocent youngster who fights with his older brother Geno (Jason Presson) and is easily influenced to go places he shouldn't by his bike-riding pals.

Rocco is particularly successful as the concerned father. Equally solid is Haas' brother, a good casting in Jason Presson, who turns out to be much less precocious than his younger sibling. This probably is as good a nightmare as any impressionable boy could have and still be suspenseful enough to get most adults' hearts going.

• •

■ LADY IS WILLING, THE

1942, 93 MINS, US
Dir Mitchell Leisen   *Prod* Charles K. Feldman
Scr James Edward Grant, Albert McCleery   *Ph* Ted Tetzlaff   *Ed* Eda Warren   *Mus* W. Frank Harling
● Marlene Dietrich, Fred MacMurray, Aline MacMahon, Arline Judge, Stanley Ridges, Roger Clark (Columbia/Feldman Group)

The Lady Is Willing is a racy and sophisticated marital comedy that carries a good share of amusement for adult audiences.

Picture carries light and breezy tempo in the first portion, with adoration of cute baby as motivating factor in holding interest. An inconclusive finish, with the oldy situation of an emergency operation necessary to save the child's life, and the pendulum-swinging problem of life-and-death crisis, allows the tale to sluff off with elemental formula convenience.

Familiar banter is apparent throughout. Despite this, strong performances by both principals succeed in holding up interest until the tale swings into heart-tug cliches. The baby's crisis is too extended and not handled in manner to hold audience attention on the dramatic elements attempted.

• •

■ LADY JANE

1986, 142 MINS, UK/US ◇ ⓥ ⊙
Dir Trevor Nunn   *Prod* Peter Snell   *Scr* David Edgar
Ph Douglas Slocombe   *Ed* Anne V. Coates
Mus Stephen Oliver   *Art Dir* Allan Cameron
● Helena Bonham Carter, Cary Elwes, John Wood, Michael Hordern, Jil Bennett, Jane Lapotaire (Paramount)

With its emphasis on youthful idealism despoiled by treacherous, manipulative adults, *Lady Jane* emerges as a tragic historical romance tinged with a strong 1960s feeling.

In 1553, six years after the death of King Henry VIII and upon the death of his 16-year-old son, Edward VI, some extraordinary maneuverings brought to the English throne Henry's 15-year-old great-niece, the scholarly but unprepared Lady Jane Grey. She ruled for only nine days, after which she was toppled, imprisoned and finally executed by the Catholic Mary.

Lady Jane's parents and the Duke of Northumberland scheme to force a marriage between Jane and the latter's dissolute 17-year-old son, Guilford Dudley, to keep Britain free of the Pope's influence.

Very much centerstage, however, is the unlikely love story of Jane and Guilford. A grimly serious, exceedingly virginal girl at the outset, Jane is very quickly liberated in body and mind. The pair rhapsodize about a socialist-type utopia where all citizens would have equal rights.

Trevor Nunn has brought little of his tremendous theatrical flair to the screen here. Pic belongs squarely within the traditions of good taste and literate dialog one assocoates with the British cinema from the 1930s onwards. Performances are all top-drawer, beginning with newcomer Helena Bonham Carter in the title role.

• •

■ LADY KILLER

1933, 67 MINS, US ⓥ ⊙
Dir Roy Del Ruth   *Prod* Henry Blanke   *Scr* Ben Markson, Lillie Hayward   *Ph* Tony Gaudio   *Ed* George Amy
Art Dir Robert Haas
● James Cagney, Mae Clarke, Leslie Fenton, Margaret Lindsay, Henry O'Neill, Willard Robertson (Warner)

This James Cagney picture has the treat-'em-rough star drag his girl friend by the hair across the room, pitch her, emphatically through the door, climaxing with an enthusiastic sample of booting. Whole picture goes on a rampage with the you-be-damned personality that Cagney has so assiduously developed.

Story [*The Finger Man* by Rosalind Keating Shaffer] has other objectionable elements. Cagney plays an underworld crook who by accident crashes a Hollywood studio and earns his way to picture fame.

Crook angle is handled with a cheerful style of humor and there is a certain spirit about the Cagney character, played in his energetic way that carries its own persuasive charm. Comedy is first rate.

Mae Clarke does extremely well as the gang girl with Margaret Lindsay in attractive contrast in the straight role of a real picture actress.

• •

■ LADYKILLERS, THE

1955, 96 MINS, UK ◇ ⓥ
Dir Alexander Mackendrick   *Prod* Michael Balcon
Scr William Rose   *Ph* Otto Heller   *Ed* Jack Harris
Mus Tristram Cary   *Art Dir* Jim Morahan
● Alec Guinness, Cecil Parker, Herbert Lom, Peter Sellers, Katie Johnson, Danny Green (Ealing)

This is an amusing piece of hokum, being a parody of American gangsterdom interwoven with whimsy and exaggeration that makes it more of a macabre farce. Alec Guinness sinks his personality almost to the level of anonymity. Basic idea of thieves making a frail old lady an unwitting accomplice in their schemes is carried out in ludicrous and often tense situations.

A bunch of crooks planning a currency haul call on their leader, who has temporarily boarded with a genteel widow near a big London rail terminal. They pass as musicians gathering for rehearsals, but wouldn't deceive a baby.

Guinness tends to overact the sinister leader while Cecil Parker strikes just the right note as a conman posing as an army officer. Herbert Lom broods gloomily as the most ruthless of the plotters, with Peter Sellers contrasting well as the dumb muscle man. Danny Green completes the quintet.
□ 1956: Nomination: Best Original Screenplay

• •

■ LADY L

1965, 124 MINS, US/ITALY ◇
Dir Peter Ustinov   *Prod* Carlo Ponti   *Scr* Peter Ustinov
Ph Henri Alekan   *Ed* Roger Dwyre   *Mus* Jean Francaix

L

● Sophia Loren, Paul Newman, David Niven, Claude Dauphin, Philippe Noiret, Michel Piccoli (M-G-M/Ponti)

Experiment of starting and ending this pic with Sophia Loren as an 80-year-old, an alleged aristocrat with a somewhat simpering tedious voice, doesn't come off. Not till the Italian dish reverts to her own radiant, lush self will her followers settle down comfortably. David Niven is immaculately debonair and wittily amusing, but Paul Newman, though turning in a thoroughly competent performance, is not happily cast – his role calling out for the dependable mixture of solidity and lightness.

Film, from Romain Gary's novel, was originally planned as a straight drama, but things misfired. Ustinov was later brought in to do a doctoring job. But, despite the cost, he took on the chore only on the proviso that he could wipe the slate clean and start afresh. His nimble brain and characteristics have since clearly shaped the entire project.

Story, set in Paris and Switzerland at the turn of the century, has Loren as an aging, allegedly aristocratic mystery woman recounting her life story for the benefit of a biographer (Cecil Parker).

Ustinov weighs in with a choice cameo as the doddering Prince Otto.

LADY OF BURLESQUE
(UK: Striptease Lady)

1943, 89 MINS, US ⓥ

Dir William Wellman   Prod Hunt Stromberg   Scr James Gunn   Ph Robert de Grasse   Ed James Newcom   Mus Arthur Lange
● Barbara Stanwyck, Michael O'Shea, J. Edward Bromberg, Iris Adrien, Marion Martin, Pinky Lee (United Artists)

Although Lady of Burlesque is based on Gypsy Rose Lee's novel, G-String Murders, story plows an obvious straight line in generating the whodunit angles, and two gal burlesque performers are knocked off in succession before the culprit is disclosed. But gallant trouping by Barbara Stanwyck, colorful background provided by Stromberg, and speedy direction by William Wellman, carry picture through for good entertainment for general audiences.

Story centers around a burlesque stock company established in an old opera house. Stanwyck is the striptease star in process of buildup by manager J. Edward Bromberg, with Michael O'Shea the lowdown comedian who's continually making romantic pitches to the girl.

Picture gets off to zestful start, with stage show background in which Stanwyck socks over 'Take off the E String, Play It on the G String', and Frank Fenton deliberately off-keys 'So This Is You'. There's a sudden raid and wagon backup; release on bail and then showdown to generate various motives for the coming murders. After swinging into the strange use of a G string for strangulation of the victims, it's just a matter of time before the windup.

□ 1943: Nomination: Best Scoring of a Dramatic Picture

LADY ON A TRAIN

1945, 96 MINS, US

Dir Charles David   Prod Felix Jackson   Scr Edmund Beloin, Robert O'Brien   Ph Woody Bredell   Ed Ted Kent   Mus Miklos Rozsa   Art Dir John B. Goodman, Robert Clatworthy
● Deanna Durbin, Ralph Bellamy, Edward Everett Horton, Dan Duryea, George Coulouris, Allen Jenkins (Universal)

Lady on a Train is a mystery comedy containing plenty of fun for both whodunnit and laugh fans. Melodramatic elements in the Leslie Charteris original are flippantly

treated without minimizing suspense, and the dialog contains a number of choice quips that are good for hefty laughs.

Deanna Durbin sings three tunes as well as handling herself excellently in the comedy role. Songs are all delivered against a background of menace. Actress is seen as a murder mystery addict who witnesses a murder from her train window while arriving in Grand Central station. Police discount her story and she turns to David Bruce, mystery writer, for help. Her pursuit of the writer to enlist his aid is good funning and accounts for some hilarious sequences.

□ 1945: Nomination: Best Sound

LADY OSCAR

1979, 122 MINS, JAPAN ◇ ⓥ

Dir Jacques Demy   Prod Mataichiro Yamamoto   Scr Jacques Demy, Patricia Louisiana Knop   Ph Jean Penzer   Ed Paul Davies   Mus Michel Legrand   Art Dir Bernard Evein
● Catriona Maccoll, Barry Stokes, Christina Bohm, Jonas Bergstrom, Terence Budd, Constance Chapman (Kitty Music)

French filmmaker Jacques Demy has given this international project, delving into French history, an opulent, posey, disarming naivete in keeping with its adaptation from a very popular Japanese comic strip [Rose of Versailles by Riyoko Ikeda], also a stage show in Japan.

The film has a historical charm that recalls the innocence of early Hollywood epics. Story takes place in 19th century France where a girl is brought up like a boy by her noble martinet father fed up with a long line of girls. She becomes the bodyguard of the flighty queen of France, Marie Antoinette, and wears a man's uniform and is known as Oscar. The girl grew up with the family housekeeper's son. The latter loves her but she sees him only as a brother. This is to change as France heads for revolution.

The unknown British cast is acceptable. Catriona Maccoll is worth further attention for her lovely limning of Oscar, a woman waiting to burst out of a man's clothing.

Film has fine art direction, costuming, music and technical qualities. The actual attack on the Bastille is a bit pithy for the reported $4 million outlay. Shooting on actual location in Versailles is an asset.

LADY SINGS THE BLUES

1972, 144 MINS, US ◇ ⓥ ⊙

Dir Sidney J. Furie   Prod Jay Weston, James S. White   Scr Terence McCloy, Chris Clark, Suzanne De Passe   Ph John Alonzo   Ed Argyle Nelson   Mus Michel Legrand   Art Dir Carl Anderson
● Diana Ross, Billy Dee Williams, Richard Pryor, James Callahan, Paul Hampton, Sid Melton (Paramount)

Individual opinions about Lady Sings The Blues may vary markedly, depending on a person's age, knowledge of jazz tradition and feeling for it, and how one wishes to regard the late Billie Holiday as both a force and a victim of her times. However, the film serves as a very good screen debut vehicle for Diana Ross, supported strongly by excellent casting, handsome 1930s physical values, and a script which is far better in dialog than structure.

Basis for the script is Holiday's autobiog Lady Sings the Blues, written with William Dufty only three years before her death in 1959 at age 44. Given that the script and production emphasis is on Ross as Holiday (and not on Holiday's life as interpreted by Ross), it still requires a severe gritting of teeth to overlook the truncations, telescoping and omissions.

Holiday's personal romantic life herein is restricted to Billy Dee Williams as Louis McKay, her third husband. Williams makes an excellent opposite lead, and Richard Pryor

registers strongly as her longtime piano-playing friend who eventually is beaten to death in LA by hoods who want him to pay for the dope he procured for her.

□ 1972: Nominations: Best Actress (Diana Ross), Original Story & Screenplay, Costume Design, Art Direction, Adapted Score

LADY VANISHES, THE

1938, 96 MINS, UK ⓥ ⊙

Dir Alfred Hitchcock   Prod [Edward Black]   Scr Sidney Gilliat, Frank Launder   Ph Jack Cox   Ed R.E. Dearing   Mus Louis Levy (dir.)   Art Dir Alex Vetchinsky
● Margaret Lockwood, Michael Redgrave, Paul Lukas, May Whitty, Cecil Parker, Linden Travers (Gainsborough/Gaumont-British)

An elderly English governess, homeward bound, disappears from a transcontinental train, and a young girl, who says she recently received a blow on the head, is confronted by numerous other passengers who say they never saw the governess. This becomes so persistent the girl finally thinks she has gone nuts.

The story [from The Wheel Spins by Ethel Lina White] is sometimes eerie and eventually melodramatic, but it's all so well done as to make for intense interest. It flits from one set of characters to another and becomes slightly difficult to follow, but finally all joins up.

This film, minus the deft and artistic handling of the director, Alfred Hitchcock, despite its cast and photography, would not stand up for Grade A candidacy. Margaret Lockwood is the central femme character; Michael Redgrave, as the lead, is a trifle too flippant. Naunton Wayne, Basil Radford, Paul Lukas (as a credibly villainous doctor), May Whitty, (as the governess) and Catherine Lacey (a villainess disguised as a nun are excellent.

LADY VANISHES, THE

1979, 99 MINS, UK ◇ ⓥ ⊙

Dir Anthony Page   Prod Tom Sachs   Scr George Axelrod   Ph Douglas Slocombe   Ed Russell Lloyd   Mus Richard Hartley   Art Dir Wilfrid Shingleton
● Elliott Gould, Cybill Shepherd, Angela Lansbury, Herbert Lom, Ian Carmichael, Arthur Lowe (Hammer)

The Lady Vanishes is a midatlantic mish-mash with some moderately amusing moments but no cohesive style.

The production has Cybill Shepherd as a madcap Yank heiress and Elliott Gould as a Life mag photographer foiling a political conspiracy aboard a train outbound from prewar Germany. Slapstick suspense and mystery elements that will fool almost no one add up to a heavy-handed affair. The script from an Ethel Lina White novel is best when dwelling on English eccentricity to make the film's most endearing impression.

Shepherd and Gould stack up as contrived cliches, characters that jar rather than complement.

Alfred Hitchcock's original version, circa 1938, had pretty much everything the remake doesn't.

LADY WITHOUT PASSPORT, A

1950, 72 MINS, US

Dir Joseph H. Lewis   Prod Samuel Marx   Scr Howard Dimsdale   Ph Paul C. Vogel   Ed Fredrick Y. Smith   Mus David Raksin   Art Dir Cedric Gibbons, Edward Carfagno
● Hedy Lamarr, John Hodiak, James Craig, George Macready, Steven Geray, Bruce Cowling (M-G-M)

Beginning is a bit too cryptic for quick understanding, but when plotline [adapted by Cyril Hume from a suggested story by Lawrence Taylor] does take shape, the story builds and holds attention. Joseph H. Lewis' direction spins it along expertly, neatly pacing the suspenseful sequences.

Hedy Lamarr is the lady of the title. Lingering in Cuba, she is used by an undercover immigration agent to set up a trap for the smuggling ring operated by George Macready. A complication is the romantic development between the lady and the agent.

Footage lensed in Cuba helps to supply an authentic touch. Cuban street scenes and Latin musical strains, an earthy rhumba by cafe dancer Nita Bieber, are among the good touches backing the plot runoff.

．．．．．．．．．．．．．．．．．．．．．．．

■ LADY WITH THE LAMP, THE

1951, 110 MINS, UK

Dir Herbert Wilcox   *Prod* Herbert Wilcox   *Scr* Warren Chetham-Strode   *Ph* Austin Dempster   *Ed* Bill Lewthwaite   *Mus* Anthony Collins   *Art Dir* William C. Andrews
● Anna Neagle, Michael Wilding, Gladys Young, Felix Aylmer, Dame Sybil Thorndyke, Arthur Young (Wilcox-Neagle/British Lion)

In the *Lady with the Lamp*, Anna Neagle adds another portrait to her screen gallery of famous women. Her characterization of Florence Nightingale is a sincerely moving study.

The script, taken from Regginald Berkeley's stage play, focuses attention on the more exciting and colorful aspects of Florence Nightingale's campaign. Main theme is told against a political background which brings in such famous characters as Gladstone, Lord Palmerston, and Sidney Herbert.

The story opens shotly before the Crimean war when Florence Nightingale, with a training in nursing, refuses to be a member of the leisure class into which born, but insists on continuing her work. The Minister of War, a steadfast believer in Nightingale's theories, gets her to organize a band of nurses to tend the wounded at Scutari.

Michael Wilding is not too happily cast as Sidney Herbert, War Minister. Within limitations, he makes the best of this part. The strong feature cast includes Felix Aylmer, with an exceptionally good study of Lord Palmerston. Herbert Wilcox, as always, directs in a plain, straightforward manner.

．．．．．．．．．．．．．．．．．．．．．．．

■ LAIR OF THE WHITE WORM, THE

1989, 93 MINS, UK ◇ ⊛ ⊙

Dir Ken Russell   *Prod* Ken Russell   *Scr* Ken Russell   *Ph* Dick Bush   *Ed* Peter Davies   *Mus* Stanislas Syrewicz   *Art Dir* Anne Tilby
● Amanda Donohoe, Hugh Grant, Catherine Oxenberg, Sammi Davis, Peter Capaldi, Stratford Johns (White Lair/Vestron)

Adapted from a tale by Bram Stoker, creator of Dracula, *Lair*, a rollicking, terrifying, post-psychedlic headtrip, features a fangy vampiress of unmatched erotic allure. Lady Sylvia Marsh (Amanda Donohoe) lives in a sprawling mansion not far from the state-of-the-art castle inhabited by Lord James D'Ampton (Hugh Grant).

On the day of a big party, just before nightfall, archaeology student Angus (Peter Capaldi) finds a bizarre, unclassifiable skull. The castle party is celebrating Lord James' inheritance of the estate as well as a family holiday commemorating a legendary ancestor said to have slain a dragon. In the Lampton clan mythology, the dragon is represented as an overblown, jawsy white worm.

Soon the duke and the digger divine an eerie connection between the mysteriously burgled skull, the white worm legend and cases of snakebite plus more strange disappearances close by the Lady's mansion. Then things start to get scary.

Donohoe as the vampire seductress projects a beguiling sexuality that should suck the resistance out of all but the most cold-blooded critics. She is also hilarious, a virtue shared by everyone and everything in *The Lair of the White Worm*.

．．．．．．．．．．．．．．．．．．．．．．．

■ LA LUNA

1979, 145 MINS, ITALY ◇

Dir Bernardo Bertolucci   *Prod* Giovanni Bertolucci   *Scr* Giuseppe Bertolucci, Bernardo Bertolucci, Clare Peploe   *Ph* Vittorio Storaro   *Ed* Gabriella Cristiani
● Jill Clayburgh, Matthew Barry, Renato Salvatori, Tomas Milian, Fred Gwynne, Veronica Lazar (20th Century-Fox/Fiction)

La Luna is a spectacle-sized melodrama filled with a variety of themes – plots and subplots that merge asymmetrically into a melodramatic mold.

The saga is of Jill Clayburgh as Yank lyric star afflicted with professional neuroses, fading pipes, a son on drugs and a close-to-incest mother-son development.

Sudden death of singer's spouse and decision to resume singing in Italy with son Joe accompanying, moves the scene from Brooklyn Heights to Rome where the mother-son cleft takes over from Verdi appearances. Her battle to break down his detachment and drug habit is the core of the film – with her own career at stake as the voice gives under stress.

Clayburgh is hard pressed to sustain the melodramatics of *Luna*.

．．．．．．．．．．．．．．．．．．．．．．．

■ LAMBADA

1990, 98 MINS, US ◇ ⊛ ⊙

Dir Joel Silberg   *Prod* Peter Shepherd   *Scr* Joel Silberg, Sheldon Renan   *Ph* Roberto D'Ettore Piazzoli   *Ed* Marcus Manton   *Mus* Greg Manton   *Art Dir* Bill Cornford
● J. Eddie Peck, Melora Hardin, Shabba-Doo, Ricky Paull Goldin, Basil Hoffman (Cannon)

Lambada's peripheral dance segs don't add up to $7 worth of lambada. Still, director/cowriter Joel Silberg keeps the story lively on a cartoonish-level.

Eddie Peck plays the Beverly Hills teacher by day, East LA lambada dancer by night, his sculpted dancer's physique straining the credibility of this most unlikely of teen fantasy scenarios. He forgoes evenings at home with his wife and son to motorbike over to the lambada club where he teaches math in the back room to a gang of east side dropouts.

His lambada prowess intrigues one of the BH highschoolers, sexually precocious Sandy (Melora Hardin), who stumbles onto the scene and sets out to seduce or blackmail him, unaware of his real, noble reason for leading this double life.

The dancing occupies little screen time compared to the sudsy intrigue Sandy stirs up on the school front, and what lambadaing there is, is photographed mostly in tight titillating shots that lack context.

．．．．．．．．．．．．．．．．．．．．．．．

■ LANA IN LOVE

1991, 85 MINS, CANADA ◇ ⊛

Dir Bashar Shbib   *Prod* Bashar Shbib   *Scr* Bashar Shbib, Daphna Kastner   *Ph* Stephen Reizes   *Ed* Bashar Shbib, Meiyen Chan   *Mus* Harry Mayronne Jr   *Art Dir* Janet Cunningham
● Daphna Kastner, Clark Gregg, Susan Eyton-Jones, Ivan E. Roth, Michael Gillis, Cheryl Platt (Oneira)

This love story has its comical moments but gets massacred midway by thesp Daphna Kastner overplaying the sexually repressed, emotionally hungry businesswoman, Lana.

Lana in Love begins as an amusing tale of mistaken identities but quickly falls apart as Kastner's shrill voice belittles love interest

Marty, stifling both their budding romance and pic.

But legit thesp Clark Gregg makes an impressive screen debut as the plumber Marty who arrives at the wrong address. Lana is waiting for a podiatrist she found through the classified ads and assumes Marty is her mystery man.

．．．．．．．．．．．．．．．．．．．．．．．

■ LANCELOT AND GUINEVERE

(US: Sword of Lancelot)

1963, 116 MINS, UK ◇ ⊛

Dir Cornel Wilde   *Prod* Cornel Wilde, Bernard Luber   *Scr* Richard Schayer, Jefferson Pascal   *Ph* Harry Waxman   *Ed* Frederick Wilson   *Mus* Ron Goodwin   *Art Dir* Maurice Carter
● Cornel Wilde, Jean Wallace, Brian Aherne, George Baker, John Longden, Iain Gregory (Emblem/Universal)

This version of the much-told tale of King Arthur and the Knights of the Round Table is an elaborately mounted production that generates fair amounts of interest and excitement when the fighting's going on but barely rises above the routine in story-telling the legend.

It's Cornel Wilde most of the way, he having coproduced, directed and costarred with his wife, Jean Wallace, latter making a beautiful Guinevere.

This outing smacks of modernization in terms of plot situation. But not filmmaking technique. King Arthur eagerly awaits his Guinevere at the altar in his Camelot and she's escorted by the gallant Lancelot (Wilde). The marriage takes place, but despite the affection Lancelot feels for his king, he shares a bed with the lady whose name he reduces in the dialog to just plain Guin.

The outdoor scenes, which were filmed in Yugoslavia with native cavalrymen, are in some measure pictorially effective but at times director Wilde is just focusing on so much confused action. No telling how much footage was left on the plains of Titoland or the cutting-room floor of Pinewood Studios, London, where the interiors were lensed.

An accomplished job is turned in by Brian Aherne, as King Arthur, who's able to give a good reading even when dialog is stilted. Wilde and Wallace are believable, John Longden is properly sinister as Arthur's rival for the crown and Iain Gregory is appealing as a young knight fighting side by side with Lancelot.

．．．．．．．．．．．．．．．．．．．．．．．

■ LAND BEFORE TIME, THE

1988, 66 MINS, US ◇ ⊛ ⊙

Dir Don Bluth   *Prod* Don Bluth, Gary Goldman, John Pomeroy   *Scr* Stu Krieger   *Ph* Jim Mann   *Ed* Dan Molina, John K. Carr   *Mus* James Horner   *Art Dir* Don Bluth
● (Sullivan-Bluth/Amblin)

Sure, kids like dinosaurs, but beyond that, premise doesn't find far to go. Story is about Littlefoot (Gabriel Damon), an innocent dinosaur tyke who gets separated from his family and after a perilous journey finds them again in a new land.

In this case it's a journey from a dried-up part of the land to another, known as the Great Valley, where the herds frolic in abundant greenery.

After Littlefoot's mother dies, he has to make the journey alone, dodging hazards like earthquakes, volcanoes and a predatory carnivore named Sharptooth. Along the way, he pulls together a band of other little dinosaurs of different species who've been brought up not to associate with each other.

Idea develops that surviving in a changing environment depends on achieving unity among the species.

For the most part, pic is about as engaging as what's found on Saturday morning TV.

．．．．．．．．．．．．．．．．．．．．．．．

L

■ LANDLORD, THE

1970, 112 MINS, US ◊
Dir Hal Ashby   *Prod* Norman Jewison   *Scr* William
Gunn   *Ph* Gordon Willis   *Ed* William Abbott Sawyer,
Edward Warschilka   *Mus* Al Kooper   *Art Dir* Robert
Boyle
● Beau Bridges, Lee Grant, Diana Sands, Pearl Bailey,
Marki Bey, Louis Gossett (United Artists/Mirisch)

Beau Bridges heads the uniformly excellent
cast as a bored rich youth who buys a black
ghetto apartment building and learns something about life.

A novel by Kristin Hunter has been scripted
into what is essentially a two-part story. First,
Bridges and his economically secure family
are played off and against the black tenants
whom he inherits in his ghetto building.
Then, Bridges' sexual encounter with married Diana Sands results in a mixed race baby
and a confrontation with some hard facts of
life.

The film is most successful when people are
interacting with people. Pearl Bailey's performance is a terrific showpiece for her talents.
Sands makes a powerful impression as a flirtatious but loving wife to Louis Gossett.
□ 1970: Nomination: Best Supp. Actress (Lee
Grant)

■ LAND OF THE PHARAOHS

1955, 103 MINS, US ◊ ⊙
Dir Howard Hawks   *Prod* Howard Hawks   *Scr* William
Faulkner, Harry Kurnitz, Harold Jack Bloom   *Ph* Lee
Garmes, Russell Harlan, Rudi Fehr
Mus Dimitri Tiomkin   *Art Dir* Alexandre Trauner
● Jack Hawkins, Joan Collins, Dewey Martin, Alexis
Minotis, James Robertson Justice (Continental/Warner)

Egypt of 5,000 years ago comes to life in *Land
of the Pharaohs*, a tremendous film spectacle.
From the opening shot of a great pharaoh
and his thousands of soldiers returning from
successful battle laden with vast treasure, an
audience is constantly overwhelmed with
spectacle, either in the use of cast thousands,
tremendously sized settings or the surging
background score by Dimitri Tiomkin.

The story tells of a great pharaoh, ably
played by Jack Hawkins, who for 30 years drives his people to build a pyramid in which his
body and treasure shall rest secure for evermore, and of a woman, portrayed by Joan
Collins, a captivating bundle of s.a., who conspires to win his kingdom and riches for herself.

When the viewing senses begin to dull from
the tremendous load of spectacle, the script
and Hawks' direction wisely switch to sex and
intrigue.

Alexis Minotis, Greek actor, lends the picture a fine performance as Hamar, the high
priest.

■ LAND THAT TIME FORGOT, THE

1975, 91 MINS, UK ◊
Dir Kevin Connor   *Prod* John Dark   *Scr* James
Cawthorn, Michael Moorcock   *Ph* Alan Hume   *Ed* John
Ireland   *Mus* Douglas Gamley   *Art Dir* Bert Davey
● Doug McClure, John McEnery, Susan Penhaligon,
Keith Barron, Anthony Ainley, Godfrey James (American
International)

Adapted from Edgar Rice Burroughs' *The
Land That Time Forgot*, the 'land' in question is
an unchartered island, icy on the outside and
smoldering within, that's populated with all
sorts of big critters.

This island of Caprona is reached by a
German submarine which torpedoes an
English ship. The survivors, led by Doug
McClure, come aboard and capture the sub.
But McEnery gets it back. Then McClure
takes over again. By this time, it's no wonder
the sub is lost in the Antarctic. Luckily, they
spot Caprona, easing the sub through an
underground tunnel where it's attacked by a
Mososaurus.

Somebody identifies the problem immediately. 'This can't be. These creatures have
been extinct for millions of years.'

■ LASER MAN, THE

1988, 92 MINS, US/HONG KONG ◊
Dir Peter Wang   *Prod* Peter Wang   *Scr* Peter Wang
Ph Ernest Dickerson   *Ed* Grahame Weinbren
Mus Mason Daring   *Art Dir* Lester Cohen
● Marc Hayashi, Maryann Urbano, Tony Leung, Peter
Wang, Joan Copeland, Sally Yeh (Wang/Film
Workshop)

The Laser Man is a quirky, cross-cultural, high-
tech comedy about serious matters from
Peter Wang, who made an impression with *A
Great Wall*. Self-consciously implausible story
concerning the manipulation of a laser expert
by big business serves as a pegboard on which
Wang hangs any number of amusing observations about the The Melting Pot, 1988, particularly where Chinese-Americans are concerned.

Laser researcher Arthur Weiss (Marc
Hayashi) accidentally kills a colleague in an
experiment, and is instantly rendered so un-
employable that he is forced to sign on with a
suspicious firm involved in space age weaponry and arms smuggling.

Weiss has a Jewish mother (Joan Copeland)
who happens to believe she has a Chinese
soul and persists in cooking perfectly dreadful
Chinese meals. Joey Chung (Tony Leung),
Arthur's best friend, is married to a Jewish
woman and reveals that he has never slept
with a Chinese, never, that is, until he meets
Susu (Sally Yeh) a stunning, newly arrived
immigrant who lives and works in a massage
parlor and dreams of going to Las Vegas.
Last, but certainly not least, there is Janet
(Maryann Urbano), a Caucasian woman obsessed with things Oriental, who, to Arthur's
distinct frustration, would rather meditate
than make love.

Unfortunately, the plotting is not always
hospitable to the engagingly flippant tone
Wang mostly maintains, especially when one
of the major characters becomes the victim of
the fancy gun, only to be casually resurrected
later on. Scenes with the women are invariably the most human, humorous and resonant in the film.

■ LASSITER

1984, 100 MINS, US ◊ ⊙
Dir Roger Young   *Prod* Albert S. Ruddy   *Scr* David
Taylor   *Ph* Gil Taylor   *Ed* Allan Jacobs, Benjamin
Weissman   *Mus* Ken Thorne   *Art Dir* Peter Mullins
● Tom Selleck, Jane Seymour, Lauren Hutton, Bob
Hoskins, Joe Regalbuto, Ed Lauter (Golden Harvest)

Set in London in 1934, *Lassiter* is part caper
picture, part intrigue story. Nick Lassiter
(Tom Selleck) is an elegant jewel thief who is
blackmailed by a coalition of the FBI and
English police to liberate $10 million in Nazi
diamonds passing through London. Selleck resists, but really isn't given much choice since
the alternative is a stay in a British prison.

The diamonds are to be transported out of
London by none other than Lauren Hutton,
playing German agent Countess Kari von
Fursten.

Hutton is totally unbelievable with her
Germanic accent and evil habits. As the girlfriend, Jane Seymour is wasted. Her role is
basically to stand by as Selleck races about
trying to grab the diamonds and run.

■ LAST ACTION HERO

1993, 130 MINS, US ◊ ⊙
Dir John McTiernan   *Prod* Steve Roth, John McTiernan
Scr Shane Black, David Arnott, [William Goldman]
Ph Dean Semler   *Ed* John Wright   *Mus* Michael Kamen
Art Dir Eugenio Zanetti
● Arnold Schwarzenegger, F. Murray Abraham, Art
Carney, Charles Dance, Anthony Quinn, Austin O'Brien
(Columbia/Oak)

Last Action Hero is a joyless, soulless machine
of a movie, an $80 million-plus mishmash of
fantasy, industry in-jokes, self-referential parody, film-buff gags and too-big action set-
pieces.

Arnold Schwarzenegger plays indestructible
screen superhero Jack Slater, whose
prophetic signature phrase to his enemies
when they try to harm him is, 'Big Mistake'.
That's what he's made here.

The central problem is that the picture is
based on a gimmick [from a screen story by
Zack Penn and Adam Leff] rather than a
story, so the viewer is presented with a succession of arbitrary scenes in which nothing is
at stake because, in context, it's almost all
'fiction' anyway.

Little 11-year-old Danny Madigan (Austin
O'Brien) is invited by projectionist friend
Nick (Robert Prosky) to a midnight private
screening of Slater's latest picture, simply titled *Jack Slater IV*. Nick presents Danny with
a golden magic ticket, a 'passport to another
world' handed down from Houdini, with
which Danny passes into the world onscreen.

Benedict (Charles Dance), sinister triggerman of a mobster (Anthony Quinn), comes
into possession of the magic ticket and takes
his evil ways into the 'real' world of Times
Square, followed by Danny and Slater, who is
dismayed to discover that violence can actually hurt and that his entire life has been
lived in movies.

It's all heavy, empty and exceptionally
noisy. On a character level, Arnold is Arnold.
Everyone else seems to have checked in for a
nice payday. Jabbering incessantly and always
badgering his hero, O'Brien, onscreen most
of the time, delivers a one-note performance.

■ LAST AMERICAN HERO, THE

1973, 95 MINS, US ◊
Dir Lamont Johnson   *Prod* William Roberts, John Cutts
Scr William Roberts   *Ph* George Silano   *Ed* Tom Rolf,
Robbe Roberts   *Mus* Charles Fox   *Art Dir* Lawrence
Paull
● Jeff Bridges, Valerie Perrine, Geraldine Fitzgerald,
Ned Beatty, Art Lund, Gary Busey (20th Century-Fox)

After a fumbling start which looks like bad
editing for TV, *The Last American Hero* [based
on two articles by Tom Wolfe] settles into
some good, gritty, family Americana, with Jeff
Bridges excellent as a flamboyant auto racer
determined to succeed on his own terms and
right a wrong to his father, played expertly by
Art Lund.

Bridges and Gary Busey are moonshiner
Lund's boys, with Geraldine Fitzgerald a concerned wife and mother. Bridges' backroad
hot-rodding outrages a revenuer into busting
Lund, who gets time for illegal liquor distill-
ing. Bridges takes to the racing circuit to buy
Lund some prison privileges.

Between the script, Lamont Johnson's sure
direction, and the excellent performances, all
but the early choppy scenes add up to a well-
told story.

■ LAST ANGRY MAN, THE

1959, 100 MINS, US ◊
Dir Daniel Mann   *Prod* Fred Kohlmar   *Scr* Gerald
Green, Richard Murphy   *Ph* James Wong Howe
Ed Charles Nelson   *Mus* George Duning
● Paul Muni, David Wayne, Betsy Palmer, Luther Adler,
Joby Baker, Nancy Pollock (Columbia)

The Last Angry Man is as pungent and indelible as Brooklyn on a hot summer afternoon.
It has faults: but it is possible to overlook
whatever imperfections stud the production

because so much of it is so good and, add, so rare.

The film is taken from Gerald Green's best-selling novel about a Jewish doctor, a character based on Green's own father. Director Daniel Mann had his problems in getting the story on film, shooting much of it on Brooklyn locations, but the finished product is worth the labor.

The conflict in the story arises from the life-time of selfless service by the doctor (Paul Muni) when placed in conjunction with the commercial demands of contemporary television. Television wants to exploit the Jewish doctor, to associate with him so it can claim some of his virtues. Muni is an immigrant who has absorbed his Americanism from Jefferson, from Emerson and Thoreau, and he believes what they said.

Muni gives a superlative performance. Someone chides him at one point for thinking of himself as an Albert Schweitzer. A Schweitzer he isn't, but in Muni's character delineation it's apparent it's the men like him who keep the world going. David Wayne, as his abrasive agent, is allowed no histrionics, but his conviction must be absolute. Wayne is as persuasive as his narrow lapels and button-down collars.

☐ 1959: Nominations: Best Actor (Paul Muni), B&W Art Direction

● ●

■ LAST BOY SCOUT, THE

1991, 105 MINS, US ◇ ⊗ ☉

Dir Tony Scott   *Prod* Joel Silver, Michael Levy
Scr Shane Black   *Ph* Ward Russell   *Ed* Mark Goldblatt, Mark Helfrich   *Mus* Michael Kamen   *Art Dir* Brian Morris
● Bruce Willis, Damon Wayans, Chelsea Field, Noble Willingham, Taylor Negron, Danielle Harris (Geffen/Silver)

Despite the bidding war surrounding Shane Black's script (and its ultimate seven-figure purchase price), there's really nothing special about this entertaining if mindless shoot-'em-up other than an ample supply of amusing juvenile put-downs and elaborate action sequences. Black should know the territory, having penned *Lethal Weapon* and the first draft of its sequel.

Equipped with a persona suited to his gifts, Bruce Willis limns a former Secret Service agent whose devotion to justice (accounting-for pic's title) put him out on the street scrounging for work as a sleazy p.i. Willis plays the part as a world-weary Bogart wannabe, grounded in domestic trappings by partial estrangement from his wife and daughter.

The plot [story by Black and Greg Hicks] is a haze of barely connected story lines about political corruption, pro-football, gambling, infidelity, and blackmail – a sort of poor man's *The Big Sleep*, but here all the questions are answered by another car chase, smashing someone in the face or shooting someone in the forehead.

Willis gets yanked into the action when he's asked to protect a stripper (Halle Berry), g.f. of a former pro quarterback (Damon Wayans) banned from the game for gambling. There's not a lot of chemistry between Willis and Wayans, but both can be flat-out funny, and the script provides them plenty of opportunity to zing each other as well as the cartoonish bad guys.

● ●

■ LAST COMMAND, THE

1928, 90 MINS, US ⊗ ☉

Dir Josef von Sternberg   *Prod* Joseph Bachman
Scr John F. Goodrich, Herman J. Mankiewicz   *Ph* Bert Glennon   *Art Dir* Hans Dreier
● Emil Jannings, Evelyn Brent, William Powell, Nicholas Soussanin, Michael Visaroff (Paramount)

Russia in the early days of the First World War and the revolution. Emil Jannings is the commander-in-chief of the czar's armies in the field. (The picture's working title was *The General*.) The general, overthrown and overwhelmed by the revolutionists, drifts to Hollywood, to become a $7.50-a-day extra waiting in a rooming house for a call.

It comes when a Russian picture director requiring a movie army recognizes a photo of the general as the same who whipped him in Russia in 1914, when the director then was a starving actor-revolutionist. They make him a general again, at $7.50 daily, with many studio scenes, to lead a movie army of Russians.

Plenty of direction and as much photography. There doesn't appear to be a miss or skip either. Herman Mankiewicz's titles [from an original by Lajos Biro] are no small part of the interest, always perfectly placed and phrased. They lack a couple of laughs, although the subject matter limits that.

☐ 1927/28: Best Actor (Emil Jennings).
☐ Nominations: Best Picture, Original Story

● ●

■ LAST DAYS OF CHEZ NOUS, THE

1992, 96 MINS, AUSTRALIA ◇ ⊗ ☉

Dir Gillian Armstrong   *Prod* Jan Chapman   *Scr* Helen Garner   *Ph* Geoffrey Simpson   *Ed* Nicholas Beauman   *Mus* Paul Grabowsky   *Art Dir* Janet Patterson
● Lisa Harrow, Bruno Ganz, Kerry Fox, Miranda Otto, Kiri Paramore, Bill Hunter (Chapman/AFFC)

This post-feminist drama about two sisters involved with the same man is beautifully acted and crafted, despite some script problems.

Fortyish Beth (Lisa Harrow) works hard as a writer, bosses people around, lacks emotion and finds it difficult to 'be part of a couple,' which is hard on her French husband, J.P. (Bruno Ganz). Beth's daughter by her first marriage, Annie (Miranda Otto), is a gangly teen on the brink of her first love affair.

Despite tension in the household, which also includes a lodger (Kiri Paramore) who romances Annie, everyone gets along until the return from overseas of Vicki (Kerry Fox), Beth's younger sister who's sometimes mistaken for her daughter.

The plot line isn't very original, but the femme characters are observed and played with notable depth.

● ●

■ LAST DAYS OF MAN ON EARTH, THE

See: *The Final Programme*

● ●

■ LAST DAYS OF POMPEII, THE

1935, 96 MINS, US ☉

Dir Ernest B. Schoedsack   *Prod* Merian C. Cooper
Scr Ruth Rose   *Ph* J. Roy Hunt   *Ed* Archie Marshek   *Mus* Roy Webb   *Art Dir* Van Nest Polglase, Al Herman
● Preston Foster, Basil Rathbone, David Holt, Alan Hale, Louis Calhern, Dorothy Wilson (RKO)

The Last Days of Pompeii is a spectacle picture, full of action and holds a good tempo throughout.

What is presented is a behind-the-scenes of Roman politics and commerce, both of which are shown as smeared with corruption and intrigue. [An opening caption claims the characters and plot have no relation to those in Edward Bulwer-Lytton's novel of the same name. Original story is credited to James Ashmore Creelman and Melville Baker, adapted by Ruth Rose and Boris Ingster.]

Basil Rathbone comes very close to stealing the picture with his playing of Pontius Pilate. Jesus crosses the path of Marcus (Preston Foster) one time gladiator who is in Judea on a little business deal (horse stealing) which he carries out as the silent partner of Pilate.

Foster has the central role. He carries through from the boyish blacksmith of the opening sequence to the rich man who in the end sees his beloved son face probable death in the arena (just before the volcano erupts). On the way he is a gladiator, slave trader, horse-stealer and general tough guy, but more the victim of a fierce semi-barbaric environment than of any personal cruelty trait.

● ●

■ LAST DETAIL, THE

1973, 103 MINS, US ◇ ⊗ ☉

Dir Hal Ashby   *Prod* Gerald Ayres   *Scr* Robert Towne   *Ph* Michael Chapman   *Ed* Robert C. Jones   *Mus* Johnny Mandel   *Art Dir* Michael Haller
● Jack Nicholson, Otis Young, Randy Quaid, Clifton James, Michael Moriarty, Carol Kane (Columbia)

The Last Detail is a salty, bawdy, hilarious and very touching story about two career sailors escorting to a naval prison a dumb boot sentenced for petty thievery. Jack Nicholson is outstanding at the head of a superb cast.

Robert Towne's outstanding adaptation of Darryl Ponicsan's novel has caught the flavor of noncombat military life. The dialog vulgarisms are simply part of the eternal environment of men in uniform.

Randy Quaid is cast as a teenage misfit. A bungled ripoff of some charity money has gotten him eight years in Portsmouth. Nicholson and Otis Young, awaiting new assignments at a receiving station, draw escort duty. With several days of transit time allowed, Nicholson decides to set a leisurely pace. The essence of the story is the exchange of compassion between the guards and prisoner, and the latter's effect on his escorts.

☐ 1973: Nominations: Best Actor (Jack Nicholson), Supp. Actor (Randy Quaid), Adapted Screenplay

● ●

■ LAST EMBRACE

1979, 103 MINS, US ◇ ⊗

Dir Jonathan Demme   *Prod* Michael Taylor, Dan Wigutow   *Scr* David Shaber   *Ph* Tak Fujimoto   *Ed* Barry Malkin   *Mus* Miklos Rozsa   *Art Dir* Charles Rosen
● Roy Scheider, Janet Margolin, Christopher Walken, Sam Levene, John Glover, Charles Napier (United Artists)

Director Jonathan Demme proves conclusively that he can handle a strictly commercial assignment, while embellishing it with the creative touches that mark a firstrate filmmaker.

Last Embrace tells of a government agent being phased out after a nervous breakdown, triggered by his wife's murder. Roy Scheider is the paranoid subject of more attention than he'd prefer, especially when it comes from Janet Margolin, a wigged-out grad student. Story is from Murray Teigh Bloom's novel, *The 13th Man*. The Hitchcock references are frequent.

Scheider delivers a convincing, nerve-tingling perf that reaffirms he can handle a romantic lead. Margolin is highly appealing as the revenge-minded femme. Christopher Walken is seen briefly in a cameo performance as Scheider's boss.

● ●

■ LAST EMPEROR, THE

1987, 160 MINS, UK/ITALY ◇ ⊗ ☉

Dir Bernardo Bertolucci   *Prod* Jeremy Thomas
Scr Mark Peploe, Bernardo Bertolucci   *Ph* Vittorio Storaro   *Ed* Gabriella Cristiani   *Mus* Ryuichi Sakamoto, David Byrne, Cong Su   *Art Dir* Ferdinando Scarfiotti
● John Lone, Joan Chen, Peter O'Toole, Ying Ruocheng, Victor Wong, Dennis Dun (Thomas/Columbia)

A film of unique, quite unsurpassed visual splendor, *The Last Emperor* makes for a fascinating trip to another world, but for the most part also proves as remote and untouchable as its subject, the last imperial ruler of China. A prodigious production in every respect,

L

Bernardo Bertolucci's film is an exquisitely painted mural of 20th-century Chinese history as seen from the point of view of a hereditary leader who never knew his people.

In 1908, the three-year-old Pu Yi is installed as Lord of Ten Thousand Years, master of the most populous nation on earth. Shortly, he is forced to abdicate, but is kept on as a symbolic figure, educated by his English tutor and tended to by a court that includes 1,500 eunuchs and countless other manipulative advisers.

Finally booted out by the new government, Pu Yi, by now in his late 20s, moves with his two wives to Tientsin and lives like a Western playboy, wearing tuxedos at elegant dances while gradually coming under the influence of the Japanese, who eventually install him as puppet emperor of Manchuria, home of his ancestors.

After World War II, he is imprisoned for 10 years by the communists, during which time he writes his memoirs, and ends his life as a gardener and simple citizen in Mao's China.

At every moment, the extraordinary aspects of both the story and the physical realization of it are astonishing to witness. For virtually the first 90 minutes, Bertolucci makes full use of the red-dominatd splendor of the Forbidden City, which has never before been opened up for use in a Western film.

John Lone, who plays Pu Yi from age 18 to 62, naturally dominates the picture with his carefully judged, unshowy delineation of a sometimes arrogant, often weak man. Joan Chen is exquisite and sad as his principal wife who almost literally fades away, and Peter O'Toole, as Lone's tutor, doesn't really have that much to do but act intelligently concerned for the emperor's well-being.

☐ 1987: Best Picture, Director, Adapted Screenplay, Cinematography, Art Direction, Sound, Original Score, Editing, Costume Design

••••••••••••••••••••••••••••••••••••••

■ LAST EXIT TO BROOKLYN

1989, 102 MINS, W. GERMANY ◇ ⍟ ▣ ☉
Dir Uli Edel   *Prod* Bernd Eichinger, Herman Weigel
Scr Desmond Nakano   *Ph* Stefan Czapsky   *Ed* Peter Przygodda   *Mus* Mark Knopfler   *Art Dir* David Chapman
● Stephen Lang, Jennifer Jason Leigh, Burt Young, Peter Dobson, Jerry Orbach, Alexis Arquette (Neue Constantin/Bavaria/Allied)

Last Exit to Brooklyn is a bleak tour of urban hell, a $16 million Stateside-lensed production of Hubert Selby Jr's controversial 1964 novel. But it doesn't hold a scalpel to the lacerating torrential prose that made the book so cringingly urgent.

Director Uli Edel, whose international reputation was made on the 1980 teen drug drama *Christiane F.*, proves himself an accomplished professional. What he lacks is that fundamental gift of empathy that would make these damned souls more than just figures under a cinematic microscope.

Action is set in a working-class section of Brooklyn in 1952, close by the navy yards where young Americans are embarking for the Korean War. Many residents are engaged in a bitter six month strike against a local factory. Film's spectacular centerpiece is a well-staged riot pitting strikers against police when factory management uses scab labour to break the picket lines.

One of the protagonists is Stephen Lang, a venal married shop steward and secretary of the strike office who has been dipping into the union till to subsidize his first homosexual affair. When union boss Jerry Orbach boots him out, Lang is dropped by his mercenary lover. A subhuman band of local goons thrashes Lang to within an inch of his life (and 'crucifies' him on a wooden crossbeam).

Other major character is a tawdry, hard-drinking teen hooker named Tralala (Jennifer Jason Leigh), who lures unsuspecting bar-hopping servicemen to a back lot where they are mugged and robbed by the band. One night she gets drunk and defiantly declares herself open for sexual services to the neighbourhood bar's entire clintele.

The resulting gangbang, one of the most horrific passages in Selby Jr's book, is here sanitized and given a hopeful finish.

••••••••••••••••••••••••••••••••••••••

■ LAST HARD MEN, THE

1976, 103 MINS, US ◇ ⍟
Dir Andrew V. McLaglen   *Prod* Walter Seltzer, Russell Thacher   *Scr* Guerdon Trueblood   *Ph* Duke Callaghan   *Ed* Fred Chulack   *Mus* Jerry Goldsmith   *Art Dir* Edward Carfagno
● Charlton Heston, James Coburn, Barbara Hershey, Jorge Rivero, Michael Parks, Larry Wilcox (20th Century-Fox)

The Last Hard Men is a fairly good actioner with handsome production values and some thoughtful overtones. Charlton Heston and James Coburn are both fine as a retired lawman and his half-Indian nemesis matching their wits in 1909 Arizona along the way to one last bloody confrontation.

Coburn escapes from a Yuma prison gang to wreak carefully planned revenge on Heston, who killed his wife years ago in a scatter-shot shootout. Recruiting a motley gang Coburn lures the anxious Heston out of Tucson by kidnapping and molesting his daughter (Barbara Hershey).

The details of life at a crucial transition point in American history are well captured in the script and in the art direction.

••••••••••••••••••••••••••••••••••••••

■ LAST HURRAH, THE

1958, 121 MINS, US ⍟ ☉
Dir John Ford   *Prod* John Ford   *Scr* Frank Nugent
Ph Charles Lawton Jr   *Ed* Jack Murray   *Art Dir* Robert Peterson
● Spencer Tracy, Jeffrey Hunter, Dianne Foster, Pat O'Brien, Basil Rathbone, James Gleason (Columbia)

Edwin O'Connor's novel has been transmuted to the screen in slick style. Spencer Tracy makes the most of the meaty role of the shrewd politician of the 'dominantly Irish-American' metropolis in New England (unmistakably Boston but not Boston).

Tracy's resourcefulness in besting the stuffy bankers who nixed a loan for a much needed low-rent housing development; his foiling of the profiteering undertaker when a constituent is buried (the wake is transformed into a political rally); the passionate loyalty of his political devotees; the rivalry between the 'respectable' elements in combating the direct-approach tactics of the Irish-American politicos; the pride in defeat when the 're-form' candidate bests Tracy at the polls; and Tracy's own 'last hurrah' as he tells off the fatuous banker (Willis Bouchey) – with a parting 'like hell I would!' – in reviewing his gaudy career, make for a series of memorable scenes.

Jeffrey Hunter is the shrewd mayor's favored nephew who, despite his ties to the opposition sheet, perceives the old codger's humaneness.

••••••••••••••••••••••••••••••••••••••

■ LAST MARRIED COUPLE IN AMERICA, THE

1980, 103 MINS, US ◇ ⍟
Dir Gilbert Cates   *Prod* Edward S. Feldman, John Herman Shaner   *Scr* John Herman Shaner   *Ph* Ralph Woolsey   *Ed* Peter E. Berger   *Mus* Charles Fox
Art Dir Gene Callahan
● George Segal, Natalie Wood, Richard Benjamin, Dom DeLuise, Valerie Harper (Universal)

The Last Married Couple In America is basically a 1950s comedy with cursing. John Herman Shaner's script offers not a single new idea about divorce in suburbia and doesn't even develop the cliches well.

Gilbert Cates' direction consists largely of letting his stars reenact favorite roles of the past. So Wood plays the nice pretty lady who wants a happy, faithful marriage to George Segal, who plays the nice, handsome husband befuddled by the world around him.

Richard Benjamin is again the neurotic modern male and Dom DeLuise the likable, nutty fat guy, while Valerie Harper is essentially Rhoda running rampant, tresses turned blonde from the sheer excitement of it all.

••••••••••••••••••••••••••••••••••••••

■ LAST MOVIE, THE

1971, 110 MINS, US ◇ ⍟
Dir Dennis Hopper   *Prod* Paul Lewis   *Scr* Stewart Stern
Ph Laszlo Kovacs   *Ed* David Berlatsky   *Art Dir* Leon Erickson
● Dennis Hopper, Stella Garcia, Sam Fuller, Daniel Ades, Tomas Milian, Don Gordon (Universal)

The narrative fluidity, using of myths for a statement on youth, so effective in Dennis Hopper's *Easy Rider* are here overdone and film suffers from a multiplicity of themes, ideas and its fragmented style with flash-forwards intertwined.

Film begins with Hopper wandering all bloody among Peruvian Indians playing at filmmaking with cameras, booms, etc., made of rattan. A local priest complains of the violence the film people have left behind among his people whose playing at it leads to a kind of passion play and the hunted and finally crucified figure becomes Hopper.

Then a scene from the film shot there, a gun battle with horses falling and men bloodied. Sam Fuller plays a no-nonsense director with aplomb in these scenes. Hopper has the canteen, plays stuntman and stays on with a native girl, dreaming of building a resort and using the set for other productions. This does not pan out.

Stella Garcia is effective as the native girl who is not moved by the dead she does not know while Hopper has an American innocence tempered with violent rage when things go beyond his ken.

••••••••••••••••••••••••••••••••••••••

■ LAST OF ENGLAND, THE

1987, 87 MINS, UK/W. GERMANY ◇ ⍟
Dir Derek Jarman   *Prod* James Mackay, Don Boyd
Scr [uncredited]   *Ph* Derek Jarman, Christopher Hughes, Cerith Wyn Evans, Richard Heslop   *Ed* Peter Cartwright, Angus Cook, Sally Yeadon, John Maybury   *Mus* Simon Turner, Andy Gill, Mayo Thompson, Albert Oehlen, Barry Adamson, El Tito   *Art Dir* Christopher Hobbs
● Tilda Swinton, Spencer Leigh, Spring, Gay Gaynor, Matthew Hawkins, Gerard McArthur (British Screen/Film Four/ZDF/Anglo-International)

The Last of England has the rare ability to envelop one in its swirling images and bleak comedy one moment, and send a viewer off to sleep the next.

Following the avant-garde helmer's most accessible film to date, the 1986 *Caravaggio*, he returns with a blatantly personal vision which combines documentary-style footage of ruined streets, home movies, and a segment with glimpses of a screen story. All is filmed and linked abstractly, but without the glimmer of plot or narrative line.

The Last of England is a self-indulgent number, opening with an actor (Spring) kicking and abusing a Caravaggio painting, 'Profane Love', and proceeding with a tirade of images of urban destruction and deprived youth. Interspersed are extracts from the Jarman family's home movies, which make an interesting contrast to the abrasive images with their views of colonial and RAF life.

••••••••••••••••••••••••••••••••••••••

■ LAST OF MRS CHEYNEY, THE

1929, 94 MINS, US
Dir Sidney Franklin   *Ph* William Daniels
● Norma Shearer, Basil Rathbone, George Barraud, Herbert Bunston, Hedda Hopper, Moon Carroll (M-G-M)

Whole story [from the play by Frederick Lonsdale] is sentimental, a deftly manipulated series of the bunk about the good girl drawn into associations with a band of crooks, getting herself accepted into society so they can prey upon the rich, the girl all the time retaining the chaste and delicate spirit of a nun.

It's bum literature but great theatre, particularly here with a splendid group of players. Norma Shearer does extremely well with the heroine. She most successfully plays the role of elegance and high breeding, the two qualities which are the key to making Mrs Cheyney plausible.

Basil Rathbone falls into a role for his casual, easy stage style, and the character of Lord Elton, composite of stupidity and meanness and the whole trick of the play's sentimental punch, is happily in the hands of Herbert Bunston, to whom it is pie.

The picture's finish could be made brisker.

■ LAST OF MRS. CHEYNEY, THE

1937, 95 MINS, US
Dir Richard Boleslawski   *Prod* Lawrence Weingarten
Scr Leon Gordon, Samson Raphaelson, Monckton Hoffe
Ph George Folsey   *Ed* Frank Sullivan   *Mus* William Axt
● Joan Crawford, William Powell, Robert Montgomery, Frank Morgan, Jessie Ralph, Nigel Bruce (M-G-M)

The Last of Mrs Cheyney is a a Metro remake of its own dialog film made in 1929 with Norma Shearer. it's from the [Frederick] Lonsdale play which Ina Claire, Roland Young and A.E. Matthews first did on Broadway in 1925. Present filmization more nearly approximates a picture than the 1929 film which was, then, more a straight transmutation of the play in celluloid form.

This is Richard Boleslawski's post-mortem release. Another director wound up the perfunctory details, but Boleslawski gets, and merits, the sole directorial billing. His hand is evident in a number of fine scenes, pacing this society crook comedy-drama with effective contrasts of suspense and laughs.

Scenes which are outstanding are made so by a rare combination of pace, scripting and direction. The sequence, for example, where the snooty English household is wondering what will happen to the crooks (Joan Crawford and her accomplice, William Powell) is a double-broadside in deft comedy painting.

In similar vein, the weekenders' truth-game less pointedly, but not too subtly, mirrors the foibles of the same group – the two-timing wife who has had 14 'cousins' (male) for constant companionship; her stupid husband; another lady of easy virtue; the engagingly lecherous male (Robert Montgomery), but frankly so: the duchess-hotesss (capably played by Jessie Ralph), who confesses she came into royalty via the London Gayety chorus-line, etc.

■ LAST OF SHEILA, THE

1973, 120 MINS, US ◇ ⑨
Dir Herbert Ross   *Prod* Herbert Ross   *Scr* Stephen Sondheim, Anthony Perkins   *Ph* Gerry Turpin
Ed Edward Warschilka   *Mus* Billy Goldenberg
Art Dir Ken Adam
● Richard Benjamin, Dyan Cannon, James Coburn, Joan Hackett, James Mason, Raquel Welch (Warner)

The Last of Sheila is a major disappointment. Result is far from the bloody *All About Eve* predicted and is simply a confused and cluttered demi *Sleuth*, grossly overwritten and underplayed.

Co-scripters Stephen Sondheim and Anthony Perkins are puzzle game fanatics, and the plot constructed for their first feature is self-indulgent camp at its most deadly.

The *Sheila* of the title is the luxury yacht named after the late wife of a Hollywood producer (James Coburn) killed by a hit-and-run driver shortly after exiting a raucous Beverly Hills party. A year later, Coburn asks six of those party guests for a week's Riviera cruise aboard the *Sheila*. Invitees include a glamorous Hollywood star (Raquel Welch), her business agent husband (Ian McShane), a fading director (James Mason), a struggling scriptwriter (Richard Benjamin), his wife (Joan Hackett) and an aggressive femme talent agent (Dyan Cannon).

On board, Coburn initiates a week-long game in which each guest is given a card indicating a secret which is to be discovered by the others. Since one of the cards reads 'I am a hit-and-run driver' the mystery concerns the person responsible for Sheila's demise.

Flashbacks, premature confessions and more murders flesh out the overlong running time. Cast is generally superior to the material with Cannon walking away with the honors as a recognizable femme talent packager with a vulgar, acid tongue.

■ LAST OF THE FINEST, THE

1990, 106 MINS, US ◇ ⑨ ⊙
Dir John Mackenzie   *Prod* John A. Davis   *Scr* Jere Cunningham, Thomas Lee Wright, George Armitage
Ph Juan Ruiz-Anchia   *Ed* Graham Walker   *Mus* Jack Nitzsche, Michael Hoenig   *Art Dir* Laurence G. Paull
● Brian Dennehy, Joe Pantoliano, Jeff Fahey, Bill Paxton, Deborra-Lee Furness, Guy Boyd (Davis/Orion)

The Last of the Finest belongs to a rarely attempted brand of pastiche film. The central characters are Brian Dennehy and his band of dedicated cops who tumble upon a bunch of corrupt characters (who parallel the Iran-Contra protagonists) while working on a drug bust.

Despite the deficiencies of a script that unwisely mixes tongue-in-cheek elements with soapbox messages, Scottish director John Mackenzie keeps the pic moving and enjoyable on a strictly thriller level. Its unsubtle references to Iran-Contra are more fun for film historians than action fans.

Dennehy is excellent in delivering a liberal message in the form of a free-thinking independent who's tired of the expediency and greed of a system riddled with phony patriots. Guy Boyd ably leads the group of Machiavellian villains and Aussie thesp Deborra-Lee Furness makes a good impression as Dennehy's wife.

■ LAST OF THE MOHICANS, THE

1936, 91 MINS, US ⑨
Dir George B. Seitz   *Prod* Edward Small, Harry M. Goetz   *Scr* Philip Dunne   *Ph* Robert Planck   *Ed* Jack Dennis   *Mus* Roy Webb   *Art Dir* John Ducasse Schulze
● Randolph Scott, Binnie Barnes, Heather Angel, Hugh Buckler, Henry Wilcoxon, Bruce Cabot (United Artists)

The James Fenimore Cooper historical fiction story [adapted by John Balderston, Paul Perez and Daniel Moore] is transferred to the screen with surprising fidelity, though the two love stories are accentuated, quite naturally. Locale is the wide open spaces of eastern America when England and the French were battling all through New York state to see which one was to be boss of this country. Story moves swiftly so that phase in the campaign when the British were rushing to the defense of Fort William Henry on Lake George (upper N.Y. state).

Hawkeye, the colonial scout, is set up as the typical American frontiersman of that day, willing to aid the British, but first interested in defending courageous colonists. Picture is hardly 15 minutes old before the first brush with the cruel Huron Indian tribe. From then it is a series of carefully conceived and deftly executed climaxes, starting with the siege and surrender of the fort.

Randolph Scott gives a virile interpretation as the scout without going overboard at any time. Henry Wilcoxon, as the snobbish British major, vies for honors on the male side. Binnie Barnes, the English girl in love with Hawkeye, further enhances her reputation as a fascinating actress. Heather Angel has less to do as the sister whose romance with a young Mohican ends tragically.
☐ 1936: Nomination: Best Assistant Director (Clem Beauchamp)

■ LAST OF THE MOHICANS, THE

1992, 122 MINS, US ◇ ⑨ ⊙
Dir Michael Mann   *Prod* Michael Mann, Hunt Lowry
Scr Michael Mann, Christopher Crowe   *Ph* Dante Spinotti, Doug Milsome   *Ed* Dov Hoenig, Arthur Schmidt
Mus Trevor Jones, Randy Edelman, Daniel Lanois
Art Dir Wolf Kroeger
● Daniel Day-Lewis, Madeleine Stowe, Russell Means, Eric Schweig, Jodhi May, Steven Waddington (20th Century-Fox)

The Last of the Mohicans benefits from rich source material (James Fenimore Cooper's classic [and the screenplay for the 1936 United Artists version]) and good performances. Adventure tale of life in the British colonies in America is a great ode to freedom and self-determination played out against codes of honor and loyalty, c. 1757. Lensed in South Carolina, pic blends pure adventure with a compelling central romance.

Sisters Alice (Jodhi May) and Cora (Madeleine Stowe) Munro are escorted through hostile country to join their colonel dad (Maurice Roeves), British commander of a fort under French siege. Rigid English soldier Duncan Heyward (Steven Waddington) is courting Cora sans success.

After an ambush leaves the Munro girls and Heyward unprotected, Hawkeye (Daniel Day-Lewis) and his adopted Mohican father (Russell Means) and brother (Eric Schweig) come to the rescue.

Lean and intense, with a dashing mane of hair, Day-Lewis brings his usual concentration to the role of the courageous woodsman at one with nature. He and Stowe spark a convincing attraction arising from shared ideals and piqued by the excitement of life-and-death ordeals.

Modern lensing techniques allow the camera to run alongside Hawkeye and accompany the trajectory of a bullet or the flight of a spinning tomahawk. Well-staged battle sequences are brutal and bloody.
☐ 1992: Best Sound

■ L.A. STORY

1991, 95 MINS, US ◇ ⑨ ⊙
Dir Mick Jackson   *Prod* Daniel Melnick, Michael Rachmil
Scr Steve Martin   *Ph* Andrew Dunn   *Ed* Richard A. Harris   *Mus* Peter Melnick   *Art Dir* Lawrence Miller
● Steve Martin, Victoria Tennant, Richard E. Grant, Marilu Henner, Sarah Jessica Parker, Susan Forristal (Carolco/Indieprod/LA Films)

Goofy and sweet, *L.A. Story* constitutes Steve Martin's satiric valentine to his hometown and a pretty funny comedy in the bargain.

Martin is in typically nutty form as an LA TV meteorologist who doesn't hestitate to take the weekends off since the weather isn't bound to change. What he can't predict, however, is the lightning bolt that hits him in the form of Brit journalist Victoria Tennant, who arrives to dish up the latest English assessment of America's new melting pot.

Martin's relationship with his snooty long-

L

time g.f. Marilu Henner is essentially over and, convinced that nothing can ever happen with his dreamgirl, he stumblingly takes up with ditzy shopgirl Sarah Jessica Parker.

Even after Martin and Tennant have gotten together and he has declared the grandest of romantic intentions, the future looks impossible, as she has promised her ex (Richard E. Grant) to attempt a reconciliation.

Despite the frantic style, the feeling behind Martin's view of life and love in LA comes through, helped by the seductively adoring treatment of Tennant (actually Martin's wife).

....

■ **LAST PICTURE SHOW, THE**

1971, 118 MINS, US ⓦ ⊙
Dir Peter Bogdanovich   *Prod* Stephen J. Friedman
Scr Larry McMurty, Peter Bogdanovich   *Ph* Robert Surtees   *Ed* Donn Cambern   *Art Dir* Walter Scott Herndon
● Timothy Bottoms, Jeff Bridges, Cybill Shepherd, Ben Johnson, Cloris Leachman, Ellen Burstyn (BBS)

Notre Dame professor Edward Fischer has said that 'the best films, like the best books, tell how it is to be human under certain circumstances'. Larry McMurtry did a beautiful job of this in his small novel (which he transferred to the screen), *The Last Picture Show*.

Timothy Bottoms and Jeff Bridges portray the pair of youths who complement each other's limited potential. Physically, they're much alike – football-playing, lanky, likable products of the Texas plains; mentally, or emotionally, they move on different planes. Bridges is the high school hero, more aggressive; Bottoms is the more sensitive, hence the more lonely, of the pair.

The boys grow a bit, some good people die, a few more secrets are revealed, and another 'nothing' decade has passed. Bridges, spurned by his girl, joins the army; Bottoms matures a bit. Not much else happens.

The best, most solid, most moving performances in the film are given by Ben Johnson, that old John Ford regular, as Sam The Lion, the owner of the picture show and pool room where the town boys spend most of their time; and Cloris Leachman as the football coach's wife, who introduces Bottoms to sex.

Peter Bogdanovich elected to shoot the film in black and white, artistically appropriate for the dust-blown, tired little community, but Robert Surtees (who's a master with color) doesn't bring off the tones of gray. There is excellent use of many pop tunes of the period and only introduced in a natural manner – a nickel in a jukebox, a car radio, or an early television set.
☐ 1971: Best Supp. Actor (Ben Johnson), Supp. Actress (Cloris Leachman).
☐ Nominations: Best Picture, Director, Supp. Actor (Jeff Bridges), Supp. Actress (Ellen Burstyn), Adapted Screenplay, Cinematography

....

■ **LAST REMAKE OF BEAU GESTE, THE**

1977, 84 MINS, US ◇ ⓦ
Dir Marty Feldman   *Prod* William S. Gilmore
Scr Marty Feldman   *Ph* Gerry Fisher   *Ed* Jim Clark, Arthur Schmidt   *Mus* John Morris   *Art Dir* Brian Eatwell
● Ann-Margret, Marty Feldman, Michael York, Peter Ustinov, James Earl Jones, Trevor Howard (Universal)

Marty Feldman's directorial debut on *The Last Remake of Beau Geste* emerges as an often hilarious, if uneven, spoof of Foreign Legion adventure films. An excellent cast, top to bottom, gets the most out of the stronger scenes, and carries the weaker ones.

Feldman stars [in a story by him and Sam Bobrick] as the ugly duckling brother of Michael York (as Beau Geste), both adopted sons of Trevor Howard, an aging lech whose marriage to swinger Ann-Margret causes

York to join the Foreign Legion and Feldman to serve time for alleged theft of a family gem.

Feldman joins York in the desert, where sadistic Peter Ustinov and bumbling Roy Kinnear run the garrison for urbane Henry Gibson, in the character of the Legion general.

....

■ **LAST RUN, THE**

1971, 92 MINS, US ◇ ⓦ
Dir Richard Fleischer   *Prod* Carter de Haven   *Scr* Alan Sharp   *Ph* Sven Nykvist   *Ed* Russell Lloyd   *Mus* Jerry Goldsmith   *Art Dir* Roy Walker, Jose Maria Tapiador
● George C. Scott, Tony Musante, Trish Van Devere, Colleen Dewhurst (M-G-M)

The Last Run is a suspense melodrama with a set of criminal characters to keep action lively but its story line is so blurred by unexplained elements that it emerges little more than an ordinary actioner. George C. Scott gives certain authority to a hardhitting role.

Produced in Spain by Carter De Haven and directed by Richard Fleischer, taking over from John Huston, who ankled the assignment, film gains in pictorial interest from constant shrewd use of colorful backgrounds. Original screenplay by Alan Sharp is designed as a saga of a man on the run after his escape from a prison van, and an old hand directing this flight. What comes out on screen militates against ready acceptance of this premise due to haphazard writing.

Scott plays a retired American mobster who once drove for criminals in fast getaways. He returns to activity after nine years to aid an escaped con and whisk him across the Spanish border into France. It's all pretty fuzzy and audience is at a loss to understand the whys and wherefores of the action.

....

■ **LAST STARFIGHTER, THE**

1984, 100 MINS, US ◇ ⓦ ⊙
Dir Nick Castle   *Prod* Gary Adelson, Edward O. Denault
Scr Jonathan Betuel   *Ph* King Baggot   *Ed* C. Timothy O'Meara   *Mus* Craig Safan   *Art Dir* Ron Cobb
● Lance Guest, Robert Preston, Dan O'Herlihy, Catherine Mary Stewart, Barbara Bosson, Norman Snow (Universal/Lorimar)

With *The Last Starfighter*, director Nick Castle and writer Jonathan Betuel have done something so simple it's almost awe-inspiring: they've taken a very human story and accented it with sci-fi special effects, rather than the other way around.

Lance Guest is a teenager with a talent for a lone video game that was somehow dropped off at his mother's rundown, remote trailer park when it should have been delivered to Las Vegas. And when he breaks the record for destroying alien invaders, Guest not only excites the whole trailer park, he attracts a visit from Robert Preston.

There is never a moment that all of this doesn't seem quite possible, accompanied by plenty of building questions about what's going to happen next.

....

■ **LAST SUMMER**

1969, 97 MINS, US ◇ ⓦ
Dir Frank Perry   *Prod* Frank Perry   *Scr* Eleanor Perry
Ph Gerald Hirschfeld   *Ed* Sidney Katz   *Mus* John Simon
● Barbara Hershey, Richard Thomas, Bruce Davison, Cathy Burns, Ralph Waite, Conrad Bain (Allied Artists/Alsid)

A solid insight into a quartet during a summer that also has fine acting and sensitive direction and writing.

A pretty, vivacious, headstrong girl finds a dying sea gull on the beach. She beseeches two youths to help her. They remove a hook from its throat and the three become friends.

The boys are expertly played by Bruce Davison and Richard Thomas, and Cathy Burns is engaging and touching as the lonely, homely little girl, drawn to those more emancipated friends, but finally appalled by their cowardice and cruelty, only to be the victim of their pent-up inarticulate needs.

Nicely hued, film has a frankness that is not forced and Eleanor Perry's dialog, if sometimes taking precedence over more visual revelations, is just and makes a statement about fairly-affluent youth.
☐ 1969: Nomination: Best Supp. Actress (Cathy Burns)

....

■ **LAST TANGO IN PARIS**

1972, 130 MINS, ITALY/FRANCE ◇ ⓦ ⊙
Dir Bernardo Bertolucci   *Prod* Alberto Grimaldi
Scr Bernardo Bertolucci, Franco Arcalli   *Ph* Vittorio Storaro   *Ed* Franco Arcalli, Roberto Perpignani
Mus Gato Barbieri, Oliver Nelson (arr.)
Art Dir Ferdinando Scarfiotti
● Marlon Brando, Maria Schneider, Maria Michi, Jean-Pierre Leaud, Massimo Girotti, Catherine Allegret (PEA/Artistes Associes)

Bernardo Bertolucci's *Last Tango in Paris* is an uneven, convoluted, certainly dispute-provoking study of sexual passion in which Marlon Brando gives a truly remarkable performance.

Brando plays an aging Lothario trailing the debris of a failed life who has wound up in Paris married to an unfaithful hotelkeeper. Pic opens on the day of his wife's suicide when the distraught Brando meets a young girl (Maria Schneider) while both are inspecting a vacant apartment. After a sudden, almost savage sexual encounter, Brando proposes that they meet in the apartment on a regular basis. Brando insists that no names or personal information be exchanged, that the affair remain purely carnal.

Plot has all the ingredients of a 1940s meller. Bertolucci uses it to explore the psyche of a man at the end of his emotional and sexual tether and at the same time to investigate on the most primitive level the chemistry of romantic love.

Schneider is standout as the girl, a difficult role played semi-tart, but one whose motivations remain cloudy through the murderous finale.
☐ 1973: Nominations: Best Director, Actor (Marlon Brando)

....

■ **LAST TEMPTATION OF CHRIST, THE**

1988, 164 MINS, US ◇ ⓦ ⊙
Dir Martin Scorsese   *Prod* Barbara De Fina   *Scr* Paul Schrader   *Ph* Michael Ballhaus   *Ed* Thelma Schoonmaker   *Mus* Peter Gabriel   *Art Dir* John Beard
● Willem Dafoe, Harvey Keitel, Barbara Hershey, Harry Dean Stanton, David Bowie, Verna Bloom (Universal/ Cineplex Odeon)

A film of challenging ideas, and not salacious provocations, *The Last Temptation of Christ* is a powerful and very modern reinterpretation of Jesus as a man wracked with anguish and doubt concerning his appointed role in life. Pic was lensed on Moroccan locations for a highly restrictive $6.5 million.

As a written prolog simply states, *Last Temptation* aims to be a 'fictional exploration of the eternal spiritual conflict,' 'the battle between the spirit and the flesh,' as Nikos Kazantzakis summarized the theme of his novel.

After rescuing Mary Magdalene from the stone-throwers, Jesus tentatively launches his career as religious leader. But only after his return from the desert and his hallucinatory exposure to representations of good and evil, is he transformed into a warrior against Satan, finally convinced he is the son of God.

Blondish and blue-eyed in the Anglo-Saxon

tradition, Willem Dafoe offers an utterly compelling reading of his character. Harvey Keitel puts across Judas' fierceness and loyalty, and only occasionally lets a New York accent and mannered modernism detract from total believability.

Barbara Hershey, adorned with tattoos, is an extremely physical, impassioned Mary Magdalene. One could have used more of David Bowie's subdued, rational Pontius Pilate.

☐ 1988: Nomination: Best Director

. . . .

■ LAST TIME I SAW PARIS, THE

1954, 116 MINS, US ◇ ⊛
Dir Richard Brooks   *Prod* Jack Cummings   *Scr* Julius J. Epstein, Philip G. Epstein   *Ph* Joseph Ruttenberg   *Ed* John Dunning   *Mus* Conrad Salinger
● Elizabeth Taylor, Van Johnson, Walter Pidgeon, Donna Reed, Eva Gabor, Kurt Kasznar (M-G-M)

The Last Time I Saw Paris is an engrossing romantic drama that tells a good story with fine performances and an overall honesty of dramatic purpose.

F. Scott Fitzgerald's short story, *Babylon Revisited* was updated and revised as the basis for the potent screenplay. Elizabeth Taylor's work as the heroine shows a thorough grasp of the character, whhich she makes warm and real. Richard Brooks' direction also gets a sock response from Van Johnson.

Plot is laid in Paris in the reckless, gay period that followed V-E Day of World War II. There, Johnson meets and marries Taylor and starts a struggling existence as a daytime reporter for a news service and wouldbe author at night. Even the faith of his wife cannot balance the brand of failure he assumes after too many rejection slips and when some supposedly worthless Texas oil property suddenly gushes into wealth he becomes a playboy himself.

Threading through the footage is the Jerome Kern-Oscar Hammerstein II title song, hauntingly sung by Odette.

. . . .

■ LAST TRAIN FROM GUN HILL

1959, 94 MINS, US ◇ ⊛
Dir John Sturges   *Prod* Hal Wallis   *Scr* James Poe   *Ph* Charles Lang Jr   *Ed* Warren Low   *Mus* Dimitri Tiomkin
● Kirk Douglas, Anthony Quinn, Carolyn Jones, Earl Holliman, Brad Dexter, Brian Hutton (Paramount/Bryna)

Last Train from Gun Hill, is a top western. Although there are some psychological undertones, it is a film that plays for almost pure action.

Kirk Douglas' Indian wife is raped and killed by two young brutes (Earl Holliman and Brian Hutton). Douglas, marshal of the town of Pauley, finds a clue that leads him to the neighboring community of Gun Hill. He discovers his fugitive (Holliman) is the son of his old friend (Anthony Quinn). His problem is how to get Holliman away to justice on that 'last train', with Quinn and his hired gunhands determined to thwart him.

James Poe's screenplay slips into a few cliches in dialog, but it is remarkable in that it avoids more. It is refreshing in its ability to shut up when action should take over, when a gesture or look completely conveys meaning.

Cameraman Charles Lang also employs an unusual number of very long shots in his sunbaked exteriors, with the human figures barely discernible black miniatures on the raw, yellow landscape.

Douglas and Quinn, by performances in depth, give the film the inevitability of tragedy. Carolyn Jones delivers impressively. Earl Holliman is most effective and sympathetic as the weakling son.

. . . .

■ LAST TYCOON, THE

1976, 122 MINS, US ◇ ⊛ ⊙
Dir Elia Kazan   *Prod* Sam Spiegel   *Scr* Harold Pinter   *Ph* Victor Kemper   *Ed* Richard Marks   *Mus* Maurice Jarre   *Art Dir* Gene Callahan
● Robert De Niro, Tony Curtis, Robert Mitchum, Jeanne Moreau, Jack Nicholson, Donald Pleasence (Paramount)

The Last Tycoon is a handsome and lethargic film, based on F. Scott Fitzgerald's unfinished Hollywood novel of the 1930s, as adapted by Harold Pinter. Producer Sam Spiegel's contribution is admirable, but Elia Kazan's direction of the Pinter plot seems unfocussed though craftsmanlike. Robert De Niro's performance as the inscrutable boy-wonder of films is mildly intriguing.

In an apparent attempt to avoid making a nostalgia film, the few choice bits of environmental interest emerge mostly as awkward interruptions in the main plot.

Ingrid Boulting is the elusive charmer who penetrates somewhat into De Niro's interior, but since her own expressions are limited in scope, we don't really know what she finds there. So, too, Theresa Russell, as Robert Mitchum's daughter, tries for De Niro, but at least she emerges as perhaps the only credible principal character in the piece.

☐ 1976: Nomination: Best Art Direction

. . . .

■ LAST UNICORN, THE

1982, 84 MINS, US ◇ ⊛
Dir Arthur Rankin Jr, Jules Bass   *Prod* Arthur Rankin Jr, Jules Bass   *Scr* Peter S. Beagle   *Ph* Hiroyasu Omoto   *Ed* Tomoko Kida   *Mus* Jimmy Webb   *Art Dir* Arthur Rankin Jr.
● (Rankin-Bass/ ITC)

The Last Unicorn represents a rare example of an animated kids' pic in which the script and vocal performances outshine the visuals.

Quest framework provided by Peter S. Beagle's adaptation of his own novel ideally serves an animated musical film's need to introduce an assortment of colorful characters who can deliver specialty numbers. Continuing thread is the search of the fabled last unicorn, in this case a beautiful white mare, for the rest of her breed, which has reportedly been vanquished by the terrible red bull.

However vapid the unicorn may appear to the eye, Mia Farrow's voice brings an almost moving plaintive quality to the character which sees the entire film through. Alan Arkin also scores as the bumbling magician, as do Christopher Lee as the evil king and, in a show-stopping turn, Paul Frees as a peglegged, eye-patched cat.

. . . .

■ LAST VALLEY, THE

1971, 125 MINS, UK/US ◇ ⊛
Dir James Clavell   *Prod* James Clavell   *Scr* James Clavell   *Ph* John Wilcox   *Ed* John Bloom   *Mus* John Barry   *Art Dir* Peter Mullins
● Michael Caine, Omar Sharif, Florinda Bolkan, Nigel Davenport, Per Oscarsson, Arthur O'Connell (ABC/ Season)

The Last Valley is a disappointing 17th-century period melodrama about the fluid and violent loyalties attendant on major civil upheaval. Shot handsomely abroad for about $6 million and top-featuring Michael Caine and Omar Sharif in strong performances, James Clavell's film emerges as heavy cinematic grand opera in tab version format, too literal in historical detail to suggest artfully the allegories intended and, paradoxically, too allegorical to make clear the actual reality of the Thirty Years War.

Clavell adapted a J.B. Pick novel in which Sharif, neither peasant nor nobleman, is fleeing the ravages of war and finds a valley still spared from cross-devastation. Caine, hardbitten leader of mercenaries, also discovers the locale. At Sharif's urging Caine decides to live in peace for the winter with the residents, headed by Nigel Davenport and an uneasy truce develops.

The fatuous political and religious and social rationalizations of behavior get full exposition. But the whole entity doesn't play well together as Clavell's script often halts for declamations.

. . . .

■ LAST WAGON, THE

1956, 98 MINS, US ◇
Dir Delmer Daves   *Prod* William B. Hawks   *Scr* James Edward Grant, Delmer Daves, Gwen Bagni Gielgud   *Ph* Wilfrid Cline   *Ed* Hugh S. Fowler   *Mus* Lionel Newman
● Richard Widmark, Felicia Farr, Susan Kohner, Tommy Rettig, Stephanie Griffin, George Mathews (20th Century-Fox)

The mounting menace of Indian attack as the survivors of a wagon train massacre make their way through hostile Apache country provides stirring motivation for this excellent production. Its suspenseful plot and rugged characterization by Richard Widmark as a Comanche-reared white man are admirably backdropped by the magnificent Northern Arizona scenery. Under Delmer Daves' shrewd direction, film comes off as an interesting enterprise far off the beaten path of routine westerns.

Widmark is seen in a forceful role, a man who killed to avenge the murder of his Comanche wife and two sons, and has none of the refinements of civilization until he meets Felicia Farr, who is one of the survivors.

Farr leads off the lineup of new talent and makes an engaging impression, as does young Rettig in his hero-worship of Widmark. Susan Kohner scores as the half-breed sister of Stephanie Griffin, an interesting newcomer, and Nick Adams and Ray Stricklyn both show promise.

. . . .

■ LAST WALTZ, THE

1978, 115 MINS, US ◇ ⊛
Dir Martin Scorsese   *Prod* Robbie Robertson   *Ph* Michael Chapman, Laszlo Kovacs, Vilmos Zsigmond, David Myers, Bobby Byrne, Michael Watkins, Hiro Narita   *Ed* Yeu-Bun Lee, Jan Roblee   *Art Dir* Boris Leven
● Bob Dylan, Joni Mitchell, Neil Diamond, Van Morrison, Eric Clapton, The Band (United Artists)

The Last Waltz is an outstanding rock documentary of the last concert by The Band on Thanksgiving 1976 at Winterland in San Francisco.

By itself The Band performs 12 numbers. The group backs up guest artists on another dozen. They include Ronnie Hawkins, Dr. John, Neil Young, the Staples, Neil Diamond, Joni Mitchell, Paul Butterfield, Muddy Waters, Eric Clapton, Emmylou Harris, Van Morrison, Bob Dylan, Ringo Starr and Ron Wood.

Director Martin Scorsese has succeeded on a number of fronts. First, he recognized that this concert deserved cinematic preservation. The Band was an important and intelligent force in rock music on its own and as a backup group for Bob Dylan and Ronnie Hawkins.

This film is a chronicle of one important group very much a part of the music of the late 1960s and 1970s and it's also a commentary on those times. It's 90% concert film and 10% history. Unlike so many of their colleagues, the members of The Band are competent musicians and spokesmen.

. . . .

■ LAST WAVE, THE

1977, 106 MINS, AUSTRALIA ◇ ⊛
Dir Peter Weir   *Scr* Tony Morphett, Petru Popescu, Peter Weir   *Ph* Russell Boyd   *Ed* Max Lemon   *Mus* Charles Wain

L

● Richard Chamberlain, Olivia Hamnett, David Gulpilil, Frederick Parslow, Nandjiwarra Amagula (Ayer/SAFC/AFC)

Australian director Peter Weir's film about the possibility of a coming tidal wave that may destroy the country or the world. Richard Chamberlain is highly effective as a young lawyer caught up in a case of an aborigine murdered by some others in town.

The lawyer has strange dreams that involve one of the accused men trying to give him some sort of sacred stone. He takes their case and tries to insist it was tribal but the man he has dreamed of, who at first tries to help him, begs off when an old patriarch seems to exert power on him.

Film builds, and though it sometimes falters in narrative, picks up again as Chamberlain turns out to be a sort of psychic member of a mysterious people who supposedly came to Australia long ago and disappeared.

■ **LAST WINTER, THE**

1990, 103 MINS, CANADA ◇
Dir Aaron Kim Johnston   *Prod* Jack Clements, Ken Rodeck, Joe MacDonald, Aaron Kim Johnston *Ph* Ian Elkin   *Ed* Lara Mazur   *Mus* Victor Davies *Art Dir* Perri Gorrare
● Gerard Parkes, Joshua Murray, David Ferry, Wanda Cannon (Rode/Aaron)

This vivid, imaginative tale of a Manitoba farmboy's coming of age captures a uniquely Canadian heartland experience. Writer-director Aaron Kim Johnson has crafted a tribute to his childhood in a tale seen through the eyes of a 10-year-old Will (Joshua Murray) as he resists his family's move to the city.

Beset with growing pains and upset by the prospect of being uprooted, Will creates a fantasy shield between himself and reality, hallucinating a white horse named Winter who charges across the farmland bearing some mysterious message. His closest ties are to his Grampa Jack (Gerard Parkes) and his cousin Kate, whom he's in love with.

The overwhelming presence of the land and weather are captured in Ian Elkin's clean, crisp photography, and the winter storms and snowdrifts painstakingly evoked by the art department. Johnston draws lovely performances from the children, especially Murray. Parkes forges a convincing link with the young actor as his elderly confidant.

■ **LATE FOR DINNER**

1991, 92 MINS, US ◇ ⓥ
Dir W.D. Richter   *Prod* Dan Lupovitz, W.D. Richter *Scr* Mark Andrus   *Ph* Peter Sova   *Ed* Richard Chew, Robert Leighton   *Mus* David Mansfield   *Art Dir* Lilly Kilvert
● Brian Wimmer, Peter Berg, Marcia Gay Harden, Colleen Flynn, Kyle Secor, Michael Beach (Castle Rock/Granite)

A tale about time travel and the transcendent power of love, *Late for Dinner* lays on the whimsicality with a trowel. After the initial promise of the early, quirky scenes, pic lapses into tiresome metaphysical vaudeville with a predictable emotional hook.

Offbeat prolog, which features the best timing and compositions in the picture, introduces Willie (Brian Wimmer), a solid, responsible young fellow, and his slow, earnest brother-in-law Frank (Peter Berg). It is 1962, and the two are making their way through the desert from Sante Fe to Southern California after Willie has been shot in a ludicrous altercation stemming from a nasty real estate transaction and an alleged kidnaping.

Seeking treatment in Pomona, the pair instead get a heavy dose of cryonics from some local medics, which puts them in a deep freeze for 29 years. Upon thawing out, the

buddies stumble into the audio blare and visual blight of downtown Los Angeles, 1991. The still-boyish Willie must confront the fact that his wife Joy (Marcia Gay Harden) is now in her 50s, and that their daughter Jessica (Colleen Flynn) has grown into womanhood not knowing him.

With both Wimmer and Berg wearing out their welcome long before fadeout, and offering no star voltage in the bargain, interest falls naturally to the women in the film's final third. Flynn comes off best as the grownup Jessica, the abandoned daughter who learned how to cope.

■ **LATE SHOW, THE**

1977, 94 MINS, US ◇ ⓥ ⊙
Dir Robert Benton   *Prod* Robert Altman   *Scr* Robert Benton   *Ph* Chuck Rosher   *Ed* Lou Lombardo *Mus* Kenn Wannberg   *Art Dir* Bob Gould
● Art Carney, Lily Tomlin, Bill Macy, Eugene Roche, Joanna Cassidy, John Considine (Warner)

Art Carney and Lily Tomlin make an arresting screen duo in *The Late Show*, a modest meller and a tribute to the private eye yarns of the 1940s.

The process has given Carney and Tomlin the freedom to create two extremely sympathetic characters. Both performances are knockout.

Carney plays an aging private detective trying to maintain his dignity while scratching out a living on the sordid underbelly of Los Angeles. When his onetime partner (Howard Duff in an opening cameo) is murdered, Carney, in the best Sam Spade tradition, vows to get the killer.

The trail begins with Tomlin whose stolen cat Duff had been hired to find. Top-heavy plot unwinds with the usual potboiler ingredients – blackmail, murder, philandering wives and double-cross.
☐ 1977: Nomination: Best Original Screenplay

■ **LAUGHTER IN PARADISE**

1951, 94 MINS, UK
Dir Mario Zampi   *Prod* Mario Zampi   *Scr* Michael Pertwee, Jack Davies   *Ph* William McLeod   *Ed* Giulio Zampi   *Mus* Stanley Black   *Art Dir* Ivan King
● Alastair Sim, Fay Compton, Guy Middleton, George Cole, Beatrice Campbell, Audrey Hepburn (Associated British)

Producer-director Mario Zampi very nearly succeeds in bringing off an outstanding comedy with *Laughter in Paradise*. Plot describes what happens after a practical joker leaves $140,000 to each of four relatives provided they fulfill certain stipulated conditions.

His sister (Fay Compton), who has always been tough on housemaids, has to hold a job as a domestic for 28 days. A cousin (Alastair Sim), who secretly writes trashy thrillers, has to get himself sentenced to 28 days in jail. A distant relative (George Cole), a timid bank clerk, has to hold up his bank manager, while another relation (Guy Middleton), who is something of a philanderer, has to marry the first single girl he meets.

The plum comedy part is undoubtedly Sim's, his endeavors to land in jail being loaded with chuckles.

■ **LAUGHTER IN THE DARK**

1969, 101 MINS, UK/FRANCE ◇
Dir Tony Richardson   *Prod* Neil Harley   *Scr* Edward Bond   *Ph* Dick Bush   *Ed* Charles Rees   *Art Dir* Julia Oman
● Nicol Williamson, Anna Karina, Jean-Claude Drouot, Sheila Burrell, Sian Phillips, Kate O'Toole (Gershwin-Kastner/Marceau/Woodfall)

Fascinating attempt to transpose the Nabokov novel to the screen. Director Tony

Richardson is able to capture the novel's profound human insights, and, as in *Lolita*, the compulsions and perversities that for Nabokov are the very stuff of the psyche.

The intricate story centers on a wealthy, titled young art dealer, Edward (Nicol Williamson) who is attracted to usherette Margot (Anna Karina), continues to return to the theatre and finally arranges to meet her.

Richardson's direction ranges from brilliantly evocative to confusing. During some of the most humorous scenes one suspects Richardson is actually serious.

Williamson, who replaced Richard Burton in the lead role, is the perfect physical type and so good as to be almost difficult to watch. Both Karina and Drouot are also excellent.

■ **LAURA**

1944, 88 MINS, US ⓥ ⊙
Dir Otto Preminger   *Prod* Otto Preminger   *Scr* Jay Dratler, Betty Reinhardt, Samuel Hoffenstein   *Ph* Joseph LaShelle   *Ed* Louis Loeffler   *Mus* David Raksin *Art Dir* Lyle R. Wheeler, Leland Fuller
● Gene Tierney, Dana Andrews, Clifton Webb, Vincent Price, Judith Anderson, Dorothy Adams (20th Century-Fox)

The film's deceptively leisurely pace at the start, and its light, careless air, only heighten the suspense without the audience being conscious of the buildup. What they are aware of as they follow the story [from the novel by Vera Caspary] is the skill in the telling. Situations neatly dovetail and are always credible. Developments, surprising as they come, are logical. The dialog is honest, real and adult.

The yarn concerns an attractive femme art executive who has been brutally murdered in her New York apartment, and the attempts of a police lieutenant to solve the case. Beginning by interviewing the girl's intimates, the sleuth's trail leads him from one friend to another, all becoming suspect in the process.

Clifton Webb makes a debonair critic-columnist. Dana Andrews' intelligent, reticent performance as the lieutenant gives the lie to detectives as caricatures. Gene Tierney makes an appealing figure as the art executive and Vincent Price is convincing as a weak-willed ne'er-do-well.
☐ 1944: Best B&W Cinematography.
☐ Nominations: Best Director, Supp. Actor (Clifton Webb), Screenplay, B&W Art Direction

■ **LAVENDER HILL MOB, THE**

1951, 81 MINS, UK ⓥ ⊙
Dir Charles Crichton   *Prod* Michael Balcon, Michael Truman   *Scr* T.E.B. Clarke   *Ph* Douglas Slocombe *Ed* Seth Holt   *Mus* Georges Auric   *Art Dir* William Kellner
● Alec Guinness, Stanley Holloway, Sidney James, Alfie Bass, Marjorie Fielding, Ronald Adam (Ealing)

With *The Lavender Hill Mob*, Ealing clicks with another comedy winner.

Story is notable for allowing Alec Guinness to play another of his w.k. character roles. This time, he is the timid escort of bullion from the refineries to the vaults. For 20 years he has been within sight of a fortune, but smuggling gold bars out of the country is a tough proposition. Eventually, with three accomplices, he plans the perfect crime. Bullion worth over £1 million is made into souvenir models of the Eiffel Tower and shipped to France.

One of the comedy highspots of the film is a scene at a police exhibition where Guinness and his principal accomplice (Stanley Holloway) first become suspect. They break out of the cordon, steal a police car, and then radio phony messages through headquarters.

This sequence and the other action scenes are crisply handled, with a light touch.

Guinness, as usual, shines as the trusted escort, and is at his best as the mastermind plotting the intricate details of the crime. Holloway is an excellent aide, while the two professional crooks in the gang (Sidney James and Alfie Bass) complete the quartet with an abundance of cockney humor.

☐ 1952: Best Story & Screenplay.
☐ Nomination: Best Actor (Alec Guinness)

■ **LAW AND DISORDER**

1958, 76 MINS, UK ⓥ
Dir Charles Crichton   *Prod* Paul Soskin   *Scr* T.E.B. Clarke, Patrick Campbell, Vivienne Knight   *Ph* Ted Scaife   *Ed* Oswald Hafenrichter   *Mus* Humphrey Searle   *Art Dir* Allan Harris
● Michael Redgrave, Robert Morley, Ronald Squire, George Coulouris, Joan Hickson, Lionel Jeffries (Hotspur)

Law and Disorder is a highly amusing off-beat comedy [from the novel *Smugglers' Circuit* by Derek Roberts] which notches guffaws and giggles with disarming ease. It has more than a little of the Ealing stamp. There is also a certain amount of confusion due to over-drastic editing. Running at 76 minutes, it lost 15 minutes in the final version and the hacking has left at least a couple of scenes in mid-air.

Michael Redgrave is a con man who does rather well financially in his racket even though Robert Morley, a strict and pompous judge, is constantly sending him to the cooler. His only problem is to keep his profession away from his young son, who grows up in the belief that his dad is a missionary away for long stretches in far-off lands. All's well until the boy becomes a barrister and, worse still, marshal to Morley. So Redgrave retires to a quiet seacoast village. But old habits die hard and he becomes involved with the villagers in an ingenious brandy-smuggling racket.

■ **LAWLESS, THE**
(UK: The Dividing Line)

1950, 81 MINS, US
Dir Joseph Losey   *Prod* William H. Pine, William C. Thomas   *Scr* Geoffrey Homes   *Ph* Roy Hunt   *Ed* Howard Smith   *Mus* Mahlon Merrick
● Macdonald Carey, Gail Russell, Lalo Rios, Martha Hyer, Tab Hunter (Paramount)

Racial tolerance gets a working over in *The Lawless*, but the producers don't soapbox the message, using it, instead, as a peg on which to produce a hard-hitting drama, equipped with action and fast pace.

Joseph Losey has a compact story to tell and he does it in a swift 81 minutes. Performances all stack up as topnotch, with several being standout. Plot concerns itself with so-called 'fruit tramps' who make a skimpy living harvesting California's various crops. They are scorned by the whites and subjected to physical abuse by bullies.

Macdonald Carey strides easily through his assignment as the editor who takes up the cudgels for justice after first trying to steer a middle course. Gail Russell does a fine piece of work. Lalo Rios wallops home his role as the fruit worker.

■ **LAWLESS BREED, THE**

1952, 83 MINS, US ◇
Dir Raoul Walsh   *Prod* William Alland   *Scr* Bernard Gordon   *Ph* Irving Glassberg   *Ed* Frank Gross   *Art Dir* Bernard Herzbrun, Richard H. Riedel
● Rock Hudson, Julie Adams, Mary Castle, John McIntire, Hugh O'Brian, Dennis Weaver (Universal)

Early-west gunman, John Wesley Hardin, has his life put on film in *The Lawless Breed*. Presumably based on Hardin's actual story of his career, published when he was released from a Texas prison after serving 16 years for killing a law man, the production has plenty of robust action stirred up by Raoul Walsh's direction.

The plot unfolds episodically and swiftly, telling how Hardin earned his reputation as a killer after getting his first victim in self defense, goes on the lam from the law and vengeance-seeking kinfolks, is forced into more killings, loses his sweetheart (Mary Castle) to a posse's bullets and acquires a new one in Julie Adams, the girl who later becomes his wife.

Rock Hudson does a very good job of the main character, and Adams makes much of her femme lead. John McIntire scores in dual roles, one as Hardin's overly-righteous, preacher father, and the other as the gunman's uncle.

■ **LAWMAN**

1971, 98 MINS, UK ◇
Dir Michael Winner   *Prod* Michael Winner   *Scr* Gerald Wilson   *Ph* Bob Paynter   *Ed* Freddie Wilson   *Mus* Jerry Fielding   *Art Dir* Stan Jolley
● Burt Lancaster, Robert Ryan, Lee J. Cobb, Sheree North, Joseph Wiseman, Robert Duvall (Scimitar)

Michael Winner, an exuberant British director, led with his chin in deciding to go to the States (Mexico) to make a western – his first.

Burt Lancaster, with cold eyes, strong chin, stiff behavior, minimal talk and a swift line on the draw, plays a marshall so dedicated to being a lawman that he is inflexible and even arrogant in his intepretation of it. He rides into a nearby town to pick up a bunch of locals who, on a drunken spree, were responsible for the death of an old man. He finds that they all work for the local bossman, played by Lee J. Cobb. Cobb's a guy who enjoys local power but hates violence. Robert Ryan is the town's weak marshal, who in the end is swayed to action with Lancaster.

Point of the story is just how far a man can compromise with his conscience and whether the end justifies the means.

Lancaster, as usual, is a highly convincing marshal, tough and taciturn. Ryan is also excellent as the faded, weak marshal with only memories. But it's Cobb who quietly steals the film as the local boss who, however, unlike in many such films, is no ruthless villain.

■ **LAWNMOWER MAN, THE**

1992, 105 MINS, US ◇ ⓥ ⊙
Dir Brett Leonard   *Prod* Gimel Everett   *Scr* Brett Leonard, Gimel Everett   *Ph* Russell Carpenter   *Ed* Alan Baumgarten   *Mus* Dan Wyman   *Art Dir* Alex McDowell
● Jeff Fahey, Pierce Brosnan, Jenny Wright, Mark Bringleson, Geoffrey Lewis, Jeremy Slate (Allied Vision/Lane Pringle)

Dazzling computer animation and special effects overcome *The Lawnmower Man*'s mundane story.

Loosely adapted from Stephen King, story has a mentally retarded gardener's assistant (Jeff Fahey) becoming the guinea pig for a scientist (Pierce Brosnan) experimenting with 'virtual reality.' The concept involves creating a computer simulation that seems real to nearly all the senses and in all directions. As Fahey's intelligence improves, he begins to rebel against those who have been abusing him, and eventually against the relatively benign Brosnan as well.

Tale has various literary influences from Daniel Keyes' *Flowers for Algernon* (Charly) to Arthur C. Clarke's *Dial F for Frankenstein*. The melodramatic elements are vintage King, and they are the pic's weakest parts. When Fahey's powers slip over into the extra-sensory, he wreaks revenge on his tormentors, and pic's dangerously close to *Carrie* territory.

The stunning visuals for the 'virtual reality' sequences really put *The Lawnmower Man* over. The computer animation doesn't necessarily break new ground, but it marks the first time it has been so well integrated into a live-action story.

The much ballyhooed animated sex sequence is imaginative and surreal, but all too brief, providing barely enough for a subplot.

■ **LAWRENCE OF ARABIA**

1962, 222 MINS, UK ◇ ⓥ ⊙
Dir David Lean   *Prod* Sam Spiegel   *Scr* Robert Bolt, [Michael Wilson]   *Ph* Freddie Young   *Ed* Anne V. Coates   *Mus* Maurice Jarre   *Art Dir* John Box
● Peter O'Toole, Alec Guinness, Anthony Quinn, Jack Hawkins, Omar Sharif, Anthony Quayle (Horizon)

Some $15 million, around three years in time, much hardship, and incredible logistics have been poured into this kingsize adventure yarn. Made in Technicolor and Super Panavision 70 it is a sweepingly produced, directed and lensed job. Authentic desert locations, a stellar cast and an intriguing subject combine to put this into the blockbuster league.

It had best be regarded as an adventure story rather than a biopic, because Robert Bolt's well written screenplay does not tell the audience anything much new about Lawrence of Arabia, nor does it offer any opinion or theory about the character of this man or the motivation for his actions. So he remains a legendary figure and a shadowy one. Another cavil is that clearly so much footage has had to be tossed away that certain scenes are not developed as well as they might have been, particularly the ending. Storyline concerns Lawrence as a young intelligence officer in Cairo in 1916. British Intelligence is watching the Arab revolt against the Turks with interest as a possible buffer between Turkey and her German allies. Lawrence (Peter O'Toole) is grudgingly seconded to observe the revolt at the request of the civilian head of the Arab bureau. Lawrence sets out to find Prince Feisal, top man of the revolt. From then on his incredible adventures begin.

He persuades Feisal to let him lead his troops as guerrilla warriors. He tackles intertribal warfare but still they arduously take the Turkish port of Aqaba. Lawrence is given the task of helping the Arabs to achieve independence and he becomes a kind of desert Scarlet Pimpernel. He reaches Deraa before the British Army is in Jerusalem, he is captured by the Turks, tortured and emerges a shaken, broken and disillusioned man. Yet still he takes on the job of leading a force to Damascus.

Lean and cameraman F.A. Young have brought out the loneliness and pitiless torment of the desert with an artistic use of color and with almost every frame superbly mounted. Maurice Jarre's musical score is always contributory to the mood of the film.

Peter O'Toole, after three or four smallish, but effective, appearances in films, makes a striking job of the complicated and heavy role of Lawrence. His veiled insolence and contempt of high authority, his keen intelligence and insight, his gradual simpatico with the Arabs and their way of life, his independence, courage, flashy vanity, withdrawn moments, pain, loneliness, fanaticism, idealism and occasional foolishness.

Jack Hawkins plays General Allenby with confidence and understanding and Arthur Kennedy provides a sharp portrayal of a cynical, tough American newspaperman. The two top support performances come from Alec Guinness as Prince Feisal and Anthony Quayle as a stereotyped, honest, bewildered staff officer. Only Anthony Quinn, as a larger-than-life, proud, intolerant Arab chief seems to obtrude overmuch and tends to turn

L

the performance into something out of the Arabian Nights.
□ 1962: Best Picture, Director, Color Cinematography, Color Art Direction, Sound, Original Music Score, Editing.
□ Nominations: Best Actor (Peter O'Toole), Supp. Actor (Omar Sharif), Adapted Screenplay

....

■ **LEAGUE OF GENTLEMEN, THE**

1960, 116 MINS, UK ⚄
Dir Basil Dearden *Prod* Michael Relph, Basil Dearden *Scr* Bryan Forbes *Ph* Arthur Ibbetson *Ed* John Guthridge *Mus* Philip Green
● Jack Hawkins, Nigel Patrick, Roger Livesey, Richard Attenborough, Bryan Forbes, Kieron Moore (Allied Film Makers)

The first entry from Allied Film Makers – consisting of actors Jack Hawkins, Richard Attenborough and Bryan Forbes, producer Michael Relph and director Basil Dearden – is a smooth piece of teamwork.

Hawkins, disgruntled at being axed from the army which he has faithfully served for many years, decides to have a go at a bank robbery. He picks up the idea from an American thriller and recruits seven broke and shady ex-officers, all experts in their own line in the army. The gang goes into hiding while every phase of the operation is planned down to the last detail. As a military exploit, the entire gang would have earned medals. As it is pulled off they are eventually tripped up by a slight, unforeseen happening.

Forbes has written a strong, witty screenplay from John Boland's novel. It takes time to get under way, but once the gang is formed, the situations pile up to an exciting and funny finale. Dearden's direction is sure and Arthur Ibbetson has turned in some excellent camerawork. The eight members of the gang all give smooth, plausible performances, with Hawkins and Patrick, as his second-in-command, having the meatiest roles.

....

■ **LEAGUE OF THEIR OWN, A**

1992, 128 MINS, US ◇ ⚄ ⊙
Dir Penny Marshall *Prod* Robert Greenhut, Elliot Abbott *Scr* Lowell Ganz, Babaloo Mandel *Ph* Miroslav Ondricek *Ed* George Bowers, Adam Bernardi *Mus* Hans Zimmer *Art Dir* Bill Groom
● Tom Hanks, Geena Davis, Madonna, Lori Petty, Jon Lovitz, Garry Marshall (Parkway/Columbia)

Awash in sentimentality and manic energy but only occasionally bubbling over with high humor, *A League of Their Own* hits about .250 with a few RBI but more than its share of strikeouts.

A comic look at the first season of the women's baseball league in 1943 [based on a story by Kim Wilson and Kelly Candaele], Penny Marshall's gangly third film benefits from a fresh, unusual subject, the joy of baseball being played by women having the time of their lives and a wonderful central performance by Geena Davis. Downside includes contrived plotting, obvious comedy and heart-tugging, some hammy thesping and a general hokiness.

Once the teams are picked, most of the obvious plotting possiblities pop up: the attempts of the women to skirt the strict behavior code, the marriage and departure of one of them, the death of another's husband at war, the gradual improvement of their play and resulting growth of popularity and respect, and the inevitable, cornball showdown between rival sisters.

Adding a little testosterone to the recipe is Tom Hanks, a former big-league star who sees life from so deep in the bottle that he virtually sleeps through practice and the initial games.

Of the large cast, Rosie O'Donnell stand out as the brash, smooth-fielding third base-woman, and Megan Cavanagh makes an impression as the dumpy slugger who finds unexpected romance on the road. A brunette Madonna plays a predictably sassy and irreverent type who shows her underwear whenever she can, and Lori Petty is irritatingly petulant as Davis' cry-baby little sister.

Despite the lavish budget, period feel isn't fully realized, as locations are pretty much restricted to ballparks and boardinghouses. An extraordinary effect is created by the appearance of Davis' character as an older woman at the beginning and end. Davis reportedly dubbed the line readings.

....

■ **LEAP OF FAITH**

1992, 108 MINS, US ◇ ⚄ ⊙
Dir Richard Pearce *Prod* Michael Manheim, David V. Picker *Scr* Janus Cercone *Ph* Matthew F. Leonetti *Ed* Don Zimmerman, Mark Warner, John F. Burnett *Mus* Cliff Eidelman *Art Dir* Patrizia Von Brandenstein
● Steve Martin, Debra Winger, Lolita Davidovich, Liam Neeson, Lukas Haas, Meat Loaf (Paramount)

Steve Martin gives a showy but sober performance as a phony faith healer in *Leap of Faith*, well-made but muddled in its aims.

The foremost problem is that the film waffles as to what it's about, never embarking on a full-scale indictment of charlatans and TV ministries and never unabashedly embracing any higher power, despite its cryptic ending.

The story begins when minister Jonas Nightengale's (Martin) traveling motorcade is forced to make an unscheduled stop-over in a small, depressed Kansas town. The entourage includes Martin's assistant (Debra Winger).

The act starts to unravel, however, as Winger becomes enamored with the local sheriff (Liam Neeson), who isn't fooled by Martin's act, while the ersatz preacher gets entangled with a pretty waitress (Lolita Davidovich) and her crippled brother (Lukas Haas), who were previously victimized by one of his brethren.

First-time writer Janus Cercone's script proves intriguing at first as it goes about debunking the faith-healing mystique. But there's also little insight into Martin and Winger's relationship.

Most other roles are equally under-developed, and the budding romance between Winger and Neeson is reduced to scenes that rely more on schmaltzy settings than character.

....

■ **LEARNING TREE, THE**

1969, 106 MINS, US ◇ ⚄
Dir Gordon Parks *Prod* Gordon Parks *Scr* Gordon Parks *Ph* Burnett Guffey *Ed* George R. Rohrs *Mus* Gordon Parks *Art Dir* Ed Engoron
● Kyle Johnson, Alex Clarke, Estelle Evans, Dana Elcar, Mira Waters (Warner/Seven Arts)

The Learning Tree is a sentimental, sometimes awkward, but ultimately moving film about the growing-up of a black teenager in rural Kansas during the 1920s. It is, apparently, the first film financed by a major company to be directed by a Negro.

Film recounts, in short, episodic passages, how a talented and perceptive 15-year-old boy learns about life from a variety of characters, situations and personal encounters.

The worst moments occur when director Gordon Parks interpolates small sermonettes. Also, the film cannot quite carry the large helping of melodrama which occurs near the end. But on the whole this is an impressive, strong film. The 1963 novel of his on which it is based is purportedly semi-autobiographical.

....

■ **LEATHER BOYS, THE**

1964, 108 MINS, UK ⚄
Dir Sidney J. Furie *Prod* Raymond Stross *Scr* Gillian Freeman *Ph* Gerry Gibbs *Ed* Reginald Beck *Mus* Bill McGuffie *Art Dir* Arthur Lawson
● Rita Tushingham, Colin Campbell, Dudley Sutton, Gladys Henson, Avice Landon, Betty Marsden (British Lion/Garrick)

Main theme is the doomed marriage of a couple of immature kids. Reggie (Colin Campbell), who spends a riotous leisure as a motorcyclist, hitches up with Dot (Rita Tushingham), who sees the union as a release from parental control.

The crackup comes when Dot turns out an incompetent wife, chary of making beds and relying on a daily diet of canned beans. This dampens Reggie's sex urge and he departs to live with grandma and takes up with a 'buddy' called Peter (Dudley Sutton).

Despite Pete's insistent affection, his reluctance to associate with girls, and his housekeeping ability, Reggie does not wise up to the fact that he's a homosexual. As the audience gets the drift early, this somewhat punctures the plot.

Virtues of the pic lie in Sidney Furie's direction and in the two male performances. Furie has a sharp eye for sleazy detail, and he uses the underprivileged backgrounds to telling visual effect. Gillian Freeman's screenplay, culled from a novel by Eliot George, is also capable in its ear for verbal mannerisms, but it doesn't give coherence to the characters. Little sympathy can be stirred up for any of them.

Dudley Sutton, however, registers strongly as the spry, loyal Pete.

....

■ **LEAVE ALL FAIR**

1985, 88 MINS, NEW ZEALAND ◇
Dir John Reid *Prod* John O'Shea *Scr* Stanley Harper, Maurice Pons, Jean Betts, John Reid *Ph* Bernard Lutic *Ed* Ian John *Mus* Stephen McCurdy *Art Dir* Joe Bleakley
● John Gielgud, Jane Birkin, Feodor Atkine, Simon Ward (Pacific/Goldeneye/Challenge)

Lensed entirely in France, this elegiac story about the husband of New Zealand writer Katherine Mansfield, who died in 1922 while returning to places where they'd lived together to oversee the publishing of a book based on her letters to him, is a sober, affecting experience.

John Gielgud, playing another elderly man of letters, returns to France to meet his publisher (Feodor Atkine). The trip brings back memories of his life with Mansfield (Jane Birkin), memories made more painful when he meets Atkine's mistress, Marie (also played by Birkin), who not only resembles his long-dead wife, but is also a New Zealander.

Lushly photographed pic is as gentle and nuanced as Mansfield's own writings, and the scenes between Gielgud and Birkin play with subtlety and insight.

....

■ **LEAVING NORMAL**

1992, 110 MINS, US ◇ ⚄ ⊙
Dir Edward Zwick *Prod* Lindsay Doran *Scr* Edward Solomon *Ph* Ralf D. Bode *Ed* Victor Du Bois *Mus* W.G. Snuffy Walden *Art Dir* Patricia Norris
● Christine Lahti, Meg Tilly, Patrika Darbo, Lenny Von Dohlen, Maury Chaykin, Eve Gordon (Universal/Mirage)

Cocktail waitress Christine Lahti and battered housewife Meg Tilly meet in a parking lot, immediately bond and are soon headed from the small western town of Normal to Alaska where Lahti will claim her inherited home and land. First they stop off to visit Tilly's relatives in Portland and get an eyeful of the dreaded 'perfect homemaker' existence (nicely caricatured by Eve Gordon as a sister).

After Lahti's GTO breaks down and is ransacked, they get a ride from friendly truckers Maury Chaykin and Lenny Von Dohlen. Lahti's distrust of all men after having been burned too often nips this relationship in the bud, but Tilly is determined to pursue Von Dohlen some day.

Edward Solomon's episodic screenplay has the duo's route and key decisions left to chance. Director Edward Zwick, who previously piloted the quite dissimilar, nearly all-male war pic *Glory*, uses optical effects, matte shots and other fantasy touches from the outset to avoid realism in depicting the women's fanciful saga.

Though Lahti dominates much of the film as a brassy, tough-as-nails character, the waif-like Tilly gets to blossom in the final reel when she finally finds a home in Alaska and becomes the small town's cheerful mascot.

● ●

■ **LEFT-HANDED GUN, THE**

1958, 105 MINS, US ⓥ
Dir Arthur Penn *Prod* Fred Coe *Scr* Leslie Stevens
Ph Peverell Marley *Ed* Folmar Blangsted
Mus Alexander Courage *Art Dir* Art Loel
● Paul Newman, Lita Milan, Hurd Hatfield, James Congdon, James Best, John Dehner (Warner)

The Left-Handed Gun is another look at Billy the Kid, probably America's most constantly celebrated juvenile delinquent. In this version he's Billy, the crazy, mixed-up Kid. The picture is a smart and exciting western paced by Paul Newman's intense portrayal.

The screenplay is based on a [1955] teleplay by Gore Vidal called *The Death of Billy the Kid*. The action is concerned with the few events that led up to the slaying of the Brooklyn boy by lawman Pat Garrett. Stevens emphasizes the youthful nature of the desperado by giving him two equally young companions, James Best and James Congdon. The three team after Newman's mentor, cattleman Colin Keith-Johnston, is shot by a crooked officer of the law. Newman is determined to avenge the cattleman's death, and the plot becomes a crusade in which Newman, Best and Congdon are all killed, the death of a badman and the birth of a legend.

The best parts of the film are the moments of hysterical excitement as the three young desperados rough-house with each other as feckless as any innocent boys and in the next instant turn to deadly killing without flicking a curly eyelash.

In his first picture, director Arthur Penn shows himself in command of the medium. Newman dominates but there are excellent performances from others, including Lita Milan in a dimly-seen role as his Mexican girl friend, John Dehner as the remorseless Pat Garrett, and Hurd Hatfield, a mysterious commentator on events.

● ●

■ **LEFT HAND OF GOD, THE**

1955, 87 MINS, US ◇ ⓥ
Dir Edward Dmytryk *Prod* Buddy Adler *Scr* Alfred Hayes *Ph* Franz Planer *Ed* Dorothy Spencer
Mus Victor Young *Art Dir* Lyle Wheeler, Maurice Ransford
● Humphrey Bogart, Gene Tierney, Lee J. Cobb, Agnes Moorehead, E.G. Marshall, Carl Benton Reid (20th Century-Fox)

Based on the novel by William E. Barrett, the film is somewhat provocative, in that its central character is a man who masquerades as a priest. Carrying on this deception is Yank flier Humphrey Bogart, who believes it to be the sole way he can escape as prisoner of Chinese warlord Lee J. Cobb.

What transpires in a remote Chinese province after Bogart dons the ecclesiastical robes in 1947 largely adds up to character studies of the fake priest and his immediate

colleagues at a Catholic mission, where all are stationed. For the drama and suspense aren't to be found in whether the flier escapes from China but in the soul-searching he subjects himself in continuing the masquerade.

Besides Bogart, others who have their own mental conflicts are Gene Tierney, E.G. Marshall, and Agnes Moorehead.

● ●

■ **LEGACY, THE**

1979, 100 MINS, US ◇ ⓥ
Dir Richard Marquand *Prod* David Foster *Scr* Jimmy Sangster, Patric Tilley, Paul Wheeler *Ph* Dick Bush, Alan Hume *Ed* Anne V. Coates *Mus* Michael J. Lewis
Art Dir Disley Jones
● Katharine Ross, Sam Elliott, Hildegard Neil, Roger Daltrey, John Standing, Charles Gray (Universal/Turman-Foster)

Using the hoary convention of stranding a young couple in the mansion of a reclusive millionaire whose guests are progressively bumped off in an assortment of gruesome ways, *The Legacy* tries for an added dimension of satanic possession, but winds up a tame, suspenseless victim of its own lack of imagination.

Katharine Ross and Sam Elliott play the Yank couple, a pair of architects mysteriously summoned for an assignment in England. When they're accidentally forced off a country road by a chauffeured Rolls, owner John Standing invites them back for 'tea'. They find themselves trapped in the house for the weekend.

The film, directed with no tension or suspenseful pacing by former TV director Richard Marquand, takes an eternity to get down to business.

● ●

■ **LEGAL EAGLES**

1986, 114 MINS, US ◇ ⓥ ⊙
Dir Ivan Reitman *Prod* Ivan Reitman *Scr* Jim Cash, Jack Epps Jr. *Ph* Laszlo Kovacs *Ed* Sheldon Kahn, Pem Herring, William Gordean *Mus* Elmer Bernstein
Art Dir John DeCuir
● Robert Redford, Debra Winger, Daryl Hannah, Brian Dennehy, Terence Stamp, Steven Hill (Northern Lights)

Loss of intrigue with a scattered plot involving art fraud and murder is made up for by an often witty, albeit lightweight dialog led by the ever-boyish star Robert Redford.

Lavish production opens with charmer Redford as one of the d.a.'s office's winningest attorneys, Tom Logan, assigned to prosecute the daughter of a famous artist for trying to steal one of her dead father's paintings.

He faces the opposing counsel of Laura Kelly (Debra Winger), a court-appointed defense attorney known for daffy courtroom antics to get her clients off.

It's when the burglary charges are suddenly dropped against the unbalanced defendant Chelsea Deardon (Daryl Hannah) that he decides to go over to Winger's side to discover why.

Winger and Redford work well as an attorney team, but in true yuppie form become more friends attracted by each others' professional acumen than by each other's bodies.

● ●

■ **LEGEND**

1986, 94 MINS, US ◇ ⓥ ⊙
Dir Ridley Scott *Prod* Arnon Milchan *Scr* William Hjortsberg *Ph* Alex Thomson *Ed* Terry Rawlings
Mus Jerry Goldsmith [US version: Tangerine Dream]
Art Dir Assheton Gorton
● Tom Cruise, Mia Sara, Tim Curry, David Bennent, Alice Playten, Billy Barty (Legend/20th Century-Fox)

Legend is a fairytale produced on a grand scale, set in some timeless world and peopled with fairies, elves and goblins, plus a spectac-

ularly satisfying Satan. At the same time, the basic premise is alarmingly thin, a compendium of any number of ancient fairytales.

Plot concerns a heroic young peasant, Jack, who takes his sweetheart, Princess Lili, to see the most powerful creatures on earth, the last surviving unicorns. Unknown to the young Lovers, Darkness (i.e. The Devil) is using the innocence of Lili as a bait to trap and emasculate the unicorns.

Kids of all ages should be entranced by the magnificent make-up effects of Rob Bottin and his crew, from the smallest elves to the giant Darkness. The latter is unquestionably the most impressive depiction of Satan ever brought to the screen. Tim Curry plays him majestically with huge horns, cloved feet, red leathery flesh and yellow eyes, plus a resonantly booming voice.

Also registering strongly is David Bennent as a knowing pixie with large, pointed ears.

Ironically, for a film that celebrates nature, *Legend* was almost entirely lensed on the large Bond set at Pinewood (production was interrupted by a fire which destroyed the set).
□ 1956: Nomination: Best Makeup

● ●

■ **LEGEND OF HELL HOUSE, THE**

1973, 94 MINS, UK ◇ ⓥ ⊙
Dir John Hough *Prod* Albert Fennell, Norman T. Herman *Scr* Richard Matheson *Ph* Alan Hume
Ed Geoffrey Foot *Mus* Brian Hodgson, Delia Derbyshire
Art Dir Robert Jones
● Pamela Franklin, Roddy McDowall, Clive Revill, Gayle Hunnicutt, Roland Culver, Peter Bowles (Academy)

Richard Matheson's scripting of his novel *Hell House* builds into an exceptionally realistic and suspenseful tale of psychic phenomena. John Hough's direction maintains this spirit as his cast of characters arrive at the deserted Hell House with an assignment from its present tycoon owner to learn the truth about survival after death, a secret he believes the house with its terrifying history may hold.

Sent on the mission are a physicist, a femme mental medium and a physical medium. Latter is the only survivor of a similar investigation 20 years before when eight scientists were either killed or driven to insanity. Wife of the physicist also is a member of the party. Shock value is an important element as audience literally feels the unseen power that exists in the house.

Clive Revill, the physicist, who attempts to clear the house of its evil, Pamela Franklin, the mental medium and Roddy McDowall the survivor of the previous incursion, are all first-rate.

● ●

■ **LEGEND OF LYLAH CLARE, THE**

1968, 127 MINS, US ◇
Dir Robert Aldrich *Prod* Robert Aldrich *Scr* Hugo Butler, Jean Rouverol *Ph* Joseph Biroc *Ed* Michael Luciano *Mus* Frank DeVol *Art Dir* George W. Davis, William Glasgow
● Kim Novak, Peter Finch, Ernest Borgnine, Milton Selzer, Rossella Falk, Gabriele Tinti (M-G-M)

Script spotlights the making of a film about Lylah Clare, a world famous pic star who died some time before under mysterious circumstances.

Her onetime producer-discoverer, who is 'fighting the big C' after a visit to the Mayo clinic, wants as his swan song to revive the Clare legend via a biopic, and succeeds in convincing Lewis Zarkan, the director who made her and was briefly in love with her, to coach look-alike Elsa Brinkman into capturing the departed star's mannerisms.

Pic is at its best when it spotlights the dilemma of the girl reincarnating the defunct star, especially when Elsa grotesquely switches to Lylah's vulgar German accented tones and phrases or when she imagines the scenes of her predecessor's violent death.

Though only intermittently given a challenging scene or two, Kim Novak brings off her dual role as Elsa-Lylah well. Peter Finch is very good as the director who's her doing and undoing, and there's a very amusing and talented performance by Ernest Borgnine as a studio boss.

● ●

■ LE MANS

1971, 108 MINS, US ◊ ⊛

Dir Lee H. Katzin, [John Sturges] *Prod* Jack N. Reddish
Scr Harry Kleiner *Ph* Robert B. Hauser, Rene Guissart Jr
Ed Donald W. Ernst *Mus* Michel Legrand
● Steve McQueen, Siegfried Rauch, Elga Andersen, Ronald Leigh-Hunt (Solar/Cinema Center)

Marked by some spectacular car-racing footage, *Le Mans* is a successful attempt to escape the pot-boiler of prior films on same subject. The solution was to establish a documentary mood. Steve McQueen stars (and races).

Filmed abroad on actual French locales, the project began under director John Sturges. Creative incompatibilities brought McQueen, his Solar Prods indie, and Cinema Center Films to the mat, and as the dust settled Sturges was out and Lee H. Katzin finished the film and gets solo screen credit.

The spare script finds McQueen returning to compete in the famed car race a year after he has been injured. Elga Andersen, wife of a driver killed in the same accident, also returns, somewhat the worse for emotional wear. Siegfried Rauch is McQueen's continuing rival in racing competition.

The film establishes its mood through some outstanding use of slow motion, multiple-frame printing, freezes, and a most artistic use of sound – including at times no sound. The outstanding racing footage not only enhances the effects, but stands proudly on its own feet in straight continuity.

● ●

■ LEMON DROP KID, THE

1951, 91 MINS, US ⊛ ⊙

Dir Sidney Lanfield *Prod* Robert L. Welch *Scr* Edmund Hartmann, Robert O'Brien, Frank Tashlin, Irving Elinson
Ph Daniel L. Fapp *Ed* Archie Marshek *Mus* Victor Young *Art Dir* Hal Pereira, Franz Bachelin
● Bob Hope, Marilyn Maxwell, Lloyd Nolan, Jane Darwell, Andrea King, Fred Clark (Paramount)

The Lemon Drop Kid is neither true Damon Runyon, from whose short story of the same title it was adapted [story by Edmund Beloin], nor is it very funny Bob Hope.

Although Hope is the principal interest and gets most of the laughs, his comedy style, and particularly his wise-cracking lines, are at the root of the picture's failure. It not only destroys the Runyonesque sentimental flavor but actually pulls the props from under the inherent humor of the story.

Marilyn Maxwell is decorative as the sophisticated and therefore un-Runyon love interest, and she teams neatly with the star in the catchy incidental songs [by Jay Livingston and Ray Evans]. Other members of the cast are generally excellent, primarily because they conform to the Runyon requirements. Thus, Lloyd Nolan is passable though a trifle over-suave as a racketeer, while Jane Darwell, Fred Clark, Jay C. Flippen, William Frawley, Harry Bellaver, Sid Melton and various others are properly intense and therefore genuinely comic as assorted minor hoodlums.

● ●

■ LEMON POPSICLE

1978, 100 MINS, ISRAEL ◊ ⊛

Dir Boaz Davidson *Prod* Menahem Golan, Yoram Globus *Scr* Boaz Davidson, Eli Tabor *Ph* Adam Greenberg *Ed* Alain Jakubowicz
● Yiftach Katzur, Anat Atzmon, Jonathan Segal, Zachi Noy (Noah)

Lemon Popsicle takes place in Tel Aviv in the late 1950s. Three youths – Benz, Momo, and Yudaleh – have only girls on their mind, while the hit-parade on the radio (Elvis Presley) reflects their own emotional engagement in the world.

Benz, a shy, sensitive lad, falls in love with Nili, who prefers his best chum, Momo. Momo gets Nili pregnant, then drops her as the summer vacation starts; Benz stays behind to arrange the necessary abortion. He confesses his love and things appear running his way, when the school term starts and Nili is back again in the arms of Momo.

The schoolboy romance also has a funnier side to it. It's in the search for an initial sexual experience – first with a middle-age nympho where Benz delivers ice, then with a prostitute who gives them the crabs – both handled with appropriate gags to put the scenes over.

● ●

■ LENNY

1974, 111 MINS, US ⊛ ⊙

Dir Bob Fosse *Prod* Marvin Worth *Scr* Julian Barry *Ph* Bruce Surtees *Ed* Alan Heim *Mus* Ralph Burns *Art Dir* Joel Schiller
● Dustin Hoffman, Valerie Perrine, Jan Miner, Stanley Beck, Gary Morton, Rashel Novikoff (United Artists)

Lenny Bruce was one of the precursors of social upheaval, and like most pioneers, he got clobbered for his foresight. Bob Fosse's remarkable film version of Julian Barry's legit play, *Lenny*, stars Dustin Hoffman in an outstanding performance.

Production was photographed in black and white, lending not only a slight period influence but also capturing the grit and the sweat, as well as the private and public tortures of its principal character in uncompromising terms.

Barry's excellent script takes the form of flashback, but with some partial flashforward scenes. Three key figures in Bruce's life – wife Valerie Perrine in a sensational performance, hardcharger mother Jan Miner in a beautiful characterization, and Stanley Beck in top form as Bruce's agent – are being tape-interviewed after his death by an unseen party, whose motives are never clear.

□ 1974: Nominations: Best Picture, Director, Actor (Dustin Hoffman), Actress (Valerie Perrine), Adapted Screenplay, Cinematography

● ●

■ LEON THE PIG FARMER

1993, 103 MINS, UK ◊ ⊛ ⊙

Dir Vadim Jean, Gary Sinyor *Prod* Gary Sinyor, Vadim Jean *Scr* Gary Sinyor, Michael Norman *Ph* Gordon Hickie *Ed* Ewa J. Lind *Mus* John Murphy, David Hughes *Art Dir* Simon Hicks
● Mark Frankel, Janet Suzman, Brian Glover, Connie Booth, David de Keyser, Maryam D'Abo (Leon the Pig Farmer)

A London Jewish kid finds his real dad is in the bacon trade in *Leon the Pig Farmer*, a good-humored riff on Jewish-gentile stereotypes.

Billing itself as 'the first Jewish comedy feature film to come out of Britain,' pic is very different in feel to Yank equivalents. Sitcom elements and British scatological humor keep peeking through the comic fabric. Pacing, too, is milder.

Opening has Leon (Mark Frankel) finding he and his brothers are actually the products of artificial insemination, as Dad has a low sperm count. His real father is gentile pig farmer Chadwick (Brian Glover) up north in the wilds of Yorkshire.

Surprised but delighted, Chadwick and his wife (Connie Booth) go 200% Jewish to make Leon feel at home. Twist comes when Leon, helping out on the farm, accidentally injects a pig with sheep's semen, producing the world's first kosher porker.

Playing of the uneven script is broad all round, with Glover dominating all his scenes and well supported by Booth. Maryam D'Abo livens up the London segs as a horny gentile with the hots for Jewish boys. Franklin is okay as the bemused Leon.

● ●

■ LEOPARD MAN, THE

1943, 63 MINS, US ⊛ ⊙

Dir Jacques Tourneur *Prod* Val Lewton *Scr* Ardel Wray *Ph* Robert de Grasse *Ed* Mark Robson *Mus* Roy Webb
● Dennis O'Keefe, Margo, Jean Brooks, Isabel Jewell (RKO)

Both script [from the novel *Black Alibi* by Cornell Woolrich] and direction noticeably strain to achieve effects of *Cat People* but fall far short of latter standard and follow too many confusing paths. After brief introduction, it's a series of chases and murders, with a tame leopard blamed for the latter until strange happenings are pinned on one of the players. It's all confusion, in fact too much for an audience to follow.

Dennis O'Keefe is press agent for a New Mexican nitery and rents a tame black leopard for a publicity stunt which backfires when the cat escapes and a girl is presumably killed by the fugitive. Yarn then spins through regulation eerie channels with two other strange murders enacted – one being in the timeworn setting of a cemetery and windstorm combined. O'Keefe and Margo stick around long enough to trip the real culprit by time for the fadeout to come along.

● ●

■ LEO THE LAST

1970, 103 MINS, UK ◊

Dir John Boorman *Prod* Robert Chartoff, Irwin Winkler *Scr* William Stair, John Boorman *Ph* Peter Suschitzky *Ed* Tom Priestley *Mus* Fred Myrow *Art Dir* Tony Wollard
● Marcello Mastroianni, Billie Whitelaw, Calvin Lockhart, Glenna Forster-Jones, Vladek Sheybal, Gwen Ffrangcon-Davis (United Artists)

An absurd satire on dethroned European royalty with a neo-realistic view of the London ghetto.

Marcello Mastroianni, the last of his line, lives in exile in a magnificent London townhouse at the end of a cul-de-sac in a black ghetto area. He is a totally ineffectual, sheltered sickly man, whose only human contacts are a flock of parasitic social magpies.

Footage on the ghetto comings and goings, as orchestrated by director John Boorman, has a gritty documentary feel.

There is a grotesquely hilarious scene of a mass nude water therapy of Mastroianni's entourage led by society doctor David de Keyser.

But the two sequences are all that work in *Leo*. The rest is at best silly, at worst pretentious allegory and unsuccessful social comment.

● ●

■ LES GIRLS

1957, 114 MINS, US ◊ ⊛ ⊙

Dir George Cukor *Prod* Sol C. Siegel *Scr* John Patrick *Ph* Robert Surtees *Ed* Ferris Webster *Mus* Cole Porter *Art Dir* William A. Horning, Gene Allen
● Gene Kelly, Mitzi Gaynor, Kay Kendall, Taina Elg, Jacques Bergerac, Leslie Phillips (M-G-M)

Les Girls is an exceptionally tasty musical morsel that is in the best tradition of the Metro studio. It's an original and zestful entry that would have been greeted with critical handsprings if it had been originally presented on the Broadway stage.

The musical is set in London, Paris and Granada, Spain. It's the story of a song-and-dance team made up of Gene Kelly and Mitzi Gaynor, Kay Kendall and Taina Elg. Known as 'Barry Nichols and Les Girls', they are a popular Continental act. Many years after the act has broken up, Kendall, now the wife of an English peer, has written a book of reminiscences that lands her in a London court, the defendant in a libel suit brought by Elg, now married to a French industrialist. The court trial provides the setting for a series of flashbacks. Each gives a different version of what happened.

The excursion into the past provides the setting for a number of Cole Porter tunes and dances brightly staged by Jack Cole as 'Les Girls' appear in niteries in France and Spain. Porter created seven new songs for the picture.

Kendall emerges as a delightful comedienne in her first American picture. Elg, a Finnish actress-ballerina who portrays a French girl, has a quality that is exceedingly appealing. Gaynor is the wholesome, uncomplicated member of the troupe.
□ 1957: Best Costume Design.
□ Nominations: Best Art Direction, Sound

■ LES MISERABLES

1935, 109 MINS, US ⓥ ⊙
Dir Richard Boleslawski   *Prod* Darryl F. Zanuck
Scr W.P. Lipscomb   *Ph* Gregg Toland   *Ed* Barbara McLean   *Mus* Alfred Newman (dir.)   *Art Dir* Richard Day
● Fredric March, Charles Laughton, Cedric Hardwicke, Rochelle Hudson, John Beal, Frances Drake (20th Century)

Les Miserables will satisfy the most exacting Victor Hugo followers, and at the same time please those looking only for entertainment, regardless of literary backgrounds. The task of boiling down the lengthy Hugo novel is accomplished by W.P. Lipscomb with no loss of flavor. The essence of the original is faithfully retained.

Fredric March makes the screen Jean Valjean a living version of the panegyrical character. He is the same persecuted, pursued, pitiable, but always admirale man that all readers of the book must visualize. Side by side with March, throughout the picture, is Charles Laughton, as Javert, the cop. His performance is much more on the quiet side, but equally powerful and always believable.

Valjean's service in the galley, to which he is sentenced for stealing a loaf of bread; Javert's pursuit of Valjean and his foster-daughter; the revolt of the French students; the race of Valjean, with the injured Marius on his shoulders, through the stinking sewers of Paris, all breath-taking action passages, are brilliantly managed.
□ 1935: Nominations: Best Picture, Cinematography, Editing, Assistant Director (Eric Stacey)

■ LES MISERABLES

1952, 105 MINS, US
Dir Lewis Milestone   *Prod* Fred Kohlmar   *Scr* Richard Murphy   *Ph* Joseph La Shelle   *Ed* Hugh Fowler
Mus Alex North   *Art Dir* Lyle Wheeler, J. Russell Spencer
● Michael Rennie, Debra Paget, Robert Newton, Edmund Gwenn, Sylvia Sidney, Cameron Mitchell (20th Century-Fox)

Victor Hugo's somber classic was previously lensed by the Fox Film Co in 1919, again by Universal in 1927, United Artists had a release out in 1935 and there was a French production in 1936.

In the first episode, when Valjean is sentenced to 10 years as a galley slave for stealing a loaf of bread, director Lewis Milestone permits the players and scenes to cry out flamboyantly against such injustice and the stark miseries of a prison ship existence.

The film actually gets going when Valjean, released under parole, becomes a successful

pottery owner after getting his first lesson in humanity from a kindly bishop, beautifully played by Edmond Gwenn. It is during this time that he aids Sylvia Sidney, a poor, dying woman, and takes in her daughter (Debra Paget).

Rennie does exceptionally well with his role, particularly after the convict ship episode.

■ LESS THAN ZERO

1987, 98 MINS, US ◇ ⓥ ⊙
Dir Marek Kanievska   *Prod* Jon Avnet, Jordan Kerner
Scr Harley Peyton   *Ph* Edward Lachman   *Ed* Peter E. Berger, Michael Tronick   *Mus* Thomas Newman
Art Dir Barbara Ling
● Andrew McCarthy, Jami Gertz, Robert Downey Jr, James Spader, Michael Bowen, Tony Bill (20th Century-Fox)

If it's possible, *Less Than Zero* is even more specious and shallow than the Bret Easton Ellis book it is based on. There's a story somewhere tracking the dissipated lifestyles of the super-rich, super-hip kids and their LA haunts.

Drugs take over Julian (Robert Downey Jr), Clay (Andrew McCarthy) avoids the scene by attending an eastern college, and his g.f. Blair (Jami Gertz) loses her identity, which was never much to begin with. This is where they are at the beginning of the film – and pretty much where they are at the end.

Perhaps this wasn't the best subject matter for British director Marek Kanievska (*Another Country*) to make his American debut. The feel for this distinctly Southern California story escapes him.

Only Downey elicits the kind of sympathy to distinguish this drama from a photojournalist essay of the kind that might run in *Vanity Fair*. Of the secondary roles, James Spader as Downey's pusher is terrifically smarmy. Unfortunately, this sick relationship doesn't become involving until the last third of the film, when Downey really begins to fall apart and is forced into male whoring to pay his drug debts. Visually the picture is a treat.

■ LETHAL WEAPON

1987, 110 MINS, US ◇ ⓥ ⊙
Dir Richard Donner   *Prod* Richard Donner, Joel Silver
Scr Shane Black   *Ph* Stephen Goldblatt   *Ed* Stuart Baird
Mus Michael Kamen, Eric Clapton   *Art Dir* J. Michael Riva
● Mel Gibson, Danny Glover, Gary Busey, Mitchell Ryan, Tom Atkins, Darlene Love (Warner/Silver)

Lethal Weapon is a film teetering on the brink of absurdity when it gets serious, but thanks to its unrelenting energy and insistent drive, it never quite falls.

Danny Glover is a family-man detective who gets an unwanted partner in the possibly psychotic Mel Gibson. Story is on the back burner as the two men square off against each other, more as adversaries than partners.

Gibson is all live wires and still carries Vietnam with him 20 years after the fact. Though he's 15 years his senior and also a Nam vet, Glover is meant to be a sensitive man of the 1980s. Gibson simmers while Glover worries about his pension.

While the film is trying to establish its emotional underpinnings, a plot slowly unfolds involving a massive drug smuggling operation headed by the lethal Vietnam vet Joshua (Gary Busey).

Ultimately, the common-ground for Glover and Gibson is staying alive as the film attempts to shift its buddy story to the battlefields of LA.

Gibson, in one of his better performances, holds the fascination of someone who may truly be dangerous. Glover, too, is likable and

so is Darlene Love as his wife, but he and Gibson come from two different worlds the film never really reconciles.
□ 1987: Nomination: Best Sound

■ LETHAL WEAPON 2

1989, 113 MINS, US ◇ ⓥ ⊙
Dir Richard Donner   *Prod* Richard Donner, Joel Silver
Scr Jeffrey Boam   *Ph* Stephen Goldblatt   *Ed* Stuart Baird   *Mus* Michael Kamen, Eric Clapton, David Sanborn   *Art Dir* J. Michael Riva
● Mel Gibson, Danny Glover, Joe Pesci, Joss Ackland, Derrick O'Connor, Patsy Kensit (Warner/Silver)

Loaded with the usual elements, *Lethal Weapon 2* benefits from a consistency of tone that was lacking in the first film. This time, screenwriter Jeffrey Boam [working from a story by Shane Black and Warren Murphy] and director Richard Donner have wisely trained their sights on humor and the considerable charm of Mel Gibson and Danny Glover's onscreen rapport.

They've also dreamed up particularly nasty villains and incorporated enough chases and shootouts to hold the attention of a hyperactive nine-year-old.

Plot sets the duo after South African diplomats using their shield of immunity to smuggle drugs. Tagging along for the ride in a hilarious comic turn is Joe Pesci as an unctuous accountant who laundered the baddies' money and now needs witness protection to stay out of the washing machine himself.

There's also a fleeting entanglement between Riggs (Mel Gibson) and the lead villain's secretary (the sparkling Patsy Kensit) that adds some welcome sex appeal.

■ LETHAL WEAPON 3

1992, 118 MINS, US ◇ ⓥ ⊙
Dir Richard Donner   *Prod* Joel Silver, Richard Donner
Scr Jeffrey Boam, Robert Mark Kamen   *Ph* Jan De Bont
Ed Robert Brown, Battle Davis   *Mus* Michael Kamen, Eric Clapton, David Sanborn   *Art Dir* James Spencer
● Mel Gibson, Danny Glover, Joe Pesci, Rene Russo, Stuart Wilson, Steve Kahan (Warner/Silver)

The recipe again works here, producing a pic that's really more about moments – comic or thrilling – than any sort of cohesive whole. The plot [by Jeffrey Boam] hinges on a wispy premise about an ex-cop (Stuart Wilson) providing confiscated guns to gangs.

This time, the emotional focus is on Danny Glover's Roger Murtaugh, who counts down the days to his retirement even as he grapples with whether hanging up his gun will make him an old man. Murtaugh and gonzo partner Martin Riggs (Mel Gibson) stumble onto the gun racket, bringing them into contact with high-kicking investigator Lorna Cole (Rene Russo), a woman who wins Riggs' heart by demonstrating that she can inflict as much damage as he can.

The pic manages to be highly entertaining and sanctions all its violence by making the bad guys so despicable that death seems to be the only solution. The broad scope of the action also brings a requisite make-believe quality to the narrative.

■ LET HIM HAVE IT

1991, 115 MINS, UK ◇ ⓥ ⊙
Dir Peter Medak   *Prod* Luc Roeg, Robert Warr
Scr Neal Purvis, Robert Wade   *Ph* Oliver Stapleton
Ed Ray Lovejoy   *Mus* Michael Kamen   *Art Dir* Michael Pickwood
● Chris Eccleston, Paul Reynolds, Tom Courtenay, Tom Bell, Eileen Atkins, Clare Holman (Vivid)

Let Him Have It takes one of the most controversial murder trials in postwar Brit history and comes up with a powerful mix of social conscience and solid entertainment. Pic reconstructs the events leading to the 1952 rooftop shoot-out in south London between local cops and cocky, gun-crazy Chris Craig. At age 16, Craig was legally too young to be hanged so his 19-year-old partner, Derek Bentley, went to the gallows instead, despite public petitions and last-minute appeals.

Though innocent of any shooting, Bentley was heard to cry 'Let him have it' to the rod-wielding Craig. The defense argued the words meant hand over the gun rather than shoot. Craig, released in 1963 and living a reformed life, played no part in the present production, though the filmmakers tried to contact him.

Pic studiously avoids a docu approach. The dramatic focus begins and ends on a tragic figure of Bentley (Chris Eccleston), an epileptic with the mental age of an 11-year-old and a distant relationship with his working-class father (Tom Courtenay) and reticent mother (Eileen Atkins). After a spell in an approved school, he's coaxed out of his shell by older sister (Clare Holman) and comes under the sway of swaggering Craig (Paul Reynolds) and Craig's crooked brother (Mark McGann).

Script is sometimes overladen with exposition, especially in the family scenes and after-trial seg. But it succinctly captures the feel of suburban postwar Britain, and its younger characters' search for thrills through Hollywood movies, flash cars and pop music. Peter Medak directs fluidly and with an eye for bigscreen values.

LET IT BE

1970, 80 MINS, UK ◇ ⊛
Dir Michael Lindsay-Hogg *Prod* Neil Aspinall *Ph* Tony Richmond, Les Parrott, Paul Bond *Ed* Tony Lenny, Graham Gilding
● Paul McCartney, John Lennon, George Harrison, Ringo Starr, Yoko Ono (Apple)

As a 16mm cinema verite of four rock musicians in a studio jamming a bit, trying to get their music together, clowning and rapping a little, and finally doing a brief concert, *Let It Be* is a relatively innocuous, unimaginative piece of film. But the musicians are the Beatles.

Through the studio session, Lennon's wife Yoko Ono is always present – close at hand, silent, not participating, yet somehow distracting Lennon, splitting his attention. The Beatles' past togetherness, the chummy camaraderie, the quickness to seize on a line and build a series of gags, is no longer there.

After the prolonged musical teasing, the film finally settles into a studio concert with 'Two of Us' and Paul McCartney's 'Let It Be'. Then the concert moves onto a London roof with a half-dozen numbers while cameras cutaway to the gathering traffic jam in the street below.

The outdoor photography, shot with available light under an overcast sky, is muddy, and the long lens close-ups shot from the surrounding roofs, are off-focus.

LET'S DO IT AGAIN

1975, 112 MINS, US ◇ ⊛
Dir Sidney Poitier *Prod* Melville Tucker *Scr* Richard Wesley *Ph* Donald M. Morgan *Ed* Pembroke J. Herring *Mus* Curtis Mayfield *Art Dir* Alfred Sweeney
● Sidney Poitier, Bill Cosby, Calvin Lockhart, John Amos, Jimmie Walker, Ossie Davis (Warner)

A Timothy March story has been scripted into a loosely-strung series of sketches which amiably advance the story. Sidney Poitier, who has a mysterious hex power, and Bill Cosby, whose versatility herein seems as great as that of Peter Sellers, hie to New Orleans to parlay a bankroll into big winnings for their lodge, presided over by a patriarchal Ossie Davis.

With wives Lee Chamberlin and Denise

Nicholas in tow, the pair confound oldtime gangster John Amos and new-wave hood Calvin Lockhart.

The secret weapon Poitier uses is his hypnotic transformation of puny Jimmie Walker from a 'before' gymnasium advertisement into a pugilistic dynamo. The film could have been a nightmare of lethargy, but it's a good mixture of broad comedy.

LET'S GET HARRY

1986, 107 MINS, US ◇ ⊛ ⊙
Dir Alan Smithee [= Stuart Rosenberg] *Prod* Daniel H. Blatt, Robert Singer *Scr* Charles Robert Carner *Ph* James A. Contner *Ed* Ralph E. Winters, Rick R. Sparr *Mus* Brad Fiedel *Art Dir* Mort Rabinowitz, Agustin Ituarte
● Michael Schoeffling, Tom Wilson, Glenn Frey, Gary Busey, Robert Duvall, Ben Johnson (Tri-Star/Delphi IV & V)

Let's Get Harry is a well made but utterly routine action picture, worth catching for two excellent (as usual) support performances by Robert Duvall and Gary Busey. Director Stuart Rosenberg took his name off the credits, reportedly due to a contretemps during post-production (pic was lensed in Mexico and Illinois in 1985).

Project was planned as a film by Samuel Fuller, writing and directing, in 1981; he is credited with co-writing the story [with Mark Feldberg]. It's the trite concept of a group of young guys, led by Michael Shoeffling, deciding to take matters into their own hands to go to Colombia to rescue Schoeffling's brother Harry (Mark Harmon), kidnaped along with the US ambassador (Bruce Gray) by terrorists.

Picture follows rigidly the cliches of this mini-genre, such as the old hand mercenary (Robert Duvall) who takes the youngsters under his wing. There's even a totally illogical female role written in, played by Elpidia Carrillo, who is cast in virtually every south-of-the-border Hollywood opus.

Film is redeemed somewhat by Duvall, as a gung-ho medal-of-honor winner. Busey is also delightful as a smooth-talking car dealer who agrees to bankroll the mission if he can come along for a 'hunting trip.'

LET'S MAKE LOVE

1960, 118 MINS, US ◇ ⊛
Dir George Cukor *Prod* Jerry Wald *Scr* Norman Krasna, Hal Kanter *Ph* Daniel L. Fapp *Ed* David Bretherton *Mus* Lionel Newman (dir.) *Art Dir* Lyle R. Wheeler, Gene Allen
● Marilyn Monroe, Yves Montand, Tony Randall, Frankie Vaughan, Wilfrid Hyde White (20th Century-Fox)

After the film has been underway about 12 minutes, the screen goes suddenly dark (the scene is rehearsal of an off-Broadway show) and a lone spotlight picks up Marilyn Monroe wearing black tights and a sloppy wool sweater. She announces, with appropriate musical orchestration, that her name is Lolita and that she isn't allowed to play (pause) with boys (pause) because her heart belongs to daddy (words and music by Cole Porter).

This not only launches the first of a series of elegantly designed (by Jack Cole) production numbers and marks one of the great star entrances ever made on the screen, but is typical of the entire film – which has taken something not too original (the Cinderella theme) and dressed it up like new.

Monroe, of course, is a sheer delight in the tailor-made role of an off-Broadway actress who wants to better herself intellectually (she is going to night school to study geography), but she also has a uniquely talented co-star in Yves Montand. Latter gives a sock performance, full of both heart and humour, as the richest man in the world who wants to find a

woman who'll love him for himself alone.

Whenever the story threatens to intrude with tedium, there's a knockout Cole Porter musical number.
□ 1960: Nomination: Best Scoring of a Musical Picture

LETTER, THE

1940, 95 MINS, US ⊛ ⊙
Dir William Wyler *Prod* Hal B. Wallis *Scr* Howard Koch *Ph* Tony Gaudio *Ed* George Amy, Warren Low *Mus* Max Steiner *Art Dir* Carl Jules Weyl
● Bette Davis, Herbert Marshall, James Stephenson, Gale Sondergaard, Sen Yung (Warner)

The Letter has a history running back to 1927. Twice before it has been seen in legit and once before (1929) in films, each time with a top femme star in the principal role. Yet never has [the W. Somerset Maugham play] been done with greater production values, a better all-around cast or finer direction. Its defect is its grimness. Director William Wyler, however, sets himself a tempo which is in rhythm with the Malay locale.

Story is essentially a mystery. It opens with Bette Davis shooting a man dead as he runs from her plantation house. The question mark from there to the climax is why? She explains to her planter-husband (Herbert Marshall) and an attorney friend (James Stephenson) that the mudered man, an old family intimate, had made advances to her and in her angry resentment she picked up a revolver. It's evident from the coolness of her recital that she's not telling the truth.

Stephenson's smart native assistant, excellently played by Sen Yung, brings him word of a letter she has written. It was to the man she killed and was in the hands of his wife, a Malay gal (Gale Sondergaard). Through it, it is revealed that for 10 years the murderess has been having an affair with her victim and the fatal triggerwork resulted when she discovered he had thrown her over for the beauteous native.

Davis' frigidity at times seems to go even beyond the characterization. On the other hand, Marshall never falters. Virtually stealing thesp honors in the pic, however, is Stephenson as the attorney, while Sondergaard is the perfect mask-like threat.

Set is of tremendous proportions and the music by Max Steiner is particularly noteworthy in creating and holding a mood, as well as in pointing up the drama.
□ 1940: Nominations: Best Picture, Director, Actress (Bette Davis), Supp. Actor (James Stephenson), B&W Cinematography, Editing, Original Score

LETTER FROM AN UNKNOWN WOMAN

1948, 84 MINS, US ⊛ ⊙
Dir Max Ophuls *Prod* John Houseman *Scr* Howard Koch *Ph* Franz Planer *Ed* Ted J. Kent *Mus* Daniele Amfitheatrof *Art Dir* Alexander Golitzen
● Joan Fontaine, Louis Jourdan, Mady Christians, Marcel Journet, Art Smith, Carol Yorke (Rampart/Universal)

Picture teams Joan Fontaine and Louis Jourdan as co-stars and they prove to be a solid combination. Both turn in splendid performances in difficult parts that could easily have been overplayed.

Story [based on a novel by Stefan Zweig] follows a familiar patttern but the taste with which the film has been put together in all departments under John Houseman's production supervision makes it a valid and interest-holding drama. The mounting has an artistic flavor that captures the atmosphere of early-day Vienna [about 1900] and has been beautifully photographed.

Story unfolds in flashback, a device that makes plot a bit difficult to follow at times, but Max Ophuls' direction holds it together. He doesn't rush his direction, adopting a leisurely pace that permits best use of the story. Film is endowed with little touches that give it warmth and heart while the tragic tale is being unfolded.

It concerns a young girl who falls in love with a neighbor, a concert pianist. Years later she again meets her only love but he fails to remember. Story is told as he reads a letter from the girl, written after the second meeting.

• •

■ LETTER TO BREZHNEV

1985, 95 MINS, UK ◇ ⓥ ⊙
Dir Chris Bernard   *Prod* Janet Goddard   *Scr* Frank Clark   *Ph* Bruce McGowan   *Ed* Lesley Walker   *Mus* Alan Gill   *Art Dir* Lez Brotherston, Nick Englefield, Jonathan Swain
● Alexandra Pigg, Alfred Molina, Peter Firth, Margi Clarke, Tracy Lea, Ted Wood (Yeardream/Film Four/Palace)

This is a farce, penned with wit and acted with appropriate deadpan honesty by all the principals. Picture a Russian ship docking in Liverpool. Two sailors go ashore for a night on the town, both primed with Beatles folklore and one speaking enough English to get them both by with the lasses in a dancehall.

As for the girls, one works in a chicken-factory and does little else than look forward to the weekend conquests. The other is on the dole, but has a romantic view in regard to her bed partners.

Elaine, the Liverpool innocent, meets Peter, the Russian romantic from the Black Sea. They fall in love at first sight.

When they part, the naive Elaine finds it unfair that the world's political stage should prove a hindrance to their ever seeing each other again. So she writes a letter to Brezhnev – and gets an answer. To wit: if you really love your Russian sailor, come to the Soviet Union to marry him and settle down as an adopted citizen.

Alexandra Pigg (Elaine) and Margi Clarke (Teresa) are a tickling pair of working girl types right out of that British tradition going back to 'Free Cinema' days.

• •

■ LETTER TO THREE WIVES, A

1948, 108 MINS, US ⓥ ⊙
Dir Joseph L. Mankiewicz   *Prod* Sol C. Siegel   *Scr* Joseph L. Mankiewicz   *Ph* Arthur Miller   *Ed* J. Watson Webb Jr   *Mus* Alfred Newman   *Art Dir* Lyle R. Wheeler, J. Russell Spencer
● Jeanne Crain, Linda Darnell, Ann Sothern, Kirk Douglas, Paul Douglas, Barbara Lawrence (20th Century-Fox)

While the picture is standout in every aspect, there are two factors mainly responsible for its overall quality. One is the unique story, adapted from a John Klempner novel Vera Caspary and given a nifty screenplay by Joseph L Mankiewicz.

Idea has three young housewives in Westchester, NY (much of the film was shot on location in the east), all jealous of the same she-wolf who grew up with their husbands. The 'other woman' addresses a letter to all three wives explaining that she has run away with one of their spouses but without identifying which one. The audience is then given a chance to figure out which one it is, before a surprise denouement explains all.

Other standout aspect is the fine film debut of legit actor Paul Douglas. His role in *Wives* is that of a big, blustering but slightly dumb tycoon and he really gives it a ride with some neat character shading. He's equally good in the more serious romantic moments with Linda Darnell.

Rest of the cast is equally good. Jeanne Crain, Darnell and Ann Sothern, as the three fraus, each turns in a job as good as anything

they've done. Kirk Douglas, playing Sothern's husband, is fine as the serious-minded literature prof who can't take his wife's soap-opera writing.

Story is bridged by the off-screen voice of the she-wolf, who is built into a character resembling every man's dream gal by the dialog. Mankiewicz, wisely, never shows her.
□ 1949: Best Director, Screenplay.
□ Nomination: Best Picture

• •

■ LEVIATHAN

1989, 98 MINS, US ◇ ⓥ ⊙
Dir George Pan Cosmatos   *Prod* Luigi De Laurentiis, Aurelio De Laurentiis   *Scr* David Peoples, Jeb Stuart   *Ph* Alex Thomson   *Ed* Roberto Silvi, John F. Burnett   *Mus* Jerry Goldsmith   *Art Dir* Ron Cobb
● Peter Weller, Richard Crenna, Amanda Pays, Daniel Stern, Ernie Hudson, Lisa Eilbacher (De Laurentiis/Gordon/M-G-M)

Breed an *Alien* with a *Thing*, marinate in salt water, and you get a *Leviathan*. It's a soggy recycling [story by David Peoples] of gruesome monster attacks unleashed upon a crew of macho men and women confined within a far-flung scientific outpost.

A stock team of six ethnically mixed men and two alluring women is working out of a mining camp 16,000 feet down on the Atlantic floor, and only has a short time to go until heading back to the surface.

In the meantime, one of the crew, the randy Daniel Stern takes ill after investigating the sunken remains of a Russian ship named Leviathan, dies, and begins transforming into a grotesque, eel-like creature.

The same fate awaits Lisa Eilbacher, and medic Richard Crenna quickly deduces that some genetic transferal is going on. Remainder of the action sees crew members doing fierce battle with the ever-growing creature and being horrifically eliminated one by one.

Shot on elaborate sets in Rome, pic boasts impressive production design by Ron Cobb.

• •

■ LIANNA

1983, 110 MINS, US ◇ ⓥ
Dir John Sayles   *Prod* Jeffrey Nelson   *Scr* John Sayles   *Ph* Austin de Besche   *Ed* John Sayles   *Mus* Mason Daring   *Art Dir* Jeanne McDonnell
● Linda Griffiths, Jane Hallaren, Jon DeVries, Jo Henderson, Jesse Solomon, John Sayles (Winwood)

John Sayles again uses a keen intelligence and finely tuned ear to tackle the nature of friendship and loving in *Lianna*.

Story of a 33-year-old woman (Linda Griffiths), saddled with an arrogant and unsupportive professor-husband (John DeVries) who constricts her life until she finds herself falling in love, for the first time, with a woman teacher (Jane Hallaren).

Particularly well-drawn are her husband's doubly-hurt sense of sexual betrayal, the half-formed understandings of her children, who've only just become aware of conventional sexual realities, and the ambivalence of once-close women friends.

Paced by Griffiths' excellent pivotal performance, the film is marked by fine acting overall, particularly Hallaren as the catalytic lover scared off by the intensity of Griffiths' feelings; DeVries as the acerbic, insecure academic mate; Jo Henderson as the retroactively frightened best girlfriend; and Jesse Solomon as the wise-beyond-years pubescent son. Sayles himself appears to good effect as a supportive friend.

• •

■ LIBEL

1959, 100 MINS, UK ◇
Dir Anthony Asquith   *Prod* Anatole de Grunwald   *Scr* Anatole de Grunwald, Karl Tunberg   *Ph* Robert

Krasker   *Ed* Frank Clarke   *Mus* Benjamin Frankel
● Dirk Bogarde, Olivia de Havilland, Paul Massie, Robert Morley, Wilfrid Hyde White, Richard Wattis (M-G-M)

Based on a 25-year-old play by Edward Wooll, Libel has been turned into a stylish and holding film. The idea is simple enough. Is Sir Mark Loddon (Dirk Bogarde), owner of one of the stately homes of England, really Loddon or an unscrupulous imposter, as alleged by a wartime comrade?

The case is sparked off when a young Canadian airman sees a TV program introducing Loddon. He is convinced that he is really Frank Welney, a small part actor. The three were in prison camp together and he is confident that Loddon was killed during a prison break. He exposes the alleged phoney in a newspaper and Loddon is persuaded by his wife to sue.

Bogarde carries much of the onus since he plays both Loddon (during the war and at the time of the trial) and Welney. He does a standout job, suggesting the difference in the two characters remarkably well with the aid of only a slight difference in hair style. Paul Massie gives a likeable, though somewhat even-key, performance as the young man whose suspicions trigger the drama. Olivia de Havilland, as Bogarde's wife, has two or three very good scenes which she handles well.

Because much of the off-court scenes were actually shot at Woburn Abbey, stately home of the Duke of Bedford, the production is given much budget-value.
□ 1959: Nomination: Best Sound

• •

■ LIBELED LADY

1936, 85 MINS, US ⓥ ⊙
Dir Jack Conway   *Prod* Lawrence Weingarten   *Scr* Maurine Watkins, Howard Emmett Rogers, George Oppenheimer   *Ph* Norbert Brodine   *Ed* Frederick Y. Smith   *Mus* William Axt   *Art Dir* Cedric Gibbons, William A. Horning, Edwin B. Willis
● Jean Harlow, William Powell, Myrna Loy, Spencer Tracy, Walter Connolly, Charley Grapewin (M-G-M)

Even though *Libeled Lady* goes overboard on plot and its pace snags badly in several spots, Metro has brought in a sockeroo of a comedy. It's broad farce for the most part, and the threesome consisting of William Powell, Spencer Tracy and Jean Harlow lend themselves perfectly to the task.

Of the starring foursome Myrna Loy's is the only behavior which is kept pretty much on a serious plane. As the much misunderstood poor little rich girl, she projects an effective performance and, with Powell in the later reels, accounts for plenty romantic arias.

Story [by Wallace Sullivan] takes for itself a Park Avenue plus newspaper row theme. Picture seeks to tell of what befalls Powell when, as the trouble-shooter for a newspaper, he undertakes to frame a young millionairess and thereby compel her to drop a $5 million libel suit. The expected occurs; he falls in love with her.

Concerned with Powell in the frame are Tracy, managing editor of the sheet, and the latter's fiancee (Harlow). Latter turns out a corking straight for the sophisticated, suave manner of Powell and she frequently steals the picture when the opportunities for cutting loose fall her way.

Tracy has the least juicy assignment, but the characterization is right up his alley. Walter Connolly registers in crack fashion, as usual, in the part of Loy's father.
□ 1936: Nomination: Best Picture

• •

■ LIBERATION OF L.B. JONES, THE

1970, 102 MINS, US ◇ ⓥ
Dir William Wyler   *Prod* Ronald Lubin   *Scr* Sterling Silliphant, Jesse Hill Ford   *Ph* Robert Surtees   *Ed* Robert

L

Swink, Carl Kress   *Mus* Elmer Bernstein
Art Dir Kenneth A. Reid
● Lee J. Cobb, Anthony Zerbe, Roscoe Lee Browne, Lola Falana, Lee Majors, Barbara Hershey (Columbia)

This story of a glossed-over Negro's murder by a Dixie policeman is, unfortunately, not much more than an interracial sexploitation film.

Story kicks off as Lee Majors and bride Barbara Hershey come to live with Majors' uncle Lee J. Cobb, while Yaphet Kotto comes home to murder bestial cop Arch Johnson. Roscoe Lee Browne is town's Negro funeral director, the title character who seeks a divorce (the liberation) from unfaithful wife Lola Falana. Her lover is Anthony Zerbe, Johnson's police buddy.

The well-structured plot [from the novel *The Liberation of Lord Byron Jones* by Jesse Hill Ford] finds lawyer Cobb trying to avoid an open-court revelation that a white married cop is a Negro woman's lover.

● ●

■ LICENCE TO KILL

1989, 133 MINS, UK ◇ ⑫ ⊙
Dir John Glen   *Prod* Albert R. Broccoli, Michael G. Wilson   *Scr* Richard Maibaum, Michael G. Wilson   *Ph* Alec Mills   *Ed* John Grover   *Mus* Michael Kamen   *Art Dir* Peter Lamont
● Timothy Dalton, Carey Lowell, Robert Davi, Talisa Soto, Anthony Zerbe, Wayne Newton (United Artists/Eon)

The James Bond production team has found its second wind with *Licence to Kill*, a cocktail of high-octane action, spectacle and drama.

Presence for the second time of Timothy Dalton as the suave British agent clearly has juiced up scripters, and director John Glen.

Out go the self-parodying witticisms and over-elaborate high-tech gizmos that showed pre-Dalton pics to a walking pace. Dalton plays 007 with a vigor and physicality that harks back to the earliest Bond pics, letting full-bloodied actions speak louder than words.

The thrills-and-spills chases are superbly orchestrated as pic spins at breakneck speed through its South Florida and Central American locations. Bond survives a series of underwater and mid-air stunt sequences that are above par for the series.

He's also pitted against a crew of sinister baddies (led by Robert Davi and Frank McRae) who give the British agent the chance to use all his wit and wiles. Femme elements in the guise of Carey Lowell and Talisa Soto add gloss but play second fiddle to the action.

● ●

■ LIEBESTRAUM

1991, 102 MINS, US ◇ ⑫ ⊙
Dir Mike Figgis   *Prod* Eric Fellner   *Scr* Mike Figgis   *Ph* Juan Ruiz Anchia   *Ed* Mark Hunter   *Mus* Mike Figgis   *Art Dir* Waldemar Kalinowski
● Kevin Anderson, Pamela Gidley, Bill Pullman, Kim Novak, Thomas Kopache, Catherine Hicks (M-G-M/Initial)

Writer-director Mike Figgis returns to the territory of his earlier success, *Stormy Monday*, with plenty of mood but not a lot of plot.

Pic is set in a grimy town hoping for an economic turnaround via demolition of a defunct department store and the construction of a shopping mall. The town continues to have repercussions of a murder that took place 30 years before (and shown during the opening credits). Figgis gets good use of his Binghamton, NY, locations, including the old building that's the focus of much of the film.

The story proper begins with the arrival of architectural writer Kevin Anderson, summoned to the bedside of his dying mother (Kim Novak) whom he has never known. While in town he runs into old college buddy

Bill Pullman, who's in charge of the demolition. He soon meets Pullman's wife (Pamela Gidley), who is suffering in a sexless marriage due to hubby's playing around, and they become involved.

Figgis' problem here is the confused script, which doesn't seem to have a point. Biggest waste is Novak, who spends virtually the entire film bedridden and moaning her few lines. Rest of the thesping is professional, but unmemorable.

[In the UK pic was released in a 113-minute version featuring a sequence in which the local sheriff takes Anderson to a brothel.]

● ●

■ LIES MY FATHER TOLD ME

1975, 103 MINS, CANADA ◇ ⑫
Dir Jan Kadar   *Prod* Anthony Bedrich, Harry Gulkin   *Scr* Ted Allan   *Ph* Paul Van Der Linden   *Ed* Edward Beyer, Richard Marks   *Mus* Sol Kaplan   *Art Dir* Francois Barbeau
● Yossi Yadin, Len Birman, Marilyn Lightstone, Jeffrey Lynas, Ted Allan, Barbara Chilcott (Pentimento/Pentacle VIII)

Set in Montreal in the 1920s, this centres on an emotional relationship between a young boy, portrayed by newcomer Jeffrey Lynas, and his aged, peddler grandfather, played by Israeli actor Yossi Yadin. Threatening this relationship at all times is the boy's hard luck, no talent father, etched by a ruggedly vigorous Len Birman, and his long-suffering mother, a dramatic leavening force played by Marilyn Lightstone.

The grandfather spins fanciful tales for the boy, and takes him on his peddling rounds, while the father tries to wheedle money from him for various unsuccessful invention schemes.

Czech director Jan Kadar has assembled a topnotch, uniformly handsome cast and his lingering over certain moments is a decided virtue. *Lies My Father Told Me* is an absorbing nostalgic trip for anyone who has ever felt close to a grandparent, and it is a powerful but never pushy statement.

☐ 1975: Nomination: Best Original Screenplay

● ●

■ LIEUTENANT WORE SKIRTS, THE

1956, 98 MINS, US ◇
Dir Frank Tashlin   *Prod* Buddy Adler   *Scr* Albert Beich, Frank Tashlin   *Ph* Leo Tover   *Ed* James B. Clark   *Mus* Cyril J. Mockridge   *Art Dir* Lyle Wheeler, Leland Fuller
● Tom Ewell, Sheree North, Rita Moreno, Rick Jason, Les Tremayne, Jean Wiles (20th Century-Fox)

This amusing comedy affair whiles away a pleasant 98 minutes of screen time. Sassy dialogue and situations predominate and make for sly fun. Footage occasionally strains into slapstick with the frenetics forcing chuckles, but the plot idea is enough to carry the show along at an amusing pace.

Story pits Tom Ewell against the Air Force, and he wins, with an assist from nature. He's an aging World War II hero now a TV writer, and Sheree North, his wife, is an ex-WAC considerably younger. The comedy of errors tees off when she rejoins the service because he is recalled. However, he's rejected, and then dejected because she likes her uniform. From then on comedy hinges on his efforts to get her discharged.

Ewell makes with the facial expressions for some solid comedy scoring. North mostly acts her role with her legs and hips. It's a performance with which no one should quarrel as she's equipped for such physical thesping. Rita Moreno captures the fancy in a girl-upstairs takeoff from *The Seven Year Itch*. Beverly Hills and Honolulu serve as backgrounds for the story.

● ●

■ LIFE AND DEATH OF COLONEL BLIMP, THE

1943, 163 MINS, UK ◇ ⑫ ⊙
Dir Michael Powell, Emeric Pressburger   *Prod* Michael Powell, Emeric Pressburger   *Scr* Michael Powell, Emeric Pressburger   *Ph* Georges Perinal   *Ed* John Seabourne   *Mus* Allan Gray   *Art Dir* Alfred Junge
● Roger Livesey, Deborah Kerr, Anton Walbrook, Roland Culver, Albert Lieven, James McKechnie (Archers/Independent)

Here is an excellent film whose basic story could have been told within normal feature limits, but which, instead, is extended close to three hours. Longer or shorter, this panorama of British army life is depicted with a technical skill and artistry that marks it as one of the really fine pix to come out of a British studio.

It's a clear, continuous unreeling of events in the life of an English military man, from the Boer War, through World War I and up to the completion of the training and equipment of England's Home Guard. Story revolves around an officer (Clive Candy) who has spent all his life in the army and still feels the German people as a whole are decent human beings, and that they're only tools of their war lords.

The role of Candy is spasmodically well enacted by Roger Livesey, who looks a little too mature in the scenes of his younger days and a bit too virile at the finish. More generous praise should go to Anton Walbrook as an Uhlan officer. This is an excellent characterization depicted with delicacy and sensitiveness. Deborah Kerr contributes attractively as the feminine lead in three separate characters through the generations, and a score of other artists leave little to criticize from the histrionic side.

Title is based on the symbolic figure of the old-time English officers who have been axed, not only due to age but because of their contempt for present methods of warfare as compared with 'the good old days'. Cartoonist Low, in the *Evening Standard*, christened them 'Colonel Blimps'.

● ●

■ LIFE AND TIMES OF JUDGE ROY BEAN, THE

1972, 120 MINS, US ◇ ⑫
Dir John Huston   *Prod* John Foreman   *Scr* John Milius   *Ph* Richard Moore   *Ed* Hugh S. Fowler   *Mus* Maurice Jarre   *Art Dir* Tambi Larsen
● Paul Newman, Victoria Principal, Anthony Perkins, Ned Beatty, John Huston, Ava Gardner (First Artists)

The Life and Times of Judge Roy Bean has a title card to the effect: 'Maybe this isn't the way it was . . . it's the way it should have been'. For some, perhaps, that will set up this $4 million freedom freeway spoof.

The two-hour running time is not fleshed out with anything more than scenic vignettes, sometimes attempting to recreate the success of *Butch Cassidy and the Sundance Kid*, with an Alan and Marilyn Bergman-lyriced tune and Maurice Jarre's music sometimes attempting honest spoofing of westerns, and sometimes trying to play the story historically straight. The overkill and the underdone do it in.

Newman (Bean) arrives in Texas badlands, draws a moustache on his wanted poster and announces himself at the saloon. He is promptly beaten, robbed, tied to a horse and run out over the prairie to die. Mexican town-girl Victoria Principal saves him. He returns to the saloon, massacres everyone there and then sits down to wait to 'kill all of your kind'.

Newman is good as Bean, injecting charm into the character along with the rough exterior. Principal is impressive in her first major role.

☐ 1972: Nomination: Best Song ('Marmalade, Molasses and Honey')

● ●

■ LIFE AT THE TOP

1965, 118 MINS, UK
Dir Ted Kotcheff   *Prod* James Woolf   *Scr* Mordecai
Richler   *Ph* Oswald Morris   *Ed* Derek York
Mus Richard Addinsell   *Art Dir* Ted Marshall
● Laurence Harvey, Jean Simmons, Honor Blackman,
Michael Craig, Donald Wolfit, Robert Morley (Romulus)

Some of the gloss of *Room at the Top* rubs off
on this follow-up, but the film lacks both the
motivation and rare subtlety which elevated
its predecessor.

Based upon a second novel by John Braine,
the sombre, sometimes dreary but usually
honest drama picks up its narrative 10 years
later. The Mordecali Richler screenplay continues the story of the young, designing opportunist who rose to the top in social and
business standing, but at loss of his self-
respect, as limned in *Room*. Now, however,
after having enjoyed the position he sought
for a decade, he is even more aware of the
necessity of clinging to his ideals and tries to
do something about a life he has found
empty.

Laurence Harvey continues in the mood of
his character in *Room*, now sales chief of his
millionaire father-in-law's woolen mills in a
sooty Yorkshire town. Jean Simmons as his
wife (replacing Heather Sears in original
role) has a rather unsympathetic character
which she nonetheless enacts persuasively.

■ LIFEBOAT

1944, 86 MINS, US
Dir Alfred Hitchcock   *Prod* Kenneth Macgowan   *Scr* Jo
Swerling   *Ph* Glen MacWilliams   *Ed* Dorothy Spencer
Mus Hugo Friedhofer   *Art Dir* James Basevi, Maurice
Ransford
● Tallulah Bankhead, William Bendix, Walter Slezak,
John Hodiak, Hume Cronyn, Canada Lee (20th Century-
Fox)

John Steinbeck's devastating indictment of
the nature of Nazi bestiality, at times an almost clinical, dissecting room analysis,
emerges as powerful adult motion picture
fare.

The picture is based on an original idea of
director Alfred Hitchcock's. Hitchcock, from
accounts, first asked Steinbeck to write the
piece for book publication, figuring that if it
turned out a big seller the exploitation value
for film purposes would be greatly enhanced.
The author, however, would not undertake
the more ambitious assignment and wrote
the story for screen purposes only, with Jo
Swerling handling the adaptation.

Patterned along one of the simplest, most
elementary forms of dramatic narration, the
action opens and closes on a lifeboat. It's a
lusty, robust story about a group of survivors
from a ship sunk by a U-boat. One by one the
survivors find precarious refuge on the
lifeboat. Finally they pick up a survivor from
the German U-boat. He is first tolerated and
then welcomed into their midst. And he repays their trust and confidence with murderous treachery.

Walter Slezak, as the German, comes
through with a terrific delineation. Henry
Hull as the millionaire, William Bendix
as the mariner with a jitterbug complex
who loses a leg, John Hodiak as the tough,
bitter, Nazi-hater, and Canada Lee as the
colored steward, deliver excellent characterizations.

Hitchcock pilots the piece skillfully, ingeniously developing suspense and action.
Despite that it's a slow starter, the picture,
from the beginning, leaves a strong impact
and, before too long, develops into the type of
suspenseful product with which Hitchcock
has always been identified.

□ 1944: Nominations: Best Director,
Original Story, B&W Cinematography

■ LIFEFORCE

1985, 101 MINS, US ◇ ⓥ ⊙
Dir Tobe Hooper   *Prod* Menahem Golan, Yoram Globus
Scr Dan O'Bannon, Don Jakoby   *Ph* Alan Hume
Ed John Grover   *Mus* Henry Mancini, Michael Kamen,
James Guthrie   *Art Dir* John Graysmark
● Steve Railsback, Peter Firth, Frank Finlay, Mathilda
May, Patrick Stewart, Michael Gothard (Cannon)

For about the first 10 minutes, this $22.5 mil-
lion pic indicates it could be a scary sci-fier as
Yank and British space travelers discover
seemingly human remains in the vicinity of
Halley's Comet and attempt to bring home
three perfectly preserved specimens.

The astronauts don't make it back but the
humanoids do, and one of them, Space Girl
(Mathilda May), is possessed of such a spectacularly statuesque physique that she could
probably have conquered all of mankind even
without her special talents, which include a
form of electroshock vampirism and the ability to inhabit other bodies.

Pic [from the novel *The Space Vampires* by
Colin Wilson] descends into subpar Agatha
Christie territory, as fanatical inspector Peter
Firth and surviving astronaut Steve Railsback
scour the countryside for the deadly Space
Girl and make a pit stop at an insane asylum
to provide for further hysteria.

Even though she turns millions of
Londoners into fruitcakes and threatens the
entire world, Railsback just can't get the
naked Space Girl out of his mind.

In the meantime, Firth makes his way
through scores of zombies in a burning
London in hopes of nailing Space Girl.

■ LIFE FOR RUTH
(US: Walk in the Shadow)

1962, 91 MINS, UK
Dir Basil Dearden   *Prod* Michael Relph   *Scr* Janet
Green, John McCormick   *Ph* Otto Heller   *Ed* John
Guthridge   *Mus* William Alwyn   *Art Dir* Alex
Vetchinsky
● Michael Craig, Patrick McGoohan, Janet Munro, Paul
Rogers, Megs Jenkins, Frank Finlay (Allied Film Makers)

First problem that confronts an honest working man (Michael Craig) occurs when his
eight-year-old daughter and her next door
playmate are involved in a boating accident.
His daughter is clinging to the boat and is not
in such immediate danger as the drowning
boy. Which should he try first to save?

He rescues both, but by then his daughter is
gravely ill. Only a blood transfusion can save
her. Because of his strict religious principles
(he is a member of the Jehovah's witness sect,
though it is not stated in the film) he ada-
mantly refuses, and the child dies. That was
his second distressing problem.

The doctor who urged the transfusion is so
irate that he gets the father tried for manslaughter. This is good telling stuff for drama
and it brings up isues about religion, the law,
conscience, marital relationship all posed
with intelligence and conviction.

Thesping is crisp all around, with Craig surmounting a gloomy type of role as the dogged
religionist, and Janet Munro as his baffled
dismayed young wife. Patrick McGoohan is
excellent in a tricky role [the doctor] which is
not so clearly defined as the other top jobs.
Otto Heller's bleak photography of the
North of England setting and William
Alwyn's unobtrusive musical score all lend
aid to Dearden's adroit direction.

■ LIFEGUARD

1976, 96 MINS, US ◇ ⓥ
Dir Daniel Petrie   *Prod* Ron Silverman   *Scr* Ron Koslow
Ph Ralph Woolsey   *Ed* Argyle Nelson Jr   *Mus* Dale
Menten
● Sam Elliott, Anne Archer, Stephen Young, Parker
Stevenson, Kathleen Quinlan, Steve Burns (Paramount)

Lifeguard is an unsatisfying film, of uncertain
focus on a 30-ish guy who doesn't yet seem to
know what he wants. Script takes Sam Elliott
through another Southern California beach
summer as a career lifeguard, encountering
the usual string of offbeat characters found in
the type of made-for-TV feature which this
project resembles.

There are, of course, some advantages –
like periodic playmate Sharon Weber;
Kathleen Quinlan, supposedly underage (but
looking far more mature) teenager who has a
crush on him; and Anne Archer, long-ago
high-school sweetheart now divorced.

Elliott, who has some beefcake value, projects a character who is mostly a passive reac-
tor rather than a person in sure command of
his fate.

■ LIFE IS CHEAP . . .
. . . BUT TOILET PAPER IS EXPENSIVE

1990, 90 MINS, US ◇ ⓥ
Dir Wayne Wang, Spencer Nakasako   *Prod* Winnie
Fredriksz   *Scr* Spencer Nakasako   *Ph* Amir M. Mokri
Ed Chris Sanderson, Sandy Nervig   *Mus* Mark Adler
Art Dir Collete Koo
● Spencer Nakasako, Cora Miao, Victor Wong, John K.
Chan, Chan Kim Wan (Far East Stars)

Audaciously stylish and visually mesmerizing,
Life Is Cheap aims to evoke the uncertain
mood of present-day Hong Kong as viewed
from the perspective of an Asian-American
naif. Director Wayne Wang's tart take on
the conundrum of Chinese identity has
all the narrative logic of a tilted pinball
machine.

Screenwriter-star Spencer Nakasako is a
half-Chinese, half-Japanese, all-American sta-
blehand from San Francisco who has agreed
to act as a courier for a San Francisco Triad,
the Chinese mafia, in return for an all-ex-
penses-paid sojourn in Hong Kong. The
black-Stetsoned, cowboy-booted hero wants to
see the legendary port before its takeover by
China. In the wake of Tiananmen Square, it's
a city of '5½ million sitting ducks'.

Handcuffed to an attache case destined for
the 'Big Boss' in Hong Kong, the hero seeks
to unlock the enigma of '5,000 years of
Chinese culture'. Wang skewers the lofty notion of Chinese self-superiority by populating
his film with a widely variegated gallery of
funny and flawed characters.

■ LIFE IS SWEET

1991, 102 MINS, UK ◇ ⓥ ⊙
Dir Mike Leigh   *Prod* Simon Channing-Williams
Scr Mike Leigh   *Ph* Dick Pope   *Ed* John Gregory
Mus Rachel Portman   *Art Dir* Alison Chitty
● Alison Steadman, Jim Broadbent, Timothy Spall,
Claire Skinner, Jane Horrocks, David Thewlis (Thin Man)

Mike Leigh's third pic is a highly sympathetic
comedy, embroidered by a superb performance from helmer's wife Alison Steadman.

Steadman is ideally cast as a suburban
housewife and mother who sells baby clothes,
supports her husband (Jim Broadbent), and
attempts to look after her twin teen daughters (one a plumber, the other an anorexic
rebel). She still finds time to help a friend
(Timothy Spall) open a new restaurant, acting as a waitress on his disastrous opening
night.

Her husband falls at work, arriving home in
plaster. Her rebel daughter veers towards
breakdown, and almost everything that could
go wrong does. But she is a survivor, who
helps others survive too.

As a precise observation of British types
and a virtuoso piece of carefully observed ensemble playing, the film would be hard to
beat.

LIFE OF BRIAN

1979, 93 MINS, UK ◇ ⊙

Dir Terry Jones   *Prod* John Goldstone   *Scr* Graham
Chapman, John Cleese, Terry Gilliam, Eric Idle, Terry
Jones, Michael Palin   *Ph* Peter Biziou   *Ed* Julian Doyle
Mus Geoffrey Burgon   *Art Dir* Terry Gilliam
● Terry Jones, Michael Palin, John Cleese, Eric Idle,
Spike Milligan, George Harrison (Warner/Orion)

Monty Python's *Life Of Brian*, utterly irreverent tale of a reluctant messiah whose impact proved somewhat less pervasive than that of his contemporary Jesus Christ, is just as wacky and imaginative as their earlier film outings. Film was shot using stunning Tunisian locales.

As an adult in Roman-occupied Palestine, Brian's life parallels that of Jesus, as he becomes involved in the terrorist Peoples Front of Judea, works as a vendor at the Colosseum, paints anti-Roman graffiti on palace walls, unwittingly wins a following as a messiah and is ultimately condemned to the cross by a foppish Pontius Pilate.

Tone of the film is set by such scenes as a version of the sermon on the mount in which spectators shout out that they can't hear what's being said and start fighting amongst themselves.

LIFE OF EMILE ZOLA, THE

1937, 123 MINS, US ⊙

Dir William Dieterle   *Prod* Henry Blanke   *Scr* Heinz
Herald, Geza Herczeg, Norman Reilly Raine   *Ph* Tony
Gaudio   *Ed* Warren Low   *Mus* Max Steiner
Art Dir Anton Grot
● Paul Muni, Gloria Holden, Gale Sondergaard, Joseph
Schildkraut, Robert Warwick, Robert Barrat (Warner)

The Life of Emile Zola is a vibrant, tense and emotional story about the man who fought a nation with his pen and successfully championed the cause of the exiled Capt Alfred Dreyfus. With Paul Muni in the title role, supported by distinguished players, the film is finely made.

The picture is Muni's all the way, even when he is off screen. Covering a period of the last half of the past century, action [from a story by Heinz Herald and Geza Herczeg] is laid in Paris, except for short interludes in England and on Devil's Island, whither Dreyfus was banished by court-martial after conspiracy charges that he betrayed military secrets to Germany. Although the release of Dreyfus is made the principal dramatic incident of the picture, the development of the character and career of Zola remains dominant.

Thus, the audience is informed of the derivation of his earlier novels of *Nana*, in which he stripped the Paris underworld of its glitter and laid it bare, and his other crusading works. In his late years he takes up the fight to free Dreyfus and purge the French army general staff of deceit and conspiracy.

Joseph Schildkraut as Dreyfus, Gale Sondergaard as his wife, and Erin O'Brien-Moore in a lesser role, as the inspiration for the conception of *Nana*, leave deep impressions. Racial theme is lightly touched upon, but impressive notwithstanding.

□ 1937: Best Picture, Supp. Actor (Joseph Schildkraut), Screenplay.
□ Nominations: Best Director, Actor (Paul Muni), Original Story, Score, Sound, Assistant Director (Russ Saunders)

LIFE STINKS

1991, 95 MINS, US ◇ ⊙

Dir Mel Brooks   *Prod* Mel Brooks   *Scr* Mel Brooks, Rudy
De Luca, Steve Haberman   *Ph* Steven Poster   *Ed* David
Rawlins, Anthony Redman, Michael Mulconery
Mus John Morris   *Art Dir* Peter Larkin
● Mel Brooks, Lesley Ann Warren, Jeffrey Tambor,
Stuart Pankin, Howard Morris, Rudy De Luca (Brooksfilms)

Mel Brooks' *Life Stinks* is a fitfully funny vaudeville caricature about life on Skid Row. Premise of a rich man who chooses to live among the poor for a spell feels sorely undeveloped, and suffers from the usual gross effects and exaggerations.

Pic gets off to a good start with Brooks' callous billionaire Goddard Bolt informing his circle of yes-men of his plans to build a colossal futuristic development on the site of Los Angeles' worst slums, the plight of its residents be damned.

Tycoon Jeffrey Tambor bets his rival that he can't last a month living out in the neighborhood he intends to buy.

In a series of vignettes that play like blackout routines, Bolt, renamed Pepto by a local denizen, tries various survival tactics, such as dancing for donations. After being robbed of his shoes, he encounters baglady Lesley Ann Warren, a wildly gesticulating man-hater who slowly comes to admit Pepto is the only person she can stand.

Some effective bug-eyed, free-wheeling comedy is scattered throughout, much of it descending to the Three Stooges level of sophistication. But distressingly little is done with the vast possibilities offered by the setting and the characters populating it.

LIFE WITH FATHER

1947, 118 MINS, US ◇ ⊙

Dir Michael Curtiz   *Prod* Robert Buckner   *Scr* Donald
Ogden Stewart   *Ph* Peverell Marley, William V. Skall
Ed George Amy   *Mus* Max Steiner   *Art Dir* Robert M.
Haas
● Irene Dunne, William Powell, Elizabeth Taylor,
Edmund Gwenn, ZaSu Pitts, Jimmy Lydon (Warner)

Irene Dunne and William Powell have captured to a considerable extent the charm of the play by Howard Lindsay and Russel Crouse [based on the book by Clarence Day Jr]. The major humor of the story, based on Father's eccentric characteristics and Mother's continual mollifying of his tantrums, is still evident in the pic. The Day children are not as effectively projected as in the play, but this, too, has been shrouded by the lesser intimacy of the pic.

Elizabeth Taylor, as the vis-a-vis for Clarence Day Jr, is sweetly feminine as the demure visitor to the Day household, while Jimmy Lydon, as young Clarence, is likewise effective as the potential Yale man. Edmund Gwenn, as the minister, and ZaSu Pitts, a constantly visiting relative, head the supporting players who contribute stellar performances.

□ 1947: Nominations: Best Actor (William Powell), Color Cinematography, Color Art Direction, Scoring of a Dramatic Picture

LIFE WITH MIKEY

1993, 91 MINS, US ◇ ⊙

Dir James Lapine   *Prod* Teri Schwartz, Scott Rudin
Scr Marc Lawrence   *Ph* Rob Hahn   *Ed* Robert Leighton
Mus Alan Menken   *Art Dir* Adrianne Lobel
● Michael J. Fox, Christina Vidal, Nathan Lane, Cyndi
Lauper, David Krumholtz, David Huddleston (Touchstone)

A better version of *Curly Sue*, this Michael J. Fox vehicle screams 'cute' from every pore but should play well with kids and won't insult the intelligence of adults.

Michael Chapman (Fox) was once the star of his own sitcom, *Life with Mikey*, making him one of the best-known tykes in America. Unfortunately, he topped out at age 15, and now suffers from a serious case of Peter Panitis, while his patient brother (Nathan Lane) runs their business.

Then a streetwise 10-year-old (newcomer Christina Vidal) steals Michael's wallet and puts on a Meryl Streep-quality performance when caught. She quickly lands a major commercial gig and moves in with Michael, compelling him to confront some of his own inadequacies.

This is all very stock, predictable stuff, but director James Lapine and writer/co-producer Marc Lawrence bring an easy charm to most of the proceedings. Fox turns in an extremely likable, believable performance sans camp or melodramatics.

LIGHT AT THE EDGE OF THE WORLD, THE

1971, 120 MINS, US ◇ ⊙

Dir Kevin Billington   *Prod* Kirk Douglas   *Scr* Tom Rowe,
Rachel Billington, Paquita Villanova, Bertha Dominguez
Ph Henri Decae   *Ed* Bert Bates   *Mus* Piero Piccioni
Art Dir Enrique Alarcon
● Kirk Douglas, Yul Brynner, Samantha Eggar, Jean
Claude Drouot, Fernando Rey, Renato Salvatori (National
General)

Jules Verne's *The Light at the Edge of the World* shapes up as good action-adventure escapism. The stars are Kirk Douglas, who produced on Spanish locations, as the sole survivor on an island captured by pirate Yul Brynner, with Samantha Eggar as a shipwrecked hostage.

Douglas is a bored assistant to lighthouse-keeper Fernando Rey on a rock off the tip of South America in 1865. Massimo Ranieri, a young man rounding out the group, is brutally killed with Rey when Brynner's pirate ship takes over the island. Douglas escapes and ekes out a passive survival. When Brynner's men darken the regular beacon and erect a false light to snare Cape Horn vessels, Douglas rescues Renato Salvatori from slaughter and begins to fight back.

Eggar, saved from the shipwreck, is used by Brynner as a look-alike of Douglas' old secret love. From this point on, it's all downhill until the exciting confrontation between Douglas and Brynner atop the burning lighthouse.

LIGHTHORSEMEN, THE

1987, 128 MINS, AUSTRALIA ◇ ⊙

Dir Simon Wincer   *Prod* Ian Jones, Simon Wincer
Scr Ian Jones   *Ph* Dean Semler   *Ed* Adrian Carr
Mus Mario Millo   *Art Dir* Bernard Hides
● Jon Blake, Peter Phelps, Tony Bonner, Bill Kerr, John
Walton, Anthony Andrews (RKO/Picture Show)

Toward the end of this epic about Aussie cavalry fighting in the Middle East in 1917, there's a tremendously exciting and spectacular 14-minute sequence in which soldiers of the Light Horse charge on German/Turkish-occupied Beersheba. It's a pity writer and co-producer Ian Jones couldn't come up with a more substantial storyline to build around his terrific climax.

Focus of attention is on Dave Mitchell, very well played by Peter Phelps. Opening sequence, which is breathtakingly beautiful, is set in Australia and involves young Dave deciding to enlist in the Light Horse after seeing wild horses being mustered for shipment to the Middle East.

Main story involves four friends (Jon Blake, John Walton, Tim McKenzie, Gary Sweet) who are members of the Australian cavalry, chaffing because the British, who have overall command of allied troops in the area, misuse the cavalry time and again, forcing the Australians to dismount before going into battle.

The principal leads are very well played, with Phelps a standout as the most interesting of the young soldiers. Walton scores as the quick-tempered leader of the group, while McKenzie creates a character out of very little material. Topbilled Blake is thoroughly charming as Scotty.

LIGHT IN THE PIAZZA

1962, 102 MINS, US ◇

Dir Guy Green   *Prod* Arthur Freed   *Scr* Julius J. Epstein
Ph Otto Heller   *Ed* Frank Clarke   *Mus* Mario
Nascimbene   *Art Dir* Frank White

● Olivia de Havilland, Rossano Brazzi, Yvette Mimieux, George Hamilton, Barry Sullivan (M-G-M)

Discerningly cast and deftly executed under the imaginative guidance of director Guy Green, the Arthur Freed production, filmed in the intoxicatingly visual environments of Rome and Florence, is an interesting touching drama based on a highly unusual romantic circumstance created in prose by Elizabeth Spencer. The film has its flaws, but they are minor kinks in a satisfying whole.

Epstein's concise and graceful screenplay examines with reasonable depth and sensible restraint the odd plight of a beautiful, wealthy 26-year-old American girl (Yvette Mimieux) who, as a result of a severe blow on the head in her youth, has been left with a permanent 10-year-old mentality.

It is, too, the story of her mother's (Olivia de Havilland) dilemma – whether to commit the girl to an institution, as is the wish of her husband (Barry Sullivan), who superficially sees in the measure a solution to his marital instability, or pave the way for the girl's marriage to a well-to-do young Florentine fellow (George Hamilton) by concealing knowledge of the child's retarded intelligence.

It's Mimieux's picture. The role requires an aura of luminous naivete mixed with childish vacancy and a passion for furry things and kind, attractive people. That's precisely what it gets. Hamilton acceptably manages the Italian flavor and displays more animation than he normally has. De Havilland's performance is one of great consistency and subtle projection.

■ LIGHT OF DAY

1987, 107 MINS, US ◇ ▽ ⊙
Dir Paul Schrader   *Prod* Rob Cohen, Keith Barish   *Scr* Paul Schrader   *Ph* John Bailey   *Ed* Jacqueline Cambas   *Mus* Thomas Newman   *Art Dir* Jeannine Claudia Oppewall
● Michael J. Fox, Gena Rowlands, Joan Jett, Michael McKean, Thomas G. Waites, Cherry Jones (Taft/Barish)

At heart, *Light of Day* is a tortured family melodrama with a rock 'n' roll beat. Renegade daughter Patti Rasnick (Joan Jett) and her younger brother Joe (Michael J. Fox) play in the Barbusters, a talented but routine bar band that performs in taverns around Ohio.

Director Paul Schrader, who also wrote the screenplay, has spread enough guilt around this family to fill a book. Jett has a four-year-old son (Billy Sullivan) but won't tell anyone who the father is. She hates her mother (Gena Rowlands) despite mom's attempts to show her God's way. With the passive father (Jason Miller) and the dutiful son (Fox), this could be anyfamily USA as written by Eugene O'Neill.

Everyone wears their emotions on his sleeve, except Jett who wears them on her shoulder. Escape hatch from all this backbiting is supposed to be rock 'n' roll but when one talks too much about the saving grace of music, as Jett does, it tends to come out as childish and silly.

Despite the over-the-edge quality of her character, Rowlands makes even the most ludicrous lines seem feasible. Fox is basically miscast as the good-natured brother who idolizes his sister and tries to cover for her. Jett looks the part and even manages to hit the mark from time to time, but for every hit there's a miss.

■ LIGHTSHIP, THE

1985, 89 MINS, US ◇ ▽
Dir Jerzy Skolimowski   *Prod* Bill Benenson, Moritz Borman   *Scr* William Mai, David Taylor   *Ph* Charly Steinberger   *Ed* Barry Vince   *Mus* Stanley Myers   *Art Dir* Holger Gross

● Robert Duvall, Klaus Maria Brandauer, Tom Bower, Robert Costanzo, Badja Djola, William Forsythe (CBS)

Jerzy Skolimowski's *The Lightship* is based on a novella by the highly regarded German writer Siegfried Lenz. It was filmed in West Germany on the island of Sylt with an all English-speaking cast, the story transferred from its North Sea setting to the coastal waters off Norfolk.

The setting is the only seaworthy lightship left, and it's on this precarious wreck that everything takes place. The other major plus is the acting duel between Robert Duvall and Klaus Maria Brandauer, both with thespian styles of their own and in direct contrast to each other. Since the roles of the hijacker Caspary and the Coast Guard captain Miller had to be switched before shooting began, one senses a battle of wits all the way down the line.

Further, Skolimowski is notorious for improvisation himself, so the script reportedly went through three changes – in addition to adding a saving narrative commentary on the editing table.

As a psychological thriller, *The Lightship* has its tense entertainment moments, but the narrative line takes so many detours that the problem is trying to figure out the non sequiturs as they surface out of nowhere.

■ LIGHT SLEEPER

1992, 100 MINS, US ◇ ▽ ⊙
Dir Paul Schrader   *Prod* Linda Reisman   *Scr* Paul Schrader   *Ph* Ed Lachman   *Ed* Kristina Boden   *Mus* Michael Been   *Art Dir* Richard Hornung
● Willem Dafoe, Susan Sarandon, Dana Delaney, David Clennon, Mary Beth Hurt, Victor Garber (Seven Arts)

Paul Schrader has created a pointed companion piece to his earlier portraits of lonely outcasts (*Taxi Driver*, *American Gigolo*). Contemplative and violent by turns, this quasi-thriller about a long-time drug dealer leaving the business has a great deal to recommend it but could have been significantly better had Schrader done some fresh plotting and not relied on his standby gunplay to resolve issues.

A former heavy user himself, LeTour (Willem Dafoe) has long worked as a drug delivery boy for Ann (Susan Sarandon), who sees the handwriting on the wall and gives up the coke trade for cosmetics. With four months to go before Ann packs it in, LeTour continues to drop off packets to characters who look like pathetic 1980s throwbacks.

He runs into the love of his life, Marianne (Dana Delaney), who has gone clean with difficulty and now wants nothing to do with him. When Marianne slips off the wagon to an untimely demise, script becomes more melodramatic.

A superb Dafoe contributes crucially to the degree of success the film achieves. In two bracing and amusing scenes he goes to a psychic (Mary Beth Hurt) to try to see into the future. Sarandon's role is a bit archly written, but she's lively and quick-witted as usual. Delaney is rather bland as the old flame. Better is Jane Adams as her sympathetic sister.

■ LIGHTS OF NEW YORK

1928, 57 MINS, US
Dir Bryan Foy   *Scr* Hugh Herbert, Murray Roth   *Ph* E.H. Dupar
● Helene Costello, Cullen Landis, Gladys Brockwell, Mary Carr, Wheeler Oakman, Eugene Pallette (Warner)

This picture got pretty billing in Warners describing it as 'The first 100 per cent all-talking picture'. Every character speaks, more or less. But it's not an expensively made picture in appearance, either in sets or cast.

This is an open-face story with roll-your-own dialog. It's underworld, starting in a small town and moving to a nite club on the Giddy Wild Way. There are bootleggers and gunmen, cops and muggs, the latter a couple of simps falling for con men back home in a hotel about twice the size of the town – from the looks of the set.

The cast of nearly all vaudeville actors talks the best they may, in lieu of legits or picture actors who can't talk. Gladys Brockwell, as the mistress, runs ahead and far, with Robert Elliott as the detective second. Bryan Foy directed – his first full-length talker. And there's some credit in that for him, considering there's no class to story or picture.

Helene Costello, in the fem lead, is a total loss. For talkers she had better go to school right away. Cullen Landis, opposite, seems to talk with much effort. Wheeler Oakman as the legger gets through fairly, burdened with much of the bad dialog. Mary Carr in a bit as the mother gives an illustration of what may be accomplished from experience. Tom McGuire nicely plays and looks a police chief, with hardly anything to say.

■ LI'L ABNER

1959, 113 MINS, US ◇ ▽
Dir Melvin Frank   *Prod* Norman Panama, Melvin Frank   *Scr* Norman Panama, Melvin Frank   *Ph* Daniel L. Fapp   *Ed* Arthur P. Schmidt   *Mus* Nelson Riddle, Joseph L. Lilley (dir.)   *Art Dir* Hal Pereira, J. McMillan Johnson
● Peter Palmer, Leslie Parrish, Stubby Kaye, Howard St John, Julie Newmar, Stella Stevens (Paramount)

The Norman Panama-Melvin Frank filmization of their [1956] Broadway hit is lively, colorful and tuneful, done with smart showmanship in every department.

Congress plans to use L'il Abner's hometown of Dogpatch for an atom bomb testing ground, it being the most worthless locale in the US. Dogpatchers must prove the town has some value so it will be spared. The item found is Mammy Yokum's Yokumberry Tonic, a stimulant to health and wealth and romance. The plot then thickens as private enterprise and the US government compete for the celebrated syrup.

The plimsoll mark on Alvin Colt's costumes for the female members of the cast is notably low throughout, and some of the humor is strongly Chic Sale. The songs, by Gene De Paul and Johnny Mercer, are breezy and amusing.

DeeDee Wood's dances, based on Michael Kidd's stage choreography, move more freely than usual, unconfined by conventional limits, and have considerable dazzle. The vocal numbers tend to get bunched up, as if the missing stage footlights were still imposing their limitations.

Characterizations are as deliberately unreal as the costumes and settings. Because of this, the principals don't have much chance to display anything but the broadest sort of caricature. Peter Palmer, who created the role on Broadway of Li'l Abner, repeats his assignment here. Leslie Parrish, a delectable dish, essays Daisy Mae, and although delectable, the dish could do with a dash of spice. Stubby Kaye, another Gotham original, creates the most fun with a brisk portrayal of Marryin' Sam. Howard St John, still another of the originals, has the best scene in the film as General Bullmoose. Julie Newmar and Stella Stevens are handsome and amusing as sexy sirens.
□ 1959: Nomination: Best Scoring of a Dramatic Picture

■ LILI

1953, 80 MINS, US ◇ ▽
Dir Charles Walters   *Prod* Edwin H. Knopf   *Scr* Helen Deutsch   *Ph* Robert Planck   *Ed* Ferris Webster   *Mus* Bronislau Kaper   *Art Dir* Cedric Gibbons, Paul Groesse

● Leslie Caron, Mel Ferrer, Jean-Pierre Aumont, Zsa Zsa Gabor, Kurt Kasznar, Amanda Blake (M-G-M)

Leslie Caron is a young French orphan who turns to a fascinating carnival magician, Jean-Pierre Aumont, for help [in this version of a story by Paul Gallico]. He's a Gallic wolf, but Lili's naive, 16-year-old innocence is too much for him, so he brushes her off with a waitress job with the show. Mel Ferrer, a puppeteer, uses his little friends to woo her from her sorrow.

The impromptu performance is so successful, Ferrer makes it part of the act he does with Kurt Kasznar and four puppets. Gruff and moody in his dealings with the girl, the puppet master actually loves her and is jealous over her continuing infatuation for Aumont. This jealousy leads him to slap her just at the time she is again desperate, after having discovered that Aumont is married to his assistant, Zsa Zsa Gabor. The girl packs her things and leaves.

Caron's metamorphosis from the forlorn little ugly duckling to a pixie-faced, attractive young lady is well-handled. Ferrer goes through most of the film in a pout, both from jealousy and because his dancing career was halted by a war injury. Aumont is delightful as the magician and his act with Gabor, staged almost as a production piece, is a highlight.
□ 1953: Best Scoring of a Dramatic Picture.
□ Nominations: Best Director, Actress (Leslie Caron), Screenplay, Color Cinematography, Color Art Direction

- -

■ LILIES OF THE FIELD

1963, 94 MINS, US Ⓥ
Dir Ralph Nelson *Prod* Ralph Nelson *Scr* James Poe *Ph* Ernest Ha ller *Ed* John McCafferty *Mus* Jerry Goldsmith
● Sidney Poitier, Lilia Skala, Lisa Mann, Stanley Adams, Dan Frazer (Rainbow/United Artists)

Made on a modest budget and filmed entirely on location in Arizona, *Lilies* reveals Sidney Poitier as an actor with a sharp sense of humor. He is a journeyman laborer, touring the countryside in his station wagon, working when the fancy moves him, and traveling on when he feels the need for a change. That is his philosophy until he stops one day at a lonely farm to refill his radiator, but he meets his match in the five women who run the place.

They are all members of a holy order from East Germany, and are working arid land that has been bequeathed them. As the Mother Superior sets eyes on Poitier she is convinced that God has answered her prayers and sent a strong healthy man, to fix the roof of their farmhouse.

Many factors combine in the overall success of the film, notably the restrained direction by Ralph Nelson, a thoroughly competent screenplay by James Poe [from a novel by William E. Barrett], and, of course, Poitier's wn standout performance. There are a number of diverting scenes that remain in the memory, such as Poitier giving the Sisters an English lesson, with gestures to demonstrate the meaning of the phrases, and later leading them in the singing of 'Aymen'.
□ 1963: Best Actor (Sidney Poitier).
□ Nominations: Best Picture, Supp. Actress (Lilia Skala), Adapted Screenplay, B&W Cinematography

- -

■ LILITH

1964, 110 MINS, US Ⓥ
Dir Robert Rossen *Prod* Robert Rossen *Scr* Robert Rossen *Ph* Eugen Shuftan *Ed* Aram Avakian *Mus* Kenyon Hopkins *Art Dir* Richard Sylbert
● Warren Beatty, Jean Seberg, Peter Fonda, Kim Hunter, Jessica Walter, Gene Hackman (Centaur)

Lilith is the story of a young man who becomes an occupational therapist in a private mental institution where patients share three conditions – schizophrenia, wealth and uncommon intelligence. Untrained in medicine, he nevertheless takes the job because he feels he can help suffering humanity.

Whatever clarity the narrative has in its early reels is shrouded in mist as his relations with a beautiful young patient begin to develop. Unfoldment is complex and often confusing. Robert Rossen as producer-scripter-director frequently fails to communicate to the spectator. Audience is left in as much of a daze as the hero is throughout most of the film.

Warren Beatty undertakes lead role with a hesitation jarring to the watcher. His dialog generally is restricted to no more than a single, or at most two sentences, and often the audience waits uncomfortably for words which never come while Beatty merely hangs his head or stares into space. As he finds himself falling in love with Jean Seberg, a fragile girl who lives in her own dream-world and wants love, the change of character from one fairly definitive in the beginning to the gropings of a sexually-obsessed mind never carries conviction.

In adapting the J.R. Salamanca novel, Rossen approaches his task with obvious attempt to shock.

- -

■ LIMELIGHT

1936, 80 MINS, UK
Dir Herbert Wilcox *Prod* Herbert Wilcox *Scr* Laura Whetter *Ph* Henry Harris
● Anna Neagle, Arthur Tracy, Ellis Jeffreys, Tilly Losch, Alexander Field (Wilcox/GFD)

The high spots of this picture are the graceful dancing in it and Arthur Tracey's fine voice. Anna Neagle is natural in the role of an ambitious chorus girl who dries up so completely when her big moment comes.

There is too much repetition; too much flashing back to the same stage set and recurrence of song scenes. But withal there is an air of sincerity that makes the story pleasing, if not epoch-making.

A chorine hears a down-and-outer singing in the street, and when the star singer of her show loses his voice within a half hour of the first night she drags the boy in and pleads with the management to give him a chance. He becomes a riot and, despite the amorous leanings of a wealthy society girl, remains faithful to the girl who discovered him.

Tilly Losch bestows a few scenes of exotic dancing, with Robinson & Martin responsible for some charming and graceful steps.

- -

■ LIMELIGHT

1952, 135 MINS, US Ⓥ
Dir Charles Chaplin *Prod* Charles Chaplin *Scr* Charles Chaplin *Ph* Karl Struss *Ed* Joe Inge *Mus* Charles Chaplin *Art Dir* Eugene Lourie
● Charles Chaplin, Claire Bloom, Sydney Chaplin, Nigel Bruce, Norman Lloyd, Buster Keaton (Celebrated/United Artists)

Charlie Chaplin's production is probably derivative of his personal career over the years. Its backdrop is the British Stage. Departing from most forms of Hollywood stereotype, the film has a flavor all its own in the sincere quality of the story anent the onetime great vaudemine and his rescue of a femme ballet student from a suicide attempt and subsequently from great mental depression.

Production-wise, *Limelight* is a one-man show since Chaplin does almost everything but grow his own rawstock. The British music hall milieu of 1917 and the third-rate rooming house, where a good deal of the story unfolds, come through as honest reproductions.

While Chaplin is the star, he must surrender some spotlight to Claire Bloom, recruited from the British stage, for the second lead. As the frustrated terper, the delicately beautiful young actress gives a sensitive and memorable performance.

Chaplin's real-life son, Sydney, is gentle and shy as the composer in love with Bloom.
□ 1972 [*sic*]: Best Original Score

- -

■ LINEUP, THE

1958, 85 MINS, US
Dir Don Siegel *Prod* Jaime Del Valle *Scr* Stirling Silliphant *Ph* Hal Mohr *Ed* Al Clark *Mus* Mischa Bakaleinikoff *Art Dir* Ross Bellah
● Eli Wallach, Robert Keith, Warner Anderson, Richard Jaeckel, Mary LaRoche, William Leslie (Columbia)

The Lineup is based on a popular teleseries [1954-60] and has some of the same characters. But the screenplay is original material. The production is a moderately exciting melodrama based on dope smuggling in San Francisco, but short on action until the final, well-plotted and photographed, climax.

The action centers around the attempt by a narcotics gang to get the heroin it has planted abroad in the possession of travelers debarking in San Francisco. Eli Wallach heads the gang's pickup squad, aided by brains Robert Keith and driver Richard Jaeckel.

The best part of the action is its background, the Mark Hopkins motel, a Nob Hill mansion, Sutro's museum, the Opera House. There is also a good chase sequence at the end on an unfinished freeway. But the early parts of the film waste too much time on police procedure and lingo.

Wallach is wasted in the leading role. He seems an ordinary heavy, competent but not particularly interesting.

- -

■ LINK

1986, 103 MINS, UK ◇ Ⓥ
Dir Richard Franklin *Prod* Richard Franklin *Scr* Everett DeRoche *Ph* Mike Molloy *Ed* Andrew London *Mus* Jerry Goldsmith *Art Dir* Norman Garwood
● Terence Stamp, Elizabeth Shue, Steven Pinner, Richard Garnett (Thorn EMI)

You know right off the film is in trouble when the chimpanzees outperform their human counterparts.

Credit here goes to animal trainer Ray Berwick for getting a full range of expressions out of the primates that director Richard Franklin couldn't get out of the actors.

Film plods along for almost an hour at an isolated English coastal manor house where pre-eminent primatologist Dr Steven Phillip (Terence Stamp) conducts rudimentary experiments on a handful of chimps.

The chimps' malevolent ringleader, Link, takes the lead from the first time he is seen as the tuxedoed butler – even though he never utters a word.

Presumably, it's when we find out that Link, is not the dutiful cigar-smoking house servant that things are supposed to get scary.

- -

■ LIONHEART

1987, 104 MINS, US ◇ Ⓥ ⊙
Dir Franklin J. Schaffner *Prod* Stanley O'Toole, Talia Shire *Scr* Menno Meyjes, Richard Outten *Ph* Alec Mills *Ed* David Bretherton, Richard Haines *Mus* Jerry Goldsmith *Art Dir* Gil Parrondo
● Eric Stoltz, Gabriel Byrne, Nicola Cowper, Dexter Fletcher, Deborah Barrymore, Nicholas Clay (Taliafilm II/Orion)

The Children's Crusade of the 12th century is the subject of Franklin J. Schaffner's *Lionheart*, a flaccid, limp kiddie adventure yarn with little of its intended grand epic sweep realized. Based partly on myth, partly on historical accounts, the story concerns bands of medieval tykes who set out to search for the elusive King Richard II on his quest to recapture the Holy Land from the Moslems.

Young knight Robert Nerra (Eric Stoltz) rides off disillusioned from his first battle and meets up with mystical Blanche (pretty Nicola Cowper) and her brother Michael (Dexter Fletcher), two teen circus performers who convince him to travel to Paris and join King Richard's crusade.

The dark threat of the Black Prince looms overhead in all corners of the misty forest. Gabriel Byrne plays him like an ennui-stricken Darth Vader. His goal is to recruit all the kids and sell them into slavery.

● ●

■ **LION IN WINTER, THE**

1968, 135 MINS, UK ◇ ▣ ⊙
Dir Anthony Harvey   *Prod* Martin H. Poll   *Scr* James Goldman   *Ph* Douglas Slocombe   *Ed* John Bloom   *Mus* John Barry   *Art Dir* Peter Murton
● Peter O'Toole, Katharine Hepburn, Jane Merrow, John Castle, Timothy Dalton, Anthony Hopkins (Avco Embassy)

The Lion in Winter, based on James Goldman's play (1966) about treachery in the family of England's King Henry II, is an intense, fierce, personal drama put across by outstanding performances of Peter O'Toole and Katharine Hepburn. Director Anthony Harvey has done excellent work with a generally strong cast and a literate adaptation.

Title refers to the late period in the life of Henry II, when a decision on succession is deemed advisable. His exiled, embittered and imprisoned wife, Eleanor of Aquitaine, and three legitimate male offspring, are gathered, along with his mistress and her brother, youthful king Philip of France.

In one day, the seven characters are stripped bare of all inner torments, outward pretensions and governing personality traits.

Goldman has blended in his absorbing screenplay elements of love, hate, frustration, fulfillment, ambition and greed. O'Toole scores a bullseye as the king, while Hepburn's performance is amazing.

☐ 1968: Best Actress (Katharine Hepburn), Adapted Screenplay, Original Score.
☐ Nominations: Best Picture, Director, Actor (Peter O'Toole), Costume Design

● ●

■ **LION IS IN THE STREETS, A**

1953, 87 MINS, US ◇ ▣
Dir Raoul Walsh   *Prod* William Cagney   *Scr* Luther Davis   *Ph* Harry Stradling   *Ed* George Amy   *Mus* Franz Waxman   *Art Dir* Wiard Ihnen
● James Cagney, Barbara Hale, Anne Francis, Warner Anderson, John McIntire, Jeanne Cagney (Warner)

The Adria Locke Langley novel was a long time coming to the screen since first purchased by the Cagneys for filming. Along the way it lost a lot of the shocker quality and emerges as just an average drama of a man's political ambitions.

The production deals with a backwoods politician who nearly forces his ambitions on a cotton-growing state. The novel had him succeeding in doing so for a long time, but the film thwarts his drive for power before he can be elected governor.

Teel against which Raoul Walsh's direction has its problems.

James Cagney plays the swamp peddler who tries to ride into the governor's mansion by making a crusade of the plight of poor share-croppers. The portrayal has an occasional strength, but mostly is a stylized performance done with an inconsistent southern dialect that rarely holds through a complete line of dialog.

Barbara Hale is sweet and charming as the

schoolteacher who marries him. The fiery Flamingo of the book has been watered down considerably and doesn't give Anne Francis much opportunity.

● ●

■ **LION OF THE DESERT**

1981, 162 MINS, LIBYA/UK ◇ ▣
Dir Moustapha Akkad   *Prod* Moustapha Akkad   *Scr* H.A.L. Craig   *Ph* Jack Hildyard   *Ed* John Shirley   *Mus* Maurice Jarre   *Art Dir* Mario Garbuglia
● Anthony Quinn, Oliver Reed, Rod Steiger, John Gielgud, Irene Papas, Raf Vallone (Falcon International)

Filmed as *Omar Mukhtar* in 1979 at a cost reportedly exceeding $30 million, *Lion of the Desert* is a very well-produced, frequently-stirring war film about a Libyan anti-colonial hero.

Functional script by H.A.L. Craig concentrates on the Italians' efforts in 1929–31 to conquer Libya. Mussolini (Rod Steiger in two effective scenes as the strutting fascist leader) sends his general Graziani (Oliver Reed) to put down the Bedouins led by Omar Mukhtar (Anthony Quinn). Quinn is a white-bearded old teacher and freedom fighter who has been battling the Italians for 20 years.

Film's many large-scale battle scenes include two ingenious ambushes where Mukhtar succeeds in beating the better-equipped Italian forces. Producer-director Moustapha Akkad stages such action with laudable scope, but much of the battle footage is impersonal.

While never explicit, the overtones of the Bedouins' desire for international recognition, Mukhtar's insistence that confiscated lands must be returned (with new Italian settlements on them not to be tolerated) and other militant dialog emphasize parallels with today's Palestinians.

Quinn is well cast as Omar Mukhtar and brings warmth and dimension to a stock national hero assignment.

● ●

■ **LIONS LOVE**

1969, 115 MINS, US ◇
Dir Agnes Varda   *Prod* Agnes Varda   *Scr* Agnes Varda   *Ph* Stefan Larner   *Ed* Robert Dalva   *Mus* Joseph Byrd   *Art Dir* Jack Wright III
● Viva, Gerome Ragni, James Rado, Shirley Clarke, Carlos Clarens (Raab)

Actors in Hollywood were once called lions. Occupying a Hollywood house Viva, Gerome Ragni and James Rado are actors in love. Hence the title.

Into this menage a trois comes filmmaker Shirley Clarke come to Hollywood to make a movie. During a period of about a week, these four plus assorted producers, actors, children and film buffs play themselves in facsimiles of their real lives. Director Agnes Varda presents her fascination with the banal myth and mania that is Southern California.

The result is a pleasant, sometimes humorous blend of style and technique that ultimately is unsuccessful.

Viva playing Viva in one of the Andy Warhol exercises can be hugely revealing of her humor and personality. But Viva playing an actress called Viva as written by Agnes Varda loses much of her meaning. Similarly with Shirley Clarke.

● ●

■ **LIPSTICK**

1976, 89 MINS, US ◇ ▣ ⊙
Dir Lamont Johnson   *Prod* Freddie Fields   *Scr* David Rayfiel   *Ph* Bill Butler, William A. Fraker   *Ed* Marion Rothman   *Mus* Michel Polnareff, Jimmie Haskell   *Art Dir* Robert Luthardt
● Margaux Hemingway, Chris Sarandon, Perry King, Anne Bancroft, Robin Gammell, Mariel Hemingway (Paramount/De Laurentiis)

Lipstick has pretensions of being an intelligent treatment of the tragedy of female rape. But by the time it's over, the film has shown its true colors as just another cynical violence exploitationer.

David Rayfiel's script tells how high-fashion model Margaux Hemingway is brutally assaulted by mild-mannered music teacher Chris Sarandon.

The early-on rape sequence (coming less than 20 minutes into the film) is really the dramatic highlight. Somehow one just knows that society's procedures will degrade the rape victim and that the ending of the film will contrive some opportunity for partially justified violence.

Margaux Hemingway's dramatic limitations lend more believability to the role. Sarandon's performance is powerful in its quiet menace.

● ●

■ **LIQUIDATOR, THE**

1966, 104 MINS, UK ◇ ▣
Dir Jack Cardiff   *Prod* Jon Pennington   *Scr* Peter Yeldham   *Ph* Ted Scaife   *Ed* Ernest Walter   *Mus* Lalo Schifrin   *Art Dir* John Blezard
● Rod Taylor, Trevor Howard, Jill St. John, Wilfrid Hyde White, David Tomlinson, Akim Tamiroff (M-G-M)

This spy yarn features Boysie Oakes, a creation of John Gardner. Peter Yeldham's screenplay and Jack Cardiff's direction combine plenty of action and some crisp wise-cracking.

Where Boysie Oakes (Rod Taylor) is different from his [1960s] counterparts is that he is neither a pro undercover agent nor an enthusiastic amateur with a flair. In fact, he is a vulnerable sort of guy who hates killing. An ex-sergeant who accidentally saves Trevor Howard's life, he is conned into joining the service by Howard (Security's No 2).

He compromises by hiring a professional killer to do the dirty work for him, an angle which has promise as a film plot. But this fairly quickly gets sidetracked when Oakes takes 'No 2's' lush secretary for a dirty weekend on the Riviera.

There are plenty of holes in the plot, but no matter. The vulnerable Oakes is played with plenty of charm and guts by Taylor, though he hardly suggests a character with such fundamental failings and frailties as Boysie.

● ●

■ **LIQUID SKY**

1982, 118 MINS, US ◇ ▣ ⊙
Dir Slava Tsukerman   *Prod* Slava Tsukerman   *Scr* Slava Tsukerman, Nina Kerova, Anne Carlisle   *Ph* Yuri Neyman   *Ed* Sharyn Leslie Ross   *Mus* Slava Tsukerman, Brenda Hutchinson, Clive Smith   *Art Dir* Marina Levikova
● Anne Carlisle, Paula Sheppard, Susan Doukas, Otto Von Wernherr, Bob Brady, Elaine Grove (Z Films)

Liquid Sky is an odd, yet generally pleasing mixture of punk rock, science fiction, and black humor. Story centers on Anne Carlisle, a new wave fashion model who inhabits a world of high-decibel noise, drug addicts (title is slang expression for heroin) and casual sex. Although Carlisle is part of the scene, she doesn't embrace any of its vices.

Unbeknownst to the crowd, a pie-plate sized flying saucer takes up residence in the neighborhood. The creature proceeds to eliminate Carlisle's lovers as they reach orgasm. Carlisle assumes she's developed some strange curse. At first she uses this power for revenge but later attempts to warn her skeptical friends.

Created by Russian emigrees living in New York City, *Liquid Sky* possesses a sophisticated sense of humor. It's view of a changing society is offered up in fiercely black comic tones. Neither the new guard nor the old escapes the filmmakers' barbed observations.

● ●

LIST OF ADRIAN MESSENGER, THE

1963, 98 MINS, US ⓥ
Dir John Huston *Prod* Edward Lewis *Scr* Anthony
Veiller *Ph* Joe MacDonald, Ted Scaife *Ed* Terry O.
Morse *Mus* Jerry Goldsmith *Art Dir* Alexander
Golitzen, Stephen Grimes, George Webb
● George C. Scott, Dana Wynter, Clive Brook, Gladys
Cooper, Herbert Marshall, Jacques Roux (Universal)

Anthony Veiller's screenplay, based on a story
by Philip MacDonald, is a kind of straight-
laced version of *Kind Hearts and Coronets*. It is
the story of a retired British Intelligence officer's efforts to nab a killer who has ingeniously murdered 11 men who represent
obstacles to his goal – the acquisition of a
huge fortune to which he will become heir as
soon as he eliminates the 12th obstacle, the
12-year-old grandson of his aged uncle, the
wealthy Marquis of Gleneyre.

The film hums along smoothly and captivatingly until the killer shows up at the estate of
the Marquis. Here the story begins to fall
apart. Since both Scotland Yard and our principal investigator (George C. Scott) are at
this time fully aware of who and where their
man is, and what he is up to, it is an incredibly contrived story distortion to suppose that
they would let him roam about freely for several days.

An even more damaging miscue is the uti-
lization of stars who are hidden behind facial
disguises in fundamentally inconsequential
roles. Of the five stars who 'guest,' Kirk
Douglas has the major assignment and carries it off colorfully and credibly. The others
are Tony Curtis, Burt Lancaster, Robert
Mitchum and Frank Sinatra. Only Mitchum
is easily recognizable beneath the facial
stickum.

Huston directs the film with style and flair.
Credit is due makeup man Bud Westmore for
his concealment of several of the most familiar faces of the 20th century.

LISZTOMANIA

1975, 104 MINS, UK ◇ ⓥ ⊙
Dir Ken Russell *Prod* Roy Baird, David Puttnam
Scr Ken Russell *Ph* Peter Suschitzky *Ed* Stuart Baird
Mus Rick Wakeman (arr.) *Art Dir* Philip Harrison
● Roger Daltrey, Sara Kestelman, Paul Nicholas, Fiona
Lewis, Veronica Quilligan, Ringo Starr (Goodtimes)

Ken Russell's *Lisztomania*, combines his customary zany and bawdy artfulness with a style
close to *Tommy*.

Liszt is depicted as somewhat of a self-indulgent professional hustler, outdone only by
Wagner, whose added ambition of unifying
Germany lends the kind of 'meaningful commitment' so often necessary to put over otherwise mediocre pop music. Daltrey and Paul
Nicholas handle their parts with flair.

LITTLE BIG MAN

1970, 147 MINS, US ◇ ⓥ ⊙
Dir Arthur Penn *Prod* Stuart Millar *Scr* Calder
Willingham *Ph* Dean Tavoularis *Ed* Dede Allen
Mus John Hammond *Art Dir* Angelo Graham
● Dustin Hoffman, Faye Dunaway, Martin Balsam,
Richard Mulligan, Chief Dan George, Jeff Corey (Cinema
Center)

Little Big Man is a sort of vaudeville show,
framed in fictional biography, loaded with
sketches of varying degrees of serious and
burlesque humor, and climaxed by the Indian
victory over Gen George A. Custer at Little
Big Horn in 1876.

The story strand [from the novel by
Thomas Berger] is Dustin Hoffman's long life
(he is over 120 at prolog and epilog brackets),
especially his years as an adopted Indian who
witnessed Custer's megalomaniacal massacre
attempt that backfired.

Might it be a serious attempt to right some

unretrievable wrong via gallows humor which
avoids the polemics? This seems to be the
course taken; the attempt at least can be respected in theory.

Chief Dan George, is outstanding as an
Indian chief who provides periodic inputs of
philosophy. Faye Dunaway is first the
preacher's over-sexed wife, later a prostitute
admired by Wild Bill Hickok, played well by
Jeff Corey; and Martin Balsam is a swindling
traveling beggar.

☐ 1970: Nomination: Best Supp. Actor (Chief
Dan George)

LITTLE CAESAR

1931, 77 MINS, US ⓥ ⊙
Dir Mervyn LeRoy *Scr* Francis E. Faragoh, Robert W.
Lee *Ph* Tony Gaudio *Ed* Ray Curtiss *Mus* Erno
Rapee (dir.) *Art Dir* Anton Grot
● Edward G. Robinson, Douglas Fairbanks Jr., Glenda
Farrell, Sidney Blackmer, Thomas Jackson, Ralph Ince
(Warner)

There are enough killings herein to fill the
quota for an old time cowboy-Indian thriller.
And one tough mugg, in the title part, who is
tough all the way from the start, when he's a
bum with ambition, to the finish, when he's a
bum again, but a dead one.

For a performance as 'Little Caesar' no director could ask for more than Edward G.
Robinson's contribution. Here, no matter
what he has to say, he's entirely convincing.

Young Douglas Fairbanks is splendid as the
gunman's friend. Another junior, William
Collier Jr. contributes real trouping to a part
that seemed out of his line. There are no off-
key performances in the picture.

No new twists to the gunman stuff [from
the novel by W.R. Burnett] same formula and
all the standard tricks, but Mervyn LeRoy, directing, had a good yarn to start with and
gives it plenty of pace besides astute handling.

☐ 1930/31: Nomination: Best Adaptated
Screenplay

LITTLE DARLINGS

1980, 92 MINS, US ◇ ⓥ ⊙
Dir Ronald F. Maxwell *Prod* Stephen J. Friedman
Scr Kimi Peck, Dalene Young *Ph* Fred Batka
Ed Pembroke J. Herring *Mus* Charles Fox
Art Dir William Hiney
● Tatum O'Neal, Kristy McNichol, Matt Dillon, Armande
Assante, Krista Errickson, Nicholas Coster (Paramount)

Little Darlings makes an honest effort to deal
with the sexual stirrings of two teenage girls,
but many adults are likely to dismiss the effort as puppy love with appeal to prurient interests.

Tatum O'Neal and Kristy McNichol are
both excellent as virgins of widely different
social backgrounds who meet at summer
camp. O'Neal is a sheltered rich girl and
McNichol the poor, streetwise urchin but
their different upbringings do not release
their shared hesitancy about making love for
the first time.

In his feature debut, director Ronald F.
Maxwell isn't perfect. But he gets several fine
scenes from his performers, especially when
O'Neal deals with her love interest, when
NcNichol deals with her love interest, and
best of all, when O'Neal and McNichol finally
level with each other.

LITTLE DORRIT

1987, 360 MINS, UK ◇ ⓥ ⊙
Dir Christine Edzard *Prod* Richard Goodwin, John
Brabourne *Scr* Christine Edzard *Ph* Bruno de Keyzer
Ed Oliver Stockman, Fraser Maclean *Mus* Michel
Sanvoisin (arr.)
● Alec Guinness, Derek Jacobi, Cyril Cusack, Sarah
Pickering, Joan Greenwood, Max Wall (Sands/Cannon)

Little Dorrit is a remarkable achievement. For
writer/director Christine Edzard the epic project [from the novel by Charles Dickens] was
obviously a labor of love, and what she has accomplished on a small budget is astounding.

The project is in fact two films, each three
hours long [I: *Nobody's Fault*, 177 mins; II:
Little Dorrit's Story, 183 mins], with the latter
being virtually a remake of the former. A
large cast of uniformly excellent British actors is topped off by quite brilliant portrayals
by Alec Guinness as William Dorrit, and
Derek Jacobi as Arthur Clennam.

In the second part you see from a different
angle the story of the family's plight, and why
they are in prison. Sarah Pickering bestows
Amy Dorrit with the gentle firmness to look
after her father, brother and sister, and when
Jacobi appears on the scene slowly falls in
love with him.

The family travels abroad and during a
plush dinner in Rome to celebrate the marriage of Fanny Dorrit (Amelda Brown) and
Sparkler (Simon Dormandy), Guinness finally
goes mad, and delivers a speech as if he were
still in the Marshalsea.

Pic then follows Pickering discovering
Jacobi is in prison and her efforts to raise the
money to free him.

Six hours of viewing obviously allows full
characterization and depth of story – though
some characters from the novel are still missing – but the style of showing virtually the
same story through two people [Clennam and
Amy] allows charming reinterpretations of
certain scenes, and presents a fully rounded
piece as never usually found in the cinema.

The pic, which is set in the 1820s, was shot
entirely in a studio owned by Sands Films in
the middle of Dickens territory, in
Rotherhithe close to the Thames, and the
painted sets give the film a rich theatrical
texture while not deflecting from the story.

☐ 1988: Nominations: Best Supp. Actor (Alec
Guinness), Adapted Screenplay

LITTLE DRUMMER GIRL, THE

1984, 130 MINS, US ◇ ⓥ ⊙
Dir George Roy Hill *Prod* Robert L. Crawford
Scr Loring Mandel *Ph* Wolfgang Treu *Ed* William
Reynolds *Mus* Dave Grusin *Art Dir* Henry Bumstead
● Diane Keaton, Yorgo Voyagis, Klaus Kinski, Sami
Frey, Michael Cristofer, David Suchet (Pan Arts)

George Roy Hill has made a disappointingly
flat film adaptation of one of John Le Carre's
top novels, *The Little Drummer Girl*. Overlong
and, for the most part, Indifferently staged on
a multitude of foreign locales, pic can't help
but intrigue due to the intense subject matter, that of complex Israeli and Palestinian
espionage and terrorism.

Diane Keaton plays the role of Charlie, in
the book a virulently pro-Palestinian British
actress generally agreed to have been inspired by Vanessa Redgrave.

No matter, though, for events quickly take
Keaton out of the UK. A team of Israeli oper-
atives, led by the supremely self-confident
Klaus Kinski, recruits her in Greece, breaks
down Her Arab sympathies and eventually
puts her in place as an ideal agent.

Keaton's loud, pushy, erratic showbiz character isn't all that easy to warm up to.

LITTLE FAUSS AND BIG HALSY

1970, 98 MINS, US ◇ ⓥ
Dir Sidney J. Furie *Prod* Albert S. Ruddy *Scr* Charles
Eastman *Ph* Ralph Woolsey *Ed* Argyle Neson Jr
Mus Johnny Cash, Bob Dylan, Carl Perkins
Art Dir Lawrence G. Paul
● Robert Redford, Michael J. Pollard, Lauren Hutton,
Noah Beery, Lucille Benson, Ray Ballard (Paramount)

Little Fauss and Big Halsy is an uneven, sluggish story of two motorcycle racers – Robert

Redford playing a callous heel and Michael J. Pollard as a put-upon sidekick who eventually (in modified finale) surpasses his fallen idol.

Hampered by a thin screenplay, film is padded further by often-pretentious direction by Sidney J. Furie against expansive physical values.

What is very disappointing is the lack of strong dramatic development. Redford's character is apparent in his very first scene; it never changes. It is in effect the carrier frequency on which Pollard and others must beat, the end result is erratic.

Pollard is very good in lending depth to his character, though his dialect often obscures his dialog.

....

■ LITTLE FOXES, THE

1941, 115 MINS, US ⓥ ⊙
Dir William Wyler   *Prod* Samuel Goldwyn   *Scr* Lillian Hellman, Dorothy Parker, Arthur Kober, Alan Campbell   *Ph* Gregg Toland   *Ed* Daniel Mandell   *Mus* Meredith Wilson   *Art Dir* Stephen Goosson
● Bette Davis, Herbert Marshall, Teresa Wright, Richard Carlson, Patricia Collinge, Dan Duryea (RKO/Goldwyn)

From starring Bette Davis down the line to the bit roles portrayed by minor Negroes the acting is well nigh flawless. And standing out sharply in Lillian Hellman's searing play about rapacious people are several performers who appeared in the 1939 Broadway stage version, i.e. Patricia Collinge, Carl Benton Reid, Dan Duryea and Charles Dingle.

In the natural padding out of the story permitted by a screenplay permits the injection of romance between Teresa Wright, as Davis' daughter, and Richard Carlson, playing a young newspaperman.

The story is about the Hubbard family of the deep south – as mercenary a foursome as has never emerged from fact or fiction. In this picture Davis also murders her husband, played by Herbert Marshall, but with the unique weapon of disinterest. When Marshall, in the throes of a heart attack, crashes a bottle of medicine that can save his life, Davis sits by and watches him do a dying swan. That's her way of killing the man who had refused to help finance the get-rich scheme of her brothers.

Marshall turns in one of his top performances in the exacting portrayal of a suffering, dying man.

On top of the smooth pace, Wyler has handled every detail with an acutely dramatic touch.

□ 1941: Nominations: Best Picture, Actress (Bette Davis), Supp. Actress (Patricia Collinge, Teresa Wright), Screenplay, B&W Art Direction, Editing, Scoring of a Dramatic Picture

....

■ LITTLE GIRL WHO LIVES DOWN THE LANE, THE

1977, 91 MINS, CANADA/FRANCE ◇ ⓥ ⊙
Dir Nicholas Gessner   *Prod* Zev Braun   *Scr* Laird Koenig   *Ph* Rene Verzier   *Ed* Yves Langlois   *Mus* Christian Gaubert   *Art Dir* Robert Prevost
● Jodie Foster, Martin Sheen, Alexis Smith, Mort Shuman, Scott Jacoby, Dorothy Davis (ICL/Filmel)

This film, about a homicidal orphan girl, is farfetched nonsense with precious little to appease shriek freaks. Laird Koenig's screenplay from his novel is riddled with unsuspended disbelief – coincidences, gimmicks.

Jodie Foster plays an all-alone sangfroid little liar of 13 going on 23 who, true to her late daddy's counsel, isn't about to let herself be pushed around or dominated by crummy grownups. Martin Sheen plays a sicko with a thing for little girls who harasses the kid. Alexis Smith is a snoopy big deal in the small local community.

One of the few agreeable angles is the relationship between Foster and Scott Jacoby, wary at first but which ripens into a boudoir romance. As a simpatico lad with a gamy leg from polio, Jacoby's performance has nice verve.

Foster's poise is impressive enough as the cool, calculating adolescent with a passion for Chopin records. But it's a one-note character. Film was shot on locations in Canada.

....

■ LITTLE HUT, THE

1957, 90 MINS, US ◇
Dir Mark Robson   *Prod* F. Hugh Herbert, Mark Robson   *Scr* F. Hugh Herbert   *Ph* Freddie Young   *Ed* Ernest Walter   *Mus* Robert Farnon   *Art Dir* Elliot Scott
● Ava Gardner, Stewart Granger, David Niven, Walter Chiari, Finlay Currie, Jean Cadell (Herbson/M-G-M)

Sex is incessantly hinted at in this saucy triangle [from Andre Roussin's play and Nancy Mitford's English stage adaptation] which keeps husband and wife intact for the moral code. It all takes place on a South Pacific island with Ava Gardner down to her lace BVDs and much sly innuendo about her husband's preoccupation with everything else but her gender.

Government business has left Stewart Granger with little time to practise the arts of a husband, so Gardner turns to hubby's best friend (David Niven) for companionship. Transfer this situation to a deserted tropical isle after a shipwreck, feed the principals a stimulating seafood diet, mostly oysters, and something has to give.

As the choice feminine tidbit who fires the masculine libido, Gardner is ideal casting. Equally adept and effective is Granger as Gardner's too-busy-to-love husband. Matching the above two is Niven, in a very amusing takeoff on a proper Englishman who wants to preempt Granger's marital rights with Gardner.

....

■ LITTLE LORD FAUNTLEROY

1921, 120 MINS, US ⊗
Dir Alfred E. Green, Jack Pickford   *Scr* Bernard McConville   *Ph* Charles Rosher   *Mus* Louis F. Gottschalk
● Mary Pickford, Claude Gillingwater, Joseph Dowling, James Marcus, Kate Price, Rose Dione (Pickford/United Artists)

Little Lord Fauntleroy is a perfect Pickford picture. It exploits the star in dual roles, one of them one of the immortal and classic boy parts of all times. Mary Pickford shows a range of versatility, between the blue-blooded and sombre mother and the blue-blooded but mischievous kid, that is almost startling. She meets herself many times in double exposures, and she is taller than herself and different from herself, and incredibly true to each.

Only director Jack Pickford could have introduced the whimsical and always amusing touches of raw boyishness in the fighting, grimacing, scheming, lovable kid that Pickford again turns out to be. She jumps off high perches onto other boys' backs, she wrestles and does trick ju-jitsus, she dodges and climbs and leans and tumbles and hand-stands.

While *Fauntleroy* is not sensational, it is a human and appealing story.

....

■ LITTLE LORD FAUNTLEROY

1936, 98 MINS, US ⓥ
Dir John Cromwell   *Prod* David O. Selznick   *Scr* Hugh Walpole   *Ph* Charles Rosher   *Mus* Max Steiner   *Art Dir* Sturges Carne
● C. Aubrey Smith, Freddie Bartholomew, Dolores Costello Barrymore, Henry Stephenson, Guy Kibbee, Mickey Rooney (Selznick/United Artists)

As his first for Selznick International after leaving Metro, David O. Selznick turns in a fine, sensitive picture in *Little Lord Fauntleroy*, which may well rank with his *David Copperfield* and *A Tale of Two Cities*. It's a transmutation of Frances Hodgson Burnett's mid-Victorian saga.

A theme as prissy as *Fauntleroy*, where the earl-to-be calls his mother 'Dearest', might have proved quite hazardous in anything but the most expert hands. As Hugh Walpole adapts it. John Cromwell directs it and a sterling cast troups it – all under Selznick's keen aegis – it's very palatable cinematic. fare.

Young Freddie Bartholomew is capital in the title role and Dolores Costello Barrymore, marking her film comeback, as 'Dearest', his young and widowed mother, are an ideal coupling in the two principal roles. C. Aubrey Smith as the gruff and grumpy earl who blindly hates his daughter-in-law just because she's American, well-nigh steals the picture in a characterization setup that's a match for this vet thespian. Henry Stephenson as the English barrister is on a par in a role that calls for much restraint.

....

■ LITTLE MALCOLM AND HIS STRUGGLE AGAINST THE EUNUCHS

1974, 112 MINS, UK ◇
Dir Stuart Cooper   *Prod* Gavrik Losey   *Scr* Derek Woodward   *Ph* John Alcott   *Ed* Ray Lovejoy   *Mus* Stanley Myers
● John Hurt, John McEnery, Raymond Platt, Rosalind Ayres, David Warner (Apple)

Adapted by Derek Woodward from a mid-1960s play by David Halliwell, item emerges as a frequently hilarious, generally thought-provoking and sobering, beautifully acted, but a trifle overlong and repetitious film of uncertain destination.

On one level, story dealing with a carefully-plotted sham uprising by a trio of students draws laughs in its Mitty-ish mock evocations of socio-political tirades, while subsurface the conclusions drawn are frightening as evidenced in the climactic scene of useless violence against a girl.

There's a trace of *Clockwork Orange* here and there (and not only because pix share same lenser, John Alcott), and it's grimly amusing in a similar way, but there the resemblance ends. Performances are all tops.

....

■ LITTLE MAN TATE

1991, 99 MINS, US ◇ ⓥ ⊙
Dir Jodie Foster   *Prod* Scott Rudin, Peggy Rajski   *Scr* Scott Frank   *Ph* Mike Southon   *Ed* Lynzee Klingman   *Mus* Mark Isham   *Art Dir* Jon Hutman
● Jodie Foster, Dianne Wiest, Adam Hann-Byrd, Harry Connick Jnr, David Pierce, P.J. Ochlan (Orion)

Jodie Foster makes an appealing, if modest, directorial debut with *Little Man Tate*. Scott Frank (*Dead Again*) penned this nicely observed tale of a year in the life of a seven-year-old genius.

An accomplished painter, poet and pianist in addition to being a math wizard, Fred Tate (Adam Hann-Byrd) is being raised by his single mother, a mildly tough working-class woman whom he, along with the rest of the world, calls Dede (played with a vulgar accent by Foster).

Before long Fred comes to the attention of wealthy Jane Grierson (Dianne Wiest), a child psychologist and teacher of the gifted. Fred moves in with her when he is invited to attend a summer college course, and strikes up an engaging relationship with a somewhat older, titanically arrogant math genius named Damon (memorably impersonated by P.J. Ochlan).

Most of the film's emotional power lies in the open, alert, eager-to-please face of Hann-

Byrd, making his acting debut. Filled with small, telling moments rather than big events, film never really gets inside Fred's head, but it neatly sketches the external aspects of his predicament.

••••••••••••••••••••••••••••••

■ **LITTLE MERMAID, THE**

1989, 82 MINS, US ◇ ⓥ ⊙
Dir John Musker, Ron Clements *Prod* Howard Ashman, John Musker *Scr* John Musker, Ron Clements *Ed* John Carnochan *Mus* Alan Menken *Art Dir* Michael A. Peraza Jr, Donald A. Towns
● (Walt Disney)

Borrowing liberally from the studio's classics, *The Little Mermaid* may represent Disney's best animated feature since the underrated *Sleeping Beauty* in 1959. That should come as no surprise to admirers of *The Great Mouse Detective*, writer-director collaborators John Musker and Ron Clements' 1986 animation feature that helped salvage the art form at the studio after it had nearly sunk into *The Black Cauldron*.

The source material is a Hans Christian Andersen tale. The mermaid princess Ariel (voiced by newcomer Jodi Benson) lives in her sea-lord father Triton's (Kenneth Mars) undersea kingdom but yearns for a life above, made all the more haunting to her when she rescues handsome young prince Sebastian (Samuel E. Wright) from the sea. Disobeying her father, she makes a pact with seawitch Ursula (Pat Carroll) enabling her to go ashore and get the prince to fall in love with her – her soul hanging in the balance, her beautiful voice as collateral.

Ursula alone proves a visual feast, a thick-jawed nightmare who swishes about on eight octopus legs in one of the film's more inspired inventions.

The animation proves lush and fluid, augmented by the use of shadow and light as elements like fire, sun and water illuminate the characters. Key contributions are made by lyricist Howard Ashman (who co-produced with Musker) and composer Alan Menken, whose songs frequently begin slowly but build in cleverness and intensity.

□ 1989: Best Song ('Under the Sea'), Original Score.
□ Nomination: Best Song ('Kiss the Girl')

••••••••••••••••••••••••••••••

■ **LITTLE MISS BROADWAY**

1938, 70 MINS, US ⓥ
Dir Irving Cummings *Prod* David Hempstead *Scr* Harry Tugent, Jack Yellen *Ph* Arthur Miller *Ed* Walter Thompson *Mus* Louis Silvers (dir.)
● Shirley Temple, George Murphy, Jimmy Durante, Phyllis Brooks, Edna May Oliver, George Barbier (20th Century-Fox)

In *Little Miss Broadway*, Shirley Temple shows an improvement in her tap dancing, her singing and her ability to turn on at will whatever emotional faucet is demanded by the script.

With Jimmy Durante, George Murphy, Edna Mae Oliver, George Barbier, Donald Meek and El Brendel in featured roles, something approaching hilarity is expected. The result is far short of the promise. Shirley is a standout, but the others through faulty cutting of the film and undeveloped opportunities in the script never quite get their openings to score.

Shirley is introduced as a ward in an orphan asylum. She is discharged into the care of an uncle (Edward Ellis) who manages a theatrical hotel near Broadway called Variety. Edna May Oliver, who owns the building and lives close by, is annoyed by the constant rehearsing of the acts and decides to close the place by demanding immediate payment of past due rent.

Her nephew (George Murphy) intercedes at the behest of Shirley Temple, but the issue finds its way to court where the acts give a dress rehearsal of a musical revue, which they hope will earn enough money to meet the financial obligation.

Walter Bullock and Harold Spina have written six songs which Shirley sings, some solo, others with chorus.

••••••••••••••••••••••••••••••

■ **LITTLE MISS MARKER**

1980, 103 MINS, US ◇ ⓥ
Dir Walter Bernstein *Prod* Jennings Lang *Scr* Walter Bernstein *Ph* Philip Lathrop *Ed* Eve Newman *Mus* Henry Mancini *Art Dir* Edward C. Carfagno
● Walter Matthau, Julie Andrews, Tony Curtis, Sara Stimson, Bob Newhart (Universal)

There is something irresistible about the story of a darling little girl left in the care of colorfully kind gamblers, which explains why this is the fourth attempt to bring Damon Runyon's story to the screen. But writer-director Walter Bernstein blows his directorial debut completely.

It's a shame, because seemingly if ever there was an actor who should play 'Sorrowful Jones' it's Walter Matthau and Bob Newhart should have been a wonderful 'Regret', while Tony Curtis could have been a respectable antagonist.

But they are all flat in their parts and that has to be Bernstein's fault. Even worse, Julie Andrews is woefully miscast with her British accent and Lee Grant gets no more than a bit part as a judge. The only really decent thing about the picture is little Sara Stimson.

••••••••••••••••••••••••••••••

■ **LITTLE MURDERS**

1971, 110 MINS, US ◇ ⓥ
Dir Alan Arkin *Prod* Jack Brodsky, Elliott Gould *Scr* Jules Feiffer *Ph* Gordon Willis *Ed* Howard Kuperman *Mus* Fred Kaz
● Elliott Gould, Marcia Rodd, Vincent Gardenia, Elizabeth Wilson, Donald Sutherland, Alan Arkin (20th Century-Fox)

Alan Arkin, making a most impressive directorial debut, has made a film that is not only funny but devastating in its emotional impact.

Arkin's actors play very broadly, just at the edge of the caricatures they are in Jules Feiffer's screenplay. But they fill in the outlines with such a wealth of human detail that it's impossible not to identify with them. Both comedy and horror, therefore, hit closer to home.

Coproducer Elliott Gould plays a photographer who was successful until he began to 'lose the people' in his pictures, and found it unnecessary or impossible either to fight or really 'feel'. Into his life comes Marcia Rodd, a girl who would like to mold him into 'a strong, vital, self-assured man, that I can protect and take care of'.

Then the world gets in the way, and Feiffer once and for all stops being the amiably satiric cartoonist, and hurtles towards a painful conclusion: that the only way for the 'mad' and the 'alienated' to get back into the world is to adopt its insanity.

Vincent Gardenia, Elizabeth Wilson and Jon Korkes are excellent as Rodd's extraordinary family. Juicy 'bits' are played by Arkin as a paranoid detective, Lou Jacobi, as a judge who remembers his days on the Lower East Side; and Donald Sutherland, as a hip minister.

••••••••••••••••••••••••••••••

■ **LITTLE NIGHT MUSIC, A**

1977, 124 MINS, AUSTRIA/US/W. GERMANY ◇ ⓥ ⊙
Dir Hal Prince *Prod* Elliott Kastner *Scr* Hugh Wheeler *Ph* Arthur Ibbetson *Ed* John Jumpson *Mus* Jonathan Tunick (dir.)
● Elizabeth Taylor, Diana Rigg, Len Cariou, Hermione Gingold, Lesley-Ann Down, Laurence Guittard (Sascha-Wien/Kastner)

A Little Night Music is based on an earlier film by Ingmar Bergman [*Smiles of a Summer Night*, 1955] that was turned into a [1973] hit Broadway musical with music and lyrics by Stephen Sondheim. In this refilming Hal Prince repeats as director.

All this fuses into an elegant looking, period romantic charade.

There is one sprightly number as the assorted characters set out for a country dinner that will resolve their complicated love problems. There is a noted promiscuous actress ready to settle down with a steady man and her teenage daughter, a staid lawyer with a young wife of 18 whose marriage has yet to be consummated, plus his son and a fiery army lieutenant, lover of the actress, and his jealous but submissive wife.

Uneven and sometimes slow, pic has good looks.

□ 1977: Best Adapted Scoring.
□ Nomination: Best Costume Design

••••••••••••••••••••••••••••••

■ **LITTLE NIKITA**
(UK: *The Sleepers*)

1988, 98 MINS, US ◇ ⓥ ⊙
Dir Richard Benjamin *Prod* Harry Gittes *Scr* John Hill, B. Goldman *Ph* Laszlo Kovacs *Ed* Jacqueline Cambas *Mus* Marvin Hamlisch *Art Dir* Gene Callahan
● Sidney Poitier, River Phoenix, Richard Jenkins, Caroline Kava, Richard Bradford, Loretta Devine (Columbia)

Little Nikita never really materializes as a taut espionage thriller and winds up as an unsatisfying execution of a clever premise – a teen's traumatic discovery that his parents are Soviet spies.

Film opens strongly as parallel storylines unfold and audience is drawn in by the need to decipher the link between the mission of a Soviet agent and an all-American family in the mythical San Diego suburb of Fountain Grove.

Poised at the juncture of these developments is FBI agent Sidney Poitier, whose natural intensity seems just right for the role.

Poitier encounters River Phoenix, a youngster who decides to apply for the Air Force Academy, on a routine FBI check. When some peculiar data turns up on Phoenix' parents – convincingly portrayed by Richard Jenkins and Caroline Kava – Poitier begins an investigation that leads to an almost avuncular bonding with Phoenix.

••••••••••••••••••••••••••••••

■ **LITTLE PRINCE, THE**

1974, 88 MINS, UK ◇ ⓥ ⊙
Dir Stanley Donen *Prod* Stanley Donen *Scr* Alan Jay Lerner *Ph* Christopher Challis *Ed* Peter Boita, John Guthridge *Mus* Frederick Loewe *Art Dir* John Barry
● Richard Kiley, Steven Warner, Bob Fosse, Gene Wilder, Joss Ackland, Clive Revill (Paramount)

Handsome production plus excellent photography and effects cannot obscure the limited artistic achievement of *The Little Prince*. Alan Jay Lerner's adaptation of the book by Antoine De Saint-Exupery is flat and his lyrics are unmemorable, as are Frederick Loewe's melodies. Richard Kiley is cast as the childman, and Steven Warner is the man-child, who ruminate on the meaning of a good life. Some okay cameo appearances by Bob Fosse, Gene Wilder, and others lend transient sparkle.

Kiley, who never forgot his youthful fantasies, makes a forced landing in a desert, where Warner, an interspace traveler, comes upon him and his grounded airplane. A series of vignettes, delicate in their import and rendered opaque by the script, supposedly make Kiley a better man for the experience.

☐ 1979: Nominations: Best Adapted Score, Song ('Little Prince')

•••••••••••••••••••••••••••••••••

■ **LITTLE ROMANCE, A**

1979, 108 MINS, US/FRANCE ◇ ▼ ⊙
Dir George Roy Hill   *Prod* Yves Rousset-Rouard, Robert L. Crawford   *Scr* Allan Burns   *Ph* Pierre-William Glenn   *Ed* William Reynolds   *Mus* Georges Delerue   *Art Dir* Henry Bumstead
● Laurence Olivier, Arthur Hill, Sally Kellerman, Diane Lane, Thelonious Bernard, Broderick Crawford (Orion/Pan Arts/Trinacra)

Scripter Allan Burns has craftily kept the point of view of the youngsters, Diane Lane and Thelonious Bernard, while the adults, with certain exceptions, are seen as suitably grotesque and ridiculous, giving *Romance* a crest of humor on which to ride.

Lane is the offspring of flighty jet-setter Sally Kellerman, who spends the film mooning over auteur director David Dukes, rather than hubby Arthur Hill. The teenagers are drawn to one another, persevere in the face of family pressure, and eventually take off in pursuit of a romantic ideal.

Fulcrum in script is the beneficent boulevardier, limned by Laurence Olivier in a modern refashioning of the old Maurice Chevalier role. The prototypical lovable scoundrel, Olivier hams it up unmercifully.
☐ 1979: Best Original Score.
☐ Nomination: Best Adapted Screenplay

•••••••••••••••••••••••••••••••••

■ **LITTLE SHOP OF HORRORS, THE**

1961, 70 MINS, US ▼ ⊙
Dir Roger Corman   *Prod* Roger Corman   *Scr* Charles B. Griffiths   *Ph* Archie Dalzell   *Ed* Marshall Neilan Jr   *Mus* Fred Katz   *Art Dir* Daniel Haller
● Jonathan Haze, Jackie Joseph, Mel Welles, Myrtle Vail, Leola Wendorff, Jack Nicholson (FilmGroup)

Reportedly only two shooting days and $22,500 went into the making of this picture, but limited fiscal resources didn't deter Roger Corman and his game, resourceful FilmGroup from whipping up a serviceful parody of a typical screen horror number.

Little Shop of Horrors is kind of one big sick joke, but it's essentially harmless and good-natured. The plot concerns a young, goofy florist's assistant who creates a talking, blood-sucking, man-eating plant, then feeds it several customers from skid row before sacrificing himself to the horticultural gods.

There is a fellow who visits the Skid Row flower shop to munch on purchased bouquets ('I like to eat in these little out-of-the-way places'). There is also the Yiddish proprietor, distressed by his botanical attraction ('we not only got a talking plant, we got one dot makes smart cracks'), but content to let it devour as the shop flourishes. And there are assorted quacks, alcoholics, masochists [Jack Nicholson, as a dental patient], sadists and even a pair of private-eyes who couldn't solve the case of the disappearing fly in a hothouse for Venus Fly-Traps.

The acting is pleasantly preposterous. Mel Welles, as the proprietor, and Jonathan Haze, as the budding Luther Burbank, are particularly capable, and Jackie Joseph is decorative as the latter's girl. Horticulturalists and vegetarians will love it.

•••••••••••••••••••••••••••••••••

■ **LITTLE SHOP OF HORRORS**

1986, 88 MINS, US ◇ ▼ ⊙
Dir Frank Oz   *Prod* David Geffen   *Scr* Howard Ashman   *Ph* Robert Paynter   *Ed* John Jympson   *Mus* Miles Goodman   *Art Dir* Roy Walker
● Rick Moranis, Ellen Greene, Vincent Gardenia, Steve Martin, Jim Belushi, John Candy (Warner/Geffen)

Little Shop of Horrors is a fractured, funny production transported rather reluctantly from

the stage to the screen. Almost nothing is left besides the setting and story outline from the 1961 Roger Corman film that inspired the 1982 stage musical.

Living a rather mundane life, working in Mushnik's flower shop are Seymour (Rick Moranis) and Audrey (Ellen Greene), that is until lightning strikes and the natural order of things is turned upside down. Through a chain of events just silly enough to be fun, Seymour becomes the proud owner of Audrey II, a rare breed of plant that makes him famous and his boss (Vincent Gardenia) prosperous. Audrey II develops an insatiable appetite for human flesh.
☐ 1986: Nominations: Best Song ('Mean Green Mother from Outer Space'), Visual Effects

•••••••••••••••••••••••••••••••••

■ **LITTLEST REBEL, THE**

1935, 70 MINS, US ▼
Dir David Butler   *Prod* Darryl F. Zanuck   *Scr* Edwin Burke   *Ph* John Seitz   *Ed* Irene Morra   *Mus* Cyril Mockridge (arr.)   *Art Dir* William Darling
● Shirley Temple, John Boles, Jack Holt, Karen Morley, Bill Robinson, Guinn Williams (20th Century-Fox)

The Littlest Rebel is a good Shirley Temple picture. It happens to be very similar in title, plantation locale, Negro comedy, and in general mechanics to *The Little Colonel* (1935).

Shrewdly playing both sides, as between the north and the south, script [from the play by Edward Peple] throws a lot of dialog to the Confederacy. All bitterness and cruelty has been rigorously cut out and the Civil War emerges as a misunderstanding among kindly gentlemen with eminently happy slaves and a cute little girl who sings and dances through the story.

Picture opens just before war is declared. The tot is giving a party to all the well-mannered children of the Virginia aristocracy and a good deal of sly comedy is slipped in at the table, and later when the children skip the minuet with genteel dignity. War brings successive losses culminating in the death of the mother (Karen Morley).

Bill Robinson and the child again dance. Robinson is once more the trusty family butler who guards little missy. John Boles, Jack Holt and Karen Morley are just routine adults who react to the charm of a little girl.

•••••••••••••••••••••••••••••••••

■ **LITTLE WOMEN**

1933, 117 MINS, US ▼
Dir George Cukor   *Prod* Merian C. Cooper   *Scr* Sarah Y. Mason, Victor Heerman   *Ph* Henry Gerrard   *Ed* Jack Kitchin
● Katharine Hepburn, Joan Bennett, Paul Lukas, Frances Dee, Jean Parker, Edna May Oliver (RKO)

Little Women is a profoundly moving history of youth and in this celluloid transcription [of the novel by Louisa M. Alcott] its deeply spiritual values are revealed with a simple earnestness.

Katharine Hepburn as Jo creates a new and stunningly vivid character; strips the Victorian hoyden of her syrupy goody-goodiness; and endows the role with awkwardly engaging youth energy that it makes it the essence of flesh and blood reality.

Story is full of tearfully sentimental passages, but they are managed with beautiful restraint. There is the heavily tearful episode of Beth's sickroom scene, in which the pathetic possibilities are realized to last extreme by the rigid restriction of obvious acting.

A notable company of standard screen names supports the star. Joan Bennett, Frances Dee and Jean Parker (as Beth) complete the feminine quartet, all playing with a persuasive charm. Paul Lukas contributes a characteristic portrait as Prof Bhaer and

Spring Byington is a conspicuous point of casting strength.
☐ 1932/33: Best Adaptation.
☐ Nominations: Best Picture, Director

•••••••••••••••••••••••••••••••••

■ **LITTLE WOMEN**

1949, 121 MINS, US ◇ ▼ ⊙
Dir Mervyn LeRoy   *Prod* Mervyn LeRoy   *Scr* Andrew Solt, Sarah Y. Mason, Victor Heeman   *Ph* Robert Planck, Charles Schoenbaum   *Ed* Ralph E. Winters   *Mus* Adolph Deutsch   *Art Dir* Cedric Gibbons, Paul Groesse
● June Allyson, Peter Lawford, Margaret O'Brien, Elizabeth Taylor, Janet Leigh, Rossano Brazzi (M-G-M)

Metro has combined a star constellation for its unstinting re-make of Louisa May Alcott's *Little Women*, the old-lace classic of a quartet of daughters and their strivings in Civil War years.

The tender story, with its frank and unashamed assault on the emotions, still has its effective moments at times when the sentiment doesn't grow a little too thick.

Playing Jo, the part which won critical plaudits for Katharine Hepburn in 1933, June Allyson's thesping dominates the film.

As Beth, the youngest of the group, Margaret O'Brien is peculiarly subdued except for one touching scene in which she speaks of her nearing death. In the two other most important parts, Elizabeth Taylor and Janet Leigh neatly counterfoil Allyson's irrepressible cavortings.
☐ 1949: Best Color Art Direction.
☐ Nomination: Best Color Cinematography

•••••••••••••••••••••••••••••••••

■ **LIVE AND LET DIE**

1973, 121 MINS, UK ◇ ▼ ⊙
Dir Guy Hamilton   *Prod* Albert R. Broccoli, Harry Saltzman   *Scr* Tom Mankiewicz   *Ph* Ted Moore   *Ed* Bert Bates, Raymond Poulton, John Shirley   *Mus* George Martin   *Art Dir* Syd Cain, Bob Laing, Peter Lamont
● Roger Moore, Yaphet Kotto, Jane Seymour, Clifton James, Julius W. Harris, Geoffrey Holder (United Artists/Eon)

Live and Let Die, the eighth Cubby Broccoli-Harry Saltzman film based on Ian Fleming's James Bond, introduces Roger Moore as an okay replacement for Sean Connery. The script reveals that plot lines have descended further to the level of the old Saturday afternoon serial.

Here Bond's assigned to ferret out mysterious goings on involving Yaphet Kotto, diplomat from a Caribbean island nation who in disguise also is a bigtime criminal. The nefarious scheme in his mind: give away tons of free heroin to create more American dopers and then he and the telephone company will be the largest monopolies. Jane Seymour, Kotto's tarot-reading forecaster, loses her skill after turning on to Bond-age.

The comic book plot meanders through a series of hardware production numbers. These include some voodoo ceremonies; a hilarious airplane-vs-auto pursuit scene; a double-decker bus escape from motorcycles and police cars; and a climactic inland waterway powerboat chase. Killer sharks, poisonous snakes and man-eating crocodiles also fail to deter Bond from his mission.
☐ 1973: Nomination: Best Song ('Live and Let Die')

•••••••••••••••••••••••••••••••••

■ **LIVE NOW PAY LATER**

1962, 104 MINS, UK
Dir Jay Lewis   *Prod* Jack Hanbury   *Scr* Jack Trevor Story   *Ph* Jack Hildyard   *Ed* Roger Cherrill   *Mus* Ron Grainer   *Art Dir* Lionel Couch
● Ian Hendry, June Ritchie, John Gregson, Liz Fraser, Geoffrey Keen, Andrew Cruickshank (Woodlands)

Jack Trevor Story's screenplay [from Jack Lindsay's novel, *All on the Never-Never*] has many amusing moments, but overall it is untidy and does not develop the personalities of some of the main characters sufficiently. Extraneous situations are dragged in without helping the plot development overmuch.

Ian Hendry plays a smart aleck, philandering, doublecrossing tallyman who, with two illegitimate babies to his discredit, still finds that the easiest way to bluff his femme patrons into getting hocked up to their eyebrows in installment buying is via the boudoir. The character has a certain brash, breezy assurance, but no charm. And that's the way Hendry plays it, to the point of irritation.

In most of the film he is trying to patch up a row that he has had with his steady girl friend. For the remainder, he is cheating his employer (John Gregson), a real estate agent and a string of creditors.

June Ritchie, as the main girl in the case, confirms the promising impression she made in her debut in *A Kind of Loving*, but she can do little in this cardboard role of wronged young mistress.

■ LIVES OF A BENGAL LANCER, THE

1935, 110 MINS, US ⓦ

Dir Henry Hathaway *Prod* Louis D. Lighton *Scr* Waldemar Young, John L. Balderston, Achmed Abdullah, Grover Jones, W.S. McNutt *Ph* Charles Lang, Ernest Schoedsack, Ellsworth Hoagland *Mus* Milan Roder *Art Dir* Hans Dreier, Roland Anderson
● Gary Cooper, Franchot Tone, Richard Cromwell, Guy Standing, C. Aubrey Smith, Akim Tamiroff (Paramount)

Work on *Lancer* commenced four years earlier when Ernest Schoedsack went to India for exteriors and atmosphere. Some of the Schoedsack stuff is still in, but in those four years the original plans were kicked around until lost. Included in the scrapping was the Francis Yeats-Brown novel.

From the book only the locale and title have been retained. With these slim leads five studio writers went to work on a story, and they turned in a pip. In theme and locale *Lancer* is of the *Beau Geste* school. A sweeping, thrilling military narrative in Britain's desert badlands.

There is a stirring emotional conflict between father and son, the former a traditional British commander with whom discipline and loyalty to the service come first, and the boy rebelling at his father's cold-blooded attitude.

Gary Cooper and Franchot Tone, as a pair of experienced officers, are not directly involved in the main theme beyond being actuated by it, but they are the picture's two most important characters and provide the story with its dynamite.

Story concerns their rescue of the colonel's son after the latter's disillusionment over his father's reception of him in a setup for capture by a warring native chieftain.

Tone establishes himself as a first-rate light comedian. But in their own way Cooper, Sir Guy Standing, Richard Cromwell, C. Aubrey Smith and Douglas Dumbrille also turn in some first-rate trouping.
□ 1935: Best Assistant Directors (Clem Beauchamp, Paul Wing).
□ Nominations: Best Picture, Director, Screenplay, Art Direction, Editing, Sound

■ LIVING DAYLIGHTS, THE

1987, 130 MINS, UK ◇ ⓦ ⊙

Dir John Glen *Prod* Albert R. Broccoli, Michael G. Wilson *Scr* Richard Maibaum, Michael G. Wilson *Ph* Alec Mills *Ed* John Grover, Peter Davies *Mus* John Barry *Art Dir* Peter Lamont
● Timothy Dalton, Maryam d'Abo, Jeroen Krabbe, Joe Don Baker, John Rhys-Davies, Art Malik (United Artists/Eon)

Timothy Dalton, the fourth Bond, registers beautifully on all key counts of charm, machismo, sensitivity and technique. In *The Living Daylights* he's abetted by material that's a healthy cut above the series norm of super-hero fantasy.

There's a more mature story of its kind, too, this one about a phony KGB defector involved in gunrunning and a fraternal assassination plot.

There are even some relatively touching moments of romantic contact between Dalton and lead femme Maryam d'Abo as Czech concert cellist. Belatedly, the Bond characterization has achieved appealing maturity.

D'Abo, in a part meant to be something more than that of window-dressed mannikin, handles her chores acceptably. Able support is turned in by Joe Don Baker as a nutcase arms seller, Jeroen Krabbe and John Rhys-Davies as respective KGB bad and good types (a little less arch than the usual types), and Art Malik as an Oxford-educated Afghan freedom fighter.

■ LIVING FREE

1972, 90 MINS, UK ◇ ⓦ

Dir Jack Couffer *Prod* Paul Radin *Scr* Millard Kaufman *Ph* Wolfgang Suschitzky *Ed* Don Deacon *Mus* Sol Kaplan *Art Dir* John Stoll
● Nigel Davenport, Susan Hampshire, Geoffrey Keen, Edward Judd (Open Road/Highroad)

The same loving care that characterized *Born Free*, based on the true-life experiences of a British couple in Kenya and their pet lioness Elsa, is evident in the sequel.

Sensitive screenplay, based on the Joy Adamson book of her and her gamewarden-husband's efforts to assure that the cubs, following the death of their mother, shall live free and not be sent to a zoo, often carries a dramatic pitch. Possibly the most remarkable facet of picture is the animal photography of the cubs and other beasts that they encounter.

Some slight confusion exists in opening reels as the past of Elsa is reviewed briefly, but script develops logically as Nigel Davenport and Susan Hampshire, as the couple, are faced with the problem of the cubs' future after they turn to raiding natives' goat herds. Davenport resigns as a warden to devote himself entirely to capturing cubs and transporting them to a game preserve 700 miles distant.

■ LOCAL HERO

1983, 111 MINS, UK ◇ ⓦ ⊙

Dir Bill Forsyth *Prod* David Puttnam *Scr* Bill Forsyth *Ph* Chris Menges *Ed* Michael Bradsell *Mus* Mark Knopfler *Art Dir* Roger Murray-Leach
● Burt Lancaster, Peter Riegert, Fulton MacKay, Denis Lawson, Norman Chancer, Peter Capaldi (Enigma/Goldcrest)

While modest in intent and gentle in feel, *Local Hero* is loaded with wry, offbeat humor.

Basic story has Peter Riegert, rising young executive in an enormous Houston oil firm, sent to Scotland to clinch a deal to buy up an entire village, where the company intends to construct a new oil refinery. Far from being resistant to the idea of having their surroundings ruined by rapacious, profit-minded Yankees, local Scots can hardly wait to sign away their town, so strong is the smell of money in the air.

Back in Houston, oil magnate Burt Lancaster keeps up to date on the deal's progress with occasional phone calls to Riegert, but is more concerned with his prodding, sadistic psychiatrist and his obsessive hobby of astronomy, which seems to dictate everything he does.

Riegert's underplaying initially seems a bit inexpressive, but ultimately pays off in a droll performance. As his Scottish buddy, the gangling Peter Capaldi is vastly amusing, and Denis Lawson is very good as the community's chief spokesman.

■ LOCKET, THE

1947, 83 MINS, US ⓦ

Dir John Brahm *Prod* Bert Granet *Scr* Sheridan Gibney *Ph* Nicholas Musuraca *Ed* J.R. Whittredge *Mus* Roy Webb *Art Dir* Albert S. D'Agostino, Alfred Herman
● Laraine Day, Brian Aherne, Robert Mitchum, Gene Raymond, Richard Cortez (RKO)

The Locket is a case history of a warped mind and its effect on the lives of those it touches intimately. Vehicle is a strong one for Laraine Day and she does much with the role of Nancy, a girl with an abnormal obsession that wrecks the lives of four men who love her.

Nancy is a young woman, marked in childhood by the cruel misunderstanding of a rich lady in whose home her mother is housekeeper. The misunderstanding, over a missing locket, influence Nancy to strange acts in her adult life.

Story carries the flashback technique to greater lengths than generally employed. The writing by Sheridan Gibney displays an understanding of the subject matter and proves a solid basis for the able performances achieved by John Brahm's direction. Latter gears his scenes for full interest and carefully carries forward the doubt – and audience hope – that Nancy is not the villainess.

■ LOCK UP

1989, 105 MINS, US ◇ ⓦ ⊙

Dir John Flynn *Prod* Lawrence Gordon, Charles Gordon *Scr* Richard Smith, Jeb Stuart, Henry Rosenbaum *Ph* Michael N. Thorin *Ed* Michael N. Knue, Donald Brochu *Mus* Bill Conti *Art Dir* Bill Kenney
● Sylvester Stallone, Donald Sutherland, John Amos, Sonny Landham, Tom Sizemore, Frank McRae (White Eagle/Carolco)

Lock Up is made in the same, simplistic vein as most other Sylvester Stallone pics – putting him, the blue-collar protagonist, against the odds over which he ultimately prevails.

Emotional guy that he is, Stallone couldn't wait for his six-month prison term to be up because in the meantime his foster father may die, so he escapes to see him one last time. It seems his cold-hearted warden (Donald Sutherland) wouldn't allow him a supervised furlough to make the trip.

As revealed through the monosyllabic posturing, Sutherland is the vengeful, sadistic type.

The rest of the film is Stallone trying to survive 'hell' that Sutherland, as the Devil, has diabolically allowed to run amok.

Short of ordering, 'kill, kill,' Sutherland allows certain of his uniformed henchmen backed up by lifer prisoner/ringleader Chink (Sonny Landham) to bring Stallone down.

Darlanne Fluegel, as his faithful girlfriend, shows up occasionally to present the soft side of things but her character's only interesting attribute is that she's not a man.

■ LOCK UP YOUR DAUGHTERS!

1969, 102 MINS, UK ◇ ⓦ

Dir Peter Coe *Prod* David Deutsch *Scr* Keith Waterhouse, Willis Hall *Ph* Peter Suschitzky *Mus* Ron Grainer *Art Dir* Tony Woollard
● Christopher Plummer, Susannah York, Glynis Johns, Ian Bannen, Tom Bell, Elaine Taylor (Columbia/Domino)

Much of the wit and satire in this portrait of the permissive morals and the corruptive

451

decay of the 18th century is blunted, making it a noisy, bawdy, slapstick yarn about three sex-starved sailors on the rampage.

The scrappy storyline, drawn from Henry Fielding's *Rape Upon Rape* and John Vanbrugh's Restoration comedy *The Relapse*, plus the Mermaid Theatre musical written by Bernard Miles, can hardly be defined. It centers around the romantic entanglements of three wenches and their sailors which, after many misfortunes, complications and misunderstandings, land practically everybody in court.

Christopher Plummer as Lord Foppington hardly does his screen reputation much good. He plays the effete aristocrat in a mannered way but extracts only exaggerated humor from it.

■ LODGER, THE
(US: The Phantom Fiend)

1932, 85 MINS, UK
Dir Maurice Elvey *Prod* Julius Hagen *Scr* Ivor Novello, Miles Mander, Paul Rotha, H. Fowler Mear *Ph* Basil Emmott, Sydney Blythe
● Ivor Novello, Elizabeth Allan, Jack Hawkins, A. W. Baskcomb, Barbara Everest, Peter Gawthorne (Twickenham)

The Lodger, from the novel by Mrs Belloc Lowndes, was made as a silent some years previously. Despite its subject of Jack the Ripper, this is an eerie, absorbing story without being morbid.

Running parallel with the narration of the frightful murders is a sweet love story, gentle and poetic. Ivor Novello plays a sensitive musician with a sorrow so great he is unable to confide in anyone, not even the girl he loves, and who tells him she would believe anything he told her. Novello has an arresting personality, which photographs romantically.

Love scenes are ably supported by Elizabeth Allan, whose depiction of a working girl carried off her feet by a romantic, soulful musician is a fine piece of acting.

■ LODGER, THE

1944, 84 MINS, US
Dir John Brahm *Prod* Robert Bassler *Scr* Barre Lyndon *Ph* Lucien Ballard *Ed* J. Watson Webb *Mus* Hugo Friedhofer *Art Dir* James Basevi, John Ewing
● Merle Oberon, George Sanders, Laird Cregar, Cedric Hardwicke, Sara Allgood, Aubrey Mather (20th Century-Fox)

With a pat cast, keen direction and tight scripting, 20th-Fox has an absorbing and, at times, spine-tingling drama concocted from Marie Belloc Lowndes' novel *The Lodger*. It's a super chiller-diller in its picturization of a Scotland Yard manhunt for London's Jack the Ripper.

Director John Brahm and scripter Barre Lyndon make it as much a psychological study of the halfcrazed 'Lodger' (Laird Cregar), as if in a deftly-paced horrific whodunit in trying to outline some explanation for the repeated throatslashings of London stage women, neither has even slightly deviated from the swift weaving of events. Aside from preliminary steps, sequence of events mounts in rapid succession with suspense injected time after time with telling effect.

It is Laird Cregar's picture. As 'The Ripper' he gives an impressive performance. It is a relentless, at times pathetic character as he pursues his self-appointed task of avenging his brother. His precise diction and almost studied poise make his characterization all the more impressive.

Merle Oberon is highly effective as Kitty, the dancer, of respectable family whose stardom is nearly abruptly ended. Stage sequences show her a graceful dancer in abbreviated skirt and provide the bright

contrast to somber and melodramatic passages. Kept more or less in the background initially, her scene in the dressing room, when she pleads for her life, is the high dramatic spot of the production. George Sanders, cast as a sleuth, is strong.

■ LOGAN'S RUN

1976, 118 MINS, US ◇ ⊕ ⊙
Dir Michael Anderson *Prod* Saul David *Scr* David Zelag Goodman *Ph* Ernest Laszlo *Ed* Bob Wyman *Mus* Jerry Goldsmith *Art Dir* Dale Hennesy
● Michael York, Richard Jordan, Jenny Agutter, Roscoe Lee Browne, Farrah Fawcett, Michael Anderson Jr (M-G-M)

Logan's Run is a rewarding futuristic film that appeals both as spectacular-looking escapist adventure as well as intelligent drama.

Heading the cast are Michael York and Richard Jordan, two members of a security guard force which supervises the life of a domed-in hedonistic civilization all comprised of persons under the age of 30; after that, the civilization's tribal rules call for a ceremony called 'renewal', though nobody's quite sure what that entails.

York, intrigued and abetted by Jenny Agutter, decides to flee, with Jordan. Peter Ustinov is featured as a withered old man living alone on the outside, in the ruins of Washington, DC.

The three young principals and Ustinov come off very well.
□ 1976: Honorary Award (visual effects).
□ Nominations: Best Cinematography, Art Direction

■ LOLITA

1962, 152 MINS, US ⊕ ⊙
Dir Stanley Kubrick *Prod* James B. Harris *Scr* Vladimir Nabokov *Ph* Oswald Morris *Ed* Anthony Harvey *Mus* Nelson Riddle *Art Dir* Bill Andrews, Syd Cain
● James Mason, Shelley Winters, Peter Sellers, Sue Lyon, Gary Cockrell, Jerry Stovin (M-G-M)

Vladimir Nabokov's witty, grotesque novel is, in its film version, like a bee from which the stinger has been removed. It still buzzes with a sort of promising irreverence, but it lacks the power to shock and, eventually, makes very little point either as comedy or satire. The novel has been stripped of its pubescent heroine and most of its lively syntax, graphic honesty and sharp observations on people and places in a land abundant with cliches.

The result is an occasionally amusing but shapeless film about a middleaged professor who comes to no good end through his involvement with a well-developed teenager. The fact that the first third of the picture is so good, bristling with Nabokovisms – a gun, for example, referred to as a tragic treasure – underscores the final disappointment.

There is much about the film that is excellent. James Mason has never been better than he is as erudite Humbert Humbert, driven by a furious passion for a rather slovenly, perverse 'nymphet' (a term, incidentally, which is used only once in the entire film). He is especially good in the early sequences as he pursues Lolita to the point where he even marries her mother, whom Shelley Winters plays to bumptious perfection.

Matching these two performances is that of Peter Sellers who, as a preposterously smug American playwright (Mason's rival for Lolita's affections), gets a chance to run through several hilarious changes of character.

Sue Lyon makes an auspicious film debut as the deceitful child-woman who'd just as soon go to a movie as romp in the hay. It's a difficult assignment and if she never quite registers as either wanton or pathetic it may be due as much to the compromises of the script as to her inexperience.

□ 1962: Nomination: Best Adapted Screenplay

■ LOLLY-MADONNA WAR, THE
See: Lolly-Madonna XXX

■ LOLLY-MADONNA XXX
(UK: The Lolly-Madonna War)

1973, 105 MINS, US ◇
Dir Richard C. Sarafian *Prod* Rodney Carr-Smith *Scr* Rodney Carr-Smith, Sue Grafton *Ph* Philip Lathrop *Ed* Tom Rolf *Mus* Fred Myrow *Art Dir* Herman Blumenthal
● Rod Steiger, Robert Ryan, Jeff Bridges, Scott Wilson, Katherine Squire, Tresa Hughes (M-G-M)

Sue Grafton's novel, *The Lolly-Madonna War*, has been handsomely and sensitively filmed. Excellent performances abound by older and younger players in a mountain-country clan feud story which mixes extraordinary human compassion with raw but discreet violence.

It doesn't take much extrapolation effort to lift the story from its down-home setting and transpose it to the level of national and international politics.

Rod Steiger heads one clan, which also includes Katherine Squire in outstanding performance as his wife, plus Scott Wilson, Timothy Scott, Ed Lauter, Randy Quaid and Jeff Bridges as the sons. The opposition clan is headed by Robert Ryan, with Tresa Hughes also outstanding as his wife. A land dispute has brought the families to the edge of violence.

Trigger for the explosion is a fake postcard sent by Kiel Martin, signed by a non-existent, apparent bride-to-be named Lolly-Madonna with three X's appended in the childish manner. Wilson and Lauter, having glommed the postcard as Martin knew they would, kidnap Season Hubley, a traveler who arrives at the moment when the fake bride was to have met her husband-to-be.

Steiger and Ryan dominate the film through their children's actions, and director Richard C. Sarafian has endowed the picture with a moody, menacing atmosphere.

■ LONDON KILLS ME

1991, 107 MINS, UK ◇ ⊕ ⊙
Dir Hanif Kureishi *Prod* Tim Bevan *Scr* Hanif Kureishi *Ph* Ed Lachman *Ed* Jon Gregory *Mus* Mark Springer, Sarah Sarhandi *Art Dir* Stuart Walker
● Justin Chadwick, Steven Mackintosh, Emer McCourt, Roshan Seth, Fiona Shaw, Brad Dourif (Polygram/Working Title)

Hanif Kureishi's *London Kills Me*, a flabby slice of London street life among pushers and hustlers, drags itself across the screen for 107 minutes and collapses in a dramatic mess on the sidewalk. First directorial outing by the Anglo-Pakistani scripter of *My Beautiful Laundrette* and *Sammy and Rosie Get Laid* shows the same interest in London's culturally mixed sub-life, sans anti-Thatcherism subtext.

Main character is the Candide-like Clint (Justin Chadwick), who hangs out with a group led by small-time dealer Muffdiver (Steven Mackintosh). To raise the cash for a job in a swank local eatery, Clint joins in Muffdiver's plans to go big time and helps himself to latter's hidden stash. He's also got eyes for Muffdiver's heroin-hooked g.f. Sylvie (Emer McCourt).

Loose plot trawls in a host of other characters, including a sex-obsessed liberal (Fiona Shaw), an Indian (Roshan Seth) who runs a Sufi center and Clint's mom (Eleanor David), who lives in the country with a thuggish, middle-aged Elvis freak (Alun Armstrong).

What was obviously meant as an ironic look at lost souls in 1990s London rapidly blurs

L

into a string of undramatic incidents. Pic recalls free-living late 1960s items, but without their buzz and color. Result, under Kureishi's unfocused helming, is drab.

••••••••••••••••••••••••••••

■ **LONELINESS OF THE LONG DISTANCE RUNNER, THE**

1962, 104 MINS, UK ⑰ ⊙
Dir Tony Richardson   *Prod* Tony Richardson   *Scr* Alan Sillitoe   *Ph* Walter Lassally   *Ed* Antony Gibbs
Mus John Addison   *Art Dir* Ralph Brinton
● Tom Courtenay, Michael Redgrave, James Bolam, Avis Bunnage, Alec McCowen, Julia Foster (Woodfall)

It is difficult to conjure up much sympathy for the young 'hero' who comes out as a disturbed young layabout (he seems thoroughly to deserve his fate of landing in Borstal, the corrective establishment for British juve delinquents). Yet the performance of Tom Courtenay and the imaginative, if sometimes overfussy, direction of Tony Richardson, plus some standout lensing by Walter Lassally makes this a worthwhile pic.

Alan Sillitoe has written a sound screenplay for his own short story. Though there are obvious signs of padding, it remains a thoroughly professional job. The flashback technique is used ingeniously, though perhaps overmuch.

Courtenay plays a young man from an unhappy home in the Midlands. Apparently on the ground that the world owes him a living, he seems not interested in work and, inevitably drifts into petty crime and gets sent to Borstal.

He is resentful about 'the system' and takes a strange way of getting back at it. A natural born runner ('we had plenty of practice in running away from the police in our family,' he says bitterly), he is selected to represent Borstal in a long distance race against a public school team. It is the ambition of the governor (Michael Redgrave) to win the cup for Borstal.

Michael Redgrave as the rather pompous, stuffy governor who, to Courtenay's jaundiced eye, represents the system, brings his polished touch to a role that could have become irritating.

••••••••••••••••••••••••••••

■ **LONELY ARE THE BRAVE**

1962, 107 MINS, US ⑰
Dir David Miller   *Prod* Edward Lewis   *Scr* Dalton Trumbo   *Ph* Philip Lathrop   *Ed* Leon Barsha   *Mus* Jerry Goldsmith   *Art Dir* Alexander Golitzen, Robert E. Smith
● Kirk Douglas, Gena Rowlands, Walter Matthau, Michael Kane, Carroll O'Connor, Bill Bixby (Universal)

Often touching, and well served by its performances and photography, *Lonely Are the Brave* ultimately blurs its focus on the loner fenced in and bemused by the encroachments and paradoxes of civilization. Its makers have approached the misfit theme with a skittishness not unlike that exhibited by cowboy Kirk Douglas's horse. They have settled for surface instead of substance.

The failure of the Dalton Trumbo screenplay from an Edward Abbey novel [*Brave Cowboy*] is that it does not provide viewers with a sustained probing of the hero's perplexity.

The plot is sparing enough. Douglas, the footloose, arrives back at the New Mexico homestead of old friends Michael Kane and Gena Rowlands. Kane is in the Albuquerque jail on an aid-and-comfort to wetbacks rap, and good guy Douglas contrives to get himself tossed into the same pokey from where he plans to bust out with Kane. The buddy opts to stay, however – his ways are changed, and there is the wife and a son to consider – but Douglas, not one for the year's confinement he faces, makes off and takes to the hills ringing town.

As the loner, Douglas is extremely likable and understands his part within its limitations, as written. Most beguiling performance, however, is turned in by Walter Matthau as the laconic and harassed sheriff, who has never faced his quarry but develops an intuitive sympathy for him.

••••••••••••••••••••••••••••

■ **LONELY GUY, THE**

1984, 90 MINS, US ◇ ⑰ ⊙
Dir Arthur Hiller   *Prod* Arthur Hiller   *Scr* Ed Weinberger, Stan Daniels   *Ph* Victor J. Kemper
Ed William Reynolds, Raja Gosnell   *Mus* Jerry Goldsmith
Art Dir James D. Vance
● Steve Martin, Charles Grodin, Judith Ivey, Steven Lawrence, Robyn Douglass, Merv Griffin (Universal)

Derived from a comic tome by Bruce Jay Friedman, premise has Steve Martin bounced by sexpot girlfriend Robyn Douglass and thereby banished to the world of Lonely Guys. He meets and commiserates with fellow LG Charles Grodin, who gets Martin to buy a fern with him and throws a party attended only by Martin and a bunch of life-sized cardboard cutouts of celebs like Dolly Parton and Tom Selleck.

Finally, Martin meets cute blonde Judith Ivey, who, having been previously married to six Lonely Guys, instantly falls for him.

Martin's trademark wacky humor is fitfully in evidence, but seems much more repressed than usual in order to fit into the relatively realistic world of single working people.

••••••••••••••••••••••••••••

■ **LONELY HEARTS**

1982, 95 MINS, AUSTRALIA ◇ ⑰ ⊙
Dir Paul Cox   *Prod* John B. Murray   *Scr* Paul Cox, John Clarke   *Ph* Yuri Sokol   *Ed* Tim Lewis   *Mus* Norman Kaye   *Art Dir* Neil Angwin
● Wendy Hughes, Norman Kaye, Jon Finlayson, Julia Blake, Jonathan Hardy (Adams-Packer)

A slowly-developing romance between a 50-ish bachelor piano tuner and a 30-ish spinsterly bank clerk hardly seems the stuff from which viable motion pictures are made. Director Paul Cox's treatment of his own story is dull, plodding and uninspiring fare.

Norman Kaye plays Peter, a nervous, vapid character who is so weak he nearly recedes into the woodwork. Wendy Hughes is Patricia, dowdy, sexually repressed, and, smothered by her parents. They meet through a dating service after his mother dies, and embark on possibly the world's longest and dreariest courtship.

Both Kaye and Hughes struggle to make their characters interesting or engaging. A few all-too-rare lively moments are provided by Julia Blake as Peter's overbearing sister, Jon Finlayson as a camp theatre director, and Ronald Falk as a twee wig salesman.

••••••••••••••••••••••••••••

■ **LONELY PASSION OF JUDITH HEARNE, THE**

1987, 110 MINS, UK ◇ ⑰
Dir Jack Clayton   *Prod* Peter Nelson, Richard Johnson
Scr Peter Nelson   *Ph* Peter Hannan   *Ed* Terry Rawlings
Mus Georges Delerue   *Art Dir* Michael Pickwood
● Maggie Smith, Bob Hoskins, Wendy Hiller, Marie Kean, Ian McNeice, Prunella Scales (HandMade/United British Artists)

An ensemble of sterling performances highlights *The Lonely Passion of Judith Hearne*, an intelligent, carefully crafted adaptation of Brian Moore's well-regarded first novel. Film's centerpiece is Maggie Smith's exceptionally detailed portrait of the title character, a middle-aged Irish spinster who tragically deludes herself into imagining herself involved in a great romance.

Judith is a fragile bird, a part-time piano teacher in 1950s Dublin who has every reason

to be desperate about life but still manages to look on the bright side. Moving into a new boarding house, she takes a liking to her landlady's brother James (Bob Hoskins), a widower recently returned from 30 years in New York, and begins stepping out with him.

Once James takes her to a fancy dinner at the Shelbourne Hotel, Judith is sure his intentions are serious. Unfortunately, she allows a misunderstanding between them to assume traumatic proportions, and her heartbreak and disappointment lead her down a spiraling road of despair, alcoholism, ostracism and religious rejection.

Hoskins, laying a brash New York accent over a hint of the Irish, brings great energy and creative bluster to the irrepressible dreamer who has been instilled with Yankee get-up-and-go.

••••••••••••••••••••••••••••

■ **LONE WOLF McQUADE**

1983, 107 MINS, US ◇ ⑰
Dir Steve Carver   *Prod* Yoram Ben-Ami, Steve Carver
Scr B.J. Nelson   *Ph* Roger Shearman   *Ed* Anthony Redman   *Ph* Francesco De Masi   *Art Dir* Norm Baron
● Chuck Norris, David Carradine, Barbara Carrera, Leon Isaac Kennedy, Robert Beltran, L.Q. Jones (1818 Production/Orion)

Fans of *Soldier of Fortune* magazine will think they've been ambushed and blown away to heaven by *Lone Wolf McQuade*. Every conceivable type of portable weapon on the world market is tried out by the macho warriors on both sides of the law in this modern western [story by H. Kaye Dyal and B. J. Nelson], which pits Texas Ranger Chuck Norris and his cohorts against multifarious baddies who like to play rough.

Opening sequence, showing the grizzled Norris busting up a gang of Mexican horse rustlers, makes it clear that film's primary source of inspiration is Sergio Leone.

Vile David Carradine is in the business of hijacking US Army weapons shipments and selling them to Central American terrorist groups. Norris and FBI agent Leon Isaac Kennedy finally locate Carradine's secret airstrip, and after a setback there, track him down at a compound loaded with all manner of armaments.

••••••••••••••••••••••••••••

■ **LONG AGO TOMORROW**

See: The Raging Moon

••••••••••••••••••••••••••••

■ **LONG AND THE SHORT AND THE TALL, THE**

(US: Jungle Fighters)

1961, 105 MINS, UK ⑰
Dir Leslie Norman   *Prod* Michael Balcon   *Scr* Wolf Mankowitz   *Ph* Erwin Hillier   *Ed* Gordon Stone
Mus Stanley Black   *Art Dir* Terence Verity, Jim Morahan
● Richard Todd, Laurence Harvey, Richard Harris, Ronald Fraser, David McCallum, John Meillon (Associated British)

Director and scriptwriter have not been able to resist the temptation to take a great deal of Willis Hall's war play into the open air of the jungle. This is a pity. It loses the sense of pent-in suspense that marked the play so effectively and it also shows up the fact that the Elstree 'jungle' is rather phoney.

Film depends on characterization rather than on the thinnish plot. It's set in the Far East jungle during the Japanese campaign. A small patrol led by a sergeant (Richard Todd) is cut off. Suddenly 'sparks' makes radio contact and jabbering Japanese voices nearby cause them to realize that they're in a spot.

A lone Japanese scout moves into their position and Todd insists that they must get him back to base alive as a source of information. The remainder want to bump him off with the solitary, surprise exception of a loud-mouthed and brash private (Laurence Harvey).

Standout performance comes from Harvey. It is dramatic license that enables him to behave in a way that would undoubtedly have had him up on a charge in a real situation.

The bewildered Jap, subtly played by Kenji Takaki, is another very sound performance. In fact there is no weak link in the cast. Todd is a dogged, worried sergeant; Richard Harris shapes very good as his righthand man, and Ronald Fraser is fine as a dour Scot.

••••••••••••••••••••••••••••••

■ LONG DAY CLOSES, THE

1992, 83 MINS, UK ◇ ⓦ ⊙
Dir Terence Davies   *Prod* Olivia Stewart   *Scr* Terence Davies   *Ph* Michael Coulter   *Ed* William Diver   *Mus* Bob Last, Robert Lockhart   *Art Dir* Christopher Hobbs
● Marjorie Yates, Leigh McCormack, Anthony Watson, Nicholas Lamont, Ayse Owens, Tina Malone (BFI/Film Four)

Terence Davies' *The Long Day Closes* is a technically elaborate, dryly witty moodpiece centered on a shy young daydreamer in mid-1950s working-class Liverpool. Pic builds on the basic elements of Davies' 1988 *Distant Voices, Still Lives*, with a free-form ride down the helmer's memory lane of family, friends, Catholicism and cinema.

Central character is Bud (movingly limned by 13-year-old newcomer Leigh McCormack), a shy loner who's given a hard time at school, idolizes his mom (Marjorie Yates) and elder sister (Ayse Owens), and finds escape from the greyness of Britain in movie theaters. There's little resolution in conventional terms: Davies simply builds a kaleidoscope out of memory fragments and shakes it every which way in a series of visual vignettes.

Pic's major weakness is its stop-go tempo. Individual segs are stunningly mounted but there is a lack of a longer dramatic line, a reluctance to go with the flow. Davies is still a miniaturist working in a feature-length format.

Nonbuffs could be flummoxed by the soundtrack, a knowing mix of popular melodies, snatches of movie dialog and M-G-M baubles. But strength of Davies' vision is the crux, and holds the line to the final, confident fadeout. Perfs by the no-name cast are all on the money.

••••••••••••••••••••••••••••••

■ LONG DAY'S DYING, THE

1968, 93 MINS, UK ◇
Dir Peter Collinson   *Prod* Harry Fine, Peter Collinson   *Scr* Charles Wood   *Ph* Brian Probyn   *Ed* John Trumper   *Art Dir* Disley Jones
● David Hemmings, Tom Bell, Tony Beckley, Alan Dobie (Paramount)

The Long Day's Dying is a bore. In tracing the steps of three British soldiers and their German captive during a single day of weary trekking through the European countryside, it adds nothing in the way of insight or impact to the dreary platitudes of countless previous anti-war pix.

Charles Wood's script is lacking in dramatic momentum and fails to clarify the four protagonists' characters. Even worse, no sympathy or interest is developed for any of the men.

Script's use of interior monologs is clumsy, frequently counterpointing the various men's thoughts in an archly poetic way and never helping to define their inner natures.

Direction by Peter Collinson is lackluster. When not relying on established tricks of documentary filmmaking or more up-to-date visual affectations, he holds on closeups of his 'thinking' actors. Fact that all four players register little beyond grim impassivity hardly lightens the pace of this lethargic film.

••••••••••••••••••••••••••••••

■ LONG DAY'S JOURNEY INTO NIGHT

1962, 176 MINS, US ⓦ
Dir Sidney Lumet   *Prod* Ely Landau   *Ph* Boris Kaufman   *Ed* Ralph Rosenbaum   *Mus* Andre Previn   *Art Dir* Richard Sylbert
● Katharine Hepburn, Ralph Richardson, Jason Robards, Dean Stockwell, Jeanne Barr (Landau)

This is an excellent film adaption of the late Eugene O'Neill's lengthy stage work. It has power in its characters and their tortured introspective lives. There have been a few cuts but otherwise it is as O'Neill wrote it. And his powerful language manages to overcome the limited sets and dependence on the spoken word.

It takes a family through the probing of themselves, their relations and their relative reasons for acting as they do. It all develops when the mother one day begins to sink back to drug addiction.

Katharine Hepburn's beautifully boned face mirrors her anguish and needs. She makes the role of the mother breathtaking and intensely moving. There is balance, depth and breadth in her acting. Ralph Richardson brings his authority to the part of the miserly father who had made money as a theatrical matinee idol but can't shake his skinflint habits because of a childhood of poverty. Jason Robards has flair and insight as the tortured older brother while Dean Stockwell is effective as the younger brother.

Made reportedly for $400,000, since the principals took minimum pay because of their desire to do the property.
□ 1962: Nomination: Best Actress (Katharine Hepburn)

••••••••••••••••••••••••••••••

■ LONG DUEL, THE

1967, 115 MINS, UK ◇
Dir Ken Annakin   *Prod* Ken Annakin   *Scr* Peter Yeldham   *Ph* Jack Hildyard   *Ed* Bert Bates   *Mus* John Scott   *Art Dir* Alex Vetchinsky
● Yul Brynner, Trevor Howard, Harry Andrews, Andrew Keir, Charlotte Rampling, Virginia North (Rank)

Produced and directed by Ken Annakin at Pinewood and on location in Granada, Spain, this is an ambitious actioner which has plenty of punch.

But the yarn, though based on fact, unfolds with little conviction and is repeatedly bogged down by labored dialog and characterization in Peter Yeldham's screenplay [based on a story by Ranveer Singh].

Story is set on the Indian Northwest Frontier during the 1920s and basically hinges on the uneasy relationship and lack of understanding between most of the British top brass and the native tribes. Trevor Howard, an idealistic police officer, is very conscious of the need for tact and diplomacy when handling the touchy natives.

When he is ordered to track down the Bhanta tribe leader (Yul Brynner), who is trying to lead his people from the bondage of the British, Howard recognizes Brynner as a fellow idealist and an enemy to respect.

••••••••••••••••••••••••••••••

■ LONGEST DAY, THE

1962, 180 MINS, US ⓦ ⊙
Dir Ken Annakin, Andrew Marton, Bernhard Wicki   *Prod* Darryl F. Zanuck   *Scr* Cornelius Ryan, Romain Gary, James Jones, David Pursall, Jack Seddon   *Ph* Jean Bourgoin, Henri Persin, Walter Wottitz   *Ed* Samuel E. Beetley   *Mus* Maurice Jarre   *Art Dir* Ted Haworth, Leon Barsacq, Vincent Korda
● John Wayne, Robert Mitchum, Henry Fonda, Robert Ryan, Richard Todd, Richard Burton (Zanuck/20th Century-Fox)

Darryl F. Zanuck achieves a solid and stunning war epic. From personal vignettes to big battles, it details the first day of the D-Day Landings by the Allies on 6 June 1944.

The savage fury and sound of war are ably caught on film. It emerges as a sort of grand scale semi-fictionalized documentary concerning the overall logistics needed for this incredible invasion. It carries its three hour length by the sheer tingle of the masses of manpower in action, peppered with little ironic, sad, silly actions that all add up to war.

The use of over 43 actual star names in bit and pivotal spots helps keep up the aura of fictionalized documentary. But it is the action, time and place, and the actual machinery of war, that are the things.

The battles ably take their places among some of the best ever put on the screen. A German strafing the beach, Yanks scaling a treacherous cliff only to find that there was no big gun there, British commandos taking a bridge, Yanks blowing up a big bunker, the French taking a town, all are done with massive pungent action. The black and white and CinemaScope screen help keep the focus on surge and movement.
□ 1962: Best B&W Cinematography, Special Effects.
□ Nominations: Best Picture, B&W Art Direction, Editing

••••••••••••••••••••••••••••••

■ LONGEST YARD, THE
(UK: The Mean Machine)

1974, 121 MINS, US ◇ ⓦ ⊙
Dir Robert Aldrich   *Prod* Albert S. Ruddy   *Scr* Tracy Keenan Wynn   *Ph* Joseph Biroc   *Ed* Michael Luciano   *Mus* Frank DeVol   *Art Dir* James S. Vance
● Burt Reynolds, Eddie Albert, Ed Lauter, Michael Conrad, Jim Hampton, Bernadette Peters (Paramount/Long Road)

The Longest Yard is an outstanding action drama, combining the brutish excitement of football competition with the brutalities of contemporary prison life. Burt Reynolds asserts his genuine star power, here as a former football pro forced to field a team under blackmail of warden Eddie Albert.

In contrast to most hard-action films, this is quality action drama, in which brute force is fully motivated and therefore totally acceptable. At the same time, the metaphysics of football are neatly interwoven with the politics and bestialities of totalitarian authority.

Script, from a story credited to producer Albert S. Ruddy, finds Reynolds arriving at Albert's prison. Ed Lauter, his chief guard, also coaches the guards' clumsy football team. Reynolds is forced to form an inmates' team from a ragtag bunch of cons, with a no-win payoff: if he loses, Lauter's guards will rub it in; if he wins, Albert's vengeance is certain.
□ 1974: Nomination: Best Editing

••••••••••••••••••••••••••••••

■ LONG GOODBYE, THE

1973, 112 MINS, US ◇ ⓦ ⊙
Dir Robert Altman   *Prod* Jerry Bick   *Scr* Leigh Brackett   *Ph* Vilmos Zsigmond   *Ed* Lou Lombardo   *Mus* John Williams
● Elliott Gould, Nina van Pallandt, Sterling Hayden, Henry Gibson, Mark Rydell, Jim Bouton (United Artists)

Robert Altman's film version of Raymond Chandler's novel is an uneven mixture of insider satire on the gumshow film genre, gratuitous brutality, and sledgehammer whimsy.

Leigh Brackett adapted the Chandler book; she, Jules Furthman and William Faulkner scripted Chandler's *The Big Sleep* [1946]. Herein, the Philip Marlowe character becomes embroiled in a Malibu murder, stolen money, the apparent death of his best friend, and compounded double-cross.

No longer the sardonic idealist, Marlowe has become part Walter Mitty. Elliott Gould keeps a low dramatic profile throughout as a passive catalyst. Nina van Pallandt makes an American film bow as the wife of dried-up author Sterling Hayden (Dan Blocker was to have been cast, and his passing is tributed in an end title card 'with special remembrance'), whose periodic disappearances include a visit to Henry Gibson's high-priced sanatorium.

Mark Rydell returns to acting after a decade of directing to play a kooky criminal, whose twisted mind runs to bashing in the face of Jo Ann Brody with a soft drink bottle.

■ **LONG GOOD FRIDAY, THE**

1981, 114 MINS, UK ◇ ⊛
Dir John Mackenzie *Prod* Barry Hanson *Scr* Barrie Keeffe *Ph* Phil Meheux *Ed* Mike Taylor *Mus* Francis Monkman *Art Dir* Vic Symonds
● Bob Hoskins, Helen Mirren, Eddie Constantine, Dave King, Brian Hall, Pierce Brosnan (Calendar/Black Lion)

In many respects a conventional thriller set in London's underworld, *The Long Good Friday* is much more densely plotted and intelligently scripted than most such yarns.

Bob Hoskins displays natural, and sizable, big-screen presence, and works out first-rate in the anchor role of a gangland boss faced with a series of seemingly gratuitous reprisals by unknown ill-wishers against his waterfront empire.

He starts as a larger-than-life figure, confidently negotiating American finance for a massive land development project. But Hoskins' overweening exterior crumbles as some of his best men are murdered.

When it becomes clear that his adversary is the provisional Irish Republican Army, he pits his Mafia-style muscle against the IRA's professional terrorism.

The narrative is steered competently, but visual style is too stolid to lend due gut-impact.

■ **LONG GRAY LINE, THE**

1955, 135 MINS, US ◇
Dir John Ford *Prod* Robert Arthur *Scr* Edward Hope *Ph* Charles Lawton Jr *Ed* William Lyon *Mus* George Duning *Art Dir* Robert Peterson
● Tyrone Power, Maureen O'Hara, Robert Francis, Ward Bond, Donald Crisp (Columbia)

The Long Gray Line is a standout drama on West Point.

For Tyrone Power the role of Marty Maher, Irishman through whose eyes the story is told, is a memorable one. Maureen O'Hara brings to the role of Maher's wife her Irish beauty and seldom displayed acting ability. Both are very fine.

Robert Arthur's exceptionally well-fashioned production is based on *Bringing Up the Brass*, the autobiography of Maher's 50 years at the Point which he wrote with Nardi Reeder Campion. A screenplay that is full of wonderfully human touches gives just the right foundation for John Ford to show his love for country (and the Irish) with his direction. Story oscillates between unashamed sniffles and warm chuckles, Ford not being afraid to bring a tear or stick in a laugh.

■ **LONG RIDERS, THE**

1980, 100 MINS, US ◇ ⊛ ⊙
Dir Walter Hill *Prod* Tim Zinnemann *Scr* Bill Bryden, Steven Phillip Smith, Stacy Keach, James Keach *Ph* Ric Waite *Ed* David Holden, Freeman Davies *Mus* Ry Cooder *Art Dir* Jack T. Collis
● David Carradine, Keith Carradine, Stacy Keach, James Keach, Dennis Quaid, Randy Quaid (United Artists)

The Long Riders is striking in several ways, not the least of which being the casting of actor brothers as historical outlaw kin, but narrative is episodic in the extreme.

Yarn opens in bang-up fashion with a bank robbery, after which trigger-happy Dennis

Quaid is kicked out of the Younger-James-Miller gang for needlessly murdering a man during stick-up. With no time frame provided, pic proceeds by alternating scenes of further crimes, the men at play in whorehouses and courting women, and the law bungling initial attempts to capture the troublemakers.

Director Walter Hill resolutely refuses to investigate the psychology or motivations of his characters, explaining away men's life of banditry as a 'habit' acquired in wake of the Civil War.

What's ultimately missing is a definable point of view which would tie together the myriad events on display and fill in the blanks which Hill has imposed on the action by sapping it of emotional or historical meaning.

■ **LONG SHADOW, THE**

1992, 89 MINS, US/HUNGARY/ISRAEL ◇ ⊛
Dir Vilmos Zsigmond *Prod* Janos Edelenyi, Paul Salamon *Scr* Paul Salamon, Janos Edelenyi *Ph* Gabor Szabo *Ed* Mari Miklos *Mus* Gyorgy Selmeczi *Art Dir* Avi Avivi, Laszlo Szoter
● Michael York, Liv Ullmann, Oded Teomi, Ava Haddad, Babi Neeman, Zoltan Gera (Prolitera)

Lush lensing and some eye-filling Israeli locations can't rescue *The Long Shadow*, a trite semi-meller sabotaged by the blah script and some dubious casting.

Michael York toplines weakly as a Hungarian Jew working out an Oedipus-Schmoedipus complex on a trip to the Holy Land. Directorial bow by Oscar-winning Magyar cinematographer Vilmos Zsigmond is strictly inflight fare.

Yarn opens in modern-day Budapest where famous legit actor Gabor (York) gets a letter telling him his father has died in Israel. There he bumps into his father's second wife, Katherine (Liv Ullmann), a Christian German who's stayed on in her adopted country. After some initial head-butting, the pair soon settle down into some heart-to-heart stuff at her mountainside retreat.

In the dual role of Gabor and his own father (seen in vid clips), York is seriously lightweight and even has trouble with a convincing Hungarian accent. Ullmann gives her best shot in an underwritten part.

■ **LONG SHIPS, THE**

1964, 124 MINS, UK/YUGOSLAVIA ◇ ⊛
Dir Jack Cardiff *Prod* Irving Allen *Scr* Berkely Mather, Beverley Cross *Ph* Christopher Challis *Ed* Geoff Foot *Mus* Dusan Radic *Art Dir* John Hoesli
● Richard Widmark, Sidney Poitier, Russ Tamblyn, Rosanna Schiaffino, Beba Loncar, Oscar Homolka (Columbia/Warwick/Avala)

Any attempt to put this into the epic class falls down because of a hodge-podge of a storyline, a mixture of styles and insufficient development of characterization.

The plot, which has obviously suffered in both editing and in censorial slaps, is a conglomeration of battles, double-crossing, seastorms, floggings, unarmed combat with occasional halfhearted peeks at sex. Throughout there's a great deal of noise and the very long drag.

Film [based on the novel by Frans G. Bengtsson] concerns the rivalry of the Vikings and the Moors in search of a legendary Golden Bell, the size of three men and containing 'half the gold in the world'. Leaders of the rival factions are Richard Widmark, an adventurous Viking con man, who plays strictly tongue in cheek, and Sidney Poitier, dignified, ruthless top man of the Moors. In contrast to Widmark, he seeks to take the film seriously. The clash in styles between these two is a minor disaster.

■ **LONGTIME COMPANION**

1990, 96 MINS, US ◇ ⊛
Dir Norman Rene *Prod* Stan Wlodkowski *Scr* Craig Lucas *Ph* Tony Jannelli *Ed* Katherine Wenning *Mus* Greg DeBelles *Art Dir* Andrew Jackness
● Bruce Davison, Campbell Scott, Stephen Caffrey, Mark Lamos, Patrick Cassidy, Mary-Louise Parker (American Playhouse)

The first feature film to tell the story of how AIDS devastated and transformed the gay community, *Longtime Companion* is simply an excellent film, with a graceful, often humorous script and affecting performances.

Story begins during the carefree pre-AIDS party days on Fire Island, where Willy (Campbell Scott) and Fuzzy (Stephen Caffrey) meet and begin a relationship that brings together an extended circle of friends. It's the same day a *New York Times* article announces a rare disease spreading among gay men. A year later, Willy's best friend John (Dermont Mulroney) becomes violently ill and dies. It's only the beginning. One by one, this community of actors, writers and lawyers is affected.

Among the most piercing events is the deterioration of a TV scripter, Sean (Mark Lamos), who is cared for by his lover, David (Bruce Davison), who owns the beach house where the friends always have gathered.

Strength of Craig Lucas' script is the way it weaves emotional and informational material together.
□ 1990: Nomination: Best Supp. Actor (Bruce Davison)

■ **LONG VOYAGE HOME, THE**

1940, 105 MINS, US ⊛ ⊙
Dir John Ford *Prod* Walter Wanger *Scr* Dudley Nichols *Ph* Gregg Toland *Ed* Sherman Todd *Mus* Richard Hageman *Art Dir* James Basevi
● John Wayne, Thomas Mitchell, Ian Hunter, Barry Fitzgerald, Wilfrid Lawson, Mildred Natwick (Wanger/United Artists)

Combining dramatic content of four Eugene O'Neill one-act plays, John Ford pilots adventures of a tramp steamer from the West Indies to an American port, and then across the Atlantic with cargo of high explosives. Picture is typically Fordian, his direction accentuating characterizations and adventures of the voyage.

Story plods along at slow tempo, making onlookers wonder when ship will finally make an English port safely. There's a rather confusing passage in which Ian Hunter, as a deckhand, is pictured as an enemy spy, and although he is finally cleared, nothing explains his actions that lead to original suspicions.

Aside from explosive cargo aboard, little interest is generated in final safety of crew, as yarn points out they are all men of the sea, who will ship out again soon as pay evaporates; all but John Wayne, who wants a nestegg for a farm in Sweden.

Along the voyage there's plenty of dialog and action in the crew's quarters, with Thomas Mitchell the accepted leader of the group. Storm at sea, in which ship's anchor breaks loose, is particularly realistic. Passage through the submarine zone with blackout restrictions is more informative than dramatic. Stuka-bombing and machine-gunning of the ship in sight of land is a dramatic excuse for heroic death of Hunter just before landing.

Mitchell hits a high mark in the seaman's character – two-fisted, domineering, and still kindly and loyal to his pals. Wayne's role is submerged among the sailor characters.
□ 1940: Nominations: Best Picture, Screenplay, B&W Cinematography, Editing, Original Score

■ LONG WALK HOME, THE

1990, 97 MINS, US ◊ ⑩ ⊙

Dir Richard Pearce   *Prod* Howard W. Koch Jr   *Scr* John Cork   *Ph* Roger Deakins   *Ed* Bill Yahraus   *Mus* George Fenton   *Art Dir* Blake Russell

● Sissy Spacek, Whoopi Goldberg, Dwight Schultz, Ving Rhames, Dylan Baker, Erika Alexander (New Visions)

Set in Montgomery, Alabama, during the 1955 civil rights bus boycott, *The Long Walk Home* is an effectively mounted drama about the human impact of changing times on two families, with sturdy performances by Sissy Spacek as an uppercrust white housewife and Whoopi Goldberg as her maid.

Spacek's Miriam Thompson is a prim model of upper-middle-class Southern womanhood who cannot run her household without her indispensable maid Odessa.

Racist jokes are commonplace during cocktail parties and family dinners, where Spacek's brother-in-law (Dylan Baker) espouses hard-line segregationist attitudes.

Goldberg's hard-working husband (Ving Rhames) and three well-mannered kids make a loving family, but the household's mood is tense because of external events. Local black leaders call for a bus boycott to end segregated seating. As the black boycott stiffens, so does white resistance, which turns ugly with the bombing of Martin Luther King's house. Afraid of change, the town establishment refuses to compromise.

The film resists the temptation to succumb to sentimentality and offers believable characterizations in the context of its time and place.

....

■ LOOK BACK IN ANGER

1959, 115 MINS, UK ⑩

Dir Tony Richardson   *Prod* Gordon L.T. Scott   *Scr* Nigel Kneale, John Osborne   *Ph* Oswald Morris   *Ed* Richard Best   *Mus* John Addison (sup.), Chris Barber and His Band   *Art Dir* Peter Glazier

● Richard Burton, Claire Bloom, Mary Ure, Edith Evans, Gary Raymond, Donald Pleasence (Woodfall)

Tony Richardson, who staged the play, *Look Back in Anger*, which helped to hoist John Osborne into the bigtime, tackles the same subject as his first directorial chore. Richardson's is a technical triumph, but somewhere along the line he has lost the heart and the throb that made the play an adventure. The film simultaneously impresses and depresses.

In the play, Jimmy Porter was a rebel – but a mixed-up weakling of a rebel. In the film, as played by Richard Burton, he is an arrogant young man who thinks the world owes him something but cannot make up his mind what it is – and certainly doesn't deserve the handout.

Burton glowers sullenly, violently and well as Porter and it is not his fault that the role gives him little opportunity for variety. Mary Ure (repeating her London & Broadway stage role) as the downtrodden, degraded young wife is first-class. Claire Bloom plays the 'other woman' with a neat variation of bite and comehitherness. Gary Raymond makes an instant impact as the cosy, kindly friend of the unhappy couple.

....

■ LOOKER

1981, 94 MINS, US ◊ ⑩ ⊙

Dir Michael Crichton   *Prod* Howard Jeffrey   *Scr* Michael Crichton   *Ph* Paul Lohmann   *Ed* Carl Kress   *Mus* Barry DeVorzon   *Art Dir* Dean Edward Mitzner

● Albert Finney, James Coburn, Susan Dey, Leigh Taylor-Young, Tim Rossovich, Daryl Hickman (Ladd/Warner)

Writer-director Michael Crichton has used interesting material, public manipulation by computer-generated TV commercials, to create *Looker*, a silly and unconvincing contempo sci-fi thriller.

Albert Finney, sporting a neutral American accent, heads the cast as Dr Larry Roberts, a leading Los Angeles plastic surgeon being set up as the fall guy in a string of murders of beautiful models who happen to be his patients. Bypassing the police detective (Dorian Harewood) on the case, Roberts teams with model Cindy (Susan Dey) to track down the real killers, with Cindy infiltrating a suspicious research institute run by Jennifer Long (Leigh Taylor-Young) as part of the conglomerate Reston Industries headed by John Reston (James Coburn).

Long has been developing the perfect TV commercials, using plastic surgery-augmented beautiful women as models and expanding into computer-generated simulation techniques. Reston has used these experiments to go beyond subliminal advertising to create hypnotic messages that can sell products or even political candidates.

With numerous lapses in credibility, Crichton falls back upon motifs better used in his *Westworld* picture: computer simulations (for robots), TV blurb soundstages (for film backlots) and assorted fancy chases.

....

■ LOOKING FOR MR GOODBAR

1977, 135 MINS, US ◊ ⑩ ⊙

Dir Richard Brooks   *Prod* Freddie Fields   *Scr* Richard Brooks   *Ph* William A. Fraker   *Ed* George Grenville   *Mus* Artie Kane   *Art Dir* Edward Carfagno

● Diane Keaton, Tuesday Weld, William Atherton, Richard Kiley, Richard Gere, Tom Berenger (Paramount)

In *Looking for Mr Goodbar*, writer-director Richard Brooks manifests his ability to catch accurately both the tone and subtlety of characters in the most repellant environments – in this case the desperate search for personal identity in the dreary and self-defeating world of compulsive sex and dope. Diane Keaton's performance as the good/bad girl is excellent.

Judith Rossner's novel was the basis for Brooks' fine screenplay about a girl who flees from a depressing home environment into the frantic world of singles bars and one-night physical gropings. The Jekyll-Hyde character caroms from sincere concern for teaching children to night-crawling of the seamiest sort.

At its best, the film, through Tuesday Weld's great performance as Keaton's sister who wanders from trend to trend, suggests dimly some alternatives.

□ 1977: Nominations: Best Supp. Actress (Tuesday Weld), Cinematography

....

■ LOOKING GLASS WAR, THE

1970, 106 MINS, UK ◊ ⑩

Dir Frank R. Pierson   *Prod* John Box   *Scr* Frank R. Pierson   *Ph* Austin Dempster   *Ed* Willy Kemplen   *Mus* Wally Stott   *Art Dir* Terence Marsh

● Christopher Jones, Pia Degermark, Ralph Richardson, Paul Rogers, Anthony Hopkins, Susan George (Columbia/Frankovich)

Based on the John le Carre novel about Cold War espionage, *The Looking Glass War* is most notable as the feature directorial debut of writer Frank R. Pierson.

Christopher Jones and Pia Degermark head a featured cast which also includes excellent performances by Ralph Richardson and Paul Rogers.

Jones, a ship-jumping Polish seaman, is recruited by Richardson and Rogers, two old hands in British espionage, to enter East Germany to verify some missile sites.

Anthony Hopkins, a younger undercover agent, is a key character as he shares many youthful reservations in an atmosphere charged with memories of an earlier, simpler spy game.

Pierson's adaptation has some superior dialog and structuring.

....

■ LOOKIN' TO GET OUT

1982, 104 MINS, US ◊ ⑩

Dir Hal Ashby   *Prod* Robert Schaffel   *Scr* Al Schwartz, Jon Voight   *Ph* Haskell Wexler   *Ed* Robert C. Jones   *Mus* Johnny Mandel   *Art Dir* Robert Boyle

● Jon Voight, Ann-Margret, Burt Young, Bert Remsen, Jude Farese, Allen Keller (Northstar International/Lorimar)

Hal Ashby's *Lookin' to Get Out* is an ill-conceived vehicle for actor (and co-writer) Jon Voight to showcase his character comedy talents in a loose, semi-improvised environment.

Alex (Jon Voight) and Jerry (Burt Young) are the central figures, who flee New York to Las Vegas to escape thugs Harry (Jude Farese) and Joey (Allen Keller) whose $10,000 Alex has dropped in a poker game. In an increasingly contrived and unconvincing series of coincidences and turns of luck, duo set up shop in the *Doctor Zhivago* suite of the M-G-M Grand Hotel and use a false identity to obtain unlimited credit from the casino.

Occasionally amusing, picture often has the feel of being improvised, with director Ashby giving Voight a loose rein to inject physical business and odd dialog into a scene. Interplay between Voight and Young is the film's raison d'etre.

....

■ LOOKS AND SMILES

1983, 104 MINS, UK

Dir Ken Loach   *Prod* Irving Teitelbaum   *Scr* Barry Hines   *Ph* Chris Menges   *Art Dir* Martin Johnson

● Graham Green, Carolyn Nicholson, Tony Pitts, Phil Askham, Cilla Mason, Arthur Davies (Black Lion/Kestrel/MK2)

Ken Loach's *Looks and Smiles* is a somber but dramatically right tale of teenagers running into unemployment and broken families in a northern industrial town. The three protagonists are played by non-pros, and very well too.

Mick, played like a young James Cagney by Graham Green, cannot find a mechanical job he covets and spends his time getting into fights. He meets Karen (Carolyn Nicholson) and something develops, but is stymied by his love for soccer, his joblessness and own problems of divorced parents. Mick's friend, Alan (Tony Pitts), joins the army and gets sent to Ireland and come home at times with gory tales.

The film certainly has a feel for its characters, and place, helped by a sharply dramatic use of b&w lensing which fits the milieu and theme.

....

■ LOOK WHO'S TALKING

1989, 90 MINS, US ◊ ⑩ ⊙

Dir Amy Heckerling   *Prod* Jonathan D. Krane   *Scr* Amy Heckerling   *Ph* Thomas Del Ruth   *Ed* Debra Chiate   *Mus* David Kitay   *Art Dir* Graeme Murray

● John Travolta, Kirstie Alley, Olympia Dukakis, George Segal, Abe Vigoda, Bruce Willis (Tri-Star/MCEG)

Like a standup comic pouring 'flopsweat', this ill-conceived comedy about an infant whose thoughts are given voice by actor Bruce Willis palpitates with desperation. *Look Who's Voice-Overing* would be a far more appropriate moniker, as Willis isn't heard by the film's other characters.

The camera simply homes in on one of the four strikingly dissimilar babies who play the leading role and Willis lets fly with asides to match their 'cute' expressions.

Kirstie Alley does the best she can as the child's mother – an accountant whose married boyfriend (George Segal) gets her

L

pregnant. Convinced he'll leave his wife for her and the child, she spurns the attention of the sweet, earnest cab driver (John Travolta) who helped her at the hospital when she was going into labor.

••••••••••••••••••••••••••••••

■ LOOK WHO'S TALKING TOO

1990, 81 MINS, US ◇ ⊛ ⊙
Dir Amy Heckerling   *Prod* Jonathan D. Krane   *Scr* Amy Heckerling, Neal Israel   *Ph* Thoms Del Ruth   *Ed* Debra Chiate   *Mus* David Kitay, Maureen Crowe   *Art Dir* Reuben Freed
● John Travolta, Kirstie Alley, Olympia Dukakis, Elias Koteas, Twink Caplan, Neal Israel (Tri-Star)

This vulgar sequel to 1989's longest-running sleeper hit looks like a rush job. Joined by her husband Neal Israel (who also appears as star Kirstie Alley's mean boss) in the scripting, filmmaker Amy Heckerling overemphasizes toilet humor and expletives to make the film appealing mainly to adolescents rather than an across-the-board family audience.

Unwed mom Alley and cabbie John Travolta are married for the sequel, with her cute son Mikey metamorphosed into Lorne Sussman, still voiceovered as precocious by Bruce Willis. First mutual arrival is undeniably cute Megan Milner, unfortunately voiced-over by Roseanne Barr. Comedienne gets a couple of laughs but is generally dull, leaving Willis to again carry the load in the gag department with well-read quips.

Plotline revolves around the bickering of Alley and Travolta whose jobs (accountant and would-be airline pilot) and personalities clash, as well as the rites of passage of the two kids. New characters, notably Alley's obnoxious brother Elias Koteas, are added to ill effect. Mel Brooks is enlisted to voice-over Mr Toilet Man, a fantasy bathroom bowl come to life, spitting blue water and anxious to bite off Mikey's privates.

••••••••••••••••••••••••••••••

■ LOOPHOLE

1981, 105 MINS, UK ◇ ⊛
Dir John Quested   *Prod* David Korda, Julian Holloway   *Scr* Jonathan Hales   *Ph* Michael Reed   *Ed* Ralph Sheldon   *Mus* Lalo Schifrin   *Art Dir* Syd Cain
● Albert Finney, Martin Sheen, Susannah York, Colin Blakely, Jonathan Pryce, Robert Morley (Brent Walker)

A clever plan to knock off a rich London bank is about the only thing that works in *Loophole*. The caper, filmed in and around the British capital, squanders some fine talent on a trite, low-voltage script.

Albert Finney as the mastermind of the heist, and Martin Sheen as an honest architect who lends the gang his talents in order to bail himself out of hock to his own bank, perform okay with little room to flex their histrionic skills.

As scripted from a Robert Pollock novel, the plot isn't exactly mint new, with Finney & Co utilizing the rat infested sewer tunnels under mid-town London for access to and getaway from the bank's vault. A downpour almost wreaks its own brand of providential justice in the only sequence with any kind of charge for action or suspense fans.

••••••••••••••••••••••••••••••

■ LOOSE CANNONS

1990, 93 MINS, US ◇ ⊛ ⊙
Dir Bob Clark   *Prod* Aaron Spelling, Alan Greisman   *Scr* Richard Christian Matheson, Richard Matheson, Bob Clark   *Ph* Reginald H. Morris   *Ed* Stan Cole   *Mus* Paul Zaza   *Art Dir* Harry Pottle
● Gene Hackman, Dan Aykroyd, Dom DeLuise, Ronny Cox, Nancy Travis, Paul Koslo (Tri-Star)

Dan Aykroyd's dexterous multipersonality schtick is the only redeeming feature of this chase-heavy comedy, up on the homevid heap.

Director Bob Clark manages to make his low-brow comedy *Porky's* look like *Amadeus*

with this latest salvo into the police-buddy genre, while Gene Hackman continues his befuddling penchant for sprinkling his overflowing resume with shameful losers.

Loose Cannons may be best remembered for its unbelievably convoluted screenplay – a concoction of elements from *Lethal Weapon 2*, *Midnight Run* and *Beverly Hills Cop*, all played at the speed of Warner Bros cartoon.

Plot involves gruesome murders, a secret 45-year-old porno film, a candidate for the chancellorship of West Germany and a horde of Uzi-brandishing neo-Nazis. All of that is irrelevant to the main plot, which pairs the gruff Mac (Hackman) with the Sybil-like Ellis (Aykroyd) – recently (and apparently prematurely) reactivated by his police-captain uncle after suffering a nervous breakdown that causes him to lapse into multiple personalities.

••••••••••••••••••••••••••••••

■ LOOSE CONNECTIONS

1983, 99 MINS, UK ◇ ⊛
Dir Richard Eyre   *Prod* Simon Perry   *Scr* Maggie Brooks   *Ph* Clive Tickner   *Ed* David Martin   *Mus* Dominic Muldowney, Andy Roberts
● Stephen Rea, Lindsay Duncan, Jan Niklas, Carole Harrison, Gary Olsen, Frances Low (Umbrella/Greenpoint)

Richard Eyre's second theatrical feature is an exceedingly amiable comic battle of the sexes.

Sally (Lindsay Duncan), together with two girlfriends, has built a jeep in which to drive from London to a feminist conference in Munich, but at the last moment she is left on her own. She takes a newspaper ad for a fellow driver, seeking a female non-smoking vegetarian, who speaks German and knows something about car engines. The only applicant is Harry (Stephen Rea), who claims to fill all the requirements except sex, and furthermore claims he's gay. Needless to say, Harry's a liar.

The trip to Munich is one comic disaster after another. But the odd couple are drawn to each other, and the inevitable happens.

Both roles are played to perfection. It's not a film of hearty laughs, but of continual quiet chuckles.

••••••••••••••••••••••••••••••

■ LOOT

1970, 101 MINS, UK ◇ ⊛
Dir Silvio Narizzano   *Prod* Arthur Lewis   *Scr* Ray Galton, Alan Simpson   *Ph* Austin Dempster   *Ed* Martin Charles   *Mus* Keith Mansfield, Richard Willing-Denton   *Art Dir* Anthony Pratt
● Richard Attenborough, Lee Remick, Hywel Bennett, Roy Holder, Milo O'Shea, Dick Emery (British Lion)

Joe Orton's macabre black comedy has transferred uneasily to the screen, the opening-out in the script having robbed the yarn of much of its comic tension. Nevertheless, it has enough speed, inventiveness and sharp, acid, irreverent comedy to satisfy many.

Story has Hywel Bennett and Roy Holder as two shiftless chums who, anxious to get rich quick, decide to blow a bank. They pull off the raid and elect to hide the loot in the coffin of Holder's mother, who has conveniently died. But there's no room for the cash and the corpse, so the poor woman's hidden in the lavatory.

The hotel belonging to Holder's father (Milo O'Shea) becomes a bedlam of frenzied rushing around, complicated by the arrival of an eccentric, pompous and venal inspector (Richard Attenborough) and Lee Remick, as a gold-digging sexpot of a private nurse.

Attenborough appears to be trying far too hard to get his effects. O'Shea is amiably amusing and bewildered. Remick is coolly efficient as the femme fatale, and Bennett and Holder keep their body-and loot-snatching roles to a high pitch of energetic activity.

••••••••••••••••••••••••••••••

■ LORD JIM

1965, 154 MINS, UK/US ◇ ⊛
Dir Richard Brooks   *Prod* Richard Brooks   *Scr* Richard Brooks   *Ph* Freddie Young   *Ed* Alan Osbiston   *Mus* Bronislau Kaper   *Art Dir* Geoffrey Drake
● Peter O'Toole, James Mason, Curt Jurgens, Jack Hawkins, Eli Wallach, Daliah Lavi (Columbia/Keep)

Many may be disappointed with Richard Brooks' handling of the Joseph Conrad novel. The storyline is often confused, some of the more interesting characters emerge merely as shadowy sketches. Brooks, while capturing the spirit of adventure of the novel, only superficially catches the inner emotional and spiritual conflict of its hero. In this he is not overly helped by Peter O'Toole whose performance is self-indulgent and lacking in real depth.

The story concerns a young merchant seaman. In a moment of cowardice he deserts his ship during a storm and his life is dogged throughout by remorse and an urge to redeem himself. His search for a second chance takes him to South Asia. There he becomes the conquering hero of natives oppressed by a fanatical war lord.

Brooks has teetered between making it a fullblooded, no-holds-barred adventure yarn and the fascinating psychological study that Conrad wrote. O'Toole, though a fine, handsome figure of a man, goes through the film practically expressionless and the audience sees little of the character's introspection and soul searching.

Of the rest of the cast the two who stand out, mainly because they are provided with the best opportunities, are Eli Wallach and Paul Lukas.

••••••••••••••••••••••••••••••

■ LORD LOVE A DUCK

1966, 105 MINS, US
Dir George Axelrod   *Prod* George Axelrod   *Scr* Larry H. Johnson, George Axelrod   *Ph* Daniel L. Fapp   *Ed* William A. Lyon   *Mus* Neal Hefti   *Art Dir* Malcolm Brown
● Roddy McDowall, Tuesday Weld, Lola Albright, Martin West, Ruth Gordon, Harvey Korman (Charleston/United Artists)

Some may call George Axelrod's *Lord Love a Duck* satire, others way-out comedy, still others brilliant, while there may be some who ask, what's it all about?

Whatever the reaction, there is no question that the film [based on Al Hire's novel] is packed with laughs, often of the truest anatomical kind, and there is a veneer of sophistication which keeps showing despite the most outlandish goings-on. Some of the comedy is inspirational, a gagman's dream come true, and there is bite in some of Axelrod's social commentary beneath the wonderful nonsense.

The characters are everything here, each developed brightly along zany lines, topped by Roddy McDowall as a Svengali-type high school student leader who pulls the strings on the destiny of Tuesday Weld, an ingenuish-type sexpot whose philosophy is wrapped up in her words 'Everybody's got to love me'.

McDowall is in good form as the mastermind of the school, and he has a strong contender for interest in blonde Weld in a characterization warm and appealing. Scoring almost spectacularly is Lola Albright as Weld's mother, a cocktail bar 'bunny' who commits suicide when she thinks she's ruined her daughter's chances for marriage.

••••••••••••••••••••••••••••••

■ LORD OF THE FLIES

1963, 90 MINS, UK ⊛
Dir Peter Brook   *Prod* Lewis Allen, Dana Hodgdon   *Scr* Peter Brook   *Ph* Tom Hollyman   *Ed* Peter Brook, J.C. Griel, M. Lubtchansky   *Mus* Raymond Leppard
● James Aubrey, Tom Chapin, Hugh Emwards, Roger Elwin, Tom Gaman (Two Arts)

The theme of young boys reverting to savagery when marooned on a deserted island has its moments of truth, but this pic rates as a near-miss on many counts.

Titles adequately indicate that evacuation in some future war has a group of youngsters surviving an air crash on a tropical island. They meet, and one boy is elected chief, but with dissent from another. Latter says his group will become hunters and they are soon drawing blood from some wild pigs and evolving tales of a monster on the island. The last-named is a dead paratrooper swaying on a ledge. But soon the hunting group goes completely native and persecutes and even exterminates those of the other group.

Peter Brook has coaxed fairly natural performances from his group of English youths. But he has drawn out his tale on a seemingly too schematic level to emerge more than illustration of the William Golding best-selling book than a film version standing on its own.

Lensing is curiously metallic but the on-the-spot shooting in the Puerto Rican jungles and beaches helps. Pic was made with US and Puerto Rican funds but with a British director and thesps.

■ **LORD OF THE FLIES**

1990, 90 MINS, US ◇ ⦿ ⊙
Dir Harry Hook *Prod* Ross Milloy, David V. Lester *Scr* Sara Schiff *Ph* Martin Fuhrer *Ed* Tom Priestley *Mus* Philippe Sarde *Art Dir* Jamie Leonard
● Balthazar Getty, Chris Furth, Danuel Pipoly, Badgett Dale, Edward Taft, Andrew Taft (Jack's Camp/Signal Hill)

The notion that the story of civilized boys reverting to savagery on a desert isle would be improved by shooting in color and substituting American actors for British child thesps is an odd one indeed.

Peter Brook's black and white version of William Goldings's *Lord of the Flies* is no classic, but it stands miles above this thoroughly undistinguised and unnecessary remake. Lewis Allen, one of the producers of the earlier version and exec producer of the remake with Peter Newman, made this film 'to protect the first film and to prevent television movie-of-the-week imitations after Golding received the Nobel Prize for literature.'

Here, director Harry Hook's literal, unimaginative visual approach makes the tale seem mundane and tedious.

The flat screenplay makes all the boys seem like dullards and does little to help differentiate the cast members, most of whom seem cut from the same mold, of bland cuteness. Nor do these boys seem to be living through the kind of gritty physical experience that would make the allegory spring to life.

■ **LORD OF THE RINGS, THE**

1978, 131 MINS, US ◇ ⦿
Dir Ralph Bakshi *Prod* Saul Zaentz *Scr* Chris Conkling, Peter S. Beagle *Mus* Leonard Rosenman
● (Fantasy)

Students of animated technique and Tolkien story-telling will find a lot to like in what Ralph Bakshi has done with *Lord of the Rings*. Unquestionably, Bakshi has perfected some outstanding pen-and-ink effects while translating faithfully a portion of J.R.R. Tolkien's trilogy. But in his concentration on craft and duty to the original story – both admirable in themselves – Bakshi overlooks the uninitiated completely.

Quite simply, those who do not know the characters of Middle Earth going in will not know them coming out. The introductory narration explaining the Rings is confusing, making the rest of the quest seem pointless in many places. Boring is an equally good word, especially toward the end of two hours.

■ **LORDS OF DISCIPLINE, THE**

1983, 102 MINS, US ◇ ⦿ ⊙
Dir Franc Roddam *Prod* Herb Jaffe, Gabriel Katzka *Scr* Thomas Pope, Lloyd Fonvielle *Ph* Brian Tufano *Ed* Michael Ellis *Mus* Howard Blake *Art Dir* John Graysmark
● David Keith, Robert Prosky, G.D. Spradlin, Barbara Babcock, Michael Biehn, Rick Rossovich (Paramount)

The Lords of Discipline laces a military school Watergate saga with heavy doses of sadism, racism and macho bullying. Designed as an expose of the corruption to be found within the hallowed walls of a venerable American institution, pic wants to have it both ways.

Set around 1964, drama follows cadet David Keith through his senior year at the Carolina Military Institute. Year in question is a notable one for the school because the first black cadet in its history has been enrolled.

As far as the new recruits are concerned, the poop hits the fan on 'hell night', which is just as bad as it sounds. With the full sanction of the faculty, upper classmen are permitted, even encouraged, to turn strong young men into oatmeal, running them through an evening of physical horrors under the guise of building character. One boy dies as a result, which leads outsider type Keith onto the existence of The Ten, a secret society to ferret out undesirables.

British director Franc Roddam had to wait over three years to make his American directorial debut and, ironically, ended up doing most of this film in Britain when no US school would allow lensing on its grounds.

■ **LORD'S OF FLATBUSH, THE**

1974, 86 MINS, US ◇ ⦿ ⊙
Dir Stephen F. Verona, Martin Davidson *Prod* Stephen F. Verona *Scr* Stephen F. Verona, Gayle Gleckler, Martin Davidson *Ph* Joseph Mangine, Edward Lachman *Ed* Stan Siegel, Muffie Meyer *Mus* Joe Brooks *Art Dir* Glenda Miller
● Perry King, Sylvester Stallone, Henry Winkler, Paul Mace, Susan Blakely, Maria Smith (Columbia)

Life among the leather-jacket high school set of Flatbush is the subject of this indie filmed in Brooklyn, NY, locale. Pic is episodic in narrative, particularly in first few reels burdened mostly by irrelevant action, but when actual story line is reached focuses on two of the members of a social club called Lords of Flatbush.

Perry King and Sylvester Stallone play a couple of would-be toughies who occasionally leave their pals for some dating. Stallone's romancing leads to getting his pal (Maria Smith) pregnant, and King to getting the final brushoff from femme (Susan Blakely) he pursues. Not too much finesse distinguishes the script, which carries neither warmth nor particular interest for the various characters. Both actors do well enough by their roles.

■ **LORENZO'S OIL**

1992, 135 MINS, US ⦿ ⊙
Dir George Miller *Prod* Doug Mitchell, George Miller *Scr* George Miller, Nick Enright *Ph* John Seale *Ed* Richard Francis-Bruce, Marcus D'Arcy, Lee Smith *Mus* Christine Woodruff (sup.) *Art Dir* Kristi Zea
● Nick Nolte, Susan Sarandon, Peter Ustinov, Kathleen Wilhoite, Gerry Bamman, Zack O'Malley Greenburg (Universal)

Lorenzo's Oil is as grueling a medical case study as any audience would ever want to sit through. A true-life story brought to the screen intelligently and with passionate motivation by George Miller, pic details in a very precise way how a couple raced time to save the life of their young son after he contracted a rare, always fatal disease.

A practising physician himself before forging his filmmaking career with the *Mad Max*

actioners, Miller has, from all accounts, scrupulously adhered to the facts in relating the harrowing but inspiring tale of Augusto and Michaela Odone.

In 1984, their five-year-old son Lorenzo was diagnosed with adrenoleukodystrophy (ALD), a condition occurring only in boys that leads to seizures, paralysis and, within two years, certain death. The Odones took it upon themselves to research the subject from scratch and try to find a cure for Lorenzo.

First section, which details the discovery of Lorenzo's ailment, is the most effective and visually striking. As the film progresses, however, its single-mindedness is such one is not surprised to see an 800 number for ALD info on the end credits, and some other elements have gotten out of hand or lost in the shuffle.

Among the irritants is an acting style that is generally cranked up to full throttle or beyond. As Augusto, Nick Nolte sports an accent unrecognizable until being identified as Italian. As Michaela, Susan Sarandon fares better, as she convincingly conveys a fierceness and tenacity that is almost frightening. The character never lets up, and neither does the film.
□ 1992: Nomination: Best Actress (Susan Sarandon), Original Screenplay

■ **LORNA**

1965, 78 MINS, US
Dir Russ Meyer *Prod* Russ Meyer *Scr* James Griffith *Ph* Russ Meyer *Ed* Russ Meyer *Mus* Hal Hooper, James Griffith
● Lorna Maitland, Mark Bradley, James Rucker, Hal Hooper, Doc Scortt, James Griffith (Eve)

A sort of sex morality play, *Lorna* is Russ Meyer's first serious effort after six nudie pix.

Myer's story concerns Lorna Maitland as the buxom wife of James Rucker, a handsome young clod who each day joins Hal Hopper and Doc Scott in commuting to work at a salt mine. (Latter is not the first Biblical overtone, since Griffith portrays a firebrand preacher-Greek chorus who greets audience via clever subjective camera intro with ominous foreboding of sin and payment therefor.)

Mark Bradley, escaped con and vicious killer, encounters Maitland in the fields with predictable results, after which she takes him home for encores.

Maitland has a sensual voice although vocal projection is her least asset. Bradley has rugged looks, a voice to match, and a bigger future in films. His role requires expressions of fear, boredom, tenderness and amoral viciousness, and he is up to them all. Griffith is a two-time loser, having overacted a trite part which he himself wrote.

■ **LOSERS, THE**

1970, 95 MINS, US ◇ ⦿
Dir Jack Starrett *Prod* Joe Solomon *Scr* Alan Caillou *Ph* Nonong Rasca *Ed* James Moore *Mus* Stu Phillips
● William Smith, Bernie Hamilton, Adam Roarke, Daniel Kemp, Houston Savage, Gene Cornelius (Fanfare)

Director Jack Starrett took his motley crew of actors to the Philippines which is supposed to pass, on the screen, as Vietnam. The viewer is asked to believe that a contingent of motor cycle bums would be hired by the US to rescue a CIA agent, held prisoner in Cambodia by the North Vietnamese or Red Chinese, it's never really made clear.

The script is so inane, with not even a feeble attempt at logic, that what are intended as serious moments come off as funny.

Some of the acting is excellent – Bernie Hamilton makes his army captain a human being; Adam Roarke's Duke is better than the part deserves; Paul Koslo, as one of the cycle riders who falls for a native girl (Ana Korita) he meets in a brothel is very effective.

LOSIN' IT

1983, 104 MINS, US ◇ ⓥ ⊙

Dir Curtis Hanson   *Prod* Bryan Gindoff, Hannah
Hempstead   *Scr* B.W.L. Norton   *Ph* Gil Taylor
Ed Richard Halsey   *Mus* Ken Wannberg   *Art Dir* Robb
Wilson King
● Tom Cruise, Jackie Earle Haley, John Stockwell,
Shelley Long, John P. Navin Jr, Hector Elias (Embassy)

As often noted, the problem with porno is
that there are only so many ways to show people having sex; the problem with films like
Losin' is that there are only so many ways to
show teenagers not having sex.

But director Curtis Hanson makes a commendable effort with a rather obvious story
about three teenage boys who head for a wild
weekend in Tijuana, hoping to trade hard
cash for manly experience.

Though none is really very experienced,
each is sophisticated to a stereotyped degree.
There's the high-school hunk (John
Stockwell) who's actually had a girl; the blustering faker (Jackie Earle Haley), whose experience is limited to his own imagination;
and the sensitive innocent (Tom Cruise), who
isn't sure he wants it, but is destined for the
best time to be had by all.

Naturally, they are accompanied by wimpy
John P. Navin Jr, brought along only because
he has the necessary cash to make the trip
possible. And along the way they pick up
crazy – but nice – Shelley Long, on the lam
from her husband.

This doesn't sound like much and it isn't,
but the picture is a solid credit for all involved.

LOSS OF INNOCENCE

See: The Greengage Summer

LOST ANGELS

1989, 116 MINS, US ◇ ⓥ ⊙

Dir Hugh Hudson   *Prod* Howard Rosenman, Thomas
Baer   *Scr* Michael Weller   *Ph* Juan Ruiz-Anchia
Ed David Gladwell   *Mus* Philippe Sarde
Art Dir Assheton Gorton
● Donald Sutherland, Adam Horovitz, Amy Locane, Don
Bloomfield, Celia Weston (Orion)

Lost Angels suffers from some of the communication problems which bedevil its young, inarticulate hero. Hugh Hudson's wannabe *Rebel
without a Cause* update tries to be a serious exploration of throwaway middle-class teens in
the San Fernando Valley, but despite some
gripping moments it's often cliched and incoherent.

Adam Horovitz of the Beastie Boys rap
band has a sympathetic presence but not
enough to do as the troubled lead.

It's another of those films about mental illness that tries to have it both ways, perhaps
for fear of turning off the audience by presenting a lead who is truly disturbed.

The film powerfully conveys the latent violence just below the brooding surface of
Horovitz' quiet demeanor. Whether it's the
prelude to a freakout as he learns he's being
locked up, or a fistfight with shrink Donald
Sutherland, or a nightmarish violence-seek-
ing trip to a Latino area, Horovitz has the
ability to impersonate a stick of dynamite.

Sutherland brings subtlety to his occasional
scenes as a scruffy shrink who has enough
emotional problems to be empathetic.

LOST BOYS, THE

1987, 92 MINS, US ◇ ⓥ ⊙ ⊙

Dir Joel Schumacher   *Prod* Harvey Bernhard
Scr Janice Fischer, James Jeremias, Jeffrey Boam
Ph Michael Chapman   *Ed* Robert Brown   *Mus* Thomas
Newman   *Art Dir* Bo Welch
● Jason Patric, Corey Haim, Dianne Wiest, Barnard
Hughes, Kiefer Sutherland, Jami Gertz (Warner)

The Lost Boys is a horrifically dreadful vampire
teensploitation entry [story by Janice Fischer
and James Jeremias] that daringly advances
the theory that all those missing children pictured on garbage bags and milk cartons are
actually the victims of bloodsucking bikers.

Arriving in a Santa Cruz-like community
that is dominated by a huge amusement park,
Dianne Wiest and her sons check in at
grandpa's creepy house, and the boys quickly
fall in with the wrong crowd.

Latter includes some unhealthy looking
punks, led by Kiefer Sutherland, who take
older brother Jason Patric back to their lair
and through the foxy but wasted Jami Gertz,
tempt him into the ways of the undead.

Getting wind of the vampire problem, little
brother Corey Haim teams up with two pint-
sized Rambos to combat the plague on their
houses, and it all ends in a colossal battle
with bats, punks, froth, spears and blood flying through the air in a frenzy of nonsensical
action.

LOST COMMAND

1966, 129 MINS, US ◇ ⓥ

Dir Mark Robson   *Prod* Mark Robson   *Scr* Nelson
Gidding   *Ph* Robert Surtees   *Ed* Dorothy Spencer
Mus Franz Waxman   *Art Dir* John Stoll
● Anthony Quinn, Alain Delon, George Segal, Michele
Morgan, Maurice Ronet, Claudia Cardinale (Columbia)

Lost Command is a good contemporary action-
melodrama about some French paratroopers
who survive France's humiliation and defeat
in Southeast Asia, only to be sent to rebellious Algeria. Filmed in Spain, the Mark
Robson production [based on a novel by Jean
Larteguy] has enough pace, action and exterior eye appeal to overcome a sometimes routine script.

Anthony Quinn heads the players as the
gruff, low-born soldier who has risen to field
grade rank because of the attrition of Indo-
Chinese guerrilla warfare which decimated
the ranks of the French army.

Providing a two-way contrast, and exempli-
fying the extremes to which the Quinn character never extends, are Alain Delon and
Maurice Ronet. Delon is the sensitive, quiet
but effective assistant who, at fadeout, leaves
military service, since fighting in itself has become meaningless. Ronet is brutal, sadistic
and callous, yet with enough fighting effectiveness to be needed in battle.

This very meaty and pathetic plot irony will
strike some as underdeveloped, in that Quinn
and Segal never effect a personal confrontation until latter is needlessly killed by Ronet,
but by then it is too late.

LOST HORIZON

1937, 125 MINS, US ⓥ ⊙

Dir Frank Capra   *Prod* Frank Capra   *Scr* Robert Riskin
Ph Joseph Walker   *Ed* Gene Havlick, Gene Milford
Mus Dimitri Tiomkin   *Art Dir* Stephen Goosson
● Ronald Colman, Edward Everett Horton, H.B. Warner,
Jane Wyatt, Sam Jaffe, Margo (Columbia)

So canny are the ingredients that where
credulity perhaps rears its practical head, audiences will be carried away by the histrionic
illusion, skill and general Hollywood ledger-
demain which so effectively capture the best
elements in this $2.5 million saga of Shangri-
La.

Ronald Colman, with fine restraint, conveys
the metamorphosis of the foreign diplomat
falling in with the Arcadian idyll that he be-
holds in the Valley of the Blue Moon.

Sam Jaffe is capital as the ancient Belgian
priest who first founded Shangri-La some 300
years ago – a Methuselah who is still alive,
thanks to the Utopian philosophy of the community he has nurtured.

As H.B. Warner (the venerable Chang and

oldest disciple of the High Lama) expounds it,
the peaceful valley's philosophy of moderation
in work, food, drink, pleasure, acquisition and
all other earthly wants, is cannily scripted for
audience appeal. Whether it's James Hilton's
original novel or Robert Riskin's celluloid
transmutation, the scripting contribution is
one of the picture's strongest assets.

It opens vigorously in Bakul, showing the
English community evacuating under the onslaught of Chinese bandits. The last plane
out throws Colman together with the fuss-
budget archaeologist (Edward Everett
Horton), the Ponzi plumber (Thomas
Mitchell), the ailing waif of the world (Isabel
Jewell), and Colman's screen brother (well
played by John Howard). It's in Shangri-La
that Jane Wyatt so vigorously establishes herself as Colman's vis-a-vis, looking decidedly
comely and handling her romance opportunities with definite understanding.
□ 1937: Best Interior Decoration (Stephen
Goosson), Editing.
□ Nominations: Best Picture, Supp. Actor
(H.B. Warner), Score, Sound, Assistant
Director (C.C. Coleman Jr)

LOST HORIZON

1973, 150 MINS, US ◇ ⊙

Dir Charles Jarrott   *Prod* Ross Hunter   *Scr* Larry Kramer
Ph Robert Surtees   *Ed* Maury Winetrobe   *Mus* Burt
Bacharach   *Art Dir* Preston Ames
● Peter Finch, Liv Ullmann, Sally Kellerman, George
Kennedy, Michael York, Olivia Hussey (Columbia)

Some 36 years after Frank Capra's filmization
of James Hillton's *Lost Horizon* novel premiered comes producer Ross Hunter's lavish
updated and musical adaptation. The form is
that of filmed operetta in three acts, superbly
mounted, and cast with an eye to international markets.

The script structure parallels that of the
Capra film – opening after the majestic main
title landscape of snowy mountains with the
tumultous escape from rioting Asians in a
kidnapped plane; the crash in the uncharted
Himalayas rescued by an inscrutable major
domo who takes the disparate survivors to the
nestled Utopia of Shangri-La, where the outsiders resolve their personal destinies.

Peter Finch heads the cast as Conway, an
international statesman selected by high
lama Charles Boyer to succeed to rule of
Shangri-La, where the world's wisdom is being preserved against the foreseen Apocalypse. Sir John Gielgud is the high lama's
chief aide who reveals the mystery of the
place to Finch.

Only Michael York, in a dramatically-crip-
pled supporting banana role, and Olivia
Hussey, an awkwardly exotic soubrette, fail to
get off the ground.

LOST IN AMERICA

1985, 91 MINS, US ◇ ⓥ

Dir Albert Brooks   *Prod* Marty Katz   *Scr* Albert Brooks,
Monica Johnson   *Ph* Eric Saarinen   *Ed* David Finfer
Mus Arthur B. Rubinstein   *Art Dir* Richard Sawyer
● Albert Brooks, Julie Hagerty, Garry Marshall, Art
Frankel, Michael Greene, Tom Tarpey (Geffen)

Film opens on Albert Brooks and wife Julie
Hagerty in bed on eve of their move to a
$450,000 house and also what Brooks pre-
sumes will be his promotion to a senior exec
slot in a big ad agency. Brooks is a nervous
mess, made worse when vaguely bored
Hagerty tells him their life has become 'too
responsible, too controlled.'

Her suppressed wish for a more dashing life
comes startlingly true the next day when a
confident Brooks glides into his boss' LA office only to hear that his expected senior v.p.
stripes are going to someone else and he's being transferred to New York.

Brooks quits his job and convinces his wife to quit her personnel job. The pair will liquidate their assets, buy a Winnebago, and head across America.

Brooks, who directed and cowrote with Monica Johnson, is irrepressible but always very human.

- -

■ **LOST IN YONKERS**

1993, 112 MINS, US ◇ ▼ ⊙
Dir Martha Coolidge   *Prod* Ray Stark   *Scr* Neil Simon
Ph Johnny E. Jensen   *Ed* Steven Cohen   *Mus* Elmer Bernstein   *Art Dir* David Chapman
● Richard Dreyfuss, Mercedes Ruehl, Irene Worth, Brad Stoll, Mike Damus, David Strathairn (Columbia/Rastar)

Lost in Yonkers is a carefully rendered, ultimately unexciting screen version of Neil Simon's 1991 Pulitzer Prize-winning play.

Story of a domineering old woman's tyranny over two generations of offspring is set in the summer of '42. Tale begins as Eddie Krunitz (Jack Laufer) attempts to deposit his two sons with his mother, who lives above her Yonkers candy store and soda fountain. She is sufficiently tended to by her somewhat backward 36-year-old daughter Bella (Mercedes Ruehl), but she finally has little choice.

The two boys, 15-year-old Jay and Arty, two years younger, are bright, presentable, well-behaved kids, and much of the pleasure of the film lies in watching the alert, bright-eyed perfomances of Brad Stoll and Mike Damus. Still, they are susceptible to the brash appeal of their uncle Louie (Richard Dreyfuss), a small-time hood.

Simon has gently opened up the pic by adding a number of characters who didn't appear in the play, and setting quite a few scenes outside the apartment and store. Despite this, the film still seems bound by its theatrical origins in the way everything is stated and spelled out. Performances by the leads could have been brought down a notch or two.

- -

■ **LOST PATROL, THE**

1934, 74 MINS, US ▼
Dir John Ford   *Prod* Cliff Reid (assoc.)   *Scr* Dudley Nichols, Garrett Fort   *Ph* Harold Wenstrom   *Ed* Paul Weatherwax   *Mus* Max Steiner   *Art Dir* Van Nest Polglase, Sidney Ullman
● Victor McLaglen, Boris Karloff, Wallace Ford, Reginald Denny, J. M. Kerrigan, Alan Hale (RKO)

Not a woman in the cast and substantially little as to story, but under the weight of suspense, dialog and competency of direction *Lost Patrol* tips the scales favorably as entertainment.

All of the action [from the story *Patrol* by Philip MacDonald] takes place in the Mesopotamian desert during the campaign of the English against militant Arabs in 1917. Outside of the bleak desert, the only other change of scene throughout the picture's length is the oasis which a patrol, lost after the commanding officer has been killed, discovers. It is here where one by one the men either die or are bumped off by Arabs, until Victor McLaglen is the last.

McLaglen, the sergeant who inherits command of the patrol, turns in a good job in the kind of a part that's particularly suited to this actor. As a Bible nut, Boris Karloff is on a somewhat different assignment. He gives a fine account of himself.
□ 1934: Nomination: Best Score

- -

■ **LOST SQUADRON, THE**

1932, 80 MINS, US ▼ ⊙
Dir George Archainbaud   *Scr* Wallace Smith, Herman J. Mankiewicz, Robert S. Presnell   *Ph* Leo Tover, Edward Cronjager   *Ed* William Hamilton   *Mus* [uncredited]   *Art Dir* Max Ree

● Richard Dix, Mary Astor, Erich von Stroheim, Dorothy Jordan, Joel McCrea, Robert Armstrong (RKO)

Squadron glorifies the cinematic stunt flyer. [From the *Liberty* magazine story] by Dick Grace, the most illustrious of the Hollywood aerial daredevils, it is not without authority, even though the dramatics are a bit strained.

The 'behind the scenes' of an aerial film production is the best appeal *Squadron* has. It's a story-within-a-story. Although the basic premise might be regarded as trite and familiar, the detail of the skullduggery of a jealous husband-director, along with his fanatical zeal in injecting realism into the aerial crash stuff, is 100% new for the screen.

Erich von Stroheim plays the director (alias Arnold von Furst in the picture) to the hilt, i.e. the role of a domineering, militaristic Prussian film director who is a martinet on location, callous to all else but the box-office effect of his celluloid production.

Action takes Richard Dix, Joel McCrea, Robert Armstrong and Hugh Herbert from an aviation corps right after the war to Hollywood, where Armstrong has preceded them and won some standing as an aerial stuntist.

With the quartet reunited as Hollywoodian stunt flyers (Dick Grace, Art Gobel, Leo Nomis and Frank Clark get the billing for the actual aerial stunting), Stroheim as the jealous director motivates the action toward a realistic crack-up by putting acid on the control wires of the ship which Dix has screen antagonist, was supposed to have piloted.

Mary Astor is unhappily cast as an ambitious actress who first throws over Dix while he's on the other side for a sinecure under a masculine protector, and who later marries von Furst to further her career on the screen.

- -

■ **LOST WEEKEND, THE**

1945, 104 MINS, US ▼ ⊙
Dir Billy Wilder   *Prod* Charles Brackett   *Scr* Charles Brackett, Billy Wilder   *Ph* John F. Seitz   *Ed* Doane Harrison   *Mus* Miklos Rozsa   *Art Dir* Hans Dreier, Earl Hedrick
● Ray Milland, Jane Wyman, Howard da Silva, Philip Terry, Doris Dowling, Frank Faylen (Paramount)

The filming by Paramount of *The Lost Weekend* marks a particularly outstanding achievement in the Hollywood setting. The psychiatric study of an alcoholic, it is an unusual picture. It is intense, morbid – and thrilling.

Weekend is the specific story [from the novel by Charles R. Jackson] of a quondam writer who has yet to put down his first novel on paper. He talks about it continuously but something always seems to send him awry just when he has a mind to work. Booze. Two quarts at a time. He goes on drunks for days. And his typewriter invariably winds up in the pawnshop.

Ray Milland has certainly given no better performance in his career. Drunks may frequently excite laughter, but at no time can there be even a suggestion of levity to the part Milland plays. Only at the film's end is the character out of focus, but that is the fault of the script. The suggestion of rehabilitation should have been more carefully developed.

Jane Wyman is the girl, Philip Terry the brother. They help make the story overshadow the characters. The entire cast, in fact, contributes notably. And that goes especially for Howard da Silva as the bartender. Billy Wilder's direction is always certain, always conscious that the characters were never to over-state the situations.
□ 1945: Best Picture, Director, Actor (Ray Milland), Screenplay.
□ Nominations: Best B&W Cinematography, Editing, Scoring of a Dramatic Picture

- -

■ **LOST WORLD, THE**

1960, 97 MINS, US ◇ ▼
Dir Irwin Allen   *Prod* Irwin Allen   *Scr* Charles Bennett, Irwin Allen   *Ph* Winton Hoch   *Ed* Hugh S. Fowler   *Mus* Paul Sawtell, Bert Shefter   *Art Dir* Duncan Cramer, Walter M. Simonds
● Michael Rennie, Jill St John, David Hedison, Claude Rains, Fernando Lamas, Richard Haydn (20th Century-Fox)

Watching *The Lost World* is tantamount to taking a trip through a Coney Island fun house. The picture's chief attraction is its production gusto. Emphasis on physical and pictorial values makes up, to some extent, for its lack of finesse in the literary and thespic departments.

In translating the Arthur Conan Doyle story to the screen for the second time (after a lapse of 36 years since the first, silent version), Irwin Allen and Charles Bennett have constructed a choppy, topheavy, deliberately-paced screenplay that labors too long with exposition and leaves several loose ends dangling. Allen's direction is not only sluggish but has somehow gotten more personality into his dinosaurs than into his people.

Among the curious individuals who venture into this treacherous hidden area at the headwaters of the Amazon are Claude Rains, overly affected as Professor George Edward Challenger; Michael Rennie, a bit wooden as a titled playboy with a notorious reputation; Jill St John, ill-at-ease as an adventuress who chooses tight pink capri pants as suitable garb for an Amazonian exploration; David Hedison, bland as a newsman-photog; and Fernando Lamas, unconvincing as a Latin guitar-player and helicopter-operator.

With the exception of one or two mighty ineffectual prehistoric spiders and a general absence of genuine shock or tension, the production is something to behold. The dinosaurs are exceptionally lifelike (although they resemble horned toads and alligators more than dinosaurs) and the violent volcanic scenery (like hot, bubbling chili sauce) and lush vegetation form backdrops that are more interesting and impressive than the action taking place in front of them.

- -

■ **LOUDEST WHISPER, THE**
See: The Children's Hour

- -

■ **LOUISIANA STORY**

1948, 77 MINS, US ▼
Dir Robert Flaherty   *Prod* Robert Flaherty   *Scr* Robert Flaherty, Frances Flaherty   *Ph* Richard Leacock   *Ed* Helen Van Dongen   *Mus* Virgil Thomson
● Joseph Boudreaux, Lionel Le Blanc, Mrs. E. Bienvenu, Frank Hardy, C.T. Guedry (Lopert Films)

Louisiana Story is a documentary-type story told almost purely in camera terms. It has a slender, appealing story, moments of agonizing suspense, vivid atmosphere and superlative photography.

Filmed entirely in the bayou country of Louisiana, the picture tells of the Cajun (Acadian) boy and his parents, who live by hunting and fishing in the alligator-infested swamps and streams, and of the oil-drilling crew that brings its huge derrick to sink a well.

There probably aren't more than 100 lines of dialog in the entire picture – long sequences being told by the camera, with eloquent sound effects and Virgil Thomson's expressive music as background. There are no real heroes or villains (unless the terrifying alligators could be considered the latter). The simple Cajun family is friendly, and the oil-drilling crew is pleasant and likable.

Standard Oil of NJ contributed the necessary $200,000 production coin to Flaherty.
□ 1948: Nomination: Best Motion Picture Story

- -

L

LOVE

1927, 84 MINS, US ⊗ ⓥ
Dir Edmund Goulding   *Prod* Edmund Goulding
Scr Frances Marion, Marian Ainslee, Ruth Cummings,
Lorna Moon   *Ph* William Daniels   *Ed* Hugh Wynn
Mus Ernst Luz   *Art Dir* Cedric Gibbons, Alexander
Toluboff
● Greta Garbo, John Gilbert, George Fawcett, Emily
Fitzroy, Brandon Hurst, Philippe De Lacy (M-G-M)

What is there to tell about the Tolstoy story
Anna Karenina? Its locale is Russia in the time
of the Czars. Anna (Greta Garbo) has a husband and a young son; Vronsky (John
Gilbert), a military heritage and a desire for
Anna. For screen purposes it's enough that
both are of the aristocracy, which permits
Garbo long, stately gowns and Gilbert a series of uniforms that would make a buck private out of the student prince.

There are rich interiors, appropriate exteriors and an excellent officers' steeplechase
to get the action figuratively off of a couch for
a while. Besides which Garbo and Gilbert
supposedly care for each other in the script.

Anyway, director Edmund Goulding hasn't
let the title run away with his sense of discretion. Possibly has leaned over backwards to
the extent of keeping this picture from becoming a rave. When all is said and done, *Love*
is a cinch because it has Gilbert and Garbo.

LOVE AFFAIR

1939, 87 MINS, US ⓥ
Dir Leo McCarey   *Prod* Leo McCarey   *Scr* Delmer
Daves, Donald Ogden Stewart   *Ph* Rudolph Mate
Ed Edward Dmytryk, George Hiveley   *Art Dir* Jack
Otterson, Martin Obzina
● Irene Dunne, Charles Boyer, Maria Ouspenskaya, Lee
Bowman, Astrid Allwyn, Maurice Moscovich (RKO)

Leo McCarey's initial production for RKO as
a producer-director offers an entirely new approach to accepted technique. Basically, it's
the regulation formula of boy-meets-girl
[story by McCarey and Mildred Cram]. But
first half is best described as romantic comedy, while second portion switches to drama
with comedy.

Aboard boat sailing from Naples to New
York, Charles Boyer starts a flirtation with
Irene Dunne. He is engaged to heiress Astrid
Allwyn, and she to Lee Bowman. They sepa-
rate on docking with pact to meet six months
later atop the Empire State building.

Dunne slips to Philadelphia to sing in a
night club, while Boyer applies himself to
painting. While on her way to keep tryst on
appointed day, Dunne is injured in a traffic
accident. Faced with life of a cripple, girl refuses to contact Boyer to explain.

Dunne is excellent in a role that requires
both comedy and dramatic ability. Boyer is
particularly effective as the modern
Casanova. Maria Ouspenskaya provides a
warmly sympathetic portrayal as Boyer's
grandmother in Madeira.
□ 1939: Nominations: Best Picture, Actress
(Irene Dunne), Supp. Actress (Maria
Ouspenskaya), Original Story, Art Direction

LOVE AND BULLETS

1979, 95 MINS, UK ◇ ⓥ
Dir Stuart Rosenberg   *Prod* Pancho Kohner
Scr Wendell Mayes, John Melson   *Ph* Fred Koenekamp,
Anthony Richmond   *Ed* Michael Anderson   *Mus* Lalo
Schifrin   *Art Dir* John DeCuir
● Charles Bronson, Rod Steiger, Jill Ireland, Strother
Martin, Bradford Dillman, Michael Gazzo (ITC/Grade)

Slowly and predictably, script plots Charles
Bronson's mission, on behalf of the FBI, to pick
up a mobster's moll (Jill Ireland) who's got separated from her paramour and is presumed to
be a mine of incriminating information.

Bronson's personal obsession with bringing

down the gangland king is accentuated when
he discovers the girl knows nothing after all,
and then falls for her. When the mob, equally
Convinced she'll shop them, have her killed,
he takes private revenge.

Rod Steiger's performance as the effete
Mafia boss is tantalizing. So too is the emergent love affair between Bronson and Ireland,
her comic talent largely starved for lack of
material.

Director Stuart Rosenberg could have
glossed over the plot's less believable twists
with a brisker style and a lot more attack.

LOVE AND DEATH

1975, 85 MINS, US ◇ ⓥ ⊙
Dir Woody Allen   *Prod* Charles H. Joffe   *Scr* Woody
Allen   *Ph* Ghislain Cloquet   *Ed* Ralph Rosenblum
Mus Felix Giglio (sup.)   *Art Dir* Willy Holt
● Woody Allen, Diane Keaton (United Artists)

Woody Allen and Diane Keaton invade the
land and spirit of Anton Chekhov. *Love and
Death* is another mile-a-minute visual-verbal
whirl by the two comedy talents, this time
through Czarist Russia in the days of the
Napoleonic Wars.

Allen's script traces his bumbling adventures with distant cousin Keaton, latter outstanding as a prim lady of both philosophical
and sexual bent. Between malaprop battlefield heroics and metaphysical deliberations,
Allen eventually combines with Keaton in an
assassination attempt on Napoleon himself. It
is impossible to catalog the comedic blue-
print; suffice to say it is another zany product
of the terrific synergism of the two stars.

About 54 supporting players have roles
which range from a few feet to a few frames.
Joffe's location production was shot in France
and Germany, where some gorgeous physical
values serve as a backdrop to the kooky
antics.

LOVE AND MONEY

1982, 90 MINS, US ◇
Dir James Toback   *Prod* James Toback   *Scr* James
Toback   *Ph* Fred Schuler   *Ed* Dennis Hill   *Mus* Aaron
Copland   *Art Dir* Lee Fischer
● Ray Sharkey, Ornella Muti, Klaus Kinski, Armand
Assante, King Vidor, Susan Heldfond (Lorimar/
Paramount)

Love and Money is an arresting romantic suspense film which, in spite of several good performances and well-crafted individual scenes,
fails to ignite.

Ray Sharkey toplines as Byron Levin, a
case of arrested development who works in an LA
bank and lives with his senile grandpa (King
Vidor) and librarian girl friend Vicky (Susan
Heldfond). He comes out of his robot-like
shell upon meeting the beautiful Catherine
(Ornella Muti), young wife of multinational
business magnate Stockheinz (Klaus Kinski).

Following an intense romance with
Catherine, Levin becomes involved in an international plot masterminded by Stockheinz
to help him deal with Latin American dictator Lorenzo Prado (Armand Assante), not coincidentally Levin's former college roommate.

Muti makes a strong US picture debut, aug-
menting her famous exotic beauty with some
powerful thesping.

LOVE AND PAIN AND THE WHOLE
DAMN THING

1973, 110 MINS, US ◇
Dir Alan J. Pakula   *Prod* Alan J. Pakula   *Scr* Alvin
Sargent   *Ph* Geoffrey Unsworth   *Ed* Russell Lloyd
Mus Michael Small   *Art Dir* Enrique Alarcon
● Maggie Smith, Timothy Bottoms, Jaime de Mora y
Aragon, Emiliano Redondo, Charles Baxter, Margaret
Modlin (Columbia)

For almost three-quarters of its overlong running time, *Love and Pain. . .* etc works as a
modest, affecting romantic comedy about two
mismatched neurotics stumbling into love
during a Spanish tour. But pic succumbs to a
fatal attack of *Love Story*itis, and goes down
for the count.

Timothy Bottoms plays the shy, asthmatic
son of a professor packed off to Spain for the
summer. Bottoms joins a tourist bus where he
is seated next to Maggie Smith, a jumpy lady
of middle age who frequently bumps into her
own shadow. For most of the film they trip
over each other, explore the countryside and
gradually accept a warmth and companionship that leads to a believable affair. Then
Smith reveals she's dying.

Smith, as ever, is luminous, and Bottoms
tackles a difficult role with ease. One only
wishes the scripter had left well enough
alone.

LOVE AT FIRST BITE

1979, 96 MINS, US ◇ ⓥ ⊙
Dir Stan Dragoti   *Prod* Joel Freeman   *Scr* Robert
Kaufman   *Ph* Edward Rosson   *Ed* Mort Fallick, Allan
Jacobs   *Mus* Charles Bernstein   *Art Dir* Serge Krizman
● George Hamilton, Susan Saint James, Richard
Benjamin, Dick Shawn, Arte Johnson, Sherman Hemsley
(American International)

'What would happen if' Dracula was victimized by life in modern New York City?

It's a fun notion and George Hamilton
makes it work. In the first place, he's funny
just to watch. Veteran make-up artist
William Tuttle, who created Lugosi's Dracula
look in 1934, retains the grey, drained visage
while adding a nutty quality that Hamilton
accents with the arch of an eyebrow.

Story evicts Dracula from his Transylvania
castle and takes him in pursuit of Susan Saint
James, a fashion model he loves from an old
photo. In the care of his bumbling manservant, slightly overplayed by Arte Johnson,
Hamilton's coffin is naturally misrouted by
the airline, winding up in a black funeral
home.

Director Stan Dragoti keeps the chuckles
coming, spaced by a few good guffaws.

LOVE AT LARGE

1990, 97 MINS, US ◇ ⓥ ⊙
Dir Alan Rudolph   *Prod* David Blocker   *Scr* Alan
Rudolph   *Ph* Elliot Davis   *Ed* Lisa Churgin   *Mus* Mark
Isham   *Art Dir* Steven Legler
● Tom Berenger, Elizabeth Perkins, Anne Archer, Ted
Levine, Annette O'Toole, Kate Capshaw (Orion)

Alan Rudolph's film is a tongue-in-cheek take
on the gumshoe genre that mostly seeks to
explore the perplexing possibilities of love.

Wealthy and idle Dolan (Anne Archer)
hires rumpled cheap detective Harry Dobbs
(Tom Berenger) to trail a lover she underde-
scribes. Berenger picks the wrong guy and
ends up pursuing a quarry far more interesting than the intended – this one's not only
married, he's got two separate families.
Meanwhile, he's being followed by novice detective Stella (Elizabeth Perkins), who's been
hired by his unreasonably jealous, crockery-
throwing girlfriend, Doris (Ann Magnuson).

It's the endless round of illogical but irresistible liaisons and the characters' own unfathomable peculiarities that form the basis
of this dizzy sendup of romance. Berenger,
with his squashed hat and growling delivery,
is slyly amusing as Dobbs, while Perkins exudes a flinty, provocative chemistry.

LOVE BUG, THE

1969, 108 MINS, US ◇ ⓥ ⊙
Dir Robert Stevenson   *Prod* Bill Walsh   *Scr* Bill Walsh,
Don DaGradi   *Ph* Edward Colman   *Ed* Cotton

Warburton *Mus* George Bruns *Art Dir* Carroll Clark, John B. Mansbridge
● Dean Jones, Michele Lee, David Tomlinson, Buddy Hackett, Joe Flynn (Walt Disney)

This is a cutie, the story of a little foreign car whose philosophy is 'be nice to me and I'll be nice to you'. Because Dean Jones, a second-rate racing driver, objects to David Tomlinson, a wealthy, but stuffy, racer, kicking it, the little car – a Volkswagen – adopts Jones and wins a flock of races for him.

For sheer inventiveness of situation and the charm that such an idea projects, *The Love Bug* rates as one of the better entries of the Disney organization.

Treatment is light and imaginative, and Herbie gradually takes on all the attributes of a human. Herbie is all heart, while having a will of iron, muscles of steel, the strength of 10 and a stubborn streak.

Direction by Robert Stevenson, who also helmed the classic *Mary Poppins*, is fast and fanciful, warmly attuned to the demands of the premise and getting the most from his cast.

Jones delivers well as the driver who thinks it's his driving which wins him all those races.

■ LOVE CHILD

1982, 97 MINS, US ◇ ⦾
Dir Larry Peerce *Prod* Paul Maslansky *Scr* Anne Gerard, Katherine Specktor *Ph* James Pergola *Ed* Bob Wyman *Mus* Charles Fox *Art Dir* Don Ivey
● Amy Madigan, Beau Bridges, Mackenzie Phillips, Albert Salmi, Joanna Merlin, Margaret Whitton (Ladd/Warner)

Love Child, subtitled 'a true story', is a tasteful and sincere filmization of young Ohioan Terry Jean Moore's battle to have and keep her baby (fathered by a guard) while serving a 20-year robbery term in Broward Correctional Institution in Florida.

In a strong screen debut, freckled Amy Madigan toplines as Moore, who while hitch-hiking with her wild cousin Jesse (Lewis Smith), takes the rap when Jesse robs their driver of $5 while trying to steal the the car.

Possessing a wild temper and perennial chip on her shoulder, Moore looks headed for doom in stir. Befriended by a personable, guard, Jack Hansen (Beau Bridges) and a sympathetic young lesbian, J.J. (Mackenzie Phillips), she adjusts and even seems en route to legal freedom.

Targeting the picture squarely at a femme audience, script [from a story by Anne Gerard] emphasizes Moore's self-reform as catalyzed by her awareness of the baby growing inside her and the new responsibility it represents. Madigan is excellent in the physically demanding central role.

■ LOVE CRAZY

1941, 97 MINS, US ⦾
Dir Jack Conway *Prod* Pandro S. Berman *Scr* William Ludwig, Charles Lederer, David Hertz *Ph* Ray June *Ed* Ben Lewis *Mus* David Snell *Art Dir* Cedric Gibbons, Paul Groesse
● William Powell, Myrna Loy, Gail Patrick, Jack Carson, Florence Bates, Sidney Blackmer (M-G-M)

William Powell and Myrna Loy romp merrily through another marital comedy loaded with solid comedy, compactly set up and tempoed at a zippy pace. *Love Crazy* is a standout laugh hit of top proportions, a happy successor to previous Powell-Loy teamings.

Under most expert piloting of Jack Conway, pair take advantage of every opportunity to create maximum of laughs from every situation offered and even dip into broad slapstick and Sennettized chase.

Story [by David Hertz and William Ludwig] is light. It's the happily-married pair's fourth anniversary, and they plan to repeat happen-

ings of their wedding night, but mother-in-law arrives to send plans awry. Meeting of Powell with a former flame (Gail Patrick) prompts jealousy, separation, and plans for a divorce.

To gain time, in endeavor to reconcile with his wife, Powell simulates insanity, and lands in a private sanatorium. Escaping, he returns home to masquerade as his sister.

There's a wealth of comedy material in the script for director Jack Conway to capably transform to the screen.

■ LOVE CRIMES

1992, 85 MINS, US ◇ ⦾
Dir Lizzie Borden *Prod* Lizzie Borden, Randy Langlais *Scr* Allan Moyle, Laurie Frank *Ph* Jack N. Green *Ed* Nicholas C. Smith, Mike Jackson *Mus* Graeme Revell, Roger Mason *Art Dir* Armin Ganz
● Sean Young, Patrick Bergin, Arnetia Walker, James Read, Ron Orbach, Wayne Shorter (Sovereign)

Love Crimes is a poorly constructed thriller suffering from a bad lead performance by Sean Young, as a mannishly styled Atlanta assistant district attorney who disobeys her superior's orders and accompanies cops on their stakeouts and arrests.

She becomes obsessed with women's charges against a con man (Patrick Bergin) posing as a famous fashion photographer. He picks up plain-looking women, snaps semi-nude Polaroids, sexually dominates them and then robs them. Young travels to Savannah to capture Bergin herself.

Screenplay (from Allan Moyle's story based on a real-life 1970s case involving a Richard Avedon impersonator) initially dangles an intriguing issue: many of the women in retrospect seem to enjoy Bergin's treatment. But director Lizzie Borden stacks the deck, showing Bergin mistreating the women but giving the actresses (other than Young) limited screen time in which to develop their characters.

Bergin delivers a near-duplicate of his villainous role in *Sleeping with the Enemy*. Young is ice-cold as the assistant d.a. Unusual teaming of black femme cop Arnetia Walker, as Young's best friend, and Jewish cop Ron Orbach is pic's best thing.

■ LOVED ONE, THE

1965, 119 MINS, US ⦾
Dir Tony Richardson *Prod* Martin Ransohoff, John Calley, Haskell Wexler *Scr* Christopher Isherwood, Terry Southern *Ph* Haskell Wexler *Ed* Antony Gibbs, Hal Ashby, Brian Smedley-Aston *Mus* John Addison *Art Dir* Rouben Ter-Arutunian
● Robert Morse, Anjanette Comer, Jonathan Winters, Rod Steiger, James Coburn, John Gielgud (M-G-M)

Poor taste is prominent in the Terry Southern-Christopher Isherwood script, based on Evelyn Waugh's scathing 1948 satire of the mortuary business in California.

Most of the subtlety of Waugh's approach is lost in an episodic screenplay bearing only a wavering story line and given often to sight gags.

Story centers around the pomp and ceremony attendant upon the daily operation of a posh mortuary and a climaxing idea (not in the book) by a sanctimonious owner of a Southern California cemetery of orbiting cadavers into space so he can convert to a senior citizens' paradise for additional profit.

Robert Morse as the poet who falls in love with the lady cosmetician (later promoted to embalmer) while making arrangements for his uncle's interment, plays it light and airy, like a soul apart. Anjanette Comer, whose life is dedicated to her work and Whispering Glades Memorial Park gives almost ethereal portraiture to her embalmer character.

Jonathan Winters appears in a dual role,

shining both as the owner of Whispering Glades and his twin brother, who operates the nearby pet graveyard and is patron of a 13-year-old scientific whiz who invents a rocket capable of projecting bodies into orbit.

■ LOVE FIELD

1992, 104 MINS, US ◇ ⦾ ⦿
Dir Jonathan Kaplan *Prod* Sarah Pillsbury, Midge Sanford *Scr* Don Roos *Ph* Ralf Bode *Ed* Jane Kurson *Mus* Jerry Goldsmith *Art Dir* Mark Freeborn
● Michelle Pfeiffer, Dennis Haysbert, Stephanie McFadden, Brian Kerwin, Louise Latham, Peggy Rea (Orion)

Love Field is a sincere, not fully realized 1960s drama that is yet another variation on the 'where were you when you heard JFK was shot' theme.

Story introduces Lurene Hallett (Michelle Pfeiffer), a rather dim Dallas hairdresser with a 100-watt platinum coif who imagines a kinship with Jacqueline Kennedy, since both lost infant children.

Against her husband's (Brian Kerwin) wishes, Lurene hops a Greyhound north to attend the state funeral. On board she meets and gradually befriends a 'Negro' man, Paul (Dennis Haysbert), with something to hide. With Paul is his traumatized young daughter, Jonell (Stephanie McFadden). The three are thrown together and must fend for themselves in the all-too-predictable American South.

Pfeiffer notches yet another memorable characterization, although her attempt at defining a not terribly bright woman skirts condescension. Haysbert, in a role that Denzel Washington relinquished over 'creative differences', is solid and likable, but the part needed more gradation. The real find is six-year-old McFadden, in her acting debut.
□ 1992: Nomination: Best Actress (Michelle Pfeiffer)

■ LOVE HAPPY

1949, 91 MINS, US ⦾ ⦿
Dir David Miller *Prod* Lester Cowan *Scr* Frank Tashlin, Mac Benoff *Ph* William C. Mellor *Ed* Basil Wrangell, Al Joseph *Mus* Ann Ronell *Art Dir* Gabriel Scognamillo
● Groucho Marx, Harpo Marx, Chico Marx, Ilona Massey, Vera-Ellen, Raymond Burr (United Artists)

The story [based on one by Harpo Marx], such as it is, deals with a chase for a priceless necklace. Involved are a private eye (Groucho Marx), a blonde Continental who would stop at nothing to get the gems (Ilona Massey), a mute klepto (Harpo), plus varied others, including a shoestring musicomedy troupe whom Harpo feeds from his daily excursions to a nearby grocer.

The major portion of the film is centered around Harpo and there are a number of his pantomimic scenes that are typically in the Harpo idiom. And some of it too is obviously contrived but plenty laugh-provoking.

There is a Times Square chase involving Harpo and Groucho, in which Harpo is pursued along rooftops, through blinking electric-light advertising signs, that gets its share of laughs. It's in situations like this that the Marx Bros. can get away with almost anything.

■ LOVE HAS MANY FACES

1965, 104 MINS, US ◇ ⦾
Dir Alexander Singer *Prod* Jerry Bresler *Scr* Marguerite Roberts *Ph* Joseph Ruttenberg *Ed* Alma Macrorie *Mus* David Raksin *Art Dir* Alfred Sweeney
● Lana Turner, Cliff Robertson, Hugh O'Brian, Ruth Roman, Stefanie Powers, Virginia Grey (Columbia)

L

High life among American beach bums in Acapulco is lavishly dramatized in this Jerry Bresler production starring Lana Turner, Cliff Robertson and Hugh O'Brian.

Turner portrays a millionairess surrounded by moochers – including her husband, Robertson – and desperately striving for unfound happiness in her own particular brandy-swilling world. Narrative concerns the love affairs – the many faces of love – at the glamorous resort.

Alexander Singer's direction gets the utmost in values from his story and cast, although none of latter is particularly sympathetic. O'Brian is an expert in the art of sharing his company for money and as a sideline indulges in friendly blackmail, in this case Ruth Roman, a wealthy divorcee.

Turner lends conviction in a demanding part and Robertson is forceful as her husband who married her for her money but finds his life distasteful. O'Brian turns in a good job as a beach parasite who sells his wares to avid young touristas.

....

■ LOVE IN THE AFTERNOON

1957, 126 MINS, US ⊛
Dir Billy Wilder *Prod* Billy Wilder *Scr* Billy Wilder, I.A.L. Diamond *Ph* William Mellor *Ed* Leonid Azar *Mus* Franz Waxman (adapt.) *Art Dir* Alexandre Trauner
● Gary Cooper, Audrey Hepburn, Maurice Chevalier, John McGiver, Van Doude, Lise Bourdin (Allied Artists)

Title-wise, *Love in the Afternoon* is fitting, being far more communicative of the film's content than the original [Claude Anet novel] *Ariane*. It is all about romance before nightfall, in Paris, with Audrey Hepburn and Gary Cooper as the participants. Under Billy Wilder's alternately sensitive, mirthful and loving-care direction, and with Maurice Chevalier turning in a captivating performance as a private detective specializing in cases of amour, the production holds enchantment and delight in substantial quantity.

Love in the Afternoon, though, is long and the casting of Cooper as the eager beaver Romeo is curious. Consider this wealthy American businessman (Cooper) constantly as the woo merchant in his lavish Parisian hotel suite, first with Madame X and then Ariane (Hepburn). Several scenes spill out before Cooper comes on camera, and then on it's love in the afternoon.

It's in Chevalier's files that his daughter, the lovely, wistful Hepburn, as a cello student, comes upon knowledge of Cooper's international conquests, runs to him with the warning that his current passion (Madame X) has a husband (Mr X) bent on murder, and finds herself soon to become a candidate for one of her own father's file cards.

Mr X is John McGiver, suitably frenzied as the husband suspecting his mate has taken to play with another. It's a floating-in-air kind of story. And being innocent of earthiness there is no offensiveness in the content.

....

■ LOVE IS A MANY-SPLENDORED THING

1955, 102 MINS, US ◇ ⊛ ⊙
Dir Henry King *Prod* Buddy Adler *Scr* John Patrick *Ph* Leon Shamroy *Ed* William Reynolds *Mus* Alfred Newman *Art Dir* Lyle R. Wheeler, George W. Davis
● William Holden, Jennifer Jones, Torin Thatcher, Isobel Elsom, Virginia Gregg, Candace Lee (20th Century-Fox)

Love, as portrayed and dramatized in this fine and sensitive production based on the Han Suyin bestseller, is indeed a many-splendored thing. It's an unusual picture in many ways, shot against authentic Hong Kong backgrounds and offbeat in its treatment, yet a simple and moving love story.

William Holden as the American correspondent, and Jennifer Jones as the Eurasian doctor, make a romantic team of great appeal.

But it must also be said that, up to the middle of the film, things go rather slowly. Director Henry King makes this into a love story that allows little else to intrude. Both he and writer John Patrick apparently thought a romantic theme should be enough.

King and lenser Leon Shamroy do a magnificent job in utilizing the Hong Kong backgrounds.

☐ 1955: Best Color Costume Design, Song ('Love is a Many-Splendored Thing'), Scoring of a Dramatic Picture.

☐ Nominations: Best Picture, Actress (Jennifer Jones), Color Cinematography, Color Art Direction, Sound

....

■ LOVE LAUGHS AT ANDY HARDY

1946, 93 MINS, US ⊛
Dir Willis Goldbeck *Prod* Robert Sisk *Scr* Harry Ruskin, William Ludwig *Ph* Robert Planck *Ed* Irvine Warburton *Mus* David Snell *Art Dir* Cedric Gibbons, Harry McAfee
● Mickey Rooney, Lewis Stone, Bonita Granville, Fay Holden (M-G-M)

This pic doesn't vary much from the basic formula used in the numerous predecessors in the Hardy family saga, but why should it?

Mickey Rooney is a couple of years older but doesn't look it, and certainly doesn't act it. A diminutive dynamo, Rooney bounces through his paces with his usual zest, capering, mugging and energetically stealing every scene he's in – and he's in practically every one.

Always a pillar of strength, Lewis Stone is back at his old stand as Judge Hardy, still playing the grave, distinguished, and ideally understanding dad. Other cast regulars in the series include Fay Holden, who does a convincing job as Andy's anxious mother, and Sara Haden, in a walk-on part as Aunt Milly. Filling in as Andy's heart throb is Bonita Granville, who registers nicely as the campus siren but who had better watch her waist and chin line for the future.

Bowing to the fact that Rooney is growing older, if no larger, story lines pushes him to the brink of a marital plunge. Back from the wars, Andy picks up his academic career as a college freshman and falls badly for Granville, who trips him up by marrying someone else. Heartbroken, Andy is set to pack up for exile in South America until he's diverted back to normal by the chili wiles of Lina Romay, a south-of-the-border chick who happens to be visiting the town of Carvel.

....

■ LOVE LETTERS

1983, 98 MINS, US ◇ ⊛ ⊙
Dir Amy Jones *Prod* Roger Corman *Scr* Amy Jones *Ph* Alec Hirschfeld *Ed* Wendy Greene *Mus* Ralph Jones *Art Dir* Jeannine Oppewall
● Jamie Lee Curtis, James Keach, Amy Madigan, Bud Cort, Matt Clark, Bonnie Bartlett (New World)

Love Letters is a fine intimate drama from writer-director (and former editor) Amy Jones. Although overly schematic and lacking a certain humor that might have been welcome, film is much closer to the tradition of personal filmmaking.

Although in no way intended to seem typical, Jamie Lee Curtis is seen living a life that is certainly shared by many young contempo women.

Suddenly, barely past ago 40, Curtis' mother dies, and the daughter discovers a collection of old letters which reveal the secret love of her mother's life, a love which can stand as a pure ideal to Curtis.

While pouring over the missives, Curtis meets prosperous photographer James Keach, a 40-ish married man with two kids.

Also believable are the intense and sweaty sex scenes, into which Curtis throws herself

with increasing abandon, and the exchanges with her best friend (Amy Madigan) who delivers conventional put-downs of modern men by way of rationalizing a vow of celibacy.

....

■ LOVELY WAY TO DIE, A
(UK: *A Lovely Way to Go*)

1968, 103 MINS, US ◇
Dir David Lowell Rich *Prod* Richard Lewis *Scr* A.J. Russell *Ph* Morris Hartzband *Ed* Sidney Katz *Mus* Kenyon Hopkins *Art Dir* Willard Levitas
● Kirk Douglas, Sylva Koscina, Eli Wallach, Kenneth Haigh, Gordon Peters, Martyn Green (Universal)

This is the kind of hard-hitting polished murder-mystery meller that Kirk Douglas can play in his sleep. Cast with the cool, aloof Sylva Koscina and Eli Wallach, the screenplay is crisp and tangy, though the plotline wavers at a few spots.

Douglas is a cop whose belief is that hands are made for shooting, punching, holding drinks and caressing dames. As a protest at the mollycoddling of hoods by the police he turns in his badge, to be hired by Wallach, a shrewd homespun attorney, to protect Koscina, being defended by Wallach on a rap of murdering her husband.

As a male bodyguard Douglas is intrigued by the girl. As an ex-cop he's intrigued by the murder mystery.

Douglas plays the confident, flip, resourceful he-man with a suave winning way with the femmes, in his customary easy-going fashion and Koscina's hot-and-cold attitude to his boudoir advances are both amusing and helpful to the atmosphere of the mystery yarn.

....

■ LOVELY WAY TO GO, A
See: A Lovely Way to Die

....

■ LOVE ME TENDER

1956, 94 MINS, US ⊛
Dir Robert D. Webb *Prod* David Weisbart *Scr* Robert Buckner *Ph* Leo Tover *Mus* Lionel Newman *Art Dir* Lyle R. Wheeler, Maurice Ransford
● Richard Egan, Debra Paget, Elvis Presley, Robert Middleton, William Campbell, Neville Brand (20th Century-Fox)

Appraising Presley as an actor, he ain't. Not that it makes much difference. There are four songs, and lotsa Presley wriggles thrown in for good measure.

Screenplay from a story by Maurice Geraghty is synthetic. Story line centers on Presley, the youngest of four brothers, who stayed on their Texas farm while the older three are away fighting the Yankees. The older brother (Richard Egan) left a gal (Debra Paget) and, when word comes that he's been killed in battle, she weds Presley. When the three boys come home to resume their civvy ways, it's hard to keep Egan down on the farm because he's still in love with Paget, now his brother's wife.

Egan is properly stoic as the older brother while Paget does nothing more than look pretty and wistful throughout. Mildred Dunnock gets sincerity into the part of mother of the brood, an achievement. Nobody, however, seems to be having as much fun as Presley especially when he's singing the title song, 'Poor Boy', 'We're Gonna Move' and 'Let Me'. Tunes were written by Presley and Vera Matson.

....

■ LOVE ME TONIGHT

1932, 90 MINS, US
Dir Rouben Mamoulian *Scr* Samuel Hoffenstein, Waldemar Young, George Marion Jr. *Ph* Victor Milner
● Maurice Chevalier, Jeanette MacDonald, Charlie Ruggles, Charles Butterworth, Myrna Loy, C. Aubrey Smith (Paramount)

Treatment takes on the color of a musical comedy frolic, whimsical in its aim and deliciously carried out in its pattern, in its playing and in its direction. Effect is altogether delightful. Gives Jeanette MacDonald an excellent opportunity for quiet comedy playing, which she rises charmingly to meet.

Story has to do with Maurice Chevalier, a Paris tailor, going to a great French castle to collect a bill run up by a scapegrace scion of the family, and being introduced as Baron Courtelin and held as an honored guest to keep his mission secret. Fun of the situation arises from the presence of the lively young Parisian commoner among a crowd of fossilized old nobles of both sexes.

The comedy [from a French play by Leopold Marchant and Paul Armont] is exquisitely amusing, particularly in all too brief sequences involving Charlie Ruggles and Charles Butterworth. Adapters also have given the dialog a number of swift and spicy sallies that count for solid laughs. And the production throughout has stunning pictorial beauty. Here is seen the fine hand of director Rouben Mamoulian.

Musical numbers [by Richard Rodgers and Lorenz Hart] are as amusing for once in their lyrics as they are attractive in their melodies, and are blended in smoothly with the action

■ **LOVE PARADE, THE**

1929, 107 MINS, US
Dir Ernst Lubitsch *Scr* Guy Bolton, Ernst Vajda
Ph Victor Milner *Mus* Victor Schertzinger *Art Dir* Hans Dreier
● Maurice Chevalier, Jeanette MacDonald, Lupino Lane, Lillian Roth, Eugene Pallette, Edgar Norton (Paramount)

In *The Love Parade*, second starring talker for Maurice Chevalier, Paramount has its first original screen operetta production whose story is more than made up in magnificence of sets and costumes, tuneful music, subtlety of direction, comedy and general appeal. It's a fine, near-grand entertainment.

At the outset the Chevalier personality is put to the fore in the manner the Parisian music-hall star knows best.

In Jeanette MacDonald, ingenue prima donna from Broadway, Chevalier has an actress opposite who all but steals the picture.

The story says that the philandering Parisian, brought back to Sylvania, ruled by MacDonald, because of his scandalous affairs as a military attache in France's capital, must, in accepting marriage to the queen, keep his fingers out of all matters of state and be subject to her own commands.

The wedding is an extravaganza, with one of the largest sets ever built, but musically lacks the punch of other scenes.

Guy Bolton wrote the libretto for *Love Parade* [from the play *The Prince Consort* by Leon Xanrof and Jules Chancel].

It can be said that this is the first true screen musical.

☐ 1929/30: Nominations: Best Picture, Director, Actor (Maurice Chevalier), Cinematography, Art Direction, Sound

■ **LOVER, THE**

1992, 110 MINS, FRANCE/UK ◇ ⓥ ⊙
Dir Jean-Jacques Annaud *Prod* Claude Berri
Scr Gerard Brach, Jean-Jacques Annaud *Ph* Robert Fraisse *Ed* Noelle Boisson *Mus* Gabriel Yared
Art Dir Thanh At Hoang
● Jane March, Tony Leung, Frederique Meininger, Arnaud Giovaninetti, Melvil Poupaud, Lisa Faulkner (Renn/Films AZ/Burrill)

The Lover, a sophisticated adaptation of Marguerite Duras' bestselling memoir about her love affair as a 15-year-old with a rich, older Chinese man, lacks the distinctive voice and ambiance of the book, but the abundant

sex – soft-core and tasteful – and the splendid sets make up for the film's banal style.

No expense has been spared – the film cost $22 million – in Jean-Jacques Annaud's evocation of the pungent atmosphere of the story's 1920s Vietnam setting.

Part of the fault lies with Jane March, a pretty 17-year-old English actress who plays the young Duras. She pouts to perfection but does not convey the jaded spirit of the girl. Tony Leung is excellent as the shiftless scion whose love for the girl makes him emotionally naked and vulnerable.

In the film's well-handled subplot, Frederique Meininger is superb as the girl's exhausted schoolteacher mother. Most powerful scene deals with the mother's farewell to her son (Arnaud Giovaninetti), who is being sent back to France.

☐ 1992: Nomination: Best Cinematography

■ **LOVER COME BACK**

1961, 107 MINS, US ◇ ⓥ
Dir Delbert Mann *Prod* Stanley Shapiro, Martin Melcher
Scr Stanley Shapiro, Paul Henning *Ph* Arthur E. Arling
Ed Marjorie Fowler *Mus* Frank DeVol
Art Dir Alexander Golitzen, Robert Clatworthy
● Rock Hudson, Doris Day, Tony Randall, Edie Adams, Jack Oakie, Jack Kruschen (Universal)

This is a funny, most-of-the-time engaging, smartly produced show. Farce has Rock Hudson as would-be conqueror of Doris Day, who as the victim of a who's-who deception plays brinkmanship with surrender. There's a bed scene but this is all right because the two, while not remembering the Maryland ceremony (due to being stoned under preposterous circumstances), were legally hitched.

Hudson and Day are rival Madison Avenue ad account people. He deceives her into thinking he's a scientist working on an actually non-existent product called VIP. She undertakes to wrest the VIP account from the masquerading Hudson. He meanwhile is trying to maneuver her into romantic conquest.

Tony Randall draws yocks consistently as head of an agency he inherited but doesn't really helm because he can't make decisions. Jack Oakie plays broadly and humorously the part of a floor-wax maker who goes to the agency offering him the best girls and bourbon. Edie Adams clicks as a chorus girl trying to get ahead, and Jack Kruschen, as a partly screwball scientist, also wins laughs.

☐ 1961: Nomination: Best Original Story & Screenplay

■ **LOVERS AND OTHER STRANGERS**

1970, 104 MINS, US ◇ ⓥ
Dir Cy Howard *Prod* David Susskind *Scr* Renee Taylor, Joseph Bologna, David Zelag *Ph* Andy Laszlo
Ed David Bretherton, Sidney Katz *Mus* Fred Karlin
Art Dir Ben Edwards
● Bea Arthur, Bonnie Bedelia, Michael Brandon, Richard Castellano, Robert Dishy, Harry Guardino (ABC)

Lovers And Other Strangers tells in a delightful way of the marriage of a young couple who have been making it on the sly for over a year. Comedy vignettes reveal amusing and compassionate fashion the assorted marital foibles of members of both families.

Bonnie Bedelia and Michael Brandon, the couple in question, have their own life style which rubs against but does not destroy relations with their respective parents. Gig Young and Cloris Leachman are her folks, while Richard Castellano and Bea Arthur are his.

Screenplay [from the play by Joseph Bologna and Renee Taylor] is essentially a string of intercut vignettes about the young couple's relatives. On the girl's side of things, Young has been having a side affair with Anne Jackson for some years; she is perfect.

☐ 1970: Best Song ('For All We Know').

☐ Nominations: Best Supp. Actor (Richard Castellano), Adapted Screenplay

■ **LOVESICK**

1983, 95 MINS, US ◇ ⓥ ⊙
Dir Marshall Brickman *Prod* Charles Okun
Scr Marshall Brickman *Ph* Gerry Fisher *Ed* Nina Feinberg *Mus* Philippe Sarde *Art Dir* Philip Rosenberg
● Dudley Moore, Elizabeth McGovern, Alec Guinness, John Huston, William Shawn, Alan King (Ladd/Warner)

An engaging idea – Dudley Moore as a successful, married shrink who becomes obsessed with a beautiful patient (Elizabeth McGovern) – is rendered inoperable by Marshall Brickman's witless script and uninspired direction.

Perhaps most descriptive of the script's desperation is the gimmicky inclusion of Sigmund Freud, who mystically materializes in the person of Alec Guinness whenever Moore seeks professional help. Guinness properly plays it straight and slightly aloof, telling Moore that his obsession with McGovern 'reminds us what we really are – animals – take it or leave it.' Pure Freud.

Ron Silver is fine as an arrogant actor but Gene Sacks as a suicidal patient, John Huston and Alan King as stuffy doctors, and Renee Taylor, as a patient, are all embarrassing.

■ **LOVES OF ISADORA, THE**

See: Isadora

■ **LOVES OF JOANNA GODDEN, THE**

1947, 91 MINS, UK
Dir Charles Frend *Prod* Michael Balcon *Scr* H.E. Bates
Ph Douglas Slocombe *Ed* Michael Truman *Mus* Ralph Vaughan Williams *Art Dir* Duncan Sutherland
● Googie Withers, Jean Kent, John McCallum, Derek Bond, Chips Rafferty (Ealing)

As a record of sheep farming in a corner of England in 1905, this picture [based on *Joanna Godden* by Sheila Kaye-Smith, adapted by Angus MacPhail] may have its points. But as a story of a high-spirited, lovely young woman who inherits a farm and is expected to marry and let her husband do the job, the picture falls short of its intentions. So enamored did producer and director become with their location, that they were determined to teach audiences all they had learned about sheep breeding.

Set against the background of the Romney Marshes in Kent, Joanna (Googie Withers), impetuous and self-willed, is bequeathed one of the leading farms on the Marsh. A codicil in her father's will expresses the hope that she will marry neighbor-farmer Arthur Alce (John McCallum). Determined to defy the conventions of the time, she outrages the countryside by running the farm herself and by her experiments in cross-breeding and ploughing. Stinting herself and luxury, she sends her young sister, Ellen (Jean Kent), to a finishing school, from which the girl returns an accomplished golddigger.

Joanna has a mild affair with Collard (Chips Rafferty), the man engaged to look after her sheep, before she falls for a local aristocrat, Martin Trevor (Derek Bond). The banns are put up, but Martin is drowned. Meanwhile Ellen has bewitched Arthur Alce, Joanna's 'old faithful,' marries him, and deserts him for an old man with money.

Withers looks as attractive as she has ever done, but her characterization of the name part has a soporific monotony.

The men fare somewhat better, although McCallum is given little to lighten his dourness. Bond gives a natural and pleasant performance as Martin, and Rafferty disappears far too early.

L

■ LOVE STORY

1970, 99 MINS, US ◇ ⬥ ⊙
Dir Arthur Hiller   *Prod* Howard G. Minsky, David
Golden   *Scr* Erich Segal   *Ph* Dick Kratina   *Ed* Robert
C. Jones   *Mus* Francis Lai   *Art Dir* Robert Gundlach
● Ali MacGraw, Ryan O'Neal, John Marley, Ray
Milland, Russell Nype, Katherine Balfour (Paramount)

Love Story is an excellent film. Made for about
$2.2 million the Paramount release is gener-
ally successful on all artistic levels, propelled
by the best-selling Erich Segal novel written
from the original screenplay.

Ali MacGraw is a girl of poor origins who
has worked her way to high academic status;
Ryan O'Neal, restive in his identity, but at
the outset just another rich man's athletic-
oriented son at the old family college, develops true manliness from his love for her,
through their marriage and the severe challenge of her terminal illness.

John Marley is excellent as MacGraw's father and Ray Milland is outstanding as
O'Neal's cold father. Both men go way beyond the superficial trappings of their roles
and make the characters vital.

It's O'Neal's picture by a good margin.
☐ 1970: Best Original Score.
☐ Nominations: Best Picture, Director, Actor
(Ryan O'Neal), Actress (Ali MacGraw), Supp.
Actor (John Marley), Original Story &
Screenplay

■ LOVE STREAMS

1984, 136 MINS, US ◇ ⬥
Dir John Cassavetes   *Prod* Menahem Golan, Yoram
Globus   *Scr* John Cassavetes, Ted Allan   *Ph* Al Ruban
Ed George Villasenor   *Mus* Bo Harwood
● Gena Rowlands, John Cassavetes, Diahnne Abbott,
Seymour Cassel, Margaret Abbott, Jakob Shaw (Cannon)

John Cassavetes' *Love Streams* shapes up as
one of the filmmaker's best, both artistically
and commercially, in some time, emotionally
potent, technically assured and often brilliantly insightful.

Reflecting the title, the plot begins with two
separate flows. Robert Harmon (Cassavetes)
is a successful writer from the Gay Talese
school currently researching the subject of
love for sale on a first-hand basis. Inter-cut is
Sarah Lawson's (Gena Rowlands) story – an
emotionally erratic woman proceeding
through a divorce and custody case.

One can nit-pick about the picture's length
and use of repetition but these are minor
points in the overall strength of the production. The dramatic rollercoaster ride of
frightening and funny moments leave little
room for indifference.

■ LOVE WALTZ, THE

1930, 70 MINS, GERMANY
Dir Wilhelm Thiele   *Prod* Erich Pommer   *Scr* Hans
Muller, Robert Liebmann   *Ph* Werner Brandes,
Konstantin Tschet   *Mus* Werner Heymann
● Lilian Harvey, John Batten, Georg Alexander (UFA)

The all-English dialog version of this UFA
talker is a presentable piece of work, even allowing for blemishes. Film errs somewhat in
starting off as snappy comedy and ending up
as the usual Ruritanian romance, being much
more entertaining first half than in the final
reels. Production is a mixture of imitation
American slickness and Germanic artistry,
with the result much of the footage is very
easy to the eye.

Story is the usual sugary mixture expected
of the species, telling how a bored youngster
rivets himself on an equally bored archduke,
who is due to get engaged to an even more
bored princess.

Usual Erich Pommer touches are noticeable. Lilian Harvey isn't photographed to the
best advantage and John Batten hasn't much

difficulty in getting honors among the leads,
although Georg Alexander's work as the duke
is a smooth job, nicely rounded off.

The English version was done under the supervision of Carl Winston, who went to
Berlin. Harvey, being of English extraction,
plays her role in both versions, and young
Englishman Batten handles the Willi Fritsch
character.

■ LOVE WITH THE PROPER STRANGER

1963, 102 MINS, US ⬥ ⊙
Dir Robert Mulligan   *Prod* Alan J. Pakula   *Scr* Arnold
Schulman   *Ph* Milton Krasner   *Ed* Aaron Stell
Mus Elmer Bernstein   *Art Dir* Hal Pereira, Roland
Anderson
● Natalie Wood, Steve McQueen, Edie Adams,
Herschel Bernardi, Tom Bosley (Paramount)

Proper Stranger is a somewhat unstable picture,
fluctuating between scenes of a substantial,
lifelike disposition and others where reality is
suspended in favor of deliberately exaggerated hokum. Fortunately the film survives
these shortcomings through its sheer breezy
good nature and the animal magnetism of its
two stars.

Arnold Schulman's scenario describes the
curious love affair that evolves between two
young New York Italians – a freedom-loving
freelance musician (Steve McQueen) and a
sheltered girl (Natalie Wood) – when she becomes pregnant following their one-night
stand at a summer resort.

Wood plays her role with a convincing mixture of feminine sweetness and emotional
turbulence. McQueen displays an especially
keen sense of timing. Although he's probably
the most unlikely Italian around (the character could and should obviously have been altered to Irish Catholic), he is an appealing
figure nevertheless.

Fine supporting work is contributed by Edie
Adams as an accommodating stripper,
Herschel Bernardi asWood's overly protective
older brother and Tom Bosley as a jittery
suitor.

Robert Mulligan's direction runs hot and
cold, like the screenplay and the film itself.
☐ 1963: Nominations: Best Actress (Natalie
Wood), Original Story & Screenplay, B&W
Cinematography, B&W Costume Design,
B&W Art Direction

■ LOVING

1970, 89 MINS, US ◇ ⬥
Dir Irvin Kershner   *Prod* Don Devlin, Raymond Wagner
Scr Don Devlin   *Ph* Gordon Willis   *Ed* Robert Lawrence
Mus Bernardo Segall   *Art Dir* Walter Scott Herndon
● George Segal, Eva Marie Saint, Sterling Hayden,
Keenan Wynn, Nancie Phillips, Janis Young (Columbia)

A good story about marriage crackups among
the fortyish set in suburbia.

A novel by J. M. Ryan was basis for the script,
which is handicapped by a protagonist who,
while not supposed to be sympathetic, isn't even
interesting in his selfishness and immaturity.

George Segal is the character, an aging
commercial artist who would seem in reality
to have been long-since crushed by the forces
against which he continually rails. Eva Marie
Saint is quite outstanding as the slightly-nag-
ging but steadfast wife. Her character is also
hampered by some incredulity of premise, but
she more than overcomes the liability.

Within script limitations, cast delivers well,
Saint in the extreme, Segal however never
quite believable.

■ LOVING COUPLES

1980, 97 MINS, US ◇ ⬥
Dir Jack Smight   *Prod* Renee Valente   *Scr* Martin
Donovan   *Ph* Philip Lathrop   *Ed* Grey Fox, Frank
Urioste   *Mus* Fred Karlin   *Art Dir* Jan Scott

● Shirley MacLaine, James Coburn, Susan Sarandon,
Sally Kellerman, Stephen Collins (20th Century-Fox)

Loving Couples opens with a snappy cute meet.
Shirley MacLaine is riding a horse and
Stephen Collins, driving along in a sports car,
stares at her, misses a turn in the road and
crashes. She rides over to the prone Collins
and rips open his pants. Well, she's a doctor.

Young stud Collins tries to put the make on
her. Not too long after he gets it. She's not
getting much attention from her work-
obsessed doctor husband (James Coburn) who
learns of her affair from Collins' live-in friend
(Susan Sarandon). And they, in turn, fall into
a motel bed.

It's all fun and sexual games. Direction by
Jack Smight is assured and never lags.
MacLaine is in top form, sassy and sweet in
turn. Coburn delivers a casually effective
light comedy performance. Sarandon is topnotch.

■ LOVING YOU

1957, 101 MINS, US ◇ ⬥ ⊙
Dir Hal Kanter   *Prod* Hal B. Wallis   *Scr* Herbert Baker,
Hal Kanter   *Ph* Charles Lang   *Ed* Howard Smith
Mus Walter Scharf (arr.)   *Art Dir* Hal Pereira, Albert
Nozaki
● Elvis Presley, Lizabeth Scott, Wendell Corey, Dolores
Hart, James Gleason (Paramount)

Elvis Presley's second screen appearance is a
simple story, in which he can be believed,
which has romantic overtones and exposes
the singer to the kind of thing he does best,
i.e. shout out his rhythms, bang away at his
guitar and perform the strange, knee-bend-
ing, hip-swinging contortions that are his
trademark.

Apart from this, Presley shows improvement as an actor. It's not a demanding part
and, being surrounded by a capable crew of
performers, he comes across as a simple but
pleasant sort. Film introes Dolores Hart, in
an undemanding role as Presley's girl.

Story has Presley picked up by Lizabeth
Scott, a publicity girl touring with a hillbilly
band on a whistlestop tour. She gets Wendell
Corey, the leader of the outfit, to take on
Presley, and they stunt him into a rock 'n' roll
personality. Of course, there are complications and Presley takes himself off just as he's
supposed to go on a national TV show.

■ LOVIN' MOLLY

1974, 98 MINS, US ◇
Dir Sidney Lumet   *Prod* Stephen Friedman   *Scr* Stephen
Friedman   *Ph* Edward Brown   *Ed* Joanne Burke
Mus Fred Hellerman   *Art Dir* Gene Coffin
● Anthony Perkins, Beau Bridges, Blythe Danner,
Edward Binns, Susan Sarandon, Conrad Fowkes
(Columbia)

The film version of Larry McMurtry's novel,
Leaving Cheyenne emerges as a misguided,
heavy-handed attempt to span 40 years in the
lives of three Texas rustics and their bizarre
but homey menage a trois.

Divided into three main sections, *Lovin'
Molly* opens in 1925 and sets up the situation
in which two farmboy friends (Anthony
Perkins, Beau Bridges) wage amicable war for
the affections of a liberated earth mother
(Blythe Danner) who loves them both in her
fashion. Jumping to 1945 with a voiceover
bridge, Danner has been married and widowed to a third young man (Conrad Fowkes)
while continuing her sidebar relationships
and bearing two children by a married
Perkins and still-bachelor Bridges.

Pic's final section takes place in 1964 as the
three find their time running out. Perkins
dies of a heart attack and the ever-ready
Bridges beds down with the accommodating
Danner for what must be the 4,160th time.

L-SHAPED ROOM, THE

1962, 142 MINS, UK ⓦ
Dir Bryan Forbes   *Prod* James Woolf, Richard
Attenborough   *Scr* Bryan Forbes   *Ph* Douglas Slocombe
Ed Anthony Harvey   *Mus* John Barry   *Art Dir* Ray Simm
● Leslie Caron, Tom Bell, Brock Peters, Cicely
Courtneidge, Avis Bunnage, Bernard Lee (Romulus)

Lynne Reid Banks' bestseller novel seemed,
on the surface, to be unlikely material for a
film. Largely set in the restricted area of a
faded lodging house the novel had little
enough glamour or strength of plot to recommended it, excellently written though it was.
But Bryan Forbes' screenplay and his tactful,
sensitive direction create a tender study in
loneliness and frustrated love.

Yarn concerns a girl (Leslie Caron) with a
background of provincial France who, in
London, has a brief affair resulting in pregnancy. Rejecting the idea of an abortion she
decides to live it out on her own. And, in the
loneliness of her L-shaped room in a seedy
tenement, she finds a new hope and purpose
in life through meeting others who, in various
ways, suffer their own loneliness and frustration.

This brief outline gives no credit to the
film's many subtle undertones. Not a great
deal happens but it is a thoroughly holding
and intelligent film having the quality of a
film like *Marty*.

Caron and Tom Bell make a strong team.
Though they, plus Brock Peters, as Negro lad,
bear the brunt of such action as there is, the
trio are well supported by a number of others.

Vet Cicely Courtneidge make a sharp
comeback as a retired vaude artist, living
with her cat and her faded press clippings.
Other notable jobs are done by Avis Bunnage
(a landlady who prides herself on the respectability of her house, despite two of her
lodgers being prosties) and Bernard Lee, as
her boozey, hearty gentleman friend.
□ 1963: Nomination: Best Actress (Leslie
Caron)

LUCK OF GINGER COFFEY, THE

1964, 100 MINS, US/CANADA
Dir Irvin Kershner   *Prod* Leon Roth   *Scr* Brian Moore
Ph Manny Wynn   *Ed* Anthony Gibbs   *Mus* Bernardo
Segall   *Art Dir* Harry Horner
● Robert Shaw, Mary Ure, Liam Redmond, Tom Harvey,
Libby McClintock, Leo Leyden (Roth)

The Luck of Ginger Coffey is a well-turned-out
drama based on a Brian Moore novel.

Robert Shaw and Mary Ure are a married
couple who have found the going in Montreal
rough since they arrived from Dublin six
months before to make their new home in
Canada. The husband, who cannot keep a job,
has spent the passage money on which the
wife was depending to return them to Ireland
should they not make the grade. A marital
crisis therefore arises, since the wife believes
that with her husband's superior attitude he
will always be unable to hold a job in Canada.

Shaw plays his brash Irishman with sincerity and Ure lends credence to the wife, both
scoring strongly.

LUCKY JIM

1957, 95 MINS, UK ⓦ
Dir John Boulting   *Prod* Roy Boulting   *Scr* Patrick
Campbell, Jeffrey Dell   *Ph* Max Greene   *Ed* Max
Benedict   *Mus* John Addison   *Art Dir* Elliott Scott
● Ian Carmichael, Terry-Thomas, Hugh Griffith, Sharon
Acker, Clive Morton, Kenneth Griffith (Charter/British
Lion)

Kingsley Amis' novel has been built up into a
farcical comedy which, though slim enough in
idea, provides plenty of opportunity for
smiles, giggles and belly laughs. John
Boulting directs with a lively tempo and even
though the comedy situations loom up with
inevitable precision, they are still irresistible.

The lightweight story spotlights Ian
Carmichael as a junior history lecturer at a
British university in the sticks who becomes
disastrously involved in such serious college
goings-on as a ceremonial lecture on 'Merrie
England' and a procession to honor the new
university chancellor. There are also some
minor shenanigans such as a riotous car
chase, a slaphappy fist fight, a tipsy entry into
a wrong bedroom containing a girl he is trying to shake off and a number of other happy-
go-lucky situations.

The screenplay veers from facetiousness to
downright slapstick but never lets up on its
irresistible attack on the funnybone.
Carmichael is a deft light-comedy performer
who proves that he also can take hold of a
character and make him believable.

LUCKY LADY

1975, 177 MINS, US ◇
Dir Stanley Donen   *Prod* Michael Gruskoff   *Scr* Willard
Huyck, Gloria Katz   *Ph* Geoffrey Unsworth   *Ed* Peter
Boita, George Hively, Tom Rolf   *Mus* Ralph Burns
Art Dir John Barry
● Gene Hackman, Liza Minnelli, Burt Reynolds, Geoffrey
Lewis, John Hillerman, Bobby Benson (20th Century-Fox)

What appears to have been conceived as a
madcap Prohibition-era action comedy, combined with an amusing romantic menage,
emerges as forced hokum.

Successive vignettes take the stars through
a series of expansive smuggling routines.
Burt Reynolds, a gringo on the lam in
Mexico, figures he can assume the dual role
of major smuggler and lover of Liza Minnelli
when her husband dies. Gene Hackman, also
on the run, assumes a leadership role and the
trio begin running hooch.

They encounter the likes of Michael
Hordern, an urbane ship captain; John
Hillerman, a feisty hood and Geoffrey Lewis,
trigger-happy Coast Guard.

Some smart-looking production work survives the plot (admitted budget was $12.6
million).

LUCKY LUCIANO

1973, 113 MINS, ITALY/FRANCE ◇ ⓦ
Dir Francesco Rosi   *Prod* Franco Cristaldi
Scr Francesco Rosi, Lino Jannuzzi, Tonino Guerra
Ph Pasqualino De Santis   *Ed* Ruggero Mastroianni
Mus Piero Piccioni   *Art Dir* Andrea Crisanti
● Gian Maria Volonte, Rod Steiger, Charles Siragusa,
Edmond O'Brien, Vincent Gardenia, Charles Cioffi
(Vides/La Boetie)

Most films by Francesco Rosi probe well under the surface of people and events to establish a constant link between the legal and
illegal exercise of power. In *Lucky Luciano* the
search is expanded to embrace an interde-
pendent crime empire operating in America
and Italy, with roots in many other points on
the map. But Rosi takes crime kingpin Lucky
Luciano as his main clinical study, objective
enough throughout to question his own facts,
legendary accusations and hearsay.

Crime action is condensed in first few reels
in sharply-paced scenes and montage escalating Luciano to the Mafia throne, his arrest
and conviction in the mid-1930s, with his deportation to Italy after serving nine years of a
30 to 50-year prison term.

LUDWIG

1973, 186 MINS, ITALY/FRANCE/W. GERMANY ◇
Dir Luchino Visconti   *Prod* Ugo Santalucia   *Scr* Luchino
Visconti, Enrico Medioli, Suso Cecchi D'Amico
Ph Armando Nannuzzi   *Ed* Ruggero Mastroianni
Mus Franco Mannino (sup.)   *Art Dir* Mario Chiari, Mario
Scisci
● Helmut Berger, Romy Schneider, Trevor Howard,
Silvana Mangano, Gert Frobe, Helmut Griem
(Mega/Cinetel/Divina)

As his 12th feature film, and third project
based on German history and personages,
Luchino Visconti chose King Ludwig II
(Helmut Berger), the so-called 'mad' monarch of Bavaria. *Ludwig* bears the Visconti
stamp of dazzling, tasteful opulence and an
operatic style. However, story construction is
at first confusing.

To its credit the English version [translated
by William Weaver] is literate, free of arch
transliteration, and dotted with occasional
brilliant aphorism. But it barely helps the
limitations of the overall structure.

Major phases of Ludwig's life include his
patronage of composer Richard Wagner, portrayed effectively by Trevor Howard; the
spendthrift erection of castles; the introverted indifference to his responsibilities as
king; a long platonic love affair with Empress
Elisabeth of Austria, played with great compassion by the spectacularly beautiful Romy
Schneider; and a pervading atmosphere of latent, then overt homosexuality.

The score utilizes themes of Wagner,
Schumann and Offenbach, with piano solos
and orchestra conducting by Franco Mannino.
Wagner's last original piano composition is
performed publicly for first time herein.
□ 1973: Nomination: Best Costume Design

LULLABY OF BROADWAY

1951, 91 MINS, US ◇ ⓦ ⊙
Dir David Butler   *Prod* William Jacobs   *Scr* Earl
Baldwin   *Ph* Wilfrid M. Cline   *Ed* Irene Morra
Mus Ray Heindorf (dir.)   *Art Dir* Douglas Bacon
● Doris Day, Gene Nelson, S.Z. Sakall, Billy De Wolfe,
Gladys George, Florence Bates (Warner)

Mounted in gorgeous Technicolor, and displaying the song-and-dance talents of co-stars
Doris Day and Gene Nelson, *Lullaby of
Broadway* has a solid comedy story line, deft
direction and a capable cast.

Film gets away from the regular practice of
injecting too many elaborate production
numbers. Most of the tunes are hits of the
previous two decades. Day scores with her
solo song-and-dance routines, including 'Just
One of Those Things' and 'You're Getting to
Be a Habit with Me'. She teams with Nelson
for tune-and-terping of 'Somebody Loves Me',
'I Love the Way You Say Goodnight' and
'Lullaby of Broadway'.

Story has Day returning from several years
in England to meet her mother (Gladys
George) former stage headliner who hit the
skids due to drink. Girl arrives at supposed
mansion of her mother, and is taken in tow by
Billy De Wolfe and Anne Triola, two at-lib-
erty vaudevillians working as butler and
maid. Sakall, elderly owner of the house,
takes an interest in the girl and gets involved
in ensuing complications when his wife suspects an affair.

LUNATIC, THE

1992, 93 MINS, US ◇ ⓦ
Dir Lol Creme   *Prod* Paul Heller, John Pringle
Scr Anthony C. Winkler   *Ph* Richard Greatrex
Ed Michael Connell   *Mus* Wally Badarou
Art Dir Giorgio Ferrari
● Julie T. Wallace, Paul Campbell, Reggie Carter, Carl
Bradshaw, Winston Stona, Linda Gambrill (Island)

Novelist-scripter Anthony C. Winkler turns a
colorful phrase but billboards all his themes
unsubtly in this Jamaican-lensed tale of an innocent black lad Aloysius (Paul Campbell in a
winning interpretation) who talks to flora and
fauna. Everyone brands him a lunatic, but visiting German photographer Inga (British
thesp Julie T. Wallace) makes him her love
slave. Soon a menage a trois is set up when

L

she takes a fancy to a butcher (Carl Bradshaw).

Debuting director Lol Creme, who has made many music vids with Kevin Godley, fails to keep a lid on pic's cuteness. Best efforts here are by Campbell as the naive hero and Reggie Carter as an oddly sympathetic major domo. Surprise is that the booming voice of Campbell's best friend, a tree, is provided by Carter as well.

••••••••••••••••••••••••••••••••

■ **LUST FOR LIFE**

1956, 122 MINS, US ◇ ⑫ ⊙
Dir Vincente Minnelli   *Prod* John Houseman
Scr Norman Corwin   *Ph* Freddie Young, Russell Harlan
Ed Adrienne Fazan   *Mus* Miklos Rozsa   *Art Dir* Cedric Gibbons, Hans Peters, Preston Ames
● Kirk Douglas, Anthony Quinn, James Donald, Pamela Brown, Everett Sloane, Niall MacGinnis (M-G-M)

This is a slow-moving picture whose only action is in the dialog itself. Basically a faithful portrait of Van Gogh, *Lust for Life* is nonetheless unexciting. It misses out in conveying the color and entertainment of the original Irving Stone novel. It's a tragic recap that Stone penned, but still there was no absence of amusing incidents.

Lensed in Holland and France, *Lust for Life* is largely conversation plus expert tint photography, and both on a high level.

Kirk Douglas plays the title role with undeniable understanding of the artist. He's a competent performer all the way, conveying the frustrations which beset Van Gogh in his quest for knowledge of life and the approach to putting this on canvas.

But somehow the measure of sympathy that should be engendered for the genius who was to turn insane is not realized. To draw a comparison, Jose Ferrer in *Moulin Rouge* made Toulouse-Lautrec 'closer' to the audience.
□ 1956: Best Supp. Actor (Anthony Quinn).
□ Nominations: Best Actor (Kirk Douglas), Adapted Screenplay, Color Art Direction

••••••••••••••••••••••••••••••••

■ **LUST IN THE DUST**

1984, 87 MINS, US ◇ ⑫
Dir Paul Bartel   *Prod* Allan Glaser, Tab Hunter
Scr Philip Taylor   *Ph* Paul Lohmann   *Ed* Alan Toomayan
Mus Peter Matz, Karen Hart   *Art Dir* Walter Pickette
● Tab Hunter, Divine, Lainie Kazan, Geoffrey Lewis, Henry Silva, Cesar Romero (Fox Run)

Lust In The Dust is a saucy, irreverent, quite funny send-up of the Western. Film takes some of the old-time conventions – the silent stranger, the saloon singer with a past, the motley crew of crazed gunslingers, the missing stash of gold – and stands them on their head with outrageous comedy and imaginative casting.

Prevailing attitude is established immediately via some florid narration and the sight of the outsized Divine making his way across the desert in full drag on a donkey. Upon meeting Tab Hunter, the epitome of the straight-arrow hero of few words, Divine's character, Rosie, explains to him, in flashback, she's just been gang-raped by Geoffrey Lewis' bunch of Third World outlaws (and outlasted them all).

Duo arrives in the squalid little town of Chili Verde, where the entire populace seems to hang out at the cantina of Lainie Kazan.

Outrageous tale is handled with fine high humor by director Paul Bartel. Picture is Divine's for the taking, and take it he does with a vibrant, inventive comic performance.

••••••••••••••••••••••••••••••••

■ **LUSTY MEN, THE**

1952, 112 MINS, US ⑫ ⊙
Dir Nicholas Ray   *Prod* Jerry Wald   *Scr* Horace McCoy, David Dortort   *Ph* Lee Garmes   *Ed* Ralph

Dawson   *Mus* Roy Webb   *Art Dir* Albert S. D'Agostino, Alfred Herman
● Susan Hayward, Robert Mitchum, Arthur Kennedy, Arthur Hunnicutt, Frank Faylen, Walter Coy (Wald-Krasna/RKO)

Robert Mitchum is a faded rodeo champion who has fallen on bad days after an accident. Returning broke to the tumbledown ranch where he spent his boyhood, he finds the property desired by Arthur Kennedy, poor cowpoke, and his wife (Susan Hayward). Tales of Mitchum's past glory light a fire under Kennedy, who sees a chance at quick realization of his ranch-owning yen via rodeoing prizes.

As the days pass, Kennedy wins money and develops a taste for the glory that goes with success but Mitchum has a growing interest in Hayward.

A lot of actual rodeo footage is used to backstop the story [suggested by one by Claude Stanush]. A somewhat slow starter, once underway it is kept playing with growing interest under Nicholas Ray's firm direction.

••••••••••••••••••••••••••••••••

■ **LUV**

1967, 93 MINS, US ◇ ⑫ ⊙
Dir Clive Donner   *Prod* Martin Manulis   *Scr* Elliott Baker
Ph Ernest Laszlo   *Ed* Harold F. Kress   *Mus* Gerry Mulligan   *Art Dir* Al Brenner
● Jack Lemmon, Peter Falk, Elaine May, Nina Wayne, Eddie Mayehoff, Paul Hartman (Columbia)

As a play, Murray Schisgal's *Luv* was a hit comedy which ran more than two years on Broadway. Many of the beguiling qualities are lost in its transference to the screen. Where the legiter was wildly absurd and deliciously outlandish much of the humor of the picture is forced, proving that a sophisticated stage comedy isn't always ideal fare for the screen.

Opening on Manhattan Bridge, where Jack Lemmon, a self-proclaimed failure, is about to commit suicide, story takes form as Peter Falk, a self-proclaimed success, comes along and saves him. Falk recognizes in Lemmon an old school friend and takes him home to meet his wife, whom he immediately tries to palm off on Lemmon so he can get a divorce and marry the girl of his dreams, a gymnasium instructor named Linda.

Clive Donner's direction fits the frantic overtones of unfoldment, but in this buildup occasionally goes overboard for effect. Lemmon appears to over-characterize his role, a difficult one for exact shading. Falk as a bright-eyed schemer scores decisively in a restrained comedy enactment for what may be regarded as pic's top performance.

••••••••••••••••••••••••••••••••

■ **LYDIA**

1941, 103 MINS, US ⑫
Dir Julien Duvivier   *Prod* Alexander Korda   *Scr* Ben Hecht, Samuel Hoffenstein   *Ph* Lee Garmes   *Ed* William Hornbeck   *Mus* Miklos Rozsa   *Art Dir* Vincent Korda
● Merle Oberon, Edna May Oliver, Alan Marshal, Joseph Cotten, Hans Yaray, Sara Allgood (Korda)

A man loves 'em and leaves 'em but a woman carries the torch for an early romance down through the years. Proceeding on this premise *Lydia* displays the life span of a woman from 20 to 60, and her torching for a lover whose promises and memories are forgotten 35 years later.

Original story, by Julien Duvivier and Ladislas Bush-Fekete, carries on romantic frustration in a minor key. It's strictly a character study of a gal pursued and loved by three men of various standings – football hero, famous doctor, and blind musical genius – but who holds in her heart through the years the brief, but hot, romance with a seafarer-lover.

Dialog and narrative, with frequent use of

cutbacks for the story telling, does not add to the speed of the unreeling under the leisurely direction by Duvivier.

Merle Oberon takes full advantage of her prominent role to turn in an excellent performance. Makeup for the span of years is particularly excellent.
□ 1941: Nomination: Best Scoring of a Dramatic Picture

••••••••••••••••••••••••••••••••

M*m*

■ M

1951, 88 MINS, US ⓥ ⊙
Dir Joseph Losey   *Prod* Seymour Nebenzal   *Scr* Leo
Katcher, Norman Reilly Raine, Waldo Salt   *Ph* Ernest
Laszlo   *Ed* Edward Mann   *Mus* Michel Michelet
Art Dir Martin Obzina
● David Wayne, Luther Adler, Howard da Silva, Martin
Gabel, Raymond Burr, Glenn Anders (Columbia)

M is a remake of picture produced in
Germany by Seymour Nebenzal in 1933.
Principal change is its shift in locale, presumably to California.

David Wayne, as the killer of small children, is effective and convincing. Luther
Adler, as a drunken lawyer member of a
gangster mob, turns in an outstanding performance, as do Martin Gabel, the gang-leader,
and Howard da Silva and Steve Brodie as police officials.

Story is that of a killer (Wayne), whose only
victims are children. The city is up in arms
over failure of the police to nab the murderer.
A series of raids by police is hampering the
activities of a crime syndicate headed by
Gabel. Mob knows it cannot continue with its
floating dice games, bookie joints and other
enterprises until the killer is caught. To protect its rackets, Gabel orders his gang to
catch the killer.

Joseph Losey's direction has captured the
gruesome theme skilfully.

■ MAC

1992, 117 MINS, US ◇ ⓥ
Dir John Turturro   *Prod* Nancy Tenenbaum, Brenda
Goodman   *Scr* John Turturro, Brandon Cole   *Ph* Ron
Fortunato   *Ed* Michael Berenbaum   *Mus* Richard
Termini, Vin Tese   *Art Dir* Robin Standefer
● John Turturro, Michael Badalucco, Carl Capotorto,
Katherine Borowitz, Ellen Barkin, John Amos (Macfilms)

John Turturro's intense, offbeat personality
as an actor comes through equally clearly in
his directorial debut, *Mac*. A tribute to the notion of craftsmen loving their work, as well as
an expression of quirky humor among three
Italian-American brothers, pic is appealing in
an idiosyncratic way.

Dedicated to Turturro's father, and inspired by his career as a carpenter, film is
centered on the title character, the oldest of
three brothers who live in Queens during the
1950s. In the wake of their father's death, the
temperamental Mac leaves his construction
job to start his own business.

In its eccentric character humor and passionate eruptions of emotion, *Mac* follows in
the vein of American cinema arguably started
by John Cassavetes and taken up, most
prominently, by Martin Scorsese.

Performances are sharp, led by Turturro's
own as the headstrong leader of the clan.
Michael Badalucco and Carl Capotorto are
both distinctive and entirely complementary
as the brothers, and Katherine Borowitz, as
Turturro's wife, and Ellen Barkin, as a suburban beatnik, are vibrant as the main women
on hand.

■ MACAO

1952, 81 MINS, US ⓥ ⊙
Dir Josef von Sternberg, [Nicholas Ray]   *Prod* Alex
Gottlieb   *Scr* Bernard C. Schoenfeld, Stanley Rubin
Ph Harry J. Wild   *Ed* Samuel E. Beetley, Robert Golden
Mus Anthony Collins   *Art Dir* Albert S. D'Agostino,
Ralph Berger

● Robert Mitchum, Jane Russell, William Bendix, Thomas
Gomez, Gloria Grahame, Brad Dexter (RKO)

Macao pairs Jane Russell and Robert
Mitchum; contains the cliche elements of adventure, romance and intrigue; and is set in
the mysterious Orient.

Story is set in the Portuguese colony south
of Hong Kong. It opens with the arrival of
three Americans Russell, a cynical, wisecracking chirper; Mitchum, an ex-GI running
away from a minor shooting scrape; and
William Bendix, disguised as a salesman but
in reality a New York detective entrusted
with the job of bringing back to the States
Brad Dexter, local gambling kingpin.

Dexter engages Russell to sing at his club
and makes a play for her, to the displeasure
of his girl friend (Gloria Grahame). Believing
Mitchum to be the New York cop, Dexter
fails in an attempt to bribe him to leave the
island and resorts to more drastic means.

■ MACARONI

1985, 104 MINS, ITALY ◇ ⓥ ⊙
Dir Ettore Scola   *Prod* Luigi De Laurentiis, Aurelio De
Laurentiis, Franco Committeri   *Scr* Ruggero Maccari,
Furio Scarpelli, Ettore Scola   *Ph* Claudio Ragona
Ed Carla Simoncelli   *Mus* Armando Trovaioli
Art Dir Luciano Ricceri
● Jack Lemmon, Marcello Mastroianni, Daria Nicolodi,
Isa Danieli, Maria Luisa Santella, Patrizia Sacchi
(Filmauro/Massfilm)

Macaroni is a mild comedy drama teaming the
formidable talents of Jack Lemmon and
Marcello Mastroianni. Lemmon toplines as
Bob Traven, a v.p. visiting Naples as a consultant to Aeritalia. It's his first time back since
1946 when, as a GI, he was stationed there.

An acquaintance from that period, Antonio
Jasiello (Marcello Mastroianni) looks Traven
up and takes the at-first unwilling (too busy)
American around town to meet the family
and friends.

Jasiello has been surreptitiously writing letters using Traven's name over the years to his
own sister Maria, who had a brief romance in
1946 with the American. She's long since been
married and now has adult grandchildren.

Relying too heavily on its two stars, at first
abrasive adverseries but later best of friends as
Lemmon unbends to Mastroianni's exuberant
joie de vivre, *Macaroni* rarely achieves the
comedic heights of director Ettore Scola's previous work. There simply isn't an abundance of
funny situations or witty dialogue here.

English language film is hampered by the
dialogue, with merely okay readings by
Mastroianni, artificial dubbing of Isa Danieli
as his emphatic wife and rote, direct-sound
speeches by Daria Nicolodi as Aeritalia's p.r.
officer.

■ MACARTHUR

1977, 128 MINS, US ◇ ⓥ ⊙
Dir Joseph Sargent   *Prod* Frank McCarthy   *Scr* Hal
Barwood, Matthew Robbins   *Ph* Mario Tosi   *Ed* George
Jay Nicholson   *Mus* Jerry Goldsmith   *Art Dir* John J. Lloyd
● Gregory Peck, Ed Flanders, Dan O'Herlihy, Marj Dusay,
Sandy Kenyon, Nicolas Coster (Universal/Zanuck-Brown)

MacArthur is as good a film as could be made,
considering the truly appalling egomania of
its subject. Film stars Gregory Peck in an excellent and remarkable characterization.

Screenplay depicts the public aspects of
Douglas MacArthur's life from Corregidor in
1942 to dismissal a decade later in the midst of
the Korean War, all framed between segments
of his farewell address to West Point cadets.

Unlike *Patton*, which was loaded with emotional and physical action highlights,
MacArthur is a far more introspective and introverted story. There are moments when,
despite all evidence to the contrary, one actually can believe that MacArthur thought he

possessed the only true vision of battle strategy; yet a second later, the vibrations of a
brassbound poseur come across all too clearly.

■ MACBETH

1948, 106 MINS, US ⓥ ⊙
Dir Orson Welles   *Prod* Orson Welles   *Scr* Orson
Welles   *Ph* John L. Russell   *Ed* Louis Lindsay
Mus Jacques Ibert   *Art Dir* Fred Ritter
● Orson Welles, Jeanette Nolan, Dan O'Herlihy, Roddy
McDowall, John Dierkes (Republic/Mercury)

Welles' idea of Shakespeare is such a personalized version. Production was comparatively
inexpensive and looks it. Mood is as dour as
the Scottish moors and crags that background
the plot. Film is crammed with scenery-chewing theatrics in the best Shakespearean manner with Welles dominating practically every
bit of footage.

Only a few of the Bard's best lines are audible. The rest are lost in strained, dialeetic
gibbering that is only sound, not prose. At
best, Shakespeare dialog requires close attention; but even intense concentration can't
make intelligible the reading by Welles and
others in the cast.

Macbeth, the play, devotes considerable time
to depicting femme influence on the male to
needle his vanity and ambition into murder
for a kingdom. *Macbeth*, the film, devotes that
footage to the male's reaction to the femme
needling. Several Shakespeare characters
have been turned into a Welles-introduced
one, a Holy Father.

Welles introduces Jeanette Nolan as Lady
Macbeth. Her reading is best in the 'out,
damned spot' scene. Dan O'Herlihy fares best
as Macduff, his reading having the clearest
enunciation.

■ MACBETH

1972, 140 MINS, UK ◇ ⓥ ⊙
Dir Roman Polanski   *Prod* Andrew Braunsberg
Scr Roman Polanski, Kenneth Tynan   *Ph* Gil Taylor
Ed Alastair McIntyre   *Mus* The Third Ear Band
Art Dir Wilfrid Shingleton
● Jon Finch, Francesca Annis, Martin Shaw, Nicholas
Selby, John Stride, Stephan Chase (Playboy)

Macbeth receives a most handsome treatment
by Roman Polanski and artistic adviser
Kenneth Tynan, both of whom adapted this
production for the entry of Playboy Enterprises into feature filming. Rugged in its
telling, raw in its motivated violence, and rich
in its appropriate physical trappings, this is
the 16th known film version of the story. The
players are very good, though Jon Finch's
Macbeth is a serious weakness.

Does Polanski's *Macbeth* work? Not especially, but it was an admirable try. The film is
traditional in the sense that there are no
forced sociological overtones, no Freudianisms, and no pop-art formula-epic 'production
numbers'. Atmospherically it is a heavy trip
through a time machine.

The prominent surrounding characters
have been cast and directed with the same
care. In such heady surroundings Francesca
Annis as Lady Macbeth often pales in impact,
and Finch as Macbeth completely fades in effectiveness. Both seem almost to be of another time and place: she closer to Sherwood
Forest and pampered gentility; he, almost a
20th-century drawing room psychotic.

■ MACHINE GUN KELLY

1958, 84 MINS, US ⓥ
Dir Roger Corman   *Prod* Roger Corman   *Scr* R. Wright
Campbell   *Ph* Floyd Crosby   *Ed* Ronald Sinclair
Mus Gerald Fried   *Art Dir* Daniel Haller
● Charles Bronson, Susan Cabot, Morey Amsterdam,
Jack Lambert, Connie Gilchrist (American-International)

Machine Gun Kelly beats out a tattoo of the 1930s in its account of the criminal career of one of that decade's most notorious outlaws. Roger Corman has taken a good screenplay and made a first-rate little picture out of the depressing but intriguing account of a bad-man's downfall.

Charles Bronson plays Kelly, shown as an undersized sadist who grows an extra foot or so as soon as he gets a submachine gun tucked under his arm. His exploits, proceeding from penny ante robbery to bigtime kidnapping, are adroitly and swiftly shown.

Bronson gives a brooding, taut performance. Susan Cabot is good as the woman behind his deeds, and Morey Amsterdam contributes an offbeat portrayal of a squealer who has the final revenge of turning Kelly in. Gerald Fried, using piano and taps for an unusual and striking combination, has done a fine progressive jazz score.

....

■ MACKENNA'S GOLD

1969, 128 MINS, US ◇ ⓦ ⊙

Dir J. Lee Thompson   *Prod* Carl Foreman   *Scr* Carl Foreman   *Ph* Joseph MacDonald   *Ed* Bill Lenny   *Mus* Quincy Jones   *Art Dir* Geoffrey Drake

● Gregory Peck, Omar Sharif, Telly Savalas, Julie Newmar, Camilla Sparv, Keenan Wynn (Columbia)

Mackenna's Gold is a standard western. The plot is good, the acting adequate. But it's the scenery, the vastness of the west, the use of cameras, and of horses, and the special effects which keep the viewer involved and entertained.

There are a few plot twists, but for the most part the story is predictable. Mackenna (Gregory Peck) has memorized a map, now destroyed, which will lead to a canyon of gold. The gold belongs to the Apaches, and it has been decreed by the Apache Gods that the gold remain untouched.

But now the young Apache warriors want the gold to support them in their fight against the white men. The Mexican bandit Colorado (Omar Sharif) wants the gold so he can emigrate to Paris and become a gentleman.

Sharif captures Peck and forces him to lead them to the gold.

....

■ MACKINTOSH MAN, THE

1973, 98 MINS, UK ◇ ⓦ

Dir John Huston   *Prod* John Foreman   *Scr* Walter Hill   *Ph* Oswald Morris   *Ed* Russell Lloyd   *Mus* Maurice Jarre   *Art Dir* Terry Marsh

● Paul Newman, Dominique Sanda, James Mason, Harry Andrews, Ian Bannen, Michael Hordern (Warner)

The Mackintosh Man is a tame tale of British espionage and counter-espionage, starring Paul Newman as a planted assassin, James Mason as a cynical right-wing politician in reality a spy, and Dominique Sanda as a combo semi-romantic interest and foreign-market star bait.

Walter Hill has adapted Desmond Bagley's novel, *The Freedom Trap*, into a serviceable meller form. Harry Andrews, a British secret agent, recruits Newman to pull a jewel heist by mail, in order to establish his criminal credentials, so that he may escape with Ian Bannen, a state secrets betrayer, and thereby ferret out Mason, who has carried on a 25-year career as a politician but has been a foreign agent.

There's a whole lot of nothing going on here.

....

■ MACOMBER AFFAIR, THE

1947, 89 MINS, US

Dir Zoltan Korda   *Prod* Benedict Bogeaus   *Scr* Casey Robinson, Seymour Bennett   *Ph* Karl Struss   *Ed* George Feld, Jack Wheeler   *Mus* Miklos Rozsa   *Art Dir* Erno Metzner

● Gregory Peck, Robert Preston, Joan Bennett , Reginald Denny, Carl Hardboard (United Artists)

The Macomber Affair, with an African hunt background, isn't particularly pleasant in content, even though action often is exciting and elements of suspense frequently hop up the spectator. Certain artificialities of presentation, too, and unreal dialog are further strikes against picture [based on a short story by Ernest Hemingway], although portion of footage filmed in Africa is interesting.

Robert Preston enacts role of Francis Macomber, a rich American with an unhappy wife (Joan Bennett), who arrives at Nairobi and hires Gregory Peck, a white hunter, to take him lion hunting. On the safari, this time in cars, Macomber can't stand up under a lion charge and his wife sees him turn coward. The white hunter kills the lion. Thereafter, Macomber broods over his shame and his wife falls for the hunter.

African footage is cut into the story with showmanship effect, and these sequences build up suspense satisfactorily. There are closeups of lions and other denizens of the veldt, and scenes in which lion and water buffalo charge, caught with telescopic lenses by camera crew sent to Africa from England, will stir any audience. These focal points of the story out-interest the human drama as developed in scripters' enmeshing trio of stars.

....

■ MAD ABOUT MUSIC

1938, 98 MINS, US

Dir Norman Taurog   *Prod* Joe Pasternak   *Scr* Bruce Manning, Felix Jackson   *Ph* Joseph Valentine   *Ed* Philip Kahn

● Deanna Durbin, Herbert Marshall, Arthur Treacher, Gail Patrick, William Frawley, Jackie Moran (Universal)

Mad about Music has a genuine and enthralling, if somewhat obvious story [by Marcella Burke and Frederick Kohner]. Idea is a simple one. So as not to risk her popularity as a glamour girl, a beauteous widowed film star unwillingly hides her 14-year-old daughter away in a Swiss boarding school. Although the youngster is inordinately proud of her illustrious mother, she must cherish her affection in secret.

When the other girls talk about their parents, the youngster takes refuge in telling of the fabulous exploits of her imaginary father, whom she describes as an explorer and big game hunter. When circumstances force her to make good the yarns, she imposes on a vacationing British composer to pretend to be her legendary father.

As evidence that Deanna Durbin is growing up, in this film she is given a beau for the first time. It's still purely in the puppy-love status. She has acquired more varied technique before the camera, without losing her ingenuous charm nor her luminous screen personality.

As the adopted-by-surprise father, Herbert Marshall plays with unaccustomed warmth. Although her part is important to the story, Gail Patrick gets comparatively little footage as the actress-mother.

□ 1938: Nominations: Best Original Story, Cinematography, Art Direction, Score

....

■ MADAME BOVARY

1949, 114 MINS, US ⓦ ⊙

Dir Vincente Minnelli   *Prod* Pandro S. Berman   *Scr* Robert Ardrey   *Ph* Robert Planck   *Ed* Ferris Webster   *Mus* Miklos Rozsa   *Art Dir* Cedric Gibbons, Jack Martin Smith

● Jennifer Jones, James Mason, Van Heflin, Louis Jourdan, Christopher Kent, Gene Lockhart (M-G-M)

As a character study, *Madame Bovary* is interesting to watch, but hard to feel. It is a curiously unemotional account of some rather basic emotions. However, the surface treatment of Vincente Minnelli's direction is slick and attractively presented.

Jennifer Jones is the daring Madame Bovary. The character is short on sympathy, being a greedy woman so anxious to better her position in life that sin and crime do not shock her moral values. Jones answers to every demand of direction and script.

Van Heflin portrays her doctor husband, an essentially weak man whose evident flaws in abiding with a greedy wife are not too satisfactorily explained away by his love for her.

The Bovary quest for something better than she has is brought to light at the trial of Gustave Flaubert, author of the realistically treated novel that brought about his arrest. James Mason is excellent as the author.

□ 1949: Nomination: Best B&W Art Direction

....

■ MADAME CURIE

1943, 125 MINS, US ⓦ

Dir Mervyn LeRoy   *Prod* Sidney Franklin   *Scr* Paul Osborn, Paul Rameau   *Ph* Joseph Ruttenberg   *Ed* Harold F. Kress   *Mus* Herbert Stothart   *Art Dir* Cedric Gibbons, Paul Groesse

● Greer Garson, Walter Pidgeon, Robert Walker, Van Johnson, Margaret O'Brien, Henry Travers (M-G-M)

Every inch a great picture. *Madame Curie* absorbingly tells of the struggle and heartaches that ultimately resulted in the discovery of radium.

Sidney Franklin, producer, and Mervyn LeRoy, director, have instilled into the story of Madame Curie and her scientist-husband a particularly high degree of entertainment value where in less-skilled hands the romance of radium and its discovery may have struck out.

While the events leading up to the discovery of radium and the fame it brought Madame Curie are of the greatest underlying importance to the picture as entertainment, it's the love story that dominates all the way. Thus, this is not just the saga of a great scientist nor just a story of test tubes and laboratories.

Film is based on the book *Madame Curie*, written by Eve Curie, daughter of the Polish teacher-scientist who quite by accident came upon the source of the element. It is adapted with great skill by Paul Osborn and Paul H. Rameau, with a few stretches of narration by James Hilton. It throws Greer Garson and Walter Pidgeon together immediately after the opening and, as the romance between them ripens, it gathers terrific momentum.

□ 1943: Nominations: Best Picture, Actor (Walter Pidgeon), Actress (Greer Garson), B&W Cinematography, B&W Art Direction, Scoring of a Dramatic Picture, Sound

....

■ MADAME DUBARRY

1934, 75 MINS, US

Dir William Dieterle   *Scr* Edward Chodorov   *Ph* Sol Polito

● Dolores Del Rio, Reginald Owen, Victor Jory, Osgood Perkins, Verree Teasdale, Anita Louise (Warner)

Madame Dubarry is a Hollywood idea of Versailles. Under William Dieterle's directorial aegis, the decadent court of Louis XV becomes even more so in its broad well-nigh travesty version of the comtesse's influence on the doddering Louie.

Script is a chameleon affair. It emphasizes the stupid extravagances of a former street waif who wants to go sleighing in the midst of summer; and in another moment seeks to suggest that perhaps some of her devious ways achieved some good. Such as when the English ambassador opines that getting rid of the French prime minister (caught in Dubarry's boudoir) has achieved something which his Brittanic majesty and other diplomats in the French court long tried but heretofore couldn't accomplish.

Dolores Del Rio's Dubarry is rarely believable. It's a theatrical conception eclipsed by the performances of Reginald Owen, who is capital as the senile Louie, and Victory Jory as d'Aiguillon. Osgood Perkins' Richelieu doesn't register.

Dubarry as a production is very Busby Berkeley. In its tinsel, costuming, and general pretentiousness it's more musical comedy than history.

....

■ **MADAME SOUSATZKA**

1988, 122 MINS, UK/US ◇ ⚉ ⊙
Dir John Schlesinger   *Prod* Robin Dalton   *Scr* Ruth Prawer Jhabvala   *Ph* Nat Crosby   *Ed* Peter Honess   *Mus* Gerald Gouriet   *Art Dir* Luciana Arrighi
● Shirley MacLaine, Navin Chowdhry, Peggy Ashcroft, Twiggy, Shabana Azmi, Leigh Lawson (Sousatzka/Cineplex Odeon)

Although essentially a rather old-fashioned British pic, *Madame Sousatzka* is filled with pleasures, not the least of them being Shirley MacLaine's effervescent performance.

Setting is London where middle-aged Mme Sousatzka, of Russian parentage but raised in New York, teaches piano to only the most gifted students. She insists her pupils not only learn to play, but also to live the kind of traditional cultured lifestyle which she herself does.

Her latest protege is a 15-year-old Indian youth, Manek (Navin Chowdhry) whose mother (Shabana Azmi) left Calcutta years before to get away from her husband.

Sousatzka lives in a crumbling house owned by old Lady Emily (Peggy Ashcroft). Besides Sousatzka, her tenants include a model and would-be pop singer (delightfully played by Twiggy) who looks much younger than she is; and a middle-aged gay osteopath (Geoffrey Bayldon).

Crucial, though, is the central relationship between MacLaine, who's seldom been better than she is here, and the youngster, warmly played by Chowdry. All their scenes have great charm, with the piano playing effectively handled.

....

■ **MADAME X**

1929, 95 MINS, US
Dir Lionel Barrymore   *Scr* Willard Mack   *Ph* Arthur Reed   *Art Dir* Cedric Gibbons
● Ruth Chatterton, Lewis Stone, Raymond Hackett, John P. Edington, Ullric Haupt, Sidney Toler (M-G-M)

This is Lionel Barrymore's first full-length directorial effort on a talker. Taking *X* as an actor-proof meller and conceding its author, the Frenchman Alexandre Bisson, knew emotion well enough to make it do somersaults in this tale, Barrymore had no difficult job with the story and cast.

But Barrymore excels in the minor bits and roles: the above-par park scene; the immensely human bit in the hotel's corridor with the landlord wanting his room rent from the besotted Jacqueline (Ruth Chatterton); or the superb scene wholly dominated by the doctor (John P. Edington).

The two big moments are Jacqueline killing her small-time blackmailing companion to prevent her son discovering what a horror his mother has become; the other the famous trial scene, the grand finale which made *Madame X* on the stage.

Chatterton has not a flaw in her performance or make up. Next to Chatterton and Edington are Raymond Hackett as the son.

☐ 1928/29: Nominations: Best Director, Actress (Ruth Chatterton)

....

■ **MADAME X**

1937, 75 MINS, US
Dir Sam Wood   *Prod* James Kevin McGuinness   *Scr* John Meehan   *Ph* John Seitz   *Ed* Frank E. Hull

Mus David Snell   *Art Dir* Cedric Gibbons, Urie McCleary, Edwin B. Willis
● Gladys George, John Beal, Warren William, Reginald Owen, William Henry, Henry Daniell (M-G-M)

This is a reverent handling of the Alexandre Bisson play, chosen by M-G-M as a vehicle to demonstrate the dramatic and emotional talent of Gladys George. It's a quiet, comforting sniffle.

Script follows with devotion the familiar developments, and the dialog is as modern as the action permits. Sam Wood's direction is conventionally sound and the production is of the best.

George's performance is effective, and her characterization of the tipsy, defeated and maudlin old woman is faithful and moving. Warren William plays the hard-hearted husband who refuses to forgive his wife's indiscretions; Reginald Owen is the friend, Douvel; Henry Daniell is the villain, Lerocle.

John Beal has the prize spot of Raymond, youthful public defender of his mother, whose identity is unknown to him. His address to the court is recited with conviction and emotion.

....

■ **MADAME X**

1966, 99 MINS, US ◇ ⚉
Dir David Lowell Rich   *Prod* Ross Hunter   *Scr* Jean Holloway   *Ph* Russell Metty   *Ed* Milton Carruth   *Mus* Frank Skinner   *Art Dir* Alexander Golitzen, George Webb
● Lana Turner, John Forsythe, Ricardo Montalban, Burgess Meredith, Constance Bennett, Keir Dullea (Universal/Hunter)

Latest time out for Alexandre Bisson's now-classic 1909 drama of mother love is an emotional, sometimes exhausting and occasionally corny picture. Lana Turner takes on the difficult assignment of the frustrated mother, turning in what many will regard as her most rewarding portrayal. Producer Ross Hunter draws generally on the original plot but has changed the locale from Paris to the US for pic's opening and climax.

Screenplay now has femme star very much in love with her husband, instead of running away from her spouse, as in the original, to join her lover. However, following an affair with a rich playboy, who is accidentally killed while she is in his apartment, she is talked by her mother-in-law into disappearing in a phony drowning episode to save her politically-minded husband and young son from scandal.

John Forsythe excels as the husband, whose political career forces him to absent himself from home for long periods of time and thus lays the ground for his lonely wife's indiscretion. Ricardo Montalban is persuasive as the playboy who falls to his death, and Constance Bennett in her last film appearance before her death endows the mother-in-law role with quiet dignity and strength.

....

■ **MAD AT THE MOON**

1992, 97 MINS, US ◇ ⚉
Dir Martin Donovan   *Prod* Michael Kastenbaum, Cassian Elwes, Matt Devlen   *Scr* Martin Donovan, Richard Pelusi   *Ph* Ronn Schmidt   *Ed* Penelope Shaw   *Mus* Gerald Gouriet   *Art Dir* Stephen Greenberg
● Mary Stuart Masterson, Hart Bochner, Fionnula Flanagan, Cec Verrell, Stephen Blake, Daphne Zuniga (Jaffe/Spectacor)

Miscasting and klutzy plot development take the shine out of *Mad at the Moon*, a Wild West amour fou movie that sprouts hairs half-way and turns into a werewolf pic. The second picture by Argentinian-born Martin Donovan, who staked a cult film claim with the quirky *Apartment Zero*, shows the same glee in blending genres and going for broke. The main problems here are accepting topliner Mary

Stuart Masterson as a 25-year-old virgin and figuring out a storyline that takes a left turn 50 minutes in.

Pretty but repressed Jenny (Masterson) has a backstreets rendezvous with charismatic bum Miller Brown (Hart Bochner), whom she's had the hots for since childhood. Despite her secret desires, she bows to the wishes of her mom (Fionnula Flanagan) and marries local milquetoast James Miller (Stephen Blake), the bum's half-brother.

Things begin to go awry (with the pic, too) as soon as the couple settle in James' remote farmhouse. The marriage is unconsummated. Miller haunts the plains outside and Jenny experiences hubby's 'moonsickness', during which he starts howling and turns partly vulpine.

Still, Donovan shows he has talent to spare as a pure technician. Pic works best when no one's talking and Donovan can stoke up the atmosphere via sound, music and images alone.

....

■ **MAD DOG AND GLORY**

1993, 96 MINS, US ◇ ⚉ ⊙
Dir John McNaughton   *Prod* Barbara De Fina, Martin Scorsese   *Scr* Richard Price   *Ph* Robby Muller   *Ed* Craig McKay, Elena Maganini   *Mus* Elmer Bernstein   *Art Dir* David Chapman
● Robert De Niro, Uma Thurman, Bill Murray, David Caruso, Mike Starr, Kathy Baker (Universal)

A pleasurably offbeat picture that manages the rare trick of being both charming and edgy, *Mad Dog and Glory* represents a refreshing, unexpected change of pace for all the major talents concerned.

Amusing premise – a poor schmoe saves a gangster's life and is given a beautiful woman for a week as thanks – ends up taking on unexpected dramatic and romantic dimensions, and leads are played to the hilt by its stellar trio.

Bill Murray plays Frank Milo, a dapper hoodlum in the modern mode. Robert De Niro's Wayne Dobie, ironically nicknamed 'Mad Dog,' is a retiring middle-aged loner who photographs crime scenes at night for the Chicago Police Dept.

Wayne has greatness thrust upon him when he interrupts an armed robbery in a convenience store and saves Milo from almost certain death. Club bartender Glory (Uma Thurman) turns up at his apartment and announces that she's staying for a week, courtesy of Milo.

What follows could easily have been cute, contrived, exploitative, crude or any combination of same. Instead, scriptwriter Richard Price deepens his characters and, with the aid of the exceptional actors, the story takes on a resonance and emotional urgency that aren't initially indicated. The key to the film lies in the intimate scenes involving Wayne and Glory.

....

■ **MADE IN AMERICA**

1993, 110 MINS, US ◇ ⚉ ⊙
Dir Richard Benjamin   *Prod* Arnon Milchan, Michael Douglas, Rick Bieber   *Scr* Holly Goldberg Sloan   *Ph* Ralf Bode   *Ed* Jacqueline Cambas   *Mus* Mark Isham   *Art Dir* Evelyn Sakash
● Whoopi Goldberg, Ted Danson, Will Smith, Nia Long, Paul Rodriguez, Jennifer Tilly (Stonebridge/Kalola/Milchan)

Made in America has the distinction of being better than the last movie involving a sperm bank, *Frozen Assets*, though at times the humor – overplayed to nearly shrill levels – seems to come from the same test tube.

The plot has Zora (Nia Long), a high-school honors student, discovering her mother Sarah (Whoopi Goldberg) conceived her after her father's death using a donor from a sperm bank. Zora finds the name of Hal Jackson (Ted Danson) – a Cal Worthington-like car salesman who cavorts on-air with elephants, bears and chimps and turns out to be white. Hostile toward each other at first, an unlikely relationship develops between Hal and Sarah.

In an effort to bring Sarah and Hal's relationship to a crisis point, the action [from a screen story by Marcia Brandwynne, Nadine Schiff and scripter Holly Goldberg Sloan] suddenly veers into a heavy-handed, semi-serious mode that doesn't mesh with the screwball opening. If there's chemistry between Danson and Goldberg, it's certainly not allowed to unfold adequately or with any sense of pacing in the script. The race issue, for example, quickly dissipates.

It's the supporting players who end up stealing much of the film, particularly rapper Will Smith as Zora's nerdy friend and a golden-locked Jennifer Tilly as Hal's air-headed aerobics instructor girlfriend.

....

■ MADE IN HEAVEN

1987, 103 MINS, US ◇ ⓥ ⊙
Dir Alan Rudolph *Prod* Raynold Gideon, Bruce A. Evans, David Blocker *Scr* Bruce A. Evans, Raynold Gideon *Ph* Jan Kiesser *Ed* Tom Walls *Mus* Mark Isham *Art Dir* Steve Legler
● Timothy Hutton, Kelly McGillis, Maureen Stapleton, Don Murray, Ellen Barkin, Debra Winger (Lorimar)

A gentle comedy which could have been integrated in the romantic fantasy genre along with classics such as *Angel on My Shoulder* and *Here Comes Mr. Jordan*, the script obviously held material that was too abundant for one single feature film.

Mike Shea (Timothy Hutton) is a nice smalltown boy who dies and goes to heaven. There he is introduced to eternal life by his long deceased aunt Lisa (Maureen Stapleton), he meets the solicitous Annie (Kelly McGillis), a beautiful guide with whom he falls in love, and finally encounters Emmett (Debra Winger), the strange person who is not God but is in charge of seeing that everything proceeds smoothly, as ordained.

Before Mike and Annie can establish a valid union, she is sent to do her stint on Earth. He begs Emmett to let him go back as well and is granted 30 years to find his love again down below.

The nature of the story invites obviously all sorts of religious and philosophical speculations, which are pretty much ignored here, even on the narrative level.

If Hutton and McGillis are likeable, it is mostly through their own personalities that this quality comes out.

Ellen Barkin plays a hellcat who almost deprives Hutton's character of his pure innocence, but she refused a credit. Winger, Hutton's spouse, assumed the part of Emmett on condition that it be kept a secret.

....

■ MADE IN PARIS

1966, 103 MINS, US ◇
Dir Boris Sagal *Prod* Joe Pasternak *Scr* Stanley Roberts *Ph* Milton Krasner *Ed* William McMillin *Mus* George Stoll *Art Dir* George W. Davis, Preston Ames
● Ann-Margret, Louis Jourdan, Richard Crenna, Edie Adams, Chad Everett, John McGiver (Euterpe/M-G-M)

A Parisian setting and some snazzy femme costumes provide the major props for this otherwise weak and formula comedy programmer. Sexy plot overtones are too protracted in scripting, and become boring via heavy-handed direction. Ann-Margret and Louis Jourdan top the list of adequate players.

Stanley Roberts' dull script, strongly reminiscent of yesteryear Doris Day-Rock Hudson-Cary Grant plots (but less effective), finds fashion buyer Ann-Margret rushed to

Paris from the lecherous arms of her employer's son (Chad Everett). Jourdan is the French designer, who, it appears, has had what is usually called an adult arrangement with Edie Adams, whom Ann-Margret has replaced. Richard Crenna is a foreign correspondent who bobs from time to time.

Plotting permits Ann-Margret to essay some wild terpery, which David Winters choreographed to the desired effect. Mongo Santamaria and band provide a solid beat for the bumps.

....

■ MADEMOISELLE

1967, 100 MINS, UK/FRANCE
Dir Tony Richardson *Prod* Oscar Lewenstein *Scr* Jean Genet *Ph* David Watkin *Ed* Anthony Gibbs *Art Dir* Jacques Saulnier
● Jeanne Moreau, Ettore Manni, Keith Skinner, Jeanne Beretta, Mony Rey (United Artists/Woodfall/Procinex)

French-British coproduction mixes Tony Richardson's free-wheeling style and the script of the controversial French writer-playwright Jean Genet. It has two versions, one English and one French, since French star Jeanne Moreau is bilingual.

A small French farming town is the locale. Story is about an arsonist who is terrorizing the people. A poisoned drinking well, and opened irrigation ditches which flood the farms, finally lead the populace to form a lynching mob.

The ingrained suspicion regarding a foreigner makes an Italian woodcutter (Ettore Manni), living in the town, the scapegoat.

Moreau's presence manages to make her schoolmarm character quite plausible in revealing her lurking lusts. But the remainder is somewhat sketchy, even though Manni has the virility to bring on hatreds from the other men and finally his own demise. The script seemingly needed more depth and background to the characters. Either that or almost surrealistic playing and treatment.

....

■ MADIGAN

1968, 101 MINS, US ◇ ⓥ
Dir Don Siegel *Prod* Frank P. Rosenberg *Scr* Henri Simoun, Abraham Polonsky *Ph* Russell Metty *Ed* Milton Shifman *Mus* Don Costa *Art Dir* Alexander Golitzen, George C. Webb
● Richard Widmark, Henry Fonda, Inger Stevens, Harry Guardino, James Whitmore, Susan Clark (Universal)

Abraham Polonsky's screenplay adaptation of Richard Dougherty's novel *The Commissioner* is tough and to the point, bringing out the side issue problems but without dallying with them overmuch.

Pic gets away to a flying start, with Richard Widmark as a dedicated cop who isn't above using his badge for some fringe benefits, and sidekick Harry Guardino bursting into a sleazy bedroom to pick up a wanted killer for questioning.

Momentarily distracted by the nude broad in the room Widmark and Guardino are taken off guard and the psychopathic killer, played with menacing hysteria by Steve Ihnat, goes on the lam. Cops are given 72 hours to pick him up.

This is a good solid big-city adventure yarn with Widmark at his best. Guardino tags along satisfactorily as his buddy. Henry Fonda plays the commissioner with the cool austerity and deceptive slowness that he made peculiarly his own and James Whitmore is a tower of strength as the chief inspector.

....

■ MAD MAX

1979, 90 MINS, AUSTRALIA ◇ ⓥ ⊙
Dir George Miller *Prod* Byron Kennedy *Scr* George Miller, James McCausland *Ph* David Eggby *Ed* Tony

Paterson, Cliff Hayes *Mus* Brian May *Art Dir* Jon Dowding
● Mel Gibson, Joanne Samuel, Hugh Keays-Byrne, Steve Bisley, Roger Ward, Tim Burns (Roadshow)

Mad Max is an all-stops-out, fast-moving exploitation pic in the tradition of New World/American International productions. The plot [from an original story by George Miller and Byron Kennedy] is extremely simple. A few years from now (opening title), the Australian countryside is terrorized by marauders who create mayhem on the roads. A crack police force opposes the villains.

Mad Max is one of the fastest and most ruthless of these cops of the future. Max quits the force to take a vacation with his wife and baby. But when The Toecutter's gang kills his wife and child, he dons his leather uniform again to hunt them down.

Stunts themselves would be nothing without a filmmaker behind the camera and George Miller, a doctor and film buff making his first feature, shows he knows what cinema is all about.

The film belongs to the director, cameraman and stunt artists: it's not an actor's piece, though the leads are all effective.

....

■ MAD MAX 2

1981, 94 MINS, AUSTRALIA ◇ ⓥ ⊙
Dir George Miller *Prod* Byron Kennedy *Scr* George Miller, Terry Hayes, Brian Hannant *Ph* Dean Semler *Ed* David Stiven, Tim Wellburn, Michael Balson *Mus* Brian May *Art Dir* Graham 'Grace' Walker
● Mel Gibson, Bruce Spence, Mike Preston, Emil Minty, Max Phipps, Vernon Wells (Kennedy Miller)

Uncomplicated plot has Max (Mel Gibson), a futuristic version of the western gunslinger, reluctantly throwing in his lot with a communal group whose lifesupport system is a rudimentary refinery in the desert (he needs the gas).

Western parallel continues as the compound is under continual attack from a bunch of marauders led by the gravel-voiced, metal-visored villain Humungus (Kjell Nilsson).

Ever-the-loner Max decides to strike out on his own again, and is saved by his friend the Gyro Captain (Bruce Spence) who swoops down from the clouds, and takes him back to the safety of the compound.

The climactic chase has Max at the wheel of a super-tanker in a desperate flight to Paradise 2,000 miles away (the promised land is the tourist resort on the Queensland Gold Coast, an unexpected touch of black humour). It's a dazzling demolition derby, as men and machines collide and disintegrate, featuring very fine stunt work and special effects.

Director Miller keeps the pic moving with cyclonic force, photography by Dean Semler is first class, editing is supertight, and Brian May's music is stirring.

....

■ MAD MAX BEYOND THUNDERDOME

1985, 106 MINS, AUSTRALIA ◇ ⓥ ⊙
Dir George Miller, George Ogilvie *Prod* George Miller *Scr* Terry Hayes, George Miller *Ph* Dean Semler *Ed* Richard Francis-Bruce *Mus* Maurice Jarre *Art Dir* Graham 'Grace' Walker
● Mel Gibson, Tina Turner, Angelo Rossitto, Helen Buday, Bruce Spence, Frank Thring (Kennedy Miller)

The third in the series opens strong with Mel Gibson being dislodged from his camel train by low-flying Bruce Spence in an airborne jalopy (providing as much fun here as he did as the gyro Captain in the earlier *Max* films, this time accompanied by Adam Cockburn as his daredevil son).

To retrieve his possessions, Gibson has to confront Tina Turner, the improbably named Aunty, mistress of Bartertown, a bizarre bazaar where anything up to and including human lives is traded as the only form of commerce in the post-apocalyptic world.

Turner throws him a challenge: engage in a fight to the death with a giant known as The Blaster (Paul Larsson) in the Thunderdome, a geometric arena which serves as a kind of futuristic Roman Colosseum for the delectation of the locals.

Gibson impressively fleshes out Max, Tina Turner is striking in her role as Aunty (as well as contributing two topnotch songs, which open and close the picture) and the juves are uniformly good.

●●●●●●●●●●●●●●●●●●●●●●●●●●●●●●●

■ MAD ROOM, THE

1969, 93 MINS, US ◇

Dir Bernard Girard   *Prod* Norman Maurer   *Scr* Bernard Girard, A.Z. Martin   *Ph* Harry Stradling Jr.   *Ed* Pat Somerset   *Mus* Dave Grusin   *Art Dir* Sidney Litwack
● Shelley Winters, Stella Stevens, Barbara Sammeth, Michael Burns, Skip Ward (Columbia)

Weak story which pretends to be a psycho-suspense yarn. Screenplay is based on the 1940 play, *Ladies in Retirement*, filmed in 1941 by Columbia, with Ida Lupino, Elsa Lanchester, Edith Barrett.

Shelley Winters, surrounded by an able cast, thin plot, good color and some magnificent scenery on and near Vancouver Island, is the better part of the pic.

Barbara Sammeth and Michael Burns, playing brother and sister recently released from a mental institution, are the focus of the story which is long on melodramatics. Script has a patent mystery plot in which the real murderer isn't exposed until the film's end but any astute filmgoer will perceive the twist long before it comes on the screen.

Winters plays a wealthy widow living with young companion Stella Stevens. The young brother and sister of Stevens have been released from a mental institution where they were confined, supposedly for the murder of their parents.

●●●●●●●●●●●●●●●●●●●●●●●●●●●●●●●

■ MADWOMAN OF CHAILLOT, THE

1969, 142 MINS, US ◇ ⓥ ⊙

Dir Bryan Forbes   *Prod* Ely Landau   *Scr* Edward Anhalt   *Ph* Claude Renoir, Burnett Guffey   *Ed* Roger Dwyre   *Mus* Michael J. Lewis   *Art Dir* Georges Petitot
● Katharine Hepburn, Richard Chamberlain, Yul Brynner, Margaret Leighton, John Gavin, Giulietta Masina (Warner/Seven Arts)

Story of struggle between good and evil becomes audience's struggle against tedium. Margaret Leighton with her imaginary dog and Giulietta Masina with her imaginary amours ricochet around the Chaillot district of Paris sharing a phantom world of the past with Katharine Hepburn.

Hepburn, as equally disturbed Countess Aurelia, the madwoman of Chaillot, measures life somewhere between a lover lost years ago and a missing feathered boa. Richard Chamberlain, an active pacifist, and Danny Kaye, a local ragpicker, rattle the countess into the present with the news that there's a plot afoot or underfoot to destroy Paris.

Film doesn't come off. Hepburn fails to capture the fantasy-spirit of the countess. Her performance suffers because of indecision.

●●●●●●●●●●●●●●●●●●●●●●●●●●●●●●●

■ 'MAGGIE', THE

(US: High and Dry)

1954, 93 MINS, UK ⓥ

Dir Alexander Mackendrick   *Prod* Michael Truman   *Scr* William Rose   *Ph* Gordon Dines   *Ed* Peter Tanner   *Mus* John Addison   *Art Dir* Jim Morahan
● Paul Douglas, Alex Mackenzie, James Copeland, Abe Barker, Tommy Kearins, Hubert Gregg (Ealing)

One of the small coastal colliers which ply in Scottish waters provides the main setting for this Ealing comedy. The story [by director Alexander Mackendrick] of a hustling American businessman who gets involved with a leisurely-minded but crafty skipper gives the film an Anglo-US flavor.

The yarn has been subtly written as a piece of gentle and casual humor. The pace is always leisurely, and the background of Scottish lakes and mountains provides an appropriate backcloth to the story.

The skipper of the *Maggie* is a crafty old sailor, short of cash to make his little coaster seaworthy. By a little smart practice he gets a contract to transport a valuable cargo but when a hustling American executive realizes what has happened, he planes from London to Scotland to get his goods transferred to another vessel.

There is virtually an all-male cast with only minor bits for a few femme players. Paul Douglas, playing the American executive, provides the perfect contrast between the old world and the new. His is a reliable performance which avoids the pitfall of overacting.

●●●●●●●●●●●●●●●●●●●●●●●●●●●●●●●

■ MAGIC

1978, 106 MINS, US ◇ ⓥ ⊙

Dir Richard Attenborough   *Prod* Joseph E. Levine, Richard P. Levine   *Scr* William Goldman   *Ph* Victor J. Kemper   *Ed* John Bloom   *Mus* Jerry Goldsmith   *Art Dir* Terence Marsh
● Anthony Hopkins, Ann-Margret, Burgess Meredith, Ed Lauter, E.J. Andre, Jerry Houser (20th Century-Fox)

The premise is that of a dummy slowly taking over the personality of its ventriloquist-master. In adapting his own best-seller, William Goldman has opted for an atmospheric thriller, a mood director Richard Attenborough fleshes out to its fullest.

The dilemma of *Magic* is that the results never live up to the standards established in the film's opening half-hour. Through flashbacks and claustrophic editing, the relationship between Anthony Hopkins and his eerily-realistic dummy, Fats, is well-documented. So is the introduction of Burgess Meredith, well cast as a Swifty Lazar-type of superagent.

When Hopkins declines a lucrative TV contract because of insecurity, and flees to his boyhood Catskills home, where a high school girl on whom he had a crush (Ann-Margret) is enmeshed in a disastrous marriage to redneck Ed Lauter, *Magic* becomes disappointingly transparent. Goldman has Hopkins becoming involved in the standard love triangle that inevitably leads to disaster for all parties concerned.

The ventriloquism and magic stunts are expertly done by Hopkins, with the aid of tech advisor Dennis Alwood.

But as the Meredith character notes early on, 'Magic is misdirection'. That sentiment applies equally to the film.

●●●●●●●●●●●●●●●●●●●●●●●●●●●●●●●

■ MAGIC BOX, THE

1951, 118 MINS, UK ◇

Dir John Boulting   *Prod* Ronald Neame   *Scr* Eric Ambler   *Ph* Jack Cardiff   *Ed* Richard Best   *Mus* William Alwyn   *Art Dir* T. Hopewell Ash
● Robert Donat, Margaret Johnston, Maria Schell, Robert Beatty, James Kenney, Bernard Miles (Festival/British Lion)

The Magic Box is a picture of great sincerity and integrity, superbly acted and intelligently directed. Biopic of William Friese-Greene, the British motion picture pioneer, is charged with real life drama.

Eric Ambler's screenplay is taken from Ray Allister's biography, *Friese-Greene: Close-up of an Inventor*. And the script pinpoints all the major triumphs and tragedies in the life of this pioneer, from his youthful beginnings as a photographer's assistant, to his death in 1921 at a film industry meeting with only the price of a cinema ticket in his pocket.

The selection of Robert Donat as Friese-Greene is an excellent one. Always a polished performer, he brings a new depth of sincerity and understanding to the role. His two wives are portrayed with infinite charm by Maria Schell and Margaret Johnston. Schell, as the ailing girl from Switzerland, shares the inventor's first and greatest triumph. Johnston shares only his failures.

Many front ranking stars have little more than walk-on bits, and quite a few just make a brief appearance without even dialog. Mention must be made of a fine cameo from Laurence Olivier as a policeman who is the first to see the inventor's moving picture.

●●●●●●●●●●●●●●●●●●●●●●●●●●●●●●●

■ MAGIC CHRISTIAN, THE

1969, 95 MINS, UK ◇ ⓥ ⊙

Dir Joseph McGrath   *Prod* Denis O'Dell   *Scr* Terry Southern, Joseph McGrath, Peter Sellers   *Ph* Geoffrey Unsworth   *Ed* Kevin O'Connor   *Mus* Ken Thorne   *Art Dir* Assheton Gorton
● Peter Sellers, Ringo Starr, Richard Attenborough, Christopher Lee, Raquel Welch, Laurence Harvey (Commonwealth United/Grand)

A spotty, uneven satire (from the novel by Terry Southern) with a number of good yocks, but insufficient sustained wit or related action. As Peter Sellers & Co swipe at the Establishment, authority, blimpishness and sacred cows, there's a great dismal feeling of self-indulgence as of a pic created merely to please an assorted bunch of chums. Much of it is too 'clever' by half.

Sellers gives a very bright and stylish performance as the posh Sir Guy Grand, richest man in the world, who adopts a young fallout hobo (Ringo Starr) and then sets out to prove to him man's venality.

Though Sellers gives one of his brightest and best-observed appearances, Ringo Starr's effort to project himself as a non-Beatle actor is a distinct non-event.

●●●●●●●●●●●●●●●●●●●●●●●●●●●●●●●

■ MAGNIFICENT AMBERSONS, THE

1942, 88 MINS, US ⓥ ⊙

Dir Orson Welles   *Prod* Orson Welles   *Scr* Orson Welles   *Ph* Stanley Cortez   *Ed* Robert Wise, Mark Robson   *Mus* Bernard Herrmann, Roy Webb   *Art Dir* Mark Lee Kirk
● Joseph Cotten, Dolores Costello, Anne Baxter, Tim Holt, Agnes Moorehead, Ray Collins (RKO/Mercury)

In *The Magnificent Ambersons*, Orson Welles devotes 9,000 feet of film to a spoiled brat who grows up as a spoiled, spiteful young man. This film hasn't a single moment of contrast; it piles on and on a tale of woe, but without once striking at least a true chord of sentimentality. [Novel by Booth Tarkington.]

The central character is Tim Holt, who is portrayed first as the spoiled, curly-haired darling of the town's richest family, and then for the major portion as a conceited, power-conscious, insufferable youth.

Welles comes up with a few more tricks in the direction of the dialog. He plays heavily on the dramatic impact of a whisper, and on the threatened or actual hysterics of a frustrated woman as played by Agnes Moorehead.
☐ 1942: Nominations: Best Picture, Supp. Actress (Agnes Moorehead), B&W Cinematography, B&W Art Direction

●●●●●●●●●●●●●●●●●●●●●●●●●●●●●●●

■ MAGNIFICENT DOLL

1946, 93 MINS, US

Dir Frank Borzage   *Scr* Irving Stone   *Ph* Joseph Valentine   *Ed* Ted J. Kent   *Mus* H. J. Salter   *Art Dir* Alexander Golitzen

M

● Ginger Rogers, David Niven, Burgess Meredith, Stephen McNally, Peggy Wood (Universal/Hallmark)

Dolly Madison has always been considered one of the most colorful figures in this country's early history and her true life story would probably have been a natural for films. It's difficult to understand, therefore, why Irving Stone, who's credited with both the original story and screenplay, went out of his way to slough off facts in favor of fiction. Incident in which Dolly salvaged important government documents from under the noses of the British in the War of 1812, for example, is given a quick brushoff. In its place, Stone has substituted such obvious fiction as having Aaron Burr, with a crush on Dolly, give up his claims to the presidency just because Dolly talked him out of it.

Picture's chief graces result from the fine work of the cast under Frank Borzage's competent direction. Ginger Rogers gives expert handling to the title role, making the transition from one emotion to another in good fashion.

David Niven plays the scoundrelly Burr, sneering when he has to and being tender in his love scenes with Rogers. He hams up several sequences but he couldn't do otherwise with the script. Burgess Meredith shines as James Madison, making the idealistic president convincing enough.

Story is told by Dolly in retrospect, with her monolog bridging the gaps. It picks her up as a young girl on her father's plantation in Virginia, carries through her first unhappy marriage, then her love affair with Burr and eventual marriage to Madison.

....

■ MAGNIFICENT OBSESSION

1935, 110 MINS, US
Dir John M. Stahl   *Prod* John M. Stahl   *Scr* George O'Neil, Sarah Y. Mason, Victor Heerman   *Ph* John Mescall   *Ed* Milton Carruth   *Mus* Franz Waxman
● Irene Dunne, Robert Taylor, Charles Butterworth, Betty Furness, Sara Haden, Ralph Morgan (Universal)

If its 110 minutes' running time makes it appear a bit sluggish, the sensitive and intelligent development (from the novel by Lloyd C. Douglas) ultimately makes the initiallethargic progression appear justified. With its metaphysical theme of godliness and faith, the spiritual background of *Magnificent* is magnificent.

It's patent that Irene Dunne and Robert Taylor, co-starred, must clinch for the finale, even though it was a drunken mishap by the wastrel (Taylor) which had something to do with the death of the venerable Dr Hudson. Dunne is the widow of Dr Hudson, and Taylor's ultimate reformation is achieved because of the romantic attachment for her.

That he becomes a Nobel prize-winner and a surgical marvel in six or seven years, finally achieving the restoration of her sight (after a high-powered battery of medical savants had previously failed to accomplish anything) is rather deftly skirted, for all the theatricalism of the basic elements.

Besides the stellar pair, Charles Butterworth and Betty Furness in secondary prominence scintillate.

....

■ MAGNIFICENT OBSESSION

1954, 107 MINS, US ◇ ⑰
Dir Douglas Sirk   *Prod* Ross Hunter   *Scr* Robert Blees   *Ph* Russell Metty   *Ed* Milton Carruth   *Mus* Frank Skinner   *Art Dir* Bernard Herzbrun, Emrich Nicholson
● Jane Wyman, Rock Hudson, Barbara Rush, Agnes Moorehead, Otto Kruger, Gregg Palmer (Universal)

The same inspirational appeal which marked the 1935 making of Lloyd C. Douglas' bestseller is again caught in this version of *Magnificent Obsession*, with Jane Wyman and Rock Hudson undertaking the roles previously enacted by Irene Dunne and Robert Taylor. It is a sensitive treatment of faith told in terms of moving, human drama which packs emotional impact.

As megged by Douglas Sirk from Robert Blees' moving and understanding screenplay [adaptation by Wells Root, based on the 1935 screenplay], the Ross Hunter production, impressively mounted, commands dramatic attention. Characters become alive and vital and infuse spiritual theme with a rare sort of beauty.

Hudson is the rich playboy responsible for Wyman's blindness who renounces his past existence to devote himself to study and work, hoping as a surgeon to cure her.

Film takes its title from the 'magnificent obsession' which possessed a doctor for whose death Hudson is indirectly responsible.
☐ 1954: Nomination: Best Actress (Jane Wyman)

....

■ MAGNIFICENT SEVEN

1960, 128 MINS, US ◇ ⑰ ⊙
Dir John Sturges   *Prod* John Sturges   *Scr* William Roberts   *Ph* Charles Lang Jr   *Ed* Ferris Webster   *Mus* Elmer Bernstein   *Art Dir* Edward FitzGerald
● Yul Brynner, Eli Wallach, Steve McQueen, Horst Buchholz, Charles Bronson, Robert Vaughan (United Artists)

Until the women and children arrive on the scene about two-thirds of the way through, *The Magnificent Seven* is a rip-roaring rootin' tootin' western with lots of bite and tang and old-fashioned abandon. The last third is downhill, a long and cluttered anti-climax in which 'The Magnificent Seven' grow slightly too magnificent for comfort.

Odd foundation for the able screenplay is the Japanese film, *Seven Samurai*. The plot, as adapted, is simple and compelling. A Mexican village is at the mercy of a bandit (Eli Wallach), whose recurrent 'visits' with his huge band of outlaws strip the meek peasant people of the fruits of their labors. Finally, in desperation, they hire seven American gunslingers for the obvious purpose.

There is a heap of fine acting and some crackling good direction by John Sturges mostly in the early stages, during formation of the central septet. Wallach creates an extremely colorful and arresting figure as the chief antagonist. Of the big 'Seven', Charles Bronson, James Coburn and Steve McQueen share top thespic honors, although the others don't lag by much, notably Horst Buchholz and Brad Dexter. Bronson fashions the most sympathetic character of the group. Coburn, particularly in an introductory sequence during which he reluctantly pits his prowess with a knife against a fast gun in an electrifying showdown, is a powerful study in commanding concentration.

Elmer Bernstein's lively pulsating score, emphasizing conscious percussion, strongly resembles the work of Jerome Moross for *The Big Country*.
☐ 1960: Nomination: Best Scoring of a Dramatic Picture

....

■ MAGNIFICENT SHOWMAN, THE
See: Circus World

....

■ MAGNUM FORCE

1973, 122 MINS, US ◇ ⑰ ⊙
Dir Ted Post   *Prod* Robert Daley   *Scr* John Milius, Michael Cimino   *Ph* Frank Stanley   *Ed* Ferris Webster   *Mus* Lalo Schifrin   *Art Dir* Jack Collis
● Clint Eastwood, Hal Holbrook, Mitchell Ryan, Felton Perry, David Soul, Robert Urich (Malpaso/Warner)

Magnum Force is an intriguing followup to *Dirty Harry* [1971] in that nonconformist Frisco detective Clint Eastwood is faced with tracking down a band of vigilante cops headed by Hal Holbrook, his nominal superior and career nemesis. The story contains the usual surfeit of human massacre for the yahoo trade, as well as a few actual thoughts.

In *Harry* there was a script loaded in favor of the end justifying the means by those pledged to law enforcement. The interesting twist in *Magnum Force* is that Eastwood stumbles on a group of bandit cop avengers. The plot [based on a story by John Milius] thus forces Eastwood to render a judgement in favor of the present system.

Eastwood and new partner Felton Perry are helping investigate a number of bloody murders of local crime leaders, but the evidence finally begins to point at four rookie cops David Soul, Tim Matheson, Robert Urich and Kip Niven who eventually tip their hand to Eastwood.

....

■ MAGUS, THE

1969, 117 MINS, UK ◇
Dir Guy Green   *Prod* Jud Kinberg, John Kohn   *Scr* John Fowles   *Ph* Billy Williams   *Ed* Max Benedict   *Mus* John Dankworth   *Art Dir* Don Ashton
● Michael Caine, Anthony Quinn, Candice Bergen, Anna Karina, Paul Stassino, Julian Glover (20th Century-Fox/Blazer)

The Magus is an esoteric, talky, slowly-developing, sensitively-executed, and somewhat dull film. Adapted by John Fowles from his novel, the production, filmed largely on Majorca (although setting is Greece), is a black tragedy-drama of self-realization. Michael Caine stars, in one of his better performances, along with Anthony Quinn, Candice Bergen and Anna Karina.

This near-miss is not without many notable virtues. Fowles' script sustains interest in its convolutions; direction is resourceful and sensitive; Caine is far more dynamic than usual and Quinn and the two femme stars register strongly.

Caine is an English teacher dispatched to a Greek island as replacement for a suicide. On the island, he meets Quinn, who is a mystic, or a wealthy spiritual hedonist playing God, or a film producer, or a recluse.

Those eager to shift intellectual planes for sheer enjoyment may find the pacing too expository and pedantic: those willing enough to be drawn along might crave more optical effects..

....

■ MAHLER

1974, 115 MINS, UK ◇ ⑰
Dir Ken Russell   *Prod* Roy Baird   *Scr* Ken Russell   *Ph* Dick Bush   *Ed* Michael Bradsell   *Mus* John Forsythe (co-ord.)   *Art Dir* Ian Whittaker
● Robert Powell, Georgina Hale, Richard Morant, Lee Montague, Rosalie Crutchley, Antonia Ellis (Goodtimes)

Mahler is another maddening meeting of Russellian extremes, brilliant and irritating, inventive and banal, tasteful and tasteless, exciting and disappointing.

Flashbacks during composer Gustav Mahler's 1911 train ride to a Vienna deathbed give us glimpses of oppressed youth, childhood memories mirrored in his work, early frustrations as he is forced to conduct so that he can buy time in which to compose, a love-hate relationship with his young wife, a conversion from Judaism to ease his nomination to an important musical post, his constant obsession with death, and so on.

At its frequent best, it mirrors admirably, movingly and even excitingly, the moments of (musical) creation and inspiration, and the torment and basic loneliness of the artist.

....

■ MAIN EVENT, THE

1979, 112 MINS, US ◇ Ⓦ
Dir Howard Zieff   *Prod* Jon Peters   *Scr* Gail Parent,
Andrew Smith   *Ph* Mario Tosi   *Ed* Edward Warschika
Mus Gary Le Mel   *Art Dir* Charles Rosen
● Barbra Streisand, Ryan O'Neal, Paul Sand, Patti
D'Arbanville, Rory Calhoun, Ernie Hudson (Warner/First
Artists/Barwood)

Instead of a comic knockout, this is more of a cream puff.

Situation of a bankrupt perfume queen left with a sore-handed fighter as her only asset has comic potential, but producers Barbra Streisand and Jon Peters, and director Howard Zieff, pad the story unmercifully.

Streisand is the garrulous yenta, after the passive and resistant Ryan O'Neal to resume his championship form and win her back the $60,000 she unknowingly wasted on him in her plush days.

Zieff has chosen to emphasize sexual innuendo and result is a low-blow effort that evokes more titters than guffaws. Romantic aspects, which should be chief draw of *Main Event*, are also blunted, until a final seduction scene instigated by Streisand that gives the pic its only resonance.

■ MAJOR AND THE MINOR, THE

1942, 100 MINS, US
Dir Billy Wilder   *Prod* Arthur Hornblow Jr   *Scr* Charles
Brackett, Billy Wilder   *Ph* Leo Tover   *Ed* Doane Harrison
Mus Robert Emmett Dolan   *Art Dir* Roland Anderson,
Hans Dreier
● Ginger Rogers, Ray Milland, Diana Lynn, Robert
Benchley, Rita Johnson, Norma Varden (Paramount)

The Major and the Minor is a sparkling and effervescing piece of farce-comedy. Story [suggested by the play *Connie Goes Home* by Edward Childs Carpenter and the story *Sunny Goes Home* by Fannie Kilbourne] is light, fluffy, and frolicsome. Ginger Rogers, disillusioned by New York, decides to head back home to Iowa. Her savings are not sufficient for ticket, she dolls up as a youngster under 12 to ride on half rate. But complications arise that throw her into compartment of Ray Milland, major at a boys' military academy, and into the school for a three-day layover.

During the interim, there's a Cinderella-esque romance developed while Rogers, in the moppet getup, is pursued by the adolescent cadet officers for some rousing laugh episodes.

Both script and direction swing the yarn along at a consistent pace, with the laughs developing naturally and without strain.

■ MAJOR BARBARA

1941, 113 MINS, UK Ⓦ
Dir Gabriel Pascal, [Harold French, David Lean]
Prod Gabriel Pascal   *Scr* George Bernard Shaw
Ph Ronald Neame, [Freddie Young]   *Ed* Charles Frend,
David Lean   *Mus* William Walton   *Art Dir* Vincent
Korda, John Bryan
● Wendy Hiller, Rex Harrison, Robert Morley, Robert
Newton, Emlyn Williams, Deborah Kerr (Pascal)

Major Barbara is the second film from the partnership of George Bernard Shaw and Gabriel Pascal. Adapted from an old Shaw play, circa 1905, it still carries the lightning thrusts of Shavian caustic satire at any and all levels of society.

The script, prepared by Shaw, closely follows his original. Wendy Hiller, daughter of a multi-millionaire sincerely works to save souls as the Salvation Army major in the Limehouse slums. Pecunious Rex Harrison, Greek scholar, falls in love at first sight.

Hiller is suddenly disillusioned in the Army soul-saving when heavy financial aid is gladly accepted from her munitions-making father and a rich distiller. It's then that the father takes his odd family and stranger menage through his factories, demonstrating he is doing more to improve conditions of his workers than could be accomplished in Limehouse.

Hiller, lead in *Pygmalion*, delivers an excellent and personable performance throughout, and does much to carry the story along through some rather dull and weighty passages. Harrison does well as the Greek scholar but secondary acting honors are shared by Robert Morley, as the father, and Robert Newton, a tough limey whose soul is finally saved.

■ MAJOR DUNDEE

1965, 134 MINS, US ◇ Ⓦ
Dir Sam Peckinpah   *Prod* Jerry Bresler   *Scr* Harry Julian
Fink, Oscar Saul, Sam Peckinpah   *Ph* Sam Leavitt
Ed William A. Lyon, Don Starling, Howard Kunin
Mus Daniele Amfitheatrof
● Charlton Heston, Richard Harris, Jim Hutton, James
Coburn, Michael Anderson Jr, Senta Berger (Columbia)

Somewhere in the development of this Jerry Bresler production the central premise was sidetracked and a maze of little-meaning action substituted. What started out as a straight story-line (or at least, idea) a troop of US Cavalry chasing a murderous Apache and his band into Mexico to rescue three kidnapped white children and avenge an Indian massacre devolves into a series of sub-plots and tedious, poorly edited footage in which much of the continuity is lost.

Sam Peckinpah's direction of individual scenes is mostly vigorous but he cannot overcome the weakness of screenplay of whose responsibility he bears a share with Harry Julian Fink and Oscar Saul. Use of offscreen narration, ostensibly from the diary of one of the troopers on the march, reduces impact and is a further deterrent to fast unfoldment.

Charlton Heston delivers one of his regulation hefty portrayals and gets solid backing from a cast headed by Richard Harris as the rebel captain, who presents a dashing figure. Jim Hutton as an energetic young lieutenant and James Coburn an Indian scout likewise stand out.

■ MAJOR LEAGUE

1989, 107 MINS, US ◇ Ⓦ ⊙
Dir David S. Ward   *Prod* Chris Chesser, Irby Smith
Scr David S. Ward   *Ph* Reynaldo Villalobos   *Ed* Dennis
M. Hill   *Mus* James Newton Howard   *Art Dir* Jeffrey
Howard
● Tom Berenger, Charlie Sheen, Corbin Bernsen,
Margaret Whitton, James Gammon, Rene Russo (Morgan
Creek/Mirage)

Major League lacks the subtlety of *Bull Durham* or the drama of *Eight Men Out*, but for sheer crowd-pleasing fun it belts one high into the left-field bleachers. Writer-director David S. Ward creates an adult version of *The Bad News Bears* in this R-rated baseball comedy about a squad of misfits who rally together to bring the pennant back to Cleveland.

Though the plot turns are mostly predictable, they are executed with wit and style. There's a lot of rooting interest for the audience in the sad sacks cynically assembled by new Indians owner Margaret Whitton with the secret hope that they'll draw so poorly that she'll be able to break the stadium lease and head for Miami.

Naturally, when the guys get wind of this maneuver, they recover their lost pride and bring off the pennant miracle. The cast is a fine ensemble, leading off with Tom Berenger as the battered, world-weary catcher and Charlie Sheen as the juve delinquent pitcher with punk hair-do who fully merits his nickname of 'Wild Thing'.

As long as it sticks to the field and the clubhouse, the script doesn't falter, but there's time to go out for popcorn during the cliched love scenes of Berenger trying to jumpstart his broken-down romance with yuppie librarian Rene Russo.

Milwaukee County Stadium fills in for the much larger (and contrastingly circular) Cleveland ballpark, which is unconvincingly used for establishing shots.

■ MAKE MINE MINK

1960, 101 MINS, UK Ⓦ
Dir Robert Asher   *Prod* Hugh Stewart   *Scr* Michael
Pertwee, Peter Blackmore   *Ph* Reginald Wyer   *Ed* Roger
Cherrill   *Mus* Philip Green   *Art Dir* Carmen Dillon
● Terry-Thomas, Athene Seyler, Hattie Jacques, Billie
Whitelaw, Elspeth Duxbury, Jack Hedley (Rank)

Based on Peter Coke's West End comedy *Breath of Spring*, plot concerns the blundering excursions into crime of a bunch of pinheaded amateurs, who specialize in lifting valuable furs and devoting the loot to charity.

Dame Beatrice Appleby (Athene Seyler) takes in lodgers to help out her income and also to provide money for her charitable work. The idea of crimes comes to her when she is able safely to return a fur which has been given to her as a present by her devoted maid Lily (Billie Whitelaw), a reformed thief who is now going steady with a policeman.

Her 'gang' consists of Albert (Terry-Thomas), a retired officer who plans the raids along strictly military lines, a daffy spinster (Elspeth Duxbury), and Nanette (Hattie Jacques), a heavyweight teacher of deportment. This unlikely quartet carry off several daring raids.

The humor is episodic, but Robert Asher has directed the lively screenplay briskly enough, and the camerawork is okay. The four members of the gang do their chores admirably, with Seyler outstanding.

■ MAKE WAY FOR TOMORROW

1937, 91 MINS, US
Dir Leo McCarey   *Prod* Leo McCarey   *Scr* Vina Delmar
Ph William Mellor   *Ed* LeRoy Stone   *Mus* Boris Morros
(dir.)   *Art Dir* Hans Dreier, Bernard Herzbrun
● Victor Moore, Beulah Bondi, Fay Bainter, Thomas
Mitchell, Ray Mayer, Barbara Read (Paramount)

Rugged simplicity marks this Leo McCarey production [from a novel by Josephine Laurence and a play by Helen and Nolan Leary]. It is a tear-jerker, obviously grooved for femme fans.

McCarey, who also directed, has firmly etched the dilemma in which an elderly married couple find themselves when they lose their old dwelling place and their five grown-up children are non-receptive. He keeps audience interest focused on old Lucy Cooper and Pa Cooper as they are separated, each finding themselves in the way and not fitting in with the two households (one with a son and the other with a daughter).

Victor Moore essays a serious role as Pa Cooper without firmly establishing himself in the new field. He continues to be more Victor Moore than an old grandfather, and he makes the biggest impression in the lighter, more whimsical moments. Beulah Bondi, as the aged Lucy is standout from the viewpoint of clever character work and make-up. She has some of the meaty scenes and makes them real.

Fay Bainter does splendidly as the wife of George Cooper, one of the sons to whose house the mother goes to live. Maurice Moscovitch, as the ardent listener to the old man's woes and who understands him better than his own children, contributes a neat portrayal.

■ MAKING LOVE

1982, 111 MINS, US ◇ Ⓦ
Dir Arthur Hiller   *Prod* Allen Adler, Daniel Melnick
Scr Barry Sandler   *Ph* David M. Walsh   *Ed* William H.

M

Reynolds   *Mus* Leonard Rosenman   *Art Dir* James D. Vance
● Michael Ontkean, Kate Jackson, Harry Hamlin, Wendy Hiller, Arthur Hill, Nancy Olson (20th Century-Fox/Indie)

This homosexual-themed domestic drama of a married man's 'coming out' stands up well on all counts, emerging as an absorbing tale.

First half-hour presents Michael Ontkean and Kate Jackson as a successful young LA couple, he a medic and she a fast-rising TV exec. Then Ontkean meets Harry Hamlin, a gay writer whose good looks provide him with enough easy one-night stands to do without any emotional commitment. Ontkean takes the plunge with Hamlin and finds he likes it, so much so that he quickly knows his marriage is finished.

Working from a story by A. Scott Berg, Barry Sandler has penned a fine, aware screenplay.

Director Arthur Hiller has elicited strong performances from his three principals, and he also carries off the device of having the trio directly address the audience with their thoughts from time to time.

■ MAKING MR. RIGHT

1987, 95 MINS, US ◇ ⊕ ⊙
Dir Susan Seidelman   *Prod* Mike Wise, Joel Tuber   *Scr* Floyd Byars, Laurie Frank   *Ph* Edward Lachman   *Ed* Andrew Mondshein   *Mus* Chaz Jankel   *Art Dir* Jack Blackman
● John Malkovich, Ann Magnuson, Glenne Headly, Ben Masters, Laurie Metcalf, Polly Bergen (Orion/Barry & Enright)

Susan Seidelman has taken nearly every wrong turn in *Making Mr. Right*, a desperately unfunny romance between an android and a New Wave 'image consultant.' The actors nearly suffocate delivering stiff dialog, with jokes that are bad or vulgar (or both) in scenes that reek of contrivance.

Sharing in the blame should be scripters Floyd Byars and Laurie Frank, who have taken Frankenstein and turned him into Frankie Stone (Ann Magnuson). Her world is Melrose Avenue Miami style, where she's a very unlikely whiz-bang publicist with a punk 'do and very ordinary sensibilities who practically moves in with an android and his creator (John Malkovich in both roles) to get the best handle on how to sell the invention to the American public before he's launched into space.

She's supposed to be teaching the android, Ulysses, social graces, but he ends up learning emotions instead.

Malkovich takes to his role of Ulysses very earnestly, considering he has to utter such gooey lines as 'Why do people fall in love?' and suffer mutterings from Magnuson and her horny girlfriend (Glenne Headly) whether he's anatomically correct.

■ MALCOLM X

1992, 201 MINS, US ◇ ⊕ ⊙
Dir Spike Lee   *Prod* Marvin Worth, Spike Lee   *Scr* Arnold Perl, Spike Lee   *Ph* Ernest Dickerson   *Ed* Barry Alexander Brown   *Mus* Terence Blanchard   *Art Dir* Wynn Thomas
● Denzel Washington, Angela Bassett, Albert Hall, Al Freeman Jr, Delroy Lindo, Spike Lee (Warner/40 Acres & a Mule)

Spike Lee has made a disappointingly conventional and sluggish film in *Malcolm X*. The pic comes up short in several departments, notably in pacing and in giving a strong sense of why this man became a legend. This is one long sit.

Despite Denzel Washington's forceful, magnetic, multilayered lead performance, the film only clicks sporadically.

The screenplay [based on *The Autobiography*

of Malcolm X as told to Alex Haley] by the late Arnold Perl and Lee (James Baldwin's name, often invoked during production, is nowhere mentioned) tellingly begins with the 'war years.' The initial hour chronicles Malcolm's misadventures in clubs and bars, his affair with a white woman, numbers running, involvement in drugs, and the burglary ring that eventually lands him in the pen.

The subsequent 25 minutes detail Malcolm's prison introduction to Islam and the beliefs of Elijah Muhammad. The next hour presents Malcolm as the rising star of the Nation of Islam.

Malcolm's gradual break with Elijah Muhammad is handled in rather a muddled fashion, and the final, short act of Malcolm's life isn't given the dramatic substance it deserves, despite the time lavished upon it.

Various periods from the 1940s through the mid-1960s have been elaborately evoked by production designer Wynn Thomas, cinematographer Ernest Dickerson, costume designer Ruth Carter and the multitude of behind-the-scenes craftspeople (the end credits last nine minutes).
□ 1992: Nominations: Best Actor (Denzel Washington), Costume Design

■ MALE AND FEMALE

1919, 107 MINS, US ⊗
Dir Cecil B. DeMille   *Prod* Jesse L. Lasky   *Scr* Jeanie MacPherson   *Ph* Alvin Wyckoff   *Art Dir* Wilfrey Buckland
● Thomas Meighan, Gloria Swanson, Lila Lee, Bebe Daniels, Theodore Roberts, Raymond Hatton (Paramount)

Cecil B. DeMille's picturization of J.M. Barrie's play, *The Admirable Crichton*, is impressive. The production places DeMille on a par with D.W. Griffith as a far as Babylonian stuff is concerned, and there are several scenes where DeMille steps a little beyond the great Grif.

The result on the screen shows that there was no stinting on money. The cast is a pippin and Thomas Meighan does good work. Gloria Swanson and Lila Lee divide the women honors of the piece.

Swanson plays the role of Lady Mary, while Lee is the little slavey, Tweeny. The former appears to advantage in both the London and the desert island scenes, looking beautiful at all times, and especially so as she slips into the sunken bath, while little Lee displays an artistry that is far greater than she showed in any of her previous productions. Bebe Daniels is also in the cast for a small bit in one of the Babylonian scenes, and certainly is good to look upon.

■ MALTA STORY

1953, 103 MINS, UK ⊕
Dir Brian Desmond Hurst   *Prod* Peter de Sarigny   *Scr* William Fairchild, Nigel Balchin   *Ph* Robert Krasker   *Ed* Michael Gordon   *Mus* William Alwyn   *Art Dir* John Howell
● Alec Guinness, Jack Hawkins, Anthony Steel, Muriel Pavlow, Flora Robson, Renee Asherson (Rank)

This is an epic story of the courage and endurance of the people and defenders of the island of Malta. It is handled in grimly realistic but not over-dramatic style. Camerawork is excellent, and some vivid war scenes of attacks on convoys are genuine newsreel shots.

Alec Guinness plays a camera reconnaissance pilot enroute to Egypt. His plane is blown up, leaving him stranded in Malta. He is roped in to continue his activities during the siege of 1942 since his pictures disclose freight trains in Italy packed with gliders obviously intended for an invasion of the island. Jack Hawkins is the air officer in command who stands helplessly by while his airfields are blasted night and day.

A dual love interest impinges rather apologetically upon this war scarred scene, with Muriel Pavlow giving an endearing performance as a Maltese girl in love with her chief, played in a forthright manner by Anthony Steel. Flora Robson gives a distinguished characterization of a steadfast, sorrowing Maltese mother stoically facing the prospect of her son's execution for treason.

Bulk of the acting laurels go to Guinness, who here forsakes his chameleon-like whimsicality for the shy diffident charm of an inexperienced lover.

■ MALTESE FALCON, THE

1931, 80 MINS, US ⊕
Dir Roy Del Ruth   *Scr* Maude Fulton, Lucien Hubbard, Brown Holmes   *Ph* William Rees
● Bebe Daniels, Ricardo Cortez, Dudley Digges, Una Merkel, Robert Elliot, Thelma Todd (Warner)

Bringing *The Maltese Falcon* to the screen as Warners have done was no easy job. But director Roy Del Ruth lets things take their course and, with a naturally nonchalant although extremely odd private detective in Ricardo Cortez, takes his audience out of the screen story rut for a series of surprise incidents and a totally different finis.

Although four men are murdered and two corpses revealed to the audience, the story treatment [from Dashiell Hammett's novel] and the Cortez smile are such that a quick thrill is permitted, a laugh, and then, through the first 75% of the footage, additionally interest to well-sustained curiosity.

It can't be called naughty, even though Bebe Daniels as Ruth Wonderly spends the second night in the elaborate apartment of this unusual private detective.

The mystery element is so flung about that not until the last reel or so does the most studious follower know who did any of the killings. Meantime a number of clever gags happen through Sam Spade in disarming people, then apologizing; taking money and then having it taken from him; making love one minute and turning the girl over to the police the next.

■ MALTESE FALCON, THE

1941, 100 MINS, US ⊕ ⊙
Dir John Huston   *Prod* Hal B. Wallis (exec.)   *Scr* John Huston   *Ph* Arthur Edeson   *Ed* Thomas Richards   *Mus* Adolph Deutsch   *Art Dir* Robert Haas
● Humphrey Bogart, Mary Astor, Peter Lorre, Sydney Greenstreet, Barton MacLane, Gladys George (Warner)

This is one of the best examples of actionful and suspenseful melodramatic story telling in cinematic form. Unfolding a most intriguing and entertaining murder mystery, picture displays outstanding excellence in writing, direction, acting and editing.

John Huston, makes his debut as a film director. He also wrote the script solo, endowing it with well-rounded episodes of suspense and surprise and carrying along with consistently pithy dialog.

Humphrey Bogart gives an attention-arresting portrayal that not only dominates the proceedings throughout but is the major motivation in all but a few minor scenes. Mary Astor skillfully etches the role of an adventuress. Sydney Greenstreet, prominent member of the Lunt-Fontaine stage troupe, scores heavily in his first screen appearance.

Story in Dashiell Hammett's best style details the experiences of private detective Bogart when called in to handle a case for Astor shortly finding himself in the middle of double-crossing intrigue and several murders perpetrated by strange characters bent on obtaining possession of the famed bejeweled Maltese Falcon. Keeping just within bounds of the law, and utilizing sparkling ingenuity in gathering up the loose ends and finally piecing them together, Bogart is able to solve the series of crimes for the benefit of the police.

☐ 1941: Nominations: Best Picture, Supp. Actor (Sydney Greenstreet), Screenplay

■ **MAMBO**

1954, 94 MINS, ITALY/US ⓥ
Dir Robert Rossen *Prod* Carlo Ponti, Dino De Laurentiis
Scr Robert Rossen, Guido Piovene, Ivo Perilli, Ennio De Concini *Ph* Harold Rosson *Ed* Adriana Novelli
Mus Bernardo Noriega, Dave Gilbert
● Silvana Mangano, Michael Rennie, Vittorio Gassman, Shelley Winters, Katherine Dunham, Eduardo Cianelli (Ponti-De Laurentiis/Paramount)

Story is near soap opera, and involves the trials of a girl who wants to be a dancer. She is torn between the pure love for a dying prince and the passionate embraces of an adventurer. For a while Giovanna (Silvana Mangano) is happy with the dance group led by Tony (Shelley Winters), and soon becomes star of the show. But despite her success on returning to her home town of Venice, she falls once more under the adventurer's (Vittorio Gassman) spell while turning down a marriage proposal by the prince (Michael Rennie).

Like the story, the film is not for the discriminating. Reportedly, it was re-cut several times and is said to bear little resemblance to the original.

Performances are generally good, with Rennie copping honors in a smooth, sympathetic effort as the doomed prince. Winters contributes ably despite a vaguely drawn character, while Gassman effectively overacts his villain role in keeping with the picture's spirit. Katherine Dunham and Eduardo Cianelli liven up some minor roles, with the former also contributing the pic's choreography.

■ **MAMBO KINGS, THE**

1992, 101 MINS, US ◇ ⓥ ⊙
Dir Arne Glimcher *Prod* Arnon Milchan, Arne Glimcher
Scr Cynthia Cidre *Ph* Michael Ballhaus *Ed* Claire Simpson *Mus* Robert Kraft *Art Dir* Stuart Wurtzel
● Armand Assante, Antonio Banderas, Cathy Moriarty, Maruschka Detmers, Desi Arnaz Jr, Roscoe Lee Browne (Warner)

The Mambo Kings is an ambitious, old-fashioned Hollywood film that lovingly recreates the Latino ambience of its Pulitzer Prize-winning source material. With impeccable period sets and costumes and striking cinematography, pic beautifully evokes 1950's New York. Arne Glimcher, an art gallery owner and producer, makes a strong directing debut.

Oscar Hijuelos' novel [*The Mambo Kings Play Songs of Love*] proved a challenge to adapt, and Glimcher and screenwriter Cynthia Cidre pared down the 407-page book to its essential story about the rise and fall of two Cuban immigrant musicians. Most striking sequences take place in smoky, crowded clubs, from the opening in Havana to final image of Cesar Castillo (Armand Assante) singing in a New York club.

Assante makes a likable skirt chaser and later conveys Cesar's downward spiral with great economy. But he occasionally slips into a New York accent and never sounds anything like brother Antonio Banderas, a Spanish actor in Pedro Aldomovar's films. As the tormented Nestor, Banderas gives a sensitive performance.

Final scenes pass too quickly, with the sexual tension between Banderas' wife Maruschka Detmers and Assante left unexplored despite one steamy scene.

☐ 1992: Nomination: Best Song ('Beautiful Maria of My Soul')

■ **MAME**

1974, 132 MINS, US ◇ ⓥ ⊙
Dir Gene Saks *Prod* Robert Fryer, James Cresson
Scr Paul Zindel *Ph* Philip Lathrop *Ed* Maury Winetrobe *Mus* Jerry Herman
● Lucille Ball, Robert Preston, Beatrice Arthur, Kirby Furlong, Bruce Davison, Joyce Van Patten (Warner/ABC)

The Lucille Ball version, or reincarnation, of *Mame*, lavishly costumed by Theadora van Runkle, with Jerry Herman's [1966] musical numbers smartly choreographed by Onna White is a fantasy of the good old days of prohibition, the depression and the world travel folders.

The narrative pretty much follows the familiar sequence of events. Mame is first discovered in the midst of prohibition, the Charleston and progressive education. She goes down with the market in 1929, tackles show business, then clerking, is rescued by the romantic Beauregard and spends the rest of her life travelling.

A comedy with songs, not a musical comedy, per se, this *Mame* climaxes with its foxhunting number in Georgia.

■ **MAMMY**

1930, 83 MINS, US ◇ ⊙
Dir Michael Curtiz *Scr* L.G. Rigby, Joseph Jackson
Ph Barney McGill *Mus* Irving Berlin
● Al Jolson, Lois Moran, Louise Dresser, Lowell Sherman, Hobart Bosworth, Mitchell Lewis (Warner)

A lively picture [from the musical *Mr Bones*], with Al Jolson singing new and old songs, including among the Irving Berlin new numbers a couple of melodious hits.

Here is a minstrel show on the stage and on the street the parade, the blacking up in the dressing room, and the semi-circle with its white face interlocutor, songs by the quartet, jokes by the end men, and dancing. The one section where Technicolor is employed is on the extended semi-circle minstrel scene.

Jolson is one of the ends and Mitchell Lewis the other. Lowell Sherman is the interlocutor, William West. It's Sherman who starts and bawls up the works. The show owner's daughter (Lois Moran) is in love with him, but he's just fooling around. Sherman does not resent it even when Jolson makes a jealous play to help along Moran, leaving the impression he wants the girl himself.

[When Sherman is accidentally shot during a performance,] Jolson runs away, going home to see mammy. When mammy tells her boy to always hold his head up, he rides the next freight back.

■ **MAN, THE**

1972, 93 MINS, US ◇
Dir Joseph Sargent *Prod* Lee Rich *Scr* Rod Serling
Ph Edward C. Rosson *Ed* George Nicholson *Mus* Jerry Goldsmith *Art Dir* James G. Hulsey
● James Earl Jones, Martin Balsam, Burgess Meredith, Lew Ayres, William Windom, Barbara Rush (ABC Circle)

The Man is a compelling and sometimes explosive adaptation of the Irving Wallace bestseller. James Earl Jones portrays the black man who ascends so unexpectedly and without precedent to the presidency of the United States.

He gains his top position through the rules of succession. As president pro tem of the Senate, he automatically is elevated when the president and speaker of the House are killed in the collapse of a building in Germany, and the vice-president, incapacitated by a stroke, announces he cannot take over the office of president.

Jones delivers an honest, forceful characterization of the president who accepts his fate with humility but discovers his own strength

as a man through learning his own powers to cope.

■ **MAN ALONE, A**

1955, 95 MINS, US ◇ ⓥ
Dir Ray Milland *Prod* Herbert J. Yates *Scr* John Tucker Battle *Ph* Lionel Lindon *Ed* Richard L. Van Enger
Mus Victor Young *Art Dir* Walter Keller
● Ray Milland, Mary Murphy, Ward Bond, Raymond Burr, Lee Van Cleef, Alan Hale (Republic)

Western suspense, combined with action and drama, shape *A Man Alone* as an okay offering.

Ray Milland turns director with *Man* and acquits himself fairly well in the new chore. He's a mite too deliberate with his pacing, particularly in handling the character he plays, but shows plenty of promise in his guidance of the other players and in an ability to develop dramatics [from a story by Mort Briskin] beyond the level of the usual outdoor feature.

Quarantined in her Arizona desert town home where her father, the sheriff (Ward Bond), is ill with yellow fever, Nadine Corrigan (Mary Murphy) suddenly finds the house has become sanctuary for a notorious gunman Wes Steele (Milland), who is being hunted by a lynch mob for several brutal murders. In this isolation, a drama of love and regeneration is developed, leading eventually to the exposure of the guilty parties.

Production rounds up a good array of sight values to backstop for the action and drama, with Lionel Lindon's TruColor photography doing its share.

■ **MAN AND HIS MATE**
See: One Million B.C.

■ **MAN BETWEEN, THE**

1953, 101 MINS, UK
Dir Carol Reed *Scr* Harry Kurnitz *Ph* Desmond Dickinson *Ed* A.S. Bates *Mus* John Addison
Art Dir Andre Andrejew
● James Mason, Claire Bloom, Hildegarde Neff, Geoffrey Toone, Dieter Krause (London)

Carol Reed picks war-torn Berlin for a story of political intrigue, capitalizing on the obvious potentialities of the divided capital.

From an original story by Walter Ebert, Harry Kurnitz fashions a script crammed with lively suspense values. Atmosphere is created almost from the opening shot although it takes some time for the plot of sinister intrigue to emerge clearly.

It is virtually a battle of wits between east and west, with the Red Zone police striving to end the trafficking of human bodies into the Western Zone. The plot is woven around Claire Bloom, an English girl, who comes to spend a holiday with her brother, an army major, and her sister-in-law, a German girl, and James Mason, an East Berliner who rescues her after she is mistakenly picked up by Red police.

Best suspense derives from the plot by Mason to get the girl back to her brother. The familiar screen chase is heightened by the contrasting locales.

■ **MAN CALLED HORSE, A**

1970, 114 MINS, US ◇ ⓥ
Dir Elliot Silverstein *Prod* Sandy Howard *Scr* Jack De Witt *Ph* Robert Hauser *Ed* Philip Anderson
Mus Leonard Rosenman *Art Dir* Dennis Lynton Clark
● Richard Harris, Judith Anderson, Jean Gascon, Manu Tupou, Corinna Tsopei, Dub Taylor (Cinema Center)

A Man Called Horse is said to be an authentic depiction of American Indian life in the Dakota territory of about 1820. Authentic it may be, but an absorbing film drama it is not.

Sandy Howard's Durango-lensed production stars Richard Harris as an English nobleman captured by the Sioux. Captivity segues to understanding and finally to tribal membership.

Jack DeWitt's spare-dialog adaptation of a 1950 Dorothy M. Johnson story, features a lot of non-subtitled Sioux lingo, broken up by Harris' expository passages with half-breed Jean Gascon.

Performances are generally good, especially that of Gascon, while Judith Anderson lends both pathos and broad comedy in her rendition. Harris is unevenly stiff.

....

■ MANCHURIAN CANDIDATE, THE

1962, 126 MINS, US ⓦ ⊙

Dir John Frankenheimer   *Prod* George Axelrod, John Frankenheimer   *Scr* George Axelrod   *Ph* Lionel Lindon   *Ed* Ferris Webster   *Mus* David Amram   *Art Dir* Richard Sylbert
● Frank Sinatra, Laurence Harvey, Janet Leigh, Angela Lansbury, Henry Silva, Leslie Parrish (United Artists)

George Axelrod and John Frankenheimer's jazzy, hip screen translation of Richard Condon's bestselling novel works in all departments.

Its story of the tracking down of a brainwashed Korean war 'hero' being used as the key figure in an elaborate Communist plot to take over the US government is, on the surface, one of the wildest fabrications any author has ever tried to palm off on a gullible public. But the fascinating thing is that, from uncertain premise to shattering conclusion, one does not question plausibility the events being rooted in their own cinematic reality.

Manchurian Candidate gets off to an early start (before the credits) as a dilemma wrapped in an enigma: a small American patrol in Korea is captured by the Chinese Communists. Shortly thereafter, the sergeant of the group, Laurence Harvey, is seen being welcomed home in Washington as a Congressional Medal of Honor winner, having been recommended for that award by his captain, Frank Sinatra, who led the illfated patrol.

But something is obviously wrong. Harvey himself admits to being the least likely of heroes, and Sinatra, though he testifies that the sergeant is 'the bravest, most honorable, most loyal' man he knows, realizes this is completely untrue. But why?

The captain's subsequent pursuit of the truth comprises the bizarre plot which ranges from the halls of Congress, New York publishing circles and an extremely unlikely Communist hideout in mid-Manhattan, to a literally stunning climax at a Madison Square Garden political convention.
☐ 1962: Nominations: Best Supp. Actress (Angela Lansbury), Editing

....

■ MANDALAY

1934, 65 MINS, US

Dir Michael Curtiz   *Prod* Robert Presnell   *Scr* Austin Parker, Charles Kenyon   *Ph* Tony Gaudio   *Ed* Thomas Pratt   *Art Dir* Anton Grot
● Kay Francis, Lyle Talbot, Ricardo Cortez, Warner Oland, Lucien Littlefield, Ruth Donnelly (Warner)

Kay Francis is a girl of doubtful past, present and future who eventually casts her lot with an outcast doctor in what an extra reel may have developed as possible reformation for both.

Picture trips along at a nice pace and except for one spot, toward the end, invites no adverse reaction. This is in connection with the faked suicide of Ricardo Cortez, a gunrunner who leaves an empty poison bottle and an open window in his ship's cabin as evidence of his act.

The audience is let in on the phony suicide, whereas it would have been more effective to spring the surprise and the explanation on the audience the same as on people in the cast, notably Francis.

Much of the action [from a story by Paul Hervey Fox] occurs on a boat bound from Rangoon for Mandalay. Earlier sequences are in the former seaport, where the heroine has been forced into a life of doubtful purity when her gun-runner boyfriend takes a run-out powder. This portion of the story isn't as convincing as it might be. Manner in which Warner Oland browbeats her into working for his joint is anything but convincing, either.

....

■ MANDINGO

1975, 126 MINS, US ◇ ⓦ ⊙

Dir Richard Fleischer   *Prod* Dino De Laurentiis   *Scr* Norman Wexler   *Ph* Richard H. Kline   *Ed* Frank Bracht   *Mus* Maurice Jarre   *Art Dir* Boris Leven
● James Mason, Susan George, Percy King, Richard Ward, Branda Sykes, Ken Norton (Paramount)

Based on Kyle Onstott's novel of sexploitation sociology, *Mandingo* is an embarrassing and crude film which wallows in every cliche of the slave-based white society in the pre-Civil War South.

The cornball adaptation is exceeded in banality only by the performances of James Mason, slave-breeder father of son Percy King, who in turn develops what passes for genuine affection for Brenda Sykes, while wife Susan George descends into revenge with Ken Norton, stud slave whom King also has befriended for purposes of pugilistic gambling. Lots of cardboard tragedy ensues.

....

■ MANDY
(US: The Crash of Silence)

1952, 92 MINS, UK

Dir Alexander Mackendrick   *Prod* Leslie Norman   *Scr* Nigel Balchin, Jack Whittingham   *Ph* Douglas Slocombe   *Ed* Seth Holt   *Mus* William Alwyn   *Art Dir* Jim Morahan
● Phyllis Calvert, Jack Hawkins, Terence Morgan, Mandy Miller, Godfrey Tearle, Marjorie Fielding (Ealing)

This story of a deaf-and-dumb child has obvious tear-jerking angles which have been freely exploited.

Central character in the yarn, which is based on a novel by Hilda Lewis, *The Day Is Ours*, is a young child who was born deaf and is, inevitably, dumb. Against a background of parental disagreement, the plot traces the methods used in teaching youngsters the art of lip-reading and expression.

The dominating performance comes from little Mandy Miller in the title role. The best adult performance comes from Jack Hawkins who makes the headmaster a vital and sincere character. Godfrey Tearle and Marjorie Fielding as the child's grandparents top a sound supporting cast.

....

■ MAN FOR ALL SEASONS, A

1966, 120 MINS, UK ◇ ⓦ ⊙

Dir Fred Zinnemann   *Prod* Fred Zinnemann   *Scr* Robert Bolt   *Ph* Ted Moore   *Ed* Ralph Kemplen   *Mus* Georges Delerue   *Art Dir* John Box
● Paul Scofield, Wendy Hiller, Leo McKern, Robert Shaw, Orson Welles, Susannah York (Highland/Columbia)

Producer-director Fred Zinnemann has blended all filmmaking elements into an excellent, handsome and stirring film version of *A Man for All Seasons*. Robert Bolt adapted his 1960 play, a timeless, personal conflict based on the 16th century politico-religious situation between adulterous King Henry VIII and Catholic Sir Thomas More.

Basic dramatic situation is that of a minister of the crown and his conscience being challenged by the imperious point of view which maintains that the lack of explicit support to an erring king is equivalent to disloyalty. This is the usual human dilemma whenever expediency confronts integrity.

Paul Scofield delivers an excellent performance as More, respected barrister, judge and chancellor who combined an urbane polish with inner mysticism. Faced with mounting pressure to endorse publicly the royal marriage of Henry VIII to Anne Boleyn, but armed with legalistic knowhow, More outfoxed his adversaries until 'perjury' was used to justify a sentence of death.

Robert Shaw is also excellent as the king, giving full exposition in limited footage to the character: volatile, educated, virile, arrogant, yet sensitive (and sensible) enough to put the squeeze on More via subordinates, mainly Thomas Cromwell, played by Leo McKern. Orson Welles in five minutes (here an early confrontation, as Cardinal Wolsey, with More) achieves outstanding economy of expression.
☐ 1966: Best Picture, Director, Actor (Paul Scofield), Adapted Screenplay, Color Cinematography, Color Costume Design.
☐ Nominations: Best Supp. Actor (Robert Shaw), Supp. Actress (Wendy Hiller)

....

■ MAN FRIDAY

1975, 115 MINS, UK ◇ ⓦ

Dir Jack Gold   *Prod* David Korda   *Scr* Adrian Mitchell   *Ph* Alex Phillips   *Ed* Anne V. Coates   *Mus* Carl Davis   *Art Dir* Peter Murton
● Peter O'Toole, Richard Roundtree, Peter Cellier, Christopher Cabot, Joel Fluellen, Sam Sebroke (Keep/ABC/ITC)

Another variation of Daniel Defoe's classic has Crusoe (Peter O'Toole) discovering his Friday (Richard Roundtree) after the shipwrecked mariner has brutally shot and killed the black's companions, washed up on 'his' island after a storm.

O'Toole's Crusoe proceeds to subdue and then teach and indoctrinate the 'savage', with missionary zeal, into the manners and mores of western society, not forgetting the master-slave relationship.

Slowly, however, Friday begins to question him, his theories and teachings, soon in effect himself becoming the teacher of newer, freer, more open-minded ideas and ideals.

O'Toole speaks his lighter lines with panache and humor, but becoming very moving indeed when seized by loneliness and despair.

....

■ MAN FROM HONG KONG, THE

1975, 99 MINS, HONG KONG/AUSTRALIA ◇ ⓦ

Dir Brian Trenchard-Smith   *Prod* Raymond Chow, John Fraser   *Scr* Brian Trenchard-Smith   *Ph* Russell Boyd   *Ed* Ron Williams   *Mus* Noel Quinlan   *Art Dir* David Copping, Chien Sun
● Jimmy Wang Yu, George Lazenby, Ros Spiers, Hugh Keays-Byrne, Roger Ward, Rebecca Gilling (Golden Harvest/Movie)

A Hong Kong policeman (Wang Yu) is sent to Australia to extradite a Chinese courier who works for an international drug syndicate. He gets involved with the syndicate, and, as per usual wipes it out in a final battle that ends with Wang escaping from a towering inferno.

Wang, though lacking the charisma of the late Bruce Lee, does have an aura of realism about him. George Lazenby does little for his image as an actor by appearing as a heavy Mr Big, although he does die well at Wilton.

The Hong Kong-Australian James Bond hybrid, the first coproduction of its kind, comes off well for a kung-fu pic. There are the usual chases around Sydney, with an unusual kite chase sequence. There is also some excellent aerial photography of both Hong Kong and Sydney.

....

MAN FROM LARAMIE, THE

1955, 102 MINS, US ◇ Ⓥ
Dir Anthony Mann   *Prod* William Goetz   *Scr* Philip Yordan, Frank Burt   *Ph* Charles Lang   *Ed* William Lyon   *Mus* George Duning   *Art Dir* Cary Odell
● James Stewart, Arthur Kennedy, Donald Crisp, Cathy O'Donnell, Alex Nichol, Aline MacMahon (Columbia)

Basically, the plot concerns the search by James Stewart, army captain on home from leave, for the man guilty of selling repeating rifles to an Apache tribe. The rifles had been used to wipe out a small cavalry patrol to which Stewart's younger brother had been attached so there is a motive of personal vengeance.

Violence gets into the act early and repeats with regularity as Stewart's trail crosses with a number of warped sadistic characters.

Stewart goes about his characterization with an easy assurance. Arthur Kennedy, Donald Crisp and Alex Nicol are firstrate in their delineations of the twisted people on the ranch. Distaff characters are done by Cathy O'Donnell, good as the girl who wants to escape the influence of the ranch, and Aline MacMahon, who gives a socko portrayal of a tough old rancher.

MAN FROM SNOWY RIVER, THE

1982, 102 MINS, AUSTRALIA ◇ Ⓥ ⊙
Dir George Miller   *Scr* John Dixon, Fred Cullen   *Ph* Keith Wagstaff   *Ed* Adrian Carr   *Mus* Bruce Rowland   *Art Dir* Leslie Binns
● Kirk Douglas, Jack Thompson, Tom Burlinson, Sigrid Thornton, Lorraine Bayly (Edgley/Cambridge)

Here is a rattling good adventure story, inspired by a legendary poem [by A.B. 'Banjo' Paterson] which nearly every Australian had drummed into him as a child, filmed in spectacularly rugged terrain in the Great Dividing Ranges in Victoria.

Kirk Douglas plays two brothers who have had a terrible falling-out for reasons explained late in the narrative. While one brother, the wealthy autocratic landowner Harrison fits him like a glove, the actor is less believable as Spur, a gruff, grizzled, out-of-luck prospector.

Apparently, Douglas wrote or rewrote some of the dialog; hopefully not some of Spur's groaners like 'It's a hard country, made for hard men'.

Tom Burlinson shines in his first feature film role as Jim, well matched by Sigrid Thornton as Harrison's high-spirited daughter. Jack Thompson shares top billing with Douglas as Clancy, the crack horseman who becomes Jim's mentor.

MAN FROM THE ALAMO, THE

1953, 79 MINS, US Ⓥ
Dir Budd Boetticher   *Prod* Aaron Rosenberg   *Scr* Steve Fisher, D.D. Beauchamp   *Ph* Russell Metty   *Ed* Virgil Vogel   *Mus* Frank Skinner   *Art Dir* Alexander Golitzen, Emrich Nicholson
● Glenn Ford, Julie Adams, Chill Wills, Hugh O'Brian, Victor Jory, Jeanne Cooper (Universal)

This basic outdoor feature has a rousing climax, good performances and beautifully photographed outdoor values. Glenn Ford and Victor Jory are particularly good in the rugged scenes and the former's performance helps to carry things during some midway story slowness.

Plot is hung on the supposed escape of one man (Ford) from the Alamo before its valiant defenders fell to Santa Ana's forces. He finds his own and the other families wiped out by renegades posing as Mexican soldiers, is branded a coward for deserting the fort, and spends the rest of the footage proving himself and getting revenge on Jory for his assault against the families of the Alamo heroes.

High spot of the footage is the climactic battle between good and evil, with Ford protecting a wagon train against Jory's gang of renegades. It's a sequence that Budd Boetticher's direction fills with violent, but believeable, action. Plotting in the script is generally good and was based on a story by Niven Busch and Oliver Crawford.

Julie Adams is gracious as a girl who helps Ford. Chill Wills is a one-armed pioneer editor stubborn about accepting the hero, as is Hugh O'Brian, army lieutenant.

MANHATTAN

1979, 96 MINS, US Ⓥ ⊙
Dir Woody Allen   *Prod* Charles H. Joffe   *Scr* Woody Allen, Marshall Brickman   *Ph* Gordon Willis   *Ed* Susan E. Morse   *Mus* Tom Pierson (arr.)   *Art Dir* Mel Bourne
● Woody Allen, Diane Keaton, Michael Murphy, Mariel Hemingway, Meryl Streep, Anne Byrne (United Artists)

Woody Allen uses New York City as a backdrop for the familiar story of the successful but neurotic urban over-achievers whose relationships always seem to end prematurely. The film is just as much about how wonderful a place the city is to live in as it is about the elusive search for love.

Allen has, in black and white, captured the inner beauty that lurks behind the outer layer of dirt and grime in Manhattan.

The core of the story revolves around Allen as Isaac Davis, an unfulfilled television writer and his best friends, Yale and Emily, an upper-middle class, educated Manhattan couple. Isaac has lately taken up with Tracy (Mariel Hemingway), a gorgeous 17-year-old, but the age difference is becoming too much of an obstacle for him.

That's especially the case when he meets Yale's girlfriend, Mary, a fast-talking, pseudo-intellectual, expertly played by Diane Keaton, to whom Isaac is instantly attracted.

□ 1979: Nominations: Best Supp. Actress (Mariel Hemingway), Original Screenplay

MANHATTAN MELODRAMA

1934, 93 MINS, US Ⓥ ⊙
Dir W. S. Van Dyke   *Prod* David O. Selznick   *Scr* Oliver H. P. Garrett, Joseph L. Mankiewicz   *Ph* James Wong Howe   *Ed* Ben Lewis
● Clark Gable, William Powell, Myrna Loy, Leo Carrillo, Nat Pendleton, Mickey Rooney (Cosmopolitan/M-G-M)

Apart from the Clark Gable-William Powell stellar duo and Myrna Loy, who does an excellent job as the principal femme, the Arthur Caesar story is replete with punchy popularly-appealing ingredients. The fast, crisp, intelligent dialog further enhances it.

True there is much to *Manhattan Melodrama* that's very ten-twent-thirt. There are a couple of spots where perhaps Gable as the too suave hoodlum is glorified a bit, but there are also many offsetting speeches by Powell as the DA as he charges the jury to remember that there's no longer public sympathy with bootleggers.

There are also a couple of somewhat banal spots such as Papa Rosen (George Sidney) adopting the two tough mick kids (Gable and Powell) because his own Morris was drowned in the Slocum disaster. Or, for example, where Papa Rosen is the first to deride the Russian red agitator (and gets trampled to death by the riot squad for his patriotism).

The captiousness embraces such incidents as the Governor's wife (Loy) visiting the prisoner (Gable) in the Tombs. Or the inevitable *Last Mile* business in the death house with the colored convict, the surcharged atmosphere of bravado, etc. But in toto *Manhattan Melodrama* will never bore, and please generally.

Mickey Rooney and Jimmy Butler in the juve portions are tiptop. Shirley Ross is the colored warbler who handles the lone

Rodgers-Hart song in the picture (which means little) in the Cotton Club setting.
□ 1934: Best Original Story

MANHATTAN PROJECT, THE

1986, 117 MINS, US ◇ Ⓥ ⊙
Dir Marshall Brickman   *Prod* Jennifer Ogden, Marshall Brickman   *Scr* Marshall Brickman, Thomas Baum   *Ph* Billy Williams   *Ed* Nina Feinborg   *Mus* Philippe Sarde   *Art Dir* Philip Rosenberg
● John Lithgow, Christopher Collet, Cynthia Nixon, Jill Eikenberry, John Mahoney, Sully Boyar (Gladden)

Marshall Brickman's *The Manhattan Project* is a warm, comedy-laced doomsday story.

Premise has 16-year-old student Paul Stevens (Christopher Collet) tumbling to the fact that the new scientist in town, Dr Mathewson (John Lithgow), is working with plutonium in what fronts as a pharmaceutical research installation. While Mathewson is romancing Stevens' mom (Jilly Eikenberry), the genius kid is plotting with his helpful girl-friend Jenny (Cynthia Nixon) to steal a canister of plutonium and build an atomic bomb. Their goal: to expose the danger of the secret nuclear plant placed in their community.

Using clever one-liners and many humorous situations, Brickman manages successfully to sugarcoat the story's serious message.

MAN HUNT

1941, 100 MINS, US
Dir Fritz Lang   *Prod* Kenneth Macgowan (assoc.)   *Scr* Dudley Nichols   *Ph* Arthur Miller   *Ed* Allen McNeil   *Mus* Alfred Newman   *Art Dir* Richard Day, Wiard B. Ihnen
● Walter Pidgeon, Joan Bennett, George Sanders, John Carradine, Roddy McDowall, Ludwig Stossel (20th Century-Fox)

Extended operations of the Gestapo are displayed in this film version of Geoffrey Household's novel, *Rogue Male*.

Household's tale of an English big game hunter and adventurer who invades the closely guarded precincts of Berchtesgaden to draw a bead on Hitler with an unloaded rifle, his capture and torture by the Gestapo; escape and return to England and further hounding by German agents; and final dropping back into Germany with a rifle for a future crack at Hitler, fails to sustain adventurous excitement on screen.

Walter Pidgeon is the Englishman hounded by the Gestapo. He does a good job of the assignment throughout. Joan Bennett is the Limey girl who befriends him, but her attempts at affected cockney accents are always synthetic. George Sanders is generally menacing as the Gestapo chief.

Fritz Lang's direction maintains excellent suspense in the first half, but yarn hits the skids for the second section to wind up with a series of overdrawn and inconclusive sequences.

MANHUNTER

1986, 119 MINS, US ◇ Ⓥ ⊙
Dir Michael Mann   *Prod* Richard Roth   *Scr* Michael Mann   *Ph* Dante Spinotti   *Ed* Dov Hoenig   *Mus* The Reds, Michel Rubini   *Art Dir* Mel Bourne
● William L. Petersen, Kim Greist, Joan Allen, Brian Cox, Dennis Farina, Tom Noonan (De Laurentiis)

Manhunter is an unpleasantly gripping thriller that rubs one's nose in a sick criminal mentality for two hours.

Pic is based upon Thomas Harris' well-received novel *Red Dragon* and deals with a southern former FBI agent (William L. Petersen) who is summoned from retirement to work on a particularly perplexing case, that of a mass murderer who appears to stalk and select his victims with particular care.

Petersen's excellent deductive talents are due, in large measure, to his tendency to deeply enter the minds of killers, to begin thinking like them.

This trick takes the film into interesting Hitchcockian guilt transference territory and Mann's grip on his material is tight and sure. Director is at all times preoccupied by visual chic.

Tom Noonan cuts a massive swath as the killer, who late in the game is surprisingly humanized by a blind girl, played in enormously touching fashion by Joan Allen.

■ **MAN IN A COCKED HAT**
See: Carlton-Browne of the F.O.

■ **MAN IN THE GRAY FLANNEL SUIT, THE**

1956, 152 MINS, US ◇ ⓥ
Dir Nunnally Johnson   Prod Darryl F. Zanuck
Scr Nunnally Johnson   Ph Charles G. Clarke
Ed Dorothy Spencer   Mus Bernard Hermann
● Gregory Peck, Jennifer Jones, Fredric March, Marisa Pavan, Lee J. Cobb, Ann Harding (20th Century-Fox)

This is the story of a young American suburbanite who gets a chance to become a big shot and turns it down because he realizes that he's a nine-to-five man to whom family means more than success.

It's also the story of a man with a conscience, who had a love affair in Rome which resulted in a child. When he tells his wife about it, their marriage almost breaks up.

As the 'Man in the Gray Flannel Suit', Gregory Peck is handsome and appealing, if not always convincing. It is only really in the romantic sequences with Marisa Pavan, who plays his Italian love, that he takes on warmth and becomes believable. Pavan is human and delightful.

Playing opposite Peck as his wife is Jennifer Jones, and her concept of the role is faulty to a serious degree. Jones allows almost no feeling of any real relationship between her and Peck. They never come alive as people.

As the broadcasting tycoon, Fredric March is excellent, and the scenes between him and Peck lift the picture high above the ordinary.

■ **MAN IN THE IRON MASK, THE**

1939, 110 MINS, US
Dir James Whale   Prod Edward Small   Scr George Bruce   Ph Robert Planck   Ed Grant Whytock
Mus Lucien Moraweck   Art Dir John DuCasse Schulze
● Louis Hayward, Joan Bennett, Joseph Schildkraut, Alan Hale, Warren William (United Artists/Small)

Alexander Dumas' classic, presented for the first time in film form, is a highly entertaining adventure melodrama. Story has a verve in its tale of dual heirship to the throne of France, used by Dumas as basis of his novel. D'Artagnan and the Three Musketeers reappear as stalwart supporters of Philippe, twin brother of Louis XIV, who is tossed into the Bastille with a fiendishly designed locked iron mask.

Louis Hayward, carrying the dual role of the arrogant Louis XIV and the vigorously self-assured Philippe, gives one of the finest dual characterizations of the screen. He vividly contrasts the king's personality, with its slight swish, with the manly and romantic attitude of twin brother Philippe.

Joan Bennett, is capably romantic. Warren William is carefree and colorful.

☐ 1939: Nomination: Best Original Score

■ **MAN IN THE MOON, THE**

1991, 99 MINS, US ◇ ⓥ
Dir Robert Mulligan   Prod Mark Rydell   Scr Jenny Wingfield   Ph Freddie Francis   Ed Trudy Ship

Mus James Newton Howard   Art Dir Gene Callahan
● Sam Waterston, Tess Harper, Gail Strickland, Reese Witherspoon, Jason London, Emily Warfield (M-G-M)

A bucolic coming-of-age story set in 1957 Louisiana, The Man in the Moon follows Reese Witherspoon, the 14-year-old daughter of Sam Waterston and Tess Harper. She's envious of her college-bound sister (Emily Warfield) and moons over pictures of Elvis Presley. All that changes with the arrival of Jason London, 17-year-old son of a family that moves in next door.

London, the man of the house since his father's death, becomes friendly with Witherspoon against his better judgment. Inevitable conflict arises when London meets the older sister, and he quickly relegates Witherspoon to the status of kid sister.

Unfortunately, vet director Robert Mulligan and tyro screenwriter Jenny Wingfield could not come up with a dramatic resolution to this triangle, and resort to a melodramatic device that at once brings the conflict between the two sisters to a head while removing the source of it.

The performances are all on the money, but two are outstanding. Newcomer Witherspoon manages to strike exactly the right note as the tomboy on the verge of womanhood while Waterston works on several levels at once.

Shot on location in Natchitoches, La, film is aided by cinematography of Freddie Francis, who catches the summer light and warmth important to the story.

■ **MAN IN THE WHITE SUIT, THE**

1951, 97 MINS, UK ⓥ ⊙
Dir Alexander Mackendrick   Prod Michael Balcon, Sidney Cole   Scr Roger MacDougall, John Dighton, Alexander Mackendrick   Ph Douglas Slocombe   Ed Bernard Gribble   Mus Benjamin Frankel   Art Dir Jim Morahan
● Alec Guinness, Joan Greenwood, Cecil Parker, Michael Gough, Ernest Thesiger, Vida Hope (Ealing)

The plot is a variation of an old theme, but it comes out with a nice fresh coat of paint. A young research scientist invents a cloth that is everlasting and dirt resisting. The textile industry sees the danger signal and tries to buy him out, but he outwits them.

Particular tribute must be paid to the sound effects department. The bubbly sound of liquids passing through specially prepared contraptions in the lab is one of the most effective running gags seen in a British film.

Alec Guinness, as usual, turns in a polished performance. His interpretation of the little research worker is warm, understanding and always sympathetic. Joan Greenwood is nicely provocative as the mill-owner's daughter who encourages him with his work, while Cecil Parker contributes another effective character study as her father. Michael Gough and Ernest Thesiger represent the textile bosses who see disaster. Vida Hope makes a fine showing as one of the strike leaders who fears unemployment returning to the mills.

☐ 1952: Nomination: Best Screenplay

■ **MANITOU, THE**

1978, 104 MINS, US ◇ ⓥ ⊙
Dir William Girdler   Prod William Girdler   Scr William Girdler, Jon Cedar, Tom Pope   Ph Michel Hugo
Ed Bub Asman   Mus Lalo Schifrin   Art Dir Walter Scott Herndon
● Tony Curtis, Michael Ansara, Susan Strasberg, Stella Stevens, Jon Cedar, Burgess Meredith (Avco Embassy/Weist-Simon)

This bout between good and Satan includes some scares, camp and better than average credits.

This time the demon is a 400-year-old American Indian medicine man. He's a little devil in the literal sense, thanks to over-ex-

posure to x-rays which has shriveled him into a three-foot tall redskin monster. Until he makes a rather dramatic entrance onto the floor of a hospital bedroom, he can be found growing as a fetus on Susan Strasberg's upper back.

Michael Ansara, a modern-day medicine man, is imported from South Dakota to deliver the evil spirit and return him to the place where 400-year-old medicine men hibernate.

Tony Curtis plays a charlatan of the supernatural, reading tarot cards for rich old ladies. He's romantically involved with Strasberg and does most of the coordinating for the exorcism booking the medicine man, arranging for cooperation from the hospital, etc.

His character is a nice twist bogus genie in a situation where the unseen powers really are controlling things. But in general Curtis is too serious about it all. Only Burgess Meredith as a befuddled professor of anthropology has any fun with his part.

■ **MAN MADE MONSTER**
(UK: The Electric Man)

1941, 89 MINS, US
Dir George Waggner   Prod Jack Bernhard   Scr Joseph West   Ph Elwood Brendell   Mus Charles Previn
● Lionel Atwill, Lon Chaney Jr, Anne Nagel, Frank Albertson, Samuel S. Hinds, Ben Taggart (Universal)

Man Made Monster is a shocker that's in the groove for the horror fans. It makes no pretense of being anything but a freakish chiller, going directly to the point and proving mighty successful.

Weird events resulting from a mad scientist's lab experiments in transforming a normal human being into a monster controlled by electrical impulses could have been made mawkish. Sincere portrayals plus alert direction and deft photography span several implausible pitfalls. Near-climax when the electric man survives an electrocution for murder and goes on a rampage is a bit incredible for average consumption.

Lon Chaney Jr's excellent work as 'Dynamo' Dan McCormick, carnival electrical wizard, who's turned into a monster, is backed up by Lionel Atwill in one of his better characterizations as the crazed Dr Rigas, who believes electricity can control anything.

■ **MANNEQUIN**

1938, 92 MINS, US ⓥ
Dir Frank Borzage   Prod Joseph L. Mankiewicz
Scr Lawrence Hazard   Ph George Folsey   Ed Frederick Y. Smith   Mus Edward Ward
● Joan Crawford, Spencer Tracy, Alan Curtis, Ralph Morgan, Mary Phillips, Oscar O'Shea (M-G-M)

Mannequin is a down-to-earth story, interestingly related, excellently directed by Frank Borzage, and splendidly acted by Joan Crawford, Spencer Tracy, and a hand-picked cast. Alan Curtis, heretofore a small bit actor, has his big chance and makes the most of it.

There is nothing wrong and everything right about Mannequin. It is based on a sound story by Katherine Brush. The story is the old standby plot of the girl of the tenements who forces herself from her environment and climbs in the world.

Curtis is the ne'er-do-well and gives a properly villainous performance, best feature of which is a gradual insight of the despicable side of his nature. Tracy, as a self-made tugboat capitalist, has his serious moments. But the film is primarily director Frank Borzage's. Without the atmosphere he creates and the movement of his characters through believable situations, Mannequin would be routine entertainment.

☐ 1938: Nomination: Best Song ('Always and Always')

MANNEQUIN

1987, 89 MINS, US ◇ ⓥ ⊙
Dir Michael Gottlieb *Prod* Art Levinson *Scr* Michael
Gottlieb, Edward Rugoff *Ph* Timothy Suhrstedt
Ed Richard Halsey *Mus* Sylvester Levay *Art Dir* Josan
Russo
● Andrew McCarthy, Kim Cattrall, Estelle Getty, G.W.
Bailey, James Spader, Meshach Taylor (Gladden)

Mannequin is as stiff and spiritless as its title
suggests.

A mannequin (Kim Cattrall) is the latest
reincarnation of an Egyptian princess who has
known Christopher Colombus and
Michelangelo in her journey through time.
He's an aspiring artist working as a model
maker (Andrew McCarthy) and creator of a
mannequin which has the likeness of a woman
he could easily love if only she were real.

Night work makes strange bedfellows of
McCarthy and Hollywood (Meshach Taylor),
the flamboyant near-transvestite who dresses
the store windows, and of McCarthy and
Emmy (Cattrall), his mannequin. She comes
alive when they're alone together, but reverts
back to her cold self if anyone else appears.

McCarthy and Cattrall certainly are an attractive couple when she's alive but they
don't get to do much more than kiss and
dance around the store after hours. Comic
development is given over to the secondary
characters (Taylor, James Spader and the
night watchman, G.W. Bailey).

□ 1987: Nomination: Best Song ('Nothing's
Gonna Stop Us Now')

MANNEQUIN ON THE MOVE

1991, 95 MINS, US ◇ ⓥ ⊙
Dir Stewart Raffill *Prod* Edward Rugoff *Scr* Edward
Rugoff, David Isaacs, Ken Levine, Betsy Israel *Ph* Larry
Pizer *Ed* John Rosenberg, Joan Chapman *Mus* David
McHugh *Art Dir* William J. Creber
● Meshach Taylor, William Ragsdale, Kristy Swanson,
Terry Kiser, Stuart Pankin, Cynthia Harris (Gladden)

It took four writers to struggle with another
idea of why a mannequin would come to life
in a department store and what would happen if she did. Their solution: the dummy
(Kristy Swanson) is actually a Bavarian peasant girl hexed 1,000 years ago to prevent her
marriage to the prince.

As part of a promotion, the legendary
statue is displayed at a Philadelphia store under the care of William Ragsdale, who's the
spitting image of the prince, and jealous eye
of count Terry Kiser, a spit-on descendant of
the sorcerer who bewitched her. The hex is in
the necklace and when Ragsdale accidentally
removes it, he suddenly has a date for the
night with a wide-eyed blonde in a micro-
miniskirt who still loves him after all this
time. Since this is her first date in a thousand
years, Ragsdale doesn't rush things.

The only real movement is offered by
Meshach Taylor, a prancing decorator who
returns from the original *Mannequin* for more
stereotyped fun.

MAN OF AFRICA

1954, 73 MINS, UK ◇
Dir Cyril Frankel *Prod* John Grierson *Scr* Montagu
Slater *Ph* Denny Densham *Ed* Alvin Bailey
Mus Malcolm Arnold
● Violet Mukabureza, Frederick Bijurenda, Mattayo
Bukwirwa, Butensa, Seperiera Mpambara, Blaseo
Mbalinda (Group Three)

Struggle for existence insofar as a native
tribe is concerned is leisurely told in *Man of
Africa*, a semi-documentary filmed in the
more remote parts of Uganda. To the picture's credit it eschews the hoky aspects
found in most films lensed in 'darkest Africa',
but this British import is often languorous to
the point of becoming dull.

Producer of the Group Three picture was
noted documentarian John Grierson. It's an
interesting phase of African life that he chose
to focus upon. But one suspects that a sketchy
story contributed by director Cyril Frankel
detracts more than adds to the realism.

For, in depicting the migration of a tribe to
virgin country after the fertility of their
homeland has been exhausted, Grierson has
seen fit to include a romance between a clerk-
turned-farmer and a native belle.

On the brighter side of the ledger are
scenes which show the basic kindness of pygmies who are native to the Kigezi territory.
They aid an injured settler and later save his
child when malaria strikes the pioneers. If
anything this unassuming import shows that
even among African natives prejudice thrives
upon misunderstanding.

Dialog of the players is in English. Cast is
headed by Violet Mukabureza and Frederick
Bijurenda who do as best they can in portraying the romantic couple.

MAN OF ARAN

1934, 75 MINS, UK ⓥ
Dir Robert J. Flaherty *Prod* Michael Balcon *Scr* Robert
J. Flaherty, Frances Flaherty, John Goldman *Ph* Robert
J. Flaherty *Ed* John Goldman *Mus* John Greenwood
● Colman 'Tiger' King, Maggie Dirrane, Michael
Dillane, Pat Mullen (Gainsborough/Gaumont-British)

Colman King, Maggie Dirrane, and Michael
Dillane are the central characters. They are
not actors, but natives of the barren, sea-
beaten islands off the western coast of
Ireland, where this picture takes place. They
play themselves. The sea is the villain and the
quest for food the plot of this peasants-
among-peasants picture, which rates high artistically.

Naturally the big item in such a picture is
the camerawork. This is splendid. With only
drab grays and speckled whites to deal with,
the lens has done right by the cause of sheer
beauty and rugged grandeur. The Aran natives are pictured as brave and indomitable,
unembittered by the rigors of their lot.

Said to have been two years in the making,
the film bespeaks a canny technique and an
inspirational sympathy on the part of
Flaherty and his co-workers. There is practically no dialog except short sentences of
warning, advice, comment on the hazards of
shark-hunting.

MAN OF A THOUSAND FACES

1957, 122 MINS, US
Dir Joseph Pevney *Prod* Robert Arthur *Scr* R.Wright
Campbell, Ivan Goff, Ben Roberts *Ph* Russell Metty
Ed Ted J. Kent *Mus* Frank Skinner *Art Dir* Alexander
Golitzen, Eric Orbom
● James Cagney, Dorothy Malone, Jane Greer, Jim
Backus, Robert J. Evans, Marjorie Rambeau (Universal)

The title stems from the billing given the late
Universal, later Metro, star, Lon Chaney by
an alert publicity man. The screenplay, based
on a story by Ralph Wheelwright, is mainly
concerned with Chaney's complicated domestic problems. His achievements as a consummate artist, while woven into the story, are
secondary to his mixed-up private life.

The story, in swift sequences, takes Chaney
from his early boyhood to his death of throat
cancer. Born of deaf and dumb parents, this
is an important emotional factor in Chaney's
motivations. Screenplay ranges song-and-
dance vaudeville days, two marriages, the
birth of his son, early struggles as a Hollywood extra, eventual rise to stardom, and
tragic death.

As Chaney, James Cagney has immersed
himself so completely in the role that it is difficult to spot any Cagney mannerisms. Jane

Greer, as his second wife, is particularly appealing in her devotion to her 'difficult'
spouse. Dorothy Malone is fine as the wife
who deems her career as a singer more important than raising children. A real heart-
tug is provided by Celia Lovsky as Chaney's
deaf and dumb mother. Bud Westmore deserves special mention for the excellent
make-up jobs on the various characters portrayed by Chaney.

□ 1957: Nomination: Best Original Story &
Screenplay

MAN OF BRONZE
See: *Jim Thorpe – All-American*

MAN OF EVIL
See: *Fanny by Gaslight*

MAN OF FLOWERS

1983, 93 MINS, AUSTRALIA ◇ ⓥ ⊙
Dir Paul Cox *Prod* Jane Ballantyne, Paul Cox *Scr* Paul
Cox, Bob Ellis *Ph* Yuri Sokol *Ed* Tim Lewis
Art Dir Asher Bilu
● Norman Kaye, Alyson Best, Chris Haywood, Sarah
Walker, Julia Blake, Bob Ellis (Flowers)

Paul Cox's film, flickering between realism
and fantasy, follows the progress of Bremer, a
rich naive eccentric (Norman Kaye), whose
inherited wealth both protects him from the
coldness of the outside world and isolates him
from its warmth. He is cocooned in a childlike
innocence, dwelling on the sexual exploration
of his boyhood.

Man of Flowers opens with an astonishingly
erotic strip by Lisa, the model. She strips,
nothing more, nothing less. Is her stated affection for him genuine, or is she attracted by
his money? Cox keeps the bond teasingly ambiguous.

At times *Man of Flowers* creates Hitchcock-
like tension, but when the suspense becomes
uncomfortable Cox lets his audience off the
hook with a little wry humor. The expected
black climax is never quite allowed to occur.

Kaye delivers a wonderful, understated performance as Bremer and Alyson Best is a delightfully enigmatic Lisa.

MAN OF LA MANCHA

1972, 130 MINS, US ◇ ⓥ ⊙
Dir Arthur Hiller *Prod* Arthur Hiller *Scr* Dale
Wasserman *Ph* Giuseppe Rotunno *Ed* Robert C. Jones
Mus Laurence Rosenthal (adapt.) *Art Dir* Luciano
Damiani
● Peter O'Toole, Sophia Loren, James Coco, Harry
Andrews, John Castle, Brian Blessed (United Artists/PEA)

Man of La Mancha, produced in the style of the
[1965 Mitch Leigh-Joe Darion] musical play
from which it was adapted, is the fanciful tale
of Don Quixote, that fictional Middle Ages lunatic living in a personal world of chivalry
long-since past. The Arthur Hiller production
of Dale Wasserman's book is more a vehicle
for music than the narrative.

Peter O'Toole enacts the dual role of
Miguel de Cervantes and his classic character, a difficult assignment which the actor undertakes with heroic overtones. Sophia Loren
appears in the dual Dulcinea-Aldonza role,
and James Coco is Sancho Panza, the ever-
faithful squire.

O'Toole persuasively brings to life the demented would-be knight. Loren, no songbird
she, does her own warbling, as does Coco, but
O'Toole's numbers actually are sung by
Simon Gilbert, a London actor-singer of fine
voice.

□ 1972: Nomination: Best Adapted Score

M

MAN OF THE WEST

1958, 100 MINS, US ◇ ⊛
Dir Anthony Mann *Prod* Walter M. Mirisch
Scr Reginald Rose *Ph* Ernest Haller *Ed* Richard
Heermance *Mus* Leigh Harline *Art Dir* Hilyard Brown
● Gary Cooper, Julie London, Lee J. Cobb, Arthur
O'Connell, Jack Lord, Royal Dano (United Artists/Mirisch)

The screenplay, from a novel by Will C.
Brown, has Gary Cooper as a reformed gunman, now a respected citizen entrusted with
the savings of his community. He is on a mission to get the town a schoolteacher when he
is robbed of the money by members of his old
gang. It is also somewhat by accident that he,
and two other victims (Julie London and
Arthur O'Connell), wind up taking refuge in
the bandits' hideout, which had once been
Cooper's, too.

Superficially, the story is simply the account
of Cooper's efforts to free himself, London
and O'Connell of the outlaws. It is given dimension by the fact that to do this he must
revert to the savagery he has foresworn.

Cooper gives a characteristically virile performance, his dominance of the outlaws quietly believable, while London achieves some
touching and convincing moments in a difficult role. Lee J. Cobb, a frontier Fagan of demoniac violence and destruction, and Arthur
O'Connell, with whimsical grace and gaiety,
add considerably to the picture's interest.

MAN ON A TIGHTROPE

1953, 105 MINS, US
Dir Elia Kazan *Prod* Robert L. Jacks *Scr* Robert E.
Sherwood *Ph* Georg Krause *Ed* Dorothy Spencer
Mus Franz Waxman *Art Dir* Hans H. Kuhnert, Theo
Zwirsky
● Fredric March, Terry Moore, Gloria Grahame,
Cameron Mitchell, Adolphe Menjou, Richard Boone (20th
Century-Fox)

Man on a Tightrope is a taut 'chase' [based on a
story, *International Incident* by Neil Paterson].
The chase, in this instance, is an entire circus, a shabby enough troupe but, nonetheless,
a burdensome commodity to sneak across any
Iron Curtain frontier. But Fredric March
does achieve this as he maneuvers his one-
ring circus from Czechslovakia into freedom.

Director Elia Kazan limns his characters
with proper mood and shade, as the red-tape
of the Reds becomes mountingly obstructive.
He projects beaucoup romance against the
general background, including a willful
daughter (Terry Moore) and a flirtatious second wife (Gloria Grahame).

Moore is equally volatile in her affections
for Cameron Mitchell, an itinerant deckhand
whom March suspects as the spy for the
Czech secret police. There is effective suspense in Adolphe Menjou's interrogation, as
an officious propaganda ministry attache.
Robert Beatty is a rival circus owner.

The bold manner in which the circus, in full
calliope style, parades right by the auxiliary
frontier guards and plans its diversion tactics
for escape into the American zone is plausibly
staged by Kazan. Much of this footage was
shot in Austria and Germany.

MANPOWER

1941, 100 MINS, US
Dir Raoul Walsh *Prod* Mark Hellinger *Scr* Richard
Macauley, Jerry Wald *Ph* Ernest Haller *Ed* Ralph
Dawson *Mus* Adolph Deutsch
● Edward G. Robinson, Marlene Dietrich, George Raft,
Alan Hale, Frank McHugh, Eve Arden (Warner)

There's plenty of rough and rowdy action and
dialog in this melodrama, premised on the
triangle formula.

Zestful direction of Raoul Walsh cannot be
discounted here. He keeps things moving at a
fast clip and displays the individual talents of
Edward G. Robinson, Marlene Dietrich and
George Raft to utmost advantage.

Story tells of the adventures of a construction and maintenance crew for power lines.
Raft and Robinson are buddies in the outfit,
and when Robinson is burned by a high tension wire he's made foreman of the gang.
Dietrich is the daughter of crew-member
Egon Brecher, getting parole from a year's
stretch in prison. She works in a clip joint,
and enacts the role to perfection. Raft tabs
her immediately, but Robinson falls in love
with her for quick marriage.

First third of the picture displays racy action and spicy dialog for maximum attention,
and then drifts into formula triangle dramatics. Robinson delivers a vivid portrayal as the
foreman-lineman who manhandles the gals
too fast until he meets Dietrich. Latter provides a stereotyped performance as the clip-
joint inmate, and sings one song chorus
throatily.

MAN'S CASTLE

1933, 75 MINS, US
Dir Frank Borzage *Prod* [uncredited] *Scr* Jo Swerling
Ph Joseph August *Ed* Viola Lawrence *Mus* Frank
Harling *Art Dir* [uncredited]
● Spencer Tracy, Loretta Young, Marjorie Rambeau,
Glenda Farrell, Walter Connolly, Arthur Hohl (Columbia)

Spencer Tracy is cast in his most distasteful
role. It's a story [from the play by Lawrence
Hazard] of a worthless mug who rudely picks
up a homeless girl and transports her to a
shanty town, where he and other no-goods reside in one fashion or another. The story attempts to justify it all by reformation of the
calloused, smart-cracking hero via marriage
to the girl when she is about to become a
mother.

Some of the wisecracks Tracy is called upon
to read are of the roughest, most inconsider-
ate kind. Such things as 'Shut up or I'll pour
that stew down your back' could hardly be accepted as ever leading to true affection.

It's that way for Tracy throughout. Loretta
Young does a noble job as the little girl who
stands nearly everything.

Locale is almost entirely in a shanty village,
where little more than sheets of tin and some
garbage was necessary. The few miniatures
employed look phoney.

MAN'S FAVORITE SPORT?

1964, 120 MINS, US ◇ ⊛
Dir Howard Hawks *Prod* Howard Hawks *Scr* John
Fenton Murray, Steve McNeil *Ph* Russell Harlan
Ed Stuart Gilmore *Mus* Henry Mancini
Art Dir Alexander Golitzen, Tambi Larsen
● Rock Hudson, Paula Prentiss, Maria Perschy, John
McGiver, Charlene Holt, Roscoe Karns (Universal)

The comically ripe premise from the story
The Girl Who Almost Got Away by Pat Frank, is
what happens when a celebrated but fraudulent piscatorial authority and fishing equipment salesman for Abercrombie & Fitch who
doesn't know how to fish is suddenly ordered
by his unaware boss to compete in a fishing
tournament.

For a while, the adventures of this angler
(Rock Hudson) romp along with a kind of
breezy *Field & Stream* charm, bolstered by
some inventive slapstick ideas, cleverly devised characters and occasionally sharp dialog. But then, poof, the fish story begins to
sag under the weight of its bulky romantic
midsection and lumbers along tediously and
repetitiously to a long overdue conclusion.

Matters are helped along somewhat by an
attractive and spirited cast, but not enough to
keep the film consistently amusing.

Hawks purportedly utilized unorthodox directorial techniques, such as filming in sequence a day at a time in order to capture an
air of comic spontaneity. Since some of the
sight gag passages are uproarious, there is a
lot to be said for this technique. But it appears that the main trouble with Hawks' day-
at-a-time approach to comedy is that there
were too many days or not enough comedy or
a combination of both.

MANSLAUGHTER

1930, 82 MINS, US
Dir George Abbott *Scr* George Abbott *Ph* Archie J.
Stout *Art Dir* Otto Lovering
● Claudette Colbert, Fredric March, Emma Dunn,
Natalie Moorhead, Richard Tucker (Paramount Publix)

This is a remake of a 1922 silent with Thomas
Meighan doing the d.a. role which Fredric
March now has. Leatrice Joy in the silent version of the Alice Duer Miller *SatEvePost* story
gives way to Claudette Colbert.

George Abbott, in adapting and directing,
has endeavored to overcome some of the banalities which, in 1922, were standard. Instead
of following the original hoke situation of the
candidate-for-governor-hero previously re-en-
countering, on a breadline, the girl he sent to
prison, March is shown doing a mild stooge
bum, but coming back into private law practice without the old hokum bucket trimmings.

The aftermath of maid and mistress meeting on equal terms in jail is retained and
rather convincingly carried through, but in
between there's much that's boloney.'

Colbert follows through the original idea of
a snobbish characterization, remade by her
prison experience, although it's still a grand
excuse for a fashion-parade.

MAN TROUBLE

1992, 100 MINS, US/ITALY ◇ ⊛ ⊙
Dir Bob Rafelson *Prod* Bruce Gilbert, Carole Eastman
Scr Carole Eastman *Ph* Stephen H. Burum *Ed* William
Steinkamp *Mus* Georges Delerue *Art Dir* Mel Bourne
● Jack Nicholson, Ellen Barkin, Harry Dean Stanton,
Beverly D'Angelo, Michael McKean, Saul Rubinek
(Penta/American Filmworks/Budding Grove)

Jack Nicholson fans should feel cheated by
Man Trouble, an insultingly trivial star vehicle.

Nicholson portrays a dog trainer who meets
opera singer Ellen Barkin when she needs a
guard dog after a break-in and other harassment. In a screenplay resembling stage farce
rather than a movie, scripter Carole Eastman
drags in several pointless subplots. Main one
concerns Beverly D'Angelo, who's penned a
tell-all book about her relationship with
reclusive billionaire Harry Dean Stanton.
Barkin is getting divorced from her conduc-
tor/husband David Clennon and has been
threatened by some homicidal thug who may
be the notorious local slasher.

None of this adds up to entertainment or
even momentarily involving escapism, as the
romantic comedy/thriller genre, typified by
Charade or *Foul Play*, seems beyond the filmmakers' combined grasp. Instead there's
strenuously overacted comic set-pieces, most
of which fail.

Barkin is saddled with completely unnatural dialogue as well as some overdone physical shtick that seems left over from her last
comedy, *Switch*. D'Angelo steals a couple of
scenes as Barkin's sister.

MAN WHO CAME BACK, THE

See: Swamp Water

MAN WHO FELL TO EARTH, THE

1976, 140 MINS, UK ◇ ⊛ ⊙
Dir Nicolas Roeg *Prod* Michael Deeley, Barry Spikings
Scr Paul Mayersberg *Ph* Anthony Richmond

Ed Graeme Clifford   *Mus* John Phillips (dir.)
Art Dir Brian Eatwell
● David Bowie, Candy Clark, Rip Torn, Buck Henry, Bernie Casey, Jackson D. Kane (British Lion)

Basic plot has David Bowie descend to Earth from another planet to secure water supply for the folks at home. To help achieve this end, he soon uses his superior intelligence to accumulate vast earthbound wealth and power.

It's a story that must be seen and not told, so rich is it in subplots mirroring the 'pure' spaceman's reaction to a corrupt environment. In fact, pic is perhaps too rich a morsel, too cluttered with themes.

Visually and aurally, it's stunning stuff throughout, and Bowie's choice as the ethereal visitor is inspired.

Candy Clark, as his naive but loving mate, performs well in intimate scenes with Bowie, especially the introductory ones, which are among pic's highlights.

....

■ **MAN WHO HAUNTED HIMSELF, THE**

1970, 94 MINS, UK ◇ ⓥ
Dir Basil Dearden   *Prod* Michael Relph   *Scr* Basil Dearden, Michael Relph   *Ph* Tony Spratling   *Ed* Teddy Darvas   *Mus* Michael J. Lewis   *Art Dir* Albert Witherick
● Roger Moore, Hildegard Neil, Alastair Mackenzie, Hugh Mackenzie, Kevork Malikyan, Thorley Walters (Associated British)

Roger Moore plays a conservative, ambitious City business man who is involved in a car smash in which he was guilty of reckless, out-of-character driving. From the moment of his recovery strange things begin to happen. He is apparently in two places at once. He apparently indulges in sharp business practice. He is apparently having an affair with a girl who he has only once met, and casually.

The uncanny situation begins to prey on Moore's mind. Has he an unscrupulous double? Or is it all a figment of his imagination? These are the headaches that prey on Moore and add up to a tense riddle.

Hildegard Neil as Moore's wife has only a cardboard role, but handles the disintegration of her marriage competently.

....

■ **MAN WHO KNEW TOO MUCH, THE**

1935, 74 MINS, UK ⓥ ⊙
Dir Alfred Hitchcock   *Prod* Michael Balcon   *Scr* A.R. Rawlinson, Edwin Greenwood, Charles Bennett, D.B. Wyndham-Lewis, Emlyn Williams   *Ph* Curt Courant   *Ed* H. St. C. Stewart   *Mus* Arthur Benjamin   *Art Dir* Alfred Junge, Peter Proud
● Leslie Banks, Edna Best, Peter Lorre, Frank Vosper, Hugh Wakefield, Nova Pilbeam (Gaumont-British)

An unusually fine dramatic story handled excellently from a production standpoint. Built along gangster lines, but from an international crook standpoint, with a lot of melodramatic suspense added.

Starts at a party in St Moritz. A man is shot during a dance. He whispers to a friend that there's a message in a brush in his bathroom. Friend realizes the dying man was in the secret service and gets the message. Before he can communicate with the police he is handed a note saying his daughter has been kidnapped and will be killed if he talks.

Back to London and the cops can't make the man or his wife say anything. Finally the man locates the gang's meeting place. He discovers that an attempt will be made to kill a famous international statesman at the Albert Hall that night and manages to communicate that news to his wife, although he is held prisoner.

Scene at Albert Hall is highly exciting and beautifully handled. Acting is splendid most all of the way. Leslie Banks is a fine actor, although the assignment is a bit heavy for him. Edna Best looks well but is not convincing in

some of the toughest passages. Peter Lorre's work stands out again. He's the gang chief.

....

■ **MAN WHO KNEW TOO MUCH, THE**

1956, 119 MINS, US ◇ ⓥ ⊙
Dir Alfred Hitchcock   *Prod* Alfred Hitchcock   *Scr* John Michael Hayes   *Ph* Robert Burks   *Ed* George Tomasini   *Mus* Bernard Herrmann   *Art Dir* Hal Pereira, Henry Bumstead
● James Stewart, Doris Day, Brenda de Banzie, Bernard Miles, Daniel Gelin, Ralph Truman (Paramount)

With Alfred Hitchcock pulling the suspense strings, *The Man Who Knew Too Much* is a good thriller. Hitchcock backstops his mystery in the colorful locales of Marrakesh in French Morocco and in London. While drawing the footage out a bit long, he still keeps suspense working at all times and gets strong performances from the two stars and other cast members. Hitchcock did the same pic under the same title for Gaumont-British back in 1935.

James Stewart ably carries out his title duties he is a doctor vacationing in Marrakesh with his wife and young son. When he witnesses a murder and learns of an assassination scheduled to take place in London, the boy is kidnapped by the plotters to keep the medico's mouth shut.

Stewart's characterization is matched by the dramatic work contributed by Doris Day as his wife. Both draw vivid portraits of tortured parents when their son is kidnapped. Additionally, Day has two Jay Livingston-Ray Evans tunes to sing: 'Whatever Will Be' and 'We'll Love Again', which are used storywise and not just dropped into the plot.

Young Christopher Olsen plays the son naturally and appealingly.
□ 1956: Best Song ('Whatever Will Be, Will Be')

....

■ **MAN WHO LOVED CAT DANCING, THE**

1973, 114 MINS, US ◇ ⓥ
Dir Richard C. Sarafian   *Prod* Martin Poll, Eleanor Perry   *Scr* Eleanor Perry   *Ph* Harry Stradling Jr   *Ed* Tom Rolf   *Mus* John Williams   *Art Dir* Edward C. Carfagno
● Burt Reynolds, Sarah Miles, Lee J. Cobb, Jack Warden, George Hamilton, Bo Hopkins (M-G-M)

The Man Who Loved Cat Dancing, supposedly a period western told from a woman's viewpoint, emerges as a steamy, turgid meller, uneven in dramatic focus and development. Crucial flaw is the adaptation by Eleanor Perry.

Marilyn Durham's novel, which gets its offbeat title from fact that 'Cat Dancing' is the name of Burt Reynolds' dead Indian wife, tells how Sarah Miles, fleeing from husband George Hamilton, accidentally witnesses a train robbery and is virtually kidnapped by the gang. Reynolds has his hands full, for about two-thirds of the film, keeping brutish Jack Warden and Bo Hopkins (the latter outstanding) from raping Miles; for the last third, his hands are full of her.

The femme lead role calls less for acting ability than a willingness to be dragged, beaten, stomped on, and abused in a variety of ways.

Lee J. Cobb is the stoic Wells Fargo detective who, with Hamilton in tow, tracks down the surviving bandits to an Indian village.

....

■ **MAN WHO LOVED WOMEN, THE**

1983, 110 MINS, US ◇ ⓥ
Dir Blake Edwards   *Prod* Blake Edwards, Tony Adams   *Scr* Blake Edwards, Milton Wexler, Geoffrey Edwards   *Ph* Haskell Wexler   *Ed* Ralph E. Winters   *Mus* Henry Mancini   *Art Dir* Roger Maus
● Burt Reynolds, Julie Andrews, Kim Basinger, Marilu Henner, Barry Corbin, Cynthia Sikes (Columbia)

The Man Who Loved Women is truly woeful, reeking of production-line, big star filmmaking and nothing else.

Once again, Burt Reynolds appears as the irresistible, yet sensitive, modern man in search of something fulfilling in his life. This time, Reynolds' angst is examined in flashback from his funeral in the words of his psychiatrist (Julie Andrews). And they are terrible words, to be sure. From the start, the psychobabble she spouts is so stilted and stupid that it raises false hopes that *Women* must surely be a satire, and perhaps a promising one.

Had not director Blake Edwards been fooling around with an 'American extension' of Francois Truffaut's 1977 film of the same title, there probably was a better picture contained here in Reynolds' one really amusing sojourn into a bemused, adulterous affair with Kim Basinger.

She's great as Houston millionaire Barry Corbin's kinky wife, given to stopwatch dalliances in dangerous places.

....

■ **MAN WHO NEVER WAS, THE**

1956, 103 MINS, UK ◇ ⓥ
Dir Ronald Neame   *Prod* Andre Hakim   *Scr* Nigel Balchin   *Ph* Oswald Morris   *Mus* Alan Rawsthorne
● Clifton Webb, Gloria Grahame, Robert Flemyng, Josephine Griffin, Stephen Boyd, Andre Morell (20th Century-Fox)

Of all the fantastic stories to come out of World War II the use by British Naval Intelligence of a corpse to deceive the Germans about the planned invasion of Sicily undoubtedly out-fictions fiction.

The role of Montagu, the 'master planner', is distinctly offbeat for Clifton Webb and, on the whole, he handles it competently.

The star of this show is the corpse which, dressed up as a British marine major, is allowed to float ashore on the coast of Spain. It carries confidential letters with references to the forthcoming invasion of Greece, a ruse which actually fooled the Germans and saved many Allied lives.

Wisely realizing that this painstaking process, however unusual, lacks action and is bound to become tedious after a while, scripter Nigel Balchin (adapting the novel by Ewen Montagu) has introduced the figure of a young Irishman sent to London by the Germans to check on the identity of Major Martin. Gloria Grahame, assigned to be the girlfriend of 'Major Martin', seems an unhappy choice for the part, and she overplays it badly. By contrast, Josephine Griffin, a British newcomer, is completely believable.

....

■ **MAN WHO SHOT LIBERTY VALANCE, THE**

1962, 123 MINS, US ⓥ ⊙
Dir John Ford   *Prod* Willis Goldbeck   *Scr* James Warner Bellah, Willis Goldbeck   *Ph* William H. Clothier   *Ed* Otho Lovering   *Mus* Cyril J. Mockridge   *Art Dir* Hal Pereira, Eddie Imazu
● James Stewart, John Wayne, Vera Miles, Lee Marvin, Edmond O'Brien, Andy Devine (Paramount)

The Man Who Shot Liberty Valance is an entertaining and emotionally involving western. Yet, while it is an enjoyable film it falls distinctly shy of its innate story potential.

Director John Ford and the writers have somewhat overplayed their hands. They have taken a disarmingly simple and affecting premise, developed it with craft and skill to a natural point of conclusion, and then have proceeded to run it into the ground, destroying the simplicity and intimacy for which they have striven. The long screenplay from a short story by Dorothy M. Johnson has Stewart as a dude eastern attorney forging idealistically into lawless western territory, where he is promptly greeted by the sadistic, though sponsored, brutality of Valance (Lee Marvin), a killer who owes his allegiance to the vested interests of wealthy cattlemen opposed to statehood, law and order.

The audience instantly senses that Stewart did not fire the fatal shot that gives him his reputation and destines him for political fame. Because the audience knows that: (1) Stewart can't hit a paint can at 15 paces, (2) Stewart has won the heart of the sweetheart of John Wayne, best shot in the territory and a man of few words but heroically alert and forthright. Had the body of the film (it is told in flashback) ended at this maximum point, it would have been a taut, cumulative study of the irony of heroic destiny.

Stewart and Wayne do what comes naturally in an engagingly effortless manner. Vera Miles is consistently effective. Marvin is evil as they come. There is a portrayal of great strength and dignity by Woody Strode. But the most memorable characterization in the film is that of Edmond O'Brien as a tippling newspaper editor deeply proud of his profession.

□ 1962: Nomination: Best B&W Costume Design

....

■ MAN WHO WATCHED TRAINS GO BY, THE

(US: The Paris Express)

1952, 80 MINS, UK ◇ ▣

Dir Harold French   *Prod* Raymond Stross   *Scr* Harold French   *Ph* Otto Heller   *Mus* Benjamin Frankel
● Claude Rains, Marta Toren, Herbert Lom, Marius Goring, Anouk Aimee, Ferdy Mayne (Stross/Shaftel)

While it varies from the original Georges Simenon novel, this keeps to essentially the same main character about whom the entire plot revolves.

Main figure is Claude Rains, loyal chief clerk to a firm of Dutch merchants, whose world of honesty and integrity is shattered when he discovers that his boss has been misappropriating the company's money to keep a French woman in luxury. But this meek, dutiful servant, who all his life has watched the trains go by to alluring capitals like Brussels and Paris, turns when he discovers his boss is running off with the firm's money. He takes the cash himself and goes to Paris, where he is involved in a series of implausible but exciting adventures with the girl who was at the root of the trouble.

Rains plays the main role of the chief clerk with quiet, dignified restraint. Toren, as the unscrupulous woman, fills the part with a vivid and believable characterization. Marius Goring gives a polished performance as the French detective while Anouk Aimee has a bit as a Paris streetwalker.

....

■ MAN WHO WOULD BE KING, THE

1975, 129 MINS, US ◇ ▣ ⊙

Dir John Huston   *Prod* John Foreman   *Scr* John Huston, Gladys Hill   *Ph* Oswald Morris   *Ed* Russell Lloyd   *Mus* Maurice Jarre   *Art Dir* Alexander Trauner
● Sean Connery, Michael Caine, Christopher Plummer, Saeed Jaffrey, Shakira Caine (Columbia/Allied Artists)

Whether it was the intention of John Huston or not, the tale of action and adventure is a too-broad comedy, mostly due to the poor performance of Michael Caine.

As Peachy Carnehan, a loudmouth braggart and former soldier in the Indian army, Caine joins forces with another veteran, Daniel Dravot (Sean Connery), to make their fortunes in a mountain land beyond Afghanistan. Connery, in the title role, gives a generally credible, but not very sympathetic, portrayal of the man thrust into potential greatness.

The most redeeming aspect of the film is

the performance of Christopher Plummer as Rudyard Kipling, from whose classic story pic is a variation. Despite the small amount of footage he well deserves his star billing.

□ 1975: Nominations: Best Adapted Screenplay, Costume Design, Art Direction, Editing

....

■ MAN WITH A MILLION

See: The Million Pound Note

....

■ MAN WITH BOGART'S FACE, THE

1980, 106 MINS, US ◇ ▣

Dir Robert Day   *Prod* Andrew J. Fenady   *Scr* Andrew J. Fenady   *Ph* Richard C. Glouner   *Ed* Eddie Saeta   *Mus* George Duning   *Art Dir* Richard McKenzie
● Robert Sacchi, Franco Nero, Michelle Phillips, Olivia Hussey, Herbert Lom, Misty Rowe (20th Century-Fox)

Clearly and intentionally the picture is a gimmick. Bogart look-alike Robert Sacchi plays Bogart as Bogart himself might have portrayed private eye Sam Marlow, always relating incidents and personalities to stars and films of yesteryear. Producer Andrew J. Fenady, whose script is based on his own novel, has sprinkled his involved plot with a continuous flow of laugh lines. It adds up to a lot of fun.

As the film opens, the star has just undergone facial surgery, and immediately sets up shop as a private eye, hiring Misty Rowe as his luscious but scatterbrained secretary.

The action and there is plenty of it is played against some handsome backgrounds, including expensive yachts and the palace-like home of Turkish magnate Franco Nero, with his bevy of belly dancers.

....

■ MAN WITHIN, THE

(US: The Smugglers)

1947, 86 MINS, UK ◇

Dir Bernard Knowles   *Prod* Sydney Box   *Scr* Muriel Box, Sydney Box   *Ph* Geoffrey Unsworth   *Ed* Alfred Roome   *Mus* Clifton Parker   *Art Dir* Andrew Mazzei
● Michael Redgrave, Jean Kent, Joan Greenwood, Richard Attenborough, Francis L. Sullivan, Ronald Shiner (Gainsborough)

This adaptation of Graham Greene's novel has much to commend it. Most glaring fault is amount of talk used.

Story is told in flashback while Richard Attenborough is undergoing torture in prison. He relates how, as an orphan, he becomes the ward of Michael Redgrave, goes to sea with him and his crew of smugglers and is sharply disciplined because he is a poor sailor. He loathes the life and when he is flogged for an offense he did not commit, his love and admiration for his guardian turn to hate. He takes vengeance by giving him away to the customs men. In the ensuing fight one of the customs men is killed and several smugglers are arrested.

Attenborough flees, taking refuge in a lonely cottage the boy meets the step-daughter of the murdered man who approves his treachery and incites him to give evidence against his former shipmates.

Most mature performance comes from Redgrave who plays the gentleman-smuggler with a sure touch. Attenborough, as the coward who finds courage, has his moments, but Joan Greenwood is somewhat handicapped by a slow genuine Sussex dialect as Attenborough's real love. Jean Kent is alarmingly modern as an 1820 vamp.

....

■ MAN WITHOUT A STAR

1955, 89 MINS, US ◇ ▣

Dir King Vidor   *Prod* Aaron Rosenberg   *Scr* Borden Chase, D.D. Beauchamp   *Ph* Russell Metty   *Ed* Virgil

Vogel   *Mus* Joseph Gershenson   *Art Dir* Alexander Golitzen, Richard H. Riedel
● Kirk Douglas, Jeanne Crain, William Campbell, Claire Trevor, Richard Boone, Jay C. Flippen (Universal)

Kirk Douglas, in the title role, takes easily to the saddle as a tumbleweed cowpoke who has a way with a sixgun or the ladies. William Campbell scores as the young greenhorn who learns his cowboying from Douglas and about the wrong kind of women from Jeanne Crain.

The latter is technically skilled in her delineation of a ruthless owner of a big ranch, not above using sex in her determination to keep the range unfenced, but is not quite believable as a sexpot. Claire Trevor is in a character she does well, playing what is, by implication, the town madam with a heart of gold, and with a soft spot in it for the wandering Douglas.

The plot is basic western in this setup of open versus fenced land, but writing variations keep it fresh and the action high as things move towards the climax.

....

■ MAN WITH THE DEADLY LENS, THE

See: Wrong Is Right

....

■ MAN WITH THE GOLDEN ARM, THE

1955, 119 MINS, US ▣

Dir Otto Preminger   *Prod* Otto Preminger   *Scr* Walter Newman, Lewis Meltzer   *Ph* Sam Leavitt   *Ed* Louis Loeffler   *Mus* Elmer Bernstein   *Art Dir* Joseph Wright
● Frank Sinatra, Eleanor Parker, Kim Novak, Arnold Stang, Darren McGavin, Robert Strauss (Carlyle/United Artists)

Otto Preminger's *The Man with the Golden Arm* is a feature that focuses on addiction to narcotics. Clinical in its probing of the agonies, this is a gripping, fascinating film, expertly produced and directed and performed with marked conviction by Frank Sinatra as the drug slave.

Sinatra returns to squalid Chicago haunts after six months in hospital where he was 'cured' of his addiction. Thwarted in his attempt to land a job as a musician, he resumes as the dealer in a smalltime professional poker game.

Eleanor Parker is a pathetic figure as his wife, pretending to be chair-ridden for the sole purpose of making Sinatra stay by her side. A downstairs neighbor is Kim Novak, and the s.a. angles are not overlooked by the camera. Arnold Stang is Sparrow, Sinatra's subservient sidekick with the larcenous inclinations.

It's the story that counts most, however. Screenplay from the Nelson Algren novel, analyzes the drug addict with strong conviction. What goes on looks for real.

Novel titles are by Saul Bass, and the music by Elmer Bernstein deftly sets the mood.

□ 1955: Nominations: Best Actor (Frank Sinatra), B&W Art Direction, Scoring of a Dramatic Picture

....

■ MAN WITH THE GOLDEN GUN, THE

1974, 123 MINS, UK ◇ ▣ ⊙

Dir Guy Hamilton   *Prod* Albert R. Broccoli, Harry Saltzman   *Scr* Richard Maibaum, Tom Mankiewicz   *Ph* Ted Moore, Oswald Morris   *Ed* John Shirley, Raymond Poulton   *Mus* John Barry   *Art Dir* Peter Murton
● Roger Moore, Christopher Lee, Britt Ekland, Maud Adams, Herve Villechaize, Clifton James (United Artists/Eon)

Screenwriters' mission this ninth time around was to give the James Bond character more maturity, fewer gadgetry gimmicks, and more humor. On the last item they fumbled badly; and the comparatively spare arrays of mechanical devices seem a more cost-cutting factor.

Story diverts Bond from tracking down a missing solar energy scientist towards the mission of locating mysterious international hit man (Christopher Lee) who uses tailor-made gold bullets on his contract victims. To nobody's surprise, Lee has the solar energy apparatus installed on his Hong Kong area island hideaway. Bond naturally conquers all obstacles, and finds some fadeout sack time for Britt Ekland, the local British intelligence charmer.

■ **MAN WITH THE GREEN CARNATION, THE**
See: The Trials of Oscar Wilde

■ **MAN WITH THE X-RAY EYES, THE**
See: X

■ **MAN WITH TWO BRAINS, THE**

1983, 93 MINS, US ◇ ⓥ ⊙
Dir Carl Reiner *Prod* David V. Picker, William E. McEuen *Scr* Carl Reiner, Steve Martin, George Gipe *Ph* Michael Chapman *Ed* Bud Molin *Mus* Joel Goldsmith *Art Dir* Polly Platt
● Steven Martin, Kathleen Turner, David Warner, Paul Benedict, Richard Brestoff, James Cromwell (Aspen/Warner)

The Man with Two Brains is a fitfully amusing return by Steve Martin to the broad brand of lunacy that made his first feature, *The Jerk* [1979], so successful.

Plot is a frayed crazy quilt barely held together as if by clothespins. Ace neurosurgeon Martin almost kills beauteous Kathleen Turner in an auto accident, only to save her via his patented screwtop brain surgery technique. Turner proves to be a master at withholding her sexual favors from her frustrated husband, who decides to take her on a honeymoon to Vienna in an attempt to thaw her out.

While there, Martin visits the lab of colleague David Warner and meets the love of his life, a charming woman and marvelous conversationalist [voiced by Sissy Spacek] who also happens to be a disembodied brain suspended in a jar, her body having been the victim of a crazed elevator killer.

Much humor, of course, stems from the befuddled Martin groveling at the feet of the knockout Turner he comes to call a 'scum queen', but too much of the film seems devoted to frantic overkill to compensate for general lack of bellylaughs and topnotch inspiration.

Martin delivers all that's expected of him as a performer, and Turner is a sizzling foil for his comic and pent-up sexual energy.

■ **MAN, WOMAN AND CHILD**

1983, 99 MINS, US ◇ ⓥ
Dir Dick Richards *Prod* Elmo Williams, Elliott Kastner *Scr* Erich Segal, David, Z. Goodman *Ph* Richard H. Kline *Ed* David Bretherton *Mus* Georges Delerue *Art Dir* Dean-Edward Mitzner
● Martin Sheen, Blythe Danner, Sebastian Dungan, Arlene McIntyre, Missy Francis, David Hemmings (Paramount)

Man, Woman and Child is a sweetly dramatic picture which, unfortunately, reaches so hard for sobs at the end that all logic is suspended.

Despite the problems in the screenplay adaptation of Erich's Segal's novel by Segal and David Z. Goodman, there are still some fine performances here, tautly directed.

Martin Sheen is superb as a happily married husband of Blythe Danner and father of Arlene McIntyre and Missy Francis. But trouble arrives with news that a brief fling of the past in France (seen in flashback with Nathalie Nell) has caused a problem for the present.

Nell has been killed in an accident, leaving a son by Sheen that he never knew about. For Sheen, the only decent thing to do is confess all to Danner and invite the boy to the US for a get-acquainted visit.

Danner is also excellent in her hurt reaction, torn between love for her husband and resentment of the young intruder young Sebastian Dungan is a real discovery.

But *Man, Woman* concludes with one of those annoying film situations where the characters have several choices of what to do and select the one that makes the least sense.

■ **MAP OF THE HUMAN HEART**

1993, 106 MINS, UK/AUSTRALIA/FRANCE/CANADA ◇ ⓥ ⊙
Dir Vincent Ward *Prod* Tim Bevan *Scr* Louis Nowra *Ph* Eduardo Serra *Ed* John Scott, George Akers *Mus* Gabriel Yared *Art Dir* John Beard
● Jason Scott Lee, Robert Joamie, Anne Parillaud, Patrick Bergin, John Cusack, Jeanne Moreau (Working Title/Ward/Ariane/Sunrise)

New Zealander Vincent Ward's third film is an immensely ambitious and audacious love story spanning 30 years and two continents. Much of it is set and filmed above the Arctic Circle in northern Canada, providing breathtaking icescapes for Eduardo Serra's camera.

The story unfolds in flashback, starting in 1965 as an old Innuit Eskimo tells a Yank mapmaker (a small role for John Cusack) his life story. Back in 1931, a vintage aircraft lands on the ice near the Innuit village, bringing with it dashing Brit, Walter Russell (Patrick Bergin), who intends to chart the area. He befriends Avik (Robert Joamie) a cheerful young Innuit, who later forms a close friendship with a half-French Canadian, half-Indian girl, Albertine (Annie Galipeau).

Ten years later, in 1941, Russell returns to the Arctic on a mission to track down a German U-boat and meets Avik (Jason Scott Lee) again. Hearing that Albertine (Anne Parillaud) is in Europe, Avik enlists in the Canadian air force. Subsequently, he takes part in the notorious bombing of Dresden. Pic's last act, set in the 1960s, records Avik's encounter with the daughter he never knew he had.

Ward [who wrote the story] and celebrated Australian playwright Louis Nowra evidently aimed to create one of those sweeping romantic sagas that are from time to time popular screen fare. They almost succeed, but more romantic passion would have helped.

[Version reviewed was 126-minute 'work in progress' shown in a non-competing slot at Cannes in May 1992. Final 106-minute version featured new scenes in the middle of the pic – a romantic triangle played by Bergin, Lee and Parillaud – and a reshaped ending.]

■ **MARATHON MAN**

1976, 125 MINS, US ◇ ⓥ ⊙
Dir John Schlesinger *Prod* Robert Evans, Sidney Beckerman *Scr* William Goldman *Ph* Conrad Hall *Ed* Jim Clark *Mus* Michael Small *Art Dir* Richard MacDonald
● Dustin Hoffman, Laurence Olivier, Roy Scheider, William Devane, Marthe Keller, Fritz Weaver (Paramount)

Film spends literally half of its length getting some basic plot pieces [from the novel by William Goldman] fitted and moving. By which time it's asking a lot if anybody still cares why Dustin Hoffman's brother Roy Scheider is a mysterious globetrotter; why Laurence Olivier as an ex-Nazi disguises his appearance to leave a jungle hideaway to go to NY; why US secret agent William Devane seems in league with Olivier and his goons, Richard Bright and Marc Lawrence; why Marthe Keller throws herself at Hoffman; why the memory of Hoffman's dishonored

professor-father, a victim of the McCarthy era, relates to anything.

Hoffman, you see, is stuck in the role of a bewildered man-in-the-middle about whom bodies fall like flies; eventually he gets into the swing of things and kills a few on his own.
□ 1976: Nomination: Best Supp. Actor (Laurence Olivier)

■ **MARCH OR DIE**

1977, 106 MINS, US ◇ ⓥ ⊙
Dir Dick Richards *Prod* Dick Richards, Jerry Bruckheimer *Scr* David Zelag Goodman *Ph* John Alcott *Ed* John C. Howard, Stanford C. Allen *Mus* Maurice Jarre *Art Dir* Gil Parrondo
● Gene Hackman, Terence Hill [= Mario Girotti], Max von Sydow, Catherine Deneuve, Ian Holm, Jack O'Halloran (ITC-Associated General)

This Foreign Legion adventure caper [from a screen story by David Zelag Goodman and Dick Richards], replete with international cast and crew, has lots of actionful battle scenes, a few squeamish torture scenes, and beautiful photography on actual locations.

Terence Hill, the Italian actor with the Yankee name, shows a tongue-in-cheek approach to his role that allows him to dominate every scene he's in. Also first rate is Britisher Ian Holm, as El Krim, the fanatic Arab chieftain.

Biggest disappointment is the 'acting' of Gene Hackman who walks listlessly through the major role of a washed-out West Pointer who has given 16 years of his life to the Legion.

This is the film in which Hackman suffered a back injury but there's no indication of it. The most physical activity he undergoes is riding a horse.

■ **MARIA'S LOVERS**

1984, 100 MINS, US ◇ ⓥ ⊙
Dir Andrei Konchalovsky *Prod* Bosko Djordjevic, Lawrence Taylor-Mortorff *Scr* Gerard Brach, Andrei Konchalovsky, Paul Zindel, Marjorie David *Ph* Juan Ruiz-Anchia *Ed* Humphrey Dixon *Mus* Gary S. Remal *Art Dir* Jeannine Oppewall
● Nastassja Kinski, John Savage, Robert Mitchum, Keith Carradine, Anita Morris, Bud Cort (Cannon)

The first American feature film by Russian director Andrei Konchalovsky, *Maria's Lovers* is a turbulent, quite particularized period romance about the sometime lack of synchronization of love and sex.

Opening sequence makes use of excerpts from John Huston's great postwar US Army documentary *Let There Be Light* to introduce the phenomenon of returning soldiers with psychological disabilities. Climaxing this is a mock verite interview with vet John Savage, who survived a Japanese prison camp and is terribly glad to be home in smalltown Pennsylvania.

His grizzled father Robert Mitchum gives Savage an understated welcome, and latter then has the misfortune of dropping by the home of his great love, Nastassja Kinski, just as she turns up in the grasp of another soldier, Vincent Spano.

Spano finally backs off, leaving the childhood sweethearts free to marry in a Russian Orthodox service.

Konchalovsky's storytelling proceeds at a smooth pace and contains certain interesting wrinkles, such as Mitchum's discouraging his son from pursuing Kinski because he himself is secretly interested in her.

■ **MARIE**

1985, 112 MINS, US ◇ ⓥ
Dir Roger Donaldson *Prod* Frank Capra Jr *Scr* John Briley *Ph* Chris Menges *Ed* Neil Travis *Mus* Francis Lai *Art Dir* Ron Foreman

● Sissy Spacek, Jeff Daniels, Keith Szarabajka, Morgan Freeman, Fred Thompson, Lisa Banes (De Laurentiis)

Marie is a powerfully-made political melodrama, the many strengths of which are vitiated only by the relative familiarity of the expose, little person-vs.-the establishment framework. Sissy Spacek adds another excellent characterization to her credits.

Based on a book [*Marie: A True Story*] by Peter Maas, tale opens in 1968 with a rough scene in which Spacek and her small kids leave home after she is brutalized by her husband. Five years later, after educating herself further, she gets a job as extradition director and, before long, is appointed chairman of the parole board for the State of Tennessee.

Helping guide her up the twisting stairway of the political system is ostensible friend Jeff Daniels, a close aide of Governor Blanton who frequently comes to Spacek with overt suggestions that she speed through the parole of certain individuals.

John Briley has set the story down in cogent fashion, and director Donaldson has brought tremendous freshness to its telling.

Spacek is right at home with her role while Jeff Daniels is outstanding as her duplicitous associate.

MARIE ANTOINETTE

1938, 160 MINS, US
Dir W.S. Van Dyke   *Prod* Hunt Stromberg
Scr Claudine West, Donald Ogden Stewart, Ernest Vajda   *Ph* William Daniels   *Ed* Robert J. Kern   *Mus* Herbert Stothart   *Art Dir* Cedric Gibbons, William A. Horning, Edwin B. Willis
● Norma Shearer, Tyrone Power, John Barrymore, Robert Morley, Anita Louise, Joseph Schildkraut (M-G-M)

Produced on a scale of incomparable splendor and extravagance, *Marie Antoinette* approaches real greatness as cinematic historical literature.

What is related on the screen is a brilliant, historic tragedy the crushing of the French monarchy by revolution and terror. Stefan Zweig's biography of Marie Antoinette is the source from which the screenwriters have drawn most of their material.

First part is concerned with the vicious intrigues of the Versailles court and the power exerted by Mme du Barry and the traitorous Orleans. The ensembles, arranged by Albertina Rasch, suggest beautiful paintings. Second portion opens with the expose of the fraudulent sale of a diamond necklace, which precipitated the enmity of the nobility. With an aroused nation and the queen as the point of attack, the action moves swiftly to the pillage of the castle, the royal arrest, the unsuccessful escape to the border, the trials and execution of the rulers.

Norma Shearer's performance is lifted by skillful portrayal of physical and mental transitions through the period of a score of years. Her moments of ardor with Ferson (Tyrone Power) are tender and believable.

Outstanding in the acting, however, is Robert Morley, who plays the vacillating King Louis XVI. He creates sympathy and understanding for the kingly character, a dullard and human misfit.

John Barrymore as the aged Louis XV leaves a deep impress. Joseph Schildkraut is the conniving Duc d'Orleans and scores as a fastidious and scheming menace. Gladys George makes much from a few opportunities as Mme du Barry.

When illness prevented Sidney Franklin from assuming the direction of the film after arduous preparation, W.S. Van Dyke was assigned the task.
□ 1938: Nominations: Best Actress (Norma Shearer), Supp. Actor (Robert Morley), Art Direction, Original Score

MARIE WALEWSKA
See: Conquest

MARJORIE MORNINGSTAR

1958, 125 MINS, US
Dir Irving Rapper   *Prod* Milton Sperling   *Scr* Everett Freeman   *Ph* Harry Stradling   *Ed* Folmar Blangsted   *Mus* Max Steiner   *Art Dir* Malcolm Bert
● Gene Kelly, Natalie Wood, Claire Trevor, Everett Sloane, Martin Milner, Ed Wynn (Warner/Beachwold)

There was in the original bestseller of Herman Wouk an attempt to isolate and examine a particular segment of American life, the upper middle class Jewish stratum of Manhattan. Producer Milton Sperling has kept some aspects of the original idea, the characters are still part of their racial and religious background, but the Jewish flavor has been watered down.

Natalie Wood gives a glowing and touching performance as the title heroine. Gene Kelly is moving as her romantic vis-a-vis, Claire Trevor and Everett Sloane are strong in support and Martin Milner is an important younger leading man. Ed Wynn is the standout as Marjorie's Uncle Samson.

The title is the clue to the story. When Marjorie changes her name from Morgenstern to Morningstar, she unwittingly cuts herself off from her Jewish background and plunges without support into a world of no visible connections and even less stability. She falls in love with Kelly, one of those fascinating men of small talent who flourish in the theatrical fringe of Broadway. He has changed his name, too, and the resulting rootlessness has left him uneasy and unsatisfied, although he never truly understands why. Marjorie caroms from his rejection to a doctor (Martin Balsam). Always standing by is hardworking playwright Milner.
□ 1958: Nomination: Best Song ('A Very Precious Love')

MARKED FOR DEATH

1990, 94 MINS, US
Dir Dwight H. Little   *Prod* Michael Grais, Mark Victor, Steven Seagal   *Scr* Michael Grais, Mark Victor   *Ph* Ric Waite   *Ed* O. Nicholas Brown   *Mus* James Newton Howard   *Art Dir* Robb Wilson King
● Steven Seagal, Basil Wallace, Keith David, Tom Wright, Joanna Pacula, Elizabeth Gracen (Victor & Grais)

This dim-witted revenge yarn is the simplest of showcases for Steven Seagal – an extremely compelling action presence with his brutal martial arts fighting style, imposing size and nasty demeanor.

It would be hard to imagine a more straightforward plot: former Drug Enforcement Agency troubleshooter Hatcher (Seagal) quits his job and goes home to visit his family. At the local tavern, he crosses a group of Jamaican drug dealers who mark him and his family for death. Naturally, he has to kill the leader to protect his loved ones. The leader of the drug 'posse,' Screwface (Basil Wallace), practices voodoo and sports braids.

The twist in Seagal's pics is that there's usually some sort of liberal bent – here Hatcher's statement that the drug war has been for naught – in contrast to the right-wing leanings of many other films in the genre. He also has a penchant for black sidekicks, here a former Army buddy (Keith David).

Seagal fans aren't likely to be disappointed, since director Dwight H. Little keeps the pedal to the metal. Beyond the incumbent violence there's a fair amount of nudity in the film.

MARK OF ZORRO, THE

1940, 93 MINS, US
Dir Rouben Mamoulian   *Prod* Raymond Griffith   *Scr* John Taintor Foote   *Ph* Arthur Miller   *Ed* Robert Bischoff   *Mus* Alfred Newman   *Art Dir* Richard Day, Joseph C. Wright
● Tyrone Power, Linda Darnell, Basil Rathbone, Gale Sondergaard, Eugene Pallette, J. Edward Bromberg (20th Century-Fox)

In the 1920s Douglas Fairbanks started his series of historical super-spectacles with *The Mark of Zorro*, a tale of early California under Spanish rule, adapted from Johnston McCulley's story, *The Curse of Capistrano*. In the remake [adapted by Garrett Fort and Bess Meredyth] 20th-Fox inducts Tyrone Power into the lead spot.

The colorful background, detailing Los Angeles as little more than a pueblo settlement under the Spanish flag, is utilized for some thrilling melodramatics. In the early portion picture drags considerably, but once it gets up steam, it rolls along with plenty of action and, despite its obvious formula of hooded Robin Hood who terrorizes the tax-biting officials of the district to finally triumph for the peons and caballeros, picture holds plenty of entertainment.

Power is not Fairbanks (the original screen Hood) but, fortunately, neither the script nor direction forces him to any close comparison. He's plenty heroic and sincere in his mission.

After an extensive education in the Spanish army in Madrid, Power returns to California to find his father displaced as Alcalde of Los Angeles by thieving J. Edward Bromberg. Latter, with aid of post captain Basil Rathbone and his command, terrorizes the district and piles on burdensome taxes. Power embarks on a one-man Robinhoodian campaign of wild riding and rapier-wielding to clean up the situation and restore his father to his rightful position. And there's a sweet romance with Linda Darnell, niece of Bromberg, who is unsympathetic to his policies.

Sword duel between Power and Rathbone, running about two minutes, is a dramatic highlight.
□ 1940: Nomination: Best Original Score

MARLOWE

1969, 95 MINS, US
Dir Paul Bogart   *Prod* Gabriel Katzka, Sidney Beckerman   *Scr* Stirling Silliphant   *Ph* William H. Daniels   *Ed* Gene Ruggiero   *Mus* Peter Matz   *Art Dir* George W. Davis, Addison Hehr
● James Garner, Gayle Hunnicutt, Carroll O'Connor, Rita Moreno, Sharon Farrell, Bruce Lee (Katzka-Berne/Cherokee)

Raymond Chandler's private eye character, Philip Marlowe, is in need of better handling if he is to survive as a screen hero. *Marlowe*, is a plodding, unsure piece of so-called sleuthing in which James Garner can never make up his mind whether to play it for comedy or hardboil.

Stirling Silliphant's adaptation of *The Little Sister* comes out on the confused side, with too much unexplained action. Garner as the private eye is hired by a girl from Kansas to find her missing brother, then finds himself involved in a maze in which he's as mystified as the spectator.

Garner walks through the picture mostly with knotted brow, but Gayle Hunnicutt as the actress is nice to look at toward the end. Rita Moreno as a strip dancer delivers soundly, but a peeler does not a picture make.

MARNIE

1964, 130 MINS, US
Dir Alfred Hitchcock   *Prod* Alfred Hitchcock   *Scr* Jay Presson Allen   *Ph* Robert Burks   *Ed* George Tomasini   *Mus* Bernard Herrmann   *Art Dir* Robert Boyle

● Tippi Hedren, Sean Connery, Diane Baker, Martin Gabel, Louise Latham, Bruce Dern (Universal)

Marnie is the character study of a thief and a liar, but what makes her tick remains clouded even after a climax reckoned to be shocking but somewhat missing its point.

Tippi Hedren, whom Hitchcock intro'd in *The Birds* returns in a particularly demanding role and Sean Connery makes his American film bow, as the two principal protagonists in this adaptation of Winston Graham's best-seller. Complicated story line offers Hedren as a sexy femme who takes office jobs, then absconds with as much cash as she can find in the safe, changing color of her tresses and obtaining new employment for similar purposes. Plot becomes objective when she is recognized by her new employer, book publisher Connery, as the girl who stole $10,000 from a business associate, and rather than turn her in marries her.

That's merely the beginning, and balance of unfoldment dwells on husband's efforts to ferret mystery on why she recoils from the touch of any man himself included and why other terrors seem to overcome her.

Hedren, undertaking role originally offered Grace Kelly for a resumption of her screen career, lends credence to a part never sympathetic. It's a difficult assignment which she fulfills satisfactorily, although Hitchcock seldom permits her a change of pace which would have made her character more interesting. Connery handles himself convincingly, but here, again, greater interest would have resulted from greater facets of character as he attempts to explore femme's unexplained past.

■ MAROC 7

1967, 91 MINS, UK ◇ ▽
Dir Gerry O'Hara *Prod* John Gale, Leslie Phillips
Scr David Osborn *Ph* Kenneth Talbot *Ed* John Jympson *Mus* Kenneth V. Jones, Paul Ferris
Art Dir Seamus Flannery
● Gene Barry, Cyd Charisse, Elsa Martinelli, Leslie Phillips, Denholm Elliott, Alexandra Stewart (Cyclone/Rank)

The cops-and-robbers thriller lacks the necessary for such a subject. Writer David Osborn's main ace is to make most of his leading characters suspect, although cinemagoers will often be in doubt as to whether the characters are goodies or baddies and the answer never offers much of a kick. Performances are mainly smooth but do not engineer much excitement. On the other hand, the genuine Moroccan backgrounds give a colorful zest to the action.

Story has Cyd Charisse as a sophisticated editress of a fashionable magazine. Her frequent trips abroad with a photographic team and a bunch of leggy, photogenic models are ostensibly for magazine layouts, but actually are a front for daring jewel robberies. Her chief model (Elsa Martinelli) and her cameraman-partner (Leslie Phillips) are both in on the murky deals.

Suspecting this, special cop Gene Barry poses as a thief, uses a blackmailing technique and forces Charisse to let him tag along on her latest trip to Morocco, where she's got her predatory eye on a priceless medallion.

■ MAROONED

1969, 134 MINS, US ◇ ▽
Dir John Sturges *Prod* Mike Frankovich *Scr* Mayo Simon *Ph* Daniel Fapp *Ed* Walter Thompson
Mus (none) *Art Dir* R. Wheeler
● Gregory Peck, Richard Crenna, David Janssen, James Franciscus, Gene Hackman, Lee Grant (Columbia)

What happens when a lunar rocket fails to fire for reentry to earth's gravity? The men on

such a capsule become lost in space. Such is the situation presented in the gripping drama, *Marooned*, a film [based on a novel by Martin Cardin] which is part documentary, part science fiction. The film is superbly crafted, taut and a technological cliff-hanger.

The production's major flaw is a hokey old fashioned Hollywood Renfrew-to-the-rescue climax that is dramatically, logically and technologically unconvincing.

For the first four-fifths of his mission, director John Sturges fashions spectacular documentary footage of launchings, on location work at Cape Kennedy, special effects, studio set ups and scenes on close-circuit TV into an edge-of-the-seat drama in which personalities and human conflicts are never subordinated to the hardware.

☐ 1969: Best Special Visual Effects.
☐ Nominations: Best Cinematography, Sound

■ MARRIAGE-GO-ROUND, THE

1960, 98 MINS, US ◇
Dir Walter Lang *Prod* Leslie Stevens *Scr* Leslie Stevens
Ph Leo Tover *Ed* Jack W. Holmes *Mus* Dominic Frontiere *Art Dir* Duncan Cramer, Maurice Ransford
● Susan Hayward, James Mason, Julie Newmar, Robert Paige, June Clayworth (20th Century-Fox)

Something appears to have gone wrong somewhere between Broadway, where *The Marriage-Go-Round* sustained itself as a hit play from October 1958 to February 1960, and Hollywood, where it is just a rather tame and tedious film. There isn't a great deal of novelty or merriment in the Leslie production, which Stevens adapted from his own play.

It rotates laboriously around one joke – the idea that an amorous Amazonian doll from Sweden would match endowments, gene for gene, with a brilliant cultural anthropology professor from the US. Since the prof is a happily-married monogamist, Miss Sweden's forward pass is intercepted right in the shadow of the goal (of bed) posts.

In the role of the professor, James Mason is competent, managing to stay reasonably appealing in a perpetual state of mild flabbergastedness. Susan Hayward does exceptionally well in the role of the wife. Julie Newmar, who won the Antoinette Perry Award as best supporting actress for her Broadway performance as the gregarious glamorpuss from Scandinavia, appears to have misplaced her award-winning attributes. The intimacy of larger-than-life celluloid reveals a queen-sized heap of overacting from the blonde bombshell.

■ MARRIAGE OF A YOUNG STOCKBROKER, THE

1971, 95 MINS, US ◇ ▽
Dir Lawrence Turman *Prod* Lawrence Turman
Scr Lorenzo Semple Jr *Ph* Laszlo Kovacs *Ed* Fredric Steinkamp *Mus* Fred Karlin *Art Dir* Pato Guzman
● Richard Benjamin, Joanna Shimkus, Elizabeth Ashley, Adam West, Patricia Barry, Tiffany Bolling (20th Century-Fox)

Based on a Charles Webb novel, the Lorenzo Semple Jr adaptation features Richard Benjamin as a dull husband given to casual voyeurism, and Joanna Shimkus as his equally confused wife. The bittersweet emotional drama unfolds in parallel with some superb high and low comedy.

Benjamin and Shimkus have an all-too-true marital blandness, disrupted by his predilection for eyeing girls. The hang-up is nowhere near criminal; in fact it's rather innocent. But Shimkus has had it, and packs off to Pasadena where barracuda sister Elizabeth Ashley, who already has emasculated hubby Adam West, begins stage-managing a divorce.

Semple's script is well structured and the dialog is superb. The varying elements of farce and satire are neatly interwoven on the genuine marital tragedy in progress. No element overpowers another nor the overall feel. Lawrence Turman's direction is incisive.

■ MARRIED TO IT

1992, 110 MINS, US ◇ ▽ ⊙
Dir Arthur Hiller *Prod* Thomas Baer *Scr* Janet Kovalcik *Ph* Victor Kemper *Ed* Robert C. Jones *Mus* Henry Mancini *Art Dir* Robert Gundlach
● Beau Bridges, Stockard Channing, Robert Sean Leonard, Mary Stuart Masterson, Cybill Shepherd, Ron Silver (Orion/Three Pair)

Auds seeking the wit and polish or an Alan Alda on Neil Simon adult ensemble comedy dealing with the ups and downs of marriage will do best to move on. This Arthur Hiller-directed version unfolds with an unaccountable clumsiness.

Story brings together three couples who gain perspective on their relationships through the course of their friendship. Problem here is one can never figure out why they're friends.

Mary Stuart Masterson and Robert Sean Leonard are the baby yuppies on the move. Born in 1966, these well-heeled 'new traditionalists' actually have been a couple since they were eight years old. Stockard Channing and Beau Bridges also were born in the 1960s – ideologically. Today he's still a welfare case worker, and she's a homemaker for their teenage sons. Ron Silver and Cybill Shepherd are more of a crowd than a couple, given that his 13-year-old daughter and angry ex-wife are pretty much running their relationship – into the ground.

Pic's most effective scenes are the knock-down fights about emotional issues, which finally give the actors something to get their teeth into. Hiller's direction is often slapdash, particularly in the final reel. Film was lensed in Toronto and New York, where former mayor Ed Koch pops up in a party scene cameo.

■ MARRIED TO THE MOB

1988, 103 MINS, US ◇ ▽ ⊙
Dir Jonathan Demme *Prod* Kenneth Utt, Edward Saxon
Scr Barry Strugatz, Mark R. Burns *Ph* Tak Fujimoto
Ed Craig McKay *Mus* David Byrne *Art Dir* Kristi Zea
● Michelle Pfeiffer, Matthew Modine, Dean Stockwell, Mercedes Ruehl, Alec Baldwin, Joan Cusack (Mysterious Arts/Orion)

Fresh, colorful and inventive, *Married to the Mob* is another offbeat entertainment from director Jonathan Demme.

Storyline's basic trajectory has unhappy suburban housewife Michelle Pfeiffer taking the opportunity presented by the sudden death of her husband, who happens to have been a middle-level gangster, to escape the limitations of her past and forge a new life for herself and her son in New York City.

Opening with a hit on a commuter train and following with some murderous bedroom shenanigans, film establishes itself as a suburban gangster comedy. Demme and his enthusiastic collection of actors take evident delight in sending up the gauche excesses of these particular nouveau riches, as the men strut about in their pinstripes and polyester and the women spend their time at the salon getting their hair teased.

The enormous cast is a total delight, starting with Pfeiffer, with hair dyed dark, a New York accent and a continuously nervous edge. Matthew Modine proves winning as the seemingly inept FBI functionary who grows into his job, and Dean Stockwell is a hoot as the unflappable gangland boss, slime under silk and a fedora.

M

☐ 1988: Nomination: Best Supp. Actor (Dean Stockwell)

■ **MARRYING KIND, THE**

1952, 92 MINS, US

Dir George Cukor   *Prod* Bert Granet   *Scr* Ruth Gordon, Garson Kanin   *Ph* Joseph Walker   *Ed* Charles Nelson   *Mus* Hugo Friedhofer   *Art Dir* John Meehan

● Judy Holliday, Aldo Ray, Madge Kennedy, Sheila Bond, John Alexander, Mickey Shaughnessy (Columbia)

Judy Holliday's first film vehicle since *Born Yesterday* is a melange of marital errors. It introduces Aldo Ray, previously in *Saturday's Hero*, as Holliday's partner. He is equipped with a trick voice of the same raspy tonal quality as the actress's.

The plot gets underway in a divorce court with a kindly judge, beautifully played by Madge Kennedy, former silent screen name, trying to effect a reconciliation between Holliday and Ray, through talking out their troubles and misunderstandings. Footage then becomes a series of dialog-laden flashbacks, taking the couple back.

■ **MARRYING MAN, THE**

(UK/Australia: Too Hot to Handle)

1991, 115 MINS, US ◇ ⊙

Dir Jerry Rees   *Prod* David Permut   *Scr* Neil Simon   *Ph* Donald E. Thorin   *Ed* Michael Jablow   *Mus* David Newman   *Art Dir* William F. Matthews

● Kim Basinger, Alec Baldwin, Robert Loggia, Elisabeth Shue, Armand Assante, Paul Reiser (Hollywood/Silver Screen Partners IV)

The Marrying Man is a stillborn romantic comedy of staggering ineptitude. Author Neil Simon reportedly disowned this film. An awkward flashback structure tells of egotistical toothpaste heir Alec Baldwin falling in love with chanteuse Kim Basinger on an outing in 1948 with his buddies to Las Vegas.

Instead of marrying his beautiful g.f. back in LA (Elisabeth Shue), Baldwin is forced into a shotgun wedding with Basinger by Armand Assante as Bugsy Siegel, Basinger's main man. Key plot point is that this is Bugsy's 're-venge' for catching Baldwin in the sack with his g.f. Also unbelievable are the duo's several breakups and remarriages.

Lack of chemistry between the two principals is only the first problem with *Marrying Man*. Obvious re-shoots result in an unwieldy package that has the film climaxing with perhaps 30 minutes to go, making it play like an original and a sequel spliced together.

■ **MARTIN**

1978, 95 MINS, US ◇ ⊛ ⊙

Dir George A. Romero   *Prod* Richard Rubinstein   *Scr* George A. Romero   *Ph* Michael Gornick   *Ed* George A. Romero   *Mus* Donald Rubinstein

● John Amplas, Lincoln Maazel, Christine Forrest, Elayne Nadeau, Tom Savini (Braddock/Laurel)

Title character in *Martin* is a supposed 84-year-old vampire whose youthful visage has survived his escape from Rumania through his contemporary journey to Braddock, Pa, where grandfather Lincoln Maazel is determined to drive out 'Nosferatu', with Martin as the last remaining relative afflicted with the family curse.

This urban vampire kills not with his teeth, but with prepackaged razor blades, neatly slicing veins and arteries for his mealtime pleasure.

Pittsburgh-based auteur George A. Romero is still limited by apparently low budgets. But he has inserted some sepia-toned flashback scenes of Martin in Rumania that are extraordinarily evocative, and his direction of the victimization scenes shows a definite flair for suspense.

■ **MARTY**

1955, 93 MINS, US ⊛ ⊙

Dir Delbert Mann   *Prod* Harold Hecht   *Scr* Paddy Chayefsky   *Ph* Joseph LaShelle   *Ed* Alan Crosland Jr   *Mus* Roy Webb, George Bassman   *Art Dir* Edward S. Haworth, Walter Simonds

● Ernest Borgnine, Betsy Blair, Esther Minciotti, Augusta Ciolli, Joe Mantell, Karen Steele (Hecht-Lancaster/United Artists)

Based on Paddy Chayefsky's teleplay, and screenplayed by the author, *Marty* has been fashioned into a sock picture. It's a warm, human, sometimes sentimental and an enjoyable experience. Although filmed on a modest budget (reportedly about $300,000), there is no evidence of any stinting in the production values.

Basically, it's the story of a boy and girl, both of whom consider themselves misfits in that they are unable to attract members of the opposite sex. The boy is sensitively played by Ernest Borgnine and the girl is beautifully played by Betsy Blair.

Chayefsky has caught the full flavor of bachelor existence in a Bronx Italian neighborhood. The meetings at a bar and grill, the stag-attended dances, the discussions about girls and 'what do we do tonight?' poser ring with authenticity.

☐ 1955: Best Picture, Director, Actor (Ernest Borgnine), Screenplay.

☐ Nominations: Best Supp. Actor (Joe Mantell), Supp. Actress (Betsy Blair), B&W Cinematography, B&W Art Direction

■ **MARY OF SCOTLAND**

1936, 123 MINS, US ⊛ ⊙

Dir John Ford   *Prod* Pandro S. Berman   *Scr* Dudley Nichols   *Ph* Joseph H. August   *Ed* Jane Loring   *Mus* Nathaniel Shilkret   *Art Dir* Van Nest Polglase, Carroll Clark

● Katharine Hepburn, Fredric March, Florence Eldridge, Douglas Walton, John Carradine, Robert Barrat (RKO)

When RKO set about the task of transmuting this Maxwell Anderson-Theatre Guild play to the screen, it had two possibilities. Could have softened the story and played up the business of a woman who threw away her kingdom for love and thus sold the picture as sheer entertainment; or it could have taken the hard way, telling the story beautifully, artistically, delicately, with meticulous attention to detail and portrayal. Having decided to do it the latter way, there can be nothing but credit to the production.

The really curious point about the film is its casting. On the face of it, Katharine Hepburn would seem to be the wrong choice for the character of the Scots queen. She is nowhere as hard as she should be, she nowhere shows the strength of courage and decision that the school-books talk of. And that is all in the film's favor because it humanizes it all.

Fredric March as Hepburn's vis-a-vis in the role of the swashbuckling Bothwell is a natural and excellent choice, playing the slap-dash earl to the hilt. Florence Eldridge as Elizabeth is again a questionable choice from a strict historical standpoint. She, too, turns in such a fine acting job as to convince quite definitely of the wisdom of it.

In handling the photography and physical production, Ford put emphasis on shadows, several times achieving surprisingly strong effects.

■ **MARY POPPINS**

1964, 140 MINS, US ◇ ⊛ ⊙

Dir Robert Stevenson   *Prod* Walt Disney   *Scr* Bill Walsh, Don Da Gradi   *Ph* Edward Colman   *Ed* Cotton Warburton   *Mus* Irwin Kostal (sup.)   *Art Dir* Carroll Clark, William H. Tuntke, Tony Walton

● Julie Andrews, Dick Van Dyke, David Tomlinson, Glynis Johns, Hermione Baddeley, Ed Wynne (Walt Disney)

Disney has gone all-out in his dream-world rendition [from the books by P.L. Travers] of a magical Engish nanny who one day arrives on the East Wind and takes over the household of a very proper London banker. Besides changing the lives of everyone therein, she introduces his two younger children to wonders imagined and possible only in fantasy.

Among a spread of outstanding songs [by Richard M. and Robert B. Sherman] perhaps the most unusual is 'Chim-Chim-Cher-ee', sung by Dick Van Dyke, which carries a haunting quality. Dancing also plays an important part in unfolding the story and one number, the Chimney-Sweep Ballet, performed on the roofs of London and with Van Dyke starring, is a particular standout. For sheer entertainment, a sequence mingling live-action and animation in which Van Dyke dances with four little penguin-waiters is immense.

Julie Andrews' first appearance on the screen is a signal triumph and she performs as easily as she sings, displaying a fresh type of beauty nicely adaptable to the color cameras. Van Dyke, as the happy-go-lucky jack-of-all-trades, scores heavily, the part permitting him to showcase his wide range of talents.

☐ 1964: Best Actress (Julie Andrews), Song ('Chim-Chim-Cher-ee'), Original Musical Scoring, Editing, Visual Efects.

☐ Nominations: Best Picture, Director, Adapted Screenplay, Color Cinematography, Color Costume Design, Color Art Direction, Adapted Music Score, Sound

■ **MARY, QUEEN OF SCOTS**

1972, 128 MINS, UK ◇

Dir Charles Jarrott   *Prod* Hal B. Wallis   *Scr* John Hale   *Ph* Christopher Challis   *Ed* Richard Marden   *Mus* John Barry   *Art Dir* Terry Marsh

● Vanessa Redgrave, Glenda Jackson, Patrick McGoohan, Timothy Dalton, Nigel Davenport, Trevor Howard (Universal)

A large cast of excellent players appears to good advantage under the direction of Charles Jarrott. Superior production details and the cast help overcome an episodic, rambling story.

Mary Stuart (Vanessa Redgrave) emerges as a romantic, immature but idealistic young woman. Her perilous position was repeatedly confounded by the machinations of half-brother (later King) James Stuart (played by Patrick McGoohan), the blunt but well-meant efforts of eventual husband and lover Lord Bothwell (Nigel Davenport), the paranoid homosexual, and bisexual inclinations of second husband Henry Darnley (Timothy Dalton), and the low-key, amiable clerical advisor, David Riccio (Ian Holm).

Elizabeth (Glenda Jackson) in contrast had a well-oiled machine of intrigue: advisor William Cecil (Trevor Howard), a power-hungry, lover Robert Dudley (Daniel Massey), and the corrupt cooperation of McGoohan and other Scottish factions.

The result of such a dramatic imbalance renders Redgrave's character that of a storm-tossed waif, while Jackson benefits from a far more well-defined character.

The face-to-face confrontations between the two women are said to be historically inaccurate. The script almost has to have one, and these brief climactic encounters are electric.

☐ 1971: Nominations: Best Actress (Vanessa Redgrave), Costume Design, Art Direction, Original Score, Sound

■ **MASH**

1970, 116 MINS, US ◇ ⊛ ⊙

Dir Robert Altman   *Prod* Ingo Preminger   *Scr* Ring Lardner Jr   *Ph* Harold E. Stine   *Ed* Danford B. Greene   *Mus* Johnny Mandel   *Art Dir* Jack Martin Smith, Arthur Lonergan

● Donald Sutherland, Elliott Gould, Tom Skerritt, Sally Kellerman, Jo Ann Pflug, Robert Duvall (20th Century-Fox/Aspen)

A Mobile Army Surgical Hospital (MASH), two minutes from bloody battles on the 38th Parallel of Korea, is an improbable setting for a comedy, even a stomach-churning, gory, often tasteless, but frequently funny black comedy [from the novel by Richard Hooker].

Elliott Gould, Donald Sutherland and Tom Skerritt head an extremely effective, low-keyed cast of players whose skillful subtlety eventually rescue an indecisive union of script and technique.

Gould is the totally unmilitary but arrogantly competent, supercool young battlefield surgeon, a reluctant draftee whose credo is let's get the job done and knock off all this Army muck.

The sardonic, cynical comments of the doctors and nurses patching and stitching battle-mangled bodies and casually amputating limbs before sending their anonymous patients out may be distasteful to some. It has the sharp look of reality when professionals become calloused from working 12 hours at a stretch to keep up with the stream of casualties from the battlefield.

☐ 1970: Best Adapted Screenplay.
☐ Nominations: Best Picture, Director, Supp. Actress (Sally Kellerman), Editing

● ●

■ **MASK**

1985, 120 MINS, US ◇ ⓥ ⊙
Dir Peter Bogdanovich *Prod* Martin Starger *Scr* Anna Hamilton Phelan *Ph* Laszlo Kovacs *Ed* Barbara Ford *Art Dir* Norman Newberry
● Cher, Sam Elliott, Eric Stoltz, Estelle Getty, Richard Dysart, Laura Dern (Universal)

Based on a true story, *Mask* is alive with the rhythms and textures of a unique life. Rocky Dennis (Eric Stoltz) is a 16-year-old afflicted with a rare bone disease which has ballooned his head to twice its normal size and cast the shadow of an early death over him.

Rocky is one of those rare individuals who has a vitality and gift for life and the emphasis here is not on dying, but living. The irony of the title is that his feelings are exposed far more than is customary and his experiences are intensified rather than dulled.

One of the accomplishments of *Mask* is the fullness of the environment it creates. Foremost in that portrait is Rocky's mother Rusty (Cher) and her motorcycle-gang friends.

Both in the background and foreground, *Mask* draws a vivid picture of life among a particular type of lower middle class Southern California whites.

Much of the credit for keeping the film from tripping over must go to the cast, especially Stoltz, who, with only his eyes visible behind an elaborate makeup job, brings a lively, life-affirming personality to his role without a trace of self-pity. Equally fine is Cher, who perfectly suggests a hard exterior covering a wealth of conflicting and confused feelings.

☐ 1985: Best Make-Up

● ●

■ **MASK OF DIMITRIOS, THE**

1944, 96 MINS, US
Dir Jean Negulesco *Prod* Henry Blanke *Scr* Frank Gruber *Ph* Arthur Edeson *Ed* Frederick Richards *Mus* Adolph Deutsch *Art Dir* Ted Smith
● Sydney Greenstreet, Zachary Scott, Faye Emerson, Peter Lorre, Victor Francen, George Tobias (Warner)

Backgrounded with international intrigues, *The Mask of Dimitrios* has an occasional element of suspense, but those moments are comparatively few.

Dimitrios, which traces the year-long inter-national criminal career of one Dimitrios Makropoulos (played by Zachary Scott), has the benefit of a good cast headed by Sydney Greenstreet and Peter Lorre, but it is mostly a conversational piece that too frequently suggests action in the dialog where, actually, the film itself practically has none.

Talky script [from the novel *A Coffin for Dimitrios* by Eric Ambler] slows the pace to a walk. Greenstreet and Lorre are capital as a criminal and mystery writer, respectively, while Scott gives a plausible performance as the titular character. The rest are mainly bits.

● ●

■ **MASK OF FU MANCHU, THE**

1932, 66 MINS, US
Dir Charles Brabin *Scr* Irene Kuhn, Edgar Allan Woolf, John Willard *Ph* Tony Gaudio *Ed* Ben Lewis *Art Dir* Cedric Gibbons
● Boris Karloff, Lewis Stone, Karen Morley, Charles Starrett, Myrna Loy, Jean Hersholt (M-G-M)

Fu Manchu's latest mission is discovery of the tomb of Genghis Khan. Possession of the mask and sword of Genghis would give Fu the leadership of the East. Then he could lead his subjects on to victory in the western world, with ultimate extermination of the white race which he fanatically despises.

Fu (Boris Karloff) has a daughter (Myrna Loy) who's not so pleasant herself. After pop is through torturing the best looking white men for his own purpose, daughter gets 'em for hers. She has the biggest boudoir couch this side of Peking, and pop doesn't object.

So that Fu doesn't get to the late Genghis' paraphernalia first, Scotland Yard dispatches a museum expedition to the spot. After that it's a contest over the tomb's contents. Just as Lewis Stone, as Inspector Nayland Smith of Scotland Yard, is about to be lowered into the cavernous mouths of a troupe of starving crocodiles he manages to escape.

Everybody is handicapped by the story and situations [from the story by Sax Rohmer]. It's strange how bad such troupers as Stone and Jean Hersholt can look when up against such an assignment as this.

● ●

■ **MASQUE OF THE RED DEATH, THE**

1964, 86 MINS, UK ◇ ⓥ
Dir Roger Corman *Prod* George Willoughby *Scr* Charles Beaumont, R. Wright Campbell *Ph* Nicolas Roeg *Ed* Ann Chegwidden *Mus* David Lee *Art Dir* Robert Jones
● Vincent Price, Hazel Court, Jane Asher, David Weston, Patrick Magee, Nigel Green (Anglo Amalgamated)

Roger Corman has garmented his film, lensed in England, with production values. His color camera work, his sets, music and plot unfoldment itself – if the latter is vague and a bit involved it still fits into the pattern intended – establish an appropriate mood for pic's tale of terror and in addition it's evident Corman doesn't take his subject [based on a story by Edgar Allan Poe] too seriously.

Vincent Price is the very essence of evil, albeit charming when need be, and as film progresses the dark workings of his mind are stressed, tortuously intent on evil as a follower of the Devil. He plays Prince Prospero, a tyrannical power in Spain in the Middle Ages, who seizes a young girl and tries to make her choose between his saving the life of her beloved or her father, even as the Red Death is killing off most of his impoverished serfs. A strange and uninvited guest to the Bacchanalian orgy he is staging for his noble guests stalks through the festivities to transform the Masque Ball into a Dance of Death.

● ●

■ **MASQUERADE**

1965, 102 MINS, UK ◇
Dir Basil Dearden *Scr* William Goldman, Michael Relph *Ph* Otto Heller *Ed* John Gutheridge *Mus* Philip Green
● Cliff Robertson, Jack Hawkins, Marisa Mell, Christopher Witty, Bill Fraser, Michel Piccoli (United Artists)

Michael Relph and Basil Dearden have had themselves a ball with *Masquerade*, for once forgetting the sociological themes which they often blend with their dramas, and turning out a clever, tongue-in-cheek spoof of the cloak-and-dagger yarns.

Relph and William Goldman have jettisoned much of the earnestness of the Victor Canning novel, *Castle Minerva*, retaining mainly the plotline and characters.

The story involves kidnapping, disguised identity, macabre doings in a travelling circus, a mysterious Spanish girl and escape from an eerie castle.

The British Foreign Office hires Jack Hawkins and Cliff Robertson for a daring mission. Hawkins is an ex-war colonel and hero. In this film, he obviously relishes being able to spoof the sort of stiff upper lip roles that so often he has to play seriously. Robertson is an American soldier of fortune who is down on his luck. Their job is to abduct the young heir to the throne of a Near East state and keep him under wraps for a few weeks until he comes of age and is able to sign a favourable oil concession to Britain.

● ●

■ **MASQUERADE**

1988, 91 MINS, US ◇ ⓥ ⊙
Dir Bob Swaim *Prod* Michael I. Levy *Scr* Dick Wolf *Ph* David Watkin *Ed* Scott Conrad *Mus* John Barry *Art Dir* John Kasarda
● Rob Lowe, Meg Tilly, Doug Savant, Kim Cattrall, John Glover, Dana Delany (M-G-M/Levy)

Masquerade, set in the Hamptons among the genteel with their weathered mansions and racing yachts, is like many poor-little-rich-girl stories; a beautiful backdrop and dreamy settings aren't enough to compensate for uninvolving characters caught in an unsuspenseful scheme.

Meg Tilly's womanizing, drunkard stepfather (John Glover) is in on a plot with Rob Lowe who, unbeknownst to her, is intent upon securing her hand in marriage so that he and his buddy will be set for life.

In the beginning, Lowe is a rake, the cocky captain of the racing boat *Obsession* while at the same time making it with the boat owner's much younger wife (Kim Cattrall). Tilly's just out of a Catholic women's college, innocent and apparently chaste.

It seems the Hamptons is not the bucolic haven it's cracked up to be. The police take their oath as peace officers to hearts that is, not upsetting the influential and wealthy community that pads the wallets for off-duty cops moonlighting at ritzy parties.

That leaves the snooping to an eager rookie (Doug Savant), seemingly wanting to protect the interests of Tilly, the girl he's always loved, as she takes the fall for a murder she didn't commit.

● ●

■ **MASSACRE IN ROME**

1973, 103 MINS, ITALY ◇ ⓥ
Dir George Pan Cosmatos *Prod* Carlo Ponti *Scr* Robert Katz, George Pan Cosmatos *Ph* Marcello Gatti *Ed* Francoise Bonnot, Roberto Silvi *Mus* Ennio Morricone *Art Dir* Arrigo Berschi
● Richard Burton, Marcello Mastroianni, Leo McKern, John Steiner, Delia Boccardo (Champion)

Massacre in Rome depends on its dramatic documentary flavor for a number of spellbinding sequences and its polemical shafts at Vatican

M

reticence in resisting the massacre of 300 Italian hostages in reprisal for a partisan assault on a German storm troop detachment in Rome.

The film generally hews close to the controversial book, *Death in Rome*, by Robert Katz. Screenplay veers from the facts as Katz originally researched and presented them, with minor fictional treatment in a few characters, but does not detract from the over-riding moral treatment involved in the wholesale slaughter of innocents, many of them Jews, in the Ardeatine Caves on the outskirts of Rome.

Richard Burton as Germany security forces commander Col Kappler gets a richer portrait than his superiors and subordinates.

....

■ **MASTER GUNFIGHTER, THE**

1975, 121 MINS, US ◇
Dir Frank Laughlin [= Tom Laughlin]   *Prod* Philip L. Parslow   *Scr* Harold Lapland   *Ph* Jack A. Marta   *Ed* William Reynolds, Danford Greene   *Mus* Lalo Schifrin   *Art Dir* Albert Brenner
● Tom Laughlin, Ron O'Neal, Lincoln Kilpatrick, GeoAnn Sosa, Barbara Carrera, Victor Campos (Billy Jack)

A curious blend of amateurish plotting and slick production values, Tom Laughlin's *The Master Gunfighter* also presents an ambiguous moral attitude toward the old West. The oater, attractively lensed on northern California locations, alternates sermonizing with gunfights and sword fights.

The Laughlin character talks like a liberal but behaves like a reactionary, and therein lies the confusion. It's a throwback to an earlier age of swashbuckling, but the blend with contemporary bleeding heart attitudes makes the film seem hypocritical.

Action fans will find a good quota of kicks if they can sit through the turgid passages.

Ron O'Neal is Laughlin's chief antagonist, but doesn't arouse much interest as a character. In the lead femme roles, GeoAnn Sosa is spunky and charming, but Barbara Carrera betrays her fashion model background with her blank beauty.

Laughlin's wife Delores Taylor, gets exec producer credit, and their nine-year-old son Frank Laughlin is billed as director.

....

■ **MASTER OF THE ISLANDS**
See: The Hawaiians

....

■ **MASTER RACE, THE**

1944, 94 MINS, US ▼
Dir Herbert J. Biberman   *Prod* Robert S. Golden   *Scr* Herbert J. Biberman, Anne Froelick, Rowland Leigh   *Ph* Russell Metty   *Ed* Ernie Leadlay   *Mus* Roy Webb   *Art Dir* Albert S. D'Agostino, Jack Okey
● George Coulouris, Osa Massen, Stanley Ridges, Lloyd Bridges, Nancy Gates, Morris Carnovsky (RKO)

Eddie Golden originally selected the title as a likely one for a picture, and then searched for a yarn to pin it to in order to dramatically show the arrogance and synthetic character of the barbaric Nazis. He selected a period when the German armies were fleeing in disorder, and the final unconditional surrender of the Nazi minions.

Picture opens with clips of the D-Day invasion of June 6 for brief footage, and then swings to headquarters of George Coulouris, member of the German general staff, where he tells assemblage of German officers that the war is lost and they are to proceed according to individual instructions to points designated to create dissension among the peoples of the liberated countries to further destroy Europe so that the self-styled master race can again rise to rule the continent.

....

■ **MASTERS OF THE UNIVERSE**

1987, 106 MINS, US ◇ ▼ ⊙
Dir Gary Goddard   *Prod* Menahem Golan, Yoram Globus   *Scr* David Odell   *Ph* Hanania Baer   *Ed* Anne V. Coates   *Mus* Bill Conti   *Art Dir* William Stout
● Dolph Lundgren, Frank Langella, Meg Foster, Billy Barty, Courteney Cox, Chelsea Field (Cannon)

All elements are of epic proportions in this *Conan–Star Wars* hybrid ripoff, based on the best-selling line of children's toys. Epitome of Good takes on Epitome of Evil for nothing less than the future of the Universe, and the result is a colossal bore.

Dolph Lundgren's He-Man is an impressive physical specimen, the ultimate warrior epitomizing all that is good and defending the honor of inhabitants of the planet Eternia. On the dark side is the hideously made up Frank Langella, as Skeletor. He has captured the Sorceress of Greyskull Castle (Christina Pickles), locking her in a tubular energy field and absorbing her power, which evidently comes from Eternia's moonbeams.

Turns out the battle to control the future of universal power takes place at a used music store in a small town in California. He-Man and his allies are searching for a cosmic key that will unlock the Sorceress from her nasty gravity field. Key is discovered by Julie Winston (Courteney Cox, she of Bruce Springsteen's *Dancing in the Dark* video fame) and her musician boyfriend, Kevin (Robert Duncan McNeil).

Makeup and costuming is universally good, special effects uninspiring.

....

■ **MATA HARI**

1931, 90 MINS, US ▼
Dir George Fitzmaurice   *Prod* [uncredited]   *Scr* Benjamin Glazer, Leo Birinski, Doris Anderson, Gilbert Emery   *Ph* William Daniels   *Ed* Frank Sullivan   *Mus* [uncredited]   *Art Dir* Cedric Gibbons
● Greta Garbo, Ramon Novarro, Lionel Barrymore, Lewis Stone, C. Henry Gordon, Karen Morley (M-G-M)

Greta Garbo, Ramon Novarro, Lionel Barrymore and Lewis Stone – the Metro Tragedy Four – dominate the whole affair, making the picture, as a picture, very secondary.

It needs its cast names at all times, being a yarn which can't stand up for long on its own gams. Though Garbo is sexy and hot in a less subtle way this time, and though the plot goes about as far as it can in situation warmth, the story presents nothing sensational. Its few attempts at power are old style and all have been used before in similar trite spy stories.

Garbo does a polite cooch to Oriental music as a starter and in the same number makes a symbolic play for a huge idol, with the hips in motion all the while. The finish is a neatly masked strip with Greta's back to the lens.

Two other torrid moments later in the running are given to Garbo and Novarro. Both times they turn out the lights.

Mata Hari's method for grabbing enemy info, if this scenario is authentic, was to get 'em in the bedroom and keep 'em interested, while an assistant operative snatches the papers.

Barrymore and Stone are playing what, for them, are minor parts. Barrymore, as a broken general who loses his honor and finally his life through the glamorous Mata Hari, succeeds in inserting a punch in his moments of despair. But Stone is under wraps with a semi-villainous assignment that doesn't warrant his ability.

....

■ **MATCHMAKER, THE**

1958, 100 MINS, US ▼ ⊙
Dir Joseph Anthony   *Prod* Don Hartman   *Scr* John Michael Hayes   *Ph* Charles Lang Jr   *Ed* Howard Smith   *Mus* Adolph Deutsch   *Art Dir* Hal Pereira, Roland Anderson

● Shirley Booth, Anthony Perkins, Shirley MacLaine, Paul Ford, Robert Morse, Wallace Ford (Paramount)

Based on the Thornton Wilder Broadway hit, Shirley Booth takes the Ruth Gordon stage role of 'marriage counsellor', dominating character in this yarn of 1884. Its period unfoldment permits added opportunity for laughs, some of the belly genre. The Yonkers screenplay catches every nuance of the situation of the widowed Booth ostensibly seeking a wife for the grasping Yonkers merchant (Paul Ford) while adroitly plotting to capture him for her own. Use of 'asides' by various principals, speaking directly into the camera, peppers the action.

Most of the story unreels in New York, where Ford goes from nearby Yonkers to propose to Shirley MacLaine, a man-hungry milliner, and to meet a sexpot promised by Booth, who against his will has taken over Ford's romantic interests. Following Ford are the two over-worked clerks in his general store (Anthony Perkins and Robert Morse) who pool their resources and determine to live it up in the big city, with 10 bucks between them.

Booth is no less than superb in her role, draining part of comedic possibilities. Perkins' switch to farce is also a bright experience. Ford is immense as the romantically-inclined but tight small-towner, and MacLaine is pert and lovely. Morse, from the original Broadway cast, amusingly enacts Perkins' pardner.

....

■ **MATEWAN**

1987, 130 MINS, US ◇ ▼ ⊙
Dir John Sayles   *Prod* Peggy Rajski, Maggie Renzi   *Scr* John Sayles   *Ph* Haskell Wexler   *Ed* Sonya Polonsky   *Mus* Mason Daring   *Art Dir* Nora Chavooshian
● Chris Cooper, Will Oldham, Mary McDonnell, Bob Gunton, James Earl Jones, Kevin Tighe (Cinecom/Film Gallery/Red Dog)

Matewan is a heartfelt, straight-ahead tale of labor organizing in the coal mines of West Virginia in 1920 that runs its course like a train coming down the track.

Among the memorable characters is Joe Kenehan (Chris Cooper), a young union organizer who comes to Matewan to buck the bosses. With his strong face and Harrison Ford good-looks, Cooper gives the film its heartbeat.

Of the townfolk, 16-year-old Danny (Will Oldham) is already a righteous preacher and a seasoned union man who passionately takes up the working man's struggle. Director John Sayles adds some texture to the mix by throwing in Italian immigrants and black migrant workers who become converted to the union side.

Most notable of the black workers is 'Few Clothes' Johnson (James Earl Jones), a burly good-natured man with a powerful presence and a quick smile. Jones' performance practically glows in the dark. Also a standout is Sayles veteran David Strathairn as the sheriff with quiet integrity who puts his life on the line.
□ 1987: Nomination: Best Cinematography

....

■ **MATINEE**

1993, 99 MINS, US ◇ ▼ ⊙
Dir Joe Dante   *Prod* Michael Finnell   *Scr* Charlie Haas   *Ph* John Hora   *Ed* Marshall Harvey   *Mus* Jerry Goldsmith   *Art Dir* Steven Legler
● John Goodman, Cathy Moriarty, Simon Fenton, Omri Katz, Lisa Jakub, Kellie Martin (Universal/Renfield)

Joe Dante lovingly re-creates the monster pics of his youth in *Matinee*, an okay film geared toward buffs that should have been much better.

Matinee derives from a high concept (credited to Jerico and scripter Charlie Haas) in which the real-life fears of the 1962 Cuban missile crisis interact with the artificial fears of a horror film premiering at a Key West movie house.

Believably cast as a huckster/showman modeled after producer-director William Castle, John Goodman is previewing his new monster pic *Mant!* (Half Man, Half Ant, All Terror!) in hopes of impressing exhibitor Jesse White to book it at his 50-theater chain.

Film-in-a-film is a very accurate, hilarious black & white pastiche featuring (uncredited) genre vets Kevin McCarthy, Robert Cornthwaite (of the original *The Thing*) and William Shallert opposite Goodman's girlfriend Cathy Moriarty. Yet Dante lets his own film lapse into the excruciating cliches of both the 'good teen' romances and the j.d. sagas of the '50s.

Even when the film gets bogged down in romantic drivel, there are enough clever in-jokes and well-remembered period details to keep buffs happy. Casting is accurate.

■ **MATING GAME, THE**

1959, 97 MINS, US ◇

Dir George Marshall   *Prod* Philip Barry Jr   *Scr* William Roberts   *Ph* Robert Bronner   *Ed* John McSweeney Jr   *Mus* Jeff Alexander
● Debbie Reynolds, Tony Randall, Paul Douglas, Fred Clark, Una Merkel, Philip Ober (M-G-M)

Figure a combination of *You Can't Take It with You* and elements of *Tobacco Road*, and it is a pretty fair indication of what *The Mating Game* is about and how the jokes are played. This romantic farce is as broad as its CinemaScope projection.

The production is based on H. E. Bates' English novel, The Darling Buds of May, a light, farcical tilt at the welfare state in Britain. Adapted for the screen, it becomes an American situation chiefly involving free enterprise versus the internal revenue department.

Tony Randall plays a tax agent assigned to investigate the Maryland farm family headed by Paul Douglas and Una Merkel. Douglas gets Randall predictably drunk, and Randall is predictably smitten with one of the Douglas-Merkel offspring, hoydenish Debbie Reynolds. She is a toothsome child of nature who is taking care of the mating of the farm stock when she isn't wrestling in the hay with some of the livelier neighbor boys.

Most of this is foreseeable farce, and much of it is done with allusions to sex, regarding both humans and animals. Reynolds is very good. Randall, somewhat uncomfortable as a straight actor, is brilliant in his comedy scenes, particularly an athletic drunk sequence and its aftermath.

■ **MATING SEASON, THE**

1951, 101 MINS, US

Dir Mitchell Leisen   *Prod* Charles Brackett   *Scr* Charles Brackett, Walter Reisch, Richard Breen   *Ph* Charles B. Lang Jr.   *Ed* Frank Bracht   *Mus* Joseph J. Lilley   *Art Dir* Hal Pereira, Roland Anderson
● Gene Tierney, John Lund, Miriam Hopkins, Thelma Ritter, Jan Sterling, Larry Keating (Paramount)

Nominal stars of the piece [suggested by a play by Caesar Dunn] are Gene Tierney and John Lund, but it is Thelma Ritter who glitters the brightest, having been given the pivotal character and choicest lines.

Bolstering the comedy considerably is the fact laughs are not based on situations that are too far-fetched, even though a plot springboard that finds a mother-in-law taking a maid's job in the home of her new daughter would seem to come under that heading. Scripters make it all seem perfectly logical, and the playing and direction strengthen that effect.

Lund, a factory clerk, ties up with Tierney, world traveler and intimate of diplomatic personages, in a love-at-first-sight marriage. Ritter, Lund's mother and a hamburger stand operator, hitchhikes to visit the new bride and groom but is taken for a domestic being sent to help out at the newlyweds' first party. She goes along with the situation and then decides to continue it over the opposition of Lund. Things are working fine until Miriam Hopkins, mother of Tierney, moves in.

☐ 1951: Nomination: Best Supp. Actress (Thelma Ritter)

■ **MATTER OF INNOCENCE, A**
See: Pretty Polly

■ **MATTER OF LIFE AND DEATH, A**
(US: Stairway to Heaven)

1946, 104 MINS, UK ◇

Dir Michael Powell, Emeric Pressburger   *Prod* Michael Powell, Emeric Pressburger   *Scr* Michael Powell, Emeric Pressburger   *Ph* Jack Cardiff   *Ed* Reginald Mills   *Mus* Allan Gray   *Art Dir* Alfred Junge
● David Niven, Kim Hunter, Marius Goring, Roger Livesey, Raymond Massey, Richard Attenborough (Archers)

Like other Powell-Pressburger pictures, the striving to appear intellectual is much too apparent. Less desire to exhibit alleged learning, and more humanity would have resulted in a more popular offering.

For the first 10 minutes, apart from some pretentious poppycock, the picture looks like living up to its boosting. This is real cinema, then action gives way to talk, some of it flat and dreary. Story is set in this world (graced with Technicolor), and the Other World (relegated to dye monochrome) as it exists in the mind of an airman whose imagination has been affected by concussion.

Returning from a bomber expedition, Squadron-Leader David Niven is shot up. Last of the crew, minus a parachute, and believing the end is inevitable, before bailing out talks poetry and love over the radio to Kim Hunter, American WAC on nearby air station. Miraculously Niven falls into the sea, is washed ashore apparently unhurt, and by strange coincidence meets Kim. They fall desperately in love.

Meanwhile in the Other World there's much bother. Owing to delinquency of Heavenly Conductor Marius Goring, Niven has failed to check in, and Goring is despatched to this world to persuade Niven to take his rightful place and balance the heavenly books.

Obviously experimental in many respects, the designs for the Other World are a matter of taste, but with all their ingenuity Powell, Pressburger, and Alfred Junge could only invent a heaven reminiscent of the Hollywood Bowl and an exclusive celestial night club where hostesses dish out wings to dead pilots.

■ **MAURICE**

1987, 140 MINS, UK ◇ ⑫ ⊙

Dir James Ivory   *Prod* Ismail Merchant   *Scr* Kit Hesketh-Harvey, James Ivory   *Ph* Pierre Lhomme   *Ed* Katherine Wenning   *Mus* Richard Robbins   *Art Dir* Brian Ackland-Snow
● James Wilby, Hugh Grant, Rupert Graves, Denholm Elliott, Simon Callow, Billie Whitelaw (Merchant-Ivory)

Maurice, based on a posthumously published novel by E.M. Forster, is a well-crafted pic on the theme of homosexuality. Penned in 1914 but not allowed to be published until 1971 (a year after Forster's death) because of its subject matter, *Maurice* is not ranked among Forster's best work. Key opening scene has Maurice as a schoolboy on a beach-side outing being lectured by his teacher (Simon Callow),

in comically fastidious fashion, on the changes that will soon occur in his body with the onset of puberty.

Maurice Hall (James Wilby) is next seen grown up and attending Cambridge where, he meets handsome Clive Durham (Hugh Grant). Durham falls in love with him and though resisting at first Maurice later reciprocates, all on a platonic level.

Durham, under pressure from his mother (Judy Parfitt), gets married to a naive girl (Phoebe Nicholls) while Maurice finally physically consummates his homosexual inclination with Durham's young game-keeper Alec Scudder (Rupert Graves).

Wilby as Maurice gives a workmanlike performance, adequate to the role but never soaring. He is far outshadowed by a superlative supporting cast.

☐ 1987: Nomination: Best Costume Design

■ **MAUSOLEUM**

1983, 96 MINS, US ◇ ⑫

Dir Michael Dugan   *Prod* Robert Madero, Robert Barich   *Scr* Robert Barich, Robert Madero   *Ph* Robert Barich   *Ed* Richard C. Bock   *Mus* Jaime Mendoza-Nava   *Art Dir* Robert Burns
● Marjoe Gortner, Bobbie Bresee, Norman Burton, Maurice Sherbanee, La Wanda Page, Laura Hippe (Western International)

Mausoleum is an engaging minor film concerning demonic possession, presenting variations on *The Exorcist* format. Not the stab 'n' slab genre picture one might infer from its title, film should please aficiandos of old-fashioned B-horror films.

Bobbie Bresee toplines as Susan Farrell, a 30-year-old woman who has been possessed by a demon at age 10 after strolling into the family mausoleum, carrying on a centuries-old family curse affecting the first-born. Twenty years after, the demon has finally taken over, going on a killing spree that arouses the suspicions of her husband Oliver (Marjoe Gortner). Friend and psychiatrist Dr Andrews (Norman Burton) is enlisted to help Susan and ultimately bests the demon.

Bresee is extremely seductive here in the femme fatale role, complete with stock victims such as the shady gardener, unwary delivery boy, etc.

■ **MAX DUGAN RETURNS**

1983, 98 MINS, US ◇ ⑫ ⊙

Dir Herbert Ross   *Prod* Herbert Ross, Neil Simon   *Scr* Neil Simon   *Ph* David M. Walsh   *Ed* Richard Marks   *Mus* David Shire   *Art Dir* Albert Brenner
● Marsha Mason, Jason Robards, Donald Sutherland, Matthew Broderick, Dody Goodman, Sal Viscuso (20th Century-Fox)

Max Dugan Returns is a consistently happy comedic fable which should please romanticists drawn to a teaming of Neil Simon, Marsha Mason and Herbert Ross. Once more, Simon's pen turns to the problems of parental relationships especially reunion after long estrangement but largely leaves aside any heavy emotional involvement or rapid fire comedy.

Struggling to raise a 15-year-old son (Matthew Broderick) on a meagre teacher's salary, widow Mason maintains a wonderful attitude as her refrigerator breaks, her old car barely runs but gets stolen to boot, and life generally never quite works. Broderick is a good kid who accepts her poor-but-honest morality very well. In addition, there's a budding romance with Donald Sutherland, an exceptionally intelligent detective who's investigating the theft of her car.

Out of a dark night, however, returns Max Dugan (Jason Robards), the father who abandoned Mason when she was nine years old. Dying of a heart ailment, Robards is carrying

490

a satchel full of remorse and a suitcase crammed with cash left over from a checkered career in Las Vegas.

• •

■ **MAXIE**

1985, 90 MINS, US ◊ ⊛ ⊙
Dir Paul Aaron *Prod* Carter De Haven *Scr* Patricia Resnick *Ph* Fred Schuler *Ed* Lynzee Klingman *Mus* Georges Delerue *Art Dir* John Lloyd
● Glenn Close, Mandy Patinkin, Ruth Gordon, Barnard Hughes, Valerie Curtin, Googy Gress (Orion/Aurora)

As forgettable as it is well-meaning, *Maxie* represents a stab at an old-fashioned sort of romantic fantasy, as well as first chance at a full-blown starring role for Glenn Close. A concoction like this needs lots of fizz, but the bubbly here has gone mostly flat, and what's left evaporates quickly.

Much of the credit for keeping it alive at all must go to Mandy Patinkin, who shows himself to be a good-looking leading man with a rare light touch for romantic comedy.

Based on the novel *Marion's Wall* by Jack Finney, *Maxie* tells the story of a dead person returning to inhabit the body of a living soul. Such is what happens to Close, the normal, cheerful wife of book specialist Patinkin. When he uncovers a message on the wall from a certain 'Maxie' who lived in the 1920s, Patinkin becomes quite taken with the jazz age flapper who bore a striking resemblance to his wife.

She has some very good comic moments, but Close may be too down-to-earth an actress for foolishness of this kind. The late Ruth Gordon, in her last film role, contributes another of her patented nutty neighbor turns.

• •

■ **MAXIMUM OVERDRIVE**

1986, 97 MINS, US ◊ ⊛ ⊙
Dir Stephen King *Prod* Martha Schumacher *Scr* Stephen King *Ph* Armando Nannuzzi *Ed* Evan Lottman *Mus* AC/DC *Art Dir* Giorgio Postiglione
● Emilio Estevez, Pat Hingle, Laura Harrington, Yeardley Smith, John Short, Ellen McElduff (De Laurentiis)

Master manipulator Stephen King, making his directoral debut from his own script, fails to create a convincing enough environment to make the kind of nonsense he's offering here believable or fun.

King starts out with a small-town idyll soon disrupted by a mindless revolt of trucks. He collects a typical mix of rednecks, good old boys, restless youth, drifters and the decent folk in a small corner of North Carolina where they hole up at a truck stop as the trucks stampede.

Truck stop is run as if it were a feudal fiefdom, complete with arsenal, by redneck despot Pat Hingle who gives an amusing performance as a true screen swine. Also on hand is Emilio Estevez as a cook in bondage to Hingle by virtue of his probation from the pen, but he's gone to college and is really a good kid.

• •

■ **MAYERLING**

1968, 140 MINS, UK/FRANCE ◊ ⊛
Dir Terence Young *Prod* Robert Dorfman *Scr* Terence Young, Denis Cannan *Ph* Henri Alekan *Ed* Benedik Rayner *Mus* Francis Lai *Art Dir* Georges Wakhevitch
● Omar Sharif, Catherine Deneuve, James Mason, Ava Gardner, James Robertson Justice, Genevieve Page (Winchester/Corona)

Film misfires through a flattish script and uninspired performances by two leads, Omar Sharif and Catherine Deneuve. Director Terence Young has used two novels (*Mayerling* and *The Archduke* by Michael Arnold) and much historical background research as the basis for his theory on how

Crown Prince Rudolf of Austria and his young baroness mistress met their deaths in the Royal Hunting Lodge at Mayerling in the late 19th century.

The screenplay rarely touches any heights of romantic ecstasy. The political background the always shaky Austrian throne, the students' violent protests, court intrigue is introduced promisingly at the beginning, but later gets swamped in the romantic story which is protracted, humorless, often hesitant and plodding.

Sharif shows fire as the arrogant, ambitious son of Emperor Franz-Josef, torn between a desire to get things moving on a new progressive scale, and his loyalty to Habsburg tradition.

His romance with Catherine Deneuve is a singularly flat and prosaic affair. Deneuve's performance is too demure. Ava Gardner makes an impact throughout.

• •

■ **MAYTIME**

1937, 132 MINS, US ◊ ⊛
Dir Robert Z. Leonard *Prod* Hunt Stromberg *Scr* Noel Langley *Ph* Oliver T. Marsh *Ed* Conrad A. Nervig *Mus* Herbert Stothart (dir.) *Art Dir* Cedric Gibbons
● Jeanette MacDonald, Nelson Eddy, John Barrymore, Herman Bing, Tom Brown, Lynne Carver (M-G-M)

Maytime has so many fine qualities that its length, occasional lapses into the superfluous and betimes dull interludes will be acceptable.

The vocal piece-de-resistance, of course, is the Sigmund Romberg waltz ballad, 'Will You Remember?' perhaps better known as 'Sweetheart, Sweetheart.' This has been artfully backgrounded throughout the extended running time by Herbert Stothart.

The stars, Jeanette MacDonald and Nelson Eddy, are splendid in their vocal assignments. it's chiefly MacDonald's picture. She looks her best in the Napoleonic period costumes, and is charming in her make-up as the venerable old lady, with a slightly mysterious past, who finally opens up as she counsels the petulant Lynne Carver and Tom Brown on the wisdom of forsaking a career in favor of romance. Eddy carries through the worthy impression made by this pair in their past operetta successes. His robust baritone again nicely balances MacDonald's soprano.

Histrionically there is also John Barrymore in a fat supporting assignment as a somewhat dour mentor of the ambitious prima donna.

The 'Huguenots' operatic sequence (Meyerbeer, scored by Stothart) is one of the major vocal highlights. 'Czaritza' is the original Stothart adaptation from Tchaikovsky's Fifth Symphony into a new Russian opera, libretto by Bob Wright and Chet Forrest. This is the major operatic interlude and MacDonald, Eddy and the Don Cossacks make the most of it, singing the French lyrics by Gilles Guilbert.

The light brown sepia tinging, which Metro used in *Good Earth* (1936), is utilized in certain sequences, notably in the St Cloud carnival scene and the 'Maytime' – 'Will You Remember?' waltz finale.
☐ 1937: Nominations: Best Score, Sound

• •

■ **MCBAIN**

1991, 102 MINS, US ◊ ⊛ ⊙
Dir James Glickenhaus *Prod* J. Boyce Harman Jr *Scr* James Glickenhaus *Ph* Robert M. Baldwin Jr *Ed* Jeffrey Wolf *Mus* Christopher Franke *Art Dir* Charles C. Bennett
● Christopher Walken, Maria Conchita Alonso, Michael Ironside, Steve James, Jay Patterson, T.G. Waites (Shapiro Glickenhaus)

Boasting excellent production values, *McBain* is a silly action film that has the elements of an A-grade picture but fails to create an en-

grossing or believable narrative. Pic becomes a spoof of itself and the genre early on and never recovers.

Prolog has Chick Vennera and fellow soldiers rescuing POW Christopher Walken on the day the Vietnam War ended in 1973, so Walken owes him one. When Vennera is killed in an abortive coup of the Colombian government 18 years later, Walken agrees to help Vennera's sister (Maria Conchita Alonso) overthrow the drug cartel-run dictatorship there and let the common people come to power.

Cartoonish action is amusing but never gripping. Walken appears awkward and bored with a stiff-upper-lip assignment more suited to director James Glickenhaus' 1980 *Exterminator* leading man Robert Ginty. The extreme earnestness of Alonso as the freedom fighter is overdone. There is no romance in the pic and zero chemistry between the two leads, a glaring deficiency. Filming in the Philippines instead of South America results in Filipino extras who definitely don't look authentic.

• •

■ **MCCABE AND MRS. MILLER**

1971, 121 MINS, US ◊ ⊛ ⊙
Dir Robert Altman *Prod* David Foster, Mitchell Brower *Scr* Robert Altman, Brian McKay *Ph* Vilmos Zsigmond *Ed* Louis Lombardo *Mus* Leonard Cohen *Art Dir* Leon Ericksen
● Warren Beatty, Julie Christie, Rene Auberjonois, William Devane, Shelley Duvall, Keith Carradine (Warner)

Robert Altman's *McCabe and Mrs. Miller* is a disappointing mixture. A period story about a small northwest mountain village where stars Warren Beatty and Julie Christie run the bordello, the production suffers from overlength; also a serious effort at moody photography which backfires into pretentiousness; plus a diffused comedy-drama plot line which is repeatedly shoved aside in favor of bawdiness.

Edmund Naughton's novel, *McCabe*, was shot around Vancouver under the title, *The Presbyterian Church Wager*, named for a fictional town. Rene Auberjonois is top-featured as a saloon-bordello owner whose monopoly on fun and games is broken by roving gambler Beatty. Christie becomes Beatty's partner in the flourishing enterprise.

Beatty seems either miscast or misdirected. His own youthful looks cannot be concealed by a beard, make-up, a grunting voice and jerky physical movements; the effect resembles a high-school thesp playing Rip Van Winkle. Christie on the other hand is excellent.
☐ 1971: Nomination: Best Actress (Julie Christie)

• •

■ **MCGUIRE, GO HOME!**
See: The High Bright Sun

• •

■ **MCHALE'S NAVY**

1964, 93 MINS, US ◊
Dir Edward J. Montagne *Prod* Edward J. Montagne *Scr* Frank Gill Jr, G. Carleton Brown *Ph* William Margulies *Ed* Sam E. Waxman *Mus* Jerry Fielding *Art Dir* Russell Kimball, Alexander Golitzen
● Ernest Borgnine, Joe Flynn, Tim Conway, Carl Ballantine, George Kennedy (Universal)

One wonders how America won the war in the Pacific, if the exploits of Lt Cmdr Quinton McHale and his PT-boat crew were typical of that dark period in US history. But then, *McHale's Navy*, a full-length feature version of Revue's successful telepix series, doesn't attempt to prove any point.

Edward J. Montagne, producer and sometimes-director of the vidpix, handles both chores in this longer color rendition and pulls out all the stops.

Like its original TV counterpart, action here depends upon outlandish situations in which McHale and his crew, who do things the 'McHale' way first and the Navy's way second, get involved. In the present case, it's getting out of debt, first for getting themselves deeply in the red by restaging Australian horse race results for excitement-hungry Marines from week-old-but-track-fresh news sheets flown in, and again for dock damages inflicted by their runaway PT-boat.

Where pic is longest on yocks is the clowning of Joe Flynn, as Capt Wallace Binghampton and McHale's immediate superior, and Tim Conway's hamming – there's no other word – as McHale's own exec and as naive a gent as ever fell down a ship's ladder.

● ●

■ MCKENZIE BREAK, THE

1970, 106 MINS, US ◇ ⑰

Dir Lamont Johnson *Prod* Jules Levy, Arthur Gardner, Arnold Laven *Scr* William Norton, Brian McKay *Ph* Michael Reed *Ed* Tom Rolf *Mus* Riz Ortolani *Art Dir* Leon Ericksen

● Brian Keith, Helmut Griem, Ian Hendry, Patrick O'Connell, Caroline Mortimer, Horst Janson (United Artists)

The McKenzie Break is a taut, classically crafted World War II POW escape drama with an original twist. This time it is the Germans, a corps of crack U-boat officers, led by Helmut Griem, breaking out of a camp in Scotland.

An imaginative, intelligent script (from a novel by Sidney Shelley), crackling direction by Lamont Johnson, and strong, three-dimension portrayals by Griem and Brian Keith, as a British intelligence officer trying to out-guess and out-maneuver the Nazi, transform the film into a tense personal duel that maintains its suspense until the final frames.

Griem is hardly the stereotype brutal Nazi, but nevertheless he is a model Hitler youth risen to young U-boat captain. He runs the prison like a youth camp, keeping his British captors aat bay with riots and demonstrations planned to the split second. It is all a coverup, and training, for the escape.

● ●

■ MCLINTOCK!

1963, 127 MINS, US ◇

Dir Andrew V. McLaglen *Prod* Michael Wayne *Scr* James Edward Grant *Ph* William H. Clothier *Ed* Otho Lovering *Mus* Frank DeVol *Art Dir* Hal Pereira, Eddie Imazu

● John Wayne, Maureen O'Hara, Yvonne De Carlo, Patrick Wayne, Stefanie Powers (Batjac/United Artists)

McLintock!, most of all, is a John Wayne western. The style of the production is forked-tongue-in-cheek. Nucleus of yarn is the marital duel between Wayne, straight-shooting, rough-and-tumble, high-living, hard-drinking cattle baron whose town has been named after him, and Maureen O'Hara, who has more reservations than a Comanche real estate agent.

Wayne is in his element, or home, home on the Waynge. O'Hara gives her customary high-spirited performance, although it's never quite clear what she's so darned sore about. Yvonne De Carlo is attractive as Wayne's cook, Stefanie Powers likewise as his college educated daughter. Vying for the latter's affection are Patrick Wayne, who etches a likable characterization, and Jerry Van Dyke, who gives a skillfully oafish performance.

● ●

■ MCQ

1974, 115 MINS, US ◇ ⑰ ⊙

Dir John Sturges *Prod* Jules Levy, Arthur Gardner *Scr* Lawrence Roman *Ph* Harry Stradling Jr *Ed* William Ziegler *Mus* Elmer Bernstein

Art Dir Walter Simonds

● John Wayne, Eddie Albert, Diana Muldaur, Colleen Dewhurst, Clu Gulager, Al Lettieri (Batjac/Warner)

McQ is a good contemporary crime actioner filmed entirely in Seattle, with John Wayne discovering that his slain buddy was a member of a crooked police ring stealing dope evidence.

Featured as an aging bar waitress from whom Wayne obtains evidence, Colleen Dewhurst is outstanding in her two scenes.

McQ attracts and sustains continued interest from the opening frames, where William Bryant, after shooting two policemen, is himself revealed as one, just before being killed. Eddie Albert, as Wayne's superior, makes the usual knee-jerk response (arrest radical hippies) while Wayne suspects big time dope dealer Al Lettieri.

● ●

■ MCVICAR

1980, 111 MINS, UK ◇ ⑰ ⊙

Dir Tom Clegg *Prod* David Gideon Thomson, Jackie Curbishley *Scr* John McVicar, Tom Clegg *Ph* Vernon Layton *Ed* Peter Boyle *Mus* Jeff Wayne *Art Dir* Brian Ackland-Snow

● Roger Daltrey, Adam Faith, Cheryl Campbell, Steven Berkoff, Brian Hall, Ian Hendry (Curbishley-Baird/The Who)

Feature is a conscientious reconstruction of several crucial months in the life of John McVicar, who escaped from the high-security wing of an English prison where he was serving eight years for robbery with violence.

McVicar is the author of the book *McVicar by Himself*, which was used as the basis of the film.

Roger Daltrey projects a disquieting mix of danger and vulnerability. Moreover, his characterization goes a long way towards supplying the sense of a mind at work behind the uncompromising, bony face and the thuggish look in the eyes.

Tom Clegg's firm direction is unflamboyant. Although much of the drama certainly doesn't call for obtrusive style, there are moments when more panache would not have come amiss.

There's an excellent, humorous performance by Adam Faith as Probyn, and a chillingly manic one by Steven Berkoff, in a role modelled on an actual inmate.

● ●

■ ME AND MY GAL

1942, 94 MINS, US

Dir Busby Berkeley *Prod* Arthur Freed *Scr* Richard Sherman, Fred Fincklehoffe, Sid Silvers *Ph* William Daniels *Ed* Ben Lewis *Mus* George Stoll (dir)

● Judy Garland, George Murphy, Gene Kelly, Richard Quine, Horace McNally (M-G-M)

Story of vaudeville troupers before and during the First World War [from an original story by Howard Emmett Rogers] is obvious, naive and sentimental. It's also genuine and affectionate and lively.

Picture's title, of course, is taken from one of the song numbers, the oldie 'For Me and My Gal'. The tune that brings Judy Garland and Gene Kelly together, first as vaudeville team and ultimately as a romance, it gets a sock presentation in a song-and-dance routine by them and is used thereafter as a theme.

Garland is a knockout as the warm-hearted young song-and-dance girl, selling a number of the songs persuasively, getting by neatly in the hoofing routines with Kelly, and giving a tender, affecting dramatic performance. Kelly gives a vividly drawn portrayal of the song-and-dance man and imperfect hero.

● ●

■ MEAN MACHINE, THE

See: The Longest Yard

■ MEAN SEASON, THE

1985, 103 MINS, US ◇ ⑰ ⊙

Dir Phillip Borsos *Prod* David Foster, Larry Turman *Scr* Leon Piedmont *Ph* Frank Tidy *Ed* Duwayne Dunham *Mus* Lalo Schifrin *Art Dir* Philip Jefferies

● Kurt Russell, Mariel Hemingway, Richard Jordan, Richard Masur, Joe Pantoliano, Richard Bradford (Orion)

Based on the novel, *In the Heat of the Summer*, by former *Miami Herald* crime reporter John Katzenbach, pic establishes solid Florida heat and humidity as the 'mean' background to a series of murders that perversely link together the killer (Richard Jordan), and a Miami police reporter (Kurt Russell) who becomes the psychopath's personal spokesman.

Jordan is at his shrewdly crazed best, anchoring the movie with a felt terror, initially just through his off-screen voice as he manipulates the reporter over the phone and ultimately through his cunning.

Russell plays a reporter (production used the city room of the *Miami Herald*) who, credibly enough, gets swept away with all the national hype he's getting as the only man who can talk to the killer.

His live-in elementary school teacher, g.f., essayed rather uneventfully by Mariel Hemingway, grows outraged as the reporter succumbs to his own ego, to the killer's tantalizing calls, and to his increased stature as newsmaker.

● ●

■ MEAN STREETS

1973, 110 MINS, US ◇ ⑰ ⊙

Dir Martin Scorsese *Prod* Jonathan T. Taplin *Scr* Martin Scorsese, Mardik Martin *Ph* Kent Wakeford *Ed* Sid Levin

● Robert De Niro, Harvey Keitel, David Proval, Amy Robinson, Richard Romanus, Cesare Danova (TPS/Warner)

In essence *Mean Streets* is an updated, downtown version of *Marty* (1955), with small-time criminality replacing those long stretches of beer-drinking in a Bronx bar. Four aging adolescents, all in their mid-20s but still inclined toward prankish irresponsibility, float among the lower-class denizens of Manhattan's Little Italy, struggling to make a living out of loan-sharking, the numbers game and bartending.

The hero, competently played by Harvey Keitel, is on the verge of taking over a restaurant for his vaguely Mafioso uncle (Cesar Danova in a compelling, deglamorized interpretation), but his climb to respectability is obstructed by his kinship with the trouble-making Robert De Niro and his budding love for De Niro's epileptic cousin, played rather confusingly by Amy Robinson.

Screenplay, instead of developing these characters and their complex interactions, remains content to sketch in their day-to-day happenings. But Scorsese is exceptionally good at guiding his largely unknown cast to near-flawless recreations of types. Outstanding in this regard is De Niro.

● ●

■ MEATBALLS

1979, 92 MINS, CANADA ◇ ⑰ ⊙

Dir Ivan Reitman *Prod* Dan Goldberg *Scr* Len Blum, Dan Goldberg, Janis Allen, Harold Ramis *Ph* Don Wilder *Ed* Debra Karen *Mus* Elmer Bernstein *Art Dir* David Charles

● Bill Murray, Harvey Atkin, Kate Lynch, Russ Banham, Kristine DeBell (Paramount)

It's difficult to come up with a more cliche situation for a summer pic than a summer camp, where all the characters and plot turns are readily imaginable. That makes director Ivan Reitman's accomplishment all the more noteworthy.

Bill Murray limns a head counselor in charge of a group of misfit counselors-in-

M

training. The usual types predominate: the myopic klutz, the obese kid who wins the pig-out contest, the smooth-talking lothario, and a bevy of comely lasses.

Scripters have managed to gloss over the stereotypes and come up with a smooth-running narrative that makes the camp hijinks part of an overall human mosaic. No one is unduly belittled or mocked, and *Meatballs* is without the usual grossness and cynicism of many contempo comedy pix.

● ●

■ MECHANIC, THE

1972, 100 MINS, US ◇ ⊛

Dir Michael Winner *Prod* Robert Chartoff, Irwin Winkler, Lewis John Carlino *Scr* Lewis John Carlino *Ph* Richard Kline *Ed* Freddie Wilson *Mus* Jerry Fielding *Art Dir* Rodger Maus
● Charles Bronson, Keenan Wynn, Jan-Michael Vincent, Jill Ireland, Linda Ridgeway, Frank deKova (United Artists)

A mechanic, in underworld parlance, is a highly-skilled contract killer. Possibilities of limning such a character are realistically pointed up in this action-drenched gangster yarn burdened with an overly-contrived plot development.

For the first few reels, footage is more a series of episodes not always clear, at that than carrying a sustained story line. Credibility is sometimes further strained during first half of film when Bronson oscillates between a typical hood at work and lolling in a luxurious apartment far removed from world of crime.

Michael Winner keeps the tempo at fever-pitch despite deficiencies of feature's opening sequences.

Bronson plays the son of a former gang leader cut down in his prime, left a fortune but still associated with crime as a hired executioner.

● ●

■ MEDICINE MAN

1992, 106 MINS, US ◇ ⊛ ⊙

Dir John McTiernan *Prod* Andrew G. Vajna, Donna Dubrow *Scr* Tom Schulman, Sally Robinson, [Tom Stoppard] *Ph* Donald McAlpine *Ed* Michael R. Miller *Mus* Jerry Goldsmith *Art Dir* John Krenz Reinhart Jr
● Sean Connery, Lorraine Bracco, Jose Wilker, Rodolfo De Alexandre, Angelo Barra Moreira (Hollywood/ Cinergi)

An indelicate attempt to create some *African Queen*-style magic while curing cancer and saving the rainforests in the bargain, this jumbo-budget two-character piece suffers from a very weak script and a lethal job of miscasting.

Pony-tailed and bearded, Sean Connery portrays a maverick biochemist who's been working in the Amazon for six years when his sponsoring company sends a researcher to his remote outpost to check up on him. The woman in question is played by Lorraine Bracco, whose screeching New York accent is so pronounced that Connery immediately starts calling her Bronx, and whose manner is so abrasive that it's a wonder Connery doesn't just toss her to the crocodiles.

In search of the rare blossoms for his cancer cure, Connery takes Bracco on a major E-ticket ride up a series of counterbalanced rope riggings to the treetops, affording a breathtaking view of the jungle. Nonetheless, their personal story remains grounded by banality relieved only by a trek through the forest that sees Bracco indulging in some high-spirited substance abuse and getting stuck on a branch hundreds of feet above a gorge.

Trying to show that he can do something other than action, which he does so well, helmer John McTiernan has not proved that he can. Jerry Goldsmith's score is thunderingly overbearing.

● ●

■ MEDIUM, THE

1951, 85 MINS, US ⊛

Dir Gian-Carlo Menotti *Prod* Walter Lowendahl *Scr* Gian-Carlo Menotti *Ph* Enzo Serafin *Ed* Alexander Hammid *Mus* Gian-Carlo Menotti
● Marie Powers, Anna Maria Alberghetti, Leo Coleman, Belva Kibler, Beverly Dame, Donald Morgan (Transfilm)

Composer-librettist Gian-Carlo Menotti, who surprised Broadway by turning out two successive operas, *The Medium* and *The Consul*, that became legit hits, turns film director and makes *The Medium* into an impressive pic. The work is limited by the fact that it is stark modern opera, all in song or recitative.

Menotti filmed the opus in Rome, utilizing Marie Powers and Leo Coleman from the original legit cast, and the 15-year-old Italian coloratura find, Anna Maria Alberghetti, in her film debut, for the third principal. Menotti is too fond of the camera, and too intent on trick angles and effects. He overworks the close-ups. But he comes up with some nifty shots that dovetail with the bizarre opus.

Story is that of a shabby medium, Madame Flora (Powers), living with her daughter Monica (Alberghetti), and Toby, a mute gypsy waif they adopted (Coleman), and the seances they hold for gullible clients.

Mme Flora, who is given to drink, disrupts one seance suddenly when she fancies someone's hand at her throat trying to choke her. She accuses her customers and then Toby of the deed, and when they deny it, is distraught. Fear of some supernatural power turning on her for her shams drives her further towards the bottle.

Although the picture was filmed in Italy, it has no particular locale, and is sung entirely in English. Sets are simple and costumes and makeup properly drab. Film shows a tightened budget without cheapness of quality.

☐ 1950: Nomination: Best Scoring of a Musical Picture

● ●

■ MEDIUM COOL

1969, 110 MINS, US ◇ ⊛

Dir Haskell Wexler *Prod* Tully Friedman, Haskell Wexler *Scr* Haskell Wexler *Ph* Haskell Wexler *Ed* Verna Fields *Mus* Mike Bloomfield *Art Dir* Leon Ericksen
● Robert Forster, Verna Bloom, Peter Bonerz, Marianna Hill, Harold Blankenship, Charles Geary (Paramount/ H&J)

Photographed in Chicago against the clamor and violence of the 1968 Democratic National Convention, where cast principals were on their own as they made their way through the crowds and police lines. Buildup to these later sequences frequently is confusing and motives difficult to fathom.

Director Haskell Wexler, in his first indie production, mixes 'reality' with the 'theatrical', his two chief protagonists a realistic TV newsreel cameraman and a young hillbilly mother come to Chicago with her young son.

Wexler adopts a documentary approach which helps sustain the mood and his cast fits into this pattern.

Robert Forster is strongly cast as the lenser who refuses to become emotionally involved with any of his assignments until caught up in the injustice done to a Negro and while on TV assignment, falls in love with a young mother.

● ●

■ MEDUSA TOUCH, THE

1978, 110 MINS, UK/FRANCE ◇ ⊛

Dir Jack Gold *Prod* Anne V. Coates, Jack Gold *Scr* John Briley *Ph* Arthur Ibbetson *Ed* Anne V. Coates, Ian Crafford *Mus* Michael J. Lewis *Art Dir* Peter Mullins
● Richard Burton, Lino Ventura, Lee Remick, Harry Andrews, Marie-Christine Barrault, Michael Hordern (ITC/Coategold)

Another disaster film? Not exactly, even if at the end a London cathedral caves in, with many victims trapped underneath the rubble but with the Queen of England saved in the nick of time. These scenes, realistically treated and technically good, are among the highlights of this lavishly-produced film [from the novel by Peter Van Greenaway].

John Morlar (Richard Burton) is attacked by an unknown intruder who bashes in his skull. Why? The man didn't seem to have a single enemy. Inspector Brunel is puzzled. Why a French detective instead of British? Apparently due to French financial participation in this film. In any case, it allows Lino Ventura to make his British film debut and very good he is.

Brunel finally discovers a clue leading to a psychiatrist played by Lee Remick. She had treated Morlar for reasons not stated at once.

It turns out that Morlar is not dead at all. His mind is fighting a desperate battle to survive. Even as a child, Morlar proved a very odd number indeed. His files relate to a vast series of disasters and apparently unsolved mysteries.

Director Jack Gold controls all the angles of this improbable story. Burton has some very effective moments too as does Remick.

● ●

■ MEETING VENUS

1991, 117 MINS, UK ◇ ⊛ ⊙

Dir Istvan Szabo *Prod* David Puttnam *Scr* Istvan Szabo, Michael Hirst *Ph* Lajos Koltai *Ed* Jim Clark *Mus* Daisy Boschan (cons.) *Art Dir* Attila Kovacs
● Glenn Close, Niels Arestrup, Erland Josephson, Moscu Alcalay, Macha Meril, Johanna Ter Steege (Enigma)

Glenn Close hits the high notes as a cool diva in *Meeting Venus*, but romantic comedy set in a strife-torn Paris opera house is knocked on the head by a central love story that's dumb and uninvolving.

Yarn opens in sprightly style with Budapest conductor (Niels Arestrup) flying in for a production of Wagner's *Tannhauser* at the fictional Opera Europa. After being introduced to polyglot staff, he soon realizes that 'here you can be misunderstood in six languages.' The internal politics make old Eastern Europe look like a summer camp.

He doesn't get any help from his lead soprano (Close), who initially dismisses him. Plot grinds to a halt halfway when Close suddenly takes a liking to the humbled Arestrup, and they're soon exchanging confidences between the sheets. Film ends with the chaotic first night of *Tannhauser* back in Paris.

What must have seemed on paper like a light-hearted satire on Euro-squabbling and the multi-lingual opera scene works okay in the opening rounds. Magyar helmer Istvan Szabo directed the same opera in Paris six years earlier and makes no secret that the pic was inspired by his experiences. Things start to go wrong when the Close-Arestrup affair gets serious.

● ●

■ MEET JOHN DOE

1941, 129 MINS, US ⊛ ⊙

Dir Frank Capra *Prod* Frank Capra *Scr* Robert Riskin *Ph* George Barnes *Ed* Daniel Mandell *Mus* Dimitri Tiomkin *Art Dir* Stephen Goosson
● Gary Cooper, Barbara Stanwyck, Edward Arnold, Walter Brennan, Spring Byington, James Gleason (Capra/Warner)

Picture tells the story of the rehabilitation of a tramp ex-baseball player who assents to the role of a puppet social reformer in the hands of a young woman columnist on a metropolitan newspaper.

The heroine, having been fired from her job through a change in the sheet's ownership, regains her place by inventing a fictitious John Doe as author of a letter of protest against the prevailing injustices of a political and social system which permits hunger in a land of plenty and idleness in a world where much remains to be accomplished. As earnest of his appeal he declares he will commit suicide on Christmas Eve in expiation for the sins of society.

The synthetic fabric of the story is the weakness of the production, despite the magnificence of the Frank Capra-directed superstructure. But Robert Riskin, who wrote the screenplay from an original story by Richard Connell and Robert Presnell, leaves the audience at the finale with scarcely more than the hope that some day selfishness, fraud and deceit will be expunged from human affairs.
□ 1941: Nomination: Best Original Story

■ MEET ME AT THE FAIR

1952, 87 MINS, US ◇
Dir Douglas Sirk   *Prod* Albert J. Cohen   *Scr* Irving Wallace   *Ph* Maury Gertsman   *Ed* Russell Schoengarth   *Mus* Joseph Gershenson (dir.)   *Art Dir* Bernard Herzbrun, Eric Orborn
● Dan Dailey, Diana Lynn, Chet Allen, Scatman Crothers, Hugh O'Brian, Carole Mathews (Universal)

The production has a period flavor featuring nostalgia and schmaltz against a 1904 setting. The old-fashioned drama [from the novel *The Great Companions* by Gene Markey, adapted by Martin Berkeley] revolves around an orphan kid who runs away from a grim institution, takes up with a medicine man, with his new friend charged with kidnapping. Before it's all over, the medicine man and the kid are mixed up in a political fight and eventually bring about reforms at the orphanage.

Best in the musical department is Carole Mathews doing 'Bill Bailey' and the title number. She also works with Dan Dailey on 'Remember the Time' and generally impresses.

Dailey is very likeable as the medicine man, giving the character a good-natured flavor that helps the film.

■ MEET ME IN ST. LOUIS

1944, 118 MINS, US ◇ ◻ ⊙
Dir Vincente Minnelli   *Prod* Arthur Freed   *Scr* Irving Brecher, Fred F. Finklehoffe   *Ph* George Folsey   *Ed* Albert Akst   *Art Dir* Cedric Gibbons, Lemuel Ayers, Jack Martin Smith
● Judy Garland, Margaret O'Brien, Mary Astor, Lucille Bremer, Tom Drake, Marjorie Main (M-G-M)

Meet Me in St. Louis is wholesome in story [from the book by Sally Benson], colorful both in background and its literal Technicolor, and as American as the World's Series.

As Leon Ames plays the head of the Alonzo Smith clan it's a 1903 life-with-father. Mary Astor is the understanding and, incidentally, quite handsome mother as they worry about Judy Garland and Lucille Bremer, playing their daughters. Henry H. Daniels Jr is the self-sufficient brother, off to Princeton, but the romantic travail of the two older girls is the fundamental. Backgrounded are Marjorie Main, capital as the maid who almost bosses the household, and the still-gallant Harry Davenport, now 80-ish, who is grandpa.

It's the time of the St Louis Fair, hence the title song, and everything that makes for the happy existence of a typical American family is skillfully panoramaed.

Seasonal pastorals, from summer into the next spring, take the Smith clan through their appealing little problems. Judy Garland's plaint about 'The Boy Next Door' (played by Tom Drake); the Paul Jones dance routine to the tune of 'Skip to My Lou'; the Yuletide thematic, 'Have Yourself a Merry Christmas'; and the 'Trolley Song', en route to the Fairgrounds, are four socko musical highlights. Thhey have been intelligently

highlighted and well-paced by director Vincente Minnelli.

Garland achieves true stature with her deeply understanding performance, while her sisterly running-mate, Lucille Bremer, likewise makes excellent impact with a well-balanced performance.
□ 1944: Nominations: Best Color Cinematograhy, Scoring of a Musical Picture, Song ('The Trolley Song')

■ MEET THE APPLEGATES

(Australia: The Applegates)

1991, 82 MINS, US ◇ ◻ ⊙
Dir Michael Lehmann   *Prod* Denise Di Novi   *Scr* Redbeard Simmons, Michael Lehmann   *Ph* Mitchell Dubin   *Ed* Norman Hollyn   *Mus* David Newman   *Art Dir* Jon Hutman
● Ed Begley Jr., Stockard Channing, Cami Cooper, Bobby Jacoby, Dabney Coleman, Glenn Shadix (New World)

tIn his weird 1988 debut *Heathers*, Lehmann gave a bizarre twist to the usual portrayal of US teen life. In this pic he takes an even more extreme approach to sending up American family life. In a bid to save the Brazilian rain forest from development, a family of giant beetles is sent to infiltrate American society and blow up a nuclear power station as a warning.

Chameleon-like, they assume the form of humans, and, learning from a *Fun with Dick and Jane* reader, become the average America family. Surrounded by temptations in a community-minded town in Ohio, the family soon degenerates, with Dick (Ed Begley Jr.) having an affair, Jane (Stockard Channing) becoming obsessed with credit and alcohol, Johnny (Bobby Jacoby) turning into a dope dealer and Sally (Cami Cooper) becoming pregnant.

Such a wacky premise could derail easily, but Lehmann handles it with humor and paces it well. Begley and company play it for all it's worth, and seem to be having a ball. Scenes of the Applegates becoming bugs (usually with disastrous consequences) are cleverly done.

■ MEET WHIPLASH WILLIE

See: The Fortune Cookie

■ MELANCHOLIA

1989, 87 MINS, UK/W. GERMANY ◇ ◻
Dir Andi Engel   *Prod* Colin MacCabe, Lewis Rodia   *Ph* Denis Crossan   *Scr* Andi Engel   *Ed* Christopher Roth   *Mus* Simon Fisher Turner   *Art Dir* Jock Scott
● Jeroen Krabbe, Susannah York, Ulrich Wildgruber, Jane Gurnett, Kate Hardie, Saul Reichlin (BFI/Lichtblick)

Despite a dauntingly uninviting title, *Melancholia* proves to be a stimulating contemporary thriller about an idealist from the 1960s who decides to take violent action in support of his long-submerged beliefs.

Jeroen Krabbe plays a German, Keller, long resident in London, who works as a critic, lives alone and drinks too much. He is aroused from his inertia by a phone call from Hamburg from Manfred, who asks him to assassinate a Chilean torturer Vargas, currently visiting London.

Manfred later visits London to tell Keller the assassination is off: the Chilean can now be of use to 'our side.' Soon after, Keller is approached by Sarah Yelin (Jane Gurnett), a torture victim, whose husband was horribly murdered by Vargas. He makes up his mind and tracks down the Chilean.

The film raises questions about the use of violence to prevent further violence, and about the passivity of idealists. It doesn't play as a straight commercial thriller, but as a serious pic exploring provocative themes with intelligence.

Melancholia is the first film directed by Andi Engel, the German-born, London-based former critic who's best known as a distributor and exhibitor in Britain.

■ MELODY OF LIFE

See: Symphony of Six Million

■ MELVIN AND HOWARD

1980, 93 MINS, US ◇ ◻ ⊙
Dir Jonathan Demme   *Prod* Art Linson, Don Phillips   *Scr* Bo Goldman   *Ph* Tak Fujimoto   *Ed* Craig McKay   *Mus* Bruce Langhorne   *Art Dir* Toby Rafelson
● Paul Le Mat, Jason Robards, Mary Steenburgen, Michael J. Pollard, Dabney Coleman, Gloria Grahame (Universal)

A pungent fable about the elusiveness of the American Dream, *Melvin and Howard* is a richly textured, highly individualistic look at Melvin Dummar, a man in over his head both before and after becoming the beneficiary of $156 million via Howard Hughes' so-called Mormon will. Jonathan Demme's tour-de-force direction, the imaginative screenplay and top-drawer performances from a huge cast fuse in an unusual, original creation.

Dummar's chance encounter with a man representing himself as the reclusive tycoon occupies first reel or so and, despite Jason Robards' amusing portrait of Hughes as a grizzled old coot, pic takes awhile generating a full head of steam. As his two-time bride and divorcee Mary Steenburgen says, Melvin is a loser, and early footage focusing upon his inability to cope with family or jobs makes for somewhat uncertain p.o.v.

Film is exemplary for its rare concentration on the quality, and lack of it, in Middle American life, and incisive, if indirect, examination of the no-win syndrome for contemporary proletariat.
□ 1980: Best Supp. Actress (Mary Steenburgen), Original Screenplay.
□ Nomination: Best Supp. Actor (Jason Robards)

■ MEMOIRS OF AN INVISIBLE MAN

1992, 99 MINS, US ◇ ◻ ⊙
Dir John Carpenter   *Prod* Bruce Bodner, Dan Kolsrud   *Scr* Robert Collector, Dana Olsen, William Goldman   *Ph* William A. Fraker   *Ed* Marion Rothman   *Mus* Shirley Walker   *Art Dir* Lawrence G. Paull
● Chevy Chase, Daryl Hannah, Sam Neill, Michael McKean, Stephen Tobolowsky, Jim Norton (Warner/Cornelius)

Main problem with this mildly entertaining special effects showcase proves as transparent as its title character – namely that Chevy Chase, who can only play Chevy Chase, lacks leading-man qualities necessary to make this sort of Hitchcockian man-in-peril scenario work. Working from H.F. Saint's well-received novel, director John Carpenter and a trio of screenwriters go the espionage route with a comedy twist, but the film fails to fully satisfy on either level.

Chase is cast as a detached stock analyst turned invisible by a freak accident, who then becomes the quarry of a ruthless government agent (Sam Neill) out to exploit his unique gift for the CIA. The story plays as a cat-and-mouse game as Chase flees from his pursuers, in the process receiving help from a woman (Daryl Hannah) he met and became instantly enamored with just prior to the optical mishap.

Film departs from past explorations of the subject in two specific areas: the hero's clothes are rendered invisible as well, meaning he doesn't have to run about in the nude like cinematic predecessor Claude Rains; and anything he ingests stays visible within him, creating the rare opportunity at one point to see an invisible man upchuck.

Hannah is asked to do little but look beautiful, and she obliges admirably. Neill and Michael McKean are notably underemployed as the one-dimensional bad guy and Chase's best friend.

● ●

■ MEMOIRS OF A SURVIVOR

1981, 117 MINS, UK ◇ ⓥ
Dir David Gladwell   *Prod* Michael Medwin, Penny Clark
Scr Kerry Crabbe, David Gladwell   *Ph* Walter Lassally
Ed William Shapter   *Mus* Mike Thorn
● Julie Christie, Christopher Guard, Leonie Mellinger, Debbie Hutchins, Pat Keen, Nigel Hawthorne (EMI/Memorial/NFFC)

The film [from the novel by Doris Lessing] depicts Julie Christie as D, an attractive middle-aged woman living alone in the midst of the chaos occurring around her. She dreams of a Victorian time and can go through a wall to witness events.

A little girl, maybe her, is seen in the rich, gilded interiors adroitly given a candlelight feeling by lenser Walter Lassally. The mother is annoyed at not being able to read, work and find herself while the little girl is somewhat neglected by mom and her austere father who at one time contemplates her undraped body while she is asleep.

But reality is grim. A teenage girl is moved in with D and she takes care of her. The girl becomes involved with a young man trying to help vagrant children, living in an abandoned subway station. They have already killed one of his helpers and cannibalized others.

People are leaving the stricken city with some indications of an outside government that gives orders. Strife is not due to any atomic war but just communal life running down.

Christie emerges as a fine character player despite her still potent attractiveness. Director David Gladwell apparently did not have the budget to give a more solid look to the degenerating city.

● ●

■ MEMPHIS BELLE

1990, 106 MINS, UK ◇ ⓥ ⊙
Dir Michael Caton-Jones   *Prod* David Puttnam, Catherine Wyler   *Scr* Monte Merrick   *Ph* David Watkin   *Ed* Jim Clark   *Mus* George Fenton   *Art Dir* Stuart Craig
● Matthew Modine, Eric Stoltz, Tate Donovan, D.B. Sweeney, David Strathairn, John Lithgow (Enigma)

Offering a romanticized view of heroism drawn from the Hollywood war epic, *Memphis Belle* is unashamedly commercial. Its moral fabric is thinner than that of other David Puttnam productions.

Pic's subject is the 25th and final mission of the Memphis Belle, the most celebrated of the US Air Force B-17 bombers. The plane flew 24 perfect missions, and its 25th became part of a massive p.r. drive to boost war-bond sales and morale.

The plane and its team are sent to Germany to drop one last load, setting the scene for suspense, tension, terror and a fitting celebration when all return safe and (almost) sound.

Large chunk of the film is set on the ground, providing adequate exposition of events and character to involve the audience in the mission. Played up is the fact that these 10 guys are barely out of their teens and don't see themselves as heroes.

Original footage from the 1944 documentary *Memphis Belle* by William Wyler, father of coproducer Catherine Wyler, is used for the guaranteed tearjerking scene, with letters from dead soldiers read over it by the commanding officer, thoughtfully played by David Strathairn.

● ●

■ MEN, THE

1950, 85 MINS, US ⓥ
Dir Fred Zinnemann   *Prod* Stanley Kramer   *Scr* Carl Foreman   *Ph* Robert de Grasse   *Ed* Harry Gerstad
Mus Dimitri Tiomkin
● Marlon Brando, Teresa Wright, Everett Sloane, Jack Webb, Richard Erdman (United Artists)

In *The Men* producer Stanley Kramer turns to the difficult cinematic subject of paraplegics, so expertly treated as to be sensitive, moving and yet, withal, entertaining and earthy-humored.

From the opening shot, a tensely-played battle scene where Lieutenant Wilozek (Marlon Brando) suffers his crushing wound, *The Men* maintains its pace and interest. Thereafter, the film centers on the overwhelming problems of paralyzed vets who must be convinced that their wounds are incurable and that they must yet fight their way to a useful existence.

While the film personalizes the story of Wilozek and his fiancee (Teresa Wright), the camera's scope is broader.

Brando, who film-debuts as Wilozek, fails to deliver the necessary sensitivity and inner warmth.

□ 1950: Nomination: Best Story & Screenplay

● ●

■ ME, NATALIE

1969, 110 MINS, US ◇
Dir Fred Coe   *Prod* Stanley Shapiro   *Scr* A. Martin Zweiback   *Ph* Arthur J. Ornitz   *Ed* Sheila Bakerman
Mus Henry Mancini   *Art Dir* George Jenkins
● Patty Duke, James Farentino, Martin Balsam, Elsa Lanchester, Salome Jens, Nancy Marchand (Cinema Center)

Me, Natalie is the type of picture which might have gone overboard in contrivance and over-sentimentality, in monotonous rendition of personal feelings of its title character. Instead, it is sensitive, often-poignant drama painted with a light touch of an ugly duckling trying to find her place in the scheme of things.

Patty Duke, in title role, delivers a warm, roundly-developed characterization of a girl who all her life has tried to be pretty, and is keenly aware she isn't nor ever will be.

The title character engages in a great deal of offscreen running commentary throughout the film, explaining her feelings and her philosophy, which gives audience an insight into her feelings without slowing the pace, generally held to an interesting temp.

As the mother, Nancy Marchand delivers a tremendous performance.

● ●

■ MEN DON'T LEAVE

1990, 113 MINS, US ◇ ⓥ ⊙
Dir Paul Brickman   *Prod* John Avnet   *Scr* Barbara Benedek, Paul Brickman   *Ph* Bruce Surtees   *Ed* Richard Chew   *Mus* Thomas Newman   *Art Dir* Barbara Ling
● Jessica Lange, Chris O'Donnell, Charlie Corsmo, Arliss Howard, Tom Mason, Joan Cusack (Geffen/Warner)

Men Don't Leave is a quietly moving tale of a widow (Jessica Lange) and her struggle to support her two sons in shabby Baltimore surroundings.

Suggested by Moshe Mizrahi's 1981 French film *La vie continue* with Annie Girardot, *Men Don't Leave* is directed by Paul Brickman.

The title misleadingly suggests a feminist tract, not the warm-hearted comedy-drama this pic becomes after getting past the disjointed kitchen-sink melodrama of debt-ridden husband Tom Mason's death and Lange's selling of the family's suburban home. The move to Baltimore revives what seemed a terminally ill film and brings it compellingly to life.

Playing the role at first with an unmodulated emotional glaze, the taciturn Lange is pulled back to life by the spirited behaviour of her boys, superbly played by newcomers Chris O'Donnell and Charlie Korsmo; by O'Donnell's sweet but loopy g.f. Joan Cusack, and by the engagingly offbeat b.f. Arliss Howard.

The film's dramatic heart is a sequence showing Lange, after losing her job in a blowup against restaurant boss Kathy Bates, descending into a catatonic state and refusing to leave her bed for days as the apartment turns into a quiet vision of hell. It's a scary piece of acting by Lange, beautifully directed by Brickman, and it turns a somewhat meandering film into a memorable emotional experience.

● ●

■ MEN IN HER LIFE, THE

1941, 89 MINS, US
Dir Gregory Ratoff   *Prod* Gregory Ratoff   *Scr* Frederick Kohner, Michael Wilson, Paul Trivers   *Ph* Harry Stradling, Arthur Miller   *Ed* Francis D. Lyon   *Mus* David Raksin
● Loretta Young, Conrad Veidt, Dean Jagger, Otto Kruger, Ann Todd, John Shepperd (Columbia)

Eleanor Smith's novel of the 1860s, *Ballerina*, in providing basis for the tale, details the intensive training required to bring a ballet dancer to stardom and her love life along the way. Loretta Young comes under the stern hand of elderly ballet master Conrad Veidt, marrying him in appreciation after a sensational debut, although in love with young John Shepperd. After Veidt's death, she marries shipping magnate Dean Jagger, and honeymoon tour of Europe finds her forgetting the stage life. But she returns to dancing for separation, and bears a daughter (Ann Todd), whom Jagger eventually finds and takes back to New York for proper rearing.

Gregory Ratoff overcomes much of the story immobility through carrying various dramatic episodes to dramatic peaks, and then veering away to the next sequence without holding on the climax. Ratoff also generates strong sympathy in the latter reels with the mother-love hearttugs for the absent child.

□ 1941: Nomination: Best Sound

● ●

■ MEN IN WAR

1957, 102 MINS, US ⓥ
Dir Anthony Mann   *Prod* Sidney Harmon   *Scr* Philip Yordan   *Ph* Ernest Haller   *Ed* Richard C. Meyer
Mus Elmer Bernstein   *Art Dir* Frank Sylos
● Robert Ryan, Aldo Ray, Robert Keith, Philip Pine, Vic Morrow, Nehemiah Persoff (Security/United Artists)

A two-fisted account of what happens to an infantry platoon in Korea is told with a general air of excitement, tension and action. Battle sequences, well-staged under Anthony Mann's direction, are all small-scale, but none the less deadly, as befits the plot and its few characters. The Philip Yordan scripting from Van Van Praag's novel, *Combat*, does considerable to overcome the fact that there is much that is similar in warpix and the characters that inhabit them.

Robert Ryan, battle-weary lieutenant trying to get the remnants of his platoon back to battalion headquarters, and Aldo Ray, hostile, disrespectful sergeant from another company trying to get his combat-shocked colonel to safety, each score strongly. Robert Keith, the colonel, successfully carries off a role that requires only one word of dialog.

Where the film does stand out over the usual warpic is in its intelligent use of music. Elmer Bernstein composed and conducted the score, never trying to compete with the sounds of battle and thereby heightening the effect of many scenes.

● ●

■ MEN OF BOYS TOWN

1941, 107 MINS, US ⊕

Dir Norman Taurog   *Prod* John W. Considine Jr
Scr James Kevin McGuinness   *Ph* Harold Rosson
Ed Frederick F. Smith   *Mus* Herbert Stothart
● Spencer Tracy, Mickey Rooney, Lee J. Cobb, Larry Nunn, Bobs Watson, Daryl Hickman (M-G-M)

Like its predecessor *Boys Town*, this one carries socko entertainment for wide general appeal, including plenty of tear-jerking and sentimental episodes to blur the eyes of the most calloused, and spotlighting the life work of Father Edward J. Flanagan in his enterprise devoted to rehabilitation of wayward boys.

Spencer Tracy again presents a sincere and human portrayal of the priest, while Mickey Rooney displays plenty of restraint in handling the assignment of the completely-reformed boy who goes out briefly to practice the precepts of the school head. Lee J. Cobb, as the fund-raiser to keep the institution open, gives a fine performance.

Story introduces Larry Nunn into the institution. Kid is bitter because of the crippled back sustained in a reform school beating, and Rooney heads a group of boys to try to make him laugh again. The kindly Father Flanagan and a dog do the trick.

Picture hits a consistent gait, always pointing up the sentimental angles in its dramatic unfolding.

Direction by Norman Taurog again demonstrates his unique talents in handling boys and their varied characteristics.

■ MEN OF TWO WORLDS

(US: *Witch Doctor*)

1946, 109 MINS, UK ◇ ⊕

Dir Thorold Dickinson   *Scr* Thorold Dickinson, Herbert W. Victor   *Ph* Desmond Dickinson   *Ed* Aben Jaggs
Mus Arthur Bliss   *Art Dir* Tom Morahan
● Eric Portman, Phyllis Calvert, Orlando Martins, Robert Adams, Cyril Raymond (Two Cities)

This ambitious Two Cities production, which enters the $4 million class, is honest, dull and in Technicolor. With the best intentions, it states the case for a scientific treatment of sleeping sickness among the African tribes as opposed to witchcraft and superstition. But it is a statement of the obvious.

Film was three years in production with delays that appear to have badly dented the screenplay. It began in 1943. Eight months were spent in Tanganyika choosing locations. On the way out a U-boat sank cameras and stock. Film unit was put ashore 1,000 miles from Lagos, where its only still camera was impounded. Slow convoys, bad weather, a strike of lab men in Hollywood, delays waiting for Technicolor equipment, all brought costly handicaps to the enterprise. Director Thorold Dickinson has done his best, but the result is a long stretch of mumbo-jumbo, unrelieved by imaginative treatment or pictorial thrills.

Randall, the district commissioner, plans to evacuate an African village to save the inhabitants from the man-killing tsetse fly. His assistant is Kisenga, a noble savage who has risen from ancestral swamps, found culture in England and gone back to his tribe as a musician and composer. He takes Randall's side in the fight against sleeping sickness, but the power of black magic in the hands of the local witch doctor, Magole (played with remarkable force by Orlando Martins), is too much for him.

■ MEN'S CLUB, THE

1986, 100 MINS, US ◇ ⊕ ⊙

Dir Peter Medak   *Prod* Howard Gottfried   *Scr* Leonard Michaels   *Ph* John Fleckenstein   *Ed* Cynthia Scheider, David Dresher, Bill Butler   *Mus* Lee Holdridge
Art Dir Ken Davis

● Roy Scheider, Frank Langella, Harvey Keitel, Treat Williams, Richard Jordan, David Dukes (Atlantic)

Those who think men are immature, destructive, insensitive and basically animals may find *The Men's Club* great fun. Others are likely to balk at the film's contrived and dated treatment of the battle between the sexes.

Film is a distasteful piece of work that displays the worst in men. Leonard Michaels' screenplay (from his novel) is all warts and no insight, full of self-loathing for the gender. In addition, film making is as tired as the material. Pic plays like a stageplay, so static is Peter Medak's direction.

A group of friends nearing age 40 get together and for most of the film's 100 minutes the camera is on their heads talking. Leader of the group is Cavanaugh (Roy Scheider), supposedly a retired baseball star who looks too unhealthy to have ever played anything more strenuous than cards.

■ MEN WITHOUT WOMEN

1930, 76 MINS, US

Dir John Ford   *Scr* John Ford, James Kevin McGuinness, Dudley Nichols   *Ph* Joseph H. August   *Ed* Paul Weatherwax   *Mus* Peter Brunellin, Glen Knight
Art Dir William S. Darling
● Kenneth MacKenna, Frank Albertson, Paul Page, Warren Hymer, Walter McGrail (Fox)

Story and characters are built up with uncanny shrewdness. It opens in Shanghai with a shore party of American gobs going whoopee in an enormous establishment of entertainment of various kinds, mostly a vast bar and many fluttering petticoats and kimonos.

Back to the ship some great views of a sub streaking out to sea at night in clouds of black smoke and weird light and water reflections. Sub is run down in a collision and goes to the bottom in 90 feet of water with all escape cut off, and here begins the sledge hammer situation that lasts to the finish. Finale is a whooping bit of flagwaving.

Kenneth MacKenna, as Chief Torpedoman Burke, does nicely with a heroic lead, but the punch of the acting is the surprise comedy bits of a number of minor characters. It is these touches and the grim comedy of the lines that lift the picture out of melodrama to an illusion of reality.

■ MEPHISTO WALTZ, THE

1971, 115 MINS, US ◇ ⊕

Dir Paul Wendkos   *Prod* Quinn Martin   *Scr* Ben Maddow   *Ph* William W. Spencer   *Ed* Richard Brockway   *Mus* Jerry Goldsmith   *Art Dir* Richard Y. Hamen
● Alan Alda, Jacqueline Bisset, Barbara Parkins, Bradford Dillman, William Windom, Curt Jurgens (20th Century-Fox)

Based on the novel by Fred Mustard Stewart, pic follows in deadpan style the antics of a deranged concert pianist (Curt Jurgens), dying of leukemia whose lust for his daughter (Barbara Parkins) and devotion to devil-worship destroy the marriage of writer Alan Alda and Jacqueline Bisset.

To revive his sexual prowess, Jurgens has Alda killed, then assumes his body. A trifle slow on the uptake, Bisset finally realizes something is amiss after her daughter dies under mysterious conditions. Alda-cum-Jurgens starts getting ruthless in bed, and the ex-husband of Parkins (Bradford Dillman) tells her (before being killed) of a monster child miscarried by Parkins and sired by her father.

Main fault is a tired script with more than a full quota of arch, laughable dialog, spouted with relish by performers struggling to keep their heads above water.

■ MERCENARIES, THE

(US: *Dark of the Sun*)

1968, 106 MINS, UK ◇

Dir Jack Cardiff   *Prod* George Englund   *Scr* Quentin Werty, Adrian Spies   *Ph* Ted Scaife   *Ed* Ernest Walter
Mus Jacques Loussier
● Rod Taylor, Yvette Mimieux, Peter Garsten, Jim Brown, Kenneth More, Andre Morell (M-G-M)

Based on the Congo uprising, this is a raw adventure yarn (from a novel by Wilbur Smith) with some glib philosophizing which skates superficially over the points of view of the cynical mercenaries and the patriotic Congolese.

Rod Taylor plays a hardbitten mercenary major who's prepared to sweat through any task, however dirty, providing his fee is okay. He's assigned by Congo's president to take a train through rebel Simba-held country and bring back fugitives and a load of uncut diamonds stashed away in a beleaguered town.

The action is taken care of effectively but the rapport between some of the characters is rarely smooth nor convincing enough. Pic was filmed in Africa and at Metro's British studios.

Acting is mostly of a straightforward nature for the script does not lend itself to a subtlety of characterization. Taylor makes a robust hero while Jim Brown brings some dignity and interest to the role of the Congolese native.

■ MERMAIDS

1990, 111 MINS, US ◇ ⊕ ⊙

Dir Richard Benjamin   *Prod* Lauren Lloyd, Wallis Nicita, Patrick Palmer   *Scr* June Roberts   *Ph* Howard Atherton
Ed Jacqueline Cambas   *Mus* Jack Nitzsche
Art Dir Stuart Wurtzel
● Cher, Bob Hoskins, Winona Ryder, Michael Schoeffling, Christina Ricci, Caroline McWilliams (Orion)

As eccentric mother-daughter films go, this one [from the novel by Patty Dann] falls into the same category as *Terms of Endearment*, with many of the same comedic pleasures and dramatic pitfalls.

Set in the early 1960s, *Mermaids* begins rousingly, introducing flamboyant Mrs Flax (Cher) and her two daughters: confused Charlotte (Winona Ryder), 15, who is obsessed with Catholicism, and Kate (Christina Ricci), nine, who's obsessed with swimming.

Constantly on the move due to mother's vagabond ways, they soon relocate to a small New England town that brings with it new romantic entanglements. Mrs Flax takes up with a lovelorn shoe salesman (Bob Hoskins), while Charlotte becomes enamored with a dreamy groundskeeper (Michael Schoeffling) from the local nunnery, conveniently situated just down the road.

Since she's unable to communicate with her wanton mother, Ryder's dialog is largely limited to voiceover confessions and pleas to God, often while staring intently, wordless and wide-eyed, at her mother or Joe (Schoeffling), the unsuspecting object of her near-crazed lust.

The delightful Ryder, billing notwithstanding, is really the star. Cher is also fine as the cavalier, self-centered mom, an equally amusing if less sympathetic character.

■ MERRILL'S MARAUDERS

1962, 98 MINS, US ◇ ⊕

Dir Samuel Fuller   *Prod* Milton Sperling   *Scr* Milton Sperling, Samuel Fuller   *Ph* William Clothier   *Ed* Folmar Blangsted   *Mus* Howard Jackson
● Jeff Chandler, Ty Hardin, Peter Brown, Andrew Duggan, Luz Valdez, Claude Akins (United States)

Jeff Chandler's last role, as Brigadier General Frank Merrill, is one of his best. The rugged, gray-thatched Chandler fits this role natu-

M

rally and portrays one of World War II's most colorful personalities with a proper blend of military doggedness and personal humanity.

When Samuel Fuller he was a GI in Europe took his small cast and crew to the Philippines to shoot *Merrill's Marauders*, he did plenty of preliminary screening and, down the line, he got the results he wanted. After Chandler, this film owes much of its excellence to William Clothier's Technicolor photography, both in his feeling for cinematic design and his superb use of color.

Charlton Ogburn's book was a springboard only for the scenarists. They elaborated it into a screenplay that balances battle scenes with character-establishing vignettes and gives the subject-hero a closer contact with his men through playing his story against the background of their daily activities, their fixture of personalities.

Ty Hardin's Lieutenant Stockton is a stock character the young, still over-sensitive officer but he conveys a tenderness, a sense of truth that keeps the role from seeming stereotyped.

●●●●●●●●●●●●●●●●●●●●●●●●●●●●

■ MERRILY WE LIVE

1938, 90 MINS, US
Dir Norman Z. McLeod   *Prod* Milton H. Bren   *Scr* Eddie Moran, Jack Jevne   *Ph* Norbert Brodine   *Ed* William Terhune   *Mus* Marvin Hatley (dir.)   *Art Dir* Charles D. Hall
● Constance Bennett, Brian Aherne, Billie Burke, Alan Mowbray, Patsy Kelly, Ann Dvorak (Favorite/M-G-M)

It's all in the acting and directing. Director Norman Z. McLeod has the knack of building up gags until he has three or four racing each other to the big laugh. Most of the fun comes from a fine performance by Billie Burke, who plays a scatterbrain wife and mother in a family of irresponsibles.

Burke has a weakness for helping worthless humanity. Brian Aherne is welcomed to the fold. It happens he isn't a tramp at all, but a writer who forgot to shave on the morning his flivver broke down when he stops by to use the telephone. Once inside, he decides to stay.

In his calm and self-possessed manner he begins to bring some order out of the confusion in which the Kilbourne family lives. This leads to a romance with the elder daughter (Constance Bennett), and a timely word which clinches an important business deal for the head of the house.

Bennett gives a good performance and appears in some striking costumes. Alan Mowbray, as the family butler, contributes to the hilarity, as do Patsy Kelly, in a small part, and Bonita Granville and Tom Brown.
□ 1938: Nomination: Best Supp. Actress (Billie Burke), Cinematography, Art Direction, Sound, Song ('Merrily We Live')

●●●●●●●●●●●●●●●●●●●●●●●●●●●●

■ MERRY ANDREW

1958, 103 MINS, US ◇
Dir Michael Kidd   *Prod* Sol C. Siegel   *Scr* Isobel Lennart, I.A.L. Diamond   *Ph* Robert Surtees   *Ed* Harold F. Kress   *Mus* Saul Chaplin   *Art Dir* William A. Horning, Gene Allen
● Danny Kaye, Pier Angeli, Baccaloni, Noel Purcell, Robert Coote, Patricia Cutts (M-G-M)

Merry Andrew has a happy-go-chuckley attitude and some smart musical numbers set up by stand-out music and lyrics. Against this is the fact that the production does not always maintain its own set of very high comedy values, nor the pace of its initial scenes.

Michael Kidd, who makes his screen debut as a director, still has a lot to learn about comedy set-ups and this unsureness is made the more evident by the contrast of the narrative stretches with the brisk and imaginative manner in which Kidd has choreographed the

musical numbers. Here he is on experienced ground and he shows it.

The romance and humor of the screenplay, based on a story by Paul Gallico, are based on the fact that Andrew, played by Danny Kaye, is anything but merry in the opening sequences. He is an instructor in a stuffy British boys' school, presided over by his martinet father (Noel Purcell) and engaged to cool and detached Patricia Cutts. Via his vocation (archeology) he gets mixed up with a family circus presided over by papa Baccaloni and featuring daughter Pier Angeli. This gives Kaye an opportunity to slap on the clown makeup and do several turns with handy circus props.

●●●●●●●●●●●●●●●●●●●●●●●●●●●●

■ MERRY CHRISTMAS, MR. LAWRENCE

1983, 122 MINS, UK ◇ ⊛
Dir Nagisa Oshima   *Prod* Jeremy Thomas   *Scr* Nagisa Oshima, Paul Mayersberg   *Ph* Toichiro Narushima   *Ed* Tomoyo Oshima   *Mus* Ryuichi Sakamoto   *Art Dir* Jusho Toda
● David Bowie, Tom Conti, Ryuichi Sakamoto, Takeshi, Jack Thompson (Recorded Picture)

By no means an easy picture to deal with, this thinking man's version of *The Bridge on the River Kwai* makes no concessions to the more obvious commercial requirements, unless it is the selection of David Bowie, the pop star, for the leading dramatic role.

The strongest points of the script, penned by Nagisa Oshima and Paul Mayersberg from a novel [*The Seed and the Sower*] by South African author Laurens van der Post, are the philosophical and emotional implications, brought up in a careful and intricate comparison between Orient and Occident on every possible level. The weakest point is its construction, sturdy and compact up to the point when it has to use flashbacks in order to explain the British side of the allegory.

Set in a Japanese prisoner-of-war camp in Java, the plot has a Japanese captain, Yonoi (Ryuichi Sakamoto), trying to impose his own ideas of discipline, honor, order and obedience, in a clash with a British major, Celliers (Bowie), who represents the diametrically opposed train of thought.

The conflict between the two leading figures is better verbalized by Colonel Lawrence (Tom Conti), who lends his name to the film's title, and Hara (Takeshi), the Japanese sergeant whose popular origins allow him much more freedom of emotions.

●●●●●●●●●●●●●●●●●●●●●●●●●●●●

■ MERRY WIDOW, THE

1934, 110 MINS, US ⊛
Dir Ernst Lubitsch   *Prod* Ernst Lubitsch   *Scr* Ernest Vajda, Samson Raphaelson   *Ph* Oliver T. Marsh   *Ed* Frances Marsh   *Mus* Herbert Stothart (adapt.)   *Art Dir* Cedric Gibbons, Frederic Hope
● Maurice Chevalier, Jeanette MacDonald, Edward Everett Horton, Una Merkel, George Barbier, Minna Gombell (M-G-M)

Ernst Lubitsch has here brought the field of operetta to the level of popular taste. Besides Lubitsch, the many involved include Ernest Vajda and Samson Raphaelson on the book; Herbert Stothart on the music; Richard Rodgers, Lorenz Hart and Gus Kahn on the 1934 lyrics. They are, 26 years after, the collaborators on the original *Widow* by Franz Lehar, Victor Leon and Leo Stein. Two or three new airs have been added, but the music still stands pat on Lehar smartly so.

In his leads, Lubitsch picked a double plum out of the talent grab bag. Maurice Chevalier and Jeanette MacDonald both are aces as Danilo and Sonia. The former Paramount pair once again works beautifully in harness. Supporting players are in chiefly for comedy purposes, and include such expert vets as Edward Everett Horton, George Barbier, Una

Merkel, Sterling Holloway and Herman Bing.
□ 1934: Best Interior Decoration (Cedric Gibbons, Frederic Hope)

●●●●●●●●●●●●●●●●●●●●●●●●●●●●

■ MESSAGE, THE
(US: *Mohammed, Messenger of God*)

1976, 179 MINS, UK ◇ ⊛
Dir Moustapha Akkad   *Prod* Moustapha Akkad   *Scr* H.A.L. Craig   *Ph* Jack Hildyard   *Ed* John Bloom   *Mus* Maurice Jarre   *Art Dir* Norman Dorme, Abdel Mouneim Chukri
● Anthony Quinn, Irene Papas, Michael Ansara, Johnny Sekka, Michael Forest, Damien Thomas (Filmco)

The Message, Moustapha Akkad's $17 million saga of the birth of the Islamic religion, bears favorable comparison as a religious epic. H.A.L. Craig's screenplay is remarkably literate, sometimes witty and ironic, but ultimately and perhaps inevitably simplistic.

The action snowballs from underground cell meetings by followers of Mohammad, through brutal harassment, expulsion from Mecca, pitched battles in the desert, and the final conquering pilgrimage back to Mecca. Throughout the narrative there is uncommon respect for the mind and the eye.

Ultimately it's a triumph for Akkad who welded a logistically sprawling epic into coherence. His crowd scenes are credible and the battle scenes superbly rendered.

●●●●●●●●●●●●●●●●●●●●●●●●●●●●

■ METEOR

1979, 103 MINS, US ◇ ⊛
Dir Ronald Neame   *Prod* Arnold Orgolini, Theodore Parvin   *Scr* Stanley Mann, Edmund H. North   *Ph* Paul Lohmann   *Ed* Carl Kress   *Mus* Laurence Rosenthal   *Art Dir* Edward Carfagno
● Sean Connery, Natalie Wood, Karl Malden, Brian Keith, Martin Landau, Trevor Howard (American International)

Meteor really combines several disasters in one continuous cinematic bummer. Along with the threat of a five-mile-wide asteroid speeding towards earth, with smaller splinters preceding it, there's an avalanche, an earthquake, a tidal wave and a giant mud bath. All in all, special effects wizards Glen Robinson and Robert Staples, along with stunt coordinator Roger Greed, got a good workout.

Inevitably, topliners Sean Connery as an American scientist, Brian Keith as his Soviet counterpart, and Natalie Wood as the translator in between them, take a back seat to the effects.

Avalanche sequence is one of the best in memory, aided by the fact that producers were allowed to blow up a mountain in the Swiss Alps.
□ 1979: Nomination: Best Sound

●●●●●●●●●●●●●●●●●●●●●●●●●●●●

■ METROPOLITAN

1990, 98 MINS, US ◇ ⊛ ⊙
Dir Whit Stillman   *Prod* Whit Stillman   *Scr* Whit Stillman   *Ph* John Thomas   *Ed* Chris Tellefsen   *Mus* Mark Suozzo, Tom Judson
● Carolyn Farina, Edward Clements, Christopher Eigeman, Taylor Nichols (Westerley Film-Video)

Filmmaker Whit Stillman makes a strikingly original debut with *Metropolitan*, a glib, ironic portrait of the vulnerable young heirs to Manhattan's disappearing debutante scene. Story centers on a set of East Side friends who dub themselves the SFRP (or 'Sally Fowler Rat Pack', after the girl whose Park Avenue apartment they gather in) and, more amusingly, UHBs, for Urban Haute Bourgeoisie.

They drag into their number a newcomer, Tom (Edward Clements), who openly disapproves of them but nonetheless shows up every night for private gatherings after black-tie parties and dances. A self-serious but in-sensitive young man, Tom inspires the first-time love of Audrey (Carolyn Farina). Tom repeatedly humiliates her as he continues to pursue an old flame, Serena (Elizabeth Thompson).

Among the fine cast, Christopher Eigeman stands out as Nick, the funny, arrogant group leader who's as jovially self-aware and self-mocking as his new friend, Tom, is stilted and blind to himself.

Pic is a true independent production, fi-nanced by Stillman (who sold his Manhattan apartment) and several friends.
☐ 1990: Nomination: Best Original Screenplay

• •

■ **MIAMI BLUES**

1990, 99 MINS, US ◇ ⑰ ⊙
Dir George Armitage   *Prod* Jonathan Demme, Gary Goetzman   *Scr* George Armitage   *Ph* Tak Fujimoto   *Ed* Craig McKay   *Mus* Gary Chang   *Art Dir* Maher Ahmad
● Alec Baldwin, Fred Ward, Jennifer Jason Leigh, Nora Dunn, Charles Napier, Jose Perez (Tristes Tropiques)

Based on Charles Willeford's novel, this quirky and sometimes brutally funny film strings together terrific moments but never takes a point of view.

Junior (Alec Baldwin) blows into town, initi-ates a crime spree with a homicide detective's stolen badge and settles down with a simple-minded hooker named Susie (Jennifer Jason Leigh). The sense that Junior can go off at any time, and the explosive and graphic bursts of violence create tension throughout.

Baldwin is more than equal to the task, and his intense machismo and make-believe pos-turing bring to mind some of Robert De Niro's menace in *Taxi Driver*. Leigh also is wondrously odd, her eyebrows knitting in frustration at the simplest of questions, her drawl filled with rapture at the recipes she can concoct for her new beau.

Pic, however, is missing a key ingredient: a discernible plot. If it's the detective (Fred Ward) seeking to reclaim his badge, false teeth and gun, it's a wispy one at best.

• •

■ **MICKEY ONE**

1965, 90 MINS, US ⑰
Dir Arthur Penn   *Prod* Arthur Penn   *Scr* Alan M. Surgal   *Ph* Ghislain Cloquet   *Ed* Aram Avakian   *Mus* Eddie Sauter   *Art Dir* George Jenkins
● Warren Beatty, Hurd Hatfield, Alexandra Stewart, Teddy Hart, Jeff Corey, Franchot Tone (Florin/Tatira)

Mickey One could be described as a study in re-generation, but the screenplay is overloaded with symbolic gestures which obscure the main objectives of the plot.

Title character is a one-time top nitery comic who has been leading an extravagant life, getting mixed up with dames and gam-blers. In a bid to get away from his past and start afresh, he assumes the identity of a Pole whose name is conveniently abbreviated to Mickey One. He gradually drifts back to the world of night clubs, and in a sleazy West Chicago joint rediscovers the art of wowing an audience.

To this point, the plot develops reasonably smoothly and the few touches of symbolism are not entirely unacceptable. Thereafter, however, symbolism runs riot, occasionally to the point of pretentiousness.

Arthur Penn must accept his share of re-sponsibility for the confused style and bewil-dering nature of the more obscure sequences. But in his main intention he is powerfully backed by Warren Beatty, who gives a com-manding, though highly mannered, perfor-mance – a consistently dominating study of a man who lives in fear of his past.

• •

■ **MICKI + MAUDE**

1984, 118 MINS, US ◇ ⑰ ⊙
Dir Blake Edwards   *Prod* Tony Adams   *Scr* Jonathan Reynolds   *Ph* Harry Stradling   *Ed* Ralph E. Winters   *Mus* Lee Holdridge   *Art Dir* Rodger Maus
● Dudley Moore, Amy Irving, Ann Reinking, Richard Mulligan, George Gaynes, Wallace Shawn (Columbia-Delphi III/BEE)

Micki + Maude is a hilarious farce. For his part, Dudley Moore is in top antic form, and Amy Irving has never been better.

Debuting screenwriter Jonathan Reynolds has constructed a farce of simple, classical proportions about a man who accidentally gets his wife and new girlfriend pregnant at virtually the same time.

The host of a silly TV show which does fea-tures on things like the food at an election night celebration, Moore rarely gets to see his attorney wife (Ann Reinking) due to her hec-tic schedule, finding time only for a quickie in the back of a limousine.

On the job for his show, Moore meets comely Amy Irving, who easily seduces him on their next encounter. Premise is set up shortly thereafter, when both women an-nounce that they are pregnant.

• •

■ **MIDDLE AGE CRAZY**

1980, 89 MINS, CANADA ◇ ⑰
Dir John Trent   *Prod* Robert Cooper   *Scr* Carl Kleinschmidt   *Ph* Reginald Morris   *Ed* John Kelly   *Mus* Matthew McCauley   *Art Dir* Karen Bromley
● Bruce Dern, Ann-Margret, Graham Jarvis, Helen Hughes, Deborah Wakeham (20th Century-Fox/Tormont)

Bobby Lee (Bruce Dern) is a successful build-ing contractor on the verge of his 40th birth-day. He is getting hung up on his milestone date as a result of his wife's persistence that he's still the old stud she married.

Constant reminders from friends and family on his dependability eventually drive him to change his style. He buys a Porsche, dresses up like a drugstore cowboy, and has a brief fling with a Dallas Cowgirl (Deborah Wakeham).

He finally decides family and responsibility aren't so bad after all. The revelation is pat and steeped in sentimentality. A quick resolu-tion would have been more in keeping with the movie's acerbic wit.

Dern emerges a likable family man with deep reservations about his lot in life. The ac-tor is equally convincing dressed in three-piece suits or denim and boots. Ann-Margret as his wife is also outstanding.

• •

■ **MIDDLE AGE SPREAD**

1979, 94 MINS, NEW ZEALAND ◇
Dir John Reid   *Prod* John Barnett   *Scr* Keith Aberdein   *Ph* Alun Bollinger   *Ed* Michael Horton   *Mus* Stephen McCurdy
● Grant Tilly, Donna Akersten, Dorothy McKegg, Bridget Armstrong, Bevan Wilson, Peter Sumner (Endeavour/NZ Film Commission)

Middle Age Spread centres on Colin (Grant Tilly), a college teacher whose promotion to principal coincides with a number of personal crises.

Not least are a widening girth, which has him jogging round the streets at night, and a tentative first-and-last affair with a much younger teaching colleague, Judy (Donna Akersten).

At a dinner party he hosts, with his increas-ingly sexually-disinterested wife, Elizabeth (Dorothy McKegg), the morality and values of their tight-knit circle of friends are played out with deadly accuracy.

To his credit, director John Reid, one of the actors in the original stage presentation, has created a film that is not just a pale adapta-tion of the play.

■ **MIDNIGHT**

1939, 92 MINS, US
Dir Mitchell Leisen   *Prod* Arthur Hornblow Jr   *Scr* Charles Brackett, Billy Wilder   *Ph* Charles Lang Jr   *Ed* Doane Harrison   *Mus* Frederick Hollander   *Art Dir* Hans Dreier, Robert Usher
● Claudette Colbert, Don Ameche, John Barrymore, Francis Lederer, Mary Astor, Hedda Hopper (Paramount)

Story [from one by Edwin Justus Mayer and Franz Schulz] is light, but with a good share of humorous moments, many of them of the screwball variety. It's a slender thread, how-ever, on which to tie series of incidents in ad-ventures of a stranded showgirl in Paris.

After a flirtation with Don Ameche, Claudette Colbert crashes a musicale and poses as a countess. This leads to job for John Barrymore, in which she is to attract the amorous attentions of Francis Lederer away from Barrymore's wife, Mary Astor. For her assignment, Colbert is provided with elabo-rate wardrobe and a hotel suite.

Direction by Mitchell Leisen is generally satisfactory, although picture is slow in get-ting under way and has several spots that could be tightened. Editing shows sketchiness in several instances.

• •

■ **MIDNIGHT COWBOY**

1969, 119 MINS, US ◇ ⑰ ⊙
Dir John Schlesinger   *Prod* Jerome Hellman, John Schlesinger   *Scr* Waldo Salt   *Ph* Adam Holender   *Ed* Hugh A. Robertson   *Mus* John Barry (sup.)   *Art Dir* John Robert Lloyd
● Dustin Hoffman, John Voight, Sylvia Miles, John McGiver, Brenda Vaccaro, Bernard Hughes (United Artists)

Midnight Cowboy is the sometimes amusing but essentially sordid saga of a male prosti-tute in Manhattan. Dustin Hoffman is cast as gimp-legged, always unshaven, a cough-wracked petty chiseler who at first exploits and then befriends the stupid boy hustler from Texas. The title role is played by Jon Voight.

The film [from a novel by James Leo Herlihy] is full of unnice people from bad en-vironments. It is obsessed with mercenary sex and haunted by memories of cruel group rav-ishments. Indignity is endemic.

Voight travels north by bus through an America that is mocked in every sign along the road. After Voight's first unsuccessful at-tempts at hustling he is 'befriended' by Hoffman. The two chums hide in a tenement marked for demolition, living on canned soup cooked over canned heat.

It is never easy to work up a liking for eith-er of the two main bums in this pantheon of lost souls. The story begins by suggesting that male prostitutes offer themselves to women but the facts of the city soon establish that this is a homosexual market primarily. The boy hustler 'consents' in a movie theatre and then is deadbeat out of the agreed price. Later, desperate for money to take his dying crony to Florida, the Texan brutalizes a pa-thetic, middle-aged whimpering homosexual in a hotel room.

Midnight Cowboy has a miscellany of compe-tent bit players and a good deal of both sly and broad humor.
☐ 1969: Best Picture, Director, Adapted Screenplay.
☐ Nominations: Best Actor (Dustin Hoffman, Jon Voight), Supp. Actress (Slyvia Miles), Editing

• •

■ **MIDNIGHT EXPRESS**

1978, 120 MINS, UK ◇ ⑰ ⊙
Dir Alan Parker   *Prod* David Puttnam   *Scr* Oliver Stone   *Ph* Michael Seresin   *Ed* Gerry Hambling   *Mus* Giorgio Moroder   *Art Dir* Geoffrey Kirkland

● Brad Davis, Randy Quaid, John Hurt, Bo Hopkins, Paul Smith, Mike Kellin (Casablanca)

Midnight Express is a sordid and ostensibly true story about a young American busted for smuggling hash in Turkey and his subsequent harsh imprisonment and later escape. Cast, direction and production are all very good, but it's difficult to sort out the proper empathies from the muddled and moralizing screenplay which, in true Anglo-American fashion, wrings hands over alien cultures as though our civilization is absolutely perfect.

Oliver Stone is credited for adapting the book by Billy Hayes, young tourist who, in the midst of airline terrorism and world pressure on Turkey over drug farming, is discovered wearing a not-insignificant amount of hash strapped to his body. Brad Davis plays Hayes in a strong performance.

Acceptance of the film depends a lot on forgetting several things: he was smuggling hash; Turkey is entitled to its laws, and is no more guilty of penal corruption and brutality than, say, the US, UK, France, Germany, etc; a world tourist can't assume that a helpful father (played well by Mike Kellin) is going to have the same clout with some midwestern politicians; nor can an American expect to be treated with kid gloves everywhere.

However, the script loads up sympathy for Davis, also fellow convicts Randy Quaid (a psycho character), John Hurt (a hard doper) and Norbert Weisser (playing the obligatory gay inmate), by making the prison authorities even worse.

□ 1978: Best Adapted Screenplay, Original Score.

□ Nominations: Best Picture, Director, Supp. Actor (John Hurt), Editing

■ MIDNIGHT MAN, THE

1974, 117 MINS, US ◇
Dir Roland Kibbee, Burt Lancaster   *Prod* Roland Kibbee, Burt Lancaster   *Scr* Roland Kibbee, Burt Lancaster
Ph Jack Priestley   *Ed* Frank Morriss   *Mus* Dave Grusin   *Art Dir* James D. Vance
● Burt Lancaster, Susan Clark, Cameron Mitchell, Morgan Woodward, Harris Yulin, Joan Lorring (Universal)

The Midnight Man stars Burt Lancaster as a paroled ex-cop stumbling into a series of small-town murders. With Roland Kibbee, Lancaster adapted, produced and directed on some refreshingly different locations in South Carolina. The cluttered plot's twists and turns get tiring after 117 minutes, but the violence highlights are well motivated and discreetly executed.

Script derives from a David Anthony novel, *The Midnight Lady and the Mourning Man*. Lancaster, out on parole after killing his wife's lover, is reduced to a campus security job under the auspices of his longtime pal (Cameron Mitchell). Susan Clark is Lancaster's sexy parole officer.

The murder of Catherine Bach, whose personal trauma was committed to a tape stolen from psychologist Robert Quarry, triggers an awful lot of storytelling.

■ MIDNIGHT RUN

1988, 122 MINS, US ◇ ⓥ ⊙
Dir Martin Brest   *Prod* Martin Brest   *Scr* George Gallo   *Ph* Donald Thorin   *Ed* Billy Weber, Chris Lebenzon, Michael Tronick   *Mus* Danny Elfman   *Art Dir* Angelo Graham
● Robert De Niro, Charles Grodin, Yaphet Kotto, John Ashton, Dennis Farina, Joe Pantoliano (City Lights)

Midnight Run shows that Robert De Niro can be as wonderful in a comic role as he is in a serious one. Pair him, a gruff ex-cop and bounty hunter, with straight man Charles Grodin, his captive, and the result is one of the most entertaining, best executed, original road pictures *ever*.

It's De Niro's boyish charm that works for him every time and here especially as the scruffy bounty hunter ready to do his last job in a low-life occupation. He's to nab a philanthropically minded accountant hiding out in Gotham (Grodin) who embezzled $15 million from a heroin dealer/Las Vegas mobster and return him to Los Angeles in time to collect a $100,000 fee by midnight Friday.

Kidnapping Grodin is the easy part; getting him back to the west coast turns out to be anything but easy. The two guys, who can't stand each other, are stuck together for the duration of a journey neither particularly wants to be on.

Midnight Run is more than a string of well-done gags peppered by verbal sparring between a reluctant twosome; it is a terrifically developed script full of inventive, humorous twists made even funnier by wonderfully realized secondary characters.

■ MIDNIGHT STING

See: Diggstown

■ MIDSUMMER NIGHT'S DREAM, A

1935, 132 MINS, US ⓥ
Dir Max Reinhardt, William Dieterle   *Prod* Henry Blanke   *Scr* Charles Kenyon, Mary C. McCall Jr   *Ph* Hal Mohr   *Ed* Ralph Dawson   *Mus* Erich Wolfgang Korngold (arr.)   *Art Dir* Anton Grot
● James Cagney, Olivia de Havilland, Mickey Rooney, Victor Jory, Joe E. Brown, Dick Powell (Warner)

Question of whether a Shakespearean play can be successfully produced on a lavish scale for the films is affirmatively answered by this commendable effort. The familiar story of *A Midsummer Night's Dream*, half of which is laid in a make-believe land of elves and fairies, is right up the film alley technically.

The fantasy, the ballets of the Oberon and Titania cohorts, and the characters in the eerie sequences are convincing and illusion compelling. Film is replete with enchanting scenes, beautifully photographed and charmingly presented. All Shakespearian devotees will be pleased at the soothing treatment given to the Mendelssohn score.

The women are uniformly better than the men. They get more from their lines. The selection of Dick Powell to play Lysander was unfortunate. He never seems to catch the spirit of the play or role. And Mickey Rooney, as Puck, is so intent on being cute that he becomes almost annoying.

There are some outstanding performances, however, notably Victor Jory as Oberon. His clear, distinct diction indicates what can be done by careful recitation and good recording; Olivia de Havilland, as Hermia, is a fine artist here; others are Jean Muir, Verree Teasdale and Anita Louise, the latter beautiful as Titania but occasionally indistinct in her lines.

Jimmy Cagney, as Bottom, registers effectively mainly in the romantic passages with Anita Louise.

□ 1935: Best Cinematography, Editing.
□ Nomination: Best Picture

■ MIDSUMMER NIGHT'S SEX COMEDY, A

1982, 88 MINS, US ◇ ⓥ
Dir Woody Allen   *Prod* Robert Greenhut   *Scr* Woody Allen   *Ph* Gordon Willis   *Ed* Susan E. Morse   *Art Dir* Mel Bourne
● Woody Allen, Mia Farrow, Jose Ferrer, Julie Hagerty, Tony Roberts, Mary Steenburgen (Orion)

Woody Allen's *A Midsummer Night's Sex Comedy* is a pleasant disappointment, pleasant because he gets all the laughs he goes for in a visually charming, sweetly paced picture, a disappointment because he doesn't go for more.

The time is the turn of the century, the place a lovely old farmhouse in upstate New

York. Here, Wall St stockbroker Allen spends his spare time inventing odd devices and trying to bed his own wife (Mary Steenburgen) who has turned cold.

Arriving for a visit and also a wedding are Steenburgen's cousin Jose Ferrer, a stuffy, pedantic scholar, and his bride to be (Mia Farrow), a former near-nympho who's decided to settle down with Ferrer's intellect.

Also arriving are Allen's best friend, who else but Tony Roberts, an amorous physician and his current short-term fling (Julie Hagerty), a nurse dedicated to the study of anatomy and all its possibilities.

With this daffy assortment and Allen's gift for laugh-lines, the picture can't avoid being fun, even at a rather leisurely pace in keeping with its times.

■ MIDWAY

(UK: Battle of Midway)

1976, 132 MINS, US ◇ ⓥ ⊙
Dir Jack Smight   *Prod* Walter Mirisch   *Scr* Donald S. Sanford   *Ph* Harry Stradling Jr   *Ed* Robert Swink, Frank J. Urioste   *Mus* John Williams   *Art Dir* Walter Tyler
● Charlton Heston, Henry Fonda, James Coburn, Glenn Ford, Hal Holbrook, Toshiro Mifune (Mirisch)

The June 1942 sea-air battle off Midway Island was a turning point in World War II. However, the melee of combat was the usual hysterical jumble of noise, explosion and violent death. *Midway* tries to combine both aspects but succumbs to the confusion.

Henry Fonda's performance as Pacific Fleet Commander Chester W. Nimitz towers over everything else.

The Midway battle followed the Mames Doolittle air raid on Tokyo in April 1942. The turnback of the Japanese Navy effectively cleared the West Coast from attack, and gave the US time enough to mobilize for the long road back across the Pacific.

■ MIGHTY DUCKS, THE

(UK: Champions)

1992, 101 MINS, US ◇ ⓥ ⊙
Dir Stephen Herek   *Prod* Jordan Kerner, Jon Avnet   *Scr* Steven Brill   *Ph* Thomas Del Ruth   *Ed* Larry Bock, John F. Link   *Mus* David Newman   *Art Dir* Randy Ser
● Emilio Estevez, Joss Ackland, Lane Smith, Heidi Kling, Josef Sommer, Joshua Jackson (Walt Disney)

The Mighty Ducks is a formulaic pic meant for children but actually focusing on a yuppie's struggle for redemption.

Emilio Estevez stars as an accomplished but arrogant Minneapolis lawyer who carelessly gets nailed on drunk driving charges. His stern boss cuts a deal for him to do community service instead of suffering the humiliation of court. Once Estevez meets the undisciplined, street-wise kids whom he must shape into a winning peewee hockey team, pic becomes predictable and mighty preachy.

Political correctness informs the film from the careful ethnic and gender composition of the hockey team to pic's value system: teamwork over aggressive individualism and concentration over strength. Schematic script contains a few inspired one-liners, but not enough to distract attention from plot machinery.

Helmer Stephen Herek endows a familiar story with a crisp look and swift tempo, seldom allowing sanctimonious tale to linger too long or gags to get too tiresome. In pic's second part, the pace is accelerated by skillful montages of hockey games.

■ MIGHTY JOE YOUNG

1949, 88 MINS, US ⓥ ⊙
Dir Ernest B. Schoedsack   *Prod* John Ford, Merian C. Cooper   *Scr* Ruth Rose   *Ph* J. Roy Hunt   *Ed* Ted Cheesman   *Mus* Roy Webb   *Art Dir* James Basevi

● Terry Moore, Ben Johnson, Robert Armstrong, Frank McHugh, Douglas Fowley, Regis Toomey (Arko/RKO)

Mighty Joe Young is fun to laugh at and with, loaded with incredible corn, plenty of humor, and a robot gorilla who becomes a genuine hero. The technical skill of the large staff of experts [led by Willis O'Brien and Ray Harryhausen] gives the robot life.

Plot [by Merian C. Cooper] deals with a gorilla, raised in the African jungle by a young girl. Both the girl and the giant ape are happy with their rusticating until a safari headed by Broadway producer Robert Armstrong arrives in the jungle. Armstrong immediately sees the possibilities of the ape and the girl.

The presentation by John Ford and Cooper pulls all stops in slugging away at audience risibilities while pointing up the melodramatic phases. It's this general air of tongue-in-cheek treatment that makes the corn palatable.

☐ 1949: Best Special Effects

··

■ **MIKEY AND NICKY**

1976, 119 MINS, US ◇ ⓥ
Dir Elaine May   *Prod* Michael Hausman   *Scr* Elaine May   *Ph* Victor J. Kemper, Lucien Ballard, Jerry File, Jack Cooperman   *Ed* John Carter   *Mus* John Strauss   *Art Dir* Paul Sylbert
● Peter Falk, John Cassavetes, Ned Beatty, Rose Arrick, Carol Grace, William Hickey (Paramount)

Peter Falk and John Cassavetes star as two old friends whose relationship is falling apart; two hours later, it is apparent there never was a friendship to begin with.

Cassavetes is a low-level criminal marked for extinction by ganglord Sanford Meisner, who employs Ned Beatty as hit man. Cassavetes calls Falk to help him, though neither Cassavetes nor the audience is certain that Falk isn't part of the rubout strategy. That's the superficial hook on which hangs the real story of human relationships and mutual abuse.

The interplay between the stars is excellent, Cassavetes slowly but steadily digging his own grave as he reveals his shallowness in dealings with Falk, girl friend Carol Grace (a beautiful performance) and estranged wife Joyce Van Patten (a brief but excellent characterization).

··

■ **MILAGRO BEANFIELD WAR, THE**

1988, 117 MINS, US ◇ ⓥ ⊙
Dir Robert Redford   *Prod* Robert Redford, Moctesuma Esparza   *Scr* David Ward, John Nichols   *Ph* Robbie Greenberg   *Ed* Dede Allen, Jim Miller   *Mus* Dave Grusin   *Art Dir* Joe Aubel
● Ruben Blades, Richard Bradford, Sonia Braga, Julie Carmen, John Heard, Melanie Griffith (Universal)

The Milagro Beanfield War is a charming, fanciful little fable built around weighty issues concerning the environment, the preservation of a cultural heritage and the rights of citizens versus the might of the dollar.

The director and his screenwriters, who adapted John Nichols' 1974 novel, adeptly juggle at least a dozen major characters in telling the story of how one man's decision to cultivate his land, which is coveted by outside developers intent upon building a resort, leads to a standoff between natives of the area and the big boys.

Redford and company have put a quirky twist on the material, investing it with a quasi-mystical aspect as well as some raw comedy.

Set in modern-day New Mexico, tale is set in motion when improverished farmer Joe Mondrago (Chick Vennera) improperly diverts some water from a main irrigation channel onto his own modest plot of land in order to start up a beanfield. This little act of defiance stirs up the handful of activists in the affected village, notably garage owner Ruby Archuleta (Sonia Braga), who recruits dropped out radical attorney and newspaperman Charley Bloom (John Heard) to rally 'round the cause.

☐ 1988: Best Original Score

··

■ **MILDRED PIERCE**

1945, 109 MINS, US ⓥ ⊙
Dir Michael Curtiz   *Prod* Jerry Wald   *Scr* Ranald MacDougall   *Ph* Ernest Haller   *Ed* David Weisbart   *Mus* Max Steiner   *Art Dir* Anton Grot
● Joan Crawford, Jack Carson, Zachary Scott, Eve Arden, Ann Blyth, Bruce Bennett (Warner)

At first reading James M. Cain's novel of the same title might not suggest screenable material, but the cleanup job has resulted in a class feature, showmanly produced by Jerry Wald and tellingly directed by Michael Curtiz.

It skirts the censorable deftly, but keeps the development adult in dealing with the story of a woman's sacrifices for a no-good daughter. High credit goes to Ranald MacDougall's scripting for his realistic dialog and method of retaining the frank sex play that dots the narrative while making the necessary compromises with the blue-pencillers.

Story is told in flashback as Mildred Pierce is being questioned by police about the murder of her second husband. Character goes back to the time she separated from her first husband and how she struggled to fulfill her ambitions for her children.

The dramatics are heavy but so skillfully handled that they never cloy. Joan Crawford reaches a peak of her acting career in this pic. Ann Blyth, as the daughter, scores dramatically in her first genuine acting assignment. Zachary Scott makes the most of his character as the Pasadena heel, a talented performance.

☐ 1945: Best Actress (Joan Crawford).
☐ Nominations: Best Picture, Supp. Actress (Eve Arden, Ann Blyth), Screenplay, B&W Cinematography

··

■ **MILLER'S CROSSING**

1990, 114 MINS, US ◇ ⓥ ⊙
Dir Joel Coen   *Prod* Ethan Coen, Mark Silverman   *Scr* Joel Coen, Ethan Coen   *Ph* Barry Sonnenfeld   *Ed* Michael Miller   *Mus* Carter Burwell   *Art Dir* Dennis Gassner
● Gabriel Byrne, Albert Finney, Marcia Gay Harden, Jon Polito, John Turturro, J.E. Freeman (Circle/Pedas-Barenholtz-Durkin)

Substance is here in spades, along with the twisted, brilliantly controlled style on which filmmakers Joel and Ethan Coen made a name.

Story unspools in an unnamed Eastern city in the 1930s where dim but ambitious Italian gangster Johnny Caspar (Jon Polito) has a problem named Bernie Bernbaum (John Turturro). Caspar wants approval from the city's Irish political boss, Leo (Albert Finney), to rub out the cause of his complaint, but Leo's not giving in. He's fallen in love with Bernie's sister, Verna (Marcia Gay Harden), who wants Bernie protected.

Leo's cool, brainy aide-de-camp Tom (Gabriel Byrne) sees that Leo is making a big mistake, and it's up to Tom to save him as his empire begins to crumble. The complication is that Tom also is in love with Verna, though he's loath to admit it.

Rarely does a screen hero of Tom's gritty dimensions come along, and Irishman Byrne brings him gracefully and profoundly to life. As portrayed by screen newcomer Harden, Verna has the verve and flintiness of a glory-days Bette Davis or Barbara Stanwyck.

Also outstanding is Finney as the big-hearted political fixer who usually has the mayor and the police chief seated happily across his desk. He's as cool in a spray of bullets as he is vulnerable in affairs of the heart.

Buffs will note cameos by director Sam Raimi, with whom the Coens collaborated on his *Evil Dead*, and Frances McDormand, who made her indelible debut in *Blood Simple*.

··

■ **MILLIONAIRESS, THE**

1960, 90 MINS, UK ◇ ⓥ
Dir Anthony Asquith   *Prod* Dimitri De Grunwald   *Scr* Wolf Mankowitz   *Ph* Jack Hildyard   *Ed* Anthony Harvey   *Mus* George van Parys
● Sophia Loren, Peter Sellers, Alastair Sim, Vittorio De Sica, Dennis Price, Alfie Bass (20th Century-Fox)

This stylized pic has Sophia Loren at her most radiant, wearing a series of stunning Balmain gowns. George Bernard Shaw's Shavianisms on morality, riches and human relationship retain much of their edge, though nudged into a practical screenplay by Wolf Mankowitz.

Anthony Asquith's direction often is slow, but he breaks up the pic with enough hilarious situations to keep the film from getting tedious. A major fault is that the cutting of the film, which is mainly episodic, but against this, there is handsome artwork and the relish with which Jack Hildyard has brought his camera to work on them.

Briefly, the yarn concerns a beautiful, spoiled young heiress who has all the money in the world but can't find love. Her eccentric deceased old man has stipulated that she mustn't marry unless the man of her choice can turn $1,400 into $42,000 within three months. She cheats. Her first marriage flops, she contemplates suicide and then sets her cap for a dedicated, destitute Indian doctor runing a poor man's clinic. He's attracted to her, but scared of her money and power.

Loren is a constant stimulation. She catches many moods. Sellers plays the doctor straight, apart from an offbeat accent, but he still manages to bring in some typical comedy touches.

··

■ **MILLION DOLLAR MERMAID**

1952, 115 MINS, US ◇ ⓥ
Dir Mervyn LeRoy   *Prod* Arthur Hornblow Jr   *Scr* Everett Freeman   *Ph* George J. Folsey   *Ed* John McSweeney Jr   *Mus* Adolph Deutsch (dir.)   *Art Dir* Cedric Gibbons, Jack Martin Smith
● Esther Williams, Victor Mature, Walter Pidgeon, David Brian, Donna Corcoran, Jesse White (M-G-M)

This is a gaudy, conventional biopic based on the career of Australian swimmer Annette Kellerman, appropriately tagged 'Million Dollar Mermaid'.

Toppers of the flashy acquatics are the fountain and smoke numbers, imaginatively staged by Busby Berkeley and boldly splashed with Technicolor hues. The old New York Hippodrome is recreated for the production numbers, which include a brief ballet by Maria Tallchief as Pavlova.

Film opens with Kellerman (Esther Williams) as a crippled child in Australia who heals her legs in taking up swimming. After becoming amateur champ Down Under, she heads for London with her musician father (Walter Pidgeon), attracts the attention of Victor Mature, a sports promoter, who brings her to America.

☐ 1952: Nomination: Best Color Cinematography

··

■ **MILLION POUND NOTE, THE**
(US: Man with a Million)

1954, 92 MINS, UK ◇ ⓥ
Dir Ronald Neame   *Prod* John Bryan   *Scr* Jill Craigie   *Ph* Geoffrey Unsworth   *Ed* Clive Donner   *Mus* William

M

Alwyn   *Art Dir* Jack Maxsted, John Box
● Gregory Peck, Jane Griffiths, Ronald Squire, Joyce Grenfell, Reginald Beckwith, Maurice Denham (Group)

Mark Twain's classic story of the penniless American who is given a million pound bank note in a wager and succeeds in keeping it intact for a month, makes gentle screen satire.

With Edwardian settings providing a fascinating background, the yarn suffers from the protracted exploitation of one basic joke. It is sustaining and amusing for a time, but there are very few single gags that can successfully hold up for 92 minutes. *Note* is not an exception.

The plot is based on a bet between two brothers (Ronald Squire and Wilfrid Hyde White) that a man with a million pound bank note in his possession could live on the fat of the land for a month without having to break into it. The guinea pig for their wager is Gregory Peck, a penniless American stranded in London. And, sure enough, he finds this an open sesame to food, clothes, hotels and, naturally, society.

■ **MILLIONS LIKE US**

1943, 103 MINS, UK
Dir Frank Launder, Sidney Gilliat   *Prod* Edward Black   *Scr* Frank Launder, Sidney Gilliat   *Ph* Jack Cox, Roy Fogwell   *Ed* R.E. Dearing, Alfred Roome   *Mus* Louis Levy (dir.)   *Art Dir* John Bryan
● Eric Portman, Patricia Roc, Gordon Jackson, Anne Crawford, Basil Radford, Naunton Wayne (Gainsborough)

Film is designed as patriotic propaganda on the UK front, minus flag waving and suchlike. Acting throughout is superior to the story, and is of such a high quality it ought to make almost any film script interesting. It would not be at all surprising if the creation of this abundance of histrionic talent was due to slickness of direction.

The main star (in point of reputation) is Eric Portman, who has a relatively small part, but gives to it a dignified and intelligent portrayal. The outstanding roles are Patricia Roc and Gordon Jackson she a factory worker, and he a young airman. Their love-making is crudely simple, but so sincere as to lift it out of the commonplace.

The list of players includes a pair of prominent artists who appeared in the writers' successful *The Lady Vanishes*, when they scored smartly as a couple of silly Englishmen. An attempt is made to reproduce them in this picture, but without the same success. It really is unfair to Basil Radford and Naunton Wayne.

■ **MIND BENDERS, THE**

1963, 101 MINS, UK
Dir Basil Dearden   *Prod* Michael Relph   *Scr* James Kennaway   *Ph* Denys Coop   *Ed* John D. Guthridge   *Mus* Georges Auric   *Art Dir* James Morahan
● Dirk Bogarde, Mary Ure, John Clements, Michael Bryant, Wendy Craig, Edward Fox (Anglo-Amalgamated)

James Kennaway's original screenplay finds the peg for its bizarre plot in 'reduction of sensation' experiments reportedly done both in the US and Britain. By eliminating a subject's various senses by submerging him in an isolation tank a shortcut to brainwashing is achieved. Once the basic story pattern has been established, it moves into a fascinating study of how a man's mind can be twisted by a laboratory technique.

Suicide of elderly scientist Harold Goldblatt prompts an investigation by secret agent John Clements to determine whether military security has been violated. Clements suspects Goldblatt has turned traitor. But the scientist's associate, Dirk Bogarde, denies any treason has been committed and blames Goldblatt's death as a result of the experi-

ments. Bogarde voluntarily submits to isolation to prove his theory.

Under Basil Dearden's firm direction, the cast absorbingly captures suspense and gruesome space age qualities frequently generated by Kennaway's script. Bogarde emerges as a dedicated scientist who shades his role with lotsa realism. Mary Ure's portrayal of the spurned wife is a touching piece of thesping.

■ **MINISTRY OF FEAR**

1945, 84 MINS, US
Dir Fritz Lang   *Prod* B.G. De Sylva (exec.)   *Scr* Seton I. Miller   *Ph* Henry Sharp   *Ed* Archie Marshek   *Mus* Victor Young   *Art Dir* Hans Dreier, Hal Pereira
● Ray Milland, Marjorie Reynolds, Dan Duryea, Carl Esmond, Hillary Brooke, Alan Napier (Paramount)

Fritz Lang, a master at getting the most out of mystery, intrigue and melodrama, in his direction apparently didn't have his way from beginning to end on *Ministry of Fear*. Pic [from the novel by Graham Greene] starts out to be a humdinger, and continues that way for the most part, but when the roundup of the spy gang gets underway the situation becomes drawn out and elementary, marring the footage that preceded.

Ray Milland, in the role of an ex-asylum inmate, who is released after serving two years for the 'mercy' killing of his incurable wife, gives a forthright performance. He is tossed into the midst of a spy chase when, in purchasing a ticket to London upon leaving the asylum, he is drawn to the crowds at a British fair and wins a cake by guessing its weight. The cake contains a capsule which one of the spies is to have delivered to other enemy agents..

■ **MINIVER STORY, THE**

1950, 104 MINS, UK/US
Dir H.C. Potter   *Prod* Sidney Franklin   *Scr* Ronald Millar, George Froeschel   *Ph* Joseph Ruttenberg   *Ed* Harold F. Kress, Alfred Junge   *Mus* Miklos Rozsa   *Art Dir* Alfred Junge
● Greer Garson, Walter Pidgeon, John Hodiak, Leo Genn, Cathy O'Donnell, Peter Finch (M-G-M)

No one seriously expected a second *Mrs Miniver* when *The Miniver Story* was in the making. It is difficult to capture the magical quality of the original, and this trades on its predecessor's name and the drawing power of Greer Garson and Walter Pidgeon.

Opening with a strangely pallid reproduction of London on VE day, Mrs Miniver finds herself caught in the exuberant melee following the news that the war is over. She has just come from a doctor, realizes she has not long to live and bravely determines to keep the news from her family.

Chief laurels go to Greer Garson who, even with the unmistakable signs of illness and mental stress, makes feasible the husband's claim that she looks as lovely as ever.

John Hodiak gives a fine clear-cut performance.

■ **MINNIE AND MOSKOWITZ**

1971, 114 MINS, US ◇
Dir John Cassavetes   *Prod* Al Ruban   *Scr* John Cassavetes   *Ph* Arthur J. Ornitz, Alric Edens, Michael Margulies   *Ed* Fred Knudtson   *Mus* Bo Harwood (sup.)
● Gena Rowlands, Seymour Cassel, Val Avery, Tim Carey, Katherine Cassavetes, John Cassavetes (Universal)

Gena Rowlands and Seymour Cassel play the title roles in *Minnie And Moskowitz*, an oppressive and irritating film in which a shrill and numbing hysteria of acting and direction soon kills any empathy for the loneliness of the main characters. John Cassavetes wrote and directed in his now-familiar home-movie im-

provisational and indulgent style.

The characters in Cassavetes' script are the 'little people' who inhabit kitchen-sink dramas. When such people exist in reality, they are leasebreakers, who lower property values, create Saturday night brawls and otherwise earn the total contempt of neighbors.

Cassavetes has laid on with a trowel the silicones of borderline personal psychosis. The principals live on the knife-edge of breakdown.

Rowlands, fed up with a back-street affair with Cassavetes, unbilled as a married man whose wife Judith Roberts tries suicide, has a friend in co-worker Elsie Ames but little more. Rescuing her from a tight situation with pushy blind date Val Avery, Seymour Cassel outdoes in boorishness anything Avery might have tried. Cassel makes King Kong look like Cary Grant.

■ **MIRACLE, THE**

1959, 121 MINS, US ◇
Dir Irving Rapper   *Prod* Henry Blanke   *Scr* Frank Butler   *Ph* Ernest Haller   *Ed* Frank Bracht   *Mus* Elmer Bernstein
● Carroll Baker, Roger Moore, Walter Slezak, Vittorio Gassman, Katina Paxinou, Gustavo Rojo (Warner)

Warner Bros.' multi-million dollar spectacle, though laid in the 19th century is a 'biblical' subject with elements and approach of such films. The production has bullfights, military battles, lavish ballroom parties, music, dancing, gypsies and vaulted cathedrals echoing to choirs of nuns. It has about everything, in fact, except a genuinely spiritual story.

The Miracle was a costume special of the German stager Max Reinhardt. Its theme is the recurrent one in religious legend, of the god, goddess or angel who assumes human shape to intervene directly in the affairs of men.

According to the screenplay, based on Karl Vollmoeller's old play, Carroll Baker is a postulant at a Spanish convent when she falls in love with Roger Moore, a soldier in the future Duke of Wellington's army, then battling Napoleon in Spain. When she leaves the convent to follow Moore, the statue of the Virgin in the chapel comes down from its pedestal and assumes the form of the postulant. And Baker is off on various adventures.

Irving Rapper's direction is effective in the spacious exteriors, moving massed groupings with force and interest. It is less perceptive in the handling of individuals and their interaction. As for the theme itself, it is not exactly clear what 'The Miracle' is supposed to do, other than give Baker a chance to gallivant about Europe in a variety of costumes.

■ **MIRACLE, THE**

1991, 96 MINS, UK ◇ ⑨ ⑩ ⊙
Dir Neil Jordan   *Prod* Stephen Woolley, Redmond Morris   *Scr* Neil Jordan   *Ph* Philippe Rousselot   *Ed* Joke van Wijk   *Mus* Anne Dudley   *Art Dir* Gemma Jackson
● Beverly D'Angelo, Donal McCann, Niall Byrne, Lorraine Pilkington, J.G. Devlin, Kathleen Delaney (Palace/Promenade)

Irish writer-director Neil Jordan returns to his home turf with the small-scale romantic drama *The Miracle*, with uneven results.

Jimmy (Niall Byrne) is a musician and a dreamer who spends much of his time in the company of Rose (Lorraine Pilkington). Rose would like their relationship to become more intimate. Together they walk the streets of their small coastal town (Bray in County Wicklow), inventing romantic stories about the people who pass them by.

Jimmy never knew his mother and lives with his father (Donal McCann), a drunken musician. One day his eye is caught by an attractive American woman (Beverly D'Angelo) who's in town to perform in a local production of *Destry Rides Again*. He fantasizes a romantic liasion with her, but there are no prizes for guessing that she's really his long-lost mother.

Like everything else in the film, the incest theme is tentatively handled. More interesting is Rose's relationship with a circus animal trainer (Mikkel Gaup).

D'Angelo exudes mature sexuality as the stranger in town, but McCann makes heavy weather of his role as the perpetually drunken father.

■ **MIRACLE CAN HAPPEN, A**
See: On Our Merry Way

■ **MIRACLE IN SOHO**

1957, 98 MINS, UK ⊙
Dir Julian Amyes *Prod* Emeric Pressburger *Scr* Emeric Pressburger *Ph* Christopher Challis *Ed* Arthur Stevens *Mus* Brian Easdale *Art Dir* Carmen Dillon
● John Gregson, Belinda Lee, Cyril Cusack, Rosalie Crutchley, Ian Bannen, Billie Whitelaw (Rank)

A rather slow moving sentimental yarn has been woven around the polyglot population in central London's Soho. It is a simple story that lacks punch and gives the impression that more could have been made of the colorful material.

A small side street of shops and cafes has been shut down for road repairs and Mike, one of the working gang, proceeds to live up to his reputation as a wolf. He gets involved with an Italian family about to emigrate to Canada. The son wants to stay behind as he is in love with a barmaid. The elder daughter is reluctant to go as she has a chance to marry a prosperous cafe proprietor. The younger girl falls for Mike's charm, and stays behind, only to find he doesn't want her.

The repairing gang moves on, after their job is complete, but after the girl is left flat she prays in the nearby church, and Saint Anthony obliges with a miracle.

John Gregson never seems quite at home in rough clothes but makes a likeable personality of the roving Romeo, and Belinda Lee is simple and naive as the anglicized Italian girl in love with him.

■ **MIRACLE OF LIFE, THE**
See: Our Daily Bread

■ **MIRACLE OF MORGAN'S CREEK, THE**

1944, 101 MINS, US ⊙
Dir Preston Sturges *Prod* [uncredited] *Scr* Preston Sturges *Ph* John F. Seitz *Ed* Stuart Gilmore *Mus* Leo Shuken, Charles Bradshaw
● Eddie Bracken, Betty Hutton, Diana Lynn, William Demarest, Brian Donlevy, Akim Tamiroff (Paramount)

Morgan's Creek is the name of the town where the action takes place and the miracle, as director Preston Sturges terms it, is the birth to Eddie Bracken and Betty Hutton of a set of sextuplets.

Done in the satirical Sturges vein, and directed with that same touch, the story makes much of characterization and somewhat wacky comedy, plus some slapstick, with excellent photography figuring throughout. The Sturges manner of handling crowds and various miscellaneous characters who are almost nothing more than flashes in the picture, such as the smalltown attorney and the justice of the peace, contribute enormously to the enjoyment derived.

However, some of the comedy situations lack punch, and the picture is slow to get rolling, but ultimately picks up smart pace and winds up quite strongly on the birth of the sextuplets with the retiring Bracken and Hutton as national heroes.

Bracken is a smalltown bank clerk who yearns to get into uniform and is madly in love with Hutton. Getting out on an all-night party with soldiers, the latter wakes up to remember that she married a serviceman, but can't remember the name, what the spouse looked like, or anything except that they didn't give their right names.

Bracken does a nice job. Hutton and he make a desirable team. Among the supporting cast, largest assignment is that given William Demarest, smalltown cop father of Hutton, who has his troubles with his daughters, the other being attractive Diana Lynn.
□ 1944: Nomination: Best Original Screenplay

■ **MIRACLE ON 34TH STREET**
(UK: The Big Heart)

1947, 95 MINS, US ⊙
Dir George Seaton *Prod* William Perlberg *Scr* George Seaton *Ph* Charles Clarke, Lloyd Ahern *Ed* Robert Simpson *Mus* Cyril J. Mockridge *Art Dir* Richard Day, Richard Irvine
● Maureen O'Hara, John Payne, Edmund Gwenn, Natalie Wood, Thelma Ritter, Gene Lockhart (20th Century-Fox)

So you don't believe in Santa Claus? If you want to stay a non-believer don't see *Miracle*.

Film is an actor's holiday, providing any number of choice roles that are played to the hilt. Edmund Gwenn's Santa Claus performance proves the best in his career, one that will be thoroughly enjoyed by all filmgoers. Straight romantic roles handed Maureen O'Hara and John Payne as co-stars also display pair to advantage.

Valentine Davies' story poses question of just how valid is the belief in Santa Claus. Gwenn, old man's home inmate, becomes Santy at Macy's Department Store, events pile up that make it necessary to actually prove he is the McCoy and not a slightly touched old gent. Gwenn is a little amazed at all the excitement because he has no doubt that he's the real article.

Gene Lockhart's performance as judge is a gem, as is Porter Hall's portrayal of a neurotic personnel director for Macy's. Surprise moppet performance is turned in by little Natalie Wood as O'Hara's non-believing daughter who finally accepts Santy. It's a standout, natural portrayal.
□ 1947: Best Supp. Actor (Edmund Gwenn), Original Story, Screenplay.
□ Nomination: Best Picture

■ **MIRACLE WOMAN, THE**

1931, 90 MINS, US
Dir Frank Capra *Prod* Frank Capra *Scr* Jo Swerling, Dorothy Howell *Ph* Joseph Walker *Ed* Maurice Wright
● Barbara Stanwyck, David Manners, Sam Hardy, Beryl Mercer, Russell Hopton, Charles Middleton (Columbia)

Film has two unusual aspects. One is its basic theme of an expose on evangelism. The other is a punch sequence at the opening, perhaps the strongest scene the feature possesses.

Frank Capra's direction has practically wasted nothing as he traces the girl through her exhortatory racket to the thrill finish of a tabernacle blaze which, from the mob standpoint, has been exceedingly well handled.

There isn't much doubt that Capra can do more with Barbara Stanwyck than any other director. Her performance here is splended in unfolding plenty of fire, balanced by undertones of instinctive character softness and mood as she slowly falls in love with a blind boy who becomes one of her ardent followers [based on the play by John Mechan and Robert Riskin].

The punch start is a country church on a Sunday morning in which the ruling faction has decided to secure a new and younger minister. Stanwyck is the deposed reverend's daughter who takes the pulpit to read her father's valedictory after 20 years of service. Half way through the message she stops and sobbingly announces that her father died at this point. Follows her launching of a tirade, berating the church members for their action and shortcomings.

■ **MIRACLE WORKER, THE**

1962, 106 MINS, US ⊙ ⊙
Dir Arthur Penn *Prod* Fred Coe *Scr* William Gibson *Ph* Ernest Caparros *Ed* Aram Avakian *Mus* Laurence Rosenthal *Art Dir* George Jenkins
● Anne Bancroft, Patty Duke, Victor Jory, Inga Swenson, Andrew Prine (United Artists)

A celebrated television show, later a critical, artistic and popular hit on the stage, the Fred Coe production was directed by Arthur Penn, who staged the legit version, and stars Anne Bancroft and Patty Duke in the roles they introduced to Broadway.

Gibson's screenplay relates the story of the young Helen Keller and how, through the dedication, perseverance and courage of her teacher, Annie Sullivan, she establishes a means of communication with the world she cannot see or hear.

Where the picture really excels, outside of its inherent story values, is in the realm of photographic technique. It is here that director Penn and cameraman Ernest Caparros have teamed to create artful, indelible strokes of visual storytelling and mood-molding. The measured dissolves, focal shifts and lighting and filtering enrich the production considerably. Add to these attributes the haunting, often chilling, score by Laurence Rosenthal.
□ 1962: Best Actress (Anne Bancroft), Supp. Actress (Patty Duke).
□ Nominations: Best Director, Adapted Screenplay, B&W Costume Design

■ **MIRAGE**

1965, 108 MINS, US ⊙
Dir Edward Dmytryk *Prod* Harry Keller *Scr* Peter Stone *Ph* Joseph MacDonald *Ed* Ted J. Kent *Mus* Quincy Jones
● Gregory Peck, Diane Baker, Walter Matthau, Kevin McCarthy, Jack Weston, Leif Erickson (Universal)

Mirage starts as a mystery, unfolds as a mystery, ends as a mystery. There are moments of stiff action and suspense but plot is as confusing as it is overly-contrived.

Gregory Peck stars as an amnesiac trying to learn why he is the target for assassins. Story is about a man in NY who suddenly discovers he cannot remember any part of his past life. Returning to his apartment from a big office building which was suddenly without lights and where a prominent man plunged to his death from the 27th floor, he is confronted by a stranger holding a gun who informs him he's taking Peck to a man he has never heard of. Knocking the gunman out, he goes to the police to demand protection, only to discover he's a thoroughly confused man.

Edward Dmytryk in his taut direction keeps a tight rein on pace and manages vigorous movement in individual sequences, but cannot overcome script deficiencies. Peck's character is not clearly drawn but actor makes the most of what's offered him as a brooding man trying to save his life. Diane Baker flits in and out of plot as a mysterious figure whose true identity is never established.

■ **MIRANDA**

1948, 80 MINS, UK
Dir Ken Annakin *Prod* Betty E. Box *Scr* Peter Blackmore, Denis Waldock *Ph* Ray Elton *Ed* Gordon Hales *Mus* Temple Abady *Art Dir* George Patterson

M

● Glynis Johns, Googie Withers, Griffith Jones, John McCallum, Margaret Rutherford, David Tomlinson (Gainsborough)

Planning a holiday alone in Cornwall, Paul Marten, a fashionable doctor, is dragged out of his fishing boat to the sea bottom by Miranda, a lovely mermaid. Price for return to his home and wife is that he takes Miranda to London.

Everything [in this adaptation of Peter Blackmore's stage play] is rightly played for laughs and Glynis Johns makes the mermaid an attractive and almost credible creature. Griffith Jones is good as her serious sponsor. Googie Withers turns in a nice performance as his bewildered wife, and David Tomlinson and John McCallum do well as the love-struck swains.

■ MIRROR CRACK'D, THE

1981, 105 MINS, UK ◇ ⑰ ⊙
Dir Guy Hamilton   *Prod* John Brabourne, Richard Goodwin   *Scr* Jonathan Hales, Barry Sandler   *Ph* Christopher Challis   *Ed* Richard Mardon   *Mus* John Cameron   *Art Dir* Michael Stringer
● Angela Lansbury, Elizabeth Taylor, Kim Novak, Rock Hudson, Geraldine Chaplin, Tony Curtis (EMI)

EMI's third Agatha Christie mystery [from her novel *The Mirror Crack'd from Side to Side*] is a nostalgic throwback to the genteel British murder mystery pix of the 1950s.

Though Angela Lansbury is top-billed in the role of Christie's famed sleuth Jane Marple, the central part really is Elizabeth Taylor's. Taylor comes away with her most genuinely affecting dramatic performance in years as a film star attempting a comeback following an extended nervous breakdown.

The Taylor character and those close to her have been haunted by the memory of an apparently accidental catastrophe which proves to have been caused by one of the minor characters.

Taylor has an uproarious good time as she trades bitchy insults with Kim Novak. Adroit supporting performances are given by Tony Curtis, Rock Hudson as Taylor's husband and director, and Geraldine Chaplin.

■ MISERY

1990, 107 MINS, US ◇ ⑰ ⊙
Dir Rob Reiner   *Prod* Andrew Scheinman, Rob Reiner   *Scr* William Goldman   *Ph* Barry Sonnenfeld   *Ed* Robert Leighton   *Mus* Marc Shaiman   *Art Dir* Norman Garwood
● James Caan, Kathy Bates, Frances Sternhagen, Richard Farnsworth, Lauren Bacall, Graham Jarvis (Castle Rock/Nelson)

Misery is a very obvious and very commercial gothic thriller, a functional adaptation of the Stephen King bestseller.

Basically a two-hander, *Misery* is the name of the 19th-century heroine of a series of gothic romances penned by James Caan. During the opening credits his car crashes on slippery Colorado roads and Kathy Bates digs him out of the snow and wreckage.

A plump former nurse, she fixes up his sevrely injured legs and virtually holds him prisoner, incommunicado, for the rest of the film. As in the classic Robert Aldrich gothics like *What Ever Happened to Baby Jane?*, the fun comes from the ebb and flow nastiness of the two characters in a love/hate (often hate/hate) relationship.

Key plot gimmick is that Caan's killed off the profitable but hack-work Misery character, an act that turns adoring fan Bates against him and sets in motion her obsession that he resurrect the fictional character.

Casting of Caan is effective, as his snide remarks and grumpy attitude are backed up by a physical dimension that makes believable his inevitable fighting back. Bates has a field day with her role, creating a quirky, memorable object of hate.

Tech credits on this $21 million pic are very good, including Reno-area location shots.
□ 1990: Best Actress (Kathy Bates)

■ MISFITS, THE

1961, 124 MINS, US ⑰ ⊙
Dir John Huston   *Prod* Frank E. Taylor   *Scr* Arthur Miller   *Ph* Russell Metty   *Ed* George Tomasini   *Mus* Alex North   *Art Dir* Stephen Grimes, William Newberry
● Clark Gable, Marilyn Monroe, Montgomery Clift, Thelma Ritter, Eli Wallach (United Artists)

At face value, *The Misfits*, is a robust, high-voltage adventure drama, vibrating with explosively emotional histrionics, conceived and executed with a refreshing disdain for superficial technical and photographic slickness in favor of an uncommonly honest and direct cinematic approach. Within this framework, however, lurks a complex mass of introspective conflicts, symbolic parallels and motivational contradictions, the nuances of which may seriously confound general audiences.

Clark Gable essays the role of a self-sufficient Nevada cowboy, a kind of last of the great rugged individualists a noble misfit. Into his life ambles a woman (Marilyn Monroe) possessed of an almost uncanny degree of humanitarian compassion. Their relationship matures smoothly enough until Gable goes 'mustanging', a ritual in which wild, 'misfit' mustangs are rudely roped into captivity. Revolted by what she regards as cruel and mercenary, Monroe, with the aid of yet another misfit, itinerant, disillusioned rodeo performer Montgomery Clift, strives to free the captive horses.

The film is somewhat uneven in pace and not entirely sound in dramatic structure. Character development is choppy in several instances. The one essayed by Thelma Ritter is essentially superfluous and, in fact, abruptly abandoned in the course of the story. Eli Wallach's character undergoes a severely sudden and faintly inconsistent transition. Even Monroe's never comes fully into focus.

■ MISHIMA
A LIFE IN FOUR CHAPTERS

1985, 120 MINS, US ◇ ⑰
Dir Paul Schrader   *Prod* Mata Yamamoto, Tom Luddy   *Scr* Paul Schrader, Leonard Schrader, Chieko Schrader   *Ph* John Bailey   *Ed* Michael Chandler, Tomoyo Oshima   *Mus* Philip Glass   *Art Dir* Eiko Ishioka
● Ken Ogata, Kenji Sawada, Yasosuke Bando, Toshiyuki Nagashima (Zoetrope/Filmlink)

Paul Schrader's film *Mishima* is a boldly conceived, intelligent and consistently absorbing study of the Japanese writer and political iconoclast's life, work and death.

The most famous of contemporary Japanese novelists to Westerners, Yukio Mishima was also a film actor and director and leader of a militant right-wing cult bent upon restoring the glory of the emperor. He became forever notorious in 1970 when, accompanied by a few followers, he entered a military garrison in Tokyo, 'captured' a general, delivered an impassioned speech to an assembly and then committed *seppuku* (ritual suicide).

Instead of pretending to deliver a fully factual, detailed biopic, director Paul Schrader, his co-screenwriter and brother Leonard and other collaborators have opted to combine relatively realistic treatment of some aspects of Mishima's life, particularly his final day, with highly stylized renditions of assorted semi-autobiographical literary works (*Temple of the Golden Pavilion*, *Kyoko's House* and *Runaway Horses*) in an effort to convey key points about the man's personality and credos.

Pacing sometimes lags, particularly in the fictional interludes, and uninitiated audiences may be confused at times. Production itself,

however, is stunning, and performances, led by that of Ken Ogata as the adult Mishima, are authoritative and convincing. [Pic is in Japanese with English subtitles, and narration read by Roy Scheider.]

■ MISS FIRECRACKER

1989, 102 MINS, US ◇ ⑰ ⊙
Dir Thomas Schlamme   *Prod* Fred Berner   *Scr* Beth Henley   *Ph* Arthur Albert   *Ed* Peter C. Frank   *Mus* David Mansfield   *Art Dir* Kristi Zea
● Holly Hunter, Mary Steenburgen, Tim Robbins, Alfre Woodard, Scott Glenn, Trey Wilson (Corsair)

Holly Hunter reprises her stage role [in Beth Henley's play *The Miss Firecracker Contest*] as Carnelle, a former goodtime girl whose dream is to win the local Miss Firecracker contest in her hometown of Yazoo City, Miss. Her cousin (Mary Steenburgen) won the crown over a decade earlier, and against all odds Carnelle makes it to the finals as an alternate.

Miss Firecracker is peopled with oddball characters, notably Tim Robbins as Steenburgen's free spirit brother and Alfre Woodard as the black seamstress assigned to fabricate Carnelle's contest costume.

Putting the show over with a bang is Hunter, the epitome of energy in a tailormade feisty role. She very accurately judges the line between high and low camp in her climactic tapdance for the talent contest, entertaining but just klutzy enough to be authentic.

Steenburgen and Woodard are consistent scene-stealers here, former dead-on as a Southern belle putting on airs and latter revivifying ethnic stereotypes such as bugged-out eyes into a hilarious, original character.

■ MISSING

1982, 122 MINS, US ◇ ⑰ ⊙
Dir Constantine Costa-Gavras   *Prod* Edward Lewis, Mildred Lewis   *Scr* Constantine Costa-Gavras, Donald Stewart   *Ph* Ricardo Aronovich   *Ed* Francoise Bonnot   *Mus* Vangelis   *Art Dir* Peter Jamison
● Jack Lemmon, Sissy Spacek, Melanie Mayron, John Shea, Charles Cioffi, David Clennon (Universal)

Although the country in question is never named, the subject here is unequivocally that of US involvement in the 1973 military coup in Allende's Chile.

Based on the true story of a young American, Charles Horman, who disappeared during the Chile coup, drama [from a book by Thomas Hauser] presents John Shea and Sissy Spacek as a vaguely counter-culturish couple living in Santiago.

When Shea inexplicably disappears and Spacek can get nowhere in locating him, his father (Jack Lemmon) flies down to get heavy with US government officials.

Real jolt of the picture, which comes across on an effective personal level due to its impact on Lemmon derives from the premise that, when pressed, the US government places the interests of business above those of individual citizens.

Lemmon is superior as a man facing up to issues he never wanted to confront personally. Edgy and belligerent most of the time, Spacek is more constrained but she's fully believable.
□ 1982: Best Adapted Screenplay.
□ Nominations: Best Picture, Actor (Jack Lemmon), Actress (Sissy Spacek)

■ MISSING IN ACTION

1984, 101 MINS, US ◇ ⑰ ⊙
Dir Joseph Zito   *Prod* Menahem Golan, Yoram Globus   *Scr* James Bruner   *Ph* Joao Fernandes   *Ed* Joel Goodman   *Mus* Jay Chattaway   *Art Dir* Ladi Wilheim
● Chuck Norris, M. Emmet Walsh, Lenore Kasdorf, James Hong, David Tress, Ernie Ortega (Cannon)

With the Philippines filling in for Vietnam jungles, with Chuck Norris kicking and firing away, with a likable sidekick in the black marketeering figure of M. Emmet Walsh, and with a touch of nudity in sordid Bangkok bars, writer James Bruner and director Joseph Zito have marshalled a formula pic with a particularly jingoistic slant: even though the war is long over, the Commies in Vietnam still deserve the smack of a bullet.

Norris plays a former North Vietnamese prisoner, an American colonel missing in action for seven years, who escapes to the US and then returns to Vietnam determined to find MIAs and convince the world that Yanks are still imprisoned in Vietnam.

● ●

■ MISSION, THE

1986, 128 MINS, UK ◇ ⓥ ☉
Dir Roland Joffe   *Prod* Fernando Ghia, David Puttnam
Scr Robert Bolt   *Ph* Chris Menges   *Ed* Jim Clark
Mus Ennio Morricone   *Art Dir* Stuart Craig
● Robert De Niro, Jeremy Irons, Ray McAnally, Liam Neeson, Aidan Quinn, Ronald Pickup (Goldcrest/Kingsmere/Enigma)

The script of this $23 million pic is based on a little-known but nonetheless intriguing historical incident in mid-18th-century South America, pitting avaricious colonialists against the Jesuit order of priests.

The fillip is the presence in the leads of Robert De Niro and Jeremy Irons, a nifty combo of British classicism with American box-office appeal. The two principal actors work hard to animate their parts. But there is little to do. *The Mission* is probably the first film in which De Niro gives a bland, uninteresting performance.

The fundamental problem is that the script is cardboard thin, pinning labels on its characters and arbitrarily shoving them into various stances to make plot points.
☐ 1986: Best Cinematography.
☐ Nominations: Best Picture, Director, Costume Design, Art Direction, Editing, Original Score

● ●

■ MISSIONARY, THE

1983, 90 MINS, UK ◇ ⓥ
Dir Richard Loncraine   *Prod* Neville C. Thompson, Michael Palin   *Scr* Michael Palin   *Ph* Peter Hannan   *Ed* Paul Green   *Mus* Mike Moran   *Art Dir* Norman Garwood
● Michael Palin, Maggie Smith, Trevor Howard, Denholm Elliott, Michael Hordern, Graham Crowden (HandMade)

Turn-of-the-century English gentry targeted in *The Missionary* remains good for laughs, especially in the hands of the talented Michael Palin. But Palin's script meanders wastefully across three separate story possibilities, never making full use of any of them.

As the Anglican title character called home to England, Palin has a brief encounter on the boat with Her Ladyship Maggie Smith who exhibits a keen interest in pagan fertility symbols. But the reverend's mind is on marriage to his childhood sweetheart (Phoebe Nicholls), whose most romantic thoughts center on how well she has managed to file and crossfile his letters for 10 years.

Once in London, Palin is assigned by Bishop Denholm Elliott to start a slum mission for 'fallen women'. And here comes Smith with the seed money Palin needs, provided he's friendly in return since her married life with stuffy Trevor Howard is a bit empty.

● ●

■ MISSION TO MOSCOW

1943, 123 MINS, US
Dir Michael Curtiz   *Prod* Robert Buckner   *Scr* Howard Koch   *Ph* Bert Glennon   *Ed* Owen Marks   *Mus* Max Steiner

● Walter Huston, Ann Harding, Oscar Homolka, Gene Lockhart, Eleanor Parker, Helmut Dantine (Warner)

Film is of a highly intellectual nature, requiring constant attention and thought if it is to be fully appreciated. It is pretty much in the nature of a lengthy monolog, with little action.

It is truly a documentary; Hollywood's initial effort at living history. Every character is the counterpart of an actual person. Real names are used throughout Roosevelt, Churchill, Stalin, Davies, Litvinov, et al and the casting is aimed for physical likeness to the person portrayed. The jolting realism of the likenesses is far from the least of the picture's interesting aspects.

Outstanding in the tremendous cast are Walter Huston as Davies, Ann Harding as Mrs Davies, Oscar Homolka as Litvinov, Gene Lockhart as Molotov, Barbara Everest as Mrs Litvinov, Vladimir Sokoloff as Kalinin, and Dudley Field Malone as Churchill.

Film follows pretty much in chronological order from the time of Roosevelt's appointment of the progressively-minded, capitalist-corporation lawyer Joseph E. Davies to the post of ambassador to Russia.

Manner of presentation of the film is the use of Huston's voice off-screen, employing the first person, to describe his tours and many of the events. Then, where the action permits, the film lapses into regular direct dialog among the characters on the screen.
☐ 1943: Nomination: Best B&W Art Direction

● ●

■ MISSISSIPPI BURNING

1988, 125 MINS, US ◇ ⓥ ☉
Dir Alan Parker   *Prod* Frederick Zollo, Robert F. Colesberry   *Scr* Chris Gerolmo   *Ph* Peter Biziou
Ed Gerry Hambling   *Mus* Trevor Jones   *Art Dir* Philip Harrison, Geoffrey Kirkland
● Gene Hackman, Willem Dafoe, Frances McDormand, Brad Dourif, R. Lee Ermey, Gailard Sartain (Orion)

Though its credibility is undermined by a fanciful ending, *Mississippi Burning* captures much of the truth in its telling of the impact of a 1964 FBI probe into the murders of three civil rights workers.

Story follows the FBI men (Gene Hackman and Willem Dafoe) who've been sent down to Jessup, Miss, to investigate the disappearance of three voter activists, one black and two white Jews. The two run into resistance from both the guilty parties and the blacks, who've been terrorized into silence. It's the fearless Dafoe who wears a hole through the wall and Hackman who knows what to do on the other side.

Dafoe gives a disciplined and noteworthy portrayal of Ward, who squelches his emotions as his moral indignation burns. But it's Hackman who steals the picture as Anderson, a messily sympathetic man who connects keenly but briefly with the people. Glowing performance of Frances McDormand as the deputy's wife who's drawn to Hackman is an asset both to his role and the picture.

Parker pushes the picture along at a fervent clip, with the character scenes back-to-back with chases or violence.
☐ 1988: Best Cinematography.
☐ Nominations: Best Picture, Director, Actor (Gene Hackman), Supp. Actress (Frances McDormand), Editing, Sound

● ●

■ MISSISSIPPI MASALA

1992, 118 MINS, US ◇ ⓥ ☉
Dir Mira Nair   *Prod* Michael Nozik, Mira Nair
Scr Sooni Taraporevala   *Ph* Ed Lachman   *Ed* Roberto Silvi   *Mus* L. Subramaniam   *Art Dir* Mitch Epstein
● Denzel Washington, Sarita Choudhury, Roshan Seth, Sharmila Tagore, Charles S. Dutton, Joe Seneca (Cinecom/Mirabi)

Indian director Mira Nair's tragicomedy is less passionate and disturbing than many US pics dealing with race relations. *Mississippi Masala* is handled with a light touch.

The dramatic opening, set in Uganda in 1972, shows a middle-class Indian family forced to leave when Idi Amin takes power. A liberal lawyer (Roshan Seth) who has defended blacks in court, his wife (Sharmila Tagore) and little daughter Mina catch the last plane out under an eerie, threatening state of siege.

Story jumps to present-day Mississippi, where the family has settled. Nair skilfully depicts an interracial small town where there's a minor traffic accident involving a white redneck, black youth Demetrius (Denzel Washington) and a pretty Indian girl, the grown-up Mina (Sarita Choudhury). Mina and Demetrius are attracted to each other right away.

Washington is savvy and attractive as the enterprising carpet cleaner destined for a brighter future. Choudhury is a discovery as the Americanized Mina, who calls herself a kind of masala (mixed spices). Together, they carry the film smoothly and agreeably.

● ●

■ MISSOURI BREAKS, THE

1976, 126 MINS, US ◇ ⓥ
Dir Arthur Penn   *Prod* Elliott Kastner, Robert M. Sherman   *Scr* Thomas McGuane   *Ph* Michael Butler   *Ed* Jerry Greenberg, Stephen Rotter, Dede Allen   *Mus* John Williams   *Art Dir* Albert Brenner
● Marlon Brando, Jack Nicholson, Kathleen Lloyd, Randy Quaid, Frederic Forrest, Harry Dean Stanton (United Artists)

The environment is the Montana headlands of the Missouri River, where pioneer John McLiam is range boss, local political muscle and pretty well master of the territory. Enter Jack Nicholson, leader of the area's horse thieves, out to avenge a colleague's death while facilitating his work by buying a ranch near the McLiam property as a rest stop for stolen horses.

Finally comes Marlon Brando, vicious frontier hired gun, engaged by McLiam to ferret out the Nicholson gang.

The trouble with *The Missouri Breaks* is that one is seriously drawn to it on its upfront elements, but leaves with a depressing sense of waste. As a film achievement it's corned beef and ham hash.

● ●

■ MISS SADIE THOMPSON

1953, 90 MINS, US ◇ ⓥ ☉
Dir Curtis Bernhardt   *Prod* Jerry Wald   *Scr* Harry Kleiner   *Ph* Charles Lawton Jr   *Ed* Viola Lawrence
Mus George Duning   *Art Dir* Carl Anderson
● Rita Hayworth, Jose Ferrer, Aldo Ray, Russell Collins, Peggy Converse, Charles Bronson (Columbia/Beckworth)

Rain, the stage play which John Colton made from W. Somerset Maugham's story about sex, sin and salvation in the tropics, is back for a third try as a motion picture. This time it's a modernized version fancied up with 3-D and Technicolor.

The production uses an authentic island background for the story, the lensing having been done in Hawaii, so the presentation has a lush tropical look.

In this treatment, Sadie is a shady lady chased out of a Honolulu bawdy house by Davidson, a man determined to keep sin out of the islands. She dodges deportation to San Francisco, where she's wanted for another rap, by taking a ship for New Caledonia. Enroute, the ship is quarantined at an island occupied mostly by Marines.

The dramatic pacing of Curtis Bernhardt's direction achieves a frenzied jazz tempo, quite in keeping with the modernization, and most of the performances respond in kind, es-

pecially that of Rita Hayworth. She catches
the feel of the title character well, even to
braving completely deglamorizing makeup,
costuming and photography to fit her physical
appearance to that of the bawdy, shady lady
that was Sadie Thompson. Less effective is
Jose Ferrer's Alfred Davidson, no longer a
missionary bigot but a straight layman bigot.
Missing under the change is the religious fanaticism that motivated and made understandable the original Freudian character.

Aldo Ray, playing Sergeant O'Hara, the
Marine who makes an honest woman of
Sadie, is good.

□ 1953: Nomination: Best Song ('Blue Pacific
Blues')

■ MISS TATLOCK'S MILLIONS

1948, 99 MINS, US

Dir Richard Haydn   *Prod* Charles Brackett   *Scr* Charles
Brackett, Richard L. Breen   *Ph* Charles B. Lang Jr
Ed Everett Douglas   *Mus* Victor Young   *Art Dir* Hans
Dreier, Franz Bachelin
● John Lund, Wanda Hendrix, Barry Fitzgerald, Monty
Woolley, Robert Stack (Paramount)

Basically, story and characters are much to-
do about nothing, but the pace is fast, the dialog flip and sophisticated, and the playing
expert. This gives the material a surface
brightness that makes it look better than it is.

Haydn's directorial debut is creditable. He
sets up his characters and situations to keep
the chuckles rolling from the broad antics. Plot
[based on the play, *Oh! Brother*, by Jacques
Deval] concerns a screwball family and the idiot heir to millions, with a number of tangent
ramifications that keep the fun pot boiling.

John Lund and Wanda Hendrix team
brightly in the principal roles and film receives major assists from Barry Fitzgerald,
Monty Woolley, Ilka Chase and others.

Haydn has given considerable footage to a
display of the brawn of Lund and Robert
Stack, romantic rivals, even to the point of
neglecting Hendrix in a bathing suit. In addition to directing Haydn cuts himself in for a
very funny bit as an eccentric lawyer, using
the name of Richard Rancyd.

■ MISTER FROST

1990, 104 MINS, FRANCE/UK ◇ ⊛ ⊙

Dir Philippe Setbon   *Prod* Xavier Gelin   *Scr* Philippe
Setbon, Brad Lynch   *Ph* Dominique Brenguier   *Ed* Ray
Lovejoy   *Art Dir* Max Berto
● Jeff Goldblum, Alan Bates, Kathy Baker, Roland
Girand, Jean-Pierre Cassel, Daniel Gelin (Hugo/AAA)

Mister Frost is a tepid thriller about a mass
murderer who claims to be the devil himself.
Jeff Goldblum is a seemingly cordial country
gentleman (in England, apparently) who casually confesses to police to having tortured
and murdered no less than 24 men, women
and children, buried on his property.

Most of the story is set in a clinic 'somewere
in Europe' where Goldblum breaks his silence
to communicate with lady psychiatrist Kathy
Baker. Yes, he's Satan in person, he tells her,
and he's fuming mad because modern psychiatry has cheated him out of authorship in
20th century evil. Now he wants to make a
comeback and has chosen Baker as his agent.

None of this is particularly terrifying or gripping, especially since Gallic writer-helmer
Philippe Setbon is incapable of creating any
suspenseful doubt about whether Goldblum is
indeed Satan, or merely a dangerous schizophrenic with psychic and hypnotic powers.

■ MISTER MOSES

1965, 115 MINS, US ◇

Dir Ronald Neame   *Prod* Frank Ross   *Scr* Charles
Beaumont, Monja Danischewsky   *Ph* Oswald Morris

Ed Phil Anderson, Peter Wetherley   *Mus* John Barry
● Robert Mitchum, Carroll Baker, Ian Bannen,
Alexander Knox, Raymond St Jacques, Orlando Martins
(United Artists)

The Biblical Moses, in a manner, has been
updated for this Frank Ross production,
switching the plot to an American diamond
smuggler leading an African tribe to a
promised land. Director Ronald Neame has
taken every advantage of fascinating African
terrain for his unusual adventure yarn from
Max Catto's novel.

Film takes its motivation from orders by the
district commissioner for a village, threatened by flood waters of a new dam being constructed, to evacuate. The religious-minded
chief, who has heard the story of Moses from
a missionary and his daughter who live with
the tribe, refuses to take his people in helicopters to be provided for purpose, because
the Bible says the children of Israel, when
they went to their promised land, took their
animals with them. No animals, no go.

Robert Mitchum, a medicine-man who
smuggles diamonds, is set down in this tick-
lish situation, a guy known as Dr Moses. The
chief hails him as the true Moses who will
lead them to a special government preserve.

■ MISTER QUILP

1975, 117 MINS, UK ◇

Dir Michael Tuchner   *Prod* Helen M. Strauss   *Scr* Louis
Kamp, Irene Kamp   *Ph* Christopher Challis   *Ed* John
Jympson   *Mus* Anthony Newley   *Art Dir* Elliot Scott
● Anthony Newley, David Hemmings, David Warner,
Michael Hordern, Paul Rogers, Jill Bennett (Avco Embassy)

Mister Quilp is a sprightly musical version of
Charles Dickens' *The Old Curiosity Shop*.

Anthony Newley, a corrupt lender in league
with fringe lawyer David Warner and latter's
sister Jill Bennett, harasses shopowner Michael
Hordern and granddaughter Sarah Jane
Varley, both rescued in time by arrival of Paul
Rogers, Hordern's wealthy long-lost brother.

Peter Duncan, as Varley's admirer, David
Hemmings as a likable boulevardier, Mona
Washbourne as a delightful traveling show
operator who befriends the fleeing Varley and
Hordern, Sarah Webb as a plaintive street
urchin, Philip Davis as Newley's whipping boy
and Yvonne Antrobus as Newley's long-suffering wife all complement the main plot line.
Casting is uniformly excellent.

■ MISTER ROBERTS

1955, 120 MINS, US ◇ ⊛

Dir John Ford, Mervyn LeRoy   *Prod* Leland Hayward
Scr Frank Nugent, Joshua Logan   *Ph* Winton Hoch
Ed Jack Murray   *Mus* Franz Waxman   *Art Dir* Art Loel
● Henry Fonda, James Cagney, William Powell, Jack
Lemmon, Betsy Palmer, Ward Bond (Orange/Warner)

Thomas Heggen's salty comedy about life
aboard a Navy cargo ship had no trouble moving from the printed page to the stage [in a
play by Heggen and Joshua Logan]. Figuring
importantly in the sock manner with which it
all comes off on the screen is the directorial
credit shared by John Ford and Mervyn
LeRoy, the former having had to bow out because of illness midway in production.

Henry Fonda, who scored on the stage in
the title role, repeats in the picture as the
cargo officer who resented not being in the
thick of the fighting in the Pacific during
World War II.

James Cagney is simply great as the captain
of the ship. William Powell tackles the role of
ship's doctor with an easy assurance that
makes it stand out and Jack Lemmon is a big
hit as Ensign Pulver.

□ 1955: Best Supp. Actor (Jack Lemmon).
□ Nominations: Best Picture, Sound

■ MISUNDERSTOOD

1984, 91 MINS, US ◇ ⊛

Dir Jerry Schatzberg   *Prod* Tarak Ben Ammar
Scr Barra Grant   *Ph* Pasqualino De Santis   *Ed* Marc
Laub   *Mus* Michael Hoppe   *Art Dir* Joel Schiller
● Gene Hackman, Henry Thomas, Rip Torn, Huckleberry
Fox, Maureen Kerwin, Susan Anspach (Accent/Keith Barish)

Misunderstood, a somber and largely unsentimental study of a rift and ultimate reconciliation between father and son, is a 'remake and
adaptation' of Luigi Comencini's 1967 Italian
pic *Incompreso*.

New version places former post-war black
marketeer and now shipping magnate Gene
Hackman in a palatial home in Tunisia. His
wife has just died, and Hackman has a tough
time breaking the news to his seven-or-eight-
year-old son, Henry Thomas. In his opinion,
his other son, Huckleberry Fox, is simply too
young to comprehend what's happened.

When his relative Rip Torn suggests
Hackman is too stern with the boys, that he
expects too much of them, the latter protests
he's trying to treat Thomas like a grownup.

Ultimately, Thomas is seriously injured in a
fall, and he and Hackman finally break
through to each other.

■ MIXED BLOOD

(UK: *Cocaine*)

1984, 97 MINS, US ◇ ⊛

Dir Paul Morrissey   *Prod* Antoine Gannage, Teven
Fierberg   *Scr* Paul Morrissey   *Ph* Stefan Zapasnik
Ed Scott Vickrey   *Mus* Andy Hernandez
Art Dir Stephen McCabe
● Marilia Pera, Richard Ulacia, Linda Kerridge,
Geraldine Smith, Angel David, Ulrich Berr (Sef Saellite)

A tale of rival youth gangs tied into the city's
drug scene, *Mixed Blood* paints a colorful story
of kingdom building, corruption and revenge.
Adopting an overblown style of performance,
the picture maintains an edgy quality where
one is often wondering whether to laugh or
shudder at the proceedings.

Brazilian actress Marilia Pera arrives on
the scene like some loud, conquering hero
and with her son, Thiago (Richard Ulacia),
fashions a Hispanic ring of young teenagers
to challenge an established gang. After stealing a shipment intended for the reigning
Puerto Rican Group, Rita la Punta (Pera)
sets up her own operation.

The offbeat nature of the piece is further
reinforced by the mixture of pro and amateur
talent and a variety of acting styles.

■ MOANA

1926, 69 MINS, US ⊗ ⊛ ⊙

Dir Robert Flaherty   *Prod* R.J. Flaherty, F.H. Flaherty
Scr Robert Flaherty, Julian Johnson   *Ph* Robert Flaherty
● (Paramount)

A magnified travel film, it's interesting and
has been well done, but there's no story, and
a travelog is a travelog.

The Flahertys were responsible for *Nanook of
the North*. Here they have delved into the southern climes for their subject matter. A subtitle
states that the men lingered with the Samoans
for two years in order to win the confidence of
the tribe and get the inside native stuff.

The action contains a couple of modified
laughs and holds some exceptionally eye-filling rugged shorelines, with the surf pounding. The spearing of fish, the capture of a
giant turtle in the water by two swimmers
and the riding of the breakers by a homemade skiff provide the major 'action' scenes.

■ MOB, THE

1951, 87 MINS, US

Dir Robert Parrish   *Prod* Jerry Bresler   *Scr* William
Bowers   *Ph* Joseph Walker   *Ed* Charles Nelson

Mus George Duning *Art Dir* Cary Odell
● Broderick Crawford, Betty Buehler, Richard Kiley, Neville Brand, Ernest Borgnine, Matt Crowley (Columbia)

Broderick Crawford is fine as a cop who poses as a hood to overthrow racketeers who've been shaking down dock workers on the waterfront. Fist fights, gunfire and some salty dialog and sexy interludes involving Crawford with Lynne Baggett enliven the proceedings considerably.

Crawford, altar-bound, gets called back to track the responsible party down, the victim being a brother cop. Difficult-to-find trail leads him to New Orleans and back to his starting point, California, right into the police department itself.

Scripter William Bowers has studded the Ferguson Findley original [novel *Waterfront*] with some logically developed clues designed to throw the customers off the track. It's definitely a surprise when the true culprit is exposed.

Betty Buehler is thoroughly sympathetic as Crawford's girl friend, and Baggett and Jean Alexander as manbait planted to distract Crawford from his pursuits spark the distaff end expertly.

● ●

■ MO' BETTER BLUES

1990, 127 MINS, US ◇ ⓥ ⊙
Dir Spike Lee *Prod* Spike Lee *Scr* Spike Lee
Ph Ernest Dickerson *Ed* Sam Pollard *Mus* Bill Lee
Art Dir Wynn Thomas
● Denzel Washington, Spike Lee, Wesley Snipes, Joie Lee, Cynda Williams, Giancarlo Esposito (40 Acres & a Mule/Universal)

Personal rather than social issues come to the fore in *Mo' Better Blues*, a Spike Lee personality piece dressed in jazz trappings that puffs itself up like *Bird* but doesn't really fly. More focused on the sexual dilemmas of its main character than on musical themes, pic might well be subtitled *He's Gotta Have It*.

Pic's fabulous opening sequence, in which the camera does a sensual pan of jazz images – a horn, a man's ear, his mouth raises expectations for a definitive film on jazz and an ambitious step forward for Lee. But the script unfolds to notes from a different scale: basically the same unique but limited range Lee has drawn on before.

Contempo tale stars Denzel Washington as Bleek Gilliam, a self-absorbed New York horn player who leads a jazz quintet on a roll at a trendy Manhattan club called Beneath the Underdog. The diminutive Lee plays Giant (as in 'giant pain in the ass', one character observes), Bleek's ne'er-do-well friend who's found a precarious niche as the band's manager. Joie Lee (Lee's sister) and Cynda Williams play the women who compete for Bleek's attention. Also overlooked by the self-centered trumpeter is his sax player, Shadow (Wesley Snipes, in a standout perf).

But if *Mo' Better* is soft in the center, the characters in and around the band and the nightclub provide winning entertainment.

● ●

■ MOBSTER, THE

See: I, Mobster

● ●

■ MOBSTERS

1991, 104 MINS, US ◇ ⓥ ⊙
Dir Michael Karbelnikoff *Prod* Steve Roth *Scr* Michael Mahern, Nicholas Kazan *Ph* Lajos Koltai *Ed* Scott Smith, Joe D'Augustine *Mus* Michael Small
Art Dir Richard Sylbert
● Christian Slater, Patrick Dempsey, Richard Grieco, F. Murray Abraham, Lara Flynn Boyle, Anthony Quinn (Universal)

Mobsters resembles a cart-before-the-horse case of putting marketing ahead of filmmaking, as the seemingly can't-miss premise of teen-heartthrob gangsters gets lost in self-important direction, a shoddy script and muddled storytelling.

The narrative is amazingly confused in light of its simplicity: two Italian and two Jewish kids from the ghetto team up in the 1920s and get into organized crime, gradually finding themselves caught between two dons. Story [by Michael Mahern] is based on the real-life exploits of mob boss Lucky Luciano (Christian Slater) and confederates Meyer Lansky (Patrick Dempsey), Bugsy Siegel (Richard Grieco) and Frank Costello (Costas Mandylor).

True highlights come from its longer-toothed characters, with Anthony Quinn's lusty portrayal of Don Masseria and F. Murray Abraham as the Yiddish-spouting no-goodnik Arnold Rothstein.

First-time director Michael Karbelnikoff occasionally betrays his roots in TV commercials, particularly with a ludicrous, gauzily shot love scene between showgirl Lara Flynn Boyle and Slater that closely resembles a perfume ad.

[For pic's UK release the handles *The Evil Empire* were added to posters.]

● ●

■ MOBY DICK

1930, 70 MINS, US
Dir Lloyd Bacon *Scr* J. Grubb Alexander *Ph* Robert Kurrle
● John Barrymore, Joan Bennett, Lloyd Hughes, May Boley, Walter Long (Warner)

The Sea Beast was a money picture for Warners in 1926. [This sound remake, using the title of Herman Melville's original novel,] again stars John Barrymore.

Moby Dick is just as smart as ever, but Barrymore is smarter. He's got a better whale to work with this time. And Moby Dick deserves his finish, after Barrymore has chased him over seven seas for seven years because of that leg bite.

Back home the demure Joan Bennett, who could never grow old out in New Bedford, waits for her whaling boy friend to return.

Moby Dick is stirring, even if you don't believe in whales. And this one's said to have cost Warners $120,000, with or without teeth.

● ●

■ MOBY DICK

1956, 116 MINS, UK ◇ ⓥ ⊙
Dir John Huston *Prod* John Huston *Scr* Ray Bradbury, John Huston *Ph* Oswald Morris, Freddie Francis
Ed Russell Lloyd *Mus* Philip Stainton *Art Dir* Ralph Brinton
● Gregory Peck, Richard Basehart, Leo Genn, Harry Andrews, Orson Welles, Bernard Miles (Moulin/Warner)

Costly weather and production delays on location in Ireland and elsewhere enlarged the bring-home price on John Huston's *Moby Dick* to as high as $5 million.

Moby Dick is interesting more often than exciting, faithful to the time and text [of the Herman Melville novel] more than great theatrical entertainment. Essentially it is a chase picture and yet not escaping the sameness and repetitiousness which often dulls the chase formula.

It was astute of Huston to work out a print combining color and black-and-white calculated to capture the sombre beauties of New Bedford, circa 1840, and its whaling ways.

Orson Welles appears early and briefly as a local New Bedford preacher who delivers a God-fearing sermon on Jonah and the whale. Welles turns in an effective bit of brimstone exhortation, appropriate to time and place.

Gregory Peck hovers above the crew, grim-faced and hate-obsessed. He wears a stump leg made of the jaw of a whale and he lives only to kill the greatest whale of all, the white-hided super-monster, Moby Dick, the one which had chewed off his leg. Peck's Ahab is not very 'elemental'. It is not that he fails in handling the rhetoric. Actually he does quite well with the stylized speech in which Melville wrote and which Ray Bradbury and Huston have preserved in their screenplay. It's just that Peck often seems understated and much too gentlemanly for a man supposedly consumed by insane fury.

● ●

■ MODEL SHOP

1969, 90 MINS, US
Dir Jacques Demy *Prod* Jacques Demy *Scr* Jacques Demy, Adrien Joyce *Ph* Michel Hugo *Ed* Walter Thompson *Mus* Spirit *Art Dir* Kenneth A. Reid
● Anouk Aimee, Gary Lockwood, Alexandra Hay, Carol Cole, Severn Darden, Tom Fielding (Columbia)

French filmmaker Jacques Demy brings a fresh look at LA and American youth, plus a revealing eye for the character and feel of the sprawling California city.

And it is a work of love in its attitude towards the city and its characters. Demy can be sentimental, sans bathos or mawkishness, and comes up with a day in the life of a 26-year-old youthful drifter whose one romantic interlude is a step in coping with his life.

There is not much story here, but rather a revealing series of incidents that serve as a backdrop for a poetic tale of human disarray, fleeting comprehension and a surface gentleness that belies an underlying discontent and groping for meaning, love and aim by its disparate but well mimed characters.

● ●

■ MODERN LOVE

1990, 109 MINS, US ◇
Dir Robby Benson *Prod* Robby Benson *Scr* Robby Benson *Ph* Christopher G. Tufty *Ed* Gib Jaffe
Mus Don Peake *Art Dir* Carl E. Copeland
● Robby Benson, Karla De Vito, Rue McClanahan, Burt Reynolds, Frankie Valli, Louise Lasser (Lyric/Soisson-Murphy)

Written, produced and directed by Robby Benson, shot in South Carolina and starring Benson and his family and friends, *Modern Love* was actually put together as part of a state university media class he was teaching in Columbia, SC, where some scenes were lensed.

It follows the adventures of Greg and a ditzy urologist named Billie (Benson and wife Karla DeVito) who 'meet cute' when she examines him in her office. Their whirlwind courtship consists of dozens of shots of them kissing against pretty backdrops, followed by telling each other lame jokes and then giggling and saying 'I'm sorry.'

Pic improves as it moves into their family years, with Benson's frustrated attempts to be a handson father giving things an interesting twist and DeVito getting a more substantial role as a capable mom, peacemaker and would-be nightclub comic.

Benson, a fairly capable director, works hard at pumping energy and humor into a flat script.

● ●

■ MODERN ROMANCE

1981, 93 MINS, US ◇ ⓥ ⊙
Dir Albert Brooks *Prod* Andrew Scheinman, Martin Shafer *Scr* Albert Brooks, Monica Johnson *Ph* Eric Saarinen *Ed* David Finfer *Mus* Lance Rubin
Art Dir Edward Richardson
● Albert Brooks, Kathryn Harrold, Bruno Kirby, Jane Hallaren, James L. Brooks, George Kennedy (Columbia)

Given room to roam as star, director and cowriter, Columbia Pictures obviously hoped that comedian Albert Brooks might break through like Woody Allen. But Allen, too, started slowly and this is only Brooks' second feature after the critically acclaimed but commercially weak *Real Life*.

Simplicity and veracity of his story are a plus. Without excessive complications, he plays a nice-enough young fellow who cannot make a permanent commitment to his girl friend, sympathetically portrayed by the beautiful and talented Kathryn Harrold. At first, he dumps her, then immediately regrets it and goes crazy trying to get her back. Succeeding in that, he starts aggravating her with jealousies.

Many scenes play far beyond the laughs they're worth. At the same time, Harrold doesn't get to round out her part quite as much as she should. One thing Brooks does well, however, is pepper the bit parts with interesting characters who all have a point to make, most particularly Bruno Kirby as his best friend.

When he isn't fretting about his personal life, Brooks plays a film editor cutting a low-budget sci-fi pic with Kirby for director James L. Brooks (no relation). The brief examination of the cutting room is hilarious as they first patch up a scene with George Kennedy hamming it up in true low-budget style as Zoron the space leader.

. . . .

■ MODERNS, THE

1988, 126 MINS, US ◇ ⓥ ☉
Dir Alan Rudolph   *Prod* Carolyn Pfeiffer, David Blocker   *Scr* Alan Rudolph, Jon Bradshaw   *Ph* Toyomichi Kurita, Jan Kiesser   *Ed* Debra T. Smith, Scott Brock   *Mus* Mark Isham   *Art Dir* Steven Legler
● Keith Carradine, Linda Fiorentino, John Lone, Wallace Shawn, Genevieve Bujold, Geraldine Chaplin (Alive/Nelson)

The artistic world of Paris in the 1920s comes to life as if in a lustrous dream in *The Moderns*, a romantic's lush vision of a group of expatriate Americans at a time and place of some of the century's most tumultuous creative activity.

There is Nick Hart (Keith Carradine) who, at 33, is viewed suspiciously for not having made it yet as an artist. Oiseau (Wallace Shawn), a gossip columnist for the *Tribune*, who dreams only of going to Hollywood; Bertram Stone (John Lone), an elegant, rich, philistine art dealer with a disturbing violent streak; his wife, Rachel (Linda Fiorentino), with whom Nick has a past and, he hopes, a future; and Hemingway himself (Kevin J. O'Connor), who amusingly careens through the action in varying states of inebriation, trying out titles for a new book.

Also critical to the assorted personal equations are Libby (Genevieve Bujold), an impoverished gallery owner with values diametrically opposed to those of Stone, and Nathalie (Geraldine Chaplin), a patroness of the arts who convinces Nick to execute some spectacular forgeries.

Carradine has never been better, as he conveys the strong feelings he has for art and his estranged wife as well as the diffidence that has set in due to years of frustration and lack of recognition. Lone is the picture of disciplined decadence, a magnetic figure who commands fascination, and Fiorentino is ideal as the gorgeous American of a prosaic background over whom men may lose their hearts, mind and lives.

. . . .

■ MODERN TIMES

1936, 85 MINS, US ⓥ
Dir Charles Chaplin   *Prod* Charles Chaplin   *Scr* Charles Chaplin   *Ph* Rollie Totheroh, Henry Bergman   *Mus* Charles Chaplin
● Charles Chaplin, Paulette Goddard, Henry Bergman, Chester Conklin (United Artists)

Whatever sociological meanings some will elect to read into *Modern Times*, there's no

denying that as a cinematic entertainment Chaplin's first picture since *City Lights* (1931) is wholesomely funny.

The pathos of the machine worker who suffers temporary derangement, as he tightens the bolts on a factory treadmill to a clocklike tempo, gives way to a series of similarly winning situations. In each the victim of circumstance meets temporary frustration, almost inevitably resulting in a ride in Black Maria. When finally achieving what promises to be a semblance of economic security the menace, in the form of the law, enters to arrest Paulette Goddard as a refugee vagrant.

Modern Times is as 100% a one-man picture as probably is possible. Chaplin the pantomimist stands or falls by his two years' work. Dialogue is almost negligible. And when the music is inadequate Chaplin frankly recourses to plain titles.

Goddard, a winsome waif attired almost throughout in short, ragged dress, registers handily. Chaplin's old standbys, notably Henry Bergman (also an assistant director), Chester Conklin, Hank Mann and Allen Garcia, contribute nicely.

. . . .

■ MODESTY BLAISE

1966, 118 MINS, UK ◇ ⓥ
Dir Joseph Losey   *Prod* Joseph Janni   *Scr* Evan Jones   *Ph* Jack Hildyard   *Ed* Reginald Beck   *Mus* John Dankworth   *Art Dir* Richard MacDonald
● Monica Vitti, Terence Stamp, Dirk Bogarde, Harry Andrews, Michael Craig, Scilla Gabel (Janni)

Modesty Blaise is one of the nuttiest, screwiest pictures ever made. Not merely a spy spoof, based on a book and a comic strip about a femme James Bond type, the colorful production gives the horse laugh to many different film plots and styles. Fine direction and many solid performances are evident.

Evan Jones has concocted a wacky screenplay, most immediately derived from the English comic strip by Peter O'Donnell and Jim Holdaway, which propels Blaise, played by Monica Vitti, into a British government espionage scheme. Heading the opposition is Dirk Bogarde, an effete international criminal, while Vitti is aided by longtime sidekick, bedhopping Terence Stamp.

Vitti's English is adequate for her part; her body English, however, transcends all language barriers. Stamp is good, and appropriately animated. Bogarde's jaded urbanity is very good, and all other players register in solid support.

. . . .

■ MOGAMBO

1953, 115 MINS, US ◇ ⓥ
Dir John Ford   *Prod* Sam Zimbalist   *Scr* John Lee Mahin   *Ph* Robert Surtees, Freddie Young   *Ed* Frank Clarke   *Mus* [none]   *Art Dir* Alfred Junge
● Clark Gable, Ava Gardner, Grace Kelly, Donald Sinden, Eric Pohlmann, Laurence Naismith (M-G-M)

The lure of the jungle and romance get a sizzling workout in *Mogambo* and it's a socko package of entertainment, crammed with sexy two-fisted adventure.

While having its origin in the Wilson Collison play [*Red Dust*], this remake is fresh in locale and characterizations switching from the rubber plantations of Indo-China to the African veldt and updating the period.

John Lee Mahin's dialog and situations are unusually zippy and adult. Ava Gardner feeding a baby rhino and elephant, and her petulant storming at a pet boa constrictor to stay out of her ber, are good touches.

The romantic conflict boils up between the principals during a safari into gorilla country, where an anthropologist and his wife plan to do research. Clark Gable is the great white hunter leading the party. Gardner is the girl on the prowl for a man, and who has now set-

tled on Gable. To get him she has to offset the sweeter charms of Grace Kelly, the wife, who also has become smitten with the Gable masculinity and is ready to walk out on Donald Sinden, the unexciting anthropologist. For the second time in Metro history, a picture has been made without a music score (*King Solomon's Mines* was the first) and none is needed as the sounds of the jungle and native rhythms are all that are required.
□ 1953: Nominations: Best Actress (Ava Gardner), Supp. Actress (Grace Kelly)

. . . .

■ MOLLY MAGUIRES, THE

1970, 124 MINS, US ◇ ⓥ
Dir Martin Ritt   *Prod* Martin Ritt, Walter Bernstein   *Scr* Walter Bernstein   *Ph* James Wong Howe   *Ed* Frank Bracht   *Mus* Henry Mancini   *Art Dir* Tambi Larsen
● Sean Connery, Richard Harris, Samantha Eggar, Frank Finlay, Anthony Zerbe, Bethel Leslie (Paramount/Tamm)

The Molly Maguires, based on a Pennsylvania coal miners' rebellion of the late 19th century, is occasionally brilliant. Sean Connery, Richard Harris and Samantha Eggar head a competent cast.

Story background ('suggested' by an Arthur H. Lewis book) depicts Irish immigrants existing in the sort of company-captivity common to other American industries of the period. Employer abuses had led to unsuccessful strikes, after which the workers spawned an underground militant group.

Story is primarily that of Harris, hired by the mineowners to infiltrate the workers' ranks. Connery is a rebel leader. Eggar appears occasionally for some light romantic interludes with Harris.
□ 1970: Nomination: Best Art Direction

. . . .

■ MOM AND DAD SAVE THE WORLD

1992, 88 MINS, US ◇ ⓥ ☉
Dir Greg Beeman   *Prod* Michael Phillips   *Scr* Chris Matheson, Ed Solomon   *Ph* Jacques Haitkin   *Ed* W.O. Garret, Michael Jablow   *Mus* Jerry Goldsmith   *Art Dir* Craig Stearns
● Teri Garr, Jeffrey Jones, Jon Lovitz, Thalmus Rasulala, Wallace Shawn, Eric Idle (Warner/HBO)

Little kids will find some infantile laughs in *Mom and Dad Save the World*, but adults will be looking at their watches during this silly sci-fi comedy. Teri Garr and Jeffrey Jones gamely struggle with inane dialogue as a California couple transported to a tacky-looking 'planet of idiots.'

With garish color, goofy-looking creatures in rubbery costumes and sets parodying old Flash Gordon serials, pic flaunts its modest budget with engaging candor. Basic trouble is with the script by *Bill & Ted* writers Chris Matheson and Ed Solomon, whose dumbness jokes are stretched too far.

Pic's obvious fun-poking at San Fernando suburbanites wears thin, but not as quickly as the smarmy antics of a half-witted emperor (Jon Lovitz). The adept comic actor chews the scenery here in an overextended part as the sadistic lout who's taken over the planet from Eric Idle's imprisoned king.

Conceiving a mad passion for Garr's ditzy Earthling after spying her through his telescope, Lovitz has her transported to the planet with Jones in their station wagon by electromagnetic beam.

Garr's blithe lack of alarm over her predicament helps her survive the pic with minimal damage.

. . . .

■ MOMENT BY MOMENT

1978, 105 MINS, US ◇
Dir Jane Wagner   *Prod* Robert Stigwood   *Scr* Jane Wagner   *Ph* Philip Lathrop   *Ed* John F. Burnett

Mus Lee Holdridge   *Art Dir* Harry Horner
● Lily Tomlin, John Travolta, Andra Akers, Bert Kramer, Shelley R. Bonus, Debra Feuer (Universal)

What seemed like inspired casting on paper, the teaming of John Travolta and Lily Tomlin, fails badly in execution.

The lion's share of the blame must go to writer-director (and long-time Tomlin collaborator) Jane Wagner, who concocted this improbable story of a Beverly Hills chic housewife whose marriage has gone sour, and who meets up with an insecure young drifter, with whom he has an affair.

Insouciant and likable from the outset, Travolta pursues the distant Tomlin like a determined puppy dog once he latches on, she can't shake him loose. The first half hour of the pic, with this unusual courtship, is appealing, and only makes what follows more of a letdown.

Approaching Trisha as if she was one of her stable theatrical creations, Tomlin never varies her nasal monotone, nor her imperturbable exterior. It's a one-note performance that frustrates the entire picture.

Not helping matters is Wagner's banal script, which has cliche piled atop cliche, and dialog that evokes embarrassing laughter.

••••••••••••••••••••••••••

■ **MOMENTS**

1975, 92 MINS, UK ◇
Dir Peter Crane   *Prod* Peter Crane, Michael Sloane, David M. Jackson   *Scr* Michael Sloane   *Ph* Wolfgang Suschitzky   *Ed* Roy Watts   *Mus* John Cameron   *Art Dir* Bruce Atkins
● Keith Michell, Angharad Rees, Bill Fraser, Jeanette Sterke, Donald Hewlett, Keith Bell (Pemini)

Despite technical flaws, this item comes across as a sincere and often moving film. Yarn probes into man's loneliness and the dead-end meaninglessness of a middle-aged accountant (Keith Michell) who, after 20 years at his job and after the death of his wife and children in a car crash, decides to return to a resort hotel in the off-season where he had once lived happy moments, and put an end to his life.

Relationship between him and a young, flighty and vivacious girl (Angharad Rees) who temporarily prevents him from carrying out his project is touchingly told as director Peter Crane plays off each of the antipodic characters. At times characterization of the man, though always believable, is too turgid and self-conscious; his poses of internal suffering are a trifle too histrionic and become wearisome.

••••••••••••••••••••••••••

■ **MOMENT TO MOMENT**

1966, 108 MINS, US ◇
Dir Mervyn LeRoy   *Prod* Mervyn LeRoy   *Scr* John Lee Mahin, Alec Coppel   *Ph* Harry Stradling   *Ed* Philip W. Anderson   *Mus* Henry Mancini   *Art Dir* Alexander Golitzen, Alfred Sweeney
● Jean Seberg, Honor Blackman, Sean Garrison, Arthur Hill, Gregoire Aslan, Peter Robbins (Universal/Le Roy)

Mervyn LeRoy, who has tackled just about every type of film, returns to romantic melodrama in *Moment to Moment*, an unabashed sudser. A mild suspense story blending a wife's infidelity and amnesia, the film doesn't entirely jell for several reasons, mainly thin scripting, weak acting and LeRoy's own too-leisurely pace.

John Lee Mahin joined Alec Coppel in adapting latter's story [*Laughs with a Stranger*] about a happily-married Yank wife, increasingly neglected by headshrinker hubby who is on the lecture circuit all over Europe while she and the kid remain on the Riviera. A US naval officer has an affair with her, provoking a physical argument and a shooting.

Jean Seberg lacks dimension as the wife, even allowing for the script. In early scenes,

an overly passive limning which suggests jaded boredom instead of a well-adjusted spouse in a single fall from grace robs the role of most sympathy.

••••••••••••••••••••••••••

■ **MOMMIE DEAREST**

1981, 129 MINS, US ◇ ⑫ ⊙
Dir Frank Perry   *Prod* Frank Yablans   *Scr* Frank Yablans, Frank Perry, Tracy Hotchner, Robert Getchell   *Ph* Paul Lohmann   *Ed* Peter E. Berger   *Mus* Henry Mancini   *Art Dir* Bill Malley
● Faye Dunaway, Diana Scarwid, Steve Forrest, Howard Da Silva, Jocelyn Brando (Paramount)

This is Faye Dunaway as Joan Crawford and the results are, well, screen history. Dunaway does not chew scenery. Dunaway starts neatly at each corner of the set in every scene and swallows it whole, costars and all.

Prior to her death, Crawford once commented that Dunaway was among the best of up-and-coming young actresses. Too bad Crawford isn't around to comment now. Too bad, Crawford isn't around to comment on the whole endeavor.

Much has been written and said pro-and-con about Crawford since daughter Christina wrote the book on which this film is based. Whatever the truth, director Frank Perry's portrait here is sorry indeed, 129 minutes with a very pathetic and unpleasant individual.

The story is familiar: self-centred, insecure and pressured movie queen adopts two babies for both love and personal aggrandizement. Growing up, the kids are battered between luxurious pampering and abuse, never finding real affection with mother, who finally dies and cuts them out of the will, reaching beyond the grave for final revenge.

As Christina, Diana Scarwid is okay, but unexceptional. Much better is little Mara Hobel as Christina the child, genuinely touching at times. Rutanya Alda is also fine as Crawford's long-suffering but loving assistant.

••••••••••••••••••••••••••

■ **MO' MONEY**

1992, 89 MINS, US ⑫ ⊙
Dir Peter Macdonald   *Prod* Michael Rachmil   *Scr* Damon Wayans   *Ph* Don Burgess   *Ed* Hubert C. de la Bouillerie   *Mus* Jay Gruska   *Art Dir* William Arnold
● Damon Wayans, Marlon Wayans, Stacey Dish, Joe Santos, John Diehl, Harry J. Lennix (Columbia/Wife N' Kids)

Damon Wayans and his younger brother Marlon make a terrific comedy team in *Mo' Money*. Loosely structured film has trouble meshing its very funny gag scenes with rough action footage, but it should earn mucho change from escapist fans.

Damon casts himself as a ne'er-do-well street punk who sets a poor role model for younger brother (Marlon). Their father was a cop who died in the line of duty, with his partner Joe Santos trying in vain to set the Wayans brothers on the right track.

To pursue a lovely romantic interest (Stacey Dash), Damon gets a job in the mailroom for her credit card company. Soon the Wayanses have cooked up a scam using uncanceled credit cards to finance a shopping spree.

Coincidentally (and this is where the Wayans' script falls apart), cop Santos is investigating a murder that's linked to a much larger credit card scam at the same company. Evil exec John Diehl is the ruthless mastermind who soon blackmails Damon into becoming his reluctant henchman.

Well-staged, showy and violent finale of Damon using his street smarts to act like his late father and collar the criminal is telegraphed too many reels ahead.

••••••••••••••••••••••••••

■ **MONA LISA**

1986, 104 MINS, UK ◇ ⑫ ⊙
Dir Neil Jordan   *Prod* Stephen Woolley, Patrick Cassavetti   *Scr* Neil Jordan   *Ph* Roger Pratt   *Ed* Lesley Walker   *Mus* Michael Kamen   *Art Dir* Jamie Leonard
● Bob Hoskins, Cathy Tyson, Michael Caine, Robbie Coltrane, Kate Hardie, Sammi Davis (HandMade/Palace)

The couple at the center of this wide and wayward romantic thriller are about as odd as you could find anywhere. George (Bob Hoskins), short in stature as well as intellect, is just out of prison. Simone (Cathy Tyson) is a tall, slender black whore who plies the poshest London hotels for her up-market trade. George gets a job driving Simone to her various assignations and finds himself falling in love with her.

What follows is a pic that skillfully combines comedy and thriller, romance and sleaze. Simone takes advantage of George's feelings for her and assigns him to search for her missing girlfriend, a teenage blonde hooked on heroin and involved in the kinkier areas of the vice trade.

Hoskins gives another memorable performance as the earnest, dumb ex-con. Tyson brings charm and sensuality to the role of Simone and the rotund Robbie Coltrane is very funny as George's loyal friend. Michael Caine is around, too, in a generously self-effacing supporting role as a sinister, dangerous cockney vice king.
□ 1986: Nomination: Best Actor (Bob Hoskins)

••••••••••••••••••••••••••

■ **MONEY PIT, THE**

1986, 91 MINS, US ◇ ⑫ ⊙
Dir Richard Benjamin   *Prod* Frank Marshall, Kathleen Kennedy, Art Levinson   *Scr* David Giler   *Ph* Gordon Willis   *Ed* Jacqueline Cambas   *Mus* Michel Colombier   *Art Dir* Patrizia Von Brandenstein
● Shelley Long, Tom Hanks, Alexander Godunov, Maureen Stapleton, Joe Mantegna, Philip Bosco (Amblin)

The Money Pit is simply the pits. Shortly after the starring couple has bought a beautiful old house which quickly shows itself to be at the point of total disrepair, Tom Hanks says to Shelley Long, 'It's a lemon, honey, let's face it'. There is really very little else to be said about this gruesomely unfunny comedy.

Unofficial remake of the 1948 Cary Grant-Myrna Loy starrer *Mr Blandings Builds His Dream House* begins unpromisingly and slides irrevocably downward from there.

Most of the scenes in this demolition derby begin with something or other caving in or falling apart, an event which is invariably followed by the two leads yelling and screaming at each other for minutes on end.

••••••••••••••••••••••••••

■ **MONEY TRAP, THE**

1966, 91 MINS, US
Dir Burt Kennedy   *Prod* Max E. Youngstein, David Karr   *Scr* Walter Bernstein   *Ph* Paul C. Vogel   *Ed* John McSweeney   *Mus* Hal Schaefer   *Art Dir* George W. Davis, Carl Anderson
● Glenn Ford, Elke Sommer, Rita Hayworth, Ricardo Montalban, Joseph Cotten, Tom Reese (M-G-M)

A story of a policeman-turned-thief, *The Money Trap* is aptly named but only as far as production coin is concerned. A cliche-plotted, tritely written script that is not to be believed could not be salvaged even by far better direction and performances.

Walter Bernstein's adaptation of a Lionel White novel has the kernel of a good drama about a contemporary problem, that of an underpaid gumshoe dazzled into dishonesty by the riches of the criminals whom he encounters. Nearly all interest in this angle is snuffed out by extraneous, unbelievable subplots.

Specifically, Glenn Ford is the cop, husband

of Elke Sommer. They live in a splashy pad made possible by her father's will and stocks. When the latter pass a divvy, hard times loom. Wife's idea to economize: fire the servants.

Add Joseph Cotten, a medic who supposedly works for the Syndicate. When he kills a junkie accomplice and reports it as self-defense from a supposed burglary, Ford gets the theft idea, keeps it from Ricardo Montalban (his partner, who later finds out and wants in).

■ **MONKEY BUSINESS**

1952, 97 MINS, US 🔞 ⊙
Dir Howard Hawks   *Prod* Sol C. Siegel   *Scr* Ben Hecht, Charles Lederer, I.A.L. Diamond   *Ph* Milton Krasner   *Ed* William B. Murphy   *Mus* Leigh Harline   *Art Dir* Lyle Wheeler, George Patrick
● Cary Grant, Ginger Rogers, Charles Coburn, Marilyn Monroe, Hugh Marlowe, Larry Keating (20th Century-Fox)

Attempt to draw out a thin, familiar slapstick idea isn't carried off.

Story has Cary Grant as a matured research chemist, working on a formula to regenerate human tissue and using monkeys in his lab as guinea pigs for his elixir-of-youth experiments. Ginger Rogers is his amiable wife, still madly enough in love with him to forgive his absentmindedness.

One of the lab monkeys breaks loose, mixes up an assortment of chemical ingredients lying about, dumps the concoction into the water-cooler. First Grant, then Rogers, drink from the cooler, and immediately get teenage notions, emotions and symptoms.

Grant plays the role sometimes as if his heart isn't completely in it. Rogers, looking beautiful, makes as gay a romp of it as she can. Marilyn Monroe's sex appeal is played up for all it's worth (and that's not inconsiderable), as she appears as a nitwit secretary.

■ **MONKEY SHINES**

1988, 115 MINS, US ◇ 🔞 ⊙
Dir George A. Romero   *Prod* Charles Evans   *Scr* George A. Romero   *Ph* James A. Contner   *Ed* Pasquale Buba   *Mus* David Shire   *Art Dir* Cletus Anderson
● Jason Beghe, John Pankow, Melanie Parker, Joyce Van Patten (Orion)

Monkey Shines is a befuddled story about a man constrained from the neck down told by a director confused from the neck up.

Jason Beghe starts out as a very virile, able-bodied young man with everything going for him, an up-and-coming physical specimen much desired by girlfriend Janine Turner and fawned over by mother Joyce Van Patten.

An accident robs Beghe of all physical ability below his jawline, leaving him despondently dependent on an array of technology.

As melodrama, this is all pretty good stuff and could have continued to a convincing conclusion. But by contract, inclination and reputation (not to mention the book [by Michael Stewart] the film's based on), Romero is a horror-film director.

So here comes Beghe's best friend John Pankow, a yuppie mad scientist busy at the nearby university slicing up the brain of a dead Jane Doe and injecting the hormones into monkeys to make them smarter.

To help his friend, Pankow volunteers one of his highly intelligent, chemically dependent capuchins to be trained by Melanie Parker to serve as Beghe's companion and helper. For a while, this all works beautifully. Until something dreadful happens.

■ **MONSIEUR VERDOUX**

1947, 122 MINS, US
Dir Charles Chaplin   *Prod* Charles Chaplin   *Scr* Charles Chaplin   *Ph* Rollie Totheroh   *Ed* Willard Nico   *Mus* Charles Chaplin   *Art Dir* John Beckman
● Charles Chaplin, Martha Raye, Isobel Elsom, Marilyn Nash, Irving Bacon, William Frawley (United Artists)

Comedy based on the characterization of a modern Parisian Bluebeard treads danger shoals indeed. Even if the accent were more effective, the fundamentals are unsound when it's revealed that Chaplin has been driven to marrying and murdering middling mesdames in order to provide for his ailing wife and their son of 10 years' marriage.

Chaplin generates little sympathy. His broad-mannered antics, as a many-aliased fop on the make for impressionable matrons; the telltale technique, a hangover from his bank-teller's days, of counting the bundles of francs in the traditional nervous manner of rapid finger movement; the business of avoiding Martha Raye at that garden party, when he finally woos and wins Isobel Elsom; the neo-*American Tragedy* hokum in the rowboat-on-the-lake scene with Raye; the mixed bottles of poisoned wine [again Raye, with oldtime musicomedy star Ada-May (Weeks) as the blowsy buxom blonde of a maid in support]; and all the rest of it is only spotty.

Chaplin's endeavor to get his 'common man' ideology into the film militates against its comedy values. Point is that depressions in the economy force us into being ruthless villains and murderers, despite the fact we are actually kind and sympathetic.

Chaplin also rings in another of his favorite themes, his strong feelings against war.

Chaplin's direction is disjointed on occasion, although perhaps the natural enough result of a leisurely production schedule which ranged up to five years. Chaplin's score, however, is above par, fortifying the progression in no small measure.
□ 1947: Nomination: Best Original Screenplay

■ **MONSIGNOR**

1982, 122 MINS, US ◇ 🔞
Dir Frank Perry   *Prod* Frank Yablans, David Niven Jr.   *Scr* Abraham Polonsky, Wendell Mayes   *Ph* Billy Williams   *Ed* Peter E. Berger   *Mus* John Williams   *Art Dir* John DeCuir
● Christopher Reeve, Genevieve Bujold, Fernando Rey, Jason Miller, Joe Cortese, Adolfo Celi (20th Century-Fox/Yablans)

Lots of potential for a rare, absorbing, behind-the-scenes look at the Vatican is totally blown in *Monsignor*. Constructed as a scene-by-scene 'expose' of all sorts of nefarious goings-on in post-Second World War Rome, the self-serious $12 million pic [from the novel by Jack Alain Leger] teeters on the brink of being an all-out-hoot through much of its running time.

Introductory sequences briefly limn Brooklyn boy Christopher Reeve's ordination and subsequent service as a military chaplain on the European front, where he commits his first major priestly sin by gunning down a bunch of Nazis.

Upon reaching Rome, brash kid makes a big impression on Papal assistant Fernando Rey and is given control over the financially ailing church's commissary. Reeve makes use of his position to strike a deal with Sicilian mafioso Jason Miller to share in black market profits.

The rising opportunist meets novice nun Genevieve Bujold, and it isn't long before the two bed down.

It's amazing that neither Abraham Polonsky nor Wendell Mayes, both outstanding screenwriters, didn't spot the most gaping fundamental flaw here, namely the lack of any convincing explanation why Reeve's character became a priest in the first place.

■ **MONSTER IN A BOX**

1991, 88 MINS, UK ◇ 🔞
Dir Nick Broomfield   *Prod* Jon Blair   *Scr* Spalding Gray   *Ph* Michael Coulter   *Ed* Graham Hutchings   *Mus* Laurie Anderson   *Art Dir* Ray Oxley
● Spalding Gray (Blair)

Spalding Gray struts his anecdotal stuff once again in *Monster in a Box*, a frisky follow-up to *Swimming to Cambodia* and film rendition of his 1990 stage hit.

Titular 'Monster' is Gray's 1,800-page autobiography, *Impossible Vacation*. Starting his peregrinations in 1987, Gray recounts how celeb status after *Swimming* gave him plenty of excuses to procrastinate.

The easy laughs come at the start: East Coaster Gray's barbed comments on Tinseltown, where execs invite him to 'idea lunches' and CAA woos him in hyper meetings. Subsequent divertissements include Columbia Pictures' putting him on a US fact-finding mission to Nicaragua (a comic horror show), AIDS hysteria in New York, a flying saucer project for HBO, taking *Swimming* to the Moscow fest and Gotham critics' trashing of his perf in Gregory Mosher's Broadway production of *Our Town*.

Pic was shot at London's Riverside Studios before a live aud (seen briefly at first and occasionally heard reacting).

■ **MONTE WALSH**

1970, 99 MINS, US ◇ 🔞
Dir William A. Fraker   *Prod* Hal Landers, Bobby Roberts   *Scr* Lukas Heller, David Zelag Goodman   *Ph* David M. Walsh   *Ed* Dick Brockway   *Mus* John Barry   *Art Dir* Al Brenner
● Lee Marvin, Jeanne Moreau, Jack Palance, Mitch Ryan, Jim Davis, John 'Bear' Hudkins (Cinema Center)

Monte Walsh is a listless, wandering story of the old American West, which takes too long to get moving. Lee Marvin stars as a taciturn roughneck whose tragic romance with Jeanne Moreau comes across as irrelevant digression in a confused story.

This film [from a novel by Jack Schaefer] attempts meaningful exposition of the reality of an aging cowboy. Unfortunately, it appears that Marvin was simply playing his image, while other thesps were going through uncertain motions, and nobody had an eye out for exactly what direction the film was supposed to be taking.

Moreau's scenes are more like padded inserts than vital plot turns. The basic feeble theme is what happened to prototype pioneers when Eastern money bought up ranches and began operating long-distance.

■ **MONTH IN THE COUNTRY, A**

1987, 96 MINS, UK ◇ 🔞 ⊙
Dir Pat O'Connor   *Prod* Kenith Trodd   *Scr* Simon Gray   *Ph* Kenneth MacMillan   *Ed* John Victor Smith   *Mus* Howard Blake   *Art Dir* Leo Austin
● Colin Firth, Kenneth Branagh, Natasha Richardson, Patrick Malahide, Richard Vernon (Euston)

A Month in the Country is a gentle but moving pic [from the novel by J. L. Carr] about two men recovering from the horrors of World War I during an idyllic summer in remote rolling English countryside.

Pic opens with Birkin (Colin Firth) arriving at the remote Yorkshire village of Oxgodby to uncover a medieval wall painting in the local church. There he meets Moon (Kenneth Branagh), who is excavating a grave outside the churchyard.

Both are tormented by their war experiences, but during a beautiful summer month they experience the tranquility of the idyllic community that gradually helps them come to terms with their problems.

Birkin falls in love with the wife (Natasha Richardson) of an unfriendly local vicar, but never lets on to her about his passion, while the Branagh character turns out to be a homosexual.

Firth and Branagh are talented young actors especially Branagh who has great screen presence. Richardson looks slightly uncomfortable in a very understated role.

• •

■ MONTY PYTHON AND THE HOLY GRAIL

1975, 89 MINS, UK ◇ ⊛ ⊙
Dir Terry Gilliam, Terry Jones   *Prod* Mark Forstater
Scr Graham Chapman, John Cleese, Terry Gilliam, Eric Idle, Terry Jones, Michael Palin   *Ph* Terry Bedford
Ed John Hackney   *Mus* DeWolfe   *Art Dir* Roy Smith
● Graham Chapman, John Cleese, Terry Gilliam, Eric Idle, Terry Jones, Michael Palin (Python)

Monty Python's Flying Circus, the British comedy group which gained fame via BBC-TV, send-up Arthurian legend, performed in whimsical fashion with Graham Chapman an effective straight man as King Arthur.

Story deals with Arthur's quest for the Holy Grail and his battles along the way with various villains and is basically an excuse for set pieces, some amusing, others overdone.

Running gags include lack of horses for Arthur and his men, and a lackey clicking co-coanuts together to make suitable hoof noises as the men trot along. The extravagantly gruesome fight scenes, including one which ends with a man having all four limbs severed, will get laughs from some and make others squirm.

• •

■ MONTY PYTHON'S LIFE OF BRIAN
See: Life of Brian

• •

■ MONTY PYTHON'S THE MEANING OF LIFE

1983, 103 MINS, UK ◇ ⊛ ⊙
Dir Terry Jones   *Prod* John Goldstone   *Scr* Graham Chapman, John Cleese, Terry Gilliam, Eric Idle, Terry Jones, Michael Palin   *Ph* Peter Hannan   *Ed* Julian Doyle
Mus Eric Idle, Terry Jones, Michael Palin, Graham Chapman, John Cleese, John du Prez, Dave Howman, Andre Jacquemin   *Art Dir* Harry Lange
● Graham Chapman, John Cleese, Terry Gilliam, Eric Idle, Terry Jones, Michael Palin (HandMade)

Gross, silly, caustic, tasteless and obnoxious are all adjectives that alternately apply to *Monty Python's The Meaning of Life* though probably the most appropriate description would simply be funny.

Pic opens with an amusing short film of its own where elderly workers unite against their younger bosses and then segues to the real task finding the meaning of life. Tracing the human existence from birth through death, the group touches on such areas as religion, education, marriage, sex and war in a way it was no doubt never taught in school or in the home. Though there are some rough spots along the way (some of the passages on war don't register) most of the sections get their maximum comedic punch by not being allowed to linger for too long.

The writing truly offers bits of comedic brilliance though, like any film of this nature, has a few duds mixed in.

• •

■ MOON AND SIXPENCE, THE

1943, 89 MINS, US ◇ ⊛
Dir Albert Lewin   *Prod* David L. Loew   *Scr* Albert Lewin
Ph John F. Seitz   *Ed* George Hively, Richard L. Van Enger   *Mus* Dimitri Tiomkin   *Art Dir* Gordon Wiles
● George Sanders, Herbert Marshall, Doris Dudley, Steve Geray, Eric Blore, Florence Bates (United Artists)

Somerset Maugham's widely read novel has been made into an intriguing, distinctive screen vehicle. The story of an English stockbroker who reached for the moon and ultimately won fame as a painter, only just before his death, at times is reminiscent of *Citizen Kane*.

While Herbert Marshall figures importantly, as he retraces the story of the painter, it is really George Sanders' picture. He makes the strange life of the struggling artist live, and it's his outstanding screen role to date.

The episodes in the distant island of Tahiti are rich in tropical flavor. The Tahitian portion of the story offers startling contrast in humorous moments and in most impressive scenes of film.

Albert Lewin's direction is keenly intelligent, shifting readily from lighter, funny moments to the harshly dramatic. Camerawork of John F. Seitz is on the same high plane. Sepia tone is employed in all Tahiti parts of the film, with color used in last few scenes when Sanders' hut is burned.

☐ 1943: Nomination: Best Scoring of a Dramatic Picture

• •

■ MOONFLEET

1955, 86 MINS, US ◇ ⊛ ⊙
Dir Fritz Lang   *Prod* John Houseman   *Scr* Jan Lustig, Margaret Fitts   *Ph* Robert Planck   *Ed* Albert Akst
Mus Miklos Rozsa, Vicente Gomez   *Art Dir* Cedric Gibbons, Hans Peters
● Stewart Granger, George Sanders, Joan Greenwood, Viveca Lindfors, Jon Whiteley, Liliane Montevecchi (M-G-M)

Costumed action, well-spiced with loose ladies and dashing rakehellies, is offered in *Moonfleet*. With mood and action the keynote of the John Houseman production, the direction by Fritz Lang plays both hard, developing considerable movement in several rugged action sequences without neglecting suspense. Period of the J. Meade Falkner novel is the 1750s.

Stewart Granger was a good choice for the dubious hero of the story, a high-living dandy who heads a gang of murderous smugglers headquartering in the English coastal village of Moonfleet. Yarn opens on a Macbeth note of cold, wild-swept moors, and scary, dark shadows, establishing an eerie flavor for the kickoff.

Later, it reminds of *Treasure Island* a bit when Granger and a small boy go through some highly imaginative adventures.

• •

■ MOONLIGHTING

1982, 97 MINS, UK ◇ ⊛ ⊙
Dir Jerzy Skolimowski   *Prod* Mark Shivas, Jerzy Skolimowski   *Scr* Jerzy Skolimowski   *Ph* Tony Pierce-Roberts   *Ed* Barry Vince   *Mus* Stanley Myers
Art Dir Tony Woollard
● Jeremy Irons, Eugene Lipinski, Jiri Stanislaw, Eugeniusz Haczkiewicz (White)

Jerzy Skolimowski made this film in 18 weeks – apparently a meditation on what happened in Poland when the military took over in December 1981 as seen by a Pole in Britain at the time.

Four Poles are sent to London by their boss who owns a house there to fix it up. They go off a week before military law is declared. The boss, a corrupt Communist, owns a building company, and the four are headed by Jeremy Irons who is the only one who can speak English.

The crew want to finish, buy things for their family, and go home. Irons pushes the work but then finds out about the military coup. He decides to keep it from the others. The men finally turn against him because of his over-bearing attitude, and it develops Irons was never a member of Solidarity.

Film is inventive, though anecdotal.

• •

■ MOONLIGHT SONATA

1937, 90 MINS, UK ⊛
Dir Lothar Mendes   *Scr* Edward Knoblock, E.M. Delafield
Ph Jan Stallich

● Ignace Jan Paderewski, Charles Farrell, Marie Tempest, Barbara Green, Eric Portman, Graham Browne (Pall Mall)

Charming love story woven round the central personality of the world-famous pianist, Paderewski. For the highbrows there will probably not be enough of the maestro's genius for the lowbrows, there will certainly be too much.

Locale is Sweden, where Charles Farrell, agent for a country estate, declares his love for Ingrid, granddaughter of the baroness, by whom he is employed. Forced landing by a passenger plane bound for Paris brings into the household for temporary hospitality three men, one of them Paderewski; another, a plausible, much-traveled gent of doubtful antecedents.

Baroness is honoured by the presence of the famous musician but soon distrusts the boastful young man-about-town. He makes a play for the young girl, who, having led a hermit-like existence, gets carried away by his worldliness and is hopelessly infatuated.

Charles Farrell has little to do but look on wistfully while his lady is alienated from him; Eric Portman gives a polished, scoundrelly performance; Barbara Greene is attractive and sincere as Ingrid: Marie Tempest, in her first screen role, is her usual delightful self. Of the aged maestro there can be no criticism; they wished to weave a story around him, and artistically and unpretentiously they have succeeded.

• •

■ MOON OVER PARADOR

1988, 105 MINS, US ◇ ⊛ ⊙
Dir Paul Mazursky   *Prod* Paul Mazursky   *Scr* Leon Capetanos, Paul Mazursky   *Ph* Donald McAlpine
Ed Stuart Pappe   *Mus* Maurice Jarre   *Art Dir* Pato Guzman
● Richard Dreyfuss, Raul Julia, Sonia Braga, Jonathan Winters, Fernando Rey, Sammy Davis Jr (Universal)

Paul Mazursky's elaborate farce about the actor as imposter (here posing as dictator of the mythical Latin nation Parador) has moments of true hilarity emerging only fitfully from a ponderous production.

Pic has Richard Dreyfuss well-cast as a fairly successful stage and film actor on a location shoot in the English-speaking Parador. He's given an offer he can't refuse by police chief Raul Julia to impersonate the just-deceased dictator.

Dreyfuss reluctantly adopts the role, but soon takes on the new persona in earnest after being coached by the dictator's sexy mistress Madonna (Sonia Braga in a flamboyant, delicious turn).

Ruse comes to a climax when Dreyfuss starts instituting reforms inimical to Julia and other powerful interests.

Dreyfuss' panache carries the film most of the way, ably played off Braga's lusty and glamourous character. Julia is very convincing as the stern local despot and Jonathan Winters makes the most of his transparent Ugly American role as a CIA man in Parador.

• •

■ MOONRAKER

1979, 126 MINS, UK ◇ ⊛ ⊙
Dir Lewis Gilbert   *Prod* Albert R. Broccoli
Scr Christopher Wood   *Ph* Jean Tournier   *Ed* John Glen
Mus John Barry   *Art Dir* Ken Adam
● Roger Moore, Lois Chiles, Michael Lonsdale, Richard Kiel, Bernard Lee, Corinne Clery (United Artists/Eon)

Christopher Wood's script takes the characters exactly where they always go in a James Bond pic and the only question is whether the stunts and gadgets will live up to expectations. They do.

The main problem this time is the outer-space setting which somehow dilutes the

M

mammoth monstrosity that 007 must save the world from. One more big mothership hovering over earth becomes just another model intercut with elaborate interiors.

The visual effects, stuntwork and other technical contributions all work together expertly to make the most preposterous notions believable. And Roger Moore, though still compared to Sean Connery, clearly has adapted the James Bond character to himself and serves well as the wise-cracking, incredibly daring and irresistible hero.
□ 1979: Nomination: Best Visual Effects

....

■ MOON-SPINNERS, THE

1964, 118 MINS, UK ◇ ⊛

Dir James Neilson   *Prod* Bill Anderson   *Scr* Michael Dyne   *Ph* Paul Beeson, John Wilcox, Michael Reed   *Ed* Gordon Stone   *Mus* Ron Grainer   *Art Dir* Tony Masters
● Hayley Mills, Eli Wallach, Peter McEnery, Joan Greenwood, Irene Papas, Pola Negri (Walt Disney)

With a mixture of American, English and Greek talents, engaged in a silly but zestful tale of villainy undone, told against some photogenic landscapes, *Moon-Spinners* naturally concentrates on Hayley Mills. With action the keyword in the loosely-knit script [from Mary Stewart's novel] this keeps the young lady perpetually on the move. Her adventures into first-puppy-love and feats of derring-do are accomplished with equal amounts of energy. She's never still long enough for her virtue or her life to be in danger.

Tale chiefly concerns two English females (Mills and Joan Greenwood) becoming involved in a jewel-theft adventure that concerns the Moon-Spinners, the Cretan inn where they're staying. The intrigue includes an odd but colorful assortment of local types headed by Eli Wallach, a most hissable villain, his sister (Irene Papas) and a young, mysterious Englishman (Peter McEnery).

Wallach comes off best by playing his villainy straight vicious, unfeeling and rotten to the core. He'd willingly shoot his nephew to keep the boy's mother from ratting on him. Irene Papas, a superb Greek actress with a wonderfully expressive face, gives more dignity and feeling to her tiny role than it deserves.

....

■ MOONSTRUCK

1987, 102 MINS, US ◇ ⊛ ⊙

Dir Norman Jewison   *Prod* Patrick Palmer   *Scr* John Patrick Shanley   *Ph* David Watkin   *Ed* Lou Lombardo   *Mus* Dick Hyman   *Art Dir* Philip Rosenberg
● Cher, Nicolas Cage, Vincent Gardenia, Olympia Dukakis, Danny Aiello, Julie Bovasso (M-G-M)

Norman Jewison's film is a mostly appetizing blend of comedy and drama carried by snappy dialog and a wonderful ensemble full of familiar faces. Leads Cher and Nicolas Cage are both solid and appealing, but it's the pic's older lovers especially the splendidly controlled Olympia Dukakis who give *Moonstruck* its endearing spirit.

Cher is Loretta Castorini, a vaguely dour, superstitious widow who believes her previous marriage she was wed at City Hall, her father didn't give her away, her husband was killed when he was hit by a bus was felled by bad luck.

Film begins with her accepting a wedding proposal, on bended knee, from the altogether unprepossessing Johnny Cammareri (Tony Aiello), who shortly thereafter heads off to Sicily to be at the bedside of his dying mother. Loretta, resigned to accepting mediocrity (she admits to her mother that she doesn't love Johnny) for the sake of security, receives a shock upon meeting his kid brother. Cage's Ronny is a brooding, vital, angry, barely contained force haunted by his past.

In Rose Castorini (Loretta's mother), Dukakis fleshes out a good, tired woman who

is nothing less than mystified by the actions of her husband, and what her response should be. It's a warm, lyrical performance, that provides the finest moments in the film.
□ 1987: Best Actress (Cher), Supp. Actress (Olympia Dukakis), Original Screenplay.
□ Nominations: Best Picture, Director, Supp. Actor (Vincent Gardenia)

....

■ MOONTIDE

1942, 94 MINS, US

Dir Archie Mayo   *Prod* Mark Hellinger   *Scr* John O'Hara   *Ph* Charles Clarke   *Ed* William Reynolds   *Mus* Cyril Mockridge, David Buttolph
● Jean Gabin, Ida Lupino, Thomas Mitchell, Claude Rains, Jerome Cowan, Helen Reynolds (20th Century-Fox)

Much of the success of the film [from the 1940 bestseller by Willard Robertson] may hinge on reaction to Jean Gabin. He's a pleasing and able player, but fails to project warmth and personal feeling.

Gabin, known as an earthy player in France, is given just that type of role in *Moontide*. He's an itinerant dock-worker who for years hasn't had a home and is chiefly interested in getting drunk. Until, that is, he rescues from the surf a hash-house waitress (Ida Lupino) intent on killing herself.

Moontide is a series of incidents, although the overall impression is of a single important event in a man's life. Despite the speed with which director Archie Mayo paints each incident, the total effect is one of slowness and lacking suspense. Mayo's artistic direction is too even-paced to provide the occasional kick that any story requires.
□ 1942: Nomination: Best B&W Cinematography

....

■ MOONWALKER

1988, 93 MINS, US ◇ ⊛ ⊙

Dir Colin Chivers, Jerry Kramer, Will Vinton, Jim Blashfield   *Prod* Dennis Jones, Jerry Kramer   *Scr* David Newman   *Ph* John Hora, Frederick Elmes, Crescenzo Notarille   *Ed* David E. Blewitt   *Mus* Bruce Broughton   *Art Dir* Michael Ploog, Bryan Jones, John Walker
● Michael Jackson, Sean Lennon, Kellie Parker, Brandon Adams, Joe Pesci (Lorimar)

Moonwalker – also the title of a Michael Jackson autobiography – seems unsure of what it was supposed to be. At the center of the pic is the *Smooth Criminal* segment, a musical/dramatic piece full of dancing, schmaltzy kids, sci-fi effects and blazing machine guns [directed by Colin Chilvers, based on a story by Jackson]. Around it are really just numerous Jackson music videos with little or no linkage. Although quite enjoyable the whole affair does not make for a structured or professional movie.

Pic opens with a hi-tech concert footage of *Man in the Mirror* and then quickly switches to a rather indulgent retrospective of Michael Jackson's career featuring clips of old songs, shows and videos, this time featuring eight to ten-year-old children dancing and miming the song, with Brandon Ames playing the Jackson part.

Next segment is *Speed Demon* with Jackson disguised as a rabbit chased by fans. Next up is *Leave me Alone*, the most fascinating section, featuring comments about Jackson from the tabloids accompanied by expert animation by Jim Blashfield. *Smooth Criminal* blends into a live performance of Jackson singing the Beatles' song 'Come Together'.

....

■ MOON ZERO TWO

1969, 100 MINS, UK ◇ ⊛

Dir Roy Ward Baker   *Prod* Michael Carreras   *Scr* Michael Carreras   *Ph* Paul Besson   *Ed* Spencer Reeve   *Mus* Don Ellis   *Art Dir* Scott MacGregor

● James Olson, Catherine Schell, Warren Mitchell, Adrienne Corri, Bernard Bresslaw, Dudley Foster (Hammer)

Moon Zero Two [from an original story by Gavin Lyall, Frank Hardman and Martin Davison] never makes up its mind whether it is a spoof or a straightforward space-adventure yarn. Overall it's a fairly dull experience, despite some capable artwork and special effects.

Space travel has progressed by 2021, and the moon's virtually oldhat. First man to set foot on Mars (James Olson) declines to work as a regular passenger pilot.

Final sequence offers a spot of excitement, but the whole film tends to limp. Moon City's airport, its Wild West saloon and other amenities are presumably meant to be satire but it doesn't come off.

Olson is a melancholy hero. Mitchell plays with tongue in cheek, Bernard Bresslaw as one of his thugs seems bewildered by the entire proceedings.

....

■ MORE

1969, 115 MINS, LUXEMBOURG ◇

Dir Barbet Schroeder   *Prod* Dave Lewis, Charles Lachman   *Scr* Barbet Schroeder, Paul Gegauff   *Ph* Nestor Almendros   *Ed* Denise De Casabianca   *Mus* The Pink Floyd
● Mimsy Farmer, Klaus Grunberg, Heinz Engelmann, Michel Chanderli (Jet/Two World)

In his first pic director Barbet Schroeder shows an insight into [late 1960s] youths, be they American or Europeans, who have been labeled everything from beatnik to yippie. There is no attempt to go in for forced erotics, violence, nudity or titillating amoralism. He gives a feeling of how it is sans didactics or obviousness. Drug-taking is a part of it in this tale of a youth from Germany destroyed by it.

The German boy meets a pretty, independent American girl. They soon become lovers and he follows her to Ibiza, a Spanish island, where they have an idyll in a beach house.

Brilliantly shot in arresting hues, it escapes picturesqueness and delves into its characters with sympathy and ease, sans indulgence. Mimsy Farmer reveals a potent personality and gives her role of the girl a tension, inner hurt and alienation.

....

■ MORE AMERICAN GRAFFITI

1979, 111 MINS, US ◇ ⊛ ⊙

Dir B.W.L. Norton   *Prod* Howard Kazanjian   *Scr* B.W.L. Norton   *Ph* Caleb Deschanel   *Ed* Tina Hirsch   *Art Dir* Ray Storey
● Candy Clark, Bo Hopkins, Ron Howard, Scott Glenn, Paul Le Mat, Charles Martin Smith (Universal/Lucasfilm)

More American Graffiti may be one of the most innovative and ambitious films of the last five years, but by no means is it one of the most successful. In trying to follow the success of George Lucas' immensely popular 1973 hit, writer-director B.W.L. Norton overloads the sequel with four wholly different cinematic styles to carry forward the lives of *American Graffiti*'s original cast.

While dazzling to the eye, the flirtation with split-screen, anamorphic, 16mm and 1:85 screen sizes does not justify itself in terms of the film's content.

Part of Norton's presumed goal, of course, is to show how the 1960s fractured and split apart. But without a dramatic glue to hold the disparate story elements together, *Graffiti* is too disorganized for its own good.

....

■ MORE THAN A MIRACLE

1967, 102 MINS, ITALY/FRANCE ◇

Dir Francesco Rosi   *Prod* Carlo Ponti   *Scr* Tonino Guerra, Raffaele La Capria, Giuseppe Patroni Griffi,

Francesco Rosi   Ph Pasquale De Santis   Ed Jolanda Benvenuti   Mus Piero Piccioni   Art Dir Piero Poletto
● Sophia Loren, Omar Sharif, Dolores Del Rio, Georges Wilson, Leslie French (M-G-M)

More Than a Miracle is a real curiosity: labelled in production notes as a 'fairy tale for adults,' the production tells a Cinderella story, with some heavy-handed anti-clericalism and anti-monarchism thrown in.

Although the fairy tale approach is evident the script defeats itself in part by going too far into reality. Omar Sharif, therefore, is not only handsome, but arrogant, wilful, brutal to his servants; also, the beautiful Sophia Loren, looking a bit uneasy and out of place in peasant weeds, eventually berates Sharif publicly for oppression of the lower classes.

Pic's fatal flaw is vacillation between pure make-believe, which would have gone over to some degree, and corny political tract which is what one would imagine *Snow White* to be if produced by Russian filmmakers.

■ MORE THE MERRIER, THE

1943, 101 MINS, US ▼ ⊙
Dir George Stevens   *Prod* George Stevens   *Scr* Robert Russell, Frank Ross, Richard Flourney, Lewis R. Foster   *Ph* Ted Tetzlaff   *Ed* Otto Meyer
● Jean Arthur, Joel McCrea, Charles Coburn, Richard Gaines, Bruce Bennett, Frank Sully (Columbia)

A sparkling and effervescing piece of entertainment, *The More the Merrier*, is one of the most spontaneous farce-comedies of the wartime era. Although Jean Arthur and Joel McCrea carry the romantic interest, Charles Coburn walks off with the honors.

Story [by Frank Ross and Robert Russell] is premised on the housing conditions existing in wartime Washington. Coburn arrives in town and sublets half interest in Miss Arthur's minute apartment, and when he finds the girl without a boy friend, conveniently picks up McCrea – Air Force sergeant in town to get orders for secret mission – to become partner in his share of the housing layout. Naturally complications ensue in hilarious fashion until Coburn backs out to watch the culmination of the romance he very effectively cooks up.
□ 1943: Best Supp. Actor (Charles Coburn).
□ Nominations: Best Picture, Director, Actress (Jean Arthur), Original Story, Screenplay

■ MORE THINGS CHANGE, THE

1986, 95 MINS, AUSTRALIA ◇
Dir Robyn Nevin   *Prod* Jill C. Robb   *Scr* Moya Wood   *Ph* Dan Burstall   *Ed* Jill Bilcock   *Mus* Peter Best   *Art Dir* Josephine Ford
● Judy Morris, Barry Otto, Victoria Longley, Lewis Fitz-Gerald, Peter Carroll (Syme)

The More Things Change is a universally topical film about a modern marriage, told with humor and insight. It's also splendidly acted.

Connie (Judy Morris) and Lex (Barry Otto) are happily married with a small son. They've decided to opt out of the rat race, and have purchased a small but spectacularly beautiful farm two hours' drive from the city, but until the farm is self-sufficient one of them has to keep working. A live-in baby-sitter is the answer, and Connie engages Geraldine (Victoria Longley).

The viewer's expectations are, naturally, that Lex and Geraldine will have an affair, but Moya Wood's sharp screenplay is much more subtle than that, making this a film where all the characters are a pleasure.

■ MORGAN!
See: *A Suitable Case for Treatment*

■ MORGAN (A SUITABLE CASE FOR TREATMENT)
See: *A Suitable Case for Treatment*

■ MORITURI
(UK: The Saboteur, Code Name – 'Morituri')

1965, 118 MINS, US ▼
Dir Bernhard Wicki   *Prod* Aaron Rosenberg   *Scr* Daniel Taradash   *Ph* Conrad Hall   *Ed* Joseph Silver   *Mus* Jerry Goldsmith   *Art Dir* Jack Martin Smith, Herman A. Blumenthal
● Marlon Brando, Yul Brynner, Janet Margolin, Trevor Howard, Martin Benrath, Hans Christian Blech (20th Century-Fox)

Morituri is a Second World War sea drama of sometimes battering impact. Starring Marlon Brando and Yul Brynner, the production carries strong suspense at times and a brooding menace that communicates to the spectator.

Action takes place aboard a German blockade runner in 1942 en route from Yokohama to Bordeaux with a cargo of 7,000 tons of indispensable crude rubber for the Nazis, which the Allies also want. British put a man on the freighter with orders to disarm explosive charges by which the captain would scuttle his ship rather than allow capture.

Both Brando and Brynner contribute hard-hitting performances, Brando as the saboteur and Brynner as captain. Former, a German deserter threatened with return to Germany and certain death if he doesn't acquiesce to British demand, gives his impersonation almost tongue-in-cheek handling.

In top support, Trevor Howard is in briefly as a British Intelligence officer, and Martin Benrath makes the most of his role as exec officer, a Nazi who takes over the ship when Brynner becomes raging drunk.
□ 1965: Nominations: Best B&W Cinematography, B&W Costume Design

■ MORNING AFTER, THE

1986, 103 MINS, US ◇ ▼ ⊙
Dir Sidney Lumet   *Prod* Bruce Gilbert   *Scr* James Hicks   *Ph* Andrzej Bartkowiak   *Ed* Joel Goodman   *Mus* Paul Chihara   *Art Dir* Albert Brenner
● Jane Fonda, Jeff Bridges, Raul Julia, Diane Salinger, Richard Foronjy (Lorimar/American Filmworks)

Overwrought and implausible, *The Morning After* is a dramatic situation in search of a thriller plot. Jane Fonda stars as a boozy, washed-up actress who wakes up one morning next to a man with a dagger in his heart, and her efforts to cope with the dilemma are neither terribly suspenseful nor entertaining.

She removes any trace that she was ever present at the fellow's place, doesn't call the cops and heads for the airport, where she hooks up with friendly redneck Jeff Bridges, who gradually insinuates himself into her life.

Along the way, Fonda battles the bottle, succumbs to Bridges' charms and is forced into a divorce by estranged hubby but good chum Raul Julia, an outrageously successful Beverly Hills hairdresser who now wants to marry a Bel-Air heiress.

While attempting to build up tension, Fonda and director Sidney Lumet more often succeed in creating hysteria.
□ 1986: Nomination: Best Actress (Jane Fonda)

■ MORNING GLORY

1933, 70 MINS, US ▼ ⊙
Dir Lowell Sherman   *Prod* Pandro S. Berman   *Scr* Howard J. Green   *Ph* Bert Glennon   *Ed* George Nicholls   *Mus* Max Steiner
● Katharine Hepburn, Douglas Fairbanks Jr, Adolphe Menjou, Mary Duncan, C. Aubrey Smith (Radio)

Morning Glory isn't an entirely happy choice for Katharine Hepburn but the star provides a strong performance. This one is heavy on legit class and lacks action and sustained conflict.

Story [from the stage play by Zoe Akins] is at great pains to build up the charming character of a well-bred, utterly innocent country girl who comes to Broadway seeking footlight fame. No sooner is the thoroughly lovable figure built to completeness than the hapless little Cinderella is dragged through the mud of backstage casual amours. This happens less than midway of the footage, and thereafter the grip of an engaging story relaxes fatally. The fate of this bedraggled Cinderella becomes a matter of indifference.

Aside from its story defects, the picture is excellent in technique. Dialog is pointed and terse, and the photography is magnificent. A first-rate supporting cast gives Hepburn invaluable co-operation, notably a fine, intelligent handling of the male lead by Douglas Fairbanks Jr and a characteristically suave performance by Adolphe Menjou.
□ 1932/33: Best Actress (Katharine Hepburn)

■ MOROCCO

1930, 90 MINS, US ▼ ⊙
Dir Josef von Sternberg   *Prod* [Hector Turnbull]   *Scr* Jules Furthman   *Ph* Lee Garmes, [Lucien Ballard]   *Ed* [Sam Winston]   *Mus* [Karl Hajer]   *Art Dir* [Hans Dreier]
● Gary Cooper, Marlene Dietrich, Adolphe Menjou, Ullrich Haupt, Eve Southern, Francis McDonald (Paramount)

Morocco is too lightweight a story to be counterbalanced by the big-time direction given it. Marlene Dietrich has little opportunities in her first American talker. There's nothing to the picture, except what Josef von Sternberg gives it in direction, and that's giving it more than it's got.

The story [from the play *Amy Jolly* by Benno Vigny] is given a terrific kick early, when Dietrich arrives in Morocco to star in the concert hall. The first evening of her appearance she gives the key to her home to a legionnaire, Cooper. After that the rest is apple sauce, even to her joining the female followers of the troops to keep near her soldier.

Adolphe Menjou has a walkthrough role, done with his acknowledged suavity. Ullrich Haupt handles a minor role very nicely. Cooper plays excellently. He gets the precise spirit of his role.
□ 1930/31: Nominations: Best Director, Actress (Marlene Dietrich), Cinematography, Art Direction

■ MORTAL STORM, THE

1940, 100 MINS, US
Dir Frank Borzage   *Scr* Claudine West, Andersen Ellis, George Froeschel   *Ph* William Daniels   *Ed* Elmo Vernon   *Mus* Edward Kane   *Art Dir* Cedric Gibbons, Wade B. Rubottom
● Margaret Sullavan, James Stewart, Robert Young, Frank Morgan, Robert Stack, Bonita Granville (M-G-M)

The Mortal Storm is a slugging indictment of the political and social theories advanced by Hitler, a combination of entertainment and democratic preachment, based on a novel of the same name by Phyllis Bottome.

The locale is Germany, 1933, at the time when the paper-hanger gained control of the government. Through the lives of the members of the family of a university professor there is revealed the soul-crushing effect of Nazi regimentation. Sons turn from their parents, friends become deadly enemies, innocent elders are tossed into concentration camps.

Because the action takes place in the early years of the Hitler regime, the ending of the story provides its most potent wallop. Hero

M

and heroine plan a dangerous escape over a snowbound and unguarded frontier pass in the Austrian Alps.

Performances are excellent. James Stewart is the courageous individualist who refuses to join the Nazi party, and Robert Young is the heavy. Frank Morgan draws a fine characterization of the non-Aryan professor. Irene Rich returns to films as mother of the unhappy family. Margaret Sullavan carries the romantic interest.

Pictorially, the film is a panorama of beautiful mountain scenes and finely photographed interiors.

. . . .

■ MORTAL THOUGHTS

1991, 104 MINS, US ◇ ⓥ ⊙
Dir Alan Rudolph   *Prod* John Fielder, Mark Tarlov
Scr William Reilly, Claude Kerven   *Ph* Elliot Davis
Ed Tom Walls   *Mus* Mark Isham   *Art Dir* Howard Cummings
● Demi Moore, Glenne Headly, Bruce Willis, John Pankow, Harvey Keitel, Billie Neal (New Visions/Polar)

Two gals make a murderous mess of a bad situation in *Mortal Thoughts*. Played straight and for sympathy, tale of dark retaliation goes astray early on, despite the promise created at the outset by imaginative, energetic production and appealing performances.

Demi Moore and Glenne Headly play lifelong friends who run a blue-collar New Jersey beauty shop and remain closer to each other than to their husbands. Small wonder, since Moore's husband (John Pankow) is a boorish salesman, and Headley's wed to a thoroughly despicable, abusive lout (Bruce Willis).

Headly's running response is that he should die and she wants to kill him, but Moore never takes it seriously until Willis ends up with his throat cut and the two femmes have blood all over their hands.

Scripters play the whole thing out from a police interrogation room, where a detective (Harvey Keitel) hammers away at Moore to get at the real story, which unspools in flashbacks.

. . . .

■ MOSCOW NIGHTS

1935, 77 MINS, UK ⓥ
Dir Anthony Asquith   *Prod* Alexis Granowski, Max Schach   *Scr* Eric Seipmann, Anthony Asquith   *Ph* Philip Tannura   *Ed* William Hornbeck, Francis Lyon
Art Dir Vincent Korda
● Harry Baur, Laurence Olivier, Penelope Dudley-Ward, Athene Seyler, Hay Petrie (Denham/London)

Moscow Nights is a triumph for director Anthony Asquith in that you are actually transported to Russia in 1916, and no book could give you a more vivid spectacle of things as they existed at that time. Not once is it deemed necessary to resort to comedy relief. It is really and truly a triumph of film direction.

Plot is conventional enough, but it is the atmosphere in which it is disclosed. A handsome young Russian officer (Laurence Olivier) is carried into a hospital in a delirious condition from war wounds. Upon regaining consciousness he discovers a celestial-looking Red Cross nurse in the person of Penelope Dudley-Ward, and falls hard. She is, however, engaged to a middle-aged war profiteer who pays off the mortgage on her parents' home. The profiteer boasts he was born a peasant and is still a peasant. Part is played by Harry Baur, a Continental actor, who brings to the role a dominance that always falls short of being repellent.

Laurence Olivier has looks, charm and acting ability. This is his first big opportunity, and he takes advantage of it to the full.

The supporting cast is of a very high order, notably Athene Seyler, Kate Cutler, Morton Selten and Hay Petrie.

. . . .

■ MOSCOW ON THE HUDSON

1984, 115 MINS, US ◇ ⓥ ⊙
Dir Paul Mazursky   *Prod* Paul Mazursky   *Scr* Paul Mazursky, Leon Capetanos   *Ph* Donald McAlpine
Ed Richard Halsey   *Mus* David McHugh   *Art Dir* Pato Guzman
● Robin Williams, Maria Conchita Alonso, Cleavant Derricks, Alejandro Rey, Savely Kramarov, Elya Baskin (Columbia)

Moscow on the Hudson is a sweet, beautifully performed picture that unfortunately wanders around several patriotic themes.

Directed by Paul Mazursky with his usual unusual touches, *Moscow* would be in a lot of trouble without a superbly sensitive portrayal by Robin Williams of a gentle Russian circus musician who makes a sudden decision to defect while visiting the US.

As Mazursky sees it, Williams thus becomes one more in a flood of immigrants who still are coming to this country and discovering virtues that those already here many times forget. Of course, they also encounter the faults, as well.

The entire film is full of performers working way beyond the material. Cleavant Derricks is especially good. Maria Conchita Alonso is also spirited as Williams' Italian girlfriend.

. . . .

■ MOSES

1975, 140 MINS, UK/ITALY ◇ ⓥ
Dir Gianfranco De Bosio   *Prod* Vincenzo Labella
Scr Anthony Burgess, Vittorio Bonicelli, Gianfranco De Bosio   *Ph* Marcello Gatti   *Ed* Gerry Hambling
Mus Ennio Morricone
● Burt Lancaster, Anthony Quayle, Ingrid Thulin, Irene Papas, Mariangela Melato, William Lancaster (ITC/RAI)

Moses is another attempt at compressing a big slice of Biblical drama, and the inevitable result is superficial story telling. The film was impressively photographed in Israel and has Burt Lancaster in a restrained portrayal as the patriarch of the ancient Hebrews who leads them from Egyptian bondage to the promised land.

Pic strikes a reasonable balance between spectacle and narrative. But the net effect is one of flat earnestness, a tale more of tribute than of dimensional human saga.

Feature was 'inspired' by the TV miniseries, *Moses, the Lawgiver*. Besides recutting, the theatrical edition assertedly contains much footage not included in the TV version.

Lancaster delivers his usual polished professionalism, arrayed in seasoned if undistinguished support are Anthony Quayle and Ingrid Thulin as his brother and sister, Irene Papas as his wife, and Laurent Terzieff as the young Egyptian monarch loathe to free his Jewish serfs.

. . . .

■ MOSQUITO COAST, THE

1986, 117 MINS, US ◇ ⓥ ⊙
Dir Peter Weir   *Prod* Jerome Hellman   *Scr* Paul Schrader   *Ph* John Seale   *Ed* Thom Noble
Mus Maurice Jarre   *Art Dir* John Stoddart
● Harrison Ford, Helen Mirren, River Phoenix, Jadrien Steele, Hilary Gordon, Rebecca Gordon (Warner)

It is hard to believe that a film as beautiful as *The Mosquito Coast* [adapted from the novel by Paul Theroux] can also be so bleak, but therein lies its power and undoing. A modern variation of *Swiss Family Robinson*, it starts out as a film about idealism and possibilities, but takes a dark turn and winds up questioning the very values it so powerfully presents. There's a stunning performance by Harrison Ford with firstrate film-making by Peter Weir.

Ford's Allie Fox is a world-class visionary with the power to realize his vision. He rants and raves against pre-packaged, mass consumed American culture and packs up his wife and four kids and moves them to a remote Caribbean island the Mosquito Coast.

Fox transforms a remote outpost on the island into a thriving community equipped with numerous Rube Goldberg-like gadgets to harness the forces of nature and make life better for the inhabitants. For a while it's an idyllic little utopian community, but the seeds of its downfall are present even as it thrives.

As Fox starts to unravel so does the film. None of the outside antagonists supplied by Paul Schrader's screenplay are fitting adversaries for Fox' genius.

. . . .

■ MOST DANGEROUS GAME, THE
(UK: The Hounds of Zaroff)

1932, 61 MINS, US ⓥ
Dir Ernest B. Schoedsack, Irving Pichel   *Prod* Merian C. Cooper, Ernest B. Schoedsack   *Scr* James A. Creelman
Ph Henry Gerrard   *Ed* Archie F. Marshek   *Mus* Max Steiner   *Art Dir* Carroll Clark
● Joel McCrea, Fay Wray, Leslie Banks, Robert Armstrong, Steve Clemento, Noble Johnson (RKO)

Fantastic would-be thriller [from a story by Richard Connell] whose efforts at horrifying are not very effective.

A crazy would-be Russian count (Leslie Banks), who derives more pleasure from hunting human beings than lions and tigers since a wild bull kicked him in the head, is this one's baby-scaring Frankenstein. He operates alone on a deserted tropical isle, using shipwreck victims for game. When he gets 'em he fattens 'em up. The routine then is to send them out on the jungle-like isle with a few hours' start.

It's a foregone cinch that Joel McCrea, as a big game hunter on his way to India when tossed into the count's trap, will hand the man hunter a trimming. It looks for a moment like the count wins this one, too, when McCrea goes over the waterfall with a hunting dog at his throat.

The producers have heretofore specialized in animal films with a more or less natural background. This time they stick mostly to the studio, and although the swamp and jungle settings serve, considering the limitations, they're frequently obviously phoney.

Banks grabs everything worth grabbing among performance honors. Fay Wray has no opportunity to be anything but decorative. With McCrea and Robert Armstrong (as a booze-guzzling simpleton) miscasting is evident.

. . . .

■ MOST DANGEROUS MAN IN THE WORLD, THE
See: The Chairman

. . . .

■ MOTHER, JUGS & SPEED

1976, 95 MINS, US ◇ ⓥ
Dir Peter Yates   *Prod* Peter Yates, Tom Mankiewicz
Scr Tom Mankiewicz   *Ph* Ralph Woolsey   *Ed* Frank P. Keller   *Art Dir* Walter Scott Herndon
● Raquel Welch, Bill Cosby, Harvey Keitel, Allen Garfield, Larry Hagman, L.Q. Jones (20th Century-Fox)

The three titular characters are Bill Cosby, Raquel Welch, and Harvey Keitel, all very pleasant in their roles as ambulance drivers for company owner Allen Garfield. Their easy-going camaraderie, which provides a strong role for Welch, allows for many good behavioral moments.

The film starts off as pure farce but veers into tragedy when young driver Bruce Davison is killed by a junkie's shotgun.

Other supporting characters also suffer from the film's opportunistic grab-bag tendencies.

The film, based on a story by Stephen Manes and Tom Mankiewicz, remains oddly appealing despite its serious flaws in many ways it's an accurate reflection of what really goes on in hustling ambulance outfits.

. . . .

■ **MOTHER LODE**

1982, 101 MINS, US ◇ ⓥ
Dir Charlton Heston   *Prod* Fraser Clarke Heston
Scr Fraser Clarke Heston   *Ph* Richard Leiterman   *Ed* Eric Boyd-Perkins   *Mus* Ken Wannberg   *Art Dir* Douglas Higgins
● Charlton Heston, Nick Mancuso, Kim Basinger, John Marley, Dale Wilson (Agamemnon)

As the title indicates, the consuming issue in *Mother Lode* is a search for gold. The picture is not without shortcomings, but is long on good performances, charismatic people in the three principal roles, compelling outdoor aerial sequences in the Cassiar Mountains of British Columbia and high-level suspense throughout.

The role of Silas McGee, the disreputable Scottish miner trying to protect his great secret find, is a switch to villainy for Charlton Heston, but he relishes the role and even makes a creditable pass at a thick Scottish brogue. Nick Mancuso, as the bush-pilot protagonist who would delve the secret location of the lode at any cost, is the character around which the suspense must swirl, and he manages to keep matters tense to the very end.

Kim Basinger, the only femme in the picture, provides the reason for some unusual plot twists, and comes across as a beauteous screen personality.

. . . .

■ **MOTHER WORE TIGHTS**

1947, 107 MINS, US ◇
Dir Walter Lang   *Prod* Lamar Trotti   *Scr* Lamar Trotti
Ph Harry Jackson   *Ed* J. Watson Webb Jr   *Mus* Alfred Newman   *Art Dir* Richard Day, Joseph C. Wright
● Betty Grable, Dan Dailey, Mona Freeman, Connie Marshall, Vanessa Brown, Sara Allgood (20th Century-Fox)

Mother Wore Tights [based on the book by Mariam Young] is a familiarly styled Technicolor musical opus on the life and times of a song-and-dance team that knocked around the vaude circuits about the century's turn. Leisurely paced and loosely constructed as a series of undramatic vignettes, picture will appeal to patrons who prefer their nostalgia trowelled on thickly and sweetly.

Musical is severely limited by its long and mediocre score of tunes [by Mack Gordon, Josef Myrow], which are presented without any visual imaginative touches. Numerous hoofing sequences [staged by Seymour Felix and Kenny Williams] featuring Betty Grable and vis-a-vis Dan Dailey also fail to rate the heavy accent put on them by the footage. Chief drawback, however, is the rambling story, whose lack of both major and minor climaxes is made glaring by Walter Lang's deadpan direction and a script which pulls out all the stops in its use of cliches and sentimentalism.

Yarn, unfolding via simple flashbacks to the commentary of the hoofers' younger daughter, progresses through the various stages of the vaude team's career.
□ 1947: Best Scoring for a Musical Picture.
□ Nominations: Best Color Cinematography, Song ('You Do')

. . . .

■ **MOTOR PSYCHO**

1965, 73 MINS, US
Dir Russ Mayer   *Prod* Russ Meyer   *Scr* Russ Meyer, W. E. Sprague   *Ph* Russ Meyer   *Ed* Charles G. Schelling
Mus Igo Kantor
● Stephen Oliver, Haji, Alex Rocco, Holle K. Winters, Joseph Cellini, Thomas Scott (Eve)

Motor Psycho is a violent Russ Meyer production concerning three young bums on a rape-murder spree in a California desert town. Slick, well-made and initially absorbing, it features sex angles which kill the credibility of a script which itself is long on loose ends and short on moral compensation.

Stephen Oliver, Joseph Cellini and Thomas Scott are the vagrants who, within the first five minutes, have viciously beaten Steve Masters and raped his wife Arshalouis Aivasian. Holle K. Winters is then assaulted while hubby Alex Rocco is down the road resisting the advances of busty Sharon Lee.

At length, Coleman Francis is beaten and accidently killed when the gang moves in on his younger wife, played by a gal named Haji. Rest of pic concerns Rocco's trackdown of the trio, in which he is joined by Haji, left for dead after Oliver shoots her.

Meyer's direction is good, while his interesting and crisp camera work is excellent.

. . . .

■ **MOULIN ROUGE**

1952, 118 MINS, UK ◇ ⓥ
Dir John Huston   *Scr* John Huston, Anthony Veiller
Ph Oswald Morris   *Ed* Ralph Kemplen   *Mus* Georges Auric   *Art Dir* Paul Sheriff
● Jose Ferrer, Colette Marchand, Suzanne Flon, Zsa Zsa Gabor, Christopher Lee, Eric Pohlmann (Romulus)

Jose Ferrer endows with conviction the part of Toulouse-Lautrec, the cultured, gifted artist of Paris in the 1880s whose glaring deformity – a childhood accident impeded growth of his legs – repulses the women whom he constantly seeks.

John Huston's direction is superb in the handling of individual scenes. The can-can ribaldry, the frank depiction of streetwalkers, the smokey atmosphere of Parisian bistro life – they come through in exciting pictorial terms. Each scene has a framed appearance which richly sets off the action. And the Technicolor tinting captures the flamboyant aura of Montmartre.

But overall, the production, while of great scenic merit, requires some dramatic explosiveness. The story unfolds in a constantly minor-key tone.

Filmed in France and England, the pic is an adaptation of the best-selling novel by Pierre La Mure.
□ 1952: Best Color Art Direction, Color Costume Design.
□ Nominations: Best Picture, Director, Actor (Jose Ferrer), Supp. Actress (Colette Marchand), Editing

. . . .

■ **MOUNTAIN MEN, THE**

1980, 102 MINS, US ◇ ⓥ ⊙
Dir Richard Lang   *Prod* Martin Shafer, Andrew Scheinman
Scr Fraser Clarke Heston   *Ph* Michael Hugo   *Ed* Eva Ruggiero   *Mus* Michel Legrand   *Art Dir* Bill Kenney
● Charlton Heston, Brian Keith, Victoria Racimo, Seymour Cassel, John Glover (Columbia)

Does anyone want to see Charlton Heston as Grizzly Adams? That's the question arising from Columbia's lethargic wilderness pic *The Mountain Men*.

Screenplay by star's son Fraser Clarke Heston is loaded with vulgarities that seem excessive for the genre, and scene after scene dwells on bloody hand-to-hand battles between Indians and the grizzled trappers played by Heston and sidekick Brian Keith.

Film takes ages to drag from one plot development to another, though the Indian battles are with sufficient regularity to keep the audience from snoozing. Basic storyline is Heston's courtly protection of runaway Indian squaw Victoria Racimo and the violent attempts by her former Indian mate Stephen Macht to win her back. It's a limp feature debut for director Richard Lang.

. . . .

■ **MOUNTAINS OF THE MOON**

1990, 135 MINS, US ◇ ⓥ ⊙
Dir Bob Rafelson   *Prod* Daniel Melnick   *Scr* William Harrison, Bob Rafelson   *Ph* Roger Deakins   *Ed* Thom Noble   *Mus* Michael Small   *Art Dir* Norman Reynolds
● Patrick Bergin, Iain Glen, Fiona Shaw, Richard E. Grant, Peter Vaughan, Anna Massey (Carolco/Indieprod)

Bob Rafelson's *Mountains of the Moon* is an outstanding adventure film, adapted from William Harrison's book *Burton and Speke* and the journals of 19th-century explorers Richard Burton and John Hanning Speke. Without sacrificing the historical context this pic provides deeply felt performances and refreshing, offbeat humour.

Starting in 1854, pic documents duo's ill-fated first two expeditions to Africa, climaxing with Speke's discovery of what became named Lake Victoria, the true source of the Nile (though Speke could not prove same). Roger Deakins' gritty, realistic photography of rugged Kenyan locations contrasts with segments of cheery beauty back home in England between treks.

Rafelson brings expert detailing to the saga. The male bonding theme of the two explorers is forcefully and tastefully told. Besides its vivid presentation of the dangers posed by brutal, hostile African tribes, pic strongly develops its major themes of self-realization and self-aggrandisement.

As Speke, Scots actor Iain Glen creates sympathy for a wayward character. He resembles David Bowie on screen, a reminder that project originally was planned as a vehicle for British rock stars including Bowie until wiser heads prevailed.

. . . .

■ **MOURNING BECOMES ELECTRA**

1947, 173 MINS, US ◇ ⓥ ⊙
Dir Dudley Nichols   *Prod* Dudley Nichols   *Scr* Dudley Nichols   *Ph* George Barnes   *Ed* Roland Gross, Chandler House   *Mus* Richard Hageman   *Art Dir* Albert S. D'Agostino
● Rosalind Russell, Michael Redgrave, Raymond Massey, Katina Paxinou, Leo Genn, Kirk Douglas (RKO)

Eugene O'Neill's post-Civil War version of the ancient Greek classic was at best 'good for those who like that sort of thing'. The success of the 1931 play proved that there were plenty who did or who were drawn by the O'Neill name and/or a sense that they owed it to themselves aesthetically to see *Electra*.

Unfortunately, the picture although still laden with tense drama lacks much of the impact of the play. The five-hour play (plus an hour's intermission for dinner) seemed less long than the 2 hours and 53 minutes of picture, which is run without intermission.

Nichols, who produced, directed and wrote the adaptation for the screen, will rate a bow from the O'Neill lovers in that he has made no compromises. The picture is every bit as unrelenting in its detailing of family tragedy, brought on by the warping effect of Puritan conscience in conflict with human emotion, as was the play. Even the distorted Oedipus relationships are unflaggingly handled. Never is there concession to a smile or other relaxation from the hammering tragedy of murder, self-destruction and twisted, dramatic emotionalism. The legend has been set down in almost modern surroundings and given the locale and speech, the morals and manners of Civil War New England.

Performances are uniformly good, although they never rise beyond the drama that is inherent in the situations themselves. Too often the emoting consists of Rosalind Russell and Michael Redgrave popping their eyes. Outstanding are Raymond Massey and Henry Hull, the latter in the secondary role of an aged retainer.
□ 1947: Nominations: Best Actor (Michael Redgrave), Actress (Rosalind Russell)

M

MOUSE THAT ROARED, THE

1959, 83 MINS, UK ◇ ⑲
Dir Jack Arnold *Prod* Walter Shenson *Scr* Roger
MacDougall, Stanley Mann *Ph* John Wilcox
Ed Raymond Poulton *Mus* Edwin Astley
● Peter Sellers, Jean Seberg, David Kossoff, William
Hartnell, Leo McKern, Macdonald Parke (Open Road/
Columbia)

Screen satire can be as risky as a banana-skin
on a sidewalk. There are a few occasions
when *The Mouse That Roared* gets oversmart,
but on the whole it keeps its slight amusing
idea bubbling happily in the realms of
straightforward comedy. It's a comedy in the
old Ealing tradition.

The yarn [from the novel by Leonard
Wibberly] concerns the Grand Duchy of Grand
Fenwick, the world's smallest country, which
relies for its existence on the export of a local
wine to the US. When California bottles a
cheaper, inferior imitation, Grand Fenwick is
on verge of going broke. So the prime minister
hits on the wily scheme of going to war against
America, on the grounds that the loser in any
war is invariably on the receiving end of hefty
financial handouts from the winners.

But the invasion of NY by an army of 20
men with mail uniforms and bows and arrows
goes awry.

Peter Sellers plays three roles in the film.
He is the Grand Duchess Gloriana, the prime
minister and also the hapless field marshal
who upsets the prime minister's plans. Jean
Seberg is pretty, but makes little impact, as
the heroine. But there is useful work from
William Hartnell, David Kossoff, Leo
McKern and Macdonald Parke as a pompous
American general. The sight of the completely deserted city is an awesome one and
owes considerably to Jack Arnold's direction,
and remarkable artwork and lensing.

MOVE OVER, DARLING

1963, 103 MINS, US ◇
Dir Michael Gordon *Prod* Aaron Rosenberg, Martin
Melcher *Scr* Hal Kanter, Jack Sher *Ph* Daniel L. Fapp
Ed Robert Simpson *Mus* Lionel Newman *Art Dir* Jack
Martin Smith, Hilyard Brown
● Doris Day, James Garner, Polly Bergen, Chuck
Connors, Thelma Ritter, Fred Clark (20th Century-Fox)

Something old, something new, something
borrowed, something blue is the nature of
Move Over, Darling, a reproduction of the 1940
romantic comedy *My Favorite Wife*, which
costarred Cary Grant and Irene Dunne.

Its complicated history is revealed in the
writing credit: screenplay by Hal Kanter and
Jack Sher based on a screenplay by Bella
Spewack and Samuel Spewack from a story by
Bella Spewack, Samuel Spewack and Leo
McCarey.

The 'old' is the basic yarn about the guy
who remarries five years after his first wife is
thought to have perished only to have his first
wife turn up alive and kicking at the outset of
his honeymoon. The 'new' are the chiefly
lacklustre embellishments tagged on. The
'borrowed', to cite one example, is a telephone sequence that owes more than a little
something to Shelley Berman. The 'blue' isn't
of a really offensive nature.

Doris Day and James Garner play it to the
hilt, comically, dramatically and last, but not
least (particularly in the case of the former),
athletically. What is missing in their portrayals is a light touch – the ability to humorously
convey with a subtle eyelash-bat or eyebrow-
arch what it tends to take them a kick in the
shins to accomplish.

Others of prominence in the cast are Polly
Bergen as the sexually-obsessed second wife
(it's never really much of a contest between
her and Day), Thelma Ritter as the understanding mother-in-law, and Chuck Connors
as the male animal who shared the small island hunk of real estate alone with Day for
five years.

MOVIE MOVIE

1978, 105 MINS, US ◇ ⑲
Dir Stanley Donen *Prod* Stanley Donen *Scr* Larry
Gelbart, Sheldon Keller *Ph* Charles Rosher Jr, Bruce
Surtees *Ed* George Hively *Mus* Ralph Burns
Art Dir Jack Fisk
● George C. Scott, Barbara Harris, Eli Wallach, Trish
Van Devere, Red Buttons, Barry Bostwick (Warner)

Stanley Donen's *Movie Movie* is a clumsy attempt to spoof the kind of film fare encountered in pic houses of the 1930s and 1940s.
The idea was patronizing in its conception, is
a flatout embarrassment in its execution, and
weak vehicle for George C. Scott and other
principal talents involved.

The overlong, 105-minute feature is split
into three parts: a black-and-white sendup of
those boxing sagas where the slum youth fueled by earnest ambition gets catapulted to
fame and riches (*Dynamite Hands*); a satire of
a coming attractions trailer featuring a saga
of World War I pilots; and finally, a shot-in-
color takeoff of the making of a Flo Ziegfeld-
type Broadway musical (*Baxter's Beauties of
1933*).

But instead of gently twitting the conventions of old Hollywood pot-boilers, *Movie
Movie* tries to milk the cliches by observing
and scorning them simultaneously. The conception is a mess, and it shows.

Things are so muddied that Donen tacked
on, after the pic was shot, a prolog by George
Burns telling the audience that yes, *Movie
Movie* is intended as fun. Too bad Burns
didn't stick around for the rest of the film.

MOVING TARGET, THE

See: *Harper*

MR. & MRS. BRIDGE

1990, 124 MINS, US ◇ ⑲ ⊙
Dir James Ivory *Prod* Ismail Merchant *Scr* Ruth Prawer
Jhabvala *Ph* Tony Pierce-Roberts *Ed* Humphrey Dixon
Mus Richard Robbins *Art Dir* David Gropman
● Paul Newman, Joanne Woodward, Robert Sean
Leonard, Kyra Sedgwick, Blythe Danner, Simon Callow
(Cineplex Odeon/Merchant-Ivory/Halmi)

Mr. & Mrs. Bridge is an affecting study of an
uppercrust Midwestern family in the late
1930s. Ruth Prawer Jhabvala has adapted two
Evan S. Connell novels into a taut script.
Books *Mrs. Bridge* (1959) and *Mr. Bridge* (1969)
painted (from each spouse's point of view) a
portrait of stuffy Kansas City lawyer Walter
Bridge and his stifled wife, India, by a steady
accretion of anecdotal detail. The screenplay
presents a series of highly dramatic scenes in
their lives, the payoffs among the novels' hundreds of brief chapters.

Central theme of India Bridge's gradual realization that her life has been crushed in her
husband's shadow is strongly conveyed by
Woodward in the role.

Casting of hubby Newman as her husband
resonates in their intimate scenes, particularly a 1939 vacation to Paris when the
Bridges briefly rekindle their romance, only
to have it cut short by World War II.

Kyra Sedgwick is smashing as the Bridges'
bohemian daughter who takes off for New
York and an arts career.
□ 1990: Nomination: Best Actress (Joanna
Woodward)

MR. & MRS. SMITH

1941, 90 MINS, US ⑲ ⊙
Dir Alfred Hitchcock *Prod* Harry E. Edington (exec.)
Scr Norman Krasna *Ph* Harry Stradling *Ed* William
Hamilton *Mus* Edward Ward *Art Dir* Van Nest
Polglase, L.P. Williams
● Carole Lombard, Robert Montgomery, Gene
Raymond, Jack Carson, Philip Merivale, Lucile Watson
(RKO)

Carole Lombard and Robert Montgomery are
teamed successfully here in a light and gay
marital farce, with accent on the laugh side
through generation of continual bickering of
the pair.

The Smiths (Lombard and Montgomery)
are happily though battlingly married. A
bantering question, 'If you had to do it all
over would you marry me' and the obvious
husbandly reply of 'No', starts things going.
Advised that the three-year-old marriage is
void because of legal technicalities, Mrs
Smith tosses Mr Smith out of the house.
Then the yarn develops into a run-around
with Mr making continual stabs to recapture
his wife, while his law partner, (Gene
Raymond) is a ready victim of her advances
aimed at inspiring jealousy.

Alfred Hitchcock pilots the story in a
straight farcical groove with resort to slapstick interludes or overplaying by the characters. Pacing his assignment at a steady gait,
Hitchcock catches all of the laugh values
from the above par script of Norman Krasna.

MR ARKADIN

See: *Confidential Report*

MR. ASHTON WAS INDISCREET

See: *The Senator Was Indiscreet*

MR. BASEBALL

1992, 109 MINS, US ◇ ⑲ ⊙
Dir Fred Schepisi *Prod* Fred Schepisi, Doug Claybourne,
Robert Newmyer *Scr* Gary Ross, Kevin Wade, Monte
Merrick *Ph* Ian Baker *Ed* Peter Honess *Mus* Jerry
Goldsmith *Art Dir* Ted Haworth
● Tom Selleck, Ken Takakura, Aya Takanashi, Dennis
Haysbert, Toshi Shioya, Kohsuke Toyohara (Walt
Disney/Outlaw)

Universal's $40 million-plus pic's a tame look
at the cultural differences that erupt from a
surly Yank trying to adjust his youngsterish
frame and bad attitude to the rigid strictures
of Japanese sport and society.

Given the central character of Jack Elliot
(Tom Selleck), former Yankee World Series
MVP who's traded off to Japan to make way
for a young prospect (played by White Sox
star Frank Thomas), there's only one direction in which the story can go, and it does, as
if by prescription: he arrives in Nagoya to
play for the Chunichi Dragons, hates it, looks
down on all these little men who play such a
safe, conformist brand of baseball, bristles at
his stern manager, then finally starts getting
it together as he begins to accept the virtues
of the harmonic Japanese approach.

Also, an interracial romance between Elliot
and the beautiful, westernized Hiroko (Aya
Takanashi), daughter of the Dragons' manager (Ken Takakura), stirs up prejudicial
feelings within the family.

Selleck is utterly believable as the star, but
even his broad shoulders can't carry the
weight of the entire pic. All the Japanese remain one-dimensional.

MR. BILLION

1977, 91 MINS, US ◇ ⑲
Dir Jonathan Kaplan *Prod* Steven Bach, Ken Friedman
Scr Ken Friedman, Jonathan Kaplan *Ph* Matthew F.
Leonetti *Ed* O. Nicholas Brown *Mus* Dave Grusin
Art Dir Richard Berger
● Terence Hill [= Mario Girotti], Valerie Perrine, Jackie
Gleason, Slim Pickens, William Redfield, Chill Wills
(Pantheon)

Terence Hill is charming as an Italian mechanic who inherits a fortune and has a hell of a time getting to Frisco in time to claim it. Valerie Perrine and Jackie Gleason are among those who try to fleece the innocent of his loot. There are many loose ends in the plot, and some choppy sequences, but the pic is brisk enjoyment.

The obvious inspiration for the film was Frank Capra's classic 1936 populist comedy-fantasy, *Mr Deeds Goes to Town*, in which Gary Cooper inherited a fortune only to find himself besieged by greedy city slickers.

Director Jonathan Kaplan also borrows heavily from Alfred Hitchcock. The blend of Capra and Hitchcock doesn't always work,and the film often seems too much of an artificial film buff homage.

■ MR BLANDINGS BUILDS HIS DREAM HOUSE

1948, 93 MINS, US 🎞 ⊙
Dir H.C. Potter *Prod* Norman Panama, Melvin Frank *Scr* Norman Panama, Melvin Frank *Ph* James Wong Howe *Ed* Harry Marker *Mus* Leigh Harline *Art Dir* Albert S. D'Agostino, Carroll Clark
● Cary Grant, Myrna Loy, Melvyn Douglas, Reginald Denny, Jason Robards, Lex Barker (Selznick/RKO)

Eric Hodgins' novel of the trials and tribulations of the Blandings, while building their dream house, read a lot funnier than they filmed. Norman Panama and Melvin Frank come through with a glossy lustre in handling physical production, but fail to jell the story into solid film fare in their dual scripting.

Film's opening pulls some standard sight gags that register strongly, helped by the business injected through H.C. Potter's direction.

Script gets completely out of hand when unnecessary jealousy twist is introduced, neither advancing the story nor adding laughs.

Grant is up to his usual performance standard as Blandings, getting the best from the material, and Myrna Loy comes through with another of her screen wife assignments nicely. Melvyn Douglas, the lawyer friend of the family, gives it a tongue-in-cheek treatment. Trio's finesse and Potter's light directorial touch do much to give proceedings a lift.

■ MR. DEEDS GOES TO TOWN

1936, 115 MINS, US 🎞 ⊙
Dir Frank Capra *Prod* Frank Capra *Scr* Robert Riskin *Ph* Joseph Walker *Ed* Gene Havlick *Mus* Howard Jackson (dir.) *Art Dir* Stephen Goosson
● Gary Cooper, Jean Arthur, George Bancroft, Lionel Stander, Douglass Dumbrille, Raymond Walburn (Columbia)

Mr Deeds Goes to Town needs the marquee draught of Gary Cooper, Jean Arthur and George Bancroft to make it really go to town. With a sometimes too thin structure [from a story by Clarence Budington Kelland], the players and director Frank Capra have contrived to convert *Deeds* into fairly sturdy substance. The farce is good-humored and the trouping and production workmanlike, but there are some lapses in midriff that cause considerable uncertainty.

The native Yankee shrewdness endowed Longfellow Deeds takes a male Pollyanna tack that skirts some dangerous shoals. A mugg with a $20 million heritage should know how to be more practical about things and while scriptwriter Robert Riskin and Capra have managed to have him turn the tables more or less effectively in the trial before a lunacy commission, there are times when Cooper's impression is just a bit too scatter-brained for sympathetic comfort.

Capra's direction is more mundane than flighty. With machinating attorneys, false claimants to the estate, down-to-earth 'jest folks,' etc, it's to be expected that the general structure will be in like tune.

Deeds is a guy who plays a tuba in bed, slides down bannisters, decides to give away his $20 million just like that, after John Wray in a theatrical hokum bit waves a gun at him, fortified with a quasi-comunistic plea. Combined with some of the other lines and business accorded the male topper, audience credulity, despite the general lightness of the theme, becomes strained.
☐ 1936: Best Director.
☐ Nominations: Best Picture, Actor (Gary Cooper), Screenplay, Sound

■ MR. DESTINY

1990, 105 MINS, US 🎞 🎬 ⊙
Dir James Orr *Prod* James Orr, Jim Cruickshank, Susan B. Landau *Scr* James Orr, Jim Cruickshank *Ph* Alex Thomson *Ed* Michael R. Miller *Mus* David Newman *Art Dir* Michael Seymour
● James Belushi, Linda Hamilton, Michael Caine, Jon Lovitz, Hart Bochner, Rene Russo (Touchstone/Silver Screen Partners IV)

A heavy-handed, by-the-numbers fantasy about an ordinary Joe who thinks his life would have been different if he'd connected with that all-important pitch in a high school baseball game.

James Belushi plays smalltown white-collar working stiff Larry Burrows, who on his depressing 35th birthday stumbles into a bar where a mysterious, twinkly-eyed barman (Michael Caine) serves him up a 'spilt milk' elixir that sends him spinning back in time to take another swat at that baseball.

He hits a home run, and his whole life turns out differently, just as he expected. But guess what? He's not any happier than he was before.

So what if he's married to the dishy prom queen (Rene Russo) and has become the absurdly wealthy president of a sports equipment company – the same one he slaved for in his other life. He misses his original wife (Linda Hamilton) and their unpretentious lifestyle, and whether it makes sense or not, he sets out to win her back.

■ MR HOBBS TAKES A VACATION

1962, 115 MINS, US 🎞 🎬
Dir Henry Koster *Prod* Jerry Wald *Scr* Nunnally Johnson *Ph* William C. Mellor *Ed* Marjorie Fowler *Mus* Henry Mancini *Art Dir* Jack Martin Smith, Malcolm Brown
● James Stewart, Maureen O'Hara, Fabian, John Saxon, Reginald Gardiner, Marie Wilson (20th Century-Fox)

Togetherness, all-American family style, is given a gently irreverent poke in the ribs in *Mr Hobbs Takes a Vacation*. This is a fun picture, although it misfires, chiefly in the situation development department.

Nunnally Johnson's screenplay, based on the novel, *Hobbs' Vacation*, by Edward Streeter, is especially strong in the dialog area. The film is peppered with refreshingly sharp, sophisticated references and quips. But Johnson's screenplay falls down in development of its timely premise, leaving the cast and director Henry Koster heavily dependent on their own comedy resources in generating fun.

Hobbs (James Stewart) is a St. Louis banker who has the misfortune to spend his vacation at the seashore with 10 other members of his immediate family, setting up a series of situations roughly designed to illustrate the pitfalls of that grand old Yankee institution, the family reunion.

The picture has its staunchest ally in Stewart, whose acting instincts are so remarkably keen that he can instill amusement into scenes that otherwise threaten to fall flat. Some of the others in the cast, endowed with less intuitive gifts for light comedy, do not fare as well.

Maureen O'Hara is decorative as Mrs Hobbs. Fabian struggles along in an undernourished romantic role, and warbles, with considerable uncertainty, an uninspired ditty, tagged *Cream Puff*, by Johnny Mercer and Henry Mancini, who has composed a satisfactory score for the film. John Saxon is mired in a stereotypical role of a pompously dense intellect.

■ MR. JOHNSON

1990, 103 MINS, US 🎞 🎬
Dir Bruce Beresford *Prod* Michael Fitzgerald *Scr* William Boyd *Ph* Peter James *Ed* Humphrey Dixon *Mus* Georges Delerue *Art Dir* Herbert Pinter
● Maynard Eziashi, Pierce Brosnan, Edward Woodward, Beatie Edney, Denis Quilley (Fitzgerald)

Capitalism and colonialism intertwine like a two-headed snake in this ponderous but well-made film. Director Bruce Beresford's modestly scaled followup to Oscar winner *Driving Miss Daisy* suffers from a slow, marginally involving storyline.

Pic's foremost discovery is Nigerian actor Maynard Eziashi in the title role as a young African obsessed with British mores, resourcefully working outside the rigid limits of his colonial clerkship.

Johnson uses that knack to help his boss Rudbeck (Pierce Brosnan) build a road connecting their small outpost to the outside world, though his consistent circumvention of proper channels eventually catches up with him and proves his downfall.

Working from a 1939 novel by Joyce Carey set in the 1920s, Beresford and writer William Boyd have delivered a film strangely devoid of emotion and lacking a clear point of view.

Brosnan's straight-legged bureaucrat proves so stiff and lifeless there's no sense of caring in any direction, toward either his wife (Beatie Edney) or Johnson. Edward Woodward injects much-needed life into the staid proceedings as a vulgar expatriate English shop owner, a boozy bigot.

■ MR. LUCKY

1943, 94 MINS, US 🎬 ⊙
Dir H.C. Potter *Prod* David Hempstead *Scr* Milton Holmes, Adrian Scott *Ph* George Barnes *Ed* Theron Warth *Mus* Roy Webb *Art Dir* William Cameron Menzies
● Cary Grant, Laraine Day, Charles Bickford, Gladys Cooper, Alan Carney, Henry Stephenson (RKO)

Cary Grant is a resourceful and opportunist gambling operator, figuring on outfitting his outlawed gaming ship for trip to Havana. But coin and draft registration balk his departure. Assuming name and a draft card of a dying 4-F, he launches drive to raise the moola and runs into society heiress Laraine Day. Pursuing her for romantic pitches, he lands as member of the war relief agency and proceeds to ply his con to help the outfit with supplies and boat charters.

Picture carries an authentic ring to operations of bigtime gamblers, and it faithfully follows the professional premise of 'never give the sucker a break, but never cheat a friend'. Writer Milton Holmes, in selling his first screen original, hews closely to the lines of actual incidents rather than depending on synthetic dramatics to drop it into the groove of obvious cinematic dramatics.

■ MR. MAJESTYK

1974, 104 MINS, US 🎞 🎬
Dir Richard Fleischer *Prod* Walter Mirisch *Scr* Elmore Leonard *Ph* Richard H. Kline *Ed* Ralph E. Winters *Mus* Charles Bernstein *Art Dir* [uncredited]

● Charles Bronson, Al Lettieri, Linda Cristal, Lee Purcell, Paul Koslo, Alejandro Rey (Mirisch)

Mr Majestyk makes a first-reel pretense of dealing with the thorny subject of migrant Chicano farm laborers, but social relevance is soon clobbered by the usual Charles Bronson heroics, here mechanically navigated by director Richard Fleischer.

Bronson, in a boringly stoic performance, plays a melon-grower whose fair labor practices are rewarded with a trumped-up assault charge that lands him in jail. During a shootout engineered by Mafia gangsters to free underworld killer Al Lettieri as prisoners are being moved from one jail to another, Bronson captures the hitman and offers to return Lettieri in exchange for his own freedom. Lettieri eventually escapes and vows revenge on Bronson.

The narrative makes little sense unless viewed as a study in pathology.

••••••••••••••••••••••••••••••••

■ **MR. MOM**

1983, 91 MINS, US ◇ ⓥ ⊙
Dir Stan Dragoti *Prod* Lynn Loring, Lauren Shuler, Harry Colomby *Scr* John Hughes *Ph* Victor J. Kemper *Ed* Patrick Kennedy *Mus* Lee Holdridge *Art Dir* Alfred Sweeney
● Michael Keaton, Teri Garr, Frederick Koehler, Taliesin Jaffe, Courtney & Brittany White, Christopher Lloyd (Sherwood/20th Century-Fox)

The comic talents of Michael Keaton and Teri Garr are largely wasted in *Mr Mom*, an unoriginal romantic comedy where breadwinner-husband and homemaker wife switch roles.

Though Keaton and Garr occasionally manage to evoke some pathos and laughs, it's an uphill battle that is won solely on the strength of their individual personalities.

Keaton, close to perfection as the husband and father depressed by unemployment but always a sport with his family, is already a known bundle of comic energy. But he especially shines here in some more dramatic moments with his children.

Garr, as always, is a delight to watch though it would be nice to see her in a role where she wasn't someone's wife or mother. Still, her inspired double takes continue to say more than pages of dialog while her keen timing helps somewhat in the more beleaguered scenes.

••••••••••••••••••••••••••••••••

■ **MR. NANNY**

1993, 84 MINS, US ◇ ⓥ ⊙
Dir Michael Gottlieb *Prod* Bob Engelman *Scr* Edward Rugoff, Michael Gottlieb *Ph* Peter Stein *Ed* Earl Ghaffari, Michael Ripps, Amy Tompkins *Mus* David Johansen, Brian Koonin *Art Dir* Don DeFina
● Terry 'Hulk' Hogan, Sherman Hemsley, Austin Pendleton, Robert Gorman, Madeline Zima, David Johansen (New Line)

Cross *Uncle Buck* with *Home Alone*, stir in the Hulkster, and you've got *Mr. Nanny*, a comedy-actioner that should entertain the under-12 and couch potato sets.

Excuse for a plot has 'Hulk' Hogan as an ex-grappler whiling away days fishing in Florida. To help out his old trainer (Sherman Hemsley), he reluctantly takes a job as bodyguard to computer tycoon Austin Pendleton.

Twist is that Hogan, who loathes kids, has in reality been hired to protect Pendleton's brats (Robert Gorman, Madeline Zima), as well as double as nanny when the latest in a long line walks out. The anklebiters have been targeted for kidnapping by a psycho loon (David Johansen) who wants one of Pendleton's microchips.

Meat of the movie is the domestic war between the indestructible Hogan and the two kids, whose preferred reading is *Unusual Weapons of the Inquisition*. Telegraphed finale

has everyone learning mutual respect and taking on Johansen and his heavies in a warehouse finale.

••••••••••••••••••••••••••••••••

■ **MR. NORTH**

1988, 92 MINS, US ◇ ⓥ ⊙
Dir Danny Huston *Prod* Steven Haft, Skip Steloff, Tom Shaw *Scr* Janet Roach, John Huston, James Costigan *Ph* Robin Vidgeon *Ed* Roberto Silvi *Mus* David McHugh *Art Dir* Eugene Lee
● Anthony Edwards, Robert Mitchum, Lauren Bacall, Harry Dean Stanton, Anjelica Huston, Mary Stuart Masterson (Heritage/Goldwyn)

By cowriting and serving as executive producer, the late John Huston could be said to have passed the baton to son Danny Huston on *Mr North*. Unfortunately, Danny has not only dropped the stick but tripped over his own feet in his feature film debut, a woefully flat affair which even a stellar cast cannot bring to life.

The 1973 novel by Thornton Wilder is a resolutely old-fashioned tale about an unusually gifted young man who stirs things up among the rich folk in Newport, RI, circa 1926.

Wilder's fanciful yarn has Theophilus North, a bright Yale gradulate, arriving in the seaside bastion of old money and extravagance and making his way in society by magically curing the rich of what ails them, and charming them to boot.

All of this gains North a reputation as something of a savior, but doesn't go down too well with the pillar of the local medical community, who drags the shining fellow into court.

Anthony Edwards gives it a reasonable try in the leading role, his matter-of-factness in the face of extraordinary accomplishments proving rather appealing, but he can't single-handedly rescue this waterlogged vessel.

••••••••••••••••••••••••••••••••

■ **MR. SATURDAY NIGHT**

1992, 119 MINS, US ◇ ⓥ ⊙
Dir Billy Crystal *Prod* Billy Crystal *Scr* Billy Crystal, Lowell Ganz, Babaloo Mandel *Ph* Don Peterman *Ed* Kent Beyda *Mus* Marc Shaiman *Art Dir* Albert Brenner
● Billy Crystal, David Paymer, Julie Warner, Helen Hunt, Jerry Orbach, Ron Silver (Castle Rock/Face)

Bringing the fictional comedian he created eight years earlier to the big screen, Billy Crystal hits a double with *Mr. Saturday Night*. By turns relentlessly jokey and shamelessly schmaltzy, the actor-writer's directorial debut charts a sometimes unpleasant funnyman's long career in choppy, two-dimensional fashion, but delivers enough laughs and heart-tugging.

As a veteran who feels dead without an audience, Buddy (Crystal) says he's 'got cancer of the career. It's inoperable.' Flashbacks reveal that the stubborn comic was usually his own worst enemy, deliberately undercutting himself with his superiors and letting his emotions get the better of him.

Other than his career, the only thing of enduring importance to Buddy is his relationship with his brother Stan, a gentle, kind soul (David Paymer, in a standout performance).

After Stan retires to Florida, Buddy decides to take on a new agent (waspy blonde Helen Hunt), who has never heard of any of the old-time comedy greats but nevertheless gets Buddy a chance at some top jobs, such as a possible starring role in a film by megadirector Larry Meyerson (Ron Silver).

It's basically all Crystal and Paymer's show, and they age very convincingly through the years.
□ 1992: Nomination: Best Supp. Actor (David Paymer

••••••••••••••••••••••••••••••••

■ **MR. SKEFFINGTON**

1944, 126 MINS, US ⓥ ⊙
Dir Vincent Sherman *Prod* Philip G. Epstein, Julius J. Epstein *Scr* Philip G. Epstein, Julius J. Epstein *Ph* Ernest Haller *Ed* Ralph Dawson *Mus* Franz Waxman *Art Dir* Robert Haas
● Bette Davis, Claude Rains, Walter Abel, Richard Waring, George Coulouris, Marjorie Riordan (Warner)

Fitting Bette Davis like a silk glove, the same as the gowns which she wears to intrigue the male of the species in defiance of all the laws of good womanhood, in the part of the vainglorious, selfish wife and mother, *Mr. Skeffington* is not only another triumph for the Warner star but also a picture of terrific strength.

Philip G. and Julius J. Epstein, who have given the story fine production and backgrounds, also adapted the book [by 'Elizabeth'] but locale it in America rather than in England. The story moves steadily and smoothly, gathering much impact as it goes along, while also the dialog ranges from the smart to the trenchantly dramatic in limning the life of the woman who lived for her beauty but found that it wasn't of a lasting character.

Davis, playing the coquettish daughter of a once-wealthy family, progresses through the years from 1914 before World War I to the present, going with gradual changes from early girlhood to around 50 years when suddenly aging badly as result of illness.

Opposite Davis is the able Claude Rains, the successful Wall Street tycoon who goes blind and also prematurely ages as result of several years spent in a Nazi concentration camp following the beginning of World War II.
□ 1944: Nominations: Best Actor (Claude Rains), Actress (Bette Davis)

••••••••••••••••••••••••••••••••

■ **MRS MINIVER**

1942, 133 MINS, US ⓥ ⊙
Dir William Wyler *Prod* Sidney Franklin *Scr* Arthur Wimperis, George Froeschel, James Hilton, Claudine West *Ph* Joseph Ruttenberg *Ed* Harold F. Kress *Mus* Herbert Stothart *Art Dir* Cedric Gibbons, Urie McCleary
● Greer Garson, Walter Pidgeon, Teresa Wright, May Whitty, Reginald Owen, Henry Wilcoxon (M-G-M)

Superbly catching the warmth and feeling of Jan Struther's characters in her best-selling book of sketches, *Mrs Miniver*, Metro has created out of it a poignant story of the joys and sorrows, the humor and pathos of middle-class family life in war-time England.

Its one defect, not uncommon with Metro's prestige product, is its length. It gets about three-quarters of the way through and begins floundering, like a vaude act that doesn't know how to get off the stage.

In addition, the film, in its quiet yet actionful way, is, probably entirely unintentionally, one of the strongest pieces of propaganda against complacency to come out of the war.

When Mrs Miniver's husband is summoned from his bed at 2 a.m. to help rescue the legions of Dunkirk, when her son flies out across the Channel each night, when she frightenedly captures a sick and starving German pilot who bears resemblance to her own boy, *Mrs Miniver* truly brings the war into one's own family.

Greer Garson, with her knee-weakening smile, and Walter Pidgeon, almost equally personable, are the Minivers. Scarcely less engaging are capable are young Teresa Wright as their daughter-in-law and Richard Ney in the difficult role of their son.

It's impossible to praise too highly William Wyler's direction, which hits only one or two false notes throughout the lengthy presentation. His is clearly the understanding heart to whom these are not actors, but people living

517

genuine joy and sorrow and fear and doubt.
☐ 1942: Best Picture, Director, Actress
(Greer Garson), Supp. Actress (Teresa
Wright), Screenplay, B&W Cinematography.
☐ Nominations: Best Actor (Walter
Pidgeon), Supp. Actor (Henry Travers), Supp.
Actress (May Whitty), Editing, Sound, Special
Effects

■ MR. SMITH GOES TO WASHINGTON

1939, 126 MINS, US 🎦 ⊙
Dir Frank Capra   *Prod* Frank Capra   *Scr* Sidney
Buchman   *Ph* Joseph Walker   *Ed* Gene Havlick, Al
Clark   *Mus* Dimitri Tiomkin   *Art Dir* Lionel Banks
● Jean Arthur, James Stewart, Claude Rains, Edward
Arnold, Thomas Mitchell, Guy Kibbee (Columbia)

Frank Capra goes to Washington in unwinding the story [by Lewis R. Foster], and in so
doing provides a graphic picture of just how
the national lawmakers operate. Capra never
attempts to expose political skullduggery on a
wide scale. He selects one state political machine and after displaying its power and ruthlessness, proceeds to tear it to pieces.

Stewart is a most happy choice for the title
role, delivering sincerity to a difficult part
that introduces him as a self-conscious idealist, but a stalwart fighter when faced with a
battle to overcome the ruthles political machine of his own state. Jean Arthur is excellent as the wisely cynical senatorial secretary
who knows the political ropes of Washington.

Replica of the Senate chamber provides a
fine set for the filibustering episode.
☐ 1939: Best Original Story.
☐ Nominations: Best Picture, Director, Actor
(James Stewart), Supp. Actor (Harry Carey),
Screenplay, Art Direction, Editing, Score,
Sound

■ MRS SOFFEL

1984, 110 MINS, US ◇ 🎦
Dir Gillian Armstrong   *Prod* Edgar J. Scherick, Scott
Rudin   *Scr* Ron Nyswaner   *Ph* Russell Boyd
Ed Nicholas Beauman   *Mus* Mark Isham
Art Dir Luciana Arrighi
● Diane Keaton, Mel Gibson, Matthew Modine, Edward
Herrmann, Trini Alvarado, Jennie Dundas (M-G-M)

The potential for a moving, tragic love story
is clearly there, but *Mrs Soffel* proves distressingly dull for most of its running time.

True story is set in Pittsburgh in 1901, and
has Diane Keaton, as the wife of Allegheny
County Prison warden, Edward Herrmann,
recovering from a long illness and resuming
her rounds of quoting scripture to prisoners.
She quickly takes a special interest in two
cons on Death Row, brothers Mel Gibson and
Matthew Modine, who are waiting to be hung
for a murder they were convicted of committing during a burglary.

Defying all reason, Keaton helps the brothers escape and thereby undergoes an instant
transformation from respectable woman to
fugitive outlaw.

Final act does carry something of a charge,
but it's too long a ride getting there.

■ MR TOPAZE

(US: I Like Money)

1961, 95 MINS, UK ◇
Dir Peter Sellers   *Prod* Pierre Rouve   *Scr* Pierre Rouve
Ph John Wilcox   *Ed* Geoffrey Foot   *Mus* Georges Van
Parys   *Art Dir* Don Ashton
● Peter Sellers, Nadia Gray, Herbert Lom, Leo McKern,
Martita Hunt, Billie Whitelaw (20th Century-Fox/De
Grunwald)

Peter Sellers plays a kindly, dedicated and
very poor schoolmaster in a little French
town. His integrity is such that when he refuses to compromise over a pupil's report to
satisfy the child's rich, influential grand-

mother he is fired by the arrogant headmaster. The gullible Sellers is soft-talked into becoming the front for a swindling business
man, finds that he has been a pawn but by
then has discovered the wicked ways of the
world.

The film [from the play by Marcel Pagnol]
falls into sharply contrasting moods. The
early stages, with Sellers as the gentle, honest
schoolmaster is crammed with sly humor.

As a director Sellers brings out some slick
performances from his colleagues. Leo McKern
tends to overplay the headmaster,
yet his scenes with Sellers are lively exchanges. Billie Whitelaw, as the daughter,
who Sellers shyly woos, has limited opportunities but does well with them. Michael Gough
is splendid as a seedy schoolmaster who is devoted to Sellers. Herbert Lom plays the con
man flashily and effectively.

■ MS. 45

(Aka: Angel of Vengeance)

1981, 84 MINS, US ◇ 🎦
Dir Abel Ferrara   *Prod* Rochelle Weisberg   *Scr* N.G. St
John   *Ph* James Momel   *Ed* Christopher Andrews
Mus Joe Delia
● Zoe Tamerlis, Steve Singer, Darlene Stuto, Jack
Thibeau, Peter Yellen (Rochelle/Navaron)

Crisply-told tale deals with a mute, stunningly attractive young woman worker (Zoe
Tamerlis) in New York's garment district
who is traumatized one night by (1) being
raped in an alley on the way home and then
(2) raped a second time by a burglar waiting
in her apartment.

Killing the burglar in self-defense, she
takes his gun and embarks on a vendetta of
shooting down lecherous males. Ultimately
her killing spree becomes undiscriminating in
its victims.

By keeping the picture short and busy,
Ferrara makes its far-fetched elements play.
His shock material works mainly by suggestion but there are enough 'gross' elements to
separate thrill-seeking viewers from traditionalists.

■ MUCH ADO ABOUT NOTHING

1993, 110 MINS, UK/US ◇ 🎦 ⊙
Dir Kenneth Branagh   *Prod* Stephen Evans, David Parfitt,
Kenneth Branagh   *Scr* Kenneth Branagh   *Ph* Roger
Lanser   *Ed* Andrew Marcus   *Mus* Patrick Doyle
Art Dir Tim Harvey
● Kenneth Branagh, Michael Keaton, Robert Sean
Leonard, Keanu Reeves, Emma Thompson, Denzel
Washington (Renaissance/Goldwyn)

Kenneth Branagh returns to the high and, for
him, safe ground of Shakespeare with *Much
Ado About Nothing*, a spirited, winningly acted
rendition of one of the Bard's most popular
comedies.

Film is continuously enjoyable from its action-filled opening to the dazzling final shot.
Only real drawback is pic's visual quality,
which is unaccountably undistinguished, even
ugly, especially considering the sun-drenched
Tuscan location.

All should be well in the domain of Leonato
(Richard Briers): the righteous Don Pedro
(Denzel Washington) helps young Claudio
(Robert Sean Leonard) woo and win
Leonato's lovely daughter Hero (Kate
Beckinsale), while the proudly unmarried
Benedick (Branagh) and the feisty Beatrice
(Emma Thompson) trade barbs with such
zest their teaming is inevitable. But the fly in
the ointment is the sulky, jealous Don John
(Keanu Reeves), who falsely convinces
Claudio of Hero's unfaithfulness on the eve of
their wedding.

Branagh and Thompson bring appealing intelligence and verbal snap to their ongoing
sparring. Looking almost as weird as

Beetlejuice, Michael Keaton delivers a very
alert, surprising turn as the malapropping
constable Dogberry.

■ MUDLARK, THE

1950, 98 MINS, UK 🎦
Dir Jean Negulesco   *Prod* Nunnally Johnson
Scr Nunnally Johnson   *Ph* Georges Perinal   *Ed* Thelma
Meyers   *Mus* William Alwyn   *Art Dir* C.P. Norman
● Irene Dunne, Alec Guinness, Andrew Ray, Anthony
Steel, Finlay Currie, Wilfrid Hyde White (20th Century-
Fox)

Let there be no illusions about *The Mudlark*. It
is not a great picture. But it is a good one.

The adventures of the young mudlark – a
riverside waif who ekes out an existence by
picking up scraps left on the mud-reaches of
the Thames – who goes to Windsor in the
hope of seeing Queen Victoria, makes an appealing and tender yarn.

Rumors spread through London of a plot to
assassinate the queen, but Her Majesty, still
in mourning for her husband 15 years after
his death, denies Disraeli (Alec Guinness) the
right to make a statement in the House of
Commons. But subsequently the prime minister uses the mudlark incident to win the sympathy of Parliament for reform legislation, as
well as persuading the queen to come out of
her retirement.

It is the teamwork of the three principal
artists which is responsible, more than any
other factor, for the success of the film.
☐ 1950: Nomination: Best B&W Costume
Design

■ MUMMY, THE

1933, 63 MINS, US 🎦 ⊙
Dir Karl Freund   *Prod* Stanley Bergerman   *Scr* John L.
Balderston   *Ph* Charles Stumar   *Art Dir* Willy Pogany
● Boris Karloff, Zita Johann, David Manners, Edward
Van Sloan, Arthur Byron, Bramwell Fletcher (Universal)

The Mummy [from a story by Nina Wilcox
Putnam and Richard Schayer] has some
weird sequences and it is the first starring
film for Boris Karloff.

Revival of the mummy comes comparatively
early in the running time. The transformation of Karloff's Im-Ho-Tep from a clay-like
figure in a coffin to a living thing is the highlight.

The sequence in the museum with Im-Ho
planning to kill Helen Grosvenor, of Egyptian
heritage, to revive her ancient state, is too
stagey. The mustiness of the tombs excavated
is also over-suggestive of the Hollywood set.

Other members of the cast are made to figure as the puppets of Im-Ho and to carry over
the dialog during the few times Karloff takes
intermissions from the camera. Zita Johann is
attractive, but always role-conscious, as
Grosvenor.

■ MUMSY, NANNY, SONNY & GIRLY

(US: Girly)

1970, 101 MINS, UK ◇ 🎦
Dir Freddie Francis   *Prod* Ronald J. Kahn   *Scr* Brian
Comport   *Ph* David Muir   *Ed* Tristam Cones
Mus Bernard Ebbinghouse   *Art Dir* Maggie Pinhorn
● Michael Bryant, Ursula Howells, Pat Heywood,
Howard Trevor, Vanessa Howard, Robert Swann (Fitsroy)

An offbeat, low-key horror melodrama a
macabre combo of Disney and Hammer films,
in which a lady, her maid and two kids kidnap
and murder unsuspecting males.

Story is set in a country estate populated by
mumsy Ursula Howells, nanny Pat Heywood,
sonny Howard Trevor and girly Vanessa
Howard. It's a quaint family, mannered in the
niceties of civilized living, except that they
get their kicks from kidnapping stray males.

The domestic status quo begins to fall apart

M

after kidnapping playboy Michael Bryant, blackmailed into coming to the house on threats of accusing him of the murder of girl-friend Imogen Hassall.

Players acquit themselves admirably. Howells, Heywood and Howard are excellent, Bryant a bit less dynamic than he should have been.

. . . .

■ **MUPPET CHRISTMAS CAROL, THE**

1992, 85 MINS, US ◇ ⓥ ⊙
Dir Brian Henson *Prod* Brian Henson *Scr* Jerry Juhl
Ph John Fenner *Ed* Michael Jablow *Mus* Miles Goodman *Art Dir* Val Strazovec
● Michael Caine, Dave Goelz, Steve Whitmire, Jerry Nelson, Frank Oz, David Rudman (Walt Disney/Henson)

This adaptation of Charles Dickens' Christmas classic is not as enchanting or amusing as the previous entries in the Muppet series. But nothing can really diminish the late Jim Henson's irresistibly appealing characters.

Closely following the Dickens story, *The Muppet Christmas Carol* is structured around Scrooge's encounters with the Ghosts of Christmas Past, Present and Yet to Come.

Michael Caine is perfectly cast as the nasty Scrooge, though his role is too dominant. Muppets take the other roles: Kermit the Frog (Steve Whitmire) becomes abused book-keeper Bob Cratchit, Miss Piggy (Frank Oz) is his wife Emily, and the Great Gonzo (Dave Goelz) is transformed into Dickens himself. The latter's narration is often obtrusive, creating unnecessary distance between the viewer and the tale.

Production values are high as ever. Brian Henson does a fluid, if not spectacular, job of direction. Paul Williams' pedestrian songs are repetitious.
□ 1979: Nominations: Best Adapted Score, Song ('The Rainbow Connection')

. . . .

■ **MUPPET MOVIE, THE**

1979, 98 MINS, US ◇ ⓥ ⊙
Dir James Frawley *Prod* Jim Henson *Scr* Jerry Juhl, Jack Burns *Ph* Isidore Mankofsky *Ed* Chris Greenbury
Mus Paul Williams *Art Dir* Joel Schiller
● Charles Durning, Austin Pendleton, Scott Walker (ITC/Henson)

Jim Henson, Muppet originator, and Frank Oz, creative consultant, have abandoned the successful format of their vidshow, and inserted their creations into a well-crafted combo of musical comedy and fantasy adventure.

Result is a muppet update of *The Wizard of Oz*, with Kermit the Frog leading a motley Muppet troupe on the asphalt road to Hollywood. Script incorporates the zingy one-liners and bad puns that have become the teleseries' trade mark.

Director James Frawley has a lot of fun with cinematic sleight-of-hand, including shots of Kermit pedalling a bicycle, the Muppets driving cars and trucks, and additional full-body camerawork.

The cogent storyline runs Kermit through a gamut of emotions, from self-doubt and bashful love to a moral showdown on the old *High Noon* set.

. . . .

■ **MUPPETS TAKE MANHATTAN, THE**

1984, 94 MINS, US ◇ ⓥ ⊙
Dir Frank Oz *Prod* David Lazer *Scr* Frank Oz, Tom Patchett, Jay Tarses *Ph* Robert Paynter *Ed* Evan Lottman *Mus* Ralph Burns *Art Dir* Stephen Hendrickson
● Jim Henson, Frank Oz, Dave Goelz, Steve Whitmire, Richard Hunt, Jerry Nelson (Tri-Star/Delphi II)

The Muppets Take Manhattan is a genuinely fun confection of old-fashioned entertainment.

Feature poses a hypothetical story [by Tom Patchett and Jay Tarses] of Kermit the Frog penning a successful senior variety show, *Manhattan Melodies*, at Danhurst College and deciding to take it to Broadway. A hit show will enable him to marry his sweetheart, Miss Piggy, but the Muppets find it difficult to find backing and split up to various towns, working at odd jobs to support themselves.

Format allows director Frank Oz to poke light fun at showbiz cliches while creating some comic tension as Kermit, working among rat (literally) waiters at a luncheonette, befriends the cute human daughter (Juliana Donald) of the immigrant owner (Louis Zorich), arousing Miss Piggy's uncontrollable jealousy. A wonderful subplot has Kermit struck with amnesia and becoming a bigshot at an ad agency.

Pic boasts effective cameos (though not as potent as the first film), best of which are Joan Rivers comfortably ad libbing with Miss Piggy (played by Oz) and Dabney Coleman doing slapstick as an unscrupulous producer.
□ 1984: Nomination: Best Original Song Score

. . . .

■ **MURDER**

1930, 110 MINS, UK ⓥ
Dir Alfred Hitchcock *Prod* John Maxwell *Scr* Alfred Hitchcock, Alma Reville *Ph* Jack Cox *Ed* Emile de Ruelle, Rene Harrison *Art Dir* John Mead
● Herbert Marshall, Norah Baring, Phyllis Konstam, Edward Chapman, Miles Mander (British International)

Original title of this one was *Enter Sir John*. Based on the rather highbrow mystery yarn [by Clemence Dane], it tells how a girl is convicted of murder on circumstantial evidence and sentenced to death. One of the jurymen, an actor, sets to work to solve the crime.

Drawback of this type of development is that the biggest kick in the picture occurs in the earlier reels.

Well photographed and mounted, it contains all the gadgets of the pet Alfred Hitchcock technique, from quick cutting to skillful dialog blending.

The dialog is very well written. Long episodes have clever satirical values as attacks on the conventional and lower-class English.

Acting is very good. Herbert Marshall beats the cast to it as the knighted actor who turns amateur detective. Norah Baring is sympathetic as the suspected girl.

. . . .

■ **MURDER AT THE VANITIES**

1934, 95 MINS, US ⓥ
Dir Mitchell Leisen *Prod* E. Lloyd Sheldon *Scr* Carey Wilson, Joseph Gollomb, Sam Hellman *Ph* Leo Tover
● Carl Brisson, Victor McLaglen, Jack Oakie, Kitty Carlisle, Gertrude Michael, Gail Patrick (Paramount)

Herein they mix up the elements of a musical show and a murder mystery, with effective comedy to flavor, and come out with 95 minutes of entertainment [based on the play by Earl Carroll and Rufus King] that should genuinely satisfy.

Victor McLaglen is in charge of the investigation of a couple murders that tax his limited detective prescience. McLaglen shares with Jack Oakie the comedy burden and for each it's a strike.

Picture serves to bring out Carl Brisson, Danish actor who was brought over by Paramount to get his baptism in this quasi-musical. In addition to having an ingratiating personality and photographing well, the foreign import sells his songs for good results.

Brisson has Kitty Carlisle opposite him, but she's not one-half as important, more attention being directed to Brisson than anyone else. Together they do several numbers [lyrics and music by Arthur Johnston and Sam Coslow], the most effective being a

seashore interlude in which the Earl Carroll girls as mermaids manipulate fans that simulate rolling waves.

Murders are well planted and cast logical suspicion in several directions. All of the action occurs backstage at what is represented as the Earl Carroll theatre (now the Casino), on opening night of a Carroll show. It's a backstage musical but different.

. . . .

■ **MURDER BY DEATH**

1976, 94 MINS, US ◇ ⓥ ⊙
Dir Robert Moore *Prod* Ray Stark *Scr* Neil Simon
Ph David M. Walsh *Ed* Margaret Booth, John F. Burnett
Mus Dave Grusin *Art Dir* Stephen Grimes
● Eileen Brennan, Peter Sellers, James Coco, Peter Falk, Alec Guinness, David Niven (Columbia)

Murder by Death is a very good silly-funny Neil Simon satirical comedy, with a super all-star cast cavorting as recognizable pulp fiction detectives gathered at the home of Truman Capote, wealthy hedonist fed up with contrived gumshoe plots.

Capote makes a good theatrical feature debut as an impish Sheridan Whiteside, deploying his guests in a confusing series of sketches in which separate player teams, then the ensemble display their flair for low-key screwball nuttiness.

The cast list reveals the adroit mating of performer to send-up prototype, plus Alec Guinness as Capote's butler, Nancy Walker as mute maid. Every single player conveys a casualness and off-handedness which, of course, is the mark of comedic excellence.

. . . .

■ **MURDER BY DECREE**

1980, 120 MINS, UK/CANADA ◇ ⓥ ⊙
Dir Bob Clark *Prod* Len Herberman *Scr* John Hopkins
Ph Reg Morris *Ed* Stan Cole *Mus* Carl Zittrer, Paul Zaza *Art Dir* Harry Pottle
● Christopher Plummer, James Mason, Donald Sutherland, Genevieve Bujold, David Hemmings, Susan Clark (Ambassador/CFDC/Famous Players)

Murder by Decree is probably the best Sherlock Holmes film since the inimitable pairing of Basil Rathbone and Nigel Bruce in the 1940s series at Universal.

The film's charm derives mainly from John Hopkins' literal, deadpan script that makes no attempt either to mock or contemporize Sir Arthur Conan Doyle's literary creation.

Ironically, Christopher Plummer works against this re-creation by presenting a Holmes who looks as if he's just returned from a Caribbean vacation. Next to James Mason, who may be the most delightful Watson ever to appear on celluloid, Plummer's blonde handsomeness seems especially foreign.

Holmes and Watson are not called in to help solve a series of murders linked to Jack The Ripper. Anthony Quayle, as the new topper at Scotland Yard, has his reasons for excluding them, as does Inspector David Hemmings.

. . . .

■ **MURDERERS' ROW**

1966, 108 MINS, US ◇ ⓥ
Dir Henry Levin *Prod* Irving Allen *Scr* Herbert Baker
Ph Sam Leavitt *Ed* Walter Thompson *Mus* Lalo Schifrin
Art Dir Joe Wright
● Dean Martin, Ann-Margret, Karl Malden, Camilla Sparv, James Gregory, Beverly Adams (Meadway-Claude/Columbia)

It's a wise film producer who knows his own success formula. About the only changes made by Irving Allen in his sequel (also from a novel by Donald Hamilton) to the successful *The Silencers* are in scenery, girls and costumes. The addition of Ann-Margret is notable for some abandoned choreography and a chance to use both of her expressions the open-mouthed Monroe imitation and the slinky Theda Bara bit.

This time out, Dean Martin's secret agent has to trek to the Riviera to catch that bad old Karl Malden who's about to blow up Washington with a secret beam.

Director Henry Levin's stress on action takes the film out of the comedy range at times. Helm is, of course, given some ridiculous special weapons this time, a delayed-reaction gun is worked to death (no pun intended). But whenever the viewer begins to take things seriously, Levin cuts back to a laugh bit (Martin ripping off Ann-Margret's miniskirt, which contains an explosive, and hurling it at a wall decorated with Frank Sinatra's picture).

■ MURDER, INC.
See: The Enforcer (1951)

■ MURDER, INC.

1960, 103 MINS, US
Dir Burt Balaban, Stuart Rosenberg *Prod* Burt Balaban *Scr* Irve Tunick, Mel Barr *Ph* Gaine Rescher *Ed* Ralph Rosenblum *Mus* Frank DeVol *Art Dir* Dick Sylbert
● Stuart Whitman, May Britt, Henry Morgan, Peter Falk, Sarah Vaughan, David J. Stewart (20th Century-Fox)

Professional killers of the crime syndicate headed by Albert Anastasia and Louis 'Lepke' Buchalter were a scourge in the Depression era. They later became known as Murder, Inc. The screenplay (from the book by Burton Turkus and Sid Feder) takes a leisurely approach to its subject. The pace is too slow, the suspense only occasionally gripping. Moreover, the overall production lacks zing and tension.

Amidst the tawdry backgrounds of Brooklyn's Brownsville section, the script recounts how Lepke and the syndicate shook down the garment district, trucking business and sundry other legitimate enterprises through goon squads and hired killers. Caught in this vicious crime ring through little fault of their own are a young couple dancer May Britt and singer Stuart Whitman.

With the possible exception of Peter Falk's portrayal of killer Abe Reles, scarcely any of the cast's performances could be rated as dynamic. His delineation sharply defines the brutal nature of the thug who was killed in a 'fall' from Brooklyn's Half Moon Hotel while in 'protective' custody of the NY police.
☐ 1960: Nomination: Best Supp. Actor (Peter Falk)

■ MURDER IN THE CATHEDRAL

1952, 140 MINS, UK
Dir George Hoellering *Prod* George Hoellering *Scr* T.S. Eliot *Ph* David Kosky *Ed* Anne Allnatt *Mus* Laszlo Lajtha *Art Dir* Peter Pendrey
● John Groser, Alexander Gauge, David Ward, George Woodbridge, Basil Burton, T.S. Eliot (Hoellering)

T.S. Eliot's legit play, *Murder in the Cathedral*, has been turned into a moving but very ponderous film.

Story of the life of Thomas Becket, the martyred Archbishop of Canterbury, unfolds too statically in the picture form. Eliot scripted this from his own play, but failed to add sufficient movement.

Plot details how the Archbishop courageously returns to England after seven years of voluntary exile rather than submit to the king's ambition to dominate the church.

Father John Groser, as Archbishop Becket, is impressive amidst the welter of wordage. Mark Dignam, Michael Aldridge, Leo McKern and Paul Rogers, as the four knights sent to destroy Becket, measure up to the high standard of the Old Vic, from which they were borrowed for this film.

■ MURDER IN THORNTON SQUARE, THE
See: Gaslight (1944)

■ MURDER MOST FOUL

1964, 90 MINS, UK
Dir George Pollock *Prod* Ben Arbeid *Scr* David Pursall, Jack Seddon *Ph* Desmond Dickinson *Ed* Ernest Walter *Mus* Ron Goodwin *Art Dir* Frank White
● Margaret Rutherford, Ron Moody, Charles Tingwell, Andrew Cruickshank, Dennis Price, Francesca Annis (M-G-M)

Margaret Rutherford brings considerable assurance to the third Agatha Christie thriller to cast the doughty oldtimer in the role of Miss Marple, the eccentric amateur sleuth.

Miss Marple is the lone member of a murder jury who holds out for acquittal. Armed only with her experience in amateur mystery theatricals, she proceeds to unsnarl the case and prove herself far more professional than the investigating police.

The picture [from the novel *Mrs McGinty's Dead*] for all its comedy delight and charm does not quite hold up to its predecessors. Miss Marple begins to wear a little thin as she retraces many of the same comedy situations and even some similar dialog.

Stringer Davis again plays the confused partner with a charming personality performance and Charles Tingwell completes the trio as the young inspector who ends up with the credit for solving the crime even though he flails Miss Marple all the way.

■ MURDER, MY SWEET
(UK: Farewell, My Lovely)

1945, 92 MINS, US
Dir Edward Dmytryk *Prod* Adrian Scott *Scr* John Paxton *Ph* Harry J. Wild *Ed* Joseph Noriega *Mus* Roy Webb *Art Dir* Albert S. D'Agostino, Carroll Clark
● Dick Powell, Claire Trevor, Anne Shirley, Otto Kruger, Mike Mazurki, Miles Mander (RKO)

Murder, My Sweet, a taut thriller about a private detective enmeshed with a gang of blackmailers, is as smart as it is gripping.

Plot ramifications may not stand up under clinical study, but suspense is built up sharply and quickly. In fact, the film gets off to so jet-pulsed a start that it necessarily hits a couple of slow stretches midway as it settles into uniform groove. But interest never flags, and the mystery is never really cleared up until the punchy closing.

Director Edward Dmytryk has made few concessions to the social amenities and has kept his yarn stark and unyielding. Story [from the novel *Farewell, My Lovely* by Raymond Chandler] begins with a private dick hired by an ex-convict to find his one-time girlfriend.

Performances are on a par with the production. Dick Powell is a surprise as the hard-boiled copper. The portrayal is potent and convincing. Claire Trevor is as dramatic as the predatory femme, with Anne Shirley in sharp contrast as the soft kid caught in the crossfire.

■ MURDER ON MONDAY
See: Home at Seven

■ MURDER ON THE ORIENT EXPRESS

1974, 127 MINS, UK ◇ ⊕ ⊙
Dir Sidney Lumet *Prod* John Brabourne, Richard Goodwin *Scr* Paul Dehn *Ph* Geoffrey Unsworth *Ed* Anne V. Coates *Mus* Richard Rodney Bennett *Art Dir* Tony Walton
● Albert Finney, Lauren Bacall, Ingrid Bergman, Sean Connery, Vanessa Redgrave, Richard Widmark (EMI)

Murder on the Orient Express is an old-fashioned film. Agatha Christie's 1934 Hercule Poirot novel has been filmed for the first time in a bygone film style as it seems to be some treasure out of a time capsule. Albert Finney and a monstrously large cast of names give the show a lot of class and charm.

Finney is outstanding as Poirot, his makeup, wardrobe and performance a blend of topflight theatre. The mysterious death of Richard Widmark, triggers Finney's investigation at the behest of Martin Balsam, a railroad executive who hopes the crime can be solved before the snowbound train is reached by rescuers.

Amidst fades, repeated cuts to exterior train shots and all those other wonderful film punctuation devices Finney interrogates the passengers.
☐ 1974: Best Supp. Actress (Ingrid Bergman).
☐ Nominations: Best Actor (Albert Finney), Adapted Screenplay, Cinematography, Costume Design, Original Dramatic Score

■ MURDER SHE SAID

1961, 86 MINS, UK ⊕
Dir George Pollock *Prod* George H. Brown *Scr* David Pursall, Jack Seddon *Ph* Geoffrey Faithfull *Ed* Ernest Walter *Mus* Ron Goodwin *Art Dir* Harry White
● Margaret Rutherford, Arthur Kennedy, Muriel Pavlow, James Robertson Justice, Charles Tingwell, Thorley Walters (M-G-M)

The spectacle of a grand-motherly amateur criminologist outsleuthing the skeptical, methodical professionals provides most of the fun in this somewhat unconvincing, but most followers of the whodunit.

According to the screenplay, from an adaptation by David Osborn of the Agatha Christie novel, *4.50 from Paddington*, Margaret Rutherford witnesses a murder transpiring in the compartment of a passing train. Since the police do not believe her story, and being an avid reader of mystery fiction, she takes it upon herself to solve the case, planting herself as maid within the household of the chief suspects.

The George H. Brown production is weak in the motivation area, and there's a sticky and unnecessary parting shot in which Rutherford nixes an absurd marriage proposal from the stingy, irascible patriarch of the house (James Robertson Justice), but otherwise matters purr along at a pleasant clip.

■ MURDERS IN THE RUE MORGUE

1932, 60 MINS, US ⊕
Dir Robert Florey *Scr* Tom Reed, Dale Van Every, John Huston *Ph* Karl Freund
● Bela Lugosi, Sidney Fox, Leon Ames, Bert Roach, Brandon Hurst, Noble Johnson (Universal)

Edgar Allan Poe wouldn't recognize his story, which drops everything but the gorilla killer and the title, completely changes the characters, motives and developments, and is sexed up to the limit. In place of the cool detective whose calculating method was the model for the Sherlock Holmeses and Arsene Lupins that followed, this version's hero is a young medical student who mixes romance with science.

The cast's other scientist, a loony Dr Mirakle played in Bela Lugosi's customary fantastic manner, is an evolution bug who seeks to prove a vague fact by mixing the blood of his captive gorilla with that of Parisian women. The murders three real and one almost are the results of his fiendish transfusions.

First meeting of the young medico and his sweetheart with Dr Mirakle and his caged gorilla occurs at the doc's side show. The brute snatches the girl's bonnet and from then on by intimation it's shown that the gorilla desires her.

The real threat is the constant possiblity of the gorilla capturing the girl. Sidney Fox overdraws the sweet ingenue to the point of nearly distracting an audience from any fear it might have for her.

....

■ **MURPHY'S LAW**

1986, 100 MINS, US ◇ ⓥ ⊙
Dir J. Lee Thompson *Prod* Pancho Kohner *Scr* Gail Morgan Hickman *Ph* Alex Phillips *Ed* Peter Lee Thompson, Charles Simmons *Mus* Marc Donahue, Valentine McCallum *Art Dir* William Cruise
● Charles Bronson, Kathleen Wilhoite, Carrie Snodgress, Robert F. Lyons, Angel Tompkins, Richard Romanus (Cannon)

Murphy's Law, a very violent urban crime meller, is tiresome but too filled with extreme incident to be boring.

Title refers not only to the w.k. axiom that, 'Whatever can go wrong will go wrong,' but to Bronson's personal version of it: 'Don't **** with Jack Murphy.' Title character (played by Charles Bronson) is an LA cop who's down but not quite out, a tough loner whose main companion in life is his flask now that his wife has left him.

Murphy's life is shaken up even more when the ex-wife and numerous others around him are mowed down. Booked for the crimes, he escapes handcuffed to a foul-mouthed female street urchin (Kathleen Wilhoite), and after many more bodies hit the deck, he clears his name by tracking down killer Carrie Snodgress.

....

■ **MURPHY'S ROMANCE**

1985, 107 MINS, US ◇ ⓥ ⊙
Dir Martin Ritt *Prod* Laura Ziskin *Scr* Harriet Frank Jr, Irving Ravetch *Ph* William A. Fraker *Ed* Sidney Levin *Mus* Carole King *Art Dir* Joel Schiller
● Sally Field, James Garner, Brian Kerwin, Corey Haim, Dennis Burkley, Georgann Johnson (Columbia)

Director Martin Ritt has just the right touch to keep *Murphy's Romance*, a fairly predictable love story, from lapsing into gushy sentimentality of cliches. Unfortunately, this sweet and homey picture which casts two very decent actors (Sally Field and James Garner) in two very decent roles, falls far short of compelling filmmaking.

Field plays a divorced mother who is determined to make a living as a horse trainer on a desolate piece of property on the outskirts of a one-street town in rural Arizona. On practically her first day in the area, she meets Murphy, a widower who is the town's pharmacist and local good guy. He takes a liking to her almost immediately, but it isn't much later until her n'er-do-well former husband, Brian Kerwin, rides back into her life.

What unfolds is how the Field, Garner and Kerwin triangle is resolved with Field leaning toward Garner the whole time.

☐ 1985: Nominations: Best Actor (James Garner), Cinematography

....

■ **MURPHY'S WAR**

1971, 108 MINS, UK ◇ ⓥ
Dir Peter Yates *Prod* Michael Deeley *Scr* Stirling Silliphant *Ph* Douglas Slocombe *Ed* Frank P. Keller, John Glen *Mus* John Barry *Art Dir* Disley Jones
● Peter O'Toole, Sian Phillips, Philippe Noiret, Horst Janson, John Hallam, Ingo Mogendorf (Dimitri de Grunwald)

Peter O'Toole, playing an Irishman for the first time does so with a gleaming zest that brings nerve and style to this wartime anecdote. It was shot mainly in a remote uncom-

fortable part of Venezuela's Orinoco River and director Peter Yates has brought out every ounce of the discomfort of the location.

Film opens with World War II drawing to a sluggish close. A German U-Boat torpedoes an armed merchantman and all survivors are bumped off, except, apparently, O'Toole, one of the ship's aviation mechanics.

He is rescued by a French oil engineer (Philippe Noiret) who wants nothing more than to lie doggo till the war's over, but he takes O'Toole to a nearby Quaker mission where he's nursed by the missionary-nurse, played by Sian Phillips.

Another survivor is brought to the mission but is killed by the Germans. Before his death he pleads with O'Toole to find his wrecked plane and keep it out of enemy hands. The Mad Murphy has a better idea. He decides to patch it up and blow the submarine to the high heavens.

....

■ **MUSCLE BEACH PARTY**

1964, 94 MINS, US ◇ ⓥ ⊙
Dir William Asher *Prod* James H. Nicholson, Robert Dillon *Scr* Robert Dillon *Ph* Harold Wellman *Ed* Eve Newman *Mus* Les Baxter *Art Dir* Lucius O. Croxton
● Frankie Avalon, Annette Funicello, Luciana Paluzzi, John Ashley, Don Rickles, Jody McCrea (American International)

This is American International's followup to *Beach Party*, its click of a year earlier. The novelty of surfing has worn off, leaving in its wake little more than a conventional teenage-geared romantic farce with songs.

The clash of three factions at a beach site sets off the romantic, comedic and musical fireworks. At one end is a group of youthful surfers. At another is a band of Atlasian musclemen. Catalyst is a wealthy, fickle contessa. Whenever the story bogs down, which it does quite often, someone runs into camera range and yells 'surf up!'

Frankie Avalon and Annette Funicello top the cast and do most of the singing. The film introduces Little Stevie Wonder, a lad who can really wail. Peter Lorre puts in an unbilled appearance.

....

■ **MUSIC BOX**

1989, 123 MINS, US ◇ ⓥ ⊙
Dir Constantin Costa-Gavras *Prod* Irwin Winkler *Scr* Joe Eszterhas *Ph* Patrick Blossier *Ed* Joele Van Effenterre *Mus* Philippe Sarde *Art Dir* Jeannine Claudia Oppewall
● Jessica Lange, Armin Mueller-Stahl, Frederic Forrest, Donald Moffat, Lukas Haas, Cheryl Lynn Bruce (Carolco)

Jessica Lange plays an accomplished Chicago defense attorney, Ann Talbot, who must defend her own father (Armin Mueller-Stahl) in extradition proceedings when he's accused of having committed war crimes in Hungary during World War II.

Slowly losing her conviction as to her father's innocence, Lange's character pulls out all the stops, including the political connections of her former father-in-law, to try to exonerate her dad.

Even the film's accounts of Holocaust atrocities prove for the most part strangely unaffecting under Joe Eszterhas' limp dialog and Constantin Costa-Gavras' stodgy direction, which relies on a concussive score to try to create tension where there is none.

☐ 1989: Nomination: Best Actress (Jessica Lange)

....

■ **MUSIC LOVERS, THE**

1971, 122 MINS, UK ◇ ⓥ
Dir Ken Russell *Prod* Ken Russell *Scr* Melvyn Bragg *Ph* Douglas Slocombe *Ed* Michael Bradsell *Mus* Andre Previn (dir.) *Art Dir* Natasha Kroll

● Richard Chamberlain, Glenda Jackson, Max Adrian, Christopher Gable, Izabella Telezynska, Kenneth Colley (United Artists)

There is frequently, but not always, a thin line between genius and madness. By going over that line and unduly emphasizing the mad and the perverse in their biopic of the 19th-century Russian composer Peter Ilyich Tchaikovsky, producer-director Ken Russell and scripter Melvyn Bragg lose their audience. The result is a motion picture that is frequently dramatically and visually stunning but more often tedious and grotesque.

Richard Chamberlain, bushy-bearded and eyes constantly brimming with tears, plays the homosexual, irrationally romantic composer, and Glenda Jackson, the neurotic trollop he tragically marries. Their performances are more dramatically bombastic than sympathetic, or sometimes even believable.

Instead of a Russian tragedy, Russell seems more concerned with haunting the viewers' memory with shocking scenes and images. The opportunity to create a memorable and fluid portrait of the composer has been sacrificed for a musical Grand Guignol.

Christopher Gable plays Count Anton Chiluvsky, presumably Chamberlain's true love, as a faun-eyed social butterfly; Izabella Telezynska is the composer's patroness, a wealthy middle-aged widow who loves him but whose own romantic fantasies demand that they never meet but merely correspond by letter, although he lives in luxury on her estate.

....

■ **MUSIC MAN, THE**

1962, 151 MINS, US ◇ ⓥ ⊙
Dir Morton DaCosta *Prod* Morton DaCosta *Scr* Marion Hargrove *Ph* Robert Burks *Ed* William Ziegler *Mus* Ray Heindorf (arr.) *Art Dir* Paul Groesse
● Robert Preston, Shirley Jones, Buddy Hackett, Hermione Gingold, Paul Ford (Warner)

Allowing something of slowness at the very start and the necessities of establishing the musical way of telling a story, plus the atmosphere of Iowa in 1912, that's about the only criticism of an otherwise building, punching, handsomely dressed and ultimately endearing super-musical.

Call this a triumph, perhaps a classic, of corn, smalltown nostalgia and American love of a parade. Dreamed up in the first instance out of the Iowa memories of Meredith Willson, fashioned into his first legit offering with his long radio musicianship fully manifest therein, the transfer to the screen has been accomplished by Morton DaCosta, as producer-director.

DaCosta's use of several of the original Broadway cast players is thoroughly vindicated. Paul Ford is wonderfully fatuous as the bumptious mayor of River City. Pert Kelton shines with warmth and humanity as the heroine's earthy mother.

But the only choice for the title role, Robert Preston, is the big proof of showmanship in the casting. Warners might have secured bigger screen names but it is impossible to imagine any of them matching Preston's authority, backed by 883 stage performances.

☐ 1962: Best Adapted Music Score.
☐ Nominations: Best Picture, Color Costume Design, Color Art Direction, Editing, Sound

....

■ **MUSIC OF CHANCE, THE**

1993, 98 MINS, US ◇ ⓥ ⊙
Dir Philip Haas *Prod* Frederick Zollo, Dylan Sellers *Scr* Philip Haas, Belinda Haas *Ph* Bernard Zitzermann, Jean de Segonzac *Ed* Belinda Haas *Mus* Phillip Johnston *Art Dir* Hugo Luczyc-Wyhowski
● James Spader, Mandy Patinkin, M. Emmet Walsh, Charles Durning, Joel Grey, Samantha Mathis (IRS/American Playhouse)

521

An outstanding cast, a coolly confident style and quirky literary material turn *The Music of Chance* into an auspicious feature debut for documentary filmmaker Philip Haas. But it's ultimately more of an intellectual tease.

Based on a tome by w.k. New York writer Paul Auster, story will be called Kafkaesque because a hapless duo are caught in a mystifying, virtually inescapable web. Yet, the piece has a thoroughly American feel.

Mandy Patinkin, zipping along a rural highway in his new red BMW, offers a lift to a bloodied drifter (James Spader). Spader convinces him to put up $10,000 for a poker game with two rich pushovers.

The pair proceed to the splendid country estate of Charles Durning and Joel Gray. After initial success, Spader's luck turns and he and Patinkin are forced to agree to work off their debt by reconstructing a medieval stone wall, a job estimated to take 50 days. Intrigue involving delays, hidden agendas, escape attempts and possible murder envelop the drudgery and command involvement.

But the denouement is too pat and O. Henry-ish and the characters, too, are shallow constructs.

••••••••••••••••••••••••••••••••

■ MUTINY ON THE BOUNTY

1935, 132 MINS, US 🔞 ⊙
Dir Frank Lloyd *Prod* Irving G. Thalberg *Scr* Talbot Jennings, Jules Furthman, Carey Wilson *Ph* Arthur Edeson *Ed* Margaret Booth *Mus* Herbert Stothart
● Clark Gable, Charles Laughton, Franchot Tone, Dudley Digges, Donald Crisp, Movita (M-G-M)

This one is Hollywood at its very best. For plot the scenarists have used, with some variations, the first two books of the Charles Nordhoff–James Norman Hall trilogy on the mutiny of Fletcher Christian. Beginnings of the first book and the picture are pretty much the same, as are the details up to the arrival of the hunted mutineers on Pitcairn's Island. Picture ends there, omitting the third book almost entirely.

First hour or so of the film leads up, step by step, to the mutiny, with a flexible 'story' backgrounding some thrilling views of seamanship on a British man-o'-war in the early 18th century, and the cruel Capt Bligh's inhuman treatment of his sailors.

Bligh, through the cruelties he performs and due to the faithful portrait drawn by Charles Laughton, is as despicable a character as has ever heavied across a screen.

Laughton, Clark Gable and Franchot Tone are all that producer Al Lewin and director Frank Lloyd could have wished for in the three key roles. Laughton is magnificent. Gable, as brave Fletcher Christian, fills the doc's prescription to the letter. Tone, likeable throughout, gets his big moment with a morality speech at the finish, and makes the most of it.
☐ 1935: Best Picture.
☐ Nominations: Best Director, Actor (Clark Gable, Charles Laughton, Franchot Tone), Screenplay, Editing, Score

••••••••••••••••••••••••••••••••

■ MUTINY ON THE BOUNTY

1962, 185 MINS, US ◇ 🔞 ⊙
Dir Lewis Milestone, [Marlon Brando, Carol Reed] *Prod* Aaron Rosenberg *Scr* Charles Lederer *Ph* Robert L. Surtees *Ed* John McSweeney Jr *Mus* Bronislau Kaper *Art Dir* George W. Davis, J. McMillan Johnson
● Marlon Brando, Trevor Howard, Richard Harris, Hugh Griffith, Richard Haydn, Tarita (M-G-M/Arcola)

Metro's 1962 version of *Mutiny on the Bounty*, after some two years of gestation and strenuous labor pains, emerges a physically superlative entertainment. It may be somewhat short of genuine dramatic greatness, but it is often overwhelmingly spectacular in Technicolor and Ultra Panavision 70. The new $8 million edition is generally superior to Metro's 1935 Academy Award winner.

Marlon Brando as Fletcher Christian and Trevor Howard as Capt Bligh etch their own brilliant entries in the *Bounty*'s log. Brando in many ways gives the finest performance of his career. While Howard is always hot on his heels, the Britisher does not have the same range of character growth.

Brando boards as a foppish aristocrat, with more arrogance than true gentlemanly breeding, but underneath the veneer there is the steel of a Royal Navy officer. The struggle within Christian as he suffers humiliation by his captain before the crew is brilliantly suggested as well as projected.

Director Lewis Milestone has come up with some terrific scenes, from opening a man's back by laying on the whip to fighting wind, cold, snow, rain, towering seas and a murderous, runaway cask in the hold. This is a superb blending of direction, photography and special effects artistry.

Milestone, who often shot as Charles Lederer turned out pages of script [from the novel by Charles Nordhoff and James Norman Hall], time and again had to reshoot scenes for one reason or another. Milestone also experienced long lapses in filming and continuity but can take some pride in a job well done.

Intermission comes after the visit to Tahiti, where the native gals frolic and generously entertain their fairskinned, if not always handsome, visitors. Tarita (Taritatumi Teriipaia) is a 19-year-old native who plays the island chieftain's daughter. She is adequate to the demands of the role.

The mutiny on the homeward voyage gets the film off to a rousing second start. However, the climactic sequences on Pitcairn, where Christian determines to return home and attempt to justify seizure of Bligh's command before injuries aboard the blazing *Bounty* end his life, having a diminishing dramatic effect.

The *Bounty*'s crew includes some fine actors, notably Richard Harris as a seaman accused of stealing a head of cheese. Richard Haydn also has some good moments as the botanist in search of the breadfruit plant.
☐ 1962: Nominations: Best Picture, Color Cinematography, Color Art Direction, Editing, Original Music Score, Song ('Follow Me'), Special Effects

••••••••••••••••••••••••••••••••

■ MY BEAUTIFUL LAUNDRETTE

1985, 97 MINS, UK ◇ 🔞 ⊙
Dir Stephen Frears *Prod* Sarah Radclyffe, Tim Bevan *Scr* Hanif Kureishi *Ph* Oliver Stapleton *Ed* Mick Audsley *Mus* Hans Zimmer, Stanley Myers *Art Dir* Hugo Luczyc Wyhowski
● Daniel Day Lewis, Gordon Warnecke, Saeed Jaffrey, Roshan Seth, Shirley Anne Field, Derrick Branche (Working Title/SAF/Channel Four)

Tale of profiteering middle-class Pakistani capitalists making a fortune out of unscrupulous wheeling and dealing in an impoverished London.

Focus is on two youths, friends from schooldays. Johnny is a working-class white whose punkish mates are members of the National Front. Omar lives with his left-leaning widower father in a rundown house by the railway line.

When the film begins, Omar is given a menial job by his wealthy uncle, Nasser. He likes young Omar and gives him a rundown laundrette which he and Johnny convert into a veritable palace of a place, complete with video screens. Meanwhile, a repressed love blossoms between Omar and Johnny, adding tension to the already volatile racial situation.

As always, director Stephen Frears does a superb job of work when given a good script, and this is a very good script. It's peopled with interesting characters, allowing for a gallery of fine performances and situations.
☐ 1986: Nomination: Best Original Screenplay

••••••••••••••••••••••••••••••••

■ MY BLUE HEAVEN

1950, 96 MINS, US ◇
Dir Henry Koster *Prod* Sol C. Siegel *Scr* Lamar Trotti, Claude Binyon *Ph* Arthur E. Arling *Ed* James B. Clarke *Mus* Alfred Newman
● Betty Grable, Dan Dailey, David Wayne, Jane Wyatt, Mitzi Gaynor (20th Century-Fox)

In *My Blue Heaven* the television's theatre stage and the face of the video tube provide the locale for some highly entertaining goings-on by Betty Grable and Dan Dailey. They're unfortunately involved with an overly-sticky plot.

Yarn has the two stars just moving over from their niche on radio to TV. They are anxious for a baby. Moved by the happy Pringle family (David Wayne/Jane Wyatt), they try to adopt a baby. This gives the scripters an opportunity to get into considerable detail on both the legal and illegal sides of the adoption business.

While Grable and Dailey offer their capable standard brands of song-and-dance, the real eye-catcher of the pic is a lush brunet youngster making her initial screen appearance. She's Mitzi Gaynor. She's long on terping and vocalizing.

••••••••••••••••••••••••••••••••

■ MY BLUE HEAVEN

1990, 95 MINS, US ◇ 🔞 ⊙
Dir Herbert Ross *Prod* Herbert Ross, Anthea Sylbert *Scr* Nora Ephron *Ph* John Bailey *Ed* Stephen A. Rotter *Mus* Ira Newborn *Art Dir* Charles Rosen
● Steve Martin, Rick Moranis, Joan Cusack, Melanie Mayron, Carol Kane, Bill Irwin (Hawn-Sylbert/Warner)

Steve Martin and Rick Moranis do the mismatched pair o' guys shtick in *My Blue Heaven*, a lighthearted fairy tale. But scripter Nora Ephron's fish-out-of-water premise isn't funny enough to sustain a whole picture.

Martin plays Vinnie, an incorrigible Italian-American criminal who teaches the whitebread citizens of a suburban town how to loose up and have fun. Moranis plays Barney Coopersmith, a stiff-necked FBI agent who's assigned to settle mobster Martin into a new life 'somewhere in America' as part of a government witness-protection program.

Life in a brand-new subdivision is too placid for Vinnie, who immediately starts getting involved in illegal mischief that brings him into the jurisdiction of the ultra-straight district attorney Hannah Stubbs (Joan Cusack). It's a mess for Moranis, who has to keep getting Vinnie out of the d.a.'s clutches so that he can testify in a New York mob murder trial.

Pic takes some satirical pot-shots at life in the have-a-nice-day suburban bubble, but beyond that it twiddles its thumbs waiting for the mob trial.

••••••••••••••••••••••••••••••••

■ MY BODYGUARD

1980, 97 MINS, US ◇ 🔞
Dir Tony Bill *Prod* Don Devlin *Scr* Alan Ormsby *Ph* Michael D. Margulies *Ed* Stu Linder *Mus* Dave Grusin *Art Dir* Jackson de Govia
● Chris Makepeace, Adam Baldwin, Matt Dillon, Ruth Gordon, John Houseman, Craig Richard Nelson (20th Century-Fox/Simon/Market Street)

In his directorial debut, Tony Bill assembles a truly remarkable cast of youngsters with little or no previous acting experience.

Chris Makepeace is superb as the slightly built kid coming anew to a Chicago high school dominated by extortionist gang leader Matt Dillon, also terrific in his part.

Adam Baldwin is a standoffish, uncommu-

M

nicative brute rumored throughout the school to be a psychotic weirdo who has killed cops and other kids. Dillon and gang use the rumors to demand payment from smaller fellows for 'protection' from Baldwin.

But Makepeace will not pay up and takes his lumps until befriended by Baldwin, thereby beginning a warm friendship that leads to surprising turns in the plot.

Technically, picture sometimes shows the threads of low-budget shooting, but the distractions are minor.

••••••••••••••••••••••••

■ MY BRILLIANT CAREER

1979, 98 MINS, AUSTRALIA ◇ ⊙
Dir Gillian Armstrong   *Prod* Margaret Fink   *Scr* Eleanor Witcombe   *Ph* Don McAlpine   *Ed* Nick Beauman
Mus Nathan Waks   *Art Dir* Luciana Arrighi
● Judy Davis, Sam Neill, Wendy Hughes, Robert Grubb, Pat Kennedy, Max Cullen (New South Wales/ GUO)

This Australian film is a charming look [from the book by Miles Franklin] at 19th-century rural days in general and the stirrings of self-realization and feminine liberation in the persona of a headstrong young girl who wants to go her own way.

Judy Davis is fine as an ugly duckling who blossoms into an independent writer and refuses to give into the ritual and place reserved for women at the time which was, namely, marriage.

She resists marriage to write her book and go on with her own life. Perhaps the last part of her servitude with the farmer and his family is forced. But there is a rightness in tone in delving into the hidebound society and early flaunting of its taboos by an engaging girl.
□ 1980: Nomination: Best Costume Design

••••••••••••••••••••••••

■ MY CHAUFFEUR

1986, 97 MINS, US ◇ ⊙ ⊙
Dir David Beaird   *Prod* Marilyn J. Tenser   *Scr* David Beaird   *Ph* Harry Mathias   *Ed* Richard E. Westover
Mus Paul Hertzog   *Art Dir* C.J. Strawn
● Deborah Foreman, Sam J. Jones, Sean McClory, Howard Hesseman, E.G. Marshall (Crown)

David Beaird avowedly set out to imitate the screwball comedies of the 1930s and 1940s and has succeeded admirably, thanks to adorably spunky Deborah Foreman and her stuffy foil, Sam J. Jones. They make quite a pair.

Foreman is a real find, fitting into the mold of Goldie Hawn, Carole Lombard and Claudette Colbert. She not only can say a lot when saying nothing, she's a real pro when it comes to combining high tuned dialog with physical action.

Summoned mysteriously by a millionaire limo company owner (E.G. Marshall), Foreman takes a job as a driver, much to the objections of a wonderful assortment of chauvinistic chauffeurs who want to maintain their male-dominated domain.

She gets the impossible assignments including Jones, a spoiled, domineering industrialist who is, unknown to her, Marshall's son. Romance gradually blossoms.

••••••••••••••••••••••••

■ MY COUSIN RACHEL

1952, 98 MINS, US
Dir Henry Koster   *Prod* Nunnally Johnson   *Scr* Nunnally Johnson   *Ph* Joseph La Shelle   *Ed* Louis Loeffler
Mus Franz Waxman   *Art Dir* Lyle Wheeler, John De Cuir
● Olivia de Havilland, Richard Burton, Audrey Dalton, Ronald Squire, George Dolenz, John Sutton (20th Century-Fox)

A dark, moody melodrama, with emphasis on tragedy, has been fashioned from Daphne du Maurier's bestseller, *My Cousin Rachel*.

Olivia de Havilland endows the title role

with commanding histrionics. Opposite her is Richard Burton, debuting in Hollywood pictures. He creates a strong impression in the role of a love-torn, suspicious man.

The story, set in early 19th-century England, tells of a young man with a deep affection for the foster father who had raised him. When the foster father marries a distant cousin he has met while touring Italy to escape the rigors of winter in Cornwall, the young man is beset with jealousy. This later turns to suspicion and hate when he receives letters that indicate his beloved relative is being poisoned by the bride.
□ 1952: Nominations: Best Supp. Actor (Richard Burton), B&W Cinematography, B&W Costume Design, B&W Art Direction

••••••••••••••••••••••••

■ MY COUSIN VINNY

1992, 119 MINS, US ◇ ⊙ ⊙
Dir Jonathan Lynn   *Prod* Dale Launer, Paul Schiff
Scr Dale Launer   *Ph* Peter Deming   *Ed* Tony Lombardo
Mus Randy Edelman   *Art Dir* Victoria Paul
● Joe Pesci, Ralph Macchio, Marisa Tomei, Mitchell Whitfield, Fred Gwynne, Lane Smith (20th Century-Fox)

Joe Pesci puts in a lovable underdog turn as a hopelessly inept lawyer battling to prove himself in his first case. Tale has coarse Brooklynite Pesci called upon by family members to help his college-age cousin Bill (Ralph Macchio) out of a jam in the Deep South.

Seems Bill and his pal Stan (Mitchell Whitfield) were mistakenly nabbed for the murder of a store clerk. The lovable loser lawyer and his mouthy best girl-friend, Lisa (Marisa Tomei), must go to Alabama to extricate the pair. Their secret weapon will be Vinny's talent for argument, demonstrated for the audience in a latenight set-to with Tomei. Pic's running joke is that Vinny can't stay awake in court.

Tomei, sashaying through the proceedings as kind of a sexy hood ornament, creates a buoyant chemistry with her combative b.f. Macchio and Whitfield are stuck in poorly drawn roles. Filmed mostly in Monticello, Ga, pic is somewhat disappointing in production aspects.
□ 1992: Best Supporting Actress (Marisa Tomei)

••••••••••••••••••••••••

■ MY DARLING CLEMENTINE

1946, 97 MINS, US ⊙ ⊙
Dir John Ford   *Prod* Samuel G. Engel   *Scr* Samuel G. Engel, Winston Miller   *Ph* Joe MacDonald   *Ed* Dorothy Spencer   *Mus* Alfred Newman   *Art Dir* James Basevi, Lyle R. Wheeler
● Henry Fonda, Linda Darnell, Victor Mature, Walter Brennan, Cathy Downs, Ward Bond (20th Century-Fox)

Trademark of John Ford's direction is clearly stamped on the film with its shadowy lights, softly contrasted moods and measured pace, but a tendency is discernible towards stylization for stylization's sake. At several points, the pic comes to a dead stop to let Ford go gunning for some arty effect.

Major boost to the film is given by the simple, sincere performance of Henry Fonda. Script doesn't afford him many chances for dramatic action, but Fonda, as a boomtown marshal, pulls the reins taut on his part charging the role and the pic with more excitement than it really has. Playing counterpoint to Fonda, Victor Mature registers nicely as a Boston aristocrat turned gambler and killer.

Femme lead is held down by Linda Darnell although Cathy Downs plays the title role. As a Mexican firebrand and dancehall belle, Darnell handles herself creditably while the camera work does the rest in highlighting her looks. Downs, in the relatively minor role of Clementine, a cultured Bostonian gal who is in love with Mature, is sweet and winning.

Story opens with the killing of Fonda's brother while they are en route to California on a cattle-herding job. Fonda is offered, and takes, the post of sheriff in a bad man's town in an effort to track down the killers. Crossing paths with Mature in a saloon, Fonda suspects him at first but both become very chummy as Mature is revealed to be a talented surgeon who escaped to a dangerous life because he suffered from consumption.

••••••••••••••••••••••••

■ MY DINNER WITH ANDRE

1981, 110 MINS, US ◇ ⊙ ⊙
Dir Louis Malle   *Prod* George W. George, Beverly Karp
Scr Wallace Shawn, Andre Gregory   *Ph* Jeri Sopanen
Ed Suzanne Baron   *Mus* Allen Shawn
● Wallace Shawn, Andre Gregory (Andre)

My Dinner with Andre is something of a film stunt, consisting almost entirely of a conversation over dinner between two theatrical acquaintances. Though conforming to the aloof, cooly observant mode of director Louis Malle's previous pics, *Andre* is really authored by its two players, Wallace Shawn and Andre Gregory, doubling as screenwriters.

Shawn, a cherubic figure roughly playing himself as a sometime playwright and actor, is the audience surrogate, even bookending the film with his voiceover narration accompanying tracking shots of him on the streets of New York City. Somewhat apprehensive, he has dinner at a posh restaurant with Andre, portrayed also semi-autobiographically by theatre director Andre Gregory.

What ensues is an overlong but mainly captivating conversation, consisting largely of stream of consciousness monologs by Gregory.

Where the picture fails is in its lack of balance between the two protagonists. For the first half, Shawn is acceptable in closeup inserts, reacting or just listening to Gregory. However, in the second half Gregory begins making philosophical conclusions which require response or rebuttal and Shawn's haltingly expressed 'little guy' comebacks are inadequate and type his entire performance as comedy relief.

••••••••••••••••••••••••

■ MY FAIR LADY

1964, 170 MINS, US ◇ ⊙ ⊙
Dir George Cukor   *Prod* Jack L. Warner   *Scr* Alan Jay Lerner   *Ph* Harry Stradling   *Ed* William Ziegler
Mus Andre Previn (sup.)   *Art Dir* Cecil Beaton
● Audrey Hepburn, Rex Harrison, Stanley Holloway, Wilfrid Hyde White, Gladys Cooper, Jeremy Brett (Warner)

The great longrun stage musical made by Lerner & Loewe (and Herman Levin) out of the wit of Bernard Shaw's play *Pygmalion* has been transformed into a stunningly effective screen entertainment. *My Fair Lady* has riches of story, humor, acting and production values far beyond the average big picture. Warner paid $5.5 million for the rights alone.

Care and planning shine in every detail and thus cast a glow around the name of director George Cukor. The original staging genius of Moss Hart cannot be overlooked as a blueprint for success. But like all great films *My Fair Lady* represents a team of talents. Rex Harrison's performance and Cecil Beaton's design of costumes, scenery and production are the two powerhouse contributions.

This is a man-bullies-girl plot with story novelty. An unorthodox musical without a kiss, the audience travels to total involvement with characters and situation on the rails of sharp dialog and business. The deft segues of dialog into lyric are superb, especially in the case of Harrison.

Only incurably disputatious persons will consider it a defect of *Lady* on screen that Julie Andrews has been replaced by the better

523

known Miss H. She is thoroughly beguiling as Eliza though her singing is dubbed by Marni Nixon.

Stanley Holloway repeats from the Broadway stage version. Again and again his theatrical authority clicks. How this great English trouper takes the basically 'thin' and repetitious, 'With a Little Bit O'Luck' and makes it stand up as gaiety incarnate.

Every one in the small cast is excellent. Mona Washbourne is especially fine as the prim but compassionate housekeeper. Wilfrid Hyde White has the necessary proper gentleman quality as Pickering and makes a good foil for Harrison. Gladys Cooper brings aristocratic common sense to the mother of the phonetics wizard.

A certain amount of new music by Frederick Loewe and added lyrics by Alan Jay Lerner are part of the adjustment to the cinematic medium. But it is the original stage score which stands out.
□ 1964: Best Picture, Director, Actor (Rex Harrison), Color Cinematography, Color Art Direction, Sound, Adapted Musical Scoring, Color Costume Design.
□ Nominations: Best Supp. Actor (Stanley Holloway), Supp. Actress (Gladys Cooper), Adapted Screenplay, Editing

....

■ MY FAVORITE BLONDE

1942, 78 MINS, US
Dir Sidney Lanfield   *Prod* Paul Jones   *Scr* Don Hartman, Frank Butler   *Ph* William Mellor   *Ed* William O'Shea   *Mus* David Buttolph
● Bob Hope, Madeleine Carroll, Gale Sondergaard (Paramount)

Madeleine Carroll is ideally cast as a British agent who involves vaudevillian Bob Hope into a helter-skelter coast-to-coast hop from Broadway to Hollywood.

The blend of a secret scorpion (containing the revised flying orders for a convoy of Lockheed bombers headed for Britain) with the wacky semi-backstage atmosphere, an al fresco plumbers' picnic, Nazi spies etc., has been well kneaded by the authors (from a story by Melvin Frank and Norman Panama) and director Sidney Lanfield alike.

Producer Paul Jones and director Lanfield permit themselves a conceit when Bing Crosby is seen idling at a picnic bus station. Crosby directs the lammister Hope and Carroll toward the picnic grounds. As Hope gives Crosby one of those takes, he muses, 'No, it can't be.' That's all, and it's one of the best laughs in a progressively funny film.

....

■ MY FAVORITE BRUNETTE

1947, 87 MINS, US ⓥ ⊙
Dir Elliott Nugent   *Prod* Daniel Dare   *Scr* Edmund Beloin, Jack Rose   *Ph* Lionel Lindon   *Ed* Ellsworth Hoagland   *Mus* Robert Emmett Dolan   *Art Dir* Hans Dreier, Earl Hedrick
● Bob Hope, Dorothy Lamour, Peter Lorre, Lon Chaney, John Hoyt, Reginald Denny (Paramount/Hope)

Bob Hope, the sad sack would-be sleuth; Hope, the condemned prisoner, nerving out his imminent quietus with unhappy bravado; and Hope, the pushover, squirming uneasily under a chemical yen for the potent Dorothy Lamour charms it's familiar stuff but still grist for the yock mills.

One long flashback is the device employed. Credits segue into a scene depicting Hope as a condemned murderer being groomed for the gas chamber. To reporters gathered to record his early demise, Hope relates his tale of woe which at the outset has him as a baby photographer whose frustrated urge towards gumshoeing has inspired the invention of a special keyhole camera.

When Hope's nextdoor neighbor, a private eye, leaves town requesting Hope to tend his

office, the comic's usual pot of trouble rises to a simmer. He tangles with Lamour in a fantastic snarl involving a mysterious map (concealed by Hope in a drinking cup container) and Lamour's missing uncle who's been snatched by a gang of international criminals headed by that familiar lawbreaker, Peter Lorre.

Curtain rings down on a solid rib. Hope's impatient executioner turns out to be you guessed it Bing Crosby. To which Hope cracks: 'That guy will take any part.' Another pretty conceit that comes off is the use of Alan Ladd in a bit part as the nextdoor detective.

....

■ MY FAVORITE SPY

1951, 93 MINS, US
Dir Norman Z. McLeod   *Prod* Paul Jones   *Scr* Edmund Hartmann, Jack Sher   *Ph* Victor Milner   *Ed* Frank Bracht   *Mus* Victor Young   *Art Dir* Hal Pereira, Roland Anderson
● Bob Hope, Hedy Lamarr, Francis L. Sullivan, Arnold Moss, John Archer, Iris Adrian (Paramount)

My Favorite Spy is in the same general pattern of other Bob Hope *My Favorite* films, scattering chuckles through the footage, with an occasional howler. Ably partnering is Hedy Lamarr, lending herself to the knockabout pace with a likeable loss of dignity.

Norman Z. McLeod guides the breezy plot with a reasonably consistent speed and manages to make the zany doings fairly easy to follow. Hope, as a burley comic, is talked into doubling for an international spy so the US government can get hold of plans for a pilotless plane. Dispatched to Tangiers with $1 million in a money belt, the masquerading Hope is met by Lamarr, another spy employed by a rival government agent (Francis L. Sullivan).

From here on, the script involves the comic in a wild and woolly free-for-all of danger, escape, lovely girls and chase that help fill out the film's 93 minutes.

....

■ MY FAVORITE WIFE

1940, 88 MINS, US ⓥ ⊙
Dir Garson Kanin   *Prod* Leo McCarey   *Scr* Sam Spewack, Bella Spewack, Leo McCarey   *Ph* Rudolph Mate   *Ed* Robert Wise   *Mus* Roy Webb   *Art Dir* Van Nest Polglase, Mark-Lee Kirk
● Irene Dunne, Cary Grant, Randolph Scott, Gail Patrick, Ann Shoemaker, Scotty Beckett (RKO)

Irene Dunne and Cary Grant pick up the thread of marital comedy at about the point where they left off in *The Awful Truth*. With these two stars working again with Leo McCarey, a surefire laughing film is guaranteed. McCarey is the producer of the new picture, which is directed by Garson Kanin, who filled in for McCarey when the latter was on the hospital list after an auto smashup.

Plot of the new film [by Leo McCarey and Bella and Samuel Spewack] is pretty thin in spots and it is distinctly to the credit of the players and Kanin that they can keep the laughs bouncing along. In this connection they have able assistance from Randolph Scott and Gail Patrick.

It's a pretty hard yarn to believe at the beginning when Dunne turns up at home after seven years' absence from her husband and two small children, who were infants when she left on a South Sea exploration. She was shipwrecked and tossed up on one of those invisible Pacific islands.

She returns, therefore, as a female Enoch Arden, arriving on the day her husband has remarried. Of course, if anyone had mentioned the truth to the new wife (Patrick) the story would have been over right then and there before it gets underway. Nor does Dunne mention that Scott was the sole other

survivor of the monsoon, and that he had come back to civilization with her.
□ 1940: Nominations: Best Original Story, B&W Art Direction, Original Score

....

■ MY FAVORITE YEAR

1982, 92 MINS, US ◇ ⓥ ⊗
Dir Richard Benjamin   *Prod* Michael Gruskoff   *Scr* Norman Steinberg, Dennis Palumbo   *Ph* Gerald Hirschfeld   *Ed* Richard Chew   *Mus* Ralph Burns   *Art Dir* Charles Rosen
● Peter O'Toole, Mark Linn-Baker, Jessica Harper, Joseph Bologna, Bill Macy, Lainie Kazan (Brooksfilms/Gruskoff)

An enjoyable romp through the early days of television, *My Favorite Year* [from a story by Dennis Palumbo] provides a field day for a wonderful bunch of actors headed by Peter O'Toole in another rambunctious, stylish starring turn.

Looking exquisitely ravaged, O'Toole portrays a legendary Hollywood star in the Errol Flynn mold who, in 1954, the year of the title, agrees to make his TV debut on *The Comedy Cavalcade*. O'Toole is put in the hands of young comedy writer Mark Linn-Baker for safekeeping, latter's sole responsibility being to keep his idol sober enough to make it through the performance a few days later.

Fully cognizant of the kid's mission, flamboyant star behaves himself for awhile, but finally falls way off the wagon after enduring a dinner party at the Brooklyn home of Linn-Baker's mother. It's madcap farce from then on.

Linn-Baker is quite appealing and engagingly energetic in an excellent screen debut. Jessica Harper is fine as a spunky staffer, Joseph Bologna is wonderfully tyrannical as the show's star, Bill Macy is particularly funny as an agonized writer and Lainie Kazan hilariously overdoes the Jewish mother bit.
□ 1982: Nomination: Best Actor (Peter O'Toole)

....

■ MY FIRST WIFE

1984, 95 MINS, AUSTRALIA ◇ ⓥ
Dir Paul Cox   *Prod* Jane Ballantyne, Paul Cox   *Scr* Paul Cox, Bob Ellis   *Ph* Yuri Sokol   *Ed* Tim Lewis   *Art Dir* Asher Bilu
● John Hargreaves, Wendy Hughes, Lucy Angwin, Anna Jemison, David Cameron, Charles Tingwell (Dofine)

A lacerating, emotionally exhausting drama about a marriage breakup, *My First Wife* manages to breathe new life into familiar material.

Director Paul Cox and coscripter Bob Ellis ring a few changes. This 10-year marriage is collapsing because the wife (Wendy Hughes) not the husband (John Hargreaves) is having an affair, and it's the husband who desperately wants her back, willing to forgive and forget everything if only she'll return to him.

At the same time, Helen, who is obviously still very fond of him but no longer wants to live with him, can only stand by helplessly as he gradually loses his grip. Also at stake is their young daughter, Lucy, whom Helen unquestionably believes should live with her.

Pic rings utterly true, with no false sentimentality, no firm ending.

....

■ MY FOOLISH HEART

1949, 98 MINS, US ⓥ
Dir Mark Robson   *Prod* Samuel Goldwyn   *Scr* Julius J. Epstein, Philip G. Epstein   *Ph* Lee Garmes   *Ed* Daniel Mandell   *Mus* Victor Young   *Art Dir* Richard Day
● Dana Andrews, Susan Hayward, Kent Smith, Lois Wheeler, Jessie Royce Landis, Robert Keith (Goldwyn)

My Foolish Heart ranks among the better romantic films.

Picture gets off on the right foot with a

M

script that is honest and loaded with dialog that is alive. The screenplay [based on a story in *The New Yorker* by J. D. Salinger] progresses through several different stages of emotion.

Plotting opens in 1949, and finds Susan Hayward at the tailend of an unhappy, wartime marriage with Kent Smith. Before she has a chance to pass on a part of her unhappiness to Smith, the sight of an old gown arouses memories and takes her back to 1941 when she was enfolded in romance with Dana Andrews.

Hayward's performance is a gem, displaying a positive talent for capturing reality. Opposite her, Andrews' slightly cynical character of a young man at loose ends comes to life and earns him a strong credit.

□ 1949: Nominations: Best Actress (Susan Hayward), Song ('My Foolish Heart')

. . . .

■ **MY FRIEND FLICKA**

1943, 89 MINS, US ◇ ⊛

Dir Harold Schuster   *Prod* Ralph Dietrich   *Scr* Lillie Hayward   *Ph* Dewey Wrigley   *Ed* Robert Fritch   *Mus* Alfred Newman

● Roddy McDowall, Preston Foster, Rita Johnson, Jeff Corey, James Bell (20th Century-Fox)

Basic theme, necessarily limited in appeal since it's the story of the influence of a wild pony (Flicka) on the lives and philosophy of a small family group, required all the topnotch production values which the producer provided.

Fine color photography, capable performances by Roddy McDowall, Preston Foster, Rita Johnson and, of course, the magnificent horses, are assets.

Essentially it's the story of a daydreaming youngster's longing for a colt of his own, the boy's complete transformation once his rancher-father fulfills his desire, and the trials and tribulations in taming and nursing the filly back to health.

. . . .

■ **MY GAL SAL**

1942, 101 MINS, US ◇

Dir Irving Cummings   *Prod* Robert Masler   *Scr* Seton I. Miller, Darrell Ware, Karl Tunberg   *Ph* Ernest Palmer   *Ed* Robert Simpson   *Mus* Alfred Newman (dir)   *Art Dir* Richard Day, Joseph Wright

● Rita Hayworth, Victor Mature, Carole Landis, Phil Silvers, James Gleason, John Sutton (20th Century-Fox)

Theodore Dreiser's biography of his songwriting brother, Paul Dreiser, parades a number of popular tunes of the 1890s – several with specially-staged production numbers – to round out a fairly entertaining piece of filmusical entertainment.

Dreiser's life is far from sugar-coated in its cinematic unreeling. Young Paul (Victor Mature) is picked up as the youth who runs away from home to pursue a musical career rather than study for the ministry. After a short stretch as entertainer with a cheap medicine show, and an intimate association with Carole Landis, he finally tosses over the small time for a whirl at the big town of New York.

There's too much footage consumed in unnecessary episodes and incidents that might have been historically correct for the times, but not important to a straight line presentation of a musical drama.

Although Mature gives a solid performance as the songwriter, it's Rita Hayworth who catches major attention from her first entrance.

□ 1942: Best Color Art Direction.

□ Nomination: Best Scoring of a Musical Picture

. . . .

■ **MY GEISHA**

1962, 119 MINS, US ◇ ⊛

Dir Jack Cardiff   *Prod* Steve Parker   *Scr* Norman Krasna   *Ph* Shunichiro Nakao   *Ed* Archie Marshek

Mus Franz Waxman   *Art Dir* Hal Pereira, Arthur Lonergan, Makoto Kikuchi

● Shirley MacLaine, Yves Montand, Edward G. Robinson, Robert Cummings, Yoko Tani, Tatsuo Saito (Paramount/Sachiko)

Although hampered by a transparent plot, a lean and implausible one-joke premise and a tendency to fluctuate uneasily between comedy and drama, the picture has been richly and elaborately produced on location in Japan, cast with perception and a sharp eye for marquee juxtaposition.

A certain amount of elementary but traditionally evasive information on the Japanese geisha girl weaves helpfully through Norman Krasna's brittle screenplay about an American film actress (Shirley MacLaine) who blithely and vainly executes a monumental practical joke on her insecure director-husband (Yves Montand) by masquerading as a Geisha to win the part of 'Madame Butterfly' in his arty production of same in Japan.

Just as the comedy is about to peter out, there is a radical swerve into sentiment and moral significance. Montand, abruptly (and at long last) cognizant of what is transpiring, and deeply hurt, proposes B-girl monkeyshines, to his bewildered G-girl wife, and the marriage seems about to go to H.

MacLaine gives her customary spirited portrayal in the title role, yet skillfully submerges her unpredictably gregarious personality into that of the dainty, tranquil geisha for the bulk of the proceedings. Montand has his moments.

□ 1962: Nomination: Best Color Costume Design

. . . .

■ **MY GIRL**

1991, 102 MINS, US ◇ ⊛ ⊙

Dir Howard Zieff   *Prod* Brian Grazer   *Scr* Laurice Elehwany   *Ph* Paul Elliott   *Ed* Wendy Greene Bricmont   *Mus* James Newton Howard   *Art Dir* Joseph T. Garrity

● Dan Aykroyd, Jamie Lee Curtis, Macaulay Culkin, Anna Chlumsky, Richard Masur, Griffin Dunne (Imagine)

Plenty of shrewd commercial calculation went into concocting the right sugar coating for this story of an 11-year-old girl's painful maturation, but chemistry seems right.

Set in an idealized Anytown, USA, supposed to be in Pennsylvania but filmed in Florida, pic can afford to be relatively oblivious to events unfolding in 1972 because the man of the house (Dan Aykroyd) essentially stopped living a decade before. The widower mortician takes barely a passing interest in the doings of his daughter Vada (Anna Chlumsky), an exceedingly bright girl who enrolls in an adult education poetry course because she has a crush on the teacher (Griffin Dunne) and expresses her severe, Woody Allen-like hypochondria by regularly bursting in on a local doctor.

Things change around the funeral home when Dad hires a sexy hippie (Jamie Lee Curtis) to apply makeup to cadavers. Vada spends most of her time with an engaging neighbor (Macaulay Culkin), and although a bit young for a real romance, the two experience their first kiss together.

It's a rough summer for an 11-year-old, but director Howard Zieff paints it in the manner of a watercolor of a youthful idyll. First-time screenwriter Laurice Elehwany's script neatly handles a number of details but on larger matters falls into predictable patterns. Performers are highly simpatico.

. . . .

■ **MY HEROES HAVE ALWAYS BEEN COW-BOYS**

1991, 106 MINS, US ◇ ⊛

Dir Stuart Rosenberg   *Prod* Martin Poll, E.K. Gaylord II   *Scr* Joel Don Humphreys   *Ph* Bernd Heinl   *Ed* Dennis M. Hill   *Mus* James Horner

● Scott Glenn, Kate Capshaw, Ben Johnson, Balthazar Getty, Tess Harper, Gary Busey (Gaylord-Poll)

An earnest family drama of *Rocky*-esque inspirational values, independently produced modern oater is a predictable tale of an aging, aching cowpoke's shot at redemption. It bears many similarities to Sam Peckinpah's fine, neglected 1972 feature *Junior Bonner*.

This time, it's Scott Glenn's turn out of the gate, playing H.D. Dalton, a journeyman rider who returns from Texas to his family in Oklahoma, only to find it in a fractured state. His father, Jesse (Ben Johnson), has been moved to an old folks' home by sister Cheryl (Tess Harper) and brother-in-law Clint (Gary Busey), who hope to sell off the compound. H.D.'s former girlfriend Jolie (Kate Capshaw) has lost her husband and is faced with raising two children alone.

H.D. spirits his Dad back home, where the two men renew their lifelong tense, bickering relationship, and takes up once again with Jolie. When Jesse is injured, pressure mounts on H.D. to make some big bucks fast.

Directed in straightforward manner by Stuart Rosenberg, pic casts its lot with the underdog in true American fashion, but is bland and unexciting.

. . . .

■ **MY HUSTLER**

1967, 79 MINS, US

Dir Chuck Wein, Andy Warhol   *Prod* Andy Warhol   *Scr* Chuck Wein, Andy Warhol   *Ph* Andy Warhol

● Paul America, Ed Hood, John McDermott, Genevieve Charbon, Joseph Campbell, Dorothy Dean (Warhol)

For all the technical blunders, *My Hustler* possesses some narrative fascination for those with sufficiently strong stomachs and/or psyches. A young boy, hired for the weekend by a wealthy Fire Island homo through the 'Dial-a-Hustler Service,' is fought over by the aging deviate, a girl from next door, and another hustler well past his prime.

What makes the film morbidly absorbing is not the tenuous storyline which, in the best NY Underground tradition, is never resolved but the detail with which gay life is documented. [Shorter version premiered in 1966.]

The camera remains stationary for long stretches (one static take lasts a full 30 minutes), and what motion Warhol does employ consists of headache-inducing zooms and wobbly pans. The sound reproduction is so poor as not to deserve the epithet 'amateur'; volume level suggests an aural rollercoaster, about a third of the dialog is muffled, and lip sync is off for most of the film.

. . . .

■ **MY LEFT FOOT**
THE STORY OF CHRISTY BROWN

1989, 98 MINS, UK ◇ ⊛ ⊙

Dir Jim Sheridan   *Prod* Noel Pearson   *Scr* Shane Connaughton, Jim Sheridan   *Ph* Jack Conroy   *Ed* J. Patrick Duffner   *Mus* Elmer Bernstein   *Art Dir* Austen Spriggs

● Daniel Day Lewis, Ray McAnally, Brenda Fricker, Ruth McCabe, Fiona Shaw, Cyril Cusack (Granada)

First and foremost, *My Left Foot* is the warm, romantic and moving true story of a remarkable man: the Irish writer and painter Christy Brown born with cerebral palsy into an impoverished family. That it features a brilliant performance by Daniel Day Lewis and a fine supporting cast lifts it from mildly sentimental to excellent.

At his birth, Christy's parents are told their child would be little more than a vegetable, but through his mother's insistence that he fit in with family life, he shows intelligence and strength inside his paralyzed body.

The older Christy amazes his family by writing the word 'mother' on the floor with a piece of chalk gripped in his left foot. He goes on to become an artist still using that left foot and is helped by therapist Fiona Shaw, with whom he falls in love.

All performances are on the mark in this perfect little film [from Brown's own novel]. Brenda Fricker, as his loving and resilient mother, is excellent, as is the late Ray McAnally as his bricklayer father. *My Left Foot* is not a sad film. In fact, there is a great deal of humor in Day Lewis's Brown.
☐ 1989: Best Actor (Daniel Day Lewis), Best Supp. Actress (Brenda Fricker).
☐ Nominations: Best Picture, Director, Adapted Screenplay

● ●

■ MY LITTLE CHICKADEE

1940, 83 MINS, US ⊛ ⊙
Dir Edward F. Cline   *Prod* [Lester Cowan]   *Scr* Mae West, W.C. Fields   *Ph* Joseph Valentine   *Ed* Edward Curtiss   *Mus* Frank Skinner   *Art Dir* Jack Otterson, Martin Obzina
● Mae West, W.C. Fields, Joseph Calleia, Dick Foran, Ruth Donnelly, Magaret Hamilton (Universal)

Universal catches Mae West on a delayed rebound from Paramount, teaming her with W.C. Fields for a hefty package of lusty humor. Picture marks return of West to the screen after two years absence.

The familiar Westian swagger, drawl, wisecracks and innuendos are all included, likewise the typical Fields routines and quick-triggered comments. Sequences in which the pair work together are reduced to a minimum. Script setup is a continual series of episodes, first with West and then Fields.

Story is a reverse twist to *Destry Rides Again* and with western frontier locale, is reminiscent of *Destry*. West, returning from a complete course in a Chicago dance hall, has a way with men. A masked bandit falls in love with her, which eventually drums her out of the town. Meeting Fields, whom she believes rich, aboard the train, she promotes a fake marriage ceremony. Pair hit the next frontier settlement, where Fields is inducted into job of sheriff, and West tosses her charms around rather freely.

My Little Chickadee has been turned in on a moderate budget compared to outlays for the West starrers previously under the Paramount banner.

● ●

■ MY MAN GODFREY

1936, 93 MINS, US ⊛
Dir Gregory LaCava   *Prod* Charles R. Rogers
Scr Morrie Ryskind, Eric Hatch   *Ph* Ted Tetzlaff   *Ed* Ted Kent   *Mus* Charles Previn (dir.)   *Art Dir* Charles D. Hall
● William Powell, Carole Lombard, Alice Brady, Gail Patrick, Eugene Pallette, Alan Mowbray (Universal)

William Powell and Carole Lombard are pleasantly teamed in this splendidly produced comedy. Story is balmy, but not too much so, and lends itself to the sophisticated screen treatment of Eric Hatch's novel.

Lombard has played screwball dames before, but none so screwy as this one. Her whole family, with the exception of the old man, seem to have been dropped on their respective heads when young. Into this punchy society tribe walks Powell, a former social light himself who had gone on the bum over a woman and is trying to become a man once more in butler's livery. He straightens out the family, as well as himself.

Alice Brady, as the social mother in whom the family's psychopathic ward tendencies seemingly originate, does a bangup job with another tough part. Gail Patrick, as Lombard's sparring partner-sister, is excellent. Eugene Pallette, as the harassed father, and Mischa Auer, in a gigolo role, a beautiful piece of sustained comedy playing and writing, are both fine.
☐ 1936: Nominations: Best Director, Actor (William Powell), Actress (Carole Lombard),

Supp. Actor (Mischa Auer), Supp. Actress (Alice Brady), Screenplay

● ●

■ MY MAN GODFREY

1957, 92 MINS, US ◇
Dir Henry Koster   *Prod* Ross Hunter   *Scr* Everett Freeman, Peter Bermeis, William Bowers   *Ph* William Daniels   *Ed* Milton Carruth   *Mus* Frank Skinner   *Art Dir* Alexander Golitzen, Richard H. Riedel
● June Allyson, David Niven, Jessie Royce Landis, Robert Keith, Eva Gabor, Martha Hyer (Universal)

Updated version of *My Man Godfrey* is a pretty well turned out comedy with June Allyson and David Niven recreating the original Carole Lombard-William Powell star roles. Ross Hunter's production of the butler to an eccentric New York family of wealth who helps straighten them out, meanwhile recipient of the affections of the younger daughter, manages to pack plenty of lusty humor in the fast 92 minutes.

Where film misses is in the Niven character of butler. The screenplay drags him in by the heels in too fabricated a character a former Austrian diplomat in the US via illegal entry. Again, the scripters hit upon too ready a solution of the Allyson-Niven romance after Niven has been deported.

Director Henry Koster deftly handles his characters in their comedic paces and succeeds in establishing an aura of screwiness in keeping with the 1936 version. Niven is a particular standout in his helping the family back on their feet after bankruptcy faces them.

Jessie Royce Landis as the wacky society mother registers a definite hit, Martha Hyer as the arrogant elder sister is stunning and Robert Keith ably portrays the father faced with ruin.

● ●

■ MY NAME IS JULIA ROSS

1945, 64 MINS, US
Dir Joseph H. Lewis   *Prod* Wallace MacDonald
Scr Muriel Roy Bolton   *Ph* Burnett Guffey   *Ed* James Sweeney, Henry Batista   *Mus* Mischa Bakaleinikoff   *Art Dir* Jerome Pycha Jr
● Nina Foch, May Whitty, George Macready, Roland Varno, Anita Bolster, Doris Lloyd (Columbia)

Mystery melodrama with a psychological twist runs only 64 minutes but it's fast and packed with tense action throughout. Acting and production (though apparently modestly budgeted) are excellent.

New face is Nina Foch, who has looks and talent, while rest of cast is backed notably by May Whitty, George Macready and Roland Varno.

Story [from the novel *The Woman in Red* by Anthony Gilbert] is of gal hired fraudulently as secretary to wealthy English dowager. Purpose of hiring is to impose a murder scheme in which the dowager's son is implicated. The story has its implausibilities, but general conduct of pic negates those factors for overall click results.

Whitty gives creditable performance, so does Macready as her psychiatric son. Others in support acquit themselves well. Joseph H. Lewis directed for pace, and he achieves it all the way.

● ●

■ MY OWN PRIVATE IDAHO

1991, 102 MINS, US ◇ ⊛ ⊙
Dir Gus Van Sant   *Prod* Laurie Parker   *Scr* Gus Van Sant   *Ph* Eric Alan Edwards, John Campbell   *Ed* Curtiss Clayton   *Mus* James Newton Howard   *Art Dir* David Brisbin
● River Phoenix, Keanu Reeves, James Russo, William Richert, Rodney Harvey, Chiara Caselli (New Line)

Rather less than the sum of its often striking parts, Gus Van Sant's appealingly idiosyn-

cratic look at a pair of very different young street hustlers is one of those ambitious, overreaching disappointments that is more interesting than some more conservative successes.

Taking his title from a B-52s song, Van Sant begins his crooked yarn on a straight Idaho highway, where the scruffy outcast Mike (River Phoenix) succumbs to his affliction of narcolepsy and has visions of his lost home and mother. In Seattle, Mike is a sex-for-hire boy, a sensitive but raw youth who will go both ways but has the unfortunate habit of passing out on the job.

Mike's cohort and soon-to-be best friend is Scott (Keanu Reeves). The wealthy son of Portland's mayor, Scott is clearly hanging with the boys as an act of teenage rebellion against his family.

Then Van Sant makes a sudden, fatal shift in tone and style. The dialog begins sounding arch, the acting style becomes strangely theatrical and, for a while, the film becomes a modern, gay adaptation of Shakespeare's *Henry IV, Part I*.

Shakespearean side of the story falls short due to Reeves' very narrow range as an actor. Phoenix cuts a believable, sometimes compelling figure of a young man urgently groping for definition in his life. For a story about two gay hustlers, film deals very little with sex.

● ●

■ MY PAL GUS

1952, 83 MINS, US
Dir Robert Parrish   *Prod* Stanley Rubin   *Scr* Fay Kanin, Michael Kanin   *Ph* Leo Tover   *Ed* Robert Fritch
Mus Leigh Harline
● Richard Widmark, Joanne Dru, Audrey Totter, George Winslow, Regis Toomey, Joan Banks (20th Century-Fox)

Richard Widmark is a bon-bon manufacturer too busy to devote much time to his small son. As a result, the kid is a problem child who eventually lands in the progressive school operated by Joanne Dru. Little Winslow takes to the teacher, so does dad, and things are well on their way towards the schoolmarm becoming his new mother when Audrey Totter, Widmark's ex-wife, appears on the scene.

Totter reveals her Mexican divorce is invalid and demands Widmark give up his community property half of his wealth for a valid divorce.

Widmark is very good as the tough, rags-to-riches father, showing both good comedy feeling as well as the more touchingly dramatic flavor required in the final scenes when he tries to take his kid to a mother who doesn't want him.

● ●

■ MYRA BRECKINRIDGE

1970, 94 MINS, US ◇ ⊛
Dir Michael Sarne   *Prod* Robert Fryer   *Scr* Michael Sarne, David Giler   *Ph* Richard Moore   *Ed* Danford B. Greene   *Mus* Lionel Newman (sup.)   *Art Dir* Jack Martin Smith, Fred Harpman
● Mae West, John Huston, Raquel Welch, Rex Reed, Farrah Fawcett, Roger C. Carmel (20th Century-Fox)

The film version of Gore Vidal's Hollywood-themed transsexual satire starts off promisingly, but after a couple of reels plunges straight downhill under the weight of artless direction.

As a lecherous female agent, Mae West after an absence from the screen of over 26 years provides some funny moments though her part is very short. John Huston, as drama school promoter Buck Loner, is good, while title-roled Raquel Welch like the film, good at the beginning has been let down as story progresses to the point where she alone must (but cannot) keep it going.

With David Giler, director Michael Sarne adapted Vidal's novel in such a way as to (1)

M

create some expository interest, (2) abandon the players to carry the ball, and (3) hype the pacing by clip inserts, motivated and otherwise, as unreal and artificial as silicone injections.

●●●●●●●●●●●●●●●●●●●●●●●●●●●●●●●●

■ MY SISTER EILEEN

1942, 97 MINS, US ⊙

Dir Alexander Hall   *Prod* Max Gordon   *Scr* Joseph Fields, Jerome Chodorov   *Ph* Joseph Walker   *Ed* Viola Lawrence   *Mus* Morris Stoloff
● Rosalind Russell, Brian Aherne, Janet Blair, Richard Quine, June Havoc, Jeff Donnell (Columbia)

Adaptors Joseph Fields and Jerome Chodorov obviously liked their stage play [adapted from *New Yorker* stories by Ruth McKenney], for in translating it to the screen they've retained virtually the entire format, including all the key dialog. About all they've done has been to fill out the various chinks in the story which had been excluded by the limitations of the single-set play.

In Alexander Hall's direction, the pacing is fast and smooth, with constant use of sight gags and comedy situations. Most of the action still takes place in the Greenwich Village basement studio-apartment, with a crescendo of exaggerated events breaking out near and in the place.

Rosalind Russell's performance as authoress Ruth is an effective blend of curtness and warmth.
□ 1942: Nomination: Best Actress (Rosalind Russell)

●●●●●●●●●●●●●●●●●●●●●●●●●●●●●●●●

■ MY SISTER EILEEN

1955, 106 MINS, US ⊙

Dir Richard Quine   *Prod* Fred Kohlmar   *Scr* Blake Edwards, Richard Quine   *Ph* Charles Lawton Jr   *Ed* Charles Nelson   *Mus* Morris Stoloff (sup.), George Duning (adapt.)   *Art Dir* Walter Holscher
● Janet Leigh, Jack Lemmon, Betty Garrett, Bob Fosse, Kurt Kasznar, Richard York (Columbia)

Scripters have turned out a simplified filmusical, in that the tunes and dances come naturally to situations and are not overly staged. Thus, the problems that befall two sisters from Ohio, who come to New York to seek fame as a writer and actress respectively play naturally, even with some broadening for comedy. Richard Quine's direction keeps things gay and mostly moving at a spirited pace. Latter helps when some of the situations tend to be repetitious.

Two major assets in the trouping and funnying are Betty Garrett, as Ruth Sherwood, who pens sister's romantic adventures, and Jack Lemmon, as Bob Baker, the young publisher and wouldbe wolf who successfully romances Ruth. Seconding this pair are Janet Leigh, very attractive as the little sister, and [choreographer] Bob Fosse, the shy soda jerk.

None of the songs is from the stage tuner [*Wonderful Town*] having been cleffed by Jule Styne and Leo Robin especially for the picture. While not particularly standout, the numbers are mostly pleasant.

●●●●●●●●●●●●●●●●●●●●●●●●●●●●●●●●

■ MY STEPMOTHER IS AN ALIEN

1988, 108 MINS, US ◇ ⊚ ⊙

Dir Richard Benjamin   *Prod* Ronald Parker   *Scr* Jerico, Herschel Weingrod, Timothy Harris, Jonathan Reynolds   *Ph* Richard H. Kline   *Ed* Jacqueline Cambas   *Mus* Alan Silvestri   *Art Dir* Charles Rosen
● Dan Aykroyd, Kim Basinger, Jon Lovitz, Alyson Hannigan, Joseph Maher (Weintraub)

My Stepmother Is an Alien is a failed attempt to mix many of the film genres associated with the 'alien' idea into a sprightly romp.

Dan Aykroyd, as a rumpled, overweight, widower scientist, foils one of his own experiments using lightning and a high-powered

satellite dish which results in a signal reaching beyond our galaxy to a planet in peril.

Soon afterwards, a flying saucer lands on a Southern California beach and two aliens alight. They come in the form of quintessential American beauty Kim Basinger in a slinky red sheath dress with an alien-buddy-mentor (the snake, voice courtesy of Ann Prentiss) hiding in her purse.

Their mission is to get Aykroyd to repeat his experiment, which will save their planet.

It is the lengths to which Basinger is expected to go wending her way into Aykroyd's otherwise nerdy suburban lifestyle that is supposed to levitate this fish-out-of-water story to comedic heights.

●●●●●●●●●●●●●●●●●●●●●●●●●●●●●●●●

■ MYSTERIOUS ISLAND

1962, 100 MINS, UK ◇ ⊚ ⊙

Dir Cy Endfield   *Prod* Charles H. Schneer   *Scr* John Prebble, Daniel Ullman, Crane Wilbur   *Ph* Wilkie Cooper   *Ed* Frederick Wilson   *Mus* Bernard Herrmann   *Art Dir* Bill Andrews
● Michael Craig, Joan Greenwood, Michael Callan, Gary Merrill, Herbert Lom, Percy Herbert (Columbia)

Produced in England under Cy Endfield's vigorous direction, the film illustrates the strange plight that befalls three Union soldiers, a newspaperman and a Rebel who, in 1865, escape the siege of Richmond in the inevitable Jules Verne balloon and return to land on an island in the remote South Seas, where they encounter, in chronological order: (1) a giant crab, (2) a giant bird, (3) two lovely shipwrecked British ladies of average proportions, (4) a giant bee, (5) a band of cutthroat pirates, (6) Captain Nemo's inoperative sub, (7) Captain Nemo.

The screenplay, from Verne's novel, winds with a staple of the science-fantasy melodrama – an entire volcanic isle sinking into the sea as the heroes and heroines beat a hasty retreat.

Dramatically the film is awkward, burdened with unanswered questions and some awfully ineffectual giant animals, but photographically it is noteworthy for the Super-dynamation process and special visual effects by Ray Harryhausen.

●●●●●●●●●●●●●●●●●●●●●●●●●●●●●●●●

■ MYSTERY OF THE WAX MUSEUM, THE

1933, 78 MINS, US ◇ ⊚ ⊙

Dir Michael Curtiz   *Scr* Don Mullaly, Carl Erickson   *Ph* Ray Rennahan   *Ed* George Amy   *Art Dir* Anton Grot
● Lionel Atwill, Fay Wray, Glenda Farrell, Frank McHugh, Allen Vincent (Warner)

Technicolor horror-mystery production co-featuring Lionel Atwill, Fay Wray, Glenda Farrell and Frank McHugh who struggle about as effectively as Michael Curtiz, the director, with a loose and unconvincing story, to manage a fairly decent job along *Frankenstein* and *Dracula* lines. Loose ends never quite jell but it's one of those artificial things.

Atwill is the maniacal custodian of the London wax museum whose fanatic enterprise with his transplanted museum on American soil leads Farrell, as the sob sister, to unearth this weird yarn, McHugh this time is the city ed. Wray and Allen Vincent are almost negligible in minor romantic background.

●●●●●●●●●●●●●●●●●●●●●●●●●●●●●●●●

■ MYSTERY TRAIN

1989, 113 MINS, US ◇ ⊚ ⊙

Dir Jim Jarmusch   *Prod* Jim Stark   *Scr* Jim Jarmusch   *Ph* Robby Muller   *Ed* Melody London   *Mus* John Lurie   *Art Dir* Dan Bishop
● Masatoshi Nagase, Youki Kudoh, Nicoletta Braschi, Elisabeth Bracco, Joe Strummer, Rick Aviles (JVC/MTI)

Wholly financed by Japanese electronics giant JVC, a first for an American production,

Mystery Train is a three-episode pic handled by indie writer-director Jim Jarmusch in his usual playful, minimalist style.

It could be almost dubbed 'Memphis Stories', as this is Jarmusch's tribute to the city of Elvis and other musical greats. Characteristically, the director explores the crumbling, decaying edges of the city through the eyes of foreigners: Japanese teenagers, an Italian widow and a British punk.

Story one, *Far from Yokohama*, intros teenagers Jun (Masatoshi Nagase) and Mitzuko (Youki Kudoh), who arrive by train, do a puzzling guided tour of Sun Studio (they can't understand a word the guide says), sit awed in front of a statue of Presley and check into the Arcade Hotel.

Story two, *A Ghost*, features Nicoletta Braschi as Luisa, in Memphis to take her deceased husband's body back to Rome. She checks into the Arcade and meets talkative DeeDee (Elisabeth Bracco) in the lobby.

Final segment, *Lost in Space*, picks up the story of abandoned Brit Johnny (Joe Strummer), who goes on a drunken binge with DeeDee's brother (Steve Buscemi) and a black friend (Rick Aviles). Johnny shoots a liquor store clerk, and the trio hides out in the Arcade; next morning, trying to stop Johnny from shooting herself, Buscemi gets shot in the leg.

●●●●●●●●●●●●●●●●●●●●●●●●●●●●●●●●

■ MYSTIC PIZZA

1988, 104 MINS, US ◇ ⊚ ⊙

Dir Donald Petrie   *Prod* Mark Levinson, Scott Rosenfelt   *Scr* Amy Jones, Perry Howze, Randy Howze, Alfred Uhry   *Ph* Tim Suhrstedt   *Ed* Marion Rothman, Don Brochu   *Mus* David McHugh   *Art Dir* David Chapman
● Annabeth Gish, Julia Roberts, Lili Taylor, Vincent D'Onofrio, William R. Moses, Adam Storke (Goldwyn)

Mystic Pizza is a deftly told coming-of-age story [by Amy Jones] about three young femmes as they explore their different destinies, mostly through romance; it's genuine and moving.

Title refers to a pizza parlor in the heavily Portuguese fishing town of Mystic, Conn, where three best friends, two of them sisters, are working the summer after high-school graduation, all on the verge of pursuing different directions in life.

Jojo (Lili Taylor) apparently is headed for marriage to high school sweetheart Bill (Vincent D'Onofrio), but the idea terrifies her, while he's all for it.

Of the two sisters, Daisy (Julia Roberts) is a vamp who's after the good life and knows how to use her looks, while Kat (Annabeth Gish) is the 'perfect' one headed for college on an astronomy scholarship. Unlike her sister, she's not too savvy about men, and falls for the married man (William Moses) she babysits for, with painful results.

Script is remarkably mature in its dealings with teens. Characters are funny and vulnerable but capable of shaping their lives, and script artfully weaves in themes of class, destiny and friendship.

●●●●●●●●●●●●●●●●●●●●●●●●●●●●●●●●

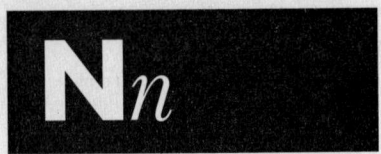

Nn

NADINE

1987, 83 MINS, US ◇ Ⓥ ⊙

Dir Robert Benton   *Prod* Arlene Donovan   *Scr* Robert Benton   *Ph* Nestor Almendros   *Ed* Sam O'Steen   *Mus* Howard Shore   *Art Dir* Paul Sylbert
● Jeff Bridges, Kim Basinger, Rip Torn, Gwen Verdon, Glenne Headly, Jerry Stiller (Tri-Star/Delphi Premier)

Nadine is an innocuous souffle from writer-director Robert Benton so lightweight that in the end one can't help wondering where the film is. Set in Austin in 1954, Benton tries to get by on Texas charm but the recipe of screwball comedy and small-town thriller fails to jell.

Jeff Bridges and Kim Basinger are husband and wife on the verge of divorce drawn together again by a suspicious killing. As Vernon Hightower, proprietor of the unsuccessful Bluebonnet saloon, Bridges has a smile and an excuse for every mishandled situation. As Nadine, Basinger is a kvetch with a twang, who gives manicures in the local beauty parlor.

Things get going when Basinger witnesses the murder of two-bit photographer Raymond Escobar (Jerry Stiller) who happens to have in his possession some 'art' shots of Nadine, thereby giving her a motive for the killing. The real meat of the matter are some photos for a proposed highway that Escobar has gotten his hands on and local mobster Buford Pope (Rip Torn) wants back at any cost.

Pope is the only truly interesting character here and the film comes alive when he's on the screen.

NAKED

1993, 131 MINS, UK ◇ Ⓥ

Dir Mike Leigh   *Prod* Simon Channing-Williams   *Scr* Mike Leigh   *Ph* Dick Pope   *Ed* Jon Gregory   *Mus* Andrew Dickson   *Art Dir* Alison Chitty
● David Thewlis, Lesley Sharp, Katrin Cartlidge, Greg Cruttwell, Claire Skinner, Peter Wight (Thin Man/Film Four)

A Stygian comedy on '90s London social angst, Mike Leigh's *Naked* will come as a major surprise to those reared on lighter fare like *Life Is Sweet* and *High Hopes*. Shot through with sudden, psychotic mood shifts, from comedy to violence to, finally, a strangely moving love story, pic dwarfs everything the director has yet done.

Center of Leigh's script – as with prior movies – is an unemployed philosopher-bum, Johnny (David Thewlis), who's fled south from Manchester and initially stays with former g.f. Louise (Lesley Sharp). After bedding her loopy flatmate, punkette Sophie (Katrin Cartlidge), he suddenly ups and leaves on a weird nocturnal odyssey on the streets of London.

Naked plays lighter than it reads, thanks to wonderful straight-faced thesping of Leigh's dry, humour-filled script. Anchored by a confident tour de force from Thewlis, perfs by the hand-chosen cast mesh splendidly, with Cartlidge (recalling the Jane Horrocks character in *Life*) delivering a wonderful array of one-liners. Dialogue is four-letter stuff all the way.

NAKED AND THE DEAD, THE

1958, 131 MINS, US ◇ Ⓥ

Dir Raoul Walsh   *Prod* Paul Gregory   *Scr* Denis Sanders, Terry Sanders   *Ph* Joseph LaShelle   *Ed* Arthur P. Schmidt   *Mus* Bernard Herrmann   *Art Dir* Ted Haworth
● Aldo Ray, Cliff Robertson, Raymond Massey, Lili St Cyr, Barbara Nichols, Richard Jaeckel (RKO)

The film bears little more than surface resemblance to the hard hitting Norman Mailer novel of the same title. It catches neither the spirit nor the intent of the original yarn and thus becomes just another war picture, weighed with some tedious dialog sporadically lifted from the book.

The characters go through the motions, hating themselves, hating each other, hating the jungle war that flares around them.

The action sequences come in spurts, but when they do, lenser Joseph LaShelle sees to it that they impress and the dangers of the jungle warfare become vividly real. Unfortunately, a good deal of the footage is taken up with the platoon moving up a mountain or down a mountain, crossing rivers, etc and, after a while, these scenes begin to wear thin.

Aldo Ray plays the frustrated, bitter and sadistic Sergeant Croft. It's not a very plausible part in the first place, and the strenuous efforts to 'explain' him (his wife, Barbara Nichols, has been unfaithful) don't help. Ray plays this beefy character with gusto and certain raw power.

As the playboy whom the general picks as his aide, Cliff Robertson turns in a slick performance. He's good in his verbal encounters with the general, whom he eventually defies, but lacks conviction once he's assigned to lead the Croft platoon on its final sortie.

NAKED CITY, THE

1948, 94 MINS, US

Dir Jules Dassin   *Prod* Mark Hellinger   *Scr* Albert Maltz, Malvin Wald   *Ph* William Daniels   *Ed* Paul Weatherwax   *Mus* Miklos Rozsa, Frank Skinner   *Art Dir* John F. DeCuir
● Barry Fitzgerald, Howard Duff, Dorothy Hart, Don Taylor, Ted De Corsia (Universal)

Naked City is a boldly fashioned yarn [by Malvin Wald] about eastside, westside; about Broadway, the elevated, Fifth Avenue; about kids playing hop-skip-and-jump; about a populace of 8 million – about a blond beaut's mysterious murder in an upper-westside apartment house.

Hellinger's off-screen voice carries the narrative. At the very opening he describes New York, with the aid of a mobile camera, and its teeming humanity. Kids at play, subway straphangers, street vendors on Orchard Street. Then that blonde with a questionable background who is mysteriously murdered. The kind of a story that Hellinger, one of the great tabloid crime reporters of the bathtub-gin era, used to write.

In this pic there are no props. A Manhattan police station scene was photographed in the police station; a lower eastside cops-and-robbers chase was actually filmed in the locale; the ghetto and its pushcarts were caught in all their realism.

Throughout, despite its omniscient, stark melodrama, there has been no sight lost of an element of humor. Barry Fitzgerald, as the film's focal point, in playing the police lieutenant of the homicide squad, strides through the role with tongue in cheek, with Don Taylor as his young detective aide.

☐ 1948: Best B&W Cinematography, Editing.
☐ Nomination: Best Motion Picture Story

NAKED EDGE, THE

1961, 99 MINS, US

Dir Michael Anderson   *Prod* Walter Seltzer, George Glass   *Scr* Joseph Stefano   *Ph* Erwin Hillier   *Ed* Gordon Pilkington   *Mus* William Alwyn   *Art Dir* Carmen Dillon
● Gary Cooper, Deborah Kerr, Eric Portman, Diane Cilento, Hermione Gingold, Peter Cushing (United Artists/Pennebaker-Baroda)

The picture that winds up Gary Cooper's long list of credits is a neatly constructed, thoroughly professional little suspense meller.

Based on Max Ehrlich's novel, *First Train to Babylon*, Joseph Stefano's screenplay casts Cooper as an American businessman living in London who, coincidentally to the murder of his business partner (and the disappearance of a couple of hundred thousand dollars), happens to make a killing on the stock-market, which funds he uses to make an even bigger fortune.

When, five years later, a blackmailer in the form of Eric Portman turns up to accuse her husband of the murder, Deborah Kerr remembers that Cooper, after all, had been the key prosecution witness at the murder trial and had come into a lot of money quite suddenly. The lady's further investigations confirm her suspicions.

Kerr suffers very prettily in a highly emotional role. Cooper, perhaps because he must appear to be enigmatic most of the time, gives a less successful performance. The picture, filmed entirely in London, utilizes some fine British supporting people.

NAKED GUN, THE
FROM THE FILES OF POLICE SQUAD!

1988, 85 MINS, US ◇ Ⓥ ⊙

Dir David Zucker   *Prod* Robert K. Weiss   *Scr* Jerry Zucker, Jim Abrahams, David Zucker, Pat Proft   *Ph* Robert Stevens   *Ed* Michael Jablow   *Mus* Ira Newborn   *Art Dir* John J. Lloyd
● Leslie Nielsen, George Kennedy, Priscilla Presley, Ricardo Montalban, O.J. Simpson, Nancy Marchand (Paramount)

The Naked Gun is crass, broad, irreverent, wacky fun – and absolutely hilarious from beginning to end.

Subtitled *From the Files of Police Squad!*, based on ill-fated too-hip-for-TV series a few seasons earlier, comedy from the crazed Jerry Zucker, Jim Abrahams, David Zucker yock factory is chockablock with sight gags.

Leslie Nielsen is the clumsy detective reprising his TV role and George Kennedy his straight sidekick who wreaks havoc in the streets of LA trying to connect shipping magnate and socialite Ricardo Montalban with heroin smuggling.

Scintilla of a plot weaves in an inspired bit of nonsense with Queen Elizabeth II lookalike Jeannette Charles as the target for assassination at a California Angels' baseball games, where she stands up and does the wave like any other foolish-looking fan, plus a May-December romance between Nielsen and vapid-acting Priscilla Presley whose exchanges of alternately drippy or suggestive dialog would make great material for a soap parody.

NAKED GUN 2½, THE
THE SMELL OF FEAR, THE

1991, 85 MINS, US ◇ Ⓥ ⊙

Dir David Zucker   *Prod* Robert K. Weiss   *Scr* David Zucker, Pat Proft   *Ph* Robert Stevens   *Ed* James Symons, Chris Greenbury   *Mus* Ira Newborn   *Art Dir* John J. Lloyd
● Leslie Nielsen, Priscilla Presley, George Kennedy, O.J. Simpson, Robert Goulet, Richard Griffiths (Paramount)

The Naked Gun 2½ is at least two-and-a-half times less funny than its hilarious 1988 progenitor. But even if the laugh machine isn't operating at top efficiency, it still cranks out a few choice bits of irreverent lunacy.

Clothesline plot, designed to make the most of director David Zucker's environmental concerns, has bad guy Robert Goulet kidnaping the president's wheelchair-bound energy czar and replacing him with a lookalike who will endorse continued heavy reliance on oil, coal and nuclear power.

Case sees Lt. Frank Drebin (Leslie Nielsen) catching up with his erstwhile inamorata (Priscilla Presley) who, we learn, dumped him two years earlier. After an amusing rendezvous in a truly blue jazz boite, pair communes soulfully over a potter's wheel in a send-up of *Ghost*, and Drebin doesn't seem threatened by a newspaper headline that announces, 'Elvis Spotted Buying Condo in Aspen.'

Nielsen seems just a tad more self-aware than he was in the original. Whereas O.J. Simpson, who reappears here as the hapless Nordberg, took the brunt of physical abuse in the first *Naked Gun*, that honor in the sequel falls to Margery Ross, whose Barbara Bush hardly goes a minute without taking a nasty fall or hit.

· ·

■ NAKED KISS, THE

1965, 90 MINS, US ⊙
Dir Samuel Fuller   *Prod* Samuel Fuller   *Scr* Samuel Fuller   *Ph* Stanley Cortez   *Ed* Jerome Thoms   *Mus* Paul Dunlap   *Art Dir* Eugene Lourie
● Constance Towers, Anthony Eisley, Michael Dante, Virginia Grey, Patsy Kelly, Marie Devereux (Allied Artists/Firks)

Good Samuel Fuller programmer about a prostie trying the straight route, *The Naked Kiss* is primarily a vehicle for Constance Towers. Hooker angles and sex perversion plot windup are handled with care, alternating with handicapped children 'good works' theme.

Action starts fast with brawl between hardened prostie Kelly (Towers) and cheating pimp who shaved her head, after which she takes to sticks, where she promptly makes it with local cop Griff. Role is played routinely throughout by Anthony Eisley.

Pic bogs down at this point in cliches, as hooker rejects berth in nearby red-lighter run by an effective hard-bitten Virginia Grey, instead taking up rehabilitation of crippled children under wing of Patsy Kelly who makes the most of her few lines.

Towers' overall effect is good, director Fuller overcoming his routine script in displaying blonde looker's acting range.

· ·

■ NAKED LUNCH

1991, 115 MINS, CANADA/UK ◇ ⓥ ⊙
Dir David Cronenberg   *Prod* Jeremy Thomas   *Scr* David Cronenberg   *Ph* Peter Suschitzky   *Ed* Ronald Sanders   *Mus* Howard Shore   *Art Dir* Carol Spier
● Peter Weller, Judy Davis, Ian Holm, Julian Sands, Roy Scheider, Monique Mercure (Thomas)

William S. Burroughs' notorious, and notoriously unfilmable, novel *Naked Lunch* has landed in the right hands. Stretching himself with each new work, David Cronenberg has come up with a fascinating, demanding, mordantly funny picture.

A cult novel since its publication in 1959, Burroughs' non-narrative novel represented the literary equivalent of a Heironymous Bosch painting, a profane, outrageous explosion of riffs dominated by drugs, gay sex and a surreal evocation of society's control mechanisms.

At the center of this chilly emotional spiral is William Lee (Burroughs' alter ego and early pseudonym), an insect exterminator in New York City circa 1953. Lee (Peter Weller) lives in quiet squalor with his wife (Judy Davis) until, on a bug drug high, he accidentally shoots her while playing *William Tell*.

Breaking into a hallucinatory state, Lee escapes to the realm of Interzone, an imaginatively demented rendition of Tangier heavily populated by artist addicts, homosexuals and secret agents where he is able to begin writing, even if what he is writing are 'reports' over which he seems to have no actual control.

Weller is a superb Burroughs stand-in, strongly holding centerscreen while not actually doing much. Supporting cast is diverse and outstanding. Dissuaded from actually shooting in Tangier by the outbreak of the 1991 Gulf War, Cronenberg's team has memorably created an artificial world almost entirely on stages.

· ·

■ NAKED PREY, THE

1966, 86 MINS, US ◇ ⓥ ⊙
Dir Cornel Wilde   *Prod* Cornel Wilde   *Scr* Clint Johnston, Don Peters   *Ph* H.A.R. Thomson   *Ed* Roger Cherrill   *Mus* Andrew Tracey (adv.)   *Art Dir* [uncredited]
● Cornel Wilde, Gert Van Der Berg, Ken Gampu, Patrick Mynhardt, Bella Randles, Morrison Gampu (Theodora/Persson)

Filmed entirely in South Africa, *The Naked Prey* is a story of a white man's survival under relentless pursuit by primitive tribesman. Told with virtually no dialog, the story embodies a wide range of human emotion, depicted in actual on-scene photography which effects realism via semi-documentary feel.

The basic story is set in the bush country of a century ago, where safari manager Cornel Wilde and party are captured by natives offended by white hunter Gert Van Der Berg. All save Wilde are tortured in some explicit footage that is not for the squeamish, while he is given a chance to survive – providing he can exist while eluding some dedicated pursuers.

Action then roves between the macroscopic and the microscopic; that is, from long shots of the varying bush country, caught in beautiful soft tones by H.A.R. Thomson's camera, where man is a spot on the landscape, all the way down to minute animal life, in which the pattern of repose, pursuit, sudden death and then repose matches that of Wilde and the natives.

Ken Gampu, film and legit actor in South Africa, is excellent as the leader of the pursuing warriors.
□ 1966: Nomination: Best Original Story & Screenplay

· ·

■ NAKED RUNNER, THE

1967, 104 MINS, UK ◇ ⓥ
Dir Sidney J. Furie   *Prod* Brad Dexter   *Scr* Stanley Mann   *Ph* Otto Heller   *Ed* Barrie Vince   *Mus* Harry Sukman   *Art Dir* Peter Proud
● Frank Sinatra, Peter Vaughan, Derren Nesbitt, Nadia Gray, Toby Robins, Inger Stratton (Warner/Sinatra)

From a Francis Clifford novel, writer Stanley Mann has fashioned a dullsville script, based on premise that British Intelligence cannot assign one of its own to murder a defector to Russia.

Instead, Frank Sinatra, a Second World War spy now a businessman-widower, is dragooned into service, and by events, deliberately staged, is goaded into killing the defector. Not only British Intelligence, but anybody's intelligence, is likely to be affronted by this potboiler.

Sinatra, whose personal magnetism and acting ability are unquestioned, is shot down by script. Peter Vaughan overacts part as the British agent.

· ·

■ NAKED SPUR, THE

1953, 91 MINS, US ◇ ⓥ
Dir Anthony Mann   *Prod* William H. Wright   *Scr* Sam Rolfe, Harold Jack Bloom   *Ph* William Mellor   *Ed* George White   *Mus* Bronislau Kaper   *Art Dir* Cedric Gibbons, Malcolm Brown
● James Stewart, Janet Leigh, Robert Ryan, Ralph Meeker, Millard Mitchell (M-G-M)

This is a taut outdoor melodrama made to order for the western action addict who likes

rugged dramatics delivered without dilution. Film has been tersely produced with no waste motion in getting the violence of the original screen story on film.

Plot deals with the violence to which greed spurs the oddly assorted characters caught up in the story. James Stewart is after Robert Ryan, an outlaw killer, so he can collect a $5,000 reward and start a ranch. As he corners the killer in the mountains after a long, arduous chase, he is joined by Millard Mitchell, an old prospector, and Ralph Meeker, who has just been dishonorably discharged from the Union Army.

They aid in the capture and determine to share in the reward, so it is a party at cross-purposes that starts the long trek back. During the journey, Ryan sets his captors against each other and, to further his aims at escape, uses Janet Leigh, an outlaw's daughter, to stir up trouble between Stewart and Meeker, both of whom are attracted to the girl.

The rugged beauty of the Colorado mountain location where film was shot is splendidly shown by William Mellor's cameras.
□ 1953: Nomination: Best Story & Screenplay

· ·

■ NAKED UNDER LEATHER

See: The Girl on a Motorcycle

· ·

■ NAME OF THE ROSE, THE

1986, 130 MINS, W. GERMANY/ITALY/FRANCE ◇ ⓥ ⊙
Dir Jean-Jacques Annaud   *Prod* Bernd Eichinger   *Scr* Andrew Birkin, Gerard Brach, Howard Franklin, Alain Godard   *Ph* Tonino Delli Colli   *Ed* Jane Seitz   *Mus* James Horner   *Art Dir* Dante Ferretti
● Sean Connery, F. Murray Abraham, Christian Slater, Michel Lonsdale, Ron Perlman, Valentina Vargas (Neue Constantin/Cristaldifilm/Ariane/ZDF)

The Name of the Rose is a sorrowfully mediocre screen version of Umberto Eco's surprise international bestselling novel.

Confusingly written and sluggishly staged, this telling of a murder mystery in a 14th-century abbey has been completely flubbed by director Jean-Jacques Annaud and his team of four (credited) screenwriters, as they struggle even to get the basics of the story up on the screen.

Tale has English Franciscan monk Sean Connery and his novice Christian Slater arriving at an Italian abbey in preparation for a conclave. After a series of murders at the massive edifice Connery, in the style of an aspiring Sherlock Holmes, undertakes an investigation of the deaths while more delegates continue to arrive.

One of the latecomers if F. Murray Abraham, an inquisitor who sees Satan behind every foul deed and who threatens to condemn his old rival Connery due to the latter's insistence on seeking a rational solution to the crimes.

Connery lends dignity, intelligence and his lovely voice to the proceedings. His performance, however, along with some tantalizing E.M. Escher-style labyrinths in the interior of the abbey, are about the only blessings.

· ·

■ NANA

1934, 87 MINS, US
Dir Dorothy Arzner   *Prod* Samuel Goldwyn   *Scr* Willard Mack, Harry Wagstaff Gribble   *Ph* Gregg Toland   *Ed* Frank Lawrence   *Mus* Alfred Newman (dir.)   *Art Dir* Richard Day
● Anna Sten, Phillips Holmes, Lionel Atwill, Richard Bennett, Mae Clarke, Muriel Kirkland (Goldwyn/United Artists)

Sam Goldwyn brilliantly launches a new star in a not so brilliant vehicle. Anna Sten has beauty, glamour, charm, histrionic ability (although there are a couple of moments which seemed a bit beyond her), and s.a.

The script is a very free adaptation of Emile Zola's famous novel. Much care is evident to make it as circumspect as possible and yet maintain its color and allure which is the basis of this transition of a Parisian gamine to music hall heights.

It ends on a tragic note with a suicide by the glorified gamine who takes this way out to reunite the two brothers, Phillips Holmes whom she loves, and Lionel Atwill, his maturer kin, who has coveted her and who subsequently patronizes her when the younger brother is transferred with his regiment to Algiers.

In between there is Richard Bennett as the great Greiner, the master showman, who decides to clay this new unglorified model into the toast of the revue halls.

Sten's likening to Marlene Dietrich becomes inevitable. Her throaty manner of singing 'That's Love' (the sole Rodgers-Hart song in the film) brings that home even more forcibly, apart from her light dialectic Teutonic brogue and the same general aura in personality. The Dorothy Arzner style of direction likewise recalls the Sternberg-Mamoulian technique employed in Dietrich's behalf.

· ·

■ NANNY, THE

1965, 93 MINS, UK ⓥ

Dir Seth Holt   *Prod* Jimmy Sangster   *Scr* Jimmy Sangster   *Ph* Harry Waxman   *Ed* James Needs, Tom Simpson   *Mus* Richard Rodney Bennett   *Art Dir* Edward Carrick

● Bette Davis, Wendy Craig, Jill Bennett, James Villiers, William Dix, Pamela Franklin (Hammer)

It's not necessary to be an astute student to guess that Bette Davis as a middle-aged Mary Poppins in a fairly fraught household will eventually be up to no good. Which immediately sets the odds against screenwriter Jimmy Sangster and director Seth Holt. But, in fairness, the balance of power between Davis, posing as a devoted nanny, and William Dix as a knowing youngster who hates Davis's innards, is so skillfully portrayed to make *The Nanny* a superior psycho-thriller.

It's an added plus to the pic [from the novel by Evelyn Piper] that neither writer nor director teeters over the edge into hysterics, and the cast has cottoned on and helped to build up the suspense gently but with a steely pricking of the nerve ends.

Yarn, briefly, concerns the relationship between nanny Davis and Master Joey (Dix) which is less than cordial. He comes out of a school for the unstable to which he has been sent when his baby sister is found drowned in the bath. He insists it was nanny's fault, but, of course, the adults don't believe him.

Davis handles her assignment with marked professionalism, and copes with plenty of knowhow competition. Wendy Craig is fine as a weak, fond young mama whose nerves are shot to pieces by the household happenings.

· ·

■ NANOOK OF THE NORTH

1922, 55 MINS, (1947 SOUND VERSION), US ⓥ

Dir Robert J. Flaherty   *Scr* Robert J. Flaherty, Carl Stearns Clancy   *Ph* Robert J. Flaherty   *Ed* Herbert Edwards (1947)   *Mus* Rudolf Schramm (1947)

● (Revillon Freres)

Nanook of the North is the granddaddy (or the Eskimo equivalent) of all documentaries and widely extolled as the classic in its field. Despite the comparatively primitive technique and the natural difficulties of shooting a film in the frozen Hudson Bay wastelands, every minute of *Nanook* lives up to its reputation.

Yarn holds tremendous interest in detailing the life of an Eskimo family through the seasons of the year.

Ralph Schoolman's narrative hits the proper note. It treats the Eskimos with dignity, yet with a sense of humor, and it never gets pompous. Berry Kroeger likewise sticks to a simple, friendly, yet thoroughly dignified style in speaking the narration.

· ·

■ NARROW MARGIN, THE

1952, 71 MINS, US ⓥ ⊙

Dir Richard Fleischer   *Prod* Stanley Rubin   *Scr* Earl Felton   *Ph* George E. Diskant   *Ed* Robert Swink   *Art Dir* Albert S. D'Agostino, Jack Okey

● Charles McGraw, Marie Windsor, Jacqueline White, Gordon Gebert, Queenie Leonard, Don Beddoe (RKO)

A standard amount of cops-and-robber melodramatics are stirred up most of the time in *The Narrow Margin*. Plot falls apart at the climax, but regulation thriller tricks, tersely played, carry the story [by Martin Goldsmith and Jack Leonard] along sufficiently.

Two Los Angeles detectives (Charles McGraw and Don Beddoe) are sent to Chicago to escort the widow of a racketeer to the Coast for testimony before the grand jury. Beddoe is killed and McGraw starts back with Marie Windsor, closely pursued by gangsters who want to keep the widow from testifying. Chase makes for some excitement aboard the train as McGraw keeps outwitting the crooks.

Trouping is competent, with McGraw showing up excellently in his tight-lipped, terse cop portrayal. Windsor impresses the most among the femmes.

□ 1952: Nomination: Best Motion Picture Story

· ·

■ NARROW MARGIN

1990, 97 MINS, US ◇ ⓥ ⊙

Dir Peter Hyams   *Prod* Jonathan A. Zimbert   *Scr* Peter Hyams   *Ph* Peter Hyams   *Ed* James Mitchell   *Mus* Bruce Broughton   *Art Dir* Joel Schiller

● Gene Hackman, Anne Archer, James B. Sikking,, J.T. Walsh, M. Emmet Walsh, Susan Hogan (Carolco)

Spectacular stunt work and Canadian locations punch up the train thriller *Narrow Margin*, but feature remake is too cool and remote to grab the viewer. Richard Fleischer's trim 1952 classic for RKO had a negative cost of only $230,000, while the remake logs in at $21 million. That extra bread shows up on screen in impressive production values but filmmaker Peter Hyams fails to make his story involving.

Basic plotline is retained in the new version. In the Charles McGraw role, Gene Hackman plays a deputy d.a. delivering key witness Anne Archer to testify against gangster Harris Yulin. Hackman's teammate, cop M. Emmet Walsh, is killed leaving Hackman and Archer to escape from a helicopter of armed heavies. They flee to a train headed across remote stretches of Canada and have to play cat and mouse with the thugs (led by evil James B. Sikking) who've boarded the train to eliminate them.

Hackman adds panache to a one-dimensional role. Archer is stuck with a nothing part, given barely one monolog to express her character's feelings. Curiously there is no sex or suggestion of romance in the film.

· ·

■ NASHVILLE

1975, 157 MINS, US ◇ ⓥ ⊙

Dir Robert Altman   *Prod* Robert Altman   *Scr* Joan Tewkesbury   *Ph* Paul Lohmann   *Ed* Sidney Levin, Dennis Hill   *Mus* Richard Baskin

● Ned Beatty, Karen Black, Keith Carradine, Geraldine Chaplin, Shelley Duvall, Henry Gibson (Paramount/ABC)

One of the most ambitious, and more artistically, successful, 'backstage' musical dramas,

Robert Altman's *Nashville* is strung on the plot thread of a George Wallace-type pre-Presidential campaign in which the interactions of 24 principal characters are followed over the period of a few days in the country music capitol of America.

Outstanding among the players are Henry Gibson, as a respected music vet with an eye on public office; Ronee Blakely, in a great film debut as a c&w femme star on the brink of nervous collapse; Gwen Welles, drawing tears from stone as a pitiably untalented waitress who undergoes the humiliation of stripping at a stag party for a chance to sing. Among some real life cameos are Elliott Gould and Julie Christie, both as themselves on p.a. tours.

Nashville is one of Altman's best films, free of the rambling insider fooling around that sometimes mars entire chunks of every second or third picture. When he navigates rigorously to defined goals, however, the results are superb.

□ 1975: Best Song ('I'm Easy').
□ Nominations: Best Picture, Director, Supp. Actress (Ronee Blakely, Lily Tomlin)

· ·

■ NASTY HABITS

1976, 98 MINS, UK ◇ ⓥ

Dir Michael Lindsay-Hogg   *Prod* Robert Enders   *Scr* Robert Enders   *Ph* Douglas Slocombe   *Ed* Peter Tanner   *Mus* John Cameron   *Art Dir* Robert Jones

● Glenda Jackson, Melina Mercouri, Geraldine Page, Sandy Dennis, Anne Jackson, Anne Meara (Bowden)

A witty, intelligent screenplay [from Muriel Spark's novella *The Abbess of Crewe*] leaves no doubts that this is the Watergate circus transposed to a convent, complete with Machiavellian intrigues and power plays, sexual hanky panky, visiting plumbers, hypocritical television chats, national and international political play, roving ambassadors, and so on.

Told straight, it's all about the battle for power in a Philly convent once the aged abbess dies, an all-stops-out dirty scrap which pits establishment against young lib 'outsiders' who want a change.

Glenda Jackson is superb, making her role as the scheming climber unerringly her own. Only one actress nearly bests her: Edith Evans in a memorable cameo, the actress' last stint in a distinguished legit/pic career.

· ·

■ NATIONAL LAMPOON'S ANIMAL HOUSE

1978, 109 MINS, US ◇ ⓥ ⊙

Dir John Landis   *Prod* Matty Simmons, Ivan Reitman   *Scr* Harold Ramis, Douglas Kenney, Chris Miller   *Ph* Charles Correll   *Ed* George Folsey Jr   *Mus* Elmer Bernstein   *Art Dir* John J. Lloyd

● John Belushi, Tom Matheson, John Vernon, Verna Bloom, Tom Hulce, Donald Sutherland (Universal)

Steady readers of the *National Lampoon* may find *National Lampoon's Animal House* a somewhat soft-pedaled, punches-pulled parody of college campus life circa 1962. However, there's enough bite and bawdiness to provide lots of smiles and several broad guffaws.

Writers have concocted a pre-Vietnam college confrontation between a scruffy fraternity and high-elegant campus society. Interspersed in the new faces are the more familiar John Vernon, projecting well his meany charisma here as a corrupt dean; Verna Bloom, Vernon's swinging wife; Cesare Danova, the Mafioso-type mayor of the college town; Donald Sutherland as the superhip young professor in the days when squares were still saying 'hep'.

Of no small and subtle artistic help is the score by Elmer Bernstein which blithely wafts 'Gaudeamus Igitur' themes amidst the tumult of beer 'orgies', neo-Nazi ROTC drills, cafeteria food fights and a climactic disruption of a traditional Homecoming street parade.

Among the younger players, John Belushi and Tim Matheson are very good as leaders of the unruly fraternity, while James Daughton and Mark Metcalf are prominent as the snotty fratmen, all of whom, quite deliberately, look like Nixon White House aides.

. . . .

■ NATIONAL LAMPOON'S CHRISTMAS VACATION

1989, 97 MINS, US ◇ ⊽ ⊙
Dir Jeremiah S. Chechik   *Prod* John Hughes   *Scr* John Hughes   *Ph* Thomas Ackerman   *Ed* Jerry Greenberg   *Mus* Angelo Badalamenti   *Art Dir* Stephen Marsh
● Chevy Chase, Beverly D'Angelo, Randy Quaid, Diane Ladd, John Randolph, E.G. Marshall (Warner/Hughes)

Solid family fare with plenty of yocks, *National Lampoon's Christmas Vacation* is Chevy Chase and brood doing what they do best. Despite the title, which links it to previous pics in the rambling *Vacation* series, this third entry is firmly rooted at the Griswold family homestead, where Clark Griswold (Chase) is engaged in a typical over-reaching attempt to give his family a perfect, old-fashioned Christmas.

Acidic contrast to his fanatical focus on family comes from next-door neighbors Todd and Margot (Nicholas Guest and Julia Louis-Dreyfus) as a pair of suave young urbanites repelled by Chase's behavior. Script gets off some zingers at their lifestyles, too.

A group piece in which the ensemble keeps growing as relatives arrive, pic really gains momentum when Randy Quaid shows up as redneck ne'er-do-well cousin, Eddie, driving an RV that looks like a septic tank on wheels.

For the most part, helmer Jeremiah S. Chechick makes an adept debut, injecting plenty of energy and spirit.

. . . .

■ NATIONAL LAMPOON'S CLASS REUNION

1982, 84 MINS, US ◇ ⊽ ⊙
Dir Michael Miller   *Prod* Matty Simmons   *Scr* John Hughes   *Ph* Phil Lathrop   *Ed* Richard C. Meyer, Ann Mills   *Mus* Peter Bernstein, Mark Goldenberg   *Art Dir* Dean Edward Mitzner
● Gerrit Graham, Michael Lerner, Fred McCarren, Miriam Flynn, Stephen Furst, Marya Small (ABC)

It took them two tries and more than four years to come up with another National Lampoon picture after the hugely successful *Animal House*. Result, *National Lampoon's Class Reunion* gets sidetracked almost immediately thanks to a harebrained lunatic-on-the-loose plot in which the 1972 graduating class' high school is turned into the semblance of a haunted house.

Motley crew here includes former wiseacre Gerrit Graham, who's now become a snooty yacht salesman; Fred McCarren, a do-gooder with such a sparkling personality that no one can remember him; Miriam Flynn, a Little Miss Prim whose mind seems best suited to ordering refreshments for a sorority punch party; Stephen Furst, who gives the late John Belushi a run for his money in the girth department but not on the laugh meter.

Coming off a bit better are Marya Small as a blind nymphomaniac and Shelley Smith, who looks smashing in her silver evening gown and gets to do Diana Ross singing 'Stop! In the Name of Love'. Even guest star Chuck Berry seems at less than his best performing a quick medley in the early going.

. . . .

■ NATIONAL LAMPOON'S EUROPEAN VACATION

1985, 94 MINS, US ◇ ⊽ ⊙
Dir Amy Heckerling   *Prod* Matty Simmons   *Scr* John Hughes, Robert Klane   *Ph* Bob Paynter   *Ed* Pembroke J. Herring   *Mus* Charles Fox   *Art Dir* Bob Cartwright

● Chevy Chase, Beverly D'Angelo, Jason Lively, Dana Hill, Eric Idle, Victor Lanoux (Warner)

Most imaginative stroke is the passport-stamped credit sequence that opens this sequel to the 1983 *National Lampoon's Vacation*. Story [by John Hughes] of a frenetic, chaotic tour of the Old World, with Chevy Chase and Beverly D'Angelo reprising their roles as determined vacationers, is graceless and only intermittently lit up by lunacy and satire.

As the family of characters cartwheel through London, Paris, Italy and Germany – with the French deliciously taking it on the chin for their arrogance and rudeness – director Amy Heckerling gets carried away with physical humor while letting her American tourists grow tiresome and predictable. Structurally, the film unfolds like a series of travel brochures.

Uneven screenplay never sails, and it's left to Chase to fire up the film. His character is actually rather sympathetic – if boorish – in his insistence on turning every Continental moment into a delight (scanning Paris, he shouts 'I want to write, I want to paint, I got a romantic urge!').

. . . .

■ NATIONAL LAMPOON'S LOADED WEAPON 1

1993, 83 MINS, US ◇ ⊽ ⊙
Dir Gene Quintano   *Prod* Suzanne Todd, David Willis   *Scr* Don Holley, Gene Quintano   *Ph* Peter Deming   *Ed* Christopher Greenbury, Neil Kirk   *Mus* Robert Folk   *Art Dir* Jaymes Hinkle
● Emilio Estevez, Samuel L. Jackson, Jon Lovitz, Tim Curry, Kathy Ireland, William Shatner (New Line)

More an imitation than a parody, this would-be comedy is very short on laughs. Premise is spoofing Richard Donner's three *Lethal Weapon* movies right down to copying their logo.

Ostensible plotline [by Don Holley and Tori Tellem] has evil general William Shatner (allowed to ham it up disturbingly by director Gene Quintano) and goofy-accented henchman Tim Curry in a scheme involving cocaine and Girl Scout (that's Wilderness Girl) cookies. Investigation begins when cop Whoopi Goldberg (one of the few uncredited cameos) is murdered. Emilio Estevez is teamed with Goldberg's ex-partner Samuel L. Jackson, earmarked for the Danny Glover role.

The re-creation of scenes from *L.W.* movies includes Jackson's pretty daughter Danielle Nicolet playing footsie with Estevez from film 1 and Estevez comparing scars with heroine Kathy Ireland a la Rene Russo in film 3.

Film digresses at length with Kathy Ireland and an uncredited actress both playing Sharon Stone in *Basic Instinct* for some cheap potshots.

. . . .

■ NATIONAL LAMPOON'S VACATION

1983, 96 MINS, US ◇ ⊽ ⊙
Dir Harold Ramis   *Prod* Matty Simmons   *Scr* John Hughes   *Ph* Victor J. Kemper   *Ed* Pem Herring   *Mus* Ralph Burns   *Art Dir* Jack Collis
● Chevy Chase, Beverly D'Angelo, Anthony Michael Hall, Imogene Coca, Randy Quaid, John Candy (Warner)

National Lampoon's Vacation is an enjoyable trip through familiar comedy landscapes.

Chevy Chase is perfectly mated with Beverly D'Angelo as an average Chicago suburban couple setting out to spend their annual two-week furlough. Determined to drive, Chase wants to take the two kids to 'Walley World' in California. She would rather fly.

Despite home-computer planning, this trip is naturally going to be a disaster from the moment Chase goes to pick up the new car. No matter how bad this journey gets – and it gets pretty disastrous – Chases perseveres in treating each day as a delight, with D'Angelo's patient cooperation. His son,

beautifully played by Anthony Michael Hall, is a help, too.

Vacation peaks early with the family's visit to Cousin Eddie's rundown farm, rundown by the relatives residing there. As the uncouth cousin, Randy Quaid almost steals the picture.

Credit director Harold Ramis for populating the film with a host of well-known comedic performers in passing parts.

. . . .

■ NATIONAL VELVET

1944, 125 MINS, US ◇ ⊽ ⊙
Dir Clarence Brown   *Prod* Pandro S. Berman   *Scr* Theodore Reeves, Helen Deutsch   *Ph* Leonard Smith   *Ed* Robert J. Kern   *Mus* Herbert Stothart   *Art Dir* Cedric Gibbons, Urie McCleary
● Mickey Rooney, Donald Crisp, Elizabeth Taylor, Anne Revere, Angela Lansbury, Reginald Owen (M-G-M)

National Velvet is a horse picture with wide general appeal. The production also focuses attention on a new dramatic find – moppet Elizabeth Taylor.

Backgrounded in England, it tells of a former jockey (Mickey Rooney) who's become embittered through circumstances and plans to steal from a family that befriends him. But the family's 11-year-old daughter, Velvet softens him.

From this point on, early in the film, Velvet becomes the dominant character in the story [from the novel by Enid Bagnold]. The kid is nuts about horses. When a neighbor raffles off an unmanageable brute he's unable to handle she wins it on tickets paid for by Rooney. Over the objections of both Rooney and her father, nag is entered in the greatest race in England, the Grand National Sweepstakes.

Story is told with warmth and understanding. There is much detail, in this direction, between husband and wife; between Velvet and her mother and between the two kids, especially when Rooney confesses to an abiding fear of horses ever since he rode in a sweepstakes which ended in another jockey's death.

☐ 1945: Best Supp. Actress (Anne Revere), Editing.

☐ Nominations: Best Director, Color Cinematography, Color Art Direction

. . . .

■ NATURAL, THE

1984, 134 MINS, US ◇ ⊽ ⊙
Dir Barry Levinson   *Prod* Mark Johnson   *Scr* Robert Towne, Phil Dusenberry   *Ph* Caleb Deschanel   *Ed* Stu Linder   *Mus* Randy Newman   *Art Dir* Angelo Graham, Mel Bourne
● Robert Redford, Robert Duvall, Glenn Close, Kim Basinger, Wilford Brimley, Barbara Hershey (Tri-Star)

The Natural is an impeccably made, but quite strange, fable about success and failure in America. Robert Redford plays an aging rookie who takes the baseball world by storm in one season while dealing with demons from his past and present.

While remaining faithful to Bernard Malamud's 1952 novel in many regards, scenarists have drastically altered some major elements. Film thereby has become the story of the redemption of a born athlete whose life didn't unfold as anticipated.

Opening sequences present farmboy Roy Hobbs showing natural skill as a ballplayer and, upon the death of his father, carving his own magical bat, dubbed 'Wonderboy' from the wood of a lightning-struck tree.

Some years later, Hobbs, now in the person of Redford, leaves for Chicago, and raises the eyebrows of ace sports-writer and cartoonist Robert Duvall when he strikes out the majors' greatest hitter (Joe Don Baker) in an impromptu exhibition.

Redford is perfectly cast as the wary, guarded Hobbs. The female characters leave behind a bad taste, however, since they schematically and simplistically stand for the archaic angel-whore syndrome. Whenever he goes for harlots like Barbara Hershey or Kim Basinger, Redford is in big trouble, from which he must be rescued by Glenn Close.

☐ 1984: Nominations: Best Supp. Actress (Glenn Close), Cinematography, Art Direction, Original Score

....

■ NAUGHTY MARIETTA

1935, 105 MINS, US ⓥ ⊙
Dir W.S. Van Dyke   *Prod* Hunt Stromberg   *Scr* J.L. Mahin, Frances Goodrich, Albert Hackett   *Ph* William Daniels   *Ed* Blanche Sewell   *Mus* Herbert Stothart (adapt.)
● Jeanette MacDonald, Nelson Eddy, Frank Morgan, Elsa Lanchester, Douglas Dumbrille, Joseph Cawthorne (M-G-M)

An adaptation of the Victor Herbert operetta [book and lyrics by Rida Johnson Young] which the singing of Jeanette MacDonald and Nelson Eddy must carry. Much of the original score, plus a couple of added tunes [lyrics by Gus Kahn], is included. There are nine songs, but only one reprise, a martial tune from Eddy and his warriors.

This operetta tells of a group of girls the French government has endowed before they sail to Louisiana, there to find husbands and build up that colony. The princess (MacDonald) escapes with this group from her tyrannical uncle and the aged suitor he has selected. In New Orleans she falls in love with the captain of the mercenaries (Eddy) and again escapes for a happy finish.

The comedy being insufficient to sustain this much footage, with no especially exciting action, provides serious handicaps. Although Marietta may have been naughty in 1910, if she's still naughty it's her secret.

MacDonald sings particularly well and is favored with fine recording and exceptional photography. She also carries her share of the story capably and in her lighter moments gives a hint of what might be.

Picture marks the full-length debut of Eddy who reveals a splendid and powerful baritone with the distinct asset for the camera of not being breathy. Eddy is a tall, nice-looking boy who previously, briefly, appeared in a couple of Metro films. In this picture he sings so often that the script calls for his kidding himself about it.

Frank Morgan does a routine governor, with an eye for an ankle, dominated by his wife. Elsa Lanchester is the wife with an unattractive tendency to mug her points.

☐ 1935: Best Sound Recording.
☐ Nomination: Best Picture

....

■ NAVIGATOR, THE

1924, 60 MINS, US ⊗
Dir Donald Crisp, Buster Keaton   *Scr* Jean Havez, Clyde Bruckman, Joe Mitchell   *Ph* Elgin Lessley, Byron Houck   *Art Dir* Fred Gabourie
● Buster Keaton, Kathryn McGuire, Frederick Vroom (Metro-Goldwyn)

Buster Keaton's comedy is spotty. That is to say it's both commonplace and novel, with the latter sufficient to make the picture a laugh getter.

The film is novel in that it has Keaton in a deep-sea diving outfit with the camera catching him under water for comedy insertions. There's a possibility of doubling during some of the action, but close-ups are registered under water that reveal Keaton, personally, behind the glass within the helmet.

There's an abundance of funny business in connection with Keaton's going overboard to fix a propellor shaft and a thrill has been inserted through the comedian getting mixed up with a devil fish.

The actual story carries little weight. It has Keaton as a wealthy young man being matrimonially rejected by the girl. Having secured passage to Hawaii, he unknowingly boards a deserted steamship selected to be destroyed by foreign and warring factions. The girl's father, owner of the vessel, visits the dock, is set upon by the rogues who are bent on casting the liner adrift, and when the girl goes to her parent's rescue she is also caught on board with no chance of a return to land. The entire action practically takes place on the deserted ship, with the girl (Kathryn McGuire) and Keaton the only figures.

....

■ NAVIGATOR, THE A MEDIAEVAL ODYSSEY

1988, 93 MINS, AUSTRALIA/NEW ZEALAND ◇ ⓥ
Dir Vincent Ward   *Prod* John Maynard   *Scr* Vincent Ward, Kelly Lyons, Geoff Chapple   *Ph* Geoffrey Simpson   *Ed* John Scott   *Mus* Davood A. Tabrizi   *Art Dir* Sally Campbell
● Bruce Lyons, Chris Haywood, Hamish McFarlane, Marshall Napier, Noel Appleby, Paul Livingston (Arenafilm/NZ Film Investment Corp)

The Navigator is remarkable because of its absorbing story that links medieval fears and fortunes to our times, while confirming director Vincent Ward as an original talent.

The story begins in Cumbria in 1348, the year of the Black Death. Young Griffin (Hamish McFarlane) is anxious for the return of his beloved, much-older brother Connor (Bruce Lyons) from the outside world. He is haunted by a dream about a journey, a quest to a great cathedral in a celestial city, and a figure about to fall from a steeple.

When his brother returns to the village with tales of impending doom, the two brothers, with four comrades, set out on the journey fired by Griffin's prophetic dream. It takes them to a city of the late 1980s and on a mission against time if their village is to be saved.

The formidable skills of Ward are shown in the way his story works, not only as adventure, but as the love story of two brothers and a parable of faith and religion.

Geoffrey Simpson's photography – stark black and white for the Cumbrian sequences, color for the enactment of Griffin's dream and visions – is of the highest order, with score by Iranian composer Davood Tabrizi (domiciled in Sydney) empathetic with the whole.

....

■ NAVY LARK, THE

1959, 82 MINS, UK
Dir Gordon Parry   *Prod* Herbert Wilcox   *Scr* Sid Colin, Laurie Wyman   *Ph* Gordon Dines   *Ed* Basil Warren   *Mus* James Moody, Tommy Reilly   *Art Dir* Jim Morahan
● Cecil Parker, Ronald Shiner, Leslie Phillips, Elvi Hale, Nicholas Phipps, Cardew Robinson (20th Century-Fox)

The Navy Lark, based on a click BBC radio series is the oldie about a 'forgotten' naval base on an island off the South Coast of Britain. They're having a high old time feathering their nests with illicit smuggling and other rackets. The skipper's involved in fishing. His No. 1 yen is a pretty Wren officer's blonde charms. Suddenly higher authority decides that the minesweeping unit is redundant and from then on chaos breaks out as they scheme to avoid being posted elsewhere.

Only occasionally does the comedy creak. Then director Gordon Parry has the good fortune to have on hand some skilled performers who hold the fort. These include Cecil Parker, a master of the art of bumbling; Nicholas Phipps, as the probing senior officer constantly on the receiving end of indignity; Ronald Shiner, who boisterously can play a wily petty officer in his sleep; Cardew Robinson, extremely good as an over-diligent war correspondent, and Leslie Phillips, as a

philandering second officer.

On the distaff side there are a number of comely femmes who are mostly around to decorate the scene. Elvi Hale, as a Wren officer who causes the love light in Phillips' eye, has the brightest opportunity.

....

■ NAVY SEALS

1990, 113 MINS, US ◇ ⓥ ⊙
Dir Lewis Teague   *Prod* Brenda Feigen, Bernard Williams   *Scr* Chuck Pfarrer, Gary Goldman   *Ph* John A. Alonzo   *Ed* Don Zimmerman   *Mus* Sylvester LeVay   *Art Dir* Guy J. Comtois, Veronica Hadfield
● Charlie Sheen, Michael Biehn, Joanne Whalley-Kilmer, Rick Rossovich, Cyril O'Reilly, Bill Paxton (Orion)

Nifty performances make this routine action flick better than it probably has a right to be. Playing to the *Rambo* mentality by focusing on an elite naval-attack group kicking tail around the globe, the film won't be a favorite of peaceniks or any Arab anti-defamation leagues.

The film begins with a full-blown assignment and repeatedly sends the group out on elaborate suicide missions, showcasing plenty of gee-whiz gimickry in the process.

That first mission involves freeing US personnel from terrorists who, it turns out, have access to hand-held stinger missiles. The Navy Seals must subsequently locate the missiles and then eliminate them, aided (preposterously) by a beautiful TV reporter (Joanne Whalley-Kilmer).

Michael Biehn displays plenty of quiet determination, while Charlie Sheen cuts loose as a borderline psycho whose maverick style and cat-and-mouse games with death occasionally endanger fellow team members.

Director Lewis Teague brings real flair to much of the action, though the messy, overlong finale – set, no less, in the ravaged streets of Beirut – gets way out of hand.

....

■ NEAR DARK

1987, 95 MINS, US ◇ ⓥ ⊙
Dir Kathryn Bigelow   *Prod* Steven-Charles Jaffe   *Scr* Eric Red, Kathryn Bigelow   *Ph* Adam Greenberg   *Ed* Howard Smith   *Mus* Tangerine Dream   *Art Dir* Stephen Altman
● Adrian Pasdar, Jenny Wright, Lance Henriksen, Bill Paxton, Jenette Goldstein, Tim Thomerson (De Laurentiis)

Near Dark achieves a new look in vampire films. High-powered but pared down, slick but spare, this is a tale that introduces the unearthly into the banality of rural American existence.

Nervous, edgy opening has sharp young cowboy Adrian Pasdar hooking up with Jenny Wright, a good-looking new girl in town not averse to some nocturnal roistering as long as she gets home by dawn.

Wright soon welcomes Pasdar into her 'family', a bunch of real low-down boys and girls that would have done Charles Manson proud. Led by the spidery Lance Henriksen, the gang hibernates by day, but at night scours the vacant landscapes in search of prey.

Script by Kathryn Bigelow and Eric Red is cool and laconic, and the evildoers essentially come off as some very nasty bikers who kill for sport as well as necessity.

Main point of interest will be the work of Bigelow, who has undoubtedly created the most hard-edged, violent actioner ever directed by an American woman.

....

■ NECESSARY ROUGHNESS

1991, 108 MINS, US ◇ ⓥ
Dir Stan Dragoti   *Prod* Mace Neufeld, Robert Rehme   *Scr* Rick Natkin, David Fuller   *Ph* Peter Stein   *Ed* John Wright, Steve Mirkovich   *Mus* Bill Conti   *Art Dir* Paul Peters

N

● Scott Bakula, Hector Elizondo, Robert Loggia, Harley Jane Kozak, Larry Miller, Fred Dalton Thompson (Paramount)

This gridiron comedy piles up cliches the way Notre Dame racks up yardage, with an option-variety screenplay that promiscuously pitches the story in multiple directions. Essentially, this is a football version of the equally contrived and only slightly less hokey baseball comedy *Major League*.

Seemingly unable to settle on a single-wing hackneyed storyline, the filmmakers float at least three – a 34-year-old quarter-back seeks to belatedly claim his college glory days, a female kicker joins a football team and a team of 'real' students is assembled after a major college program is disbanded for recruiting violations – but basically settle on the former, with Scott Bakula carrying the ball.

The hurdles Bakula faces include wooing his attractive journalism prof (Harley Jane Kozak) and outwitting the priggish dean (Larry Miller), who's intent on punting the football program off-campus once and for all.

Director Stan Dragoti, who doesn't take the material too seriously, draws several procedure penalties for the horribly corny finale, slow-motion shots during the closing football game and for letting the air out of the ball with some long lulls in the action.

■ NED KELLY

1970, 101 MINS, UK ◇ ⦾
Dir Tony Richardson *Prod* Neil Hartley *Scr* Tony Richardson, Ian Jones *Ph* Gerry Fisher *Ed* Charles Rees *Mus* Shel Silverstein *Art Dir* Jocelyn Herbert
● Mick Jagger, Diane Craig, Clarissa Kaye, Frank Thring, Mark McManus, Allen Bickford (Woodfall)

Ned Kelly is basically an outback western in which director and coscripter Tony Richardson's simplicity becomes a pretension of its own. It is a film to which one applies the damning word 'interesting'.

In the 1870s Australia was a brutal frontier, settled by Irish, English and Scots convicts and their descendants.

In the film, the convict stock are continually harassed by the English police troopers and the settlers' ranging cattle and horses impounded by the authorities on the slightest pretext. Unable to exist otherwise, Kelly and the other Irishmen turn to rustling.

Mick Jagger is a natural actor and performer with a wide range of expressions and postures at his instinctive command. Given whiskers, that gaunt, tough pop hero face takes on a classic hard bitten frontier look that is totally believable for the role. However he has no one to play to. Jagger's Clyde has no Bonnie, his Sundance Kid has no Butch Cassidy.

■ NEIGHBORS

1981, 94 MINS, US ◇ ⦾ ⊙
Dir John G. Avildsen *Prod* Richard D. Zanuck, David Brown *Scr* Larry Gelbart *Ph* Gerald Hirschfield *Ed* John G. Avildsen, Jane Kurson *Mus* Bill Conti *Art Dir* Peter Larkin
● John Belushi, Kathryn Walker, Cathy Moriarty, Dan Aykroyd (Columbia)

Essentially the story of *Neighbors* focuses on staid suburbanite John Belushi who is slowly being driven crazy by his new, nutsy neighbors – a dyed blonde, goon Dan Aykroyd and his smooth, sexually scintillating wife Cathy Moriarty. The new couple take over his car, his bank account, his house and even his family while at the same time making it seem like Belushi is a stick-in-the mud poor sport for not going along with it.

Larry Gelbart's script [from the novel by Thomas Berger] seems content to leave it at that, yet both he and director John G. Avildsen take great pains to throw in some serious reminders of just how pathetic the

lives of each of these characters are including the fun-loving neighbors. Consequently, other than a few laughs the reason for the film is a little puzzling.

Ultimately it is Belushi and Aykroyd that make the picture work. When they hit the comedic mark, as they more often than not do here, nothing else seems to matter.

■ NELSON AFFAIR, THE

See: Bequest to the Nation

■ NEPTUNE'S DAUGHTER

1949, 92 MINS, US ◇ ⦾
Dir Edward Buzzell *Prod* Jack Cummings *Scr* Dorothy Kingsley *Ph* Charles Rosher *Ed* Irvine Warburton *Mus* Frank Loesser
● Esther Williams, Red Skelton, Ricardo Montalban, Betty Garrett, Keenan Wynn, Xavier Cugat (M-G-M)

Neptune's Daughter is a neat concoction of breezy, light entertainment. It combines comedy, songs and dances into an amusing froth.

Star sparkplugs are Esther Williams and Red Skelton. Williams' bathing beauty and Skelton's comedy make for a pleasing combination that does much to get over the pleasant, but fluffy, story.

Top tune of the Frank Loesser score is 'Baby, It's Cold Outside', dueted by Williams and Ricardo Montalban, and, for comedy, by Skelton and Garrett.

Story thread holding the antics together concerns itself with a bathing suit designer-manufacturer-model, Williams; her business partner, Keenan Wynn; her dumbdora sister, Betty Garrett; and Skelton, a masseur for a polo club.

Film includes a number of beautifully staged water sequences.
☐ 1949: Best Song ('Baby It's Cold Outside')

■ NETWORK

1976, 121 MINS, US ◇ ⦾ ⊙
Dir Sidney Lumet *Prod* Howard Gottfried *Scr* Paddy Chayefsky *Ph* Owen Roizman *Ed* Alan Heim *Mus* Elliot Lawrence *Art Dir* Philip Rosenberg
● Faye Dunaway, William Holden, Peter Finch, Robert Duvall, Wesley Addy, Ned Beatty (M-G-M)

Paddy Chayefsky's absurdly plausible and outrageously provocative original script concerns media running amok. Sidney Lumet's direction is outstanding.

This is a bawdy, stops-out, no-holds-barred story of a TV network that will, quite literally, do anything to get an audience.

The fictional TV network, United Broadcasting System, has been acquired by a conglomerate headed by Ned Beatty, whose hatchet man, Robert Duvall, succeeds to operating control. Peter Finch, the passe evening news anchorman is about to get the heave. To the dismay of all, Finch announces his own axing, becoming an instant character.

Finch's on-the-air freakout suggests to Faye Dunaway that she turn the news into a gross entertainment package. It works, of course.
☐ 1976: Best Actor (Peter Finch), Actress (Faye Dunaway), Supp. Actress (Beatrice Straight), Original Screenplay.
☐ Nominations: Best Picture, Director, Actor (William Holden), Supp. Actor (Ned Beatty), Cinematography, Editing

■ NEVADA SMITH

1966, 131 MINS, US ◇ ⦾ ⊙
Dir Henry Hathaway *Prod* Henry Hathaway *Scr* John Michael Hayes *Ph* Lucien Ballard *Ed* Frank Bracht *Mus* Alfred Newman *Art Dir* Hal Pereira, Tambi Larsen, Al Roelofs
● Steve McQueen, Karl Malden, Brian Keith, Arthur Kennedy, Suzanne Pleshette, Raf Vallone (Paramount/Embassy/Solar)

A good story idea – boy avenging his murdered parents and maturing in the process – is stifled by uneven acting, often lethargic direction, and awkward sensation-shock values. Overlength serves to dull the often spectacular production values.

John Michael Hayes scripted in routine fashion a story and screenplay based on a character from Harold Robbins' *The Carpetbaggers*. Hayes' yarn is not a sequel, but a precedessor work, in that it is centered on the Nevada Smith character who acted as guardian to Jonas Cord Jr, the youthful anti-hero of *Carpetbaggers*.

Steve McQueen is the young half-Indian boy whose parents are brutally murdered by Karl Malden, Arthur Kennedy and Martin Landau. Vowing revenge, McQueen sets off to kill them all. Brian Keith plays the elder Jonas Cord, then an itinerant gunsmith, who befriends the greenhorn and teaches him armed self-defense.

Henry Hathaway's uneven direction alternates jarring, overbearing fisticuffs with exterior footage as spectacular in some cases as it is dull in others.

■ NEVER A DULL MOMENT

1950, 89 MINS, US ⦾ ⊙
Dir George Marshall *Prod* Harriet Parsons *Scr* Lou Breslow, Doris Anderson *Ph* Joseph Walker *Ed* Robert Swink *Mus* Frederick Hollander
● Irene Dunne, Fred MacMurray, William Demarest, Andy Devine, Gigi Perreau, Natalie Wood (RKO)

Never a Dull Moment doesn't always live up to its title in telling the story of a smooth femme songwriter who falls in love with a western rancher and goes to his impoverished acreage to make a home. George Marshall's direction is a great help in selling the physical business that goes with the comedy, and where scripting isn't strong he still manages chuckles for the average audience.

Incidents build to a point where Irene Dunne, as the songsmith, accidentally kills the prize bull of cantankerous William Demarest, a neighbor on whom Fred MacMurray depends for water. The married couple quarrel, she takes off for the east and tunecleffing, but finds there's no inspiration now.

Demarest has little to do other than be grumpy. Andy Devine adds some comedy as MacMurray's friend. Gigi Perreau and Natalie Wood are good as the little girls. Three songs are spotted in the footage, all written by Kay Swift, who authored the novel on which the script was based.

■ NEVER CRY WOLF

1983, 105 MINS, US ◇ ⦾ ⊙
Dir Carroll Ballard *Prod* Lewis Allen, Jack Couffer, Joseph Strick *Scr* Curtis Hanson, Sam Hamm, Richard Kletter *Ph* Hiro Narita *Ed* Peter Parasheles, Michael Chandler *Mus* Mark Isham *Art Dir* Graeme Murray
● Charles Martin Smith, Brian Dennehy, Zachary Ittimangnaq, Samson Jorah, Hugh Webster, Martha Ittimangnaq (Walt Disney)

Never Cry Wolf is a story about the life-and-times of white wolves in the Arctic. Based on a bestseller by Farley Mowat (an autobiographical account of the popular writer's experiences as a government biologist in the Canadian Northwest), pic was two years in production in the wilds of the Yukon and Alaska, and it measures up to the promise Ballard amply provided in his first feature, *The Black Stallion*.

The stretch of location shooting in and around Dawson City, Yukon, and Nome, Alaska, tried the talents of the entire crew, from the documentarist Ballard to actor Charles Martin Smith in the role of the young biologist Tyler.

The story is simple: idiotically simple. Biologist Tyler is sent to survive in the Arctic while investigating whether the predatory wolf is responsible for the gradual disappearance of the caribou herds. A friendly but reticent Eskimo, Ootek (Zachary Ittimangnaq), fortunately happens by the helpless biologist's stake-out in the dead of winter to rescue him. Then begins the study of the white wolf. Biologist Tyler, in some of the wittiest, funniest, and most human scenes in the film, comes to know his research-quarry quite intimately.

The most praise goes to the imagery of this poetic fiction-documentary as fashioned by Ballard, cameraman Hiro Narita and soundman Alan R. Splet. Yet the magic of the film is in that quaint comic performance rendered by thesp Smith. He's the Goofy of the Walt Disney nature series.

● ●

■ **NEVERENDING STORY, THE**

1984, 94 MINS, W. GERMANY ◇ ▽ ⊙
Dir Wolfgang Petersen *Prod* Bernd Eichinger, Dieter Geissler *Scr* Wolfgang Petersen, Herman Weigel *Ph* Jost Vacano *Ed* Jane Seitz *Mus* Klaus Doldinger, Giorgio Moroder *Art Dir* Rolf Zehetbauer
● Noah Hathaway, Barret Oliver, Tami Stronach, Moses Gunn, Patricia Hayes, Sydney Bromley (Neue Constantin)

Wolfgang Petersen's *The Neverending Story* is a marvelously realized flight of pure fantasy.

With the support of top German, British and US technicians and artists plus a hefty $27 million budget (highest for any film made outside US or USSR), helmer Petersen has improved on pic's immediate forebear, Jim Henson/Frank Oz' 1982 *The Dark Crystal*, by avoiding too much unrelieved strangeness.

Film opens with a little boy, Bastian (Barret Oliver) borrowing a strange-looking book at a local bookstore and holes up in the school attic to read.

Book, titled *The Neverending Story*, depicts a world known as Fantasia, threatened by an advancing force called The Nothing (represented by storms) which is gradually destroying all. To save Fantasia, an ailing empress (Tami Stronach) sends for a young warrior from among the plains people, Atreyu (Noah Hathaway) to go on a quest to find a cure for her illness.

Filming at and backed by Munich's Bavaria Studios, *Story* benefits from special effects technicians working overtime to create a new-look world.

● ●

■ **NEVERENDING STORY II, THE THE NEXT CHAPTER**

1990, 89 MINS, GERMANY ◇ ▽ ⊙
Dir George Miller *Prod* Dieter Geissler *Scr* Karin Howard *Ph* Dave Connell *Ed* Peter Hollywood, Chris Blunden *Mus* Robert Folk *Art Dir* Bob Laing, Gotz Weidner
● Jonathan Brandis, Kenny Morrison, Clarissa Burt, Alexandra Johnes, Martin Umbach, John Wesley Shiff (Geissler)

Follow-up, produced by Germans based in Munich with location filming in Canada, Argentina, Australia, France and Italy, is a natural, since first film directed by Wolfgang Petersen only covered half of Michael Ende's classic novel.

Part II utilizes a whole new cast (except for Thomas Hill, reprising as Koreander the book-seller) to depict adventures in the imaginary world of Fantasia. Main innovation is that young hero Bastian joins his fantasy counterpart Atreyu in a heroic trek in search of the childlike empress locked in her Ivory Tower in Fantasia, rather than just reading about him.

Another improvement is the inclusion of a delicious villainess, dark beauty Clarissa Burt as Xayide, who suckers Bastian into making numerous wishes, each time losing a bit of his memory in return.

Film is effective in its own right, but as with most sequels, it lacks freshness. American actress Burt is any adolescent boy's fantasy seductress. Rest of the cast is adequate, but a letdown compared with the original's.

● ●

■ **NEVER GIVE AN INCH**
See: Sometimes a Great Notion

● ●

■ **NEVER GIVE A SUCKER AN EVEN BREAK**
(UK: What a Man)

1941, 70 MINS, US ▽ ⊙
Dir Edward Cline *Scr* John T. Noville, Prescott Chaplin *Ph* Charles Van Enger *Ed* Arthur Hilton *Mus* Frank Skinner
● W.C. Fields, Gloria Jean, Margaret Dumont, Susan Miller, Franklin Pangbourn (Universal)

W.C. Fields parades his droll satire and broad comedy in this takeoff on eccentricities of film making – from personal writings of the original story by Fields under nom de plume of Otis Criblecoblis. It's a hodge-podge of razzle-dazzle episodes, tied together in disjointed fashion but with sufficient laugh content for the comedian's fans.

Story focuses attention on Fields and his presentation of an imaginative script for his next picture at Esoteric Studios. In series of cutbacks depicting wild-eyed action as read by producer Franklin Pangborn, Fields horseplays in a plane, dives out to land on a mountain plateau safely, and finally leaves the studio to embark on a crashing auto chase.

Fields is Fields throughout. He wrote the yarn for himself, and knew how to handle the assignment. Picture is studded with Fieldsian satire and cracks – many funny and several that slipped by the blue-pencil squad. Byplay and reference to hard liquor is prominent throughout.

● ●

■ **NEVER LOVE A STRANGER**

1958, 91 MINS, US ▽
Dir Robert Stevens *Prod* Harold Robbins, Richard Day *Scr* Harold Robbins, Richard Day *Ph* Lee Garmes *Ed* Sidney Katz *Mus* Raymond Scott *Art Dir* Leo Kerz
● John Drew Barrymore, Lita Milan, Robert Bray, Steve McQueen, R.G. Armstrong (Allied Artists)

This New York locationed melodrama is so ineptly, unprofessionally done, especially in its handling of such volatile subjects as race and religion, that it has nothing else to recommend it.

John Drew Barrymore plays a young man raised in a Catholic orphanage who discovers when he is almost grown that his parents were Jewish. Under the law, he must be removed to the jurisdiction of an orphanage of his own faith. Young Barrymore is already involved with hoodlum elements and, feeling rejection by the orphanage that has been his home and parents, takes the final plunge into the gangster world.

Barrymore does an able job with his role although that is repeatedly sabotaged by a story that is persistently old hat in its approach to religion, gangsterism and unwed mothers, the three chief plot threads.

● ●

■ **NEVER SAY NEVER AGAIN**

1983, 137 MINS, US ◇ ▽ ⊙
Dir Irvin Kershner *Prod* Jack Schwartzman *Scr* Lorenzo Semple Jr. *Ph* Douglas Slocombe *Ed* Robert Lawrence, Ian Crafford *Mus* Michel Legrand *Art Dir* Philip Harrison, Stephen Grimes
● Sean Connery, Klaus Maria Brandauer, Max von Sydow, Barbara Carrera, Kim Basinger, Alec McCowen (Taliafilm)

After a 12-year hiatus, Sean Connery is back in action as James Bond. The new entry marks something of a retreat from the farfetched technology of many of the later Bonds in favor of intrigue and romance.

Although it is not acknowledged as such, pic is roughly a remake of the 1965 *Thunderball*. World-threatening organization SPECTRE manages to steal two US cruise missiles and announces it will detonate their nuclear warheads in strategic areas unless their outrageous ransom demands are met.

In short order, Bond hooks up with dangerous SPECTRE agent Fatima Blush (Barbara Carrera), who makes several interesting attempts to kill her prey, and later makes the acquaintance of Domino (Kim Basinger), g.f. of SPECTRE kingpin Largo (Klaus Maria Brandauer), who enjoys the challenge presented by the secret agent as long as he thinks he holds the trump card.

What clicks best in the film is the casting. Klaus Maria Brandauer makes one of the best Bond opponents since very early in the series. Carrera lets out all the stops, while Basinger is luscious as the pivotal romantic and dramatic figure.

And then, of course, there's Connery, in fine form and still very much looking the part.

● ●

■ **NEVER SO FEW**

1959, 126 MINS, US ◇ ▽ ⊙
Dir John Sturges *Prod* Edmund Grainger *Scr* Millard Kaufman *Ph* William C. Daniels *Ed* Ferris Webster *Mus* Hugo Friedhofer
● Frank Sinatra, Gina Lollobrigida, Peter Lawford, Steve McQueen, Richard Johnson, Paul Henreid (Canterbury/M-G-M)

Never So Few is one of those films in which individual scenes and sequences play with verve and excitement. It is only when the relation of the scenes is evaluated, and their cumulative effect considered, that the threads begin to unravel like an old, worn sock.

The locale of the screenplay, based on Tom T. Chamales' book, is Burma during World War II. Frank Sinatra is the iconoclastic, ruggedly individualistic commander of a small British-American task force. The bulk of his force is made up of native Kachin troops. He is idolized by them and his Occidental troops. Chief action of the film has Sinatra leading a foray against a Japanese position near the Chinese border in which some of his men are ambushed by a Nationalist Chinese group out for plunder.

Sinatra's romantic interest is Gina Lollobrigida, looking like about $15 million, who has been the pampered mistress of mystery man Paul Henreid. She will abandon her plush life with Henreid and go back to Indianapolis with Sinatra, she says.

Steve McQueen has a good part, and he delivers with impressive style. Richard Johnson, a British actor, is also a standout.

Never So Few did its principal photography on the Metro lot and on domestic locations, but it has some effective Ceylon photography that is neatly blended.

● ●

■ **NEVER TAKE SWEETS FROM A STRANGER**

1960, 81 MINS, UK
Dir Cyril Frankel *Prod* Anthony Hinds *Scr* John Hunter *Ph* Freddie Francis *Ed* Jim Neels *Mus* Elizabeth Lutyens
● Gwen Watford, Patrick Allen, Felix Aylmer, Niall MacGinnis, Alison Leggatt, Bill Nagy (Hammer)

The yarn is set in Canada. Though filmed in Britain, the Canadian atmosphere is remarkably well conveyed. It deals with a senile, psychopathic pervert (Felix Aylmer) with a yen for little girls. When he persuades two innocent little girls to dance naked in front of him in exchange for candy, the English parents of one of them decide to take him to court.

N

Unfortunately, they do not realize that he is the local big shot, the man who has helped to build the Canadian town to its prosperity and power.

Gwen Watford and Patrick Allen, as the distraught parents, and Alison Leggatt, as a wise, understanding grandmother, lead a cast which is directed with complete sensitivity by Cyril Frankel. Both Watford and Allen are completely credible while Leggatt, well-served by John Hunter's script, is outstanding.

Aylmer, who doesn't utter a word throughout the film, gives a terrifying acute study of crumbling evil, while Bill Nagy, as his son, is equally effective.

．．．．．．．．．．．．．．．．．．．．．．．．．

■ **NEVER TOO LATE**

1965, 104 MINS, US ◇
Dir Bud Yorkin   *Prod* Norman Lear   *Scr* Sumner Long
Ph Philip Lathrop   *Ed* William Ziegler   *Mus* David Rose
Art Dir Edward Carrere
● Paul Ford, Connie Stevens, Maureen O'Sullivan, Tim Hutton, Jane Wyatt, Lloyd Nolan (Tandem/Warner)

Outstanding direction and acting give full life to this well-expanded legiter about an approaching-menopause wife who becomes pregnant to the chagrin of hubby, spoiled-brat daughter, and free-loading son-in-law. Comedy ranges from sophisticated to near-slapstick, all handled in top form.

Sumner Arthur Long adapted his play which though essentially a one-joke affair he has filled out with exterior sequences which enhance, rather than pad. While the result is a family pic, it's not a pollyanna pot pourri of fluff.

Paul Ford and Maureen O'Sullivan are smartly re-teamed in their Broadway roles of small town Massachusetts parents, settled in middle-age habits until wife's increasing fatigue is diagnosed as pregnancy. O'Sullivan looks great and handles light comedy with a warm, gracious flair.

Ford carries the pic as the flustered father-to-be, saddled with the sly grins of neighbors, the incompetency of son-in-law Jim Hutton, and the domestic bumblings of daughter Connie Stevens.

．．．．．．．．．．．．．．．．．．．．．．．．．

■ **NEW ADVENTURES OF DON JUAN, THE**
See: Adventures of Don Juan

．．．．．．．．．．．．．．．．．．．．．．．．．

■ **NEW CENTURIONS, THE**
(UK: Precinct 45 – Los Angeles Police)

1972, 103 MINS, US ◇ ⊛ ⊙
Dir Richard Fleischer   *Prod* Irwin Winkler, Robert Chartoff   *Scr* Stirling Silliphant   *Ph* Ralph Woolsey
Ed Robert C. Jones   *Mus* Quincy Jones   *Art Dir* Boris Leven
● George C. Scott, Stacy Keach, Jane Alexander, Scott Wilson, Rosalind Cash, Erik Estrada (Columbia)

The New Centurions is a somewhat unsatisfying film. Story [from Joseph Wambaugh's novel] largely avoids like the plague any real confrontation with the gray areas of modern-day citizen-police interactions which are at the seat of unrest.

George C. Scott domintes the first 76 minutes, starring as the oldtime cop with a paradoxical philosophy. He sees nothing wrong in applying some pragmatic justice at the street level (there are several good, sometimes amusing episodes in this regard); at the same time, he is obviously blind to the realization that laws are contemporary reflections of transient attitudes which every few generations undergo a major flushing out.

Also starring is Stacy Keach. The nature of the plot necessarily makes Keach second banana to Scott. After Scott retires from the force the film falls off in impact.

．．．．．．．．．．．．．．．．．．．．．．．．．

■ **NEW JACK CITY**

1991, 97 MINS, US ◇ ⊛ ⊙
Dir Mario Van Peebles   *Prod* Doug McHenry, George Jackson   *Scr* Thomas Lee Wright, Barry Michael Cooper
Ph Francis Kenny   *Ed* Steven Kemper   *Mus* Michel Colombier   *Art Dir* Charles C. Bennett
● Wesley Snipes, Ice-T, Mario Van Peebles, Allen Payne, Judd Nelson, Chris Rock (Jackson-McHenry)

Filmmakers pull off a provocative, pulsating update on gangster pics with this action-laden epic about the rise and fall of an inner city crack dealer. Strongest element is the anger and disgust directed squarely at drug dealers.

Drawn from articles about real drug kingpins in *California* magazine and the *Wall Street Journal*, pic presents the fictional story [by Thomas Lee Wright] of Nino Brown (Wesley Snipes), who in 1986 foresees the potential of crack and by 1989 has built an empire around it. Term 'New Jack' was coined by journalist Barry Michael Cooper, pic's co-writer, to describe modern urban street life.

After Nino takes over an apartment building, brutally ejecting the tenants, police detective Stone (played by the director) recruits undercover cops Scotty (rap artist Ice-T) and Peretti (Judd Nelson) to bring him in.

It's clear from the start the filmmakers are out to blow the audiences away with pic's jacked-up hyperactive pace. Camera style is restless and aggressive. Problems of narrative flow mar the second half, with events jumping around without setup. Nonetheless, pic, filmed on location mostly in Harlem and the Bronx for $8.5 million, has a seat-of-the-pants energy guaranteed to sweep its target audience along.

．．．．．．．．．．．．．．．．．．．．．．．．．

■ **NEW LEAF, A**

1971, 102 MINS, US ◇ ⊛
Dir Elaine May   *Prod* Joe Manduke   *Scr* Elaine May
Ph Gayne Rescher   *Ed* Fredric Steinkamp, Donald Guidice   *Art Dir* Richard Fried
● Walter Matthau, Elaine May, Jack Weston, George Rose, William Redfield, James Coco (Paramount)

Walter Matthau is both broad and satirically sensitive and Elaine May has gotten off some sharp and amusing dialog in her screenplay. It's sophisticated and funny, adroitly put together for the most part. May complained in a court action that final cuts were not hers and she would prefer not to have identity as the director.

Matthau is the marriage-aloof middle-ager who's running out of his inheritance because of high living and who has to come upon a rich wife to sustain himself. Rich wife turns out to be unglamorous May. The director and cosmetician have made May about as sexy as an Alsophiplia Grahamicus, which is a new leaf she has cultivated in her role as botanist. A new leaf is also something that Matthau turns over because after he weds May he decides, rather than kill her, to take care of her like the fine character he hadn't been in the past.

William Redfield fits in as the exasperated lawyer who has difficulty in conveying to Matthau that one doesn't drive a Ferrari and live in a luxurious town house when one is broke. James Coco is Uncle Harry, to whom Henry goes for a loan, which is provided on condition that Henry pay it back in six weeks or pay 10 times the principal.

．．．．．．．．．．．．．．．．．．．．．．．．．

■ **NEW LIFE, A**

1988, 104 MINS, US ◇ ⊛ ⊙
Dir Alan Alda   *Prod* Martin Bregman   *Scr* Alan Alda
Ph Kelvin Pike   *Ed* William Reynolds   *Mus* Joseph Turrin
Art Dir Barbara Dunphy
● Alan Alda, Ann-Margret, Hal Linden, Veronica Hamel, John Shea, Beatrice Alda (Paramount)

Perhaps trying to break his image as the most conscientiously nice guy of the latter half of the 20th century, Alan Alda has tried to give himself an edge in *A New Life*. As the newly divorced Steve Giardino, he is loud, obnoxious, neurotic, argumentative and manic; he also has permed hair and a beard, smokes, drinks hard liquor rather than wine, and eats red meat instead of chicken and fish.

After some 20 years of marriage, New Yorkers Alda and Ann-Margret decide to call it quits. Alda's screenplay follows the two equally as each endures the predictably excruciating blind dates, singles parties and matchups.

They are tenacious and game, and some months later each meets an attractive new prospect, she a dreamy, younger TriBeCa sculptor (John Shea), he a sharp and similarly younger doctor (Veronica Hamel).

All the actors have the upper-middle-class mannerisms down pat, and make for perfectly agreeable company despite the familiarity of the terrain. Shot mainly in Toronto, pic looks and sounds good.

．．．．．．．．．．．．．．．．．．．．．．．．．

■ **NEWS BOYS, THE**
See: Newsies

．．．．．．．．．．．．．．．．．．．．．．．．．

■ **NEWSFRONT**

1978, 110 MINS, AUSTRALIA ◇ ⊛ ⊙
Dir Phillip Noyce   *Prod* David Elfick   *Scr* Phillip Noyce
Ph Vince Monton   *Ed* John Scott   *Mus* William Motzing
Art Dir Lissa Coote
● Bill Hunter, Gerard Kennedy, Angela Punch, Wendy Hughes, Chris Hayward, John Ewart (Palm Beach)

Set in an historically turbulent period for Australia (1949-56), *Newsfront* deals with the lives of movie newsreel cameramen and uses the events in which they are involved as a sort of microcosmic view of how, in a very short period of time, the country underwent remarkable socio-political change.

The approach is interesting and the film benefits greatly from two central strengths: history and Bill Hunter (as Len Maguire). In his feature film debut, director Phillip Noyce demonstrates his ability to deal with actors, narrative, and choreograph background activity.

By clever merging of b&w newsreel footage and scenario-inspired monochromatic sequences, he moves his film into and out of actuality and fiction in such a way as often to blur the edges so well that it frequently takes a conscious effort to detect the blend-point. This is especially true in one of his major set-pieces, re-creating the disastrous floods in the Maitland area in the early 1950s.

Plot [from an original screenplay by Bob Ellis, based on a concept by David Elphick] concerns the rivalry between two competing newsreel companies: Len works for the plodding, traditionally-valued, Aussie-owned Cinetone, and ambitious brother Frank (Gerard Kennedy) has left them to run the go-ahead, pushy, Yank-owned Newsco.

Acting performances are all fine, particularly Angela Punch as the embittered wife, John Dease as the voice-over man, and Chris Hayward as the brash Britisher who gets a job as a camera assistant.

．．．．．．．．．．．．．．．．．．．．．．．．．

■ **NEWSIES**
(UK: The News Boys)

1992, 121 MINS, US ◇ ⊛ ⊙
Dir Kenny Ortega   *Prod* Michael Finnell   *Scr* Bob Tzudiker, Noni White   *Ph* Andrew Laszlo   *Ed* William Reynolds   *Mus* J.A.C. Redford   *Art Dir* William Sandell
● Christian Bale, David Moscow, Luke Edwards, Ann-Margret, Ele Keats, Robert Duvall (Walt Disney)

They should have filmed the pitch meeting for this project: 'Hey, guys, I found a story I bet nobody's ever thought of making: How about a movie on the 1899 New York newsboys' strike? Robert Duvall's got a hole in his schedule; he could play Pulitzer.' 'Great! But let's get Ann-Margret and a lot of cute kids and make a musical!'

A strange cross between *Oliver!* and Samuel Fuller's *Park Row*, *Newsies* was made with care and affection by choreographer-turned-director Kenny Ortega. But the writers have created cardboard cutouts instead of flesh-and-blood characters.

Composer Alan Menken, whose music works hard at being rousing, badly misses lyricist Howard Ashman, his late partner: Jack Feldman's lyrics here are relentlessly banal and unmemorable.

Cast has pleasant but ordinary voices, and it's only in the vigorous, *West Side Story*-style dancing, choreographed by Ortega and Peggy Holmes, that the film sporadically comes alive. Ortega avoids the MTV fragmentation that's de rigeur in musicals today.

Christian Bale plays the leader of the newsboys' walk-out against the penny-pinching Pulitzer (bearded Robert Duvall). He's a charismatic figure, with a compelling blend of brashness and vulnerability. Duvall is a cartoon figure of ranting hard-heartedness as publisher of the *N.Y. World*. Ann-Margret's Jenny Lind-like thrush, an improbable ally of the boys, is shoehorned into the film to provide s.a. in a male-dominated story.

······································

■ **NEW YEAR'S DAY**

1989, 89 MINS, US ◇ ⊚

Dir Henry Jaglom   *Prod* Judith Wolinsky   *Scr* Henry Jaglom   *Ph* Joey Forsyte

● Maggie Jakobson, Gwen Welles, Melanie Winter, Henry Jaglom, Milos Forman, Michael Emil (International Rainbow)

An undifferentiated extension of the same themes, concerns and artistic strategies featured in Henry Jaglom's previous films, *New Year's Day* is nonetheless notable for introducing a luminous new actress, Maggie Jakobson.

Jaglom again stars as a depressed Me Generation obsessive who returns to New York from Los Angeles in the midst of a midlife crisis.

Arriving on New Year's morning, Jaglom finds his apartment still occupied by three young ladies who thought they had until the end of the day to vacate the premises. Instead of booting them out, Jaglom immediately imposes himself upon their most personal concerns, especially those of Jakobson, whose boyfriend continues to fool around with other women throughout the open house the trio holds on their last day as roommates.

Lots of people show up for a drink or two in the course of the day, including Jakobson's parents and shrink, helmer's brother Michael Emil as a randy 'psychosexologist,' and director Milos Forman.

······································

■ **NEW YORK CONFIDENTIAL**

1955, 87 MINS, US

Dir Russell Rouse   *Prod* Clarence Greene   *Scr* Russell Rouse, Clarence Greene   *Ph* Edward Fitzgerald   *Ed* Grant Whytock   *Mus* Joseph Mullendore   *Art Dir* Fernando Carrere

● Broderick Crawford, Richard Conte, Marilyn Maxwell, Anne Bancroft, J. Carrol Naish (Warner)

Among crime exposes *New York Confidential* stacks up as one of the better-made entries, thanks to a well-fashioned story and good performances by a cast of familiar names. While a tough, no-punches-pulled melodrama, it relies more on logical development for effect than on unsoundly motivated bare-knuckles action.

Story [suggested by Jack Lait and Lee Mortimer's book] tells of the rise of Richard

Conte, ambitious triggerman, in the big syndicate said to control all crime under the chairmanship of Broderick Crawford.

Conte does a topnotch job of making a cold-blooded killer seem real and Crawford is good as the chairman of the crime board, as is Marilyn Maxwell as his girl friend. Anne Bancroft, showing continuing progress and talent, scores with a standout performance of Crawford's unhappy daughter.

······································

■ **NEW YORK NEW YORK**

1977, 153 MINS (1981: 164 MINS), US ◇ ⊚ ⊙

Dir Martin Scorsese   *Prod* Irwin Winkler, Robert Chartoff   *Scr* Earl MacRauch, Mardik Martin   *Ph* Laszlo Kovacs   *Ed* Irving Lerner, Marcia Lucas, Tom Rolf, B. Lovitt   *Mus* Ralph Burns (sup.)   *Art Dir* Boris Leven

● Liza Minnelli, Robert De Niro, Barry Primus, Mary Kay Place, Georgie Auld, Lionel Stander (United Artists)

Taking Liza Minnelli and Robert De Niro from their first meeting after VJ Day, film proceeds slowly and deliberately through their struggle to make it as a band singer and saxophonist and as a marriage in which her voice is early acclaimed while his music is ahead of its time. The two are making it pretty good until her pregnancy sidelines her.

Though still professing enduring love, the couple breaks up with the birth of the baby and the film lurches forward several years. Now she's a big film star, banging out the new numbers by John Kander and Fred Ebb, and the 1950s have brought his style into vogue and he's a big name, too, if not as big as she.

In a final burst from Old Hollywood, Minnelli tears into the title song and it's a wowser.

······································

■ **NEW YORK STORIES**

1989, 123 MINS, US ◇ ⊚ ⊙

Dir Martin Scorsese, Francis Coppola, Woody Allen   *Prod* Robert Greenhut   *Scr* Richard Price, Francis Coppola, Sofia Coppola, Woody Allen   *Ph* Nestor Almendros, Vittorio Storaro, Sven Nykvist   *Ed* Thelma Schoonmaker, Barry Malkin, Susan E. Morse   *Mus* Carmine Coppola, Kid Creole and the Coconuts   *Art Dir* Kristi Zea, Dean Tavoularis, Santo Loquasto

● Nick Nolte, Rosanna Arquette, Heather McComb, Talia Shire, Woody Allen, Mia Farrow (Touchstone)

New York Stories showcases the talents of three of the modern American cinema's foremost auteurs, Martin Scorsese, Francis Coppola and Woody Allen. Scorsese's is aimed at serious-minded adults, Coppola's to children, and Allen's to a more general public looking for laughs.

Scorsese's *Life Lessons* gets things off to a pulsating start, as Nestor Almendros' camera darts, swoops and circles around Nick Nolte and Rosanna Arquette as they face the end of an intense romantic entanglement. The leonine Nolte plays a an abstract painter unprepared for a major gallery opening three weeks away. Announcing that she's had a fling, Arquette, Nolte's lover and artistic protege, agrees to stay on in his loft as long as she no longer has to sleep with him.

At 33 minutes, Coppola's *Life without Zoe* is the shortest of the three, but that is still not nearly short enough. Vignette is a wispy urban fairy tale about a 12-year-old girl who, because her parents are on the road most of the time, basically lives alone at the ritzy Sherry Netherland Hotel.

Happily, Woody Allen salvages matters rather nicely with *Oedipus Wrecks*, about the Jewish mother syndrome. When Allen takes shiksa girlfriend Mia Farrow home for dinner, he winces as mama assails him for choosing a blonde with three kids. Allen's fondest wish – that his mother just disappear – comes true when a magician literally loses her in the course of a trick.

······································

■ **NEXT MAN, THE**

1976, 108 MINS, US ◇ ⊚

Dir Richard C. Sarafian   *Prod* Martin Bregman   *Scr* Mort Fine, Alan R. Trustman, David M. Wolf, Richard C. Sarafian   *Ph* Michael Chapman   *Ed* Aram Avakian, Robert Q. Lovett, Nina Feinberg   *Mus* Michael Kamen   *Art Dir* Gene Callahan

● Sean Connery, Cornelia Sharpe, Albert Paulsen, Adolfo Celi, Marco St John, Ted Beniades (Artists Entertainment)

The Next Man emerges more a slick travesty with political overtones than the cynical suspense meller it was designed to be.

The project apparently grew out of an interesting proposition – a major oil-producing nation breaks with the Middle Eastern oil cartel to join forces with Israel to assure technological development and peace.

Pic is based on an original story by Alan R. Trustman and David M. Wolf. No less than four writers compiled the screenplay and it shows.

Briefly, Sean Connery plays a peace-mongering Saudi Arabian diplomat, dispatched to the UN to plead a case for Israel cooperation. For such arrant revisionism he is plagued by a network of Arab terrorists in whose employ is a beautiful, wealthy playgirl, friskily portrayed by Cornelia Sharpe.

······································

■ **NEXT OF KIN**

1989, 108 MINS, US ◇ ⊚ ⊙

Dir John Irvin   *Prod* Les Alexander, Don Enright   *Scr* Michael Jenning   *Ph* Steven Poster   *Ed* Peter Honess   *Mus* Jack Nitzsche   *Art Dir* Jack T. Collis

● Patrick Swayze, Liam Neeson, Adam Baldwin, Helen Hunt, Andreas Katsulas, Michael J. Pollard (Lorimar/Warner)

Interesting wrinkle in Michael Jenning's screenplay, uncredited [based on a script by Jenning and pic's associate producer, Jeb Stuart], is a mixing and matching of two ethnic strains of the vendetta: backwoods Appalachian version and revenge Sicilian-style.

These plot threads are set in motion when Bill Paxton, a Kentucky boy from the hills now working in Chicago, is ruthlessly murdered by mafia enforcer Adam Baldwin as part of a strong-arm move in the vending machines racket. Paxton's older brother, Patrick Swayze, is a Chicago cop determined to find the killer.

Inferfering with Swayze's efforts is the old-fashioned 'eye for an eye' vengeance demanded by eldest brother Liam Neeson. Picture climaxes with an elaborate war in a Chicago cemetery between Baldwin's mafioso and Neeson's Kentucky kin, matching automatic weaponry with primitive (but reliable) crossbows, hatchets, snakes and knives.

······································

■ **NEXT STOP, GREENWICH VILLAGE**

1976, 111 MINS, US ◇ ⊚

Dir Paul Mazursky   *Prod* Paul Mazursky   *Scr* Paul Mazursky   *Ph* Arthur Ornitz   *Ed* Richard Halsey   *Mus* Bill Conti   *Art Dir* Phil Rosenberg

● Lenny Baker, Shelley Winters, Ellen Greene, Lois Smith, Christopher Walken, Dori Brenner (20th Century-Fox)

Next Stop, Greenwich Village is a very beautiful motion picture. Writer-director Paul Mazursky's gentle and touching film is a sort of young adult's *American Graffiti*.

An outstanding cast of New York players, plus Shelley Winters in one of the most superb characterizations of her career, gives the film a wonderful humanity and credibility.

Lenny Baker heads the cast in an excellent depiction of a young Brooklyn boy aiming for an acting career; quite naturally, pop Mike Kellin and mom Winters have their doubts – she being more than willing to articulate

N

them. But Baker, like Don Quixote, sets forth on his quest.

Baker's new life centers around a group of arresting people: Ellen Greene, his girl; Christopher Walken, lothario-playwright; Dori Brenner, the type girl who hides her sensitivities in kookiness; Antonio Fargas, the gay equivalent of Brenner's character and so on.

In dark hair, Winters has managed to escape her near-formula mother role into new creative territory.

. . . .

■ **NIAGARA**

1953, 89 MINS, US ◇ ⓥ ⊙
Dir Henry Hathaway   *Prod* Charles Brackett
Scr Charles Brackett, Walter Reisch, Richard Breen   *Ph* Joe MacDonald   *Ed* Barbara McLean   *Mus* Sol Kaplan   *Art Dir* Lyle R. Wheeler, Maurice Ransford
● Marilyn Monroe, Joseph Cotten, Jean Peters, Casey Adams, Denis O'Dea, Richard Allan (20th Century-Fox)

Niagara is a morbid, cliched expedition into lust and murder. The atmosphere throughout is strained and taxes the nerves with a feeling of impending disaster. Focal point of all this is Marilyn Monroe, who's vacationing at the Falls with hubby Joseph Cotten.

A Korean War vet, Cotten is emotionally disturbed and his eye-filling blonde wife deliberately goes out of her way to irritate him. She flaunts her physical charms upon mere strangers, taunts him with disparaging remarks and has a clandestine affair in progress with Richard Allan.

These incidents are noticed by Jean Peters and Casey Adams. A honeymooning couple, they're stopping at the same cabins, and it's only too obvious that they'll be involved in the events to come. First, a plot of Monroe and Allan to kill Cotten backfires when the latter shoves his attacker over the Falls. Cotten then hunts down Monroe and strangles her. Now, pure theatrics takes over.

The camera lingers on Monroe's sensuous lips, roves over her slip-clad figure and accurately etches the outlines of her derriere as she weaves down a street to a rendezvous with her lover. As a contrast to the beauty of the female form is another kind of nature's beauty – that of the Falls. The natural phenomena have been magnificently photographed on location.

. . . .

■ **NICE GIRL LIKE ME, A**

1969, 90 MINS, UK ◇ ⓥ
Dir Desmond Davis   *Prod* Roy Millichip   *Scr* Anne Piper, Desmond Davis   *Ph* Gil Taylor, Manny Wynn   *Ed* Ralph Sheldon   *Mus* Pat Williams   *Art Dir* Ken Bridgeman
● Barbara Ferris, Harry Andrews, Gladys Cooper, Bill Hinnant, James Villiers, Fabia Drake (Partisan/Levine)

On the death of her father, Candida (Barbara Ferris) goes to live with two gorgon aunts and escapes them to go to Paris to study languages. Her first tutor is a young student who picks her up and, after a brief idyllic affair, she is pregnant. Back home she confides in Savage (Harry Andrews), a gruff, kindly man who was caretaker to her late father.

She kids her aunts that she is minding the babe for a friend and nips off to Venice to continue her linguistic 'studies'. There, a hip young American picks her up and, pronto, she's carrying a second child.

Screenplay is light and gently amusing but not too cynically flip or gooey and director Davis keeps the film on a non-serious, yet perceptive level.

Ferris is a pleasantly attractive combo of intelligent approach and charm, Andrews is dependable as ever.

. . . .

■ **NICHOLAS AND ALEXANDRA**

1971, 185 MINS, UK ◇ ⓥ ⊙
Dir Franklin J. Schaffner   *Prod* Sam Spiegel   *Scr* James Goldman, Edward Bond   *Ph* Freddie Young   *Ed* Ernest Walter   *Mus* Richard Rodney Bennett   *Art Dir* John Box
● Michael Jayston, Janet Suzman, Harry Andrews, Irene Worth, Jack Hawkins, Laurence Olivier (Columbia)

Sam Spiegel comes up with a rarity: the intimate epic, in telling the fascinating story of the downfall of the Romanovs.

The tone is set from the opening sequences depicting the birth of the Russian Emperor and Empress' first boy and heir to the Romanov throne, followed closely by the tragic discovery that the child is haemophilic. Slowly, intrusively, the viewers get to know more about the dominant Alexandra and the frequently vacillating Nicholas, whom she influences in misguided political decisions.

Complicating factors, of course, are the growing unrest of the Russian people culminating in its confused revolution, the constant, distracting worry about the 'bleeding' Czarevitch and, most of all, the dominant influence on the Empress of Rasputin, without whose occult, hypnotic presence she feels the heir will die.

Scripter James Goldman (with an assist from Edward Bond) has provided literate, sparse dialog in fashioning a crystal-clear picture of a confused and confusing period. Certainly, as in the Robert K. Massie book, there's a feel here for tragically opposed worlds both heading blindly on a collision course towards the inevitable bloody clash.

Michael Jayston makes a most believable Nicholas, while Janet Suzman is also just right in the perhaps more difficult role of the Empress.

□ 1971: Best Art Direction, Costume Design.
□ Nominations: Best Picture, Actress (Janet Suzman), Cinematography, Orignal Music Score

. . . .

■ **NICHOLAS NICKLEBY**

1947, 108 MINS, UK ⓥ
Dir Alberto Cavalcanti   *Prod* Michael Balcon   *Scr* John Dighton   *Ph* Gordon Dines   *Ed* Leslie Norman   *Mus* Lord Berners   *Art Dir* Michael Relph
● Derek Bond, Cedric Hardwicke, Sally Ann Howes, Sybil Thorndike, Cyril Fletcher, Stanley Holloway (Ealing)

To make an entertaining film of this Dickens classic needed more courage than producer Michael Balcon shows. He should have thought first of the millions who care little or nothing whether any particular character or episode is missing as long as the picture does no violence to the author and is entertaining.

The 52 characters of the original prove too much for the scriptwriter. Some minor characters have been left out, and Gride has become amalgamated with Ralph at the end, but the screenplay is more in the nature of a condensation into a series of scenes. And that's the way it appears on the screen.

Nicholas' adventures with the Crummies family has an old ham actor grandly played by Stanley Holloway. The stage scenes are amusing, but they do little to further the main story and, as an interlude, they slow up what action there might be. Scenes in Dotheboys Hall, which should have been among the most memorable, are slovenly, untidy and cramped. For some reason, Alfred Drayton, who otherwise gives a fine performance, makes Wackford Squeers a brutish Cockney thug. His forbiding consort, played by Sybil Thorndike, obviously comes from a slightly better family.

Casting any Dickens film is an unenviable chore and Balcon has made as good a job as most producers. Derek Bond brings manly grace to the title role, but betrays inexperience. Nor does Sally Ann Howes, sweet and simple as Kate, rise to her big occasion when

her wicked uncle uses her as a decoy to attract his unmoral clients.

. . . .

■ **NICKELODEON**

1976, 121 MINS, US ⓥ
Dir Peter Bogdanovich   *Prod* Irwin Winkler, Robert Chartoff   *Scr* W.D. Richter, Peter Bogdanovich   *Ph* Laszlo Kovacs   *Ed* William Caruth   *Mus* Richard Hazard   *Art Dir* Richard Berger
● Ryan O'Neal, Burt Reynolds, Tatum O'Neal, Brian Keith, Stella Stevens, John Ritter (Columbia)

Peter Bogdanovich's film is an okay comedy-drama about the early days of motion pictures. Story begins with a group of barnstorming filmmakers in the pre-feature film era, later segues to the adolescene of the industry.

Stars include Ryan O'Neal, struggling lawyer who literally stumbles into directing; Burt Reynolds, roustabout who becomes a leading man; Tatum O'Neal, enterprising California country girl who makes money renting things to the fledgling production units sent here to escape the goon squads of the Motion Picture Patents Co trust; Brian Keith, composite pioneer mogul; and Stella Stevens as an early leading lady.

The O'Neals, Reynolds, Keith and Stevens all engage interest, attention and affection.

. . . .

■ **NIGHT AMBUSH**

See: Ill Met by Moonlight

. . . .

■ **NIGHT AND DAY**

1946, 120 MINS, US ◇ ⓥ
Dir Michael Curtiz   *Prod* Arthur Schwartz   *Scr* Charles Hoffman, Leo Townsend, William Bowers   *Ph* Peverell Marley, William V. Skall   *Ed* David Weisbart   *Mus* Ray Heindorf (arr.), Leo F. Forbstein (dir.), Max Steiner   *Art Dir* John Hughes
● Cary Grant, Alexis Smith, Monty Woolley, Jane Wyman, Dorothy Malone, Mary Martin (Warner)

Night and Day is a filmusical, based on the career of Cole Porter. It's to the credit of director Mike Curtiz and the combined scripters that they weighed the fruitful elements so intelligently, and kept it all down as much as they did. Wisely all steered clear of making this a blend of 'and then I wrote' and a Technicolored songplug unspooling.

Here's a guy to whom nothing more exciting happens than that he's born to millions and stays in a 'rut' for the rest of his career by making more money. The plot, per se, therefore is static on analysis but paradoxically it emerges into a surprisingly interesting unfolding. A real-life ambulance driver in World War I, Porter is shown with the French army. Alexis Smith plays the nurse whom he marries; she's previously introduced as of an aristocratic family. And thereafter, save for a fall off a spirited steed which caused Porter much real-life suffering because of broken legs which never set properly, the footage of *Night and Day* is a succession of hit shows and hit songs.

The tunes are chronologically mixed up a bit – a cinematic license with which none can be captious – and the romantic story line takes the accent principally in that Smith seeks to get her husband away from the mad show biz whirl of London and Broadway.
□ 1946: Nomination: Best Scoring of a Musical Picture

. . . .

■ **NIGHT AND THE CITY**

1950, 96 MINS, US
Dir Jules Dassin   *Prod* Samuel G. Engel   *Scr* Jo Eisinger   *Ph* Max Greene   *Ed* Nick De Maggio, Sidney Stone   *Mus* Franz Waxman   *Art Dir* C.P. Norman
● Richard Widmark, Gene Tierney, Googie Withers, Hugh Marlowe, Francis L. Sullivan, Herbert Lom (20th Century-Fox)

Night and the City is an exciting, suspenseful melodrama, produced in London [from a novel by Gerald Kersh], which is the story of a double-crossing heel who finally gets his just desserts. In this role, Richard Widmark scores a definite hit. And he has excellent support right down the line. Gene Tierney was cast for name value only.

Jules Dassin, in his direction, manages extraordinarily interesting backgrounds, realistically filmed to create a feeling both of suspense and mounting menace.

Widmark plays a London hustler willing to do anything to be somebody. He finally sees an opportunity in going into partnership with the father of London's top wrestling promoter – and setting up his own wrestling enterprise, depending upon promoter's love for his father to make a go of it. Idea backfires.

．．．．．．．．．．．．．．．．．．．．．．．．．．．．

■ NIGHT AND THE CITY

1992, 98 MINS, US ◇ ⓥ ⊙
Dir Irwin Winkler   *Prod* Jane Rosenthal, Irwin Winkler
Scr Richard Price   *Ph* Tak Fujimoto   *Ed* David Brenner
Mus James Newton Howard   *Art Dir* Peter Larkin
● Robert De Niro, Jessica Lange, Cliff Gorman, Alan King, Jack Warden, Eli Wallach (Tribeca)

Night and the City is a skilled, if not entirely psychologically convincing, remake of the 1950 film noir classic of the same name. Lively performances, pungent NYC atmosphere and abundance of dramatic incident keep this story of an irrepressible low-life hustler ripping along.

Playing a frenetic, wired character right up his alley, Robert De Niro stars as Harry Fabian, a longtime ambulance-chasing lawyer who conceives the big-time scheme to promote 'the return of people's boxing' with a night of fights featuring sharp locals. But boxing promoter Boom Boom Grossman (Alan King), a genial tough guy, doesn't take kindly to Harry horning in.

Harry recruits Boom Boom's estranged brother Al (Jack Warden), a grizzled former prize-fighter, and Eli Wallach's retired moneyman. He also counts on an investment from his good friend Phil (Cliff Gorman), a bar owner, but at the same time proceeds to lure away Phil's wife Helen (Jessica Lange).

Richard Widmark's Fabian in the original film (set in London) was very credibly a young American who remained in Europe after the war and tried to con his way through a foreign, hostile system. De Niro's Harry pushes just as brazenly, but fact that he's in his late 40s creates a credibility gap.

Gene Tierney's role in the first version, an add-on to the script at the behest of Darryl Zanuck, doesn't exist here. Story's ending has also been altered, to less powerful effect.

No particular sexual spark is indicated between De Niro and Lange, nor does Lange's laid-back performance suggest any reasons for her behavior.

In a nice gesture, pic is dedicated to Jules Dassin, director of the orginal film.

．．．．．．．．．．．．．．．．．．．．．．．．．．．．

■ NIGHT AT THE OPERA, A

1935, 93 MINS, US ⓥ ⊙
Dir Sam Wood   *Prod* [Irving G. Thalberg]   *Scr* George S. Kaufman, Morrie Ryskind   *Ph* Merritt B. Gerstad
Ed William LeVanway   *Mus* Herbert Stothart
Art Dir Cedric Gibbons, Ben Carre, Edwin B. Willis
● Groucho Marx, Harpo Marx, Chico Marx, Kitty Carlisle, Siegfried Rumann, Allan Jones (M-G-M)

Story [by James Kevin McGuinness] is a rather serious grand opera satire in which the comics conspire to get a pair of Italian singers a break over here. For their foils the Marxes have Walter King and Siegfried Rumann as heavies, Robert Emmett O'Connor as a pursuing flatfoot, and Margaret Dumont to absorb the regulation brand of Groucho insults.

Although King also doubles on the vocals, Kitty Carlisle and Allan Jones do most of the singing as the love interest.

Groucho and Chico in a contract-tearing bit, the Marxes with O'Connor in a bed-switching idea, and a chase finale in the opera house are other dynamite comedy sequences, along with a corking build-up by Groucho while riding to his room on a trunk. The backstage finish, with Harpo doing a Tarzan on the fly ropes, contains more action than the Marxes usually go in for, but it relieves the strictly verbal comedy and provides a sock exit.

．．．．．．．．．．．．．．．．．．．．．．．．．．．．

■ NIGHTBREED

1990, 99 MINS, US ◇ ⓥ ⊙
Dir Clive Barker   *Prod* Gabriella Martinelli   *Scr* Clive Barker   *Ph* Robin Vidgeon   *Ed* Richard Marden, Mark Goldblatt   *Mus* Danny Elfman   *Art Dir* Steve Hardie
● Craig Sheffer, Anne Bobby, David Cronenberg, Charles Haid, Hugh Ross (Morgan Creek)

Writer-director Clive Barker's *Nightbreed* is a mess. Self-indulgent horror pic [from his novel *Cabal*] could be the *Heaven's Gate* of its genre, of obvious interest to diehard monster fans but a turnoff for mainstream audiences.

Barker's inverted story premise is not explained until halfway through the picture: the last survivors of shapeshifters (legendary monsters including vampires and werewolves) are huddled below ground in a tiny Canadian cemetery near Calgary called Midian, trying to avoid final extinction.

Hero Craig Sheffer is plagued by nightmares and heads there in hopes of becoming a monster, while his nutty shrink (David Cronenberg) is on a messianic mission to destroy the undead critters. Sheffer's normal girlfriend (Anne Bobby) tags along.

Pic presents unrelated sequences of gore and slashing until the ridiculously overproduced finale.

Chief casting gimmick is giving the lead baddie role to revered Canadian director Cronenberg. Horror cultists might enjoy his soft-spoken, monotone performance and in-jokes, but others will merely wonder why a professional actor was cheated out of a salary.

．．．．．．．．．．．．．．．．．．．．．．．．．．．．

■ NIGHTCOMERS, THE

1972, 96 MINS, UK ◇ ⓥ ⊙
Dir Michael Winner   *Prod* Michael Winner
Scr Michael Hastings   *Ph* Robert Paynter   *Ed* Freddie Wilson   *Mus* Jerry Fielding
● Marlon Brando, Stephanie Beacham, Thora Hird, Verna Harvey, Christopher Ellis, Harry Andrews (Scimitar)

The Nightcomers is one of those atmosphere-drenched thrillers in which a semblance of surface decorum and respectability hides a multitude of aberrations beneath. This one, penned by Michael Hastings and inspired by the characters in Henry James' *The Turn of the Screw*, has a hand-tailored starring appearance by Marlon Brando.

Two recently-orphaned children live alone on a British country estate with their nurse, a housekeeper and a gardener, Quint. It's the last-named (played by Brando) who fascinates the boy and girl to such a degree that his instinctive actions, mysterious manners, homespun philosophising becomes their (only) guide and lifeline.

His sado-carnal affair with the otherwise prim and bourgeois nurse, glimpsed in fleshly violent action by the fascinated boy, is similarly aped by youngsters, as are other aspects of couple's love-hate relationship which, in their unknowing innocence, they adopt and idealize. When the housekeeper decides to fire both nurse and gardener, the children plot to keep them together – forever – by killing them both.

．．．．．．．．．．．．．．．．．．．．．．．．．．．．

■ NIGHT CROSSING

1981, 106 MINS, UK ◇ ⓥ
Dir Delbert Mann   *Prod* Tom Loetch   *Scr* John McGreevey   *Ph* Tony Imi   *Ed* Gordon D. Denner
Mus Jerry Goldsmith   *Art Dir* Rolf Zehetbauer
● John Hurt, Jean Alexander, Glynnis O'Connor, Beau Bridges, Ian Bannen, Kay Walsh (Walt Disney)

There's plenty of drama hiding in this tale of two families' daring escape from East to West Germany by homemade hot-air balloon, but this Disney production can't find much of it. Unbelievable mix of actors from different nations is forced to deliver one bad line after another.

Story is a dramatic natural, as two construction workers, fed up with life behind the Iron Curtain, conspire to fashion a giant balloon out of household fabric and pilot it over the forbidding, heavily guarded half-mile zone between the two Germanys. First attempt doesn't quite make it but, despite fact that the secret police begin sniffing their trail, they try again, with suspenseful, successful results.

It all happened in 1978–79 and everything about it would indicate the potential for a grippingly serious family adventure pic. But script so seriously stumbles in the exposition stage that recovery is difficult even in the close-call climax.

．．．．．．．．．．．．．．．．．．．．．．．．．．．．

■ NIGHT HAS A THOUSAND EYES

1948, 80 MINS, US
Dir John Farrow   *Prod* Endre Bohem   *Scr* Barre Lyndon, Jonathan Latimer   *Ph* John F. Seitz   *Ed* Eda Warren
Mus Victor Young   *Art Dir* Hans Dreier, Franz Bachelin
● Edward G. Robinson, Gail Russell, John Lund, Virginia Bruce, William Demarest (Paramount)

Suspense is the dominating element in this thriller which follows a man who can foresee the future. Told in flashback form, story starts with Gail Russell about to commit suicide by jumping from a trestle onto a track in front of onrushing train, in terror after having been told by Edward G. Robinson, the diviner, that she will meet a violent death within a few days.

Events in natural order then are narrated by Robinson, from time he learned he was gifted – or damned – with his inner sight to opening events, and occurrences that follow leading up to strong climax.

John Farrow's sure directorial hand is seen throughout unfolding of picture, scripted melodramatically by Barre Lyndon and Jonathan Latimer [from a novel by Cornell Woolrich].

■ NIGHTHAWKS

1981, 99 MINS, US ◇ ⓥ ⊙
Dir Bruce Malmuth   *Prod* Martin Poll   *Scr* David Shaber
Ph James A. Contner   *Ed* Christopher Holmes
Mus Keith Emerson   *Art Dir* Peter Larkin
● Sylvester Stallone, Billy Dee Williams, Rutger Hauer, Lyndsay Wagner, Persis Khambatta, Nigel Davenport (Universal)

Nighthawks is an exciting cops and killers yarn with Sylvester Stallone to root for and cold-blooded Rutger Hauer to hate.

Off and running right from the beginning, director Bruce Malmuth presents a vulnerable woman on a dark NY street about to be mugged. Suddenly the guys with the knives discover the woman is Stallone, on decoy duty and backed up by partner Billy Dee Williams.

While Stallone is doing his best to rid Gotham's streets of riff-raff, Hauer is introduced in London as one of the most wanted and most murderous terrorists in the world, a crafty, intelligent killer who has fully rationalized his cause to justify blowing up department stores full of innocent victims, including children. This is an American film debut for Holland's top actor and he plays the part ex-

N

pertly, matching Stallone scene for scene.

Hauer comes to NY accompanied by equally evil Persis Khambatta and pursued by Nigel Davenport, a terrorist expert from Interpol who recruits the assistance of Stallone and Williams.

Though there's never much doubt how the duel will end, the climax is nonetheless surprising and totally satisfying, topping the energy of the previous pursuit.

NIGHT IN CASABLANCA, A

1946, 85 MINS, US ⦿
Dir Archie Mayo *Prod* David L. Loew *Scr* Joseph Fields, Roland Kibbee *Ph* James Van Trees *Ed* Gregg C. Tallas *Mus* Werner Janssen *Art Dir* Duncan Cramer
● Groucho Marx, Harpo Marx, Chico Marx, Lisette Verea, Charles Drake (United Artists)

This isn't the best the Marx Bros have made but it's a pretty funny farce.

Postwar Nazi intrigue in Casablanca is the theme, having to do with the handsome French flyer who is under a cloud because of Nazi skullduggery dealing with European loot cached in the Hotel Casablanca. When three of the hotel's managers get bumped off in rapid succession, Groucho gets the nod. Chico runs the Yellow Camel Co. and Harpo is his mute pal who later breaks the bank in the hotel's casino and stumbles on the Nazi gold through a mishap with the lift.

Against the desert background of French provincial political bungling and Nazi chicanery the Marxes get off some effective comedy, and some of it not so. The brighter spots are the clown fencing duel; the frustrated tryst between Groucho and Lisette Verea, running from suite to suite, with portable phonograph, champagne cooler, etc; the sequence with the packing cases and clothes closet, prior to the getaway; and finally the air-autotruck chase, winding up back in the same jail from whence all escaped.

NIGHTMARE

1964, 83 MINS, UK
Dir Freddie Francis *Prod* Jimmy Sangster *Scr* Jimmy Sangster *Ph* John Wilcox *Ed* James Needs *Mus* Don Banks *Art Dir* Bernard Robinson, Don Mingaye
● David Knight, Moira Redmond, Brenda Bruce, Jennie Linden (Hammer)

Best features of this highly contrived chiller is the direction and lensing (by Freddie Francis and John Wilcox respectively) of the atmosphere of a house where eerie things happen in this way of shadows, significant noises and the fleeting appearances of a phantom-like woman in white.

Jennie Linden's mother was committed to an asylum when the child was 14, after stabbing her husband. This preys on the child's mind and she is convinced that she may have inherited a streak of madness. She certainly is the victim of bad dreams.

She is taken from school to her home where she is apparently safely guarded by the attention of an adoring housekeeper (Irene Richmond), her school mistress (Brenda Bruce), her young guardian (David Knight) and a nurse (Moira Redmond), posing as a companion. But Knight and Redmond are clandestine lovers. Their attempts to prey on the mind of the girl are elaborately worked out and, though highly incredible, serve as a workmanlike plot for such a modest thriller.

NIGHTMARE ALLEY

1947, 110 MINS, US
Dir Edmund Goulding *Prod* George Jessel *Scr* Jules Furthman *Ph* Lee Garmes *Ed* Barbara McLean *Mus* Cyril J. Mockridge *Art Dir* Lyle R. Wheeler, J. Russell Spencer
● Tyrone Power, Joan Blondell, Colleen Gray, Helen Walker, Ian Keith, Mike Mazurki (20th Century-Fox)

Nightmare Alley is a harsh, brutal story [based on the novel by William Lindsay Gresham] told with the sharp clarity of an etching.

The film deals with the roughest phases of carnival life and showmanship. Tyrone Power is Stan Carlisle, reform school graduate, who works his way from carney roustabout to bigtime mentalist and finally to important swindling in the spook racket. Ruthless and unscrupulous, he uses the women in his life to further his advancement, stepping on them as he climbs.

Most vivid of these is Joan Blondell as the girl he works for the secrets of the mind-reading act. Coleen Gray is sympathetic and convincing as his steadfast wife and partner in his act and Helen Walker comes through successfully as the calculating femme who topples Power from the heights of fortune back to degradation as the geek in the carney. Ian Keith is outstanding as Blondell's drunken husband.

NIGHTMARE ON ELM STREET, A

1984, 91 MINS, US ◇ ⦿ ⊙
Dir Wes Craven *Prod* Robert Shaye *Scr* Wes Craven *Ph* Jacques Haitkin *Ed* Rick Shaine *Mus* Charles Bernstein *Art Dir* Greg Fonseca
● John Saxon, Ronee Blakley, Heather Langenkamp, Amanda Wyss, Johnny Depp, Robert Englund (New Line/Media Home/Smart Egg)

A Nightmare on Elm Street is a highly imaginative horror film that provides the requisite shocks to keep fans of the genre happy.

Young teenagers in a Los Angeles neighborhood are sharing common nightmares about being chased and killed by a disfigured bum in a slouch hat who has knives for fingernails. It turns out that years ago, the neighborhood's parents took deadly vigilante action against a child murderer, who apparently is vengefully haunting their kids.

With original special effects, the nightmares are merging into reality, as teens are killed under inexplicable circumstances.

Writer-director Wes Craven tantalizingly merges dreams with the ensuing wakeup reality but fails to tie up his thematic threads satisfyingly at the conclusion.

NIGHTMARE ON ELM STREET, PART 2, A FREDDY'S REVENGE

1985, 84 MINS, US ◇ ⦿ ⊙
Dir Jack Sholder *Prod* Robert Shaye, Sara Risher *Scr* David Chaskin *Ph* Jacques Haitkin *Ed* Arline Garson, Bob Brady *Mus* Christopher Young *Art Dir* Mick Strawn
● Mark Patton, Kim Myers, Robert Rusler, Clu Gulager, Hope Lange, Robert Englund (New Line/Heron/Smart Egg)

Beneath its verbose, title, Jack Sholder's follow-up to Wes Craven's 1984 hit is a well-made though familiar reworking of demonic horror material.

Screenplay basically makes a sex change on Craven's original: a teenage boy Jesse Walsh (Mark Patton) is experiencing the traumatic nightmares previously suffered by a young girl, Nancy Thompson. Walsh's family has moved into Thompson's house, five years after the events outlined in the first film.

The slouch-hatted, long, steel fingernails-affixed, disfigured monster Freddy (Robert Englund) is attempting to possess Walsh's body in order to kill the local kids once more and, judging from the film's body count, is quite successful.

Episodic treatment is punched up by an imaginative series of special effects. The standout is a grisly chest-burster setpiece.

Mark Patton carries the show in the central role as not quite a nerd, but strange enough to constitute an outsider presence. Kim Myers scores as his sympathetic girl friend, surmounting her obvious teen lookalike for Meryl Streep image.

NIGHTMARE ON ELM STREET 3, A DREAM WARRIORS

1987, 96 MINS, US ◇ ⦿ ⊙
Dir Chuck Russell *Prod* Robert Shaye *Scr* Wes Craven, Bruce Wagner, Chuck Russell, Frank Darabont *Ph* Roy H. Wagner *Ed* Terry Stokes, Chuck Weiss *Mus* Angelo Badalamenti *Art Dir* Mick Strawn, C.J. Strawn
● Heather Langenkamp, Patricia Arquette, Larry Fishburne, Priscilla Pointer, Craig Wasson, Robert Englund (New Line/Heron/Smart Egg)

With input from the original's creator, Wes Craven [who also co-wrote the screen story with Bruce Wagner], *3* shifts its focus away from the homely neighborhood horror to a setting of seven nightmare-plagued teens under the care of medicos Priscilla Pointer (instantly hissable) and Craig Wasson (decidedly miscast).

Heather Langenkamp, young heroine of the first film in the series, returns as an intern assigned to the ward. She's been using an experimental dream-inhibiting drug to keep her wits about her and proposes using it on the kids.

While everyone is stewing in their juices, pic is mainly focused on the violent special effects outbursts of Freddy Krueger (ably limned under heavy makeup by Robert Englund), the child murderer's demon spirit who seeks revenge on Langenkamp and the other Elm St kids for the sins of their parents.

Debuting director Chuck Russell elicits poor performances from most of his thesps, making it difficult to differentiate between pic's comic relief and unintended howlers.

NIGHTMARE ON ELM STREET 4, A THE DREAM MASTER

1988, 93 MINS, US ◇ ⦿ ⊙
Dir Renny Harlin *Prod* Robert Shaye, Rachel Talalay *Scr* Brian Helgeland, Scott Pierce *Ph* Steven Fierberg *Ed* Michael N. Knue, Chuck Weiss *Mus* Craig Safan *Art Dir* Mick Strawn, C.J. Strawn
● Robert Englund, Lisa Wilcox, Rodney Eastman, Danny Hassel, Andras Jones, Tuesday Knight (New Line/Heron/Smart Egg)

Imaginative special effects highlight the fourth entry in the series. As before, Freddy's out for revenge on the kids of Elm Street for their parents' having murdered him after he killed several children in the first place. Freddy's conjured up in the kids' nightmares and a clever plot [by William Kotzwinkle and Brian Helgeland] has him rapidly (and unexpectedly) dispensing with the surviving kids, only to extend his mayhem to their friends, starting with Alice (Lisa Wilcox).

Wilcox in the lead role gives a solid performance ranging from vulnerable to resourceful, as she gains strength from her departed friends to do battle with Freddy.

Robert Englund, receiving star billing for the first time, is delightful in his frequent incarnations as Freddy, delivering his gag lines with relish and making the grisly proceedings Funny.

NIGHTMARE ON ELM STREET, A THE DREAM CHILD

1989, 89 MINS, US ◇ ⦿ ⊙
Dir Stephen Hopkins *Prod* Robert Shaye, Rupert Harvey *Scr* Leslie Bohem *Ph* Peter Levy *Ed* Chuck Weiss, Brent Schoenfeld *Mus* Jay Ferguson *Art Dir* C.J. Strawn
● Robert Englund, Lisa Wilcox, Kelly Jo Winter, Danny Hassel, Erika Anderson, Nick Mele (New Line/Heron/Smart Egg)

Fifth edition of the hit *Nightmare* series is a poorly constructed special effects showcase. Pic's storyline [by John Skipp, Craig Spector and Leslie Bohem] dovetails closely with Parts 3 and 4: Alice (Lisa Wilcox, surviving from last pic) learns that the vengeful monster Freddy Krueger (steady Robert Englund) is now preying on her friends, materializing through the dreams of the fetus she's carrying.

New title character is Jacob (Whitby Hertford), 10-year-old dream child who reps what Alice's child will become and is the focus of her war with Freddy. Key to battling the monster is contacting the spirit of Freddy's mom (Beatrice Boepple), a nun who committed suicide following his birth.

Unfortunately, Aussie helmer Stephen Hopkins adopts a music-video approach, delaying the boring exposition for several reels and usually cutting away from climaxes to destroy much of the film's impact. Acting is highly variable. Saving grace is the series of spectacular special effects set pieces featuring fanciful makeup, mattes, stopmotion animation and opticals.

. . . .

■ **NIGHT MOVES**

1975, 99 MINS, US ◇ ⓦ
Dir Arthur Penn   *Prod* Robert M. Sherman   *Scr* Alan Sharp   *Ph* Bruce Surtees   *Ed* Dede Allen, Stephen A. Rotter   *Mus* Michael Small   *Art Dir* George Jenkins
● Gene Hackman, Jennifer Warren, Edward Binns, Susan Clark, James Woods, Melanie Griffith (Warner)

Night Moves is a paradox: a suspenseless suspenser, very well cast with players who lend sustained interest to largely synthetic theatrical characters.

Minor LA detective Hackman, hired by faded actress Janet Ward to find runaway teenage daughter Melanie Griffith, becomes enmeshed in the Florida smuggling operations of John Crawford (Griffith's stepfather), whose classy mistress Jennifer Warren indirectly helps Hackman's own reconciliation with wife Clark, herself dallying out of loneliness with Harris Yulin. Stuntmen Edward Binns and Anthony Costello, and mechanic Woods, provide a link between the Hollywood and Florida environments.

Far more meritorious than the play are the players. Hackman works well with everyone.

. . . .

■ **NIGHT MUST FALL**

1964, 99 MINS, UK
Dir Karel Reisz   *Prod* Karel Reisz, Albert Finney   *Scr* Clive Exton   *Ph* Freddie Francis   *Ed* Philip Barnikel   *Mus* Ron Grainer   *Art Dir* Timothy O'Brien
● Albert Finney, Susan Hampshire, Mona Washbourne, Sheila Hancock, Michael Medwin (M-G-M)

Artfully composed and strikingly photographed, this British-manufactured reproduction of Metro's 1937 shock-suspense thriller lacks the restraint, clarity and subtlety of its forerunner but makes up, to some degree, in cinematic flamboyance what it lacks in dramatic tidiness and conviction.

Albert Finney's performance as the cunning madman is vivid and explosive, and it might not be too far from wrong to suppose that the entire project may have germinated out of his desire to tackle the character.

Vagueness in key dramatic junctures hampers the new version, constructed around the skeleton of Emlyn Williams' stage play.

That story lapses and irregularities seem less than drastic is a tribute to the dazzling execution and a batch of tangy performances. Finney, in the role first played so well by Robert Montgomery, is fascinating to watch as his dispositions shift with maniacal rootlessness. It's an inventive, stimulating portrayal by a gifted actor. Yet Finney's thespic thunder is often stolen by Mona

Washbourne's masterful delineation of the lonely 'invalid' who becomes his victim.

. . . .

■ **NIGHT OF THE FOLLOWING DAY, THE**

1969, 93 MINS, UK ◇
Dir Hubert Cornfield   *Prod* Hubert Cornfield   *Scr* Hubert Cornfield, Robert Phippeny   *Ph* Willi Kurout   *Ed* Gordon Pilkington   *Mus* Stanley Myers   *Art Dir* Jean Boulet
● Marlon Brando, Richard Boone, Rita Moreno, Pamela Franklin, Jess Hahn (Universal/Gina)

The Night of the Following Day begins as an intriguing, offbeat kidnap drama, but soon shifts emphasis to delineating the freaked-out characters of its principals, and ends abruptly on a cop-out note.

Lionel White's book, *The Snatchers*, has been adapted into a rambling stew of deliberate and accidental black comedy and melodrama. Pamela Franklin is the prop focal character, a young woman kidnapped for ransom by Marlon Brando, Richard Boone, Rita Moreno and Jess Hahn.

A lot of effective and moody camerawork by Willi Kurout, combined with the good promise of the first reel and Brando's excellent physical appearance and dynamism, wash out as each character loses sympathy and interest. Even Franklin, ostensibly the victim of the piece, is forgotten for long periods.

. . . .

■ **NIGHT OF THE GENERALS**

1967, 148 MINS, UK/FRANCE ◇ ⓦ ⊙
Dir Anatole Litvak   *Prod* Sam Spiegel   *Scr* Joseph Kessel, Paul Dehn   *Ph* Henri Decae   *Ed* Alan Osbiston   *Mus* Maurice Jarre   *Art Dir* Alexandre Trauner
● Peter O'Toole, Omar Sharif, Tom Courtenay, Donald Pleasence, Charles Gray, Joanna Pettet (Columbia/Horizon)

With an important theme about the nature of guilt and the promise of a teasing battle of wits, this is an interesting feature that lets the tension run slack, being afflicted with galloping inflation of its running-time.

Plot opens in Nazi-occupied Warsaw in 1942, with a prostie being brutally murdered and the killer being recognized as wearing the uniform of a German general. But that's the only clue for Major Grau (Omar Sharif), the Military Intelligence man in charge of the hunt, and he establishes that only three brasshats could have committed the crime, having insufficient alibis.

One is Tanz (Peter O'Toole), a ruthless and devoted Nazi who destroys a quarter of Warsaw as an exercise in discipline. Another is Kahlenberge (Donald Pleasence), a cynical opportunist who has few scruples, but plenty ingenuity. And the third suspect is the pompous Galber (Charles Gray).

Adapted from Hans Helmut Kirst's bitter novel, the story is told in flashback and the technique adds to the somewhat languid effect. But the chief factor militating against conviction is the central performance by O'Toole, which lacks the firm savagery Tanz seems to require.

. . . .

■ **NIGHT OF THE HUNTER, THE**

1955, 93 MINS, US ⓦ ⊙
Dir Charles Laughton   *Prod* Paul Gregory   *Scr* James Agee   *Ph* Stanley Cortez   *Ed* Robert Golden   *Mus* Walter Schumann   *Art Dir* Hilyard Brown
● Robert Mitchum, Shelley Winters, Lillian Gish, Billy Chapin, Peter Graves, James Gleason (Gregory/United Artists)

The relentless terror of Davis Grubb's novel got away from Paul Gregory and Charles Laughton in their translation of *Night of the Hunter*. This start for Gregory as producer and Laughton as director is rich in promise

but the completed product, bewitching at times, loses sustained drive via too many offbeat touches that have a misty effect.

Straight story telling without the embellishments, it would seem, might have rammed home with frightening force the horror of this man's diabolical quest of a hanged murderer's $10,000 which he wants to use in serving his fancied Lord. It builds fine with suspense ingredients to a fitting climax.

Robert Mitchum intermittently shows some depth in his interpretation of the preacher but in instances where he's crazed with lust for the money, there's barely adequate conviction.

. . . .

■ **NIGHT OF THE IGUANA, THE**

1964, 117 MINS, US ⓦ
Dir John Huston   *Prod* Ray Stark   *Scr* Anthony Veiller, John Huston   *Ph* Gabriel Figueroa   *Ed* Ralph Kemplen   *Mus* Benjamin Frankel   *Art Dir* Stephen Grimes
● Richard Burton, Ava Gardner, Deborah Kerr, Sue Lyon, James Ward, Grayson Hall (Seven Arts/M-G-M)

This Ray Stark production is rich in talents. Performances by Richard Burton, Ava Gardner and Deborah Kerr are superlative in demanding roles. Direction by John Huston is resourceful and dynamic as he sympathetically weaves together the often-vague and philosophical threads that mark Tennessee Williams' writing.

Unfoldment takes place mainly in a ramshackle Mexican seacoast hotel where Burton, an unfrocked minister and now guide of a cheap bus tour, takes refuge from his latest flock, a group of complaining American schoolteachers who refuse to believe he actually is a preacher who lost his church. Frankness in dealing with his emotional problems as first he is pursued by a young sexpot in the party, then his involvement with the aggressive, man-hungry hotel owner and a sensitive, itinerant artist travelling with her 97-year-old grandfather, produces compassionate undertones finely realized in situations evoking particular interest.

Burton has stature in the difficult portrayal of the Reverend T. Lawrence Shannon, a part without glamour yet touched with magical significant force as he progresses to the point of a near-mental crackup. Gardner, in the earthy role of Maxine Faulk, the proprietress, is a gutsy figure as she makes her play for the depraved ex-minister, turning in a colorful delineation. Kerr lends warm conviction as the spinster who lives by idealism and her selling of quick sketches, a helpless creature yet endowed with certain innate strength.
□ 1964: Best B&W Costume Design.
□ Nominations: Best Supp. Actress (Grayson Hall), B&W Cinematography, B&W Art Direction

. . . .

■ **NIGHT OF THE JUGGLER**

1980, 100 MINS, US ◇ ⓦ
Dir Robert Butler   *Prod* Jay Weston   *Scr* Bill Norton Sr, Rick Natkin   *Ph* Victor J. Kemper   *Ed* Argyle Nelson   *Mus* Artie Kane   *Art Dir* Stuart Wurtzel
● James Brolin, Cliff Gorman, Richard Castellano, Abby Bluestone, Dan Hedaya, Julie Carmen (Columbia)

Night of the Juggler is a relentlessly preposterous picture which never gives its cast a chance to overcome director Robert Butler's passion for mindless action.

This is supposed to be the story [from a novel by William P. McGivern] of James Brolin's frantic pursuit of a kidnapper who grabs his daughter and takes off with her in a car.

But who cares if the performers are never allowed to make the characters come true?

As a frustrated, racist psychotic seeking revenge for the deterioration of his Bronx neighborhood, Cliff Gorman is trapped by the

N

script's needs for him to be so loony you might actually believe in him.

Technically each individual shot was approached with intense concentration on the craft of filmmaking. Which is exactly what's wrong with the picture.

• •

■ NIGHT OF THE LIVING DEAD

1968, 90 MINS, US ⓥ ⊙
Dir George A. Romero   *Prod* Russell Streiner, Karl Hardman   *Scr* John A. Russo, George A. Romero   *Ph* George A. Romero
● Judith O'Dea, Russell Streiner, Duane Jones, Karl Hardman, Keith Wayne (Image Ten)

Although pic's basic premise is repellent – recently dead bodies are resurrected and begin killing human beings in order to eat their flesh – it is in execution that the film distastefully excels.

No brutalizing stone is left unturned: crowbars gash holes in the heads of the living dead, monsters are shown eating entrails, and – in a climax of unparalleled nausea – a little girl kills her mother by stabbing her a dozen times in the chest with a trowel.

The rest of the pic is amateurism of the first order. Pittsburgh-based director George A. Romero appears incapable of contriving a single graceful set-up, and his cast is uniformly poor.

Both Judith O'Dea and Duane Jones are sufficiently talented to warrant supporting roles in a backwoods community theatre, but Russell Streiner, Karl Hardman, Keith Wayne and Judith Ridley do not suggest that Pittsburgh is a haven for undiscovered thespians.

John A. Russo's screenplay is a model of verbal banality and suggests a total antipathy for his characters.

• •

■ NIGHT OF THE LIVING DEAD

1990, 89 MINS, US ◇ ⓥ ⊙
Dir Tom Savani   *Prod* John A. Russo, Russ Steiner   *Scr* George A. Romero   *Ph* Frank Prinzi   *Ed* Tom Dubensky   *Mus* Paul McCollough   *Art Dir* James Feng
● Tony Wood, Patricia Tallman, Tom Towles, McKee Anderson, William Butler, Katie Finnerman (21st Century)

The original producers of *Night of the Living Dead* have remade their own cult classic in a crass bit of cinematic grave-robbing. The only legitimate reason to remake the 1968 film would have been to improve its effects and sub-$200,000 budget, although the dimly shot black-&-white images were far creepier than any of its color progeny.

The story faithfully follows the original except for the bonehead decision to replace the ending with a 'meaningful' twist that reeks of pretentiousness.

The plot still involves seven people trapped in a farmhouse fending off hordes of walking corpses intent on devouring them. Never explained is what animated the bodies in the first place, although a solid bash to the brain deanimates them.

The hero still is Ben (Tony Wood), and the bad guy still is a middle-aged businessman named Harry (Tom Towles) who holes up in the basement with his wife and daughter. The one beefed-up role is that of the female lead (Patricia Tallman), who reveals a Rambo-esque bent.

• •

■ NIGHT ON EARTH

1992, 130 MINS, US ◇ ⓥ ⊙
Dir Jim Jarmusch   *Prod* Jim Jarmusch   *Scr* Jim Jarmusch   *Ph* Frederick Elmes   *Ed* Jay Rabinowitz   *Mus* Tom Waits   *Art Dir* [uncredited]
● Winona Ryder, Gena Rowlands, Giancarlo Esposito, Armin Mueller-Stahl, Roberto Benigni, Beatrice Dalle (JVC/Locus Solus)

Jim Jarmusch's existential comedy *Night on Earth* is an easy-to-take followup to his previous pic *Mystery Train*. Beginning with an outer-space shot gradually zeroing in on planet Earth, the director covers in five separate segments his favorite theme of lonely people interacting but ultimately facing the great void alone.

From this cosmic perspective he examines brief encounters between taxi drivers and their late-night fares. Opening LA segment is pic's weakest, as tomboyish cabbie Winona Ryder is matched against her patrician passenger Gena Rowlands. Contrasting with this is a powerful finale, set in Helsinki with actors from the troupe of the Kaurismaki brothers. Matti Pellonpaa is genuinely moving as a cabbie pouring out his tragic story to a trio of drunken guys. It's a tale of faith and love unrewarded.

En route to this somber finish, Jarmusch provides ebullient comedy in two winning routines: the hilarious and unlikely team (in matching floppy winter hats) of Giancarlo Esposito and Armin Mueller-Stahl in New York as well as a goofy, all-stops-out monolog by Roberto Benigni as a Roman cabbie confessing to a back-seat priest about his sexual exploits with pumpkins and a sheep named Lola.

Parisian segment is an unsettling encounter between a bitter blind woman (Beatrice Dalle) and her Ivory Coast-transplanted driver Isaach De Bankole. Filming in the languages of each city results in a feature about 60% English subtitled.

• •

■ NIGHT ON THE TOWN, A

See: Adventures in Babysitting

• •

■ NIGHT PASSAGE

1957, 90 MINS, US ◇
Dir James Neilson   *Prod* Aaron Rosenberg   *Scr* Borden Chase   *Ph* William Daniels   *Ed* Sherman Todd   *Mus* Dimitri Tiomkin   *Art Dir* Alexander Golitzen, Robert Clatworthy
● James Stewart, Audie Murphy, Dan Duryea, Dianne Foster, Elaine Stewart, Brandon de Wilde (Universal)

This taut, well-made and sometimes fascinating western is the first use of Technicolor's new widescreen, anamorphic process, Technirama. Borden Chase has fashioned a script around two brothers – James Stewart, decent, upright; Audie Murphy, wild, a deadly gunman. The Technirama process gives new depth and definition, said to combine the principles of both VistaVision and CinemaScope. Pic was lensed in the Durango-Silverton region of Colorado.

Plot carries a railroad-building backdrop. Stewart is a former railroad employee recalled to help transport the payroll to rail's-end, previous attempts to take the money through to rebelling workers having been stymied when outlaw gang conducts series of raids. He becomes involved with gang during a train holdup.

Both stars deliver sound portrayals, Murphy making up in color Stewart's greater footage. Dan Duryea is immense as outlaw chief who isn't quite certain whether he can outdraw Murphy, a wizard with a gun.

• •

■ NIGHT PORTER, THE

1974, 115 MINS, US/ITALY ◇ ⓥ ⊙
Dir Liliana Cavani   *Prod* Robert Gordon Edwards, Esae De Simone   *Scr* Liliana Cavani, Italo Moscati   *Ph* Alfio Contin   *Ed* Franco Arcalli   *Mus* Daniele Paris
● Dirk Bogarde, Charlotte Rampling, Philippe Leroy, Gabriele Ferzetti, Isa Miranda, Amedeo Amadio (United Artists)

Liliana Cavani deals with the ambivalent relationship between a concentration camp victim (Charlotte Rampling) and her torturer-lover (Dirk Bogarde) in a strange, brooding tale. There's a touch of *Last Tango in Paris* in this love affair that does not take society or other people into much account.

It has an apartment, albeit furnished and the couple trapped there, serving for their trysts in Vienna of 1957. They meet accidentally, but the past and a group of still ardent Nazis force them to revert to their camp relationship.

Bogarde is an ex-Storm Trooper who now works as a night porter. He belongs to a group which have managed to be acquitted by doing away with witnesses and destroying evidence.

It's a gritty look at concentration camp quirks, but transposed to a strange drama. Bogarde treads intelligently through his role of an unbalanced man.

• •

■ NIGHT SHIFT

1982, 105 MINS, US ◇ ⓥ ⊙
Dir Ron Howard   *Prod* Brian Grazer   *Scr* Lowell Ganz, Babaloo Mandel   *Ph* James Crabe   *Ed* Robert J. Kern, Daniel P. Hanley, Mike Hill   *Mus* Burt Bacharach   *Art Dir* Jack Collis
● Henry Winkler, Michael Keaton, Shelley Long, Gina Hecht, Pat Corley, Bobby DiCicco (Ladd)

Nerdy Henry Winkler is a meek attendant at the city morgue who is the kind of person who'd rather eat a plate of poisonous mushrooms than offend the chef who served them. His life is a mess. To compound matters, he must work the night shift with Looney Tune Michael Keaton – the type of guy who talks non-stop as he blasts rock songs on the radio while dancing up and down the aisles.

At the same time, Winkler befriends Shelley Long, the perennial 'nice girl hooker' who just happens to live next door and happens to have just lost her pimp. It's not long before Winkler and Keaton devise a scheme to act as pimps for Long using the morgue as a base of operation.

Though the plot line hardly sounds like a family film, this is probably the most sanitized treatment of pimps and prostitution audiences will ever see.

None of this much matters, because director Ron Howard and screenwriters Lowell Ganz and Babaloo Mandel, all TV veterans, are only bent on giving the audience a good time.

• •

■ NIGHT THE PROWLER, THE

1978, 90 MINS, AUSTRALIA ◇
Dir Jim Sharman   *Prod* Anthony Buckley   *Scr* Patrick White   *Ph* David Sanderson   *Mus* Cameron Alan
● Ruth Cracknell, John Frawley, Kerry Walker, John Derum, Maggie Kirkpatrick, Terry Camilleri (Chariot)

A hodge-podge of flash forwards, flashbacks, and even some flash sideways, *The Night the Prowler* tells the story, as one pundit put it, of a female slob's search for self-identification.

A young woman (Kerry Walker) moves into adulthood as an overweight, sullen, neurotic and ill-mannered daughter of a couple of middleclass stereotypes. The mother is attractive and dimwitted; the father is dull.

With flashbacks to the various stages of her youth, including the usual father fixation and an engagement to a rather boring young diplomat with a promising future, she fakes (or misinterprets) a visit from a prowler – in her version, with rape in mind.

This event, of course, lessens her chances at a marriage which she wasn't too eager about anyhow and she goes through a series of increasingly demoralizing changes, finally emerging as a leather-clad night prowler on her own.

• •

■ NIGHT THEY RAIDED MINSKY'S, THE

1968, 100 MINS, US ◇ ▽
Dir William Friedkin   *Prod* Norman Lear   *Scr* Arnold
Schulman, Sidney Michaels, Norman Lear   *Ph* Andrew
Laszlo   *Ed* Ralph Rosenblum   *Mus* Charles Strouse
Art Dir William Eckart, Jean Eckart
● Jason Robards, Britt Ekland, Norman Wisdom, Forrest
Tucker, Harry Andrews, Joseph Wiseman (United
Artists/Tandem)

Norman Lear's period peek at a peculiarly
American form of entertainment – burlesque
– is most successful in its art direction and
nostalgic recapturing of New York's lower
East Side during its most hoydenish period.

So easily does Norman Wisdom dominate
the many scenes he's in, that the other cast
members suffer by comparison, particularly
leading man Jason Robards, who's cast as the
top banana in the Minsky burlesque theatre.

One fault with this highly-colorful and fast-
moving comedy film is that it jumps about so
much in its story-telling. Characters are introduced, then never developed.

Lear was able, during NY location filming,
to talk the city into forestalling the demolishing of an entire block on the East Side until
he had used it for background footage.

Britt Ekland is lovely as the Amish girl who
not only rebels against the restrictions of her
religious background and a tyrannical father,
but does so with a strip sequence that titil-
lates the screen audience almost as much as
it does the on-screen audience.

■ NIGHT TIDE

1961, 85 MINS, US ▽
Dir Curtis Harrington   *Prod* Aram Kantarian   *Scr* Curtis
Harrington   *Ph* Vilis Lapenieks   *Ed* Jodie Copelan
Mus David Raksin   *Art Dir* Paul Mathison
● Dennis Hopper, Linda Lawson, Gavin Muir, Luana
Anders (American International/Filmgroup-Virgo)

Curtis Harrington, onetime avant-garde filmmaker and assistant to Jerry Wald, made this
first feature on an indie basis. Film mixes a
love affair with the supernatural. If
Harrington displays a good flair for narration
and mounting, his feel for mood, suspense
and atmospherics is not too highly developed.

A sailor on leave meets a girl who works as
a mermaid in a side show on the amusement
pier in Venice, California. It develops into
love but there is a strangeness in her com-
portment. Her guardian tells the sailor that
he had found her on a Greek island and
brought her to the US and that she is really a
mermaid. It also develops that two men she
had been with were found drowned. The
sailor is bewildered but when she almost kills
him during skin diving he manages to escape
while she disappears.

Dennis Hopper is acceptably bewildered by
his plight while Linda Lawson has the exotic
looks for the psychotic siren.

■ NIGHT TO REMEMBER, A

1958, 123 MINS, UK ▽
Dir Roy Ward Baker   *Prod* William MacQuitty   *Scr* Eric
Ambler   *Ph* Geoffrey Unsworth   *Ed* Sidney Hayers
Mus William Alwyn   *Art Dir* Alex Vetchinsky
● Kenneth More, Honor Blackman, Anthony Bushell,
Laurence Naismith, Kenneth Griffith, David McCallum
(Rank)

Producer and director have done an honest
job in putting the tragic sinking of the *Titanic*
in 1912 on the screen with an impressive, almost documentary flavor. With around 200
speaking roles in the pic, few of the actors are
given much chance to develop as characters.
Even Kenneth More, in the star role, is only
part of a team. The ship itself is the star.

The story tells how the 'unsinkable' new
ship set out for the US on the night of 14
April 1912, how it struck an iceberg and sank

in less than three hours with 1,302 people
drowned and only 705 survivors. The film
takes only 37 minutes less than the time of
the actual disaster.

The errors and confusion which played a
part in the drama are brought out with no
whitewashing. Although many of the passengers and crew come vividly to life, there is no
attempt to hang a fictional story on any of
them. Technically, director Roy Baker does a
superb job in difficult circumstances. His direction of some of the panic scenes during the
manning of the lifeboats – of which there
were not nearly enough to accommodate all
on board – is masterly. Eric Ambler's screenplay [from Walter Lord's book], without
skimping the nautical side of the job, brings
out how some people kept their heads and
others became cowards.

Others who manage to make impact are
Laurence Naismith as the skipper; Anthony
Bushell, captain of the rescue ship; Kenneth
Griffith and David McCallum, as a couple of
radio operators; Tucker McGuire, as a hearty
American woman; George Rose, as a bibulous
ship's baker; Michael Goodliffe, as the designer of the ship; and Frank Lawton, as the
chairman of the White Star Line.

■ NIGHT TRAIN TO MUNICH

1940, 95 MINS, UK ▽
Dir Carol Reed   *Prod* Edward Black   *Scr* Sidney Gilliat,
Frank Launder   *Ph* Otto Kanturek   *Ed* R.E. Dearing,
Michael Gordon   *Mus* Louis Levy   *Art Dir* Alex
Vetchinsky
● Margaret Lockwood, Rex Harrison, Paul Henreid, Basil
Radford, Naunton Wayne, Felix Aylmer (Gaumont-British)

Made by the same British studio that turned
out *Lady Vanishes*, the film also has the same
general subject matter, the same screenplay
writers, Margaret Lockwood in the femme
lead, and even makes similar use of Basil
Radford and Naunton Wayne as two tourist
Englishmen with a ludicrous interest in
cricket.

Much of the film's merit obviously stems
from the compact, propulsive screenplay by
Sydney Gilliat and Frank Launder, and the
razor-edge direction of Carol Reed. Story by
Gordon Wellesley opens in the tense days of
August 1939 with a Nazi espionage agent in
London recapturing two Czechs who have escaped from a concentration camp, an aged ar-
mor-plate inventor and his pretty daughter. A
British Secret Service operative follows them
to Berlin and, after an exciting sequence of
events during which war is declared, escapes
with them into Switzerland.

Yarn is not only told without a single letdown, but it actually continues to pile up suspense to a nerve-clutching pitch. The
headlong chase and escape at the end is a
time-tested melodramatic device superbly
handled.

Carol Reed's direction is worthy of the best
thrillers of Edgar Wallace, for whom he was
for many years stage manager. Lockwood is
an appealing heroine and her performance is
direct and persuasive. Rex Harrison is properly suave as the ubiquitous British operative,
while Paul Henreid is rightly cold as the
treacherous Gestapo agent, Radford and
Wayne repeat their goofy Britisher performances of *Lady Vanishes* and again click.
There are countless touches of atmosphere
and comedy that add immeasurable flavor
and zest to the picture.

■ NIGHT UNTO NIGHT

1949, 84 MINS, US
Dir Don Siegel   *Prod* Owen Crump   *Scr* Kathryn Scola
Ph Peverell Marley   *Ed* Thomas Reilly   *Mus* Franz
Waxman
● Ronald Reagan, Viveca Lindfors, Broderick Crawford,
Rosemary De Camp (Warner)

Night unto Night ventures into a dramatic
theme rarely more than hinted at on the
screen – epilepsy.

Picture's major strength comes from the
performance of Viveca Lindfors, but it is not
enough to carry the film. She projects emotion realistically, and with sex appeal. Ronald
Reagan's performance suffers in comparison
to his co-star's, and lacks depth.

Plot of the Philip Wylie novel, scripted by
Kathryn Scola, brings together a young man,
who has just learned he is suffering from
epilepsy, and a woman, still grieving over the
loss of her husband.

Don Siegel's direction is strained and
strives too much for dramatic effects with the
more mechanical elements of the production.

Broderick Crawford tops the featured players as an artist friend of the dramatic couple.

■ NIGHT WARNING

1983, 94 MINS, US ◇ ▽
Dir William Asher   *Prod* Stephen Breimer, Eugene
Mazzola   *Scr* Stephen Breimer, Alan Jay Glueckman,
Boon Collins   *Ph* Robbie Greenberg   *Ed* Ted Nicolaou
Mus Bruce Langhorne
● Jimmy McNichol, Susan Tyrrell, Bo Svenson, Marcia
Lewis, Julia Duffy, Britt Leach (S2D Associates/Royal
American)

Night Warning is a fine psychological horror
film. As the maniacally possessive aunt and
guardian of a 17-year-old boy, Susan Tyrrell
gives a tour-de-force performance.

Billy (Jimmy McNichol) is a basketball
player at high school who has been brought
up by his aunt Cheryl (Tyrrell) after his parents died in a car crash (great stunt footage)
14 years ago. An old maid, Cheryl is over-protective, opposing Billy's desire to go to college
in Denver on a hoped-for athletic scholarship
to be with his girlfriend.

Cheryl maintains a candlelit memorial to
an old boyfriend in the basement. The film's
horror content begins (replete with slow-motion violence and plenty of blood) when she
kills a young TV repairman after failing to seduce him. Cop on the case Detective Carlson
(Bo Svenson). is very closed-minded, ignoring
the facts and insisting on linking the crime to
a homosexual basketball coach, making Billy
the prime suspect instead of his aunt.

■ NIGHT WE NEVER MET, THE

1993, 99 MINS, US ◇ ⊙
Dir Warren Leight   *Prod* Michael Peyser   *Scr* Warren
Leight   *Ph* John Thomas   *Ed* Camilla Toniolo
Mus Evan Lurie   *Art Dir* Lester Cohen
● Matthew Broderick, Annabella Sciorra, Kevin
Anderson, Jeanne Tripplehorn, Justine Bateman, Michael
Mantell (Miramax)

A quintessential New York movie, *The Night
We Never Met* takes a novel premise and develops it in fits and starts.

Debuting filmmaker Warren Leight has
come up with an off-beat notion: time-sharing
a Greenwich Village apartment by days of the
week. Hissable yuppie Kevin Anderson is behind the scheme, wanting two nights out a
week with his buddies while living with patrician fiancee Justine Bateman.

One customer is Matthew Broderick, mop-
ing over losing his performance artist girlfriend Pastel (Jeanne Tripplehorn, spoofing a
familiar downtown type). Third tenant is
frustrated housewife Annabella Sciorra, who
uses it to get away from her dense husband
(Michael Mantell) and spend a couple of days
painting.

Plot is set in motion when Anderson innocently switches one of his designated days
with Broderick but doesn't update the posted
schedule, causing Sciorra to confuse the two
guys.

Wonderfully atmospheric use of New York

N

locations and familiar characters brings *Night* to life. Unfortunately, it's not really so much an ensemble piece as a film of alternating casts or vignettes.

....

■ **NIJINSKY**

1980, 125 MINS, UK ◇ ⓥ

Dir Herbert Ross   *Prod* Nora Kaye, Stanley O'Toole
Scr Hugh Wheeler   *Ph* Douglas Slocombe   *Ed* William Reynolds   *Mus* John Lanchbery   *Art Dir* John Blezard
● Alan Bates, George De La Pena, Leslie Browne, Alan Badel, Janet Suzman, Ronald Pickup (Hera)

In *Nijinsky*, Herbert Ross and scripter Hugh Wheeler have constructed nothing less than a male-to-male romantic tragedy. The film takes the form of a broad flashback covering only two critical years (1912-13) in the young dancer's early 20s.

Beginning with his mentor-lover Sergei Diaghilev (Alan Bates), the period charts Nijinsky's gradual allegiance to a wealthy homosexual patron – brilliantly etched by Alan Badel; and the successful attempt of Hungarian aristocrat Romola de Pulsky (Leslie Browne) to catch Nijinsky on his briefly heterosexual rebound from Diaghilev.

Central theme of Wheeler's script is that Diaghilev's obsessive love for Nijinsky clouded his otherwise shrewd taste, showmanship and business sense.

George De La Pena has the intensity and ambiguous sexual aura to make him a credible Nijinsky.

....

■ **NINE ½ WEEKS**

1986, 113 MINS, US ◇ ⓥ ⊙

Dir Adrian Lyne   *Prod* Antony Rufus Isaacs, Zalman King
Scr Patricia Knop, Zalman King, Sarah Kernochan
Ph Peter Biziou   *Ed* Tom Rolf, Caroline Biggerstaff
Mus Jack Nitzsche   *Art Dir* Ken Davis
● Mickey Rourke, Kim Basinger, Margaret Whitton, David Margulies, Christine Baranski, Karen Young (PSO/Kimmel/Barish/Jonesfilm/Galactic/Triple Ajaxxx)

Only and entire raison d'etre for this screen adaptation of Elizabeth McNeill's novel would be to vividly present the obsessive, all-consuming passion between a successful Wall Street type and a beautiful art gallery employee, who embark upon an intense love affair that lasts as long as the title indicates.

The film is about the crazy, overwhelming attachment they have with one another, and nothing else. Therefore, the virtual absence of anything interesting happening between them – like plausible attraction, exotic, amazing sex, or, God forbid, good dialog – leaves one great big hole on the screen for two hours.

Mickey Rourke is less than totally convincing as a big businessman, but Kim Basinger is the film's one saving grace, as she manages to retain a certain dignity.

....

■ **NINE HOURS TO RAMA**

1963, 125 MINS, US ◇

Dir Mark Robson   *Prod* Mark Robson   *Scr* Nelson Gidding   *Ph* Arthur Ibbetson   *Ed* Ernest Walker
Mus Malcolm Arnold   *Art Dir* Elliot Scott
● Horst Buchholz, Jose Ferrer, Valerie Gearon, Don Borisenko, Robert Morley, Diane Baker (20th Century-Fox)

At the core, this dramatization of circumstances surrounding the assassination of Mahatma Gandhi is an achievement of insight and impact. The success of a drama focusing its attention on the assassinator of a great man is to make the character of the killer dimensional and clearly motivated. This is achieved in the screenplay from Stanley Wolpert's novel and bolstered by Horst Buchholz's virile portrayal of the perpetrator.

Action of the drama takes place in the nine-hour span culminating with the fatal measure, with several flashback passages to

illustrate the incidents of the past that contributed to the unstable frame of mind of the young man.

The story falls down in its development and clarification of certain key secondary characters. A married woman (Valerie Gearon) for whom the killer-to-be has fallen does not make very much sense. And her abrupt metamorphosis from sophisticated lady of the world to devout woman of India in the final scene is both superfluous and dramatically awkward.

Several other important characters, too, are poorly defined, among them the assassin's unwilling accomplice (Don Borisenko), a baffling Indian politico (Robert Morley) and an impulsive prostitute (Diane Baker).

Buchholz delivers a performance of intensity and conviction. Jose Ferrer is excellent as a desperately concerned and conscientious police superintendent guarding Gandhi against disheartening odds. An astonishingly accurate personification of the latter is etched by J. S. Casshyap.

....

■ **NINE LIVES OF FRITZ THE CAT, THE**

1974, 76 MINS, US ◇ ⓥ

Dir Robert Taylor   *Prod* Steve Krantz   *Scr* Fred Halliday, Eric Monte, Robert Taylor   *Ph* Ted C. Bemiller, Greg Heschong   *Ed* Marshall M. Borden   *Mus* Tom Scott and the LA Express
● (American International)

Fritz the Cat is back again. The synthetic troublemaker and dilettante revolutionary was a trifle anachronistic when he first hit the screens in 1972. He is even more so in *The Nine Lives of Fritz the Cat*. The animated production utilizes several random flashback and flash-forward sequences within the framework of Fritz being chewed out by his wife and lapsing into reveries.

Somewhat forced and dated humor, not too well fluffed up by a frenzied and compulsive hip storytelling style, cartoon feature will please teenage mentalities.

Fact that period flashbacks – to Hitler's last days, to the Depression 1930s – and to a futuristic separate black state, among other segments, are the body of the plot, seems to suggest a lack of current timeliness.

....

■ **1984**

1956, 90 MINS, UK

Dir Michael Anderson   *Prod* N. Peter Rathvon
Scr William P. Templeton, Ralph Bettinson
Ph C. Pennington Richards   *Ed* Bill Lewthwaite
Mus Malcolm Arnold   *Art Dir* Terence Verity
● Michael Redgrave, Edmond O'Brien, Jan Sterling, David Kossoff, Mervyn Johns, Donald Pleasence (Holiday/Associated British)

A sinister glimpse of the future as envisaged by George Orwell, *1984* is a grim, depressing picture. The action takes place after the first atomic war, with the world divided into three major powers.

London, the setting for the story, is the capital of Oceania and is run by a ruthless regime, the heads of which are members of the inner party while their supporters are in the outer party. There are ministries of Love and Thought, anti-sex leagues and record divisions where the speeches of the great are rewritten from time to time to suit the needs of contemporary events.

The story is built around the illegal romance of two members of the outer party, Edmond O'Brien and Jan Sterling.

Orwell's picture of the ultimate in totalitarian ruthlessness is faithfully presented. Television 'eyes' keep a day-and-night watch on party members in their homes and TV screens are to be found everywhere, blurting out the latest reports on the endless wars with rival powers.

....

■ **NINETEEN EIGHTY-FOUR**

1984, 120 MINS, UK ◇ ⓥ ⊙

Dir Michael Radford   *Prod* Simon Perry   *Scr* Michael Radford   *Ph* Roger Deakins   *Ed* Tom Priestley
Mus Dominic Muldowney [later replaced by Eurythmics]
Art Dir Allan Cameron
● John Hurt, Richard Burton, Suzanna Hamilton, Cyril Cusack, Gregor Fisher, James Walker (Virgin/Umbrella)

In this unremitting downer, writer-director Michael Radford introduces no touches of comedy or facile sensationalism to soften a harsh depiction of life under a totalitarian system as imagined by George Orwell in 1948.

Richard Burton is splendid as inner-party official O'Brien. Ironically, his swansong performance as the deceptively gentle spur to Winston Smith's 'thought-crimes', and then as the all-knowing interrogator who takes on the attributes of a father-figure to the helpless man whom he is intent on destroying, is something new in Burton's repertoire.

Also strong is Suzanna Hamilton as Julia who is the other agent of Smith's downfall. John Hurt as Winston Smith holds center stage throughout.

....

■ **1941**

1979, 118 MINS, US ◇ ⓥ ⊙

Dir Steven Spielberg   *Prod* Buzz Feitshans   *Scr* Robert Zemeckis, Bob Gale   *Ph* William A. Fraker   *Ed* Michael Kahn   *Mus* John Williams   *Art Dir* Dean Edward Mitzner
● Dan Aykroyd, Ned Beatty, John Belushi, Toshiro Mifune, Nancy Allen, Robert Stack (Universal/Columbia/A-Team)

Billed as a comedy spectacle, Steven Spielberg's *1941* is long on spectacle, but short on comedy. The Universal-Columbia Pictures co-production is an exceedingly entertaining, fast-moving revision of 1940s war hysteria in Los Angeles.

Pic [from a story by Robert Zemeckis, Bob Gale and John Milius] is so overloaded with visual humor of a rather monstrous nature that feeling emerges, once you've seen 10 explosions, you've seen them all.

Main comic appeal resides in whatever audience enjoyment will result from seeing Hollywood Boulevard trashed (in miniature scale), paint factories bulldozed, houses toppled into the sea, and a giant ferris wheel rolling to a watery demise.

□ 1979: Nominations: Best Cinematography, Sound, Visual Effects

....

■ **1969**

1988, 90 MINS, US ◇ ⓥ ⊙

Dir Ernest Thompson   *Prod* Daniel Grodnik, Bill Badalato
Scr Ernest Thompson   *Ph* Jules Brenner   *Ed* William Anderson   *Mus* Michael Small   *Art Dir* Marcia Hinds
● Robert Downey Jr, Kiefer Sutherland, Bruce Dern, Mariette Hartley, Winona Ryder, Joanna Cassidy (Atlantic)

Affecting memories and good intentions don't always add up to good screen stories, and such is the case in *1969*, one of the murkiest reflections on the Vietnam War era yet, notwithstanding good performances all around and bright packaging of Kiefer Sutherland and Robert Downey Jr in the leads.

Director-screenwriter Ernest Thompson (*On Golden Pond*) has a wonderful feel for the relationships. It's only when it comes time to deliver a screen-size story that things go goofy.

College students and best pals Scott (Sutherland) and Ralph (Downey) have adopted a lifestyle in sharp contrast to the buttoned-down mores of their families in a small Maryland town 83 miles away. When they hitchhike home, there's conflict, particularly between Scott and his older brother Alden (Christopher Wynne, in an extremely unsympathetic turn), who's shipping out for the war.

Story is not exactly gripping. Instead, it's a mild trip down memory lane as the two hit the road in a psychedelic van to taste America in their last 'summer of innocence.'

Sutherland gives one of his best and most natural performances, and Downey is very good in a role that's similar to his *Less Than Zero* junkie, but gives him less to work with. Joanna Cassidy gives a topnotch performance as Ralph's spunky, effervescent and slightly liberated mother, and Winona Ryder is a scene-stealer as younger sister Beth, who's the only one with any ideas.

■ 9/30/55

1977, 101 MINS, US ◇
Dir James Bridges   *Prod* Jerry Weintraub   *Scr* James Bridges   *Ph* Gordon Willis   *Ed* Jeff Gourson *Mus* Leonard Rosenman   *Art Dir* Robert Luthardt
● Richard Thomas, Susan Tyrrell, Deborah Benson, Lisa Blount, Thomas Hulce, Dennis Quaid (Universal)

Title is the date of the car-crash death of James Dean, and James Bridges' original script tells of the impact on Richard Thomas, starring in an excellent performance as a smalltown Arkansas college kid whose life is permanently transformed by the incident.

Thomas is superb as the kid whose entire attitudes undergo change when news of Dean's death is heard on the radio. Girlfriend Deborah Benson partially shares the grief, but not as much as Lisa Blount, a freakier chick.

Together with chums Thomas Hulce, Dennis Quaid and Mary Kai Clark, Thomas helps commemorate Dean's demise with booze and mock-occult mysticism, leading to a prank on other students.

Susan Tyrrell is outstanding as Blount's flamboyant mother.

■ NINE TO FIVE

1980, 110 MINS, US ◇ ⓥ ⊙
Dir Colin Higgins   *Prod* Bruce Gilbert   *Scr* Colin Higgins, Patricia Resnick   *Ph* Reynaldo Villalobos *Ed* Pembroke J. Herring   *Mus* Charles Fox *Art Dir* Dean Mitzner
● Jane Fonda, Lily Tomlin, Dolly Parton, Dabney Coleman, Sterling Hayden, Elizabeth Wilson (IPC/20th Century-Fox)

Anyone who has ever worked in an office will be able to identify with the antics in *Nine to Five*. Although it can probably be argued that Patricia Resnick and director Colin Higgins' script [from a story by Resnick] at times borders on the inane, the bottom line is that this picture is a lot of fun.

Story concerns a group of office workers (Lily Tomlin the all-knowing manager who trained the boss but can't get promoted, Jane Fonda the befuddled newcomer and Dolly Parton the alluring personal secretary) who band together to seek revenge on the man who is making their professional lives miserable.

Tomlin comes off best in the most appealing role as the smart yet under-appreciated glue in the office cement.

Parton makes a delightful screen debut in a role tailored to her already well-defined country girl personality. Surprisingly, Fonda, initiator of the project, emerges as the weakest.
□ 1980: Nomination: Best Song ('Nine to Five')

■ 99 AND 44/100% DEAD

1974, 97 MINS, US ◇ ⓥ
Dir John Frankenheimer   *Prod* Joe Wizan   *Scr* Robert Dillon   *Ph* Ralph Woolsey   *Ed* Harold F. Kress *Mus* Henry Mancini   *Art Dir* Herman Blumenthal

● Richard Harris, Edmond O'Brien, Bradford Dillman, Ann Turkel, Constance Ford, Chuck Connors (20th Century-Fox)

99 and 44/100% Dead starts like a house on fire, with directorial style to burn, but self-incinerates within its first half-hour. Thereafter, audience endures a pointless hour of 'bitter ashes,' which the offended taste with spattering noise rejected' to use Milton's famous line.

Director John Frankenheimer struggles with Robert Dillon's sophomoric, repulsive screenplay about gang warfare, but pyrrhic victory eludes him.

Hired killer Richard Harris enters a mythical, futuristic city 'on the beginning of the third day of the War' and hunts down mob kingpin Bradford Dillman for rival gangster Edmond O'Brien's peace of mind.

For a short while Dillon seems to have parody on his mind. Unfortunately, Dillon has neither the wit nor the invention to sustain this tone for more than a few reels.

■ NINJA III THE DOMINATION

1984, 95 MINS, US ◇ ⓥ
Dir Sam Firstenberg   *Prod* Menahem Golan, Yoram Globus   *Scr* James R. Silke   *Ph* Hanania Baer *Ed* Michael J. Duthie, Ken Bornstein   *Mus* Udi Harpaz, Misha Segal, Buddy Royston, Mike Mercury *Art Dir* Elliot Ellentuck
● Sho Kosugi, Lucinda Dickey, Jordan Bennett, David Chung, Dale Ishimoto, James Hong (Cannon)

With *Ninja III* producers reunite members of the team that made their second entry in the martial arts series about the more deadly cousins of the Samurai. The new outing into the never-never land of the world's trickiest controlled violence is done with quite a twist.

The twist has several quite humorous aspects, the least of which being that most of the Ninja action is performed by a woman (Lucinda Dickey).

From time to time she bewilders her police officer boyfriend by unconsciously taking over the spirit of an evil Ninja on a visit to Arizona to carry on his wholesale killing of the police force.

Sho Kosugi is the Good Ninja who finally helps the American girl out of her predicament so she can return to her regular pastime.

■ NINOTCHKA

1939, 111 MINS, US ⓥ ⊙
Dir Ernst Lubitsch   *Prod* Ernst Lubitsch   *Scr* Charles Brackett, Billy Wilder, Walter Reisch   *Ph* William Daniels *Ed* Gene Ruggiero   *Mus* Werner Heymann *Art Dir* Cedric Gibbons, Randall Duell
● Greta Garbo, Melvyn Douglas, Bela Lugosi, Sig Rumann, Felix Bressart, Ina Claire (M-G-M)

Selection of Ernst Lubitsch to pilot Garbo in her first light performance in pictures proves a bull's-eye.

The punchy and humorous jabs directed at the Russian political system and representatives, and the contrast of bolshevik receptiveness to capitalistic luxuries and customs, are displayed in farcical vein, but there still remains the serious intent of comparisons between the political systems in the background [based on an original story by Melchior Lengyel].

Three Russian trade representatives arrive in Paris to dispose of royal jewels 'legally confiscated'. Playboy Melvyn Douglas is intent on cutting himself in for part of the jewel sale. Tying up the gems in lawsuit for former owner, Ina Claire, Douglas is confronted by special envoy Garbo who arrives to speed the transactions. Douglas gets romantic, while Garbo treats love as a biological problem.

□ 1939: Nominations: Best Picture, Actress (Greta Garbo), Original Story, Screenplay

■ NINTH CONFIGURATION, THE

1980, 105 MINS, US ◇ ⓥ ⊙
Dir William Peter Blatty   *Prod* William Peter Blatty *Scr* William Peter Blatty   *Ph* Gerry Fisher   *Ed* T. Battle Davis, Peter Lee-Thompson, Roberto Silvi   *Mus* Barry DeVorzon   *Art Dir* Bill Malley, J. Dennis Washington
● Stacy Keach, Scott Wilson, Jason Miller, Neville Brand, Moses Gunn, Robert Loggia (Warner)

The Ninth Configuration is an often confusing story concerning the effects of a new 'doctor' on an institution for crazed military men which manages to effectively tie itself together in the end. Problem is the William Peter Blatty film takes entirely too long to explain itself.

Blatty makes his directorial debut here in addition to performing, producing and writing from his own novel.

Stacy Keach limns an army colonel who has been brought Stateside to play psychiatrist to a compound of disturbed military men. From the beginning it's apparent Keach is infinitely more disturbed than any of the men he is supposed to be treating, making the actor's monotone, robot-like state unbearably grating on the nerves only minutes after his appearance.

■ NOAH'S ARK THE STORY OF THE DELUGE

1928, 135 MINS, US
Dir Michael Curtiz   *Prod* Darryl F. Zanuck   *Scr* Darryl F. Zanuck, Anthony Goldeway, De Leon Anthony *Ph* Hal Mohr, Barney McGill   *Mus* Louis Silvers
● Dolores Costello, George O'Brien, Noah Beery, Guinn Williams, Paul McAllister, Myrna Loy (Warner)

Noah's Ark has touches reminiscent of *Ten Commandments*, *King of Kings*, *Wings*, *The Big Parade* and quite a few other [1920s] screen epics. Better than $1.5 million was reported to have been spent on this film.

The Warner staff show everything conceivable under the sun – mobs, mobs and mobs; Niagaras of water; train wreck; war aplenty; crashes; deluges and everything. Nothing is missed from 'way back when folks thought that praying to the real God instead of Jehovah was the right thing until Noah got the message from above that it was not.

The story opens with scenes showing what is left of the world after the big deluge. It then drifts into the age where folks worshipped the Golden Calf and their lust for gold. It flashes modern to the extent of bringing to the fore the selfish motive of man. A flash is shown of the stock exchange in New York on a panicky day. A guy gets bumped off.

Then they hop to Europe. The scene is the Orient Express from Constantinople to Paris just as the First World War is in the air. There are folks of every nationality on the train. War is the topic.

Talk does not enter into the picture until after the first 35 minutes. It starts with love scene between George O'Brien and Dolores Costello and then brings in talk by Wallace Beery, Paul McAllister and Guinn Williams. The Costello voice hurts the impression made by her silent acting.

Beery is great as the Russian spy and as the King. McAllister, an old stage trouper, has a hard job with biblical quotations which are overdone. Voice okay but talk just a bit too much.

■ NOBODY'S FOOL

1986, 107 MINS, US ◇ ⓥ ⊙
Dir Evelyn Purcell   *Prod* James C. Katz, Jon S. Denny *Scr* Beth Henley   *Ph* Mikhail Suslov   *Ed* Dennis Virkler *Mus* James Newton Howard   *Art Dir* Jackson DeGovia

● Rosanna Arquette, Eric Roberts, Mare Winningham, Jim Youngs, Louise Fletcher (Island/Katz-Denny)

Nobody's Fool features kookiness without real comedy, romance without magic.

Rosanna Arquette, a smalltown western girl, attends dutifully to her burned-out mother and bratty younger brother as she tries to forget the public shame and ridicule she endured when she impulsively stabbed her old beau in a restaurant. She is as insecure as can be when Eric Roberts, the lighting technician with a visiting theatrical troupe, begins quietly noticing her.

Arquette's performance, like the film, features hits and misses, yet there is something frequently moving about the character's scattershot approach to emotional salvation. Roberts, more subdued than usual, effectively registers the impulses of a young man who thinks he can save Arquette from her prospective dismal fate.

● ●

■ NOBODY WAVED GOODBYE

1964, 80 MINS, CANADA
Dir Don Owen *Prod* Roman Kroitor, Don Owen
Scr Don Owen *Ph* John Spotton *Ed* John Spotton, Donald Ginsberg *Mus* Eldon Rathburn
● Peter Kastner, Julie Biggs, Claude Rae, Toby Tarnow, Charmion King, Ron Taylor (National Film Board of Canada)

This is a simple story, simply told, about a couple of Toronto juves, the boy typically smartalecky, the girl attractive, decent and naive. From truancy and petty offenses, the road is downhill until by fadeout the young couple is split, the girl pregnant, and the boy having to decide whether to go back and face the music for theft, while there's still time to rehabilitate himself.

It's not a flawless film by any means. Some of the dialogue is dull. The acting in instances is bordering on bush league. The camera work veers to the pretentious. By and large, however, even if the story line becomes hokey and a little soap-operaish in content, the film could be a winner.

Peter Kastner and Julie Biggs have high and low points in the leads, but they're naturally charming enough to get away with momentary lapses in their performance.

● ●

■ NO HOLDS BARRED

1989, 91 MINS, US ◇ ⓦ ⊙
Dir Thomas J. Wright *Prod* Michael Rachmil
Scr Dennis Hackin *Ph* Frank Beascoechea *Ed* Tom Pryor *Mus* Jim Johnston *Art Dir* James Shanahan
● Hulk Hogan, Kurt Fuller, Joan Severance, Tom 'Tiny' Lister, Mark Pellegrino, Bill Henderson (Shane)

No Holds Barred is a disappointing big-screen vehicle for wrestling champ Hulk Hogan. Extremely lame plotline has tyrannical TV network boss Kurt Fuller unable to coax Rip (Hogan) away from a rival web. Fuller's counter-move is to telecast live tough-guy contests, with muscular and mean black wrestler Tiny Lester emerging the winner.

In a cliched fashion, Rip must meet Lister (as Zeus) in the octagonal ring while a race against the clock goes on to find his kidnaped girlfriend (Joan Severance) or Rip will have to 'throw' the match to save her pretty neck.

Fans are bound to be disappointed by the uninteresting wrestling action on display here, poorly photographed to boot. Toilet humor abounds and far too much footage is devoted to Fuller's wimpy, bumbling henchmen (Charles Levin and David Palmer).

Best scenes are when Hogan takes his rassling into the street and applies it comic-book-style to smash up limos and anything else in his way.

● ●

■ NOISES OFF

1992, 104 MINS, US ◇ ⓦ ⊙
Dir Peter Bogdanovich *Prod* Frank Marshall *Scr* Marty Kaplan *Ph* Tim Suhrstedt *Ed* Lisa Day *Mus* Phil Marshall (adapt.) *Art Dir* Norman Newberry
● Carol Burnett, Michael Caine, Denholm Elliott, Julie Hagerty, Marilu Henner, Christopher Reeve (Touchstone/ Amblin)

Michael Frayn's [1982] play centered on a theatrical company bumbling through the British provinces in a silly sex comedy, *Nothing On*. With the first act taken up with a disastrous dress rehearsal, Frayn's coup de theatre came in the second act, when the curtain came up on the behind-the-scenes shenanigans of a feuding cast. Third act was devoted to a presentation of the play so lax that most of the lines were ad libbed.

In Marty Kaplan's smart adaptation, the company is an American troupe working toward a New York opening. Action is framed – and the acts are divided – by director Michael Caine fretting outside a Broadway theater during the opening-night performance. Otherwise, Kaplan and director Peter Bogdanovich are faithful to their source.

Thesps include Carol Burnett as a slovenly housekeeper; John Ritter as a real estate agent planning to give sexy Nicollette Sheridan a personal tour of the bedroom; Christopher Reeve and Marilu Henner as the owners of the home who slip back into Britain from their tax haven in Spain; and Denholm Elliott as an inept burglar.

Bogdanovich has judged his approach to the material astutely, resisting impulses toward comic overkill or transferring focus away from the stage. He takes his cue from the actors, and the camera is always in the right place.

● ●

■ NOMADS

1985, 100 MINS, US ◇ ⓦ
Dir John McTiernan *Prod* Elliott Kastner *Scr* John McTiernan *Ph* Stephen Ramsey *Ed* Michael John Bateman *Mus* Bill Conti *Art Dir* Marcia Hinds
● Pierce Brosnan, Lesley-Anne Down, Anna-Maria Montecelli, Adam Ant, Hector Mercado, Josie Cotton (PSO/Kastner/Cinema 7)

Nomads avoids the more obvious ripped-guts devices in favor of dramatic visual scares. Director John McTiernan even has some kind of a love interest in his story without cluttering up the plot with sticky romance or strained eroticism. In fact, everything seems to come naturally in a tale that even has the supernatural ring true.

Pierce Brosnan plays French anthropologist Pommier who intends to settle in LA with his wife Niki (Anna-Maria Montecelli), when flesh-and-blood (seemingly) Evil Spirits of nomads he once studied in arctic and desert regions materialize to haunt him. They now look like death-pale punkers.

The acting of Brosnan and Lesley-Anne Down (as a doctor) is the more effective for being restrained. Singer Adam Ant is seen as one of the Nomads.

● ●

■ NO MAN OF HER OWN

1950, 97 MINS, US
Dir Mitchell Leisen *Prod* Richard Maibaum *Scr* Sally Benson, Catherine Turney *Ph* Daniel L. Fapp *Ed* Alma Macrorie *Mus* Hugo Friedhofer *Art Dir* Hans Dreier, Henry Bumstead
● Barbara Stanwyck, John Lund, Phyllis Thaxter, Lyle Bettger, Jane Cowl, Milburn Stone (Paramount)

No Man of Her Own combines an adult love story with melodrama, runs off with the intensity of a full-bloom soap opera, and is altogether satisfying screen dramatics [from a novel by William Irish].

Barbara Stanwyck does a beautiful job of portraying the heroine, a girl who has been kicked out by her lover after becoming preg-

nant. She takes advantage of a train accident to assume the identity of a fellow passenger killed in the wreck and moves in with the latter's in-laws to assure her son a home and the love of good people. Her happiness is threatened when the ex-lover tracks her down.

John Lund wraps up his role as the man who falls in love with a girl he believes to be the widow of his dead brother. It's a fine job.

● ●

■ NO MAN'S LAND

1987, 106 MINS, US ◇ ⓦ ⊙
Dir Peter Werner *Prod* Joseph Stern, Dick Wolf *Scr* Dick Wolf *Ph* Hiro Narita *Ed* Steve Cohen *Mus* Basil Poledouris *Art Dir* Paul Peters
● Charlie Sheen, D.B. Sweeney, Randy Quaid, Lara Harris, Bill Duke, R.D. Call (Orion)

No Man's Land is a stylish thriller about a lower-class rookie cop becoming caught up in the fast-lane high life of the filthy rich car thief he's assigned to nail.

Charlie Sheen and D.B. Sweeney are both extremely effective as two young men, barely into their 20s, whose diametrically opposed backgrounds make for a dynamic and ultimately deadly relationship.

Sweeney is assigned by boss Randy Quaid to take a job at a Porsche garage that doubles as a 'chop shop,' where stolen cars are broken up and reassembled as untraceable new vehicles. Quaid suspects the wealthy owner, Sheen, of having killed another policeman, and Sweeney, despite his total inexperience, is supposed to get the goods on him.

A little joyriding and partying with the handsome, crafty Sheen easily seduces Sweeney into taking a softer view of illegal activity. He comes to like Sheen a lot and, furthermore, gets sexually involved with the latter's beautiful sister (Lara Harris).

Scenarist Dick Wolf is a vet of both *Hill Street Blues* and *Miami Vice* and both influences turn up here, as he has carefully worked out the script to offer opportunities for the character nuances of the first show and the flash of the second.

● ●

■ NO MERCY

1986, 105 MINS, US ◇ ⓦ ⊙
Dir Richard Pearce *Prod* D. Constantine Conte *Scr* Jim Carabatsos *Ph* Michel Brault *Ed* Jerry Greenberg, Bill Yahraus *Mus* Alan Silvestri *Art Dir* Patrizia Von Brandenstein
● Richard Gere, Kim Basinger, Jeroen Krabbe, George Dzundza, Gary Basaraba, William Atherton (Tri-Star Delphi IV & V)

Despite some graphically brutal violence and a fair bit of 'too-cool' police jargon, *No Mercy* turns out to be a step above most other films in this blooming genre of lone-cop-turned-vigilante stories.

Eddie Jillette (Richard Gere) and his partner Joe Collins (Gary Basaraba) get wind of a contract to kill a Louisiana crime overlord. They go undercover as the hit men, but find they are dealing with a much bigger, much deadlier fish as Collins is murdered brutally. Jillette has only one lead in tracking his partner's murder, a mysterious blond (Kim Basinger).

From the native, wild beauty of the Louisiana swamplands to the steamy, colourful French quarter of New Orleans, the film is a tightly woven piece.

Credit also goes to Gere, now sporting a noticeably older, grayer look, who manages to bring that maturity to his often typecast roles of the angry young man.

● ●

■ NONE BUT THE BRAVE

1965, 105 MINS, US/JAPAN ◇ ⓦ ⊙
Dir Frank Sinatra *Prod* Frank Sinatra, Kikumaru Okuda *Scr* John Twist, Katsuya Susaki *Ph* Harold Lipstein

Ed Sam O'Steen   *Mus* John Williams   *Art Dir* LeRoy
Deane
● Frank Sinatra, Clint Walker, Tommy Sands, Bill
Dexter, Tony Bill, Tatsuya Mihashi (Artanis/Tokyo Eiga-
Toho)

Marking the first joint screen venture actually filmed by an American and Japanese
company in the US, *None but the Brave* manages a high level of interest via its unusual
premise and action-adventure backdrop.

Frank Sinatra, who also stars with Clint
Walker and produces, makes his directorial
bow and is responsible for some good effects
in maintaining a suspenseful pace. The compact and mostly tenseful screenplay tells its
story [by Kikumaru Okuda] through the eyes
of a Japanese lieutenant, commanding a
small detachment of troops forgotten on an
uncharted South Pacific island where an
American plane carrying US Marines crash-
lands.

A truce is arranged by the Japanese commander and Walker, the American pilot and
senior officer, after Sinatra, as a pharmacist's
mate, amputates the leg of one of the
Japanese soldiers wounded in a skirmish with
the Americans. Americans' radio is believed
destroyed in the crash, and with no means of
communication for the Japanese it seems that
both sides are destined to sweat out the war
on the island.

Sinatra appears only intermittently, his
character only important in the operation
scene which he enacts dramatically.

■ **NONE BUT THE LONELY HEART**

1944, 110 MINS, US ⦿
Dir Clifford Odets   *Prod* David Hempstead   *Scr* Clifford
Odets   *Ph* George Barnes   *Ed* Roland Gross
Mus Hanns Eisler   *Art Dir* Albert S. D'Agostino, Jack
Okey
● Cary Grant, Ethel Barrymore, Barry Fitzgerald, June
Duprez, Jane Wyatt, Dan Duryea (RKO)

With the sotto voce accent on any social significance, *Heart* [from Richard Llewellyn's
novel] emerges as a medley of simple romance in London's east side, interspersed
with a little melodrama. The meller phase
doesn't bestir matters until almost an hour
and a half from scratch when the limey hoodlums hijack Ike Weber's pawnshop and beat
up the kindly loan broker.

Cary Grant starts as a shiftless cockney who
lets his struggling mother (Ethel Barrymore)
fend for herself with her small, secondhand
shop beneath their dingy home until the
pawnbroker-friend (well underplayed by
Konstantin Shayne) tips him off that his
mother is dying of cancer.

When Grant sees the light and decides to
cease vagabonding, he becomes an almost
model son. An expert clock and furniture re-
pairer and piano-tuner, he helps make his
mother's little business thrive until he himself gets mixed up with the mob, while the
mother succumbs to the temptations of dealing in stolen goods.
☐ 1944: Best Supp. Actress (Ethel
Barrymore)
☐ Nominations: Best Actor (Cary Grant),
Editing, Scoring of a Dramatic Picture

■ **NO, NO, NANETTE**

1940, 96 MINS, US
Dir Herbert Wilcox   *Prod* Herbert Wilcox   *Scr* Ken
Englund   *Ph* Russell Metty   *Ed* Elmo Williams
Mus Vincent Youmans
● Anna Neagle, Richard Carlson, Victor Mature, Roland
Young, Helen Broderick, ZaSu Pitts (Suffolk/RKO Radio)

Musical comedies rarely have much story.
That's all right. No one expects them to. Plot
is compensated for in a hit tune show by good
music. That's an elementary show business
lesson taught in a class that producer

Herbert Wilcox must have skipped. In making a film version of the 1925 Broadway hit
[by Frank Mandel, Otto Harbach, Vincent
Youmans and Emil Nyltray], Wilcox saves all
the book but very little of the music. 'Tea for
Two' and 'I Want to Be Happy', as well as the
title tune, 'No, No, Nanette' have been reduced to virtually incidental music.

Even at that, Wilcox has been fortunate.
Nanette has a pretty good plot as musical comedy plots go. He has erred, however, in complicating it instead of simplifying it, as was
needed. Wilcox has been lavish, however, in
instilling production values in *Nanette* and
there's no denying, despite their age, the lilt
of the Vincent Youmans tunes.

Anna Neagle, as the little Miss Fiix-It who
sparks the film, is passable. Roland Young,
with accustomed facility, tops the cast-appeal.
Runners-up are Helen Broderick and ZaSu
Pitts, which makes it clear that all the honors
go to the older generation. Neagle and the
youngsters, Richard Carlson, Victor Mature
and Eve Arden, show to no advantage against
such a trio of comedy vets.

Yarn finds Young a gay oldster with a penchant for making people happy, particularly
pretty girls, by promising them help to get
ahead in their fields. Neagle as Young's niece,
sets about getting each of the femmes the
things she wants, thus keeping from Young's
wife the sordid details. Mature is a theatrical
producer and Carlson an artist. Nanette
works on each to take the trouble-making females under their wings and save the family
honor.

■ **NORA PRENTISS**

1947, 110 MINS, US
Dir Vincent Sherman   *Prod* William Jacobs   *Scr* N.
Richard Nash   *Ph* James Wong Howe   *Ed* Owen Marks
Mus Franz Waxman   *Art Dir* Anton Grot
● Ann Sheridan, Kent Smith, Bruce Bennett, Robert
Alda, Rosemary De Camp, John Ridgely (Warner)

Nora Prentiss is an overlong melodrama, a
story of romance between a married man and
a girl. But it's never quite believable. Ann
Sheridan makes much of her role but the production has unsympathetic slant for leads and
a lack of smoothness. Background is San
Francisco and New York, with authentic
footage of both sites a physical aide.

Yarn [by Paul Webster and Jack Sobell]
concerns a stuffy, middle-aged doctor who
falls in love with a nightclub singer. To follow
his love to New York, the doctor fakes death,
destroying the body of a patient who had died
in his office and assuming latter's identity.
This fact traps him later when he's arrested
for killing himself. Plot is supposedly based
on actual insurance case history, but script is
full of holes that make for featherweight motivation.

Sheridan is the singer, and has two tunes to
warble. As the doctor, Kent Smith is okay
dramatically in a part that doesn't hold much
water. Bruce Bennett, co-starred, has little to
do as a medico friend of Smith's.

■ **NORMA RAE**

1979, 113 MINS, US ◇ ⦿ ⊙
Dir Martin Ritt   *Prod* Tamara Asseyev, Alex Rose
Scr Irving Ravetch, Harriet Frank   *Ph* John A. Alonzo
Ed Sidney Levin   *Mus* David Shire   *Art Dir* Walter Scott
Herndon
● Sally Field, Beau Bridges, Ron Leibman, Pat Hingle,
Gail Strickland, Lonny Chapman (20th Century-Fox)

g*Norma Rae* is that rare entity, an intelligent
film with heart.

Films about unions haven't always fared
well at the boxoffice, but that didn't deter director Martin Ritt and screenwriters from updating the traditional management-labor
struggles to a sharp contemporary setting.

Now the battle is being waged in Southern
textile mills, where the din of the machinery
is virtually unbearable, and workers either go
deaf or suffer the consumptive effects of
'brown lung' disease.

Ron Leibman arriveson the scene as a New
York-based labor organizer, who picks Sally
Field as his most likely convert. This unlikely
pairing of Jewish radicalism and Southern mi-
asma is the core of *Norma Rae*, and is made
real and touching by the individual performances of Leibman and Field.

The pacing is fresh and never laggard, and
Norma Rae virtually hums right along.
☐ 1979: Best Actress (Sally Field), Song ('It
Goes Like This').
☐ Nominations: Best Picture, Adapted
Screenplay

■ **NORTH BY NORTHWEST**

1959, 136 MINS, UK ◇ ⦿ ⊙
Dir Alfred Hitchcock   *Prod* Alfred Hitchcock   *Scr* Ernest
Lehman   *Ph* Robert Burks   *Ed* George Tomasini
Mus Bernard Herrmann   *Art Dir* Robert Boyle, William
A. Horning
● Cary Grant, Eva Marie Saint, James Mason, Jessie
Royce Landis, Leo G. Carroll, Martin Landau (M-G-M)

North by Northwest is the Alfred Hitchcock mixture – suspense, intrigue, comedy, humor.
Seldom has the concoction been served up so
delectably. Hitchcock uses actual locations –
the Plaza in New York, the Ambassador East
in Chicago, Grand Central Station, the 20th
Century, Limited, United Nations headquarters in Manhattan, Mount Rushmore
National Monument, the plains of Indiana.
One scene, where the hero is ambushed by an
airplane on the flat, sun-baked prairie, is a
brilliant use of location.

Cary Grant brings technique and charm to
the central character. He is a Madison
Avenue man-about-Manhattan, sleekly handsome, carelessly twice-divorced, debonair as a
cigaret ad. The story gets underway when
he's mistaken for a US intelligence agent by a
pack of foreign agents headed by James
Mason. The complications are staggering but
they play like an Olympic version of a three-
legged race.

Grant's problem is to avoid getting knocked
off by Mason's gang without tipping them
that he is a classic case of the innocent bystander. The case is serious, but Hitchcock's
macabre sense of humor and instinct for romantic byplay never allows it to stay grim for
too long. Suspense is deliberately broken for
relief and then skillfully re-established.

Eva Marie Saint dives headfirst into Mata
Hari and shows she can be unexpectedly and
thoroughly glamorous. She also manages the
difficult impression of seeming basically innocent while explaining how she becomes
Mason's mistress. Mason, in a rather stock
role, is properly forbidding.

Robert Burks' photography, whether in the
hot yellows of the prairie plain, or the soft
green of South Dakota forests, is lucid and
imaginatively composed. It is the first Metro
release in VistaVision. Bernard Herrmann's
score is a tingling one, particularly in the
Mount Rushmore sequences, but light where
mood requires.
☐ 1959: Nominations: Best Original Story &
Screenplay, Color Art Direction, Editing

■ **NORTH DALLAS FORTY**

1979, 119 MINS, US ◇ ⦿ ⊙
Dir Ted Kotcheff   *Prod* Frank Yablans   *Scr* Frank
Yablans, Ted Kotcheff, Peter Gent   *Ph* Paul Lohmann
Ed Jay Kamen   *Mus* John Scott   *Art Dir* Alfred Sweeney
● Nick Nolte, Mac Davis, Charles Durning, Dabney
Coleman, Dayle Haddon, Bo Svenson (Paramount)

It's no surprise that the National Football
League refused to cooperate in the making of

N

North Dallas Forty. The production is a most realistic, hard-hitting and perceptive look at the seamy side of pro football.

What distinguishes this screen adaptation of Peter Gent's bestseller is the exploration of a human dimension almost never seen in sports pix. Most people understand that modern-day athletes are just cogs in a big business wheel, but getting that across on the screen is a whole different matter. And in large measure, that success is due to a bravura performance in the lead role by Nick Nolte.

Ted Kotcheff keeps the action flowing smoothly, and has perfectly captured the locker-room intensity and post-game letdown that never shows up on the tube.

● ●

■ NORTH SEA HIJACK
(US: ffolkes)

1980, 99 MINS, UK ◇ ⓦ
Dir Andrew V. McLaglen *Prod* Elliott Kastner *Scr* Jack Davies *Ph* Tony Imi *Ed* Alan Strachan *Mus* Michael J. Lewis *Art Dir* Bert Davey
● Roger Moore, James Mason, Anthony Perkins, Michael Parks, Jack Watson (Universal)

The biggest attraction is the banter between Roger Moore and the various types with whom he comes in conflict during his preparations to save a hijacked supply ship.

A misogynistic but dedicated frogman, whose private crew of frogmen are the only seeming rescuers of the ship, Moore is today's ideal male chauvinistic pig. And delights in it. He doesn't even mind telling the British Prime Minister (a lady, of course) what he thinks of the situation.

He's ably supported by James Mason as a by-the-book admiral. Mason is also given star billing and almost builds his role into deserving it but Anthony Perkins and especially Michael Parks certainly belong below the title.

● ●

■ NORTH STAR, THE

1943, 105 MINS, US ⓦ
Dir Lewis Milestone *Prod* Samuel Goldwyn *Scr* Lillian Hellman *Ph* James Wong Howe *Ed* Daniel Mandell *Mus* Aaron Copland
● Anne Baxter, Dana Andrews, Walter Huston, Walter Brennan, Farley Granger, Erich von Stroheim (RKO)

Samuel Goldwyn as the producer and Lillian Hellman, the writer, team to tell of the Nazi invasion of the Soviet. As entertainment, however, there's too much running time consumed before the film actually gets into its story and, in parts, it is seemingly a too-obviously contrived narrative detailing the virtues of the Soviet regime.

Setting the background for the actual climax is a long and sometimes tedious one. The early parts of the film are almost always colorful in depicting the simple life of the villagers around whom this story revolves, but it's a question of too premeditatedly setting, a stage of a simple, peace-loving people who, through the bestiality of the enemy, are driven to an heroic defense that must, in time, become legendary. For this is the story of the Soviet people as seen through the eyes of a small village.

Hellman's story, when she finally gets around to it, is a parallel one, dealing with a picnic group that's suddenly called on to rush arms through the German lines to their guerrilla comrades when the sudden invasion catches them unawares while on a walking trip. It is an exciting tale from here on in.
☐ 1943: Nominations: Best Original Screenplay, B&W Cinematography, B&W Art Direction, Scoring of a Dramatic Picture, Sound, Special Effects

● ●

■ NORTH WEST FRONTIER
(US: Flame Over India)

1959, 129 MINS, UK ◇ ⓦ
Dir J. Lee Thompson *Prod* Marcel Hellman *Scr* Robin Estridge *Ph* Geoffrey Unsworth *Ed* Freddie Wilson *Mus* Mischa Spoliansky *Art Dir* Alex Vetchinsky
● Kenneth More, Lauren Bacall, Herbert Lom, Wilfrid Hyde White, I.S. Johar, Ursula Jeans (Rank)

From a smash opening to quietly confident fade, *North West Frontier* is basically the ageless chase yarn, transferred from the prairie to the sun-baked plains of India and done with a spectacular flourish [adapted from a screenplay by Frank Nugent, based on an original story by Patrick Ford and Will Price].

Handled with tremendous assurance by J. Lee Thompson, the film is reminiscent of the same director's *Ice Cold in Alex*, with an ancient locomotive replacing the ambulance in that desert war story and with hordes of beturbaned tribesmen substituting for the Nazi patrols.

Time is the turn of the century when the English still held sway in India. Kenneth More plays an officer ordered to take a boy prince, sacred figurehead to the Hindus, to safety in the teeth of Moslems. In company with an assorted group, More makes his getaway from a besieged citadel in a makeshift coach drawn by a worn-out locomotive.

Throughout, the cast serves the job expertly, More coming through as solid and dependable if a shade too unemotional. Lauren Bacall scores with a keen delineation of the prince's outspoken nurse. Herbert Lom is first-rate as a journalist. I.S. Johar is the hit of the picture as the Indian railroad man.

● ●

■ NORTH WEST MOUNTED POLICE

1940, 125 MINS, US ◇
Dir Cecil B. DeMille, Arthur Rosson, Eric Stacey *Prod* Cecil B. DeMille *Scr* Alan LeMay, Jesse Lasky Jr, C. Gardner Sullivan *Ph* Victor Milner, W. Howard Greene *Ed* Anne Bauchens *Mus* Victor Young *Art Dir* Hans Dreier, Roland Anderson
● Gary Cooper, Madeleine Carroll, Preston Foster, Paulette Goddard, Robert Preston, George Bancroft (Paramount)

The story is founded upon an incident of insurrection and bloodshed which took place in and around Regina in 1885, when Canadian troops finally subdued a settlers' discontent and revolt.

With that much fact to start from, scripters weave a story which has its exciting moments, a reasonable and convincing romance and a hero who is a pure Texan from down near the Rio Grande. Gary Cooper is the man from the South, and although Canadian uprisings are none of his business (he is one of the Texan Rangers on search for a murderer) he finds himself in the middle of gunplay before the end of the second reel.

Preston Foster as the sergeant-leader of the redcoats gets the better of Cooper in the contest for Madeleine Carroll. Foster has the girl and Cooper has George Bancroft, the heavy, tied up with his lariat and on his way back home. Before that takes place there are innumerable plot complications involving Paulette Goddard, a half-breed vixen; Robert Preston, one of the mounted who faltered in outpost duty; Walter Hampden, a big Indian chief; and Akim Tamiroff and Lynne Overman, who stage their own private duel of marksmanship, which is hilarious.

Interesting novelty is an introductory soundtrack talk by DeMille in which he recounts the historical basis for the film.
☐ 1940: Best Editing.
☐ Nominations: Best Color Cinematography, Color Art Direction, Original Score, Sound

● ●

■ NORTHWEST PASSAGE

1940, 125 MINS, US ◇ ⓦ ⊙
Dir King Vidor *Prod* Hunt Stromberg *Scr* Laurence Stallings, Talbot Jennings *Ph* Sidney Wagner, William V. Skall *Ed* Conrad A. Nervig *Mus* Herbert Stothart *Art Dir* Cedric Gibbons, Malcolm Brown
● Spencer Tracy, Robert Young, Walter Brennan, Ruth Hussey, Nat Pendleton, Donald McBride (M-G-M)

Northwest Passage, which hit a negative cost of nearly $2 million, is a fine epic adventure. The picture carries through only the first half of the novel [by Kenneth Roberts] and is so designated in the main title. The title is misleading from an historical standpoint as it only covers the one expedition through upper New York state to the St Lawrence territory where the village of a hostile tribe is wiped out.

Spencer Tracy is brilliantly impressive as the dominating and driving leader of Rogers' Rangers, a band of 160 trained settlers inducted into service to clean up the hostile tribes to make homes and families safe. Robert Young, as the Harvardian who joins the Rangers to sketch Indians, has a more virile role than others assigned him and turns in a fine performance. Walter Brennan provides a typically fine characterization as the friend of Young.

There's a peculiar fascination in the unfolding of the historical narrative and adventure of the inspired band on the march to and from the Indian village. It's a continual battle against natural hazards, possible sudden attacks by ambushing enemies, and a display of indomitable courage to drive through swamps and over mountains for days at a time without food. It's grim and stark drama of those pioneers who blazed trails through the wilderness to make living in this country safe for their families and descendants.
☐ 1940: Nomination: Best Color Cinematography

● ●

■ NO SMALL AFFAIR

1984, 102 MINS, US ◇ ⓦ ⊙
Dir Jerry Schatzberg *Prod* William Sackheim *Scr* Charles Bolt, Terence Mulcahy *Ph* Vilmos Zsigmond *Ed* Priscilla Nedd, Eve Newman, Melvin Shapiro *Mus* Rupert Holmes *Art Dir* Robert Boyle
● Jon Cryer, Demi Moore, George Wendt, Peter Frechette, Elizabeth Daily, Ann Wedgeworth (Columbia-Delphi II)

No Small Affair is an okay coming-of-age romance in which the believability of the leading characters far outweighs that of many of the situations in which the script places them.

Film is set in San Francisco and has Jon Cryer as a 16-year-old who's precocious in still photography but not much else, being difficult socially and unresponsive to girls his own age.

By chance, he snaps a shot of a sharp looking gal by the waterfront and, by chance again, he finds her singing in a seedy North Beach nightspot. In a selfless effort to give her sluggish career a boost, he spends his entire life savings and gets her photo placed on top of 175 SF taxicabs.

Ultimately, she is invited to LA by a record company and, before she leaves, the inevitable occurs.

● ●

■ NOT AS A STRANGER

1955, 135 MINS, US
Dir Stanley Kramer *Prod* Stanley Kramer *Scr* Edna Anhalt, Edward Anhalt *Ph* Franz Planer *Ed* Fred Knudtson *Mus* George Antheil *Art Dir* Rudolph Sternad, Howard Richmond
● Olivia de Havilland, Robert Mitchum, Frank Sinatra, Gloria Grahame, Broderick Crawford, Charles Bickford (United Artists)

Producer Stanley Kramer, a man with a penchant for offbeat choices, took Morton Thompson's best-selling novel of a young doctor as the occasion of his own directorial debut.

Some of the most interesting characterizations appear only in the second story (out of three). Charles Bickford comes near to stealing the picture. Gloria Grahame, as a neurotic widow with lots of money, also stands out, though the part is much changed from the novel and never too clear in her motivations.

Frank Sinatra is another of the players who comes close to doing a little picture stealing. And what about the hero of the story? He's Robert Mitchum and he's considerably over his acting depth. Though some scenes come off fairly well, Mitchum is poker-faced from start to finish.

☐ 1955: Nomination: Best Sound

....

■ NOTHING BUT THE BEST

1964, 99 MINS, UK ◇

Dir Clive Donner   *Prod* David Deutsch   *Scr* Frederic Raphael   *Ph* Nicolas Roeg   *Ed* Fergus McDonell   *Mus* Ron Grainer   *Art Dir* Reece Pemberton
● Alan Bates, Denholm Elliott, Harry Andrews, Millicent Martin (Domino/Anglo Amalgamated)

This stylish British comedy takes a sly, penetrating peek at the social climbing upper classes that use the Old School tie, social connections, well padded bank balances and the Smart Set background to further their material ambitions.

It is ruthless in its unpeeling of the dubious foibles and mannerisms of its characters, none of whom fails to have an axe to gind. It's the story of an ambitious young man of humble background who, excited by the glitter of money, business power and an entry into the fascinating world of Hunt Balls, Ascot, smart restaurants, shooting, hunting, fishin' and the rest of the trappings, lies, bluffs, smiles, cheats, loves, and smoothtalks his way to marrying the boss' daughter, and doesn't stop at murder en route.

Alan Bates, showing a previously unexplored vein of comedy, is firstclass as the dubious hero. This is a measured, confident performance that appeals even when he is behaving at his worst. Many of the top scenes are those with Denholm Elliott who, in fact, turns in the best acting of the lot.

....

■ NOTHING BUT TROUBLE

1991, 94 MINS, US ◇ ⊛ ⊙

Dir Dan Aykroyd   *Prod* Robert K. Weiss   *Scr* Dan Aykroyd   *Ph* Dean Cundey   *Ed* Malcolm Campbell, James Symons   *Mus* Michael Kamen   *Art Dir* William Sandell
● Chevy Chase, Dan Aykroyd, John Candy, Demi Moore (Warner/Applied Action)

First-time director Dan Aykroyd might have once parodied this sort of wretched excess in his 'bad-cinema' sketches on *Saturday Night Live*. Premise, stripped to the bone, had potential: a faceless drive-through town seems to have no resident except the cop who miraculously appears to pinch unsuspecting drivers.

The one-joke starter is then taken to absurd extremes as four Manhattan yuppies get shanghaied to the village of Valkenvania, where a demented old judge (Aykroyd, in heavy makeup) metes out executioner-style justice over moving violations.

The story [by Peter Aykroyd] turns into an extended maze with Chevy Chase and Demi Moore as the principal Nintendo-ized targets running through one tepid peril after another, while mouthing banal wisecracks.

It's a good bet a film is in trouble when the highlight comes from seeing John Candy in drag.

....

■ NOTHING SACRED

1937, 75 MINS, US ◇ ⊛ ⊙

Dir William A. Wellman   *Prod* David O. Selznick   *Scr* Ben Hecht   *Ph* W. Howard Greene   *Ed* James E. Newcom, Hal Kern   *Mus* Oscar Levant   *Art Dir* Lyle Wheeler
● Carole Lombard, Fredric March, Charles Winninger, Walter Connolly, Sig Rumann, Frank Fay (Selznick/United Artists)

Ben Hecht wrote the adaptation for *Sacred* from the William Street magazine story detailing the experiences of a village beauty who becomes the center of a fantastic newspaper circulation stunt which justifies itself in the belief, unfounded, that the girl has only a short time to live. Hecht handles the material breezily and pungently, poking fun in typical manner of half-scorn at the newspaper publisher, his reporter, doctors, the newspaper business, phonies, suckers, and whatnot.

For added value there is tinting by Technicolor which greatly enhances its pictorial charm. The running time is only 75 minutes, making this a meaty and well-edited piece of entertainment from start to finish. There are no lagging moments.

Fredric March does the reporter behind the dizzy ride given Carole Lombard by a sucker-victimized New York which thinks she already has one foot in the grave. Walter Connolly bristles with importance from a comedy viewpoint as March's publisher-boss. Charles Winninger does the rural medico who hates newspapers but not booze.

....

■ NO TIME FOR LOVE

1944, 83 MINS, US

Dir Mitchell Leisen   *Prod* Fred Kohlmar   *Scr* Claude Binyon   *Ph* Charles Lang Jr   *Ed* Alma Macrorie   *Mus* Victor Young
● Claudette Colbert, Fred MacMurray, Ilka Chase, Ruth Havoc, Richard Haydn, Paul McGrath (Paramount)

Escapist is the word, and *No Time for Love* is just that, in spades. Starring Claudette Colbert and Fred MacMurray in a Claude Binyon screenplay [adapted by Warren Duff from a story by Robert Lees and Fred Rinaldo] that's heavily loaded for laughs, this pic is rather obviously contrived in some of its situations, but there's no denying a sufficiency of crack dialog – and the laughs that go with it. Mitchell Leisen handles both the production and direction reins, giving *No Time* both barrels on each count.

Story concerns a famous femme photographer for a national picture magazine (Colbert), and the complications that evolve when, on an assignment to lens a tunnel construction project, she meets up with a sandhog (MacMurray).

From there on the basic story is pretty much pretense, but the laughs come fast, and the performances by Colbert and MacMurray are capital.

Colbert emphasizes her flair for comedy and doesn't spare herself either in relegating her usual sartorial elegance for the sake of serious story values, as indicated in the climactic scene when she gets spilled into a lake of spewing mud from a tunnel cave-in.

☐ 1944: Nomination: Best B&W Art Direction

....

■ NOTORIOUS

1946, 101 MINS, US ⊛ ⊙

Dir Alfred Hitchcock   *Prod* Alfred Hitchcock   *Scr* Ben Hecht   *Ph* Ted Tetzlaff   *Ed* Theron Warth   *Mus* Roy Webb   *Art Dir* Albert S. D'Agostino, Carroll Clark
● Cary Grant, Ingrid Bergman, Claude Rains, Louis Calhern, Reinhold Schunzel, Moroni Olsen (RKO)

Production and directorial skill of Alfred Hitchcock combine with a suspenseful story and excellent performances to make *Notorious* force entertainment.

The Ben Hecht scenario carries punchy dialog but it's much more the action and manner in which Hitchcock projects it on the screen that counts heaviest. Of course the fine performances by Cary Grant, Ingrid Bergman and Claude Rains also figure. The terrific suspense maintained to the very last is also an important asset.

Story deals with espionage, the picture opening in Miami in the spring of 1946. Bergman's father has been convicted as a German spy. Yarn shifts quickly to Rio de Janeiro, where Bergman, known to be a loyal American, unlike her father, is pressed into the American intelligence service with a view to getting the goods on a local group of German exiles under suspicion.

Inducted into espionage through Cary Grant, an American agent with whom she is assigned to work. Bergman, because she loves Grant, doesn't want to go through with an assignment to feign love for Claude Rains, head of the Brazilian Nazi group.

☐ 1946: Nominations: Best Supp. Actor (Claude Rains), Original Screenplay

....

■ NOTORIOUS GENTLEMAN

See: The Rake's Progress

....

■ NO TREES IN THE STREET

1959, 98 MINS, UK

Dir J. Lee Thompson   *Prod* Frank Godwin   *Scr* Ted Willis   *Ph* Gilbert Taylor   *Ed* Richard Best   *Mus* Laurie Johnson   *Art Dir* Robert Jones
● Sylvia Syms, Herbert Lom, Ronald Howard, Stanley Holloway, Joan Miller, Melvyn Hayes (Associated British)

Ted Willis is a writer with a sympathetic eye for problems of the middle and lower classes. Again teamed up with director J. Lee Thompson, his *No Trees in the Street* plays out a seamy slice of life in a London slum 20 years ago. Film is played on a violently strident note. Willis hammers home the point that people are more important than places.

The slim story line shows how the various larger-than-life characters face up to the challenge of the Street. The drab blowsy mother (Joan Miller) who has given up long ago. Her daughter (Sylvia Syms), longing to get away from it with her young brother, but lacking the resources or the courage. The boy racketeer (Herbert Lom), who has made money by shady activities and now ruthlessly rules the Street.

Syms gives a moving performance as the gentle girl who refuses to marry the cheap racketeer just to escape. Lom, as the opportunist who dominates the street, is sufficiently suave and unpleasant. Stanley Holloway is a bookmaker's tout with the cheerful philosophy that the world's gone mad.

....

■ NOT WITH MY WIFE, YOU DON'T!

1966, 118 MINS, US

Dir Norman Panama   *Prod* Norman Panama   *Scr* Norman Panama, Larry Gelbart, Peter Barnes   *Ph* Charles Lang Jr   *Ed* Aaron Stell   *Mus* John Williams   *Art Dir* Edward Carrere
● Tony Curtis, Virna Lisi, George C. Scott, Carroll O'Connor, Richard Eastham, Eddie Ryder (Warner)

Not With My Wife, You Don't! is an outstanding romantic comedy about a US Air Force marriage threatened by jealousy as an old beau of the wife returns to the scene. Zesty scripting, fine performances, solid direction and strong production values sustain hilarity throughout.

Story sets up Tony Curtis and George C. Scott as old Korean conflict buddies whose rivalry for Virna Lisi is renewed when Scott discovers that Curtis won her by subterfuge. The amusing premise is thoroughly held together

N

via an unending string of top comedy situations, including domestic squabbles, flashback, and an outstanding takeoff on foreign pix.

Curtis is excellent as the husband whose duties as aide to Air Force General Carroll O'Connor create the domestic vacuum into which Scott moves with the time-tested instincts of a proven, and non-marrying, satyr.

••••••••••••••••••••••••••••••

■ **NOT WITHOUT MY DAUGHTER**

1991, 114 MINS, US ◇ ⊛ ⊙
Dir Brian Gilbert   *Prod* Harry J. Ufland, Mary Jane Ufland   *Scr* David W. Rintels   *Ph* Peter Hannan
Ed Terry Rawlings   *Mus* Jerry Goldsmith
Art Dir Anthony Pratt
● Sally Field, Alfred Molina, Sheila Rosenthal, Roshan Seth, Sarah Badel, Mony Rey (Pathe/Ufland)

True story of Betty Mahmoody is a harrowing one by any standard. Married to Iranian doctor Moody who has lived in the US for 20 years, she reluctantly agrees to accompany him back to Teheran in 1984 to visit his family, only to be told at the end of two weeks that he has decided to remain in Iran.

As related in the by-the-numbers screenplay [from Mahmoody's book, with William Hoffer], Iran turns Moody from a civilized, sophisticated gent into an intolerant monster within a fortnight. Not only is Betty restricted to the home, but she can't use the phone, has her passport taken away, and is told that her daughter will be raised as a Muslim.

After nearly two years of staggering suffering, Betty finally manages to make contact with an underground of helpful Iranians who offer to smuggle her and her daughter over the mountains into Turkey, a perilous episode in itself.

With Israel, of all places, standing in for Iran, the film manages to strongly convey how strange and off-putting a truly alien culture can be to an average American. Biggest problem is Moody's abrupt transition from sensitive husband to violent tyrant; there is little the gifted actor Alfred Molina can do to clarify psychological issues ignored by the script.

Sally Field has the stage to herself to engage the audience's sympathy, and this she does with an earnest, suitably emotional performance as a rather typically sincere, middle-class American.

••••••••••••••••••••••••••••••

■ **NO WAY OUT**

1950, 106 MINS, US
Dir Joseph L. Mankiewicz   *Prod* Darryl F. Zanuck
Scr Joseph L. Mankiewicz, Lesser Samuels   *Ph* Milton Krasner   *Ed* Barbara McLean   *Mus* Alfred Newman
● Richard Widmark, Linda Darnell, Stephen McNally, Sidney Poitier, Joanne Smith, Harry Bellaver (20th Century-Fox)

Race riot hysteria is the theme of the original script. Story is told with words rather than action. There is one brief sequence of rioting, but that doesn't come until after 60-odd minutes of dialog buildup.

The racial question is forceably raised when two hoodlum brothers are brought into the prison ward injured in a gunfight. The Negro doctor takes over and one of the brothers dies during examination. The other brother, slumbred with all the prejudices of such an environment, charges the doctor with murder. Equally prejudiced, a group of Negroes turn on the hoods.

Richard Widmark's work as the vindictive brother is exaggerated just enough. Stephen McNally does compelling work. Sidney Poitier is splendid.

□ 1950: Nomination: Best Story & Screenplay

••••••••••••••••••••••••••••••

■ **NO WAY OUT**

1987, 116 MINS, US ◇ ⊛ ⊙
Dir Roger Donaldson   *Prod* Laura Ziskin, Robert Garland
Scr Robert Garland   *Ph* John Alcott   *Ed* Neil Travis
Mus Maurice Jarre   *Art Dir* Dennis Washington
● Kevin Costner, Gene Hackman, Sean Young, Will Patton, Howard Duff, George Dzundza (Orion)

No Way Out is an effective updating and revamping of the 1948 film noir classic *The Big Clock*, also based on Kenneth Fearing's novel of that name.

Film is set primarily in the Pentagon, with heroic Kevin Costner cast as a Lt Commander assigned to the Secretary of Defense (Gene Hackman), acting as liaison to the CIA under Hackman's righthand man Will Patton.

Costner has a torrid love affair with good-time girl Sean Young ended when she is murdered by her other lover, Hackman. Costner recognizes his boss in the shadows but Hackman sees only an unidentified figure. Hackman starts a cover-up to find the unidentified man he saw leaving the apartment. Costner is put in charge of the top-security investigation to catch himself.

Costner is extremely low key while Hackman glides through his role and Patton dominates his scenes overplaying his villainous hand. Young is extremely alluring as the heroine.

••••••••••••••••••••••••••••••

■ **NO WAY TO TREAT A LADY**

1968, 108 MINS, US ◇ ⊛
Dir Jack Smight   *Prod* Sol C. Siegel   *Scr* John Gay
Ph Jack Priestley   *Ed* Archie Marshek   *Mus* Stanley Myers   *Art Dir* Hal Pereira, George Jenkins
● Rod Steiger, Lee Remick, George Segal, Eileen Heckart, Murray Hamilton, Michael Dunn (Paramount)

Entertaining suspense film neatly laced with mordant humor. Stronger, more appropriate direction could have pushed the film into the category of minor classic.

Plotline casts Rod Steiger as a psychotic theatrical entrepreneur who takes to strangling drab middle-aged women as a means of working out his hangups over his dead mother. He employs a variety of disguises, accents and mannerisms for each murder.

Steiger relishes the multiple aspect of his part, and audiences should equally relish his droll impersonations of an Irish priest, German handyman, Jewish cop, middle-aged woman, Italian waiter and homosexual hairdresser.

Assigned to capture the lunatic ladykiller is a mother-smothered cop, played to perfection by George Segal.

With an excellent cast and a very good screenplay, *No Way to Treat a Lady* comes close to the quality of the best British films of the 1950s.

••••••••••••••••••••••••••••••

■ **NOWHERE TO RUN**

1993, 94 MINS, US ◇ ⊛ ⊙
Dir Robert Harmon   *Prod* Craig Baumgarten, Gary Adelson   *Scr* Joe Eszterhas, Leslie Bohem, Randy Feldman   *Ph* David Gribble   *Ed* Zach Staenberg, Mark Helfrich   *Mus* Mark Isham   *Art Dir* Dennis Washington
● Jean-Claude Van Damme, Rosanna Arquette, Kieran Culkin, Ted Levine, Tiffany Taubman, Joss Ackland (Columbia)

Action hero Jean-Claude Van Damme takes a career step backward in *Nowhere to Run*, a relentlessly corny and shamelessly derivative vehicle. Dog-eared project has a story credited to Joe Eszterhas and his *Jagged Edge* director Richard Marquand (who died in 1987), with its central loner role modeled after the Alan Ladd classic *Shane*.

Van Damme is a bank robber who hides out on Rosanna Arquette's farm. She's a widow (the major plot change from *Shane*) with two young kids (Kieran Culkin – younger brother of Macaulay – and Tiffany Taubman). They glimpse Van Damme bathing nude in a nearby lake, and before long mama Arquette has seduced the handsome stranger.

The next day the quartet are at the dinner table matter-of-factly discussing Van Damme's penis size and, with many reels to go, *Nowhere to Run* has self-destructed. But patchwork plot continues, with Arquette pressured by evil land developer Joss Ackland to sell her homestead.

At every key moment, Van Damme pops up, comic-strip style, to display his heroism, but his bread-and-butter fight scenes are so one-sided there's no catharsis in them.

••••••••••••••••••••••••••••••

■ **NOW, VOYAGER**

1942, 117 MINS, US ⊛ ⊙
Dir Irving Rapper   *Prod* Hal B. Wallis   *Scr* Casey Robinson   *Ph* Sol Polito   *Ed* Warren Low   *Mus* Max Steiner
● Bette Davis, Paul Henreid, Claude Rains, Bonita Granville, Gladys Cooper, Ilka Chase (Warner)

Voyager, an excursion into psychiatry, is almost episodic in its writing. It affords Bette Davis one of her superlative acting roles, that of a neurotic spinster fighting to free herself from the shackles of a tyrannical mother. A spinster still recalling the frustration of a girlhood love.

The first scenes show Davis as dowdy, plump and possessed of a phobia that fairly cries for the ministrations of a psychiatrist. Treatment by the doctor, played by Claude Rains, transforms the patient into a glamorous, modish, attractive woman who soon finds herself, after long being starved for love.

The yarn's major love crisis focuses on Davis and Paul Henreid, the latter unable to upset the conventions of a complicated marital life. The remote satisfaction of their love, via the emotionally unstable daughter of Henreid, upon whom Davis lavishes a mother's attention, is, perhaps, a rather questionable conclusion, but it's the kind of drama [from a novel by Oliver Higgins Pronty] that demands little credibility.

Henreid neatly dovetails and makes believable the sometimes-underplayed character of the man who finds love too late. As the curer of Davis' mental ills, Rains gives his usual restrained, above-par performance. Gladys Cooper is the domineering mother, weighted by Boston's Back Bay traditions and she's also within her metier.

□ 1942: Best Score for a Dramatic Picture.
□ Nominations: Best Actress (Bette Davis), Supp. Actress (Gladys Cooper)

••••••••••••••••••••••••••••••

■ **NUN AND THE BANDIT, THE**

1992, 92 MINS, AUSTRALIA ◇ ⊛
Dir Paul Cox   *Prod* Paul Ammitzboll, Paul Cox   *Scr* Paul Cox   *Ph* Nino Martinetti   *Ed* Paul Cox   *Mus* Tom E. Lewis, Norman Kaye   *Art Dir* Neil Angwin
● Gosia Dobrowolska, Chris Haywood, Victoria Eagger, Charlotte Hughes Haywood, Norman Kaye, Tom E. Lewis (Illumination/Film Victoria/AFFC)

Marking a departure for Aussie auteur Paul Cox, *The Nun and the Bandit* is adapted from a book and set in the primal Australian bush, far from the claustrophobic interiors of his earlier films. Cox has updated E.L. Grant's kidnap thriller set in the 1930s to what appears to be the '50s, playing down the thriller elements in favour of a brittle character study.

Kidnappers are led by Michael Shanley (Chris Haywood), disaffected nephew of prominent citizen George Shanley (Norman Kaye). Michael devises an impromptu, hare-brained scheme to hold the rich man's young granddaughter (played by the daughter of Haywood and Wendy Hughes, Charlotte Hughes

Haywood) for ransom. The child is snatched when she is with her aunt, Sister Lucy (Gosia Dobrowolska), a Polish nun visiting her sickly sister (Eva Sitta), the girl's mother.

The bulk of the film plays as a two-hander between the frightened, unworldly nun and the strange 'bandit' who refuses to rape his victim but demands that she 'be nice' to him. Cox leaves it up to the viewer to decide what happens between the two.

Cox regulars Dobrowolska and Haywood give their usual standout performances. Kaye excels as the charmingly unscrupulous capitalist. Pic has very fine production values belying the modest budget.

....

■ NUNS ON THE RUN

1990, 90 MINS, UK ◇ ⓥ ⊙
Dir Jonathan Lynn   *Prod* Michael White   *Scr* Jonathan Lynn   *Ph* Michael Garfath   *Ed* David Martin
Mus Yello, Hidden Faces   *Art Dir* Simon Holland
● Eric Idle, Robbie Coltrane, Camille Coduri, Janet Suzman, Doris Hare, Tom Hickey (HandMade)

Like Jack Lemmon and Tony Curtis in the Billy Wilder classic *Some Like It Hot*, Eric Idle and Robbie Coltrane are motivated by fear for their lives to dress in women's garb. New pic has rival British and Chinese gangs trying to recover two suitcases full of illicit cash.

Idle and Coltrane make a wonderful pair of dumbbells, both in and out of their habits. Both are oddly believable as nuns, even while writer/director Jonathan Lynn mines all the expected comic benefits of drag humor.

Idle and Coltrane are a lookout and a getaway driver for believable nasty London crime lord Robert Patterson. Their desire to escape their surroundings and the lure of easy cash backfire ominously, and they take refuge in a convent school run by Janet Suzman.

The constant double entendres are done with wit and the slapstick is mostly agreeable and efficiently directed, although the sight gags about Camille Coduri's extreme myopia are pushed a little far on occasion. Coduri otherwise is sweet and endearing in the Marilyn Monroe part.

....

■ NUN'S STORY, THE

1959, 149 MINS, US ◇ ⓥ ⊙
Dir Fred Zinnemann   *Prod* Fred Zinnemann   *Scr* Robert Anderson   *Ph* Franz Planer   *Ed* Walter Thompson
Mus Franz Waxman   *Art Dir* Alexander Trauner
● Audrey Hepburn, Peter Finch, Edith Evans, Peggy Ashcroft, Dean Jagger, Mildred Dunnock (Warner)

Fred Zinnemann's production is a soaring and luminous film. Audrey Hepburn has her most demanding film role, and she gives her finest performance. Despite the seriousness of the underlying theme, *The Nun's Story* [from the book by Kathryn C. Hulme] has the elements of absorbing drama, pathos, humor, and a gallery of memorable scenes and characters.

The struggle is that of a young Belgian woman (Hepburn), to be a successful member of an order of cloistered nuns. The order (not specified) is as different from the ordinary 'regular guy' motion picture conception of nuns as the army is from the Boy Scouts. Its aim is total merging of self.

Although the story is confined chiefly to three convents, in Belgium and the Congo, the struggle is fierce. Hepburn, attempting to be something she is not, is burned fine in the process.

One of the consistent gratifications is the cast. In addition to Edith Evans as the Mother Superior, who might have been a Renaissance prelate, there is Peggy Ashcroft, another convent superior, but less the dignitary, more the anchorite. Mildred Dunnock is a gentle, maiden aunt of a nun; Patricia Collinge, a gossipy cousin.

Peter Finch and Dean Jagger are the only males in the cast of any stature. Finch, as an intelligent, attractive agnostic, conveys a romantic attachment for Hepburn, but in terms that can give no offense. Jagger is Hepburn's perturbed loving father but contributes a valuable facet on the story.

Despite the seeming austerity of the story, Zinnemann has achieved a pictorial sweep and majesty. Franz Planer's Technicolor photography has a Gothic grace and muted splendor, Franz Waxman's score is a great one, giving proper place to cathedral organs and Congo drums.

□ 1959: Nominations: Best Picture, Director, Actress (Audrey Hepburn), Adapted Screenplay, Color Cinematography, Scoring of a Dramatic Picture, Sound

....

■ NUTCRACKER

1986, 84 MINS, US ◇ ⓥ
Dir Carroll Ballard   *Prod* Willard Carroll, Donald Kushner, Peter Locke,   *Scr* Kent Stowell, Maurice Sendak
Ph Stephen M. Burum   *Ed* John Mutt, Michael Silvers
Mus Tchaikovsky   *Art Dir* Maurice Sendak
● Hugh Bigney, Vanessa Sharp, Patricia Barker, Wade Walthall (Hyperion)

Despite some moments of disarray, *Nutcracker* is a wonderfully expressive and fanciful film.

This production of the timeless ballet is not only a beautiful version of the dance, but also incorporates much of the dark-natured story of E.T.A. Hoffman's original fairytale, *The Nutcracker and the Mouse King* – that of a young girl on the threshold of maturity who confronts many of her fears and hopes through a dream about sinister controller of the universe, Pasha, and her nutcracker prince.

Whereas live performances have often underplayed the sensitive storyline in preference to the dance, the film intricately and subtly delves into the story.

This version of the ballet was presented first by the Pacific Northwest Ballet in 1983. The company veers from the often-pat sugarplum ballets to a more darkly intense version.

....

■ NUTS

1987, 116 MINS, US ◇ ⓥ ⊙
Dir Martin Ritt   *Prod* Barbra Streisand   *Scr* Tom Topor
Ph Andrzej Bartkowiak   *Ed* Sidney Levin   *Mus* Barbra Streisand   *Art Dir* Joel Schiller
● Barbra Streisand, Richard Dreyfuss, Maureen Stapleton, Karl Malden, Eli Wallach, Robert Webber (Barwood/Ritt)

Based on the stageplay by Tom Topor, *Nuts* presents a premise weighted down by portentous performances. Issue of society's right to judge someone's sanity and the subjectivity of mental health is not only trite, but dated. While film ignites sporadically, it succumbs to the burden of its own earnestness.

As Claudia Draper, an uppercrust New York kid who has gone off the deep end into prostitution, Barbra Streisand is good, but it's too much of a good thing. For the most part it's a heroic performance, abandoning many of the characteristic Streisand mannerisms while she allows herself to look seedy. Streisand is flamboyantly, eccentrically crazy in a way that implies she is just a spirited woman society is trying to crush.

Richard Dreyfuss as Streisand's reluctant public defender is by far the film's most textured character, giving a performance that suggests a world of feeling and experience not rushing to gush out at the seams.

Arrested for killing her high-priced trick, it is Dreyfuss' job to convince a preliminary hearing that Streisand is mentally competent enough to stand trial with little help from her and against her parents' wishes.

....

■ NUTTY PROFESSOR, THE

1963, 107 MINS, US ◇ ⓥ ⊙
Dir Jerry Lewis   *Prod* Ernest D. Glucksman   *Scr* Jerry Lewis, Bill Richmond   *Ph* W. Wallace Kelley   *Ed* John Woodcock   *Mus* Walter Scharf   *Art Dir* Hal Pereira, Walter Tyler
● Jerry Lewis, Stella Stevens, Del Moore, Kathleen Freeman, Howard Morris (Paramount/Lewis)

The Nutty Professor is not one of Jerry Lewis' better films. Although attractively mounted and performed with flair by a talented cast, the production is only fitfully funny. Too often the film bogs down in pointless, irrelevant or repetitious business, nullifying the flavor of the occasionally choice comic capers and palsying the tempo and continuity of the story.

The star is cast as a meek, homely, accident-prone chemistry prof who concocts a potion that transforms him into a handsome, cocky, obnoxiously vain 'cool cat' type. But the transfiguration is of the Jekyll-Hyde variety in that it wears off, restoring Lewis to the original mold, invariably at critical, embarrassing moments.

Another standard characteristic of the Lewis film is its similarity to an animated cartoon, especially noticeable on this occasion in that the professor played by Lewis is a kind of live-action version of the nearsighted Mr Magoo.

Musical theme of the picture is the beautiful refrain 'Stella by Starlight'. By starlight or any other light, Stella is beautiful – Stella Stevens, that is, who portrays the professor's student admirer. Stevens is not only gorgeous, she is a very gifted actress. This was an exceptionally tough assignment, requiring of her almost exclusively silent reaction takes, and Stevens has managed almost invariably to produce the correct responsive expression. On her, even the incorrect one would look good.

....

O₀

■ OBJECTIVE, BURMA!

1945, 142 MINS, US ⓥ
Dir Raoul Walsh   *Prod* Jerry Wald   *Scr* Ranald
MacDougall, Lester Cole   *Ph* James Wong Howe
Ed George Amy   *Mus* Franz Waxman   *Art Dir* Ted Smith
● Errol Flynn, Henry Hull, William Prince, James Brown,
George Tobias, Warner Anderson (Warner)

Yarn [from an original story by Alvah Bessie]
deals with a paratroop contingent dropped
behind the Japanese lines in Burma to destroy a radar station. The chutists achieve
their objective but while returning to a designated spot to be picked up by planes and
flown back to the base they're overtaken by
Japs. Then follows a series of exciting experiences by the troopers against overwhelming
odds.

The film has considerable movement, particularly in the early reels, and the tactics of
the paratroopers are authentic in their
painstaking detail. However, while the
scripters have in the main achieved their purpose of heightening the action, there are
scenes in the final reels that could have been
edited more closely.

Flynn gives a quietly restrained perfor-
mance as the contingent's leader, while sup-
porting players who also perform capably are
Henry Hull, as a war correspondent; William
Prince, James Brown, George Tobias, Dick
Erdman and Warner Anderson.
□ 1945: Nominations: Best Original Story,
Editing, Scoring of a Dramatic Picture

■ OBJECT OF BEAUTY, THE

1991, 101 MINS, US/UK ◇ ⓥ
Dir Michael Lindsay-Hogg   *Prod* Jon S. Denny
Scr Michael Lindsay-Hogg   *Ph* David Watkin   *Ed* Ruth
Foster   *Mus* Tom Bahler   *Art Dir* Derek Dodd
● John Malkovich, Andie MacDowell, Lolita Davidovich,
Rudi Davies, Joss Ackland, Bill Paterson (Avenue/BBC)

The Object of Beauty is a throwback to the romantic comedies of Swinging London cinema,
but lacks the punch of the best of that late
1960s genre.

John Malkovich toplines as a ne'er-do-well
holed up in a swank London hotel with mate
Andie MacDowell. Everyone assumes the two
of them are married, but MacDowell is still
hitched to estranged hubbie Peter Riegert.

Plot concerns the title object, a small Henry
Moore figurine that MacDowell received from
Riegert as a present and which Malkovich
desperately wants to sell or use for an insurance scam to cover his hotel tab and ongoing
business reverses.

Key script contrivance has a deaf-mute
maid (Rudi Davies), newly hired at the hotel,
becoming obsessed with the Moore sculpture
and stealing it for a keepsake.

Malkovich ably brings out the unsympathetic nature of his antihero, but the script
doesn't help him much. The viewer will instantly side with MacDowell, whose natural
beauty is augmented here by a feisty violent
streak whenever Malkovich steps over the
line (which is frequent). Result is a mildly diverting but empty picture.

■ OBSESSION

(US: The Hidden Room)

1949, 96 MINS, UK ⓥ
Dir Edward Dmytryk   *Prod* N.A. Bronsten   *Scr* Alec
Coppel   *Ph* C. Pennington Richards, Robert Day   *Ed* Lilo
Carruthers   *Mus* Nino Rota

● Robert Newton, Sally Gray, Naunton Wayne, Phil
Brown (Rank/Independent Sovereign)

Powerful suspense is the keynote of Edward
Dymtryk's first British directional effort and
a strong dramatic situation has been developed from Alec Coppel's ill-fated stage play *A
Man about a Dog*, which ran for only a few
nights.

A straightforward situation is presented in
which a doctor plans the 'perfect' murder of
his wife's American lover. Firstly the victim is
confined in chains and the intention is to
keep him alive while the hue and cry is on. If
suspicion should fall on the doctor he could
always produce the missing person.

In the early stages the pace could be quickened but the whole atmosphere becomes
tense when the official Scotland Yard inquiries begin. Naunton Wayne as the Yard
superintendent is an example of perfect casting and his nonchalant manner deserves particular praise.

■ OBSESSION

1976, 98 MINS, US ◇ ⓥ ⊙
Dir Brian De Palma   *Prod* George Litto, Harry N. Blum
Scr Paul Schrader   *Ph* Vilmos Zsigmond   *Ed* Paul Hirsch
Mus Bernard Herrmann   *Art Dir* Jack Senter
● Cliff Robertson, Genevieve Bujold, John Lithgow,
Sylvia Kuumba Williams, Wanda Blackman (Columbia)

Obsession is an excellent romantic and non-vio-
lent suspense drama starring Cliff Robertson
and Genevieve Bujold, shot in Italy and New
Orleans.

Paul Schrader's script [from a story by
Brian De Palma] is a complex but comprehensible mix of treachery, torment and selfishness. Robertson is haunted with guilt for
the death of wife Bujold and child Wanda
Blackman, both kidnapped in 1959.

Sixteen years later, on a trip abroad, he
sees a lookalike to Bujold, and gets swept
away with this new girl. John Lithgow, as
Robertson's business partner, is not happy
with these events.

Robertson's low-key performance is as crucial to the manifold surprise impact as
Bujold's versatile, sensual and effervescent
charisma.
□ 1976: Nomination: Best Original Score

■ O.C. AND STIGGS

1987, 109 MINS, US ◇ ⓥ
Dir Robert Altman   *Prod* Robert Altman, Peter Newman
Scr Donald Cantrell, Ted Mann   *Ph* Pierre Mignot
Ed Elizabeth Kling   *Mus* King Sunny Ade & His African
Beats   *Art Dir* Scott Bushnell
● Daniel H. Jenkins, Neill Barry, Paul Dooley, Jane
Curtin, Ray Walston, Dennis Hopper (M-G-M)

Loosely based on a story in *National Lampoon*,
pic is an anarchistic jab at the insurance business and any other American institution that
happens to be handy. In his best work such as
Nashville and *M*A*S*H*, Robert Altman was
able to weave together an array of sights and
sounds into a distinctive social commentary.
In *O.C. and Stiggs* the structure comes apart
and what's left is mostly random silliness.

Plot [by Tod Carrol and Ted Mann] has
something to do with O.C. (Daniel H.
Jenkins) and Stiggs' (Neil Barry) efforts to
extract a pound of flesh from Arizona insurance magnate Randall Schwab (Paul Dooley)
in revenge for cancelling the old age insurance of O.C.'s grandfather (Ray Walston).

Along for the ride through the desert heartland is Schwab's drunken wife (Jane Curtin),
Stiggs' lecherous father (Donald May) and
bird-brained mother (Carla Borelli), a shell-
shocked Vietnam vet (Dennis Hopper) and a
horny high school nurse (Tina Louise), to
name just a few.

In spite of the shortcomings and tedium of
the production, there are moments when it

becomes evident there is a vision and talent
behind all the nonsense. Performances are
uniformly good, with Dennis Hopper once
again excelling as a madman.
[Pic was finished in 1984 but not released
until 1987.]

■ OCEAN'S ELEVEN

1960, 127 MINS, US ◇ ⓥ
Dir Lewis Milestone   *Prod* Lewis Milestone   *Scr* Harry
Brown, Charles Lederer   *Ph* William H. Daniels
Ed Philip W. Anderson   *Mus* Nelson Riddle
Art Dir Nicolai Remisoff
● Frank Sinatra, Dean Martin, Sammy Davis Jr, Peter
Lawford, Richard Conte, Cesar Romero (Warner)

Although basically a no-nonsense piece about
the efforts of 11 ex-war buddies to make off
with a multi-million dollar loot from five
Vegas hotels, the film is frequently one resonant wisecrack away from turning into a musical comedy. Laboring under the handicaps
of a contrived script, an uncertain approach
and personalities in essence playing themselves, the production never quite makes its
point, but romps along merrily unconcerned
that it doesn't.

Coincidence runs rampant in the screenplay, based on a story by George Clayton
Johnson and Jack Golden Russell. Set in motion on the doubtful premise that 11 playful,
but essentially law-abiding wartime acquaintances from all walks of life would undertake
a job that makes the Brink's hoist pale by
comparison, it proceeds to sputter and stammer through an interminable initial series of
scrambled expository sequences.

Acting under the stigma of their own flashy,
breezy identities, players such as Frank
Sinatra, Dean Martin, Sammy Davis Jr and
Peter Lawford never quite submerge themselves in their roles, nor try very hard to do
so. At any rate, the pace finally picks up when
the daring scheme is set in motion.

The dialog is sharp, but not always pertinent
to the story being told. And director Lewis
Milestone has failed to curb a tendency toward
flamboyant but basically unrealistic behaviour,
as if unable to decide whether to approach the
yarn straight or with tongue-in-cheek.

■ OCTAGON, THE

1980, 103 MINS, US ◇ ⓥ ⊙
Dir Eric Karson   *Prod* Joel Freeman   *Scr* Leigh
Chapman   *Ph* Michel Hugo   *Ed* Dann Cahn   *Mus* Dick
Halligan   *Art Dir* James Schoppe
● Chuck Norris, Karen Carlson, Lee Van Cleef, Tadashi
Yamashita, Carol Bagdasarian, Art Hindle (American
Cinema)

A bizarre plot involving the Ninja cult of
Oriental assassins with international terrorism provides plenty of chances for Chuck
Norris and other martial arts experts to do
their stuff, and pic has a nicely stylized look
with excellent lensing and music.

Screenwriter Leigh Chapman, working
from a story she wrote with Paul Aaron,
weaves a wildly incredible but entertaining
tale of retired martial arts champ Norris being recruited by wealthy Karen Carlson to
rub out the terrorists who have earmarked
her for death. Norris gets involved when he
realizes his nemesis is Tadashi Yamashita,
his sworn enemy from their youthful days as
chopsocky pupils.

The vendetta culminates in a pitched battle
at the octagonal training compound of the
Ninja cult, a school for terrorists of all types.

■ OCTOBER MAN, THE

1947, 93 MINS, UK ⓥ
Dir Roy Ward Baker   *Prod* Eric Ambler   *Scr* Eric
Ambler   *Ph* Erwin Hillier   *Ed* Alan L. Jaggs
Mus William Alwyn   *Art Dir* Alex Vetchinsky

● John Mills, Joan Greenwood, Edward Chapman, Kay Walsh, Joyce Carey, Felix Aylmer (Two Cities)

Author of many thrillers, Eric Ambler makes his debut as producer of his own script, and a fine beginning it is, with John Mills in top form and a grand all-round cast.

Unlike the usual Ambler story, this is not a whodunit or spy story. It's a study of the conflict in the mind of a mentally sick man, not absolutely certain that he hasn't committed murder.

John Mills plays Jim Ackland, an industrial chemist who suffers from a brain injury following an accident in which the child of a friend is killed. He blames himself for the child's death, and develops suicidal tendencies. Released from hospital, he is warned of a possible relapse unless he takes things easy. He returns to work and lives in a suburban hotel inhabited by a small cross-section of the community.

Molly, a fashion model (Kay Walsh), is found murdered and Jim is suspected. From then on it is the police versus Jim until, finally escaping arrest, he tracks down the murderer.

The dialog is taut and adult, and the direction by Roy Ward Baker, onetime assistant to Hitchcock, is imaginative. Only defect is the tempo. For a suspense pic it sometimes lacks pace.

■ OCTOPUSSY

1983, 130 MINS, UK ◇ ⓥ ⊙
Dir John Glen *Prod* Albert R. Broccoli *Scr* George MacDonald Fraser, Richard Maibaum, Michael G. Wilson *Ph* Alan Hume *Ed* John Grover, Peter Davies, Henry Richardson *Mus* John Barry *Art Dir* Peter Lamont
● Roger Moore, Maud Adams, Louis Jourdan, Kristina Wayborn, Kabir Bedi, Steven Berkoff (Eon/United Artists)

Storyline concerns a scheme by hawkish Russian General Orlov (Steven Berkoff) to launch a first-strike attack with conventional forces against the NATO countries in Europe, relying upon no nuclear retaliation by the West due to weakness brought about by peace movement in Europe.

Orlov is aided in his plan by a beautiful smuggler Octopussy (Maud Adams), her trader-in-art-forgeries underling Kamal (Louis Jourdan) and exquisite assistant Magda (Kristina Wayborn). James Bond (Roger Moore, in his sixth entry) is set on their trail when fellow agent 009 (Andy Bradford) is killed at a circus in East Berlin.

Trail takes Bond to India (lensed in sumptuous travelog shots) where he is assisted by local contact Vijay (tennis star Vijay Amritraj in a pleasant acting debut). Surviving an impromptu *Hounds of Zaroff* tiger hunt turned manhunt and other perils, Bond pursues Kamal to Germany for the hair-raising race against time conclusion.

Film's high points are the spectacular aerial stuntwork marking both the pre-credits teaser and extremely dangerous-looking climax.

■ ODD ANGRY SHOT, THE

1979, 90 MINS, AUSTRALIA ◇ ⓥ
Dir Tom Jeffrey *Prod* Tom Jeffrey, Sue Milliken *Scr* Tom Jeffrey *Ph* Don McAlpine *Ed* Brian Kavanagh *Mus* Michael Carlos *Art Dir* Bernard Hides
● Graham Kennedy, John Hargreaves, John Jarratt, Bryan Brown, Graeme Blundell (Samson)

Australia's involvement in the Vietnamese war created a political and moral dichotomy in the country such as hadn't been seen since the question of conscription at the time of World War I. If anything, Tom Jeffrey's *The Odd Angry Shot* could be said to be cathartic.

The film concentrates on a group of Aussie volunteers. Special Air Service troops, militarily as elite as the Yanks' Special Forces,

but in this view, at least, rather more bawdy than the Americans as depicted in *The Deer Hunter*. It is the same futile war, but what Jeffrey has expressed faithfully is the pragmatism and essential hope-of-survival of the troops on the ground.

Jeffrey has been helped immeasurably by his cameraman, Don McAlpine, who worked as a news cameraman in Vietnam.

There is no agonising political or moral message, and Jeffrey maintains the basic good humor of the guys at a very believable pitch.

■ ODD COUPLE, THE

1968, 105 MINS, US ◇ ⓥ ⊙
Dir Gene Saks *Prod* Howard W. Koch *Scr* Neil Simon *Ph* Robert B. Hauser *Ed* Frank Bracht *Mus* Neal Hefti *Art Dir* Hal Pereira, Walter Tyler
● Jack Lemmon, Walter Matthau, John Fiedler, Herbert Edelman, David Sheiner, Larry Haines (Paramount)

The Odd Couple, Neil Simon's smash legit comedy, has been turned into an excellent film starring Jack Lemmon and Walter Matthau. Simon's somewhat expanded screenplay retains the broad, as well as the poignant, laughs inherent in the rooming together of two men whose marriages are on the rocks.

Teaming of Lemmon and Matthau has provided each with an outstanding comedy partner. As the hypochondriac, domesticated and about-to-be-divorced Felix, Lemmon is excellent. Matthau also hits the bullseye in a superior characterization.

Carrying over from the legit version with Matthau are Monica Evans and Carole Shelley, the two English girls from upstairs, and John Fiedler, one of the poker game group which, until Lemmon moved in, revelled in cigarette butts, clumsy sandwiches, and other signs of disarray.

New to the plot is opening scene of Lemmon bumbling in suicide attempts in a Times Square flophouse. By the time he arrives at Matthau's apartment, his amusing misadventures have caused a wrenched back and neck. Staggered main titles help prolong this good intro.
□ 1968: Nominations: Best Adapted Screenplay, Editing

■ ODD MAN OUT
(US: Gang War)

1947, 116 MINS, UK ⓥ ⊙
Dir Carol Reed *Scr* F.L. Green, R.C. Sherriff *Ph* Robert Krasker *Ed* Fergus McDonnell *Mus* William Alwyn *Art Dir* Ralph Brinton
● James Mason, Robert Newton, Robert Beatty, Kathleen Ryan, F.J. McCormick, Cyril Cusack (Two Cities)

Accent in this film [based on the novel by F.L. Green] is on art with a capital A. Carol Reed has made his film with deliberation and care, and has achieved splendid teamwork from every member of the cast. Occasionally too intent on pointing his moral and adorning his tale, he has missed life in its telling.

Story is set in a city in Northern Ireland and takes place between 4 pm and midnight on a winter's day. Johnnie, leader of an organization, sentenced for gun running, has broken gaol and is hiding with his girl Kathleen. He plans a holdup on a mill to obtain funds, and although deprecating violence, he takes a gun. During the holdup he accidentally kills a man, is badly wounded himself, and the driver of the car panics, leaving Johnnie to fend for himself. Bleeding, he stumbles through the city trying to hide from the police.

For Mason two-thirds of the film is silent. From the moment he is wounded he has few lines and has to drag himself along, a hunted man with a fatal wound. It is hardly his fault that, in this passive character that expresses little more than various phases of pain and

occasional delirium, he is less effective than he could be.

Making her screen debut, Kathleen Ryan reveals undoubted ability and much promise. Graduate of the Abbey and Gate theatres, this 24-year-old redhead was 'discovered' in Ireland by Reed, who coached and trained her for this part.
□ 1947: Nomination: Best Editing

■ ODDS AGAINST TOMORROW

1959, 96 MINS, US
Dir Robert Wise *Prod* Robert Wise *Scr* John O. Killens, Nelson Gidding *Ph* Joseph Brun *Ed* Dede Allen *Mus* John Lewis *Art Dir* Leo Kurz
● Harry Belafonte, Robert Ryan, Shelley Winters, Ed Begley, Gloria Grahame (HarBel/United Artists)

On one level, *Odds against Tomorrow* is a taut crime melodrama. On another, it is an allegory about racism, greed and man's propensity for self-destruction. Not altogether successful in the second category, it still succeeds on its first.

The point of the screenplay, based on a novel of the same name by William P. McGivern, is that the odds against tomorrow coming at all are very long unless there is some understanding and tolerance today. The point is made by means of a crime anecdote, a framework not completely satisfactory for cleanest impact.

Harry Belafonte, Robert Ryan and Ed Begley form a partnership with plans to rob a bank with a haul estimated to total $150,000. An ill-matched trio, their optimistic plans are dependent on the closest teamwork. Belafonte, a horse-playing night club entertainer, is something of an adolescent. Ryan is a psychotic. Begley, as ex-cop fired for crookedness, has learned from this experience only not to get caught.

Director Robert Wise has drawn fine performances from his players. It is the most sustained acting Belafonte has done. Ryan makes the flesh crawl as the fanatical bigot. Begley turns in a superb study of a foolish, befuddled man who dies, as he has lived, without knowing quite what he has been involved in.

Shelley Winters etches a memorable portrait, and Gloria Grahame is poignant in a brief appearance. Joseph Brun's black and white photography catches the grim spirit of the story and accents it with some glinting mood shots. John Lewis' music backs it with a neurotic, edgy, progressive jazz score.

■ ODESSA FILE, THE

1974, 128 MINS, UK/W. GERMANY ◇ ⓥ ⊙
Dir Ronald Neame *Prod* John Woolf, John R. Sloan *Scr* Kenneth Ross, George Markstein *Ph* Oswald Morris *Ed* Ralph Kemplen *Mus* Andrew Lloyd Webber *Art Dir* Rolf Zehetbauer
● Jon Voight, Maximilian Schell, Maria Schell, Mary Tamm, Derek Jacobi, Shmuel Rodensky (Columbia)

The Odessa File is an excellent filmization of Frederick Forsyth's novel of a reporter who tracks down former Nazi SS officers still undetected in 1960s Germany.

Jon Voight's accidental reading of the diary of a suicide (a Jewish survivor of Nazi prison camps) leads to his attempted infiltration of Odessa, a secret network of SS veterans who have maintained their cover in diverse positions in postwar commerce and government.

Voight's immediate search is for Maximilian Schell, a quest inhibited by secret Odessa officials, but facilitated by Israeli intelligence agents who also get on his tail.

As Voight establishes his credentials in a superb grilling by Noel Willman, his girl (Mary Tamm) is under close surveillance by Odessa-affiliated police, and Klaus Lowitsch is dispatched to kill him.

ODE TO BILLY JOE

1976, 105 MINS, US ◇ ⑰

Dir Max Baer   *Prod* Max Baer, Roger Camras
Scr Herman Raucher   *Ph* Michel Hugo   *Ed* Frank E.
Morriss   *Mus* Michel Legrand   *Art Dir* Philip Jefferies
● Robby Benson, Glynnis O'Connor, Joan Hotchkis,
Sandy McPeak, James Best, Terence Goodman (Warner)

Ode to Billy Joe is a superbly sensitive period romantic tragedy, based on Bobbie Gentry's 1967 hit song lyric. Robby Benson is excellent as Billy Joe McAllister, and Glynnis O'Connor is outstanding as his Juliet.

The time is 1953. O'Connor and Benson are both emerging into fumbling sexual awareness, written and acted in a way to bring out all of the humor, heart and horniness that attends on such matters. O'Connor's parents, sensationally played by Sandy McPeak and Joan Hotchkis, have a wary but loving eye out for her.

The puppy love affair unfolds smoothly as it is interwoven with family, church, work and community functions, all of which establish the people as real, loving folk and create a magnificent dramatic environment.

ODETTE

1950, 123 MINS, UK

Dir Herbert Wilcox   *Prod* Herbert Wilcox   *Scr* Warren
Chetham-Strode   *Ph* Max Greene   *Ed* W. Lewthwaite
Mus Anthony Collins
● Anna Neagle, Trevor Howard, Marius Goring, Peter
Ustinov, Bernard Lee (British Lion)

The film recaptures all the essential details of Odette's adventures as a secret agent in France during the last war.

In the production of a factual story of this type, presentation inevitably tends to be a bit jerky. Herbert Wilcox's facile direction mainly succeeds in overcoming this difficulty. Logically, too, he has used French or German dialog when justified.

Acting is uniformly good. Anna Neagle puts all she's got into the playing of Odette. Trevor Howard gives a smooth and confident interpretation of Capt Peter Churchill, the British agent whom she subsequently marries. Marius Goring plays the counter-espionage officer with a genuine conviction while Peter Ustinov gives one of his best performances as the secret radio operator.

OEDIPUS THE KING

1968, 97 MINS, UK ◇

Dir Philip Saville   *Prod* Michael Luke   *Scr* Michael Luke,
Philip Saville   *Ph* Walter Lassally   *Ed* Paul Davies
Mus Yanni Christou   *Art Dir* Yanni Migadis
● Christopher Plummer, Orson Welles, Lilli Palmer,
Richard Johnson, Cyril Cusack (Rank/Crossroads)

This version of Sophocles' play deals fairly superficially with the bare bones of the tragic story of the king, dragged down to degradation after having discovered that, unwittingly, he has murdered his father and married and had children by his mother.

It is filmed with dignity, extremely well directed and excellently acted by a small cast of fine thesps.

Director Philip Saville and, indeed, the translation do not harp so melodramatically on the tragic sequences. Done with restraint, physical action is confined mainly to the assassination of Laius and a recap. Nor is the translation sonorously heavy but retains a dignified poetry.

Christopher Plummer as Oedipus gives a sterling performance. His early clashes with his brother-in-law (Richard Johnson) are striking and the latter's performance is a useful foil to Plummer's.

Lilli Palmer, as the ill-fated Jocasta, does not fully bring out the tragic personality until the final bitter scene, and Orson Welles is

unusually subdued, but all the more effective, as Tiresias, the blind prophet of doom.

The film is superbly lensed with the greens and browns making a soft, yet bleak backdrop to the sombre action.

OFF BEAT

1986, 92 MINS, US ◇ ⑰ ⊙

Dir Michael Dinner   *Prod* Joe Roth, Harry Ufland
Scr Mark Medoff   *Ph* Carlo Di Palma   *Ed* Dede Allen,
Angelo Corrao   *Mus* James Horner   *Art Dir* Woods
Mackintosh
● Judge Reinhold, Meg Tilly, Harvey Keitel, Cleavant
Derricks, Joe Mantegna, John Turturro (Touchstone)

Off Beat is a tedious comedy [from a story by Dezso Magyar] that suffers visibly from the involvement of several artists known for good work on more serious fare.

Except for Cleavant Derricks, who shows a natural comedic talent playing a New York City cop in over his head in a mixup involving a friend (Judge Reinhold) subbing for him at the annual police benefit dance auditions, cast led by Reinhold seem so conscientious about trying to be funny, they forget to lighten up.

Reinhold, a library clerk, agrees to replace friend Abe Washington (Derricks) in the chorus line where he falls instantly for a cute little policewoman (Meg Tilly). He's supposed to fail the audition, but instead woos the choreographer (National Dance Institute founder Jacques D'Amboise) so he can stick around and get to know Tilly better.

To keep up the charade for Tilly, he ends up in uniform more often than he should and unwittingly gets himself involved in a few incidents. Romance between Reinhold and Tilly is lackluster, attributable partially to some dreary dialog.

OFFENCE, THE

1973, 112 MINS, UK ◇ ⑰

Dir Sidney Lumet   *Prod* Denis O'Dell   *Scr* John Hopkins
Ph Gerry Fisher   *Ed* John Victor Smith   *Art Dir* John
Clark
● Sean Connery, Trevor Howard, Vivien Merchant, Ian
Bannen, Derek Newark, Peter Bowles (United Artists)

There's a powerful confrontation of authority and accused between police sergeant Sean Connery and suspected child molester Ian Bannen in Sidney Lumet's *The Offence*. A brilliant scene, however, does not in itself make for a brilliant overall feature.

This often cold and dreary tale is about the self realization of a veteran police officer that his own mind contains much of the evil with which he is confronted daily. Indeed, his willing accumulation of brutality and violence-packed incidents is recognized almost immediately by Bannen and it is not long before accuser becomes the accused.

However, the lengthy lead-up to this important scene is played against dreary backgrounds and with colorless people.

OFFICER AND A GENTLEMAN, AN

1982, 126 MINS, US ◇ ⑰ ⊙

Dir Taylor Hackford   *Prod* Martin Elfand   *Scr* Douglas
Day Stewart   *Ph* Donald Thorin   *Ed* Peter Zinner
Mus Jack Nitzsche   *Art Dir* Philip M. Jefferies
● Richard Gere, Debra Winger, Louis Gossett Jr, David
Keith, Lisa Blount, Lisa Eilbacher (Lorimar)

An Officer and a Gentleman deserves a 21-gun salute, maybe 42. Rarely does a film come along with so many finely-drawn characters to care about.

Officer belongs to Louis Gossett Jr, who takes a near-cliche role of the tough, unrelenting drill instructor and makes him a sympathetic hero without ever softening a whit.

The title refers to the official reward await-

ing those willing to endure 13 weeks of agony in Naval Aviation Officer Candidate School, whose initial aim – via Gossett – is to wash out as many hopefuls as possible before letting the best move on to flight training.

Pic is a bit muddled, via flashback, in setting up Richard Gere's motives for going into the training. Suffice to say he did not enjoy a model childhood. On leave, Gere meets Debra Winger, one of the local girls laboring at a paper mill and hoping for a knight in naval officer's uniform to rescue her from a life of drudgery. It's another fetching little slut role for Winger and she makes the most of it.

A secondary romance involves Gere's friend and fellow candidate (David Keith), who takes a tumble for Winger's friend (Lisa Blount), another slut but not so fetching.
□ 1982: Best Supp. Actor (Louis Gossett Jr), Original Song ('Up Where We Belong').
□ Nominations: Best Actress (Debra Winger), Original Screenplay, Editing, Original Score, Original Song ('Up Where We Belong')

OFF LIMITS

(UK: Saigon)

1988, 102 MINS, US ◇ ⑰ ⊙

Dir Christopher Crowe   *Prod* Alan Barnette
Scr Christopher Crowe, Jack Thibeau   *Ph* David Gribble
Ed Douglas Ibold   *Mus* James Newton Howard
Art Dir Dennis Washington
● Willem Dafoe, Gregory Hines, Fred Ward, Amanda
Pays, Kay Tong Lim, Scott Glenn (20th Century-Fox)

Off Limits is a well-crafted story that explores the underbelly of 1968 Saigon well enough as two undercover detectives (Willem Dafoe, Gregory Hines) go about to solve a string of prostitute murders by a high-ranking army officer. While the plot and characterizations are well worked out, what this production lacks is enough pizzazz to distinguish it from others of this genre.

Dafoe and Hines stick together like glue, working diligently in the sticky Saigon heat with equally racist attitudes about 'gooks' and 'slopes.' Dafoe is a little more hot-tempered and Hines only slightly less intense.

This is much more a civilian story that only twice puts the action out in the country where the bombs are exploding. As such, with the exception of one scene where a sadist colonel, whom Dafoe and Hines suspect of being the sicko murderer, is pushing Vietcong out of a helicopter, lensing could have been accomplished on the backlot.

Director Christopher Crowe has tried to make a tough picture with sensitivity, though it's the former that mostly prevails. Dafoe has a platonic affection for a nun (Amanda Pays) who counsels prostitutes and takes care of their children. Fred Ward is particularly good as the partners' superior, Master Sgt Dix.

OF HUMAN BONDAGE

1934, 83 MINS, US ⑰ ⊙

Dir John Cromwell   *Prod* Pandro S. Berman   *Scr* Lester
Cohen   *Ph* Henry W. Gerrard   *Ed* William Morgan
Mus Max Steiner   *Art Dir* Van Nest Polglase, Carroll
Clark
● Leslie Howard, Bette Davis, Frances Dee, Kay Johnson,
Reginald Denny, Alan Hale (Radio)

Basically, it's an obvious and familiar theme [from the novel by W. Somerset Maugham]. The unrequited love of the art-medical student, inhibited and club-footed to the degree that he stumbles physically, mentally and spiritually, commands respect and sympathy. But as the footage unreels, the feeling grows that he's pretty much of a clunk to go the hard way he does for the strumpet who treats him so shabbily.

Leslie Howard tries hard to mellow his assignment. But somehow he misses at times because the script is too much against him. Perhaps Bette Davis is to blame. She plays her free 'n' easy vamp too well, so that it negates any audience sympathy for the gentle Howard.

Reginald Denny and Alan Hale get over a couple of lusty innings as males on the hunt who know how to handle gals of her type. Reginald Owen, too, milks his assignment.

Locales are Paris and London, chiefly London, with Davis in Cockney dialect throughout.

■ OF HUMAN BONDAGE

1946, 100 MINS, US

Dir Edmund Goulding   *Prod* Henry Blanke
Scr Catherine Turney   *Ph* Peverell Marley   *Ed* Clarence Kolster   *Mus* Erich Wolfgang Korngold   *Art Dir* Hugh Reticker, Harry Kelso
● Eleanor Parker, Paul Henreid, Alexis Smith, Edmund Gwenn, Janis Paige, Patric Knowles (Warner)

Somerset Maugham story has been given excellent period mounting to fit early London background, is well-played and directed in individual sequences, but lacks overall smoothness.

Top roles go to Eleanor Parker, as the tart; Paul Henreid, the sensitive artist-doctor, and Alexis Smith, novelist. A third femme love interest is Janis Paige. Three femmes represent various loves that enter the life of Henreid, frustrated artist, but major interest is concentrated on character played by Parker and how she affects Henreid's happiness.

Edmund Goulding's direction gets good work out of the cast generally and helps interest although most of major characters carry little sympathy, Parker's work is excellent, as is Henreid's depiction of the self-pitying cripple. Smith's role has been edited to a comparatively small part.

■ OF HUMAN BONDAGE

1964, 98 MINS, UK Ⓥ

Dir Ken Hughes, Henry Hathaway   *Prod* James Woolf
Scr Bryan Forbes   *Ph* Oswald Morris   *Ed* Russell Lloyd
Mus Ron Goodwin   *Art Dir* John Box
● Kim Novak, Laurence Harvey, Robert Morley, Siobhan McKenna, Roger Livesey, Jack Hedley (Seven Arts/M-G-M)

There was the Leslie Howard/Bette Davis 1934 version of this story and the 1946 entry starring Paul Henried and Eleanor Parker. This stab, with Laurence Harvey and Kim Novak, will not erase the memories. For those who come fresh to *Of Human Bondage*, this perceptive but highly introspective yarn by Somerset Maugham may seem a hard-to-take slab of period meller.

The pic had a ruffled nascency, due primarily to clashes of opinion among top brass. Henry Hathaway quit to let in Ken Hughes as director and it's bruited that the star duo did not always see eye-to-ee on the chore in hand.

Story concerns a withdrawn, young medical student very conscious of his clubfoot who manages to become a doctor in London's East End despite being totally besotted with the tawdry charms of a promiscuous waitress.

Allowing for the fact that Bryan Forbes' screenplay is light on humor, Harvey nevertheless plays the role in such a stiff, martyred manner as to forfeit any sympathy or liking in the audience.

The role that made Davis doesn't serve the same purpose for Novak. Yet she gamely tackles a wide range of emotions and seems to be far more aware of the demands of her role than is her co-star.

Collectors of cinema trivia will notice, with interest, the fleeting appearances by highly-paid scriptwriter Forbes as a student-extra without any lines, an inexplicable throwback to his earlier business of being an actor.

■ OF HUMAN HEARTS

1938, 100 MINS, US

Dir Clarence Brown   *Prod* John W. Considine Jr
Scr Bradbury Foote   *Ph* Clyde DeVinna   *Ed* Frank E. Hull   *Mus* Herbert Stothart   *Art Dir* Cedric Gibbons, Harry Oliver, Edwin B. Willis
● Walter Huston, James Stewart, Beulah Bondi, Guy Kibbee, Charles Coburn, John Carradine (M-G-M)

Frontier life in a village on the banks of the Ohio river in the days preceding the Civil War is the background against which Clarence Brown tells the story of a mother's sacrifice for the career of an ungrateful son.

Brown is said to have cherished the idea of producing this story for some time. Screenplay is based on Honore Morrow's story *Benefits Forgot*, published nearly a score of years earlier.

A meaner, more selfish, bigoted and ornery group never existed than these villagers, into whose midst comes a preacher of the Gospel with his wife and 12-year-old son. They had promised him $400 a year to be custodian of their souls, then cut the allowance to $250 and some cast-off clothing for his dependents. The preacher accepts these terms with humility. The son, however, rebels against the petty tyranny and selfishness of the neighbors.

Latter part of the film relates the boy's brilliant success as a surgeon in the Union army, and his neglect for his mother, now widowed.

Walter Huston is the zealous circuit riding preacher, a man of uncompromising principle. Beulah Bondi is the wife and mother and she shades the transitions of age with convincing acting. Gene Reynolds first appears as the son, a role played by James Stewart in the later scenes.

Chief cause for disappointment with the film is its slow pace, and the defeatist mood of the story.

☐ 1938: Nomination: Best Supp. Actress (Beulah Bondi)

■ OF MICE AND MEN

1939, 104 MINS, US Ⓥ

Dir Lewis Milestone   *Prod* Hal Roach   *Scr* Eugene Solow   *Ph* Norbert Brodine   *Ed* Bert Jordan   *Mus* Aaron Copland   *Art Dir* Nicolai Remisoff
● Burgess Meredith, Lon Chaney Jr, Betty Field, Charles Bickford, Roman Bohnen, Bob Steele (Roach/United Artists)

Under skillful directorial guidance of Lewis Milestone, the picture retains all of the forceful and poignant drama of John Steinbeck's original play and novel, in presenting the strange palship and eventual tragedy of the two California ranch itinerants. In transferring the story to the screen, scripter Eugene Solow eliminated the strong language and forthright profanity. Despite this requirement for the Hays whitewash squad, Solow and Milestone retain all of the virility of the piece in its original form.

As in the play, all of the action takes place on the San Joaquin valley barley ranch. George and Lennie catch on as hands. Former's strange wardship of the half-wit possessed of Herculean strength is never quite explained – in fact he wonders himself just why. George keeps Lennie close to him always – continually fearful that the simpleton will kill someone with his brute power. The pair plan to buy a small ranch of their own, where Lennie can raise rabbits, when disaster strikes.

Despite the lack of box-office names in the cast set-up, the players have been excellently selected. Burgess Meredith is capital as George, and Lon Chaney Jr dominates throughout with a fine portrayal of the childlike giant. Betty Field is the sexy wife who encourages approaches from the ranch workers; Bob Steele is her jealous and hard hitting husband.

☐ 1939: Nominations: Best Picture, Original Score, Sound

■ OF MICE AND MEN

1992, 110 MINS, US ◇ Ⓥ ⊙

Dir Gary Sinise   *Prod* Russ Smith, Gary Sinise
Scr Horton Foote   *Ph* Kenneth MacMillan   *Ed* Robert L. Sinise   *Mus* Mark Isham   *Art Dir* David Gropman
● John Malkovich, Gary Sinise, Ray Walston, Casey Siemaszko, Sherilyn Fenn, John Terry (M-G-M)

Well-mounted and very traditional, *Of Mice and Men* honorably serves John Steinbeck's classic story of two Depression-era drifters without bringing anything new to it.

First published in 1937, the novel has had continued life as a Broadway play, a Hollywood film starring Lon Chaney and Burgess Meredith, and a 1980 stage piece at Chicago's Steppenwolf Theater that featured John Malkovich and Gary Sinise, who repeat their roles here.

Set in a lonely world of itinerant men in 1930, intelligent adaptation begins with George and Lennie fleeing a posse of dogs and armed men across the sun-baked California countryside. They have jobs lined up at a farm near Soledad. George (Sinise) is a quick-witted man of few but well-chosen words with no family or money to his name. His only charge is Lennie (Malkovich), a lumbering simpleton who has the mind of a child but the strength of an ox.

Dramatic gears start turning when belligerent farm boss son Curley (Casey Siemaszko) starts picking on Lennie. Before long, son's lovely, lonely wife (Sherilyn Fenn) begins hanging around the bunkhouse and barn, seemingly with an eye for George.

Captured in lovely, burnished hues by lenser Kenneth MacMillan and evocatively realized by production designer David Gropman, pic could not look more different from the studio-bound Lewis Milestone rendition of more than 50 years ago. Performances are sterling.

■ OH DAD, POOR DAD, MAMMA'S HUNG YOU IN THE CLOSET, AND I'M FEELIN' SO SAD

1967, 86 MINS, US ◇ Ⓥ

Dir Richard Quine   *Prod* Ray Stark, Stanley Rubin
Scr Ian Bernard   *Ph* Geoffrey Unsworth   *Ed* Warren Low, David Wages   *Mus* Neal Hefti   *Art Dir* Phil Jeffries
● Rosalind Russell, Robert Morse, Barbara Harris, Hugh Griffith, Jonathan Winters, Lionel Jeffries (Paramount)

Producers have labored mightily to bring forth a mouse. Rosalind Russell is the emasculating mother of Robert Morse, sired by Jonathan Winters who is dead, but stuffed and carried around by his widow as she and son travel about. Barbara Harris is the nymphet chippie who puts the make on Morse so successfully that he kills her in a psycho-substitution for his ma. Hugh Griffith is an ageing lecher eyed by Russell as her next victim.

Despite multi-colored wigs and a game attempt, Russell falls flat. Morse has an appealing, winsome quality which certain film roles will fit, but not this one. Harris does rather well, however, and Griffith is up to the demands of his role. Winters gets the best comedy material, but it clashes with the rest. Film was shot on Jamaica locations, which adds color, but to no avail.

■ O. HENRY'S FULL HOUSE

1952, 116 MINS, US

Dir Henry Hathaway, Howard Hawks, Henry King, Henry Koster, Jean Negulesco   *Prod* Andre Hakim
Scr Richard Breen, Walter Bullock, Ivan Goff, Ben Roberts, Lamar Trotti   *Ph* Lloyd Ahern, Lucien Ballard, Milton

Krasner, Joe MacDonald   *Ed* Nick De Maggio, Barbara McLean, William B. Murphy   *Mus* Alfred Newman
● Charles Laughton, Marilyn Monroe, Richard Widmark, Anne Baxter, Fred Allen, Jeanne Crain (20th Century-Fox)

This ties together five of O. Henry's classics into a full house of entertainment that has something for all tastes. The five classics are tied together by John Steinbeck's narration.

The Cop and the Anthem gets the quintet off to an enjoyable 19-minute start as Charles Laughton milks the fat part of Soapy, the gentleman bum who tries unsuccessfully to get arrested so he can spend the winter months in a warm jail.

The Clarion Call is a 22-minute excursion into melodrama with a twist. Dale Robertson plays the cop with a conscience who must arrest Richard Widmark, an old pal gone wrong and to whom he owes a debt.

The Last Leaf plunges into dramatics for 23 minutes, with Anne Baxter, Jean Peters and Gregory Ratoff keeping it emotionally sure. It's the tale of a girl, without the will to live because of an unhappy love affair, who believes she will die when the last leaf falls from a vine outside her window.

Fred Allen, Oscar Levant and young Lee Aaker keep amusing a highly burlesqued takeoff on *The Ransom of Red Chief*, the comedy saga of two city slickers who make the mistake of kidnapping for ransom the hellion son of a backwoods Alabama rich farmer. It's broad fun as directed by Howard Hawks.

Picture closes with a choice little account of that tender story of young love, *The Gift of the Magi*, splendidly trouped by Jeanne Crain and Farley Granger.

▪ **OH! FOR A MAN**

See: Will Success Spoil Rock Hunter?

▪ **OH, GOD!**

1977, 97 MINS, US ◇ ⓥ
Dir Carl Reiner   *Prod* Jerry Weintraub   *Scr* Larry Gelbert   *Ph* Victor Kemper   *Ed* Bud Molin   *Mus* Jack Elliott   *Art Dir* Jack Senter
● George Burns, John Denver, Teri Garr, Donald Pleasence, Ralph Bellamy, William Daniels (Warner)

Oh, God! is a hilarious film which benefits from the brilliant teaming of George Burns, as the Almighty in human form, and John Denver, sensational in his screen debut as a supermarket assistant manager who finds himself a suburban Moses.

Carl Reiner's controlled and easy direction of a superb screenplay and a strong cast makes the Jerry Weintraub production a warm and human comedy.

An Avery Corman novel is the basis for Larry Gelbart's adaptation which makes its humanistic points while taking gentle pokes at organized Establishment religions, in particular the kind of fund-raising fundamentalism epitomized by Paul Sorvino. Teri Garr is excellent as Denver's perplexed but loyal wife.
□ 1977: Nomination: Best Adapted Screenplay

▪ **OH, GOD! BOOK II**

1980, 94 MINS, US ◇ ⓥ
Dir Gilbert Cates   *Prod* Gilbert Cates   *Scr* Josh Greenfeld, Hal Goldman, Fred S. Fox, Seaman Jacobs, Melissa Miller   *Ph* Ralph Woolsey   *Ed* Peter E. Berger   *Mus* Charles Fox   *Art Dir* Preston Ames
● George Burns, Suzanne Pleshette, David Birney, Louanne, John Louie, Howard Duff (Warner)

Oh, God! Book II is not a sequel to the hit 1977 release but rather an alternate approach to the same basic premise: what would happen if God were to appear to an ordinary person with instructions to 'spread my message.' Absence this time of John Denver, his chem-

istry with lead George Burns, and the original's solid comedy material lead to a bland, unstimulating film.

Script [from a story by Josh Greenfeld] has a pleasant moppet (Louanne) meeting God (Burns) in the lounge of a Chinese restaurant. It seems that Burns has decided to enlist a child 'with belief in things you can't see' to remind people that God is still around. Since Louanne's dad (David Birney) is an ad-man, she sets out to concoct a slogan which will 'make God a household name.'

Burns is fine once again, a master of the throwaway line and well-suited to tone down the religious philosophy in the script. More screen time, however, is allotted to debuting Louanne, a pleasant and talented youngster who holds one's sympathy. Suzanne Pleshette and David Birney as her estranged parents are effective in limited roles.

▪ **OH, GOD! YOU DEVIL**

1984, 96 MINS, US ◇ ⓥ ☉
Dir Paul Bogart   *Prod* Robert M. Sherman   *Scr* Andrew Bergman   *Ph* King Baggot   *Ed* Randy Roberts, Andy Zall   *Mus* David Shire   *Art Dir* Peter Wooley
● George Burns, Ted Wass, Ron Silver, Roxanne Hart, Eugene Roche, Robert Desiderio (Warner)

After two turns as an amusing Supreme Being, George Burns proves to be an equally diverting demon in *Oh God! You Devil*. Director Paul Bogart and writer Andrew Bergman have let Burns loose as Lucifer and relegated Burns as God to little more than a cameo.

Bergman's plot is unashamedly Faustian: struggling musician Ted Wass is desperate for the break that will bring happiness and afford parenthood for him and wife Roxanne Hart. Bad Burns picks up Wass' wail and a deal is soon struck. Burns switches him with an already reigning rock star (Robert Desiderio) whose own pact with the devil has run out.

Unhappily, the story didn't need to get this involved and it winds up constantly trying to pull the picture apart, working against the comedy. By the time Burns as God heeds Wass' plea for salvation, it's almost too much for even Him to iron out satisfactorily.

Ron Silver does an excellent rendition of a hotshot record company executive and Eugene Roche is delightful as the hopeless agent who's originally in charge of Wass' failing career.

▪ **OH, MR. PORTER!**

1937, 84 MINS, UK ⓥ
Dir Marcel Varnel   *Prod* Edward Black   *Scr* J.O.C. Orton, Val Guest, Marriott Edgar   *Ph* Arthur Crabtree   *Ed* R.E. Dearing, Alfred Roome   *Mus* Louis Levy (dir.)   *Art Dir* Alex Vetchinsky
● Will Hay, Moore Marriott, Graham Moffatt, Sebastian Smith, Percy Walsh, Agnes Lauchlan (Gainsborough)

A railway comedy [story by Frank Launder], reminiscent of *The Ghost Train* (1931), written around the comic personality of Will Hay, supported by his very 'aged' and very 'young' foils.

An amiable misfit, with a brother-in-law in the railway company, is sent as a last resort to a tiny, obscure village in Ireland as stationmaster, where his family hope to be rid of him. Finding a decrepit clerk and fat-boy porter the only occupants of the station, where no train ever stops, the newcomer tries to convert the ramshackle dump into something worthy of his dignity.

He senses a sinister atmosphere, in that his predecessors have either disappeared mysteriously, or gone nutty. Tracking a lost excursion to a disused tunnel and derelict line, the dauntless stationmaster discovers the supposedly ghostly crew are gun-runners about to get over the border.

No love interest to mar the comedy, as far as the juvenile mind is concerned, and the whole thing is amusing, if over-long.

▪ **O.H.M.S.**

(US: *You're in the Army Now*)
1937, 87 MINS, UK
Dir Raoul Walsh   *Prod* [uncredited]   *Scr* Lesser Samuels, Ralph Bettinson, Austin Melford, Bryan Wallace   *Ph* Roy Kellino   *Ed* Charles Saunders (dir.)   *Art Dir* Edward Metzner
● Wallace Ford, John Mills, Anna Lee, Grace Bradley, Frank Cellier, Peter Croft (Gaumont-British)

Not much to get excited about. Takes off from a fetching theme, but that nothing much eventuates can largely be blamed on a dour and flabby script.

Wallace Ford is a lively enough personality in the central role. Narrative poses him as a petty American racketeer who flees to England from a threatened rap for murder. There he turns to the army as a hideout, enlisting as from Canada. With occasional touches of humor, picture relates his doings as a recruit, adding romance to the proceedings by making Ford the third corner in a play for the sergeant-major's daughter (Anna Lee). His rival, and a good natured one, is his barracks sidekick (John Mills).

Complications develop when Ford's former showgirl flame from the States pops up. Ford stows away on a ship and finds himself occupying the same vessel as his regiment bound for China. The girl is also aboard. Picture goes melodramatic for the final reel.

▪ **OH! WHAT A LOVELY WAR**

1969, 144 MINS, UK ◇ ⓥ
Dir Richard Attenborough   *Prod* Brian Duffy, Richard Attenborough   *Scr* [Len Deighton]   *Ph* Gerry Turpin   *Ed* Kevin Connor   *Mus* Alfred Ralston   *Art Dir* Don Ashton
● Ralph Richardson, Laurence Olivier, John Gielgud, John Mills, Michael Redgrave, Vanessa Redgrave (Paramount/Accord)

Richard Attenborough's debut as a film director can be labelled with such debased showbiz verbal coinage as fabulous, sensational, stupendous, etc. It also happens to be dedicated, exhilarating, shrewd, mocking, funny, emotional, witty, poignant and technically brilliant.

A satire on war in which the songs are an integral part of the message, it was shot entirely on location, in and around Brighton [based on Joan Littlewood's Theatre Workshop production, by Charles Chilton and members of the original cast, after a stage treatment by Ted Allan].

Oh! What a Lovely War is an indictment of war which never relies on violence. Sudden, brutal death in combat is omitted and far more effectively, is rammed home by the symbol of poppies for each death.

The film is a kick in the pants for jingoism, false heroics, vanity and stupidity in high places. It never lessens or denigrates the bravery of those who took part, but brilliantly pinpoints the collective stupidity that made such a holocaust possible. The familiar wartime songs, sentiment, humor and satire are all incorporated, but Attenborough has never allowed any to stretch a mood beyond its capacity.

The film is seen through the eyes and family life of the humble Smith family, whose sons all go to war and are senselessly killed.

▪ **OIL FOR THE LAMPS OF CHINA**

1935, 110 MINS, US
Dir Mervyn LeRoy   *Prod* [Robert Lord]   *Scr* Laird Doyle   *Ph* Tony Gaudio   *Ed* William Clemens   *Mus* Leo F. Forbstein (dir.)   *Art Dir* Robert M. Haas

● Pat O'Brien, Josephine Hutchinson, Jean Muir, Lyle Talbot, John Eldredge, Donald Crisp (Cosmopolitan/ Warner)

This story, in book form, was a bestseller for over a year and caused a lot of talk. In transferring it to screen the filmers have taken many liberties, so that it evolves as a choppy, long, and sometimes confused yarn.

Alice Tisdale Hobart's original was an indictment of a great oil company for its subjugation of its employees. Film switches that around to a man's blind struggle against mistreatment, dishonesty in officials, personal misfortune, and rank deception on the part of his officers, with nothing more than faith in 'the company' as his wand.

Story is laid practically entirely in China. The Atlantis Oil Company has sent Pat O'Brien over there to sell oil to the Chinese. Because he's saving the company some money, his first baby dies in childbirth. Because his best friend has lost a minor sales contract, he fires him, etc. Comes the revolution. The rebels try to take a few thousand dollars of the company's money so he risks his life, sees his assistant shot, is badly wounded himself, and is in a hospital for months. But he saves the $15,000. When he's out of the hospital he's rewarded by being demoted.

■ OKLAHOMA!

1955, 145 MINS, US ◇ ⑫ ⊙
Dir Fred Zinnemann *Prod* Arthur Hornblow Jr
Scr Sonya Levien, William Ludwig *Ph* Robert Surtees
Ed Gene Ruggiero *Mus* Jay Blackton (sup.)
Art Dir Oliver Smith
● Gordon MacRae, Shirley Jones, Gloria Grahame, Gene Nelson, Charlotte Greenwood, Rod Steiger (Magna)

The innovating musical comedy magic that Richard Rodgers and Oscar Hammerstein II first created when The Theatre Guild produced their *Oklahoma!* [in 1943] has been captured and, in some details, expanded in the film version. The tunes ring out with undiminished delight. The characters pulsate with spirit. The Agnes De Mille choreography makes the play literally leap.

The wide screen used for the Todd-AO process adds production scope and visual grandeur, capturing a vista of blue sky and green prairie that can be breathtaking.

Heading the cast, Gordon MacRae as Curly, and Shirley Jones as Laurey make a bright, romantic pair. The entire cast goes through its paces with verve and spirit. If the singing is good, the acting just fine, top honors go to De Mille and her dancers.

After all's said and done, the main burden still falls on MacRae and Jones. MacRae not only looks the part of Curly, he acts it out with a modicum of theatrics. He cuts a clean-cut figure and he delivers his songs in grand style.

□ 1955: Best Sound Recording, Scoring of a Musical Picture.
□ Nominations: Best Color Cinematography, Editing

■ OKLAHOMA CRUDE

1973, 108 MINS, US ◇ ⑫
Dir Stanley Kramer *Prod* Stanley Kramer *Scr* Marc Norman *Ph* Robert Surtees *Ed* Folmar Blangsted
Mus Henry Mancini *Art Dir* Alfred Sweeney
● George C. Scott, Faye Dunaway, John Mills, Jack Palance, William Lucking, Harvey Jason (Columbia)

Oklahoma Crude is a dramatically choppy potboiler about oil wildcatting in 1913.

Faye Dunaway plays a bitter woman determined to bring in an oil well on her own, aided by Rafael Campos, an Indian laborer. John Mills aiming to help her out after years of parental abandonment, recruits George C. Scott from the hobo jungles. The three of them (Campos is killed off early) joust with

Jack Palance, snarling provocateur of the oil trust which wants Dunaway's property.

Since Oklahoma today does not resemble 1913, director Stanley Kramer found a great location in Stockton, California, but the solid impact of that choice is often negated by erratic special effects work.

Scott hunkers around chewing the scenery, but occasionally the interplay with Dunaway is momentarily touching. Mills does well, but Palance's caricature destroys the chance for a good, tough characterization.

■ OLD ACQUAINTANCE

1943, 110 MINS, US
Dir Vincent Sherman *Prod* Henry Blanke *Scr* John Van Druten, Lenore Coffee *Ph* Sol Polito *Ed* [uncredited]
Mus Franz Waxman *Art Dir* John Hughes
● Bette Davis, Miriam Hopkins, Gig Young, John Loder, Dolores Moran, Philip Reed (Warner)

Bette Davis and Miriam Hopkins were schoolgirl chums. With former leaving home town to carve literary career, while latter settles to happy marriage to John Loder, Davis returns for lecture and, as guest of former pal, finds her with child and writer of hot sexy novels which she agrees to read and submit to publishers.

Eight years later, Hopkins is a successful pop novelist and hits New York with Loder and daughter for opening of Davis' play. Latter sees pending breakup of marriage, tries to prevent it, even though Loder tells of his walkout and real love for her.

Next episode unfolds another 10 years, with Loder now an army major, renewing acquaintance with Davis, but latter is being romanced by Gig Young, 10 years her junior. Moving swiftly to involvement, dramatics tosses young daughter into arms of Young, Loder is engaged to another woman, and the two schoolgal chums find themselves together and alone for mutual companionship.

John Van Druten and Lenore Coffee have devised fine script from the [former's 1940] original play, deftly moulding it to particular dramatic talents of Hopkins-Davis, while Vincent Sherman provides fine directing job.

■ OLD BOYFRIENDS

1979, 103 MINS, US ◇ ⑫ ⊙
Dir Joan Tewkesbury *Prod* Edward R. Pressman, Michele Rappaport *Scr* Paul Schrader, Leonard Schrader *Ph* William A. Fraker *Ed* Bill Reynolds
Mus David Shire *Art Dir* Peter Jamison
● Talia Shire, Richard Jordan, Keith Carradine, John Belushi, John Houseman, Buck Henry (Avco Embassy)

The premise of *Old Boyfriends* is an intriguing and universal one, the fantasy of revisiting lovers out of an individual's past.

Script is contemporary and grounded in realism, right down to the shifting morals which have marked male-female relationships in the past. In this case, the femme (Talia Shire) is a clinical psychologist who roots into her past after a failed suicide attempt.

Shire's odyssey takes her across America to old beaux including her college sweetheart (Richard Jordan), high school romance (John Belushi) and first adolescent love (Keith Carradine). The experience proves to be disquieting.

A protege of Robert Altman, novice director Joan Tewkesbury, who scripted his *Nashville*, employs similar loosely narrative techniques, with the Shire character holding together the series of set pieces.

■ OLD DARK HOUSE, THE

1932, 74 MINS, US
Dir James Whale *Prod* Carl Laemmle Jr *Scr* Benn W. Levy, [R. C. Sherriff] *Ph* [Arthur Edeson] *Ed* [Clarence Kolster] *Art Dir* [Charles D. Hall]

● Boris Karloff, Melvyn Douglas, Charles Laughton, Gloria Stuart, Lillian Bond, Ernest Thesiger (Universal)

The [original J.B.] Priestley novel must have been a bit more plausible than as evidenced in the cinematic transition. But regardless, it has all the elements for horror and thriller exploitation, including as it does a mad brute butler (Boris Karloff), insanity, ghosts in the family closets, sex, romance, not to mention the titular setting in a storm-torn Welsh mountain retreat.

Let one stop and think but a few seconds about what's happened on the screen and there'd be no picture; hence, it's been the somewhat too difficult task of the Laemmle studio to pile on trick after trick. For it's a certainty that the average mortal, despite the raging elements without, would have carried on in the storm at any price, or camped out in their motor, rather than sit in for an evening with the eccentric Femm family or their insane butler, Morgan.

Among the performances, Karloff with a characteristically un-drawing-room physical getup, by no means impresses as a sissy by stature, demeanor and surliness. Gloria Stuart gives excellent account of herself, although that extreme decolletage is rather uncalled for considering the locale. Charles Laughton turns in one of his usually tophole performances as the Lancashire knight. Melvyn Douglas is rather hit and miss under the circumstances, and that stable tete-a-tete with Lillian Bond, who is satisfactory up until that point, makes it a bit worse.

■ OLD DRACULA
See: *Vampira*

■ OLD ENOUGH

1984, 91 MINS, US ◇ ⑫
Dir Marisa Silver *Prod* Dina Silver *Scr* Marisa Silver
Ph Michael Ballhaus *Ed* Mark Burns *Mus* Julian Marshall *Art Dir* Jeffrey Townsend
● Sarah Boyd, Rainbow Harvest, Neill Barry, Danny Aiello, Susan Kingsley, Roxanne Hart (Silverfilm)

The tale of friendship between two young girls of widely different social backgrounds, *Old Enough* has just the right balance of humor and insight to connect with audiences.

Produced and directed by sisters Dina and Marisa Silver, the project evolved from Utah's Sundance Institute for Independent Filmmakers. Nonetheless, the simple story and modest budgeted effort need make no excuses for finished product.

Story centers on 12-year-old Lonnie Sloan (Sarah Boyd) from an upper-class New York City family and slightly older Karen Bruckner (Rainbow Harvest) from blue-collar background. Both are at important emotional turning points when they meet on the street of the widely divergent economic neighborhood. It is an easily understandable attraction of opposites.

The mix of fresh faces and a few seasoned pros in cast all register indelibly. Both Boyd and Harvest have burden of carrying the film, which they accomplish with ease.

■ OLD FASHIONED WAY, THE

1934, 69 MINS, US
Dir William Beaudine *Prod* William LeBaron
Scr Garnett Weston, Jack Cunningham *Ph* Benjamin Reynolds *Mus* Harry Revel *Art Dir* [John Goodman]
● W. C. Fields, Joe Morrison, Judith Allen, Jan Duggan, Nora Cecil, Baby LeRoy (Paramount)

Made to order for W. C. Fields and permitting him to do his old cigar-box juggling among other things, *The Old Fashioned Way* is light comedy material that will please the Fields followers.

A repertoire troupe of the days when *The

Drunkard and *East Lynne* were big draws serves as the background and the small town of Bellefontaine, O, is the locale. It is here that the Great McGonigle, who heads the rep company, runs into all kinds of difficulties, most of them of a financial origin.

At the outset the troupe is on the way to the next stand, Bellefontaine. Train sequences provide some pretty good laughs from the beginning as McGonigle skips a summons and accidentally falls heir to an upper berth, not to mention the reception at Bellefontaine he mistakingly believes to be in his honor.

Joe Morrison is worked in for songs with suitable spots provided for him during the *Drunkard* sequence. Morrison's voice registers well and on the love interest he carries himself through satisfactorily. Romantic side of the story [by Charles Bogle (= W.C. Fields)] treated lightly but has its place as fitted in, Judith Allen holding up the other end adequately.

. . . .

■ **OLD GRINGO**

1989, 119 MINS, US ◇ ▼ ⊙

Dir Luis Puenzo *Prod* Lois Bonfiglio *Scr* Aida Bortnik, Luis Puenzo *Ph* Felix Monti *Ed* Juan Carlos Macias, William Anderson, Glen Farr *Mus* Lee Holdridge *Art Dir* Stuart Wurtzel
● Jane Fonda, Gregory Peck, Jimmy Smits, Patricio Contreras, Jenny Gago (Fonda/Columbia)

Based on Carlos Fuentes' novel *Gringo Viejo*, the complex psychological tableau makes it easy to see why Jane Fonda plopped herself in the plum role of 40-ish spinster on the run Harriet Winslow. She is swept up by accident in the Mexican Revolution and swept off her feet by a charismatic general in Pancho Villa's popular front.

A rakish Jimmy Smits as Gen. Arroyo is superbly cast. He conveys the cocksure yet sensitive machismo and motivations of his character's torment between the revolution he lives and the woman he loves.

As the embittered, sardonic journalist Ambrose Bierce, Gregory Peck has found a role that suits him to a T. He portrays the world-weary Bierce with relish and wit.

The paternalistic figure in a nebulous love triangle with Fonda and Smits, Peck exudes a sympathetic mien despite his crusty exterior. His best moments come long before the denouement, and the film's wittiest lines are his alone.

. . . .

■ **OLD MAID, THE**

1939, 92 MINS, US ▼ ⊙

Dir Edmund Goulding *Prod* Hal B. Wallis *Scr* Casey Robinson *Ph* Tony Gaudio *Ed* George Amy *Mus* Max Steiner *Art Dir* Robert Haas
● Bette Davis, Miriam Hopkins, George Brent, Donald Crisp, Jane Bryan, James Stephenson (Warner)

Film version of the Pulitzer prize play [by Zoe Akins from a novel by Edith Wharton] sticks pretty close to the original development and dialog. Therein lies a handicap to success of the piece on the screen. It's stagey, sombre and generally confusing fare.

Story opens during the Civil War days. Miriam Hopkins loves George Brent, but, when he fails to return after two years, prepares to marry rich James Stephenson. Brent arrives on the wedding day and is comforted by Bette Davis, younger cousin of Hopkins. Brent goes to war and is killed, leaving Davis with a child.

Skipping over 15 years, household is presented in complex antagonism between the two cousins, now matronly.

Davis provides a strong portrayal in the title role. Hopkins provides a strong contrast as the motherly matron.

. . . .

■ **OLD MAN AND THE SEA, THE**

1958, 86 MINS, US ◇

Dir John Sturges *Prod* Leland Hayward *Scr* Peter Viertel *Ph* James Wong Howe, Floyd Crosby, Tom Tutwiler *Ed* Arthur P. Schmidt *Mus* Dimitri Tiomkin *Art Dir* Art Loel, Edward Carrere
● Spencer Tracy, Felipe Pazos, Harry Bellaver (Warner)

Ernest Hemingway's introspective one-episode novelette, *The Old Man and the Sea*, is virtually a one-character film, the spotlight being almost continuously on Spencer Tracy as the old Cuban fisherman who meets his final test in his tremendous struggle with the huge marlin.

The picture has power, vitality and sharp excitement as it depicts the gruelling contest between man and fish. It is exquisitely photographed and skillfully directed. It captures the dignity and the stubborness of the old man, and it is tender in his final defeat.

And yet it isn't a completely satisfying picture. There are long and arid stretches, when it seems as if producer and director were merely trying to fill time.

It is Tracy's picture from beginning to end. One could quarrel with his interpretation of the old man. There are moments when he is magnificent and moving, and others when he seems to move in a stupor. It is, on the whole, a distinguished and impressive performance, ranging from the old man's pursuit of the fish, to hooking him, to the long chase and the final slashing battle.

In a supporting part, Felipe Pazos plays the boy who loves the old man and understands him. It is a very appealing and tender performance. Harry Bellaver has a small role as the tavern owner who sympathizes with the old man and, with the rest of the village, learns to admire him for his catch.

John Sturges directs with a view to keeping the essential values intact. It's not his fault that the basic material simply doesn't sustain interest throughout 86 minutes.

□ 1958: Best Scoring of a Dramatic Picture.
□ Nominations: Best Actor (Spencer Tracy), Color Cinematography

. . . .

■ **OLD YELLER**

1957, 83 MINS, US ◇ ▼ ⊙

Dir Robert Stevenson *Prod* Walt Disney *Scr* Fred Gipson, William Tunberg *Ph* Charles P. Boyle *Ed* Stanley Johnson *Mus* Oliver Wallace *Art Dir* Carroll Clark
● Dorothy McGuire, Fess Parker, Tommy Kirk, Kevin Corcoran, Chuck Connors (Walt Disney)

Disney organization's flair for taking a homely subject and building a heartwarming film is again aptly demonstrated in this moving story set in 1869 of a Texas frontier family and an old yeller dog. Based on Fred Gipson's novel of same tag, this is a careful blending of fun, laughter, love, adventure and tragedy.

Emphasis is laid upon animal action, including squirrels, jackrabbits, buzzards and newborn calves as well as more rugged depictions. Packed into film's tight footage is the 115-pound dog's fight with a huge bear, its struggle with a marauding wolf and battle with a pack of wild hogs.

. . . .

■ **OLIVER!**

1968, 146 MINS, UK ◇ ▼ ⊙

Dir Carol Reed *Prod* John Woolf *Scr* Vernon Harris *Ph* Oswald Morris *Ed* Ralph Kemplen *Mus* Johnny Green (dir.) *Art Dir* John Box
● Ron Moody, Shani Wallis, Oliver Reed, Harry Secombe, Mark Lester, Jack Wild (Columbia/Romulus)

This $10 million pic is a bright, shiny, heart-warming musical, packed with songs and lively production highspots. Lionel Bart's [1960] stage musical hit is adroitly opened

out by director Carol Reed.

Oliver! goes with a cheerful swing, leading up to a strong dramatic climax when Bill Sikes gets his comeuppance. Mark Lester, as the workhouse waif who finds happiness after a basinful of scary adventures, is a frail Oliver, with a tremulous, piping singing voice, but he's vigorous and mischievous enough, and is sufficiently dewy-eyed and angelic to captivate the audience.

The youngsters are natural scene-stealers but major honors go to a diminutive 15-year-old, Jack Wild, who plays the Artful Dodger with knowing cunning and impudent self-confidence.

Ron Moody's Fagin lacks some of the malignance usually associated with the role of the wily old rascal though he shows sudden flashes of evil temper. He riotously squeezes every morsel of fun out of his tuition scenes with the little pickpockets.

Bart's familiar songs, such as 'Food, Glorious Food,' 'Consider Yourself,' 'I'd Do Anything' and 'Oom-Pah-Pah' are as fresh as ever.
□ 1968: Best Picture, Director, Art Direction, Sound, Scoring of a Musical Picture, (Honor Award (Onna White, for choreography).
□ Nominations: Best Actor (Ron Moody), Supp. Actor (Jack Wild), Adapted Screenplay, Cinematography, Costume Design, Editing

. . . .

■ **OLIVER'S STORY**

1978, 92 MINS, US ◇ ▼

Dir John Korty *Prod* David V. Picker *Scr* Erich Segal, John Korty *Ph* Arthur Ornitz *Ed* Stuart H. Pappe *Mus* Francis Lai *Art Dir* Robert Gundlach
● Ryan O'Neal, Candice Bergen, Nicola Pagett, Edward Binns, Benson Fong, Ray Milland (Paramount)

Love Story is a tough act to follow, but *Oliver's Story* manages to hold its own. The continuation of Erich Segal's tale of fated lovers gets a sensitive and moving treatment from director and coscripter (with Segal) John Korty.

Oliver's Story begins with the burial of Jenny Cavalleri Barrett, whose death closed out the first pic. Ryan O'Neal, working as a lawyer in a prestigious New York firm, is burdened by a sense of despair and loneliness, along with a liberal dose of self-pity.

Enter Candice Bergen as the Bonwit heir in Bonwit Teller, the flip side in looks and disposition to the Jenny character created by Ali MacGraw. Their meeting is one of those coincidences that only occur in films, but Korty and Segal plot the relationship with a sureness that proves to be highly endearing.

The most moving segments come, ironically, not out of the O'Neal-Bergen encounters, but from a few brief scenes between O'Neal and Ray Milland, who encores as his wealthy banker father. It's a tribute to both performances and Korty's direction that this most basic of conflicts is resolved here in a genuinely satisfying manner.

. . . .

■ **OLIVER TWIST**

1948, 116 MINS, UK ▼

Dir David Lean *Prod* Ronald Neame *Scr* David Lean, Stanley Haynes *Ph* Guy Green *Ed* Jack Harris *Mus* Arnold Bax *Art Dir* John Bryan
● Robert Newton, Alec Guinness, Kay Walsh, Francis L. Sullivan, John Howard Davies, Anthony Newley (Cineguild)

From every angle this is a superb achievement. Dickens' devotees may object to condensing of the story and omission of some of the minor characters. But what is left still runs close to two hours.

One of its merits is the absence of considerable unnecessary dialog, the child Oliver having the fewest lines ever allotted to so prominent a character. He has the wistful air of the typical Dickens waif and heads almost faultless casting.

Camerawork is on an exceptionally high level. Opening shots of a storm-swept sky and heavy clouds give an eerie quality that immediately grips the imagination. Josephine Stuart's delineation of a woman in labor pains, dragging herself across rain-sodden fields to a distant light that spells sanctuary, is unparalleled in its poignant realism.

Alec Guinness gives a revoltingly faithful portrait of Fagin and Kay Walsh extracts just the right amount of viciousness overcome by pity in her delineation of Nancy. Robert Newton is a natural for the brutish Sikes and gets every ounce out of his opportunities.

....

■ O LUCKY MAN!

1973, 176 MINS, UK ◇ ▼

Dir Lindsay Anderson *Prod* Michael Medwin, Lindsay Anderson *Scr* David Sherwin *Ph* Miroslav Ondricek *Ed* David Gladwell, Tom Priestley *Mus* Alan Price *Art Dir* Jocelyn Herbert
● Malcolm McDowell, Ralph Richardson, Rachel Roberts, Arthur Lowe, Helen Mirren, Dandy Nichols (Memorial/SAM)

No less than an epic look at society is created in Lindsay Anderson's third and most provocative film. It is in the form of a human comedy on a perky, ambitious but conformist young man using society's ways to get to the top.

Malcolm McDowell, though practically on screen throughout, displays a solid grasp of character and nuances. He is first a salesman, then guinea pig to science, assistant to a great business tycoon, railroaded to prison as a fall guy, converted to near saintliness, almost martyred and then returned to conformism by an almost mystical reaching of understanding through a Zen-Buddhist-like happening.

The film bows to various film greats but always assimilated to Anderson's own brand of epic comedy. The music and songs of AlanPrice also add by underlining and counterpointing the action.

Ralph Richardson gives his pointed aplomb to the rich man and as a wise old tailor who gives the hero a golden suit; Rachel Roberts is a sexy personnel chief, rich society mistress and a poverty row housefrau who commits suicide with expert balance in all. In fact, all are good, especially Helen Mirren as the way-out rich girl and Arthur Lowe as an unctous African potentate.

....

■ OMEGA MAN, THE

1971, 98 MINS, US ◇ ▼

Dir Boris Sagal *Prod* Walter Seltzer *Scr* John William Corrington, Joyce H. Corrington *Ph* Russell Metty *Ed* William Ziegler *Mus* Ron Grainer *Art Dir* Arthur Loel, Walter M. Simonds
● Charlton Heston, Anthony Zerbe, Rosalind Cash, Paul Koslo, Lincoln Kilpatrick, Eric Laneuville (Warner)

The Omega Man is an extremely literate science-fiction drama starring Charlton Heston as the only survivor of a worldwide bacteriological war, circa 1975. Thrust of the well-written story [adapted from Richard Matheson's novel] is Heston's running battle with deranged survivors headed by Anthony Zerbe.

The deserted streets of LA through which Heston drives by day while Zerbe's eye-sensitive mutations hide until nightfall, provide low-key but powerful emphasis on what can and does happen when the machinery of civilized society grinds to a halt.

An Oriental missile war has caused a worldwide plague. Zerbe, formerly a TV newscaster, has become the leader of the mutations, whose extreme reaction to the science which caused the disaster has led to wanton destruction of cultural and scientific objects. Rosalind Cash provides romantic interest for Heston as a member of another band of rural survivors not yet under Zerbe's control.

....

■ OMEN, THE

1976, 111 MINS, US ◇ ▼ ⊙

Dir Richard Donner *Prod* Harvey Bernhard *Scr* David Seltzer *Ph* Gilbert Taylor *Ed* Stuart Baird *Mus* Jerry Goldsmith *Art Dir* Carmen Dillon
● Gregory Peck, Lee Remick, David Warner, Billie Whitelaw, Patrick Troughton, Harvey Stephens (20th Century-Fox)

Suspenser starring Gregory Peck and Lee Remick as the unwitting parents of the anti-Christ. Richard Donner's direction is taut. Players all are strong.

There's enough exposition of the Book of Revelation to educate on the spot a person from another civilization. As for any religious commitment needed, that problem is minimal; the only premise one must accept is that the fallen Lucifer remains a very strong supernatural being.

Peck, well cast as a career American ambassador, is convinced by Italian priest Martin Benson to substitute another hospital baby for the one wife Remick lost in childbirth. Five years later, strange things begin to happen.

At various points, portents of Satanism emerge, underscored (or, rather, overscored) by Jerry Goldsmith's heavy music.
□ 1976: Best Original Score.
□ Nomination: Best Song ('Ave Satani')

....

■ ON A CLEAR DAY YOU CAN SEE FOREVER

1970, 129 MINS, US ◇ ▼ ⊙

Dir Vincente Minnelli *Prod* Howard W. Koch, Alan Jay Lerner *Scr* Alan Jay Lerner *Ph* Harry Stradling *Ed* David Bretherton *Mus* Nelson Riddle (arr.) *Art Dir* John DeCuir
● Barbra Streisand, Yves Montand, Bob Newhart, Larry Blyden, Simon Oakland, Jack Nicholson (Paramount)

[Based on the Lerner-Lane 1965 Broadway musical], the story line, without the gimmick of reincarnation, is pure soap suds. Barbra Streisand is a chain-smoker so addicted that she doesn't fly because 'I'm afraid of the No Smoking sign'. She is engaged to Larry Blyden, a business school student in the upper 2% of his class who is so square that he is selecting a future employer on the basis of the pension plan.

To stop smoking before an important dinner with the personnel recruiter from Chemical Foods Inc, Streisand crashes a medical school class in hypnotism taught by Yves Montand. He accidentally discovers that she has extra-sensory perception. Under hypnosis, she becomes an aristocratic femme fatale with whom Montand falls in love.

....

■ ONCE AROUND

1991, 114 MINS, US ◇ ▼ ⊙

Dir Lasse Hallstrom *Prod* Amy Robinson, Griffin Dunne *Scr* Malia Scotch Marmo *Ph* Theo Van De Sande *Ed* Andrew Mondsheim *Mus* James Horner *Art Dir* David Gropman
● Richad Dreyfuss, Holly Hunter, Danny Aiello, Laura San Giacomo, Gena Rowlands, Roxanne Hart (Universal/Cinecom)

Vast opportunities for unbearable quantities of sentimentality are fortunately squelched in *Once Around*, an intelligently engaging domestic comedy-drama. US debut by Lasse Hallstrom, director of the widely loved 1985 Swedish hit *My Life As a Dog*, keenly delineates how a woman finding happiness with a man for the first time paradoxically involves the serious deterioration of relations within her close-knit family.

Story is hung upon numerous family rituals – weddings, dinners, birthdays, baptisms, funerals – and opening sees thirty- something Holly Hunter being badgered about her marital prospects at the wedding of sister Laura San Giacomo.

Rebuffed by her b.f. (coproducer Griffin Dunne in a neat cameo), Hunter flees chilly Boston for the Caribbean, where she instantly is swept off her feet by irrepressible, vulgar, tireless, wealthy condominium salesman Richard Dreyfuss.

Brightest strategy is forcing the viewer to experience Hunter's family's acceptance of Dreyfuss. His sheer relentlessness darkens the mood and thickens the complexity of the situation, removing the film from the real of the feel-good Hollywood formula.

Danny Aiello (as the father), brightest in an excellent cast, invests all his scenes with evident emotional and mental deliberation. Hunter has many nice moments. San Giacomo and Gena Rowlands (as the mother) are very much on the money.

....

■ ONCE A THIEF

1965, 106 MINS, US

Dir Ralph Nelson *Prod* Jacques Bar *Scr* Zekial Marko *Ph* Robert Burks *Ed* Fredric Steinkamp *Mus* Lalo Schifrin *Art Dir* George W. Davis, Paul Groesse
● Alain Delon, Ann-Margret, Van Heflin, Jack Palance, John Davis Chandler, Jeff Corey (M-G-M)

Once a Thief packs both violence and young married love in unfoldment of its theme, aptly titled, about an ex-con trying to go straight, but constantly harassed by a vengeful cop.

Once a Thief has a San Francisco setting, where lenser Robert Burks makes interesting use of Chinatown and North Beach locations to backdrop story of $1 million platinum robbery and ultimate violent demise of each member of the five-man gang that pulled the job. Alain Delon not too unwillingly is pulled into the plot when he finds his wife, Ann-Margret working in a cheap nightclub so they may live.

Delon delivers strongly. He's the romantic type who excels also in rugged action. Ann-Margret, too, is firstrate in her role. Van Heflin, as a police inspector who thinks Delon once shot him, and Jack Palance, as Delon's gangster brother, also star.

Heflin, as Delon's nemesis effectively plays the relentless police officer, and Palance, with less footage, similarly scores.

....

■ ONCE IN PARIS

1978, 100 MINS, US ◇ ▼

Dir Frank D. Gilroy *Prod* Frank D. Gilroy, Manny Fuchs, Gerard Croce *Scr* Frank D. Gilroy *Ph* Claude Saunier *Ed* Robert Q. Lovett *Mus* Mitch Leigh
● Wayne Rogers, Gayle Hunnicutt, Jack Lenoir, Phillippe March, Clement Harari, Tanya Lopert (Gilroy)

Writer-director Frank Gilroy has come up with a highly personalized tale of a rough around-the-edges Yank screenwriter's relationship with a worldly chauffeur and a bauteous British aristocrat. Gilroy's developed the triad in subtle, believable, intelligent and often humorous fashion making *Once in Paris* a super film.

Shot entirely in Paris, with a French crew, the pic gets maximum mileage from its three principals: Wayne Rogers, Gayle Hunnicutt, and Jack Lenoir.

Michael Moore (Rogers) is a scenarist travelling to Paris for the first time to salvage a film script. He is met at the airport and immediately informed that the chauffeur (Lenoir) is a bad egg (he has served time for manslaughter) and will be replaced tout de suite.

The driver stays, of course, and develops a

strong friendship with the writer. The writer eventually has an affair with the British aristocrat (Hunnicutt) in Paris on business – she just happens to occupy the hotel suite adjoining the scripter's.

● ●

■ ONCE IS NOT ENOUGH
(Aka: Jacqueline Susann's Once Is Not Enough)

1975, 121 MINS, US ◇ ⊛
Dir Guy Green   *Prod* Howard W. Koch   *Scr* Julius J. Epstein   *Ph* John A. Alonzo   *Ed* Rita Roland   *Mus* Henry Mancini   *Art Dir* John DeCuir
● Kirk Douglas, Alexis Smith, David Janssen, George Hamilton, Melina Mercouri, Gary Conway (Paramount)

Jacqueline Susann's final novel, *Once Is Not Enough*, gallumphs to the screen as a tame potboiler. Kirk Douglas heads as a fading film producer devoted to daughter Deborah Raffin, so much so that he marries wealthy Alexis Smith to pay for the daughter's lifestyle.

Raffin resists the casual sexuality epitomized by George Hamilton, wealthy young man-about-town, and stumbles into a genuine love for David Janssen, a fading author who can't get it on in many areas of life anymore. Brenda Vaccaro plays a kooky magazine editor who tries to help Raffin.

Opulent production credits put the shallow dramaturgy even more to shame. Henry Mancini's lush romantic score is appropriate.
□ 1975: Nomination: Best Supp. Actress (Brenda Vaccaro)

● ●

■ ONCE MORE, WITH FEELING

1960, 92 MINS, US ◇
Dir Stanley Donen   *Prod* Stanley Donen   *Scr* Harry Kurnitz   *Ph* Georges Perinal   *Ed* Jack Harris   *Mus* Muir Mathieson (arr.)   *Art Dir* Alexander Trauner
● Yul Brynner, Kay Kendall, Geoffrey Toone, Maxwell Shaw, Gregory Ratoff, Mervyn Johns (Columbia)

The bright, entertaining touches of producer-director Stanley Donen breeze through *Once More, With Feeling* like an allegro, making a good Broadway play into a better motion picture. It's a smart, perfectly cast comedy.

Kay Kendall died less than three months after *Once More* was completed. Her eyes clouded with tears, Kendall blows away a kiss in her final scene, the sentiment seeming peculiarly prophetic. However, the picture of the actress through the rest of the film is one of life and of a spirited performer.

As a pompous sympathy conductor with a love of fine music that surpasses his participation in mundane existence, Yul Brynner has strength and humor, adeptly playing sly appeal against defiant arrogance. Together, he and Kendall make an overwhelming screen couple.

Harry Kurnitz wrote the screenplay from his own play, moved the setting from the United States to Europe and has come up with a scriptful of witty dialog and amusing situations.

The conflict finds Brynner at odds with the world. He makes great music, but he can't get along with his musicians or the orchestra's board of trustees, and his pretty wife (Kendall) must soothe feelings all the way around. Eventually she has enough of her egomaniac husband, leaves him and decides to marry a physicist.

In support of the stars, Gregory Ratoff is excellent as the agent, prone to absurd comparisons and remarkably able to keep the warring mates in hand.

● ●

■ ONCE UPON A CRIME

1992, 94 MINS, US ◇ ⊛ ⊙
Dir Eugene Levy   *Prod* Dino De Laurentiis   *Scr* Charles Shyer, Nancy Meyers, Steve Kluger   *Ph* Giuseppe Rotunno   *Ed* Patrick Kennedy   *Mus* Richard Gibbs   *Art Dir* Pier Luigi Basile

● John Candy, James Belushi, Cybill Shepherd, Sean Young, Richard Lewis, Ornella Muti (De Laurentiis)

SCTV alum Eugene Levy makes his feature-film directing debut with a film that, ironically, would have provided ample fodder for a Second City spoof as a group of US stars chews its way through Italy and France in search of a movie.

The action is fittingly spurred along by a dog, as an out-of-work actor (Richard Lewis) and just-jilted woman (Sean Young) find a stray dachshund and trek from Rome to Monte Carlo to collect the $5,000 reward for its return. But the pair find the dog's owner murdered and get implicated in the crime, as do a compulsive gambler (John Candy), a too-ugly American (James Belushi) and his neglected wife (Cybill Shepherd).

Tech credits are significantly better than the action, with splashy costumes and sets as well as a jaunty score by Richard Gibbs.

● ●

■ ONCE UPON A TIME IN AMERICA

1984, 227 MINS, US ◇ ⊛ ⊙
Dir Sergio Leone   *Prod* Arnon Milchan   *Scr* Leonardo Benvenuti, Piero De Bernardi, Enrico Medioli, Franco Arcalli, Franco Ferrini, Sergio Leone, Stuart Kaminsky   *Ph* Tonino Delli Colli   *Ed* Nino Baragli   *Mus* Ennio Morricone   *Art Dir* Carlo Simi, James Singelis
● Robert De Niro, James Woods, Elizabeth McGovern, Treat Williams, Tuesday Weld, Burt Young (Ladd)

Once Upon a Time in America arrives as a disappointment of considerable proportions. Sprawling $32 million saga of Jewish gangsters over the decades is surprisingly deficient in clarity and purpose, as well as excitement and narrative involvement.

Pic opens with a series of extraordinary violent episodes. It's 1933 and some hoods knock off a girlfriend and some cohorts of 'Noodles' (Robert De Niro), while trying to track down the man himself.

Then, action shifts to 1968, when the aging De Niro (superior makeup job) returns to New York after a 35-year absence and reunites with a childhood pal, Fat Moe (Larry Rapp). De Niro is clearly on a mission relating to his past, and his later discovery of a briefcase filled with loot for a contract is obviously a portent of something big to come.

Leone's pattern of jumping between time periods isn't at all confusing and does create some effective poetic echoes, but also seems arbitrary at times and, because of the long childhood section, forestalls the beginning of involvement.

Quiet and subtle throughout, De Niro and his charisma rep the backbone of the picture but, despite frequent threats to become engaging, Noodles remains essentially unpalatable.

● ●

■ ONCE UPON A TIME IN THE WEST

1969, 165 MINS, ITALY/US ◇ ⊛ ⊙
Dir Sergio Leone   *Prod* Fulvio Morsella   *Scr* Sergio Leone, Sergio Donati, Mickey Knox   *Ph* Tonino Delli Colli   *Ed* Nino Baragli   *Mus* Ennio Morricone   *Art Dir* Carlo Simi
● Henry Fonda, Claudia Cardinale, Jason Robards, Charles Bronson, Gabriele Ferzetti, Lionel Stander (Paramount/Rafran/San Marco)

Henry Fonda and Jason Robards relish each screen minute as the heavies, and Charles Bronson plays Clint Eastwood's 'man with no name' role.

Leone's story here [from one by Dario Argento, Bernardo Bertolucci and himself], presented in broad strokes through careful interconnection of set-piece action, focuses on the various reactions of four people – the three male leads, plus Claudia Cardinale, extremely effective as a fancy lady from New Orleans – to the idea of garnering extreme wealth via ownership of a crucial watertown

on the route of the transcontinental railroad.

The paradoxical, but honest 'fun' aspect of Leone's previous preoccupation with elaborately-stylized violence is here unconvincingly asking for consideration in a new 'moral' light. This means that Leone's own special talent for playing with film ideas gets lost in a no man's land of the merely initiative.

● ●

■ ON DANGEROUS GROUND

1951, 82 MINS, US ⊛ ⊙
Dir Nicholas Ray   *Prod* John Houseman   *Scr* A.I. Bezzerides   *Ph* George E. Diskant   *Ed* Roland Gross   *Mus* Bernard Herrmann   *Art Dir* Albert S. D'Agostino, Ralph Berger
● Ida Lupino, Robert Ryan, Ward Bond, Charles Kemper, Anthony Ross, Sumner Williams (RKO)

Lack of definition in characters is chief flaw in writing, with Nicholas Ray, who also directed, and A.I. Bezzerides sharing the blame for their adaptation of the Gerald Butler novel, *Mad with Much Heart*. There's not much Robert Ryan can do with the character of a cop made tough by the types with whom he is brought into contact, nor does Ida Lupino have much opportunity as a blind girl who presumably softens Ryan's character.

First half of the footage is given over to Ryan's mental travail as a city prowl car cop who favors plenty of roughness for those he arrests. In fact, this ready use of fists eventually gets him assigned out of town to aid a county sheriff hunt down a madman who has killed a little girl. Trail leads to a lonely farmhouse where Ryan and Ward Bond, playing the father of the murder victim, encounter Lupino. The killer is her mentally deficient kid brother (Sumner Williams) whom she has hidden out.

Ray manages to inject an occasional bit of excitement into the yarn, and had the psychotic touches been elimated in the script, film could have qualified as okay, even if grim, melodrama.

● ●

■ ONE BORN EVERY MINUTE
See: The Flim-Flam Man

● ●

■ ONE DAY IN THE LIFE OF IVAN DENISOVICH

1972, 100 MINS, UK/NORWAY ◇ ⊛ ⊙
Dir Caspar Wrede   *Prod* Caspar Wrede   *Scr* Ronald Harwood   *Ph* Sven Nykvist   *Ed* Thelma Connell   *Mus* Arne Nordheim   *Art Dir* Per Schwab
● Tom Courtenay, Espen Skjonberg, James Maxwell, Alfred Burke, Eric Thompson, John Cording (Group W/ Norsk)

Based on the novel by Alexander Solzhenitsyn, *One Day in the Life of Ivan Denisovich* is a tribute to the inherent dignity of man and his ability to maintain his humanity under seemingly impossible conditions. Though faithful to the novel, the film emerges as strangely unmoving.

Life chronicles a 'good' day for Ivan Denisovich, a prisoner in the eighth year of a 10-year sentence at a Siberian labor camp. The day is filled with small victories over the system. He does not fall ill, he manages to cop some extra food and tobacco, finds a hacksaw blade, builds a cinderblock wall and retires without incurring the wrath of his keepers.

Sincerity (and austerity) of the production, lensed expertly under fierce conditions in Norway by Sven Nykvist, cannot compensate for Caspar Wrede's lackluster direction and a script so sparse it almost seems nonexistent. Considering what they have to work with, the performers are fine, especially Courtenay who captures a mix of wiliness and childlike enthusiasm that is consistently convincing.

● ●

ONE-EYED JACKS

1961, 137 MINS, US ◇ ⑫ ⊙
Dir Marlon Brando   *Prod* Frank P. Rosenberg   *Scr* Guy
Trosper, Calder Willingham   *Ph* Charles Lang Jr
Ed Archie Marshek   *Mus* Hugo Friedhofer   *Art Dir* Hal
Pereira, J. McMillan Johnson
● Marlon Brando, Karl Malden, Pina Pellicer, Katy
Jurado, Ben Johnson, Slim Pickens (Paramount)

Charles Neider's novel, *The Authentic Death of
Hendry Jones*, is the source of the tellingly direct screenplay. It is the brooding, deliberate
tale of a young man (Marlon Brando) consumed by a passion for revenge after he is betrayed by an accomplice (Karl Malden) in a
bank robbery, for which crime he spends five
years (1880-85) in a Mexican prison.

His vengeful campaign leads him to the
town of Monterey, where Malden has attained respectability and the position of sheriff, but romantic entanglements with
Malden's stepdaughter (Pina Pellicer) persuade Brando to abandon his intention until
the irresistibility of circumstance and
Malden's own irrepressible will to snuff out
the living evidence of his guilt draws the two
men into a showdown.

It is an oddity of this film that both its
strength and its weakness lie in the area of
characterization. Brando's concept calls,
above all, for depth of character, for human
figures endowed with overlapping good and
bad sides to their nature. In the case of the
central characters – his own, Malden's,
Pellicer's – he is successful. But a few of his
secondary people have no redeeming qualities
– they are simply arch-villains.

Brando creates a character of substance, of
its own identity. It is an instinctively right
and illuminating performance. Another rich,
vivid variable portrayal is the one by Malden.
Katy Jurado is especially fine as Malden's
wife. Outstanding in support is Ben Johnson
as the bad sort who leads Brando to his prey.

The $5 to 6 million production, framed
against the turbulent coastline of the
Monterey peninsula and the shifting sands
and mounds of the bleak Mexican desert, is
notable for its visual artistry alone.
☐ 1961: Nomination: Best Color
Cinematography

ONE FLEW OVER THE CUCKOO'S NEST

1975, 133 MINS, US ◇ ⑫ ⊙
Dir Milos Forman   *Prod* Saul Zaentz   *Scr* Lawrence
Hauben, Bo Goldman   *Ph* Haskell Wexler, Bill Butler,
William Fraker   *Ed* Richard Chew, Lynzee Klingman,
Sheldon Kahn   *Mus* Jack Nitzsche   *Art Dir* Paul Sylbert
● Jack Nicholson, Louise Fletcher, William Redfield,
Dean Brooks, Scatman Crothers, Danny DeVito (Fantasy)

One Flew over the Cuckoo's Nest is brilliant cinema theatre. Jack Nicholson stars in an outstanding characterization of asylum anti-hero
McMurphy, and Milos Forman's direction of a
superbly-cast film is equally meritorious.

The film is adapted from Ken Kesey's novel,
the 1963 Broadway legit version of which, by
Dale Wasserman, starred Kirk Douglas.

The $3 million film traces the havoc wrecked
in Louis Fletcher's zombie-run mental ward
when Nicholson (either an illness faker or a
free spirit) displays a kind of leadership which
neither Fletcher nor the system can handle.

The major supporting players emerge with
authority: Brad Dourif (in a part played on
Broadway by Gene Wilder), the acne-marked
stutterer whose immature sexual fantasies
are clarified on the night of Nicholson's
aborted escape; Sidney Lassick, a petulant
auntie; Will Sampson, the not-so-dumb
Indian with whom Nicholson effects a strong
rapport; and William Redfield, the over-intel-
ligent inmate.

The film's pacing is relieved by a group es-
cape and fishing boat heist, right out of Mack
Sennett, and some stabs at basketball in
which Nicholson stations the tall Indian for
telling effect. This in turn make the shock
therapy sequences awesomely potent.
☐ 1975: Best Picture, Director, Actor (Jack
Nicholson), Actress (Louise Fletcher),
Adapted Screenplay.
☐ Nominations: Best Supp. Actor (Brad
Dourif), Cinematography, Editing, Original
Score

ONE FOOT IN HEAVEN

1941, 106 MINS, US
Dir Irving Rapper   *Prod* Hal B. Wallis   *Scr* Casey
Robinson   *Ph* Charles Rosher   *Ed* Warren Low
Mus Max Steiner
● Fredric March, Martha Scott, Beulah Bondi, Gene
Lockhart, Elisabeth Fraser, Harry Davenport (Warner)

A warm and human preachment for godliness, this biography of a Methodist minister
is from the best-seller by Hartzell Spence.
About the only faults with the picture are its
slowness in the first half and the tendency of
director Irving Rapper to skip over the hectic
postwar depression years. Most of the dramatic wallop is contained in the last 40 minutes, or when the Rev. Spence (Fredric
March) is in conflict with the wealthy element in his Denver congregation.

Spence, originally a medical student, comes
to religion through listening to an evangelist.
He takes his fiancee (Martha Scott) from her
opulent Canadian home to his first parish in
an Iowa mud-road town. This is the beginning
of a trek through similar parishes with the
Spences undergoing various privations. They
raise three children, likably played by Frankie
Thomas, Elisabeth Fraser and Casey Johnson.

March and Scott are both splendid in their
roles. The stars carry the brunt of the story,
although the cast is both populous and excellent.
☐ 1941: Nomination: Best Picture

ONE FROM THE HEART

1982, 101 MINS, US ◇ ⑫ ⊙
Dir Francis Coppola   *Prod* Gray Frederickson, Fred
Roos, Armyan Bernstein   *Scr* Armyan Bernstein, Francis
Coppola   *Ph* Vittorio Storaro   *Ed* Arne Goursaud, Rudi
Fehr, Randy Roberts   *Mus* Tom Waits   *Art Dir* Dean
Tavoularis
● Frederic Forrest, Teri Garr, Nastassja Kinski, Raul
Julia, Lainie Kazan, Harry Dean Stanton (Zoetrope)

Francis Coppola's *One from the Heart* is a hybrid musical romantic fantasy, lavishing giddy
heights of visual imagination and technical
brilliance onto a wafer-thin story of true love
turned sour, then sweet.

Set against an intentionally artificial fantasy version of Las Vegas – with production
designer Dean Tavoularis' studio-recreated
casino strip, desert outposts and even the
Vegas airport easily the film's best-paid and
most dazzling stars – the film quite simply
plots the break-up, separate dalliances and
eventual happy ending of a pair of five-year
lovers (Frederic Forrest and Teri Garr) over
the course of a single Independence Day.

He meets a sultry, exotic circus girl
(Nastassja Kinski); she's swept away by a
suave Latino singing waiter (Raul Julia).

With cheerful intermittent turns by Harry
Dean Stanton as Forrest's best friend and
partner, and Lainie Kazan as Garr's blowsy,
sentimental barmaid buddy, the film's focus
turns almost exclusively on Forrest's mounting efforts to win back Garr.
☐ 1982: Nomination: Best Original Song
Score

ONE GOOD COP

1991, 105 MINS, US ◇ ⑫ ⊙
Dir Heywood Gould   *Prod* Laurence Mark
Scr Heywood Gould   *Ph* Ralf Bode   *Ed* Richard Marks
Mus David Foster, William Ross   *Art Dir* Sandy
Veneziano
● Michael Keaton, Rene Russo, Anthony LaPaglia, Kevin
Conway, Rachel Ticotin, Tony Plana (Hollywood/Silver
Screen Partners IV)

Michael Keaton plays a staunchly decent cop
who's as close to his longtime partner
(Anthony LaPaglia) as he is to his fashion designer wife (Rene Russo). When widowed
LaPaglia gets killed in an heroic attempt to
save a woman's life, Keaton and Russo take in
his three orphaned little girls and decide they
want to keep them.

But the authorities seem rather eager to
take them away and Keaton's crowded digs
can't accommodate a family, so he winds up
on a wrong-side-of-the-law stunt to come up
with enough money to be a hero at home.

The drug-dealer villains and inner-city skirmishes here are standard issue, and pic's basic parameters are only a cut above telefilm
fare. Still, it's the skill with which the writer-
director works the audience into the palm of
his hand that makes this a crowd-pleaser.

Keaton demonstrates remarkable range
and dexterity, giving his best performance
since *Clean and Sober* [1988], and soulful
LaPaglia projects a toned-down version of the
same true-hearted qualities that made him so
winning in *Betsy's Wedding* [1990].

ONE HOUR TO DOOMSDAY

See: City Beneath the Sea

ONE HOUR WITH YOU

1932, 75 MINS, US
Dir Ernst Lubitsch   *Prod* Ernst Lubitsch   *Scr* Samson
Raphaelson   *Ph* Victor Milner   *Mus* Oscar Strauss,
Richard A. Whiting
● Maurice Chevalier, Jeanette MacDonald, Genevieve
Tobin, Charlie Ruggles, Roland Young, George Barbier
(Paramount)

It's a 100% credit to all concerned, principally
Ernst Lubitsch on his production and direction, which required no little courage to carry
out the continuity idea. The unorthodoxy concerns Maurice Chevalier's interpolated, confidential asides to his audience, in the *Strange
Interlude* manner, although in an altogether
gay spirit. Chevalier periodically interrupts
the romantic sequence to come downscreen
for a close-up to intimately address the 'ladies
and gentlemen' as to his amorous problems.

It starts first with the opening scene in the
Bois de Boulogne of Paris where Chevalier
and his bride (Jeanette MacDonald) of three
years are caught necking. The gendarme
won't believe it's legal so they retire to their
home where, in a boudoir scene, Chevalier interrupts just in time for that first aside to tell
the audience that they really are married.

From then on Genevieve Tobin in an obvious 'make' role completes the triangle, with
Chevalier periodically soliloquizing in a
chatty, intimate manner (taking the audience
into his marital confidence, so to speak) on
what is he to do under the circumstances.

The excellent script [from the play by
Lothar Schmidt] is replete with many niceties
and touches which Lubitsch has skillfully
dovetailed, without overdoing the detail. On
top of that, Jeanette MacDonald is a superb
vis-a-vis for the star, intelligently getting her
song lyrics over in a quiet, chatty manner.
☐ 1931/32: Nomination: Best Picture

ONE HUNDRED AND ONE DALMATIANS

1961, 79 MINS, US ◇ ⑫
Dir Wolfgang Reitherman, Hamilton S. Luske, Clyde
Geronimi   *Prod* Walt Disney   *Scr* Bill Peet   *Ed* Donald
Halliday, Roy M. Brewer Jr   *Mus* George Burns
Art Dir Ken Anderson
● (Walt Disney)

While not as indelibly enchanting or inspired as some of the studio's most unforgettable animated endeavors, this is nonetheless a painstaking creative effort. There are some adults for whom 101 – count 'em – dalmatians is about 101 dalmatians too many, but even the most hardened, dogmatic pooch-detester is likely to be amused by several passages in this story.

Bill Peet's screen yarn, based on the book by Dodie Smith, is set in London and concerned with the efforts of Blighty's four-legged population to rescue 99 dognapped pups from the clutches of one Cruella De Ville, a chic up-to-date personification of the classic witch. The concerted effort is successful thanks to a canine sleuthing network ('Twilight Bark') that makes Scotland Yard an amateur outfit by comparison.

Film purportedly is the $4 million end product of three years of work by some 300 artists. It benefits from the vocal versatility of a huge roster of 'voice' talents, including Rod Taylor, J. Pat O'Malley and Betty Lou Gerson. There are three songs by Mel Leven, best and most prominent of which is 'Cruella De Ville'.

■ ONE HUNDRED MEN AND A GIRL

1937, 85 MINS, US
Dir Henry Koster *Prod* Joe Pasternak *Scr* Bruce Manning, Charles Kenyon, James Mulhauser *Ph* Joseph Valentine *Ed* Bernard W. Burton *Mus* Charles Previn (dir.) *Art Dir* John Harkrider
● Deanna Durbin, Adolphe Menjou, Alice Brady, Eugene Pallette, Mischa Auer, Leopold Stokowski (Universal)

Deanna Durbin is a bright, luminous star in her second picture, *One Hundred Men and a Girl*. Its originality rests on a firm and strong foundation, craftsmanship which has captured popular values from Wagner, Tchaikovsky, Liszt, Mozart and Verdi.

Universal wisely gives her excellent support in Leopold Stokowski, director of the Philadelphia symphony orchestra, who plays a lengthy film role with surprising ease and conviction, and Adolphe Menjou, who is in a role quite different from his usual type of parts. In addition to these two, Alice Brady breezes thru a short sequence in high glee, and Eugene Pallette, Mischa Auer and Billy Gilbert have important things to do and do them well.

The 'hundred men' of the title are members of a symphony orchestra of unemployed musicians whom Durbin is organizing and managing. Hans Kraly is credited with the original story.

Idea is that the unemployed artists in order to get sponsorship for a radio contract must obtain a conductor with an outstanding name of wide radio appeal. Stokowski, completing his regular subscription season, is unapproachable, but rebuffs which would discourage Napoleon mean nothing to the youngster.

Durbin, to Stokowski accompaniment, sings Mozart's 'Exultate' and the aria 'Libiamo ne' from *Traviata*.
□ 1937: Best Score.
□ Nomination: Best Picture, Original Story, Editing, Sound

■ ONE IS A LONELY NUMBER

1972, 97 MINS, US ◇ ⊚
Dir Mel Stuart *Prod* Stan Margulies *Scr* David Seltzer *Ph* Michel Hugo *Ed* David Saxon *Mus* Michel Legrand *Art Dir* Walter M. Simonds
● Trish Van Devere, Monte Markham, Janet Leigh, Melvyn Douglas, Jane Elliot, Jonathan Lippe (M-G-M)

One Is a Lonely Number is an excellent contemporary drama about the big and little problems affecting a divorced woman.

Trish Van Devere is the focal point of the story [from one by Rebecca Morris]. Suddenly abandoned by husband Paul Jenkins, she is forced into self-reliance for the first time in her life. It isn't always easy.

But Van Devere does get help, principally from the kindness of old store-keeper Melvyn Douglas; professional man-hater Janet Leigh; Jane Elliot, the heroine's best friend; and Maurice Argent, manager of the neighbourhood swimming pool where she finds employment as a life guard.

Van Devere, strikingly beautiful, projects a credible warmth, depth of character and a great deal of ladylike sensuality. Her romantic scenes with Monte Markham are as tasteful as they are most arousingly erotic.

■ ONE MAGIC CHRISTMAS

1985, 88 MINS, US/CANADA ◇ ⊚ ⊙
Dir Phillip Borsos *Prod* Peter O'Brian *Scr* Thomas Meehan *Ph* Frank Tidy *Ed* Sidney Wolinsky *Mus* Michael Conway Baker *Art Dir* Bill Brodie
● Mary Steenburgen, Gary Basaraba, Harry Dean Stanton, Arthur Hill, Elizabeth Harnois, Robbie Magwood (Walt Disney/Silver Screen Partners II/Telefilm Canada)

One Magic Christmas represents an emotionally rewarding and artistically successful attempt to pull off the sort of uplifting family fare Hollywood used to do so well but lately has forgotten how to make.

Director Phillip Borsos keeps sentimentality nicely in check as he presents the sad Christmas season being faced by the Grainger family. Dad has been laid off, Mom is hardly managing to pay the bills, and they and the two kids are being evicted from their home just in time for the holidays.

Just when it appears things can't get any worse, they get very much worse indeed. The drama becomes intensely grim at midpoint, as Mom hits the absolute bottom-of-the-barrel. As has been seen periodically up to now, however, Mom has had an angel appointed to restore the proper spirit to her, and he quickly takes over to remedy matters.

Mary Steenburgen is realistically depressed for a long while, and is then very wonderfully won over to optimism and warmth.

The real find is six-year-old Elizabeth Harnois for the role of the little daughter who, while pathetically deprived of what any kid wants, doesn't give up on Mom.

■ ONE MAN MUTINY

See: The Court-Martial of Billy Mitchell

■ ONE MILLION B.C.

(UK: Man and His Mate)

1940, 80 MINS, US ⊚ ⊙
Dir Hal Roach, Hal Roach Jr *Prod* Hal Roach *Scr* Mickell Novak, George Baker, Joseph Frickert, Grover Jones *Ph* Norbert Brodine *Ed* Ray Snyder *Mus* Werner R. Heymann *Art Dir* Charles D. Hall, Nicolai Remisoff
● Victor Mature, Carole Landis, Lon Chaney Jr, John Hubbard, Mamo Clark, Nigel de Brulier (Roach/United Artists)

One Million B.C. looks something like A.D.1910; it's that corny. Except for the strange-sounding grunts and monosyllabic dialog, it is also another silent. Hal Roach, who spent a lifetime making comedies, goes to the other extreme as producer of the prehistoric spectacle, filmed in Nevada. D.W. Griffith was associated with Roach in production of the film at the beginning but withdrew following dissension concerning casting and other angles. His name does not appear in the credits.

There isn't much sense to the action nor much interest in the characters. Majority of the animals fail to impress but the fight between a couple of lizards, magnified into great size, is exciting and well photographed.

The ease with which some of the monsters are destroyed by man is a big laugh, notably the way one is subdued with a fishing spear. Knocking off a giant iguana is another audience snicker.

On occasion, also, the actions of the characters, including Victor Mature, bring a guffaw. He plays the part ox-like and the romantic interest, with Carole Landis on the other end, fails to ignite. Chaney Jr carves a fine characterization from the role of a tribal chieftain.

The story, pretty thin, relates to the way common dangers serve to wash up hostilities between the Rock and Shell clans, with a note of culture developed by the heroine (Landis) who astonishes the lads of the stone age when she sees to it that the women are to be served first, and the roast dinosaur (or whatever it is) is cut off in hunks with a rock knife, instead of torn off by the hands.
□ 1940: Nominations: Best Original Score, Special Effects

■ ONE MILLION YEARS B.C.

1966, 100 MINS, UK ◇ ⊚
Dir Don Chaffey *Prod* Michael Carreras *Scr* Michael Carreras *Ph* Wilkie Cooper *Ed* James Needs, Tom Simpson *Mus* Mario Nascimbene *Art Dir* Robert Jones
● Raquel Welch, John Richardson, Percy Herbert, Robert Brown, Martine Beswick, Jean Wladon (Hammer)

Biggest novelty gimmick is that, despite four writers on screenplay [Mickell Novak, George Baker and Joseph Frickert from 1940 screenplay *One Million B.C.*, plus producer Michael Carreras], dialog is minimal, consisting almost entirely of grunts. Raquel Welch here gets little opportunity to prove herself an actress but she is certainly there in the looks department.

Don Chaffey does a reliable job directorially, but leans heavily on the ingenious special effects in the shape of prehistoric animals and a striking earthquake dreamed up by Ray Harryhausen. Simple idea of the film is of the earth as a barren, hostile place, one million years B.C., inhabited by two tribes, the aggressive Rock People and the more intelligent, gentler Shell People.

John Richardson plays a Rock man who is banished after a fight with his gross father (Robert Brown). Wandering the land, battling off fearful rubber prehistoric monsters, he comes across the Shell People and falls for Welch, one of the Shell handmaidens. The two go off together to face innumerable other hazards.

■ ONE NIGHT OF LOVE

1934, 98 MINS, US ⊚ ⊙
Dir Victor Schertzinger *Scr* S.K. Lauren, James Gow, Edmund North *Ph* Joseph Walker *Mus* Victor Schertzinger (adapt.), Louis Silvers
● Grace Moore, Tullio Carminati, Lyle Talbot, Mona Barrie, Jessie Ralph, Luis Alberni (Columbia)

One Night of Love is basically an operatic film. It's the fact that the film is human, down to earth, that helps most. Even the operatic excerpts have all been carefully picked for popular appeal.

Story [by Dorothy Speare and Charles Beahan] is one of those convenient little yarns spun around the career of a singer (Grace Moore). She fails to win a radio contest so goes to Europe on her own, has usual student struggles, sings in a cafe, is discovered by Tullio Carminati, a great singing teacher. He drives her, mesmerises her, makes her into a star. She falls in love with him, is jealous of another girl singer, and almost upsets the applecart at the last minute of success at the Metropolitan debut in New York.

It's all handled carefully. Carminati, as the teacher-lover, is a perfect choice and manages to ease himself into a lot more attention than might be expected. Lyle Talbot is the other man for Moore and Mona Barrie is the other girl. Both do well enough. Jessie Ralph is excellent as the housekeeper.

☐ 1934: Best Score, Sound Recording.

☐ Nominations: Best Picture, Director, Actress (Grace Moore), Editing

....

■ **ONE NIGHT STAND**

1984, 94 MINS, AUSTRALIA ◇ Ⓥ

Dir John Duigan *Prod* Richard Mason *Scr* John Duigan *Ph* Tom Cowan *Ed* John Scott *Mus* William Motzing *Art Dir* Ross Major

● Tyler Coppin, Cassandra Delaney, Jay Hackett, Saskia Post, Midnight Oil (Edgley)

It's New Year's Eve on a hot summer night in Sydney. Over a transistor radio comes the news nobody thought was possible: nuclear war has broken out in Europe and North America, and bombs have already dropped on US facilities in Australia: everyone is warned to stay where they are. Thus begins a long, long night.

Pic builds inexorably to a truly shattering climax, yet doesn't rely on special effects or histrionics. Duigan seems to suggest that, in Australia at least, the world will end not with a bang nor exactly a whimper, but with a puzzled question-mark.

It's a daring approach but overall, and despite some rather strident acting early on, it does work.

....

■ **ONE OF OUR AIRCRAFT IS MISSING**

1942, 100 MINS, UK Ⓥ

Dir Michael Powell *Prod* John Corfield, Michael Powell, Emeric Pressburger *Scr* Emeric Pressburger, Michael Powell *Ph* Ronald Neame *Ed* David Lean *Art Dir* David Rawnsley

● Godfrey Tearle, Eric Portman, Hugh Williams, Bernard Miles, Pamela Brown, Hay Petrie (British National)

Aircraft is a full-length feature dealing with the flight of a crew of bombers which start from England to raid Stuttgart. The squadron all returns safely, except one which hits an obstruction and is entirely demolished. Then follows the story of what happened to the airmen.

The aforesaid bomber is returning from its raid on Stuttgart when it is hit and the crew tries to limp home. But over Holland they're compelled to bale out, landing in Dutch (occupied) territory, where the people protect them and give them disguises.

The six members of the Wellington are played by Godfrey Tearle, Eric Portman, Hugh Williams, Bernard Miles, Hugh Burden and Emrys Jones. A lot of Dutch people are recruited as natives of Holland, all of them excellent, not to mention Hay Petrie as the burgomaster. With the exception of Pamela Brown, all arrive solidly. Script, production, direction and photography are splendid.

☐ 1942: Nominations: Best Original Screenplay, Special Effects

....

■ **ONE ON ONE**

1977, 98 MINS, US Ⓥ

Dir Lamont Johnson *Prod* Martin Hornstein *Scr* Robby Benson, Jerry Segal *Ph* Donald M. Morgan *Ed* Robbe Roberts *Mus* Charles Fox *Art Dir* Sherman Loudermilk

● Robby Benson, Annette O'Toole, G.D. Spradlin, Gail Strickland, Melanie Griffith, James G. Richardson (Warner)

A trite and disappointing little film about a Los Angeles college basketball player. It follows the formula about the underdog-turned-hero but fails to ignite the emotions.

Robby Benson has an inarticulate, bumbling presence in this film as he blunders through the commercialized world of college

athletics. His awkward performance slows down the film badly and makes it hard to empathize with him, despite the usually potent plot cliche of the little guy fighting back.

It's unbelievable that this nebbish would be pursued by such mature and attractive women as Annette O'Toole and Gail Strickland, both of whom have extended and embarrassing romantic scenes with Benson.

....

■ **ONE POTATO, TWO POTATO**

1964, 102 MINS, US

Dir Larry Peerce *Prod* Sam Weston *Scr* Raphael Hayes, Orville H. Hampton *Ph* Andrew Laszlo *Ed* Robert Fritch *Mus* Gerald Fried

● Barbara Barrie, Bernie Hamilton, Richard Mulligan, Marti Merika, Robert Earl Jones (Cinema V/Weston-Bowalco)

Made in Ohio on a subscription basis for a reported $250,000, this is a tender, tactful look at miscegenation that speaks in human rather than polemic terms.

Set in a midwest US location (northern tier), it deals with a seemingly well-adjusted young Negro office worker who meets a young white divorcee who has a little girl. Their idyll grows slowly and gently as both react on normal planes with the color no apparent problem.

Then along comes the woman's first husband who has made his fortune after leaving her and demands the custody of the little girl. A sympathetic judge locates the girl in a good home, since he feels that as long as prejudice exists the little girl's life could be touched by it. All this is helped by fine delineation of character and added help from some new faces and the on-the-spot lensing.

Barbara Barrie has a striking presence and manages to mix integrity with need to etch a firm, moving character as the woman who finally finds the right man only to have her child taken away on racist principles. Bernie Hamilton is taking as the Negro husband who suddenly finds his manhood and very human liberty threatened by something that prevents him being a complete man.

Director Larry Peerce, for his first pic, has wisely told his story without many heavy symbolical and overdramatic embellishments.

☐ 1964: Nomination: Best Original Story & Screenplay

....

■ **ONE SPY TOO MANY**

1966, 101 MINS, US ◇

Dir Joseph Sargent *Prod* David Victor *Scr* Dean Hargrove *Ph* Fred Koenekamp *Ed* Henry Berman *Mus* Gerald Fried *Art Dir* George W. Davis, Merrill Pye

● Robert Vaughn, David McCallum, Rip Torn, Dorothy Provine, Leo G. Carroll, Yvonne Craig (Arena/M-G-M)

Expanded from a *Man from U.N.C.L.E.* TV two-parter, *One Spy Too Many* zips along at a jazzy spy thriller pace.

Action and gadgetry are hung on a slender plot. Alexander, played by Rip Torn, is out to take over the world in the fashion of his Greek namesake. He hoists from the US Army Biological Warfare Division a tankful of its secret 'will gas,' leaving a Greek inscription in the lab.

International espionage agents Robert Vaughn and David McCallum begin to pursue Alexander and are joined in their efforts by his wife (Dorothy Provine), who is attempting to reach her husband in order to have him sign her divorce papers.

....

■ **ONE TOUCH OF VENUS**

1948, 81 MINS, US Ⓥ ⊙

Dir William A. Seiter *Prod* Lester Cowan *Scr* Harry Kurnitz, Frank Tashlin *Ph* Franz Planer *Ed* Otto Ludwig *Mus* Ann Ronell *Art Dir* Bernard Herzbrun, Emrich Nicholson

● Robert Walker, Ava Gardner, Dick Haymes, Eve Arden, Olga San Juan, Tom Conway (Universal)

One Touch of Venus comes to the screen as a pleasant comedy fantasy. Ava Gardner steps into the top ranks as the goddess, Venus. Hers is a sock impression, bountifully physical and alluring, delivered with a delightfully sly instinct for comedy. Three of the songs from the original [1943] stage musical have been used, with new lyrics [by Ann Ronell].

Plot, briefly, covers the romantic adventures of a department store window dresser (Robert Walker), who, in a completely pixilated moment, kisses a statue of Venus and brings her to life for 24 hours. Those are eventful hours; Venus' aura of love casts a spell over all, bringing couples together and spreading happiness of romance. The script by Harry Kurnitz and Frank Tashlin [based on S.J. Perelman's book of the musical, suggested by F. Anstey's *The Tinted Venus*] is punctuated with snappy dialog and funny situation.

Walker delivers a gifted comedy performance. Eve Arden, the store owner's glib secretary, gives another of her punchy deliveries. Musical high spots please the ear and best is 'Speak Low', from the original Kurt Weill-Ogden Nash score, reprised several times.

....

■ **ONE, TWO, THREE**

1961, 115 MINS, US Ⓥ ⊙

Dir Billy Wilder *Prod* Billy Wilder *Scr* Billy Wilder, I.A.L. Diamond *Ph* Daniel L. Fapp *Ed* Daniel Mandell *Mus* Andre Previn (arr.) *Art Dir* Alexandre Trauner

● James Cagney, Horst Buchholz, Pamela Tiffin, Arlene Francis, Lilo Pulver, Lilo Pulver (Mirisch/Pyramid)

Billy Wilder's *One, Two, Three* is a fast-paced, high-pitched, hard-hitting, lighthearted farce crammed with topical gags and spiced with satirical overtones. Story is so furiously quick-witted that some of its wit gets snarled and smothered in overlap. But total experience packs a considerable wallop.

James Cagney is the chief exec of Coca-Cola's West Berlin plant whose ambitious promotion plans are jeopardized when he becomes temporary guardian of his stateside superior's wild and vacuous daughter. The girl (Pamela Tiffin) slips across the border, weds violently anti-Yankee Horst Buchholz, and before long there's a bouncing baby Bolshevik on the way. When the home office head man decides to visit his daughter, Cagney masterminds an elaborate masquerade that backfires.

The screenplay, based on a one-act play by Ferenc Molnar, is outstanding. It pulls no punches and lands a few political and ideological haymakers on both sides of the Brandenburg Gate.

Cagney proves himself an expert farceur with a glib, full-throttled characterization. Although some of Buchholz delivery has more bark than bite, he reveals a considerable flair for comedy. Pretty Tiffin scores with a convincing display of mental density.

Another significant factor in the comedy is Andre Previn's score, which incorporates semi-classical and period pop themes (like *Saber Dance* and 'Yes, We Have No Bananas') to great advantage throughout the film.

☐ 1961: Nomination: Best B&W Cinematography

....

■ **ONE WAY PENDULUM**

1965, 90 MINS, UK

Dir Peter Yates *Prod* Michael Deeley *Scr* N.F. Simpson *Ph* Denys Coop *Ed* Peter Taylor *Mus* Richard Rodney Bennett *Art Dir* Reece Pemberton

● Eric Sykes, George Cole, Julia Foster, Jonathan Miller, Peggy Mount, Mona Washbourne (Woodfall)

Adapted from his own play by N. F. Simpson, what there is of a plot deals with an eccentric

British family whose antics resemble normal behavior as Salvador Dali resembles Grandma Moses.

Papa (Eric Sykes) seeks change from his humdrum existence as an insurance clerk by erecting a do-it-yourself replica of the Old Bailey in his living room, only to find a trial underway when he gets it finished; the mother (Alison Leggatt repeating her stage role), seemingly the sane one, goes along with her oddly-behaviored family until she adds her own bit by engaging a charwoman (Peggy Mount) not to clean, but to eat the family's leftovers.

Nearly rational is daughter (Julia Foster), whose only concern is for what she considers a physical deformity – her arms don't reach her knees.

Peter Yates directs with a technique that treats comedy as deadly serious and is responsible for much of the antic spirit that keeps the film animated during most of its chaotic run.

· ·

■ ONE WILD NIGHT

See: Career Opportunities

· ·

■ ONE WOMAN'S STORY

See: The Passionate Friends

· ·

■ ON GOLDEN POND

1981, 109 MINS, US ◇ ⓥ ⊙
Dir Mark Rydell   *Prod* Bruce Gilbert   *Scr* Ernest Thompson   *Ph* Billy Williams   *Ed* Robert L. Wolfe   *Mus* Dave Grusin   *Art Dir* Stephen Grimes
● Katharine Hepburn, Henry Fonda, Jane Fonda, Dabney Coleman, Doug McKeon (Universal/ITC/IPC)

Without question, these are major, meaty roles for Katharine Hepburn and Henry Fonda, and there could have been little doubt that the two would work superbly together. Fact that Ernest Thompson's 1978 play backs away from the dramatic fireworks that might have been mutes overall impact of the piece, but sufficient pleasures remain.

Fonda, a retired professor, and Hepburn arrive at their New England cottage to spend their 48th summer together. He's approaching his 80th birthday and, while it's clear that his wife is thoroughly familiar with his crotchety act, his mostly intentional rudeness and irascibility make life difficult for others in his vicinity.

At the half-hour point, along come daughter Jane Fonda, future son-in-law Dabney Coleman and latter's son Doug McKeon. Coleman manages a stand-off with the elder Fonda, but Jane is clearly still terrified of her dad, suffering from lingering feelings of neglect and inferiority.

The film's most moving interlude, a near-death scene, is saved for the end, and both Fonda (pere) and Hepburn are miraculous together here, conveying heartrending intimations of mortality which are doubly powerful due to the stars' venerable status.
□ 1981: Best Actor (Henry Fonda), Actress (Katharine Hepburn), Adapted Screenplay.
□ Nominations: Best Picture, Director, Supp. Actress (Jane Fonda), Cinematography, Editing, Score, Sound

· ·

■ ON HER MAJESTY'S SECRET SERVICE

1969, 139 MINS, UK ◇ ⓥ ⊙
Dir Peter Hunt   *Prod* Harry Saltzman, Albert R. Broccoli   *Scr* Richard Maibaum, Simon Raven   *Ph* Michael Reed   *Ed* John Glen   *Mus* John Barry   *Art Dir* Syd Cain
● George Lazenby, Diana Rigg, Telly Savalas, Ilse Steppat, Gabriele Ferzetti, Bernard Lee (United Artists)

Film of break-neck physical excitement and stunning visual attractions in which George Lazenby replaced Sean Connery as James Bond.

Lazenby is pleasant, capable and attractive in the role, but he suffers in the inevitable comparison with Connery. He doesn't have the latter's physique, voice and saturnine, virile looks.

The baddie's hideout is perched on the peak of a Swiss alp, part Playboy Penthouse, part Frankenstein's laboratory, and part cave of the mountain troll. There Telly Savalas is experimenting with biological warfare to take over the world, under the guise of being a research institute for treating allergies.

In *Service* Bond finds his true love, Diana Rigg, coolly beautiful, intelligent, sardonic, and his equal in bed, on skis, driving hellbent on icy mountain roads, and with a few karate chops of her own.

· ·

■ ONION FIELD, THE

1979, 122 MINS, US ◇ ⓥ ⊙
Dir Harold Becker   *Prod* Walter Coblenz   *Scr* Joseph Wambaugh   *Ph* Charles Rosher   *Ed* John W. Wheeler   *Mus* Eumir Deodato   *Art Dir* Brian Eatwell
● John Savage, James Woods, Ted Danson, Ronny Cox, Franklyn Seales, Priscilla Pointer (Avco Embassy/Black Marble)

A highly-detailed dramatization of a true case, *The Onion Field* deals in its two hours with death and guilt; and the manipulation of the judicial system to pervert justice.

Set in 1963, two plainclothes cops on patrol in Hollywood stop a couple of suspicious-looking punks in a car. In a swift moment one of the bad guys pulls a gun and the cops are disarmed and kidnapped. They are taken to an onion field miles away and one is brutally murdered. The second makes his escape. The two killers are quickly arrested but each claims the other did the killing.

On this confusion the trials and re-trials drag on for years. Concurrently the survivor goes through bouts of guilt and is forced to resign from the force.

James Woods as the near-psychotic Powell is chillingly effective, creating a flakiness in the character that exudes the danger of a live wire near a puddle.

· ·

■ ONLY ANGELS HAVE WINGS

1939, 120 MINS, US ⓥ
Dir Howard Hawks   *Prod* Howard Hawks   *Scr* Jules Furthman   *Ph* Joseph Walker, Elmer Dyer   *Ed* Viola Lawrence   *Mus* Manuel Maciste, Dimitri Tiomkin
● Cary Grant, Jean Arthur, Richard Barthelmess, Rita Hayworth, Thomas Mitchell, Sig Ruman (Columbia)

In *Only Angels Have Wings*, Howard Hawks had a story to tell and he has done it inspiringly well. Cary Grant is boss of the kindly Dutchman's decrepit airline. Grant takes up the planes only when it's too hazardous for the others. If the Dutchman can fly the mails regularly he's set for a juicy contract.

Jean Arthur is an American showgirl en route to Panama. She's excellent for the assignment.

Sub-plot has Richard Barthelmess coming on the scene with Rita Hayworth as his wife.

Baranca is the basic setting of this sub-tropical aviation romance [from an original story by Hawks] where treacherous mountain crags, capricious rainstorms and the like do their utmost to worst the mail plane service.

The Grant-Arthur cynicism and unyielding romantics are kept at a high standard.
□ 1939: Nomination: Best Special Effects

· ·

■ ONLY GAME IN TOWN, THE

1970, 113 MINS, US ◇ ⓥ
Dir George Stevens   *Prod* Fred Kohlmar   *Scr* Frank D. Gilroy   *Ph* Henri Decae   *Ed* John W. Holmes, William Sands, Pat Shade   *Mus* Maurice Jarre   *Art Dir* Herman Blumenthal
● Elizabeth Taylor, Warren Beatty, Charles Braswell, Hank Henry (20th Century-Fox)

The Only Game in Town is a rather mixed blessing. Elizabeth Taylor and Warren Beatty star as two Vegas drifters who find love with each other.

Film was shot at Studios de Boulogne in Paris, with second unit work in Las Vegas for some key exteriors.

Beatty delivers an engaging performance as a gambling addict, working off his debts as a saloon pianist for Hank Henry.

Frank D. Gilroy's script [based on his play] permits both stars to shine in solo and ensemble moments of hope, despair, recrimination, and sardonic humor. But the drama develops too sluggishly.

Montage sequences of Vegas niteries, all well shot and cut, break up the pacing, but also emphasize the dramatic vamping even more so, an inevitable result.

· ·

■ ONLY THE LONELY

1991, 102 MINS, US ◇ ⓥ ⊙
Dir Chris Columbus   *Prod* John Hughes, Hunt Lowry   *Scr* Chris Columbus   *Ph* Julio Macat   *Ed* Raja Gosnell   *Mus* Maurice Jarre   *Art Dir* John Muto
● John Candy, Maureen O'Hara, Ally Sheedy, Kevin Dunn, Milo O'Shea, Anthony Quinn (20th Century-Fox/Hughes)

A lower-key *Marty* for the 1990s, *Only the Lonely* is a charming and well-observed romantic comedy about a single Chicago cop (John Candy) trying to break free from his smothering Irish mom (Maureen O'Hara, in her welcome return to the screen after 20 years). Performances are delightfully true and never descend into bathos or cheap sentiment.

O'Hara uses her native Dublin accent and her feistiest no-nonsense style to convey the mean-spirited, bigoted personality of Rose Muldoon. This flinty immigrant widow, who's bullied her son all his life, routinely spews out invective against Italians, Greeks, Poles and Jews.

Candy is a sweet-natured fellow who yearns for something more out of life but is afraid to ask for it. His best friend (James Belushi) and his brother (Kevin Dunn) want him to stay single and everyone treats him like an overgrown baby. When he meets a shy mortuary cosmetician (Ally Sheedy), Candy begins to assert himself in ways that drive his mother to new lows of tart-tongued nastiness.

The neighborhood is enjoyably populated with such serio-comic types as the silver-tongued denizens of O'Neill's pub (Bert Remsen and Milo O'Shea), and O'Hara's devastatingly sexy next-door neighbor (Anthony Quinn) whom she scorns as a 'Typical Greek' for besieging her with passion: 'Come to my bed. You will never leave.'

· ·

■ ONLY TWO CAN PLAY

1962, 106 MINS, UK ⓥ
Dir Sidney Gilliat   *Prod* Leslie Gilliat   *Scr* Bryan Forbes   *Ph* John Wilcox   *Ed* Thelma Connell   *Mus* Richard Rodney Bennett   *Art Dir* Albert Witherick
● Peter Sellers, Mai Zetterling, Virginia Maskell, Richard Attenborough, Kenneth Griffiths (British Lion)

Kingsley Amis' novel, *That Uncertain Feeling*, has had some of its cool sting extracted for the film version, but the result is a lively, middle-class variation along the lines of *The Seven Year Itch*.

Some of the humor is over-earthy and slightly lavatory, and the film never fully decides whether it is supposed to be light comedy, farce or satire. But it remains a cheerful piece of nonsense with some saucy dialog and situations capably exploited by Sellers and his colleagues.

He is a member of the staff of a Welsh public library. A white collar job. He is fed up and frustrated with the eternal prospect of living in a shabby apartment with a dispirited wife, two awful kids, peeling wallpaper, erratic plumbing and a dragon of a landlady. Into his drab life floats the bored, sexy young wife of a local bigwig and she makes a play for Sellers.

The fact that she can influence her spouse to get Sellers promotion is hardly in Sellers' mind. But what is in his mind never gets a chance of jelling. Their attempts at mutual-seduction are thwarted by babysitting problem, sudden return of the husband, intrusion of a herd of inquisitive cows when attempting a nocturnal roll.

Sellers adds another wily characterization to his gallery. His problems as frustrated lover carry greater weight because, from the beginning, he does not exaggerate or distort the role of the humble little librarian with aspirations. Mai Zetterling and Virginia Maskell provided effective contrasts as the two women in his life.

■ ONLY WHEN I LARF

1968, 103 MINS, UK ◇
Dir Basil Dearden *Prod* Len Deighton, Brian Duffy
Scr John Salmon *Ph* Anthony Richmond *Ed* Fergus McDonnell *Mus* Ron Grainer *Art Dir* John Blezard
● Richard Attenborough, David Hemmings, Alexandra Stewart, Nicholas Pennell, Melissa Stribling (Paramount)

Only When I Larf is a pleasant little joke, based on a Len Deighton novel and rather less complicated than some of his other work, with sound, unfussy direction and witty, observed thesping.

Filmed in London, New York and Beirut, it has Richard Attenborough, David Hemmings and Alexandra Stewart as a con-trio. Situation arises whereby Attenborough and Hemmings fall out and seek to doublecross each other.

Mood is admirably set with the gang pulling off a slickly-planned con trick in a New York office. Talk is minimal, though the sript opens up into a more gabby talk-fest later, but dialog is usually pointed and crisp.

Attenborough plays an ex-brigadier and takes on various guises. His brigadier is a masterly piece of observation and the whole film has Attenborough at his considerable comedy best. Hemmings is equally effective as the discontented young whiz-kid lieutenant and Stewart, with little to do, manages to look both efficient and sexy.

■ ONLY WHEN I LAUGH
(UK: It Hurts Only When I Laugh)

1981, 120 MINS, US ◇ Ⓥ ⊙
Dir Glenn Jordan *Prod* Roger M. Rothstein, Neil Simon
Scr Neil Simon *Ph* David M. Walsh *Ed* John Wright
Mus David Shire *Art Dir* Albert Brenner
● Marsha Mason, Kristy McNichol, James Coco, Joan Hackett, David Dukes, Kevin Bacon (Columbia)

Patrons expecting a skin-deep laughfest may be surprised at the unusually sombre shadows and heavy dramatics that make their way into this tale (a reworking of Simon's short-lived legit play, *The Gingerbread Lady*), though abundant humor still shines through.

Marsha Mason delivers a bravura performance as the film's centerpiece, a divorced actress who returns from a three-month drying out session at an alcoholic clinic to face a revitalized career both on the legit boards and as a mother to her long-estranged, 17-year-old daughter, well-played here by Kristy McNichol.

Core of the film is McNichol's attempt to reestablish a fulltime relationship with her mother, despite latter's previously boozy neglect and frequent social embarrassment. Storyline details Mason's juggling of those demands, along with the potential for renewed romance and career success (with former lover David Dukes, who's written their stormy affair into a strong Broadway vehicle for her).

The one-on-one encounters between Mason and McNichol, ranging from sisterly tomfoolery to intense emotional battling, are particularly strong. Their final scene of family rapprochement is not unrealistically rosy.
☐ 1981: Nominations: Best Actress (Marsha Mason), Supp. Actor (James Coco), Supp. Actress (Joan Hackett)

■ ONLY YESTERDAY

1933, 105 MINS, US
Dir John M. Stahl *Prod* Carl Laemmle Jr *Scr* Arthur Richman, George O'Neill, William Hurlbut *Ph* Merritt Gerstad *Ed* Milton Carruth *Mus* [uncredited]
Art Dir Charles D. Hall
● Margaret Sullavan, John Boles, Edna Mae Oliver, Billie Burke, Benita Hume, Reginald Denny (Universal)

Introducing to the screen Margaret Sullavan, trained in legit, this picture is as auspicious a launching as could be asked by any performer. Universal says the picture was suggested by Frederick Lewis Allen's book, a volume of contemporary reminiscences. That has nothing to do with the story except that the yarn starts in 1917 during the war, and ends in 1929 just as Wall Street laid that egg.

It is the irony of the heroine's life to be twice seduced by the same man but not recognized by him. A lapse of 12 years has wiped the man's memory clean but to the woman, in her middle 30s, her love for the man is as pristine as when she first surrendered.

A secondary role by Billie Burke glistens like a diamond. She is Aunt Julia, the broad-minded New Yorker who takes care of the girl and her child. Later, Aunt Julia takes herself a husband (Reginald Denny). A couple of delightful comedy sequences with Denny playing the piano and Burke singing offkey provide natural laughs.

The lad with the faulty memory, but okay for all of that, is John Boles, a tenor who turns out to be a dependable dramatic leading man.

■ ON MY WAY TO THE CRUSADES, I MET A GIRL WHO . . .

1968, 93 MINS, ITALY/US ◇
Dir Pasquale Festa Campanile *Prod* Francesco Mazzei
Scr Luigi Magni, Larry Gelbart *Ph* Carlo Di Palma
Ed Chas Nelson *Mus* Riz Ortolami *Art Dir* Piero Poletto
● Tony Curtis, Monica Vitti, Nino Castelnuovo, Hugh Griffith, John Richardson, Ivo Garrani (Julia/Warner/Seven Arts)

It's a mystery why Warner-Seven Arts abandoned the Italian title, *The Chastity Belt*, even briefly, for the long tongue-twisting title used outside of Italy but there's plenty of entertainment in this release.

Set in the Middle Ages, Larry Gelbart provides an extra measure of modern, romantic candor. When bumpkin-type provincial noble Guerrando (Tony Curtis) is knighted to become a crusade draftee, he gets a castle, the tax-collecting concession and the right to have affairs with all eligible soft-bosomed femininity in his fief. Only holdout is Boccadoro (Golden Lips) played by Monica Vitti, an emancipated forest wench.

To safeguard his prize, Guerrando locks his chaste spouse into a chastity belt, puts the key into his pocket and heads out across the drawbridge. The indignant medieval feminist is determined to get even.

Director Pasquale Festa Campanile fluctuates between classy ribald satire and stock burlesque.

It is safe to assume that the original English version will further lighten some of the medieval clinkers that show here and there and tighten slack moments.

Curtis and Vitti are not at their best but the latter is much more at home in her role.

■ ON OUR MERRY WAY
(Aka: A Miracle Can Happen)

1948, 107 MINS, US
Dir King Vidor, Leslie Fenton *Prod* Benedict Bogeaus, Burgess Meredith *Scr* Laurence Stallings, Lou Breslow *Ph* Edward Cronjager, Joseph Biroc, Gordon Avil, John Seitz, Ernest Laszlo *Ed* James Smith *Mus* Heinz Roemheld *Art Dir* Ernst Fegte, Duncan Cramer
● Burgess Meredith, Paulette Goddard, Fred MacMurray, James Stewart, Dorothy Lamour, Henry Fonda (United Artists)

The fact that this attempt at whimsy doesn't always come off is incidental; just look at the names! The pic opens with a pair of surefire names like Goddard and Meredith and in bed, too.

Then Stewart, Fonda, and Harry James. Plus Lamour and Victor Moore, in a Hollywood satire, or how the sarong became famous. Followed by Fred MacMurray and William Demarest. All in episodic sequences detailing what an inquiring reporter encounters when he seeks to have answered the question of how a child influenced the lives of a group of selected adults.

Meredith is the reporter, so-called. Actually he's only a classified-ad solicitor for a newspaper. But he's lied to his recent bride; he's told her he's the inquiring reporter. Through a subterfuge, however, he assumes the mantle of the paper's actual I.R., a longtime ambition, for just this one question.

The cast couldn't have been better. The story's execution falters because a scene here and there is inclined to strive too much for its whimsical effect. But Meredith responds capitally to the mood of the character he plays, being given more of a chance to do so than any of the other stars.

[Originally reviewed at a New York sneak preview under the title *A Miracle Can Happen*.]

■ ON THE BEACH

1959, 134 MINS, US ◇ Ⓥ
Dir Stanley Kramer *Prod* Stanley Kramer *Scr* John Paxton *Ph* Giuseppe Rotunno *Ed* Frederic Knudtson
Mus Ernest Gold *Art Dir* Rudolph Sternad
● Gregory Peck, Ava Gardner, Fred Astaire, Anthony Perkins, Donna Anderson, John Tate (United Artists)

On the Beach is a solid film of considerable emotional, as well as cerebral, content. But the fact remains that the final impact is as heavy as a leaden shroud. The spectator is left with the sick feeling that he's had a preview of Armageddon, in which all contestants lost.

John Paxton, who did the screenplay from Nevil Shute's novel, avoids the usual cliches. There is no sergeant from Brooklyn, no handy racial spokesmen. Gregory Peck is a US submarine commander. He and his men have been spared the atomic destruction because their vessel was submerged when the bombs went off.

The locale is Australia and the time is 1964. Nobody remembers how or why the conflict started. 'Somebody pushed a button,' says nuclear scientist Fred Astaire. Australia, for ill-explained reasons, is the last safe spot on earth. It is only a matter of time before the radiation hits the continent and its people die as the rest of the world has died.

In addition to Peck and Astaire, the other chief characters include Ava Gardner, a pleasure-bent Australian; and a young Australian naval officer and his wife, Anthony Perkins and Donna Anderson. All the personal stories are well-presented. The trouble is it is almost impossible to care with the implicit question ever-present – do they live?

The cast is almost uniformly excellent. Peck and Gardner make a good romantic team in the last days of the planet. Perkins and Anderson evoke sympathy as the young couple. Fred Astaire, in his first straight dramatic role, attracts considerable attention.

□ 1959: Nominations: Best Editing, Scoring of a Dramatic Picture

••••••••••••••••••••••••••••••••••••

■ ON THE BLACK HILL

1988, 116 MINS, UK ◇ ⦾

Dir Andrew Grieve   *Prod* Jennifer Howarth
Scr Andrew Grieve   *Ph* Thaddeus O'Sullivan   *Ed* Scott Thomas   *Mus* Robert Lockhart   *Art Dir* Jocelyn James
● Mike Gwilym, Robert Gwilym, Bob Peck, Gemma Jones, Nesta Harris (BFI/Film Four/British Screen)

A low-budget drama about Welsh hill farmers may not sound broadly appealing, but Andrew Grieve's *On the Black Hill* is a remarkably moving and entertaining film [from the novel by Bruce Chatwin] offering a fascinating view of life in the border country between Wales and England.

Pic follows the Jones family from 1895–1980, but mainly centers around twin brothers Benjamin and Lewis Jones (played by brothers Mike and Robert Gwilym). It is through their inseparability, and the traumas and humor that inspires, that the story is told.

Bob Peck and Gemma Jones are excellent as the Welsh farming couple, and the pic ably displays the hardship of their life. The Gwilyms perform well and are especially good in the twins' later years.

••••••••••••••••••••••••••••••••••••

■ ON THE TOWN

1949, 97 MINS, US ◇ ⦾ ⦿

Dir Gene Kelly, Stanley Donen   *Prod* Arthur Freed
Scr Adolph Green, Betty Comden   *Ph* Harold Rosson
Ed Ralph E. Winters   *Mus* Lennie Hayton (dir.)
Art Dir Cedric Gibbons, Jack Martin Smith
● Gene Kelly, Frank Sinatra, Betty Garrett, Ann Miller, Jules Munshin, Vera-Ellen (M-G-M)

The pep, enthusiasm and apparent fun the makers of *On the Town* had in putting it together comes through to the audience and gives the picture its best asset.

Gene Kelly, Frank Sinatra and Jules Munshin are the three sailors on a 24-hour leave in New York. Betty Garrett, Ann Miller and Vera-Ellen are the three femmes who wind up with the navy.

Picture is crammed with songs and dance numbers. Picture kicks off and ends with 'New York, New York'. Tune is used in the beginning as a musical backing for a montage of three curious sailors prowling the city's points of interest. It gets the film off to a fascinating start and the style and pacing is continued.

Based on their 1944 musical play [from an idea by Jerome Robbins], the Adolph Green-Betty Comden script puts the players through light story paces as a setup for 10 tunes and dances.

Roger Edens, associate producer, did the music for the six new tunes and lyrics are by Green and Comden. Latter team, with Leonard Bernstein, did the four original numbers ['New York, New York,' 'Miss Turnstiles' dance, 'Come Up to My Place,' and 'A Day in New York' ballet].

□ 1949: Best Scoring of a Musical Picture

••••••••••••••••••••••••••••••••••••

■ ON THE WATERFRONT

1954, 108 MINS, US ⦾ ⦿

Dir Elia Kazan   *Prod* Sam Spiegel   *Scr* Budd Schulberg
Ph Boris Kaufman   *Ed* Gene Milford   *Mus* Leonard Bernstein   *Art Dir* Richard Day
● Marlon Brando, Karl Malden, Lee J. Cobb, Rod Steiger, Pat Henning, Eva Marie Saint (Columbia/Horizon)

Longshore labor scandals serve as the takeoff point for a flight into fictionalized violence concerning the terroristic rule of a dock union over its coarse and rough, but subdued, members.

Budd Schulberg's script was based on his own original which in turn was 'suggested' by the Malcolm Johnson newspaper articles. Schulberg greatly enhanced the basic story line with expertly-turned, colorful and incisive dialog.

Under Elia Kazan's direction, Marlon Brando puts on a spectacular show, giving a fascinating, multi-faceted performance as the uneducated dock walloper and former pug, who is basically a softie with a special affection for his rooftop covey of pigeons and a neighborhood girl back from school. Eva Marie Saint has enough spirit to escape listlessness in her characterization.

Story opens with Brando unwittingly setting the trap for the murder of a longshoreman who refuses to abide by the 'deaf and dumb' code of the waterfront.

Lee J. Cobb is all-powerful as the one-man boss of the docks. He looks and plays the part harshly, arrogantly and with authority. Another fine job is executed by Karl Malden as the local Catholic priest who is outraged to the point that he spurs the revolt against Cobb's dictatorship.

Rod Steiger is a good choice as Brando's brother for both incline toward the hesitant manner of speech that has been especially identified with Brando. Steiger is Cobb's 'educated' lieutenant who is murdered when he fails to prevent Brando from blabbing to the crime probers.

□ 1954: Best Picture, Director, Actor (Marlon Brando), Supp. Actress (Eva Marie Saint), Story & Screenplay, B&W Cinematography, B&W Art Direction, Editing

□ Nominations: Best Supp. Actor (Lee J. Cobb, Carl Malden, Rod Steiger), Scoring of a Dramatic Picture

••••••••••••••••••••••••••••••••••••

■ OPENING NIGHT

1978, 144 MINS, US ◇

Dir John Cassavetes   *Prod* Al Ruban   *Scr* John Cassavetes   *Ph* Tom Ruban   *Ed* Tom Cornwell   *Mus* Bo Harwood   *Art Dir* Brian Ryman
● Gena Rowlands, Ben Gazzara, John Cassavetes, Joan Blondell, Paul Stewart, Zohra Lampert (Faces)

With *Opening Night*, John Cassavetes, the cinematic poet of middle-class inner turmoil, explores the angst-ridden world of a famous actress on the brink of breakdown. Preparing a difficult role in a Broadway play, she witnesses the accidental death of a devoted fan, a traumatic event which causes her to re-examine her personal and professional relationships.

Gena Rowlands turns in a virtuoso performance as the troubled actress.

As with his other films, Cassavetes, who wrote and directed, puts a slice of life under the microscope. Across the board, he culls stunning performances from the entire cast, especially Joan Blondell as the writer whose play is being mounted. But it is such a demanding work.

••••••••••••••••••••••••••••••••••••

■ OPERATION CROSSBOW

1965, 118 MINS, US ◇ ⦾

Dir Michael Anderson   *Prod* Carlo Ponti   *Scr* Richard Imrie, Derry Quinn, Ray Rigby   *Ph* Erwin Hillier
Ed Ernest Walter   *Mus* Ron Goodwin   *Art Dir* Elliot Scott
● Sophia Loren, George Peppard, Trevor Howard, John Mills, Tom Courtenay, Richard Johnson (M-G-M)

Operation Crossbow is a sometimes suspenseful war melodrama said to be based upon British attempts to find and destroy Germany's development of new secret weapons – long-range rockets – in the early days of the Second World War. Ambitiously filmed in Europe and boasting production values which may seem to catch the spirit of the monumental effort, what the Carlo Ponti produc-

tion lacks primarily is a cohesive story line [by Duilio Coletti and Vittorio Petrilli].

Sophia Loren is in for little more than a bit, albeit a key character in one sequence. George Peppard plays the chief protagonist in this rambling tale of a British espionage mission, whose members impersonate German scientists believed dead, sent to locate and transmit information on the underground installation where Nazis are working on their deadly project.

Peppard acquits himself satisfactorily although unexplained is his flawless command of German so he can impersonate a German scientist.

••••••••••••••••••••••••••••••••••••

■ OPERATION PETTICOAT

1959, 124 MINS, US ◇ ⦾ ⦿

Dir Blake Edwards   *Prod* Robert Arthur   *Scr* Stanley Shapiro, Maurice Richlin   *Ph* Russell Harlan   *Ed* Ted J. Kent, Frank Gross   *Mus* David Rose   *Art Dir* Alexander Golitzen, Robert E. Smith
● Cary Grant, Tony Curtis, Joan O'Brien, Dina Merrill, Gene Evans, Arthur O'Connell (Granart/Universal)

Operation Petticoat has no more weight than a sackful of feathers, but it has a lot of laughs. Cary Grant and Tony Curtis are excellent, and the film is directed by Blake Edwards with a slam-bang pace.

The time is December 1941, and the locale is the Philippines. Grant is the commander of a wheezy old submarine which he gets operational through his conniving junior officer (Curtis). In a series of improbable but acceptable situations [suggested by a story by Paul King and Joseph Stone], the sub takes on as passengers five army nurses, a couple of Filipino families (including expectant mothers) and a goat.

Grant is a living lesson in getting laughs without lines. In this film, most of the gags play off him. Curtis is a splendid foil, and his different style of playing meshes easily with Grant's. David Rose's score is especially bright, helping the comedy without getting coy.

□ 1959: Nomination: Best Original Story & Screenplay

••••••••••••••••••••••••••••••••••••

■ OPERATION UNDERCOVER

See: Report to the Commissioner

••••••••••••••••••••••••••••••••••••

■ OPPORTUNITY KNOCKS

1990, 105 MINS, US ◇ ⦾ ⦿

Dir Donald Petrie   *Prod* Mark R. Gordon, Christopher Meledandri   *Scr* Mitchel Katlin, Nat Bernstein
Ph Steven Poster   *Ed* Marion Rothman   *Mus* Miles Goodman   *Art Dir* David Chapman
● Dana Carvey, Robert Loggia, Todd Graff, Julia Campbell, Milo O'Shea, James Tolkan (Imagine/Brad Grey/Melendandri-Gordon)

Television and standup comic Dana Carvey's deft mimicry and physical comedy are used to the max in *Opportunity Knocks*, but pic's routine venture into action and romance genres subtracts from the laughs.

Carvey and con accomplice Todd Graff break, enter and take up residence in a luxurious suburban house. Carvey is mistaken for a housesitting friend by the mother of the house's owner (Doris Belack). Carvey heeds the advice of semiretired con artists Milo O'Shea and Sally Gracie, and starts a 'love con' with Julia Campbell, the earthy doctor daughter of Belack and Robert Loggia. Naturally, they fall in love.

Fortunately, the conventional screenplay and direction are frequently interrupted by Carvey's winsome shticking. Later, however, Carvey is expected to be a romantic lead, and the audience is expected to believe it. Filmmakers err on both counts.

••••••••••••••••••••••••••••••••••••

■ OPTIMISTS OF NINE ELMS, THE

(US: The Optimists)

1974, 110 MINS, UK ◇ ◉

Dir Anthony Simmons *Prod* Adrian Gaye, Victor Lyndon
Scr Anthony Simmons, Tudor Gates *Ph* Larry Pizer
Ed John Jympson *Mus* George Martin *Art Dir* Robert Cartwright

● Peter Sellers, Donna Mullane, John Chaffey, David Daker, Marjorie Yates (Cheetah/Sagittarius)

Pic is a romanticized, Anglicized variant on [Vittorio De Sica's 1952 Italian classic] *Umberto D*, with Peter Sellers playing an aging vaudevillian whose meager income derives from sidewalk minstrelling with his equally-weary trained mutt. He tentatively befriends an eleven-year-old girl and her six-year-old brother, opening their poverty-clouded eyes to a world of magical dreams while they offer him the blessing of human contact.

It all sounds like goo, and the film's last half-hour verges perilously close. But even at its worst *The Optimists* is acceptable family fare, and for much of its first 80 minutes it engagingly achieves a sense of fantasy.

Director-coscripter Anthony Simmons (on whose novel *The Optimists of Nine Elms* screenplay is based) obviously understands and relishes the unique world of childhood.

■ ORCA

1977, 92 MINS, US ◇ ◉ ⊙

Dir Michael Anderson *Prod* Luciano Vincenzoni
Scr Luciano Vincenzoni, Sergio Donati *Ph* Ted Moore
Ed Ralph E. Winters, John Bloom, Marion Rothman
Mus Ennio Morricone *Art Dir* Mario Garbuglia

● Richard Harris, Charlotte Rampling, Will Sampson, Bo Derek, Keenan Wynn, Robert Carradine (De Laurentiis)

Orca is man-vs-beast nonsense. Some fine special effects and underwater camera work are plowed under in dumb story-telling.

Richard Harris is a shark-hunting seafarer who incurs the enmity of a superintelligent whale after harpooning the whale's pregnant mate.

We learn all about the whales from Charlotte Rampling, ever at the ready with scientific exposition, occasional voiceover and arch posing.

Assorted supporting players include Will Sampson, who complements Rampling's pedantic dialog with ancient tribal lore; Peter Hooten, Bo Derek and Keenan Wynn, a part of the Harris boat crew; Scott Walker as menacing leader of village fishermen who wish Harris would just leave their whale-harassed town.

■ ORDINARY PEOPLE

1980, 123 MINS, US ◇ ◉ ⊙

Dir Robert Redford *Prod* Ronald L. Schwary *Scr* Alvin Sargent *Ph* John Bailey *Ed* Jeff Kanew *Mus* Marvin Hamlisch *Art Dir* Phillip Bennett, J. Michael Riva

● Donald Sutherland, Mary Tyler Moore, Judd Hirsch, Timothy Hutton, Elizabeth McGovern, M. Emmet Walsh (Paramount/Wildwood)

A powerfully intimate domestic drama, *Ordinary People* represents the height of craftsmanship across the board. Robert Redford stayed behind the camera to make a remarkably intelligent and assured directorial debut that is fully responsive to the mood and nuances of the astute adaptation of Judith Guest's best seller.

While not ultimately downbeat or despairing, tale of a disturbed boy's precarious tightrope walk through his teens is played out with tremendous seriousness. Pic possesses a somber, hour-of-the-wolf mood, with characters forced to definitively confront their own souls before fadeout.

Dilemma is of a youth who has recently attempted suicide in remorse for not having saved his older brother from drowning.

Redford keenly evokes the darkly serene atmosphere of Chicago's affluent North Shore and effectively portrays this WASP society's predilection for pretending everything is okay even when it's not.

□ 1980: Best Picture, Director, Supp. Actor (Timothy Hutton), Adapted Screenplay.
□ Nominations: Best Actress (Mary Tyler Moore), Supp. Actor (Judd Hirsch)

■ ORGANIZATION, THE

1971, 105 MINS, US ◇ ◉

Dir Don Medford *Prod* Walter Mirisch *Scr* James R. Webb *Ph* Joseph Biroc *Ed* Ferris Webster *Mus* Gil Melle *Art Dir* George B. Chan

● Sidney Poitier, Barbara McNair, Gerald S. O'Loughlin, Sheree North, Fred Beir, Allen Garfield (United Artists)

Sidney Poitier is back for third time around as Virgil Tibbs, the San Francisco homicide lieutenant, faced this time with combatting a worldwide dope syndicate.

The screenplay, generally highly polished, is a bit hazy occasionally in development, and Don Medford establishes a fast tempo in his lively direction. Pic's opening is a gem as stage is set for consequent action, skillfully enacted and drivingly constructed.

It's a heist of a furniture factory – front for crime ring – and seizure of $5 million in heroin by a group of young people taking law into their own hands to try to halt the drug sale that has been ruining the lives of relatives and friends. Tibbs is assigned case when the murdered body of the factory manager is found.

Poitier is confronted by a serious problem in police ethics as group calls him in, admitting robbery but denying the murder. Group asks his assistance, leaving them free to operate while they try their own methods.

■ ORLANDO

1993, 93 MINS, UK/RUSSIA/ITALY/FRANCE/NETHERLANDS ◇ ◉ ⊙

Dir Sally Potter *Prod* Christopher Sheppard *Scr* Sally Potter *Ph* Alexei Rodionov *Ed* Herve Schneid
Mus Bob Last *Art Dir* Ben van Os, Jan Roelfs

● Tilda Swinton, Billy Zane, Lothaire Bluteau, John Wood, Charlotte Valandrey, Quentin Crisp (Adventure/Lenfilm/Mikado/Rio/Sigma)

Overcoming European co-production pitfalls, *Orlando* provides exciting, wonderfully witty entertainment with glorious settings and costumes and Tilda Swinton's sock performance in the title role.

Virginia Woolf's 1928 novel is structured around the intriguing notion of a character who lived for 400 years, changing sex in the course of time. Orlando is a youth who, in 1600, becomes the favorite of the aging Queen Elizabeth I and lives to tell the tale well into the 20th century.

Though she's really too feminine to pass for a man in pic's first half, Swinton is extraordinary as the eponymous Orlando, who frequently, in witty asides to the camera, takes the audience into his/her confidence.

The cast is uniformly strong, with Billy Zane very effective as a manly Yank and Quentin Crisp looking exactly right as the aging Queen Elizabeth.

Logistically, pic looks rich and expensive, with St. Petersburg locations standing in for medieval London in winter. Pic was also shot in Uzbekistan.

■ ORPHANS

1987, 120 MINS, US ◇ ◉ ⊙

Dir Alan J. Pakula *Prod* Alan J. Pakula *Scr* Lyle Kessler *Ph* Donald McAlpine *Ed* Evan Lottman
Mus Michael Small *Art Dir* George Jenkins

● Albert Finney, Matthew Modine, Kevin Anderson, John Kellogg (Lorimar)

The inherent dramatic insularity of Lyle Kessler's play about two urban outcast brothers and the Mephisphelian gangster who transforms their hermetic world is driven by the inspired energies of its principal cast.

Treat (Matthew Modine) and Phillip (Kevin Anderson) live in isolated squalor. Treat is a violent sociopath who ventures into New York to steal and scavenge. Phillip is a recluse terrified of the world outside the house and the physically dominant older brother who keeps him there, a virtual prisoner of fear.

Control of self and one's destiny is the gospel of Harold (Albert Finney), a hard-drinking mobster whom Treat lures from a saloon to the house one night with the intention of holding him hostage for ransom. The tables are quickly turned, however, when the mysterious but expansive gunman offers these destitute marginals an opportunity for big money and a spiffy new life.

Modine does all he can to dominate the picture in a tangibly physical performance that seems to use madness as its method and to succeed on these terms more often than not. Anderson portrays Phillip with great sensitivity and an aching pathos that's free of mannered affectation. Finney permits himself to anchor the center between these two extremes.

■ ORPHANS OF THE STORM

1921, 170 MINS, US ⊗ ◉ ⊙

Dir D.W. Griffith *Prod* D.W. Griffith *Scr* Marquis de Trolignac [= D.W. Griffith] *Ph* Hendrik Sartov, Paul Allen, G.W. Bitzer *Ed* James Smith, Rose Smith
Art Dir Charles M. Kirk, Edward Scholl

● Lillian Gish, Dorothy Gish, Joseph Schildkraut, Frank Losee, Katherine Emmett, Morgan Wallace (Griffith/United Artists)

D.W. Griffith has tossed two orphans onto the tempestuous sea of the French Revolution and uses the ride-to-the-rescue for a finale, with an orphan under the guillotine and 'Danton five miles away'. This scene is drawn out agonizingly but does not let down in any spot.

The cavalry ride through the town, the storming of the moated guillotine gates, the last-minute reprieve and the hesitating release trigger on the guillotine all make for a dramatic final reel with a Griffith thrill that will compensate those who are not won by the unbelievable fidelity of the entire film historically.

The plot [based on the French play *Les Deux Orphelines*, by D'Ennery and Cormon] carries the two orphan girls, one blind, into Paris. Dorothy Gish is the blind girl, and this step from comedienne roles into a role of unlimited emotional possibilities reveals new capabilities in the less famous of the two Gish girls.

■ OSCAR, THE

1966, 122 MINS, US ◇ ◉

Dir Russell Rouse *Prod* Clarence Greene *Scr* Harlan Ellison, Russell Rouse, Clarence Greene *Ph* Joseph Ruttenberg *Ed* Chester W. Schaeffer *Mus* Percy Faith
Art Dir Hal Pereira, Arthur Lonegan

● Stephen Boyd, Elke Sommer, Milton Berle, Eleanor Parker, Joseph Cotten, Jill St John (Greene-Rouse)

This is the story of a vicious, bitter, first-class heel who rises to stardom on the blood of those close to him. Without a single redeeming quality, part played by Stephen Boyd is unsympathetic virtually from opening shots.

Clarence Green as producer and Russell Rouse as director are unrelenting in their development of the character, in screenplay on which they collabed with Harlan Ellison [based on Richard Sale's novel], and they make handsome use of the Hollywood background.

Boyd is surrounded by some offbeat casting which adds an interesting note. Milton Berle switches to dramatic role as a top Hollywood agent, and Tony Bennett, the singer, portrays a straight character, Boyd's longtime friend victimized by the star in his battle for success.

Boyd makes the most of his part, investing it with an audience-hate symbol which he never once compromises. Elke Sommer, as his studio-designer wife who is another of his victims, is chief distaff interest in a well-undertaken portrayal. Eleanor Parker excels in the rather thankless role of a studio talent scout and dramatic coach who discovers Boyd in NY.

An arresting impression is made by Hedda Hopper, playing herself.

☐ 1966: Nominations: Best Color Costume Design, Color Art Direction

• •

■ OSCAR

1991, 109 MINS, US ◇ ⓥ ⊙
Dir John Landis   *Prod* Leslie Belzberg   *Scr* Michael Barrie, Jim Mulholland   *Ph* Mac Ahlberg   *Ed* Dale Beldin   *Mus* Elmer Bernstein   *Art Dir* Bill Kenney
● Sylvester Stallone, Ornella Muti, Don Ameche, Peter Riegert, Tim Curry, Vincent Spano (Touchstone)

Oscar is an intermittently amusing throwback to gangster comedies of the 1930s. While dominated by star Sylvester Stallone and heavy doses of production and costume design, pic is most distinguished by sterling turns by superb character actors.

Verbally adept script by TV comedy writers Michael Barrie and Jim Mulholland is based on a 1958 French play of the same name by Claude Magnier that was turned into a 1967 film starring Louis de Funes and directed by Edouard Molinaro. Set virtually entirely in Stallone's mansion, antics have an inescapably stagebound feel.

Manic proceedings unfold within a four-hour time period on the morning when legendary hood Angelo 'Snaps' Provolone (Stallone) will officially go straight by entering the banking business. Snaps is rudely awakened on his big day by his young accountant (Vincent Spano), who brashly announces he needs a big raise so he can afford to marry the gangster's daughter (Marisa Tomei).

This sets in motion a domestic tempest involving two more potential husbands for the daughter, her surprise announcement she's pregnant, the arrival of another woman who claims to be Snaps' daughter and the mixing up of three identical black bags.

Stallone does no more than a serviceable job in getting across the humor. But pic's a pleasure around the edges through the casting of Don Ameche and Eddie Bracken, not to mention Yvonne DeCarlo and, in an opening scene cameo as Snaps' father, Kirk Douglas.

• •

■ OSCAR WILDE

1960, 98 MINS, UK
Dir Gregory Ratoff   *Prod* William Kirby   *Scr* Jo Eisinger   *Ph* Georges Perinal   *Ed* Tony Gibbs   *Mus* Kenneth V. Jones
● Robert Morley, Phyllis Calvert, John Neville, Ralph Richardson, Dennis Price, Alexander Knox (Vantage)

This black-and-white version of the story of the poet-playwright-wit whose tragic downfall on homosexual charges was a scandal in Victorian times hit London screens just five days before *The Trials of Oscar Wilde*, a color job. It was produced swiftly but shows no signs of technical shoddiness, even though it was being edited up to a couple of hours before screening for the press.

Georges Perinal's lensing is effective and the atmosphere of Victorian London, Paris and the court scenes has been faithfully caught. The literate screenplay draws heavily on both Wilde's own epigrams and wisecracks but also on the actual documented evidence in the two celebrated court cases.

The picture starts unsatisfactorily but comes vividly to life when the court proceedings begin. The opening sequences are very sketchy and merely set the scene of Wilde as a celebrated playwright and his first meeting with the handsome father-hating young Lord Alfred Douglas, an association which was to prove his downfall.

Gregory Ratoff, as director, swiftly gets into his stride after the aforesaid uneasy start and, though the film is over-talky and over-stagey, it is a good and interesting job of work.

Robert Morley, who once made an effective stage Oscar Wilde, looks perhaps a little too old for the role but he gives a very shrewd performance, not only in the rich relish with which he delivers Wilde's bon mots but also in the almost frighteningly pathetic way in which he crumbles and wilts in the dock.

Ralph Richardson is also in memorable form as the brilliant Queen's Counsel, Sir Edward Carson, who mercilessly strips Wilde in court with his penetrating questions.

• •

■ OSTERMAN WEEKEND, THE

1983, 102 MINS, US ◇ ⓥ ⊙
Dir Sam Peckinpah   *Prod* Peter S. Davis, William N. Panzer   *Scr* Alan Sharp, Ian Masters   *Ph* John Coquillon   *Ed* Edward Abroms, David Rawlins   *Mus* Lalo Schifrin   *Art Dir* Robb Wilson King
● Rutger Hauer, John Hurt, Craig T. Nelson, Dennis Hopper, Chris Sarandon, Burt Lancaster (Davis-Panzer/20th Century-Fox)

Sam Peckinpah's *The Osterman Weekend* is a competent, professional but thoroughly impersonal meller which reps initial adaptation of a Robert Ludlum tome for the big screen.

CIA chief Burt Lancaster, who harbors presidential ambitions, recruits operative John Hurt to convince powerful TV journalist Rutger Hauer that several of his closest friends are actually Soviet agents. Hauer is about to host an annual weekend get-together with his buddies and their wives.

After Hurt has equipped the California ranch house with a warehouse-full of sophisticated surveillance gear, Hauer warily bids welcome to his guests, who include: hot-tempered financier Chris Sarandon and his sexually unsatisfied wife (Cassie Yates); writer and martial arts expert Craig T. Nelson; doctor Dennis Hopper, and his wife, cocaine addict Helen Shaver.

After a videotape foul-up, the pals get wind of Hauer's suspicions of them, and the domestic situation rapidly deteriorates.

Hauer is solid as the off-balance but determined protagonist. Hurt effectively plays most of his role isolated from the others in his video command post, and Lancaster socks over his bookend cameo as the scheming CIA kingpin.

• •

■ OTHELLO

1952, 91 MINS, MOROCCO
Dir Orson Welles   *Prod* Orson Welles   *Scr* Orson Welles   *Ph* Anchise Brizzi, G.R. Aldo, Georgo Fanto, Obadan Troiani, Roberto Fusi   *Ed* Jean Sacha, Renzo Lucidi, John Shepridge   *Mus* Angelo Francesco Lavagnino, Alberto Barberis   *Art Dir* Alexandre Trauner
● Orson Welles, Micheal MacLiammoir, Suzanne Cloutier, Robert Coote, Hilton Edwards, Fay Compton (Mercury)

After three years in the making, Orson Welles unveiled his *Othello* at the Cannes Film Festival in April 1952 to win the top award. Film is an impressive rendering of the Shakespearean tragedy.

Beginning is catchy in lensing, plasticity and eye appeal, but a bit murky in development. After the marriage of Othello and Desdemona over the protests of her father, the film takes a firm dramatic line and crescendos as the warped Iago brings on the ensuing tragic results. The planting of the jealousy seed in Othello is a bit sudden, but once it takes hold, the pic builds in power until the final death scene.

Micheal MacLiammoir is good as Iago, the jealous, twisted friend whose envy turns to hate and murder. Orson Welles gives the tortured Moor depth and stature.

Footage shot in Italy and Morocco is well matched photographically. Standout scenes are the murder of Roderigo in a Moroccan bath as the chase weaves through the steamy air and ends in general skewering and mayhem.

• •

■ OTHER, THE

1972, 108 MINS, US ◇ ⓥ
Dir Robert Mulligan   *Prod* Robert Mulligan   *Scr* Tom Tryon   *Ph* Robert L. Surtees   *Ed* Folmar Blangsted, O. Nicholas Brown   *Mus* Jerry Goldsmith   *Art Dir* Albert Brenner
● Uta Hagen, Diana Muldaur, Chris Udvarnoky, Martin Udvarnoky, Norma Connolly, Victor French (20th Century-Fox)

The apparently sluggish opening reels of *The Other* subsequently justify themselves among many other mind-engrossing plot twists in this occult shocker. The film [written by actor Tom Tryon from his first novel] is an outstanding example of topflight writing structure and dialog, enhanced to full fruition by a knowing director.

On a small Connecticut farm in 1935 a tragedy-stricken family is plagued further with a series of deaths. The story unfolds around, and from the viewpoint of, Diana Muldaur's two young identical-twin sons, expertly played by 10-year-olds Chris and Martin Udvarnoky. Martin is aloof, introverted, and a downbeat influence on Chris, whose more normal juvenile attributes and fantasies are nurtured lovingly by Hagen.

Tryon and Mulligan have seeded the story with many clues and visible occasions for misjudgment.

• •

■ OTHER PEOPLE'S MONEY

1991, 101 MINS, US ◇ ⓥ ⊙
Dir Norman Jewison   *Prod* Norman Jewison, Ric Kidney   *Scr* Alvin Sargent   *Ph* Haskell Wexler   *Ed* Lou Lombardo   *Mus* David Newman   *Art Dir* Philip Rosenberg
● Danny DeVito, Gregory Peck, Penelope Ann Miller, Piper Laurie, Dean Jones, Tom Aldredge (Warner/Yorktown)

Danny DeVito does a very entertaining star turn as a delicious personification of the greedy and heartless 1980s, but there is a softening of Jerry Sterner's biting theatrical success and problematic casting.

First produced in 1987 and launched on a long run off-Broadway two years later with Kevin Conway and Mercedes Ruehl in the leads, acidly comic play effectively illustrated the vulnerability of old-fashioned virtues embodied in family-run, locally owned companies when preyed upon by takeover vultures looking for asset-rich firms.

Bigtime Wall Street operator Lawrence Garfield (DeVito) sets his sights on a venerable old company run by folksy 'Jorgy' Jorgenson (Gregory Peck) amid the beautiful turning leaves of Rhode Island. Jorgy is inclined to ignore the threat but is convinced to call in Kate Sullivan (Penelope Ann Miller), a sharp young lawyer and daughter of his longtime assistant and companion (Piper Laurie).

Winning the game is the bottom line for the wily Larry, but he is also extremely taken with the foxy, deliberately provocative Kate, and the two perform a teasing tango in which he holds the upper hand in biz smarts, but she holds the sexual reins. Constant maneuvers and one-upsmanship ploys constitute good, peppery drama, and the strongly etched settings, both in Manhattan and New England, provide a vivid backdrop for this drama of capitalistic conflict.

Peck and Laurie give perfectly good performances. More crucially, Miller comes off about 10 years too young to play Kate. She looks more like a law student than an experienced corporate attorney.

■ OTHER SIDE OF MIDNIGHT, THE

1977, 165 MINS, US ◇ ▼
Dir Charles Jarrott *Prod* Frank Yablans *Scr* Herman Raucher, Daniel Taradash *Ph* Fred J. Koenekamp *Ed* Donn-Cambern, Harold F. Kress *Mus* Michel Legrand *Art Dir* John DeCuir
● Marie-France Pisier, John Beck, Susan Sarandon, Raf Vallone, Clu Gulager, Christian Marquand (20th Century-Fox)

The film, is directed in somewhat predictable style by Charles Jarrott. The script [from the novel by Sidney Sheldon] seems awkwardly pulled together, making for some weird time jumps in the 1939-47 period even with the help of sequence subtitles.

Inducted early into a life of making it on her body, Marie-France Pisier sleeps her way up to international film star status, all the while paying out money to follow John Beck.

Beck meanwhile meets Susan Sarandon in Washington, DC, whom he marries before going off to the Pacific theater of war. Sarandon has enough troubles in his absence, but when he comes back, her pull with boss Clu Gulager lands Beck lots of jobs.

Pisier, from the mansions of rich Greek Raf Vallone, fixes it so Beck has to turn to work abroad, hiring on as her pilot so she can degrade him.

Players, script and director have not failed the project in this regard; Michel Legrand's score is appropriately goopy.
□ 1977: Nomination: Best Costume Design

■ OTHER SIDE OF THE MOUNTAIN, THE
(UK: Window in the Sky)

1975, 101 MINS, US ◇ ▼
Dir Larry Peerce *Prod* Edward S. Feldman *Scr* David Seltzer *Ph* David M. Walsh *Ed* Eve Newman *Mus* Charles Fox *Art Dir* Philip Abramson
● Marilyn Hassett, Beau Bridges, Belinda J. Montgomery, Nan Martin, William Bryant, Dabney Coleman (Universal/Filmways)

This is a heartwarming love story – the true-life tale of a desperately-injured 19-year-old girl skier with such love for life she beats her way back to a future of hope.

It's based on the tragic experience of Jill Kinmont, a Bishop, Calif, girl who was a shoo-in for a berth on the 1956 Winter Olympics team until she suffered her near-fatal accident while racing down the slopes in the Snow Cup Race at Alta, Utah.

Script is from the biographical book, *A Long Way Up*, by E.G. Valens, and personal reminiscences of the victim.

Film is a standout in every department, perfect casting, fine acting, sensitive direction, imaginative photography and general overall production all combining to give unusual strength to subject matter.
□ 1975: Nomination: Best Song ('Richard's Window')

■ OTLEY

1969, 90 MINS, UK ◇ ▼
Dir Dick Clement *Prod* Bruce Cohn Curtis *Scr* Ian La Frenais *Ph* Austin Dempster *Ed* Richard Best *Mus* Stanley Myers *Art Dir* Carmen Dillon
● Tom Courtenay, Romy Schneider, Alan Badel, James Villiers, Leonard Rossiter (Columbia)

Otley seeks to break away from over-done Ian Fleming-like spy tales [of the period]. It focuses on exploits of bumbling 'everyman type' thrust into the espionage game.

Storyline is pegged around Tom Courtenay unfortuitously present at an acquaintance's London flat, when the latter is bumped off. It soon evolves that the recently deceased was a defector from a gang of state-secret smugglers, and now all parties concerned think that Courtenay somehow knew as much as his late friend.

Because of this, he is first kidnapped and beaten up by Romy Schneider and her cohorts, then after bumbling his way out of their clutches, he is caught by the opposing side and bounced about by them.

In seeking to avoid overheroics as well as the pitfalls of parody, the film has an uneasy lack of a point of view and fails to focus viewer's attention on any particular character or plotline philosophy.

■ OUR DAILY BREAD
(UK: The Miracle of Life)

1934, 74 MINS, US ▼ ⊙
Dir King Vidor *Prod* King Vidor *Scr* King Vidor, Elizabeth Hill Vidor *Ph* Robert Planck *Ed* Lloyd Nossler *Mus* Alfred Newman
● Karen Morley, Tom Keene, John Qualen, Barbara Pepper (Viking/United Artists)

King Vidor, who has the nerve to do unusual things, has here brought to the screen a story which deals with a throng of unemployed who take up squatter rights on an abandoned farm and turn it into a thriving communal collective project. On the way they have various difficulties chiefly from that ghoulish visitor of farmlands, the drought.

When the drought has just about withered the corn, and the young leader (Tom Keene) of the collectives is nuts over a blonde strumpet (Barbara Pepper), the colony is aroused from the abyss of despondency for one last effort.

It's a glorification of human will power driving man beyond ordinary feats of endurance. Primitive, forceful, real and moving.

■ OUR GIRL FRIDAY
(US: The Adventures of Sadie)

1953, 88 MINS, UK ◇
Dir Noel Langley *Prod* George Minter, Noel Langley *Scr* Noel Langley *Ph* Wilkie Cooper *Ed* John Seabourne *Mus* Ronald Binge *Art Dir* Fred Pusey
● Joan Collins, George Cole, Kenneth More, Robertson Hare, Hermione Gingold, Hattie Jacques (Renown)

Three men and a girl stranded on a desert island should be an obvious vehicle for a spicy, sexy comedy, but this British effort does not quite come up to expectations. The story [from Norman Lindsay's novel, *The Cautious Amorist*] has its moments of fun but the dialog is often flat and forced. Much of the film was lensed in the Spanish island of Mallorca.

After a collision at sea, Joan Collins finds herself on a desert island with George Cole, a journalist; Kenneth More, a ship's stoker; and Robertson Hare, an insufferable professor. For the sake of harmony, the three men make a pact not to make a pass at the girl, but two of them, Cole and Hare, rapidly succumb to her charms.

There is some lively competition among the two swains for the privilege of being alone with the girl. These incidents are the mainstay of the film's humor and inevitably the joke to be a little protracted. There is a delightful guest portrayal, taking only a couple of minutes of screen time, from Hermione Gingold.

■ OUR MAN FLINT

1966, 107 MINS, US ◇ ▼ ⊙
Dir Daniel Mann *Prod* Saul David *Scr* Hal Fimberg, Ben Starr *Ph* Daniel L. Fapp *Ed* William Reynolds *Mus* Jerry Goldsmith *Art Dir* Jack Martin Smith, Ed Graves
● James Coburn, Lee J. Cobb, Gila Golan, Edward Mulhare, Benson Fong, Shelby Grant (20th Century-Fox)

This Saul David production is a dazzling, action-jammed swashbuckling spoof [from a story by Hal Fimberg] of Ian Fleming's valiant counter-spy, he's given more tools and gimmicks to pursue his craft as he tracks down and destroys the perpetrators of a diabolical scheme to take over the world.

James Coburn takes on the task of being surrounded by exotically-undraped beauts and facing dangers which would try any man. But he comes through unscathed, helped by a dandy little specially-designed lighter which has 83 separate uses, including such items as being a derringer, two-way radio carrying across oceans, blow-torch, tear gas bomb, dart gun, you- name-it.

Assignment comes to him when three mad scientists threaten the safety of the world by controlling the weather, and he's selected by ZOWIE (Zonal Organization on World Intelligence Espionage) as the one man alive who can ferret them out before they can put their final threatened plan into work.

Lee J. Cobb has a field day as the exasperated American rep and head of ZOWIE who cannot keep Flint in line according to recognized standards for espionage.

■ OUR MAN IN HAVANA

1960, 111 MINS, UK
Dir Carol Reed *Prod* Carol Reed *Scr* Grahame Greene *Ph* Oswald Morris *Ed* Bert Bates *Mus* Hermand Deniz *Art Dir* John Box
● Alec Guinness, Burl Ives, Maureen O'Hara, Ernie Kovacs, Noel Coward, Ralph Richardson (Columbia)

Based on the Graham Greene novel, scripted by that author, directed by Carol Reed, shot mainly in colorful Cuba and acted by a star-loaded cast headed by Alec Guinness, this turns out to be polished, diverting entertainment, brilliant in its comedy but falling apart towards the end when undertones of drama, tragedy and message crop up.

Story concerns a mild-mannered and not very successful vacuum-cleaner salesman in Havana who needs extra money to send his daughter to finishing school in Switzerland. Against his will he is persuaded to become a member of the British secret service. To hold down his job, he is forced to invent mythical sub-agents and concoct highly imaginative, fictitious reports which he sends back to London. They are taken so seriously that two assistants are sent to help him, and the web of innocent deceit that he has spun gradually mounts up to sinister and dramatic consequences.

Greene has scripted his novel fairly faithfully, though the Catholic significance is only lightly brought into the film. Reed sometimes lets the story become woolly but has expert control of a brilliant cast. Guinness is a perfect choice for the reluctant spy role, giving one of his usual subtle, slyly humorous studies.

But the standout thesping comes from Noel Coward. From his first entrance, which is immediately after the credits, he dominates every scene in which he appears. He plays the boss of the Caribbean network.

Another performance which steals a lot of thunder from Guinness is that of Ralph Richardson, who is Coward's boss stationed in London.

OUR MOTHER'S HOUSE

1967, 104 MINS, UK/US ◇
Dir Jack Clayton *Prod* Jack Clayton *Scr* Jeremy
Brooks, Haya Harareet *Ph* Larry Pizer *Ed* Tom
Priestley *Mus* Georges Delerue *Art Dir* Reece
Pemberton
● Dirk Bogarde, Margaret Brooks, Pamela Franklin,
Louis Sheldon Williams, John Gugolka, Mark Lester
(Heron/M-G-M)

Our Mother's House, a film about children but
not to be considered in any way a kiddie pic,
is a well-made look at family life and parenthood by seven destitute moppets. Dirk
Bogarde stars in an excellent performance as
their long-lost legal father, who is not the total heel he seems; nor, for that matter are the
kids all angels.

Julian Gloag's novel has been adapted into a
good screenplay which develops neatly the accelerated maturing of children after the death
of their long-ailing mother (Annette Carell).

Latter, object of adulation, is buried in the
back yard, eldest child Margaret Brooks imposing her belief on others that this will eliminate orphanage fears. To all except eldest
son Louis Sheldon Williams, she conceals existence of a father, Bogarde.

OUR TOWN

1940, 89 MINS, US ⓥ
Dir Sam Wood *Prod* Sol Lesser *Scr* Thornton Wilder,
Frank Craven, Harry Chandlee *Ph* Bert Glennon
Ed Sherman Todd *Mus* Aaron Copland
Art Dir William Cameron Menzies, Harry Horner
● William Holden, Martha Scott, Fay Bainter, Beulah
Bondi, Thomas Mitchell, Frank Craven (Lesser/United
Artists)

The film version of Thornton Wilder's
Pulitzer prize play *Our Town* is an artistic offering, utilizing the simple and philosophical
form of the stage piece, excellently written,
directed, acted and mounted.

The film version retains the story and essentials of the play. Developed at a deliberately slow tempo, the simple and unhurried
life of a rural New England village of 2,200
souls is unfolded without attempt to point up
dramatic highlights.

The tale is divided into three periods, 1901,
1904, and 1913. It's a plain and homey exposition of life, romance, marriage and death in
the New Hampshire town. More explicitly, it
concerns the intimacies of two families, the
adolescent and matured romance and married life of a boy and girl. Tragic ending of
the play is switched for picture purposes, the
girl taking a nightmare excursion through
the village graveyard and visions of death
while going through childbirth. The ethereal
expedition, running about five minutes, is the
one false note in the picture.

Lesser drew heavily on the original stage
cast for the film version. Martha Scott delivers a sincerely warm portrayal as the girl, displaying a wealth of ability and personality. In
addition, Arthur Allen and Doro Merande are
from the stage group in their original roles,
Allen particularly effective in his brief professor appearance describing the geographic
structure of the countryside.

William Holden is fine as the boy; Fay
Bainter and Beulah Bondi provide excellent
mother portrayals; while Thomas Mitchell
and Guy Kibbee are prominent as heads of
the two households.
□ 1940: Nominations: Best Picture, Actress
(Martha Scott), B&W Art Direction, Original
Score, Sound

OUTCAST OF THE ISLANDS

1952, 102 MINS, UK
Dir Carol Reed *Prod* Carol Reed *Scr* William
Fairchild, Edward Scaife *Ph* John Wilcox *Ed* Bert
Bates *Mus* Brian Easdale *Art Dir* Vincent Korda

● Ralph Richardson, Trevor Howard, Robert Morley,
Kerima, Wendy Hiller, George Coulouris (London/British
Lion)

Picture is based on the Joseph Conrad story,
but the screenplay fails to capture the authentic atmosphere of the Far East in which
the story is set. The backgrounds are genuine
enough, but the plot is loosely constructed
and the editing occasionally episodic.

The outcast is played by Trevor Howard. He
is saved from the police, after being involved
in a swindle, by the captain of a trading vessel
who takes him to his island outpost. There,
he doublecrosses his friend, tricks his partner
and falls in love with the daughter of the
blind tribal chief.

Within that outline, the film concentrates
on developing the shifting character of the
outcast as a man without honor, without principle and without friends, yet having a devouring passion for the native girl.

Ralph Richardson, polished and dignified as
usual, gives a sterling performance as the
captain of the trading boat. Robert Morley
chalks up another success as the captain's
partner.

OUTFIT, THE

1973, 102 MINS, US ◇ ⓥ
Dir John Flynn *Prod* Carter De Haven *Scr* John Flynn
Ph Bruce Surtees *Ed* Ralph E. Winters *Mus* Jerry
Fielding *Art Dir* Tambi Larsen
● Robert Duvall, Karen Black, Joe Don Baker, Robert
Ryan, Timothy Carey, Richard Jaeckel (M-G-M)

In *The Outfit* two relatively small time outside-
the-law characters, stylishly handled by
Robert Duvall and Joe Don Baker, drive off
into the credits laughing gleefully. In their
wake they leave countless stiffs, including
crime-syndicate topper Robert Ryan, Duvall's
girl friend (Karen Black), and a batch of
other broken-boned face-smashed individuals
who were caught up in pair's vengeance-moti-
vated assault on organized crime.

John Flynn's simple screenplay [from a
novel by Richard Stark, pen name for Donald
E. Westlake] focuses on Duvall's explosive
compulsion to square things with the mobsters who killed his brother as reprisal for
their ripping off a bank controlled by the syndicate.

Flynn keeps the pace extremely fast and engaging. Duvall and Baker work smoothly together. Joanna Cassidy makes an attractive
screen bow as Ryan's wife.

OUT FOR JUSTICE

1991, 91 MINS, US ◇ ⓥ
Dir John Flynn *Prod* Steven Seagal, Arnold Kopelson
Scr David Lee Henry *Ph* Ric Waite *Ed* Robert A.
Ferretti, Donald Brochu *Mus* David Michael Frank
Art Dir Gene Rudolf
● Steven Seagal, William Forsyth, Jerry Orbach, Jo
Champa, Shareen Mitchell, Sal Richards (Warner)

Out for Justice harbors an incredibly simple
vengeance plot loaded with enough macho
sadism to satiate the action genre's bloodthirsty fans.

This time Steven Seagal plays an Italian
cop pursuing the killer of his partner, who's
gunned down in broad daylight just after the
opening credits. Seagal relentlessly pursues
the murderous, drugged-out Richie (William
Forsythe), dispatching his henchmen in brutal encounters in a butcher shop, pool hall
and his own apartment that make the
LAPD's brutality seem tame.

Director John Flynn does a fair job of keeping the minimal storyline crawling along well
enough to justify all the mayhem. Too bad
the climactic confrontation doesn't justify the
build-up. Stuntwork, however, is first rate, and
Seagal remains a convincing action figure.

OUTLAND

1981, 109 MINS, US ◇ ❖ ⊙
Dir Peter Hyams *Prod* Richard A. Roth *Scr* Peter
Hyams *Ph* Stephen Goldblatt *Ed* Stuart Baird
Mus Jerry Goldsmith *Art Dir* Philip Harrison
● Sean Connery, Peter Boyle, Frances Sternhagen, Kika
Markham, James B. Sikking, Clarke Peters (Warner/Ladd)

Outland is something akin to *High Noon* in
outer space, a simple good guys-bad guys yarn
set in the future on a volcanic moon of
Jupiter.

While there are several mile-wide plot holes
and one key under-developed main character,
the film emerges as a tight, intriguing old-
fashioned drama that gives audiences a hero
worth rooting for.

It's clear from the beginning that newly arrived marshal Sean Connery is going to have
his hands full. Soon into the action, a miner
takes it upon himself to enter the deadly
moon atmosphere without his spacesuit and
literally fries before the audience's eyes.

Connery soon finds out that the miners are
growing crazy due to an amphetamine they
are taking that makes them produce more,
but eventually destroys their brains. It
doesn't take long to figure out that his rival
(Peter Boyle), the smug general manager
who basically runs the colony's operations, is
involved in supplying the drug.

Writer-director Peter Hyams falls just short
of providing the exciting payoff to the conflicts he so painstakingly sets up throughout
the picture.
□ 1981: Nomination: Best Sound

OUTLAW, THE

1943, 124 MINS, US ⓥ ⊙
Dir Howard Hughes *Prod* Howard Hughes *Scr* Jules
Furthman *Ph* Gregg Toland *Ed* Wallace Grissell
Mus Victor Young
● Jack Buetel, Jane Russell, Thomas Mitchell, Walter
Huston (Howard Hughes)

Beyond sex attraction of Jane Russell's
frankly displayed charms, picture, according
to accepted screen entertainment standards,
falls short. Plot is based on legend Billy the
Kid wasn't killed by the law but continued to
live on after his supposed death.

Pace is series of slow-moving incidents making up continuous chase as directed by
Howard Hughes and isn't quickened by the
two hours running time, but slowness is not
so much a matter of length as a lack of tempo
in individual scenes.

This variation of the checkered film career
of Billy the Kid has the outlaw joining forces
with legendary Doc Holliday, played by
Walter Huston, to escape the pursuing
Sheriff Pat Garrett (Thomas Mitchell).
Mixing strangely into the kid's life is Rio,
Latin charmer, as portrayed by Russell.

Sex seldom rears its beautiful head in si-
monpure prairie dramas, but since this is an
unorthodox, almost burlesque, version of
tried and true desert themes, anything can
and often does happen.

OUTLAW BLUES

1977, 100 MINS, US ◇ ⓥ
Dir Richard T. Heffron *Prod* Steve Tisch *Scr* B.W.L.
Norton *Ph* Jules Brenner *Ed* Danford B. Greene, Scott
Conrad *Mus* Charles Bernstein, Bruce Langhorne
Art Dir Jack Marty
● Peter Fonda, Susan Saint James, John Crawford,
James Callahan, Michael Lerner, Steve Fromholz
(Warner)

Script takes Peter Fonda from prison, where
he has developed a musical ability, to Texas
in pursuit of James Callahan, C&W name
who has stolen the title song from Fonda.

Accidental shooting of Callahan in a scuffle
launches a manhunt for Fonda by police chief

John Crawford, mayoral candidate not about to be embarrassed at election time. Susan Saint James, one of Callahan's singing group, beds and befriends Fonda and, by clever p.r., makes him a major new platter star to be reckoned with by Michael Lerner, a music biz sharpie.

The film revolves into a series of chases, interleaved with some okay songs which Fonda is said to have sung himself. Story opts for the laughs and smiles which come easily in abundance.

....

■ **OUTLAW JOSEY WALES, THE**

1976, 135 MINS, US ◇ 🅥 ⊙

Dir Clint Eastwood   *Prod* Robert Daley   *Scr* Phil Kaufman, Sonia Chernus   *Ph* Bruce Surtees   *Ed* Ferris Webster   *Mus* Jerry Fielding   *Art Dir* Tambi Larsen
● Clint Eastwood, Chief Dan George, Sondra Locke, Bill McKinney, John Vernon, Paula Trueman (Warner)

The screenplay [based on the book *Gone to Texas* by Forrest Carter] is another one of those violence revues, with carnage production numbers slotted every so often and intercut with Greek chorus narratives by John Vernon and Chief Dan George.

Clint Eastwood is a Civil War era farmer whose family is murdered by brigands led by Bill McKinney; Vernon is a fellow counter-guerrilla who is tricked into surrendering his men; George is an old Indian whom Eastwood encounters on the long trail of earthly retribution.

Eastwood's character meanders through the Middle West, disposing of antagonists by the dozen aided at times by George, Sam Bottoms, romantic interest Sondra Locke, latter's granny Paula Trueman and others.
☐ 1976: Nomination: Best Original Score

....

■ **OUT OF AFRICA**

1985, 150 MINS, US ◇ 🅥 ⊙

Dir Sydney Pollack   *Prod* Sydney Pollack   *Scr* Kurt Luedtke   *Ph* David Watkin   *Ed* Fredric Steinkamp, William Steinkamp, Pembroke Herring, Sheldon Kahn   *Mus* John Barry   *Art Dir* Stephen Grimes
● Meryl Streep, Robert Redford, Klaus Maria Brandauer, Michael Kitchen, Malick Bowens, Joseph Thiaka (Universal)

At two-and-a-half hours, *Out of Africa* certainly makes a leisurely start into its story. Just short of boredom, however, the picture picks up pace and becomes a sensitive, enveloping romantic tragedy.

Getting top billing over Robert Redford, Meryl Streep surely earns it with another engaging performance. Still, the film rarely comes to life except when Redford is around.

Ably produced and directed by Sydney Pollack, *Africa* is the story of Isak Dinesen, who wrote her experiences in Kenya. Though Dinesen (real name: Karen Blixen) remembered it lovingly, hers was not a happy experience. Pic opens in 1914.

With one landscape after another, Pollack and lenser David Watkin prove repeatedly, however, why she should love the land so, but at almost travelog drag.

Eventually, Streep and husband Klaus Maria Brandauer split, leaving an opening for Redford to move in. True love follows, but not happiness because he's too independent to be tied down by a marriage certificate.
☐ 1985: Best Picture, Director, Adapted Screenplay, Cinematography, Art Direction, Sound, Original Score.
☐ Nominations: Best Actress (Meryl Streep), Supp. Actor (Klaus Maria Brandauer), Costume Design, Editing

....

■ **OUT OF SEASON**

1975, 90 MINS, UK ◇ 🅥

Dir Alan Bridges   *Prod* Eric Bercovici, Reuben Bercovitch   *Scr* Eric Bercovici, Reuben Bercovitch   *Ph* Arthur Ibbetson

Ed Peter Weatherly   *Mus* John Cameron   *Art Dir* Robert Jones
● Vanessa Redgrave, Cliff Robertson, Susan George, Edward Evans, Frank Jarvis (EMI/Lorimar)

Virtually a three-hander, *Out of Season* boasts topnotch performances by Vanessa Redgrave, Cliff Robertson and Susan George, a taut script and firstrate direction.

Though basic plot is that old chestnut about the dark stranger returning – after 20 years away – to visit an isolated hotel in an English seaside town, its handling is expert enough to avoid most of the pitfalls of the genre. And so is the acting.

Director Alan Bridges displays his ability to develop and hold obsessive situations, all hints and innuendos, and this ping pong match of the affections often has the suspense of a whodunit as audience tries to guess next move by the entangled mother, daughter, lover trio.

....

■ **OUT OF THE BLUE**

1980, 94 MINS, CANADA ◇ 🅥

Dir Dennis Hopper   *Scr* Leonard Yakir, Gary Jules Jouvenat   *Ph* Marc Champion   *Ed* Doris Dyck   *Mus* Tom Lavin
● Linda Manz, Sharon Farrell, Dennis Hopper, Raymond Burr, Don Gordon (Robson Street)

Dennis Hopper directs and stars in this terse drama of what the 1970s drug culture and dregs of the counter-culture would have wrought on those easy riders who got off their bikes and tried to conform.

Linda Manz has tart authority as a streetwise 15-year-old. She had been in a terrible accident while driving with Hopper, her father, who plowed into a school bus stalled in the middle of the road, killing many of the kids.

Hopper has been sentenced to five years in prison. He has become a hero to his daughter, who has fantasised the late Elvis Presley into another hero.

Dramatically economical, pic captures urban overcrowding, personal problems and violence but sans excess. Hopper reportedly took over direction after film started but worked with the writer on changes to fit his own personal outlooks.

....

■ **OUT OF THE PAST**
(UK: Build My Gallows High)

1947, 95 MINS, US 🅥 ⊙

Dir Jacques Tourneur   *Prod* Warren Duff   *Scr* Geoffrey Homes [= Daniel Mainwaring]   *Ph* Nicholas Musuraca   *Ed* Samuel E. Beetley   *Mus* Roy Webb   *Art Dir* Albert S. D'Agostino, Jack Okey
● Robert Mitchum, Jane Greer, Kirk Douglas, Rhonda Fleming, Richard Webb, Steve Brodie (RKO)

Out of the Past is a hardboiled melodrama [from the novel by Geoffrey Homes] strong on characterization. Direction by Jacques Tourneur pays close attention to mood development, achieving realistic flavor that is further emphasized by real life settings and topnotch lensing by Nicholas Musuraca.

Plot depicts Robert Mitchum as a former private detective who tries to lead a quiet, small-town life. Good portion of story is told in retrospect by Mitchum when his past catches up with him. Hired by a gangster to find a girl who had decamped with $40,000 after shooting the crook, Mitchum crosses her path in Acapulco, falls for her himself and they flee the gangster together.

Mitchum gives a very strong account of himself. Jane Greer as the baby-faced, charming killer is another lending potent interest. Kirk Douglas, the gangster, is believable and Paul Valentine makes role of henchman stand out effectively. Rhonda Fleming is in briefly but effectively.

....

■ **OUT-OF-TOWNERS, THE**

1970, 97 MINS, US ◇ 🅥 ⊙

Dir Arthur Hiller   *Prod* Paul Nathan   *Scr* Neil Simon   *Ph* Andrew Laszlo   *Ed* Fred Chulack   *Mus* Quincy Jones   *Art Dir* Charles Bailey
● Jack Lemmon, Sandy Dennis, Sandy Baron, Anne Meara, Robert Nichols, Ann Prentiss (Paramount/Jalem)

The Out-of-Towners is a total delight. Neil Simon's first modern original screen comedy stars Jack Lemmon and Sandy Dennis, an Ohio couple who become disillusioned with big-city life, New York style.

Lemmon and Dennis come to NY on one of those expense paid executive suite job interviews. In the course of 24 hours, they are stacked-up over the airport; diverted to Boston; lose their luggage; ride a food-less train to strike-bound and rainy NY; lose their Waldorf reservations; get held up; become involved in a police chase; escape mugging in Central Park; flee a mounted cop; and are asked to leave a church because of a TV rehearsal. Among other things.

Dennis and Lemmon are superb in comedy characterizations.

....

■ **OUT ON A LIMB**

1992, 82 MINS, US ◇ 🅥 ⊙

Dir Francis Veber   *Prod* Michael Hertzberg   *Scr* Daniel Goldin, Joshua Goldin   *Ph* Donald E. Thorin   *Ed* Glenn Farr   *Mus* Van Dyke Parks   *Art Dir* Stephen Marsh
● Matthew Broderick, Jeffrey Jones, Heidi Kling, John C. Reilly, Marian Mercer, Larry Hankin (Interscope)

Matthew Broderick sinks with the ship in *Out on a Limb*, a moronic comedy about a fish-out-of-water yuppie.

Planning to finalize a $140 million company takeover over the weekend, he's drawn instead to the small California town of Buzzsaw to rescue his young sister Marci (Courtney Peldon) from the clutches of a mad villain (Jeffrey Jones).

Evidently rewritten and reshot repeatedly, film makes no sense and develops not an iota of credibility. It's crudely framed as a 'how I spent my summer vacation' tall tale told in school by Peldon, despite the fact that she's not present for 99% of the incidents she narrates in such great detail.

In the release version the leading lady, played by Heidi Kling, is never given a character. Kling enters the film on the run, kidnaps and torments Broderick for several reels and finally wins him romantically with no explanation of who she is or why she's running.

Intervening segments consist of well-staged but pointless car chases and stunts, as well as a boring story of Jones playing demented twin brothers.

Director Francis Veber, known for his hit French farces, is out of luck here.

....

■ **OUTRAGE**

1950, 79 MINS, US

Dir Ida Lupino   *Prod* Collier Young, Malvin Wald   *Scr* Collier Young, Malvin Wald, Ida Lupino   *Ph* Archie Stout   *Ed* Harvey Manger   *Mus* Paul Sawtell
● Mala Powers, Tod Andrews, Robert Clarke, Raymond Bond, Lilian Hamilton, Rita Lupino (RKO/Filmakers)

Rape and its effect on the victim and her loved ones set up the melodramatic plot. However, handling of the theme is more interested in the events that transpire afterwards.

Mala Powers impresses as the victim. She is a young girl, engaged to a cleancut young man. After working late one night, she is violated while going home. The whispering and knowing looks that come later from the smalltown folks force her to run away.

Ida Lupino directed from a script written with Collier Young and Malvin Wald, co-producers. Her handling of the earlier sequences packs a hefty punch. In the latter sequences, when Powers is beginning to find herself, the pace is deliberate, almost idyllic.

While made on a tight budget, the production manages very good values.

••••••••••••••••••••••••••••••

■ **OUTRAGE, THE**

1964, 95 MINS, US ⑰
Dir Martin Ritt   *Prod* A. Ronald Lubin   *Scr* Michael Kanin   *Ph* James Wong Howe   *Ed* Frank Santillo   *Mus* Alex North   *Art Dir* George W. Davis, Tambi Larsen
● Paul Newman, Laurence Harvey, Claire Bloom, Edward G. Robinson, William Shatner, Howard da Silva (M-G-M)

The Outrage is adapted from the Fay and Michael Kanin Broadway play, *Rashomon*, which in turn was based on the Japanese film production of same tab. It is the story of a killing of a Southern gentleman and the rape of his wife by a bloodthirsty bandit, told through the eyes of the three protagonists and then by a disinterested eye witness, each version differing.

Script unfolds in the American Southwest in the 1870s, a neat metamorphosis from the 12th-century Japan of the play and original Nipponese pic. Bandit character is retained, but the samurai character becomes a Southern gentleman of fine family (Laurence Harvey) who is travelling through the West with his wife (Claire Bloom) when set upon by a Mexican outlaw (Paul Newman).

Plot takes its form, opening on platform of a deserted railroad station as a prospector and a preacher, who is leaving the town a disillusioned man, recite to con-man Edward G. Robinson the trial of the outlaw a few days previously, when three people testify to three totally different accounts of what 'actually' happened.

Newman as the violent and passionate killer plays his colorful character with a flourish and heavy accent. Harvey has little to do in first three accounts except remain tied to a tree, his turn coming in fourth when the prospector tells how he and bandit are shamed by the wife into fighting for her. Bloom, who appeared in Broadway play, has her gamut during the four versions of her ravishment, running from pure innocence to her demand to the outlaw to kill her husband so she can go away with her new lover. In all, she delivers strongly, turning glibly from drama to comedy.

••••••••••••••••••••••••••••••

■ **OUTRAGEOUS FORTUNE**

1987, 100 MINS, US ◇ ⑰ ⊙
Dir Arthur Hiller   *Prod* Ted Field, Robert Cort   *Scr* Leslie Dixon   *Ph* David M. Walsh   *Ed* Tom Rolf   *Mus* Alan Silvestri   *Art Dir* James D. Vance
● Shelley Long, Bette Midler, Peter Coyote, Robert Prosky, John Schuck, George Carlin (Touchstone/ Interscope)

Outrageous Fortune is well crafted, old-fashioned entertainment that takes some conventional elements, shines them up and repackages them as something new and contemporary. It's a traditional male buddy film that has substituted women and the main plot device is that the two heroines are sleeping with the same man. Bette Midler and Shelley Long collide even before their affections do in an acting class given by the eminent Russian director Stanislov Korenowski (Robert Prosky). Long is a wealthy, spoiled dilettante while Midler last starred in *Ninja Vixens*. When the audience learns they're sharing the same man (Peter Coyote) before they do, it's a delicious moment complete with one image-shattering sight gag.

The film takes off as a chase picture with the girls following Coyote to New Mexico to demand a decision. They're not the only ones looking for him. It seems the CIA is hot on his trail as is the KGB. To top things off, it turns out Korenowski is a Russian agent first and a director second.

Even when Leslie Dixon's script sags and becomes a bit repetitious in the long New Mexico chase section, Midler and Long are never less than fun to watch.

••••••••••••••••••••••••••••••

■ **OUTSIDER, THE**

1979, 128 MINS, US ◇
Dir Tony Luraschi   *Scr* Tony Luraschi   *Ph* Ricardo Aronovitch   *Ed* Catherine Kelber   *Mus* Ken Thorne   *Art Dir* Franco Fumagalli
● Craig Wasson, Sterling Hayden, Patricia Quinn, Niall O'Brien, T.P. McKenna, Ray McAnally (Paramount/ Cinematic Arts)

The Outsider represents the first attempt to get behind the incessant headlines and into the minds and motives at work on one of the longest-fought terrorist campaigns of the times – through an intelligent fictional story with an Irish setting.

A measure of the effectiveness of Craig Wasson's performance, as a young Irish-American inflamed to join the IRA by his grandfather's (Sterling Hayden) tales of fighting the Brits in the religion-charged cause of Irish nationalism, is that by the time he finally leaves Ireland as a disillusioned fugitive he looks – without artifice – 10 years older. What he's escaped is a neatly-plotted double trap by both the IRA and British army.

The strength of Tony Luraschi's features debut lies in its restraint.

••••••••••••••••••••••••••••••

■ **OUTSIDERS, THE**

1983, 91 MINS, US ◇ ⑰ ⊙
Dir Francis Coppola   *Prod* Fred Roos, Gray Frederickson   *Scr* Kathleen Knutsen Rowell   *Ph* Stephen H. Burum   *Ed* Anne Goursaud   *Mus* Carmine Coppola   *Art Dir* Dean Tavoularis
● C. Thomas Howell, Matt Dillon, Ralph Macchio, Patrick Swayze, Rob Lowe, Emilio Estevez (Zoetrope)

Francis Coppola has made a well acted and crafted but highly conventional film out of S.E. Hinton's popular youth novel, *The Outsiders*. Although set in the mid-1960s, pic feels very much like a 1950s drama about problem kids.

Screenplay is extremely faithful to the source material, even down to having the film open with the leading character and narrator, C. Thomas Howell, reciting the first lines of his literary effort while we see him writing them.

But dialog which reads naturally and evocatively on the page doesn't play as well on screen, and there's a decided difficulty of tone during the early sequences, as Howell and his buddies (Matt Dillon and Ralph Macchio) horse around town, sneak into a drive-in and have an unpleasant confrontation with the Socs, rival gang from the well-heeled part of town.

When the Socs attack Howell and Macchio in the middle of the night, latter ends up killing a boy to save his friend, and the two flee to a hideaway in an abandoned rural church. It is during this mid-section that the film starts coming to life, largely due to the integrity of the performances by Howell and Macchio.

Howell is truly impressive, a bulwark of relative stability in a sea of posturing and pretense. Macchio is also outstanding as his doomed friend, and Patrick Swayze is fine as the oldest brother forced into the role of parent.

••••••••••••••••••••••••••••••

■ **OVERBOARD**

1987, 112 MINS, US ◇ ⑰ ⊙
Dir Garry Marshall   *Prod* Anthea Sylbert, Alexandra Rose   *Scr* Leslie Dixon   *Ph* John A. Alonzo   *Ed* Dov Hoenig, Sonny Baskin   *Mus* Alan Silvestri   *Art Dir* James Shanahan, Jim Dultz
● Goldie Hawn, Kurt Russell, Edward Herrmann, Katherine Helmond, Michael Hagerty, Roddy McDowall (M-G-M)

Overboard is an uninspiring, unsophisticated attempt at an updated screwball comedy that is brought down by plodding script and a handful of too broadly drawn characters. Only element that occasionally lifts pic is the work of the redoubtable Goldie Hawn, who gives a gem of a performance.

Hawn plays Joanna Stayton, a millionaire wife who decides it's time to have her yacht's closet remodeled. On deck comes Kurt Russell as carpenter Dean Proffitt, whose performance doesn't seem to go beyond affable or angry. She fires him and, shortly thereafter, pushes him overboard.

Her comeuppance is the kind of revenge only found in film – Joanna falls off the boat trying to retrieve her wedding rock, and washes back on the Elk Cove shore with a nasty case of amnesia. Proffitt sees her on TV and devises a scheme to claim her as his wife Annie.

There is little to do but sit back and admire Hawn's performance, as she splendidly transforms herself from rich bitch to caring wife. Supporting roles are mostly pedestrian, except for a sweet, funny turn by Michael Hagerty, as Russell's best friend and a graduate of the John Candy School of Cinematic Oafishness.

••••••••••••••••••••••••••••••

■ **OVERLANDERS, THE**

1946, 91 MINS, UK/AUSTRALIA ⑰
Dir Harry Watt   *Prod* Michael Balcon   *Scr* Harry Watt   *Ph* Osmond Borradaile   *Ed* Leslie Norman   *Mus* John Ireland
● Chips Rafferty, John Nugent Hayward, Daphne Campbell, Jean Blue (Ealing)

Producer Michael Balcon sent director Harry Watt to Australia with a mandate to make a picture representative of that continent. Watt spent five months soaking up the atmosphere. In the Federal Food Office, Controller Murphy explained of the greatest mass migration of cattle the world has ever known to get them out of reach of a probable Jap landing. Across 2,000 miles of heat and dust, drovers had battled with 500,000 head of cattle. Watt decided this would be the film's theme.

Story begins in 1942 at the tiny town of Wyndham, where meat works are destroyed, personnel evacuated, and Chips Rafferty, boss cattle drover, is told to shoot 1,000 head of prime beasts. He decides instead to overland them across 2,000 miles of tough going.

Epic trip lasts 15 months, and the adventures are graphic. Highlights are the breaking in of wild horses when their own had died from poison weed; the stampede with the men facing a charge of maddened cattle and the forced march across a mountain path with a sheer drop on one side.

••••••••••••••••••••••••••••••

■ **OVERLORD**

1975, 85 MINS, UK ⑰
Dir Stuart Cooper   *Prod* James Quinn   *Scr* Stuart Cooper, Christopher Hudson   *Ph* John Alcott   *Ed* Jonathan Gili   *Mus* Paul Glass
● Brian Stirner, Davyd Harries, Nicholas Ball, Julie Neesam, Sam Sewell (Imperial War Museum)

Overlord concentrates on a British youngster's World War II blitztime induction into the army, his brief training period and his early D-day death.

Pic has a lovely reminiscent feel for its period and the deceptively peaceful at-home backdrop to the war in the buildup phase to the Allied invasion of the Continent, with bombers taking off from the green fields of England, convoys of invasion troops crossing silent villages and, as a foretaste of deadlier things to come, rarely seen footage of dummy run rehearsals conducted along the coasts of Britain, eerily dramatic when glimpsed in hindsight on later events.

Youth's indoctrination, is very skillfully melded with real footage.

US director Stuart Cooper gives it the right understated, unheroic feel.

. . . .

■ OVER THE BROOKLYN BRIDGE

1984, 106 MINS, US ◇ ⓥ
Dir Menahem Golan *Prod* Menahem Golan, Yoram Globus *Scr* Arnold Somkin *Ph* Adam Greenberg *Ed* Mark Goldblatt *Mus* Pino Donaggio *Art Dir* John Lawless
● Elliott Gould, Margaux Hemingway, Sid Caesar, Burt Young, Shelley Winters, Carol Kane (City)

Over the Brooklyn Bridge is producer-director Menahem Golan's love letter to New York City: a warm and pleasant romance similar to the type of films topliner Elliott Gould used to make in the early 1970s. Screenplay by Arnold Somkin is short on laughs but very effective.

Gould stars as Alby Sherman, owner of a Brooklyn eatery who dreams of buying a posh restaurant on the East Side in midtown Manhattan. His love affair with an aristocratic Catholic girl from Philadelphia (Margaux Hemingway) raises the ire of his Jewish family, particularly the patriarch Uncle Benjamin (Sid Caesar), a women's underwear manufacturer who would rather have Alby marry his fourth cousin Cheryl (Carol Kane).

Gould and Hemingway are solid in the central roles, with standout support from a large cast. Caesar is very funny as a man who tries to run everyone else's lives for them. Kane is delightfully droll as the virginal intellectual whose demure exterior hides a rather kinky fantasy-sex life.

. . . .

■ OVER THE TOP

1987, 93 MINS, US ◇ ⓥ ⊙
Dir Menahem Golan *Prod* Menahem Golan, Yoram Globus *Scr* Stirling Silliphant, Sylvester Stallone *Ph* David Gurfinkel *Ed* Don Zimmerman, James Symons *Mus* Giorgio Moroder *Art Dir* James Schoppe
● Sylvester Stallone, Robert Loggia, Susan Blakely, Rick Zumwalt, David Mendenhall, Chris McCarty (Cannon)

Sylvester Stallone muscles his way to the top of the heap in a beefy world of armwrestling in *Over the Top*. Routinely made in every respect, melodrama [from a story by Gary Conway and David C. Engelbach] concerns itself as much with a man's effort to win the love of his son as it does with macho athletics.

Stallone, as a down-on-his-luck trucker named Lincoln Hawk, appears out of the blue to fetch his son when the latter graduates from military academy. Absent from both the kid's and mama Susan Blakely's lives for years, Stallone proposes a get-to-know-you truck ride back home to Los Angeles.

Little Michael (David Mendenhall) doesn't make things especially easy for his papa, his military rigidity and formality providing a formidable barrier. At truckstops along the way, Stallone introduces his son to the thrills of armwrestling, and Michael's transformation from spoiled intellectual snot to future regular guy is well underway.

Stallone is sincere and soulful as a 'father who messed up pretty bad' and just wants his kid back, Mendenhall is a likable tyke, and justice is served in the end.

. . . .

■ OWL AND THE PUSSYCAT, THE

1970, 98 MINS, US ◇ ⓥ ⊙
Dir Herbert Ross *Prod* Ray Stark *Scr* Buck Henry *Ph* Harry Stradling *Ed* Margaret Booth *Mus* Richard Halligan *Art Dir* Robert Wightman

● Barbra Streisand, George Segal, Robert Klein, Allen Garfield, Roz Kelly, Jacques Sandulescu (Columbia)

A zany, laugh-filled story of two modern NY kooks who find love at the end of trail of hilarious incidents.

Bill Manhoff's 1954 play, adapted here by Buck Henry, has been altered in that, as originally cast, one of the principals was white, the other black (on Broadway, Alan Alda and Diana Sands). Here it's two Bronx-Brooklyn Caucasian types, with Barbra Streisand giving it a Jewish Jean Arthur treatment and George Segal as an amiable, low-key foil.

The story is basically that of the out-of-work quasi-model and the struggling writer who cut up and down apartment corridors and in public to the astonishment of all others.

Streisand is a casual hooker, who first confronts Segal after he has finked on her activities to building superintendent Jacques Sandulescu. Their harangues then shift to apartment of buddy Robert Klein who decides it is better to leave with gal Evelyn Lang than lie awake listening.

One of her old scores turns out to be Jack Manning, Segal's intended father-in-law, but that plot turn blows up his affair and leads into the excellent climax we have been waiting for.

. . . .

■ OX-BOW INCIDENT, THE

1943, 75 MINS, US ⓥ ⊙
Dir William A. Wellman *Prod* Lamar Trotti *Scr* Lamar Trotti *Ph* Arthur Miller *Ed* Allen McNeil *Mus* Cyril J. Mockridge
● Henry Fonda, Dana Andrews, Mary Beth Hughes, Anthony Quinn, Jane Darwell, Harry Davenport (20th Century-Fox)

Screen version of the best-selling book [by Walter Van Tilburg Clark] depends too much on the hanging theme, developing this into a brutal closeup of a Nevada necktie party. Hardly a gruesome detail is omitted. Where the pleading by the three innocent victims doubtlessly was exciting on the printed page, it becomes too raw-blooded for the screen. Chief fault is that the picture over-emphasizes the single hanging incident of the novel, and there's not enough other action.

Western opus follows the escapades of two cowboys, played by Henry Fonda and Henry Morgan, in town after a winter on the range. They are tossed into the turmoil of the usually quiet western community which is aroused by the report of a cattleman's slaying by rustlers. A buddy of the supposedly slain rancher stirs the pot-boiling, and a posse is formed to get the culprits and handle them 'western style'. Remainder of story concerns efforts of the few law-abiding gentry to halt the lynching.

Fonda measures up to star rating, as one of the few level-headed cowhands. His brief scene with Mary Beth Hughes, the flashy belle of the village, following her sudden marriage, is topflight. He helps hold together the loose ends of the rather patent plot.

□ 1943: Nomination: Best Picture

. . . .

■ OXFORD BLUES

1984, 93 MINS, UK/US ◇ ⓥ ⊙
Dir Robert Boris *Prod* Cassian Elwes, Elliott Kastner *Scr* Robert Boris *Ph* John Stanier *Ed* Patrick Moore *Mus* John DuPrez *Art Dir* Terry Pritchard
● Rob Lowe, Ally Sheedy, Amanda Pays, Julian Sands, Julian Firth, Alan Howard (Winkast/M-G-M)

At heart, *Oxford Blues* is really *Rocky Goes to College*. Though source material is M-G-M's 1938 Robert Taylor starrer, *A Yank at Oxford*, treatment is decidedly modern. Director-writer Robert Boris fails to establish a consistent tone to make his fairytale story believable.

In the original film, Lionel Barrymore bor-

rows the cash to send athlete son Taylor over to Oxford. In *Oxford Blues*, Lowe, a valet at the Dunes Hotel in Vegas, hustles the money at the crap table from a stake put up by an older woman (Gail Strickland) who picks him up. Nick's real reason for going to England is not to crew and certainly not for an education (students never seem to study in this film), but to chase his dreamgirl, aristocrat covergirl Lady Victoria (Amanda Pays). Climax proves the hero has the right stuff to get the girl. Only the girl turns out to be another American (Ally Sheedy). Must be a moral in there somewhere.

Lowe is suitably nasty as the streetwise Nick in a way that often passes for charm in films like this.

. . . .

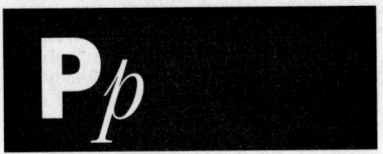

Pp

■ PACIFIC HEIGHTS

1990, 102 MINS, US ◇ ⓥ ⊙
Dir John Schlesinger *Prod* Scott Rudin, William
Sackheim *Scr* Daniel Pyne *Ph* Dennis E. Jones
Ed Mark Warner *Mus* Hans Zimmer *Art Dir* Neil
Spisak
● Melanie Griffith, Matthew Modine, Michael Keaton,
Mako, Nobu McCarthy, Laurie Metcalf (Morgan Creek)

The specter of a menace who invades one's
home turf and can't be ousted is universally
disturbing, and director John Schlesinger
goes all out to make this creepy thriller-
chiller as unsettling as it needs to be.

Story has babes-in-the-woods home buyers
Patty (Melanie Griffith) and Drake (Matthew
Modine) spending their every dime to restore
an 1883 Victorian house in San Francisco,
counting on the income from two downstairs
apartments to meet the mortgage.

A nice Asian couple takes the one-bedroom,
but the studio falls to reptilian Michael
Keaton, who smoothtalks Modine into handing over a key without money up front. After
he 'takes possession', it becomes clear they'll
never see a dollar from this unnerving man.
They encounter the shock of a legal system
that's always on the renter's side.

First-time film scripter Daniel Pyne sets up
a menacing cat-and-mouse game as sociopath
Keaton plays the system to his advantage, finally provoking Modine into attacking him so
he can go after his assets with a lawsuit. But
pic loses its grip when it tips over into psycho-
chiller territory.

Griffith lights up the screen as the kittenish
but in-control Patty who lets her instincts be
her guide when she takes off after Keaton on
a one-woman crusade for justice.

■ PACIFIC PALISADES

1990, 94 MINS, FRANCE ◇
Dir Bernard Schmitt *Prod* Bernard Verley, Lise Fayolle
Scr Marion Vernoux, Bernard Schmitt *Ph* Martial
Barrault *Ed* Gilbert Namiand *Mus* Jean-Jacques
Goldman, Roland Romanetti
● Sophie Marceau, Adam Coleman Howard, Anne
Curry, Virginia Capers, Toni Basil (BVF/Sandor)

Pacific Palisades is a transatlantic romance
bringing Sophie Marceau to America for a
change of climate (physical and emotional).
She's in for some surprises, but the audience
isn't. First feature by prize-winning vidclip
helmer Bernard Schmitt sinks into the tar
pits of culture shock cliches.

Marceau is a dissatisfied Parisian waitress
who heads for LA on a bum job offer and finds
herself living alone in a large modern suburban house. She's quickly exasperated and
bored. Then she gets involved with the
Canadian boyfriend (Adam Coleman
Howard) of a Yank actress she initially was to
have flown in with.

Despite the platitudes and plot inconsistencies, film is charmingly acted by Marceau in
her first (mostly) English-lingo role. Howard
is okay as the romantic interest whose idea of
a hot date is a group outing to a hockey game.

■ PACK, THE

1977, 99 MINS, US ◇ ⓥ
Dir Robert Clouse *Prod* Fred Weintraub, Paul Heller
Scr Robert Clouse *Ph* Ralph Woolsey *Ed* Peter E.
Berger *Mus* Lee Holdridge
● Joe Don Baker, Hope Alexander-Willis, Richard B.
Shull, R.G. Armstrong, Ned Wertimer, Bibi Besch (Warner)

The Pack is a well-made and discreetly violent
story of a pack of wild dogs menacing residents of a remote island.

The production, with Robert Clouse scripting Dave Fisher's novel and also directing,
stars Joe Don Baker as a marine biologist who
leads the humans' defense.

Strong story peg is habit of summer vacationers to abandon pets, but in this case, the
stranded mutts band together in ferocious attack on people.

Clouse's attention to lighting and shadow
adds an extra eerie feel to the proceedings.
Fast cutaways from dog attacks create an unseen horror that makes for more fear than explicit footage otherwise might have achieved.

Given the simplistic script demands, Baker
is very good. Hope Alexander-Willis, in film
debut, comes across okay.

■ PACKAGE, THE

1989, 108 MINS, US ◇ ⓥ ⊙
Dir Andrew Davis *Prod* Beverly J. Camhe *Scr* John
Bishop *Ph* Frank Tidy *Ed* Don Zimmerman, Billy Weber
Mus James Newton Howard *Art Dir* Michael Levesque
● Gene Hackman, Joanna Cassidy, Tommy Lee Jones,
John Heard, Dennis Franz, Pam Grier (Orion)

Smartly written, sharply played and directed
at a cracking pace that never sacrifices clarity
for speed, *The Package* is an enormously satisfying political thriller.

Poised and professional as ever, Gene
Hackman is perfectly cast as a career army
officer, escorting a troublesome soldier
(Tommy Lee Jones) Stateside to stand trial.
When this 'package' (the military term for
the person being delivered) takes a powder,
Hackman visits the man's estranged wife –
and soon realizes the package is posing as
someone he's not.

When the woman turns up murdered – and
Hackman's under house arrest for the killing
– the action really heats up. He turns to his
ex-wife (Joanna Cassidy), also an army officer. Soon she finds herself behind the eight
ball along with her ex.

The film's grand finale – in which various
forces are seen converging on a Chicago hotel
to either kill or prevent a killing – is very effective. You know exactly where each character is in relation to the other in this very
complex piece of staging.

In the brief but pivotal title role, Jones
shows it's possible to play an out-of-control
psychopath without turning into a gargoyle.
Cassidy is as smooth as ever.

■ PACK UP YOUR TROUBLES

1932, 70 MINS, US ⓥ
Dir George Marshall, Raymond McCarey *Prod* Hal
Roach *Scr* H.M. Walker *Ph* Art Lloyd *Ed* Richard
Currier
● Stan Laurel, Oliver Hardy, Donald Dillaway, Jacquie
Lyn, Mary Carr, James Finlayson (M-G-M)

Seventy minutes of slapstick is a tall order for
Laurel & Hardy and they hardly fill it. It's one
of those hokum war farces with the numbskull L&H jazzing up the army as hapless
rookies.

There's also a wartime buddy's girl baby
whom the well-meaning L&H endeavor to return to her grandparents, a Mr and Mrs
Smith. Trying to identify the Smiths through
the city directory constitutes a major portion
of that sort of pseudo-comedy.

One wonders why it wasn't kept to the confines of the usual twin-reeler as in the past.

■ PAD (AND HOW TO USE IT), THE

1966, 86 MINS, US ◇
Dir Brian G. Hutton *Prod* Ross Hunter *Scr* Thomas C.
Ryan, Ben Starr *Ph* Ellsworth Fredericks *Ed* Milton
Carruth *Mus* Russ Garcia *Art Dir* Alexander Golitzen

● Brian Bedford, Julie Sommars, James Farentino, Edy
Williams, Nick Navarro, Pearl Shear (Universal)

The Private Ear, which made up one half of the
Peter Shaffer play, *The Private Ear and the
Public Eye*, was a short but observant look at
loneliness and the aborted effort of one shy
male to communicate with the opposite sex.
Ross Hunter's screen adaptation, thanks almost entirely to Shaffer's original dialog and
the recreation by Brian Bedford of the shy
young man he played in the New York production, recaptures much of the humor, compassion and wisdom of the legit production.

While the setting has been switched from
an English flat to a Los Angeles rooming
house, there is, basically, little difference between the storyline of the play and the film.
Necessary expansion shows scenes only referred to in the play and adds a few extraneous characters. There is first rate playing by
Julie Sommars as the gauche girl he covets
and James Farentino as the Lothario friend
who wrecks the timid type's plans.

■ PAGE MISS GLORY

1935, 92 MINS, US
Dir Mervyn LeRoy *Prod* Robert Lord *Scr* Delmer
Daves, Robert Lord *Ph* George Folsey *Ed* William
Clemens *Mus* Leo F. Forbstein (dir.) *Art Dir* Robert
Haas
● Marion Davies, Pat O'Brien, Dick Powell, Mary Astor,
Frank McHugh, Patsy Kelly (Cosmopolitan/Warner)

Same deficiency as in the play [by Joseph
Schrank and Philip Dunning] occurs – the obvious. The farcical situations telegraph each
ensuing denouement yards ahead. But the
same fast and furious tempo, as in the play,
does much to offset this fault. It's really a
comedy Cinderella theme.

Marion Davies is the hotel chambermaid
who is catapulted into being 'Down Glory',
the mythical non-existent, composite beauty
who cops a contest. Pat O'Brien and Frank
McHugh are the broken-down promoters
(slang for chiselers, although harmless guys
in the main) who engineer the photographic
compo girl into a $2,500 cash prize and a flock
of offers.

When besieged by commercial sponsors for
endorsements and newspapermen for interviews, Davies unconsciously walks from the
metamorphosis from the femme de chambre
into the No. 1 US beaut. The farcical complications pile on with O'Brien (Chick Wiley)
extricating himself ingeniously with each
turn.

Davies does well by her generous comedy
opportunities. Dick Powell, as a goofy stunt
flyer, is well nigh wasted, virtually dragged in
for his 'Page Miss Glory' title song [by Harry
Warren and Al Dubin] duet with the star.

■ PAINTED VEIL, THE

1934, 83 MINS, US ⓥ
Dir Richard Boleslavski *Prod* Hunt Stromberg *Scr* John
Meehan, Salka Viertel, Edith Fitzgerald *Ph* William
Daniels *Ed* Hugh Wynn *Mus* Herbert Stothart
Art Dir Cedric Gibbons, Alexander Toluboff, Edwin B.
Willis
● Greta Garbo, Herbert Marshall, George Brent,
Warner Oland, Jean Hersholt, Beulah Bondi (M-G-M)

From almost any standpoint, *The Painted Veil*
is a bad picture. It's clumsy, dull and long-
winded. It's mostly the fault of the scripters.
Yarn is so confused in the telling as to be almost hopeless. It deviates considerably from
the original W. Somerset Maugham tale; that
wouldn't be so bad if well done, but it
emerges as neither film nor novel.

Yarn has Greta Garbo as the daughter of a
Viennese professor (Jean Hersholt). A doctor
in China (Herbert Marshall) comes a-visiting,
asks her to marry him and she does, largely,
it's indicated, because she wants to see

573

China. Once they get to China she sits down to a constant and dangerous routine of wearing cockeyed hats that are an absolute menace

She meets George Brent, who doesn't seem to mind the hats. He flatters her for a while, then manages to get in a kiss. Hubby Marshall finds out, so he goes into the interior of China to clear up a bad cholera plague and drags her along, the idea seemingly being that may be both of them will catch the disease and die.

Garbo is but fair, although she doesn't get much chance to emote. Acting honors really go to Marshall.

●●●●●●●●●●●●●●●●●●●●●●●●●●●●

■ PAINT YOUR WAGON

1969, 166 MINS, US ◇ ▼ ⊙
Dir Joshua Logan   *Prod* Alan Jay Lerner   *Scr* Alan Jay Lerner, Paddy Chayevsky   *Ph* William A. Fraker   *Ed* Robert Jones   *Mus* Nelson Riddle (arr.)   *Art Dir* John Truscott
● Lee Marvin, Clint Eastwood, Jean Seberg, Ray Walston, Harve Presnell, Tom Ligon (Paramount)

Paint Your Wagon is the tale of a gold mining town in California in the 1840s – before it became a state and before there were many 'good' women in the territory.

Main story centres around a menage a trois. Lee Marvin, his pardner Clint Eastwood, and Marvin's wife (Jean Seberg) are the trio.

Director Joshua Logan has captured best the vastness and beauty of the country; the loneliness of men in womenless societies.

What the $17 million-plus film (from the 1951 Lerner-Loewe Broadway musical) lacks in a skimpy story line it makes up in the music and expert choreography. There are no obvious 'musical numbers'. All the songs, save one or two, work neatly, quietly and well into the script. The actors used their own voices, which are pleasant enough and add to the note of authenticity.
□ 1969: Nomination: Best Adapted Music Score

●●●●●●●●●●●●●●●●●●●●●●●●●●●●

■ PAJAMA GAME, THE

1957, 101 MINS, US ◇ ▼ ⊙
Dir George Abbott, Stanley Donen   *Prod* George Abbott, Stanley Donen   *Scr* George Abbott, Richard Bissell   *Ph* Harry Stradling   *Ed* William Ziegler   *Mus* Nelson Riddle, Buddy Bregman (arr.)   *Art Dir* Malcolm Bert
● Doris Day, John Raitt, Carol Haney, Eddie Foy Jr, Reta Shaw, Barbara Nichols (Warner)

The inherent mobility and fluidity of *Pajama Game* as a stage property was such that this almost faithful transmutation into celluloid required little physical enhancement [of the Richard Adler-Jerry Ross 1954 musical]. But the filmmakers have not slighted the opportunities for size and scope when occasion warranted.

If the film version contains a shade more of social significance in the labor-engagement hassle, which was the springboard of the original Richard Bissell novel, *7-1/2 Cents*, from which stems the romantic conflict between pajama factory superintendent John Raitt (who created the original stage role) and 'grievance committee chairman' Doris Day, it is a plus value because of the sturdy book.

Raitt is properly serious as the earnest factory executive and earnestly smitten with the blonde and beauteous Day. Day, always authoritative with a song, makes her chore even a shade more believable than Raitt. Carol Haney, recreating her soubret role opposite Eddie Foy Jr (also of the original stage cast), whams with 'Steam Heat', aided by Buzz Miller (stage original) and Kenneth LeRoy (substituting for Peter Gennaro of the Broadway cast).

●●●●●●●●●●●●●●●●●●●●●●●●●●●●

■ PAJAMA PARTY

1964, 82 MINS, US ◇ ▼
Dir Don Weis   *Prod* James H. Nicholson, Samuel Z. Arkoff, Anthony Carras   *Scr* Louis M. Heyward   *Ph* Floyd Crosby   *Ed* Fred Feitshans, Eve Newman   *Mus* Les Baxter   *Art Dir* Daniel Haller
● Tommy Kirk, Annette Funicello, Elsa Lanchester, Jody McCrea, Buster Keaton, Dorothy Lamour (American International)

Exuberance of youth guns the action which twirls around a personable young Martian – Tommy Kirk – arriving on earth to pave the way for an invasion. He lands during a swimming party tossed by an eccentric wealthy widow (Elsa Lanchester), and immediately falls for Annette Funicello, girl-friend of widow's lug nephew (Jody McCrea).

Funicello displays an engaging presence and registers solidly. Kirk likewise shows class and Lanchester projects a rather zany character nicely, McCrea hams it up the way he should for such a part. Buster Keaton, playing an Indian, and Dorothy Lamour, dress store manager, sock over their roles.

●●●●●●●●●●●●●●●●●●●●●●●●●●●●

■ PALEFACE, THE

1948, 91 MINS, US ◇ ▼ ⊙
Dir Norman Z. McLeod   *Prod* Robert L. Welch   *Scr* Edmund Hartmann, Frank Tashlin, Jack Rose   *Ph* Ray Rennahan   *Ed* Ellsworth Hoagland   *Mus* Victor Young   *Art Dir* Hans Dreier, Earl Hedrick
● Bob Hope, Jane Russell, Robert Armstrong, Iris Adrian, Robert Watson (Paramount)

The Paleface is a smart-aleck travesty on the west, told with considerable humor and bright gags. Bob Hope has been turned loose on a good script.

Hope isn't all the film has to sell. There's Jane Russell as Calamity Jane, that rough, tough gal of the open west whose work as a government agent causes Hope's troubles, but whose guns save him from harm and give him his hero reputation. She makes an able sparring partner for the Hope antics, and is a sharp eyeful in Technicolor.

'Buttons and Bows' is top tune of the score's three pop numbers. Jay Livingston and Ray Evans cleffed and Hope renders as a plaintive love chant to Russell.

Script poses an amusing story idea – Hope as a correspondence school dentist touring the west in a covered wagon. He's having his troubles, but they're nothing compared to the grief that catches up with him when Calamity Jane seduces him into marriage so she can break up a gang smuggling rifles to the Indians.
□ 1948: Best Song ('Buttons and Bows')

●●●●●●●●●●●●●●●●●●●●●●●●●●●●

■ PALE RIDER

1985, 115 MINS, US ▼ ⊙
Dir Clint Eastwood   *Prod* Clint Eastwood   *Scr* Michael Butler, Dennis Shryack   *Ph* Bruce Surtees   *Ed* Joel Cox   *Mus* Lennie Niehaus   *Art Dir* Edward Carfagno
● Clint Eastwood, Michael Moriarty, Carrie Snodgress, Christopher Penn, Richard Dysart, Richard Kiel (Malpaso/ Warner)

As he did in his Sergio Leone trilogy, Clint Eastwood portrays a nameless drifter, here called 'Preacher', who descends into the middle of a struggle between some poor, independent gold prospectors and a big company intent upon raping the beautiful land for all it's worth.

Borrowing from *Shane*, 'Preacher', so dubbed because he initially appears wearing a clerical collar, moves in with a group consisting of earnest Michael Moriarty, his somewhat reluctant lady friend Carrie Snodgress and her pubescent daughter Sydney Penny.

Preach pulls the threatened community together and inspires them to fight for their

rights to the land rather than give up.

It's all been seen before, but Eastwood serves it up with authority, fine craftsmanship and a frequent sense of fun. This film is graced not only by an excellent visual look and confident storytelling, but by a few fine performances, led by Eastwood's own.

●●●●●●●●●●●●●●●●●●●●●●●●●●●●

■ PAL JOEY

1957, 112 MINS, US ◇ ▼ ⊙
Dir George Sidney   *Prod* Fred Kohlmar   *Scr* Dorothy Kingsley   *Ph* Harold Lipstein   *Ed* Viola Lawrence, Jerome Thoms   *Mus* Morris Stoloff (sup.)   *Art Dir* Walter Holscher
● Rita Hayworth, Frank Sinatra, Kim Novak, Barbara Nichols, Bobby Sherwood, Hank Henry (Columbia)

Pal Joey is a strong, funny entertainment. Dorothy Kingsley's screenplay, from John O'Hara's book, is skillful rewriting, with colorful characters and solid story built around the Richard Rodgers and Lorenz Hart songs. Total of 14 tunes are intertwined with the plot, 10 of them being reprised from the original. Others by the same team of cleffers are 'I Didn't Know What Time It Was', 'The Lady Is a Tramp', 'There's a Small Hotel' and 'Funny Valentine'.

Kingsley pulled some switches in shaping the [1940] legiter for the screen. Given a buildup to star status is the chorine from Albuquerque who becomes Joey's prey; Rita Hayworth (in the Vivienne Segal role) does the 'Zip' number that had been done by the herein-eliminated newspaper gal. There's not much terping, and the finale is happy ending stuff.

Frank Sinatra is potent. He's almost ideal as the irreverent, free-wheeling, glib Joey, delivering the rapid-fire cracks in a fashion that wrings out the full deeper-than-pale blue comedy potentials. Point might be made, though, that it's hard to figure why all the mice fall for this rat. Kim Novak is one of the mice (term refers to the nitery gals) and rates high as ever in the looks department but her turn is pallid in contrast with the forceful job done by Sinatra.

Hayworth, no longer the ingenue, moves with authority as Joey's sponsor and does the 'Zip' song visuals in such fiery, amusing style as to rate an encore. Standout of the score is 'Lady Is a Tramp'. It's a wham arrangement and Sinatra gives it powerhouse delivery.
□ 1957: Nominations: Best Costume Design, Art Direction, Editing, Sound Recording

●●●●●●●●●●●●●●●●●●●●●●●●●●●●

■ PALM BEACH STORY, THE

1942, 96 MINS, US ▼ ⊙
Dir Preston Sturges   *Prod* Paul Jones   *Scr* Preston Sturges   *Ph* Victor Milner   *Ed* Stuart Gilmore   *Mus* Victor Young   *Art Dir* Hans Dreier, Ernst Fegte
● Claudette Colbert, Joel McCrea, Mary Astor, Rudy Vallee, William Demarest, Sig Arno (Paramount)

This Prestton Sturges production is packed with delightful absurdities. Claudette Colbert comes through with one of her best light comedy interpretations. She's strikingly youthful and alluring as the slightly screwball wife of five years standing, who, after seeing husband Joel McCrea out of debt, suddenly decides to seek a divorce, adventure and a bankroll for the husband she leaves behind.

Tongue-in-cheek spoofing of the idle rich attains hilarious proportions in scenes where Rudy Vallee, as John D. Hackensacker the Third, proposes to the errant wife and later woos her by singing to her to the accompaniment of a privately hired symphony orch big enough to fill the Radio City Music Hall pit.

McCrea plays it straight, for the most part, as the husband intent on winning his wife back.

●●●●●●●●●●●●●●●●●●●●●●●●●●●●

P

PANDORA AND THE FLYING DUTCHMAN

1951, 122 MINS, UK ◇

Dir Albert Lewin *Prod* Albert Lewin *Scr* Albert Lewin
Ph Jack Cardiff *Ed* Ralph Kemplen *Mus* Alan
Rawsthorne *Art Dir* John Bryan
● James Mason, Ava Gardner, Nigel Patrick, Sheila
Sim, Marius Goring, Mario Cabre (Kaufman/Lewin)

Albert Lewin produced, directed and did the
story and script, keeping this film on an
almost unrelieved level of sombre
depression.

Lewin set his story in 1930 and filmed it on
the coast of Spain. He gets into it with a
flashback to explain the bodies of a man and
woman found by fishermen off the coast.

Thanks to the pesence of James Mason, the
film has at least one distinctive histrionic
touch. He plays the Dutchman of the title, a
sea captain who, back in the 17th century,
had been condemned to sail the oceans of the
world until he found a woman willing to die
for love. When this miracle occurs, his soul
can find salvation.

Ava Gardner fares less distinctively as the
girl who falls in love with this restless shade
during one of the occasional brief periods allotted him to take on human form. Standout
quality of the production is Jack Cardiff's
color photography.

PANIC IN NEEDLE PARK, THE

1971, 110 MINS, US ◇ ⓥ

Dir Jerry Schatzberg *Prod* Dominick Dunne *Scr* Joan
Didion, John Gregory Dunne *Ph* Adam Holender
Ed Evan Lottman *Art Dir* Murray P. Stern
● Al Pacino, Kitty Winn, Alan Vint, Richard Bright, Kiel
Martin, Michael McClanathan (20th Century-Fox)

The Panic in Needle Park is a total triumph.
Gritty, gutsy, compelling, and vivid to the
point of revulsion, it is an overpowering
tragedy about urban drug addiction. Director
Jerry Schatzberg in only his second film becomes a major talent, while Al Pacino and
Kitty Winn are terrific as a heroin-doomed
couple.

Dominick Dunne produced on the streets of
NY a drama so real that the persons and situations seem to have been caught in a documentary. James Mills' novel has been
superbly adapted. The dialog is raw and uncompromising, yet artistic in its tragic-sar-
donic-ironic context.

Winn, introduced as a post-abortion discard
of artist Raul Julia, takes up with Pacino, a
drug pusher whose pretense of non-addiction
soon fades away. She learns, and fast, the
ropes of a strung-out world filled with young
derelicts who steal, love, cheat, befriend and
betray. This world is a jungle, ruled by instinctive addiction and passion, and it's just
around everyone's corner now.

Pacino, after a brief mannered introduction, settles into his key role with terribly effective results. Winn is smash.

PANIC IN THE CITY

1968, 96 MINS, US ◇

Dir Eddie Davis *Prod* Earle Lyon *Scr* Eddie Davis,
Charles E. Savage *Ph* Alan Stensvold *Ed* Terrell O.
Morse *Mus* Paul Dunlap *Art Dir* Paul Sylos Jr
● Howard Duff, Linda Cristal, Stephen McNally,
Nehemiah Persoff, Anne Jeffries, Oscar Beregi (United)

Panic in the City posits that a Communist operative in the US, acting independently of his
Russian superiors, should be able to collect
the material to construct an atomic bomb in
Los Angeles. The panic of the title – there is
talk of evacuating the city – never really happens thanks to the ingenious efforts of
Howard Duff, an agent of the 'National'
Bureau of Investigation.

It's all done perfunctorily and without any
real distinction, but the low budget, necessi-

tating real locations, makes possible the use
of a great deal of LA.

Nehemiah Persoff rather hysterically portrays the Commie fanatic, while Anne
Jeffreys is his accomplice.

There are some sparks from Oscar Beregi's
Czech scientist who assembles the bomb.
Motorcycle vet Dennis Hooper has brief role
of a murderer.

Development of the story is workmanlike
enough, but disbelief sets in after Persoff
goes batty by disobeying his superiors and deciding to explode the bomb.

PANIC IN THE STREETS

1950, 92 MINS, US ⓥ

Dir Elia Kazan *Prod* Sol C. Siegel *Scr* Richard Murphy
Ph Joe MacDonald *Ed* Harmon Jones *Mus* Alfred
Newman *Art Dir* Lyle Wheeler, Maurice Ransford
● Richard Widmark, Paul Douglas, Barbara Bel Geddes,
Jack Palance, Zero Mostel (20th Century-Fox)

This is an above-average chase meller.
Tightly scripted and directed, it concerns the
successful attempts to capture a couple of
criminals, who are germ carriers, in order to
prevent a plague and panic in a large city.
The plague angle is somewhat incidental to
the cops-and-bandits theme.

Story [by Edna and Edward Anhalt, adapted
by Daniel Fuchs] opens harshly with three
thieves stalking a man for his money and
killing him to obtain it. The man has just arrived in New Orleans illegally and is suffering
from a bubonic plague. His murderers, unknown to themselves, pick it up from him.
The plot then concerns the efforts of the police, prodded by an alert Health Service officer, to locate and capture the slayers.

There is vivid action, nice human touches
and some bizarre moments. Jack Palance
gives a sharp performance.
☐ 1950: Best Motion Picture Story

PANIC IN YEAR ZERO

1962, 92 MINS, US

Dir Ray Milland *Prod* Lou Rusoff, Arnold Houghland
Scr Jay Simms, John Morton *Ph* Gil Warrenton
Ed William Austin *Mus* Les Baxter *Art Dir* Daniel
Haller
● Ray Milland, Jean Hagen, Frankie Avalon, Mary
Mitchel, Joan Freeman (American-International)

The aftermath of a nuclear attack is the subject pursued by this serious, sobering and engrossing film. The screenplay advances the
theory that, in the event of a sudden wholesale outbreak of nuclear warfare, civilization
will swiftly deteriorate into a decentralized
society of individual units, each necessarily
hostile in relations with all others as part of a
desperate struggle for self-preservation.

A family unit of four – father, mother and
two teenaged children – is followed here in
the wake of an series of initial nuclear blasts
destroying Los Angeles and four other major
US cities (excluding Washington – a rather
astonishing oversight on the part of the unspecified enemy). The family is followed to an
isolated cave in the hills where, thanks to the
father's negative ingenuity, it remains until it
is safe to come out.

Ray Milland manages capably in the dual
task of director and star (he's the resourceful
father), but it's safe to observe that he'd
probably have done twice as well by halving
his assignment, one way or the other.

PAPER CHASE, THE

1973, 111 MINS, US ◇ ⓥ ⊙

Dir James Bridges *Prod* Robert C. Thompson, Rodrick
Paul *Scr* James Bridges *Ph* Gordon Willis *Ed* Walter
Thompson *Mus* John Williams *Art Dir* George Jenkins
● Timothy Bottoms, Lindsay Wagner, John Houseman,
Graham Beckel, Edward Herrmann (20th Century-Fox)

The Paper Chase has some great performances,
literate screenwriting, sensitive direction and
handsome production.

The tale of a young law school student, confused by his professional calling vs his inner
evolution as a human being, seems timeless
yet dated, too narrowly defined for broad audience empathy, and too often a series of
sideways moving (though entertaining) thespian declamations.

James Bridges directs his own adaptation of
the novel by John Jay Osborn Jr. Timothy
Bottoms is excellent as the puzzled law student, Lindsay Wagner is very good as his girl,
and John Houseman, the veteran legit and
film producer-director-writer, is outstanding
as a hard-nosed but urbane law professor.

The three players constitute the pervading
plot triangle – Houseman the classroom dictator, Bottoms the uncertain supplicant, and
Wagner, who plays Houseman's daughter.
☐ 1973: Best Supp. Actor (John Houseman).
☐ Nominations: Best Adapted Screenplay,
Sound

PAPER HEARTS

1993, 90 MINS, US ◇ ⓥ ⊙

Dir Rod McCall *Prod* Rod McCall, Catherine Wanek
Scr Rod McCall *Ph* Barry Markowitz *Ed* Curtis Edge
Mus George S. Clinton *Art Dir* Susan Brand
● Sally Kirkland, James Brolin, Pamela Gidley, Kris
Kristofferson, Laura Johnson, Michael Moore (King-
Moonstone)

A feminist streak informs Rod McCall's directorial feature debut *Paper Hearts*, a modest,
sensitive and often touching family drama
that poignantly dissects the effects of a dissolving marriage.

Sally Kirkland stars as Jenny Stevenson, an
attractive, middle-aged woman separated
from her scoundrel womanizer of a husband,
Henry (James Brolin), who left her a mountain of debts. Jenny tries to hold onto the
house she inherited, now on the verge of foreclosure.

The family's disparate members reunite for
one stormy and fateful weekend, during
which Kirkland's youngest daughter (Renee
Estevez) gets married. Brolin is actually
scheming to get the house. The oldest daughter (Pamela Gidley), a music student in New
York, also shows up.

McCall acquits himself better as writer
than as director, endowing his story with a coherent female point of view. The moody, often somber film consists of brief scenes,
usually confrontations between two characters. Regrettably, the big climactic scene is
overly melodramatic.

PAPERHOUSE

1989, 92 MINS, UK ◇ ⓥ ⊙

Dir Bernard Rose *Prod* Sarah Radclyffe, Tim Bevan
Scr Matthew Jacobs *Ph* Mike Southon *Ed* Dan Rae
Mus Hans Zimmer, Stanley Myers *Art Dir* Frank Walsh,
Ann Tilby
● Charlotte Burke, Ben Cross, Glenne Headly, Elliott
Spears, Gemma Jones, Sarah Newbold (Working Title)

Paperhouse is the thinking person's *A Nightmare
on Elm Street*. A riveting fantasy film, centering on the vivid dreams and nightmares of an
11-year-old girl [from Catherine Starr's
novel], it heralds a new director of talent in
Bernard Rose.

Anna (Charlotte Burke), psychologically
disturbed, perhaps because of the frequent
long absences from home of her beloved father (Ben Cross), has become a discipline
problem at school via her bossy, unappealing
ways. While undergoing minor punishment,
she faints and finds herself by a strange house
on a cliff-top, a house similar to one she'd
earlier drawn on paper.

Gradually, she discovers that as she embellishes the drawing, she can enter the house in her dreams. Between her dreams, Anna discovers her kindly doctor (Gemma Jones) is treating a dying boy who seems to be identical to a boy in the house.

There's no violence in this film, but there's considerable suspense and tension. Crucial to the film's success is a superb soundtrack, with a strong music score, but also heightened sound effects of great impact.

■ PAPER MARRIAGE

1993, 84 MINS, UK/POLAND ◇ ⊙
Dir Krzysztof Lang *Prod* Mark Forstater, Raymond Day
Scr Krzysztof Lang, Marek Kreutz, Debbie Horsfield, Lise Mayer *Ph* Grzegorz Kediersky *Ed* Elzbieta Kurkowski
Mus Stanislas Syrewicz *Art Dir* Allan Starski
● Gary Kemp, Joanna Trepechinska, Rita Tushingham, Richard Hawley, David Horovitch, William Ilkley (Forstater/Zodiak)

Paper Marriage is an amiable enough variation on the *Green Card* template given more charm than the script deserves by leads Gary Kemp *The Krays* and Polish thesp Joanna Trepechinska.

Story opens in Warsaw, where beautiful young Pole Alicja (Trepechinska) is fixing her entry visa to Blighty in hope of marrying a young doc (Martin McKellen) she's fallen for. Arriving in Newcastle, northern England, she's rapidly dumped and arranges a marriage of convenience with small-time crook Aiden (Kemp), who needs the cash to pay off some hoods he's on the run from.

The movie takes a while to get going, with the inevitable sack scene (handled, in the event, with delicacy and some originality) almost an hour in. The pair (Trepechinska holding her own in English) bond well on screen when the script gives them a chance, and there's an off-the-wall perf by Rita Tushingham as Trepechinska's landlady.

Interiors, mostly shot in Poland, blend seamlessly with Newcastle exteriors, which are often given a fresh look.

■ PAPER MASK

1990, 118 MINS, UK ◇ ⊛ ⊙
Dir Christopher Morahan *Prod* Christopher Morahan
Scr John Collee *Ph* Nat Crosby *Ed* Peter Coulson
Mus Richard Harvey *Art Dir* Caroline Hanania
● Paul McGann, Amanda Donohoe, Frederick Treves, Tom Wilkinson, Barbara Leigh-Hunt, Jimmy Yuill (Film Four/Granada/British Screen)

Christopher Morahan's taut suspense thriller, from John Collee's novel about a young man who gets away with posing as an emergency room doctor in a British hospital, raises provocative questions about human pretense and the ruses of professional survival.

Pic focuses on a dissatisfied hospital worker, Matthew (Paul McGann), who seizes the chance to assume the identity of a promising young doctor after the other man dies in a car crash and his papers fall into Matthew's hands. Befriended by a competent and sympathetic nurse (Amanda Donohoe), he survives day by day. But the stakes are dramatically raised when he accidentally kills a doctor's wife with an overdose of anesthesia. To his astonishment, the hospital protects him, and in turn, itself.

Highly entertaining as a thriller-chiller, film is equally engrossing on a psychological level as it is always some aspect of the typically self-absorbed beings surrounding him that allows Matthew to pull off his deception.

■ PAPER MOON

1973, 101 MINS, US ⊛ ⊙
Dir Peter Bogdanovich *Prod* Peter Bogdanovich
Scr Alvin Sargent *Ph* Laszlo Kovacs *Ed* Verna Fields
Art Dir Polly Platt

● Ryan O'Neal, Tatum O'Neal, Madeline Kahn, John Hillerman, P.J. Johnson, Randy Quaid (Directors/Paramount/Saticoy)

Ryan O'Neal stars as a likeable con artist in the Depression midwest, and his real-life daughter, Tatum O'Neal, is outstanding as his nine-year-old partner in flim-flam. Joe David Brown's novel, *Addie Pray*, was the basis for Alvin Sargent's adaptation.

O'Neal arrives late at the funeral of a woman who was, or wasn't (as he claims), his wife, who has left a child of undetermined parentage but most determined character. Figuring to promote some fast money from locals for the kid, O'Neal finds the child more than adept in the shifty arts of selling Bibles to widows. Locked in uneasy but increasingly affectionate partnership, the O'Neals wend their way through the Kansas-Missouri farmlands.

Prominent among the large cast is Madeline Kahn, excellent as a carny stripper who captivates Ryan O'Neal. Tatum O'Neal makes a sensational screen debut.
□ 1973: Best Supp. Actress (Tatum O'Neal).
□ Nominations: Best Supp. Actress (Madeline Kahn), Adapted Screenplay, Sound

■ PAPER TIGER

1975, 101 MINS, UK ◇ ⊛
Dir Ken Annakin *Prod* Euan Lloyd *Scr* Jack Davies
Ph John Cabrera *Ed* Alan Pattillo *Mus* Roy Budd
Art Dir Herbert Smith
● David Niven, Toshiro Mifune, Hardy Kruger, Ando, Jeff Corey, Irene Tsu (Shalako/Maclean)

Paper Tiger recalls the plots of vintage Shirley Temple vehicles in its cutesy relationship between English tutor David Niven and an 11-year-old Japanese moppet (Ando), kidnapped together during turmoil in [Kulagong, a fictitious] Southeast Asian country.

Ando, like Temple, is dimpled, plucky, clever, and more resourceful than any of the adults in the story. He has a fresh, engaging personality, and it isn't his fault the camera moons over him at every opportunity.

Niven tries hard to breathe subtlety into his coward-turned-hero role, but is impeded by the lame screenplay and plodding direction. Toshiro Mifune, playing Ando's ambassador father, acts like his mind is elsewhere.

■ PAPILLON

1973, 150 MINS, US ◇ ⊛ ⊙
Dir Franklin J. Schaffner *Prod* Robert Dorfmann, Franklin J. Schaffner *Scr* Dalton Trumbo, Lorenzo Semple Jr *Ph* Fred Koenekamp *Ed* Robert Swink
Mus Jerry Goldsmith *Art Dir* Anthony Masters
● Steve McQueen, Dustin Hoffman, Victor Jory, Don Gordon, Anthony Zerbe, Robert Deman (Allied Artists)

Henri Charriere's story of confinement in, and escape from, the infamous French Guiana prison colony was that of an ordeal. So is Franklin J. Schaffner's film version. For 150 uninterrupted minutes, the mood is one of despair, brutality, and little hope.

The script is very good within its limitations, but there is insufficient identification with the main characters. Steve McQueen, for example, says he has been framed for murdering a pimp; we do not see the injustice occur, hence have insufficient empathy.

Dustin Hoffman plays an urbane counterfeiter, a white collar criminal whose guilt is beyond question. Hoffman does an excellent job in portraying his character's adaptation to the corruptibilities of prison life.

The film begins with co-adaptor Dalton Trumbo (in an unbilled bit) addressing the latest shipload of prisoners consigned to the South American jungle horrors. He informs them they are henceforth nonhuman baggage. The oppressive atmosphere is so absolutely established within the first hour of

the film that, in a sense, it has nowhere to go for the rest of the time.

The $13 million film was shot mostly in Spain and in Jamaica.
□ 1973: Nomination: Best Original Score

■ PARADINE CASE, THE

1947, 131 MINS, US ⊛
Dir Alfred Hitchcock *Prod* David O. Selznick
Scr David O. Selznick *Ph* Lee Garmes *Ed* Hal C. Kern
Mus Franz Waxman *Art Dir* J. McMillan Johnson
● Gregory Peck, Ann Todd, Charles Laughton, Charles Coburn, Louis Jourdan, Alida Valli (RKO/Selznick)

The Paradine Case offers two hours and 11 minutes of high dramatics.

Plot concerns murder of a blind man by his wife so she can marry her lover. Her attorney, believing in her not guilty plea, fights for her life. Himself infatuated with his client, the barrister plots and schemes to defeat justice but as dramatic events are brought out the truth is revealed. There are no flashback devices to clutter the trial and the audience gradually is let in on the facts as is the court as the hearing proceeds and emotions take hold. Charles Laughton gives a revealing portrait of a gross, lustful nobleman who presides at the trial.

Alfred Hitchcock's penchant for suspense, unusual atmosphere and development get full play. There is a deliberateness of pace, artful pauses and other carefully calculated melodramatic hinges upon which he swings the story and players. Selznick wrote the screenplay, adapted from the Robert Hichens novel by Alma Reville and James Bridie. It is a job that puts much emphasis on dialog and it's talk that punches. A very mobile camera helps give a feeling of movement to majority of scenes confined to the British courtroom as Hitchcock goes into the unfoldment of the highly dramatic murder trial.

Gregory Peck's stature as a performer of ability stands him in good stead among the extremely tough competition. As the barrister who defends Alida Valli, charged with the murder of her husband, he answers every demand of a demanding role. Ann Todd delights as his wife, giving the assignment a grace and understanding that tug at the emotions.
□ 1947: Nomination: Best Supp. Actress (Ethel Barrymore)

■ PARADISE

1991, 110 MINS, US ◇ ⊛ ⊙
Dir Mary Agnes Donoghue *Prod* Scott Kroopf, Patrick Palmer *Scr* Mary Agnes Donoghue *Ph* Jerzy Zielinski
Ed Eva Gardos, Debra McDermott *Mus* David Newman
Art Dir Evelyn Sakash, Marcia Hinds
● Melanie Griffith, Don Johnson, Elijah Wood, Thora Birch, Sheila McCarthy, Louise Latham (Touchstone)

Writer Mary Agnes Donoghue debuts as a film director with her careful adaptation of a 1987 French drama *Le grand chemin* [written and directed by Jean-Loup Hubert]. Story focuses on 10-year-old Elijah Wood, sent by his pregnant mom (Eve Gordon) to spend a school vacation in the sleepy town of Paradise. Melanie Griffith and husband Don Johnson, who are mysteriously cold to each other, take care of the boy. There's a third reel revelation that the death of their three-year-old son in 1987 has driven a wedge between them.

The boy is befriended by nine-year-old Thora Birch, and film gently follows their pranks and adventures in an idyllic natural setting. Duo have in common the absence of a father; Wood's is supposedly away at sea while Birch's is a roller-skating instructor in a nearby town.

Donoghue shows impressive self-assurance

for a first-time helmer in not rushing the pace or overdoing the maudlin elements of this material. Birch is irresistible as the wise little girl, whose gestures and body language are a treat throughout the picture. Wood underplays and is very natural.

Johnson and Griffith co-star for the first time with effective overtones of a longstanding off-screen relationship (married twice). Both are deglamorized for their character roles and are convincing as a rustic, unsophisticated couple.

. . . .

■ **PARADISE ALLEY**

1978, 107 MINS, US ◇ ⑦ ⊙

Dir Sylvester Stallone *Prod* John F. Roach, Ronald A. Suppa *Scr* Sylvester Stallone *Ph* Laszlo Kovacs *Ed* Eve Newman *Mus* Bill Conti *Art Dir* John W. Corso
● Sylvester Stallone, Kevin Conway, Anne Archer, Armand Assante, Lee Canalito, Tom Waits (Force Ten/Universal)

Paradise Alley is *Rocky* rewritten by Damon Runyon. Set in New York's Hell's Kitchen area during the 1940s, it tells the uplifting tale of three brothers, played by Sylvester Stallone, Armand Assante, and Lee Canalito, and how they literally wrestle their way out of the ghetto.

It's an upbeat, funny, nostalgic film populated by colorful characters, memorable more for their individual moments than for their parts in the larger story.

Stallone proves a number of points with this film. First that he's a very capable director with a keen eye for casting. Second, he has a charming comic presence.

Paradise Alley shows off, once again, Stallone's ability as a writer. His sense of plot is old-fashioned – but it's also very commercial. The basic element is a hopeful loser who wants desperately to be a winner and triumphs.

The plot of this film is almost a throwaway. Three brothers, a dumb, beefy ice man (Canalito), a bitter crippled war veteran (Assante) and Stallone, the conman, all want to escape the slums. Stallone decides that Canalito's muscles in a wrestling ring are their ticket uptown.

. . . .

■ **PARADISE, HAWAIIAN STYLE**

1966, 87 MINS, US ◇ ⑦

Dir Michael Moore *Prod* Hal Wallis *Scr* Allan Weiss, Anthony Lawrence *Ph* W. Wallace Kelley *Ed* Warren Low *Mus* Joseph J. Lilley *Art Dir* Hal Pereira, Walter Tyler
● Elvis Presley, Suzanna Leigh, James Shigeta, Donna Butterworth, Marianna Hill, Irene Tsu (Paramount)

Hal Wallis, who first brought Elvis Presley to the screen in 1956 and once before locationed in Hawaii (*Blue Hawaii*, 1961), returns singer to the island state in this gaily-begarbed and flowing musical.

Light script by Allan Weiss and Anthony Lawrence, based on former's original, serves more as a showcase for Presley's wares than as plottage but suffices to sock over the Presley lure. Star plays an airplane pilot with girl trouble, who loses one job after another when he becomes innocently embroiled. His troubles continue after he and James Shigeta team up for inter-island ferrying, with usual romanantic entanglements, fights and outbursts of song.

Michael Moore, making his directional bow after seven years with Wallis as an assistant, maintains a breezy pace and manages good performances from his cast.

. . . .

■ **PARADISE LAGOON**
See: The Admirable Crichton

. . . .

■ **PARALLAX VIEW, THE**

1974, 102 MINS, US ◇ ⑦

Dir Alan J. Pakula *Prod* Alan J. Pakula *Scr* David Giler, Lorenzo Semple Jr *Ph* Gordon Willis *Ed* John W. Wheeler *Mus* Michael Small *Art Dir* George Jenkins
● Warren Beatty, Hume Cronyn, William Daniels, Paula Prentiss, Anthony Zerbe, Kenneth Mars (Paramount)

The Parallax View is a partially-successful attempt to take a serious subject – a nationwide network of political guns for hire – and make it commercially palatable to the popcorn trade – via chases, fights, and lots of exterior production elements.

The adaptation of Loren Singer's novel follows newshawk Warren Beatty in his discovery of an assassination complex involving a security organization (called the Parallax Corp) which deliberately seeks out social misfits, dispatched by clients to murder political figures of various persuasions.

The story begins with the murder of Senator Bill Joyce, followed by the official investigation, after which many witnesses begin to die.

Paula Prentiss, very good as a prototype TV newshen, finally gets Beatty's interest aroused before her mysterious death.

Pakula's production and direction are lavish in physical details.

. . . .

■ **PARAMOUNT ON PARADE**

1930, 101 MINS, US ◇

Dir Dorothy Arzner, Victor Heerman, Ernst Lubitsch, Edward Sutherland, Otto Brower, Edwin H. Knopf, Lothar Mendes, Edmund Goulding, Rowland V. Lee, Victor Schertzinger, Frank Tuttle *Ph* Harry Fishbeck, Victor Milner *Ed* Merrill White *Art Dir* John Wenger
● Maurice Chevalier, Jean Arthur, Gary Cooper, Clara Bow, Jack Oakie, George Bancroft (Paramount)

Paramount on Parade links together with almost incredible smoothness achievements from the smallest technical detail to the greatest artistic endeavor. Interspersed throughout the 20 numbers are 11 songs, the work of 13 writers. Technicolor is used in seven of the numbers.

In color, setting and gracefulness of players and direction, the 'Dream Girl' number is outstanding.

But even with all the competition Maurice Chevalier comes through in first place. He is featured in three numbers and in two of these renders the song hits of the production. 'Sweeping the Clouds Away' is sung by him. Before this Chevalier appears in a sketch called 'A Park in Paris' which presents him as a gendarme among springtime activities.

Jack Oakie and Zelma O'Neal do a tapping special, in a gym. Clara Bow, in sailor garb, does her regular on the navy.

. . . .

■ **PARANOIAC**

1963, 80 MINS, UK

Dir Freddie Francis *Prod* Anthony Hinds *Scr* Jimmy Sangster *Ph* Arthur Grant *Ed* James Needs *Mus* Elizabeth Lutyens *Art Dir* Bernard Robinson
● Janette Scott, Oliver Reed, Liliane Brousse, Alexander Davion, Maurice Denham (Hammer)

Paranoiac marks the directorial debut of Freddie Francis, British cameraman. Lack of experience proves no handicap for Francis, however, as he sculpts a suspenseful and smartly-paced opus out of Jimmy Sangster's effective screenplay.

Plot is a reworking of the imposter-heir swindle bit in which someone poses as a long-lost member of a family who just happens to turn up in time to claim a tidy inheritance. The phoney is impersonating a young man believed by members of his family to have committed suicide when a boy, following the death of his parents. His sister deeply misses him but his brother wouldn't mind it at all if

the sister vanished too so he could have all the loot for himself. In fact he tries to convince his sister and their aunt that she's nuts so they'll pack her off and leave him with the inheritance all to himself.

Oliver Reed plays the scheming brother with demonic skill, blending bits of spoiled brat and sneaky madman for a menacing portrayal. Janette Scott is pretty and disarming as the sister and emotes credibly. Alexander Davion makes a fine baddie-turned-hero, thesping with ease and believability.

. . . .

■ **PARASITE**

1982, 85 MINS, US ◇ ⑦

Dir Charles Band *Prod* Charles Band *Scr* Alan Adler, Michael Shoob, Frank Levering *Ph* Mac Ahlberg *Ed* Brad Arensman *Mus* Richard Band *Art Dir* Pamela Warner
● Robert Glaudini, Demi Moore, Luca Bercovici, James Davidson, Al Fann, Vivian Blaine (Embassy)

Parasite is a low-budget monster film which utilizes the 3-D process to amplify its shock effects.

Set in 1992, tale has a skimpy sci-fi peg of scientist Dr Paul Dean (Robert Glaudini) attempting to neutralize a strain of parasite he has developed for the government. Morbid premise is that the large, worm-like parasite is in his abdomen growing while he studies another specimen, racing to somehow avert his own death and save the world from millions of offspring.

Pic's raison d'etre is a set of frightening mechanical and sculpted monster makeup effects by Stan Winston. Convincing gore and sudden plunges at the camera are enhanced by Stereo Vision 3-D filming. Otherwise *Parasite* is lethargic between its terror scenes, making it a test of patience for all but the fanatical followers of horror cheapies.

. . . .

■ **PARDON MY SARONG**

1942, 83 MINS, US

Dir Erle C. Kenton *Prod* Jules Levey *Scr* True Boardman, Nat Perrin, John Grant *Ph* Milton Krasner *Ed* Arthur Hilton *Mus* Charles Previn (dir.)
● Bud Abbott, Lou Costello, Virginia Bruce, Lionel Atwill, Robert Paige, William Demarest (Universal/Mayfair)

Abbott and Costello starrer is one continual chase, with the boys displaying their familiar routines and antics for plenty of laughs en route. In addition to the broad horseplay of the two comedians, picture has six song numbers.

Chase gets away right at the opening, with the two comics heading west in a Chicago municipal bus bound for the Coast. Gags and routines are dropped plentifully along the route, until boys switch to a sailing yacht. This lands them on a South Sea island as locale for further horseplay.

Despite the fact that many of the gag sequences have been filmed many times before, the spontaneous and expertly timed deliveries by Abbott and Costello dress them up in new regalia for cinch laugh reaction. Director Erle Kenton, veteran of Hollywood's comedy scene, pulls many an oldie out of the files for the boys to romp around with merrily.

. . . .

■ **PARENTHOOD**

1989, 124 MINS, US ◇ ⑦ ⊙

Dir Ron Howard *Prod* Brian Grazer *Scr* Lowell Ganz, Babaloo Mandel *Ph* Donald McAlpine *Ed* Michael Hill, Daniel Hanley *Mus* Randy Newman *Art Dir* Todd Hallowell
● Steve Martin, Mary Steenburgen, Dianne Wiest, Jason Robards, Rick Moranis, Tom Hulce (Imagine/Universal)

An ambitious, keenly observed, and often very funny look at one of life's most daunting passages, *Parenthood*'s masterstroke is that it covers the range of the family experience, offering the points of view of everyone in an extended and wildly diverse middle-class family.

At its centre is over-anxious dad Steve Martin, who'll try anything to alleviate his eight-year-old's emotional problems, and Mary Steenburgen, his equally conscientious but better-adjusted wife.

Rick Moranis is the yuppie extreme, an excellence-fixated nerd who forces math, languages, Kafka and karate on his three-year-old girl, to the distress of his milder wife (Harley Kozak).

Dianne Wiest is a divorcee and working mother whose rebellious teens (Martha Plimpton and Leaf Phoenix) dump their anger in her lap.

Jason Robards is the acidic patriarch of the family whose neglectful fathering made his eldest son (Martin) grow up with an obsession to do better. The old man is forced to take another shot at fatherhood late in life when his ne'er-do-well, 27-year-old son (Tom Hulce) moves back in.
□ 1989: Nominations: Best Supp. Actress (Dianne Wiest), Song ('I Love to See You Smile')

■ PARENTS

1989, 82 MINS, US ◇ ⑩ ⊙
Dir Bob Balaban   *Prod* Bonnie Palef   *Scr* Christopher Hawthorne   *Ph* Ernest Day, Robin Vidgeon   *Ed* Bill Pankow   *Mus* Angelo Badalamenti, Jonathan Elias   *Art Dir* Andris Hausmanis
● Randy Quaid, Mary Beth Hurt, Sandy Dennis, Bryan Madorsky, Juno Mills-Cockell, Kathryn Grody (Vestron)

Parents is your typical anthropological analysis of cannibalism in 1950s suburbia. First feature from actor Bob Balaban, who has worked behind the camera on shorts and in TV, delights in its evocation of plastic suburbia, highlighting the bad-taste clothes and furniture that look vaguely fashionable today.

Most of the action takes place in the home of the Laemles, where Dad (Randy Quaid) lords it over little Michael (Bryan Madorsky) while Mom (Mary Beth Hurt) mostly busies herself in the kitchen. Michael suffers from recurring nightmares, and is sent to see the in-house psychologist-social worker (Sandy Dennis).

It's pretty clear to the viewer early on that Mom and Dad are up to something very nasty, so it's only a matter of time, quite laboriously spent, until the folks attempt to indoctrinate little Michael in their peculiar tastes.

There is not enough weight or complexity to the material to justify the serious approach, and while the potential for considerable black comedy exists, Balaban only scratches the surface. The laughs never come. Shot in Toronto, pic conveys the desired look.

■ PARENT TRAP, THE

1961, 129 MINS, US ◇ ⑩ ⊙
Dir David Swift   *Prod* Walt Disney   *Scr* David Swift   *Ph* Lucien Ballard   *Ed* Philip W. Anderson   *Mus* Paul Smith   *Art Dir* Carroll Clark, Robert Clatworthy
● Hayley Mills, Maureen O'Hara, Brian Keith, Charlie Ruggles, Una Merkel, Leo G. Carroll (Walt Disney)

David Swift, whose writing, direction and appreciation of young Hayley Mills' natural histrionic resources contributed so much to *Pollyanna*, repeats the three-ply effort on this excursion, with similar success. Swift's screenplay, based on Erich Kastner's book, *Das doppelte Lottchen*, describes the nimble-witted method by which identical twin sisters (both played by Mills) succeed in reuniting their estranged parents after a 14-year separation during which the sisters were parted, unbeknownst to them, in opposite parental camps.

Mills seems to have an instinctive sense of

comedy and an uncanny ability to react in just the right manner. Overshadowed, but outstanding in his own right, is Brian Keith as the father. Maureen O'Hara's durable beauty makes the mother an extremely attractive character.
□ 1961: Nominations: Best Editing, Sound

■ PARIS BLUES

1961, 98 MINS, US ⑩
Dir Martin Ritt   *Prod* Sam Shaw   *Scr* Walter Bernstein, Irene Kamp, Jack Sher   *Ph* Christian Matras   *Ed* Roger Dwyre   *Mus* Duke Ellington   *Art Dir* Alexandre Trauner
● Paul Newman, Joanne Woodward, Sidney Poitier, Louis Armstrong, Diahann Carroll, Serge Reggiani (United Artists/Pennebaker)

This reflects to some extent in form and technique the influence of the restless young Paris cinema colony, the environment in which the film was shot. But within its snappy, flashy veneer is an undernourished romantic drama of a rather traditional screen school.

The screenplay, based on a novel by Harold Flender, relates the romantic experiences of two expatriate US jazz musicians (Paul Newman and Sidney Poitier) and two American girls (Joanne Woodward and Diahann Carroll) on a two-week vacation fling in Paris. The men fall in love with the girls, then must weigh their philosophies and careers against their amour.

The screenplay fails to bring any true identity to the four characters. As a result, their relationships are vague and superficial. The film is notable for Duke Ellington's moody, stimulating jazz score. There are scenes when the drama itself actually takes a back seat to the music, with unsatisfactory results insofar as dialog is concerned. Along the way there are several full-fledged passages of superior Ellingtonia such as 'Mood Indigo' and 'Sophisticated Lady', and Louis Armstrong is on hand for one flamboyant interlude of hot jazz.
□ 1961: Nomination: Best Scoring of a Musical Picture

■ PARIS BY NIGHT

1989, 101 MINS, UK ◇ ⑩
Dir David Hare   *Prod* Patrick Cassavetti   *Scr* David Hare   *Ph* Roger Pratt   *Ed* George Akers   *Mus* Georges Delerue   *Art Dir* Anthony Pratt
● Charlotte Rampling, Michael Gambon, Robert Hardy, Iain Glen, Jane Asher, Niamh Cusack (British Screen/Zenith/Film Four/Greenpoint-Pressman)

David Hare's second feature as a director is a handsomely produced, rather cold drama about the fall of a femme politician.

Although Clara Paige is at the top of the ladder, a high-profile, pro-Thatcher, Tory politico and member of the European parliament, she still finds other people's lives more attractive han her own. Her husband, Gerald (an MP) is a drunk she's come to despise.

On a high-level trip to Paris she meets with a young British businessman, Wallace, and starts an affair with him. Late at night, by the Seine, she's walking along when she sees Michael. Certain he's followed her, and that he's her anonymous caller, she tips him into the river, where he drowns.

What follows involves Clara's attempts to cover up her crime and her gradual realization that Michael, after all, was neither a blackmailer nor her telephone caller.

Hare handles it all with dry, often witty, precision, but with a slightly academic style. Iain Glen is miscast as the lover, and hardly comes across as a candidate for a passionate love affair.

■ PARIS EXPRESS

See: The Man Who Watched Trains Go By

■ PARIS, TEXAS

1984, 150 MINS, W. GERMANY/FRANCE ◇ ⑩ ⊙
Dir Wim Wenders   *Prod* Don Guest   *Scr* Sam Shepard   *Ph* Robby Muller   *Ed* Peter Przygodda   *Mus* Ry Cooder   *Art Dir* Kate Altman
● Harry Dean Stanton, Nastassja Kinski, Dean Stockwell, Aurore Clement, Hunter Carson, Bernhard Wicki (Road/Argos)

Paris, Texas is a 'road movie' – an odyssey, if you will. It's a man's journey to self-recognition. But what really impresses is the vision of writer-playwright Sam Shepard, upon whose *Motel Chronicles* short stories the original script was inspired and partially based.

Pic is the story of a man, Travis, wandering aimlessly along the Texas-Mexican border. Travis' brother in Los Angeles, Walt, is a billboard artist who took in the hero's boy four years ago when the mother literally left him on their doorstep.

Travis decides to win back the love of his son. Once he has done so, the pair's then off to Houston to find the missing mother, who works in a lonely-hearts kind of strip-joint.

Dean Stockwell as Walt is a standout, while Harry Dean Stanton as Travis only comes alive in the interim segments when he recovers his taste for humanity. Nastassja Kinski is hampered in a part that drags the film out interminably during a duolog with Stanton at the end.

■ PARIS TROUT

1991, 100 MINS, US ◇ ⑩ ⊙
Dir Stephen Gyllenhaal   *Prod* Frank Konigsberg, Larry Sanitsky   *Scr* Pete Dexter   *Ph* Robert Elswit   *Ed* Harvey Rosenstock   *Mus* David Shire   *Art Dir* Richard Sherman
● Dennis Hopper, Barbara Hershey, Ed Harris, Ray McKinnon, Tina Lifford, Darnita Henry (Viacom)

Pete Dexter's haunting novel about an unspeakable crime in a simple Southern town circa 1949 is brought masterfully to life in *Paris Trout*, a mesmerizing, morbidly fascinating tale, with outstanding performances by Dennis Hopper, Barbara Hershey and Ed Harris.

Trouble begins when a young black man (Eric Ware) signs a note to buy a used car from Trout (Hopper). When the worthless car is wrecked the same day, he drops it off at Trout's store, declaring he won't pay. Trout and a hired gun head out to the 'hollow' to settle the debt. When the black man runs off, they enter the house and unload their pistols into his terrified mother and 12-year-old sister.

After his horrified wife (Hershey) visits the dying child at the clinic, Trout begins to humiliate and abuse her. He hires the town's crack lawyer (Harris) to defend him, but the attorney becomes more and more disturbed by the case and Trout's lack of remorse.

Hopper, beefy and aged for the role and sporting a clipped redneck haircut, gives an extraordinary portrayal of the tortured madman. Hershey is marvelous in a mature, nuanced perf as the compassionate spouse struggling to maintain dignity.

■ PARIS WHEN IT SIZZLES

1964, 108 MINS, US ◇ ⑩
Dir Richard Quine   *Prod* Richard Quine, George Axelrod   *Scr* George Axelrod   *Ph* Charles Lang Jr   *Ed* Archie Marshek   *Mus* Nelson Riddle   *Art Dir* Jean D'Eaubonne
● William Holden, Audrey Hepburn, Gregoire Aslan, Raymond Bussieres, Christian Duvaleix (Paramount)

Paris When It Sizzles fizzles. The Richard Quine-George Axelrod production is a romantic comedy that, as Axelrod himself describes the story - within - a story that weaves through the film, is 'contrived, utterly preposterous and totally unmotivated'.

Axelrod's 108-minutes of marsh mallow-weight hokum is concerned with the evolution of a romantic relationship between a somewhat broken down, middleaged screenwriter (William Holden) and his Tessie the Typist, an adorable Givenchy wenchy also known as Audrey Hepburn. Their affair is more or less paralleled in the creative ramblings of Holden's mind as he dreams up an artificial cloak-and-dagger screenplay.

The basic error in this film seems to be the artificiality of the shell in which the takeoffs are encased.

Prettiest image by far is Hepburn, a refreshingly individual creature in an era of the exaggerated curve. Holden handles his assignment commendably. Both give a lot more than they have gotten. Chipping in extended, uncredited cameos are Tony Curtis and Noel Coward, with smaller bits in the same vein by Mel Ferrer and Marlene Dietrich. The singing voices of Fred Astaire and Frank Sinatra are heard, former in a chorus of 'That Face', latter singing one line of a tune in a parody of main titles that is one of the more amusing passages of the film.

●●●●●●●●●●●●●●●●●●●●●●●●●●●●●●●

■ PARRISH

1961, 140 MINS, US ◇
Dir Delmer Daves *Prod* Delmer Daves *Scr* Delmer Daves *Ph* Harry Stradling Sr *Ed* Owen Marks *Mus* Max Steiner *Art Dir* Leo K. Kuter
● Troy Donahue, Claudette Colbert, Karl Malden, Dean Jagger, Connie Stevens, Diane McBain (Warner)

Parrish is a long, plodding account of man vs monopoly in Connecticut's tobacco game.

Based on the novel by Mildred Savage, director Delmer Daves' screenplay is something of a cross between a rich man's *Tobacco Road* and a poor man's *A Place in the Sun*. Troy Donahue essays the title role of a poor young man who emerges from a laborer's toil in the Connecticut tobacco fields to challenge the dynasty of mighty land baron Karl Malden.

A number of romantic entanglements crop up to complicate this basic conflict, not the least of which are Donahue's bat-of-an-eyelash love affairs with Malden's daughter (Sharon Hugueny), his arch rival's (Dean Jagger's) daughter (Diane McBain) and a loose field girl (Connie Stevens) who gives illegitimate birth to the child of Malden's son (Hampton Fancher). Then there is the supreme complication: Malden's marriage to Donahue's mother (Claudette Colbert).

Donahue is handsome and has his moments, but lacks the animation and projection that is required to bring the title character, curiously vacant and elusive as written, into clearer focus. The picture's three principal veterans – Colbert, Malden and Jagger – do well, particularly Malden in spite of the exaggerated nature of his role.

●●●●●●●●●●●●●●●●●●●●●●●●●●●●●●●

■ PARTING GLANCES

1986, 90 MINS, US ◇ ⑰
Dir Bill Sherwood *Prod* Yoram Mandel, Arthur Silverman *Scr* Bill Sherwood *Ph* Jacek Laskus *Ed* Bill Sherwood *Art Dir* John Loggia
● Richard Ganoung, John Bolger, Steve Buscemi, Adam Nathan, Patrick Tull (Rondo)

Parting Glances is bracingly forthright and believable in its presentation of an all-gay world within contempo New York City.

Set within a 24-hour period, Bill Sherwood's highly sophisticated pic centers around a series of farewell events for Robert (John Bolger), good-looking boyfriend of ultra-yuppie Michael (Richard Ganoung).

Robert, for reasons finally discovered by his lover, is leaving for a stint in Kenya, which will bring about the interruption, if not the end, of a six-year relationship.

Intertwined with this is Michael's very re-sponsible dealing with his former lover Nick (Steve Buscemi), a caustic, cynical rock musician who has recently learned that he has AIDS.

Fortunately, film indulges in no special pleading, merely regarding the disease as another fact of gay life.

●●●●●●●●●●●●●●●●●●●●●●●●●●●●●●●

■ PARTNERS

1976, 96 MINS, CANADA ◇ ⑰
Dir Dan Owen *Prod* Chalmers Adams, Dan Owen *Scr* Norman Snider, Dan Owen *Ph* Marc Champion *Ed* George Appleby *Mus* Murray McLauchlan
● Denholm Elliott, Hollis McLaren, Michael Margotta, Lee Broker, Judith Gault, Robert Silverman (Clearwater)

Partners is a love story played off against a background of unscrupulous methods used by an American multi-national firm interested in buying out a large Canadian pulp and paper firm controlled by a very old moneyed family. Dan Owen brings it off with elan and a few mystifying moments along the way.

A thief and dope smuggler, played with macho vigor by Michael Margotta, gets romantically and sexually involved with the daughter of the pulp and paper firm's owner and takes her along running dope across the US-Canada border.

Aside from Margotta, a fine performance by Denholm Elliott, and a jail scene vignette by actress Jackie Burroughs as a prostitute, the acting rarely rises above the superficial.

●●●●●●●●●●●●●●●●●●●●●●●●●●●●●●●

■ PARTNERS

1982, 93 MINS, US ◇ ⑰
Dir James Burrows *Prod* Aaron Russo *Scr* Francis Veber *Ph* Victor J. Kemper *Ed* Danford B. Greene *Mus* Georges Delerue *Art Dir* Richard Sylbert
● Ryan O'Neal, John Hurt, Kenneth McMillan, Robyn Douglass, Jay Robinson, Denise Galik (Paramount)

Screenwriter/exec producer Francis Veber, who scored by spoofing one segment of the homosexual life-style in *La Cage aux Folles* and its sequel, this time tries to transfer his approach to a contemporary American setting. This production could loosely be termed *The Odd Couple Turns Gay and Joins the Police Force*, ultimately runs one very tired joke into the ground.

Essentially, this is the story of straight, macho detective Ryan O'Neal and closeted gay police office clerk John Hurt – an odd pair forced by their superior to go undercover and pose as a homosexual couple in order to trap the murderer of a male model.

Naturally, all the gays they encounter seem to either putter around displaying their limp wrists or swoon the moment O'Neal walks into a room. Hurt tries to be a crime solver, but is infinitely more content to bake a souffle or stare doe-eyed at O'Neal as he adoringly serves him breakfast in bed.

●●●●●●●●●●●●●●●●●●●●●●●●●●●●●●●

■ PARTY, THE

1968, 98 MINS, US ◇ ⑰ ⊙
Dir Blake Edwards *Prod* Blake Edwards *Scr* Blake Edwards, Tom Waldman, Frank Waldman *Ph* Lucien Ballard *Ed* Ralph Winters *Mus* Henry Mancini *Art Dir* Fernando Carrere
● Peter Sellers, Claudine Longet, Marge Champion, Steve Franken, Fay McKenzie (United Artists)

All the charm of two-reel comedy, as well as all the resulting tedium when the concept is distended to 10 reels, is evident in *The Party*.

The one-joke script, told in laudable, if unsuccessful, attempt to emulate silent pix technique, is dotted with comedy ranging from drawing-room repartee to literally, bathroom vulgarity.

Peter Sellers is a disaster-prone foreign thesp, who, in an amusing eight-minute prolog to titles, fouls up an important Bengal Lancer-type film location. His outraged producer (Gavin MacLeod) blackballs him to studio chief J. Edward McKinley, but, in a mixup, Sellers gets invited to a party at McKinley's home.

Production designer Fernando Carrere has done an outstanding job in creating, on the one set used, a super-gauge house of sliding floors, pools, centralized controls and bizarre trappings.

Besides Sellers, most prominent thesps are Claudine Longet, the romantic interest, and Steve Franken as a tipsy butler. Eventually it all becomes a big yawn.

●●●●●●●●●●●●●●●●●●●●●●●●●●●●●●●

■ PARTY GIRL

1958, 99 MINS, US ◇ ⑰ ⊙
Dir Nicholas Ray *Prod* Joe Pasternak *Scr* George Wells *Ed* Robert Bronner *Ed* John McSweeney Jr *Mus* Jeff Alexander *Art Dir* William A. Horning, Randall Duell
● Robert Taylor, Cyd Charisse, Lee J. Cobb, John Ireland, Claire Kelly, Corey Allen (Euterpte/M-G-M)

Party Girl is a straight melodrama of gangster days in [early 1930s] Chicago, played straight. There is no effort to understand the phenomenon or to relate it to the times.

Robert Taylor plays a crippled lawyer, mouthpiece for gangster boss Lee J. Cobb. Taylor uses his disability to play on the sympathies of juries to get the mobster underlings, such as John Ireland, free of murder and mayhem charges he knows they are guilty of. He begins to be disturbed about his way of life when he meets Cyd Charisse, a dancer at a nightclub who picks up a little money occasionally at parties. Taylor sees he cannot censure Charisse for making money out of the mobs when he is doing the same thing himself. Taylor's breaking point comes when he is called on by Cobb to defend a psychopath mobster (Corey Allen).

The screenplay, based on a story by Leo Katcher, is intelligent and convincing, and Nicholas Ray's direction is good within the limits of the action.

Taylor carries considerable conviction as the attorney, suave and virile. Charisse's character has little background to supply her with any acting exercise, but she is interesting and, in two fine dance numbers, exciting. Lee J. Cobb contributes another of his somewhat flamboyant characterizations.

●●●●●●●●●●●●●●●●●●●●●●●●●●●●●●●

■ PARTY'S OVER, THE

1965, 94 MINS, UK
Dir Guy Hamilton *Prod* Anthony Perry *Scr* Mark Behm *Ph* Larry Pizer *Ed* John Bloom *Mus* John Barry
● Oliver Reed, Clifford David, Ann Lynn, Catherine Woodville, Louise Sorel, Eddie Albert (Tricastle)

Censorship problems delayed release of *The Party's Over* for two years.

The tawdry yarn, loosely scripted by Mark Behm, concerns a young American girl, daughter of a tycoon, who comes to London and gets involved with a group of young Chelsea layabouts known as the 'Pack', a disillusioned bunch which lives only for kicks.

Eventually the girl disappears after one of the wildest parties, and is found dead. How she met her death, the events leading up to it and immediately after, which involve a mock funeral, a hint of necrophilia and a young man's suicide all merge into a pseudo-psychological and phony finale.

Performances are mostly routine, but there are a few that show distinct promise, notably Oliver Reed, as the arrogant, womanizing young misfit leader of the 'Pack', Clifford David, as a likeable American boy with a tricky role to which he brings a sense of humor, and Catherine Woodville, a standout as one of the few of the 'Pack' with any decent instincts left. Louise Sorel as the heroine is overly fey.

●●●●●●●●●●●●●●●●●●●●●●●●●●●●●●●

■ PASCALI'S ISLAND

1989, 104 MINS, UK ◇ ☺ ⊙
Dir James Dearden   *Prod* Eric Fellner, Paul Raphael
Scr James Dearden   *Ph* Roger Deakins   *Ed* Edward
Marnier   *Mus* Loek Dikker   *Art Dir* Andrew Mollo
● Ben Kingsley, Charles Dance, Helen Mirren, George
Murcell, Sheila Allen, Nadim Sawalha (Avenue/Initial)

Intrigue on a Turkish-occupied Greek island
in 1908 is the theme of this mildly exotic
British pic [based on the novel by Barry
Unsworth] which, despite an eye-catching but
mannered central performance from Ben
Kingsley, looms as too languid and remote to
make much impact.

Kingsley plays Pascali, a seedy little
Turkish spy who's lived on the small island of
Nisi for 20 years. The ever-watchful agent is a
very minor cog in the crumbling Ottoman
Empire, yet is filled with self-importance.
Sexually ambivalent, he carries a half-hearted
torch for a comely, middle-aged Austrian
painter, Lydia (Helen Mirren).

Enter Charles Dance as Bowles, a bronzed
British adventurer professing to be an archeologist, actually planning to loot the island of
its ancient treasures. Before long he's involved in an affair with Lydia, observed by the
frustrated and jealous Pascali who is, perhaps, even more attracted to Bowles than to
the woman. The stage is set for a final-reel
tragedy.

Kingsley gives a technically impressive performance as the frustrated, bitter spy, but his
mannerisms are becoming bothersome. Best
is Mirren who still can disrobe to play a love
scene with elegance and style; she brings
much-needed warmth to an otherwise cold
pic.

■ PASSAGE TO INDIA, A

1985, 163 MINS, UK ◇ ☺ ⊙
Dir David Lean   *Prod* John Brabourne, Richard Goodwin
Scr David Lean   *Ph* Ernest Day   *Ed* David Lean
Mus Maurice Jarre   *Art Dir* John Box
● Judy Davis, Victor Banerjee, Peggy Ashcroft, James
Fox, Alec Guinness, Nigel Havers (Columbia/HBO)

Fourteen years after his last film, David Lean
returned to the screen with *A Passage to India*,
an impeccably faithful, beautifully played and
occasionally languorous adaptation of E.M.
Forster's classic novel about the clash of East
and West in colonial India.

Tale is set in 1928, a curious fact in that
Forster's enduring novel was penned four
years earlier. A young woman, Judy Davis, is
taken from England to India by Peggy
Ashcroft with the likely purpose of marrying
the older woman's son Nigel Havers, the city
magistrate of fictitious Chandrapore.

Intelligent and well brought up, Davis is not
exactly a rebel, but chafes at the limitations
and acute snobbery of the ruling British community.

Breaking the general rule against racial intermingling, local medic Victor Banerjee invites the ladies on an expedition to the
nearby Marabar caves, an excursion which
ends in tragedy when a bloodied Davis returns to accuse the bewildered, devastated
Banerjee of having attempted to rape her in
one of the caves.

Lean has succeeded to a great degree in the
tricky task of capturing Forster's finely edged
tone of rational bemusement and irony.

The outstanding set of performances here
is led by Ashcroft, a constant source of delight
as the wonderfully independent and frank
Mrs Moore, and Davis, an Australian actress
who has the rare gift of being able to look
very plain (as the role calls for) at one moment and uncommonly beautiful at another.

□ 1984: Best Supp. Actress (Peggy Ashcroft),
Original Score.
□ Nominations: Best Picture, Director,
Actress (Judy Davis), Adapted Screenplay,

Cinematography, Costume Design, Art
Direction, Editing, Sound

■ PASSAGE TO MARSEILLE

1944, 110 MINS, US ☺
Dir Michael Curtiz   *Prod* Hal B. Wallis   *Scr* Casey
Robinson, Jack Moffitt   *Ph* James Wong Howe
Ed Owen Marks   *Mus* Max Steiner   *Art Dir* Carl Jules
Weyl
● Humphrey Bogart, Michele Morgan, Claude Rains,
Sydney Greenstreet, Peter Lorre, Philip Dorn (Warner)

Yarn [from a novel by Charles Nordhoff and
James Norman Hall], dedicated to the
Fighting French, unwinds in a series of flashbacks, as related by a French liaison officer
(Claude Rains) to an American newspaperman (John Loder), who seeks background for
a story dealing with activities of these
Frenchmen who are fighting, and flying, on
the side of the Allies. Rains goes back many
months in the telling, when a ship he was on
picked up a group of men in a lifeboat in the
Atlantic. The survivors admit, when pressed,
that they are escaped prisoners from Devil's
Island, who wish to return to France to fight
for their country.

After the rescue, the freighter settles down
to its normal routine, continuing back to
Marseille, its destination, only to be disturbed
again when the wireless crackles with the
news of French surrender to the Nazis. The
captain of the ship (Victor Francen) secretly
orders its course changed toward England,
but not before the fascist wireless operator
radios the ship's position to a German patrol
bomber.

Humphrey Bogart, as Matrac, a journalist
whose opposition to the appeasers at the time
of Munich resulted in his conviction on a
trumped up charge of murder and treason
and his banishment to Devil's Island, gives a
forthright performance as one of the escaped
convicts rescued by the freighter.

But the best job of all is done by Rains. Not
only does he have the biggest part in the picture, but he captures practically all the acting
honors in a film filled with good acting.

■ PASSED AWAY

1992, 96 MINS, US ◇ ☺ ⊙
Dir Charlie Peters   *Prod* Larry Brezner, Timothy Marx
Scr Charlie Peters   *Ph* Arthur Albert   *Ed* Harry
Keramidos   *Mus* Richard Gibbs   *Art Dir* Catherine
Hardwicke
● Bob Hoskins, Jack Warden, William Petersen,
Maureen Stapleton, Tim Curry, Peter Riegert (Hollywood)

A rich ensemble cast of true-to-life eccentrics
makes *Passed Away* a constant delight.
Debuting director Charlie Peters' lively original script is full of unpredictable touches and
droll humor, capturing the off-kilter behavior
of a family gathered for the funeral of their
paterfamilias (Jack Warden).

Pic's tone is set early on when star Bob
Hoskins utters an Irish malapropism akin to
Victor McLaglen lines in John Ford films:
'We'll give Dad a wake he'll never forget.'

Warden's widow (Maureen Stapleton) has
reached some transcendent level of resignation and when a mysterious young woman
(Nancy Travis) appears at the wake, she isn't
the old man's mistress Hoskins at first thinks
she is. Quirky, oblique plot line leads Hoskins
into a fervent declaration of love for Travis,
who gently rebuffs him and sends him back to
his wife (the underutilized Blair Brown).

Ebullient, warm-hearted Hoskins is always
a pleasure to watch, but his bumptious
British accent keeps popping through despite
his best efforts at middle-American speech.
Travis also turns in a splendid performance,
gradually revealing depths behind her illusory
good-time-girl facade.

■ PASSENGER, THE

1975, 123 MINS, US ◇ ☺
Dir Michelangelo Antonioni   *Prod* Carlo Ponti
Scr Mark Peploe, Peter Wollen, Michelangelo Antonioni
Ph Luciano Tovoli   *Ed* Franco Arcali, Michelangelo
Antonioni   *Art Dir* Piero Poletto
● Jack Nicholson, Maria Schneider, Jennie Runacre, Ian
Hendry (M-G-M)

Jack Nicholson plays a seasoned TV newsman, adjusted to established limits yet conscious of his inadequacy in probing through
the grim truth. Death of a British adventurer
in a small north African hotel becomes a last
chance for the newsman to scrap his own anguished identity and take on the mission of
the dead man.

His new probe becomes a showdown with
the merciless revolutionary currents and
countercurrents in today's world.

It is not quite clear what part of Nicholson
is courageous involvement in third world liberation, what part is a reaction to the disinterested passion of youth for justice or the
ironic attrition of feared exposure by his estranged wife in London.

Nicholson plays the character with personal
flair, as penetrating as Antonioni's handling
of the film.

■ PASSENGER 57

1993, 83 MINS, US ◇ ☺ ⊙
Dir Kevin Hooks   *Prod* Lee Rich, Dan Paulson, Dylan
Sellers   *Scr* David Loughery, Dan Gordon   *Ph* Mark
Irwin   *Ed* Richard Nord   *Mus* Stanley Clarke
Art Dir Jaymes Hinkle
● Wesley Snipes, Bruce Payne, Tom Sizemore, Alex
Datcher, Bruce Greenwood, Elizabeth Hurley (Warner)

Passenger 57 is a reasonably saucy action tale
that runs out of gas before landing.

At least the filmmakers have the good sense
to acknowledge the scenario's absurdity when
an airline exec questions the logic, after the
fact, of transporting a known hijacker (Bruce
Payne) by air.

With his henchmen disguised as crew members, Payne seizes the jet, murdering the FBI
agents and pilot. That leaves it to newly hired
airline security expert Wesley Snipes (cutting
his teeth as a big-time action hero) to try and
stop them, however burdened by the inconve-
nient emotional baggage of having watched
his wife's murder under similar circumstances.

Snipes seems to relish his opportunity to
play this cross between John Shaft and *Die
Hard*'s John McClane, but script [from
Stewart Raffill and Dan Gordon's story]
doesn't give him much room to operate.
Payne's hissable villain contributes greatly to
maintaining the film's intensity.

■ PASSIONATE FRIENDS, THE
(US: One Woman's Story)

1949, 91 MINS, UK
Dir David Lean   *Prod* Ronald Neame   *Scr* Eric Ambler
Ph Guy Green   *Ed* Geoffrey Foot   *Mus* Richard
Addinsell   *Art Dir* John Bryan
● Anne Todd, Claude Rains, Trevor Howard, Betty Ann
Davies, Isabel Dean (Cineguild)

Polished acting, masterly direction and an excellent script put *The Passionate Friends* in the
top rank of class British productions. Eric
Ambler's screenplay takes many liberties with
the original H. G. Wells novel [adapted by
David Lean and Stanley Haymes], but he has
built up a powerful dramatic situation on the
triangle drama.

For the first half hour the story is related by
means of a series of flashbacks, which inclines
to some confusion, but it soon settles down to
straightforward presentation with none of the
dramatic effect being lost in the telling.

Ann Todd rises to new heights as the girl

P

who forswears love for security and wealth. Hers is a flawless portrayal and ranks with the best seen in British pictures. Claude Rains, in the role of the banker husband, is a model of competence and Trevor Howard brings vigor and polish to the part of the lover.

. . . .

■ **PASSION FISH**

1992, 134 MINS, US ◇ Ⓥ ⊙
Dir John Sayles   *Prod* Sarah Green, Maggie Renzi
Scr John Sayles   *Ph* Roger Deakins   *Ed* John Sayles
Mus Mason Daring   *Art Dir* Dan Bishop, Diana Freas
● Mary McDonnell, Alfre Woodard, David Strathairn, Vondie Curtis-Hall, Nora Dunn, Sheila Kelley (Atchafalaya)

John Sayles charts the long road back from physical and emotional debilitation in *Passion Fish*, a sympathetic if somewhat deliberate and over-long intimate study of two women emerging from their protective shells.

Mary McDonnell plays May-Alice, a TV soap star who becomes paralyzed from the waist down in an accident she suffers en route to getting her legs waxed in New York. Retreating to her childhood womb, she installs herself in the deserted family home in Louisiana's Cajun Country and nastily rejects a succession of nurses until Chantelle (Alfre Woodard) comes along.

Understandably bitter, May-Alice sinks into a daily grind of drinking and non-stop TV watching. Not for long willing to tolerate maid status, Chantelle soon throws out the booze and forces her employer to shape up. But Chantelle is fighting demons of her own.

Interludes between the two men (David Strathairn and Vondie Curtis-Hall) invigorate the picture and provide a way to introduce a welcome dose of local color. Other relief, comic and otherwise, comes in the form of visits from a couple of bird-brained former schoolmates of May-Alice, three soap actresses from Gotham and the show's producer.

Sayles edited this one solo, and might have profited by advice to keep this small-scaled drama under two hours. Title refers to some tiny fish that Strathairn's character finds in the belly of a large fish he catches.

☐ 1992: Nominations: Best Actress (Mary McDonnell), Original Screenplay

. . . .

■ **PASSOVER PLOT, THE**

1976, 108 MINS, US/ISRAEL ◇ Ⓥ
Dir Michael Campus   *Prod* Wolf Schmidt   *Scr* Millard Cohan, Patricia Knop   *Ph* Adam Greenberg   *Ed* Dov Hoenig   *Mus* Alex North   *Art Dir* Kuli Sander
● Harry Andrews, Hugh Griffith, Zalman King, Donald Pleasence, Scott Wilson, Dan Ades (Atlas/Golan-Globus)

A disappointing film based on Hugh J. Schonfield's tampering-with-orthodoxy revisionist 1960s book on the life of Jesus Christ, *The Passover Plot*. The physically handsome production drains the vitality out of the Christ story through verbiage and overacting.

Schonfield's retelling of the New Testament depicts Jesus (or 'Yeshua', the Hebraic name used in the book and film) as a political revolutionary who contrives his own crucifixion as a plot against the Roman establishment.

Zalman King's Yeshua is an angry young man with little of the warmth and folk humor the character displays in the Bible texts. Far from seeming disrespectful, the film in fact errs on the side of excessive respect.

☐ 1976: Nomination: Best Costume Design

. . . .

■ **PASSPORT TO FAME**

See: The Whole Town's Talking

. . . .

■ **PASSPORT TO PIMLICO**

1949, 84 MINS, UK Ⓥ
Dir Henry Cornelius   *Prod* Michael Balcon   *Scr* T.E.B. Clarke   *Ph* Lionel Banes   *Ed* Michael Truman
Mus Georges Auric   *Art Dir* Roy Oxley
● Stanley Holloway, Barbara Murray, Raymond Huntley, Paul Dupuis, Jane Hylton, Hermione Baddeley (Ealing)

Sustained, lightweight comedy scoring a continual succession of laughs.

Story describes what happens when a wartime unexploded bomb in a London street goes off and reveals ancient documents and treasure which make the territory part of the duchy of Burgundy. Ration cards are joyfully torn up and customs barriers are put up by British.

The theme is related with a genuine sense of satire and clean, honest humor. The principal characters are in the hands of experienced players with Stanley Holloway leading the new government, Raymond Huntley the bank manager turned Chancellor of the Exchequer, Hermione Baddeley as the shopkeeper and Sydney Tafler as the local bookmaker.

☐ 1949: Nomination: Best Story & Screenplay

. . . .

■ **PASSWORD IS COURAGE, THE**

1962, 116 MINS, UK
Dir Andrew Stone   *Prod* Andrew Stone, Virginia Stone
Scr Andrew Stone   *Ph* Davis Boulton   *Ed* Noreen Ackland, Virginia Stone
● Dirk Bogarde, Maria Perschy, Alfred Lynch, Nigel Stock, Reginald Beckwith (M-G-M)

Stone's screenplay, based on a biog of Sergeant-Major Charles Coward by John Castle, has pumped into its untidy 116 minutes an overdose of slapstick humour. Result is that what could have been a telling tribute to a character of guts and initiative, the kind that every war produces, lacks conviction.

Coward (Dirk Bogarde), a breezy, likeable character, becomes a prisoner of war and is dedicated to sabotaging and humiliating his German captors. As senior soldier in Stalag 8B, he rallies the other men to escape so that they can get back to fighting the Nazis. Coward's main problem is to make contact with the Polish underground to get maps, money, etc., before escaping through a 280-foot tunnel which the prisoners have laboriously built.

Bogarde gives a performance that is never less than competent, but never much more. The best male performance comes from Lynch, as Corporal Pope, a philosophical soldier devoted to Coward. He is a composite of several characters in Coward's actual story. Maria Perschy, a personable Hungarian girl making her first appearance in a British film, brings some glamor to the film as the underground worker.

. . . .

■ **PAT AND MIKE**

1952, 94 MINS, US Ⓥ ⊙
Dir George Cukor   *Prod* Lawrence Weingarten
Scr Ruth Gordon, Garson Kanin   *Ph* William Daniels
Ed George Boemler   *Mus* David Raksin   *Art Dir* Cedric Gibbons, Urie McCleary
● Spencer Tracy, Katharine Hepburn, Aldo Ray, William Ching, Sammy White, George Mathews (M-G-M)

The smooth-working team of Spencer Tracy and Katharine Hepburn spark the fun in *Pat and Mike*. Hepburn is quite believable as a femme athlete taken under the wing of promoter Tracy. Actress, as a college athletic instructor engaged to eager-beaver prof William Ching, enters an amateur golf tournament to prove to herself and to Ching that she is good. Deed attracts the attention of

Tracy, who quick-talks her into signing a pro contract for a number of sports.

Film settles down to a series of laugh sequences of training, exhibitions and cross-country tours in which Hepburn proves to be a star.

Tracy is given some choice lines in the script and makes much of them in an easy, throwaway style that lifts the comedy punch.

☐ 1952: Nomination: BestStory & Screenplay

. . . .

■ **PATCH OF BLUE, A**

1965, 105 MINS, US Ⓥ
Dir Guy Green   *Prod* Pandro S. Berman   *Scr* Guy Green   *Ph* Robert Burks   *Ed* Rita Roland   *Mus* Jerry Goldsmith   *Art Dir* George W. Davis, Urie McCleary
● Sidney Poitier, Shelley Winters, Elizabeth Hartman, Wallace Ford, Ivan Dixon, Elisabeth Fraser (M-G-M/Berman)

A Patch of Blue is a touching contemporary melodrama, relieved at times by generally effective humor, about a blind white girl, rehabilitated from a dreary home by a Negro. Film has very good scripting plus excellent direction and performances, including an exceptional screen debut by Elizabeth Hartman as the gal.

Director Guy Green adapted Elizabeth Kata's *Be Ready with Bells and Drums*, and the ending, while positive, isn't sudsy. Hartman gives a smash interpretation to the role, and progresses most believably from an uneducated, unwanted and home-anchored maiden, to an upbeat, firmer grasp on what is to be her sightless maturity.

Sidney Poitier is excellent as he becomes her first true friend and gives her some self-assurance. She, of course, doesn't know he is Negro.

The domestic situation is grim, with Shelley Winters very good as Hartman's sleazy mother. Vet character actor Wallace Ford, Winters' dad, effectively blends personal frustration, shame and disappointment in his own daughter and pity for Hartman in limited footage.

☐ 1965: Best Supp. Actress (Shelley Winters).
☐ Nominations: Best Actress (Elizabeth Hartman), B&W Cinematography, B&W Art Direction, Original Music Score

. . . .

■ **PATERNITY**

1981, 94 MINS, US ◇ Ⓥ ⊙
Dir David Steinberg   *Prod* Lawrence Gordon, Hank Moonjean   *Scr* Charlie Peters   *Ph* Bobbie Byrne
Ed Donn Cambern   *Mus* David Shire   *Art Dir* Jack Collis
● Burt Reynolds, Beverly D'Angelo, Paul Dooley, Elizabeth Ashley, Lauren Hutton (Paramount)

There are several funny bits in *Paternity* a harmless enough romantic comedy that strangely has its strongest laughs in its least important scenes. But the basic story of a successful 44-year-old man who decides to fulfill his desire for fatherhood by pacting with a woman to have his child never comes across with much punch.

The idea behind the film is a charming one and Reynolds manages to evoke the sensitivity needed to make his character's desires seem believable. Charlie Peters' script comes through in odd moments, usually in the form of witty visual asides superfluous to the primary action. Much of the latter is also due to the hand of first time director David Steinberg, whose style clearly owes to his wonderfully snide point of view as a successful standup comic.

While Reynolds and D'Angelo make a nice enough onscreen couple, they just don't provide the sparks needed to light up a romantic comedy.

. . . .

■ PAT GARRETT & BILLY THE KID

1973, 106 MINS [1989: 122 MINS], US ◇ ⊙
Dir Sam Peckinpah   *Prod* Gordon Carroll   *Scr* Rudy
Wurlitzer   *Ph* John Coquillon   *Ed* Roger Spottiswoode,
Garth Craven, Robert L. Wolfe, Richard Halsey, David
Berlatsky, Tony de Zarraga   *Mus* Bob Dylan
Art Dir Ted Haworth
● James Coburn, Kris Kristofferson, Bob Dylan, Richard
Jaeckel, Katy Jurado, Jason Robards (M-G-M)

'It feels like times have changed,' mutters
James Coburn as gunman-turned-sheriff Pat
Garrett, now hot on the trail of erstwhile
buddy, Billy the Kid (Kris Kristofferson).

Coburn offers more of his smiles as testimony to the wizardry of Old West dentistry,
while Kristofferson ambles through his role
with solid charm. Neither conveys the psychological tension felt between the two men
whose lives diverge after years of camaraderie.

Bob Dylan makes his dramatic film debut in
a part so peripheral (or so abridged by six
film editors) as to make his appearance a trivial cameo. His acting is limited to an embarrassing assortment of tics, smirks, shrugs,
winks and smiles.

The editing, faulted by the director, conceals the reported postproduction tinkering
but also reduces such players as Jason
Robards, Richard Jaeckel and Katy Jurado to
walk-on status. [Peckinpah's original cut was
finally released in 1989.]

■ PATHS OF GLORY

1957, 87 MINS, US ⑫ ⊙
Dir Stanley Kubrick   *Prod* James B. Harris   *Scr* Stanley
Kubrick, Calder Willingham, Jim Thompson   *Ph* George
Krause   *Ed* Eva Kroll   *Mus* Gerald Fried
Art Dir Ludwig Reiber
● Kirk Douglas, Ralph Meeker, Adolphe Menjou,
George Macready, Wayne Morris, Richard Anderson
(Bryna/Harris-Kubrick/United Artists)

Paths of Glory [based on the novel by
Humphrey Cobb] is a starkly realistic recital
of French army politics in 1916 during World
War I. While the subject is well handled and
enacted in a series of outstanding characterizations, it seems dated and makes for grim
screen fare.

Story nub revolves around decision of the
General Staff for a military unit commanded
by George Macready, a general of the old
school, to take an objective held for two years
by the Germans. Knowing full well the impossibility of such an assault because of lack of
manpower and impregnability of the position,
the general nevertheless orders Kirk Douglas,
colonel in command of the regiment, to make
the suicidal attempt.

When his men either are driven back by enemy fire or are unable to leave the trenches,
an unjust charge of cowardice against the
men is lodged by the general and Douglas is
ordered to arrange for three men to be selected to stand courtmartial, as an object lesson to whole army.

Stanley Kubrick in his taut direction
catches the spirit of war with fine realism,
and the futile advance of the French is exciting. He draws excellent performances, too,
right down the line. Douglas scores heavily in
his realization that his is a losing battle
against the system, and Macready as the relentless general instilled with the belief that
an order is an order, even if it means the
death of thousands, socks over what may be
regarded his most effective role to date.

■ PATRICK

1978, 110 MINS, AUSTRALIA ◇ ⑫
Dir Richard Franklin   *Prod* Antony I. Ginnane, Richard
Franklin   *Scr* Everett de Roche   *Ph* Don McAlpine
Ed Edward Queen-Mason   *Mus* Brian May
Art Dir Leslie Binns

● Susan Penhaligon, Robert Helpmann, Rod Mullinar,
Bruce Barry, Julia Blake, Helen Heminway (Australian
International)

Psychokinesis is a subject that can usually be
relied upon to create some spectacular effects
on screen, and as a result, occasionally the
story and characters become subordinated.
No so with *Patrick*, which is more a study in
character reactions.

The denominative Patrick is introduced as
a matricide who, after having done away with
mom and her lover, is next seen in the intensive care section in a state of chronic, advanced – and, we're told – irreversible
catatonic reaction: '160 pounds of limp meat
hanging off a comatosed brain', says Dr Roget
(Robert Helpmann).

Jathy Jacquard (Susan Penhaligon) is a recently estranged wife who returns to nursing
to support herself. At Roget's clinic, as the
newest member of the staff, she's given
Patrick to watch over.

The patient falls in love with his nurse,
which would be okay if he only had tonsillitis
and was normal: Patrick is polyplegic and
homicidal and possessed of this really terrific
sixth sense which he uses spitefully.

The inert (and uncredited) lead, with help
from Richard Franklin's shrewd direction,
creates an incredible menace while the thesps
surrounding him go through their action.

■ PATRIOT, THE

1928, 108 MINS, US
Dir Ernst Lubitsch   *Scr* Hans Kraley, Julian Johnson
Ph Bert Glennon   *Mus* Domenico Savino, Gerard
Carbonara   *Art Dir* Hans Dreier
● Emil Jannings, Lewis Stone, Florence Vidor, Neil
Hamilton, Harry Cording, Vera Voronina (Paramount)

Many elements combine to give *The Patriot* a
valid claim to greatness. The magnificent performance of Emil Jannings as the mad Czar
Paul alone. Besides Jannings the production
has a whole array of assets. Story value is excellent, cast is almost flawless and the physical production is rich in beauty and fine
graphic background.

Time is the late 18th century, and locale
the richly picturesque atmosphere of the
Russian court under Czar Paul, the insane
emperor of all the Russias, idiot-monster of
Nero-like proportions. Surrounded by murderous plots, the only creature the madman
trusts is his minister of war, Count Pahlen
(Lewis Stone).

The role of Pahlen is really the star part,
and it is only Jannings' genius that holds up
the character of the Czar. Stone gives a balanced and polished performance. Pahlen is
pictured as a suave man of the world rather
than the paragon of virtue as legendary heroes are usually presented. Character comes
on the screen without heroics.

Pictorially the production is full of magnificent bits. One of the sets is the vast palace
courtyard and long shots of soldiers moving
through its intricate vistas, columns of foot
soldiers with galloping horsemen weaving
around dim corners and streaking across the
snow-covered spaces, are stunning effects.

Sound effects are managed inconspicuously.
There is no dialog.
□ 1928/29: Best Writing.
□ Nominations: Best Picture, Director, Actor
(Lewis Stone), Art Direction

■ PATRIOT GAMES

1992, 116 MINS, US ◇ ⑫ ⊙
Dir Philip Noyce   *Prod* Mace Neufeld, Robert Rehme
Scr W. Peter Iliff, Donald Stewart   *Ph* Donald M.
McAlpine, Stephen Smith, James Devis   *Ed* Neil Travis,
William Hoy   *Mus* James Horner   *Art Dir* Joseph
Nemec III
● Harrison Ford, Anne Archer, Patrick Bergin, Sean
Bean, Thora Birch, James Fox (Paramount)

Mindless, morally repugnant and ineptly directed to boot, *Patriot Games* is a shoddy follow-up to Par's 1990 hit *The Hunt for Red
October*. Also based on a bestselling Tom
Clancy novel about intrepid CIA analyst Jack
Ryan, the ultra-violent, fascistic, blatantly
anti-Irish film stars a dour Harrison Ford.

Ford's Ryan, at the onset, has left the CIA
to teach naval history at Annapolis. A visit to
London makes him a family places him in the middle of an attack on a high British official
(James Fox) by what Ford later identifies as
'some ultra-violent faction of the IRA.' His
rescue of Fox and killing of one attacker
makes him the quarry of a revengeful, ice-
blooded IRA man (Sean Bean).

The case is sentimentally loaded by painting the IRA faction as monsters who don't
hesitate to attack Ford's wife (Anne Archer)
and daughter (Thora Birch) as part of Bean's
vendetta.

Director Philip Noyce is way out of his
depth here, relying on tight close-ups that
eliminate visual and social context and incoherently handling action sequences in the
would-be spectacular climax.

■ PATSY, THE

1964, 100 MINS, US ◇ ⑫ ⊙
Dir Jerry Lewis   *Prod* Ernest D. Glucksman   *Scr* Jerry
Lewis, Bill Richmond   *Ph* Wallace Kelley   *Ed* John
Woodcock   *Mus* David Raksin   *Art Dir* Hal Pereira,
Cary Odell
● Jerry Lewis, Ina Balin, Everett Sloane, Phil Harris,
Keenan Wynn, Peter Lorre (Paramount)

The Patsy's slim story line has it ups and downs,
sometimes being hilarious, frequently unfunny.

Premise of a group of film professionals – a
producer, director, writer-gagman, press
agent and secretary – who have lost their star
in a plane disaster and find another meal
ticket by grabbing a hotel bellboy and building him to stardom, is an okay device for situations but lacks development – which might
have made a better comedy.

Jerry Lewis also directs in the part, and as
the patsy of this pack of hangers-on he indulges
in his usual mugging and clowning, good for
guffaws and enough nonsensical anticking to
appeal to juve audiences especially.

Lewis as the simple-minded Stanley, 'discovered' as he is delivering ice to the forlorn
group wondering how to salvage their own positions, socks over his customary brand of
broad and nutty humor and gets good backing
right down the line. Everett Sloane as the
producer, Peter Lorre the director, Phil
Harris the gagman, Keenan Wynn the p.a.,
and Ina Balin the secretary, deliver soundly.

Hedda Hopper plays herself in a nice scene,
and others playing themselves in cameo roles
are Ed Wynn, Rhonda Fleming, George Raft,
Mel Torme.

■ PATTON

1970, 173 MINS, US ◇ ⑫ ⊙
Dir Franklin J. Schaffner   *Prod* Frank McCarthy
Scr Francis Coppola, Edmund H. North   *Ph* Fred
Koenekamp   *Ed* Hugh S. Fowler   *Mus* Jerry Goldsmith
Art Dir Urie McCleary, Gil Parrondo
● George C. Scott, Karl Malden, Michael Bates, Karl
Michael Vogler, Edward Binns, Lawrence Dobkin (20th
Century-Fox)

War is hell, and *Patton* is one hell of a war picture.

George C. Scott's title-role performance is
outstanding and the excellent direction of
Franklin J. Schaffner lends realism, authenticity, and sensitivity without ever being visually offensive, excessive or overdone in any
area.

Patton is an amazingly brilliant depiction of
men in war, revealing all facets of their character.

Film begins in North Africa, just before Gen George S. Patton Jr. takes over command in 1943 of an American component of an Anglo-American unit, decimated by German attack. It ends after the surrender of Germany, and Patton's relief from an occupation command because of embarrassing statements contrary to civilian and Allied policy.
□ 1970: Best Picture, Director, Actor (George C. Scott, declined award), Original Story & Screenplay, Art Direction, Sound, Editing.
□ Nominations: Best Cinematography, Original Score, Visual Effects

■ **PATTY HEARST**

1988, 108 MINS, US ◇ ⊚ ⊙
Dir Paul Schrader   *Prod* Marvin Worth   *Scr* Nicholas Kazan   *Ph* Bojan Bazelli   *Ed* Michael R. Miller   *Mus* Scott Johnson   *Art Dir* Jane Musky
● Natasha Richardson, William Forsythe, Ving Rhames, Frances Fisher, Jodi Long (Atlantic/Zenith)

Patty Hearst puts forth much less than its pretensions. Frequently wrapped in surrealistic stylization, film manages only to tell Hearst's side of her kidnapping ordeal.

Paralleling Hearst's book *Every Secret Thing*, on which Nicholas Kazan based the script, story quickly recounts Hearst's early life and picks up cinematically with her kidnapping.

Stuffed into a closet and blindfolded for nearly 50 days, Hearst is subjected to verbal abuse by the deranged band of self-styled revolutionaries that called themselves the Symbionese Liberation Army.

By the time Hearst is offered her freedom or membership in the SLA, one is bound to accept that the latter was chosen at least as much for survival as for any other motive.

In portraying Hearst, Natasha Richardson – daughter of Vanessa Redgrave and director Tony Richardson – is quite effective. She manages to convey all the sympathy clearly intended.

■ **PAWNBROKER, THE**

1965, 112 MINS, US ⊚ ⊙
Dir Sidney Lumet   *Prod* Roger H. Lewis, Philip Langner   *Scr* Morton Fine, David Friedkin   *Ph* Boris Kaufman   *Ed* Ralph Rosenblum   *Mus* Quincy Jones   *Art Dir* Richard Sylbert
● Rod Steiger, Geraldine Fitzgerald, Brock Peters, Thelma Oliver, Jaime Sanchez, Marketta Kimbrell (Landau/Allied Artists)

The Pawnbroker [based on the novel by Edward Lewis Wallant] is a painstakingly etched portrait of a man who survived the living hell of a Nazi concentration camp and encounters further prejudice when he runs a pawnshop in Harlem.

Rod Steiger plays the embittered pawnbroker, and his personal credo is a reflection of his past experiences. He has lost his faith in God, the arts and sciences, he has no discriminatory feelings against white or colored man, but regards them all as human scum. Such is the character of the man whose pawnshop is actually a front for a Negro racketeer, whose main income comes from the slums and brothels.

There is little plot in the regular sense, but a series of episodes spanning just a few days of the present, which recall many harrowing experiences of the past. Some are absorbing, but others seem to lack the dramatic punch for which the director must have strived.

By the very nature of the subject, the pic is dominated by Steiger, and indeed virtually must stand or fall by his performance. He knows most of the tricks of the trade, and puts them to good use.

Although appearing only in three scenes, Geraldine Fitzgerald makes a deep impression as a welfare worker who almost succeeds

in getting through to him, but at the last moment he refuses to weaken.
□ 1965: Nomination: Best Actor (Rod Steiger)

■ **PEACEMAKER**

1990, 90 MINS, US ◇ ⊚ ⊙
Dir Kevin S. Tenney   *Prod* Andrew Lane, Wayne Crawford   *Scr* Kevin S. Tenney   *Ph* Thomas Jewitt   *Ed* Dan Duncin   *Mus* Dennis Michael Tenney   *Art Dir* Rob Sissman
● Robert Forster, Lance Edwards, Hilary Shephard, Robert Davi, Bert Remsen (Gibraltar/Mentone)

Peacemaker is an unexpected gem, a sci-fi action thriller that really delivers the goods despite an apparent low budget.

Inventive plot is a tale of two humanoid aliens (Robert Forster and Lance Edwards) who crash-land on Earth. One is an intergalactic serial killer, the other a police officer, or peacemaker. A simple set-up, except for one complication: both claim to be the cop.

Both aliens attempt to enlist the aid of assistant medical examiner Hilary Shepard, hoping she can help them find the key to the one functional space rover that survived their crash landing.

Peacemaker is a stunt extravaganza, a nonstop, fast-paced assemblage of chases, shootouts and explosions building to an impressive climax. Pic has a big-budget look throughout.

■ **PEEPER**

1975, 87 MINS, US ◇
Dir Peter Hyams   *Prod* Irwin Winkler, Robert Chartoff   *Scr* W.D. Richter   *Ph* Earl Rath   *Ed* James Mitchell   *Mus* Richard Clements   *Art Dir* Albert Brenner
● Michael Caine, Natalie Wood, Kitty Winn, Thayer David, Liam Dunn, Dorothy Adams (20th Century-Fox)

Peeper is flimsy whimsy. In the can for a year after being made under the title *Fat Chance*, director Peter Hyams' limp spoof of a 1940s private-eye film stars Michael Caine as a fumbling gumshoe and Natalie Wood as a member of a mysterious wealthy family. Even in the cutdown 87-minute release version, the extremely handsome production shows far more care in physical details than artistic ones.

Keith Laumer's novel *Deadfall* (not to be confused with a 1968 Bryan Forbes film of that name, coincidentally starring Caine) was altered in tone and time by scripter W.D. Richter. Mimic artist Guy Marks opens the film by a Humphrey Bogart reading of the main credits over footage of a mysterious figure in an alley.

Story gets underway with Michael Constantine hiring Caine to find his long lost daughter so she will get his money. But comic assassins Timothy Agoglia Carey and Don Calfa keep popping up doing bad numbers on people.

Caine's search involves him with the odd Prendergast family, where bedridden neurotic mother Dorothy Adams, daughters Wood and Kitty Winn (one of whom may be Constantine's kid), and uncle Thayer David and household fixture Liam Dunn complicate the plot.

■ **PEEPING TOM**

1960, 109 MINS, UK ◇ ⊚
Dir Michael Powell   *Prod* Michael Powell   *Scr* Leo Marks   *Ph* Otto Heller   *Ed* Noreen Ackland   *Mus* Brian Easdale, Wally Stott   *Art Dir* Arthur Lawson
● Carl Boehm, Moira Shearer, Anna Massey, Maxine Audley, Shirley Ann Field, Jack Watson (Anglo-Amalgamated/Powell)

Anglo-Amalgamated unloaded around $560,000 on making *Peeping Tom*, the biggest load of coin it had ever invested in one pic-

ture. It's as well, for stripped of its color and some excellent photography plus imaginative direction by Michael Powell, the plot itself would have emerged as a shoddy yarn.

Story concerns a young man who, as a boy, was used a guinea-pig by his father [played by Powell himself], a noted professor studying the symptoms of fear. The boy grows up to become an insane killer obsessed with the desire to photograph the terror on the faces of his victims as he kills them. He also has an unhealthy craving for peeping at young lovers, hence the title. In between these activities, he has a regular job as an assistant cameraman in a film studio and a part time job of photographing saucy pictures.

This mixed-up young man is played rather stolidly by Carl Boehm. It is more the fault of the screenplay than the actor himself that one gets only a very superficial glimpse into the workings of his mind. Anna Massey is charming as the girl who is one of his tenants and befriends him before she realizes that he is a killer. Maxine Audley, as her blind mother, tackles a difficult, unrewarding role very well.

Brenda Bruce has a few good moments at the beginning of the film as a streetwalker who is his first victim while Moira Shearer is effective as another of his victims, an ambitious bit player who is murdered while he is pretending to give her a screen test on a deserted studio lot.

Powell has directed with imagination but he might well have tightened up the story line. The standout feature of *Peeping Tom* is some fascinating photography by Otto Heller, particularly in the film studio sequences. His use of color and shadow is most effective. Heller does much to give *Peeping Tom* a veneer which the story by Leo Marks does not entirely deserve.

■ **PEE-WEE'S BIG ADVENTURE**

1985, 90 MINS, US ◇ ⊚ ⊙
Dir Tim Burton   *Prod* Robert Shapiro, Richard Gilbert Abramson   *Scr* Phil Hartman, Paul Reubens, Michael Varhol   *Ph* Victor J. Kemper   *Ed* Billy Weber   *Mus* Danny Elfman   *Art Dir* David L. Snyder
● Pee-wee Herman [= Paul Reubens], Elizabeth Daily, Mark Holton, Diane Salinger, Judd Omen, Jon Harris (Aspen/Shapiro)

Children should love the film and adults will be dismayed by the light brushstrokes with which Paul Reubens (one of three credited screenwriters, but star-billed under his stage name, Pee-wee Herman) suggests touches of Buster Keaton and Eddie Cantor.

Pee-wee wakes up in a children's bedroom full of incredible toys, slides down a fire station-like brass pole, materializing in his trademark tight suit with white shoes and red bow-tie, proceeds to make a breakfast a la Rube Goldberg, and winds up in a front yard that looks like a children's farm.

It's a delicious bit, with Reubens making noises like a child, walking something like Chaplin, and remarkably drawing for adult viewers the joys and frustrations of being a kid. Rest of narrative deals with Pee-wee's unstoppable pursuit of his prized lost bicycle, a rambling kidvid-like spoof.

■ **PEGGY SUE GOT MARRIED**

1986, 104 MINS, US ◇ ⊚ ⊙
Dir Francis Coppola   *Prod* Paul R. Gurian   *Scr* Jerry Leichtling, Arlene Sarner   *Ph* Jordan Cronenweth   *Ed* Barry Malkin   *Mus* John Barry   *Art Dir* Dean Tavoularis
● Kathleen Turner, Nicolas Cage, Barry Miller, Catherine Hicks, Joan Allen, Kevin J. O'Connor (Rastar/Tri-Star Delphi IV & V)

First-time scriptwriters have written a nice mix of sap and sass for Peggy Sue's (Kathleen

Turner) character, a melancholy mother of two facing divorce who gets all dolled up in her 1950s-style ballgown to make a splash at her 25th high school reunion.

Sure enough, she's selected Prom Queen. In all the excitement, she collapses on stage – finding herself revived as an 18-year-old high school senior of the class of 1960.

Almost immediately, she realizes she's returned to her youth with all the knowledge and experience learned as an adult, quickly figuring out that she can alter the course of her future life by changing certain crucial decisions she made as a teenager.

The most important relationship for her is with steady boyfriend Charlie (Nicolas Cage), who she eventually marries, has two children by and only later seeks to divorce because of his infidelity.

What makes this treatment unique is that the jokes aren't so much derivative of pop culture, but are instead found in the learned wisdom of a middle-aged woman reacting to her own teenage dilemmas.

☐ 1986: Nominations: Best Actress (Kathleen Turner), Cinematography, Costume Design

•••••••••••••••••••••••••••••••••

■ **PEKING EXPRESS**

1951, 85 MINS, US
Dir William Dieterle   *Prod* Hal Wallis   *Scr* John Meredyth Lucas   *Ph* Charles B. Lang Jr   *Ed* Stanley Johnson   *Mus* Dimitri Tiomkin   *Art Dir* Hal Pereira, Franz Bachelin
● Joseph Cotten, Corinne Calvet, Edmund Gwenn, Marvin Miller, Benson Fong (Paramount)

An excellent coating of intrigue and action against an Oriental background provides *Peking Express* with enough thriller melodramatics to satisfy action-minded audiences.

Considerable of the action [from a story by Harry Hervey, adapted by Jules Furthman] takes place aboard the Peking Express on a run between Shanghai and Peking. Aboard are Joseph Cotten, UN doctor on his way to operate on the head of the Nationalist underground; Corinne Calvet, adventuress and old flame of Cotten's; Edmund Gwenn, a priest; Marvin Miller, black market operator; and Benson Fong, rabid Commie newspaperman.

Action becomes rapid when Miller tips his hands, has his bandits seize the train and the principal passengers to hold as hostages so he can secure the release of his son from the underground.

Cotten does a credible job of his character, keeping it unassuming but forceful. Calvet makes an interesting charmer, and Gwenn is excellent as the old priest. Miller's Chinese heavy is expertly forced for hisses. Fong impresses strongly as the reporter, a role that takes him away from his usual light-comedy characters.

•••••••••••••••••••••••••••••••••

■ **PENDULUM**

1969, 101 MINS, US ◇ ⑨ ⊙
Dir George Schaefer   *Prod* Stanley Niss   *Scr* Stanley Niss   *Ph* Lionel Lindon   *Ed* Hugh S. Fowler   *Mus* Walter Scharf   *Art Dir* Walter M. Simonds
● George Peppard, Jean Seberg, Richard Kiley, Charles McGraw, Madeleine Sherwood, Robert F. Lyons (Columbia)

Although the end result is a somewhat routine crime meller, *Pendulum* attacks head-on the issue of individual liberties under the US Constitution vs society as a whole. An excellent basic plot strain has been weakened by potboiler elements.

The root idea is a nifty. George Peppard is a police hero who rode to fame on the rape-murder conviction of Robert F. Lyons. But some sloppy gumshoe work precipitated a US Supreme Court reversal, and ultimate dismissal of charges against the accused.

Then, Peppard himself is suspected of the murder of his wife (Jean Seberg) and becomes a victim of a society, and its keepers, who, while mouthing the principle that an accused is innocent until he's proven guilty, tends to think along reverse lines.

•••••••••••••••••••••••••••••••••

■ **PENELOPE**

1966, 94 MINS, US ◇
Dir Arthur Hiller   *Prod* Arthur Loew Jr   *Scr* George Wells   *Ph* Harry Stradling   *Ed* Rita Roland   *Mus* John Williams   *Art Dir* George W. Davis, Preston Ames
● Natalie Wood, Ian Bannen, Dick Shawn, Peter Falk, Jonathan Winters, Lila Kedrova (M-G-M)

Penelope is one of those bright, delightfully-wacky comedies. It's got a good – if light – basic plot premise and plenty of glib laugh lines and situations.

Script by George Wells [from a novel by E.V. Cunningham] gives full sway to the story of a young wife whose hobby is larceny. Arthur Hiller's deft direction takes advantage of the intended spirit and seizes upon every opportunity for a romp.

Film opens with a little old lady holding up a bank and getting away with $60,000 a few hours after bank's official opening. She turns out to be Natalie Wood, married to the bank's prexy (Ian Bannen) and disguised with a rubber mask which she doffs, along with a distinguishing yellow suit, in ladies' washroom.

Wood does a nimble job and turns in a gay performance as well as being a nice clotheshorse for Edith Head's glamorous fashions. Bannen is properly stuffy as her spouse. As the psychoanalyst Dick Shawn is in his element in one of his zany characterizations and Peter Falk socks over his role as police lieutenant assigned to the bank case.

•••••••••••••••••••••••••••••••••

■ **PENITENTIARY**

1979, 99 MINS, US ◇ ⑨
Dir Jamaa Fanaka   *Prod* Jamaa Fanaka   *Scr* Jamaa Fanaka   *Ph* Marty Ollstein   *Ed* Betsy Blankett   *Mus* Frankie Gaye   *Art Dir* Adel Mazen
● Leon Isaac Kennedy, Thommy Pollard, Hazel Spears, Badja Djola, Gloria Delaney, Chuck Mitchell (Gross)

A tough, disturbing and relatively uncompromising look at contemporary prison life, *Penitentiary* is a solid third feature for Jamaa Fanaka and rates as one of the 'blackest' pictures to come along since the blaxploitation trend waned.

Circumstantial evidence lands lanky, streetwise Leon Isaac Kennedy in prison. Balance of power in his cell block, largely inhabited by blacks, is dictated by brute force, with the meanest, toughest inmates lording it over the smaller (read sensitive) ones with their fists. Bottom line in prison relationships is sexual power, and Kennedy avoids the dreaded fate of being used as a 'girl' only by beating up his cellmate.

The brutal realities of prison life are rendered with extreme believability, and a welcome lack of preachiness or liberal posturing.

•••••••••••••••••••••••••••••••••

■ **PENNIES FROM HEAVEN**

1981, 107 MINS, US ◇ ⑨ ⊙
Dir Herbert Ross   *Prod* Nora Kaye, Herbert Ross   *Scr* Dennis Potter   *Ph* Gordon Willis   *Ed* Richard Marks   *Art Dir* Ken Adam, Fred Tuch, Bernie Cutler
● Steve Martin, Bernadette Peters, Christopher Walken, Jessica Harper, Tommy Rall, John McMartin (M-G-M/Hera)

Adapted by Dennis Potter from his acclaimed six-part, 1978 BBC series of the same name, film deliberately alienates viewer from the first scene, which presents an unpleasant Steve Martin attempting to force morning sex on his mousy, unhappy wife, Jessica Harper.

Martin is a sheet-music salesman in Depression-ridden Chicago of 1934 whose 'real' life consists of one squalid little scene after another: he makes virginal schoolteacher Bernadette Peters pregnant, after which she loses her job and becomes a streetwalker in the employ of pimp Christopher Walken.

Worked into this lugubrious, neo-Brechtian tragedy are more than a dozen musical numbers of grave opulence. Purpose is to illustrate the idealism and innocence to which Martin presumably aspires, with the vivid contrast between the sunny escapism of 1930s song lyrics and the somber dispiritedness of the era from whence they came.

Almost as if he were directing Pinter, Herbert Ross has actors speak a line, then wait two beats before delivering the next phrase. Technique smothers such ordinarily lively performers as Martin, Peters and Harper.

In short, this reportedly $19 million esoteric item is *Penny Gate*.

☐ 1981: Nominations: Best Adapted Screenplay, Costume Design, Sound

•••••••••••••••••••••••••••••••••

■ **PENNY SERENADE**

1941, 110 MINS, US ⑨
Dir George Stevens   *Prod* George Stevens   *Scr* Morrie Ryskind   *Ph* Joseph Walker   *Ed* Otto Meyer   *Mus* Morris Stoloff
● Irene Dunne, Cary Grant, Beulah Bondi, Edgar Buchanan, Ann Doran (Columbia)

Here's the story. Irene Dunne and Cary Grant adopt a six weeks' old baby and raise her until she is six, when she dies, after a brief illness. Then they adopt a boy of two.

That's all, but the telling of it from an excellently written screenscript by Morrie Ryskind, who found inspiration from a *McCall's Magazine* story by Martha Cheavens, occupies nearly two hours, in the course of which there are tenderness, heart-throb, comedy and good, old-fashioned, gulping tears. Half a dozen times the yarn approaches the saccharine, only to be turned back into sound, human comedy-drama.

Produced with less skill and acted with less sincerity, *Penny Serenade* might have missed the mark by a mile, but George Stevens' direction and the excellence of the stars' playing make the film.

☐ 1941: Nomination: Best Actor (Cary Grant)

•••••••••••••••••••••••••••••••••

■ **PENTHOUSE, THE**

1967, 90 MINS, UK ◇
Dir Peter Collinson   *Prod* Harry Fine   *Scr* Peter Collinson   *Ph* Arthur Lavis   *Ed* John Thumper   *Mus* John Hawksworth   *Art Dir* Peter Mullins
● Suzy Kendall, Terence Morgan, Tony Beckley, Norman Rodway, Martine Beswick (Tahiti-Twickenham/Compton)

Story is one of those claustrophobic items which find hero and heroine trapped in an isolated apartment with a pair of deranged hoodlums alternating physical and mental bouts of sadism as they break down the couple's resistance.

But it's not what goes on but how it's developed that raised this item above the level of other orgy-chiller entries. Peter Collinson's script [from the play *The Meter Man* by C. Scott Forbes] and direction work hand-in-hand like a precision watch in milking a situation or line to the utmost before seguing, after a pause for breath, to the next crescendo built-up.

The quality of the lines and the subtle yet powerful impact of their content, plus the superbly controlled delivery by the cast, make this a compelling – if at times inevitably distasteful – glimpse at some of the seamier characteristics of the human being.

•••••••••••••••••••••••••••••••••

■ PEOPLE AGAINST O'HARA, THE

1951, 101 MINS, US
Dir John Sturges *Prod* William H. Wright *Scr* John Monks Jr *Ph* John Alton *Ed* Gene Ruggiero *Mus* Carmen Dragon *Art* Cedric Gibbons, James Basevi
● Spencer Tracy, Pat O'Brien, Diana Lynn, John Hodiak, Eduardo Ciannelli, James Arness (M-G-M)

A basically good idea for a film melodrama [from a novel by Eleazar Lipsky] is cluttered up with too many unnecessary side twists and turns, and the presentation is uncomfortably overlong.

Plot premise finds Spencer Tracy, practicing civil law after pressure of criminal cases had driven him to the bottle, taking on the defense of James Arness, a young man he has known since a boy, who has been charged with murder. Arness has been neatly framed for the killing, and asst district attorney John Hodiak sees it as a cinch case. Despite careful work by Tracy, he loses the case to Hodiak.

Arness is convicted, but Tracy does not give up and finally convinces Hodiak and homicide policeman Pat O'Brien there is still a chance to prove the frame.

The picture has a number of very good performances, sparked by the always sound Tracy. O'Brien, Hodiak and Diana Lynn, latter doing Tracy's daughter, have comparatively shorter footage, but each comes through excellently.

■ PEOPLE THAT TIME FORGOT, THE

1977, 90 MINS, US ◇ ⓥ
Dir Kevin Connor *Prod* John Dark *Scr* Patrick Tilley *Ph* Alan Hume *Ed* John Ireland, Barry Peters *Mus* John Scott *Art* Maurice Carter
● Patrick Wayne, Doug McClure, Sarah Douglas, Dana Gillespie, Thorley Walters, Shane Rimmer (American International)

Story of a small party headed by Patrick Wayne seeking a marooned World War I naval hero north of the ice barrier in the Arctic. Film is second in Edgar Rice Burroughs' *Lost World* trilogy lensed in the Canary Islands and in Britain.

Special effects predominate the action as Wayne and his group leave their ship in a 1918 amphibian through ice-cluttered water and perilously lift over towering ice peaks, are attacked by a giant pterodactyl and forced to crash-land on the dusty island of Caprona.

Again, special effects add to the suspense as the group encounter all manner of hair-raising beasties and erupting fire in braving the dangers of the cavemen in an attempt to find their quarry.

■ PEOPLE UNDER THE STAIRS, THE

1991, 102 MINS, US ◇ ⓥ ⊙
Dir Wes Craven *Prod* Marianne Maddalena, Stuart M. Besser *Scr* Wes Craven *Ph* Sandi Sissel *Ed* James Coblentz *Mus* Don Peake *Art* Bryan Jones
● Brandon Adams, Everett McGill, Wendy Robie, A.J. Langer, Ving Rhames, Sean Whalen (Alive)

A pretense of social responsibility and most of the necessary tension get lost in a combination of excessive gore and over-the-top perfs in *The People Under the Stairs*. Writer-director Wes Craven sneaks in a post-Reagan era message about haves and have-nots by making his hero a 13-year-old ghetto kid. Pic's still an old-style haunted house film with spooky couple Everett McGill and Wendy Robie terrorizing their teen daughter (A.J. Langer) and keeping a horde of ashen youths locked in the basement.

Stumbling into the ample vulgarity within those walls is the aptly nicknamed Fool (Brandon Adams), brought along by his sister's b.f. to rob the place since the strange couple also are the boy's landlords on the verge of evicting the family.

House of horrors includes cannibalism, McGill cavorting around in a leather suit and a blood-crazed Rottweiler. Cartoonish villains quickly thaw pic's initial chill, in the process trivializing the more serious issues (child abuse, poverty) that might have been raised.

■ PEOPLE WILL TALK

1951, 109 MINS, US
Dir Joseph L. Mankiewicz *Prod* Darryl F. Zanuck *Scr* Joseph L. Mankiewicz *Ph* Milton Krasner *Ed* Barbara McLean *Mus* Alfred Newman (dir.) *Art Dir* Lyle Wheeler, George W. Davis
● Cary Grant, Jeanne Crain, Finlay Currie, Hume Cronyn, Walter Slezak, Sidney Blackmer (20th Century-Fox)

Curt Goetz's play and film, *Dr Praetorius*, was used by Joseph L. Mankiewicz as the basis for his screenplay, and the script reflects his construction skill at melding drama. Serious aspects of the play, concerning a doctor who believes illness needs more than just medicinal treatment, have been brightened with considerable humor, and the camera adds enough scope to help overcome the fact that the picture's legit origin is still sometimes apparent.

Cary Grant is the doctor and Jeanne Crain the medical student who are the principals mixed up in the plot. Grant, facing charges of conduct unbecoming to his profession, finds time to become interested in Crain when she faints during a classroom lecture. He discovers she is pregnant, but when she tries to commit suicide, he proclaims the diagnosis a mistake and marries her.

Climax is hung on Grant's trial by the college board, and its more serious touches are carefully leavened with a lightness that makes it more effective.

Grant and Crain turn in the kind of performances expected of them and their work receives top support from the other members of the largish cast.

■ PERFECT

1985, 120 MINS, US ◇ ⓥ ⊙
Dir James Bridges *Prod* James Bridges *Scr* Aaron Latham, James Bridges *Ph* Gordon Willis *Ed* Jeff Gourson *Mus* Ralph Burns *Art* Michael Haller
● John Travolta, Jamie Lee Curtis, Anne De Salvo, Marilu Henner, Laraine Newman, Jann Wenner (Columbia/Delphi III)

Perfect pretends to be an old-fashioned love story dressed up in leotards, but more than anything else, it's a film about physical attraction. Set in the world of journalism, pic is guilty of the sins it condemns – superficiality, manipulation and smugness.

Formula is really quite simple – a man must prove his worth to a reluctant woman – but problems with the plot and profession it's set in keep the affair from flowering.

Jamie Lee Curtis is an ex-Olympic-class swimmer turned aerobics instructor who was burned by a reporter and must be thawed out before she can enter into a relationship with star Travolta.

John Travolta is the heat, but before she can accept him, he must prove himself a decent fellow, something the film never really succeeds in doing. Character is a semi-autobiographical version of writer Aaron Latham, who based the script on a searing story he originally wrote for *Rolling Stone* and now seems to be exorcising here, feeling guilty for his ruthlessness.

Travolta cannot rescue his character, and he remains basically an unsympathetic figure. Curtis does cut quite a figure in her numerous aerobic outfits, and she does communicate a certain wounded pride and appeal.

■ PERFECT COUPLE, A

1979, 110 MINS, US ◇
Dir Robert Altman *Prod* Robert Altman *Scr* Robert Altman, Allan Nicholls *Ph* Edmond L. Koons *Ed* Tony Lombardo *Mus* Allan Nicholls (prod.)
● Paul Dooley, Marta Heflin, Titos Vandis, Belita Moreno, Henry Gibson, Dimitra Arliss (20th Century-Fox/Lion's Gate)

Immensely likeable in some parts, and a complete turn-off in others *Perfect Couple* reaffirms both Robert Altman's intelligence and his inaccessibility. The same theme turns up again here: the struggle of individuals to deal with forces and circumstances beyond their control.

In this instance, it's two different family structures. The linear family has Alex Theodopoulos (Paul Dooley) imprisoned in a suffocating, old-world Greek clan. Flip side is Sheila Shea (Marta Heflin), an elfin singer locked into a rock group/commune.

The couple meets through a videotape dating service (the kind of institution Altman loves to poke fun at) and have an on-again, off-again relationship complicated by both families.

■ PERFECT FRIDAY

1970, 94 MINS, UK ◇ ⓥ
Dir Peter Hall *Prod* Jack Smith *Scr* Anthony Grenville² Bell, C. Scott Forbes *Ph* Alan Hume *Ed* Rex Pyke *Mus* John Dankworth *Art* Terence Marsh
● Ursula Andress, David Warner, Stanley Baker, Patience Collier, T.P. McKenna, David Waller (De Grunwald)

No one else can steal $1 million with quite the flair of the British. A caper in point is *Perfect Friday* with Ursula Andress, Stanley Baker, and David Warner as a triangle of totally amoral thieves in a charming, ingenious and sexy bank job, tightly masterminded to the split-second, by director Peter Hall.

Andress and Warner play a casually-married couple, a vain, self-centered, modish and jet-setting playboy English lord and his Swiss wife, who live now, pay later, but at the moment are thoroughly bankrupt.

The gorgeously undressed Andress spends a great deal of the footage at maximum exposure, but also demonstrates a flair for low-key comedy. Warner is superb as the foppish young lord.

■ PERFECT STRANGERS

1945, 100 MINS, US
Dir Alexander Korda *Prod* Alexander Korda *Scr* Clemence Dane, Anthony Pelissier *Ph* Georges Perinal *Ed* E.B. Jarvis *Mus* Clifton Parker *Art* Vincent Korda
● Robert Donat, Deborah Kerr, Glynis Johns, Ann Todd, Roland Culver (London)

Perfect Strangers is a perfect stranger to modern technique, real life and smooth running. It appears too much like a museum piece.

The story is that of a young worker and his suburban wife, who find themselves respectively in the Royal Navy and the Wrens with the war's outbreak. Both benefit physically and mentally from the change. Donat shaves his moustache; Deborah Kerr puts on lipstick. Neither expects to like the other when they meet again but they do.

It's the type of yarn [an original story by Clemence Dane] that offers many possibilities of drama and situation, but all have been missed in this film. First you see Donat getting fit; then you see Kerr getting fit. Then you see Donat dancing; then you see Kerr dancing. Then you hear Donat telling his friends how dreary Kerr is; then you hear Kerr telling her friends how dreary Donat is. It seems to go on and on like this.

■ PERFECT STRANGERS

1950, 87 MINS, US ⓥ
Dir Bretaigne Windust   *Prod* Jerry Wald   *Scr* Edith Sommer   *Ph* J. Peverell Marley   *Ed* David Weisbart   *Mus* Leigh Harline
● Ginger Rogers, Dennis Morgan, Thelma Ritter, Margalo Gillmore, Anthony Ross (Warner)

Cramming the Ben Hecht-Charles MacArthur legiter, *Ladies and Gentlemen*, into a fast-stepping film was a tough trick. It has been done admirably by scripter Edith Sommer and slammed home forcefully by director Bretaigne Windust.

Stars are spotted as jurors in a murder trial. Dennis Morgan is a married man with two children, Ginger Rogers a divorcee. They fall in love. Margalo Gillmore, whose husband has deserted her, holds out for the death sentence because the accused had asked his wife for a divorce before she was pushed, or fell, from a cliff. Suspense mounts neatly, hand-in-glove with the love story, to a gripping climax.

Picture is a top credit for producer Jerry Wald – different, provocative, adult. Morgan and Rogers are in top form.

■ PERFORMANCE

1971, 102 MINS, UK ◇ ⓥ ⊙
Dir Donald Cammell, Nicolas Roeg   *Prod* Sandy Lieberson   *Scr* Donald Cammell   *Ph* Nicolas Roeg   *Ed* Antony Gibbs, Brian Smedley-Aston   *Mus* Jack Nitzsche   *Art Dir* John Clark
● James Fox, Mick Jagger, Anita Pallenberg, Michele Breton, Ann Sidney, John Bindon (Goodtimes/Warner)

James Fox, Mick Jagger and Anita Pallenberg star in a crime meller, laced with needless, boring sadism and dull, turnings-off sex angles.

Fox is a hood who finally gets the heat put on him; he hides in a house owned by Jagger, entrenched in freaky atmosphere with Pallenberg and Michele Breton. Fox finally is found out, there's a phony sadness to the climax, and it all runs out after a too-long 102 minutes.

Randy Newman conducted the Jack Nitzsche music, overall a good sound. Co-director Nicolas Roeg's lensing is tricky, the characters gamey, the dialog dull, performances flat, impact none.

■ PERILS OF PAULINE, THE

1947, 93 MINS, US ◇ ⓥ
Dir George Marshall   *Prod* Sol C. Siegel   *Scr* P. J. Wolfson, Frank Butler   *Ph* Ray Rennahan   *Ed* Arthur Schmidt   *Mus* Robert Emmett Dolan   *Art Dir* Hans Dreier, Roland Anderson
● Betty Hutton, John Lund, Constance Collier, William Demarest, Billy de Wolfe, Frank Faylen (Paramount)

Betty Hutton is tiptop in the title role, giving distinction to antics of early day picture-making and four bright tunes [by Frank Loesser]. It's a funfest for the actress and she makes the most of it.

Pointing up many solid laughs are sequences depicting old open-air stages on which all variety of entertainment was ground out side by side in utter confusion. George Marshall draws heavily on his long picture experience to make it all authentic and garners himself a top credit for surefire direction.

Screenplay [from a story by P.J. Wolfson, 'with a salute to Charles W. Goddard who wrote the original serial'] purports to show how Pearl White, early-day serial queen, got her start in silent films. Scripters carry her from a New York sweatshop to a traveling stock company and then into pictures with credible writing. Romance angle is the only apparent hoke factor in script but it, too, blends well with overall high entertainment level.

John Lund co-stars as a ham stock actor who is loved by the cliffhanger queen. Choice performances are delivered by Constance Collier, as the character actress, and William Demarest, as the silent director.
☐ 1947: Nomination: Best Song ('I Wish I Didn't Love You So')

■ PERIOD OF ADJUSTMENT

1962, 112 MINS, US
Dir George Roy Hill   *Prod* Lawrence Weingarten   *Scr* Isobel Lennart   *Ph* Paul C. Vogel   *Ed* Fredric Steinkamp   *Mus* Lyn Murray   *Art Dir* George W. Davis, Edward Carfagno
● Anthony Franciosa, Jane Fonda, Jim Hutton, Lois Nettleton, John McGiver (M-G-M)

Period of Adjustment is lower case Tennessee Williams, but it also illustrates that lower case Williams is superior to the upper case of most modern playwrights.

Jane Fonda-Jim Hutton and Lois Nettleton-Anthony Franciosa are two teams whose emotional instability is explored. The togetherness of the first couple – newlyweds – is threatened by the insecurity of the afflicted groom, whose periodically severe outbreaks of the shakes are the manifestation of a long-standing complex wherein he feels compelled to hide behind a false he-man facade for fear of being found inadequate or below par at the supreme sexual moment.

Relations of the second pair are impaired by a more routine issue – in-law interference – coupled with the wife's accurate knowledge she was wed for money, not love – an original mercenary motive dissolved, however, after six years of marriage. Doesn't sound very funny, but there are spurts and flashes of good fun, both in dialog and situation.

Fonda gives an animated performance and makes an impression, but there are times when animation lapses into over-animation, stripping the character of believability. Hutton does generally well by the part of the afflicted husband. Franciosa has the meatiest part, and plays it to the hilt, creating an appealing, attractive, masculine person. Nettleton is solid as the gradually more desirable wife. George Roy Hill's direction has peaks and valleys.
☐ 1962: Nomination: Best B&W Art Direction

■ PERMANENT RECORD

1988, 91 MINS, US ◇ ⓥ ⊙
Dir Marisa Silver   *Prod* Frank Mancuso Jr   *Scr* Jarre Fees, Alice Liddle, Larry Ketron   *Ph* Frederick Elmes   *Ed* Robert Brown   *Mus* Joe Strummer   *Art Dir* Michel Levesque
● Alan Boyce, Keanu Reeves, Michelle Meyrink, Jennifer Rubin, Pamela Gidley, Lou Reed (Paramount)

A look at how a bunch of high schoolers try to deal with the suicide of their class' most promisng member, pic is populated by profoundly unrewarding characters doing and saying utterly uninteresting things.

The only potentially distinguished one of the lot is David (Alan Boyce), who is the best-looking, smartest and possibly a talented composer. At the same time, David is prone to inexplicable bouts of doubt, anguish and indecision, until he finally just plunges off a cliff into the sea.

Shocking event forces everyone to face their own insecurity and vulnerability, but it is especially painful to Chris, David's best friend, who looked up to him as a shining example for his own comparatively aimless, irresponsible life.

Chris' gradual coming to grips with his sense of self gives the film its only point of interest, largely due to Keanu Reeves' performance, which opens up nicely as the drama progresses. Boyce is appealing enough as the doomed bright boy, and Richard Bradford contributes a highly sympathetic turn as the school principal. All the girls are vapid dips.

■ PERSONAL BEST

1982, 122 MINS, US ◇ ⓥ
Dir Robert Towne   *Prod* Robert Towne   *Scr* Robert Towne   *Ph* Michael Chapman   *Ed* Bud Smith, Ned Humphreys, Jere Huggins, Jacqueline Cambas, Walt Mulconery   *Mus* Jack Nitzsche, Jill Fraser   *Art Dir* Ron Hobbs
● Mariel Hemingway, Scott Glenn, Patrice Donnelly, Kenny Moore, Jim Moody, Luana Anders (Geffen/Warner)

Personal Best offers audiences a lot to like in solid characterizations, plus some shock that is a Robert Towne trademark. What they probably won't share, however, is his tedious fascination with physical perfection.

At his best, Towne handily overcomes the surface distractions of a lesbian relationship between two track stars (Mariel Hemingway and Patrice Donnelly). Though sometimes graphic, their intimacy is never self-conscious and Towne's sensitive pen creates two entirely believable characters in search of affection.

Towne is equally adept at drawing the two male characters, Scott Glenn as tough, domineering coach, and Kenny Moore, an ex-Olympic jock who becomes Hemingway's cushion once her crush on Donnelly is done.

Unfortunately, the vibrant personal scenes among these four are set against various track-and-field preparations for the Olympic trials. Towne has a love of slow motion that's employed as if he's afraid you might miss one, rippling muscle. Worse than that, when people aren't exercising, they are often talking about exercising.

■ PERSONALS, THE

1982, 90 MINS, US ◇ ⓥ ⊙
Dir Peter Markle   *Prod* Patrick Wells   *Scr* Peter Markle   *Ph* Peter Markle, Greg Cummins   *Ed* Stephen E. Rivkin   *Mus* Will Sumner
● Bill Schoppert, Karen Landry, Paul Elding, Michael Laskin, Vicki Dakil, Chris Forth (New World)

With a neutral title and a cast of unknowns, *The Personals* has little going for it other than that it's a terrific little picture.

Entire cast make their feature film debut, along with writer-director Peter Markle. Markle's story really isn't all that profound, but it's told with sincerity and humor.

Bill Schoppert is a true discovery as an average, balding, career-minded and funny fellow whose equally nice wife feels neglected and leaves him for another man. Reluctantly tossed back into the singles world. Schoppert resorts to placing a personal ad in a newspaper.

Initial result is a hilarious date with pushy Vicki Dakil, but he perseveres until he connects with Karen Landry, another neatly unassuming actress, and the result is love.

■ PERSONAL SERVICES

1987, 105 MINS, UK ◇ ⓥ ⊙
Dir Terry Jones   *Prod* Tim Bevan   *Scr* David Leland   *Ph* Roger Deakins   *Ed* George Akers   *Mus* John Du Prez   *Art Dir* Hugo Luczyc Wyhowski
● Julie Walters, Alec McCowen, Shirley Stelfox, Danny Schiller, Tim Woodward, Peter Cellier (British Screen/Zenith)

For a pic about sex, *Personal Services* is remarkably unerotic. It deals with society's two-faced attitude to sex-for-sale in a humorous but essentially sad way, and is excellently acted and directed. Film is based on a real madam who became a household name as a result of a trial in 1986.

P

Pic tells the story of the transition of Christine Painter (a dominating performance by Julie Walters) from waitress to madam of Britain's most pleasant brothel, where the perversions are served up with a cooked breakfast and a cup of tea to follow. She looks after the aged and infirm along with eminent clients, none of whom has a kink her girls can't cater to.

Julie Walters plays Christine as a charmingly vulgar yet benign madam, whose brothel-keeping career seemingly comes to an end when the police raid her London house during a Christmas party. At her trial she recognizes the judge as one of her regular clients.

Alec McCowen is excellent as her friend and business partner, a former pilot who proudly boasts of a World War II record of 207 missions over enemy territory in 'bra and panties'.

••••••••••••••••••••••••••••••

■ PETE KELLY'S BLUES

1955, 95 MINS, US ◇ ⓥ ⊙
Dir Jack Webb   *Prod* [uncredited]   *Scr* Richard L. Breen
Ph Hal Rosson   *Ed* Robert M. Leeds   *Mus* Matty Matlock (arr.)   *Art Dir* Harper Goff
● Jack Webb, Janet Leigh, Edmond O'Brien, Peggy Lee, Andy Devine, Lee Marvin (Mark VII/Warner)

Jazz addicts (usually highly opinionated) may have a special interest in the musical frame. Beyond this special-interest factor is a melodramatic story that catches the mood of the Prohibition era. Jack Webb enacts a cornet player in a 1927 Kansas City speakeasy. Mostly it develops as a gangster picture (without the cops) with a Dixieland accompaniment.

Plot around which the music is woven has to do with the move-in into the band field by Edmond O'Brien, smalltime bootlegger-racketeer, and the abortive efforts at resistance made by Webb to protect his small outfit. Webb's understatement of his character is good and Peggy Lee scores a personal hit with her portrayal of a fading singer taken to the bottle.

□ 1955: Nomination: Best Supp. Actress (Peggy Lee)

••••••••••••••••••••••••••••••

■ PETE 'N' TILLIE

1972, 100 MINS, US ◇ ⓥ
Dir Martin Ritt   *Prod* Julius J. Epstein   *Scr* Julius J. Epstein   *Ph* John Alonzo   *Ed* Frank Bracht   *Mus* John Williams   *Art Dir* George Webb
● Walter Matthau, Carol Burnett, Geraldine Page, Barry Nelson, Rene Auberjonois, Lee H. Montgomery (Universal)

Pete 'n' Tillie is a generally beautiful, touching and discreetly sentimental drama-with-comedy, starring Walter Matthau and Carol Burnett as two lonely near-middleagers whose courtship, marriage, breakup and reunion are told with compassion through producer Julius J. Epstein's fine script and Martin Ritt's delicate direction.

Based on a Peter De Vries novella, *Witch's Milk*, screenplay neatly establishes the two main characters – Matthau as an awkward, pun-prone market researcher who covers his gaucheries with a sardonic veneer; and Burnett as a maturing woman beginning to harden into uneasy spinsterhood.

In particular, Burnett is the key to the film's viability by largely playing straight man to Matthau's ironies, so there is a smooth credible transition to the drama of later reels.

□ 1977: Nominations: Best Supp. Actress (Geraldine Page), Adapted Screenplay

••••••••••••••••••••••••••••••

■ PETER IBBETSON

1935, 83 MINS, US
Dir Henry Hathaway   *Prod* Louis D. Lighton
Scr Vincent Lawrence, Waldemar Young   *Ph* Charles

Lang   *Ed* Stuart Heisler   *Mus* Ernst Toch   *Art Dir* Hans Dreier, Robert Usher
● Gary Cooper, Ann Harding, John Halliday, Ida Lupino, Douglass Dumbrille, Doris Lloyd (Paramount)

From a technical standpoint, picture is just about tops, gaining so much weight in beauty and serenity that it almost overbears the incredulity of the story. George du Maurier wrote this story two generations earlier. It followed on his already successful first novel *Trilby* and was an even greater success. [Script also draws on the play by John Nathaniel Raphael.] Wallace Reid made a click film of it in the silent days.

Casting is not of the happiest. Gary Cooper was never meant to be a dreamy love-sick boy. When he tells the Duchess of Towers that she can't have things the way she wants them but the way he wants them, he's fine. When he lies dying in a stinking jail and dreams of wandering in Elysian lanes with his sweetheart – he's just not believable.

Ann Harding, on the other hand, as the duchess, is splendid. Ringlets have replaced the part down the center and the effect is startling.

John Halliday is the duke, a bit here but expertly played. Ida Lupino has a bit as Agnes and most definitely impresses.

□ 1935: Nomination: Best Score

••••••••••••••••••••••••••••••

■ PETER PAN

1953, 76 MINS, US ◇ ⓥ ⊙
Dir Hamilton Luske, Clyde Geronimi, Wilfred Jackson
Prod Walt Disney   *Scr* Ted Sears, Bill Peat, Joe Rinaldi, Erdman Penner, Winston Hibler, Milt Banta, Ralph Wright
Mus Oliver Wallace
● (Walt Disney)

James M. Barrie's childhood fantasy, *Peter Pan*, many times legit-staged, and previously filmed with live actors, is a feature cartoon of enchanting quality.

The music score is fine, highlighting the constant buzz of action and comedy, but the songs are less impressive than usually encountered in such a Disney presentation.

The Barrie plot deals familiarly with a little boy (Peter Pan) who refused to grow up, preferring to remain a pixie in Never Never Land, and a little girl (Wendy) under paternal orders to pass into young ladyhood.

Before she does, however, she has one more night of childhood and, with Peter, Tinker Bell, and her two young brothers, John and Michael, pays a visit to the land of chimerical fantasy wherein dwell the comically-dreadful Captain Hook; the toadying Smee, who fawningly tends the pirate; the basso-voiced Indian chief; the popeyed, tick-tocking crocodile; and the beautiful mermaids and lost boys.

The voice of young Bobby Driscoll, and cartoon animation in his likeness, sell the Peter Pan character. Equally good are the voices of Kathryn Beaumont as Wendy; Hans Conried as the villainous Hook and the exasperated father, Mr Darling and Bill Thompson as the fawning Smee. Tom Conway dulcetly intones the narrated story bridges.

••••••••••••••••••••••••••••••

■ PETERSEN

1974, 103 MINS, AUSTRALIA ◇ ⓥ
Dir Tim Burstall   *Prod* Tim Burstall   *Scr* David Williamson   *Ph* Robin Copping   *Ed* David Bilcock
Mus Peter Best   *Art Dir* Bill Hutchinson
● Jack Thompson, Jacki Weaver, Joey Hohenfels, Amanda Hunt, George Mallaby, Arthur Dignam (Hexagon)

Tony Petersen (Jack Thompson) is an ex-electrician at university in pursuit of an arts degree. Married with two children, he's carrying on an affair with Patricia who, besides being a tutor in English at the university is also the wife of Associate Professor of English who is responsible for Petersen's studies.

Women find Petersen irresistible, and the

attraction is mutual. He even actively participates in a public sex act protest by the University Women's Liberationists.

Plotwise pic is not too strong but has several meaningful meanderings. It contains some of playwright David Williamson's best writing yet. He's more disciplined and doesn't let the action get farcically out of hand and displays depths of sensitivity, humanity and gentleness mostly lacking previously.

••••••••••••••••••••••••••••••

■ PETER'S FRIENDS

1992, 100 MINS, UK/US ◇ ⓥ ⊙
Dir Kenneth Branagh   *Prod* Kenneth Branagh   *Scr* Rita Rudner, Martin Bergman   *Ph* Roger Lanser   *Ed* Andrew Marcus   *Mus* Gavin Greenaway (dir.)   *Art Dir* Tim Harvey
● Kenneth Branagh, Emma Thompson, Stephen Fry, Hugh Laurie, Rita Rudner, Imelda Staunton (Renaissance/Channel 4/Goldwyn)

Already called a British *Big Chill*, Kenneth Branagh's third feature is a sometimes funny, often cloying entertainment about old friends who experience a year's worth of crises in two days.

Script confines the action almost entirely to the country estate of Peter (Stephen Fry), a witty, charmingly dissolute young aristocrat who invites his college theatrical friends for a New Year's reunion. In a manner that smacks of both stage comedy and sitcoms, the various characters are paraded forward with their most humorous traits front and center.

Playing an insecure egotist and fitness freak who secretly raids the fridge, co-writer Rita Rudner has given herself a lion's share of the good bits and she carries off the Joan Collins-ish role in high style. As her tag-along hubby who has deserted the UK for L.A., Branagh is slyly humorous, but a hollow character.

Most appealing are the ditzy Thompson, whose sudden transformation into a glamorpuss by Rudner and subsequent quickie affair are nevertheless jarring; Phyllida Law as the mansion's dignified, longtime housekeeper; and Fry as the affable host.

••••••••••••••••••••••••••••••

■ PETE'S DRAGON

1977, 134 MINS, US ◇ ⓥ ⊙
Dir Don Chaffey   *Prod* Ron Miller   *Scr* Malcolm Marmorstein   *Ph* Frank Phillips   *Ed* Gordon D. Brenner
Mus Irwin Kostal (sup.)   *Art Dir* John B. Mansbridge, Jack Martin Smith
● Helen Reddy, Jim Dale, Mickey Rooney, Red Buttons, Shelley Winters, Sean Marshall (Walt Disney)

Pete's Dragon is an enchanting and humane fable which introduces a most lovable animal star (albeit an animated one). Budgeted at $11 million it was the most expensive film in the history of the Disney Studios, besting *Mary Poppins* by $4.5 million.

The pic's storyline is just a shell. This is a star vehicle and the headliner has been created with love and care by Disney animators headed by Ken Anderson and Don Blyth.

Elliott, the dumpy, clumsy, 12-foot tall mumbling dragon with the ability to go instantly invisible and the misfortune of setting the idyllic Maine town of Passamaquoddy even further back into the early 20th century, is a triumph.

□ 1977: Nominations: Best Adapted Score, Song ('Candle on the Water')

••••••••••••••••••••••••••••••

■ PETRIFIED FOREST, THE

1936, 75 MINS, US ⓥ
Dir Archie L. Mayo   *Scr* Charles Kenyon, Delmer Daves
Ph Sol Polito   *Ed* Owen Marks   *Art Dir* John Hughes
● Leslie Howard, Bette Davis, Humphrey Bogart, Genevieve Tobin, Dick Foran, Joseph Sawyer (Warner)

The picture sticks closely to the legit script by Robert E. Sherwood. Playing the roles they created in the stage version are Leslie Howard and Humphrey Bogart – the former a soul-broken, disillusioned author, seeking, by wayfaring, to find some new significance in living, and the latter a killer, harried and surrounded by pursuers, revealing in his last moments a bewildered desperation which is not far removed from that of the writer.

The scenes in which the desperado holds court, as he awaits his own doom, over the group in the little Arizona gas station-barbecue stand are packed with skillfully etched drama and embroidered with appropriate touches of comedy.

Impressively enacted is the romance between Howard and Bette Davis which comes to flowering under the lowering brows and guns of the killer. The girl, daughter of the desert oasis' owner, longs for foreign climes and a chance to develop her talents as a painter. Howard, wishing to make this longing a reality, strikes a bargain with the gunman.

Davis gives a characterization that fetches both sympathy and admiration. Bogart's menace leaves nothing wanting. Well placed are the comedy relief bits which are allotted Charles Grapewin.

Warners made two endings for this picture. The happy ending had Howard recovering.

....

■ PET SEMATARY

1989, 102 MINS, US ◇ ⊙ ⊙
Dir Mary Lambert   *Prod* Richard P. Rubinstein
Scr Stephen King   *Ph* Peter Stein   *Ed* Michael Hill, Daniel Hanley   *Mus* Elliot Goldenthal   *Art Dir* Michael Z. Hanan
● Dale Midkiff, Fred Gwynne, Denise Crosby, Brad Greenquist, Michael Lombard (Paramount)

Pet Sematary marks the first time Stephen King has adapted his own book for the screen, and the result is undead schlock dulled by a slasher-film mentality – squandering its chilling and fertile source material.

The story hinges on a small family that comes to New England, moving into a vintage Americana house alongside a truck route. When Louis Creed (Dale Midkiff) finds his daughter's cat dead along the road, his elderly neighbor Jud (Fred Gwynne) takes him to a hidden Indian burial ground that brings the beast back to life.

The quiet madness that gradually leads Louis to try and bring a person back via the same process – despite the repeated warnings of a friendly ghost – isn't apparent in Mary Lambert's hastily assembled narrative.

King appears in a cameo as a minister presiding over a funeral. He also introduces some wan, recurrent humor in the form of the reappearing and grisly ghost (Brad Greenquist).

....

■ PET SEMATARY TWO

1992, 100 MINS, US ◇ ⊙ ⊙
Dir Mary Lambert   *Prod* Ralph S. Singleton   *Scr* Richard Outten   *Ph* Russell Carpenter   *Ed* Tom Finan
Mus Mark Governor   *Art Dir* Michelle Minch
● Edward Furlong, Anthony Edwards, Clancy Brown, Jared Rushton, Darlanne Fluegel, Lisa Waltz (Paramount)

Pet Sematary Two is about 50% better than its predecessor, which is to say it's not very good at all. The latest incarnation relies more on gore than genuine chills and is sorely lacking in subtlety.

The story opens with the accidental death of an actress (Darlanne Fluegel) in front of her teenage son (Edward Furlong). Dad (Anthony Edwards) and son move to a small town, where the boy has to grapple with his loneliness and the obligatory school bully (Jared Rushton).

Jeff (Furlong) befriends another boy (Jason McGuire) whose tyrannical stepfather (Clancy Brown) guns down the kid's dog. Duo take the beast to the 'pet sematary,' an an-

cient Indian burial ground rumored to revive the dead, subsequently repeating the process on the stepfather and setting up the inevitable question about tempting the forces of nature by awakening mom.

Director Mary Lambert (reprising her duties from the 1989 release) again errs by setting much of the action around the cemetery in daylight, although the pacing is significantly better than the first pic. Makeup and special effects are topnotch.

....

■ PETTICOAT PIRATES

1961, 87 MINS, UK ◇ ⊙
Dir David Macdonald   *Prod* Gordon L.T. Scott   *Scr* Lew Schwarz, Charlie Drake   *Ph* Gilbert Taylor   *Ed* Ann Chegwidden   *Mus* Don Banks   *Art Dir* Robert Jones
● Charlie Drake, Anne Heywood, Cecil Parker, John Turner, Maxine Audley, Thorley Walters (Associated British)

Film has a flimsy, screwball but acceptable theme for a comedy-farce. Wren Officer Anne Heywood and the 150 girls under her command are piqued. On the grounds that anything men can do, Wrens can do better they maintain the right to serve at sea in warships. When the plan is turned down by the authorities they raid a frigate, imprison the skeleton crew and set off to sea, where they take part in an exercise between British and US fleets.

These goings-on are mainly an excuse for pocket-sized television comedian Charlie Drake (in his second cinema vehicle) to masquerade as a Wren and for the main decks of the frigate to be turned into a sun-bathing parade, with the girls stripped down to their scanties.

The screenplay [from a story by T.J. Morrison] is flabby and dialog mainly flat. Heywood looks pretty, but unconvincing as the chief raider. Cecil Parker offers another of his well-timed studies in pomposity while John Turner makes a stalwart, pleasant hero.

....

■ PETULIA

1968, 103 MINS, UK ◇ ⊙
Dir Richard Lester   *Prod* Raymond Wagner
Scr Lawrence B. Marcus   *Ph* Nicolas Roeg   *Ed* Antony Gibbs   *Mus* John Barry   *Art Dir* Tony Walton
● Julie Christie, George C. Scott, Richard Chamberlain, Arthur Hill, Shirley Knight, Pippa Scott (Petersham-Wagner)

Petulia is an excellent romantic drama featuring the brief encounter of Julie Christie and George C. Scott. The bittersweet story vies for prominence with much commentary on materialistic aspects of society. Producer Raymond Wagner has complemented the story with strong production values, mainly from the Frisco locations.

Based on a John Haase novel, *Me and the Arch Kook Petulia*, the plot turns on the hectic, sometimes ecstatic affair between Christie, unhappy wife of sadistically weak Richard Chamberlain and Scott, just divorced from Shirley Knight and currently squiring Pippa Scott.

Arthur Hill and Kathleen Widdoes play a couple who try to patch things up between Knight and Scott, and Joseph Cotten has a few key scenes as Chamberlain's indulgent, overpowering father.

Scott's performance, in the face of a plot and film structure which could have relegated him to a reactive posture, is excellent. The natural emphasis is on Christie, who turns in a vital, versatile performance.

....

■ PEYTON PLACE

1957, 166 MINS, US ◇ ⊙
Dir Mark Robson   *Prod* Jerry Wald   *Scr* John Michael Hayes   *Ph* William Mellor   *Ed* David Bretherton
Mus Franz Waxman

● Lana Turner, Hope Lange, Lee Philips, Lloyd Nolan, Arthur Kennedy, Russ Tamblyn (20th Century-Fox)

In leaning backwards not to offend, producer and writer have gone acrobatic.

On the screen is not the unpleasant sex-secret little town against which Grace Metalious set her story. These aren't the gossiping, spiteful, immoral people she portrayed. There are hints of this in the film, but only hints.

Under Mark Robson's direction, every one of the performers delivers a topnotch portrayal. Performance of Diane Varsi particularly is standout as the rebellious teenager Allison, eager to learn about life and numbed by the discovery that she is an illegitimate child. Also in top form in a difficult role is Hope Lange, stepdaughter of the school's drunken caretaker. As Varsi's mother, Lana Turner looks elegant and registers strongly.

Lee Philips is another new face as Michael Rossi, the school principal who courts the reluctant Turner. Pleasant looking, Philips has a voice that is at times high and nasal. Opposite Varsi, Russ Tamblyn plays Norman Page, the mama's boy, with much intelligence and appealing simplicity.

Robson's direction is unhurried, taking best advantage of the little town of Camden, Me, where most of the film was shot.
□ 1957: Nominations: Best Picture, Director, Actress (Lana Turner), Supp. Actor (Arthur Kennedy, Russ Tamblyn), Supp. Actress (Hope Lange, Diana Varsi), Adapted Screenplay, Cinematography

....

■ PHANTASM

1979, 90 MINS, US ◇ ⊙
Dir Don Coscarelli   *Prod* D.A. [= Don] Coscarelli
Scr Don Coscarelli   *Ph* Don Coscarelli   *Ed* Don Coscarelli   *Mus* Fred Myrow, Malcolm Seagrave
Art Dir S. Tyer
● Michael Baldwin, Bill Thornbury, Reggie Bannister, Kathy Lester, Angus Scrimm (Avco Embassy)

Pic opens with 13-year-old Mike Pearson (Michael Baldwin), who foolishly disobeys his older brother's orders not to attend the funeral of a close friend who, unbeknownst to everyone, was really stabbed by a woman after the two made love in a cemetery. Mike hides in the bushes during the ceremony and later happens to eye the villainous tall man (Angus Scrimm) loading the casket into a car.

Once inside the mausoleum, the fun begins, with Mike treated to a quite grisly murder courtesy of a futuristic flying silver sphere and the wrath of the tall man, who doesn't cotton to the kid's curiosity. Film then follows Mike, brother Jody (Bill Thornbury) and company as they attempt to unravel exactly what is going on.

Strong point of the feature is that it's played for both horror and laughs.

....

■ PHANTASM II

1988, 90 MINS, US ◇ ⊙ ⊙
Dir Don Coscarelli   *Prod* Robert. A. Quezada   *Scr* Don Coscarelli   *Ph* Daryn Okada   *Ed* Peter Teschner
Mus Fred Myrow   *Art Dir* Philip J.C. Duffin
● James Le Gros, Reggie Bannister, Angus Scrimm, Paula Irvine, Samantha Phillips (Universal)

Phantasm II is an utterly unredeeming, full-gore sequel to the original nine years earlier. The special effects horrors run amok here, with slimy, hissing apparitions constantly erupting from the bodies of the afflicted.

Story involves the morbid obsessions of two psychically connected teens, Mike (James Le Gros) and Liz (Paula Irvine). The pair are tortured in their dreams by The Tall Man (Angus Scrimm, reprising the role), a ghoulish mortician who wreaks evil via flying spheres that carve up people's faces.

Working out of his Morningside Mortuary,

The Tall Man robs graves and hauls away corpses via a band of dwarves whose costumes look suspiciously like those of the Jawas in *Star Wars*.

All of this might be a hoot if molded in the right spirit, but in writer-director Don Coscarelli's hands it's incredibly morbid and meaningless.

. . . .

■ PHANTOM LADY

1944, 83 MINS, US
Dir Robert Siodmak   *Prod* Milton Feld (exec.)
Scr Bernard C. Schoenfeld   *Ph* Woody Bredell
Ed Arthur Hilton   *Mus* Hans J. Salter   *Art Dir* John B.
Goodman, Robert Clatworthy
● Franchot Tone, Ella Raines, Alan Curtis,, Elisha Cook
Jr (Universal)

Phantom Lady [based on the novel by Cornell Woolrich] is an expertly contrived, suspenseful mystery meller developing along unusual cinematic lines. Catching and holding attention at the opening sequence, it rolls through a maze of episodes to allow a femme amateur detective to unravel a strange murder.

Plot has Alan Curtis picking up a strange woman in a bar, and he takes her to a show. During the evening his wife is murdered, and he eventually is convicted on circumstantial evidence when he cannot find or identify his woman companion of the night, whose main distinguishing feature is an odd hat creation. While Curtis is facing execution, secretary Ella Raines embarks on sleuthing tour to find the woman with the hat.

Picture is the first producer chore for Joan Harrison, who was associated with producer-director Alfred Hitchcock for eight years as secretary, reader and scripter. *Phantom Lady* demonstrates that the pupil absorbed much of Hitchcock's technique in displaying screen suspense.

. . . .

■ PHANTOM OF THE OPERA, THE

1925, 101 MINS, US ◇ ⊗ ⑩
Dir Rupert Julian   *Scr* Raymond Schrock, Elliott J.
Clawson, Tom Reed   *Ph* Virgil Miller   *Ed* Maurice Pivar
Art Dir Charles D. Hall
● Lon Chaney, Mary Philbin, Norman Kerry, Arthur
Edmund Carewe, Gibson Gowland (Universal)

It's reported the production cost approached $1 million, including over $50,000 for retakes, far above Universal's expectations. It's not a bad film from a technical viewpoint, but revolving around the terrifying of all inmates of the Grand Opera House in Paris by a criminally insane mind (Lon Chaney) behind a hideous face, the combination (from the novel by Gaston Leroux) makes a welsh rarebit look foolish as a sleep destroyer.

The love angle is in the persons of an understudy (Mary Philbin) whom the Phantom cherishes while she is also the sole thought of her military lover (Norman Kerry).

The girl is twice abducted by the Phantom to his cellar retreat, and the finish is built up by the pulling of levers, concealed buttons etc to make active secret doors, heat chambers, flooding passages and other appropriate devices. However, the kick of the picture is in the unmasking of the Phantom by the girl. It's a wallop.

Kerry is a colorless hero, Philbin contents herself with being pretty and becoming terrorized at the Phantom, and Chaney is either behind a mask or grimacing through his fiendish makeup.

. . . .

■ PHANTOM OF THE OPERA, THE

1930, 89 MINS, US ◇ ⑩
Dir Rupert Julian, Edward Sedgwick, (sound sequences)
Ernst Laemmle   *Scr* Elliott J. Clawson, Frank McCormack,
Tom Reed   *Ph* Charles Van Enger   *Ed* Gilmore Walker,
Edward Sedgwick   *Art Dir* Charles D. Hall, Ben Carre

● Lon Chaney, Mary Philbin, Norman Kerry, Snitz
Edwards, Arthur Edmund Carewe, Virginia Pearson
(Universal)

In taking the old negative of *Phantom of the Opera*, U has even reproduced off-screen the voice of Lon Chaney in a few spots, besides scenes with Norman Kerry, Mary Philbin and others.

Dialog starts at the beginning. The big scene leading to the finish and capture of the Phantom is silent action. Synchronized score accompanies throughout with sound effects added to former silent scenes and singing obviously dubbed in for solos. This is particularly noticeable in a sequence where Philbin does a *Faust* favorite. Only scenes in color are a few of the opera and a masque ball but they are okay.

Only substitution in cast is Edward Martindel, talking the part played formerly by John Sainpolis. Others who appeared in the original picture, including John Miljan, are out through cutting of lesser scenes.

. . . .

■ PHANTOM OF THE OPERA

1943, 92 MINS, US ◇ ⑩ ⊙
Dir Arthur Lubin   *Prod* George Waggner   *Scr* Eric
Taylor, Samuel Hoffinstein   *Ph* Hal Mohr   *Mus* Edward
Ward   *Art Dir* Alexander Golitzen, John B. Goodman
● Nelson Eddy, Susanna Foster, Claude Rains, Jane
Farrar, Hume Cronyn, J. Edward Bromberg (Universal)

Phantom of the Opera is far more of a musical than a chiller, though this element is not to be altogether discounted, and holds novelty appeal. Story is about the mad musician who haunts the opera house and kills off all those who are in his protege's way towards becoming the headliner.

Tuneful operatic numbers and the splendor of the scenic settings in these sequences, combined with excellent group and solo vocalists, count heavily. Nelson Eddy, Susanna Foster and Jane Farrar (niece of operatic star Geraldine Farrar) score individually in singing roles and provide marquee dressing. Third act from [Friedrich von Flotow's opera] *Martha* and two original opera sketches based on themes from Chopin and Tchaikovsky have been skillfully interwoven.

Outstanding performance is turned in by Claude Rains as the musician who, from a fixation seeking to establish the heroine as a leading opera star, grows into a homicidal maniac. Eddy, Foster, and Edgar Barrier, as the Parisian detective, are awkward in movement and speech, though much like opera performers restricted by their medium.
□ 1943: Best Color Cinematography, Color Art Direction.
□ Nominations: Best Scoring of a Musical Picture, Sound

. . . .

■ PHANTOM OF THE OPERA, THE

1962, 84 MINS, UK ◇ ⑩
Dir Terence Fisher   *Prod* Anthony Hinds   *Scr* John Elder
Ph Arthur Grant   *Ed* James Needs, Alfred Cox
Mus Edwin Astley   *Art Dir* Bernard Robinson, Don
Mingaye
● Herbert Lom, Heather Sears, Thorley Walters, Michael
Gough, Edward De Souza (Hammer)

Herbert Lom somewhat precariously follows in the macabre footsteps of Lon Chaney and Claude Rains. Switched to a London Opera House background, lushed up in color, with a new character, a dwarf rather confusingly brought in to supplement the sinister activities of The Phantom, it still provides a fair measure of goose pimples to combat some potential unwanted yocks.

Basically, the story remains the same. Baleful goings on backstage at the opera which suggest that the place is invaded by evil spirits. The evil spirit is, of course, the Phantom but he turns out to be a rather more

sympathetic character than of old and much of his malignance is now switched to a new character, the dwarf, played effectively by Ian Wilson.

However, the atmosphere of brooding evil still works up to some effective highlights, with the terror of the heroine (Heather Sears) paramount, the bewilderment of the hero (Edward De Souza) and the eerie personality of the Phantom still motivating the action.

. . . .

■ PHANTOM OF THE OPERA, THE

1989, 90 MINS, US ◇ ⑩ ⊙
Dir Dwight H. Little   *Prod* Harry Alan Towers   *Scr* Duke
Sandefur   *Ph* Elemer Ragalyi   *Ed* Charles Bornstein
Mus Misha Segal   *Art Dir* Tivada Bertalan
● Robert Englund, Jill Schoelen, Alex Hyde-White, Bill
Nighy, Stephanie Lawrence (21st Century)

Not only are audiences unlikely to confuse this competent but flatly directed in Budapest production with Andrew Lloyd Webber's stage musical, or the classic Lon Chaney's silent, it also has precious little to do with Gaston Leroux's novel.

Opening in contemporary New York, this *Phantom* [based on a screenplay by Gerry O'Hara] starts with its heroine being hit on the head by a sandbag and mentally transported back to the mid-19th century for the bulk of the plot.

Set in London, rather than the Paris of Phantom tradition, this rendition seems faithful in broad outline to the original, save for the fact that its tragic antihero is a Jack the Ripper-style maniac who apparently would rather kill the young soprano to whom he's devoted than kiss her.

Running about encased in makeup that makes him appear a kind of Jack Palance gone to seed, Robert England is his usual broad self. Yet gorehounds are bound to be disappointed. As the object of his decidedly mixed emotions, Jill Schoelen is pretty but vapid.

. . . .

■ PHANTOM OF THE PARADISE

1974, 91 MINS, US ◇ ⑩ ⊙
Dir Brian De Palma   *Prod* Edward R. Pressman
Scr Brian De Palma   *Ph* Larry Pizer   *Ed* Paul Hirsch
Mus Paul Williams   *Art Dir* Jack Fisk
● Paul Williams, William Finley, Jessica Harper, George
Memmoli, Gerrit Graham (Pressman-Williams/20th
Century-Fox)

Phantom of the Paradise is a very good horror comedy-drama about a disfigured musician haunting a rock palace. Brian De Palma's direction and script makes for one of the very rare 'backstage' rock story pix, catching the garishness of the glitter scene in its own time.

The story takes novice songwriter William Finley through the despair of being ripped off by Paul Williams (excellent as a composite rock entrepreneur mogul), framed into prison, disfigured by an accident, and nearly betrayed anew by Williams who ostensibly sought reconciliation with Finley after the latter began haunting the Paradise rock house.

Part of phantom Finley's motivation is his distant love of Jessica Harper, whom he wants to sing his music in Williams' rock cantata production.

All the principals come across extremely well, especially Harper.
□ 1974: Nomination: Best Adapted Score

. . . .

■ PHANTOM OF THE RUE MORGUE

1954, 83 MINS, US ◇
Dir Roy Del Ruth   *Prod* Henry Blanke   *Scr* Harold
Medford, James R. Webb   *Ph* J. Peverell Marley
Ed James Moore   *Mus* David Buttolph
● Karl Malden, Claude Dauphin, Patricia Medina, Steve
Forrest, Allyn McLerie, Veola Vonn (Warner)

The horror in *Phantom of the Rue Morgue* is more to be taken lightly than seriously, since the shocker quality in Edgar Allen Poe's chiller tale, *Murders in the Rue Morgue*, has been dimmed considerably by the passage of time.

Murders and gory bodies abound in the Henry Blanke production, which gives fulsome attention to the bloody violence loosed by the title's phantom.

The script follows regulation horror lines in getting the Poe yarn on film and Roy Del Ruth's direction also is standard. Performances by Karl Malden, Claude Dauphin, Patricia Medina, Steve Forrest and the others fall into the same groove and none manages to rise above the material.

Malden is the mad scientist who has his trained ape destroy all pretty girls who spurn him. After Allyn McLerie, Veola Vonn and Dolores Dorn have died violent deaths, the rather stupid police inspector played by Dauphin figures Forrest, young professor of psychology, is the guilty party.

The 3-D color lensing by J. Peverell Marley is good, and puts the turn-of-the-century Paris scenes on display to full advantage.

. . . .

■ PHAR LAP

1983, 118 MINS, AUSTRALIA ◇ ⓥ
Dir Simon Wincer   *Prod* John Sexton   *Scr* David Williamson   *Ph* Russell Boyd   *Ed* Tony Paterson   *Mus* Bruce Rowland   *Art Dir* Lawrence Eastwood
● Tom Burlinson, Martin Vaughan, Judy Morris, Ron Leibman, Celia de Burgh, Vincent Ball (Edgley)

Phar Lap was a champion Australian racehorse, a legend in his own lifetime, who met a mysterious death in California in 1932.

Film's one flaw is its opening: it begins with Phar Lap's illness and death, and while every schoolboy in Australia knows this is how the story ended, a little suspense might have been retained for overseas viewers. However, once the flashbacks begin and Phar Lap's story is told, the film takes off.

Tom Burlinson is very effective as the shy stable-boy who becomes devoted to the courageous horse. Martin Vaughan is impressive as the grimly determined trainer who leases the horse in the first place, as is Celia de Burgh, luminous as his loyal but neglected wife. Ron Leibman practically walks away with the picture as Davis, the smooth American horse-owner, and Judy Morris is quietly effective as his naive, talkative wife.

. . . .

■ PHASE IV

1974, 93 MINS, US ◇ ⓥ ⊙
Dir Saul Bass   *Prod* Paul B. Radin   *Scr* Mayo Simon   *Ph* Dick Bush, Ken Middleton   *Ed* Willy Kemplen   *Mus* Brian Gascoigne   *Art Dir* John Barry
● Nigel Davenport, Michael Murphy, Lynne Frederick, Alan Gifford, Robert Henderson, Helen Horton (Alced)

This one didn't get the bugs worked out before release. It's another in the Hollywood cycle of films based on every kind of creature enlarged by radiation. Today, the hot topic is ecology and the beasties have returned to normal size, but still bent on getting back at mankind.

In *Phase IV*, the ants are it. A couple of scientists (Nigel Davenport and Michael Murphy) set up an elaborate outpost in the desert to find out what the ants are up to and why.

Despite endless conversation and dial twirling, Davenport and Murphy never focus the story in any dramatic direction. Joining them as an ant attack refugee, Lynne Frederick only adds to the confusion.

Cinematically, the ants are never very menacing. Pic opens with an interminable segment inside an anthill. But photography is poor quality, looking like outtakes rejected by National Geographic.

. . . .

■ PHENIX CITY STORY, THE

1955, 87 MINS, US
Dir Phil Karlson   *Prod* Samuel Bischoff, David Diamond   *Scr* Crane Wilbur, Dan Mainwaring   *Ph* Harry Neumann   *Ed* George White   *Mus* Harry Sukman   *Art Dir* Stanley Fleischer
● John McIntire, Richard Kiley, Kathryn Grant, Edward Andrews, Lenka Peterson, Biff McGuire (Allied Artists/Bischoff)

Vice, Southern style, gets the expose treatment in *Phenix City Story*. Production mostly hews to provable incident, with some coloring or rearrangement for dramatic emphasis. There's quite a bit of violence.

Contemporary headlines and magazine articles have up-pointed conditions in this Alabama town, just across the Chattahoochee River from Columbus, Georgia, and the army's Fort Benning. Proximity of the latter contributed to the label of 'the wickedest city in the U.S.' hung on the southern town, particularly during World War II.

A 13-minute prolog features radio-TV's Clete Roberts doing on-the-scene interviews with actual participants in the 1954 events, including the widow of Albert Patterson, the murdered candidate. This prolog stretches show's running time to 100 minutes, but it's up to the exhibitor whether or not it is used.

The downfall of Phenix City sin is woven around the return from overseas service of Richard Kiley with wife and two children to find his hometown still living up to its wicked reputation. Kiley plays John Patterson, the son of the murdered candidate, who was elected to the attorney general post by an aroused citizenry after the death of the father, ably depicted by John McIntire.

Edward Andrews plays Rhett Tanner, a menacing, entirely believable crime czar. Kathryn Grant is another who scores as Ellie Rhodes, a dealer in Tanner's joint.

Picture was lensed almost entirely in the actual locale, with hometown talent seen to quite an extent.

. . . .

■ PHFFFT

1954, 91 MINS, US ⓥ
Dir Mark Robson   *Prod* Fred Kohlmar   *Scr* George Axelrod   *Ph* Charles Lang   *Ed* Charles Nelson   *Mus* Frederick Hollander   *Art Dir* William Flannery
● Judy Holliday, Jack Lemmon, Jack Carson, Kim Novak, Luella Gear, Donald Randolph (Columbia)

Title is the product of Walter Winchell's shell game with words – put 'rift' under one cover, shake well, and it emerges 'phffft' from another. Pic originally was written as a play (unproduced) by George Axelrod and was fashioned for the screen by the same author.

Phffft is a lightweight farce running from bed to verse. Judy Holliday and Jack Lemmon are the married couple whose bickering leads to the great divide of Reno. Each seeks to put the newly-found freedom to exciting use via romantic pursuits in other directions.

Kim Novak gets across a zesty show as an accessible blonde out to cure Lemmon of the post-conubial blues. Jack Carson, as a bachelor wont to boast of his success in free-wheeling romance, registers colorfully. Holliday and Lemmon make an attractive combo. Femme star's bouts with the French language and psychiatry in addition to the agressive Carson are smartly-played comedy.

. . . .

■ PHILADELPHIA EXPERIMENT, THE

1984, 102 MINS, US ◇ ⓥ
Dir Stewart Raffill   *Prod* Douglas Curtis, Joel B. Michaels   *Scr* William Gray, Michael Janover   *Ph* Dick Bush   *Ed* Neil Travis   *Mus* Ken Wannberg   *Art Dir* Chris Campbell
● Michael Pare, Nancy Allen, Eric Christmas, Bobby Di Cicco, Kene Holliday, Louise Latham (New World/Cinema Group)

The Philadelphia Experiment had a lot of script problems in its development that haven't been solved yet, but final result is an adequate sci-fi yarn [story by Wallace Bennett, Don Jakoby].

Problems with the pic are common to all stories with a time-warp twist but director Stewart Raffill and writers have kept *Philadelphia* reasonably simple.

In 1943, Michael Pare and Bobby Di Cicco are sailors aboard a destroyer that's the center of a secret radar experiment which goes awry, throwing them into 1984, seemingly cross-circuited into another experiment.

Befriended in the future by Nancy Allen, the pair obviously are a bit bemused at their surroundings before Di Cicco fades again into the past, leaving Pare to develop a romance with Allen and try to find his own way back in time.

. . . .

■ PHILADELPHIA STORY, THE

1940, 112 MINS, US ⓥ ⊙
Dir George Cukor   *Prod* Joseph L. Mankiewicz   *Scr* Donald Ogden Stewart   *Ph* Joseph Ruttenberg   *Ed* Frank Sullivan   *Mus* Franz Waxman   *Art Dir* Cedric Gibbons, Wade B. Rubottom
● Cary Grant, Katharine Hepburn, James Stewart, Ruth Hussey, John Howard, Roland Young (M-G-M)

It's Katharine Hepburn's picture, but with as fetching a lineup of thesp talent as is to be found, she's got to fight every clever line of dialog all of the way to hold her lead. Pushing hard is little Virginia Weidler, the kid sister, who has as twinkly an eye with a fast quip as a blinker light. Ruth Hussey is another from whom director George Cukor has milked maximum results to get a neat blend of sympathy-winning softness under a python-tongued smart-aleckness. As for Cary Grant, James Stewart and Roland Young, there's little to be said that their reputation hasn't established. John Howard, John Halliday and Mary Nash, in lesser roles, more than adequately fill in what Philip Barry must have dreamt of when he wrote the 1939 play.

The perfect conception of all flighty but characterful Main Line socialite gals rolled into one, Hepburn has just the right amount of beauty, just the right amount of disarray in wearing clothes, just the right amount of culture in her voice – it's no one but Hepburn.

Story is localed in the very social and comparatively new (for Philly, 1860) Main Line sector in the suburbs of Quakertown. Hepburn, divorced from Grant, a bit of rather useless uppercrust like herself, is about to marry a stuffed-bosom man of the people (Howard). Grant, to keep Henry Daniell, publisher of the mags *Dime* and *Spy* (*Time* and *Life*, get it?) from running a scandalous piece about Hepburn's father (Halliday), agrees to get a reporter and photog into the Hepburn household preceding and during the wedding. Stewart and Hussey are assigned and Grant, whose position as ex-husband is rather unique in the mansion, manages to get them in under a pretext. Everyone, nevertheless, knows why Stewart and Hussey are there and the repartee is swift.

When the acid tongues are turned on at beginning and end of the film it's a laugh-provoker from way down. When the discussion gets deep and serious, however, on the extent of Hepburn's stone-like character, the verbiage is necessarily highly abstract and the film slows to a toddle.

☐ 1940: Best Actor (James Stewart), Screenplay.

☐ Nominations: Best Picture, Director, Actress (Katharine Hepburn), Supp. Actress (Ruth Hussey)

. . . .

PHYSICAL EVIDENCE

1989, 99 MINS, US ◇ Ⓥ ⊙
Dir Michael Crichton *Prod* Martin Ransohoff *Scr* Bill Phillips *Ph* John A. Alonzo *Ed* Glenn Farr *Mus* Henry Mancini *Art Dir* Dan Yarhi
● Burt Reynolds, Theresa Russell, Ned Beatty, Kay Lenz, Ted McGinley, Tom O'Brien (Columbia)

Burt Reynolds plays Joe Paris, a suspended detective who wakes up from a drunken binge to find himself the lead suspect in a murder investigation. His case is given to an assertive debutante (Theresa Russell) working in the public defender's office, whose obsession with the case begins to wreack havoc on her relationship with her yuppie, hot-tubbing fiance stockbroker (Ted McGinley).

Beyond that it's really anybody's guess as to what's going on, since the film [story by Steve Ransohoff] is so choppily assembled none of the various clues and innumerable suspects ever seem to lead anywhere.

Another major shortcoming is the woeful miscasting of Russell as the young attorney. Even with her hair tightly pulled back into an unflattering bun (to be literally and symbolically let down in quieter moments), Russell's uncommon onscreen beauty proves a distraction.

PIANO, THE

1993, 120 MINS, AUSTRALIA/FRANCE ◇ Ⓥ ⊙
Dir Jane Campion *Prod* Jan Chapman *Scr* Jane Campion *Ph* Stuart Dryburgh *Ed* Veronika Jenet *Mus* Michael Nyman *Art Dir* Andrew McAlpine
● Holly Hunter, Harvey Keitel, Sam Neill, Ana Paquin, Kerry Walker, Genevieve Lemon (Chapman/Ciby 2000)

Jane Campion's fourth feature is a visually sumptuous and tactile tale of adultery set during the early European colonization of New Zealand, with Harvey Keitel daringly cast in the role of a passionately romantic lover, and Holly Hunter knockout as a woman physically unable to articulate her feelings.

Ada McGrath (Hunter) can hear, and can communicate in sign language through her young daughter, Fiona (Ana Paquin), but she can't talk. Apart from her child, Ada's most treasured possession is her piano. She's to marry a man she's never met, a pioneer settler (Sam Neill) in far-off New Zealand.

The marriage gets off to a bad start when Neill refuses to transport Ada's piano to his settlement. Later, he allows George Baines (Keitel) to take the piano. Baines, who has 'gone native', offers to return the piano to her – if she gives him some lessons. These become stages in an increasingly erotic courtship.

Campion unfolds this striking story with bold strokes, including flashes of unexpected humor. The settlement is a chilly, muddy, rainswept place where civilization is barely making an impact. Hunter herself played solo piano and acted as piano coach on the production.

PICCADILLY

1929, 92 MINS, UK
Dir E.A. Dupont *Scr* Arnold Bennett *Ph* Werner Brandes *Ed* J.N. McConaughty *Mus* Eugene Contie
● Gilda Gray, Jameson Thomas, Anna May Wong, King Ho Chang, Cyril Ritchard, Charles Laughton (British International)

Piccadilly is virtually silent despite a useless prolog. It may have been added and contains its only dialog, badly done there.

This Arnold Bennett story is set in a cabaret in Piccadilly. The owner of the class joint digs up a dancer from the scullery. It's Anna May Wong, a dishwasher whom the proprietor catches dancing for her companions.

In the cabaret are a couple of ballroom dancers, with Gilda Gray one of them.

Business commences to fade and the house staff concludes the male dancer must have been the draw. With trade shot, the proprietor remembers the girl downstairs, calls her up and dresses her up, then falls for her.

Gray is so peeved she calls upon the Chinese dancer. The two women meet after the owner leaves. The audience apparently sees Gray shoot Wong, as the latter unsheaths a dagger.

Music is the usual medley of pop dance stuff, with the cabaret set about the best thing in the production. Camerawork on close-ups is excellent.

PICKLE, THE

1993, 103 MINS, US ◇ Ⓥ
Dir Paul Mazursky *Prod* Paul Mazursky *Scr* Paul Mazursky *Ph* Fred Murphy *Ed* Stuart Pappe *Mus* Michel Legrand *Art Dir* James Bissell
● Danny Aiello, Dyan Cannon, Clotilde Courau, Shelley Winters, Barry Miller, Jerry Stiller (Columbia)

The Pickle is a vegetarian turkey. Self-indulgent story about a depressed, dispirited, middle-aged film director aims for comedy and poignance that never come, and feels wearily disenchanted and out of touch.

More than 20 years earlier, Paul Mazursky made *Alex in Wonderland*, an appealingly personal look at a creatively blocked filmmaker with a hit behind him. By contrast, the director in *The Pickle*, Harry Stone (Danny Aiello), has made a string of flops and is suffering convulsions of remorse over having sold out for the first time in his career.

Mazursky once again summons up memories of Fellini's *8 1/2* by surrounding his melancholy protagonist with two ex-wives, a 22-year-old French girlfriend, daughter, son, granddaughter, mother, predatory female fan, publicist and journalist, among others. Harry abuses almost all of his loved ones.

Mazursky layers the mirthless tale with black and white flashbacks to Harry's youth in 1940s Brooklyn, as well as with bizarre snatches from the dreaded film-within-a-film, which concerns a space trip embarked upon by a giant pickle grown and launched by farm kids.

PICK-UP ARTIST, THE

1987, 81 MINS, US ◇ Ⓥ ⊙
Dir James Toback *Prod* David L. MacLeod *Scr* James Toback *Ph* Gordon Willis *Ed* David Bretherton, Angelo Corrao *Mus* Georges Delerue *Art Dir* Paul Sylbert
● Molly Ringwald, Robert Downey, Dennis Hopper, Danny Aiello, Mildred Dunnock, Harvey Keitel (20th Century-Fox)

As long as this film sticks to what its title suggests, *The Pick-Up Artist* is a tolerably amusing comedy. But as soon as the compulsive skirt-chaser gets hooked on one girl, James Toback's long-gestating portrait of a one-track mind becomes bogged down in unconvincing plot mechanics.

Opening reels possess considerable buoyancy and zip, as makeout king Robert Downey cruises the streets of New York trying out his shtick on every pretty woman who crosses his path. Downey hits on Ringwald and quickly scores in his convertible, but predictably becomes intrigued by her apparent lack of interest in seeing him again.

Suddenly, he's got blinders on and finds himself assuming personal responsibility for some enormous gambling debts the mob expects delivered by high noon. Dennis Hopper once again plays a drunken, washed-up shell of his former self as Ringwald's irresponsible father, and Harvey Keitel is the threatening collector.

More responsible for the picture's deterioration than the unnecessary melodrama is

Ringwald's thinly conceived character. Toback never lets the viewer in on what she really thinks and feels. Downey, in his first starring role, is brashly likeable, if perhaps too young, as the indefatigable but sincere ladies' man.

Warren Beatty developed the project and was listed as producer during shooting, but producer-of-record credit goes to Beatty's cousin, David L. MacLeod.

PICKUP ON SOUTH STREET

1953, 80 MINS, US Ⓥ
Dir Samuel Fuller *Prod* Jules Schermer *Scr* Samuel Fuller *Ph* Joe MacDonald *Ed* Nick De Maggio *Mus* Leigh Harline *Art Dir* Lyle R. Wheeler, George Patrick
● Richard Widmark, Jean Peters, Thelma Ritter, Murvyn Vye, Richard Kiley, Willis B. Bouchey (20th Century-Fox)

If *Pickup on South Street* makes any point at all, it's that there is nothing really wrong with pickpockets, even when they are given to violence, as long as they don't play footsie with Communist spies. Since this is at best a thin theme, *Pickup* for the most part falls flat on its face and borders on presumably unintended, comedy.

Film's assets are partly its photography, which creates an occasional tense atmosphere, and partly the performance of Thelma Ritter, the only halfway convincing figure in an otherwise unconvincing cast. As Moe, the tired but sharp-tongued old woman who sells ties and habitually informs on her underworld pals in order to collect enough money for a decent 'plot and stone', Ritter is both pathetic and amusing.

Story [by Dwight Taylor] has Richard Widmark picking Jean Peters' purse in the subway. In the wallet he lifts are films of a secret chemical formula obtained by a Commie spy ring. Widmark's act is observed by two Federal agents who are shadowing Peters. Latter is instructed by her boyfriend-boss Richard Kiley to trace Widmark and get back the film.

Widmark is given a chance to repeat his snarling menace characterization followed by a look-what-love-can-do-to-a-bad-boy act as Widmark's hard-boiled soul melts before Peters' romancing.
☐ 1953: Nomination: Best Supp. Actress (Thelma Ritter)

PICKWICK PAPERS, THE

1952, 109 MINS, UK Ⓥ
Dir Noel Langley *Prod* George Minter *Scr* Noel Langley *Ph* Wilkie Cooper *Ed* Anne V. Coates *Mus* Antony Hopkins
● James Hayter, James Donald, Nigel Patrick, Kathleen Harrison, Joyce Grenfell, Donald Wolfit (Langley-Minter/Renown)

The adventures of Mr Pickwick (James Hayter) and his henchmen have been deftly adapted for the screen by Noel Langley. By its adherence to the original, the film is naturally episodic in character.

The picture follows the members of the Pickwick Club on their adventurous tour across England in search of knowledge and human understanding. The encounter with Mr Jingle (Nigel Patrick), the unscrupulous ne'er-do-well with the stilted turn of phrase; the famous literary fancy dress breakfast; the engagement of Sam Weller (Harry Fowler); the breach of promise suit brought against Mr Pickwick by his former housekeeper and his subsequent sojourn in Fleet prison are among the incidents.

In manner and appearance Hayter gives the impression of being the genuine article. His fellow members of the Pickwick Club are admirably played.

■ PICNIC

1955, 115 MINS, US ◇ ⓥ ⊙

Dir Joshua Logan   *Prod* Fred Kohlmar   *Scr* Daniel
Taradash   *Ph* James Wong Howe   *Ed* Charles Nelson,
William A. Lyon   *Mus* George Duning   *Art Dir* Jo
Mielziner, William Flannery

● William Holden, Rosalind Russell, Kim Novak, Betty
Field, Susan Strasberg, Cliff Robertson (Columbia)

This is a considerably enlarged *Picnic*, introducing new scope and style in flow of presentation without dissipating the mood and
substance of the legiter by William Inge. The
boards-to-screen transplanters correctly re-
frained from making any basic changes. It's
the story of a robust and shiftless showoff
who, looking up an old college chum in a
small town in Kansas, sets off various emotional responses among the small group of local inhabitants he encounters.

William Holden is the drifter, sometimes
ribald, partly sympathetic and colorful and
giving a forceful interpretation all the way.

Kim Novak is the town's No. 1 looker, and
an emotional blank until muscle-man (and, to
her, downtrodden) Holden proves an awakening force. Novak does right well.

Rosalind Russell, the spinster school
teacher boarding with Novak's family, is
standout.

□ 1955: Best Color Art Direction, Editing.
□ Nominations: Best Picture, Director, Supp.
Actor (Arthur O'Connell), Scoring of a
Dramatic Picture

•••••••••••••••••••••••••••••

■ PICNIC AT HANGING ROCK

1975, 115 MINS, AUSTRALIA ◇ ⓥ

Dir Peter Weir   *Prod* Jim McElroy, Hal McElroy
Scr Cliff Green   *Ph* Russell Boyd   *Mus* Bruce Smeaton
Art Dir David Copping

● Rachel Roberts, Dominic Guard, Vivian Gray, Helen
Morse, Kirsty Child, Anne Lambert (SAFC)

On a warm St Valentine's Day in 1900 some
schoolgirls from a boarding school in Victoria
picnic at nearby Hanging Rock. Four girls
venture forth on their own; one, Edith, falls
asleep and wakes to find the other three have
taken off their shoes and stockings and are
climbing higher.

The police are called to make an unsuccessful search. A young Englishman, Michael,
also searches, spends the night alone by the
rock and next day is found with a mysterious
head wound but no memory of happenings.
Later, one of the girls, Irma, is also found
with a similar head wound and no memory of
events.

Visually it probably is one of the most beautiful pix ever seen, with Aussie flora and
fauna and wonderful blue skies. Everything
has been carefully re-created with loving ex-
actitude.

•••••••••••••••••••••••••••••

■ PICTURE OF DORIAN GRAY, THE

1945, 107 MINS, US ◇ ⓥ ⊙

Dir Albert Lewin   *Prod* Pandro S. Berman   *Scr* Albert
Lewin   *Ph* Harry Stradling   *Ed* Ferris Webster
Mus Herbert Stothart (dir.), [Mario Castelnuovo-Tedesco,
Franz Waxman]   *Art Dir* Cedric Gibbons, Hans Peters

● George Sanders, Hurd Hatfield, Donna Reed, Angela
Lansbury, Peter Lawford, Lowell Gilmore (M-G-M)

The Picture of Dorian Gray, based upon the
Oscar Wilde novel, represents an interesting
experiment by Metro, reported to have cost
over $2 million.

The morbid theme of the Wilde story is
built around Gray: his contempt for the
painting that was made of him, the fears of
not retaining youth and, of course, the unre-
generate depths to which Gray sinks.

In the adaptation by Albert Lewin, much of
the offscreen narration, explaining among
other things what is going on in Gray's mind
may be too much for most to grasp.

Hurd Hatfield is pretty-boy Gray. He plays
it with little feeling, as apparently intended,
though he should have aged a little toward
the end. George Sanders, misogynistic of
mind and a cynic of the first water, turns in a
very commendable performance. It's he who
upsets the romance, ostensibly serious on
Gray's part, which has developed with a
cheap music hall vocalist. She's Angela
Lansbury, who registers strongly and very
sympathetically.

[Original release prints included inserts in
Technicolor.]

□ 1945: Best B&W Cinematography
□ Nominations: Best Supp. Actress (Angela
Lansbury), B&W Art Direction

•••••••••••••••••••••••••••••

■ PICTURE SHOW MAN, THE

1977, 99 MINS, AUSTRALIA ◇

Dir John Power   *Prod* Joan Long   *Scr* Joan Long
Ph Geoff Burton   *Ed* Nick Beauman   *Mus* Peter Best
Art Dir David Copping

● Rod Taylor, John Meillon, John Ewart, Harold
Hopkins, Patrick Cargill, Yelena Zigon (Limelight)

The Picture Show Man has an old-fashioned endearing quality. The story of an itinerant pur-
veyor of motion picture entertainment in the
country areas of Australia in the 1920s, it's
cute without being cloying, and episodic without being disjointed.

Based on an unpublished manuscript, Joan
Long's script has enough characterization to
allow the actors a fair go at establishing
themselves, yet keeps them well ordered
enough to maintain the forward movement of
the plot.

John Power's direction is firm without being
thwarting and the result is that the good
times being had on screen are conveyed to
the audience and are affecting.

Rod Taylor's portrayal of the heavy is definitely lightweight.

•••••••••••••••••••••••••••••

■ PIED PIPER, THE

1972, 90 MINS, UK ◇ ⓥ

Dir Jacques Demy   *Prod* David Puttnam, Sandy
Lieberson   *Scr* Andrew Birkin, Jacques Demy, Mark
Peploe   *Ph* Peter Suschitzky   *Ed* John Trumper
Mus Donovan   *Art Dir* Assheton Gorton

● Jack Wild, Donald Pleasence, John Hurt, Donovan,
Michael Hordern, Roy Kinnear (Sagittarius/Goodtimes)

The Pied Piper, based on the 14th-century legend from Hamelin, has been filmed by the sensitive Jacques Demy as a sort of somber fairy
tale and allegory. The results are commendable in ambition but uneven in execution.

In recreating the story of the minstrel who
leads the rats out of Hamelin, but then leads
its children away when the politicians fail to
keep a promise, the writers started with one of
folklore's greatest pre-sold subjects.
However, the script seems more a series of
broad, arch, low-comedy vignettes without a
clear emphasis.

As a result, Donovan, in the title role, is in
and out of the story, as is Jack Wild, cast as
the crippled boy whose alchemist patron,
Michael Hordern, cannot convince the town's
elders of the connection between Black
Plague and rats.

•••••••••••••••••••••••••••••

■ PIGEON THAT TOOK ROME, THE

1962, 101 MINS, US

Dir Melville Shavelson   *Prod* Melville Shavelson
Scr Melville Shavelson   *Ph* Daniel L. Fapp   *Ed* Frank
Bracht   *Mus* Allessandro Cicognini   *Art Dir* Hal Pereira,
Roland Anderson

● Charlton Heston, Elsa Martinelli, Harry Guardino,
Salvatore Baccaloni, Gabriella Pollotta, Brian Donlevy
(Paramount)

Melville Shavelson functions as producer, director and writer and shows good control in

all three categories. This is a good-fun comedy and there's no incongruity in the fact that
the setting is authentic-looking World War II
Italy. His adaptation of *The Easter Dinner*, a
novel by Donald Downes, has a wacky story
that plays out amusingly well.

Interesting casting has to do with Charlton
Heston who's an American infantry officer assigned to a cloak-and-dagger role in Rome before the Nazis decide to leave and the Yanks
walk in. It comes to be that homing pigeons
represent his contact with the Allies. His
birds provide an Easter dinner for a local and
friendly family who do not know they're par-
taking of a part of 'the American Air Force',
as stated by one of the characters. Heston becomes replenished with German pigeons,
gives them ankle bracelets with false war information, and one of these messengers
heads unexpectedly to the Allies, instead of
the enemy.

Heston plays the bewildered American officer with enough effectiveness to suggest that
he can be at home with cinematic mischief.
Harry Guardino is Heston's radio man, a sort
of funny fellow sidekick who becomes enamored of a local girl who happens to be pregnant by previous misfortune.

Elsa Martinelli is Heston's romantic vis-a-
vis, not one easily won over but eventually, of
course, they go hand in hand.

□ 1962: Nomination: Best B&W Art
Direction

•••••••••••••••••••••••••••••

■ PILLOW TALK

1959, 105 MINS, US ◇ ⓥ

Dir Michael Gordon   *Prod* Ross Hunter, Martin Melcher
Scr Stanley Shapiro, Maurice Richlin   *Ph* Arthur E. Arling
Ed Milton Carruth   *Mus* Frank DeVol   *Art Dir* Richard
H. Riedel

● Rock Hudson, Doris Day, Tony Randall, Thelma Ritter,
Nick Adams, Julia Meade (Arwin/Universal)

Pillow Talk is a sleekly sophisticated production that deals chiefly with s-e-x. The principals seem to spend considerable time in bed
or talking about what goes on in bed, but the
beds they occupy are always occupied singly.
There's more talk than action natch.

The plot (slight) of the amusing screenplay,
from a story by Clarence Greene and Russell
Rouse, is based on the notion that a telephone shortage puts Doris Day and Rock
Hudson on a party line. Hudson is here a sophisticated man about town. Day displays a
brace of smart Jean Louis gowns, and delivers
crisply.

There is a good deal of cinema trickery in
Pillow Talk. There are split screens; spoken
thoughts by the main characters; and even introduction of background music orchestration
for a laugh. It all registers strongly.

□ 1959: Best Story & Screenplay.
□ Nominations: Best Actress (Doris Day),
Supp. Actress (Thelma Ritter), Color Art
Direction, Scoring of a Dramatic Picture

•••••••••••••••••••••••••••••

■ PINK FLAMINGOS

1974, 95 MINS, US ◇ ⓥ

Dir John Waters   *Scr* John Waters   *Ph* John Waters
Ed John Waters

● Divine, David Lochary, Mink Stole, Mary Vivian
Pearce, Edith Massey, Danny Mills (Dreamland)

Divine, also known as Babs Johnson, is a 300 lb
drag queen of grotesque proportions who
holds the title 'the filthiest person in the
world'. Vying for the title are Connie and
Raymond Marble, who kidnap girls, impreg-
nate them, and sell the children to lesbian
couples in order to finance 'an inner city
heroin ring' catering to high school students.

Around the above premise spins the nitwit
plot of the poorly lensed 16mm picture *Pink
Flamingos* – one of the most vile, stupid and
repulsive films ever made.

Divine's Mama Edie, a huge mountain of adipose tissue, inhabits a playpen in the mobile home and performs coprophagy on the fresh product of a miniature poodle while 'How Much Is That Doggie in the Window' toodles on the soundtrack.

PINK FLOYD THE WALL

1982, 99 MINS, UK ◇ ⑰ ⑨
Dir Alan Parker   *Prod* Alan Marshall   *Scr* Roger Waters
Ph Peter Biziou   *Ed* Gerry Hamblyn   *Art Dir* Gerald Scarfe
● Bob Geldof, Christine Hargreaves, James Laurenson, Eleanor David, Bob Hoskins (M-G-M/United Artists/Tin Blue)

This $12 million production is not a concert film but an eye-popping dramatization of an audio storyline. Being a visual translation of a so-called 'concept' album, pic works extremely well in carrying over the somber tone of the LP.

The music is the core of the film, vocals subbing for the usual film dialog. But there's little need for dialog, since the visual treats offered by animation director Gerald Scarfe and photography director Peter Biziou tell the story.

Story centers around a frustrated, burned-out but successful rock star (Pink) who is near-suicidal and on the verge of insanity. His wife has left him for another man because of the interminable amount of time Pink spends on the road. When he contacts her by telephone, only to have the other man answer, his self-destruct mechanism begins its slow burn.

Powerful performance of Boomtown Rats lead singer Bob Geldof as Pink works to the pic's overall believability, despite its fantasy aura.

PINK PANTHER, THE

1964, 115 MINS, US ◇ ⑰ ⑨
Dir Blake Edwards   *Scr* Blake Edwards, Maurice Richlin
Ph Philip Lathrop   *Ed* Ralph E. Winters   *Mus* Henry Mancini   *Art Dir* Fernando Carrere
● David Niven, Peter Sellers, Robert Wagner, Capucine, Claudia Cardinale, Brenda DeBanzie (United Artists/Mirisch/GE)

This is film making as a branch of the candy trade, and the pack is so enticing that few will worry about the jerky machinations of the plot.

Quite apart from the general air of bubbling elegance, the pic is intensely funny. The yocks are almost entirely the responsibility of Peter Sellers, who is perfectly suited as a clumsy cop who can hardly move a foot without smashing a vase or open a door without hitting himself on the head.

The Panther is a priceless jewel owned by the Indian Princess Dala (Claudia Cardinale), vacationing in the Swiss ski resort of Cortina. The other principals are introduced in their various habitats, before they converge on the princess and her jewel.

Sellers' razor-sharp timing is superlative, and he makes the most of his ample opportunities. His doting concern for criminal wife (Capucine), his blundering ineptitude with material objects, and his dogged pursuit of the crook all coalesce to a sharp performance, with satirical overtones.

David Niven produces his familiar brand of debonair ease. Robert Wagner has a somewhat undernourished role. Capucine, sometimes awkward and over-intense as if she were straining for yocks, is nevertheless a good Simone Clouseau.
□ 1964: Nomination: Best Original Music Score

PINK PANTHER STRIKES AGAIN, THE

1976, 103 MINS, UK ◇ ⑰ ⑨
Dir Blake Edwards   *Prod* Blake Edwards   *Scr* Frank Waldman, Blake Edwards   *Ph* Harry Waxman

Ed Alan Jones   *Mus* Henry Mancini   *Art Dir* Peter Mullins
● Peter Sellers, Herbert Lom, Colin Blakely, Leonard Rossiter, Lesley-Anne Down, Burt Kwouk (United Artists)

The Pink Panther Strikes Again is a hilarious film about the further misadventures of Peter Sellers as Inspector Clouseau. Herbert Lom, Clouseau's nemesis in the police bureau, has had his character expanded into a Professor Moriarty-type fiend, which works just fine.

This time around, Lom is introduced nearly cured of his nervous collapse. But Sellers has assumed Lom's old chief inspector job, and when Lom escapes, Sellers is assigned to the case. Lom kidnaps scientist Richard Vernon who has a disappearing ray device; pitch is that Lom threatens world destruction unless Sellers is handed over to him for extermination.

Action proceeds smartly through plot-advancing action scenes, interleaved with excellent non-dialog sequences featuring Sellers and underscored superbly by Henry Mancini.
□ 1976: Nomination: Best Song ('Come to Me')

PINK STRING AND SEALING WAX

1945, 93 MINS, UK
Dir Robert Hamer   *Prod* Michael Balcon   *Scr* Diana Morgan, Robert Hamer   *Ph* Richard S. Pavey, R. Julius
Ed Michael Truman   *Mus* Norman Demuth
Art Dir Duncan Sutherland
● Mervyn Johns, Mary Merrall, Gordon Jackson, Sally Ann Howes, Googie Withers, Catherine Lacey (Ealing)

Bringing the England of the Victorian period to life is the best thing *Pink String and Sealing Wax* accomplishes. The black, high-necked, rustling Sunday-best bombazines which the church-going women wear contrast violently with the billowing cleavages of the bad women. The unrelenting tyranny of the lord and master of the respectable family is offset by the free-and-easy beatings-up the naughty gals receive at the hands of Cagney-ish husbands and sweethearts. In giving this side of English life, the picture (based on the West End stage hit by Roland Pertwee) is tops.

The bit players turn in performances so bright one wonders how come they aren't in the top billing. Catherine Lacey as a gin drunkard is superb. John Carol's warned-off jockey who loves 'em and leaves 'em without batting an eye is as smooth as the greasy cowlick draped over his forehead. Garry Marsh as the booze hound proprietor of the pub whom Withers rubs out with strychnine is Bill Sykes come to life.

PINKY

1949, 102 MINS, US ⑰
Dir Elia Kazan   *Prod* Darryl F. Zanuck   *Scr* Philip Dunne, Dudley Nichols   *Ph* Joe MacDonald
Ed Harmon Jones   *Mus* Alfred Newman
● Jeanne Crain, Ethel Barrymore, Ethel Waters, William Lundigan (20th Century-Fox)

Pinky is the tag hung by Negroes on a member of their own race who is light-skinned enough to pass for white. In this case it is made clear that Jeanne Crain had passed herself off as ofay for a number of years while studying in Boston. However, when she returns to the home of her grandmother (Ethel Waters) in the south, the scripters always have her quickly reveal herself as Negro. That's what leads to the complications, romantic and dramatic.

'Pinky' is in love with a young doctor (William Lundigan) from New England who wants to marry her despite the color line.

Scripters have put a load of dramatic punch and a share of humor in the yarn [from a novel by Cid Ricketts Sumner].

Crain brings proper dignity and sincerity to her role, although she's not always convincing.

□ 1949: Nominations: Best Actress (Jeanne Crain), Supp. Actress (Ethel Barrymore, Ethel Waters)

PINOCCHIO

1940, 87 MINS, US ◇ ⑰ ⑨
Dir Ben Sharpsteen, Hamilton Luske   *Prod* Walt Disney
Scr Ted Sears, Webb Smith, Joseph Sabo, Otto Englander, William Cottrell, Aurelius Battaglia, Erdman Penner   *Mus* Leigh Harline
● (Walt Disney/RKO)

Pinocchio is a substantial piece of entertainment for young and old. Both animation and photography are vastly improved over Walt Disney's first cartoon feature, *Snow White*. Animation is so smooth that cartoon figures carry impression of real persons and settings rather than drawings.

Extensive use of the Disney-developed multiplane camera (first used moderately for *Snow White*) provides some ingenious cartoon photography, allowing for camera movement similar to dolly shots. Most startling effect is the jumpy landscape as seen through the eyes of a leaping Jiminy Cricket.

Opening is similar to *Snow White*, establishing at the start that this is a fairy tale. Jiminy, witty, resourceful and effervescing cricket, displays the title cover and first illustrations of the book with a dialog description introducing the old woodcarver, Geppetto, and his workshop. Place abounds with musical clocks and gadgets, pet kitten and goldfish – and the completed puppet whom he names Pinocchio. Geppetto's wish for a son on the wishing star is granted when the blue fairy appears and provides life for the puppet; with Jiminy Cricket appointed guardian of latter's conscience. Pinocchio soon encounters villainous characters and his impetuous curiosity gets him into a series of escapades.

Cartoon characterization of Pinocchio is delightful, with his boyish antics and pranks maintaining constant interest. Jiminy Cricket is a fast-talking character providing rich humor with wisecracks and witticisms. Kindly old Geppetto is a definitely drawn character while several appearances of Blue Fairy are accentuated by novel lighting effects. Picture stresses evil figures and results of wrongdoing more vividly and to greater extent than *Snow White*, and at times somewhat overplays these factors for children. This is minor, however.
□ 1940: Best Song ('When You Wish Upon a Star'), Original Score

PIN UP GIRL

1944, 85 MINS, US ◇ ⑰ ⑨
Dir Bruce Humberstone   *Prod* William LeBaron
Scr Robert Ellis, Helen Logan, Earl Baldwin   *Ph* Ernest Palmer   *Ed* Robert Simpson   *Mus* Emil Newman, Charles Henderson (dir.)   *Art Dir* James Basevi, Joseph C. Wright
● Betty Grable, John Harvey, Martha Raye, Joe E. Brown (20th Century-Fox)

This is one of those escapist filmusicals which makes no pretenses at ultra-realism, and if you get into the mood fast that it's something to occupy your attention for an hour and a half. It's all very pleasing and pleasant.

Producer William LeBaron, director Bruce Humberstone and the cast, scripters, et al. have treated *Pin Up Girl* in uniform spirit. The Missouri gal who crashes the party of a welcome-to-a-Guadalcanal-hero (John Harvey) in one of New York's top niteries brooks no plot examination.

Right from the start, when Betty Grable is almost trapped in her gate-crashing she poses as a musicomedy actress, mounts the rostrum pronto and Charlie Spivak picks up the music cue and it all comes out all right. Just like that!

Joe E. Brown as the cafe prop and Martha Raye as his jealous star carry the low comedy against which are backgrounded expert hoofology by the Condos Bros, Spivak's stuff, rollerskating routines and the military finale.

In Technicolor Grable is a looker in pastel shades and spades. The costumes of the spec numbers have likewise been contrived for ultra-sartorial resplendence. All combined it makes for merry movie moments.

● ●

■ PIRANHA

1978, 92 MINS, US ◇ ⓥ

Dir Joe Dante *Prod* Jon Davison *Scr* John Sayles
Ph Jamie Anderson *Ed* Mark Goldblatt, Joe Dante
Mus Pino Donaggio *Art Dir* Bill Mellin, Kerry Mellin
● Bradford Dillman, Heather Menzies, Kevin McCarthy, Keenan Wynn, Dick Miller, Barbara Steele (New World)

Since the title characters in *Piranha* are never actually seen (there's lots of speeded-up nibbling, but no closeups of the deadly Brazilian river munchers), the pic utilizes a lot of red dye in the water, and an auditory effect for the gnawing that sounds like an air-conditioner on the fritz.

What is different about *Piranha* is the unusual number of victims. Not only is the requisite slew of cameo performers dispatched quickly (Keenan Wynn, Kevin McCarthy, Bruce Gordon), but an entire camp full of school children, and a holiday crowd at a lakeside resort get chomped. This is one film where the fish win.

Heather Menzies plays an aggressive femme searching for missing persons, who enlists backwoods recluse Bradford Dillman in her cause. When they stumble on mad doctor McCarthy's mountain-top lab, they unwittingly release a generation of super-hardy piranhas McCarthy was breeding for use in the Mekong Delta during the Vietnam war.

Barbara Steele turns up as a government scientist who hints the piranhas may be back for a sequel. Menzies is attractively competent, and Dillman does what he's supposed to, which isn't much. One yearns to have seen more of McCarthy and his lab, where a scaly homunculus is seen lurking about, but never explained.

● ●

■ PIRANHA II
THE SPAWNING
(Aka: Piranha 2: Flying Killers)

1983, 95 MINS, ITALY ◇ ⓥ ☉

Dir James Cameron *Prod* Chako van Leuwen, Jeff Schectman *Scr* H.A. Milton *Ph* Roberto D'Ettore Piazzoli *Ed* Roberto Silvi *Mus* Steve Powder
● Tricia O'Neil, Steve Marachuk, Lance Henriksen, Ricky G. Paul, Ted Richert, Leslie Graves (Chako)

Made in 1981, this is a routine monster film, unrelated to Joe Dante's 1978 *Piranha*. Idiotic premise has US government genetic engineering experiments creating a deadly form of grunions (hinted at being used in the Vietnam war). A missing canister of fertile eggs of these mutant fish (called piranha for horror fans' sake) turns up in the Caribbean resort of Club Elysium and the beasties start chewing up vacationers.

Film's title refers to the grunions' annual mating ritual of spawning on the beach. Lame script pokes fun at the match of human and fishy mating rites. Nominal human interest plot has Club Elysium scuba diver Anne (Tricia O'Neil) teaming up with incognito biochemist Tyler (Steve Marachuk) to discover and blow up the fish, while her estranged husband Steve (Lance Henriksen) looks out for the welfare of the locals as the film's Roy Scheider-esque cop.

Exec producer Ovidio G. Assonitis follows up his similar made-in-America horror pics *Beyond the Door*, *Tentacles*, and *The Visitor* with an Italian-crewed film which easily passes as All-American. Special effects experts come up with convincing gore for the victims, but the monsters are laughably phoney.

● ●

■ PIRATE, THE

1948, 101 MINS, US ◇ ⓥ

Dir Vincente Minnelli *Prod* Arthur Freed *Scr* Albert Hackett, Frances Goodrich *Ph* Harry Stradling
Ed Blanche Sewell *Mus* Lennie Hayton (dir.), Conrad Salinger (arr.) *Art Dir* Cedric Gibbons, Jack Martin Smith
● Judy Garland, Gene Kelly, Walter Slezak, Gladys Cooper, Reginald Owen, George Zucco (M-G-M)

The Pirate is escapist film fare. It's an eye and ear treat of light musical entertainment, garbing its amusing antics, catchy songs and able terping in brilliant color.

Gene Kelly and Judy Garland team delightfully in selling the dances and songs, scoring in both departments. The Cole Porter score is loaded with tunes that get over to the ear and the foot.

Adapted from the S. N. Behrman play, picture tells of the cloistered Latin girl about to fulfill an arranged wedding when she meets a travelling troupe of entertainers headed by Kelly. Title springs from fact that gal yearns for a fabulous pirate and sees him in the actor.

Vincente Minnelli's direction is light and seems to poke subtle fun at the elaborate musical ingredients and plot. The fact that *The Pirate* never takes itself too seriously adds to enjoyment, giving sharp point to some of the dialog in the script.
☐ 1948: Nomination: Best Scoring of a Dramatic Picture

● ●

■ PIRATES

1986, 124 MINS, FRANCE/TUNISIA ◇ ⓥ

Dir Roman Polanski *Prod* Tarak Ben Ammar
Scr Gerard Brach, Roman Polanski, John Brownjohn
Ph Witold Sobocinski *Ed* Herve de Luze, William Reynolds *Mus* Philippe Sarde *Art Dir* Pierre Guffroy
● Walter Matthau, Damien Thomas, Richard Pearson, Cris Campion, Charlotte Lewis, Olu Jacobs (Carthago/Accent-Cominco)

Roman Polanski's *Pirates* is a decidedly underwhelming comedy adventure adding up to a major disappointment.

Pirates first was announced as a 1976 Polanski feature to star Jack Nicholson and Isabelle Adjani, before finally being produced (commencing in 1984) in Tunisia, Malta and the Seychelles, costing in excess of $30 million.

Walter Matthau gainfully essays the central role of Capt Thomas Bartholomew Red, a peg-legged British pirate captain with plenty of Long John Silver in his manner. Teamed with a handsome young French sailor (Cris Campion), Red is captured by Don Alfonso (Damien Thomas), captain of the Spanish galleon *Neptune*.

In a series of turnabout adventures, Red causes the *Neptune*'s crew to mutiny, takes the niece (Charlotte Lewis) of the governor of Maracaibo hostage, and steals a golden Aztec throne from the Spaniards.

Casting is unimpressive, with Matthau unable to carry the picture singlehandedly. Newcomer Campion projects a pleasant personality, more than can be said for Polanski's discovery Charlotte Lewis, thoroughly inexpressive here.
☐ 1986: Nomination: Best Costume Design

● ●

■ PIRATES OF PENZANCE, THE

1983, 112 MINS, US ◇ ⓥ ☉

Dir Wilford Leach *Prod* Joseph Papp, Timothy Burrill
Scr Wilford Leach *Ph* Douglas Slocombe *Ed* Anne V. Coates *Mus* William Elliott (arr.) *Art Dir* Elliot Scott
● Kevin Kline, Angela Lansbury, Linda Ronstadt, George Rose, Rex Smith, Tony Azito (Pressman/Universal)

Gilbert & Sullivan's durable *The Pirates of Penzance* has been turned into an elaborate screen musical by basically the same hands

responsible for Joseph Papp's smash New York Shakespeare Festival and Broadway stage production, and result is a delight.

For the film, shot at Shepperton Studios in England, a charming artificiality of style was arrived at, which is most immediately apparent in Elliot Scott's beautifully witty production design.

Simple tale has orphan Rex Smith leaving, upon turning 21, the band of pirates with whom he's been raised. Upon hitting land, he encounters eight sisters and becomes smitten with one of them, Linda Ronstadt, Pirate King Kevin Kline is not about to let Smith go straight so easily, however, and informs him that, having been born on 29 February, he's actually only had five birthdays, and will therefore be obliged to remain with the gang until 1940 or so.

With the exception of Angela Lansbury, entertaining as the pirates' nursemaid and *aide-de-combat*, all principal cast members have repeated their Broadway performances here, and in exemplary fashion.

● ●

■ PIT AND THE PENDULUM

1961, 85 MINS, US ◇ ⓥ

Dir Roger Corman *Prod* Roger Corman *Scr* Richard Matheson *Ph* Floyd Crosby *Ed* Anthony Carras
Mus Les Baxter *Art Dir* Daniel Haller
● Vincent Price, John Kerr, Barbara Steele, Luana Anders, Antony Carbone, Patrick Westwood (American International)

Pit and the Pendulum is an elaboration of the short Poe classic about blood-letting in 16th-century Spain. The result is a physically stylish, imaginatively photographed horror film which, though needlessly corny in many spots, adds up to good exploitation.

The main problem is that Poe furnished scriptwriter Richard Matheson with only one scene – the spine-tingling climax – and Matheson has been hard put to come up with a comparably effective build-up to these last 10 or so minutes. He has removed the tale one generation beyond the time of the Spanish Inquisition (for reasons best known to himself) and contrived a plot involving an ill-fated nobleman slowly losing his mind because he thinks he accidentally buried his wife alive, just like his father did some years before – on purpose.

Actually Matheson's plotting isn't at all bad, but he has rendered it in some fruity dialog. If audiences don't titter, it's only because veteran star Vincent Price can chew scenery while keeping his tongue in his cheek.

While Matheson's script takes a good deal of time, including three extended flashbacks, to get to the denouement, it's almost worth it. The last portion of the film builds with genuine excitement to a reverse twist ending that might well have pleased Poe himself.

● ●

■ PLACE FOR LOVERS, A

1969, 88 MINS, ITALY/FRANCE ◇

Dir Vittorio De Sica *Prod* Carlo Ponti, Arthur Cohn
Scr Julian Halevy, Peter Baldwin, Ennio De Concini, Tonino Guerra, Cesare Zavattini *Ph* Pasquale De Santis
Ed Adriana Novelli *Mus* Maurice De Sica
Art Dir Piero Poletto
● Faye Dunaway, Marcello Mastroianni, Caroline Mortimer, Karin Engh (M-G-M/Ponti-Cohn)

With five scripters freely adapting a play [*Amanti*, by Brunello Rondi and Renaldo Cabieri] the result is bound to lack decision and this romantic drama comes out at times as somewhat sudsy and flabby. But with Vittorio De Sica's direction, the eye-pleasing atmosphere of the Italian Alps and Marcello Mastroianni and Faye Dunaway a good team as a pair of ill-starred lovers, there's enough pull.

Dunaway arrives to stay at a deserted ele-

P

gant villa near Venice. She phones Mastroianni and he hotfoots it to the villa. Without quite understanding what gives, he is in the sack with Dunaway before the night's out.

Situations are often lethargically introduced and dialog is frequently stagey and mannered. But De Sica gets full measure out of the love interest with its moody background. Dunaway looks beautiful and enticing and Mastroianni is pleasantly cast as the infatuated lover.

....

■ PLACE IN THE SUN, A

1951, 118 MINS, US ⑱ ⊙
Dir George Stevens   *Prod* George Stevens   *Scr* Michael Wilson, Harry Brown   *Ph* William C. Mellor
Ed William Hornbeck   *Mus* Franz Waxman
Art Dir Hans Dreier, Walter Tyler
● Montgomery Clift, Elizabeth Taylor, Shelley Winters, Anne Revere, Fred Clark, Raymond Burr (Paramount)

Theodore Dreiser's much-discussed novel of the 1920s, *An American Tragedy*, is here transposed to the screen for the second time by Paramount. The first version was made in 1930 by Josef Von Sternberg under the original title. This version, brought completely up to date in time and settings [and also based on Patrick Kearney's play from the novel], is distinguished beyond its predecessor in every way. Montgomery Clift, Shelley Winters and Elizabeth Taylor give wonderfully shaded and poignant performances.

Tale is of a poor and lonely boy and girl who find comfort in each other. Unhappily, while the girl progresses to real love of the boy, he finds love elsewhere in a wealthy lass of a social set to which he'd like to become a part. His first attachment is not easily broken off, however, because the girl discovers herself pregnant. When she appears at a mountain lake resort where he is spending his vacation with the femme who has by this time become his fiancee, his confused emotions lead him to take her into a boat with intention of drowning her.

Winters plays the poor gal, Taylor the rich one. Clift at times seems overly-laconic.
☐ 1951: Best Director, Screenplay, B&W Cinematography, Scoring of a Dramatic Picture, Editing, B&W Costume Design.
☐ Nominations: Best Picture, Actor (Montgomery Clift), Actress (Shelley Winters)

....

■ PLACES IN THE HEART

1984, 102 MINS, US ◇ ⑱ ⊙
Dir Robert Benton   *Prod* Arlene Donovan   *Scr* Robert Benton   *Ph* Nestor Almendros   *Ed* Carol Littleton
Mus John Kander   *Art Dir* Gene Callahan
● Sally Field, Lindsay Crouse, Ed Harris, Amy Madigan, John Malkovich, Danny Glover (Tri-Star)

Places in the Heart is a loving, reflective homage to his hometown by writer-director Robert Benton. Flawlessly crafted, Benton creates a full tapestry of life in Waxahachie, Texas circa 1935, but filmgoers may find his understated naturalistic approach lacking in dramatic punch.

Obviously drawing on his personal experiences and people he knew growing up, Benton remembers the rituals of everyday life: love, in all of its forms, birth and death.

Sally Field is solid in the lead role as a widowed mother, but she is not the strong unifying character that can tie the strands of Benton's script together.

Nestor Almendros' photography is not pretty, but high on feeling and atmosphere. It radiates a lived-in autumnal light.
☐ 1984: Best Actress (Sally Field), Original Screenplay.
☐ Nominations: Best Picture, Director, Actor (John Malkovich), Supp. Actress (Lindsay Crouse), Costume Design

....

■ PLAINSMAN, THE

1937, 112 MINS, US ⑱ ⊙
Dir Cecil B. DeMille   *Prod* Cecil B. DeMille
Scr Waldemar Young, Lynn Riggs, Harold Lamb
Ph Victor Milner, George Robinson   *Ed* Anne Bauchens
Mus George Anthei   *Art Dir* Hans Dreier, Roland Anderson
● Gary Cooper, Jean Arthur, James Ellison, Charles Bickford, Helen Burgess, Porter Hall (Paramount)

The Plainsman is a big and a good western. It's cowboys and Indians on a broad, sweeping scale; not a *Covered Wagon* (1923) but majestic enough. Gary Cooper is Hickok, Jean Arthur is the historic Calamity Jane of his immediate associations, and James Ellison is a rather aggrandized Buffalo Bill. Opposite the latter is Helen Burgess as his bride. This perforce casts him as something of a musical comedy version of the plains scout whom history has pictured a much more grisly personality.

The spec appeal is in the redskin warfare. The sequence with the near burning-at-the-stake of Hickok in Yellow Hand's camp is tingling and the soldiers' holding out for several days against an almost overwhelming horde of Comanches, with some corking charging-through-the-water action, is another. Scripting [based on data from stories by Courtney Ryley Cooper and Frank J. Wilstack] and editing stand out favorably. Arthur is particularly endowed with some punch lines and pungent expletives as the hardy daughter.

....

■ PLANES, TRAINS & AUTOMOBILES

1987, 93 MINS, US ◇ ⑱ ⊙
Dir John Hughes   *Prod* John Hughes   *Scr* John Hughes
Ph Don Peterman   *Ed* Paul Hirsch   *Mus* Ira Newborn
Art Dir John W. Corso
● Steve Martin, John Candy, Laila Robins, Michael McKean, Kevin Bacon, Dylan Baker (Paramount)

John Hughes has come up with an effective nightmare-as-comedy in *Planes, Trains & Automobiles*. Disaster-prone duo of Steve Martin and John Candy repeatedly recall a contemporary Laurel & Hardy as they agonizingly try to make their way from New York to Chicago by various modes of transport.

Man versus technology has been one of the staples of screen comedy since the earliest silent days, and Hughes makes the most of the format here packing as many of the frustrations of modern life as he can into this calamitous travelog of roadside America.

An ultimte situation comedy, tale throws together Martin, an ad exec, and Candy, a shower curtain ring salesman, as they head home from Manhattan to their respective homes in Chicago two days before Thanksgiving.

The problems start before they even get out of midtown. From there, it's a series of ghastly motel rooms, crowded anonymous restaurants, a sinister cab ride, an abortive train trip, an even worse excursion by rented car, some hitchhiking by truck, and, finally, a hop on the 'El' before sitting down to turkey.

....

■ PLANET OF THE APES

1968, 112 MINS, US ◇ ⑱ ⊙
Dir Franklin J. Schaffner   *Prod* Arthur P. Jacobs
Scr Michael Wilson, Rod Serling   *Ph* Leon Shamroy
Ed Hugh S. Fowler   *Mus* Jerry Goldsmith   *Art Dir* Jack Martin Smith, William Creber
● Charlton Heston, Roddy McDowall, Kim Hunter, Maurice Evans, James Whitmore, Linda Harrison (Apjac/20th Century-Fox)

Planet of the Apes is an amazing film. A political-sociological allegory, cast in the mold of futuristic science-fiction, it is an intriguing blend of chilling satire, a sometimes ludicrous juxtaposition of human and ape mores, optimism and pessimism.

Pierre Boulle's novel, in which US space explorers find themselves in a world dominated by apes, has been adapted by Michael Wilson and Rod Serling.

The totality of the film works very well, leading to a surprise ending. The suspense, and suspension of belief, engendered is one of the film's biggest assets.

Charlton Heston, leader of an aborted space shot which propels his crew 20 centuries ahead of earth, is a cynical man who eventually has thrust upon him the burden of reasserting man's superiority over all other animals. At fadeout, he is the new Adam.

Key featured players – all in ape makeup – include Roddy McDowall and Kim Hunter, Maurice Evans, James Whitmore and James Daly.
☐ 1968: Honorary Award (John Chambers, for makeup design).
☐ Nominations: Best Costume Design, Original Music Score

....

■ PLATINUM BLONDE

1931, 82 MINS, US
Dir Frank Capra   *Scr* Jo Swerling, Dorothy Howell, Robert Riskin   *Ph* Joseph Walker   *Ed* Gene Milford
● Loretta Young, Robert Williams, Jean Harlow, Louise Closser Hale, Donald Dillaway, Reginald Owen (Columbia)

It's entertaining, has a lot of light, pleasing comedy and carries a cast that's tops. Robert Williams is a very likable character as a reporter who marries himself off to a snobbish society frail, and he plays it like a champ. Always displaying a fine screen presence and manner, Williams quickly ingratiates himself.

The newspaper background is prominent, and for once its 100% natural. The managing editor (Edmund Breese) with his hollering, swearing, affability and pride is aces.

The picture is with Williams all the way. It gives him a great break, and a pip scene, when after marrying the snooty plat (Jean Harlow) he renounces the whole gang in stiff language, taking ozone with the sob sister who all along has wanted it that way. Loretta Young runs third on footage and is somewhat missed.

....

■ PLATOON

1986, 120 MINS, US ◇ ⑱
Dir Oliver Stone   *Prod* Arnold Kopelson   *Scr* Oliver Stone   *Ph* Robert Richardson   *Ed* Claire Simpson
Mus Georges Delerue   *Art Dir* Bruno Rubeo
● Tom Berenger, Willem Dafoe, Charlie Sheen, Forest Whitaker (Hemdale)

Platoon is an intense but artistically distanced study of infantry life during the Vietnam War. Writer-director Oliver Stone seeks to immerse the audience totally in the nightmare of the United States' misguided adventure, and manages to do so in a number of very effective scenes.

A Vietnam vet himself, Stone obviously had urgent personal reasons for making this picture, a fact that emerges instantly as green volunteer Charlie Sheen is plunged into the thick of action along the Cambodian border in late 1967.

Willem Dafoe comes close to stealing the picture as the sympathetic sergeant whose drugged state may even heighten his sensitivity to the insanity around him, and each of the members of the young cast all have their moments to shine.
☐ 1986: Best Picture, Director, Sound, Editing.
☐ Nominations: Best Supp. Actor (Tom Berenger, Willem Dafoe), Original Screenplay, Cinematography

....

■ PLAYBOYS, THE

1992, 110 MINS, US ◇ ⊛
Dir Gillies MacKinnon   *Prod* William P. Cartlidge
Scr Shane Connaughton, Kerry Crabbe   *Ph* Jack Conroy
Ed Humphrey Dixon   *Mus* Jean-Claude Petit
Art Dir Andy Harris
● Albert Finney, Aidan Quinn, Robin Wright, Milo
O'Shea, Alan Devlin, Niamh Cusack (Goldwyn)

Pic started off with a hitch when originally
cast star Annette Bening dropped out on the
eve of production. Replacement Robin
Wright (Mrs Sean Penn) was a felicitous
choice, in her best film acting to date. Story
by Shane Connaughton, who co-scripted *My
Left Foot*, concerns an Irish lass (Wright) in
1957 who's shamed by her fellow townsfolk
for being an unwed mother.

A new love enters her life with the arrival of
Milo O'Shea's troupe of traveling actors, The
Playboys. Newest thesp in the company
(Aidan Quinn) immediately impresses
Wright and eventually beds her. Fly in the
ointment is the local constable (Albert
Finney) who has always been in love with
Wright and explodes into violence.

This familiar pattern of headstrong girl and
passions brimming beneath the surface is
well directed by first time Scottish helmer
Gillies MacKinnon, though the pace slows in
middle reels as plot gives way to the troupe's
enjoyable stage performances.

■ PLAY DIRTY

1969, 117 MINS, UK ◇
Dir Andre de Toth   *Prod* Harry Saltzman   *Scr* Lotte
Colin, Melvyn Bragg   *Ph* Ted Scaife   *Ed* Alan Osbiston
Mus Michel Legrand   *Art Dir* Tom Morahan
● Michael Caine, Nigel Davenport, Nigel Green, Harry
Andrews, Bernard Archer (United/Lowndes)

Play Dirty is mainly the story of a small unit
detailed to blow up a vital enemy fuel dump
in the desert.

Main disappointment about the film [from
an original story by George Marton] which
has occasional crisp dialog and situations and
two or three lively skirmishes is the performance of lead Michael Caine, who plays with
an often tired and flat lack of expression
which doesn't pump much blood into the dialog or action. He handles his role with intelligence but comes out second best to Nigel
Davenport, a resourceful rogue with style.

Caine is cast as an inexperienced British
army captain, detailed to lead reluctantly a
small band of mercenaries into the desert to
dispose of a vital enemy fuel dump.

Clash between Caine and Davenport is the
main thread of the story and results in a fascinating relationship beween the two.

■ PLAYER, THE

1992, 123 MINS, US ◇ ⊛ ⊙
Dir Robert Altman   *Prod* David Brown, Michael Tolkin,
Nick Wechsler   *Scr* Michael Tolkin   *Ph* Jean Lepine
Ed Geraldine Peroni   *Mus* Thomas Newman
Art Dir Stephen Altman
● Tim Robbins, Greta Scacchi, Fred Ward, Whoopi
Goldberg, Peter Gallagher, Vincent D'Onofrio (Avenue)

The Player is the deep dish on Hollywood,
1992. Mercilessly satiric yet good-natured,
this enormously entertaining slam dunk quite
possibly is the most resonant Hollywood saga
since the days of *Sunset Blvd.* and *The Bad and
the Beautiful*.

Brilliantly scripted by Michael Tolkin from
his own novel, plot hinges on a series of
threatening postcards received by hotshot
studio executive Griffin Mill (Tim Robbins)
from an ignored screenwriter. Mill tracks
down the man he suspects of being the sender
– the garrulous writer David Kahane
(Vincent D'Onofrio) – has a few drinks with
the man and, in a fit of anger, accidentally

kills him. Mill is able to continue his normal
life of worrying about being edged out of the
studio by the newly hired Larry Levy (Peter
Gallagher).

The postcards keep coming, but Mill initiates a romance with his victim's sexy girlfriend, June (Greta Scacchi), then maneuvers
brilliantly on a film project that provides *The
Player* with its showstopping capper.

Centerscreen throughout, Robbins is superb
as Mill. Whoopi Goldberg brings cheerful
vigor to her surprising role of a Pasadena police detective. Scacchi gives the unfearful girlfriend a contemporary, ambiguous amorality.

Glimpsed at restaurants, galas, parties, on
the lot and just around, celebs from Cher,
Nick Nolte, Anjelica Huston, Burt Reynolds,
Susan Sarandon and Harry Belafonte to Jack
Lemmon, Lily Tomlin, Elliott Gould, Rod
Steiger and, hilariously, Julia Roberts and
Bruce Willis, keep turning up. Made indepen-
dently on a modest $8 million, the picture
looks like plenty more.
☐ 1992: Nomination: Best Director,
Screenplay Adaptation, Editing

■ PLAYERS

1979, 120 MINS, US ◇ ⊛
Dir Anthony Harvey   *Prod* Robert Evans   *Scr* Arnold
Schulman   *Ph* James Crabe   *Ed* Randy Roberts
Mus Jerry Goldsmith   *Art Dir* Richard Sylbert
● Ali MacGraw, Dean-Paul Martin, Maximilian Schell,
Pancho Gonzales, Steve Guttenberg (Paramount)

Another love story in disguise, this time backgrounded against the tennis world, *Players* is
disqualified by exec producer Arnold
Schulman's wobbly script, a simpering performance by Ali MacGraw, and a preponderance
of tennis footage.

Via backward glances, it's explained that
Dean-Paul Martin, who at the film's begin-
ning is pitted against Guillermo Vilas in the
Wimbledon championships, rescues socialite
Ali MacGraw from a car accident, is adopted
by her, and eventually falls in love with her.

Only ace in *Players* is casting of Martin, who,
in his first film role proves highly believable
in both his tennis and dramatic scenes.
Excellent support is offered by Pancho
Gonzales in a re-creation of his real-life role
as a pro-turned-teacher.

■ PLAY IT AGAIN, SAM

1972, 84 MINS, US ◇ ⊛ ⊙
Dir Herbert Ross   *Prod* Arthur P. Jacobs   *Scr* Woody
Allen   *Ph* Owen Roizman   *Ed* Marion Rothman
Mus Billy Goldenberg   *Art Dir* Ed Wittstein
● Woody Allen, Diane Keaton, Tony Roberts, Jerry Lacy,
Susan Anspach, Jennifer Salt (Paramount/Apjac)

Woody Allen's 1969 legit comedy-starrer, *Play
It Again, Sam*, has become on the screen 84
minutes of fragile fun. Allen and other key
players from the stage version encore to good
results. The placid direction of Herbert Ross
keeps Allen in the spotlight for some good
laughs, several chuckles and many smiles.

Allen's adaptation showcases his self-deprecating, and sometimes erratic, comedy personality. Ditched by wife Susan Anspach, who
cannot stand his vicarious living of old
Humphrey Bogart films, Allen is consoled by
Diane Keaton and Tony Roberts, to the point
that Keaton begins to fall for Allen. The interlude ends with a recreation of the final
scene from Warners' *Cassablanca*. Jerry Lacy
is most effective as the Bogart phantom who
drops in from time to time.

■ PLAY MISTY FOR ME

1971, 102 MINS, US ◇ ⊛ ⊙
Dir Clint Eastwood   *Prod* Robert Daley   *Scr* Jo Heims,
Dean Riesner   *Ph* Bruce Surtees   *Ed* Carl Pingitore
Mus Dee Barton   *Art Dir* Alexander Golitzen

● Clint Eastwood, Jessica Walter, Donna Mills, John
Larch, Clarice Taylor, Don Siegel (Universal/Malpaso)

When it's not serving as an overdone travelog
for the Monterey Peninsula-Carmel home environment of star, producer and debuting director Clint Eastwood, *Play Misty for Me* is an
often fascinating suspenser about psychotic
Jessica Walter, whose deranged infatuation
for Eastwood leads her to commit murder.
For that 80% of the film which constitutes the
story, the structure and dialog create a mood
of nervous terror which the other 20% nearly
blows away.

Walter gives a superior performance as an
unusual woman whose eccentricities are
killing. Eastwood has selected excellent support: John Larch as a detective who nearly
solves the case; Clarice Taylor, outstanding
as a housekeeper; James McEachin as
Eastwood's fellow-deejay on a (real) local radio station; Irene Hervey as a potential benefactor driven off by Walter's insults and
director Don Siegel as a friendly bartender.

■ PLAZA SUITE

1971, 114 MINS, US ◇ ⊛ ⊙
Dir Arthur Hiller   *Prod* Howard W. Koch   *Scr* Neil
Simon   *Ph* Jack Marta   *Ed* Frank Bracht   *Mus* Maurice
Jarre   *Art Dir* Arthur Lonergan
● Walter Matthau, Maureen Stapleton, Barbara Harris,
Lee Grant, Louise Sorel (Paramount)

Neil Simon's excellent adaptation of his 1968
Broadway hit stars Walter Matthau in three
strong characterizations of comedy-in-depth,
teamed separately with Maureen Stapleton,
Lee Grant and Barbara Harris.

Film opens with a 44-minute sketch featuring Stapleton as a nervous suburban wife who
has taken her bridal suite at NY's Plaza Hotel
while the paint dries at home. Hubby
Matthau is a cool, jaded mate whose affair
with secretary Louise Sorel is intuitively di-
vined by the wife. Segment is the most dramatic, though filled with nervous comedy.

Middle episode is 33 minutes of lecherous
farce, as Hollywood producer Matthau puts
the make on Harris, a flame of 15 years past.
She has become a reluctant matron of
Tenafly, NJ. Some of the best laughs of the
whole piece occur here.

Final 37 minutes involve father-of-the-bride
Matthau, trying to coax frightened daughter
Jenny Sullivan out of a locked hotel bathroom
and into marriage to Thomas Carey. Grant is
the harried mother. The comedy emphasis
here is generally slapstick: rain-drenched
clothes; torn tails and stockings; broken furniture.

Each of the femme stars is given much
screen time and the result not only is excellent spotlighting of their own talents, but also
an adroit restraint on Matthau's presence.

■ PLEASE DON'T EAT THE DAISIES

1960, 111 MINS, US ◇ ⊛
Dir Charles Walters   *Prod* Joe Pasternak   *Scr* Isobel
Lennart   *Ph* Robert Bronner   *Ed* John MacSweeney
Mus David Rose   *Art Dir* George W. Davis, Hans Peters
● Doris Day, David Niven, Janis Paige, Spring Byington,
Richard Haydn, Patsy Kelly (M-G-M)

Please Don't Eat The Daisies is a light and frothy
comedy, and boff family fare. Pic is episodic –
as was the book by Jean Kerr – a series of
highly amusing incidents strung together by a
rather loose story thread, but this circumstance doesn't militate against interest.
Charles Walters' direction maintains terrific
pace.

Plotline is based on the adventures of Doris
Day and David Niven after he turns to newspaper drama criticking during which they are
forced out of their Gotham apartment and
buy a monstrosity in the country – 70 miles
from Broadway – where Day takes on commu-

nity life while trying to modernize and make their new home livable. Janis Paige enters scene as a Broadway actress whom Niven pans in his very first review, which also incurs the enmity of his best friend, producer Richard Haydn.

Day delivers lustily and Niven makes hay with his critic's portrayal, for whom Paige goes on the make in a big way. Jack Weston also is good as a play-writing cabby.

••••••••••••••••••••••••••••••••

■ PLEASURE PRINCIPLE, THE

1992, 98 MINS, UK ◇ ⓥ
Dir David Cohen   *Prod* David Cohen   *Scr* David Cohen
Ph Andrew Spellar   *Ed* Joe McAllister   *Mus* Sonny Southon   *Art Dir* Cecelia Bretherton
● Colin Firth, Lynsey Baxter, Haydn Gwynne, Lysette Anthony, Sara Mair-Thomas, Ian Hogg (Psychology News)

An amiable *Alfie* for the postfeminist 1990s, *The Pleasure Principle* is a refreshing light comedy that simply asks its audience to lie back and enjoy. First feature of Haifa-born, British-based director David Cohen sports dapper ensemble playing.

A womanizing journalist (Colin Firth) is divorced from a raving gay feminist (Sara Mair-Thomas), and his current mate is the unpredictable brain surgeon (Haydn Gwynne) who keeps an Alsatian dog in her bedroom and answers the phone in mid-orgasm. Firth's sexual roundlay gathers steam when he also starts canoodling with a mousy divorcee (Lynsey Baxter) and beautiful yuppie lawyer (Lysette Anthony). Finally, the surgeon springs the trap and brings him to his senses.

Much of the action is of a superior bedroom farce type, with Firth desperately juggling his women and being given a hard time in return. Dialogue is sharp and candid and the sack scenes funny and natural. Indie pic was shot on a budget of £200,000 but looks solidly pro.

••••••••••••••••••••••••••••••••

■ PLENTY

1985, 124 MINS, US ◇ ⓥ ☉
Dir Fred Schepisi   *Prod* Edward R. Pressman, Joseph Papp   *Scr* David Hare   *Ph* Ian Baker   *Ed* Peter Honess   *Mus* Bruce Smeaton   *Art Dir* Richard Macdonald
● Meryl Streep, Charles Dance, Tracey Ullman, John Gielgud, Sting, Ian McKellen (RKO/Pressman)

A picture possessing a host of first-class pedigrees, *Plenty* emerges as an absorbing and fastidiously made adaptation of David Hare's acclaimed play, but also comes off as cold and ultimately unaffecting.

Hare's ambitious drama, first staged in London in 1978, charts the growing social malaise of Western Europe and, specifically, Great Britain, over the years following World War II. He does this through the character of Susan Traherne, a difficult, unsettled, neurotic young woman who moves from idealism to frustration and madness in her passage through a succession of bleak political and personal events.

Pic opens with Susan, played by Meryl Streep, involved in derring-do with the Resistance in France during the war. She has a brief affair with commando Sam Neill, and no man can ever displace Neill from her mind.

Personally and historically, it's all downhill from there. Action is set principally in the British diplomatic world, and moves across a stage backdropped by post-war economic difficulties, Coronation Year, the Suez crisis and further developments in the Middle East.

••••••••••••••••••••••••••••••••

■ PLOT AGAINST HARRY, THE

1989, 80 MINS, US ⓥ
Dir Michael Roemer   *Prod* Robert Young, Michael Roemer   *Scr* Michael Roemer   *Ph* Robert Young

Ed Terry Lewis, Georges Klotz   *Mus* Frank Lewin
Art Dir Howard Mandel
● Martin Priest, Ben Lang, Henry Nemo (King Screen)

The Plot against Harry is hilarious and often poignant. It was shot in 1969 but was held up because of a lack of completion funding. B&w pic is a sociological fossil of manners, mores and life in the 1960s.

Harry Plotnick (Martin Priest), a smalltime Jewish numbers racketeer, gets released from prison and expects to pick up the gambling circuit he ran in his old neighborhood. His loyal schlemiel assistant/chauffeur Max, in cruising through his old turf in Manhattan, makes him realize the world has changed, and blacks and Hispanics now have dibs on his area.

In a farcical accident, Harry hits the rear end of a car carrying his ex-wife Kay and his ex-brother-in-law Leo and wife. Without missing a beat, Kay introduces Harry to the daughter he never saw, Margie (now pregnant), and her husband Mel, in an almost touching encounter.

As the story unfolds, Harry is faced with a new world and the gnawing lures of the solid middle-class family life that he's always eschewed.

The Plotnick family is boisterous, upfront, multilayered and Jewish in a way that Philip Roth would savor parodying. The cast is uniformly solid, delivering their sparklingly crisp dialog straight.

••••••••••••••••••••••••••••••••

■ PLOUGH AND THE STARS, THE

1937, 72 MINS, US ◇ ⓥ
Dir John Ford   *Prod* Cliff Reid, Robert Sisk   *Scr* Dudley Nichols   *Ph* Joseph H. August   *Ed* George Hiveley   *Mus* Roy Webb
● Barbara Stanwyck, Preston Foster, Barry Fitzgerald, Denis O'Dea, Arthur Shields, Una O'Conner (RKO)

Story is an account of the Irish rebellion in 1916, a sanguinary outburst which failed of its purpose because the people were divided in allegiance, many Irish at the time fighting in France. It depicts the Irish character in various shadings of comedy, tragedy, sacrifice, selfishness and stupidity.

So many changes have been made in adapting this Sean O'Casey play to the screen that the tragic original has been modified into a romantic melodrama. Primarily the screen version is a woman's starring picture calling for an actress of considerably more gifts than Barbara Stanwyck here possesses. The altered story is the familiar theme that the men do the fighting and the women the weeping.

The opening shows the struggle and grief in a young bride's heart when her husband is selected by the citizen army to be the commandant of the fighting forces in Dublin. She has no interest in the uprising to free Ireland. Her world is her home.

These Irish boys are good looking, earnest and sincere. They take a tough licking but they're not quitters. Sympathy therefore is with the lads, which is one of the reasons Stanwyck has such a hard time holding up her end of the story.

In between there is humor and amusing characterization. Barry Fitzgerald has a joyful time in the role of Fluther, an Irish braggart. He is teamed with J.M. Kerrigan who is up to his usual high standard.

Preston Foster, opposite Stanwyck, fits nicely and his brogue comes easily. Only Stanwyck, of the entire cast, does not go Irish.

••••••••••••••••••••••••••••••••

■ PLOUGHMAN'S LUNCH, THE

1983, 100 MINS, US ◇ ⓥ
Dir Richard Eyre   *Prod* Simon Relph, Ann Scott
Scr Ian McEwan   *Ph* Clive Tickner   *Ed* David Martin   *Mus* Dominic Muldowney   *Art Dir* Luciana Arrighi

● Jonathan Pryce, Tim Curry, Rosemary Harris, Frank Finlay, Charlie Dore, Bill Paterson (Greenpoint/ Goldcrest/White)

Pic is set in the heartland of bourgeois England among its media creators and academic pontificators, and runs the period from the first spark of 1982's Falklands warlet to the victory speech of Prime Minister Margaret Thatcher at her party's gungho autumn shindig.

But those events are only a backdrop to the multi-layered story of a group of people who are either off the rails or suffering an acute lack of human commitment. It's a plot that could have turned out over-schematic, but Richard Eyre's strong directorial hand shows in delicately ambivalent performances from all players.

The film evidently springs from its author Ian McEwan's heart in characterizing the radio journalist played by Jonathan Pryce as lacking in virtue and understanding. His sins include political convictions that blow with the wind; neglect of a dying mother, leading on an older woman, and a fruitless infatuation with the TV researcher played by Charlie Dore.

Film reaches an astonishing climax during the Conservative party conference, where crew and cast filmed undercover.

••••••••••••••••••••••••••••••••

■ PLYMOUTH ADVENTURE

1952, 104 MINS, US ◇
Dir Clarence Brown   *Prod* Dore Schary   *Scr* Helen Deutsch   *Ph* William Daniels   *Ed* Robert J. Kern   *Mus* Miklos Rozsa   *Art Dir* Cedric Gibbons, Urie McCleary
● Spencer Tracy, Gene Tierney, Van Johnson, Leo Genn, Lloyd Bridges, Dawn Adams (M-G-M)

Metro has made *Plymouth Adventure*, the story of the Mayflower's perilous voyage to America [from a novel by Ernest Gebler], a large-scale sea spectacle.

The production, ably executed, puts more emphasis on the voyage itself and the attendant dangers than on developing the characters into flesh-and-blood people.

To Spencer Tracy falls the chore of enacting Captain Christopher Jones, the tough, earthy master of the Mayflower. Gene Tierney is the tragic Dorothy Bradford and Leo Genn her husband, the William Bradford later to become the first governor of the new colony. Van Johnson is John Alden, the carpenter who ships on the voyage and later marries Priscilla Mullins, played by Dawn Adams. They are all competent.
☐ 1952: Best Special Effects

••••••••••••••••••••••••••••••••

■ POCKETFUL OF MIRACLES

1961, 136 MINS, US ◇ ⓥ ☉
Dir Frank Capra   *Prod* Frank Capra   *Scr* Hal Kanter, Harry Tugend   *Ph* Robert Bronner   *Ed* Frank P. Keller   *Mus* Walter Scharf   *Art Dir* Hal Pereira, Roland Anderson
● Glenn Ford, Bette Davis, Hope Lange, Arthur O'Connell, Peter Falk, Edward Everett Horton (Franton)

The scenario, which alternates uneasily between wit and sentiment, is based on the 1933 *Lady for a Day*, which was adapted by Robert Riskin from a Damon Runyon story, and also directed by Frank Capra. It has to do with an impoverished apple-vender (Bette Davis) who would have her long lost daughter (Ann-Margret) believe that she is a lady of means. This is simple enough when the daughter is on the other side of the globe, but when she comes trotting over for a look-see, mama is in trouble.

Enter mama's favorite apple-polisher, influential Dave the Dude (Glenn Ford), who hastily sets up an elaborate masquerade with the aid of a horde of typical 1930s Runyonesque hoodlums who are hard as nails on the surface, but all whipped cream on the inside.

The picture seems too long, considering that there's never any doubt as to the outcome, and it's also too lethargic, but there are sporadic compensations of line and situation that reward the patience. Fortunately Capra has assembled some of Hollywood's outstanding character players for the chore.

For the romantic leads, he has Ford and Hope Lange. As a comedy team, they are no James Stewart-Jean Arthur (probably Capra's most formidable star-pairing), but they get by – particularly Ford. Lange is more suitable for serious roles. Davis has the meaty role of 'Apple Annie' and, except for a tendency to overemote in closeups, she handles it with depth and finesse.

The best lines in the picture go to Peter Falk, who just about walks off with the film when he's on.

☐ 1961: Nomination: Best Supp. Actor (Peter Falk); Color Costume Design, Song ('Pocketful of Miracles')

■ **POINT BLANK**

1967, 92 MINS, US ◇ ⓥ
Dir John Boorman *Prod* Judd Bernard, Robert Chartoff *Scr* Alexander Jacobs, David Newhouse, Rafe Newhouse *Ph* Philip H. Lathrop *Ed* Henry Berman *Mus* Johnny Mandel *Art Dir* George W. Davis, Albert Brenner
● Lee Marvin, Angie Dickinson, Keenan Wynn, Carroll O'Connor, John Vernon, Sharon Acker (M-G-M)

Point Blank is a violent, dynamic, thinly-scripted film. Lee Marvin stars as a double-crossed thief seeking vengeance, only to find he has again been used. Britisher John Boorman's first Hollywood pic is a textbook in brutality and a superior exercise in cinematic virtuosity.

Richard Stark's novel *The Hunter* is the basis for the screenplay, in which first five minutes recap Marvin's betrayal by best pal John Vernon and wife (Sharon Acker). The space-time jumps are lucid, effective, inventive, fluid – and repetitive. A hurry-and-wait sensation grows on a viewer as, once transposed from one scene to another, a dramatic torpor ensues at times, except for the hypo of choreographed brutality.

The futility of revenge is exemplified by the cyclic pattern of Marvin's movements, and Boorman's frequent cuts to the past overmake the point.

■ **POINT BREAK**

1991, 122 MINS, US ◇ ⓥ ⊙
Dir Kathryn Bigelow *Prod* Peter Abrams, Robert L. Levy *Scr* W. Peter Iliff *Ph* Donald Peterman *Ed* Howard Smith *Mus* Mark Isham *Art Dir* Peter Jamison
● Patrick Swayze, Keanu Reeves, Gary Busey, Lori Petty, John McGinley, James LeGros (Largo)

A hare-brained wild ride through big surf and bad vibes, *Point Break* acts like a huge, nasty wave, picking up viewers for a few major thrills but ultimately grinding them into the sand via overkill and absurdity. What it lacks is subtlety, logic or any redeeming grace. 'Too much testosterone here,' says a femme surfer (Lori Petty), walking disdainfully away from a crude party. Comment fits.

Keanu Reeves plays a 25-year-old ex-footballer turned FBI agent who is assigned to penetrate the Southern California surf culture in search of some highly successful bank robbers. Partnered with a cranky veteran fed (Gary Busey), who naturally doesn't like him, Reeves has to first learn to surf, then gain the trust of a radical dude named Bodhi (Patrick Swayze) who mixes mystical vibes with fearless thrill-seeking.

Script [from a story by Rick King and W. Peter Iliff] tries to ride on the cockeyed relationship between these two rocketheads, but since they spend most of the pic trying to

throttle or maim each other, it's not very interesting.

Director Kathryn Bigelow (*Blue Steel*) affects a hyperkinetic, agitated visual style that generates plenty of excitement. Actors, especially John McGinley as an FBI boss, behave as if injected with rocket fuel. One wonders if their heads had to be unscrewed from the ceiling after each take.

■ **POINT OF NO RETURN**
(UK: The Assassin)

1993, 109 MINS, US ◇ ⓥ ⊙
Dir John Badham *Prod* Art Linson *Scr* Robert Getchell, Alexandra Seros *Ph* Michael Watkins *Ed* Frank Morriss *Mus* Hans Zimmer *Art Dir* Philip Harrison
● Bridget Fonda, Gabriel Byrne, Dermot Mulroney, Miguel Ferrer, Anne Bancroft, Harvey Keitel (Warner)

For those who saw Luc Besson's high-tech thriller *Nikita*, about a female criminal transformed into a government assassin, this soulless, efficiently slavish remake [of the 1990 French pic] is almost like watching it all over again.

But the premise remains a strong hook on which to peg a taut, straight-line action narrative. Sentenced to death for killing a cop in a robbery, a young drug-addicted punk (Bridget Fonda), here named Maggie, is given a chance to live, under the supervision of an agent named Bob (Gabriel Byrne). The elegant Amanda (Anne Bancroft) adds the feminine touch.

Having won her stripes, she is transferred from Washington to Venice, California, where she instantly seduces J.P. (Dermot Mulroney), the friendly young caretaker of her boardwalk apartment building. The nasty assignments keep coming, though, until her jobs get in the way of her pleasant personal life. Ending is a shade more upbeat and conventional than the French version.

Fonda acquits herself admirably in all departments. Byrne is low-key as Maggie's lovestruck Pygmalion, and Mulroney endows Maggie's beach-dwelling boyfriend with welcome humor and a comfortable naturalism. Most amusing turn comes from Harvey Keitel, who plays a ruthless hitman nicknamed the Cleaner as if pretending to be the Terminator.

Director John Badham offers no interpretation or distinctive p.o.v., but does get the requisite action up on the screen in a straightforward manner that's a degree less stylized and poetic than the original.

■ **POISON**

1991, 85 MINS, US ◇ ⓥ
Dir Todd Haynes *Prod* Christine Vachon *Scr* Todd Haynes *Ph* Maryse Alberti, Barry Ellsworth *Ed* James Lyons, Todd Haynes *Mus* James Bennett *Art Dir* Sarah Stollman
● Edith Meeks, Millie White, Larry Maxwell, Susan Norman, Scott Renderer, James Lyons (Bronze Eye)

Todd Haynes' *Poison* is a conceptually bold, stylistically audacious first feature, a compelling study of different forms of deviance. Point of departure is the works of the late French writer Jean Genet: *Our Lady of the Flowers*, *Miracle of the Rose* and *Thief's Journal*. Haynes has composed three distinctive stories that constitute case studies of antisocial aberrations, shot them in three strikingly different styles and intercut them in surprisingly successful ways.

Hero takes up the case of a seven-year-old boy who, in blandest suburbia, murders his father. Arguably the weakest of the three story strands, but amusing enough withal, section features straight-on TV documentary-style interviews with the lad's mother, neighbors, teachers and classmates.

The vastly effective *Horror* uses a 1950s B-pic sci-fi approach to relate the sad story of a

scientist who isolates the source of human sex drive, but, upon drinking the fluid, becomes horribly disfigured and murderous.

A direct representation of the Genet universe, *Homo* scrutinizes an obsessive relationship between a hardened criminal and a new arrival in a 1940s French prison. A mood of seething, violent homoeroticism permeates the proceedings, as one prisoner stalks another in an episode spiked with multiple glimpses of rear-entry intercourse and one of genital fondling.

■ **POLICE ACADEMY**

1984, 95 MINS, US ◇ ⓥ ⊙
Dir Hugh Wilson *Prod* Paul Maslansky *Scr* Neal Israel, Pat Proft, Hugh Wilson *Ph* Michael D. Margulies *Ed* Robert Brown, Zach Staenberg *Mus* Robert Folk *Art Dir* Trevor Williams
● Steve Guttenberg, G.W. Bailey, George Gaynes, Michael Winslow, Kim Cattrall, Bubba Smith (Warner/Ladd)

Police Academy at its core is a harmless, innocent poke at authority that does find a fresh background in a police academy. Women in the film, such as Kim Cattrall as an Ivy League-type and Leslie Easterbrook as a busty sergeant, have almost nothing to do. Marion Ramsey as a timid-voiced trainee is fine in the film's most vivid female part.

Co-writer Hugh Wilson, makes his feature film debut as director, and his scenes are short and fragmentary. He gets a fresh comic performance from Michael Winslow as a walking human sound effects system (the film's most appealing turn).

Through it all, Steve Guttenberg is a likeable rogue in a role that's too unflappable to set off any sparks.

■ **POLICE ACADEMY 2**
THEIR FIRST ASSIGNMENT

1985, 87 MINS, US ◇ ⓥ ⊙
Dir Jerry Paris *Prod* Paul Maslansky *Scr* Barry Blaustein, David Sheffield *Ph* James Crabe *Ed* Bob Wyman *Mus* Robert Folk *Art Dir* Trevor Williams
● Steve Guttenberg, Bubba Smith, David Graf, Michael Winslow, Bruce Mahler, Marion Ramsey (Warner/Ladd)

Follow-up features much of the original's cast but none of its key behind-the-scenes creative talent, save producer Paul Maslansky. Only actor to get any mileage out of this one is series newcomer Art Metrano, as an ambitious lieutenant bent upon taking over the department.

With the recruits assigned to saving the neighborhood from the grasp of marauding punks, Metrano does everything he can to make them fail, whereupon they exact some faintly amusing revenge upon him. Metrano somehow manages to shine in these murkiest of circumstances, and Michael Winslow has a couple of good moments doing his patented sound effects and engaging in some kung fu, complete with unsynchronized yells and screams.

■ **POLICE ACADEMY 3**
BACK IN TRAINING

1986, 82 MINS, US ◇ ⓥ ⊙
Dir Jerry Paris *Prod* Paul Maslansky *Scr* Gene Quintano *Ph* Robert Saad *Ed* Bud Molin *Mus* Robert Folk *Art Dir* Trevor Williams
● Steve Guttenberg, Bubba Smith, David Graf, Michael Winslow, Marion Ramsey, Leslie Easterbrook (Warner)

Cast of cartoon misfits is still basically intact and if *Police Academy 3* has any charm it's in the good-natured dopeyness of these people. No bones about it, these people are there to laugh at.

Leading the charge for the third time is Steve Guttenberg turning in another likable boy-next-door performance. His role, however, as the cute straight man seems a bit abbreviated, with the comic burden spread out among the cast. New additions Tim Kazurinsky and Bobcat Goldhwait as cadets are only intermittently amusing.

Plot has something to do with one of the two rival police academies being shut down by the penny-pinching governor (Ed Nelson). Bad guys led by Commandant Mauser (Art Metrano) try to sabotage the forces of virtue led by Commandant Lassard (George Gaynes).

●●●●●●●●●●●●●●●●●●●●●●●●●●●●●●

■ **POLICE ACADEMY 4
CITIZENS ON PATROL**

1987, 87 MINS, US ◊ ⓥ ⊙
Dir Jim Drake   *Prod* Paul Maslansky   *Scr* Gene Quintano   *Ph* Robert Saad   *Ed* David Rawlins   *Mus* Robert Folk   *Art Dir* Trevor William
● Steve Guttenberg, Bubba Smith, Michael Winslow, David Graf, Sharon Stone, Leslie Easterbrook (Warner)

Police Academy 4 carries the banner of tasteless humor raised in the first three installments to new heights of insipidity. As usual, Steve Guttenberg leads the proceedings as Mahoney, the cute cop. Instead of just resembling a puppy dog, he actually imitates one at one point.

Most of the regulars are back with Bobcat Goldthwait assuming a larger role as the moronic cop Zed, who spends most of his time chasing birdlike Officer Sweetchuck (Tim Kazurinsky). Bubba Smith growls his way through a few scenes and Leslie Easterbrook as the statuesque Officer Callahan gets to show off her talents as well.

Plot, such as it is, has something to do with Commandant Lassard's (George Gaynes) Citizens On Patrol program and attempts by archrival Captain Harris (G.W. Bailey) to make him look bad, a truly difficult task since collectively this police force barely has a triple digit IQ. Script is merely a collection of gags tied together by the slightest suggestion of a story.

●●●●●●●●●●●●●●●●●●●●●●●●●●●●●●

■ **POLICE ACADEMY 5
ASSIGNMENT: MIAMI BEACH**

1988, 90 MINS, US ◊ ⓥ ⊙
Dir Alan Myerson   *Prod* Paul Maslansky   *Scr* Stephen J. Curwick   *Ph* Jim Pergola   *Ed* Hubert De La Bouillerie   *Mus* Robert Folk   *Art Dir* Trevor Williams
● Matt McCoy, Janet Jones, George Gaynes, G.W. Bailey, Rene Auberjonois, Bubba Smith (Warner)

Miami field trip only brings a pastel backdrop to the insipid infighting of the boobs in blue.

The jokes are all on Capt. Harris (G.W. Bailey) this time out, as he makes a disastrous attempt to unseat Cmdt Lassard (George Gaynes), aging leader of this dunce-cap police academy, by pulling out a mandatory retirement clause. Lassard's last act is to address a Miami police convention, which gives his downhearted but loyal graduates an excuse to follow him there for some surfside antics.

At Miami airport, Lassard crosses paths with some excitable crooks, and in the old luggage switcheroo, ends up in possession of some diamonds they've heisted. The trio of baddies, led by Rene Auberjonois, spends the rest of the film trying to get them back from the blissfully unaware, graciously idiotic Lassard.

The usual crew – minus Steve Guttenberg or Bobcat Goldthwait, but with Tab Thacker, a Fat Albert lookalike, taking both seats – is ostensibly on vacation while in Miami.

●●●●●●●●●●●●●●●●●●●●●●●●●●●●●●

■ **POLICE ACADEMY 6
CITY UNDER SIEGE**

1989, 83 MINS, US ◊ ⓥ ⊙
Dir Peter Bonerz   *Prod* Paul Maslansky   *Scr* Stephen J. Curwick   *Ph* Charles Rosher Jr   *Ed* Hubert De La Bouillerie   *Mus* Robert Folk   *Art Dir* Thomas E. Azzari

● Bubba Smith, David Graf, Michael Winslow, Leslie Easterbrook, Marion Ramsay, Lance Kinsey (Warner)

Commandant Lassard (George Gaynes) and his crack team are assigned to stop a wave of robberies, much to the chagrin of the cartoonish Captain Harris (G.W. Bailey). The crimes are committed by a trio with circus-like skills, keyed by a not-so-mysterious Mr. Big.

Director Peter Bonerz and writer Stephen J. Curwick (the latter taking his second *Academy* shift) both cut their teeth on TV sitcoms, and it shows. Rarely has a film cried out so desperately for a laughtrack.

Michael Winslow still has the funniest shtick with his seemingly limitless ability to perform vocal gymnastics – the film's only truly amusing moment coming when he nails one of the bad guys, first as a badly dubbed ninja, then a herky-jerky robot.

●●●●●●●●●●●●●●●●●●●●●●●●●●●●●●

■ **POLLYANNA**

1960, 133 MINS, US ◊ ⓥ ⊙
Dir David Swift   *Prod* George Golitzin (assoc.)
Scr David Swift   *Ph* Russell Harlan   *Ed* Frank Gross   *Mus* Paul Smith   *Art Dir* Carroll Clark, Robert Clatworthy
● Jane Wyman, Hayley Mills, Richard Egan, Karl Malden, Nancy Olson, Adolphe Menjou (Walt Disney)

In Walt Disney's *Pollyanna* Hayley Mills' work more than compensates for the film's lack of tautness and, at certain points, what seems to be an uncertain sense of direction. That the incredibly pre-World War I confectionary character (the glad girl, she was called) emerges normal and believably lovable is a tribute to Mills' ability and to writer-director David Swift's sane sensible approach to the familiar character from Eleanor H. Porter's novel.

Pollyanna is the tale of the little 12-year-old girl who plays the 'glad game' so well that she's soon got everyone she knows playing it. She's an orphan who lives with her aunt (Jane Wyman), the richest, most influential woman in a town which bears her name and sheepishly takes her advice and her charity. That is, until Pollyanna arrives.

Wyman, Richard Egan, Donald Crisp, Adolphe Menjou, Agnes Moorehead and Karl Malden are more than competent in key roles.

☐ 1960: Honorary Award (Hayley Mills)

●●●●●●●●●●●●●●●●●●●●●●●●●●●●●●

■ **POLTERGEIST**

1982, 114 MINS, US ◊ ⓥ ⊙
Dir Tobe Hooper   *Prod* Steven Spielberg, Frank Marshall
Scr Steven Spielberg, Michael Grais, Mark Victor
Ph Matthew F. Leonetti   *Ed* Michael Kahn   *Mus* Jerry Goldsmith   *Art Dir* James H. Spencer
● Craig T. Nelson, JoBeth Williams, Beatrice Straight, Dominique Dunne, Oliver Robins, Heather O'Rourke (M-G-M/United Artists)

Given the talents, *Poltergeist* is an annoying film because it could have been so much better. Certainly, the subject is interesting, a persistent parapsychological phenomenon that defies scientific explanation, yet refuses to go away.

But producer Steven Spielberg and the director Tobe Hooper, don't really care. They're fully content to demonstrate how well they can create the physical manifestations, plus a lot of standard sideshow horrors.

But the story is truly stupid, though well-acted. Craig T. Nelson and JoBeth Williams are the parents, living almost wall-to-wall with their neighbors in a suburban development. But when the furniture starts to fly around the room and the big tree in the yard gets hungry for the kids nobody ever seems to notice. Here you have a house in the middle of the street going berserk in Dolby Stereo and nobody calls the cops. But Williams is terrific as the mother, at first amused by the

strange goings-on in her kitchen and later terrified when cute little Heather O'Rourke disappears into the walls. And Zelda Rubinstein walks off with the film as the miniature lady who comes to cleanse the house.
☐ 1982: Nominations: Best Original Score, Sound Effects Editing, Visual Effects

●●●●●●●●●●●●●●●●●●●●●●●●●●●●●●

■ **POLTERGEIST II**

1986, 90 MINS, US ◊ ⓥ ⊙
Dir Brian Gibson   *Prod* Mark Victor, Michael Grais
Scr Mark Victor, Michael Grais   *Ph* Andrew Laszlo
Ed Thom Noble   *Mus* Jerry Goldsmith   *Art Dir* Ted Haworth
● JoBeth Williams, Craig T. Nelson, Heather O'Rourke, Oliver Robins, Zelda Rubinstein, Will Sampson (M-G-M)

It's another horrifying house party at the Freelings' in *Poltergeist II*. Sequel finds the poor Freeling family a year later penniless and slightly crazed after their Cuesta Verde house was obliterated by poltergeists.

When Gramma dies, little Carol Anne's play telephone spontaneously rings with a call from 'the other side'.

This time around, co-scripters Mark Victor and Michael Grais (who wrote the first *Poltergeist* with Steven Spielberg) have the focus of evil in human form, in the perfectly cast, since deceased, Julian Beck.

Unlike the first film that focused all the action around the innocent blond and persecuted Carol Anne (Heather O'Rourke), juiciest moments in 'II' revolve around Craig Nelson playing a soppy drunk, a lustful husband (again to the warm JoBeth Williams), a loving father and a ghoulie-spewing monster.
☐ 1986: Nomination: Best Visual Effects

●●●●●●●●●●●●●●●●●●●●●●●●●●●●●●

■ **POLTERGEIST III**

1988, 97 MINS, US ◊ ⓥ ⊙
Dir Gary Sherman   *Prod* Barry Bernardi   *Scr* Gary Sherman, Brian Taggert   *Ph* Alex Nepomniaschy
Ed Ross Albert   *Mus* Joe Renzetti   *Art Dir* Paul Erads
● Tom Skerritt, Nancy Allen, Heather O'Rourke, Zelda Rubinstein, Lara Flynn Boyle, Richard Fire (M-G-M)

As the third chapter unfolds, poor little Carol Anne (the late Heather O'Rourke) has had to move again. Her parents have shipped her off to live with her aunt and uncle (Nancy Allen and Tom Skerritt) in a brand-new Chicago high-rise. No sooner does Carol Anne move in than the mirrors start to crack and icebergs begin to form, not to mention the noise in her bedroom and the smoke that follows her down the hallway.

The family relationships are somewhat confused, but there's a teenage daughter (Lara Flynn Boyle) and her boyfriend (Kip Wenz) who get dragged into the basement floor with Carol Anne and a know-it-all school psychiatrist (Richard Fire), who may or may not have been dropped down the elevator shaft. Zelda Rubinstein is back as Tangina, the friendly psychic.

Director/co-writer Gary Sherman demonstrates absolutely no interest in whether this film ever has a modicum of meaning as he rushes from one special effect to another. Even there, Sherman arrives too late.

●●●●●●●●●●●●●●●●●●●●●●●●●●●●●●

■ **POLYESTER**

1981, 94 MINS, US ◊ ⓥ
Dir John Waters   *Prod* John Waters   *Scr* John Waters
Ph David Insley   *Ed* Charles Roggero   *Mus* Chris Stein
Art Dir Vincent Peranio
● Divine, Tab Hunter, Edith Massey, Mary Garlington, David Samson, Stiv Bators (New Line)

Baltimore-based underground filmmaker John Waters, famous for his midnight circuit hits like *Pink Flamingos*, surfaces in the pro ranks with *Polyester*, a fitfully amusing comedy of not so ordinary people. Waters' fabled shock tactics are toned down here.

Transvestite thesp Divine never steps out of character essaying the role of a housewife stuck with horrid children (Mary Garlington and Ken King) an unsympathetic husband (David Samson) and a truly evil mother (Joni Ruth White). As the episodic situation comedy unfolds, camp followers may enjoy Divine's eyerolling reactions but to the uninitiated most scenes play as overacted melodrama.

After a couple of silent teaser shots, Tab Hunter finally enters the picture after a full hour has elapsed. He is unable to fit into Waters' world, straining to overact and pull faces as the rest of the troupe and even extras do. His kissing Divine is about as offensive as film gets.

With nudity and explicit sex and violence absent, *Polyester* strains for a marketing gimmick by introducing 'Odorama.' After a cute scientist-in-lab prolog explaining the process, cheap gimmick turns out to be a scratch and sniff card handed out to the viewer, keyed manually to numbers flashed on the screen periodically during the film. It's a far cry from the fumes in the theatre gimmicks of Walter Reade's 1959 AromaRama and Mike Todd Jrs 1960 Smell-O-Vision.

■ **POOKIE**
See: The Sterile Cuckoo

■ **POOL OF LONDON**

1951, 85 MINS, UK
Dir Basil Dearden *Prod* Michael Relph *Scr* Jack Whittingham, John Eldridge *Ph* Gordon Dines *Ed* Peter Tanner *Mus* John Addison *Art Dir* Jim Morahan
● Bonar Colleano, Susan Shaw, Renee Asherson, Earl Cameron, Moira Lister, Max Adrian (Ealing)

The story of *Pool of London* spans just 48 hours when a cargo ship is in the London docks. The plot goes off at various tangents before finally converging on the basic dramatic theme of a manhunt following a holdup, murder and jewel robbery.

The central character, played by Bonar Colleano, is an over-confident, over-exuberant seaman who makes a bit of side money by small-time smuggling. He is tempted into the big coin by a gang of jewel thieves. Before he gets back to his boat, he finds that he has become implicated in a murder hunt and that he has landed his best friend, a colored boy, with the incriminating evidence.

While the main story is being developed, the film traces the warm attachment of the Negro seaman for a white girl. Although this is tastefully done, it has no bearing on the plot.

Colleano's role is a natural for him. He lives the part of the swaggering sailor, sure of himself until the moment of crisis. Earl Cameron gives a restrained and dignified performance as his friend.

■ **POOR COW**

1967, 101 MINS, UK ◇ ⊛
Dir Ken Loach *Prod* Joseph Janni *Scr* Nell Dunn, Ken Loach *Ph* Brian Probyn *Ed* Roy Watts *Mus* Donovan *Art Dir* Bernard Sarron
● Carol White, Terence Stamp, John Bindon, Kate Williams, Queenie Watts, Malcolm McDowell (Vic/Anglo Amalgamated)

The film has a jolting opening, with Joy, the hapless heroine, shown in full detail giving birth to a baby, with the infant emerging from the womb in its natural state. This leads into a portrait of Joy, who has married a brutal crook (John Bindon) and, after he is nabbed by the cops, shacks up with another

thief (Terence Stamp), a gentler type who is himself put inside.

The incidents of the plot are an excuse for an examination of promiscuous Joy. Left to fend for herself, she snatches happiness where she can find it.

Kenneth Loach uses an improvisatory technique in all this, and it largely works. Thesps were given the gist and trend of the dialog, and permitted to embroider it with their own words.

It is Carol White's film, and she scores with a flow of varied emotion, ranging from fetching happiness to a sudden spurt of tears in the final minutes, when she recalls straight to camera her affection for her baby.

■ **POPE JOAN**

1972, 101 MINS, UK ◇ ⊛
Dir Michael Anderson *Prod* Kurt Unger *Scr* John Briley *Ph* Billy Williams *Ed* Bill Lenny *Mus* Maurice Jarre *Art Dir* Elliot Scott
● Liv Ullmann, Trevor Howard, Lesley-Anne Down, Franco Nero, Olivia de Havilland, Maximilian Schell (Columbia/Big City)

Pope Joan deals with a female head of the Roman Catholic Church. Thanks to a screenplay that uses a modern-day story counterpart to suggest, apparently, that the theme is timely, this is too disjointed and rambling to make much sense.

The story is told as the ancient prototype of a modern female evangelist, torn between sex and salvation, whose religious fervor and bedroom capers more or less match those of her earlier counterpart.

She's 'adopted' in more ways than one by an artist-monk who eventually takes her to Greece as a male. They eventually wind up in Rome where her street preaching brings her to the attention of Leo XII, who takes her (him) on as a papal secretary, upped to cardinal and eventually his successor.

Liv Ullmann as Pope Joan carries the film with Maximilian Schell and Franco Nero trailing behind.

[Version reviewed above is 132-minute trade one shown in New York. The 101-minute UK version omits all modern sequences.]

■ **POPE MUST DIE, THE**

(US: The Pope Must Diet)

1991, 97 MINS, UK ◇ ⊛
Dir Peter Richardson *Prod* Stephen Woolley *Scr* Peter Richardson, Pete Richens *Ph* Frank Gell *Ed* Katherine Wenning *Mus* Anne Dudley, Jeff Beck *Art Dir* John Ebden
● Robbie Coltrane, Beverly D'Angelo, Herbert Lom, Paul Bartel, Salvatore Cascio, Alex Rocco (Palace/British Screen)

Say no prayers for *The Pope Must Die*, a barbed comedy about an honest goofball who boots the mob out of the Vatican when he's mistakenly made top banana.

Scots comic Robbie Coltrane toplines as a priest who doubles as a car mechanic and rock musician in a rural Italian orphanage. When the pope kicks it in Rome, Father Dave Albinizi's name comes up thanks to a clerical error, and next thing he's riding around in the popemobile and dispensing blessings.

First to hit the cobblestones is the finance director (Alex Rocco), mob boss Herbert Lom's main inside man. But when Coltrane's ex-g.f. (Beverly D'Angelo) turns up and reveals they have a long-lost rock star son (Balthazar Getty), Rocco and his accomplice (Paul Bartel) inform the press.

Loosely based (like *The Godfather Part III*) on the Roberto Calvi banking scandal, yarn broadens out into a breezy satire of mob pictures and religious pics. Coltrane is solid (and physically right) as the ingenuous lead, but

pace slackens when he's left to make the running. Rest of the cast play it in the fast lane.

Pic lensed in Yugoslavia under the dummy title *Sleeping with the Fishes*. End roller includes the blithe note: 'Filmed entirely on location in Europe, not far from the Vatican.'

■ **POPE MUST DIET, THE**
See: The Pope Must Die

■ **POPE OF GREENWICH VILLAGE, THE**

1984, 120 MINS, US ◇ ⊛ ⊙
Dir Stuart Rosenberg *Prod* Gene Kirkwood *Scr* Vincent Patrick *Ph* John Bailey *Ed* Robert Brown *Mus* Dave Grusin *Art Dir* Paul Sylbert
● Eric Roberts, Mickey Rourke, Daryl Hannah, Geraldine Page, Kenneth McMillan, Tony Musante (United Artists)

The Pope of Greenwich Village, set in Manhattan's Italian community, is a near-miss in its transition from novel [by Vincent Patrick] to film, setting forth an offbeat slice-of-life tale of small-time guys involved in big trouble.

Key protagonists are two young buddies (distantly related), Charlie (Mickey Rourke), a supervisor in a restaurant where Paulie (Eric Roberts) works as a waiter. Both are heavily in debt and headed nowhere, with the usual pipe dreams of escape.

Fired from their jobs at film's outset due to a misdeed by Paulie, the two of them seek a way out via a crime caper initiated by Paulie, involving an older man Barney (Kenneth McMillan) as safecracker.

□ 1984: Nominations: Best Supp. Actress (Geraldine Page)

■ **POPEYE**

1980, 114 MINS, US ◇ ⊛ ⊙
Dir Robert Altman *Prod* Robert Evans *Scr* Jules Feiffer *Ph* Giuseppe Rotunno *Ed* Tony Lombardo *Mus* Harry Nilsson *Art Dir* Wolf Kroeger
● Robin Williams, Shelley Duvall, Ray Walston, Paul L. Smith, Paul Dooley, Linda Hunt (Paramount/Walt Disney)

It is more than faint praise to say that *Popeye* is far, far better than it might have been, considering the treacherous challenge it presented. But avoiding disaster is not necessarily the same as success.

To the eye, Robin Williams is terrifically transposed into the squinting sailor with the bulging arms. But to the ear, his mutterings are not always comprehensible.

Popeye comes to the quaint village of Sweethaven in search of a father who abandoned him and this is his underlying motivation as he first meets Olive Oyl and acquires his own abandoned baby, Swee'pea.

That's just too much for a cartoon to carry, even with some generally good songs and a wacky, colorfully created town. Shelley Duvall makes a delightful Olive Oyl and Paul L. Smith a perfectly jealous Bluto.

■ **POPI**

1969, 115 MINS, US ◇ ⊛
Dir Arthur Hiller *Prod* David B. Leonard *Scr* Tina Pine, Lester Pine *Ph* Andrew Laszlo *Ed* Anthony Ciccolini *Mus* Dominic Frontiere *Art Dir* Robert Gundlach
● Alan Arkin, Rita Moreno, Miguel Alejandro, Ruben Figueroa, John Harkins (United Artists)

Alan Arkin is cast as a Puerto Rican father, living in Spanish Harlem, whose fantastic plan to improve the lot of his two small sons backfires.

Arkin is given too much free rein for his very personal style, and is sometimes guilty of working a scene, meant to be poignant or even dramatic, for a laugh, which he usually gets. The undecided mood of the film works against it for any lasting impression on the viewer.

P

The character played by Arkin is the little man vs the big odds and he does what he can with it but the story is too much for him.

Script is riddled with illogical loopholes, some of which, hopefully, will only be apparent to those familiar with the Spanish Harlem scene.

Moreno is dropped midway through the film, but makes a good impression while she's on scene. If any viewer believes that Arkin would turn down such a doll, they'll believe the rest of the story.

POPPY

1936, 75 MINS, US
Dir A. Edward Sutherland   *Prod* William LeBaron
Scr Waldemar Young, Virginia Van Upp   *Ph* William Mellor   *Ed* Stuart Heisler   *Mus* Gerard Carbonera
Art Dir Hans Dreier, Bernard Herzbrun
● W.C. Fields, Rochelle Hudson, Richard Cromwell, Lynne Overman, Catherine Doucet (Paramount)

There's one thing that W.C. Fields will never be, and that's unfunny. He could get laughs with Hamlet's soliloquy, which is just about what he does in *Poppy* [from a play by Dorothy Donnelly]. Amidst the 19th-century melodramatics and the considerable sob stuff that goes with it, Fields manages to shake off the ill effects and get his laughs.

The role of Prof Eustace McGargle, carnival guy, three-shell operator, medicine man and beloved rogue, is a setup for Fields. The juvenile romance, calling for mostly starry-eyed mutual admiration close-ups by Richard Cromwell and Rochelle Hudson, is just a series of interruptions between the Fields comedy business. The section of the plot which provides the complications, via villainy, is more helpful, for it ushers in Catherine Doucet as a first rate contrasting foil for Fields in some of his best moments.

PORGY AND BESS

1959, 136 MINS, US ◇
Dir Otto Preminger   *Prod* Samuel Goldwyn
Scr N. Richard Nash   *Ph* Leon Shamroy   *Ed* Daniel Mandell   *Mus* Andre Previn (dir.)   *Art Dir* Oliver Smith
● Sidney Poitier, Dorothy Dandridge, Sammy Davis Jr, Pearl Bailey, Brock Peters, Diahann Carroll (Columbia)

As screen entertainment, Porgy and Bess retains most of the virtues and some of the libretto traits of the folk opera.

A novel [by DuBose and Dorothy Heyward] first in 1925 it became a play in 1927, running 217 performances for the Theatre Guild. The opera version of 1935, also for the Guild, eked out only 124 performances. It was not until the revival, after composer George Gershwin's death, that Porgy and Bess came into its own. The melodrama of a 1905 Charleston waterfront slum, which might otherwise have been forgotten, was elevated into a world favorite.

Sidney Poitier makes him thoroughly believable though when he opens his voice to sing it is Robert McPherrin. Bess, the incompletely regenerate floozie, is Dorothy Dandridge, but the voice is Adele Addison. (Neither voice gets screen credit.)

The love affair of this oddly-assorted pair has considerable humanity though Dandridge is perhaps too 'refined' to be quite convincing as the split-skirt, heroin-sniffing tramp.

Otto Preminger manipulates the characters in the Catfish Row to develop as much tension and pathos as the screenplay (fairly close to the original text) allows.

Many of the old slum life details of the stage production have been faded down. The racial stereotype dangers have been sterilized.

The handling of the music by conductor Andre Previn, including a three-minute overture before the story opens, is professional.

Some liberties with the arrangements, in the de-operatizing direction, may irritate loyal followers of Gershwin who notice such matters.
□ 1959: Best Scoring of a Musical Picture.
□ Nominations: Best Color Cinematography, Color Costume Design, Sound

PORK CHOP HILL

1959, 97 MINS, US Ⓥ
Dir Lewis Milestone   *Prod* Sy Bartlett   *Scr* James H. Webb   *Ph* Sam Leavitt   *Mus* Leonard Rosenman
Art Dir Nicolai Remisoff
● Gregory Peck, Harry Guardino, Rip Torn, George Peppard, George Shibata, Woody Strode (United Artists/Melville)

Pork Chop Hill is a grim, utterly realistic story that drives home both the irony of war and the courage men can summon to die in a cause which they don't understand and for an objective which they know to be totally irrelevant.

King Company, commanded by Gregory Peck as Lt. Joe Clemons, is ordered to take Pork Chop Hill from the Chinese Reds and to hold it against attack. The time is the Korean War, and the irony of the situation is that (1) armistice negotiations at Panmunjon are virtually concluded, and (2) Pork Chop has absolutely no tactical importance. It must be taken simply because its loss means a loss of face on the part of the Americans in the eyes of the Communist negotiators.

Peck's performance as the company commander is completely believable. He comes through as a born leader, and yet it is quite clear that he has his moments of doubt and of uncertainty.

The accent on the combat is such that, besides Peck, the other men barely emerge as people. They look real, they sound real, but there's no chance to get to know them, though the picture makes it very clear that they all know that their objective is secondary at best.

PORKY'S

1981, 94 MINS, CANADA ◇ Ⓥ ⊙
Dir Bob Clark   *Prod* Don Carmody, Bob Clark   *Scr* Bob Clark   *Ph* Reginald H. Morris   *Ed* Stan Cole   *Mus* Carl Zittrer, Paul Zaza   *Art Dir* Reuben Freed
● Dan Monahan, Mark Herrier, Wyatt Knight, Kim Cattrall, Alex Karras, Susan Clark (Simon/Astral Bellevue/Pathe)

If, by chance, *Porky's* should prove to be Melvin Simon's swan song in the film industry, it will either be perceived as a thunderously rude exit or a titanic raspberry uttered to audiences everywhere.

Virtually every scene and dialog exchange constitutes a new definition of lewdness. Locker room humor reaches new heights (depths) here. Film cannot be faulted for lack of a driving force – simply, all these young Florida boys are itching to score and most of their time is spent in pursuit of said goal.

Title refers to a redneck establishment out in the Everglades known for its available women. After being embarrassingly turned away on their first visit, the boys return to wreak havoc on the joint, proving once and for all that violence will result when the sex drive is repressed.

PORKY'S II
THE NEXT DAY

1983, 95 MINS, US ◇ Ⓥ ⊙
Dir Bob Clark   *Prod* Don Carmody, Bob Clark
Scr Roger E. Swaybill, Alan Ormsby, Bob Clark
Ph Reginald H. Morris   *Ed* Stan Cole   *Mus* Carl Zittrer
Art Dir Fred Price
● Dan Monahan, Wyatt Knight, Mark Herrier, Roger Wilson, Cyril O'Reilly, Tony Ganios (Simon-Reeves-Landsburg/Astral Bellevue/Pathe)

Plot follows in the grand tradition of many early rock 'n' roll quickies, in which self-righteous upholders of comic morality attempted to stomp out the threat posed by the new primitive music. Replacing Chuck Mitchell's Porky as the heavy here is Bill Wiley's bigoted Rev. Bubba Flavel, who makes a crusade out of shutting down the school's Shakespeare festival due to the lewdness he finds strewn throughout the Bard's work.

Enlisted in his cause is the ample girls' gym teacher Miss Balbricker and the local contingent of the Ku Klux Klan, who are each the victims of two of the film's three 'big scenes'. Everyone who saw it remembers 'that scene' from the original. Here, some of the boys get back at Balbricker by sending a snake up into her toilet.

Director Bob Clark has not allowed success lead him astray into the dreaded realm of good taste.

PORTNOY'S COMPLAINT

1972, 101 MINS, US ◇ Ⓥ
Dir Ernest Lehman   *Prod* Ernest Lehman, Sidney Beckerman   *Scr* Ernest Lehman   *Ph* Philip Lathrop
Ed Sam O'Steen, Gordon Scott   *Mus* Michel Legrand
Art Dir Robert F. Boyle
● Richard Benjamin, Karen Black, Lee Grant, Jack Somack, Jeannie Berlin, Jill Clayburgh (Warner/Chenault)

The film version of *Portnoy's Complaint* is *not* trashy, tawdry, cheap, offensively vulgar, and pruriently titillating. Instead, it is a most effective, honest in context, necessarily strong and appropriately bawdy study in ruinous self-indulgence.

Besides adapting the Philip Roth novel into a lucid, balanced and moral screenplay, and producing handsomely on various locations, Ernest Lehman makes an excellent directorial debut. Richard Benjamin heads an outstanding cast.

Alexander Portnoy's hangup derives from heterosexual masturbation fantasies, and the first 44 minutes constitute the slap-happy, kinky exposition of his development. But what the story then pulls an audience into is the inevitable consequence.

PORTRAIT OF JENNIE

1948, 86 MINS, US ◇ Ⓥ
Dir William Dieterle   *Prod* David O. Selznick   *Scr* Paul Osborn, Peter Berneis   *Ph* Joseph August   *Ed* [William Morgan, Gerald Wilson]   *Mus* Dimitri Tiomkin
Art Dir J. McMillan Johnson, Joseph B. Platt
● Joseph Cotten, Jennifer Jones, Ethel Barrymore, David Wayne, Lillian Gish, Cecil Kellaway (RKO/Selznick)

Portrait of Jennie is an unusual screen romance. The story of an ethereal romance between two generations is told with style, taste and dignity.

William Dieterle has given the story sensitive direction and his guidance contributes considerably toward the top performances from the meticulously cast players.

The script, by Paul Osborn and Peter Berneis, taken from Robert Nathan's novel, deals sympathetically with an artist living in New York in the 1930s. His work lacks depth and it is only when he meets a strange child in the park one day that inspiration to paint people comes. The elfish quality of the child stimulates a sketch. It is appreciated by art dealers and he builds the child's physical being in his mind until the next time she appears he sees her as a girl just entering her teens. Her growth moves into college years and then as a graduate while he, meantime, is discovering she is a person who has been dead for years.

Jennifer Jones' performance in standout. Her miming ability gives a quality to the four ages she portrays – from a small girl through the flowering woman. Ingenuity in makeup also figures importantly in sharpening the portrayal.

Joseph Cotten endows the artist with a top performance, matching the compelling portrayal by Jones.

[Original release prints featured a Technicolor sequence in the final reel.]

□ 1948: Best Special Effects.

□ Nomination: Best B&W Cinematography

....

■ POSEIDON ADVENTURE, THE

1972, 117 MINS, US ◇ ⓥ ⊙

Dir Ronald Neame   *Prod* Irwin Allen   *Scr* Stirling Silliphant, Wendell Mayes   *Ph* Harold E. Stine   *Ed* Harold F. Kress   *Mus* John Williams   *Art Dir* William Creber

● Gene Hackman, Ernest Borgnine, Red Buttons, Carol Lynley, Roddy McDowall, Stella Stevens (20th Century-Fox)

The Poseidon Adventure is a highly imaginative and lustily-produced meller that socks over the dramatic struggle of 10 passengers to save themselves after an ocean liner capsizes when struck by a mammoth tidal wave created by a submarine earthquake.

It is a case of everything being upside down; in this reversed world of twisted ruin the principals' goal is the vessel's bottom where to break through may be some hope of survival.

The adaptation of the Paul Gallico novel plays up the tragic situation with a set of values which permits powerful action and building tension.

Chief protagonist is played by Gene Hackman, as a free-talking minister who keeps his cool and assumes leadership of the small group.

□ 1972: Best Song ('The Morning After'), Honorary Award (special visual effects).

□ Nominations: Best Supp. Actress (Shelley Winters), Cinematography, Costume Design, Art Direction, Editing, Original Score, Sound

....

■ POSSE

1975, 92 MINS, US ◇ ⓥ ⊙

Dir Kirk Douglas   *Prod* Kirk Douglas   *Scr* William Roberts, Christopher Knopf   *Ph* Fred J. Koenekamp   *Ed* John W. Wheeler   *Mus* Maurice Jarre   *Art Dir* Lyle Wheeler

● Kirk Douglas, Bruce Dern, Bo Hopkins, James Stacy, Luke Askew, David Canary (Paramount/Bryna)

Posse is a good western, with Kirk Douglas as a cynical US marshal who eventually stumbles on his own political ambitions while tracking thief Bruce Dern under a strident law-and-order platform.

Story is a sort of conluted *High Noon*, in which self-assured Douglas, complete with his own gang of deputies, manipulates a cowardly town which in the end turns its back on him. Dern, very effective as an escaped robber, ultimately capitalizes on Douglas' disloyalty to his men and escapes anew with a fully-trained crew which easily adapts to lawlessness.

Bo Hopkins, Luke Askew, Bill Burton, Louie Elias and Gus Greymountain are good as Douglas' assistants whom he plans to dump after becoming a US Senator from Texas.

....

■ POSSE

1993, 109 MINS, US/UK ◇ ⓥ ⊙

Dir Mario Van Peebles   *Prod* Preston Holmes, Jim Steele   *Scr* Sy Richardson, Dario Scardapane   *Ph* Peter Menzies Jr   *Ed* Mark Conte   *Mus* Michel Colombier   *Art Dir* Catherine Hardwicke

● Mario Van Peebles, Stephen Baldwin, Charles Lane, Tiny Lister Jr, Big Daddy Kane, Billy Zane (PolyGram/Working Title)

Begin with a reliable pursuit-and-revenge plotline, lay on a Sergio Leone look and flashback structure, stir in some John Ford community values and Sam Peckinpah violence, tag *The Magnificent Seven* on at the end and paint it black, and you've got *Posse*.

Engaged in the Spanish-American War in Cuba in 1898, a ragtag band including strong silent type Mario Van Peebles, bespectacled Charles Lane, giant Tiny Lister Jr., cigar-chomping Tone Loc and irreverent white boy Stephen Baldwin, is betrayed by vicious, swashbuckling commanding officer Billy Zane, and flees the regiment with a large stash of gold. They also pick up a laconic riverboat gambler, Father Time (Big Daddy Kane).

The band finally arrives at Freemansville, a utopian black township. But venal nearby sheriff Richard Jordan and his Ku Klux Klan goons suddenly covet Freemansville since it lies along a future railway route.

Eventful script packs in enough confrontations, fights and shootouts for several films, which will keep action fans happy. But neither the writers nor Van Peebles, in his second directorial outing, modulate the drama to maximize its impact.

....

■ POSSESSED

1947, 108 MINS, US ⓥ ⊙

Dir Curtis Bernhardt   *Prod* Jerry Wald   *Scr* Silvia Richards, Ranald MacDougall   *Ph* Joseph Valentine   *Ed* Rudi Fehr   *Mus* Franz Waxman   *Art Dir* Anton Grot

● Joan Crawford, Van Heflin, Raymond Massey, Geraldine Brooks, Stanley Ridges (Warner)

Joan Crawford cops all thesping honors in this production with a virtuoso performance as a frustrated woman ridden into madness by a guilt-obsessed mind. Actress has a self-assurance that permits her to completely dominate the screen even vis-a-vis such accomplished players as Van Heflin and Raymond Massey.

Heflin's part of a footloose engineer who romances his ladies with one eye on the railroad schedule is now drawn with equal sharpness. By sheer power of personal wit, however, Heflin infuses his role with charm and degree of credibility despite a lack of clear motivation for his behavior.

Unfolding via flashback technique, film opens with a terrific bang as the camera picks up Crawford wandering haggard and dazed through Los Angeles until she collapses. In the psychiatric ward of the local hospital, under narco-hypnosis, she relives the series of personal blows that ultimately reduced her to schizophrenia.

Despite its overall superiority, *Possessed* is somewhat marred by an ambiguous approach in Curtis Bernhardt's direction. Film vacilates between being a cold clinical analysis of a mental crackup and a highly surcharged melodramatic vehicle for Crawford's histrionics.

□ 1947: Nomination: Best Actress (Joan Crawford)

....

■ POSSESSION

1981, 127 MINS, FRANCE/W. GERMANY ◇ ⓥ

Dir Andrzej Zulawski   *Prod* Marie-Laure Reyre   *Scr* Andrzej Zulawski, Frederic Tuten   *Ph* Bruno Nuytten   *Ed* Marie-Sophie Dubus   *Mus* Andrzej Korzynski   *Art Dir* Holger Gross

● Isabelle Adjani, Sam Neill, Heinz Bennent, Margit Carstensen, Michael Hogben (Oliane/Marianne/Soma)

Possession starts on a hysterical note, stays there and surpasses it as the film progresses. There are excesses on all fronts: in supposedly ordinary married life and then occult happenings, intricate political skulduggery with the infamous Berlin Wall as background – they all abound in this horror-cum-political-cum – psychological tale.

Sam Neill, New Zealand actor, returns home after a long absence. He has been on some sort of secret mission. After an ambiguous report to a commission he goes home to find his wife (Isabelle Adjani) acting strangely.

Neill hires a detective who tracks Adjani to an old house and a strange apartment. The detective gains entry and sees some sort of monster [special effects by Caro Rambaldi] before Adjani slashes his throat with a broken bottle. Another sleuth gets the same treatment, and a bizarre mass of entrails encompass the men after they are killed.

Adjani is game as she plays the deranged, obsessed woman in high gear throughout. Pic's mass of symbols and unbridled, brilliant directing meld this disparate tale into a film that could get cult following on its many levels of symbolism and exploitation.

....

■ POSSESSION OF JOEL DELANEY, THE

1972, 105 MINS, UK ◇ ⓥ

Dir Waris Hussein   *Scr* Matt Robinson, Grimes Grice   *Ph* Arthur Ornitz   *Ed* John Victor Smith   *Mus* Joe Raposo   *Art Dir* Peter Murton

● Shirley MacLaine, Michael Hordern, Edmundo Rivera Alvarez, Robert Burr, Miriam Colon, David Elliott (ITC)

The Possession of Joel Delaney is an unusual occult thriller [based on Ramona Stewart's novel]. Pic centers on a chic East Side society divorcee (Shirley MacLaine) who harbors an inordinate affection for her brother, Joel (Perry King), and attempts to save him when he is possessed by the spirit of a Puerto Rican friend fond of ritual beheadings.

Script eschews any serious attempt to explain the subject matter in conventional psychiatric terms, coming down on the side of ethnically-originated spiritualism. You believe it or you don't, ditto the rather murky sociological overtones that seem needlessly overemphasized.

Script overextends the build-up, making the final quarter a bit anti-climactic and slowing the pace, but the presence of MacLaine smooths over the rough spots.

....

■ POSTCARDS FROM THE EDGE

1990, 101 MINS, US ◇ ⓥ ⊙

Dir Mike Nichols   *Prod* Mike Nichols, John Calley   *Scr* Carrie Fisher   *Ph* Michael Ballhaus   *Ed* Sam O'Steen   *Mus* Howard Shore (sup.), Carly Simon   *Art Dir* Patrizia Von Brandenstein

● Meryl Streep, Shirley MacLaine, Dennis Quaid, Gene Hackman, Richard Dreyfuss, Rob Reiner (Columbia)

Mike Nichols' film of Carrie Fisher's novel *Postcards from the Edge* packs a fair amount of emotional wallop in its dark-hued comic take on a chemically dependent Hollywood mother and daughter (Shirley MacLaine and Meryl Streep).

Streep's tour through Hollywood hell is signposted with many recognizable, on-target types: predatory macho creep (Dennis Quaid), sleazy business manager (Gary Morton), oafish producer (Rob Reiner), airheaded and roundheeled actress (Annette Bening) and sternly paternalistic director (Gene Hackman).

Refreshingly guileless in a role requiring casual clothing and no accent, Streep plays an overgrown child who's spent her life in her mother's shadow and has resorted to drugs to blunt her pain and boredom.

While casting of MacLaine in the role of an arch, ditzy, impossible stage mother is somewhat predictable, the actress gradually makes it her own until, stripped of her glamour in the climactic scene, she abandons the rampant egotism of the character to reveal the frightened creature underneath.

(Nichols insists, for the record, that the character isn't based on Fisher's mom, Debbie Reynolds, even though MacLaine's

wickedly salacious memories of life at Louis B. Mayer's M-G-M might suggest otherwise.)
□ 1990: Nominations: Best Actress (Meryl Streep), Song ('I'm Checkin' Out')

● ●

■ POSTMAN ALWAYS RINGS TWICE, THE

1946, 110 MINS, US Ⓥ ⊙

Dir Tay Garnett   *Prod* Carey Wilson   *Scr* Harry Ruskin, Niven Busch   *Ph* Sidney Wagner   *Ed* George White   *Mus* George Bassman   *Art Dir* Cedric Gibbons, Randall Duell
● Lana Turner, John Garfield, Cecil Kellaway, Hume Cronyn, Audrey Totter, Leon Ames (M-G-M)

The Postman Always Rings Twice is a controversial picture. The approach to lust and murder is as adult and matter-of-fact as that used by James M. Cain in his book from which the film was adapted.

It was box-office wisdom to cast Lana Turner as the sexy, blonde murderess, and John Garfield as the foot-loose vagabond whose lust for the girl made him stop at nothing. Each give to the assignments the best of their talents. Development of the characters makes Tay Garnett's direction seem slowly paced during first part of the picture, but this establishment was necessary to give the speed and punch to the uncompromising evil that transpires.

As in Cain's book, there will be little audience sympathy for the characters, although plotting will arouse moments of pity for the little people too weak to fight against passion and the evil circumstances it brings. The script is a rather faithful translation of Cain's story of a boy and girl who murder the girl's husband, live through terror and eventually make payment for their crime. The writing is terse and natural to the characters and events that transpire.

Cecil Kellaway, the husband, is a bit flamboyant at times in interpreting the character. Hume Cronyn is particularly effective as the attorney who defends the couple for murder.

● ●

■ POSTMAN ALWAYS RINGS TWICE, THE

1981, 123 MINS, US ◇ Ⓥ ⊙

Dir Bob Rafelson   *Prod* Charles Mulvehill, Bob Rafelson   *Scr* David Mamet   *Ph* Sven Nykvist   *Ed* Graeme Clifford   *Mus* Michael Small   *Art Dir* George Jenkins
● Jack Nicholson, Jessica Lange, John Colicos, Anjelica Huston, Christopher Lloyd, John P. Ryan (Paramount)

James M. Cain's 1934 novel attracted notoriety for its adulterous murder story, spiced with some fairly daring sequences for its day.

Because of the Hays Office, Hollywood couldn't touch the property until 1946, when MGM released a sanitized version with Lana Turner and John Garfield – and even that was greeted by some shock. For this remake, Bob Rafelson said he would shoot as an X but cut to an R.

But the final cut is limited to some fairly heavy groping, explicit shots of Jack Nicholson massaging the front of Jessica Lange's panties and a view of his head between her legs, suggesting more than is ever witnessed.

Stripped of its excess, Cain's yarn is essentially a morality tale of a Depression drifter who comes to work for a beautiful young woman and her older Greek husband. Falling madly in lust, they murder the old man, escape justice and then get their desserts in an ironical twist at the end.

In the key roles, Nicholson and Lange are excellent, as is Michael Lerner as their defense attorney.

In Cain's novel, once the couple escape punishment in court, she dies in an auto accident and he is wrongly executed for her murder, thus providing the justice. Rafelson throws this away for an ending that's not so neat.

● ●

■ POT CARRIERS, THE

1962, 84 MINS, UK

Dir Peter Graham Scott   *Prod* Gordon L.T. Scott   *Scr* T.J. Morrison, Mike Watts   *Ph* Erwin Hillier   *Ed* Richard Best   *Mus* Stanley Black   *Art Dir* Robert Jones
● Ronald Fraser, Paul Massie, Carol Lesley, Dennis Price, Davy Kaye, Alfred Burke (Associated British)

This lively slice of life in jail is a moderately unpretentious job but it shrewdly captures the atmosphere of the locale, neatly blends comedy and drama and offers some sharp thesping. Screenplay has been adapted by T. J. Morrison and Mike Watts from the latter's play. Pic title is used to spotlight one of the supreme indignities of prison.

Paul Massie plays a first offender sentenced to a year's jail for grievous bodily harm, after slugging another man in a jealous tiff with his girl friend. Assigned to the Kitchen Gang, he quickly settles down to the routine and joins in the 'fiddling' which is highly organized among the prisoners, which mainly consists of stealing chow from the kitchens and swapping it for luxuries which another member of the gang lifts from the officers' mess.

In a large, mainly male cast, there are some notable bits of thesping, biggest impact being made by Ronald Fraser as the 'trusty' who is the kingpin among the fiddlers. Paul Massie is a likeable, straightforward hero.

● ●

■ POWER, THE

1968, 108 MINS, US ◇

Dir Bryon Haskin   *Prod* George Pal   *Scr* John Gay   *Ph* Ellsworth Fredricks   *Ed* Thomas J. McCarthy   *Mus* Miklos Rozsa   *Art Dir* George W. Davis, Merrill Pye
● George Hamilton, Suzanne Pleshette, Richard Carlson, Yvonne De Carlo, Earl Holliman, Arthur O'Connell (M-G-M)

Somewhere along the way something misfired. What started out as an ingenious, imaginative sci-fi premise developed into a confusing maze of cloudy characters, motivations and events in its development.

George Pal production carries plenty of suspense as audience hopefully awaits a logical conclusion, but in final wrapup the spectator is left wondering what it's all about.

Screenplay, based on the Frank M. Robinson novel, is set among a group of scientists engaged in human endurance research. It is discovered that one among them has a super-intelligence, possibly a mind of the next evolution, so strong it controls the others' minds. As murder starts, George Hamilton, one of the scientists, undertakes to learn the identity of The Power, while himself a suspect by the police.

Byron Haskin's direction is limited by script but he manages tension as yarn builds to its finale. Hamilton is okay in his role and Suzanne Pleshette, in part of his geneticist girlfriend, is easy on the eye. Balance of cast are as good as roles will allow.

● ●

■ POWER

1986, 111 MINS, US ◇ Ⓥ ⊙

Dir Sidney Lumet   *Prod* Reene Schisgal, Mark Tarlov   *Scr* David Himmelstein   *Ph* Andrzej Bartkowiak   *Ed* Andrew Mondshein   *Mus* Cy Coleman   *Art Dir* Peter Larkin
● Richard Gere, Julie Christie, Gene Hackman, Kate Capshaw, Denzel Washington, E.G. Marshall (Lorimar/Polar)

Not so much about power as about p.r., this facile treatment of big-time politics and media, featuring Richard Gere as an amoral imagemaker, revolves around the unstartling premise that modern politicians and their campaigns are calculatedly packaged for TV. In spite of relentless jet-propelled location

hopping that helps to stave off boredom, *Power* never gets airborne.

Pete St John (Gere) is a peripatetic public relations wiz whose services practically guarantee political success. His ex-wife (Julie Christie) and alcoholic former mentor Wilfred Buckley (Gene Hackman) both remember Pete when the kid had ideals. He's dumped them both but they still care for him. All that remains to be seen is if Pete will find some sort of redemption.

● ●

■ POWER AND THE GLORY, THE

1933, 73 MINS, US

Dir William K. Howard   *Prod* Jesse L. Lasky   *Scr* Preston Sturges   *Ph* James Wong Howe   *Mus* Louis De Francesco (dir.)   *Art Dir* Max Parker
● Spencer Tracy, Colleen Moore, Ralph Morgan, Helen Vinson, Clifford Jones, Henry Kolker (Fox)

Jesse L. Lasky's production for Fox, is unique through its 'narratage' style of cinematurgy. Its treatment has been consummately developed by director William K. Howard and scenarist Preston Sturges. The four principal characters are performed by Spencer Tracy, who has never done better; Colleen Moore, whose come-back is distinguished; Ralph Morgan, ever-effective; and Helen Vinson, at her best.

Film starts with its ending – the ecclesiastic services for the dead. Showing the finale of the life span of your central character is something that is by no means easy to offset. And that's where the 'narratage' comes in. Morgan is the narrator, detailing the highlights in the career of his friend (Tracy) who, even in death, is much maligned.

Morgan undertakes to show that Tracy, who fought his way up from an ignorant, unschooled trackwalker to the presidency of railroads, and a tycoon of industry, was not the bad egg everybody painted. He argues that his strike-breaking methods, which cost many railroad workers' lives, had another element to it; that his turning out his first wife (Moore) in favor of Vinson might have had extenuating circumstances, etc.

It's well done in every respect. Casting right down the line is punchy for performance. Howard's direction is truly unique and distinguished. His favorite camera-man. James Wong Howe, manifests indubitable artistry.

● ●

■ POWER OF ONE, THE

1992, 111 MINS, US ◇ Ⓥ ⊙

Dir John G. Avildsen   *Prod* Arnon Milchan   *Scr* Robert Mark Kamen   *Ph* Dean Semler   *Ed* John G. Avildsen   *Mus* Hans Zimmer   *Art Dir* Roger Hall
● Stephen Dorff, Armin Mueller-Stahl, Morgan Freeman, John Gielgud, Maria Marais, Simon Fenton (Regency/Canal Plus/Alcor)

Bryce Courtenay's South African coming-of-age novel is brought to the screen with mixed success in this lushly mounted production. On the one hand a captivating and inspiring tale of a boy's journey to courage amid searing injustice, pic often gives way to scenes of intense violence that are likely to bludgeon the very sensibilities it seeks to awaken.

In 1930s Zimbabwe, young white P.K. is orphaned and sent to a boarding school. The only English boy among Afrikaaners, he is treated brutally, a victim of the bitter struggle among the two colonizing groups for control of South Africa. Kindly German composer and botanist Doc (Armin Mueller-Stahl) educates his mind, and dignified black prisoner Geel Piet (Morgan Freeman) teaches P.K. to defend himself in the boxing ring.

Piet molds P.K. into a boxing champion and spreads word among the hundreds of other black prisoners that he's the legendary Rainmaker, come to make peace. As P.K.

grows up (played admirably at age 18 by Californian Stephen Dorff), he decides to fulfill that destiny, defying the brutally racist regime.

Beautifully produced and gorgeously shot on location in Zimbabwe by lenser Dean Semler, picture has depth, dimension and first-rate casting.

• •

■ POWER OF THE PRESS

1928, 62 MINS, US ⊗
Dir Frank Capra *Scr* Fred C. Thompson
Ph Ted Tetzlaff
● Douglas Fairbanks Jr, Jobyna Ralston, Robert Edeson, Mildred Harris, Dell Henderson, Wheeler Oakman (Columbia)

Exciting and insistently engaging melodrama with a light touch that lifts it out of the stencil class. While theatricalizing to an extent, the newspaper atmosphere is exceptionally restrained and reasonable for Hollywood.

Story hinges about a mayoralty election in which the candidate of the w.k. party of intelligence and morality is maneuvered into a disastrous political position by the candidate of vice and corruption. Having by his story ruined the virtuous candidate and disgraced the daughter, a young reporter (Douglas Fairbanks Jr), upon meeting the daughter socially, goes after the hidden aspects of the scandal and ends by exposing the whole kaboodle.

Fairbanks in ease and confidence belies his age and takes after his famous pop, never an introvert in the matter of self-assurance. Jobyna Ralston is attractive as the girl. A very suave and cold-blooded henchman of corruption is ably played by Wheeler Oakman.

• •

■ PRAGUE

1992, 88 MINS, UK/FRANCE ◇
Dir Ian Sellar *Prod* Christopher Young *Scr* Ian Sellar
Ph Darius Khondji *Ed* John Bloom *Mus* Jonathan Dove
Art Dir Jiri Matolin
● Alan Cumming, Sandrine Bonnaire, Bruno Ganz (BBC/Constellation/Young/UGC/Hachette Premiere)

This leisurely paced lightweight effort for scripter/helmer Ian Sellar comes across like a collection of ideas for a Euro co-production to be lensed in a photogenic city rather than an accomplished and vital picture.

On his maiden journey to Prague, young Alexander (Alan Cumming) arrives from the UK in search of newsreel film supposedly stored at Czech film archives. Alex knows exactly what he's looking for but has not anticipated the sluggish serendipity of the archive and its two key employees, Elena (Sandrine Bonnaire) and Josef (Bruno Ganz).

Alex, whose Czechoslovakian-born mother survived the war thanks to a bold family gesture, is looking for visual clues to his past. Elena, romantically linked to Josef, is looking for a key ingredient in her future.

Individual characters have endearing quirks, but no one is strong enough to carry the film; Cumming is too doughy and nebulous. Bonnaire and Ganz are convincing as Czechs, but much of what they do and say is either too arbitrary or too obvious.

• •

■ PRAYER FOR THE DYING, A

1988, 107 MINS, UK/US ◇ ⑨ ⊙
Dir Mike Hodges *Prod* Peter Snell *Scr* Edmund Ward, Martin Lynch *Ph* Mike Garfath *Ed* Peter Boyle
Mus Bill Conti *Art Dir* Evan Hercules
● Mickey Rourke, Bob Hoskins, Alan Bates, Sammi Davis, Liam Neeson, Alison Doody (PFD/Goldwyn)

A Prayer for the Dying is a disappointing thriller adapted from Jack Higgins' novel. Release version has been disowned by director Mike Hodges, who joined the project on short no-

tice, succeeding Franc Roddam before shooting commenced. Pic was originally planned to be filmed a decade earlier, with Edward Dmytryk to direct and Robert Mitchum to star.

Mickey Rourke, styled with red hair and Irish brogue, portrays Martin Fallon, an IRA hitman who sees the light and flees to London. He reluctantly agrees to carry out a mob hit for gangster Jack Meehan (Alan Bates), but the killing is witnessed by priest Father Da Costa (Bob Hoskins).

Fallon confesses the murder to the priest, who refuses to identify Fallon to the police. Film becomes rather conventional at this point, with Fallon outwitting the gangsters, police and IRA hitmen (Liam Neeson, Alison Doody) hot on his case, aided by the sympathetic, blind niece of the priest, Anna (Sammi Davis).

Dying emerges as a cold, unexciting affair, lightened up only by Bates' funny overplaying of the villain. Rourke is convincing as the antihero and ably supported by Davis. As an IRA hit-lady, Doody looks more like a fashion model.

• •

■ PRECINT 45 – LOS ANGELES POLICE
See: The New Centurions

• •

■ PREDATOR

1987, 107 MINS, US ◇ ⑨ ⊙
Dir John McTiernan *Prod* Lawrence Gordon, Joel Silver, John Davis *Scr* Jim Thomas, John Thomas *Ph* Donald McAlpine *Ed* John F. Link, Mark Helfrich *Mus* Alan Silvestri *Art Dir* John Vallone
● Arnold Schwarzenegger, Carl Weathers, Elpidia Carrillo, Bill Duke, Jesse Ventura, Sonny Landham (20th Century-Fox)

Predator is a slightly above-average actioner that tries to compensate for tissue-thin-plot with ever-more-grisly death sequences and impressive special effects.

Arnold Schwarzenegger plays Dutch, the leader of a vaguely defined military rescue team that works for allied governments. Called into a US hot spot somewhere in South America, he encounters old buddy Dillon (Carl Weathers), who now works for the CIA.

The unit starts to get decimated in increasingly garish fashion by an otherworldly Predator. Enemy is a nasty, formidable foe with laser powers.

Schwarzenegger, while undeniably appealing, still has a character who's not quite real. While the painted face, cigar, vertical hair and horizontal eyes are all there, none of the humanity gets on the screen, partly because of the sparse dialog.

Weathers can't breathe any life into the cardboard character of Dillon, who goes from being unbelievably cynical to unbelievably heroic in about five minutes.

Director John McTiernan relies a bit too much on special effects 'thermal vision' photography, in looking through the Predator's eyes, while trying to build tension before the blood starts to fly.
☐ 1987: Nomination: Best Visual Effects

• •

■ PREDATOR 2

1990, 108 MINS, US ◇ ⑨ ⊙
Dir Stephen Hopkins *Prod* Lawrence Gordon, Joel Silver, John Davis *Scr* Jim Thomas, John Thomas
Ph Peter Levy *Ed* Mark Goldblatt *Mus* Alan Silvestri
Art Dir Lawrence G. Paull
● Danny Glover, Gary Busey, Ruben Blades, Maria Conchita Alonso, Bill Paxton, Kevin Peter Hall (20th Century-Fox)

While the film doesn't achieve the same thrills of the final 45 minutes of *Predator* in terms of overall excitement, it outdoes its

first safari in start-to-finish hysteria. The real star is the pic's design. Writers don't waste much time on character development.

The setting is Los Angeles, 1997, where outgunned cops face hordes of Jamaican, Colombian and other assorted drug dealers who rule the streets. It's a balmy 109 degrees in the globally warmed basin, where Danny Glover heads a dedicated, ethnically mixed group of cops who are more than a little confused as the drug dealers start turning up dead in droves. The plot thickens when a fed (Gary Busey) comes in to take charge of the investigation.

Centerpiece is, again, a massive alien gifted with the strange weaponry and camouflage abilities like his kinsman that, it's told, had visited the planet 10 years earlier.

The pace of the film is absolutely frenetic. An awe-inspiring set in the closing sequence recalls the climactic moment in *Aliens*.

• •

■ PRELUDE TO A KISS

1992, 106 MINS, US ◇ ⑨ ⊙
Dir Norman Rene *Prod* Michael Gruskoff, Michael I. Levy *Scr* Craig Lucas *Ph* Stefan Czapsky *Ed* Stephen A. Rotter *Mus* Howard Shore *Art Dir* Andrew Jackness
● Alec Baldwin, Meg Ryan, Kathy Bates, Ned Beatty, Patty Duke, Sydney Walker (20th Century-Fox)

Thanks to a magnetic cast and intelligent adaptation, *Prelude to a Kiss* has made a solid transfer to stage to screen. Craig Lucas' 1988 fairytale play about commitment and transcendent romantic love enjoyed a nice run on Broadway in 1990 after a limited period off-Broadway engagement with Alec Baldwin toplined.

Zippy opening reel nicely conveys the headiness of love's first stage. Peter (Baldwin) and Rita (Meg Ryan) meet sexily at a party and combust so quickly that they are in bed before they've even had a proper date.

They soon tie the knot at a lovely lakeside ceremony that turns curious with the arrival of a mysterious old man who asks to kiss the bride. Strangely drawn to the oldster, Rita agrees, then scarely knows what hit her.

During their Jamaica honeymoon, Rita doesn't seem at all like her old self. She flees back to her parents, leaving Peter to track down the old man whose ailing body now contains his wife's personality, and then to effect a retransference.

Lucas' overarching theme has to do with the spiritual prevailing over the physical, of the primacy of love no matter what the temporal obstacles.

Baldwin is a romantic lead both men and women can enjoy watching. Cuter-than-cute Ryan rambunctiously embodies the life force even when playing a basically aimless young woman, and pic suffers during her prolonged absence in the later stages.

Pic's title is derived from the Duke Ellington standard, and Howard Shore's original compositions have been combined with more than a dozen tunes of varied vintage to outstanding effect.

• •

■ PRESENTING LILY MARS

1943, 106 MINS, US ⑨
Dir Norman Taurog *Prod* Joseph Pasternak
Scr Richard Connell, Gladys Lehman *Ph* Joseph Ruttenberg *Ed* Albert Akst *Mus* George Stoll (dir.)
● Judy Garland, Van Heflin, Fay Bainter, Marta Eggerth, Richard Carlson (M-G-M)

Presenting Lily Mars spotlights Judy Garland and Van Heflin in a stage Cinderella yarn that supplies minor switches to regulation formula, but mainly depends on performances, direction and musical mounting, to carry it through.

Story is a typical Cinderella tale, with

Garland an aspiring and stagestruck young-ster who attempts to catch attention of pro-ducer Van Heflin in a small Indiana town. She makes a pest of herself for 40 minutes of the running time until she follows him into New York, gets a job in his new show, and eventually falls in love with the producer.

Heflin adequately handles the asignment of the young producer who eventually falls in love with Garland. Latter delivers in her usual effective style as the aspiring actress, putting across her numbers in top fashion.

Bob Crosby band is on for one tune in a nightspot where Garland heads for the mike to sing a song, while Tommy Dorsey and his ork appears for the finale accompaniment to song and dance by Miss Garland.

....

■ **PRESIDENT'S ANALYST, THE**

1967, 103 MINS, US ◇ ⓥ

Dir Theodore J. Flicker   *Prod* Stanley Rubin
Scr Theodore J. Flicker   *Ph* William A. Fraker   *Ed* Stuart Pappe   *Mus* Lalo Schifrin   *Art Dir* Pato Guzman
● James Coburn, Godfrey Cambridge, Severn Darden, Joan Delaney, Pat Harrington, Barry Maguire (Paramount/Panpiper)

The President's Analyst is a superior satire on some sacred cows, principally the lightly cam-ouflaged FBI, hippies, psychiatry, liberal and conservative politics – and the telephone company.

Inventive story peg – James Coburn star-ring as the personal analyst to the President of the US – is fleshed out with hilarious inci-dents which zero in on, and hit, their targets.

William Daniels scores as an upper-middle class compulsive liberal, whose family prac-tices marksmanship, karate and eaves-drop-ping because of right-wing neighbours.

Barry Maguire and Jill Banner are hippies, and Banner's sex scene with Coburn – in fields of flowers right out of some cosmetics teleblurb – is a comedy highlight in which several foreign and domestic spies kill each other off as they plot Coburn's demise.

....

■ **PRESIDENT'S LADY, THE**

1953, 96 MINS, US ⓥ

Dir Henry Levin   *Prod* Sol C. Siegel   *Scr* John Patrick
Ph Leo Tover   *Ed* William B. Murphy   *Mus* Alfred Newman   *Art Dir* Lyle R. Wheeler, Leland Fuller
● Susan Hayward, Charlton Heston, John McIntire, Fay Bainter, Ralph Dumke (20th Century-Fox)

The dramatic story of a lady's influence on the life of a great man invariably makes for interesting filming, and in the case of Andrew Jackson, the seventh president of the United States, 20th-Fox has created a particularly moving narrative. Based on Irving Stone's bestselling novel, *Lady* covers more than 40 years in the life of the famed Indian fighter and general.

It covers the period when the young Tennessee lawyer is Attorney General, through his battles with the Indians – and, more importantly, through the period of courting and marriage with Rachel Donelson Robards. It is the story of Jackson being forced to fight his way up the political ladder with the stigma of adultery plaguing him along the way.

Through it all, Charlton Heston supplies the kind of ammunition to this film that is as loaded as any carbine slung across his broad shoulders. It is a forthright steely-eyed por-trayal. Susan Hayward gives the pic a simple, sustained performance in addition to physical beauty. John McIntire plays Jackson's long-time friend and law partner, and he gives the role neat shading in a distinctly lesser role.
□ 1953: Nominations: Best B&W Costume Design, B&W Art Direction

....

■ **PRESIDIO, THE**

1988, 97 MINS, US ◇ ⓥ ⊙

Dir Peter Hyams   *Prod* D. Constantine Conte   *Scr* Larry Ferguson   *Ph* Peter Hyams   *Ed* James Mitchell
Mus Bruce Broughton   *Art Dir* Albert Brenner
● Sean Connery, Mark Harmon, Meg Ryan, Jack Warden, Mark Blum (Paramount)

Sean Connery and Mark Harmon go head to head as an Army provost marshal and a San Francisco cop who clash jurisdictions and styles in the investigation of an MP's murder.

Naturally, there's a backstory – they'd locked horns earlier when Connery was Harmon's c.o. in the military – and a compli-cation – Harmon gets involved with Connery's frisky and equally willful daughter (Meg Ryan).

Tug-of-war for dominance among the trio provides the interest in an otherwise ordinary crime story, as Harmon and Connery end up working to piece together clues in a convo-luted smuggling caper.

Along the way there are three very splashy action sequences – a car chase through the army base and the streets of S.F., a footrace through crowded Chinatown and the final, treacherous shootout in a water bottling plant that becomes as hairy as the swamps of 'Nam.

....

■ **PRESUMED INNOCENT**

1990, 127 MINS, US ◇ ⓥ ⊙

Dir Alan J. Pakula   *Prod* Sydney Pollack, Mark Rosenberg   *Scr* Frank Pierson, Alan J. Pakula
Ph Gordon Willis   *Ed* Evan Lottman   *Mus* John Williams
Art Dir George Jenkins
● Harrison Ford, Brian Dennehy, Raul Julia, Bonnie Bedelia, Paul Winfield, Greta Scacchi (Mirage/Warner)

Honed to a riveting intensity by director Alan Pakula and featuring the tightest script imag-inable, *Presumed Innocent* is a demanding, dis-turbing javelin of a courtroom murder mystery.

Hewing closely to Scott Turow's bestselling 1987 novel, the harrowing tale unfolds with nary a wasted step, as deputy prosecutor and family man Rusty Sabich (Harrison Ford) ar-rives at work to learn his beautiful colleague Carolyn Polhemus (Greta Scacchi) has been brutally murdered. Forced to lead the investi-gation by his longtime boss Raymond Horgan (Brian Dennehy), who's in a deep sweat over his re-election campaign, Sabich can scarcely admit he'd had an affair with the dead attor-ney. But his pained, steely cool wife (Bonnie Bedelia) knows, and she's none too sympa-thetic or forgiving about it.

Sabich is then confronted by rat-like ex-col-league Tommy Molto (Joe Grifasi), who's part of an opposing campaign for the chief prosecutor's office. Molto swears Sabich was at Carolyn's apartment the night of the mur-der. Before long Sabich is embroiled in a grand jury investigation that spurs his politi-cally frightened boss to turn on him. With a sly, magnetic Raul Julia brought in as Sabich's crafty defense lawyer, one never knows, until pic's astonishing denouement, whether Sabich did the deed or not.

Ford, in a very mature, subtle, lowkey per-formance, pulls off the difficult feat of mak-ing it impossible to be sure. Bedelia is wondrously controlled, and Scacchi, sans any hint of a European accent, is convincing and seductive.

....

■ **PRETTY BABY**

1978, 109 MINS, US ◇ ⓥ ⊙

Dir Louis Malle   *Prod* Louis Malle   *Scr* Polly Platt
Ph Sven Nykvist   *Ed* Suzanne Baron, Suzanne Fenn
Mus Jerry Wexler   *Art Dir* Trevor Williams
● Keith Carradine, Susan Sarandon, Brooke Shields, Frances Faye, Antonio Fargas, Gerrit Graham (Paramount)

The Louis Malle-Polly Platt collaboration on *Pretty Baby* has yielded an offbeat depiction of life in New Orleans' Storyville red-light dis-trict circa 1917, as experienced by a lifelong resident – a 12-year-old girl. The film is hand-some, the players nearly all effective, but the story highlights are confined within a narrow range of ho-hum dramatization.

The time of the plot is just before Josephis Davids, Secretary of the US Navy, closed Storyville as a bad influence; the black musi-cians who found employment in the brothels there drifted north to Kansas City, Memphis and Chicago, later east to NY, and thereby changed forever the direction and the fabric of American popular music. But that poten-tially strong film plot is not what's here.

Instead, Malle and Platt [using material in *Storyville* by Al Rose] have created a placid milieu in the barrelhouse owned by Frances Faye. There, Susan Sarandon is one of the girls who, in residence, has given birth to a child, in this case Brooke Shields, who gives either an extraordinarily subtle or else a to-tally perplexed performance as a pre-teenager whose entire world is that of the brothel.

Keith Carradine is cast as a catatonic pho-tographer who only likes to shoot portraits of the girls. Eventually Shields and Carradine live together, but the relationship ends when Sarandon, who left to marry a customer, re-turns in respectability to claim the underage child. That's it.
□ 1978: Nomination: Best Adapted Score

....

■ **PRETTY BOY FLOYD**

1960, 96 MINS, US

Dir Herbert J. Leder   *Prod* Monroe Sachson
Scr Herbert J. Leder   *Ph* Chuck Austin   *Ed* Ralph Rosenblum   *Mus* Del Sirino, William Sanford
● John Ericson, Barry Newman, Joan Harvey, Carl York, Phil Kenneally (Le-Sac)

This is a grim, almost sadistic reworking of the tale of the Oklahoma farm boy who won fame and ill-fortune in the early 1930s. It points a glib moral (crime does not pay) with-out ever presenting anything more than a few superficial reasons for the phenomenon that Pretty Boy Floyd represented. Script says Floyd had a bad temper and was ignorant. Period.

John Ericson does a good job in the role and is backed by a competent group of New York actors, few of whom have been on the screen before. (Film was shot entirely at Gold Medal Studios in the Bronx.) Low budget of the pic shows through from time to time, but actually seems to help create an appropriately seedy and sordid atmosphere.

Script first picks up Floyd when he is mak-ing a desultory attempt to go straight as an oil-field worker. Bounced when it's revealed that he served time for armed robbery in St Louis, Floyd picks up a life of crime again with an old cellmate. He soon branches out on his own and becomes the terror of the Middle West.

The film shows numerous of Floyd's bank holdups, as well as the famous 'Kansas City Massacre', in which Floyd and two others gunned to death two FBI men and a police-man who were transferring a brother hood to prison. Same incident, as well as Floyd's even-tual demise at the hands of the G-Men, are in *The FBI Story*.

....

■ **PRETTY IN PINK**

1986, 96 MINS, US ◇ ⓥ ⊙

Dir Howard Deutch   *Prod* Lauren Shuler   *Scr* John Hughes   *Ph* Tak Fujimoto   *Ed* Richard Marks
Mus Michael Gore   *Art Dir* John W. Corso
● Molly Ringwald, Harry Dean Stanton, Jon Cryer, Andrew McCarthy, Annie Potts, James Spader (Paramount)

Pretty in Pink is a rather intelligent (if not terribly original) look at adolescent insecurities.

Like scores of leading ladies before her, Molly Ringwald is the proverbial pretty girl from the wrong side of the tracks, called to a motherless life with down-on-his-luck dad (Harry Dean Stanton) and the misfortune to have to attend high school where the rich kids lord it over the poor.

That's enough to make any young lady insecure, even before the wealthy nice guy (Andrew McCarthy) asks her to the senior prom. Teased by his rich pals for slumming, McCarthy is also a bundle of uncertainties.

Moving predictably, none of this is unique drama. In the end, the wrong guy still gets the girl, which is a lesson youngsters might as well learn early.

● ●

■ PRETTY MAIDS ALL IN A ROW

1971, 95 MINS, US ◇

Dir Roger Vadim   *Prod* Gene Roddenberry   *Scr* Gene Roddenberry   *Ph* Charles Rosher   *Ed* Bill Brame   *Mus* Lalo Schifrin   *Art Dir* George W. Davis, Preston Ames

● Rock Hudson, Angie Dickinson, Telly Savalas, John David Carson, Roddy McDowall, Keenan Wynn (M-G-M)

Pretty Maids All in a Row, Roger Vadim's first US-made film, is apparently intended as a sort of genteel black murder-sex comedy. Gene Roddenberry's production careers through 95 minutes of juvenile double entendre and pratfall. Rock Hudson stars as a married high-school guidance counsellor who gets to know his girl students in the academic and Biblical sense, and eventually has to kill several to keep them quiet.

The unravelling of the murders (but not to an audience, which knows early what's up) parallels another story line: John David Carson's post-acne, pre-adult shy-guy character which blossoms under the careful attention of Angie Dickinson, the constant nymph. Carson does extremely well in the best developed characterization in the script.

Whatever substance was in the original [novel by Francis Pollini] or screen concept has been plowed under, leaving only superficial, one-joke results.

● ●

■ PRETTY POISON

1968, 89 MINS, US ◇ ⓦ

Dir Noel Black   *Prod* Marshal Backlar, Noel Black   *Scr* Lorenzo Semple Jr   *Ph* David Quaid   *Ed* William Ziegler   *Mus* Johnny Mandel   *Art Dir* Jack Martin Smith, Harold Michelson

● Anthony Perkins, Tuesday Weld, Beverly Garland, John Randolph, Dick O'Neill, Clarice Blackburn (20th Century-Fox)

Pretty Poison is an attempt at low-key psychological terror. Anthony Perkins, a mentally unhealthy resident of his own fantasies, finds in Tuesday Weld a more than willing pupil. Awkwardly begun and tediously developed, the film [from a novel by Stephen Geller] goes too much off the track.

A prolog and a quasi-epilog sequence establish Perkins as a disobedient parolee from confinement for arson-murder. Main body of the story, all shot on location in Massachusetts, concerns his play-acting and sexual playing with Weld, restless daughter of the widowed Beverly Garland.

From an innocent-looking teenager, Weld progresses to a cold, pathological killer and betrayor, escaping justice while pitiable Perkins, probably less deranged than she, falls victim to her superior depravity.

Perkins does a creditable job in a difficult part. So much of his earlier dialog might lead to disastrous guffaws that merely avoiding this trap must be credited to him and the director.

● ●

■ PRETTY POLLY
(US: A Matter of Innocence)

1967, 102 MINS, UK ◇

Dir Guy Green   *Prod* George W. George, Frank Granat   *Scr* Willis Hall, Keith Waterhouse   *Ph* Arthur Ibbetson   *Ed* Frank Clarke   *Mus* Michel Legrand   *Art Dir* Peter Mullins

● Hayley Mills, Trevor Howard, Shashi Kapoor, Brenda de Banzie, Dick Patterson, Kalen Lui (Universal)

Hayley Mills (as Polly) goes on vacation with a rich, disagreeable aunt to Singapore. Frumpish, bespectacled and lumpily dressed, she timidly obeys her aunt's constant demands for attention and looks suitably badgered.

But the relation dies from taking a swim too soon after a heavy lunch, and this sparks off the transformation scene. Polly is encouraged by an Indian acting as guide and helpmate to have her hair done, exchange her glasses for contact lenses, and indulge in a riot of makeup. She emerges as a siren.

Derived from a Noel Coward short story – itself written in the vein of Somerset Maugham – the script goes all out for sentiment, and, on its undemanding level, achieves it.

● ●

■ PRETTY WOMAN

1990, 117 MINS, US ◇ ⓦ ⊙

Dir Garry Marshall   *Prod* Arnon Milchan, Steven Reuther   *Scr* J.F. Lawton   *Ph* Charles Minsky   *Ed* Priscilla Nedd   *Mus* James Newton Howard   *Art Dir* Albert Brenner

● Richard Gere, Julia Roberts, Ralph Bellamy, Jason Alexander, Laura San Giacomo, Hector Elizondo (Touchstone)

J.F. Lawton's formula screenplay owes plenty to *Pygmalion*, *Cinderella* and *The Owl and the Pussycat* in limning a fairy tale of a prostitute with a heart of gold who mellows a stuffy businessman.

Pic's first two reels are weak, as corporate raider Richard Gere is unconvincingly thrown together with streetwalker Julia Roberts when he seeks directions to Beverly Hills. Seducing this reluctant john, she's improbably hired by Gere to spend the week with him as his escort since he's split up with his girlfriend. Her price tag is $3,000; film's cryptic shooting title was *3000*.

Film blossoms along with Roberts, when she doffs her unflattering Carol Channing blond wig to get natural and embark on a massively entertaining (and class conscious) shopping adventure on Rodeo Drive. Roberts handles the transition from coarse and gawky to glamorous with aplomb.

Pic's casting is astute, with Gere underplaying like a sturdy ballet star who hoists the ballerina Roberts on his shoulders. Sexiest routine has Gere playing solo-jazz piano late at night in the hotel ballroom and joined for a tryst by Roberts. Supporting cast is outstanding.

□ 1990: Nomination: Best Actress (Julia Roberts)

● ●

■ PRICK UP YOUR EARS

1987, 108 MINS, UK ◇ ⓦ ⊙

Dir Stephen Frears   *Prod* Andrew Brown   *Scr* Alan Bennett   *Ph* Oliver Stapleton   *Ed* Mick Audsley   *Mus* Stanley Myers   *Art Dir* Hugo Luczyc Wyhowski

● Gary Oldman, Alfred Molina, Vanessa Redgrave, Wallace Shawn, Julie Walters, Frances Barber (Civilhand/Zenith)

Though selling itself as a biography of controversial young British playwright Joe Orton, who was murdered in 1967, *Prick Up Your Ears* actually says very little about Orton the author, but deals almost totally with his relationship with Kenneth Halliwell, his lover and bludgeon killer.

Orton and Halliwell met at the Royal Academy of Dramatic Art. The inarticulate Orton fell for the seemingly sophisticated Halliwell, and for a while the pic dwells on Orton's promiscuity, at a time when homosexuality was still illegal in the UK. Suddenly, after years of obscurity, Orton becomes an overnight success.

The script [based on the biography by John Lahr] is witty, the direction fluid, with one of the homosexual orgy scenes in a public toilet almost balletic, and the depiction of the lovers' life in their flat suitably claustrophobic.

Gary Oldman is excellent as Orton, right down to remarkable resemblance, while Alfred Molina creates both an amusing and tormented Halliwell. Vanessa Redgrave takes top honors, though, as a compassionate and benign agent.

● ●

■ PRIDE AND PREJUDICE

1940, 117 MINS, US ⓦ

Dir Robert Z. Leonard   *Prod* Hunt Stromberg   *Scr* Aldous Huxley, Jane Murfin   *Ph* Karl Freund   *Ed* Robert J. Kern   *Mus* Herbert Stothart   *Art Dir* Cedric Gibbons, Paul Groesse

● Greer Garson, Laurence Olivier, Mary Boland, Edna May Oliver, Edmund Gwenn, Maureen O'Sullivan (M-G-M)

Metro reaches into the remote corners of the library bookshelf for this old-time novel about English society and the vicissitudes of a British mother faced with the task of marrying off five daughters in a limited market. *Pride and Prejudice* was written by Jane Austen in 1793. As a film it possesses little of general interest, except as a co-starring vehicle for Greer Garson and Laurence Olivier.

Any novel which survives more than a century possesses unusual qualities, and *Pride and Prejudice* qualifies chiefly because of the characterization of Elizabeth Bennet (Garson), eldest of the eligible sisters and a rather daring young woman with ideas of feminism far in advance of her contemporaries. In the screenplay she is trimmed to fit into a yarn about a family, rather than about an unusual and courageous girl. In consequence, the film is something less than satisfactory entertainment, despite lavish settings, costumes, and an acting ensemble of unique talent.

Olivier appears very unhappy in the role of Darcy, rich young bachelor, who is first spurned and then forgiven for his boorishness, conceit and bad manners.

There are some good performances. Mary Boland is a fluttering, clucking mother of a brood of young women whose aim is matrimony. Edna May Oliver, as the dominant Lady Catherine, comes on the scene late in the story and makes for some much needed merriment. Melville Cooper does a good comedy bit and the other Bennet sisters, as played by Maureen O'Sullivan, Ann Rutherford, Marsha Hunt and Heather Angel, provide charm and pulchritude.

□ 1940: Best B&W Interior Decoration

● ●

■ PRIDE AND THE PASSION, THE

1957, 132 MINS, US ◇ ⓦ

Dir Stanley Kramer   *Prod* Stanley Kramer   *Scr* Edna Anhalt, Edward Anhalt   *Ph* Franz Planer   *Ed* Frederic Knudson, Ellsworth Hoagland   *Mus* George Antheil   *Art Dir* Fernando Carrere

● Cary Grant, Frank Sinatra, Sophia Loren, Theodore Bikel, John Wengraf (United Artists)

This is Stanley Kramer's powerful production of C.S. Forester's sweeping novel, *The Gun*, about the Spanish 'citizens' army' that went to battle against the conquering legions of the French in 1810. The picture was in preparation and production in Spain for a year and a half.

It is the story of the band of guerillas who

P

come upon an oversized cannon that is abandoned by the retreating Spanish army. All things revolve around the huge weapon; it becomes symbolic of the spirit and courage of the Spanish patriots and their leader (Frank Sinatra).

From this point on *Passion* focuses on this unlikely army seeking to make its way to the French stronghold at Avila against incredibly tall odds. Their ally is Cary Grant, a British naval officer assigned to retrieve the gun for use against Napoleon's forces.

Sophia Loren is Sinatra's sultry and inflammable mistress with beaucoup accent on the decollete. At first hostile toward Grant, she comes to recognize his pro-Spanish motives and veers to him romantically. They make for an engaging trio.

Top credit must go to the production. The panoramic, longrange views of the marching and terribly burdened army, the painful fight to keep the gun mobile through ravine and over waterway – these are major plusses.

■ PRIDE OF THE MARINES
(UK: Forever in Love)

1945, 119 MINS, US

Dir Delmer Daves *Prod* Jerry Wald *Scr* Albert Maltz, Marvin Borowsky *Ph* Peverell Marley, Robert Burks *Ed* Owen Marks *Mus* Franz Waxman *Art Dir* Leo Kuter

● John Garfield, Eleanor Parker, Dane Clark, Ann Doran, John Ridgely, Rosemary De Camp (Warner)

Pride of the Marines is a two-hour celluloid saga [from a story by Roger Butterfield] which as an entertainment film with a forceful theme, so punchy that its 'message' aspects are negligible, is a credit to all concerned.

The simple story of Al Schmid, real-life marine-hero of Guadalcanal, is the story of American patriotism and heroism which is unheroic in its simple forthrightness; American pride in defending our way of life; American guts; and also a distorted sense of foolish pride, born of stubbornness, when the blinded Al Schmid rebels at returning to his loved ones because he 'wants nobody to be a seeing-eye dog for me'.

As unfolded it's a heart-tugging, sentimentally heroic tale. John Garfield as the brittle Al Schmid, ex-machinist now Marine-hero, albeit blinded, gives a vividly histrionic performance. He is buoyed plenty by Dane Clark and Anthony Caruso, with Eleanor Parker as the No 1 femme.
□ 1945: Nomination: Best Screenplay

■ PRIDE OF THE YANKEES, THE

1942, 120 MINS, US ▽ ⊙

Dir Sam Wood *Prod* Sam Goldwyn *Scr* Jo Swerling, Herman J. Mankiewicz *Ph* Rudolph Mate *Ed* Daniel Mandell *Mus* Leigh Harline *Art Dir* William Cameron Menzies

● Gary Cooper, Teresa Wright, Babe Ruth, Walter Brennan, Dan Duryea, Elsa Jansen (RKO/Goldwyn)

Sam Goldwyn has produced a stirring epitaph on Lou Gehrig. For baseball and non-baseball fan alike, this sentimental, romantic saga of the NY kid who rose to the baseball heights and later met such a tragic end is well worth seeing. Clever fictionizing and underplaying of the actual sport in contrast to the more human, domestic side of the great ballplayer make the film good for all audiences.

Gary Cooper makes his Gehrig look and sound believable from the screen.

To the credit of the screenwriters, and Paul Gallico who wrote the original, no attempt is made to inject color into the characterization of Gehrig. He's depicted for what he was, a quiet, plodding personality who strived for and achieved perfection in his profession.
□ 1942: Best Editing.

□ Nominations: Best Picture, Actor (Gary Cooper), Actress (Teresa Wright), Original Story, Screenplay, B&W Cinematography, B&W Art Direction, Scoring of a Dramatic Picture, Sound, Special Effects

■ PRIEST OF LOVE

1981, 125 MINS, UK ◇ ▽

Dir Christopher Miles *Prod* Christopher Miles, Andrew Donally *Scr* Alan Plater *Ph* Ted Moore *Ed* Paul Davies *Mus* Joseph James *Art Dir* Ted Tester, David Brockhurst

● Ian McKellen, Janet Suzman, Ava Gardner, Penelope Keith, Jorge Rivero, John Gielgud (Milesian)

Priest of Love is an impressively mounted and acted biopic [from a book by Harry T. Moore] dealing with the later years in the life of author D.H. Lawrence. Reunited with screenwriter Alan Plater who wrote his filmization of Lawrence's *The Virgin and the Gypsy*, director Christopher Miles takes a somewhat removed and cool look at his subject.

Picture opens in 1924 with Lawrence (Ian McKellen), wife Frieda (Janet Suzman) and their friend Dorothy Brett (Penelope Keith) enroute to Taos, New Mexico, for a self-imposed exile at the home of art patroness Mabel Dodge Luhan (Ava Gardner). Back in Britain, his books have been banned by the censor Herbert Muskett (an effetively stern cameo by John Gielgud).

Key scenes involve the fearless duo pushing relentlessly for the truth in a sexual manifesto in literature and tasteful scenes indicating his bisexuality (with a youth nude bathing at an Italian seashore) and relentless selfishness in inviting Dorothy to bed and then spurning her suddenly.

Too infrequently seen in films, McKellen gives a bravura performance, all the more remarkable for its avoidance of easy empathy. Veteran of a one-woman show on stage as Frieda, Janet Suzman is given her head by Miles and turns in a flamboyant, explosive turn which prevents the film from being dominated by McKellen.

■ PRIME CUT

1972, 86 MINS, US ◇ ▽

Dir Michael Ritchie *Prod* Joe W izan *Scr* Robert Dillon *Ph* Gene Polito *Ed* Carl Pingitore *Mus* Lalo Schifrin *Art Dir* Bill Malley

● Lee Marvin, Gene Hackman, Angel Tompkins, Gregory Walcott, Sissy Spacek, Janit Baldwin (Cinema Center)

Prime Cut is another contemporary underworld bloodletting, which is drawn, quartered and ground according to an overused recipe for hash. Lee Marvin and Gene Hackman provide the dressing along with the scenery of Calgary.

Writer Robert Dillon sends collection-agent Marvin to Eddie Egan, a Chi gangster who no longer is getting his cut from Hackman, a Kansas cattle king who also deals in dope and girls, among whom are Sissy Spacek and Janit Baldwin.

Director Michael Ritchie moves the pawns about inventively and with sterile precision.

There are no serious dramatic demands made of the players. Marvin and Hackman do this sort of thing all the time. Spacek and Baldwin look good in their feature debut and Gregory Walcott is most effective as a supersadist.

■ PRIME OF MISS JEAN BRODIE, THE

1969, 116 MINS, UK ◇ ▽

Dir Ronald Neame *Prod* Robert Fryer *Scr* Jay Presson Allen *Ph* Ted Moore *Ed* Norman Savage *Mus* Rod McKuen *Art Dir* John Howell

● Maggie Smith, Robert Stephens, Pamela Franklin, Gordon Jackson, Celia Johnson, Jane Carr (20th Century-Fox)

Maggie Smith's tour-de-force performance as a school-teacher slipping into spinsterhood is one of several notable achievements in this sentimental and macabre personal tragedy.

Jay Presson Allen adapted her own play [based on a novel by Muriel Spark]. The story, set in 1930s Edinburgh, treats in a tenderly savage way the decline of an age-resisting school-marm who lives too vicariously through a select group of prodigy-stooges. The telling involves elements of warm humor, biting sarcasm, pity, contempt, betrayal, and despair.

Smith's performance is a triumph. Other cast principals, all of whom project excellent performances, include Robert Stephens, the art teacher, Pamela Franklin, cast as a mysteriously-adult child and the eventual betrayer of Smith, and Gordon Jackson is impressive as the pitiable, gutless music teacher. Celia Johnson's key adversary role as the school head-mistress comes off magnificently.
□ 1969: Best Actress (Maggie Smith).
□ Nomination: Best Song ('Jean')

■ PRINCE AND THE PAUPER, THE

1937, 115 MINS, US ▽

Dir William Keighley *Prod* Robert Lord *Scr* Laird Doyle *Ph* Sol Polito *Ed* Ralph Dawson *Mus* Erich Wolfgang Korngold

● Errol Flynn, Claude Rains, Henry Stephenson, Barton MacLane, Billy Mauch, Bobby Mauch (Warner)

Of all his stories, Mark Twain loved best *The Prince and the Pauper*. Produced with sincerity and lavishness, this film [from a dramatised version by Catherine C. Cushing] is a costume picture minus any romance whatsoever.

In this film are the Mauch Twins, in addition to Errol Flynn, who is at his best in romantic, swashbuckling roles. But there is no girl opposite Flynn. So it's just the story of the Tudor Prince who exchanges places with a beggar boy, and regains his throne on Coronation Day through the heroism of a dashing soldier of fortune.

Such interest as the film contains could have been heightened by some drastic trimming in the early scenes, so that Flynn's entrance might have been moved up. He does Miles Hendon with the proper dash and spirit. The Mauch boys play their contrasting parts with earnestness if not too much skill. Claude Rains as Hertford; Montagu Love as Henry VIII, and Barton MacLane as John Canty, are fiercely melodramatic.

It doesn't seem that William Keighley, in his direction, has captured sufficient sympathy for the two youngsters to compensate for the romantic loss in having no fiancee for Flynn. The fragile plot scarcely holds together a full-length screenplay.

■ PRINCE AND THE PAUPER, THE

1977, 121 MINS, UK ◇ ▽

Dir Richard Fleischer *Prod* Pierre Spengler *Scr* George Macdonald Frazer *Ph* Jack Cardiff *Ed* Ernest Walter *Mus* Maurice Jarre *Art Dir* Tony Pratt

● Oliver Reed, Raquel Welch, Mark Lester, Ernest Borgnine, George C. Scott, Rex Harrison (Salkind)

Some of the irony and wit of Mark Twain's original fable about an English prince's switch with his poor lookalike has been lost or subdued, but this edition of *The Prince and the Pauper* [from an original screenplay by Berta Dominguez and Pierre Spengler, based on Twain's novel] still makes for satisfactory entertainment.

Lester as the prince trades identities with Mark Lester the pauper and is then banished from the castle and launched into an eye- and heart-opening odyssey around medieval England, finding it to be no Camelot but a land of wretched poor and persecuted.

As the pauper, meantime, he not only

swoons over young Lady Jane but also breathes a refreshing humanity into the court of ruthless King Henry.

● ●

■ **PRINCE AND THE SHOWGIRL, THE**

1957, 117 MINS, US ◇ ⓥ
Dir Laurence Olivier   *Prod* Laurence Olivier
Scr Terence Rattigan   *Ph* Jack Cardiff   *Ed* Jack Harris
Mus Richard Addinsell   *Art Dir* Roger Furse
● Marilyn Monroe, Laurence Olivier, Sybil Thorndike, Richard Wattis, Jeremy Spenser, Paul Hardwick (Monroe/Warner)

This first indie production of Marilyn Monroe's company is a generally pleasant comedy, but the pace is leisurely. Filmed in London with a predominantly British cast, the film is not a cliche Cinderella story as its title might indicate.

Based on Terence Rattigan's play *The Sleeping Prince*, the story takes place in London in 1911 at the time of the coronation of King George V. Laurence Olivier and his entourage, including his son, the boy king of the Balkan country, and the queen dowager, Olivier's mother-in-law, come to London for the ceremonies. The regent's roving eye alights on Monroe and the British Foreign Office, apprehensive of the delicate balance of power in the Balkan area, makes a determined effort to give the regent what he wants.

To Olivier's credit as producer, director and performer, he achieves the utmost from his material. His own performance as the stuffy regent is flawless. The part of the seemingly naive showgirl is just right for Monroe; she shows a real sense of comedy and can command a laugh with her walk or with an expression.

Sybil Thorndike is excellent as the hard-of-hearing not-quite-there dowager; Jeremy Spenser, who bears a remarkable resemblance to Sal Mineo, is appropriately serious as the young king, and Richard Wattis is properly harassed as the British Foreign office representative.

● ●

■ **PRINCE JACK**

1984, 100 MINS, US ◇ ⓥ
Dir Bert Lovitt   *Prod* Jim Milio   *Scr* Bert Lovitt   *Ph* Hiro Narita   *Ed* Janice Hampton   *Mus* Elmer Bernstein
Art Dir Michael Corenblith
● Robert Hogan, James F. Kelly, Kenneth Mars, Lloyd Nolan, Cameron Mitchell, Robert Guillaume (LMF)

Prince Jack is an ambiguous little indie mock documentary about key events and private encounters during the Kennedy years. The ambiguity lies in writer-director Bert Lovitt's wavering between depicting Jack Kennedy as a tough wheeler-dealer and a politician of the grandest vision.

Towards the end, the Cuban missile crisis is solved with Martin Luther King as a go-between.

King is made to be the only thoroughly likable and almost all-around popular guy in this feature, and he is played with cool and quiet charm by Robert Guillaume.

It would seem that the greater policy decisions are depicted fairly correctly (Ole Miss, The Bay of Pigs), while most of the Inner Sanctum private talks in the Oval Office of the White House are obviously based on hearsay and guesswork.

● ●

■ **PRINCE OF DARKNESS**

1987, 101 MINS, US ◇ ⓥ ⊙
Dir John Carpenter   *Prod* Larry Franco   *Scr* Martin Quatermass [= John Carpenter]   *Ph* Gary B. Kibbe
Ed Steve Mirkovich   *Mus* John Carpenter, Alan Howarth
Art Dir Daniel Lomino
● Donald Pleasence, Jameson Parker, Victor Wong, Lisa Blount, Dennis Dun, Susan Blanchard (Alive/Universal)

The Great Satan doesn't just reside in man's heart of darkness. Instead he lives in an opposite dimension, and manifests himself in this world in. . .bugs. That's about the extent of the horror that John Carpenter conjures up in *Prince of Darkness*.

Carpenter spends so much time turning the screws on the next scare that he completely forsakes his actors, who are already stranded with a shoddy script.

Story takes place in LA, where physics prof Birack (Victor Wong) takes his graduate class to an abandoned church in the middle of the city. He's summoned there by a priest (Donald Pleasence, who seems to have some secret sorrow), who has discovered inside the church a secret canister, guarded for hundreds of years by a forgotten sect of the Catholic church, the Brotherhood of Sleep.

Canister itself, which is supposed to be the embodiment of all evil, mostly looks like a green slime lava lamp. It starts sliming various students and turning them into zombies, so they ccan go out and wreak even more havoc.

None of the ensemble really stand out, with lovers Jameson Parker and Lisa Blount never getting a real chance to develop their relationship, and Dennis Dun's Walter completely robbed of his charm through his stilted delivery of equally wooden lines.

● ●

■ **PRINCE OF FOXES**

1949, 107 MINS, US ⓥ
Dir Henry King   *Prod* Sol C. Siegel   *Scr* Milton Krims
Ph Leon Shamroy   *Ed* Barbara McLean   *Mus* Alfred Newman   *Art Dir* Lyle Wheeler, Mark-Lee Kirk
● Tyrone Power, Orson Welles, Wanda Hendrix, Everett Sloane, Katina Paxinou, Felix Aylmes (20th Century-Fox)

Prince of Foxes actually is a fictional incident in the history of the Italian Renaissance general Cesare Borgia, but too often it is slow and plodding in its exposition and execution.

Prince tells of Borgia's lust for power and desire to expand his empire. This he does with all the intrigue and knife-in-the-back knavery at his command.

The Borgiastic episode, despite its 16th-century background, has been conceived and executed in true Capone and Chicago tradition. As the murderous Cesare, Orson Welles is alternately glowering, reposing and diabolical.

Tyrone Power plays Orsini, who assumes the mantle of nobility to achieve social stature and ultimately bests Borgia when he deserts him to join the invaded duchy of the elderly Varano. Wanda Hendrix, as Varano's young wife, gives the weakest of the performances.

□ 1949: Nominations: Best B&W Cinematography, B&W Costume Design

● ●

■ **PRINCE OF THE CITY**

1981, 167 MINS, US ◇ ⓥ ⊙
Dir Sidney Lumet   *Prod* Burtt Harris   *Scr* Jay Presson Allen, Sidney Lumet   *Ph* Andrzej Bartkowiak   *Ed* John J. Fitzstephens   *Mus* Paul Chihara   *Art Dir* Tony Walton
● Treat Williams, Jerry Orbach, Bob Balaban, Lindsay Crouse, James Tolkan, Lance Henrickson (Warner/Orion)

The film is a concentrated, unrelievedly serious and cerebrally involving entry, exhaustively detailing the true-life saga of a Gotham detective who turned Justice Dept informer to eke out widespread corruption in his special investigating unit during the 1960s.

Treat Williams is outstanding as the young, gung-ho cop who is courted by federal investigators and finds himself on a conscience-wracking approach-avoidance track that finally leads him to accept the informant role.

As Federal pressure for indictments mounts, however, matters quickly careen out of control and Williams is cajoled, manipu-

lated and ultimately blackmailed into spilling everything, while friends spurn him or commit suicide, his protectors are promoted upstairs, Mafiosi attempt buying him off, then try bumping him off, and the Feds barely agree not to prosecute him for his own past sins.

Within a nightmarish, frequently Kafkaesque atmosphere of intense danger and uncontrollable conscience, the film paints a world where law and morality are only relative commodities.

Director Sidney Lumet is in firm control of the sprawling canvas, showing in spades his ability to harness intense energy and almost uniformly top-rate performances from a cannily-cast stable of solid character actors.

□ 1981: Nomination: Best Adapted Screenplay

● ●

■ **PRINCE OF TIDES, THE**

1991, 132 MINS, US ◇ ⓥ ⊙
Dir Barbra Streisand   *Prod* Barbra Streisand, Andrew Karsch   *Scr* Pat Conroy, Becky Johnston   *Ph* Stephen Goldblatt   *Ed* Don Zimmerman   *Mus* James Newton Howard   *Art Dir* Paul Sylbert
● Nick Nolte, Barbra Streisand, Blythe Danner, Kate Nelligan, Jeroen Krabbe, Melinda Dillon (Columbia/Barwood-Longfellow)

A deeply moving exploration of the tangled emotions of a dysfunctional Southern family, this lovingly crafted (though unevenly scripted) film of Pat Conroy's novel centers on Nick Nolte's performance of a lifetime. Bringing her usual strengths of character to her role as Nolte's psychiatrist/lover, Barbra Streisand marks every frame with the intensity and care of a filmmaker committed to heartfelt, unashamed emotional involvement with her characters.

Ex-teacher/coach Nolte is in a midlife crisis unusually chaotic even for a Nolte character. He's jobless, drinking too much and struggling with a disintegrating marriage to Blythe Danner.

Nolte's disturbed sister Melinda Dillon, a NY poet of some repute, has attempted suicide, and she lies catatonic in hospital restraints. Her brother is summoned north to help Streisand piece together the splintered mirror of her past. In the process, this emotionally guarded doctor finds herself not only becoming Nolte's surrogate mother but also crossing the professional line to emotional and sexual involvement.

Screenwriters underdevelop some characters (especially Dillon) while overdoing the boorishness of Streisand's musician husband (Jeroen Krabbe) and the 'Golden Boy' subplot involving her violin-playing son (Jason Gould), who learns football from Nolte. But the heart of the film is the relationship between Nolte and Streisand, a creative sparring match doomed to go nowhere but leaves an indelible imprint on each.

□ 1991: Nominations: Best Picture, Actor (Nick Nolte), Supp. Actress (Kate Nelligan), Adapted Screenplay, Cinematography, Original Score, Art Direction

● ●

■ **PRINCESS BRIDE, THE**

1987, 98 MINS, US ◇ ⓥ ⊙
Dir Rob Reiner   *Prod* Andrew Scheinman, Rob Reiner
Scr William Goldman   *Ph* Adrian Biddle   *Ed* Robert Leighton   *Mus* Mark Knopfler   *Art Dir* Norman Garwood
● Cary Elwes, Mandy Patinkin, Chris Sarandon, Christopher Guest, Robin Wright, Peter Falk (Act III/20th Century-Fox)

Based on William Goldman's novel, this is a post-modern fairy tale that challenges and affirms the conventions of a genre that may not be flexible enough to support such horseplay.

It also doesn't help that Cary Elwes and

Robin Wright as the loving couple are nearly comatose and inspire little passion from each other, or the audience.

Bound together by their love at tender age, young Westley (Elwes) then stableboy, falls in love with his beautiful mistress (Wright), but they're separated when he goes off to sea on a mission. After years of grieving for him she becomes betrothed to the evil Prince Humperdinck (Chris Sarandon) who masterminds her kidnaping to strengthen his own position in the kingdom.

First off, Westley must defeat a trio of kidnapers headed by the diminutive, but slimy, Wallace Shawn. His accomplices are the kind-hearted giant Fezzik (Andre The Giant) and Inigo Montoya, a Spanish warrior (Mandy Patinkin) out to avenge the murder of his father.

Patinkin especially is a joy to watch and the film comes to life when his longhaired, scruffy cavalier is on screen.

□ 1987: Nomination: Best Song ('Storybook Love')

■ **PRINCE VALIANT**

1954, 100 MINS, US ◇ ▽
Dir Henry Hathaway *Prod* Robert L. Jacks *Scr* Dudley Nichols *Ph* Lucien Ballard *Ed* Robert Simpson *Mus* Franz Waxman
● James Mason, Janet Leigh, Robert Wagner, Debra Paget, Sterling Hayden, Victor McLaglen (20th Century-Fox)

The cartoon strip hero comes to the screen as a good offering for fans who dote on the fanciful derring-do of the Arthurian period.

Harold Foster's King Features strip gives an imaginative action basis for Robert L. Jacks' production guidance and the direction by Henry Hathaway. Although the picture comes in a bit overlength, the direction and Dudley Nichols' scripting combine to bring it off acceptably against some rather dazzling settings, including authentic castles and sites actually lensed in England.

Heading the star list is James Mason, who plays Sir Brack, pretender to King Arthur's throne. His dirty work is excellent, whether thinking up ambushes for Robert Wagner, in the title role, or engaging the young hero in joust or broadsword combat. The way he and Mason have at each other in the climaxing duel puts a topnotch action capper on the tale.

The plot finds Wagner in exile with his royal parents after their throne was seized by Primo Carnera. The Viking prince goes to King Arthur's court, becomes a squire to Sir Gawain, falls in love with Janet Leigh and, eventually, is able to put the finger on Mason as the mysterious Black Knight.

■ **PRISON**

1988, 102 MINS, US ◇ ▽ ⊙
Dir Renny Harlin *Prod* Irwin Yablans *Scr* C. Courtney Joyner *Ph* Mac Ahlberg *Ed* Ted Nicolaou *Mus* Richard Band *Art Dir* Phillip Duffin
● Lane Smith, Viggo Mortensen, Chelsea Field, Andre De Shields, Lincoln Kilpatrick (Empire)

Starring as the prison in this rough penal pic with its special effects-laden horror story is the 87-year-old Wyoming State Penitentiary, which has attracted tourists rather than cons since 1981. The structure takes on all the menace of the house in *Amityville Horror* or hotel in *The Shining*.

The crumbling stone fortress is grounds for revenge because, as aged inmate Cresus (Lincoln Kilpatrick) points out toward the end, 'things won't stay buried.' It turns out that in 1964 guard Ethan Sharpe (Lane Smith) watched an innocent man fry in the electric chair.

Sharpe, now a warden, is appointed to the

prison's helm despite recurrent nightmares brought on by a guilty conscience. The wronged convict's evil spirit is mad enough to eliminate a few of the new guards and inmates.

Viggo Mortensen plays Burke, a James Dean type antihero spared death but not a lot of bumps and bruises. His resemblance to the electrocuted con apparently is just a coincidence in the screenplay of producer Irwin Yablans' story.

■ **PRISONER, THE**

1955, 94 MINS, UK ▽
Dir Peter Glenville *Prod* Vivian A. Cox *Scr* Bridget Boland *Ph* Reginald Wyer *Ed* Freddie Wilson *Mus* Benjamin Frankel *Art Dir* John Hawkesworth
● Alec Guinness, Jack Hawkins, Wilfrid Lawson, Jeannette Sterke, Ronald Lewis, Raymond Huntley (Columbia)

Closely following the Bridget Boland play, this British filmization retains the essentials of this stark and dramatic narrative with Alec Guinness repeating his original role of the cardinal held on a phoney charge of treason.

In her own adaptation, Boland has broadened the canvas of her subject, particularly to include background atmosphere of unrest in the capital while the cardinal is held without charge.

Peter Glenville's studied direction is a technical achievement, although the film just fails to achieve the anticipated emotional impact. The acting, however, is exceptionally high. The flawless performance by Guinness is matched by a superb portrayal by Jack Hawkins. But both of these stars find their equal in Wilfrid Lawson's interpretation of the jailor.

■ **PRISONER OF SECOND AVENUE, THE**

1974, 98 MINS, US ◇ ▽
Dir Melvin Frank *Prod* Melvin Frank *Scr* Neil Simon *Ph* Philip Lathrop *Ed* Bob Wyman *Mus* Marvin Hamlisch *Art Dir* Preston Ames
● Jack Lemmon, Anne Bancroft, Gene Saks, Elizabeth Wilson, Florence Stanley, Macine Stuart (Warner)

Neil Simon's play *The Prisoner of Second Avenue* has Jack Lemmon and Anne Bancroft as a harried urban couple. The film is more of a drama with comedy, for the personal problems as well as the environmental challenges aren't really funny, and even some of the humor is forced and strident.

Lemmon has done prior Simon plots on the screen, and he has the same basic character down cold. Bancroft demonstrates a fine versatility in facing the script demands. Atop the couple's problems in their apartment comes Lemmon's axing after many years on the job.

Gene Saks, Elizabeth Wilson and Florence Stanley do well as Lemmon's brother and sisters, while Ed Peck, the hostile upstairs neighbor, and Ivor Francis, Lemmon's taciturn shrink, head a good supporting cast.

■ **PRISONER OF SHARK ISLAND, THE**

1936, 95 MINS, US ▽
Dir John Ford *Prod* Darryl F. Zanuck *Scr* Nunnally Johnson *Ph* Bert Glennon *Ed* Jack Murray *Mus* Hugo Friedhofer, R.H. Bassett *Art Dir* William Darling
● Warner Baxter, Gloria Stuart, Claude Gillingwater, Arthur Byron, Harry Carey, Francis Ford (20th Century-Fox)

Warner Baxter as Dr Samuel A. Mudd, 'America's Jean Valjean' of the post-Civil War hysteria, turns in a capital performance as the titular prisoner of 'America's Devil's Island'.

The sympathetic trouping of Gloria Stuart as Dr Mudd's plucky wife who constantly en-

deavors to win back biased public favor for her unjustly condemned husband, plus the effective injection of a new kid charmer (Joyce Kay) as their baby daughter does much to achieve some mixed sympathies, but by and large it's a film for the men.

Not wholly a figment of Hollywood imagination, the saga of Dr Mudd is founded on fact. Baxter's woes start when he unknowingly sets the broken leg of John Wilkes Booth, Lincoln's assassin. Accused of con- spiracy in the crime, he is court-martialed and, of eight co-defendants, three are hung and Dr Mudd is among those committed to Shark Island for life.

Casting is tiptop. John Carradine stands out as a new face among especially sinister heavies, a highly effective villyun. Frank McGlynn Sr, in his Abraham Lincoln personation is, as ever, realistic in dignified portrayal and uncanny resemblance to the martyred liberator.

■ **PRISONER OF ZENDA, THE**

1922, 130 MINS, US ⊗
Dir Rex Ingram *Prod* Rex Ingram *Scr* Mary O'Hara *Ph* John F. Seitz
● Lewis Stone, Alice Terry, Robert Edeson, Stuart Holmes, Barbara La Marr, Lois Lee (Metro)

To say that Rex Ingram and a remarkably good company of screen players have made the very utmost of the possibilities of Anthony Hope's novel about sums up this venture. It is the kind of romance that never stales – fresh, genuine, simple and wholesome. Indeed this screen translation is more profoundly interesting than either the novel or the Edward Rose stage play.

Ingram built a spacious ballroom with an atmosphere of unobtrusive splendor. For once you get the illusion that it is a royal ball and not a movie mob scene.

Another bit of finesse is the choice of the hero and heroine, in Lewis Stone, who makes no pretence to Apollo-like beauty, and Alice Terry who makes a Princess Flavia of surpassing blonde loveliness in her regal robes.

The close-ups of all the characters are done in a misty dimness that gives them a remoteness that inspires the imagination. Some of the landscapes are handled in like manner and throughout the photography is marked.

■ **PRISONER OF ZENDA, THE**

1937, 100 MINS, US ▽
Dir John Cromwell *Prod* David O. Selznick *Scr* John L. Balderston, Donald Ogden Stewart *Ph* James Wong Howe *Ed* Hal C. Kern, James E. Newcom *Mus* Alfred Newman *Art Dir* Lyle Wheeler
● Ronald Colman, Madeleine Carroll, Douglas Fairbanks Jr, Mary Astor, David Niven, Raymond Massey (Selznick/United Artists)

Zenda is hokum of the 24-carat variety [from Anthony Hope's novel, dramatized by Edward Rose; script adaptation by Wells Root]; a sheer piece of romantic nonsense about a mythical European kingdom, a struggle for possession of a throne between a dissolute true heir and an ambitious step-brother with larcenous inclinations; a lovely blonde princess; a swashbuckling duke, who bends with the political wind, and a young Englishman, on his annual outing, who is persuaded to impersonate the king.

Cromwell's direction is excellent. His opening scenes in the Balkan capital are as casual as a travelog, and his players assume lifelike characterizations through a series of intimate, human situations.

Colman (who plays the dual role of Englishman and King) has the ability to make a full dress court uniform appear as comfortable as a suit of pajamas. He never trips over his sword, or loosens his collar for air. Madeleine Carroll in all her blonde loveliness is quite receptive to impassioned protestations, so the romance has a touch of verity.

It's a close race between Colman and Fairbanks Jr, who plays Rupert of Hentzau for top acting honours. Best femme part is the scheming Antoinette, which Mary Astor is inclined to underplay.

☐ 1937: Nomination: Best Art Direction, Score

■ PRISONER OF ZENDA, THE

1952, 100 MINS, US ◇ ⊛

Dir Richard Thorpe   *Prod* Pandro S. Berman   *Scr* John L. Balderston, Noel Langley   *Ph* Joseph Ruttenberg   *Ed* George Boemler   *Mus* Alfred Newman   *Art Dir* Cedric Gibbons, Hans Peters
● Stewart Granger, Deborah Kerr, James Mason, Louis Calhern, Jane Greer, Lewis Stone (M-G-M)

Fanciers of costumed swashbucklers will find this remake of the venerable *Prisoner of Zenda* a likeable version. The third time around for the yarn [adapted by Wells Root from the novel by Anthony Hope and dramatization by Edward Rose] this time it wears Tehnicolor dress, and has lavish physical appurtenances.

Plot deals with an Englishman who goes on a holiday to the small kingdom of Ruritania and gets involved in a royal impersonation and a love affair with a beautiful princess. Stewart Granger is the hero, dualing as the Englishman and the king he impersonates, and gives the roles the proper amount of dashing heroics.

Opposite him is Deborah Kerr, the lovely princess, and her looks and ability to wear period gowns are just what the part requires. James Mason scores as Rupert of Hentzau, making the character a rather likeable heavy.

Lewis Stone, who played the dual role in the original 1922 version of the story, appears briefly in this one as a cardinal.

■ PRIVATE AFFAIRS OF BEL AMI, THE

1947, 110 MINS, US ◇ ⊛

Dir Albert Lewin   *Prod* David L. Loew   *Scr* Albert Lewin   *Ph* Russell Metty   *Ed* Albrecht Joseph   *Mus* Darius Milhaud   *Art Dir* Gordon Wiles
● George Sanders, Angela Lansbury, Ann Dvorak, Frances Dee, John Carradine, Susan Douglas (Loew-Lewin)

Confronted with the old problem of cleaning up a classic novel to conform to strict censorship codes, the production outfit has come up with a scrubbed-face version of the complete scoundrel depicted in Guy de Maupassant's novel *Private Affairs of Bel Ami*. The title character pays for his sins by being killed in a duel which he brought on himself, in strict compliance with the Production Code's 'crime doesn't pay' edict. Prosties, which had a feature part in the story, emerge as dancers of questionable character.

Entire tempo of the story is slow-paced. Director Albert Lewin's script builds up little sympathy for George Sanders, the Bel Ami of the piece, who climbs to the top of Paris social and political circles in the 1880s over the broken hearts of five women whom he uses to advance himself and then discards.

Cast is exceptionally strong and, under Lewin's skilled direction, is mostly responsible for the film's merits. Sanders plays it with the correct hammy touch, emoting with de Maupassant epigrams for sock effect. Angela Lansbury is beauteous and competent as the young widow with whom he's probably in love all the time. Ann Dvorak, Frances Dee, Susan Douglas, Katherine Emery and Marie Wilson all show well as the other women in his path. John Carradine, as the comrade, and Hugo Haas and Albert Basserman handle the male roles in okay fashion.

Painting of *The Temptation of Saint Anthony*,

by Max Ernst, which forms one of the focal points of the story a la *Dorian Gray*, is flashed on the screen the first time it's shown in brilliant Technicolor for good effect. Darius Milhaud's score is excellent and Russell Metty's camera work, spotlighting shadows and gas-lit interiors, is good.

■ PRIVATE BENJAMIN

1980, 109 MINS, US ◇ ⊛ ⊙

Dir Howard Zieff   *Prod* Nancy Meyers, Charles Shyer, Harvey Miller   *Scr* Nancy Meyers, Charles Shyer, Harvey Miller   *Ph* David M. Walsh   *Ed* Sheldon Kahn   *Mus* Bill Conti   *Art Dir* Robert Boyle
● Goldie Hawn, Eileen Brennan, Armand Assante, Sam Wanamaker, Harry Dean Stanton, Robert Webber (Warner/Meyers-Shyler-Miller)

Goldie Hawn's venture in producing her own film is actually a double feature – one is a frequently funny tale of an innocent who is conned into joining the US Army and her adventures therein; the other deals with the same innocent's personality problems as a Jewish princess with only an intermittent chuckle to help out.

The trouble may be with the use of too many screenwriters who have been told to always keep their star's image uppermost in their scribblings. But she's not so gifted that she can carry a heavy load of indifferent material on her own two little shoulders, without considerable sagging.

Another script problem is that the supporting characters are, even when they start out sympathetically, turned into unlikeable types.

☐ 1980: Nominations: Best Actress (Goldie Hawn), Supp. Actress (Eileen Brennan), Original Screenplay

■ PRIVATE FILES OF J. EDGAR HOOVER, THE

1977, 112 MINS, US ⊛

Dir Larry Cohen   *Prod* Larry Cohen   *Scr* Larry Cohen   *Ph* Paul Glickman   *Ed* Christopher Lebenzon   *Mus* Miklos Rozsa   *Art Dir* Cathy Davis
● Broderick Crawford, Jose Ferrer, Michael Parks, Ronee Blakely, Rip Torn, Celeste Holm (Larco)

According to Larry Cohen, who wrote, produced and directed this $3 million look at America's top cop, J. Edgar Hoover was a public relations gimmick. As a vindictive, puritanical paranoid he shipped agents off to Knoxville for reading *Playboy* magazine. Privately, he was a mama's boy and a homosexual who got his jollies by sitting in the dark with a bottle of bourbon and a tape recorder playing the sounds of a powerful government official's hotel liaisons.

This may be the motion picture industry's first historical horror story. Cohen has adopted two visual styles. There's the 'backlot look' used to reenact great moments in J. Edgar Hoover's life, like the shooting of John Dillinger in front of the Biograph Theatre in Chicago and Hoover's first arrest.

Then there's the documentary look: Hoover in the FBI building; that's the real FBI building. Hoover in the apartment of his lifelong friend Lionel McCoy; that's the real McCoy's apartment.

He also knew enough to cast Broderick Crawford in the lead. As Hoover, the jowly Crawford turns in a fine performance. However, the remainder of the performances, starting with Michael Parks' Robert Kennedy, are grotesque attempts to mimic well known public officials.

■ PRIVATE FUNCTION, A

1984, 93 MINS, UK ◇ ⊛

Dir Malcolm Mowbray   *Prod* Mark Shivas   *Scr* Alan Bennett   *Ph* Tony Pierce-Roberts   *Ed* Barrie Vince   *Mus* John Du Prez   *Art Dir* Stuart Walker

● Michael Palin, Maggie Smith, Liz Smith, Denholm Elliott, Richard Griffiths, John Normington (HandMade)

Pic is set in 1947, at a time of national rejoicing over a royal wedding and hardship caused by food rationing. Plot evolves out of a plan hatched by a group of town notables to fatten up a secret pig for festive devouring on the wedding night.

Central characters are a husband and wife team played by Maggie Smith and Michael Palin. She's a bullying wife anxious to reach the social highspots in the Yorkshire village where he works as a foot doctor. Their domestic crises are made more complex and amusing by the presence of a greedy mother (Liz Smith) who lives in terror of being put away.

Director Malcolm Mowbray neatly orchestrates the resulting drama, and points up the class antagonisms at play.

■ PRIVATE LESSONS

1981, 87 MINS, US ◇ ⊛ ⊙

Dir Alan Myerson, [James Fargo]   *Prod* R. Ben Efraim   *Scr* Dan Greenburg   *Ph* Jan De Bont   *Ed* Fred Chulack
● Sylvia Kristel, Howard Hesseman, Ron Foster, Eric Brown, Pamela Bryant, Ed Begley Jr (Jensen Farley)

Private Lessons is a novelty comedy limning an adolescent boy's introduction to sex via his worldly European housekeeper. Suffering from a rickety structure that reflects extensive production problems (James Fargo directed additional footage sans credit), picture has a sustained air of amorality which is quite unusual for US films.

Story is set at a ritzy mansion in idyllic Arizona during summer vacation, with premise of Mr Fillmore (Ron Foster) leaving orders that his beautiful housekeeper (Sylvia Kristel) initiate his 15-year-old son Philly (Eric Brown) to sex before he returns from a business trip.

Dan Greenburg's script from his own novel [*Philly*] is very effective in presenting an innocent youth's point-of-view confronted with the sexual stimuli that pervade modern society. Inability to flesh out this central notion into a feature-length screenplay is a pity, but *Private Lessons* should satisfy general audiences with its diversions of frequent nudity, softcore sex, dominant rock music score and gags.

As Philly, Brown successfully carries the picture with a warm performance. Kristel is a beautiful dream-woman, but play-acting role here does not tap her thesping abilities. Although Kristel bares her breasts frequently, an unmatched stunt double [Judy Helden] is used for her disconcertingly in several of the nude scenes.

■ PRIVATE LIFE OF DON JUAN, THE

1934, 89 MINS, UK ⊛

Dir Alexander Korda   *Prod* Alexander Korda   *Scr* Frederick Lonsdale, Lajos Biro   *Ph* Georges Perinal, Robert Kras007   *Ed* Harold Young, Stephen Harrison   *Mus* Mischa Spoliansky, Arthur Wimperis, Arthur Benjamin   *Art Dir* Vincent Korda
● Douglas Fairbanks, Merle Oberon, Binnie Barnes, Joan Gardner, Benita Hume, Barry Mackay (London/ United Artists)

Douglas Fairbanks' prime portrayal is as the antiquated knight who is finally disillusioned as the arch-heartbreaker when he must bow to his years and recognize that his amorous porch-climbing career is finis.

But the film holds more than that. There are many fine lights and shadings to get over the fact that the susceptible Seville femmes, who were not loath to two-timing their senors, had glorified Don Juan into an almost mythical figure.

Fairbanks is first introduced as a bit weary and slightly ill cavalier. All the faithful illusion is maintained to impress upon the viewer that he is still the potent Don Juan of history,

P

excepting that he happens to have become a bit fatigued. His faithful retainer, his cook, his masseur, all his aides, are shown jealously watching over him.

There's even planted the premise of Fairbanks being irked with the wife (Benita Hume) whom, he complains, has been too possessive of late; so much so that it's been cramping his style.

Fairbanks, stacked beside some nifty lookers – Merle Oberon, Binnie Barnes, Joan Gardner, Hume, Patricia Hilliard, Diana Napier, Natalie Lelong (Princess Paley), Betty Hamilton, Toto Koopman, Spencer Trevor, Nancy Jones and Florence Wood – makes for an incongruous impression.

Georges Perinal, Rene Clair's ace camera-grinder, in this, his first away from French productions, has fashioned some fine stuff.

■ PRIVATE LIFE OF HELEN OF TROY, THE

1927, 87 MINS, US ⊗
Dir Alexander Korda   *Prod* Carey Wilson   *Scr* Carey Wilson   *Ph* Lee Garmes, Sid Hickox   *Ed* Harold Young
● Maria Corda, Lewis Stone, Ricardo Cortez, George Fawcett, Alice White (First National)

Helen [based on the novel by John Erskine] is all comedy. Satirizing ancient myth in general and Helen's affairs particularly, the titles are topical, while the music is mainly based on pop dance tunes. Wheeling the giant wooden horse inside the gates of Troy is accomplished to the strains of 'Horses, Horses, Horses', etc.

The film kids the husband-wife complex throughout, the king, following the conquest of Troy, making a beeline for Helen's dress-maker to destroy the shop. Meanwhile, he has been trying to go fishing since nine o'clock. When it looks as if Helen is about to take another vacation with her second prince, the king is convinced he's going to get in his trip, and that finishes the picture.

No battles and no slow spots. The action is lively all the way, with Maria Corda in various stages of slight clothing.
☐ 1927/28: Nomination: Best Engineering Effects

■ PRIVATE LIFE OF HENRY VIII, THE

1933, 96 MINS, UK Ⓥ ⊙
Dir Alexander Korda   *Prod* Alexander Korda   *Scr* Lajos Biro, Arthur Wimperis   *Ph* Georges Perinal   *Ed* Stephen Harrison   *Mus* Kurt Schroeder (dir.)   *Art Dir* Vincent Korda
● Charles Laughton, Binnie Barnes, Merle Oberon, Elsa Lanchester, Wendy Barrie, Robert Donat (London/United Artists)

Unquestionably the perfect pick for the part, it must also be said that Charles Laughton is aided no little by the script, more generous to the character of Henry VIII than most of his biographers. The corpulent ruler is here made rather a jolly old soul and, for those who may have forgotten, it can be said that he had six wives, of whom the picture concerns itself with five. A couple are inclined to beat about the royal bush, so they thereby lose their heads for being promiscuous.

Laughton is happily supported right down the line, especially by Merle Oberon, Binnie Barnes, Robert Donat and Elsa Lanchester. The fair Barnes shares with Lanchester the major portion of footage devoted to the wives while Oberon is a British edition of Fay Wray.

Of comedy highlights audiences will probably like best the card game between Henry and Anne of Cleves (Lanchester), in which she takes him for almost half his kingdom, and the ruler at the banquet table. It being the open season for belching, Laughton demonstrates that he is equally as adept in this as at giving the 'berry [*If I Had a Million* 1932].

☐ 1932/33: Best Actor (Charles Laughton).
☐ Nomination: Best Picture

■ PRIVATE LIFE OF SHERLOCK HOLMES, THE

1970, 125 MINS, UK ◇ Ⓥ
Dir Billy Wilder   *Prod* Billy Wilder   *Scr* Billy Wilder, I.A.L. Diamond   *Ph* Christopher Challis   *Ed* Ernest Walter   *Mus* Miklos Rozsa   *Art Dir* Tony Inglis
● Robert Stephens, Colin Blakely, Irene Handl, Stanley Holloway, Christopher Lee, Genevieve Page (United Artists)

Billy Wilder's enterprise is a strange one because of its shift in directions from quite good satire to straight spy stuff. It is in large part old-fashioned, in that it's mile-wide and ancient-history Sherlock Holmes, but it's also handsomely produced and directed with incisiveness by Wilder.

Robert Stephens is the detective consultant, the man from Baker Street who fakes a story about his being not all masculine to duck out on an assignment from a Russian ballerina. But is he really faking? Stephens plays Sherlock in rather gay fashion under Wilder's tongue-in-cheek direction. Colin Blakely is Dr John H. Watson; a performer who plays it broad and bright.

The dialog is crisp and amusing, Wilder and I.A.L. Diamond having a way with such matters.

■ PRIVATE LIVES OF ELIZABETH AND ESSEX, THE

1939, 106 MINS, US ◇ Ⓥ
Dir Michael Curtiz   *Prod* Hal B. Wallis (exec.)
Scr Norman Reilly Raine, Aeneas MacKenzie   *Ph* Sol Polito, W. Howard Greene   *Ed* Owen Marks   *Mus* Erich Wolfgang Korngold   *Art Dir* Anton Grot
● Bette Davis, Errol Flynn, Olivia de Havilland, Vincent Price, Donald Crisp, Alan Hale (Warner)

The Private Lives of Elizabeth and Essex is a lavishly-produced historical drama, the first picture to be released using the new fast Technicolor negative, and improved processing methods.

Bette Davis dominates the production at every turn as Elizabeth, virgin queen of England. Her delineation would indicate that Davis did much personal research.

Picture is a film version of Maxwell Anderson's [stage play] *Elizabeth the Queen*. Story details the intimate May-and-December love affair of youthful Lord Essex (Errol Flynn) and matronly Queen Elizabeth. Both are headstrong and stubborn; each is ambitious to rule England.

Picture has its slow spots, particularly the excursion of Essex to Ireland to subdue Tyrone (Alan Hale). At times the dialog becomes brittle, and direction grooves into stagey passages that could have been lightened. Minor shortcomings, however, in the general excellence of the production.
☐ 1939: Nominations: Best Color Cinematography, Color Art Direction, Score, Sound, Special Effects

■ PRIVATE NAVY OF SGT. O'FARRELL, THE

1958, 92 MINS, US ◇
Dir Frank Tashlin   *Prod* John Beck   *Scr* Frank Tashlin   *Ph* Alan Stensvold   *Ed* Eda Warren   *Mus* Harry Sukman   *Art Dir* Bob Kinoshita
● Bob Hope, Phyllis Diller, Jeffrey Hunter, Mylene Demongeot, Gina Lollobrigida, Mako (NAHO)

The Private Navy of Sgt. O'Farrell is an okay, but crudely plotted comedy set in World War II, routinely directed by Frank Tashlin from his awkward screenplay.

Tashlin's script, from a John L. Greene-Robert M. Fresco story, has Bob Hope as one of these stock all-knowing, all-wise paternal non-coms, herein looking out for the morale of his troops. Site is a South Pacific island, around which the war and the action have detoured. Seems a cargo ship loaded with beer has been torpedoed, and Hope fears a dip in morale unless the booze is found.

Diller is a daffy civilian nurse, not quite the morale-lifter Hope had anticipated. Jeffrey Hunter is a junior naval officer. Gina Lollobrigida is an old Hope sweetie with whom he split in a flashback to a Hawaiian beach rendezvous, moments before the Pearl Harbor attack. She pops up again – goddess-ex-machina – adrift on a raft, with niece Mylene Demongeot.

References to Bing Crosby (appearing in an old clip), a takeoff on the Burt Lancaster-Deborah Kerr beach scene in *From Here to Eternity* and satirical sub-titles, plus occasional good gags from assorted players, make the 92 minutes sporadically enjoyable.

■ PRIVATE POTTER

1963, 89 MINS, UK
Dir Caspar Wrede   *Prod* Ben Arbeid   *Scr* Ronald Harwood, Caspar Wrede   *Ph* Arthur Lavis   *Ed* John Pomeroy   *Mus* George Hall
● Tom Courtenay, James Maxwell, Ralph Michael, Brewster Mason, Ronald Fraser, Mogens Wieth (M-G-M)

This film is an egghead pic that doesn't quite come off. Yarn has a strong, imaginative idea but tails away inconclusively and falls between two stools, not quite arty, not quite commercial.

Tom Courtenay plays an inexperienced young soldier who screams in terror while on patrol that is tracking down a terrorist leader on a Mediterranean island. As a result, the mission misfires and a colleague is killed. The young soldier excuses himself with the plea that he saw a vision of God. Question that arises is whether he is to be court-martialled for cowardice or whether, in fact, he did have this religious experience. And, if so, whether or not he should be punished.

It is the conflicting clash of army regulations and men's consciences which intrigue. But the young solider's character is never clearly defined and the film eventually flounders in speculation and conjecture.

Courtenay acts with some imagination but best performance comes from James Maxwell, as his commanding officer. Gradually he begins to believe in the lad's story and then his own conscience starts to interfere. Ralph Michael, as the padre; Brewster Mason, as the brigadier, who lives by army regulations; and Ronald Fraser, as a cheery doctor, also give vivid performances.

■ PRIVATE'S PROGRESS

1956, 102 MINS, UK Ⓥ
Dir John Boulting   *Prod* John Boulting, Roy Boulting   *Scr* Frank Harvey, John Boulting   *Ph* Eric Cross   *Ed* Anthony Harvey   *Mus* John Addison
● Richard Attenborough, Dennis Price, Terry-Thomas, Ian Carmichael, Peter Jones, William Hartnell (Charter/British Lion)

As a lighthearted satire on British army life during the last war, *Private's Progress* has moments of sheer joy based on real authenticity. But it is not content to rest on satire alone and introduces an unreal melodramatic adventure which robs the story of much of its charm. The Boulting Brothers obviously felt there must be some point to the plot and they've added an adventure tailpiece in which a War Office brigadier invades enemy territory to bring back valuable art treasures to Britain.

The basic comedy, however, derives from the depiction of the typical misfit into the army way of life. Ian Carmichael is shown as the earnest university student who interrupts his studies to join the forces. He is a lamentable failure.

Many weaknesses of the yarn are surmounted by the allround performances of the cast. Carmichael does remarkably well. Richard Attenborough is in confident mood as a private who soon gets to know his way around. Dennis Price gives a smooth study as the brigadier.

●●●●●●●●●●●●●●●●●●●●●●●●●●●●●●●●

■ **PRIVILEGE**

1967, 103 MINS, UK ◇ ▣

Dir Peter Watkins *Prod* John Heyman *Scr* Norman Bogner *Ph* Peter Suschitzky *Ed* John Trumper *Mus* Mike Leander *Art Dir* Bill Brodie
● Paul Jones, Jean Shrimpton, Mark London, William Job (Rank-Universal/World-Film/Memorial)

In *Privilege*, Paul Jones, erstwhile singer with the Manfred Mann Group, makes his acting debut. Maybe it's the fault of writer, director or both but Jones plays the role of the bewildered, disillusioned singer on one note of unanimated distaste.

Trouble with *Privilege* is that it cannot make up its mind whether it's a crusading film for the intelligentsia or a snide, 'with it' comedy.

A coalition government encourages the violence of the act of pop idol Steve Shorter (Jones) as a means of guiding the violence of Britain's youth into controllable channels. Then, cynically, it's decided that his image must be changed and he is taken from the ordinary scene of putting over national-interest commercials and selling consumer-goods to his worshipping fans and exploited by the Church as a kind of godlike hot gospeller.

But the best angles of the pic are those which turn a cynical and only too accurate searchlight on the pop music scene and those who batten on a minimal talent, plus the gullibity of the fans.

●●●●●●●●●●●●●●●●●●●●●●●●●●●●●●●●

■ **PRIZE, THE**

1963, 135 MINS, US ◇ ▣

Dir Mark Robson *Prod* Pandro S. Berman *Scr* Ernest Lehman *Ph* William H. Daniels *Ed* Adrienne Fazan *Mus* Jerry Goldsmith *Art Dir* George W. Davis, Urie McCleary
● Paul Newman, Edward G. Robinson, Elke Sommer, Diane Baker, Micheline Presle, Gerard Oury (M-G-M/Roxbury)

Stockholm during Nobel week is the setting for Irving Wallace's smorgasbord novel. In Ernest Lehman's Hitchcockeyed screenplay, seven selected prizewinners convene to receive the award. The man from literature (Paul Newman) senses something amiss in the behavior and physique of the man from physics (Edward G. Robinson), proceeds to snoop around for clues and ends up in a wild goose chase, with himself as the goose who almost gets cooked.

The Prize is a suspense melodrama played for laughs. Trouble is the basic comedy approach clashes with the political-topical framework of the story. Although limited as a comic actor and confronted here with a rather difficult and unsubstantial character to portray, Newman tackles his task with sufficient vivacity to keep an audience concerned for his welfare and amused by his antics. Robinson achieves a persuasive degree of contrast in his dual role.

Elke Sommer, as an attache who gets attached to Newman, hasn't a very scintillating role, but has the looks to make that a secondary issue.

Mark Robson's direction generates a lot of excitement, humor and suspense in spots, but this is offset by hokey elements, occasional exaggerations and stripping of dramatic gears as the film fluctuates between its incompatible components.

●●●●●●●●●●●●●●●●●●●●●●●●●●●●●●●●

■ **PRIZE OF ARMS, A**

1962, 105 MINS, UK

Dir Cliff Owen *Prod* George Maynard *Scr* Paul Ryder *Ph* Gilbert Taylor, Gerald Gibbs *Ed* John Jympson *Mus* Robert Sharples *Art Dir* Jim Morahan, Bernard Sarron
● Stanley Baker, Helmut Schmid, Tom Bell, Tom Adams, Anthony Bate (RLC/British Lion)

Stanley Baker's carefully laid scheme for knocking off a $700,000 army payroll seems unnecessarily complicated. This seems to shriek out for mishaps. But Paul Ryder's screenplay [from an original story by Nicolas Roeg and Kevin Kavanagh] is smoothly efficient even though audiences are too often left in the dark about detail. Baker plays an exarmy captain who has been cashiered for Black Market activities in Hamburg. While in the army he has dreamed up a perfect plan for revenge (and to get rich). He has enlisted the help of Helmut Schmid, an explosives expert, and Tom Bell, a daring but edgy young man.

Baker learns that an army is preparing to go abroad at the time of the Suez crisis. He realizes that when troops are on the move abroad they have to take money with them. The trio plan to hijack the dough while the forces are moving towards the docks.

Baker, Schmid and Bell play the three leads confidently, with Baker particularly on the ball in the type of harsh tough part that he plays so often and so well. But the thesping of the three stars is given greater impact by the strength of a long list of character and feature actors as officers, other ranks, detectives, etc.

●●●●●●●●●●●●●●●●●●●●●●●●●●●●●●●●

■ **PRIZE OF GOLD, A**

1955, 96 MINS, UK ◇

Dir Mark Robson *Prod* Irving Allen, Albert R. Broccoli *Scr* John Paxton *Ph* Ted Moore *Ed* William Lewthwaite *Mus* Malcolm Arnold
● Richard Widmark, Mai Zetterling, Nigel Patrick, George Cole, Donald Wolfit, Joseph Tomelty (Warwick/Columbia)

A Prize of Gold is a taut suspense thriller unfolded against vividly interesting Berlin-London backgrounds.

Based on Max Catto's novel of the same title, the script details the hijacking of gold bullion being air-transported from Berlin to London. The writing lays a good foundation for the climaxing action, switching from lightly humorous handling in the first half to tight excitement in the latter half and Mark Robson's direction projects it all strongly with the aid of the topnotch cast.

Richard Widmark is an American sergeant stationed in the British sector of Berlin who turns larcenous when Mai Zetterling, a refugee with whom he has fallen in love, needs funds to transport a group of war-displaced children for whom she is caring to South America and a new life.

●●●●●●●●●●●●●●●●●●●●●●●●●●●●●●●●

■ **PRIZZI'S HONOR**

1985, 129 MINS, US ◇ ▣ ⊙

Dir John Huston *Prod* John Foreman *Scr* Richard Condon, Janet Roach *Ph* Andrzej Bartkowiak *Ed* Rudi Fehr, Kaja Fehr *Mus* Alex North *Art Dir* Dennis Washington
● Jack Nicholson, Kathleen Turner, Robert Loggia, William Hickey, John Randolph, Anjelica Huston (ABC)

John Huston's *Prizzi's Honor* packs love, sex, and murder – and dark comedy – into a labyrinthine tale.

Based on the novel by Richard Condon, plot centers on the tragic-comedy that results when a hit man for a powerful crime family (Jack Nicholson) falls hard for a svelte blonde (Kathleen Turner) who turns out to be his female counterpart in hired killings.

Picture is a stretch for Nicholson, who speaks in a street-tough, accented gangsterese that initially takes some getting used to, but shortly becomes totally convincing. Turner manages to use her loveliness to jolting results when she finally turns her gun on a pair of victims in an apartment hallway.

Even more monstrous, in a deceptive way, is the character played by Anjelica Huston, who is the black sheep of the powerful clan, but who maneuvers the plot in insidious ways, all of them tied to the fact that she harbors a lost love for Nicholson.
☐ 1985: Best Supp. Actress (Anjelica Huston).
☐ Nominations: Best Picture, Director, Actor (Jack Nicholson), Supp. Actor (William Hickey), Adapted Screenplay, Costume Design, Editing

●●●●●●●●●●●●●●●●●●●●●●●●●●●●●●●●

■ **PROBLEM CHILD**

1990, 81 MINS, US ◇ ▣ ⊙

Dir Dennis Dugan *Prod* Robert Simonds *Scr* Scott Alexander, Larry Karaszewski *Ph* Peter Lyons Collister *Ed* Daniel Hanley, Michael Hill *Mus* Miles Goodman *Art Dir* George Costello
● John Ritter, Jack Warden, Michael Oliver, Gilbert Gottfried, Amy Yasbeck, Michael Richards (Imagine)

Universal took a step in the right direction by whittling *Problem Child* down to just 81 minutes but didn't go far enough. The studio should have excised another 75 minutes and released this unbelievable mess as a short. (Several characters listed in the credits never show upon screen.)

John Ritter and Amy Yasbeck play a yuppie couple determined to have a child, primarily so they can be invited to the neighbors' birthday parties for their own kids. Unable to conceive themselves, they get suckered into adopting round-faced Junior (Michael Oliver), a child repulsive enough to make nuns cheer when he's taken from their care.

The major subplot has Junior becoming pen pals with a serial killer (Michael Richards) who busts out of prison to see him, leading to a kidnaping and chase that makes *Smokey and the Bandit* look like *Citizen Kane*.

The film marks an atrocious bigscreen debut for actor and episodic TV director Dennis Dugan. The most offensive character is Yasbeck's shrill, status-conscious wife.

●●●●●●●●●●●●●●●●●●●●●●●●●●●●●●●●

■ **PROBLEM CHILD 2**

1991, 91 MINS, US ◇ ▣

Dir Brian Levant *Prod* Robert Simonds *Scr* Scott Alexander, Larry Karaszewski *Ph* Peter Smokler *Ed* Lois Freeman-Fox *Mus* David Kitay *Art Dir* Maria Caso
● John Ritter, Michael Oliver, Jack Warden, Laraine Newman, Amy Yasbeck, Ivyann Schwan (Universal/Imagine)

At times this poor version of a sitcom seems written by five-year-olds for five-year-olds, so much so that one suspects its script was fingerpainted.

The plot has Ben (John Ritter) and Junior (Michael Oliver) moving to a new town of cloying divorcees, as Junior grapples with his fear of losing his adopted dad by reverting to various revolting if not terribly funny habits.

A second 'problem child', a little girl (Ivyann Schwan, from *Parenthood*), eventually teams up with Junior to try to bring his lonely dad together with her sheepish mom (Amy Yasbeck).

The most depressing aspect of the film stems from seeing Ritter and Laraine Newman, playing a rich femme fatale with her own desires on Ben, struggling against such fastidiously inane material. Oliver remains an annoying child actor who mugs constantly.

Pic also suffers from a cheap look all the

P

way around, including jokes using a stuffed dog that's supposed to be a real dog and an obviously styrofoam rock.

....

■ PRODUCERS, THE

1968, 100 MINS, US ◇ ⓦ ⊙
Dir Mel Brooks   *Prod* Sidney Glazier   *Scr* Mel Brooks
Ph Joseph Coffey   *Ed* Ralph Rosenblum   *Mus* John Morris   *Art Dir* Charles Rosen
● Zero Mostel, Gene Wilder, Kenneth Mars, Estelle Winwood, Dick Shawn, Christopher Hewett (Embassy)

Mel Brooks has turned a funny idea into a slapstick film, thanks to the performers, particularly Zero Mostel.

Playing a Broadway producer of flops who survives (barely) by suckering little old ladies, he teams with an emotionally retarded accountant portrayed by Gene Wilder in a scheme to produce a flop. By selling 25,000% of production, they figure to be rich when it flops. For the twist, the musical comedy *Springtime for Hitler*, penned by a shell-shocked Nazi, is a smash.

The film is unmatched in the scenes featuring Mostel and Wilder alone together, and several episodes with other actors are truly rare. When the producers approach the most atrocious director on Broadway, they find Christopher Hewett in drag exchanging catty comments with his secretary (Andreas Voutsinas).

Estelle Winwood is a winner as a salacious little old lady, and Kenneth Mars has his moments as the Nazi scripter.
□ 1968: Best Original Story & Screenplay.
□ Nomination: Best Supp. Actor (Gene Wilder)

....

■ PROFESSIONALS, THE

1966, 116 MINS, US ◇ ⓦ ⊙
Dir Richard Brooks   *Prod* Richard Brooks   *Scr* Richard Brooks   *Ph* Conrad Hall   *Ed* Peter Zinner
Mus Maurice Jarre   *Art Dir* Edward Haworth
● Burt Lancaster, Lee Marvin, Robert Ryan, Jack Palance, Claudia Cardinale, Ralph Bellamy (Columbia)

The Professionals is a well-made actioner, set in 1917 on the Mexican-US border, in which some soldiers of fortune rescue the reportedly kidnapped wife of an American businessman. Exciting explosive sequences, good overall pacing and acting overcome a sometimes thin script.

Richard Brooks' adaptation of Frank O'Rourke's novel, *A Mule for the Marquesa*, depicts the strategy of Lee Marvin and cohorts, sent by gringo Ralph Bellamy into the political turmoil of Mexico to rescue his missing wife, Claudia Cardinale, known to be secreted in the brigand village of Jack Palance. Latter only a few years earlier had achieved a transient victory in the Revolution with the help of Marvin and Burt Lancaster.

Quiet and purposeful, Marvin underplays very well as the leader of the rescue troop. Robert Ryan, who loves animals, is in the relative background, as is Woody Strode, Negro-Indian scout and tracker. Lancaster is the most dynamic of the crew, as a light-hearted but two-fisted fighter.
□ 1966: Nominations: Best Director, Adapted Screenplay, Color Cinematography

....

■ PROJECT X

1987, 108 MINS, US ◇ ⓦ ⊙
Dir Jonathan Kaplan   *Prod* Walter F. Parkes, Lawrence Lasker   *Scr* Stanley Weiser   *Ph* Dean Cundey   *Ed* O. Nicholas Brown   *Mus* James Horner   *Art Dir* Lawrence G. Paull
● Matthew Broderick, Helen Hunt, Bill Sadler, Johnny Ray McGhee, Jonathan Stark, Robin Gammell (20th Century-Fox)

If nothing else, *Project X* is the ultimate film for monkey lovers. Some quite endearing chimpanzees share center stage with Matthew Broderick for nearly two hours here, and while they, and he, are engaging enough to watch, picture lets its manipulative strings show too clearly.

Broderick plays a wayward air force pilot who, as punishment, is sent to play zookeeper at the Strategic Weapons Research Center, where intelligent chimps are trained for top secret and, it transpires, fatal experiments involving the effects of radiation.

Brightest of the little hairy ones is Virgil, an orphan who was taught sign language under a university program. When Virgil is put on the line, Broderick feels compelled to act and end the seemingly needless experiments.

Director Jonathan Kaplan keeps the proceedings [from a screen story by Stanley Weiser and Lawrence Lasker] amiable enough, and has covered the monkeys' actions with loving care and skillful attention, which cannot have been easy. Broderick is rightly more subdued here than in some recent performances, and supporting cast is discreetly effective.

....

■ PROMISE, THE

(Aka: Face of a Stranger)

1979, 97 MINS, US ◇ ⓦ
Dir Gilbert Cates   *Prod* Fred Weintraub, Paul Heller
Scr Gary Michael White   *Ph* Ralph Woolsey   *Ed* Peter E. Berger   *Mus* David Shire   *Art Dir* William Sandell
● Kathleen Quinlan, Stephen Collins, Beatrice Straight, Laurence Luckin, Michael O'Hare, Bibi Besch (Universal)

The title of this romantic melodrama, has to do with a buried necklace and the promise of undying love and faith in each other made by a young architectural student and a girl student.

The girl is severely injured in an auto accident and the boy is unconscious for some time, during which his mother – a female building tycoon – persuades the girl to undergo some very expensive plastic surgery and seek a new life elsewhere. She tells her son the girl is dead.

The scene changes to California. The girl, a promising artist, has for reasons known only to herself, switched to photography. She's an overnight success and is sought by the young architect who's building a medical center. Does he recognize her?

Kathleen Quinlan is pretty convincing as the painter/photographer and a new, very handsome, young leading man is added to the Hollywood scene with Stephen Collins as the architect.
□ 1979: Nomination: Best Song ('I'll Never Say Goodbye')

....

■ PROMISE HER ANYTHING

1966, 96 MINS, UK/US ◇
Dir Arthur Hiller   *Prod* Stanley Rubin   *Scr* William Peter Blatty   *Ph* Douglas Slocombe   *Ed* John Shirley
Mus Lyn Murray   *Art Dir* Wilfrid Shingleton
● Warren Beatty, Leslie Caron, Bob Cummings, Keenan Wynn, Hermione Gingold, Lionel Stander (Seven Arts/Stark)

Promise Her Anything is a light, refreshing comedy-romance, set in Greenwich Village but filmed in England, which satirizes both child psychology and nudie pix in a tasteful, effective manner. Well-paced direction of many fine performances, generally sharp scripting and other good production elements add up to a satisfying comedy.

An Arne Sultan-Marvin Worth story has been adapted into what is basically a romantic triangle. Leslie Caron, with a precocious baby boy but no hubby, hopes to connect with her employer, child psychologist Bob Cummings who, in private life, abhors mop-

pets. Caron's neighbor (Warren Beatty) wants her, although he is careful to conceal his profession – making mail-order nudie films.

Director Arthur Hiller has overcome a basic problem: specifically, that Caron and Beatty are not known as film comics. His fine solution has been to spotlight baby Michael Bradley in the first 30 minutes, when Caron is establishing an easy audience rapport, while Beatty slides into a likeable groove via energetic tumbles and other manifestations of youthful enthusiasm.

....

■ PROMISES IN THE DARK

1979, 115 MINS, US ◇ ⓦ
Dir Jerome Hellman   *Prod* Jerome Hellman   *Scr* Lorin Mandel   *Ph* Adam Holender   *Ed* Bob Wyman
Mus Leonard Rosenman   *Art Dir* Walter Scott Herndon
● Marsha Mason, Kathleen Beller, Ned Beatty, Susan Clark, Michael Brandon, Paul Clemens (Orion)

Producer-director Jerome Hellman has admirably attempted to focus attention on the death of a young cancer victim. Major problem remains not the promises physician Marcia Mason makes to her terminally-ill patient (Kathleen Beller) but the premise itself. No matter how well acted (and thesping here is superior) or mounted, a story that spends two hours watching a pretty young girl expire is just not most people's idea of a good time.

Screenplay pulls no punches, and medical realism is heightened to an extent that damages the film more than it helps. Beller injures her leg in the pic's opening sequence, and after that, it's an endless array of emergency rooms, surgery theatres and bed-ridden shots as the cancer spreads throughout her body.

Set up as counterpoint to the distress Beller, boyfriend Paul Clemens, and parents Ned Beatty and Susan Clark undergo is the courtship of divorced Mason by radiologist Michael Brandon. Mason, who is given the central focus by Helman's serivative direction, never really allows the audience to share in her conflicting emotions.

Rest of cast is first-rate, particularly Beller (whose 'why me' speech is heart-wrenching). Hellman's direction seems to have been inspired by two colleagues he's frequently worked with, Hal Ashby and John Schlesinger.

....

■ PROM NIGHT

1980, 91 MINS, US ◇ ⓦ ⊙
Dir Paul Lynch   *Prod* Peter Simpson   *Scr* William Gray
Ph Robert New   *Ed* Brian Ravok   *Mus* Carl Zittrer, Paul Zaza   *Art Dir* Reuben Freed
● Leslie Nielsen, Jamie Lee Curtis, Casey Stevens, Eddie Benton (Simcom)

Borrowing shamelessly from *Carrie* and any number of gruesome exploitations pic [from a story by Robert Gunza Jr] manages to score a few horrific points amid a number of sagging moments.

It opens with the falling death of a 10-year-old girl brought on by unmerciful teasing on the part of four of her peers. It's six years later and prom night for the surviving kiddies and each is slated to meet an unsavory fate due to past exploits – unbeknownst to anyone.

Once the masked killer gets going it becomes a guessing game of who is the ax-wielding avenger and which, if any, victims will escape.

Director Paul Lynch seems to capture the spirit of the genre here, but spends a little too much time setting up each murder, thus eliminating some suspense.

....

■ PROMOTER, THE

See: The Card

....

■ PROOF

1991, 86 MINS, AUSTRALIA ◇ ⓥ
Dir Jocelyn Moorhouse   *Prod* Lynda House   *Scr* Jocelyn Moorhouse   *Ph* Martin McGrath   *Ed* Ken Sallows   *Mus* Not Drowning, Waving   *Art Dir* Patrick Reardon
● Hugo Weaving, Genevieve Picot, Russell Crowe, Heather Mitchell, Jeffrey Walker, Frank Gallacher (House & Moorhouse)

Proof is an intriguing psychological drama structured around the contradictory character of a blind photographer, a striking debut from writer-director Jocelyn Moorhouse.

Intriguing premise has a blind man required to rely on the information of others, and what if those people don't tell the truth? Blind from birth, Martin (Hugo Weaving) never really believed his mother (Heather Mitchell) was telling him the truth about the world around him. Now in his 30s, Martin lives alone, his only company a seeing-eye dog and Celia (Genevieve Picot), the young woman who comes to clean his house and do his shopping.

She has become infatuated with Martin, but he keeps her firmly at arm's length. Enter Andy (Russell Crowe), a guileless young man who works in an Italian restaurant Martin frequents. Celia decides to get at Martin through Andy.

Moorhouse builds up a good deal of sexual tension among the three characters, aided by a trio of excellent performances. Pic is also not without humor.

. . . .

■ PROPHECY

1979, 102 MINS, US ◇ ⓥ
Dir John Frankenheimer   *Prod* Robert L. Rosen   *Scr* David Seltzer   *Ph* Harry Stradling Jr   *Ed* Tom Rolf   *Mus* Leonard Rosenman   *Art Dir* William Craig Smith
● Talia Shire, Robert Foxworth, Armand Assante, Richard Dysart, Victoria Racimo, Tom McFadden (Paramount)

Director John Frankenheimer has made a frightening monster movie that people could laugh at for generations to come, complete with your basic big scary thing, cardboard characters and a story so stupid it's irresistible.

Once again, the real villain is Careless Mankind. Only this time, it isn't Atomic Fallout that's creating giant ants and killer cockroaches but Industrial Pollution.

Among the performers, only Armand Assante as an Indian leader gets half-a-chance to show his talent and Talia Shire is reduced to a whining wimp. Leonard Rosenman's score cheats constantly, building to frightening moments that don't happen.

. . . .

■ PROSPERO'S BOOKS

1991, 124 MINS, UK/FRANCE ◇ ⓥ
Dir Peter Greenaway   *Prod* Kees Kasander   *Scr* Peter Greenaway   *Ph* Sacha Vierny   *Ed* Marina Bodbyl   *Mus* Michael Nyman   *Art Dir* Ben Van Os, Jan Roelfs
● John Gielgud, Michael Clark, Michel Blanc, Roland Josephson, Isabelle Pasco, Tom Bell (Allarts/Cinea/Camera/Penta)

With more visual stimulation than a dozen normal films, Peter Greenaway's *Prospero's Books* is an intellectually and erotically rampaging meditation on the arrogance and value of the artistic process. The product of a feverish, overflowing imagination, this almost impossibly dense take on *The Tempest* displays both the director's audacious brilliance and lewd extravagance at full tilt.

The playwright's tale is presented basically intact, but Greenaway's underlying gambit is to make Prospero (John Gielgud) the author of his own story. Through the use of exquisite calligraphy, the old man's writing is made vivid on the screen, and the device opens the way to Gielgud himself to supply the voices

for many of the supporting characters, who are sometimes also voiced by Gielgud and another thesp simultaneously.

Shot entirely indoors in Amsterdam, the production is stunning from every physical point of view. As always, Michael Nyman's vaulting, repetitive, lyrical score plays a major part in the effectiveness of a Greenaway film. Greenaway here ventures into new cinematic territory through the use of high-definition video (which accounts for the unusual 1.77:1 aspect ratio) and the Quantel Paintbox.

. . . .

■ PROTECTOR, THE

1985, 95 MINS, US ◇ ⓥ
Dir James Glickenhaus   *Prod* David Chan   *Scr* James Glickenhaus   *Ph* Mark Irwin   *Ed* Evan Lottman   *Mus* Ken Thorne   *Art Dir* William F. De Seta, Oliver Wong
● Jackie Chan, Danny Aiello, Roy Chiao, Victor Arnold, Kim Bass, Richard Clarke (Golden Harvest/Warner)

Jackie Chan and Danny Aiello head for Hong Kong to track down a drug kingpin who has kidnapped the daughter of his estranged business partner.

A furious barroom shootout at the outset is immediately followed by a speedboat chase in New York harbor that rivals James Bond pictures for elaborate thrills.

What also puts matters on the right track is the tongue-in-cheek humor running throughout. Chan and Aiello both sail through the farfetched action with insouciance and aplomb as they infuriate their superiors by wreaking havoc wherever they go and knock off enough baddies to momentarily put a dent in Hong Kong's population figures.

Chan indulges in almost superhuman acrobatics every 15 minutes or so, running up walls, pole-vaulting and swinging from sampan to sampan in the harbor and generally putting his karate expertise to good use.

. . . .

■ PROTOCOL

1984, 96 MINS, US ◇ ⓥ ⊙
Dir Herbert Ross   *Prod* Anthea Sylbert   *Scr* Buck Henry   *Ph* William A. Fraker   *Ed* Paul Hirsch   *Mus* Basil Poledouris   *Art Dir* Bill Malley
● Goldie Hawn, Chris Sarandon, Richard Romanus, Andre Gregory, Gail Strickland, Cliff De Young (Warner)

Goldie Hawn's insistence on Saying Something Important takes a lot of the zip out of *Protocol*, but the light comedy still has its moments for the forgiving.

One big problem here is an oh-so-obvious effort to reinvent the formula that boosted *Private Benjamin* to the heights. Here she's a sweet, unsophisticated cocktail waitress hurled into the unfamiliar world of Washington diplomacy and Mideast travail.

In *Benjamin*, Hawn's main adversary was a woman captain (Eileen Brennan) and ill-intentioned men; here, it's Gail Strickland as a devious, plotting protocol officer and more ill-intentioned men.

Formula doesn't work as well in *Protocol*, partly because Strickland and gang aren't as much fun to foil as Brennan's bunch was.

. . . .

■ PROUD REBEL, THE

1958, 100 MINS, US ◇ ⓥ
Dir Michael Curtiz   *Prod* Samuel Goldwyn Jr   *Scr* Joe Petracca, Lillie Hayward   *Ph* Ted McCord   *Ed* Aaron Stell   *Mus* Jerome Moross   *Art Dir* McClure Capps
● Alan Ladd, Olivia de Havilland, Dean Jagger, David Ladd, Cecil Kellaway, John Carradine (Buena Vista)

Warmth of a father's love and faith, and the devotion of a boy for his dog, are the stand-out ingredients of this suspenseful and fast-action post-Civil War yarn. Michael Curtiz, too, has achieved fine feeling in his direction

of the screenplay, based on an original by James Edward Grant, and is backed by some fine color photography.

It's the characterizations that hold forth most strongly, topped perhaps by the very appealing performance of David Ladd, star's 11-year-old son who plays Alan Ladd's boy in the pic. Youngster has been shocked mute during Union forces' sacking of Atlanta during the war, when he saw his mother killed and his home destroyed by fire, and it's Alan Ladd's dogged wandering of the land to find a doctor who can cure his son which motivates plot.

Action unfolds in a small Southern Illinois community, where Ladd is drawn into a fight with the two sons of Dean Jagger, a big sheep-raiser; the payment of his fine after his arrest by Olivia de Havilland, a lonely farm-woman whose property is coveted by Jagger; and Ladd working out this fine on the farm.

. . . .

■ PROVIDENCE

1977, 110 MINS, FRANCE ◇ ⓥ
Dir Alain Resnais   *Prod* Action Films-SFP   *Scr* David Mercer   *Ph* Ricardo Arnovitch   *Ed* Albert Jurgenson   *Mus* Miklos Rozsa   *Art Dir* Jacques Saulnier
● Dirk Bogarde, Ellen Burstyn, John Gielgud, David Warner, Elaine Stritch, Cyril Luckham (Action/SFP)

A striking amalgam of the literary and theatrical approach in scripting; that is, sharp talk, highblown scenes of personal revelation and general politico asides; has been turned into an unusual visual tour-de-force by French director Alain Resnais.

It is a riveting pic pictorially, offering dense insights into the flights of imagination of a supposedly dying writer of perhaps some faddish fame.

The style is impeccable as the film sashays from the novelist's feverish, drunken ramblings about his new novel, putting his family into it, and commenting on them.

John Gielgud's mellifluous or impassioned delivery as the writer is extraordinary; as well as Dirk Bogarde as the son, a cold, internally-wounded man who cannot show emotion.

. . . .

■ PROWLER, THE

1951, 92 MINS, US
Dir Joseph Losey   *Prod* S.P. Eagle [= Sam Spiegel]   *Scr* Hugo Butler   *Ph* Arthur Miller   *Ed* Paul Weatherwax   *Mus* Lyn Murray   *Art Dir* Boris Leven
● Van Heflin, Evelyn Keyes, John Maxwell, Katherine Warren, Emerson Treacy, Madge Blake (Horizon/ United Artists)

Combination of illicit love, murder and premarital relations makes *The Prowler* a bawdy, daring story [from an original by Robert Thoeren and Hans Wilhelm].

Van Heflin makes the most of an unsympathetic role, that of a cop who steals the love of a woman (Evelyn Keyes) who had called the police when she saw a prowler peering through her bathroom window. Keyes, as the woman, wife of an all-night disk jockey, also has an unsympathetic part, as a gal wooed and won by Heflin behind her husband's back.

Pic builds to an exciting climax in a desert ghost town, where Heflin has taken Keyes, now his wife, to have her baby in order to avoid publicity.

. . . .

■ PRUDENCE AND THE PILL

1968, 92 MINS, US ◇
Dir Fielder Cook   *Prod* Kenneth Harper, Ronald J. Kahn   *Scr* Hugh Mills   *Ph* Ted Moore   *Ed* Norman Savage   *Mus* Bernard Ebbinghouse   *Art Dir* Wilfrid Shingleton
● Deborah Kerr, David Niven, Judy Geeson, David Dundas, Vickery Turner, Hugh Armstrong (20th Century-Fox)

Deborah Kerr and David Niven team as a couple which winds up married to others.

Hugh Mills wrote the book, and adapted it for films. Basic flaw in the screenplay, which the generally excellent acting and direction cannot entirely overcome, is the rambling from one set of interesting characters to another.

Obvious attempt was to incorporate a lot of unique personalities, all affected by the pill and changing sex customs, but the result is a lack of unity. The whole film, then, is less than the sum of its parts.

Film is more than a one-joke script – the secret switching of birth control pills so that the wrong people get pregnant – and to the credit of the pic, this is not a tasteless recurring incident.

Title art designed by Richard Williams is a great sendoff to the film, in its semi-Victorian atmosphere on which modern characters intrude. The parallel between old-fashioned genteel marriage and contemporary assaults thereon, is drawn most cleverly.

■ **PSYCHO**

1960, 109 MINS, US ⓥ ⊙
Dir Alfred Hitchcock *Prod* Alfred Hitchcock *Scr* Joseph Stefano *Ph* John L. Russell *Ed* George Tomasini *Mus* Bernard Herrmann *Art Dir* Joseph Hurley, Robert Clatworthy
● Anthony Perkins, Janet Leigh, Vera Miles, John Gavin, Martin Balsam, John McIntire (Paramount)

Alfred Hitchcock is up to his clavicle in whimsicality and apparently had the time of his life in putting together *Psycho*. He's gotten in gore, in the form of a couple of graphically-depicted knife murders, a story that's far out in Freudian motivations, and now and then injects little amusing plot items that suggest the whole thing is not to be taken seriously.

Anthony Perkins is the young man who doesn't get enough exorcise (repeat exorcise) of that other inner being. Among the victims are Janet Leigh, who walks away from an illicit love affair with John Gavin, taking with her a stolen $40,000, and Martin Balsam, as a private eye who winds up in the same swamp in which Leigh's body also is deposited.

John McIntire is the local sheriff with an unusual case on his hands, and Simon Oakland is the psychiatrist. Perkins gives a remarkably effective in-a-dream kind of performance as the possessed young man. Others play it straight, with equal competence.

Joseph Stefano's screenplay, from a novel by Robert Bloch, provides a strong foundation for Hitchcock's field day. And if the camera, under Hitchcock's direction, tends to overemphasize a story point here and there, well, it's forgivable.
□ 1960: Nominations: Best Director, Supp. Actress (Janet Leigh), B&W Cinematography, B&W Art Direction

■ **PSYCHO II**

1983, 113 MINS, US ◇ ⓥ
Dir Richard Franklin *Prod* Hilton A. Green *Scr* Tom Holland *Ph* Dean Cundey *Ed* Andrew London *Mus* Jerry Goldsmith *Art Dir* John W. Corso
● Anthony Perkins, Vera Miles, Meg Tilly, Robert Loggia, Dennis Franz, Hugh Gillin (Universal/Oak Industries)

Psycho II is an impressive, 23-years-after followup to Alfred Hitchcock's 1960 suspense classic.

New story, set 22 years later, has Norman Bates (Anthony Perkins) released from a mental institution on the petition of his psychiatrist, Dr Raymond (Robert Loggia), over the objections of Lila Loomis (Vera Miles) whose sister he murdered (Janet Leigh in the first film).

Securing a job as cook's assistant at a local diner, Bates is befriended by a young waitress Mary (Meg Tilly) who moves into his house as

an empathetic companion. A series of mysterious murders ensue, beginning with the killing of the obnoxious manager Toomey (Dennis Franz), who has turned the Bates family business into a hot-sheets motel.

Director Richard Franklin deftly keeps the suspense and tension on high while dolling out dozens of shock-of-recognitions shots drawn from the audience's familiarity with *Psycho*.

Reprising his famous role, Perkins is very entertaining, whether stammering over the pronunciation of 'cutlery' or misleading the audience in both directions as to his relative sanity.

■ **PSYCHO III**

1986, 96 MINS, US ◇ ⓥ ⊙
Dir Anthony Perkins *Prod* Hilton A. Green *Scr* Charles Edward Pogue *Ph* Bruce Surtees *Ed* David Blewitt *Mus* Carter Burwell *Art Dir* Henry Bumstead
● Anthony Perkins, Diana Scarwid, Jeff Fahey, Roberta Maxwell, Hugh Gillin, Lee Garlington (Universal)

A few amusing little notions are streched to the point of diminishing returns in *Psycho III*.

Opening sequence is a full-fledged homage to Alfred Hitchcock's *Vertigo* and helps set the comic, in-joke tone of the rest of the picture. Unhappy novice Diana Scarwid is all set to jump from a church belltower but, in an effort to save her, one of the nuns falls to her death instead.

Scarwid flees in distress, is given a ride through the desert by aspiring musician Jeff Fahey, and where should the unlikely and unsuspecting duo wind up but the Bates Motel.

The whole enterprise is dependent almost entirely upon self-referential incidents and attitudes for its effect, and it eventually becomes wearying.

Main pleasure of the picture stems from Anthony Perkins' amusing performance.

■ **PSYCHOMANIA**

1964, 90 MINS, US ⓥ
Dir Richard L. Hilliard *Prod* Del Tenney *Scr* Robin Miller *Ph* Louis McMahon *Ed* Robert Q. Lovett *Mus* W.L. Holcombe
● Lee Philips, Shepperd Strudwick, James Farentino, Jean Hale, Lorraine Rogers, Sylvia Miles (Emerson)

Psychomania is a low-budget, well-done shocker with a tightly-knit plot and a believable surprise ending.

Lee Philips does a fine acting job as the karate-expert artist from a family with a psychotic background, who gets involved in a pair of bizarre murders. Shepperd Strudwick and James Farentino are believable as the lawyer and tough motorcycle hood respectively.

Richard Hilliard's realistic direction and Louis McMahon's excellent camerawork help build the suspense of Robin Miller's screenplay to a satisfyingly real ending. Some of the dialog shows good imagination.

Probably with a bigger budget, film could have been an excellent psychodrama.

■ **PSYCH-OUT**

1968, 88 MINS, US ◇ ⓥ ⊙
Dir Richard Rush *Prod* Dick Clark *Scr* E. Hunter Willett, Betty Ulius *Ph* Leslie Kovacs *Ed* Ken Reynolds *Mus* Ronald Stein *Art Dir* Leon Ericksen
● Susan Strasberg, Dean Stockwell, Jack Nicholson, Bruce Dern, Adam Roarke, Henry Jaglom (American International)

Psych-Out is an above average programmer about San Francisco hippies. Thin story line – girl seeking lost brother – is sufficient as the medium for a series of incidents, including drug-induced hallucinations, all directed in excellent fashion by Richard Rush.

Production is strong on realistic location values, as well as special effects.

Script follows Susan Strasberg on her search for far-out brother Bruce Dern. Dean Stockwell is a disenchanted hippie, while Jack Nicholson is a swinger tending towards a romantic interest in Strasberg.

Most principals register strong impact, Strasberg via reaction, Nicholson via action, and Stockwell through a combination of both. Dern's flamboyant performance is partly justified by script.

Rush's direction is quite exceptional. Considering what coin he had to play with, it is worthy of 20 times the apparent budget.

There are a lot of songs in the film, many quite good, by The Strawberry Alarm Clock and The Seeds.

■ **PUBERTY BLUES**

1981, 97 MINS, AUSTRALIA ◇ ⓥ
Dir Bruce Beresford *Prod* John Long *Scr* Margaret Kelly *Ph* Don McAlpine *Ed* Bill Anderson *Mus* Les Gock *Art Dir* David Copping
● Nell Schofield, Jad Capelja, Geoff Rhoe, Tony Hughes, Sandy Paul (Limelight)

Puberty Blues is a leisurely, entertaining tale about a group of teenagers fumbling, fighting and fretting their way through adolescence.

Puberty Blues is based on a book of the same name, published in 1979, by Sydney teenagers Kathy Lette and Gabrielle Carey, who also wrote for local newspapers and magazines under the intriguing pseudonym, the Salami Sisters.

Set in the middle-class suburb of Cronulla, one of Sydney's southern beaches, the story focusses on Debbie and Sue, two girls of fairly average looks, intelligence and upbringing. Opening passages show them falling in with one of the school gangs, cheating in exams, smoking in the toilets, getting drunk, and pairing off with boyfriends.

Film gains more momentum when Debbie fears she is pregnant, her boyfriend Garry cannot cope, he seeks refuge in heroin, and dies of an overdose. To offset the bleakness, the pic is laced with Debbie's witty observations and humorous interludes.

Working with a young, inexperienced cast, Beresford has drawn some remarkable performances. Nell Schofield, 17, is particularly impressive as Debbie, an intuitive player with tangible screen presence.

■ **PUBLIC ENEMY, THE**
(UK: Enemies of the Public)

1931, 83 MINS, US ⓥ ⊙
Dir William Wellman *Scr* Harvey Thew *Ph* Dev Jennings *Ed* Edward M. McDermott *Mus* David Mendoza (dir.) *Art Dir* Max Parker
● James Cagney, Edward Woods, Donald Cook, Joan Blondell, Jean Harlow, Beryl Mercer (Warner)

There's no lace on this picture. It's raw and brutal. It's low-brow material given such workmanship as to make it high-brow. To square everything there's a foreword and postscript moralizing on the gangster as a menace to the public welfare.

Pushing a grapefruit into the face of the moll (Mae Clarke) with whom he's fed up, socking another on the chin for inducing him to her for the night while he's drunk, and spitting a mouthful of beer into the face of a speakeasy proprietor for using a rival's product are a few samples of James Cagney's deportment as Tom, a tough in modern gangster's dress.

The story [by Kubec Glasmon and John Bright] traces him and Matt (Edward Woods) from street gamins in 1909 as a couple of rowdy neighbourhood boys. Titles then designate lapses in time of 1915, 1917 and finally 1920. During this interim they've killed a cop on their first big job, and both kids are set to go the hard way.

The comedy in the picture, as well as the rough stuff, is in the dialog and by-play with the dames who include, besides Clarke, Joan Blondell and Jean Harlow. Harlow better hurry and do something about her voice. She doesn't get the best of it alongside Clarke and Blondell, who can troupe.

☐ 1930/31: Nomination: Best Original Story

. . . .

■ **PUBLIC EYE, THE**

1992, 98 MINS, US ◇ ⓦ ☉
Dir Howard Franklin   *Prod* Sue Baden-Powell
Scr Howard Franklin   *Ph* Peter Suschitzky   *Ed* Evan Lottman   *Mus* Mark Isham   *Art Dir* Marcia Hinds-Johnson
● Joe Pesci, Barbara Hershey, Stanley Tucci, Jerry Adler, Jared Harris, Gerry Becker (Universal)

A down-and-dirty subject gets the velvet glove treatment in *The Public Eye*. Playing a 1940s tabloid crime photographer (based on w.k. shutterbug Weegee) who yearns for respectability and a little love, Joe Pesci creates an involving character, but almost everything about Howard Franklin's solo directorial debut is muted and moody where it should be bold and brash.

Franklin wrote the screenplay nine years earlier before making a name for himself with scripts to *Someone to Watch Over Me*, *The Name of the Rose* and *Quick Change*, which he co-directed with Bill Murray.

Called in to do a favor for beautiful Kay Levitz (Barbara Hershey), a glamorpuss who has inherited an exclusive nightclub from her wealthy late husband, Bernzy (Pesci) is flattered by her apparent serious interest in his book proposal. As a result, he allows himself to get involved in a power struggle between two N.Y. mob factions when his whole career has been based on a philosophy of not playing favorites.

In all respects, the film looks great, but that's the main problem. With terrific production design evoking wartime N.Y. (location work was done in Cincinnati and Chicago) and gorgeous lensing, pic approaches physical beauty of a Coen Bros. or David Cronenberg film. Unfortunately, this is entirely counterproductive to the style that would have been appropriate for the tabloid subject matter.

. . . .

■ **PULP**

1972, 95 MINS, UK ◇ ⓦ
Dir Mike Hodges   *Prod* Michael Klinger   *Scr* Mike Hodges   *Ph* Ousama Rawi   *Ed* John Glen
Mus George Martin   *Art Dir* Patrick Downing
● Michael Caine, Mickey Rooney, Lionel Stander, Lizabeth Scott, Nadia Cassini, Dennis Price (United Artists)

A crime fictionalist (Michael Caine) reluctantly enters the reality of his own fantasies in *Pulp*, a reasonably entertaining piece of rococo recall [shot on Malta], at its best as visual camp. The joke isn't an easy one to sustain, but it's part of the film's appeal that writer-director Mike Hodges doesn't flog it.

Caine is hired by a faded screen tough guy (Mickey Rooney) to ghost his memoir, and the plottage thereafter hinges on a scandal in the star's past involving elements of the local shady set. Having previously hushed things up, they now fear Rooney means to spill the beans in his book, hence they contract his murder. Caine is naturally compelled not to turn tail but to see the mystery and danger through.

Hodges' dialog is appropriately crisp and often witty, though it's the sight gags that work best – a throwaway salute to Bogart or the camp interior of Rooney's island villa, fitted out for the insecure narcissist that he was.

Caine, solo billed above the title, delivers his usual attractive turn, albeit with more than a whiff of hangover from one of Len Deighton's spy plots. There's also a deft bit by Dennis Price as a shaggy Englishman, and newcomer Nadia Cassini is featured as Rooney's sexy satrap.

. . . .

■ **PUMPING IRON**

1977, 85 MINS, US ◇ ⓦ ☉
Dir George Butler, Robert Fiore   *Prod* George Butler, Jerome Gary   *Scr* George Butler   *Ph* Robert Fiore
Ed Larry Silk, Geof Bartz   *Mus* Michael Small
● Arnold Schwarzenegger, Lou Ferrigno, Matty Ferrigno, Ken Waller, Franco Columbu, Mike Katz (Cinema 5)

The life of a bodybuilder who takes himself seriously is, ultimately, as lonely as that of a ballet dancer. He knows that if he's serious about his profession it means a daily, dedicated routine of exercises so that any gains won are not lost.

What this film documentary, based on George Butler and Charles Gaines' book, *Pumping Iron*, does not tell the viewer, however, is what lies beyond the peak of success.

The most fascinating aspect of this film is the dedicated training that turns average-built young men (frequently they refer to themselves as weaklings in their early youth) into superbly-created physical edifices.

The film, while spotlighting Arnold Schwarzenegger, also treats with other competitors, preparing for the Mr Universe and Mr Olympia contests.

. . . .

■ **PUMPING IRON II
THE WOMEN**

1985, 107 MINS, US ◇ ⓦ ☉
Dir George Butler   *Prod* George Butler   *Scr* Charles Gaines, George Butler   *Ph* Dyanna Taylor, Craig Perry
Ed Paul Barnes, Susan Crutcher, Jane Kurson
Mus David McHugh, Michael Montes
● Lori Bowen, Carla Dunlap, Bev Francis, Rachel McLish, Kris Alexander, Lydia Cheng (Pumping Iron/White Mountain/Bar Belle)

This enjoyable, slickly conceived documentary on the subculture of women's bodybuilding could have been better had director George Butler tempered his penchant for camera's eye detachment with some analytical and repertorial sweat.

Although he succeeds fairly well in exploiting the inherent drama of the 1983 Caesars Palace World Cup Championship for women bodybuilders, Butler is too content to let the alluring amazons speak for themselves on the film's central question: what is femininity and how far many women go in liberating themselves from stereotypes before confronting immovable cultural resistance?

The question is embodied graphically by Australian power-lifter Bev Francis, whose awesome, spectacularly mannish physique will be matched in a great flex-off against the wiry, compelling developed bodies of the best 'feminine' bodybuilders. These include smug, shrewd defending champ Rachel McLish; the appealingly articulate Carla Dunlap, who's the only black woman in the group; and Lori Bowen, a humble girl from Texas who idolizes the aloof McLish and plans to use her prize money to free her boyfriend from his male go-go dancer's gig.

. . . .

■ **PUMPKIN EATER, THE**

1964, 118 MINS, UK
Dir Jack Clayton   *Prod* James Woolf   *Scr* Harold Pinter
Ph Oswald Morris   *Ed* James Clark   *Mus* Georges Delerue   *Art Dir* Edward Marshall
● Anne Bancroft, Peter Finch, James Mason, Cedric Hardwicke, Richard Johnson, Eric Porter (Columbia/Romulus)

Harold Pinter's screenplay is based on a witty novel by Penelope Mortimer, and his script vividly brings to life the principal characters in this story of a shattered marriage, though Pinter's resort to flashback technique is confusing in the early stages. Jack Clayton's direction gets off to a slow, almost casual start, but the pace quickens as the drama becomes more intense.

Anne Bancroft is exceptionally good. She plays the mother of several young children who leaves her second husband to marry Peter Finch, a scriptwriter with a promising career ahead. And as he succeeds in his work, so she becomes aware of his increasing infidelities and she becomes a case for psychiatric treatment. The role may sound conventional enough, but not as played by Bancroft; she adds a depth and understanding which puts it on a higher plane.

Peter Finch's performance is a mature intrepretation, and always impressive. To him, casual infidelities are the natural prerequisites of a successful writer.

Notwithstanding the scope offered by those two roles, James Mason stands out in a much smaller part. He plays a deceived husband with a sinister, malevolent bitterness, to provide one of the acting highlights of the picture.

☐ 1964: Nomination: Best Actress (Anne Bancroft)

. . . .

■ **PUMP UP THE VOLUME**

1990, 105 MINS, US/CANADA ◇ ⓦ ☉
Dir Allan Moyle   *Prod* Rupert Harvey, Sandy Stern
Scr Allan Moyle   *Ph* Walt Lloyd   *Ed* Wendy Bricmont, Ric Keeley, Kurt Hathaway   *Art Dir* Bruce Bolander
● Christian Slater, Samantha Mathis, Ellen Greene, Scott Paulin, Cheryl Pollack, Annie Ross (New Line/SC Entertainment)

Writer-director Allan Moyle's story about a shy high school student who galvanizes an Arizona suburb with a rebellious pirate radio show has rambunctious energy and defiant attitude.

Christian Slater is first-rate as a bright but alienated student who feels trapped and disconnected in a suburban 'whitebread land' where 'everything is sold out.' Everything includes his father (Scott Paulin), a former 1960s radical who has bought into the yuppie dream.

Slater's rebellious late-night broadcasts soon make him a hero and stir up the dormant anger of other alienated kids. But one night his talk-radio antics go out of control.

Moyle resolves things in favor of love and justice, but his ending resolutely refuses to sell out the movie's angry stance against complacency. Slater handles numerous monolog scenes with conviction and charisma. Newcomer Samantha Mathis (as Nora, who falls in love with Slater's disembodied voice) and Paulin show a good grasp of their characters.

. . . .

■ **PUNCH AND JUDY MAN, THE**

1963, 96 MINS, UK
Dir Jeremy Summers   *Prod* Gordon L. T. Scott
Scr Philip Oakes, Tony Hancock   *Ph* Gilbert Taylor
Ed Gordon Pilkington   *Mus* Derek Acott, Don Banks
● Tony Hancock, Sylvia Syms, Ronald Fraser, Barbara Murray, John Le Mesurier, Hugh Lloyd (Macconkey)

Tony Hancock's second film produces many amusing sequences, but it fails to jell. Story line is too slight. Result is a series of spasmodic incidents which Hancock has, largely, to carry on his own personality, despite being surrounded by some firstclass character actors.

Hancock plays a Punch and Judy man at a seaside resort which is ruled over by a snobbish mayor. Hancock's marriage is foundering, since he fights the snobbery while his social climbing wife (Sylvia Syms) is anxious for him to mend his ways so that she can move into the local big league. Climax is the gala held to celebrate the 60th anni of the resort.

Director Jeremy Summers makes good use of the closeup to put over Hancock's expressive mug, and devotees of the comic will get a generous quota of giggles. But either Summers or the editor, or maybe both, have failed to keep the film on a taut and even keel.

Syms, as Hancock's disgruntled wife, takes her few opportunities avidly. Ronald Fraser shines as the officious mayor. Eddie Byrne chips in with a neat cameo as an ice cream assistant and Barbara Murray, as a socialite and guest of honor at the gala, pin-points once more that she is a sadly underrated femme in pix.

■ **PUNISHER, THE**

1990, 90 MINS, US/AUSTRALIA ◇ ⓦ ⊙

Dir Mark Goldblatt   *Prod* Robert Kamen   *Scr* Boaz Yakin   *Ph* Ian Baker   *Ed* Tim Wellburn   *Mus* Dennis Dreith   *Art Dir* Norma Moriceau
● Dolph Lundgren, Louis Gossett Jr, Jeroen Krabbe, Kim Miyori, Bryan Marshall, Nancy Everhard (New World)

With origins in a Marvel Comics character, *The Punisher* is, as might be expected, two-dimensional. The Punisher has killed 125 people before the film even begins, and the ensuing 90 minutes are crammed with slaughters of every conceivable kind. Pic was the only product of the New World offshoot Down Under.

Story involves an ex-cop whose wife and children were murdered by the mafia in New York. He hides from civilization in the city's sewers and for five years he's been killing the various heads of the mob families in nonstop vengeance.

Another party comes to play – the Japanese mafia headed by the glamorous, stony cold Lady Tanaka. The Punisher is quite content to see his enemies slaughter each other until the Japanese kidnap the locals' children.

Dolph Lundgren looks just as if he's stepped out of a comic book. Thankfully, he breezes through the B-grade plot with tongue firmly placed in cheek.

■ **PUNISHMENT PARK**

1971, 88 MINS, US ◇

Dir Peter Watkins   *Scr* Peter Watkins   *Ph* Joan Churchill   *Ed* Peter Watkins   *Mus* Paul Motian
● Paul Alelyanes, Carmen Argenziano, Stan Armsted, Harold Beaulieu, Jim Bohan, Kerry Cannon (Francoise)

Like the same director's *The War Game*, this pic apparently is set in the indeterminate future. It is presented in the guise of a live TV documentary complete with camera jerks, microphones and lights in full view.

Escalation of Asian wars is pre-supposed with intensified tensions between the larger international powers and the increase of anti-war propaganda and demonstrations of draft evaders.

Those youthful rebels coming before tribunals on conscientious and other grounds are given the choice of serving penal sentences or a three-days endurance test in Punishment Park, situated in Southern California.

The rules are that 'corrective groups' are given three days to reach, on foot, an American flag 57 miles away. They are allowed two to three hours' start, after which the National Guard hounds them out. If they manage to reach the flag in the alloted time they will be given their freedom. The journey they have to traverse is over desert territory in temperatures rising above the 100-degree mark by day and cold by night.

The pic deftly switches back and forth from the members of one such corrective group, the armed forces and seven different offenders being tried by a quasi-judicial tribunal.

■ **PUNK, THE**

1993, 96 MINS, UK ◇ ⓦ

Dir Mike Sarne   *Prod* Mike Sarne   *Scr* Mike Sarne   *Ph* Alan M. Trow   *Ed* Gwyn Jones
● Charlie Creed-Miles, Vanessa Hadaway, David Shawyer, Jess Conrad (Videodrome)

After a long absence from the screen, director Mike Sarne, best known for *Myra Breckinridge*, makes an impressive comeback with *The Punk*, a gritty, contempo take on *Romeo and Juliet*. Theatrical prospects are excellent for the vibrant, visually stunning movie, clearly made with an eye on the youth market.

Sarne's script is based on Gideon Sams' 1976 book, originally scribbled as an essay in an English class. The irony is that Sams, who died in New York from pneumonia when he was 21, reputedly never read Shakespeare.

The Montagues and Capulets are transformed into the Punks and the Rockers. David (Charlie Creed-Miles), a working-class punk, calls himself Adolph just to annoy his obnoxious policeman father (David Shawyer). He accidentally meets Rachel (Vanessa Hadaway), a product of a rich and pompous family, in a local theater where she is performing Shakespeare.

Set for the most part around Notting Hill Gate, Sarne brings a narrative looseness and immediacy to his love story. But the portraiture of the adult world comes off as a stereotypical caricature.

■ **PUPPET ON A CHAIN**

1971, 98 MINS, UK ◇ ⓦ

Dir Geoffrey Reeve   *Prod* Kurt Unger   *Scr* Alistair MacLean   *Ph* Jack Hildyard   *Ed* Bill Lenny   *Mus* Piero Piccioni
● Sven-Bertil Taube, Barbara Parkins, Alexander Knox, Patrick Allen, Vladek Sheybal, Penny Casdagli (Unger)

Puppet on a Chain could be remembered as the film with the speedboat chase. Don Sharp, who was engaged specially to direct this sequence, has in no way spared the boats as the hero relentlessly pursues the villain through the canals of Amsterdam. Regrettably the standard of this sequence is not reflected in the rest of the film.

Sven-Bertil Taube plays a US narcotics agent seeking the headquarters of a drug syndicate in Amsterdam aided by his undercover assistant, Maggie (Barbara Parkins). Wherever they go sudden death is never far behind. The trail leads to a religious order and an island castle.

Alistair MacLean scripted his own story. There is all the action, implausible happenings, violent rough housing and mystery that distinguishes so much of his work, but he has created little sympathy for the characters.

■ **PURE COUNTRY**

1992, 112 MINS, US ◇ ⓦ

Dir Christopher Cain   *Prod* Jerry Weintraub   *Scr* Rex McGee   *Ph* Richard Bowen   *Ed* Jack Hofstra, Robin Katz   *Mus* Steve Dorff   *Art Dir* Jeffrey Howard
● George Strait, Lesley Ann Warren, Isabel Glasser, Kyle Chandler, John Doe, Rory Calhoun (Warner/Weintraub)

Though this slick-looking paean to down-home values often undercuts its own message, *Pure Country* is an effective vehicle for amiable country star George Strait. Screenplay mingles corn with knowing satire of the hollowness of stardom, but the heartfelt romantic chemistry between Strait and Texas ranch gal Isabel Glasser carries the day.

Strait's Dusty feels like a sham in his gussied-up show and wants to get back to basics, while his desperate manager Lesley Ann Warren fools the public by having her young stud (Kyle Chandler) lip-sync in his place.

Strait, who looks like a more wholesome version of the late Warren Oates, doesn't have much acting range, but he is convincing as someone who would just as soon chuck it all to settle down on Glasser's ranch.

Glasser's freshly scrubbed, weatherbeaten beauty and forthright country charm stand in starkly loaded contrast to the twitchy, overheated neuroticism of Warren, who archly vamps in a role that cries out for Elizabeth Ashley to camp it up.

■ **PURE HELL OF ST. TRINIAN'S, THE**

1960, 94 MINS, UK ⓦ

Dir Frank Launder   *Prod* Frank Launder, Sidney Gilliat   *Scr* Sidney Gilliat, Frank Launder, Val Valentine   *Ph* Gerald Gibbs   *Ed* Thelma Connell   *Mus* Malcolm Arnold
● Cecil Parker, Joyce Grenfell, George Cole, Thorley Walters, Irene Handl, Eric Barker (Hallmark/Tudor)

Ronald Searle's familiar cartoon characters come to life in yet another St Trinian's School romp, which is well up to standard.

Current yarn gets of to a flying start with the girls burning down the school and being brought to trial at the Old Bailey. But to the horror of the police and the Ministry of Education they are acquitted. This is partly because the judge does not miss the most beautiful blonde in the sixth form (Julie Alexander), but also because of the intervention of a strange professor who offers to start a new St Trinian's and give the girls a fresh start. He turns out to be a dubious character mixed up with a racket for supplying glamor girls to an Oriental Emir as wives for his numerous sons.

Dialog is brisk and the film is directed at a sufficiently swift pace to keep the fun moving steadily.

In a large cast, Cecil Parker, as the professor; Irene Handl, as his assistant; Dennis Price, Thorley Walters, Eric Barker and Raymond Huntley all provide polished comedy studies. Joyce Grenfell is once again the prim policewoman in love with the superintendent. George Cole repeats his familiar performance as Flash Harry, who runs a matrimonial agency on behalf of the Sixth Form

■ **PURE LUCK**

1991, 96 MINS, US ◇ ⓦ

Dir Nadia Tass   *Prod* Lance Hool, Sean Daniel   *Scr* Herschel Weingrod, Timothy Harris   *Ph* David Parker   *Ed* Billy Weber   *Mus* Jonathan Scheffer   *Art Dir* Peter Wooley
● Martin Short, Danny Glover, Sheila Kelley, Sam Wanamaker, Scott Wilson, Harry Shearer (Universal/Daniel)

Purely lucky pairing of Martin Short and Danny Glover creates a sprinkling of good laughs in this light, likeable comedy remake of the 1982 French film *La chevre*. Nonetheless, this banana-peel souffle enjoys more *bon chance* in the hands of director Nadia Tass, whose flair for offbeat comedy (*Ricky & Pete*) keeps the one-joke premise afloat, than did the earlier, less amusing *Three Fugitives* from Touchstone, also a French remake starring Short and exec produced by Francis Veber.

Short plays a disastrously unlucky accountant who's hired by his wealthy boss (Sam Wanamaker) to lead an investigation to find the boss' extraordinarily klutzy daughter (Sheila Kelley), who's disappeared during a Mexican vacation. He's paired with Glover, a logic-driven, hardbitten p.i. who's gravely unamused at the prospect of being subordinate to the jinxed accountant.

Pair sets out for Acapulco and Puerto Vallarta on the trail already trodden unsuccessfully by Glover, but this time mishaps keep leading them into the same pitfalls the daughter stumbled into.

Hard-working Short keeps the energy up with mugging and temper tantrums, while the ultra-low-key Glover strikes a nice contrast as he struggles to adapt to the weird dynamic by which things come together in Short's world.

■ PURPLE HEARTS

1984, 115 MINS, US ◇ ⊛

Dir Sidney J. Furie   *Prod* Sidney J. Furie   *Scr* Rick Natkin, Sidney J. Furie   *Ph* Jan Kiesser   *Ed* George Grenville   *Mus* Robert Folk   *Art Dir* Francisco Balangue
● Ken Wahl, Cheryl Ladd, Stephen Lee, David Harris, Cyril O'Reilly, Lane Smith (Ladd)

Purple Hearts is a systematically simple love story set against the Vietnam War, with the action largely overwhelming the romantic time-outs.

Ken Wahl is a handsome young and dedicated doctor in Vietnam where he meets a beautiful young and dedicated nurse (Cheryl Ladd). They fall in love. Between kisses, they assure each other that they hope one day to return Stateside and do medical good together forever. But then he's killed – but no he isn't – and then she's killed – but (fill in the blank) – and it looks like they may never live happily ever after.

Wahl is solid in the lead and Ladd hangs in there in a less demanding part.

■ PURPLE PLAIN, THE

1954, 100 MINS, UK ◇

Dir Robert Parrish   *Prod* John Bryan   *Scr* Eric Ambler   *Ph* Geoffrey Unsworth   *Ed* Clive Donner   *Mus* John Veale   *Art Dir* Jack Maxstead
● Gregory Peck, Win Min Than, Bernard Lee, Maurice Denham, Lyndon Brook, Brenda De Banzie (Two Cities)

The combined writing talents of novelist H.E. Bates and scripter Eric Ambler produce a fine dramatic vehicle for Gregory Peck's second British-made film which is set in the Burmese jungle in the last days of the war.

After vividly establishing the atmosphere and developing the principal characters, the action switches from the airstrip to mountainous terrain held by the Japs into which Peck has crashed his plane while on a routine flight with his navigator (Lyndon Brook) and a fellow officer (Maurice Denham). From that point the entire incident concentrates on their attempts to get out with Peck in an obstinate mood and insisting that they should not wait by the wreckage for help but should try and reach water.

There are some very tender scenes played in a neighbouring village community in which Peck begins a romantic entanglement with Win Min Than, an exotic yet restrained Burmese beauty. The backgrounds, filmed in Ceylon, are lensed in lush Technicolor.

■ PURPLE RAIN

1984, 104 MINS, US ◇ ⊛ ⊙

Dir Albert Magnoli   *Prod* Robert Cavallo, Joseph Ruffalo, Steven Fargnoli   *Scr* Albert Magnoli, William Blinn   *Ph* Donald E. Thorin   *Ed* Albert Magnoli, Ken Robinson   *Mus* Michel Colombier   *Art Dir* Ward Preston
● Prince, Apollonia Kotero, Morris Day, Olga Karlatos, Clarence Williams III, Jerome Benton (Warner/Purple)

Playing a character rooted in his own background, and surrounded by the real-life members of his Minneapolis-based musical 'family', rock star Prince makes an impressive feature film debut in *Purple Rain*, a rousing contemporary addition to the classic backstage musical genre.

Director Albert Magnoli gets a solid, appealing performance from Prince, whose sensual, somewhat androgynous features are as riveting on film as they are on a concert stage. Femme love interest Apollonia Kotero is a beautiful, winsome presence.

Custom-tailored vehicle for the rocker spins the familiar tale of a youngster who escapes the sordid confines of his family life through music, ultimately becoming the better man and musician.
□ 1984: Best Original Song Score

■ PURPLE ROSE OF CAIRO, THE

1985, 82 MINS, US ◇ ⊛ ⊙

Dir Woody Allen   *Prod* Robert Greenhut   *Scr* Woody Allen   *Ph* Gordon Willis   *Ed* Susan E. Morse   *Mus* Dick Hyman   *Art Dir* Stuart Wurtzel
● Mia Farrow, Jeff Daniels, Danny Aiello, Dianne Wiest, Van Johnson, Zoe Caldwell (Orion)

Tale is a light, almost frivolous treatment of a serious theme, as Woody Allen here confronts the unalterable fact that life just doesn't turn out the way it does (or did) in Hollywood films. For all its situational goofiness, pic is a tragedy, and it's too bad Allen didn't build up the characters and drama sufficiently to give some weight to his concerns.

Allen introduces Depression-era waitress Mia Farrow, a hopeless film buff so consumed by motion picture gossip and fantasies she can barely hold down her job.

Her husband (Danny Aiello) is a complete boor, so she spends all her free time seeing films over and over again until Tom Baxter (Jeff Daniels), a character in a fictional RKO epic *The Purple Rose of Cairo*, stops the action, starts speaking to Farrow directly from the screen, and, fed up with repeating the same action time after time, steps out of the film and asks to be shown something of real life.

Mia Farrow is excellent again under Allen's direction, and at certain times (especially when lying to her husband) begins to sound like him. Jeff Daniels is okay as the bland 1930s adventurer come to life, although he's rather restricted by role's unavoidable thinness.
□ 1985: Nomination: Best Original Screenplay

■ PURSUED

1947, 100 MINS, US ⊛

Dir Raoul Walsh   *Prod* Milton Sperling   *Scr* Niven Busch   *Ph* James Wong Howe   *Ed* Christian Nyby   *Mus* Max Steiner   *Art Dir* Ted Smith
● Teresa Wright, Robert Mitchum, Judith Anderson, Dean Jagger, Harry Carey Jr (Warner/United States)

Pursued is potent frontier days western film fare. Standout in picture is suspense generated by the original script and Raoul Walsh's direction. It builds the western gunman's death walk to high moments of thrill and action. Strong casting also is a decided factor in selling the action wares. Production makes use of natural outdoor backgrounds supplied by New Mexico scenery, lending air of authenticity that is fully captured by the camera.

There are psychological elements in the script, depicting the hate that drives through a man's life and forces him into unwanted dangers. Robert Mitchum is the victim of that hate, made to kill and fear because of an old family feud. His role fits him naturally and he makes it entirely believable. Teresa Wright upholds the femme lead with another of her honestly valued, talented portrayals that register sincerity.

Plot motivation stems from feuding between the Callums and the Rands. Feud starts when Dean Jagger, a Callum, wipes out Mitchum's family because a Callum girl dared love Mitchum's father.

Among memorable moments is the stalking of Mitchum by the Callums as he spends his wedding night with a bride who also had just tried to kill him.

■ PURSUIT OF THE GRAF SPEE
See: The Battle of the River Plate

■ PUSSYCAT ALLEY
See: The World Ten Times Over

■ PUTNEY SWOPE

1969, 84 MINS, US ◇ ⊛

Dir Robert Downey   *Scr* Robert Downey   *Ph* Gerald Cotts   *Ed* Bud Smith   *Mus* Charley Cuva   *Art Dir* Gary Weist
● Stanley Gottlieb, Allan Garfield, Arnold Johnson, Laura Greene, Ramon Gordon (Herold)

What happens when black militants take over a large Manhattan advertising agency is the basis for a comic satire on black racial identity and the dollar sign on the American altar of success.

The situations include political caricature, but disappointingly nothing much beyond marginal interest occurs. The comedy is only intermittently funny and the satire is mostly shallow and obvious.

Putney Swope is the only black member of an ad agency. By happenstance he is elected to head the firm after the previous chairman dies.

Director Robert Downey's sense of the ridiculous is employed in a spotty, punchline kind of comic usage. The sharp individual parts do not build to anything and the film, as a piece, is more often dull than exciting, less revealingly witty then merely clever.

■ PUZZLE OF A DOWNFALL CHILD

1970, 104 MINS, US ◇

Dir Jerry Schatzberg   *Prod* Paul Newman, John Foreman   *Scr* Adrien Joyce [= Carolyn Eastman]   *Ph* Adam Holender   *Ed* Evan Lottman   *Mus* Michael Small   *Art Dir* Richard Bianchi
● Faye Dunaway, Barry Primus, Viveca Lindfors, Barry Morse, Roy Scheider (Universal)

Puzzle of a Downfall Child, stars Faye Dunaway as a confused high-fashion model with severe emotional problems, most never resolved. Unfortunately, the film is marked by cinema-verite chic though Dunaway makes the most of a tour-de-force opportunity.

Plot takes a riches-to-rags course, Dunaway entering as the latest hot model, insecure in frustrating relationships with photographer Barry Primus and well-to-do Roy Scheider. Dunaway tells her story to Primus in flashback in her seacoast cabin refuge from mental breakdown, professional decline and personal unfulfillment.

The character first garners wholesome pity, but the plot development soon banishes her to bathos and finally boredom.

■ PYGMALION

1938, 96 MINS, UK ⊛ ⊙

Dir Anthony Asquith, Leslie Howard   *Prod* Gabriel Pascal   *Scr* George Bernard Shaw, W.P. Lipscomb, Cecil Lewis, Ian Dalrymple   *Ph* Harry Stradling   *Ed* David Lean   *Mus* Arthur Honegger   *Art Dir* Laurence Irving, John Bryan
● Wendy Hiller, Leslie Howard, Wilfrid Lawson, Marie Lohr, Scott Sunderland, Jean Cadell (Pascal)

Smartly produced, this makes an excellent job of transcribing George Bernard Shaw, retaining all the key lines and giving freshness to the theme. The speed of the first half contrives to show up the anti-climax, the play subsequently petering out in a flood of clever talk. But it's still a Cinderella story, which is

P

one of the most reliable subjects for drama.

Leslie Howard's performance is excellent in its comedy. It's vital and at times dominating. Wendy Hiller carries off a difficult part faultlessly. She never loses sight of the fact that this is a guttersnipe on whom culture has been imposed; the ambassador's reception, where she moves like a sleepwalker, is eloquent of this, and even in the final argument the cockney is always peeping through the veneer.

Wilfred Lawson's Doolittle is only a shadow of the part G.B.S. wrote, but his moral philosophies could obviously not have been put on the screen in toto without gumming up the action. As it is he presents a thoroughly enjoyable old reprobate.
□ 1938: Best Adaptation, Screenplay (George Bernard Shaw).
□ Nominations: Best Picture, Actor (Leslie Howard), Actress (Wendy Hiller)

■ **Q**
(UK: Q – The Winged Serpent; aka: The Winged Serpent)

1982, 92 MINS, US ◇ ⓥ
Dir Larry Cohen   *Prod* Larry Cohen   *Scr* Larry Cohen
Ph Fred Murphy   *Ed* Armand Lebowitz   *Mus* Robert O. Ragland
● Michael Moriarty, David Carradine, Candy Clark, Richard Roundtree, Malachi McCourt (Arkoff)

Q– The Winged Serpent is a delightful science-fiction winner. Larry Cohen's tale of a religious bird of prey terrorizing New York City has wit, style and an above average script for the genre.

Story centers on Michael Moriarty, an ex-junkie who drives getaway cars for the mob. He takes refuge in the Chrysler Building's summit, where he stumbles onto the title character's lair complete with a large unhatched egg.

In the meantime, the green bird has been having a merry feed of workmen and apartment dwellers in the city's high rises. Policeman David Carradine links the arrival of the monster to a series of bizarre ritual killings where the victims are literally skinned alive.

The Winged Serpent has great fun mixing realistic settings with political satire and a wild yarn. Writer-director Cohen has a bagful of tricks and a wild sense of the bizarre to lend the project.

The picture belongs to the bird and Moriarty, and the latter assays his loser with relish.

■ **Q&A**

1990, 132 MINS, US ◇ ⓥ ⊙
Dir Sidney Lumet   *Prod* Arnon Milchan, Burtt Harris
Scr Sidney Lumet   *Ph* Andrzej Bartkowiak   *Ed* Richard Cirincione   *Mus* Ruben Blades   *Art Dir* Philip Rosenberg
● Nick Nolte, Timothy Hutton, Armand Assante, Patrick O'Neal, Lee Richardson, Jenny Lumet (Regency/Odyssey)

Director Sidney Lumet grabs a tiger by the tail with *Q&A*, a hard-hitting thriller that takes on weighty topics of racism and corruption in the New York City justice system.

Working from Edwin Torres' novel, Lumet has scripted in concise, suspenseful fashion, opening with cop Nick Nolte ruthlessly killing a Latino drug dealer outside an after-hours club and then intimidating witnesses on the scene. As his first job as a new assistant d.a., Timothy Hutton is summoned by his cooly evil boss Patrick O'Neal (a man with unbridled political ambitions) to do a routine investigation, writing up a Q&A with Nolte and other principal players. He's obviously the fall guy. Key to film's success is how the case gradually uncovers new layers of corruption and insidious racism, with escalating awareness (and danger) for Hutton.

Nolte is outstanding, bringing utter conviction to the stream of racist and sexist epithets that pour from his good ole boy lips.

■ **Q PLANES**

1939, 82 MINS, UK
Dir Tim Whelan   *Prod* Irving Asher, Alexander Korda
Scr Ian Dalrymple, Brock Williams, Jack Whittingham, Arthur Wimperis   *Ph* Harry Stradling   *Mus* Muir Mathieson (dir.)   *Art Dir* Vincent Korda
● Laurence Olivier, Ralph Richardson, Valerie Hobson (Harefield/London)

Q Planes is an aviation picture, but not heavy on heroics. Even in the final rescue sequence,

melodramatically carried to the timber line of hokum, there is a refreshing tongue-in-cheek attitude. Whole thing is bright, breezy and flavorsome. Starts off as a newsreel, showing government buildings and streets in London.

The acting honors go – and at a gallop – to Ralph Richardson, playing a Scotland Yard eccentric. Director Tim Whelan is entitled to full credit for a generally fast-paced and well-integrated entertainment.

Plot concerns the use of a salvage ship anchored at sea to capture army airplanes on their test flights. All of the crew speak with German accents and little doubt is left as to who the villains are.

Valerie Hobson, as a newspaper-woman and sister of the Scotland Yard eccentric, provides the romantic touch.

■ **Q – THE WINGED SERPENT**
See: Q

■ **QUADROPHENIA**

1979, 120 MINS, UK ◇ ⓥ ⊙
Dir Franc Roddam   *Prod* Roy Baird, Bill Curbishley
Scr Dave Humphries, Martin Stellman, Franc Roddam
Ph Brian Tufano   *Ed* Mike Taylor   *Mus* Pete Townshend
Art Dir Simon Holland
● Phil Daniels, Mark Wingett, Toyah Wilcox, Sting, Leslie Ash (The Who)

Set in 1963, when rival image-cults among young Britishers led to a wave of crowd-fights in normally staid seaside resorts, the picture [based on the record album *Quadrophenia* by Pete Townshend] plots the plight of one pill-popping, fashion-mad 'Mod' who abandons himself completely to the gang-identity.

After fighting the enemy 'Rockers' (denoted by black leather, motorbikes and beer) in a disorderly clash on Brighton beach, and being arrested for the cause, he swiftly discovers the hollowness of the whole image thing.

It's a tribute to helmer Franc Roddam's simple, restrained direction that the downbeat ending, when the jobless, exhausted kid is left in the advanced state of schizophrenia implied by the title, succeeds in being climactic.

Sting, as the weekend super-Mod whose image collapses when he's revealed to work as a bellhop, cuts a slick dash in the dancehall sequences.

■ **QUALITY STREET**

1937, 84 MINS, US ⓥ ⊙
Dir George Stevens   *Prod* Pandro S. Berman
Scr Mortimer Offner, Allan Scott   *Ph* Robert de Grasse
Ed Henry Berman   *Mus* Roy Webb
● Katharine Hepburn, Franchot Tone, Eric Blore, Fay Bainter, Cora Witherspoon, Joan Fontaine (RKO)

Of a dramatic texture which never was too strong even in the theatre, *Quality Street* is a theatrical memory involving Maude Adams in a J.M. Barrie piece. It was not rated among her best. Incredibly romantic and farcical, the idea of a 30-year-old woman deceiving her sweetheart into believing she is her own niece of 16 was tough going for the horse-and-buggy patrons of 1901.

It is a film full of effort. The settings are of a charming London residential spot, the gardens are charmingly arranged, and the costumes are charming beyond description. The dialog tries to be charming, too. The men in the cast, headed by Franchot Tone, are soldiers in England's army which smashed Napoleon. They're not so charming as quaint. Napoleon must have been a pushover and history is all wrong.

Working from a script possessing neither imagination nor ingenuity, George Stevens is limited in his direction.
□ 1937: Nomination: Best Score

■ QUARE FELLOW, THE

1962, 90 MINS, UK
Dir Arthur Dreifuss   *Prod* Anthony Havelock-Allan
Scr Arthur Dreifuss   *Ph* Peter Hennessy   *Ed* Gitta Zadek
Mus Alexander Faris   *Art Dir* Ted Marshall
● Patrick McGoohan, Sylvia Syms, Walter Macken,
Harry Brogan, Dermot Kelly, Marie Kean (British Lion)

Based on Brendan Behan's play [adapted by
Jacqueline Sundstrom and director Arthur
Dreifuss], this is an all-out protest against capital punishment. It is downbeat entertainment
but honest and has the benefit of a sterling
cast, virtually all Irish. It has also been shot entirely in a Dublin prison and on location.

Patrick McGoohan is a young man from the
Irish backwoods who takes up his first appointment as a jail warder with lofty ideals.
Criminals must be punished for the sake of society is his inflexible theory and that also embraces capital punishment. But when he
arrives he is shaken by the prison atmosphere.

Two men are awaiting the noose. One is reprieved but hangs himself. That shakes
McGoohan. He meets the young wife (Sylvia
Syms) of the other murderer and his convictions totter still more when he hears precisely
what caused her husand to murder his
brother. Mostly, though, he is influenced by a
veteran warder (Walter Macken) who believes that capital punishment is often a
worse crime than the original offence.

The Quare Fellow (Irish prison slang for a guy
due to be topped) is mostly a study of men's
conscience and convictions. Such thin storyline as there is hinges on whether the murderer will be reprieved.

The film, a mixture of grim humor and cynical starkness, brings out the clamminess and
misery of prison life, and is helped by the grey
lensing of Peter Hennessy.

■ QUARTET

1948, 120 MINS, UK ⓥ
Dir Ken Annakin, Arthur Crabtree, Harold French, Ralph
Smart   *Prod* Anthony Darnborough   *Scr* R.C. Sherriff
Ph Ray Elton, Reg Wyer   *Ed* A. Charles Knott, Jean
Barker   *Mus* John Greenwood   *Art Dir* George Provis,
Cedric Dalve
● Basil Radford, Naunton Wayne, Dirk Bogarde,
Bernard Lee, Cecil Parker, Nora Swinburne (Rank/
Gainsborough)

Of the four stories [from originals by
Somerset Maugham] that make up the film,
the first and last are the most intriguing. *The
Facts of Life* [directed by Ralph Smart] is a superbly told piece of a 19-year-old who disregards his father's advice on his first trip to
Monte Carlo and outwits an obvious adventuress, and *The Colonel's Lady* [directed by Ken
Annakin] is a delightful yarn of a colonel's
wife (Nora Swinburne) who causes much embarrassment to her husband (Cecil Parker) by
the publication of a book of verse purporting
to describe her romantic experiences.

The intermediate two, while lacking the
high level of the first and last, are certainly
more than potboilers. An undergraduate son
(Dirk Bogarde) of a member of the landed
gentry, who hopes to become a professional
pianist, provides the melodramatic theme of
The Alien Corn [directed by Harold French],
while *The Kite* [directed by Arthur Crabtree]
is an unusual story of a simple young man
(George Cole), very much under his mother's
domination, who put his kite-flying before his
wife and cheerfully goes to gaol when she
wrecks his latest invention.

■ QUARTET

1981, 100 MINS, UK/FRANCE ◇ ⓥ
Dir James Ivory   *Prod* Ismael Merchant, Jean-Pierre
Mahot de la Querantonnais   *Scr* Ruth Prawer Jhabvala
Ph Pierre Lhomme   *Ed* Humphrey Dixon   *Mus* Richard
Robbins   *Art Dir* Jean-Jaques Caziot

● Alan Bates, Maggie Smith, Isabelle Adjani, Anthony
Higgins, Suzanne Flon, Pierre Clementi (Merchant
Ivory/Lyric)

Quartet is an elegant tale of a pretty, innocent
but resilient woman set in the Paris of the
late 1920s. Director James Ivory takes his
usual aloofly observant distance and the film's
love triangle loses some drastic impetus. The
seething Paris bohemian backdrop of the era
is used only in a token way.

Isabelle Adjani is married to a young Pole
who, arrested when he gets mixed up in nefarious art dealings, is sentenced to a year in
prison.

She is left alone and penniless. A noted
English agent, played by Alan Bates with
massive solemnity, had taken a shine to her
after meeting her in the expatriate circles of
Paris residents. He asks her to move in with
him and his wife.

The latter is an edgy, middle-aged painter
limned with asperity by Maggie Smith. Other
girls had stayed there and she indulged her
husband's sensuality to keep him. Adjani at
first spurns Bates's advances but gives in
though she still loves her husband.

Overall, a lowkey film. Based on Jean Rhys'
book, the script uses her spare style.

■ QUATERMASS AND THE PIT

(US: 5,000,000 Years to Earth)

1968, 98 MINS, UK ◇
Dir Roy Ward Baker   *Prod* Anthony Nelson Keys
Scr Nigel Kneale   *Ph* Arthur Grant   *Ed* James Needs,
Spencer Reeve   *Mus* Tristram Cary   *Art Dir* Bernard
Robinson, Ken Ryan
● James Donald, Andrew Keir, Barbara Shelley, Julian
Glover, Duncan Lamont, Bryan Marshall (Hammer)

A long-dormant tribe from Mars, accidentally
liberated by a London excavation, forms a
good story peg but routine, somewhat distended development blunts impact of this
British-made programmer.

Nigel Kneale's original script again turns
on the Prof. Quatermass character, essayed
by Andrew Keir, this time embroiled with a
stuffy colonel (Julian Glover) when a scientist
(James Donald) discovers skeletons in a
London subway expansion. Evil demons, brain
waves and sketchy visions of a dying Mars civilization, plus some great special effects work,
provide plot complications. Given the predictable science-vs-military conflicts, and the
introduction of Barbara Shelley as a female
scientist (like Jean Parker and Ellen Drew in
other years), film manages to retain interest
through suspenseful (if not always clear) exposition of the mysterious creatures. Roy
Ward Baker's direction is professional.

■ QUATERMASS EXPERIMENT, THE

(US: The Creeping Unknown)

1955, 81 MINS, UK ⓥ
Dir Val Guest   *Prod* Anthony Hinds   *Scr* Val Guest,
Richard Landau   *Ph* Jimmy Harvey   *Ed* James Needs
Mus James Bernard   *Art Dir* J. Elder Wills
● Brian Donlevy, Jack Warner, Richard Wordsworth,
David King-Wood, Gordon Jackson, Lionel Jeffries
(Hammer)

Taken from a BBC television play, *The
Quatermass Experiment* is an extravagant piece
of science fiction, based on the after-effects of
an assault on space by a rocket ship. Despite
its obvious horror angles, production is
crammed with incident and suspense.

Brian Donlevy (in the title role) is the scientist
who designs a new rocket that is sent hurtling
into space with three men on board. It crash
lands in a small English village, with only one
survivor. The mystery is what happened to the
other two who have disappeared without trace
although the rocket ship remained air sealed.

This is unrelieved melodrama. It draws its
entertainment from a series of wildly improb-

able happenings. There is an occasional overplus of horror closeups of the victims.

Donlevy plays the scientist with a grim and
ruthless conviction.

■ QUATERMASS 2

(US: Enemy from Space)

1957, 84 MINS, UK ⓥ ⊙
Dir Val Guest   *Prod* Anthony Hinds   *Scr* Nigel Kneale,
Val Guest   *Ph* Gerald Gibbs   *Ed* James Needs
Mus James Bernard   *Art Dir* Bernard Robinson
● Brian Donlevy, John Longden, Sydney James, Bryan
Forbes, William Franklyn, Vera Day (Hammer)

Production stars Brian Donlevy as an English
scientist engaged in interplanetary research. He
suddenly stumbles upon a hush-hush government project on the moorlands where it's announced that synthetic food is being produced,
but actually its operations are being directed by
an enemy from space, working to take over the
earth. Yarn unfolds in fine confusion, Donlevy in
some way managing to destroy the project.

Val Guest's direction is as uncertain as
script on which he collabs with Nigel Kneale
[author of original story], with the result that
all characters are stodgy. Donlevy is supported by John Longden, as a Scotland Yard
inspector trying to help; Sidney James, a
newspaper reporter; William Franklyn, a lab
assistant, and Bryan Forbes, another assistant
who comes under the out-of-this-world spell.

Special effects are imaginative.

■ QUEEN CHRISTINA

1933, 100 MINS, US ⓥ ⊙
Dir Rouben Mamoulian   *Prod* Walter Wanger   *Scr* S.
N. Behrman, Salka Viertel, H. M. Harwood   *Ph* William
Daniels   *Ed* Blanche Sewell   *Mus* Herbert Stothart
Art Dir Alexander Toluboff
● Greta Garbo, John Gilbert, Ian Keith, Lewis Stone,
Elizabeth Young, C. Aubrey Smith (M-G-M)

Chief fault with *Christina* is its lethargy. It is
slow and ofttimes stilted. This is perhaps good
cinematic motivation to establish the contrast
between the queen, who has been reared as a
boy to succeed to the Swedish throne, and the
episode in the wayside inn where she shares
her room with the new Spanish envoy who had
mistaken her for a flip Nordic youth.

The buildup of the romance fol-de-rol, after
the major climactic clinch, is a bit DeMille-Stroheim. Greta Garbo, in this sequence, for
example, consumes beaucoup footage caressing sundry pieces of furniture, fixtures and
plaques in the room, in a self-expressed purpose of memorizing every aspect thereof and
when John Gilbert asks her, 'What are you
doing?' sympathetically, the audience isn't
quite as understanding.

The background is an obviously romantic admixture of history and fiction [story by Salka
Viertel and Margaret P. Levino], touching
lightly on the protestations of the A.D. 1600
Protestant Sweden's nationals against their
queen's alliance with a Catholic from Spain.
Gilbert is the Spanish envoy who has come to
Stockholm on the expressly diplomatic and
amorous mission of asking for the queen's hand
in marriage to his king, the Spanish ruler.

Garbo's performance is too often apace of
the script's lethargy, but as often, and more,
in glamorous keeping with the romantic highlights. Her regal impression is convincing,
which counts for plenty.

That goes for almost every character, from
the humble peasants who are called upon to
manifest their deep-rooted loyalty to the Crown
in words, to the members of the royal court.

■ QUEEN KELLY

1929, 96 MINS, US ⓥ ⊙
Dir Erich Von Stroheim   *Prod* Gloria Swanson
Scr Erich Von Stroheim   *Ph* Gordon Pollock, Paul Ivano

Ed Viola Lawrence   *Mus* Adolph Tandler
Art Dir Harold Miles
● Gloria Swanson, Seena Owen, Walter Byron, Wilhelm von Brincken, Madge Hunt, Wilson Benge (Gloria/United Artists)

Queen Kelly, which Erich von Stroheim originally wrote as *The Swamp*, was the director's eighth silent picture and was undertaken at the behest of Gloria Swanson. Best guess is that Stroheim's full scenario would have played for at least five hours' running time. Film was in production less than three months, from 1 November 1928 to 21 January 1929, when Swanson, finally fed up with her director's excesses, told financier Joseph Kennedy to shut it down after an expenditure of $800,000.

Since *Queen Kelly* was shot in sequence, what exists of it plays very smoothly and coherently up through its arbitrary, but dramatically valid, conclusion. Set in the sort of fin-de-siecle Ruritanian principality usually favored by the director, tale presents the mad young Queen Regina (Seena Owen) forcing the playboy Prince Wolfram (Walter Byron) into a royal marriage.

Far from resigned to a life of amorous activity, Wolfram encounters a troup of convent girls while on cavalry drill in the country and, in a legendary scene, meets Kitty Kelly (Gloria Swanson).

As planned by the director, film would have continued ever-deeper into grand melodrama until, coming full circle, Kitty would truly have become Queen Kelly along with Wolfram, displacing Regina on the throne.

Version of the film released minimally in Europe and South America in the early 1930s ended with Kitty successfully committing suicide. Footage of her in a bordello in German East Africa was not discovered until 1963. The music score by Adolph Tandler, which was written for Swanson's 1931–32 version, was discovered on a nitrate soundtrack for use in this edition. [Version reviewed is a complete-as-possible reconstruction in 1985.]
....

■ QUEEN OF OUTER SPACE

1958, 80 MINS, US ◇ ⓦ
Dir Edward Bernds   *Prod* Ben Schwalb   *Scr* Charles Beaumont   *Ph* William Whitley   *Ed* William Austin   *Mus* Marlin Skiles   *Art Dir* David Milton
● Zsa Zsa Gabor, Eric Fleming, Laurie Mitchell, Paul Birch, Patrick Waltz, Barbara Darrow (Allied Artists)

Most of the female characters in *Queen of Outer Space* look like they would be more at home on a Minsky runway than the Cape Canaveral launching pad, but Ben Schwalb's production [based on a story by Ben Hecht] is a good-natured attempt to put some honest sex into science-fiction.

The year is 1985, and Eric Fleming, Patrick Waltz and Dave Willock are US officers in charge of a space ship assigned to check on an American satellite space station. They are deflected from their course by mysterious energy rays from the planet Venus, where their ship is eventually wrecked. Taken prisoner by a malignant queen (Laurie Mitchell), they are about to be destroyed, when they are rescued by a pro-masculine group headed by Zsa Zsa Gabor.

The cast is predominantly feminine and attractively garbed in the brief raiment that appears to be customary on other planets. Gabor makes a handsome leading lady, romanced by Fleming and the others lend the necessary ingredients to their roles.
....

■ QUEEN OF SPADES, THE

1949, 95 MINS, UK ⓦ
Dir Thorold Dickinson   *Prod* Anatole de Grunwald   *Scr* Rodney Ackland, Arthur Boys   *Ph* Otto Heller, Gus Drisse, Val Stewart   *Ed* Hazel Wilkinson   *Mus* Georges Auric   *Art Dir* Oliver Messel

● Anton Walbrook, Edith Evans, Yvonne Mitchell, Ronald Howard (Associated British Pathe)

Opulence of Imperial Russia at the beginning of the 19th century provides a colorful background for this filmization of Alexander Pushkin's short story, which brings to the screen a legend of gambling and intrigue.

Central character in the story is a captain of the Engineers. He cannot afford to gamble but is prepared to stake his all on a secret formula believed to have been passed on to a certain countess. Countess dies, but believing he has received a message from the dead, the captain goes to a gambling table and challenges his rival in love.

Outstanding performance comes from Edith Evans, making her screen debut. Her interpretation of the old grotesque countess is almost terrifying in its realism, and she dominates the screen from her first entry until her death. Anton Walbrook, and Ronald Howard as his rival in love, lack color.
....

■ QUERELLE

1982, 120 MINS, W. GERMANY/FRANCE ◇ ⓦ
Dir Rainer Werner Fassbinder   *Scr* Rainer Werner Fassbinder   *Ph* Xaver Schwarzenberger   *Ed* Juliane Lorenz   *Mus* Peer Raben   *Art Dir* Rolf Zehetbauer
● Brad Davis, Franco Nero, Jeanne Moreau, Laurent Malet, Hanno Poschl, Gunther Kaufman (Planet/Gaumont)

The last film of Rainer Werner Fassbinder is, unfortunately, disappointing. His attempt to put the mystical homosexual world of French writer Jean Genet on film is ultimately tedious.

There is curio value in this strange tale of a young sailor, Querelle, who fascinates all who come in contact with him but who seems more absorbed in himself.

It seems to be set in the 1930s but is timeless and stylized. A boat on which Querelle works pulls into a port in Brest, France. Film is all studio work without any pretense at realism. It ties up at a jetty which has a bar and a bordello run by Jeanne Moreau. Querelle, played with a sort of dreamlike intensity by Brad Davis, is soon mixed up in this strange world.
....

■ QUEST FOR FIRE

1981, 97 MINS, FRANCE/CANADA ◇ ⓦ ⊙
Dir Jean-Jacques Annaud   *Prod* Denis Heroux, John Kemeny, Jacques Dorfmann   *Scr* Gerard Brach   *Ph* Claude Agostini   *Ed* Yves Langlois   *Mus* Philippe Sarde   *Art Dir* Brian Morris
● Everett McGill, Rae Dawn Chong, Ron Perlman, Nameer El Kadi, Gary Schwartz, Kurt Schiegel (ICC/Belstar/Stephan)

Jean-Jacques Annaud's *Quest for Fire* is an engaging prehistoric yarn that happily never degenerates into a club and lion skin spinoff of *Star Wars* and resolutely refuses to bludgeon the viewer with facile or gratuitous effects.

Despite four years of effort, a $12 million budget, grueling location shooting in Kenya, Scotland, Iceland and Canada, hundreds of masks and costumes and a herd of difficult elephants (making their screen apperance as mammoths), Annaud and his collaborators have brought off a polished entertainment.

Technical advisor Anthony Burgess invented special primitive jargons for the occasion, which are used in moderation and don't jar comically on the ears.

Gerard Brach's screenplay is loosely based on Jean-Henri Rosny the Elder's *La guerre du feu* (1911), a classic of French language popular literature. He also introduces a female character as a major dramatic and emotional pivot.

Three warriors of a primitive homo sapiens tribe are sent out to find a source of fire after

their old pilot lights are extinguished during an attack by a group of unneighborly Neanderthals. After numerous adventures they find a fire amongst a cannibal tribe, but also learn how to produce it when they are led to an advanced human community by a young girl whom they've saved from the cannibals.

Annaud wisely uses mimes, dancers, acrobats and stuntmen for many of the secondary and extra roles. Under the guidance of anthropologist Desmond Morris, they provide credible physical expression under their excellent masks and makeup.

Everett McGill, New York stage actor Ron Perlman, and Turkish-born Nameer El Kadi etch engaging portraits as the three early homo sapiens, but the best performance comes from 20-year-old Rae Dawn Chong (daughter of comic Tommy Chong), unaffectedly radiant as the tribal nymphet who teaches them how to make a fire and eventually mates with McGill (after showing him how to make love face-to-face).
□ 1982: Best Make-Up
....

■ QUICK CHANGE

1990, 88 MINS, US ◇ ⓦ ⊙
Dir Howard Franklin, Bill Murray   *Prod* Robert Greenhut, Bill Murray   *Scr* Howard Franklin   *Ph* Michael Chapman   *Ed* Alan Heim   *Mus* Randy Edelman   *Art Dir* David Gropman
● Bill Murray, Geena Davis, Randy Quaid, Jason Robards, Bob Elliott, Philip Bosco (Warner/Devoted)

Bill Murray delivers a smart, sardonic and very funny valentine to the rotten Apple in *Quick Change*. Pic became Murray's directing debut (he shares the chores with screenwriter Howard Franklin) after he and Franklin became too attached to the project to bring anyone else in. Material, based on Jay Cronley's book, is neither ambitious nor particularly memorable, but it's brought off with a sly flair that makes it most enjoyable.

Murray plays a fed-up New Yorker who enlists his girlfriend (Geena Davis) and lifelong pal (Randy Quaid) in a bank heist so they can get outta town. Hold-up, which nets $1 million and a very nice watch, sets off a carnival of police and crowd reaction in the New York streets, but none of it flaps the dynamite-rigged Murray.

With Jason Robards as a crusty police inspector who's as crazily sharp as *Twin Peaks* agent Cooper, pic offers some crazy little set-pieces in a manic game of chase. Pic is so thick with gritty, tired, scuzzy NY atmosphere viewer wants to scrape it off the skin.

Only in the final reel do things feel broadly contrived, concurrent with pic's move from NY locations to a Florida soundstage for airport shooting.
....

■ QUICK MILLIONS

1931, 69 MINS, US
Dir Rowland Brown   *Scr* Courtenay Terrett, Rowland Brown, John Wray   *Ph* Joseph August   *Ed* Harold Schuster   *Art Dir* Duncan Cramer
● Spencer Tracy, Marguerite Churchill, Sally Eilers, Robert Burns, John Wray, Warner Richmond (Fox)

Another gangster story, but written down to the bone and directed for everything it contains.

For continuity and cutting the studio handed Brown a bonus of $1,000. It's Rowland Brown's first picture. Previously he was a Fox contract writer. His co-author on this story, like himself, is a former newspaper reporter. Courtenay Terrett once wrote a story called *Only Saps Work*, and Paramount took it along with Terrett.

The background of *Quick Millions* is similar and takes the eye through a cleverly-knit panorama of racketeering as the yoke is laid on big business interests.

Story, after a fashion, gives an inside on how racketeers prey on organized business. In brief, it recounts the tale of a tough truck driver, with ideas, who climbs to the top, even socially, through forcing contractors into the right corner, only to topple from his throne at the hands of rival gangsters after turned down by the girl, a contractor's daughter. Simple, but the force, interest, suspense and the benefit of capable workmanship.

Spencer Tracy is excellent. Sally Eilers looks well at all times, and that's about all she has to do. Marguerite Churchill, as the former sweetheart, has the better of it from a script viewpoint. Robert Burns, Warner Richmond and George Raft are good gangster types. Contractor racket victim John Wray, who did the added dialog, oke.

■ QUIET AMERICAN, THE

1958, 120 MINS, US

Dir Joseph L. Mankiewicz *Prod* Joseph L. Mankiewicz
Scr Joseph L. Mankiewicz *Ph* Robert Krasker
Ed William Hornbeck *Mus* Mario Nascimbene
Art Dir Rino Mondinello
● Audie Murphy, Michael Redgrave, Claude Dauphin, Giorgia Moll, Kerima, Bruce Cabot (United Artists/Figaro)

In adapting Graham Greene's bitter and cynical *The Quiet American* into a motion picture, Joseph L. Mankiewicz has allowed himself the luxury of turning the screen into a debating society. It might have paid off had he retained the central character of the American in the book who, in Greene's version, represented all the determined bungling of Ameican foreign policy. As it turns out, the film – shot in Vietnam and at Cinecitta Studios in Rome – is an overlong, overdialogued adaptation, concerned with the pros and cons of a Third Force in Asia.

Story follows the line of the book, but with the all-important difference that the character of the American, played without much depth by Audie Murphy, has been drained of meaning, giving the whole picture a pro-American slant. Murphy here doesn't represent the US government, but merely works for a private US aid mission. In other words, his ideas of a Third Force standing between Communism and French Colonialism are his own.

It's one long flashback from the moment Murphy is found murdered and Michael Redgrave, playing a British correspondent, is asked by French inspector Claude Dauphin to identify him. Dauphin gradually unspools the sometimes obscure story.

Love interest in the film is pretty newcomer Giorgia Moll who lives with Redgrave but leaves him for the younger Murphy. Running throughout is the clashing of views between Redgrave and Murphy.

Redgrave's moody portrayal of the neurotic aging Britisher hiding personal anxieties under a mask of cynicism makes the whole thing worthwhile.

The Quiet American has been photographed skillfully, though the number of scenes showing off Vietnam (the story is laid in 1952, before the partition) isn't very large.

■ QUIET DAYS IN CLICHY

1970, 100 MINS, DENMARK

Dir Jens-Jorgen Thorsen *Scr* Jens-Jorgen Thorsen
Ph Jesper Hom *Ed* Anker *Mus* Country Joe McDonald, Ben Webster, Andy Sunstrom
● Louise White, Paul Valjean, Wayne John Rodda, Ulla Lemvig-Muller, Susanne Krage (SBA)

This is a true-to-the-letter re-telling of Henry Miller's memoir about Montmartre life, with very little food and many, many women.

Director Jens-Jorgen Thorsen shows both technical skill and madcap humor and, furthermore, knows more than a little about the loneliness dimension of Miller's work.

Paul Valjean looks like the popular image of Henry Miller, easygoing, nice, lecherous, hungry and full of fun. Among the girls who indulge in unlimited frontal nudity, Louise White, Ulla Lemvig-Muller and Susanne Krage have the rather spectacular achievement of making the audience remember their faces as well as their bodies.

■ QUIET EARTH, THE

1985, 100 MINS, NEW ZEALAND

Dir Geoff Murphy *Prod* Don Reynolds, Sam Pillsbury
Scr Bill Baer, Bruno Lawrence, Sam Pillsbury *Ph* James Bartle *Ed* Michael Horton *Mus* John Charles
Art Dir Rick Kofoed
● Bruno Lawrence, Alison Routledge, Peter Smith (Cinepro/Pillsbury)

One of Neww Zealand's top directors, Geoff Murphy has taken a man-alone theme and turned it imaginatively to strong and refreshing effect in *The Quiet Earth*.

Plot centers on scientist Zac Hobson (Bruno Lawrence) who wakes one morning to discover he is alone in the world. A global top-secret energy project he has been working on has malfunctioned and altered the fabric of the universe. While humanity appears to be wiped out, all its materialistic trappings remain. For a time, Zac lives out his fantasies.

Then begins a search for other survivors. He finds two – a woman, Joanne (Alison Routledge), and a man, Api (Peter Smith). The emotions unleashed by this trio in their struggle for survival propels the story, which has an intriguing mystical dimension, to a shattering conclusion.

The film is notable for high production values. Acting isn't far behind. Lawrence, a veteran of NZ films turns in a performance that is funny and moving, while Maori actor Smith makes a bold debut. But it is Alison Routledge who is the real find. Possessing a special, delicate, Madonna-like beauty, she invests Joanne with sparky intelligence and strength.

■ QUIET MAN, THE

1952, 129 MINS, US

Dir John Ford *Prod* John Ford, Merian C. Cooper
Scr Frank S. Nugent *Ph* Winton C. Hoch *Ed* Jack Murray *Mus* Victor Young *Art Dir* Frank Hotaling
● John Wayne, Maureen O'Hara, Victor McLaglen, Barry Fitzgerald, Ward Bond, Mildred Natwick (Argosy/Republic)

This is a robust romantic drama of a native-born's return to Ireland. Director John Ford took cast and cameras to Ireland to tell the story [by Maurice Walsh] against actual backgrounds.

Wayne is the quiet man of the title, returning to the land of his birth to forget a life of struggle and violence. In Inisfree, Wayne buys the cottage where he was born, immediately arousing the ire of Victor McLaglen, a well-to-do farmer who wanted the property himself.

His next mistake is to fall for Maureen O'Hara, McLaglen's sister. Custom decrees the brother must give consent to marriage, so Wayne's suit is hopeless until newly-made friends are able to trick McLaglen long enough to get the ceremony over with. Safely married, Wayne finds himself with a bride but not a wife.

Despite the length of the footage, film holds together by virtue of a number of choice characters, the best of which is Barry Fitzgerald's socko punching of an Irish type. Wayne works well under Ford's direction, answering all demands of the vigorous, physical character.

□ 1952: Best Director, Color Cinematography.

□ Nominations: Best Picture, Supp. Actor (Victor McLaglen), Screenplay, Color Art Direction, Sound

■ QUIGLEY DOWN UNDER

1990, 119 MINS, US

Dir Simon Wincer *Prod* Stanley O'Toole *Scr* John Hill
Ph David Eggby *Ed* Adrian Carr, Peter Burgess
Mus Basil Poledouris *Art Dir* Ross Major
● Tom Selleck, Laura San Giacomo, Alan Rickman, Chris Haywood, Ron Haddrick, Tony Bonner (M-G-M/Pathe)

Quigley Down Under is an exquisitely crafted, rousing western made in Oz.

Script was written for Steve McQueen in the 1970s, then developed in 1984, Rick Rosenthal to helm; project was reactivated in 1986 with Lewis Gilbert scheduled to direct.

Tom Selleck is in the title role as a sharp-shooter from the American West who answers villain Alan Rickman's ad and heads to Fremantle in Western Australia. Quigley is informed that he's been hired to kill aborigines with his long-range, custom-made rifle as part of Rickman's campaign of genocide, encouraged by the local authorities.

Sellec's violent response to the request begins a vendetta is which Rickman has him left for dead in the middle of nowhere. Along for the ensuing survival trek is Laura San Giacomo, a fellow American haunted by the death of her child in a Comanche raid.

Selleck has his best bigscreen casting so far here (not counting the missed opportunity to be Indiana Jones). He's thoroughly convincing with his custom-made rifle and low-key manner. San Giacomo comes into her own as the feisty heroine. Rickman is a perfectly cast hissable villain.

■ QUILLER MEMORANDUM, THE

1966, 103 MINS, UK

Dir Michael Anderson *Prod* Ivan Foxwell *Scr* Harold Pinter *Ph* Erwin Hiller *Ed* Freddie Wilson *Mus* John Barry *Art Dir* Maurice Carter
● George Segal, Alec Guinness, Max von Sydow, Senta Berger, George Sanders, Robert Helpmann (Rank)

The Quiller Memorandum, based on a novel by Adam Hall (pen name for Elleston Trevor) and with a screenplay by Harold Pinter, deals with the insidious upsurge of neo-Nazism in Germany. It relies on a straight narrative storyline, simple but holding, literate dialog and well-drawn characters.

Set largely on location in West Berlin, it has George Segal brought back from vacation to replace a British agent who has come to a sticky end at the hands of a new infiltrating group of Nazis. His job is to locate their headquarters. He does this in a lone-wolf way, refusing to be hampered by bodyguards. En route he has some edgy adventures.

Segal plays Quiller with a laconic but likeable detachment, underlining the loneliness and lack of relaxation of the agent, who cannot even count on support from his own side. Alec Guinness never misses a trick in his few scenes as the cold, witty fish in charge of Berlin sector investigations. Max von Sydow plays the Nazi chief quietly but with high camp menace.

■ QUINTET

1979, 118 MINS, US

Dir Robert Altman *Prod* Robert Altman *Scr* Frank Barhydt, Robert Altman, Patricia Resnick *Ph* Jean Boffety
Ed Dennis M. Hill *Mus* Tom Pierson *Art Dir* Leon Ericksen
● Paul Newman, Vittorio Gassman, Fernando Rey, Bibi Andersson, Brigitte Fossey, Nina Van Pallandt (Lion's Gate)

Here's another one for Robert Altman's inner circle.

In one of the few obvious points about the picture [based on a story by Altman, Lionel Chetwynd and Patricia Resnick], the title refers to a game popular in some future city (Montreal?) that's slowly dying in a new Ice Age. Though the finer details are anybody's guess, the game involves five players trying to eliminate each other, plus a sixth who comes late to the board.

Paul Newman arrives in the city with his young pregnant bride (Brigitte Fossey) and finds some of the citizens playing the game for real, with Fernando Rey as referee. After losing his bride to a bomb, Newman is drawn into the game.

Before it's over, there have been two bloody throat slashings, a hand bursting open in a fire and one vigorous stabbing.

· ·

■ QUO VADIS

1951, 171 MINS, US ◇ ⓥ

Dir Mervyn LeRoy   *Prod* Sam Zimbalist   *Scr* John Lee Mahin, S. H. Behrman, Sonya Levien   *Ph* Robert Surtees, William V. Skall   *Ed* Ralph E. Winters   *Mus* Miklos Rozsa   *Art Dir* Cedric Gibbons, William Horning, Edward Carfagno, Hugh Hunt
● Robert Taylor, Deborah Kerr, Leo Genn, Peter Ustinov, Patricia Laffan, Finlay Currie (M-G-M)

Quo Vadis is a super-spectacle in all its meaning. That there are shortcomings [in this fourth version of the tale] even Metro must have recognized and ignored in consideration of the project's scope. The captiousness about the story line, some of the players' wooden performances in contrast to the scenery-chewing of Peter Ustinov (Nero), are part and parcel of any super-spectacular.

The contrast, of course, is sharp in that Leo Genn's slick underplaying makes Ustinov's sybarite conception of Nero that much more out of focus with realities. But the Polish novelist, Henryk Sienkiewicz, intended to contrast the glory that was Rome and the splendor that was Nero's court with the travails of the early Christians.

While the Romans worship their idols and vestal virgins, while Nero rules a still-lush if decadent court in its final stage of cowardice, wickedness and degeneracy, Robert Taylor is shown leading his victorious Roman troops down the Appian Way. Deborah Kerr, as a Christian hostage, is the vis-a-vis. Genn, as the suave Petronius, who constantly derides the stupid Nero, has Marina Berti, a beauteous slave girl, as his romantic opposite.

There are no ups and downs on the spectacular values that comprise the Circus of Nero, the profligate court scenes, the marching armies, the racing chariots, the burning of Rome, the shackled captives under Roman rule, the pagan ceremonies, the secret Christian meetings, the gladiators unto the death to amuse Nero's court, and the climax as the Christian martyrs face the unleashed lions in the great Circus of Nero.
□ 1951: Nominations: Best Picture, Supp. Actor (Leo Genn, Peter Ustinov), Color Cinematography, Color Costume Design, Color Art Direction, Editing, Scoring of a Dramatic Picture

· ·

■ RABID

1977, 91 MINS, CANADA ◇ ⓥ

Dir David Cronenberg   *Prod* John Dunning   *Scr* David Cronenberg   *Ph* Rene Verzier   *Ed* Jean Lafleur   *Mus* Ivan Reitman (sup.)   *Art Dir* Claude Marchand
● Marilyn Chambers, Frank Moore, Joe Silver, Howard Ryshpan, Patricia Gage, Susan Roman (Cinema Entertainment)

Rabid, as the dictionary explains means both 'affected with rabies' and 'extremely violent'. Using both definitions, *Rabid*, is so accurately titled that this one word tells all. Here is an extremely violent, sometimes nauseating, picture about a young woman affected with rabies, running around Montreal infecting others.

Marilyn Chambers, the Whilone Procter & Gamble Ivory Snow girl turned porno film actress, plays the infected one – sort of a cross between Typhoid Mary with rabies and a vampire.

On the one side in the urban jungle are human animals, foaming at the mouth, biting each other in shopping malls, operating rooms and subway cars. On the other side are animals of another sort shooting down those salivating the green foam.

· ·

■ RACE WITH THE DEVIL

1975, 88 MINS, US ◇ ⓥ

Dir Jack Starrett   *Prod* Wes Bishop   *Scr* Wes Bishop, Lee Frost   *Ph* Robert Jessup   *Ed* Alan Jacobs   *Mus* Leonard Rosenman
● Peter Fonda, Warren Oates, Loretta Swit, Lara Parker, R.G. Armstrong, Clay Tanner (20th Century-Fox)

A followup to *Dirty Mary Crazy Larry*, this meller includes the requisite road chases and other hyped-up thrills, some of them slickly executed by director Jack Starrett. Otherwise the production is a sloppy, cynical blend of second-hand plot elements.

Patchwork screenplay also uses story elements from horror pix as it pits vacationing Peter Fonda, Warren Oates and their wives Lara Parker and Loretta Swit against a horde of rampaging Satanists in the Texas backwoods. Pic seems to be trying at times for an archetypal confrontation between middle-American values, as repped by the couples in their fortress-like motor home, and bizarre counter-culture elements.

The film's action highlight is a slam-bang duel between the camper and several trucks, but generally the pic is done with perfunctory TV-like stylelessness.

Oates does his usual believably gritty job with the meagre character material here. Fonda is less dreamy than usual, though still without evoking much interest.

· ·

■ RACHEL AND THE STRANGER

1948, 92 MINS, US ⓥ ⊙

Dir Norman Foster   *Prod* Richard H. Berger   *Scr* Waldo Salt   *Ph* Maury Gertsman   *Ed* Les Millbrook   *Mus* Roy Webb   *Art Dir* Albert S. D'Agostino, Jack Okey, Walter E. Keller
● Loretta Young, William Holden, Robert Mitchum, Gary Gray, Tom Tulley, Sara Haden (RKO)

Mood of the picture is pleasant but is so even that interest isn't too strong. Dangers of pioneering in a wilderness, vaguely referred to as the northwest, could have been more excitingly depicted. Single incident of excitement – a strong one – is put off until the finale and has a socko Indian raid on a settler's homestead in the wilds.

Otherwise, narrative maintains its even pace in telling story of a pioneer who buys a bride to do the chores and teach niceties of life to his motherless son. The bride is only a servant until a hunter, friend of the groom, appears and makes a play for her.

William Holden enacts the dour settler, so deeply in love with his dead wife he fails to appreciate, or even notice, the charms of his new bondswoman bride. Loretta Young has only two costume changes and her makeup is true to role, but she makes some glamour shine through. Robert Mitchum is the aimlessly wandering hunter.

· ·

■ RACHEL PAPERS, THE

1989, 95 MINS, UK ◇ ⓥ

Dir Damian Harris   *Prod* Andrew S. Karsch   *Scr* Damion Harris   *Ph* Alex Thomson   *Ed* David Martin   *Mus* Chaz Jenkel   *Art Dir* Andrew McAlpine
● Dexter Fletcher, Ione Skye, Jonathan Pryce, James Spader, Bill Patterson, Michael Gambon (Initial/Longfellow)

Charles Highway is a 19-year-old with no money problems who maps out his sexual conquests via his desktop. He meets beautiful American Rachel Noyce, also 19. It's love at first sight, but she already has a boyfriend.

After a bit of frustration, he sends her a funny love message on videotape, and she comes around. They have a steamy, passionate affair, of which he tires all too soon. They part. End of story.

The basic material is as old as the hills, but Martin Amis, who wrote the original novel some 15 years earlier, explored it in fresh directions. Director Damian Harris isn't able to capture the book's special charms, and resorts to having his young hero address the camera to keep the viewer in the picture. Unfortunately, Dexter Fletcher is rather too self-conscious here, and makes Charles a less than endearing hero. On the other hand, Ione Skye seizes her chances as Rachel and gives a glowingly sensual performance. Their lengthy loves scenes together, often in a bathtub, are certainly steamy.

· ·

■ RACHEL, RACHEL

1968, 101 MINS, US ◇ ⓥ

Dir Paul Newman   *Prod* Paul Newman   *Scr* Stewart Stern   *Ph* Gayne Rescher   *Ed* Dede Allen   *Mus* Jerome Moross   *Art Dir* Robert Gundlach
● Joanne Woodward, James Olson, Kate Harrington, Estelle Parsons, Donald Moffatt, Terry Kiser (Warner/Seven Arts)

Rachel, Rachel is a low-key melodrama starring Joanne Woodward as a spinster awakening to life. Produced austerely by Paul Newman, who also directs with an uncertain hand, it marks Newman's feature debut in these nonacting capacities. Offbeat film moves too slowly to an upbeat, ironic climax.

Margaret Laurence's novel, *A Jest of God*, has been adapted into an episodic, halting screenplay which not only conveys the tedium of Woodward's adult life but also, unfortunately, takes its time in so doing.

There is very little dialog – most of which is very good – but this asset makes a liability out of the predominantly visual nature of the development, which in time seems to become redundant, padded and tiring.

James Olson, a childhood friend who has returned for a visit, provides Woodward with an alternative. Believing herself pregnant by Olson, she determines to have the child.

Direction is awkward. Were Woodward not there film could have been a shambles.
□ 1968: Nominations: Best Picture, Actress (Joanne Woodward), Supp. Actress (Estelle Parsons), Adapted Screenplay

· ·

■ RACING WITH THE MOON

1984, 108 MINS, US ◇ ⓥ ⊙

Dir Richard Benjamin   *Prod* Alain Bernheim, John Kohn   *Scr* Steven Kloves   *Ph* John Bailey   *Ed* Jacqueline

Cambas *Mus* Dave Grusin *Art Dir* David L. Snyder
● Sean Penn, Elizabeth McGovern, Nicolas Cage, John Karlen, Rutanya Alda, Kate Williamson (Paramount)

Racing with the Moon is a sweet, likable film that doesn't contain the usual commercial elements normally expected these days in youth pics. Working in a more straightforward, serious mode, Richard Benjamin confirms the directorial promise he dipslayed in *My Favorite Year*, and Sean Penn and Elizabeth McGovern are good as the romantic leads.

Time frame is Christmas of 1942, and Penn and his rowdy buddy Nicolas Cage have just a few weeks left until they join the Marines. Penn becomes dazzled by a new face (McGovern) in the California coastal town, whom he takes to be a rich girl since she lives up in the 'Gatsby' mansion. While Cage, a wrong-side-of-the-tracks type, gets his g.f. pregnant, and after a disastrous, but wonderfully staged, attempt to hustle some sailors at pool, Penn forces himself to enlist McGovern's help in raising $150 for an abortion for his friend's gal.

First-time scenarist Steven Kloves has created two nice leading characters, nicely essayed by Penn and McGovern.

Benjamin shows a consistently generous attitude toward his characters and an inclination to emphasize their most exemplary traits.

● ●

■ RACKET, THE

1928, 70 MINS, US ⊗
Dir Lewis Milestone *Prod* Howard Hughes *Scr* Harry Behn, Del Andrews, Bartlett Cormack, Eddie Adams *Ph* Tony Gaudio *Ed* Tom Miranda
● Thomas Meighan, Marie Prevost, Louis Wolheim, George Stone, John Darrow, Richard 'Skeets' Gallagher (Paramount/Caddo)

A good story, plus good direction, plus a great cast and minus dumb supervision, is responsible for another great underworld film.

Thomas Meighan has his best role in years as Captain McQuigg, and Louis Wolheim, as Nick Scarsi, adds to a screen rep that has already labeled him the best character heavy, the one-eyed monster has ever pecked at.

The Racket, like all great pictures, started with a great yarn [from Bartlett Cormack's play] and a director alive to its possibilities. It grips your interest from the first shot to the last, and never drags for a second. It's another tale of the underworld, a battle of wills and cunning between an honest copper and a gorilla who has the town in his lap.

Tom Miranda was given wide latitude with slang and gun chatter and the result is the most authentic set of titles that have graced an underworld picture to date. The gorillas talk as they should and not act as some lame-brained obstructionist thinks they should. They don't go to jail – they go to the can – and without those diagrams the average super wants with any title in vernacular.

And shades of Beverly Hills, there's no love interest! Imagine a hero who doesn't cop a moll in the last ten feet.

Boy, page the millenium!
☐ 1927/28: Nomination: Best Picture

● ●

■ RACKET, THE

1951, 89 MINS, US ⓥ ⊙
Dir John Cromwell *Prod* Edmund Grainger *Scr* William Wister Haines, W.R. Burnett *Ph* George E. Diskant *Ed* Sherman Todd *Mus* Constantin Bakaleinikoff (dir.) *Art Dir* Albert S. D'Agostino
● Robert Mitchum, Lizabeth Scott, Robert Ryan, William Talman, Ray Collins, Joyce MacKenzie (RKO)

This remake of Bartlett Cormack's old play has been handled to emphasize clearcut action and suspense and the casting is just right to stress the rough and ready toughness in the script.

Robert Mitchum is the honest police captain pitted against Robert Ryan, the mobster, and both dominate the picture with forceful

credible performances that add a lot of interest. Further masculine attention is gained through the strong work of William Talman as a rookie cop, the pairing of Ray Collins and William Conrad as crooked politicians, and other assorted male castes.

Development is enlivened with some solid thriller sequences, such as a rooftop fight between Mitchum and a gunman, careening autos and crashes, and gunplay between the forces of good and evil.

Femme interest is at a minimum, but Lizabeth Scott, as a nitery singer does what she has to do well.

● ●

■ RADIO DAYS

1987, 85 MINS, US ◇ ⓥ ⊙
Dir Woody Allen *Prod* Robert Greenhut *Scr* Woody Allen *Ph* Carlo Di Palma *Ed* Susan E. Morse *Mus* Dick Hyman (sup.) *Art Dir* Santo Loquasto
● Mia Farrow, Seth Green, Julie Kavner, Josh Mostel, Michael Tucker, Dianne Wiest (Orion)

Although lacking the bite and depth of his best work, *Radio Days* is one of Woody Allen's most purely entertaining pictures. It's a visual monolog of bits and pieces from the glory days of radio and the people who were tuned in.

Rockaway Beach, a thin strip of land on the outskirts of New York City is where young Joe (Seth Green) and his family live in not-so splendid harmony and for entertainment and escape to listen to the radio. Set at the start of World War II, it's a world of aunts and uncles all living on top of each other and the magical events and people, real and imagined, that forever shape one's young imagination.

Radio Days is not simply about nostalgia, but the quality of memory and how what one remembers informs one's present life.

Dianne Wiest is delicious as an aunt who is desperate to find a husband but somehow keeps meeting Mr Wrong. The robust Masked Avenger is, in real life, the diminutive Wallace Shawn. Mia Farrow is a none-too-bright cigaret girl with a yen for stardom who magically transforms her life.
☐ 1987: Nominations: Best Original Screenplay, Art Direction

● ●

■ RADIO FLYER

1992, 113 MINS, US ◇ ⓥ ⊙
Dir Richard Donner *Prod* Lauren Schuler-Donner *Scr* David Mickey Evans *Ph* Laszlo Kovacs *Ed* Stuart Baird *Mus* Hans Zimmer *Art Dir* J. Michael Riva
● Lorraine Bracco, John Heard, Adam Baldwin, Elijah Wood, Ben Johnson, Tom Hanks (Columbia/Stonebridge)

Radio Flyer is a film one would like to like more. Underdeveloped screenplay about two boys' fantasy of escape from an abusive stepfather is sometimes moving but too often distant and literal-minded.

David Mickey Evans started the pic in June 1990 with Rosanna Arquette as the mother, but the first time writer-director was soon fired. Production shut down before new director Richard Donner moved the setting of the late 1960s story from LA to rustic northern California.

Film builds a quiet sense of dread as the boys, who feel they can't confide in their distracted mother (Lorraine Bracco), spend as little time as possible in a home that has become a purgatory. Elijah Wood, the older, has a believable mixture of strength and timidity in his attempts to protect Joseph Mazzello from the (mostly off-screen) beatings by their drunken stepfather (Adam Baldwin). Mazzello, terrific as Baldwin's stoic victim, gives the film much of its intermittent emotional power.

Pic, however, has a feeling of distance reinforced by some major screenplay gaps and by heavy-handed narration read by unbilled Tom Hanks. As the grown-up Wood, Hanks bookends the film by telling his own sons what

happened to their uncle. Only pic's last part, with the boys building and launching their flying machine, has a magical feeling.

● ●

■ RAFFERTY AND THE GOLD DUST TWINS

1975, 91 MINS, US ◇ ⓥ
Dir Dick Richards *Prod* Michael Gruscoff, Art Linson *Scr* John Kaye *Ph* Ralph Woolsey *Ed* Walter Thompson *Mus* Artie Butler *Art Dir* Joel Schiller
● Alan Arkin, Sally Kellerman, Mackenzie Phillips, Alex Rocco, Charles Martin Smith, Harry Dean Stanton (Warner)

Rafferty and the Gold Dust Twins is another sterile Warner Bros. comedy-drama about the 'little people' of America, as seen through the eyes of Beverly Hills and Upper Manhattan. Alan Arkin stars as a loutish bumbler, fraudulently kidnapped by Sally Kellerman and teenager Mackenzie Phillips, into an odyssey through many lower class southwest locations.

Arkin's stereotyped Everyman clod meshes awkwardly with spaced-out Kellerman's formula characterization, thereby throwing interest by default to Phillips (the mature moppet of *American Graffiti*) in another good streetwise role.

Harry Dean Stanton in a very good part as an embittered yahoo, and Charlie Martin Smith (also from *Graffiti*) are among the more effective supporting players.

● ●

■ RAFFLES

1930, 70 MINS, US
Dir Harry D'Arrast, George Fitzmaurice *Prod* Samuel Goldwyn *Scr* Sidney Howard *Ph* George Barnes, Gregg Toland *Ed* Stuart Heisler *Art Dir* William Cameron Menzies, Park French
● Ronald Colman, Kay Francis, David Torrence, Frances Dade, Alison Skipworth, Bramwell Fletcher (Goldwyn)

The old-fashioned artifices of the [original 1899 novel *The Amateur Cracksman* by E.W. Hornung and its subsequent dramatization] are incidental. The essence of its interest is a rascal so captivating that you are pleased to see him emerge triumphant, though guilty, from his brush with Scotland Yard.

Picture version capitalizes such instinctive feeling, by actually having the defeated Inspector K. McKenzie take his final trimming with a philosophical grin.

Kay Francis is a happy choice – an actress with that suggestion of reserve vitality that makes her stand out strongly.

Comedy sequences supplied by Alison Skipworth and Frederick Kerr, the sentimental British dowager and her absurd spouse, have a good deal of freshness and reality. In like manner, the picture's atmosphere impresses as thoroughly authentic.
☐ 1929/30: Nomination: Best Sound

● ●

■ RAGE

1966, 103 MINS, US/MEXICO ◇ ⓥ
Dir Gilberto Gazcon *Prod* Gilberto Gazcon *Scr* Teddi Sherman, Gilberto Gazcon, Fernando Mendez *Ph* Rosalio Solano *Ed* Carlos Savage, Walter Thompson *Mus* Gustavo Cesar Carreon
● Glenn Ford, Stella Stevens, David Reynoso, Armando Silvestre, Ariadna Wellter, Jose Elias Moreno (Schenck/Jalisco)

Rage, a joint Mexican-American production lensed entirely below the Border, is a moderately interesting story of a doctor's frantic race against time to reach a hospital for the Pasteur treatment against rabies.

Glenn Ford and Stella Stevens are the only Americans in cast, balance recruited wholly from Mexican ranks. Although Mexican-made, pic was shot in English.

Ford plays a guilt-ridden physician half-bent upon self-destruction, haunted by memory of the death of his wife and child, for which he blames himself. His base of operations is a

R

construction camp practically in the wilderness. Nipped by his pet dog, he finds later it has rabies, and figures he has only about 48 hours to reach a medical center where he may be treated. With Stevens, a hooker who has been in the camp, he races thru desert and mountain in an attempt to reach the hospital.

Good suspense is worked up in situation and writer-director Gilberto Gazcon maintains mood realistically. Ford etches a rugged characterization, particularly as panic begins to take hold in what appears to be a hopeless effort in reaching the hospital in time.

....

■ **RAGE**

1972, 99 MINS, US ◇ ⑰

Dir George C. Scott   *Prod* Fred Weintraub   *Scr* Philip Friedman, Dan Kleinman   *Ph* Fred Koenekamp   *Ed* Michael Kahn   *Mus* Lalo Schifrin   *Art Dir* Frank Sylos
● George C. Scott, Richard Basehart, Martin Sheen, Barnard Hughes, Nicolas Beauvy, Paul Stevens (Warner/Weintraub)

Rage is a sluggish, tried and tiring melodrama, starring George C. Scott, in his directorial debut, as a father wreaking vengeance for the death of his son after a chemical warfare experimental accident. Though largely a western states exterior film, the plot is a stagey, talky effort reminiscent of a 1950s TV anthology drama.

Writers start on a promising track – establishing widower Scott's relationship with son Nicolas Beauvy, and engendering suspense when the boy and the family cattle suddenly begin to drop like flies. Even further, the efforts of the US Army and other government officials to hush the goof from press and Scott are dramatized in an all-too-credible way. But the story resolution becomes a shambles as Scott begins killing and blowing up installations.

....

■ **RAGE IN HARLEM, A**

1991, 108 MINS, US ◇ ⑰ ⊙

Dir Bill Duke   *Prod* Stephen Woolley, Kerry Boyle   *Scr* John Toles-Bey, Bobby Crawford   *Ph* Toyomichi Kurita   *Ed* Curtiss Clayton   *Mus* Elmer Bernstein   *Art Dir* Steven Legler
● Forest Whitaker, Gregory Hines, Robin Givens, Zakes Mokae, Danny Glover, John Toles-Bey (Palace/Miramax)

Director Bill Duke has brought a stylish sheen to *A Rage in Harlem*, but his mix of comedy and violence in the Chester Himes period crime tale is dubious. Many will be turned off by the excessive bloodshed, but the fine cast keeps the pic watchable.

Though not promoted as such, *Rage* is a followup to the Himes film adaptations *Cotton Comes to Harlem* (1970) and *Come Back, Charleston Blue* (1972). Here the novelist's cynical police detective protagonists Coffin Ed Johnson and Grave Digger Jones are relegated to secondary parts as the criminals take centerstage.

The raffish humor that made *Cotton Comes to Harlem* so delightful is only fitfully present. Co-producer Forest Whitaker, as an innocent mortuary accountant sucked into a plot involving stolen gold transported to 1956 Harlem from Mississippi, provides amiable but overdone antics in the lead role.

Pudgy mama's boy Whitaker keeps large pictures of Jesus and his stolid mother framed over his bed, occasioning jokes that become progressively less funny. And when he falls for Southern siren Robin Givens, he falls predictably hard. Givens holds the screen with assurance, though she works a bit too hard at the coy and sultry bits.

....

■ **RAGE TO LIVE, A**

1965, 101 MINS, US

Dir Walter Grauman   *Prod* Lewis J. Rachmil   *Scr* John T. Kelley   *Ph* Charles Lawton   *Ed* Stuart Gilmore   *Mus* Nelson Riddle   *Art Dir* James Sullivan

● Suzanne Pleshette, Bradford Dillman, Ben Gazzara, Peter Graves, Bethel Leslie, James Gregory (Mirisch/United Artists)

In this banal transfer from tome to film, the characters in John O'Hara's *A Rage to Live* have retained their two-dimensional unreality in a country-club setting. Nympho heroine goes from man to man amidst corny dialog and inept direction which combine to smother all thesps.

Director Walter Grauman achieves little with the players, nor does he attempt to hypo visual interest via technical gimmicks.

Thesps share the guilt. Suzanne Pleshette misses as the nympho who is dressed to the nines in an eye-catching Howard Shoup wardrobe. Bradford Dillman, the love in her life (as opposed to the men in her bed), is wasted on Rover-boy lines. Ben Gazzara, the boy-who-worked-his-way-up, has little of the animal magnetism which is supposed to have rocked the pair's marriage boat.
□ 1965: Nomination: Best B&W Costume Design

....

■ **RAGGEDY MAN**

1981, 94 MINS, US ◇ ⑰ ⊙

Dir Jack Fisk   *Prod* Burt Weissbourd, William D. Wittliff   *Scr* William D. Wittliff   *Ph* Ralf Bode   *Ed* Edward Warschilka   *Mus* Jerry Goldsmith   *Art Dir* John Lloyd
● Sissy Spacek, Eric Roberts, Sam Shepard, William Sanderson, Tracey Walter, Henry Thomas (Universal)

Directed by husband Jack Fisk (his first feature), Sissy Spacek plays a spunky divorcee, struggling to raise two young boys and stuck in a hopeless job as a small-town telephone operator tied to the switchboard in her house.

The setting is Texas in 1944 and Fisk, along with art director John Lloyd and costumer Joe I. Tompkins, has done a superb job in creating a faithful environment, down to the smallest detail. (Fisk was previously an art director.)

Enter sailor Eric Roberts in a rainstorm, knocking on the door to use the phone. After a night on the porch, Roberts spends a warm-hearted day with Spacek and the lads (Henry Thomas and Carey Hollis Jr). Gradually, warmth turns to heat in Spacek's bed.

Roberts is a terrific match for Spacek and their building romance sparkles. But she abruptly sends him packing and, after a tearful farewell, Roberts is seen no more.

With Roberts gone, the film turns mean as William Sanderson and Tracey Walter – both ably playing their redneck roles – make their move on Spacek. This is standard stuff and hardly worth Spacek's talents.

....

■ **RAGGEDY RAWNEY, THE**

1988, 102 MINS, UK ◇ ⑰

Dir Bob Hoskins   *Prod* Bob Weis   *Scr* Bob Hoskins, Nicole De Wilde   *Ph* Frank Tidy   *Ed* Alan Jones   *Mus* Michael Kamen   *Art Dir* Jiri Matolin
● Bob Hoskins, Dexter Fletcher, Zoe Nathanson, Dave Hill, Ian Dury, Zoe Wanamaker (HandMade)

Bob Hoskins brings to the screen an intriguing and particularly insightful perspective on the horrors suffered by the innocent amidst warfare.

Heading an ensemble cast as Darky, Hoskins plays the gritty leader of a gypsy-like band of refugees on the run from a war purposely set in an unspecified period somewhere in Europe.

A young soldier named Tom (Dexter Fletcher) deserts after an attack on his unit sends him into a panic.

By the time he catches up with Darky, et al, Tom is deemed to be a 'rawney' – a person who is half-mad and half-magic. The film then opens its direct passageway into this closed community of near medieval attitudes, with fears of evil spirits and the unknown.

....

■ **RAGING BULL**

1980, 119 MINS, US ◇ ⑰ ⊙

Dir Martin Scorsese   *Prod* Irwin Winkler, Robert Chartoff, Peter Savage   *Scr* Paul Schrader, Mardik Martin   *Ph* Michael Chapman   *Ed* Thelma Schoonmaker   *Art Dir* Gene Rudolf
● Robert De Niro, Cathy Moriarty, Joe Pesci, Frank Vincent, Nicholas Colasanto (United Artists)

Martin Scorsese makes pictures about the kinds of people you wouldn't want to know. In his mostly b&w biopic of middleweight boxing champ Jake La Motta, *Raging Bull*, the La Motta character played by Robert De Niro is one of the most repugnant and unlikeable screen protagonists in some time.

But the boxing sequences are possibly the best ever filmed, and the film captures the intensity of a boxer's life with considerable force.

Scorsese excels at whipping up an emotional storm but seems unaware that there is any need for quieter, more introspective moments in drama.

The relentless depiction of the downward slide of La Motta from a trim contender in 1941 to a shockingly bloated slob introducing strippers in a sleazy nightclub in 1964 has the morbid quality of a German expressionist film. By the time De Niro – who actually gained 50 pounds for the latter scenes – sits at a dressing-room mirror looking at his puffy face, he's become as grotesque as Emil Jannings in *The Blue Angel*.

Aside from the customary genre plot of a boxer selling out to the mob, what seems to be on the minds of Scorsese and his screenwriters is an exploration of an extreme form of Catholic sado-masochism.
□ 1980: Best Actor (Robert De Niro), Editing.
□ Nominations: Best Picture, Director, Supp. Actor (Joe Pesci), Supp. Actress (Cathy Moriarty), Cinematography, Sound

....

■ **RAGING MOON, THE**
(US: Long Ago Tomorrow)

1971, 110 MINS, UK ◇ ⑰

Dir Bryan Forbes   *Prod* Bruce Cohn Curtis   *Scr* Bryan Forbes   *Ph* Tony Imi   *Ed* Timothy Gee   *Mus* Stanley Myers   *Art Dir* Robert Jones
● Malcolm McDowell, Nanette Newman, Georgia Brown, Bernard Lee, Gerald Sim, Michael Flanders (M-G-M/EMI)

The Raging Moon is a tender love story [from a novel by Peter Marshall] woven round a delicate situation, but it has some good tangy dialog and some funny situations.

Early situations are broad and a bit bawdy but purpose is to establish the rough-and-ready character of the young hero (a bit of a yobbo, though with a yearning to write) and his background. He's a carefree boy with the birds, crazy about football and with little respect for his elders. Injured in a football match he loses the use of his legs. He lands up in a home for cripples. He's surly, resentful and a pain to the rest of the inmates who've learned to live with their misfortune.

But at the home he meets and falls in love with a girl who has been wheelchaired for six years. Slowly, their relationship blossoms.

Bryan Forbes' dialog is punchy, perceptive and very understanding of human problems. He has also worked on an excellent cast. Malcolm McDowell handles the two or three facets of the hero with strong facility. Nanette Newman has a stunning warmth and radiance that communicates.

....

■ **RAGMAN'S DAUGHTER, THE**

1972, 94 MINS, UK ◇

Dir Harold Becker   *Prod* Harold Becker, Souter Harris   *Scr* Alan Sillitoe   *Ph* Michael Seresin   *Ed* Antony Gibbs   *Mus* Kenny Clayton   *Art Dir* David Brockhurst

● Simon Rouse, Victoria Tennant, Patrick O'Connell, Leslie Sands, Rita Howard, Brian Murphy (Penelope/Harpoon)

Slow-paced but poignant pic based on an Alan Sillitoe novel which captures both the lyricism and grime of the Nottingham area. Carefully avoiding the pitfalls of the motorcycle thug genre, director Harold Becker weaves a bitter-sweet love affair between a petty teenage thief and the daughter of a wealthy rag dealer. Touches of humor and implied social comment, plus imaginative location lensing, give a ring of authenticity and honesty.

Both Simon Rouse and Patrick O'Connell, as the younger and older Tony, put in superb, convincing jobs of thesping as outcasts of society. Sillitoe steers clear of moralizing, and even social issues inherent in the relationship between the protagonists is made subservient to a broader concern for lost youth and the joys of yesteryear.

■ RAGTIME

1981, 155 MINS, US ◇ ⑫ ⊙
Dir Milos Forman   *Prod* Dino De Laurentiis   *Scr* Michael Weller   *Ph* Miroslav Ondricek   *Ed* Anne V. Coates, Antony Gibbs, Stanley Warnow   *Mus* Randy Newman   *Art Dir* John Graysmark
● James Cagney, Brad Dourif, Elizabeth McGovern, Pat O'Brien, Donald O'Connor, Mandy Patinkin (Paramount/De Laurentiis)

The page-turning joys of E.L. Doctorow's bestselling *Ragtime*, which dizzily and entertainingly charted a kaleidoscopic vision of a turn-of-century America in the midst of intense social change, have been realized almost completely in Milos Forman's superbly crafted screen adaptation.

Within a myriad of characters who include the likes of Evelyn Nesbit, Stanford White, Booker T. Washington and J. Pierpont Morgan, the film charts the syncopated social forces that truly ushered in 20th-century America by pivoting them around a nameless upper-crust family unexpectedly caught up in the maelstrom.

Overriding focus of the film is on the travails of a fictional black ragtime pianist (Howard E. Rollins), whose common-law wife (Debbie Allen) is taken in by The Family after she abandons her newborn child in their garden.

Juggling the scores of characters that Doctorow intertwined in his quirky blend of historical and fictional people and events, Forman and scripter Michael Weller were forced into some occasional truncation and short-cutting, but ultimately win the chess game hands down.
□ 1981: Nominations: Best Supp. Actor (Howard E. Rollins), Supp. Actress (Elizabeth McGovern), Adapted Screenplay, Cinematography, Costume Design, Art Direction, Score, Song ('One More Hour')

■ RAIDERS OF THE LOST ARK

1981, 115 MINS, US ◇ ⑫ ⊙
Dir Steven Spielberg   *Prod* Frank Marshall   *Scr* Lawrence Kasdan   *Ph* Douglas Slocombe   *Ed* Michael Kahn   *Mus* John Williams   *Art Dir* Norman Reynolds
● Harrison Ford, Karen Allen, Denholm Elliott, Paul Freeman, Wolf Kahler, Ronald Lacey (Paramount)

Raiders of the Lost Ark is the stuff that raucous Saturday matinees at the local Bijou once were made of, a crackerjack fantasy-adventure.

Steeped in an exotic atmosphere of lost civilizations, mystical talismans, gritty mercenary adventurers, Nazi arch-villians and ingenious death at every turn, the film is largely patterned on the serials of the 1930s, with a large dollop of Edgar Rice Burroughs.

Story [by George Lucas and Philip Kaufman] begins in 1936 as Indiana Jones (Harrison Ford), an archeologist and university professor who's not above a little mercenary activity on the side, plunders a South American jungle tomb. He secures a priceless golden Godhead, only to have it snatched away by longtime archeological rival Paul Freeman, now employed by the Nazis.

Back in the States, Ford is approached by US intelligence agents who tell him the Nazis are rumored to have discovered the location of the Lost Ark of the Covenant (where the broken 10 Commandments were sealed). The ark is assumed to contain an awesome destructive power. Ford's mission is to beat the Germans to the ark.

Director Steven Spielberg has deftly veiled proceedings in a sense of mystical wonder that makes it all the more easy for viewers to suspend disbelief and settle back for the fun.
□ 1981: Best Art Direction, Sound, Editing, Visual Effects, Sound Effects Editing.
□ Nominations: Best Picture, Director, Cinematography, Score

■ RAILWAY CHILDREN, THE

1970, 108 MINS, UK ◇ ⑫
Dir Lionel Jeffries   *Prod* Robert Lynn   *Scr* Lionel Jeffries   *Ph* Arthur Ibbetson   *Ed* Teddy Darvas   *Mus* Johnny Douglas   *Art Dir* John Clark
● Dinah Sheridan, Bernard Cribbins, William Mervyn, Iain Cuthbertson, Jenny Agutter, Sally Thomsett (EMI)

Story, from E. Nesbit's w.k. novel set in the Edwardian age, concerns a well-to-do family whose life's turned upside down when the father (something in the Foreign Office) is unjustly jailed. The family, in straitened circumstances, go to live on the Yorkshire moors.

They soon adapt to the new life, make friends with the goodhearted villagers, and particularly with a well-to-do gent whom they enlist to help clear their father.

The village is near a railway and this becomes the centre of their activities with the local porter and general railway factotum becoming one of their most useful allies.

Much of the film's success depends on the trio of children. Eldest is played with grave confidence by snub-nosed Jenny Agutter.

■ RAIN

1932, 92 MINS, US ⑫
Dir Lewis Milestone   *Prod* Lewis Milestone   *Scr* Maxwell Anderson, Lewis Milestone   *Ph* Oliver Marsh   *Ed* W. Duncan Mansfield   *Art Dir* Richard Day
● Joan Crawford, Walter Huston, William Gargan, Guy Kibbee, Walter Catlett, Beulah Bondi (Milestone/United Artists)

It turns out to be a mistake to have assigned the Sadie Thompson role to Joan Crawford. The dramatic significance of it all is beyond her range. As for producer-director Lewis Milestone's shortcomings as an entrepreneur, the outcome is equally to be laid at his doorstep [in this version of the play by John Cotton and C. Randolph from the story by W. Somerset Maugham].

The 92 minutes to achieve the climactic finale, where the salvationist succumbs to the flesh, is too long a period to reach the fairly obvious. It then becomes the burden of the Sadie Thompson, Davidson (Walter Huston) and other characters to sustain matters through their own personal impressions. And it's all so talky.

Apart from that, Milestone goes in for the impressionistic rain thing too much with camera angles.

Huston must have felt as ridic as were some of his lines when he had to utter them during production.

Joan Crawford's getup as the light lady is

extremely bizarre. Pavement pounders don't quite trick themselves up as fantastically as all that.

■ RAINBOW, THE

1989, 112 MINS, US ◇ ⑫ ⊙
Dir Ken Russell   *Prod* Ken Russell   *Scr* Ken Russell, Vivian Russell   *Ph* Billy Williams   *Ed* Peter Davies   *Mus* Carl Davis   *Art Dir* Luciana Arrighi
● Sammi Davis, Paul McGann, Amanda Donohoe, Christopher Gable, David Hemmings, Glenda Jackson (Vestron)

The Rainbow was D. H. Lawrence's fourth novel and concludes with the sexual awakening of Ursula Brangwen, whose story was continued in *Women in Love*. The current film reps a prequel to director Ken Russell's earlier one, in which Jennie Linden played Ursula, and Glenda Jackson won an Oscar as her sister Gudrun.

Concentrating on the last section of the novel, Russell charts the spasmodic, often brutal maturation of Ursula (Sammi Davis), a country girl at the turn of the century. Ursula's very out-of-the-ordinary sexual initiation comes at the persuasive hands of her swimming instructor, the strikingly beautiful Winnifred (Amanda Donohoe), one of Lawrence's patented free spirits.

Rebelling against her parents, Ursula moves to London to take a lowly position as a grade school teacher. Before long, she finds herself attracted to a man, the career soldier Anton (Paul McGann), who is mostly occupied fighting the Boer War. Despite the rough deflowering, Ursula's feelings grow into love before coming to grips with her full nature and rushing off to the adventures that will be *Women in Love*.

The Rainbow finds Russell working in a most restrained, classical style. The director, who wrote the script with his wife Vivian, plainly identifies and sympathizes with his heroine's fierce search for independence.

Davis, who came to the fore as the man-hungry teenager in *Hope and Glory*, throws herself into Ursula with all the physical and emotional energy she can muster. Donohoe is absolutely on the money as the liberated Winnifred. McGann makes Anton too languid and remote to get excited about

■ RAINING STONES

1993, 90 MINS, UK ◇ ⑫
Dir Ken Loach   *Prod* Sally Hibbin   *Scr* Jim Allen   *Ph* Barry Ackroyd   *Ed* Jonathan Morris   *Mus* Stewart Copeland   *Art Dir* Martin Johnson
● Bruce Jones, Julie Brown, Ricky Tomlinson, Tom Hickey, Gemma Phoenix, Jonathan James (Parallax/Film Four)

Repeating more or less the same formula as their 1991 success *Riff-Raff*, director Ken Loach and writer Jim Allen come up trumps with *Raining Stones*, a sad-funny portrayal of working class stiffs battling the recession in northern England.

Pic, set in Manchester suburb of Middleton, centers on Bob (Bruce Jones), an out-of-work plumber who desperately needs money to pay for the expensive white dress he feels his small daughter deserves for her first communion. His attempts to earn much-needed cash include the bizarre (rustling a sheep and selling pieces of mutton at the local pub) to the comic (going door to door offering to fix faulty drains) to the dangerous (borrowing money from a loan shark).

Loach and Allen alternate comedy (some of it spoken in broad enough Manchester accents to warrant the use of subtitles) with suspense and tragedy. Jones is perfectly cast as the rumpled hero and Ricky Tomlinson (the guy caught in the bath in *Riff-Raff*) is a scream as his loyal, sardonic friend.

R

The title is derived from a comment made by Bob's socialist father-in-law: 'When you're a worker, it rains stones seven days a week.'

....

■ RAINMAKER, THE

1956, 121 MINS, US ◇ ⊛ ☉
Dir Joseph Anthony *Prod* Hal Wallis *Scr* N. Richard Nash *Ph* Charles Lang Jr *Ed* Warren Low *Mus* Alex North *Art Dir* Hal Pereira, Walter Tyler
● Burt Lancaster, Katharine Hepburn, Wendell Corey, Lloyd Bridges, Earl Holliman, Cameron Prud'homme (Paramount)

The N. Richard Nash play has been fashioned into a solid screen entertainment. With Burt Lancaster turning in perhaps his most colorful performance and Katharine Hepburn offering a free-wheeling interpretation of a spinster in search of romance, the adaptation is a click show all around.

Nash's own screenplay stays close to the original, establishing the title character right at the start and then moving into the story of how the smooth-talking fraud pretends to bring rain to a drought-stricken ranch area. It's humorously and imaginatively done against unusually effective sets.

Locale is the southwestern town of Three Point where Lancaster sets out to pick up $100 on his promise of bringing a vitally-needed downpour. He comes into contact with rancher Cameron Prud'homme and his family, comprising Hepburn as the daughter, two sons, Lloyd Bridges, who's stern and practical, and Earl Holliman, a clumsy, likeable youngster.

That's the setup. Lancaster, although he's obviously a con artist, is permitted to live in Prud'homme's tack house and work his rain magic. He convinces Hepburn that she's pretty, and not plain as Bridges insists.
□ 1956: Nominations: Best Actress (Katharine Hepburn), Scoring of a Dramatic Picture

....

■ RAIN MAN

1988, 140 MINS, US ◇ ⊛ ☉
Dir Barry Levinson *Prod* Mark Johnson *Scr* Ronald Bass, Barry Morrow *Ph* John Seale *Ed* Stu Linder *Mus* Hans Zimmer *Art Dir* Ida Random
● Dustin Hoffman, Tom Cruise, Valeria Golino, Jerry Molen, Jack Murdock (Guber-Peters/United Artists)

Raymond Babbitt (Dustin Hoffman) is an autistic savant, a person extremely limited in some mental areas and extremely gifted in others. His younger brother, hard-driving luxury car dealer Charlie Babbitt (Tom Cruise), has his limitations too – mostly in the areas of kindness and understanding.

Unaware of Raymond's existence until his estranged father dies, Charlie is brought up short when he learns the old man's entire $3 million fortune has been willed to his brother.

Charlie shanghais him, without regard for his welfare, into a cross-country trip to LA, dangling a Dodger game as bait. Meanwhile, he threatens Raymond's guardian, the bland Dr. Bruner (Jerry Molen), with a custody battle unless he hands over half the fortune.

Director Barry Levinson lingers long on the road trip segment, building the relationship between the brothers degree by degree. Result is lightly engrossing.

By the last third, pic [based on a story by Barry Morrow] becomes quite moving as these two very isolated beings discover a common history and deep attachment.

It's a mature assignment for Cruise and he's at his best in the darker scenes. Hoffman achieves an exacting physical characterization of Raymond, from his constant nervous movements to his rigid, hunched shoulders and childish gait.

□ 1988: Best Picture, Director, Actor (Dustin Hoffman), Original Screenplay
□ 1988: Nominations: Best Cinematography, Editing, Original Score, Art Direction

....

■ RAIN PEOPLE, THE

1969, 101 MINS, US ◇ ⊛
Dir Francis Coppola *Prod* Bart Patton, Ronald Colby *Scr* Francis Coppola *Ph* Wilmer Butler *Ed* Blackie Malkin *Mus* Ronald Stein *Art Dir* Leon Ericksen
● James Caan, Shirley Knight, Robert Duvall, Marya Zimmet, Tom Aldredge (Warner/Seven Arts/Coppola)

Writer-director Francis Coppola, scrutinizing the flight of a neurotic young woman and her efforts to assist a brain-damaged ex-football player, has developed an overlong, brooding film incorporating some excellent photography. Often lingering too long on detail to build effects, he manages to lose character sympathy.

Shirley Knight, in a neurotic panic because she dreads the ties of domesticity, runs away from her Long Island home and husband. She phones him from the Pennsylvania Turnpike to tell him she is pregnant and has to get away from home.

She picks up James Caan, an ex-football hero whose brain was damaged in a college game, who is hitchhiking to West Virginia to work for the father of a girlfriend from school.

....

■ RAINS CAME, THE

1939, 100 MINS, US
Dir Clarence Brown *Prod* Darryl F. Zanuck *Scr* Philip Dunne, Julien Josephson *Ph* Arthur Miller *Ed* Barbara McLean *Mus* Alfred Newman *Art Dir* William Darling, George Dudley
● Myrna Loy, Tyrone Power, George Brent, Brenda Joyce, Nigel Bruce, Maria Ouspenskaya (20th Century-Fox)

Liberties have been taken with [Louis Bromfield's] original novel, resulting in switching some of the original characterizations or intent, but under production code restrictions, and to conform with the mass market of film entertainment, it merges as a competent job.

Newcomer Brenda Joyce, cast as the daughter of social-climbing missionaries, rings the bell throughout with a consistent performance as a forthright romantic adolescent, stuck on George Brent. Latter is the wastrel, of good British family, who has been dawdling in Ranchipur for years on an art assignment.

His best friend is the enlightened young Dr-Major Rama Safti, who is blind to any romantic deviations, in his intensive medical duties, until Myrna Loy comes on the scene.
□ 1939: Best Special Effects.
□ Nominations: Best Art Direction, Editing, Sound, Original Score

....

■ RAINS OF RANCHIPUR, THE

1955, 104 MINS, US ◇
Dir Jean Negulesco *Prod* Frank Ross *Scr* Merle Miller *Ph* Milton Krasner *Ed* Dorothy Spencer *Mus* Hugo Friedhofer *Art Dir* Lyle Wheeler, Addison Hehr
● Lana Turner, Richard Burton, Fred MacMurray, Joan Caulfield, Michael Rennie, Eugenie Leontovich (20th Century-Fox)

Louis Bromfield's *The Rains Came*, brought to the screen once before by 20th-Fox in 1939, is filmed this time with Lana Turner as the titled trollop.

However, the cast itself hardly comes alive. Only sturdy performances are turned in by Richard Burton and Eugenie Leontovich.

Turner, as Edwina (Lady Esketh), has the role of a temptress down pat, perhaps too much so. She's good in a couple of scenes, indifferent in most of them and almost

embarrassing in some. Burton's portrayal of Dr Safti, the dedicated Indian doctor, who falls in love with Turner, has strength and conviction and is underplayed intelligently. As the Maharani, Leontovich has dignity, and the scenes between her and Burton are definite assets to the picture.
□ 1955: Nomination: Best Special Effects

....

■ RAINTREE COUNTY

1957, 187 MINS, US ◇ ⊛
Dir Edward Dmytryk *Prod* David Lewis *Scr* Millard Kaufman *Ph* Robert Surtees *Ed* John Dunning *Mus* Johnny Green *Art Dir* William A. Horning, Urie McCleary
● Montgomery Clift, Elizabeth Taylor, Eva Marie Saint, Nigel Patrick, Lee Marvin, Rod Taylor (M-G-M)

Raintree County, one of the biggest and costliest (estimated at $5 million) productions from Metro since its release of *Gone with the Wind*, was lensed via the Camera 65 process (65 mm negative is used and reduced to 35 mm for release prints). It is a study of emotional conflicts set against the Civil War turmoil, and done with pictorial sweep.

Story unfolds against a background of historic events – the war, Abraham Lincoln's election, the Northern abolition movement, Southern secession, etc. Metro shot on location near Danville, Ky, for the most part.

The settings at the start is Raintree County, Indiana, where Montgomery Clift and Eva Marie Saint are blissfully in love and looking ahead to life together. Elizabeth Taylor, whose troubled mind is later revealed, comes as a visitor from New Orleans and woos Clift away from Saint and into marriage.

They take up residence in the Deep South where the slavery issue is exposed to Clift, who abhors it, and the couple return to Raintree. At first distressed by the upheaval of the times, Taylor eventually becomes insane. Taking her young son with her, she runs again to her native Dixie. Clift enters the Union Army.

Under Edward Dmytryk's direction, this adaption of Ross Lockridge Jr's novel unfolds fairly interestingly but slowly. Picture lacks highlight material; even the war scenes don't quite have the necessary impact and the relationship between Taylor and Clift could have been charged up more.
□ 1957: Nominations: Best Actress (Elizabeth Taylor), Costume Design, Art Direction, Score

....

■ RAISE THE TITANIC

1980, 102 MINS, UK ◇ ⊛ ☉
Dir Jerry Jameson *Prod* William Frye *Scr* Adam Kennedy *Ph* Matthew F. Leonetti *Ed* J. Terry Williams, Robert F. Shugrue *Mus* John Barry *Art Dir* John F. DeCuir
● Jason Robards, Richard Jordan, Alec Guinness, David Selby, Anne Archer, M. Emmet Walsh (ITC)

Raise the Titanic wastes a potentially intriguing premise with dull scripting, a lackluster cast, laughably phony trick work, and clunky direction. Half of the running time (at least) is devoted to underwater miniature shots of submarines and other apparatus trying to dislodge the long-lost luxury liner *Titanic* from its deepsea resting place.

The ridiculously expository screenplay [adapted by Eric Hughes from the novel by Clive Cussler] repeatedly explains what will happen, why it's happening, and how it's going to happen.

The actors adopt various strategies for coping with their unspeakable dialog and cardboard characterizations. Alec Guinness provides a dramatic highlight with a lovely scene as a retired old salt who served on the *Titanic*'s crew.

....

■ RAISING ARIZONA

1987, 94 MINS, US ◇ [V] ⊙

Dir Joel Coen *Prod* Ethan Coen, Mark Silverman *Scr* Ethan Coen, Joel Coen *Ph* Barry Sonnenfeld *Ed* Michael R. Miller *Mus* Carter Burwell *Art Dir* Jane Musky

● Nicolas Cage, Holly Hunter, Trey Wilson, John Goodman, William Forsythe, Frances McDormand (Circle/Pedas-Barenholtz)

Pic is the Coen Brothers' twisted view of family rearing in the American heartlands and as full of quirky humor and off-the-wall situations as their debut effort, *Blood Simple*. The film captures the surrealism of everyday life. Characters are so strange here that they seem to have stepped out of late-night television, tabloid newspapers, talk radio and a vivid imagination.

Nicolas Cage and Holly Hunter are the off-center couple at the center of the doings. Cage is a well-meaning petty crook with a fondness for knocking off convenience stores. Hunter is the cop who checks him into prison so often that a romance develops.

They soon learn marriage is 'no Ozzie and Harriet Show' and when she learns she can't have kids or adopt them, they do the next logical thing – steal one.

Loosely structured around a voice-over narration by Cage, *Raising Arizona* is as leisurely and disconnected as *Blood Simple* was taut and economical. While film is filled with many splendid touches and plenty of yocks, it often doesn't hold together as a coherent story.

While Cage and Hunter are fine as the couple at sea in the desert, pic sports at least one outstanding performance from John Goodman as the con brother who wants a family too.

■ RAISING CAIN

1992, 95 MINS, US ◇ [V] ⊙

Dir Brian De Palma *Prod* Gale Anne Hurd *Scr* Brian De Palma *Ph* Stephen H. Burum *Ed* Paul Hirsch, Bonnie Koehler, Robert Dalva *Mus* Pino Donaggio *Art Dir* Doug Kraner

● John Lithgow, Lolita Davidovich, Steven Bauer, Frances Sternhagen, Gregg Henry, Mel Harris (Universal/Pacific Western)

Brian De Palma's modest-budget ($11 million) thriller *Raising Cain* is a superficial, often risible, exercise in pure aesthetics. As a showcase for John Lithgow's acting talents and a visual tour de force, the film may delight the director's most camp followers.

Though there are plenty of nods to Hitchcock's 1960 *Psycho* here, De Palma's point of departure is Michael Powell's classic *Peeping Tom* (also released in 1960), in which a scientist experimented on his young son, causing him to grow up as a psychotic killer.

Lithgow portrays both scientist and son, among several other contrasting roles, in an impressive display of surface acting skills.

Film begins promisingly with daylit horror, as the meek Carter (Lithgow) turns suddenly sinister, attacking a family friend (Teri Austin) to kidnap her young son. Out of nowhere his alter ego, twin brother Cain, pops up to save the day and take over Carter's identity. Carter and Cain are rounding up five kids, including Carter's daughter, for their dad who's returned to America to complete his experiments.

Pic loses its footing midway through with the introduction of a spoofed romantic subplot involving Carter's wife Lolita Davidovich and her old flame, Steven Bauer. Using awkwardly inserted (on purpose) and very showy flashbacks, De Palma deconstructs his narrative and has trouble gaining momentum.

■ RAKE'S PROGRESS, THE

(US: Notorious Gentleman)

1945, 110 MINS, UK [V]

Dir Sidney Gilliat *Prod* Sidney Gilliat, Frank Launder *Scr* Sidney Gilliat, Frank Launder *Ph* Wilkie Cooper, Jack Asher *Ed* Thelma Myers *Mus* William Alwyn *Art Dir* Norman Arnold

● Rex Harrison, Lilli Palmer, Godfrey Tearle, Jean Kent, Griffith Jones (Individual)

This is probably one of the finest films to come out of a British studio. Superb as Rex Harrison and Lilli Palmer are, their individual performances are equalled by many others in the big cast. The script is racy in dialogue.

Direction by Sidney Gilliat who with Frank Launder, also wrote [from a story by Val Valentine] and produced the picture, is virtually flawless. The independent company [Individual Productions] was formed by Gilliat and Launder when these two experienced scriptwriters got tired of working for a salary and threw up their jobs with Gainsborough.

■ RALLY 'ROUND THE FLAG, BOYS!

1958, 106 MINS, US ◇

Dir Leo McCarey *Prod* Leo McCarey *Scr* Claude Binyon, Leo McCarey *Ph* Leon Shamroy *Ed* Louis Loeffler *Mus* Cyril J. Mockridge *Art Dir* Lyle Wheeler, Leland Fuller

● Paul Newman, Joanne Woodward, Joan Collins, Jack Carson, Dwayne Hickman, Tuesday Weld (20th Century-Fox)

This is a bedroom farce of split-level thinking in split-level housing. The film version of Max Shulman's bestseller is unmistakably a Leo McCarey picture. Some of the gags are elaborate and as carefully timed as a dance sequence.

The plot is simple. Paul Newman and Joanne Woodward are the couple (two children), living in Fairfield County, Conn. They have, in the delicate phrase, drifted apart. Newman is all for drifting right back, but Woodward is so busy organizing their town into a community as neat, tidy and efficient as their modern kitchen, she can't find the time. Enter the Temptress, or third angle of triangle. She is Joan Collins.

McCarey is working here with players – Newman, Woodward and Collins – who did only incidental film comedy up to this one. They are called upon to slam into opening doors, swing from chandeliers, do the dropped pants bit (in Newman's case), takes and double-takes. Jack Carson, of course, is a past-master at the slow burn and volcanic reaction, and more than holds his own.

■ RAMBLING ROSE

1991, 113 MINS, US ◇ [V] ⊙

Dir Martha Coolidge *Prod* Renny Harlin *Scr* Calder Willingham *Ph* Johnny Jensen *Ed* Steven Cohen *Mus* Elmer Bernstein *Art Dir* John Vallone

● Laura Dern, Robert Duvall, Diane Ladd, Lukas Haas, John Heard, Kevin Conway (Midnight Sun)

Calder Willingham's memoir [novel] of the South, *Rambling Rose* is a funny and moving tale of an oversexed young woman from the wrong side of the tracks.

Rose (Laura Dern) starts her life as maid to the family of Robert Duvall and Diane Ladd in a small Georgia town in 1935. It turns out that rumors of her having been forced into prostitution at a tender age are true. Both Duvall and his 13-year-old son Lukas Haas are immediately taken by Dern's raw sexuality, yet it is the boy who nearly has his first conquest with her when Dern innocently gets in bed with him one night in a funny and risque scene.

Duvall is a proper gentleman, rejecting Dern's attempt at seduction and quickly adopting a fatherly concern for her. Family matriarch Ladd (Dern's real-life mom) is a Yankee educated at Columbia U who also takes Dern under her wing. Main source of conflict is Dern's promiscuous activities, which cause young men to loiter outside the house at all hours.

Dern's naturalness in a very eccentric role confirms the promise of her earlier work. Duvall and Ladd play off each other to perfection. Director Martha Coolidge and her technical crew have re-created the detail and texture of Southern life with great feeling at Carolco's Wilmington, NC, studio.

☐ 1991: Nominations: Best Actress (Laura Dern), Supporting Actress (Diane Ladd)

■ RAMBO FIRST BLOOD PART II

1985, 95 MINS, US ◇ [V] ⊙

Dir George Pan Cosmatos *Prod* Buzz Feitshans *Scr* Sylvester Stallone, James Cameron *Ph* Jack Cardiff *Ed* Mark Goldblatt, Mark Helfrich *Mus* Jerry Goldsmith *Art Dir* Bill Kenney

● Sylvester Stallone, Richard Crenna, Charles Napier, Julia Nickson, Steven Berkoff, Martin Kove (Tri-Star)

This overwrought sequel to the popular *First Blood* (1982) is one mounting fireball as Sylvester Stallone's special operations veteran is sprung from a prison labor camp by his former Green Beret commander (Richard Crenna) to find POWs in Vietnam.

That the secret mission is a cynical ruse by higher-ups which is meant to fail heightens Stallone's fury while touching off a provocative political theme: a US government that wants to forget about POWs and accommodate the public at the same time.

The charade on the screen, which is not pulled off, is to accept that the underdog Rambo character, albeit with the help of an attractive machine-gun wielding Vietnamese girl (Julia Nickson), can waste hordes of Vietcong and Red Army contingents enroute to hauling POWs to a Thai air base in a smoking Russian chopper with only a facial scar (from a branding iron-knifepoint) marring his tough figure.

Steven Berkoff is a twisted and nominally chilly Russian advisor, but his performance is essentially the same nasty thing he did in *Octopussy* and *Beverly Hills Cop*.

☐ 1985: Nomination: Best Sound Effects Editing

■ RAMBO III

1988, 101 MINS, US ◇ [V] ⊙

Dir Peter Macdonald *Prod* Buzz Feitshans *Scr* Sylvester Stallone, Sheldon Lettich *Ph* John Stanier *Ed* James Symons, Andrew London, O. Nicholas Brown, Edward A. Warschilka *Mus* Jerry Goldsmith *Art Dir* Billy Kenney

● Sylvester Stallone, Richard Crenna, Marc de Jonge, Kurtwood Smith, Spiros Focas (Carolco)

Rambo III stakes out a moral high ground for its hero missing or obscured in the previous two pictures. In the Soviets' heinous nine-year occupation of Afghanistan, this mythic commando and quintessential outsider is enlisted in a cause that – glasnost notwithstanding – is indisputably righteous.

Indeed, as this chapter opens, the character of John Rambo has been demilitarized and transported to exotic self-exile in Thailand, where he lives in a Buddhist monastery and supports himself by engaging in slam-bang mercenary martial arts contests.

Richard Crenna has come halfway around the world to Bangkok to ask Stallone for payback – Rambo's participation in a clandestine operation to destroy a 'brutal' Russian general who rules a remote province in occupied Afghanistan.

The battle scenes in *Rambo III* are explosive, conflagratory tableaux that make for wrenching, frequently terrifying viewing. Always at ground zero in the chaos is Rambo – gloriously, inhumanly impervious to fear and danger – whose character is inhabited by Stallone with messianic intensity.

■ **RAMPAGE**

1987, 97 MINS, US ◇ ⓥ
Dir William Friedkin *Prod* David Salven *Scr* William Friedkin *Ph* Robert D. Yeoman *Ed* Jere Huggins *Mus* Ennio Morricone *Art Dir* Buddy Cone
● Michael Biehn, Alex McArthur, Nicholas Campbell, Deborah Van Valkenburgh, John Harkins, Art Lafleur (De Laurentiis)

Anthony Fraser (Michael Biehn) is the assistant district attorney in charge of the major crimes division and is handed a grisly murder case by his boss with orders to go for the death penalty. The case involves a psychopath named Charles Reece (Alex McArthur) who has killed five people, mutilating four of them and drinking their blood. Fraser doesn't want the case because he's against the death penalty.

Writer-director William Friedkin [adapting the novel by William P. Wood] elects to explore the frustration of the legal system's insanity defense. He refuses to present an easy out to the dilemma. Even Dr Keddie (John Harkins), as the defense's chief psychiatrist, is given his moment to defend his position.

The cast is top notch all around with Biehn (once cast as a crazed killer in *The Fan*) suggesting the anguish beneath the cool exterior of his prosecutor. Deborah Van Valkenburgh brings some depth to the supporting role of Biehn's wife. As Reece, McArthur appears dangerous and unstable but remains opaque, so we – like the lawyers and the doctors – can never be completely sure if he knew what he was doing when he committed the murders.

■ **RANCHO DELUXE**

1975, 93 MINS, US ◇ ⓥ
Dir Frank Perry *Prod* Elliott Kastner *Scr* Thomas McGuane *Ph* William A. Fraker *Ed* Sid Katz *Mus* Jimmy Buffett *Art Dir* Michael Haller
● Jeff Bridges, Sam Waterston, Elizabeth Ashley, Charlene Dallas, Slim Pickens, Harry Dean Stanton (United Artists)

Rancho Deluxe becomes an amiable, lightweight comedy featuring Bridges and Waterston as two modern day drifters living hand-to-mouth on illegal pickings from bigtime rancher Clifton James.

Perry's location film has a very good cast and an easy charm. But the humor is too throwaway when it isn't laid on with a trowel.

Script has Bridges and Waterston (his Indian pal) besting pompous James in minor ripoffs. James hires Pickens to roust the rustlers, while the boys corrupt ranch hands Dean Stanton and Richard Bright into a major heist plan.

The film has a kind of relaxed pointlessness and a measure of dainty bawdiness, and the presence of some good players. Bridges' indefatigable charisma is in good shape to the very end.

■ **RANCHO NOTORIOUS**

1952, 89 MINS, US ◇ ⓥ ⊙
Dir Fritz Lang *Prod* Howard Welsch *Scr* Daniel Taradash *Ph* Hal Mohr *Ed* Otto Ludwig *Mus* Emil Newman *Art Dir* Wiard Ihnen
● Marlene Dietrich, Arthur Kennedy, Mel Ferrer, Gloria Henry, William Frawley, Jack Elam (Fidelity)

This Marlene Dietrich western has some of the flavor of the old outdoor classics (like the actress's own onetime *Destry Rides Again* without fully capturing their quality and magic. The characters play the corny plot [original

story by Silvia Richards] straight; directing keeps the pace lively and interesting, and the outdoor shots, abetted by the constant splash of color, are eye-arresting. Dietrich is as sultry and alluring as ever.

Plot, starting off in a little Wyoming town in the 1870s, finds a young femme brutally assaulted and killed on the eve of her wedding and her embittered cowboy lover (Arthur Kennedy) riding off to find and kill the unknown murderer. The trail first leads to Frenchy Fairmount (Mel Ferrer), a flashy outlaw, and then to Chuck-a-Luck, the ranch run by Altar Keane (Dietrich), one-time fabulous saloon entertainer.

Dietrich is a dazzling recreation of the old-time saloon mistress, and handles her song, 'Get Away, Young Man', with her usual throaty skill.

■ **RANDOM HARVEST**

1942, 125 MINS, US ⓥ ⊙
Dir Mervyn LeRoy *Prod* Sidney Franklin *Scr* Claudine West, George Froeschel, Arthur Wimperis *Ph* Joseph Ruttenberg *Ed* Harold F. Kress *Mus* Herbert Stothart *Art Dir* Cedric Gibbons, Randall Duell
● Ronald Colman, Greer Garson, Philip Dorn, Susan Peters, Henry Travers, Reginald Owen (M-G-M)

The film transcription of James Hilton's novel *Random Harvest*, under Sidney Franklin's production and Mervyn LeRoy's direction, achieves much more than average importance.

Ronald Colman plays Charles Rainier, prosperous Briton who loses his memory as result of shellshock in the First World War. As the film opens he is a mental case in an asylum where efforts are being made to restore his memory. He wanders off, eluding officers of the sanatorium.

Colman gives a fine performance but is not quite the romantic type that he was years ago. In fact, he looks older than he should have been for film expediency.

Greer Garson, more charming and seductive than ever, is an important mainstay of the picture. Essaying a highly sympathetic role, she overshadows Colman.
□ 1942: Nominations: Best Picture, Director, Actress (Susan Peters), Screenplay, B&W Art Direction, Scoring of a Dramatic Picture

■ **RANSOM**
(US: The Terrorists)

1975, 97 MINS, UK ◇ ⓥ
Dir Casper Wrede *Prod* Peter Rawley *Scr* Paul Wheeler *Ph* Sven Nykvist *Ed* Thelma Connell *Mus* Jerry Goldsmith *Art Dir* Sven Wickman
● Sean Connery, Ian McShane, Norman Bristow, John Cording, Isabel Dean, William Fox (Lion/20th-Century Fox)

Sean Connery is billed above the title as the head of a government security agency trying to cope with plane-hijacking terrorists. Rather curiously, Connery works for the government of 'Scandinavia', not Norway where most of the pic was filmed, but in any event at no time does he lose his Scottish brogue.

The terrorists are holding the British ambassador in exchange for their own release and that of some cohorts held by Britain. A squad of accomplices headed by Ian McShane commandeer a loaded passenger jet as it lands at Oslo, and the cat and mouse game begins.

As a match of wits, the ensuing tale doesn't amount to much. But along with plot ingenuity, what's glaringly missing is even the briefest of exploration of the terrorists and their psychology.

■ **RAPE OF MALAYA, THE**
See: A Town Like Alice

■ **RAPID FIRE**

1992, 95 MINS, US ◇ ⓥ ⊙
Dir Dwight H. Little *Prod* Robert Lawrence *Scr* Alan McElroy *Ph* Ric Waite *Ed* Gib Jaffe *Mus* Christopher Young *Art Dir* Ron Foreman
● Brandon Lee, Powers Boothe, Nick Mancuso, Raymond J. Barry, Kate Hodge, Tzi Ma (20th-Century Fox)

Brandon Lee, American-born son of the legendary chopsocky hero Bruce Lee, acquits himself well in his first lead role in a U.S. film, *Rapid Fire*, as a pacifist college student forced to become a killing machine. Director Dwight H. Little expertly handles implausible but entertaining action sequences that keep the pic lively despite a schlocky plot [from a story by Cindy Cirile and Alan McElroy] and cardboard characterizations.

Thankfully devoid of standard hunk narcissism, young Lee manages to maintain audience sympathy despite having to surrender his ideals and annihilate hordes of bad guys (stock Mafia and Oriental types) on behalf of Chicago cop Powers Boothe.

Boothe, enjoyable as a lower-budget Clint Eastwood type, works out of an abandoned bowling alley, does illegal wiretapping and coldly uses Lee as bait in his 10-year-old vendetta against heroin-dealing bigwigs Tzi Ma and Nick Mancuso.

The script unwisely does away with Mancuso after only an hour. The tension slackens in the last section and even a budding sexual relationship between Lee and Boothe's macho female partner Kate Hodge can't make up for it.

■ **RAPTURE, THE**

1991, 102 MINS, US ◇ ⓥ ⊙
Dir Michael Tolkin *Prod* Nick Wechsler, Nancy Tenenbaum, Karen Koch *Scr* Michael Tolkin *Ph* Bojan Bazelli *Ed* Suzanne Fenn *Mus* Thomas Newman *Art Dir* Robin Standefer
● Mimi Rogers, Patrick Bauchau, David Duchovny, Kimberly Cullum, Dick Anthony Williams, Will Patton (New Line)

An unexpectedly serious investigation into spiritual malaise and religious fanaticism, *The Rapture* has difficulty walking the line between profundity and pretentiousness. Film nevertheless stands as a singular feature debut for writer-director Michael Tolkin, who demonstrates more talent than judgment.

Mimi Rogers plays Sharon, a beautiful young woman with no direction. She lives on the sexual edge in LA with her amoral b.f. (Patrick Bauchau), and in one of their group gropes meets Randy (David Duchovny).

Her hot affair with him pushes her to peer into the spiritual abyss, which leads her to the Bible, prayer and ultimate acceptance of the Lord. Six years later, now a fervently devout married couple, Sharon and Randy are raising their daughter in the belief that the end is nigh. Sharon absconds with her daughter to the desert, where she awaits the rapture, the ultimate fulfillment of her religious beliefs that will unite her with her husband and God.

Centerscreen throughout, Rogers reduces everyone else in range to pawns and delivers one of those soul-baring turns that is both impressive and almost too much. Also notable is Bojan Bazelli's luminous lensing.

■ **RARE BREED, THE**

1966, 97 MINS, US ◇ ⓥ
Dir Andrew V. McLaglen *Prod* William Alland *Scr* Ric Hardman *Ph* William H. Clothier *Ed* Russell F. Schoengarth *Mus* John Williams *Art Dir* Alexander Golitzen, Alfred Ybarra
● James Stewart, Maureen O'Hara, Brian Keith, Juliet Mills, Don Galloway, David Brian (Universal)

Based on the actual intro of white-faced

Hereford cattle from England to the US western ranges, *The Rare Breed* is a generally successful fictionalized blend of violence, romance, comedy, inspiration and oater Americana.

Ric Hardman's good – if overly wide-ranging – script takes as a point of departure the phasing out of the longhorn by the 'rare' (circa 1884) Hereford stock from England. As the drama unfolds, rugged animal survival problems dissolve into human conflicts.

For almost half of the running time the plot concerns the stubborn determination of widowed Maureen O'Hara and daughter Juliet Mills to deliver a bull for breeding purposes. Opposing factors include James Stewart, initially a drifter who agrees, although reluctantly, to swindle the gals via Alan Caillou's bribe, with two conspirators, Jack Elam and Harry Carey Jr.

Second half is virtually another pic, with quietly-stubborn O'Hara pitted against Brian Keith in a sort of Anna-and-the-King-of-Siam byplay.

....

■ **RASPUTIN THE MAD MONK**

1966, 92 MINS, UK ◇ Ⓥ

Dir Don Sharp   *Prod* Anthony Nelson-Keys   *Scr* John Elder [= Anthony Hinds]   *Ph* Michael Reed   *Ed* James Needs, Roy Hyde   *Mus* Don Banks   *Art Dir* Bernard Robinson
● Christopher Lee, Barbara Shelley, Richard Pasco, Francis Matthews, Suzan Farmer, Renee Asherson (Hammer)

Producer Anthony Nelson-Keys had scripter John Elder take a somewhat fanciful (and unbelievable) approach to the subject of Russia's bad boys. As a result, the dastardly villain has been given some attributes that are certainly colorful. Christopher Lee's Rasputin is completely in character – huge, deep-voiced, compelling stare. He's a proper rascal.

Religious aspects of l'affaire Rasputin are skimmed over, the only two dignitaries portrayed as colorless and dull. Of the Russian court, the Czarina (Renee Asherson) and the Czarevitch (Robert Duncan) are the only Romanoffs shown, the plot revolving (after the monk's entry into court affairs, accredited to his hypnotic influence over a lady-in-waiting) on a revenge plot by the would-be fiance (Nicholas Pennell) of the seduced lady-in-waiting (Barbara Shelley). His principal accomplices are an alcoholic doctor (Richard Pasco), and an Army officer (Francis Matthews), whose sister (Suzan Farmer) has been lined up as Rasputin's next victim.

....

■ **RATBOY**

1986, 104 MINS, US ◇ Ⓥ

Dir Sondra Locke   *Prod* Fritz Manes   *Scr* Rob Thompson   *Ph* Bruce Surtees   *Ed* Joel Cox   *Mus* Lennie Niehaus   *Art Dir* Edward Carfagno
● Sondra Locke, Robert Townsend, Christopher Hewett, Larry Hankin, Sydney Lassick, Gerrit Graham (Malpaso)

Yet another picture about how a semi-human, quasi-alien being just can't fit in among earthlings, *Ratboy* can boast of some modest virtues, but is simply too mild on all counts to carry much impact. Oddball first feature from Sondra Locke, who also stars as an out-of-work journalist, deals with eccentric, desperate individuals but in a rather straightforward, unobsessed manner.

The origins of the title character are never investigated or explained. Indeed, after the terrified little bugger is trapped by some transients, he is just blithely manipulated and used by a succession of hustlers who can't put their greed and self-interests on hold long enough to even inquire where the tiny one came from or how he got that way.

Acting tends to the broad side, and Ratboy's nose twitching is cute.

....

■ **RATTLE OF A SIMPLE MAN**

1964, 96 MINS, UK Ⓥ

Dir Muriel Box   *Prod* William Gell   *Scr* Charles Dyer   *Ph* Reg Wyer   *Ed* Frederick Wilson   *Mus* Stanley Black   *Art Dir* Robert Jones
● Harry H. Corbett, Diane Cilento, Thora Hird, Michael Medwin, Charles Dyer, Hugh Futcher (Associated British)

Most of the charm and tenderness that occasionally illuminated Charles Dyer's successful play has been lost in this coarsened, fatuous film. Only a lively, vivid performance by Diane Cilento in a contrived role holds much interest, though a sound cast does spartan work in juggling the sparse material. Dyer, has broadened his intimate little play for the benefit of the screen and has heaved most of its values into the trash can.

A bunch of football fans from the North of England, characteristically drawn as noisy, boozing, lecherous nitwits, comes to London for the Cup Final and a night out among the sleazy bright lights. One of them (Harry H. Corbett), a particuarly gormless, repressed, mother-ridden oaf, is conned into a bet with his pals. He wagers his motorbike that he'll have an affair with a goodlooking, blonde tart that he picks up in Soho drinking club.

The bedroom rendezvous is a pitiable farce in which he fails to take the opportunities cheerfully flung at him by the goodtime girl. Instead he weaves dreams of real love about the goldenhearted little prostie.

....

■ **RAVEN, THE**

1963, 85 MINS, US ◇ Ⓥ ☉

Dir Roger Corman   *Prod* Roger Corman   *Scr* Richard Matheson   *Ph* Floyd Crosby   *Ed* Ronald Sinclair   *Mus* Les Baxter   *Art Dir* Daniel Haller
● Vincent Price, Peter Lorre, Boris Karloff, Hazel Court, Olive Sturgess, Jack Nicholson (American International)

Edgar Allan Poe might turn over in his crypt at this nonsensical adaptation of his immortal poem, but audiences will find the spooky goings-on of a flock of 15th century English sorcerers a corn-pop of considerable comedic dimensions.

The screenplay is a skillful, imaginative narrative of what comes to pass when there comes a rapping at magician Vincent Price's chamber-door by a raven – who else but Peter Lorre, a fellow magician, transformed by another sorcerer (Boris Karloff).

Roger Corman as producer-director takes this premise and develops it expertly as a horror-comedy climaxing with Price and Karloff engaging in a duel to the death in the black arts, each a master of the craft. Special effects figure prominently.

Hazel Court as Price's sexy and conniving spouse, Olive Sturgess, his daughter, and Jack Nicholson, Lorre's son, lend effective support.

....

■ **RAW DEAL**

1986, 106 MINS, US ◇ Ⓥ ☉

Dir John Irvin   *Prod* Martha Schumacher   *Scr* Gary M. DeVore, Norman Wexler   *Ph* Alex Thomson   *Ed* Anne V. Coates   *Mus* Cinemascore   *Art Dir* Giorgio Postiglione
● Arnold Schwarzenegger, Kathryn Harrold, Sam Wanamaker, Paul Shenar, Robert Davi, Ed Lauter (De Laurentiis/International)

Comic book crime meller suffers from an irredeemably awful script, and even director John Irvin's engaging sense of how absurd the proceedings are can't work an alchemist's magic.

Bald exposition sees former FBI man, Arnold Schwarzenegger, now rather implausibly a southern sheriff, recruited to infiltrate Chicago's biggest mob, which has been rubbing out men scheduled to testify against it. The big man impresses kingpin Sam Wanamaker with his brain and lieutenant

Paul Shenar (as well as tarty Kathryn Harrold) with his brawn, and soon wins himself a job with the gang.

Cast members do what's necessary, but have all been seen to better advantage on other occasions.

....

■ **RAWHIDE**

1951, 87 MINS, US Ⓥ

Dir Henry Hathaway   *Prod* Samuel G. Engel   *Scr* Dudley Nichols   *Ph* Milton Krasner   *Ed* Robert Simpson   *Mus* Sol Kaplan   *Art Dir* Lyle Wheeler, George W Davis
● Tyrone Power, Susan Hayward, Hugh Marlowe, Dean Jagger, Edgar Buchanan, Jack Elam (20th Century-Fox)

Maximum suspense for a western is generated in this Tyrone Power-Susan Hayward costarrer. Despite a strongly-told story, however, picture isn't the proper vehicle for Power, who is wasted in part and comes off second best to a number of other players.

Power and Hayward are held prisoners at a stagecoach station in the early west by Hugh Marlowe, an escaped murderer from a prison in the territory, and his three companions, who are waiting to rob the eastbound stage next day which carries $100,000 in gold. Power is employed at station, and Hayward is there with her infant niece only until she can catch the next stage east.

Acting honors are about evenly divided between femme star and Marlowe, both in hardboiled parts. Jack Elam, too, fares particularly favorably as woman-hungry escaped con, member of Marlowe's pack, and Edgar Buchanan, Dean Jagger and George Tobias likewise are effective. Power is never permitted a chance as a hero.

....

■ **RAZORBACK**

1984, 94 MINS, AUSTRALIA ◇ Ⓥ

Dir Russell Mulcahy   *Prod* Hal McElroy   *Scr* Everett De Roche   *Ph* Dean Semler   *Ed* Bill Anderson   *Mus* Iva Davies   *Art Dir* Bryce Walmsley
● Gregory Harrison, Arkie Whiteley, Bill Kerr, Chris Haywood, David Argue, Judy Morris (McElroy & McElroy)

A razorback is a particularly nasty species of feral pig, vicious and brainless, which is found in Australia's outback. Production involves a giant of the species which runs amok with spectacular abandon.

Screenplay by Everett De Roche, an experienced writer of thrillers, from a book by Peter Brennan, starts with a bang: Jake Cullen (Bill Kerr) is minding his grandchild in his isolated homestead when the place is attacked by the unseen porker who wounds the old man and disappears with the infant.

The distraught granddad is brought to trial for killing the kid, but acquitted, and he becomes obsessed with getting the giant beast.

Enter Judy Morris who plays an American TV journalist who arrives in this remote spot to do a story on the slaughter of the kangaroos.

She becomes the next victim of the razorback. But her husband, Carl (Gregory Harrison), doesn't believe she fell down a mine shaft, the story put out by the locals.

The plot may be a bit familiar, but *Razorback* is no quickie: it's an extremely handsome production, beautifully shot by Dean Semler.

....

■ **RAZOR'S EDGE, THE**

1946, 146 MINS, US Ⓥ

Dir Edmund Goulding   *Prod* Darryl F. Zanuck   *Scr* Lamar Trotti   *Ph* Arthur Miller   *Ed* J. Watson Webb   *Mus* Alfred Newman   *Art Dir* Richard Day, Nathan Juran
● Tyrone Power, Gene Tierney, John Payne, Anne Baxter, Clifton Webb, Herbert Marshall (20th Century-Fox)

R

The Razor's Edge has everything for virtually every type of film fan. Fundamentally it's all good cinematurgy. It's a moving picture that moves.

The romance is more than slightly on the sizzling side. Tyrone Power, as the flyer who can't find himself, is always seeking goodness and spurns the easy life offered him by the more than casually appealing Gene Tierney. It reaches a climax after they play the Paris nitery belt from Montmartre to Montparnasse, and when back in Chicago she loses sight of him and marries John Payne there is the unashamed confession of a lasting love which Power spurns.

For all its pseudo-ritualistic aura the film is fundamentally a solid love story. Tierney is the almost irresistibly appealing femme and completely depicts all the beauty and charm endowed her by Maugham's characterization. Anne Baxter walks off with perhaps the film's personal bit as the dipso, rivaled only by Clifton Webb's effete characterization as the dilettante rich uncle.

Herbert Marshall introduces a new cine-matic technique – as it was in the original novel – of playing the author W. Somerset Maugham who thus integrates himself into the story by name identity instead of the conventional first-person (but invariably fictiously identified) characterization.

☐ 1946: Best Supp. Actress (Anne Baxter).
☐ Nominations: Best Picture, Supp. Actor (Clifton Webb), B&W Art Direction

. . . .

■ RAZOR'S EDGE, THE

1984, 128 MINS, US ◇ ⓥ ⊙
Dir John Byrum   *Prod* Robert P. Marcucci, Harry Brenn   *Scr* John Byrum, Bill Murray   *Ph* Peter Hannan   *Ed* Peter Boyle   *Mus* Jack Nitzsche   *Art Dir* Philip Harrison
● Bill Murray, Theresa Russell, Catherine Hicks, Denholm Elliott, James Keach, Peter Vaughan (Columbia)

Conceived as a major career departure for comic star Bill Murray, *The Razor's Edge* emerges as a minimally acceptable adaptation of W. Somerset Maugham's superb 1944 novel. Tonally inconsistent and structurally awkward, film does develop some dramatic interest in the second half, but inherent power of the material is never realized. This is the film that Columbia let him make if he appeared in *Ghost Busters*.

Film opens with a happy-go-lucky Murray preparing to set sail for the European conflict. When it's over, he is no longer certain he wants to marry his intended, pretty chatterbox Catherine Hicks. While his old friends are being destroyed by the stock market crash, he's finally finding inner peace in the Himalayas.

The full-fledged arrival of Theresa Russell into the story livens things up considerably. A former friend from the States, Russell has descended to a routine of drugs, drink and hooking in Paris' underworld, from which Murray resolves to rescue her. Hicks conspires to wreck their planned marriage, and ends by doing much worse than that.

Most of the time, it seems that director John Byrum and Murray have all they can handle just getting the basic plot developments up on the screen. Regretfully absent is any sense of time passing, of spiritual and emotional feeling being deepened.

Chicago-area scenes were shot in Europe, and Paris locationing has yielded little in the way of local color or atmosphere. The trip to India was worth it, though.

. . . .

■ REACH FOR GLORY

1962, 80 MINS, UK
Dir Philip Leacock   *Prod* John Kohn, Jud Kinberg   *Scr* John Kohn, Jud Kinberg   *Ph* Bob Huke   *Ed* Freddie Wilson   *Mus* Bob Russell   *Art Dir* John Blezard
● Michael Anderson Jr., Martin Tomlinson, Oliver Grimm, Harry Andrews, Kay Walsh (Gala/Blazer)

In this tale about a group of adolescent boys at a military school in Britain during the last war, the themes of racism, war hate and its effect on youth, conscientious objection and the consequences of parental weakness on youth are all touched on.

Film is well meaning, tightly and economically made but still lacks the edge of the necessary impact. Result is a diffuse pic which is interesting but does not emerge a heavyweight.

A group of London youths chafe in a country school to which they have been evacuated. The war fills them with dreams of glory and a desire for action that is unfortunately turned to gang warfare, spartan, cabalistic rituals, antisemitism and general unruliness. Into this comes a refugee Jewish boy from Germany.

Shame at conscientious objectors is also worked in via a brother of one of the boys and false accusations of budding homosexuality.

. . . .

■ REACH FOR THE SKY

1956, 136 MINS, UK ⓥ
Dir Lewis Gilbert   *Prod* Daniel M. Angel   *Scr* Lewis Gilbert   *Ph* Jack Asher   *Ed* John Shirley   *Mus* John Addison   *Art Dir* Bernard Robinson
● Kenneth More, Muriel Pavlow, Lyndon Brook, Lee Patterson, Alexander Knox, Dorothy Alison (Rank/Pinnacle)

First and foremost, this is a story of courage, showing a man's triumph over physical disability and every obstacle raised to curtail his normal activities. Adapted from the biography [*The Story of Douglas Bader*] by his fellow pilot Paul Brickhill, it covers the career of Douglas Bader who, after losing both legs in a plane crash while stunting, succeeds in rejoining the RAF to become a Wing Commander in the last world war and one of the aces in the Battle of Britain.

From the cocky young recruit's first day at the training station through all the gay comradeship and hazards of flying, Kenneth More (Bader) depicts with unerring skill the humor, friendliness and supreme fortitude of one of the war's most honored heroes.

His determination to take up life where it nearly left off and return to the only job he knows, is shown without heroics. And this enhances its dramatic value. Every Air Force taboo on his disability is finally overcome and he gets airborne again with the outbreak of war.

Lyndon Brook plays the staunch friend who has to break the news to Bader of his affliction. Alexander Knox is quietly effective as the surgeon.

. . . .

■ REAL GENIUS

1985, 104 MINS, US ◇ ⓥ ⊙
Dir Martha Coolidge   *Prod* Brian Grazer   *Scr* Neal Israel, Pat Proft, Peter Torokvei   *Ph* Vilmos Zsigmond   *Ed* Richard Chew   *Mus* Thomas Newman   *Art Dir* Josan F. Russo
● Val Kilmer, Gabe Jarret, Michelle Meyrink, William Atherton, Jonathan Gries, Patti D'Arbanville (Tri-Star)

Real Genius is *Police Academy* with brains. Setting the proceedings at a think tank for young prodigies seems a curious choice as most of the humor of the film comes out of character rather than place. Val Kilmer, punning his way through his senior year at Pacific Tech, is hardly convincing as a world-class intellect.

Plot [by Neal Israel, Pat Proft] about creating a portable laser system for the Air Force under the tutelage of campus creep Professor Hathaway (William Atherton) has the authority of an old Abbott and Costello film. Theme about the exploitation of these youthful minds is lost in a sea of sight gags.

What lifts the production above the run-of-the-mill is swift direction by Martha Coolidge, who has a firm grasp over the manic material.

. . . .

■ RE-ANIMATOR

1985, 86 MINS, US ◇ ⓥ ⊙
Dir Stuart Gordon   *Prod* Brian Yuzna   *Scr* Dennis Paoli, William J. Norris, Stuart Gordon   *Ph* Mac Ahlberg   *Ed* Lee Percy   *Mus* Richard Band   *Art Dir* Robert A. Burns
● Jeffrey Combs, Bruce Abbott, Barbara Crampton, Robert Sampson, David Gale, Gerry Black (Re-Animated)

Re-Animator is based on an H.P. Lovecraft tale [*Herbert West – The Re-Animator*] about a crazy scientist who brings dead bodies back to life with a special serum. Trouble is, they come back violent and ready to kill.

Herbert West (Jeffrey Combs) is the inventor who, like horror film scientists from time immemorial, is too batty to realize the consequences of his actions. Romantic leads are Bruce Abbott and Barbara Crampton, latter a looker who, at the pic's climax, is strapped naked to a lab table as an object of the lusts of a hateful admirer, who by this time literally has lost his head.

Pic has a grisly sense of humor, and sometimes is *so* gross and over the top the film tips over into a bizarre comedy.

. . . .

■ REAP THE WILD WIND

1942, 124 MINS, US ⓥ
Dir Cecil B. DeMille   *Prod* Cecil B. DeMille   *Scr* Alan LeMay, Charles Bennett, Jesse Lasky Jr   *Ph* Victor Milner, William V. Skall   *Ed* Anne Bauchens   *Mus* Victor Young   *Art Dir* Hans Dreier, Roland Anderson
● Ray Milland, John Wayne, Paulette Goddard, Raymond Massey, Robert Preston, Susan Hayward (Paramount)

Reap the Wild Wind is a melodrama of Atlantic coastal shipping in the windjammer days, 100 years ago. It is a film possessing the spectacular sweep of colorful backgrounds which characterize the Cecil DeMille type of screen entertainment.

After a short foreword by DeMille, the picture opens with scenes of a hurricane, shipwreck and struggle for bounty among the salvage workers. This melodramatic tempo is too swift to be maintained. Various angles of plot and contest necessarily must be introduced. The pacing is uneven.

Towards the end, however, the action quickens. There is a unique filming of an undersea battle between a giant squid, of octopus descent, and the two male protagonists. Despite its obvious make-believe, it is shrewd filming, realistic and thrilling.

The production is a visual triumph. Some of the marine scenes are breathtaking. There is skillful blending of process photography.

☐ 1942: Best Special Effects.
☐ Nominations: Best Color Cinematography, Color Art Direction

. . . .

■ REAR WINDOW

1954, 112 MINS, US ◇ ⓥ ⊙
Dir Alfred Hitchcock   *Prod* Alfred Hitchcock   *Scr* John Michael Hayes   *Ph* Robert Burks   *Ed* George Tomasini   *Mus* Franz Waxman   *Art Dir* Hal Pereira, Joseph MacMillan Johnson
● James Stewart, Grace Kelly, Wendell Corey, Thelma Ritter, Raymond Burr, Judith Evelyn (Paramount)

A tight suspense show is offered in *Rear Window*, one of Alfred Hitchcock's better thrillers. Hitchcock combines technical and artistic skills in a manner that makes this an unusually good piece of murder mystery entertainment. A sound story by Cornell Woolrich and a cleverly dialoged screenplay provide a solid basis for thrill-making.

Hitchcock confines all of the action to a single apartment-courtyard setting and draws nerves to snapping point in developing the thriller phases of the plot.

James Stewart portrays a news photographer confined to his apartment with a broken leg. He passes the long hours by playing peeping-tom on the people who live in the other apartments overlooking the courtyard. In one of the apartments occupied by Raymond Burr and his invalid, shrewish wife Stewart observes things that lead him to believe Burr has murdered and dismembered the wife.

Adding to the grip the melodrama has on the audience is the fact that virtually every scene is one that could only be viewed from Stewart's wheelchair, with the other apartment dwellers seen in pantomime action through the photog's binoculars or the telescopic lens from his camera.

The production makes clever use of natural sounds and noises throughout.

☐ 1954: Nominations: Best Director, Screenplay, Color Cinematography, Sound

●●●●●●●●●●●●●●●●●●●●●●●●●●●

■ REBECCA

1940, 130 MINS, US ⑫ ⊙
Dir Alfred Hitchcock *Prod* David O. Selznick
Scr Robert E. Sherwood, Joan Harrison *Ph* George Barnes *Ed* Hal C. Kern, James E. Newcom *Mus* Franz Waxman *Art Dir* Lyle Wheeler
● Laurence Olivier, Joan Fontaine, George Sanders, Judith Anderson, Nigel Bruce, Reginald Denny (Selznick/United Artists)

Picture is noteworthy for its literal translation of Daphne du Maurier's novel to the screen, presenting all of the sombreness and dramatic tragedy of the book.

Alfred Hitchcock pilots his first American production with capable assurance and exceptional understanding of the motivation and story mood. Despite the psychological and moody aspects of the tale throughout its major footage, he highlights the piece with several intriguing passages that display inspired direction.

Laurence Olivier provides an impressionable portrayal as the master of Manderley, unable to throw off the memory of his tragic first marriage while trying to secure happiness in his second venture. Joan Fontaine is excellent as the second wife, carrying through the transition of a sweet and vivacious bride to that of a bewildered woman marked by the former tragedy she finds hard to understand.

Supporting cast has been selected with careful attention to individual capabilities. Judith Anderson is the sinister housekeeper and confidante of the former wife; George Sanders is personable in portrayal of the despicable Jack Flavell; and Reginald Denny is Crawley, the estate manager and pal of Olivier. Florence Bates provides many light moments in the early portion as a romantically-inclined dowager.

☐ 1940: Best Picture, B&W Cinematography.
☐ Nominations: Best Director, Actor (Laurence Olivier), Actress (Joan Fontaine), Supp. Actress (Judith Anderson), Screenplay, B&W Art Direction, Editing, Original Score, Special Effects

●●●●●●●●●●●●●●●●●●●●●●●●●●●

■ REBECCA OF SUNNYBROOK FARM

1917, 74 MINS, US ⊗ ⊙
Dir Marshall Neilan *Scr* Frances Marion *Ph* Walter Stradling
● Mary Pickford, Eugene O'Brien, Helen Jerome Eddy, Charles Ogle, Marjorie Daw, Mayme Kelso (Artcraft)

Rebecca of Sunnybrook Farm moves along in perfect unison, devoid of padding, minus the wastage of one foot of film, engrossing and impressive, yet with perfect accord in its relation to suspense and cumulative appeal.

In adapting the Kate Douglas Wiggin book for the screen, Frances Marion wrought well. The original story has been retained, with the necessary elaboration. Compared with the dramatic production, which was excellently done, the screen version seems magnitudinous. The story is of Rebecca, a member of a large family, who is sent to the home of her aunts for rearing, ultimately inheriting their estate, and, incidentally, marrying the finest young man in the town. It attained its great popularity through its fidelity in picturing the atmosphere of New England.

Mary Pickford plays as she never played before, varying lights and shades to elicit the major interest, tearful at one moment and laughing the next. Her support is flawless, embodying many artists of repute.

●●●●●●●●●●●●●●●●●●●●●●●●●●●

■ REBECCA OF SUNNYBROOK FARM

1938, 80 MINS, US ⑫ ⊙
Dir Allan Dwan *Prod* Raymond Griffith *Scr* Karl Tunberg, Don Ettlinger *Ph* Arthur Miller *Ed* Allen McNeil *Mus* Arthur Lange (dir.) *Art Dir* Bernard Herzbrun, Hans Peters
● Shirley Temple, Randolph Scott, Jack Haley, Gloria Stuart, Helen Westley, Bill Robinson (20th Century-Fox)

Shirley Temple proves she's a great little artist in this one. The rest of it is synthetic and disappointing. Why they named it *Rebecca of Sunnybrook Farm* is one of those mysteries. The only resemblance to Kate Douglas Wiggins' charming comedy is a load of hay, a litter of pigs and Bill Robinson's straw hat.

More fitting title would be *Rebecca of Radio City*. The story is about a talented stage child who wins a broadcasting moppet contest, then is lost to the advertising agency in the shuffle and rediscovered at Aunt Mirandy's farm. The supporting characters, mostly unsympathetic, over-drawn and exaggerated, are familiar types.

Randolph Scott and Jack Haley try to get some excitement and suspense into the search for Shirley. Slim Summerville and Helen Westley manage a few laughs from the old situation of sulking sweethearts.

●●●●●●●●●●●●●●●●●●●●●●●●●●●

■ REBECCA'S DAUGHTERS

1992, 94 MINS, GERMANY/UK ◇ ⑫
Dir Karl Francis *Prod* Chris Sievernich *Scr* Guy Jenkin *Ph* Russ Walker *Ed* Roy Sharman *Mus* Rachel Portman *Art Dir* Ray Price
● Peter O'Toole, Paul Rhys, Joely Richardson, Keith Allen, Simon Dormandy, Dafydd Hywel (Astralma Erste/Rebecca's Daughters/Delta)

Peter O'Toole goes way over the top and stays there in *Rebecca's Daughters*, an irresistible period romp about Welsh peasants taking on the English taxmen. Script is based on a screenplay commissioned in 1948 from Dylan Thomas but never produced.

Set in southern Wales in 1843, yarn opens with Anthony Raine (Paul Rhys) returning from service in India with thoughts of childhood sweetheart Rhiannon (Joely Richardson) uppermost on his mind. He soon gets wise, however, to the peasants' problems, including a tollgate tax levied by drunken lord of the manor (O'Toole).

With Rhiannon playing hard to get, he dresses up as a mysterious masked avenger, Rebecca (modeled on the Bible figure whose offspring rose up against their oppressors), to win her back and right local wrongs. He's soon leading a hit squad of yokels in drag who turn the tables on a snotty English captain (Simon Dormandy) in nocturnal raids.

Main competition to O'Toole in the histrionics department is Dormandy, excellent as the crazed English captain. Bulk of pic's $6 million budget was raised by producer from private German investors.

●●●●●●●●●●●●●●●●●●●●●●●●●●●

■ REBEL, THE
(US: Call Me Genius)

1961, 105 MINS, UK ◇
Dir Robert Day *Prod* W.A. Whittaker *Scr* Alan Simpson, Ray Galton *Ph* Gilbert Taylor *Ed* Richard Best *Mus* Frank Cordell *Art Dir* Robert Jones
● Tony Hancock, George Sanders, Paul Massie, Margit Saad, Gregoire Aslan, Irene Handl (Associated British)

Tony Hancock's TV writers, Alan Simpson and Ray Galton, scripted this, and they knew their man's idiosyncracies intimately. He's the little man, slightly at war with himself and his fellows, but quick to grasp an opportunity for getting on.

In *The Rebel*, he is a downtrodden London city clerk, fed up with the daily round, and with a yen to be a sculptor. Unfortunately, he's very unskilled. Eventually, he blows his top, throws up his job and sets up shop as an existentialist painter in Paris. He talks himself into being accepted on the Left Bank as the leader of a new movement in art. Then an art connoisseur boobs. He exhibits the paintings of Hancock's roommate, thinking they are Hancock's work. The misfit becomes a national figure.

Among several amusing scenes are those when Hancock revolts against his office boss, an existentialist Left Bank party, Hancock's visit to the yacht of a Greek millionaire where he is commissioned to sculpt the tycoon's vamp wife, a colorful carnival party aboard the yacht and Hancock 'painting' a picture by daubing paint on a canvas and then bicycling over it.

☐ 1955: Nominations: Best Supp. Actor (Sal Mineo), Supp. Actress (Natalie Wood), Motion Picture Story

●●●●●●●●●●●●●●●●●●●●●●●●●●●

■ REBEL WITHOUT A CAUSE

1955, 111 MINS, US ◇ ⑫ ⊙
Dir Nicholas Ray *Prod* David Weisbart *Scr* Stewart Stern *Ph* Ernest Haller *Ed* William Zeigler *Mus* Leonard Rosenman *Art Dir* William Wallace
● James Dean, Natalie Wood, Corey Allen, Sal Mineo, Dennis Hopper, Jim Backus (Warner)

Here is a fairly exciting, suspenseful and provocative, if also occasionally far-fetched, melodrama of unhappy youth on another delinquency kick. The film presents a boy whose rebellion against a weakling father and a shrewish mother expresses itself in boozing, knife-fighting and other forms of physical combat and testing of his own manhood.

Although essentially intent upon action, director Nicholas Ray, who sketched the basic story, does bring out redeeming touches of human warmth. There is as regards the hero, if not as regards the highschool body generally, a better-than-average-for-a-psychological thriller explanation of the core of confusion in the child.

James Dean is very effective as a boy groping for adjustment to people. His actor's capacity to get inside the skin of youthful pain, torment and bewilderment is not often encountered.

Natalie Wood as the girl next door also shows teenage maladjustment. She, too, asks more of her father than he can give.

●●●●●●●●●●●●●●●●●●●●●●●●●●●

■ RECKLESS

1935, 95 MINS, US ⑫
Dir Victor Fleming *Prod* David O. Selznick *Scr* P.J. Wolfson *Ph* George Folsey *Ed* Margaret Booth *Mus* Herbert Stothart (sup.) *Art Dir* Cedric Gibbons, Merrill Pye, Edwin B. Willis
● Jean Harlow, William Powell, Franchot Tone, May Robson, Rosalind Russell, Mickey Rooney (M-G-M)

Reckless is a hodge-podge of melodrama, backstage and quasi-musical. It includes a cinematic recreation [from a story by Oliver Jeffries] of a recent newspaper melodrama involving a torch songstress and a posthumous heir to a tobacco fortune, but it's a rambling affair in toto.

Direction is as haphazard as the story. The showfolk are ridiculously white-washed and the socialites are made out consistently caddish. It's one of those things.

From the moment the infatuated Franchot Tone buys out the whole evening's performance and sops up champagne in the audience while solo-appreciating the performance, up until the elopement, which culminates in his suicide, it's ever make-believe. William Powell is an equally vague character. A combination sportsman-philanthropist, he's subsequently influential enough to b.r. and angel the musical comedy which spell the girl's professional comeback.

Instead of a torcher, Jean Harlow is a dancer, yet for the climatic situation she's the fulcrum of a dramatic song number – strongly reminiscent of the real-life counterpart. Rosalind Russell as a jilted girl and Robert Light as her brother alone make their chores ring true.

. . . .

■ RECKLESS KELLY

1993, 94 MINS, AUSTRALIA ◇ ▼ ⊙

Dir Yahoo Serious *Prod* Yahoo Serious, Warwick Ross *Scr* Yahoo Serious, David Roach, Warwick Ross, Lulu Serious *Ph* Kevin Hayward *Ed* Yahoo Serious, David Roach, Robert Gibson, Antony Gray *Mus* Yahoo Serious, Tommy Tycho *Art Dir* Yahoo Serious, Graham 'Grace' Walker
● Yahoo Serious, Melora Hardin, Alexei Sayle, Hugo Weaving, Kathleen Freeman, John Pinette (Serious)

Australian comic Yahoo Serious' second outing, produced on a far larger budget, is full of ideas and nonsense but short on geniune laughs and zest.

Starting from the engaging premise that the spirit of Australia's legendary outlaw Ned Kelly (1855-80) lives on in one of his descendents, Serious puts the new Ned Kelly (himself) and family on an island paradise.

Kelly motorbikes to Sydney, where he robs the bank owned by evil Sir John (Hugo Weaving), who hires Brit military expert Alexei Sayle and plots to sell Kelly's island to the Japanese. Needing a quick $1 million, Kelly heads for the 'land of opportunity for outlaws,' America, accompanied by actress girlfriend Robin Banks (get it?), charmingly played by Melora Hardin. In Hollywood, they are spotted by schlock producer (John Pinette) and starred in a Vegas-based B-picture.

There are a lot of ideas here and a brash, go-for-it style. But star-helmer-co-writer-editor-designer Serious seems to have taken on too many chores: his own perf suffers and the script continually builds to punchlines that, when they come, fall flat.

. . . .

■ RECKLESS MOMENT, THE

1949, 81 MINS, US

Dir Max Ophuls *Prod* Walter Wanger *Scr* Henry Garson, Robert W. Soderberg *Ph* Burnett Guffey *Ed* Gene Havlick *Mus* Hans J. Salter *Art Dir* Cary Odell
● James Mason, Joan Bennett, Geraldine Brooks, Henry O'Neill, Shepperd Strudwick, David Bair (Columbia)

A tense melodrama projecting good mood and suspense has been fashioned out of Elisabeth Sanxay Holding's *Ladies Home Journal* yarn, *The Blank Wall* [adaptation by Mel Dinelli and Robert E. Kent]. Matter-of-fact technique used in the script and by Max Ophuls' direction doesn't permit much warmth to develop for the characters. Production gains in authentic values by using the seaside resort of Balboa and commercial sections of Los Angeles.

Plot wrings out suspense in its concern with a mother who becomes involved in murder and blackmail to save her daughter from the consequences of a romance with an unsavory older man.

James Mason's ability as an actor makes his assignment as a blackmailer very substantial and Joan Bennett shows up exceptionally well in a part that is tinged with coldness despite the fact it deals with a mother's concern and Henry O'Neill is good as the grandfather.

. . . .

■ RECKONING, THE

1970, 109 MINS, UK ◇

Dir Jack Gold *Prod* Ronald Shedlo *Scr* John McGrath *Ph* Geoffrey Unsworth *Ed* Peter Weatherley *Mus* Malcolm Arnold *Art Dir* Ray Simm
● Nicol Williamson, Rachel Roberts, Ann Bell, Zena Walker, Paul Rogers, Gwen Nelson (Columbia)

The Reckoning is the story of a ruthless man, who rises from a Liverpool slum to the upper strata of cutthroat big business in London. Actually a character study of a man totally without morals or ethics, it is interesting in its treatment and for Nicol Williamson's performance in a hard-hitting role.

Filmed in story's actual locale, script is based on Patrick Hall's novel, *The Harp That Once*.

Scene segues from fashionable London, where Williamson, as an ambitious and aggressive businessman, is married to a woman he doesn't love and is stymied from rising in his job by politics, to Liverpool. He is called there when his father is dying.

Williamson is entirely believable in his part, displaying a dominant personality and a flair for punching over his role.

Rachel Roberts is realistic as a married woman Williamson picks up at a wrestling match the night his father dies.

. . . .

■ RED BADGE OF COURAGE, THE

1951, 68 MINS, US ▼

Dir John Huston *Prod* Gottfried Reinhardt *Scr* John Huston *Ph* Harold Rosson *Ed* Ben Lewis *Mus* Bronislau Kaper *Art Dir* Cedric Gibbons, Hans Peters
● Audie Murphy, Bill Mauldin, John Dierkes, Royal Dano, Arthur Hunnicutt, Douglas Dick (M-G-M)

This is a curiously moody, arty study of the psychological birth of a fighting man from frightened boy, as chronicled in Stephen Crane's novel *The Red Badge of Courage*.

Pic follows two figures during the days of the War Between the States. They are Audie Murphy, the youth who goes into his first battle afraid but emerges a man, and Bill Mauldin, on whom the same fears and misgivings have less sensitive impact.

Rather than any clearly defined story line, picture deals with a brief few hours of war and the effect it has on the few characters with which the script is concerned. Within the limited format, director John Huston artfully projects the characters to capture a seemingly allegorical mood of all wars and the men involved in them. His battle scene staging has punch and action, and his handling of the individual players makes them stand out. Narration, taken directly from the text of Crane's story, does a great deal to make clear the picture's aims.

There is an unbilled guest appearance by Andy Devine as a cheery soldier who lets God do his worrying, and it makes a single scene stand out.

. . . .

■ RED DANUBE, THE

1950, 119 MINS, US

Dir George Sidney *Prod* Carey Wilson *Scr* Gina Kaus, Arthur Wimperis *Ph* Charles Rosher *Ed* James E. Newcom *Mus* Miklos Rozsa
● Walter Pidgeon, Ethel Barrymore, Peter Lawford, Angela Lansbury, Janet Leigh, Louis Calhern (M-G-M)

In *The Red Danube* [from the novel *Vespers in Vienna* by Bruce Marshall], Metro aims a haymaker at Soviet repatriation methods in Europe and general Communist ideology, but the punch lands short of the mark.

Film might have been rescued by a more winning portrayal of its pro-democratic forces. But Walter Pidgeon, who limns a British army colonel engaged in fulfilling the western allies' commitment to repatriate forcibly all refugees from Russia, is hamstrung for too many reels by calloused and blundering doings. His adjutant, Peter Lawford, is depicted as a peculiarly capri cious character.

Scene of the struggle is Vienna, circa 1945, where Pidgeon is billeted in a convent. Here much tedious religious talk is generated between the colonel, a professed unbeliever, and the mother-superior (Ethel Barrymore) on the pros and cons of organized religion.

Chief pawn is a ballerina (Janet Leigh) beloved by Lawford. Pidgeon turns over the ballerina on the promise she will not be mistreated.

□ 1950: Nomination: Best B&W Art Director

. . . .

■ RED DAWN

1984, 114 MINS, US ◇ ▼ ⊙

Dir John Milius *Prod* Buzz Feitshans, Barry Beckerman *Scr* Kevin Reynolds, John Milius *Ph* Ric Waite *Ed* Thom Noble *Mus* Basil Poledouris *Art Dir* Jackson De Govia
● Patrick Swayze, C. Thomas Howell, Ron O'Neal, William Smith, Powers Booth, Charlie Sheen (United Artists/Valkyrie)

Red Dawn charges off to an exciting start as a war picture and then gets all confused in moralistic handwriting, finally sinking in the sunset.

Sometime in the future, the United States stands alone and vulnerable to attack, abandoned by its allies. Rather than an all-out nuclear war Soviet and Cuban forces bomb sel-ectively and then launch a conventional invasion across the southern and northwest borders.

Dawn takes place entirely in a small town taken by surprise by paratroopers. Grabbing food and weapons on the run, a band of teens led by Patrick Swayze and C. Thomas Howell makes it to the nearby mountains as the massacre continues below.

Swayze, Howell and the other youngsters are all good in their parts.

. . . .

■ RED DUST

1932, 83 MINS, US ▼

Dir Victor Fleming *Prod* [uncredited] *Scr* John Lee Mahin *Ph* Harold Rosson *Ed* Blanche Sewell *Mus* [uncredited] *Art Dir* Cedric Gibbons
● Clark Gable, Jean Harlow, Gene Raymond, Mary Astor, Donald Crisp, Tully Marshall (M-G-M)

Familiar plot stuff, but done so expertly it almost overcomes the basic script shortcomings and the familiar hot-love-in-the-isolated-tropics theme [from the play by Wilson Collison].

This time it's a rubber plantation in Indo-China, bossed by Clark Gable. Jean Harlow is the Sadie Thompson of the territory. Enter Gene Raymond and Mary Astor on Raymond's initial engineering assignment. Gable makes a play for Astor and it looks like the young husband will have his ideals shattered when circumstances cause Gable to send them both back to a more civilized existence, with more conventional standards, leaving Harlow as a more plausible (and, for audience purposes, more acceptable) playmate.

It's as simple as all that, basically. Astor is oke in the passive virtuous moments, but falls down badly on the clinches, sustained only by Gable. As the putteed, unshaven he-man rubber planter Gable's in his element, sustaining an unsympathetic assignment until it veers about a bit.

Harlow's elementary conception of moral standards, so far as the decent kid explorer (Raymond) is concerned, sort of gilds her lily of the fields assignment. She plays the light lady to the limit, however, not overdoing anything.

. . . .

■ RED-HEADED WOMAN

1932, 74 MINS, US ⓥ

Dir Jack Conway   *Scr* Anita Loos   *Ph* Harold Rosson
Ed Blanche Sewell
● Jean Harlow, Chester Morris, Lewis Stone, Leila
Hyams, Una Merkel, Henry Stephenson (M-G-M)

The outstanding fact is that M-G-M has
turned out an interesting dissertation on a
thoroughly provocative subject. Jean Harlow,
hitherto not highly esteemed as an actress,
gives an electric performance.

Ethics of the subject are sufficient to make
a church deacon gulp and stammer. Heroine
(Harlow) is a home wrecker, a vicious vamp
and a destroyer of peace, and the wages of sin
in her case are paid in the final close-up in
strange and wonderful coin.

Picture is handled with a curious blending
of bluntness and subtlety. Some of the 'vamping' sequences, and there are plenty of them,
are torrid. But the overall effect is conveyed
with a great deal of fancy skating over very
thin ice and its very candor is disarming.

■ RED HEAT

1988, 103 MINS, US ◇ ⓥ ⊙

Dir Walter Hill   *Prod* Walter Hill, Gordon Carroll
Scr Harry Kleiner, Walter Hill, Troy Kennedy Martin
Ph Matthew F. Leonetti   *Ed* Freeman Davies, Carmel
Davies, Donn Aron   *Mus* James Horner   *Art Dir* John
Vallone
● Arnold Schwarzenegger, James Belushi, Peter Boyle,
Ed O'Ross, Larry Fishburne, Gina Gershon (Carolco/Lone
Wolf/Oak)

Red Heat [from a screen story by Walter Hill]
has earned a place in the history books as the
first entirely American-produced film to have
been permitted to lens in the USSR, even if
location work was essentially limited to establishing shots.

Entire early Moscow section (shot mostly in
Budapest) establishes the notion that one of
the prices the East will pay for opening up is
an increase in the Western disease of drug
dealing. A particularly loathesome practitioner in the field named Viktor (Ed O'Ross)
manages to slip through the fingers of the
Red Army's top enforcer (guess who) and
heads for Chicago.

In full uniform, Arnold Schwarzenegger arrives at O'Hare Airport, where he is greeted
by two working stiffs from the Chicago Police
Dept, James Belushi and Richard Bright.
Belushi is assigned to keep tabs on the terminator as the latter tracks down Viktor.

Schwarzenegger, who when he dons a green
suit is dubbed 'Gumby' by Belushi, is right on
target with his characterization of the iron-
willed soldier, and Belushi proves a quicksilver foil.

■ RED HOUSE, THE

1947, 100 MINS, US ⓥ

Dir Delmer Daves   *Prod* Sol Lesser   *Scr* Delmer Daves
Ph Bert Glennon   *Ed* Merrill White   *Mus* Miklos Rozsa
Art Dir McClure Capps
● Edward G. Robinson, Lon McCallister, Judith
Anderson, Allene Roberts, Julie London, Rory Calhoun
(United Artists)

The Red House is an interesting psychological
thriller [based on the novel by George Agnew
Chamberlain], with its mood satisfactorily
sustained throughout the pic. Film, however,
has too slow a pace, so that the paucity of incident and action stands out sharply, despite
good performances by Edward G. Robinson,
Judith Anderson, Allene Roberts, Lon
McCallister and others.

Film has a simple, rustic quality in scripting, setting and characterization.

Pic, however, is built on a single thread, and
takes too long in getting to its climax. It ends
on something of a macabre note, and

throughout it has several false touches – a
muscle-brained young woodsman being in
possession of $750; entrusting the money to a
flighty girl to buy him a bond with it, etc.

Robinson has supplied himself with a fat
part that suits his talents and to which he
gives his best efforts. He's cast as a farmer,
living with a sister and an adopted daughter
in an isolated area of a small community, further withdrawn from the community by his
strange, gloomy moods. Part of his property is
a wooded area to which no one can go; the
farmer even employs a young woodsman to
keep trespassers out by gunfire if necessary. A
young hired hand comes to work on the farm,
is intrigued by the wooded area, and enters it,
to meet with several mishaps.

■ RED LINE 7000

1965, 118 MINS, US ◇ ⓥ

Dir Howard Hawks   *Prod* Howard Hawks   *Scr* George
Kirgo   *Ph* Milton Krasner   *Ed* Stuart Gilmore, Bill Brame
Mus Nelson Riddle
● James Caan, Laura Devon, Gail Hire, Charlene Holt,
John Robert Crawford, Marianna Hill (Paramount)

Script by George Kirgo, based on a story by
director Howard Hawks, centers on three sets
of characters as they go about their racing
and lovemaking. Trio of racers are members
of a team operating out of Daytona, Fla, their
individual lives uncomplicated until three
femmes fall in love with them. In a thrilling
climax, one of the drivers, overcome with
jealousy, causes another to crash but miraculously his life is saved.

Making excellent impressions are Laura
Devon, Gail Hire and Marianna Hill, as girl-
friends of the three daredevils of the track.
James Caan, John Robert Crawford and
James Ward in these roles are effective.

Hawks is on safe ground while his cameras
are focused on race action. His troubles lie in
limning his various characters in their more
intimate moments. Title refers to an engine
speed beyond which it's dangerous to operate
a race car, perhaps symbolic of what Hawks
wanted to achieve in the emotions of his players.

■ RED PONY, THE

1949, 89 MINS, US ◇ ⓥ ⊙

Dir Lewis Milestone   *Prod* Charles K. Feldman, Lewis
Milestone   *Scr* John Steinbeck   *Ph* Tony Gaudio
Ed Harry Keller   *Mus* Aaron Copland
● Myrna Loy, Robert Mitchum, Louis Calhern, Shepperd
Strudwick, Peter Miles, Beau Bridges (Republic)

Lewis Milestone's filmization of a novelette
by John Steinbeck has been pieced together
with taste and fidelity. It has, however, stumbled over one obstacle. The secondary theme,
an attempt to etch the emotional complexities of the grownups that surround the boy is
slack-paced and sketchily drawn.

Boy-and-pony theme owes much of its compassion and winning graces to a fine and sensitive performance by Peter Miles. As Billy
Buck, the hired man, Robert Mitchum underscores a likeable role.

Neither Myrna Loy nor Shepperd Strudwick
are as satisfactory as the boy's parents. Since
it is their lot to go through some pretty tedious bits of business, script and direction are
undoubtedly more at fault than their thesping efforts.

■ RED RIVER

1948, 126 MINS, US ⓥ ⊙

Dir Howard Hawks   *Prod* Charles K. Feldman
Scr Borden Chase, Charles Schnee   *Ph* Russell Harlan
Ed Christian Nyby   *Mus* Dimitri Tiomkin   *Art Dir* John
Datu Arensma
● John Wayne, Montgomery Clift, Joanne Dru, Walter
Brennan, Coleen Gray, John Ireland (United Artists)

Howard Hawks' production and direction
give a masterful interpretation to a story of
the early west and the opening of the
Chisholm Trail, over which Texas cattle were
moved to Abilene to meet the railroad on its
march across the country.

Also important to *Red River* is the introduction of Montgomery Clift. Clift brings to the
role of Matthew Garth a sympathetic personality that invites audience response.

Hawks has loaded the film with mass spectacle and earthy scenes. His try for naturalness in dialog between principals comes off
well. The staging of physical conflict is
deadly, equalling anything yet seen on the
screen. Picture realistically depicts trail hardships; the heat, sweat, dust, storm and marauding Indians that bore down on the
pioneers. Neither has Hawks overlooked sex,
exponents being Joanne Dru and Coleen
Gray.

Picture is not all tough melodrama. There's
a welcome comedy relief in the capable hands
of Walter Brennan. He makes his every scene
stand out sharply, leavening the action with
chuckles while maintaining a character as
rough and ready as the next.

Sharing co-director credit with Hawks is
Arthur Rosson. The pair have staged high excitement in the cattle stampedes and other
scenes of mass action.
□ 1948: Nominations: Best Motion Picture
Story, Editing

■ REDS

1981, 200 MINS, US ◇ ⓥ ⊙

Dir Warren Beatty   *Prod* Warren Beatty   *Scr* Warren
Beatty, Trevor Griffiths   *Ph* Vittorio Storaro   *Ed* Dede
Allen, Craig McKay   *Mus* Stephen Sondheim, Dave
Grusin   *Art Dir* Richard Sylbert
● Warren Beatty, Diane Keaton, Jerzy Kosinski, Jack
Nicholson, Maureen Stapleton, Edward Herrmann
(Paramount)

Warren Beatty's *Reds* is a courageous and uncompromising attempt to meld a high-level
socio-political drama of ideas with an intense
love story, but it is ultimately too ponderous.

More than just the story of American jour-
nalist-activist John Reed's stormy romantic
career with writer Louise Bryant, a kinetic affair backdropped by pre-World War I radicalism and the Russian Revolution, the film is
also, to its eventual detriment, structured as
a Marxist history lesson.

First half of the film, though it takes an inordinate amount of time and detail to do it,
does an intelligent job of setting both the political and emotional scene. Beginning in
1915, Reed (Beatty) is introduced as an idealistic reporter of decidedly radical bent who
meets Portland writer Bryant (Diane Keaton)
and persuades her to join him in New York
within a tight-knit radical intellectual salon
that includes the likes of playwright Eugene
O'Neill (Jack Nicholson), anarchist-feminist
Emma Goldman (Maureen Stapleton) and
radical editor Max Eastman (Edward
Herrmann).

Their on-again, off-again affair – which
challenges their respective claims of emotional liberation – survives Keaton's brief
fling with Nicholson and they marry.

But Beatty's inability to resist the growing
socialist bandwagon strains them yet again
and Keaton ships off to cover the French bat-
tlefront and begin life afresh. En route to
cover the upcoming conflagration in Russia,
Beatty persuades her to join him – in professional, not emotional status – and in
Petrograd, the revolutionary fervor rekindles
their romantic energies as well.

Reds bites off more than an audience can
comfortably chew. Constant conflicts between
politics and art, love and social conscience, individuals versus masses, pragmatism against
idealism, take the form of intense and eventually exhausting arguments that dominate

R

the script by Beatty and British playwright Trevor Griffiths.

As director, Beatty has harnessed considerable intensity into individual confrontations but curiously fails to give the film an overall emotional progression.

☐ 1981: Best Director, Supp. Actress (Maureen Stapleton), Cinematography.

☐ Nominations: Best Picture, Actor (Warren Beatty), Actress (Diane Keaton), Supp. Actor (Jack Nicholson), Original Screenplay, Costume Design, Art Direction, Editing, Sound

••••••••••••••••••••••••••••••••••••

■ **RED SALUTE**

(Aka: Runaway Daughter; Her Enlisted Man; Arms and the Girl)

1935, 77 MINS, US

Dir Sidney Lanfield   *Prod* Edward Small   *Scr* Humphrey Pearson, Manuel Seff   *Ph* Robert Planck   *Ed* Grant Whytock   *Mus* [uncredited]   *Art Dir* John DuCasse Schulze

● Barbara Stanwyck, Robert Young, Hardie Albright, Ruth Donnelly, Cliff Edwards, Gordon Jones (Reliance)

Stripped of its anti-Red angle, *Red Salute* resolves itself down to a weak take-off of *It Happened One Night*. While it is studded here and there with pungent humor, after the first few rounds the rough, wisecracking exchange between Barbara Stanwyck and Robert Young begins to pall.

Preachment which *Salute* seeks to espouse stems from the agitation against war by student groups on various college campuses. Into this topical idea is woven the story of a young radical orator (Hardie Albright) who is loved by the general's daughter (Stanwyck), the efforts of her father to keep them apart, and the new romance that comes into her life when an enlisted man (Young) goes AWOL to help her escape from Mexico and back to her lover.

Stanwyck does a crack job at holding interest. Another telling performance is that of Young as the reckless soldier who pulls many a misdemeanor, including the kidnaping of a tourist trailer and its owner, while pursued by border police. Showing by Albright is as all-sided as the political arguments that the script [from a story by Humphrey Pearson] assigns him to voice on the platform.

During the first day's showing at the Rivoli, NY, patriots and youths allied with the anti-war National Student League climaxed their contending rounds of applause, hissing and booing with several fist fights. Out on the sidewalk girl and boy Student Leaguers distributed handbills urging a boycott of the picture

••••••••••••••••••••••••••••••••••••

■ **RED SCORPION**

1989, 102 MINS, US ◇ ⊛ ⊙

Dir Joseph Zito   *Prod* Jack Abramoff   *Scr* Arne Olsen   *Ph* Joao Fernandes   *Ed* Daniel Loewenthal   *Mus* Jay Chattaway   *Art Dir* Ladislav Wilheim

● Dolph Lundgren, M. Emmet Walsh, Al White, T.P. McKenna, Carmen Argenziano, Alex Colon (Shapiro Glickenhaus)

Red Scorpion is a dull, below-average action pic, lensed in Swaziland.

Out-of-date screenplay has Scandinavian star Dolph Lundgren playing a Russian special services officer ordered by his nasty commander (Irish thesp T.P. McKenna) to kill the rebel leader of a fictional African country. Lundgren fails in his mission and is tortured by Cubans.

Under the guidance of a knowing, mystical bushman (Regopstaan, obviously patterned on the hero of *The Gods Must Be Crazy*) who tattoos a scorpion on Dolph's chest, Lundgren realizes the commies are oppressing the Africans. Anticlimax has this Nordic giant leading the otherwise defeated rebels to defeat the combined Russian/Cuban might.

Joseph Zito's sluggish direction lingers on nonessentials. Tediousness could have been alleviated by dropping at least a reel's worth of trekking across the African desert. Lundgren provides little more than sustained beefcake.

••••••••••••••••••••••••••••••••••••

■ **RED SHOES, THE**

1948, 134 MINS, UK ◇ ⊛ ⊙

Dir Michael Powell, Emeric Pressburger   *Prod* Michael Powell, Emeric Pressburger   *Scr* Michael Powell, Emeric Pressburger   *Ph* Jack Cardiff   *Ed* Reginald Mills   *Mus* Brian Easdale   *Art Dir* Hein Heckroth, Arthur Lawson

● Anton Walbrook, Marius Goring, Moira Shearer, Leonide Massine, Robert Helpmann, Ludmilla Tcherina (Archers)

For the first 60 minutes, this is a commonplace backstage melodrama, in which temperamental ballerinas replace the more conventional showgirls. Then a superb ballet of the Red Shoes, based on a Hans Andersen fairy tale, is staged with breathtaking beauty out-classing anything that could be done on the stage. It is a colorful sequence, full of artistry, imagination and magnificence. The three principal dancers, Moira Shearer, Leonide Massine and Robert Helpmann, are beyond criticism.

Then the melodrama resumes, story being about the love of a ballerina for a young composer thus incurring the severe displeasure of the ruthless Boris Lermontov, guiding genius of the ballet company.

Although the story may be trite, there are many compensations, notably the flawless performance of Anton Walbrook, whose interpretation of the role of Lermontov is one of the best things he has done on the screen. Shearer, glamorous redhead, shows that she can act as well as dance, while Marius Goring, polished as ever, plays the young composer with enthusiasm.

Other assets that can be chalked up are the wide variety of interesting locations – London, Paris, Monte Carlo, magnificent settings, firstclass Technicolor and some brilliant musical scores played by the Royal Philharmonic Orchestra with Thomas Beecham as conductor.

☐ 1948: Best Color Art Direction, Score for a Dramatic Picture.

☐ Nominations: Best Picture, Motion Picture Story, Editing

••••••••••••••••••••••••••••••••••••

■ **RED SONJA**

1985, 89 MINS, US ◇ ⊛ ⊙

Dir Richard Fleischer   *Prod* Christian Ferry   *Scr* Clive Exton, George MacDonald Fraser   *Ph* Giuseppe Rotunno   *Ed* Frank J. Urioste   *Mus* Ennio Morricone   *Art Dir* Danilo Donati

● Brigitte Nielsen, Arnold Schwarzenegger, Sandahl Bergman, Paul Smith, Ernie Reyes Jr, Ronald Lacey (De Laurentiis/Famous)

Red Sonja [based on stories by Robert E. Howard] returns to those olden days when women were women and the menfolk stood around with funny hats on until called forth to be whacked at.

Except, of course, for Arnold Schwarzenegger, whose Kalidor creation has just enough muscles to make him useful to the ladies, but not enough brains to make him a bother, except that he talks too much.

To her credit in the title role, Brigitte Nielsen never listens to a word he has to say, perhaps because he has an unfortunate tendency to address her as 'Sony-uh.' Nielsen wants to revenge her sister and find the magic talisman all on her own with no help from Kalidor, though she does think it's kind of cute when he wades into 80 guys and wastes them in an effort to impress her.

••••••••••••••••••••••••••••••••••••

■ **RED SUN**

1971, 115 MINS, FRANCE ◇ ⊛

Dir Terence Young   *Prod* Robert Dorfmann   *Scr* L. Koenig, D.B. Petitclerc, W. Roberts, L. Roman   *Ph* Henri Alekan   *Ed* Johnny Dwyre   *Mus* Maurice Jarre

● Charles Bronson, Ursula Andress, Toshiro Mifune, Alain Delon, Capucine (Corona/Oceania)

East is East and West is West, but the twain meet in this actionful oater with Japanese actor Toshiro Mifune matching sword and wits with Yank Charles Bronson and Frenchman Alain Delon.

Mifune is a Samurai accompanying the Japanese ambassador in a trek across the West to Washington in the mid-19th century to deliver a jeweled, golden sword to the US president. On the way the train is held up by Bronson and Delon, but the latter doublecrosses Bronson and also kills a samurai friend of Mifune and takes the sword. Mifune's code requires he find the sword and kill Delon.

Mifune is his towering, glowering self in his rich samurai garb and his sword matches the guns. Bronson is relaxed and effective as the bandit with some honor within his own life. Ursula Andress is decorative as the wily prostie, out to make a killing to get out of her life of bondage.

Young lays on the action and blood with some interludes in the growing friendship between Bronson and Mifune.

••••••••••••••••••••••••••••••••••••

■ **RED TENT, THE**

1971, 121 MINS, ITALY/USSR ◇ ⊛ ⊙

Dir Mikhail Kalatozov   *Prod* Franco Cristaldi   *Scr* Ennio De Concini, Richard Adams   *Ph* Leonid Kalashnikov   *Ed* Peter Zinner   *Mus* Ennio Morricone   *Art Dir* Giancarlo Bartolini Salimbeni, David Vinitsky

● Sean Connery, Claudia Cardinale, Hardy Kruger, Peter Finch, Massimo Girotti, Luigi Vannucchi (Vides/Mosfilm)

This first Italo-Russian co-production deals with the 1928 rescue of an Italian Polar expedition stranded by a dirigible crash. Some spectacularly beautiful Arctic footage, plus an exciting personal story of survival, make the production compelling and suspenseful.

Framework of the script is metaphysical; a sort of rugged adventure yarn in a Jean-Paul Sartre setting. Peter Finch plays General Nobile, an Italian Arctic explorer who is lost in the North Atlantic wastes. Years later, his nightmares about the incident summon up phantoms of those involved with him.

Sean Connery plays Roald Amundsen, a fellow explorer who died in search of Finch; Claudia Cardinale plays a nurse who was in love with one of Finch's crew; and Hardy Kruger is a daredevil rescue pilot whose motivations in rescuing Finch before his men creates an international scandal.

Connery plays an aged man very convincingly. Kruger and Cardinale supply key plot motivations, but the heaviest burden is on Finch; he is excellent in a characterization which demands many moods, many attitudes.

••••••••••••••••••••••••••••••••••••

■ **REFLECTIONS IN A GOLDEN EYE**

1967, 109 MINS, US ◇ ⊛

Dir John Huston   *Prod* Ray Stark   *Scr* Chapman Mortimer, Gladys Hill   *Ph* Aldo Tonti   *Ed* Russell Lloyd   *Mus* Toshiro Mayuzumi   *Art Dir* Stephen Grimes

● Elizabeth Taylor, Marlon Brando, Brian Keith, Julie Harris, Robert Forster, Zorro David (Warner/Seven Arts)

Carson McCullers' novel, *Reflections in a Golden Eye*, about a latent homosexual US Army officer in the pre Second World War period, has been turned into a pretentious melodrama by director John Huston.

Adaptation features six disparate characters: Marlon Brando, the latent homosexual;

his wife, Elizabeth Taylor, a practicing heterosexual – practicing with Brian Keith, whose own wife, Julie Harris, once cut off her breasts with scissors after unfortunate childbirth; Robert Forster, young fetishist and exhibitionist; Zorro David, Harris' fey houseboy. Also prominent are a host of sex symbols, and some salty expressions.

Brando struts about and mugs as the stuffy officer, whose Dixie dialect is often incoherent. Taylor is appropriately unaware of her husband's torment. Her dialect also obscures some vital plot points.

The most outstanding and satisfying performance is that of Brian Keith. This versatile actor is superb as the rationalizing and insensitive middle-class hypocrite.

■ REFORM SCHOOL GIRLS

1986, 94 MINS, US ◇ ⓥ ⊙
Dir Tom deSimone   *Prod* Jack Cummins   *Scr* Tom deSimone   *Ph* Howard Wexler   *Ed* Michael Spence   *Mus* Tedra Gabriel   *Art Dir* Becky Block
● Linda Carol, Wendy O. Williams, Pat Ast, Sybil Danning, Charlotte McGinnis, Sherri Stoner (New World)

Reform School Girls don't have it so bad. For one thing, they don't have to wear uniforms – or much else for that matter. They talk dirty, play dirty and are allowed to take long, long showers.

Busty Wendy O. Williams, who made a name for herself as the headbanging lead singer of the rock group, The Plasmatics, continues her trashy theatrics here as a leather-clad lesbian who reigns terror over the other girls serving time at Pridemore Juvenile Facilities.

Supported by her gang of 'death rockers,' Williams intimidates each new arrival into submission until she encounters fresh-faced Jenny (Linda Carol), who is bent on countering corruption at Pridemore.

Every character is a caricature, from the rifle-toting, Bible-quoting warden (Sybil Danning) to the lineup of lovelies who parade as reform school girls.

Pat Ast, as the cantankerous and corpulent head matron, and Williams play their rotten roles to the hilt and get most of the juicy lines.

■ REGARDING HENRY

1991, 107 MINS, US ◇ ⓥ ⊙
Dir Mike Nichols   *Prod* Mike Nichols, Scott Rudin   *Scr* Jeffrey Abrams   *Ph* Giuseppe Rotunno   *Ed* Sam O'Steen   *Mus* Hans Zimmer   *Art Dir* Tony Walton
● Harrison Ford, Annette Bening, Bill Nunn, Mikki Allen, Donald Moffat, Nancy Marchand (Paramount)

A subtle emotional journey impeccably orchestrated by director Mike Nichols and acutely well acted, *Regarding Henry* has a back-to-basics message that's bound to strike a responsive chord in the troubled aftermath of the 1980s. In a way, the pic is a variation on the old story of the husband who goes down to the corner for a pack of cigarettes and never comes back.

The controlling, intolerant Henry Turner (Harrison Ford) who steps out of his Manhattan brownstone late one night for a pack of Merits, only to become the victim of a mindless, hysterical violence, is certainly not the same man who has to be coaxed back home from the hospital after a lengthy rehabilitation. Henry has to start from scratch to regain such basic capacities as how to read, take a walk or make love to his wife.

The grace of the script by 23-year-old Jeffrey Abrams is that it doesn't contrive a practical alternative for Henry. The change in his character is story enough. On the other hand, there is the dimension contributed by Annette Bening's interpretation of an elegant society wife who bravely becomes Henry's

truest friend when his former confidence deserts him.

In a role as far removed as possible from her cunning Myra in *The Grifters*, Bening sets a shining new standard of performance. Ford operates with his usual firstrate precision, pushing the super-competent Henry slyly into the realm of humor, and suggesting the physical timidity and mental struggles of the debilitated Henry without overdoing it.

■ REINCARNATION OF PETER PROUD, THE

1975, 104 MINS, US ◇ ⓥ ⊙
Dir J. Lee Thompson   *Prod* Frank P. Rosenberg   *Scr* Max Ehrlich   *Ph* Victor J. Kemper   *Ed* Michael Anderson   *Mus* Jerry Goldsmith   *Art Dir* Jack Martin Smith
● Michael Sarrazin, Jennifer O'Neill, Margot Kidder, Cornelia Sharpe, Paul Hecht, Tony Stephano (American International)

Reincarnation of Peter Proud embodies all the thrills of Max Ehrlich's bestseller, plus an outstandingly rich performance from Margot Kidder. Only weakness still is story's sudden and unsatisfactory ending.

Michael Sarrazin from the start almost, realizes that some unknown person is within him. Tracing scenes from his dreams, he ventures to small Massachusetts town where Kidder had murdered philandering husband, briefly but ably played by Stephano.

Sarrazin is best in contending with the semi incestuous love affair that develops between him and Jennifer O'Neill. Her best moments, too, come in the clinches that do-don't take place between two obviously attracted, and otherwise eligible, young lovers.

■ REIVERS, THE

1969, 107 MINS, US ◇ ⓥ
Dir Mark Rydell   *Prod* Irving Ravetch   *Scr* Irving Ravetch, Harriet Frank Jr   *Ph* Richard Moore   *Ed* Thomas Stanford   *Mus* John Williams   *Art Dir* Charles Bailey, Joel Schiller
● Steve McQueen, Sharon Farrell, Rupert Crosse, Mitch Vogel, Clifton James, Will Geer (Duo)

The Reivers is a nice bawdy film, sort of Walt Disney with an adult rating. Imagine a charming nostalgia-soaked family-type film about a winsome 11-year-old in turn-of-the-century Mississippi who gets himself cut up in a Memphis bordello defending the good name of a lovely professional lady. The film is an adaptation [narrated by Burgess Meredith] of William Faulkner's last novel.

Mitch Vogel, as the kid, is appealing, subtle and sensitive, hovering between freckle-faced moppet and sexual puberty.

He is led astray by the family handy man and resident rogue Steve McQueen who gives a lively ribald characterization. Completing the triumvirate of 'Reivers', an old word that means 'thieves', is Rupert Crosse. He is a humorously light-hearted but sardonically mocking dude.

In a gleaming gold Winton Flyer the three steal off to Memphis, and the end of innocence for the boy.
☐ 1969: Nominations: Best Supp. Actor (Rupert Crosse), Original Music Score

■ RELUCTANT DEBUTANTE, THE

1958, 96 MINS, US ◇ ⓥ
Dir Vincente Minnelli   *Prod* Pandro S. Berman   *Scr* William Douglas Home   *Ph* Joseph Ruttenberg   *Ed* Adrienne Fazan   *Mus* Eddie Warner (arr.)   *Art Dir* A.J. d'Eaubonne
● Rex Harrison, Kay Kendall, John Saxon, Sandra Dee, Angela Lansbury, Diane Clare (M-G-M/Avon)

The Reluctant Debutante is refreshing and prettily dressed, a colorful, saucy film version of the William Douglas Home stage trifle.

Debutante is the story of London's social 'season', a time when bright and not-too-bright 17-year-olds make their debuts in society, carrying on at one deb's ball after another. Rex Harrison and Kay Kendall, as newly married on screen as off, invite his American daughter (by a former marriage) for a British visit that results in the girl's coming out socially.

As played by Sandra Dee, the teenager is bored with English stiffs but falls madly for an American drummer (John Saxon) who's tabbed with a most dubious reputation. Mixed-up telephone calls, embarrassing situations and advances – both wanted and unwanted – follow with rapidity.

Harrison is suavely disturbed as the father. Dee proves a rather good actress who maintains a lively character throughout, and Saxon lends a fine boyish charm to the proceedings. But it's really Kendall's picture, and she grabs it with a single wink. She's flighty and well-meaning, snobbish and lovable.

■ RELUCTANT DRAGON, THE

1941, 73 MINS, US ◇
Dir Alfred L. Werker, Hamilton Luske   *Prod* Walt Disney   *Scr* Ted Sears, Al Perkins, Larry Clemmons, Bill Cottrell, Harry Clork   *Ph* Bert Glennon, Winton Hoch   *Ed* Paul Weatherwax   *Mus* Frank Churchill, Larry Morey   *Art Dir* Gordon Wiles
● Robert Benchley, Frances Gifford, Buddy Pepper, Nana Bryant, Claud Allister, Barnett Parker (Walt Disney)

Ever a trail-hewer, Walt Disney has once more created a film entirely different from anything before. The film, in its essentials, is a trip through the Disney plant – interspersed with cartoon shorts to insure the picture's appeal. Aside from the introductory sequences in Disney's *Fantasia*, this is the first film to combine cartoons and humans on a large scale.

Pic opens with Robert Benchley's wife (Nana Bryant) reading Kenneth Grahame's famed fairy tale, *The Reluctant Dragon*. She rags Benchley into calling on Disney to sell it to him. Even after he is admitted to the studio, Benchley 'escapes' from his guide (Buddy Pepper) so that he won't have to face Disney.

His 'escape' takes him into strange doors and strange rooms. In his stumbling through the plant, Benchley (and the audience) sees some eight operations in the making of cartoons, plus three full shorts and hunks of a number of other Disney features in work, notably *Bambi*.

Cartoons [directed by Hamilton Luske] include *Baby Weems*, *How to Ride a Horse* and *The Reluctant Dragon*. Many of the performers in the live action portions are Disney employees doing their actual jobs, although virtually all of the speaking parts are handled by professionals.

Beginning of the film is in black and white. It cleverly shifts into Technicolor [photographed by Winton Hoch] when Benchley gets to the camera room where the color work is done. Direction keeps the live action zipping along. If there's any slowness, it's in the cartoon division.

■ REMBRANDT

1936, 85 MINS, US ⓥ
Dir Alexander Korda   *Prod* Alexander Korda   *Scr* Carl Zuckmayer, June Head, Arthur Wimperis   *Ph* Georges Perinal   *Ed* Francis Lyon, William Hornbeck   *Mus* Geoffrey Toye   *Art Dir* Vincent Korda
● Charles Laughton, Gertrude Lawrence, Elsa Lanchester, Walter Hudd, Roger Livesey, John Bryning (London)

An idealized film biography of the life of the famous painter. Story begins at the height of Rembrandt's fame, during his lifetime, and carries on to his solitary, poverty-stricken old age. Despite a cast of two score principals, it is a one-part production, with but one scene in the entire film in which the star does not play the central character.

It was an inspiration to film many of the scenes with a suggestion of the lighting for which Rembrandt is famous in his paintings.

Forty principals were requisitioned from the best artists the British legitimate stage has to offer. If some of them, like Gertrude Lawrence and Elsa Lanchester, stand out from the others, it is only because they have more extensive and showier roles.

Despite all this artistic and technical assistance, Charles Laughton is far from satisfactory. According to the story, he is never interested in anything relating to finance or the ordinary rules of domestic economy. The only tragic things in his life are the deaths of his two wives. On neither occasion does Laughton express the overwhelming sorrow the story calls for.

....

■ REMEMBER MY NAME

1978, 95 MINS, US ◇

Dir Alan Rudolph *Prod* Robert Altman *Scr* Alan Rudolph *Ph* Tak Fujimoto *Ed* Thomas Walls, William A. Sawyer *Mus* Alberta Hunter
● Geraldine Chaplin, Anthony Perkins, Moses Gunn, Berry Berenson, Jeff Goldblum, Timothy Thomerson (Lion's Gate)

Remember My Name is an attempt to make what Alan Rudolph calls a 'contemporary blues fable'. Whatever the generic goal, the end product is an incomprehensible melange of striking imagery, obscure dialog, a powerful score, and a script that doesn't know how to go from A to B.

Anthony Perkins is a construction worker married to Berry Berenson. Geraldine Chaplin arrives on the scene and begins a petty harassment of the couple, which gradually turns more sinister.

It develops that Chaplin is an ex-convict, recently sprung from a 12-year sentence for murder. She got a job in a nearby five-and-dime store managed by Jeff Goldblum (whose mother is still doing time), where she terrorizes store clerk Alfre Woodard and Goldblum. Chaplin also gets a room in a rundown apartment building managed by Moses Gunn, with whom she has a brief liaison.

If done on a traditional, linear level, *Remember My Name* might have induced some interest as a moderate chiller with emotional undertones. In Rudolph's infuriatingly oblique style, however, it becomes an irritating and puzzling affair that insults, rather than teases, the viewer.

....

■ REMEMBER THE NIGHT

1940, 93 MINS, US

Dir Mitchell Leisen *Prod* Mitchell Leisen *Scr* Preston Sturges *Ph* Ted Tetzlaff *Ed* Doane Harrison *Mus* Frederick Hollander *Art Dir* Hans Dreier, Roland Anderson
● Barbara Stanwyck, Fred MacMurray, Beulah Bondi, Elizabeth Patterson, Williard Robertson, Sterling Holloway (Paramount)

Preston Sturges' original screenplay depends mainly on individual sequences and bright situations rather than the overall effect of the story itself. Here is a tale of a girl crook (Barbara Stanwyck) who becomes enmeshed in the law after lifting a bracelet from a store. Deputy district attorney Fred MacMurray is assigned to prosecute, even though he plans to leave for Xmas holidays with his mother in Indiana.

When defense attorney pulls a surprise, young d.a. has trial continued for two weeks, and girl has to remain in jail in the interim. MacMurray suffers pangs of conscience and gets her out on bail. When he finds her home is also in Indiana, he takes her along on the trip.

Picture is highlighted in numerous instances by some deft telling in the script and fine piloting by director Mitchell Leisen to lift the yarn from commonplace and trite category.

Stanwyck turns in a fine performance. MacMurray is impressive as the serious-minded prosecutor, but loosens up for the comedy stretches. Beulah Bondi and Elizabeth Patterson, MacMurray's mother and aunt, respectively, provide good characterizations, and Sterling Holloway scores as the hick hired hand.

....

■ REMO WILLIAMS
THE ADVENTURE BEGINS . . .
(UK: Remo Williams – Unarmed and Dangerous)

1985, 121 MINS, US ◇ ⑫ ⊙

Dir Guy Hamilton *Prod* Larry Spiegel *Scr* Christopher Wood *Ph* Andrew Laszlo *Ed* Mark Melnick *Mus* Craig Safan *Art Dir* Jackson De Govia
● Fred Ward, Joel Grey, Wilford Brimley, J.A. Preston, Kate Mulgrew, Charles Cioffi (Orion)

Remo Williams: The Adventure Begins . . . is a poor man's James Bond with a dash of two or three other popular genres thrown in for good measure. The film [based on *The Destroyer* series by Richard Sapir and Warren Murphy] never seems to know where it's going and, when the smoke has cleared, doesn't seem to have got there either.

Williams (Fred Ward) is sort of a proletarian Bond – a New York City cop recruited for some secret government agency (headed by Wilford Brimley) supposedly working undercover for the President himself. What levity occurs in the film is mostly reserved for the long middle section in which Remo is placed under the tutelage of the last living master of the Korean martial art Sinanju.

The relationship between Remo and Chiun (Joel Grey) is an adult version of *The Karate Kid*. Small feats such as walking on water and dodging bullets are simply routine for the great man.

Charles Cioffi as an arms manufacturer in cahoots with the military is a cardboard heavy surrounded by a supply of bumbling bad guys. Thrown in for a slight romantic interest is Kate Mulgrew as an honest officer stumbling on the nefarious plot.

□ 1985: Nomination: Best Makeup

....

■ REMO WILLIAMS
UNARMED AND DANGEROUS
See: Remo Williams – The Adventure Begins . . .

....

■ RENEGADES

1989, 106 MINS, US ◇ ⑫ ⊙

Dir Jack Sholder *Prod* David Madden *Scr* David Rich *Ph* Phil Meheux *Ed* Caroline Biggerstaff *Mus* Michael Kamen *Art Dir* Carol Spier
● Kiefer Sutherland, Lou Diamond Phillips, Jami Gertz, Rob Knepper, Bill Smitrovich, Floyd Westerman (Morgan Creek/Interscope)

Renegades offers some rollercoaster thrills thanks to Jack Sholder's full-throttle direction but ultimately exhausts itself with unrelenting bedlam.

Kiefer Sutherland plays Buster, an undercover cop chasing a baddie who's stolen $2 million in diamonds. In the process, Marino (Rob Knepper) kills the brother of Hank (Lou Diamond Phillips) and makes off with an ancient spear, an artifact sacred to their Lakota Indian tribe.

Phillips must recover it to satisfy his father, throwing him together with Sutherland, who's intent on exposing the 'dirty cop' working with the gang because *his* father was ousted from the force with a blemished record.

Story resembles an earlier quest film, *Red Sun*, which cast Charles Bronson as a gunslinger shackled with a stone-faced samurai

(Toshiro Mifune) jointly pursuing the bad guy who swiped Mifune's ceremonial sword.

There's some terrific action, to be sure, which should come as no surprise to anyone who saw Sholder's impressive sleeper *The Hidden*. The frenetic pace, however, provides scant opportunity to flesh out the two leads, let alone any of the supporting cast.

....

■ RENT-A-COP

1988, 95 MINS, US ◇ ⑫ ⊙

Dir Jerry London *Prod* Raymond Wagner *Scr* Dennis Shryack, Michael Blodgett *Ph* Giuseppe Rotunno *Ed* Robert Lawrence *Mus* Jerry Goldsmith *Art Dir* Tony Masters
● Burt Reynolds, Liza Minelli, James Remar, Richard Masur, Dionne Warwick, Bernie Casey (Kings Road)

Pic, a cheesy little crime thriller, starts off promisingly as a sort of followup to Burt Reynolds' *Sharky's Machine*, with him working again with fellow cop Bernie Casey on a big drug bust. Nutcase James Remar wipes everybody out except Reynolds, who is suspected of being crooked and bounced from the force.

He gets work as a 'rent-a-cop', undercover (dressed as a Santa Claus) in a department store. In an awkwardly staged but key subplot, Liza Minnelli, as a Chicago hooker, has been saved from Remar by Reynolds and now attaches herself to him for protection.

Reynolds looks bored and is boring here, with an ill-fitting toupe that is downright embarrassing from one closeup angle. Minnelli is a lot of fun as the flamboyant prostie. Dionne Warwick is thoroughly wasted here as head of a callgirl ring. Remar is laughably hammy as the narcissistic killer.

....

■ REPO MAN

1984, 94 MINS, US ◇ ⑫ ⊙

Dir Alex Cox *Prod* Jonathan Wacks, Peter McCarthy *Scr* Alex Cox *Ph* Robby Muller *Ed* Dennis Dolan *Mus* Steven Hufsteter, Humberto Larriva *Art Dir* J. Rae Fox, Lynda Burbank
● Harry Dean Stanton, Emilio Estevez, Olivia Barash, Tracey Walter, Sy Richardson, Vonetta McGee (Edge City)

Repo Man has the type of unerring energy that leaves audiences breathless and entertained. While the title, referring to the people who repossess cars from those behind on their payments, might suggest a low-budget, gritty, realistic venture, the truth exists somewhat on the other end of the spectrum.

The more conventional aspects of the script deal with an aimless young man, wonderfully underplayed by Emilio Estevez, who falls in with a crowd of repo men and takes to the 'intense' lifestyle with ease.

Director-writer Alex Cox establishes the offbeat nature of the film from the start. In the opening scene, a state trooper stops a speeder and on a routine check of his trunk is blasted by a flash of light leaving him merely a smoldering pair of boots. This aspect of the story, centering on a 1964 Chevy Malibu, begins to have significance only later.

The initial plot thrust involves Otto Maddox (Estevez) and Bud (Harry Dean Stanton), the veteran repo man who teaches him the ropes. However, these are certainly tame facets as a story of alien invaders evolves.

The ever reliable Stanton turns in yet another indelible portrait of a seamy lowlife while Estevez registers as a charismatic and talented actor.

....

■ REPORT TO THE COMMISSIONER
(UK: Operation Undercover)

1975, 112 MINS, US ◇ ⑫

Dir Milton Katselas *Prod* Mike Frankovich *Scr* Abby Mann, Ernest Tidyman *Ph* Mario Tosi *Ed* David Blewitt *Mus* Elmer Bernstein *Art Dir* Robert Clatworthy

● Michael Moriarty, Yaphet Kotto, Susan Blakely, Hector Elizondo, William Devane, Richard Gere (United Artists)

Report to the Commissioner is a superb suspense drama of the tragic complexities of law enforcement.

Based on the novel by James Mills, it tells in flashback why Michael Moriarty, an idealistic new detective, is being harassed to provide an alibi for the death of Susan Blakely, an undercover narc killed accidentally in the pad she shares with bigtime dealer Tony King.

Hector Elizondo and Michael McGuire are medium-level detectives whose ambitions overcome their adherence to procedure, and lay the foundations for Moriarty's unexpected fate. Yaphet Kotto, in an outstanding performance, is Moriarty's senior partner. Richard Gere is very good as a smalltime pimp.

■ REPOSSESSED

1990, 84 MINS, US ◇ ⓥ ⊙
Dir Bob Logan   *Prod* Steve Wizan   *Scr* Bob Logan
Ph Michael Margulies   *Ed* Jeff Freeman   *Mus* Charles Fox   *Art Dir* Shay Austin
● Linda Blair, Ned Beatty, Leslie Nielsen, Anthony Starke, Lana Schwab, Thom J. Sharp (New Line)

Nonstop silliness keeps this frightless spoof of *The Exorcist* entertaining enough to keep an undemanding audience happy. Linda Blair, her teeth and hair encrusted with green gunk, once again plays the devil's host. Leslie Nielsen plays the priest pulled out of retirement to battle Satan. This time the rematch is staged on national TV.

Blair is a housewife who prepares (what else?) split-pea soup for her suburban family until Satan flies out of the television during an evangelist show and takes possession of her soul. Earnest young priest Anthony Starke is called in to help, but he's no match for swivel-neck, so Nielsen has to be persuaded.

No joke is too tasteless, no gag too weak, as the script romps along trying to pad its thin premise out to feature-length. Starke more than holds up his end as the timid clergyman, and Ned Beatty and Lana Schwab are a hoot as the evangelists. Production values are fairly generous.

■ REPULSION

1965, 104 MINS, UK ⓥ
Dir Roman Polanski   *Prod* Gene Gutowski   *Scr* Roman Polanski, Gerard Brach, David Stone   *Ph* Gilbert Taylor
Ed Alastair McIntyre   *Mus* Chico Hamilton
Art Dir Seamus Flannery
● Catherine Deneuve, Ian Hendry, John Fraser, Patrick Wymark, Yvonne Furneaux, Renee Houston (Compton/Tekli)

Repulsion is a classy, truly horrific psychological drama in which Polish director Roman Polanski draws out a remarkable performance from young French thesp, Catherine Deneuve. Polanski, who wrote the original screenplay with Gerard Brach, uses his technical resources and the abilities of his thesps to build up a tense atmosphere of evil.

A notable plus is Polanski's use of sound. There are two brief sequences, for instance, when the young heroine tosses in her bed as she listens to the muted sound of her sister and her lover in the next room. The moans and ecstatic whimperings of the love act is a dozen times more effective and sensual than any glimpse of the lovers in bed.

Deneuve is a youngster working in a beauty shop, a deliberately sharp contrast to the drab apartment which she shares with her flighty elder sister. The girl is sexually repressed, deeply attracted to the thought of men but at the same time loathing the thought of them. Her daydreaming grows into erotic sexual fantasies, and when her sister and boyfriend leave her for a few days

while they go on an Italian vacation, her loneliness and imagination take hold and insanity sets in.

Deneuve, without much dialog, handles a very difficult chore with insight and tact. John Fraser plays her would-be boyfriend likeably.

■ REQUIEM FOR A HEAVYWEIGHT
(UK: Blood Money)

1962, 85 MINS, US
Dir Ralph Nelson   *Prod* David Susskind   *Scr* Rod Serling   *Ph* Arthur J. Ornitz   *Ed* Carl Lerner
Mus Laurence Rosenthal   *Art Dir* Burr Smidt
● Anthony Quinn, Jackie Gleason, Mickey Rooney, Julie Harris, Stan Adams, Cassius Clay (Columbia)

Rod Serling's poignant portrait of the sunset of a prizefighter has lost some of its dramatic weight in the transition from the very small to the very large screen. However, it still packs considerable punch as a character study, although its action has slowed to where the plot padding is often obvious.

Some of the casting, no doubt done for authenticity and atmosphere, has boomeranged. Julie Harris plays her employment counselor as though she never really believed in the character. Casting actual boxing personalities is atmospheric but distracting and often ludicrous, particularly an amateurish bit by Jack Dempsey.

The performances of Quinn and Gleason are equally matched and carry the picture, no small chore. Quinn's punchy, inarticulate behemoth is so painfully natural that one winces when he feels pain, whether to his body or his feelings. Gleason is amazingly fine. He's weak, crafty, shifty and still a little pathetic.

Mickey Rooney, hampered with some bad makeup, is warm and sympathetic as Army, the trainer, but doesn't really shine except for one card-playing scene. It's the only funny bit in the pic and he steals it from under Gleason's nose. The plot contains some glaring implausibilities.

■ RESCUERS, THE

1977, 76 MINS, US ◇ ⓥ
Dir Wolfgang Reitherman, John Lounsbery, Art Stevens
Prod Wolfgang Reitherman   *Scr* Larry Clemmons, Ken Anderson, Vance Gerry, David Michener, Burny Mattinson, Frank Thomas, Fre   *Ed* James Melton, Jim Koford   *Mus* Artie Butler   *Art Dir* Don Griffith
● (Walt Disney)

Four years of work were invested on this $7.5 million production and the expense, care, and expertise shows.

An admirably simple story [suggested by *The Rescuers* and *Miss Bianca* by Margery Sharp] about two mice (voiced by Bob Newhart and Eva Gabor) who embark on a quest to rescue a kidnapped orphan girl (Michelle Stacy) from the clutches of an evil witch (Geraldine Page).

There's real terror in the story, and the Gothic setting of the swamp where the girl is held captive; the maudlin pitfalls of the plot are avoided through deft use of humor, and the plucky character of the young captive.

Among the most memorable sequences are two hilarious ascents by a goofy bird named Orville, who takes the mice on their rescue mission.

☐ 1977: Nomination: Best Song ('Someone's Waiting For You')

■ RESCUERS DOWN UNDER, THE

1990, 74 MINS, US ◇ ⓥ ⊙
Dir Hendel Butoy, Mike Gabriel   *Prod* Thomas Schumacher   *Scr* Jim Cox, Karey Kirkpatrick, Byron Simpson, Joe Ranft   *Ph* John Aardal, Chris Beck, Mary E. Lescher, Gary W. Smith, Chuck Warren   *Ed* Michael Kelly   *Mus* Bruce Broughton   *Art Dir* Maurice Hunt
● (Walt Disney)

This sort-of sequel to the 1977 hit *The Rescuers* boasts reasonably solid production values and fine character voices. Too bad they're set against such a mediocre story that adults may duck.

The bare-bones storyline hinges on a little boy who inexplicably cavorts with animals in Dolittle-esque fashion, including a huge golden eagle, a species apparently indigenous to the Aussie Outback. The bird is the prey of an evil hunter, McLeach (voiced by George C. Scott), who kidnaps the boy, resulting in a round-the-world call for those fearless mice of the Rescue Aid Society to come a-runnin'.

From there it's a simple quest pic, as mice Bernard (Bob Newhart), Miss Bianca (Eva Gabor) and guide Jake (Tristan Rogers) fumble their way through the jungle, with Bernard poised to pop the question to his rodent love only to be interrupted by one threat after another.

The film is not a musical. Instead, the producers have gone the action-adventure route, adding comic relief based largely on an awkward albatross named Wilbur (John Candy). Bruce Broughton augments the action immeasurably with his strongest score since *Silverado*.

■ RESTLESS YEARS, THE

1958, 86 MINS, US
Dir Helmut Kautner   *Prod* Ross Hunter   *Scr* Edward Anhalt   *Ph* Ernest Laszlo   *Ed* Al Joseph   *Mus* Joseph Gershenson   *Art Dir* Alexander Golitzen, Philip Barber
● John Saxon, Sandra Dee, Teresa Wright, James Whitmore, Luana Patten, Margaret Lindsay (Universal)

A touching account of adolescence and some of its problems as compounded by adult density, *The Restless Years* is based on Patricia Joudry's play, *Teach Me How to Cry*. In almost the first line of dialog, Sandra Dee is described as an illegitimate child. Her problems arise out of this and the fact that her unwed mother (Teresa Wright) has never recovered from the desertion by the father.

Everyone in town, apparently, knows the story except Dee. The girl begins to grow up when a new boy in town (John Saxon), who doesn't know or doesn't care about local gossip and prejudice, meets her and falls in love. His life is complicated by his luckless father (James Whitmore) who has come back to his home town to achieve the success that has eluded him elsewhere.

It is a period piece, with the dressmaker mother of an illegitimate child, and would have been more plausible if it had been played in period. But granting this, it has a feeling of poetry and sensitivity. Dee gives the picture its strongest sense of reality.

■ RESURRECTION

1980, 103 MINS, US ◇ ⓥ
Dir Daniel Petrie   *Prod* Renee Missel, Howard Rosenman   *Scr* Lewis John Carlino   *Ph* Mario Tosi   *Ed* Rita Roland   *Mus* Maurice Jarre   *Art Dir* Paul Sylbert
● Ellen Burstyn, Sam Shepard, Richard Farnsworth, Roberts Blossom (Universal)

Resurrection, an unusual supernatural drama about a faith healer, gives Ellen Burstyn a shot at a tour-de-force performance, but never comes into strong enough focus dramatically or philosophically.

The overly prosaic style of director Daniel Petrie and the underdeveloped screenplay inhibit her from exerting her full range of emotions.

She begins as a housewife who gives her husband a sports car, only to have it cause his death in a crash which leaves her legs paralyzed. During her laborious recovery period, she discovers that her close brush with death has given her the power of healing by the laying on of hands.

R

There is commendably little sensationalism, but not enough thoughtful exploration. Petrie's filming makes the pic resemble a soap opera.

☐ 1980: Nominations: Best Actress (Ellen Burstyn), Supp. Actress (Eva Le Gallienne)

■ **RETURN FROM THE ASHES**

1965, 108 MINS, UK

Dir J. Lee Thompson   *Prod* J. Lee Thompson   *Scr* Julius Epstein   *Ph* Christopher Challis   *Ed* Russell Lloyd   *Mus* John Dankworth   *Art Dir* Michael Stringer
● Maximilian Schell, Samantha Eggar, Ingrid Thulin, Herbert Lom, Talitha Pol, Vladek Sheybal (Mirisch)

Return from the Ashes does not always reach its mark as a thriller. The production, filmed in England, carries the makings of a suspenseful melodrama but in development is early contrived.

The screenplay based on a novel by Hubert Monteilhet builds around a plot for the perfect murder by an unscrupulous Polish chess master married to one woman and in love with her stepdaughter. Set in Paris at the close of Second World War, when the wife, a Jewess, returns from tortured internment in Dachau to find her husband living with the younger woman, plottage concerns the Pole's passion for money as he does away first with one, then the other femme, to accomplish his goal.

Thompson, who also directs, establishes a tense mood frequently, but level of interest suffers from character fuzziness which occasionally clouds the issue.

Maximilian Schell delivers strongly in a blackhearted role, lending credence to the character through constantly underplaying his scenes. Samantha Eggar displays dramatic aptitude as the amoral stepdaughter, Fabi, whose entry into her bath provides one of the highlights of the film.

■ **RETURN FROM WITCH MOUNTAIN**

1978, 93 MINS, US ◇ ⓦ

Dir John Hough   *Prod* Ron Miller, Jerome Courtland   *Scr* Malcolm Marmorstein   *Ph* Frank Phillips   *Ed* Bob Bring   *Mus* Lalo Schifrin   *Art Dir* John B. Mansbridge, Jack Senter
● Bette Davis, Christopher Lee, Kim Richards, Ike Eisenmann, Jack Soo, Anthony James (Walt Disney)

Kim Richards and Ike Eisenmann reprise their roles from *Escape to Witch Mountain* (1975) as sister and brother from another world, this time back on Earth for a vacation, courtesy of space traveler Uncle Bene (Denver Pyle). Siblings get a quick test of their psychic powers as mad scientist Christopher Lee and accomplice Bette Davis are testing their mind-control device on henchman Anthony James – when Eisenmann saves James from falling off a building by anti-gravity display, Lee sees the youngster as his meal ticket to world power.

Film is basically a chase caper, as Richards tries to find her brother, aided by a junior bunch of Dead End kids, Christian Juttner, Brad Savage, Poindexter and Jeffrey Jacquet. Despite an extrasensory link between the siblings (they communicate via telepathy, and can also make objects move at will), Lee has Eisenmann strait-jacketed with his device, so he can use youngster's 'molecular reorganization' powers to his own purposes.

Eisenmann and Richards have matured considerably since original. Lee makes one of the best Disney villains in years, but Davis doesn't quite click as his partner in crime.

■ **RETURN HOME**

1990, 87 MINS, AUSTRALIA ◇

Dir Ray Argall   *Prod* Cristina Pozzam   *Scr* Ray Argall   *Ph* Mandy Walker   *Ed* Ken Sallows   *Mus* Joe Camilleri   *Art Dir* Kerith Homes

● Dennis Coard, Frankie J. Holden, Ben Mendelsohn, Micki Camilleri, Rachel Rains (Musical)

Cinematographer Ray Argall makes an assured crossover to the director's chair with *Return Home*. The low-key performances perfectly fit the mood Argall is aiming for.

Newcomer Dennis Coard plays Noel, a successful big city insurance broker, whose personal life appears to be in tatters after a recent divorce. He decides to go home, back to the beachside suburb in Adelaide where he grew up at his father's gas station with older brother, Steve.

Steve (Frankie J. Holden) still runs the gas station, in partnership with his hard-working wife, Judy (Micki Camilleri), but things aren't going well. The other principal character in the film is Gary (Ben Mendelsohn), Steve's teenage mechanic, a well-meaning, awkward youth who's had a falling out with Wendy (Rachel Rains), his girlfriend.

Noel hangs out with Steve, Gary and Judy; he observes their lives, and evidently sees in them what he's lost in his own world of the rat race.

■ **RETURN OF A MAN CALLED HORSE, THE**

1976, 125 MINS, US ◇ ⓦ

Dir Irvin Kershner   *Prod* Terry Morse Jr   *Scr* Jack De Witt   *Ph* Owen Roizman   *Ed* Michael Kahn   *Mus* Laurence Rosenthal   *Art Dir* Stewart Campbell
● Richard Harris, Gale Sondergaard, Geoffrey Lewis, Bill Lucking, Jorge Luke, Claudio Brook (United Artists)

The Return of a Man Called Horse is a visually stunning sequel, again starring Richard Harris as an English nobleman who this time returns to the American west to save his adopted Indian tribe from extinction.

Irvin Kershner's film is handsome, leisurely, placid to the point of being predictable but dotted with some action highlights; in particular, Harris encores a physical torture-ritual, explicit enough to drive some audiences to the concession stand.

Jack De Witt wrote the original *Horse* script from a Dorothy M. Johnson story, published in 1950 in the old *Collier's* mag.

De Witt herein has extended the story, bringing Harris back west again to find his tribe wasted and dispossessed by land poacher Geoffrey Lewis.

■ **RETURN OF DR. FU MANCHU, THE**

1930, 73 MINS, US

Dir Rowland V. Lee   *Scr* Florence Ryerson, Lloyd Corrigan   *Ph* Archie J. Stout
● Warner Oland, Neil Hamilton, Jean Arthur, O.P. Heggie, William Austin, Evelyn Hall (Paramount)

Another chapter in the lurid melodramatic series made more or less from the detective stories by Sax Rohmer, English writer. As a picture it's absurd.

Picture has a brisk opening. Fu Manchu (Warner Oland) having been apparently killed in the previous picture, it became necessary to bring him to life again in an elaborate Chinese funeral. The archdemon escapes from his own coffin by a spring door, while an Oriental attendant is sealing the casket with molten lead. He takes up the trail of Dr Petrie all over and the story becomes a checker game between the wily Celestial and the super detective, Nayland Smith.

Picture has a nicely staged wedding scene with Jean Arthur looking remarkably beautiful as the bride. Neil Hamilton does all that is possible to hold up the puppet role of the hero and O.P. Heggie is once more the superhuman cool Inspector Nayland Smith.

■ **RETURN OF FRANK JAMES, THE**

1940, 92 MINS, US ◇ ⓦ ⊙

Dir Fritz Lang   *Prod* Kenneth Macgowan   *Scr* Sam Hellman   *Ph* George Barnes, William V. Skall

Ed Walter Thompson   *Mus* David Buttolph   *Art Dir* Richard Day, Wiard B. Ihnen
● Henry Fonda, Gene Tierney, Jackie Cooper, John Carradine, Henry Hull, J. Edward Bromberg (20th Century-Fox)

Jesse James, under the sponsorship of 20th Century-Fox, was murdered a year ago by those cowards, the Ford brothers. This season, with vengeance rankling in his breast, Jesse's older brother, Frank, returns to even the score. That he does, in obedience to Sam Hellman's script, but it's pretty slow stuff in the telling. Frank's no cinematic match for Jesse, which appears to be Will Hays' fault more than anyone else's. Rule 16a in the book is that a bad man can't be a hero. Which leaves Hellman in the paradoxical position of having Frank responsible for deaths of three men who never so much as tasted a single slug from his six-shooter. Effort to put wings on Frank is too much. Angelic aspect bogs the plot and instead of flying it can do no better than plod for a slow 92 minutes.

From standpoint of production and cast, Darryl Zanuck has spared nary a horse. It's filled with ah-evoking outdoor scenes and nostalgically-impressive western streets and indoor sets. Henry Fonda, underplaying Jesse James' older brother, Frank, in typical quiet style, is impressive; Jackie Cooper, as his kid buddy, shows a maturing dramatic sense although the pout is still there; Henry Hull, as a southern newspaper editor, overacts like no one else can, but is tremendously appealing despite it; John Carradine is a duly hissable villain as Bob Ford; J. Edward Bromberg earns laughs as a dumb railroad detective; and Donald Meek, Eddie Collins and George Barbier are, as usual, good for smiles.

Only member of the cast with whom fault can be found is Gene Tierney, making her film debut. Tierney's plenty pretty but for oomph she just isn't. Playing the role of a naive gal reporter to whom Frank takes a fancy, she seems to just lack what it takes to make an impression on the screen.

■ **RETURN OF SWAMP THING, THE**

1989, 88 MINS, US ◇ ⓦ ⊙

Dir Jim Wynorski   *Prod* Ben Melniker, Michael Uslan   *Scr* Derek Spencer, Grant Morris   *Ph* Zoran Hochstalter   *Ed* Leslie Rosenthal   *Mus* Church Cirino   *Art Dir* Robb Wilson King
● Louis Jourdan, Heather Locklear, Sarah Douglas, Dick Durock, Ace Mask, Joey Sagal (Lightyear)

The Return of Swamp Thing is scientific hokum without the fun. Second attempt to film the DC Comics character will disappoint all but the youngest critters.

They may be entertained by watching crossbred creatures squirm helplessly or buy into the Swamp Thing's (Dick Durock) instant love for Heather Locklear. He's a plant; she's a vegetarian.

Pic is set against a backdrop of evil where Dr Arcane (Louis Jourdan) has turned the disco-looking basement of his ante-bellum mansion into a mutant lab inhabited by failed experiments as he tries to discover the genetic equivalent of the Fountain of Youth.

The Swamp Thing escaped, but most of his more unfortunate distant cousins of the Petri dish have not, like the cockroach/man stuck on his back flailing his legs while Drs Lana Zurrell and Rochelle (Sarah Douglas and Ace Mask, respectively) lament another misfire.

Locklear arrives at the scene to confront Jourdan, her evil stepfather, who has never quite adequately explained her mother's mysterious death.

It doesn't take a genius to figure out Mom's fate, though it take the dense Locklear character an hour and a half.

■ RETURN OF THE JEDI

1983, 133 MINS, US ◇ ⚑ ⊙
Dir Richard Marquand   *Prod* Howard Kazanjian
Scr Lawrence Kasdan, George Lucas   *Ph* Alan Hume
Ed Sean Barton, Marcia Lucas, Duwayne Dunham
Mus John Williams   *Art Dir* Norman Reynolds
● Mark Hamill, Harrison Ford, Carrie Fisher, Billy Dee
Williams, Anthony Daniels, Peter Mayhew
(Lucasfilm/20th Century-Fox)

Jedi is the conclusion of the middle trilogy of George Lucas' planned nine-parter and suffers a lot in comparison to the initial *Star Wars* [1977], when all was fresh. One of the apparent problems is neither the writers nor the principal performers are putting in the same effort.

Telegraphed in the preceding *The Empire Strikes Back* [1980], the basic dramatic hook this time is Mark Hamill's quest to discover – and do something about – the true identity of menacing Darth Vader, while resisting the evil intents of the Emperor (Ian McDiarmid).

Hamill is not enough of a dramatic actor to carry the plot load here, especially when his partner in so many scenes is really little more than an oversized gas pump, even if splendidly voiced by James Earl Jones.

Even worse, Harrison Ford, who was such an essential element of the first two outings, is present more in body than in spirit this time, given little to do but react to special effects. And it can't be said that either Carrie Fisher or Billy Dee Williams rise to previous efforts.

But Lucas and director Richard Marquand have overwhelmed these performer flaws with a truly amazing array of creatures, old and new, plus the familiar space hardware.
□ 1983: Best Special Visual Effects
□ Nominations: Best Art Direction, Original Score, Sound, Sound Editing

■ RETURN OF THE LIVING DEAD, THE

1985, 90 MINS, US ◇ ⚑ ⊙
Dir Dan O'Bannon   *Prod* Tom Fox   *Scr* Dan O'Bannon
Ph Jules Brenner   *Ed* Robert Gordon   *Mus* Matt Clifford
Art Dir William Stout
● Clu Gulager, James Karen, Don Calfa, Thom
Mathews, Beverly Randolph, John Philbin (Hemdale/Fox)

Early on here, one character asks another if he's seen the original *Night of the Living Dead*, then goes on to explain that the 1968 film altered the facts concerning a real-life zombie attack on the local populace.

Virtually the entire action of the rather threadbare production [from a story by Rudy Ricci, John Russo and Russell Streiner] shuttles among three locations – a medical supply warehouse, where numerous zombies have been sent by the Army; a nearby mortuary; and an adjacent cemetery, where a bunch of punks frolic before being chased out by corpses risen from their graves.

From then on, it's the same old story, as unusually vigorous, athletic zombies besiege the motley bunch of human beings holed up in the vicinity and eat the brains of anyone they get their hands on.

Director Dan O'Bannon deserves considerable credit for creating a terrifically funny first half-hour of exposition, something in which he is greatly aided by the goofball performance of James Karen as a medical supply know-it-all.

■ RETURN OF THE MUSKETEERS, THE

1989, 94 MINS, UK/FRANCE/SPAIN ◇ ⚑
Dir Richard Lester   *Prod* Pierre Spengler   *Scr* George
MacDonald Fraser   *Ph* Bernard Lutic   *Ed* John Victor
Smith   *Mus* Jean-Claude Petit   *Art Dir* Gil Arrondo
● Michael York, Oliver Reed, Frank Finlay, C. Thomas
Howell, Richard Chamberlain, Kim Cattrall (Burrill/
Filmdebroc/Cine 5/Iberoamericana)

In 1974 Richard Lester boosted his then-flagging career with *The Three Musketeers* and its sequel *The Four Musketeers*, lavish swashbucklers with a comic touch. His attempt at a comeback is, sadly, a stillborn event which looks as tired as its re-assembled cast.

It's 20 years since the four musketeers ordered the execution of the evil Milady De Winter. But now King Charles is dead, and his son Louis, a 10-year-old, reigns with his mother (a reprise by Geraldine Chaplin).

D'Artagnan (Michael York) is assigned to bring together his three former comrades to fight for the Queen and Cardinal. He quickly recruits Porthos (Frank Finlay) and Athos (Oliver Reed), together with the latter's son, Raoul (C. Thomas Howell); however, Aramis (Richard Chamberlain), now a womanizing Abbe, is reluctant to join the band.

There follows a complicated and sometimes hard to follow plot [from Alexandre Dumas' *Twenty Years After*] involving a failed attempt to rescue King Charles I of England from execution. According to this, the executioner of the king was actually Justine (Kim Cattrall), evil daughter of Milady, who's intent on avenging herself on the four musketeers who she blames for the death of her mother.

Pic is dedicated to Roy Kinnear, whose accidental death during production must have cast a pall over the entire project.

■ RETURN OF THE PINK PANTHER, THE

1975, 115 MINS, UK ◇ ⚑ ⊙
Dir Blake Edwards   *Prod* Blake Edwards   *Scr* Frank
Waldman, Blake Edwards   *Ph* Geoffrey Unsworth
Ed Tom Priestley   *Mus* Henry Mancini   *Art Dir* Peter
Mullins
● Peter Sellers, Christopher Plummer, Catherine Schell,
Herbert Lom, Peter Arne, Gregoire Aslan (United Artists)

The Return of the Pink Panther establishes Peter Sellers once again as the bane of the existence of chief detective Herbert Lom, who is forced to reinstate Sellers when the Pink Panther diamond is stolen from its native museum by a mysterious burglar.

Suspicion falls on Christopher Plummer, ostensibly retired phantom jewel thief who decides he must catch the real culprit to save himself. Catherine Schell plays Plummer's wife, who turns out to be a decoy in more ways than one.

Sellers' work takes him into contact with Peter Arne and Gregoire Aslan, native police under pressure from general Peter Jeffrey to find the gem: with befuddled concierge Victor Spinetti and perplexed bellboy Mike Grady, both at a posh Swiss resort hotel; and periodically with his valet Cato, played by Burt Kwouk.

All hands seem to be having a ball, especially Schell, whose unabashed amusement at Clouseau's seduction attempts often matches an audience's hilarity.

■ RETURN OF THE SECAUCUS SEVEN

1980, 110 MINS, US ◇ ⚑
Dir John Sayles   *Prod* Jeffrey Nelson, William Aydelott
Scr John Sayles   *Ph* Austin de Besche   *Ed* John Sayles
Mus K. Mason Daring
● Mark Arnott, Gordon Clapp, Maggie Cousineau,
Brian Johnston, Adam LeFevre, John Sayles (Salsipuedes)

John Sayles has fashioned an admirable postmortem of the 1960s student left. Virtually the whole cast and crew make their feature debut here, and while not all the work is on an entirely professional level, earnestness and intelligence of the enterprise carry the day.

Structured like a well-built three-act play, drama is set at eight-year reunion of seven student activists who were arrested together in Secaucus, NJ on their way to a Washington demonstration. As old cohorts and a few new companions gather at the New Hampshire farm of one of the couples, complicated history of romantic relationships within the group begins to be unravelled. A diagram of past and present liaisons would prove as dense as that for any soap opera.

Film is virtually wall-to-wall talk, all of it interesting and much of it rather witty.

■ RETURN OF THE SEVEN

1966, 95 MINS, US ◇ ⚑
Dir Burt Kennedy   *Prod* Ted Richmond   *Scr* Larry Cohen
Ph Paul Vogel   *Ed* Bert Bates   *Mus* Elmer Bernstein
Art Dir Jose Alguero
● Yul Brynner, Robert Fuller, Julian Mateos, Warren
Oates, Claude Akins, Elisa Montes (Mirisch)

Filmed in Spain by Mirisch, *Return of the Seven* is an unsatisfactory followup to John Sturges' *The Magnificent Seven*. Yul Brynner, sole holdover thesp, stars in a plodding cliche-ridden script.

Dreary screenplay reunites Brynner and two other members of the Sturges septet – Robert Fuller evidently in the old Steve McQueen part, and Julian Mateos filling the former Horst Buchholz role – when the latter is dragooned by Emilio Fernandez, psychotic Mexican rancher who enslaves local farmers to rebuild a village. Four new characters are recruited – girl-chasing Warren Oates, brooding Claude Akins, suave Virgilio Texeira and juvenile Jordan Christopher, latter in a dim dramatic feature debut.

Under Burt Kennedy's limp direction, players walk through their predictable dialog while rescuing Mateos, and provoking the long-awaited showdown with Fernandez. Elisa Montes is okay as Mateos' wife, and Fernando Rey is competent in a thankless role of a prayer-mumbling priest.

■ RETURN OF THE SOLDIER, THE

1982, 102 MINS, UK ◇ ⚑
Dir Alan Bridges   *Prod* Anne Skinner, Simon Relph
Scr Hugh Whitemore   *Ph* Stephen Goldblatt
Ed Laurence Mery Clark   *Mus* Richard Rodney Bennett
Art Dir Luciana Arrighi
● Julie Christie, Alan Bates, Glenda Jackson, Ann-
Margret, Ian Holm, Frank Finlay (Brent Walker)

Alan Batess comes home from World War I with shell shock and is partly amnesiac. He does not remember his wife, played by Julie Christie with overdone snobbishness, but does recall a lower-class girl (Glenda Jackson) he loved as a young man and his doting cousin, latter played with feeling by Ann-Margret.

Christie allows Bates to see Jackson, now married and a bit dowdy. However the love is still there. A psychiatrist warns that bringing Bates back to normal might be dangerous, for he is probably concealing the tragedy of the death of his child from himself.

Stereotyped characters may have been more alive when the book [by Rebecca West] was written castigating the hollowness of a certain British class system. Today it is more quaint than anything else and fails to find the depth in these people to make them timeless.

■ RETURN TO OZ

1985, 110 MINS, US ◇ ⚑ ⊙
Dir Walter Murch   *Prod* Paul Maslansky   *Scr* Walter
Murch, Gill Dennis   *Ph* David Watkin   *Ed* Leslie
Hodgson   *Mus* David Shire   *Art Dir* Norman Reynolds
● Nicol Williamson, Jean Marsh, Fairuza Balk, Piper
Laurie, Matt Clark, Sean Barrett (Walt Disney/Silver
Screen Partners II)

Return to Oz is an astonishingly somber, melancholy and, sadly, unengaging trip back to a favorite land of almost every American's youth. Straight dramatic telling of little Dorothy's second voyage to the Emerald City [based on *The Land of Oz* and *Ozma of Oz* by L. Frank Baum] employs an amusement park-

R

full of imaginative characters and special effects, but a heaviness of tone and absence of narrative drive prevent the flights of fancy from getting off the ground.

Opening finds Dorothy back at home in Kansas but unable to sleep because of disturbing memories of her recent trip. Reacting harshly, Aunt Em and Uncle Henry decide the girl has become deranged and send her to a clinic to receive electroshock therapy from sinister nurse Jean Marsh and doctor Nicol Williamson.

After nearly a half-hour of these nightmarish goings-on, Dorothy and her talking chicken Billina are delivered to Oz, but not a very inviting section of it. Landed on the edge of the Deadly Desert, Dorothy soon discovers the Yellow Brick Road in disrepair, the Emerald City in ruins and her companions from the previous trip turned to stone.

Along the way, as before, Dorothy accumulates some helpful friends.

☐ 1985: Nomination: Best Visual Effects

■ RETURN TO PARADISE

1953, 90 MINS, US ◇

Dir Mark Robson *Prod* Theron Warth *Scr* Charles Kaufman *Ph* Winton C. Hoch *Ed* Daniel Mandell *Mus* Dimitri Tiomkin

● Gary Cooper, Roberta Haynes, Barry Jones, Moira MacDonald, John Hudson (Aspen)

The simplicity of authentic Samoan settings provides a strong, appealing background for this leisurely, idyllic, romantic drama, based on the *Mr Morgan* portion of James A. Michener's bestselling *Return to Paradise*.

Gary Cooper protrays Morgan, a casual soldier of fortune taking his ease in the unhurried life of the island paradises. On one atoll where he decides to stay awhile, an island beauty attracts his attention to set the romance of the piece. For conflict there is the domination of the island and the natives by a missionary, a man who has forgotten the Bible teaches more than hellfire and damnation.

Cooper's delivery of the foot-loose South Seas wanderer is in his easy-going, understated style of histrionics and just right for the character and for the mood aimed by Mark Robson's direction. Opposite him is Roberta Haynes as the native girl, Maeva. Barry Jones makes his portrayal of the zealot, Pastor Cobbett, a performance gem. Moira MacDonald, three-quarters Polynesian and recruited in Samoa for the role, has natural appeal as the daughter.

Music is an important part of the production both in the native numbers recorded in the islands, where all of the lensing took place, and that cleffed by Dimitri Tiomkin.

■ RETURN TO PEYTON PLACE

1961, 123 MINS, US ◇ ⓦ

Dir Jose Ferrer *Prod* Jerry Wald *Scr* Ronald Alexander *Ph* Charles G. Clarke *Ed* David Bretherton *Mus* Franz Waxman *Art Dir* Jack Martin Smith, Hans Peters

● Carol Lynley, Jeff Chandler, Eleanor Parker, Mary Astor, Tuesday Weld, Robert Sterling (20th Century-Fox)

Basically *Return to Peyton Place* is a high-class soap opera. The screenplay preserves the nature of Grace Metalious' novel, alternately building three or four separate but related story veins into individual crescendos, then welding the moving parts into a single grand climax in which everything falls neatly into place.

The basic stories are: (1) Carol Lynley's, as they tyro novelist whose close-to-home fiction produces civic repercussions and whose romantic relations with her editor-publisher (Jeff Chandler) accelerate her maturity; (2) Tuesday Weld's, as the emotionally-troubled girl whose past misfortunes are soothed when Lynley's book sheds new light into the matter; and (3) Mary Astor's, as a super-possessive Peyton Place mother who attempts to wreck the marriage of her son.

Jose Ferrer's direction of this material is deliberate, but restrained and perceptive. The cast is a blend of polished veterans and young players. The lovely Lynley does a thoroughly capable job, although a shade more animation would have been desirable. But it is the veteran Astor who walks off with the picture.

■ RETURN TO THE BLUE LAGOON

1991, 100 MINS, US ◇ ⓦ

Dir William A. Graham *Prod* William A. Graham *Scr* Leslie Stevens *Ph* Robert Steadman *Ed* Ronald J. Fagan *Mus* Basil Poledouris *Art Dir* Jon Dowding

● Milla Jovovich, Brian Krause, Lisa Pelikan, Courtney Phillips, Garette Patrick Ratcliff, Nana Coburn (Columbia/Price)

Return to the Blue Lagoon is a pointless spinoff of the 1980 hit, which was itself a remake of a 1949 British pic. Leslie Stevens' script [based on Henry DeVere Stacpoole's novel *The Garden of God*] has the original's leading characters found dead in a tiny boat along with their young son, who has survived the journey in fine shape.

But the tyke is soon put out to sea again to escape an outbreak of cholera on board the rescue ship and, along with straightlaced American Lisa Pelikan and her little daughter, washes up on the same tropical island his parents inhabited. Once the budding beauties hit adolescence and assume the bodies of international model Milla Jovovich and TV hunk Brian Krause, they are disturbed to find that 'nothing's the same'.

For propriety's sake, they marry, then they splash about a lot as they begin what promises to be a very long honeymoon. Only conflict crops up in the form of a visiting ship, which provides all sorts of trouble.

Vet TV director William A. Graham is content to stick to pretty pictures rather than create a strong feeling for isolated life through the accretion of telling detail. Jovovich manages to project some good sense and resilience along with her cover girl beauty; the 15-year-old Soviet native makes a decent impression in her first bigscreen leading role. Krause looks like he's straight off the Southern California beaches. Pic was lensed on Taveuni in the Fiji archipelago.

■ REUBEN, REUBEN

1983, 101 MINS, US ◇ ⓦ

Dir Robert Ellis Miller *Prod* Walter Shenson, Julius J. Epstein *Scr* Julius J. Epstein *Ph* Peter Stein *Ed* Skip Lusk *Mus* Billy Goldenberg *Art Dir* Peter Larkin

● Tom Conti, Kelly McGillis, Roberts Blossom, Cynthia Harris, E. Katherine Kerr, Joel Fabiani (20th Century-Fox/Taft Entertainment)

About a leching, alcoholic Scottish poet making the New England campus circuit, *Reuben, Reuben* is exceptionally literate, with lines that carom with wit from the superb adaptation by Julius J. Epstein of a 1964 Peter De Vries novel [and the play *Spofford* by Herman Shumlin]. Epstein, with De Vries' blessing, merged three separate stories in the novel into the character of the rascal poet on the slide.

Helmsman Robert Ellis Miller draws solid performances from debuting actress Kelly McGillis, whose chic blonde Vassar looks interestingly contrast, in this case, with her character's farmyard roots. She becomes the all-consuming obsession of Tom Conti as he lurches from one bottle and bed to another. Two of his sexual conquests on the poet's college town Circuit are nicely and avariciously played by Cynthia Harris and E. Katherine Kerr.

But the film is a tour-de-force act for Conti (in his first US-made film) and he captures the vulnerability of a man whose plunge into darkness suggests the emotional time most closely associated with 4 a.m.

☐ 1983: Nominations: Best Actor (Tom Conti), Adapted Screenplay

■ REUNION

1989, 110 MINS, FRANCE/W. GERMANY/UK ◇ ⓦ

Dir Jerry Schatzberg *Prod* Anne Francois *Scr* Harold Pinter *Ph* Bruno de Keyzer *Ed* Martine Barraque *Mus* Philippe Sarde *Art Dir* Alexandre Trauner

● Jason Robards, Christian Anholt, Samuel West, Francois Fabian, Maureen Kewin, Barbara Jefford (Ariane/FR3/NEF/Vertriebs/CLG/Tac/Arbo/Maran)

This enormously impressive film ranks as one of the best of countless pics dealing with the rise of Nazism in Germany in the early 1930s.

Based on Fred Uhlman's autobiographical novel, drama is set in Stuttgart in 1933 and deals with the growing friendship between two schoolboys from different backgrounds: Hans (Christian Anholt), son of a Jewish doctor and World War I vet who, till now, was considered a pillar of the community; and the aristocratic Konrad (Samuel West), who's led a sheltered life, taught by private tutors, and who finds himself stimulated by the intelligent, sensitive Hans.

At the beginning of the year, portents of what's to come are few: small groups of Nazis march in the streets; a friend advises Hans' father to leave before Hitler takes over. Gradually, as the year progresses, the Fascist movement takes hold.

The long central part of the film is framed by a present-day narrative in which Hans, now Henry Strauss (Jason Robards), decides to return to Stuttgart to locate his parents' grave and to discover what happened to his old friend.

Director Jerry Schatzberg has made what probably is his best film to date, a sober, thoughtful pic that recreates a seemingly authentic world of 56 years ago.

■ REVENGE

1990, 124 MINS, US ◇ ⓦ ⊙

Dir Tony Scott *Prod* Hunt Lowry, Stanley Rubin *Scr* Jim Harrison, Jeffrey Fiskin *Ph* Jeffrey Kimball *Ed* Chris Lebenzon *Mus* Jack Nitzsche *Art Dir* Michael Seymour, Benjamin Fernandez

● Kevin Costner, Anthony Quinn, Madeleine Stowe, Sally Kirkland, James Gammon, Miguel Ferrer (Rastar)

This far-from-perfect rendering of Jim Harrison's shimmering novella has a romantic sweep and elemental power that ultimately transcend its flaws. It's a contempo tale of a doomed love triangle in lawless Mexico.

As J. Cochran, a hotshot Navy pilot who retires after 12 years, Kevin Costner heads down to Puerto Vallarta for recreation at the home of a wealthy sportsman friend, Tibey (Anthony Quinn) and is right away smitten with his host's gorgeous and unhappy wife Miryea (Madeleine Stowe). Despite his friend's graciousness and reputation as a cold-blooded killer, Cochran takes the suicide plunge into passion, running off with Miryea for a sexual idyll.

The much-fiddled-with footage was eventually pasted into its current form, and though much is lost, the tale's simplicity, grace and subtlety shine through. All three elements of the love triangle are compelling, and as a crucial fourth character Mexico performs radiantly.

Stowe is a great screen beauty and is certainly a match for Costner's charisma. The magnificent Quinn as a political puppeteer is so rich and sympathetic that he threatens to steal away the audience despite his brutality.

■ REVENGE OF FRANKENSTEIN, THE

1958, 89 MINS, UK ◇ ▼

Dir Terence Fisher *Prod* Anthony Hinds *Scr* Jimmy
Sangster, H. Hurford Janes *Ph* Jack Asher *Ed* Alfred
Cox, James Needs *Mus* Leonard Salzedo
Art Dir Bernard Robinson
● Peter Cushing, Francis Matthews, Eunice Gayson,
Michael Gwynn, John Welsh, Lionel Jeffries (Hammer)

Made by the same team as *The Curse of
Frankenstein*, this is a high grade horror film.

Peter Cushing, as the famed medical experimenter, is still determined to make a monster, although that is not how he would put it. Despite official pressure, Frankenstein is again collecting bits of bone and tissue, muscle and blood, to put together a man of his creation. Again he succeeds, but again something goes wrong and his creature – through brain damage – becomes a cannibal, slavering blood and saliva.

The production is a rich one. The screenplay is well-plotted, peopled with interesting characters, aided by good performances from Francis Matthews as Cushing's chief assistant and others.

■ REVENGE OF THE CREATURE

1955, 82 MINS, US

Dir Jack Arnold *Prod* William Alland *Scr* Martin
Berkeley *Ph* Charles S. Welbourne *Ed* Paul
Weatherwax *Mus* Herman Stein *Art Dir* Alexander
Golitzen, Alfred Sweeney
● John Agar, Lori Nelson, John Bromfield, Robert P.
Williams, Nestor Paiva (Universal)

Revenge of the Creature, sequel to U's *Creature
from the Black Lagoon*, is a routine shocker that doesn't get much of a boost from the 3-D treatment.

The fellow who plays the scaly monster in the film certainly rates top billing. Expertly made up, he's the only one who looks and acts believable. Fact that he only roars and has no speaking lines helps since the script cooked up by Martin Berkeley is hardly on the expert side. There's an unusual volume of dialog that serves mostly to bridge the gaps between the action sequences.

There are too few of those, but some of them are staged with sock effect, with or without 3-D. Underwater scenes involving the gillman, have been directed by Jack Arnold for shock value and they build up tension nicely. Cast performs its routine chores in routine fashion.

■ REVENGE OF THE NERDS

1984, 90 MINS, US ◇ ▼ ⊙

Dir Jeff Kanew *Prod* Ted Field, Peter Samuelson
Scr Steve Zacharias, Jeff Buhai *Ph* King Baggot
Ed Alan Baisam *Mus* Thomas Newman *Art Dir* James
L. Schoppe
● Robert Carradine, Anthony Edwards, Ted McGinley,
Bernie Casey, Julia Montgomery (Interscope)

Simple-minded romp about a group of freshmen outcasts doesn't quite qualify for the dean's list, but *Revenge of the Nerds* shows more than enough smarts to deserve passing grades.

From the outset the nerds, who have learned to feel more at home talking computers and grade point average, get a 'real-world' education from the upperclass fraternity of jocks. They suffer constant humiliations from the older students and ultimately decide to fight back.

Led by hometown buddies Lewis (Robert Carradine) and Gilbert (Anthony Edwards), the nerds rent a house and form their own frat. But breaking into the school's Greek fraternity group will not come easily because the council is chaired by Stan (Ted McGinley), a member of the jock frat, and his g.f. Betty (Julie Montgomery), enemies of the nerds and sticklers for the rules.

Though the picture features extensive cardboard stereotypes, belching and other bad taste humor, director Jeff Kanew moves the action [from a screen story by Tim Metcalfe, Miguel Tejeda-Flores, Steve Zacharias and Jeff Buhai] swiftly to a convincing payoff. There's also ample t&a along the way.

■ REVENGE OF THE NINJA

1983, 88 MINS, US ◇ ▼

Dir Sam Firstenberg *Prod* Menahem Golan, Yoram
Globus *Scr* James R. Silke *Ph* David Gurfinkel
Ed Michael J. Duthie, Mark Helfrich *Mus* Rob Walsh,
W. Michael Lewis, Laurin Rinder *Art Dir* Paul Staheli
● Sho Kosugi, Keith Vitali, Virgil Frye, Arthur Roberts,
Mario Gallo, Grace Oshita (Cannon)

Revenge of the Ninja is an entertaining martial arts actioner, following up *Enter the Ninja* (1981) but lacking that film's name players and Far East locale.

After a brief intro set in Japan, where Cho Osaki (Sho Kosugi) witnesses most of his family wiped out by black-clad ninjas, action shifts to an unidentified US locale (filmed in Salt Lake City) six years later. Osaki, with his surviving child and its grandma, runs a gallery featuring imported Japanese dolls, which unbeknownst to him is a front for heroin smuggling run by his pal Braden (Arthur Roberts). Braden is involved with an unscrupulous US mobster Caifano (Mario Gallo).

Revenge occurs when Braden kills grannie, kidnaps the child Kane (Kane Kosugi) and later kills Osaki's best friend, martial arts expert Dave Hatcher (Keith Vitali). Fine fight choreography by Kosugi, including fast and often funny moves by him, keeps the film cooking.

■ REVENGE OF THE PINK PANTHER

1978, 98 MINS, US ◇ ▼ ⊙

Dir Blake Edwards *Prod* Blake Edwards *Scr* Frank
Waldman, Ron Clark, Blake Edwards *Ph* Ernest Day
Ed Alan Jones *Mus* Henry Mancini *Art Dir* Peter
Mullins
● Peter Sellers, Herbert Lom, Dyan Cannon, Robert
Webber, Burt Kwouk, Paul Stewart (United Artists)

Revenge of the Pink Panther isn't the best of the continuing film series, but Blake Edwards and Peter Sellers on a slow day are still well ahead of most other comedic filmmakers.

This time out, Sellers tracks down an international drug ring. Herbert Lom also encores as Sellers' nemesis and Dyan Cannon is delightful as the resourceful discarded mistress of dope smuggler industrialist Robert Webber.

The screenplay, from an Edwards story, is a paradoxical embarrassment of riches: Sellers, faithful servant Burt Kwouk, Lom, Cannon, etc, each alone and also in various combinations, are too much for a simple story line. The result is that the plot roams all over the map, trying to cover all the bases but in totality adding up to less than the parts.

■ REVERSAL OF FORTUNE

1990, 120 MINS, US ◇ ▼ ⊙

Dir Barbet Schroeder *Prod* Edward R. Pressman, Oliver
Stone, Elon Dershowitz *Scr* Nicholas Kazan
Ph Luciano Tovoli *Ed* Lee Percy *Mus* Mark Isham
Art Dir Mel Bourne
● Jeremy Irons, Glenn Close, Ron Silver, Anabella
Sciorra, Uta Hagen, Fisher Stevens (Warner/Shochiku
Fuji/Sovereign)

Reversal of Fortune turns the sensational Claus von Bulow case into a riveting film. The story [from the book by Alan Dershowitz] of the Newport society figure's trial, conviction and acquittal on appeal for the attempted murder of his wealthy wife is presented here in an ab-

sorbing, complex mosaic.

Jeremy Irons gives a memorable performance as the inscrutable European blueblood emigre. Cast in perfect apposition is Ron Silver, seizing with dynamic gusto the role of a career as von Bulow's passionately idealistic but streetwise defense attorney, Harvard law professor Dershowitz.

Glenn Close is typically excellent in the smaller but pivotal role of Sunny von Bulow, who narrates the story and appears in flashbacks.

On one level, *Reversal of Fortune* deals with the impossibility of knowing the truth about the unknowable. Was von Bulow guilty of injecting his wife with a near-fatal dose of insulin? Was he framed by Sunny's maid (Uta Hagen) or family? Or did the profoundly unhappy woman attempt suicide?

On other levels, it is a finely detailed manners study of the superwealthy, a drama of conflicting principles and values and an engrossing legal detective story.
☐ 1990: Best Actor (Jeremy Irons).
☐ Nominations: Best Director, Adapted Screenplay

■ REVOLUTION

1986, 125 MINS, UK/NORWAY ◇ ▼ ⊙

Dir Hugh Hudson *Prod* Irwin Winkler *Scr* Robert
Dillon *Ph* Bernard Lutic *Ed* Stuart Baird *Mus* John
Corigliano *Art Dir* Assheton Gorton
● Al Pacino, Donald Sutherland, Nastassja Kinski, Joan
Plowright, Steven Berkoff, Annie Lennox
(Goldcrest/Viking)

Watching *Revolution* is a little like visiting a museum – it looks good without really being alive. The film doesn't tell a story so much as it uses characters to illustrate what the American Revolution has come to mean. Despite attempting to reduce big events to personal details, *Revolution* rarely works on a human scale.

While intimate story of Tom Dobb (Al Pacino) and his son Ned (Dexter Fletcher, Sid Owen as young Ned) and Tom's love for renegade aristocrat Daisy McConnahay (Nastassja Kinski) is full of holes, the larger canvas is staged beautifully.

Unfortunately, against this well-drawn background the small story that is meant to serve as a way into the drama for viewers looks too much like an historical reenactment.

Performances fail to elevate the material with only Pacino, Fletcher and Owen giving their characters a personal touch. Donald Sutherland is wasted and distant as an English officer, partially because it is nearly impossible to understand what he's saying through his thick brogue.

■ REWARD, THE

1965, 91 MINS, US ◇

Dir Serge Bourguignon *Prod* Aaron Rosenberg
Scr Serge Bourguignon, Oscar Millard *Ph* Joe
MacDonald *Ed* Robert Simpson *Mus* Elmer Bernstein
Art Dir Jack Martin Smith, Robert Boyle
● Max von Sydow, Yvette Mimieux, Efrem Zimbalist Jr,
Gilbert Roland, Emilio Fernandez, Nino Castelnuovo
(Arcola/20th Century-Fox)

The Reward for a fugitive and its effects on a group thrown together by fate comprise the theme of this moody, somewhat uneven, desert meller. Some good acting and excellent production values bolster a plot that fizzes out in final reel.

Director Serge Bourguignon and Oscar Millard adapted Michael Barrett's tome which crash lands crop-duster Max von Sydow in a boondocks Mexican town coincident with the passing through of Efrem Zimbalist Jr, latter on the lam from a murder rap and accompanied by Yvette Mimieux. Sydow cues

R

police inspector Gilbert Roland to the price on Zimbalist's head, and the slow chase is on, leading to uneventful and unresisted capture.

About 40 per cent of the film has elapsed before plot begins to move when brutal, sadistic police sergeant Emilio Fernandez finds out there's a reward and starts to dominate the group.

Sydow gives a lethargic performance despite a role that is basically passive. He talks little, then in gutteral tones, but mostly reacts sluggishly to events.

....

■ RHAPSODY IN BLUE

1945, 130 MINS, US 🎬 ⊙
Dir Irving Rapper   *Prod* Jesse L. Lasky   *Scr* Howard Koch, Elliot Paul   *Ph* Sol Polito, Merritt Gerstad   *Ed* Folmer Blangsted   *Mus* Leo F. Forbstein (dir.)   *Art Dir* Anton Grot, John B. Hughes
● Robert Alda, Joan Leslie, Alexis Smith, Charles Coburn, Oscar Levant, Albert Basserman (Warner)

Those who knew George Gershwin and the Gershwin saga may wax slightly vociferous at this or that miscue, but as cinematurgy, designed for escapism and entertainment, no matter the season, *Rhapsody in Blue* can't miss.

The years have certainly lent enhancement to his music, and the glib interplay of names such as Otto Kahn, Jascha Heifetz, Maurice Ravel, Walter Damrosch and Rachmaninov (all of whom are impersonated) lend conviction to the basic yarn [from a story by Sonya Levien] of the New York East Side boy whose musical genius was to sweep the world.

Robert Alda plays Gershwin and makes him believable. Herbert Rudley as Ira Gershwin is perhaps more believable to the initiate, looking startlingly like the famed lyricist brother of the composer, but young Alda, a newcomer, makes his role tick as the burningly ambitious composer who is constantly driving himself.

Oscar Levant as Oscar Levant can't miss, and he doesn't here. He has the meatiest, brilliant lines and whams over the titular *Rhapsody in Blue* and Concerto in F with virtuosity and authority as befits a real-life confidante of the late composer.
□ 1945: Nominations: Best Scoring of a Musical Picture, Sound

....

■ RHINESTONE

1984, 111 MINS, US ◇ 🎬 ⊙
Dir Bob Clarke   *Prod* Howard Smith, Marvin Worth   *Scr* Phil Alden Robinson, Sylvester Stallone   *Ph* Timothy Galfas   *Ed* Stan Cole, John Wheeler   *Mus* Dolly Parton   *Art Dir* Robert Boyle
● Sylvester Stallone, Dolly Parton, Richard Farnsworth, Ron Leibman, Tim Thomerson, Steven Apostle Pec (20th Century-Fox)

Effortlessly living up to its title, *Rhinestone* is as artificial and synthetic a concoction as has ever made its way to the screen.

Directed in low-down, good-spirited vulgar fashion by Bob Clark, film is a genuine oddball. Sylvester Stallone's character, that of a Gotham cabbie whom singer Dolly Parton bets she can turn into a convincing country crooner in two weeks' time, is like no one ever encountered on earth before.

Uncouth loudmouth, has no discernible talents whatsoever, so it's an uphill battle when Parton takes him down home to Tennessee to try to pump some real country feeling into his bulging veins.

Neither Stallone nor Parton stray at all from their past personae.

....

■ RICH AND FAMOUS

1981, 117 MINS, US ◇ 🎬 ⊙
Dir George Cukor   *Prod* William Allyn   *Scr* Gerald Ayres   *Ph* Don Peterman   *Ed* John F. Burnett   *Mus* Georges Delerue   *Art Dir* Jan Scott

● Jacqueline Bisset, Candice Bergen, Meg Ryan, David Selby, Hart Bochner, Michael Brandon (M-G-M)

While not without its problems, *Rich and Famous* is an absorbing drama of some notable qualities, the greatest of which is a gutsy, fascinating and largely magnificent performance by Jacqueline Bisset. Tale delineating the friendship of two smart, creative ladies over a period of two decades makes for 'women's picture' in the best sense of the term.

Plot dynamics of Gerald Ayres' imaginative, very modern updating of John Van Druten's 1940 play *Old Acquaintance* rather closely follow those of Warner Brothers' solid 1943 film version, which starred Bette Davis and Miriam Hopkins. Bisset and Bergen essay college chums whose lives intersect at crucial points over the years.

A recurrent spot in which the pic seems to miss its potential is the occasional confrontation scene in which the ladies have at it in shouting cat fights. These abusive sessions invariably deal with the essence of their relationship, but they have been directed at such a fast pace that the emotional depthcharges fizzle out on the surface.

For a bright, sophisticated piece such as this, particularly one under the guidance of the irrepressibly elegant Goerge Cukor, the somewhat harsh, murky visual style is suprising. Cukor took over the production on short notice when original director Robert Mulligan was replaced after four days' lensing (none of the latter's footage remains).

....

■ RICHARD III

1955, 160 MINS, UK ◇ 🎬
Dir Laurence Olivier, Anthony Bushell   *Prod* Laurence Olivier   *Scr* Laurence Olivier   *Ph* Otto Heller   *Ed* Helga Cranston   *Mus* William Walton   *Art Dir* Roger Furse, Carmen Dillon
● Laurence Olivier, John Gielgud, Claire Bloom, Ralph Richardson, Alec Clunes, Stanley Baker (London)

The Bard pulled no punches in his dramatization of *Richard III*, and Laurence Olivier's filmization likewise portrays him as a ruthless and unscrupulous character, who stops at nothing to obtain the throne. The murder of his brother Clarence (John Gielgud), the betrayal of his cousin, Buckingham (Ralph Richardson), the suffocation of the princes in the Tower are among the unscrupulous steps in the path of Richard's crowning, which are staged with lurid, melodramatic conviction.

At all times Shakespeare's poetry, impeccably spoken by this outstanding cast, heightens the dramatic atmosphere. The production, and notably Roger Furse's decor, is consistently spectacular. The climactic battle sequences rival the pageantry of *Henry V*.

Running Olivier's performance a very close second is Richardson's scheming Buckingham. Another distinguished performance is contributed by Gielgud as Clarence.
□ 1956: Nomination: Best Actor (Laurence Olivier)

....

■ RICHARD PRYOR . . . HERE & NOW

1983, 94 MINS, US ◇ 🎬
Dir Richard Pryor   *Prod* Bob Parkinson, Andy Friendly   *Scr* Richard Pryor   *Ph* Vincent Singletary, Kenneth A. Patterson, Joe Epperson, Tom Geren, Johnny Simmons, Dave Landry   *Ed* Raymond Bush   *Art Dir* Anthony Sabatino, William Harris
● Richard Pryor (Columbia/Indigo)

As a concert film, *Richard Pryor . . . Here & Now* should attract and please those who appreciate him as a standup comic. But beyond the ample laughs, there is a beautiful monolog that's so painfully acute it would entrance even those who never laugh at his other stuff.

His third concert film, *Here & Now* is a mixture of the ones done before and after the fire that almost killed him. Drug-free and still

grateful for a second chance, Pryor remains much more mellow, but less self-examining and contemplative than in *Live on the Sunset Strip* (1982).

Some of the hostility and bite have returned, though well under control. On top of the laughs, he also displays a deepening sympathy for those doomed by substances.

....

■ RICHARD PRYOR LIVE ON THE SUNSET STRIP

1982, 82 MINS, US ◇ 🎬 🎥
Dir Joe Layton   *Prod* Richard Pryor   *Scr* Richard Pryor   *Ph* Haskell Wexler   *Ed* Sheldon Kahn   *Mus* Harry R. Betts   *Art Dir* Michael Baugh
● Richard Pryor (Columbia/Rastar)

This is not a film in any respect, except to note the medium Richard Pryor's stand-up routine was captured on in two nights at the Palladium in 1981. Director Joe Layton and cameraman Haskell Wexler make no noticeable contributions and often fail to solve the problems of concert lensing.

But Pryor is truly amazing and that's all that counts. After a number of roles in successful pictures, he brings an acting ability to his stage routine that enhances his well-established talent for caricature. What this allows him to do is pull the audience into moments of genuine emotion, then clobber them suddenly with a hilarious switch.

By far the best comes with a candid discussion of his drug addiction that culminates in the freebase explosion that almost killed him.

....

■ RICH IN LOVE

1993, 105 MINS, US ◇ 🎬 ⊙
Dir Bruce Beresford   *Prod* Richard D. Zanuck, Lili Fini Zanuck   *Scr* Alfred Uhry   *Ph* Peter James   *Ed* Mark Warner   *Mus* Georges Delerue   *Art Dir* John Stoddart
● Albert Finney, Jill Clayburgh, Kathryn Erbe, Kyle MacLachlan, Piper Laurie, Ethan Hawke (M-G-M/Zanuck)

The creative team that brought *Driving Miss Daisy* to the screen fails to conjure up similar magic with *Rich in Love*. Despite a luminous performance by Kathryn Erbe, the story of a South Carolina teen's coming of age in a dysfunctional family seems overly familiar and dramatically diffuse.

Daisy playwright/scriptwriter Alfred Uhry, recruited by producers to adapt a novel by Josephine Humphreys, has a fine ear for Southern dialog that's colorful but not too arch. But this languidly paced film follows a meandering narrative line that seems to have trouble coming to its point.

Is it a story about the shattering effect of divorce on Erbe and her aimless, recently retired father (Albert Finney)? Not really, since they eventually adapt quite well to life without mom (Jill Clayburgh), who briefly pops in and out of the film without making much of an impression.

Finney fits into his Charleston accent like an old shoe, but he's working here with an unfocused character and using his technical virtuosity to carry it along. The unglamorized but compellingly watchable Erbe commendably avoids punching obvious emotional buttons.

A brief romantic interlude with Kyle MacLachlan, Yankee husband of her neurotic older sister (Suzy Amis), never develops into much of anything because his character is so amorphous.

Pic is dedicated to composer Georges Delerue, who died shortly after completing this score.

....

■ RICOCHET

1991, 97 MINS, US ◇ 🎬 ⊙
Dir Russell Mulcahy   *Prod* Joel Silver, Michael Levy   *Scr* Steven de Souza   *Ph* Peter Levy   *Ed* Peter Honess   *Mus* Alan Silvestri   *Art Dir* Jaymes Hinkle

● Denzel Washington, John Lithgow, Ice T, Kevin Pollak, Lindsay Wagner, Victoria Dillard (HBO/Silver)

A taut, twisty urban suspenser powered by the spring-loaded performance of Denzel Washington in his first major action role, *Ricochet* has a nasty streak and a tendency toward implausible excess.

Washington plays an ambitious young cop who nails a vicious hitman (John Lithgow), putting him behind bars just as his own career begins an upward spiral. The pathological killer plots his revenge for seven years, watching the gifted cop become district attorney and acquire a loving family and a promising political future. When Lithgow finally breaks out of jail, he's armed with a diabolical plan to wreak havoc on everything his nemesis has attained.

Tension is sustained by skillful cutting between the two opposite lives and full-bore performances on both ends of the seesaw. Plot kicks into high gear once the killer gets loose to pursue his prey.

Screenplay [from a story by Fred Dekker and Menno Meyjes] offers unusually good dialog for the smooth-talking Washington and a number of scenes to savor. Pic threatens to become truly absorbing as Lithgow's brilliant revenge scheme unfolds, but *Ricochet* soon abandons cleverness in favor of spectacle.

．．．．．．．．．．．．．．．．．．．．．．．．．．

■ RIDE IN THE WHIRLWIND

1966, 82 MINS, US ◇ ⊛ ⊙
Dir Monte Hellman   *Prod* Monte Hellman, Jack Nicholson   *Scr* Jack Nicholson   *Ph* Gregory Sandor   *Mus* Robert Drasnin   *Art Dir* James Campbell
● Cameron Mitchell, Jack Nicholson, Millie Perkins, Katherine Squire, George Mitchell, Harry Dean Stanton (Proteus)

Monte Hellman's *Ride in the Whirlwind* is a flat, woodenly acted western with mild suspense that never grabs. Part of the fault is with Jack Nicholson's script, which is little more than a promising plot line rather than a fully developed scenario. Nicholson also plays the lead, but since Nicholson the writer has little to say, Nicholson the actor has even less.

Hellman never exploits the full potential of the situations. A trio of uncommunicative saddle tramps – Nicholson, Cameron Mitchell, Tom Filer – stumble on a motley gang holed up in a mountain shack after a stage coach robbery. For reasons never adequately explained, the one-eyed gang leader is downright cordial to the cow pokes.

They spend the night, and in the morning find themselves surrounded by a posse of vigilantes that is going to string them up first and ask questions later.

In the getaway Filer is shot down and Mitchell and Nicholson have to climb up a sheer canyon.

Not one of the characters emerges from the flatness of the screen, and to a man they move and talk like animated cigar store Indians.

．．．．．．．．．．．．．．．．．．．．．．．．．．

■ RIDE LONESOME

1959, 74 MINS, US ◇
Dir Budd Boetticher   *Prod* Budd Boetticher   *Scr* Burt Kennedy   *Ph* Charles Lawton Jr   *Ed* Jerome Thoms   *Mus* Heinz Roemheld   *Art Dir* Robert Peterson
● Randolph Scott, Karen Steele, Pernell Roberts, James Best, Lee Van Cleef, James Coburn (Ranown/Columbia)

Ride Lonesome has Randolph Scott as a bounty hunter whose interest in a young murderer (James Best) seems to be solely the money he will collect for his delivery. Along the way, he picks up a young widow (Karen Steele), and two feckless outlaws (Pernell Roberts and James Coburn). Soon Best's brother (Lee Van Cleef) is trailing them with his own band, intent on rescuing Best.

Ride Lonesome has several good plots and sub-plots going for it, creating a chase melodrama that is often a chase-within-a-chase. Scriptwriter Burt Kennedy has used genuine speech of the frontier and some offhand, often rather grim humor, to give the screenplay additional interest where the pursuit portions necessarily lag. Boetticher and his cast handle it well, only occasionally overreaching in brief scenes where Steele's sex seems stressed beyond reason.

Scott does a good job as the taciturn and misunderstood hero, but the two standouts are Best as the giggling killer and Roberts as the sardonic outlaw who wants to get away to a new start.

．．．．．．．．．．．．．．．．．．．．．．．．．．

■ RIDE THE HIGH COUNTRY

1962, 94 MINS, US ◇ ⊛ ⊙
Dir Sam Peckinpah   *Prod* Richard E. Lyons   *Scr* N.B. Stone Jr   *Ph* Lucien Ballard   *Ed* Frank Santillo   *Mus* George Bassman   *Art Dir* George W. Davis, Leroy Coleman
● Randolph Scott, Joel McCrea, Mariette Hartley, Edgar Buchanan, Ron Starr, Warren Oates (M-G-M)

The old saying 'you can't make a silk purse out of a sow's ear' rings true for Metro-Goldwyn-Mayer's artistic western *Ride the High Country*. It remains a standard story, albeit with an interesting gimmick and some excellent production values.

Scott and McCrea play their ages in roles that could well be extensions of characters they have each played in countless earlier films. They are quick-triggered ex-lawmen, former famed 'town-tamers' whom life has passed by and who are now reduced to taking jobs as guards for a gold shipment. They engage in one last battle – over a woman and involving a youth who epitomizes their own youth.

It is Sam Peckinpah's direction, however, that gives the film greatest artistry. He gives N. B. Stone Jr.'s script a measure beyond its adequacy, instilling bright moments of sharp humor and an overall significant empathetic flavor.

．．．．．．．．．．．．．．．．．．．．．．．．．．

■ RIDE, VAQUERO

1953, 91 MINS, US ◇
Dir John Farrow   *Prod* Stephen Ames   *Scr* Frank Fenton   *Ph* Robert Surtees   *Ed* Harold F. Kress   *Mus* Bronislau Kaper   *Art Dir* Cedric Gibbons, Arthur Lonergan
● Robert Taylor, Ava Gardner, Howard Keel, Anthony Quinn, Kurt Kasznar, Jack Elam (M-G-M)

Locale of the production is southwest Texas, a territory around Brownsville, that is under the thumb of a group of outlaw gangs controlled by Anthony Quinn and his lieutenant (Robert Taylor). When Howard Keel tries to found a cattle empire and brings in settlers, the outlaws fight back, knowing they will be through if civilization comes to the land.

John Farrow's direction stirs up plenty of violent action as he plays off the story. While the script is a bit vague in development of some of the personalities, overall effect is okay for the outdoor fan, although more critical audiences would have liked less obscurity. Keel brings Ava Gardner, his bride, to his new homestead, only to find it a smoking ruin as the result of a Quinn-directed raid. Keel builds again, stronger this time, after he fails to unite the townspeople and the sheriff against the outlaw. When the new home is ready, Quinn's forces attack.

Taylor is very good in selling the quiet menace of his character, and Quinn stands out as the flamboyant outlaw leader. Gardner provides physical beauty to a character that is not as well stated as it could have been. Keel does well by his determined, foolhardy character.

．．．．．．．．．．．．．．．．．．．．．．．．．．

■ RIFF-RAFF

1991, 92 MINS, UK ◇ ⊛
Dir Ken Loach   *Prod* Sally Hibbin   *Scr* Bill Jesse   *Ph* Barry Ackroyd   *Ed* Jonathan Morris   *Mus* Stewart Copeland   *Art Dir* Martin Johnson
● Robert Carlyle, Emer McCourt, Jimmy Coleman, Ricky Tomlinson, Willie Ross, Derek Young (Parallax/Film Four)

Riff-Raff, a sprightly ensemble comedy about workers on a London building site, will surprise those who think Brit helmer Ken Loach can crank out only political items. Semi-improvised pic is strong on yocks and easy to digest.

Central character is Stevie (Robert Carlyle), a young Glaswegian just out of stir, who's come south and got a job converting a closed-down hospital into luxury apartments. His co-workers are from all over – Liverpudlians, Geordies (natives of Newcastle), West Indians. They're breaking every regulation in the book and running scams on the side. Home is a squat in a dingy council block.

After Stevie meets Susan (Emer McCourt), a drifter from Belfast who's trying to make it as a singer, they move in together and make a go of it in the big city. Story yo-yos between their fragile relationship and the shenanigans on the building site.

Fruity script by onetime laborer Bill Jesse (who died in 1990 just before the pic was completed) catches the wisecracking flavor of navvy repartee. Comedic tone also spills over into the love story. Thesping by no-name cast is strong and clearly benefits from Loach's insistence that all actors have building-site experience.

．．．．．．．．．．．．．．．．．．．．．．．．．．

■ RIGHT STUFF, THE

1983, 192 MINS, US ◇ ⊛ ⊙
Dir Philip Kaufman   *Prod* Robert Chartoff, Irwin Winkler   *Scr* Philip Kaufman   *Ph* Caleb Deschanel   *Ed* Glenn Farr, Lisa Fruchtman, Stephen A. Rotter, Tom Rolf, Douglas Stewart   *Mus* Bill Conti   *Art Dir* Geoffrey Kirkland
● Sam Shepard, Scott Glenn, Ed Harris, Dennis Quaid, Fred Ward, Barbara Hershey (Ladd Company)

The Right Stuff is a humdinger. Full of beauty, intelligence and excitement, this big-scale look at the development of the US space program and its pioneering aviators provides a fresh, entertaining look back at the recent past. Film version of Tom Wolfe's best selling revisionist history was some three years in the making.

Tale spans 16 years, from ace test pilot Chuck Yeager's breaking of the sound barrier over the California desert to Vice-President Johnson's welcoming of the astronauts to their new home in Houston with an enormous barbecue inside the Astrodome. Telling takes over three hours, but it goes by lickity-split under Philip Kaufman's direction and is probably the shortest-seeming film of its length ever made.

Emblematic figure here is Yeager, played by a taciturn Sam Shepard. As the ace of aces who was passed by for astronaut training due to his lack of college degree, Yeager, for Kaufman as for Wolfe, is the embodiment of 'the right stuff', that ineffable quality which separates the men from the boys, so to speak.
☐ 1983: Best Original Score, Editing, Sound (Mark Berger Tom Scott, Randy Thom, David MacMillan), Sound Editing.
☐ Nominations: Best Picture, Supp. Actor (Sam Shepard), Cinematography, Art Direction

．．．．．．．．．．．．．．．．．．．．．．．．．．

■ RIKKY AND PETE

1988, 101 MINS, AUSTRALIA ◇ ⊛ ⊙
Dir Nadia Tass   *Prod* Nadia Tass, David Parker   *Scr* David Parker   *Ph* David Parker   *Ed* Ken Sallows   *Mus* Phil Judd, Eddie Rayner   *Art Dir* Josephine Ford

R

● Stephen Kearney, Nina Landis, Tetchie Agbayani, Bill Hunter, Bruno Lawrence, Bruce Spence (United Artists/Cascade)

Rikky and Pete has a clutch of potentially interesting characters and a promising storyline; but the characters are inadequately developed, and the plotting doesn't live up to expectations.

Pete is an inventor in Melbourne. For reasons barely specified, Pete is in the middle of a vendetta with a burly police officer (Bill Hunter) who's out to get him; his sister, Rikky, meanwhile, is tired of her latest beau (Lewis Fitzgerald) and of singing to unappreciative audiences in a bar. They take off in their mother's magnificent Bentley for the outback.

They arrive in a mining town and strike it rich. Pete has an affair with a pretty Filipino girl (Tetchie Agbayani), but winds up in prison where the pursuing cop finally locates him.

Stephen Kearney gives Pete plenty of raffish charm, and Nina Landis has a warm personality as Rikky. Unfortunately, their roles remain sketchy. Landis suffers particularly, since a romance with miner Bruno Lawrence is suggested but never followed through, leaving a void in the film. Nadia Tass directs with a very deliberate pace, which drags the film down.

● ●

■ RING, THE

1952, 79 MINS, US Ⓦ

Dir Kurt Neumann *Scr* Irving Shulman *Ph* Russell Harlan *Ed* Bruce B. Pierce *Mus* Herschel Burke Gilbert
● Gerald Mohr, Rita Moreno, Lalo Rios, Robert Arthur, Robert Osterloh, Jack Elam (King Bros/United Artists)

Efforts of a young boxer to fight his way up from preliminaries to main bout stature provides a sock setting for a well-spun yarn [from a novel by Irving Shulman] of discrimination on the Coast against the Mexican-Americans.

Accent is on realism. Pic pinpoints the discriminatory line without relying on any hysterical sequences. The message hits home with such effectively underplayed scenes as tourists gazing at 'those lazy Mexicans', brushoff of a group of Mexican-American boys by a waitress in a Beverly Hills eatery and the turndown of a young couple at a skating rink gate because it wasn't 'Mexican Night'. The prizefighting scenes, too, are executed graphically.

Cast is headed by Gerald Mohr, the manager; Lalo Rios, the boxer, and Rita Moreno.

● ●

■ RING OF BRIGHT WATER

1969, 107 MINS, UK ◇ Ⓦ

Dir Jack Couffer *Prod* Joseph Strick *Scr* Jack Couffer, Bill Travers *Ph* Wolfgang Suschitzky *Ed* Reginald Mills *Mus* Frank Cordell *Art Dir* Ken Ryan
● Bill Travers, Virginia McKenna, Roddy McMillan, Jameson Clark, Jean Taylor-Smith (Palomar)

Bill Travers and Virginia McKenna followed up their success in *Born Free* with an engaging film about an otter. It is a semi-documentary, based on Gavin Maxwell's autobiographical bestseller, *Ring of Bright Water*.

Story concerns a London civil servant, anxious to get out of the rat race to write. He makes his decision when he acquires Mij, a young otter, as a pet and finds that keeping the charming but mischievous mammal in a London apartment is frought with headaches. So he and Mij depart for a lonely coastal village in the Highlands where they settle down contentedly in a ramshackle crofter's cottage.

Travers and McKenna unselfishly subdue their performances to the star demands of the lolloping young rascal, Mij, but keep the interest firmly alive by their tactful playing.

● ●

■ RIO BRAVO

1959, 140 MINS, US ◇ Ⓥ ⊙

Dir Howard Hawks *Prod* Howard Hawks *Scr* Jules Furthman, Leigh Brackett *Ph* Russell Harlan *Ed* Folmar Blangsted *Mus* Dimitri Tiomkin *Art Dir* Leo K. Kuter
● John Wayne, Dean Martin, Ricky Nelson, Angie Dickinson, Walter Brennan, Ward Bond (Armada)

Rio Bravo is a big, brawling western. Script, based on the B. H. McCampbell short story, gets off to one of the fastest slam-bang openings on record. Within 90 seconds Wayne, a fast-shooting sheriff, is clubbed, another man knocked out and a third man murdered.

Plot thereafter revolves around Wayne's attempts to hold the murderer, brother of the most powerful rancher in the area, until the arrival some days hence of the US marshal. He's up against the rancher utilizing gunman tactics to free the jailed killer.

Producer-director Howard Hawks makes handsome use of force in logically unravelling his hard-hitting narrative, creating suspense at times and occasionally inserting lighter moments to give variety. Wayne delivers a faithful portrayal of the peace officer who must fight his battle with the aid of only two deputies. One of these is Dean Martin, his ex-deputy who attempts to kick off a two-year drunk to help his friend. The other deputy is Walter Brennan, a cantankerous old cripple assigned to guard the prisoner in the jail.

In for distaff interest and with more legitimate footage than usual in a western is Angie Dickinson, a looker fashioned into an important key character who delivers in every way.

● ●

■ RIO CONCHOS

1964, 105 MINS, US ◇ Ⓦ

Dir Gordon M. Douglas *Prod* David Weisbart *Scr* Joseph Landon, Clair Huffaker *Ph* Joe MacDonald *Ed* Joseph Silver *Mus* Jerry Goldsmith *Art Dir* Jack Martin Smith, William Geber
● Richard Boone, Stuart Whitman, Anthony Franciosa, Wende Wagner, Warner Anderson, Edmond O'Brien (20th Century-Fox)

Rio Conchos is a big, tough, action-packed slam-bang western with as tough a set of characters as ever rode the sage. It is Old West adventure at its best.

Producer David Weisbart has woven fanciful movement along with lush settings via on-the-spot color lensing in Arizona. To this, Gordon Douglas has added his own version of what a lusty western should be in the direction, getting the most from a batch of colorful characters. Music score by Jerry Goldsmith is a particularly valuable asset in striking a fast mood from the opening scene.

Script by Joseph Landon and Clair Huffaker, adapted from latter's novel, limns the quest of four men for 2,000 stolen repeating rifles that a group of former Confederate soldiers have been running to the Apaches. Quartet is composed of Stuart Whitman, a cavalry captain, who heads the party; Richard Boone, an ex-reb who hates Apaches; Tony Franciosa, a Mexican gigolo-type killer whom the army was about to hang; and Jim Brown, a cavalry corporal. Their destination is the camp of a demented Confederate gun-runner (Edmond O'Brien) who wants vengeance on the North for the South's defeat.

Whitman acquits himself excellently in his tough role but interest principally lies in characters played by Boone and Franciosa, both killers and a director's dream. Brown, too, handles himself well, and Vito Scotti, as a laughing bandit, registers particularly in his brief menacing role before being killed.

● ●

■ RIO GRANDE

1950, 105 MINS, US Ⓦ

Dir John Ford *Prod* John Ford, Merian C. Cooper *Scr* James Kevin McGuinness *Ph* Bert Glennon

Ed Jack Murray *Mus* Victor Young *Art Dir* Frank Hotaling
● John Wayne, Maureen O'Hara, Ben Johnson, Claude Jarmon Jr, Harry Carey Jr, Victor McLaglen (Republic/Argosy)

Rio Grande is filmed outdoor action [based on a *SatEvePost* story by James Warner Bellah] at its best, delivered in the John Ford manner.

John Wayne's devotion to military oath had led him, some 15 years back, to destroy the plantation home of his southern-born wife during the war between the states. He is now a lonely man, fighting Indians in the west. To his fort comes his young son, Claude Jarman Jr whom he has not seen in 15 years.

Into this setup of rugged living, endangered daily by marauding Indians, comes Maureen O'Hara, Wayne's estranged wife, determined to take the son back.

Comedy touches are introduced by Victor McLaglen as the top sergeant, a role he has performed in other Ford pictures.

● ●

■ RIO LOBO

1970, 114 MINS, US ◇ Ⓥ ⊙

Dir Howard Hawks *Prod* Howard Hawks *Scr* Leigh Brackett, Burton Wohl *Ph* William Clothier *Ed* John Woodcock *Mus* Jerry Goldsmith *Art Dir* Robert Smith
● John Wayne, Jorge Rivero, Jennifer O'Neill, Jack Elam, Chris Mitchum, Victor French (Malabar/Cinema Center)

Rio Lobo is the sort of western that John Wayne and producer-director Howard Hawks do in their sleep. But by no stretch of nostalgia does it match such previous Wayne-Hawks epics as *Red River* or *Rio Bravo*.

Leigh Brackett and Burton Wohl's script, based on Wohl's story, is by the numbers. In the Civil War, Wayne is a Union colonel – an ex-Texas Ranger, of course – who keeps losing army gold shipments to Confederate guerrillas led by Jorge Rivero and Chris Mitchum. He captures them, but they won't tell him who the traitors are who have been tipping them off about the gold.

From than on it is the same plot that has been worked over since the silent days of Bronco Billy with no new surprises.

Hawks' direction is as listless as the plot.

● ●

■ RIO RITA

1942, 91 MINS, US Ⓦ

Dir S. Sylvan Simon *Prod* Pandro S. Berman *Scr* Richard Connell, Gladys Lehman *Ph* George Folsey *Ed* Ben Lewis *Mus* Herbert Stothart (dir)
● Bud Abbott, Lou Costello, Kathryn Grayson, John Carroll, Patricia Dane, Tom Conway (M-G-M)

Like all Abbott and Costello entries. Without them it would be so much celluloid. So far as the oft-filmed version of the former Ziegfeld stage musical is concerned, Metro uses but the original title song and the 'Rangers' number.

Script relies principally on a Nazi espionage story. The plot has to do with mysterious radiocasts to a foreign power; the manager (Tom Conway) of the heroine's (Kathryn Grayson) hotel is really a Nazi spy; his girl friend Patricia Dane is (or isn't) a G-woman in disguise (the plot's confusing on this point), and Abbott and Costello, along with hero John Carroll, save the day in the nick. It's that kind of a plot.

Director S. Sylvan Simon has spaced the A&C nonsensities with a good sense of timing to properly break up the hoke. There are a couple of reprises on some of the business, but withal the 91 minutes pace well.

● ●

■ RIOT

1968, 96 MINS, US ◇

Dir Buzz Kulik *Prod* William Castle *Scr* James Poe *Ph* Robert B. Hauser *Ed* Edwin H. Bryant *Mus* Christopher Komeda *Art Dir* Paul Sylbert

● Jim Brown, Gene Hackman, Mike Kellin, Gerald S. O'Loughlin, Ben Carruthers (Paramount)

Riot is a good prison programmer produced with authenticity inside Arizona State Prison. Jim Brown and Gene Hackman are leaders of a convict revolt which paralyzes prison routine and unleashes some violent passions. Buzz Kulik's direction is better in the forward plot thrusts than in the many repetitious stretches, not at all alleviated by a pedestrian ballad reprised much too often.

Ex-convict Frank Elli's book, *The Riot*, has been adapted into a wandering script which lacks a definite cohesion. Concept vacillates between apparent attempt to tell a straight-forward escape story, and temptation to linger and exploit violence. No social document, this; but not a potboiler, either.

Hackman, Mike Kellin and a freaked-out psychotic con, played by Ben Carruthers, launch a minor riot as prelude to escape.

Brown's immensely strong screen presence is manifest. Hackman gives the best performance as an equivocating, cynical manipulator of crowd psychology. Carruthers is too unrestrained.

■ RIOT IN CELL BLOCK 11

1954, 80 MINS, US Ⓥ
Dir Don Siegel *Prod* Walter Wanger *Scr* Richard Collins *Ph* Russell Harlan *Ed* Bruce B. Pierce *Mus* Herschel Burke Gilbert
● Neville Brand, Emile Meyer, Frank Faylen, Leo Gordon, Robert Osterloh, Paul Frees (Allied Artists)

Riot in Cell Block 11 is a hard-hitting, suspenseful prison thriller.

The pros and cons of prison riots are stated articulately in the Richard Collins screen story, and producer Walter Wanger uses a realistic, almost documentary, style to make his point for needed reforms in the operation of penal institutions.

The picture doesn't use formula prison plot. There's no inmate reformed by love or fair treatment, nor unbelievable boy-meets-girl, gets-same angle. Nor are there any heroes and heavies of standard pattern. Instead, it deals with a riot, how it started and why, what was done to halt it, the capitulations on both sides.

The points for reform made in the Wanger production cover overcrowding housing, poor food, the mingling of mentally well and mentally sick prisoners, the character-corroding idleness of men caged in cell blocks.

A standout performance is given by Emile Meyer, the warden who understands the prisoners' problems.

■ RISE OF CATHERINE THE GREAT, THE

(US: Catherine the Great)

1934, 95 MINS, UK Ⓥ ⊙
Dir Paul Czinner *Prod* Alexander Korda *Scr* Arthur Wimperis, Lajos Biro, Melchior Lengyel *Ph* Georges Perinal *Ed* Harold Young, Stephen Harrison *Mus* Muir Mathieson *Art Dir* Vincent Korda
● Douglas Fairbanks Jr, Elisabeth Bergner, Flora Robson, Gerald du Maurier, Irene Vanbrugh, Joan Gardner (London)

A nice rather than a good-looking girl, with beautiful eyes, Elisabeth Bergner charms as she progresses and is altogether believable as the minor German princess of moderate circumstances summoned to Russia by the Empress Elizabeth to wed her erratic nephew, the Grand Duke Peter, sometimes called Peter the Impossible. The throne needs an heir.

Theatrical license has been liberally taken. This story makes the marriage the culmination of the blue-blooded Cinderella's childhood dream and almost places her upon the throne despite herself, except that she rises to meet the obligation upon realizing how un-

equipped her dissolute husband is to meet the responsibility.

Bergner's scene with the dying empress (Flora Robson) is a gem of expert playing by both women and there are other highlight sequences, particularly a banquet, which stand out for direction, portrayal and dialog. The story is principally in the hands of Bergner, Robson and Douglas Fairbanks. Robson gives a fine performance, while Fairbanks' definition of the fuming Peter is one of the best he has ever done.

Catherine is reported to have cost close to $400,000 which, for England, is the theoretical equivalent of a $1 million Hollywood effort. It is certainly one of the most expensive pictures ever made there.

■ RISKY BUSINESS

1983, 96 MINS, US ◇ Ⓥ ⊙
Dir Paul Brickman *Prod* Jon Avnet *Scr* Paul Brickman *Ph* Reynaldo Villalobos, Bruce Surtees *Ed* Richard Chew *Mus* Tangerine Dream *Art Dir* William J. Cassidy
● Tom Cruise, Rebecca DeMornay, Curtis Armstrong, Bronson Pinchot, Raphael Sbarge, Joe Pantoliano (Geffen)

Risky Business is like a promising first novel, with all the pros and cons that come with that territory.

High schooler Tom Cruise could literally be a next-door neighbor to Timothy Hutton in *Ordinary People* on Chicago's affluent suburban North Shore. That changes virtually overnight, however, when he meets sharp-looking hooker Rebecca DeMornay. On the lam from her slimy pimp, she shacks up in Cruise's splendid home while his parents are out of town and, since he's anxious to prove himself as a Future Enterpriser in one of his school's more blatantly greed-oriented programs, convinces him to make the house into a bordello for one night.

Ultimately, pic seems to endorse the bottom line, going for the big buck. In fact, not only is Cruise rewarded financially for setting up the best little whorehouse in Glencoe, but it gets him into Princeton to boot. Writer-director Paul Brickman can therefore be accused of trying to have it both ways, but there's no denying the stylishness and talent of his direction.

■ RITA, SUE AND BOB TOO

1987, 95 MINS, UK ◇ Ⓥ ⊙
Dir Alan Clarke *Prod* Sandy Lieberson *Scr* Andrea Dunbar *Ph* Ivan Strasburg *Ed* Stephen Singleton *Mus* Michael Kamen *Art Dir* Leo Huntingford
● Michelle Holmes, Siobhan Finneran, George Costigan, Lesley Sharp, Willie Ross, Patti Nicholls (Film Four/Umbrella/British Screen)

Rita, Sue and Bob Too is a sad-funny comedy about sex and life in the Yorkshire city of Bradford.

Rita and Sue are two schoolgirls who sometimes babysit for a well-off couple, Bob and Michelle. In the film's opening sequence, the odious yet somehow charming Bob, a real-estate agent, gives the girls a lift home, but stops off first on the moors above the city and without preliminaries, proposes sex with them. The girls are agreeable, with Sue taking the first turn on the reclining seat in Bob's Rover.

Immediately screenwriter Andrea Dunbar [who adapted the film from her own plays *The Arbor* and *Rita, Sue and Bob Too*] injects a completely convincing mixture of raunchy comedy and sadness.

Rita and Sue, splendidly played by Siobhan Finneran and Michelle Holmes, are pathetic figures as they trip along in their tight miniskirts, but they're lively and funny. George Costigan makes Bob a charming character, despite his ingrained seediness.

■ RITZ, THE

1976, 90 MINS, US ◇ Ⓥ
Dir Richard Lester *Prod* Denis O'Dell *Scr* Terrence McNally *Ph* Paul Wilson *Ed* John Bloom *Mus* Ken Thorne *Art Dir* Phillip Harrison
● Jack Weston, Rita Moreno, Jerry Stiller, Kaye Ballard, F. Murray Abraham, Paul B. Price (Warner)

Depending on where one's taste lies, *The Ritz* is either esoteric farce for the urban cosmopolite, or else one long tasteless and anachronistic 1950-ish 'gay' joke, shot at England's Twickenham Studios in 25 days.

Terrence McNally adapted his 1975 play about assorted mistaken identities and hangups in a NY gay steambath (including Broadway cast originals).

McNally's story has Weston fingered for rubout by dying father-in-law George Coulouris. Escaping from the midwest, Jack Weston heads for a notorious Gotham gay bath, figuring that avenging brother-in-law Jerry Stiller will never find him.

But the plan doesn't figure on the gangland family's diversified business interests, nor on the ingenuity of Weston's wife, played by Kaye Ballard.

Classic farce construction provides the expected physical action.

■ RIVER, THE

1938, 30 MINS, US
Dir Pare Lorentz *Scr* Pare Lorentz *Ph* Stacy Woodward, Floyd Crosby, Willard Van Dyke *Ed* Pare Lorentz *Mus* Virgil Thompson
● (Farm Security Administration)

This is the second film produced by the Farm Security Administration, previous one having been *The Plough That Broke the Plains*, also written and directed by Pare Lorentz, with musical score by Virgil Thomson. It's a more arresting, more compelling job than the previous effort, although still failing to encompass the subject entirely.

Documentary pic seeks to tell the story of the Mississippi river, its sources, its majestic course, its destination, its uses and abuse by heedless man, and its relentless retaliation. As the narrator [Thomas Chalmers] states, the Mississippi is the most nearly perfect river in the world, and something of that mighty quality infests the film. Film impressively depicts the beauty and the power of the river, how it has been squandered and destroyed, how terrible has been the inevitable result. But it fails to tie its interrelated parts into a whole that is entirely clear or convincing. It skips from fact to fact, argument to argument, but doesn't quite weave a perfect pattern.

Thomson's score, blended from symphonic sources, ballads, spirituals and original compositions, highlights the film dramatically. Narrative is vividly effective, being a composite of straight description and exposition and poetic prose.

■ RIVER, THE

1951, 99 MINS, INDIA/US ◇ Ⓥ ⊙
Dir Jean Renoir *Prod* Kenneth McEldowney *Scr* Rumer Godden, Jean Renoir *Ph* Claude Renoir *Ed* George Gale *Mus* M.A. Partha Sarathy *Art Dir* Eugene Lourie, Bansi Chandragupta
● Nora Swinburne, Esmond Knight, Arthur Shields, Thomas E. Breen, Patricia Walters, Adrienne Corri (Oriental-International/United Artists)

Jean Renoir's *The River* is a sort of animated geographic, in color, of life on the Ganges River in West Bengal. It is a distinctive story of adolescent love, with a philosophy that life flows on just as the river.

This is a beautiful picture, and certainly neither Technicolor nor India ever looked better. Throughout it is ablaze with vivid, contrasting colors. But one never feels the real India and rather suspects that this is a highly glamorized version.

The story tells how the life of a British family (the family runs a jute mill) is interrupted by the appearance of one Capt John on a visit to his cousin, Mr John, a neighbor. Two young teenagers fall as madly in love with Capt John, who lost a leg in the last war, as their newly-awakened emotions will allow. But Capt John is too busy being a lost soul to take them seriously.

Although the drama too frequently seems merely an afterthought, a sort of excuse upon which to build a lush panorama of India, the characters are completely credible. Exception is Thomas Breen as Capt John. He has the appearance of one who might excite the immature emotions of the three young ladies, but hasn't the ability to appear convincing. Outstanding is Radha, whose ritual dance of love with the god Krishna highlights the pic.

....

■ RIVER, THE

1984, 122 MINS, US ◇ ⑩ ⊙
Dir Mark Rydell   *Prod* Edward Lewis, Robert Cortes
Scr Robert Dillon, Julian Barry   *Ph* Vilmos Zsigmond
Ed Sidney Levin   *Mus* John Williams   *Art Dir* Charles Rosen
● Mel Gibson, Sissy Spacek, Shane Bailey, Becky Jo Lynch, Scott Glenn, Don Hood (Universal)

The River puts fundamental American values to the test in a society that has come unglued. Stripped down to the bare essentials few people actually ever come into contact with, pic remains a rather private ordeal observed from the outside looking in. There is a victory at the end, but not a sense of lasting triumph.

Setting the tone is the Garvey family battling the flood waters of the river to save their farm. Farmers are forced to sell off their land with hungry wolf businessman Joe Wade (Scott Glenn) waiting to pick up the pieces.

Glenn, as the silver-spoon kid and Spacek's former lover, is the film's most complex creation. Though he is the malignancy behind much of the farmers' troubles, director Mark Rydell allows him to maintain a level of humanity.
□ 1984: Nominations: Best Actress (Sissy Spacek), Cinematography, Original Score, Sound, Special Achievement Award (Sound Effects Editing)

....

■ RIVER OF NO RETURN

1954, 90 MINS, US ◇ ⑩ ⊙
Dir Otto Preminger   *Prod* Stanley Rubin   *Scr* Frank Fenton   *Ph* Joseph LaShelle   *Ed* Louis Loeffler
Mus Cyril J. Mockridge
● Robert Mitchum, Marilyn Monroe, Rory Calhoun, Tommy Rettig, Murvyn Vye, Douglas Spencer (20th Century-Fox)

The striking beauties of the Canadian Rockies co-star with the blonde charms of Marilyn Monroe and the masculine muscles of Robert Mitchum in *River of No Return*.

The competition between scenic splendors of the Jasper and Banff National Parks and entertainment values finds the former finishing slightly ahead on merit, although there's enough rugged action and suspense moments to get the production through its footage. In between the high spots, Otto Preminger's directorial pacing is inclined to lag, so the running time seems overlong.

Mitchum and Tommy Rettig, playing father and son, pull Monroe and Rory Calhoun from a river that races by their wilderness farm. Calhoun is trying to get to a settlement to file a gold claim he has won dishonestly at cards and Monroe is along because she expects to marry him. Calhoun steals Mitchum's horse and gun and rides off, leaving the others at the mercy of warring Indians. Man, woman

and boy take to the river on a raft to escape the redskins.

....

■ RIVER RUNS THROUGH IT, A

1992, 123 MINS, US ◇ ⑩ ⊙
Dir Robert Redford   *Prod* Robert Redford, Patrick Markey
Scr Richard Friedenberg   *Ph* Philippe Rousselot
Ed Lynzee Klingman, Robert Estrin   *Mus* Mark Isham
Art Dir Jon Hutman
● Craig Sheffer, Brad Pitt, Tom Skerritt, Brenda Blethyn, Emily Lloyd, Edie McClurg (Columbia)

A skilled, careful adaptation of a much-admired story, *A River Runs Through It* is a convincing trip back in time to a virtually vanished American West, as well as a nicely observed family study. Old-fashioned, literary and restrained, it's Robert Redford's third directorial outing.

Published in 1976, the poetic, elegiac novella traces Norman Maclean's relationship with his wilder, younger brother Paul in Montana against the backdrop of fly fishing, used as a metaphor for achieving a state of grace in life.

Arcing gracefully from 1910 to 1935, tale reveals the love and stability within the proud Maclean family, but also the inability to transform that love into the help Paul needs to save his life.

Performances are thoughtful and well-judged. Craig Sheffer brings well-tempered nuances to Norman. With the showiest role, Brad Pitt shines, his smoldering James Deanish looks and recklessness encompassing both Paul's charm and doom. Tom Skerritt discreetly reveals the loving core inside the reedy exterior of the boys' preacher father.

Exquisitely lit and lensed, pic gives a strong physical sense of the majestic mountains and brilliant rivers of Montana.
□ 1992: Best Cinematography.
□ Nominations: Best Screenplay Adaptation, Original Score

....

■ RIVER'S EDGE

1986, 99 MINS, US ◇ ⑩ ⊙
Dir Tim Hunter   *Prod* Sarah Pillsbury, Midge Sanford
Scr Neal Jimenez   *Ph* Frederick Elmes   *Ed* Howard Smith, Sonya Sones   *Mus* Jurgen Knieper   *Art Dir* John Moto
● Crispin Glover, Keanu Reaves, Ione Skye, David Roebuck, Dennis Hopper, Leo Rossi (Hemdale)

Tim Hunter's *River's Edge* is an unusually downbeat and depressing youth pic.

The setting is a small town, presumably in Oregon. Pic opens with 12-year-old Tim destroying his kid sister's doll and then spotting high-schooler Samson sitting on the river bank With the naked body of a girl he's just murdered. Tim's reaction is to steal a couple of cans of beer for the killer.

But they're really nice at heart, the film seems to be saying. They have to cope with broken homes and the threat of the Bomb, otherwise they wouldn't be so hopeless.

As group leader Layne, Crispin Glover could have used more restraint: he gives a busy, fussy performance. Others in the cast are more effective, with young Joshua Miller particularly Striking as the awful child, Tim.

....

■ ROAD GAMES

1981, 100 MINS, AUSTRALIA ◇ ⑩
Dir Richard Franklin   *Prod* Richard Franklin   *Scr* Everett DeRoche   *Ph* Vincent Monton   *Ed* Edward McQueen-Mason   *Mus* Brian May   *Art Dir* Jon Dowding
● Stacy Keach, Jamie Lee Curtis, Marion Edward, Grant Page, Bill Stacey (Quest)

Road Games is an above-average suspenser concerning an offbeat truck driver who winds up stalking a murderer. Stacy Keach's characterization of the amusing, poetry-spouting

man is particularly endearing but the film builds all too effectively to a rather disappointing climax.

Keach limns an independent trucker in Melbourne assigned to deliver a major shipment of pork to Perth. Amid cracking jokes, concocting stories about the inhabitants of passing cars and fantasizing about pretty girls (all to the deadpan of his pet dog), he becomes suspicious of the driver of a green van.

Through a series of clues he begins to realize the guy is actually a killer of young women the police have been looking for. Neither the police nor anyone else will listen to Keach so he eventually decides to get the guy himself.

Jamie Lee Curtis appears midway through as an heiress hitchhiker who befriends Keach while looking for some diversion from everyday life.

....

■ ROAD HOUSE

1948, 95 MINS, US ⑩
Dir Jean Negulesco   *Prod* Edward Chodorov
Scr Edward Chodorov   *Ph* Joseph LaShelle   *Ed* James B. Clark   *Mus* Cyril J. Mockridge   *Art Dir* Lyle R. Wheeler, Maurice Ransford
● Ida Lupino, Cornel Wilde, Celeste Holm, Richard Widmark, O. Z. Whitehead, Robert Karnes (20th Century-Fox)

Framed within a realistically intimate roadhouse setting, yarn [by Margaret Gruen and Oscar Saul] reconstructs the triangle with an arrestingly psychotic twist supplied by Richard Widmark. For most of the way, director Jean Negulesco hurdles the script's overlength and internal weaknesses by building up conflict out of character studies of the principals. But the film finally bogs down in a lack of incident until a climatic shot-in-the-arm revives interest.

At the center of the story, turning in one of the best performances of her career, is Ida Lupino, playing a lowdown blues warbler who finds herself in the middle between Widmark and Cornel Wilde. Widmark, the roadhouse operator, has a powerful yen for the singer but she prefers his general manager, Wilde.

Lupino's standout performance is highlighted by her firstrate handling of a brace of blues numbers. Her graveltoned voice lacks range but has the more essential quality of style, along the lines of a femme Hoagy Carmichael.

....

■ ROAD HOUSE

1989, 114 MINS, US ◇ ⑩ ⊙
Dir Rowdy Herrington   *Prod* Joel Silver   *Scr* David Lee Henry, Hilary Henkin   *Ph* Dean Cundey   *Ed* Frank Urioste, John LInk   *Mus* Michael Kamen
● Patrick Swayze, Kelly Lynch, Sam Elliott, Ben Gazzara, Marshall Teague, Julie Michaels (United Artists/Silver)

With *Road House*, United Artists hotwires Patrick Swayze a star vehicle shackled by a couple of flat tires in the script department. Ill-conceived and unevenly executed, pic essentially is a Western - a loner comes in to clean up a bar, of all things, and ends up washing and drying the whole town - but its vigilante justice, lawlessness and wanton violence feel ludicrous in a modern setting.

A club owner (Kevin Tighe) recruits Dalton (Swayze) to clean up his bar, which is frequented by lowlifes and bikers. At first, Dalton avoids fighting when possible yet carries a big rep – including the label of having killed a man.

Road House degenerates into a seemingly endless series of fistfights, egged on by bad guy Brad Wesley (Ben Gazzara), who runs the town. The wispy subplot involves a flat romantic attachment for Dalton by a leggy and beautiful local doctor (Kelly Lynch) who turns up with thick glasses and her hair in a bun.

Director Rowdy Herrington has a flair for lensing the fisticuffs – especially a particularly brutal encounter between Swayze and Wesley's top mugger (Marshall Teague). But there's just far too much of it.

. . . .

■ ROAD TO BALI

1952, 91 MINS, US ◇ Ⓥ
Dir Hal Walker *Prod* Harry Tugend *Scr* Frank Butler, Hal Kanter, William Morrow *Ph* George Barnes *Ed* Archie Marshek *Mus* Joseph J. Lilley (dir.) *Art Dir* Hal Pereira, Joseph McMillan Johnson
● Bob Hope, Bing Crosby, Dorothy Lamour, Murvyn Vye, Peter Coe, Leon Askin (Paramount)

Bing Crosby, Bob Hope and Dorothy Lamour are back again in another of Paramount's highway sagas, with nonsensical amusement its only destination. Five songs are wrapped up in the production.

Needing a job, Crosby and Hope hire out to Murvyn Vye, a South Seas island prince, as divers, sail for Vye's homeland and meet Princess Lamour, which is excuse enough for her to sing 'Moonflowers', later reprised as the finale tune.

There's no story to speak of in the script [from a story by Frank Butler and Harry Tugend] but the framework is there on which to hang a succession of amusing quips and physical comedy dealing with romantic rivalry and chuckle competition between the two male stars. It also permits some surprise guest star appearances, such as the finale walkon of Jane Russell; Humphrey Bogart pulling the African Queen through Africa.

. . . .

■ ROAD TO HONG KONG, THE

1962, 91 MINS, UK/US Ⓥ
Dir Norman Panama *Prod* Melvin Frank *Scr* Norman Panama, Melvin Frank *Ph* Jack Hildyard *Ed* Alan Osbiston, John Victor Smith *Mus* Robert Farnon *Art Dir* Roger Furse
● Bing Crosby, Bob Hope, Joan Collins, Dorothy Lamour, Robert Morley, Felix Aylmer (United Artists/Melnor)

The seventh *Road* comedy, after a lapse of seven years, takes the boys on a haphazard trip to a planet called Plutonius, though this only happens as a climax to some hilarious adventures in Ceylon and Hong Kong.

It's almost useless to outline the plot. But it involves Crosby and Hope as a couple of flop vaudevillians who turn con men. Somewhere along the line, Hope loses his memory and that, in a mysterious manner, leads them to involvement with a mysterious spy (Joan Collins) a secret formula and a whacky bunch of thugs called the Third Echelon, led by Robert Morley.

The script is spiced with a number of private jokes (golf, Hope's nose, Crosby's dough, reference to gags from previous *Road* films) but not enough to be irritating. Major disappointment is Joan Collins, who though an okay looker, never seems quite abreast of the comedians. Lamour plays herself as a vaude artist who rescues the Crosby-Hope team from one of their jams.

As guest artists, Frank Sinatra and Dean Martin help to round off the film. David Niven appears for no good reason, while the best interlude is that of Peter Sellers. He plays a native medico, examining Hope for amnesia and it is a brilliantly funny cameo.

. . . .

■ ROAD TO MOROCCO

1942, 83 MINS, US Ⓥ
Dir David Butler *Prod* Paul Jones (assoc.) *Scr* Frank Butler, Don Hartman *Ph* William C. Mellor *Ed* Irene Morra *Art Dir* Hans Dreier, Robert Usher
● Bing Crosby, Bob Hope, Dorothy Lamour, Anthony Quinn, Vladimir Sokoloff, Dona Drake (Paramount)

Morocco is a bubbling spontaneous entertainment without a semblance of sanity; an uproarious patchquilt of gags, old situations and a blitz-like laugh pace that never lets up for a moment. It's Bing Crosby and Bob Hope at their best, with Dorothy Lamour, as usual, the pivotal point for their romantic pitch.

The story's absurdities, all of which are predicated on Crosby and Hope as shipwrecked stowaways cast ashore on the coast of North Africa, at no time weave a pattern of restraint. It's just a madcap holiday for the fun-makers.

The scripters, along with everyone else associated with the production, must surely have realized, of course, that the yarn couldn't be played straight. The result is some unorthodox film-making that finds both male stars making dialogistic asides that kid, for instance, some of the film's 'weaknesses' or, in other cases, poke fun at various objects that aren't even remotely associated with the picture.

☐ 1942: Nominations: Best Original Screenplay, Sound

. . . .

■ ROAD TO RIO

1947, 100 MINS, US Ⓥ
Dir Norman Z. McLeod *Prod* Daniel Dare *Scr* Edmund Beloin, Jack Rose *Ph* Ernest Laszlo *Ed* Ellsworth Hoagland *Mus* Robert Emmett Dolan (dir.) *Art Dir* Hans Dreier, Earl Hedrick
● Bing Crosby, Bob Hope, Dorothy Lamour, Gale Sondergaard, Frank Faylen, Joseph Vitale (Paramount)

There are no talking animals in this to prep uproarish see-hear gags, but a capable substitute is a trumpet that blows musical bubbles. Stunt pays off as one of a number of top, hard-punching laugh-getters. Norman Z. McLeod's direction blends the music and comedy into fast action and sock chuckles that will please followers of the series.

Bing Crosby and Bob Hope repeat their slaphappy characters in the Edmund Beloin-Jack Rose plot. Opening establishes the boys, as usual, in trouble and broke. When they set a circus on fire, pair escape by taking refuge on a ship heading for Rio. It doesn't take them long to discover a damsel in distress (Dorothy Lamour) and action centers around their efforts to save her from a wicked aunt and a forced marriage.

☐ 1947: Nomination: Best Scoring of a Musical Picture

. . . .

■ ROAD TO SINGAPORE

1940, 84 MINS, US Ⓥ
Dir Victor Schertzinger *Prod* Harlan Thompson *Scr* Don Hartman, Frank Butler *Ph* William C. Mellor *Ed* Paul Weatherwax *Mus* Victor Young (dir.) *Art Dir* Hans Dreier, Robert Odell
● Bing Crosby, Dorothy Lamour, Bob Hope, Charles Coburn, Anthony Quinn, Jerry Colonna (Paramount)

Initial teaming of Bing Crosby and Bob Hope in *Road to Singapore* provides foundation for continuous round of good substantial comedy of rapid-fire order, swinging along at a zippy pace. Contrast is provided in Crosby's leisurely presentation of situations and dialog, in comparison to the lightning-like thrusts and parries of Hope. Neat blending of the two brands accentuates the comedy values for laugh purposes.

Story [by Harry Hervey] is a light framework on which to drape the situations for Crosby and Hope, with Dorothy Lamour providing decorative character of a native gal in sarong-like trappings. Crosby is the adventurous son of a shipping magnate, who refuses to sit behind a desk. He walks out on both father and a socialite fiancee to ship to the South Seas with sailor-buddy Hope. Lamour moves in with the pair, and from there on it's a happy mixture of both making passes for the

native beauty, while they struggle to raise the necessary coin to live in comfort on the island. Crosby eventually gets the girl, but not until the trio romps through some zany adventures.

. . . .

■ ROAD TO UTOPIA

1946, 90 MINS, US Ⓥ
Dir Hal Walker *Prod* Paul Jones *Scr* Norman Panama, Melvin Frank *Ph* Lionel Lindon, Gordon Jennings, Farciot Edouart *Ed* Stuart Gilmore *Mus* Leigh Harline *Art Dir* Hans Dreier, Roland Anderson
● Bing Crosby, Bob Hope, Dorothy Lamour, Robert Benchley, Hillary Brooke, Douglass Dumbrille (Paramount)

Bob Benchley is cut into an upper corner of various shots making wisecracks, first being that 'this is how not to make a picture'. Others are in the same groove, while additional off-the-path gags include Bob Hope and Dorothy Lamour in a kissing scene, topped by Hope's aside to the audience: 'As far as I'm concerned the picture is over right now'. Another is a guy walking across a scene asking Bing Crosby and Hope where Stage 8 is.

Action is laid in the Klondike of the gold rush days. On their way there, scrubbing decks because they'd lost their money, Crosby and Hope come upon a map leading to a rich gold mine. It had been stolen from Lamour's father by two of the toughest badmen of Alaska. Lamour goes to the Klondike in search of them.

Technically picture leaves nothing to be desired. Paul Jones, producer, and Hal Walker, who directed, make a fine combination in steering and in the production value provided. Performances by supporting cast are all good.

☐ 1946: Nomination: Best Original Screenplay

. . . .

■ ROAD TO ZANZIBAR

1941, 89 MINS, US Ⓥ
Dir Victor Schertzinger *Prod* Paul Jones *Scr* Frank Butler, Don Hartman *Ph* Ted Tetzlaff *Ed* Alma Macrorie *Mus* Victor Young (dir.) *Art Dir* Hans Dreier, Robert Usher
● Bing Crosby, Bob Hope, Dorothy Lamour, Una Merkel, Jean Marsh, Eric Blore (Paramount)

Zanzibar is Paramount's second coupling of Bing Crosby, Bob Hope and Dorothy Lamour. Although picture has sufficient comedy situations and dialog between its male stars, it lacks the compactness and spontaneity of its predecessor.

The story framework [by Don Hartman, Sy Bartlett] is pretty flimsy foundation for hanging the series of comedy and thrill situations concocted for the pair. It's a fluffy and inconsequential tale, with Crosby-Hope combo, doing valiant work to keep up interest.

Pair are stranded in South Africa, with Crosby the creator of freak sideshow acts for Hope to perform. With his saved passage money back to the States, Crosby buys a diamond mine, which is quickly sold by Hope for profit. Then pair start out on strange Safari with Lamour and Una Merkel, pair of Brooklyn entertainers, pursuing a millionaire hunter.

Comedy episodes generally lack sparkle and tempo, and musical numbers [staged by Le Roy Prinz] are also below par for a Crosby picture.

. . . .

■ ROAR

1981, 102 MINS, US ◇
Dir Noel Marshall *Prod* Noel Marshall, Charles Sloan, Jack Rattner *Scr* Noel Marshall *Ph* Jan De Bont *Mus* Dominic Frontiere *Art Dir* Joel Marshall
● Tippi Hedren, Noel Marshall, John Marshall, Melanie Griffith, Jerry Marshall, Kyalo Mativo (Marshall)

The noble intentions of director-writer-producer Noel Marshall and his actress-wife Tippi Hedren shine through the faults and short-comings of *Roar*, their 11-year, $17 million project – touted as the most disaster-plagued pic in Hollywood history.

Given the enormous difficulties during production – a devastating flood, several fires, an epidemic that decimated the feline cast and numerous injuries to actors and crew, it's a miracle that the pic was completed.

Here is a passionate plea for the preservation of African wildlife meshed with an adventure-horror tale which aims to be a kind of *Jaws* of the jungle. If it seems at times more like *Born Free* gone berserk, such are the risks of planting the cast in the bush (actually the Marshalls' ranch in Soledad Canyon in California), surrounded by 150 untrained lions, leopards, tigers, cheetahs and other big cats, not to mention several large and ill-tempered elephants.

Thin plot has Hedren and her three children trekking to Africa to reunite with Marshall, an eccentric scientist who's been living in a three-story wooden house in the jungle with his feline friends, an experiment to show that humans and beasts can happily coexist.

Hedren and her daughter Melanie Griffith have proved their dramatic ability elsewhere: here they and their costars are required to do little more than look petrified.

••

■ ROARING TWENTIES, THE

1939, 106 MINS, US ⚉ ⊙
Dir Raoul Walsh *Prod* Samuel Bischoff *Scr* Jerry Wald, Richard Macaulay, Robert Rossen *Ph* Ernest Haller *Ed* Jack Killifer *Mus* Heinz Roemheld *Art Dir* Max Parker
● James Cagney, Humphrey Bogart, Priscilla Lane, Gladys George, Frank McHugh, Paul Kelly (Warner)

This is a partially true gangster melodrama from the pen of Mark Hellinger. As a seasoned Broadway columnist Hellinger well remembered the dizzy times that gave birth to such illegal hot spots as the Hotsy-Totsy, Dizzy, Black Bottom, etc. Above all, he had intimate knowledge of the El Fay, the Del Fey and the Guinan clubs, and the Texas Guinan-Larry Fay operation thereof. He has thinly disguised them as the central figures of this yarn, in a good many instances spilling some inside facts, but the blow-off (for the sake of better picture entertainment) is certainly fictionized.

Because of James Cagney and the story's circumstances, *The Roaring Twenties* is reminiscent of *Public Enemy*. Story and dialog are good. Raoul Walsh turns in a fine directorial job; the performances are uniformly excellent.

••

■ ROBBERY

1967, 114 MINS, UK ◇ ⚉
Dir Peter Yates *Prod* Stanley Baker, Michael Deeley *Scr* Edward Boyd, Peter Yates, George Markstein *Ph* Douglas Slocombe *Ed* Reginald Beck *Mus* Johnny Keating *Art Dir* Michael Seymour
● Stanley Baker, Joanna Pettet, James Booth, Frank Finlay, Barry Foster, William Marlowe (Oakhurst)

This precision-tooled suspense thriller turns many of the traditional ingredients that usually go into this kind of film inside out and manages to come up with a tight, well paced, highly entertaining pic[from a treatment by Gerald Wilson].

For a brisk start there's a car robbery and the maneuvres of the robbers in London streets consume the first 20 minutes, during which there is [virtually] no dialog but a thumping good score by Johnny Keating which adds to the unexplained incidents. The cleverly executed theft is followed by a roller-coaster car chase.

Peter Yates directs with a sense of authenticity and detail which makes the viewer both detached and increasingly curious concerning the various incidents involved in blueprinting and executing the robbery of £3 million from a British mail train.

••

■ ROBBERY UNDER ARMS

1957, 99 MINS, UK ◇ ⚉
Dir Jack Lee *Prod* Joseph Janni *Scr* Alexander Baron, W.P. Lipscomb *Ph* Harry Waxman *Ed* Manuel Del Campo *Mus* Matyas Seiber *Art Dir* Alex Vetchinsky
● Peter Finch, Ronald Lewis, Laurence Naismith, Maureen Swanson, David McCallum, Jill Ireland (Rank)

Set in Australia of a 100 years earlier, *Robbery under Arms* is a well-made straightforward drama. The story, based on a Victorian novel [by Rolf Boldrewood] has Peter Finch as Captain Starlight, a virile, likeable rogue who runs a gang of bushrangers. In search of adventure, Ronald Lewis and David McCallum join the gang which includes their father. When the two attempt to break away and lead honest lives they find that they've lost their chance.

Jack Lee's direction splendidly captures the Australian atmosphere. He indulges in no frills. Lee is admirably supported by lenser Harry Waxman who fills the screen with sweeping camerawork, suggesting the vastness of the Australian canvas.

In the star role, Finch has a comparatively small role but he plays it with a swagger which is highly effective. Good opportunities are given to the brothers, Lewis and McCallum. The distaff side plays second fiddle to the men in this action meller, but Maureen Swanson, in an undeveloped role as a fiery, possessive young woman who sets her amorous sights on Lewis, has a real opportunity.

••

■ ROBE, THE

1953, 135 MINS, US ◇ ⚉ ⊙
Dir Henry Koster *Prod* Frank Ross *Scr* Philip Dunne *Ph* Leon Shamroy *Ed* Barbara McLean *Mus* Alfred Newman *Art Dir* Lyle R. Wheeler, George W. Davis
● Richard Burton, Jean Simmons, Victor Mature, Michael Rennie, Jay Robinson, Dean Jagger (20th Century-Fox)

The Robe was 10 years coming, first under RKO aegis when producer Frank Ross was there. It is a big picture in every sense of the word. One magnificent scene after another, under the [new] anamorphic CinemaScope technique, unveils the splendor that was Rome and the turbulence that was Jerusalem at the time of Christ on Calvary.

The homespun robe worn by Jesus is the symbol of Richard Burton's conversion when the Roman tribune realizes he carried out the crucifixion of a holy man at Pontius Pilate's orders. Victor Mature is the Greek slave for whom Burton outbid the corrupt Caligula (Jay Robinson), the Roman prince regent.

Lloyd C. Douglas' original bestseller is a fictionized novel of Scriptural times, and thus Jean Simmons is cast as the love interest who, as the ward of the Emperor Tiberius (Ernest Thesiger), spurns her destiny as the betrothed of the Prince Regent for the love of Marcellus Gallio (Burton).

The performances are consistently good. Simmons, Burton and Mature are particularly effective, and Betta St John, Dean Jagger, Michael Rennie, Torin Thatcher and Ernest Thesiger likewise standout in the other more prominent roles. Jeff Morrow's heavy is good, and the sword duel between him and Burton a highlight.

The slave market, the freeing of the Greek slave from the torture rack, the Christians in the catacombs, the dusty plains of Galilee, the Roman court splendor and that finale 'chase' (with the four charging white steeds head-on into the camera creating a most effective 3-D illusion) are standouts.

The Robe reportedly cost $4.5 million, of which close to $1 million may date back to producer Frank Ross' investiture under the original RKO banner. With or without the hidden charges it looks almost all of it.
□ 1953: Best Color Art Direction, Color Costume Design.
□ Nominations: Best Picture, Actor (Richard Burton), Color Cinematography

••

■ ROBIN AND MARIAN

1976, 106 MINS, UK ◇ ⚉
Dir Richard Lester *Prod* Denis O'Dell *Scr* James Goldman *Ph* David Watkin *Ed* John Victor Smith *Mus* John Barry *Art Dir* Michael Stringer
● Sean Connery, Audrey Hepburn, Robert Shaw, Richard Harris, Nicol Williamson, Denholm Elliott (Columbia/Rastar)

Robin and Marian is a disappointing and embarrassing film: disappointing, because Sean Connery, Audrey Hepburn, the brilliant Robert Shaw, Richard Harris and a screenplay by James Goldman ought to add up to something even in the face of Richard Lester's flat direction; embarrassing, because the incompatible blend of tongue-in-cheek comedy, adventure and romance gives the Robin Hood-revisited film the grace and energy of a geriatrics' discotheque.

Connery's Robin and Nicol Williamson's Little John return to England after Harris' King Richard dies abroad; back home, Shaw's Sheriff of Nottingham is still in office, now nominally subservient to nobleman Kenneth Haigh who was appointed by Ian Holm's bad King John. Hepburn's Marian has retired to a nunnery, eventually becoming Mother Superior there when Robin didn't return from the Crusades.

The idea of picking up the Robin Hood legend 20 years later seems okay at first consideration, but Goldman and Lester never got beyond the premise.

••

■ ROBIN AND THE 7 HOODS

1964, 123 MINS, US ◇ ⚉ ⊙
Dir Gordon Douglas *Prod* Frank Sinatra *Scr* David R. Schwartz *Ph* William H. Daniels *Ed* Sam O'Steen *Mus* Nelson Riddle (dir.) *Art Dir* LeRoy Deane
● Frank Sinatra, Dean Martin, Sammy Davis Jr, Peter Falk, Bing Crosby, Barbara Rush (Warner/P-C)

Robin and the 7 Hoods is a spoof on gangster pix of bygone days sparked by the names of Frank Sinatra, Dean Martin and Bing Crosby. The daffy doings of Chicago's hoodlums during the Prohibition era in a battle for leadership of the rackets backdrops action which usually is on the slightly wacky side.

Scripter David R. Schwartz takes the legend of Robin Hood and his merrie men and retailors it loosely to the frolickings of Sinatra and his pack. In some measure the parallel is successful, at least as basis for a premise which gives the plot a gimmick springboard as Sinatra, as Robbo, the good-hearted hood, takes from the rich to give to the poor.

Yarn opens in 1928 with the gangster king-pin of the day – Edward G. Robinson doing a cameo bit here – guest of honor at a lavish birthday party. After a sentimental rendition of 'For He's a Jolly Good Fellow' by the assembled company of hoods, they shoot Robinson dead.

Thereafter it's for grabs as Peter Falk has himself elected as the new Number One, and Sinatra arrives to warn him to keep out of his territory.

Performance-wise, Falk comes out best. His comic gangster is a pure gem. Sinatra, of course, is smooth and Crosby in a 'different' type of role rates a big hand.
□ 1964: Nominations: Best Adapted Musical Score, Song ('My Kind of Town')

••

■ ROBIN HOOD

1922, 120 MINS, US ⊗ ⓥ

Dir Allan Dwan *Prod* Douglas Fairbanks *Scr* Elton
Thomas [= Douglas Fairbanks], Lotta Woods *Ph* Arthur
Edeson *Ed* William Nolan *Art Dir* Wilfred Buckland,
Irvin J. Martin, Edward M. Langley
● Douglas Fairbanks, Wallace Beery, Sam De Grasse,
Enid Bennett, Paul Dickey, William Lowery (Fairbanks/
United Artists)

Archery, and when knights were bold while
villains were cold, and that is *Robin Hood*.

Robin Hood is a great production but not a
great picture. It just misses being great
through a slow long opening. In the days of
Richard the Lionheart and his First Crusade.

The prettiness of the sets of Robin Hood's
lair in Sherwood Forest, the picturesqueness
of his band of outlaws who were for their
King and against his villainous brother,
Prince John; the breadth of the settings
throughout; the stunts by Douglas Fairbanks
when he gets going; the superb supporting
cast, the castle – that's *Robin Hood* and why it
is a good picture. It holds you tense in the
Robin Hood portion and lets you down badly
when it's about Richard.

■ ROBIN HOOD

1991, 104 MINS, US/UK ◇ ⓥ ⊙

Dir John Irvin *Prod* Sarah Radclyffe, Tim Bevan
Scr Mark Allen Smith, John McGrath *Ph* Jason Lehel
Ed Peter Tanner *Mus* Geoffrey Burgon *Art Dir* Austen
Spriggs
● Patrick Bergin, Uma Thurman, Jurgen Prochnow,
Edward Fox, Jeroen Krabbe, Owen Teale (Working
Title/20th Century-Fox)

Despite solid production values and a few extremely good moments, this awkwardly depicted *Robin Hood* may disturb those
sentimentally attached to the original 1938
Michael Curtiz-directed classic. Tinkering
with the lore, the pic's tone unflatteringly recalls the worst flippant aspects of Richard
Lester's *Musketeers* films.

This story has nobleman Robert Hode
(Patrick Bergin) giving spoils to the poor as
an afterthought. Having already turned to
crime, he thinks the gesture could be just the
one to protect his hide. The one wrinkle that
does work is Uma Thurman's scrappy, sexy
Maid Marian, a woman who battles alongside
the men.

The reworked legend has Saxon noble Hode
disenfranchised by his onetime friend
Deguerre (Jeroen Krabbe), the Norman who
holds sway over the area. After an encounter
with Little John (David Morrissey), Hode and
his compatriot (Owen Teal) join the ranks of
a group of thieves – hidden in caves rather
than the trees of Sherwood Forest – ultimately leading the group in rebellion against
Deguerre and Prochnow's foppish baron.

The lack of major action sequences is surprising in light of the resumes of director
John Irvin and exec producer John
McTiernan. Costumes and sets solidly capture the 12th-century time period, muted
with autumnal tones.

[Version reviewed was the 180-minute telemovie broadcast on US TV May 13, 1991.]

■ ROBIN HOOD
PRINCE OF THIEVES

1991, 138 MINS, US ◇ ⓥ ⊙

Dir Kevin Reynolds *Prod* John Watson, Pen Densham,
Richard B. Lewis *Scr* Pen Densham, John Watson
Ph Doug Milsome *Ed* Peter Boyle *Mus* Michael Kamen
Art Dir John Graysmark
● Kevin Costner, Morgan Freeman, Mary Elizabeth
Mastrantonio, Christian Slater, Alan Rickman, Sean
Connery (Morgan Creek)

Kevin Costner's *Robin Hood* is a Robin of
wood. Murky and uninspired, this $50 million

rendition bears evidence of the rushed and
unpleasant production circumstances that
were much reported upon. At the same time,
this seriously intended, more realistically motivated revision of the Robin myth may have
diminished the hero, but it hasn't destroyed
him.

Lackluster script, from a story by Pen
Densham, begins in the year 1194 in
Jerusalem, where Robin leads a prison upris-
ing and escapes with a Moor, Azeem (Morgan
Freeman). Retreating from the Crusades, the
pair head for England, where they find that
Robin's father has been slain by the Sheriff of
Nottingham (Alan Rickman), who is attempt-
ing to eliminate all resistance and perhaps
make a play for the throne in the absence of
King Richard.

To avenge his father's death, Robin joins up
with Little John and the latter's band of outsiders in a safe enclave in Sherwood Forest.
Major setpiece is the sheriff's attack on the
outlaws' hippie-like compound, which deci-
mates the group. But Robin is able to lead a
counterattack on Nottingham Castle.

The best that can be said for Costner's performance is that it is pleasant. At worst, it
can be argued whether it is more properly described as wooden or cardboard.

Looking beautiful and sporting an accent
that comes and goes, Mary Elizabeth
Mastrantonio makes a sprightly, appropriately feisty Marian. Of the Americans,
Christian Slater is most successful at putting
on an English accent, and he has some spirited moments as Will Scarlett.

As the 'painted man' who accompanies
Robin in gratitude for his life having been
saved, Freeman is a constant, dominant presence. As the sheriff, Rickman goes way over
the top, emoting with facial and vocal leers.
It's a relief whenever this resourceful thesp is
on-screen, such as the energy and brio he
brings to the proceedings. An unbilled Sean
Connery shows up at the very end as King
Richard to give his blessing to Robin and
Marian's marriage.

☐ 1991: Nomination: Best Original Song
('(Everything I Do) I Do It For You')

■ ROBOCOP

1987, 103 MINS, US ◇ ⓥ ⊙

Dir Paul Verhoeven *Prod* Arne Schmidt *Scr* Edward
Neumeier, Michael Miner *Ph* Jost Vacano *Ed* Frank J.
Urioste *Mus* Basil Poledouris *Art Dir* William Sandell
● Peter Weller, Nancy Allen, Ronny Cox, Kurtwood
Smith, Daniel O'Herlihy, Miguel Ferrer (Davison)

RoboCop is a comic book movie that's definitely not for kids. The welding of extreme violence with four-letter words is tempered
with gut-level humor and technical wizardry.

Roller-coaster ride begins with the near-dis-
memberment of recently transferred police
officer Murphy (Peter Weller), to the southern precinct of the Detroit Police Dept in the
not-too-distant future.

There are three organizations inextricably
wound into Detroit's anarchical society – the
police, a band of sadistic hoodlums, and a
multinational conglomerate which has a contract with the city to run the police force.

Weller is blown to bits just at the time an
ambitious junior exec at the multinational is
ready to develop a prototype cyborg – half-
man, half-machine programmed to be an indestructable cop. Thus Weller becomes
RoboCop, unleashed to fell the human scum
he encounters, not the least among them his
killers.

As sicko sadists go, Kurtwood Smith is a
well-cast adversary. Nancy Allen as Weller's
partner (before he died) provides the only
warmth in the film, wanting and encouraging
RoboCop to listen to some of the human
spirit that survived inside him. *RoboCop* is as
tightly worked as a film can be, not a moment
or line wasted.

☐ 1987: Special Award (sound effects editing)
☐ Nominations: Best Editing, Sound

■ ROBOCOP 2

1990, 118 MINS, US ◇ ⓥ ⊙

Dir Irvin Kershner *Prod* Jon Davison *Scr* Frank Miller,
Walon Green *Ph* Mark Irwin *Ed* William Anderson
Mus Leonard Rosenman *Art Dir* Peter Jamison
● Peter Weller, Nancy Allen, Daniel O'Herlihy, Belinda
Bauer, Tom Noonan, Galyn Gorg (Orion/Tobor)

This ultraviolent, nihilistic sequel has
enough technical dazzle to impress hardware
fans, but obviously no one in the Orion front
office told filmmakers that less is more.

The future is represented by a crumbling
Detroit (actually filmed like the original in
Texas), dominated by Dan O'Herlihy's Omni
Consumer Products company. He's set to
foreclose on loans and literally take possession of Motown. Standing in his way is a loose
cannon, drug magnate/user Tom Noonan,
whose goal is to flood society with designer
versions of his drug Nuke.

Peter Weller as RoboCop must defeat both
factions while effeminate mayor Willard
Pugh gets in the way. Noonan is reconstituted
as Robocop 2 by O'Herlihy's sexy assistant
Belinda Bauer, providing the film's final half
hour of great special effects as an end in
themselves.

Gabriel Damon as a precocious 12-year-old
gangster is the best thing in the picture.

■ ROBOT MONSTER

1953, 62 MINS, US ⓥ ⊙

Dir Phil Tucker *Prod* Phil Tucker *Scr* Wyott Ordung
Ph Jack Greenhalgh *Ed* Bruce Schoengarth *Mus* Elmer
Bernstein
● George Nader, Claudia Barrett, Selena Royle,
Gregory Moffett, John Mylong, Pamela Paulson (Three
Dimensional)

Judged on the basis of novelty, as a showcase
for the Tru-Stereo Process, *Robot Monster*
comes off surprisingly well, considering the
extremely limited budget ($50,000) and
schedule on which the film was shot.

The Tru-Stereo Process (3-D) utilized here
is easy on the eyes, coming across clearly at
all times. To the picture's credit no 3-D gimmicks were employed.

Beating Arch Oboler's *Five* [1951] by one
survivor, yarn here concerns itself with the
last six people on earth – all pitted against a
mechanical monster called Ro-Man, sent
from another planet whose 'people' are disturbed by strides being made on earth in the
research fields of atomic development and
space travel.

Sextet – a famed scientist, his wife, assistant, daughter and two children – are protected from Ro-Man's supersonic death ray by
anti-biotic serum.

Of the principals, George Nader, as the
aide who falls in love with and eventually
marries the scientist's daughter in a primitive
ceremony, fares the best. Selena Royle also
comes across okay, but of the others the less
said the better.

■ ROCK AROUND THE CLOCK

1956, 76 MINS, US ⓥ

Dir Fred F. Sears *Prod* Sam Katzman *Scr* Robert Kent,
James B. Gordon *Ph* Benjamin H. Kline *Ed* Saul A.
Goodkind, Jack W. Ogilvie *Mus* Fred Karger (sup.)
● Bill Haley and The Comets, The Platters, Tony Martinez
and His Band, Freddie Bell and His Bellboys, Alan Freed,
Lisa Gaye (Clover/Columbia)

Rock around the Clock takes off to a bouncy little beat and never lets up for 76 minutes of
foot-patting entertainment. Bill Haley and
The Comets set the beat with nine of their

R

record favorites, including the title tune, 'Razzle Dazzle', 'Happy Baby', 'See You Later, Alligator', 'Rudy's Back' and others. Freddie Bell and His Bellboys are on for two solid numbers, 'Giddy Up, Ding Dong' and 'We're Gonna Teach You to Rock'.

Fred F. Sears' direction has excellent pace and keeps interest going with a story that tells how a band manager finds the Haley Comets in the mountains and brings dancing back to ballrooms throughout the country.

Johnny Johnston is likeable as the manager, while Alix Talton is a cool chick as a big band booker who tries unsuccessfully to get his matrimonial hooks in him. Film is a particularly strong showcasing for Lisa Gaye, who plays the rock and roll dancer with The Comets. Her terping's good and that figure the dance costumes display commands added interest.

....

■ **ROCKETEER**
(Australia: The Adventures of the Rocketeer)

1991, 108 MINS, US ◇ ⊙ ⊙
Dir Joe Johnston *Prod* Lawrence Gordon, Charles Gordon, Lloyd Levin *Scr* Danny Bilson, Paul De Meo *Ph* Hiro Narita *Ed* Arthur Schmidt *Mus* James Horner *Art Dir* Jim Bissell
● Bill Campbell, Jennifer Connelly, Alan Arkin, Timothy Dalton, Paul Sorvino, Ed Lauter (Touchstone/Gordon)

Based on a comic ['graphic novel'] by Dave Stevens] unveiled in 1981, this $40 million adventure fantasy puts a shiny polish on familiar elements: airborne hero, damsel in distress, Nazi villains, 1930s Hollywood glamor, and dazzling special effects.

Elaborate opening sequence has an ace pilot (Bill Campbell) testing a new racing plane over LA skies in 1938 while, on the ground below, hoods and Feds in speeding cars shoot it out after robbery of a mysterious device.

Developed by none other than Howard Hughes, the invention makes its way into the pilot's hands, but it's coveted by a dashing star of swashbuckling films who also happens to be a dedicated Nazi (Timothy Dalton). Although he has hired thugs led by Paul Sorvino to recover the priceless device, Dalton has his own ideas about getting at Campbell through his gorgeous g.f. (Jennifer Connelly).

The object of intense interest is a portable rocket pack which, if strapped to one's back, can send its wearer zipping around almost as fast, if not as quietly, as Superman.

Newcomer Campbell exhibits the requisite grit and all-American know-how, but the lead role is written with virtually no humor or subtext. Those around him come off to better advantage, notably Dalton as the deliciously smooth, insidious Sinclair; Sorvino and Alan Arkin, with the latter as the Rocketeer's mentor; Terry O'Quinn as Hughes; and the lovely, voluptuous Connelly.

....

■ **ROCKING HORSE WINNER, THE**

1949, 96 MINS, UK ⊙
Dir Anthony Pelissier *Prod* John Mills *Scr* Anthony Pelissier *Ph* Desmond Dickinson *Ed* John Seabourne *Mus* William Alwyn
● Valerie Hobson, John Howard Davies, Ronald Squire, John Mills, Hugh Sinclair, Charles Goldner (Two Cities)

There has rarely been a more faithful adaptation of an original, with the exception of the ending, which was added at the request of the censor.

In following the original D. H. Lawrence short story, Anthony Pelissier, who scripted as well as directed, has developed the story of an extravagant mother as seen through the eyes of a sensitive child. How to raise the cash to bring the family out of debt and anxiety is the problem preying on the youngster's mind.

Then, gradually, the boy realizes he has a

facility for picking winners in horse races and in secret association with the family handyman, later joined by a sporting uncle, has an astonishing run of good luck.

John Howard Davies plays the sensitive lad with a skill and sincerity which would do credit to a seasoned trouper. Valerie Hobson is fine as the mother.

....

■ **ROCKY**

1976, 119 MINS, US ◇ ⊙ ⊙
Dir John G. Avildsen *Prod* Irwin Winkler *Scr* Sylvester Stallone *Ph* James Crabe *Ed* Richard Halsey, Scott Conrad *Mus* Bill Conti *Art Dir* Bill Cassidy
● Sylvester Stallone, Talia Shire, Burt Young, Carl Weathers, Burgess Meredith, Thayer David (United Artists)

Sylvester Stallone stars in his own screenplay about a minor local boxer who gets a chance to fight a heavyweight championship bout.

Stallone's title character is that of a near-loser, a punchy reject scorned by gym owner Burgess Meredith, patronized by local loan shark Joe Spinell, rebuffed by plain-Jane Talia Shire whose brother, Burt Young, keeps engineering a romantic match.

Rocky would have remained in this rut, had not heavyweight champ Carl Weathers come up with the Bicentennial gimmick of fighting a sure-ringer, thereby certifying the American Dream for public consumption.

En route all this, Stallone brings out the best in Shire, exposes the worst in Young and generally gets his life together.
☐ 1976: Best Picture, Director, Editing.
☐ Nominations: Best Actor (Sylvester Stallone), Actress (Talia Shire), Supp.Actor (Burgess Meredith, Burt Young), Story & Screenplay, Best Song ('Gonna Fly Now'), Sound

....

■ **ROCKY II**

1979, 119 MINS, US ◇ ⊙ ⊙
Dir Sylvester Stallone *Prod* Irwin Winkler, Robert Chartoff *Scr* Sylvester Stallone *Ph* Bill Butler *Ed* Danford B. Greene *Mus* Bill Conti *Art Dir* Richard Berger
● Sylvester Stallone, Talia Shire, Burt Young, Carl Weathers, Burgess Meredith (United Artists)

Rocky II follows much the same theme as its predecessor – that is fighter Rocky Balboa's path to a stab at the heavyweight crown. In its boxing and training scenes *Rocky II* packs much of the punch the original did, complete with an exciting pugilistic finale that's even better than its predecessor.

However, in an attempt to tell the new story – that of Rocky's adjustment to near-success and an attempt to lead a non-boxing life – the plot tends to drag and the picture takes on a murky quality.

Luckily, director, actor and scripter Sylvester Stallone and producers Irwin Winkler and Robert Chartoff know from experience audiences love to root for the underdog and have concocted an irresistible final 30 minutes.
☐ 1982: Nomination: Best Original Song ('Eye of the Tiger')

....

■ **ROCKY III**

1982, 99 MINS, US ◇ ⊙ ⊙
Dir Sylvester Stallone *Prod* Irwin Winkler, Robert Chartoff *Scr* Sylvester Stallone *Ph* Bill Butler *Ed* Don Zimmerman, Mark Warner *Mus* Bill Conti *Art Dir* Ronald Kent Foreman
● Sylvester Stallone, Carl Weathers, Mr T, Talia Shire, Burt Young, Burgess Meredith (United Artists)

The real question with *Rocky III* was how Sylvester Stallone could twist the plot to make an interesting difference. He manages.

Revisiting the champ three years after the

big victory, we find him and wife Talia Shire happily married with a son, a big house, lots of money and media attention after successfully defending his title 10 times.

But Clubber Lang, menacingly and beautifully played by Mr T, is also tough and hungry for a title shot. Ailing Burgess Meredith tells Stallone he's no longer a match for T and should retire gracefully. But Stallone insists on proving himself and quickly goes down for the count under T's hammering.

Though lion-hearted and iron-jawed, it's obvious now that Stallone has never been a very skilled boxer. But Carl Weathers steps in to teach and train him, if Stallone can work up the will.

As usual, Stallone the writer-director is less successful in handling all the dramatic interims than staging the battles.

....

■ **ROCKY IV**

1985, 91 MINS, US ◇ ⊙ ⊙
Dir Sylvester Stallone *Prod* Robert Chartoff, Irwin Winkler *Scr* Sylvester Stallone *Ph* Bill Butler *Ed* Don Zimmerman, John W. Wheeler *Mus* Vince DiCola *Art Dir* Bill Kenney
● Sylvester Stallone, Talia Shire, Burt Young, Carl Weathers, Brigitte Nielsen, Dolph Lundgren (United Artists)

Sylvester Stallone is really sloughing it off shamelessly in *Rocky IV*, but it's still impossible not to root for old Rocky Balboa to get up off the canvas and whup that bully one more time.

Beyond its visceral appeal, *Rocky IV* is truly the worst of the lot, though Stallone himself is more personable in this one and that helps. Dolph Lundgren is the most contrived opponent yet and that hurts.

Lundgren, an almost inhuman giant fighting machine created in Russian physical-fitness labs, comes to the US to challenge the champ, but is first taken on by Apollo Creed (Carl Weathers), anxious to prove himself one last time.

So it's on to Moscow where, surprise, surprise, it's going to take a lot of training to get Stallone in shape for the Soviet. Though it really makes no difference, the story gets truly dumb at this point.

Lundgren, according to the digital readout, has developed a punch of 2,000 p.s.i., which should be enough to send Rocky back to Philadelphia without a plane. Once the fight starts, however, there's no way Rocky fans can resist getting caught up in it, predictable and preposterous though it be.

....

■ **ROCKY V**

1990, 104 MINS, US ◇ ⊙ ⊙
Dir John G. Avildsen *Prod* Irwin Winkler, Robert Chartoff *Scr* Sylvester Stallone *Ph* Steven Poster *Ed* John G. Avildsen, Michael N. Knue *Mus* Bill Conti *Art Dir* William J. Cassidy
● Sylvester Stallone, Talia Shire, Burt Young, Sage Stallone, Burgess Meredith, Tommy Morrison (United Artists)

When the underdog always wins he's not much of an underdog anymore, and the narrative cartwheels Sylvester Stallone has turned over the years to put Rocky in that position have peeled away the novelty.

So it is with *Rocky V*. Stallone again scripted and continues to evince a thudding lack of storytelling subtlety, sinking to a new low with the ending, which seems inspired by championship wrestling.

Stallone positively goes wild with cliches here: Rocky left broke by mismanagement of his fortune, a Don King-like promoter (Richard Gant) pressuring Rocky to fight again, strained relations between Rocky and his son (real-life son Sage) because of Rocky's tutelage of a young boxer (Tommy Morrison) who ultimately turns on him.

The central problem is that Rocky suffers brain damage from his various beatings in the ring, making it risky for him ever to fight again.

Burt Young has his moments as the slobbish Paulie. Talia Shire has become shrill and annoying as Adrian. Gant is perfectly hissable as Duke. Boxer-turned-actor Morrison is serviceable as the ham-fisted heavy. Bill Conti's score remains the series' greatest asset.

• •

■ **ROCKY HORROR PICTURE SHOW, THE**

1975, 100 MINS, UK ◇ ⑨

Dir Jim Sharman   *Prod* Michael White   *Scr* Jim Sharman, Richard O'Brien   *Ph* Peter Suschitzky   *Ed* Graeme Clifford   *Mus* Richard Hartley (arr.)   *Art Dir* Brian Thomson

● Tim Curry, Susan Sarandon, Barry Bostwick, Richard O'Brien, Jonathan Adams, Little Nell [= Nell Campbell] (White/20th Century-Fox)

The Rocky Horror Picture Show is adapted from a rock stage musical of same title [by Richard O'Brien] set in a spooky castle deep in the heart of Ohio. Into it on a rain-swept night stumble affianced Janet and Brad, wholesome straights, hoping to find a telephone, but finding instead the earthy lair of some weirdos from the planet Transylvania. Chief freak therein is the bisexual Frank N. Furter, played with relish by Tim Curry, who first seduces Janet (Susan Sarandon) and then conquers Brad (Barry Bostwick).

The plot mixture also includes Curry's 'monster' creation, rippling-muscled Rocky; a revenging scientist; Riff Raff (O'Brien), Curry's hunch-backed lackey; and assorted groupies of which Magenta and Columbia (Patricia Quinn and Nell Campbell) are most prominent.

Overall, however, most of the jokes that might have seemed jolly fun on stage now appear obvious and even flat. The sparkle's gone.

• •

■ **ROGER AND ME**

1989, 90 MINS, US ◇ ⑨ ⊙

Dir Michael Moore   *Prod* Michael Moore   *Ph* Chris Beaver, John Prusak, Kevin Rafferty, Bruce Schermer   *Ed* Wendey Stanzler, Jennifer Berman

● (Dog Eat Dog)

Roger and Me is a cheeky and smart indictment against General Motors for closing its truck plant in Flint, Mich, throwing 30,000 employees out of work and, as a result, leaving many neighborhoods abandoned.

Michael Moore, a Flint native who recalls the prosperous 'Great American Dream' days of his 1950s childhood, launches a one-man documentary crusade to bring GM chairman Roger Smith back to town. He wants Smith to see the human tragedy caused by the plant closing.

He interviews fired workers, shows decaying houses across the city and two grandiose schemes to reactivate the town: the opening of a Hyatt Regency hotel and a huge shopping mall. Both fail quickly for lack of business. Tourists don't come to Flint.

Intercut are scenes of the town's rich, who seem oblivious to the plight of their fellow citizens and wonder what the fuss is about.

Pic is one-sided, for sure, but Moore makes no pretense otherwise. The irony of the title pervades the piece.

• •

■ **ROLLERBALL**

1975, 129 MINS, US ◇ ⑨ ⊙

Dir Norman Jewison   *Prod* Norman Jewison   *Scr* William Harrison   *Ph* Douglas Slocombe   *Ed* Antony Gibbs   *Mus* Andre Previn (sup.)   *Art Dir* John Box

● James Caan, John Houseman, Maud Adams, John Beck, Moses Gunn, Pamela Hensley (United Artists)

Norman Jewison's sensational futuristic drama about a world of Corporate States stars James Caan in an excellent performance as a famed athlete who fights for his identity and free will. The $5 million film was made in Munich and London.

The year is 2018, and the world has been regrouped politically to a hegemony of six conglomerate cartels. There is total material tranquility: no wars, no poverty, no unrest – and no personal free will and no God.

The ingenious way of ventilating human nature's animal-violence residual content is the world sport of rollerball, a combination of roller derby, motorcycle racing and basketball where violent death is part of the entertainment. Caan is a long-standing hero of the sport, becoming dangerously popular. He is ordered to retire. He refuses. Tilt.

The very fine music track was supervised and conducted by Andre Previn, utilizing excerpts from Bach, Shostakovich, Tchaikovsky and Albinoni/Giazotto, plus original Previn work which included the corporate anthems which begin each game.

The performances of the principals are uniformly tops. Besides the great work of Caan, John Houseman and Ralph Richardson (as head of the corporation), John Beck is excellent as the model yahoo jock. As the women in Caan's life, Maud Adams, Pamela Hensley and Barbara Trentham step right out of today's deodorant and cosmetics teleblurbs – just the way they're supposed to be when life imitates consumer advertising imagery.

• •

■ **ROLLERCOASTER**

1977, 119 MINS, US ◇ ⑨

Dir James Goldstone   *Prod* Jennings Lang   *Scr* Richard Levinson, William Link   *Ph* David M. Walsh   *Ed* Edward A. Biery, Richard Sprague   *Mus* Lalo Schifrin   *Art Dir* Henry Bumstead

● George Segal, Richard Widmark, Timothy Bottoms, Henry Fonda, Harry Guardino, Susan Strasberg (Universal)

Timothy Bottoms is a subdued maniac with a plan to blackmail $1 million from a group of amusement park owners.

Pic's plot is simple and uncluttered. There is a madman on the loose, one with a thorough knowledge of bombs, rollercoasters and electronics. From a short scene early on, there is a hint that he served in Vietnam, which is supposed to partly account for his instability. His sole objective is cash.

Bottoms and the man trying to outsmart him (George Segal) are adversaries who develop a mutual respect and, in a sense, a rapport.

Pic's taut opening 20 minutes depict the major catastrophe – bombing of a rollercoaster track and the subsequent derailing of the cars.

The rollercoaster rides are the picture's highlights and they are fabulous.

• •

■ **ROLLING THUNDER**

1977, 99 MINS, US ◇ ⑨ ⊙

Dir John Flynn   *Prod* Lawrence Gordon   *Scr* Paul Schrader, Heywood Gould   *Ph* Jordon Croneweth   *Ed* Frank P. Keller   *Mus* Barry DeVorzon   *Art Dir* Steve Berger

● William Devane, Tommy Lee Jones, Linda Haynes, Lisa Richards, Dabney Coleman, James Best (AIP)

Excellent cast performs well, but not well enough and Paul Schrader's story is strong, but not strong enough. In sum, it neither rolls nor thunders.

With co-scripter Heywood Gould, Schrader follows an embittered loner to a bloody conclusion. After eight years of torture as a prisoner of war, William Devane returns to a grateful San Antonio where he receives a hero's welcome, except at home where wife

Lisa Richards has fallen in love with his friend Lawrason Driscoll.

But neither the good nor the ill has much impact on Devane, who left all emotion behind in the prison camp. And even though he has a hard time animating a wooden character, Devane succeeds in making the first half of the picture the best, creating a believable reflection of the difficult adjustments of real POWs.

• •

■ **ROLLOVER**

1981, 118 MINS, US ◇ ⑨

Dir Alan J. Pakula   *Prod* Bruce Gilbert   *Scr* David Shaber   *Ph* Giuseppe Rotunno   *Ed* Evan Lottman   *Mus* Michael Small   *Art Dir* George Jenkins

● Jane Fonda, Kris Kristofferson, Hume Cronyn, Josef Sommer, Bob Gunton, Jodi Long (Orion/Warner)

Although elegantly appointed and possessed of a provocative theme, *Rollover* is a fundamentally disappointing political-romantic thriller [from a story by David Shaber, Howard Kohn and David Weir] set in the rarified world of international high finance.

Coiffed and gowned to the hilt, Jane Fonda plays a former film star whose corporate big-wheel husband is mysteriously murdered. Bank troubleshooter Kris Kristofferson is called in to try to right the ailing firm, quickly begins consoling the widow by night as well as by day and soon accompanies her to Saudi Arabia to firm a deal for venture capital, which, while giving Fonda the board chairmanship, also hands the Arabs the final financial trump card.

Eventually transpires that the Arabs decide not to 'rollover', or redeposit, their huge sums in the bank, which sends the banking community, Wall Street and the entire international financial network into chaos.

It's a scary theme, and Pakula's previously displayed expertise at conveying pervasive paranoia triggered by massive conspiracies at high levels is perfectly in tune with the story's aims. But there's a certain lack of reality, cued in part by numerous melodramatic contrivances.

• •

■ **ROMANCING THE STONE**

1984, 105 MINS, US ◇ ⑨ ⊙

Dir Robert Zemeckis   *Prod* Michael Douglas, Jack Brodsky, Joel Douglas   *Scr* Diane Thomas   *Ph* Dean Cundey   *Ed* Donn Cambern, Frank Morriss   *Mus* Alan Silvestri, Eddy Grant   *Art Dir* Lawrence G. Paull

● Michael Douglas, Kathleen Turner, Danny DeVito, Zack Norman, Alfonso Arau, Manuel Ojeda (El Corazon/20th Century-Fox)

Living alone with her cat, Kathleen Turner writes romantic novels and cries over the outcome, assuring friend Holland Taylor that one day the writer's life will pick up for real.

Naturally, Turner receives a package mailed from South America just ahead of sister's phone call that she's been kidnapped and will die if Turner doesn't deliver the contents of the package south of the border as soon as possible.

Heading for the jungles in her high heels, Turner is like a lot of unwitting screen heroines ahead of her, guaranteed that her drab existence is about to be transformed – probably by a man, preferably handsome and adventurous. Sure enough, Michael Douglas pops out of the jungle.

The expected complications are supplied by the kidnappers, Danny DeVito and Zack Norman.

☐ 1984: Nomination: Best Editing

• •

■ **ROMAN HOLIDAY**

1953, 118 MINS, US ⑨ ⊙

Dir William Wyler   *Prod* William Wyler   *Scr* Ian McLellan Hunter, John Dighton   *Ph* Franz Planer, Henri

R

Alekan   *Ed* Robert Swink   *Mus* Georges Auric
Art Dir Hal Pereira, Walter Tyler
● Gregory Peck, Audrey Hepburn, Eddie Albert, Hartley Power, Harcourt Williams, Margaret Rawlings (Paramount)

This William Wyler romantic comedy-drama [from a story by Dalton Trumbo] is the Graustarkian fable in modern dress, plus the Cinderella theme in reverse. He times the chuckles with a never-flagging pace, puts heart into the laughs, endows the footage with some boff bits of business and points up some tender, poignant scenes in using the smart script and the cast to the utmost advantage.

The aged face of the Eternal City provides a contrast to the picture's introduction of a new face, Audrey Hepburn, British ingenue who made an impression with the legit-goers in *Gigi*. Gregory Peck, in the role of American newspaperman, figures importantly in making the picture zip along engrossingly. Eddie Albert makes a major comedy contribution as a photog who secretly lenses the princess during the 24 hours she steals away from the dull court routine.

The fine script deals with a princess who rebels against the goodwill tour she is making of Europe after arriving in Rome. The adventures she encounters with Peck during the day and evening are natural and amusing. After this day of fun is over the princess and the reporter are in love, but each knows nothing can come of the Roman holiday.

All the interiors, except those in the Palazzos Brancaccio and Colonna, were lensed in Rome's Cinecitta Studios, while exteriors put on film many landmarks of the city.

□ 1953: Best Actress (Audrey Hepburn), Motion Picture Story [awarded to Ian McLellan hunter, in place of blacklisted Dalton Trumbo], B&W Costume Design (Edith Head)

□ Nominations: Best Picture, Director, Supp. Actor (Eddie Albert), Screenplay, B&W Cinematography, B&W Art Direction, Editing

● ●

■ ROMANOFF AND JULIET

1961, 103 MINS, US ◇
Dir Peter Ustinov   *Prod* Peter Ustinov   *Scr* Peter Ustinov
Ph Robert Krasker   *Ed* Renzo Lucidi   *Mus* Mario Nascimbene   *Art Dir* Alexandre Trauner
● Peter Ustinov, Sandra Dee, John Gavin, Akim Tamiroff, Suzanne Cloutier, John Phillips (Universal)

Some of the satiric toxin has gone out of Peter Ustinov's *Romanoff and Juliet* in its cinematamorphosis, but enough of the comic chemistry remains. Ustinov has managed not only to retain the lion's share of his tongue-in-cheek swing at political hyprocisy, diplomatic pomposity and general 20th-century lack of harmony or philosophical perspective, but he has added several noteworthy observations.

His performance as the general of Concordia, a tiny mock republic feverishly wooed by Russia and the US to solicit its vital UN vote, is a beautiful blend of outrageous mugging and sly comment. When he's on, the picture's at its best. Sandra Dee and John Gavin costar as daughter and son of the US and Russian ambassadors to Concordia, whose romance and marriage ultimately blots out the political crisis, representing Ustinov's love-and-laughter platform for harmonious international relations.

● ●

■ ROMAN SCANDALS

1933, 93 MINS, US ⓥ
Dir Frank Tuttle, Busby Berkeley   *Prod* Samuel Goldwyn
Scr George S. Kaufman, Robert Sherwood, William Anthony McGuire, Arthur Sheekman, Nat Perrin, George

Oppenheimer   *Ph* Ray June, Gregg Toland   *Ed* Stuart Heisler   *Art Dir* Richard Day
● Eddie Cantor, Ruth Etting, Gloria Stuart, David Manners, Verree Teasdale, Edward Arnold (Goldwyn/United Artists)

Comedy high spots and moments of exotic beauty in production retrieve a sometimes ineffective Eddie Cantor vehicle. Subject matter is the hokiest kind of hoke.

Best of the bits has Cantor as the Roman emperor's food taster trying to stall off the queen's plot to poison her royal spouse and struggling at the same time with a stubborn attack of hiccoughs. Hilarity of Cantor's buffoonery lies in the dignity of the stately surroundings of the Roman court and the straight playing of the supporting cast.

Background of imperial Rome is made to order for spectacle, and the producer has made the most of it. There is a long sequence in a swank Roman women's bath, elaborated and built for pictorial effect to the last extreme. This sequence is the elaborate incidental to one of the song numbers, 'Keep Young and Beautiful', which gets a remarkably intricate build-up for the Cantor rendering in blackface.

Cantor is almost constantly on the screen for all of the hour and a half, and it's practically impossible for any funmaker to sustain top speed that length of time.

David Manners stands out in the cast, one of the few Hollywood actors who can look genuine in Roman toga. His satisfying playing of the leading straight role does a lot to sharpen the comedy angle. Gloria Stuart and Verree Teasdale in the top femme parts make an eyeful, the one blonde and the other brunette.

● ●

■ ROMAN SPRING OF MRS. STONE, THE

1962, 103 MINS, UK ◇ ⓥ
Dir Jose Quintero   *Prod* Louis de Rochemont   *Scr* Gavin Lambert   *Ph* Harry Waxman   *Ed* Ralph Kemplen
Mus Richard Addinsell   *Art Dir* Roger Furse
● Vivien Leigh, Warren Beatty, Coral Browne, Jill St John, Lotte Lenya, Jeremy Spenser (Warner)

Vivien Leigh is the star of this gloomy, pessimistic portrait of the artist as a middle-aged widow, from Tennessee Williams' only novel. She portrays a lonely, uncertain ex-actress who has given up her profession and her past to settle in Rome following the sudden death of her wealthy husband. However reluctantly, she soon falls prey to the interests of the fortune-hunting parasites and pimps of Rome who seek monetary rewards in return for romantic favors.

But Leigh has the misfortune to fall in love with her 'young man' (Warren Beatty), who convincingly feigns amour, then flutters away on another attractive assignment provided by agent-panderer Lotte Lenya.

Leigh gives an expressive, interesting delineation – projecting intelligence and femininity, as always. Mrs Stone, however, is no Blanche DuBois. There's less to work with. Although every once in a while a little Guido Panzini creeps into his Italo dialect and Marlon Brando into his posture and expression, Beatty gives a fairly convincing characterization of the young, mercenary punk-gigolo. Lenya is frighteningly sinister as the cunning pimpette.

□ 1962: Nomination: Best Supp. Actress (Lotte Lenya)

● ●

■ ROMANTIC ENGLISHWOMAN, THE

1975, 115 MINS, UK/FRANCE ◇ ⓥ
Dir Joseph Losey   *Prod* Daniel M. Angel   *Scr* Thomas Wiseman, Tom Stoppard   *Ph* Gerry Fisher
Mus Richard Hartley   *Art Dir* Richard MacDonald
● Glenda Jackson, Michael Caine, Helmut Berger, Beatrice Normand, Nathalie Delon, Michel Lonsdale (DIAL/Meric-Matalon)

Joseph Losey has concocted a low-key, sit-com-type pic [from the book by Thomas Wiseman] using the familiar theme of an unsatisfied, well-heeled married woman with a child on a romantic escapade.

Glenda Jackson plays in her clipped, cold way as she is off to the German bath and gambling site of Baden-Baden at the start of the pic. There she notices Helmut Berger who is noted as smuggling in heroin which he inanely stashes in a rain drain and which is later washed away.

In Britain the husband, Michael Caine, invites him to stay. Eventually she and Berger are caught necking by Caine and she runs off after Berger.

Pic remains disappointing in its cocktail of satire, intrigue and romantic comedy-drama that do not quite jell.

● ●

■ ROME EXPRESS

1932, 94 MINS, UK
Dir Walter Forde   *Prod* Michael Balcon   *Scr* Sidney Gilliat, Clifford Grey, Frank Vosper, Ralph Stock
Ph Gunther Krampf   *Ed* Frederick Y. Smith   *Art Dir* A. L. Mazzei
● Conrad Veidt, Esther Ralston, Joan Barry, Cedric Hardwicke, Frank Vosper, Hugh Williams (Gaumont-British)

The acting and casting call attention to *Rome Express*. A combination of *Grand Hotel* and *Shanghai Express*, nevertheless it is original in conception and execution. Casting is superb and the players all excellent.

Conrad Veidt does an unusually good job as Zurta, a criminal, and Frank Vosper makes a human being of Jolif, the head of the French Surete.

Story is laid entirely on a train which travels out of Paris. Veidt and Hugh Williams are adventurers chasing Donald Calthrop, who double-crossed them after stealing a famous painting. Also on the train are Joan Barry and Harold Huth, married but not traveling with their legal mates; Esther Ralston, a film star, and her American manager, Finlay Currie; as also Cedric Hardwicke, a philanthropist, and his secretary (Eliot Makeham); and Vosper, head of the French police. Search for the picture leads to murder, with all those above named involved. Theft, murder and explanation unravel before the train ends its run.

● ●

■ ROMEO AND JULIET

1936, 130 MINS, US ⓥ
Dir George Cukor   *Prod* Irving Thalberg   *Scr* Talbot Jennings   *Ph* William Daniels   *Ed* Margaret Booth
Mus Herbert Stothart   *Art Dir* Cedric Gibbons, Oliver Messel
● Norma Shearer, Leslie Howard, John Barrymore, Edna May Oliver, Basil Rathbone, C. Aubrey Smith (M-G-M)

Romeo and Juliet is a faithful and not too imaginative translation to the screen of the William Shakespeare play.

Romeo and Juliet is a love-story tragedy, requiring precise pace in order that the beauty of its poetry shall be thoroughly grasped. The fine lyric qualities have been retained, and from that point of view there is every reason to laud the production as successful. In accomplishing this worthy purpose, however, the tempo is a beat or two slower than the familiar methods of modern story telling.

Surprisingly few liberties have been taken with the original text. Preparation for the screen was confined chiefly to condensation.

Norma Shearer adds an important portrait to her gallery of roles. She never conveys the impression that she is getting a great kick out of the part, and her restraint aids her conception of the characterization of the daughter of the Capulets, a child of 14.

The famous balcony love scene with Leslie

653

Howard is played sincerely and beautifully. She makes the final tragic moments of the play convincing and moving.

Against her child-like figure, Howard and Ralph Forbes, rival suitors, appear years her senior. Howard's Romeo is a forthright young man of considerable determination, rather than a headstrong, impassioned young lover. But what illusion is lost in looks, Howard adequately makes up in speech. His lines are clearly spoken.

After a rather hesitant beginning John Barrymore makes a real, live person out of Mercutio. His opening scenes are hurried, noisy and indistinct. But the passages preceding and following the fatal duel with Basil Rathbone (Tybalt) are exciting and thrilling. Barrymore plays in the grand manner, which the part allows.

□ 1936: Nominations: Best Picture, Actress (Norma Shearer), Supp. Actor (Basil Rathbone), Art Direction

■ **ROMEO AND JULIET**

1968, 152 MINS, ITALY/UK ◇ ⓦ ⊙
Dir Franco Zeffirelli   *Prod* Dino De Laurentiis
Scr Franco Brusati, Masolino D'Amico   *Ph* Pasquale de Santis   *Ed* Reginald Mills   *Mus* Nino Rota
Art Dir Luciano Puccini
● Olivia Hussey, Leonard Whiting, Milo O'Shea, Michael York, John McEnery, Pat Heywood (Verona/De Laurentiis/British Home Entertainments)

Shot entirely in Italy, director Franco Zeffirelli has conjured up a very good eyeful, with splendid use of color in costumes and back-grounds.

Street and fight sequences give film plenty of movement, allied with bold effective cuts in the Bard's text. Zeffirelli has tried, and often succeeds, in giving the film an up-to-date feeling.

Neither Olivia Hussey nor Leonard Whiting has the experience, looks or vital personality to rise to the pinnacles of the star-cross'd lovers. Dramatic highlights are stilted and much of the verse flat to the ear. Rarely will audiences be moved to throat-gulping by the plight of the young couple.

For all Hussey's prettiness and Whiting's shy charm it is clear that they do not understand one tenth of the meaning of their lines and it is a drawback from which the film cannot recover. The young leads are surrounded by some excellent pro performers, which helps them, but also shows up their inadequacies.

□ 1968: Best Cinematography, Costume Design.
□ Nominations: Best Picture, Director (Danilo Donati).

■ **ROMMEL – DESERT FOX**
See: The Desert Fox

■ **ROMPER STOMPER**

1992, 92 MINS, AUSTRALIA ◇ ⓦ ⊙
Dir Geoffrey Wright   *Prod* Daniel Scharf, Ian Pringle
Scr Geoffrey Wright   *Ph* Ron Hagen   *Ed* Bill Murphy
Mus John Clifford White   *Art Dir* Steven Jones-Evans
● Russell Crowe, Daniel Pollock, Jacqueline McKenzie, Alex Scott, Leigh Russell, Daniel Wyllie (Seon)

Romper Stomper is a *Clockwork Orange* without the intellect. In many ways genuinely appalling, pic centers on a gang of moronic neo-Nazi skinheads who regularly do battle with Melbourne's Vietnamese community.

Russell Crowe gives a powerful performance as skinhead leader Hando, a brute with a veneer of charm whose bible is *Mein Kampf*. The late Daniel Pollock is also impressive as Davey, his friend and lieutenant. Gang is joined by Gabe (Jacqueline McKenzie), a spaced-out drug addict whose father (Alex

Scott) has abused her in an incestuous relationship.

When gang attacks Vietnamese in the process of purchasing the skinheads' favorite bar, the 'gooks' (as they're called) counter-attack with a large force, driving the skinheads from their warehouse base in a long, brutally violent battle sequence.

Pic is well acted and directed with a certain slickness.

■ **ROOKIE, THE**

1990, 121 MINS, US ◇ ⓦ ⓥ ⊙
Dir Clint Eastwood   *Prod* Howard Kazanjian, Steven Siebert, David Valdes   *Scr* Boaz Yakin, Scott Spiegel
Ph Jack N. Green   *Ed* Joel Cox   *Mus* Lennie Niehaus
Art Dir Judy Cammer
● Clint Eastwood, Charlie Sheen, Raul Julia, Sonia Braga, Tom Skerritt, Lara Flynn Boyle (Malpaso/Warner)

Overlong, sadistic and stale even by the conventions of the buddy pic genre, Clint Eastwood's The Rookie is actually Dirty Harry 5½ since Eastwood's tough-as-nails cop Nick Pulovski could just as easily be named Harry Callahan, and his penchant for breaking in partners (and getting them killed) is a holdover from Harry's first three patrols.

This time, however, the troubles lie in partner Charlie Sheen, a rich kid working out childhood guilt and hostility against his parents by playing policeman. Pair pursues a stolen-car ring operated by ruthless thief Raul Julia and sweaty henchwoman Sonia Braga (in a nearly non-verbal role). Pulovski is taken hostage, and Sheen's character has to find himself by, essentially, disregarding all conventional legal channels and destroying as much property as possible.

The normally brilliant Julia lapses into and out of a bad German accent, Braga has just a window-dressing bad-girl role, and *Twin Peaks*' Lara Flynn Boyle is Sheen's blandly drawn girlfriend. Eastwood the actor seems rightfully bored with the material, while Sheen continues to hammer away at his own toughguy rep with only marginal success.

■ **ROOKIE OF THE YEAR**

1993, 103 MINS, US ◇ ⓦ ⊙
Dir Daniel Stern   *Prod* Robert Harper   *Scr* Sam Harper
Ph Jack N. Green   *Ed* Donn Cambern, Raja Gosnell
Mus Bill Conti   *Art Dir* Steven Jordan
● Gary Busey, Albert Hall, Amy Morton, Dan Hedeya, Bruce Altman, Eddie Bracken (20th Century-Fox)

Rookie of the Year aspires to be a pint-sized 'It's a Wonderful Field of Dreams', and largely succeeds in minor league fashion.

The premise is engaging. Pre-teen Henry Rowengarter (Thomas Ian Nicholas) is your typical single-parented, enthusiastic baseball-playing Chicago kid who's unaware of life's cruelties. Then the accident happens. When a school bully goads him into going for a high pop fly, in his headlong zeal Henry fails to notice a loose baseball in his path. Tripping on the orb, he's sent skyward, falling with a thud and breaking his arm.

Months later, when his cast is removed, Henry discovers the fracture has healed in a curious way. His tendons have tightened, allowing him to hurl a ball faster than a speeding bullet. Circumstance brings this to the attention of his beloved Chicago Cubs. Soon the contracts are signed and the pee-wee player is rapidly on his way to delivering his franchise a berth in the World Series.

Essentially a one gag premise, Sam Harper's screenplay valiantly attempts to enhance the yarn by fleshing out the characters and injecting broad splashes of madcap comedy. It connects more often than it fans in the hands of rookie director Daniel Stern, who lack seasoning to ground the fantasy in a realistic setting.

The principal cast shines. Youngster Thomas Ian Nicholas has a winning personality. Also strong are the ever-reliable Gary Busey as the pitcher edging into over-the-hill status, and Amy Morton, who, with little script help, provides the modern mum with old-fashioned warmth and new-era independence. John Candy provides an uncredited turn as an announcer.

■ **ROOM AT THE TOP**

1959, 117 MINS, UK ⓥ
Dir Jack Clayton   *Prod* John Woolf, James Woolf
Scr Neil Paterson   *Ph* Freddie Francis   *Ed* Ralph Kemplen   *Mus* Mario Nascimbene
● Laurence Harvey, Simone Signoret, Heather Sears, Donald Wolfit, Donald Houston, Hermione Baddeley (Remus)

Room at the Top, based on John Braine's best-selling novel, is an adult, human picture. Neil Paterson's literate, well-molded screenplay is enhanced by subtle, intelligent direction from first-timer Jack Clayton and a batch of top-notch performances.

Laurence Harvey takes a job as an accountant in the local government offices of a North Country town. He is an alert young man with a chip on his shoulder because of his humble background. He quickly finds that the small town is virtually controlled by a self-made millionaire and is dominated by those with money and power. Harvey is determined to break down this class-consciousness and sets his cap at the millionaire's daughter. At the same time he is irresistibly drawn to an unhappily married Frenchwoman (Simone Signoret) with whom he has a violent affair.

The Clayton touch produces some fine scenes. These include the young girl's first capitulation to Harvey, the manner in which the millionaire stresses his power over the young upstart, the love scenes between Harvey and Simone Signoret and their quarrel and parting. Above all, Clayton never loses the authentic 'small town' atmosphere.

Harvey makes a credible figure of the young man, likeable despite his weaknesses, torn between love and ambition, and he brings strength and feeling to his love scenes with Signoret. She gives perhaps, the best performance in a capital all-round cast. Heather Sears has less opportunity as the young girl.

□ 1959: Best Actress (Simone Signoret), Adapted Screenplay.
□ Nominations: Best Picture, Director, Actor (Laurence Harvey), Supp. Actress (Hermione Baddeley)

■ **ROOM SERVICE**

1938, 76 MINS, US ⓦ ⊙
Dir William A. Seiter   *Prod* [Pandro S. Berman]
Scr Morrie Ryskind   *Ph* J. Roy Hunt   *Ed* George Crone
Mus Roy Webb (dir.)   *Art Dir* Van Nest Polglase, Al Herman
● Groucho Marx, Chico Marx, Harpo Marx, Lucille Ball, Ann Miller, Frank Albertson (RKO)

Room Service with the Marx Bros will satisfy on the laugh score. There may be captious ones who'll miss (1) Groucho's standard rasslin' with a femme via-a-vis; (2) Harpo's harp solo; (3) Chico's equally standard pianology. But the Marxes have a more staple story structure upon which to hang their buffoonery.

The minimization of the musical highlights naturally points up Groucho's comedy all the more. But running a close second is Donald MacBride, from the original George Abbott play production [by John Murray and Allen Boretz] re-creating his role of the bombastic hotel executive. MacBride well nigh steals all of his scenes, adroitly foiled by Cliff Dunstan (also of the Broadway original) as the distrait hotel manager who has permitted the shoestring impresario (Groucho Marx) to camp a stranded troupe of 22 in his hostelry and run up a $1,200 tab.

Frank Albertson is the trusting young playwright from Oswego; Lucille Ball and Ann Miller are virtually walk-throughs as the femme vis-a-vis to Groucho and Albertson.

ROOM WITH A VIEW, A

1986, 115 MINS, UK ◇ ⏀ ⊙
Dir James Ivory *Prod* Ismail Merchant *Scr* Ruth Prawer Jhabvala *Ph* Tony Pierce-Roberts *Ed* Humphrey Dixon *Mus* Richard Robbins *Art Dir* Gianni Quaranta, Brian Ackland-Snow
● Maggie Smith, Helena Bonham Carter, Denholm Elliott, Julian Sands, Daniel Day Lewis, Simon Callow (Merchant-Ivory/Goldcrest)

A thoroughly entertaining screen adaptation of novelist E.M. Forster's comedy of manners about the Edwardian English upper class at home and abroad, distinguished by superb ensemble acting, intelligent writing and stunning design.

Set in 1907, *A Room with a View* moves between a pensione in Florence, Italy where a well-to-do young English lady, Lucy Honeychurch (Helena Bonham Carter) is traveling on the type of compulsory horizon-broadening tour that was the prerogative of her class, chaperoned by her fussy, punctilious aunt Charlotte (Maggie Smith), and the insular Surrey countryside where she lives with her mother (Rosemary Leach).

James Ivory's direction makes what might have been a talky period piece in lesser hands a consistently engaging study of the mores and morality of a bygone time.
□ 1986: Best Adapted Screenplay, Art Direction, Costume Design (Jenny Beavan, John Bright).
□ Nominations: Best Picture, Director, Supp. Actor (Denholm Elliott), Supp. Actress (Maggie Smith), Cinematography

ROOSTER COGBURN

1975, 107 MINS, US ◇ ⏀ ⊙
Dir Stuart Millar *Prod* Hal B. Wallis *Scr* Martin Julien *Ph* Harry Stradling Jr *Ed* Robert Swink *Mus* Laurence Rosenthal *Art Dir* Preston Ames
● John Wayne, Katharine Hepburn, Anthony Zerbe, Richard Jordan, John McIntyre, Strother Martin (Universal)

Roosterr Cogburn has the exciting charisma of John Wayne and Katharine Hepburn, plus the memories of Wayne's Oscar-winning performance in *True Grit*.

The title is based on the character from Charles Portis' novel *True Grit*, which picks up judge John McIntyre after another trigger-happy foulup. But outlaw Richard Jordan and gang, aided by Anthony Zerbe, Wayne's one-time scout, is acting up, causing several deaths including that of preacher Jon Lormer, survived by spinster daughter Hepburn and Indian lad Richard Romancito. Latter pair join reinstated marshal Wayne to track down the bad guys.

A little artfulness, a little creativity, a little subtlety could work wonders. Like Jordan not chewing up the scenery like a silent pix heavy. Like Hepburn and Wayne not doing a frontier version of The Bickersons. Like not shoe-horning *The African Queen* plot line into this script.

ROOTS OF HEAVEN, THE

1958, 130 MINS, US ◇
Dir John Huston *Prod* Darryl F. Zanuck *Scr* Romain Gary, Patrick Leigh-Fermor *Ph* Oswald Morris *Ed* Russell Lloyd *Mus* Malcolm Arnold *Art Dir* Stephen Grimes, Raymond Gabutti
● Errol Flynn, Juliette Greco, Trevor Howard, Eddie Albert, Orson Welles, Herbert Lom (20th Century-Fox)

The Roots of Heaven has striking pictorial aspects, some exciting performances and builds to a pulsating climax of absorbing tension. Unfortunately, these plus factors almost all come in the second half of the picture.

The locale of the screenplay, from Romain Gary's novel, is French Equatorial Africa. Trevor Howard, whose presence is never completely explained, is launching a campaign to save the elephants of Africa. He believes they are threatened with extinction from big game hunters, ivory poachers and the encroachment of civilization. When he tries to get signers of his petition to outlaw the killings, he is rebuffed on all fronts.

Howard gets only two signatures. One is from Errol Flynn, an alcoholic British ex-officer, and the other is from Juliette Greco, a prostitute. So Howard decides on a campaign of harassment of the huntes and his counter-attack attracts the attention of a safari-ing American TV personality, Orson Welles; a Danish scientist, Friedrich Ledebur; a German nobleman, Olivier Hussenot, and some natives who propose to use Howard as a symbol of their own resistance to colonial law and practice.

Director John Huston has staged his exterior scenes superbly. Full advantage is taken here of the arduous African locations. Howard gives a fine performance and is responsible for conveying as much as comes across of the tricky theme. Flynn plays the drunken officer competently but without suggesting any latent nobility or particular depth. Greco is interesting without being very moving. Orson Welles in a brief bit (reportedly done as a favor to producer Darryl F. Zanuck) is a pinwheel of flashing vigor, his evil to be lamented.

ROPE

1948, 80 MINS, US ⏀ ⊙
Dir Alfred Hitchcock *Prod* Alfred Hitchcock, Sidney Bernstein *Scr* Arthur Laurents *Ph* Joseph Valentine, William V. Skall *Ed* William H. Ziegler *Mus* [David Buttolph] *Art Dir* Perry Ferguson
● James Stewart, John Dall, Farley Granger, Cedric Hardwicke, Constance Collier, Joan Chandler (Transatlantic)

Hitchcock could have chosen a more entertaining subject with which to use the arresting camera and staging technique displayed in *Rope*. Theme is of a thrill murder, done for no reason but to satisfy a sadistical urge and intellectual vanity. Plot has its real-life counterpart in the infamous Loeb-Leopold case, and is based on the play by Patrick Hamilton [adapted by Hume Cronyn].

Feature of the picture is that story action is continuous without time lapses. Action takes place within an hour-and-a-half period and the film footage nearly duplicates the span, being 80 minutes. It is entirely confined to the murder apartment of two male dilettantes, intellectual morons who commit what they believe to be the perfect crime, then celebrate the deed with a ghoulish supper served to the victim's relatives and friends from atop the chest in which the body is concealed.

To achieve his effects, Hitchcock put his cast and technicians through lengthy rehearsals before turning a camera.

James Stewart, as the ex-professor who first senses the guilt of his former pupils and nibbles away at their composure with verbal barbs, does a commanding job. John Dall stands out as the egocentric who masterminds the killing and ghoulish wake. Equally good is Farley Granger as the weakling partner in crime.

ROSARY MURDERS, THE

1987, 105 MINS, US ◇ ⏀ ⊙
Dir Fred Walton *Prod* Robert G. Laurel, Michael Mihalich *Scr* Elmore Leonard, Fred Walton *Ph* David Golia *Ed* Sam Vitale *Mus* Bobby Laurel, Don Sebesky
● Donald Sutherland, Charles Durning, Josef Sommer, Belinda Bauer, James Murtaugh, John Danelle (First Take)

A string of a half-dozen murders committed by someone with a grudge against the Catholic Church, his victims being nuns and priests in a Detroit parish, is lacking in suspense or dramatic buildup, and what should have been the final climatic sequences are as flat as a holy wafer.

Pic [from the novel by William X. Kienzle] revolves mostly around a priest, Father Koesler, who sets about trying to solve the murders while the police seem to be twiddling their thumbs. The priest turns sleuth after the murderer drops a few clues to him during a confessional box session. As a man of the cloth, latter can't tip off the police or probable victims because of his secrecy vows.

Donald Sutherland puts in a good performance as the liberal-minded investigating priest, and Charles Durning is fine as the hard-line father superior.

ROSE, THE

1979, 134 MINS, US ◇ ⏀ ⊙
Dir Mark Rydell *Prod* Marvin Worth *Scr* Bill Kerby, Bo Goldman *Ph* Vilmos Zsigmond *Ed* Robert L. Wolfe *Mus* Paul A. Rothchild *Art Dir* Richard MacDonald
● Bette Midler, Alan Bates, Frederic Forrest, Harry Dean Stanton, Barry Primus, David Keith (20th Century-Fox)

Producers haven't flinched from picking the scabs off the body of 1960s rock-and-roll. While there are certainly similarities to the tragic story of Janis Joplin, *The Rose* emerges as its own self-contained tale.

What's puzzling is that the screenwriters have chosen to dwell solely on the downward career spiral of Bette Midler's character, known on and off-stage as The Rose.

Revolving around the star are various satellites, including boyfriend Frederic Forrest, manager Alan Bates and road manager Barry Primus.

Result is an ultra-realistic look at the infusion of money, sex, drugs and booze into the simple process of singing a song, a chore Midler does faultlessly in several excellent concert sequences.
□ 1979: Nominations: Best Actress (Bette Midler), Supp. Actor (Frederic Forrest), Editing, Sound

ROSEBUD

1975, 126 MINS, US ◇
Dir Otto Preminger *Prod* Preminger *Scr* Erik Lee Preminger *Ph* Denys Coop *Ed* Peter Thornton *Mus* Laurent Petitgirard *Art Dir* Michael Seymour
● Peter O'Toole, Richard Attenborough, Cliff Gorman, Claude Dauphin, John V. Lindsay, Peter Lawford (United Artists)

Political tumult story, involving Palestine Liberation Organization terrorist kidnapping, is a bland and unexciting film. Peter O'Toole heads the cast as a Briton, secret agenting for the U.S., who sorts out the crisis.

An episodic collage of long sequences which cross cut between the yacht heist of five young wealthy girls, and the efforts of their families and police to track down their kidnappers. O'Toole (who replaced Robert Mitchum after shooting began) is recruited from his CIA cover as a *Newsweek International* reporter to locate the girls and the PLO group.

O'Toole's is among the few strong performances, but that isn't saying much. As a foreign policy document, *Rosebud* at least will not cause controversy, because as a motion picture, it's a crashing bore.

ROSELAND

1977, 103 MINS, US ◇ ⏀
Dir James Ivory *Prod* Ismail Merchant *Scr* Ruth

Prawer Jhabvala   *Ph* Ernest Vincze   *Ed* Humphrey Dixon, Richard Schmiechen   *Mus* Michael Gibson
● Teresa Wright, Lou Jacobi, Christopher Walken, Louise Kirtland, Geraldine Chaplin, Helen Gallagher (Merchant-Ivory)

There is romance to the notion that our buildings will outlast us, that our passions will be seen and remembered within the walls while we go on our way to our just desserts. That is the emotional underpinning of *Roseland*, a clean, well-lighted ballroom of New York's West Side.

Standout is Lilia Skala, playing an elderly German woman with the bearing of Bismarck, who confides to her sleepy Peabody (a Roseland dance) partner, David Thomas, that she has had to do cleaning and work as a cook at Schrafft's to pay her way.

Second tale of a gigolo, nicely crafted by Christopher Walken, is of his failure to separate himself from Joan Copeland, excellent in her portrayal of a lonely and dying woman now buying what her faded glamor once commanded.

■ **ROSE-MARIE**

1936, 110 MINS, US ⓦ ⊙
Dir W.S. Van Dyke   *Prod* Hunt Stromberg   *Scr* Frances Goodrich, Albert Hackett, Alice Duer Miller   *Ph* William Daniels   *Ed* Blanche Sewell   *Mus* Rudolf Friml, Herbert Stothart (dir.)   *Art Dir* Cedric Gibbons, Joseph Wright, Edwin B. Willis
● Jeanette MacDonald, Nelson Eddy, James Stewart, Reginald Owen, Allan Jones, Alan Mowbray (M-G-M)

Strong impression left by the Jeanette MacDonald-Nelson Eddy twain in *Naughty Marietta* (1935) is surpassed in *Rose-Marie*, Metro's operatic western. Sturdy stage libretto by Otto Harbach and Oscar Hammerstein II is further enhanced by the scope of the cinematic treatment. There is a wholly satisfying blend of sophisticated behind-the-opera-scenes temperament with the Great Outdoors stuff which comprises much of the ensuing footage as Eddy pursues MacDonald's scapegrace brother.

Score by Rudolf Friml and Herbert Stothart, the latter also Metro studio musical director (also contributing the maestro-ing on this production), has survived more than a decade since its premiere at the Imperial Theatre on Broadway September 2 1924. The classic 'Indian Love Call' as it re-echoes through the 'Canadian' woodlands (actual location at Lake Tahoe on the Cal-Nev border, and very beautiful) means more than it ever did in its stage original. Eddy's balladeering of the titular 'Rose-Marie' as he paddles MacDonald on the trek for the escaped criminal (her brother) is likewise photographically and in other respects enhanced.

The waltz song from *Romeo and Juliet* is the legit operatic opener [staged by William von Wymetal], wherein Allan Jones, who warbles a nifty tenor on his own, is MacDonald's vocal vis-a-vis. Femme star has a solo opportunity with 'Pardon Me, Madame' (Gus Kahn's lyric interpolation).

■ **ROSEMARY'S BABY**

1968, 134 MINS, US ◇ ⓦ ⊙
Dir Roman Polanski   *Prod* William Castle   *Scr* Roman Polanski   *Ph* William Fraker   *Ed* Sam O'Steen, Bob Wyman   *Mus* Christopher Komeda   *Art Dir* Richard Sylbert
● Mia Farrow, John Cassavetes, Ruth Gordon, Sidney Blackmer, Maurice Evans, Ralph Bellamy (Paramount)

Several exhilarating milestones are achieved in *Rosemary's Baby*, an excellent film version of Ira Levin's diabolical chiller novel. Writer-director Roman Polanski has triumphed in his first US-made pic. The film holds attention without explicit violence or gore.

Mia Farrow and John Cassavetes, a likeable young married couple, take a flat in a run-down New York building. Ralph Bellamy, an obstetrician prescribing some strange pre-natal nourishment for Farrow and Maurice Evans, Farrow's sole ally, who dies a mysterious death, as well as Charles Grodin, enter the plot at adroit intervals.

The near-climax – Farrow has been drugged so as to conceive by Satan – and the final wallop make for genuine cliff hanger interest.

Farrow's performance is outstanding. Cassavetes handles particularly well the difficult projection of a husband as much in love with his wife as with success. Neighbour Ruth Gordon is pleasantly unrestrained in her pushy self-interest, quite appropriate herein, while other principals score solidly.
□ 1968: Best Supp. Actress (Ruth Gordon)
□ Nomination: Best Adapted Screenplay

■ **ROSENCRANTZ AND GUILDENSTERN ARE DEAD**

1991, 118 MINS, UK ◇ ⓦ ⊙
Dir Tom Stoppard   *Prod* Michael Brandman, Emanuel Azenberg   *Scr* Tom Stoppard   *Ph* Peter Biziou   *Ed* Nicolas Gaster   *Mus* Stanley Myers   *Art Dir* Vaughan Edwards
● Garry Oldman, Tim Roth, Richard Dreyfuss, Iain Glen, Joanna Roth, Donald Sumpter (Brandenberg)

Marking his debut as director, playwright Tom Stoppard takes two marginal characters from Shakespeare's *Hamlet*, and places them at the center of a comedy-drama, while the major characters of the play – Hamlet, Ophelia, Claudius and the rest – are only part of the background.

Rosencrantz and Guildenstern are never certain about what's going on in Elsinore. They overhear crucial conversations and encounters, they talk briefly to the King and to Hamlet, and, in the end, they accompany Hamlet on a voyage to England, but they're never a part of the central drama.
NP>Stoppard's 1967 play has been seen as a mixture of Samuel Beckett and Shakespeare, but on film, he adds cinematic references so that the two protagonists, with their endless word games, come across as a mixture of Abbott & Costello (the 'Who's On First' routine) and Laurel and Hardy (with the clumsy Rosencrantz forever annoying and frustrating the superior Guildenstern). There's also a touch of Monty Python in the zaniness of the characters and their verbal and visual antics.

Gary Oldman and Tim Roth are splendid in their roles. Oldman plays his character as a shrewd simpleton, and Roth plays his as a man who thinks he's clever, but really isn't. Also giving a formidable performance is Richard Dreyfuss as the leader of a band of strolling players.

■ **ROSE OF WASHINGTON SQUARE**

1939, 90 MINS, US
Dir Gregory Ratoff   *Prod* Nunnally Johnson (assoc.)
Scr Nunnally Johnson   *Ph* Karl Freund   *Ed* Louis Loeffler   *Mus* Louis Silvers (dir.)   *Art Dir* Richard Day, Rudolph Sternad
● Tyrone Power, Alice Faye, Al Jolson, William Frawley, Joyce Compton, Hobart Cavanaugh (20th Century-Fox)

Of the three co-stars this is Al Jolson's picture. But it's not much of a filmusical. It's primarily a story deficiency. Nunnally Johnson did the screenplay and production, although original by John Larkin and Jerry Horwin is as much to blame.

A major, solo title emphasizes that the plot structure is fictional. However, the Fannie Brice-Nicky Arnstein saga is an incidental to a show business romance where Al Jolson (billed as Ted Cotter, but he might just as well have been called Jolson) is the altruistic patron of the beauteous and talented Alice Faye. She in turn is stuck on the wrong-guy character played by Tyrone Power.

Faye is still plenty on the s.a. side, excepting for a few camera angles that don't flatter her chin-line. Power's vacillating characterization is a missout.

■ **ROSE TATTOO, THE**

1955, 117 MINS, US ⓦ ⊙
Dir Daniel Mann   *Prod* Hal Wallis   *Scr* Tennessee Williams   *Ph* James Wong Howe   *Ed* Warren Low   *Mus* Alex North   *Art Dir* Hal Pereira, Tambi Larsen
● Anna Magnani, Burt Lancaster, Marisa Pavan, Ben Cooper, Jo Van Fleet, Virginia Grey (Paramount)

The Rose Tattoo creates a realistic Italiano atmosphere in the bayou country of the south, establishes vivid characters with one glaring exception and dwells upon a story that is important only because it gives its key character a jumping-off point for fascinating histrionics.

Anna Magnani gives *Tattoo* its substance; she's spellbinding as the signora content with the memory of the fidelity of her husband until she discovers he had a blonde on the side before his banana truck carried him to death.

The characters inspire little sympathy. Magnani has animalistic drive and no beauty. Burt Lancaster, as the village idiot by inheritance, is called upon to take on a role bordering on the absurd.

Otherwise Daniel Mann does fine in the directing. He provides pace where some situations might have been static.
□ 1955: Best Actress (Anna Magnani), B&W Cinematography, B&W Art Direction.
□ Nominations: Best Picture, Supp. Actress (Marisa Pavan), B&W Costume Design), Editing, Scoring of a Dramatic Picture

■ **ROTTEN TO THE CORE**

1965, 89 MINS, UK
Dir John Boulting   *Prod* Roy Boulting   *Scr* Jeffrey Dell, Roy Boulting, John Warren, Len Heath   *Ph* Freddie Young   *Ed* Teddy Darvas   *Mus* Michael Dress   *Art Dir* Alex Vetchinsky
● Anton Rodgers, Eric Sykes, Charlotte Rampling, Ian Bannen, Avis Bunnage, Dudley Sutton (BLC/Boulting)

Bigtime crime is the main target of the Boulting Brothers' latest piece of satirical joshing, with army and police figuring in the story. It provides a reasonable ration of yocks and amusing situations but these have to struggle against some dim passages. The Boulting Brothers' knives are less sharp than customary.

Idea hinges on the appeal of Prime Minister Harold Wilson to adapt scientific methods to 1965 big business and industry. And this the Boultings have applied to the activities of a gang of crooks whose young boss (Anton Rodgers) has set his beady eye on hijacking an army payroll worth nearly $3 million. Rodgers, known as 'Duke,' assembles his gang under the front of running a health resort hospital near the army camp.

Rodgers shows versatility in four or five characterizations but it needed a comedy character actor to dominate the laugh sequences. Eric Sykes is largely wasted in the role of a private eye, which fails to jell.

The Boultings put their faith in an unknown girl (Charlotte Rampling) as the Duke's moll. She is quite easy on the eye but lacks the experience and personality.

■ **ROUGH CUT**

1980, 112 MINS, US ◇ ⓦ ⊙
Dir Don Siegel   *Prod* David Merrick   *Scr* Francis Burns [= Larry Gelbart]   *Ph* Freddie Young   *Ed* Doug Stewart   *Mus* Nelson Riddle   *Art Dir* Ted Haworth
● Burt Reynolds, Lesley-Anne Down, David Niven, Patrick Magee, Joss Ackland, Timothy West (Paramount)

R

Rough Cut emerges as an undistinctive, frothy romantic comedy that will charm a few and probably miss the eye of many. Love match of Burt Reynolds and Lesley-Anne Down works only in selected spots and frame of the story, intrigue over a $30 million diamond heist, is hard-pressed to sustain interest.

Blake Edwards was originally scheduled to direct the picture for David Merrick in 1977 with Larry Gelbart scripting and Reynolds top-lining. Edwards eventually bowed out and Reynolds took on other films until Don Siegel was signed to helm in 1979. Siegel was fired and rehired by Merrick and pic finally wound.

Trouble began when Merrick decided he wanted a new ending and Siegel insisted he had the final cut. Result was Merrick hiring Robert Ellis Miller to shoot a fourth finale.

Problem seems to lie in much of the dialog, which comes across as both wooden and contrived. Reynolds and Down do what they can but their attempts at witty banter never appear natural.

ROUGH NIGHT IN JERICHO

1967, 102 MINS, US ◇
Dir Arnold Laven *Prod* Martin Rackin *Scr* Sydney Boehm, Marvin H. Albert *Ph* Russell Metty *Ed* Ted J. Kent *Mus* Don Costa *Art Dir* Alexander Golitzen, Frank Arrigo
● Dean Martin, George Peppard, Jean Simmons, John McIntire, Slim Pickens, Don Galloway (Universal)

Most unusual aspect about this production is offbeat casting of Dean Martin as a heavy without a single redeeming quality. George Peppard is the hero. Both are embroiled in a bloody and violent western.

Plotwise, *Rough Night in Jericho* frequently carries a nebulous story line, particularly in limning the actions of Martin, onetime lawman turned vicious town boss. Screenplay, an adaptation of Marvin H. Albert's novel *The Man in Black*, is lacking in the suspense one expects from a big league western but regulation action is there in good measure.

Peppard plays a former deputy US marshal who becomes involved in the affairs of the town of Jericho – and Martin – when he arrives with John McIntire, onetime marshal whom he once served under. Latter has come to help Jean Simmons save her stage line, coveted by Martin, who also wants its femme owner.

'ROUND MIDNIGHT

1986, 133 MINS, FRANCE/US ◇ ⊙
Dir Bertrand Tavernier *Prod* Irwin Winkler
Scr Bertrand Tavernier, David Rayfiel *Ph* Bruno de Keyzer *Ed* Armand Psenny *Mus* Herbie Hancock
Art Dir Alexandre Trauner
● Dexter Gordon, Francois Cluzet, Gabrielle Haker, Sandra Reaves-Phillips, John Berry, Martin Scorsese (Little Bear/PECF/Warner)

'Round Midnight is a superbly crafted music world drama in which Gallic director Bertrand Tavernier pays a moving dramatic tribute to the great black musicians who lived and performed in Paris in the late 1950s. The $3 million film is dedicated to jazz giants Bud Powell and Lester Young, the composite inspiration for the story's central personage.

With his American co-scripter, David Rayfiel, Tavernier has placed deftly the themes of cultural roots, affinities and distances at the heart of the screenplay ['inspired by incidents in the lives of Francis Paudras and Bud Powell'], which dramatizes the friendship between an aging jazz saxophonist, who has accepted an engagement at the legendary Blue Note club in Saint-Germain-des-Pres, and a passionate young French admirer who is ready to make personal sacrifices to help his idol.

Tavernier cast a non-professional in the central role: Dexter Gordon, the 63-year-old jazz veteran whom Tavernier has long admired. With his hoarse, hesitant diction and his lanky shuffle, Gordon fills the part of the world-weary artist with his own jagged warmth.

Film is no less a treat for the eye as for the ear. Shot almost entirely in the Epinay studios north of Paris, production is vividly designed by veteran Alexandre Trauner.
□ 1986: Best Original Score.
□ Nomination: Best Actor (Dexter Gordon)

ROXANNE

1987, 107 MINS, US ◇ ⊙ ⊙
Dir Fred Schepisi *Prod* Michael Rachmil, Daniel Melnick
Scr Steve Martin *Ph* Ian Baker *Ed* John Scott
Mus Bruce Smeaton *Art Dir* Jack DeGovia
● Steve Martin, Daryl Hannah, Rick Rossovich, Shelley Duvall, Michael J. Pollard, Damon Wayans, Fred Willard, Michael J. Pollard (Columbia/Melnick/LA Films)

As a reworking of Edmond Rostand's play *Cyrano de Bergerac*, the only reason to see the film is for a few bits of inspired nonsense by Steve Martin as the nosey lover. Written by Martin to suit his special talent for sight gags, this Cyrano, called CB here, is just a wild and crazy guy with a big nose and a gift for gab.

The central plot device of the play, in which a true love writes letters to help another suitor with the same woman he doesn't love as much, is here adapted to a small ski community in Washington State where Martin is fire chief.

The film is barely underway when Roxanne (Daryl Hannah) is out of her clothes and locked out of her house. When CB comes to the rescue it's love at first sight, but his enlarged proboscis disqualifies him as a serious suitor, or so he thinks.

Instead, Roxanne turns her attentions to Chris (Rick Rossovich), a new recruit on the fire department who is all but rendered dumb in front of women. Eventually, Roxanne learns Rossovich is only after her body and realizes Martin loves her truly.

Aussie director Fred Schepisi, who has elsewhere handled much rougher material, does a professional job of creating a breezy atmosphere, but in the end it's hopelessly sappy stuff.

ROXIE HART

1942, 72 MINS, US
Dir William A. Wellman *Prod* Nunnally Johnson
Scr Nunnally Johnson *Ph* Leon Shamroy *Ed* James B. Clark *Mus* Alfred Newman
● Ginger Rogers, Adolphe Menjou, George Montgomery, Lynne Overman, Nigel Bruce, Phil Silvers (20th Century-Fox)

Maurine Watkins' play [*Chicago*] of a girl who basks in the publicity spotlight for a brief period when accused of murder is broadly embellished via the screenplay by Nunnally Johnson and direction by William Wellman.

Picture aims solely for adult attention. Ginger Rogers is the girl who stands trial for murder committed by her husband, after getting buildup on publicity values by cynical crime reporter Lynne Overman. Banner-lined all over town, Roxie becomes an enthusiastic stooge for the press, court and slick mouthpiece (Adolphe Menjou).

Ginger Rogers does well as the tough girl who is dazzled by the sudden attention, but seems to overdo her characterization at several points. Menjou is excellent as the theatric and wily criminal mouthpiece who craftily steers the judge and jury to the proper verdict.

ROYAL FLASH

1975, 121 MINS, UK ◇ ⊚
Dir Richard Lester *Prod* David B. Picker, Denis O'Dell
Scr George McDonald Fraser *Ph* Geoffrey Unsworth
Ed John Victor Smith *Mus* Ken Thorne *Art Dir* Terence Marsh
● Malcolm McDowell, Alan Bates, Florinda Bolkan, Oliver Reed, Britt Ekland, Lionel Jeffries (20th Century-Fox)

Royal Flash is a royal pain. Richard Lester's formula period comedy style [adapted by George MacDonald Fraser from his novel], as enduring as it is not particularly endearing, achieves its customary levels of posturing silliness.

Malcolm McDowell, fleeing a bordello raid, falls in with Florinda Bolkan, playing Lola Montez, in turn alienating Oliver Reed's Otto von Bismarck. The latter, with accomplice Alan Bates and hit-men Lionel Jeffries and Tom Bell, force McDowell to impersonate a Prussian nobleman for purposes of marriage to duchess Britt Ekland. Complex political, sexual and survival strategies lurch the plot forward.

The players are as competent as the film allows, and their work in other films is proof of their talent.

ROYAL HUNT OF THE SUN, THE

1969, 121 MINS, UK ◇
Dir Irving Lerner *Prod* Eugene Frenke, Philip Yordan
Scr Philip Yordan *Ph* Roger Barlow *Ed* Peter Parasheles *Mus* Marc Wilkinson *Art Dir* Eugene Lourie
● Robert Shaw, Christopher Plummer, Nigel Davenport, Michael Craig, Leonard Whiting, Andrew Keir (Rank)

Based on Peter Shaffer's rich, imaginative play, *Royal Hunt of the Sun* is a film that's striking in many ways, visually and literately.

It has many plusses, notably a standout duo of performances by Robert Shaw and Christopher Plummer and some very sound supporting and an intelligent top-drawer script by Philip Yordan.

Story concerns General Francisco Pizarro, Spanish soldier of fortune who, for the third time penetrates Peru, the Land of the Sun, in search of the Kingdom of Gold. He leads a small, ill-equipped band with which to tackle the forces of the Inca.

Shaw powerfully portrays the conquistador and his varying and complicated moods of violence, sadness, despair, anger and puzzlement. Plummer is particularly outstanding in the tricky role of King Atahuallpa, though not always entirely audible due to the curious accent he affects.

ROYAL SCANDAL, A

1945, 94 MINS, US
Dir Otto Preminger *Prod* Ernst Lubitsch *Scr* Edwin Justus Mayer, Bruno Frank *Ph* Arthur Miller
Ed Dorothy Spencer *Mus* Alfred Newman *Art Dir* Lyle R. Wheeler, Mark-Lee Kirk
● Tallulah Bankhead, Charles Coburn, Anne Baxter, William Eythe, Vincent Price, Mischa Auer (20th Century-Fox)

A Royal Scandal is a highly hilarious comedy with superb performances by Tallulah Bankhead and Charles Coburn, in particular, and the wit of the original play by Lajos Biro and Melchior Lengyel.

This version of Catherine the Great's saga turns out to be a farce of real proportions, although never eclipsing the Czarina as an extremely vigorous personality, surrounded by palace intrigue and a parade of lovers. Ernst Lubitsch and director Otto Preminger have neatly interwoven the court intrigue with her w.k. amorous proclivities. The stream of captains of the palace guards is pointed up somewhat briskly.

Yarn concentrates on impetuous William Eythe, who has ridden three days and nights to warn the Czarina about two plotting generals. Because he admittedly is not tired after his strenuous ride, Catherine ignores his impetuosity and slight dumbness to have him await a nocturnal interview. That this interview is successful is borne out by subsequent events.

....

■ **ROYAL WEDDING**
(UK: Wedding Bells)

1951, 93 MINS, US ◇ ⓥ ⊙
Dir Stanley Donon   *Prod* Arthur Freed   *Scr* Alan Jay Lerner   *Ph* Robert Planck   *Ed* Albert Akst   *Mus* Johnny Green (dir.)
● Fred Astaire, Jane Powell, Peter Lawford, Sarah Churchill, Keenan Wynn, Albert Sharpe (M-G-M)

This is an engaging concoction of songs and dances in a standard musical framework, brightly dressed in color to show off its physical attributes.

Score uses up nine tunes to back the singing and terping, and two of the numbers are sock enough to almost carry the picture by themselves. They are Astaire's solo dance on a ceiling, upside-down, and the teaming with Powell in a sort of Frankie-and-Johnny-apache-hepcat presentation that will click with audiences.

The ceiling stepping to the Burton Lane-Alan Jay Lerner 'You're All the World to Me' combines technical magic and Astaire's foot wizardry into a potent novelty. 'How Could You Believe Me' sets up the earthy Astaire-Powell delivery of the other outstanding musical sequence.

Light plot sees Astaire and Powell as a brother-sister team of Broadway musical stars. They go to London to open their show during the period when preparations are being made for the royal marriage. In between presentation of the musical numbers, Astaire falls in love with Sarah Churchill, show hoofer, and Powell catches the love bug from Peter Lawford, an English lord-romeo.
□ 1951: Nomination: Best Song ('Too Late Now')

....

■ **R.P.M.**
REVOLUTIONS PER MINUTE

1970, 92 MINS, US ◇ ⓥ
Dir Stanley Kramer   *Prod* Stanley Kramer   *Scr* Erich Segal   *Ph* Michel Hugo   *Ed* William A. Lyon   *Mus* Barry DeVorzon, Perry Botkin Jr   *Art Dir* Robert Clatworthy
● Anthony Quinn, Ann-Margret, Gary Lockwood, Paul Winfield, Graham Jarvis, Alan Hewitt (Columbia)

Subtitled 'Revolutions Per Minute', this campus crisis meller slowly spins its improbable wheels to the climactic production number involving a student riot.

Anthony Quinn stars as an harassed college president, Ann-Margret is his plot-irrelevant young mistress, and Gary Lockwood is a student radical. The treatment is deja vu, Eric Segal's script is replete with glib one-liners but lacking real story fibre, and Kramer's direction is dull.

Quinn is introduced as a 53-year-old professor, risen to his post from Spanish Harlem and popular with his students. At the outset, the current college head has thrown in the towel as students have occupied the Administration Bldg, housing a big computer.

Lockwood, along with Paul Winfield, are the radical student leaders.

....

■ **RUBY**

1977, 84 MINS, US ◇ ⓥ
Dir Curtis Harrington   *Prod* George Edwards
Scr George Edwards, Barry Schneider   *Ph* William

Mendenhall   *Ed* Bill Magee   *Mus* Don Ellis
Art Dir Tom Rasmussen
● Piper Laurie, Stuart Whitman, Roger Davis, Janit Baldwin, Crystin Sinclaire, Paul Kent (Dimension/Krantz)

In the cookbook school of filmmaking *Ruby* is strictly leftovers. Begin with a hunk of the occult. Add a cup of 1950s nostalgia, some hard-boiled detective, a dash of camp from old horror movies and sprinkle with violence.

Most of the pic's action takes place around Ruby's Drive-In. Piper Laurie is the one-time gun moll and wife of a big-time mobster. She now owns a drive-in staffed by 'associates' of her dead husband. He was gunned down 16 years ago when someone finked on him, but his spirit is back to haunt the drive-in.

He gets the job done: a projectionist is strangled with film; a concession stand attendant stuffed into a soda machine; and the dead mobster's daughter afflicted with a case of the shaking bed.

Performances are generally poor.

....

■ **RUBY**

1992, 110 MINS, US ◇ ⓥ ⊙
Dir John Mackenzie   *Prod* Sigurjon Sighvatsson, Steve Golin   *Scr* Stephen Davis   *Ph* Phil Meheux   *Ed* Richard Trevor   *Mus* John Scott   *Art Dir* David Brisbin
● Danny Aiello, Sherilyn Fenn, Arliss Howard, Tobin Bell, David Duchovny, Richard Sarafian (Polygram/Propaganda)

Danny Aiello and Sherilyn Fenn's earnest, first-rate performances can't overcome strewed story elements of this otherwise well-put-together drama [from Stephen Davis' play *Love Field*]. Highly fictionalized bio of the club owner and small-time hood who killed Lee Harvey Oswald points a finger at organized crime and rogue elements within the CIA as the parties responsible for bringing Camelot to a crashing end.

The fiction stems in large part from Ruby's relationship with a stripper (Fenn) who, it's revealed at the end, is a composite of various characters. Ruby starts to be drawn in when he's sent to Cuba to kill an imprisoned Mafia don (Marc Lawrence) but instead turns on the con who sent him, in the process being drawn back into big-league mob activities.

The problem with *Ruby* is that it plays too much like TV docudrama and, to paraphrase Winston Churchill, ends up a mystery wrapped in a riddle.

Aiello is terrific as Ruby, a tough outsider who never quite was. Fenn turns in a performance hotter than a cup of *Twin Peaks* java as the power-seeking stripper, looking Monroe-like with her platinum blond locks and classic features.

....

■ **RUBY CAIRO**

1993, 110 MINS, US/JAPAN ◇ ⓥ ⊙
Dir Graeme Clifford   *Prod* Lloyd Phillips, Haruki Kadokawa   *Scr* Robert Dillon, Michael Thomas   *Ph* Laszlo Kovacs   *Ed* Caroline Biggerstaff, Paul Rubell   *Mus* John Barry, Robert Randles   *Art Dir* Richard Sylbert
● Andie MacDowell, Liam Neeson, Viggo Mortensen, Jack Thompson, Jeff Corey, Miriam Reed (Kadokawa)

Ruby Cairo is an old-fashioned Yank-in-Europe mystery-adventure [from a screen story by Robert Dillon] that squanders an interesting cast headed by Andie MacDowell and Liam Neeson. Too bad everyone forgot to pack a script along with their passports and sunscreen.

MacDowell plays the wife of Viggo Mortensen, who runs an aircraft salvage company directly under a flightpath to LAX. One day, while he's off in Mexico, she receives a packet with some teeth inside, and hotfoots it to Veracruz to inspect the remains of his plane and supposed body.

Realizing he's still alive and done a runner, she sets off tracking him down. The trail

leads from Panama and the Bahamas to Berlin, Athens and Cairo, where with the help of food aid worker Liam Neeson she uncovers a scam smuggling a chemical for making poison gas inside grain shipments.

This could have played either as a romantic comedy-thriller or as a long-limbed drama of betrayed love. Under Graeme Clifford's unfocused direction, it keeps promising both but ends up neither. Where the reported $24 million budget went is anyone's guess.

....

■ **RUBY GENTRY**

1952, 82 MINS, US ⓥ
Dir King Vidor   *Prod* Joseph Bernhard   *Scr* Silvia Richards   *Ph* Russell Harlan   *Ed* Terry Morse   *Mus* Heinz Roemheld
● Jennifer Jones, Charlton Heston, Karl Malden, Tom Tully, James Anderson, Josephine Hutchinson (Bernhard-Vidor/20th Century-Fox)

This is a bold, adult drama laying heavy stress on sex, a story of fleshy passions in the tidewater country of North Carolina.

Vidor belts over the blatantly sensual Arthur Fitz-Richard story. It's a sordid type of drama, with neither Jennifer Jones nor Charlton Heston gaining any sympathy in their characters.

Story starts with the animal attraction between Jones, from the wrong side of the tracks, and Heston, purse-poor southern gent who willingly trifles in the swamp but for marriage chooses Phyllis Avery's wealthy, properly-bred girl, so he can rebuild his family fortunes.

With a legal mating with Heston impossible, Jones turns to the friendship of Malden and his bedridden wife (Josephine Hutchinson). After the latter dies, she accepts Malden's proposal and they are married. Society refuses to accept his bride.

Jones goes through much of the footage in skin-tight levis, of which she and careful camera angles and lighting make the most.

....

■ **RUGGLES OF RED GAP**

1923, 89 MINS, US ⊗
Dir James Cruze   *Scr* Walter Woods, Anthony Coldeway   *Ph* Karl Brown
● Edward Everett Horton, Ernest Torrence, Lois Wilson, Fritzi Ridgeway, Charles Ogle, Louise Dresser (Paramount)

Here is a great comedy novel [by Harry Leon Wilson] made into a delightful feature picture. The adaptation is literal in that it reproduces the effect of the original story with no forced interpolations and a full use of the material. The acting is a triumph of team work.

Ernest Torrance's Cousin Egbert is a gem, a bit of comic characterization that hasn't a suspicion of clowning. Edward Horton's Ruggles is a fitting companion piece. This most British of British valets is almost as good fun in the film as was in the book.

One of the things that go to make the whole picture delightful is the absence of hokum. Ruggles is as far from the familiar comic picture of the English valet as could be. He is just an embarrassed automaton hedged about by his own class consciousness and prejudices and stunned by the strange people he is thrown among. He is actually a likeable human being.

Lois Wilson plays 'the Kenner woman' with her invariable charm while Louise Dresser is abundantly convincing as the formidable Mrs Ellie, wife and general manager of Cousin Egbert.

....

■ **RUGGLES OF RED GAP**

1935, 90 MINS, US ⓥ
Dir Leo McCarey   *Prod* Arthur Hornblow Jr   *Scr* Walter De Leon, Harlan Thompson, Humphrey Pearson

R

Ph Alfred Gilks   *Ed* Edward Dmytryk   *Mus* Ralph Rainger   *Art Dir* Hans Dreier, Robert Odell
● Charles Laughton, Mary Boland, Charles Ruggles, ZaSu Pitts, Roland Young, Leila Hyams (Paramount)

Leo McCarey has turned out a fast and furiously funny film which is a perfect example of what smart handling behind the camera can do. Original novel [by Harry Leon Wilson] has been made as a film twice before, once by Essanay (1918) and by Paramount (1923). But this time the yarn is handled from a completely fresh standpoint – with gratifying results.

Story is a bit dated. It plants Elmer (Charlie Ruggles) and his wife (Mary Boland) in Paris. They play poker with the Earl of Burnstead (Roland Young) and win his butler, Ruggles (Charles Laughton). They take him back to Red Gap, state of Washington. There Ruggles is mistaken for a British army captain and becomes a celebrity. That gives him the idea of freedom and standing on his own. He falls in love with Mrs Judson (ZaSu Pitts) and opens a restaurant.

Laughton turns in a performance that will surprise some and widen his appeal by far. He's played comedy before (*Henry VIII*), but here he is doing it differently. It's not satire; it's not a pathological character study. Just plain comedy.
□ 1935: Nomination: Best Picture

■ RULING CLASS, THE

1972, 154 MINS, UK ◇ ⑰ ⊙
Dir Peter Medak   *Prod* Jules Buck, Jack Hawkins
Scr Peter Barnes   *Ph* Ken Hodges   *Ed* Ray Lovejoy
Mus John Cameron   *Art Dir* Peter Murton
● Peter O'Toole, Alastair Sim, Arthur Lowe, Harry Andrews, Coral Browne, Michael Bryant (Keep)

Peter Medak's *Ruling Class*, based on Peter Barnes' play of same name and scripted by the author, is a biting indictment of the so-called upper strata (British and/or other) of the old school tie thing.

Barnes' amusing but hardhitting script doesn't tell as well as it plays in recounting the rise to the House of Lords of the allegedly insane 14th Earl of Gurney, who very topically believes he's J.C. and whose unamused family wants wants him back in the nuthouse – once he's fathered the child through which they hope to get their greedy hands back on the estate the Earl has unexpectedly inherited.

Symbols are up for grabs, of course, but pic avoids usual message film pitfalls in coming across almost throughout with amusing tongue-in-cheek finesse alternating with hilarious stretches.
□ 1972: Nomination: Best Acotr (Peter O'Toole)

■ RUMBLE FISH

1983, 94 MINS, US ◇ ⑰
Dir Francis Coppola   *Prod* Fred Roos, Doug Claybourne
Scr S. E. Hinton, Francis Coppola   *Ph* Stephen H. Burum
Ed Barry Malkin   *Mus* Stewart Copeland   *Art Dir* Dean Tavoularis
● Matt Dillon, Mickey Rourke, Diane Lane, Dennis Hopper, Diana Scarwid, Vincent Spano (Zoetrope)

Rumble Fish is another Francis Coppola picture that's overwrought and overthought with camera and characters that never quite come together in anything beyond consistently interesting. Beautifully photographed in black and white by Stephen H. Burum, the picture [from the novel by S. E. Hinton] really doesn't need all the excessive symbolism Coppola tries to cram into it.

For those who want it, however, *Fish* is another able examination of teenage alienation, centered around two brothers who are misfits in the ill-defined urban society they inhabit.

One, Matt Dillon, is a young tough inspired to no good purposes by an older brother,

Mickey Rourke, once the toughest but now a bit of an addled eccentric, though remaining a hero to neighborhood thugs.

Dillon and Rourke turn in good performances as does Dennis Hopper as their drunken father and Diane Lane as Dillon's dumped-on girlfriend.

Title and a lot of the symbolism stem from Siamese fighting fish (photographed in color composite shots) which are unable to coexist with their fellows, or even an image of themselves.

■ RUNAWAY

1984, 100 MINS, US ◇ ⑰ ⊙
Dir Michael Crichton   *Prod* Michael Rachmil
Scr Michael Crichton   *Ph* John A. Alonzo   *Ed* Glenn Farr   *Mus* Jerry Goldsmith   *Art Dir* Douglas Higgins
● Tom Selleck, Cynthia Rhodes, Gene Simmons, Kirstie Alley, Stan Shaw, Joey Cramer (Tri-Star/Delphi III)

Tom Selleck, with a cop's short haircut and playing a workaday stiff who's afraid of heights, cuts a less dashing but more accessible figure in *Runaway* than in prior pictures. However, this Michael Crichton robotic nightmare is so trite that the story seems lifted from Marvel Comics, with heat-seeking bullets and a villain so bad he would be fun if the film wasn't telling us to take this near-futuristic adventure with a straight face.

Selleck's femme police partner Cynthia Rhodes, is an over-achiever and formula romantic foil to Selleck, who's a single parent raising a son. Departure may be fresh for Selleck but the comparative lack of his trademarked sardonic humor does cost the pic.

■ RUNAWAY DAUGHTER
See: Red Salute

■ RUNAWAY TRAIN

1985, 111 MINS, US ◇ ⑰ ⊙ ⑪
Dir Andrei Konchalovsky   *Prod* Menahem Golan, Yoram Globus   *Scr* Djordje Milicevic, Paul Zindel, Edward Bunker   *Ph* Alan Hume   *Ed* Henry Richardson
Mus Trevor Jones   *Art Dir* Stephen Marsh
● Jon Voight, Eric Roberts, Rebecca DeMornay, Kyle T. Heffner, John P. Ryan, T.K. Carter (Cannon/Northbrook)

Runaway Train is a sensational picture. Wrenchingly intense and brutally powerful, Andrei Konchalovsky's film rates as a most exciting action epic and is fundamentally serious enough to work strongly on numerous levels.

An exercise in relentless, severe tension, tale begins with a prison drama, then never lets up as it follows two escaped cons as they become inadvertent passengers on some diesel units that run out of control through the Alaskan wilderness.

The two desperate men who find themselves joined by a young lady, are tracked throughout their headlong journey by railroad officials bent on avoiding a crash.

Jon Voight brilliantly portrays a two-time loser determined never to return to prison after his third breakout.

Pic is based upon [an unfilmed] screenplay by Akira Kurosawa, and bears imprint of the renowned Japanese director.

Younger con Eric Roberts impressively manages to hold his own under the demanding circumstances, and Rebecca DeMornay works herself well into the essentially all-male surroundings.
□ 1985: Nominations: Best Actor (Jon Voight), Supp. Actor (Eric Roberts), Editing

■ RUNESTONE, THE

1992, 101 MINS, US ◇ ⑰ ⊙
Dir Willard Carroll   *Prod* Harry E. Gould Jr, Thomas L. Wilhite   *Scr* Willard Carroll   *Ph* Misha Suslov

Ed Lynne Southerland   *Mus* David Newman
Art Dir Jon Gary Steele
● Peter Riegert, Joan Severance, William Hickey, Tim Ryan, Mitchell Laurance, Lawrence Tierney (Hyperion/Signature)

The Runestone is a horror film with a difference. First-time writer-director Willard Carroll has brought an unusual amount of wit and intelligence to the genre, and has enlisted a classy cast.

Pic's premise [from Mark E. Rogers' novella] is as hokey as that of any other scarefest that ever came down the pike. In a Western Pennsylvania mine is found a runestone, a large 6th-century Norse rock engraved with inscrutable lettering and a carving of a monster. Group of characters whose lives become entwined with the discovery include foundation head Mitchell Laurance; his ex-flame, artist Joan Severance; her b.f., archaeologist Tim Ryan; nutty Norse expert William Hickey; clockmaker Alexander Godunov; and a film revival house manager partial to a double bill of Dreyer's *Ordet* and *Gertrud*.

Before long, Laurance, who keeps the runestone in his loft, begins behaving belligerently and then disappears altogether, to be replaced on the scene by a ghastly beast that stalks the streets of New York. As the death count quickly mounts, sarcastic detective Peter Riegert takes on the case.

As usual, Riegert brings very welcome, self-conscious humor to the proceedings, and remainder of the cast is capable and agreeably grown-up. Technically, low-budget production is highly accomplished. Filmmakers have done an expert job making mostly LA locations convince as NY, with only a bit of Gotham second unit work.

■ RUN FOR THE SUN

1956, 98 MINS, US ◇
Dir Roy Boulting   *Prod* Harry Tatelman   *Scr* Dudley Nichols, Roy Boulting   *Ph* Joseph LaShelle   *Ed* Fred Knudtsen   *Mus* Fred Steiner
● Richard Widmark, Trevor Howard, Jane Greer, Peter Van Eyck, Carlos Henning, Juan Garcia (Russ-Field)

Film is a chase feature in practically all phases. Jane Greer, news mag staffer, comes to Mexico to find Richard Widmark, writer-adventurer, to find why he's given up writing. She falls for her news quarry and then the plane in which she is flying with him crashes in the jungle.

The couple is rescued by Trevor Howard and Peter Van Eyck, a mysterious pair. When Widmark discovers their true identities as war criminals hiding out from trial and punishment, it becomes a murderous game through the jungle.

The four principals enact their roles exceptionally well. Pic is based on Richard Connell's story *The Most Dangerous Game* [filmed in 1932], but there is virtually no resemblance to that old thriller in the final results.

■ RUNNERS

1983, 110 MINS, UK ◇ ⑰
Dir Charles Sturridge   *Prod* Barry Hanson   *Scr* Stephen Poliakoff   *Ph* Howard Atherton   *Ed* Peter Coulson
Mus George Fenton   *Art Dir* Arnold Chapkis
● James Fox, Jane Asher, Kate Hardie, Robert Lang, Eileen O'Brien, Ruti Simon (Hanstoll/Goldcrest)

There are a lot of interesting ideas in *Runners*, but they're never really shaped into a coherent film. It's evident that directing *Brideshead Revisited*, the rambling TV series with which helmer Charles Sturridge secured international acclaim, was not the best education in cinematic structure.

The meandering plot follows a father, played by James Fox, who searches for his daughter long after everyone else, including his wife, have given up. Tracking her down to a car hire firm, rather than some perverse religious sect as he had expected, he is horrified at her reluctance to return.

Along the way, the father strikes up with a woman from a different social class who is hunting for her son. There are some interesting nuances in this relationship, but eventually it is the trival details of the hunt that dominate the screen.

One is two thirds of the way through the film before the question is even raised of why this girl fled. Fox and Jane Asher give as much to the roles as they can.

. . . .

■ **RUNNER STUMBLES, THE**

1979, 99 MINS, US ◇ ▼
Dir Stanley Kramer   *Prod* Stanley Kramer   *Scr* Milan Stitt   *Ph* Laszlo Kovacs   *Ed* Pembroke J. Herring   *Mus* Ernest Gold   *Art Dir* Al Sweeney Jr
● Dick Van Dyke, Kathleen Quinlan, Maureen Stapleton, Ray Bolger, Tammy Grimes, Beau Bridges (Stanley Kramer)

Based on an actual murder case in 1927 where a priest was accused of killing a nun he was in love with, subject matter is celibacy in the Catholic church, and presented in such a way that, at times, it appears like the best of the old-fashioned 1940s tear jerkers complete with overly lush sound track.

Yet *Runner* ultimately emerges as more than melodrama because director Stanley Kramer puts equal emphasis on the priest (Dick Van Dyke) and how he grapples with his love for God and this woman (Kathleen Quinlan) in his life.

Throughout, the film is paced by fine performances, especially Van Dyke as Father Rivard, Quinlan as Sister Rita and Maureen Stapleton as Van Dyke's housekeeper.

. . . .

■ **RUNNING MAN, THE**

1963, 103 MINS, UK ◇
Dir Carol Reed   *Prod* Carol Reed   *Scr* John Mortimer   *Ph* Robert Krasker   *Ed* Bert Bates   *Mus* William Alwyn
● Laurence Harvey, Lee Remick, Alan Bates, Felix Aylmer, Eleanor Summerfield (Columbia)

The story of the man who poses as dead in order that his 'widow' can pick up the insurance money is not exactly new. But director Carol Reed makes it holding entertainment.

Based on Shelley Smith's novel *Ballad of a Running Man*, John Mortimer has written a smart script, with the three principal characters well delineated. Interiors were shot at Ardmore Studios, Ireland, but main locations were lensed in Spain.

Film opens with a memorial service for Laurence Harvey, believed drowned following a glider accident. Solemnly his wife (Lee Remick) accepts the sympathy of friends. But soon Harvey turns up, larger than life, and sets in motion their plan to collect $140,000.

The claim goes through and the wife joins Harvey in Spain where she finds that he has assumed the identity of an Australian millionaire and is already plotting to pull off another insurance swindle.

Harvey has a role that suits him admirably, allowing him to run the gamut of many moods. Remick is also admirable as the young, pretty wife. Hers is a difficult part suggesting acute tension as she wavers between Harvey and Alan Bates, who has fallen for her and to whom she gives in one afternoon.

Bates, in the less flashy role of an insurance agent, ostensibly playing detective, is first-class. He plays on a quiet, yet strong, note and is a most effective contrast to the flamboyance of Harvey.

. . . .

■ **RUNNING MAN, THE**

1987, 101 MINS, US ◇ ▼ ⊙
Dir Paul Michael Glaser   *Prod* Tim Zinnemann, George Linder   *Scr* Stephen E. de Souza   *Ph* Tom Del Ruth

Ed Mark Roy Warner, Edward A. Warschilka, John Wright   *Mus* Harold Faltermeyer   *Art Dir* Jack T. Collis
● Arnold Schwarzenegger, Maria Conchita Alonso, Richard Dawson, Yaphet Kotto, Jim Brown, Jesse Ventura (Tri-Star/Taft/Barish/HBO

Pic, based on a novel by Richard Bachman (Stephen King), opens in 2017 when the world, following a financial collapse, is run by a police state, with TV a heavily censored propaganda tool of the government. Arnold Schwarzenegger is Ben Richards, a helicopter pilot who disobeys orders to fire on unarmed people during an LA food riot. He's slapped in prison and escapes 18 months later with pals Yaphet Kotto and Marvin J. McIntyre.

Producer-host of the popular TV gameshow *The Running Man* Damon Killian (Richard Dawson) orders Richards up as his next contestant and he is duly captured and made a runner in this lethal (and fixed) gladiatorial contest for the masses.

Format works only on a pure action level, with some exciting, but overly repetitious, roller-coaster style sequences of runners hurtling into the game through tunnels on futuristic sleds. Bloated budget was $27 million.

Schwarzenegger sadistically dispatches the baddies, enunciating typical wisecrack remarks (many repeated from his previous films), but it's all too easy, despite the casting of such powerful presences as Jim Brown and former wrestlers Jesse Ventura and Prof. Toru Tanaka.

. . . .

■ **RUNNING ON EMPTY**

1988, 116 MINS, US ◇ ▼ ⊙
Dir Sidney Lumet   *Prod* Amy Robinson, Griffin Dunne   *Scr* Naomi Foner   *Ph* Gerry Fisher   *Ed* Andrew Mondshein   *Mus* Tony Mottola   *Art Dir* Philip Rosenberg
● Christine Lahti, River Phoenix, Judd Hirsch, Martha Plimpton, Jonas Arby (Lorimar/Double Play)

The continuing shock waves emitted by the cataclysmic events of the 1960s are dramatized in fresh and powerful ways in *Running On Empty*, a complex, turbulent tale told with admirable simplicity. Film successfully operates on several levels – as study of the primacy of the family unit, an anguished teen romance, a coming-of-age story and a look at what happened to some political radicals a generation later.

The two central adult characters are Weathermen-like urban bombers who have been living underground since 1971.

Arthur and Annie Pope (Judd Hirsch and Christine Lahti) have been on the FBI's most-wanted list since bombing a university defense research installation, an act that blinded a janitor. Their life since then has required them to be as unobtrusively middle-class as possible, and to be able to pick up and leave for a new destination on a moment's notice.

Son Danny (River Phoenix), now 17, is quickly recognized by the local music teacher as an exceptionally promising pianist, and is nudged along toward an eventual audition for Juilliard. At the same time, Danny slowly commences an edgy but potent first love with the teacher's daughter Lorna (Martha Plimpton).

Superior screenplay keeps the focus intimate, forcing the head of the family to face the prospect of the family's breakup so that his son can pursue his own talents and interests.

□ 1988: Nominations: Supp. Actor (River Phoenix), Original Screenplay

. . . .

■ **RUNNING SCARED**

1986, 106 MINS, US ◇ ▼ ⊙
Dir Peter Hyams   *Prod* David Foster, Lawrence Turman   *Scr* Gary DeVore, Jimmy Huston   *Ph* Peter Hyams

Ed James Mitchell   *Mus* Rod Temperton   *Art Dir* Albert Brenner
● Gregory Hines, Billy Crystal, Steven Bauer, Darlanne Fleugel, Joe Pantoliano, Jimmy Smits (M-G-M/Turman-Foster)

Set in dead of winter in Chicago, *Running Scared* is an ultra-hip cop picture, shot in gritty style by Peter Hyams, that plays like a combination of *Beverly Hills Cop* and *Hill Street Blues*.

Gregory Hines and Billy Crystal are undercover cops too cool for words, guys who risk their necks by the hour without a hint of fear, chase women together at night and feel smugly superior to their cohorts in the force. Hines and Crystal are concerned particularly with aborting the career of aspiring Spanish godfather Jimmy Smits, a ruthless thug whose favorite film undoubtedly would be *Scarface*.

Plot is no more original or eventful than an average police TV show, so it must sink or swim on the moment-by-moment cleverness of the dialog and the behavioral talents of Hines and Crystal. Fortunately, these elements prove formidable. Nonstop banter between the two stars is rowdy, intimate, natural and often very funny. Hyams keeps most of it fresh, including the action ending, staged within one of Chicago's architectural spectacles, the cavernous, glass-enclosed Illinois State Building.

. . . .

■ **RUN OF THE ARROW**

1957, 86 MINS, US ◇ ▼
Dir Samuel Fuller   *Prod* Samuel Fuller   *Scr* Samuel Fuller   *Ph* Joseph Biroc   *Ed* Gene Fowler Jr   *Mus* Victor Young   *Art Dir* Albert S. D'Agostino, Jack Okey
● Rod Steiger, Sarita Montiel, Brian Keith, Ralph Meeker, Jay C. Flippen, Charles Bronson (RKO)

Yankee-hatting Southerner goes west after the Civil War to join the Sioux in their uprising against the US. Slow in takeoff, action becomes pretty rough at times.

Production is strong on visual values to bolster Samuel Fuller's sometimes meandering screenplay highlighting Rod Steiger as Southerner taken into the tribe after he survives the run-of-the-arrow torture ordeal. Forceful use is made of Indians and their attacks on the whites to give unusual color to feature, which additionally has Sarita Montiel, Spanish actress, in as Steiger's Indian wife [dubbed by Angie Dickinson].

On debit side, Steiger frequently lapses from Southerner into Irish dialect, and footage occasionally is impeded by irrelevant sequences. Steiger is never sympathetic and character itself is not clearly defined, though actor endows his character with vigor.

. . . .

■ **RUN SILENT, RUN DEEP**

1958, 93 MINS, US ▼
Dir Robert Wise   *Prod* Harold Hecht   *Scr* John Gay   *Ph* Russell Harlan   *Ed* George Boemler   *Mus* Franz Waxman   *Art Dir* Edward Carrere
● Clark Gable, Burt Lancaster, Jack Warden, Brad Dexter, Don Rickles, Nick Cravat (United Artists/Hecht-Hill-Lancaster)

Run Silent, Run Deep is a taut, exciting drama of submarine warfare in the Pacific during the Second World War. Observant viewers may recognize overtones of *Moby Dick* and *The Caine Mutiny* in the screenplay from the novel by Capt Edward L. Beach. Clark Gable is seen as a staunchly-dedicated, hard-driving submarine commander with a single-minded purpose – to seek out and destroy a Japanese Akikaze destroyer which he holds responsible for sinking his previous sub.

His one-track dedication leads to charges of cowardice and incompetency which results in what seems like a 'mutiny' on the part of Burt

R

Lancaster, his tough executive officer who is resentful of Gable for taking over the command he had expected and who is in disagreement with Gable's tactics.

The submarine action is particularly effective and provides a sense of participation as the men sweat out depth charges and fire from enemy destroyers and planes. The miniature photography is especially good.

■ RUN WILD, RUN FREE

1969, 100 MINS, UK ◇
Dir Richard C. Sarafian   *Prod* John Danischewsky
Scr David Rook   *Ph* Wilkie Cooper   *Ed* Geoffrey Foot
Mus David Whitaker   *Art Dir* Ted Tester
● John Mills, Sylvia Syms, Bernard Miles, Mark Lester, Gordon Jackson, Fiona Fullerton (Irving Allen)

This sensible and sensitive film, is handled with care and obvious affection. Heavy on the melodrama and profound in the study of characters through outstanding performances by John Mills and Mark Lester, feature is an honestly moving film.

Young Lester registers an excellent performance as an introverted, psychosomatically mute lad growing up on the moors of England.

Lester's meeting with a wild, white colt concurrent with his initial acquaintance with moorman Mills, a retired army colonel, provides a setup for interaction beween the three that is basis for the film.

David Rook's film adaptation of his own novel [*The White Colt*] is particularly good in that it sentimentalizes without getting sticky and his concise dialog and sensible placement of incidents eliminates any story lag.

■ RUSH

1991, 120 MINS, US ◇ ⓥ ⊙
Dir Lili Fini Zanuck   *Prod* Richard D. Zanuck   *Scr* Pete Dexter   *Ph* Kenneth MacMillan   *Ed* Mark Warner
Mus Eric Clapton   *Art Dir* Paul Sylbert
● Jason Patric, Jennifer Jason Leigh, Sam Elliott, Max Perlich, Gregg Allman, William Saddler (Zanuck)

Moral ambiguity that has plagued America since the 1960s is given a harrowing probe in this tale of undercover narcs who succumb to the temptation in their midst. Head-swiveling directorial debut of Lili Fini Zanuck lays out a tough masculine scenario [based on Kim Wozencraft's book] in a way that is always emotionally riveting.

A bearded Jason Patric stars as Jim, an earthy, direct, Texas narcotics cop who sees a spark in rookie Kristen (Jennifer Jason Leigh), a fresh-scrubbed comer who's serious about making a difference. Kristen soon finds Jim has a disturbing way of getting too involved in his work.

Kirsten tries to draw the line, but she's already too emotionally involved with Jim, who's become her lover, and the strange, secret and intoxicating rituals of drug buys and the underworld.

Set in the early 1970s, when America was struggling to reinvent itself after the shattering events of the 1960s, pic depicts a culture in which morality is one big gray area. *Rush* benefits from outstanding lead performances and an uncannily accurate picture of its time and place.

■ RUSH TO JUDGMENT

1967, 122 MINS, US
Dir Emile de Antonio   *Prod* Mark Lane, Emile de Antonio
Scr Mark Lane   *Ph* Robert Primes   *Ed* Daniel Drasin
● (Impact Films/Judgment)

Lawyer Mark Lane, whose 'brief for the defense' of Lee Harvey Oswald was in the no 1 non-fiction best-seller position for several months, converted his material into a film of the same name, *Rush to Judgment*. For many it will seem a convincing pic, opening up severe doubts about the thoroughness and even integrity of the Warren Commission's [investigation into the assassination of President Kennedy].

Rush to Judgment is sober and unexcited, making its points with quiet and controlled definiteness, sans hysterics or frenzied accusations. Lane and collaborator Emile de Antonio have let their material present itself, utilizing wryness as their main weapon to sow seeds of doubt.

Point of the film is neatly summed up by one interviewee: 'The Warren Commission, I think, had to report in their book what they wanted the world to believe. . .It had to read like they wanted it to read. They had to prove that Oswald did it alone.'

■ RUSSIA HOUSE, THE

1990, 123 MINS, US ◇ ⓥ ⊙
Dir Fred Schepisi   *Prod* Paul Maslansky, Fred Schepisi
Scr Tom Stoppard   *Ph* Ian Baker   *Ed* Peter Honess
Mus Jerry Goldsmith   *Art Dir* Richard MacDonald
● Sean Connery, Michelle Pfeiffer, Roy Scheider, James Fox, Klaus Maria Brandauer, Ken Russell (Pathe)

John Le Carre's glasnost-era espionage novel has been turned into intelligent adult entertainment, but somber tone, utter lack of action and sex, and complexity of plot tilts this mainly to upscale audience.

The film is the first US non-coproduction to be shot substantially in the USSR.

Sean Connery plays Barley Blair, a boozy, inconoclastic London publisher to whom a highly sensitive manuscript is sent via a Moscow book editor named Katya (Michelle Pfeiffer). Intercepted by British authorities, the text, authored by a leading physicist, purports to lay out the facts about Soviet nuclear capabilities in devastating detail.

Over his protestations, Blair is sent to Moscow in his role as prospective publisher to meet the writer, the mysterious Dante (Klaus Maria Brandauer), determine his reliability and put more questions to him. His intermediary is the beautiful Katya with whom he falls in love.

As the flawed, unreliable publisher, Connery is in top form. Pfeiffer's Katya is a much more guarded figure. Her Russian accent proves very believable but she has limited notes to play.

Most of the supporting roles are one-dimensional British or US intelligence types, but James Fox, Roy Scheider, John Mahoney and Michael Kitchen embody them solidly and with wit when possible. Director Ken Russell amusingly hams it up as an impishly aggressive spy master. Brandauer is strong as always in his brief appearance as the charismatic Dante.

■ RUSSIANS ARE COMING! THE RUSSIANS ARE COMING!, THE

1966, 124 MINS, US ◇ ⓥ
Dir Norman Jewison   *Prod* Norman Jewison
Scr William Rose   *Ph* Joseph Biroc   *Ed* Hal Ashby, J. Terry Williams   *Mus* Johnny Mandel   *Art Dir* Robert F. Boyle
● Carl Reiner, Eva Marie Saint, Alan Arkin, Brian Keith, Jonathan Winters, Theodore Bikel (Mirisch/United Artist)

The Russians Are Coming! The Russians Are Coming! is an outstanding cold-war comedy depicting the havoc created on a mythical Massachusetts island by the crew of a grounded Russian sub.

Nathaniel Benchley's novel *The Off-Islanders* got its title from New England slang for summer residents, herein top-featured Carl Reiner, wife Eva Marie Saint, and their kids, Sheldon Golomb and Cindy Putnam.

Basically, story concerns aftermath of an accidental grounding of the Russian sub by overly curious skipper Theodore Bikel, who sends Alan Arkin ashore in charge of a landing party to get a towing boat. The wild antics which follow center around sheriff Brian Keith, sole resident who manages to keep cool except when arguing with Paul Ford, firebrand civil defense chief (self appointed) who arms himself to repel the 'invasion' with a sword and an American Legion cap.

Arkin, in his film bow, is absolutely outstanding as the courtly Russian who kisses a lady's hand even as he draws a gun.

English music hall vet Tessie O'Shea, also in film debut, is very good as the island's telephone operator who contributes to the spread of the 'invasion' rumors, and her scenes with Reiner, in which they are lashed together and attempt to escape, is a comedy highlight.

□ 1966: Nominations: Best Picture, Actor (Alan Arkin), Adapted Screenplay, Editing

■ RUTHLESS

1948, 104 MINS, US ⓥ
Dir Edgar G. Ulmer   *Prod* Arthur S. Lyons   *Scr* S.K. Lauren, Gordon Kahn   *Ph* Bert Glennon   *Ed* Francis D. Lyon   *Mus* Werner Janssen   *Art Dir* Frank Sylos
● Zachary Scott, Louis Hayward, Diana Lynn, Sydney Greenstreet, Lucille Bremer, Martha Vickers (Producing Artists)

Despite a sextet of name players, *Ruthless* is a victim of cliched and outmoded direction and of weary dialog to which no actor could do justice.

Practically the entire yarn stems from the mental reflections of Louis Hayward, one-time partner of powerful financier Zachary Scott. Early sequences show how Scott moved from a poor environment to a position of prestige and wealth by a 'what-makes-Zachary-run' technique. Picture boils down to a character study of Scott.

Performances are handicapped by the direction of Edgar G. Ulmer. Adaptation from the Dayton Stoddart novel, *Prelude to Night*, is involved and confusing. Plot's denouement is also telegraphed long before the finale.

Hayward contribs a fair interpretation of Scott's associate, who eventually breaks from him. Diana Lynn, in a dual role, is wistful and appealing as a pawn in Scott's affections. Sydney Greenstreet, cast as a utilities magnate who's ousted by Scott, tends to overact.

■ RUTHLESS PEOPLE

1986, 93 MINS, US ◇ ⓥ ⊙
Dir Jim Abrahams, David Zucker, Jerry Zucker
Prod Michael Peyser   *Scr* Dale Launer   *Ph* Jan DeBont
Ed Arthur Schmidt   *Mus* Michel Colombier
Art Dir Donald Woodruff
● Danny DeVito, Bette Midler, Judge Reinhold, Helen Slater, Anita Morris, Bill Pullman (Touchstone)

Ruthless People is a hilariously venal comedy about a kidnapped harridan whose rich husband won't pay for her return.

In short, impoverished couple Judge Reinhold and Helen Slater kidnap Bel-Air princess Bette Midler because her mercenary husband, played by Danny DeVito, has ripped off Slater's design for spandex miniskirts.

There is much, much more to it than that, as screenwriter Dale Launer cleverly builds twist upon complication to a point where practically everyone in the cast is writhing in frustration and mystification as they wonder whether their latest opportunistic scheme is going to work.

Midler, when first glimpsed, is an absolute fright who looks like a cross between Cyndi Lauper and Divine. After terrorizing her kidnappers, she embarks upon an energetic self-improvement program, and not surprisingly emerges with the upper hand.

RYAN'S DAUGHTER

1970, 194 MINS, UK ◇ ▼ ⊙
Dir David Lean   *Prod* Anthony Havelock-Allan
Scr Robert Bolt   *Ph* Freddie Young   *Ed* Norman Savage
Mus Maurice Jarre   *Art Dir* Stephen Grimes
● Robert Mitchum, Trevor Howard, Sarah Miles, Christopher Jones, John Mills, Leo McKern (M-G-M/Faraway)

Ryan's Daughter is a brilliant enigma, brilliant, because director David Lean achieves to a marked degree the daring and obvious goal of intimate romantic tragedy along the rugged geographical and political landscape of 1916 Ireland; an enigma, because overlength of perhaps 30 minutes serves to magnify some weaknesses of Robert Bolt's original screenplay, to dissipate the impact of the performances, and to overwhelm outstanding photography and production.

Robert Mitchum gives a stolid performance as an aloof widower, a schoolteacher returning from a Dublin trip to whom Sarah Miles pours out her conception of love. United in marriage, pair never achieve a full sexual-spiritual union – he is 20 years her senior, she is immature. Arrival of shell-shocked Christopher Jones to take over the British occupation garrison cues an illicit affair.

As the townsfolk become more scandalized by the affair between Jones and Miss Miles, she is eventually stripped and shorn as an adulterer and a wrongly-convicted informer.

Trevor Howard gives an assured performance as a knowing local priest; John Mills might be a technical tour de force as a Quasimodo-like town idiot, but the character is overdrawn and often jarring to storytelling; other supporting players, many drawn from the Irish stage, are very good.
□ 1970: Best Supp. Actor (John Mills), Cinematography.
□ Nominations: Best Actress (Sarah Miles), Sound

• •

Ss

SABOTAGE

1936, 76 MINS, UK ▼ ⊙
Dir Alfred Hitchcock   *Prod* Michael Balcon   *Scr* Charles Bennett, Ian Hay, Helen Simpson, E.V.H. Emmett
Ph Bernard Knowles   *Ed* Charles Frend   *Mus* Louis Levy
Art Dir Otto Werndorff, Albert Jullion
● Sylvia Sydney, Oscar Homolka, Desmond Tester, John Loder, Joyce Barbour, Matthew Boulton (Gaumont-British)

Competent and experienced hand of the director is apparent throughout this production, which is a smart one and executed in a business-like manner from start to finish.

But the story, somehow, seems outmoded. Joseph Conrad was never a dramatist, and his novels were dependent altogether upon his genius for descriptive writing. Film play [from Conrad's novel *The Secret Agent*] is, therefore, more or less obscure in plot.

It revolves around a secret organization which hires people to plant bombs in crowded sections of London, but the reason for their desire to systematically blow up innocent persons is not made clear. Film thus just misses being great.

Oscar Homolka's performance of the harassed victim of the sabotage organization into whose clutches he has fallen is a brilliant piece of character acting. Sylvia Sydney seems to have been circumscribed by plot deficiency.

• •

SABOTEUR

1942, 100 MINS, US ▼ ⊙
Dir Alfred Hitchcock   *Prod* Frank Lloyd   *Scr* Peter Viertel, Joan Harrison, Dorothy Parker   *Ph* Joseph Valentine   *Ed* Otto Ludwig   *Mus* Frank Skinner
Art Dir Jack Otterson
● Priscilla Lane, Robert Cummings, Norman Lloyd, Otto Kruger, Murray Alper, Alma Kruger (Universal)

Saboteur is a little too self-consciously Hitchcock. Its succession of incredible climaxes, its mounting tautness and suspense, its mood of terror and impending doom could have been achieved by no one else. That is a great trib- ute to a brilliant director. But it would be a greater tribute to a finer director if he didn't let the spectator see the wheels go round, didn't let him spot the tricks – and thus shatter the illusion, however momentarily.

Like all Hitchcock films, *Saboteur* is excellently acted. Norman Lloyd is genuinely plausible as the ferret-like culprit who sets the fatal airplane factory on fire. Robert Cummings lacks variation in his performance of the thick-headed, unjustly accused worker who crosses the continent to expose the plotters and clear himself; but his directness and vigor partly redeem that short-coming.

There is the customary Hitchcock gallery of lurid minor characters, including a group of circus freaks, a saboteur whose young son has the macabre habit of breaking his toys, and a monstrous butler with a sadistic fondness for a blackjack.

• •

SABOTEUR, CODE NAME – 'MORITURI', THE

See: *Morituri*

• •

SABRINA

(UK: *Sabrina Fair*)

1954, 112 MINS, US ▼ ⊙
Dir Billy Wilder   *Prod* Billy Wilder   *Scr* Billy Wilder, Samuel Taylor, Ernest Lehman   *Ph* Charles Lang
Ed Arthur Schmidt   *Mus* Frederick Hollander
Art Dir Hal Pereira, Walter Tyler

● Humphrey Bogart, Audrey Hepburn, William Holden, Walter Hampden, John Williams, Martha Hyer (Paramount)

A slick blend of heart and chuckles makes *Sabrina* a sock romantic comedy. Script is long on glibly quipping dialog, dropped with a seemingly casual air, and broadly played situations. The splendid trouping delivers them style. Leavening the chuckles are tugs at the heart.

Basically, the plot's principal business is to get Audrey Hepburn, daughter of a chauffeur in service to an enormously wealthy family, paired off with the right man. She's always been in love with playboy William Holden, but ends up with Humphrey Bogart, the austere, businessman brother.

The fun is in the playing. Bogart is sock as the tycoon with no time for gals until he tries to get Hepburn's mind off Holden. The latter sells his comedy strongly, wrapping up a character somewhat offbeat for him. Hepburn again demonstrates a winning talent for being 'Miss Cinderella'.
□ 1954: Best B&W Costume Design
□ Nominations: Best Director, Actress (Audrey Hepburn), Screenplay, B&W Cinematography, B&W Art Direction, Costume Design (Edith Head)

• •

SABRINA FAIR

See: *Sabrina*

• •

SADIE MCKEE

1934, 90 MINS, US ▼
Dir Clarence Brown   *Prod* Lawrence Weingarten
Scr John Meehan   *Ph* Oliver T. Marsh   *Ed* Hugh Wynn
Mus William Axt (dir.)   *Art Dir* Cedric Gibbons, Fredric Hope, Edwin B. Willis
● Joan Crawford, Gene Raymond, Franchot Tone, Edward Arnold, Esther Ralston, Akim Tamiroff (M-G-M)

Sadie McKee is the Cinderella theme all over again, plus an s.a. angle through the stellar player of the titular role encountering three major romances in the persons of the featured male trio in support – Franchot Tone, Gene Raymond and Edward Arnold.

Basically it's the story [from the *Liberty* magazine serial by Vina Delmar] of the housemaid (Joan Crawford) who marries the boss of the manor, but not until after he comes humbly to her, and after she has experienced turbulent affairs with the other two.

That her major attachment to Arnold is obviously a mercenary marriage is sufficiently well built up to make it almost sympathetic, in view of the goading of the supercilious young master (Tone) of the house hold in which Sadie's mother is the cook.

Raymond is cast as the No. 1 sweetie who, according to Tone, is a no-good guy, but who is the major romance interest even after he runs out with a vaudeville single (well played by Esther Ralston).

The playing is expert throughout, so much so that in its realism it perhaps makes the star suffer a bit, particularly at the hands of Arnold whose bluff, constantly inebriated performance almost steals the picture.

• •

SADIE THOMPSON

1928, 94 MINS, US ⊗ ▼ ⊙
Dir Raoul Walsh   *Scr* Raoul Walsh, C. Gardner Sullivan
Ph Oliver Marsh, George Barnes, Robert Kurrle   *Ed* C. Gardner Sullivan   *Art Dir* William Cameron Menzies
● Lionel Barrymore, Gloria Swanson, Blanche Friderici, Raoul Walsh, Charles Lane, Florence Midgley (United Artists)

Program credits make no reference to *Rain* the play, the picture having been adapted from the 'original story' by W. Somerset Maugham. However, the presentation conveys the idea of *Rain* by a stereoptican downpour effect prior to and through the opening titles.

The scene in which Hamilton enters Sadie's room during the night is not more than barely hinted at, finishing with Lionel Barrymore standing at the door. For a few previous feet is shown his mental struggle to overcome Sadie's physical attraction for him, but nothing more than a faltering hand reaching out to stroke her hair is flashed.

Sadie's costume, her struggle to articulate above and over a wad of rum and her familiarity with the Marines is sufficient to establish her character at the beginning. But there's likely to be a wide difference of opinion on Gloria Swanson's interpretation of the role.

Barrymore's performance is okay and Raoul Walsh, assuming the double duties of actor and director, does well by both. He plays O'Hara with whom Sadie eventually sails away. Charles Lane makes a minor bit count, and Blanche Friderici rises to her occasion late in the running.

□ 1927/8: Nominations: Best Actress (Gloria Swanson), Cinematography

● ●

■ SAFE PLACE, A

1971, 94 MINS, US ◇
Dir Henry Jaglom   *Prod* Bert Schneider   *Scr* Henry Jaglom   *Ph* Dick Kratina   *Ed* Pieter Bergema
● Tuesday Weld, Orson Welles, Jack Nicholson, Philip Proctor, Gwen Welles, Dov Lawrence (BBS/Columbia)

Tuesday Weld is the child-like woman in whose silly pussycat consciousness the backward, forward, now it's now, now it isn't now action takes place. In her one clear decision she is casually cruel to the young man (Philip Proctor) who adores her while receptive to the curiously charming drop-by-without-calling stud played by Jack Nicholson.

Weld has many scenes in the park with an itinerant magician, supposedly a father image. Of the many weirdo roles played in his time by Orson Welles this may be the prize example.

Unrelated to the story in Weld's head is hippie girl's rambling account of her feelings adroitly soliloquized by Gwen Welles. This is rather touching, quite lucid and uninterrupted, though wildly neurotic.

All this deliberate experimentation puts a heavy burden upon the viewer. Hardly a scene is fully played out, hardly an explanation provided. It would seem that writer-director Henry Jaglom has plunged in over his own depth. It is like a gymnastic symphony conductor over-personalizing the music.

● ●

■ SAFETY LAST

1923, 77 MINS, US ⊗ Ⓥ
Dir Fred Newmeyer, Sam Taylor   *Scr* Hal Roach, Sam Taylor, Tim Whelan, H.M. Walker   *Ph* Walter Lundin   *Ed* Thomas J. Crizer   *Art Dir* Fred Guiol
● Harold Lloyd, Mildred Davis, Bill Strother, Noah Young, Westcott B. Clarke, Mickey Daniels (Roach)

This Harold Lloyd high-class low comedy has thrills as well as guffaws. It leads up to big shrieks through Lloyd apparently climbing the outside wall to the top or 12th floor of a building, probably in Los Angeles. This bit is chockerblock with trick camera work but skilfully done.

The comedy business of the department store where Lloyd is a clerk nearly equals the remainder.

Lloyd as a small town boy leaves his sweetheart in the country, going to the city and obtains a $15-a-week position as a counter jumper. Back home the girl receives a little cheap piece of jewelry and believes Lloyd has made the great success he said he would in the big city. Upon the advice of her mother she goes there.

Lloyd, in an attempt to have her think he is the boss instead of a clerk, wanders into all kinds of complications. It leads up to the building climbing, a plan suggested by the clerk to the general manager as a means of obtaining publicity for the firm.

● ●

■ SAHARA

1943, 85 MINS, US Ⓥ ⊙
Dir Zoltan Korda   *Prod* Harry Joe Brown   *Scr* John Howard Lawson, Zoltan Korda   *Ph* Rudolph Mate   *Ed* Charles Nelson   *Mus* Miklos Rozsa
● Humphrey Bogart, Bruce Bennett, Lloyd Bridges, Rex Ingram, J. Carrol Naish, Dan Duryea (Columbia)

Story background displays Libyan desert fighting in 1942, when the British were hurled back to the El Alamein line. It vividly focuses attention on exploits of an American tank crew headed by Humphrey Bogart to escape the onrushing Nazis, and battles against desert sands and lack of water.

Picture gets off to a fast start, with Bogart heading his 28-ton tank south on the desert in drive to regain the British lines. Along the way he picks up six Allied stragglers; Sudenese soldier Rex Ingram with latter's Italian prisoner, J. Carrol Naish; and a downed Nazi pilot (Kurt Krueger). Bogart pushes on with his assorted passengers to reach a water hole at an old desert fort which provides a trickle but enough to sustain the group. Nazi motorized battalion also heads for the water supply.

Script [adapted by James O'Hanlon from a story by Philip MacDonald] is packed with pithy dialog, lusty action and suspense, and logically and well-devised situations avoiding ultra-theatrics throughout. It's an all-male cast, but absence of romance is not missed in the rapid-fire unfolding of vivid melodrama.

□ 1943: Nominations: Best Supp. Actor (J. Carrol Naish), B&W Cinematography, Sound

● ●

■ SAHARA

1983, 104 MINS, US ◇ Ⓥ
Dir Andrew V. McLaglen   *Prod* Menahem Golan, Yoram Globus   *Scr* James R. Silke   *Ph* David Gurfinkel   *Mus* Ennio Morricone   *Art Dir* Luciano Spadoni
● Brooke Shields, Lambert Wilson, Horst Buchholz, John Rhys-Davies, Ronald Lacey, John Mills (Cannon)

Coproducer Menahem Golan reportedly hatched the idea for *Sahara* when Mark Thatcher, son of the British prime minister, disappeared in the desert during an international car rally.

An old fashioned B-grade romantic adventure, directed in pedestrian fashion by Andrew V. McLaglen, *Sahara* is lamentably low on excitement, laughs and passion.

Screenplay, set in 1927, has Brooke Shields as heiress to a car company who promises her dying daddy that she'll win the world's toughest endurance rally driving the car he designed. Wily Brooke disguises herself as a man, complete with wig and moustache.

Soon after the race starts, she discards her disguise and reverts to Brooke the beautiful, only to receive a beating and a mouthful of sand when she's captured by Arab thug John Rhys-Davies. Handsome sheikh Lambert Wilson saves her from his clutches and falls mildly in love with her.

Director McLaglen and most everyone else treat it all tongue in cheek.

● ●

■ SAIGON

See: Off Limits

● ●

■ SAILOR FROM GIBRALTAR, THE

1967, 89 MINS, UK
Dir Tony Richardson   *Prod* Oscar Lewenstein, Neil Hartley   *Scr* Christopher Isherwood, Don Magner, Tony Richardson   *Ph* Raoul Coutard   *Ed* Anthony Gibbs   *Mus* Antoine Duhamel   *Art Dir* Marilena Aravantinou
● Jeanne Moreau, Ian Bannen, Vanessa Redgrave, Zia Moyheddin, Hugh Griffith, Orson Welles (Lopert Pictures)

The novels of Marguerite Duras are frequently no more than lengthy short stories – and not too strong on the narrative side. With such interpreters as Christopher Isherwood and Tony Richardson (neither famous for clarity of intent) plus Don Magner, the ensuing screenplay is replete with repetitive sequences.

A Britisher (Ian Bannen) and his mistress (Vanessa Redgrave) are on an Italian holiday which quickly becomes evident will be their last. She's still hungry for him but he can't stand her but isn't brave enough to send her away.

When a mysterious woman on a yacht (Jeanne Moreau) crosses their path, his greed (both sexual and practical) provides the impetus to ditch his mistress and make a fast pass at the yachtswoman.

Orson Welles is wasted on a brief bit as an information peddler and Hugh Griffith is only slightly better as a white hunter and guide. Redgrave is touching and believably irritating in her brief role. The rest of the cast walk through their parts like somnambulists.

● ●

■ SAILOR'S RETURN, THE

1978, 112 MINS, UK ◇
Dir Jack Gold   *Prod* Otto Plaschkes   *Scr* James Saunders   *Mus* Carl Davis
● Tom Bell, Shope Shodeinde, Mick Ford, Paola Dionisotti, George Costigan, Clive Swift (Ariel/NFFC)

Set in the early reign of Queen Victoria (1819-1901), story, adapted from David Garnett's novel, is about a sailor who returns home to England with a bride from the black Kingdom of Dahomey in West Africa.

It's her dowry, a treasure of pearls, that sets them up in business with an inn for thirsty passers-by in a lush English countryside. But her color and the presence of a black son set them off from intolerant neighbors, despite some support from friends in the area.

Conflicts with the sailor's sister, the local pastor (who preaches hell fire), and prejudiced visitors to the inn lead to slow alienation in a foreign land.

Tom Bell scores as the sailor Targett, and Shope Shodeinde (a native Nigerian) as the African princess brings credibility but hardly sparkle to Tulip, a lively flower that must slowly wither in a foreign climate with the accumulation of disappointments and unawaited hostility.

● ●

■ SAILOR TAKES A WIFE, THE

1946, 92 MINS, US
Dir Richard Whorf   *Prod* Edwin H. Knopf   *Scr* Chester Erskine, Anne Morrison Chapin, Whitfield Cook   *Ph* Sidney Wagner   *Ed* Irvine Warburton   *Mus* Johnny Green   *Art Dir* Cedric Gibbons, Edward Carfagno
● Robert Walker, June Allyson, Hume Cronyn, Audrey Totter, Eddie 'Rochester' Anderson (M-G-M)

The Sailor Takes a Wife stage play has been given light, broad screen treatment. Production isn't elaborate but has polish, the direction is smooth, and the cast gets the best from the comedy situations.

Robert Walker and June Allyson head the funning, making the antics and complications around which the plot revolves delightful. Story is on the light side and laughs are mostly situation, but Richard Whorf's direction keeps it on the move. Plot deals with a sailor and a girl who meet and marry, all in one evening, and subsequent efforts to adjust themselves to marital status.

Bride's first disappointment comes when her husband is discharged almost immediately, leaving her with a civilian instead of the hero she expected. Further complications develop when Walker, searching for a job, becomes entangled innocently with a romantically-inclined foreign femme menace, brightly played by Audrey Totter.

▪ **SAILOR WHO FELL FROM GRACE WITH THE SEA, THE**

1976, 104 MINS, UK ◇ ⓥ
Dir Lewis John Carlino   *Prod* Martin Poll   *Scr* Lewis John Carlino   *Ph* Douglas Slocombe   *Ed* Anthony Gibbs   *Mus* John Mandel   *Art Dir* Ted Haworth
● Sarah Miles, Kris Kristofferson, Jonathan Kahn, Margo Cunningham, Earl Rhodes, Paul Tropea (Avco Embassy)

With a quartet of fine characters and performances, *The Sailor Who Fell from Grace with the Sea* could have ventured just about anywhere – except where writer-director Lewis John Carlino takes it in an effort to remain faithful to Yukio Mishima's novel.

Cultural differences still remain in this increasingly homogenized world and the prime problem with *Sailor* is trying to transfer decidedly Oriental ideas about honor, order and death into an English countryside.

Mishima's novel was about a Japanese widow who falls in love with a sailor. At first attracted to the sailor as an honorable symbol, her 13-year-old son defends him before his gang of idealistic schoolmates. But when the sailor leaves the sea to marry, the boy and his gang feel betrayed and plot to kill him to restore his purity.

On film, the story won't settle down with these upper-class young English lads.

▪ **SAINT IN LONDON, THE**

1939, 72 MINS, UK ⓥ
Dir John Paddy Carstairs   *Prod* William Sistrom   *Scr* Lynn Root, Frank Fenton   *Ph* Claude Friese-Greene   *Ed* Douglad Robertson   *Mus* Harry Acres (dir.)   *Art Dir* C. Wilfred Arnold
● George Sanders, Sally Gray, David Burns, Athene Seyler, Gordon McLeod, Henry Oscar (RKO)

This is a workmanlike job. Previous *Saint* pix, with George Sanders in his standard role, were made in Hollywood.

Plot [from the story *The Million Pound Day* by Leslie Charteris] revolves around an organization of international counterfeiters. The Saint aids Scotland Yard in rounding up a gang that's ready to foist upon the public $5 million worth of banknotes printed in England for a Continental country. The Saint's chief assistants are Sally Gray and David Burns. Burns almost steals the picture with another inimitable hick crook role. Sanders is excellent, as usual.

Direction is alert, with some photography being excellent.

▪ **SAINT JACK**

1979, 112 MINS, US ◇ ⓥ
Dir Peter Bogdanovich   *Prod* Roger Corman   *Scr* Howard Sackler, Paul Theroux, Peter Bogdanovich   *Ph* Robby Muller   *Ed* William Carruth   *Art Dir* David Ng
● Ben Gazzara, Denholm Elliott, James Villiers, Joss Ackland, Rodney Bewes, Lisa Lu (New World/Playboy/Shoals Creek-Copa de Oro)

Shot entirely on location in Singapore, the film (produced by Roger Corman, who gave Bogdanovich his start of *The Wild Angels* in 1964) is extremely well crafted, finely acted, and conjures up a positively intriguing milieu.

At bottom line, though, it's essentially a character study – Ben Gazzara excels as a pimp with a heart of gold – told in a mood that begins with a twinkling-eyed bawdiness, but becomes progressively more sombre and even nihilistic.

Based on Paul Theroux's novel, the film is

laid in 1971, putting its exclusive focus on Gazzara, an expatriate US hustler-type who jumps ship and uses the cover of a local provision broker to operate a freelance prostitution ring.

The script is a good one, gutsy and sometime very funny.

▪ **SAINT JOAN**

1957, 110 MINS, US ⓥ
Dir Otto Preminger   *Prod* Otto Preminger   *Scr* Graham Greene   *Ph* Georges Perinal   *Ed* Helga Cranston   *Mus* Mischa Spoliansky   *Art Dir* Roger Furse
● Jean Seberg, Richard Widmark, Richard Todd, Anton Walbrook, John Gielgud, Felix Aylmer (United Artists)

Otto Preminger showed courage when he decided to make G.B. Shaw's *Saint Joan* into a film and to star an unknown of next to no theatrical experience in the title role. Jean Seberg of Marshalltown, Iowa, makes a sincere effort, but her performance rarely rises above the level of the Iowa prairie.

Seberg is helped most by her appealing looks. She has a fresh, unspoiled quality and she photographs well. But Shaw's Joan is more than just an innocent country maiden.

In vivid contrast, Preminger surrounds her with a supporting cast that performs brilliantly. Richard Widmark plays the idiot Dauphin with gusto though he at times overacts the part. Richard Todd as Dunois; Anton Walbrook as Cauchon, the Bishop of Beauvais, and Felix Aylmer, the Inquisitor.

It is John Gielgud who stands out with a brilliant performance as the politically-minded Earl of Warwick, determined to get Joan to the stake, though contemptuous of the Church's winded arguments of 'heretic' vs 'witch'.

Graham Greene wrote the screenplay, and while it is somewhat toned down, and probably less anti-clerical than the Shaw original, it still retains the essentials of the Shaw classic.

▪ **SALLY IN OUR ALLEY**

1931, 77 MINS, UK
Dir Maurice Elvey   *Scr* Basil Dean   *Ph* Miles Malleson, Alma Reville, Archie Pitt
● Gracie Fields, Ian Hunter, Florence Desmond, Fred Groves, Gibb McLaughlin (Associated Talking Pictures/Radio)

Gracie Fields doesn't exactly suggest sufficient sympathy to hold the romantic lead, but her eccentric singing and dialect-gagging records well.

Story [from the play *The Likes of 'Er* by Charles McEvoy] tells how a Lancashire girl refuses to marry because her boy friend is reported killed in the war, although actually he isn't dead but pretends to be because he's crippled. She makes a hit serving and singing in a coffee shop.

Atmosphere is good generally. Introduction of the songs is resourceful and some of the gags are quite good. Dialog is pert on English comedy lines. But the whole canvas is very small aand the footage seems very long.

Fields is just Fields as in vaude, but lacking aggressiveness. Ian Hunter has more repose and acting ability than the rest, while newcomer Florence Desmond troupes well in an utterly unsympathetic role.

▪ **SALLY, IRENE AND MARY**

1938, 86 MINS, US
Dir William A. Seiter   *Prod* Darryl F. Zanuck   *Scr* Harry Tugend, Jack Yellen   *Ph* Peverell Marley   *Ed* Walter Thompson   *Mus* Arthur Lange (dir.)   *Art Dir* Bernard Herzbrun, Rudolph Sternad
● Alice Faye, Tony Martin, Fred Allen, Jimmy Durante, Gregory Ratoff, Joan Davis (20th Century-Fox)

Sally, Irene and Mary is another in the Darryl F. Zanuck formula of vaudscreen musicals,

skillfully blending the variety components and dovetailing them into an amiable entertainment [from an original story by Karl Tunberg and Don Ettlinger, suggested by a play by Edward Dowling and Cyrus Wood].

Fred Allen marks his second big league picture work since he became a radio name. He foils with and for Jimmy Durante, both proving an efective team throughout with a running gag sequence.

It's the vocal prowess of Tony Martin and Alice Faye, Mr and Mrs in private life and the romance interest here, that does much to sustain the interest.

Gregory Ratoff as an amorous baron, the gangling Joan Davis with her standard comedy hokum, notably a gypsy sequence, Durante as a white wing gone impresario, and a runaway show boat (finale) are the comedy highlights. Plus of course Allen's own stacato line-reading, cast as a shoestring agent. He's foiled principally in this respect by Louise Hovick, nee Gypsy Rose Lee, doing a sleeker, brunet Mae West.

▪ **SALOME**

1922, 75 MINS, US ⊗
Dir Charles Bryant   *Scr* Peter M. Winters   *Ph* Charles Van Enger   *Mus* Ulderico Marcelli   *Art Dir* Natacha Rambova
● Nazimova, Rose Dione, Mitchell Lewis, Nigel De Brulier (Nazimova/Allied)

A highly fantastic *Salome* is that which Nazimova presents on the screen. It is far from the *Salome* Oscar Wilde penned.

The picture is done with a decidedly modernistic touch. Picturesquely it is very pretty as to lightings, setting and photography, but there ends about all that can be said in praise. *Nazimova in Facial Expressions*, with Salome as the background, would have been much better billing for the picture.

Other than the facial contortions there is little to the picture, likewise little to her costume. The heroic figures are given a decided appearance of effeminacy and the slaves of color are beefy instead of muscular. The settings, however, are well worked out and make a really worth background for the action, such as it is.

▪ **SALOME**

1953, 102 MINS, US ◇ ⓥ
Dir William Dieterle   *Prod* Buddy Adler   *Scr* Harry Kleiner   *Ph* Charles Lang   *Ed* Viola Lawrence   *Mus* George Duning, Daniele Amfitheatrof   *Art Dir* John Meehan
● Rita Hayworth, Stewart Granger, Judith Anderson, Cedric Hardwicke, Alan Badel, Charles Laughton (Columbia/Beckworth)

The story by Jesse L. Lasky Jr and the screenplay by Harry Kleiner, change and embroider the Biblical tale of the girl who danced for King Herod and caused the beheading of John the Baptist. More their own interpretation than a factual chronicle of the religious story, it is a vehicle especially slanted for Rita Hayworth.

Film opens by establishing King Herod's superstitious fear of John the Baptist and his protection of the prophet, despite the insistence of his queen, Herodias, that the holy man be slain for talking against the throne. Opening also finds Salome, Herod's stepdaughter, banished from Rome because Caesar's nephew wants to marry her. During the trip back to Galilee, she vents her spite against all Romans on Commander Claudius, played by Stewart Granger, even though they are attracted to each other. Salome finds Galilee in a state of unrest and, egged on by her wicked mother, Herodias, tries to enlist Claudius' aid in doing away with the prophet.

Hayworth, who has never been better pho-

S

tographed, injects excellent dramatic values and wears the clinging Roman costumes to advantage. Her dance, staged by Valerie Bettis, packs plenty of s.a. Granger gives an easy, assured masculine portrayal to his central role, and when he and Miss Hayworth are on together the picture has a decided lift.

• •

■ **SALT OF THE EARTH**

1954, 94 MINS, US ⊗
Dir Herbert J. Biberman *Prod* Paul Jarrico *Scr* Michael Wilson *Ph* [uncredited] *Ed* [uncredited] *Mus* Sol Kaplan
● Rosaura Revueltas, Juan Chacon, Will Geer, David Wolfe, Mervin Williams, David Sarvis (Independent/International Union of Mine, Mill & Smelter Workers)

Salt of the Earth is a good, highly dramatic and emotion-charged piece of work that tells its story straight. It is, however, a propaganda picture which belongs in union halls rather than theatres.

It is a bitter tale that Michael Wilson has concocted and the large cast acts it out with a conviction that obviously didn't require much prompting. The story concerns Mexican miners in a small New Mexican mining community, Zinc Town. A series of mine accidents prompts a strike. The company attempts to break it via acts of intimidation that include arrest and brutality.

Director Herbert J. Biberman was one of the Unfriendly Ten who served a five-months jail sentence for contempt of Congress. Producer Paul Jarrico also was in trouble with Congress.

Yet as a piece of film artistry, *Salt* achieves moments of true pictorial excellence. Rosaura Revueltas, a Mexican actress playing the wife of the strike leader, gives a taut, impressive performance that has real dimension. Juan Chacon, a union leader in real life, turns in a creditable acting job.

Biberman's direction achieves distinctive quality. He concentrates on misery and violence and anger with a stark determination and a flair for realism that is designed to do much more than rouse sympathy.

• •

■ **SALT ON OUR SKIN**

1993, 110 MINS, GERMANY/FRANCE/CANADA ◇ ⊗ ⊙
Dir Andrew Birkin *Prod* Bernd Eichinger, Martin Moszkowicz *Scr* Andrew Birkin, Bee Gilbert *Ph* Dietrich Lohmann *Ed* Dagmar Hirtz *Mus* Klaus Doldinger *Art Dir* Jean-Baptiste Tard
● Greta Scacchi, Vincent D'Onofrio, Anais Jenneret, Petra Berndt, Claudine Auger, Rolf Illig (Constantin)

Salt on Our Skin is an old-fashioned weepie about mismatched lovers whose rare, passionate encounters over 30 years make both their lives worth living.

Couple's odyssey is told in flashback and v.o. by the 40ish Greta Scacchi. Refreshing twist here is that Scacchi follows her heart as well as her intellect.

Shortly after discovering true ecstasy in Vincent D'Onofrio's arms in the late 1950s, Scacchi discovers Camus, Sartre and – bingo! – Simone de Beauvoir's *The Second Sex*. When D'Onofrio proposes, Scacchi assures him it could never work: she's a restless intellectual, he's a hunky fisherman, and a future cannot be built on sex alone. They part but end up trysting every so often.

Based on Benoite Groult's 1988 bestseller [*Les vaisseaux du coeur*], which was hailed for its frank descriptions of female sexual desire, conventional pic relies on the two leads' personalities and does not innovate. The heat and devotion between the real-life couple are convincing. (They also starred in Gillian Armstrong's 1991 *Fires Within*.)

• •

■ **SALT TO THE DEVIL**
See: Give Us This Day

• •

■ **SALUTE OF THE JUGGER, THE**
(US: The Blood of Heroes)

1989, 102 MINS, AUSTRALIA ◇ ⊗
Dir David Peoples *Prod* Charles Roven *Scr* David Peoples *Ph* David Eggby *Ed* Richard Francis-Bruce *Mus* Todd Boekelheide *Art Dir* John Stoddart
● Rutger Hauer, Joan Chen, Vincent D'Onofrio, Anna Katarina, Delroy Lindo, Hugh Keays-Byrne (Kings Road)

It's the first feature directed by screenwriter David Peoples (*Blade Runner*, *Leviathan*) and he's provided himself with a murky, familiar screenplay about a band of wandering 'juggers.' They're futuristic gladiators, led by the deeply scarred Sallow (Rutger Hauer), who was once a member of the League, the ruling elite, but who was banished over a misdemeanor. Now Sallow is determined to challenge the League's juggers and regain his position.

His own team (which includes Vincent D'Onofrio, Delroy Lindo and Anna Katarina) is augmented by a feisty peasant girl, Kidda (Joan Chen), who proves invaluable in the climactic confrontation with the League's team, which is headed by the giant Gonzo (Max Fairchild).

Plot development is slim. Much of running time is given over to the game itself, which seems to have no rules except that the winning team places the skull of a dog atop a pointed stick.

Hauer, whose character loses an eye halfway through the pic, gives Sallow a certain presence, but doesn't extend himself. Chen comes off best with a graceful performance as Kidda: her moves in the game sequences are often quite beautiful in the midst of all the ugliness.

Pic was shot on desert locations near the mining town of Coober Pedy, South Australia, as well as in studios in Sydney.

• •

■ **SALVADOR**

1986, 123 MINS, US ◇ ⊗ ⊙
Dir Oliver Stone *Prod* Gerald Green, Oliver Stone *Scr* Oliver Stone, Richard Boyle *Ph* Robert Richardson *Ed* Claire Simpson *Mus* Georges Delerue *Art Dir* Bruno Rubeo
● James Woods, James Belushi, Michael Murphy, John Savage, Elpedia Carrillo, Tony Plana (Hemdale)

The tale of American photojournalist Richard Boyle's adventures in strife-torn Central America, *Salvador* is as raw, difficult, compelling, unreasonable, reckless and vivid as its protagonist.

James Woods portrays the real-life Boyle, who at the outset is shown to be at his lowest ebb as a virtual bum and professional outcast in San Francisco.

With no particular prospects, he shanghais fun-loving buddy James Belushi for the long drive down to (El) Salvador, where Woods has left behind a native girlfriend and where he thinks he might be able to pick up some freelance work.

The film has an immediacy, energy and vividness that is often quite exciting, and the essential truth of much of what director Oliver Stone has put on display will prove bracing for many viewers.
☐ 1986: Nominations: Best Actor (James Woods), Original Screenplay

• •

■ **SAME TIME, NEXT YEAR**

1978, 119 MINS, US ◇ ⊗ ⊙
Dir Robert Mulligan *Prod* Walter Mirisch, Morton Gottlieb *Scr* Bernard Slade *Ph* Robert Surtees *Ed* Sheldon Kahn *Mus* Marvin Hamlisch *Art Dir* Henry Bumstead
● Ellen Burstyn, Alan Alda, Ivan Bonar (Universal)

Same Time, Next Year is a textbook example of how to successfully transport a stage play to the big screen. The production of Bernard Slade's play, sensitively directed by Robert Mulligan, is everything you'd want from this kind of film. And it features two first class performances by Ellen Burstyn and Alan Alda.

The picture opens in 1951 at a resort in northern California. Burstyn, a 24-year-old Oakland housewife, and Alda, a 27-year-old accountant from New Jersey, meet over dinner, get along and have a fling. The next morning they wake up in the same bed, talk about what's happened, realize that while they're both happily married with six children between them, they're in love.

They make a pact to meet at the same resort every year, which is just what they do and is just what the film is about. We see the two every five or six years as they adjust to the changes time brings.

What always remains through the years is the deep affection the two share. It's nice to see a film about two people who like each other this deeply.
☐ 1978: Nominations: Best Actress (Ellen Burstyn), Adapted Screenplay, Cinematography, Song ('The Last Time I Felt Like This')

• •

■ **SAMMY AND ROSIE GET LAID**

1987, 100 MINS, UK ◇ ⊗ ⊙
Dir Stephen Frears *Prod* Tim Bevan, Sarah Radclyffe *Scr* Hanif Kureishi *Ph* Oliver Stapleton *Ed* Mick Audsley *Mus* Stanley Myers *Art Dir* Hugo Lyczyc Wyhowski
● Shashi Kapoor, Frances Barber, Claire Bloom, Ayub Khan Din, Roland Gift, Wendy Gazelle (Working Title)

Cynical and brutally unsentimental in outlook, *Sammy and Rosie Get Laid*, brings the force of an accelerated cinematic attack to bear upon its complex thematic juxtaposition of sexual warfare, cross-cultural dislocation, racism and the ruthlessness of power.

With relentless momentum director Stephen Frears unfolds the story of Sammy, (Ayub Khan Din), the hedonistic, thoroughly English son of a prominent Pakistani politician. Sammy, who scrapes out a living as an accountant, lives in a dangerous and decaying black neighborhood with his wife Rosie (Frances Barber), a sexually adventurous feminist journalist.

Change enters their lives with the arrival of Rafi (Shashi Kapoor), Sammy's long-lost father who has been forced to flee his political enemies in Pakistan. Rafi attempts to buy his way back into the affection of his son and that of a beautiful and sensitive Englishwoman, Alice (Claire Bloom) whom he also cruelly abandoned in his self-centered quest for power in the East.

Frears levitates the film's harsh realism with a fantastical counterpoint in touches like the ghost of a tortured labor leader who haunts Rafi from the outset, and a band of gypsy buskers who serenade the ongoing anarchy.

• •

■ **SAMMY GOING SOUTH**
(US: A Boy Ten Feet Tall)

1963, 128 MINS, UK ◇
Dir Alexander Mackendrick *Prod* Michael Balcon *Scr* Denis Cannan *Ph* Edwin Hillier *Ed* Jack Harris *Mus* Tristram Cary
● Edward G. Robinson, Fergus McClelland, Constance Cummings, Harry H. Corbett, Paul Stassino, Zia Moyheddin (British Lion/Bryanston Seven Arts)

Pic is based on an uneasy, incredible idea [from a novel by W.H. Canaway]. A 10-year-old youngster (Fergus McClelland) is orphaned when his parents are killed in an air raid during the Suez crisis. In a blur he remembers that he has an Aunt Jane in Durban and that Durban is in the South. So he sets out, armed only with a toy compass.

He meets a Syrian peddler who sees in the kid a chance of a reward from Aunt Jane. He meets a rich American tourist but escapes her greedy clutches. Not until he meets up with a grizzled old diamond smuggler (Edward G. Robinson) does the film flicker into some spark of human interest. The old man and the moppet strike up a splendid friendship.

Mackendrick's films usually strike an attitude and have intuition on points of views. Relationships between his key characters are usually more clearly defined and worked on than in this. With the exception of Robinson, looking like a slightly junior Ernest Hemingway, and Paul Stassino, as a glib crook of a guide, the others are cardboard.

....

■ **SAMSON AND DELILAH**

1950, 120 MINS, US ◇ ⓥ ⊙
Dir Cecil B. DeMille   *Prod* Cecil B. DeMille   *Scr* Jesse L. Lasky Jr, Fredric M. Frank   *Ph* George Barnes   *Ed* Anne Bauchens   *Mus* Victor Young   *Art Dir* Hans Dreier, Walter Tyler
● Hedy Lamarr, Victor Mature, George Sanders, Angela Lansbury, Henry Wilcoxon, Russ Tamblyn (Paramount)

Cecil B. DeMille has again dipped into the Bible for his material, made appropriately dramatic revisions in the original, and turned up with a DeMille-size smash.

The scriptwriters have woven from the abbreviated biblical telling of the Samson legend [from original treatments by Harold Lamb and Vladimir Jabotinsky] a lusty action story with a heavy coating of torrid-zone romance. Dozens of bit players and extras in tremendous, sweeping sets give size to the picture.

Victor Mature fits neatly into the role of the handsome but dumb hulk of muscle that both the Bible and DeMille make of the Samson character. Hedy Lamarr never has been more eye-filling and makes of Delilah a convincing minx. George Sanders gives a pleasantly light flavor of satirical humor to the part of the ruler, while Henry Wilcoxon is duly rugged as the military man.

The picture is claimed to have cost $3 million and looks well like it might have run considerably more than that.
☐ 1950: Best Color Art Direction, Color Costume Design (Edith Head)
☐ Nominations: Best Color Cinematogrphy, Scoring of a Dramatic Picture, Special Effects
....

■ **SAND CASTLE, THE**

1961, 70 MINS, US ◇
Dir Jerome Hill   *Prod* Jerome Hill   *Scr* Jerome Hill   *Ph* Lloyd Ahern   *Ed* Julia Knowlton, Henri A. Sundquist   *Mus* Alec Wilder
● Barrie Cardwell, Laurie Cardwell, George Dunham, Maybelle Nash, Erica Speyer (De Rochemont/Noel)

This delightful, fanciful look at the world and its people as we might like them to be is the complete work of Jerome Hill who previously made the notable documentary *Albert Schweitzer*.

A little boy and his sister (Barrie and Laurie Cardwell) start the day's activities as their mother leaves them on the beach to play. Slowly but in ever-increasing numbers, other people begin to arrive: the painter (George Dunham) who must change his picture as the people obscure his view; the eccentric old lady (Maybelle Nash) who brings her bird in its cage and sits beneath a large canopy; the angler, the diver, the fat man and the blonde who worship the sun.

Oblivious to them all, the boy starts to build a large sand castle in the shape of a fort, helped by his sister who fetches driftwood and shells. The others gather round and admire his work. There is no dialog, only incidental and amusing conversation.

Nothing is overstated and none of the characters is overdrawn or derivative. The mood is always one of gentleness, charm and tranquility. As the afternoon ends everyone goes home and the boy and his sister fall asleep by their castle to dream (in color) of being within its walls where they meet cut-out puppets (also the work of Hill) of the people who were on the beach.

....

■ **SAN DEMETRIO–LONDON**

1943, 93 MINS, UK
Dir Charles Frend   *Prod* Michael Balcon   *Scr* Robert Hamer, Charles Frend   *Ph* Ernest Palmer   *Ed* Eily Boland   *Mus* John Greenwood
● Walter Fitzgerald, Mervyn Johns, Ralph Michael, Robert Beatty, Gordon Jackson (Ealing)

Whether wittingly or accidentally, the presentation of this epic tale of the British Merchant Marine omits the customary cast of characters in the screen credits. Thus does it emphasize the genuineness of the personalities concerned in the unfolding of a gripping drama.

So one prefers to believe the man who plays the skipper of the *San Demetrio* is Captain Waite in person, just as the tough, nameless Texan who joins the tanker in Galveston is a tough Texan imbued with the idea of Britain's needing help to win the war.

If the chief engineer – who performs miracles in the half-flooded, fire-swept engine room by not only restarting the engines, but by cooking a pailful of potatoes in live steam from a leaking valve – is not a c.e. in real life, it really doesn't make any difference. And this goes for all of them, from the bosun to the kid apprentice whose first voyage it is.

Much credit must go to Michael Balcon, the producer, and Charles Frend, who directed. How much F. Tennyson Jesse's official account on salvaging the *San Demetrio*, after she had been abandoned for two days and nights 900 miles from her port, helped Robert Hamer and the director in their writing of the script can only be surmised, but the dialog is unvaryingly authentic.

....

■ **SANDERS OF THE RIVER**

1935, 98 MINS, UK ⓥ
Dir Zoltan Korda   *Prod* Alexander Korda   *Scr* Lajos Biro, Jeffrey Dell   *Ph* Georges Perinal   *Ed* Charles Crichton   *Mus* Mischa Spoliansky   *Art Dir* Vincent Korda
● Leslie Banks, Paul Robeson, Nina Mae McKinney, Robert Cochran, Martin Walker, Allan Jeayes (London/United Artists)

Story of an African colony is an immense production, done for the greater part with deft direction, played with distinction by two main characters. Leslie Banks and Paul Robeson carry the greater part of this tale of a British commissioner who rules an African sector through commanding both fear and respect.

The story [from an original by Edgar Wallace] is simple. Sanders (Banks) is in charge of a large section in the British African possessions. He makes a minor chief of Bosambo (Robeson), an engaging fugitive from prison, revealing the excellence of his judgment of men. Mofolabo, known as 'the old king', is in an inaccessible section of the district and gives much trouble. When Sanders goes out on leave to get married, rum runners send word through the district that Sanders is dead, inciting the king to fresh depredations. But Sanders has gone only as far as the coast when he hears of the trouble, and comes back.

There are some nicely staged mob scenes, mostly ceremonials, with a remarkable male muscle dancer and a small regiment of natives who appear to be genuine. Robeson gets two of the songs [lyrics by Arthur Wimperis], with the third going to Nina Mae McKinney, a lullaby set against a humming harmonic background.

....

■ **SANDLOT, THE**

1993, 101 MINS, US ◇ ⓥ ⊙
Dir David Mickey Evans   *Prod* Dale de la Torre, William S. Gilmore   *Scr* David Mickey Evans, Robert Gunter   *Ph* Anthony Richmond   *Ed* Michael A. Stevenson   *Mus* David Newman   *Art Dir* Chester Kaczenski
● Tom Guiry, Mike Vitar, Patrick Renna, Chauncey Leopardi, Karen Allen, James Earl Jones (20th Century-Fox)

The Sandlot is yet another wallow in the coming-of-age stakes circa 1962. Sweet and sincere, the film is also remarkably shallow, rife with incident and slim on substance.

Scotty Smalls (Tom Guiry) arrives in some quiet piece of Americana and is recruited into the neighborhood's ad-hoc baseball team despite – to use the boys' most withering reference – the fact he 'plays like a girl'.

Scotty's mentor is Benny Rodriguez (Mike Vitar), the most charismatic and best player on the block. Running beneath the surface is the promise of some cataclysmic event, foreshadowed in voiceover by the older Scotty (silently played by Arliss Howard and voiced by director David Mickey Evans, both uncredited) 30 years later.

The Sandlot pretends to be about something when it really just strings together loosely connected vignettes. Worse, the setpieces are familiar retreads. The adult roles provide solid cameos for James Earl Jones and Karen Allen.

....

■ **SAND PEBBLES, THE**

1966, 193 MINS, US ◇ ⓥ
Dir Robert Wise   *Prod* Robert Wise   *Scr* Robert Anderson   *Ph* Joseph MacDonald   *Ed* William Reynolds   *Mus* Jerry Goldsmith   *Art Dir* Boris Leven
● Steve McQueen, Richard Attenborough, Richard Crenna, Candice Bergen, Marayat Andriane, Mako (Argyle/Solar/20th Century-Fox)

Out of the 1926 political and military turmoil in China, producer-director Robert Wise has created a sensitive, personal drama, set against a background of old style US Navy gunboat diplomacy. *The Sand Pebbles*, based on the novel by Richard McKenna, is a handsome production, boasting some excellent acting characterizations.

Steve McQueen looks and acts the part he plays so well – that of a machinist's mate with nine years of navy service. Richard Crenna likewise is authentic as the gunboat captain, a young lieutenant who speaks the platitudes of leadership with a slight catch in his throat, due to lack of practical experience.

The title derives from a language perversion of San Pablo, formal name of the gunboat on Yangtze river patrol. Among the crew is Richard Attenborough, very believable in his role as a sailor who falls in love with newcomer Marayat Andriane in a tragic bi-racial romance. Her performance is sensitive.

The major drawback to the film as a whole is a surfeit of exposition, mainly in the second half. Every scene is in itself excellent, but unfortunately the overall dramatic flow of the pic suffers in the end.
☐ 1966: Nominations: Best Picture, Actor (Steve McQueen), Supp. Actor (Mako), Color Cinematography, Color Art Direction, Editing, Original Music Score, Sound

....

■ **SANDPIPER, THE**

1965, 115 MINS, US ◇ ⓥ
Dir Vincente Minnelli   *Prod* Martin Ransohoff   *Scr* Dalton Trumbo, Michael Wilson   *Ph* Milton Krasner

Ed David Bretherton   *Mus* Johnny Mandel
Art Dir George W. Davis, Urie McCleary
● Elizabeth Taylor, Richard Burton, Eva Marie Saint,
Charles Bronson, Robert Webber, James Edwards
(M-G-M/Filmways)

The Sandpiper is the story of a passing affair between an unwed nonconformist and a married Episcopalian minister who is headmaster of a private boys school attended by femme's nine-year-old son. Original by Martin Ransohoff, who produced, is trite and often ponderous in its philosophizing by the two principals, and picture is further burdened by lack of any fresh approach. [Story adaptation by Irene and Louis Kamp.]

Under Vincente Minnelli's leisurely but dramatic direction, the screenplay opens on Elizabeth Taylor as a budding artist whose young son is taken away from her after lad's brush with the law and sent to the school run by Richard Burton. Latter becomes interested in her although ostensibly happily wed to Eva Marie Saint, mother of his twin teenage sons.

Burton probably comes off best with a more restrained performance, although Taylor plays well enough a role without any great acting demands.

Saint gets the most out of a comparatively brief appearance, most of her drama confined to her reaction upon Burton's confession. Morgan Mason, son of Pamela and James Mason, makes a nice impression as Taylor's son.

□ 1965: Best Song ('The Shadow of Your Smile')

■ SANDS OF IWO JIMA

1949, 110 MINS, US ⊛ ⊙
Dir Allan Dwan   *Prod* Edmund Grainger   *Scr* Harry Brown, James Edward Grant   *Ph* Reggie Lanning
Ed Richard L. Van Enger   *Mus* Victor Young
● John Wayne, John Agar, Adele Mara, Forrest Tucker, Wally Cassell, Richard Webb (Republic)

This is a vast saga [by Harry Brown] of a marine platoon whose history is traced from its early combat training through its storming of Iwo Jima's beaches to the historic flag-raising episode atop the sandy atoll. It's loaded with the commercial ingredients of blazing action, scope and spectacle, but it falls short of greatness because of its sentimental core and its superficial commentary on the war.

Best portions of this pic are the straight battle sequences, many of which were made up of footage taken at the actual fighting at Tarawa and Iwo Jima.

John Wayne stands head and shoulders above the rest of the cast, and not only physically, as the ruthlessly efficient marine sergeant. He draws a powerful portrait of a soldier with the job of making plain joes into murdering machines.

□ 1949: Nominations: Best Actor (John Wayne), Motion Picture Story, Editing, Sound

■ SANDS OF THE KALAHARI

1965, 119 MINS, UK ◊
Dir Cy Endfield   *Prod* Cy Endfield, Stanley Baker
Scr Cy Endfield   *Ph* Erwin Hillier   *Ed* John Jympson
Mus John Dankworth   *Art Dir* Seamus Flannery, George Provis
● Stuart Whitman, Stanley Baker, Susannah York, Harry Andrews, Theodore Bikel, Nigel Davenport (Paramount/Levine)

Cy Endfield, co-producer, director and scripter of the long film (made almost entirely on location in Africa), wisely makes the camera as important as anyone in the cast, emphasizing the savagery that is throughout. Although Endfield has been lucky with his casting, some members too quickly betray symptoms of scenery chewing.

A planeload of assorted types crashes in the desert and the rest of the film deals with their efforts to survive. It's some time before a villain is unveiled and, even then, the viewer's faith gets a few shakes. Susannah York, as the only female in the cast, gets plenty of exposure. Stuart Whitman, a gunhappy survivalist, and Stanley Baker, a nondescript loser, are the only main characters. Unbilled but colorful are assorted natives, animals and insects.

Entertainment, pure and simple [from a novel by William Mulvihill], was evidently what the filmmakers aimed for and that's the target they hit.

■ SANDWICH MAN, THE

1966, 95 MINS, UK ◊ ⊛
Dir Robert Hartford-Davis   *Prod* Peter Newbrook
Scr Michael Bentine, Robert Hartford-Davis   *Ph* Peter Newbrook   *Ed* Peter Taylor   *Mus* Mike Vickers
● Michael Bentine, Dora Bryan, Harry H. Corbett, Bernard Cribbins, Diana Dors, Ian Hendry (Titan)

The Sandwich Man is like a documentary in drag. Michael Bentine, who wrote the screenplay with the director, Robert Hartford-Davis, seeks to give a picture of London and some of the wayout, curious behaviour of its inhabitants through the eyes of a sandwich-board man who, wandering the streets, has a load of opportunity of observing, and of getting implicated. Not a bad idea and, filmed on location entirely, it gives director and cameraman Peter Newbrook a swell chance of bringing London to life. But in the countdown, a film has either got to be a feature pic or a 'doc' primarily.

A loosely scribed romance between a young car salesman and a model, and the fact that on this day Bentine's prize racing pigeon is competing in an important race are the only two highly slim 'plotlines'. For the remainder, Bentine (dressed as a dude sandwich-board man) wanders around observing the odd things happening around him.

Bentine has an amiable personality that deserves further screen exposure.

■ SAN FRANCISCO

1936, 115 MINS, US ⊛ ⊙
Dir W.S. Van Dyke   *Prod* John Emerson, Bernard Hyman   *Scr* Anita Loos   *Ph* Oliver T. Marsh   *Ed* Tom Held   *Mus* Herbert Stothart   *Art Dir* Cedric Gibbons, Arnold Gillespie, Harry McAfee
● Clark Gable, Jeanette MacDonald, Spencer Tracy, Jack Holt, Jessie Ralph, Ted Healy (M-G-M)

An earthquake noisy and terrifying, is *San Francisco*'s forte. Quake occurs after more than an hour and up to then the picture is distinguished chiefly for its corking cast and super-fine production.

Story basically follows the outline traced previously by Warner's *Frisco Kid* and Goldwyn's *Barbary Coast* [both 1935] although this one tends more to the musical through the constant singing of Jeanette MacDonald.

Lone incongruous note is the remarkable survival of Clark Gable after a whole wall has toppled over on him. His survival is necessary, to complete the picture, but it might have been made easier to believe.

As were James Cagney and Edward G. Robinson before him, Gable is 'king' of the Barbary Coast, and like his predecessors, his reformation is the essence of the plot [story by Robert Hopkins]. Only this guy is tougher; it takes the earthquake to cure him. As Blackie Norton he operates a prosperous gambling joint and beer garden. The closest friend of this godless soul is a priest, who doesn't try to reform Blackie but always hopes for the best.

MacDonald enters as a Denver choir singer who's in Frisco looking for work. From the show at Blackie Norton's she graduates to grand opera under the sponsorship of Blackie's political rival.

Spencer Tracy plays a priest, and it's the most difficult role in the picture. His slang – he calls Gable 'mug' and 'sucker' good naturedly – is the sort usually associated with men of lesser spiritual quality.

□ 1936: Best Sound Recording.
□ Nominations: Best Director, Actor (Spencer Tracy), Original Story, Assistant Director (Joseph Newman)

■ SAN QUENTIN

1946, 66 MINS, US
Dir Gordon M. Douglas   *Prod* Martin Mooney
Scr Lawrence Kimble, Arthur A. Ross, Howard J. Green   *Ph* Frank Redman   *Ed* Marvin Coil   *Mus* Paul Sawtell   *Art Dir* Albert S. D'Agostino, Lucius O. Croxton
● Lawrence Tierney, Barton MacLane, Harry Shannon, Marian Carr, Carol Forman, Richard Powers (RKO)

Gordon M. Douglas whips together this tale of reformation leagues within prisons with plenty of movement, spotting action and development without a slow moment. Lawrence Tierney, as a prisoner of San Quentin, now reformed and just discharged from honorable army service, acquits himself capably, making role believable all the way.

Plot frames its melodramatics around efforts of Harry Shannon, San Quentin warden, to keep his prisoners' welfare league going in the face of opposition. Taking a group of prisoners to San Francisco to speak to a newspaper club, Shannon is wounded and others killed when a supposedly reformed inmate arranges an escape. To clear the warden's plan and make life better for majority of prisoners Tierney goes on a manhunt for Barton MacLane, the killer.

■ SANTA CLAUS

1985, 112 MINS, US ◊ ⊛ ⊙
Dir Jeannot Szwarc   *Prod* Ilya Salkind, Pierre Spengler   *Scr* David Newman   *Ph* Arthur Ibbetson   *Ed* Peter Hollywood   *Mus* Henry Mancini   *Art Dir* Anthony Pratt
● David Huddleston, Dudley Moore, John Lithgow, Judy Cornwell, Christian Fitzpatrick, Carrie Kei Heim (Salkind/Santa Claus)

Santa Claus is a film for children of all ages, but will probably skew best toward infancy or senility.

Oddly enough, even Scrooge himself might adore the first 20 minutes when *Santa* develops a charming attitude, lovely special effects and a magical feeling that the audience may indeed be settling down for a warm winter's eve.

After that, however, the picture becomes *Santa Meets Son of Flubber* or something in a mad rush to throw in whatever might appeal to anybody. Bah, humbug.

David Huddleston is a perfect Claus, first introduced several centuries ago as a woodcutter who delights in distributing Christmas gifts to village children. Wondrously, Mr and Mrs Claus awake to discover they are at the North Pole, where their arrival is excitedly hailed by elves led by Dudley Moore.

Moore manufactures a batch of bad toys and, sorry to have disappointed Santa, flees to 20th Century New York City, where he ends up working in a crooked toy factory run by John Lithgow, saddled with an absolutely horrible, cigar-sucking performance as a greedy corporate monster.

■ SAPPHIRE

1959, 92 MINS, UK ◊ ⊛
Dir Basil Dearden   *Prod* Michael Relph   *Scr* Janet Green, Lukas Heller   *Ph* Harry Waxman   *Ed* John D. Guthridge   *Mus* Philip Green   *Art Dir* Carmen Dillon
● Nigel Patrick, Yvonne Mitchell, Michael Craig, Paul Massie, Bernard Miles, Earl Cameron (Rank)

Sapphire is a well-knit pic showing how the police patiently track down a murderer. But, though obviously inspired by 1958's outbreak of color-bar riots in London and Nottingham, it ducks the issue, refusing to face boldly up to the problem. It eventually adds up merely to another whodunit.

Victim of a savage murder in a London open space is attractive music student Sapphire (Yvonne Buckingham). The girl is revealed as having a dual personality. As well as being a student, she is also a good-time girl with a love for the bright lights. She is pregnant after an affair with a young man with a brilliant career as architect awaiting him.

Director Basil Dearden has a very effective cast. Nigel Patrick is fine as a suave, polite but ruthlessly efficient cop. Michael Craig, his assistant, is equally good as a less tolerant man who, for some unexplained reason, loathes coloured people. But perhaps the best performance of all is that of Earl Cameron as an intelligent, tolerant Negro doctor who is the brother of the slain girl. Cameron brings immense dignity to a small role.

....

■ **SARABAND**

See: Saraband for Dead Lovers

....

■ **SARABAND FOR DEAD LOVERS**
(US: Saraband)

1948, 96 MINS, UK ◇
Dir Basil Dearden, Michael Relph *Prod* Michael Balcon
Scr John Dighton, Alexander Mackendrick *Ph* Douglas Slocombe *Ed* Michael Truman *Mus* Alan Rawsthorne
Art Dir Jim Morahan, William Kellner
● Stewart Granger, Joan Greenwood, Flora Robson, Francoise Rosay, Anthony Quayle, Frederick Valk (Ealing)

Colorful production, magnificent settings and costumes enhanced by unobtrusive use of Technicolor and a powerful melodramatic story of court intrigue at the House of Hanover in the early 18th century, add up to a firstrate piece of hokum entertainment.

Taken from Helen Simpson's novel, the screenplay sincerely captures the atmosphere of the period. It tells the poignant story of the unhappy Princess Dorothea, compelled to marry against her will the uncouth Prince Louis to strengthen his title to the kingship of England.

Without undue sentiment, and with emotion in the right key, the plot unfolds against the fascinating background of the Hanoverian court, with its intrigue and tragedies, its romances and miseries.

Reality is established by the excellent characterization of a well-chosen cast. Stewart Granger, as the Swedish Count Konigsmark, gives a performance that ranks with his best. Joan Greenwood is charming and colorful as the hapless Dorothea. Flora Robson is merciless as the arch intriguer at the court.
□ 1949: Nomination: Best Color Art Direction

....

■ **SARAFINA!**

1992, 115 MINS, SOUTH AFRICA ◇ ⊛
Dir Darrell James Roodt *Prod* Anant Singh
Scr William Nicholson, Mbongeni Ngema *Ph* Mark Vicente *Ed* Peter Hollywood, Sarah Thomas
Mus Stanley Myers *Art Dir* David Barkham
● Leleti Khumalo, Whoopi Goldberg, Miriam Makeba, John Kani, Mbongeni Ngema (Distant Horizon/Ideal)

Opening up *Sarafina!* for the screen has given the popular musical a dimension it never had onstage. Powerfully lensed on location in Soweto, emotionally and politically impassioned piece effectively registers the anti-apartheid movement's anger and hope in an infectious musical context, and has been imaginatively reconceived for film.

Mbongeni Ngema's theatrical production, a Broadway hit in 1988, was set principally at the township high school. Institution still serves as the symbolic center of the action.

Pic clicks in as students try to pursue such normal activities as getting an education and putting on a show under the strictures of emergency rule. Inspiring teacher Whoopi Goldberg gives an amusingly apt history lesson, but casting a pall over everything is a firebombing of the school.

The beautiful Sarafina, who idolizes Nelson Mandela, sees a fellow student she may fancy shot dead by police, participates in the rioting following the shooting of more blacks, takes part in the torching of a black officer who works for the whites, and is tortured in prison.

Terrific songs by Ngema and Hugh Masekela propel the work at a fine clip and are exceedingly well performed and staged. Technical side of the film matches anything Hollywood could have done with much more money.

....

■ **SARATOGA**

1937, 90 MINS, US
Dir Jack Conway *Prod* Bernard H. Hyman, John Emerson *Scr* Anita Loos, Robert Hopkins *Ph* Ray June
Ed Elmo Veron *Mus* Edward Ward *Art Dir* Cedric Gibbons, John S. Detlie
● Jean Harlow, Clark Gable, Lionel Barrymore, Frank Morgan, Walter Pidgeon, Una Merkel (M-G-M)

Saratoga, a story of the thoroughbreds and the men and women who follow the horses around the circuit, is a glamorous comedy-drama which the late Jean Harlow was completing, as co-star with Clark Gable. The few scenes remaining to be made at the time of her death were photographed with an alternate in her part, and done with such skill that audiences will not easily distinguish the substitution.

Anita Loos and Robert Hopkins, who collaborated on *San Francisco*, have gone behind the scenes at racetracks and breeding farms to tell a story of human interest. Gable plays a bookmaker in a breezy, horsey manner. Harlow is the daughter in a family which has bred and raced horses for generations. She takes her small inheritance and wagers on the horses. She is prompted to this in an effort to win enough to repurchase the family breeding farm from Gable, who holds the mortgage to cover losses incurred by her father.

Harlow's performance is among her best. She has several rowdy comedy passages with Gable which are excellently done. The performances of Lionel Barrymore (as the grandfather), Una Merkel (an itinerant follower of the horses), and Frank Morgan (as a turf neophyte) are splendid.

....

■ **SARATOGA TRUNK**

1943, 135 MINS, US
Dir Sam Wood *Prod* Hal B. Wallis *Scr* Casey Robinson *Ph* Ernest Haller *Ed* Ralph Dawson
Mus Max Steiner *Art Dir* Joseph St. Amand
● Gary Cooper, Ingrid Bergman, Flora Robson, Jerry Austin, John Warburton, Florence Bates (Warner)

Story has color, romance, adventure, and not a little s.a. Ingrid Bergman is the beautiful albeit calculating Creole, and Gary Cooper is very effective in the plausible role of a droll, gamblin' Texan who has the romantic hex on the headstrong Creole. Flora Robson is capitally cast as her body-servant and Jerry Austin does a bangup job as the dwarf who, with the mulatto servant, make a strange entourage.

The 1875 period, and the New Orleans and Saratoga locales, combine into a moving story [from Edna Ferber's novel] as Bergman returns from Paris to avenge her mother's 'shame'. That this is a spurious sentimentality, considering she was born out of wedlock, and her father's family sought to banish her virtually to France, is beside the point.

Bergman, as fetching in a brunette wig as in her natural lighter tresses, takes command in every scene. She sparks the cinematurgy, a vital plus factor considering Cooper's laconic personation, and the sultry reticence of her two curious servants.

The two major geographical segments – her native NO and the fertile Saratoga – are replete with basic action and never pall.
□ 1946: Nomination: Best Supp. Actress (Flora Robson)

....

■ **SATAN BUG, THE**

1965, 114 MINS, US ◇ ⊛
Dir John Sturges *Prod* John Sturges *Scr* James Clavell, Edward Anhalt *Ph* Robert Surtees *Ed* Ferris Webster
Mus Jerry Goldsmith
● George Maharis, Richard Basehart, Anne Francis, Dana Andrews, Edward Asner, Frank Sutton (Mirisch-Kappa)

The Satan Bug is a superior suspense melodrama and should keep audiences on the edge of their seats despite certain unexplained, confusing elements which tend to make plot at times difficult to follow.

Based on a novel by Ian Stuart (nom de plume for Britisher Alistair MacLean), producer-director John Sturges builds his action to a generally chilling pace after a needlessly-slow opening which establishes America's experiments in bacteriological warfare at a highly-secret top-security research installation in the desert. The scientist who develops the deadly virus known as the Satan Bug, so lethal it can cause instant death over great areas, is murdered and flasks containing the liquid mysteriously spirited out of the lab.

Script projects George Maharis as a former Army Intelligence officer recalled to find the virus before it can be put to the use threatened by a millionaire paranoiac who masterminded the theft and claims to hate war.

Maharis makes a good impression as the investigator, although his character isn't developed sufficiently – a fault also applying to other principals – due to overspeedy editing in an attempt to narrate story at fever pitch.

....

■ **SATAN MET A LADY**

1936, 74 MINS, US ⊛
Dir William Dieterle *Scr* Brown Holmes *Ph* Arthur Edeson *Ed* Warren Low *Art Dir* Max Parker
● Bette Davis, Warren William, Alison Skipworth, Arthur Treacher, Winifred Shaw, Marie Wilson (Warner)

This is an inferior remake of *The Maltese Falcon*, which Warner produced in 1931. Many changes have been made [to the novel by Dashiell Hammett], in story structure as well as title, but none is an improvement.

Bette Davis is dropped to featured billing rank in this one, on an equal basis with Warren William, and both under the title. But as for importance in the story, Davis has much less to do than at least one other femme member of the cast.

Where the detective of *Maltese Falcon* and his activities were natural and amusing, he and his satiric crime detection are now forced and unnatural.

Among items changed are the names of the characters as well as a few of the characters themselves. Sam Spade, played by Ricardo Cortez in the original, is now Ted Shane as played by Warren William. The plaster bird is now a ram's horn. There's hardly any mystery in this version. The comedy isn't strong enough to fill the bill.

William tries hard to be gay as the eccentric private cop and his performance is all that keeps the picture moving in many lagging moments. Marie Wilson has a tendency to muff her best chances through overstressing.

....

■ SATAN NEVER SLEEPS

(UK: The Devil Never Sleeps)

1962, 133 MINS, US ◇
Dir Leo McCarey   *Prod* Leo McCarey   *Scr* Claude
Binyon, Leo McCarey   *Ph* Oswald Morris   *Ed* Gordon
Pilkington   *Mus* Richard Rodney Bennett   *Art Dir* Tom
Morahan
● William Holden, Clifton Webb, France Nuyen, Athene
Seyler, Martin Benson, Weaver Lee (20th Century-Fox)

China in its critical year of 1949 is the setting
of the screenplay, from a novel by Pearl S.
Buck. Cornered in this moment of imminent
national alteration to Communism are two
Catholic priests, played by Clifton Webb and
William Holden, the latter adoringly but
hopelessly pursued by a Chinese maiden
(France Nuyen). The priests are soon impris-
oned by the local People's Party leader
(Weaver Lee), who also rapes the girl.

Lee eventually see the light when: (1)
Nuyen given birth to his child, (2) his parents
are murdered by the Reds, (3) he is reprimanded and demoted for personal ambition
and leniency. More occurs in the final 15 minutes of this picture than in the preceding 118.

Holden is a kind of leather-jacketed varia-
tion of Bing Crosby's sweatshirted Father
O'Malley and Webb a wry, caustic version of
Barry Fitzgerald's Father Fitzgibbon in Leo
McCarey's *Going My Way* (1944). Nuyen plays
vivaciously as the sweet nuisance. The villains
are absurdly all black. Outdoor locations in
England and Wales pass acceptably for
China.

■ SATURDAY NIGHT AND SUNDAY MORNING

1960, 89 MINS, UK ▽
Dir Karel Reisz   *Prod* Tony Richardson, Harry Saltzman
Scr Alan Sillitoe   *Ph* Freddie Francis   *Ed* Seth Holt
Mus Johnny Dankworth
● Albert Finney, Shirley Anne Field, Rachel Roberts,
Hylda Baker, Norman Rossington, Bryan Pringle
(Woodfall/Bryanston)

Alan Sillitoe's novel is produced, directed and
acted with integrity and insight. This is a
good, absorbing but not very likeable film.

The hero is a Nottingham factory worker
who refuses to conform. He hates all authority but protests so blunderingly. His attitude
is simple: 'What I want is a good time. The
remainder is all propaganda.' Through the
week he works hard at his lathe. In his spare
time – Saturday night and Sunday morning
(and a couple of evenings) – he comes into his
own. Liquor and women.

Sillitoe does a good job with his first screenplay, though, necessarily, much of the motive
and the thinking of his characters has been
lost in the adaptation. Director Karel Reisz'
experience in documentaries enables him to
bring a sharp tang and authenticity to the
film. The locations and the interiors have
caught the full atmosphere of a Midland industrial town.

The central figure is cocky, violent and selfish, yet at times almost pathetically likeable.
Albert Finney, in his first major screen performance, handles scenes of belligerence and
one or two love scenes with complete confidence and is equally effective in quieter moments. On a par is the performance of Rachel
Roberts as the married woman carrying on a
hopeless affair with Finney. Shirley Anne
Field, as the conventional young woman who
eventually snares Finney, is appropriately pert.

■ SATURDAY NIGHT FEVER

1977, 119 MINS, US ◇ ▽ ⊙
Dir John Badham   *Prod* Robert Stigwood   *Scr* Norman
Wexler   *Ph* Ralph D. Bode   *Ed* David Rawlins
Mus David Shire (adapt.)   *Art Dir* Charles Bailey
● John Travolta, Karen Lynn Gorney, Barry Miller,
Joseph Cali, Paul Pape, Bruce Ornstein (Paramount)

John Travolta stars as an amiably inarticulate NY kid who comes to life only in
a disco environment. The clumsy story
lurches forward through predictable travail
and treacle, separated by phonograph records
(or vice versa). John Badham's direction is
awkward.

Coloring-book plot lines [based on a story
by Nik Cohn] give Travolta a bad homelife
(Val Bisoglio's father is an ethnic horror
story), a formula gang of buddies, an available 'bad' girl (Donna Pescow), an elusive
'good' girl (Karen Lynn Gorney) plus lots of
opportunity to boogie on the dance floor and
make out in automobile back seats.

Between original music by Barry, Robin and
Maurice Gibb plus David Shire, and familiar
platter hits, the film usually has some rhythm
going on in the background.
□ 1977: Nomination: Best Actor (John
Travolta)

■ SATURN 3

1980, 88 MINS, UK ◇ ▽ ⊙
Dir Stanley Donen   *Prod* Stanley Donen   *Scr* Martin
Amis   *Ph* Billy Williams   *Ed* Richard Marden
Mus Elmer Bernstein   *Art Dir* Stuart Craig
● Farrah Fawcett, Kirk Douglas, Harvey Keitel, Ed
Bishop, Douglas Lambert (Grade-Kastner)

Somewhere in deepest, darkest space, Kirk
Douglas and Farrah Fawcett jog around
through a space station that looks suspiciously like Bloomingdale's after closing. The
pair are scientists doing important work,
when bad guy Harvey Keitel shows up.

Douglas is sprightly, but he has to handle
some pretty awful lines in this Martin Amis
script [from a story by John Barry]. Keitel's
dialog, if quoted, would be on a par.

Life goes on in this shopping mall of lights
till Keitel builds Hector, the mad robot,
whose tubes and hubcaps develop goose-
bumps for Farrah.

Best scene in the entire effort is Hector's
resurrection after he has been dismantled for
being randy. The parts find each other and
reconnect which is more than this film does.

■ SAVAGE, THE

1953, 95 MINS, US ◇
Dir George Marshall   *Prod* Mel Epstein   *Scr* Sydney
Boehm   *Ph* John F. Seitz   *Ed* Arthur Schmidt   *Mus* Paul
Sawtell   *Art Dir* Hal Pereira, William Flannery
● Charlton Heston, Susan Morrow, Peter Hanson, Joan
Taylor, Richard Rober, Donald Porter (Paramount)

This tale of Indian fighting travels in
fairly devious circles to relate a standard
story [from a novel by L.L. Foreman].
However, it has excellent outdoor photography and liberal amounts of Indian fighting
scenes.

Charlton Heston has a fairly confused role
which forces the story to travel unnecessarily
in circles. He plays Warbonnet, a white lad
who has been brought up as an Indian following the massacre of his father by Crow
Indians. Living with a tribe in the Sioux con-
federation, Heston knows how to knock off a
Crow scalp, but his major problem comes
when he has to choose on which side he'll
fight in the impending war between the paleface and the Indians.

The femme interest is slight, with Susan
Morrow as the belle of the army fort. Joan
Taylor as an Indian maid is Morrow's major
competition for Heston's affection.

Peter Hanson and Richard Rober do well in
major white roles while Indians are staunchly
portrayed by Ian MacDonald and Donald
Porter. One of the more colorful enactments
is by Milburn Stone as a corporal who befriends Heston.

■ SAVAGE EYE, THE

1959, 68 MINS, US
Dir Ben Maddow, Sidney Meyers, Joseph Strick
Prod Edward Harrison   *Ph* Jack Couffer, Helen Leavitt,
Haskell Wexler   *Mus* Leonard Rosenman
● Barbara Baxley, Herschel Bernardi, Jean Hidey,
Elizabeth Zemach (City)

Fascinating and uncompromising semi-documentary impressively put together as an obvious labor of love by three talented American
filmmakers.

Story of a divorced woman's attempts to
readjust to a single life affords an excellent
opportunity to dissect some frightening and
depressing panoramas of modern existence.
From the woman's first arrival at a big-city
airport (site of most of shooting is Los
Angeles, but no effort has been made to establish a specific locale), pic moves into her
first visual impressions of the city, its seamy
side, its bars and drunks, its beauty parlors
lined with elderly women, its store windows,
and above all, its people.

Subsequent portions of the film feature,
among other things, the detailed horror of a
nose-bobbing operation, the bloodthirsty behaviour of men and women at boxing and
wrestling matches, a detailed and critically
observed striptease sequence, complete with
leering spectators, a cruelly fascinating sequence shot during a faith-healing service,
and a harrowing and nightmarish bit depicting a pervert's party.

Wealth of material is linked by presence of
the key character, caught on her search for
warmth and companionship, and by a spoken
commentary (well-mouthed by Gary Merrill)
in the form of a dialogue between the woman
and an imaginary poet.

Footage, shot over a span of several years,
boasts much expertly and realistically photographed (some of it hidden-camera) material. It's slickly integrated and matched with
recreated sequences to bring about a true-
looking patina.

■ SAVAGE INNOCENTS, THE

1960, 111 MINS, UK/ITALY/US ◇ ▽
Dir Nicholas Ray   *Prod* Joseph Janni, Maleno Malenotti
Scr Nicholas Ray   *Ph* Aldo Tonti, Peter Hennessy
Ed Ralph Kemplen   *Mus* Angelo Francesco Lavagnino
Art Dir Don Ashton
● Anthony Quinn, Yoko Tani, Marie Jang, Marie Jang,
Francis De Wolff, Peter O'Toole (Rank/Appia/
Paramount)

The Savage Innocents is a polyglot pic. Financial
responsibility was carved up between Britain,
America and Italy. Rank chipped in with a
third of the $1.5 million budget and Pinewood
studios and British technicians were used;
Italy, through producer Maleno Malenotti,
has a third stake; America (Paramount release) supplied the remainder. There's a
Yank director and screenplay writer, Nicholas
Ray; America's Anthony Quinn is the main
star, while the [Japanese] femme lead Yoko
Tani comes from Paris.

Remainder of the cast is drawn from vari-
ous countries. Shooting, apart from
Pinewood, took place in Hudson Bay and
Greenland. Somewhere along the line
Denmark gets an honorable mention among
the credits.

Two undeniable things stand out. Art director and editor have done a standout job in
matching and cutting so that it is virtually
impossible to decide where Pinewood began
and Canada came in. Secondly, the chief
lensers have turned out some brilliant camerawork with color sweeping superbly across the
widescreen.

The problem is whether the yarn [based on
Hans Ruesch's novel *Top of the World*] stands
up. For long sessions it is a documentary of
life in the Eskimo belt. The story line is sim-

ple. It concerns a powerful, good humored hunter (Quinn) who spends the early stages of the film deciding which of two young women he wishes to make his wife. Second half becomes melodrama when he accidentally murders a missionary.

The memorable moments are those of Quinn hunting down foxes, bears, seals, walruses and the majesty of the bleak wastes, the ice, the storms and primitive living conditions. The human element doesn't come out of it quite so well.

Quinn, mainly talking pidgin English-cum-Eskimo, comes out as an authentic Eskimo. Tani is a delight as the woman. Peter O'Toole is firstrate as a tough trooper.

....

■ SAVAGE MESSIAH

1972, 100 MINS, UK ◇
Dir Ken Russell *Prod* Ken Russell *Scr* Christopher Logue *Ph* Dick Bush *Ed* Michael Bradsell *Mus* Michael Garrett *Art Dir* George Lack, Derek Jarman
● Dorothy Tutin, Scott Antony, Helen Mirren, Lindsay Kemp, Michael Gough, John Justin (Russfilm/M-G-M)

Offbeat in subject matter (the platonic yet deeply affectionate love of an extrovert young French sculptor, Henri Gaudier, for an introverted older woman, set early in this century) pic is distinctively Russellian in treatment as well, showing that the British director has lost none of his filmic impudence.

Not unexpectedly played with most stops out, and soundtrack decibels at upper limits, a potentially introverted tale [from H.S. Ede's book] is instead played broadly and with considerable panache, especially in having the artist portrayed as a physically strong and agile extrovert, and young to boot. A virtual unknown in his first pic role, Scott Antony rises beautifully to the challenge.

More expected, but enjoyable nevertheless, is Dorothy Tutin's astute and measured delivery as the object of the sculptor's affection, a would-be writer whose somber reasoning acts as counterpoint to his ebullience, while lending him inner strength. Helen Mirren is eye-filling and able as a women's lib type (and, incongruously, improvised full-frontal nude model as well), while a number of backdrop roles are colorfully filled by a large back-up cast.

As usual, there's more style than warmth in Russell's character relationships. It is only at the end, when one is brought up sharply by the (true-to-life) news of the sculptor's precocious demise, aged 23, in a World War II battle that some deep-down feeling comes into play.

....

■ SAVAGES

1972, 105 MINS, US ◇ ⓥ
Dir James Ivory *Prod* Ismail Merchant *Scr* James Ivory, George Swift Trow, Michael O'Donoghue *Ph* Walter Lassally *Ed* Kent McKinney *Mus* Joe Raposo *Art Dir* Charles E. White III, Michael Doret
● Louis J. Stadlen, Anne Francine, Thayer David, Susan Blakely, Russ Thacker, Salome Jens (Angelika/Merchant-Ivory)

Savages, first US film by producer Ismail Merchant and director James Ivory, is about members of a primitive tribe who are lured by the appearance of a rolling croquet ball to an old deserted mansion where they dress in clothes and take on 'civilized' societal behavior, only to return to the forest and their primitive behavior the following morning.

The playing has flair and grace, sans woodenness from everyone, with Walter Lassally's excellently balanced b&w lensing for the primitive days and color for the so-called civilized times a great asset, as are the editing and music. The only carp might be a tendency to overplay an act.

But no denying an almost hypnotic charm and fascination in this offbeat, insouciant look at mankind and his climb to civilization and fall.

....

■ SAVAGE STREETS

1984, 93 MINS, US ◇ ⓥ ⊙
Dir Danny Steinmann *Prod* John C. Strong III *Scr* Norman Yonemoto, Danny Steinmann *Ph* Stephen Posey *Ed* Bruce Stubblefield, John O'Conner *Mus* Michael Lloyd, John D'Andrea *Art Dir* Ninkey Dalton
● Linda Blair, John Vernon, Robert Dryer, Johnny Venocur, Sal Landi, Scott Mayer (Savage Street)

Linda Blair toplines as Brenda, an LA girl who turns vigilante when her mute younger sister Heather (Linnea Quigley) is brutally gang-raped by a local gang of toughs.

Pic unfolds as a tough update of the juvenile delinquency B-pictures of the 1950s, incorporating ineffectual adult authorities (John Vernon as the hardnosed but powerless high school principal), warring groups of dislikeable good kids and gangs of punks.

The uncensored approach pays off in deliciously vulgar dialog and well-directed confrontation scenes.

Blair emerges here as a tawdry, delightfully trashy sweater girl in a league with 1950s B-heroines such as Beverly Michaels, Juli Reding and Mamie Van Doren.

....

■ SAVE THE TIGER

1973, 99 MINS, US ◇ ⓥ ⊙
Dir John G. Avildsen *Prod* Steve Shagan *Scr* Steve Shagan *Ph* Jim Crabe *Ed* David Bretherton *Mus* Marvin Hamlisch *Art Dir* Jack Collis
● Jack Lemmon, Jack Gilford, Laurie Heineman, Norman Burton, Patricia Smith, Thayer David (Filmways)

Save the Tiger is an intellectual exploitation film which ostensibly lays bare the crass materialism of the age. Producer-writer Steve Shagan's script stars Jack Lemmon in an offbeat casting as a pitiable businessman trapped in his own life-style.

Partnered with Jack Gilford in the garment business, Lemmon finds his finances so strapped that he decides to hire a professional arsonist to have what used to be called 'a successful fire' in one of his factories. This trauma occurs on fashion-show day, when lecherous out-of-town buyer Norman Burton demands some call-girl kinkiness and has a coronary attack.

The closest thing to a point of reference is in Gilford's character, who, after the successful fashion line showing, berates Lemmon's ethics. Latter makes a facile comeback, thereby returning the plot to its free-form, floating exploitation of seaminess.

There is a lot of mature, untapped ability on display in Lemmon's performance. Gilford delivers an outstanding performance, beyond the fact that his is the sole voice of sanity. Patricia Smith is excellent as Lemmon's wife.
□ 1973: Best Actor (Jack Lemmon).
□ Nominations: Best Supp. Actor (Jack Gilford), Original Story & Screenplay

....

■ SAVING GRACE

1986, 112 MINS, US ◇ ⓥ ⊙
Dir Robert M. Young *Prod* Herbert F. Solow *Scr* David S. Ward *Ph* Reynaldo Villalobos *Art Dir* Giovanni Natalucci
● Tom Conti, Fernando Rey, Erland Josephson, Giancarlo Giannini, Donald Hewlett, Angelo Evans (Embassy)

This may be the first comedy ever about a Pope running away from office – for a short, private spree in the country among the real people whose shepherd he is supposed to be, sans the bureaucratic interference of the Vatican hierarchy.

Tom Conti may be a little young and literally too light on his feet to play a Pope, but he is too good an actor not to make the best of it, eliciting lots of personal sympathy even when not quite convincing as a High Pontiff.

Fernando Rey and Erland Josephson and Donald Hewlett are an amusing trio of Cardinals covering for their boss in his absence. Giancarlo Giannini is effective as a mysterious goat-herd of few words, and Angelo Evans displays plenty of vitality as a tough-acting kid with a good heart.

....

■ SAY ANYTHING . . .

1989, 100 MINS, US ◇ ⓥ ⊙
Dir Cameron Crowe *Prod* Polly Platt *Scr* Cameron Crowe *Ph* Laszlo Kovacs *Ed* Richard Marks *Mus* Richard Gibbs, Anne Dudley, Nancy Wilson *Art Dir* Mark Mansbridge
● John Cusack, Ione Skye, John Mahoney, Lili Taylor, Amy Brooks, Lois Chiles (20th Century-Fox/Gracie)

Say Anything . . . is a half-baked love story, full of good intentions but uneven in the telling. Appealing tale of an undirected army brat proving himself worthy of the most exceptional girl in high school elicits a few laughs, plenty of smiles and some genuine feeling.

On the eve of high school graduation, bright but unremarkable student John Cusack decides he's just got to go out with 'Miss Priss' (Ione Skye). Skye is doted upon by her divorced father (John Mahoney) and is headed for studies in England on a fellowship.

Cusack, who bunks with his nephew and sister (an unbilled appearance by real-life sister Joan Cusack), starts a friendship that slowly grows into something more. Conflict rears its head in a conventional way when Skye becomes torn between leaving for England and staying with her boyfriend.

Cusack and Skye's relationship develops nicely and believably, but Crowe has not written an entirely convincing character for the latter to play. Pic also has considerable structural problems, as many scenes feel unachieved.

Lois Chiles (unbilled) plays a scene as Skye's mother, and Eric Stoltz pops up briefly at a teen party.

....

■ SAYONARA

1957, 147 MINS, US ◇ ⓥ
Dir Joshua Logan *Prod* William Goetz *Scr* Paul Osborn *Ph* Ellsworth Fredricks *Ed* Arthur P. Schmidt, Philip W. Anderson *Mus* Franz Waxman *Art Dir* Ted Haworth
● Marlon Brando, Red Buttons, Ricardo Montalban, Patricia Owens, Martha Scott, James Garner (Warner)

Sayonara, based on the James A. Michener novel, is a picture of beauty and sensitivity. Amidst the tenderness and the tensions of a romantic drama, it puts across the notion that human relations transcend race barriers. Joshua Logan's direction is tops.

Though strongly supported, particularly by Red Buttons, it's Marlon Brando who carries the production. As Major Gruver, the Korean war air-ace, Brando affects a nonchalant Southern drawl that helps set the character from the very start. He is wholly convincing as the race-conscious Southerner whose humanity finally leads him to rebel against army-imposed prejudice.

Story has combat-fatigued Brando transferred to Kobe for a rest and to meet his State-side sweetheart (Patricia Owens), daughter of the commanding general of the area. They find things have changed and the sensitive, well-educated girl is no longer sure she wants to marry Brando. He in turn is upset because Airman Joe Kelly, played by Buttons, wants to marry a Japanese (Miyoshi Umeki).

Brando meets a beautiful Japanese actress-

S

dancer (Miiko Taka) and gradually falls deeply in love with her. When Buttons and his wife, in desperation, commit suicide, Brando realizes that, regardless of the consequences, he must marry Taka.

Taka plays the proud Hana-ogi, the dedicated dancer, who starts by hating the Americans whom she sees as robbing Japan of its culture and ends in Brando's arms. Apart from being beautiful she's also a distinctive personality and her contribution rates high.
□ 1957: Best Supp. Actor (Red Buttons), Supp. Actress (Miyoshi Umeki), Art Direction, Sound (Warner Bros. Sound Dept)
□ Nominations: Best Picture, Director, Actor (Marlon Brando), Adapted Screenplay, Cinematography, Editing

● ●

■ SCALPHUNTERS, THE

1968, 102 MINS, US ◇ ⓥ
Dir Sydney Pollack   *Prod* Jules Levy   *Scr* William Norton   *Ph* Duke Callaghan, Richard Moore   *Ed* John Woodcock   *Mus* Elmer Bernstein   *Art Dir* Frank Arrigo
● Burt Lancaster, Shelley Winters, Telly Savalas, Ossie Davis, Armando Silvestre, Dabney Coleman (United Artists)

In artistic terms, *The Scalphunters* is hard to describe: a satirical, slapstick, intellectual drama, laced with civil rights overtones, and loaded with recurring action scenes. Burt Lancaster and Shelley Winters provide marquee dressing.

Story topcasts Lancaster as a fur trapper, robbed of his skins by Indian chief Armando Silvestre who swaps cultured Negro ex-slave Ossie Davis. Telly Savalas heads a crew of scalphunters, with Winters as mistress to Savalas. Lancaster and Davis pursue the scalphunters.

The whole ensemble works to a remarkable degree. Lancaster and Davis work particularly well together, ditto Savalas and Winters. There are talky periods of slow pace, but they are terminated before undue damage has been done.

● ●

■ SCAMP, THE

1957, 88 MINS, UK
Dir Wolf Rilla   *Prod* James Lawrie   *Scr* Wolf Rilla   *Ph* Freddie Francis   *Ed* Bernard Gribble   *Mus* Francis Chagrin   *Art Dir* Elven Webb
● Richard Attenborough, Terence Morgan, Dorothy Alison, Jill Adams, Colin Petersen, Geoffrey Keen (Minter)

Based on Charlotte Hastings' play *Uncertain Joy*, this emerges as a run-of-mill domestic drama. It has a touch too much of sentimentality and many situations are implausible.

Richard Attenborough is a schoolmaster, and he and his doctor wife befriend a youngster (Colin Petersen) whose father, a drunken vaudeville actor, neglects the child and leaves him to run wild. When he goes on a tour of South America, he reluctantly leaves his son with Attenborough and his wife who try to show the kid a new way of life. But he can't live down his background and the authorities order that he should be returned to his father who has returned from tour with a new wife.

While there is plenty of scope in such a story for a good, meaty drama, *The Scamp* suffers from unimaginative direction by Wolf Rilla and a somewhat pedestrian script. But no praise can be too high for Petersen (who sprang to prominence in the film *Smiley*) as the 10-year-old scamp. Here is a natural.

● ●

■ SCANDAL

1989, 114 MINS, UK ◇ ⓥ ⊙
Dir Michael Caton-Jones   *Prod* Stephen Woolley   *Scr* Michael Thomas   *Ph* Mike Molloy   *Ed* Angus Newton   *Mus* Carl Davis   *Art Dir* Simon Holland
● John Hurt, Joanne Whalley-Kilmer, Bridget Fonda, Ian McKellen, Leslie Phillips, Britt Ekland (Palace)

In 1963 the sensational revelations that a good-time girl had been having affairs with a British cabinet minister and a Soviet naval attache shocked the UK and helped bring down the Conservative government. *Scandal* reexamines the controversy.

Man-about-town Stephen Ward (John Hurt) meets young showgirl Christine Keeler (Joanne Whalley-Kilmer) and decides to transform her into a glamorous sophisticate.

Ward is delighted when Soviet naval attache Ivanov (Jeroen Krabbe) takes a shine to Whalley-Kilmer, though at the same time cabinet minister John Profumo (Ian McKellen), the secretary of state for war, falls for her.

Profumo is forced to resign and Ward is eventually arrested and charged with living on the earnings of prostitutes.

Hurt is excellent as the charming but shallow Ward. Whalley-Kilmer looks the part, but seems happier with the humorous and ironic parts of the script. American Bridget Fonda – with an admirable British accent – is perfect.

● ●

■ SCANNERS

1981, 102 MINS, CANADA ◇ ⓥ ⊙
Dir David Cronenberg   *Prod* Claude Heroux   *Scr* David Cronenberg   *Ph* Mark Irwin   *Ed* Ron Sanders   *Mus* Howard Shore   *Art Dir* Carol Spier
● Stephen Lack, Jennifer O'Neill, Patrick McGoohan, Michael Ironside, Lawrence Dane (Filmplan)

Scanners offers at least one literally eye-popping moment and another that can only be called mind-blowing.

A variation on the pod people of *Invasion of the Body Snatchers* in that they cannot readily be distinguished from normal humans, scanners are telepathic curiosities who, like Sissy Spacek's Carrie, are able to zap people and things at will.

There are good scanners and bad scanners and one, Stephen Lack, who is in between and finds himself recruited by scientist Patrick McGoohan to infiltrate the evil group and track down the chief baddie, who has Hitlerian aspirations for his band of psychic gangsters.

Following the pattern of many effects-oriented low-budgeters, story settles into low gear after the opening reel, in which a man's head explodes on camera.

All this should give fans of David Cronenberg's previous pix their money's worth, although lack of any rooting interest vitiates any possible suspense and highly elegant visual style works against much shock value. Ending is also a bit puzzling.

● ●

■ SCARAMOUCHE

1952, 115 MINS, US ◇ ⓥ ⊙
Dir George Sidney   *Prod* Carey Wilson   *Scr* Ronald Millar, George Froeschel   *Ph* Charles Rosher   *Ed* James E. Newcom   *Mus* Victor Young   *Art Dir* Cedric Gibbons, Hans Peters
● Stewart Granger, Eleanor Parker, Janet Leigh, Mel Ferrer, Henry Wilcoxon, Nina Foch (M-G-M)

Metro's up-to-date version of *Scaramouche* bears only the most rudimentary resemblance to its 1923 hit or to the Rafael Sabatini novel on which they both were based. Pic never seems to be quite certain whether it is a costume adventure drama or a satire on one.

The highly-complex Sabatini plot has been greatly simplified for present purposes. It finds the French Revolution all but eliminated from the story, because of the inevitable Red analogy were the hero allowed to spout the 1789 theme of 'Liberty, Equality, Fraternity'.

Granger is a brash young man who is determined to avenge the death of a friend at the hand of nobleman Mel Ferrer, the best swordsman in France. Stewart Granger has to keep under cover until he gets in enough

lessons with the weapon to take on Ferrer. Just in the nick, (a) he's elected to the French assembly, so he doesn't have to hide out anymore; (b) he discovers Janet Leigh is not his sister, so he can grab her, and (c) the marquis is really his brother. That leaves everyone mildly happy except Eleanor Parker, who, when last seen is being hauled into a bedroom by Napoleon.

● ●

■ SCARECROW

1973, 112 MINS, US ◇ ⓥ
Dir Jerry Schatzberg   *Prod* Robert M. Sherman   *Scr* Garry Michael White   *Ph* Vilmos Zsigmond   *Ed* Evan Lottman   *Mus* Fred Myrow   *Art Dir* Al Brenner
● Gene Hackman, Al Pacino, Dorothy Tristan, Ann Wedgeworth, Richard Lynch, Eileen Brennan (Warner)

Scarecrow is a periodically interesting but ultimately unsatisfying character study of two modern drifters. Gene Hackman is excellent as a paroled crook with determined plans for the future, but Al Pacino is shot down by the script which never provides him with much beyond freaky second-banana status.

Script seems an attempt to update Runyonesque characters and situations to the seamy 1970s.

Hackman and Pacino meet in the California countryside. The former is gruff, eccentric, crude and volatile. The latter is likeable, weak, but sufficiently put together to return to Detroit to the wife and child he abandoned years earlier.

In their travels, pair encounter several extremely well-cast and most effective characters.

● ●

■ SCARECROW, THE

1982, 87 MINS, NEW ZEALAND ◇
Dir Sam Pillsbury   *Prod* Rob Whitehouse   *Scr* Sam Pillsbury, Michael Heath   *Ph* James Bartle   *Ed* Ian John   *Mus* Andrew Hagen, Morton Wilson, Phil Broadhurst   *Art Dir* Neil Angwin
● Jonathan Smith, Daniel McLaren, Stephen Taylor, Des Kelly, Tracy Mann, John Carradine (Oasis/NZNFU)

As did the novel on which it is based, *The Scarecrow* sets up its own category, which is a kind of hillbilly Gothic thriller. The bizarre events are seen through the eyes of Ned, and the impact on a small New Zealand country township, circa 1953, of the quintessential evil stranger, embodied by the smooth-talking itinerant side-show magician and hypnotist, Salter.

Evil the stranger may be, but he is also the flame that brings to the boil the town's stew of lust and perversion that has been simmering all along.

Events are commented upon by the off-screen voice of Ned, now grown older but still talking in the overblown phrases of a lad who has read too many cheap adventure thrillers. It is an effective part of this device, however, carried over from the original novel by Ronald Hugh Morrieson, that highly unpleasant undertones exist, such as necrophilia and senile sexuality.

The central role of Salter himself is given the full saturnine treatment by John Carradine, abetted by ominous lighting and sound effects at every turn.

● ●

■ SCARED STIFF

1953, 106 MINS, US ⓥ
Dir George Marshall   *Prod* Hal B. Wallis   *Scr* Herbert Baker, Walter De Leon, Ed Simmons, Norman Lear   *Ph* Ernest Laszlo   *Ed* Warren Low   *Mus* Leith Stevens   *Art Dir* Hal Pereira, Franz Bachelin
● Dean Martin, Jerry Lewis, Lizabeth Scott, Carmen Miranda, Dorothy Malone, George Dolenz (Paramount)

Dean Martin & Jerry Lewis provide a free-wheeling round of slapstick hilarity – the kind they do so well – in *Scared Stiff*, new version of the old Paul Dickey-Charles W. Goddard play [*The Ghost Breakers*]. Script has its chief setting on a lonely, zombie-haunted island off the coast of Cuba.

Preliminaries are concerned with Martin, a cabaret singer, and his awkward chum (Lewis) back in New York, where they get mixed up with a gangster's girl (Dorothy Malone) and, in fleeing a gangland ride, meet up with Lizabeth Scott, hieress to the island. M&L decide to go along with her as protection against mysterious men who are attempting to keep her from claiming her inheritance.

Oddly enough, a comedy highlight in the picture is handled by uncredited Frank Fontaine, playing a drunk who thinks Martin is a ventriloquist when he is caught talking to Lewis, hidden in a trunk at dock-side. The comedy team is in its element in the story's slap-stick harum-scarum. Scott handles herself niftily and Carmen Miranda shows up well. Malone's chores in the early footage are carried out delightfully as a gal who likes to kiss, even if it does displease her gangster boyfriend.

● ●

■ **SCARFACE**

1932, 90 MINS, US Ⓥ ⊙
Dir Howard Hawks *Prod* Howard Hughes *Scr* Ben Hecht, W. R. Burnett, John Lee Mahin, Seton I. Miller *Ph* Lee Garmes, L. William O'Connell *Ed* Edward Curtiss *Mus* Adolph Tandler, Gustav Arnheim *Art Dir* Harry Olivier
● Paul Muni, Ann Dvorak, Karen Morley, George Raft, Boris Karloff, Osgood Perkins (Hughes/United Artists)

Scarface contains more cruelty than any of its gangster picture predecessors, but there's a squarer for every killing. The blows are always softened by judicial preachments and sad endings for the sinners.

There is none of the *Public Enemy*'s tracing the mug from boyhood to blame the environment for the cause this time. Paul Muni is a bad one in the first spin of the spindle, murdering a gent while he (Muni) is still just an introductory shadow on the wall. He whistles an operatic aria before shooting his cannon, which signalizes when he's going to kill somebody from then on.

Plot traces the rise of Scarface from the position of bodyguard for an early district beer baron to the booze chief of the whole city. Along the way he overthrows his employer and later has him slain. He even cops the boss' girl. She's a wicked blonde with a love for gunmen and gunfire, and she of all the gang is left unpunished at the finish.

George Raft gets most of the sympathy for his Rinaldo. He talks little and habitually tosses a coin while doing most of his pal's private gat work. Karen Morley has to fight an apparently natural air of refinement to get into the moll atmosphere, but she makes her part sit up and talk. Ann Dvorak is okay as Scarface's kid sister.

● ●

■ **SCARFACE**

1983, 170 MINS, US ◇ Ⓥ ⊙
Dir Brian De Palma *Prod* Martin Bregman, Peter Saphier *Scr* Oliver Stone *Ph* John A. Alonzo *Ed* Jerry Greenberg, David Ray *Mus* Giorgio Moroder *Art Dir* Ed Richardson
● Al Pacino, Steven Bauer, Michelle Pfeiffer, Mary Elizabeth Mastrantonio, Robert Loggia, F. Murray Abraham (Universal)

Scarface is a grandiose modern morality play, excessive, broad and operatic at times. Film's origins lie in the 1932 Howard Hughes production directed by Howard Hawks and adapted by Ben Hecht from the novel by Armitage Trail. Contours of the saga are very similar to those of the original, as the nearly three-hour effort charts the rise and fall of an ambitious young thug who for awhile becomes the biggest shot in gangsterdom, but ultimately is just too dumb to stay at the top.

Docu prolog recounts how some 25,000 criminals entered the United States in 1980 during the boatlift from Mariel Harbor in Cuba. Among them, per this fiction, was one Tony Montana (Al Pacino), who impresses local Miami kingpin Robert Loggia. Thanks to the fact that he has nerves of steel and ice in his veins, Pacino moves up fast in the underworld and establishes a crucial personal link with Bolivian cocaine manufacturer Paul Shenar.

All this is brought off by scripter Oliver Stone and director Brian De Palma in efficient, sometimes stylish fashion.

Performances are all extremely effective, with Pacino leading the way. Michelle Pfeiffer does well with a basically one-dimensional role as blonde WASP goddess. Shenar is outstanding as the cool, well-bred Bolivian.

● ●

■ **SCARLET BUCCANEER, THE**
See: Swashbuckler

● ●

■ **SCARLET EMPRESS, THE**

1934, 104 MINS, US
Dir Josef von Sternberg *Scr* Manuel Komroff *Ph* Bert Glennon *Mus* John M. Leopold, W. Frank Harling (arr.) *Art Dir* Hans Dreier, Peter Ballbusch, Richard Kollorsz
● Marlene Dietrich, John Lodge, Sam Jaffe, Louise Dresser, Maria Sieber, C. Aubrey Smith (Paramount)

The greatest trouble with *Scarlet Empress* is, at the same time, its greatest weakness. Josef von Sternberg becomes so enamoured of the pomp and flash values that he subjugates everything else to them. That he succeeds as well as he does is a tribute to his artistic genius and his amazingly vital sense of photogenic values.

Marlene Dietrich has never been as beautiful as she is here. Again and again she is photographed in closeups, under veils and behind thin mesh curtains and always breathtakingly. But never is she allowed to become really alive and vital. She is as though enchanted by the immense sets through which she stalks.

She is first picked up as a baby and a cute touch has this sequence being acted by her baby, Maria Sieber. Then she's the young German princess affianced to the far-off Russian and sent to the foreign court. She is innocent, wide-eyed, unsuspecting. And, of course, she is an easy mark for all the viciousness and grossness she soon finds herself surrounded with. Wedded to the mad crown prince she is slowly driven into the arms of other men.

Film is claimed based on a diary of Catherine II which, perhaps, forgives its choppiness and episodic quality. Sternberg uses a minimum of dialog and goes back to the silent film method of titles to explain action.

● ●

■ **SCARLET PIMPERNEL, THE**

1934, 98 MINS, UK Ⓥ ⊙
Dir Harold Young *Prod* Alexander Korda *Scr* S.N. Behrman, Robert Sherwood, Arthur Wimperis, Lajos Biro *Ph* Harold Rosson *Ed* William Hornbeck *Mus* Arthur Benjamin *Art Dir* Vincent Korda
● Leslie Howard, Merle Oberon, Raymond Massey, Nigel Bruce, Bramwell Fletcher, Joan Gardner (London Films/United Artists)

An intriguing adaptation of a noted novel, the English-made *Pimpernel* is distinguished by a splendid cast and productional mounting that rates with Hollywood's best.

Leslie Howard's performance in the title role is not only up to the Howard standard, but so fine that an extraordinary production job was required to prevent this from being a monolog film.

As the Scarlet Pimpernel, an English nobleman who seeks to rescue the aristocrats of France from Robespierre's guillotine, Howard essays what amounts to a dual role. At home a foppish, affected clotheshorse; abroad, a gallant adventurer playing a dangerous game.

With the story in his favor, Howard has the acting edge all the way, so it was only by their own efforts that the supporting players could stand out. As Chauvelin, the villain of the piece, Raymond Massey turns in a gem of a performance.

Co-starred with Howard is Merle Oberon, the slant-eyed knockout. Portraying Lady Blakeley, a tragic young woman who nearly betrays her husband, Oberon is confined by script limitations to sad moments only.

Enough of Baroness Orczy's novel is retained to make the picture plot recognizable to the book readers.

● ●

■ **SCARLET STREET**

1945, 96 MINS, US Ⓥ
Dir Fritz Lang *Prod* Walter Wanger *Scr* Dudley Nichols *Ph* Milton Krasner *Ed* Arthur Hilton *Mus* Hans J. Salter *Art Dir* Alexander Golitzen
● Edward G. Robinson, Joan Bennett, Dan Duryea, Margaret Lindsay, Rosalind Ivan, Jess Barker (Universal/Diana)

Fritz Lang's production and direction ably project the sordid tale of the romance between a milquetoast character and a gold-digging blonde. Script [based on the French novel and play *La Chienne* by Georges la Fouchardière] is tightly written by Dudley Nichols and is played for sustained interest and suspense by the cast.

Edward G. Robinson is the mild cashier and amateur painter whose love for Joan Bennett leads him to embezzlement, murder and disgrace. Two stars turn in top work to keep the interest high, and Dan Duryea's portrayal of the crafty and crooked opportunist whom Bennett loves is a standout in furthering the melodrama.

● ●

■ **SCENES FROM A MALL**

1991, 87 MINS, US ◇ Ⓥ ⊙
Dir Paul Mazursky *Prod* Paul Mazursky *Scr* Roger L. Simon, Paul Mazursky *Ph* Fred Murphy *Ed* Stuart Pappe *Mus* Marc Shaiman *Art Dir* Pato Guzman
● Bette Midler, Woody Allen, Bill Irwin, Daren Firestone, Rebecca Nickels, Paul Mazursky (Touchstone/Silver Screen Partners IV)

Paul Mazursky's 14th film as director is a cozy, insular middle-aged marital comedy that's about as deep and rewarding as a day of mall-cruising.

Talents of Bette Midler and Woody Allen seem misspent in roles as cuddly but squabbling spouses. Pic's title, a takeoff on Ingmar Bergman's *Scenes from a Marriage*, should be consumers' first clue as to what's in store.

Midler and Allen are a Hollywood Hills-dwelling twin-career couple of the 1990s. He's a successful sports lawyer; she's a psychologist who's written a high-concept book on how to renew a marriage. They pack their kids off for a ski weekend and head for the Beverly Center mall to spend their 16th anniversary indulging their every whim.

Allen drops the bombshell that he's just ended a six-month affair with a 25-year-old. Midler confesses to an ongoing affair with a Czechoslovakian colleague, played by Mazursky. These emotional storms never achieve any veracity. They seem like just another indulgence on the part of the pampered, secure spouses.

Pic shot exteriors at the Beverly Center and moved to a mall in Stamford, Conn, for two weeks of interior filming. For the remainder, a huge, two-story replica mall was constructed at Kaufman Astoria Studios, NY, and 2,600 New York extras were outfitted in LA garb.

....

■ SCENES FROM THE CLASS STRUGGLE IN BEVERLY HILLS

1989, 102 MINS, US ◇ ⊚ ⊙

Dir Paul Bartel   *Prod* J. C. Katz   *Scr* Bruce Wagner
Ph Steven Fierberg   *Ed* Alan Toomayan   *Mus* Stanley Myers   *Art Dir* Alex Tavoularis
● Jacqueline Bisset, Ray Sharkey, Robert Beltran, Mary Woronov, Ed Begley Jr, Wallace Shawn (North Street)

Scenes from the Class Struggle in Beverly Hills is a lewd delight. In top form here, director Paul Bartel brings a breezy, sophisticated touch to this utterly outrageous sex farce and thereby renders charming even the most scabrous moments in Bruce Wagner's very naughty screenplay [from a story by him and Bartel].

Script is structured in the manner of a classical French farce, and features more seductions and coitus interuptus than a season of soap operas. Hoity-toity divorcee Mary Woronov is having her house fumigated and so, with her sensitive son, checks in for the weekend next door at the home of former sitcom star Jacqueline Bisset, whose husband has just kicked the bucket.

Joining the menagerie of the filthy rich are Woronov's pretentious playwright brother Ed Begley Jr, his brand-new sassy black wife Arnetia Walker, Woronov's crazed ex-husband Wallace Shawn, Bisset's precocious daughter Rebecca Schaeffer, 'thinologist' Bartel and, in a surprisingly real apparition, Bisset's late hubby, Paul Mazursky.

Droll tone is set at the outset by the quaintly 1950s titles and Stanley Myers' witty score, and the comic champagne is kept bubbly with only the most momentary of missteps.

....

■ SCENT OF A WOMAN

1992, 157 MINS, US ◇ ⊚ ⊙

Dir Martin Brest   *Prod* Martin Brest   *Scr* Bo Goldman
Ph Donald E. Thorin   *Ed* William Steinkamp, Michael Tronick, Harvey Rosenstock   *Mus* Thomas Newman
Art Dir Angelo Graham
● Al Pacino, Chris O'Donnell, James Rebhorn, Gabrielle Anwar, Philip S. Hoffman, Richard Venture
(Universal/City Light)

Of note for Al Pacino's theatrical, virtuoso star turn as a blind ex-military officer who introduces a greenhorn to the things of life, *Scent of a Woman* indulgently stretches a modest conceit well past the breaking point.

Universal release is based on a 1974 Italian film directed by Dino Risi [from Giovanni Arpino's novel *Il buio e il miele*], it stands more as a reconceptualization than a remake. Oddly, original title was kept when it has next to nothing to do with anything.

Script takes the p.o.v. of teenager Charlie Simms (Chris O'Donnell), a straight-arrow student at a snooty Eastern boarding school. While the other boys head for Vermont to ski during Thanksgiving vacation, O'Donnell is obliged to earn a few bucks by caring for a sightless lieutenant colonel (Pacino) whose family is leaving for the long weekend.

Frank Slade is a feisty, combative, irascible, remarkably insightful character who holds on to a genuine, if embittered, lust for life. He whisks the reluctant Charlie to New York, where he intends to savor some of his favorite things one last time. Most of the action is confined to the pair's suite at the Waldorf-Astoria.

O'Donnell does pretty well holding his own, although for dramatic purposes the character stays the same.

Reportedly, two shorter versions of the film were tested at previews but went over less well with auds than the release cut.

☐ 1992: Best Actor (Al Pacino).
☐ Nominations: Best Picture, Director, Screenplay Adaptation

....

■ SCENT OF MYSTERY

1960, 125 MINS, US ◇

Dir Jack Cardiff   *Prod* Michael Todd Jr   *Scr* William Roos   *Ph* John Von Kotze   *Mus* Mario Nascimbene
● Denholm Elliott, Peter Lorre, Paul Lukas, Peter Arne, Beverley Bentley, Leo McKern (Todd)

Scent of Mystery is carefully planned to synchronize scents with action in the film. Unlike Aromarama, which hit the market (in Manhattan) first, the script is designed with the smells in mind. In the Aromarama presentation, a documentary dealing with Red China, the odors were added as an afterthought.

The dispensing systems are different. In Smell-O-Vision, developed by the Swiss-born Hans Laube, the odors are piped via plastic tubing – a mile of tubing at Chicago's Cinestage Theatre – to individual seats, the scents being triggered automatically by signals on the film's soundtrack. The Aromarama smells are conveyed through the theatre's regular air ventilating system. The Smell-O-Vision odors are more distinct and recognizable and do not appear to linger as long as those in Aromarama.

Reaction of those at the Smell-O-Vision premiere was mixed. Of those queried, not all claimed to have whiffed the some 30 olfactions said to have been distributed during the course of the film. A number of balcony smellers said the aroma reached them a few seconds after the action on the screen. Other balcony dwellers said they heard a hissing sound that tipped off the arrival of a smell. Among the smells that clicked were those involving flowers, the perfume of the mystery girl in the film, tobacco, orange, shoe polish, port wine (when a man is crushed to death by falling casks), baked bread, coffee, lavender, and peppermint.

Utilizing the 70 mm Todd Process, a similar but technically different process, from Todd-AO, the picture – with or without the smells – is a fun picture, expertly directed by Jack Cardiff. It has many elements that are derivative of a Hitchcock chase film, the late Mike Todd's *Around the World in 80 Days*, and the Cinerama travelog technique.

wanders all over the Spanish landscape, covering fiestas, the running of the bulls ceremony, native dances, street scenes of Spanish cities and towns. The travelog is neatly integrated as part of the chase as Denholm Elliott, as a very proper Englishman on Spanish holiday, plays a sort of Don Quixote character who boldly stumbles through the cities and countryside as a self-appointed protector of a damsel in distress. He is accompanied by a philosophical taxi driver, neatly portrayed by Peter Lorre. Paul Lukas is properly sinister as a mysterious hired assassin.

Cardiff has wisely directed the film with a tongue-in-cheek quality. Diana Dors is seen briefly (time and costume) on a Spanish beach and Elizabeth Taylor is present at the denoument in a non-speaking role. Although smell plays an important part in Elliott's uncovering of the villain, the audience need not necessarily be involved in the odor – the recognition of a man's tobacco.

....

■ SCHOOL DAZE

1988, 120 MINS, US ◇ ⊚ ⊙

Dir Spike Lee   *Prod* Spike Lee   *Scr* Spike Lee
Ph Ernest Dickerson   *Ed* Barry Alexander Brown
Mus Bill Lee   *Art Dir* Wynn Thomas
● Larry Fishburne, Giancarlo Esposito, Tisha Campbell, Kyme, Joe Seneca, Spike Lee (40 Acres & a Mule/ Columbia)

Filmgoers who admired the freshness and energy of Spike Lee's *She's Gotta Have It* are bound to be thrown by his followup *School Daze*. A loosely connected series of musical set-pieces exploring the experience of blackness at an all-black university, film is a hybrid of forms and styles that never comes together in a coherent whole. Surprising, too, is the almost dour tone of the film.

Story, such as it is, focuses on the conflict between the militant activists on campus and the goodtime boys of Gamma Phi Gamma fraternity which comes to a head during homecoming week. Leading the freshman pledges class and begging for acceptance is the diminutive Half-Pint (Spike Lee), caught between the demands of fraternity life and the responsibilities of being black advanced by his cousin Dap Dunlap (Larry Fishburne).

Making life miserable for Half-Pint is his pledge-master and Dap's arch-rival Julian Eaves (Giancarlo Esposito). On the female side, it's the Gamma Rays vs the Jigaboos illustrating the tensions between the light-skinned, straight-haired blacks and the dark-skinned sisters.

As a director, Lee fails to strike the right note between realism and fantasy, and the heavy subject matter just falls with a thud. As an actor, however, Lee does a good job creating a sort of black babe in the woods.

....

■ SCHOOL FOR SCOUNDRELS OR HOW TO WIN WITHOUT ACTUALLY CHEATING

1960, 94 MINS, UK ⊚

Dir Robert Hamer   *Prod* Hal E. Chester (exec.)
Scr Patricia Moyes, Hal E. Chester, Peter Ustinov
Ph Erwin Hillier   *Ed* Richard Best   *Mus* John Addison
Art Dir Terence Verity
● Ian Carmichael, Terry-Thomas, Alastair Sim, Janette Scott, Dennis Price, Peter Jones (Guardsman)

The gentle art of getting and remaining 'one up' on the next fellow, so painstaking chronicled by British humorist Stephen Potter in his series of books, is engagingly translated to the screen in this delicate English comedy. Those familiar with Potter's spoofs (*Lifemanship*, *Gamesmanship*, *Oneupmanship*) will get the biggest boot out of *School for Scoundrels*.

Although it is virtually impossible to capture Potter's many intimate ironies, the scenarists have successfully caught the essence of the author's maxim – 'How to Win Without Actually Cheating' (as the film is subtitled).

Alastair Sim personifies the master lifeman down to the minutest detail – a brilliant performance. Ian Carmichael is a delight as the pitifully inept wretch who undergoes metamorphosis at Sim's finishing school for social misfits, and Terry-Thomas masterfully plummets from one-up to one-down as his exasperated victim.

Janette Scott, a fresh, natural beauty, charmingly plays the object of their attention. Unfortunately for Dennis Price and Peter Jones, they are involved in the weakest passage of the film – a none-too-subtle used car sequence that will disturb Potter purists.

....

■ SCHOOL TIES

1992, 107 MINS, US ◇ ⊚ ⊙

Dir Robert Mandel   *Prod* Stanley R. Jaffe, Sherry Lansing
Scr Dick Wolf, Darryl Ponicsan   *Ph* Freddie Francis
Ed Jerry Greenberg, Jacqueline Cambas   *Mus* Maurice Jarre   *Art Dir* Jeannine Claudia Oppewall
● Brendan Fraser, Matt Damon, Chris O'Donnell, Randall Batinkoff, Andrew Lowery, Amy Locane
(Paramount/Jaffe-Lansing)

Anti-Semitism is treated forthrightly and intelligently in Paramount's 1955-set *School Ties*. Brendan Fraser is superb in the lead role of a scholarship student painfully hiding his Jewishness to assimilate in an elite Eastern prep school.

Following the well-meaning but misguided advice of his father (Ed Lauter) to 'fit in' among his gentile schoolmates, Fraser quickly becomes a big man on campus. He's fully alive and aware, with a growing sense of irony, unlike the other boys, who struggle grimly under the burden of their families' often unreasonable expectations.

But Fraser's principal antagonist (Matt Damon) has it worse: he's doomed to a life of mediocrity and he knows it. The cancerous growth of anti-Semitic reaction against Fraser, engendered by his rivalry with Damon for a sweet but vapid shiksa Amy Locane, leads to a bitter split in the school.

Rather than neatly tying up the dramatic threads with a simple triumph-over-adversity ending, the filmmakers [working from a story by Dick Wolf] send the audience out thinking about the gray areas of life. Crisp, classical lensing gives the film a suitably '50s elegance, meshing beautifully with director Robert Mandel's subdued visual style.

● ●

■ SCORCHERS

1992, 88 MINS, UK ◇ ⓥ ⊙

Dir David Beaird *Prod* Morrie Eisenman, Richard Hellman *Scr* David Beaird *Ph* Peter Deming *Ed* David Garfield *Mus* Carter Burwell *Art Dir* Bill Eigenbrodt

● Emily Lloyd, Jennifer Tilly, Leland Crooke, Faye Dunaway, James Earl Jones, Denholm Elliot (Goldcrest)

Writer-director David Beaird's beguiling stage play about a bawdy, rollicking wedding night in the Louisiana bayou makes an uneven transfer to film. Despite some pungent performances, *Scorchers* is hampered by a nervous visual tone and inexplicable production flaws.

Emily Lloyd plays a nervous 20-year-old virgin bride whose cajun wedding night jitters are exacerbated by the community's lusty interest in the goings on. Jennifer Tilly plays a preacher's daughter who can't get her husband to prefer her to the town whore (Faye Dunaway).

Film's flighty story eventually finds two successful places to roost – a bar and the bedroom in which Lloyd and her madly frustrated young husband (James Wilder) are counseled by Lloyd's father (Leland Crooke).

Film suffers from a murky sound mix obscuring initial dialog, which already is difficult to make out with the Cajun accents.

● ●

■ SCORPIO

1973, 114 MINS, US ◇ ⓥ

Dir Michael Winner *Prod* Walter Mirisch *Scr* David W. Rintels, Gerald Wilson *Ph* Robert Paynter *Ed* Freddie Wilson *Mus* Jerry Fielding *Art Dir* Herbert Westbrook

● Burt Lancaster, Alain Delon, Paul Scofield, John Colicos, Gayle Hunnicutt, J.D. Cannon (Scimitar/United Artists)

Despite its anachronistic emulation of mid-1960s cynical spy mellers, *Scorpio* might have been an acceptable action programmer if its narrative were clearer, its dialog less 'cultured' and its visuals more straightforward.

Pic opens with the assassination of an Arab government official, but his identity and relationship to the protagonists remain puzzles beyond the film's conclusion. Even more irritating is nearly total confusion about other characters' occupations or moral positions.

Ultimately, pic settles down into the usual is-he-or-isn't-he-a-double-agent gimmick, with CIA-blackmailed Alain Delon pursuing supposed Soviet defector Burt Lancaster from Washington to Europe. While ducking his

would-be assassin, Lancaster takes refuge in the Viennese home of Paul Scofield, a Russian agent.

● ●

■ SCOTT JOPLIN

1977, 96 MINS, US ◇

Dir Jeremy Paul Kagan *Prod* Stan Hough *Scr* Christopher Knopf *Ph* David M. Walsh *Ed* Patrick Kennedy *Mus* Scott Joplin *Art Dir* William H. Hiney

● Billy Dee Williams, Clifton Davis, Margaret Avery, Eubie Blake, Godfrey Cambridge, Seymour Cassel (Motown/Universal)

Universal Pictures owed a large debt to Scott Joplin – whose ragtime music was a key factor in the enormous success of *The Sting* – and the studio paid back the debt with *Scott Joplin*, a biopic starring Billy Dee Williams originally intended for TV.

Williams is fine, and the film has a lot of verve and intensity, but the story of Joplin's life is so grim it makes the film a real downer.

Scott Joplin is buoyant fun for the first half but then becomes a harrowing ordeal when Joplin learns he has syphilis. He turns into a desperate wreck, forsaking his popular ragtime tunes to write an opera, 'Treemonisha,' which wasn't performed until 1975.

But the second half of the film makes too many wobbly jumps over periods of Joplin's life to satisfy dramatically.

● ●

■ SCOTT OF THE ANTARCTIC

1948, 111 MINS, UK ◇ ⓥ

Dir Charles Frend *Prod* Michael Balcon *Scr* Walter Meade, Ivor Montagu, Mary Hayley Bell *Ph* Jack Cardiff, Osmond Borrodaile, Geoffrey Unsworth *Ed* Peter Tanner *Mus* Ralph Vaughan Williams *Art Dir* Arne Akermark

● John Mills, Harold Warrender, Derek Bond, Reginald Beckwith, James Robertson Justice, Kenneth More (Ealing)

Scott of the Antarctic should be not only a magnificent eye-filling spectacle but also a stirring adventure. But the director's affinity to the documentary technique robs the subject of much of its intrinsic drama.

Pic's greatest asset is the superb casting of John Mills in the title role. Obviously playing down the drama on directorial insistence, Mills' close resemblance to the famous explorer makes the character come to life.

Scott's discovery that he has been beaten in the race to the South Pole should be a piece of poignant and moving drama. Instead, the five members of the expedition look very resolute, and very British, and philosophically begin the long trail home. Although depicted with fidelity, the agonies of the explorers on their homeward trek are presented with inadequate dramatization, with the result that the audience isn't emotionally affected.

● ●

■ SCOUNDREL, THE

1935, 75 MINS, US

Dir Ben Hecht, Charles MacArthur *Prod* Ben Hecht, Charles MacArthur *Scr* Ben Hecht, Charles MacArthur *Ph* Lee Garmes *Ed* Arthur Ellis *Mus* George Antheil *Art Dir* Walter E. Keller

● Noel Coward, Julie Haydon, Stanley Ridges, Martha Sleeper, Hope Williams, Ernest Cossart (Paramount)

The film is something of an audible novel. Beaucoup dialog and much palaver, with a minimum of action. It's a talky, slow exposition for the first three reels or so, all tending to indicate what a rat Anthony Mallare (Noel Coward), publisher, is.

When Julie Haydon becomes the latest romantic vis-a-vis, the motivation illustrates the same shabby technique which sends a real romance into the gutter. Coward meets destruction when an equally self-centred, cynical individual (Hope Williams) treats him

in kind, and he thus becomes the victim of a NY-Bermuda plane wreck.

Histrionically Coward has his moments, but there are others when most film fans may find it a bit difficult to remain content with just an English accent and a Continental flair of character. The illusion isn't always wholly there.

□ 1935: Nomination: Best Original Story

● ●

■ SCREAM OF STONE

1991, 105 MINS, GERMANY/FRANCE/CANADA ◇ ⓥ

Dir Werner Herzog *Prod* Walter Saxer *Scr* Hans-Ulrich Klenner, Walter Saxer *Ph* Rainer Klausmann, Herbert Raditschnig *Ed* Suzanne Baron *Mus* Ingram Marshall, Alan Lamb, Sarah Hopkins, Atahualpa Yupanqui *Art Dir* Juan Santiago

● Vittorio Mezzogiorno, Mathilda May, Stefan Glowacz, Brad Dourif, Donald Sutherland, Al Waxman (SERA/Molecule/Stock)

Ever in search of new mad adventurers to catch his fancy, Werner Herzog has found them among mountain climbers for his latest South American epic, *Scream of Stone*. While it does feature some spectacular mountain photography in an area of the world few will ever see first-hand, the dramatic and psychological aspects remain so obscure as to become silly.

Clumsy prolog introduces two champion climbers. Martin (Vittorio Mezzogiorno) is a young hotshot who, for two years running, has won a televised indoor event by scaling an artificial cliff. Roger (Stefan Glowacz), an older man and a quintessentially Herzogian figure, is the world-class climbing master who scoffs at Martin as a mere 'acrobat'.

Roger accepts a challenge to climb what he regards as the toughest peak in the world, a needlelike peak in Patagonia that he has tried and failed to conquer twice before. Accompanied by journalist Donald Sutherland, the rivals and their entourages assemble in Argentina and commence to wait around for ideal conditions for their climb.

Pic is poorly, sometimes laughably acted by an international cast playing uniquely dour, shallow, self-absorbed characters. But once the cameras get above ground level, Herzog offers quite a bit worth looking at.

● ●

■ SCREWBALLS

1983, 90 MINS, US ◇ ⓥ

Dir Rafal Zielinski *Prod* Maurice Smith *Scr* Jim Wynorski, Linda Shayne *Ph* Miklos Lente *Ed* Brian Ravok *Mus* Tim McCauley *Art Dir* Sandra Kybartas

● Peter Keleghan, Lynda Speciale, Alan Daveau, Kent Deuters, Jason Warren, Linda Shayne (New World)

Screwballs is a poor man's *Porky's*. This compendium of horny high school jokes set in 1965 is full of youthful exuberance and proves utterly painless to watch, but it is so close in premise and tone to its model that negative comparisons can't help but be drawn.

Five lads receive detentions for such infractions as posing as a doctor during girls' breast examinations and straying into the gals' locker room. Responsible for the boys' plight is snooty homecoming queen Purity Busch, evidently the only female virgin left at the school. Five guys dedicate themselves to depurifying her, and remainder of the film describes their goonlike attempts on her innocence.

Film was lensed in Toronto, which can only make one wonder why all these studies of randy young Americans come from north of the border.

● ●

■ SCROOGE

1970, 118 MINS, UK ◇ ⓥ ⊙

Dir Ronald Neame *Prod* Robert H. Solo *Scr* Leslie Bricusse *Ph* Oswald Morris *Ed* Peter Weatherley *Mus* Leslie Bricusse *Art Dir* Terry Marsh

Albert Finney, Alec Guinness, Edith Evans, Kenneth More, Laurence Naismith, Michael Medwin (Cinema Center/Waterbury)

Scrooge is a most delightful film in every way, made for under $5 million in direct costs at England's Shepperton Studios. Albert Finney's remarkable performance in the title role; executive producer Leslie Bricusse's fluid adaptation of the Charles Dickens classic, *A Christmas Carol*, plus his unobtrusive complementary music and lyrics; and Ronald Neame's delicately controlled direction which conveys, but does not force, all the inherent warmth, humor and sentimentality.

An excellent cast of key supporting players enhances both the artistry of the film and its universal appeal: Alec Guinness, as Marley's ghost and, Edith Evans and Kenneth More, respectively, as the Ghosts of Christmas Past and Present.

Finney's performance as cold-hearted Scrooge is a professional high-water mark.
□ 1970: Nominations: Best Costume Design, Art Direction: Song Score, Song ('Thenk You Very Much')

■ SCROOGED

1988, 101 MINS, US ◇ ⓦ
Dir Richard Donner *Prod* Richard Donner *Scr* Mitch Glazer, Michael O'Donoghue *Ph* Michael Chapman *Ed* Fredric Steinkamp, William Steinkamp *Mus* Danny Elfman *Art Dir* J. Michael Riva
● Bill Murray, Karen Allen, John Forsythe, John Glover, Carol Kane, Robert Mitchum (Paramount)

Scrooged is an appallingly unfunny comedy, and a vivid illustration of the fact that money can't buy you laughs. Its stocking spilling with big names and production values galore, this updating of Dickens' *A Christmas Carol* into the world of cutthroat network television is, one episode apart, able to generate only a few mild chuckles.

Scrooge here is an utterly venal network chief whose taste runs beneath the lowest common denominator, has no friends, sacks any underlings who dare to disagree with him and possesses a personal history based entirely upon having watched TV since infancy. Unfortunately for the film, things ring false from the start because Bill Murray's cruelty seems very arbitrary, unfunny and ultimately unconvincing.

Murray's network IBC is preparing to broadcast a live version of *A Christmas Carol* (with, in a good bit, Buddy Hackett as Scrooge), so it is against this backdrop that Murray's own journey through his past and toward his personal salvation takes place.

Lunatic taxi driver David Johansen spirits Murray back to his deprived childhood in 1955. By 1968, Murray is working as an office boy when he bumps into the idealistic Karen Allen and takes up with her. Within three years, however, the love of his life has left, and so starts Murray's ascent from portraying a dog on a kiddies' show into the top executive suite at the company.

Pic's comic highlight unquestionably is Carol Kane's appearance as the Ghost of Christmas Present. Kane dispenses verbal and physical punishment on her victim with sadistic glee.
□ 1988: Nomination: Best Makeup

■ SCUM

1979, 96 MINS, UK ◇ ⓦ
Dir Alan Clarke *Prod* Davina Belling *Scr* Roy Minton *Ph* Phil Meheux *Ed* Mike Bradsell *Art Dir* Mike Porter
● Ray Winstone, Mick Ford, John Judd, Phil Daniels (Boyd's)

Given that *Scum*, a relentlessly brutal slice of British reform school life, is strongly directed by Alan Clarke, and acted with admirable conviction, it is a pity that the hard-hitting

screenplay is more passionate tract than powerful entertainment.

Its appeal could have been wider with more dramatic light and shade, and its message more likely to find its mark if the basic point – that a youth penitentiary can kill, not cure – had been made through more investigative character-study, instead of via a catalog of horrific events.

Significantly, the plot of a 'trainee' (young offender) whose means of survival in the corrupt reformatory is to become top dog by meeting violence with violence started life as a BBC-TV play. Although filmed, it was never aired on account of its alleged bias and unpalatability.

■ SEA GULL, THE

1968, 141 MINS, UK ◇
Dir Sidney Lumet *Prod* Sidney Lumet *Ph* Gerry Fisher *Ed* Alan Heim *Art Dir* Tony Walton
● James Mason, Vanessa Redgrave, Simone Signoret, David Warner, Harry Andrews, Denholm Elliott (Warner/Seven Arts)

The Sea Gull is a sensitive, well-made and abstractly interesting period pic. Downbeat eternal verities – frustration, unrequited love, etc. – are projected admirably by a cast featuring James Mason, Simone Signoret (both in memorable performances), Vanessa Redgrave and David Warner.

Setting is a rural Russian house, where bailiff Ronald Radd, his wife Eileen Herlie and daughter Kathleen Widdoes seek to create a pleasant climate for the final years of Harry Andrews, a retired official who apparently has endured a life of frustration. Andrews herein is a cliche, crotchety old fool. His performance is the poorest one in the film.

Signoret, Andrews' sister, has descended for a visit, trailed by her current lover, Mason, a popular hack writer. Redgrave, a neighborhood girl, becomes entranced with Mason.

The deliberate adherence to the Chekhov's script necessarily retains the somewhat old-fashioned character motivations and plot structures.

Director Sydney Lumet has created an appropriately somber mood.

■ SEA GYPSIES, THE

(UK: *Shipwreck*)

1978, 101 MINS, US ◇ ⓦ
Dir Stewart Raffill *Prod* Joseph C. Raffill *Scr* Stewart Raffill *Ph* Thomas McHugh *Ed* Dan Greer *Mus* Fred Steiner
● Robert Logan, Mikki Jamison-Olsen, Heather Rattray, Cjon Damitri Patterson, Shannon Saylor (Raffill)

The Sea Gypsies is a sometimes touching, sometimes frightening adventure tale about a father, his two daughters, a female photojournalist, and a stowaway who set off on a round-the-world sail and wind up stranded on a desert island off the coast of Alaska.

It's a superior effort in every way – credible story, effective acting, first rate technical credits. Thomas McHugh's photography is worthy of picture postcards and Stewart Raffill's direction is expertly paced.

Loosely adapted by the director from a true story about a group of animal trainers and actors sailing from Jamaica to California, the plot opens with Robert Logan about to embark on his voyage with his two daughters (Heather Rattray and Shannon Saylor).

The trip is being financed partly by a magazine and Logan is waiting for the correspondent to arrive – the male correspondent who is also a crack sailor – when his replacement shows up. She's an attractive, ambitious female journalist (Mikki Jamison-Olsen).

A storm hits, the ship goes down and suddenly it's survival time off the coast of Alaska.

■ SEA HAWK, THE

1924, 129 MINS, US ⊗
Dir Frank Lloyd *Scr* J.G. Hawks, Walter Anthony *Ph* Norbert Brodine *Ed* Edward M. Roskam *Art Dir* Stephen Goosson, Fred Gabourie
● Milton Sills, Enid Bennett, Lloyd Hughes, Wallace MacDonald, Marc MacDermott, Wallace Beery (First National)

This picture has no end of entertainment value. It is just as thrilling and gripping as reading one of Rafael Sabatini's books; all of the punch of that author's writings has been brought to the screen.

There's action aplenty. It starts in the first reel and holds true to the last minute. Milton Sills, who is featured together with Enid Bennett, comes into his own in this production, and Bennett also scores tremendously. One must, however, not overlook Wallace Beery, a low comedy ruffian, who wades right through the story.

Frank Lloyd, who directed, is to be considered with the best that wield a megaphone. *The Sea Hawk* cost around $800,000. The properties used alone cost $135,000. The picture looks it.

■ SEA HAWK, THE

1940, 127 MINS, US ⓥ ☉
Dir Michael Curtiz *Prod* Hal B. Wallis, Henry Blanke *Scr* Howard Koch, Seton I. Miller *Ph* Sol Polito *Ed* George Amy *Mus* Erich Wolfgang Korngold *Art Dir* Anton Grot
● Errol Flynn, Brenda Marshall, Claude Rains, Flora Robson, Donald Crisp, Alan Hale (Warner)

The Sea Hawk retains all of the bold and swashbuckling adventure and excitement of its predecessor, turned out for First National by Frank Lloyd in 1923. But the screenplay of the new version is expanded to include endless episodes of court intrigue during the reign of Queen Elizabeth that tend to diminish the effect of the epic sweep of the high seas dramatics. When the script focuses attention on the high seas and the dramatic heroics of the sailors who embarked on daring raids against Spanish shipping, the picture retains plenty of excitement.

Story traces the adventures of the piratical sea fighter (Errol Flynn), commander of a British sailing ship that preys on Spanish commerce in the late 16th century. Colorful and exciting sea battle at the start, when Flynn's ship attacks and sinks the galleon of the Spanish ambassador, comes too early and is never topped by any succeeding sequences. Then follows extensive internal politics of Elizabeth's court, with the queen secretly condoning Flynn's buccaneering activities.

Little credit can be extended to the overwritten script, with long passages of dry and uninteresting dialog, or to the slow-paced, uninspiring direction by Michael Curtiz. Errol Flynn fails to generate the fire and dash necessary to successfully put over the role of the buccaneer leader, although this lack might partially be attributed to the piloting. Flora Robson gets attention in the role of Queen Elizabeth.

The Sea Hawk is a big budget production with reported cost set around $1.75 million. Expenditure is easily seen in the large sets, sweeping sea battles and armies of extras used with lavish display. From a production standpoint, the picture carries epic standards, but same cannot be said for the story.
□ 1940: Nominations: Best B&W Art Direction, Score, Sound, Special Effects

■ SEALED CARGO

1951, 90 MINS, US
Dir Alfred Werker *Prod* Samuel Bischoff, Warren Duff *Scr* Dale Van Every, Oliver H.P. Garrett, Roy Huggins *Ph* George E. Diskant *Ed* Ralph Dawson *Mus* Roy Webb

675

● Dana Andrews, Claude Rains, Carla Balenda, Philip Dorn, Onslow Stevens, Skip Homeier (RKO)

Story of adventure at sea during the Second World War [from Edmund Gilligan's *Gaunt Woman*], involving Yankee fishermen and Nazi submarines, has some fanciful exploits and not-too-believable intrigue, but it hangs together for most of the pic.

Dana Andrews plays the skipper of a New England fishing ship which comes across a shell-riddled square-rigger, *The Gaunt Woman*, off Newfoundland. Master of the floundering craft (Claude Rains) gets the smaller boat to tow his vessel to an isolated village in Newfoundland, where Andrews discovers that it is actually crammed with torpedoes and serves as the mother ship for German U-boats. Problem is one of blowing up the *Woman* without at the same time wiping out the village. Further complication is that Carla Balenda, one of Andrews' passengers, has been taken as hostage by Rains.

Andrews handles his role in convincing fashion. Rains clicks in his characterization of the German officer, getting across his menacing aspect underneath his quiet, cultured front.

● ●

■ SEANCE ON A WET AFTERNOON

1964, 116 MINS, UK ⊛
Dir Bryan Forbes   *Prod* Richard Attenborough, Bryan Forbes   *Scr* Bryan Forbes   *Ph* Gerry Turpin   *Ed* Derek York   *Mus* John Barry   *Art Dir* Ray Simms
● Kim Stanley, Richard Attenborough, Nanette Newman, Patrick Magee, Mark Eden (Rank/Allied Film Makers)

This is a skillful and, on many counts, admirable picture. Bryan Forbes' writing and direction create an aptly clammy atmosphere and he's backed by some shrewd thesping.

Onus of the acting falls heavily on Kim Stanley and Richard Attenborough. Yet though she is an exciting actress to watch, she is much Method, and technicalities occasionally get in the way.

It throws extra responsibility on Attenborough as her weak, loving and downtrodden husband. Here is a splendid piece of trouping which rings true throughout.

The star is a medium of dubious authenticity, who inveigles her spouse into a nutty plan which she confidently believes will give her the recognition due to her. Idea is to 'borrow' a child, make out it has been kidnapped, collect the ransom loot and wait for the story to pump up to front page sensation. Then she aims to hold a seance and reveal clues which will enable the cops to find the child unharmed.

The film throughout is pitched in sombre key with much macabre reference to a son that the couple never had but in whom Stanley implicitly believes. The dankness of the house in which her shabby machinations evolve is well caught, thanks to deft artwork and Gerry Turpin's searching camera.

Forbes' well-written, imaginative script [from the novel by Mark McShane] is a study in grey, abetted by the fine lensing of Turpin. An exciting, ingenious highspot involves complicated production when Attenborough is due to collect the ransom money. It was shot with hidden cameras in Leicester Square and Piccadilly at London's busiest hour. Result is an air of intense, exciting realism. So realistic, in fact, that parts of it had to be reshot. Without realizing that a film was being shot, the negative revealed several w.k. characters such as John Gielgud captured while strolling in London about their daily business.

□ 1964: Nomination: Best Actress (Kim Stanley)

● ●

■ SEA OF GRASS, THE

1947, 122 MINS, US ⊛
Dir Elia Kazan   *Prod* Pandro S. Berman
Scr Marguerite Roberts, Vincent Lawrence   *Ph* Harry Stradling   *Ed* Robert J. Kern   *Mus* Herbert Stothart
Art Dir Cedric Gibbons, Paul Groesse
● Spencer Tracy, Katharine Hepburn, Robert Walker, Melvyn Douglas, Phyllis Thaxter, Edgar Buchanan (M-G-M)

Film is loaded with very superior acting and spectacular imaginative photography. Camerawork by Harry Stradling is particularly breathtaking in the outdoor sequences for the sense of space and correct feeling it gives to this drama of the New Mexico prairielands.

Story [from the novel by Conrad Richter] is built around the traditional American feud between cattlemen and farmers, with Spencer Tracy perfect as the iron-jawed leader in the ranchers' determined stand against the inevitable surge westward of the agriculturists whose hoes and fences cut into the ranges on which the huge herds are dependent.

Katharine Hepburn is pictured as a cultured St Louis belle who goes to New Mexico to marry range-baron Tracy. His attachment is so great for the 'sea of grass' that he has no understanding of his wife's feeling for the farm families whom he is forcing to starvation by illegally keeping them from the land. Melvyn Douglas, a lawyer and judge, not only has a feeling for the farmers, but for Hepburn as well, and a natural amity grows between them.

Long arm of coincidence enters in when she finally leaves Tracy and runs into Douglas in Denver. In despair and confusion she gives herself up to him, only to turn remorseful the following day and decide to return to Tracy. A child is born and all concerned realize it is Douglas' not Tracy's. Tracy forces his wife to leave. There's never a surprise. Likewise, the cliched dialog is frequently hard to accept.

● ●

■ SEA OF LOVE

1989, 112 MINS, US ◇ ⊛ ⊙
Dir Harold Becker   *Prod* Martin Bregman, Louis A. Stoller   *Scr* Richard Price   *Ph* Ronnie Taylor   *Mus* Trevor Jones   *Art Dir* John Jay Moore
● Al Pacino, Ellen Barkin, John Goodman, Michael Rooker, William Hickey, Richard Jenkins (Universal)

Sea of Love is a suspenseful film noir boasting a superlative performance by Al Pacino as a burned-out Gotham cop.

Handsome production benefits from a witty screenplay limning the bittersweet tale of a 20-year veteran NYC cop (Pacino) assigned to a case tracking down the serial killer of men who've made dates through the personal columns.

He teams up with fellow cop John Goodman to set a trap for the murderer. Clues point to a woman being the killer.

Early on, Ellen Barkin appears as one of the suspects, but after an initial rebuff Pacino is smitten with her and crucially decides not to get her fingerprints for analysis. Pic builds some hair-raising twists and turns as the evidence mounts pointing to her guilt, climaxing in a surprising revelation.

Pacino here brings great depth to the central role. A loner with retirement after 20 years facing him, this cop is a sympathetic, self-divided individual and Pacino makes his clutching at a second chance with femme fatale Barkin believable.

● ●

■ SEA OF SAND

(US: Desert Patrol)

1958, 97 MINS, UK
Dir Guy Green   *Prod* Robert S. Baker, Monty Berman
Scr Robert Westerby   *Ph* Wilkie Cooper   *Ed* Gordon Pilkington   *Mus* Clifton Parker   *Art Dir* Maurice Pelling, Alastair McIntyre

● Richard Attenborough, John Gregson, Michael Craig, Vincent Ball, Percy Herbert, Barry Foster (Tempean)

Sea of Sand, it's claimed, is based on an original story by Sean Fielding, but there is nothing very original about it. It is a routine war adventure, with excellent all-round acting and taut direction by Guy Green.

Pic deals with the Long Range Desert Group on the eve of Alamein [in 1942]. Y Patrol is given the arduous task of blowing up one of the Nazis' biggest petrol dumps. Mission accomplished, the nine men fight their way back to base.

Shot entirely on location [in Tripolitania, Libya], director Green and cameraman Wilkie Cooper splendidly capture the remote loneliness of the vast desert, the heat, the boredom and the sense of pending danger. The screenplay is predictable, but the dialog is reasonably natural and the various characters are well drawn.

● ●

■ SEARCH, THE

1948, 105 MINS, US ⊛
Dir Fred Zinnemann   *Prod* Lazar Wechsler   *Scr* Richard Schweizer, David Wechsler, Paul Jarrico   *Ph* Emile Berna   *Ed* Hermann Haller   *Mus* Robert Blum
● Montgomery Clift, Aline MacMahon, Jarmila Novotna, Ewart G. Morrison, Ivan Jandl, Wendell Corey (M-G-M)

This simple film was made in the American zone of Germany, principally in and around the rubbled remains of Nuremberg. Only four of its actors are professionals, the others having been recruited on the spot.

The story is the familiar one of a family torn apart by the Nazis. This time the family is Czech. Only survivors are the mother and a nine-year-old boy, who are separated. Unable to differentiate between the beatings suffered from the Germans and the good intent of UNRRA's displaced persons workers, the lad runs away. His cap is found by a river bank and it is assumed he has drowned. Actually, he lives amongst the rubble until hunger tempts him close enough to a GI for the soldier to catch him.

The four professionals in the cast are Montgomery Clift, as the GI, making his film debut following a Broadway break-in; Aline MacMahon, as the camp official, and as typical a social worker as one could put a finger on anywhere; Jarmila Novotna, Metropolitan Opera singer and herself a Czech, who plays the mother, and Wendell Corey.

□ 1948: Best Motion Picture Story, Special Award (Ivan Jandl)
□ Nominations: Best Director, Actor (Montgomery Clift), Screenplay

● ●

■ SEARCHERS, THE

1956, 119 MINS, US ◇ ⊛ ⊙
Dir John Ford   *Prod* C.V. Whitney   *Scr* Frank S. Nugent   *Ph* Winton C. Hoch   *Ed* Jack Murray   *Mus* Max Steiner
Art Dir Frank Hotaling, James Basevi
● John Wayne, Jeffrey Hunter, Vera Miles, Ward Bond, Natalie Wood, Hank Worden (Whitney/Warner)

The Searchers is a western in the grand scale – handsomely mounted and in the tradition of *Shane*. The VistaVision-Technicolor photographic excursion through the southwest – presenting in bold and colorful outline the arid country and areas of buttes and giant rock formations – is eyefilling and impressive.

Yet *The Searchers* is somewhat disappointing. There is a feeling that it could have been so much more. Overlong and repetitious, there are subtleties in the basically simple story that are not adequately explained. There are, however, some fine vignettes of frontier life.

The picture [from the novel by Alan LeMay] involves a long, arduous trek through primitive country by two men in search of nine-year-old girl kidnaped by hostile Comanche Indians.

Wayne, the uncle of the kidnaped girl, is a bitter, taciturn individual throughout and the reasons for his attitude are left to the imagination of the viewer. His bitterness towards the Indians is understandable. They massacred his brother's family (except for the kidnaped girl) and destroyed the ranch. He feels the girl has been defiled by the Indians during her years with them and is determined to kill her. Wayne's partner in the search is Jeffrey Hunter, who is also involved in labored attempts at comic relief.

Wayne is fine in the role of hard-bitten, misunderstood, and mysterious searcher and the rest of the cast acquits itself well, notably Hunter and Vera Miles.

☐ 1969: Nominations: Best Editing, Original Musical Score

■ SEARCH FOR PARADISE

1957, 120 MINS, US ◇
Dir Otto Lang   *Prod* Lowell Thomas   *Scr* Lowell Thomas, Otto Lang, Prosper Buranelli   *Ph* Harry Squire, Jack Priestley   *Ed* Lovel S. Ellis, Harvey Manger   *Mus* Dimitri Tiomkin
● Lowell Thomas, James S. Parker, Christopher Young (Cinerama)

The fourth Cinerama sticks almost slavishly to established formulae. Once more strange lands are 'seen' by two selected 'tourists' this time a make-believe air force major (Christopher Young) and sergeant (James S. Parker) who, at the payoff, decide that they'll sign up for another hitch, the air force itself being the ultimate paradise.

The beginning of the picture is cornily contrived. An Associated Press newsmachine is seen ticking out a bulletin that Lowell Thomas is one of three ambassadors just appointed to represent Washington at the coronation durbar of King Mahendra of Nepal.

The several stops of *Search* are all way-stations en route to Nepal. The picture centres upon the approach to and environs of the Himalayas, world's greatest peaks, truthfully described as a region of mystery, age, mysticism and Communistic intrigue.

Lowell picks up the major and the sarge in the Vale of Kashmir, a plausible paradise indeed, especially its Shalimar Gardens. The visit at Nepal is the big sequence. And a stunning display of oriental pomp it is. This segment is a genuine peep into dazzling fantasy and a true coup for Cinerama and Thomas.

■ SEA WOLF, THE

1941, 98 MINS, US
Dir Michael Curtiz   *Prod* Henry Blanke (assoc.)
Scr Robert Rossen   *Ph* Sol Polito   *Ed* George Amy   *Mus* Erich Wolfgang Korngold   *Art Dir* Anton Grot
● Edward G. Robinson, Ida Lupino, John Garfield, Alexander Knox, Gene Lockhart, Barry Fitzgerald (Warner)

Jack London's famous hellship sails for another voyage over the cinematic seas in this version of *The Sea Wolf*. Edward G. Robinson steps into the role of the callous and inhuman skipper, Wolf Larsen.

John Garfield signs on to the sailing schooner to escape the law. Ida Lupino (also a fugitive) and the mild-mannered novelist (Alexander Knox) are rescued from a sinking ferryboat in San Francisco bay. Robinson is the dominating and cruel captain who takes fiendish delight in breaking the spirits of his crew and unwilling passengers.

Robinson provides plenty of vigor and two-fisted energy to the actor-proof role of Larsen, and at times is over-directed. Garfield is the incorrigible youth whose spirit cannot be broken, and is grooved to his familiar tough characterization of previous pictures.

Lupino gives a good account of herself in the rough-and-tumble goings on, but the romantic angle is under-stressed in this version.

Michael Curtiz directs in a straight line, accentuating the horrors that go on during the voyage of the *Ghost*.

■ SEA WOLVES, THE
THE LAST CHARGE OF THE CALCUTTA LIGHT HORSE

1980, 120 MINS, UK ◇ Ⓥ
Dir Andrew V. McLaglen   *Prod* Euan Lloyd
Scr Reginald Rose   *Ph* Tony Imi   *Ed* John Glen   *Mus* Roy Budd   *Art Dir* Syd Cain
● Gregory Peck, Roger Moore, David Niven, Trevor Howard, Barbara Kellermann, Patrick Macnee (Lorimar)

How a band of pip-pip British civilians rallied to King and country, tucked in their pot bellies and knocked out a German spy nest that was playing havoc with wartime Allied shipping in the Indian Ocean.

Touted as 'the last great untold action story of the war', film was scripted by Reginald Rose from James Leasor's novel *Boarding Party*.

Sea Wolves is unabashed flag-waving, a salute to the Calcutta Light Horse, a part-time regiment whose membership consisted mainly of colonial business types way past draft age but recruited as volunteers for the destruction of three German freighters interned in coastal waters off the then-neutral Portuguese colony of Goa.

Gregory Peck's a Britisher in this one, but the affected accent won't fool anyone. He and Roger Moore are regular army. The stiff-uppered civvy retreads, headed by David Niven, include Trevor Howard and Patrick Macnee.

■ SEBASTIAN

1968, 100 MINS, UK ◇ Ⓥ
Dir David Greene   *Prod* Herbert Brodkin, Michael Powell   *Scr* Gerald Vaughn-Hughes   *Ph* Gerry Fisher   *Ed* Brian Smedley-Aston   *Mus* Jerry Goldsmith   *Art Dir* Wilfrid Shingleton
● Dirk Bogarde, Susannah York, Lilli Palmer, John Gielgud, Janet Munro, Ronald Fraser (Paramount/Maccius)

Very good direction, acting and dialog are apparent in *Sebastian*, but a fatal flaw in basic plotting makes this production just a moderately entertaining Cold War comedy-drama.

The amusing, and not so amusing, pressures on persons who break foreign government secret codes are potent angles for a strong film, but, herein, story touches so many bases that it never really finds a definite concept.

Leo Marks' original screen story, scripted by Gerald Vaughn-Hughes, depicts Dirk Bogarde as a daffy math genius in cryptography. Susannah York, a new recruit to the code force, breaks down his romantic reserve.

Lilli Palmer, as a politically-suspect coder, and John Gielgud, an Intelligence chief, add lustre. Janet Munro scores very well as a boozy fading pop singer who, with Ronald Fraser, attempts to compromise Bogarde's security clearance.

Despite all the plus elements, film wanders about in its unfolding. Short, tight scenes of good exposition are broken by recurring transitional sequences which add up to an apparent padding effect.

■ SECONDS

1966, 108 MINS, US
Dir John Frankenheimer   *Prod* John Frankenheimer, Edward Lewis   *Scr* Lewis John Carlino   *Ph* James Wong Howe   *Ed* Ferris Webster, David Webster   *Mus* Jerry Goldsmith   *Art Dir* Ted Howarth
● Rock Hudson, Salome Jens, John Randolph, Will Geer, Jeff Corey, Richard Anderson (Paramount)

US suburbia boredom is treated in an original manner in this cross between a sci-fi opus, a thriller, a suspense pic and a parable on certain aspects of American middle-class life.

A middle-aged man has lost contact with his wife. His only daughter is married and gone. Even his work, which was his mainstay in life, seems to pall. Into this comes a strange call from a supposedly dead friend to come to a certain place.

He finds himself in a mysterious big business surgery corporation with some disquieting features of a room full of listless men. He is told he can be redone surgically to become a young man and start life over again. He decides to go through with it and after surgery wakes up as Rock Hudson.

This has some intriguing aspects on the yearning for youth and a chance to live life over again by many men. But this Faustian theme is barely touched on and the hero's tie with the past is also somewhat arbitrary. Film [from the novel by David Ely] does not quite come off as a thriller, sci-fi adjunct or philosophical fable.

■ SECRET AGENT, THE

1936, 83 MINS, UK Ⓥ ⊙
Dir Alfred Hitchcock   *Prod* Michael Balcon   *Scr* Charles Bennett, Ian Hay, Jesse Lasky Jr   *Ph* Bernard Knowles   *Ed* Charles Frend   *Mus* Louis Levy   *Art Dir* Otto Wrendorff, Albert Jullion
● Madeleine Carroll, Peter Lorre, John Gielgud, Robert Young, Percy Marmont, Lilli Palmer (Gaumont-British)

Secret Agent dallies much on the way but rates as good spy entertainment, suave story telling, and, in one particular case, brilliant characterization. This is the role of the Mexican hired killer as played by Peter Lorre. Director Alfred Hitchcock has done well at lending the tale's grim theme [from the play by Campbell Dixon, based on the novel *Ashenden* by W. Somerset Maugham] with deftly fashioned humor, appropriate romantic interplay and some swell outdoor photography.

More critical element will find the part of Madeleine Carroll somewhat straining credulity. The film has her philandering at the game of espionage and out of sheer ineptitude pulling one of the major coups of the service. Likewise unconvincing is the overly sensitive conduct in which her co-spy (John Gielgud) indulges once he is bitten by love.

Production maintains an easy-going pace almost throughout, with most of the action cast against the background of the Swiss Alps. Gielgud is assigned to Switzerland to prevent a German spy from getting back into pro-German territory. To do the actual killing, Lorre, a Mexican with a juvenile sense of fun but a boundless enthusiasm for playing the knife upon humans, is sent along. Arriving on the scene, Gielgud finds that Carroll had been matched with him for the job, with the pair to pose as man and wife.

■ SECRET BEYOND THE DOOR . . .

1947, 98 MINS, US Ⓥ
Dir Fritz Lang   *Prod* Fritz Lang   *Scr* Silvia Richards   *Ph* Stanley Cortez   *Ed* Arthur Hilton   *Mus* Miklos Rozsa   *Art Dir* Max Parker
● Joan Bennett, Michael Redgrave, Anne Revere, Barbara O'Neil, Natalie Schafer (Universal/Diana)

Film carries the Diana Productions label, a combo of Walter Wanger, Fritz Lang and Joan Bennett who have been responsible for several other Diana thrillers. It is arty, with almost surrealistic treatment in camera angles, story-telling mood and suspense, as producer-director Lang hammers over his thrill points.

Co-starring with Bennett is Michael Redgrave. He disappoints as the man with an anti-woman complex who nearly murders his wife before finding out what his trouble is. Bennett is good as the rich, useless society girl who finds a love so strong she would rather die than give it up.

Mental complexities of the principals makes it sometimes hard to sort out the various motivations used to spin the tale. It's based on a story by Rufus King, scripted by Silvia Richards. Such psychiatric tricks as mental cases who recoil at locked doors, lilacs, or become oddly stimulated by physical combat and looks are some of the suspense devices.

■ **SECRET CEREMONY**

1968, 109 MINS, UK ◇ ⑲

Dir Joseph Losey   *Prod* John Heyman, Norman Priggen   *Scr* George Tabori   *Ph* Gerald Fisher   *Ed* Reginald Beck   *Mus* Richard Rodney Bennett   *Art Dir* Richard MacDonald

● Elizabeth Taylor, Mia Farrow, Robert Mitchum, Peggy Ashcroft, Pamela Brown (Universal)

Robert Mitchum is featured in this macabre tale [from a short story by Marco Denevi] of mistaken identity, psychological and sexual needs, ultimate suicide and murder. Moody, leisurely developed and handsomely produced, it was made at England's Elstree Studios.

Mia Farrow, playing a wealthy, demented and incest-prone nympho, appears to have kidnapped Elizabeth Taylor, in the role of an aging prostitute. As things turn out, Taylor does not mind being mistaken for Farrow's deceased mother; instead, she gradually, but fitfully, eases into the child's desired mold.

Only the return of Mitchum, the girl's stepfather with a libertine reputation, cues the revelation that Farrow is a sexual psychotic whose seduction of Mitchum helped ruin her mother's marriage.

Performances are generally good: Farrow's via an emphasis on facial expressions, Taylor's via a salutary toning down of her shrieking-for-speaking tendencies, and Mitchum's casual, stolid projection.

■ **SECRET FOUR, THE**

See: The Four Just Men

■ **SECRET FOUR, THE**

See: Kansas City Confidential

■ **SECRET LIFE OF AN AMERICAN WIFE, THE**

1968, 93 MINS, US ◇

Dir George Axelrod   *Prod* George Axelrod   *Scr* George Axelrod   *Ph* Leon Shamroy   *Ed* Harry Gerstad   *Mus* Billy May   *Art Dir* Jack Martin Smith

● Walter Matthau, Anne Jackson, Patrick O'Neal, Edy Williams, Richard Bull (20th Century-Fox/Charlton)

The Secret Life of an American Wife, as the title might indicate, is a light sophisticated marital farce. Basic idea, which sometimes takes on the aspect of a French romp, takes a comedy look at sex in the person of a 34-year-old Connecticut wife who thinks she's gone to pot and lost all her appeal. More skillful development might have heightened impact of her deciding to do something about it, but overall the tale is amusing.

George Axelrod production, which he also wrote and directed, actually is a one-woman show with a couple of male characters tossed in for necessary consequence.

Even when such a past master at comedy as Walter Matthau, in role of a top film star on whom Anne Jackson tries her wiles, enters, the unfoldment is focused on her.

Jackson is enticing as the wife of a public relations man, Patrick O'Neal, who must cater to his top client, Matthau, whenever latter comes to NY from Hollywood for a round of frolic.

Matthau turns on all the faucets in his delineation of the thesp, who spends most of his scenes in pajama bottoms and a towel.

■ **SECRET LIFE OF WALTER MITTY, THE**

1947, 108 MINS, US ◇ ⑲ ⊙

Dir Norman Z. McLeod   *Prod* Samuel Goldwyn   *Scr* Ken Englund, Everett Freeman   *Ph* Lee Garmes   *Ed* Monica Collingwood   *Mus* David Raksin   *Art Dir* George Jenkins, Perry Ferguson

● Danny Kaye, Virginia Mayo, Boris Karloff, Fay Bainter, Ann Rutherford, Florence Bates (RKO/Goldwyn)

Some of the deepest-dyed Thurber fans may squeal since there's naturally considerable change from the famed short story on which the screenplay is built. There's a basic switch in the plot that has been concocted around the Mitty daydreams. Thurber's whole conception of Mitty was an inconsequential fellow from Perth Amboy, NJ, to whom nothing – but nothing – ever happened and who, as a result, lived a 'secret life' via his excursions into daydreaming. In contrast, the picture builds a spy-plot around Mitty that is more fantastic than even his wildest dream.

Danny Kaye reveals a greater smoothness and polish thespically and a perfection of timing in his slapstick than has ever been evident in the past.

Exceedingly slick job is done on the segues from the real-life Mitty into the dream sequences. Mitty's fantasies carry him through sessions as a sea captain taking his schooner through a storm, a surgeon performing a next-to-impossible operation, an RAF pilot, a Mississippi gambler, a cowpuncher and a hat designer. They're all well-loaded with satire, as is the real-life plot with pure slapstick.

Virginia Mayo is the beautiful vis-a-vis in both the real-life spy plot, and the dreams. She comes a commendable distance thespically in this picture. Karloff wins heftiest yaks in a scene in which he plays a phony psychiatrist convincing Mitty he's nuts.

■ **SECRET OF MY SUCCE$S, THE**

1965, 112 MINS, UK ◇

Dir Andrew L. Stone   *Prod* Virginia Stone, Andrew L. Stone   *Scr* Andrew L. Stone   *Ph* David Boulton   *Ed* Virginia Stone, Noreen Ackland   *Mus* Lucien Cailliet, Derek New, Joao Baptista Laurenco, Christopher Stone

● Shirley Jones, Stella Stevens, Honor Blackman, James Booth, Lionel Jeffries, Amy Dolby (M-G-M)

There are several capable players in *Secret of My Succe$s*, many of them from the British studios. But the screenplay Andrew L. Stone has whipped up is too much of a handicap, and what might have been a bright, little British comedy turns out to be neither comedy nor melodrama.

Three almost separate yarns are employed to trace the rise of a lowly English town constable to position of ruler in a mythical Latin-American country.

Initial episode details how his understanding of a comely, little village dressmaker (Stella Stevens), while only a town constable, wins a promotion to police inspector. The curvaceous, red-haired Stevens puts this across despite all its implausibilities, such as hiding the body of her slain husband.

Booth's first big job as police inspector shows him becoming involved with a baroness. This little tale tells about the breeding of giant spiders until they become as big as over-sized bulldogs – and large enough to crush a man to death.

Another sharp maneuver by his mother wins Booth the job of liaison officer to the president of Guanduria, Latin-American mythical land. By helping Shirley Jones, who is secretly plotting a revolution, he winds up as new ruler of this country.

■ **SECRET OF MY SUCCESS, THE**

1987, 110 MINS, US ◇ ⑲ ⊙

Dir Herbert Ross   *Prod* Herbert Ross   *Scr* Jim Cash, Jack Epps, A.J. Carothers   *Ph* Carlo Di Palma   *Ed* Paul Hirsch   *Mus* David Foster   *Art Dir* Edward Pisoni, Peter Larkin

● Michael J. Fox, Helen Slater, Richard Jordan, Margaret Whitton, John Pankow, Christopher Murney (Rastar)

The Secret of My Success is a bedroom farce with a leaden touch, a corporate comedy without teeth. What it does have is Michael J. Fox in a winning performance as a likable hick out to hit the big time in New York.

Fresh off the bus from Kansas, Brantley Foster (Fox) doesn't want to return until he has a penthouse, jacuzzi, a beautiful girlfriend and a private jet he can go home in. His ideals are a yuppie's dream.

Fox encounters the predictable crime-infested corners of New York and his squalid apartment is furnished with roaches and rats. When he meets his dream girl (Helen Slater), he is literally thunderstruck.

After young Brantley lands a job in the mailroom of an anonymous NY corporation his big chance comes when he takes over an abandoned office and sets himself up as a young exec.

Fox, in spite of his inherent charm, lacks a genuine personality and is neither country bumpkin nor city sharpie. Consequently, the film lacks a consistent tone or style.

■ **SECRET OF NIMH, THE**

1982, 82 MINS, US ◇ ⑲ ⊙

Dir Don Bluth   *Prod* Don Bluth, Gary Goldman, John Pomeroy   *Scr* Don Bluth, Gary Goldman, John Pomeroy, Will Finn   *Ed* Jeffrey Patch   *Mus* Jerry Goldsmith

● (M-G-M/United Artists)

The Secret of NIMH is a richly animated and skillfully structured film created by former Disney animators Don Bluth, Gary Goldman and John Pomeroy. As craft, their first feature film is certainly an homage to the best of an age ago. Every character moves fluidly and imaginatively against an extravaganza of detailed background and dazzling effects, all emboldened by fascinating colored textures.

The story is simple. A mother mouse (voiced by Elizabeth Hartman) is simply trying to find a new home for her brood before the old one is destroyed by spring plowing. Her task is complicated by the severe illness of a son, too sick to move.

Beyond that, the layers pile high. On the light side there's the comedy of Dom DeLuise as a clumsy crow who tries to help. At the worst are a pack of rats led for good and ill by Derek Jacobi, Peter Strauss and Paul Shenar, all influenced by some modern-day sci-fi mind-bending, mixed with old-fashioned sorcery. John Carradine also serves well as a menacing but helpful great owl, full of wisdom and woe.

■ **SECRET OF SANTA VITTORIA, THE**

1969, 134 MINS, US ◇

Dir Stanley Kramer   *Prod* Stanley Kramer   *Scr* William Rose, Ben Maddow   *Ph* Giuseppe Rotunno   *Ed* William Lyon, Earle Herdan   *Mus* Ernest Gold   *Art Dir* Robert Clatworthy

● Anthony Quinn, Anna Magnani, Virna Lisi, Hardy Kruger, Sergio Franchi, Giancarlo Giannini (United Artists)

The Secret of Santa Vittoria comes near being a dramatic knockout, so tempered with humor and understanding that it also becomes an idyll of war and Italian peasantry. Carrying charm, suspense, romance, the production offers Anthony Quinn at his seasoned best, a plot and unfoldment that holds the spectator.

Based on the Robert Crichton bestseller, its story – said to be true and to have become a legend – is simple. The people of a hill town in northern Italy are suddenly thrown into shock when apprised that a detachment of the retreating German army is to descend on their town to confiscate all their wine, their very life blood.

Screenplay painstakingly develops this conflict, to which Stanley Kramer's direction adds fascinating character evolvement and ingenious invention.

. . . .

■ SECRET PEOPLE

1952, 96 MINS, UK

Dir Thorold Dickinson *Prod* Sidney Cole *Scr* Thorold Dickinson, Wolfgang Wilhelm *Ph* Gordon Dines *Ed* Peter Tanner *Mus* Roberto Gerhard *Art Dir* William Kellner

● Valentina Cortese, Serge Reggiani, Charles Goldner, Audrey Hepburn, Megs Jenkins, Athene Seyler (Ealing)

Secret People is a hackneyed story of political agents working against a tyrannical dictator, dressed up with all the familiar cliches to make a dull and rather confusing offering.

The yarn has a prewar setting, opening in London in 1930 with the arrival of two girls whose father has been killed by a European dictator. Story skips seven years, when the two girls together with the Italian cafe owner who has adopted them, spend a weekend in Paris. There, the older girl runs into the boy she left behind at home to carry on her father's work. He follows her to London, and compels her to act as an accomplice in an attempt on the dictator's life.

Audrey Hepburn, in a minor role combines beauty with skill, particularly in two dance sequences.

. . . .

■ SECRET PLACES

1984, 96 MINS, UK ◇ ⓥ

Dir Zelda Barron *Prod* Simon Relph, Ann Skinner *Scr* Zelda Barron *Ph* Peter MacDonald *Ed* Laurence Mery-Clark *Mus* Michel Legrand *Art Dir* Eileen Diss

● Marie-Therese Relin, Tara MacGowran, Claudine Auger, Jenny Agutter, Cassie Stuart, Anne-Marie Gwatkin (Skreba/Virgin)

Secret Places is a pleasing evocation of schoolgirl life in England during World War II.

Based on a novel by Janice Elliott, the film recounts the initially hostile response of a group of adolescents to the enrollment of Laura Meister, a German refugee, in their all-girl school. Gradually her exotically winning ways and intelligence secure her enrollment in the select circle which gathers in 'secret places'. Things turn sour, however, when a girl's father is killed in battle.

The plot relates the psychological pressures which lead to Laura's attempted suicide.

Marie-Therese Relin captures the gestures and looks of a girl whose emotional resilience conceals suffering. Tara MacGowran is right on as a repressed English girl.

. . . .

■ SECRET POLICEMAN'S BALL, THE

1980, 91 MINS, UK ◇ ⓥ ⊙

Dir Roger Graef *Prod* Roger Graef, Thomas Schwalm *Ph* Ernest Vincze, Clive Tickner, Pascoe MacFarlane *Ed* Thomas Schwalm

● John Cleese, Peter Cook, Eleanor Bron, Pete Townshend, Rowan Atkinson, Michael Palin (Document/Amnesty International)

Roger Graef's film record of the 1979 Amnesty International benefit show at Her Majesty's Theatre, London, is primarily aimed at the tube.

John Cleese, Michael Palin and Terry Jones of the *Monty Python* team appear in various sketches; guitarist Pete Townshend plays acoustic versions of a couple of The Who's repertoire, joined on one by classical picker John Williams; Peter Cook (sans Dudley

Moore) renders a takeoff of one of the local hits of 1979 – the judge's summing-up in the trial of Liberal politician Jeremy Thorpe; and Billy Connolly, Clive James and Eleanor Bron, among others, contribute solo spots. All gave their services free.

There is no backstage material in *The Secret Policeman's Ball*, which is a disappointment. The earlier such venture, *Pleasure at Her Majesty's* [1976], included footage of hasty rehearsals and dressing-room neurosis, which leavened the laugh-lump with an extra dimension.

. . . .

■ SECRET POLICEMAN'S OTHER BALL, THE

1982, 99 MINS, UK ◇ ⓥ ⊙

Dir Julian Temple *Prod* Martin Lewis, Peter Walker *Scr* Marty Feldman, Michael Palin, Martin Lewis, and members of the cast *Ph* Oliver Stapleton *Ed* Geoff Hogg

● Rowan Atkinson, Alan Bennett, John Cleese, Billy Connolly, Victoria Wood, Eric Clapton (Amnesty International)

The second filmed record of the bi-annual Amnesty International fundraiser in London. *The Secret Policeman's Other Ball* is a thoroughly entertaining concert pic. As irreverent and clever as its title, show boasts comic talents from *Monty Python, Beyond the Fringe* and *Not the Nine O'Clock News* and therefore does require a taste for British humor.

Some of the humor slides over into tastelessness, but most of it is rousing fun in the tradition of the groups from which these performers have sprung. Particularly hilarious are a *Top of the Form* quiz show take-off in which the moderator gets the correct answers mixed up, and a deadpan, coming-out-of-the-closet sexual confession by Alan Bennett.

. . . .

■ SECRET WAR OF HARRY FRIGG, THE

1968, 110 MINS, US ◇

Dir Jack Smight *Prod* Hal Chester *Scr* Peter Stone, Frank Tarloff *Ph* Russell Metty *Ed* Terry Williams *Mus* Carlo Rustichelli *Art Dir* Alexander Golitzen, Henry Bumstead

● Paul Newman, Sylva Koscina, Tom Bosley, Andrew Duggan, John Williams, Werner Peters (Universal/Albion)

The Secret War of Harry Frigg is an amusing World War II comedy starring Paul Newman as a dumb army private sent to rescue five Axis-held Allied generals. Strong story premise, excellent supporting cast and generally good dialog work to smooth over sometimes static direction and sluggish pacing.

Frank Tarloff's original story, scripted by author and Peter Stone, concerns the exploits of the title character as he effects the eventual rescue of five top brass from Italian-German incarceration. Newman plays a perennial goof-off, who achieves a measure of self-confidence and maturity under pressure. Sympathy is with him all the way.

Carrying the main comedy load are the five captured generals – Andrew Duggan, Tom Bosley, John Williams, Charles D. Gray, Jacques Roux – plus their Italo captor, Vito Scotti, and James Gregory, the US general.

There are many smiles, and some strong laughs, in the pic, result of which audience will probably emerge feeling lifted, if never consistently nor hilariously diverted.

. . . .

■ SECRET WAYS, THE

1961, 112 MINS, US

Dir Phil Karlson *Prod* Richard Widmark *Scr* Jean Hazlewood *Ph* Max Greene *Ed* Aaron Stell *Mus* John Williams *Art Dir* Werner Schlichting, Isabella Schlichting

● Richard Widmark, Sonja Ziemann, Charles Regnier, Walter Rilla, Howard Vernon, Senta Berger (Universal)

The Secret Ways emerges a ludicrous, imitative, unintentional parody of dozens of cloak-and-dagger pictures. Filmed in Europe by producer-star Richard Widmark, the production amounts to a sort of poor man's *Third Man*.

The undistinguished, astonishingly uninformative screenplay was adapted from the novel by Alistair MacLean. Widmark stars as an American adventurer-for-hire who hires out to rescue a noted scholar from behind the Iron Curtain in Hungary. He has a running skirmish with the Budapestiferous AVO (Hungarian Secret Police), but ultimately gets his man.

As directed by Phil Karlson, there are a few lively chase sequences but most of the film is burdened with suspicious eye-balling and unrealistically theatrical behavior.

. . . .

■ SEDUCTION OF JOE TYNAN, THE

1979, 107 MINS, US ◇ ⓥ ⊙

Dir Jerry Schatzberg *Prod* Martin Bregman *Scr* Alan Alda *Ph* Adam Holender *Ed* Evan Lottman *Mus* Bill Conti *Art Dir* David Chapman

● Alan Alda, Barbara Harris, Meryl Streep, Rip Torn, Melvyn Douglas (Universal)

Adroitly combining humor and intimate drama, *Joe Tynan* joins that list of exemplary Washington-set pix, including *Advise and Consent* and *The Best Man*.

In large part, the credit goes to Alan Alda, whose portrayal in the title role is no less complex and multi-faceted than his screenplay. Joe Tynan is a familiar political figure: the young, handsome liberal Senator who rides upward on the coat-tails of a few big media victories. Alda assumes the pasted-on smile, the hearty handshake and breezy confidence of a politico with immense ease. He seems to have been born for the role.

Less often explored is the price paid for such double-edged success, and this is where *Joe Tynan* excels. As Alda's intelligent and frustrated wife, Barbara Harris gives the performance of her career.

. . . .

■ SEE NO EVIL
(UK: Blind Terror)

1971, 87 MINS, US ◇ ⓥ

Dir Richard Fleischer *Prod* Martin Ransohoff, Leslie Linder *Scr* Brian Clemens *Ph* Gerry Fisher *Ed* Thelma Connell *Mus* Elmer Bernstein *Art Dir* John Hoesli

● Mia Farrow, Dorothy Alison, Robin Bailey, Diane Grayson, Brian Rawlinson, Norman Eshley (Filmways)

Brian Clemens' script has Mia Farrow recuperating from a blinding horse riding accident at the home of Robin Bailey, his wife Dorothy Alison and daughter Diane Grayson. An innocently-offended young punk slays the household while Farrow is riding with fiance Norman Eshley. Extremely good suspense is built and maintained as Farrow discovers the senseless murders, then outwits the murderer who has returned to recover a wrist bracelet.

Paul Nicholas, the murderer, is not seen facially until the climax though Gerry Fisher's lensing puts the mysterious character in an emphatic dramatic posture throughout via shooting his boots and arrogant bodily mannerisms. Clemens' script seeds the plot with a thousand sock red herrings, but Farrow's lengthy travails in time become rather heavy on the meller side; all that's missing is for her to be trapped on an ice floe.

Farrow's performance as a blind girl is very convincing, grabbing and maintaining audience sympathy for her character.

. . . .

■ SEE NO EVIL, HEAR NO EVIL

1989, 103 MINS, US ◇ ⓥ ⊙

Dir Arthur Hiller *Prod* Marvin Worth *Scr* Earl Barret, Arne Sultan, Eliot Wald, Andrew Kurtzman, Gene Wilder

Ph Victor J. Kemper *Ed* Robert C. Jones *Mus* Stewart Copeland *Art Dir* Robert Gundlach
● Richard Pryor, Gene Wilder, Joan Severance, Kevin Spacey, Kirsten Childs, Anthony Zerbe (Tri-Star)

With Richard Pryor and Gene Wilder in the lead roles, *See No Evil, Hear No Evil* could only be a broadly played, occasionally crass, funny physical comedy.

How the blind Pryor ends up working for the deaf Wilder at a Manhattan lobby newsstand really is inconsequential, since neither their first encounter, nor anything that follows, is believable for a minute, including the thing that binds them in the first place – how each denies his limitations.

While Wilder's back is turned, a customer is shot in the back. Pryor is out on the curb listening for the New York *Daily News* to make its morning drop – so he misses hearing anything inside.

By the time Wilder turns around, he's only able to catch a glimpse of the assailant's (Joan Severance) sexy gams. Pryor has missed it all, though he does manage to catch a whiff of Severance's perfume before she slips by him onto the crowded street.

The cops arrive and, in predictable fashion, arrest the only suspects around, the two numbskulls who couldn't possibly coordinate anything, much less a murder.

■ SEE YOU IN THE MORNING

1989, 119 MINS, US ◇ ⓥ ⊙
Dir Alan J. Pakula *Prod* Alan J. Pakula *Scr* Alan J. Pakula *Ph* Donald McAlpine *Ed* Evan Lottman *Art Dir* George Jenkins
● Jeff Bridges, Alice Krige, Farrah Fawcett, Drew Barrymore, Lukas Haas, Macaulay Culkin (Lorimar)

See You in the Morning is a bad dream for those who've admired Alan J. Pakula's best work.

Pakula produced, wrote and directed the semi-autobiographical story of a man torn between two families and two marriages.

Jeff Bridges is a Manhattan psychiatrist who tries earnestly to fit in with his new life with second wife Beth (Alice Krige) and her two kids, while remaining the most decent of dads to his own two kids. Their mother is played by Farrah Fawcett.

As dull as this sounds, it's even more boring to watch. At just under two hours, it seems nearly interminable.

Pakula tried too hard to make this into a romantic comedy. Bridges' character jokes to avoid talking about his feelings (some shrink!) while Krige is the guilt-ridden martyr type.

■ SEIZE THE DAY

1986, 93 MINS, US ◇ ⓥ ⊙
Dir Fielder Cook *Prod* Chiz Schultz *Scr* Ronald Ribman *Ph* Eric Van Haren Noman *Ed* Sidney Katz *Mus* Elizabeth Swados *Art Dir* John Robert Lloyd
● Robin Williams, Jerry Stiller, Joseph Wiseman, Glenne Headley, William Hickey, Tony Roberts (Learning in Focus)

The first film ever made based upon a Saul Bellow novel, *Seize the Day* can boast of earnest performances and intent, but is swamped in obviousness and the broadness of its brush strokes. Overwrought piece was made for television.

Having lost his job as a salesman, disappointed his girl friend and allowed himself to be bled dry by his estranged wife, Tommy (Robin Williams in a 'serious' starring role), who's pushing 40, returns to New York City to appeal to his father in an attempt at a new start.

Tommy finds heartlessness everywhere he turns. His father (Joseph Wiseman) is a successful doctor forever disappointed that his son didn't follow in his footsteps. The only one to take a positive interest in poor Tommy is Doc (Jerry Stiller), a physician of great alleged healing powers who in fact spends most of his time playing the commodities market.

The world of power here, in 1956, is made up exclusively of crusty old Jewish men who play cards and hang out at the steam bath, and it is not a pretty picture. Williams throws himself entirely into his character, and his desperation is palpable. Fielder Cook's direction is extremely literal, and lack of modulation is a major problem.

■ SEMI-TOUGH

1977, 107 MINS, US ◇ ⓥ ⊙
Dir Michael Ritchie *Prod* David Merrick *Scr* Walter Bernstein *Ph* Charles Rosher Jr *Ed* Richard A. Harris *Mus* Jerry Fielding *Art Dir* Walter Scott Herndon
● Burt Reynolds, Kris Kristofferson, Jill Clayburgh, Robert Preston, Bert Convy, Roger E. Mosley (United Artists)

Semi-Tough begins as a bawdy and lively romantic comedy about slap happy pro football players, then slows down to a too-inside putdown of contemporary self-help programs.

Stars Burt Reynolds, Kris Kristofferson and Jill Clayburgh are all excellent within the limits of the zigzag Walter Bernstein script and Michael Ritchie's ambivalent direction.

Dan Jenkins' book was adapted by Bernstein to tell of pals Reynolds and Kristofferson, members of a flashy team owned by eccentric Robert Preston, whose daughter (Clayburgh) roommates with the two guys. She tilts romantically towards Kristofferson, whose personality has become more assured after undergoing training by Bert Convy.

■ SENATOR WAS INDISCREET, THE

(UK: Mr Ashton Was Indiscreet)

1947, 86 MINS, US ⓥ
Dir George S. Kaufman *Prod* Nunnally Johnson *Scr* Charles MacArthur *Ph* William Mellor *Ed* Sherman A. Rose *Mus* Daniele Amfitheatrof *Art Dir* Bernard Herzbrun, Boris Leven
● William Powell, Ella Raines, Arleen Whelan, Charles D. Brown, Peter Lind Hayes, Myrna Loy (Universal)

Director George S. Kaufman manifests pace and polish in a fast-moving bit of fluff [story by Edwin Lanham] about a flannel-mouth Solon whose presidential aspirations become complicated when he loses an incriminating diary wherein he had recorded every step taken by his political backers in the past 30 days. Topper finds William Powell (in the title role) in native South Seas garb and his 'queen' is the unbilled Myrna Loy – a frank takeoff on the Crosby-Hope technique of 'surprise' tongue-in-cheek fadeouts.

Powell does a fine job as the stuffy dimwit of a senator who was not stupid enough not to record his political machine's machinations. He uses that as a club over Charles D. Brown, who does a capital job as the bullying political boss. Ella Raines is the newspaper gal who rightly suspects Arleen Whelan got away with the diary as a favor to her beau, who too has political ambitions in opposition to the senator.

Casting is good down the line, and there are many nice little touches (such as that autographed, oversize postage stamp whereon George Washington 'thanks' p.a. Peter Lind Hayes for 'putting me on the stamp').

■ SENDER, THE

1983, 91 MINS, US ◇ ⓥ ⊙
Dir Roger Christian *Prod* Edward S. Feldman *Scr* Thomas Baum *Ph* Roger Pratt *Ed* Alan Strachan *Mus* Trevor Jones *Art Dir* Malcolm Middleton
● Kathryn Harrold, Zeljko Ivanek, Shirley Knight, Paul Freeman, Sean Hewitt, Harry Ditson (Paramount)

The Sender is a superbly-crafted modern horror picture, credibly using telepathic communication as its premise for creating nightmarish situations.

Thomas Baum's screenplay concerns a suicidal young amnesiac (Zeljko Ivanek) near the fictional town of Corinth, Georgia. Taken to a psychiatric clinic, he establishes a telepathic link with his psychiatrist Gail Farmer (Kathryn Harrold), causing her to experience involuntarily his violent nightmares.

The 'sender' cannot control his telepathic powers, and when Dr Denman (Paul Freeman), Farmer's superior, subjects him to shock treatment and surgical experiments, he sends telepathic images of horror which disrupt the entire hospital. Farmer, who is visited by the sender's mysterious mother Jerolyn (Shirley Knight), tries to cure him.

Cast is good within script limitations, as Harrold represents an attractive, sympathetic heroine and Ivanek a mesmerizing, troubled youngster.

■ SEND ME NO FLOWERS

1964, 100 MINS, US ◇ ⓥ
Dir Norman Jewison *Prod* Harry Keller *Scr* Julius Epstein *Ph* Daniel L. Fapp *Ed* J. Terry Williams *Mus* Frank DeVol *Art Dir* Alexander Golitzen, Robert Clatworthy
● Rock Hudson, Doris Day, Tony Randall, Paul Lynde, Hal March, Edward Andrews (Universal)

Send Me No Flowers doesn't carry the same voltage, either in laughs or originality, as Doris Day and Rock Hudson's two previous entries, *Pillow Talk* (1959) and *Lover Come Back* (1961).

Adapted from the Broadway play by Norman Barasch and Carroll Moore, the thin story line romps around Hudson, a hypochondriac, overhearing his doctor discussing the fatal symptoms of another patient and believing them to be his own. In the belief he has only a few weeks to live, he sets about trying to find a suitable man to take his place as Day's husband.

Norman Jewison in his direction weaves his characters in and out of this situation as skillfully as the script will permit, having the benefit, of course, of seasoned thesps in such roles. Day is quite up to the demands of her part, indulging in a bit of slapstick in the opening sequence as she's locked out of the house in her nightgown, arms loaded with eggs and milk bottles. Hudson plays his character nobly.

Tony Randall, costarred with the pair in the other two films, again plays Hudson's pal, this time his next door neighbor, who takes his friend's expected fate even harder than the soon-to-be-deceased and goes on a three-day drunk.

■ SENTINEL, THE

1977, 91 MINS, US ◇ ⓥ
Dir Michael Winner *Prod* Michael Winner *Scr* Michael Winner *Ph* Dick Kratina *Ed* Bernard Gribble, Terence Rawlings *Mus* Gil Melle *Art Dir* Philip Rosenberg
● Chris Sarandon, Cristina Raines, Martin Balsam, John Carradine, Jose Ferrer, Ava Gardner (Universal)

The Sentinel is a grubby, grotesque excursion into religioso psychodrama, notable for uniformly poor performances by a large cast of familiar names and direction that is hysterical and heavy-handed.

The story [from Jeffrey Knovitz' novel] is based on the familiar device of taking some innocent (in this case, Cristina Raines, whose performance is miserable), confronted with kooky situations and characters whose motives are unclear except that the innocent seems to be losing mental control.

Raines, cast as a fashion model, has some mighty formidable plot adversaries: fiance Chris Sarandon, amusingly trying to play a

successful lawyer; weird neighbors like
Burgess Meredith, in ludicrous overacting
job; also pushy lesbian Sylvia Miles and lover
Beverly D'Angelo.

••••••••••••••••••••••••••••••••••

■ **SEPARATE TABLES**

1958, 98 MINS, US ⊛
Dir Delbert Mann *Prod* Harold Hecht *Scr* Terence
Rattigan, John Gay *Ph* Charles Lang Jr *Ed* Marjorie
Fowler, Charles Ennis *Mus* David Raksin
Art Dir Edward Carrere
● Rita Hayworth, Deborah Kerr, David Niven, Wendy
Hiller, Burt Lancaster, Gladys Cooper (United Artists/
Hecht-Hill-Lancaster)

As a play, *Separate Tables* consisted of two separate vignettes set against the same English
boarding house and served as an acting tour
de force for Eric Portman and Margaret
Leighton. Much of the appeal of Terence
Rattigan's play was due to the remarkable
change in characterization they were able to
make as they assumed different roles in each
of the segents. Rattigan and John Gay have
masterfully blended the two playlets into one
literate and absorbing full-length film.

Basically, story is a character study of a
group of residents of the small British seaside
town of Bournemouth, described in the film
as a tourist spot in the summer and haven for
the lonely and the desperate in the winter.
The majority of the residents are tortured by
psychological problems and unhappy pasts. As
a phoney major, with a makeup Sandhurst
background, David Niven gives one of the
best performances of his career. Deborah
Kerr is excellent as a plain, shy girl completely cowed by a domineering and strong
mother, finely portrayed by Gladys Cooper.

A separate but integrated story concerns
Burt Lancaster, Rita Hayworth and Wendy
Hiller. As a writer hurt by life and living a
don't-care existence at the out-of-the-way hotel, Lancaster turns in a shaded performance.
Hayworth is equally good as his former wife
whose narcissism and desire to dominate men
leads to Lancaster's downfall. Hiller is the efficient manager of the hotel who finds her romance with Lancaster shattered on the
arrival of his physically attractive and fashionable ex-wife.
□ 1958: Best Actor (David Niven), Supp.
Actress (Wendy Hiller).
□ Nominations: Best Picture, Actress
(Deborah Kerr), Adapted Screenplay, B&W
Cinematography, Scoring of a Dramatic
Picture

••••••••••••••••••••••••••••••••••

■ **SEPTEMBER**

1987, 82 MINS, US ◇ ⊛ ⊙
Dir Woody Allen *Prod* Robert Greenhut *Scr* Woody
Allen *Ph* Carlo D. Palma *Ed* Susan E. Morse
Art Dir Santo Loquasto
● Denholm Elliott, Dianne Wiest, Mia Farrow, Elaine
Stritch, Sam Waterston, Jack Warden (Orion)

September sees Woody Allen in a compellingly
melancholy mood, as he sends four achingly
unhappy younger people and two better adjusted older ones through a grim story
drenched with Chekhovian overtones.

Set entirely within the lovely Vermont
country home of Mia Farrow at summer's
end, tale is constructed around a pattern of
unrequited, mismatched infatuations that
drive the high-strung, intellectual characters
to distraction. Neighbor Denholm Elliott
loves Farrow, Farrow is a goner for guest-
house occupant Sam Waterston, and
Waterston is nuts for Farrow's best friend
Dianne Wiest, who is married.

Also visting are Farrow's mother, a former
screen star and great beauty played by Elaine
Stritch, and the latter's husband, physicist
Jack Warden.

So it goes, a merry-go-round of frustration,

resentment, heartbreak, disappointment and
bitterness, described in brittle, often piercing
terms in Allen's dialog. Happily, the air is
cleared on occasion by the outrageous Stritch,
whose rowdy, forthright comments never fail
to lighten the mood and provide genuine
amusement.

This is the film Allen largely reshot with a
significantly altered cast after feeling dissatisfied with his first version. Originally,
Maureen O'Sullivan, Farrow's real mother,
played the role finally filled by Stritch. Sam
Shepard, then, briefly, Christopher Walken,
had Waterston's part, and Elliott was first
cast as the actress' husband, with Charles
Durning in the role of the neighbor.

••••••••••••••••••••••••••••••••••

■ **SERGEANT, THE**

1968, 107 MINS, US ◇
Dir John Flynn *Prod* Richard Goldstone *Scr* Dennis
Murphy *Ph* Henri Persin *Ed* Charles Nelson, Francoise
Diot *Mus* Michel Magne *Art Dir* Willy Holt
● Rod Steiger, John Phillip Law, Ludmila Mikael, Frank
Latimore, Elliott Sullivan (Warner/Seven Arts)

Dennis Murphy's novel reaches the screen as
a moving production, filmed with sensitivity
by debuting director John Flynn, and with robust, appropriately grim physical values. Rod
Steiger's title-role performance is generally
excellent, and John Phillip Law hits the mark,
as the would-be mark.

To say that this is a story about a homosexual is like claiming that an iceberg floats
completely on the surface of water. The pic is
about a total, pervading enslavement of one
person to another.

A five-minute prolog, in black-and-white for
good contrast, establishes Steiger as a hero
during the 1944 liberation of France. The
heroic deed included the strangling of a helpless, disarmed German soldier. His death grip
on the younger man betrays a latent homosexuality.

Time shifts under titles to 1952, with
Steiger reporting as first sergeant at a US
base in rural France. He effectively seizes
command, and works to shape up the slovenly
unit. Law attracts Steiger's attention.
Practically dragooned into the company office, Law falls increasingly under the thrall of
Steiger.

Story threads are strongly woven, through
Murphy's own fine adaptation of his book as
well as Flynn's incisive direction.

••••••••••••••••••••••••••••••••••

■ **SERGEANT RUTLEDGE**

(Aka: *The Trial of Sergeant Rutledge*)

1960, 111 MINS, US ◇
Dir John Ford *Prod* Willis Goldbeck, Patrick Ford
Scr James Warner Bellah, Willis Goldbeck *Ph* Bert
Glennon *Ed* Jack Murray *Mus* Howard Jackson
Art Dir Eddie Imazu
● Jeffrey Hunter, Constance Towers, Billie Burke, Woody
Strode, Carleton Young, Juano Hernandez (Warner)

Give John Ford a troop of cavalry, some hostile Indians, a wisp of story and chances are
the director will come galloping home with an
exciting film. *Sergeant Rutledge* provides an extra plus factor in the form of an offbeat and
intriguing screenplay which deals frankly, if
not too deeply, with racial prejudice in the
post-Civil War era. Ford expertly blends the
action-pictorial and the story elements to create lively physical excitement as well as sustained suspense about the fate of a Negro
trooper who is accused of rape and double
murder. Original tag on this picture was
Captain Buffalo.

As the giant-sized Negro 1st sgt who is
eventually proven to be a victim of circumstantial evidence, Woody Strode gives an unusually versatile performance.

The screenplay is said to have a historical

basis in that the US 9th and 10th Cavalry of
Negro troopers, commanded by white officers,
fought skirmishes with the Apaches in
Arizona after the Civil War. Whether the actual incident which forms the plot structure –
the murder of the Commanding Officer of
the 9th Cavalry and the rape-murder of his
daughter – also is factual is not quite as important as that it plays well.

Story unfolds via a series of flashbacks from
the court martial of Strode as witnesses
describe his friendship with the dead white
girl, his panicky desertion, the circumstances
of his capture by the lieutenant (Jeffrey
Hunter) who later volunteers as defense
counsel.

Most of the action flows out of the testimony of Constance Towers, the only sympathetic witness, whom Strode has saved from
an Indian ambush.

••••••••••••••••••••••••••••••••••

■ **SERGEANTS 3**

1962, 113 MINS, US ◇
Dir John Sturges *Prod* Frank Sinatra *Scr* W.R. Burnett
Ph Winton Hoch *Ed* Ferris Webster *Mus* Billy May
Art Dir Frank Hotaling
● Frank Sinatra, Dean Martin, Sammy Davis Jr, Peter
Lawford, Joey Bishop (United Artists)

Sergeants 3 is warmed-over *Gunga Din* a westernized version of that screen epic, with
American-style Indians and Vegas-style
soldiers of fortune. The essential differences
between the two pictures, other than the
obvious one of setting, is that the emphasis
in *Gunga* was serious, with tongue-in-cheek
overtone, whereas the emphasis in *Sergeants* is
tongue-in-cheek, with serious overtones.

Although, unaccountably, no mention is
made of the obvious source in the screen
credits. W. R. Burnett's screenplay not only
owes its existence to that story, but adheres
to it faithfully, with one noteworthy exception
– *Gunga* does not die for his heroism. It's
peaches and cream all the way.

The 'Big Three' of Sinatra, Martin and
Lawford reenact the parts played in the original by Cary Grant, Victor McLaglen and
Douglas Fairbanks Jr. Of the three, Martin
seems by far the most animated and comfortable, Sinatra and Lawford coming off a trifle
too businesslike for the irreverent, look-ma-
we're-cavalrymen approach.

••••••••••••••••••••••••••••••••••

■ **SERGEANT YORK**

1941, 134 MINS, US ⊛
Dir Howard Hawks *Prod* Jesse L. Lasky, Hal B. Wallis
Scr Abem Finkel, Harry Chandlee, Howard Koch, John
Huston *Ph* Sol Polito *Ed* William Holmes *Mus* Max
Steiner *Art Dir* John Hughes
● Gary Cooper, Walter Brennan, Joan Leslie, Ward
Bond, Margaret Wycherly, George Tobias (Warner)

For more than 20 years authors sought permission to film the heroic World War deeds of
Sergeant York. And for as long a period York
refused the necessary cooperation for a film
of his heroism on the early morning of 8
October 1918, when he single-handed killed
20 Germans and compelled the surrender of
132 of the enemy in the Argonne sector.

Lauded, praised, awarded the Congressional Medal of Honor, York side-stepped all
proffers to benefit from the acclaim. He returned from army service to his home in Pall
Mall, Tenn, where he devoted himself to
farming and educational work.

It is film biography at its best. The writers
have paid more attention to character, and
the backgrounds and associations which create it, than to incident.

For Gary Cooper the role is made to order.
He convincingly portrays the youthful backwoodsman, unruly as a youth, who in time
gains mastery over his wildness. The romantic passages played with Joan Leslie are ten-

der and human. But Cooper is best, perhaps, in the scenes of early camp training when his marksmanship, learned in the woods, attracts attention. Among the featured players the reliable Walter Brennan is splendid as the combination village pastor and storekeeper.
□ 1941: Best Actor (Gary Cooper), Editing.
□ Nominations: Best Picture, Director, Supp. Actor (Walter Brennan), Supp. Actress (Margaret Wycherly), Original Screenplay, B&W Cinematography, B&W Art Direction, Scoring of a Dramatic Picture, Sound

• •

■ SERPENT AND THE RAINBOW, THE

1988, 98 MINS, US ◇ ▣ ⊙
Dir Wes Craven   *Prod* David Ladd, Doug Claybourne
Scr Richard Maxwell, A.R. Simoun   *Ph* John Lindley
Ed Glenn Farr, Peter Amundson   *Mus* Brad Fiedel
Art Dir David Nichols
● Bill Pullman, Cathy Tyson, Zakes Mokae, Paul Winfield, Brent Jennings, Michael Gough (Universal)

Wes Craven's *The Serpent and the Rainbow* is a better-than-average supernatural tale [inspired by Wade Davis' book] that offers a few good scares but gets bogged down in special effects. Film is intriguingly eerie as long as it explores the secrets of voodoo in a lush Haitian setting alive with mysteries of the spirit.

Dennis Alan (Bill Pullman), a Harvard anthropologist looking for a magic zombie powder at the behest of an American drug company, is sort of a second-rate Indiana Jones.

In Haiti, Alan gets involved with psychiatrist Marielle Celine (Cathy Tyson) who is battling the cumulative effects of deep-rooted black magic, religion and everyday mental illness.

Opposing the more progressive Marielle are the reactionary political and supernatural forces of police chief Dargent Peytraud, played with evil zeal by Zakes Mokae. Speaking out of the side of his gold-toothed mouth, Mokae walks a narrow line between being truly frightening and truly hilarious.

Special effects are well done, but fail to capture the creepy undercurrents of voodoo.

• •

■ SERPENT OF THE NILE

1953, 81 MINS, US ◇
Dir William Castle   *Prod* Sam Katzman   *Scr* Robert E. Kent   *Ph* Henry Freulich   *Ed* Gene Havlich
Mus Mischa Bakaleinikoff   *Art Dir* Paul Palmentola
● Rhonda Fleming, William Lundigan, Raymond Burr, Jean Byron, Michael Ansara, Julie Newmar (Columbia)

Producer Sam Katzman dusts off some incidents in the life and loves of Cleopatra for mediocre results in *Serpent of the Nile*. Much of the difficulty is the lack of credibility in the script. Its treatment of Mark Anthony's rise to power following Caesar's assassination and subsequent fall, when subjected to the wiles of Cleopatra, is seldom convincing. This slice of Roman history is played straight.

Yarn has Raymond Burr, as Anthony, proposing an alliance between Rome and wealthy Egypt, which is ruled by Rhonda Fleming as Cleopatra. Thoroughly unscrupulous, she schemes to eliminate Burr and place herself on the throne of Rome. Her plan, however, is nipped by William Lundigan, Burr's lieutenant, who brings the Roman legions to Alexandria.

Burr's Anthony is a wishywashy individual whose love for drink and infatuation for Fleming makes him lose his sense of logic. She, on the other hand, fails to impress as the Egyptian beauty, primarily due to the stilted dialog. Lundigan, too, has his moments of vacillation. But, fortunately, his portrayal shows enough virility and drive to meet the combat requirements the role demands.

• •

■ SERPENT'S EGG, THE

1977, 120 MINS, W. GERMANY/US ◇ ▣
Dir Ingmar Bergman   *Prod* Dino De Laurentiis
Scr Ingmar Bergman   *Ph* Sven Nykvist   *Ed* Petra von Oelffen   *Mus* Rolf Wilhelm   *Art Dir* Rolf Zehetbauer
● Liv Ullmann, David Carradine, Gert Frobe, Heinz Bennent, James Whitmore (Rialto/De Laurentiis)

The Serpent's Egg, Ingmar Bergman's first English-language feature and his first film made outside his home country, bears the master's stamp right from the beginning in a superior collaboration with cinematographer Sven Nykvist and production designer Rolf Zehetbauer.

The latter has recreated a Berlin of a poverty-ridden, fear-stricken early 1920s that is much more than paint-deep. Also, Bergman makes his actors, with one fatal exception (David Carradime), work their individualities into the grandest of ensemble playing.

The Serpent's Egg lacks both the strength and depth of Bergman's major work. By going outwardly international, the master becomes perilously close to becoming shallow as well.

• •

■ SERPICO

1973, 129 MINS, US ◇ ▣ ⊙
Dir Sidney Lumet   *Prod* Martin Bregman   *Scr* Waldo Salt, Norman Wexler   *Ph* Arthur J. Ornitz   *Ed* Dede Allen, Richard Marks   *Mus* Mikis Theodorakis
Art Dir Charles Bailey
● Al Pacino, John Randolph, Jack Kehoe, Biff McGuire, Barbara Eda-Young, Cornelia Sharpe (De Laurentiis/Artists Entertainment)

Serpico is based on the actual experiences of an honest NY policeman who helped expose corruption. Al Pacino's performance is outstanding. Sidney Lumet's direction adeptly combines gritty action and thought-provoking comment.

The real-life Frank Serpico, who climaxed an 11-year police career by blowing the lid on departmental corruption, told his story first through a book collaboration with Peter Maas.

Pacino dominates the entire film. His inner personal torment is vividly detailed, manifested first in the breakup of an affair with Cornelia Sharpe and later, much more terribly, in the wreck of his love for Barbara Eda-Young.

A very large cast exemplifies the assorted attitudes with which Pacino must deal.
□ 1973: Nominations: Best Actor (Al Pacino), Adapted Screenplay

• •

■ SERVANT, THE

1963, 117 MINS, UK ▣
Dir Joseph Losey   *Prod* Joseph Losey, Norman Priggen
Scr Harold Pinter   *Ph* Douglas Slocombe   *Ed* Reginald Mills   *Mus* John Dankworth   *Art Dir* Ted Clements
● Dirk Bogarde, Sarah Miles, Wendy Craig, James Fox, Catherine Lacey, Patrick Magee (Springbok)

The Servant is for the most part strong dramatic fare, though the atmosphere and tension is not fully sustained to the end. Harold Pinter's screenplay based on the Robin Maugham novel is distinguished by its literacy and sharp incisive dialog.

Dirk Bogarde plays a manservant who is hired by a young and elegant man about town to run a house he has just bought in a fashionable part of London, and who, almost imperceptibly, begins to dominate his master.

Up to the point where the servant gains supremacy, Joseph Losey's direction is first class, despite a few conventional shots which are used to gain effect. The last segment of the story, which puts some strain on credibility, is less convincing and, therefore, less satisfying. But the relationship of master and servant, with its underlying suggestion of homosexuality is sensitively handled.

Bogarde not only looks the part, but plays it with natural assurance. There is also a noteworthy performance from James Fox, who assuredly suggests the indolent young man about town. The two main femme roles are also expertly played, Sarah Miles making a highly provocative and sensuous maid, and Wendy Craig giving a contrasting study as the fiancee who is overwhelmed by events she cannot control.

• •

■ SET-UP, THE

1949, 72 MINS, US ▣
Dir Robert Wise   *Prod* Richard Goldstone   *Scr* Art Cohn
Ph Milton Krasner   *Ed* Roland Gross   *Mus* Constantin Bakaleinikoff (dir.)   *Art Dir* Albert S. D'Agostino, Jack Okey
● Robert Ryan, Audrey Totter, George Tobias, Alan Baxter, Wallace Ford (RKO)

Compact and suspenseful is RKO's *The Set-Up*, a boxing film which shows the seamier side of the fight racket [from the poem by Joseph Moncure March].

It throws the spotlight on 35-year-old washed-up heavyweight (Robert Ryan). Feeling that it's his lucky night, he wades through a four-rounder to kayo his opponent and spoil a match that had been fixed.

But the story itself is not the peg that integrates *Set-Up* into a biting, pictorial analysis of pugilism; the film's values primarily lie in its unmerciless character studies. Under Robert Wise's skillful direction, the assorted ringside audience 'types' give an added lustre of realism. Dressing-room hangers-on, rubdown boys and other pugs on the bill also come in for scalpel-like scrutiny.

• •

■ SEVEN BRIDES FOR SEVEN BROTHERS

1954, 102 MINS, US ◇ ▣ ⊙
Dir Stanley Donen   *Prod* Jack Cummings   *Scr* Albert Hackett, Frances Goodrich, Dorothy Kingsley
Ph George Folsey   *Ed* Ralph E. Winters   *Mus* Adolph Deutsch (dir.)   *Art Dir* Cedric Gibbons, Urie McCleary
● Howard Keel, Jeff Richards, Russ Tamblyn, Tommy Rall, Jane Powell, Julie Newmar (M-G-M)

This is a happy, hand-clapping, foot-stomping country type of musical with all the slickness of a Broadway show. Johnny Mercer and Gene de Paul provide the slick, showy production with eight songs, all of which jibe perfectly with the folksy, hillbilly air maintained in the picture. Howard Keel's robust baritone and Jane Powell's lilting soprano make their songs extremely listenable.

A real standout is the acrobatic hoedown staged around a barn-raising shindig, during which six of the title's seven brothers vie in love rivalry with the town boys for the favor of the mountain belles.

With tunes and terping taking up so much of the footage there isn't too much for Stanley Donen to do except direct the story bridges between the numbers.

It's the story of seven brothers living on a mountain farm. The eldest gets a bride and the others decide likewise, steal their maidens and after a snowed-in winter, the girls' parents mastermind a mass shot-gun wedding.

The long and the short of the teaming of Keel and Powell is that the pairing comes off very satisfactorily, vocally and otherwise. The brothers are all good, with Russ Tamblyn standing out in particular for performance and his dance work.
□ 1954: Best Scoring of a Musical Picture.
□ Nominations: Best Picture, Screenplay, Color Cinematography, Editing

S

■ SEVEN DAYS IN MAY

1964, 120 MINS, US 📺 ⊙

Dir John Frankenheimer   *Prod* Edward Lewis   *Scr* Rod Serling   *Ph* Ellsworth Fredricks   *Ed* Ferris Webster   *Mus* Jerry Goldsmith   *Art Dir* Cary Odell

● Burt Lancaster, Kirk Douglas, Fredric March, Ava Gardner, Edmond O'Brien, Martin Balsam (Seven Arts/Joel)

A combination of competents has drawn from the novel of the same title a strikingly dramatic, realistic and provocatively topical film in *Seven Days in May*. Fletcher Knebel-Charles W. Bailey II's book detailed a military plot to overthrow the government of the United States 'in the not-too-distant future'.

What *Seven Days in May* undertakes is the proposition that extremists could reach the point where they'd try to uproot the present form of government. Such a man is Gen. James M. Scott, played with authority by Burt Lancaster. He's a member of the Joint Chiefs of Staff, burning with patriotic fervor and seeking to 'save' the country from the perils of a just-signed nuclear pact with Russia. He enlists the support of fellow chiefs. Their plan of seizure is to be consummated in seven days in May.

The performances are excellent down the line, under the taut and penetrating directorial guidance of John Frankenheimer. Kirk Douglas is masterfully cool and matter of fact as Scott's aide, utterly devoted until he comes to be suspicious. He goes to the president with information that has got to be checked out in those fateful seven days.

Edmond O'Brien is standout as a southern senator with an addiction to bourbon and an unfailing loyalty to the president. Ava Gardner works out well enough as the Washington matron who has had an affair with Lancaster and is amenable to a go with Douglas.

☐ 1964: Nominations: Best Supp. Actor (Edmund O'Brien), B&W Art Direction

■ SEVEN DAYS TO NOON

1950, 94 MINS, UK

Dir John Boulting   *Prod* Roy Boulting   *Scr* Frank Harvey, Roy Boulting   *Ph* Gilbert Taylor   *Ed* Roy Boulting   *Mus* John Addison

● Barry Jones, Olive Sloane, Andre Morell, Sheila Manahan, Hugh Cross, Joan Hickson (London/Boulting)

Much of the pic was lensed on location in the London area. Focal point of the plot [by Paul Dehn and James Bernard] is an ultimatum sent to the prime minister by an atom scientist who becomes mentally deranged because his work is being used for destruction, not for mankind's benefit. He warns that unless atomic bomb production ceases by noon the following Sunday (the letter is received on the Monday morning), he will, himself, blow up all of London with a bomb he has stolen.

Barry Jones' interpretation of the scientist is intelligent. His clearly defined portrait of the man no one understands is a moving piece of acting. Principal female role, which is generously filled with comedy lines, is taken by Olive Sloane. She plays a former showgirl with rare gusto.

☐ 1951: Best Motion Picture Story

■ 711 OCEAN DRIVE

1950, 102 MINS, US

Dir Joseph H. Newman   *Prod* Frank N. Seltzer   *Scr* Richard English, Francis Swann   *Ph* Franz Planer   *Ed* Bert Jordan   *Mus* Sol Kaplan   *Art Dir* Perry Ferguson

● Edmond O'Brien, Joanne Dru, Donald Porter, Sammy White, Otto Kruger, Dorothy Patrick (Columbia)

Story concerns a telephone worker (Edmond O'Brien) with a knack for electrons who joins a syndicate and expands its operations with

his inventions. When the syndicate chief is killed, he takes charge of the organization, and runs into the opposition of an eastern syndicate. The bigger outfit makes overtures which he rejects until he meets Joanne Dru, the wife of one of the eastern leaders.

Operations of the syndicates are given a realistic touch by the screenplay, and Joseph H. Newman's direction keeps action at a fast pace. O'Brien is excellent as the hot-tempered, ambitious young syndicate chief.

■ SEVEN LITTLE FOYS, THE

1955, 92 MINS, US ◇ 📺

Dir Melville Shavelson   *Prod* Jack Rose   *Scr* Melville Shavelson, Jack Rose   *Ph* John F. Warren   *Ed* Ellsworth Hoagland   *Mus* Joseph J. Lilley   *Art Dir* Hal Pereira, John Goodman

● Bob Hope, James Cagney, Milly Vitale, Angela Clarke, George Tobias, Herbert Hayes (Paramount)

Bob Hope abandons the buffoon to go straight actor in biopicturing Eddie Foy, song-and-dance man of the vaudeville age.

From the opening when Foy vows he will always remain a single, professionally and maritally, even an audience unfamiliar with his life will know it won't be long. It isn't, and Milly Vitale, Italian film actress who does a fine job of portraying the Italian ballerina who marries Foy, is reason enough for him to change his mind. Their hit-and-miss life together is told with heart in the performances of Hope and Vitale.

A standout sequence is the appearance of James Cagney as George M. Cohan, a characterization he created with 1942 Academy Award-winning success in *Yankee Doodle Dandy*. He and Hope, in a Friars Club scene, toss the Shavelson-Rose lines back and forth for sock results and then turn in some mighty slick hoofing.

☐ 1955: Nomination: Best Story & Screenplay

■ SEVEN NIGHTS IN JAPAN

1976, 104 MINS, UK/FRANCE ◇ 📺

Dir Lewis Gilbert   *Prod* Lewis Gilbert   *Scr* Christopher Wood   *Ph* Henri Decae   *Ed* John Glen   *Mus* David Hentschel

● Michael York, Hidemi Aoki, Charles Gray, Ann Lonnberg, Eleonore Hirt, James Villiers (EMI/Paramount)

Seven Nights in Japan is a beautifully-photographed pastiche bearing little true resemblance to the enigmatic life of bustling Tokyo, where it was lensed.

Simplistic plot details the implausible romance between a royal prince (Michael York) who is serving as a naval officer, and a petite Japanese bus guide (Hidemi Aoki) whom he meets when his ship visits Japan. There are also some ludicrous attempts to kill the prince made by a fanatical gang of bungling political cut-throats.

Christopher Wood's script is sadly lacking in humor and pace and the storyline can only be labeled corny and unreal. York's acting is suitably princelike although never exceptional while Aoki has occasional moments.

■ SEVEN-PER-CENT SOLUTION, THE

1976, 113 MINS, UK ◇ 📺 ⊙

Dir Herbert Ross   *Prod* Herbert Ross   *Scr* Nicholas Meyer   *Ph* Oswald Morris   *Ed* William Reynolds, Chris Barnes   *Mus* John Addison   *Art Dir* Ken Adam

● Alan Arkin, Vanessa Redgrave, Robert Duvall, Nicol Williamson, Laurence Olivier, Joel Grey (Universal)

The Seven-Per-Cent Solution is an outstanding film. Producer-director Herbert Ross and writer Nicholas Meyer, adapting his novel, have fashioned a most classy period crime drama.

The concept is terrific, in that Sherlock

Holmes (Nicol Williamson), while a patient of Sigmund Freud (Alan Arkin), becomes his analyst's partner as both apply their specialized abilities in the parallel solution of a kidnap crime. Simultaneously, there is resolved Holmes' own childhood trauma which has motivated his lifelong enmity towards Professor Moriarty.

The title takes its name from a dope mixture used by Holmes in his addiction. Dr Watson, faithful friend, gets Holmes' brother Mycroft (Charles Gray) and mild-mannered Moriarty (Laurence Olivier) to trick Holmes to Vienna where Freud can treat him.

Holmes agrees to a powerful withdrawal regimen, which dissolves story wise into the introduction of Vanessa Redgrave, a former Freud patient cured of her own addiction, but now apparently in relapse. Holmes becomes intrigued with Redgrave's plight, as does Freud, and both pursue the matter.

☐ 1976: Nominations: Best Adapted Screenplay, Costume Design

■ SEVENTH CROSS, THE

1944, 111 MINS, US 📺

Dir Fred Zinnemann   *Prod* Pandro S. Berman   *Scr* Helen Deutsch   *Ph* Karl Freund   *Ed* Thomas Richards   *Mus* Roy Webb   *Art Dir* Cedric Gibbons, Leonid Vasian

● Spencer Tracy, Signe Hasso, Hume Cronyn, Jessica Tandy, Agnes Moorehead, George Macready (M-G-M)

Cross tells the story of seven men who escape from a concentration camp, and it follows the death or capture of six of them. Upon their escape the camp's commandant has ordered seven trees stripped and crosses nailed to them. It is his plan, as each fugitive is caught, to pinion them to the crosses and let them die of exposure.

And so this becomes the story of the seventh cross – the one that was never occupied. It is the story of George Heisler, who makes good his escape amid a web of almost unbelievable circumstances. The sheer fancy, as he eludes the Gestapo at every turn, is gripping drama.

This is a film of fine performances. There are one or two characterizations that might possibly eclipse that of the central one, played by Spencer Tracy, who, as usual, underplays and gives one of his invariably creditable portrayals.

☐ 1944: Nomination: Best Supp. Actor (Hume Cronyn)

■ 7TH DAWN, THE

1964, 123 MINS, UK ◇

Dir Lewis Gilbert   *Prod* Charles K. Feldman, Karl Tunberg   *Scr* Karl Tunberg   *Ph* Freddie Young   *Ed* John Shirley   *Mus* Riz Ortolani   *Art Dir* John Stoll

● William Holden, Susannah York, Capucine, Tetsuro Tamba, Michael Goodliffe, Allan Cuthbertson (United Artists)

Set in the Malayan jungle, circa 1945, the pic uses as its background a three-way struggle between Communist-inspired Malayan terrorists, British governors and the people of Malaya along with outsiders who have vested interests in the country. All are interested in freedom for the place but their motives vary considerably.

Pivotal characters in the film each represent a faction, a fact which leads to some rather predictable problems and solutions as time passes. Personal relationships aren't helped much either by co-producer Karl Tunberg's screenplay, based on Michael Keon's novel *The Durian Tree*. Although the script moves fairly fluently through the action passages, harmful slowdowns develop during personal moments between the characters.

William Holden handles himself in credible fashion as a Yank co-leader of local guerilla forces during World War II who stays on after the war's end to become a major local land owner and who gets involved in the new politics because of his old-time friendshp for the leader of the Red terrorists, played by Tetsuro Tamba. Holden is further involved because of his mistress, a Malayan loyalist portrayed by Capucine. These three had worked together on the same side during the previous combat. For further plot there's the blonde and attractive daughter of the British governor, a role essayed by Susannah York.

• •

■ **7TH HEAVEN**

1927, 115 MINS, US ⊗

Dir Frank Borzage *Scr* Benjamin Glazer, Katherine Hilliker, H.H. Caldwell *Ph* Ernest Palmer *Ed* Katherine Hilliker, H.H. Caldwell *Art Dir* William Darling, David Hall
● Janet Gaynor, Charles Farrell, Ben Bard, David Butler, Marie Mosquini, Albert Gran (Fox)

7th Heaven [based on Austin Strong's play] is a great big romantic, gripping and red-blooded story told in a straight-from-the-shoulder way.

Director Frank Borzage is entitled to the blue ribbon for this one. He has made a great picture. Secondly, he has brought to the fore a little girl who has been playing parts in pictures for two years and made a real star out of her overnight – Janet Gaynor.

Borzage can also take credit for bringing Charles Farrell over the hurdles. David Butler comes into his own as Gobin. George Stone has his first shot at a part in the cinema. He plays the rat in the devoted and cringing fashion it should be.

There is not more than 2,500 feet of actual warfare in the film. Balance of the story is romance. A big punch is the march of the taxi cabs and trucks and pleasure cars with troops 30 from Paris to the Marne to stem the advance of the Germans.

This one cost Fox around $1.3 million and took over six months to make. .
☐ 1927/28: Best Director, Actress (Janet Gaynor), Adaptation.
☐ Nominations: Best Picture, Interior Direction

• •

■ **SEVENTH VEIL, THE**

1945, 94 MINS, UK ⍟

Dir Compton Bennett *Prod* Sydney Box *Scr* Muriel Box, Sydney Box *Ph* Reginald Wyer, Bert Mason *Ed* Gordon Hales *Mus* Benjamin Frankel *Art Dir* Jim Carter
● James Mason, Ann Todd, Herbert Lom, Albert Lieven, Hugh McDermott (Sydney Box/Ortus)

Title refers to the screen every human uses to hurdle his innermost thoughts. Like Salome, ordinary people will remove one or two – or more veils for the benefit of friends, sweethearts, spouses. But unlike Salome, nobody ever sheds the seventh veil. How Ann Todd is made to do this is the backbone of the pic – and its achievement is filmed magnificently.

Apart from the engrossing story (of the merciless discipline to which a teenage, sensitive orphan is subjected by a grim bachelor guardian) as it surges swiftly to its tremendous climax, there is a feast of harmony by the London Symphony Orchestra, conducted by Muir Mathieson, accompanying an unidentified piano virtuoso [Eileen Joyce] – ostensibly Todd.
☐ 1946: Best Original Screenplay

• •

■ **7TH VOYAGE OF SINBAD, THE**

1958, 89 MINS, UK ◇ ⍟ ⊙

Dir Nathan Juran *Prod* Charles H. Schneer *Scr* Kenneth Kolb *Ph* Wilkie Cooper *Ed* Edwin Bryant, Jerome Thoms *Mus* Bernard Herrmann *Art Dir* Gil Parrondo

● Kerwin Mathews, Kathryn Grant, Richard Eyer, Torin Thatcher, Alec Mango, Danny Green (Morningside/Columbia)

Just about every trick in the book – including one called Dynamation, i.e. the animation of assorted monsters, vultures, skeletons, etc – has been used to bring a vivid sort of realism to the various and terrifying hazards which Sinbad encounters on his voyage and in his battle with Sokurah the magician. Add to this a love story, interrupted when the princess Parisa is shrunk to inch-size by the magician, and what emerges is a bright, noisy package.

Kerwin Mathews makes a pleasant Sinbad, acting the part with more restraint than bravura; Kathryn Grant is pretty as the princess; Torin Thatcher has a fittingly evil look as the magician; Richard Eyer is cute as the Genie; Alec Mango has dignity as the Caliph.

But this isn't the sort of film in which performances matter much. It's primarily entertainment for the eye, and the action moves swiftly and almost without interruption. Ray Harryhausen, who was responsible for visual effects, emerges as the hero of this piece.

• •

■ **SEVEN UPS, THE**

1973, 103 MINS, US ◇ ⍟ ⊙

Dir Philip D'Antoni *Prod* Philip D'Antoni *Scr* Albert Ruben, Alexander Jacobs *Ph* Urs Furrer *Ed* Jerry Greenberg, Stephen A. Rotter, John C. Horger *Mus* Don Ellis *Art Dir* Ed Wittstein
● Roy Scheider, Victor Arnold, Jerry Leon, Ken Kercheval, Tony Lo Bianco, Larry Haines (20th Century-Fox)

The Seven Ups is a serviceable dualer about some underground cops who get caught in a series of gangland kidnappings. Produced by debuting director Philip D'Antoni in NY, the film features, at midpoint, a complicated and extravagant car chase which must have taxed the ingenuity of the director and that of stunt coordinator Bill Hickman. Roy Scheider heads an okay cast in a fair script.

Plot finds Scheider, Victor Arnold, Jerry Leon and Ken Kercheval members of a special NYPD unit which operates in unorthodox methods. Tony Lo Bianco plays an informant who uses Scheider's loan shark list to set up his own kidnap operation.

Scheme backfires with Kercheval's surprise death. That event sets off Scheider into a spree of lawless law enforcement which on the screen always turns out right.

• •

■ **7 WOMEN**

1965, 88 MINS, US ◇ ⊙

Dir John Ford *Prod* Bernard Smith *Scr* Janet Green, John McCormick *Ph* Joseph LaShelle *Ed* Otho S. Lovering *Mus* Elmer Bernstein *Art Dir* George W. Davis, Eddie Imazu
● Anne Bancroft, Sue Lyon, Margaret Leighton, Flora Robson, Mildred Dunnock, Eddie Albert (M-G-M)

7 Women is a run-of-the-mill story of an isolated American mission in North China whose serenity is rudely shattered by a ravaging Mongolian barbarian and his band of cutthroats. Production is set in 1935, when the Chinese-Mongolian border was a lawless, violent land dominated by bandits, and takes its title from the seven femmes trapped in mission and subjected to gross indignities.

John Ford directs from script based on a short story *Chinese Finale* by Norah Lofts and manages regulation treatment. While yarn attempts to tell the relationships of the septet – generally an uninteresting lot – most of the attention focuses necessarily upon Anne Bancroft, a recently-arrived doctor whose worldly cynicism brings her into conflict with the rigid moral concepts of mission's head, portrayed by Margaret Leighton. Bancroft endows character with some author-

ity, and Mike Mazurki is properly brutal as the huge bandit leader.

Leighton acquits herself well in an intolerant, self-righteous role.

• •

■ **7 WONDERS OF THE WORLD**

1956, 120 MINS, US ◇

Dir Ted Tetzlaff, Andrew Marton, Tay Garnett, Paul Mantz, Walter Thompson *Prod* Lowell Thomas *Scr* Prosper Buranelli, William Lipscomb *Ph* Harry Squire, Gayne Rescher *Ed* Harvey Manger, Jack Murray *Mus* Emil Newman, David Raksin, Jerome Moross
● (Stanley Warner/Cinerama)

While the titular *7 Wonders of the World* might be pointed to captiously as a misnomer, [this third Cinerama production] is a resourceful kickoff for an airlift from Manhattan through 32 countries in 120 minutes. The Sphinx and the Pyramids are pointed to as the sole remainders of the seven ancient wonders and the unfolding is a modern odyssey.

Emerging from the aerial hedgehop of local geographical closeups is a religioso pageantry which includes an exposition of Israel's renaissance; the final ceremonies of the Marian Year, culminating in the Papal blessing and a first-time lighting of Saint Peter's for motion pictures; and a curtsy to the Protestant church, back in the US with a typical American countryside scene. Buddhist priests and Benares (India) temple dancers blend with scenes of African tribal dances and a glorified Japanese geisha line that looks more Leonidoff than authentic Fujiyama.

7 Wonders of the World is at its best when the old and the modern are shown in sharp juxtaposition.

• •

■ **SEVEN YEAR ITCH, THE**

1955, 105 MINS, US ◇ ⍟ ⊙

Dir Billy Wilder *Prod* Billy Wilder, Charles K. Feldman *Scr* George Axelrod, Billy Wilder *Ph* Milton Krasner *Ed* Hugh S. Fowler *Mus* Alfred Newman *Art Dir* Lyle Wheeler, George W. Davis
● Marilyn Monroe, Tom Ewell, Evelyn Keyes, Sonny Tufts, Robert Strauss, Victor Moore (20th Century-Fox)

The film version of *The Seven Year Itch* bears only a fleeting resemblance to George Axelrod's play of the same name on Broadway. The screen adaptation concerns only the fantasies, and omits the acts, of the summer bachelor, who remains totally, if unbelievably, chaste. Morality wins if honesty loses, but let's not get into that. What counts is that laughs come thick and fast, that the general entertainment is light and gay.

The performance of Marilyn Monroe is baby-dollish as the dumb-but-sweet number upstairs who attracts the eye of the guy, seven years married and restless, whose wife and child have gone off for the summer. The acting kudos belongs to Tom Ewell, a practiced farceur and pantomimist who is able to give entire conviction to the long stretches of soliloquy, a considerable test of Ewell's technique.

• •

■ **SEVERED HEAD, A**

1971, 98 MINS, UK ◇

Dir Dick Clement *Prod* Alan Ladd Jr *Scr* Frederic Raphael *Ph* Austin Dempster *Ed* Peter Weatherley *Mus* Stanley Myers *Art Dir* Richard Macdonald
● Lee Remick, Richard Attenborough, Ian Holm, Claire Bloom, Jennie Linden, Clive Revill (Winkast)

This is a very upper-class and intellectually snobbish film about 'civilized copulation'. It's based on Iris Murdoch's novel (subsequently dramatized by Murdoch and J.B. Priestley).

It's the writing, direction (by Dick Clement) and acting that gives it stylish panache. The mattress merry-go-round has a great game of musical chairs among its cast.

S

Ian Holm plays Martin Lynch-Gibbon, a wine taster, with a mistress played by Jennie Linden. Holm's wife (Lee Remick), a predatory nympho, is having an affair with her husband's best friend, psychologist Richard Attenborough, who is also sexually involved with his sister, Claire Bloom ('She's only my half sister,' he explains apologetically, but with little conviction).

Cast, all round, is very good, with Holm, the fall guy, excellent. Attenborough gives the psychiatrist a nicely humored pomposity, and Clive Revill, as Holm's sculptor brother, brings his usual breeziness to one of the few extrovert roles.

On the distaff side Remick makes the least impact, at times becoming tediously fluffy. Linden is strong and loving as the mistress who's shuffled around like a pawn and Bloom scores heavily as the menacing, enigmatic egghead.

SEX AND THE SINGLE GIRL

1964, 114 MINS, US ◇ ⑦ ⊙
Dir Richard Quine *Prod* Richard Quine *Scr* Joseph Heller, David R. Schwartz *Ph* Charles Lang *Ed* David Wages *Mus* Neal Hefti *Art Dir* Cary Odell
● Tony Curtis, Natalie Wood, Henry Fonda, Lauren Bacall, Mel Ferrer, Edward Everett Horton (Quine-Reynard/Warner)

Helen Gurley Brown's how-to-do-it book for single girls is takeoff point for story by Joseph Hoffman, scripted by Joseph Heller and David R. Schwartz. Natalie Wood is Dr Helen Brown of International Institute of Advanced Marital and Pre-Marital Studies, who is target of scandal mag editor Tony Curtis. Curtis is bent on exposing her to be 23-year-old virgin without background for advising single girls about sex.

Curtis poses as his neighbor, Henry Fonda, who has monumental wife trouble, and goes to Wood for advice. Inevitably, they fall for one another with Wood ignorant of Curtis' identity as ogre out to ruin her career.

As usual in this type of farce, male and female leads have fewer comic lines than supporting players. But Curtis registers exceptionally well when detailing supposed marital problems to adviser. His timing in confessing to 'inadequacies' shows great comic talent. And one of funniest bits in pic comes when poised, self-assured 'Dr Brown' finds she has romantic problem of own, crumples into tears and places long-distance call to 'Mother'.

Fonda and Bacall as warring husband and wife also serve up effective scenes as they battle over Fonda's non-existent wild life as head of Sexy Sox Inc.

Edward Everett Horton shines as boss of Curtis' mag, who harangues aides to make publication 'the most disgusting scandal sheet the human mind can recall'.

SEX, LIES, AND VIDEOTAPE

1989, 101 MINS, US ◇ ⑦ ⊙
Dir Steven Soderbergh *Prod* Robert Newmyer, John Hardy *Scr* Steven Soderbergh *Ph* Walt Lloyd *Ed* Steven Soderbergh *Mus* Cliff Martinez *Art Dir* Joanne Schmidt
● James Spader, Andie MacDowell, Peter Gallagher, Laura San Giacomo (Outlaw)

This is a sexy, nuanced, beautifully controlled examination of how a quartet of people are defined by their erotic impulses and inhibitions.

Imaginatively presented opening intercuts the embarrassed therapy confessions of young wife Andie MacDowell with the impending arrival in town of James Spader, a mysterious stranger type who was a college chum of MacDowell's handsome husband (Peter Gallagher).

Given MacDowell's admissions that she and Gallagher are no longer having sex, it would seem that Spader is walking into a potentially provocative situation.

He drops a bombshell by revealing that he is impotent, seemingly scratching any developments on that end. Meanwhile Gallagher has been conducting a secret affair with his wife's sexy wild sister (Laura San Giacomo).

Pic is absorbing and titillating because nearly every conversation is about sex and aspects of these attractive people's relationships. Several steamy scenes between Gallagher and San Giacomo, and some extremely frank videotapes featuring women speaking about their sex lives, turn the temperature up even more.

Lensed on location in Baton Rouge, La, for $1.2 million, production looks splendid.
□ 1989: Nomination: Best Original Screenplay

SEXTETTE

1978, 91 MINS, US ◇ ⑦
Dir Ken Hughes *Prod* Daniel Briggs, Robert Sullivan *Scr* Herbert Baker *Ph* James Crabe *Ed* Argyle Nelson *Mus* Artie Butler *Art Dir* James F. Claytor
● Mae West, Timothy Dalton, Dom DeLuise, Tony Curtis, Ringo Starr, George Hamilton (Briggs-Sullivan)

Sextette is a cruel, unnecessary and mostly unfunny musical comedy. Mae West made the mistake in 1970 of returning to the screen after a 26-year absence in *Myra Breckenridge*, and she's blundered again.

The screenplay, based on a play by West, concerns a sexy Hollywood movie star who has married a young British nobleman. It's her sixth marriage and in the course of attempting to consummate the liaison she's interrupted by numbers four and five, fans, newspapermen, Rona Barrett, an American gymnastic team and a group of international diplomats meeting at her London hotel.

She's also in the middle of dictating her memoirs when the tape of her recorded autobiography gets out of her hands, a fate which could shorten her latest marriage.

West is on screen for most of the film, mostly attempting Mae West imitations and lip-syncing a series of undistinguished musical numbers. It's an embarrassing attempt at camp from the lady who helped invent the word.

Only Dom DeLuise is occasionally amusing as West's agent. The remainder of the cast – Tony Curtis as a Soviet delegate to the peace conference, Timothy Dalton as West's new husband, Ringo Starr and George Hamilton as former husbands, among others – hardly enhance their reputations.

SGT. PEPPER'S LONELY HEARTS CLUB BAND

1978, 111 MINS, US ◇ ⑦ ⊙
Dir Michael Schultz *Prod* Robert Stigwood *Scr* Henry Edwards *Ph* Owen Roizman *Ed* Christopher Holmes *Art Dir* Brian Eatwell
● Peter Frampton, Barry Gibb, Robin Gibb, Maurice Gibb, Frankie Howerd, Paul Nicholas (Universal)

Sgt. Pepper's Lonely Hearts Club Band will attract some grown-up flower children of the 1960s who will soon find the Michael Schultz film to be a totally bubblegum and cotton candy melange of garish fantasy and narcissism. The production crams nearly 30 songs, largely by The Beatles, into newly-recorded versions tailored for stars Peter Frampton and The Bee Gees.

Plot has Frampton as the grandson of the earlier Sgt Pepper who carries on the family band tradition with a modern-sound in partnership with The Bee Gees. Story introduces a lot of freakish characters out to steal the band's instruments which, somehow, make

Heartland, USA, a dream of a small town. They don't succeed, though there's enough teeny-bopper-teasing naughtiness to amuse and thrill the target audience. Donald Pleasance, one of the heavies, plays a music biz wizard whose fictional trademark is that of producer Robert Stigwood's organization.

Near the end of the 111-minute film, when all wrongs have been righted, there's a celebrity olio in which many familiar names appear to be singing happily. The sound of this isn't any more lifelike than much of the preceding singing.

SHADOW MAKERS
See: Fat Man and Little Boy

SHADOW OF A DOUBT

1943, 106 MINS, US ⑦
Dir Alfred Hitchcock *Prod* Jack H. Skirball *Scr* Thornton Wilder, Sally Benson, Alma Reville *Ph* Joseph Valentine *Ed* Milton Carruth *Mus* Dimitri Tiomkin *Art Dir* John B. Goodman, Robert Boyle
● Joseph Cotten, Teresa Wright, Macdonald Carey, Henry Travers, Patricia Collinge, Hume Cronyn (Skirball/Universal)

The suspenseful tenor of dramatics associated with director Alfred Hitchcock is utilized here to good advantage in unfolding a story [by Gordon McDonell] of a small town and the arrival of what might prove to be a murderer. Hitchcock poses a study in contrasts when the world-wise adventurer (Joseph Cotten) eludes police in Philadelphia to journey to his sister's home and family in the small California town of Santa Rosa. His debage niece (Teresa Wright), is not only named young Charlie after her uncle, but knows there's a mental contact somewhere along the line. Amid the typical small-town family life, she intuitively feels that Cotten has a guilty conscience, and finally ties the ends together to cast suspicion on him as a murderer and fugitive.

Hitchcock deftly etches his small-town characters and homey surroundings. Wright provides a sincere and persuasive portrayal as the girl, while Cotten is excellent as the motivating factor in the proceedings. Strong support is provided by Henry Travers, Patricia Collinge, Edna May Wonacott and Charles Bates. Hume Cronyn gets attention as the small-town amateur sleuth.
□ 1943: Nomination: Best Original Story

SHADOW OF THE THIN MAN

1941, 97 MINS, US ⑦ ⊙
Dir W.S. Van Dyke *Prod* Hunt Stromberg *Scr* Irving Brecher, Harry Kurnitz *Ph* William Daniels *Ed* Robert J. Kern *Mus* David Snell *Art Dir* Cedric Gibbons, Paul Groesse
● William Powell, Myrna Loy, Barry Nelson, Donna Reed, Sam Levene, Alan Baxter (M-G-M)

Much of the farcical flavor which characterized the earlier *Thin Man* films is reclaimed in the new picture. On the sentimental side, William Powell and Myrna Loy get a great deal of fun from their first appearance as parents of a four-year son, who has a way of asking embarrassing questions. For excitement the couple find themselves in the middle of an investigation into racetrack gambling, in the course of which there are three homicides, half a dozen suspects and a bit of gunplay.

Harry Kurnitz has fashioned the story with a good deal of ingenuity, using the characters of the private detective and his wife, as created in the original yarn by Dashiell Hammett.

Sam Levene, as a police lieutenant, is particularly amusing. Stella Adler is a stunning blonde heavy, and the character bits by Lou

Lubin, Joseph Anthony, Alan Baxter and Loring Smith add some reality to the seamy side of the action. With much to work with, W.S. Van Dyke has directed with speed.

....

■ **SHADOW OF THE WOLF**

1993, 112 MINS, CANADA/FRANCE ◇ ⓥ
Dir Jacques Dorfmann *Prod* Claude Leger *Scr* Rudy Wurlitzer, Evan Jones *Ph* Billy Williams *Ed* Francoise Bonnot *Mus* Maurice Jarre *Art Dir* Wolf Kroeger
● Lou Diamond Phillips, Toshiro Mifune, Jennifer Tilly, Bernard-Pierre Donnadieu, Donald Sutherland (Vision)

A story of survival, revenge and murder in the frozen north, *Shadow of the Wolf* has all the subtlety of a silent movie serial. Reportedly, at $30-plus million, the costliest Canadian production ever, this wilderness epic's oddball international cast enacts the tragic confrontation of native Americans and encroaching whites in the Arctic, circa 1935.

As fashioned here from the much honored source novel [Yves Theriault's *Agaguk*, adapted by David Milhaud], tale relates the maturation of a young Inuit Eskimo hunter (Lou Diamond Phillips) who, out of violent hatred for whites, is banished by his shaman father, impetuously kills a trader and, in company with the local beauty, forges a difficult life on the tundra. Eventually, everything comes full circle and Agaguk returns to the village to accept the mantle of maturity from his father.

Unfortunately, the film borders on the laughable throughout due to dialogue that erases the distinction between simple and simple-minded. One notable sequence has Agaguk jumping on board a speeding whale to escape his foes.

Phillips acts with a heavy seriousness that compounds the problems. As the compromised father, Japanese great Toshiro Mifune lends his imposing presence, but is obviously dubbed.

....

■ **SHADOWS**

1961, 84 MINS, US
Dir John Cassavetes *Prod* Maurice McEndree, Seymour Cassel *Ph* Erich Kolmar *Ed* Len Appleson, Maurice McEndree *Mus* Charlie Mingus, Shifi Hadi *Art Dir* Randy Liles, Bob Reeh
● Lelia Goldoni, Ben Carruthers, Tony Ray, Hugh Hurd, Rupert Crosse, Tom Allen (McEndree-Cassel)

First made in 16mm as an exercise in improvisation by a group of actors directed by John Cassavetes, a w.k. thesp himself, *Shadows* was then filled out and blown up to 35mm under the supervision of two producers. It came in for $40,000, and a showing at the British Film Institute got it raves and an advance from British Lion of $25,000.

A brother and sister who look white have a brother who is completely Negro. The film dwells on the dramatic interludes in their lives and the inevitable race problems. The girl is 20 and unsure of her emotions until her first affair is marred by a cowardly reaction to the revelation of her color by her lover. The white-looking brother drifts through various adventures with too unanchored white friends, and the Negro brother is a singer accepting his fate of trying to work in low dive shows and getting along with his edgy sister and brother.

Nothing rings false in the film. Though the narrative is rambling it strikes solid truths and dimension in showing people living and reacting in a manner which is dictated from within rather than forced on them by a script. Pic, in its improvised form, has actors working from general situations within an agreed outline.

Lelia Goldoni has nervous charm, guile and vulnerability as the girl, Ben Carruthers possesses the sullen violence of solitude and indecision, and Hugh Hurd has warmth and understanding as the breadwinning brother. Cassavetes has given this form and a point of view without trying to solve anything but letting the characters express themselves. There is no attempt at technique but the story and action carries itself and New York is an essential part of this unique film.

....

■ **SHADOWS AND FOG**

1992, 86 MINS, US ⓥ ⊙
Dir Woody Allen *Prod* Jack Rollins, Charles H. Joffe *Scr* Woody Allen *Ph* Carlo Di Palma *Ed* Susan E. Morse *Art Dir* Santo Loquasto
● Woody Allen, Mia Farrow, John Malkovich, Madonna, Donald Pleasence, Jodie Foster (Orion)

Exquisitely shot in black & white, Woody Allen's *Shadows and Fog* is a sweet homage to German expressionist filmmaking and a nod to the content of socially responsible tales since narrative film began. Allen's fans will regard this as a nice try that falls short.

Mia Farrow and boyfriend John Malkovich are part of a traveling circus that has pitched its tent near an unnamed European town where rival bands of vigilantes roam the nighttime streets in search of a marauding strangler. When Farrow catches Malkovich cheating on her with the strongman's wife (Madonna in a murky cameo), she walks out into the fog where she is befriended by streetwalker Lily Tomlin.

Helmer throws in some Kafka (Allen's persecuted character is never sure what he's supposed to do), some evil (there's a killer on the loose, casting shadows in the fog), a spunky counterbalancing force (Mia Farrow) and a little magic.

Tomlin is good, and Julie Kavner also scores as a former Allen paramour. John Cusack hits all the right notes as a college student who cajoles Farrow into selling herself just once. Several top thesps, including Jodie Foster and Kathy Bates, have been caught in surprisingly ordinary (and brief) perfs.

....

■ **SHAFT**

1971, 98 MINS, US ◇ ⓥ
Dir Gordon Parks *Prod* Joel Freeman *Scr* John D.F. Black *Ph* Urs Furrer *Ed* Hugh A. Robertson *Mus* Isaac Hayes
● Richard Roundtree, Moses Gunn, Gwenn Mitchell, Christopher St John, Charles Cioffi, Lawrence Pressman (M-G-M)

Take a formula private-eye plot, update it with all-black environment, and lace with contemporary standards of on-and off-screen violence, and the result is *Shaft*. It is directed by Gordon Parks with a subtle feel for both the grit and the humanity of the script.

Ernest Tidyman's novel, adapted by himself and John D.F. Black, concerns the kidnap by the Mafia of Sherri Brewer, daughter of Harlem underworld boss Moses Gunn. Richard Roundtree, as a black Sam Spade, is hired by Gunn to find her. Understanding but tough white cop Charles Cioffi, whose outstanding characterization singlehandedly upgrades the plot from strictly racial polemic, works with Roundtree in avoiding a gangland confrontation which, to outsiders, would appear to be a racial war.

In his second feature film after a long career as a still photographer, Parks shows some excellent story-telling form, with only minor clutter of picture-taking-for-its-own-sake.
☐ 1971: Best Song ('Theme from Shaft')
☐ Nomination: Best Original Score

....

■ **SHAFT IN AFRICA**

1973, 112 MINS, US ◇ ⓥ
Dir John Guillermin *Prod* Roger Lewis *Scr* Stirling Silliphant *Ph* Marcel Grignon *Ed* Max Benedict *Mus* Johnny Pate *Art Dir* John Stoll
● Richard Roundtree, Frank Finlay, Vonetta McGee, Neda Arneric, Debebe Eshetu, Spiros Focas (M-G-M)

Shaft in Africa, third in the series, takes a new story-telling direction which gets it out of the well-plowed inner-city ghetto rut. Richard Roundtree again stars as the black private eye, now infiltrating an Africa-to-Europe slave smuggling ring.

Script, from the Ernest Tidyman character trove, is surprisingly good. Dragooned by diplomat Cy Grant into cracking the slave ring, run by Frank Finlay and his nympho mistress Neda Arneric, Roundtree embarks on a series of journeys, in which he successively kills all assassins dispatched by Finlay through Debebe Eshetu, Grant's aide who is also in Finlay's employ. Vonetta McGee is Grant's daughter with whom Roundtree eventually connects, though her character is most awkwardly interwoven in the script.

....

■ **SHAFT'S BIG SCORE**

1972, 105 MINS, US ◇ ⓥ
Dir Gordon Parks *Prod* Roger Lewis, Ernest Tidyman *Scr* Ernest Tidyman *Ph* Urs Furrer *Ed* Harry Howard *Mus* Gordon Parks *Art Dir* Emanuel Gerard
● Richard Roundtree, Moses Gunn, Drew Bundini Brown, Joseph Mascolo, Kathy Imrie, Julius W. Harris (M-G-M)

Richard Roundtree again heads the cast as a swinging black private eye, caught between opposing criminal forces. This time around, there is a lot more production and nurturing of the project, not all of which is to the good, however.

Script finds Roundtree trapped in the double-dealings of Wally Taylor, who has killed partner Robert Kya-Hill for money. Moses Gunn is again excellent as a black mobster, and Joseph Mascolo is a white mobster eyeing Taylor's territory for a move-in. Julius W. Harris is a police detective who gives Roundtree his head to unravel the mess.

The first *Shaft* had a running-scared excitement not only in the characters, but also throughout the whole picture. The new film seems more self-conscious, contrived, ambitious, and sluggish.

....

■ **SHAG**

1988, 100 MINS, UK/US ◇ ⓥ ⊙
Dir Zelda Barron *Prod* Stephen Wooley, Julia Chasman *Scr* Robin Swicord, Lanier Laney, Terry Sweeney *Ph* Peter Macdonald *Ed* Laurence Mery-Clark *Art Dir* Buddy Cone
● Phoebe Cates, Scott Coffey, Bridget Fonda, Annabeth Gish, Page Hannah, Robert Rusler (Palace/Hemdale)

As a dance flick, *Shag* suffers from an unexciting dance-style and so-so choreography but compensates with a fine young cast and likable story.

Pic is set in South Carolina in 1963 and opens with three girls, Page Hannah, Annabeth Gish and Bridget Fonda, picking up pal Phoebe Cates for her last summer fling with the girls before she marries dull Tyrone Power Jr.

They head for Myrtle Beach and the Sun Fun Festival, full of boys, beer, a beauty parade and shagging – the current dance craze. Within hours of their arrival Cates becomes fascinated by hunky Robert Rusler and plump Gish falls for preppy Scott Coffey.

The four female leads are excellent, though it is Fonda who exudes confidence and star quality and looks destined for great things. Of the guys, Coffey's character is the only one with any depth; the rest seem to play hunks, wimps or louts.

Acting-family connections are strong in *Shag*, including Bridget Fonda (daughter of Peter), Page Hannah (sister of Daryl) and Tyrone Power Jr (billed as 'Junior' but son of star Tyrone Power and grandson of Tyrone

Power Sr.), though Annabeth Gish is no relation to the thesp sisters.

■ **SHAGGY D.A., THE**

1976, 91 MINS, US ◇ ⓥ
Dir Robert Stevenson *Prod* Bill Anderson *Scr* Don Tait
Ph Frank Phillips *Ed* Bob Bring, Norman Palmer
Mus Buddy Baker *Art Dir* John B. Mansbrough, Perry Ferguson
● Dean Jones, Tim Conway, Suzanne Pleshette, Keenan Wynn, JoAnne Worley, Dick Van Patten (Walt Disney)

In *The Shaggy Dog*, teenager Tommy Kirk came into possession of a magical ring which periodically changed him into a sheepdog. Here, in Don Tait's script drawn from the same material, Felix Salten's *The Hound of Florence*, fledgling d.a. candidate Dean Jones suffers the same fate. Most of the brisk 91-minute film is physical comedy as Jones tries to escape embarrassing situations and to outwit villainous d.a. Keenan Wynn.

Jones is a pleasant light comedian whose style is perfectly suited to the WASPish world of Disney. As his wife, Suzanne Pleshette has her first film role in five years, and her beauty and intelligence livens a part that might have been dull without her.

Rounding out a large and able supporting cast are such people as Tim Conway, JoAnne Worley (in her film debut), Dick Van Patten, Hans Conreid, and in an unbilled cameo as a dogcatcher, the late Liam Dunn, who died before completing his part. Conway is particularly droll as a cloddish ice-cream salesman.

■ **SHAGGY DOG, THE**

1959, 101 MINS, US ⓥ ⊙
Dir Charles Barton *Prod* Walt Disney *Scr* Bill Walsh, Lillie Hayward *Ph* Edward Colman *Ed* James D. Ballas *Mus* Paul Smith
● Fred MacMurray, Jean Hagen, Tommy Kirk, Annette Funicello, Tim Considine, Kevin Corcoran (Walt Disney)

The Shaggy Dog, said to be the first live action film by Walt Disney set in the present, is about what's called 'shape-shifting'. According to the screenplay suggested by Felix Salten's The Hound of Florence, there used to be a great deal of shifting of shapes, from man to beast and sometimes back.

There are a good many laughs on this simple premise and the script's exploitation of them. The only time the film falters badly is in its choice of a gimmick to get the boy-who-turns-into-a-dog turned back, for good and all, into a boy. According to the legend, it takes an act of heroism on the part of the shifting shape to be restored.

Fred MacMurray plays the father of the two boys, Tommy Kirk and Kevin Corcoran. MacMurray himself is a mailman physically allergic to dogs. Young Kirk accidentally transforms himself into a large, shaggy sheep dog when he comes into possession of a spell-casting ring once owned by the Borgias.

Where MacMurray has a good line, he shows that he has few peers in this special field of comedy. Jean Hagen, as his wife, is pretty and pleasant in a more or less straight role, while the two boys handle their comedy nicely.

■ **SHAKE HANDS WITH THE DEVIL**

1959, 104 MINS, US
Dir Michael Anderson *Prod* Michael Anderson
Scr Ivan Goff, Ben Roberts *Ph* Erwin Hillier *Ed* Gordon Pilkington *Mus* William Alwyn *Art Dir* Tom Morahan
● James Cagney, Don Murray, Dana Wynter, Glynis Johns, Michael Redgrave, Sybil Thorndike (United Artists/Pennebaker)

A strong and unusual story has been diluted in its telling. The theme is that those who 'shake hands with the devil' often find they

have difficulty getting their hands back. Two such, in the screenplay from the novel by Rearden Conner, are James Cagney and Don Murray.

Against a background of the 1921 Irish Rebellion, Cagney is a professor of medicine at a Dublin university, and Murray, an American veteran of World War I, is his student. Cagney is also a 'commandant' of the underground, and Murray's father, an Irish patriot, was killed while working with Cagney.

It is Cagney who wants to continue the terror when the leader of the Irish independence movement (Michael Redgrave) works out a treaty with the British that eventually leads to freedom.

The principals, paced by Cagney, are interesting and sometimes moving. But they seem posed against the Irish background, rather than part of it. The supporting cast looms larger than it should. Sybil Thorndike, for instance, as a titled Irish lady lending her name and fierce old heart to the cause, is fine. Redgrave has dignity and strength in his few scenes.

Erwin Hillier's camerawork is good, creating a grim, gray Ireland that is a natural setting for the sanguine struggle.

■ **SHAKESPEARE WALLAH**

1965, 125 MINS, INDIA/US ⓥ
Dir James Ivory *Prod* Ismail Merchant *Scr* Ruth Prawer Jhabvala, James Ivory *Ph* Subrata Mitra *Ed* Amit Bose *Mus* Satyajit Ray
● Shashi Kapoor, Felicity Kendal, Geoffrey Kendal, Laura Liddell, Madhur Jaffrey (Merchant-Ivory)

Shakespeare Wallah is officially designated an Indian-American coproduction, though the official credits do not name the US associates, apart from the Californian-born director, James Ivory.

The English language production is the story of a touring theatrical company specializing in Shakespearean production which has seen better days. It's a struggle to keep the company going which was founded by Tony and Carla Buckingham (Geoffrey Kendal and Laura Liddell) who are totally dedicated, and expect the same from all around, and particularly from their daughter Lizzie, who is currently enamored of an Indian playboy, who is also indulging in some extra-curricular activities with an Indian actress in the company.

The pace of the production is always too leisurely, and some of the Shakespearean excerpts could advantageously be cut. Nevertheless, there is a naive charm to the production.

There is also a very confident performance by Shashi Kapoor, as the Indian playboy. Felicity Kendal is a pert newcomer with an ingenuous style. Madhur Jaffrey ably completes the cast as the Indian actress.

■ **SHALAKO**

1968, 118 MINS, UK ◇ ⓥ
Dir Edward Dmytryk *Prod* Euan Lloyd *Scr* J.J. Griffith, Hal Hopper, Scot Finch *Ph* Ted Moore *Ed* Bill Blunden *Mus* Robert Farnon
● Sean Connery, Brigitte Bardot, Peter Van Eyck, Stephen Boyd, Honor Blackman, Jack Hawkins (Kingston/Palomar)

Though purporting to take place in New Mexico during the 19th century, this $5 million film was actually shot on location in Almeria, Spain, but doesn't look it.

Based on Louis L'Amour's novel, it's a 19th-century story of an aristocratic, 'dude' hunting safari from Europe which is led into Apache territory by its double crossing 'white' hunter and given a hard time by the redskins.

Shalako (Sean Connery) comes across the camp when he rescues one of them (Brigitte

Bardot) from Indians and has to pit his wits and resource, not only against the Apaches but against members of the expedition, before he manages to save the party from complete destruction.

Jealousy, obstinacy, greed and roguery all emotionally stir up trouble for the hunters.

The film is a slow starter while the various characters are being established and has an over-abrupt and inconclusive ending. Intriguing are the relationships between members of the hunting party.

■ **SHALL WE DANCE**

1937, 101 MINS, US ⓥ ⊙
Dir Mark Sandrich *Prod* Pandro S. Berman *Scr* Allan Scott, Ernest Pagano *Ph* David Abel *Ed* William Hamilton *Mus* Nathaniel Shilkret (dir.) *Art Dir* Van Nest Polglase, Carroll Clark
● Fred Astaire, Ginger Rogers, Edward Everett Horton, Eric Blore, Jerome Cowan, Ketti Gallian (RKO)

Shall We Dance, the seventh in the Astaire-Rogers series, is a standout because the script affords Astaire a legitimate excuse for a change of pace in his dancing, the comedy is solid, and this is the best cutting job an Astaire picture has enjoyed in a long time. This latter item is important as it had begun to look as if the studio couldn't decide whether Astaire was making musicals or operettas.

There have been others in the string which have had stronger tunes, superior punch laughs, and packed more dynamite in Astaire's own specialties, yet seldom have these ingredients been made to fit so evenly. All six songs [by George and Ira Gershwin], one more than usual, have been nicely spotted with no attempt to overplay any of them. Nor is there a bad ditty in the batch.

Basically the story [*Watch Your Step* by Lee Loeb and Harold Buchman, adapted by P.J. Wolfson] is of a ballet dancer (Astaire) who would rather be a hoofer. Romantically the script ties him into a complicated affinity with Ginger Rogers who is a musical comedy star. The rumors of their marriage grow to such proportion it forces them to secretly wed with the understanding of an immediate divorce. In locale the yarn starts in Paris, spends some time en route to the US and finishes in New York.

Astaire's stock company has been reassembled, hence the comedy is in the hands of Edward Horton, as Astaire's manager, and Eric Blore, as a Manhattan maitre d'hotel.
□ 1937: Nomination: Best Song ('They Can't Take That Away From Me')

■ **SHAMPOO**

1975, 109 MINS, US ◇ ⓥ ⊙
Dir Hal Ashby *Prod* Warren Beatty *Scr* Robert Towne, Warren Beatty *Ph* Laszlo Kovacs *Ed* Robert C. Jones *Mus* Paul Simon *Art Dir* Richard Sylbert
● Warren Beatty, Julie Christie, Goldie Hawn, Lee Grant, Jack Warden, Tony Bill (Columbia)

Late 1960s story about the ultimate emotional sterility and unhappiness of a swinger emerges as a mixed farcical achievement.

Warren Beatty is a Beverly Hills hairdresser who turns onto all his customers including Lee Grant, bored wife of Jack Warden (latter in turn keeping Julie Christie on the side), while Beatty's current top trick is Goldie Hawn.

All the excellent creative components do not add up to a whole. There are, however, strong elements in the film. Warden's performance is outstanding. He makes the most of a script and direction which gives his character much more dimension than the prototype cuckold. Also, Hawn's excellent delineation of a bubbly young actress has a solid undertone of sensitivity which culminates in her quiet dismissal of Beatty from her home and her heart.

□ 1975: Best Supp. Actress (Lee Grant)
□ Nominations: Best Supp. Actor (Jack Warden), Original Screenplay, Art Direction

....

■ **SHAMUS**

1973, 98 MINS, US ◇ ⑫ ⊙
Dir Buzz Kulik   *Prod* Robert M. Weitman   *Scr* Barry Beckerman   *Ph* Victor J. Kemper   *Ed* Walter Thompson   *Mus* Jerry Goldsmith   *Art Dir* Philip Rosenberg
● Burt Reynolds, Dyan Cannon, John Ryan, Joe Santos, Georgio Tozzi, Ron Weyand (Columbia)

Shamus is a confusing, hardbiting meller of a tough private eye. Burt Reynolds plays a rough-hewn and alert character who has turned to private investigation in his tough Brooklyn neighborhood instead of laying in with the mob. Filming was done on actual locations, which lends an emphatic authenticity to backgrounds.

Star carries the narrative niftily as he's called in by a multi-millionaire to ferret out the indentity of the person who bumped off a man who stole a fortune in diamonds owned by a tycoon. But thereafter scripter Barry Beckerman drags in an assortment of mostly-unexplained characters but some dandy rough work – and finales in a fine fog. Perhaps something was lost in translation to the screen.

....

■ **SHANE**

1953, 118 MINS, US ◇ ⑫ ⊙
Dir George Stevens   *Prod* George Stevens   *Scr* A.B. Guthrie Jr, Jack Sher   *Ph* Loyal Griggs   *Ed* William Hornbeck, Tom McAdoo   *Mus* Victor Young   *Art Dir* Hal Pereira, Walter Tyler
● Alan Ladd, Jean Arthur, Van Heflin, Brandon de Wilde, Jack Palance, Ben Johnson (Paramount)

This is by no means a conventional giddyap oater feature, being a western in the truer sense and ranking with some of the select few that have become classics in the outdoor field.

Director George Stevens handles the story and players with tremendous integrity. Alan Ladd's performance takes on dimensions not heretofore noticeable in his screen work. Van Heflin commands attention with a sensitive performance, as real and earnest as the pioneer spirit he plays. The screenplay is A.B. Guthrie Jr's first, as is the novel of Jack Schaefer.

Plot is laid in early Wyoming, where a group of farmer-settlers have taken land formerly held by a cattle baron. Latter resents this intrusion on the free land and the fences that come with the setting down of home roots. His fight is against Heflin chiefly, who is the driving force that keeps the frightened farmers together. Just when it seems the cattle man may eventually have his way, a stranger, known only as Shane, rides on to Heflin's homestead, is taken in and becomes one of the settlers, as he tries to forget his previous life with a gun.

Jean Arthur plays the role of Heflin's wife, who is attracted to the stranger. A standout is the young stage actor, Brandon de Wilde, who brings the inquisitiveness and quick hero worship of youth to the part of Heflin's son. Jack Palance, with short but impressive footage, is the hired killer.

Wyoming's scenic splendors against which the story is filmed are breathtaking. Sunlight, the shadow of rain storms and the eerie lights of night play a realistic part in making the picture a visual treat.

□ 1953: Best Color Cinematography.
□ Nominations: Best Picture, Director, Supp. Actor (Brandon de Wilde, Jack Palance), Screenplay

....

■ **SHANGHAI EXPRESS**

1932, 80 MINS, US
Dir Josef von Sternberg   *Prod* [uncredited]   *Scr* Jules Furthman   *Ph* Lee Garmes   *Ed* [uncredited]   *Mus* W. Franke Harling   *Art Dir* Hans Dreier
● Marlene Dietrich, Clive Brook, Anna May Wong, Warner Oland, Eugene Pallette, Lawrence Grant (Paramount)

Josef von Sternberg, the director, has made this effort interesting through a definite command of the lens. As to plot structure and dialog, *Shanghai Express* runs much too close to old meller and serial themes to command real attention. The finished product is an example of what can be done with a personality and photogenic face such as Marlene Dietrich possesses to circumvent a trashy story.

The script [from a story by Harry Hervey] relates how the heroine became China's most famed white prostitute, who meets her former English fiance (Clive Brook) on board train. The man has become a medical officer in the British Army. With a revolution going on, Warner Oland turns out to be the rebel leader, has the train held up and in looking for a hostage, to guarantee the return of his chief lieutenant captured by the Chinese forces, he picks Brook.

To save Brook's eyes being burned from his head, Shanghai Lily promises to become mistress of the revolutionary, leading to further misunderstandings between the central pair.

For counter-interest there is Eugene Pallette as an American gambler among the passengers, Louise Closser Hale as a prim boarding housekeeper, Gustav von Seyffertitz as a dope smuggling invalid, Lawrence Grant as a fanatical missionary, and Emile Chautard as a disgraced French officer wearing his uniform without authority.

It can't be said that either Dietrich or Brook gives an especially good performance. The British actor is unusually wooden, while Dietrich's assignment is so void of movement as to force her to mild but consistent eye rolling.

□ 1931/32: Best Cinematography.
□ Nominations: Best Picture, Director

....

■ **SHANGHAI GESTURE, THE**

1942, 97 MINS, US ⑫ ⊙
Dir Josef von Sternberg   *Prod* Arnold Pressburger   *Scr* Karl Vollmoeller, Geza Herczeg, Jules Furthman, Josef von Sternberg   *Ph* Paul Ivano   *Ed* Sam Winston   *Mus* Richard Hageman   *Art Dir* Boris Leven
● Gene Tierney, Victor Mature, Ona Munson, Walter Huston, Phyllis Brooks, Albert Basserman (United Artists)

Thirty-one film treatments on [John Colton's play] *Shanghai Gesture* were submitted without success to the Hays Office. Producer Arnold Pressburger finally slipped through a treatment for a go-ahead signal – to at least bring the original title and the Oriental background of the polyglot Asiatic metropolis to the screen.

Stripped of the sensational elements of *Gesture* at the time it was produced on the stage, the resultant film version is a rather dull and hazy drama of the Orient.

Mother Gin Sling (Ona Munson) is the operating brains of a gambling casino, case-hardened through her struggles up the ladder. When property in the district is bought up by Walter Huston, English financier, and the Mother is told to fold, she goes out to get the goods on her enemy in typical Oriental fashion. Result is Gin Sling's manipulation of Huston's daughter (Gene Tierney) onto a downward path; Gin Sling's accusation of his desertion years before; and his rebuttal that the girl she has ruined is actually their daughter.

Victor Mature, as the matter-of-fact Arab despoiler of Tierney's honor, provides a standout performance. Huston's abilities are lost in the jumble, while Munson cannot penetrate the mask-like makeup arranged for her characterization.

□ 1942: Nominations: Best B&W Art Direction, Scoring of a Dramatic Picture

....

■ **SHANGHAI SURPRISE**

1986, 97 MINS, UK/US ◇ ⑫ ⊙
Dir Jim Goddard   *Prod* John Kohn   *Scr* John Kohn, Robert Bentley   *Ph* Ernie Vincze   *Ed* Ralph Sheldon   *Mus* George Harrison, Michael Kamen   *Art Dir* Peter Mullins
● Sean Penn, Madonna, Paul Freeman, Richard Griffiths, Philip Sayer (M-G-M/Handmade/Vista)

Tale [from the novel *Faraday's Flowers* by Tony Kenrick] is a phony, thoroughgoing concoction. A missionary (Madonna) enlists the services of a down-and-out, would-be adventurer (Sean Penn) to help her track down a substantial supply of opium that disappeared under mysterious circumstances a year before, in 1937, during the Japanese occupation of China.

The blood-stirring premise provides the excuse for any number of encounters with exotic and shady characters who would have been right at home in Warner Bros foreign intrigue mellers of the 1940s.

But centerstage is the completely illogical relationship between the hustler and missionary. Penn seems game and has energy while Madonna can't for a moment disguise that her character makes no sense at all.

....

■ **SHARKY'S MACHINE**

1981, 119 MINS, US ◇ ⑫ ⊙
Dir Burt Reynolds   *Prod* Hank Moonjean   *Scr* Gerald Di Pego   *Ph* William A. Fraker   *Ed* William Gardeau   *Mus* Al Capps   *Art Dir* Walter Scott Herndon
● Burt Reynolds, Vittorio Gassman, Rachel Ward, Charles Durning, Brian Keith, Earl Holliman (Orion/Warner)

Directing himself in *Sharky's Machine*, Burt Reynolds has combined his own macho personality with what's popularly called mindless violence to come up with a seemingly guaranteed winner [from a novel by William Diehl].

Not surprisingly, Reynolds is 'Sharky' and the 'machine' is police parlance for a team of fellow cops working with him. They are all good policemen, but for one reason or another have been relegated to unchallenging assignments, mainly in the cesspool of the vice squad.

But a hooker's murder brings Reynolds within sniffing distance of big time shenanigans involving gubernatorial candidate Earl Holliman, crime boss Vittorio Gassman and high-priced call girl Rachel Ward.

Staking out Ward's apartment, actor Reynolds surrenders to an infatuation with her that director Reynolds has an intersting time developing.

By the time Reynolds gets a couple of fingers sliced off by Darryl Hickman & Co, all characterization is gone and it's just a matter then of who runs out of bullets first.

....

■ **SHATTERED**

1991, 98 MINS, US ◇ ⑫ ⊙
Dir Wolfgang Petersen   *Prod* Wolfgang Petersen, John Davis, David Korda   *Scr* Wolfgang Petersen   *Ph* Laszlo Kovacs   *Ed* Hannes Nikel, Glenn Farr, Richard Byard   *Mus* Alan Silvestri   *Art Dir* Gregg Fonseca
● Tom Berenger, Bob Hoskins, Greta Scacchi, Joanne Whalley-Kilmer, Corbin Bernsen, Theodore Bikel (Bodo Scriba/Baer/Capella)

Shattered goes to pieces almost instantly. A far-fetched thriller about unlikable characters, Wolfgang Petersen's debut American feature aspires to Hitchcockian suspense and surprise, but the parade of hokey implausibilities puts the viewer off rather than drawing one in.

Petersen assembled an attractive cast to populate his adaptation of Richard Neely's novel *The Plastic Nightmare*, a project he was contemplating even before his breakthrough success with *Das Boot* 10 years earlier. Unfortunately, the roles the actors fill are nearly all unappetizing or uninteresting, leaving the audience with no emotional investment in their fates.

A devastating car wreck leaves an upscale Bay Area real estate developer (Tom Berenger) a disfigured mess, although his wife (Greta Scacchi) escapes virtually unscathed. Although plastic surgery restores his good looks, husband's memory is a blank. Berenger eventually learns that he and his wife weren't getting along well before the accident and that she was having an affair with a certain Jack Stanton. Enter a private detective (Bob Hoskins), enlisted to help Berenger try to figure everything out.

Berenger manages character's outward anguish and bafflement but is not one who makes himself vulnerable enough to invite the viewer into his skin or mind. The ever-gorgeous Scacchi has the meatiest role, that of a scheming liar accustomed to always getting her way, but full, Bette Davis-style impact of the role is missed. Hoskins enlivens things as a p.i. who works out of a pet shop.

• •

■ SHE

1965, 104 MINS, UK ◇

Dir Robert Day   *Prod* Michael Carreras   *Scr* David T. Chantler   *Ph* Harry Waxman   *Ed* James Needs, Eric Boyd-Perkins   *Mus* James Bernard   *Art Dir* Robert Jones
● Ursula Andress, Peter Cushing, Bernard Cribbins, John Richardson, Christopher Lee, Andre Morell (Seven Arts/Hammer)

Fourth filming of H. Rider Haggard's fantasy adds color and widescreen to special effects, all of which help overcome a basic plot no film scripter has yet licked.

Ursula Andress is sole-starred as the immortal She, cold-blooded queen Ayesha of a lost kingdom who pines for return of the lover she murdered eons ago. In David T. Chantler's okay script, it turns out that John Richardson is the look-alike lover, footloose in Palestine after the First World War with buddies Peter Cushing and Bernard Cribbins.

High priest Christopher Lee and servant girl Rosenda Monteros are emissaries who spot Richardson's resemblance, triggering a desert trek by the three men to Kuma land. Cushing and Cribbins keep their senses, while Richardson falls under Andress' spell.

Director Robert Day's overall excellent work brings out heretofore unknown depths in Andress' acting. Role calls for sincere warmth as a woman in love, also brutal cruelty as queen, and she convinces.

All other players are good in routine roles, particularly Monteros as the competing love interest who loses her man and her life. Christopher Lee is also effective as the loyal priest whom Ayesha kills.

• •

■ SHE-DEVIL

1989, 99 MINS, US ◇ ⊙

Dir Susan Seidelman   *Prod* Jonathan Brett, Susan Seidelman   *Scr* Barry Strugatz, Mark R. Burns   *Ph* Oliver Stapleton   *Ed* Craig McKay   *Mus* Howard Shore   *Art Dir* Santo Loquasto
● Meryl Streep, Roseanne Barr, Ed Begley Jr, Linda Hunt, Sylvia Miles, Elizabeth Peters (Orion)

A dark and gleeful revenge saga set in a world of unfaithful husbands and unfair standards of beauty, *She-Devil* [from Fay Weldon's novel *The Life and Loves of a She Devil*] offers a unique heroine in Ruth Patchett (Roseanne Barr), a dumpy but dedicated housewife

afflicted with a conspicuous facial mole and an uninterested husband (Ed Begley Jr).

When Begley, an accountant, strays into the arms of a fabulously wealthy and affected romance novelist (Meryl Streep), Barr puts up with it – to a point.

However, when Begley, bags more or less packed, sets her blood boiling with crude put-downs, Barr clicks into an inspired attack mode, first by blowing up the house, then by dumping off the children at his love nest on her way to Whereabouts Unknown, then by ingeniously dismantling his career.

The casting is a real coup, with Barr going her everywoman TV persona one better by breaking the big screen heroine mold, and Streep blowing away any notion that she can't be funny.

• •

■ SHE DONE HIM WRONG

1933, 65 MINS, US ▾

Dir Lowell Sherman   *Prod* [uncredited]   *Scr* Harvey Thew, John Bright   *Ph* Charles Lang   *Ed* [uncredited]   *Mus* Ralph Rainger   *Art Dir* [uncredited]
● Mae West, Cary Grant, Owen Moore, Gilbert Roland, Noah Beery Sr, David Landau (Paramount)

Atmospherically, *She Done Him Wrong* is interesting since it takes audiences back to the 1890s and inside a Bowery free-and-easy, but mostly following a few highlights in the career of Diamond Lou, nee Lil.

Director Lowell Sherman turns in a commendable job. He tackles the script with a tongue-in-cheek attitude that takes nothing too seriously, and he restrains Mae West from going too far.

The locale, the clothes and the types are interesting, and so is West in her picture hats, straight jacket gowns and with so much jewelry that she looks like a Knickerbocker ice plant.

Deletions in the script from its original 1928 legit form [*Diamond Lil* by Mae West] are few, with only the roughest of the rough stuff out. White slavery angle is thinly disguised, with the girls instead shipped to Frisco to pick pockets. Character titles are changed only slightly, such as from Lil to Lou, etc. The swan bed is in, but for a flash only, with West doing her stuff on the chaise lounge in this version.

Numerous ex-vaudevillians besides West in the cast, including Cary Grant, the soul-saver; Fuzzy Knight, who whips a piano, and Grace La Rue. The latter, who headlined when West was chasing acrobats in the No. 2 spot, has a bit. Rafaela Ottiano, who does Rita, is a carry-over from the original legit cast.

With this strong line-up and others, including Gilbert Roland, Noah Beery, David Landau and Owen Moore as background, they're never permitted to be anything more than just background. West gets all the lens gravy and full figure most of the time.
☐ 1932/33: Nomination: Best Picture

• •

■ SHEIK, THE

1921, 100 MINS, US ⊗ ▾

Dir George Melford   *Scr* Monte M. Katterjohn   *Ph* William Marshall
● Agnes Ayres, Rudolph Valentino, Adolphe Menjou, Walter Long, Lucien Littlefield, George Waggner (Paramount)

Edith M. Hull's novel, preposterous and ridiculous as it was, won out because it dealt with every caged woman's desire to be caught up in a love clasp by some he-man who would take the responsibility and dispose of the consequences, but Monte M. Katterjohn's scenario hasn't even that to recommend it. He has safely deleted most of the punch, and what they missed George Melford manages by inept direction of the big scenes.

Lady Diana has gone alone into the desert with a native guide only to be captured by a young sheik and he detains her in his palace of a tent, and that is all.

The acting could not be worse than the story, but it is bad enough. Valentino is revealed as a player without resource. He depicts the fundamental emotions of the Arabian sheik chiefly by showing his teeth and rolling his eyes, while Agnes Ayres looks too matronly to lend much kick to the situation in which she finds herself.

• •

■ SHELF LIFE

1993, 83 MINS, US ◇ ▾

Dir Paul Bartel   *Prod* Bradley Laven, Anne Kimmel   *Scr* O-Lan Jones, Andrea Stein, Jim Turner   *Ph* Philip Holahan   *Ed* Judd Maslansky   *Mus* Andy Paley   *Art Dir* Alex Tavoularis
● O-Lan Jones, Andrea Stein, Jim Turner, Paul Bartel, Justin Houchin, Shelby Lindley ((?????))

Sprightly, compact and quickly paced, *Shelf Life* is a nifty little allegorical number about second-hand life in a fallout shelter where two sisters and their brother have spent nearly their entire lives.

With the skeletons of mom and pop lying nearby, Tina, Pam and Scotty, now well into their 30s, go through the motions of real life as they have learned it from TV, which they have managed to receive uninterrupted over the years. A fair amount of the dialogue is chanted in unison and/or rhythmically, with the characters expressing joint or contrapuntal meanings within prescribed formats.

Based on an original stage piece created by the performers, who repeat their roles on screen, pic represents something of a departure from helmer Paul Bartel's usual outrageous comedies, but features some of his best direction.

• •

■ SHE'LL BE WEARING PINK PAJAMAS

1985, 90 MINS, UK ◇ ▾

Dir John Goldschmidt   *Prod* Tara Prem, Adrian Hughes   *Scr* Eva Hardy   *Ph* Clive Tickner   *Ed* Richard Key   *Mus* John du Prez   *Art Dir* Colin Pocock
● Julie Walters, Anthony Higgins, Jane Evers, Janet Henfrey, Paula Jacobs, Penelope Nice (Film Four/Pink Pajamas)

She'll Be Wearing Pink Pajamas is about a group of British women from mixed backgrounds who gather together, awkwardly at first, but eventually confide in each other and reveal their innermost secrets and problems.

After a slightly off-key opening, in which the characters are introed, we're into the setting of an outdoor survival course for women only, a week-long exercise designed to push the participants physically as far as they can go. The intimate discussions that follow take place against outdoor backgrounds, filmed in England's beautiful Lake District, as the women ford streams, climb mountains, canoe, swing on ropes, or go on a marathon hike.

There's one man around (Anthony Higgins), but he's almost an intrusion. The women are a lively and well-differentiated lot, and there is a bevy of fine actresses playing them. Standout is Julie Walters as a bouncy type who proves surprisingly weak in the crunch.

• •

■ SHELTERING SKY, THE

1990, 137 MINS, UK/ITALY ◇ ▾ ⊙

Dir Bernardo Bertolucci   *Prod* Jeremy Thomas   *Scr* Mark Peploe, Bernardo Bertolucci   *Ph* Vittorio Storaro   *Ed* Gabriella Cristiani   *Mus* Ryuichi Sakamoto, Richard Horowitz   *Art Dir* Gianni Silvestri
● John Malkovich, Debra Winger, Campbell Scott, Jill Bennett, Timothy Spall, Eric Vu-An (Thomas)

Paul Bowles' classic 1949 novel of a journey into emptiness has been visualized with intense beauty by the creative team of *The Last Emperor*. But those who haven't read the book will be left bewildered.

John Malkovich and Debra Winger play Port and Kit Moresby, Americans traveling without destination or itinerary in postwar North Africa. Their 10-year marriage is unraveling while their opportunistic companion, Tunner (Campbell Scott), looks on.

They press on through Tangiers, Niger and Algeria, moving with a perverse sense of purpose further from comfort, ego and the signposts of the familiar. Pic boils down to the existential love story between Kit and Port, who are groping through the ruins of their infidelities toward whatever is left between them when all is lost.

In a marvelous directorial conceit, Bowles himself, 80 years old, watches his characters from a seat in a Tangiers cafe.

Malkovich is an excellent choice as Port, his shifting, centaur-like physicality filling in for the interior life the screen can't provide. Aside from her resemblance to writer Jane Bowles, who inspired Kit, Winger is less interesting to watch.

At the end, familiar language completely disappears, as shell-shocked Kit wanders into the desert and becomes a sex slave to the wandering Tuareg leader Belqassim (played by Eric Vu-An of the Paris Ballet).

■ SHENANDOAH

1965, 105 MINS, US ◇ ▼ ⊙
Dir Andrew V. McLaglen   *Prod* Robert Arthur
Scr James Lee Barrett   *Ph* William H. Clothier   *Ed* Otho Lovering   *Mus* Frank Skinner   *Art Dir* Alexander Golitzen, Alfred Sweeney
● James Stewart, Doug McClure, Glenn Corbett, Patrick Wayne, Rosemary Forsyth, Katharine Ross (Universal)

Shenandoah centers upon one person, a sort of behind-the-scenes glimpse of one man's family in Virginia during the Civil War.

Screenplay focuses on Stewart, a prosperous Virginia farmer in 1863 who completely ignores the strife raging around him. A widower, he has raised his family of six sons and one daughter to be entirely self-contained. Not believing in slavery, he wants no part in a war based upon it, providing the conflict does not touch either his land or his family. When his youngest, a 16-year-old boy whose mother died giving birth and who therefore occupies a particular spot in the father's heart, is captured as a Reb by Unionists, the farmer then makes the war his own business.

Stewart, seldom without a cigar butt in the corner of his mouth, endows his grizzled role with warm conviction.

Battle sequences are well integrated with the family's efforts to lead a normal life, and Andrew McLaglen is responsible for some rousing hand-to-hand action between the Blue and the Grey.

□ 1965: Nomination: Best Sound

■ SHERIFF OF FRACTURED JAW, THE

1958, 100 MINS, UK ◇ ▼
Dir Raoul Walsh   *Prod* Daniel M. Angel   *Scr* Arthur Dales   *Ph* Otto Heller   *Ed* John Shirley   *Mus* Robert Farnon   *Art Dir* Bernard Robinson
● Kenneth More, Jayne Mansfield, Robert Morley, Ronald Squire, Henry Hull, Bruce Cabot (20th Century-Fox)

The starring combo of Jayne Mansfield and Kenneth More merge like bacon and eggs, and the result is a wave of yocks. Raoul Walsh directs this cheerful skit about the wild, woolly west with vigor and pace. He gives little time to remind the audience that many of the situations are predictable and that the brisk screenplay [from a short story by Jacob Hay] occasionally needs an upward jolt from the skill of the leading thesps.

Yarn starts off in London at the turn of the century. More has inherited a fading gunsmith business. Reading that there is a spot of bother in the Wild West he decides that that's the place to sell his guns. So this dude salesman (walking stick, brown derby and strictly West End suiting) nonchalantly sets off with some samples, and all the confidence in the world.

It's not long before he is up to his surprised eyebrows in trouble. He becomes involved with Injuns, two warring sets of cowboys and with Mansfield, the pistol-packing boss of a saloon. He is conned into becoming the sheriff of the one-horse town of Fractured Jaw.

More's immaculate throwaway line of comedy gets full rein. With polite manners, impeccable accent and a brash line of action, he leaves the locals in doubt as to whether he is the biggest fool or the bravest man ever to hit their territory. Mansfield gives More hearty support, looks attractive in a big, bosomy way and sings two or three numbers very well. The film was made in Spain and at Pinewood, but the locations have an authentic western air.

■ SHERLOCK, JR.

1924, 48 MINS, US ⊗
Dir Buster Keaton   *Scr* Jean Havez, Joseph Mitchell, Clyde Bruckman   *Ph* Elgin Lessley, Byron Houck   *Art Dir* Fred Gabourie
● Buster Keaton, Kathryn McGuire, Ward Crane, Joseph Keaton (Keaton/Metro)

This Buster Keaton feature length comedy is about as unfunny as a hospital operating room.

The picture has all the old hoke in the world in it. That ranges from a piece of business with a flypaper to a money-changing bit and, for added good measure, a chase. There are, in fact, two chases; but neither can for a single second hold a candle to Harold Lloyd. In comparison they appear child's play.

There is one piece of business, however, that is worthy of comment. It is the bit where Buster as a motion-picture machine operator in a dream scene walks out of the booth and into the action that is taking place on the screen of the picture that he is projecting. That is clever. The rest is bunk.

■ SHE'S GOTTA HAVE IT

1986, 100 MINS, US ▼ ⊙
Dir Spike Lee   *Prod* Shelton J. Lee   *Scr* Spike Lee
Ph Ernest Dickerson   *Ed* Spike Lee   *Mus* Bill Lee
Art Dir Wynn Thomas
● Tracy Camilla Johns, Redmond Hicks, John Terrell, Spike Lee, Raye Dowell, Joie Lee (40 Acres & a Mule)

This worthy but flawed attempt to examine an independent young woman of the 1980s was lensed, in Super 16mm, in 15 days but doesn't appear jerrybuilt.

All the elements of an interesting yarn are implicit here – save one: a compelling central figure (played by Tracy Camilla Johns). The young woman who's the focus of pic is, clearly, trying to find herself. She juggles three beaus, fends off a lesbian's overtures and consults a shrink to determine if she's promiscuous or merely a lady with normal sexual appetites.

The three beaus, an upscale male model, a sensitive sort and a funny street flake, all essayed nicely by, respectively, John Terrell, Spike Lee and Redmond Hicks, serve to keep the scenario moving with interest.

■ SHE'S HAVING A BABY

1988, 106 MINS, US ◇ ▼ ⊙
Dir John Hughes   *Prod* John Hughes   *Scr* John Hughes
Ph Don Peterman   *Ed* Alan Heim   *Mus* Stewart Copeland, Nicky Holland   *Art Dir* John W. Corso

● Kevin Bacon, Elizabeth McGovern, Alec Baldwin, Isabel Lorca, William Windom, Cathryn Damon (Paramount)

She's Having a Baby is an oddly uneven and quasi-serious look into the angst of the early years of a contemporary marriage that parallels TV's *thirtysomething*. There are many comedic setups which, if they were with less architypically drawn characters, might have delivered the laughs with the refreshingly innocent joy that has been the hallmark of other John Hughes pics.

In the lead role, Kevin Bacon is enthusiastic and believable, but even his energy can't carry what boils down to a fairly limp story told from his p.o.v. about buying into the confortable suburban dream possibly before his time.

Bacon ties the knot with teenage sweetheart Kristy (Elizabeth McGovern) and begins to fantasize about what he's going to be missing out on as a married man from the moment they take their vows. It soon becomes evident why Bacon is endlessly dreaming: take away his imaginings and his home life is dull indeed.

For one thing, he's got a stepford wife for a mate. McGovern is so uncomplicated and unabashedly adoring towards her husband, it gets one wondering what such a bright guy is doing with her. Bacon's wayward buddy Davis (Alec Baldwin) shows up too infrequently to spar with his good chum and ruffle McGovern's feathers by bringing along just the kind of girl she would loathe.

■ SHE'S OUT OF CONTROL

1989, 95 MINS, US ◇ ▼ ⊙
Dir Stan Dragoti   *Prod* Stephen Deutsch   *Scr* Seth Winston, Michael J. Nathanson   *Ph* Donald Peterman   *Ed* Dov Hoenig   *Mus* Alan Silvestri   *Art Dir* David L. Snyder
● Tony Danza, Catherine Hicks, Ami Dolenz, Wallace Shawn, Dick O'Neill, Laura Mooney (Weintraub)

Somewhere lurking behind the scenes of *She's Out of Control* is the germ of a good idea. Despite some funny scenes, the sitcomish treatment of a father's anxiety over his teenage daughter's budding sexuality is mostly shallow and uneven.

The widowed g.m. of an LA rock radio station, Tony Danza is no square, but he freaks out when his g.f. Catherine Hicks decides to transform his daughter Ami Dolenz from a studious wallflower into an airheaded sexpot. After a shaky opening, film picks up some wit and steam when Danza begins consulting a shrink, played with his customary sly intelligence by Wallace Shawn.

Naturally, everything Shawn tells Danza to do backfires. It's not long before the daughter dumps punker Dana Ashbrook and he begins clinging to Danza as the dad he's never had.

There's also some fun in the parade of eager boys Danza has to keep turning away from the door, Laura Mooney is terrif as Danza's precocious younger daughter, and the episode of Dolenz' attempted seduction by Matthew L. Perry is also a standout.

■ SHE WORE A YELLOW RIBBON

1949, 103 MINS, US ◇ ▼ ⊙
Dir John Ford   *Prod* John Ford, Merian C. Cooper
Scr Frank Nugent, Laurence Stallings   *Ph* Winton Hoch   *Ed* Jack Murtay   *Mus* Richard Hageman   *Art Dir* James Basevi
● John Wayne, Joanne Dru, John Agar, Ben Johnson, Victor McLaglen, Mildred Natwick (RKO/Argosy)

She Wore a Yellow Ribbon is a western meller done in the best John Ford manner.

Drama [from James Warner Bellah's story] of the undermanned US Cavalry post far out in the Indian country is centered on a veteran captain about to retire. It develops into a saga of the cavalry, its hard-bitten men, loyal wives and usual intrigues. The tale moves along easily as it shows how the troop surmounts the Indian peril. There's hardly a breather from the time the audience is tipped that John Wayne is soon retiring as cavalry captain til he finalizes his last dramatic moment.

Wayne wears well in this somewhat older characterization. He makes the officer an understanding, two-fisted guy without overdoing it. Victor McLaglen gives the production tremendous lift as the whisky-nipping noncom.

□ 1949: Best Color Cinematography

······························

■ SHINING, THE

1980, 146 MINS, US ◇ ⓥ ⊙
Dir Stanley Kubrick   *Prod* Stanley Kubrick   *Scr* Stanley Kubrick, Diane Johnson   *Ph* John Alcott   *Ed* Ray Lovejoy   *Mus* Wendy Carlos, Rachel Elkind   *Art Dir* Roy Walker
● Jack Nicholson, Shelley Duvall, Danny Lloyd, Scatman Crothers, Barry Nelson, Anne Jackson (Warner)

With everything to work with, director Stanley Kubrick has teamed with jumpy Jack Nicholson to destroy all that was so terrifying about Stephen King's bestseller.

In his book, King took a fundamental horror formula – an innocent family marooned in an evil dwelling with a grim history – and built layers of ingenious terror upon it. The father is gradually possessed by the demonic, desolate hotel.

With dad going mad, the only protection mother and child have is the boy's clairvoyance – his 'shining' – which allows him an innocent understanding and some ability to outmaneuver the devils. But Kubrick sees things his own way, throwing 90% of King's creation out.

The crazier Nicholson gets, the more idiotic he looks. Shelley Duvall transforms the warm sympathetic wife of the book into a simpering, semi-retarded hysteric.

[Pic was cut to 142 minutes by Kubrick soon after the premiere.]

······························

■ SHINING THROUGH

1992, 132 MINS, US ◇ ⓥ ⊙
Dir David Seltzer   *Prod* Howard Rosenman, Carol Baum   *Scr* David Seltzer   *Ph* Jan De Bont   *Ed* Craig McKay   *Mus* Michael Kamen   *Art Dir* Anthony Pratt
● Michael Douglas, Melanie Griffith, Liam Neeson, Joely Richardson, John Gielgud, Francis Guinan (20th Century-Fox)

An old-fashioned women's picture that could pass for a television movie except for its lavish trappings, this oddly titled melodrama [from Susan Isaac's novel] turns out to be little more than a big, brassy Hallmark card with a World War II backdrop, combining shameless romance with predictable spy intrigue.

Melanie Griffith plays Linda Voss, a half-Jewish, half-Irish woman, circa 1940, who goes to work for a mysterious attorney (Michael Douglas) who turns out to be a spy for the US government. The two become lovers, and despite his reluctance, Linda, a lower-class girl hired because of her fluent German, is ultimately sent to Berlin, as a spy, infiltrating the house of a German honcho (Liam Neeson).

Along the way, she hooks up with several Germans working undercover for the US, including the code-named Sunflower (John Gielgud) and a young woman of privilege (Joely Richardson).

There's a fair degree of tension as the spy antics draw to a close, but the flashback structure diffuses some of it because it's the aged Linda, after all, who's recounting the tale.

The dialog doesn't make any effort to capture that era, and Griffith's spunky secretary,

despite appealing moments, seems more a 1990s working girl than a 1940s working-class girl.

Douglas has less to work with as the robotic soldier whose heart is turned to mush.

······························

■ SHIP OF FOOLS

1965, 148 MINS, US ⓥ ⊙
Dir Stanley Kramer   *Prod* Stanley Kramer   *Scr* Abby Mann   *Ph* Ernest Laszlo   *Ed* Robert C. Jones   *Mus* Ernest Gold   *Art Dir* Richard Clatworthy
● Vivien Leigh, Simone Signoret, Jose Ferrer, Lee Marvin, Oskar Werner, Elizabeth Ashley (Columbia)

Director-producer Stanley Kramer and scenarist Abby Mann have distilled the essence of Katherine Anne Porter's bulky novel in a film that appeals to the intellect and the emotions.

As screen entertainment *Ship of Fools* is intelligent and eminently satisfying most of the time. The human cargo aboard the German ship *Vera* sailing from Vera Cruz to Bremerhaven (1933) is a cross-section of mass humanity that a landlubber can encounter in any metropolis.

All of the principals give strong performances from the aggressive interpretation by Jose Ferrer as a loathsome disciple of the emerging Hitlerian new order to Vivien Leigh as a fading American divorcee who gets her kicks out of leading on admirers and throwing cold water on their burning desires.

Of equal importance to the main stream of this drama, and also astutely attuned, are the contributions by Simone Signoret in the role of La Condesa and Oskar Werner as Dr Schumann, the ship's doctor.

Also impressive are George Segal and Elizabeth Ashley as young lovers whose intellects and emotions seem to be always warring against the animal magnetism that draws them together.

□ 1965: Best B&W Cinematography, B&W Art Direction.
□ Nominations: Best Picture, Actor (Oskar Werner), Actress (Simone Signoret), Supp. Actor (Michael Dunn), Adapted Screenplay, B&W Costume Design

······························

■ SHIP WAS LOADED, THE

See: Carry On Admiral

······························

■ SHIPWRECK

See: The Sea Gypsies

······························

■ SHIRLEY VALENTINE

1989, 108 MINS, UK ◇ ⓥ ⊙
Dir Lewis Gilbert   *Prod* Lewis Gilbert   *Scr* Willy Russell   *Ph* Alan Hume   *Ed* Lesley Walker   *Mus* George Hadjinasios, Willy Russell   *Art Dir* John Stoll
● Pauline Collins, Tom Conti, Alison Steadman, Julia McKenzie, Joanna Lumley, Bernard Hill (Paramount)

Shirley Valentine is an uneven but generally delightful romantic comedy that has as its lead the irresistible Pauline Collins.

Collins *is* Shirley Valentine, the perfect match of actress and character. She starred in the one-woman show for more than a year on stage, first in a London West End production, then on Broadway.

The legit work was a monolog in which Collins, a middle-aged Liverpool housewife who yearns to drink 'a glass of wine in a country where the grape is grown,' described other characters and gave them life through her fanciful imagery.

In Willy Russell's film adaptation, *Shirley Valentine* becomes a full-blown location shot with those and other characters now cast as separate speaking parts, mostly by other terrific British actors. Tom Conti is barely recognizable here playing a very convincing

swarthy Greek tavern keeper whose specialty is the romantic sail to a secluded cove.

Shirley Valentine-Bradshaw, the mildly sour Liverpool housewife, was more entertaining than Shirley Valentine, the contented reborn woman. Even so, it would be impossible not to smile along with this very happy person as the curtain/sunset falls.

□ 1989: Nominations: Best Actress (Pauline Collins), Song ('The Girl Who Used To Be Me')

······························

■ SHIVERS

(Aka: They Came from Within)

1975, 88 MINS, CANADA ◇ ⓥ
Dir David Cronenberg   *Prod* Ivan Reitman   *Scr* David Cronenberg   *Ph* Robert Saad   *Ed* Patrick Dodd   *Mus* Ivan Reitman (sup.)   *Art Dir* Erla Gliserman
● Paul Hampton, Joe Silver, Lynn Lowry, Alan Migicovsky, Susan Petrie, Barbara Steele (DAL/Reitman)

Shivers, a low-budget Canadian production, is a silly but moderately effective chiller about creeping parasites that systematically (and comically) 'infect' an entire highrise population with nothing less than sexual hysteria.

Premise of pic is a bit shaky. A mad doctor who believes in matter over mind has implanted in his teenage mistress a strange parasite that brings out the basest of human impulses. He's not the only one she fools around with, so before long, the 'disease' is spreading like crazy.

The star of the movie is special effects and makeup man Joe Blasco, whose bloody, disgusting-looking crawlers are seen climbing out of people's throats as well as highrise plumbing to attack innocents.

······························

■ SHOCK CORRIDOR

1963, 101 MINS, US ⓥ ⊙
Dir Samuel Fuller   *Prod* Samuel Fuller   *Scr* Samuel Fuller   *Ph* Stanley Cortez, [Samuel Fuller]   *Ed* Jerome Thoms   *Mus* Paul Dunlap   *Art Dir* Eugene Lourie
● Peter Breck, Constance Towers, Gene Evans, James Best, Hari Rhodes, Larry Tucker (Allied Artists)

Samuel Fuller's thin plot has a newspaperman (Peter Breck) contriving, with the aid of a psychiatrist no less, to get himself committed to a mental ward in order to identify a murderer known only to the inmates and whom the police have been unable to detect.

Within all this lurks three points about Americana, each embodied in characters the fourth-estater encounters in the hospital. A Communist-brainwashed and subsequently disgraced Korean war vet (James Best) is the mouthpiece through which Fuller pleads for greater understanding of such unfortunate individuals.

Likewise, a Negro (Hari Rhodes) supposed to have been the first to attend an all-white Southern university serves to make the point that it takes enormous emotional stamina to play the role of the martyr in social progress. And the character of a renowned physicist (Gene Evans) whose mind has deteriorated into that of a six-year-old enables Fuller to get in some digs against bomb shelters and America's participation in the space race.

But all these points go for naught because the film is dominated by sex and shock superficialities. Among the gruelling passages are a striptease and an attack on the hero in a locked room by half-a-dozen nymphos.

The dialog is unreal and pretentious, and the direction is heavyhanded, often mistaking sordidness for realism. The performers labor valiantly, but in vain. Those most prominent are Breck, who really gets his lumps and earns his pay, and Constance Towers as his stripper girlfriend. [Orignal prints include documentary color sequencees shot on 16mm by Fuller himself.]

······························

■ SHOCKER

1989, 110 MINS, US ◇ Ⓥ Ⓒ

Dir Wes Craven *Prod* Marianne Maddalena, Barin Kumar *Scr* Wes Craven *Ph* Jacques Haitkin *Ed* Andy Blumental *Mus* William Goldstein *Art Dir* Cynthia Kay

● Michael Murphy, Peter Begg, Mitch Pileggi, Cami Cooper, Richard Brooks, Dr Timothy Leary (Alive/Universal)

At first glance (or at least for the first 40 minutes) *Shocker* seems a potential winner, an almost unbearably suspenseful, stylish and blood-drenched ride courtesy of writer-director Wes Craven's flair for action and sick humour.

As it continues, however, the camp aspects simply give way to the ridiculous while failing to establish any rules to govern the mayhem. The result is plenty of unintentional laughs.

The obtuse story has Horace Pinker (Mitch Pileggi), already a mass killer of several families, slaying the foster family of Jonathan (Peter Berg) and his police captain father (Michael Murphy). Jonathan 'sees' the events in a prescient dream that indicates he's linked to the murderer.

That leads the police to Pinker's door, and after a series of misadventures he's caught and executed. But Horace lives on after the execution as a disembodied malevolent spirit who strikes out by possessing others.

....

■ SHOCKPROOF

1949, 78 MINS, US

Dir Douglas Sirk *Scr* Helen Deutsch, Samuel Fuller *Ph* Charles Lawton Jr *Ed* Gene Havlick *Mus* George Duning

● Cornel Wilde, Patricia Knight, John Baragrey, Esther Minciotti, Howard St John (Columbia)

Shockproof is a patly told tale of the parole system with a strong romantic thread.

Yarn is wrapped up in a good production dress that uses Los Angeles locales to stress semi-documentary flavor. While never credible, story does point up the standard melodramatics and good playing to keep it all interesting.

Douglas Sirk's direction moves at an excellent pace. Plot deals with probationary work, with Cornel Wilde as one of the officers in the local bureau. A paroled murderess, Patricia Knight, is assigned to his care, and story is based on what happens to him and the girl when love moves into their lives.

Situations come together with pat coincidences that don't make for credence.

Wilde does well by his assignment, and Knight brings a strong personality and s.a to her part.

....

■ SHOCK TO THE SYSTEM, A

1990, 87 MINS, US ◇ Ⓥ Ⓒ

Dir Jan Egleson *Prod* Patrick McCormick *Scr* Andrew Klavan *Ph* Paul Goldsmith *Ed* Peter C. Frank, William A. Anderson *Mus* Gary Chang *Art Dir* Howard Cummings

● Michael Caine, Elizabeth McGovern, Peter Riegert, Swoosie Kurtz, Will Patton, John McMartin (Corsair)

A Shock to the System is a very dark comedy about escaping the current rat race via murder. Unsympathetic, poorly motivated central character [from a novel by Simon Brett] and flat direction nullify Michael Caine's reliable thesping.

Caine is cast as a Britisher working for a NY firm who's passed over for the post of marketing department head when John McMartin (in an affecting performance) is forced to take early retirement. Upstart Peter Riegert (way too sympathetic for the role) gets the job instead and starts throwing his weight around.

After doing away with wife Swoosie Kurtz by rigging faulty electric wiring in the basement, he blows up Riegert (and obnoxious assistant Philip Moon) on his sailboat. Plodding Connecticut cop Will Patton discovers plenty of clues.

Jan Egleson's direction slows to a snail's pace during the middle reels and lacks the style of the classics in this genre.

....

■ SHOES OF THE FISHERMAN, THE

1968, 162 MINS, US ◇ Ⓥ

Dir Michael Anderson *Prod* George Englund *Scr* John Patrick, James Kennaway *Ph* Erwin Hillier *Ed* Ernest Walter *Mus* Alex North *Art Dir* George W. Davis, Edward Carfagno

● Anthony Quinn, Laurence Olivier, Oskar Werner, David Janssen, Vittorio De Sica, Leo McKern (M-G-M)

Anthony Quinn plays a future Pope of Russian extraction who would, if necessary, strip the Roman Catholic Church of its material wealth in order to avoid nuclear world war. Occasionally awkward script structure and dialog, and overall sluggish pacing do not substantially blunt the impact of the basic story (from Morris L. West's novel), as interpreted by an excellent international cast.

It starts with Quinn as a 20-year inmate of a Siberian slave labor camp, and ends with his public Coronation promise as the new Pope to spend the Church's wealth.

Laurence Olivier, as the Russian premier, had ordered Quinn's release from religious persecution, and ultimate dispatch to Rome.

Quinn's performance is excellent. That experience-lined face suggests 20 years of Siberian enslavement, even if the script has him returning to urbane society with a bit too much facility.

Olivier, along with Frank Finlay and Clive Revill, are superior in projecting not unsympathetic Russian politicians.

☐ 1968: Nominations: Best Art Direction, Original Music Score

....

■ SHOGUN

1981, 150 MINS, US ◇ Ⓥ Ⓒ

Dir Jerry London *Prod* Eric Bercovici *Scr* Eric Bercovici *Ph* Andrew Laszlo *Ed* Bill Luciano, Jerry Young, Benjamin A. Weissman, Donald R. Rode *Mus* Maurice Jarre *Art Dir* Joseph R. Jennings

● Richard Chamberlain, Toshiro Mifune, Yoko Shimada, Alan Badel, Michael Hordern, John Rhys-Davies (Paramount)

In *Shogun*, East meets West in a period clash of swords and culture, but with scarcely the wit, style, dramatic tension or plausibility to justify a running time of 150 tiresome minutes for this spinoff from the James Clavell novel as recut from the eight-hour Paramount TV miniseries.

Richard Chamberlain and Toshiro Mifune are top-featured in this bilingual (and subtitled) tale of 17th-century Japanese political intrigue with praiseworthy professioal dignity, the former as a shipwrecked Englishman, the latter as one of the tribal chieftains vying for the title and power of shogun, or supreme Godfather. The whole shebang was lensed on locations in Japan.

Yoko Shimada projects a Dresden-doll appeal as an aristocratic lady who, besides helping Chamberlain bridge the culture gap, enters into forbidden love, thereby telegraphing her doom.

Producer Eric Bercovici's script on the big screen proves only too diffuse and confusing to do anything like justice to either the romance, any other relationship or indeed the wider canvas of betrayal, barbarism and warlord ritual posturing.

....

■ SHOOTING PARTY, THE

1984, 106 MINS, UK ◇ Ⓥ

Dir Alan Bridges *Prod* Geoffrey Reeve *Scr* Julian Bond *Ph* Fred Tammes *Ed* Peter Davies *Mus* John Scott *Art Dir* Morley Smith

● Edward Fox, Cheryl Campbell, James Mason, Dorothy Tutin, John Gielgud, Frank Windsor (Reeve)

A handsome historical homage to the proprieties and values of pre-First World War landed aristocracy in England, *The Shooting Party* revolves around a holiday spent on an estate in 1913, as an era ends.

Julian Bond's adaptation of the novel [by Isabel Colegate] incorporates enough to make a promising miniseries.

James Mason as Sir Randolph is as world-weary as he is tired of his genuinely tiresome guests. Thesp credits resemble a Who's Who of the British stage, with John Gielgud eclipsing the gentry in a brief appearance as a pamphleteering defender of animal rights, opposed to slaughter as amusement.

Director Alan Bridges is very good at handling a story that tries to distinguish between the nobility and what is truly noble.

....

■ SHOOTIST, THE

1976, 99 MINS, US ◇ Ⓥ Ⓒ

Dir Don Siegel *Prod* Mike Frankovich, William Self *Scr* Miles Hood Swarthout, Scott Hale *Ph* Bruce Surtees *Ed* Douglas Stewart *Mus* Elmer Bernstein *Art Dir* Robert Boyle

● John Wayne, Lauren Bacall, Ron Howard, Bill McKinney, James Stewart, Richard Boone (De Laurentiis)

The Shootist stands as one of John Wayne's towering achievements. Don Siegel's terrific film is simply beautiful, and beautifully simple, in its quiet, elegant and sensitive telling of the last days of a dying gunfighter at the turn of the century. Wayne and Lauren Bacall are both outstanding.

The time is 1901. Wayne a prairie-hardened gunfighter, rides into the new century where Carson City is in segue to modern civilization. Saloon shootouts still occur; Hugh O'Brian's card dealing is still not to be challenged.

Wayne's trip is to town doctor James Stewart, who confirms a cancer diagnosis. Atop this comes an emerging tenderness between Wayne and Bacall which is articulated in careful politeness and the artful exchange of expressions that evoke memories of great silent films.

☐ 1976: Nomination: Best Art Direction

....

■ SHOOT THE MOON

1982, 124 MINS, US ◇ Ⓥ

Dir Alan Parker *Prod* Alan Marshall *Scr* Bo Goldman *Ph* Michael Seresin *Ed* Gerry Hambling *Art Dir* Geoffrey Kirkland

● Albert Finney, Diane Keaton, Karen Allen, Peter Weller, Dana Hill, Viveka Davis (M-G-M)

A number of high-powered artists fail to coalesce their talents in *Shoot the Moon* a grim drama of marital collapse which proves disturbing and irritating by turns.

Noisy pic belongs almost entirely to toplined Albert Finney and Diane Keaton, who play affluent serious writer and housewife, respectively, and parents of four girls. First act is devoted to couple hitting absolute rock bottom, with nothing to do but for Finney to walk out into the arms of g.f. Karen Allen.

Attempting to handle the situation in civilized fashion, pair agrees that Finney can spend a reasonable amount of time with the girls, which allows Finney to catch glimpses of his wife's slow-cooking affair with a construction worker.

Forced to 'control' himself much of the time, Finney is a walking time bomb, exploding horrendously on one occasion before the climax when he beats his most troublesome daughter. Stripped of most of her charm and sometimes brutally photographed, Keaton is more erratic.

. . . .

■ SHOOT TO KILL
(UK: Deadly Pursuit)

1988, 110 MINS, US ◇ ⓥ ⊙
Dir Roger Spottiswoode   *Prod* Ron Silverman, Daniel Petrie Jr.   *Scr* Harv Zimmel, Michael Burton, Daniel Petrie Jr.   *Ph* Michael Chapman   *Ed* Garth Craven, George Bowers   *Mus* John Scott   *Art Dir* Richard Sylbert
● Sidney Poitier, Tom Berenger, Kirstie Alley, Clancy Brown, Richard Masur, Andrew Robinson (Touchstone/ Silver Screen Partners III)

Everybody, including the audience, gets a good workout in *Shoot to Kill*, a rugged, involving manhunt adventure [story by Harv Zimmel] in which a criminal leads his pursuers over what is perhaps the most challenging land route out of the United States.

Sidney Poitier establishes his authority immediately as a veteran FBI man in San Francisco who, despite handling the crisis with calm assuredness, cannot prevent the getaway of a jewel thief who kills hostages on a foggy night on Frisco Bay.

Another shooting of a similar type takes Poitier up to the Pacific Northwest, where he is forced to engage the services of tough backwoodsman Tom Berenger to lead him up into the mountains to apprehend the villain before he makes it over the border into Canada.

A self-styled macho hermit, Berenger considers Poitier a cityfied softy incapable of making it in the mountains. This sets up a cliched enmity between the two men that one knows will have to be broken down, but not without some predictable jibes at Poitier's awkwardness outdoors and some revelations of Berenger's own vulnerabilities.

Poitier, 63 when the film was shot, looks little more than 40. The actor's directness and easiness on the screen are refreshing, his humor self-deprecating and understated.

Berenger solidly fills the bill as the confident mountain man, and Kirstie Alley, despite the extreme limitations of her role, proves entirely believable as his female counterpart. British Columbia locations give the film tremendous scenic impact.

. . . .

■ SHOP AROUND THE CORNER, THE

1940, 97 MINS, US ⓥ ⊙
Dir Ernst Lubitsch   *Prod* Ernst Lubitsch   *Scr* Samson Raphaelson   *Ph* William Daniels   *Ed* Gene Ruggiero   *Mus* Werner R. Heymann   *Art Dir* Cedric Gibbons, Wade B. Rubottom
● Margaret Sullavan, James Stewart, Frank Morgan, Joseph Schildkraut, Sara Haden, Felix Bressart (M-G-M)

Although picture carries the indelible stamp of Ernst Lubitsch at his best in generating humor and human interest from what might appear to be unimportant situations, it carries further to impress via the outstanding characterizations by Margaret Sullavan and James Stewart in the starring spots. Sullavan's portrayal is light and fluffy – in contrast to the seriousness of Stewart in both business and romance.

The supporting cast is very well-balanced. In the compact group is Frank Morgan, as the owner-operator of the small gift shop in Budapest, and his staff including Joseph Schildkraut, Sara Haden, Felix Bressart, William Tracy, Inez Courtney and Charles Smith.

The story [based on Nikolaus Laszlo's play] might be termed a small edition of *Grand Hotel*, with practically all of the action taking place in the small shop. Stewart, senior clerk, confides to Bressart that he is corresponding

with a girl (Sullavan) through a newspaper ad, and takes the affair with the unknown very seriously. Sullavan arrives to apply for a job and, after being turned down by Stewart, is hired by Morgan.

From that point on it's an intimate tale of the store and its workers. Story swings along at fast pace.

. . . .

■ SHOPWORN ANGEL, THE

1928, 80 MINS, US
Dir Richard Wallace   *Scr* Howard Estabrook, Albert Shelby LeVino
● Nancy Carroll, Gary Cooper, Paul Lukas (Paramount)

Once in a long while the formula picture factories in Hollywood turn out a glamorous gem such as this [from a story by Dana Burnet], stirring, finely drawn, and so beautifully presented that the critical faculties declare a holiday. Nancy Carroll and Gary Cooper contribute excellent work. Both seem natural and lifelike.

As the showgirl Daisy living with the worldly sophisticate (Paul Lukas), with nothing to worry over except booze headaches and bawling the dance director when asked to come to rehearsals on time, Carroll never strays from type. She's hard, smart and strong-willed.

The soldier boy, William Tyler (Cooper), is from Texas where he never saw a show girl or a skyscraper first hand. He bumps into Daisy accidentally, is driven to camp in her limousine, and then brags to the gang. She later weakens enough to get the soldier out of the mess.

Only two dialog sequences in the picture, both highly effective. First is the marriage ceremony; Cooper has a few brief lines. In the second the dance director is putting the chorus through the paces; Carroll has a few lines here and also sings. The girl's voice records surprisingly well.

Lukas, a Hungarian imported by Paramount over a year ago, is a smooth, most nonchalant and likeable heavy.

. . . .

■ SHOPWORN ANGEL, THE

1938, 85 MINS, US
Dir H.C. Potter   *Prod* Joseph L. Mankiewicz   *Scr* Waldo Salt   *Ph* Joseph Ruttenberg   *Ed* W. Donn Hayes   *Mus* Edward Ward   *Art Dir* Cedric Gibbons, Joseph C. Wright, Edwin C. Willis
● Margaret Sullavan, James Stewart, Walter Pidgeon, Hattie McDaniel, Nat Pendleton, Alan Curtis (M-G-M)

Original of *Shopworn Angel* first appeared about 20 years earlier as a *Sat Eve Post* story by Dana Burnet. Paramount filmed it (partly in sound) in 1928, with Nancy Carroll, Gary Cooper and Paul Lukas.

In general, this remake follows the original story with reasonable faithfulness. It's still the wartime yarn about the crafty Broadway chorine who meets a Texas rookie on his way to France and, when he falls for her, marries him rather than disillusion him. Latter pair had their first strong parts in the production and it established their reps as well as cleaned up financially. The present version seems a softer one, without the stark edges of the original and as a result less absorbing. Instead of the cool schemer played by Nancy Carroll, the chorine is now generous and warm-hearted. The girl's lover is no longer the menace of the earlier version, but is now the typical Walter Pidgeon man-who-doesn't-get-the-girl.

It is only occasional credible screen drama. As the girl, Margaret Sullavan turns in a powerful performance. Her playing is pliant, has depth and eloquence.

James Stewart is a natural enough rookie but there's little characterization in his performance.

. . . .

■ SHORT CIRCUIT

1986, 98 MINS, US ◇ ⓥ ⊙
Dir John Badham   *Prod* David Foster, Lawrence Turman   *Scr* S.S. Wilson, Brent Maddock   *Ph* Nick McLean   *Ed* Frank Morriss   *Mus* David Shire   *Art Dir* Dianne Wager
● Ally Sheedy, Steve Guttenberg, Fisher Stevens, Austin Pendleton, G.W. Bailey, Brian McNamara (Tri-Star/PSO)

Short Circuit is a hip, sexless sci-fi sendup featuring a Defense Dept robot who comes 'alive' to become a pop-talking peacenik.

Robot is the one-dimensional No. 5, the ultimate weapon designed by playful computer whiz Dr Newton Crosby (Steve Guttenberg).

By a fluke, No. 5 gets short-circuited and begins to malfunction. It finds itself outside the high-security Nova compound in a chase that lands it on top of a natural foods catering truck and under the influence of its sweet but tough animal-loving owner, Stephanie (Ally Sheedy). Scripters get credit for some terrific dialog that would have been a lot less disarming if not for the winsome robot and Sheedy's affection for it. Guttenberg plays his best goofy self.

. . . .

■ SHORT CIRCUIT 2

1988, 110 MINS, US ◇ ⓥ ⊙
Dir Kenneth Johnson   *Prod* David Foster, Lawrence Turman, Gary Foster   *Scr* S.S. Wilson, Brent Maddock   *Ph* John McPherson   *Ed* Conrad Buff   *Mus* Charles Fox   *Art Dir* Bill Brodie
● Fisher Stevens, Michael McKean, Cynthia Gibb, Jack Weston, Tim Blaney, Dee McCafferty (Turman-Foster/Tri-Star)

Mild and meek, *Short Circuit 2* has an uncomplicated sweetness as a successful followup to the original robot kiddie comedy.

'Johnny Five' makes his way to the Big City, where protector Fisher Stevens struggles to make ends meet hawking toy models of his mechanical wonder on the street.

Cutie-pie store employee Cynthia Gibb needs to bring a novel item to her shelves, and sends Stevens and self-styled entrepreneur Michael McKean into instant action by ordering 1,000 of the little of the little buggers for the Christmas season. Underhanded banker Jack Weston has some other ideas for the tireless automaton, scheming to kidnap it and press it into service stealing some priceless jewels from a safe deposit box.

Although derivative, the robot, made up of all manner of spare electronic parts, remains charming, and kids will undoubtedly find delightful scenes in which Number Five jumps around from place to place and sails through the air amid the skyscrapers of Toronto.

The film is set in a generic US metropolis, complete with American flags and a citizenship swearing-in ceremony. However, the city is constantly recognizable as Toronto.

. . . .

■ SHORT CUT TO HELL

1957, 89 MINS, US
Dir James Cagney   *Prod* A.C. Lyles   *Scr* Ted Berkman, Raphael Blau   *Ph* Haskell Boggs   *Ed* Tom McAdoo   *Mus* Irvin Talbot   *Art Dir* Hal Pereira, Roland Anderson
● Robert Ivers, Georgann Johnson, William Bishop, Jacques Aubuchon (Paramount)

Updated version of the 1942 *This Gun for Hire* comes off as a crackling melodrama. Marking James Cagney's first pitch as a director and A.C. Lyles' initial full producer chore, film packs enough gutsy action.

Cagney socks over his helming in expected style from one who has specialized in hard-boiled characters, and gives parts plenty of meaning. Pair of unknowns take over the two top roles, Robert Ivers in the original Alan Ladd role and Georgann Johnson (with two eyes showing) the Veronica Lake, both doing yeoman service and handling themselves expertly. The screenplay, based on W.R. Burnett script [adapted from Graham Greene's novel, *A Gun for Sale*], carries fast pace and holds up generally through final climax.

Yarn is motivated by the search of Ivers, a ruthless young gunman, for the man who has paid him off in stolen money for two murders. Police have the numbers of the bills, which makes it impossible for gun to pass them. He picks up Johnson, girl friend of William Bishop, detective in charge of the murders, and forcibly keeps her with him during the police hunt.

● ●

■ SHORT TIME

1990, 97 MINS, US ◇ ▣ ⊙
Dir Gregg Champion   *Prod* Todd Black   *Scr* John Blumenthal, Michael Berry   *Ph* John Connor   *Ed* Frank Morriss   *Mus* Ira Newborn   *Art Dir* Michael Bolton
● Dabney Coleman, Matt Frewer, Teri Garr, Barry Corbin, Joe Pantoliano (Gladden)

Anyone trying to make a black comedy should be made to watch the classic *Harold & Maude* about 20 times before venturing into what too often is a sorely misused genre. Gregg Champion's extensive work as a second-unit director evidently hasn't prepared him for dealing with the nuances of human emotion. His idea of humor in this uneasy cross between farce and disease-of-the-week melodrama is to pile the desperate Dabney Coleman into a police car and have him crash into about half of the vehicles in Seattle before angrily stepping out in one piece.

Champion wants to turn Coleman's dilemma from farce into genuine emotion as the film progresses, but the character's callous disregard of other people's lives in his own quest for death makes him impossible to care about when the soapy music begins. He's otherwise a seemingly decent guy who has alienated wife Teri Garr, typecast as a drab but understanding featherhead.

The real problem is the subplot about a black bus driver (Deejay Jackson), whose urine sample has been mixed up with Coleman's, and who's really the one dying of a rare blood disorder but doesn't realize it.

● ●

■ SHOT IN THE DARK, A

1964, 103 MINS, US ◇ ▣ ⊙
Dir Blake Edwards   *Prod* Blake Edwards   *Scr* Blake Edwards, William Peter Blatty   *Ph* Christopher Challis   *Ed* Ralph E. Winters, Bert Bates   *Mus* Henry Mancini   *Art Dir* Michael Stringer
● Peter Sellers, Elke Sommer, Herbert Lom, George Sanders, Graham Stark, Douglas Wilmer (Mirisch/United Artists)

Based upon the French farce authored by Marcel Achard and adapted to the American stage by Harry Kurnitz, director Blake transforms Peter Sellers' role from a magistrate, whose activities were limited to judicial chambers, into Inspector Clouseau, where more movement and greater area are possible. 'Give me 10 men like Clouseau, and I could destroy the world!' his superior exclaims in despair, summing up the character played by Sellers, sent to investigate a murder in the chateau of a millionaire outside Paris.

When this chief inspector, portrayed by Herbert Lom, attempts to take him off the case, powers above return him to his investigations which revolve about chief suspect Elke Sommer, a French maid, whom the dick is convinced is innocent.

The chores takes him to a nudist camp, a tour of Parisian nightclubs, where dead bodies are left in his wake, and to his apartment, where one of the funniest seduction scenes ever filmed unfolds to the tune of three in a

bed and an exploding time bomb. It's never completely clear whether the detective solves his case in a windup that doesn't quite come off.

Sometimes the narrative is subordinated to individual bits of business and running gags but Sellers' skill as a comedian again is demonstrated, and Sommer, in role of the chambermaid who moves all men to amorous thoughts and sometimes murder, is pert and expert. Lom gives punch and humor to star's often distraught superior, George Sanders lends polish as the millionaire and Graham Stark excels as Sellers' dead-pan assistant.

● ●

■ SHOULDER ARMS

1918, 36 MINS, US ⊗
Dir Charles Chaplin   *Prod* Charles Chaplin   *Scr* Charles Chaplin   *Ph* Rollie Totheroh   *Mus* Charles Chaplin
● Charles Chaplin, Edna Purviance, Sydney Chaplin, Loyal Underwood, Henry Bergman, Albert Austin (First National)

In *Shoulder Arms* Chaplin is a doughboy. At the finish he captures the Kaiser, Crown Prince and Hindenburg.

At the opening he is the most awkward member of an awkward drilling squad. His trouble with his feet is terrific. After a long hike, Chaplin has heroic dreams of what he accomplishes as a private in the trenches over there.

Chaplin wrote and directed the story. His camouflage as a small tree, during which he runs through a wood is one of the best and most original pieces of comedy work ever put on a screen. There is some slapstick, laughably worked in, also pie-throwing with limburger cheese substituted. That occurs in the trenches.

The trenches are good production bits. There is fun also in the dug-out, with the water, and a floating candle burning one of the boys' exposed toes.

Shoulder Arms includes much more action than generally found in a Chaplin comedy. With Chaplin in uniform without his derby hat and cane, it says that Charlie Chaplin is a great film comedian.

● ●

■ SHOUT, THE

1978, 87 MINS, UK ◇ ▣
Dir Jerzy Skolimowski   *Prod* Jeremy Thomas   *Scr* Michael Austin, Jerzy Skolimowski   *Ph* Mike Molloy   *Ed* Barrie Vince   *Mus* Rupert Hine, Anthony Banks, Michael Rutherford   *Art Dir* Simon Holland
● Alan Bates, Susannah York, John Hurt, Robert Stephens, Tim Curry, Julian Hough (Recorded Picture)

Polish director Jerzy Skolimowski has been able to create a gripping film [from a story by Robert Graves] that holds attention most of the way through its economical length. It probes a couple beset by a catalyst that breaks their seemingly surface contentment. Film is told by Alan Bates during a cricket match in an asylum.

Bates, a tramp-like figure, accosts a man (John Hurt) outside a church one day. It is a small town and Bates gets invited to dinner and stays. He tells strange tales of how he lived with Australian aborigines and killed his own children when he left and how he learned how to cast various spells, especially a shout that can kill.

Flash forwards indicate Bates will disrupt the couple with one problem of the man apparently dallying with the wife of the local shoemaker.

Hurt is an electronic music composer and his work counterpoints Bates's shout in a way. The story builds as the listener becomes apprehensive. It crescendos as Bates, in the tale, reduces the wife to his whims.

● ●

■ SHOUT

1991, 89 MINS, US ◇ ▣ ⊙
Dir Jeffrey Hornaday   *Prod* Robert Simonds   *Scr* Joe Gayton   *Ph* Robert Brinkmann   *Ed* Seth Flaum   *Mus* Randy Edelman   *Art Dir* William F. Matthews
● John Travolta, James Walters, Heather Graham, Richard Jordan, Linda Fiorentino, Scott Coffey (Universal)

Shout is a 1950s rock'n'roll fantasy that tries to have it all ways at once and winds up sorely out of tune. Set in an isolated hamlet on the Texas plains, film purports to be about the liberating effect of the birth of rock'n'roll, but as producers have not secured rights to any signature songs of that era, musical mix sounds wildly inauthentic.

Broadly etched tale is about a home for wayward and orphaned boys. Kid with the worst attitude (James Walters) clashes with the grim and heavy-handed headmaster (Richard Jordan), who espouses a regimen of hard labor and calisthenics.

Along comes a music teacher (John Travolta), a hepcat ahead of his time who indoctrinates the boys in the forbidden pleasures of rock'n'roll. On the side, he's making time with the owner (Linda Fiorentino) of a dance club on the wrong side of the tracks and former flame of the town sheriff.

It's the kind of hokey scenario that would fly only if aided by a camp sense of humor or the promise of a good musical number about to break out, and neither of these are present. Music and dance elements are used naturalistically, as in *La Bamba*, but rather sparingly.

Only Travolta bothers to put on a Texas accent, and his thick, nuanced emoting clashes with the unadorned delivery of the others. In all, ill-thunk scenario seems slung together by amateurs. The culprits are producer Robert Simonds (both *Problem Child* pics) and first-time director Jeffrey Hornaday (*Flashdance* choreographer).

● ●

■ SHOUT AT THE DEVIL

1976, 147 MINS, UK ◇ ▣ ⊙
Dir Peter Hunt   *Prod* Michael Klinger   *Scr* Wilbur Smith, Stanley Price, Alastair Reid   *Ph* Mike Reed   *Ed* Michael Duthie   *Mus* Maurice Jarre   *Art Dir* Syd Cain
● Lee Marvin, Roger Moore, Barbara Parkins, Ian Holm, Rene Kolldehoff, Horst Janson (Hemdale)

A nice sprawling, basic, gutsy and unsophisticated film, which displays its reported $7 million budget on nearly every frame.

Based on a Wilbur Smith (*Gold*) novel, the script is a pastiche of almost every basic action-suspense ingredient known to the cinema.

Exotic tropical settings, man-eating crocodiles, air and sea combat, shipwreck, big game hunting, natives on a rampage, ticking time bombs, rape and fire, malaria, they're all there and then some.

Basic ingredients have to do with a successful attempt to put permanently out of action a crippled World War I German battle cruiser holed up for repairs in a remote South East African river delta.

The oddball opposites-attract relationship between Lee Marvin and Roger Moore generally works very well indeed, and the constantly imbibing Irisher and the contrastingly 'straight' Britisher make good foils. The motivating love story linking Moore and Barbara Parkins is rarely involving and convincing.

● ●

■ SHOW BOAT

1936, 110 MINS, US ▣ ⊙
Dir James Whale   *Prod* Carl Laemmle Jr   *Scr* Oscar Hammerstein II   *Ph* John J. Mescall   *Ed* Ted Kent, Bernard Burton   *Mus* Victor Baravelle (dir.)   *Art Dir* Charles D. Hall
● Irene Dunne, Allan Jones, Charles Winninger, Paul Robeson, Helen Morgan, Helen Westley (Universal)

S

Show Boat, Universal's second talkerized version, is a smash filmusical. Basic tender romance [from Edna Ferber's novel] between Magnolia (Irene Dunne) and Gaylord Ravenal (Allan Jones), romantic wastrel of the Mississippi river banks, has been most effectively projected by this reproduction of the classic [1927] Edna Ferber-Oscar Hammerstein II-Jerome Kern operetta.

The now classic songs, 'Make Believe', 'Ol' Man River', 'Can't Help Lovin' That Man', 'Why Do I Love You', 'Bill' and 'You Are Love', as the duet thematic have been retained and three new numbers, all in a novelty vein, have been added.

Dunne and Jones are superb in the roles originally created by Norma Terriss and Howard Marsh. Charles Winninger in his original Captain Andy role is, as ever, engaging; Helen Morgan is the same Julie as in the Ziegfeld original; Paul Robeson has Jules Bledsoe's basso opportunities with 'Ol' Man River'; Helen Westley has the original Edna Mae Oliver assignment and delivers adequately, if a bit morosely, lacking the subtle brittleness of the Oliver interpretation.

Dunne maintains the illusion of her Magnolia throughout – from her own secluded girlhood; into sudden stardom on the Cotton Blossom; and later, as a more mature artist, carrying the torch for the disappeared Ravenal and rearing her own child into professional prominence.

Robeson's 'Ol' Man river' is perhaps the single song highlight, although some may be captious a bit over the camera angles illustrating 'totin' the bales' and 'landing in jail'.
□ 1951: Nominations: Best Color Cinematography, Scoring of a Musical Picture

■ SHOW BOAT

1951, 107 MINS, US ◇ ⑳ ⊙
Dir George Sidney   *Prod* Arthur Freed   *Scr* John Lee Mahin   *Ph* Charles Rosher   *Ed* John Dunning   *Mus* Adolph Deutsch (dir.)   *Art Dir* Cedric Gibbons, Jack Martin Smith
● Kathryn Grayson, Howard Keel, Ava Gardner, Joe E. Brown, Marge Champion, Gower Champion (M-G-M)

Show Boat started beguiling audiences back in 1927, when it was first brought to the Broadway stage after a Philadelphia tryout. Since then, in many legit versions and in two previous film treatments, it has continued that beguilement.

There has been no tampering with the basic line of the Edna Ferber novel, from which Jerome Kern and Oscar Hammerstein II did the original musical. There are a few changes in this latest film version, the first in color, and an introduction of the finale in a time span much shorter than the original.

'Ol' Man River', 'Make Believe', 'Why Do I Love You', 'You Are Love', 'My Bill', and 'Can't Help Lovin' That Man' are Kern tunes that lose nothing in the passing of the years. With voices of such show-tune ableness as Kathryn Grayson and Howard Keel to sing them they capture the ear and tear at the emotions.

Grayson is a most able Magnolia, the innocent show boat girl who runs off with the dashing gambler (Keel), finds her marriage wrecked by his love of lady chance, goes back to the show boat to have her child and then reconciles with the wandering mate after a few years.

Ava Gardner is the third star, bringing to her role of Julie, the mulatto who is kicked off the Cotton Blossom because of early southern prejudice, all the physical attributes it needs to attract attention.

There is an amazing amount of freshness instilled into the picture by Marge and Gower Champion, young dance team who handle the roles of Ellie May and Frank Schultz, show boat terpers. The other big song moment is William Warfield's rich baritoning of 'Ol' Man River'.

■ SHOWDOWN IN LITTLE TOKYO

1991, 76 MINS, US ◇ ⑳
Dir Mark L. Lester   *Prod* Mark L. Lester, Martin E. Caan   *Scr* Stephen Glantz, Caliope Brattlestreet   *Ph* Mark Irwin   *Ed* Steven Kemper, Robert A. Ferretti   *Mus* David Michael Frank   *Art Dir* Craig Stearns
● Dolph Lundgren, Brandon Lee, Carey-Hiroyuki Tagawa, Tia Carrere, Toshiro Obata (Warner)

Story is all by-the-numbers revenge stuff, although screenplay skips a lot of numbers, the better to focus on nonstop and generally unimaginative action sequences. The Japanese mafia (yakuza) provide the cardboard cutout villains for the good guys to knock over. Dolph Lundgren, whose parents top mobster Carey-Hiroyuki Tagawa sliced and diced during his boyhood, plays a raised-in-Japan supercop. Brandon Lee (son of Bruce Lee) is his preppy, comic relief Eurasian partner.

Lundgren can hold his own with other action leads as an actor and could easily be Van Damme-marketable if only he'd devote as much attention to quality control as he does to pectoral development. Editing also proves choppy, with some seemingly out-of-sequence cuts. Lee, making his US feature debut, has a gee-whiz delivery that seems plucked from another film.

■ SHOW PEOPLE

1928, 63 MINS, US ⑳
Dir King Vidor   *Scr* Wanda Tuchock, Ralph Spence   *Ph* John Arnold   *Ed* Hugh Wynn   *Art Dir* Cedric Gibbons
● Marion Davies, William Haines, Dell Henderson, Paul Ralli, Tenen Holtz, Harry Gribbon (M-G-M)

As an entertainment *Show People* is a good number. It has laughs, studio atmosphere galore, intimate glimpses of various stars, considerable Hollywood geography, and just enough sense and plausibility to hold it together.

As a document of Hollywood it presents some peculiar angles. When Peggy Pepper (Marion Davies) gets the w.k. swell head she is seen to be the complacent girlfriend of her leading man, an insufferably conceited stuffed shirt. The odd part of this leading man character is that he (Paul Ralli) looks, dresses and acts like John Gilbert, star of the company which produced the picture. The satire seems pretty sharply pointed at times.

Davies is obviously mimicking the peculiar pucker of the lips identified with Mae Murray, former M-G-M star. However, at other times the story suggests the career of Gloria Swanson, particularly with emphasis upon the custard pie gal becoming an emotional actress. Bebe Daniels is also suggested.

■ SHUTTERED ROOM, THE

1966, 99 MINS, UK ◇ ⑳
Dir David Greene   *Prod* Phillip Hazelton   *Scr* D.B. Ledrov, Nathaniel Tanchuck   *Ph* Ken Hodges   *Ed* Brian Smedley-Aston   *Mus* Basil Kirchin   *Art Dir* Brian Eatwell
● Gig Young, Carol Lynley, Oliver Reed, Flora Robson, William Devlin, Bernard Kay (Seven Arts)

With a good quota of shudders and a neat suggestion of evil throughout, this is an efficient entry in a somewhat oldfashioned vein of melodrama. Although supposedly taking place in New England, the locations are blatantly British scenery.

Susannah Kelton (Carol Lynley) has inherited an old millhouse on a remote island, and turns up there with husband Mike (Gig Young) to take possession. A prolog already has warned that there's a mad dame locked up in an upper story. Ethan (Oliver Reed), who heads a mischievous gang of layabouts, surveys her with a morose and lascivious eye.

The script is adequate in the plotting but feeble in the dialog department, sparking off untoward laffs in the wrong places. Lynley is competently scared throughout. And Reed brings a brooding touch of lechery to the over-excited Ethan.

■ SHY PEOPLE

1987, 118 MINS, US ◇ ⑳ ⊙
Dir Andrei Konchalovsky   *Prod* Menahem Golan, Yoram Globus   *Scr* Gerard Brach, Andrei Konchalovsky, Marjorie David   *Ph* Chris Menges   *Ed* Alain Jakubowicz   *Mus* Tangerine Dream   *Art Dir* Steve Marsh
● Jill Clayburgh, Barbara Hershey, Martha Plimpton, Merritt Butrick, John Philbin, Don Swayze (Cannon)

Cosmopolitan writer Diana Sullivan (Jill Clayburgh) lives in splendid disharmony in New York with her teenage daughter Grace (Martha Plimpton). Clayburgh is totally in her element as a spoiled middle-age woman trying to cope with her too-hip daughter.

They are soon out of their element, though, when they travel to Louisiana. It is not simply a case of invaders from civilization soiling a pure culture; story is deepened by the exploration of family ties.

What they find when they arrive is Ruth Sullivan (Barbara Hershey), the matriarch of a family of three sons, one of whom is kept in a cage and another retarded, plus a pregnant daughter (Mare Winningham).

Director Andrei Konchalovsky and cinematographer Chris Menges offer a slow and seductive descent into this world of alligators and primordial beauty.

Clayburgh gives one of her best performances and seems right at home with the ticks and self-centered mannerisms of a modern woman. Plimpton nearly steals the show with her mixture of girlish brashness and suggestive sexuality.

■ SIBLING RIVALRY

1990, 88 MINS, US ◇ ⑳ ⊙
Dir Carl Reiner   *Prod* David V. Lester, Don Miller, Liz Glotzer   *Scr* Martha Goldhirsh   *Ph* Reynaldo Villalobos   *Ed* Bud Molin   *Mus* Jack Elliott   *Art Dir* Jeannine Claudia Oppewall
● Kirstie Alley, Bill Pullman, Carrie Fisher, Jami Gertz, Scott Bakula, Sam Elliott (Castle Rock/Nelson)

In her first solo-starring vehicle, Kirstie Alley – who plays the creatively stifled wife of a stuffy young doctor (Scott Bakula) – comes into her own with a flamboyant, highly physical performance.

Her adulterous hop in the sack with mystery hunk Sam Elliott results in his death by heart attack after strenuous lovemaking. What follows involves three sets of siblings: Alley and her slightly ditzy younger sister and rival (Jami Gertz); weird vertical blinds salesman Bill Pullman as the black sheep younger brother of upwardly mobile cop Ed O'Neil; and the massive clan of doctors comprising Bakula, his sister (Carrie Fisher) and brother (Elliott).

The surprise that Elliott turns out to be Alley's brother-in-law is effectively developed and launches several hilarious setpieces. Pullman and Alley are united in crime after Pullman thinks *he* accidentally killed Elliott with his vertical blinds equipment. Both he and Alley attempt to cover up the fatality as a suicide.

Though the rushed happy ending doesn't ring true, *Sibling Rivalry* creates a cheerful mood from morbid material. Carl Reiner directs swiftly and efficiently, getting maximum yocks out of borderline vulgar content.

■ SICILIAN, THE

1987, 115 MINS, US ◇ ⑫ ⊙

Dir Michael Cimino *Prod* Michael Cimino, Joann Carelli
Scr Steve Shagan *Ph* Alex Thomson *Ed* Francoise
Bonnot *Mus* David Mansfield *Art Dir* Wolf Kroeger
● Christopher Lambert, Terence Stamp, Joss Ackland,
John Turturro, Barbara Sukowa, Ray McAnally
(Gladden/Beckerman)

The Sicilian represents a botched telling of
the life of postwar outlaw leader Salvatore
Giuliano. Just who contributed to what parts
of the botching remain a mystery, since uncredited hands cut 30 minutes from the version director Michael Cimino delivered. [The
145-minute version was later released on
video, and theatrically in Europe.]

Cimino seems to be aiming for an operatic
telling of the short career of the violent 20th-
century folk hero [based on Mario Puzo's
novel], but falls into an uncomfortable middle
ground between European artfulness and
stock Hollywood conventions.

Saga served as the basis of Francesco Rosi's
1962 *Salvatore Giuliano*, and has at its core a
popular young man who, working from the
mountains, employs increasingly excessive
means to further his dream of achieving radical land distribution from the titled estate
owners to the peasants.

Giuliano unhesitatingly kills anyone he
thinks has betrayed him, and maintains a
semi-adversarial, curiously equivocal relationship with both the Catholic Church and the
all-powerful Mafia.

In the lead, Christophe (billed in US projects as Christopher) Lambert betrays little
inner conflict or sense of thought, and simply
does not make Giuliano interesting.

Coming off by far the best is Joss Ackland,
who makes the Mafia chieftain a warm, sympathetic man one enjoys being around.
Richard Bauer makes a strong impression as
an adviser and go-between for Giuliano and
the Mafia, and Giulia Boschi is strikingly, seriously beautiful as the hero's wife.

■ SID AND NANCY

1986, 111 MINS, UK ◇ ⑫ ⊙

Dir Alex Cox *Prod* Eric Fellner *Scr* Alex Cox, Abbe
Wool *Ph* Roger Deakins *Ed* David Martin *Mus* The
Pogues, Pray for Rain *Art Dir* Andrew McAlpine
● Gary Oldman, Chloe Webb, David Hayman, Drew
Schofield, Debby Bishop, Tony London (Embassy/
Zenith/Initial)

Sid and Nancy is the definitive pic on the punk
phenomenon. The sad, sordid story of Sid
Vicious, a lead member of The Sex Pistols,
and his relationship with his American girlfriend, Nancy Spungen, is presented by Alex
Cox without flinching. Authenticity is the
film's major asset.

It's a world of drugs and booze, with sex
lagging behind in interest for the most part.
But grim as much of the film is, it's not without humor.

With his unwashed hair sticking out at all
angles, his pale face and brash British accent,
Gary Oldman fits the part like a glove. Chloe
Webb doesn't spare her looks as the ravaged,
shrill Nancy. Both actors are beyond praise.

The film's dialog is extremely rough, the
settings sordid, the theme of wasted lives
(and talent?) depressing. But *Sid and Nancy* is
a dynamic piece of work, which brings audiences as close as possible to understanding its
wayward heroes.

■ SIDDHARTHA

1972, 95 MINS, US ◇

Dir Conrad Rooks *Prod* Conrad Rooks *Scr* Conrad
Rooks *Ph* Sven Nykvist *Ed* Willy Kemplen
Mus Hemanta Kumar *Art Dir* Malcolm Golding
● Shashi Kapoor, Simi Garewal, Romesh Sharma,
Pincho Kapoor, Zul Vellani, Amrik Singh (Lotus)

Conrad Rooks' second pic, *Siddhartha*, based on
the 1922 book by Hermann Hesse, takes place
2,500 years ago in India. It is about a well-to-
do young Brahmin who feels he must leave
home and find himself and also echoes a man
questing for nirvana in a confused society.

Rooks has chosen to give this a surface elegance which sometimes robs the film of its
needed earthiness and sensuality in its love
angle and more robustness in detailing the
vagaries of social aspects and values at the
time. But it does have a fine photographic
beauty in the hands of Swedish lenser Sven
Nykvist.

Siddhartha, after leaving his father, roams
with a friend for years, with a group of holy
men. Then he meets a great teacher who
preaches the need for one's own way to inner
harmony who may be the Buddha himself.

■ SIDEKICKS

1993, 100 MINS, US ◇ ⑫ ⊙

Dir Aaron Norris *Prod* Don Carmody *Scr* Don
Thompson, Lou Illar *Ph* Joao Fernandes *Ed* David
Rawlins, Bernard Weiser *Mus* Alan Silvestri
Art Dir Reuben Freed
● Chuck Norris, Beau Bridges, Jonathan Brandis, Mako,
Julia Nickson-Soul, Joe Piscopo (Gallery)

Imagine a cross between *The Karate Kid* and
The Secret Life of Walter Mitty, and you'll know
what to expect from *Sidekicks*, an off-beat
family-audience opus from, of all people, action star Chuck Norris.

Norris' presence dominates pic, but the
lead character is a day-dreaming teen
(Jonathan Brandis), an asthmatic outsider
who's mocked by many of his peers, harassed
by most of his teachers, and ignored by his
computer-programmer dad (Beau Bridges).
So the boy seeks refuge in heroic fantasies
where he is the brave and resourceful sidekick of his favorite action movie hero
(Norris).

Film is peppered with moderately clever
daydream sequences modeled after (and featuring brief excerpts from) such Norris
movies as *Missing in Action*, *Lone Wolf McQuade*
and *The Hit Man*.

Coached by the sage uncle (Mako) of his
only compassionate teacher (Julia Nickson-
Soul), Brandis quickly picks up enough martial arts skill to compete in a karate
tournament against his school's worst bully (a
punkish John Buchanan).

Brandis is appealing and persuasively intense; Danica McKellar is passably sweet as a
classmate who feels sorry for, then falls for
him.

■ SIEGE OF SIDNEY STREET, THE

1960, 93 MINS, UK

Dir Robert S. Baker, Monty Berman *Prod* Robert S.
Baker, Monty Berman *Scr* Jimmy Sangster, Alexander
Baron *Ph* Robert S. Baker, Monty Berman *Ed* Peter
Bezencenet *Mus* Stanley Black *Art Dir* William Kellner
● Donald Sinden, Nicole Maurey, Kieron Moore, Peter
Wyngarde, Leonard Sachs, T.P. McKenna (Mid-Century)

This turns out to be quite a lively version of a
gangster episode that had the East End of
London on its ears early in 1911. It's a re-
vamp [from a story by Jimmy Sangster] of the
celebrated incident when a gang of Russians
brought out the police and the army before
they could be smoked out of their hideout in
Sidney Street.

In straightforward fashion, this shows
Donald Sinden as a dedicated police officer
who patiently tracks down the gang of
Russian patriots, led by a character named
Peter the Painter (Peter Wyngarde). They
robbed allegedly to gain funds for their cause,
which was anarchy. By disguising himself as a
down-and-outer, Sinden eventually gets the
thugs penned up.

The result was one of the bloodiest gangster scenes that London has ever known. The
East End of London in 1911 is vividly brought
to life, direction is sound without being over-
emphasized while the final siege is an exciting sock climax.

Wyngarde gives an alert, strong portrayal of
the quiet but ruthless top gangster. Kieron
Moore, a trigger-happy lieutenant, and
Leonard Sachs, as an older but equally devoted member of the cause, are also first-rate.

Sinden, as the cop, tends to play much on
same note, but his is a comparatively colorless role compared with those of the Russo
thugs.

■ SIESTA

1987, 97 MINS, US/UK ◇ ⑫ ⊙

Dir Mary Lambert *Prod* Gary Kurfirst, Chris Brown
Scr Patricia Louisianna Knop *Ph* Bryan Loftus
Ed Glenn A. Morgan *Mus* Marcus Miller *Art Dir* John
Beard
● Ellen Barkin, Gabriel Byrne, Julian Sands, Isabella
Rossellini, Martin Sheen, Jodie Foster (Lorimar/Siren/
Palace)

First feature film by Mary Lambert, best
known for her Madonna videos, is a densely
packed portrait of a beautiful, disturbed
woman at the end of her rope. Told in a fragmented, time-jumping style, this subjective,
hallucinatory recollection of a five-day descent into hell sustains intense interest
throughout, to a great extent because of
Ellen Barkin's extravagantly fine performance in the leading role.

In its elaborate, jigsaw-puzzle way, film
[from the novel by Patrice Chaplin] tells of
how Barkin, a daredevil skydiver, impulsively
leaves her home and husband in Death Valley
for a quick trip to Spain to find the man she
still loves, trapeze artist Gabriel Byrne, who
also has married someone else, Isabella
Rossellini.

Although due back in California imminently
for a big commercial payday, Barkin lets her
desire for Byrne prolong her Spanish sojourn
past the deadline. She falls in with a dissolute,
aimless English crowd led by Julian Sands and
Jodie Foster and finally becomes utterly lost
and delirious, helpless at the hands of filthy-
minded taxi driver Alexei Sayle.

Byrne puts on a continuous smoldering act
as the sought-after lover, Martin Sheen is all
congenial American hype as Barkin's abandoned husband, and Jodie Foster, as a snooty
but friendly socialite, has fun with a British
accent.

■ SIGN OF THE CROSS, THE

1932, 115 MINS, US

Dir Cecil B. DeMille *Prod* Cecil B. DeMille
Scr Waldemar Young, Sidney Buchman *Ph* Karl Struss
Ed Anne Bauchens *Mus* Rudolph Kopp
● Fredric March, Claudette Colbert, Elissa Landi,
Charles Laughton, Ian Keith (Paramount)

Religion triumphant over paganism. And the
soul is stronger than the flesh. Religion gets
the breaks, even though its followers all get
killed in this picture. It's altogether a moral
victory.

For example, the handsome Prefect of
Rome (Fredric March) sees that he can't get
to first base with the Christian maiden
(Elissa Landi), so he calls in the village
temptress, Ancaria (Joyzelle Joyner), for help.
Ancaria is described as the hottest gal in
town. 'The most versatile' is the phrase used.
She uses her arts on Landi. In the street the
other Christian martyrs are marching to
their doom, singing hymns bravely as they go.
Their chants disrupts and finally drowns out
the temptress' routine, and she strikes the
unmoved Landi in the face. Then, having lost,
she walks.

Besides Ancaria, there is Charles Laughton's expert Nero, who doubles as the degenerate emperor and musical pyromaniac as Rome burns. Most of the last half is taken up with a bloody festival staged by crazy Caesar in the arena.

Cast is uniformly good, but only one exceptional performance is registered. That's Laughton's. With utmost subtlety and a minimum of effort he manages to get over his queer character before his first appearance is a minute old.

Claudette Colbert [as Poppaea] and Landi and March and Ian Keith [as Tigellinus] are called upon chiefly to look their parts, and they manage. Frequently some badly written and often silly dialog holds them down.

□ 1932/3: Nomination: Best Cinematography

··

■ SIGN OF THE PAGAN

1954, 91 MINS, US ◇

Dir Douglas Sirk   *Prod* Albert J. Cohen   *Scr* Oscar Brodney, Barre Lyndon   *Ph* Russell Metty   *Ed* Al Clark   *Mus* Frank Skinner, Hans J. Salter   *Art Dir* Alexander Golitzen, Emrich Nicholson
● Jeff Chandler, Jack Palance, Ludmilla Tcherina, Rita Gam, Jeff Morrow, George Dolenz (Universal)

Unlike most screen spectacles, *Sign of the Pagan*'s running time is a tight 91 minutes, in which the flash of the Roman Empire period is not permitted to slow down the telling of an interesting action story.

Plot [from a story by Oscar Brodney] deals with Attila the Hun, the Scourge of God, and his sweep across Europe some 1,500 years ago. Particularly noteworthy is the treatment of the barbarian in writing and direction, and in the manner in which Jack Palance interprets the character. Instead of a straight, all-evil person, he is a human being with some good here and there to shade and make understandable the bad.

Douglas Sirk's direction of the excellent script catches the sweep of the period portrayed without letting the characters get lost in spectacle. Representing good in the plot is Jeff Chandler, centurion made a general by his princess, Ludmilla Tcherina, to fight off Attila's advancing hordes.

With Palance scoring so solidly in his role of Attila, he makes the other performers seem less colorful, although Chandler is good as Marcian.

··

■ SIGN O' THE TIMES

1987, 85 MINS, US ◇ ⓥ

Dir Prince   *Prod* Robert Cavallo, Joseph Ruffalo, Steven Fragnoli   *Ph* Peter Sinclair, Jerry Watson   *Ed* Steve Purcell   *Mus* Billy Youdelman, Susan Rogers (sup.)   *Art Dir* Leroy Bennett
● (Cavallo Ruffalo & Fragnoli)

Following his disastrous, hubris-drenched fling as a leading man in the non-musical, glossy b&w fantasy *Under the Cherry Moon*, Prince Rogers Nelson of Minneapolis wisely has returned with a polychromatic concert performance film that should draw anyone who got a charge of out his classic rock 'n' roll romance pic *Purple Rain*.

Shot on location at a music hall in Rotterdam and at the musician's studio in Minnesota, *Sign O' the Times* is a filmed treatment of Prince's touring show of 14 songs from his hit lp of the same name. Defiantly carnal in the face of AIDS-era safe sexiness, the Prince revue is set in a *film noir* fantasy zone where the come-hither blinking of gaudy neon honky-tonk signs flashes over an idealized back-alley netherworld. There, strong-willed, Nautilus-sinewed, lascivious women – lissom gladiatrixes of rock 'n' roll bloodsport – challenge the sexual imperatives of Princely machismo.

Posing, pouting and pirouetting with an-

drogynous abandon, pushing his guitar into ethereal, upper-register soundstorms and giving supple voice to songs of sensual and emotional free-fall in an anomic contemporary world, Prince provides musicvideo addicts with a pure fix of visual and aural synchronicity.

··

■ SILENCE OF THE LAMBS, THE

1991, 118 MINS, US ◇ ⓦ ⊙

Dir Jonathan Demme   *Prod* Edward Saxon, Kenneth Utt, Ron Bozman   *Scr* Ted Tally   *Ph* Tak Fujimoto   *Ed* Craig McKay   *Mus* Howard Shore   *Art Dir* Kristi Zea
● Jodie Foster, Anthony Hopkins, Scott Glenn, Ted Levine, Brooke Smith, Diane Baker (Orion/Strong Heart)

Skillful adaptation of Thomas Harris' bestseller intelligently wallows in the fascination for aberrant psychology and pervese evil.

Sharp script charts tenacious efforts of young FBI recruit Clarice Starling (Jodie Foster) to cope with the appalling challenges of her first case. Confounded by a series of grotesque murders committed by someone known only as 'Buffalo Bill', bureau special agent Jack Crawford (Scott Glenn) asks his female protege to seek the help of the American prison system's No. 1 resident monster in fashioning a psychological profile of the killer.

Dr Hannibal Lecter (Anthony Hopkins) has been kept in a dungeon-like cell for eight years, and while officious doctors and investigators can get nothing out of him, he is willing to play ball with his attractive new inquisitor. Lecter gives Starling clues as to the killer's identity in exchange for details about her past.

Just as it seems the noose is tightening around the killer, Lecter, in a remarkably fine suspense sequence, manages an unthinkable escape.

Plot is as tight as a coiled rattler. Foster fully registers the inner strength her character must summon up. Scott Glenn is a very agreeable surprise as the FBI agent who takes a chance by putting his young charge on the case. Hopkins, helped by some highly dramatic lighting, makes the role the personification of brilliant, hypnotic evil, and the screen jolts with electricity whenever he is on.

□ 1991: Best Picture, Director, Actor (Anthony Hopkins), Actress (Jodie Foster), Adapted Screenplay
□ Nominations: Best Editing, Sound

··

■ SILENCER, THE

1992, 84 MINS, US ◇ ⓥ

Dir Amy Goldstein   *Prod* Brian J. Smith   *Scr* Scott Kraft, Amy Goldstein   *Ph* Daniel Berkowitz   *Ed* Rick Blue   *Mus* Carole Pope, Ron Sures   *Art Dir* John Myhre
● Lynette Walden, Chris Mulkey, Paul Ganus, Brook Parker (Marimark)

As slick as an ad for designer biker wear, *The Silencer* presses all the right buttons. Knowing mix of softcore tease and style-trash visuals is wrapped around a *Nikita* rip-off plot.

Lynette Walden is a professional hit woman lured out of retirement by former employer The Agency to waste five sleazebags behind an LA child-slave ring. Hot on her trail is former lover Chris Mulkey, who follows her exploits on an arcade vidgame called 'The Silencer.'

Pic quickly settles down into a series of set pieces, with Walden changing her wardrobe for each hit and working off her frustrations between times with bemused b.f. Paul Ganus. Computer-generated script's only other subplot is Walden's female solidarity with a black street girl (Brook Parker).

Debuting director Amy Goldstein delivers the goods on every level, with occasional up-front humor adding to the knowing tone. In her first leading role, Walden, tops in the s.a.

department, maintains her femininity in the action sequences, cut and framed to show her 'Madonna with a pistol' to best effect. Nudity and violence are relatively restrained.

··

■ SILENCERS, THE

1966, 103 MINS, US ◇ ⓥ

Dir Phil Karlson   *Prod* Irving Allen   *Scr* Oscar Saul   *Ph* Burnett Guffey   *Ed* Charles Nelson   *Mus* Elmer Bernstein   *Art Dir* Joe Wright
● Dean Martin, Stella Stevens, Daliah Lavi, Victor Buono, Arthur O'Connell, Cyd Charisse (Meadway/Claude)

Dean Martin – as Matt Helm, ace of the American counter-espionage agency, ICE – succeeds in a kind of lover-boy way in taking his place up there with such stalwarts as Sean Connery, James Coburn and David Niven.

Produced by Irving Allen and directed by Phil Karlson, both utilizing shock technique, the fastdriving screenplay is based on two of Donald Hamilton's Matt Helm books, *The Silencers* and *Death of a Citizen*.

Plot focuses on a Chinese agent (Victor Buono) who masterminds a ring that plans to divert a US missile so it will destroy Alamogordo, New Mexico, thus creating wide devastation and atomic fallout leading perhaps to global war. All Matt Helm has to do is halt this catastrophe.

Starring with Martin are Stella Stevens and Daliah Lavi. Stevens does herself proud as a mixed-up living doll who can stumble over her own shadow. Lavi is a femme fatale, Martin's ever-lovin' spymate who comes up with a big surprise for him. The glamor department is further repped by Cyd Charisse as a dancer killed by the mob as she's dancing.

··

■ SILENT ENEMY, THE

1958, 112 MINS, UK ⓥ

Dir William Fairchild   *Prod* Bertram Ostrer   *Scr* William Fairchild   *Ph* Otto Heller   *Ed* Alan Osbiston   *Mus* William Alwyn   *Art Dir* Bill Andrews
● Laurence Harvey, Dawn Addams, Michael Craig, John Clements, Gianna Maria Canale, Arnoldo Foa (Romulus)

The Silent Enemy [from the book *Commander Crabb* by Marshall Pugh] tells the remarkable story of Lieutenant Crabb, a young naval bomb disposal officer, whose exploits in leading frogmen against the Italians earned him a George Medal. It makes smooth, impressive drama, done without heroics, but with excitement.

Laurence Harvey arrives in Gibraltar in 1941 to tackle the Italian menace that is striking successfully at key shipping in the area. With courage and determination, he becomes an experienced diver. Harvey is brash, intolerant of red tape, but fired with drive.

Without permission, Harvey and Michael Craig, one of the seamen, slip across to Spain and discover that the enemy base is in an interned Italian ship. The hull has been converted so that the frogmen can come and go underwater without being seen.

The impatience of the men as they wait to strike, the rigorous training and, above all, the feeling of men doing a thankless and arduous job with a quiet sense of duty are all admirably portrayed. The remarkable underwater scenes give this polished film a sock impact.

··

■ SILENT MOVIE

1976, 86 MINS, US ◇ ⓥ ⊙

Dir Mel Brooks   *Prod* Michael Hertzberg   *Scr* Mel Brooks, Ron Clark, Rudy DeLuca, Barry Levinson   *Ph* Paul Lohmann   *Ed* John C. Howard, Stanford C. Allen   *Mus* John Morris   *Art Dir* Al Brenner
● Mel Brooks, Marty Feldman, Dom DeLuise, Bernadette Peters, Sid Caesar, Harold Gould (20th Century-Fox)

It took a lot of chutzpah for Mel Brooks to make *Silent Movie* a film with only one word of dialog in an almost non-stop parade of sight gags.

Brooks, Marty Feldman, and Dom DeLuise head the cast as a has-been director and his zany cronies, conning studio chief Sid Caesar into making their silent film as a desperate ploy to prevent takeover of the studio by the Engulf & Devour conglomerate, headed by villainous Harold Gould. The parallels with realities are drolly satiric.

The slender plot of *Silent Movie* [from a story by Ron Clark] is basically a hook for slapstick antics, some feeble and some very fine (notably a wonderful nightclub tango with Anne Bancroft). Harry Ritz, Charlie Callas, Henny Youngman, and the late Liam Dunn are standouts.

. . . .

■ SILENT PARTNER, THE

1979, 103 MINS, CANADA ◇ ▼ ⊙
Dir Daryl Duke   *Prod* Joel B. Michaels, Stephen Young
Scr Curtis Hanson   *Ph* Billy Williams   *Mus* Oscar Peterson   *Art Dir* Trevor Williams
● Susannah York, Christopher Plummer, Elliott Gould, Celine Lomez, Ken Pogue, John Candy (EMC)

The *Silent Partner* is one of the films that run the gamut from intrigue to violence. Filmed entirely in Toronto, it's an independently financed film which won six Canadian Film Awards.

Christopher Plummer plays the villain for a change – a bank robber. Elliott Gould is a bank clerk who finds out that Plummer, dressed in a Santa Claus suit, plans a robbery. Susannah York is a bank employee under pressure from Plummer and newcomer Celine Lomez is a cohort of Plummer.

The story [from the novel *Think of a Number* by Anders Bodelson] has Gould, a teller in a branch office, get suspicious when it is the Christmas season and the bank is filled with shoppers. The robber hits and Gould's alertness inspires him to hide $50,000 in a lunch box with the police believing that the robber has all the loot.

. . . .

■ SILENT PLAYGROUND, THE

1964, 75 MINS, UK
Dir Stanley Goulder   *Prod* George Mills   *Scr* Stanley Goulder   *Ph* Martin Curtis   *Ed* Peter Musgrave
Mus Tristram Cary   *Art Dir* Maurice Pelling
● Roland Curram, Bernard Archard, Jean Anderson, Ellen McIntosh (Focus/British Lion)

Brought in in 24 days at a modest $75,000, with entire location shooting and a little known cast, this is quality production. Writer-director Stanley Goulder had documentary experience but this is his first feature work. His screenplay is taut, economic and natural in dialog and his direction is unfussy and alert.

The story, which has a useful reminder to parents and moppets, 'never take sweets from a stranger', concerns a mentally retarded youth who loves kids. Returning from the hospital where he is an out-patient he hands out highly colored barbiturate tablets to youngsters in a cinema matinee queue. End of show finds a number of unconscious children slumped in their seats. All are dangerously ill. Then begins the patient fight for their lives at the local hospital, while the police hunt for the donor of the tablets.

. . . .

■ SILENT RAGE

1982, 100 MINS, US ◇ ▼ ⊙
Dir Michael Miller   *Prod* Anthony B. Unger   *Scr* Joseph Fraley   *Ph* Robert Jessup, Neil Roach   *Ed* Richard C. Meyer   *Mus* Peter Bernstein, Mark Goldenberg
Art Dir Jack Marty
● Chuck Norris, Ron Silver, Steven Keats, Toni Kalem, William Finley, Brian Libby (Unger/Topkick)

Silent Rage seems as if it were made with a demographics sampler entitled '10 Sleazy Ways to Cash in on the Exploitation Market'. The result is a combination horror-kung fu-oater-woman in peril-mad scientist film with more unintentional laughs than possible in the space of 100 minutes.

The scenario goes something like this – a sweaty, crazy young man chops a woman and another man to death. Our hero of the day, Chuck Norris (the sheriff), catches him but the guy is shot by some over-anxious law enforcers.

The run-of-the-mill crime story? Of course not. One of the hospital surgeons happens to be a mad scientist who has been working on a formula to speed up the human healing process. All he needs is a human guinea pig. Now we have a murderer who is not only crazy but indestructible.

. . . .

■ SILENT RUNNING

1972, 89 MINS, US ◇ ▼ ⊙
Dir Douglas Trumbull   *Prod* Michael Gruskoff   *Scr* Deric Washburn, Michael Cimino, Steven Bocho   *Ph* Charles F. Wheeler   *Ed* Aaron Stell   *Mus* Peter Schickele
● Bruce Dern, Cliff Potts, Ron Rifkin, Jesse Vint (Universal)

Silent Running depends on the excellent special effects of debuting director Douglas Trumbull and his team and on the appreciation of a literate but broadly entertaining script. Those being the highlights, they are virtually wiped out by the crucial miscasting of Bruce Dern. As a result, the production lacks much dramatic credibility and often teeters on the edge of the ludicrous.

Dern and three clod companions man a space vehicle in a fleet of airships containing vegetation in case the earth again can support that type of life. But the program is scuttled, all hands are recalled, but Dern decides to mutiny. In the process, he kills his three shipmates and goes deeper into space. His only companions are two small robots, whose life-like qualities are rather touching.

. . . .

■ SILENT TONGUE

1993, 106 MINS, FRANCE/US ◇ ▼ ⊙
Dir Sam Shepard   *Prod* Carolyn Pfeiffer, Ludi Boeken
Scr Sam Shepard   *Ph* Jack Conroy   *Ed* Bill Yahraus
Mus Patrick O'Hearn   *Art Dir* Cary White
● Alan Bates, Richard Harris, Dermot Mulroney, River Phoenix, Sheila Tousey, Jeri Arredondo (Canal Plus/Belbo/Alive)

Sam Shepard transplants a couple of his famously dysfunctional families to the Old West in *Silent Tongue*, a bizarre, meandering and, finally, maddening mystic-oater, the first Western financed entirely with French money.

The sins of the fathers are distinctly visited upon the sons in this loosely knit yarn, with the characters literally haunted by the ghosts of those they wronged. Result is an unpalatable combination of prairie melodrama, Greek tragedy, Japanese ghost tale and traveling minstrel show, staged with little sense of style and cinematic rhythm.

Richard Harris arrives in search of Alan Bates, a drunken Irish charlatan of the first order. Bates had sold Harris his half-Indian daughter (Sheila Tousey), who married Harris' son (River Phoenix). Tousey has since died in childbirth, driving Phoenix to the brink of madness. Hoping to cure his son's delirium, Harris kidnaps Bates' second daughter (Jeri Arredondo) and takes her back to Phoenix.

The dialogue is mostly rambling and unmemorable and, in the case of Bates and his brogue-tinted blustering, indecipherable.

. . . .

■ SILENT TOUCH, THE

1993, 100 MINS, UK/POLAND/DENMARK ◇ ▼ ⊙
Dir Krzysztof Zanussi   *Prod* Mark Forstater   *Scr* Peter Morgan, Mark Wadlow   *Ph* Jaroslav Zamojda
Ed Marek Denys   *Mus* Wojciech Kilar   *Art Dir* Ewa Braun
● Max von Sydow, Lothaire Bluteau, Sarah Miles, Sofie Grabol, Aleksander Bardini, Peter Hesse Overgaard (Forstater/Tor/Metronome)

After years of directing brilliant and complex Polish films, Krzysztof Zanussi has helmed a simple and moving breakthrough pic about a crotchety old composer coaxed out of retirement by an inspired musicologist and a sweet young muse.

Max von Sydow delivers a definitive performance as a silenced classic composer and Holocaust survivor who re-blossoms from a miserable old drinker into a meticulous artist when Stefan (Lothaire Bluteau) arrives as 'guardian angel.' Casting is superb, though Sarah Miles' stiff delivery (in the wife role) is pic's drawback.

Bluteau (*Jesus of Montreal*) does his usual low-key routine to perfection as the Polish music student who becomes obsessed with a melody he hears in his sleep (thesp's Quebecois accent is a non-issue in the film).

Stefan tracks down von Sydow in Copenhagen and, after much (believable) resistance, convinces him to compose a complex symphony on his neglected piano. Love interests take fascinating twists as loyal wife Miles reluctantly accepts her husband's music secretary (Danish thesp Sophie Grabol, a fresh screen presence) as his young lover.

. . . .

■ SILK STOCKINGS

1957, 117 MINS, US ◇ ▼ ⊙
Dir Rouben Mamoulian   *Prod* Arthur Freed
Scr Leonard Gershe, Leonard Spigelgass   *Ph* Robert Bronner   *Ed* Harold F. Kress   *Mus* Cole Porter
Art Dir William A. Horning, Randall Duell
● Fred Astaire, Cyd Charisse, Janis Paige, Peter Lorre, Joseph Buloff, Jules Munshin (M-G-M)

Silk Stockings has Fred Astaire and Cyd Charisse, the music of Cole Porter and comes off as a top-grade musical version of Metro's 1939 *Ninotchka*. Adapted from the [1955] Broadway musical adaptation of same tag, film has two new Porter songs and a total of 13 numbers. Astaire enacts an American film producer in Paris who falls for the beautiful Commie when she arrives from Moscow to check on the activities of three Russian commissars.

Rouben Mamoulian in his deft direction maintains a flowing if over-long course. Musical numbers are bright, inserted naturally, and both Astaire and Charisse shine in dancing department, together and singly. Choreography is by Hermes Pan (Astaire numbers) and Eugene Loring (others).

Janis Paige shares top honors with the stars for a knock-'em-dead type of performance, George Tobias has a few good moments as a Commie chief, and commissar trio Peter Lorre, Jules Munshin and Joseph Buloff are immense.

. . . .

■ SILKWOOD

1983, 128 MINS, US ◇ ▼ ⊙
Dir Mike Nichols   *Prod* Mike Nichols, Michael Hausman
Scr Nora Ephron, Alice Arlen   *Ph* Miroslav Ondricek
Ed Sam O'Steen   *Mus* Georges Delerue
Art Dir Patrizia Von Brandenstein
● Meryl Streep, Kurt Russell, Cher, Craig T. Nelson, Diana Scarwid, Fred Ward (ABC)

A very fine biographical drama, *Silkwood* concerns Karen Silkwood, a nuclear materials factory worker who mysteriously died just before she was going to blow the whistle on her company's presumed slipshod methods and cover-ups.

A lowdown, spunky and seemingly uneducated Southern gal whose three kids live elsewhere with their father, Silkwood works long hours at a tedious job which presents the constant threat of radiation contamination.

Her home life is rather more unconventional, as she shares a rundown abode with two coworkers, b.f. Kurt Russell and a lesbian friend, Cher.

The complexion of their domestic life takes a turn when blonde cowgirl beautician Diana Scarwid moves in with Cher, and at work, Silkwood finds herself increasingly at odds with management after she becomes involved with a union committee fighting decertification of the union at the plant.

Silkwood's death in 1974 was officially ruled an accident, but the story became a cause celebre in the media and among anti-nuke proponents.

☐ 1983: Nominations: Best Director, Actress (Meryl Streep), Supp. Actress (Cher), Original Screenplay, Editing

....

■ SILVERADO

1985, 132 MINS, US ◇ ⑩ ⊙
Dir Lawrence Kasdan   *Prod* Lawrence Kasdan
Scr Lawrence Kasdan, Mark Kasdan   *Ph* John Bailey
Ed Carol Littleton   *Mus* Bruce Broughton   *Art Dir* Ida Random
● Kevin Kline, Scott Glenn, Kevin Costner, Danny Glover, John Cleese, Rosanna Arquette (Columbia)

Rather than relying on legendary heroes of Westerns past, writer-director Lawrence Kasdan with his brother Mark have used their special talent to create a slew of human scale characters against a dramatic backdrop borrowing from all the conventions of the genre. *Silverado* strikes an uneasy balance between the intimate and naturalistic with concerns that are classical and universal.

Drifters Paden (Kevin Kline) and Emmett (Scott Glenn) join fates in the desert and follow their destiny to Silverado where they tangle with the McKendrick clan. Along the way they meet up with Glenn's gun happy brother Jake (Kevin Costner) who they break from a jail guarded by Sheriff Langston (John Cleese).

Modern element in the stew is introduction of Danny Glover, an itinerant black returning to Silverado to rejoin what's left of his family.

On the other side of the fence is arch villain Cobb, sheriff of Silverado and puppet of the McKendricks. As Cobb, Brian Dennehy is an actor born to be in Westerns, so powerful is his sense of destruction. Other performances, especially Kline and Glenn, are equally strong.

Real rewards of the film are in the visuals and rarely has the West appeared so alive, yet unlike what one carries in his mind's eye. Ida Random's production design is thoroughly convincing in detail.

☐ 1985: Best Original Score, Sound

....

■ SILVER BEARS

1978, 113 MINS, US ◇ ⑩
Dir Ivan Passer   *Prod* Alex Winitsky, Arlene Sellers
Scr Peter Stone   *Ph* Anthony Richmond   *Ed* Bernard Gribble   *Mus* Claude Bolling   *Art Dir* Edward Marshall
● Michael Caine, Cybill Shepherd, Louis Jourdan, Stephane Audran, Tom Smothers, David Warner (Columbia)

Director Ivan Passer has assembled a rather talented squad of performers, then marched them through a minefield, losing all hands in an attack on an uncertain objective.

Michael Caine goes to Switzerland to set up a bank for mobster Martin Balsam, with the help of Louis Jourdan running swindle one against the other. Caine and Jourdan get involved with Stephane Audran and David Warner's swindle two silver-mine in Iran.

Adapted from Paul E. Erdman's novel about international finance, Peter Stone's script keeps the air filled with multi-million dollar figures, confounded hourly but yielding no interest.

Unceasingly cynical, the film lacks a single sympathetic character worth caring about. Everybody lies; everybody swindles; and all the bad guys – and girl – win in the end.

....

■ SILVER CHALICE, THE

1954, 142 MINS, US ◇
Dir Victor Saville   *Prod* Victor Saville   *Scr* Lesser Samuels   *Ph* William V. Skall   *Ed* George White
Mus Franz Waxman   *Art Dir* Rolf Gerard, Boris Leven
● Virginia Mayo, Pier Angeli, Jack Palance, Paul Newman, Natalie Wood, Joseph Wiseman (Warner)

Like the Thomas B. Costain book, the picture is overdrawn and sometimes tedious, but producer-director Victor Saville still manages to instill interest in what's going on, and even hits a feeling of excitement occasionally.

The picture introduces Newman who handles himself well before the cameras. Helping his pic debut is Pier Angeli, and it is their scenes together that add the warmth to what might otherwise have been a cold spectacle.

The plot portrays the struggle of Christians to save for the future the cup from which Christ drank at the Last Supper. On the side of the Christians is a Greek sculptor, played by Newman, who is fashioning a silver chalice to hold the religious symbol. On the side of evil are the decadent Romans, ruled over by an effete Nero, and Simon, the magician (a real character), played by Jack Palance, who wants to use the destruction of the cup to further his own rise to power.

☐ 1954: Nominations: Best Color Cinematography, Scoring of a Dramatic Picture

....

■ SILVER CITY

1984, 101 MINS, AUSTRALIA ◇ ⑩
Dir Sophia Turkiewicz   *Prod* Joan Long   *Scr* Thomas Keneally, Sophia Turkiewicz   *Ph* John Seale   *Ed* Don Saunders   *Mus* William Motzig   *Art Dir* Igor Nay
● Gosia Dobrowolska, Ivar Kants, Anna Jemison, Steve Bisley, Debra Lawrance, Ewa Brok (Limelight)

A passionate love story set against a background of post-war European immigration into Australia is the theme of *Silver City*, an extremely handsome production which introduces vibrant new actress Gosia Dobrowolska.

She plays Nina, a young Polish girl who arrives, bereaved and alone, in Australia in 1948 and becomes one of thousands of citizens of so-called Silver City, a migrant camp outside Sydney. There she meets a fellow Pole, Julian, a former law student, and falls in love with him although he's married to one of her best friends.

This is a film for anyone who has ever left the country of their birth to start a new life in a strange land.

The background to this affair is vividly etched in. Director Sophia Turkiewicz, came to Australia from Poland aged three with her mother, which has provided her with rich material for her first feature.

....

■ SILVER DREAM RACER

1980, 111 MINS, UK ◇ ⑩
Dir David Wickes   *Prod* Rene Dupont   *Scr* David Wickes   *Ph* Paul Beeson   *Ed* Peter Hollywood
Mus David Essex, John Cameron (dir.)   *Art Dir* Malcolm Middleton
● David Essex, Beau Bridges, Cristina Raines, Harry H. Corbett, Diane Keen, Lee Montague (Rank)

It's about motorcycle racing. But among all the biking footage in a yarn about a 'revolutionary' prototype which challenges and,

natch, licks all world championship comers, there's not one memorable shot of the machine in action.

That's a big pity, as the model – a genuine prototype built by Britisher Barry Hart – will certainly whet the appetites of two-wheel fans. But the film's action sequences prove generally disappointing.

Plot [from an original story by Michael Billington] is routine, but no worse than many, and the acting does favors for the dialog. Popstar David Essex is a natural as the ingenuous-looking Cockney fellow who can turn on a sneer when needed. Beau Bridges is fine as the loud-mouthed American Goliath against whom David pits his derided British mount.

....

■ SILVER STREAK

1976, 113 MINS, US ◇ ⑩ ⊙
Dir Arthur Hiller   *Prod* Thomas L. Miller, Edward K. Milkis   *Scr* Colin Higgins   *Ph* David M. Walsh
Ed David Bretherton   *Mus* Henry Mancini
Art Dir Alfred Sweeney
● Gene Wilder, Jill Clayburgh, Richard Pryor, Patrick McGoohan, Ned Beatty, Clifton James (20th Century-Fox)

While falling short of its comedy promise (except when Richard Pryor is on the screen), *Silver Streak* is an okay adventure comedy starring Gene Wilder on the lam from crooked art thieves aboard a trans-continental train.

Wilder, mild-mannered book executive, boards a train for a leisurely trip from Los Angeles to Chicago. Jill Clayburgh, in adjoining compartment, works for an art scholar whose research will expose the fakery of Patrick McGoohan, urbane and despicable villain of the George Sanders-Basil Rathbone school.

Only when Pryor enters the film is there some long-overdue snap and zest. Wilder and Pryor are great together.

☐ 1976: Nomination: Best Sound

....

■ SIMPLE MEN

1992, 106 MINS, US ◇ ⑩
Dir Hal Hartley   *Prod* Ted Hope, Hal Hartley   *Scr* Hal Hartley   *Ph* Michael Spiller   *Ed* Steve Hamilton
Mus Ned Rifle   *Art Dir* Dan Ouellette
● Robert Burke, William Sage, Karen Sillas, Elina Lowensohn, Martin Donovan, Mark Chandler Bailey (Zenith/American Playhouse/True Fiction)

Hal Hartley's *Simple Men* is a beautifully realized American art film. Tale of two brothers' search for their renegade father, and the major life change one of them experiences, possesses exceptional literary and cinematic qualities, as well as emotional resonance new for the director.

Startling opening sequence has small-time criminal Bill McCabe (Robert Burke) doubly betrayed by his g.f., who runs off with their mutual partner and stiffs him of his loot. Meanwhile Bill's father, a radical anarchist on the run, has apparently escaped somewhere on Long Island. Bill's younger brother Dennis (William Sage) is anxious to track the old man down.

Bill announces to his brother how he plans to behave with the next woman he meets. He will calculatedly remain aloof. But the drama takes on a significant new dimension when the fellows meet Kate (Karen Sillas), a lovely, divorced earth mother type who runs a homey rural inn. At the same time, Dennis encounters a sexy young Romanian woman (Elina Lowensohn) who turns out to be his father's lover.

Thesps are a constant pleasure to watch. No matter how arbitrary or bizarre some of Hartley's ploys seem at first, pic is so carefully constructed that they all resurface to pay off in the end.

....

■ SINBAD AND THE EYE OF THE TIGER

1977, 112 MINS, US ◇ ⓦ ⊙
Dir Sam Wanamaker   *Prod* Charles H. Schneer, Ray
Harryhausen   *Scr* Beverley Cross   *Ph* Ted Moore
Ed Roy Watts   *Mus* Roy Budd   *Art Dir* Geoffrey Drake
● Patrick Wayne, Taryn Power, Margaret Whiting, Jane
Seymour, Patrick Troughton, Kurt Christian (Columbia)

The plot [by Beverley Cross and Raqy
Harryhausen] takes Patrick Wayne, as
Sinbad, on a quest to free a prince (Damien
Thomas) from the spell of evil sorceress
Margaret Whiting. Thomas has quite a
dilemma, in that he's turned into a baboon
and is fast losing all vestiges of human
behavior.

Along for the odyssey are a couple of young
cuties (Taryn Power and Jane Seymour) who
keep their modest demeanor while wearing
scanty outfits.

The plot scenes are hammy beyond belief.
Whiting is a particular offender with her all-
stops-out villainy.

When the fantasy creatures have center
stage, the film is enjoyable to watch. Such
beasties as skeletons, a giant bee and an outsized walrus, are marvelously vivified by Ray
Harryhausen.

Most of the studio work was done in
England, with locations in Spain, Malta, and
the Mediterranean.

■ SINBAD THE SAILOR

1947, 116 MINS, US ◇ ⓦ ⊙
Dir Richard Wallace   *Prod* Stephen Ames   *Scr* John
Twist   *Ph* George Barnes   *Ed* Sherman Todd, Frank
Doyle   *Mus* Roy Webb   *Art Dir* Albert S. D'Agostino,
Carroll Clark
● Douglas Fairbanks Jr, Maureen O'Hara, Walter
Slezak, Anthony Quinn, Jane Greer, George Tobias
(RKO)

The sterling adventures of Sinbad as a sailing
man and as a romancer are garbed in brilliant color in this RKO production.

Cast values match production elegance.
Douglas Fairbanks Jr matches do-and-dare
antics of his father. He measures up to the
flamboyance required to make Sinbad a dashing fictional hero. Maureen O'Hara lends
shapely presence as the heroine.

Story concerns Sinbad's mythical eighth adventure wherein he seeks a fabulously rich island and the love of an Arabian Nights
beauty. Major production fault is that dialog
and main story points are obscure, making intelligent following of plot difficult. Principal
opponents to Sinbad's search are Walter
Slezak and Anthony Quinn. Former's character is never clearly explained, and latter's role
also is obscured in the writing.

■ SINCE YOU WENT AWAY

1944, 158 MINS, US ⓦ ⊙
Dir John Cromwell   *Prod* David O. Selznick   *Scr* David
O. Selznick   *Ph* Stanley Cortez, Lee Garmes   *Ed* Hal C.
Kern   *Mus* Max Steiner   *Art Dir* William L. Pereira
● Claudette Colbert, Jennifer Jones, Joseph Cotten,
Shirley Temple, Monty Woolley, Robert Walker (Selznick)

As David O. Selznick screenplayed his own
production, from Margaret Buell Wilder's
[adaptation of her own] book, *Since You Went
Away* is a heart-warming panorama of human
emotions, reflecting the usual wartime frailties of the thoughtless and the chiseler, the
confusion and uncertainty of young ideals
and young love, all of it projected against a
background of utterly captivating home love
and life in the wholesome American
manner.

Claudette Colbert is the attractive, understanding mother of Jennifer Jones, 17, and
Shirley Temple, in her earliest teens, all of
whom adore their absent husband and father,
Timothy, a captain off to the wars. The father

is never shown; only his photo in officer's uniform, along with closeups of other domestic
memorabilia.

True, Selznick's continuity has given director John Cromwell an episodic script, but it is
this narrative form which makes for so much
audience-appeal. Each sequence is a closeup,
a character study, a self-contained dramalet.
□ 1944: Best Score for a Dramatic Picture.
□ Nominations: Best Picture, Actress
(Claudette Colbert), Supp. Actor (Monty
Woolley), Supp. Actress (Jennifer Jones),
B&W Cinematography, B&W Art Direction,
Editing, Special Effects

■ SINFUL DAVEY

1969, 95 MINS, UK ◇
Dir John Huston   *Prod* William N. Graf   *Scr* James R.
Webb   *Ph* Freddie Young, Edward Scaife   *Ed* Russel
Lloyd   *Mus* Ken Thorne   *Art Dir* Stephen Grimes
● John Hurt, Pamela Franklin, Nigel Davenport, Ronald
Fraser, Robert Morley, Anjelica Huston (Mirisch)

Sinful Davey is a bland, lethargic period comedy about a 19th-century teenage highwayman. A competent cast and a good James R.
Webb screenplay are shot down by the club-
footed, forced direction of John Huston, who
seems to think that comedy is chatter,
alternating with pratfall running and
jumping.

Webb, it is said, discovered the ancient diary of David Haggart, subject of the piece,
and the writer has, indeed, fashioned a good
episodic story.

John Hurt has the title role, and other principal players include Nigel Davenport, a dedicated cop and Ronald Fraser and Fidelma
Murphy, as Hurt's two genial associates in a
series of daring robberies.

The script and cast, plus uniformly excellent below-the-line staffers are present, but
the project founders on Huston's work.

■ SINGER NOT THE SONG, THE

1961, 132 MINS, UK ◇ ⓦ
Dir Roy Ward Baker   *Prod* Roy Ward Baker   *Scr* Nigel
Balchin   *Ph* Otto Heller   *Ed* Roger Cherrill   *Mus* Philip
Green   *Art Dir* Alex Vetchinsky
● Dirk Bogarde, John Mills, Mylene Demongeot,
Laurence Naismith, Eric Pohlmann, John Bentley, Leslie
French (Rank)

As a dialectic discussion hinged on the
Roman Catholic religion, this can only be accepted as flippant. As a romantic drama, it
must be agreed that it is glossy, but over-
contrived. Yet, somehow, the thesping of
the two principals, John Mills and Dirk
Bogarde, prevents the screen version of
Audrey Erskine Lindop's novel (shot in Spain)
from falling between these two spacious
schools.

Mills is a dedicated Roman Catholic priest
who comes to the tiny community of
Quantana, Mexico, to replace an older priest
who is worn out from battling with the murderous, marauding gang of bandits led by
Anacleto (Bogarde). To intimidate the newcomer, Bogarde's gang sets out on a series of
murders by the alphabetical method.

Priest Mills, resolutely deciding to break
Bogarde's power, shows a struggle in which
the two gain mutual respect, though their religious opinions clash badly. The unscrupulous, cynical bandit realizes, though in a
manner not explained very convincingly, that
a local belle (Mylene Demongeot) is in love
with the priest and he with her. He uses this
knowledge to create a situation that puts the
priest in a moral dilemma.

Mills and Bogarde have some excellent acting encounters, though their accents, like
those of many others, strike odd notes in the
Mexican atmosphere.

■ SINGING NUN, THE

1966, 96 MINS, US ◇
Dir Henry Koster   *Prod* John Beck, Hayes Goetz
Scr Sally Benson, John Furia Jr   *Ph* Milton Krasner
Ed Rita Roland   *Mus* Harry Sukman   *Art Dir* George
W. Doris, Urie McCleary
● Debbie Reynolds, Ricardo Montalban, Greer Garson,
Agnes Moorehead, Chad Everett, Katharine Ross
(M-G-M)

The Singing Nun, patently designed to cash in
on the story of the Belgian nun Soeur Sourire
and her song 'Dominique', carries an expectancy not always realized. Fictionized approach to the truelife character –
necessitated by agreement with Catholic
church authorities not to make pictures autobiographical – resultantly loses in the transition, and while there are engaging musical
interludes what emerges is slight and frequently slow-moving.

The production unfolds mostly in the small
Samaritan House, situated in a slum section
of Brussels, where the young Dominican nun
carries on her work with children and study
preparatory to an African missionary assignment. In this role, Debbie Reynolds expertly
warbles a dozen numbers to her own guitar
accompaniment, some nine of the songs composed by the Belgian sister.
□ 1966: Nomination: Best Adapted Musical
Score

■ SINGIN' IN THE RAIN

1952, 102 MINS, US ◇ ⓦ ⊙
Dir Gene Kelly, Stanley Donen   *Prod* Arthur Freed
Scr Betty Comden, Adolph Green   *Ph* Harold Rosson
Ed Adrienne Fazan   *Mus* Lennie Hayton (dir.)
Art Dir Cedric Gibbons, Randall Duell
● Gene Kelly, Donald O'Connor, Debbie Reynolds, Jean
Hagen, Millard Mitchell, Cyd Charisse (M-G-M)

Musical has pace, humor and good spirits a-
plenty, in a breezy, good-natured spoof at the
film industry itself. The 1927 era, with advent
of the talkies, lends itself to some hilarious
slapstick, of which the film takes excellent advantage.

Story has Gene Kelly and Jean Hagen as a
team of romantic film favorites of the silents,
and the studio's problem of translating their
popularity to the talkies because of Hagen's
high-pitched, squeaky voice. Problem is complicated further by Kelly falling in love with a
nitery chorine (Debbie Reynolds), and
Hagen's jealous tantrums and knifings.
Donald O'Connor plays the boyhood pal and
early-vaude days teammate of Kelly, as well
as his present studio mentor.

Kelly's dancing is standout, whether in the
'Singin' in the Rain' and other solos; in the
duo dance numbers with O'Connor, such as
the vaudeville routine, 'Fit As a Fiddle', or
the diction lesson, or in trios with O'Connor
and Reynolds as in 'Good Morning'. Reynolds
is a pretty, pert minx, with a nice singing
voice and fine dancing ability. O'Connor has
the film's highspot with a solo number, 'Make
'Em Laugh'. The guy appears to kill himself
with his acrobatics and pratfalls over a cluttered studio set.
□ 1952: Nominations: Best Supp. Actress
(Jean Hagen), Scoring of a Musical Picture

■ SINGLES

1992, 99 MINS, US ◇ ⓦ ⊙
Dir Cameron Crowe   *Prod* Cameron Crowe, Richard
Hashimoto   *Scr* Cameron Crowe   *Ph* Ueli Steiger
Ed Richard Chew   *Mus* Paul Westerberg   *Art Dir* Mark
Haack
● Bridget Fonda, Campbell Scott, Kyra Sedgwick, Sheila
Kelley, Jim True, Matt Dillon (Atkinson-Knickerbocker/
Warner)

This younger version of *The Big Chill* is a
straightforward story about young adults who

live separate and intertwined lives in a Seattle apartment building. They often share their secrets directly with the audience and their bodies with each other.

Linda (superbly played by Kyra Sedgwick) becomes the link between the audience and parallel comedies. Her first romantic catastrophe sets the stage for the many hilarious horror stories – and feats of desperation – that follow, including her budding love story with honest, earnest, cool dude Steve (Campbell Scott).

Bridget Fonda turns in a stunning performance as dipsy Janet, in love with hopelessly bad guitar player Cliff (Matt Dillon, doing a great job as a brain-dead, self-centered, second-rate musician). Their story unfolds amidst various singles' crises, including Debbie Hunt's (Sheila Kelley) dating video search for a man. Any man.

There's no shortage of tender moments in this comedy, and former rock journalist Cameron Crowe cleverly transforms 'real' problems into crackerjack material.

SINGLE WHITE FEMALE

1992, 107 MINS, US ◇ ⑩ ⊙
Dir Barbet Schroeder   *Prod* Barbet Schroeder   *Scr* Don Roos   *Ph* Luciano Tovoli   *Ed* Lee Percy   *Mus* Howard Shore   *Art Dir* Milena Canonero
● Bridget Fonda, Jennifer Jason Leigh, Steven Weber, Peter Friedman, Stephen Tobolowsky (Columbia)

Director Barbet Schroeder has made a calculated attempt to cross an acutely observed character study with a slasher pic. But despite excellent lead performances and numerous memorable scenes, *Single White Female* feels like two different movies in one.

Giving her unfaithful b.f. the heave, smart, upwardly mobile designer/software expert Bridget Fonda takes waify Jennifer Jason Leigh in to share her attractive Upper West Side flat. They become instant best friends, and the needy Leigh seems reassured by Fonda's vow she'll never take her cheating man back.

Even after Fonda returns to her errant lover (Steven Weber) and becomes engaged, the ways in which Leigh tries to nicely insinuate herself into the 'family' remain beautifully observed and psychologically true.

But pic [from John Lutz's novel *SWF Seeks Same*] gradually tilts in the direction of a production line thriller, until finally assuming the full personality of a Hollywood killing machine. Turning point arrives when Leigh gets her hair cut and dyed just like Fonda's pert carrot-top.

Most of pic's virtues are subtle, while the flaws are blatant. Under Schroeder's careful guidance, both Fonda and Leigh play with an ease and unselfconsciousness that are bracingly refreshing. Some of their scenes together feature a casual intimacy rare in U.S. films.

SINK THE BISMARCK!

1960, 97 MINS, UK ⑩ ⊙
Dir Lewis Gilbert   *Prod* John Brabourne   *Scr* Edmund H. North   *Ph* Christopher Challis   *Ed* Peter Hunt   *Mus* Clifton Parker   *Art Dir* Arthur Lawson
● Kenneth More, Dana Wynter, Carl Mohner, Laurence Naismith, Geoffrey Keen, Michael Hordern (20th Century-Fox)

Sink The Bismarck! is a first-rate film re-creation of a thrilling historical event. The screenplay is taken from a book by C. S. Forester. It concentrates almost entirely on three playing areas. These are the subterranean London headquarters of the British admiralty, where the battle is plotted and directed; aboard the Germans' 'unsinkable' battleship, the *Bismarck;* and on board the various British vessels called into pursuit of the Nazi raider.

The film opens with the chilling news that the *Bismarck* has escaped the British naval blockade and is loose in the North Atlantic. After it sinks the *Hood*, considered the greatest battleship in the world, it appears nothing can stop it from rendezvousing with its sister ships holed up at Brest.

Some of the dialog is a little high-flown, with the British at times too aware of the historical importance of the event. The Germans, on the other hand, tend to be Nazi caricatures.

Kenneth More plays the British captain who directs the battle to catch the *Bismarck* with his customary and effective taciturnity. Dana Wynter is a helpful note as the WREN officer who is his aide. Carl Mohner manages some character as the German officer commanding the Bismarck.

SIN OF HAROLD DIDDLEBOCK, THE

1947, 90 MINS, US ⑩
Dir Preston Sturges   *Prod* Preston Sturges   *Scr* Preston Sturges   *Ph* Robert Pittock   *Ed* Tom Neff   *Mus* Werner Heymann   *Art Dir* Robert Usher
● Harold Lloyd, Raymond Walburn, Franklin Pangborn, Margaret Hamilton, Edgar Kennedy (California)

Attired in the same strawhat and black-rimmed specs of his silent flickers, neither Harold Lloyd's person nor his comedy has changed much. As an added lure, director Preston Sturges has incorporated into the first 10 minutes of the film an actual sequence from Lloyd's *The Freshman* which the comedian made in 1923.

Film segues expertly from the *Freshman* footage to the new product, showing Raymond Walburn, as an enthusiastic alumnus now head of a top ad agency, promising Lloyd a job for having won the game. Lloyd takes the job after graduation but is stuck immediately into a minor bookkeeper's niche, where he remains forgotten for 22 years. Walburn finally remembers him long enough to fire him – which is where the fun starts.

Abetted by some excellent dialog from Sturges' pen, Lloyd handles his role in his usual funny fashion. One sequence, in which he dangles from a leash 80 stories above the sidewalk, with the other end of the leash tied to a nervous lion, is standout.

SISTER ACT

1992, 100 MINS, US ◇ ⑩ ⊙
Dir Emile Ardolino   *Prod* Teri Schwartz   *Scr* Joseph Howard   *Ph* Adam Greenberg   *Ed* Richard Halsey   *Mus* Marc Shaiman   *Art Dir* Jackson DeGovia
● Whoopi Goldberg, Maggie Smith, Kathy Najimy, Wendy Makkena, Mary Wickes, Harvey Keitel (Touchstone)

Blessed with the from-on-high concept of Whoopi Goldberg bringing rock 'n' roll to a nuns' chorus, this infectious little throwaway – originally seen as a vehicle for Bette Midler – has a warm-hearted story and engaging premise.

Goldberg plays Deloris, a Reno lounge singer who witnesses a murder by her mobster b.f. Vince (Harvey Keitel) and ends up on the lam. The detective (Bill Nunn) trying to bust Vince pops Deloris into a San Francisco convent for safekeeping, where one-time Catholic school girl promptly outrages the mother superior (Maggie Smith).

Deloris and the movie find their respective callings about halfway in when she's asked to take over the convent's dreadful choir, introducing 1960s rock to the nuns through adapted renditions of 'My Guy' (becoming 'My God').

It's a divine concept, and after a weak start director Emile Ardolino (*Dirty Dancing*, *Three Men and a Little Lady*) milks it for all the laughs it's worth, while deriving requisite warmth from Goldberg and Smith's solid performances.

SISTERS

See: Some Girls

SISTERS, THE

1938, 95 MINS, US
Dir Anatole Litvak   *Prod* Anatole Litvak   *Scr* Milton Krims   *Ph* Tony Gaudio   *Ed* Warren Low   *Mus* Max Steiner   *Art Dir* Carl Jules Weyl
● Errol Flynn, Bette Davis, Anita Louise, Ian Hunter, Donald Crisp, Beulah Bondi (Warner)

Adapted from Myron Brinig's bestseller, this film has the sweep of a virtual cavalcade of early 20th-century American history. Plot starts out with three sisters, daughters of a small Montana town druggist, getting ready for a dance, staged to hear returns on the national election that swept Roosevelt into a second term as president. It closes four years later as the same family prepares again for another election ball, this time to hail Taft as new president.

Totally different marriages of the three girls are clearly set out, with highlights in their wedded lives taking the happy sisters often close to the brink of matrimonial smash-up but always managing to surmount trying difficulties.

Most of the interest centres on Louise (Bette Davis) who elopes with Frank Medlin (Errol Flynn), sports scribe. This case of love-at-first sight works out satisfactorily until the newspaperman, hampered by domestic ties and unwillingness to buckle down as an author, takes to heavy imbibing.

Davis turns in one of her most scintillating performances. Flynn's happy-go-lucky reporter is a vivid portrayal although his slight English accent seems incongruous. Anita Louise makes a delightful flirty daughter who finally weds the elderly wealthy man in her commmunity while Jane Bryan is adequate as the more conservative sister who decides that safety in matrimony is represented by the dull town banker's son.

SISTERS

1973, 92 MINS, US ◇ ⑩
Dir Brian De Palma   *Prod* Edward R. Pressman   *Scr* Brian De Palma, Louisa Rose   *Ph* Gregory Sandor   *Ed* Paul Hirsch   *Mus* Bernard Herrmann   *Art Dir* Gary Weist
● Margot Kidder, Jennifer Salt, Charles Durning, Bill Finley, Lisle Wilson, Bernard Hughes (American International)

Sisters is a good psychological murder melodrama, starring Margot Kidder as the schizoid half of Siamese twins, and Jennifer Salt as a news hen driven to terror in her investigation of a bloody murder. Brian De Palma's direction emphasizes exploitation values which do not fully mask script weakness.

Kidder, paired with Lisle Wilson on a TV game show (neatly satirized in opening scene), later invites him over for the night. Next morning, in a nervous state and after a voiceover dialog in French with another person never seen, Kidder slashes Wilson with a butcher knife.

Salt views the murdered man's agonies from a nearby window, and doggedly pursues the case despite incredulity of detective Dolph Sweet but with assistance of private eye Charles Durning.

SITTING DUCKS

1979, 90 MINS, US ◇ ⑩
Dir Henry Jaglom   *Prod* Meira Attia Dor   *Scr* Henry Jaglom   *Ph* Paul Glickman   *Mus* Richard Romanus
● Michael Emil, Zack Norman, Patrice Townsend, Richard Romanus, Irene Forrest, Henry Jaglom (Sunny Side Up)

Rather loopy story serves basically to provide a framework for several fabulous character riffs and to give a little momentum to any number of enjoyable crazy situations.

Two small-time hustlers make off with loot siphoned off from a gambling syndicate for which one works, and majority of the running time is devoted to their haphazard drive down the eastern seaboard to reach a plane that will carry them to a life of kings in Central America.

Along the way, hyped-up pair, acted in a marvel of improvisational style by Michael Emil and Zack Norman, meet up with two young ladies who hitch on for the wild ride.

Interplay among the four constitutes the meat of the film, and every line and every scene springs spontaneously off the screen as if they're being played for the first time.

■ SITTING PRETTY

1933, 80 MINS, US
Dir Harry Joe Brown   *Prod* Charles R. Rogers   *Scr* Jack McGowan, S. J. Perelman, Lou Breslow   *Ph* Milton Krasner
● Jack Oakie, Jack Haley, Ginger Rogers, Thelma Todd, Gregory Ratoff, Lew Cody (Paramount)

Sitting Pretty's assets are a youthful trio of leads, some fast dialog, a swell score and direction that hits a pace from the start and sustains it to the finish.

The good old triangle provides a foundation for the action [from a story suggested by Nina Wilcox Putnam]. But that foundation is neatly upholstered by the cast, the music, the girls and the staging. Story takkes Jack Oakie and Jack Haley to Hollywood as a songwriting team. Back in New York they're told to go west by Mack Gordon, who plays a music publisher in the film and who, with his partner Harry Revel, wrote the score. Ginger Rogers slips in as a kindhearted lunch-wagon proprietress whom the boys happen to touch while hitch-hiking westward.

For Oakie it's quite familiar ground; again he's the fresh guy who goes swell-headed from success, then becomes a nice but deflated fellow at the finish. For Haley this is his first really important screen assignment. Rogers hasn't an opportunity to get a good lick at the ball, being hemmed in by story limitations, but she looks good.

Gregory Ratoff plays a Hollywood agent, and through this dialectician and Lew Cody, as a picture producer, the dialog gets in some satirical inside studio stuff that's broad enough to be understood by almost anybody.

■ SITTING TARGET

1972, 93 MINS, UK
Dir Douglas Hickox   *Prod* Barry Kulick   *Scr* Alexander Jacobs   *Ph* Ted Scaife   *Ed* John Glen   *Mus* Stanley Myers   *Art Dir* Jonathan Barry
● Oliver Reed, Jill St John, Ian McShane, Edward Woodward, Frank Finlay, Freddie Jones (M-G-M)

Sitting Target is a picture of brutish violence. Its story of a British prison break by a hardened, jealousy-ridden convict to kill the wife he believes unfaithful has been recounted with no holds barred.

The screenplay [from a novel by Laurence Henderson] sometimes is difficult to follow, but Douglas Hickox' tense direction keeps movement at top speed. Obsession of con to get to his wife, who has revealed she is pregnant and wants a divorce, is a motivating theme – built with growing suspense. Jill St John becomes the sitting target for Oliver Reed as the convicted murderer who smashes his way to freedom and stalks his prey.

Actual scenes lensed in two Irish prisons give film a grimly authentic atmosphere and the escape of Reed and two other cons is spectacularly depicted.

■ SIXTEEN CANDLES

1984, 93 MINS, US ◇ ⓥ ☉
Dir John Hughes   *Prod* Hilton A. Green   *Scr* John Hughes   *Ph* Bobby Byrne   *Ed* Edward Warschilka   *Mus* Ira Newborn   *Art Dir* John W. Corso
● Molly Ringwald, Anthony Michael Hall, Michael Schoeffling, Paul Dooley, Justin Henry, Liane Curtis (Universal)

Cream puff of a teen comedy about the miseries of a girl turning 16 turns out to be an amiable, rather goldilocked film. Tone of the film, despite some raw language, brief nudity in the shower and carnage at a high school party, actually suggests the middle America of a Norman Rockwell *Saturday Evening Post* cover.

For the girls, there's Molly Ringwald as the film's angst-ridden centerpiece. Ringwald is engaging and credible. For the boys, there's a bright, funny performance by Anthony Michael Hall, a hip freshman called Ted the Geek. There's also a darkly handsome high school heartbreak kid (Michael Schoeffling), a merciful brisk pace, some quick humor (visual and verbal), and a solid music track.

■ SIXTH AND MAIN

1977, 103 MINS, US ◇
Dir Christopher Cain   *Prod* Christopher Cain   *Scr* Christopher Cain   *Ph* Hilyard John Brown   *Ed* Ken Johnson   *Mus* Bob Summers
● Leslie Nielsen, Roddy McDowall, Beverly Garland, Leo Penn, Joe Maross, Bard Stevens (National Cinema)

Sixth and Main is a very professionally made lowbudgeter which succeeds to a great extent in exploring the emotions underneath the skin of the cliche skid row character. Christopher Cain wrote, produced and directed the pic, starring Leslie Nielsen as a talented dropout and Roddy McDowall as a crippled street person.

The film is earthy without being vulgar, though script at times veers too far into the preachy and meller realm.

Plot stars Beverly Garland, a slumming literary type, to downtown LA to absorb atmosphere for a book. She stumbles onto Nielsen, who hardly ever speaks but lives in a junked trailer full of promising manuscripts. With help from literary critic Joe Maross, she tries to promote Nielsen as a new find.

■ 633 SQUADRON

1964, 94 MINS, UK ⓥ
Dir Walter E. Grauman   *Prod* Cecil F. Ford   *Scr* James Clavell, Howard Koch   *Ph* Ted Scaife, John Wilcox   *Ed* Bert Bates   *Mus* Ron Goodwin   *Art Dir* Michael Stringer
● Cliff Robertson, George Chakiris, Maria Perschy, Harry Andrews, Donald Houston, Michael Goodliffe (Mirisch)

Cinematically, *633 Squadron* is a spectacular achievement, a technically explosive depiction of an RAF unit's successful but costly mission to demolish an almost impregnable Nazi rocket fuel installation in Norway. The production, filmed in its entirety in England, contains some rip-roaring aerial action. Unfortunately, this technical prowess is not matched by the drama it adorns.

The characters of the scenario from the novel by Frederick E. Smith are somewhat shallowly drawn and fall into rather familiar war story molds and behavior patterns.

Cliff Robertson skillfully rattles off the leading assignment, that of a Yank wing commander whose squadron is chosen for the dangerous mission. George Chakiris is adequate though miscast and rather colorless as a Norwegian resistance leader who is to pave the way for the vital bombing raid. Maria Perschy supplies decorative romantic interest

as Chakiris' sister and eventually Robertson's girl.

■ SIX WEEKS

1982, 107 MINS, US ◇ ⓥ ☉
Dir Tony Bill   *Prod* Peter Guber, Jon Peters   *Scr* David Seltzer   *Ph* Michael D. Margulies   *Ed* Stu Linder   *Mus* Dudley Moore
● Dudley Moore, Mary Tyler Moore, Katherine Healy, Shannon Wilcox, Bill Calvert, Joe Regalbuto (PolyGram/Universal)

A sort of moppet *Love Story, Six Weeks* is an unabashed tearjerker aimed directly at the hearts of the mass audience.

Story [from the novel by Fred Mustard Stewart] for the most part takes place in the rarified, monied atmosphere of upper-class LA and NY as leukemia-stricken Katherine Healy is the 12-year-old daughter of cosmetics tycoon Mary Tyler Moore and has admittedly had all the advantages in life, except for a father.

Daddy figure comes along in the person of California Congressional candidate Dudley Moore. Healy takes an immediate shine to the likable politician, so much so that she insists upon working for his campaign.

In the middle of his campaign, Moore chucks everything for a whirlwind weekend in Gotham, where he 'miraculously' manages to get ballet-addict Healy cast in a children's production of *The Nutcracker*.

Such material could have been insufferable, but scripter David Seltzer and Tony Bill, displaying growing assurance in his second directorial outing, have generally stayed on the tightrope between shameless emotional manipulation and undue restraint.

■ SKIN DEEP

1978, 103 MINS, NEW ZEALAND ◇ ⓥ
Dir Geoff Steven   *Prod* John Maynard   *Scr* Piers Davies, Roger Horrocks, Geoff Steven   *Ph* Leon Narby
● Jim Macfarlane, Ken Blackburn, Alan Jervis, Grant Tilly, Bill Johnson, Arthur Wright (Phase Three)

Skin Deep, New Zealand's long-awaited breakthrough film, is a soberly-paced but absorbing tale of a small country town which is making its bid, via a publicity campaign, to attract tourists and industry.

When a masseuse is imported from the nearest big city and Vic's Gym becomes a massage parlor and sauna the inevitable happens. Many local males are anxious to try the parlor-style sex that previously they had only read about, and the respectable matrons pressure the police to shutter the den of vice.

An excellent script and three-dimensional characters flesh out this skeleton. Central to the theme and payoff is Sandra Ray (Deryn Cooper), the masseuse who, though she still emits plenty of erotic voltage, has had enough of the sex side of the business.

Leading the parade of straying husbands on the prowl for parlor extras is Bob Warner, (Ken Blackburn) chairman of the fund-raising group, the town's leading business man and the first to run for cover when the squeeze comes on the massage establishment.

■ SKIN DEEP

1989, 101 MINS, US ◇ ⓥ ☉
Dir Blake Edwards   *Prod* Tony Adams   *Scr* Blake Edwards   *Ph* Isidore Mankofsky   *Ed* Robert Pergament   *Mus* Ivan Neville, Don Grady   *Art Dir* Rodger Maus
● John Ritter, Vincent Gardenia, Alyson Reed, Joel Brooks, Julianne Phillips, Raye Hollitt (Morgan Creek/BECO)

Blake Edwards' *Skin Deep* finds the director centering again on the trials and tribulations of his favourite kind of character – the charming, womanizing sot. Fortunately, he freshens up his trademark formula by satirizing the most contemporary of current social practices: safe sex.

John Ritter is a dissipated writer with writer's block who is always to be found with a drink in his hand and an eye on a potential sexual conquest.

Ritter is married to a pretty (and pretty dull) newscaster (Alyson Reed) who is smart enough, however, to boot her husband out when she finds him in bed with her hairdresser (Julianne Phillips).

Revenge is sweet and Ritter gets his due in any number of silly and embarrassing situations which he handles with nearly perfect comic timing.

....

■ SKIPPY

1931, 85 MINS, US

Dir Norman Taurog   *Scr* Joseph L. Mankiewicz, Norman McLeod, Don Marquis
● Jackie Cooper, Robert Coogan, Mitzi Green, Jackie Searl, Willard Robertson, Enid Bennett (Paramount)

All credit to the kid players, director Norman Taurog, and the adapters for taking Percy Crosby's newspaper comic strip [co-written with Sam Mintz] and making it readable and moving in scenario form.

When Skippy (Jackie Cooper) is so sorely depressed over the death of his poor kid-pal's dog, he turns down supper and goes up to his bed to cry. The two kids had tried so hard to dig up the coin for his release from the moronic dogcatcher's pound.

To get the $3 for the license they tried everything from staging a show and running out on the musicians after promoting a buck from Mitzi Green to let her play the lead, to selling lemonade for a cent a drink.

When Skippy's father gives him the promised bike to ease his sorrow, Skippy trades it for Mitzi's dog. Sooky (Robert Coogan) already had gotten a new mutt meanwhile, making it a bad deal for Skippy, but Skippy's father makes the ending happy.

Cooper's playing could not be improved upon. He does everything well, never camera-conscious and never suggesting it's only a picture. The small and young Coogan boy is cute in every sense. His voice jibes with his looks and manner so well it makes him doubly cute. In contributing some valuable 'heavy' aid to this talker, Jackie Searl plays his boyish assignment as well as John Barrymore ever played a lover.

☐ 1930/31: Best Director.
☐ Nominations: Best Picture, Actor (Jackie Cooper), Adapted Screenplay, Writing (Joseph L. Mankiewicz, Sam Mintz).

....

■ SKIP TRACER

1977, 93 MINS, CANADA

Dir Zale Dalen   *Prod* Laara Dalen   *Ph* Ron Oreiux
● David Petersen (Highlights/CFDC)

Skip Tracer, as its title implies, is an account of the methods of persons employed to recover automobiles, television sets, furniture or whatever on which the time-purchase buyers have defaulted.

Film emerges as one of the best ever turned out in British Columbia, though none of the players are known and all were recruited from Vancouver legit stage troupes. Film was made on a low budget of $145,000.

David Petersen is the central figure, the poker-faced, epitome of a hardhearted, alibi-contemptuous sleuth. Supporting players also believable.

There is a slow pace and a lack of action, but the film involves the viewer.

....

■ SKYJACKED

1972, 100 MINS, US

Dir John Guillermin   *Prod* Walter Seltzer   *Scr* Stanley R. Greenberg   *Ph* Harry Stradling Jr   *Ed* Robert Swink   *Mus* Perry Botkin Jr   *Art Dir* Edward C. Carfagno
● Charlton Heston, Yvette Mimieux, James Brolin, Claude Akins, Jeanne Crain, Susan Dey (M-G-M)

Charlton Heston and Yvette Mimieux star as pilot and stewardess respectively of a jetliner seized by James Brolin. John Guillermin's fastpaced direction makes the most of a large group of top performers.

Stanley R. Greenberg's adaptation of David Harper's novel, *Hijacked*, establishes early and sustains throughout the diverse personal interactions of literally dozens of characters. The dramatic device of trapping a motley group is a venerable but effective blue-print, herein made all the more compelling by a contemporary social phenomenon.

Heston is a most effective leader as the plane captain suddenly faced with a lipstick-scrawled demand for a course change to Anchorage, Alaska, where Claude Akins as a ground controller heightens the suspense of a delicate landing maneuver.

....

■ SKY RIDERS

1976, 91 MINS, US

Dir Douglas Hickox   *Prod* Terry Morse Jr   *Scr* Jack DeWitt, Stanley Mann, Garry Michael White   *Ph* Ousama Rawi   *Ed* Malcolm Cooke   *Mus* Lalo Schifrin   *Art Dir* Terry Ackland-Snow
● James Coburn, Susannah York, Robert Culp, Charles Aznavour, Werner Pochath, Zou Zou (20th Century-Fox)

Hang gliding stunts provide most of the interest in *Sky Riders* filmed in Greece. The political terrorism story line is a familiar one and the screenplay is synthetic formula stuff, but the stunt work is good.

The simple plot has footloose pilot James Coburn masterminding the rescue of Susannah York and her two children after bungling police operation led by Charles Aznavour doesn't produce results.

The film provoked an international incident when a Greek electrician died in an explosion accident. Ironically, no one was seriously injured in the aerial scenes. Producer Terry Morse Jr was arrested, exec producer Sandy Howard was detained in Greece for several weeks, and a $250,000 out-of-court settlement was made.

....

■ SKY WEST AND CROOKED

(US: Gypsy Girl)

1966, 102 MINS, UK

Dir John Mills   *Prod* Jack Hanbury   *Scr* Mary Hayley Bell, John Prebble   *Ph* Arthur Ibbetson   *Ed* Gordon Hales   *Mus* Malcolm Arnold   *Art Dir* Carmen Dillon
● Hayley Mills, Ian McShane, Laurence Naismith, Geoffrey Bayldon, Annette Crosbie, Norman Bird (Rank)

It's a family affair with Hayley Mills starring, poppa John Mills doing his first directorial stint and his wife Mary (who writes professionally as Mary Hayley Bell), sharing the screenplay with John Prebble from her own story.

Hayley Mills portrays a village girl who is a misfit because of simplicity, the result of an accident which resulted in the death of her boy playmate and her own wounding.

The adults around the village tolerantly regard her as slightly idiotic, with her morbid obsession with death which causes her to be at her happiest when playing in the local graveyard and in burying dead pets in consecrated ground.

This naive yarn is rescued from bathos by the evident sincerity of both star and director and by a very convincing portrayal of village life, highlighted by some excellent photography by Arthur Ibbetson. John Mills has played

safe in his first directing experiment and the result, while often stodgy, suggests that he knows his way around a directorial chair.

....

■ SLAM DANCE

1987, 99 MINS, US/UK ◇ ⑩

Dir Wayne Wang   *Prod* Rupert Harvey, Barry Opper   *Scr* Don Opper   *Ph* Amir Mokri   *Ed* Lee Percy   *Mus* Mitchell Froom   *Art Dir* Eugenio Zanetti
● Tom Hulce, Mary Elizabeth Mastrantonio, Virginia Madsen, Millie Perkins, Adam Ant, Harry Dean Stanton (Island/Zenith/Sho)

Slam Dance is like junk food. It's brightly packaged, looks good and satisfies the hunger for entertainment, but it isn't terribly nourishing or well-made.

Tom Hulce is underground cartoonist C.C. Drood, a man whose life has come apart cheerfully at the seams. He's separated from his wife (Mary Elizabeth Mastrantonio) and daughter (Judith Barsi), though he still imagines them back together as a family.

Drood's the kind of man who never lets a little thing like marriage stand in the way of a good time or a hot romance with the beautiful and mysterious Yolande (Virginia Madsen). Only one day Yolande turns up dead and Drood's the prime suspect.

Mastrantonio is lovely as always, but without direction. Madsen fares even worse and has virtually nothing to do but look glamorous in a few scenes.

Adam Ant decorates the screen as Drood's two-timing buddy, but basically he's just along for the ride. What really holds the film together is Hulce's loosey-goosey performance which sets the tempo for the action.

....

■ SLAP SHOT

1977, 123 MINS, US ◇ ⑩ ⊙

Dir George Roy Hill   *Prod* Robert J. Wunsch, Stephen Friedman   *Scr* Nancy Dowd   *Ph* Victor Kemper   *Ed* Dede Allen   *Mus* Elmer Bernstein   *Art Dir* Henry Bumstead
● Paul Newman, Strother Martin, Michael Ontkean, Jennifer Warren, Lindsay Crouse, Jerry Houser (Universal)

Like the character played by Paul Newman in *Slap Shot*, director George Roy Hill is ambivalent on the subject of violence in professional ice hockey. Half the time Hill invites the audience to get off on the mayhem, the other half of the time he decries it.

Screenwriter Nancy Dowd, who drew on the experiences of her hockey-playing brother Ned Dowd (pic's tech advisor and a bit player), had the originality to deal with an offbeat milieu that has been rarely treated by American films.

What Dowd seems to have had in mind was a satire of American rowdyism, as brought out in the adolescent antics of this sleazy minor league Pennsylvania hockey team, of which Newman is player-coach.

Interspersed with the roughhouse rink action are scenes delineating the confused sexual liaisons of Newman and the others.

....

■ SLAUGHTERHOUSE-FIVE

1972, 104 MINS, US ◇ ⑩ ⊙

Dir George Roy Hill   *Prod* Paul Monash   *Scr* Stephen Geller   *Ph* Miroslav Ondricek   *Ed* Dede Allen   *Mus* Glenn Gould   *Art Dir* Alexander Golitzen, George Webb
● Michael Sacks, Ron Leibman, Eugene Roche, Sharon Gans, Valerie Perrine, Roberts Blossom (Universal/Vanadas)

Slaughterhouse-Five is a mechanically slick, dramatically sterile commentary about World War II and afterward, as seen through the eyes of a boob Everyman. Director George Roy Hill's arch achievement emphasizes the diffused cant to the detriment of characterizations, which are stiff, unsympathetic and skin-deep.

Stephen Geller's adaptation of Kurt Vonnegut Jr's novel *Slaughterhouse-Five or The Children's Crusade* is in an academic sense fluid and lucid. Michael Sacks in his screen debut plays Billy Pilgrim, the luckless loser who always seems to be in the wrong place at the wrong time.

The story jumps around from its beginning in World War II where as a dumb draftee Pilgrim becomes a prisoner of war in Germany.

In the postwar period, Pilgrim moves into the orbits of overweight wife and predictable offspring.

■ SLAUGHTER ON TENTH AVENUE

1957, 103 MINS, US
Dir Arnold Laven *Prod* Albert Zugsmith *Scr* Lawrence Roman *Ph* Fred Jackman *Ed* Russell F. Schoengarth *Mus* Herschel Burke Gilbert (arr.) *Art Dir* Alexander Golitzen, Robert E. Smith
● Richard Egan, Jan Sterling, Dan Duryea, Julie Adams, Walter Matthau, Charles McGraw (Universal)

Slaughter on Tenth Avenue, the title of Richard Rodgers' ballet music from *On Your Toes*, is effectively employed for a hard-hitting and commendable film about racketeering on the New York waterfront. The picture is adapted from a book entitled *The Man Who Rocked the Boat* by William J. Keating and Richard Carter.

Since Keating was a NY assistant district attorney whose true-life experiences with waterfront gangs are recorded in the book, the film has a quiet, documentary flavor and contains a minimum of the false heroics that usually appear in pictures of this type.

The story presents Richard Egan as Keating, a young assistant DA who has been assigned to a shooting case stemming from waterfront conflicts. Mickey Shaughnessy, an honest longshoreman, is shot because of his efforts to eliminate the gangster elements from the docks. Shaughnessy, his wife (Jan Sterling) and his supporters at first follow the underworld code of not revealing the identity of the triggermen. However, Keating is persistent.

Egan is convincing as the at-first-wide-eyed and then tough assistant DA from the Pennsylvania coal country. Sterling is excellent as Shaughnessy's tough yet tender and understanding wife.

■ SLEEPER

1973, 88 MINS, US ◇ ⓥ ⊙
Dir Woody Allen *Prod* Jack Grossberg *Scr* Woody Allen, Marshall Brickman *Ph* David M. Walsh *Ed* Ralph Rosenblum *Mus* Woody Allen *Art Dir* Dale Hennesy
● Woody Allen, Diane Keaton, John Beck, Mary Gregory, Don Keefer, Don McLiam (United Artists)

Woody Allen's *Sleeper*, is a nutty futuristic comedy, with Allen brought back to life 200 years hence to find himself a wanted man in a totally regulated society. Diane Keaton again plays his foil, and both are hilarious. The Dixieland music score [played by Allen with the Preservation Hall Jazz Band and New Orleans Funeral & Ragtime Orchestra] is just one more delightful non sequitur.

Story opens with Bartlett Robinson and Mary Gregory, two underground scientists, restoring Allen to life from a two-century deep freeze after sudden death from a minor operation. Allen is hunted as an alien. In the course of avoiding capture he becomes first a robot servant to Keaton, later her captor, then rescuer, finally her lover in a fadeout clinch.

The film is loaded with throwaway literacy

and broad slapstick, and while it fumbles the end, the parade of verbal and visual amusement is pleasant as long as it lasts.

The star teaming resembles, on a much more advanced basis, the Bob Hope pix of the 1940s in which he starred with some gorgeous leading women in a series of improbable but delightful escapades.

■ SLEEPERS, THE
See: Little Nikita

■ SLEEPING BEAUTY

1959, 75 MINS, US ◇ ⓥ ⊙
Dir Clyde Geronimi *Prod* Walt Disney *Scr* Erdman Penner *Ed* Roy M. Brewer Jr, Donald Halliday *Mus* George Bruns (adapt.)
● (Walt Disney)

Sleeping Beauty, adapted from the Charles Perrault version of the fairy tale (and reportedly costing $6 million), is no surprise in its familiar outlines. It's the story of Princess Aurora, who is put under a spell at birth by the bad fairy, Maleficent. She is to prick her finger on a spinning wheel and die before she grows up. But the good fairies, Flora, Fauna and Merryweather, are able to amend the curse. The princess shall not die, but shall fall into a deep sleep. She will be awakened by her true love, Prince Philip.

Mary Costa's rich and expressive voice for the title character gives substance and strength to it. The music is an adaptation of Tchaikovsky's Sleeping Beauty ballet, and it is music – where adapted for song – that requires something more than just a pleasant voice. Bill Shirley, as the prince, contributes some good vocal work. His cartoon character is considerably more masculine than Disney heroes usually are.

Some of the best parts of the picture are those dealing with the three good fairies, spoken and sung by Verna Felton, Barbara Jo Allen and Barbara Luddy.

The picture was shot in Technirama and Technicolor, and then, when completed, printed for 70mm on special printer lenses developed for Disney by Panavision. Disney gives credit to more than 70 contributors on Sleeping Beauty. Clyde Geronimi was supervising director, and Eric Larson, Wolfgang Reitherman and Les Clark, the sequence directors.
□ 1959: Nomination: Best Scoring of a Musical Picture

■ SLEEPING CITY, THE

1950, 85 MINS, US
Dir George Sherman *Prod* Leonard Goldstein *Scr* Jo Eisinger *Ph* William Miller *Ed* Frank Gross *Mus* Frank Skinner *Art Dir* Bernard Herzbrun, Emrich Nicholson
● Richard Conte, Coleen Gray, Richard Taber, Peggy Dow, Alex Nicol (Universal)

The production, storied in the corridors of NY's Bellevue hospital – and actually filmed at Bellevue – recruited a New York stage cast in the main to back up the stars, Richard Conte and Coleen Gray, in telling a yarn of intrigue and murder. Only, as Conte points up in a foreword, none of these actually happened at Bellevue.

Sleeping City tells of two deaths in which the hospital is involved. Both victims are interns. Both, because of meagre wages that all interns receive, are forced to steal narcotics from the hospital stocks and sell them to pay off gambling debts. Both have become linked with an unknown bookmaker. Conte plays a member of the police confidential squad who is planted in the hospital as an intern to uncover the mystery.

Conte gives his usually plausible perfor-

mance. Gray looks attractive as the nurse, though her characterization doesn't call for much thesping ability.

■ SLEEPING DOGS

1977, 107 MINS, NEW ZEALAND ◇ ⓥ
Dir Roger Donaldson *Prod* Roger Donaldson *Scr* Ian Mune, Arthur Baysting *Ph* Michael Sarasin *Ed* Ian John *Mus* Murray Grindlay
● Sam Neill, Bernard Kearns, Nevan Rowe, Ian Mune, Ian Watkin, Don Selwyn (Aardvark)

Sleeping Dogs has sharp directional flair evident, particularly in the action segments, taut performances by the large cast and a handsome technical gloss in all departments.

When the pictures are left to tell the story they do it with great visual impact. The script is less successful.

The story is a political thriller [from the novel *Smith's Dream* by Karl Stead], set in New Zealand of the near future, and sees the small democracy taken over by the rightist party in power, via rigged shooting at a street demonstration. Overnight a police state is set up, and a counter-revolutionary force of freedom-fighters starts hitting back.

As Smith, Sam Neill is natural. He projects the right intensity for a man caught up in an Orwellian nightmare.

■ SLEEPING WITH THE ENEMY

1991, 98 MINS, US ◇ ⓥ ⊙
Dir Joseph Ruben *Prod* Leonard Goldberg *Scr* Ronald Bass *Ph* John W. Lindley *Ed* George Bowers *Mus* Jerry Goldsmith *Art Dir* Doug Kraner
● Julia Roberts, Patrick Bergin, Kevin Anderson, Elizabeth Lawrence, Kyle Secor (20th Century-Fox)

In *Sleeping with the Enemy*, a chilling look at marital abuse gives way to a streamlined thriller [from the novel by Nancy Price] delivering mucho sympathy for imperiled heroine Julia Roberts and screams aplenty as she's stalked by her maniacal husband.

Laura (Roberts) appears to be a perfect doll wife dwelling in an isolated Cape Cod beach manse with successful financial consultant Martin (Patrick Bergin). In fact, he's an overbearing control freak.

She's actually been plotting her escape for a long time. One night she gets her chance, slipping off a sailboat during a storm and swimming ashore while her husband believes she's drowned.

But Martin comes up with enough peculiar clues to believe he's been had. Soon after Laura, who's renamed herself Sara Wates, is ensconced in an idyllic Iowa college town and forging a friendship with a sweet-natured drama teacher (Kevin Anderson), the menacing Martin is on the trail.

Ironically, it's Laura's poor, blind, stroke-ridden mother (Elizabeth Lawrence) who points Martin toward her door, and once there he indulges in some unique forms of fetishistic terrorism.

Roberts is terrific in a layered part. Anderson brings an edge to the nice-guy-next-door role, and the dark, dashing Bergin is chillingly twisted.

■ SLEEPLESS IN SEATTLE

1993, 104 MINS, US ◇
Dir Nora Ephron *Prod* Gary Foster *Scr* Nora Ephron, David S. Ward, Jeff Arch *Ph* Sven Nykvist *Ed* Robert Reitano *Mus* Marc Shaiman *Art Dir* Jeffrey Townsend
● Tom Hanks, Meg Ryan, Bill Pullman, Ross Malinger, Rosie O'Donnell, Gaby Hoffmann (Tri-Star)

Having achieved her greatest success writing *When Harry Met Sally . . .* , director-cowriter Nora Ephron tries a slightly new riff on that theme in this shamelessly romantic comedy [from a screen story by Jeff Arch]. Pic delivers ample warmth and some explosively funny moments.

Sam (Tom Hanks) is still grieving over the death of his wife (Carey Lowell, seen in flashback) when his son Jonah (Ross Malinger) phones a latenight radio call-in show saying he thinks the solution is for dad to remarry. Sam reluctantly gets on the line and ends up spilling his guts.

Among those listening is Annie (Meg Ryan), a just-engaged newspaper reporter whose husband-to-be, Walter (Bill Pullman), is sensible but not very exciting. She finds herself increasingly obsessed with 'Sleepless in Seattle,' Sam's on-air handle.

For all the enjoyable flourishes, and there are many, Ephron keeps pausing to remind us that this is a movie, making it hard for anyone to really get lost in the story. And since the big question isn't 'if', but 'when' and 'how', the film loses considerable momentum about two-thirds through before rallying for a heart-tugging finale.

Hanks certainly figures to increase his stock as a well-rounded actor and not just a comic, while Ryan essentially plays the same character as *Sally*, with pleasing if predictable results.

• •

■ SLEEPWALKERS

1992, 91 MINS, US ◇ ⓥ ⊙
Dir Mick Garris *Prod* Mark Victor, Mark Grais, Nabeel Zahid *Scr* Stephen King *Ph* Rodney Charters *Ed* O. Nicholas Brown *Mus* Nicholas Pike *Art Dir* John DeCuir Jr
● Brian Krause, Madchen Amick, Alice Krige, Jim Haynie, Cindy Pickett, Ron Perlman (Ion/Victor & Grais)

Stephen King's *Sleepwalkers* is an idiotic horror potboiler. New approach to the vampire legend is really a variation on TriStar's 1988 flop *The Kiss*. Brian Krause and mom Alice Krige are incestuous monsters called Sleepwalkers who survive by draining the life force from virgin girls.

Film takes place in sleepy Travis, Ind, where Krause is the new kid in school claiming to be a transfer student. He romances beautiful classmate Madchen Amick, resulting in a pretentious date-rape scene in which Amick is saved from a fate worse than death *and* worse than rape.

King's screenplay has no internal logic and relies wholly on stupid gimmicks like the monsters' ability to become invisible and their vulnerability to cats. The potential pathos of Krause and Krige as perhaps the last lonely members of their breed is undeveloped.

Many noted genre directors (Joe Dante, Tobe Hooper) as well as King himself have pointless cameo roles. Even Amick's name 'Tanya Robertson' seems like a pun on sexy actress Tanya Roberts. Cast is physically appealing and could have generated some sympathy if permitted.

• •

■ SLENDER THREAD, THE

1965, 98 MINS, US
Dir Sydney Pollack *Prod* Stephen Alexander
Scr Stirling Silliphant *Ph* Loyal Griggs *Ed* Thomas Stanford *Mus* Quincy Jones *Art Dir* Hal Pereira, Jack Poplin
● Sidney Poitier, Anne Bancroft, Telly Savalas, Steven Hill, Edward Asner, Indus Arthur (Athene/Paramount)

The Slender Thread, suggested by a 29 May 1964 *Life* article by Shana Alexander (wife of producer) of an actual ocrurence, is supercharged with emotion and dramatic overtones. As a showy vehicle for talents of Sidney Poitier adn Anne Bancroft, the production offers mounting tension, but good as the picture is it could have been improved through more lucid writing. Story is of a distraught woman who has taken an overdose of barbitu-

rates and phones a clinic. Film takes its title fromt he telephone line which suddenly becomes a slender thread by means of Poitier, a college student volunteer who answers femme's call, must try to save her life without breaking the connection.

Poitier, who remains on the telephone almost the entire unreeling of the picture, delivers a compelling performance, matched by Bancroft as the tortured wife and mother who attempts suicide when she sees her marriage of 12 years going down the drain.

Film is kept on a realistic level. The two stars never meet, their sole contact strictly telephonic.
□ 1965: Nominations: Best B&W Costume Design, B&W Art Direction

• •

■ SLEUTH

1973, 138 MINS, UK ◇ ⓥ ⊙
Dir Joseph L. Mankiewicz *Prod* Morton Gottlieb
Scr Anthony Shaffer *Ph* Oswald Morris *Ed* Richard Marden *Mus* John Addison *Art Dir* Ken Adam
● Laurence Olivier, Michael Caine (Palomar/20th Century Fox)

Joseph L. Mankiewicz' film version of *Sleuth* is terrific. Anthony Shaffer's topnotch screenplay of his legit hit provides Laurence Olivier and especially Michael Caine with two of their best roles.

Olivier is outstanding as the famed mystery novelist and society figure who is galled at the prospect of losing his wife to Caine. Latter is sensational as the lower-class tradesman (hairdresser) who eventually proves himself worthy of playing the game of cat-and-mouse with which Olivier seeks to avenge his honor.

Ken Adam's outstanding production design, replete with the automated gadgetry with which Olivier's character enjoys his private games, contributes mightily to the overall achievement.
□ 1972: Nominations: Best Director, Actor (Michael Caine, Lawrence Olivier), Original Score

• •

■ SLIPPER AND THE ROSE, THE STORY OF CINDERELLA

1976, 146 MINS, UK ◇ ⓥ
Dir Bryan Forbes *Prod* Stuart Lyons *Scr* Bryan Forbes, Richard M. Sherman, Robert B. Sherman *Ph* Tony Imi
Ed Timothy Gee *Mus* Richard M. Sherman, Robert B. Sherman *Art Dir* Raymond Simm
● Richard Chamberlain, Gemma Craven, Annette Crosbie, Edith Evans, Christopher Gable, Michael Hordern (Paradine)

What script has managed to do so surprisingly well is first of all to modernize the classic Cinderella tale, making it entertaining and (almost) believable for adults while preserving basic pattern and texture of the original for the youngsters.

Richard Chamberlain makes a believable, feet-on-the-ground Prince, Gemma Craven is a pretty and very effective Cinderella.

Michael Hordern steals many a scene as the king, in a very good performance; Kenneth More has great moments as the chamberlain; while Edith Evans thefts the scenes she's in with some irresistible windup oneliners.

Physical facets, from eye-popping Pinewood Studio sets to the lushly romantic Austrian exteriors, are standout.
□ 1977: Nomination: Best Adapted Score, Song

• •

■ SLIPSTREAM

1989, 101 MINS, UK ◇ ⓥ ⊙
Dir Steven Lisberger *Prod* Gary Kurtz *Scr* Tony Kayden *Ph* Frank Tidy *Ed* Terry Rawlings *Mus* Elmer Bernstein *Art Dir* Andrew McAlpine
● Mark Hamill, Bob Peck, Bill Paxton, Kitty Aldridge, Ben Kingsley, F. Murray Abraham (Entertainment)

British-made sci-fi adventure romp *Slipstream* is one of those films that had potential, but unfortunately it doesn't make the grade.

Slipstream seems to be making some kind of ecological message; the film's version of Earth [from a story by Sam Clemens] is a place ruined by pollution with the planet washed clean by a river of wind called the 'Slipstream.'

Lawman Mark Hamill and his partner Kitty Aldridge capture Bob Peck, who's wanted for murder. When adventurer Bill Paxton discovers there is a price on Peck's head he snatches him and makes his escape down the Slipstream.

They come across a cult of religious fanatics who worship the wind, led by Ben Kingsley. One of the cult (Eleanor David) falls for Peck – even though it turns out he is an android.

Strong points are the stunning locations (Turkey and the Yorkshire moors), the performances by Hamill and Aldridge, plus impressive aircraft and technical effects. Kingsley and F. Murray Abraham have virtual walk-on parts.

• •

■ SLITHER

1973, 98 MINS, US ◇ ⓥ
Dir Howard Zieff *Prod* Jack Sher *Scr* W.D. Richter
Ph Laszlo Kovacs *Ed* David Bretherton *Mus* Tom McIntosh *Art Dir* Dale Hennesy
● James Caan, Peter Boyle, Sally Kellerman, Louise Lasser, Allen Garfield, Richard B. Shull (M-G-M)

Slither is, in effect, an excellent, live-action, feature-length counterpart to a great old Warner Bros cartoon. That is to say, a combination of physical and visual madness overlaid with satirical, throwaway sophistication which ends up its caper plot while nourishing it to the full.

W.D. Richter's first produced script is a smash achievement in structure and dialog. James Caan is superb as a likeable paroled car thief whose incidental friendship with Richard B. Shull, an embezzler, leads him into contact with a bizarre set of characters, some in search of a concealed fortune, others determined to thwart the treasure hunt.

The characters road-run over the countryside, where a couple of ominous black vans and several ordinary-looking businessmen create a mood of latent terror.

• •

■ SLIVER

1993, 106 MINS, US ◇ ⓥ ⊙
Dir Phillip Noyce *Prod* Robert Evans *Scr* Joe Eszterhas
Ph Vilmos Zsigmond *Ed* Richard Frances-Bruce, William Hoy *Mus* Howard Shore *Art Dir* Paul Sylbert
● Sharon Stone, William Baldwin, Tom Berenger, Polly Walker, Colleen Camp, Martin Landau (Paramount)

After ratings board strife and last-minute reshoots, *Sliver* proves all flash and no sizzle – a thriller that simply changes gender on the *Basic Instinct* formula to 'did he or didn't he?'

Working from Ira Levin's novel, writer Joe Eszterhas and director Phillip Noyce have crafted a cold, inaccessible yarn about murder and voyeurism that's too leisurely about getting where it needs to go and doesn't fully develop what should be its core: a just-divorced woman (Sharon Stone) drawn into a kinky, voyeuristic relationship with mysterious younger man (William Baldwin).

Carly (Stone) is a book editor who moves into a new building and catches the eye of both Zeke (Baldwin), a computer whiz, and Jack (Tom Berenger), a burned-out writer who comes on strong right away. Carly discovers Zeke owns the building, has each unit wired with intrusive video cameras and that there's been a series of murders there – including a woman to whom she bears an unerring resemblance and who occupied her unit.

Blame it on the editing and reediting, but

even the sex scenes aren't all that steamy, and the movie suffers from some choppy moments and highrise-size lapses in logic.

For Stone fans, the actress shows a lot less here, both literally and figuratively, than she did in her menacing and alluring turn in *Basic Instinct*. Baldwin brings the requisite creepy-yet-alluring quality to the role, while Berenger sleepwalks through an underdeveloped character.

■ SLOW DANCING IN THE BIG CITY

1978, 101 MINS, US ◇

Dir John G. Avildsen   *Prod* Michael Levee, John G. Avildsen   *Scr* Barra Grant   *Ph* Ralf Bode   *Ed* John G. Avildsen   *Mus* Bill Conti   *Art Dir* Henry Shrady
● Paul Sorvino, Anne Ditchburn, Nicolas Coster, Anita Dangler, Hector Jaime Mercado, Thaao Penghlis (United Artists)

Slow Dancing in the Big City has so much heart John Avildsen's aorta is showing.

Barra Grant's story is a simple boy meets girl tale, or in this case, dancer meets columnist. Anne Ditchburn, a lovely dancer and choreographer, meetsPaul Sorvino, the columnist.

Sorvino seems to do a good job in any picture under any conditions and he's just terrific here. Ditchburn is promising, but the post-production looping is downright dreadful and interferes not just with her performance but with the flow of the film.

A number of dancing scenes featuring Ditchburn – performances, rehearsals and a solo on the roof of a Manhattan apartment – are among the production's high points.

The film has two plots moving along side by side although the focus clearly is on the Ditchburn-Sorvino relationship. The second genuinely touching plot concerns a young ghetto kid Sorvino is writing about and his struggle to overcome the harsh city.

What's a shame about *Slow Dancing* is that somewhere on the cutting room floor probably is a fine film.

■ SLUMBER PARTY MASSACRE
(UK: Slumber Party Murders)

1982, 84 MINS, US ◇

Dir Amy Jones   *Prod* Amy Jones, Aaron Lipstadt   *Scr* Rita Mae Brown   *Ph* Steve Posey   *Ed* Wendy Allan   *Mus* Ralph Jones   *Art Dir* Pam Canzano
● Michele Michaels, Robin Stille, Michael Villela, Andre Honore (Santa Fe)

Besides its obviously catchy title, *Slumber Party Massacre* is an entertaining terror thriller, with the switch that distaff filmmakers handle the 'young women in jeopardy' format.

Set in Venice, Cal, pic concerns high school girls having a sleep-over party, with 'let's scare 'em' antics by the boyfriends. Meanwhile, a mad killer is in the vicinity, wasting kids of both sexes in bloody fashion with a portable drill and various wicked knives.

Out of traditional horror material consisting of red herrings, sudden shock movements into frame, etc, helmer Amy Jones develops some very stylish sequences. Notable is a complex mid-film montage mixing (with matched compositions) a horror film on TV, actual killings by the nut, and the sister chatting humorously on the phone.

■ SLUMBER PARTY MURDERS
See: Slumber Party Massacre

■ SMALL BACK ROOM, THE
(US: Hour of Glory)

1949, 106 MINS, UK

Dir Michael Powell, Emeric Pressburger   *Prod* Michael Powell, Emeric Pressburger   *Scr* Michael Powell, Emeric

Pressburger, Nigel Balchin   *Ph* Christopher Challis   *Ed* Clifford Turner, Reginald Mills   *Mus* Brian Easdale   *Art Dir* Hein Heckroth
● David Farrar, Kathleen Byron, Jack Hawkins, Cyril Cusack, Michael Gough, Leslie Banks (London/Archers)

Central character in the plot [from a novel by Nigel Balchin] is Sammy Rice, scientist and research worker, whose lame foot has made him a complex individual. Although becoming extremely unpopular by his frank and adverse comments on a new type of anti-tank gun, he redeems himself by dismantling a booby bomb which is the enemy's latest secret weapon.

It is this latter scene which is by far the high spot of the production, and although it is a long time coming it is handled to extract every ounce of suspense from it. In scenes like that the drama becomes real and satisfying but the same reaction isn't forthcoming in the highly imaginative sequence in which the complex Sammy seeks solace in whisky.

■ SMALLEST SHOW ON EARTH, THE
(US: Big Time Operators)

1957, 81 MINS, UK

Dir Basil Dearden   *Prod* Michael Relph   *Scr* William Rose, John Eldridge   *Ph* Douglas Slocombe   *Ed* Oswald Hafenrichter   *Mus* William Alwyn   *Art Dir* Allan Harris
● Bill Travers, Virginia McKenna, Leslie Phillips, Peter Sellers, Margaret Rutherford, Bernard Miles (British Lion)

William Rose, who scripted *Genevieve*, has fashioned a shrewd and bright comedy around the exhibition side of motion pictures. The centre of interest is a small, derelict picture house inherited by a young struggling writer.

The theatre, in a small, smelly provincial town, is adjacent to the mainline railroad station. The staff comprises three ancients – Margaret Rutherford, who played the piano in the silent days, but now sits at the cash desk; Peter Sellers, the boothman with a weakness for whisky; and Bernard Miles, a doorman and general handyman.

When Bill Travers and Virginia McKenna inherit the theatre, their immediate reaction is to sell out to the opposition, who had made a substantial offer to the previous owner. But the offer now forthcoming would not even be adequate to meet the inherited debts, so they set about on a big bluff, pretending to re-open in the hope that the bids will be bettered.

The film is loaded with delightful touches, and there's one prolonged laughter sequence when the projectionist is on a drinking bout and Bill Travers takes over the booth.

■ SMALL TOWN GIRL

1936, 95 MINS, US

Dir William Wellman   *Prod* Hunt Stromberg   *Scr* John Lee Mahin, Edith Fitzgerald   *Ph* Charles Rosher   *Ed* Blanche Sewell   *Mus* Herbert Stothart, Edward Ward   *Art Dir* Cedric Gibbons, Arnold Gillespie
● Janet Gaynor, Robert Taylor, Binnie Barnes, Lewis Stone, Andy Devine, James Stewart (M-G-M)

Small Town Girl is romance with nice comedy sequences and with a well-balanced cast headed by Janet Gaynor and Robert Taylor.

Ben Ames Williams' novel gives a few neat twists to the ancient plot of the obscure Cinderella who marries into the wealthy family. All the time-tested and easy-to-foresee elements are present, including the hoity-toity sweetheart who is bad for the character and the career of the silver-spoon kid who is ultimately brought onto the right track by the wholesome influence exponent.

Picture has tempo and humanity. There is a skillful blending of the sentimentality and the giggles. On the acting end it's a smacko assignment for Gaynor and she displays considerable authority in her performance.

Taylor looks like the dames like him to look, and he acts like the boys can okay him. Binnie Barnes makes a provocative off-type vixen.

□ 1953: Nomination: Best Song ('My Flaming Heart')

■ SMALL TOWN GIRL

1953, 93 MINS, US ◇

Dir Leslie Kardos   *Prod* Joe Pasternak   *Scr* Dorothy Cooper, Dorothy Kingsley   *Ph* Joseph Ruttenberg   *Ed* Albert Akst   *Mus* Andre Previn (dir.)   *Art Dir* Cedric Gibbons, Hans Peters
● Jane Powell, Farley Granger, Ann Miller, S.Z. Sakall, Robert Keith, Bobby Van (M-G-M)

Small Town Girl packages an engaging round of light musical comedy and a plot [from a story by Dorothy Cooper] with just enough substance to hold the attention without wearing. Jane Powell and Farley Granger are the chief exponents of young love and both carry a major portion of the entertainment to excellent results. However, it is the spotlighting of young Bobby Van in a song-dance-comedy spot that impresses the most.

However, Van doesn't grab all the dance footage. Shapely Ann Miller exposes her gams in two hot production pieces. 'I've Gotta Hear That Beat', flashily staged by Busby Berkeley, and 'My Gaucho', a piece of south-of-the-border rhythm that she makes pay off. Both tunes were written by Nicholas Brodszky and Leo Robin.

Granger is a rich playboy who makes the mistake of speeding through a small town in which Robert Keith is judge. He's jailed for 30 days, thus breaking up his elopement with showgirl Miller. Granger makes happy time, though, with Powell, Keith's daughter, even talking her and Chill Wills, jailer, into letting him out for a night in New York. She goes along to insure his return, and love blooms, breaking up the hopes of S.Z. Sakall that his son, Van, will eventually marry the gal and settle down to clerking job instead of dreaming of the NY stage.

■ SMALL TOWN IN TEXAS, A

1976, 95 MINS, US ◇

Dir Jack Starrett   *Prod* Joe Solomon   *Scr* William Norton   *Ph* Bob Jessup   *Ed* John C. Horger, Larry L. Mills, Jodie Copelan   *Mus* Charles Bernstein   *Art Dir* Elayne Ceder
● Timothy Bottoms, Susan George, Bo Hopkins, Art Hindle, John Karlen, Morgan Woodward (CoCaCo)

Plot picks up Timothy Bottoms en route home from a prison stretch to reunite with girl friend Susan George and their out of wedlock son, also to contemplate revenge on Bo Hopkins, who busted him on a pot charge and is now involved with George.

The film jettisons believability to concentrate on stunt crashes and explosions. Bottoms' character is overly obtuse even for an embittered ex-con and pointlessly risks the lives of George and their son.

Bo Hopkins acts rings around Bottoms. He does an excellent job of conveying the sheriff's unsettling mixture of boyish charm and viciousness. George is okay in another overwrought part. Buck Fowler is a standout in the supporting cast as a grizzled old moonshiner who gleefully joins the chase.

■ SMALL WORLD OF SAMMY LEE, THE

1963, 107 MINS, UK

Dir Ken Hughes   *Prod* Frank Godwin   *Scr* Ken Hughes   *Ph* Wolfgang Suschitzky   *Ed* Henry Richardson   *Mus* Kenny Graham
● Anthony Newley, Julia Foster, Robert Stephens, Wilfrid Brambell, Warren Mitchell, Miriam Karlin (British Lion/Bryanston Seven Arts)

Originally an award-winning teleplay by Ken Hughes the film has been pumped up to feature length, perhaps at overlength. Though highly overcoloured, it remains a sharp, snide commentary on the sleazy side of Soho, and emerges as a firstclass vehicle for Anthony Newley.

Newley, a fugitive from the East End, is the smart-aleck emcee of one a shabby strippery. Between churning out tired, near-blue gags and introducing the peelers, he is an inveterate poker and horse player. The story consists entirely of his efforts to raise $840 in five hours to pay off a gangster-bookie who is threatening to cut him up if he doesn't deliver the loot on time.

Hughes' uninhibited screenplay is incisive and tart while his direction has the deft assurance of a man who is reeling with his own idea and knows what he wants as the end product. His cameras stray restlessly around the seamier parts of Soho and the East End.

Newley gives a restless, intelligent and perceptive performance. Few of the supporting actors have much opportunity to make great impact but some register brilliantly, notably Warren Mitchell as Newley's East End delicatessen store-owner brother.

■ SMASHING TIME

1967, 96 MINS, UK ◇
Dir Desmond Davis   *Prod* Roy Millichip, Carlo Ponti
Scr George Melly   *Ph* Manny Wynn   *Ed* Barry Vince
Mus John Addison   *Art Dir* Ken Bridgeman
● Rita Tushingham, Lynn Redgrave, Michael York, Anna Quayle, Irene Handl, Ian Carmichael (Paramount/Solmur)

Starring Rita Tushingham and Lynn Redgrave as a pair of girls from the north of England who go to London to explore its glittery side – and have themselves a smashing time – the writer and producers display an amazing memory of Hollywood film.

Femmes play Laurel and Hardy characters, Tushingham as the bewildered Stan, Redgrave the aggressive Oliver. George Melly's original screenplay might be the further misadventures of the Hollywood comics in change-of-sex garb.

Extensive use is made of a swinging London background, with many of its characters, particularly the fey. Desmond Davis' direction, when it isn't focusing on hoary routines, is fast in limning the conglomerate situations in which femmes are plunged, Lynn becoming a recording star, Rita a top fashion photographer's model. With their usual flair for disaster, both find themselves out.

■ SMASH PALACE

1981, 100 MINS, NEW ZEALAND ◇ ⊙
Dir Roger Donaldson   *Prod* Roger Donaldson
Scr Roger Donaldson   *Ph* Graeme Cowley   *Ed* Mike Horton   *Mus* Sharon O'Neill   *Art Dir* Reston Griffiths
● Bruno Lawrence, Anna Jemison, Greer Robson, Keith Aberdein, Les Kelly (Aardvark)

Smash Palace is a thoroughly remarkable drama about a marital break-up which erupts into an impulsive kidnapping of a child by its father and a totally-believable escalation to the brink of tragedy.

Roger Donaldson's handling of actors is excellent, and his visual control constantly enthralling. The eponymous location is a vast junk-yard of cars, established by Al Shaw's father, and now the panier of hope for Al, a former Grand Prix driver, returned to a remote New Zealand country town with a pregnant French wife.

However, his wife has, during the ensuing eight years, grown increasingly dissatisfied, and the early scenes economically establish the deeper reasons. The script's expositional sequences are neatly handled, making the character development logically part of the narrative.

With strong performances by both Bruno Lawrence and Anna Jemison to work with, the director has effectively created a reality to the tension that goes beneath the surface – or as it might be said: has re-created real life on film.

■ SMILE

1975, 113 MINS, US ◇ ⊙
Dir Michael Ritchie   *Prod* Ritchie   *Scr* Jerry Belson
Ph Conrad Hall   *Ed* Richard Harris   *Mus* Daniel Osborn, Leroy Holmes, Charles Chaplin
● Bruce Dern, Barbara Feldon, Michael Kidd, Geoffrey Lewis, Nicholas Pryor, Colleen Camp (United Artists)

Smile is a hilarious but ultimately shallow put-down of teenage beauty contests. Jerry Belson's original script depicts the climactic days of a statewide beauty competition, where a group of adolescent girls get caught up in the melange of mercantilism, boosterism and backstage politics attendant to such tribal rites.

The uniformly excellent performances come from Bruce Dern, a compulsively upbeat smalltown mobile home dealer and chief judge of the contest; Barbara Feldon, perfect as an 'active' woman whose marriage to Nicholas Pryor is in a shambles; Geoffrey Lewis, very effective as pageant president; and Michael Kidd, imported bigtime choreographer whose career is in a slump.

Titles employ Nat 'King' Cole's old hit record of 'Smile'.

■ SMILING LIEUTENANT, THE

1931, 88 MINS, US
Dir Ernst Lubitsch   *Prod* Ernst Lubitsch   *Scr* Ernest Vaida, Samson Raphaelson, Ernst Lubitsch   *Ph* George Folsey   *Mus* Oscar Straus
● Maurice Chevalier, Claudette Colbert, Miriam Hopkins, Charles Ruggles, George Barbier (Paramount)

Ernst Lubitsch, Ernest Vajda and Samuel Raphaelson form a plenty smart trio working behind a camera. Any script or treatment springing from this source is bound to hold many things that are good and very few that are not.

The film's real weakness is not theirs. The drought is in the disappointing Oscar Straus score of four numbers.

Its story is a pert yarn of free morals and makes no attempt to be otherwise. Maurice Chevalier steals Claudette Colbert, a violinist, from Charles Ruggles. She moves in and stays until the officer becomes circumstantially embroiled with Miriam Hopkins as the unsophisticated and plain but willing princess whom he has to marry. Thereafter it's something of a contest to lure the lieutenant into the princess' chamber.

On performance Hopkins ranks equally with Colbert in doing the unattractive princess who sees her lieutenant and wants him at any cost. Colbert also plays well but lacks the opportunity to make the foremost impression. Neither of the girls seems happy when singing.

No question as to George Barbier's valiant assistance as the king. He makes everything count and handles many a laugh on his own.
☐ 1931/32: Nomination: Best Picture

■ SMILIN' THROUGH

1932, 96 MINS, US
Dir Sidney Franklin   *Scr* Ernest Vajda, James Bernard Fagan   *Ph* Lee Garmes   *Ed* Margaret Booth
Mus William Axt
● Norma Shearer, Fredric March, Leslie Howard, O. P. Heggie, Ralph Forbes (M-G-M)

In interpretation, in acting and in the fine presentation of all its poetically romantic qualities, this version is a worthy successor to the earlier transcription, first the stage play

by Jane Murfin and Jane Cowl, the 1922 silent screenplay with Norma Talmadge, and now with Norma Shearer, who reveals a fine feeling for this old-fashioned but perennial romantic role.

Story is about as sentimetal as it could be without spilling over, and the literary trick of casting the dialog in the love scenes in the patter of the day serves to emphasize by its very nonchalance the depth of the feeling it thus indirectly conveys.

The cutting has not been done as expertly as the other details. Many sequences are a bit overdone, for no good reason save that of pictorial effect and the episode of the tragic wedding is held a fatal instant too long.
☐ 1932/33: Nomination: Best Picture

■ SMOKEY AND THE BANDIT

1977, 96 MINS, US ◇ ⊙
Dir Hal Needham   *Prod* Mort Engelberg   *Scr* James Lee Barrett, Charles Shyer, Alan Mandel   *Ph* Bobby Byrne
Ed Walter Hanneman, Angelo Ross   *Mus* Bill Justis, Jerry Reed, Dick Feller   *Art Dir* Mark Mansbridge
● Burt Reynolds, Sally Field, Jerry Reed, Jackie Gleason, Mike Henry, Paul Williams (Universal/Rastar)

Burt Reynolds stars as a bootlegger-for-kicks who, with Jerry Reed and Sally Field, outwit zealous sheriff Jackie Gleason.

The plot is simple: rich father-son team of blowhards Pat McCormick and Paul Williams offer a reward if Reynolds will truck a load of Coors beer from Texas to Georgia; Reynolds and buddy Reed race to meet the deadline; Field complicates matters as a not-yet-bride who flees beau Mike Henry, son of outraged Gleason, who then chases them all across the southeast.

There is a parade of roadside set pieces involving many different ways to crash cars. Overlaid is citizens band radio jabber (hence, the title) which is loaded with downhome gags. Field is the hottest element in the film.

■ SMOKEY AND THE BANDIT II

1980, 101 MINS, US ◇ ⊙
Dir Hal Needham   *Prod* Hank Moonjean   *Scr* Jerry Belson, Brock Yates   *Ph* Michael Butler   *Ed* Donn Cambern, William Gordean   *Mus* Snuff Garrett (sup.)
Art Dir Henry Bumstead
● Burt Reynolds, Jackie Gleason, Sally Field, Dom DeLuise, Jerry Reed, Paul Williams (Universal/Rastar)

Sally Field tells Burt Reynolds in *Smokey and the Bandit II* that he is no longer having fun doing what used to come naturally. This stale sequel seems to be evidence of going through the motions for money instead of fun.

Smokey II [from a story by Michael Kane] concentrates on sluggish and mostly overdone attempts at roadside comedy skits, and it doesn't even bother to have Reynolds and Field play the same characters they played so engagingly in the original.

Here, Reynolds is hired to haul a pregnant elephant to the Republican convention. The heavy reliance on elephant gags quite literally slows down the film.

Ironically, the best part of the film is the unusual end credit sequence, which shows the actors having fun when they blow lines in outtakes.

■ SMOKEY AND THE BANDIT PART 3

1983, 88 MINS, US ◇ ⊙
Dir Dick Lowry   *Prod* Mort Engelberg   *Scr* Stuart Birnbaum, David Dashev   *Ph* James Pergola   *Ed* Byron 'Buzz' Brandt, David Blewitt, Christopher Greenbury
Mus Larry Cansler   *Art Dir* Ron Hobbs
● Jackie Gleason, Paul Williams, Pat McCormick, Jerry Read, Mike Henry, Colleen Camp (Universal)

Filmmakers, including first-time theatrical director Dick Lowry, have wisely returned to the non-stop car-chasing destruction derby of the first movie. But the sense of fun in that original is missing and the countless smashups and near-misses are orchestrated randomly.

Result is a patchwork of arbitrary mayhem as Jackie Gleason's sheriff Budford T. Justice, who tires of retirement in Florida, pursues Jerry Reed and sidekick Colleen Camp through the South. Except for the closing and opening moments, film is so devoid of structure that reels could be shown in reverse order without any loss of coherence.

Gleason, in a testament to endurance, remains funny, and his dimwit son is still humorously parlayed by Mike Henry. All Reed has to do is grin a lot and he's fast becoming a parody of former film roles. Pat McCormick and Paul Williams, reprising their rich and nasty father-son combo, are tiresome caricatures.

....

■ SMUGGLERS, THE

See: The Man Within

....

■ SNAKE PIT, THE

1948, 107 MINS, US

Dir Anatole Litvak *Prod* Anatole Litvak, Robert Bassler *Scr* Frank Partos, Millen Brand *Ph* Leo Tover *Ed* Dorothy Spencer *Mus* Alfred Newman *Art Dir* Lyle R. Wheeler, Joseph C. Wright

● Olivia de Havilland, Mark Stevens, Leo Genn, Celeste Holm, Helen Craig, Leif Erickson (20th Century-Fox)

The Snake Pit is a standout among class melodramas. Based on Mary Jane Ward's novel, picture probes into the processes of mental illness with a razor-sharp forthrightness, giving an open-handed display of the make-up of bodies within minds and the treatments used to restore intelligence. Clinical detail is stated with matter-of-fact clarity and becomes an important part of the melodramatics.

Olivia de Havilland is a young bride who goes insane and is committed to an institution for treatment. An understanding medico (Leo Genn) uses kindness and knowledge of mental ills to restore her. Just as a cure seems possible, she again plunges into a mental snake pit and starts all over on the road to insanity.

De Havilland's performance is top gauge. Genn goes about his part of the doctor with a quietness that gives it strength and Mark Stevens is excellent as De Havilland's husband.

□ 1948: Best Sound Recording.
□ Nominations: Best Picture, Director, Actress (Olivia de Havilland), Screenplay, Scoring of a Dramatic Picture

....

■ SNEAKERS

1992, 125 MINS, US ◇ ⓥ ⊙

Dir Phil Alden Robinson *Prod* Walter F. Parkes, Lawrence Lasker *Scr* Phil Alden Robinson, Lawrence Lasker, Walter F. Parkes *Ph* John Lindley *Ed* Tom Rolf *Mus* James Horner *Art Dir* Patrizia von Brandenstein

● Robert Redford, Dan Aykroyd, Ben Kingsley, Mary McDonnell, River Phoenix, Sidney Poitier (Universal)

A slick, hip, liberal, hi-tech, all-star buddy spy comic caper pic, *Sneakers* serves up a breezy good time in the vein of some of toplined Robert Redford's 1970s hits.

Film gets off to a good start with a mock break-in demonstrating the skill of Redford's company in cracking security systems. His gang of underpaid but fun-loving experts sports a full complement of shady backgrounds: Sidney Poitier was fired from the CIA, Dan Aykroyd is an ex-con, David Strathairn is a blind wiretapping and audio expert, and River Phoenix changed his school grades by computer.

Two alleged agents from the top-secret National Security Agency enlist Redford's services to recover a mysterious black box that turns out to contain a device that can penetrate the computer systems of vital services.

It turns out the boys are up against Redford's criminal college cohort Ben Kingsley, who sees the box as a way to accomplish their student dream of changing the world, and to take revenge on Redford in the bargain.

When issues grow into matters of life and death, viewer can be expected to take matters more seriously as well. Unfortunately, script's second half can't support a more sober examination, as too many issues are ignored or glossed over.

The film looks exceedingly expensive, and no doubt was. The big-time cast provides sterling company.

....

■ SNIPER

1993, 98 MINS, US ◇ ⓥ ⊙

Dir Luis Llosa *Prod* Robert L. Rosen *Scr* Michael Frost Beckner, Crash Leyland *Ph* Bill Butler *Ed* Scott Smith *Mus* Gary Chang *Art Dir* Herbert Pinter

● Tom Berenger, Billy Zane, J.T. Walsh, Aden Young, Ken Radley, Reinaldo Arenas (Baltimore/Tri-Star)

Sniper is an expertly directed, yet ultimately unsatisfying psychological thriller. Luis Llosa's first-rate action direction is undermined by underdeveloped characters and pedestrian dialogue.

Tom Berenger essays a Marine sniper, oddly named Thomas Beckett, on assignment in Panama. Pic quickly establishes sniping as a lonely profession shunned even by other gung-ho Marines. On his latest assignment he's accompanied by an ambitious young Washington bureaucrat, Richard Miller (Billy Zane), who is so green he doesn't really need camouflage.

The hostile interplay between the emotionally detached veteran and the cocky youngster is strictly textbook, as is their eventual male bonding. This would be okay if they weren't virtually the only characters in the film.

Action scenes – and there are a good number of them – range from good to edge-of-your-seat. Audiences will see the finale coming from a mile away, but the pace only flags when the characters stop to make sense of their actions.

The tropical forests of Queensland, Australia, stood in for Panama.

....

■ SNOWBALL EXPRESS

1972, 99 MINS, US ◇ ⓥ

Dir Norman Tokar *Prod* Ron Miller *Scr* Don Tait, Jim Parker, Arnold Margolin *Ph* Frank Phillips *Ed* Robert Stafford *Mus* Robert F. Brunner *Art Dir* John B. Mansbridge, Walter Tyler

● Dean Jones, Nancy Olson, Harry Morgan, Keenan Wynn, Johnny Whitaker, Kathleen Cody (Walt Disney)

The Disney trademark of wholesome entertainment is immediately discernible in this comedy focusing on a young family man inheriting a derelict resort hotel in Colorado.

Dean Jones, a veteran of Disney films, plays the insurance accountant who quits the Manhattan rat race when he's informed he has been willed the estate of a distant uncle in the Rockies, principal asset of which is the Grand Imperial Hotel.

Based on the book *Chateau Bon Vivant*, by Frankie and John O'Rear, narrative under Norman Tokar's deft direction follows Jones' efforts at making a go of a bad deal. Highlights of film are the various ski sequences and a nightmarish snowmobile race.

Jones delivers as usual in a slightly frustrated character and Nancy Olson, as his wife, lends piquancy as she gradually throws in with Jones on his project.

....

■ SNOWS OF KILIMANJARO, THE

1952, 113 MINS, US ◇ ⓥ

Dir Henry King *Prod* Darryl F. Zanuck *Scr* Casey Robinson *Ph* Leon Shamroy *Ed* Barbara McLean *Mus* Bernard Herrmann *Art Dir* Lyle Wheeler, John DeCuir

● Gregory Peck, Susan Hayward, Ava Gardner, Hildegarde Neff, Leo G. Carroll, Torin Thatcher (20th Century-Fox)

A big, broad screen treatment has been given to Ernest Hemingway's *The Snows of Kilimanjaro*. The script broadens the 1927 short story considerably without losing the Hemingway penchant for the mysticism behind his virile characters and lusty situations.

Ava Gardner makes the part of Cynthia a warm, appealing, alluring standout. Gregory Peck delivers with gusto the character of the writer who lies dangerously ill on the plain at the base of Kilimanjaro, highest mountain in Africa, and relives what he believes is a misspent life. Susan Hayward is splendid, particularly in the dramatic closing sequence, in the less colorful role of Peck's wife.

The location-lensed footage taken in Paris, Africa, the Riviera and Spain add an important dress to the varied sequences. The Paris street and cafe scenes, the music and noise, are alive. The African-lensed backgrounds are brilliant, as are those on the Riviera and in Spain.

□ 1952: Nominations: Best Color Cinematography, Color Art Direction

....

■ SNOW WHITE AND THE SEVEN DWARFS

1937, 80 MINS, US ◇

Dir David Hand *Prod* Walt Disney *Scr* Ted Sears, Otto Englander, Earl Hurd, Dorothy Ann Blank, Richard Credon, Dick Rickard, Merrill De Maris, Webb Smith *Mus* Frank Churchill, Paul Smith, Leigh Harline (arr.) *Art Dir* Charles Philippi, High Hennesy, Terrell Stapp, McLaren Stewart, Harold Miles, Tom Codrick, Gustaf Tenggren, Kenneth Anderson, Kendall O'Connor, Hazel Sewell

● (Disney/RKO)

Wal Disney's *Snow White and the Seven Dwarfs*, seven reels of animated cartoon in Technicolor, unfolds an absorbingly interesting and, at times, thrilling entertainment.

More than two years and $1 million were required by the Disney staff, under David Hand's supervision, to complete the film. In a foreword Disney pays a neat compliment to animators, designers and musical composers whose united efforts have produced a work of art. No less than 62 staff names are flashed in the credit titles as being responsible for various divisions of the job.

The opening shows the cover of Grimm's book of tales. Soon all the characters assume lifelike personalities. Snow White is the embodiment of girlish sweetness and kindness, exemplified in her love for the birds and the small animals of the woods that are her friends and, as it subsequently develops, her rescuers. The queen is a vampish brunet, of homicidal instincts, who consorts with black magic and underworld forces of evil. And the seven little dwarfs, Doc, Grumpy, Dopey, Sleepy, Happy, Sneezy and Bashful, are the embodiments of their nametags, a merry crew of masculine frailities.

Pastel shades predominate in the Technicolor and there is an absence of garish, brilliant colorings.

Sound plays an important part in the production and the synchronization of words to the moving lips of the characters is worked out perfectly.

□ 1938: Special Award (significant screen innovation)
□ 1937: Nomination: Best Score

....

■ SOAPDISH

1991, 95 MINS, US ◇ ⓥ ⊙
Dir Michael Hoffman   *Prod* Aaron Spelling, Alan
Greisman   *Scr* Robert Harling, Andrew Bergman
Ph Ueli Steiger   *Ed* Garth Craven   *Mus* Alan Silvestri
Art Dir Eugenio Zanetti
● Sally Field, Kevin Kline, Robert Downey Jr, Cathy
Moriarty, Whoopi Goldberg, Carrie Fisher (Paramount)

Soapdish aims at a satiric target as big as a
Macy's float and intermittently hits it. Sally
Field and Kevin Kline play a feuding pair of
romantically involved soap opera stars in this
broad but amiable sendup of daytime TV.

Field, the reigning 'queen of misery' on the
sudser *The Sun Also Sets*, is at the peak of her
glory but is going to pieces emotionally.
Amazonian harpy Cathy Moriarty is scheming to take over the show by using her sexual
wiles to convince the slimy producer (Robert
Downey Jr) to have Field's character destroy
her popularity by committing some unspeakable crime.

To drive Field even more off the edge,
Downey surprises her by bringing back her
long-ago flame, Kevin Kline, whom she had
thrown off the show in 1973. Whoopi
Goldberg, the show's jaded head writer, flips
when told Kline is coming back because his
character was written out by having him decapitated in a car crash.

Field works hard and shows an expert sense
of comic timing, but the grittily down-to-
earth acting persona Field has developed now
makes her seem a bit too reasonable for the
zany demands of this script.

Kline is utterly marvelous as a sort of low-
rent John Barrymore type, boozing and
carousing his way through the ranks of wor-
shipful young actresses. Moriarty, who acts as
if she's been staying up late studying Mary
Woronov pics, is a scream as Field's deep-
voiced, hate-consumed rival.

■ S.O.B.

1981, 121 MINS, US ◇ ⓥ ⊙
Dir Blake Edwards   *Prod* Blake Edwards, Tony Adams
Scr Blake Edwards   *Ph* Harry Stradling   *Ed* Ralph E.
Winters   *Mus* Henry Mancini   *Art Dir* Roger Maus
● Julie Andrews, William Holden, Marisa Berenson,
Larry Hagman, Robert Loggia, Robert Vaughn
(Paramount/Lorimar)

S.O.B. is one of the most vitriolic – though
only occasionally hilarious – attacks on the
Tinseltown mentality ever.

Taking its core from part of director Blake
Edwards' own battle-weary Hollywood career,
pic is structured as an arch fairy tale, spinning the chronicle of a top-grossing producer
(Richard Mulligan) whose latest $30 million
musical extravaganza is hailed by the world
as the b.o. turkey of the century, relegating
him to has-been status overnight.

With Julie Andrews as his pure-as-driven
snow imaged wife prompted finally to leave
him for good, while production chief Robert
Vaughn plots how to salvage the pic by massive, contract-bending recutting, Mulligan
tries several failed variations on the suicide
route until a mid-orgy epiphany tells him to
cut and reshoot the G-rated failure into an
opulent softcore porno fantasy.

Black comedy is a tough commodity to sustain and, after a broad start, Edwards quickly
finds a deft balance that paints a cockeyed,
self-contained world that comfortably supports its exaggerated characters. Unhappily,
about midway through the pic, the tone becomes less certain (especially when it strains
for seriousness) and styles begin to switch
back and forth.

■ SO BIG

1953, 101 MINS, US
Dir Robert Wise   *Prod* Henry Blanke   *Scr* John Twist

Ph Ellsworth Fredericks   *Ed* Thomas Reilly   *Mus* Max
Steiner   *Art Dir* John Beckman
● Jane Wyman, Sterling Hayden, Nancy Olson, Steve
Forrest, Elizabeth Fraser, Martha Hyer (Warner)

This is the third time around for Edna
Ferber's Pulitzer Prize-winning novel. It was
made as a silent film by First National back in
1925 and as a talker by Warner Bros in 1932.
Jane Wyman handles the emotional histrionics in this re-make.

So Big is big and sprawling, covering a period of some 25 years. Its basic flaw is that it
attempts to cover too much, resulting in an
episodic quality and flat surface characters.

Wyman is superb in transition from the
young girl with the aristocratic background to
the widow of a Dutch truck farmer. Nothing
stops Selina's nobility from the time she arrives in the Dutch community outside of
Chicago as a young schoolteacher to the moment her son decides to return to his drawing
board. She takes poverty, back-breaking farm
work, widowhood and disappointment
serenely, philosophically and with dignity.

Sterling Hayden scores as the unlearned,
rugged but gentle farmer who wins the
schoolteacher. Nancy Olson is appropriately
flippant and understanding as the Paris-
trained artist who values true creativeness
over financial success. Steve Forrest, as
Selina's architect-son, wrestles neatly with
the money versus art problem.

Ellsworth Fredericks' camera has successfully captured the drudgery of the farm, the
excitement of the market place, and the
splendor and gaudiness of the rich in 1900
Chicago.

■ SOCIETY

1989, 99 MINS, US ◇ ⓥ ⊙
Dir Brian Yuzna   *Prod* Keith Walley   *Scr* Woody Keith,
Rick Fry   *Ph* Rick Fichter   *Ed* Peter Teschner   *Mus* Mark
Ryder, Phil Davies   *Art Dir* Matthew C. Jacobs
● Billy Warlock, Devin Devasquez, Evan Richards, Ben
Meyerson, Connie Danese, Patrice Jennings (Wild Street)

Society is an extremely pretentious, obnoxious
horror film that unsuccessfully attempts to
introduce kinky sexual elements into extravagant makeup effects.

Teen Billy Warlock is thought to be paranoid by everyone, including his shrink, when
he starts suspecting not only that he must
have been adopted but also that his parents
are having incestuous orgies with his sister.

Following many strange occurrences, red
herrings and repetitive nudges about the
class system and 'fitting into society', it's finally revealed that rich and powerful folk really are some sort of undead monsters
preying on Billy and all us other have-nots.

Sickening climax, notable for its poor continuity, is a sexual orgy called shunting, in
which makeup expert Screaming Mad George
indulges in what's credited as 'surrealistic
makeup effects.'

Sole bright spot is a very sexy turn by former *Playboy* magazine model Devin
Devasquez.

■ SO DARK THE NIGHT

1946, 71 MINS, US
Dir Joseph H. Lewis   *Prod* Ted Richmond   *Scr* Martin
Berkeley, Dwight Babcock   *Ph* Burnett Guffey
Ed Jerome Thoms   *Mus* Hugo Friedhofer   *Art Dir* Carl
Anderson
● Steven Geray, Micheline Cheirel, Eugene Borden, Ann
Codee, Egon Brecher, Helen Freeman (Columbia)

Around the frail structure of a story [by
Aubrey Wisberg] about a schizophrenic Paris
police inspector who becomes an insane killer
at night, a tight combination of direction,
camerawork and musical scoring produce a
series of isolated visual effects that are subtle
and moving to an unusual degree.

Paradoxically, the film seems to collapse
under the weight of its technical niceties as
director Joseph H. Lewis continuously takes
time out to make his points through the indi-
rection of cinematic imagery rather than directly through the spoken word.

Settings for the pic, which unfolds in an obscure French village, are outstanding for their
density and accuracy of detail. Despite the
obvious budget limitations, the layout of the
streets, interior decorations and landscape
shots define France as it exists in our imagination.

Story revolves around the ill-fated romance
between a middle-aged Parisian detective and
a young country girl who is already betrothed
to a neighboring farmer. On the wedding eve,
the farmer in a well-portrayed dramatic encounter, threatens the detective and stalks
out of the party, the girl following in a frenzy
of mixed emotions. Several days later, both
the girl and farmer are found to have been
strangled to death.

■ SODOM AND GOMORRAH

1962, 153 MINS, ITALY ◇ ⓥ ⊙
Dir Robert Aldrich   *Prod* Goffredo Lombardo, Joseph E.
Levine   *Scr* Hugo Butler, Giorgio Prosperi   *Ph* Silvano
Ippoliti, Mario Montuori, Cyril Knowles   *Ed* Peter Tanner
Mus Miklos Rozsa   *Art Dir* Ken Adam
● Stewart Granger, Pier Angeli, Stanley Baker, Anouk
Aimee, Rossana Podesta, Claudia Mori (20th Century-
Fox/Titanus)

Director Robert Aldrich has said, 'Every director ought to get one Biblical film out of his system, but there's not very much that you can do
about this sort of picture.' Too true. Net:
Sodom and Gomorrah has many of the faults of
the Biblical epic, but many good qualities.

Storyline concerns Lot's pilgrimage to the
Valley of Jordan with the Hebrews. They set
up camp in the valley but are almost immediately involved in a bitter clash between the
Helamites, who covet the wealth of Sodom
and Gomorrah, two cesspools of depravity,
ruled over by the cold, beautiful, unscrupulous
Queen Bera who, incidentally, is being dou-
blecrossed for power by her scheming brother.

Stewart Granger makes a distinguished,
solemn and sincere figure of Lot and Stanley
Baker, as the treacherous Prince of Sodom, is
sufficiently sneaky though he has only a couple of highspots in his role. Anouk Aimee is
an impressively sinister Queen, Pier Angeli
has some moments of genuine emotion as
Lot's wife and Rosanna Podesta and Claudia
Mori play the shadowy roles of Lot's daughters adequately.

■ SO FINE

1981, 91 MINS, US ◇ ⓥ
Dir Andrew Bergman   *Prod* Mike Lobell   *Scr* Andrew
Bergman   *Ph* James A. Contner   *Ed* Alan Heim
Mus Ennio Morricone   *Art Dir* Santo Loquasto
● Ryan O'Neal, Jack Warden, Mariangela Melato,
Richard Kiel, Fred Gwynne (Warner)

So Fine is quite all right. Andrew Bergman,
screenwriter on *Blazing Saddles* and *The In-
Laws*, has come up with a somewhat less zany
concoction this time but makes an impressively sharp directorial debut highlighted by
some good bedroom farce.

Ryan O'Neal is a Shakespeare-spouting
English professor implausibly recruited into
his father Jack Warden's faltering dressmaking firm upon the unchallengable demand of
Big Eddie, played by the 7'2" Richard Kiel.

Latter's petite wife, Mariangela Melato,
quickly corrals O'Neal into the sack (while
Kiel's in it too, no less) and, in his best bumbling manner, O'Neal inadvertantly hits upon
a new fashion discovery – skin tight jeans
with seethrough behinds.

Despite his smashing success in the garment district, O'Neal retreats to the world of academia but is pursued by Melato, who in turn is followed by the jealous Big Eddie. It all ends up in a slapstick, amateur-hour operatic production of Verdi's *Otello* remindful of, among other things, *A Night at the Opera*.

. . . .

■ SOFT TOP HARD SHOULDER

1993, 93 MINS, UK ◇ ▽

Dir Stefan Schwartz   *Prod* Richard Holmes   *Scr* Peter Capaldi   *Ph* Henry Braham   *Ed* Derek Trigg   *Mus* Chris Rea   *Art Dir* Sonja Klaus
● Peter Capaldi, Elaine Collins, Frances Barber, Simon Callow, Phyllis Logan, Richard Wilson (Gruber Bros./Road Movies)

Scotland gets its first road movie with *Soft Top Hard Shoulder*, a wafer-thin but likable addition to the genre.

Gavin Bellini (scripter Peter Capaldi) is a crazy Italo-Scot trying to make it as an illustrator down south in London. Meeting his Uncle Sal (witty Richard Wilson) by chance, he learns he has 36 hours to make it to his father's surprise 60th birthday party in Glasgow if he's to collect a chunk of family money.

Hitting the highways in a bronchial old auto, he quickly meets kooky hitchhiker Yvonne (Elaine Collins), a resourceful Glaswegian. Rest of pic follows the familiar route of the pair's love-hate relationship, stopovers and breakdowns, capped by a happy ending.

Capaldi's script comes up with plenty of incident. When it's good, it's very good, with plenty of dry Scots humor, but other sections lack zing.

. . . .

■ SOLDIER BLUE

1970, 112 MINS, US ◇ ▽

Dir Ralph Nelson   *Prod* Harold Loeb, Gabriel Katzka   *Scr* John Gay   *Ph* Robert Hauser   *Ed* Alex Beaton   *Mus* Roy Budd   *Art Dir* Frank Arrigo
● Candice Bergen, Peter Strauss, Donald Pleasence, John Anderson, Jorge Rivero, Dana Elcar (Avco Embassy)

Screenplay, from Theodore V. Olsen's novel, *Arrow in the Sun*, deals with the attempt of US soldier Honus Gant (Peter Strauss), the 'soldier blue' of the title, and a white woman who had been captured by Indians two years before (Candice Bergen) to stay alive until they can reach an army outpost. The paymaster's party, with which they have been traveling, is ambushed and slaughtered by the Cheyennes.

The major portion of the film deals with the pair's trek. Their misadventures include encountering white man Isaac Cumber (Donald Pleasence) who is en route to the Cheyennes to sell them guns for the gold they stole from the paymaster and who takes the pair prisoner.

Finally, Bergen goes on ahead for help when Strauss is wounded, but discovers the Army's plot to wipe out the Indians. She rides out to warn them.

The climax of the film makes the Army the complete villain and the Cheyennes the complete innocents. The seemingly handful of warriors are quickly wiped out, the women raped, children mutilated and, in many cases, murdered.

It would appear obvious that director Ralph Nelson is trying to correlate this allegedly historical incident with more contemporous events.

. . . .

■ SOLDIER IN THE RAIN

1963, 87 MINS, US ▽

Dir Ralph E. Nelson   *Prod* Martin Jurow   *Scr* Maurice Richlin, Blake Edwards   *Ph* Philip Lathrop   *Ed* Ralph Winters   *Mus* Henry Mancini   *Art Dir* Phil Barber
● Jackie Gleason, Steve McQueen, Tuesday Weld, Tony Bill, Tom Poston, Ed Nelson (Allied Artists/Cedars-Solar)

One might classify the film a fairy tale in khaki. The screenplay out of a novel by William Goldman relates the bittersweet tale of two modern army buddies – a smooth operating master sergeant (Jackie Gleason) who has found a home in the service, and his hero-worshipping protege (Steve McQueen), a supply sergeant who is about to return to civvies and hopes Gleason will join him in private enterprise on the outside.

There are several sudden, and vigorous, bursts of comedy dialog, principally exchanges between Gleason, who has a complex about his bulk, and Tuesday Weld, who plays a basically sweet but dumb and ingeniously tactless 18-year-old whose idea of a compliment is to refer to him as a 'fat Randolph Scott'. But such mirth is only spasmodic and is snowed under by a sentimental approach that misfires.

McQueen is a kind of southern-fried boob who reminds one of Clem Kadiddlehoffer. The style of portrayal is exaggerated and unnatural. Gleason fares better with a restrained approach, through which his natural endomorphic vitality seeps through. Weld is a standout with her convincing portrait of the classic dizzy blonde as a teenager. Tony Bill scores as McQueen's screwball sidekick.

. . . .

■ SOLDIER'S STORY, A

1984, 101 MINS, US ◇ ▽ ⊙

Dir Norman Jewison   *Prod* Norman Jewison, Ronald L. Schwary, Patrick Palmer   *Scr* Charles Fuller   *Ph* Russell Boyd   *Ed* Mark Warner, Caroline Bigglestaff   *Mus* Herbie Hancock   *Art Dir* Walter Scott Herndon
● Howard E. Rollins Jr., Adolph Caesar, Dennis Lipscomb, Art Evans, Denzil Washington, Larry Riley (Caldix)

A Soldier's Story is a taut, gripping film which features many of the old fashioned virtues of a good Hollywood production – brilliant ensemble acting, excellent production values, a crackling script (adapted from the Pulitzer Prize winning *A Soldier's Play* [1981] by its author, Charles Fuller), fine direction and a liberal political message.

Howard Rollins Jr plays Captain Davenport, a prideful black army attorney called into Fort Neal, La, to investigate the murder of Sgt Waters (Adolph Caesar). Rollins' arrival at this holding tank for black soldiers is cause for racial strife on both sides of the fence – the white officers are contemptuous and the black soldiers are proud.

Film is structured around a series of flashbacks as Rollins interviews the team members who represent a variety of black experience and attitudes.

☐ 1984: Nominations: Best Picture, Supp. Actor (Adolph Caesar), Adapted Screenplay

. . . .

■ SOLDIERS THREE

1951, 91 MINS, US

Dir Tay Garnett   *Prod* Pandro S. Berman   *Scr* Marguerite Roberts, Tom Reed, Malcolm Stuart Boylan   *Ph* William Mellor   *Ed* Robert J. Kern   *Mus* Adolph Deutsch   *Art Dir* Cedric Gibbons, Malcolm Brown
● Stewart Granger, Walter Pidgeon, David Niven, Robert Newton, Cyril Cusack, Greta Gynt (M-G-M)

Three scripters worked on the story, loosely based on Rudyard Kipling, but come up with nothing more than a string of incidents involving three soldiers in India (Stewart Granger, Robert Newton and Cyril Cusack). Trio's off-limits antics, such as drunken brawling, add to the hot water in which their colonel (Walter Pidgeon) finds himself and do nothing to calm the colonel's aide (David Niven). Antics do, however, enliven the film's footage and save it from missing altogether.

Granger is very likeable in his comedy role, and his two cohorts, Newton and Cusack, do their full share in getting laughs. Niven also

is good as the slightly stuffy aide who leads the pants-losing patrol. Pidgeon, as a colonel with worries, forgets his broad British bumbling occasionally, but this fits with general development.

. . . .

■ SOLID GOLD CADILLAC, THE

1956, 99 MINS, US ◇

Dir Richard Quine   *Prod* Fred Kohlmar   *Scr* Abe Burrows   *Ph* Charles Lang   *Ed* Charles Nelson   *Mus* Cyril J. Mockridge   *Art Dir* Ross Bellah
● Judy Holliday, Paul Douglas, Fred Clark, John Williams, Neva Patterson, Ralph Dumke (Columbia)

Original George S. Kaufman-Howard Teichmann Broadway script was changed to fit an older stage actress, Josephine Hull, and is now changed back in the Columbia film version for a younger comedienne, Judy Holliday. The satire on minority stockholder gadfly treatment of vested interests and pompous executives makes for hilarity.

It's a broad treatment of big corporation board members who get their comeuppance from a femme who owns only 10 shares of common in the company. As the dizzy blonde with some native, and naive, common sense, Holliday is a delight. The man's Paul Douglas, who does much to make the comedy click.

Fred Kohlmar's production achieves a plushy look without the use of colour or bigscreen assists. There is a flash of color at the tale's wrapup to show off that creampuff auto of the title, but the comedy is such that no one will miss a dye job elsewhere.

Film has a narration by George Burns, although it serves no particular purpose as far as the comedy is concerned. In the stage original the late Fred Allen officiated similarly.

. . . .

■ SOLOMON AND SHEBA

1959, 141 MINS, US ◇ ▽

Dir King Vidor   *Prod* Ted Richmond   *Scr* Anthony Veillier, Paul Dudley, George Bruce   *Ph* Freddie Young   *Ed* John Ludwig   *Mus* Mario Nascimbene   *Art Dir* Richard Day, Alfred Sweeney, Luis Perez Espinosa
● Yul Brynner, Gina Lollobrigida, George Sanders, David Farrar, Marisa Pavan, Alejandro Rey (United Artists)

The tab for this expensive production was unexpectedly hiked when Tyrone Power died in mid-production (although insurance covered much) and the subsequent hiring of Yul Brynner necessitated new writing as well as new shooting. A figure of over $5 million, judging by the spectacle, color and location expenses in Spain seems a reasonable one.

The story concerns the clash between Solomon and his brother Adonijah when King David crowns the poet-philosopher instead of the warrior. From then on it's political intrigue, with Egypt conniving with Sheba to bring down Israel, which is flourishing under the wise rule of Solomon, and the treacherous manner in which the Queen of Sheba undermines Solomon but falls in love with him in the process.

The fascinating clash between the two brothers is only spasmodically developed and, inevitably, plays second fiddle to the relationship between the queen and her infatuated target. Often what should have been a moving, gripping romance turns out to be little more than an affair between a couple of people at the local golf club.

There are some magnificent production scenes. Three startlingly effective battle sequences, the stoning of Sheba, her arrival in Jerusalem, the terrifying wrath of God which razes the Temple of Jehova and Sheba's God of Love, the scene where Solomon gives judgment over the baby, the sight of the plains of Israel made bleak and arid and, above all, the startling dance-ritual to the God of Love which develops into an orgy.

S

Gina Lollobrigida virtually portrays three different Shebas. First, the arrogant, fiery, ambitious Queen; then the voluptuous, wily, seductress; finally, the Sheba who involuntarily falls in love with the King and risks all by denouncing her own gods.

Lollobrigida not only looks stunning but shows the queen to be a woman of sharp brain as well as sensual beauty. Brynner, surprisingly subdued, also does a fine job in presenting a Solomon who credibly suggests a singer of songs, yet finally is a man of ordinary flesh and blood who cannot resist Sheba.

....

■ SO LONG AT THE FAIR

1950, 84 MINS, UK ▼
Dir Terence Fisher, Antony Darnborough   *Prod* Sidney Box   *Scr* Anthony Thorne, Hugh Mills   *Ph* Reginald Wyer   *Ed* Gordon Hales   *Mus* Benjamin Frankel
● Jean Simmons, Dirk Bogarde, David Tomlinson, Honor Blackman, Cathleen Nesbitt, Felix Aylmer (Gainsborough/Rank)

The pic is a good workmanlike British thriller, not in the top bracket. Setting for the film is the Paris exhibition of 1889.

The story opens as Vicky Barton (Jean Simmons) arrives in Paris with her brother (David Tomlinson). After a festive first night, they return to their hotel eager to participate in the revels of the following day. But the next morning, the brother disappears. At the hotel they insist the girl came alone and both the British consul and the chief of police find it hard to accept her story.

Despite the strong plot, the film never succeeds in developing a tense atmosphere. Picture has a good all-round cast. Simmons turns in a smooth performance. Dirk Bogarde displays a keen determination as the young artist who helps her unravel the mystery.

....

■ SOMEBODY UP THERE LIKES ME

1956, 112 MINS, US ▼
Dir Robert Wise   *Prod* Charles Schnee   *Scr* Ernest Lehman   *Ph* Joseph Ruttenberg   *Ed* Albert Akst   *Mus* Bronislau Kaper   *Art Dir* Cedric Gibbons, Malcolm Brown
● Paul Newman, Pier Angeli, Everett Sloane, Eileen Heckart, Sal Mineo, Harold J. Stone (M-G-M)

Somebody Up There Likes Me is a superbly done, frank and revealing film probe of Rocky Graziano, the East Side punk who overcame a lawless beginning to win respect and position as middle-weight champion of the world.

Paul Newman's talent is large and flexible, revealing an approach to the Graziano character that scores tremendously.

In the latter half, when Norma Unger, played with beautiful sensitivity by Pier Angeli, comes into his life, the audience is back on his side, pulling for him to shake off the past, and literally cheering him on in that potently staged championship match with Tony Zale. Credit for this stirring climax and its authenticity must be shared by technical adviser Johnny Indrisano and Courtland Shepard, who fights like a true-to-life Zale.

Numbered among the featured and supporting cast are Everett Sloane, great as the manager Irving Cohen; Eileen Heckart, exceptionally fine as Graziano's mother; Harold J. Stone, almost uncomfortably real as the wine-sodden father; and Sal Mineo, excellent as the street chum who shared Graziano's early ways.
□ 1956: Best B&W Cinematography, B&W Art Direction
□ Nomination: Best Editing

....

■ SOME CAME RUNNING

1958, 137 MINS, US ◇ ▼ ☉
Dir Vincente Minnelli   *Prod* Sol C. Siegel   *Scr* John Patrick, Arthur Sheekman   *Ph* William H. Daniels   *Ed* Adrienne Fazan   *Mus* Elmer Bernstein   *Art Dir* William A. Horning, Urie McCleary
● Frank Sinatra, Dean Martin, Shirley MacLaine, Martha Hyer, Arthur Kennedy, Nancy Gates (M-G-M)

The story is pure melodrama, despite the intention of the original novel's author, James Jones, to invest it with greater stature. But the integrity with which the film is handled by all its contributors lifts it at times to tragedy. Jones' novel has been stripped to essentials in the screenplay, and those are presented in hard clean dialog and incisive situations.

Frank Sinatra is an ex-serviceman and ex-novelist who returns to his home town, unwitting and unwilling, when he gets drunk in Chicago and is shipped back unconscious on a bus. Accompanying him is Shirley MacLaine who is generally unwitting but never unwilling, a good-natured tart with no pretensions.

Sinatra can't stand his brother (Arthur Kennedy) or the brother's wife (Leora Dana) but he falls deeply in love with a friend of theirs (Martha Hyer). He meets a pal (Dean Martin) who becomes an ally, and he becomes involved in the personal life of his niece (Betty Lou Keim).

The title, incidentally, is taken from St Mark, and is construed to mean that some have come running to find the meaning of life, but are prevented from finding it by obsession with materialism.

Sinatra gives a top performance, sardonic and compassionate, full of touches both instinctive and technical. It is not easy, either, to play a man dying of a chronic illness and do it with grace and humor, and this Martin does without faltering.

MacLaine isn't conventionally pretty. Her hair looks like it was combed with an eggbeater. But she elicits such empathy and humor that when she offers herself to Sinatra she seems eminently worth taking.
□ 1958: Nominations: Best Actress (Shirley MacLaine), Supp. Actor (Arthur Kennedy), Supp. Actress (Martha Hyer), Costume Design, Song ('To Love and Be Loved')

....

■ SOME GIRLS
(UK: Sisters)

1988, 94 MINS, US ◇ ▼
Dir Michael Hoffman   *Prod* Rick Stevenson   *Scr* Rupert Walters   *Ph* Ueli Steiger   *Ed* David Spiers   *Mus* James Newton Howard   *Art Dir* Eugenio Zanetti
● Patrick Dempsey, Florinda Bolkan, Jennifer Connelly, Lance Edwards, Ashley Greenfield, Lila Kedrova (Oxford/Wildwood)

A cross-cultural teen sex farce with some good moments, *Some Girls* hinges on the deadpan comic timing of Patrick Dempsey, who plays Michael, an American student invited by his college sweetheart Gabby (Jennifer Connelly) to spend Christmas with her family in Quebec City. The architecturally stately city is presented as a snow-covered fairyland in the eyes of the Yank visitor.

Gabby informs Michael that she doesn't love him anymore and that sleeping arrangements will be separate. Fortunately for Michael, Gabby has two fetching sisters who each show more than a passing interest in him.

Eccentric spice is provided by the girls' father, a head-in-the-clouds scholar with a proclivity for working in the nude, portrayed by Andre Gregory in a little gem of a performance. There's also a sweet, batty grandmother (Lila Kedrova), who's convinced Michael is her long-dead husband.

Director and screenwriter have fun mixing and mismatching these comic elements and succeed in springing a few flashes of wacky hilarity.

....

■ SOME KIND OF HERO

1982, 97 MINS, US ◇ ▼ ☉
Dir Michael Pressman   *Prod* Howard W. Koch   *Scr* James Kirkwood, Robert Boris   *Ph* King Baggot   *Ed* Christopher Greenbury   *Mus* Patrick Williams   *Art Dir* James L. Schoppe
● Richard Pryor, Margot Kidder, Ray Sharkey, Ronny Cox, Lynne Moody, Olivia Cole (Paramount)

Some Kind of Hero is yet another example of how Richard Pryor can take a mediocre film and elevate it to the level of his extraordinary talents.

Something went awry in the adaptation of James Kirkwood's novel to the screen, for Pryor's performance is truly a class piece of acting, playing a likable enough fellow who loses everything but his sense of humor during five years in a Vietnamese prison camp.

During this tenure, he establishes a loving friendship with hot-tempered POW Ray Sharkey. When Sharkey becomes deathly ill, Pryor signs a denouncement of US activities in the war to get the North Vietnamese to provide proper medical attention. Action then shifts to Pryor's return to the US, where the act comes back to haunt him.

Pryor's only luck is meeting Beverly Hills prostitute Margot Kidder, who gives him some loving encouragement and considers him something more than just another customer.

With Kidder's role almost as limited as Sharkey's, latter portion of the story pretty much falls apart as Pryor is torn between good and bad.

....

■ SOME KIND OF WONDERFUL

1987, 93 MINS, US ◇ ▼ ☉
Dir Howard Deutch   *Prod* John Hughes   *Scr* John Hughes   *Ph* Jan Kiesser   *Ed* Bud Smith, Scott Smith   *Mus* Stephen Hague, John Musser   *Art Dir* Josan Russo
● Eric Stoltz, Mary Stuart Masterson, Lea Thompson, Craig Sheffer, John Ashton, Elias Koteas (Paramount)

Some Kind of Wonderful is a simple, lovely and thoughtful teenage story that occasionally shines due to fine characterizations and lucid dialog. Writer-producer John Hughes and director Howard Deutch, who collaborated on *Pretty in Pink*, return here for an empathetic portrayal of dilemmas on such weighty matters as individuality, genuine friendship and love.

Film is set in LA's San Pedro area and centers on high school senior Eric Stoltz, who is a sensitive young man struggling to develop his artistic talent while juggling school, part-time work as a car mechanic and the distraction of the immensely popular Lea Thompson that he can't quite pick up on the emotions of Mary Stuart Masterson, whom Stoltz dismisses early on as just a tomboy friend.

As Thompson fights with her wealthy and arrogant b.f. (Craig Sheffer), Stoltz manages to get her to accept a date amidst the furor and stage is set for the inevitable confrontation with Sheffer. It's especially satisfying to watch the bond deepen between Stoltz and longtime friend Masterson.

Masterson is so adept and appealing in her role that she becomes the most interesting character of all. Fortunately, however, Stoltz has the substance to maintain his lead role. Maddie Corman as one of his younger sisters is just precocious enough to avoid being unlikable.

....

■ SOME LIKE IT HOT

1959, 105 MINS, US ▼ ☉
Dir Billy Wilder   *Prod* Billy Wilder   *Scr* Billy Wilder, I.A.L. Diamond   *Ph* Charles Lang Jr   *Art Dir* Arthur P. Schmidt   *Mus* Adolph Deutsch   *Art Dir* Ted Haworth
● Marilyn Monroe, Tony Curtis, Jack Lemmon, George Raft, Pat O'Brien, Joe E. Brown (Ashton/Mirisch)

Some Like It Hot is a whacky, clever, farcical comedy [suggested by a story by R. Thoeren and M. Logan] that starts off like a fire-cracker and keeps on throwing off lively sparks till the very end.

Story revolves around the age-old theme of men masquerading as women. Tony Curtis and Jack Lemmon escape from a Chicago nightclub that's being raided, witness the St. Valentine's Day massacre and 'escape' into the anonymity of a girl band by dressing up as feminine musicians. This leads to the obvious complications, particularly since Curtis meets Marilyn Monroe (ukulele player, vocalist and gin addict) and falls for her. Lemmon, in turn, is propositioned by an addle-brained millionaire (Joe E. Brown).

A scene on a train, where the 'private' pull-man berth party of Lemmon and Monroe in her nightie is invaded by guzzling dames, represents humor of Lubitsch proportions. And the alternating shots of Monroe trying to stimulate Curtis on a couch, while Lemmon and Brown live it up on the dance floor, rate as a classic sequence.

Marilyn has never looked better. Her performance as Sugar, the fuzzy blonde who likes saxophone players 'and men with glasses', has a deliciously naive quality. It's a tossup whether Curtis beats out Lemmon or whether it goes the other way round. Both are excellent.

Curtis has the upper hand because he can change back and forth from his femme role to that of a fake 'millionaire' who woos Monroe. He employs a takeoff on Cary Grant, which scores with a bang at first, but tends to lose its appeal as the picture progresses.

Lemmon draws a choice assignment. Some of the funniest bits fall to him, such as his announcement that he's 'engaged' to Brown.

But, in the final accounting, this is still a director's picture and the Wilder touch is indelible. If the action is funny, the lines are there to match it.
□ 1959: Best B&W Costume Design (Corry Kelly)
□ Nominations: Best Director, Actor (Jack Lemmon), Adapted Screenplay, B&W Cinematography, B&W Art Direction

■ **SOMEONE TO LOVE**

1987, 109 MINS, US ◇ ⓥ ⊙
Dir Henry Jaglom *Prod* M.H. Simonsons *Scr* Henry Jaglom *Ph* Hanania Baer
● Orson Welles, Henry Jaglom, Andrea Marcovicci, Michael Emil, Sally Kellerman, Oja Kodar (Rainbow)

Someone To Love represents Henry Jaglom's alternately engaging and chaotic rumination on loneliness and aloneness in the 1980s. A serio-comic psycho-drama in which the filmmaker calls upon his friends to explore why he and they have problems with commitment or finding the right mate, pic is blessed with an almost overwhelming final screen appearance by Orson Welles.

Jaglom plays himself, a director so frustrated at his girlfriend Andrea Marcovicci's unwillingness to settle down he decides to devote an entire feature to what he perceives as a general malaise of his generation.

Without revealing his intentions, Jaglom invites many friends to a St Valentine's Day party who are somewhat taken aback by their host's desire to scrutinize their innermost feelings and insecurities with a camera, and some bow out.

Orson Welles, who appeared in Jaglom's first feature, *A Safe Place* (1971), returns here to act as the younger man's mentor and provocateur as he sits in the back of the theater smoking a cigar and delivering stunningly perceptive and intellectually far-ranging comments.

Also notable is Welles' longtime companion Oja Kodar, who portrays a visiting

Yugoslavian woman with particularly sensitive and personal things to say about being a woman alone. Marcovicci gets to sing impressively and aggravate Jaglom, Sally Kellerman gives a vivid account of what one imagines Sally Kellerman to be like, and Michael Emil here gets his usual humorous philosophical ramblings thrown back in his face for a change.

■ **SOMEONE TO WATCH OVER ME**

1987, 106 MINS, US ◇ ⓥ ⊙
Dir Ridley Scott *Prod* Thierry de Ganay *Scr* Howard Franklin *Ph* Steven Poster *Ed* Claire Simpson *Mus* Michael Kamen *Art Dir* Jim Bissell
● Tom Berenger, Mimi Rogers, Lorraine Bracco, Jerry Orbach, John Rubinstein, Andreas Katsulas (Columbia)

Someone to Watch Over Me is a stylish and romantic police thriller which manages, through the sleek direction of Ridley Scott and persuasive ensemble performances, to triumph over several hard-to-swallow plot developments.

Tom Berenger portrays Mike Keegan, a happily married NY cop from the Bronx who has just been promoted to detective and finds himself assigned on the night shift to protect socialite Claire Gregory (Mimi Rogers), witness to a brutal murder.

Heinous killer Joey Venza, played with economical nuance and menace by Andreas Katsulas, tracks Gregory down at the Guggenheim Museum and terrorizes her in the ladies' room while Keegan is distracted. Though he subsequently chases Venza down and effects the collar, failure to read the goon his rights results in Venza back on the street and Gregory marked for death.

Berenger carries the film handily, utterly convincing as the working class stiff out of his element accompanying Rogers through her elegant apartment or posh parties. Rogers is alluring as the romantic interest, recalling the sharpness and beauty of Laraine Day, while wife, Lorraine Bracco is fully sympathetic and easily has the viewer siding against the two leads during their hanky-panky segments.

■ **SOME PEOPLE**

1962, 93 MINS, UK ◇
Dir Clive Donner *Prod* James Archibald *Scr* John Eldridge *Ph* John Wilcox *Ed* Fergus McDonell *Mus* Ron Grainer *Art Dir* Reece Pemberton
● Kenneth More, Ray Brooks, Annika Wills, Angela Douglas, David Andrews, David Hemmings (Anglo Amalgamated)

This one is something of a hybrid. It is designed as a feature entertainment film, a peek at the problems of modern youth in danger of becoming delinquents. As such it stands up as reasonable entertainment. But also planted firmly in the film, some unabashed propaganda for the Duke of Edinburgh's Award Scheme for youth.

The pic is set in the industrial town of Bristol. Three lads are part of a gang of ton-up motorcyclists. Involved in an accident, they are banned from driving. Then, out of sheer boredom, they become potential young hoods. Luckily, they become involved with Kenneth More, playing a voluntary church choirmaster. He gives them the opportunity of rehearsing their rock 'n' roll combo. And gradually, they become interested in the new pursuits that the Duke's scheme has to offer youngsters of initiative.

John Eldridge's storyline is loose. Clive Donner's direction is leisurely but affectionate.

More handles the role of the sympathetic choirmaster with his usual, easy charm. But the revelation is in the performances of some of the youngsters. Ray Brooks, David Andrews

and David Hemmings play the three main teenagers with authority. Angela Douglas is pretty provocative as a young blonde who can handle a song and a boy with equal assurance.

■ **SOMETHING WICKED THIS WAY COMES**

1983, 94 MINS, US ◇ ⓥ ⊙
Dir Jack Clayton *Prod* Peter Vincent Douglas *Scr* Ray Bradbury *Ph* Stephen H. Burum *Ed* Argyle Nelson *Mus* James Horner *Art Dir* Richard MacDonald
● Jason Robards, Jonathan Pryce, Diane Ladd, Pam Grier, Royal Dano, Vidal Peterson (Walt Disney/Bryna)

Film version of Ray Bradbury's popular novel *Something Wicked This Way Comes* must be chalked up as something of a disappointment. Possibilities for a dark, child's view fantasy set in rural America of yore are visible throughout the $20 million production but various elements have not entirely congealed into a unified achievement.

Location scenes shot in an astonishingly beautiful Vermont autumn stand in for early 20th century Illinois, where two young boys are intrigued by the untimely arrival of a mysterious carnival troupe. By day, fairgrounds seem innocent enough, but by night they possess a strange allure which leads local inhabitants to fall victim to their deepest desires.

Thanks to the diabolical talents of carnival leader Mr Dark, played by the suitably sinister Jonathan Pryce, these wishes can be granted, but at the price of becoming a member of the traveling freak show. Mr Dark decides that little Will and Jim would make excellent recruits and pursues them vigilantly until the apocalyptic finale.

■ **SOMETHING WILD**

1986, 113 MINS, US ◇ ⓥ ⊙
Dir Jonathan Demme *Prod* Jonathan Demme, Kenneth Utt *Scr* E. Max Frye *Ph* Tak Fujimoto *Ed* Craig McKay *Mus* John Cale, Laurie Anderson *Art Dir* Norma Moriceau
● Jeff Daniels, Melanie Griffith, Ray Liotta, Margaret Colin, Tracey Walter, Dana Preu (Religioso Primitiva)

Conceptually and stylistically compelling under Jonathan Demme's sometimes striking direction, this offbeat thriller is about an unlikely couple on the run.

First-time screenwriter E. Max Frye's story sees superyuppie Jeff Daniels being picked up by hot number Melanie Griffith at a luncheonette, driven out to New Jersey and, before he knows what's happening, being handcuffed to a bed and ravished by this crazy lady.

Everything changes at her highschool reunion, however, as Griffith's ex-con husband makes an unexpected appearance and proceeds to change the couple's joyride into a nightmare. From this point on, Demme and Frye adroitly tighten the screws as the focus shifts from Griffith to the showdown between the two utterly different men vying for her attentions.

Daniels does a good job in transforming himself from straitlaced good boy to loosened up, wised-up man. Griffith is provocative enough, but falls a little short in putting across all the aspects of this complicated woman.

■ **SOMETIMES A GREAT NOTION**
(UK: *Never Give an Inch*)

1971, 114 MINS, US ◇ ⓥ
Dir Paul Newman *Prod* John C. Foreman *Scr* John Gay *Ph* Richard Moore *Ed* Bob Wyman *Mus* Henry Mancini *Art Dir* Philip Jefferies
● Paul Newman, Henry Fonda, Lee Remick, Michael Sarrazin, Richard Jaeckel, Linda Lawson (Universal)

Sometimes a Great Notion is a good, if plot-sprawling, outdoor action film set in

Northwest lumber country, about a family of individualists fighting a town and a union. Paul Newman directed, produced, and stars as the crown prince to family patriarch Henry Fonda.

John Gay's adaptation of Ken Kesey's novel tries to balance the intellectual angles – Fonda's rigorous adherence to a principle, Newman's unending follow-through after disaster, and Michael Sarrazin's maturity from a self-indulgent drop-out. The result is rather good – a sort of contemporary 'western' in the timber territory.

Fonda's performance is perhaps his first in a crotchety characterization; there is an artistic overrun, however, which makes the character seem semi-senile instead of rock-ribbed noble. Lee Remick is too chic and sophisticated for her nothing part as Newman's concerned wife.

Sarrazin and Newman come off the best, the latter again in the kind of believable melodramatic role which first made him a star, the former in a demanding role which begins with drop-out petulance mixed with fraternal enmity.

□ 1971: Nominations: Best Supp. Actor (Richard Jaekel), Song ('All His Children')

● ●

■ SOMEWHERE IN TIME

1980, 103 MINS, US ◇ ⓥ ⊙
Dir Jeannot Szwarc   *Prod* Stephen Deutsch   *Scr* Richard Matheson   *Ph* Isidore Mankofsky   *Ed* Jeff Gourson   *Mus* John Barry   *Art Dir* Seymour Klate
● Christopher Reeve, Jane Seymour, Christopher Plummer, Teresa Wright, Bill Erwin, Sean Hayden (Universal/Rastar)

A charming, witty, passionate romantic drama about a love transcending space and time, *Somewhere In Time* is an old-fashioned film in the best sense of that term. Which means it's carefully crafted, civilized in its sensibilities, and interested more in characterization than in shock effects.

In the finely wrought screenplay by veteran fantasy writer Richard Matheson, based on his own novel *Bid Time Return*, Christopher Reeve is a young Chicago playwright who becomes mysteriously fascinated by a 1912 photo of a stage actress (Jane Seymour).

Reeve is drawn to a hotel on Mackinac Island in Michigan, where it transpires they actually did meet and have an affair at the time the photo was taken.

Seymour is lovely and mesmerizing enough to justify Reeve's grand romantic obsession with her.

□ 1971: Nomination: Best Costume Design

● ●

■ SOMMERSBY

1993, 112 MINS, US ◇ ⓥ ⊙
Dir Jon Amiel   *Prod* Arnon Milchan, Steven Reuther   *Scr* Nicholas Meyer, Sarah Kernochan   *Ph* Philippe Rousselot   *Ed* Peter Boyle   *Mus* Danny Elfman   *Art Dir* Bruno Rubeo
● Richard Gere, Jodie Foster, Lanny Flaherty, Wendell Wellman, Bill Pullman, James Earl Jones (Warner/Canal Plus/Regency/Alcor)

Sommersby is an unabashedly romantic and morally intricate Civil War-era tale splendidly acted by Richard Gere and Jodie Foster. It's one of those rare occasions that the Americanization of a foreign property (here Daniel Vigne's *The Return of Martin Guerre*) works as well as the original.

The missing-in-action and presumed dead Jack Sommersby (Gere) suddenly reappears two years after the end of the Civil War and attempts to start life anew with his wife, Laurel (Foster), and young son. Foster breaks off her relationship with the righteous Orin (Bill Pullman) and tentatively resumes her place alongside her husband.

Sommersby returns a new man, as tender

and committed to his wife as he had once been distant and cruel. Naturally, this arouses suspicion about his identity.

The movie keeps the question beautifully balanced in mid-air. Nicholas Meyer and Sarah Kernochan's screenplay (from Meyer and Anthony Shaffer's story) is cogent and elegantly literate. The film's ending is entirely appropriate but will be much debated.

Foster isa compelling actress, telegraphing layer after layer of emotional subtext. But Gere, whose production company developed the film, comes close to stealing the picture.

● ●

■ SONG IS BORN, A

1948, 112 MINS, US ◇ ⓥ
Dir Howard Hawks   *Prod* Samuel Goldwyn   *Scr* [uncredited]   *Ph* Gregg Toland   *Ed* Daniel Mandell   *Mus* Don Raye, Gene De Paul   *Art Dir* George Jenkins, Perry Ferguson
● Danny Kaye, Virginia Mayo, Benny Goodman, Hugh Herbert, Steve Cochran, Louis Armstrong (RKO/Goldwyn)

Picture is a remake of Goldwyn's *Ball of Fire* (1941) starring Gary Cooper and Barbara Stanwyck. Most of Goldwyn's production crew worked on both films, including director, cameraman and editor. Charles Brackett and Billy Wilder screenplayed *Ball* from an original story, *From A to Z*, by Wilder and Thomas Monroe, but there's no screenplay credit given on *Song*.

While *Ball* dealt with a group of stodgy old professors writing a new dictionary and the way a burlesque stripper tossed a bombshell into their work, *Song* presents a similar group of professors, only this time they're compiling a history of music and the stripper is a nitery thrush. When Danny Kaye is working with them before the cameras, in fact, the picture is standout entertainment. Last half of the picture, though, in which they get a semi-brushoff as Kaye becomes involved with a group of gangsters, drags by comparison.

Kaye himself does his usual neat thesping job as the youngest of the bachelor pendants, who gets his first intro to feminine wiles at the hands of a worldlywise nitery singer, played engagingly by Virginia Mayo.

Script makes good use of the various musicians involved. They're spotlighted neatly at the beginning, as Kaye tours various Broadway niteries to get an idea of swing and jazz, which is completely unknown to the professorial group.

● ●

■ SONG OF BERNADETTE, THE

1943, 158 MINS, US ⓥ ⊙
Dir Henry King   *Prod* William Perlberg   *Scr* George Seaton   *Ph* Arthur Miller   *Ed* Barbara McLean   *Mus* Alfred Newman   *Art Dir* James Basevi, William Darling
● Jennifer Jones, Charles Bickford, Gladys Cooper, Vincent Price, Lee J. Cobb, Anne Revere (20th Century-Fox)

Song of Bernadette is an absorbing, emotional and dramatic picturization of Franz Werfel's novel. Film version is a warming and intimate narrative of godly visitation on the young girl of Lourdes which eventuated in establishment of the Shrine at Lourdes, a grotto for the divine healing of the lame and halt.

Sensitively scripted and directed in best taste throughout, *Bernadette* unfolds in leisurely fashion with attention held through deft characterizations and incidents, rather than resort to synthetic dramatics. Many times during the extended running time there are sideline episodes inserted, but even these fail to lessen intense attention to the major theme.

Cast is expertly selected, and even the one-shot bits click solidly in fleeting footage. Jennifer Jones, in title role, delivers an inspirationally sensitive and arresting perfor-

mance. Wistful, naive, and at times angelic, Jones takes command early to hold control as the motivating factor through the lengthy unfolding.

Despite the deeply religious tone of the dramatic narrative, theme is handled with utmost taste and reverence.

□ 1943: Best Actress (Jennifer Jones), B&W Cinematography, B&W Interior Decoration (James Basevi, William Darling), Score for a Dramatic Picture.
□ Nominations: Best Picture, Director, Supp. Actor (Charles Bickford), Supp. Actress (Gladys Cooper, Anne Revere), Screenplay, Editing, Sound

● ●

■ SONG OF CEYLON

1935, 39 MINS, UK
Dir Basil Wright   *Prod* John Grierson   *Ph* Basil Wright   *Mus* Walter Leigh
● (Ceylon Tea Production Board)

This thoroughgoing four-reel travelog on Ceylon attempts to dig down deep and cinematically explain the country and its people in more thorough manner than customarily encountered. Unfortunately it is just a shade too arty.

Had some of the hard-headed realistic *March of Time* approach been used, film would have come off much better. As it stands, the fancy and at time fantastic treatment will largely mystify audiences. In view of the splendid camerawork and some of the sequences, notably the native dances and religious devotions to Buddha, pic should have been aimed at the general public.

Effort to explain the economics and commerce of Ceylon is badly muddled through extensive use of vague or bewildering symbolisms. [Film is narrated by Lionel Wendt.]

● ●

■ SONG OF NORWAY

1970, 138 MINS, US ◇ ⓥ
Dir Andrew L. Stone   *Prod* Andrew L. Stone, Virginia Stone   *Scr* Andrew L. Stone   *Ph* Davis Boulton   *Ed* Virginia Stone   *Mus* Roland Shaw (sup.)   *Art Dir* William Albert Havemeyer
● Toralv Maurstad, Florence Henderson, Christina Schollin, Harry Secombe, Robert Morley, Edward G. Robinson (ABC/Stone)

Production and staging, the Robert Wright-George Forrest music and lyrics based on Norwegian composer Edvard Grieg's music, and wide screen photography make *Song of Norway* a magnificent motion picture. Unfortunately, Andrew L. Stone's screenplay imparts a frequently banal, two-dimensional note featuring a wooden performance by Norwegian actor Toralv Maurstad in this musical biopic.

It is not another *Sound of Music* but screenplay, even with its faults, is superior to the original stage play by Homer Curran.

Maurstad as Grieg, Florence Henderson as the cousin he marries and Frank Porretta as composer Rikard Nordraak, Grieg's closest friend, are primarily required to sing – not bring deep psychological sensitivity to their roles.

Stone shot *Song of Norway* totally on location in Europe at an announced cost of $3.9 million and scenes follow scenes with an irresistible richness. Choreographer Lee Theodore's staging of the musical numbers is smashing.

Harry Secombe gives a hearty, warm portrayal of the Norwegian playwright Bjornson, one of Grieg's early benefactors, displaying a rich, strong voice; Robert Morley imparts a delicate villainy to a role as Schollin's father; and Edward G. Robinson is kindly and concerned as the kindly and concerned old piano teacher.

● ●

SONG OF SCHEHERAZADE

1947, 105 MINS, US ◇
Dir Walter Reisch *Prod* Edward Kaufman *Scr* Walter Reisch *Ph* Hal Mohr, William V. Skall *Ed* Frank Goss *Mus* Miklos Rozsa (adapt.) *Art Dir* Jack Olterson
● Yvonne De Carlo, Brian Donlevy, Jean-Pierre Aumont, Eve Arden, Philip Reed (Universal)

The music of Rimsky-Korsakov and eye value of brilliant color give *Song of Scheherazade* entertainment elements not otherwise found in the fluffy, ineptly directed and played story. Score contains 10 Rimsky-Korsakov tunes, ably adapted to the screen by Miklos Rozsa.

Basis for display of composer's muscle is his supposed escapades during a week in Spanish Morocco. Story has a comic-opera flavor, and Walter Reisch's direction of his own script often wavers in the treatment of plot elements and characters. Adding to ludicrous spots are a variety of accents, topped by the Broadwayese and 20th-century flippancy tossed into the 1865 period by Eve Arden. Plot purports to be based on an incident in Rimsky-Korsakov's life, when he was a midshipman in the Russian Navy, and is aimed at showing the influence the background had on his music.

Jean-Pierre Aumont plays the young composer. Yvonne De Carlo is the Spanish dancer with whom he falls in love during the week's adventuring. Brian Donlevy does a chain-smoking captain of the training ship who tries to make his students the pride of the Russian navy.

SONG OF THE ISLANDS

1942, 73 MINS, US ◇ ⊕ ⊙
Dir Walter Lang *Prod* William Le Baron *Scr* Joseph Schrank, Robert Pirosh, Robert Ellis, Helen Logan *Ph* Ernest Palmer *Ed* Robert Simpson *Mus* Mack Gordon
● Betty Grable, Victor Mature, Jack Oakie, Thomas Mitchell, Hilo Hattie (20th Century-Fox)

Song of the Islands is a spontaneous and breezy mixture of comedy, song, dance and romance – set in Hawaiian atmosphere.

There's plenty of color, a load of romance, and sufficient comedy ladled out in generally broad style to carry audience interest.

Story is only a light and fragile framework on which to hang the various sequences. Betty Grable is the daughter of Thomas Mitchell, philosophical Irish beachcomber, who owns a portion of a small island in the Hawaiian group and treats the natives with consideration.

Victor Mature sails in to visit his father's cattle ranch on the other side of the island, and immediately romance gets under way.

Liberal potions of surefire comedy are supplied by Jack Oakie, who has a field day in byplay with buxom native maid (Hilo Hattie). Fast-paced script is commandeered by consistently zippy direction by Walter Lang.

SONG TO REMEMBER, A

1945, 110 MINS, US ◇ ⊕ ⊗
Dir Charles Vidor *Prod* Sidney Buchman, Louis F. Edelman *Scr* Sidney Buchman *Ph* Tony Gaudio *Ed* Charles Nelson *Mus* Miklos Rozsa (adapt.) *Art Dir* Lionel Banks, Van Nest Polglase
● Paul Muni, Merle Oberon, Cornel Wilde, Stephen Bekassy, George Coulouris, Sig Arno (Columbia)

Based on the colorful – though brief – life of Polish composer Frederic Chopin, picture is a showmanly presentation of intimate drama and music.

Plot [from a story by Ernst Marischka] introduces Chopin as a prodigy at 11, with Paul Muni the old music master who easily recognizes his genius. When 22, the student and teacher flee to Paris after Chopin refuses to perform for the Russian governor. Young Franz Liszt befriends the newcomer and is directly responsible in getting him recognition.

Brilliant performances are generally turned in by the cast, with Muni provoking maximum interest with his portrayal of the music teacher. Cornel Wilde is spotlighted as Chopin and establishes himself as a screen personality. Merle Oberon clicks as the cold and calculating writer.

Jose Iturbi contributes importantly in the overall with his background playing of numerous Chopin compositions. Wilde does a fine job of keyboard manipulations and the visual and sound components blend accurately for realist effect.

Reproduction of the piano passages is the best of its kind that has so far been accomplished, and credit for the achievement must go to John Livadary and the entire Columbia sound department.
☐ 1945: Nominations: Best Actor (Cornel Wilde), Original Story, Color Cinematography, Editing, Scoring of a Musical Picture, Sound

SONG WITHOUT END

1960, 145 MINS, US ◇
Dir Charles Vidor, George Cukor *Prod* William Goetz *Scr* Oscar Millard *Ph* James Wong Howe *Ed* William A. Lyons *Mus* Harry Sukman (arr.) *Art Dir* Walter Holscher
● Dirk Bogarde, Capucine, Genevieve Page, Patricia Morison, Ivan Desny, Martita Hunt (Columbia)

Song Without End dramatizes the story of pianist-composer Franz Liszt. It is a must-see motion picture for music lovers, an enriching experience for family audiences, and a particularly compelling attraction for social security eligibles.

A complex central character, Liszt is depicted as a man tragically embroiled in overlapping romantic, religious and professional conflicts. His relations with the opposite sex are stormy, illicit and ill-fated. Discarding the irreligious mother of his two children, he discovers happiness and the germ of artistic fulfillment during his affair with the devout wife of a Russian prince, only to have it dissolve abruptly on the eve of their wedding.

Where the screenplay is never quite clear is in its concept of Liszt's creative ability. Peerless keyboard technician and interpreter of the genius of his contemporaries, he is regarded as a victim of his own virtuosity.

It is in the production itself that the film attains stature. It is a feast of sight and sound put together by a battery of expert cinema craftsmen. Lensman James Wong Howe zeroes in on the authentic settings with athletic dexterity.

All these skills have been integrated into an impressive physical whole by directors Charles Vidor and George Cukor, but they were not as uniformly successful in commandeering a matching dramatic spirit from the cast.

Vidor died on June 4 1959, having filmed about 15% of the picture. He got full director's title at request of Cukor who took a smaller screen credit.
☐ 1960: Best Scoring of a Musical Picture

SONGWRITER

1984, 94 MINS, US ◇ ⊕ ⊙
Dir Alan Rudolph *Prod* Sydney Pollack *Scr* Bud Shrake *Ph* Matthew Leonetti *Ed* Stuart Pappe *Mus* Larry Cansler *Art Dir* Joel Schiller
● Willie Nelson, Kris Kristofferson, Melinda Dillon, Rip Torn, Lesley Ann Warren, Richard C. Sarafian (Tri-Star)

Songwriter is a good-natured film that rolls along on the strength of attitudes and poses long ago established outside the picture by its stars, Willie Nelson and Kris Kristofferson, basically playing themselves disguised as fictional characters.

Brief opening collage establishes the younger days of Doc Jenkins (Nelson) and Blackie Buck (Kristofferson) as a performing duo before they go their semi-separate ways and revert to character.

Doc Jenkins is the saint of country music, loved and respected by everyone. Luckily Nelson has enough of a screen presence to support his deification. As Blackie Buck, Kristofferson is still the outlaw with a heart of gold, but who will probably never grow up and settle down.

Director Alan Rudolph, who took over for Steve Rash two weeks into the filming, is best at working with actors, and Lesley Ann Warren, in particular, is radiant as an up-and-coming, but reluctant country & western singer.
☐ 1984: Nomination: Best Original Song Score

SON OF PALEFACE

1952, 95 MINS, US ◇ ⊕ ⊙
Dir Frank Tashlin *Prod* Robert L. Welch *Scr* Frank Tashlin, Robert L. Welch, Joseph Quillan *Ph* Harry J. Wild *Ed* Eda Warren, Ellsworth Hoagland *Mus* Lyn Murray *Art Dir* Hal Perira, Roland Anderson
● Bob Hope, Jane Russell, Roy Rogers, Bill Williams, Lloyd Corrigan, Paul E. Burns (Paramount)

A free-wheeling, often hilarious, rambunctious followup to *The Paleface*. It is the broadest kind of slapstick, drawing advantageously on the silent-day masters of the pratfalls.

Plot finds Roy Rogers and Lloyd Corrigan, government agents, assigned to the case of running down 'The Torch', a bandit and gang that is looting gold shipments and then mysteriously disappearing. The job is complicated by the appearance in the small western town of Sawbuck Pass of Hope, the Harvard grad son of the late Paleface Potter.

A supercilious, cowardly braggart, Hope complicates matters temporarily until the agents decide to use him to confirm their suspicions that Jane Russell, the long-legged, amorous keeper of the Dirty Shame saloon, is the leader of the robbers.
☐ 1952: Nomination: Best Song ('Am I in Love?')

SONS AND LOVERS

1960, 99 MINS, UK
Dir Jack Cardiff *Prod* Jerry Wald *Scr* Gavin Lambert, T.E.B. Clarke *Ph* Freddie Francis *Ed* Gordon Pilkington *Art Dir* Tom Morahan
● Trevor Howard, Dean Stockwell, Wendy Hiller, Mary Ure, Heather Sears, William Lucas (20th Century-Fox)

Sons and Lovers is a well-made and conscientious adaptation of D. H. Lawrence's famed novel, smoothly directed by Jack Cardiff and superbly acted by a notable cast.

Gavin Lambert and T. E. B. Clarke collaborated in producing a literate screenplay, though not entirely recapturing the atmosphere of the Nottinghamshire mining village so vividly described in the original. Also there is a tendency to portray the mother as an overly selfish, possessive and nagging woman. Even Wendy Hiller's flawless performance cannot make her a sympathetic character.

Many of the exteriors were filmed on location outside Nottingham, and their authenticity is a plus factor. Against the background of the grimy mining village is unfolded the story of a miner's son with promising artistic talents who is caught up in continual conflict between his forthright father and possessive mother. He sacrifices a chance to study art in London, gives up the local farm girl he loves, and eventually becomes entangled with a married woman separated from her husband.

Easily the outstanding feature of the production is the powerful performance by Trevor Howard, as the miner. He gives a moving and wholly believable study of a man equally capable of tenderness as he is of being tough. He looks the character, too. Dean Stockwell puts up a good showing as the son, and makes a valiant try to cope with the accent.

□ 1960: Best B&W Cinematography.
□ Nominations: Best Picture, Director, Actor (Trevor Howard), Supp. Actress (Mary Ure), Adapted Screenplay, B&W Art Direction

■ SONS OF KATIE ELDER, THE

1965, 120 MINS, US ◇ ⊕ ⊙
Dir Henry Hathaway *Prod* Hal Wallis *Scr* William H. Wright, Allan Weiss, Harry Essex *Ph* Lucien Ballard *Ed* Warren Low *Mus* Elmer Bernstein *Art Dir* Hal Pereira, Walter Tyler
● John Wayne, Dean Martin, Martha Hyer, Michael Anderson Jr, Earl Holliman, Denis Hopper (Paramount)

Talbot Jennings' story tells of four brothers – John Wayne a notorious gunslinger, Dean Martin a gambler – who return to their Texas home to attend their mother's funeral and remain to fight the town.

Two stars are joined by Earl Holliman and Michael Anderson Jr, latter the kid brother, in family setup. The three older brothers are prodigals who left home years before. The mother is never shown, but her influence is felt throughout the film as the three seniors decide that the best monument they can erect for their mother is to send her last-born back to college.

Drama takes form as the brothers decide to stay long enough to learn who murdered their father six months previously, look into the situation of their mother losing her ranch to a townsman, and a grim young deputy sheriff learning Martin is wanted for murder and deciding to bring the brothers in.

Wayne delivers one of his customary rugged portrayals, a little old, perhaps, to have such a young brother as Anderson but not so old that he lacks the attributes of a gunman. Martin, who plays his part with a little more humor than the others, is equally effective in a hardboiled characterization.

■ SOPHIE'S CHOICE

1982, 157 MINS, US ◇ ⊕ ⊙
Dir Alan J. Pakula *Prod* Alan J. Pakula, Keith Barish *Scr* Alan J. Pakula *Ph* Nestor Almendros *Ed* Evan Lottman *Mus* Marvin Hamlisch *Art Dir* George Jenkins
● Meryl Streep, Kevin Kline, Peter MacNicol, Rita Karin, Stephen D. Newman, Josh Mostel (ITC)

Sophie's Choice is a handsome, doggedly faithful and astoundingly tedious adaptation of William Styron's best-seller.

Set in 1947, tale has young aspiring writer Stingo (Peter MacNicol), a southern lad, taking a room in a comfortable house in which also dwell Sophie (Meryl Streep), a Polish former Catholic, and her exuberant, changeable, Jewish lover, Nathan Landau (Kevin Kline). Three become best of friends, although at times Nathan turns on the other two, leaving Stingo to console Sophie and hear some of her painful confessions about her pre-war life and incarceration by the Nazis.

Ever so slowly, it comes clear that Sophie has lied about many things, notably her father. After 90 minutes, film flips into a halfhour, subtitled, sepiatoned flashback to portray Sophie's tenure as secretary to the commanding officer at Auschwitz.

Streep, Kline and MacNicol all give it a good shot individually, but they never coalesce into the close, warm trio called for by the story.

□ 1982: Best Actress (Meryl Streep)
□ Nominations: Best Screenplay Adaptation, Cinematography, Costume Design, Original Score

■ SO PROUDLY WE HAIL!

1943, 126 MINS, US
Dir Mark Sandrich *Prod* Mark Sandrich *Scr* Allan Scott *Ph* Charles Lang *Ed* Ellsworth Hoagland *Mus* Miklos Rozsa
● Claudette Colbert, Paulette Goddard, Veronica Lake, George Reeves, Barbara Britton, Sonny Tufts (Paramount)

Mark Sandrich's *So Proudly We Hail!* is a saga of the war-front nurse and her heroism under fire. As such it glorifies the American Red Cross and presents the wartime nurse, in the midst of unspeakable dangers, physical and spiritual, in a new light.

Director-producer Sandrich and scripter Allen Scott have limned a vivid, vital story. It's backgrounded against a realistic romance of how a group of brave American Nightingales came through the hellfire to Australia and thence back to Blighty.

Done in flashback manner, with Claudette Colbert rapidly sinking physically, the saga of their travail pitches to the situation where, out of the past, a love letter from her officer-lover finally brings her back on the road to recovery. Paulette Goddard does a capital job as running mate, and Veronica Lake is the sullen nurse who finally sees the light.

Sonny Tufts walks off with the picture every time he's on. As Kansas, the blundering ex-footballer, he's Goddard's vis-a-vis. George Reeves isn't as effective as the romantic opposite to Colbert.

□ 1943: Nomination: Best Supp. Actress (Paulette Goddard), Original Screenplay, B&W Cinematography, Special Effects

■ SORCERER
(UK: Wages of Fear)

1977, 121 MINS, US ◇ ⊕ ⊙
Dir William Friedkin *Prod* William Friedkin *Scr* Walon Green *Ph* John M. Stephens, Dick Bush *Ed* Bud Smith *Mus* Charlie Parker *Art Dir* John Box
● Roy Scheider, Bruno Cremer, Francisco Rabal, Amidou, Ramon Bieri, Peter Capell (Universal/Paramount)

William Friedkin's *Sorcerer* is a painstaking, admirable, but mostly distant and uninvolving suspenser based on the French classic *The Wages of Fear* [from the novel by Georges Arnaud]. Friedkin vividly renders the experience of several men driving trucks loaded with nitro through the South American jungle. The drivers are Roy Scheider, Bruno Cremer, Amidou and Francisco Rabal.

The story has a strong existential feeling, desperate men staking their lives on a suicidal mission because they have no other way of making a living.

But despite the opening scenes – of Scheider involved in a New Jersey robbery, Cremer in a French bank scandal, and Amidou in an Arab terrorist incident – the film fails to bring them alive as people.

□ 1977: Nomination: Best Sound

■ SORCERERS, THE

1967, 86 MINS, UK ◇ ⊕
Dir Michael Reeves *Prod* Patrick Curtis, Tony Tenser *Scr* Michael Reeves, Tom Baker *Ph* Stanley Long *Ed* Ralph Sheldon *Mus* Paul Ferris *Art Dir* Tony Curtis
● Boris Karloff, Catherine Lacey, Ian Ogilvy, Elizabeth Ercy, Victor Henry, Susan George (Tigon)

Boris Karloff brings his familiar adroit horror touch to the role of an aging somewhat nutty ex-stage mesmerist who aims to complete his experiments by dominating the brain of a young subject. Karloff himself is dominated by his wife (Catherine Lacey), who was his stage assistant.

Karloff persuades Ian Ogilvy, who plays a feckless, slightly moody youth, to become the subject for his experiments. Initial experiments work well as Karloff sees in the youth a tool who may be able to benefit mankind un-

der his influence. But Karloff's wife, motivated by greed, insists that the lad should work for their benefit for a while.

■ SORRY, WRONG NUMBER

1948, 89 MINS, US ⊕
Dir Anatole Litvak *Prod* Hal B. Wallis, Anatole Litvak *Scr* Lucille Fletcher *Ph* Sol Polito *Ed* Warren Low *Mus* Franz Waxman *Art Dir* Hans Dreier, Earl Hedrick
● Barbara Stanwyck, Burt Lancaster, Ann Richards, Wendell Corey, Ed Begley (Wallis/Paramount)

Sorry, Wrong Number is a real chiller. Film is a fancily dressed co-production by Hal B. Wallis and Anatole Litvak. Pair has smoothly coordinated efforts to give strong backing to the Lucille Fletcher script, based on her radio play.

Plot deals with an invalid femme who overhears a murder scheme through crossed telephone lines. Alone in her home, the invalid tries to trace the call. She fails, and then tries to convince the police of the danger. She gradually comes to realize that it is her own death that is planned.

Barbara Stanwyck plays her role of the invalid almost entirely in bed. Her reading is sock, the actress giving an interpretation that makes the neurotic, selfish woman understandable. Same touch is used by Burt Lancaster to make audiences see through the role of the invalid's husband and how he came to plot her death.

Considerable emphasis is placed on the score by Franz Waxman to heighten the gradually mounting suspense. Sol Polito uses an extremely mobile camera for the same effect, sharpening the building terror with unusual angles and lighting.

□ 1948: Nomination: Best Actress ((Barbara Stanwyck)

■ SOUL MAN

1986, 101 MINS, US ◇ ⊕ ⊙
Dir Steve Miner *Prod* Steve Tisch *Scr* Carol Black *Ph* Jeffrey Jur *Ed* David Finfer *Mus* Tom Scott *Art Dir* Gregg Fonseca
● C. Thomas Howell, Arye Gross, Rae Dawn Chong, James Earl Jones, Melora Hardin, Leslie Nielsen (Balcour/Tisch)

This social farce is excellently written, fast paced and intelligently directed.

Film is hilarious throughout as initial screenplay by Carol Black consistently engages via fable-like tale of a white man (C. Thomas Howell) darkening his skin in order to win a law-school scholarship intended for a black.

Director Steve Miner skillfully guides pic through visually compelling scenes, producing a comedic review of the state of America's racist attitudes.

Howell as the white-turned-black law student is just effective enough to be believable. As Howell's close buddy, Arye Gross delivers gifted and energized screen humor. Rae Dawn Chong is wholly natural and intellectually appealing. Her reluctant romantic involvement with Howell focuses his ultimate moral dilemma over the skin deception.

■ SOUND AND THE FURY, THE

1959, 115 MINS, US
Dir Martin Ritt *Prod* Jerry Wald *Scr* Irving Ravetch, Harriet Frank Jr *Ph* Charles G. Clarke *Ed* Stuart Gilmore *Mus* Alex North
● Yul Brynner, Joanne Woodward, Margaret Leighton, Stuart Whitman, Ethel Waters, Jack Warden (20th Century-Fox)

Considerable talents have gotten together to make *The Sound and the Fury* a work of cinematic stature. It is a mature, provocative and sensitively executed study of the decadent remnants of an erstwhile eminent family of a small southern town, from the William Faulkner allegorical novel.

The Compsons are two brothers, one a weak alcoholic and the other a mute idiot (John Beal and Jack Warden), and a sister (Margaret Leighton) who has a long history of promiscuity. Their father, before his own death, had taken on a stepson (Yul Brynner). Latter in turn has taken on the Compson name and rules as master over a decrepit estate and his wretched second-hand relatives.

Subject to his control also is Joanne Woodward, cast as Leighton's youthful, illegitimate daughter. A Negro servant family, headed by Ethel Waters, completes the cast of residents.

Woodward gives firm conviction to the part of the girl who, somewhat giddily, takes up with a crude mechanic (lecherous, barechested type) who's in town with a traveling carnival (Stuart Whitman).

Leighton is remarkably realistic as the washed-out hag. Brynner is every inch the household tyrant. The Mississippi settings are unusually effective in communicating atmosphere.

■ SOUND BARRIER, THE
(US: Breaking the Sound Barrier)

1952, 118 MINS, UK ⊗
Dir David Lean *Prod* David Lean *Scr* Terence Rattigan *Ph* Jack Hildyard *Ed* Geoffrey Foot *Mus* Malcolm Arnold *Art Dir* Vincent Korda
● Ralph Richardson, Ann Todd, Nigel Patrick, John Justin, Dinah Sheridan, Joseph Tomelty (London)

Technically, artistically and emotionally, this is a topflight British offering.

Dwarfing the individual performers, good though they are, are the magnificent air sequences, with impressive and almost breathtaking dives by the jet as it attempts to crash the sound barrier.

The visionary in the film is superbly played by Ralph Richardson. His ambition to make the first faster-than-sound plane has brought him nothing but grief and disaster. He sees his only son killed in his first solo try; he accepts the estrangement of his daughter (Ann Todd) when his son-in-law (Nigel Patrick) crashes while making the first attempt to crash the barrier.

Ann Todd's portrayal of the daughter correctly yields the emotional angle. David Lean's direction is bold and imaginative.
□ 1952: Best Sound Recording (London Film Sound Dept)
□ Nomination: Best Story & Screenplay

■ SOUNDER

1972, 105 MINS, US ◇ ⊗ ⊙
Dir Martin Ritt *Prod* Robert B. Radnitz *Scr* Lonne Elder III *Ph* John Alonzo *Ed* Sid Levin *Mus* Taj Mahal *Art Dir* Walter Herndon
● Cicely Tyson, Paul Winfield, Kevin Hooks, Carmen Mathews, Taj Mahal, Janet MacLachlan (20th Century Fox)

Sounder is an outstanding film. The superb production depicts the heart-warming and character-building struggles of a poor black sharecropper family in the Depression era. Martin Ritt's masterful direction, an excellent adaptation [from William H. Armstrong's novel], and a uniformly terrific cast make this a film which transcends space, race, age and time. Ritt's sensitive, gentle and delicate style is mated well with script and cast.

Appearing in his first major theatrical role is Kevin Hooks, excellent as the eldest son who assumes the challenges of manhood when his father (Paul Winfield) is sentenced to a year at hard labor for stealing some food for his family.

Winfield is a smash in combining youth and mature virility into a figure of parental authority and parental love. His scenes with Hooks are magnificent, as are his interactions with Cicely Tyson as his wife.
□ 1972: Nominations: Best Picture, Actor (Paul Winfield), Actress (Cicely Tyson), Adapted Screenplay

■ SOUND OF MUSIC, THE

1965, 173 MINS, US ◇ ⊗ ⊙
Dir Robert Wise *Prod* Robert Wise *Scr* Ernest Lehman *Ph* Ted McCord, Paul Beeson *Ed* William Reynolds *Mus* Irwin Kostal (arr.) *Art Dir* Boris Leven
● Julie Andrews, Christopher Plummer, Eleanor Parker, Richard Haydn, Peggy Wood, Charmian Carr (20th Century-Fox)

The magic and charm of the Rodgers-Hammerstein-Lindsay-Crouse 1959 stage hit are sharply blended in this filmic translation. The Robert Wise production is a warmly-pulsating, captivating drama set to the most imaginative use of the lilting R-H tunes, magnificently mounted and with a brilliant cast headed by Julie Andrews and Christopher Plummer.

Wise drew on the same team of creative talent associated with him on *West Side Story* to convert the stage property, with its natural physical limitations, to the more expansive possibilities of the camera.

For the story of the Von Trapp family singers, of the events leading up to their becoming a top concert attraction just prior to the Second World War and their fleeing Nazi Austria, Wise went to the actual locale, Salzburg, and spent 11 weeks limning his action amidst the pageantry of the Bavarian Alps.

Against such background the tale of the postulant at Nonnberg Abbey in Salzburg who becomes governess to widower Captain Von Trapp and his seven children, who brings music into a household that had, until then, been run on a strict naval office regimen, with no frivolity permitted, takes on fresh meaning.

Andrews endows her role of the governess who aspires to be a nun, but instead falls in love with Navy Captain Von Trapp and marries him, with fine feeling and a sense of balance which assures continued star stature. Plummer also is particularly forceful as Von Trapp, former Austrian Navy officer who rather than be drafted into service under Hitler prefers to leave his homeland.

Playing the part of the baroness, whom the captain nearly married, Eleanor Parker acquits herself with style.
□ 1965: Best Picture, Director, Sound (20th Century-Fox Sound Dept), Adapted Musical Scoring, Editing.
□ Nominations: Best Actress (Julie Andrews), Supp. Actress (Peggy Wood), Color Cinematography (Ted McCord), Color Art Direction, Color Costume Design

■ SOURSWEET

1989, 110 MINS, UK ◇ ⊗
Dir Mike Newell *Prod* Roger Randall-Cutler *Scr* Ian McEwan *Ph* Michael Gerfath *Ed* Mick Audsley *Mus* Richard Hartley *Art Dir* Adrian Smith
● Sylvia Chang, Danny Dun, Jodi Long, Soon-Teck Oh, William Chow (First/British Screen/Zenith)

Soursweet is an aptly titled charmer about a Chinese family living in a dismal suburb of London. Pic sympathetically explores the insidious ways in which Chinese emigrants have to adapt to life in Britain after moving to London from Hong Kong.

Adapted from Timothy Mo's novel, the film opens with an elaborate wedding ceremony for a young couple (Sylvia Chang, Danny Dun) held on the outskirts of Hong Kong. Shortly after, the couple moves to London,

where Dun finds work as a waiter in a crowded Chinatown restaurant.

Dun goes through a period in which he becomes indebted to a seedy moneylender who works for one of the two gangs who seem to control the Chinatown underworld. The couple soon moves to the suburbs, where they start a modest Chinese restaurant in a rented house. After a slow start, the place prospers, and gradually friendly links are formed with the locals.

It's the small details that are most significant. The way a little boy discovers at school that the Chinese way of fighting, taught to him by his mother, is considered unfair. Or the way traditional Chinese customs give way in the face of British culture and lifestyle; french fries replace noodles.

■ SOUTH CENTRAL

1992, 99 MINS, US ◇ ⊗ ⊙
Dir Steve Anderson *Prod* Janet Yang, William B. Steakley *Scr* Steve Anderson *Ph* Charlie Lieberman *Ed* Steve Nevius *Mus* Tim Truman *Art Dir* David Brian Miller, Marina Kieser
● Glenn Plummer, Byron Keith Minns, Lexie D. Bigham, Vincent Craig Dupree, LaRita Shelby, Kevin Best (Warner/Ixtlan)

As a cautionary tale about the nihilistic life of street gangs, *South Central* speaks eloquently to black kids desperately in need of straight talk. A profoundly moving story of a father's attempt to save his son from his own mistakes, Steve Anderson's film has performances by Glenn Plummer and young Christian Coleman that will touch any viewer.

Based on a novel by an LA teacher [Donald Bakeer's *Crips*], starting in 1981, pic picks up Plummer as a hardened gang leader getting out of jail and drifting back into the clutches of charismatic Deuces boss Byron Keith Minns, who wants to take over the local drug business from ruthless pusher/pimp Kevin Best.

Since Best has appropriated Plummer's PCP-addict wife (LaRita Shelby), Plummer is easily manipulated into murdering the pusher, which sends him to prison for 10 years. While in the slammer, Plummer is transformed into a man of reason and idealism by his Muslim cellmate (Carl Lumbly).

The direction is suitably unobtrusive and tech credits are pro.

■ SOUTHERN COMFORT

1981, 100 MINS, US ◇ ⊗ ⊙
Dir Walter Hill *Prod* David Giler *Scr* Michael Kane, Walter Hill, David Giler *Ph* Andrew Laszlo *Ed* Freeman Davies *Mus* Ry Cooder *Art Dir* John Vallone
● Keith Carradine, Powers Boothe, Fred Ward, Franklyn Seales, T.K. Carter, Peter Coyote (20th Century-Fox)

An arresting exercise in visual filmmaking and a tautly told suspenser about men out of their depths in the Louisiana swamps, *Southern Comfort* is hardly a cinematic equivalent of the libation of the same name. It's an elemental drama of survival in a threatening environment, and the traditional themes of group camaraderie and mutual support are turned inside out.

Set in 1973, tale presents nine National Guard members, weekend soldiers, heading out into the bayou for practice maneuvers. They make the mistake of appropriating some canoes belonging to local Cajuns, and when the densest of the group commits the lunacy of firing (blanks) at some native pursuers the ill-prepared unit finds itself in a virtual state of war with forbidding area's inhabitants.

Pic is most exciting as a visual experience, as Walter Hill once again proves himself a

S

consummate filmmaker with a great talent for mood, composition and action choreography. Also outstanding is Ry Cooder's unusual score, which makes use of spare, offbeat instrumentation as well as some authentic Cajun music. Acting-wise, this is an ensemble piece, and all hands contribute strongly.

. . . .

■ SOUTHERNER, THE

1945, 91 MINS, US ▼

Dir Jean Renoir *Prod* David L. Loew, Robert Hakim
Scr Jean Renoir *Ph* Lucien Andriot *Ed* Gregg G. Tallas
Mus Werner Janssen *Art Dir* Eugene Lourie
● Zachary Scott, Betty Field, Beulah Bondi, Percy Kilbride, J. Carrol Naish, Jay Gilpin, Charles Kemper
(Producing Artists)

There is something distressing about the haphazards of the soil's human migrants, and all the squalor that one associates with their condition is brought to *The Southerner*. An adaptation [by Hugo Butler] from the George Sessions Perry novel, *Hold Autumn in Your Hand*, this film conjures a naked picture of morbidity. It may be trenchant realism, but these are times when there is a greater need. Escapism is the word.

The Southerner creates too little hope for a solution to the difficulties of farm workers who constantly look forward to the day when they can settle forever their existence of poverty with a long-sought harvest – a harvest that invariably never comes.

This is, specifically, the story of Sam and Nona, and their struggle to cultivate the rich earth of their mid-west farm. It is a farm beset by liabilities, of which lack of money and food are no small factors. Their home is a patchwork of sagging planks and misguided faith.

Zachary Scott and Betty Field give fine performances, as do Beulah Bondi, the grandmother, Percy Kilbride, Charles Kemper and J. Carrol Naish.

□ 1945: Nominations: Best Director, Scoring of a Dramatic Picture, Sound

. . . .

■ SOUTH PACIFIC

1958, 170 MINS, US ◇ ▼ ☉

Dir Joshua Logan *Prod* Buddy Adler *Scr* Paul Osborn
Ph Leon Shamroy *Ed* Robert Simpson *Mus* Alfred Newman (dir.) *Art Dir* Lyle R. Wheeler, John DeCuir
● Rossano Brazzi, Mitzi Gaynor, John Kerr, Ray Walston, Juanita Hall, France Nuyen (20th Century-Fox/South Pacific Enterprises/Magna)

South Pacific is a compelling entertainment. The songs, perennial favorites, are mated to a sturdy James A. Michener story. Combination boffo.

Mitzi Gaynor is no Mary Martin but there are millions who never saw the original Nellie Forbush. Rossano Brazzi may be no Ezio Pinza but the late, great Metropolitan Opera basso profundo hasn't the global b.o. impact of the Italian film-star-gone-Hollywood. Besides, Giorgio Tozzi's dubbed basso has been skillfully integrated into the Brazzi brand of romantic antics.

The histrionics are effective throughout and of high standard. John Kerr (vocally dubbed by Bill Lee) is the right romantic vis-a-vis for Eurasian beauty France Nuyen, daughter of the bawdy 'Bloody Mary' whom Juanita Hall recreates for the screen. She's of the Broadway original and like most of the other principals has been given a vocal stand-in (Muriel Smith, but unbilled; Tozzi alone gets screen credit as Brazzi's ghost voice). Ray Walston is capital as the uninhibited seabee Luther Billis, recreating the role he did in the road company and in London.

Gaynor is uneven in her overall impact. She is in her prime with 'Honey-Bun' in that captivating misfit sailor's uniform, and she is properly gay and buoyant and believable in

'Wonderful Guy'. In other sequences she is conventional. No dubbee she, Gaynor's song-and-dance is essentially very professional.

Brazzi is properly serious of mien and earnest in his love protestations. The seabees are forthrightly dame-hungry; and there is enough cheesecake among the nurses corps to decorate the beachhead. Their treatment of 'Nothing Like a Dame' is standout.

From 'Some Enchanted Evening' to 'My Girl Back Home', it's a surefire score. It's probably the greatest galaxy of popular favorites from a single show in the history of musical comedy. 'Home' was originally in the legit score, was eliminated for show's length but, a favorite with R&H, reinstated into the film version.

All the other credits are topflight – the Alfred Newman baton, the Ken Darby musical assist, and all that goes with this $5 million spectacle.

□ 1958: Best Sound (Todd-AO Sound Dept)
□ Nominations: Best Color Cinematography, Scoring of a Musical Picture

. . . .

■ SOUTH RIDING

1938, 91 MINS, UK ▼

Dir Victor Saville *Prod* Victor Saville *Scr* Ian Dalrymple, Donald Bull *Ph* Harry Stradling *Ed* Hugh Stewart, Jack Dennis *Mus* Richard Addinsell
Art Dir Lazare Meerson
● Edna Best, Ralph Richardson, Edmund Gwenn, Ann Todd, John Clements, Marie Lohr (London)

There are enough requisites in this English melodrama [from a novel by Winifred Holtby] to excite attention. It is fairly familiar matter – the spoiled child whose father fears she will grow up to be like her stark-mad mother, the conniving contractor and real estate operator, and the country gentleman whose intense love of his estate nearly enables the crooked plot to hatch. But all of this has been heightened by original twirls of acting and direction.

Many incidental plot threads are dragged in at the sacrifice of more vital episodes. An example is the flashback to show how the estate owner's wife became demented, obviously to display Ann Todd's histrionics.

The affair the week-kneed councilman is supposed to have had with a country damsel is not obvious enough for average American audiences.

Edna Best is tops in the film as the school teacher. Ralph Richardson contributes one of his finer thespian jobs as the country gentleman. John Clements, who resembles Gary Cooper, also is top flight as the ambitious young councilman. Glynis Johns, in the role of the headstrong daughter of the wealthy estate holder, shows promise.

Title of film, derives from a supposed judicial district. Actually there is no 'South' Riding, the other divisions being East, West and North.

. . . .

■ SOUTH SEAS ADVENTURE

1958, 120 MINS, US ◇

Dir Carl Dudley, Richard Goldstone, Francis D. Lyon, Walter Thompson, Basil Wrangell *Prod* Carl Dudley, Richard Goldstone *Scr* Charles Kaufman, Joseph Ansen, Harold Medford *Ph* John F. Warren, Paul Hill
Ed Frederick Y. Smith, Walter Stern *Mus* Alex North
Art Dir Dan Cathcart, Ray Morris, Eric Thompson
● (Cinerama)

If *South Seas Adventure* were not No. 5 in a sequence of [three-camera Cinerama] travelogs its merits would no doubt seem more estimable. Here again is the airplane ride over the snow, the ocean, the endless prairie. Glacial and other geologic wonders, raging waters and smouldering volcanic mud are again glanced. There is even once again the ride in the amusement park.

Yet the voyage by liner, schooner and air-

craft adds up to a fairly diverting if not very exciting journey. Cinerama still conveys its unique brand of pictorial experience, though distortion and seams persist.

Continuity is pretty straightforward, dotted with a few giggles but eschewing the purple prose, and especially the built-in songplugs and private exploitation which marred *Search for Paradise*.

Some confusion results from the use of a main narrator, Orson Welles, but spelled off in different sequences by three other narrators, Shepherd Menken, Walter Coy, Ted de Corsia. Alex North's score stays in the background, where it belongs, most of the time, but in some of the flying and Australian scenes, notably the demented steeplechase of the kangaroos, the music comes forward strongly and imaginatively.

This is an updated and primarily respectable South Seas in which Paul Gauguin is only a name and cannibalism, beach-combing, Somerset Maugham, Robert Louis Stevenson and J.C. Furnas tales are not on the screen. Big physical thrill among the islands is the jump off the bamboo tower by the natives of the New Hebrides, the fall being broken by vine ropes attached to the men's ankles.

. . . .

■ SOYLENT GREEN

1973, 97 MINS, US ◇ ▼ ☉

Dir Richard Fleischer *Prod* Walter Seltzer, Russell Thatcher *Scr* Stanley R. Greenberg *Ph* Richard H. Kline *Ed* Samuel E. Boetley *Mus* Fred Myrow
Art Dir Edward C. Carfagno
● Charlton Heston, Leigh Taylor-Young, Chuck Connors, Joseph Cotten, Brock Peters, Edward G. Robinson
(M-G-M)

The somewhat plausible and proximate horrors in the story of *Soylent Green* carry the production over its awkward spots to the status of a good futuristic exploitation film.

The year is 2022, the setting NY City, where millions of over-populated residents exist in a smog-insulated police state, where the authorities wear strange-looking foreign uniforms (not the gray flannel suits which is more likely the case), and where real food is a luxury item. Charlton Heston is a detective assigned to the assassination murder of industrialist Joseph Cotten, who has discovered the shocking fact that the Soylent Corp, of which he is a director, is no longer capable of making synthetic food from the dying sea. The substitute – the reconstituted bodies of the dead.

The character Heston plays is pivotal, since he is supposed to be the prototype average man of the future who really swallows whole the social system. Edward G. Robinson, his investigative aide, reminisces about the old days – green fields, flowers, natural food, etc. But the script bungles seriously by confining Heston's outrage to the secret of Soylent Green.

. . . .

■ SPACEBALLS

1987, 96 MINS, US ◇ ▼ ☉

Dir Mel Brooks *Prod* Mel Brooks *Scr* Mel Brooks, Thomas Meehan, Ronny Graham *Ph* Nick McLean
Ed Conrad Buff IV, Nicholas C. Smith *Mus* John Morris
Art Dir Terence Marsh
● Mel Brooks, John Candy, Rick Moranis, Bill Pullman, Daphne Zuniga, John Hurt, Dick Van Patten (M-G-M/Brooksfilms)

Mel Brooks will do anything for a laugh. Unfortunately, what he does in *Spaceballs*, a misguided parody of the *Star Wars* adventures, isn't very funny.

Pic features Bill Pullman as Lone Starr and Daphne Zuniga as Princess Vespa, former a composite of Harrison Ford and Mark Hamill, latter a Carrie Fisher clone.

Pullman's partner is John Candy as Barf, a half-man, half-dog creature who is his own best friend. Equipped with a constantly wagging tale and furry sneakers, Barf is one of the better comic creations here.

The plot about the ruthless race of Spaceballs out to steal the air supply from the planet Druidia is more cliched than the original. Brooks turns up in the dual role of President Skroob of Spaceballs and the all-knowing, all-powerful Yogurt.

Brooks' direction is far too static to suggest the sweeping style of the *Star Wars* epics and pic more closely resembles Flash Gordon programmers. Aside from a few isolated laughs *Spaceballs* is strictly not kosher.

■ **SPACECAMP**

1986, 107 MINS, US ◇ ⑨ ⊙
Dir Harry Winer *Prod* Patrick Bailey *Scr* W.W. Wicket, [= Clifford Green, Ellen Green], Casey T. Mitchell *Ph* William A. Fraker *Ed* John W. Wheeler, Timothy Board *Mus* John Williams *Art Dir* Richard MacDonald
● Kate Capshaw, Lea Thompson, Kelly Preston, Larry B. Scott, Leaf Phoenix, Tate Donovan (ABC)

SpaceCamp is a youthful view of outer space set at the real-life United States Space Camp in Huntsville, Alabama for aspiring young astronauts. Pic never successfully integrates summer camp hijinks with outer space idealism to come up with a dramatically compelling story.

Hampered by cliche-ridden dialog, performances suffer from a weightlessness of their own. Kate Capshaw as the instructor and one trained astronaut to make the flight neither looks nor acts the part of a serious scientist.

As for the kids, Tate Donovan as the shuttle commander-in-training is uninteresting and Lea Thompson as his would-be girlfriend is too young and naive for words, even the ones she's given.

■ **SPACEHUNTER**
ADVENTURES IN THE FORBIDDEN ZONE

1983, 90 MINS, US ◇ ⑨ ⊙
Dir Lamont Johnson *Prod* Don Carmody, John Dunning, Andre Link *Scr* Edith Rey, David Preston, Dan Goldberg, Len Blum *Ph* Frank Tidy *Ed* Scott Conrad *Mus* Elmer Bernstein *Art Dir* Jackson DeGovia
● Peter Strauss, Molly Ringwald, Ernie Hudson, Andrea Marcovicci, Michael Ironside, Beeson Carroll (Columbia/Delphi)

Columbia's big-budget ($12-13 million) 3-D entry is a muddled science fiction tale set in the mid-21st century on planet Terra Eleven of a double-star sysem, an Earth colony reduced to *Road Warrior*-style rubble by wars and a plague.

Weak story premise, lacking urgency of any sense of importance, has salvage ship pilot Wolff (Peter Strauss) and other 'Earthers' including orphaned waif Niki (Molly Ringwald) and Wolff's former training school colleague, now sector chief Washington (Ernie Hudson), searching the planet for three shipwrecked, later kidnaped girls.

Episodic treatment pits them against many local dangers including a well-executed set of puffy monsters, en route to a showdown at the lair of local tyrant McNabb, known as Overdog (Michael Ironside, in skull-like makeup reminiscent of actor Reggie Nalder).

Technical highlights are the vast metal sculpture sets, plus impressive and well-matched miniatures and explosions. Director Lamont Johnson, who entered the picture midstream after original helmer Jean LaFleur [author of screen story with Stewart Harding] was bounced, handles the action scenes well but editing opposes viewer involvement, taking one out of each hectic action scene before its impact can be enjoyed.

■ **SPANISH GARDENER, THE**

1957, 97 MINS, UK ◇ ⑨
Dir Philip Leacock *Prod* John Bryan *Scr* Lesley Storm, John Bryan *Ph* Christopher Challis *Ed* Reginald Mills *Mus* John Veale *Art Dir* Maurice Carter
● Dirk Bogarde, Jon Whiteley, Michael Hordern, Cyril Cusack, Maureen Swanson, Bernard Lee (Rank)

A.J. Cronin's novel of a minor diplomat with considerable academic qualifications, but without human understanding, translates into absorbing screen entertainment. It is a leisurely told story with colorful Spanish backgrounds.

Michael Hordern is the diplomat separated from his wife, continually passed up for promotion, who insists that his son is delicate, cannot join other children in games or at school and is denied every form of companionship. Dirk Bogarde is hired as a gardener and his friendly attitude to the kid sparks a violent jealousy in the father.

Bogarde gives a polished, restrained study as the Spanish gardener whose motives in befriending the boy are completely misunderstood. Jon Whiteley's moppet is a keenly sensitive portrayal. Cyril Cusack, as a sinister valet, and Maureen Swanson, as the gardener's girl friend, top a good supporting cast.

■ **SPARROWS CAN'T SING**

1963, 94 MINS, UK ⑨
Dir Joan Littlewood *Prod* Donald Taylor *Scr* Joan Littlewood, Stephen Lewis *Ph* Max Greene, Desmond Dickinson *Ed* Oswald Hafenrichter *Mus* Stanley Black
● James Booth, Barbara Windsor, Roy Kinnear, Avis Bunnage, George Sewell, Barbara Ferris (Carthage)

For her first essay in pix, Joan Littlewood plays fairly safe. The film is based on a play that she staged at the Theatre Workshop. She and the author of the play (Stephen Lewis) collaborated on the loose screenplay and Littlewood surrounds herself with most of the Workshop cast. She also operates almost entirely on location in the East End that she knows and clearly loves so well.

The storyline is disarmingly slight. James Booth plays a tearaway merchant seaman who comes back to his East End home after two years afloat to find that his home had been torn down during replanning and his wife (Barbara Windsor) has found herself another nest with a local bus driver. His arrival strikes uneasiness in the hearts of the locals, who know his uncertain temper. But Booth sets out to find his wife and collect his conjugal rights.

This could have been played for drama or even tragedy. The screenplay writers and Littlewood's direction beckon to the brighter and breezier slant and, though there is a sober side to the film, this is mostly played for yocks. Much of the dialog, which is rather salty, appears to have been made up off the cuff of the players. This shows up dangerously in the intimate scenes, but gives gusto to others.

Booth is a striking personality, a punchy blend of toughness, potential evil and irresistible charm. Barbara Windsor (who also chants the Lionel Bart title song) is a cute young blonde who teeters delightfully through her role, on stiletto heels and with a devastating sense of logic.

■ **SPARTACUS**

1960, 197 MINS, US ◇ ⑨ ⊙
Dir Stanley Kubrick, [Anthony Mann] *Prod* Edward Lewis *Scr* Dalton Trumbo *Ph* Russell Metty, Clifford Stine *Ed* Robert Lawrence *Mus* Alex North *Art Dir* Alexander Golitzen
● Kirk Douglas, Laurence Olivier, Jean Simmons, Charles Laughton, Peter Ustinov, Tony Curtis (Universal/Bryna)

It took a lot of moolah – U says $12 million – and two years of intensive work to bring *Spartacus* to the screen. Film justifies the effort. There is solid dramatic substance, purposeful and intriguingly contrasted character portrayals and, let's come right out with it, sheer pictorial poetry that is sweeping and savage, intimate and lusty, tender and bitter sweet.

Director Stanley Kubrick had a remarkably good screenplay with which to work by Dalton Trumbo, whose name appears on the film for the first time in about a decade since he served a prison sentence for contempt of Congress because he refused to declare whether or not he was a member of the Communist party.

Spartacus is a rousing testament to the spirit and dignity of man, dealing with a revolt by slaves against the pagan Roman Empire [from the novel by Howard Fast]. In terms of spectacle the clash between the slave army led by Kirk Douglas and the Romans commanded by Laurence Olivier is nothing short of flabbergasting.

Douglas is the mainstay of the picture. He is not particularly expressive – not in contrast with the sophisticated Olivier, the conniving parasite of a gladiator ring operator portrayed by Peter Ustinov, or the supple and subtle slave maiden represented by Jean Simmons. But Douglas succeeds admirably in giving an impression of a man who is all afire inside. Tony Curtis as the Italian slave, Antoninus, who serves as houseboy to Olivier before running away to join Spartacus, gives a nicely balanced performance.

Charles Laughton is superbly wily and sophisticated as a Republican senator who is outwitted by Olivier in attempting to gain control of Rome through sponsorship of the young Julius Caesar. John Gavin plays the latter adequately.

Some 8,000 Spanish soldiers became Roman legionaries for the massive battle sequences filmed outside Madrid, but the rest of the picture was made in Hollywood.

[Version reviewed was the complete one, before censor cuts. Initial release version ran for 192 minutes. Complete version was finally released in 1991.]

□ 1960: Best Supp. Actor (Peter Ustinov), Color Cinematography, Color Art Direction, Color Costume Design (Valles, Bill Thomas)
□ Nominations: Best Editing, Scoring of a Dramatic Picture

■ **SPAWN OF THE NORTH**

1938, 105 MINS, US
Dir Henry Hathaway *Prod* Albert Lewin *Scr* Jules Furthman, Talbot Jennings *Ph* Charles Lang *Ed* Ellsworth Hoagland *Mus* Dimitri Tiomkin
● George Raft, Henry Fonda, Dorothy Lamour, Akim Tamiroff, John Barrymore, Louise Platt (Paramount)

Impressive scenes of the Alaskan waters, backgrounded by towering glaciers which drop mighty icebergs into the sea, imperiling doughty fishermen and their frail craft, lift *Spawn of the North* into the class of robust out-of-door films where the spectacular overshadows the melodrama.

The plot [story by Barrett Willoughby] recounts the battles between licensed fishermen and pirates who steal the catch from the traps which are set for salmon at spawning time. George Raft and Henry Fonda, boyhood friends, are members of opposing factions, the former having fallen in with Russian thieves.

Merit of the film is in the persuasive and authentic photographic record of Alaskan life and customs. Akim Tamiroff is a truly menacing pirate with a black heart and no regard for law and order. John Barrymore is an amusing small town editor and Lynne Overman makes a cynical role standout by his gruff humor.

□ 1938: Special Award (special photographic and sound effects)

SPEAKING PARTS

1989, 92 MINS, CANADA ◇ Ⓦ ⊙
Dir Atom Egoyan   *Scr* Atom Egoyan   *Ph* Paul Sarossy
Ed Bruce McDonald   *Mus* Mychael Danna
Art Dir Linda Del Rosario
● Michael McManus, Arsinee Khanjian, Gabrielle Rose, David Hemblen, Patricia Collins (Ego)

Speaking Parts, the third feature from Toronto's Atom Egoyan, is a brooding, personal effort, adroitly blending film and video, but with mixed results overall.

Hero cleans hotel rooms, sexually services female clients off screen on orders from the housekeeper, but seeks a speaking part in films after playing extra roles.

He spurns advances from an equally brooding hotel laundry worker and persuades a scriptwriter guest to advance him for the role as her dead brother in a forthcoming pic. That she does to a producer, who is seen almost throughout on a video screen communicating with his staff.

Meanwhile, the laundry worker replays videos of the would-be-actor's bit part scenes at home and attaches herself to a vidstore owner who tapes a sexual orgy and a wedding.

SPECIAL AGENT

1949, 70 MINS, US
Dir William C. Thomas   *Prod* William H. Pine, William C. Thomas   *Scr* Lewis R. Foster, Whitman Chambers
Ph Ellis Carter   *Ed* Howard Smith   *Mus* Lucien Cailliet
● William Eythe, George Reeves, Laura Elliot, Paul Valentine (Paramount)

Special Agent draws its melodramatic meat from an actual case in the files of the railroads' special agent division. Script tells of a daring express car robbery by two brothers and the painstaking way the special agents go about bringing the crooks to justice. Direction by William C. Thomas achieves a good documentary flavor in the thrills, concentrating footage mostly on the agents and their work.

William Eythe pleases as the young agent stationed in a small California town. For romance there is Laura Elliot, daughter of the engineer killed in the robbery.

George Reeves and Paul Valentine depict the heavies who, in tackling their first major crime, loot a train of a $100,000 payroll. Reeves is good but Valentine is a bit too mannered as the trigger-happy killer.

SPECTER OF THE ROSE

1946, 90 MINS, US Ⓦ
Dir Ben Hecht   *Prod* Ben Hecht, Lee Garmes   *Scr* Ben Hecht   *Ph* Lee Garmes   *Ed* Harry Keller   *Mus* George Antheil
● Judith Anderson, Michael Chekhov, Ivon Kirov, Viola Essen, Lionel Stander (Republic)

Ben Hecht, to say the least, has done the expected by coming up with the unusual. *Specter of the Rose* was obviously a conscious attempt by Hecht to prove on how small a budget he could produce an acceptable picture. Reports are that it cost in the neighborhood of $160,000. The serious defect productionwise is a general lack of polish that is at times disturbing.

Yarn concerns a ballet troupe in which the top male dancer has gone berserk. Okay mentally for periods, he at times has hallucinations in which he hears music which forces him to dance the ballet *Spectre de la Rose* and, while terpin, he gets a desire to slit his wife's throat.

This he has already done to one wife when the picture opens. One of the ballerinas is nevertheless in love with him and is sure she can cure him. She marries him, his mind remains clear and the ballet goes on. But, as is expected, the hallucinations suddenly return.

All this is against a serio-comic and satirical background of the ballet company's travails, financial and otherwise in staging a tour. Judith Anderson is the troupe's mentor, Michael Chekhov the comic impresario, and two actual ballet dancers, Ivan Kirov and Viola Essen, the boy and girl. Stander is a Greenwich Village poet who seems to be in the film for no other reason than to mouth Hechtisms.

Hecht's direction and dialog give the acting a stylized artificiality that grows on the spectator as the picture progresses. Satire of the characterizations makes many of the film's people virtually caricatures.

SPELLBOUND

1945, 116 MINS, US Ⓦ ⊙
Dir Alfred Hitchcock   *Prod* David O. Selznick   *Scr* Ben Hecht, Angus MacPhail   *Ph* George Barnes   *Ed* William Ziegler, Hal C. Kern   *Mus* Miklos Rozsa   *Art Dir* James Basevi, John Ewing
● Ingrid Bergman, Gregory Peck, Rhonda Fleming, Leo G. Carroll, Norman Lloyd, Michael Chekhov (United Artists)

David O. Selznick devised unique production values for this Alfred Hitchcock-directed version of a psychological mystery novel [*The House of Dr Edwardes*, written by Hilary St George Saunders].

The story, employing as it does psychiatry and psychoanalysis in a murder mystery, would not lend itself for anything but a skillfully blended top budget production.

Gregory Peck, suffering from amnesia, believes that he committed a murder but has no memory of the locale or circumstances surrounding the crime. Ingrid Bergman as a psychiatrist in love with Peck tries desperately to save him from punishment for the crime she is certain he could not have committed, and in doing so risks her career and almost her life.

Salvador Dali designed the dream sequence with all the aids of futurism and surrealism in his sets. The sets, chairs and tables have human legs and roofs slope at 45-degree angles into infinity.

Alfred Hitchcock handles his players and action in suspenseful manner and, except for a few episodes of much scientific dialogue, maintains a steady pace in keeping the camera moving.

□ 1945: Best Score for a Dramatic Picture.
□ Nominations: Best Picture, Director, Supp. Actor (Michael Chekhov), B&W Cinematography, Special Effects

SPENCER'S MOUNTAIN

1963, 121 MINS, US ◇ ⊙
Dir Delmer Daves   *Prod* [uncredited]   *Scr* Delmer Daves   *Ph* Charles Lawton   *Ed* David Wages   *Mus* Max Steiner   *Art Dir* Carl Anderson
● Henry Fonda, Maureen O'Hara, James MacArthur, Donald Crisp, Wally Cox, Mimsy Farmer (Warner)

Delmer Daves chooses the majestic Grand Teton's to background a quite ordinary, but generally enjoyable and often emotionally moving comedy-drama about a large, simple, hardworking family and its joys and disappointments from the cradle to the grave.

Daves, working from a novel (laid in Blue Ridge Mountain Country) by Earl Hamner Jr, views the Spencers idealistically – the family that pulls together and walks straight.

Daves' script plays better than it sounds in synopsis for it is the interplay and incidents that spark humor and warmth, sentiment and a bit of boisterousness in the story which is motivated by the desire of uneducated parents to fulfill their son's desire for a college education when all that the father earns is required to keep food on the table for a brood of nine youngsters, plus husband-wife and grandparents.

With less ingratiating and expert performers than Henry Fonda and Maureen O'Hara as the central characters the chances are Daves might have found himself in trouble. Fonda, in particular, can take what easily could have been an ordinary hayseed and invest such a role with depth, purposefulness and dignity.

SPHINX

1981, 117 MINS, US ◇ Ⓦ
Dir Franklin J. Schaffner   *Prod* Stanley O'Toole
Scr John Byrum   *Ph* Ernest Day   *Ed* Robert E. Swink, Michael F. Anderson   *Mus* Michael J. Lewis
Art Dir Terence Marsh
● Lesley-Anne Down, Frank Langella, Maurice Ronet, John Gielgud, Saeed Jaffrey, John Rhys-Davies (Orion)

This film is an embarrassment. Contempo *Perils of Pauline* sees earnest, dedicated Egyptologist Lesley-Anne Down through countless situations of dire jeopardy as she travels from Cairo to Luxor's Valley of the Kings in pursuit of a mysterious tomb of riches, which also holds great interest for black marketeers.

Along the way, lovely Lesley-Anne is almost murdered after witnessing John Gielgud's demise, caught off guard not once, not twice, but three times in her hotel room, shot at as a matter of course, nearly raped by a prison guard, held at knifepoint, thrown into a dark dungeon inhabited by decomposed corpses, attacked by bats, chased by a car, shot at again and finally nearly buried as the tomb's ceiling comes crashing down.

In all, she screams, gasps and exclaims 'My God!' more often than any heroine since Jamie Lee Curtis in her collected horror films.

Franklin J. Schaffner's steady and sober style is helpless in the face of the mounting implausibilities.

SPIES LIKE US

1985, 109 MINS, US ◇ Ⓦ ⊙
Dir John Landis   *Prod* Brian Grazer, George Folsey Jr
Scr Dan Aykroyd, Lowell Ganz, Babaloo Mandel
Ph Robert Paynter   *Ed* Malcolm Campbell   *Mus* Elmer Bernstein   *Art Dir* Peter Murton
● Chevy Chase, Dan Aykroyd, Steve Forrest, Donna Dixon, Bruce Davison, Bernard Casey (Paramount)

Teamed together for the first time in *Spies Like Us*, Chevy Chase and Dan Aykroyd need a subteen audience for their juvenile humor.

Spies is not very amusing. Though Chase and Aykroyd provide moments, the overall script thinly takes on eccentric espionage and nuclear madness, with nothing new to add.

Chase and Aykroyd are a couple of bumbling bureaucrats with aspirations for spy work, but no talent for the job. They unknowingly are chosen for a mission, however, because they will make expendable decoys for a real spy team headed by pretty Donna Dixon.

Much of the time, Aykroyd is fooling with gadgets, Chase is fooling with Dixon and director John Landis is fooling with half-baked comedy ideas.

SPINSTER

See: Two Loves

SPIRAL ROAD, THE

1962, 145 MINS, US ◇
Dir Robert Mulligan   *Prod* Robert Arthur   *Scr* Neil Paterson, John Lee Mahin   *Ph* Russell Harlan   *Ed* Russell F. Schoengarth   *Mus* Jerry Goldsmith
Art Dir Alexander Golitzen, Henry Bumstead

● Rock Hudson, Burl Ives, Gena Rowlands, Geoffrey Keen, Neva Patterson, Will Kuvula (Universal)

Being uninspired, *The Spiral Road* is the uninspiring tale of an atheist's conversion to God. The picture, moreover, takes the devil's own time getting down to cases and the resolution; and of its numerous defects, prolonged length is a major infirmity of this chronicle of jungle medicine in Java as practiced by the Dutch.

A novel by Dutch author Jan de Hartog is the source for the flabby screenplay. It concerns an opportunitist, gainsaying freshman medic (Rock Hudson) and his determination to ride to scientific fame on the research of a seasoned jungle physician (Burl Ives). Hudson's arrogance and cynicism are played against sundry goodhearts – his suffering wife (Gena Rowlands), the Salvation Army man (Geoffrey Keen), and highminded types who constitute his superiors in the government medical mission.

● ●

■ SPIRAL STAIRCASE, THE

1946, 83 MINS, US ®
Dir Robert Siodmak   *Prod* Dore Schary   *Scr* Mel Dinelli
Ph Nicholas Musuraca   *Ed* Harry Marker, Harry Gerstad
Art Dir Albert S. D'Agostino, Jack Okey
● Dorothy McGuire, George Brent, Ethel Barrymore, Kent Smith, Rhonda Fleming (RKO)

This is a smooth production of an obvious, though suspenseful murder thriller, ably acted and directed. Mood and pace are well set, and story grips throughout.

Mel Dinelli has done a tight, authentic-sounding script of a mass-murder story [based on Ethel Lina White's novel, *Some Must Watch*] set in a small New England town of 1906. Director Robert Siodmak has retained a feeling for terror throughout the film by smart photography, camera angles and sudden shifts of camera emphasis, abetted in this job by a choice performance of his cast. Film lacks the leaven of a little humor, but interest never wanes.

Dorothy McGuire's stature as actress is increased by her performance as a maidservant bereft of speech by a shock since childhood, and Ethel Barrymore's list of pic-portraits will get another gold-framer from her role of bedridden wealthy eccentric. McGuire's portrayal of a tongue-tied girl in love; the pathos of her dream wedding-scene; her terror when pursued by the murderer – are all etched sharply for unforgettable moments. Barrymore's awareness from her bedchamber of the insanity and murder going on about her is also acutely set, to give distinction to her part.

□ 1946: Nomination: Best Supp. Actress (Ethel Barrymore)

● ●

■ SPIRIT OF ST. LOUIS, THE

1957, 135 MINS, US ◇ ®
Dir Billy Wilder   *Prod* Leland Hayward   *Scr* Billy Wilder, Wendell Mayes   *Ph* Robert Burks, J. Peverell Marley   *Ed* Arthur P. Schmidt   *Mus* Franz Waxman
Art Dir Art Loel
● James Stewart, Murray Hamilton, Patricia Smith, Bartlett Robinson (Warner)

Although lacking the elaborate production trappings that would automatically mirror a multi-million dollar budget, an extensive shooting schedule and painstaking care went into this picture. It's Class A picture-making yet doesn't manage to deliver entertainment wallop out of the story about one man in a single-engine plane over a 3,610-mile route.

Spirit is a James Stewart one-man show. He portrays Charles Lindbergh with a toned-down performance intended as consistent with the diffident (i.e. non-communicative) nature of the famed aviator. The story development tends to focus on the personal side of

the 1927 hero, as much as it does on the flight itself, and Stewart comes off with sort of an appropriate, shy amiability.

The flashback technique is used frequently to convey some of Lindbergh's background, such as his days as a mail pilot, an amusing bit re his first encounter with the air force, his barnstorming stunts, etc.

□ 1957: Nomination: Best Special Effects

● ●

■ SPITFIRE
See: The First of the Few

● ●

■ SPLASH

1984, 111 MINS, US ◇ ® ⊙
Dir Ron Howard   *Prod* Brian Grazer   *Scr* Lowell Ganz, Babaloo Mandel, Bruce Jay Friedman   *Ph* Don Peterman   *Ed* Daniel P. Hanley, Michael Hill   *Mus* Lee Holdridge
Art Dir Jack T. Collis
● Tom Hanks, Daryl Hannah, John Candy, Eugene Levy, Dody Goodman, Shecky Greene (Touchstone)

Touchstone Films takes the plunge with surprisingly charming mermaid yarn notable for winning suspension of disbelief and fetching by-play between Daryl Hannah and Tom Hanks.

Although film is a bit uneven, production benefits from a tasty look, an airy tone, and a delectable, unblemished performance from Hannah who couldn't be better cast if she were Neptune's daughter incarnate. Hanks, as a Gotham bachelor in search of love, makes a fine leap from sitcom land, and John Candy as an older playboy brother is a marvelous foil.

The mermaid's fin materializes into human legs when she leaves the water and, a la Lady Godiva, blonde tresses covering her breasts.

Screenplay is marred by some glaring loopholes in its inner structure but story is a sweet takeoff on the innocence mythology and sensuality associated with mermaids.

□ 1984: Nomination: Best Original Screenplay

● ●

■ SPLENDOR

1935, 77 MINS, US
Dir Elliott Nugent   *Prod* Samuel Goldwyn   *Scr* Rachel Crothers   *Ph* Gregg Toland   *Ed* Margaret Clancey   *Mus* Alfred Newman   *Art Dir* Richard Day
● Miriam Hopkins, Joel McCrea, Paul Cavanaugh, Helen Westley, Billie Burke, David Niven (Goldwyn/United Artists)

Here is a rare combination of a well-written story, interpreted in skilled and sympathetic action under able and understanding direction. This is the film Rachel Crothers specially authored for Goldwyn on a royalty and guarantee basis.

Miriam Hopkins marries Joel McCrea while he is south on a business trip, and he proudly bring her home, not realizing that his ambitious mother (Helen Westley) is looking to a marriage with an heiress (Ruth Weston).

Hopkins gets small welcome from her in-laws, and even McCrea is a bit impatient with her because of his own perplexities. His father and grandfather amassed money, apparently without effort. He doesn't seem able to realize why he cannot.

Paul Cavanaugh, a distant relative, takes an interest in the young wife and things become easier for her. The old lady looks to her to use her influence in behalf of McCrea. She virtually forces the girl into an affair.

Helen Westley, as the mother, is the dominant figure. Her cold-blooded, merciless nagging of the girl is as well played as it has been written. Hopkins is not altogether at ease as the sweet young thing in the first few scenes, but later she doesn't miss a chance. Paul Cavanaugh is admirable.

● ●

■ SPLENDOR IN THE GRASS

1961, 124 MINS, US ◇ ® ⊙
Dir Elia Kazan   *Prod* Elia Kazan   *Scr* William Inge   *Ph* Boris Kaufman   *Ed* Gene Milford   *Mus* David Amram   *Art Dir* Richard Sylbert
● Natalie Wood, Warren Beatty, Pat Hingle, Audrey Christie, Barbara Loden, Fred Stewart (Warner)

Elia Kazan's production of William Inge's original screenplay covers a forbidding chunk of ground with great care, compassion and cinematic flair. Yet there is something awkward about the picture's mechanical rhythm. There are missing links and blind alleys within the story. Too much time is spent focusing on characters of minor significance.

Inge's screenplay deals with a young couple deeply in love but unable to synchronize the opposite polarity of their moral attitudes. Their tragedy is helped along by the influence of parental intervention. The well-meaning parents (his father, her mother, both of whom completely dominate their more perceptive mates), in asserting their inscrutable wills upon their children, lead them into a quandary. The children cannot consummate their relationship, either sexually or maritally.

Natalie Wood and Warren Beatty (whom the picture 'introduces') are the lovers. Although the range and amplitude of their expression is not always as wide and variable as it might be, both deliver convincing, appealing performances. The real histrionic honors, though, belong to Audrey Christie, who plays Wood's mother, and Pat Hingle, as Beatty's father. Both are truly exceptional, memorable portrayals.

Barbara Loden does an interesting job in a role (Beatty's flapper sister) that is built up, only to be sloughed off at the apex of its development. Fred Stewart is excellent as Wood's father.

Exteriors for the picture were shot in New York State, and the countryside looks a little lush for Kansas, which is the setting of the drama. David Amram's romantic theme is hauntingly beautiful. There's an exceptional job of costuming by Anna Hill Johnstone. The clothes are not only faithful to the two eras (late 1920s, early 1930s) covered, but they are attractive on the people who wear them.

□ 1961: Best Original Story & Screenplay.
□ Nomination: Best Actress (Natalie Wood)

● ●

■ SPLITTING HEIRS

1993, 86 MINS, UK/US ◇ ® ⊙
Dir Robert Young   *Prod* Simon Bosanquet, Redmond Morris   *Scr* Eric Idle   *Ph* Tony Pierce-Roberts   *Ed* John Jympson   *Mus* Michael Kamen   *Art Dir* John Beard
● Rick Moranis, Eric Idle, Barbara Hershey, Catherine Zeta Jones, John Cleese, Sadie Frost (Prominent/Universal)

Splitting Heirs is a minor royalty *King Ralph*, a breezy but lightweight comedy topling Rick Moranis as a phony Yank heir to a Brit dukedom.

Moranis plays a motormouth Yank who becomes the 15th Duke of Bournemouth and head of the family bank when his father suddenly drowns. Unbeknownst to him, the real heir to the fortune is bank underling Eric Idle, who's become his best pal.

Source of the confusion is Idle's mom (Barbara Hershey) who left him in a restaurant during the Swinging Sixties and claimed the wrong baby at the police station. When Idle stumbles across the truth he tries every means to deep-six Moranis and claim his rightful fortune, in between fighting off the foxy Hershey who doesn't realise he's her son.

Even though it's short of true belly-laughs, the dumb-sounding storyline plays better than it reads, thanks to brisk pacing, all-out playing by the main leads, and some okay sight gags once the plot cranks up into revenge mode.

● ●

SPRING AND PORT WINE

1970, 101 MINS, UK ◇

Dir Peter Hammond   *Prod* Michael Medwin   *Scr* Bill Naughton   *Ph* Norman Warwick   *Ed* Fergus McDonell   *Mus* Douglas Gamley   *Art Dir* Reece Pemberton
● James Mason, Susan George, Diana Coupland, Rodney Bewes, Hannah Gordon, Len Jones (Memorial)

Set in the mill area of Lancashire and its moors (though lacking most of the cliche Lancashire gags and mannerisms), this is the story [from the play by Bill Naughton] of a generation clash in a small family and the points of view of both parents and children are fairly, compassionately and interestingly brought out.

James Mason plays the patriarch of the family, a kindly but stubborn man who brings up his family with a startling strictness. Remembering his own youth he is determined the house he reigns over shall not be such a mess.

Chief rebel is the high-spirited Susan George whose refusal to eat a herring for tea sparks off a handful of situations that remind Mason that 'you can spend a lifetime creating a family and break it up in a weekend.'

SPRING IN PARK LANE

1948, 91 MINS, UK

Dir Herbert Wilcox   *Prod* Herbert Wilcox   *Scr* Nicholas Phipps   *Ph* Max Greene   *Ed* F. Clarke   *Mus* Robert Farnon   *Art Dir* Bill Andrews
● Anna Neagle, Michael Wilding, Tom Walls, Peter Graves, Nicholas Phipps, Nigel Patrick (British Lion)

Great merit of the story is that it seems like a happy improvisation. None of the elaborate and necessary scaffolding is apparent, and when Michael Wilding as a younger son of a noble family, needing money for a return trip to New York, becomes a temporary footman in a Park Lane mansion, he is immediately accepted as such by the audience. And since Anna Neagle plays a secretary in the same house, everybody knows it will be love at first sight and that sooner or later the two will march altarwards.

It's a story in which the trimmings and incidentals are all-important. The gay harmless fun poked at the film stars, the dinner party bore, the housekeeper to whom bridge is a religion, the footman cutting in to dance or discussing art with his boss – incident upon incident carry merry laughter through the picture.

SPY IN BLACK, THE

(US: U-Boat 29)

1939, 82 MINS, UK

Dir Michael Powell   *Prod* Irving Asher   *Scr* Emeric Pressburger   *Ph* Bernard Browne   *Ed* William Hornbeck, Hugh Stewart   *Mus* Miklos Rozsa   *Art Dir* Vincent Korda
● Conrad Veidt, Sebastian Shaw, Valerie Hobson, Marius Goring, June Duprez, Mary Morris (Harefield/Korda)

The Spy in Black is a praiseworthy film on international espionage during World War I.

The plot [adapted by Roland Pertwee from a novel by J. Storer Clouston], while necessarily melodramatic, is always within the range of possibility. Conrad Veidt, as captain of a German submarine, receives instructions to proceed to the Orkney Islands, where he's to meet a woman spy, from whom he's to take orders. She instructs him to sink 15 British ships cruising off the coast of Scotland, and contacts him with a discharged traitorous lieutenant of the British Navy.

Veidt has a strong role for which he's admirably suited. Sebastian Shaw is excellent as the English naval officer. Valerie Hobson, as the other spy, is credible.

SPY WHO CAME IN FROM THE COLD, THE

1966, 112 MINS, UK

Dir Martin Ritt   *Prod* Martin Ritt   *Scr* Paul Dehn, Guy Trosper   *Ph* Oswald Morris   *Ed* Anthony Harvey   *Mus* Sol Kaplan   *Art Dir* Hal Pereira, Tambi Larsen
● Richard Burton, Claire Bloom, Oskar Werner, Sam Wanamaker, George Voskovec, Rupert Davies (Salem/Paramount)

The Spy Who Came in from the Cold is an excellent contemporary espionage drama of the Cold War which achieves solid impact via emphasis on human values, total absence of mechanical spy gimmickry, and perfectly controlled underplaying. Filmed at Ireland's Ardmore Studios and England's Shepperton complex, the production boasts strong scripting, acting, direction and production values.

Film effectively socks over the point that East-West espionage agents are living in a world of their own, apart from the day-to-day existence of the millions whom they are serving.

Other fictional spies operate with such dash and flair that the erosion of the spirit is submerged in picturesque exploits and intricate technology. Not so in this adaptation of John Le Carre's novel in which Richard Burton 'comes in from the cold' – meaning the field operations – only to find himself used as a pawn in high-level counter-plotting.

Burton fits neatly into the role of the apparently burned out British agent, ripe for cultivation by East German Communist secret police as a potential defector.

☐ 1965: Nominations: Best Actor (Richard Burton), B&W Art Direction

SPY WHO LOVED ME, THE

1977, 125 MINS, UK ◇

Dir Lewis Gilbert   *Prod* Albert R. Broccoli   *Scr* Christopher Wood, Richard Maibaum   *Ph* Claude Renoir   *Ed* John Glen   *Mus* Marvin Hamlisch   *Art Dir* Peter Lamont
● Roger Moore, Barbara Bach, Curt Jurgens, Richard Kiel, Caroline Munro, Walter Gotell (United Artists/Eon)

As always, story and plastic character are in the service of comic strip parody, an excuse to star the prop department, set designer, stunt arrangers, the optical illusion chaps, and such commercial suppliers as the maker of the sporty Lotus car, a lethal job that also converts to an underwater craft.

When British and Russian nuclear subs start to mysteriously vanish, two agents are assigned by their collaborating governments to jointly crack the case.

Curt Jurgens' arsenal includes the film's gimmick character, a monster human known as 'Jaws', played with robotic finesse by Richard Kiel.

The big action sequences were shot on a specially-built stage with tank at Pinewood Studios outside London.

☐ 1977: Nominations: Art Direction, Original Score, Song ('Nobody Does It Better')

SPY WITH MY FACE, THE

1966, 86 MINS, US ◇

Dir John Newland   *Prod* Sam Rolfe   *Scr* Clyde Ware, Joseph Calvelli   *Ph* Fred Koenekamp   *Ed* Joseph Dervin   *Mus* Morton Stevens   *Art Dir* George W. Davis, Merrill Pye
● Robert Vaughn, Senta Berger, David McCallum, Leo G. Carroll, Michael Evans, Sharon Farrell (M-G-M/Arena)

The Spy With My Face, new version of an old *Man From U.N.C.L.E.* episode, is perhaps most garbled, plotwise, of any entry in the [mid-1960s] spymelodrama cycle. Thrush, that band of murderous renegades that would rule the world and is constantly combating U.N.C.L.E., fixes up one of its agents to be the exact double of Napoleon Solo, the goodguy, and nearly succeeds in its purpose – whatever that is.

New footage was added to the original TV segment hour's length to bring it up to 86 minutes for theatrical release.

Film loses sight of story line, which has something to do with transporting a new combination to a vault in Switzerland containing a scientific secret of world import. Vaughn plays his double role straight, and Senta Berger is in as a beauteous she-spy. Femme honors, however go to Sharon Farrell as a cute sexpot. David McCallum appears in his familiar sidekick role, as does Leo G. Carroll as U.N.C.L.E. topper, and Michael Evans is the smooth heavy.

SQUEAKER, THE

1937, 79 MINS, UK

Dir William K. Howard   *Prod* Alexander Korda   *Scr* Edward O. Berkman   *Ph* Georges Perinal   *Ed* Jack Dennis, Russell Lloyd   *Mus* Miklos Rozsa   *Art Dir* Vincent Korda
● Edmund Lowe, Sebastian Shaw, Ann Todd, Tamara Desni, Robert Newton, Alastair Sim (London)

Typically fine Korda production, starring Edmund Lowe in an adaptation from the Edgar Wallace play. Despite the fact that Wallace's son Bryan is credited with the scenario, the screenplay is by Edward O. Berkman, and there now remains not a single line, joke or wisecrack by the original author.

Barest framework of Wallace Sr remains, but it has been changed from a whodunit to a newer formula, that of revealing early the identity of the arch-criminal who for years baffled Scotland Yard, and interest in the film is wholly dependent on how the Yard unravels the crime.

Role of Inspector Barrabal has been built up into a romantic lead for Edmund Lowe and he fulfills this purpose to a nicety. That of the villain, played by Sebastian Shaw, is not carried through convincingly. Audience is asked to believe that a ruthless criminal, who doesn't even stop at murder, breaks down and confesses in a cowering, hysterical manner when confronted with the corpse of his victim.

There are only two feminine roles of consequence in the cast. Ann Todd is the lead in a colorless part, and Tamara Desni is a cabaret singer in love with the murdered man. Fine piece of character work on the part of Robert Newton, eventually murdered, is outstanding.

SQUEEZE, THE

1977, 106 MINS, UK ◇

Dir Michael Apted   *Prod* Stanley O'Toole   *Scr* Leon Griffiths   *Ph* Dennis Lewiston   *Ed* John Shirley   *Mus* David Hentschel   *Art Dir* William McCrow
● Stacy Keach, Freddie Starr, Edward Fox, Stephen Boyd, David Hemmings, Carol White (Warner)

There's nothing to distinguish *The Squeeze* from routine crime drama in which retribution triumphs. Stacy Keach plays a busted cop fighting the booze habit and some murderous thugs at the same time.

Keach suffers some nasty lumps and sundry humiliations, all in the cause of Edward Fox as a security film exec whose wife and kid are hostages against a million-dollar-plus payoff. Carol White is the terrorized wife, with the complication that she's also Keach's former spouse.

Directed on locations in London by Michael Apted, pic has little in the way of style and no great surprises. It does, however, have a kind of gratuitous nasty tone, as evidenced when the thugs holding White captive force her to perform a strip.

■ SQUIRM

1976, 93 MINS, US ◇ Ⓥ
Dir Jeff Lieberman   *Prod* George Manasse   *Scr* Jeff
Lieberman   *Ph* Joseph Mangine   *Ed* Brian Smedley
Mus Robert Prince   *Art Dir* Henry Shrady
● John Scardino, Patricia Pearcy, R.A. Dow, Jean
Sullivan, Peter MacLean, Fran Higgins (American
International)

Squirm is an average shock meller about some
rampaging sand worms in the Georgia sticks,
claimed to be derived from an actual occur-
rence on September 29 1975. Some genuine
creepy special effects are offset by clumsy and
amateurish low-budget location production,
yet there is an admirable earnestness to the
effort.

Story kicker is an electrical storm which
downs power lines, with runaway juice charging the wet mud and driving out the 10-18-
inch sand worms of the area. They are hungry
and angry. They are also effective.

City slicker John Scardino visits local
Patricia Pearcy, eldest daughter of widow
Jean Sullivan. Sheriff Peter MacLean doesn't
believe in the worm plague, but becomes one
of its victims.

. . . .

■ STAGECOACH

1939, 95 MINS, US Ⓥ ⊙
Dir John Ford   *Prod* Walter Wanger   *Scr* Dudley
Nichols   *Ph* Bert Glennon   *Ed* Dorothy Spencer, Walter
Reynolds   *Mus* Leo Shuken, John Leipold, Richard
Hageman, W. Franke Harling, Louis Gruenberg
Art Dir Alexander Toluboff
● Claire Trevor, John Wayne, Andy Devine, Thomas
Mitchell, George Bancroft, John Carradine (United Artists)

Directorially, production [based on Ernest
Haycox' *Collier's* magazine story, *Stage to
Lordsburg*] is John Ford in peak form, sustain-
ing interest and suspense throughout, and
presenting exceptional characterizations.
Picture is a display of photographic grandeur.

It's the adventures of a group aboard a
stagecoach between two frontier settlements
during the sudden uprising of the Apaches.
Situation is a *Grand Hotel* on wheels.

There's Claire Trevor, dance hall gal forced
to leave town; driver, Andy Devine; gambler,
John Carradine; inebriated frontier medic,
Thomas Mitchell; marshall, George Bancroft;
wife of an army officer en route to his post,
Louise Platt; whiskey salesman, Donald
Meek, and absconding banker, Berton
Churchill. John Wayne, recently escaped
from prison, is picked up on the road shortly
after the start.

In maintaining a tensely dramatic pace all
the way, Ford still injects numerous comedy
situations, and throughout sketches his characters with sincerity and humaneness. It's absorbing drama without the general theatrics
usual to picturizations of the early west.

The running fight between the stagecoach
passengers and the Apaches has been given
thrilling and realistic presentation by Ford. In
contrast, the hacienda sequence is an extremely tender episode.
□ 1939: Best Score, Supp. Actor (Thomas
Mitchell).
□ Nominations: Best Picture, Director, B&W
Cinematography, Art Direction, Editing
. . . .

■ STAGECOACH

1966, 114 MINS, US ◇
Dir Gordon M. Douglas   *Prod* Martin Rackin
Scr Joseph Landon   *Ph* William H. Clothier   *Ed* Hugh S.
Fowler   *Mus* Jerry Goldsmith   *Art Dir* Jack Martin
Smith, Herman A. Blumenthal
● Ann-Margret, Red Buttons, Michael Connors, Alex
Cord, Bing Crosby, Bob Cummings (Rackin/20th Century-
Fox)

New version of *Stagecoach* derives from a 1939
Walter Wanger production for United Artists,

written by Dudley Nichols from a 1937 short
story by Ernest Haycox.

Film kicks off with a gory two-minute sequence establishing the brutality of Indians
on the warpath, the menace which hangs over
subsequent developments, after which the
stagecoach starts loading its motley passenger crew. Ann-Margret is quite good as the
saloon floozy bad-mouthed out of town under
US Army pressure by John Gabriel. Bing
Crosby, the boozy medic, is a similar victim of
Gabriel's incorrect evaluation of a drunken
brawl.

Bob Cummings, the gutless bank clerk absconding with a large payroll, is excellent.
Cummings delivers much depth, evoking pity
and sympathy. He makes an excellent heavy.

To Alex Cord goes the choice John Wayne
role of Ringo, framed into prison by landgrab-
bing Keenan Wynn. Cord underplays very
well, and conveys the stubborn determination
to avenge his dead father and brother, killed
by Wynn, which sustained him during a sadistic incarceration from which he has escaped
to join the stage.

Artist Norman Rockwell, who designed pic's
logo and painted the perceptive talent portraits used in end titles and exploitation, appears briefly in an early saloon scene.

. . . .

■ STAGE DOOR

1937, 83 MINS, US/UK Ⓥ
Dir Gregory La Cava   *Prod* Pandro S. Berman
Scr Morrie Ryskind, Anthony Veiller   *Ph* Robert de
Grasse   *Ed* William Hamilton   *Mus* Roy Webb
● Katharine Hepburn, Ginger Rogers, Adolphe Menjou,
Gail Patrick, Constance Collier, Andrea Leeds (RKO)

It isn't *Stage Door*, as written [for the stage]
by Edna Ferber and George S. Kaufman.
Instead, it is a hall bedroom view of aspiring
young actresses who live in a New York theatrical boarding house and vent their bitterness against the economic uncertainties of
legit employment in sharp and cutting repartee. It is funny in spots, emotionally effective
occasionally, and generally brisk and entertaining.

Whether it was Gregory La Cava or Pandro
S. Berman, the producer, who decided to
throw away the play and write a new script on
the old idea that there is a broken heart for
every light on Broadway, is beside the point.

Story revolves around one of the minor
characters, a talented young actress of
promise unable to withstand the pressure of
constant casting disappointment. Part is
played for all it's worth by Andrea Leeds.

Opening shows the inhabitants of a rooming house in the West 40s. They're a high
strung, noisy bevy of showgirls, nightclub
dancers and embryo dramatic timber. Dialog
is caustic as they comment on each other and
the passing world of show business. Ginger
Rogers does a floor specialty in a night club
which gives her an introduction to Adolphe
Menjou, a hardboiled theatrical producer and
femme despoiler.

Katharine Hepburn, stagestruck daughter
of a wealthy westerner, becomes Ginger's
roommate at the boarding house. Former's
father, in the hope he can discourage her theatrical career, anonymously finances a
Menjou dramatic production, with Hepburn
in the lead.

Rogers has more to do than Hepburn, but her
part is less clearly defined. As a sharpshooter
with the snappy reply she scores heavily. Her
dancing is limited to a short floor number.
□ 1937: Nominations: Best Picture, Director,
Supp. Actress (Andrea Leeds), Screenplay
. . . .

■ STAGE DOOR CANTEEN

1943, 132 MINS, US Ⓥ ⊙
Dir Frank Borzage   *Prod* Sol Lesser   *Scr* Delmer Daves
Ph Harry Wild   *Ed* Hal Kern   *Mus* Freddie Rich

● Cheryl Walker, William Terry, Marjorie Riordan, Lon
McCallister, Margaret Early, Michael Harrison (United
Artists)

What stood a good chance of emerging a 'big
short' under less skillful hands than Sol
Lesser proves a sock filmusical of great
stature. It has a cast that reads like an out-of-
this-world benefit, and a romance as simple
as Elsie Dinsmore – and the blend is plenty
boffo.

Stage Door Canteen is a skilful admixture by
two casts, in itself a departure. One cast projects the simple love story – Eileen and her
'Dakota'; Jean and her 'California'; Ella Sue
and her 'Texas'; Mamie and her 'Jersey'.
Another cast comprises the Stars of the Stage
Door Canteen, and but few of them do walk-
through parts.

Plausibly and smoothly, these stars are introduced into their natural habitat, the Stage
Door Canteen on West 44th Street, just off
Broadway, where Lunt and Fontanne and
Vera Gordon, Sam Jaffe, George Raft and
Allen Jenkins, Ned Sparks, Ralph Morgan and
Hugh Herbert – these, among others, are
shown doing their menial back-in-the-kitchen
chores. Then, up front, performing for the
visiting men in uniform, gobs, doughboys,
marines – no officers – is paraded a galaxy of
talent that's a super-duper, all-star array
which reads like a casting agent's dream of
paradise.

Thus are paraded six bands – Basie, Cugat,
Goodman, Kyser, Lombardo and Martin, in
sock specialties all.

And, to project the mechanics of the canteen, showing the officer-of-the-day, the senior hostesses, the dancing junior hostesses,
or as part of the plot motivation (as with
Katherine Cornell's skillful bit of *Romeo and
Juliet*, and Paul Muni's part as rehearsing his
own play) there are introduced another array
of stars and legit personalities: Helen Hayes,
Ina Claire, Tallulah Bankhead, Vinton
Freedley, Merle Oberon, Brock Pemberton,
Katherine Hepburn and the others are intertwined into the lonely-soldier-boy-meets-ro-
mantic-stage-girl plot.

Scripter Delmer Daves does a deft writing
job, and Frank Borzage's direction smoothly
splices the sum total into a very palatable cohesive entity.
□ 1943: Nominations: Best Scoring of a
Musical Picture, Song ('We Mustn't Sya
Goodbye')
. . . .

■ STAGE FRIGHT

1950, 110 MINS, US/UK Ⓥ ⊙
Dir Alfred Hitchcock   *Prod* Alfred Hitchcock
Scr Whitfield Cook   *Ph* Wilkie Cooper   *Ed* Edward
Jarvis   *Mus* Leighton Lucas   *Art Dir* Terence Verity
● Jane Wyman, Marlene Dietrich, Michael Wilding,
Richard Todd, Kay Walsh, Alistair Sim (Warner/
Associated British)

Alfred Hitchcock doesn't stress melodrama
throughout. He plays a surprising number of
sequences strictly for lightness. Also, he has a
choice cast to put through its paces, and
there's not a bad performance anywhere [In
this adaption by Alma Reville of a novel by
Selwyn Jepson]. The dialog has purpose, either for a chuckle or a thrill, and the pace is
good.

Jane Wyman is a drama student who is
sought out by a friend (Richard Todd) who is
fleeing from the charge of murdering
Marlene Dietrich's husband. Wyman and
her father (Alistair Sim) hide Todd and
attempt to prove Dietrich is guilty of the
crime.

Wyman is delightful as embryo actress but
the choice femme spot goes to Dietrich.
Michael Wilding clicks as a debonair
detective.
. . . .

STAGESTRUCK

1936, 90 MINS, US ⓥ
Dir Busby Berkeley *Scr* Tom Buckingham, Pat C. Flick
Ph Byron Haskin
● Dick Powell, Joan Blondell, Warren William, Frank McHugh, Jeanne Madden, Carol Hughes (Warner)

Even though it makes an attempt to poke fun at the show-must-go-on thing, *Stage Struck* is cut from the same old pattern, gravitating between moments of sizzling comedy and long stretches of dull palaver.

Picture takes a pretzel-like course in recounting the conventional yarn [by Robert Lord] about the unknown kid who makes good as the last-minute fill-in for the show's star. Musical interludes [songs by E.Y. Harburg and Harold Arlen] are kept down to the minimum.

With her material anything but surefire, Joan Blondell unlimbers a likable grade of comedy. Hers is the part of the dame whose only claim to fame is a penchant for drilling her troublesome boy friends and the newsprint attention that goes with such incidents. She backs herself to the lead part in a musical show where Dick Powell functions as director. A clash of temperaments ends that venture and the pair meet again in her next bit of angeling.

Paired with Powell for the romantic byplay, Jeanne Madden does okay for a starter.

STAGE STRUCK

1958, 95 MINS, US ◇ ⓥ ⊙
Dir Sidney Lumet *Prod* Stuart Millar *Scr* Ruth Goetz, Augustus Goetz *Ph* Franz Planer, Maurice Hartzband *Ed* Stuart Gilmore *Mus* Alex North *Art Dir* Kim Edgar Swados
● Henry Fonda, Susan Strasberg, Joan Greenwood, Herbert Marshall, Christopher Plummer, Patricia Englund (RKO)

Stage Struck weaves another variation on the wellworn tale of the eager young actress who can't persuade anyone on Broadway to give her a job until the star flounces out on the eve of opening night. The tyro steps into the star's shoes, knocks the audience right out of its red plush seats; veterans backstage murmur, 'that's showbiz,' and the camera pans slowly away from a solitary figure standing in the middle of an empty theatre; music up and out. It's a remake of *Morning Glory*, a yesteryear [1933] Katharine Hepburn starrer.

Susan Strasberg plays the would-be actress who hounds producer Henry Fonda for a chance. He is intrigued by the girl but not as an actress and turns her down. Not so his playwright (Christopher Plummer), who sees her both as actress and romantic opposite. When the star of their show (Joan Greenwood) makes a temperamental exit, Plummer has Strasberg set to take over her role and she does with plot-predictable ease and success.

Strasberg occupies a major portion of the footage in this screenplay from a Zoe Akins play. She is not a conventional screen beauty but her face is expressive and lively. Fonda plays with his customary quiet authority and disarming command and Herbert Marshall limns a warming portrait as a stage veteran. Greenwood gives the rampaging star the Bankhead bit and very funny she is. Plummer has considerable depth to his playing.

Camerawork is striking, notably in the Central Park scene, a setting of a Greenwich Village street, dawn in Times Square, and the interiors of the theatre (actually the National on 41st Street).

STAIRCASE

1969, 101 MINS, US ◇ ⓥ
Dir Stanley Donen *Prod* Stanley Donen *Scr* Charles Dyer *Ph* Christopher Challis *Ed* Richard Marden *Mus* Dudley Moore *Art Dir* Willy Holt

● Richard Burton, Rex Harrison, Cathleen Nesbitt, Beatrix Lehmann, Avril Angers, Stephen Lewis (20th Century-Fox)

Staircase, investigating lonely, desperate lives of two aging male homosexuals in a drab London suburb, comes uncomfortably close to being depressing. Caustic wit, splendid photography and fine direction serve only to point up weary plight of the middleaged pair who cling to one another even while they clash.

Homosexuality, though predominant influence of storyline [from the play by Charles Dyer], is not central theme of screenplay. Its basis is urgent need of neurotic individuals for consolation.

Harrison as the flighty dagger-tongued roommate of fellow 'hair stylist' Burton offers portrait of a bitter, disenchanted man living in terror of being alone. Burton, almost stoic, commands respect and, at the same time, sympathy. Harrison and Burton have dared risky roles and have triumphed.

STAIRWAY TO HEAVEN
See: A Matter of Life and Death

STAKEOUT

1987, 115 MINS, US ◇ ⓥ ⊙
Dir John Badham *Prod* Jim Kouf, Cathleen Summers *Scr* Jim Kouf *Ph* John Seale *Ed* Tom Rolf, Michael Ripps *Mus* Arthur B. Rubinstein *Art Dir* Philip Harrison
● Richard Dreyfuss, Emilio Estevez, Madeleine Stowe, Aidan Quinn, Dan Lauria, Forest Whitaker (Touchstone)

StakeOut is a slick, sure-footed entertainment, one part buddy comedy and one part police actioner stitched together with a dash of romance.

Richard Dreyfuss is a reck¹less cop whose life is unraveling slowly. While he's on familiar ground talking his way out of tight spots and jousting with partner Emilio Estevez, when the plot calls for rough stuff, it's a stretch he doesn't make.

As the more stable, but still mischievous anchor of the pair, Estevez is likable, if a bit flat. He's not an actor with a great gift for comedy, and many of his exchanges with Dreyfuss lack chemistry.

As Seattle cops (the film was shot in Vancouver), the wisecracking duo is assigned to a routine stakeout where they are supposed to wait for an escaped con (Aidan Quinn) to contact his ex-girlfriend (Madeleine Stowe). Dreyfuss is not a man to wait around for something to happen and, as he barrels into the case, he falls in love with Stowe.

STALAG 17

1953, 119 MINS, US ⓥ ⊙
Dir Billy Wilder *Prod* Billy Wilder *Scr* Billy Wilder, Edwin Blum *Ph* Ernest Laszlo *Ed* George Tomasini *Mus* Franz Waxman *Art Dir* Hal Pereira, Franz Bachelin
● William Holden, Don Taylor, Otto Preminger, Robert Strauss, Harvey Lembeck, Peter Graves (Paramount)

The legit hit about GI internees in a Nazi prison camp during the Second World War is screened as a lusty comedy-melodrama, loaded with bold, masculine humor and as much of the original's uninhibited earthiness as good taste and the Production Code permit.

Producer-director Billy Wilder, who did the screen adaptation of the Donald Bevan-Edmund Trzcinski play with Edwin Blum, uses a suspense approach with plenty of leavening humorous byplay springing from the confinement of healthy young males. Nub of the plot is the uncovering of an informer among the GIs in a particular barracks and up to the time his identity is revealed there is plenty of tenseness in the footage.

Opening shows the death of two GIs while attempting a well-plotted escape and the sudden realization there is an informer in their midst. Suspicion fastens on William Holden, a cynical character trying to make the best of his prison lot. When Don Taylor is temporarily moved into the barracks and just as quickly revealed as the American who blew up an ammunition train, the prisoners decide Holden is their man and beat him unmercifully.

Otto Preminger is the third star, playing the camp commander, with obvious relish for its colorful cruelty. Laugh standouts are Robert Strauss, the dumb Stosh of the play and Harvey Lembeck as Harry, the only slightly brighter pal of Stosh.
☐ 1953: Best Actor (William Holden).
☐ Nominations: Best Director, Supp. Actor (Robert Strauss)

STALKING MOON, THE

1969, 109 MINS, US ◇ ⓥ
Dir Robert Mulligan *Prod* Alan J. Pakula *Scr* Alvin Sargent *Ph* Charles Lang *Ed* Aaron Stell *Mus* Fred Karlin *Art Dir* Roland Anderson, Jack Poplin
● Gregory Peck, Eva Marie Saint, Robert Forster, Noland Clay (National General/Stalking Moon)

The Stalking Moon seemingly was meant to be a chilling suspenser, framed in a western environment. It does not achieve this goal, because of clumsy plot structuring and dialog and limp direction, which produces tedious pacing.

Theodore V. Olsen's novel, scripted by Alvin Sargent, has Gregory Peck retiring as a vet Indian scout with the US Army. In an Indian round-up, Eva Marie Saint appears, with son Noland Clay. Years before, she was kidnapped and impressed into squaw service by Nathaniel Narcisco. Peck takes her and the boy to his retirement ranch, but the Indian brave stalks them.

Forgetting the oater atmosphere (which is supposed to be secondary) film doesn't cut it as a suspenser. Saint, although perhaps as stolid as a frightened Indian slave-woman might be, is not able to project her determined flight from the range territory.

Kid Clay just stares at everything. Dialog is spare and vapid.

STAND BY ME

1986, 87 MINS, US ◇ ⓥ ⊙
Dir Rob Reiner *Prod* Bruce A. Evans, Raynold Gideon, Andrew Scheinman *Scr* Raynold Gideon, Bruce A. Evans *Ph* Thomas Del Ruth *Ed* Robert Leighton *Mus* Jack Nitzsche *Art Dir* Dennis Washington
● Wil Wheaton, River Phoenix, Corey Feldman, Jerry O'Connell, Richard Dreyfuss, Kiefer Sutherland (Act III)

Stand by Me falls somewhat short of being a firstrate 'small' picture about adventurous small-town adolescent boys, although director Rob Reiner is to be lauded for coming close. Formerly titled *The Body*, based on a novella of the same name by Stephen King, it is the experiences of four youths on a two-day trek through the woods around their home-town of Castle Rock, Oregon, to find the yet-undiscovered body of a dead teenager reported missing for several days.

Film opens very slowly with the extraneous narration of grownup writer Richard Dreyfuss reminiscing on that certain summer of 1959 between sixth and seventh grades that he spent with three close buddies as they sought to become heroes in each other's and the town's eyes.

Scripters have written inspired dialog for this quartet of plucky boys at that hard-to-capture age when they're still young enough to get scared and yet old enough to want to sneak smokes and cuss.

Leading the cast is the introspective, sensitive 'brain' of the bunch, Gordie Lachance (Wil Wheaton). His somber personality is matched by best friend Chris Chambers (River Pheonix), a toughie who is an abused child; Teddy Dechamp (Corey Feldman), the loony kid of an institutionalized father; and the perfectly named wimp, Vern Tessie, the chubby kid who everyone else enjoys poking fun at.

☐ 1986: Nomination: Best Adapted Screenplay

....

■ STANLEY & IRIS

1990, 102 MINS, US ◇ ⑫ ⊙
Dir Martin Ritt   *Prod* Arlene Sellers, Alex Winitsky   *Scr* Harriet Frank Jr, Irving Ravetch   *Ph* Donald McAlpine   *Ed* Sidney Levin   *Mus* John Williams   *Art Dir* Joel Schiller
● Jane Fonda, Robert De Niro, Swoosie Kurtz, Martha Plimpton, Harley Cross, Jamey Sheridan (Lantana/M-G-M)

The elements are in place but they don't add up to great drama in this well-meant effort to personalize the plight of illiterate people.

Project reunites director Martin Ritt with screenwriting team that produced the Oscar-winning *Norma Rae*, which also had a working-class setting and underdog social concern. *Stanley & Iris* [from the novel *Union Street* by Pat Barker] features Robert De Niro's plight as an illiterate cook but proves too small for a feature film framework.

Jane Fonda plays Iris, a recent widow still struggling with grief while trying to support a whole household. She catches the eye of Stanley Cox, a cafeteria cook who at middle age has never learned to read or write. Fired by his boss for being potentially dangerous, Stanley no longer can afford to care properly for the aging father who lives with him. When the old man dies, Stanley finally confronts his fears and asks Iris to teach him to read.

Fonda has some trouble evoking a woman whose life would have dropped her off at such a humble station. De Niro, as a quiet, prideful man who feels foolish and like 'a big dummy' trying to learn, does in fact come across as self-consciously awkward and a tad silly, though his performance includes some muted, winning comedy.

....

■ STAR, THE

1952, 90 MINS, US ⑫
Dir Stuart Heisler   *Prod* Bert E. Friedlob   *Scr* Katherine Albert, Dale Eunson   *Ph* Ernest Laszlo   *Ed* Otto Ludwig   *Mus* Victor Young   *Art Dir* Boris Levin
● Bette Davis, Sterling Hayden, Natalie Wood, Warner Anderson, Minor Watson, June Travis (Friedlob/20th Century-Fox)

A strong performance by Bette Davis, in a tailor-made role, gives a lift to *The Star* that it might not have had otherwise.

There is a 'tradey' feel to the story, as befits the backstage Hollywood plot. Opening finds Davis sulking outside an auction house that is selling her last possessions to pay her creditors. A meeting there with her agent-friend (Warner Anderson) and a pitch for him to get her another picture fails. She gets drunk, is arrested and bailed out by a boating man (Sterling Hayden).

Hayden tries to get her to forget a film career and become a normal, natural woman. She tries, but fails at holding a department store job, and wangles a screen test from a kindly producer.

With most of the footage concentrating on Davis' character, there isn't too much for the other players to do.

☐ 1952: Nomination: Best Actress (Bette Davis)

....

■ STAR!

(Aka: Those Were the Happy Days)

1968, 165 MINS, US ◇ ⑫ ⊙
Dir Robert Wise   *Prod* Saul Chaplin   *Scr* William Fairchild   *Ph* Ernest Laszlo   *Ed* William Reynolds   *Mus* Lennie Hayton (arr.)   *Art Dir* Boris Leven
● Julie Andrews, Richard Crenna, Michael Craig, Daniel Massey, Robert Reed, Bruce Forsyth (20th Century-Fox)

Julie Andrews' portrayal of the late, great musicomedy idol, Gertrude Lawrence, occasionally sags between musical numbers but the cast and team of redoubtable technical contributors have helped to turn out a pleasing tribute to one of the theatre's most admired stars.

It gives a fascinating coverage of Lawrence's spectacular rise to showbiz fame, and also a neatly observed background of an epoch now gone.

The film has, as its framework, the star sitting in with a TV producer watching a supposed black-and-white TV documentary of her career.

It's a tricky but meaty role, but even those intimate with Lawrence's work and personality will quickly settle for accepting, in Andrews' carefully built-up performance, the illusion that they're watching Lawrence. Andrews, however, tends to overdo the cockney hoydenishness in the early stages.

Humor is more witty than boisterously funny, while the 17 musical numbers are staged in polished fashion [by Michael Kidd].

☐ 1968: Nominations: Best Supp. Actor (Daniel Massey), Cinematography, Costume Design, Art Direction, Adapted Musical Score, Song ('Star!'), Sound

....

■ STAR CHAMBER, THE

1983, 109 MINS, US ◇ ⑫ ⊙
Dir Peter Hyams   *Prod* Frank Yablans   *Scr* Roderick Taylor, Peter Hyams   *Ph* Richard Hannah   *Ed* Jim Mitchell   *Mus* Michael Small   *Art Dir* Bill Malley
● Michael Douglas, Hal Holbrook, Yaphet Kotto, Sharon Gless, James B. Sikking, Yaphet Kotto (20th Century-Fox)

Producer and director exhibit an excess of faith in today's educational system if they think the bulk of today's filmgoing audience will know the title's 15th-century derivation as an extra-judicial body.

Chamber does start out on an important note. The US criminal justice system is not only collapsing but what's left has been perverted until the victims of crime have no hope of satisfaction nor protection.

As a decent, conscientious judge, Michael Douglas deals with the problem daily, forced by straining legal precedent to free the obviously 'guilty'.

Severely stricken by one event, Douglas turns to his friend and mentor, Hal Holbrook, who is secretly part of a group of judges who mete out their own fatal sentences on criminals who've been through their real courts and gone free.

Getting to this point in the film, there's a pleasure in rediscovering intelligent dialog, ably provided by Hyams and Roderick Taylor. But the talk is haunted by concern that this intellectual morass cannot be solved within the confines of cinema.

....

■ STARDUST

1974, 113 MINS, UK ◇ ⑫
Dir Michael Apted   *Prod* David Puttnam, Sandy Lieberson   *Scr* Ray Connolly   *Ph* Tony Richmond   *Ed* Mike Bradsell   *Mus* Dave Edmunds, David Puttnam (arr.)
● David Essex, Adam Faith, Larry Hagman, Ines Des Longchamps, Rosalind Ayres, Marty Wilde (EMI/Goodtimes)

Several members of the team that put together the highly successful *That'll Be the Day* [1973] are associated with this much more

elaborate and ambitious followup.

Singer-guitarist Jim Maclaine (David Essex), seen on the verge of maturity and foretasting fame and fortune at the end of *Day*, is followed here on his rapid rise and fall as the eventual star of a heterogeneous pop group, the Stray Cats, as it makes it first in the nabes, then in the UK, US and the world.

En route, pic details the loves, joys and tribulations, hardships and achievements, jealousies, superficialities and hypocrisies, as well as – and importantly – the damning effect of drugs, of the music scene glimpsed from the lowest beginnings to number one position in the global charts.

....

■ STARDUST MEMORIES

1980, 89 MINS, US ⑫ ⊙
Dir Woody Allen   *Prod* Robert Greenhut   *Scr* Woody Allen   *Ph* Gordon Willis   *Ed* Susan E. Morse   *Art Dir* Mel Bourne
● Woody Allen, Charlotte Rampling, Marie-Christine Barrault, Jessica Harper, Amy Wright, Tony Roberts (United Artists)

While Woody Allen teased with autobiography in *Manhattan* and *Annie Hall* he drops all pretense here. No effort is made to pretend that his character of Sandy Bates is anybody but Allen himself – a filmmaker first adored for wacky comedies, then gradually appreciated as a cinematic genius.

But Bates-Allen thinks those who like his early comedies more than his later 'deeper' pictures are buffoons; he thinks those who try to sift through the meaning of his later works are intellectual lamebrains and he makes clear that any attempt to analyze *Stardust Memories* itself would be the height of pompous pretension.

Though there are laughs along the way, this is a truly mean-spirited picture. Once a sympathetic nebbish, Allen here sees himself as a put-upon, embittered genius, disdainful of everything around him.

....

■ STAR 80

1983, 102 MINS, US ◇ ⑫ ⊙
Dir Bob Fosse   *Prod* Wolfgang Glattes, Kenneth Utt   *Scr* Bob Fosse   *Ph* Sven Nykvist   *Ed* Alan Helm   *Mus* Ralph Burns   *Art Dir* Jack G. Taylor Jr.
● Mariel Hemingway, Eric Roberts, Cliff Robertson, Carroll Baker, Roger Rees, David Clennon (Ladd Company)

Bob Fosse takes another look at the underside of the success trip in *Star 80*, an engrossing, unsentimental and unavoidably depressing account of the short life and ghastly death of Playmate-actress Dorothy Stratten.

Stratten was a sweet, voluptuous blonde who became a popular Playmate of the Year in Playboy, appeared in a few films, all of which are forgettable except for Peter Bogdanovich's *They All Laughed* (1981), and was brutally killed by her estranged husband in a murder-suicide in 1980.

As played here by Mariel Hemingway, Stratten is a virginal, extremely insecure teenager – almost a baby, really – in Vancouver who is swooped down upon by smalltime hustler Paul Snider. Although doubtlessly in love with his discovery, Snider uses Stratten as his ticket to the big time in LA.

Give Stratten's passivity and pliability, histrionics fall to the Snider character, and Eric Roberts gives a startlingly fine performance as this pathetic loser.

....

■ STAR IS BORN, A

1937, 111 MINS, US ◇ ⑫ ⊙
Dir William A. Wellman   *Prod* David O. Selznick   *Scr* Robert Carson, Dorothy Parker, Alan Campbell

Ph W. Howard Greene   *Ed* Hal C. Kern   *Mus* Max
Steiner   *Art Dir* Lansing C. Holden
● Janet Gaynor, Fredric March, Adolphe Menjou, May
Robson, Andy Devine, Lionel Stander (Selznick/United
Artists)

Although not the first film which has attempted to capitalize the international reputation of Hollywood, it is unquestionably the most effective one yet made. The highly commendable results are achieved with a minimum of satiric hokum and a maximum of honest story telling.

Film is photographed throughout in Technicolor. Several scenes impress on sheer beauty and composition – a view of the California desert backed by snow-capped mountains, a garden landscape with swans in the foreground, a Pacific sunset towards which the broken screen idol swims to his tragic death. Colors of the interiors are soft and subdued.

Story [by William A. Wellman, Robert Carson] relates the experiences of a young girl who rises to cinema fame while her husband, having touched the heights, is on a swift descent. Love is the heroine; alcohol, the villain.

Janet Gaynor gives to her role, the small town girl who makes good, a characterization of sustained loveliness. She is equally as good in the comedy passages.

The same, without reservation, may be said for Fredric March and the manner in which he plays the passe star, Norman Maine. He creates a finely drawn portrait of weakness without viciousness, a demoralization which reminds of George Hurstwood in Theodore Dreiser's novel *Sister Carrie*.

Others in the cast also are excellent, including Adolphe Menjou, who plays a producer; Lionel Stander, as a studio publicity man; Andy Devine, an assistant director, and May Robson.
□ 1937: Best Original Story, Special Award (color cinematography).
□ Nominations: Best Picture, Director, Actor (Fredric March), Actress (Janet Gaynor), Screenplay, Assistant Director (Eric Stacey)

■ STAR IS BORN, A

1954, 182 MINS, US ◇ ⑫ ⊙
Dir George Cukor   *Prod* Sid Luft   *Scr* Moss Hart
Ph Sam Leavitt   *Mus* Ray Heindorf (dir.)
Art Dir Malcolm Bert
● Judy Garland, James Mason, Jack Carson, Charles
Bickford, Tom Noonan, Lucy Marlow (Warner/Transcona)

A Star Is Born was a great 1937 moneymaker and it's an even greater picture in its filmusical transmutation.

Unfolded in the showmanly adaptation is a strong personal saga which somehow becomes, in a sense, integrated into the celluloid plot. The reel and the real-life values sometimes play back and forth, in pendulum fashion, and the unspooling is never wanting for heart-wallop and gutsy entertainment values.

Judy Garland glitters with that stardust which in the plot the wastrel star James Mason recognizes. And her loyalties are as Gibraltar amidst the house of cards which periodically seem to collapse around her and upon him.

From the opening drunken debacle at the Shrine benefit to the scandalous antics of a hopeless dipsomaniac when his wife (Garland) wins the Academy Award, there is an intense pattern of real-life mirrorings.

Whatever the production delays, which allegedly piled up a near-$5 million production cost, the end-results are worth it.

[Version reviewed is the original premiere one. Pic was subsequently cut to 154 mins. A 1983 partial restoration runs 170 mins.]
□ 1954: Nominations: Best Actor (James Mason), Actress (Judy Garland), Color

Costume Design, Color Art Direction, Scoring of a Musical Picture, Song ('The Man That Got Away')

■ STAR IS BORN, A

1976, 140 MINS, US ◇ ⑫
Dir Frank Pierson   *Prod* Jon Peters   *Scr* John Gregory
Dunne, Joan Didion, Frank Pierson   *Ph* Robert Surtees
Ed Peter Zinner   *Art Dir* Polly Platt
● Barbra Streisand, Kris Kristofferson, Paul Mazursky,
Gary Busey, Oliver Clark, Vanetta Fields (Warner)

A Star Is Born has the rare distinction of being a superlative remake. Film rightfully credits the original William Wellman-Robert Carson story on which David O. Selznick mounted his 1937 version, the first to use this title.

Plot picks up Kris Kristofferson past his rock superstar prime, unable or unwilling to make his tour commitments, raising hell and alienating people. His success has become a machine, supervised by Paul Mazursky (as a smooth rock music manager), kept in line by Gary Busey, and attended to by Sally Kirkland, Joanne Linville and others who typify the coterie that comes with fame.

Barbra Streisand is discovered in a tacky nitery, singing with Vanetta Fields and Clydie King. There's a lot of music in the film, mostly by Paul Williams and Kenny Ascher, and it's important to note that, while the material is better than the rest, in the context of the story it should be that way.
□ 1976: Best Song ('Evergreen')
□ Nominations: Best Cinematography, Adapted Score, Sound

■ STARLIGHT HOTEL

1987, 93 MINS, NEW ZEALAND ◇ ⑫ ⊙
Dir Sam Pillsbury   *Prod* Finola Dwyer, Larry Parr
Scr Grant Hindin Miller   *Ph* Warrick Attewell   *Ed* Mike
Horton   *Art Dir* Mike Beacroft
● Peter Phelps, Greer Robson, Marshall Napier, The
Wizard, Alice Fraser, Patrick Smyth (Challenge)

Starlight Hotel is a road movie [from Grant Hinden Miller's 1986 novel *The Dream Monger*] centering on the friendship between a man on the run from the law and a 13-year-old girl looking for her father. Setting is the central South Island in 1930, with farmers forced to leave their land as the Depression bites. Kate (Greer Robson) runs away to try to find her father, who's looking for work in Wellington on the North Island.

She soon encounters Patrick (Peter Phelps), a man whose life was shattered by his experiences in the world war and later when his wife left him. He's wanted by the police for beating a repo man who was taking advantage during the Depression, and is trying to get to a port and then passage to Australia.

All the classic elements of this kind of film are here: jumping on trains, hiding out in barns, making friends and enemies along the way. The film benefits enormously from the charismatic performances in the leads. Phelps, an Aussie actor, gives a rugged, charming performance. Robson, the little girl in *Smash Palace*, has the required toughness and sensitivity for this role.

Title refers to the 'hotel' where the runaways sleep: under the stars.

■ STARMAN

1984, 115 MINS, US ◇ ⑫ ⊙
Dir John Carpenter   *Prod* Larry J. Franco   *Scr* Bruce A.
Evans, Raynold Gideon   *Ph* Donald M. Morgan
Ed Marion Rothman   *Mus* Jack Nitzsche   *Art Dir* Daniel
Lomino
● Jeff Bridges, Karen Allen, Charles Martin Smith,
Richard Jaeckel, Robert Phalen, Tony Edwards (Columbia-
Delphi II)

There is little that is original in *Starman*, but at least it has chosen good models. As amal-

gam of elements introduced in *Close Encounters of the Third Kind*, *E.T.* and even *The Man Who Fell to Earth*, *Starman* shoots for the miraculous and only partially hits its target.

The Starman (Jeff Bridges) arrives much like 'E.T.' – an alien in a hostile environment – but in an elaborate transformation scene he assumes human form. The body he chooses for his sojourn on Earth happens to belong to the dead husband of Jenny Hayden (Karen Allen) who lives alone in a remote section of Wisconsin.

Bridges and Allen set off on a trip across the country to a point in Arizona where the Starman must make his connection to return home.
□ 1984: Nomination: Best Actor (Jeff Bridges)

■ STAR OF MIDNIGHT

1935, 90 MINS, US ⑫ ⊙
Dir Stephen Roberts   *Prod* Pandro S. Berman
Scr Howard J. Green, Anthony Veiller, Edward Kaufman
Ph J. Roy Hunt   *Ed* Arthur Roberts   *Mus* Max Steiner
● William Powell, Ginger Rogers, Paul Kelly, Gene
Lockhart, Ralph Morgan, Leslie Fenton (RKO)

Star of Midnight is a non-camouflaged follow-up on *The Thin Man* (1934), although made by a different producer [from the novel by Arthur Somers Roche]. It hits a similar merry comedy-drama stride and attains practically the same effectiveness as screen entertainment.

William Powell is once more the happy-go-lucky master sleuth, brought into the case against his wishes and better judgment, but solving it just the same. His romance this time is not so adult, but equally humorous, and, with Ginger Rogers opposite, always interesting.

The mystery is double-barrelled, concerning the disappearance of a show's leading woman and the killing of a Broadway columnist. Powell unravels both in the customary ingenious manner, to the consternation and despite the interference of the regularly assigned policemen. As did Myrna Loy in *Thin Man*, Rogers here helps him considerably. She looks like a million, troupes splendidly and wears a pictureful of class clothes.

Smart dialog containing a good share of genuine laughs keeps Powell and Rogers occupied most of the time when they are not mystery-solving or drinking.

■ STARS AND BARS

1988, 94 MINS, US ◇ ⑫ ⊙
Dir Pat O'Connor   *Prod* Sandy Lieberson   *Scr* William
Boyd   *Ph* Jerzy Zielinski   *Ed* Michael Bradsell
Mus Stanley Myers   *Art Dir* Leslie Dilley, Stuart Craig
● Daniel Day Lewis, Harry Dean Stanton, Martha
Plimpton, Matthew Cowles, Joan Cusack, Maury Chaykin
(Columbia)

Stars and Bars represents an unfunny mixture of farce and misdirected satire. Project was developed by David Puttnam, but given to his ex-partner Sandy Lieberson to produce after Puttnam acceded to head of Columbia.

Scripted by William Boyd from his novel, thin storyline follows the misadventures of a Brit in America. Daniel Day Lewis plays the hapless hero, an art expert sent by his boss to acquire a rare Renoir painting (worth about $10 million) from hayseed Harry Dean Stanton, who claims to have bought it for $500 in France in 1946.

Bulk of pic deals with Davy Lewis' interactions with Stanton's weird brood, including Maury Chaykin as his Elvis-imitating son who has already sold the painting to unscrupulous, rival New York art dealers. Add some awkward bedroom farce (Day Lewis unconvincingly juggling his new pickup, Joan Cusack, at an Atlanta hotel with his fiancee Laurie Metcalf) and pic self-destructs rapidly.

Helmer Pat O'Connor evidences no feel for comedy. Day Lewis is downright embarrassing.

. . . .

■ **STARS LOOK DOWN, THE**

1939, 104 MINS, UK ⓥ
Dir Carol Reed   *Prod* Isadore Goldsmith   *Scr* J.B. Williams   *Ph* Mutz Greenbaum   *Ed* Reginald Beck   *Art Dir* James Carter
● Michael Redgrave, Margaret Lockwood, Emlyn Williams, Nancy Price, Edward Rigby, Cecil Parker (Grafton/Grand National)

The Stars Look Down is a visual education on British mining. A picturization of a subject long an uncomfortable wedge in the English social-political scheme, *Stars* would merit laurels alone for a faithful and gripping treatment. But film goes for more; it is a splendid dramatic portrait of those who burrow for the black diamond in England's northland. Direction is of class standing and picture is mounted with exactness of detail and technique.

Adopted from A.J. Cronin's novel of the mining town from where two sons seek different roads to success, one returning to foster misery, the other to fight on for its alleviation, film unrolls at steady pace a wealth of dramatic incident.

There are some gaps where treatment is not on par with dramatic situation. The Emlyn Williams part, the focal point of the tragedy, is under-developed, but director Carol Reed has guided well a cast that exacts the utmost generally. Michael Redgrave, as son of the strike-leader (Williams), a ne'er-do-well, and Margaret Lockwood, as a slut, share the starring honors.

. . . .

■ **STAR SPANGLED RHYTHM**

1943, 99 MINS, US
Dir George Marshall   *Prod* Joseph Sistrom   *Scr* Harry Tugend   *Ph* Leo Tover   *Ed* Arthur Schmidt   *Mus* Robert Emmett Dolan
● Victor Moore, Betty Hutton, Eddie Bracken, Anne Revere, Walter Abel (Paramount)

Except for a few gags and situations, *Rhythm* has essentially nothing new in it. But neither has a Christmas tree. Yet both bring good cheer because of the way they're dressed up. The whole thing, as Harry Tugend has written it and George Marshall directed it, is fresh, alive and full of bounce.

It's a gay and good-humored tune-pic, but on the grand scale, grand because of the personalities who wander in and out of the pic, because of the seven listenable tunes, because of the general lavishness of the production and because of the downright gaiety of the whole affair.

Best of all, most of the flock of stars do much better than the usual smile and a couple of lines. Among the names whose contribution to the film deserves more than perfunctory billing are Bing Crosby, Bob Hope, Dorothy Lamour, Paulette Goddard, Veronica Lake, Mary Martin, Victor Moore, Betty Hutton and Eddie Bracken.

Scaffolding for this galaxy is the arrival at San Pedro of Bracken and a pile of his navy shipmates. Bracken's father (Victor Moore) is a former hoss opry star who's now a gateman at the Paramount lot. Rather than disclose this comedown to Bracken, Hutton convinces Moore that he should say he's head of the studio. Bracken thereupon brings his shipmates to the lot (promising each of them a 24-karat Par blonde) and Moore has to attempt to play the big-shot that his son has billed him.

☐ 1943: Nominations: Best Scoring of a Musical Picture, Song ('Black Magic')

. . . .

■ **STAR STRUCK**

1982, 102 MINS, AUSTRALIA ◇ ⓥ ⊙
Dir Gillian Armstrong   *Prod* David Elfick, Richard Brennan   *Scr* Stephen Maclean   *Ph* Russell Boyd   *Ed* Nicholas Beauman   *Mus* Mark Moffatt   *Art Dir* Brian Thomson
● Jo Kennedy, Ross O'Donovan, Pat Evison, Margo Lee, Max Cullen, Ned Lander (Palm Beach)

Picture is a raucous, 'let's put on a show' musical with a punk rock beat. Story centers on an enterprising 14-year-old entrepreneur Ross O'Donovan who has big career plans for his cousin, singer Jo Kennedy. Grooming (?) her in the punk mode, O'Donovan has his sights on copping first prize on a New Year's television talent show.

However, he can't get the attention of a powerful Sydney disk jockey until he stages a daring balancing tightrope stunt for Kennedy. Suddenly, she's a media star quickly homogenized for home consumption. Meanwhile, the family hotel-bar is on the verge of bankruptcy. The $25,000 talent prize becomes all-important to save the failing establishment.

Script is pure fantasy material offering director Gillian Armstrong the opportunity to send-up the likes of Busby Berkeley and Garland-Rooney musicals. The film certainly doesn't lack energy. Camerawork by Russell Boyd is glossy and fluid and song-and-dance routines are loud and splashy. Regrettably, the choreography is uninspired.

. . . .

■ **STARTING OVER**

1979, 106 MINS, US ◇ ⓥ ⊙
Dir Alan J. Pakula   *Prod* Alan J. Pakula   *Scr* James L. Brooks   *Ph* Sven Nykvist   *Ed* Marion Rothman   *Mus* Marvin Hamlisch   *Art Dir* George Jenkins
● Burt Reynolds, Jill Clayburgh, Candice Bergen, Charles Durning, Frances Sternhagen, Austin Pendleton (Paramount/Brook)

Starting Over takes on the subject of marital dissolution from a comic point of view, and succeeds admirably, wryly directed by Alan J. Pakula, and featuring an outstanding cast.

In fact, *Starting Over* [from the novel by Dan Wakefield] favorably evokes the screwball comedies of the 1930s and the heyday of American screen comedy.

Burt Reynolds plays a mild-mannered writer unwillingly foisted into a 'liberated' condition by spouse Candice Bergen, feeling her feminine oats as a songwriter. Fleeing to Boston and protection of relatives Charles Durning and Frances Sternhagen, he meets spinster schoolteacher Jill Clayburgh, and the off-and-on romance begins.

With unfailing comic timing Reynolds is the core of the film, and underplays marvellously.

☐ 1979: Nominations: Best Actress (Jill Clayburgh), Supp. Actress (Candice Bergen)

. . . .

■ **STAR TREK**
THE MOTION PICTURE

1979, 132 MINS, US ◇ ⓥ ⊙
Dir Robert Wise   *Prod* Gene Roddenberry   *Scr* Harold Livingston   *Ph* Richard H. Kline   *Ed* Todd Ramsay   *Mus* Jerry Goldsmith   *Art Dir* Harold Michelson
● William Shatner, Leonard Nimoy, DeForest Kelley, Stephen Collins, James Doohan, Persis Khambatta (Paramount)

The *Enterprise* has been completely reconditioned during a two-year drydock, but must be prematurely dispatched to intercept an Earth-bound attacker.

William Shatner's Kirk is told to lead the mission along with other show regulars.

Upshot is a search-and-destroy thriller [based on a story by Alan Dean Foster] that includes all of the ingredients the TV show's fans thrive on: the philosophical dilemma wrapped in a scenario of mind control,

troubles with the space ship, the dependable and understanding Kirk, the ever-logical Spock, and suspenseful take with twist ending. Touches of romance and corn also dot this voyage.

But the expensive effects (under supervision of Douglas Trumbull) are the secret of this film, and the amazing wizardry throughout would appear to justify the whopping budget. Jerry Goldsmith's brassy score is the other necessary plus.

☐ 1979: Nominations: Best Art Direction, Original Score, Visual Effects

. . . .

■ **STAR TREK II**
THE WRATH OF KHAN

1982, 113 MINS, US ◇ ⓥ ⊙
Dir Nicholas Meyer   *Prod* Robert Sallin   *Scr* Jack B. Sowards   *Ph* Gayne Rescher   *Ed* William P. Dornisch   *Mus* James Horner, Alexander Courage   *Art Dir* Joseph R. Jennings
● William Shatner, Leonard Nimoy, DeForest Kelley, Ricardo Montalban, James Doohan, Walter Koenig (Paramount)

Star Trek II is a very satisfying space adventure, closer in spirit and format to the popular TV series than to its big-budget predecessor.

Story is nominally a sequel to the TV episode *Space Seed*, with Starship Reliant captain Terrell (Paul Winfield) and Commander Chekov (Walter Koenig) incorrectly landing on a planet on an exploration mission. This allows the evil Khan (Ricardo Montalban) who was marooned there with his family and crew 15 years before by Kirk (William Shatner), to take over the Reliant and vow revenge on Kirk.

Admiral Kirk is coaxed to take command once again of the Starship *Enterprise* on a training mission, travels to the Regula space station on a rescue mission. Dr Carol Marcus (Bibi Besch) and her (and Kirk's) son David (Merritt Butrick) have been working there on the Genesis Project, to convert barren planets into Eden-like sources of life. Khan has stolen the Genesis Effect equipment.

Final reel is a classic of emotional manipulation: Spock unhesitatingly calculates that he must sacrifice himself to save the Enterprise crew.

. . . .

■ **STAR TREK III**
THE SEARCH FOR SPOCK

1984, 105 MINS, US ◇ ⓥ ⊙
Dir Leonard Nimoy   *Prod* Harve Bennett   *Scr* Harve Bennett   *Ph* Charles Correll   *Ed* Robert F. Shugrue   *Mus* James Horner, Alexander Courage   *Art Dir* John E. Chilberg II
● William Shatner, DeForest Kelley, James Doohan, George Takei, Walter Koenig, Leonard Nimoy (Paramount)

Star Trek III is an emotionally satisfying science fiction adventure. Dovetailing neatly with the previous entry in the popular series *Star Trek II*, film centers upon a quest to seemingly bring Spock (Leonard Nimoy), the noble science officer and commander who selflessly gave his life to save 'the many', back to life.

Spock's friend, Admiral Kirk (William Shatner) is visited by Spock's Vulcan father (Mark Lenard), who informs him that Spock's living spirit may still be alive via a mindmeld with one of Kirk's crew and must be taken to the planet Vulcan to be preserved.

Kirk discovers who the 'possessed' crew member is, and with his other shipmates, steals the Enterprise out of its dock and sets off for Vulcan.

☐ 1986: Nominations: Best Cinematography, Original Score, Sound, Sound Effects Editing

S

STAR TREK IV
THE VOYAGE HOME

1986, 119 MINS, US ◇ ◐ ⊙
Dir Leonard Nimoy   *Prod* Harve Bennett   *Scr* Harve
Bennett, Steve Meerson, Peter Krikes, Nicholas Meyer
Ph Don Peterman   *Ed* Peter E. Berger   *Mus* Leonard
Rosenman   *Art Dir* Jack T. Collis
● William Shatner, Leonard Nimoy, DeForest Kelley,
James Doohan, Catherine Hicks, George Takei (Bennett)

Latest excursion is warmer, wittier, more socially relevant and truer to its TV origins
than prior odysseys.

This voyage finds the crew earthbound but
they find the galaxy dark and messages from
Earth distorted. Spock locates the source of
the trouble in the bleating, eerie sounds of an
unidentified probe and links them to a cry
from the Earth's past that has long been silenced. Scripters employ successful use of
time travel.

Spock (Leonard Nimoy) and Kirk (William
Shatner) play off each other in a sort of deadpan futuristic version of Hope and Crosby
with Nimoy, surprisingly, as the awkward one
relying on Shatner's smooth talking to win
the help of a zealous save-the-whales biologist
(Catherine Hicks) in capturing a couple of
specimens.

....

STAR TREK V
THE FINAL FRONTIER

1989, 106 MINS, US ◇ ◐ ⊙
Dir William Shatner   *Prod* Harve Bennett   *Scr* David
Loughery   *Ph* Andrew Laszlo   *Ed* Peter Berger
Mus Jerry Goldsmith   *Art Dir* Herman Zimmerman
● William Shatner, Leonard Nimoy, DeForest Kelley,
James Doohan, Nichelle Nichols, George Takei
(Paramount)

Even diehard Trekkies may be disappointed
by *Star Trek V*. Coming after Leonard Nimoy's
delightful directorial outing on *Star Trek IV*,
William Shatner's inauspicious feature directing debut is a double letdown.

A major flaw in the story [by Shatner,
Harve Bennett and David Loughery] is that it
centers on an obsessive quest by a character
who isn't a member of the Enterprise crew, a
renegade Vulcan played by Laurence
Luckinbill in Kabuki-like makeup. The crazed
Luckinbill kidnaps the crew and makes them
fly to a never-before-visited planet at the centre of the galaxy in quest of the Meaning of
Life.

Better they should have stayed home and
watched reruns of the TV series, which had a
lot more to say about the meaning of life.

Shatner, rises to the occasion, however, in
directing a dramatic sequence of the mystical
Luckinbill teaching Nimoy and DeForest
Kelley to re-experience their long-buried
traumas. The re-creations of Spock's rejection by his father after his birth and Kelley's
euthanasia of his own father are moving highlights.

....

STAR TREK VI
THE UNDISCOVERED COUNTRY

1991, 109 MINS, US ◇ ◐ ⊙
Dir Nicholas Meyer   *Prod* Ralph Winter, Steven-Charles
Jaffe   *Scr* Nicholas Meyer, Denny Martin Flinn   *Ph* Hiro
Narita   *Ed* Ronald Roose, William Hoy   *Mus* Cliff
Eidelman   *Art Dir* Herman Zimmerman
● William Shatner, Leonard Nimoy, DeForest Kelley,
Kim Cattrall, David Warner, Christopher Plummer
(Paramount)

Weighed down by a midsection even flabbier
than the long-in-the-tooth cast, director
Nicholas Meyer still delivers enough of what
Trek auds hunger for to justify the trek to the
local multiplex.

Following a Chernobyl-like disaster, a
Klingon leader seeks peace with the
Federation, the Klingon economy and envi-

ronment having been depleted by constant
warring – a not-at-all-veiled parable for the
end of the Cold War. Kirk & Co are sent, reluctantly, to escort the leader to peace talks
on earth, but conspirators seek to scuttle the
detente by assassinating him and pinning the
blame on the Enterprise.

Unfortunately, the murder is a rather tepid
mystery and the ice planet to which Kirk and
McCoy travel feels like a pale imitation of the
Star Wars films. Pace and visual trappings
pick up considerably in the final frames, when
the Enterprise rides to the rescue of the
peace talks, in the process dueling a Klingon
Vessel.

Meyer and co-scripter Denny Martin Flinn
[working from a story by Leonard Nimoy,
Lawrence Konner and Mark Rosenthal] also
have loaded the film with sentimental
touches. (Why Christian Slater turns up in an
uncredited cameo is anybody's guess.) Chris
Eidelman's terrific score manages to stand on
its own yet still evoke earlier work associated
with the pics and series. Sappy ending provides a fitting send-off (and ridiculously literal sign-off) to the ground-breaking series
and its rabid fans, reinforcing its humanistic
messages and fairy-tale trappings. [Pic is dedicated to creator Gene Roddenberry who died
in 1991.]
□ 1991: Nominations: Best Sound Effects
Editing, Makeup

....

STAR WARS

1977, 121 MINS, US ◇ ◐ ⊙
Dir George Lucas   *Prod* Gary Kurtz   *Scr* George Lucas
Ph Gilbert Taylor   *Ed* Paul Hirsch, Marcia Lucas, Richard
Chew   *Mus* John Williams   *Art Dir* John Barry
● Mark Hamill, Harrison Ford, Carrie Fisher, Peter
Cushing, Alec Guinness, Anthony Daniels (20th Century-
Fox)

Star Wars is a magnificent film. George Lucas
set out to make the biggest possible adventure fantasy out of his memories of serials
and older action epics, and he succeeded brilliantly.

The superb balance of technology and human drama is one of the many achievements:
one identifies with the characters and accepts, as do they, the intriguing intergalactic
world in which they live.

Carrie Fisher is delightful as the regal, but
spunky princess on a rebel planet who has
been kidnapped by Peter Cushing, would-be
ruler of the universe. Mark Hamill is excellent as a farm boy who sets out to rescue
Fisher in league with Alec Guinness, last survivor of a band of noble knights.

Harrison Ford is outstanding as a likeable
mercenary pilot.
□ 1977: Best Art Direction, Sound (Don
MacDougall, Ray West, Bob Minkler, Derek
Ball), Original Score, Editing, Costume
Design (John Mollo), Visual Effects, Special
Achievement Award (sound effects)
□ Nominations: Best Picture, Supp. Actor
(Alec Guinness), Original Screenplay

....

STATE FAIR

1933, 80 MINS, US
Dir Henry King   *Prod* Winfield Sheehan   *Scr* Paul
Green, Sonya Levien   *Ph* Hal Mohr   *Ed* R. W. Bischoff
Mus Ray Flynn   *Art Dir* Duncan Cramer
● Will Rogers, Janet Gaynor, Lew Ayres, Sally Eilers,
Norman Foster, Louise Dresser (Fox)

Based on Phil Stong's bestseller written
around a country fair, Henry King has nicely
caught the spirit of the simple story and has
turned in a production that has the charm of
naturalness and the virtue of sincerity.

No villain, little suspense, but a straightforward story of a rural family who find their
great moments at the state fair, where paterfamilias captures the title for his prize hog,

the mother makes a clean sweep in the pickle
entries, the boy gets his first vicarious but satisfying taste of romance, and the girl finds a
more lasting love.

Of chief interest is the debut of a new romance team in Janet Gaynor and Lew Ayres.
His rather flippant style gives a needed tang
to situations which sometimes in the past
have been too saccharine. It is a charming romance between these two. There is interest,
too, in the less wholesome romance of the boy
with the girl of the acrobatic act. Norman
Foster and Sally Eilers handle this capably,
while there is just enough of Will Rogers'
quaint humor and Louise Dresser's country
dame to temper the more hectic moments.

For a moment Victor Jory steals the screen
as the concession owner who gypped young
Frake (Foster) the year before and smilingly
prepares to repeat, only to find that his erstwhile victim has spent the twelve-month interval in practising to ring the prizes and is
practically a dead shot. There is even a humorous twist to the porcine romance of Blue
Boy, the prize hog, who comes to life only
when he meets Esmeralda, the red-headed
sow.
□ 1932/33: Nominations: Best Picture,
Adaptation

....

STATE FAIR

1945, 100 MINS, US ◇ ◐
Dir Walter Lang   *Prod* William Perlberg   *Scr* Oscar
Hammerstein II   *Ph* Leon Shamroy   *Ed* J. Watson Webb
Mus Alfred Newman, Charles Henderson (dirs.)
Art Dir Lyle R. Wheeler, Lewis Creber
● Jeanne Crain, Dana Andrews, Dick Haymes, Vivian
Blaine, Charles Winninger, Fay Bainter (20th Century-
Fox)

The Philip Stong novel, which Oscar
Hammerstein II authored for the latest
screen version [adapted by Sonya Levien and
Paul Green], is still a boy-meets-girl yarn that
has lost none of the flavor of the years. And
notably distinctive in the telling is the frequent punctuation of the story by the
Rodgers-Hammerstein tunes. Otherwise, the
yarn is still the one of midwest rustication,
concerning mainly the hoopla attendant to
the annual state fair, at which products, from
pickles to hogs, are displayed for judging and
prizes.

Jeanne Crain and Dick Haymes are the
Frake progeny, and Dana Andrews is the
newspaper reporter who covers the fair and is
the other half of the Crain romantic attachment. Haymes and Blaine handle the other
romantic situation. Fay Bainter is the
mother.

The film's top tune is 'That's for Me', featured by Vivian Blaine in a bandstand sequence. It's a sock ballad. Not too far behind
is another, 'It Might As Well Be Spring', sung
by Crain. 'It's a Grand Night for Singing', by
Haymes, is another. The tunes are whammo
from both lyrical and melody content, made
evident by the allotment of one to each of the
three singing principals.
□ 1945: Best Song ('It Might As Well Be
Spring').
□ Nomination: Best Scoring of a Musical
Picture

....

STATE FAIR

1962, 118 MINS, US ◇ ◐
Dir Jose Ferrer   *Prod* Charles Brackett   *Scr* Richard
Breen   *Ph* William C. Mellor   *Ed* David Bretherton
Mus Alfred Newman (arr.)   *Art Dir* Jack Martin Smith,
Walter M. Simonds
● Pat Boone, Bobby Darin, Pamela Tiffin, Ann-Margret,
Tom Ewell, Alice Faye (20th Century-Fox)

This marks the third time around (1933,
1945) on the screen for this vehicle. To the
five original R&H refrains retained in this

version, five new numbers with both music and lyrics by Richard Rodgers have been added. The old songs are still charming, but they are not rendered with quite the zest and feeling of the 1945 cast.

Richard Breen's updated, reset (from Iowa to Texas) scenario isn't otherwise appreciably altered from the last time out. Same three love affairs are there (involving four people and two Hampshire hogs). Same brandy-spiked mince meat episode. Fairgrounds, however, have been switched to Dallas, and there's something crass and antiseptic about the atmosphere – a significant loss.

None of the four young stars comes off especially well. Pat Boone and Bobby Darin emerge rather bland and unappealing. Pamela Tiffin's range of expression seems rather narrow on this occasion. Of the four, Ann-Margret makes perhaps the most vivid impression, particularly during her torrid song-dance rendition of 'Isn't It Kind of Fun', the film's big production number.

. . . .

■ STATE OF GRACE

1990, 134 MINS, US ◇ ⓦ ⊙
Dir Phil Joanou   *Prod* Ned Dowd, Randy Ostrow, Ron Rotholz   *Scr* Dennis McIntyre   *Ph* Jordan Cronenweth   *Ed* Claire Simpson   *Mus* Ennio Morricone   *Art Dir* Patrizia Von Brandenstein, Doug Kraner
● Sean Penn, Ed Harris, Gary Oldman, Robin Wright, John Turturro, Burgess Meredith (Cinehaus/Orion)

State of Grace is a handsomely produced, mostly riveting, but ultimately overlong and overindulgent gangster picture.

Sean Penn plays Terry, one of New York's Irish residents who grew up in Hell's Kitchen with his friends, brothers Frankie (Ed Harris) and Jackie (Gary Oldman) and their sister, Kathleen (Robin Wright), with whom he was once in love.

Terry's been away from New York for 12 years, but now he returns and signs up with the Irish mob headed by the ruthless Frankie. He also resumes his passionate relationship with Kathleen. Terry isn't all he seems, and in fact he's an undercover cop assigned to get the goods on Frankie.

Penn is excellent as Terry, who drinks too much and who ultimately gets too personally involved with his mission. Harris is a malevolent Frankie, who carries out his executions personally. Oldman is suitably manic as the unstable younger brother. Wright, though she gives a glowing performance as Kathleen, seems to belong to an altogether different movie.

. . . .

■ STATE OF THE UNION
(UK: The World and His Wife)

1948, 121 MINS, US ⓦ ⊙
Dir Frank Capra   *Prod* Frank Capra   *Scr* Anthony Veiller, Myles Connolly   *Ph* George J. Folsey   *Ed* William Hornbeck   *Mus* Victor Young   *Art Dir* Cedric Gibbons, Urie McCleary
● Spencer Tracy, Katharine Hepburn, Van Johnson, Angela Lansbury, Adolphe Menjou, Lewis Stone (M-G-M/Liberty)

The hit Broadway play by Howard Lindsay and Russel Crouse has been expanded somewhat in the screen adaptation, a broadening that makes the best use of screen technique. Dialog has headline freshness, and a stinging bite when directed at politicians, the normal voter and the election scene.

Plot deals with a power-mad femme newspaper publisher who picks a selfmade plane magnate and shoves him towards the White House to satisfy her own interests. The candidate begins to lose his commonsense when the political malarkey soaks in and only is saved by his frank and honest wife.

Cast is loaded with stalwarts who deliver in top form. The fact that it's pat casting only

helps to insure the payoff. Spencer Tracy fits his personality to the role of the airplane manufacturer who becomes a presidential aspirant. It's a sock performance. Katharine Hepburn makes much of the role of Tracy's wife, giving it understanding and warmth that register big. Van Johnson shines as the columnist turned political press agent. It's one of his better performances.

Capra's direction punches over the pictorial expose of US politics and candidate manufacturers, the indifference of the average voter, and the need for more expression of true public opinion at the polls.

. . . .

■ STATION SIX-SAHARA

1964, 97 MINS, UK
Dir Seth Holt   *Prod* Victor Lyndon   *Scr* Bryan Forbes, Brian Clemens   *Ph* Gerald Gibbs   *Ed* Alastair McIntyre   *Mus* Ron Grainer   *Art Dir* Jack Stephens
● Carroll Baker, Peter Van Eyck, Ian Bannen, Denholm Elliott, Jorg Felmy, Mario Adorf (Allied Artists)

Station Six-Sahara is a sex melodrama [from the play, *Men without a Past*, by Jacques Maret], filmed in the Libyan desert with Carroll Baker. Story premise of a sexpot arriving at an isolated desert oil pipeline station where five lonely men have only one thing in common – the nagging need for a woman – is generally well developed.

Good interest is early sustained despite fact that Baker does not appear for first 42 minutes. Limited confines of the rude station settings puts emphasis strictly upon yarn unfoldment and permits director Seth Holt to display his helming while audience awaits entrance of femme star, only woman in cast. With her entry into plot, when a car roars out of the night and eager hands, after it crashes, lift her seductive figure out of the wreckage, attention picks up perceptibly as the men react in varying degrees and kind to her presence.

Baker, in what amounts actually to a smaller role, feelingly delineates this key character and makes her work count. Peter Van Eyck, in charge of the station which he operates with typical cold Teutonic efficiency, is smooth and convincing. Jorg Felmy, another German with icy self-control, underplays his role for excellent effect. Ian Bannen, a Scotsman with a sour sense of humor, and Denholm Elliott, a paperspined Englishman who lives on memories of the desert war in World War II, persuasively portray their respective parts.

. . . .

■ STAY HUNGRY

1976, 102 MINS, US ◇ ⓦ
Dir Bob Rafelson   *Prod* Harold Schneider   *Scr* Charles Gaines, Bob Rafelson   *Ph* Victor Kemper   *Ed* John F. Link III   *Mus* Bruce Langhorne   *Art Dir* Toby Carr Rafelson
● Jeff Bridges, Sally Field, Arnold Schwarzenegger, R.G. Armstrong, Robert Englund, Helena Kallianiotes (United Artists)

Stay Hungry features an excellent Jeff Bridges as a spoiled but affable rich young Alabama boy who slums his way to maturity through relationships with street-smart characters.

Bridges gets involved in a big urban real estate scheme with Joe Spinell and cohorts, all buying up small plots for a major development. But R.G. Armstrong's second-rate gym can't be had, so Bridges decides to infiltrate.

There he falls for Sally Field and also is exposed to the barbell denizens who include real-life bodybuilding champ Arnold Schwarzenegger, good-natured staffer Robert Englund, uptight ladies instructor Helena Kallianiotes and amiable attendant Roger E. Mosely.

All these characters conflict with Bridges' family and social circle. But underneath it all is a lurching and poorly defined film concept.

. . . .

■ STAYING ALIVE

1983, 96 MINS, US ◇ ⓦ ⊙
Dir Sylvester Stallone   *Prod* Robert Stigwood, Sylvester Stallone   *Scr* Sylvester Stallone, Norman Wexler   *Ph* Nick McLean   *Ed* Don Zimmerman, Mark Warner   *Mus* The Bee Gees   *Art Dir* Robert F. Boyle
● John Travolta, Cynthia Rhodes, Finola Hughes, Steve Inwood, Julie Bovasso, Frank Stallone (Stigwood/Paramount)

The bottom line is that *Staying Alive* is nowhere as good as its 1977 predecessor, *Saturday Night Fever*.

When last heard from, John Travolta's Tony Manero had left Brooklyn for an uncertain future in Manhattan. Now, he's on the rounds of casting calls and auditions for Broadway dance shows.

He's also got a comfortable but uncommitted relationship going with fellow struggling dancer and sometime saloon singer Cynthia Rhodes, who loves him a lot. Nevertheless, Travolta doesn't think twice about her feelings when he spots alluring British dancer Finola Hughes and hooks up with her while winning a background role in a show in which she will be starring.

By close to showtime, Travolta and Hughes loathe each other, and she's none too pleased when this unknown upstart manages to replace her faltering costar in the male lead of the production. The show, entitled *Satan's Alley*, emerges as an opening night smash, and Tony Manero is a success at last.

. . . .

■ STAYING TOGETHER

1989, 91 MINS, US ◇ ⓦ
Dir Lee Grant   *Prod* Joseph Feury   *Scr* Monte Merrick   *Ph* Dick Bush   *Ed* Katherine Wenning   *Art Dir* W. Steven Graham
● Sean Astin, Stockard Channing, Melinda Dillon, Jim Haynie, Levin Helm (Feury)

Staying Together, a sincerely made coming-of-age tale, serves up familiar homilies about family values in changing small-town America and the indomitable power of love.

In a bucolic town somewhere in South Carolina, Mr and Mrs McDermott and their three strapping sons run a self-named home-cooked-chicken restaurant. Mom is a tower of strength and a paragon of understanding; dad is gruff but caring, and the brothers confine their red-blooded oats-sowing, boozing and pot-smoking to their off hours.

The yuppies have landed and pop McDermott takes an offer he can't refuse for the restaurant and its choice land site.

Middle sibling Brian (essayed by Tom Cruise-John Travolta hybrid Tim Quill) has been having an affair with an older woman who's championing the developers' cause. When his dad decides to cash in, the hot-tempered kid denounces pop, leaves home and talks his way into a job on the condo construction site.

Lee Grant and screenwriter Monte Merrick push all the preprogrammed melodrama buttons, including prodigal son Brian's too-late-to-say-goodbye dash to the hospital.

. . . .

■ STAY TUNED

1992, 87 MINS, US ◇ ⓦ ⊙
Dir Peter Hyams   *Prod* James G. Robinson   *Scr* Tom S. Parker, Jim Jennewein   *Ph* Peter Hyams   *Ed* Peter E. Berger   *Mus* Bruce Broughton   *Art Dir* Philip Harrison
● John Ritter, Pam Dawber, Jeffrey Jones, David Tom, Heather McComb, Bob Dishy (Morgan Creek)

Not diabolical enough for true black comedy, and witless in its send-up of obsessive TV viewing,

Stay Tuned is a picture with nothing for everybody. As a Seattle couple trapped in a hellish cable system run by the devil himself,

John Ritter and Pam Dawber look glum for more than plot reasons. [Screen story by Tom S. Parker, Jim Jennewein, and Richard Siegel.]

Ritter is introduced as the ultimate couch potato, a depressed plumbing-supplies salesman who's a sucker for the suave Jeffrey Jones' free cable-tryout offer. The catch is that if he and Dawber don't survive 24 hours lost inside the alternative dimension, they forfeit (what else?) their souls.

The titles of the cable shows are the only (mildly) amusing things about them: *Sadistic Hidden Videos, Three Men and Rosemary's Baby, Autopsies of the Rich and Famous, Driving Over Miss Daisy.* The crudely executed skits tend to expire as soon as they are announced.

One brief respite from the overall inanity is a six-minute cartoon interlude by the masterful Chuck Jones, with Ritter and Dawber portrayed as mice menaced by a robot cat. The animation has grace and depth.

STEALING HEAVEN

1989, 110 MINS, UK/YUGOSLAVIA ◇ ▼ ⊙
Dir Clive Donner   *Prod* Simon MacCorkindale, Andros Epaminondas   *Scr* Chris Bryant   *Ph* Mikael Salomon   *Ed* Michael Ellis   *Mus* Nick Bicat   *Art Dir* Voytek
● Derek de Lint, Kim Thomson, Denholm Elliott, Bernard Hepton, Kenneth Cranham, Rachel Kempson (Amy/Jadran)

This handsome historical pageant attempts to tell the 'true story' behind one of history's most famous romances, that of 12th-century French philosopher Pierre Abelard and his beloved Heloise which has survived through the ages in the exchange of letters between them, each of them shut off from the world in another convent.

Chris Bryant's script, based on Marion Meade's novel, pushes toward a sharp and witty, anticlerical, feminist tract. Abelard shuns emotional commitments as dangerous to his intellectual capacities. Fulbert, Heloise's uncle, is a mercenary bigot who looks for the best deal on his niece; and Heloise is the smart, intelligent and unconventional girl with the courage to assume responsibility for her feelings.

STEALING HOME

1988, 98 MINS, US ◇ ▼ ⊙
Dir Steven Kampmann, Wil Aldis   *Prod* Thom Mount, Hank Moonjean   *Scr* Steven Kampmann, Will Aldis   *Ph* Bobby Byrne   *Ed* Antony Gibbs   *Mus* David Foster   *Art Dir* Vaughan Edwards
● Mark Harmon, Blair Brown, Jodie Foster, Jonathan Silverman, Harold Ramis, John Shea (Mount)

For all the sadness and loss in *Stealing Home*, the story of how a privileged boy's love for playing baseball is gone with the sudden death of his father, the film remains too remote emotionally to elicit more than a sigh of relief at its conclusion.

In suburban Philadelphia of big homes and summer beach houses most of the kids are like Billy Wyatt (played at 10, teenage and 38 by Thacher Goodwin, William McNamara and Mark Harmon respectively) and his pal Alan Appleby (Jonathan Silverman, Harold Ramis). Around for valuable lessons on how to grow up fast is the wayward and rebellious Katie (Jodie Foster), the family friends' daughter and the irresponsible babysitter that becomes for Billy a mentor, lover and tragic figure.

For Billy, baseball takes priority. It's something he breathes for and something he cherishes sharing with his equally fanatical baseball-loving dad (John Shea).

Foster's complex and confused character would have been the better choice upon which to center this melodrama. The actress is perfect for the part and, along with Ramis'

warm and funny short screen time as the adult Alan, brings whatever emotional energy there is to the proceedings.

STEAMBOAT BILL, JR

1928, 65 MINS, US ⊗ ▼ ⊙
Dir Charles F. Reisner   *Prod* Joseph M. Schenck   *Scr* Carl Harbaugh   *Ph* Dev Jennings, Bert Haines
● Buster Keaton, Ernest Torrence, Tom McGuire, Marion Byron, Tom Lewis (United Artists)

The last comedy Buster Keaton made under his United Artists contract, it was held back for several months, getting itself concerned in several wild rumors. Whatever may have been the real reason why United Artists took its time about releasing this one, it had nothing to do with quality, for it's a pip of a comedy. It's one of Keaton's best.

The story concerns the efforts of an old hard-boiled river captain (Ernest Torrence), to survive on the river in the face of opposition from a brand new modern rival boat, put in commission by his rival (Tom McGuire). The old-timer hasn't seen his son since he was an infant. The son arrives (Keaton), and things begin to happen, fast and furiously.

The son falls in love with the daughter of the rival owner. Matters reach a climax when the old tub of Steamboat Bill is condemned. In a rage, he confronts his rival and accuses him of robbing him. A battle ensues.

An excellent cast gives Keaton and Torrence big league support. Tom Lewis as the first mate, McGuire as the rival owner and Marion Byron as the girl contribute heavily. The windstorm is a gem and the river stuff interesting and colorful.

STEAMING

1985, 95 MINS, UK ◇ ▼
Dir Joseph Losey   *Prod* Paul Mills   *Scr* Patricia Losey   *Ph* Christopher Challis   *Ed* Reginald Beck   *Mus* Richard Harvey   *Art Dir* Maurice Fowler
● Vanessa Redgrave, Sarah Miles, Diana Dors, Patti Love, Brenda Bruce, Felicity Dean (World Film Service)

On film, *Steaming* lacks the impact it had on stage. The ebullience and sheer fun of the original [play by Nell Dunn] have mostly disappeared and, although this is by no means an earnest women's lib tract, it's a lesser experience.

There's no opening out – all the action takes place in a rundown steam bath on ladies day. Here we find the manager, Violet (Diana Dors), worried that the lcoal council is going to close the place down; Josie (Patti Love), an ebullient type forever talking about her sex life; conservative Mrs Meadows (Brenda Bruce) and her daughter, Dawn (Felicity Dean); and the upper-class Sarah (Sarah Miles) who introduces her friend, Nancy (Vanessa Redgrave), to the group.

Performances are all very strong, with Redgrave probably making the least impact in the rather tight-lipped role of Nancy. Miles positively glows as Sarah, while Love seizes all her opportunities in the flashiest role. Dors, who like director Joseph Losey, died soon after the film was completed, is quietly effective as the motherly Violet.

STEEL

1980, 99 MINS, US ◇ ▼
Dir Steve Carver   *Prod* Peter S. Davis, William N. Panzer   *Scr* Leigh Chapman   *Ph* Roger Shearman   *Ed* David Blewitt   *Mus* Michel Colombier   *Art Dir* Ward & Preston
● Lee Majors, Jennifer O'Neill, Art Carney, George Kennedy, Harris Yulin (Davis-Panzer/New Line)

Steel began lensing in Lexington, Kentucky, in 1978 and during production famed stuntman A.J. Bakunis died doing a tricky maneuver (pic is dedicated to him).

Lee Majors stars and exec produced and his well-crafted, restrained portrayal as the leader of the constructioners provides a solid base for a series of involving relationships.

There is an explosion and George Kennedy, the good-hearted company owner, plunges to a tragic death. Daughter Jennifer O'Neill is then left to take on the task of completing the project. Kennedy's friend Art Carney suggests O'Neill search out Majors to coordinate the job, and he rounds up the most famous workers in the business.

What unravels is a rightly-directed story and true-to-life character study of endearing personalities interacting against outside forces.

STEEL HELMET, THE

1951, 84 MINS, US ▼
Dir Samuel Fuller   *Prod* Samuel Fuller   *Scr* Samuel Fuller   *Ph* Ernest W. Miller   *Ed* Philip Cahn   *Mus* Paul Dunlap   *Art Dir* Theobald Holsopple
● Gene Evans, Robert Hutton, Richard Loo, Steve Brodie, James Edwards, William Chun (Deputy/Lippert)

The Steel Helmet pinpoints the Korean fighting in a grim, hardhitting tale that is excellently told.

A veteran top sergeant is the sole survivor of a small patrol, bound and murdered by North Koreans. He and a young native boy, who freed him, start back for the lines. They are soon joined by a Negro medic, sole survivor of another group. Trio encounters a patrol of green GIs, help them out of an ambush and go along to establish an observation post in a Korean temple. There they help direct artillery fire and capture a North Korean major hiding out in the temple.

Film serves to introduce Gene Evans as the sergeant, a vet of World War II, a tough man who is interested in staying alive, and hardened to the impact of warfare. Robert Hutton, conscientious objector in the last war but now willing to fight against communism; Steve Brodie, the lieutenant who used pull to stay out of combat previously; James Edwards, the Negro medic, and Richard Loo, a heroic Nisei, are the other principals who add to the rugged realism.

STEEL MAGNOLIAS

1989, 118 MINS, US ◇ ▼ ⊙
Dir Herbert Ross   *Prod* Ray Stark   *Scr* Robert Harling   *Ph* John A. Alonzo   *Ed* Paul Hirsch   *Mus* Georges Delerue   *Art Dir* Gene Callahan, Edward Pisoni
● Sally Field, Dolly Parton, Shirley MacLaine, Daryl Hannah, Olympia Dukakis, Julia Roberts (Rastar/Tri-Star)

Robert Harling's play was set solely in the beauty parlor where his heroines – a group of the liveliest, warmest Southern women imaginable – gather to dish dirt, crack jokes, do hair and give one another some solid, post-feminist emotional support. In opening up his own play for the screen, Harling has made actual characters of the menfolk only talked about in the play.

As Sally Field's troubled yet ever-hopeful seriously diabetic daughter, Julia Roberts has real freshness and charm of the sort that can't be faked.

As the beauty shop owner around whom all the action swirls, Dolly Parton is thoroughly in her element. Wisely she remains in character as a particular good ole gal – with the Dolly her fans love peeking out from underneath.

Shirley MacLaine is a nicely bridled caricature as the town curmudgeon. She looks a wreck, talks trash and obviously loves every minute of it.

As her partner in hamming-as-an-art-form, Olympia Dukakis just about walks away with the picture, even though she's never the center of attention in any of the film's scenes.

Daryl Hannah, not unexpectedly, has her hands full keeping up with this company as a gawky, nerdish beautician's assistant.

Field does some spectacular underplaying through the bulk of the action, revealing layer after layer of the feelings of this kindly tempered, deeply worried mother.

☐ 1989: Nomination: Best Supp. Actress (Julia Roberts)

．．．．．．．．．．．．．．．．．．．．．．．．．．．．

■ STEEL TRAP, THE

1952, 84 MINS, US

Dir Andrew L. Stone *Prod* Bert E. Friedlob *Scr* Andrew L. Stone *Ph* Ernest Laszlo *Ed* Otto Ludwig *Mus* Dimitri Tiomkin

● Joseph Cotten, Teresa Wright, Eddie Marr, Aline Towne, Bill Hudson (Thor/20th Century-Fox)

Andrew Stone's direction of his own story emphasizes suspense that is leavened with welcome chuckles of relief in telling the improbable but entertaining events.

Joseph Cotten is a minor bank exec who succumbs to a larcenous impulse and lays plans to heist $1 million when the bank closes on Friday, take off via plane with his wife for Brazil, where there is no extradition treaty with the States. Suspense continues to mount as Cotten encounters such frustrating difficulties as passport trouble, delays in plane transportation from Los Angeles to New Orleans that cause him to miss the Saturday plane to Brazil and, finally, customs curiosity that reveals to his wife he is a thief.

Cotten is very good, and Wright is capable as the wife.

．．．．．．．．．．．．．．．．．．．．．．．．．．．．

■ STEELYARD BLUES

1973, 92 MINS, US ◇ ⓥ

Dir Alan Myerson *Prod* Tony Bill, Michael Phillips, Julia Phillips *Scr* David S. Ward *Ph* Laszlo Kovacs, Steven Larner *Ed* Donn Cambern, Robert Grovenor *Mus* Nick Gravenites, Paul Butterfield, David Shire *Art Dir* Vincent Cresciman

● Jane Fonda, Donald Sutherland, Peter Boyle, Garry Goodrow, Howard Hesseman, John Savage (Warner)

Steelyard Blues is an erratically amusing slapstick comedy about non-conformists.

Screenplay spotlights Donald Sutherland as ring-leader of some drop-outs which also include kid brother John Savage and Peter Boyle, who does a hilarious takeoff of Marlon Brando's *The Wild One* image. Jane Fonda is the town hooker whose customers include most of the city hall, including Sutherland's prime-adversary, his older brother Howard Hesseman, a politically ambitious DA.

The drop-outs focus their energies on restoring an old US Navy amphibian plane, and their search for spare parts leads to a climactic raid on a nearby naval air station.

Like many other films, this one suffers from a lingering late 1960s social-protest plot fibre, the result being an odd combination of nostalgia and anachronism.

．．．．．．．．．．．．．．．．．．．．．．．．．．．．

■ STELLA

1990, 114 MINS, US ◇ ⓥ ⊙

Dir John Erman *Prod* Samuel Goldwyn Jr *Scr* Robert Getchell *Ph* Billy Williams *Ed* Jerrold L. Ludwig *Mus* John Morris *Art Dir* James Hulsey

● Bette Midler, John Goodman, Trini Alvarado, Stephen Collins, Marsha Mason, Eileen Brennan (Touchstone/Goldwyn)

The semitragic *Stella Dallas* shows her years in this hopelessly dated and ill-advised remake.

The idea of a lower-class mother who selflessly sends her daughter off to her upper-crust dad and his new wife – all so daughter can land the right beau – must sound like nails on a blackboard to Equal Rights Amendment proponents, and Bette Midler's ballsy wit completely misses the redeeming lower-class yearning Barbara Stanwyck gave the 1937 role.

All of the significant changes in the story come early, as Stella (Midler) meets a young doctor (Stephen Collins) while tending bar and quickly gets pregnant by him. She refuses his half-hearted offfer of marriage as well as any financial help, letting him run off to New York while she raises their daughter (Trini Alvarado) on her own.

Erman and writer Robert Getchell try to inject some levity into the maudlin proceedings. On that front they largely succeed, thanks primarily to the winning performance by John Goodman as Stella's long-suffering admirer Ed as well as Midler's natural comic flair.

．．．．．．．．．．．．．．．．．．．．．．．．．．．．

■ STELLA DALLAS

1925, 108 MINS, US ⊗ ⓥ

Dir Henry King *Prod* Samuel Goldwyn *Scr* Frances Marion *Ph* Arthur Edeson *Ed* Stuart Heisler *Art Dir* Ben Carre

● Belle Bennett, Ronald Colman, Alice Joyce, Jean Hersholt, Lois Moran, Douglas Fairbanks Jr (Goldwyn/United Artists)

A mother picture. Not a great picture, but a great mother picture. Its sentiment is terrific. Henry King tells his story simply and directly without dramatics, gauging the extent to which he can play upon such an emotional subject to a nicety. In this he is helped by two magnificent performances by Belle Bennett and Lois Moran.

If ever there were a two-character picture this is it. Both characters are women, mother and daughter. It tells of a mother who eliminates herself so that her child may enjoy the advantages of which the girl will not partake while knowing that her mother has no one to whom she can turn.

Moran convinces in what practically amounts to three roles, as she plays the daughter at 10, 13 and as a young woman. Excellent in each, her performance is something of a revelation. Bennett, makes something of a cinema comeback in this release.

Alice Joyce makes a splendid contrast, while Ronald Colman is limited in his activities. Jean Hersholt is prominent among the secondary players, with young Douglas Fairbanks Jr acquitting himself creditably in his brief footage.

．．．．．．．．．．．．．．．．．．．．．．．．．．．．

■ STELLA DALLAS

1937, 104 MINS, US ⓥ ⊙

Dir King Vidor *Prod* Samuel Goldwyn *Scr* Harry Wagstaff Gribble, Gertrude Purcell *Ph* Rudolph Mate *Ed* Sherman Todd *Mus* Alfred Newman *Art Dir* Richard Day

● Barbara Stanwyck, John Boles, Anne Shirley, Barbara O'Neil, Alan Hale, Marjorie Main (Goldwyn/United Artists)

Producer Samuel Goldwyn made the film first in 1925 and did mighty well by the results. *Stella Dallas* is chiefly a tear-jerker of A ranking.

In producing this picture Goldwyn pretty much followed his original, bringing it, however, a bit more up-to-date. Thus the sock scenes are still the same ones. These are, especially, a scene between Barbara Stanwyck and Anne Shirley in a train when the former has just heard playmates of the latter criticize the mother as a millstone around the child's head; a scene between the girl and her father, and the woman he wants to marry; and a scene between the mother and daughter at a birthday party to which no one has shown up because of one of the mother's indiscretions.

The story [from the novel by Olive Higgins Prouty] itself is a simple enough one, not so much of mother love as the difficulties of a young girl whose parents are at extremes in the social world. It isn't overdone.

There are few faults to be pointed. Only one which is obvious is that Stanwyck is permitted to go entirely too far in costuming in her latter scenes. Especially when it is considered that the mother makes all the daughter's clothes and these are in rare good taste.

☐ 1937: Nominations: Best Actress (Barbara Stanwyck), Supp. Actress (Anne Shirley)

．．．．．．．．．．．．．．．．．．．．．．．．．．．．

■ ST. ELMO'S FIRE

1985, 108 MINS, US ◇ ⓥ ⊙

Dir Joel Schumacher *Prod* Lauren Shuler *Scr* Joel Schumacher, Carl Kurlander *Ph* Stephen H. Burum *Ed* Richard Marks *Mus* David Foster (sup.) *Art Dir* William Sandell

● Rob Lowe, Demi Moore, Andrew McCarthy, Judd Nelson, Ally Sheedy, Emilio Estevez (Columbia-Delphi IV/Channel)

St. Elmo's Fire is all about a group of recent college graduates in Washington who were always the best of friends but now are drifting apart as real life approaches, discovering various reasons why they are so individually obnoxious.

Rob Lowe is a saxophone player who refuses to assume any adult responsibility. The rest of the gang befriends him, especially virginal Mare Winningham, who's a social worker by trade anyway.

The other major problem is beautiful, coked-out Demi Moore who lives in a pink apartment, sleeps with her boss and calls her friends with wee-hour problems.

There's also yuppie Capitol Hill aide Judd Nelson, a Democrat turned Republican because the pay is better, and his live-in (Ally Sheedy) who won't marry him but has reason to resent his cheating.

Making them all look good by comparison is Emilio Estevez. He spots medical student Andie MacDowell and decides he must marry her despite her absolute lack of interest.

Beyond occasional mutterings of words like 'love' and 'beer,' there's never any explanation in the dialog that would hint at motivation.

．．．．．．．．．．．．．．．．．．．．．．．．．．．．

■ STEPFATHER, THE

1987, 98 MINS, US ◇ ⓥ ⊙

Dir Joseph Ruben *Prod* Jay Benson *Scr* Donald E. Westlake *Ph* John W. Lindley *Ed* George Bowers *Mus* Patrick Moraz *Art Dir* James Newton Westport

● Terry O'Quinn, Jill Schoelen, Shelley Hack, Stephen Shellen, Charles Lanyer (ITC)

The Stepfather is an engrossing suspense thriller that refreshingly doesn't cheat the audience in terms of valid clues and plot twists.

Terry O'Quinn toplines as a mild-looking guy who immediately is revealed to be a psychotic who has murdered his entire family. A year later he has started a new life as Jerry Blake, married to young Susan (Shelley Hack) who has a teenage daughter Stephanie (Jill Schoelen).

His past eventually catches up with him as his previous brother-in-law Jim (Stephen Shellen) is still researching the murder of his sister with the help of a reporter, the police and (independently) Stephanie's psychiatrist Dr Bondurant (Charles Lanyer).

What makes *The Stepfather* work is its believability, as writer Donald Westlake [from a story by him, Carolyn Lefcourt and Brian Garfield] expertly injects clues which can trip up Blake's new identity. A most ingenious plot peg has Blake carefully planning out his new identity (quitting his job, finding a new home, etc) each time before he goes completely over the edge and sets out to murder his family.

O'Quinn gives a measured, effective performance balancing the normalcy and craziness of the character, while Shoelen is powerfully empathetic as the young heroine. Helmer Joseph Ruben brings a lot more credibility to the film than his previous *Dreamscape* assignment.

....

■ **STEPFATHER II**

1989, 86 MINS, US ◇ ⑦ ⊙
Dir Jeff Burr *Prod* William Burr, Darin Scott *Scr* John Auerbach *Ph* Jacek Laskus *Ed* Pasquale A. Buba *Mus* Jim Manzie, Pat Regan *Art Dir* Bernadette Disanto
● Terry O'Quinn, Meg Foster, Caroline Williams, Jonathan Brandis, Henry Brown, Mitchell Laurance (ITC)

This dull sequel reduces the intriguing premise of the original *Stepfather* to the level of an inconsequential, tongue-in-cheek slasher film.

Terry O'Quinn as the murderous, average guy vainly trying to mimic the American Family ideal was killed off at the end of the first pic. Sequel opens with recap of previous finale (including brief footage of previous co-stars Shelley Hack and Jill Schoelen), followed by O'Quinn waking up in a Washington State asylum with several chest scars indicating his not-quite-fatal wounds.

This time, O'Quinn bamboozles the shrink (Henry Brown) at the asylum and escapes, lifts the identity of a deceased family therapist from the newspaper obituary, and moves into an LA suburb. He romances the pretty real estate divorcee who's his neighbor (Meg Foster).

Pic builds towards their impending marriage, but 13-year-old son Todd (Jonathan Brandis) is only a minor character who does not figure in the dramatics. It is another neighbor (Caroline Williams), the postal delivery woman, who is suspicious of O'Quinn.

Jeff Burr, who has horror pics under his belt, directs the piece claustrophobically and fails to whip up any atmosphere.

....

■ **STEPFORD WIVES, THE**

1975, 114 MINS, US ◇ ⑦
Dir Bryan Forbes *Prod* Edgar J. Scherick *Scr* William Goldman *Ph* Owen Roizman *Ed* Timothy Gee *Mus* Michael Small *Art Dir* Gene Callahan
● Katharine Ross, Paula Prentiss, Peter Masterson, Nanette Newman, Patrick O'Neal, Tina Louise (Palomar/Columbia)

Bryan Forbes' filmization of Ira Levin's *The Stepford Wives* is a quietly freaky suspense-horror story.

Katharine Ross (in an excellent and assured performance), husband Peter Masterson and kids depart NY's urban pressures to a seemingly bovine Connecticut existence. Trouble is, Ross and new friend Paula Prentiss (also excellent) find all the other wives exuding sticky hairspray homilies and male chauvinist fantasy responses. When Prentiss finally changes her attitude, Ross panics but cannot escape.

Patrick O'Neal heads a local men's club that somehow is involved in the unseen, sluggishly developed but eventually exciting climax.

The black humor and sophistication of the plot is handled extremely well.

....

■ **STEPKIDS**

See: Big Girls Don't Cry ... They get even

....

■ **STEPPENWOLF**

1974, 105 MINS, US ◇ ⑦ ⊙
Dir Fred Haines *Prod* Melvin Fishman, Richard Herland *Scr* Fred Haines *Ph* Tomislav Pinter *Ed* Irving Lerner *Mus* George Gruntz *Art Dir* Leo Karen
● Max von Sydow, Dominique Sanda, Pierre Clementi, Carla Romanelli, Roy Bosier, Alfred Baillou (Sprague)

Four decades after publication, *Steppenwolf* sold some 1.5 million paperbacks to a young audience suddenly attracted to Herman Hesse. Film remains just as subjective and essentially plotless as the book, but director Fred Haines seems fully in control.

Film has a rich appearance far beyond its $1.2 million budget. The weird effects produced from a sophisticated, electronic video mix allow Haines to translate Hesse's abstractions faithfully, if such a thing is at all possible.

Haines was equally careful in casting Max von Sydow as Harry Haller, the misanthrope who opts for one last try at life before reaching 50 and a preplanned suicide. Whether it's madness, drugs or love that envelopes him remains as mysterious in pic, but von Sydow makes the journey remarkable.

....

■ **STEPPING OUT**

1991, 106 MINS, US ◇ ⑦ ⊙
Dir Lewis Gilbert *Prod* Lewis Gilbert *Scr* Richard Harris *Ph* Alan Hume *Ed* Humphrey Dixon *Mus* Peter Matz *Art Dir* Peter Mullins
● Liza Minnelli, Shelley Winters, Bill Irwin, Ellen Greene, Julie Walters, Sheila McCarthy (Paramount)

It's Liza-as-you-love-her in *Stepping Out*, a modest heartwarmer about a bunch of suburban left-feeters getting it together for a charity dance spot. Fragile ensemble item often creaks under the Minnelli glitz, but results are likeable enough.

Adapted by Richard Harris from his 1984 award-winning play, action is switched from a London church hall to a Buffalo, NY, equivalent. Minnelli is a former pro hoofer who's now teaching amateur dance classes on the side.

Her current group includes a snooty Brit with a cleanliness fixation (Julie Walters), a shy plain Jane with a bossy husband (Sheila McCarthy), a pretty, disillusioned young nurse (Jane Krakowski) and a working-class pants-chaser (Robyn Stevan).

Minnelli's problems start when her grumpy accompanist (Shelley Winters) threatens to walk out. She's then invited to put together an amateur tap routine for a charity show.

Minnelli's lost none of her pizzazz. Looking as fresh-faced and gamine as ever, and in good voice and shape, she provides the pic's emotional highs in a solo dance spot and the finale's John Kander-Fred Ebb title song, but as an actress, she's one-note perky. Technically, the Toronto-lensed pic is solid.

....

■ **STEREO**

1969, 63 MINS, CANADA
Dir David Cronenberg *Prod* David Cronenberg *Scr* David Cronenberg *Ph* David Cronenberg *Ed* David Cronenberg
● Ron Mlodzik, Jack Messinger, Iain Ewing, Clara Mayer, Paul Mulholland, Arlene Mlodzik (Emergent)

Lensed for a paltry $3,500, *Stereo* is the initial feature film effort by David Cronenberg.

Shot in black-and-white wihout synch sound, *Stereo* carries built-in liabilities thanks to its technical limitations and aesthetic idiosyncracies. Basically a student effort (Cronenberg was 26), pic tests the viewer's patience and endurance even with its hour's running time due to its emphatically dry, scientific narration and deliberate emotional distancing.

Film abstractly examines the situation at the Canadian Academy for Erotic Inquiry, where eight individuals have been subjected to telepathic surgery. As the narrator drones on the operation, alternately strange and static scenes are presented which only occasionally bear any relation to the words being spoken.

....

■ **STERILE CUCKOO, THE**

(UK: *Pookie*)

1969, 108 MINS, US ◇ ⑦ ⊙
Dir Alan J. Pakula *Prod* Alan J. Pakula *Scr* Alvin Sargent *Ph* Milton R. Krasner *Ed* Sam O'Steen, John W. Wheeler *Mus* Fred Karlin *Art Dir* Roland Anderson
● Liza Minnelli, Wendell Burton, Tim McIntire, Elizabeth Harrower, Austin Green (Paramount/Boardwalk)

The Sterile Cuckoo is a kook named Pookie, a wacky, wisecracking motherless, outrageously adorable, collegiate gamin [from a novel by Jack Nichols] who comes on like gangbusters. Liza Minnelli plays the role, and her fragile, funny freshman love affair with an undergraduate entomologist (Wendell Burton in his first screen role) is in a class by itself.

A first affair in a ramshackle upstate New York motel becomes high comedy with the hot-to-trot vamp Minnelli prodding the nervous-in-the-service Burton, who keeps his mackinaw buttoned up to the chin while she strips down.

It is Minnelli's one-woman show. The 21-year-old Burton is not so much her costar as her straight man.

□ 1969: Nominations: Best Actress (Liza Minelli), Song ('Come Saturday Morning')

....

■ **STEVIE**

1978, 102 MINS, UK ◇ ⑦
Dir Robert Enders *Prod* Robert Enders *Scr* Hugh Whitemore *Ph* Freddie Young *Ed* Peter Tanner *Mus* Patrick Gowers *Art Dir* Bob Jones
● Glenda Jackson, Mona Washbourne, Alec McCowen, Trevor Howard (Bowden)

Stevie is a well-acted and literate, but also talky and claustrophobic screen biography of British poet and novelist Stevie Smith. Glenda Jackson stars in the title role and her performance – in fact, the entire style of the film – seems better suited to the stage than the big screen.

Robert Enders, who directed from Hugh Whitemore's script of his own play, has adopted a visual style better suited to a tele-film than a theatrical feature. Most of the picture takes place inside a suburban residence Smith shared with her aunt, portrayed by Mona Washbourne in a charming and sympathetic performance.

By limiting the action to that one setting the film becomes stifling. Too much of Smith's life is described by Jackson in reminiscences to her aunt, confessions into the camera, or recitations of her poetry, rather than re-enacted.

Only other characters are Alec McCowen as a boyfriend of Jackson and Trevor Howard as companion who also comments on the poet's life and work.

....

■ **STICKY FINGERS**

1988, 97 MINS, US ◇ ⑦ ⊙
Dir Catlin Adams *Prod* Catlin Adams, Melanie Mayron *Scr* Catlin Adams, Melanie Mayron *Ph* Gary Thieltges *Ed* Bob Reitano *Mus* Gary Chang *Art Dir* Jessica Scott-Justice
● Helen Slater, Melanie Mayron, Danitra Vance, Eileen Brennan, Carol Kane, Christopher Guest (Hightop)

Sticky Fingers is a snappy, offbeat urban comedy about two NY gal pals – starving artist types – who get caught up in the shopping spree of a lifetime. Too bad the money isn't theirs.

Story, cowritten by debut director Catlin Adams and Melanie Mayron, casts Mayron and Helen Slater as struggling musicians on the verge of eviction from their NY walkup until a bagful of drug money – nearly a million bucks – lands in their laps. They've been asked to 'mind it' for a spacey friend-of-a-friend (Loretta Devine) who's clearing out of town in a hurry.

Initially panicked, they wind up using it to pay their rent; then to replace their instruments. As days pass, the urge to spend becomes insatiable, and they give in with gusto.

Memorable supporting roles abound, including Danitra Vance as a fellow musician and Stephen McHattie as a tough but romantic undercover cop posing as a parking lot attendant across from their building.

Eileen Brennan is right on as the ailing landlady and Carol Kane delightful as her sister, who has a romance with the cop. Christopher Guest is near perfect as Mayron's uncertain boyfriend, a newly published novelist pursued by a spooky ex-girlfriend (Gwen Welles).

• •

■ STILL OF THE NIGHT

1982, 91 MINS, US ◇ ⓥ
Dir Robert Benton *Prod* Arlene Donovan *Scr* Robert Benton *Ph* Nestor Almendros *Ed* Jerry Greenberg *Mus* John Kander *Art Dir* Mel Bourne
● Roy Scheider, Meryl Streep, Jessica Tandy, Joe Grifasi, Sara Botsford, Josef Sommer (United Artists)

It comes as almost a shock to see a modern suspense picture that's as literate, well acted and beautifully made as *Still Of The Night*. Despite its many virtues, however, Robert Benton's film [from a story by him and David Newman] has its share of serious flaws, mainly in the area of plotting.

Roy Scheider effectively plays an introspective New York shrink whose own life becomes endangered after one of his patients is found murdered. Prime suspect may well be Meryl Streep, the neurotic mistress of the dead man whose distressed, unpredictable behavior represents the source of most of the film's mystery.

Perpetually moving around physically, mentally and emotionally, Streep slowly insinuates herself into Scheider's relatively uneventful life.

Benton has fashioned as gorgeously crafted a suspense piece as one could ask for. High marks also go to supporting players, particularly Josef Sommer as the murdered man who appears in flashback, and Joe Grifasi as the persistent cop.

• •

■ STING, THE

1973, 127 MINS, US ◇ ⓥ ⊙
Dir George Roy Hill *Prod* Tony Bill, Michael Phillips, Julia Phillips *Scr* David S. Ward *Ph* Robert Surtees *Ed* William Reynolds *Mus* Marvin Hamlisch (adapt.) *Art Dir* Henry Bumstead
● Paul Newman, Robert Redford, Robert Shaw, Charles Durning, Ray Walston, Eileen Brennan (Universal)

Paul Newman and Robert Redford are superbly re-teamed as a pair of con artists in Chicago of the 1930s, out to fleece a bigtime racketeer brilliantly played by Robert Shaw.

Script establishes Redford as a novice con artist, apprentice to Robert Earl Jones who is murdered when one of their marks turns out to be a cash runner for Shaw's regional syndicate. Ambition plus revenge leads Redford to Newman, an acknowledged master of the con trade who rounds up Eileen Brennan, Harold Gould, Ray Walston and John Heffernan to fake a bookie joint operation to snare Shaw in a major bet.

The three stars make all the difference between simply a good film and a superior one. Newman's relationship with Brennan (in a sensational supporting role) rounds out his characterization of an old pro making his last big score. Redford really turns to and works superbly. Shaw's taciturn menace commands attention even when he is simply part of a master shot.

The film comes to a series of startling climaxes, piled atop one another with zest. In the final seconds the audience realizes it has

been had, but when one enjoys the ride, it's a pleasure.
☐ 1973: Best Picture, Director, Original Story & Screenplay, Art Direction, Adapted Scoring, Editing, Costume Design (Edith Head)
☐ Nominations: Best Actor (Robert Redford), Cinematography, Sound

• •

■ STING II, THE

1983, 102 MINS, US ◇ ⓥ ⊙
Dir Jeremy Paul Kagan *Prod* Jennings Lang *Scr* David S. Ward *Ph* Bill Butler *Ed* David Garfield *Mus* Lalo Schifrin *Art Dir* Edward C. Carfagno
● Jackie Gleason, Mac Davis, Teri Garr, Karl Malden, Oliver Reed, Bert Remsen (Universal)

Stars Jackie Gleason and Mac Davis come nowhere close to evoking the charming on-screen qualities of Paul Newman and Robert Redford. Combined with the slow pace and overdone exposition, *The Sting II* is mostly just a chore to watch.

Though screenwriter David S. Ward concocts as viable a story as he did in the original, the trouble is there is still an original.

Gleason plays the master con man out to make a big score with the help of fellow huckster Davis. The chief patsy is tacky nightclub owner Karl Malden while Oliver Reed does a less than distinctive turn as a mysterious gangster watching it all happen.

So much of the intricate plot is explained in dialog that the first half of the film often seems like someone reading an instruction book. Exception is Teri Garr, who provides what little life there is as a slick, seasoned trickster who becomes involved in the scam.

The second half picks up a bit as the plan goes into effect and this is where the performances come into play.
☐ 1983: Nomination: Best Adapted Score

• •

■ STIR CRAZY

1980, 111 MINS, US ◇ ⓥ ⊙
Dir Sidney Poitier *Prod* Hannah Weinstein *Scr* Bruce Jay Friedman *Ph* Fred Schuler *Ed* Harry Keller *Mus* Tom Scott *Art Dir* Alfred Sweeney
● Gene Wilder, Richard Pryor, JoBeth Williams, Georg Stanford Brown, Craig T. Nelson, Barry Corbin (Columbia)

Story setup has down-on-their-luck New Yorkers Richard Pryor and Gene Wilder deciding to blow the city for what they think are the promising shores of California. Driving cross-country they land in a small town where they take a job dressing up as woodpeckers in a local bank in order to make some cash. Two baddies they met in a bar use the woodpecker suits to rob the bank, leaving Pryor and Wilder 120-year prison sentences and no alibi.

Majority of the action focuses on the antics of prison life, with Pryor and Wilder at the center of a group of fairly stereotypical jail characters.

Director Sidney Poitier's chief role seems to be providing enough space for Pryor and Wilder to do their schtick without going too far afield from the scant storyline.

• •

■ STITCH IN TIME, A

1963, 94 MINS, UK
Dir Robert Asher *Prod* Hugh Stewart *Scr* Jack Davies *Ph* Jack Asher *Ed* Gerry Hambling *Mus* Philip Green
● Norman Wisdom, Edward Chapman, Jeannette Sterke, Jerry Desmonde, Jill Melford (Rank)

This gains by economizing on plot, but devises a string of farcical events that put the pint-sized Norman Wisdom through the full pratfalling routine. The thin thread linking the scenes has Wisdom as a hapless butcher's assistant causing constant commotion in a

hospital, where his employer is undergoing surgery for a swallowed watch. He gets banned from the place by the hospital boss, Sir Hector (Jerry Desmonde), and the remainder of the running time is taken up by his bizarre attempts to regain entry.

The sketches follow each other thick and fast, and leave no time to brood over their naivety. Jack Davies's script is the sixth for the comedian, and he knows the strength and limitations of the star. For sophisticated palates, Wisdom is mechanical, and he plays up the sentiment of the 'little man' up against authority to cloying effect.

• •

■ ST. IVES

1976, 93 MINS, US ◇ ⓥ
Dir J. Lee Thompson *Prod* Pancho Kohner, Stanley Canter *Scr* Barry Beckerman *Ph* Lucien Ballard *Ed* Michael F. Anderson *Mus* Lalo Schifrin *Art Dir* Philip M. Jefferies
● Charles Bronson, John Houseman, Jacqueline Bisset, Maximilian Schell, Harry Guardino, Harris Yulin (Warner)

St. Ives merely confirms a point: eliminate gratuitous, offensive and overdone violence from a dull and plodding film story, and all you've got left is a dull and plodding film.

The production stars Charles Bronson as an ex-police reporter involved with wealthy crime dilettante John Houseman and partner Jacqueline Bisset. J. Lee Thompson's direction is functional.

Barry Beckerman wrote the script from an Oliver Bleeck novel, *The Procane Chronicle*. Plot injects Bronson as go-between in recovery for some stolen Houseman papers, but every time the ransom is to be delivered, somebody dies.

Plot progress is marred by lots of month-old red herrings. Film is careful to show that Bronson's character doesn't need pistols.

• •

■ STOLEN LIFE, A

1946, 100 MINS, US ⓥ
Dir Curtis Bernhardt *Prod* Bette Davis *Scr* Catherine Turney *Ph* Sol Polito, Ernest Haller *Ed* Rudi Fehr *Mus* Max Steiner *Art Dir* Robert M. Haas
● Bette Davis, Glenn Ford, Dane Clark, Walter Brennan, Charlie Ruggles, Bruce Bennett (Warner/BD)

Story [from a novel by Karel J. Benes] unfolds leisurely in telling of a sister who assumes her twin's identity in order to find love.

Bette Davis appears as a sweet, sincere, artistic girl, and as this girl's man-crazy sister. When the latter, by trickery, marries man with whom former has fallen in love and is later drowned in a boating accident, the sweet girl takes on her sister's identity in a try for happiness. Script spends a great deal of footage establishing life in New England summer resorts. Since it is a woman's story, dialog hands plenty of cliches to male players, particularly to Glenn Ford as the man in love with both sisters.

Dane Clark appears briefly in role of rude artist. Role is difficult and not a fortunate one for Clark. Walter Brennan gives a good character reading to his part of a salty old down'easter.

Special photography for dual role played by Davis is the best yet. At no time is double exposure or other tricks used to bring the characters together in scenes apparent. Credit for trick work goes to Willard Van Enger and Russell Collings.
☐ 1946: Nomination: Best Special Effects

• •

■ STONE BOY, THE

1984, 93 MINS, US ◇ ⓥ
Dir Christopher Cain *Prod* Joe Roth, Ivan Bloch *Scr* Gina Berriault *Ph* Juan Ruiz-Anchia *Ed* Paul Rubell *Mus* James Horner *Art Dir* Joseph G. Pacelli

● Robert Duvall, Jason Presson, Frederic Forrest, Glenn Close, Wilford Brimley, Gail Youngs (TLC)

Director Chris Cain, in only his second feature, draws a remarkably restrained and moving performance from debuting child actor Jason Presson, who plays central role of a 12-year-old brother who accidentally and tragically slays his older, beloved brother with a shotgun in the opening moments of the film.

Production's sorrowful subject matter as family is rendered dazed and grief-stricken by the death of the older son, while young responsible brother retreats behind a wall of guilt, never lapses into sentimentality or melodrama.

Robert Duvall unthinkingly compounds the misery of his son by fostering a family attitude that denies the boy communication.

The Stone Boy, in its inarticulate characters whose feelings tear them apart, is a singular and highly accessible film.

● ●

■ STONE KILLER, THE

1973, 95 MINS, US ◇ ⑰ ⊙
Dir Michael Winner   *Prod* Michael Winner   *Scr* Gerald Wilson   *Ph* Richard Moore   *Ed* Freddie Wilson   *Mus* Roy Budd   *Art Dir* Ward Preston
● Charles Bronson, Martin Balsam, David Sheiner, Norman Fell, Ralph Waite, Stuart Margolin (De Laurentiis)

The Stone Killer [from John Gardner's novel, *A Complete State of Death*], is a confused, meandering crime potboiler, starring Charles Bronson as a tough detective who starts out on a low-level gangster case only to find upper Mafia echelon also are involved. The story and direction reach for so many bases that the end result is a lot of cinema razzle-dazzle without substance.

Bronson is discovered killing a NY ghetto punk, his overkill enough to banish him to the LA Police Dept, a plot point which may strike some as unintentionally amusing. Eventually it becomes clear that Martin Balsam, a prototype hood of the Prohibition era, is planning massacre-revenge for a 40-year old shootout which introduced non-Sicilian elements to organized crime.

● ●

■ STOOGE, THE

1952, 100 MINS, US
Dir Norman Taurog   *Prod* Hal Wallis   *Scr* Fred F. Finklehoffe, Martin Rackin, Elwood Ullman   *Ph* Daniel L. Fapp   *Ed* Warren Low   *Mus* Joseph J. Lilley (dir.)
● Dean Martin, Jerry Lewis, Polly Bergen, Marion Marshall, Eddie Mayehoff, Richard Erdman (Paramount)

Dean Martin and Jerry Lewis venture into a straight story-line comedy in *The Stooge* as a change of pace from their usual frenetic clowning.

Martin plays a crooning, accordion-playing comic who flunks as a single and only becomes a success when he acquires a dumb stooge to work with him from the audience. He is fortunate in landing Lewis as the patsy, and it isn't long before the act, still billed as a single at Martin's insistence, becomes a big success.

Lewis scores as the wistful ugly duckling who adores the man who gave him a chance in show business. He's particularly outstanding when he subs for Martin as a single during a vaude stand, and in the mirror sequence when he admires and fancies himself as a dashing hero.

● ●

■ STOP! OR MY MOM WILL SHOOT

1992, 87 MINS, US ◇ ⑰ ⊙
Dir Roger Spottiswoode   *Prod* Ivan Reitman, Joe Medjuck, Michael C. Gross   *Scr* Blake Snyder, William Osborne, William Davies   *Ph* Frank Tidy   *Ed* Mark Conte, Lois Freeman-Fox   *Mus* Alan Silvestri   *Art Dir* Charles Rosen

● Sylvester Stallone, Estelle Getty, JoBeth Williams, Roger Rees, Martin Ferrero, Gailard Sartain (Universal/Northern Lights)

Expertly produced in the mold of slick, juvenile action comedies like Ivan Reitman's *Kindergarten Cop*, this buddy cop picture casts budding comic actor Sylvester Stallone (*Oscar*) and proven laugh-getter Estelle Getty (TV's *Golden Girls*) as a beleaguered LA lawman and his aggravating mother.

Visiting from the east coast, the hyper-meddlesome Getty, as New Jersey widow Tutti Bomowski, proves second to none in embarassing the pants off her Joey (Stallone). Knowing that her visit will be brief is alll that keeps Joey sane, but then his mother becomes a key witness in a drive-by shooting, and the cops ask her to stay on indefinitely. Before long she's pushed her way even further into Joey's business as his pistol-packing partner in some perilous escapades.

Stallone, in a slim, articulate and disciplined incarnation, is the model of the amiable, put-upon comic hero, while the tiny Getty, her familiar technique and timing honed to a cutting edge, is worth triple her weight in ticket stubs.

Director Roger Spottiswode delivers purely pro product in his adept handling of both action and comedy scenes. JoBeth Williams is typically excellent in the light comic role of the precint lieutenant who's also Joey's neglected flame.

● ●

■ STORM, THE

1930, 76 MINS, US
Dir William Wyler   *Scr* Wells Root   *Ph* Alvin Wyckoff
● Lupe Velez, Paul Cavanaugh, William Boyd, Alphonz Ethier, Ernie S. Adams (Universal)

The Storm served on two former occasions as a silent, in 1916 for Paramount and in 1922 for U. Lupe Velez is a French smuggler's daughter who is left with a friendly trapper by her father just before a bullet from a mountie's gun lays him low. She plays with an accent that is a cross between Spanish and French, half the time doing a flashing Spanish demoiselle.

Story [from a play, *Men without Skirts*, by Langdon McCormick] is that of a trapper-miner and his best friend who develop a bad jealousy between each other for the girl ward left with the forme. They both lean heavily toward the girl, finally hating each other.

Shots of the girl in the river attempting to rescue her father from Mounties are very cleverly done. The old man's leap from a cliff, and their race down the river until the canoe capsizes, is also fairly thrilling stuff expertly photographed.

● ●

■ STORM BOY

1976, 88 MINS, AUSTRALIA ◇ ⑰
Dir Henri Safran   *Prod* Matt Carroll   *Scr* Sonia Borg   *Ph* Geoff Burton   *Ed* G. Turney-Smith   *Mus* Michael Carlos   *Art Dir* David Copping
● Greg Rowe, Peter Cummins, David Gulpilil, Judy Dick, Tony Allison, Michael Moody (SAFC)

Storm Boy is a gem of a film. Modestly and carefully made, it is a skillful adaptation of a kid's book by Colin Thiele.

Mike (Greg Rowe) is the 10-year-old son of Tom (Peter Cummins), a wifeless fisherman who inhabits a shanty on the beach and ekes out a living selling his catch to the fishmonger in the nearest town.

They live near a bird sanctuary, and a chance meeting with an aborigine (David Gulpilil) affects Mike's life, and gives him the name Storm Boy. Fingerbone Bill is also a rejector of society, his tribe has cast him out and he lives a nomadic life pretty much along the lines of his ancestors. And he has retained the mystical insights of his forebears.

Storm Boy is certainly a kid-flick, but it's one that'll get to the adults, too.

For a first feature, Paris-born director Henri Safran shows a sure hand. Final kudos to composer, Michael Carlos, for an evocative score.

● ●

■ STORMY MONDAY

1988, 93 MINS, UK ◇ ⑰ ⊙
Dir Mike Figgis   *Prod* Nigel Stafford-Clark   *Scr* Mike Figgis   *Ph* Roger Deakins   *Ed* David Martin   *Mus* Mike Figgis   *Art Dir* Andrew McAlpine
● Melanie Griffith, Tommy Lee Jones, Sting, Sean Bean, Prunella Gee, Alison Steadman (Moving Picture)

The attempt to come up with a stylish British *film noir* in the vein of *Mona Lisa* comes a cropper in *Stormy Monday*. Debut theatrical pic for Mike Figgis is all visual flash and no script, with comatose performances to boot.

Melanie Griffith toplines as a sort of B-girl working for US gangster/real estate magnate Tommy Lee Jones. Jones is in Newcastle to run an American Week promotion to boost US/UK business development, and also is trying to run Sting out of business, operating a local jazz club.

Griffith soon becomes involved romantically with a handsome Irish lad (Sean Bean) who is doing odd jobs at Sting's club. Plot unfolds as a string of ridiculous coincidences, set in motion when Bean at lunch overhears two of Jones' hitmen plotting to do in Sting.

Jones walks through his idiotic role with barely hidden embarrassment. Griffith hasn't missed many meals, sporting an unbecoming figure resembling latter-day Anita Ekberg.

● ●

■ STORMY WEATHER

1943, 77 MINS, US ⑰ ⊙
Dir Andrew Stone   *Prod* William LeBaron   *Scr* Frederick Jackson, Ted Koehler   *Ph* Leon Shamroy, Fred Sersen, Benny Carter   *Ed* James B. Clark
● Lena Horne, Bill Robinson, Fats Waller, Dooley Wilson, Cab Calloway, Katherine Dunham (20th Century-Fox)

Stormy Weather is chockful of the cream-of-the-crop colored talent, with a deft story skein to hold it together. Bill Robinson and Lena Horne top the cast. It's a tribute to the affection in which Bojangles is held that the story plot is glossed over in favor of all the other components.

Story nicely spans both wars. Lt Jim Europe's band is marching up 5th Ave in a riotous homecoming. Dooley Wilson, Robinson and the others have come back from the wars. The big Harlem hoopla thus projects Lena Horne who takes a liking immediately to Robinson. Her partner (Babe Wallace) is the menace, a conceited professional.

Story is told via the flashback formula. A 25th Anniversary Number of *Theatre World* holds the plot together. The special edition is in tribute to the great trouper, Robinson. Surrounding him are the neighbors' children on his comfortable, handsome front porch.

Via the *Theatre World* anniversary number, Robinson continues crossing and re-crossing paths with Horne, in and out of shows, Hollywood filmusicals, etc, with Cab Calloway, Katherine Dunham and her expert troupe of ballet dancers, Fats Waller, the Nicholas Bros, plus others.

● ●

■ STORY OF DR. WASSELL, THE

1944, 136 MINS, US ◇
Dir Cecil B. DeMille   *Prod* Cecil B. DeMille   *Scr* Alan LeMay, Charles Bennett   *Ph* Victor Milner, William Snyder   *Ed* Anne Bauchens   *Mus* Victor Young   *Art Dir* Hans Dreier, Roland Anderson
● Gary Cooper, Laraine Day, Signe Hasso, Dennis O'Keefe, Carol Thurston, Carl Esmond (Paramount)

Because this is the factual story of Dr Wassell's heroic evacuation of 12 men, plus himself, from Java in earlier stages of the war, it packs more interest than otherwise might have been the case. The exploits of the by-now famed naval commander are brought to the screen on a lavish scale by Cecil B. DeMille, with an exceptionally fine cast and good comedy relief. The entertainment value, even had the scenario been fictional, is very strong.

There can be no quarrel with the cast. While Gary Cooper bears no particular resemblance to Commander Wassell himself, who was 60 and a weather-beaten type, the star imparts to the role much vigor, color and sympathetic interest. It's one of Cooper's best performances.

The story [by James Hilton] based upon facts as related by Commander Wassell [and 15 of the wounded sailors involved], through various cutbacks, takes Cooper from his early horse-and-buggy country doctor days in Arkansas through medical research in China before the war and, finally, to Australia after he has successfully transported wounded men to that point. Instead of being court-mar-tialed there for having disobeyed orders to leave stretcher cases behind in Java, Dr Wassell was awarded the Navy Cross and his heroic deed made the subject of a broadcast by President Roosevelt.

☐ 1944: Nomination: Best Special Effects

••••••••••••••••••••••••••••••••••••••

■ **STORY OF ESTHER COSTELLO, THE**

1957, 104 MINS, UK

Dir David Miller *Prod* Jack Clayton *Scr* Charles Kaufman *Ph* Robert Krasker *Ed* Ralph Kemplen *Mus* Georges Auric *Art Dir* George Provis, Tony Masters

● Joan Crawford, Rossano Brazzi, Heather Sears, Lee Patterson, Ron Randell, Denis O'Dea (Romulus/Valiant)

Nicholas Monsarrat's poignant best-selling novel has been shaped into a glossy, highly effective screenplay, with David Miller's direction affording his powerful cast every opportunity for an all-out assault on the emotions.

Joan Crawford is a rich American socialite who, revisiting her Irish birthplace, finds a young girl, deaf, dumb and blind as a result of an explosion when she was a child. Joan rescues the girl from her evil surroundings, takes her to the US and devotes her life to the girl's recovery. This mercy campaign sparks the interest of the world, but Crawford's estranged husband (played by Rossano Brazzi) and a slick exploitation guy turn it into a giant racket.

Apart from its gripping story, *Esther Costello* has an almost documentary quality in showing the patient way a mute can be taught to communicate with the world. So authentic are these scenes that Heather Sears, who portrays Esther, and Crawford as her tutor actually learned to 'hand-talk'.

The acting throughout is impeccable and is noteworthy for a remarkable debut by 21-year-old Heather Sears, who stands up notably to seasoned competition though faced with the tricky chore of conveying emotion without benefit of eye-play or dialog.

••••••••••••••••••••••••••••••••••••••

■ **STORY OF G.I. JOE, THE**

1945, 109 MINS, US

Dir William A. Wellman *Prod* Lester Cowan *Scr* Leopold Atlas, Guy Endore *Ph* Russell Metty *Ed* Otto Lovering, Albrecht Joseph *Mus* Ann Ronell, Louis Applebaum *Art Dir* James Sullivan, David Hall

● Burgess Meredith, Robert Mitchum, Freddie Steele, Wally Cassell (United Artists)

From where the civilian sits, this seems the authentic story of GI Joe – that superb, slugging human machine, the infantryman, with-

out whom wars cannot be won. Add to authentic story handling a production that's superb, casting and directing that's perfect, and a sock star supported by a flawless group of artists.

From the moment the infantrymen are picked out by the camera at 'blanket drill' in the African desert until the last shot on the open highway to Rome, it's the foot-slogging soldier who counts most in this film. Real-life GI diarist Ernie Pyle is there, very much. He is ever present. But as conceived by the scripters, directed by William A. Wellman, and acted by Burgess Meredith, Pyle is not the war but a commentary on it – which is as it should be.

Meredith, playing the simple little figure that's Pyle, is felt in every scene, his impact carrying over from the preceding sequences.

But without support, Meredith for all his worth could not have made this the great picture it is. Robert Mitchum is excellent as the lieutenant who, in the film, grows to a captaincy. Freddie Steele is tops as the tough sergeant who finally cracks up when he hears his baby's voice on a disc mailed from home. Wally Cassell as the Lothario of the company, and all the others – professionals as well as real-life GIs who helped make the pic – are excellent.

••••••••••••••••••••••••••••••••••••••

■ **STORY OF LOUIS PASTEUR, THE**

1936, 85 MINS, US

Dir William Dieterle *Scr* Sheridan Gibney, Pierre Collings *Ph* Tony Gaudio *Ed* Ralph Davison *Mus* Erich Wolfgang Korngold *Art Dir* Robert Haas

● Paul Muni, Josephine Hutchinson, Anita Louise, Donald Woods, Fritz Leiber, Henry O'Neill (Warner)

It couldn't have been an easy film to make, and the fact that it holds as much general interest as it does speaks volumes. But the producers couldn't avoid some dull stretches of scientific discourse.

Expert casting and splendid production are the points in the film's favor, primarily. Paul Muni in the title role is at his very top form.

Film starts out with Pasteur already somewhat established, skipping his early life and struggles. His wine and beer discoveries have already been accepted and he's propagandizing for sterilization of doctors and doctors' instruments in childbirth. Doesn't get him very far because of general medical opposition and he turns to treatment of anthrax in sheep and cattle. Gets that over and is admitted into the French Academy, although still scoffed at by the majority of his confreres. Works on a cure for rabies and hydrophobia for the rest of the picture. His reward finally is general acclaim.

Josephine Hutchinson as Pasteur's wife is splendid and believable. Anita Louise as his daughter and Donald Woods as her fiance are expected to handle the romance and almost do it. Fritz Leiber as Dr Charbonnet, Pasteur's strongest enemy, turns in an outstanding performance.

☐ 1936: Best Actor (Paul Muni), Original Story & Screenplay.

☐ Nomination: Best Picture

••••••••••••••••••••••••••••••••••••••

■ **STORY OF MANKIND, THE**

1957, 99 MINS, US ◇

Dir Irwin Allen *Prod* Irwin Allen *Scr* Irwin Allen, Charles Bennett *Ph* Nicholas Musuraca *Ed* Roland Gross, Gene Palmer *Mus* Paul Sawtell *Art Dir* Art Loel

● Ronald Colman, Vincent Price, Agnes Moorehead, Peter Lorre, Dennis Hopper, Virginia Mayo (Cambridge/Warner)

Hendrik Willem Van Loon's monumental *Story of Mankind* has been brought to the screen in a name-dropping production that provides a kaleidoscope of history from Pleistocene man to Plutonium man. In the process, however, producer-director Irwin

Allen seems unable to decide whether to do a faithful history of man's development into a thinking being, a debate on whether man's good outweighs his evil, or a compilation of historical sagas with some humor dragged in for relief.

As a peg on which to hang the panorama, screenplay convokes the 'High Tribunal of Outer Space' upon news that man has discovered the Super-H bomb 60 years too soon. The problem is whether to halt the scheduled explosion and thereby save mankind or let it go off and exterminate the human race. To reach a decision, the tribunal permits both the Devil and the Spirit of Man to give evidence as to man's fitness to continue.

In the dreary cataloguing of man's crimes against humanity, the Devil makes a much better case.

Best of the portrayals is Agnes Moorehead's Queen Elizabeth and Cedric Hardwicke turns in a good performance as the High Judge. Ronald Colman is a dignified personification of the Spirit of Man and Vincent Price is the sophisticated, sneering embodiment of Old Scratch.

Peter Lorre brings some conviction to the role of Nero, Dennis Hopper is moodily appropriate as Napoleon and Virginia Mayo looks the part of Cleopatra. Hedy Lamarr is miscast as Joan (yes, of Arc) in one of the few other key parts, some of the 'stars' being on and off the screen so rapidly as to go unrecognized.

••••••••••••••••••••••••••••••••••••••

■ **STORY OF ROBIN HOOD, THE**

(Aka: The Story of Robin Hood and His Merrie Men)

1952, 83 MINS, UK ◇ ⊛ ⊙

Dir Ken Annakin *Prod* Perce Pearce *Scr* Lawrence E. Watkin *Ph* Guy Green *Ed* Gordon Pilkington *Mus* Clifton Parker *Art Dir* Carmen Dillon, Arthur Lawson

● Richard Todd, Joan Rice, Peter Finch, James Hayter, James Robertson Justice, Martita Hunt (Walt Disney/RKO)

For his second British live-action production, Walt Disney took the legend of Robin Hood and translated it to the screen as a superb piece of entertainment, with all the action of a western and the romance and intrigue of a historical drama.

Despite his modest stature, Richard Todd proves to be a first-rate Robin Hood, alert, dashing and forceful, equally convincing when leading his outlaws against Prince John as he is in winning the admiration of Maid Marian. Although a comparative newcomer to the screen, Joan Rice acts with charm and intelligence.

James Hayter as Friar Tuck, Martita Hunt as the queen, Peter Finch as the sheriff, James Robertson Justice as Little John, Bill Owen as the poacher, and Elton Hayes as the minstrel are in the front rank.

••••••••••••••••••••••••••••••••••••••

■ **STORY OF RUTH, THE**

1960, 132 MINS, US ◇ ⊛

Dir Henry Koster *Prod* Samuel G. Engel *Scr* Norman Corwin *Ph* Arthur E. Arling *Ed* Jack W. Holmes *Mus* Franz Waxman *Art Dir* Lyle R. Wheeler, Franz Bachelin

● Stuart Whitman, Tom Tryon, Peggy Wood, Viveca Lindfors, Jeff Morrow, Elana Eden (20th Century-Fox)

The Story of Ruth is a refreshingly sincere and restrained Biblical drama, a picture that elaborates on the romantic, political and devotional difficulties encountered by the Old Testament heroine. Yet, for all its obvious high purpose, bolstered by several fine performances, there is a sluggishness that is disturbing.

The screenplay describes the heroine's activities from her youthful indoctrination as a Moabite priestess through her marriage to the Judean, Boaz. Along the way it dramatizes her romance with the kindly Mahlon, his violent death, her conversion to Judaism and flight with Mahlon's mother, Naomi, to Bethlehem, where she encounters religious persecution and becomes embroiled in a romantic triangle.

Although the screenplay wisely avoids archaic phrases, director Henry Koster has not always succeeded in side-stepping stereotyped biblical-pic posturing and mannerisms among his players, and is inclined to anticipate mysterious character knowledge in a few instances. But he has coaxed several very effective portrayals out of his principals.

The film introduces Elana Eden in the title role. She gives a performance of dignity, projecting an inner strength through a delicate veneer. The picture is helped by veteran Peggy Wood's excellent characterization of Naomi. Her timing is always sharp. Tom Tryon establishes a pleasing screen personality with a vigorous delineation of Mahlon. Franz Waxman's music is typically biblical in tone and tempo.

● ●

■ STORY OF THREE LOVES, THE

1953, 122 MINS, US ◇

Dir Gottfried Reinhardt, Vincente Minnelli   *Prod* Sidney Franklin   *Scr* John Collier, Jan Lustig, George Froeschel   *Ph* Charles Rosher, Harold Rosson   *Ed* Ralph E. Winters   *Mus* Miklos Rozsa   *Art Dir* Cedric Gibbons, Preston Ames, Edward Carfagno, Gabriel Scognamillo
● Pier Angeli, Ethel Barrymore, Leslie Caron, Kirk Douglas, James Mason, Moira Shearer (M-G-M)

Metro has put some top stars into a beautifully dressed Technicolor combination of three yarns tied together by placing the key characters aboard an ocean liner. With a strong initial entry and a suspenseful finale [directed by Gottfried Reinhardt], picture's weakness lies in the middle [section, directed by Vincente Minnelli].

Opening episode, *The Jealous Lover* [scripted by John Collier] is easily the most effective. Moira Shearer plays an aspiring ballerina prevented from dancing by a serious heart condition. When James Mason, a famous choreographer, sees her improvising on an empty stage, he asks her to perform for him.

Both Mason and Shearer score, the latter especially in her beautiful terping to the music of Rachmaninoff's *Rhapsody on a Theme of Paganini*. Credit Sadler's Wells choreographer Frederick Ashton with some topnotch dance arrangements.

Second episode, *Mademoiselle*, a fantasy [scripted by Jan Lustig and George Froeschel, from a story by Arnold Phillips], is aimless in direction and lacking in interest. A boy (Ricky Nelson), in Rome with his parents, wishes he could grow up so as to be rid of his French governess (Leslie Caron). Ethel Barrymore, as an old lady believed by children to be a witch, grants him the wish for four hours, and as a man (Farley Granger) he falls in love with the governess.

Final episode [*Equilibrium*, scripted by Collier, from a story by Ladislas Vadja and Jacques Maret, adaptation by Lustig and Froeschel] has Kirk Douglas as a trapeze artist who's retired after being accused of killing his femme partner by giving her too risky a trick. After he fishes Pier Angeli, a lonely young widow, out of the Seine, he decides she would be a good partner, since she has no will to live. Story gets off to a slow start, but it builds suspense and thrills for a solid close.

● ●

■ STORY OF VERNON AND IRENE CASTLE, THE

1939, 96 MINS, US ⓥ ⊙

Dir H.C. Potter   *Prod* George Haight   *Scr* Richard Sherman   *Ph* Robert de Grasse   *Ed* William Hamilton   *Mus* Victor Baravalle (dir.)   *Art Dir* Van Nest Polglase, Perry Ferguson

● Fred Astaire, Ginger Rogers, Edna May Oliver, Walter Brennan, Lew Fields, Etienne Girardot (RKO)

The Story of Vernon and Irene Castle is top-flight cinematic entertainment. It's another switch on the backstage story, this time dealing with a much-in-love married pair of ballroomologists catapulted from dire straits in Paris into international acclaim and fortune.

The medley of some 40 yesteryear pops is the common denominator for all types of audiences.

Irene Castle technically-advised. Her published memoirs, *My Husband* and *My Memories of Vernon Castle*, are the story background [adapted by Oscar Hammerstein II and Dorothy Yost] of the film. Her personal life story has been seemingly transmuted into celluloid with considerable faithfulness and a minimum of bombast or heroics.

Their success story dates from the time that the shrewd Maggie Sutton (Edna May Oliver) gets them an audition at the Cafe de Paris. Comes the war, however, and Castle enlists in the Canadian Royal Flying Corps, and meets untimely death as a flying instructor.

Ginger Rogers and Fred Astaire are excellent as the Castles.

● ●

■ STORYVILLE

1992, 110 MINS, US ◇ ⓥ

Dir Mark Frost   *Prod* David Roe, Edward R. Pressman   *Scr* Mark Frost, Lee Reynolds   *Ph* Ron Garcia   *Ed* B.J.Sears   *Mus* Carter Burwell   *Art Dir* Richard Hoover
● James Spader, Joanne Whalley-Kilmer, Jason Robards, Charlotte Lewis, Michael Warren, Michael Parks (Davis Entertainment/Pressman)

Storyville has a little trouble getting its story straight. A teeming cesspool of illicit sex, murder, suicide, family intrigue and political chicanery in exotic Louisiana, this would-be *Chinatown* is so overloaded with outrageous implausibilities that the temptation is very strong to consider it all a joke.

In his first big-screen direction, Mark Frost, a key force behind *Hill Street Blues* and David Lynch's partner on *Twin Peaks* for TV, has taken an Australian novel [*Juryman* by Frank Galbally and Robert Macklin] and relocated it in New Orleans, where just about anything goes.

James Spader plays Cray Fowler, a callow, good-looking kid trying to carry his rich, corrupt family's tradition of political service into a third generation. Encouraged by family patriarch Clifford Fowler (Jason Robards) in the old-boy-network school, Cray is divorcing his wife and seeking the support of black voters.

Cray is crazy enough to run off with the enticing Lee (Charlotte Lewis), a Vietnamese woman he's barely met. He is obliged to fight her maniacal father, who mysteriously winds up dead. When Lee is charged with the murder, Cray astoundingly offers his services as defense attorney. Opposing him will be a prosecutor (Joanne Whalley-Kilmer) who's his old flame.

Cray does so many apparently stupid things, and the many jaw-dropping loopholes and long-shots in the first half make the film systematically unconvincing. Whalley-Kilmer and Lewis are attractive in functional parts, and Robards serves up an old-school blowhard to a fare-thee-well.

● ●

■ STRAIGHT TALK

1992, 91 MINS, US ◇ ⓥ ⊙

Dir Barnet Kellman   *Prod* Robert Chartoff, Fred Berner   *Scr* Craig Bolotin, Patricia Resnick   *Ph* Peter Sova   *Ed* Michael Tronick   *Mus* Brad Fiedel   *Art Dir* Jeffrey Townsend
● Dolly Parton, James Woods, Griffin Dunne, Michael Madsen, Deirdre O'Connell, John Sayles (Hollywood)

Borrowing liberally from the classic *Mr. Deeds goes to Town*, with its story of a successful smalltown bumpkin conned by a big-city reporter feigning romantic interest to get material for an expose, pic has Dolly Parton in the Gary Cooper role and James Woods in Jean Arthur's. Major diff between the pics is *Straight Talk*'s relative lack of interest in social issues. But Parton's winning personality shines in the amusing, if superficial, screenplay.

After leaving Flat River, Ark, to seek a better life, former dance teacher Parton is mistakenly hired as a Chi radio psychologist and immediately captivates listeners.

She meets-cute with Woods on the Irv Kupcinet Bridge after he spies her from a window in the *Sun Times* office and mistakenly thinks she's committing suicide. He starts digging into her past, prodded by his heartless *Front Page*-style editor (Jerry Orbach).

Woods isn't a conventional leading man, but that's an asset here, since he fits effortlessly into his role and is credible in his slippery behavior as he woos the guileless Parton for a story. Barnet Kellman's TV-style direction is efficient but tends to be visually static.

● ●

■ STRAIGHT TIME

1978, 114 MINS, US ◇ ⓥ

Dir Ulu Grosbard   *Prod* Stanley Beck, Tim Zinnemann   *Scr* Alvin Sargent, Edward Bunker, Jeffrey Boam   *Ph* Owen Roizman   *Ed* Sam O'Steen, Randy Roberts   *Mus* David Shire   *Art Dir* Stephen Grimes
● Dustin Hoffman, Theresa Russell, Gary Busey, Harry Dean Stanton, M. Emmet Walsh, Rita Taggart (First Artists/Sweetwall)

Straight Time is a most unlikeable film because Dustin Hoffman, starring as a paroled and longtime criminal, cannot overcome the essentially distasteful and increasingly unsympathetic elements in the character. Ulu Grosbard's sluggish direction doesn't help.

Apparent plot peg [from Edward Banker's novel *No Beast so Fierce*] is that a parolee suffers so many indignities that a return to crime is easier.

Viewers are asked initially to believe that M. Emmet Walsh, the assigned parole officer, is a sadistic person who delights in hassling his charges. But given the circumstances, he does not emerge as a heavy. Indeed, Hoffman's too-easy lapse into his old ways absolves any blame on The System. Hoffman's character would have defied the parole supervision of a saint.

Theresa Russell is very good as Hoffman's girl; Harry Dean Stanton is excellent as a reformed hood who (nobody explains why) is being suffocated in the life of a successful suburban businessman; Gary Busey is good as a weak ex-con who bungles a climactic robbery plan.

● ●

■ STRAIT-JACKET

1963, 93 MINS, US ⓥ

Dir William Castle   *Prod* William Castle   *Scr* Robert Bloch   *Ph* Arthur Arling   *Ed* Edwin Bryant   *Mus* Van Alexander   *Art Dir* Boris Leven
● Joan Crawford, Diane Baker, Leif Erickson, Howard St John, John Anthony Hayes, George Kennedy (Columbia)

Strait-Jacket could be summoned up as a chip off the old Bloch. Writer Robert Bloch's *Psycho*, that is. In crossing the basic plot design of that 1960 Bloch-buster with the instrument of murder (the axe) and at least one of the ramifications of the celebrated Lizzie Borden case, Bloch has provided the grisly ingredients for producer-director William Castle to concoct some marketable 'chop' suey.

Heads really roll in this yarn, which commences with a dual hatchet job on a cheating husband and his lady friend who are discovered bedroominating by the wife (Joan Crawford), whose three-year-old daughter witnesses in horror the 40 some odd whacks per victim administered by her mother. Mom goes to the insane asylum and daughter grows up into Diane Baker. They are reunited 20 years later when mom is released.

Crawford does well by her role, delivering an animated performance. Baker is pretty and histrionically satisfactory as her daughter. Some of Castle's direction is stiff and mechanical, but most of the murders are suspensefully and chillingly constructed.

. . . .

■ STRANGE AFFAIR, THE

1968, 102 MINS, UK ◇

Dir David Greene   *Prod* Howard Harrison, Stanley Mann   *Scr* Stanley Mann   *Ph* Alex Thomson   *Ed* Brian Smedley-Aston   *Mus* Basil Kirchin   *Art Dir* Brian Eatwell
● Michael York, Jeremy Kemp, Susan George, Jack Watson, David Glaisyer, Richard Vanstone (Paramount)

Michael York is the 'Strange' involved in an affair which finds Scotland Yard detective Pierce (Jeremy Kemp) trying to nail a trio of dangerous criminals and drug peddlers.

Frustrated in various attempts at getting legal evidence, Kemp in desperation resorts to blackmailing Strange, who's been caught in a compromising situation with a girl, into planting a drug packet on one of the trio during a search.

Situation provides opportunities for some subsurface characterizations of the two men torn by different concepts of duty.

There are no lags in the action, with Stanley Mann's literate script [from a novel by Bernard Toms] ringing true all the way, just as it provides an amusing change of pace in the tryst linking Strange with an ebullient hippie played by Susan George.

York makes a very sympathetic person out of Strange. Kemp is suitably harassed and obsessed as the duty-first plainclothesman, while Jack Watson, David Glaisyer and Richard Vanstone are properly sneery as the baddies. It is, however, George who captures most attention in a very appealing performance.

. . . .

■ STRANGE ALIBI

1941, 63 MINS, US

Dir D. Ross Lederman   *Scr* Kenneth Gamet   *Ph* Allen G. Siegler   *Ed* Frank Magee
● Arthur Kennedy, Joan Perry, Howard da Silva, Florence Bates (Warner/First National)

This rates high among the average run of B mellers. It's an evidence of Warners' crime-and-punishment actioners working at an all-out peak. Everything in it has been seen before – particularly the sets – but the concoction has been tossed together again under director D. Ross Lederman to become a speedy and delectable dish.

Plot [from a story by Leslie T. White] is far from new. Unfortunately, Lederman has had to dive into the stock barrel for a load of trite court and prison stuff which bogs the picture right down in the center.

Arthur Kennedy plays a detective who arranges with his chief for a publicized break between them so that he can go over to the mob. Racket guys find out he's not playing them straight and kill the chief, planting the murder on Kennedy, who is sent up for life. He breaks from prison and very neatly squares himself for fadeout clinch.

Kennedy does a nice job when not stilted by the B-picture dialog.

. . . .

■ STRANGE BEDFELLOWS

1964, 99 MINS, US ◇

Dir Melvin Frank   *Prod* Melvin Frank   *Scr* Melvin Frank, Michael Pertwee   *Ph* Leo Tover   *Ed* Gene Milford

Mus Leigh Harline   *Art Dir* Alexander Golitzen, Joseph Wright
● Rock Hudson, Gina Lollobrigida, Gig Young, Edward Judd, Terry-Thomas, Arthur Haynes (Panama-Frank/Universal)

Strange Bedfellows is another of those romantic marital comedies, based primarily on misunderstandings. Critics for the thinking man may scoff at the plot, which derives much of its drama from ancient device of each character not quite understanding what the others are up to. But story line differs enough so that it isn't simple carbon of all the Rock Hudson-Tony Randall-Doris Day comedies.

Hudson is a trifle solemn as London-based US oil executive who can rise to extreme top echelon if his corporate image is whitewashed. This means he must patch up seven-year marriage to Gina Lollobrigida, who more than compensates for Hudson's stuffiness by her enthusiastic rapport with zany causes.

But the unabashed comedians steal the show. Probably the funniest bit has Arthur Haynes and David King as taxidrivers with Hudson and Gina in their respective vehicles. The estranged lovers try to communicate with one another by way of two-way cab radio, with hilarity resulting from cabbies garbling of messages.

. . . .

■ STRANGE CARGO

1940, 111 MINS, US ▼

Dir Frank Borzage   *Prod* Joseph L. Mankiewicz   *Scr* Lawrence Hazard   *Ph* Robert Planck   *Ed* Robert J. Kern   *Mus* Franz Waxman
● Joan Crawford, Clark Gable, Ian Hunter, Peter Lorre, Paul Lukas, Albert Dekker (M-G-M)

Strange Cargo is a strange melodramatic concoction [from a book by Richard Sale] that endeavors to mix the adventures of an escaping group of convicts from a tropical island prison with religious preachment through inclusion of a mysterious stranger with Christ-like attributes. The attempt is not successful. Combined with this fault is a slow, ploddy technique on the directing side, overlong footage and many dragging passages.

In accentuating the individual spiritual redemptions of the various convict members of the escaping group, story builds up with some rather strong talk and ridicule of the Bible, its passages and teachings.

Story, in attempt to dovetail stark and dangerous adventure with a religious motif, does not jell to any degree of consistency. Shortly after establishing the prison setting, the convicts escape and struggle through jungle, swamp and sand to reach a hidden boat. Clark Gable saves Joan Crawford from the clutches of a designing miner en route, and takes her along. It's a strange group aboard the small open sailboat, the stranger (Ian Hunter) dominating with his quiet though definite manner.

Crawford is provided with a particularly meaty role as the hardened dance hall gal who falls hard for the tough convict. Gable is vigorous in his portrayal of the self-appointed head of the escaping convicts, a far from sympathetic assignment, and he is overshadowed by the reserved but strong-willed Hunter as the redeemer of the tough souls assembled in the small boat.

. . . .

■ STRANGE INTERLUDE

(UK: *Strange Interval*)

1932, 110 MINS, US

Dir Robert Z. Leonard   *Scr* Bess Meredyth, C. Gardner Sullivan   *Ph* Lee Garmes   *Ed* Margaret Booth
● Norma Shearer, Clark Gable, Alexander Kirkland, Ralph Morgan, Robert Young, May Robson (M-G-M)

Norma Shearer who shoulders the brunt of the histrionic burden, somehow misses in a vacillating characterization which was made

necessarily so, for censor purposes alone, if nothing else. As for Clark Gable, he is eclipsed by Alexander Kirkland as the weak husband of the heroine and Ralph Morgan as the mawk with the mother fixation.

Through their life's span, as the story proceeds into old age, when Nina Leeds (Shearer) sees her illegitimate son moulded to conform with her life's ideas, the episodic, transitory cinematurgy is as much a credit to the hairdressers and the makeup staff on the Metro lot as to Shearer, Gable, Kirkland and Morgan. The makeup is excellent but the make-believe isn't.

No question that the devitalizing of the [1928 – 29 Pulitzer Prize play by Eugene] O'Neill has much to do with it. The formula cinematic contrivances employed to pitch emotions falsely, to misfit climaxes, are very apparent.

The O'Neill asides, in screen treatment, might be said to be somewhat of an improvement over the stage original. The actual words are uttered, and then the subconscious thoughts are voiced by the same player on the soundtrack (with a different inflection, of course).

. . . .

■ STRANGE INTERVAL

See: *Strange Interlude*

. . . .

■ STRANGE LOVE OF MARTHA IVERS, THE

1946, 113 MINS, US ▼

Dir Lewis Milestone   *Prod* Hal B. Wallis   *Scr* Robert Rossen   *Ph* Victor Milner   *Ed* Archie Marshek   *Mus* Miklos Rozsa   *Art Dir* Hans Dreier, John Meehan
● Barbara Stanwyck, Van Heflin, Lizabeth Scott, Kirk Douglas, Judith Anderson, Darryl Hickman (Wallis/Paramount)

Story is a forthright, uncompromising presentation of evil, greedy people and human weaknesses. Characters are sharply drawn in the Robert Rossen script, based on Jack Patrick's original story [*Love Lies Bleeding*], and Lewis Milestone's direction punches home the melodrama for full suspense and excitement.

Prolog opening [in 1928] establishes the murder of a bullying aunt by her young niece. Deed is witnessed by the son of the girl's tutor, but is blamed on an unknown prowler. Coverup moves the tutor and son into a position of power in the girl's household. Story then picks up 18 years later with the accidental return to the town of another of the girl's childhood friends. Return panics Barbara Stanwyck and Kirk Douglas, now grown up and married, who fear the friend was also a witness of the early killing.

Character portrayed by Stanwyck is evil and she gives it a high-caliber delineation. Douglas makes his weakling role interesting, showing up strongly among the more experienced players. Best performance honors, though, are divided between Heflin and Scott, latter as a Heflin pickup.
□ 1946: Nomination: Best Original Story

. . . .

■ STRANGER, THE

1946, 94 MINS, US ▼

Dir Orson Welles   *Prod* S.P. Eagle [= Sam Spiegel]   *Scr* Anthony Veiller, [John Huston, Orson Welles]   *Ph* Russell Metty   *Ed* Ernest Nims   *Mus* Bronislau Kaper   *Art Dir* Perry Ferguson
● Orson Welles, Edward G. Robinson, Loretta Young, Philip Merivale, Richard Long (RKO/International)

The Stranger is socko melodrama, spinning an intriguing web of thrills and chills. Director Orson Welles gives the production a fast, suspenseful development, drawing every advantage from the hard-hitting script from the Victor Trivas story. Plot moves forward at a relentless pace in depicting the hunt of the Allied Commission for Prosecution of Nazi

S

War Criminals for a top Nazi who has removed all traces of his origin and is a professor in a New England school. Edward G. Robinson is the government man on his trail. Loretta Young is the New England girl who becomes the bride of the Nazi.

Story opens in Germany, where a Nazi is allowed to escape in belief he will lead the way to former head of a notorious prison camp. Chase moves across Europe to the small New England town where Welles is marrying Young. When the escaped Nazi contacts him, Welles strangles him and buries the body in the woods. From then on the terror mounts as Robinson tries to trap Welles into revealing his true identity.

A uniformly excellent cast gives reality to events that transpire. The three stars, Robinson, Young and Welles, turn in some of their best work, the actress being particularly effective as the misled bride.
□ 1946: Nomination: Best Original Story

. . . .

■ **STRANGER AMONG US, A**
(UK: Close To Eden)

1992, 111 MINS, US ◇ ▣
Dir Sidney Lumet   *Prod* Steve Golin, Sigurjon Sighvatsson   *Scr* Robert J. Averech   *Ph* Andrzej Bartkowiak   *Ed* Andrew Mondshein   *Mus* Jerry Bock   *Art Dir* Philip Rosenberg
● Melanie Griffith, Eric Thal, John Pankow, Tracey Pollan, Lee Richardson, Mia Sara (Hollywood/ Propaganda)

Director Sidney Lumet's fish-out-of-water mystery about a case-hardened WASP female cop investigating a murder in New York's cloistered Hasidic community tries to make up in local color what it lacks in dramatic plausibility.

Melanie Griffith stars as a seen-it-all cop who, after having killed a thug who stabbed her lover-partner, is assigned to the low-pressure case of a vanished Hasidic jewelry dealer. When this fellow turns up dead in his office with $720,000 in diamonds missing, Griffith moves in with the Brooklyn group's Rebbe (Lee Richardson) and his adopted children Eric Thal – the next Rebbe designate – and Mia Sara to penetrate the community in her search for the killer.

Plot is overloaded with hard-to-take factors, while the revelation of the killer is far from surprising. More importantly, the nature of the Hasidic community effectively prevents Griffith from conducting any kind of penetrating investigation.

Griffith is at her best in the role's moments of awakening, when she realizes she is no longer satisfied with the prosaic interests of her cop b.f. and that she may have a spiritual side that has never been acknowledged.

. . . .

■ **STRANGERS**
See: Voyage to Italy

. . . .

■ **STRANGERS IN THE CITY**

1962, 80 MINS, US
Dir Rick Carrier   *Prod* Rick Carrier   *Scr* Rick Carrier   *Ph* Rick Carrier   *Ed* Stan Russell   *Mus* Bob Prince
● Robert Gentile, Camilo Delgado, Rosita De Triana, Creta Margos, Robert Corso (Embassy/Carrier)

A first film by Yank Rick Carrier, this shows a Puerto Rican family in a Manhattan slum. The father is a vain, proud man with a lack of understanding of America or his family – and he has just lost his job. His teenage son and daughter go to look for work but he orders his wife to stay home. The boy runs into local racism and general hoodlumism as a delivery boy while the girl, a beauty, is used by factory workers and then becomes a sort of call girl for a dressmaker.

It may sound overly melodramatic, but this

has a neat insight into NY life, as this producer sees it. Though this pic shows mainly bigoted people, it also depicts how their own weaknesses help betray this family. Much of the wickedness is from plain ignorance.

Some of the acting is skimpy. But Robert Gentile, as the son; Creta Margos, as his pliant comely sister; Rosita De Triana, as the anguished mother and Robert Corso, as the foppish gang leader, are standout.

. . . .

■ **STRANGER'S KISS**

1983, 94 MINS, US ◇ ▣
Dir Matthew Chapman   *Prod* Doug Dilge   *Scr* Matthew Chapman, Blaine Novak   *Ph* Mikail Suslov   *Ed* William Carruth   *Mus* Gato Barbieri
● Peter Coyote, Victoria Tennant, Blaine Novak, Dan Shor, Richard Romanus, Linda Kerridge (White)

Stranger's Kiss is a glowing homage to 1950s melodrama set in the film world. Though shot on a modest budget, picture has a lush look aided by strong artistic and technical contributions.

The love triangle tale is mirrored in both the real life and film-within-a-film structure of the production. Principals are Carole Redding (Victoria Tennant), a young woman kept by a gangster (Richard Romanus) who agrees to finance the film's film and costar, Stevie Blake (Blaine Novak, who also cowrote the script), a hustler who soon becomes consumed by Carole's mysterious background.

Stanley (Peter Coyote), the director, keeps Stevie in the dark to capitalize on his emotions. Both stories concern a boxer and a dancehall girl who fall in love but her past debt to a hoodlum threatens to destroy the relationship. Plot is reminiscent of Stanley Kubrick's *Killer's Kiss* and several other low budget items circa 1955, the setting of the picture.

Tennant is radiant as Carole with a genuine screen presence suited to her role. In sharp contrast, Novak has a forceful presence which demands our attention and eventually wins our affection.

. . . .

■ **STRANGERS ON A TRAIN**

1951, 100 MINS, US ▣ ☉
Dir Alfred Hitchcock   *Prod* Alfred Hitchcock   *Scr* Raymond Chandler, Czenzi Ormonde   *Ph* Robert Burks   *Ed* William H. Ziegler   *Mus* Dimitri Tiomkin   *Art Dir* Ted Haworth
● Farley Granger, Robert Walker, Ruth Roman, Leo G. Carroll, Patricia Hitchcock, Laura Elliott (Warner)

Given a good basis for a thriller in the Patricia Highsmith novel [script adaption by Whitfield Cook] and a first-rate script, Hitchcock embroiders the plot into a gripping, palm-sweating piece of suspense.

Story offers a fresh situation for murder. Two strangers meet on a train. One is Farley Granger, separated from his tramp wife (Laura Elliott) and in love with Ruth Roman. The other is Robert Walker, a neurotic playboy who hates his rich father. Walker proposes that he will kill Elliott if Granger will do away with the father. Granger treats the proposal as a bad joke but Walker is serious.

Latter stalks down Elliott in an amusement park and strangles her. He then starts chasing Granger to make him fulfill the other end of the bargain.

Performance-wise, the cast comes through strongly. Granger is excellent as the harassed young man innocently involved in murder. Roman's role of a nice, understanding girl is a switch for her, and she makes it warmly effective. Walker's role has extreme color, and he projects it deftly. Elliott stands out briefly as the victim, and Patricia Hitchcock (the director's daughter) also registers.
□ 1951: Nomination: Best B&W Cinematography

. . . .

■ **STRANGER'S RETURN**

1933, 88 MINS, US
Dir King Vidor   *Prod* King Vidor   *Scr* Brown Holmes, Phil Stong   *Ph* William Daniels   *Ed* Dick Fantl   *Art Dir* Frederic Hope
● Lionel Barrymore, Miriam Hopkins, Franchot Tone, Stuart Erwin, Irene Hervey, Beulah Bondi (M-G-M)

It is the story [from the novel by Phil Stong] of a New York girl who goes west after she leaves her husband, finds a new love, but loses out when the hero leaves to avoid temptation since he does not want to injure his wife and son, despite his greater love for his new idol.

Supplementing, or rather overshadowing the love interest, is a rare well-written story of a somewhat eccentric old farmer plagued by his fortune-seeking relatives who hover about the farm waiting the death of their prospective victim.

As the farmer Lionel Barrymore has a role he fits. Even his false whiskers are forgiven. Barrymore carries the bulk of the story. Miriam Hopkins is not as fortunate. She is natural for the greater part, but fails at times in the lighter phases.

Franchot Tone is a likable hero, always in command of his scenes. No faulty performance in the entire cast.

. . . .

■ **STRANGERS WHEN WE MEET**

1960, 117 MINS, US ◇ ▣
Dir Richard Quine   *Prod* Richard Quine   *Scr* Evan Hunter   *Ph* Charles Lang Jr   *Ed* Charles Nelson   *Mus* George Duning   *Art Dir* Ross Bellah
● Kirk Douglas, Kim Novak, Ernie Kovacs, Barbara Rush, Walter Matthau, Virginia Bruce (Bryna-Quine/ Columbia)

A pictorially attractive but dramatically vacuous study of modern-style infidelity, *Strangers When We Meet* is easy on the eyes but hard on the intellect. A bunch of maladjusted suburbanites are thrown together in Evan Hunter's screenplay (from his novel), and what comes out is an old-fashioned soap opera.

Brilliant architect Kirk Douglas is upset because his spouse (Barbara Rush) is overly concerned with balancing the family budget. Meanwhile, housewife Kim Novak is disturbed over being taken for granted by her undersexed mate (John Bryant). Out of this germ of marital instability, a feverishly passionate affair blossoms between Douglas and Novak via a series of trysts. But unstable, sharp-eyed neighbor Walter Matthau, putting two and two together and coming up with an odd number, decides to even things up by getting into the act.

It is a rather pointless, slow-moving story, but it has been brought to the screen with such skill that it charms the spectator into an attitude of relaxed enjoyment, much the same effect as that produced by a casual daydream fantasy. Douglas does well by his role, and Novak brings to hers that cool, style-setting attitude that is her trademark.

. . . .

■ **STRANGER THAN PARADISE**

1984, 95 MINS, US ▣ ☉
Dir Jim Jarmusch   *Prod* Sara Driver   *Scr* Jim Jarmusch   *Ph* Tom DiCillo   *Ed* Jim Jarmusch, Melody London   *Mus* John Lurie
● John Lurie, Eszter Balint, Richard Edson, Cecilia Stark (Cinesthesia-Grokenberger)

Stranger than Paradise is a bracingly original avant-garde black comedy. Begun as a short which was presented under the same title at some earlier festivals, film has been expanded in outstanding fashion by young New York writer-director Jim Jarmusch.

Simple narrative starts with self-styled New York hipster Willie (John Lurie) being paid a surprise, and quite unwelcome, visit by Hungarian cousin Eva (Eszter Balint). But when she finally leaves after 10 days, there seems to be a strange sort of affection between them.

Since plot doesn't count for much here, the style takes over, and Jarmusch has made such matters as camera placement, composition (in stunning black-and-white) and structure count for a lot.

....

■ STRANGE VENGEANCE OF ROSALIE, THE

1972, 107 MINS, US ◇

Dir Jack Starrett   *Prod* John Kohn   *Scr* Anthony Greville-Bell, John Kohn   *Ph* Ray Parslow   *Ed* Thom Noble   *Mus* John Cameron   *Art Dir* Roy Walker
● Bonnie Bedelia, Ken Howard, Anthony Zerbe (20th Century-Fox/Cinecrest)

The Strange Vengeance of Rosalie is an offbeat film, centered around the fascinating, although admittedly preposterous, situation of a lonely adolescent part-Indian girl (Bonnie Bedelia), naive and emotionally disturbed, who hitches a ride with a traveling salesman (Ken Howard) and leads him to her isolated ramshackle cabin in New Mexico, where she lets the air out of the tires of his car, breaks his leg and holds him captive.

Pic generally holds together on strength of engaging performances and a fair amount of tension throughout, but the mixture of serious suspenseful drama (tinged with an ever-present air of impending violence) and humorous repartee between the characters doesn't jell. [Based on *Chicken* by Miles Tripp.]

....

■ STRANGLER, THE

1964, 89 MINS, US ▼

Dir Burt Topper   *Prod* Samuel Bischoff, David Diamond   *Scr* Bill S. Ballinger   *Ph* Jacques Marquette   *Ed* Robert Eisen   *Mus* Marlin Skiles   *Art Dir* Hal Pereira, Eugene Lourie
● Victor Buono, David McLean, Diane Sayer, Davey Davison, Ellen Corby, James B. Sikking (Allied Artists)

Bill S. Ballinger's scenario describes the latter phases of the homicidal career of a paranoid schizophrenic (Victor Buono) whose hatred of women has been motivated by a possessive mother who has completely warped his personality. His fetish for dolls ultimately betrays him to the police just as he is in the act of applying the coup de grace to distaff victim No. 11.

Dramatically skillful direction by Burt Topper and a firm level of histrionic performances help *The Strangler* over some rough spots and keep the picture from succumbing to inconsistencies of character and contrivances of story scattered through the picture.

Bueno for Buono, a convincing menace all the way. There's always a place on the screen for a fat man who can act, and Buono has the avoirdupois field virtually to himself.

....

■ STRAPLESS

1990, 97 MINS, UK ◇ ▼ ⊙

Dir David Hare   *Prod* Rick McCallum   *Scr* David Hare   *Ph* Andrew Dunn   *Ed* Edward Marnier   *Mus* Nick Bicat   *Art Dir* Roger Hall
● Blair Brown, Bruno Ganz, Bridget Fonda, Alan Howard, Michael Gough, Hugh Laurie (Granada)

Writer-director David Hare's third feature centers on the concerns of a middle-aged professional woman whose personal problems relate to wider political and social issues in Britain today.

This time the central character is an American, Dr Lillian Hempel (Blair Brown), who's lived in Britain for 12 years. While on vacation in Portugal she meets an apparently wealthy stranger, Raymond Forbes (Bruno Ganz), who woos her but fails to get her into his bed.

Back in London, Forbes continues his courtship, begging Lillian to marry him. They marry secretly, and soon after he simply disappears. Lillian discovers he already has a wife and son, also abandoned.

Lillian's serious, well-ordered life is contrasted with her flighty younger sister Amy (Bridget Fonda), who has a series of Latin lovers and gets pregnant by one of them.

Meanwhile, Lillian gradually is being drawn toward political activism as the British government's health service cutbacks begin to hurt.

Strapless (so-named because both the sisters wind up with no visible means of support) is an intelligent, ironic, multi-layered drama that's consistently intriguing. Performances are impeccable.

....

■ STRAWBERRY BLONDE

1941, 98 MINS, US ▼

Dir Raoul Walsh   *Prod* William Cagney   *Scr* Julius J. Epstein, Philip G. Epstein   *Ph* James Wong Howe   *Ed* William Holmes   *Mus* Heinz Roemheld
● James Cagney, Olivia de Havilland, Rita Hayworth, Jack Carson, Alan Hale, George Tobias (Warner)

Warners dips into the Gay Nineties period with this second film version of James Hagan's play, *One Sunday Afternoon*. Paramount turned out the original picture back in 1933 with Gary Cooper starred.

This entry of the Hagan play switches the locale to New York; otherwise it sticks close to the original. Story is told in retrospect. James Cagney is a struggling dentist with few patients, when an emergency call comes to pull a molar of his worst enemy, and he figures to give the latter a good dose of gas. While waiting for the patient's arrival, yarn goes back 10 years, when Cagney was enamored of the neighborhood's 'strawberry blonde'.

Jilted, he conveniently marries the loving and understanding nurse (Olivia de Havilland) but through the years carries a hate for the man who victimized him and stole his first girl. But he again meets the girl of his memories, finds her a nagging nuisance, and figures his enemy has had sufficient punishment through the years. It's then that he realizes he has the perfect wife.

Cagney and de Havilland provide topnotch performances that do much to keep up interest in the proceedings. Rita Hayworth is an eyeful as the title character, while Jack Carson is excellent as the politically ambitious antagonist of the dentist.

□ 1941: Nomination: Best Scoring of a Musical Picture

....

■ STRAW DOGS

1971, 118 MINS, UK ◇ ▼ ⊙

Dir Sam Peckinpah   *Prod* Daniel Melnick   *Scr* David Zelag Goodman, Sam Peckinpah   *Ph* John Coquillon   *Ed* Paul Davies   *Mus* Jerry Fielding   *Art Dir* Ray Simms
● Dustin Hoffman, Susan George, Peter Vaughan, T.P. McKenna, Del Henney, Colin Welland (ABC)

Director Sam Peckinpah indulges himself in an orgy of unparalleled violence and nastiness with undertones of sexual repression in this production.

Dustin Hoffman appears as a quiet American mathematician who has married a lively, sexy English girl, played by Susan George, and goes to live on her isolated West Country farm. They get on reasonably well with a moronic assortment of locals, most of whom are heavy drinkers. Some are sexually repressed and the wife is seduced while her husband is hunting.

When the village dolt accidentally kills a teenage mini-skirted flirt he takes refuge at the farm. Hoffman refuses to give him to the enflamed villagers. Count is lost of the grue-

some killings and bestialities that ensue.

The script relies on shock and violence to tide it over weakness in development, shallow characterization and lack of motivation. Hoffman scores as the easy-going American who rises to heights of belligerence when he considers the dolt is being wronged.

□ 1971: Nomination: Best Original Score

....

■ STREAMERS

1983, 118 MINS, US ◇ ▼ ⊙

Dir Robert Altman   *Prod* Nick J. Mileti, Robert Altman   *Scr* David Rabe   *Ph* Pierre Mignot   *Ed* Norman Smith   *Mus* Stephen Foster   *Art Dir* Wolf Kroeger
● Matthew Modine, Michael Wright, Mitchell Lichtenstein, David Allen Grier, Albert Macklin, Guy Bond (United Artists Classics)

Streamers is a highly stylized set of theatricals describing an existentialist hell among a small group of men in a military barracks.

Apart from allowing the camera to occasionally peek through a curtain, writer David Rabe and director Robert Altman have their 1965 soldiers await orders to go to Vietnam and spending the waiting time either lying around on their bunks or returning drunk from saloon or whorehouse outings. They mostly taunt each other with tales of their own past history, but the taunts are socially, racially and sexually loaded, two of the soldiers being black, a third being an Ivy League homosexual and the fourth an intellectual 'from the sticks'.

Things explode in blood-gushing violence and general sadness when the possibilities have been exhausted in this overlong, over-emphatic film.

....

■ STREETCAR NAMED DESIRE, A

1951, 125 MINS, US ▼ ⊙

Dir Elia Kazan   *Prod* Charles K. Feldman   *Scr* Oscar Saul   *Ph* Harry Stradling   *Ed* David Weisbart   *Mus* Alex North   *Art Dir* Richard Day
● Vivien Leigh, Marlon Brando, Kim Hunter, Karl Malden, Rudy Bond, Nick Dennis (Feldman)

Tennessee Williams' exciting Broadway stage play – winner of the Pulitzer Prize and New York Drama Critics award during the 1947-48 season – has been screenplayed into an even more absorbing drama of frustration and stark tragedy. With Marlon Brando essaying the part he created for the Broadway stage, and Vivien Leigh as the morally disintegrated Blanche DuBois (originated on Broadway by Jessica Tandy). *A Streetcar Named Desire* is thoroughly adult drama, excellently produced and imparting a keen insight into a drama whose scope was, of necessity, limited by its stage setting.

Pic is a faithful adaptation from the original play. It is the story of Blanche DuBois, a faded Mississippi teacher, who seeks refuge with a sister in the old French Quarter of New Orleans. Because her presence intrudes on the husband-wife relationship, the husband, a crude brutal young Polish-American, immediately becomes hostile to the visitor. He also suspects she's lying about her past. It is this hostility that motivates the story's basic elements. Stanley Kowalski (Brando), the husband, embarks on a plan to force his sister-in-law from his home.

Leigh gives a compelling performance in telling the tragedy of Blanche DuBois. Brando at times captures strongly the brutality of the young Pole but occasionally he performs unevenly in a portrayal marked by frequent garbling of his dialog. Kim Hunter and Karl Malden are excellent, as Blanche's sister and frantic suitor.

□ 1951: Best Actress (Vivien Leigh), Supp. Actor (Karl Malden), Supp. Actress (Kim Hunter), B&W Art Direction.

☐ Nominations: Best Picture, Director, Actor (Marlon Brando), Screenplay, B&W Cinematography, B&W Costume Design, Scoring of a Dramatic Picture, Sound

●●●●●●●●●●●●●●●●●●●●●●●●●●●●●●●●

■ **STREETFIGHTER, THE**
See: Hard Times

●●●●●●●●●●●●●●●●●●●●●●●●●●●●●●●●

■ **STREETS**

1990, 83 MINS, US ◇ ⓥ
Dir Katt Shea Rubin *Prod* Andy Rubin *Scr* Katt Shea Rubin, Andy Rubin *Ph* Phedon Papamichael *Ed* Stephen Mark *Mus* Aaron Davis *Art Dir* Virginia Lee
● Christina Applegate, David Mendenhall, Eb Lottimer, Patrick Richwood, Alan Stock (Concorde)

Despite its B-film framework involving a maniacal killer stalking street kids, *Streets* transcends its genre with a gritty and affecting portrait of a teenage throwaway struggling to exist in LA's demimonde. Director Katt Shea Ruben, who scripted with her producer-husband Andy Ruben, clearly had more ambitious things in mind than just another Concorde thriller in which nubile girls are stalked and murdered.

Christina Applegate's solid performance in her first starring feature as the jaded but still sensitive Dawn, who sells sex to survive and shoots up heroin to get through the day, speaks volumes about the scuzzy side of LA life. Working with a minimal budget and a 19-day shooting sked, Ruben conjures up an impressive, subtly fantastic atmosphere.

Yet since this is a Roger Corman production, neorealism isn't enough, and there has to be a psycho killer (vampirish policeman Eb Lottimer), who preys on street kids and becomes obsessed with eliminating Applegate. Although without much insight into the character of the killer, *Streets* has a compelling pattern of visual suspense.

●●●●●●●●●●●●●●●●●●●●●●●●●●●●●●●●

■ **STREET SCENE**

1931, 80 MINS, US ⓥ
Dir King Vidor *Prod* Samuel Goldwyn *Scr* Elmer Rice *Ph* George Barnes *Ed* Hugh Bennett *Mus* Alfred Newman *Art Dir* Richard Day
● Sylvia Sidney, William Collier Jr., Estelle Taylor, Max Montor, David Landau, Russell Hopton (Goldwyn/United Artists)

Street Scene comes upon the screen in faithful reproduction of the stage play. Author Elmer Rice went to Hollywood and had a supervisory hand in the filming and nearly a dozen of the characters are played by the same actors who appeared in the first New York production.

Principal setting is almost a reproduction of the stage locale, even to the scaffolding of the construction job adjoining the tenement house in the West 60s of New York.

Picture opens on a sequence of city life with the introduction of a crashing symphonic musical setting, rather in the Gershwin manner, symbolizing the breadth and scope of the subject.

Sylvia Sidney gives an even, persuasive performance in a role for which she is particularly fitted, typifying the tragedy of budding girlhood cramped by sordid surroundings. Even her lack of formal beauty intensifies the pathos of the character. Young William Collier Jr. makes a splendid opposite to the heroine, playing his quieter scenes with true emphasis and rising to the swifter tempo with satisfying vigor.

In a purely acting sense the honors go to Beula Bondi, as the malicious scandalmonger of the tenement, playing the part she created on the stage, and playing it to the hilt.

●●●●●●●●●●●●●●●●●●●●●●●●●●●●●●●●

■ **STREETS OF FIRE**

1984, 94 MINS, US ◇ ⓥ ⊙
Dir Walter Hill *Prod* Lawrence Gordon, Joel Silver *Scr* Walter Hill, Larry Gross *Ph* Andrew Laszlo *Ed* Freeman Davies, Michael Ripps *Mus* Ry Cooder *Art Dir* John Vallone
● Michael Pare, Diane Lane, Rick Moranis, Amy Madigan, Willem Dafoe, Deborah Van Valkenburgh (Universal/RKO)

Assembled by the team that created *48HRS.* [1982], pic is a pulsing, throbbing orchestration careening around the rescue of a kidnapped young singer. The decor is urban squalor.

Movie has 10 original songs and musically the movie is continually hot, with lyrics charting the concerns of the narrative line, simplistic as it is.

Film also has undeniable texture. Smoke, neon, rainy streets, platforms of elevated subway lines, alleys and warehouses create an urban inferno in an unspecified time and place.

Diane Lane, whose singing voice is dubbed, looks great and is cast expertly. So are Willem Dafoe and Lee Ving.

Briefly seen as a stripper-dancer in the Bombers' hangout is Marine Jahan, who was the uncredited dancer in *Flashdance*.

●●●●●●●●●●●●●●●●●●●●●●●●●●●●●●●●

■ **STREETS OF GOLD**

1986, 95 MINS, US ◇ ⓥ
Dir Joe Roth *Prod* Joe Roth *Scr* Heywood Gould, Richard Price, Tom Cole *Ph* Arthur Albert *Ed* Richard Chew *Mus* Jack Nitzsche *Art Dir* Marcos Flaksman
● Klaus Maria Brandauer, Adrian Pasdar, Wesley Snipes, Angela Molina (Ufland/Roth)

Streets of Gold is a likable, but hardly compelling story of not one, but two kids trying to box their way out of the slums.

Klaus Maria Brandauer is at the center of the ring, playing a Russian Jew and former boxing champion who was banned from competing for the Soviet team because of his religion – so he emigrated to the US and now works as a dishwasher and gets drunk a lot.

A brash Irish tough named Timmy Doyle (Adrian Pasdar) is so impressed that this middle-aged and seemingly out-of-shape lunk can so easily humiliate an athlete half his age, he seeks him out the next day, and asks him to be his coach.

Streets of Gold is paved with credibly gritty scenes, but the end result comes off as a highbrow boxing training film.

●●●●●●●●●●●●●●●●●●●●●●●●●●●●●●●●

■ **STRICTLY BALLROOM**

1992, 92 MINS, AUSTRALIA ◇ ⓥ ⊙
Dir Baz Luhrmann *Prod* Tristram Miall, Ted Albert *Scr* Baz Luhrmann, Craig Pearce *Ph* Steve Mason *Ed* Jill Bilcock *Mus* David Hirshfelder *Art Dir* Catherine Martin
● Paul Mercurio, Tara Morice, Bill Hunter, Barry Otto, Pat Thompson, Gia Carides (M&A)

This bright, breezy and immensely likable musical-comedy is a remarkably confident film debut for co-writer/director Baz Luhrmann. A behind-the-scenes look at a contest for ballroom dancers, pic unfolds a classical tale of a young dance star, Scott, who wants to break the rules and the opposition he faces from the establishment.

Paul Mercurio (son of vet character actor Gus Mercurio) is a real find as Scott, a handsome leading man who, in addition, is obviously a top-flight dancer. Opposite him, Tara Morice shines as a plain Jane who turns from ugly duckling to swan when she's on the dance floor.

Scott, partnered with the lovely but waspish Liz (Gia Carides) blows the semifinals when he breaks federation rules by improvising on the floor. Enter Fran (Morice), a shy Spanish girl with bad skin and glasses. They work on a

flamenco routine they know will be anathema to the federation honchos, but, this being a wish-fulfillment pic, everything turns out fine at fadeout.

●●●●●●●●●●●●●●●●●●●●●●●●●●●●●●●●

■ **STRIKE IT RICH**

1990, 84 MINS, UK/US ◇ ⓥ ⊙
Dir James Scott *Prod* Christine Oestreicher, Graham Easton *Scr* James Scott, Richard Rayner, Julian Mitchell, Dick Vosburgh *Ph* Robert Paynter *Ed* Thomas Schwalm *Mus* Shirley Walker, Cliff Eidelman *Art Dir* Christopher Hobbs
● Robert Lindsay, Molly Ringwald, John Gielgud, Max Wall, Simon de la Brosse, Michel Blanc (Flamingo/Ideal)

Strike It Rich is a poorly directed piece of light (i.e. low calorie) entertainment. Helmer James Scott closely follows the letter of Graham Green's 1955 novella *Loser Takes All*. He adds an opening reel (shot partly in black & white) that fleshes out the romance of accountant Robert Lindsay and half-his-age Molly Ringwald, portraying a British lass raised in America after being evacuated during the Blitz.

Unfortunately, the Greene material is merely a trifle that would have needed the talents and charm of say, Stanley Donen, Kenneth More and Audrey Hepburn in the 1950s to constitute a viable theatrical feature. As executed here, it's hopelessly old-fashioned, remote and even fusty.

There's no chemistry between the stars. Ringwald's frequently flat line readings are a drag. Lindsay's screen career remains stillborn. Gielgud's role is just a brief walkthrough.

●●●●●●●●●●●●●●●●●●●●●●●●●●●●●●●●

■ **STRIKE UP THE BAND**

1940, 119 MINS, US ⊙
Dir Busby Berkeley *Prod* Arthur Freed *Scr* John Monks Jr, Fred Finklehoffe *Ph* Ray June *Ed* Ben Lewis *Mus* Arthur Freed, Roger Edens, George Gershwin
● Mickey Rooney, Judy Garland, Paul Whiteman, June Preisser, William Tracy, Ann Shoemaker (M-G-M)

Strike Up the Band is Metro's successor to *Babes in Arms*, with Mickey Rooney, assisted by major trouping on the part of Judy Garland, dominating every minute of the extended running time. Story details the enthusiastic musical talents of Rooney, who converts the high school band into a swing orchestra, and then aims for a spot on the Paul Whiteman scholastic band broadcast.

The attention-arresting abilities of Rooney are forcibly demonstrated here. Young star is a socko personality, timing every movement for most effective reaction. In addition to a standout performance, he sings, dances and plays both piano and drums in talented style.

Despite the overall dominance of Rooney, Garland catches major attention for her all-around achievements. She's right there with Rooney in much of the story as his mentoring girl friend, teams with him in the production numbers for both songs and dances, and rings the bell with several songs sold to the utmost.

Outstanding production number is a conga played by the school band and danced by a large student ensemble, with Rooney and Garland spotlighted prominently throughout. In contrast, a novel and ingenious little production number – with only Rooney and Garland participating – is one of the most original sequences ever devised for pictures. In bragging to Judy how he will arrange and lead the band for the contest, Rooney sets out the contents of a fruit dish on the table and starts his imaginary direction. The various pieces of fruit dissolve into small puppet musicians, playing their respective instruments in proper tempo.

Direction by Busby Berkeley deftly carries through the story side, despite script deficiencies, but he is in his element in the staging of the production and musical sequences.

☐ 1940: Best Sound Recording (Douglas Shearer)
☐ Nominations: Best Score, Song ('Our Love Affair')

. . . .

■ **STRIPES**

1981, 103 MINS, US ◇ ⓥ ⊙

Dir Ivan Reitman   *Prod* Ivan Reitman, Dan Goldberg
Scr Len Blum, Dan Goldberg, Harold Ramis   *Ph* Bill
Butler   *Ed* Eva Ruggiero, Michael Luciano, Harry Keller
Mus Elmer Bernstein   *Art Dir* James H. Spencer
● Bill Murray, Harold Ramis, Warren Oates, Sean
Young, John Candy, Judge Reinhold (Columbia)

Stripes is a cheerful, mildly outrageous and
mostly amiable comedy pitting a new generation of enlistees against the oversold lure of a
military hungry for bodies and not too choosy
about what it gets. There's little in the way of
art or comic subtlety here, but the film really
seems to work.

Bill Murray, who worked under Ivan
Reitman in *Meatballs*, is an aimless layabout
whose Sad Sack life prompts him to consider
the army as a last-ditch passport to the career, rromances, travels and other delights
painted in those glossy federal commercials.

Predictably, after he cons buddy Harold
Ramis into enlisting, the sexy ads quickly
prove to be Madison Avenue fiction, with basic training – under the grizzled glare of drill
sergeant Warren Oates – taking the place of
fraternity hell week as Murray heads deeper
into trouble, cued by his amiably arrogant
smart-assedness.

Apart from Murray's focal presence, Ramis
and obese John Candy are wildly funny, with
Oates treading a good balance between grizzly humor and military convictions (which the
film, surprisingly, winds up more honoring
than knocking).

. . . .

■ **STRIPPER, THE**

(UK: Woman of Summer)

1963, 95 MINS, US ⓥ

Dir Franklin J. Schaffner   *Prod* Jerry Wald   *Scr* Meade
Roberts   *Ph* Ellsworth Fredericks   *Ed* Robert Simpson
Mus Jerry Goldsmith   *Art Dir* Jack Martin Smith, Walter
M. Simonds
● Joanne Woodward, Richard Beymer, Claire Trevor,
Carol Lynley, Robert Webber, Gypsy Rose Lee (20th
Century-Fox)

This final film by Jerry Wald is an unsuccessful attempt to convert William Inge's 1959
Broadway flop, *A Loss of Roses*, into a substantial and appealing motion picture. Like the
play, the film has its merits, but they are only
flashes of magic in a lacklustre package.
Joanne Woodward's performance in a role expanded to focal prominence in the film is one
of them.

The story is set in traditional Inge country –
a small town in Kansas – more specifically the
modest residence of two characters into those
humdrum lives comes Woodward, stranded by
the abrupt deterioration of the little magician's unit of which she is a part.

She is taken in by an old friend (Claire
Trevor) now a widow who lives with her son
(Richard Beymer), an ardent but inexperienced lad. There are attempts to make something of the mother-son relationship, but the
two characters are never properly clarified,
and remain two-dimensional. At any rate,
Beymer fancies himself in love with the visitor and has a one-night affair with the fading,
desperately accommodating and romantically
vulnerable would-be actress.

Histrionic honors go hands down to the animated Woodward, who rivets attention and
compassion to herself throughout with a
farceful and vivacious portrayal of the good-
hearted but gullible girl. Beymer is adequate,
little more, in the rather baffling role of the
lad.

Lovely Carol Lynley is wasted in a thankless
role which requires mostly a photogenic rear
anatomy for walking away shots. Woodward's
rear gets a big photographic play, too.

Franklin Schaffner's direction tends to be a
bit choppy, uneven and, in spots, heavy-
handed or unobservant. Jerry Goldsmith's
score has sparkle and character, and is obtrusive in a constructive manner – when a musical lift is needed to enliven the going.
☐ 1963: Nomination: Best B&W Costume
Design

. . . .

■ **STRIPTEASE LADY**
See: Lady of Burlesque

. . . .

■ **STROMBOLI**

1950, 81 MINS, ITALY/US ⓥ

Dir Robert Rossellini   *Prod* Ingrid Bergman, Roberto
Rossellini   *Scr* Roberto Rossellini, Art Cohn, Renzo
Cesana, Sergio Amidei, Gianpaolo Callegari   *Ph* Otello
Martelli   *Ed* Roland Gross, Jolanda Benvenuti
Mus Renzo Rossellini
● Ingrid Bergman, Mario Vitale, Renzo Cesana, Mario
Sponzo (Be-Ro/RKO)

Director Roberto Rossellini purportedly denied responsibility for the film, claiming the
American version was cut by RKO beyond
recognition. Cut or not cut, the film reflects
no credit on him. Given elementary-school dialog to recite and impossible scenes to act,
Ingrid Bergman's never able to make the
lines real nor the emotion sufficiently motivated to seem more than an exercise.

So many morally-questionable scenes apparently had to be removed that RKO found
it necessary to insert a great deal of detail in
other actions to stretch the film to its 81-
minute length [from its original 107 min-
utes].

The only visible touch of the famed Italian
director is in the hard photography, which
adds to the realistic, documentary effect of
life on the rocky, lava-blanketed island.
Rossellini's penchant for realism, however,
does not extend to Bergman. She's always
fresh, clean and well-groomed.

The story is of a girl (Bergman) in an
Italian displaced persons camp who marries a
native fisherman (Mario Vitale) of Stromboli
so that she may be released. Miss Bergman
hates it from the start, but she does grow to
love her man.

Language of the pic is a bit confusing.
Bergman, on an Italian isle, speaks English
with a Swedish accent. Vitale's voice has been
dubbed and there's little strain in deciphering his English. Renzo Cesana as the priest
does the best thespic job in the pic.

. . . .

■ **STRONGEST MAN IN THE WORLD, THE**

1975, 92 MINS, US ◇

Dir Vincent McEveety   *Prod* Bill Anderson   *Scr* Joseph L.
McEveety, Herman Groves   *Ph* Andrew Jackson
Ed Cotton Warburton   *Mus* Robert F. Brunner
Art Dir John B. Mansbridge, Jack Senter
● Kurt Russell, Joe Flynn, Eve Arden, Cesar Romero, Phil
Silvers, Dick Van Patten (Walt Disney)

The students of Medfield College unintentionally zap the laws of nature with unexpected and sometimes hilarious results.
Through a lab accident, they concoct a scientific formula which gives people superhuman
strength, a spoof on vitality and energy claims
of cereal companies.

The script rivets on situation of the school's
reputation and financial stability tied in with
sale of the formula to a cereal outfit and participating in an intercollegiate weight-lifting
contest. The other team is sponsored by a rival cereal concern, acknowledged the No. 1
because of its previous success in out-publiciz-
ing the merits of its product.

Joe Flynn, who died just after pic was finished, is the sputtering college dean, faced
with the threat by the college board that he's
through unless he can create a financial turnaround and Kurt Russell is the student responsible for the formula and Cesar Romero
cops a hand as the slick heavy.

. . . .

■ **STUD, THE**

1978, 90 MINS, UK ◇ ⓥ

Dir Quentin Masters   *Prod* Ronald S. Kass   *Scr* Jackie
Collins, Dave Humphries, Christopher Stagg   *Ph* Peter
Hannan   *Ed* David Campling   *Mus* Biddu, John
Cameron (arr.)   *Art Dir* Michael Bastow
● Joan Collins, Oliver Tobias, Emma Jacobs, Sue Lloyd,
Walter Gotell, Mark Burns (Brent Walker)

The Stud goes a long way toward transcending
the softcore sexpo genre, but ultimately
doesn't quite make it. It's a shame because the
producers have obviously tried hard to avoid
low-budget seediness of routine skinflicks.

Based on the novel by Jackie Collins (sister
of Joan, who toplines) the $1 million produc-
tion has Oliver Tobias in title role as a virile
manager of a London nitery.

Joan Collins is the lady who pulls the
strings to manipulate him as her own sexual
marionette. Her husband (Walter Gotell)
owns the nightclub and if the stud wants to
keep his perquisites he must toe the line and
keep the lady happy. And quite a few others,
too.

Tobias is short on sensitivity and would-be
Lotharios seeking useful tips might be ex-
cused for wondering what, apart from rakish
good looks, is the secret of his success in persuading so many eligibles into the sack. He,
in fact, seems faintly embarrassed about the
whole thing. Collins sails through her part
giving just what was demanded but adding no
dimension.

. . . .

■ **STUDENT PRINCE, THE**

1927, 105 MINS, US ⊗ ⓥ

Dir Ernst Lubitsch   *Scr* Hans Kraly, Marian Ainslee, Ruth
Cummings   *Ph* John Mescall   *Ed* Andrew Marton
Art Dir Cedric Gibbons, Richard Day
● Ramon Novarro, Norma Shearer, Jean Hersholt,
Gustav von Seyffertitz, Philippe De Lacy (M-G-M)

Ernst Lubitsch took his tongue out of his
cheek when he directed this special [based on
the 1924 operetta by Dorothy Donnelly and
Sigmund Romberg from the novel by
Wilhelm Meyer-Forster]. He had to, and in
doing so he also took any kick right out of the
picture, if any were there in the script for
him. It's not farce and it's not drama. Just a
pretty love story of peaches and cream.

The Student Prince concerns an heir to a
throne who is forced to give up his love for a
tavern maid because of duty to his country.
And on the point of the Prince marrying the
Princess his dead uncle had selected, the film
ends.

The claim is that it took a year to make this
feature, yet this doesn't show. Productionally
there are some rich interiors counterbalanced
by a sprinkling of back drops on exteriors.

But nothing can stand off Ramon Novarro's
facial makeup. This is ghastly under certain
lighting conditions and at no time allows him
to completely spin the illusion of the character he is playing. Shearer's personal efforts
are a highlight and Jean Hersholt stands a
good chance of outlasting both in the
memory.

. . . .

■ **STUDENT PRINCE, THE**

1954, 107 MINS, US ◇

Dir Richard Thorpe   *Prod* Joe Pasternak   *Scr* William
Ludwig, Sonya Levien   *Ph* Paul C. Vogel   *Ed* Gene
Ruggiero   *Mus* Georgie Stoll (dir.)   *Art Dir* Cedric
Gibbons, Randall Duell

S

● Ann Blyth, Edmund Purdom, John Ericson, Louis Calhern, Edmund Gwenn, Betta St John (M-G-M)

The venerable operetta about a royal cutup in the beer gardens of Heidelberg has been given a brand new look in this classy Joe Pasternak production via CinemaScope and Ansco Color. This latest pic version is a fresh, beguiling musical, beautiful to hear and behold.

The voice personality of Mario Lanza doesn't jibe with the British starch of Edmund Purdom's physical appearance, but not many will mind because the latter's acting is good. Doing her own singing in a gracious, charming manner is Ann Blyth, who might not be everyone's idea of a barmaid who could charm a prince, but she's pert and pretty.

Richard Thorpe's direction keeps things moving at a likeable pace, whether the people are engaging in song, amour or duel.

To the Sigmund Romberg tunes for which Dorothy Donnelly did the original lyrics and Paul Francis Webster the revised ones used here, have been added three new songs by Webster and Nicholas Bredszky. They are 'Beloved,' 'I'll Walk With God,' that is given a standout staging, and 'Summertime in Heidelberg.'

Louis Calhern plays, with a flourish, the king who sends his grandson (Purdom) to Heidelberg to learn how to be a man. There the young prince falls in love with Blyth and is about to run away with her when the king's illness intervenes.

■ STUDS LONIGAN

1960, 103 MINS, US ⓥ
Dir Irving Lerner   *Prod* Philip Yordan   *Scr* Philip Yordan   *Ph* Arthur H. Feindel, Haskell P. Wexler   *Ed* Verna Fields   *Mus* Jerry Goldsmith   *Art Dir* Jack Poplin
● Christopher Knight, Frank Gorshin, Helen Westcott, Dick Foran, Venetia Stevenson, Jack Nicholson (United Artists)

Compressing James T. Farrell's respected trilogy into a 103-minute film doesn't come off. *Studs Lonigan* is an earnest attempt gone wrong, principally through incoherent execution complicated by undisciplined histrionics.

Philip Yordan's scenario is quite faithful to Farrell's book, which centers its attention on the essentially decent hero who struggles against slum life of Chicago's South Side district in the 1920s. Christopher Knight, as the hero, has a disquieting tendency toward facial contortion and responsive exaggeration. The role is an extremely demanding one for any actor, let alone a newcomer to the screen.

The three standouts in the large cast are Frank Gorshin, Helen Westcott and Dick Foran. Gorshin has an instinctive ability to generate a natural reaction. Westcott creates a figure of pathos and dimension, despite the fact that Yordan's screenplay leaves the character she is playing undeveloped and unexplored. Foran comes through admirably in the role of Stud's decent father.

Lensman Arthur H. Feindel and special photographic consultant Haskell P. Wexler have chosen an unusual assortment of sharp, tilted angles at which to place the camera. In combination with some unusual shading effects, this emphasis on startling composition is clever, but frequently distracting.

■ STUFF, THE

1985, 93 MINS, US ◇ ⓥ
Dir Larry Cohen   *Prod* Paul Kurta   *Scr* Larry Cohen   *Ph* Paul Glickman   *Ed* Armond Lebowitz   *Art Dir* Marleen Marta, George Stoll
● Michael Moriarty, Andrea Marcovicci, Paul Sorvino, Scott Bloom, Garrett Morris, Danny Aiello (Larco/New World)

The Stuff is sci-fi with no hardware but lots of white goo. It's a certified Larry Cohen film

that seems to fly right out of the 1950s horror genre. It also has an underlying humor about it, plays around with satirizing fast foods, and cloaks a sly little subtext about people who ingest stuff they know is not good for them.

What's not to like? The film enjoys a larky sense of innocence, some hideous gaping mouths full of a curdling, parasitic menace, and a fey performance by Michael Moriarty as an industrial saboteur who, along with Andrea Marcovicci and little Scott Bloom, track down the scourge of the countryside and the heavies.

It also benefits from a hilarious performance played straight by Paul Sorvino as a self-styled paramilitary nut. The 11-year-old Bloom is appealing, while Garrett Morris as a chocolate cookie mogul and Danny Aiello as Vickers lend flavor in support.

■ STUNT MAN, THE

1980, 129 MINS, US ◇ ⓥ ⊙
Dir Richard Rush   *Prod* Richard Rush   *Scr* Lawrence B. Marcus   *Ph* Mario Tosi   *Ed* Jack Hofstra, Caroline Ferriol   *Mus* Dominic Frontiere   *Art Dir* James Schoppe
● Peter O'Toole, Steve Railsback, Barbara Hershey, Alan Garfield, Alex Rocco, Sharon Farrell (Simon)

Offbeat tale, based on Paul Brodeur's 1970 novel, has Vietnam vet Steve Railsback on the lam and accepting refuge from both benevolent and sinister film director Peter O'Toole, who puts the fugitive through some highly dangerous paces as a stunt man while shielding him from the cops.

Lawrence B. Marcus and adaptor-director Richard Rush are least successful in making fully credible the relationship between Railsback and film-within-the-film star Barbara Hershey, with his disillusionment upon discovering that she once had a fling with O'Toole playing as particularly unconvincing.

O'Toole is excellent in his best, cleanest performance in years. He smashingly delineates an omnipotent, godlike type whose total control over those around him makes him seem almost unreal.

☐ 1980: Nominations: Best Director, Actor (Peter O'Toole), Adapted Screenplay

■ STUNTS

1977, 90 MINS, US ◇ ⓥ
Dir Mark L. Lester   *Prod* Raymond Lofaro, William Panzer   *Scr* Dennis Johnson, Barney Cohen   *Ph* Bruce Logan   *Ed* Corky Ehlers   *Mus* Michael Kamen
● Robert Forster, Fiona Lewis, Joanna Cassidy, Darrell Fetty, Bruce Glover, Jim Luisi (New Line/Fleischman)

Robert Forster is excellent as an ace stuntman who thwarts a maniac stalking a film crew making a police actioner on an oceanside location in San Luis Obispo, Calif.

This is a tight-lipped actioner about a male group involved in a dangerous trade, with sexy female camp followers admitted to the group once they accept the code of grace under pressure.

There is much emphasis on expertise, emotional control, and the details of the craft, which are shown in docu-like style. The action scenes alternate with more relaxed character interplay in a motel and a bar, where the concept of expertise is translated into personal relationships.

Fiona Lewis is the prime romantic interest, a groupie journalist who initially causes friction in the group.

■ ST. VALENTINE'S DAY MASSACRE, THE

1967, 100 MINS, US ◇ ⓥ
Dir Roger Corman   *Prod* Roger Corman   *Scr* Howard Browne   *Ph* Milton Krasner   *Ed* William B. Murphy   *Mus* Fred Steiner   *Art Dir* Jack Martin Smith, Philip Jeffries

● Jason Robards, George Segal, Ralph Meeker, Jean Hale, Clint Ritchie, Frank Silvera (20th Century-Fox)

The film is a slam-bang, gutsy recreation of *The St. Valentine's Day Massacre*, a 1929 gangland sensation of Chicago. Well-written, and presented in semi-documentary style, it features Jason Robards as Al Capone. Salty dialog and violence are motivated properly, and solid production values recreate a by-gone era.

Robards is excellent as Capone, and Ralph Meeker, as Moran, is equally chilling. A large cast spotlights George Segal, who with brother David Canary act as Meeker's ace gunmen.

Clint Ritchie, playing in very good fashion the ever-smiling, dapper Jack McGurn, one of Capone's key aides, is placed by his boss in charge of eliminating Moran and his mob. Latter – through a stroke of fate – escaped the bloodbath, and Capone was never proven the man behind it all.

■ SUBJECT WAS ROSES, THE

1968, 107 MINS, US ◇
Dir Ulu Grosbard   *Prod* Edgar Lansbury   *Scr* Frank D. Gilroy   *Ph* Jack Priestley   *Ed* Jerry Greenberg   *Mus* Lee Pockriss   *Art Dir* George Jenkins
● Patricia Neal, Jack Albertson, Martin Sheen, Don Saxon, Elaine Williams (M-G-M)

Frank D. Gilroy's Pulitzer Prize legit drama of 1964 has been translated to the screen in an outstanding way by original producer Edgar Lansbury and stager Ulu Grosbard, all three making an impressive debut in films. Joining original stars Jack Albertson and Martin Sheen is Patricia Neal, in a triumphant return to pix after near-fatal illness.

An intimate, poignant and telling drama of a young World War II vet, returning to an unhappy home, film is superior in all departments. Neal and Albertson are outstanding as a married Bronx-Irish couple who, while not happy and loving, are not unloving either. Albertson, whose rising business star fell in the Depression, and Neal, whose over-dependence on her unseen mother is a sore point with Albertson, have struggled along for years.

Return from war of only son Sheen brings the festering crisis to a head, partly by a title-inspiring gift of flowers which releases pent up emotions.

The terrific writing, which top-notch performances make more magnificent, displays a wide range of human emotions, without recourse to cheap sensationalism or dialog. Grosbard's perceptive direction keeps the bickering and banter from becoming shrill histrionics.

■ SUBURBAN COMMANDO

1991, 90 MINS, US ◇ ⓥ ⊙
Dir Burt Kennedy, Gary Davis   *Prod* Howard Gottfried   *Scr* Frank Cappello   *Ph* Bernd Heinl, Ken Lambkin, Richard Clabaugh, Charlie Lieberman   *Ed* Terry Stokes   *Mus* David Michael Frank   *Art Dir* Ivo Cristante, C.J. Strawn
● Hulk Hogan, Christopher Lloyd, Shelley Duvall, Larry Miller, William Ball, Jack Elam (New Line)

Some funny gags enliven the stupid sci-fi spoof *Suburban Commando*. Lame vehicle for wrestler Hulk Hogan is a bad 'high-concept' effort marrying two elements. Hogan is an intergalactic warrior who travels to earth for some r&r, instantly becoming a fish out of water boarding at suburbanites Christopher Lloyd and Shelley Duvall's house. Lloyd is a Casper Milquetoast architect who briefly becomes the title character by donning Hogan's muscle-enhancing power suit.

Special effects are okay in copying and spoofing the *Star Wars* films, with good stunts as Hogan battles two intergalactic bounty hunters sent to kill him. His final battle with his evil nemesis (William Ball) is an underwhelming anticlimax. Casting of top talent Lloyd and Duvall was a good idea, but both are underutilized.

• •

■ SUCCESS

See: The American Success Company

• •

■ SUDDEN IMPACT

1983, 117 MINS, US ◇ ⓥ ⊙
Dir Clint Eastwood   Prod Clint Eastwood   Scr Joseph C. Stinson   Ph Bruce Surtees   Ed Joel Cox   Mus Lalo Schifrin   Art Dir Edward Carfagno
● Clint Eastwood, Sondra Locke, Pat Hingle, Bradford Dillman, Paul Drake, Audrie J. Neenan (Warner)

The fourth entry in the lucrative Dirty Harry series, Sudden Impact is a brutally hard-hitting policier which casts Clint Eastwood as audiences like to see him, as the toughest guy in town.

Sudden Impact sends Harry out of his normal jurisdiction in San Francisco to research a case with connections to coastal San Paulo. While there, he bumps into Sondra Locke, who is extracting her own brand of vengeance on a group of individuals who, some years back, savagely raped both her and her younger sister.

Local police chief Pat Hingle tries to bar Harry from behaving as usual in his community, but that doesn't prevent a slew of shootings.

This is the first entry in the series to have been directed by Eastwood himself, and action is put over with great force, if also with some obviousness. Locke looks astonishingly like Tippi Hedren did in Hitchcock's Marnie and, with the exception of a sympathetic black cop played by Albert Popwell, nearly everyone else in the cast represents a menace to Harry in one way or another.

• •

■ SUDDENLY, LAST SUMMER

1959, 112 MINS, US ⓥ ⊙
Dir Joseph L. Mankiewicz   Prod Sam Spiegel   Scr Gore Vidal, Tennessee Williams   Ph Jack Hildyard   Ed W. Hornbeck, Thomas G. Stanford   Mus Buxton Orr, Malcolm Arnold
● Elizabeth Taylor, Katharine Hepburn, Montgomery Clift, Albert Dekker, Mercedes McCambridge, Gary Raymond (Columbia)

Perversion and greed, Tennessee Williams' recurrent themes, are worked over again in Suddenly Last Summer. The play was concerned with homosexuality and cannibalism. The cannibalism has been dropped, or muted, in the film version. It has some very effective moments, but on the whole it fails to move.

Perhaps the reason is that what was a long one-act play has been expanded in the screenplay to a longish motion picture. Nothing that's been added is an improvement on the original; they stretch the seams of the original fabric without strengthening the seamy aspects of the story.

The story is that of a doting mother (Katharine Hepburn) and her son. The son was a homosexual and his mother his procuress. When she had passed the age when she could function effectively in this capacity, he enlisted the services of his beautiful cousin, Elizabeth Taylor.

The question is whether Taylor is fancifully insane or ruthlessly sane. Hepburn wants a lobotomy performed on Taylor, to excise the memory of the son's death, by detaching a portion of the brain. It is the job of Montgomery Clift, as the neuro-surgeon who would perform the operation, to decide if Taylor is deranged as Hepburn insists.

Hepburn is dominant, making her brisk authority a genteel hammer relentlessly crush-

ing the younger woman. Taylor is most effective in her later scenes, although these have been robbed of their original theatricality. Clift is little more than straight man to the two ladies.

Although Joseph L. Mankiewiez' direction is inventive in giving the essentially static narrative some movement and rhythm, it must be faulted for blunting Taylor's final scene so it fails to match Hepburn's opening monolog. (The play was actually only two monologs of almost equal power and length.)
☐ 1959: Nominations: Best Actress (Katharine Hepburn, Elizabeth Taylor), B&W Art Direction

• •

■ SUDDEN TERROR

See: Eyewitness

• •

■ SUFFERING BASTARDS

1990, 89 MINS, US ◇ ⓥ
Dir Bernard McWilliams   Prod Tom Mangan, Neil Hodges, George F. Andrews   Scr Bernard McWilliams, John C. McGinley   Ph Neil Hodges   Ed Steve Wang   Mus Dan Di Paola
● John C. McGinley, David Warshofsky, Pam LaTesta, Rene Rivera, Eric Bogosian (Cinelux)

Bernard McWilliams' demented comedy Suffering Bastards, shot on a shoestring, soars with sheer zaniness and outrageous invention.

Womanizing Buddy Johnson (John C. McGinley) and his brother Al (David Warshofsky) sing and swing in their mother's tawdry Atlantic City nightclub. The irrepressible brothers, who bear as much resemblance to each other as Laurel did to Hardy, find the club taken over by a smooth-talking swindler.

Out of a job, but vowing to Mommy (a delectable Pam LaTesta) they'll buy the club back someday, they find employment in a sinister warehouse. Buddy's irresponsible flirting with the secretary makes a permanent enemy out of her violent boyfriend, Bernard (fine Rene Rivera), a Hispanic hitman who becomes their undefeatable, hilarious nemesis.

Scripters take galiardic humor one notch up the sophistication ladder, mixing sight gags with a deadpan offscreen narrator. McGinley and Warshofsky carry off their roles with unrepentant relish.

• •

■ SUGARLAND EXPRESS, THE

1974, 109 MINS, US ◇ ⓥ
Dir Steven Spielberg   Prod Richard D. Zanuck, David Brown   Scr Hal Barwood, Matthew Robbins   Ph Vilmos Zsigmond   Ed Edward M. Abroms, Verna Fields   Mus John Williams   Art Dir Joseph Alves Jr
● Goldie Hawn, Ben Johnson, Michael Sacks, William Atherton, Gregory Walcott, Harrison Zanuck (Universal)

The Sugarland Express begins and plays for much of its length as a hilarious madcap caper chase comedy.

Goldie Hawn stars as a young mother who helps husband William Atherton escape from prison so they may rescue their baby from involuntary adoption. Unfortunately, the film degenerates in final reels to heavy-handed social polemic and sound-and-fury shootout.

Based on an actual event in Texas in 1969, the screenplay is by Hal Barwood and Matthew Robbins, from a story by them and feature-debuting director Steven Spielberg. Besides some excellent major characterizations – Michael Sacks as a patrol car officer whom they kidnap, and Ben Johnson, outstanding as a police captain – the comedic impact is enhanced by terrific visual staging.

• •

■ SUICIDE SQUAD

See: Dangerous Moonlight

• •

■ SUITABLE CASE FOR TREATMENT, A

(US: Morgan!; aka: Morgan (A Suitable Case for Treatment))

1966, 97 MINS, UK ⓥ ⊙
Dir Karel Reisz   Prod Leon Clore   Scr David Mercer   Ph Gerry Turpin, Larry Pizer   Ed Tom Priestley   Mus Johnny Dankworth   Art Dir Philip Harrison
● Vanessa Redgrave, David Warner, Robert Stephens, Irene Handl, Bernard Bresslaw, Arthur Mullard (British Lion/Quintra)

Morgan follows the frequently funny, sometimes pathetic but relentlessly lunatic exploits of an eccentric artist to his eventual, though not inevitable, incarceration in an insane asylum. Although it is established that the title character, played with zest and skill by David Warner, was always engagingly dotty, his latest bizarre binge is triggered by his opposition to ex-wife's (Vanessa Redgrave) impending marriage to a sympathetic and likeable suitor.

Spare, straight-line plot follows Morgan's misguided but amusingly slapstick attempts to win back his mate, Leonie, who, though displaying a tolerance and protectiveness bordering on the saintly, longs for a less frenetic and wearying life with a 'normal' husband. To director Karel Reisz's credit, the suitor, well played by Robert Stephens, is never cast as a villain.

Schizophrenia seems to have infected Reisz's direction. Instead of providing the subtle, gradually disintegrating character of Morgan, Reisz dwells on the comedic aspects of each prank, cunningly milked for maximum yaks, in the process ceding any hope of the observer taking Morgan seriously.
☐ 1966: Nominations: Best Actress (Vanessa Redgrave), B&W Costume Design

• •

■ SULLIVAN'S TRAVELS

1941, 90 MINS, US ⓥ ⊙
Dir Preston Sturges   Prod Paul Jones   Scr Preston Sturges   Ph John Seitz   Ed Stuart Gilmore   Mus Leo Shuken, Charles Bradshaw   Art Dir Hans Dreier, Earl Hedrick
● Joel McCrea, Veronica Lake, William Demarest, Franklin Pangborn, Porter Hall, Eric Blore (Paramount)

Sullivan's Travels is a curious but effective mixture of grim tragedy, slapstick of the Keystone brand and smart, trigger-fast comedy.

It is written and directed by Preston Sturges, who springs a flock of surprises as he flits from slapstick to stark drama, from high comedy to a sequence of the Devil's Island prison type of stuff, into romantic spells, some philosophy and, in effect, all over the place without warning.

He ties it all together neatly, however, and keeps his audience on the go and on edge. Sturges' dialog is trenchant, has drive, possesses crispness and gets the laughs where that is desired.

Hollywood director Joel McCrea, anxious to produce Oh, Brother, Where Art Thou?, an epic of hard times and troubles, disguises himself as a hobo and goes out to look for troubles, finding plenty for himself. He picks up Veronica Lake on the way and they travel the rails together, she in boy's clothes.

A fine cast has been assembled around McCrea and Lake. Latter supplies the sex appeal and does a good acting job. McCrea, in the lap of luxury as a Hollywood director one minute, and a bum the next, turns in a swell performance.

• •

■ SUMMER AND SMOKE

1961, 120 MINS, US ◇ ⓥ ⊙
Dir Peter Glenville   Prod Hal Wallis   Scr James Poe, Meade Roberts   Ph Charles Lang Jr   Mus Elmer Bernstein   Art Dir Hal Pereira, Walter Tyler
● Laurence Harvey, Geraldine Page, John McIntire, Una Merkel, Rita Moreno, Thomas Gomez (Paramount)

Peter Glenville, who guided Tennessee Williams' play in Britain, gives this pic version a solid delineation, effectively guiding his cast, and giving several scenes heightened impact by cutting them off short, allowing effect to follow into next sequence. Throughout most of the first half, he has also successfully disengaged film from its stage format.

Performances are almost uniformly excellent, though Geraldine Page walks off with top honors in a repeat of her 1952 stage role as Alma Winemiller, the repressed spinster. Laurence Harvey, perhaps a bit young to play her opposite number, John, perhaps a bit too continental as a bayou boy, is nevertheless very good, and gives a solid and believeable rendering of the ne'er-do-well who reforms.

Una Merkel (again a repeat of her stage role) cuts herself a memorable cameo in a relatively small part, while Rita Moreno as the dance hall girl, Thomas Gomez as her father, John McIntire as the boy's pa, all give their supporting roles an effective reading. Earl Holliman is standout in a brief one-sequence appearance as the traveling salesman in the finale. An extra nod must go also to Pamela Tiffin, who as Nellie adds a pro flair to dazzling youthful beauty. It's her first screen role.

☐ 1961: Nominations: Best Actress (Geraldine Page), Supp. Actress (Una Merkel), Color Art Direction, Scoring of a Dramatic Picture

....

■ SUMMERFIELD

1977, 95 MINS, AUSTRALIA ◇

Dir Ken Hannam   *Prod* Pat Lovell   *Scr* Cliff Green
Ph Mike Molloy   *Ed* Sarah Bennet   *Mus* Bruce Smeaton
Art Dir Grace Walker
● Nick Tate, John Walters, Elizabeth Alexander, Michelle Jarman, Charles Tingwell, Geraldine Turner (Clare Beach)

A good-looking mystery, *Summerfield* is not unlike an Australian version of Hitchcock's *The Birds* in the opening sequences. It starts slowly, introducing the characters while at the same time establishing an undefined menace in the locale – a remote island community off the coast of Victoria.

Nick Tate is the replacement schoolteacher – his successor has disappeared in strange circumstances – and he unravels the intricacies of the local society. The atmosphere is heavy with xenophobic responses by the denizens of the area, and there is a generally overpowering feeling of mendacity and tightly-inbred coverup.

Gradually he picks up clues to what everybody is not talking about. And, of course, once he starts, his curiosity gets the better of him and impetus takes over.

....

■ SUMMER HOLIDAY

1948, 92 MINS, US ◇ ⑫

Dir Rouben Mamoulian   *Prod* Arthur Freed   *Scr* Frances Goodrich, Albert Hackett, Irving Brecher, Jean Holloway   *Ph* Charles Schoenbaum   *Ed* Albert Akst   *Mus* Harry Warren, Ralph Blane   *Art Dir* Cedric Gibbons, Jack Martin Smith
● Mickey Rooney, Gloria de Haven, Walter Huston, Frank Morgan, Agnes Moorehead, Marilyn Maxwell (M-G-M)

The Eugene O'Neill play, *Ah. Wilderness* with its account of a turn-of-the-century smalltown New England family, provides admirable setting, story, color and mood for the musical numbers and script. The musical numbers, tastefully chosen and skillfully staged, are not spotted arbitrarily, but stem naturally from the situations.

For example, the film is introduced by a song called 'It's Our Home Town'. Walter Huston sings the first chorus, as the newspaper publisher, with the other characters taking it up to identify themselves and plant the general story line.

The story emphasizes the puppy-love romance between the publisher's son and girl across the street. Respectively Mickey Rooney and Gloria de Haven. Except for some laughable mugging by the former, they make an appealing pair, and their musical numbers are nicely done.

Huston is fine as the understanding Nat Miller, the boy's father. Frank Morgan achieves a nice blend of comedy and pathos as Uncle Sid. Mamoulian's direction has style, is well paced and without sacrificing story credibility makes the songs stand out.

....

■ SUMMER HOLIDAY

1963, 109 MINS, UK ◇ ⑫

Dir Peter Yates   *Prod* Kenneth Harper   *Scr* Peter Myers, Ronald Cass   *Ph* John Wilcox   *Ed* Jack Slade
Mus Stanley Black
● Cliff Richard, Lauri Peters, Melvyn Hayes, Una Stubbs, The Shadows (Elstree)

Peter Myers and Ronald Cass have provided a screenplay which is short on wit but anyway is simply a valid excuse for a lighthearted jaunt through sunny Europe. Cliff Richard and three mechanic buddies set out for a European holiday in a borrowed double-decker London bus. They pick up (in quite the nicest way) three stranded girls, a cabaret act en route to Athens. The boys decide to make Athens their objective.

They also encounter a troupe of wandering entertainers and a stowaway in the shape of a young boy. 'He' turns out to be an American girl tele singer, fleeing from the professional demands of her dragon of a mother and her agent.

From this thin thread of yarn, songs, situations and dance routines arise fairly naturally. Even when dragged in, they add a lot to the excitement. Richard has a warm presence and sings and dances more than adequately.

Lauri Peters is pleasant as the young Yank heroine and romantic interest, and Melvyn Hayes has a sharp comic talent.

Highlighted throughout are production sequences which are put over shrewdly by director Peter Yates and into which choreographer Herbert Ross pumps an exuberant American expertise.

Myers and Cass have written seven numbers and others including Richard have contributed another nine. Filmed largely in France and Greece, the editing and backgrounds give an impression of a continuous trip across Europe.

....

■ SUMMER MADNESS
(US: Summertime)

1955, 100 MINS, UK/US ◇ ⑫ ⊙

Dir David Lean   *Prod* Ilya Lopert   *Scr* H.E. Bates, David Lean   *Ph* Jack Hildyard   *Ed* Peter Taylor
Mus Alessandro Cicognini   *Art Dir* Vincent Korda
● Katharine Hepburn, Rossano Brazzi, Isa Miranda, Darren McGavin, Mari Aldon, Jeremy Spenser (Lopert/London)

Summer Madness, made in Venice during the summer of 1954, is a loose adaptation of Arthur Laurents' stage play, *The Time of the Cuckoo*. With Katharine Hepburn in the role originated by Shirley Booth and with the scenic beauties of the canal city, the film stacks up as promising entertainment – with some reservations. There is a lack of cohesion and some abruptness in plot transition without a too-clear buildup. Lesser characterizations, too, are on the sketchy side.

Covering these flaws is a rich topsoil of drama as the proud American secretary who hits Venice as a tourist falls for and is disillusioned by the middle-aged Italian charmer.

Rossano Brazzi, as the attractive vis-a-vis, scores a triumph of charm and reserve. Hepburn turns in a feverish acting chore of proud loneliness.

☐ 1955: Nominations: Best Director, Actress (Katharine Hepburn)

....

■ SUMMER OF '42

1971, 102 MINS, US ◇ ⑫ ⊙

Dir Robert Mulligan   *Prod* Richard A. Roth   *Scr* Herman Raucher   *Ph* Robert Surtees   *Ed* Folmar Blangsted
Mus Michel Legrand   *Art Dir* Albert Brenner
● Jennifer O'Neill, Gary Grimes, Jerry Houser, Oliver Conant, Katherine Allentuck, Christopher Norris (Warner)

The emotional and sexual awakening of teenagers is a dramatic staple. Robert Mulligan's *Summer of '42* has a large amount of charm and tenderness; it also has little dramatic economy and much eye-exhausting photography which translates to forced and artificial emphasis on a strungout story.

Script tells of that long-ago summer, way out on Long Island, when Gary Grimes had his first sexual-romantic experience with war-widowed Jennifer O'Neill. His two pals (Jerry Houser and Oliver Conant), begin and end the film not yet matured. For Houser, the easy charms of Christopher Norris still suffice, but the younger Conant literally disappears from the plot when the prospects of action instead of talk presents itself.

The three boys come across well, particularly Grimes. Houser's character is more coarse, even obnoxious at times, and he plays it well to help set off Grimes' more introspective nature. O'Neill is wooden and stilted, though her lines are few so the handicap does not unduly mar the film.

☐ 1971: Best Original Score
☐ Nominations: Best Story & Screenplay, Cinematography, Editing

....

■ SUMMER PLACE, A

1959, 130 MINS, US ◇ ⑫ ⊙

Dir Delmer Daves   *Prod* Delmer Daves   *Scr* Delmer Daves   *Ph* Harry Stradling   *Ed* Owen Marks
Mus Max Steiner
● Richard Egan, Dorothy McGuire, Sandra Dee, Arthur Kennedy, Troy Donahue, Constance Ford (Warner)

A Summer Place is one of those big, emotional, slickly-produced pictures that bite off a great deal more than they can chew and neatly dispose of their intense, highly-dramatic melange by dropping their characters into slots clearly marked 'good' and 'bad'.

In his capacity as writer [from the novel by Sloan Wilson] and director, Delmer Daves has missed the mark by a mile. His characters, anguished most of the time, are unreal and totally devoid of depth. The film runs at least 20 minutes too long and has a tendency to use dialog to preach what should be implied.

Millionaire Richard Egan, his wife (Constance Ford) and daughter (Sandra Dee) arrive on a small island off the New England coast where, 20 years ago, Egan was a lifeguard and had an affair with Dorothy McGuire, who subsequently married Arthur Kennedy, the impoverished owner of a summer mansion. Egan has an affair with McGuire, which is discovered, and divorces result. Meanwhile, Dee and Kennedy's son (Troy Donahue) have fallen in love but are broken up by Dee's mother.

With the single exception of McGuire, who comes through with a radiant performance and is lovely to look at, the cast does an average job.

....

■ SUMMER RENTAL

1985, 88 MINS, US ◇ ⑫ ⊙

Dir Carl Reiner   *Prod* George Shapiro   *Scr* Jeremy Stevens, Mark Reisman   *Ph* Ric Waite   *Ed* Bud Molin
Mus Alan Silvestri   *Art Dir* Peter Wooley

● John Candy, Rip Torn, Richard Crenna, Karen Austin, Kerri Green, John Larroquette (Paramount)

Amusing in spots, *Summer Rental* is more a collection of bits about taking the family to the shore for the summer than a coherent story. John Candy manages to elevate some of those bits to the hilarious and therein lies the film's appeal.

With three kids, dog and a U-Haul, family sets off for r&r at the Florida shore. Things don't go as planned and Candy finds himself sunburned and with an injured leg. Script also is lame and dreams up only the most pedestrian domestic catastrophes, from a a young daughter's (Kerri Green) budding interest in boys to a gay divorcee's interest in Candy's wife (Karen Austin). After an hour meandering around the beach and environs, Candy locks horns with local denizen and resident sailing champ Richard Crenna.

Best bits in the film are supplied by Candy's wardrobe. As a modern-day pirate with a heart of gold, Rip Torn demonstrates once again that he can make any role believable regardless of how silly it is.

■ SUMMER STOCK

(UK: If You Feel Like Singing)

1950, 108 MINS, US ◇ ▣ ⊙

Dir Charles Walters   *Prod* Joe Pasternak   *Scr* George Wells, Sy Gomberg   *Ph* Robert Planck   *Ed* Albert Akst   *Mus* Johnny Green, Saul Chaplin (dirs.)   *Art Dir* Cedric Gibbons, Jack Martin Smith
● Judy Garland, Gene Kelly, Eddie Bracken, Gloria de Haven, Marjorie Main, Phil Silvers (M-G-M)

Summer Stock showcases M-G-M's two top musical stars, Judy Garland and Gene Kelly. It has a light, gay air, including nine tunes [chiefly by Harry Warren and Mack Gordon], some used for dance numbers [staged by Nick Castle]. Story portion is never allowed to intrude much.

The background is a New England farm setting. Garland is the farmerette. Her younger sister (Gloria de Haven) brings a troupe of would-be thespians to the farm and they take over the barn to stage a new musical written by Kelly. Not only is Garland upset at such an invasion, so is the whole village of New Englanders.

Setup [story by Sy Gomberg] provides ample excuse for ringing in most of the musical numbers, although not justifying the finale that sees a production that would do credit to Broadway being staged in a arn by a group of impoverished actors.

■ SUMMER STORM

1944, 103 MINS, US ▣

Dir Douglas Sirk   *Prod* Seymour Nebenzal
Scr Rowland Leigh, Robert Thoeren   *Ph* Archie J. Stout   *Ed* Gregg Tallas   *Mus* Karl Hajos   *Art Dir* Rudi Feld
● George Sanders, Linda Darnell, Anna Lee, Edward Everett Horton, Hugo Haas, Lori Lahner (United Artists)

Summer Storm is a carefully made drama of people and passion adapted from a Chekhov drama [*The Shooting Party*].

Russian background of the Kharkov district displays intimate study in contrasts of various persons – local judge, George Sanders; young and impetuous siren, Linda Darnell, who's determined to have wealth and finery; flustery and decadent Edward Everett Horton, land-owning aristocrat; estate superintendent, Hugo Haas; and Anna Lee, engaged to Sanders. All become engulfed in tragedy when Darnell marries Haas and immediately embarks on an affair with Sanders, while slyly playing Horton for the finery and jewels he can supply.

Darnell is spotlighted with her particularly effective performance. Sanders is excellent, sharing supporting prominence with Horton, Lori Lahner scores as the maid who protects Sanders' secret; Lee, Haas,

and John Philliber are strong in support.

Script, with adaptation credited to Michael O'Hara, is particularly effective despite details of characters and carefully-etched situations which consume plenty of footage and tend to slow up the tempo.

□ 1944: Nomination: Best Scoring of a Dramatic Picture

■ SUMMER STORY, A

1988, 95 MINS, UK/US ◇ ▣

Dir Piers Haggard   *Prod* Danton Rissner   *Scr* Penelope Mortimer   *Ph* Kenneth MacMillan   *Ed* Ralph Sheldon   *Mus* Georges Delerue   *Art Dir* Leo Austin
● Imogen Stubbs, James Wilby, Kenneth Colley, Sophie Ward, Susannah York, Jerome Flynn (ITC)

A Summer Story is a beautifully made pastoral romance, skillfully adapted from a John Galsworthy story, *The Apple Tree*.

Screen version is set in Devon in 1902, portraying the ill-fated romance one summer between weak-willed young barrister Ashton (James Wilby, perfectly cast) and a lovely country lass Megan (newcomer Imogen Stubbs).

Holed up at a country farm on holiday due to a sprained ankle, Ashton procrastinates, delaying his departure due to a crush on Megan. Shortly after they consummate the relationship, he heads for home via the resort at Torquay and procrastinates again, lolling with a beautiful sister (Sophie Ward) of an old school chum he meets there rater than returning quickly to fetch Megan as promised.

Stage actress Stubbs is a real find as the heartbroken heroine, bringing a modern strength to the period role, while Wilby is a sympathetic version of the archetypal weak young aristocrat.

■ SUMMERTIME

See: Summer Madness

■ SUMMER WISHES, WINTER DREAMS

1973, 87 MINS, US ◇ ▣

Dir Gilbert Cates   *Prod* Jack Brodsky   *Scr* Stewart Stern   *Ph* Gerald Hirschfeld   *Ed* Sidney Katz   *Mus* Johnny Mandel   *Art Dir* Peter Dohanos
● Joanne Woodward, Martin Balsam, Sylvia Sidney, Dori Brenner (Columbia/ Rastar)

Summer Wishes, Winter Dreams begins with idle chatter between Joanne Woodward and her mother Sylvia Sidney about lunch and tea. Fifteen minutes later the two are still debating whether to have broiled chicken and fritters. And 80 minutes later – long after mother is gone with a heart attack – Woodward and husband Martin Balsam are reminiscing about the macaroons in Atlantic City.

After one of her routine days is interrupted by the sudden death of mother, Woodward takes off for Europe with Balsam. Now the focus shifts from her woes to his as he searches for the only place his life had drama: 28 years earlier at Bastogne. He recalls the horror of two frightened days under attack, staring at the bodies of three young Germans he had killed, and the abandoned prayer he made that he would never be ungrateful for life if allowed to hold onto it.

Performances by Woodward, Balsam and Sidney (her first pic in 17 years) are first-rate, and they create genuinely tender moments. But only those past 40 and approaching 50 or more are likely to feel the depth.

□ 1973: Nominations: Best Actress (Joanne Woodward), Supp. Actress (Sylvia Sidney)

■ SUN ALSO RISES, THE

1957, 129 MINS, US ◇

Dir Henry King   *Prod* Darryl F. Zanuck   *Scr* Peter Viertel   *Ph* Leo Tover   *Ed* William Mace   *Mus* Hugo Friedhofer   *Art Dir* Lyle R. Wheeler, Mark-Lee Kirk

● Tyrone Power, Ava Gardner, Mel Ferrer, Errol Flynn, Eddie Albert, Juliette Greco (20th Century-Fox)

In undertaking the transmutation into screen fare of the novel which first escalatored Ernest Hemingway to renown, producer Darryl F. Zanuck doesn't gloss over key plot twist that Tyrone Power plays an impotent newspaperman in frustrated love with Ava Gardner, who plays Lady Brett Ashley. But the script drags along their 'love affair' instead of propelling it. Thus the yarn never comes off either as a love story or a definitive study of the 'lost generation'.

Performances are mixed. Power is on the wooden side, his character never wholly believable. Gardner turns in a far more sympathetic and credible performance. Mel Ferrer never quite achieves the hangdog aspect required of his role. Errol Flynn and Eddie Albert turn in topflight characterizations as drunken members of the gambling expatriates. Flynn registers especially well.

■ SUNBURN

1979, 99 MINS, US ◇ ▣

Dir Richard C. Sarafian   *Prod* John Daly, Gerald Green   *Scr* John Daly   *Ph* Alex Phillips Jr   *Ed* Geoff Foot   *Mus* John Cameron   *Art Dir* Ted Tester
● Farrah Fawcett, Charles Grodin, Art Carney, Joan Collins, Eleanor Parker, Keenan Wynn (Paramount)

Sunburn exists for no other reason than to provide a vehicle for Farrah Fawcett.

Confection [from the book *The Bind* by Stanley Ellin] has Fawcett as a Gotham model posing as Charles Grodin's wife as he sleuths around chic Acapulco settings investigating the mysterious death of an industrialist on behalf of an insurance company stuck with a $5 million claim.

Scenes devoted to real plot movement are few and far between in script's first hour, since Fawcett's character is mostly irrelevant and has to be given something to do, like being scared by a lizard entering her bedroom.

Grodin works overtime to carry the picture and does so marvelously, displaying a savvy low-key comedy style. Grodin and Joan Collins share a farcical seduction scene that's a small comic gem.

■ SUNDAY BLOODY SUNDAY

1971, 110 MINS, UK ◇ ▣ ⊙

Dir John Schlesinger   *Prod* Joseph Janni   *Scr* Penelope Gilliatt   *Ph* Billy Williams   *Ed* Richard Marden   *Art Dir* Norman Dorme
● Glenda Jackson, Peter Finch, Murray Head, Peggy Ashcroft, Maurice Denham, Vivian Pickles (United Artists)

John Schlesinger's *Sunday Bloody Sunday* is a low-keyed, delicately-poised recital of triangular love in which Glenda Jackson and Peter Finch share the affections of AC-DC Murray Head. The visible sexplay, however, is diffident, the storyline sparse. Observation and character are all.

The story's bi-sexual triangle differs in that it's not menage-a-trois stuff. Head goes from one pad to the other. Scripter Penelope Gilliatt with nice economy of dialog, is herein observing the emotional incompleteness of people and how they try to cope.

Jackson is a career femme on the rebound (separated from husband), Finch is a Jewish doctor, and Head, youngest of the trio, is a sculptor-designer oscillating between homo and hetero affairs and career.

Sequence after vignette after sequence larded with deft little touches, all add to this story's cumulative message, namely that half a loaf is often better than none.

□ 1971: Nomination: Best Director, Actor (Peter Finch), Actress (Glenda Jackson), Original Story & Screenplay

SUNDAY IN NEW YORK

1963, 105 MINS, US ◇

Dir Peter Tewksbury *Prod* Everett Freeman
Scr Norman Krasna *Ph* Leo Tover *Ed* Fredric
Steinkamp *Mus* Peter Nero *Art Dir* George W. Davis,
Edward Carfagno
● Cliff Robertson, Jane Fonda, Rod Taylor, Robert Culp,
Jim Backus, Jo Morrow (M-G-M)

Norman Krasna's screenplay, from his
Broadway legiter, doesn't really get rolling
until it has virtually marked time for almost
an hour, but once it gets up this head of
steam the entire complexion of the picture
seems to change.

The story has to do with the sudden arrival
at her brother's apartment in New York of an
Albany maiden (Jane Fonda) who's fretting
over that age-old puzzler – should a girl before marriage? By now, she has alienated herself from a well-heeled hometown beau
(Robert Culp) upon whom she had matrimonial designs. Big brother (Cliff Robertson),
an airline pilot, lauds the virtuous life, but
when sis subsequently discovers flimsy negligee in his closet, she impulsively attempts to
seduce the nearest male (Rod Taylor), a
young newspaperman.

The entire cast is equal to the challenge.
Best of the lot is Taylor, who delivers a warm,
flexible and appealing performance as the
young journalist. Fonda, showing more becoming restraint on this outing, scores
comedically and romantically as the forward-
thinking lass. Robertson is convincing and
chips in some highly amusing reactions as her
generally befuddled pilot-brother.

SUNDAY TOO FAR AWAY

1975, 90 MINS, AUSTRALIA ◇

Dir Ken Hannam *Scr* John Dingwall *Ph* Geoffrey
Burton
● Jack Thompson, Max Cullen, Reg Lye, John Ewart
(SAFC)

Sheep shearers are journeymen who go about
to the sheep farms, and, through a contractor, skim off the wool in backbreaking, dreary
work. This, of course, leads to a sort of rivalry
to remove some of the strain.

Foley (Jack Thompson) is a solid chap who
would like to quit after his present job. But
apparently that is not to be. The cutting of
prices for shearers leads to a strike after the
odyssey of their last contract. They finally
win it.

Pic may have resemblances to oaters in its
place and hardbitten characters, the brawls
and the landscapes. But this has a directorial
ease that gets over a rather flat intro to create an extraordinary insight into men at
work.

SUNDOWN

1941, 90 MINS, US

Dir Henry Hathaway *Prod* Walter Wanger *Scr* Barre
Lyndon *Ph* Charles Lang *Ed* Dorothy Spencer
Mus Miklos Rozsa *Art Dir* Alexander Golitzen
● Gene Tierney, Bruce Cabot, George Sanders, Harry
Carey, Joseph Calleia, Reginald Gardiner
(Wanger/United Artists)

An adventurous melodrama, unfolded in a
colonial outpost of British East Africa,
Sundown is an interesting tale of its type.
Locale is cinematically fresh, the Kenya country near the Abyssinian border. Barre
Lyndon's screenplay of own *SatEvePost* story
neatly mixes informative material of conditions with interesting drama of conditions on
East African front; while Henry Hathaway directs in straight line to hold audience attention, and accentuate the dramatic highlights
en route.

Story details the British administration of
colonies, and the far-reaching efforts of Nazi
agents to foment native uprisings against the
British. Bruce Cabot is local commissioner of
Manieka, being joined by army officer George
Sanders, who is detailed to uncover gun-run-
ning plot to natives. Carl Esmond, secret Nazi
agent, arrives posing as mining engineer; also
Gene Tierney, operator of large caravans and
network of native trading posts.
□ 1941: Nominations: Best B&W
Cinematography, B&W Art Direction,
Scoring of a Dramatic Picture

SUNDOWNERS, THE
(UK: Thunder in the Dust)

1950, 65 MINS, US ◇

Dir George Templeton *Prod* Alan LeMay *Scr* Alan
LeMay *Ph* Winton C. Hoch *Ed* Jack Ogilvie *Mus* Al
Colombo
● Robert Preston, Robert Sterling, Chill Wills, John Litel,
Cathy Downs, John Barrymore Jr (Eagle Lion/LeMay-
Templeton)

Story pits brother against brother to bring to
a conclusion its account of a feud between rival cattlemen. Before that finale, tension is
kept alive by cattle raids, gun battles and the
constant fight of wills between a brother trying to carve a ranch and home from his section of Texas land and an older brother who
dominates.

Interesting is the film debut of John
Barrymore Jr. He does well by his role of a kid
who idolizes his bad, eldest brother but is
held in line by the middle kin (Robert
Sterling). Latter makes his footage count.
Robert Preston gets his teeth into the colorful
role of the daring, dashing eldest member of
the Cloud family, and will be liked despite his
bad ways.

SUNDOWNERS, THE

1960, 133 MINS, UK ◇

Dir Fred Zinnemann *Prod* Gerry Blattner *Scr* Isobel
Lennart *Ph* Jack Hildyard *Ed* Jack Harris *Mus* Dimitri
Tiomkin *Art Dir* Michael Stringer
● Deborah Kerr, Robert Mitchum, Peter Ustinov, Glynis
Johns, Dina Merrill, Chips Rafferty (Warner)

Jon Cleary's novel is the basic source from
which director Fred Zinnemann's inspiration
springs. Between Cleary and Zinnemann lies
Isobel Lennart's perceptive, virile screenplay,
loaded with bright, telling lines of dialog and
gentle philosophical comment. But, fine as
the scenario is, it is Zinnemann's poetic
glances into the souls of his characters, little
hints of deep longings, hidden despairs, indomitable spirit that make the picture the
achievement it is.

On paper, the story sounds something short
of fascinating. It tells of a 1920s Irish-
Australian sheepdrover (Robert Mitchum)
whose fondness for the freedom of an itinerant existence clashes with the fervent hope of
settling-down shared by his wife (Deborah
Kerr) and his son (Michael Anderson Jr). The
wife, in an effort to raise funds for a down-
payment on a farm, persuades her husband to
accept stationary employment as a shearer.

Mitchum's rugged masculinity is right for
the part. There are moments when he projects a great deal of feeling with what appears
to be a minimum of effort. Kerr gives a luminous and penetrating portrayal of the faithful
wife, rugged pioneer stock on the outside,
wistful and feminine within. There is one
fleetingly eloquent scene at a train station, in
which her eyes meet those of an elegant lady
traveller, that ranks as one of the most memorable moments ever to cross a screen.

Peter Ustinov, as a whimsical, learned
bachelor who joins the family and slowly
evolves into its 'household pet,' gives a robust,
rollicking performance. Glynis Johns is a vivacious delight as a hotelkeeper who sets her
sights on matrimonially-evasive Ustinov.

Art, photographic and technical skills are
extremely well represented by the craftsmen
assembled in the bush country of Australia
and at Elstree Studios in London.
□ 1960: Nominations: Best Picture, Director,
Actress (Deborah Kerr), Supp. Actress
(Glynis Johns), Screenplay Adaptation

SUNFLOWER

1970, 105 MINS, ITALY/FRANCE ◇

Dir Vittorio De Sica *Prod* Carlo Ponti, Arthur Cohn
Scr Antonio Guerra, Cesare Zavattini, Gheorghij Mdivani
Ph Giuseppe Rotunno *Ed* Adriana Novelli *Mus* Henry
Mancini *Art Dir* Piero Poletto
● Sophia Loren, Marcello Mastroianni, Ludmila
Savelyeva, Galina Andreeva, Anna Carena (Champion/
Concordia)

Sunflower is the tragedy of an ill-starred love
destroyed by the horrors of war.

Sophia Loren reaches a new high of mature,
dramatic expression, particularly in contrast
with Ludmila Savelyeva's briefer but beautifully contained portrait of a Russion woman
who saves an Italian soldier (Marcello
Mastroianni) on the Stalingrad front, to become his wife and mother of his child. The
climactic confrontation between Loren, the
wife Mastroianni left behind, and Savelyeva is
a sterling credit to both femme performers.

Also creditable is the glimpse of postwar
Moscow and Russia, grimly objective of life
there, during and post-Stalin. The Soviets cooperated in providing the loosely integrated
but spectacular battlefield action.

It's a heart-clutcher and a four-handker-
chief hit, abetted at every turn by a Henry
Mancini theme of lyric substance that quietly
penetrates every mournful moment.
Giuseppe Rotunno's color camerawork is
firstrate.

SUNRISE

1927, 95 MINS, US ⊗

Dir F.W. Murnau *Scr* Carl Mayer, Katherine Hilliker,
H.H. Caldwell *Ph* Charles Rosher, Karl Struss
Ed Katherine Hilliker, H.H. Caldwell, Harold Schuster
Mus Hugo Riesenfeld *Art Dir* Rochus Gliese
● George O'Brien, Janet Gaynor, Margaret Livingston,
Bodil Rosing, J. Farrell MacDonald (Fox)

Sunrise is a distinguished contribution to the
screen, made in this country, but produced after the best manner of the German school. In
its artistry, dramatic power and graphic suggestion it goes a long way toward realizing
the promise of this foreign director in his former works, notably *Faust*.

What director F.W. Murnau has tried to do is
to crystallize in dramatic symbolism those conflicts, adjustments, compromises and complexities of man-and-woman mating experiences
that ultimately grow into an endearing union.

Many elements enter into the success of
this ambitious effort. Murnau reveals a remarkable resourcefulness of effects; the playing of George O'Brien and Janet Gaynor and
their associates is generally convincing.

The incidental music blends smoothly, suggesting the mood of the scene, but without intruding into the conscientiousness. In many
scenes (honking autos, when dreaming lovers
block a street, is a case in point) sound effects
are introduced. This has been managed with
skill.

All these things lay upon a story [by
Herman Sadermann] as simple as it is human. The Woman from the City snares a
young farmer. Under her hypnotism he listens to a plan to drown the young wife, sell
the farm and go off to the city.
□ 1927/28: Best Actress (Janet Gaynor),
Cinematography, Artistic Quality of
Production.
□ Nomination: Best Art Direction

SUNRISE AT CAMPOBELLO

1960, 144 MINS, US ◇ Ⓥ ☉
Dir Vincent J. Donehue *Prod* Dore Schary *Scr* Dore
Schary *Ph* Russell Harlan *Ed* George Boemler
Mus Franz Waxman *Art Dir* Edward Carrere
● Ralph Bellamy, Greer Garson, Hume Cronyn, Jean
Hagen, Ann Shoemaker, Tim Considine (Warner)

In the journey from stage to screen this chapter from the life of Franklin Delano Roosevelt
loses none of its poignant and inspirational
qualities, none of its humor and pathos. Dore
Schary, as author-producer of the play and
the film, can take just pride in this grandslam
feat. And this satisfaction is to be shared also
by Ralph Bellamy, whose brilliant portrayal
of Roosevelt, and Vincent J. Donehue, the
director, clicked so resoundingly on
Broadway.

The period is 1921, when polio shatters a
joyous family vacation on the island retreat of
Campobello, to 1924, when Roosevelt re-
emerged in public to put in Al Smith's name
as a presidential hopeful at the Democratic
convention and in the process, lit his own political star.

Campobello opened a new career for Schary
as a playwright in 1958, shortly after he ex-
ited as production head of M-G-M. The film is
also a brilliant new showcase for Greer
Garson. She comes through as Eleanor
Roosevelt with a deeply moving, multifaceted
characterization.

There is a third tower of strength in the
person of Hume Cronyn as Louis Howe, the
wizened, asthmatic, devoted friend and political Svengali to Roosevelt. There is, considering the sober nature of the subject, a
surprising amount of humor in *Campobello* and
a good measure of it is deftly generated by
Cronyn.

Franz Waxman's score makes a big contribution, notably to the convention sequence.
Pic begins with an overture, about eight minutes, of melodious oldtimers.
☐ 1960: Nominations: Best Actress (Greer
Garson), Color Costume Design, Color Art
Direction, Sound

SUNSET

1988, 106 MINS, US ◇ Ⓥ ☉
Dir Blake Edwards *Prod* Tony Adams *Scr* Blake
Edwards *Ph* Anthony B. Richmond *Ed* Robert
Pergament *Mus* Henry Mancini *Art Dir* Rodger Maus
● Bruce Willis, James Garner, Malcolm McDowell,
Mariel Hemingway, Kathleen Quinlan, Jennifer Edward
(Hudson Hawk/Tri-Star)

Sunset is a silly Hollywood fiction, unconvincing in all but a couple of its details. Premise
of teaming up righteous cowboy star Tom
Mix and real-life lawman Wyatt Earp to solve
an actual murder case may have looked good
on paper, but it plays neither amusingly nor
excitingly.

Despite the tough guy charm he has
exhibited elsewhere, Bruce Willis is one of
the least likely choices imaginable to play
Mix, perhaps the top Western star of the
1920s.

That's just the beginning of the film's lack
of plausibility, even on its own terms. The notion of English, Chaplin-like former star
(Malcolm McDowell) becoming the venal
head of a studio bears no resemblance to anything that ever occurred in Hollywood while
the idea of multiple murders taking place at
the first Academy Awards ceremony is nasty
and far-fetched.

Fortunately, there is James Garner as Earp
as relief from all the nonsense around him. In
fact, the man from Tombstone seems a little
too sophisticated and at ease in Tinseltown,
but the actor's natural charm and fine sense
of one-upmanship wins the day in virtually all
his scenes.
☐ 1988: Nomination: Best Costume Design

SUNSET BLVD.

1950, 110 MINS, US Ⓥ ☉
Dir Billy Wilder *Prod* Charles Brackett *Scr* Charles
Brackett, Billy Wilder, D.M. Marshman Jr *Ph* John F.
Seitz *Ed* Arthur Schmidt *Mus* Franz Waxman
Art Dir Hans Dreier, John Meehan
● William Holden, Gloria Swanson, Erich von Stroheim,
Nancy Olson, Cecil B. DeMille, Buster Keaton (Paramount)

Sunset Blvd. is a backstage melodrama using a
filmland, instead of a legit, locale. It is tied in
with a pseudo-expose of Hollywood.

The expose of the land of the swimming
pool opens with a shot of a dead man floating
in the plunge of a Beverly Hills mansion. The
voice of the dead man then narrates the
story, going back six months to explain why
he eventually reached such a sorry state. He
is a young writer with a few minor credits and
many creditors.

He finds refuge in what he believes to be an
abandoned mansion. It is occupied by a former great femme star. She takes a fancy to
the young man, employs him to write a script
that will return her to past glory. The association segues into an affair.

Performances by the entire cast, and particularly William Holden and Gloria Swanson,
are exceptionally fine. Swanson, returning to
the screen after a very long absence, socks
hard with a silent-day technique to put over
the decaying star she is called upon to portray. Erich von Stroheim, as her butler and
original discoverer, delivers with excellent restraint.

The other performer rating more than a
mention is Cecil B. DeMille. He plays himself
with complete assurance in one of the few
sympathetic roles.
☐ 1950: Best Story & Screenplay, B&W Art
Direction, Score for a Dramatic Picture.
☐ Nominations: Best Picture, Director, Actor
(William Holden), Actress (Gloria Swanson),
Supp. Actor (Erich von Stroheim), Supp.
Actress (Nancy Olson), B&W
Cinematography, Editing

SUNSHINE BOYS, THE

1975, 111 MINS, US ◇ Ⓥ
Dir Herbert Ross *Prod* Ray Stark *Scr* Neil Simon
Ph David M. Walsh *Ed* Margaret Booth, John F. Burnett
Mus Harry V. Lojewski (sup.) *Art Dir* Albert Brenner
● Walter Matthau, George Burns, Richard Benjamin, Lee
Meredith, Carol Arthur, Rosetta Le Noire (M-G-M)

The Sunshine Boys is an extremely sensitive
and lovable film version of Neil Simon's play,
with Walter Matthau and George Burns outstanding in their starring roles as a pair of
long-hostile vaudeville partners.

Matthau, with some complex makeup
artistry atop his own brilliant talent, gives the
Willy Clark character its full dimension of
rascality, stubborness, heart, pride and, eventually, humility. Burns, returning to pix, provides in his standout performance the right
complementing aspects to the pair's love-hate
relationship spanning 43 years.

Richard Benjamin, the nephew-agent who
is the catalyst of their reconciliation, serves to
ventilate audience responses to the principals' behavior while simultaneously creating
an independent characterization all his own.

Apart from the incidental title music, there
is no score, which seems the proper decision.
Matthau, Burns, Benjamin and the story need
no musical accent.
☐ 1975: Best Supp. Actor (George Burns).
☐ Nominations: Best Actor (Walter Matthau),
Screenplay Adaptation, Art Direction

SUN SHINES BRIGHT, THE

1953, 90 MINS, US Ⓥ
Dir John Ford *Prod* John Ford, Merian C. Cooper
Scr Laurence Stallings *Ph* Archie Stout *Ed* Jack Murray
Mus Victor Young *Art Dir* Frank Hotaling

● Charles Winninger, Arleen Wheelan, John Russell,
Stepin Fetchit, Russell Simpson, Ludwig Stossel (Argosy/
Republic)

This is a lightweight comedy-drama, poorly
plotted and overlength.

Three Irvin S. Cobb short stories [*The Sun
Shines Bright*, *The Mob from Massac* and *The Lord
Provides*] have been spliced together.
Characters are such stereotype figures as
julep-drinking southerners, comic-opera
darkies and bigoted poor white trash. Script
and John Ford's direction attempt to cloak
these hackneyed types with a generous dose
of schmaltz and a theme of 'good triumphing
over evil' but it fails to come off with any impact.

Charles Winninger makes as much as possible of his Judge Priest character, the principal
figure. It's election time in Fairfield, Ky, a
sleepy southern town back in 1905, and an
upstart Yankee state's attorney (Milburn
Stone) is threatening to unseat the judge.
Depite the damage it may do to his political
future, the judge goes his easy-going humane
way.

He talks down a mob threatening to lynch a
colored boy falsely accused of rape; aids a
woman who keeps a house of ill-fame on the
outskirts of town; and leads the town's few
substantial, right-thinking citizens in the funeral march for another fallen woman.

Players go through their chores in routine
fashion.

SUPER, THE

1991, 86 MINS, US ◇ Ⓥ ☉
Dir Rod Daniel *Prod* Charles Gordon *Scr* Sam Simon
Ph Bruce Surtees *Ed* Jack Hofstra *Mus* Miles
Goodman *Art Dir* Kristi Zea
● Joe Pesci, Vincent Gardenia, Madolyn Smith Osborne,
Ruben Blades, Stacey Travis, Carole Shelley (Largo/JVC)

Visually, *The Super* succeeds all too well in
creating a believable image of an urban hellhole. Comedically, *The Super* is a hellhole.
Aside from Joe Pesci's Dickensian caricature
of a NY slumlord ordered to live among his
miserable tenants, pic is almost unrelentingly
depressing and unbelievably schmaltzy to
boot.

Director Rod Daniel's sitcom roots are constantly evident in his sledgehammer direction
of Sam Simon's overly jokey script, and the
tone seems grotesque in light of the subject
matter.

Pesci adds another flamboyantly vile character to his gallery. While providing what is
euphemistically termed 'affordable housing
for the underprivileged,' he's the kind of
landlord who gleefully snaps 'Get a man!'
when a matron complains that her apartment
is freezing. But he seems like Gandhi next to
his father (Vincent Gardenia), a raging racist
whose ultimate solution to Pesci's problems
with tenants and the Housing Authority is to
hire an arsonist to torch the building.

SUPERFLY

1972, 96 MINS, US ◇ Ⓥ
Dir Gordon Parks Jr *Prod* Sig Shore *Scr* Phillip Fenty
Ph James Signorelli *Ed* Bob Brady *Mus* Curtis
Mayfield
● Ron O'Neal, Carl Lee, Sheila Frazier, Julius W.
Harris, Charles McGregor, Nate Adams (Warner)

Best that can be said for this quickie is its un-
pretentiousness in not seeking any pseudo-so-
ciological meaning or theme, or assuming any
airs that one is supposed to be enriched or
provoked by it all. It's strictly action-adventure, alternating, like clockwork, drugs-sex-
violence for its duration with hardly a plot
line to hold it together.

Cast handles the simple characterizations
adequately, with Ron O'Neal heading as
Superfly, sluggin', lovin', needlin' and philoso-

phizing his way through the tale of the pusher with heart of gold, wanting to get out – but only after making his easy $1 million. Supporting convincingly are Carl Lee, Julius W. Harris as Scatter and Charles McGregor as Fat Freddie.

Sheila Frazier and Polly Niles offer the sex interests, including a breast or two when things get otherwise dull.

....

■ SUPERGIRL

1984, 117 MINS, UK ◇ ⓦ ⓞ
Dir Jeannot Szwarc *Prod* Timothy Burrill *Scr* David Odell *Ph* Alan Hume *Ed* Malcolm Cooke *Mus* Jerry Goldsmith *Art Dir* Richard MacDonald
● Faye Dunaway, Helen Slater, Peter O'Toole, Hart Bochner, Peter Cook, Brenda Vaccaro (Artistry/Cantharus)

Supergirl is Kara, Superman's cousin, who journeys from her home on the planet of Argo to Earth to recover the missing Omegahedron Stone, life-force of her world, which has fallen into the clutches of the evil Selena (Fay Dunaway), a power-hungry sorceress.

Landing near an exclusive boarding school for young ladies, Kara quickly adopts the name of Linda Lee and finds herself rooming with Lois Lane's kid sister, Lucy (Maureen Teefy).

Rest of pic represents a struggle between the good of Supergirl and the evil of Selena with, as is usually the case, evil being a lot more fun.

Dunaway has a ball as Selena, and her joyably over-the-top handling of the part could merit cult attention. She's ably backed by Brenda Vaccaro as her incredulous assistant, and Peter Cook as her sometime lover and math teacher at the girls' school.

Peter O'Toole makes a modest impression as Supergirl's friend and mentor, while Mia Farrow and Simon Ward, as her parents, have even smaller roles than Susannah York and Marlon Brando in the first *Superman*.

Helen Slater is a find: blonde as Supergirl, dark-haired as Linda Lee, she's an appealing young heroine in either guise. Screenplay is filled with witty lines and enjoyable characters, but Jeannot Szwarc's direction is rather flat.

....

■ SUPERMAN

1978, 143 MINS, US ◇ ⓦ ⓞ
Dir Richard Donner *Prod* Pierre Spengler *Scr* Mario Puzo, David Newman, Leslie Newman, Robert Benton *Ph* Geoffrey Unsworth *Ed* Stuart Baird *Mus* John Williams *Art Dir* John Barry
● Marlon Brando, Gene Hackman, Christopher Reeve, Margot Kidder, Ned Beatty, Glenn Ford (Warner/Salkind)

Magnify James Bond's extraordinary physical powers while curbing his sex drive and you have the essence of *Superman*, a wonderful, chuckling, preposterously exciting fantasy.

Forget Marlon Brando who tops the credits. As Superman's father on the doomed planet Krypton, Brando is good but unremarkable.

As both the wholesome man of steel and his bumbling secret identity Clark Kent, Christopher Reeve is excellent. As newswoman Lois Lane, Margot Kidder plays perfectly off both of his personalities.

Tracing the familiar cartoon genesis, film opens with spectacular outer-space effects and the presentation of life on Krypton where nobody believes Papa Brando's warnings of doom. So he and wife Susannah York ship their baby son on his way to Earth.

Striking terra firma, the baby is found by Glenn Ford and Phyllis Thaxter who take him for their own. But the time must ultimately come when Superman's powers for good are revealed to the world and his debut becomes

a wild night, beginning with Lane's rescue from a skyscraper, the capture of assorted burglars and the salvation of the president's airplane.

Lurking in wacky palatial splendor in the sewers beneath Park Ave, supercriminal Gene Hackman views this caped arrival as a superthreat befitting his evil genius.
□ 1978: Special Achievement Award (visual effects)
□ Nominations: Best Editing, Origial Score, Sound

....

■ SUPERMAN II

1981, 127 MINS, UK ◇ ⓦ ⓞ
Dir Richard Lester *Prod* Pierre Spengler *Scr* Mario Puzo, David Newman, Leslie Newman *Ph* Geoffrey Unsworth, Robert Paynter *Ed* John Victor-Smith *Mus* Ken Thorne *Art Dir* John Barry, Peter Murton
● Christopher Reeve, Gene Hackman, Margot Kidder, Ned Beatty, Terence Stamp, Sarah Douglas (International/Salkind)

For all the production halts, setbacks, personnel changeovers and legal wrangling that paved its way to the screen, *Superman II* emerges as a solid, classy, cannily constructed piece of entertainment which gets down to action almost immediately.

Although original plans called for lensing the first two *Superman* features simultaneously, the sequel is reportedly 80% newly shot footage.

The film does an especially good job of picking up the strings of unexplored characters and plot seeds left dangling from the first pic, taking its core plot from the three Kryptonian villains – Terence Stamp, Jack O'Halloran and Sarah Douglas – briefly glimpsed in the first pic. Here, they're liberated from perpetual imprisonment in a bizarre time-warp by an H-bomb explosion in outer space.

The film builds quickly to a climactic battle between Christopher Reeve and the three supervillains in mid-town Manhattan.

....

■ SUPERMAN III

1983, 123 MINS, UK ◇ ⓦ ⓞ
Dir Richard Lester *Prod* Pierre Spengler *Scr* David Newman, Leslie Newman *Ph* Robert Paynter *Ed* John Victor Smith *Mus* Ken Thorne *Art Dir* Peter Murton
● Christopher Reeve, Richard Pryor, Robert Vaughn, Annette O'Toole, Annie Ross, Margot Kidder (Salkind/Dovemead)

Superman III emerges as a surprisingly soft-cored disappointment. Putting its emphasis on broad comedy at the expense of ingenious plotting and technical wizardry, it has virtually none of the mythic or cosmic sensibility that marked its predecessors.

The film begins with a hilarious pre-credits sequence in which Richard Pryor, an unemployed 'kitchen technician', decides to embark on a career as a computer programmer. Robert Vaughn, a crooked megalomaniac intent on taking over the world economy, dispatches Pryor to a small company subsid in Smallville, where he programs a weather satellite to destroy Colombia's coffee crop (and make a market-cornering killing for Vaughn).

Foiled by Superman (Christopher Reeve), Pryor uses the computer to concoct an imperfect form of Kryptonite – using cigarette tar to round out the formula. The screenplay opts for the novelty of using the Kryptonite to split the Clark Kent/Superman persona into two bodies, good and evil.

Most of the action relies on explosive pyrotechnics and careening stuntpersons. At the romantic level, the film does paint a nice relationship between Reeve (as Kent) and his onetime crush Annette O'Toole.

....

■ SUPERMAN IV
THE QUEST FOR PEACE

1987, 89 MINS, US ◇ ⓦ ⓞ
Dir Sidney J. Furie *Prod* Menahem Golan, Yoram Globus *Scr* Lawrence Konner, Mark Rosenthal *Ph* Ernest Day *Ed* John Shirley *Mus* John Williams *Art Dir* John Graysmark
● Christopher Reeve, Gene Hackman, Jackie Cooper, Mariel Hemingway, Jon Cryer, Margot Kidder (Cannon/Warner)

Opening sequence shows Superman has picked up the spirit of glasnost as he flies into space to rescue an imperiled cosmonaut and utters his first lines of the picture in Russian.

Superman's newly assumed mission sees him addressing the United Nations to tell the world he personally is going to remove all nuclear weapons from the face of the earth.

Meanwhile, Lex Luthor (Gene Hackman) has created an evil clone of Superman called Nuclear Man, who wreaks havoc with famous landmarks around the world and does savage battle with the hero on the face of the moon until Superman discovers his nemesis' single flaw.

The earlier films in the series were far from perfect, but at their best they had some flair and agreeable humor, qualities this one sorely lacks. Hackman gets a few laughs, but has less to work with than before, and everyone else seems to be just going through the motions and having less fun doing so.

....

■ SUPER MARIO BROS.

1993, 104 MINS, US ◇ ⓦ ⓞ
Dir Rocky Morton, Annabel Jankel *Prod* Jake Eberts, Roland Joffe *Scr* Parker Bennett, Terry Runte, Ed Solomon *Ph* Dean Semler *Ed* Mark Goldblatt *Mus* Alan Silvestri *Art Dir* David L. Snyder
● Bob Hoskins, John Leguizamo, Dennis Hopper, Samantha Mathis, Fisher Stevens, Fiona Shaw (Hollywood Pictures/Lightmotive/Allied Filmmakers)

The task of converting a non-narrative Nintendo videogame [and characters created by Shigeru Miyamoto and Takashi Tezuka] into a $50 million motion picture was too much for a trio of scripters, a pair of (married) directors and a couple of high-profile producers. What set them in motion was obviously the success of the *Teenage Mutant Ninja Turtles* movies, which *Mario* imitates when it's not into *Star Wars* riffs or *Batman* pastiche.

Awkwardly constructed pic, featuring two prologues and two epilogues, starts with the premise of a parallel world to New York created 65 million years ago by a meteorite that also killed off the dinosaurs. A miscast (he's not the only one) Dennis Hopper is intent upon retrieving a meteorite fragment and a young princess (Samantha Mathis) sent with it to our world.

Mathis is kidnapped by Hopper's bumbling assistants and pursued into his world by the Mario Bros., two Brooklyn plumbers. If you're over the age of five and can believe that Bob Hoskins and John Leguizamo are brothers, let alone Italian, the rest of the film's leaps of faith are child's play.

As stiffly directed by Annabel Jankel and Rocky Morton, *Mario* occasionally attempts to career along like a videogame with chases, fireballs and narrow escapes. However, the action is generally photographed in unexciting closeups and telephoto shots.

....

■ SUPERVIXENS

1975, 105 MINS, US ◇ ⓦ
Dir Russ Meyer *Prod* Russ Meyer *Scr* Russ Meyer *Ph* Russ Meyer *Ed* Russ Meyer *Mus* William Loose *Art Dir* Michael Levesque
● Shari Eubank, Charles Pitts, Charles Napier, Uschi Digard, Henry Rowland, Christy Hartburg (September 19)

Russ Meyer's *Supervixens* is an overlong and overly violent skin pic whose interest lies in its pretentions to be more than a skin film.

The story involves a gas-station attendant, Clint (Charles Pitts) whose foul-mouthed girlfriend is, successively stabbed, beaten, drowned and electrocuted by a brutish cop (Charles Napier) with Clint getting the blame. Fleeing town, he has sexual encounters with a succession of busty amazons, then falls for Supervixen (Shari Eubank) whom he must eventually rescue from a sick cop (Napier again). It's all very low on camp and high on blood.

The film is technically slick and the acting is competent.

. . . .

■ SUPPORT YOUR LOCAL GUNFIGHTER

1971, 92 MINS, US ◇ ⓥ
Dir Burt Kennedy *Prod* Bill Finnegan *Scr* James Edward Grant *Ph* Harry Stradling *Ed* Bill Gulick *Mus* Jack Elliot, Allyn Ferguson *Art Dir* Phil Barber
● James Garner, Suzanne Pleshette, Jack Elam, Joan Blondell, Harry Morgan, Marie Windsor (Cherokee/Brigade)

Burt Kennedy's follow-up to *Support Your Local Sheriff* has James Garner escaping from the clutches of Marie Windsor, only to become mistaken by competing mine-owners Harry Morgan and John Dehner for a hired gun, played in finale cameo by Chuck Connors. Jack Elam again is excellent in role of a befuddled but willing accomplice to Garner's maneuvers. Joan Blondell is good as a bordello queen, and Henry Jones scores as a nosy gossip.

Suzanne Pleshette starts out a bit too strong as a tom-boy, but eventually settles in. There are a few hefty laughs, many chuckles, a few smiles, and some cold gags.

A.D. Flowers' special explosive effects punch up some of the action sequences, and Elam's curtain-narration speech, where he describes how he went on to become a big star of Italian westerns, brings the 92 minutes to a good finish.

. . . .

■ SUPPORT YOUR LOCAL SHERIFF

1969, 96 MINS, US ◇ ⓥ
Dir Burt Kennedy *Prod* William Bowers *Scr* William Bowers *Ph* Harry Stradling *Ed* George Brooks *Mus* Jeff Alexander *Art Dir* Leroy Coleman
● James Garner, Joan Hackett, Walter Brennan, Harry Morgan, Jack Elam, Bruce Dern (United Artists/Cherokee)

Support Your Local Sheriff uses as the basis for its comedy the many cliches that have become part and parcel of the Western genre.

Whether it's the town dominated by a tyrant, the never-missing gunfighter, the absolutely pure hero, the chaste but unchased maiden, the growth of the territory – they're all dealt with and done under, by demolishing dialogue or just enough exaggeration to point up the ridiculous in even the most respectable circumstances.

James Garner is delightful as the 'stranger' riding into town on his way to Australia, so modest, yet so perfect in his various abilities – never missing a shot, turning the town derelict into his deputy, outthinking the Danbys (a superb quartet of villains) outwitting the attempts of the mayor's daughter to land him until he's ready.

The action almost never moves beyond the tiny town's limits, and the community itself seems just enough exaggerated to let the audience know that it's not to be taken seriously.

. . . .

■ SUPPOSE THEY GAVE A WAR AND NOBODY CAME?

1970, 113 MINS, US ◇ ⓥ
Dir Hy Averback *Prod* Fred Engel *Scr* Don McGuire, Hal Captain *Ph* Burnett Guffey *Ed* John F. Brunett *Mus* Jerry Fielding *Art Dir* Jack Poplin

● Brian Keith, Tony Curtis, Ernest Borgnine, Ivan Dixon, Suzanne Pleshette, Tom Ewell (ABC)

A meandering comedy about three old-time army tankmen in a non-combatant missile base at war with the southern redneck town in which it is located.

Main problem is that Hy Averback's direction and the screenplay, both of which have their moments, never focus and decide if it is a comedy, serious drama or farce.

Ernest Borgnine is the heavy-handed southern sheriff. Tony Curtis keeps it lighthearted, but nevertheless convincing, as 'a middle-aged, paunchy garrison soldier who thinks he is Warren Beatty'.

Suzanne Pleshette, a wise-cracking, self-proclaimed 'beer hustler', is very real, and her handling of tough snappy dialog makes her appearances some of the best scenes in the film, especially in those with Curtis.

. . . .

■ SURE THING, THE

1985, 94 MINS, US ◇ ⓥ ⊙
Dir Rob Reiner *Prod* Roger Birnbaum *Scr* Steven L. Bloom, Jonathan Roberts *Ph* Robert Elswit *Ed* Robert Leighton *Mus* Tom Scott *Art Dir* Lilly Kilvert
● John Cusack, Daphne Zuniga, Boyd Gaines, Tim Robbins, Lisa Jane Persky, Viveca Lindfors (Embassy/Monument)

The Sure Thing is at heart a sweetly old-fashioned look at the last lap of the coming-of-age ordeal in which the sure thing becomes less important than the real thing. Realization may not be earth shattering, but in an era of fast food and faster sex, return to the traditional is downright refreshing.

Gib (John Cusack) is a beer guzzling junk food devotee with a flair for the outrageous, but he is not having much luck with the opposite sex in his freshman year at an eastern Ivy League college. One of the women he strikes out with is Alison (Daphne Zuniga), a prim and proper coed who thinks that spontaneity is a social disease.

The plot thickens as they both arrange a ride, unbeknownst to each other, with a California bound couple for the Christmas break. Gib is off to score with the sure thing (Nicollette Sheridan) while Alison is visiting her boorish boyfriend (Boyd Gaynes). Stranded together, the two travelers mix like oil and water, volatile at first and gradually realizing that their different personalities complement each other.

Chemistry between Cuzack and Zuniga is a plus as they change and grow together as the film progresses. Off-key serenade of showtunes from Tim Robbins and Lisa Jane Persky in the car heading west supplies the same daffy humor director Rob Reiner brought to his mock documentary, *This Is Spinal Tap*.

. . . .

■ SURF NAZIS MUST DIE

1987, 80 MINS, US ◇ ⓥ ⊙
Dir Peter George *Prod* Robert Tinnell *Scr* Jon Ayre *Ph* Rolf Kestermann *Ed* Craig Colton *Mus* Jon McCallum *Art Dir* Bernadette Disanto
● Barry Brenner, Gail Neely, Michael Sonye, Dawn Wildsmith, Tom Shell, Bobbie Bresee (Troma/Institute)

A sort of *Clockwork Orange* meets *Mad Max* on the beach, pic hasn't one redeeming feature. Time is the near future and California's social fabric has been torn apart by a devastating earthquake. It's hell out there on the beaches.

Striving for supremacy are the Surf Nazis, who live in a beach bunker, own beweaponed surf boards, bristle with knives and swastika tattoos, and are fueled by a surfing Fuhrer – Adolf – who has a dream of owning the 'new beach.'

Not much else is clear until a revenge-seeking mother takes on the Nazis after they kill her son; prior to this there are various and of-

ten bloody fights between the Nazis and the other gangs, and there's even regular surf footage interspersed. The hulking mother, played by Bobbie Bresee, turns out to be quite a handful and wreaks gory retribution on each of the nasty Nazis.

Pic looks like most of its budget went on its titles, a not unlikeable score, and a surprisingly punchy and facetious trailer.

. . . .

■ SURRENDER

1987, 95 MINS, US ◇ ⓥ ⊙
Dir Jerry Belson *Prod* Aaron Spelling, Alan Greisman *Scr* Jerry Belson *Ph* Juan Ruiz Anchia *Ed* Wendy Greene Bricmont *Mus* Michel Colombier *Art Dir* Lilly Kilvert
● Sally Field, Michael Caine, Steve Guttenberg, Peter Boyle, Jackie Cooper, Julie Kavner (Cannon)

Surrender is a '50s sitcom dressed up in modern clothes. The issues are somewhat updated but the characters still think like Doris Day and Rock Hudson. As the confused lovers, Michael Caine and Sally Field are good for a couple of laughs along the way, but production runs out of steam early.

Caine is a casualty of too many marriages and too much success as a pop novelist. Field is a would-be artist who takes the easy way out in the form of a rich and indulgent but unchallenging boy friend (Steve Guttenberg).

Opening skirmish is love at first fight. But once they've coupled, the series of complications concocted by writer-director Jerry Belson can only lead to an inevitable happy ending. Things at least move fast and Belson does have an ear for modern courtship and the silly things people say to each other.

Although their acting styles don't quite mesh and there isn't a great deal of chemistry between them, both Caine and Field are strong enough presences to make them entertaining to observe.

. . . .

■ SURVIVORS, THE

1983, 102 MINS, US ◇ ⓥ ⊙
Dir Michael Ritchie *Prod* William Sackheim *Scr* Michael Leeson *Ph* Billy Williams *Ed* Richard A. Harris *Mus* Paul Chihara *Art Dir* Gene Callahan
● Walter Matthau, Robin Williams, Jerry Reed, James Wainwright, Kristen Vigard, Annie McEnroe (Delphi/Rastar)

An aimless, unfocused social comedy, *The Survivors* misfires on just about every level, finding what laughs it has to offer solely in the personal performing talents of Walter Matthau and Robin Williams.

Exec Williams and gas station owner Matthau both become unemployed at the outset, and through a bizarre coincidence are thrown together as intended victims of professional hitman Jerry Reed.

Confronted with the threat of another attack by Reed, Williams becomes a maniacal gun enthusiast and joins a survival training unit run in the snowy mountains by James Wainwright.

It feels as though the script, such as it was, was tossed out the window once action moves to the New Hampshire compound. All of Williams' dialog from this point on sounds like lifts from crazed comic monologs he might deliver onstage. Matthau at least makes things watchable thanks to his masterful comic timing.

. . . .

■ SUSAN AND GOD
(UK: *The Gay Mrs Trexel*)

1940, 115 MINS, US
Dir George Cukor *Prod* Hunt Stromberg *Scr* Anita Loos *Ph* Robert Planck *Ed* William H. Terhune *Mus* Herbert Stothart *Art Dir* Cedric Gibbons, Randall Duell

● Joan Crawford, Fredric March, Ruth Hussey, John Carroll, Rita Hayworth, Nigel Bruce (M-G-M)

Film version of Rachel Crothers' play, with Joan Crawford in the role played by Gertrude Lawrence on the stage, is smartly cast, deftly directed and elaborately mounted. In contrast to the original piece, picture builds up parts of the husband (Fredric March) and young daughter (Rita Quigley) to the equals of Susan (Crawford). In fact, when everything is over, sympathy tends strongly to the former pair rather than the latter.

Crawford returns from abroad a shallow and scatter-brained disciple of a 'new thought', or Oxford, movement. In expounding her views strongly amongst her socialite friends, she upsets several happy couples; but is faced with reconstructing her own marital happiness through personal practice of her tenets. Persistence of her husband to keep her in line and sincerity of the couple's youngster finally bring her to reason.

Crawford provides a strong portrayal of Susan – a mature matron characterization, which is a marked departure for the player. March provides a polished and capital presentation of the bewildered husband who battles through to reestablish happiness in his household. Quigley, as the daughter, is excellent.

George Cukor's direction highlights the characterizations he unfolds, and his weakness in piloting can be attributed to the slow pace at which he develops the story.

■ SUSAN LENOX HER FALL AND RISE

1931, 75 MINS, US Ⓥ
Dir Robert Z. Leonard   *Scr* Wanda Tuchock, Zelda Sears, Leon Gordon, Edith Fitzgerald   *Ph* William Daniels   *Ed* Margaret Booth
● Greta Garbo, Clark Gable, Jean Hersholt, John Miljan, Alan Hale (M-G-M)

Not the least of this film's assets is the title, carrying the prestige of a novel that was a sensation upon its publication. What David Graham Phillips wrote as a protest against narrow-minded respectability has evolved in the filming into a hot romance based on sexual antagonism.

The picture provides Greta Garbo with a role of destiny-hounded woman, not altogether unlike her Anna Christie, and adds to the Garbo gallery another impressive portrait.

The Garbo Susan is a glamorous figure, a vital Swedish immigrant girl who flees her ignorant, self-righteous foster parents in a raging storm to take refuge with a prepossessing young engineer (Clark Gable). The young pair fall in love. Out of the curious sexual antagonism that seems to be generated by their passion she goes her errant way to become a famous courtesan, while he sinks from bad to worse to the finality of a South Seas beachcomber.

Teaming with the great Garbo, of course, marks the peak of Gable's vogue. He appears to excellent purpose here, playing with agreeable urbanity and giving a performance that blends effectively into the whole atmosphere.

■ SUSAN SLADE

1961, 116 MINS, US ◇
Dir Delmer Daves   *Prod* Delmer Daves   *Scr* Delmer Daves   *Ph* Lucien Ballard   *Ed* William Ziegler   *Mus* Max Steiner   *Art Dir* Leo K. Kuter
● Troy Donahue, Connie Stevens, Dorothy McGuire, Lloyd Nolan, Bert Convy (Warner)

Susan Slade, though slickly produced and attractively peopled, weighs in as little more than a plodding and predictable soap opera. It is, however, a telling showcase for Connie Stevens.

The screenplay by Delmer Daves, who also

produced and directed as is his custom, is from the novel by Doris Hume. Yarn has a chicken way of evading its real issues by ushering in devastatingly convenient melodramatic swerves at key moments.

Stevens enacts the innocent, virginal daughter of a devoted family man and engineer (Lloyd Nolan) who returns with his brood to luxury in the States after 10 years of service on a project in remote Chile. The girl promptly falls madly in love and finds herself with child but without husband.

The family then tries a fake by moving to Guatemala, where Nolan dies and his wife (Dorothy McGuire) supposedly bears the child. The story returns to the US and boils down to the inevitable triangle. Who is worthy of Stevens' love – junior tycoon Bert Convy or poor stable operator Troy Donahue?

Pretty Stevens comes on like gangbusters, and Lucien Ballard's misty, flattering close-up photography is her ally from start to finish. Donahue gives a wooden performance. Veterans Nolan and McGuire emote with sincerity.

The film was lensed in dazzlingly scenic places such as the Carmel coastline and San Francisco.

■ SUSAN SLEPT HERE

1954, 97 MINS, US ◇ Ⓥ ⊙
Dir Frank Tashlin   *Prod* Harriet Parsons   *Scr* Alex Gottlieb   *Ph* Nicholas Musuraca   *Ed* Harry Marker   *Mus* Leigh Harline   *Art Dir* Albert S. D'Agostino, Carroll Clark
● Dick Powell, Debbie Reynolds, Anne Francis, Alvy Moore, Glenda Farrell, Horace McMahon (RKO)

Some 97 minutes of well-farced escapism is offered in *Susan Slept Here*. Romantic comedy is imaginatively developed, brightly trouped under Frank Tashlin's smart direction most of the way. Alex Gottlieb script, based on Gottlieb-Steve Fisher play [*Susan*], involves Hollywood writer Dick Powell with juve delinquent Debbie Reynolds in sort of May-October romantic affair.

Tashlin handling, and players, score strongest in scenes played strictly for pantomime. One sure laugh getter scene is Powell watching old movie he dialoged on television. Other has Debbie watching home movies, grimacing cattily at love rival Anne Francis.

Some of material approaches frankness of *Moon Is Blue*. Some chuckles are sly type since battle-of-sexes stuff is open to assorted interpretations. For [Production] Code purposes, Debbie remains pure through all (her delinquency only that of being left homeless by mother gone off to remarry), she manages to spoil Francis' courtship of Powell and gets him for herself.

□ 1954: Nominations: Best Song ('Hold My Hand'), Sound

■ SUSPECT, THE

1944, 85 MINS, US
Dir Robert Siodmak   *Prod* Islin Auster   *Scr* Bertram Millhauser   *Ph* Paul Ivano   *Ed* Arthur Hilton   *Mus* Frank Skinner   *Art Dir* John B. Goodman, Martin Obzina
● Charles Laughton, Ella Raines, Rosalind Ivan, Stanley C. Ridges (Universal)

Film is a murder mystery lacking much mystery but with all the suspense of a super-whodunnit. More than that, this production actually is a keen character study of a man whose married life has been a hell-on-earth and who sacrifices all to protect the one happiness in his middle-age, a sensible young stenographer who later becomes his wife.

In Charles Laughton's accomplished hands, this character becomes fascinating. Withal,

he makes it a typical home-loving storekeeper accustomed to the simple things in London of the gaslight era.

There is less of the bluster and none of the villainy of Laughton's previous vehicles. He gives an impeccable performance as the kindly, law-abiding citizen. Matching his deft portrayal is Ella Raines as the youthful steno he weds after his wife's demise.

■ SUSPECT

1987, 121 MINS, US ◇ Ⓥ ⊙
Dir Peter Yates   *Prod* Daniel A. Sherkow   *Scr* Eric Roth   *Ph* Billy Williams   *Ed* Ray Lovejoy   *Mus* Michael Kamen   *Art Dir* Stuart Wurtzel
● Cher, Dennis Quaid, Liam Neeson, John Mahoney, Joe Mantegna, Philip Bosco (Tri-Star)

Art imitates art – and not very well – in Peter Yates' gimmicky suspense drama sabotaged by a flimsy script full of cliches. Dennis Quaid valiantly struggles to breathe life into the matter, but comes up short when a surprise ending packs little punch because the audience knows in the first five minutes the prime suspect can't be guilty.

Cher stars as Kathleen Riley, a hard-working Washington, DC public defender unlike any ever seen before. A day before taking a long-needed vacation, she's given a defendant charged with the brutal murder of a Justice Dept staffer. Carl Wayne Anderson (Liam Neeson) has everything working against him: a Vietnam vet, he was rendered deaf and speechless by the psychological toll of the war, and he's homeless – he *has* to be innocent.

Just when it seems the entire film is going to be suffocated by liberal piety, Quaid shows up as Dairy State lobbyist Eddie Sanger, so persuasive that he's 'dangerous'. Sanger is called in for jury duty and sparks begin to fly when he faces off against Cher in the courtroom. Scenes with the two of them are the best in the film, but there aren't enough.

■ SUSPICION

1941, 102 MINS, US Ⓥ ⊙
Dir Alfred Hitchcock   *Prod* [Alfred Hitchcock]
Scr Samson Raphaelson, Joan Harrison, Alma Reville   *Ph* Harry Stradling   *Ed* William Hamilton   *Mus* Franz Waxman   *Art Dir* Van Nest Polglase, Carroll Clark
● Cary Grant, Joan Fontaine, Cedric Hardwicke, Nigel Bruce, May Whitty, Isabel Jeans (RKO)

Alfred Hitchcock's trademarked cinematic development of suspenseful drama, through mental emotions of the story principals, is vividly displayed in *Suspicion*, a class production [from the novel *Before the Fact* by Francis Iles] provided with excellence in direction, acting and mounting.

Joan Fontaine successfully transposes to the screen her innermost emotions and fears over the wastrel and apparently-murderous antics of her husband. Cary Grant, turns in a sparkling characterization as the bounder who continually discounts financial responsibilities and finally gets jammed over thefts from his employer.

Unfolded at a leisurely pace, Hitchcock deftly displays the effect of occurrences on the inner emotions of the wife. Protected girl of an English country manor, Fontaine falls in love and elopes with Grant, an impecunious and happy-go-lucky individual, who figured her family would amply provide for both of them. Deeply in love, she overlooks his monetary irresponsibilities until discovery that he has stolen a large sum from an estate, and prosecution and exposure looms.

□ 1941: Best Actress (Joan Fontaine).
□ Nominations: Best Picture, Scoring of a Dramatic Picture

SVENGALI

1931, 79 MINS, US

Dir Archie Mayo   *Scr* J.G. Alexander   *Ph* Barney McGill   *Art Dir* Anton Grot
● John Barrymore, Marian Marsh, Bramwell Fletcher, Donald Crisp, Lumsden Hare, Carmel Myers (Warner)

Formerly well known as *Trilby* via famed novel [by George Du Maurier] and stage interpretations, the studio renamed it to designate the villainous hypnotist as the leading character.

Story, of course, is well known, but Svengali (John Barrymore) here makes it clear that Trilby (Marian Marsh), the model has been the house guest of several artists so that her desire to become legally attached to the pursuing young Englishman is not going to be without family difficulties. He hypnotizes her into running away with him and also into a career as a concert star.

Barrymore's playing is interesting, sterling and in broad strokes. Marsh takes a change for the better on looks in the late footage, but flashes nothing unusual histrionically.

☐ 1930/31: Nominations: Best Cinematography, Art Direction

••••••••••••••••••••••••••••••••••

SWALLOWS AND AMAZONS

1974, 92 MINS, UK ◇ ⓥ

Dir Claude Whatham   *Prod* Richard Pilbrow   *Scr* David Wood   *Ph* Denis Lewiston   *Ed* Michael Bradsell   *Mus* Wilfred Josephs   *Art Dir* Simon Holland
● Virginia McKenna, Ronald Fraser, Brenda Bruce, Jack Woolgar, John Franklyn-Robbins, Simon West (EMI/Theatre Projects)

This charming, delightful, beautifully-made film for both adults and children is faithfully based on the 1929 children's classic by Arthur Ransome. In the deft screenplay by David Wood, the essential plot involving four children (the Swallows) on holiday in the Lake District, and their friendly rivalry with two tomboy girls (the Amazons) is simple but absorbing, and captures the spirit of the period.

Their activities take place on and around the water, with the picturesque landscape caught in pastel shades by Denis Lewiston. Virginia McKenna and Ronald Fraser are seen briefly but register well, especially Fraser as the peppery but sympathetic uncle, living on a houseboat. The main burden is carried by the child actors, who all enter into the spirit of the proceedings with naturalness and enthusiasm.

••••••••••••••••••••••••••••••••••

SWAMP THING

1982, 90 MINS, US ◇ ⓥ ⊙

Dir Wes Craven   *Prod* Benjamin Melniker, Michael E. Uslan   *Scr* Wes Craven   *Ph* Robin Goodwin   *Ed* Richard Bracken   *Mus* Harry Manfredini   *Art Dir* Robb Wilson King
● Louis Jourdan, Adrienne Barbeau, Ray Wise, David Hess, Nicholas Worth, Don Knight (United Artists)

Writer-director Wes Craven's adaptation of the DC Comics book, *Swamp Thing*, to live-action feature filming is a childish programmer, short on thrills and laughs.

Sci-fi premise has scientist Alec Holland (Ray Wise) working with his sister in a lab in the bayous on a secret government project. He's developing a vegetable cell with an animal nucleus. With a government agent Alice Cable (Adrienne Barbeau) inspecting the operation, all hell breaks loose when evil genius Arcane (Louis Jourdan) has his henchmen break in to steal the scientific formula.

The green mixture is accidentally poured on Holland who, catching fire (in pic's best special effects scene), runs off into the swamp, later emerging as a big, green dude in a rubber suit, the Swamp Thing (Dick Durock). Pic disintegrates at this point into a series of contrived chases, pitting Arcane vs.

Cable in a battle to obtain the formula and the creature.

Craven tries in vain, through old-fashioned characters and dialog, to re-create the '50s B-monster movie. The film's only asset for adult audiences is Barbeau, who is thoroughly believable and a feisty, rough 'n' tumble heroine, able to beat up most bad guys or outrun them through the swamp.

••••••••••••••••••••••••••••••••••

SWAMP WATER
(UK: The Man Who Came Back)

1941, 90 MINS, US

Dir Jean Renoir   *Prod* Irving Pichel   *Scr* Dudley Nichols   *Ph* Peverell Marley   *Ed* Walter Thompson   *Mus* David Buttolph
● Walter Brennan, Walter Huston, Anne Baxter, Dana Andrews, Virginia Gilmore, John Carradine (20th Century-Fox)

Too bad that this picture's story does not match its excellent cast. Another of the hillbilly dramas, *Swamp Water* is an unflattering reflection upon Dudley Nichols' usually facile pen. The scenarist has failed to spark Vereen Bell's *SatEvePost* serial.

French director Jean Renoir's first job for an American company, it's something less than an auspicious beginning. Giving him a story dealing with a segment of the US population with whom not even many Americans are familiar appears open to debate. The background is the Georgia swamps.

All the ingredients of an oldtime meller have been thrown into the plot. Story has Walter Brennan hiding in a swamp after escaping hanging for a murder. Dana Andrews, Huston's son by a previous marriage, finds him while searching for his dog. Brennan first threatens to kill the boy, but then convinces the kid of his innocence. They enter a fur-trapping partnership, the boy to give Brennan's share to the latter's daughter. But the lad's girl gets hep to what's going on and in a fit of jealousy, gives the secret away.

••••••••••••••••••••••••••••••••••

SWAN, THE

1956, 107 MINS, US ◇ ⓥ

Dir Charles Vidor   *Prod* Dore Schary   *Scr* John Dighton   *Ph* Joseph Ruttenberg, Robert Surtees   *Ed* John Dunning   *Mus* Bronislau Kaper
● Grace Kelly, Alec Guinness, Louis Jourdan, Agnes Moorehead, Jessie Royce Landis, Brian Aherne (M-G-M)

Delightful make-believe of Ferenc Molnar's venerable play *The Swan* makes for a genteel picture about genteel people in a never-never world of crowns, titles and luxury living. There's subtle humor and broad humor, and several scenes that reach right into the heart.

Co-starring with Grace Kelly is Alec Guinness, who adds the correct, modified comedy touch to his role of the crown prince who, regardless of what audiences might want, must end up with the princess, and Louis Jourdan, who adds a feeling romantic flavor to his character of the commoner-tutor who dares to love the princess. Kelly shines right along with her male stars as the princess.

A standout romantic sequence occurs during a ball welcoming the crown prince. The tutor and Kelly fall in love right before your eyes as they dance to 'The Swan Waltz'.

Abetting the star trio with sock support in featured roles are Jessie Royce Landis, Kelly's mother; Brian Aherne, as the monk; Estelle Winwood, the pixilated, not-bright old maid sister of Landis and Agnes Moorehead, the strident queen mother.

••••••••••••••••••••••••••••••••••

SWARM, THE

1978, 116 MINS, US ◇ ⓥ

Dir Irwin Allen   *Prod* Irwin Allen   *Scr* Stirling Silliphant   *Ph* Fred J. Koenekamp   *Ed* Harold F. Kress   *Mus* Jerry Goldsmith   *Art Dir* Stan Jolley

● Michael Caine, Katharine Ross, Richard Widmark, Richard Chamberlain, Olivia de Havilland, Ben Johnson (Warner)

Killer bees periodically interrupt the arch writing, stilted direction and ludicrous acting in Irwin Allen's disappointing and tired non-thriller.

Stirling Silliphant gets writing credit, based on an Arthur Herzog novel. It's the kind of screenplay where characters who supposedly are familiar with certain technical work spend most of their time explaining it to each other.

Then there's the sub-plot romance between schoolmarm Olivia de Havilland (with the worst phony southern accent imaginable) and either Fred MacMurray or Ben Johnson.

Michael Caine heads the cast as a scientist who must contend with killer bees as well as with Richard Widmark, once again playing one of those cardboard military officers. Lots of other familiar names crop up.

Allen was smarter on *The Towering Inferno* to have a partner handling the dramatic sequences. By the time the bees get to Houston, and the city is torched, few will care.

☐ 1978: Nomination: Best Costume Design

••••••••••••••••••••••••••••••••••

SWASHBUCKLER
(UK: The Scarlet Buccaneer)

1976, 101 MINS, US ◇ ⓥ ⊙

Dir James Goldstone   *Prod* Jennings Lang   *Scr* Jeffrey Bloom   *Ph* Philip Lathrop   *Ed* Edward A. Biery   *Mus* John Addison   *Art Dir* John Lloyd
● Robert Shaw, James Earl Jones, Peter Boyle, Genevieve Bujold, Beau Bridges, Anjelica Huston (Universal)

An uneven picture which is splotchy in the form it tries to emulate, and vacuous in the substance.

Jeffrey Bloom is given sole screenplay credit and Paul Wheeler sole story credit, for the coloring-book plot and formula characters as follows: genial lead pirates, Robert Shaw and James Earl Jones; wicked colonial governor, Peter Boyle; wronged nob_elady, Genevieve Bujold; wronged noblelady's noble father, Bernard Behrens; and foppish soldier, Beau Bridges.

There's no sincerity in *Swashbuckler*. There's not even a consistent approach. This tacky pastepot job can't make up its mind whether it is serious, tongue-in-cheek, satirical, slapstick, burlesque, parody or travesty; but be assured it's all of the above.

••••••••••••••••••••••••••••••••••

SWEENEY!

1977, 97 MINS, UK ◇ ⓥ

Dir David Wickes   *Prod* Ted Childs   *Scr* Ranald Graham   *Ph* Dusty Miller   *Ed* Chris Burt   *Mus* Denis King   *Art Dir* Bill Alexander
● John Thaw, Dennis Waterman, Barry Foster, Ian Bannen, Colin Welland, Diane Keen (Euston)

Regular TV series topliners John Thaw and Dennis Waterman as two cops drift through Ranald Graham's occasionally witty screenplay with no special flair following the unlikely storyline.

Oil and its sway on the world's political and economic situation is the plot. Ian Bannen plays a steely-eyed alcoholic government minister and easily gives the best performance of the pic, while Barry Foster, an English actor, is unconvincing as an American press agent whose accent-slip is constantly showing.

David Wickes' direction and Chris Burt's editing produce a dull package. The TV show [created by Ian Kennedy Martin] packed a certain authenticity. This theatrical version, must put the concept back into the realms of the fairy story class.

••••••••••••••••••••••••••••••••••

■ **SWEENEY 2**

1978, 108 MINS, UK ◇ ⚏

Dir Tom Clegg   *Prod* Ted Childs   *Scr* Troy Kennedy
Martin   *Ph* Dusty Miller   *Ed* Chris Burt   *Mus* Tony
Hatch   *Art Dir* Bill Alexander
● John Thaw, Dennis Waterman, Denholm Elliott,
Georgina Hale, Nigel Hawthorne, Lewis Fiander (Euston)

Sweeney 2 is excellent British cops and robbers
stuff in which a special squad of Scotland
Yard detectives ultimately crack and demolish a gang of bank robbers whose hallmarks
include goldplated shotguns. Good action
well-spaced and paced; good characterization
played with finesse; a witty script and stylish
direction all lend the production a degree of
distinction.

Thesping is good to excellent. John Thaw is
credible and appealing as the hardbitten cop
who leads the police team on the case. Also
notably fine are Denholm Elliott as a corrupt
police officer who lands in the jug, Dennis
Waterman as Thaw's number two, and
Georgina Hale as a pickup promoted by the
unattached Thaw.

■ **SWEET BIRD OF YOUTH**

1962, 120 MINS, US ◇ ⚏ ⊙

Dir Richard Brooks   *Prod* Pandro S. Berman
Scr Richard Brooks   *Ph* Milton Krasner   *Ed* Henry
Berman   *Mus* Harold Gelman (sup.)   *Art Dir* George
W. Davis, Urie McCleary
● Paul Newman, Geraldine Page, Shirley Knight, Ed
Begley, Rip Torn, Mildred Dunnock (M-G-M)

Sweet Bird of Youth is a tamer and tidied but
arresting version of Tennessee Williams'
Broadway play. It's a glossy, engrossing hunk
of motion picture entertainment, slickly produced by Berman.

In altering the playwright's Dixie climax
(castration of the hero) Brooks has slightly
weakened the story by damaging character
consistency and emotional momentum. But
he has accomplished this revision as if winking his creative eye at the 'in' audience.

Four members of the original Broadway
cast re-create their roles: Newman, Page,
Torn and Sherwood. Newman brings thrust
and vitality to the role, but has some overly-
mannered moments that distract.

But this is Page's picture. She draws the
best, wittiest and most acid lines and the
most colorful character and what she does
with this parley is a lesson in the art of acting. Her portrayal of the fading actress seeking substitute reality in drink, sex and what
have you to offer is a histrionic classic. Shirley
Knight is sympathetic and attractive as the
distraught daughter of a corrupt political
boss, and Ed Begley is outstanding in a perceptive portrayal of the latter.
□ 1962: Best Supp. Actor (Ed Begley).
□ Nominations: Best Actress (Geraldine
Page), Supp. Actress (Shirley Knight)

■ **SWEET CHARITY**

1969, 148 MINS, US ◇ ⚏ ⊙

Dir Bob Fosse   *Prod* Robert Arthur   *Scr* Peter Stone
Ph Robert Surtees   *Ed* Stuart Gilmore   *Mus* Cy Coleman
Art Dir Alexander Golitzen, George C. Webb
● Shirley MacLaine, John McMartin, Ricardo
Montalban, Sammy Davis Jr, Chita Rivera, Paula Kelly
(Universal)

Sweet Charity is, in short, a terrific musical
film. Based on the 1966 legituner, extremely
handsome and plush production accomplishes
everything it sets out to do.

Elements of comedy, drama, pathos and
hope blend superbly with sure fire entertainment values, stylishly and maturely planned
and executed.

The story involves a gullible woman, of relatively low station in life, who refuses to believe that tomorrow does not hold a promise

of happiness. [Pic was made available with
both 'sad' and 'happy' endings.]

Shirley MacLaine is a dance-hall hostess
who, at the outset, has just been sloughed off
by a gigolo. An accidental encounter with an
Italian screen idol, played superbly by
Ricardo Montalban, precedes a blossoming
romance with John McMartin.

MacLaine's unique talents as a comic tragedienne are set off to maximum impact.

The film strikes the correct balance between escapist fantasy and hard reality.
MacLaine's working environment is sleazy,
but romantic adventures occur in believable
settings – a lavish apartment, a street, a
rooftop, a restaurant, a discotheque.

Fosse's staging of the musical numbers is
outstanding. Atop his remembered style is a
brilliant, film-oriented appreciation of the
emphasis possible only with camera and
movieola.
□ 1969: Nominations: Best Costume Design,
Art Direction, Adapted Musical Score

■ **SWEET DREAMS**

1985, 115 MINS, US ◇ ⚏ ⊙

Dir Karel Reisz   *Prod* Bernard Schwartz, Charles
Mulvehill   *Scr* Robert Getchell   *Ph* Robbie Greenberg
Ed Malcolm Cooke   *Mus* Charles Gross   *Art Dir* Albert
Brenner
● Jessica Lange, Ed Harris, Ann Wedgeworth, David
Clennon, James Staley, Gary Basabara (HBO/Silver
Screen)

Clearly the coal miner's daughter's cousin by
both birthright and ambition, *Sweet Dreams*
upholds the family honor quite well, with
Jessica Lange's portrayal of country singer
Patsy Cline certainly equal to Sissy Spacek's
Oscar-winning recreation of Loretta Lynn.

The film slants Cline's biography toward romance as likeable redneck Harris meets
Lange at a roadside inn and their initially
blissful marriage tackles the rough, upward
climb to stardom, with many a shabby waystop. Apart from the deftly interwoven
singing sequences, most of Cline's career
takes place off-camera.

Instead, *Dreams* deals with what could have
been any marriage of its time and place: an
ambitious, independent wife – a bit too sassy
and sharp-tongued at times – versus an essentially loving working stiff, whose macho insecurities inspire him to too much booze, a
little infidelity and boorish brutality.
□ 1985: Nomination: Best Actress (Jessica
Lange)

■ **SWEET HUNTERS**

1969, 115 MINS, PANAMA [FRANCE] ◇

Dir Ruy Guerra   *Prod* Claude Giroux   *Scr* Ruy Guerra,
Philippe Dumarcay, Gerard Zinzz   *Ph* Ricardo
Arnonovitch   *Ed* Kenout Peltier   *Art Dir* Bernard Evein
● Sterling Hayden, Maureen McNalley, Susan
Strasberg, Stuart Whitman, Andrew Hayden (General)

A moody, brooding tale of a growingly alienated family on an isolated island whose actions are catalyzed by the news that an
escaped prisoner could be heading for the
isle. Pic tries for interior landscapes to be reflected by the bleak natural surroundings but
falters between romantic mannerism and lit-
erary-hued melodrama.

Film does have stunning lensing and visual
intensity and some good acting. But direction
has a tendency to linger too lovingly on isolated scenes.

Maureen McNalley plays the wife with chilling lassitude. Her husband is played by
Sterling Hayden who seems so taken by his
interest in migrating birds that when he
finds his wife with the prisoner he can only
talk about the birds to the exhausted, dying
man.

[Though carrying a Panamanian tag, pic
was made by Claude Giroux's company, entirely in France.]

■ **SWEETIE**

1989, 97 MINS, AUSTRALIA ◇ ⚏ ⊙

Dir Jane Campion   *Prod* John Maynard, William
MacKinnon   *Scr* Jane Campion, Gerard Lee   *Ph* Sally
Bongers   *Ed* Veronika Haussler   *Mus* Martin Armiger
Art Dir Peter Harris
● Genevieve Lemon, Karen Colston, Tom Lycos, Jon
Darling, Dorothy Barry (Arenafilm)

Sweetie is an original, audacious tragicomedy
about two sisters, one who's afraid of trees
but believes in fortune tellers, the other who's
plump and plain and eager to make her mark
in showbiz.

At the beginning, focus is on Kay (Karen
Colston) who works in an undefined factory in
the inner city. She becomes convinced that a
man described by a fortune teller as the man
of her life is Louis (Tom Lycos), who just became engaged to a workmate. Kay sets about
seducing him (in the factory parking lot) and
before long they're living together in a rundown house in an unfashionable part of town.

Enter Dawn (Genevieve Lemon), known as
Sweetie, Kay's sister, who with her drugged-
out boyfriend Bob (Michael Lake) simply
breaks into the house and moves into the
spare room.

Genevieve Lemon is so good as the overweight, slow-witted Sweetie that her part
seems too small. Karen Colston is fine as the
sensitive, constantly nervous Kay. As
Sweetie's tacky, somnolent boyfriend,
Michael Lake steals his scenes.

■ **SWEET LIBERTY**

1986, 107 MINS, US ◇ ⚏ ⊙

Dir Alan Alda   *Prod* Martin Bregman   *Scr* Alan Alda
Ph Frank Tidy   *Ed* Michael Economou   *Mus* Bruce
Broughton   *Art Dir* Ben Edwards
● Alan Alda, Michael Caine, Michelle Pfeiffer, Bob
Hoskins, Lise Hilboldt, Lillian Gish (Universal)

Comedic potential is too rarely realized in
this story of a college professor who watches
filming of his historical tome become bas-
tardized by Hollywood into a lusty romp.

Playing their true ages are Alan Alda as college professor Michael Burgess who teaches
history of the American Revolution, and
Michael Caine as boxoffice draw Elliot James.

When the film company arrives on location
in bucolic Sayeville, Alda falls for leading lady
Faith Healy (Michelle Pfeiffer), at the same
time stringing along girlfriend Gretchen
Carlsen (Lise Hilboldt).

The Hollywood cast and crew look and act
the part, notably the macho stuntmen out to
strut their stuff, as do the townsfolk who appear eager to do something other than endure another stifling Southern summer.

■ **SWEET MOVIE**

1974, 99 MINS, FRANCE/CANADA ◇ ⚏

Dir Dusan Makevejev   *Scr* Dusan Makevejev   *Ph* Pierre
Lhomme   *Ed* Yann Dedet   *Mus* Manos Hadjidakis
● Carole Laure, Pierre Clementi, Anna Pruchnal, Sami
Frey, Jane Mallet, John Vernon (VM/Mojack)

Sweet Movie is literally sweet, with lovemaking
in a bed of sugar and a girl being bathed in
chocolate for advertising purposes. But it also
has an underpinning of scatology and a zany
look at sensuality. Neither hard nor softcore.
Yugoslav filmmaker Dusan Makevejev's first
pic in the West, is provocative but also arbitrary.

It begins as broad funny satire on the richest man in the world looking for a virgin to
marry and then goes into the girl's hegira as
she finds personal sensual liberation with a

revolutionary type woman who plows the rivers in a boat called Survival with a giant head of Karl Marx on its prow.

The virgin, played with winsome innocence and then phlegmatism and eventual awakening by Carole Laure, finds her rich husband has a golden phallus.

••••••••••••••••••••••••••••••••

■ **SWEET NOVEMBER**

1968, 114 MINS, US ◇
Dir Robert Ellis   *Prod* Jerry Gershwin, Elliott Kastner
Scr Herman Raucher   *Ph* Daniel L. Fapp   *Ed* James Heckett   *Mus* Michael Legrand   *Art Dir* John Lloyd
● Sandy Dennis, Anthony Newley, Theodore Bikel, Burr DeBenning, Sandy Baron, Marj Dusay (Warner/Seven Arts)

Sweet November is a love story with a charming, almost fragile and slightly nebulous premise.

Sandy Dennis and Anthony Newley are the stars and each is outstanding in a strongly characterized role. They are called upon to engage in what some may regard as an overabundance of dialog, which lends more an aspect of a stage play than a motion picture, but this fits the mood and the tenor of the plot. Plot itself, which deals with a quixotic Brooklyn girl, is curiously motivated but interesting in its fulfillment.

Herman Raucher's original screenplay focuses on the girl who takes to her heart – and her flat – for a month at a time some man with a problem. In doing so, she seeks to ease her own troubles, which may mean the end of her life at any time, but the man always leaves her as a changed human being.

Dennis is delightful in role of the kindly femme and Newley shades his performance with subtle comedy.

••••••••••••••••••••••••••••••••

■ **SWEET REVENGE**

1990, 93 MINS, US/FRANCE ◇ ▼
Dir Charlotte Brandstrom   *Prod* Monique Annaud
Scr Janet Bromwell   *Ph* Olivier Gueneau   *Ed* Marie-Sophie Gally   *Mus* Didier Vasseur   *Art Dir* Francoise Benoit-Fresco
● Rosanna Arquette, Carrie Fisher, John Sessions, Francois Eric Gendron, Myriam Moszko, John Hargreaves (Chrysalide/Canal Plus)

Sweet Revenge is a stab at old-fashioned screwball romantic comedy that comes off only half-heartedly because Americanized Swedish-French helmer Charlotte Brandstrom works from a screenplay that relies on squeaky contrivances in every twist of its convoluted plot.

Carrie Fisher plays Linda Michaels, a Paris-based corporation lawyer, who pays out-of-work actress Kate Williams (Rosanna Arquette) to trap her ex-husband John (England's dark and curly-headed John Sessions), a struggling writer, into a mock marriage so that Linda can get out of paying him the alimony awarded him. The actress and the writer, of course, fall in real love right away.

Sweet Revenge has a neat production dress but uses the attractions of its Paris locations in a distracted way. Romance, in other words, is served up pretty cold throughout although Arquette and Sessions do kindle a flickering flame convincingly for a few moments.

••••••••••••••••••••••••••••••••

■ **SWEET RIDE, THE**

1968, 111 MINS, US ◇
Dir Harvey Hart   *Prod* Joe Pasternak   *Scr* Tom Mankiewicz   *Ph* Robert B. Hauser   *Ed* Philip W. Anderson   *Mus* Pete Rugolo   *Art Dir* Jack Martin Smith, Richard Day
● Anthony Franciosa, Michael Sarrazin, Jacqueline Bisset, Bob Denver, Michael Wilding, Michael Carey (20th Century-Fox)

The Sweet Ride could sum up as *Hell's Angels' Bikini Beach Party in Valley of the Dolls near Peyton Place.* Though well-mounted and inter-

esting in the spotlighting of Michael Sarrazin and Jacqueline Bisset, overall result is a flat programmer, with ragged scripting, papier mache characters and routine direction.

Tony Franciosa is a beach-bum tennis hustler who is a sort of god to Malibu pad-mates Sarrazin and draft-dodging musician Bob Denver. Their life is a ball, we are told, interrupted only by neighbor Lloyd Gough, who keeps yelling about the decline of morals.

Enter Bisset, who has a running, masochistic affair with producer Warren Stevens. She takes to Sarrazin, though Charles Dierkop, a recurring motorcycle bum, gets an inordinate amount of attention from Bisset.

William Murray's novel has been adapted by Tom Mankiewicz into a contrived, unbelievable script about the Malibu-Hollywood young set, which supposedly 'tells it like it is.' It succeeds both in talking down to young people, and talking up to older folks.

••••••••••••••••••••••••••••••••

■ **SWEET SMELL OF SUCCESS**

1957, 96 MINS, US ▼ ⊙
Dir Alexander Mackendrick   *Prod* James Hill
Scr Clifford Odets, Ernest Lehman   *Ph* James Wong Howe   *Ed* Alan Crosland Jr   *Mus* Elmer Bernstein
Art Dir Edward Carrere
● Burt Lancaster, Tony Curtis, Susan Harrison, Marty Milner, Sam Levene, Barbara Nichols (Norma-Curtleigh/United Artists)

James Hill's production, locationed in Manhattan, captures the feel of Broadway and environs after dark. It's a no-holds-barred account of the sadistic fourth estater played cunningly by Burt Lancaster [from the novelette *Tell Me About It* by Ernest Lehman].

Failure to comply with his wishes means a broken career. Breaks in his column sustain the pressagent but for the mentions there are certain favors to be granted. To the p.a., the columnist's dictates are law; if the favors include framing a young musician on a narcotics rap, that's all right, too.

Flaw in *Success* concerns the newspaperman's devotion to his sister. It's not clear why he rebels at her courtship with a guitarist, who appears to be a nice kid.

Tony Curtis as the time-serving publicist comes through with an interesting performance, although somehow the character he plays is not quite all the heel as written.

Susan Harrison is 'introduced' in the picture and comes off well as the sister. She has a fetching beauty and shows easiness in handling the assignment.

••••••••••••••••••••••••••••••••

■ **SWEET WILLIAM**

1980, 92 MINS, UK ◇ ▼
Dir Claude Whatham   *Prod* Jeremy Watt, Don Boyd
Scr Beryl Bainbridge   *Ph* Les Young   *Ed* Peter Coulson
Art Dir Eileen Diss
● Sam Waterston, Jenny Agutter, Anna Massey, Tim Pigott-Smith, Geraldine James, Arthur Lowe (Kendon)

Nice, ordinary English girl Jenny Agutter meets wild, charming Scots divorcee Sam Waterston. Sadly for her – though the tone is never more than just slightly bitter-sweet – his romantic nature includes having a wildly on-off relationship with the truth. He's a wolf with two not-so-ex-wives, and a compulsion to bed down her friends, neighbors and anything else he sees move.

Adapted from her own novel by Beryl Bainbridge, the screenplay is diligent without being distinguished. The same goes for Claude Whatham's direction, which tends to prefer lingering realism to dramatic pace, and thus to set up apparent significance where there is none.

Agutter is well cast, and good in that her seduction by the outlandish Waterston is entirely believable.

••••••••••••••••••••••••••••••••

■ **SWIMMER, THE**

1968, 94 MINS, US ◇ ▼ ⊙
Dir Frank Perry   *Prod* Frank Perry, Roger Lewis
Scr Eleanor Perry   *Ph* David L. Quaid, Michael Nebbia
Ed Sidney Katz, Carl Lerner, Pat Somerset   *Mus* Marvin Hamlisch   *Art Dir* Peter Dohanos
● Burt Lancaster, Janet Landgard, Janice Rule, Diana Van Der Vlis, Tony Bickley, Joan Rivers (Columbia/Horizon-Dover)

Burt Lancaster stars as a suburban bum who, in retracing his steps from pool to pool, illuminates the causes of his downfall. The stylized, episodic, moody film, based on John Cheever's dramatic fantasy, is something of a minor triumph in collaborative filmmaking.

Lancaster, in swim trunks throughout, pops up on a sunny Sunday morning at a suburban poolside, miles away from his house, and decides to 'swim' home by visiting at each neighbor's house. Each self-contained sequence adds indirect light to Lancaster himself; he is compulsively gregarious, compulsively youthful, compulsively sexual, compulsively self-deluded. Film is the story of a moral hangover, with the sobered-up bewildered man retracing his steps to see what he has done.

Without detailing the large cast, suffice it to say that performances, direction and writing hit the target. Lancaster emerges with a strong achievement, that of a pitiable middle-aged Joe College.

••••••••••••••••••••••••••••••••

■ **SWIMMING TO CAMBODIA**

1987, 87 MINS, US ◇ ▼ ⊙
Dir Jonathan Demme   *Prod* R.A. Shafransky
Scr Spalding Gray   *Ph* John Bailey   *Ed* Carol Littleton
Mus Laurie Anderson   *Art Dir* Sandy McLeod
● Spalding Gray (Demme)

Witnessed in its original SoHo incarnation as a staged monolog, Spalding Gray's free- associating recollection of his experiences in Thailand during the making of *The Killing Fields* had an exhilarating immediacy which is mostly absent in this compressed filmed performance of *Swimming to Cambodia.*

Addressing an audience from a seat at a bare table, the emotionally expansive, anti-heroic raconteur skillfully fosters an illusion of spontaneous, confessional intimacy.

Recreating a dislocating culture-shocked odyssey that takes him from the surreal flesh-pots of Bangkok to a nearly suicidal quest for a 'perfect moment' at a spectacularly paradisical Thai beach, Gray elicits compassion and universal recognition for his serio-comic search for self.

••••••••••••••••••••••••••••••••

■ **SWINGER, THE**

1966, 81 MINS, US ◇
Dir George Sidney   *Prod* George Sidney   *Scr* Lawrence Roman   *Ph* Joseph Biroc   *Ed* Frank Santillo
Mus Marty Paich   *Art Dir* Hal Pereira, Walter Tyler
● Ann-Margret, Anthony Franciosa, Robert Coote, Yvonne Romain, Horace McMahon, Nydia Westman (Paramount)

The Swinger is a very amusing original screen comedy which satirizes nudie books and magazines. The colorful, tuneful George Sidney production utilizes outstanding post-production skills to enhance impact of hip scripting and good performances.

Ann-Margret's best screen work derives from Sidney's direction, which herein spotlights her singing-dancing talents. She is an aspiring mag writer who, unable to sell straight material, fakes her autobiog in the form of a mish-mash of lurid paperback plots. Tony Franciosa, the editor, swallows the bait and tries to reform her, while nudie mag publisher Robert Coote seeks to exploit the gal.

A two-minute terp scene by Ann-Margret, to a rhythmic title tune by Andre and Dory

Previn, precedes main title. Pic then opens with a hilarious tour of L.A., featuring non-sequitur narration by Coote to some jazzy picture editing. David Winters choreographed the terp sequences, one of which is a rather sexy bit in which Ann-Margret, in a fake orgy, rolls about on canvas with her body covered with paint.

• •

■ SWING HIGH, SWING LOW

1937, 92 MINS, US ⓥ

Dir Mitchell Leisen   *Prod* Arthur Hornblow Jr
Scr Virginia Van Upp, Oscar Hammerstein II   *Ph* Ted Tetzlaff   *Ed* Eda Warren   *Mus* Boris Morros (dir.)
● Carole Lombard, Fred MacMurray, Charles Butterworth, Jean Dixon, Dorothy Lamour, Franklyn Pangborn (Paramount)

Swing High, Swing Low is a switch on the old George Manker Watters-Arthur Hopkins play, *Burlesque*. Instead of the burlesque comic, Skid Johnson, of the putty-nose, whom the late Hal Skelly glorified in the Broadway original and in the first filmization (called *Dance of Life*, 1929), the switch to a Panama honky-tonk and a class NY cafe is as ultramodern as the sweet-hot trumpeting which is the keynote of Fred MacMurray's expert performance.

As an ex-Canal Zone soldier who can toot a mean horn, which carries him from Mama Murphy's Panama joint to the Hollywood version of an El Morocco type of class place, MacMurray, ably foiled by Carole Lombard, does much to sustain a story, which, in spots, looms as a bit dated.

Sagas about kings of the nite clubs who, when they start to skid, go down fast, have become a bit familiar, as has also the basic triangle situation when MacMurray goes the whoopee route and Lombard ultimately comes back to resurrect him from the sloughs. However, expert trouping by both more than sustains the story requirements.

MacMurray's off-screen hot lips are two boys from Victor Young's band, Frank Zinziv and William Candreva, and their triple-tongue and other horn intricacies are somethin'! Young with Phil Boutelje, of the Par musical corps, does an expert job on the arrangements.

• •

■ SWING KIDS

1993, 112 MINS, US ◇ ⓥ

Dir Thomas Carter   *Prod* Mark Gordon, John Bard Manulus   *Scr* Jonathan Marc Feldman   *Ph* Jerzy Zielinski   *Ed* Michael R. Miller   *Mus* James Horner
Art Dir Allan Cameron
● Robert Sean Leonard, Christian Bale, Frank Whaley, Barbara Hershey, Kenneth Branagh, Tushka Bergen (Hollywood Pictures)

A fascinating footnote to WWII Nazi Germany is trivialized and sanitized in this odd concoction of music and politics.

Screenplay plays fast and loose with historical fact and chronology as it chronicles the development of a trio of young men whose passion for such American pop music favorites as Benny Goodman, Artie Shaw and Count Basie puts them in the unusual dilemma of embracing officially forbidden 'decadent art.'

Peter's (Robert Sean Leonard) situation provides the narrative line. His family lives under a cloud of suspicion only relieved by the intervention of a seemingly generous SS official (an uncredited Kenneth Branagh) who has romantic intentions on Peter's mother (Barbara Hershey).

The more upwardly mobile Thomas (Christian Bale) finds his musical ardor dampened after joining the Hitler Youth. Initially, he signs up to pal around with Peter (who was forced to join after committing a petty crime), but Thomas soon gives way to

total conformity. The third, the physically crippled Arvid (Frank Whaley), remains unrepentant: the least capable of standing against the tide, he is the fiercest in devotion to jazz.

• •

■ SWING SHIFT

1984, 100 MINS, US ◇ ⓥ ⊙

Dir Jonathan Demme   *Prod* Jerry Bick   *Scr* Rob Morton [= Ron Nyswaner, Bo Goldman, Nancy Dowd, Robert Towne]   *Ph* Tak Fujimoto   *Ed* Craig McKay
Mus Patrick Williams   *Art Dir* Peter Jamison
● Goldie Hawn, Kurt Russell, Christine Lahti, Fred Ward, Ed Harris, Holly Hunter (Lantana/Warner)

With all the heartwarming heroics to choose from on the homefront in World War II, *Swing Shift* tries instead to twist some consequence out of a tawdry adulterous tryst by a couple of self-centered sneaks. But the writing and acting are too flat for the challenge.

Goldie Hawn and Ed Harris are your basic nice young couple living modestly in a Santa Monica cottage until Pearl Harbor demands he immediately volunteer. Hawn fretfully sees him off to war and somewhat timidly goes to work at an aircraft factory where she draws the immediate romantic interest of Kurt Russell.

Bearded by Hawn's neighbor/coworker Christine Lahti, the lovers spend the war having loads of fun, dancing, smooching, bedding and riding with the top down.

But Harris eventually comes home for a happy ending.
□ 1984: Nomination: Best Supp. Actress (Christine Lahti)

• •

■ SWING TIME

1936, 103 MINS, US ⓥ ⊙

Dir George Stevens   *Prod* Pandro S. Berman
Scr Howard Lindsay, Allan Scott   *Ph* David Abel
Ed Henry Berman   *Mus* Nathaniel Shilkret (dir.)
Art Dir Van Nest Polglase, Carroll Clark
● Fred Astaire, Ginger Rogers, Victor Moore, Helen Broderick, Eric Blore, Betty Furness (RKO)

Swing Time is another winner for the Fred Astaire-Ginger Rogers combo. It's smart, modern, and impressive in every respect, from its boy-loses-girl background to its tunefulness, dancipation, production quality and general high standards.

There are six Jerome Kern tunes (Dorothy Fields' clever lyrics don't retard the motivation, either) and while perhaps a bit more sprightly in general tenor than the quasi-operetta score of Kern's previous *Roberta* (1935) for the same team, the tunes as usual have substance and quality.

'The Way You Look Tonight' is the ballad outstander, although not over-plugged and first introduced in her boudoir after Astaire and his pop (Victor Moore) are shown picketing Ginger Rogers and Helen Broderick's rooms as being 'unfair' to them.

Finale number, after the pash maestro (Georges Metaxa) seemingly breaks up the romance, is 'Never Gonna Dance', perhaps the best tune of the score, with its sweet-swing tempo.

This is George Stevens' first directorial chore for Astaire-Rogers and also his first film musical on the RKO lot. Young megger (nephew of Ashton Stevens, the Chicago dramatic critic) does a highly competent job considering everything. He's also credited for suggesting the *Swing Time* title which Astaire's personal endorsement finally clinched after *Never Gonna Dance* was agreed upon, more or less officially, as the release title.
□ 1936: Best Song ('The Way You Look Tonight').
□ Nomination: Best Dance Direction ('Bo Jangles')

• •

■ SWISS FAMILY ROBINSON

1960, 126 MINS, US ◇ ⓥ ⊙

Dir Ken Annakin   *Prod* Bill Anderson   *Scr* Lowell S. Hawley   *Ph* Harry Waxman   *Ed* Peter Boita
Mus William Alwyn   *Art Dir* John Howell
● John Mills, Dorothy McGuire, James MacArthur, Janet Munro, Sessue Hayakawa, Cecil Parker (Walt Disney)

The rather modest 1813 Johann Wyss tale has been blown up to prodigious proportions. The essence and the spirit of the simple, intriguing story of a marvelously industrious family is all but snuffed out, only spasmodically flickering through the ponderous approach.

The Robinson family seems to be enjoying a standard of living that would be the envy of an average modern family. Their famous tree house is almost outrageously comfortable (running water, no less), and seems to pop up overnight with virtually no effort. In fact, the element of time and realistic effort, so vital to the overall perspective, is consistently vague in this version. It seems to bbe happening in a matter of days, not decades. The climactic scrape with a band of Oriental buccaneers is the crushing blow to any semblance of credulity.

Photographically, it isa striking achievement. Through Harry Waxman's lens have been captured some compelling views of Tobago island in the West Indies. Several sequences have a heap of genuine excitement, particularly the opening raft scene in which the family battles treacherous ocean currents to get from wrecked ship to island. These aspects add excitement and interest but don't make up for the all-important loss of the story's basic values. The acting is generally capable, but hardly memorable.

• •

■ SWITCH

1991, 103 MINS, US ◇ ⓥ ⊙

Dir Blake Edwards   *Prod* Tony Adams   *Scr* Blake Edwards   *Ph* Dick Bush   *Ed* Robert Pergament
Mus Henry Mancini   *Art Dir* Roger Maus
● Ellen Barkin, Jimmy Smits, JoBeth Williams, Lorraine Bracco, Tony Roberts, Lysette Anthony (HBO/Cinema Plus)

Switch is a faint-hearted sex comedy that doesn't have the courage of its initially provocative convictions. Undemanding audiences will get a few laughs from the notion of a man parading around in Ellen Barkin's body. Ladykiller Steve Brooks (Perry King) accepts an invitation for a hot tub frolic with three of his old girlfriends, only to be murdered by them for his innumerable emotional crimes against women over the years. Steve is given a chance to escape a fiery fate by returning to Earth and finding just one woman who genuinely likes him. Only catch is that he will henceforth inhabit the body of a woman, and that of an uncommonly sexy one.

Masquerading as the disappeared man's long-lost half-sister, 'Amanda' manages to hold on to Steve's old job at a high-powered ad agency, hangs out with Steve's best friend Jimmy Smits and intimidates the murder ringleader, JoBeth Williams, into assisting her in dressing.

Things look like they'll shift into high gear when Amanda meets cosmetics queen Lorraine Bracco, a lesbian, and decides to seduce her into transferring her big account to the agency. Unfortunately, pic chickens out from this point on, to dismaying ends.

Barkin is clearly game for anything the director wants her to do, including extensive physical clowning, but mugs and overdoes the grimacing and macho posturing. Smits and Bracco are smooth enough.

• •

■ SWITCHING CHANNELS

1988, 105 MINS, US ◇ ⓥ ⊙

Dir Ted Kotcheff   *Prod* Martin Ransohoff   *Scr* Jonathan Reynolds   *Ph* Francois Protat   *Ed* Thom Noble
Mus Michel Legrand   *Art Dir* Anne Pritchard

● Kathleen Turner, Burt Reynolds, Christopher Reeve, Ned Beatty, Henry Gibson, Al Waxman (Tri-Star)

Switching Channels is a broad, sometimes silly transfer of *The Front Page* or, more specifically, *His Girl Friday*, from the old world of smoke-filled newspaper offices to the gleaming modern setting of a satellite TV news station. This is the least distinguished rendition of the classic Ben Hecht-Charles MacArthur piece on record.

Ace anchor-woman Kathleen Turner leaves Chicago for a much-needed Canadian vacation and is swept off her feet by the dashing and obscenely rich Christopher Reeve. Upon her return, Turner announces to her crafty, manipulative boss (Burt Reynolds) that she is through with the news game and intends to settle down in New York with her new love.

Reynolds also is her ex-husband and, though he'd never admit it, still is in love with her, so he launches into a frantic campaign to keep her on the station. As in *The Front Page*, this involves her in covering the scheduled execution of a hapless man, played in a nice touch by Henry Gibson, who escapes just as his electrocution is about to be covered live.

Reynolds is good at his part's sardonic insincerity, but isn't really intimidating. Reeve comes off as the last word in confident swank in the seduction scenes. Unfortunately, he turns into a wimp almost from the moment he meets Reynolds, making it no contest. Turner suits her superstar news-hen role to a T.

Lensed mostly in Toronto, production looks a little thin around the edges and makes the setting, Chicago, look more like a suburb than a metropolis.

■ SWOON

1992, 90 MINS, US ◊ ⓥ

Dir Tom Kalin   *Prod* Christine Vachon
Hilton Als   *Ph* Ellen Kuras   *Ed* Tom Kalin   *Mus* James
Bennett   *Art Dir* Therese Deprez
● Daniel Schlachet, Craig Chester, Ron Vawter, Michael Kirby, Michael Stumm (Intolerance)

A dramatization of the 1924 Leopold and Loeb murder case unlike any before it, *Swoon* is a studied, ultra-arty look at a notorious crime as seen through a thick filter of sexual politics.

Sensational story revolves around Nathan Leopold Jr. and Richard Loeb, two wealthy, brilliant, Jewish teenage lovers whose crime spree culminated in the murder of a kidnaped boy in their native Chicago. Having left behind a trail of evidence, pair was quickly caught and later convicted in a massively publicized trial. Tale previously inspired Alfred Hitchcock's *Rope* and Richard Fleischer's *Compulsion*.

Tom Kalin, in his first feature after making short films and videos, has taken another tack entirely, one specifically informed by gay politics, essentially equating gayness with outlaw status in a hostile society. Kalin mixes in archival footage with his staged material and has used actual texts (diary entries, court-room testimony and the like) for a substantial portion of the script.

■ SWORD AND THE SORCERER, THE

1982, 100 MINS, US ◊ ⓥ ⊙

Dir Albert Pyun   *Prod* Brandon Chase, Marianne Chase, Tom Karnowski,   *Scr* Albert Pyun, Tom Karnowski, John Stuckmeyer   *Ph* Joseph Mangine   *Ed* Marshall Harvey
Mus David Whitaker   *Art Dir* George Costello
● Lee Horsley, Kathleen Beller, Simon MacCorkindale, George Maharis, Richard Lynch, Nina Van Pallandt (Chase)

Combine beaucoup gore and an atrocity-a-minute action edited in fastpace style. Then, toss in a scantily clad cast of none-too-talented performers mouthing dimwitted dialog and garnish with a touch of medieval gibberish. The result would be something resembling *The Sword and the Sorcerer*.

The plot is needlessly complicated by a truly lackluster script. Stripped to essentials, which the cast often does in this pseudo epic, *Sword* is about the retaking by a group of rag-tag medievalists of a once peaceable kingdom sadistically ruled by an evil knight named Cromwell.

Lee Horsley grins a lot as the leader of the rebels, who turns out to be the long-banished son of the old and virtuous king. Simon MacCorkindale grimaces a good deal as a royal pretender.

For trivia fans, Nina Van Pallandt plays the good queen who's dispatched quickly and mercifully since her performance is nothing to boast of.

■ SWORD OF LANCELOT

See: *Lancelot and Guinevere*

■ SYLVIA

1965, 115 MINS, US

Dir Gordon Douglas   *Prod* Martin H. Poll   *Scr* Sydney Boehm   *Ph* Joseph Ruttenberg   *Ed* Frank Bracht
Mus David Raksin   *Art Dir* Hal Pereira, Roland Anderson
● Carroll Baker, George Maharis, Joanne Dru, Peter Lawford, Viveca Lindfors, Edmond O'Brien (Paramount)

Sylvia is the story of a prostitute who turns to decency. The production is episodic until its closing reels, covering a period of 14 to 15 years as a private investigator digs into her obscure past to learn who she really is; consequently, considerable dramatic impact is lost due to film's rambling flashback treatment.

Carroll Baker is joined in stellar spot by George Maharis as the private eye who ultimately falls in love with the woman he is tracing. Actually, although hers is the motivating character, top honours go to Maharis for a consistently restrained performance that builds, while actress suffers somewhat from the spotty nature of her haphazard part.

Under Gordon Douglas' telling direction of Sydney Boehm's screenplay based on the E.V. Cunningham novel, sequences limning title character's part are generally individually strongly etched.

Ann Sothern is a definite standout; Viveca Lindfors likewise scores as a Pittsburgh librarian.

■ SYLVIA SCARLETT

1936, 90 MINS, US ⓥ ⊙

Dir George Cukor   *Prod* Pandro S. Berman   *Scr* Gladys Unger, John Collier, Mortimer Offner   *Ph* Joseph August
Ed Jane Loring   *Mus* Roy Webb
● Katharine Hepburn, Cary Grant, Brian Aherne, Edmund Gwenn, Natalie Paley, Dennie Moore (Radio)

Silvia Scarlett is puzzling in its tangents and sudden jumps, plus the almost poetic lines that are given to Katharine Hepburn. At moments the film [from the novel by Compton MacKenzie] skirts the border of absurdity.

Mistake seems to have been in not sticking to a broad vein of comedy. In the serious passages, notably the half-crazy jealousy of the father (Edmund Gwenn) for his young and helter-skelter wife (Dennie Moore) there is little preparation in the audience's mind for anything so serious as a suicide.

Perhaps it is not valid to ask whether anybody would really fail to suspect the true sex of such a boy as Hepburn looks and acts. But while carrying this off well enough, she shines brightest and is most likeable in the transition into womanhood inspired by her meeting with an artist (Brian Aherne).

Cary Grant, doing a petty English crook with a Soho accent, practically steals the picture. This is especially true in the earlier sequences. A scene in an English mansion to which Hepburn, Grant and Gwenn have gone for purposes of robbery is dominated by Grant.

The picture is half-whimsical, almost allegorical, and with the last half having a dream-worldish element that's hard to define, and equally hard to understand.

■ SYMPHONY OF SIX MILLION

(UK: *Melody of Life*)

1932, 92 MINS, US

Dir Gregory La Cava   *Prod* David O. Selznick, Pandro S. Berman   *Scr* Bernard Schubert, J. Walter Ruben, James Seymour   *Ph* Leo Tover   *Ed* Archie Marshek
Mus Max Steiner   *Art Dir* Carroll Clark
● Irene Dunne, Ricardo Cortez, Gregory Ratoff, Anna Appel, Lita Chevret, Noel Madison (RKO)

This is a story [by Fannie Hurst] of a brilliant Jewish surgeon who loses his nerve when his family virtually forces him to operate on his father for a brain tumor. The father dies on the table and the boy goes to pieces, vowing he will never touch an instrument again. His faith in himself is restored when he successfully performs a delicate spinal operation on the girl he loves. She has deliberately endangered her own life to force him to action.

It is an all-Jewish film which could have stood more attention as to racial contrasts for general appeal. Only now and then do the characters become human, but all have at least one fine moment of sincerity. Gregory Ratoff gets his big chance in the scene of the redemption of the firstborn. Anna Appel, as the mother, gets her scene early in the play when she persuades her son to move uptown to a fashionable practice and wealth.

Ricardo Cortez is generally good as the young surgeon. Irene Dunne is meaningless, appearing but seldom and then always in forced and unreal situations.

■ SYNANON

(UK: *Get off My Back*)

1965, 105 MINS, US

Dir Richard Quine   *Prod* Richard Quine   *Scr* Ian Bernard, S. Lee Pogostin   *Ph* Harry Stradling   *Ed* David Wages   *Mus* Neal Hefti
● Edmond O'Brien, Chuck Connors, Stella Stevens, Alex Cord, Richard Conte, Eartha Kitt (Columbia)

Synanon is a fictionized semi-documentary of a rehabilitation home for drug addicts on the beachfront of Santa Monica, Calif, where almost miraculous cures are said to be achieved. As backdrop for a dramatic story it is grim, hard-hitting and sometimes shocking.

Producer-director Richard Quine moved his cameras to the actual locale to ensure authenticity in this story of Synanon House, established by Charles E. Dederich, an ex-alcoholic, in 1958.

Edmond O'Brien enacts the character of Dederich (who acted as technical advisor), plagued by debts and civil opposition as he goes about his seemingly thankless task of trying to bring lives back from the brink.

O'Brien's performance is smooth and convincing and lends strength to the character he portrays. Cord registers decisively in an unsympathetic role, and Stella Stevens is persuasive as a hooker, with a great love for her five-year-old son.

■ SYSTEM, THE

(US: *The Girl-Getters*)

1964, 90 MINS, UK

Dir Michael Winner   *Prod* Kenneth Shipman   *Scr* Peter Draper   *Ph* Nicolas Roeg   *Ed* Fred Burnley
Mus Stanley Black   *Art Dir* Geoffrey Tozer
● Oliver Reed, Jane Merrow, Barbara Ferris, Julia Foster, David Hemmings, Derek Nimmo (BLC/Bryanston)

S

The System is a slight anecdote, not explored as fully as it might have been, but made worthwhile by some bright direction, lensing and acting from young, eager talent.

Screenplay concerns the activities of a bunch of local lads at a seaside resort who every summer work a system by which they 'take' the holidaying femmes for a light-hearted emotional ride. There's nothing vicious about it. It's simply young men in search of goodtime romances that will have to make do in their memories during the dreary offseason winter months.

Tinker (Oliver Reed), a young beach photographer, is leader of the 'come up and see my pad' gang. The film tells how, one summer, he himself gets taken. He falls heavily in love with a well-loaded, well-stacked fashion model, and that's against the 'rules', even when the girl reciprocates.

This thin yarn is an adroitly spun concoction of comedy, sentiment and pathos which, however, needs a strong sub-plot to sustain interest. Scripter Peter Draper has decked out his situations with some neat dialog, mostly of the flip-talk variety, but there are one or two moments of genuine emotional depth between the young lovers.

• •

■ TABLE FOR FIVE

1983, 122 MINS, US ◇ ⑰ ⊙
Dir Robert Lieberman   *Prod* Robert Schaffel   *Scr* David Seltzer   *Ph* Vilmos Zsigmond   *Ed* Michael Kahn   *Mus* Miles Goodman, John Morris   *Art Dir* Robert F. Boyle
● Jon Voight, Richard Crenna, Marie-Christine Barrault, Millie Perkins, Roxana Zal, Robby Kiger (CBS Theatrical)

Well-written drama concerns an errant father who takes his three children on an ocean voyage in an effort to close the gap that's grown between them. Pic earns most of its emotional points honestly and will touch most anyone who's ever taken the responsibilities of parenting seriously, either in fact or theoretically.

At the opening, Jon Voight's kids have lived with their mother (Millie Perkins) and her new man, attorney Richard Crenna, for several years. Voight swoops into New York to take the moppets off on a luxurious sea cruise with the promise of a new-found sense of responsibility.

But Voight quickly realizes that he really doesn't know how to communicate with the kids who, for their part, resent the fact he's more interested in chasing blondes in the bar than hanging out with them.

Despite the attempted interference of his sharp daughter, Voight manages to initiate a shipboard romance with a sympathetic French woman, Marie-Christine Barrault.

• •

■ TABU

1931, 81 MINS, US ⑰ ⊙
Dir F.W. Murnau   *Prod* Robert J. Flaherty, F.W. Murnau   *Scr* Robert J. Flaherty, F.W. Murnau   *Ph* Floyd Crosby, Robert J. Flaherty   *Mus* Hugo Riesenfeld
● Reri, Matahi, Hitu, Jean, Jules, Kong Ah (Paramount)

A strong love story in a South Seas background, with South Sea natives rather than regular actors.

The title, *Tabu*, means death. It's the fate that hangs over the romantic leads who flee from a distant isle and its barbaric customs after a girl has been handed over to Tabu, ruler of one of the islands, as 'the chosen one'. Along with her goes the dictum, 'no man must touch her or cast eyes of desire upon her'.

Matahi rescues the girl, Reri, from a schooner at the propitious moment, just as she is to be taken away. They flee to an island that flourishes in the pearl trade and has been penetrated to a greater extent by white men. Here Matahi becomes famous as a pearl diver, but finally Tabu turns up to claim the girl, threatening the Tabu sign (or death) on Matahi if she doesn't come along with him.

About 90% of the footage is devoted to the romantic leads, their happiness, troubles, heartaches, etc. Against this, there is a little native life – fishing, diving, waterfalls, mode of living, etc, as was brought but to a far greater extent in *Moana*.

Tabu is a silent, with synchronization and sound effects, but difficult to figure out whether some of the effects and the singing, as well as native music, were dubbed over or not.
☐ 1930/31: Best Cinematography

• •

■ TAI-PAN

1986, 127 MINS, US ◇ ⑰ ⊙
Dir Daryl Duke   *Prod* Raffaella De Laurentiis   *Scr* John Briley, Stanley Mann   *Ph* Jack Cardiff   *Mus* Maurice Jarre   *Art Dir* Tony Masters
● Bryan Brown, Joan Chen, John Stanton, Tom Guinee, Bill Leadbitter, Russell Wong (De Laurentiis)

Tai-Pan is a historical epic [from James Clavell's novel] lost somewhere between 19th-century Hong Kong and 20th-century Hollywood. Despite flashes of brilliance and color, *Tai-Pan* fails to evoke a mysterious and moving world as a back-drop to its romantic drama. Director Daryl Duke and his team have made an attractive shell but failed to put in any heart.

As the Tai-Pan, or trade leader of the European community, first in Canton and then later in Hong Kong, Aussie thesp Bryan Brown looks the part well enough, but lacks charisma.

Within the exotic setting the story is actually rather conventional. Brown is opposed by arch villains Brock (John Stanton) and his son Gorth (Bill Leadbitter) for the control of the trading rights. At the same time there is considerable politicking going on with the Chinese over the opium trade and the British over trade regulations.

Film presents a good deal of romancing, between Brown and his lovely Chinese concubine May-May (Joan Chen) and several other women who seem to have a bottomless supply of revealing costumes.

• •

■ TAKE A GIRL LIKE YOU

1970, 101 MINS, UK ◇ ⑰
Dir Jonathan Miller   *Prod* Hal Chester   *Scr* George Melly   *Ph* Dick Bush   *Ed* Jack Harris   *Mus* Stanley Myers
● Noel Harrison, Oliver Reed, Hayley Mills, Sheila Hancock, John Bird, Aimi MacDonald (Columbia)

Take a movie like this. It's about a virgin (Hayley Mills) and a guy (Oliver Reed) who is trying to make her, can't, and is obsessed about it. That's all there is to it.

Basically, it is not a bad little English kitchen-sink drama with some strong but low-key performances, but a lack of sense of humor, generally wearisome development, and a downbeat ending.

At the core of George Melly's script, based on Kingsley Amis' novel, is the whole dreary ritual of a boy and girl in conflict about sex.

Jonathan Miller's direction iss competent, not without its occasional humor and bright spots, but they are too occasional, and what should be a comedy is essentially heavy and melodramatic.

• •

■ TAKE A HARD RIDE

1975, 103 MINS, US ◇ ⑰
Dir Anthony M. Dawson [= Antonio Margheriti]   *Prod* Harry Bernsen   *Scr* Eric Bercovici, Jerry Ludwig   *Ph* Riccardo Pallotini   *Ed* Stanford C. Allen   *Mus* Jerry Goldsmith   *Art Dir* Julio Molina
● Jim Brown, Lee Van Cleef, Fred Williamson, Catherine Spaak, Jim Kelly, Barry Sullivan (20th-Century Fox)

Take a Hard Ride is a poly-formula period western dual bill item for the popcorn belt. Jim Brown heads cast as a wrangler hunted for the $86,000 in cash he is returning to his late employer's widow. Lots and lots of people get killed in Harry Bernsen's location production shot in the Canary Islands.

The script mixes several potboiler genres: Brown, gambler Fred Williamson and mute Jim Kelly contribute black and karate elements; Lee Van Cleef provides the Italoater menace as a callous bounty hunter; Catherine Spaak is briefly encountered and dropped on the trail, not before adding a Continental touch; crooked sheriff Barry Sullivan and Dana Andrews, in a cameo as Brown's boss, are in more conventional oater roles.

Second unit director and stunt boss Hal Needham jazzes up the pace with several offbeat highlights.

• •

■ TAKE HER, SHE'S MINE

1963, 98 MINS, US ◇
Dir Henry Koster   *Prod* Henry Koster   *Scr* Nunnally
Johnson   *Ph* Lucien Ballard   *Ed* Marjorie Fowler
Mus Jerry Goldsmith   *Art Dir* Jack Martin Smith,
Malcolm Brown
● James Stewart, Sandra Dee, Audrey Meadows, Robert
Morley, Philippe Forquet, John McGiver (20th Century-
Fox)

The screen version of *Take Her, She's Mine* is
an improvement over the Phoebe and Henry
Ephron stage play from which it springs, even
though several of the revisions and additions
dreamed up by scenarist Nunnally Johnson
are contrived and far from fresh.

The difficulty encountered by an older generation in comprehending the behavior of a
younger generation is the business explored
in this comedy. More specifically, one father's
(James Stewart) trials and tribulations when
he packs his precious daughter (Sandra Dee)
off to college and observes, in long distance
dismay with an occasional globe-trot for
closer inspection, her transition from adolescent to young woman.

An occasional dash of the *Tammy* whammy
seeps into Dee's characterization, but on the
whole she's effective. Audrey Meadows, a
gifted comedienne, is wasted in the bland and
barren role of Stewart's wife. Robert Morley,
though in the somewhat irrelevant role of a
jaded Britisher, has some of the best lines in
the film. Jerry Goldsmith contributes a whimsical score, especially helpful in a costume
party sequence that needs all the help it can
get.

■ TAKE ME OUT TO THE BALL GAME

(UK: Everybody's Cheering)

1949, 83 MINS, US ◇ ⊚ ⊙
Dir Busby Berkeley   *Prod* Arthur Freed   *Scr* Harry
Tugend, George Wells   *Ph* George Folsey   *Ed* Blanche
Sewell   *Mus* Adolph Deutsch (dir.)   *Art Dir* Cedric
Gibbons, Daniel B. Cathcart
● Frank Sinatra, Esther Williams, Gene Kelly, Betty
Garrett, Edward Arnold, Jules Munshin (M-G-M)

Take Me Out to the Ball Game, backgrounded by
an early-day baseball yarn, is short on story,
but has some amusing moments – and Gene
Kelly.

Aided by Technicolor, Esther Williams is an
eyeful, and Frank Sinatra cavorts pleasantly
as shortstop Kelly's second baseman. Jules
Munshin and Betty Garrett are the comedy
relief, and the overall combination of talents
is actually worthier of better material.

The yarn [by Kelly and Stanley Donen, who
both staged the musical numbers] is about a
couple of singing-dancing major league ball-
players and the complications in which they
become involved when they meet some gamblers and Williams, owner of the club. There
is no pretense that *Ball Game* is anything
more than a romp for Kelly's virtuosity.

■ TAKE THE HIGH GROUND

1953, 100 MINS, US ◇
Dir Richard Brooks   *Prod* Dore Schary   *Scr* Millard
Kaufman   *Ph* John Alton   *Ed* John Dunning
Mus Dimitri Tiomkin   *Art Dir* Cedric Gibbons, Edward
Carfagno
● Richard Widmark, Karl Malden, Elaine Stewart, Russ
Tamblyn, Carleton Carpenter, Steve Forrest (M-G-M)

Take the High Ground is an absorbing study of
the training that makes tough, fighting GIs
out of raw civilians. It has meticulous attention to detail and authenticity of incident.

There's the strictly general-issue top
sergeant intent on making fighting men out
of callow youths; the non-com who uses a
softer, more understanding good fellow,
approach to the fresh recruits; the mixed-up
girl whose drinking covers a great sorrow; and

the assorted trainee types, brash, shy, cowardly.

In the script treatment and under Brooks'
direction, however, these standard forms take
on new life and become interesting people
whose careers through the plot attract the attention and hold it.

Richard Widmark comes over very strongly
as the tough top sarg. Karl Malden is the understanding sergeant and he too gives the
character life and feeling. Elaine Stewart is
the mixed-up girl and, as the only credited
femme in the cast, makes much of her part.
□ 1953: Best Story & Screenplay

■ TAKE THE MONEY AND RUN

1969, 85 MINS, US ◇ ⊚ ⊙
Dir Woody Allen   *Prod* Charles H. Joffe   *Scr* Woody
Allen, Mickey Rose   *Ph* Lester Shorr   *Ed* Ralph
Rosenblum, James T. Heckert   *Mus* Marvin Hamlisch
Art Dir Fred Harpman
● Woody Allen, Janet Margolin, Marcel Hillaire,
Jacquelyn Hyde, Lonny Chapman (Palomar)

A few good laughs in an 85-minute film do
not a comedy make. Woody Allen's *Take the
Money and Run*, basically a running gag about
hero Allen's ineptitude as a professional
crook, scatters its fire in so many directions it
has to hit at least several targets. But satire
on documentary coverage of criminal flop is
over-extended and eventually tiresome.

Bright spots are interviews with parents-in-
disguise Ethel Sokolow and Henry Leff; Janet
Margolin, as wife, and prison psychiatrist Don
Frazier also deliver yocks.

Margolin turns in a neat performance as
Allen's wife. Allen, both as director and actor,
sustains his own characterization. In such
scenes as robbery when he can't convince
bank personnel they are being robbed, or in
chain gang's visit to farmhouse, he creates
genuinely funny moments.

■ TAKING CARE OF BUSINESS

(UK: Filofax)

1990, 103 MINS, US ◇ ⊚ ⊙
Dir Arthur Hiller   *Prod* Geoffrey Taylor   *Scr* Jill
Mazursky, Jeffrey Abrams   *Ph* David M. Walsh
Ed William Reynolds   *Mus* Stewart Copeland
Art Dir Jon Hutman
● James Belushi, Charles Grodin, Anne DeSalvo, Loryn
Locklin, Veronica Hamel, Hector Elizondo
(Hollywood/Silver Screen Partners IV)

Charles Grodin and James Belushi come together too late in the plot to prevent a poky
start for *Taking Care of Business*, but their mutual chemistry eventually kicks in some jovial
jousting. Brash Belushi and befuddled Grodin
are perfect casting for yarn about a likable escaped con who assumes the identity of a
stuffy, overworked ad agency exec.

At the start, Belushi is still in county jail,
and there's some fun as he high-fives it with
fellow inmates and torments warden Hector
Elizondo. Mostly familiar schtick. Ditto
Grodin's intro as he fusses with his workload
and neglects wife Victoria Hamel. Though
Belushi is set for release in days, he can't wait
to see the World Series so he escapes just as
Grodin arrives in LA to pitch his agency to a
Japanese tycoon.

At the airport, Grodin loses his time-plan-
ning book – *Business* is one long commercial
itself for a particular brand (Filofax, as pic is
titled in the UK) – and Belushi finds it.
Setting himself up in a Malibu mansion,
Belushi proceeds to live Grodin's life just the
opposite of how the businessman would do it,
romancing the boss's daughter (played with
sexy feistiness by Loryn Locklin), beating the
potential client (Mako) at tennis, criticizing
his products and making sexist remarks to
fierce, feminist exec (Gates McFadden).

Inevitably, Grodin catches up with Belushi

and the farcical convolutions multiply with
the arrival of Hamel. As the action picks up,
so does the dialog.

■ TAKING OFF

1971, 92 MINS, US ◇ ⊚
Dir Milos Forman   *Prod* Alfred W. Crown   *Scr* Milos
Forman, John Guare, Jean-Claude Carriere
Ph Miroslav Ondricek   *Ed* John Carter   *Art Dir* Robert
Wightman
● Lynn Carlin, Buck Henry, Linnea Heacock, Georgia
Engel, Tony Harvey, Audra Lindley (Universal)

Taking Off is a very compassionate, very amusing contemporary comedy about a NY couple
whose concern for a drop out daughter is
matched by her astonishment at their social
mores. Milos Forman's first US-made film
shows him to be a director who can depict the
contradictions of human nature while avoiding
tract, harangue and polemics.

The plot peg is the flight to Greenwich
Village of Linnea Heacock, who's seeking
something not provided in her home life.
Lynn Carlin and Buck Henry (as the parents)
enliven the many motivated and developing
sequences: initial search for the girl conducted with friends Tony Harvey and Georgia
Engel; a large meeting of discarded parents
where Vincent Schiavelli turns them all on to
marijuana; and a funny strip poker game at
home which ends abruptly when the runaway
girl calmly appears from her bedroom.

Henry tackles his first big screen role and
achieves superb results. Carlin seems not an
actress in a part, but a real mother, caught by
candid camera, who doesn't know whether to
laugh or cry about a family crisis.

■ TAKING OF PELHAM ONE TWO THREE, THE

1974, 104 MINS, US ◇ ⊚ ⊙
Dir Joseph Sargent   *Prod* Gabriel Katzka, Edgar J.
Scherick   *Scr* Peter Stone   *Ph* Owen Roizman
Ed Jerry Greenberg   *Mus* David Shire   *Art Dir* Gene
Rudolf
● Walter Matthau, Robert Shaw, Martin Balsam, Hector
Elizondo, Earl Hindman, James Broderick (Palomar/
Palladium)

The Taking of Pelham One Two Three is a good
action caper about a subway car heist under
the streets of Manhattan. Walter Matthau
heads the cast as a Transit Authority detective matching wits with the hijackers headed
by Robert Shaw. Joseph Sargent's direction is
fast but the major liability is Peter Stone's
screenplay [from novel by John Godey] which
develops little interest in either Matthau or
Shaw's gang, nor the innocent hostages.

Shaw, Martin Balsam, Hector Elizondo and
Earl Hindman seize a subway car, named for
the starting station on the line and its time of
departure, and demand $1 million. Matthau
is on duty at subway communications h.q. and
deals with Shaw over voice radio all the while
fending off the Archie Bunker types with
whom he works.

A sidebar characterization is that of Lee
Wallace as the mayor, a travesty of a role
played for silly laughs.

Shaw is superb in another versatile characterization.

■ TALE OF TWO CITIES, A

1936, 121 MINS, US ⊚
Dir Jack Conway   *Prod* David O. Selznick   *Scr* W.P.
Lipscomb, S.N. Behrman   *Ph* Oliver T. Marsh
Ed Conrad A. Nervig   *Mus* Herbert Stothart
Art Dir Cedric Gibbons, Frederic Hope, Edwin B. Willis
● Ronald Colman, Elizabeth Allan, Edna May Oliver,
Reginald Owen, Basil Rathbone, Blanche Yurka (M-G-M)

Metro achieves in *A Tale of Two Cities* a screen
classic. The two yawning pitfalls of spectacle

T

and dialog have been adroitly evaded. The fall of the Bastille [directed by Val Lewton and Jacques Tourneur] is breathtaking but it is given no greater valuation than its influence on the plot [from the novel by Charles Dickens] warrants.

The rabble at the guillotine is blood-chilling in its ferocity, but not for a moment does it overlie the principals, waiting in the shadow of the bloody platform for their turn to come. In the dialog the lines are neither the often stilted phrases of the book, nor yet the colloquial language of today.

Ronald Colman makes his Carton one of the most pathetic figures in the screen catalog. Gone are his drawing room mannerisms, shaved along with his moustache. Henry B. Walthall is good as Manette and Blanche Yurka magnificent as the vengeful Mme De Farge.

The others all are good, each in proportion to assignment, with Elizabeth Allan suffering somewhat from necessity for being so typically a Dickens' heroine.

□ 1936: Nominations: Best Picture, Editing

••••••••••••••••••••••••••••••

■ TALE OF TWO CITIES, A

1958, 117 MINS, UK Ⓥ
Dir Ralph Thomas   *Prod* Betty E. Box   *Scr* T.E.B. Clarke   *Ph* Ernest Steward   *Ed* Alfred Roome   *Mus* Richard Addinsell   *Art Dir* Carmen Dillon
● Dirk Bogarde, Dorothy Tutin, Cecil Parker, Marie Versini, Stephen Murray, Athene Seyler (Rank)

Set against the Storming of the Bastille, *Cities* is primarily a character study of a frustrated young lawyer who fritters his life away in drink until the moment when he makes everything worthwhile by a supreme sacrifice for the girl he loves. Dirk Bogarde brings a lazy charm and nonchalance to the Sydney Carton role but tends to play throughout in a surprisingly minor key.

Leading femme is Dorothy Tutin, whose role does not strain her thesping ability. Cecil Parker, as a banker; Athene Seyler, as Tutin's fussy companion; and Stephen Murray, as Dr Manette, all have meaty portrayals which they handle with authority.

But it is among some of the other characterizations that there is most to admire, notably new young actress Marie Versini. Playing a young servant girl who becomes a victim of Madame Guillotine, Versini brings a beautiful restraint and appeal to her task.

Among other standout performances are those by Donald Pleasence, as an unctuous spy; Christopher Lee, as a sadistic aristocrat; and Duncan Lamont, as one of the leaders of the revolution. Rosalie Crutchley also makes notable impact with a brilliant study in malevolence as his vengeful wife.

••••••••••••••••••••••••••••••

■ TALES FROM THE DARKSIDE THE MOVIE

1990, 93 MINS, US ◇ Ⓥ ⊙
Dir John Harrison   *Prod* Richard P. Rubinstein, Mitchell Galin   *Scr* Michael McDowell, George A. Romero   *Ph* Robert Draper   *Mus* Donald A. Rubinstein, Jim Manzie, Pat Regan, Chaz Jankel, John Harrison   *Art Dir* Ruth Ammon
● Deborah Harry, Christian Slater, Rae Dawn Chong, James Remar, David Johansen, Steve Buscemi (Paramount)

Tales from the Darkside is significantly gorier than its namesake TV series, and has better production values.

Structure is a lift from Scheherazade in *1,001 Nights*, as Deborah Harry prepares to cook little boy Matthew Lawrence, he delays his fate by telling her a trio of horror stories.

Most ambitious segment, *Beetlejuice* writer Michael McDowell's *Lover's Vow* is saved for last: Gotham artist James Remar witnessing a barman's extremely gory murder by a gar-

goyle come to life. To save his skin he vows to the gargoyle not to tell anyone what happened, but after meeting beautiful Rae Dawn Chong, romancing her and marrying her, 10 years later he spills the beans with tragic results. Sexy and sinister Chong is a delight in this one.

Other segments are more routine. George A. Romero's adaptation of a Stephen King story is punched up by casting David Johansen as a hit man assigned to kill a black cat by drug tycoon William Hickey. Curtain-raiser is a corny but effective tale from the creator of Sherlock Holmes: college student Steve Buscemi bringing an ancient mummy back to life for revenge with ironic results.

••••••••••••••••••••••••••••••

■ TALES OF BEATRIX POTTER
(Aka: Peter Rabbit and Tales of Beatrix Potter)

1971, 90 MINS, UK ◇ Ⓥ
Dir Reginald Mills   *Prod* John Brabourne, Richard Goodwin   *Scr* Richard Goodwin, Christine Edzard   *Ph* Austin Dempster   *Ed* John Rushton   *Mus* John Lanchbery   *Art Dir* John Howell
● Frederick Ashton, Alexander Grant, Ann Howard, Wayne Sleep, Michael Coleman, Lesley Collier (M-G-M/EMI)

The production partners, John Brabourne and Richard Goodwin and director Reginald Mills, conceived the happy notion of having Beatrix Potter's animals represented by members of the Royal Ballet and the result is 90 minutes of style, fun and enchantment.

Film's opener introduces Erin Geraghty as the introverted young Beatrix in her gloomy Victorian home. But then the animals take over. There's little point in detailing the various stories – the adventures of The Bad Mice, the jaunty capers of Jeremy Fisher, how Jemima Puddle-Duck escapes a fate worse than death at the paws of The Fox, etc. The point is that the episodes skip merrily along, the choreography by Frederick Ashton blends splendidly with Reginald Mills' direction and John Lanchbery's bright, if tinkly, music has the right lilting note. But the whole thing might have fallen apart but for the life-like masks designed by Rostislav Doboujinsky and Christine Edzard's gay costumes.

••••••••••••••••••••••••••••••

■ TALES OF HOFFMAN, THE

1951, 138 MINS, UK ◇
Dir Michael Powell, Emeric Pressburger   *Prod* Michael Powell, Emeric Pressburger   *Scr* Michael Powell, Emeric Pressburger   *Ph* Christopher Challis   *Ed* Reginald Mills   *Art Dir* Arthur Lawson
● Moira Shearer, Robert Rounseville, Robert Helpmann, Pamela Brown, Frederick Ashton, Leonide Massine (Archers/London)

Michael Powell and Emeric Pressburger follow up their sock *Red Shoes* ballet picture with as distinguished an opera-ballet film in *Tales of Hoffman*. The Jacques Offenbach fantasy opera has been transformed to the screen with great imagination and taste, with an unusual amount of inventiveness and effects, for a lush, resplendent production that's a treat to eye and ear.

Hoffman is a better picture than *Shoes*, with more imagination and story structure. But the story lines in the second and third episodes are confusing, except perhaps to the inveterate operagoer. *Hoffman* lacks the everyday romance of *Shoes*, is sung throughout instead of having spoken dialog, and lacks humor.

Film is a brilliant integration of dance, story and music. Fantastic nature of its story is brought out more sharply by the excellent use of Technicolor.

Prolog has Hoffman (Robert Rounseville) watching a ballet and in love with the prima ballerina, Stella (Moira Shearer), who ap-

pears to him as the embodiment of his past loves. When he thinks Stella has spurned him, he moons in a tavern, and relates to a group of students 'the three tales of my folly of love'.

One concerns the time, in Paris, when he fancied himself in love with Olympia (Shearer), who turned out to be a life-size doll created by a magician. Second act, set in Venice, has Hoffman bewitched by a beautiful courtesan, Giulietta (Ludmilla Tcherina), whose master is trying to acquire Hoffman's soul through the girl. Third act, set on a Grecian isle, has Hoffman in love with Antonia (Ann Ayars), daughter of a singer and conductor, who is in danger of dying from consumption if she herself attempts to sing.

Shearer, Robert Helpmann, Ludmilla, Tcherina and Leonide Massine, all of them dancers who appeared in *Red Shoes*, are distinguished again here.

□ 1951: Nominations: Color Costume Design, Color Art Direction

••••••••••••••••••••••••••••••

■ TALES OF MANHATTAN

1942, 117 MINS, US
Dir Julien Duvivier   *Prod* Boris Morros, S.P. Eagle [= Sam Spiegel]   *Scr* Ben Hecht, Ferenc Molnar, Donald Ogden Stewart, Samuel Hoffenstein, Alan Campbell, Ladislas Fodor, L. Vadnai, L. Gorog, Lamar Trotti, Henry Blankfort   *Ph* Joseph Walker   *Ed* Robert Bischoff   *Mus* Sol Kaplan   *Art Dir* Richard Day, Boris Leven
● Charles Boyer, Rita Hayworth, Ginger Rogers, Henry Fonda, Charles Laughton, Edward G. Robinson (20th Century-Fox)

In *Tales of Manhattan* the hero is an expensive dress coat, which bears a curse, and the film recounts the fortunes and misfortunes of those who wear or come in possession of it. It was originally made for Charles Boyer, playing a Broadway matinee idol, and winds up as scarecrow on a poor old Negro's farm.

The expanse of acting and writing talent may have been too much for Julien Duvivier, a fine foreign director, for he comes up with very few original touches in this picture. Some of the sequences he appears to have permitted to go along on their momentum.

Despite the plenitude of costly stars, featured players and writers, Boris Morros and S.P. Eagle [= Sam Spiegel] brought the film in for slightly more than $1 million, not high considering all the credits.

••••••••••••••••••••••••••••••

■ TALES OF ORDINARY MADNESS

1981, 107 MINS, ITALY ◇ Ⓥ
Dir Marco Ferreri   *Scr* Sergio Amidei, Marco Ferreri, Anthony Fourtz   *Ph* Tonino Delli Colli   *Ed* Ruggero Mastroianni   *Mus* Philippe Sarde
● Ben Gazzara, Ornella Muti, Susan Tyrrell, Tanya Lopert (23 Giugno/Ginis)

Marco Ferreri, the anarchically-inclined 'Italo' filmmaker who has delved into the human psyche often in its mainly frustrated, exploited aspects in today's world, seems to have found a kindred spirit in the stories of the 1960s Yank sub-culture writer-poet Charles Bukowski. Film is a distillation of Ferreri's themes.

Ben Gazzara, in a knowing characterization of a poet (Charles) searching for the essence of love though primarily self-destructive and half believing in its redemptive powers, is first seen giving a philosophical comic talk in some foreign university on a tour. Going back to a dressing room, he finds a Lolita-like runaway who steals his money when he falls asleep.

He goes back to LA to write, drink and keep searching for women in a sort of adventurous series of escapades reminiscent of Henry Miller but not as self-indulgent and sex-for-its-own sake as the writings of Miller.

One day a sexy-looking blonde catches his

eye in the street and he follows her. He finds her house and goes in to be suddenly devoured by her sexually but then turned over to the police for molesting her. Susan Tyrrell is effective in her sexual quirkiness.

Charles is freed and joins the tramp wino world for a while. Then home again to write and dry out. He also comments on the action along the way.

. . . .

■ TALK OF THE TOWN

1942, 110 MINS, US 🎬 ⊙

Dir George Stevens   *Prod* George Stevens   *Scr* Irwin Shaw, Sidney Buchman   *Ph* Ted Tetzlaff   *Ed* Otto Meyer   *Mus* Frederick Hollander   *Art Dir* Lionel Banks, Rudolph Sternad

● Cary Grant, Jean Arthur, Ronald Colman, Edgar Buchanan, Glenda Farrell, Rex Ingram (Columbia)

Case of Cary Grant, the outspoken factory town, soapbox 'anti' worker, being tried for arson and the death of factory foreman in the blaze, serves as a vehicle to introduce a pert schoolteacher (Jean Arthur) and a law school dean (Ronald Colman) in a procession of comedy dissertations on law, in theory and practice. Plot has Grant escaping before his trial is completed and seeking refuge in the schoolmarm's home.

Story [from one by Sidney Harmon, adapted by Dale Van Every] doesn't give Grant quite enough to do, with plenty of meaty lines and situations handed Colman, who manages the transition from the stuffy professor to a human being with the least amount of implausibility.

George Stevens' direction is topflight for the most part. Transition from serious or melodramatic to the slap-happy and humorous sometimes is a bit awkward, but in the main it is solid escapist comedy.
□ 1942: Nominations: Best Picture, Original Story & Screenplay, B&W Cinematography, B&W Art Direction, Editing, Scoring of a Dramatic Picture

. . . .

■ TALK RADIO

1988, 110 MINS, US ◇ 🎬 ⊙

Dir Oliver Stone   *Prod* Edward R. Pressman, A. Kitman Ho   *Scr* Eric Bogosian, Oliver Stone   *Ph* Robert Richardson   *Ed* David Brenner   *Mus* Stewart Copeland   *Art Dir* Bruno Rubeo

● Eric Bogosian, Alec Baldwin, Ellen Greene, Leslie Hope, John C. McGinley, John Pankow (Cineplex Odeon/Ten Four)

Talk Radio casts a spotlight on the unpalatable underside of American public opinion, and turns up an unlimited supply of anger, hatred and resentment in the process.

Known in theatrical circles as a monologist and performance artist, Eric Bogosian debuted the initial incarnation of *Talk Radio* in Portland, Ore, in 1985. For the screenplay, he and director Oliver Stone worked in material relating to Alan Berg, the Denver talkshow host murdered by neo-Nazis in 1984, and also created a flashback to illuminate their antihero's personal background and beginnings in the radio game.

Most of the film, however, unfolds in the modern studio of KGAB, a Dallas station from which the infamous Barry Champlain (Bogosian) holds forth. Young, caustic, rude, insulting, grandstanding, flippant and mercilessly cruel, the talkshow host spews vitriol impartially on those of all races, colors and creeds and spares the feelings of no one.

Champlain draws out the nighttime's seamiest denizens from under their rocks, fringe characters with access to the airwaves.

A dramatic structure has been imposed on the proceedings by the arrival of a radio syndicator who wants to take Champlain's show nationwide. At the same time, Champlain's ex-wife Ellen (Ellen Greene) arrives in town,

which occasions a look back at the man's origins.

Bogosian commands attention in a patented tour-de-force. Supporting performances are all vividly realized, notably Michael Wincott's drug-crazed Champlain fan invited to the studio for a tete-a-tete with the host.

. . . .

■ TALL GUY, THE

1989, 92 MINS, UK ◇ 🎬 ⊙

Dir Mel Smith   *Prod* Paul Webster   *Scr* Richard Curtis   *Ph* Adrian Biddle   *Ed* Dan Rae   *Mus* Peter Brewis   *Art Dir* Grant Hicks

● Jeff Goldblum, Emma Thompson, Rowan Atkinson, Emil Wolk, Geraldine James, Anna Massey (LWT/Virgin)

The Tall Guy is a cheery, ingratiating romantic comedy with Jeff Goldblum putting in a stellar performance as a bumbling American actor in London whose career and romantic tribulations are suddenly transformed into triumphs.

At the outset, Yank thesp Goldblum has been performing in the West End for several years as straight man to popular comic Rowan Atkinson. The insecure goof-ball is earning a living but going nowhere fast when he comes under the care of hospital nurse Emma Thompson.

Immediately smitten, Goldblum spends the time between weekly visits for injections desperately concocting ways to ask her out.

Throughout the entire film, the relationship evolves winningly, with so much believable give-and-take, mutual ribbing and support that one roots for it heavily.

As soon as he has discovered domestic bliss, however, Goldblum is sacked by Atkinson, who resents anyone else in his show getting a laugh, and is thrust into the forbidding world of the unemployed actor.

The fresh, alert performances add enormously to the polished sparkle of the script. Goldblum is in splendid form as the eternally naive American abroad. Thompson makes a wonderfully poised foil for her leading man's volubility. British favorite Atkinson has a great time enacting the most vain and meanspirited of stars, and Hugh Thomas elicits quite a few laughs in his brief appearance as a wild-eyed medic.

. . . .

■ TALL MEN, THE

1955, 122 MINS, US ◇ 🎬

Dir Raoul Walsh   *Prod* William A. Bacher, William B. Hawks   *Scr* Sydney Boehm, Frank Nugent   *Ph* Leo Tover   *Ed* Louis Loeffler   *Mus* Victor Young   *Art Dir* Lyle Wheeler, Mark-Lee Kirk

● Clark Gable, Jane Russell, Robert Ryan, Cameron Mitchell, Emile Meyer, Harry Shannon (20th Century-Fox)

They must have had *The Tall Men* in mind when they invented CinemaScope. It's a big, robust western that fills the wide screen with a succession of panoramic scenes of often incredible beauty.

This is the Clark Gable of old in a role that's straight up his alley – rough, tough, quick on the draw and yet with all the 'right' instincts. The vet actor seems to enjoy himself thoroughly and he is equally at ease in the saddle as in his swap-a-quip dialog with Jane Russell.

There's no use quibbling about Russell. She goes through most of the film taunting both Gable and Robert Ryan. It's probably only fair to assume that her pancake-flat acting is a secondary consideration. She does show a sense of comedy in a couple of scenes and the pic benefits from it.

Story has brothers Gable and Cameron Mitchell working for Ryan and they become partners in a venture that calls for them to drive a large herd of cattle from Texas to Montana. On the way south, the trio runs

into Russell, and Gable saves her from an Indian attack.

. . . .

■ TALL T, THE

1957, 78 MINS, US ◇ 🎬

Dir Budd Boetticher   *Prod* Randolph Scott, Harry Joe Brown   *Scr* Burt Kennedy   *Ph* Charles Lawton Jr   *Ed* Al Clark   *Mus* Heinz Roemheld   *Art Dir* George Brooks

● Randolph Scott, Richard Boone, Maureen O'Sullivan, Arthur Hunnicutt, Skip Homeier, Henry Silva (Columbia)

An unconventional western, *The Tall T* passes up most oater cliches. There's a wealth of suspense in the screenplay based on a story [*The Captives*] by Elmore Leonard. From a quiet start the yarn acquires a momentum which explodes in a sock climax.

Modest and unassuming, Randolph Scott is a rancher who's been seized by a trio of killers led by Richard Boone. Also captured are newlyweds Maureen O'Sullivan and John Hubbard. Originally the outlaws planned a stage robbery, but are urged privately by the craven Hubbard to hold his heiress-wife for ransom in the hope that this move might save his skin.

Under Budd Boetticher's direction the story develops slowly, but relentlessly toward the action-packed finale. Scott impresses as the strong, silent type who ultimately vanquishes his captors. Boone is crisply proficient as the sometimes remorseful outlaw leader. His psychopathic henchmen are capably delineated by Skip Homeier and Henry Silva.

. . . .

■ TAMARIND SEED, THE

1974, 123 MINS, UK ◇ 🎬

Dir Blake Edwards   *Prod* Ken Wales   *Scr* Blake Edwards   *Ph* Freddie Young   *Ed* Ernest Walter   *Mus* John Barry   *Art Dir* Harry Pottle

● Julie Andrews, Omar Sharif, Anthony Quayle, Dan O'Herlihy, Sylvia Syms, Oscar Homolka (ITC/Jewel/Lorimar)

Blake Edwards, whose forte usually is comedy, has turned Evelyn Anthony's novel, *The Tamarind Seed*, into what some will see as a love story against an espionage background and others as an excellent spy effort involving two people in love.

Julie Andrews as a British civil servant on vacation in the Caribbean meets and becomes fond of (but keeps at arm's length) a handsome Russian (Omar Sharif), also on leave. The Russian also has thoughts of enlisting her as an agent.

Sharif's importance lessens and he's slated for recall to Moscow, so he decides to defect. His bargaining point is the disclosure of a Britisher of high rank who is a Russian spy.

A major strong point of the film is the convincing performances of Andrews and Sharif as a pair of unlikely romantics.

. . . .

■ TAMING OF THE SHREW, THE

1967, 122 MINS, UK/ITALY ◇ 🎬 ⊙

Dir Franco Zeffirelli   *Prod* Richard Burton, Elizabeth Taylor   *Scr* Paul Dehn, Suso Cecchi D'Amico, Franco Zeffirelli   *Ph* Oswald Morris, Luciano Trasatti   *Ed* Peter Taylor   *Mus* Nino Rota   *Art Dir* Renzo Mongiardino, John F. De Cuir

● Richard Burton, Elizabeth Taylor, Michael York, Michael Hordern, Victor Spinetti, Cyril Cusack (Columbia/Royal Films International/F.A.I.)

The Taming of the Shrew offers the interesting situation of Richard Burton fictionally taming Elizabeth Taylor, although the version is a boisterous, often over-stagey frolic. It will strike many as a fair compromise for mass audiences between the original Shakespeare and, say, *Kiss Me Kate*.

Screenwriters have done neat job, infusing dialog without rocking Bard's memory overmuch. The two stars pack plenty of wallop making their roles meaty and flamboyant with a larger-than-life Burton playing for plenty of sly laughs in the uninhibited wife-beating lark.

Taylor tends to over-exploit an 'earthy' aspect in early footage and switch to the subdued attitude comes too abruptly. But against that she's a buxom delight when tamed. Comedy is sustained in witty wedding ceremony.

Shrewd casting of experienced players pays off with Michael Hordern, Victor Spinetti, Cyril Cusack, Alfred Lynch and Giancarlo Cobelli standouts.

....

■ **TANGO & CASH**

1989, 98 MINS, US ◇ ⓦ ⊙
Dir Andrei Konchalovsky, [Albert Magnoli] *Prod* John Peters, Peter Guber, Larry Franco *Scr* Randy Feldman *Ph* Donald E. Thorin *Ed* Huber De La Bouillerie, Robert Forretti *Mus* Harold Faltermeyer *Art Dir* David Klassen, Richard Berger
● Sylvester Stallone, Kurt Russell, Teri Hatcher, Jack Palance, Brion James, Michael J. Pollard (Guber-Peters/Warner)

Tango & Cash is a mindless buddy cop pic, loaded with nonstop action that's played mostly for laughs and delivers too few of them. Inane and formulaic, the film relies heavily on whatever chemistry it can generate between Sylvester Stallone and Kurt Russell, who repeatedly trade wisecracks while facing life-or-death situations.

Jack Palance re-creates down to each gasp his role from *Batman* as a snarling crime boss who decides to bring down the two cops who have separately plagued his drug-dealing schemes.

Framed and sent to prison, the two rival cops (named Tango and Cash) become a reluctant team to exonerate themselves. Along the way, they hitch up with Tango's bombshell sister (Teri Hatcher), who happens to be an exotic dancer at some *Star Wars*-esque nightspot.

The thinking seems to be if you're going to be ridiculous you might as well go at it full throttle, and director Andrei Konchalovsky does just that. Albert Magnoli, helmer of *Purple Rain*, directed the final two weeks of lensing after Konchalovsky quit in a dispute over pic's ending.

....

■ **TANK**

1984, 113 MINS, US ◇ ⓦ ⊙
Dir Marvin Chomsky *Prod* Irwin Yablans *Scr* Dan Gordon *Ph* Don Brinkrant *Ed* Donald R. Rede *Mus* Lalo Schifrin *Art Dir* Bill Kenney
● James Garner, G.D. Spradlin, Shirley Jones, C. Thomas Howell, James Cramwell, Jenilee Harrison (Lorimar)

The audience appeal of loners-against-corruption is here refashioned with the hero inside a marauding Sherman tank, taking on a maniacal southern sheriff in defense of integrity and family.

James Garner's persona gives the events a soft, human, and at times bemused edge.

First 10 minutes, showing Garner's arrival on an army base are terribly slow; relationship is ploddingly established with wife Shirley Jones and teenage son C. Thomas Howell.

Pace finally picks up when Garner gets in trouble for bashing a deputy who had slapped around a prostitute in a bar. The action triggers outrage by the local sheriff, another signature role by G.D. Spradlin, who gets even with Garner by framing his son and sending the boy to a despicable work farm.

....

■ **TAP**

1989, 110 MINS, US ◇ ⓦ ⊙
Dir Nick Castle *Prod* Gary Adelson, Richard Vane *Scr* Nick Castle *Ph* David Gribble *Ed* Patrick

Kennedy *Mus* James Newton Howard *Art Dir* Patricia Norris
● Gregory Hines, Suzzanne Douglas, Sammy Davis Jr, Savion Glover, Joe Morton, Terrence McNally (Tri-Star)

Tap is a surprisingly rich and affecting blend of dance and story that transcends its respectful deference toward the great hoofers of a bygone era to deliver plenty of glowing contemporary entertainment.

Impassioned by the twin personal commitments of writer-director Nick Castle (whose father choreographed Fred Astaire and Gene Kelly) and star Gregory Hines (whose tap career began at five at Harlem's Apollo Theater), project benefits from a dream cast and crew.

Hines plays Max, an ex-con torn between the high style and fast money of his former career as a jewel thief and the more deeply felt pleasures of tap dance, learned from his dead father. Trying to spark up an old romance with a dance teacher (Suzzanne Douglas), whose father, Lil Mo (Sammy Davis Jr), was his dad's pal, Max gets pulled unwillingly into the world of the oldtime hoofers, who occupy the exalted third floor of Sonny's, a dance studio and shabby shrine to the all-but-forgotten form.

Much like blues music, the dancing in this pic seems a heartfelt and exuberant response to urban struggle. Another big asset is pic's introduction in final dance seg of Tap-Tronics, a blend of tap and electric rock in which dancer's taps are connected with synthesizers that allow him to make both rhythmic and melodic music.

....

■ **TAPS**

1981, 118 MINS, US ◇ ⓦ
Dir Harold Becker *Prod* Stanley R. Jaffe, Howard B. Jaffe *Scr* Darryl Ponicsan, Robert Mark Kamen *Ph* Owen Roizman *Ed* Maury Winetrobe *Mus* Maurice Jarre *Art Dir* Stan Jolley, Alfred Sweeney
● George C. Scott, Timothy Hutton, Ronny Cox, Sean Penn, Tom Cruise, Brendan Ward (20th Century-Fox/Jaffe)

A heavy dramatic portrait of military school education with a disturbing shoot 'em up climax, *Taps* labors at an unbearably slow pace to an inevitable, depressing conclusion.

Plot [based on Devery Freeman's novel *Father Sky*, adapted by James Lineberger] centers on a military academy whose students are angered that their school and its traditions are being sold out from under them in order to build a bunch of condominiums.

Timothy Hutton tries to lend some humanity to the headstrong cadet who leads his fellow students in forcibly taking over the school (weapons and all) in a last ditch effort to save it, but he just appears too nice a guy. George C. Scott makes a brief but convincing appearance as a slightly deranged general.

Much of the supporting cast fare better, especially Sean Penn as Hutton's humane best friend, Tom Cruise as a trigger-happy cadet and Ronny Cox as the reasonable colonel who tries to talk Hutton out of his mission.

....

■ **TARANTULA**

1955, 80 MINS, US ◇
Dir William Alland *Prod* Jack Arnold *Scr* Robert M. Fresco, Martin Berkeley *Ph* George Robinson *Ed* William M. Morgan *Mus* Henry Mancini *Art Dir* Alexander Golitzen, Alfred Sweeney
● John Agar, Mara Corday, Leo G. Carroll, Nestor Paiva, Ross Elliott, Clint Eastwood (Universal)

A tarantula as big as a barn puts the horror into this well-made program science-fictioner and it is quite credibly staged and played, bringing off the far-fetched premise with a maximum of believability.

Some scientists, stationed near Desert Rock, Ariz, are working on an automatically

stabilized nutritional formula that will feed the world's ever-increasing population when the natural food supply becomes too small. Through variously staged circumstances, a tarantula that has been injected with the yet unstabilized formula escapes and, while continuously increasing in size starts living off cattle and humans.

Leo G. Carroll is excellent in his scientist role, while John Agar, young town medico, and Mara Corday carry off the romantic demands very well.

....

■ **TARAS BULBA**

1962, 123 MINS, US ◇ ⓦ
Dir J. Lee Thompson *Prod* Harold Hecht *Scr* Waldo Salt, Karl Tunberg *Ph* Joseph MacDonald *Ed* William Reynolds, Gene Milford, Eda Warren, Folmar Blangsted *Mus* Franz Waxman *Art Dir* Edward Carrere
● Tony Curtis, Yul Brynner, Christine Kaufmann, Sam Wanamaker, Brad Dexter, Guy Rolfe (United Artists)

For many minutes of the two hours it takes director J. Lee Thompson to put Gogol's tale of the legendary Cossack hero on the screen, the panorama of fighting men and horses sweeping across the wide steppes (actually the plains of Argentina) provides a compelling sense of pageantry and grandeur.

As powerful as they are, the spectacular features of *Taras Bulba* do not quite render palatable the wishy-washy subplot, seemingly devised to give Tony Curtis as much screen time as the far more colorful title-role of Yul Brynner.

Curtis, an excellent actor when properly supervised or motivated, was seemingly neither inspired nor irritated sufficiently by his talented credits-sharer to do more than kiss and kill on cue.

Brynner's Taras Bulba is an arrogant, proud, physically powerful Cossack chief. Even though the actor follows the habit of running his lines together, his actions are always unmistakably clear. He's allowed plenty of space in which to chew the scenery and there's precious little of it in which he doesn't leave teethmarks.

The battle sequences and, to a lesser extent, the Cossack camp scenes, are the picture's greatest assets. Some of cameraman Joseph MacDonald's long shots of hordes of horsemen sweeping across the plains, as countless others pour over every hillside, are breathtakingly grand and fully utilize the wide screen. Franz Waxman's score, Russian derived, for the battles and his czardas-like themes for the Cossacks are among his best work.

□ 1962: Nomination: Best Original Music Score

....

■ **TARGET**

1985, 117 MINS, US ◇ ⓦ ⊙
Dir Arthur Penn *Prod* Richard D. Zanuck, David Brown *Scr* Howard Berk, Don Petersen *Ph* Jean Tournier *Ed* Stephen A. Rotter, Richard P. Cirincione *Mus* Michael Small *Art Dir* Willy Holt
● Gene Hackman, Matt Dillon, Gayle Hunnicutt, Victoria Fyodorova, Josef Sommer, Guy Boyd (CBS)

Target is a spy thriller that's not only completely understandable and involving throughout, but also continually surprising along the way. It also strangely contains a few scenes of dreadful writing, acting and direction.

Gene Hackman is a seemingly dull lumberyard owner in Dallas and Matt Dillon is his sporty roughneck son. Loving but a bit bored, too, mother Gayle Hunnicutt finally has decided to vacation in Paris alone because Hackman has an odd aversion to visiting Europe. While away, she hopes the two will make an effort to get to like each other. Then comes news that Mom has been kidnapped.

Although there are the obligatory preposterous auto chases, the action overall is supportive of the plot rather than a substitute. Ditto bloodshed and pyromania.

•••••••••••••••••••••••••••••••••

■ TARGETS

1968, 90 MINS, US ◊ ▨
Dir Peter Bogdanovich   *Prod* Peter Bogdanovich
Scr Peter Bogdanovich   *Ph* Laszlo Kovacs   *Ed* [uncredited]   *Art Dir* Polly Platt
● Boris Karloff, Tim O'Kelly, Nancy Hsueh, James Brown, Peter Bogdanovich (Saticoy)

A good programmer, within low budget limitations, about a sniper and his innocent victims. A separate, concurrent sub-plot features Boris Karloff as a horror film star who feels he is washed up. Both plot lines converge in an exciting climax.

Peter Bogdanovich has made a film of much suspense and implicit violence. It opens with a typical horror pic finale, which in a neat switcheroo turns out to be just that, as producer Monte Landis, o.o.'s the film. Karloff declares he is through with films and exits. A sidewalk scene introduces Tim O'Kelly, all-American boy who has drawn a bead on Karloff from a nearby gun shop.

Plot then picks up O'Kelly, a gun-loving, disturbed youth who 'had everything to live for'. One night, his mind snaps. He hides in the screen tower of a drive-in theatre, whence he terrorizes the audience. A press stunt has drawn Karloff to the ozoner for the climax.

As any newspaper or TV newsreel shows, mass murderers look just like anyone else. O'Kelly's projection of blandness is most appropriate to the suspense.

Aware of the virtue of implied violence, Bogdanovich conveys moments of shock, terror, suspense and fear.

•••••••••••••••••••••••••••••••••

■ TARNISHED ANGELS, THE

1957, 87 MINS, US
Dir Douglas Sirk   *Prod* Albert Zugsmith   *Scr* George Zuckerman   *Ph* Irving Glassberg   *Ed* Russell F. Schoengarth   *Mus* Frank Skinner   *Art Dir* Alexander Golitzen, Alfred Sweeney
● Rock Hudson, Robert Stack, Dorothy Malone, Jack Carson, Robert Middleton, Troy Donahue (Universal)

The Tarnished Angels is a stumbling entry. Characters are mostly colorless, given static reading in drawn-out situations, and story line is lacking in punch. Film is designed as a follow-up to *Written on the Wind*, to take advantage of the principals both before and behind the camera.

The production is based on William Faulkner's novel *Pylon*, and screenplay carries an air circus setting. Rock Hudson is intro'd as a seedy, but idealistic, New Orleans reporter covering a barnstorming show in that city. He falls for Dorothy Malone, trick parachutist-wife of Robert Stack, speed flyer and World War I ace, still living in his past glory as he and his small unit cruises about the country participating in air events.

Hudson appears in an unrealistic role to which he can add nothing and Stack spends most of the time with eagles in his eyes.

•••••••••••••••••••••••••••••••••

■ TARZAN AND HIS MATE

1934, 92 MINS, US ▨ ⊙
Dir Cedric Gibbons   *Scr* Howard Emmett Rogers, Leon Gordon, James Kevin McGuinness   *Ph* Charles Clarke, Clyde De Vinna
● Johnny Weissmuller, Maureen O'Sullivan, Neil Hamilton, Paul Cavanagh, Forrester Harvey, Nathan Curry (M-G-M)

In *Tarzan and His Mate*, second of the Metro series with Johnny Weissmuller, the monkeys do everything but bake cakes and the very human elephants always seem on the verge of sitting down for a nice, quiet game of chess; yet the picture has a strange sort of power that overcomes the total lack of logic.

Tarzan No. 1 ended with Tarz and the white girl from England at peace in their jungle kingdom. They're again at peace as No. 2 ends, but in the 92 minutes between the two fade-outs they're almost in pieces, several times. Trouble starts soon as the domain of Mr and Mrs Tarzan (Weissmuller and Maureen O'Sullivan) is trespassed upon by Neil Hamilton and Paul Cavanagh, a couple of heels from Mayfair. Boys are after the fortune in ivory which lies in a pachyderm graveyard.

Tarzan and his mate spend most of their time swinging through the branches. The Tarzans also do some fancy swimming, particularly during a tank sequence when Weissmuller and a lady swimmer doubling for O'Sullivan, perform some artistic submarine formations. The lady is brassiere-less, but photographed from the side only.

•••••••••••••••••••••••••••••••••

■ TARZAN AND THE SLAVE GIRL

1950, 74 MINS, US
Dir Lee Sholem   *Prod* Sol Lesser   *Scr* Hans Jacoby, Arnold Belgard   *Ph* Russell Harlan   *Ed* Christian Nyby   *Mus* Paul Sawtell   *Art Dir* Harry Horner
● Lex Barker, Vanessa Brown, Robert Alda, Denise Darcel, Hurd Hatfield, Arthur Shields (RKO/Lesser)

Lex Barker, as Tarzan, takes to the jungle on the trail of some femme natives who are being held prisoners by a group of lost tribesmen [led by Hurd Hatfield]. With him on the trek are a doctor (Arthur Shields), searching for the source of a jungle disease; a comely half-breed nurse with a yen for men; a drunken jungle beachcomber (Robert Alda), and sundry native carriers. Enroute, the safari fights off natives disguised as bushes and armed with deadly blowguns.

Vanessa Brown makes her bow in the Jane role and fills the bill on all counts. Denise Darcel is the nurse, adding plenty of s.a. spice.

•••••••••••••••••••••••••••••••••

■ TARZAN ESCAPES

1936, 90 MINS, US ▨
Dir Richard Thorpe   *Prod* Sam Zimbalist (assoc.)
Scr Cyril Hume   *Ph* Leonard Smith   *Ed* W. Donn Hayes   *Mus* [uncredited]   *Art Dir* Elmer Sheeley
● Johnny Weissmuller, Maureen O'Sullivan, John Buckler, Benita Hume, William Henry, Herbert Mundin (M-G-M)

This plot permits Tarzie's idyllic romance with his mate (Maureen O'Sullivan) to be rudely interrupted by a couple of the missus' relatives from London. Mrs Tarzan has unknowingly become the heir to a late uncle's large fortune, and the relatives try to bring her back to civilization so that she may grab the coin and help them grab some of it also.

It so happens, however, that their jungle guide is a dastardly rat who sees in Tarzan a cinch freak show attraction for up north, and it takes not only Tarz himself but also a big zoo full of animal friends to clear up the mess, save the lives of the white folks, give the villyan his just dues, and restore Tarzan's mate to Tarzan.

Johnny Weissmuller once again looks good as the jungle boy. And O'Sullivan is also okay once more as the loving wife, but considerably more covered up in clothing this time. A female ape called Cheetah is the Tarzans' pet and houseworker, and some expert handling of the monk provides the picture with its most legitimately comical and best moments.

•••••••••••••••••••••••••••••••••

■ TARZAN FINDS A SON

1939, 81 MINS, US
Dir Richard Thorpe   *Prod* Sam Zimbalist   *Scr* Cyril Hume   *Ph* Leonard Smith   *Ed* Frank Sullivan, Gene Ruggiero   *Art Dir* Cedric Gibbons, Urie McCleary
● Johnny Weissmuller, Maureen O'Sullivan, Johnnie Sheffield, Ian Hunter, Laraine Day, Frieda Inescort (M-G-M)

Tarzan Finds a Son carries more credulity and believable jungle adventure than the long list of preceding Tarzan features.

Tarzan and the Missus save a baby in plane that crashes in the jungle. Tarzan is proudly teaching his accepted son the jungle lore, when a searching party arrives to establish death of the baby, who has come into heavy inheritance. Ian Hunter and Frieda Inescort are out to grab the inheritance for themselves, and start plotting death of Tarzan and snatch of the youngster.

Johnny Weissmuller athletically runs and swims through as the ape-man in okay fashion. Maureen O'Sullivan is the jungle wife, and gets in some good dramatic work in battling against herself to give up the youngster. Tarzan's boy, little Johnnie Sheffield, does nicely and performs his athletic chores satisfactorily.

•••••••••••••••••••••••••••••••••

■ TARZAN'S GREATEST ADVENTURE

1959, 90 MINS, UK ◊
Dir John Guillermin   *Prod* Sy Weintraub   *Scr* Berne Giler, John Guillermin   *Ph* Ted Scaife   *Ed* Bert Rule   *Mus* Douglas Gamley   *Art Dir* Michael Stringer
● Gordon Scott, Anthony Quayle, Sara Shane, Niall MacGinnis, Sean Connery, Scilla Gabel (Solar)

Tarzan finally steps away from Hollywood's process screens to pound his chest amid authentic terrors in the heart of Africa. Death and trauma are the stars, and the supporting players are bullets, arrows, knives, hatchets, dynamite, neck-choking paraphernalia, crocodiles, lions, snakes, spiders, boulders, spikes, pits, quicksand and prickly cactus. It's a furious affair, with an exciting chase or two.

Tarzan (Gordon Scott) is a modern he-man, still adorned in loincloth but more conversational than Edgar Rice Burroughs pictured him. Scott puts little emotion into his greatest adventure, but he swings neatly from tree to tree, takes good care of a crocodile, even if it does appear dead from the start, deciphers with ease the sounds of his animal friends and, more than anything else, looks the part.

Film's storyline [by Les Crutchfield] has Tarzan and another white man as mortal enemies. The antagonist (Anthony Quayle) is leading a five-member boat expedition to get rich in diamonds, and Tarzan, knowing of his bestial attitude, follows in hot pursuit. An approximately beautiful female (Sara Shane) drops out of the sky to tag along with Tarzan and turns out to be quite handy in helping the apeman through a bad time or two.

Quayle is excellent as the scarfaced villain, and Niall MacGinnis as a nearly blind diamond expert is equally fine. Sean Connery and Al Mulock, the two other male members of the expedition, are okay, and Scilla Gabel, looking like a miniature Sophia Loren, is easy to look at.

•••••••••••••••••••••••••••••••••

■ TARZAN'S PERIL

1951, 79 MINS, US
Dir Byron Haskin, Phil Brandon   *Prod* Sol Lesser
Scr Samuel Newman, Francis Swann, John Cousins
Ph Karl Struss, Jack Whitehead   *Ed* Jack Murray
Mus Michel Michelet   *Art Dir* John Meehan
● Lex Barker, Virginia Huston, George Macready, Douglas Fowley, Glenn Anders, Dorothy Dandridge (Lesser/ RKO)

This latest entry in the *Tarzan* series has the familiar ingredients of jungle adventure, plus good background footage actually lensed in Africa.

Lex Barker is a capable hero in his Tarzan character. Script could have made him even more of a superman, but otherwise does not let down the fans of the Edgar Rice Burroughs creation.

Tarzan is called upon to mete out jungle justice to a gun-runner who supplies forbidden weapons to a tribe of would-be warriors. The script has the hero swinging through trees, swimming rivers, surviving a plunge over a waterfall and taking on a whole tribe in battle before establishing peace and quiet again in his native heath.

Virginia Huston has only a few scenes as Tarzan's mate, Jane, in the footage. There's more emphasis on Dorothy Dandridge, queen of a tribe that is saved by Tarzan from its warring rivals. George Macready is the able villain.

. . . .

■ TARZAN THE APE MAN

1932, 70 MINS, US Ⓥ
Dir W. S. Van Dyke   *Prod* [uncredited]   *Scr* Cyril Hume, Ivor Novello   *Ph* Harold Rosson, Clyde De Vinna   *Ed* Ben Lewis, Tom Held   *Mus* [uncredited]   *Art Dir* Cedric Gibbons
● Johnny Weissmuller, Maureen O'Sullivan, Neil Hamilton, C. Aubrey Smith, Doris Lloyd, Forrester Harvey (M-G-M)

A jungle and stunt picture, done in deluxe style, with tricky handling of fantastic atmosphere, and a fine, artless performance by the Olympic athlete that represents the absolute best that could be done with the character [created by Edgar Rice Burroughs].

Footage is loaded with a wealth of sensational wild animal stuff. Suspicion is unavoidable that some of it is cut-in material left over from the same producer's *Trader Horn* (by the same director).

Some of the stunt episodes are grossly overdone, but the production skill and literary treatment in other directions compensates. Tarzan (Johnny Weissmuller) is pictured as achieving impossible feats of strength and daring. One of them has him battling singlehanded, and armed only with an inadequate knife, not only with one lion but with a panther and two lions, and saved at the last minute from still a third big cat only by the friendly help of an elephant summoned by a call of distress in jungle language.

Story that introduces the Tarzan character is slight. An English trader (C. Aubrey Smith) and his young partner (Neil Hamilton) are about to start in search of the traditional elephants' graveyard where ivory abounds, when the elder man's daughter from England (Maureen O'Sullivan) appears at the trading post and insists upon going along. The adventures grow out of their travels.

. . . .

■ TARZAN, THE APE MAN

1981, 112 MINS, US ◇ Ⓥ ⊙
Dir John Derek   *Prod* Bo Derek   *Scr* Tom Rowe, Garry Goddard   *Ph* John Derek   *Ed* James B. Ling   *Mus* Perry Botkin   *Art Dir* Wolfgang Dickman
● Bo Derek, Richard Harris, John Phillip Law, Miles O'Keeffe, Wilfred Hyde White (M-G-M/Svengali)

This endless romp through the jungle, lacking any focus, fun or excitement (sexual or otherwise), seems to exist merely as a reason for husband John to find another 1001 ways to photograph wife Bo in varying stages of undress.

With about three minutes shaved as a result of a court decision stating that the Dereks and M-G-M went beyond the remake rights bought from the Burroughs estate, this opus will disappoint both Tarzan fans and Bo admirers.

A supposed remake of the 1932 *Tarzan the Ape Man*, the Derek version has less to do with the jungle man (who doesn't show his face until halfway through the picture) than it does in dealing with Jane's (Bo's) rediscovery of her long-lost explorer father Richard Harris.

The father-daughter relationship doesn't have a chance here with Bo's wooden recitation of her lines and Harris' ranting through any number of dreary, confusing speeches.

Although John Derek's direction remains loose and uninspired (the few action shots of Tarzan are ruined with corny slow motion footage), he does know how to shoot pretty pictures of Sri Lanka and, more particularly, Bo. If *Tarzan* were a magazine layout, he'd probably be nominated for something.

. . . .

■ TASTE OF HONEY, A

1961, 100 MINS, UK Ⓥ
Dir Tony Richardson   *Prod* Tony Richardson   *Scr* Shelagh Delaney, Tony Richardson   *Ph* Walter Lassally   *Ed* Antony Gibbs   *Mus* John Addison   *Art Dir* Ralph Brinton
● Dora Bryan, Rita Tushingham, Robert Stephens, Murray Melvin, Paul Danquah (Woodfall)

Shelagh Delaney's play, which clicked both in the West End and on Broadway, has an earthy gusto and sincerity that lift its somewhat downbeat theme and drab surroundings. It has humor, understanding and poignance. Oddly enough the dialog, though pointedly couched in the semi-illiterate vernacular of the lower-class North Country working folk, archives at times a halting and touching form of poetry.

The film faithfully follows the narrative of the play. But the camera effectively gets into the streets and captures the gray drabness of the locals as well as the boisterous vulgarity of Blackpool, saloons and dance-halls. Yarn primarily concerns five people and their dreams, hopes and fears. They are Jo (Rita Tushingham); her flighty, sluttish neglectful mother; the fancy man her mother marries; a young Negro ship's cook with whom Jo has a brief affair which leaves her pregnant; and a sensitive young homosexual who gives her the tenderness aand affection lacking in her relationship with her mother.

Film introduces 19-year-old Rita Tushingham as the 16-year-old schoolgirl. She plays with no makeup, her hair is untidy, her profile completely wrong by all accepted standards; but her expressive eyes and her warm, wry smile are haunting.

Dora Bryan tackles the role of the flighty, footloose mother with confidence and zest. The three men in the lives of daughter and mother are also played with keen insight by Robert Stephens, Paul Danquah and Murray Melvin. Perhaps the most difficult role is that of Melvin. He repeats the success he made of the part of the young homosexual in the play.

. . . .

■ TASTE THE BLOOD OF DRACULA

1970, 95 MINS, UK ◇ Ⓥ
Dir Peter Sasdy   *Prod* Aida Young   *Scr* John Elder [= Anthony Hinds]   *Ph* Arthur Grant   *Ed* Chris Barnes   *Mus* James Bernard   *Art Dir* Scott MacGregor
● Christopher Lee, Geoffrey Keen, Gwen Watford, Linda Hayden, Peter Sallis, Anthony Corlan (Hammer)

The setting is in Victorian England, on London's fringes and concerns three hypocritical, erotic old buffers who, sated by their dingy little orgies in the East End, look for bigger, more lustful thrills.

They get entangled with one of Dracula's disciples and, with the aid of the blood of Dracula and some of his 'props', sold to them by a wise peddler, they start to dabble in Black Mass and Satanic ritual. They bump off Dracula's messenger in terror and Dracula swears to dispose of the three men.

From then on, it's the old routine of Dracula causing death and disaster, upsetting the families by abducting daughters and turning one of them into a vampire and generally making himself a thundering evil nuisance.

. . . .

■ TATTOO

1981, 102 MINS, US ◇ Ⓥ
Dir Bob Brooks   *Prod* Joseph E. Levine, Richard P. Levine   *Scr* Joyce Bunuel   *Ph* Arthur Ornitz   *Ed* Thom Noble   *Mus* Barry DeVorzon   *Art Dir* Stuart Wurtzel
● Bruce Dern, Maud Adams, Leonard Frey, Rikke Borge, John Getz (20th Century-Fox)

In this 20th-Century release, Bruce Dern appears as a congenital cuckoo, who loves to paint permanent pictures on people's bodies. Becoming enamored of fashion model Maud Adams, Dern decides she could be life's perfect companion, given a new paint job.

So he kidnaps her. Such is Bob Brooks' direction and Joyce Bunuel's script that the problem of getting the unconscious Adams from her NY highrise apartment to an abandoned house on the New Jersey seashore isn't difficult at all. In one scene, they are in NY. In the next, cut to NJ. Filmmaking is simple.

Anyway, once Dern has her in his drawing room, he begins to doodle on her bare body. Finally, the work is finished and Dern takes his own clothes off to reveal that he, too, is a work of art. This seems to turn Adams on and they make love until she stabs him to death with the tattoo machine. Yes, she does.

. . . .

■ TAXI DRIVER

1976, 113 MINS, US ◇ Ⓥ ⊙
Dir Martin Scorsese   *Prod* Michael Phillips, Julia Phillips   *Scr* Paul Schrader   *Ph* Michael Chapman   *Ed* Marcia Lucas, Tom Rolf, Melvin Shapiro   *Mus* Bernard Herrmann   *Art Dir* Charles Rosen
● Robert De Niro, Cybill Shepherd, Peter Boyle, Albert Brooks, Leonard Harris, Harvey Keitel (Columbia)

Assassins, mass murderers and other freakish criminals more often than not turn out to be the quiet kid down the street. *Taxi Driver* is Martin Scorsese's frighteningly plausible case history of such a person. It's a powerful film and a terrific showcase for the versatility of star Robert De Niro.

The pic has a quasi-documentary look, and Bernard Herrmann's final score is superb (a final credit card conveys 'Our gratitude and respect').

Paul Schrader's original screenplay is in fact a sociological horror story. Take a young veteran like Travis Bickle. A night cabbie, he prowls the NY streets until dawn, stopping occasionally for coffee, killing offduty time in porno theatres.

What prods Travis are a series of rejections: among others by Cybill Shepherd, adroitly cast as the tele-heroine lookalike working for the presidential campaign of Leonard Harris, and by Jodie Foster, teenage prostitute.

In a climactic sequence, the madman exorcises himself. It's a brutal, horrendous and cinematically brilliant sequence, capped by the irony that he becomes a media hero for a day.

De Niro gives the role the precise blend of awkwardness, naivete and latent violence.

□ 1976: Nominations: Best Picture, Actor (Robert De Niro), Supp. Actress (Jodie Foster), Original Score

. . . .

■ TAZA, SON OF COCHISE

1954, 79 MINS, US ◇
Dir Douglas Sirk   *Prod* Ross Hunter   *Scr* George Zuckerman, Gerald Drayson Adams   *Ph* Russell Metty   *Ed* Milton Carruth   *Mus* Frank Skinner
● Rock Hudson, Barbara Rush, Gregg Palmer, Bart Roberts, Morris Ankrum, Gene Iglesias (Universal)

Taza, Son of Cochise is a colorful 3-D Indian – US Cavalry entry alternating between hot action and passages of almost pastoral quality. The spectacular scenery of Moab, Utah, furnishes a particularly apropos background for unfoldment of the script, and Douglas Sirk's direction is forceful, aimed at making every scene an eye-filling experience.

This is the story of the great Apache chief's son, who promises at his father's deathbed he will try to keep the peace that Cochise so painstakingly made with the whites. He is opposed here by his younger brother, who attempts to win the tribe over to Geronimo and take to the warpath again.

Rock Hudson suffices in action demands of his role of Taza, but character is none too believable. Barbara Rush, co-starring as the daughter of Morris Ankrum, one of Geronimo's followers, is in for romantic purposes and handles part well.

Jeff Chandler, who was Cochise in studio's *Battle at Apache Pass*, repeats character for the single death-bed scene, without screen credit.

● ●

■ TEA AND SYMPATHY

1956, 122 MINS, US ◇ ▽ ⊙
Dir Vincente Minnelli   *Prod* Pandro S. Berman
Scr Robert Anderson   *Ph* John Alton   *Ed* Ferris
Webster   *Mus* Adolph Deutsch   *Art Dir* William A.
Horning, Edward Carfagno
● Deborah Kerr, John Kerr, Leif Erickson, Edward
Andrews, Darryl Hickman, Norma Crane (M-G-M)

This is the story of a youngster regarded by fellow students as 'not regular' (i.e. not manly). The spotlight is on clearly implied homosexuality.

Robert Anderson's adaptation of his own legiter keeps the essentials in proper focus. The pivotal role of the misunderstood sensitive boy is an excellently drawn characterization. The part is played with marked credibility by John Kerr. The housemaster's wife is a character study of equal sensitivity and depth. Deborah Kerr gives the role all it deserves.

The housemaster part, played with muscle-flexing exhibitionism by Leif Erickson, loses some of its meaning in the tone-down. On the stage his efforts at being 'manly' carried the suggestion that he was trying to compensate a fear of a homo trend in his own makeup. The suggestion is diluted to absence in the picture.

Edward Andrews, as John Kerr's father, is the brash and understanding parent who would prefer to see his son carry on with the town tart to erase his 'sister-boy' reputation.

● ●

■ TEACHERS

1984, 106 MINS, US ◇ ▽ ⊙
Dir Arthur Hiller   *Prod* Aaron Russo   *Scr* W.R.
McKinney   *Ph* David M. Walsh   *Ed* Don Zimmerman
Mus Sandy Gibson (sup.)   *Art Dir* Richard MacDonald
● Nick Nolte, JoBeth Williams, Judd Hirsch, Ralph
Macchio, Lee Grant, Richard Mulligan (United Artists)

Teachers stars Nick Nolte as a burned-out teacher who's drawn back to his ideals. Social drama and irreverent, often broad comedy underscore this story of a zoo-like urban high school that's run like an asylum. Pic makes stinging, important points about the mess of secondary public education, but those points are diluted gradually by an overload of comic absurdity.

Catalyst to dark comedy is a lawsuit brought against the school district for awarding a diploma to a student who can't read or write. JoBeth Williams plays the attorney serving notice on the school.

Filmmakers engaged a large cast of well-known performers: Lee Grant as calculating, ruthless school superintendent; Allen Garfield as a teacher afraid of his student but who turns heroic; Royal Dano as a glum disciplinarian; and, in the central student role, Ralph Macchio as a street-smart but illiterate kid who triggers Nolte's reemergence.

Nolte nicely captures the image of a rather shaggy 10-year veteran of the classroom, and Williams is okay as his zealous nemesis.

Script was written by 27-year-old debuting screenwriter W.R. McKinney from a story conceived by producer Aaron Russo and his brother and exec producer Irwin Russo. Latter capitalized on his 10 years' experience as a teacher in New York.

● ●

■ TEACHER'S PET

1958, 120 MINS, US ▽ ⊙
Dir George Seaton   *Prod* William Perlberg   *Scr* Fay
Kanin, Michael Kanin   *Ph* Haskell Boggs   *Ed* Alma
Macrorie   *Mus* Roy Webb   *Art Dir* Hal Pereira, Earl
Hedrick
● Clark Gable, Doris Day, Gig Young, Mamie Van
Doren, Nick Adams, Vivian Nathan (Perslea/Paramount)

There is rich new life and liveliness, and even a fresh approach with humor and heartiness, in Fay and Michael Kanin's original screenplay. Clark Gable is one of those crusty, old-line newspapermen who believes that nothing good comes out of colleges, certainly not out of schools of journalism. When he is invited to lecture by journalism professor Doris Day, he discovers his ideas about female professors were wrong.

For various reasons he must pretend he is not a city editor but a pupil. In trying to get this straightened out, his emotional relations with Day become more involved and they finally arrive at the expected conclusion.

This is the straight story line, but the Kanins have decorated the framework with some hilarious comedy lines and scenes which director George Seaton has set up with skill and delivered with gusto. There is the sequence of Gable's reactions to a strip-tease by Mamie Van Doren; another between Gable and his rival for Day, Gig Young, where Young is suffering from the grandfather of all hangovers. These and a dozen other bright gags spark the story. It runs long (two hours) for a comedy but it holds up.

Gable frankly mugs through many of his comedy scenes and it is effective low comedy. Day is as bright and fresh as a newly set stick of type. Young gives the picture its funniest moments, milking the scenes with the expertness of a master.

☐ 1958: Nominations: Best Supp. Actor (Gig Young), Original Story & Screenplay

● ●

■ TEA FOR TWO

1950, 97 MINS, US ◇ ▽ ⊙
Dir David Butler   *Prod* William Jacobs   *Scr* Harry
Clork   *Ph* Wilfrid M. Cline   *Ed* Irene Morra
Mus Ray Heindorf (dir.)   *Art Dir* Douglas Bacon
● Doris Day, Gordon MacRae, Gene Nelson, Eve
Arden, Billy De Wolfe, S.Z. Sakall (Warner)

A generous sprinkling of songs, dances and comedy makes *Tea for Two* the type of beguiling musical nonsense that practically always finds a ready reception. It wears its Technicolor dress well, the nostalgic numbers from the 1929 *No, No, Nanette* and other cleffing of the period listen well, the pacing is smooth and the cast able.

Suggested by the *Nanette* book by Frank Mandel, Otto Harbach, Vincent Youmans and Emil Nyitray, the script is spiced with dialog and situations that permit easy introduction of the variety of dance numbers [directed by LeRoy Prinz, staged by Eddie Prinz and Al White].

Flashback technique to get 1929 period on the screen has the capable help of S.Z. Sakall, playing Doris Day's uncle, who is telling the story to the children of the two singers.

● ●

■ TEAHOUSE OF THE AUGUST MOON, THE

1956, 123 MINS, US ◇ ▽ ⊙
Dir Daniel Mann   *Prod* Jack Cummings   *Scr* John
Patrick   *Ph* John Alton   *Ed* Harold F. Kress

Mus Saul Chaplin, Kikuko Kanai   *Art Dir* William A.
Horning, Eddie Imazu
● Marlon Brando, Glenn Ford, Machiko Kyo, Eddie
Albert, Paul Ford, Harry Morgan (M-G-M)

Teahouse retains the basic appeal that made it a unique war novel and a legit hit. There is some added slapstick for those who prefer their comedy broader. Adding to its prospects are some top comedy characterizations, notably from Glenn Ford, plus the offbeat casting of Marlon Brando in a comedy role.

In transferring his play based on the Vern Sneider novel to the screen, John Patrick has provided a subtle shift in the focal interest.

Deft screenplay provides an interesting filip in retaining the stage device of a narrative prolog and epilog by Brando and the warmly humorous verbiage has been left intact. Story line also is unsullied as the film unspools the tribulations of Ford, the young army officer assigned to bring the benefits of democracy and free enterprise to the little Okinawan town of Tobiki.

The role of Capt Fisby represents a romp for Glenn Ford, who gives it an unrestrained portrayal that adds mightily to the laughs. Brando is excellent as the interpreter, limning the rogueish character perfectly. Physically, he seems a bit too heavy for the role.

Japanese actress Machiko Kyo is easy on the eyes as the geisha girl and there is excellent support from Eddie Albert, who sparkles as the psychiatrist who yearns to be an agricultural expert.

● ●

■ TED AND VENUS

1991, 100 MINS, US ◇ ▽
Dir Bud Cort   *Prod* Randolf Turrow, William Talmadge
Scr Paul Ciotti, Bud Cort   *Ph* Dietrich Lohmann
Ed Katina Zinner, Peter Zinner   *Mus* David Robbins
Art Dir Lynn Christopher
● Bud Cort, Jim Brolin, Kim Adams, Carol Kane,
Pamella D'Pella, Brian Thompson (Gondola/LA Dreams)

In his directorial debut, Bud Cort attempts to recapture some of the eccentric appeal of his 1971 starrer *Harold and Maude* but he's picked the wrong story and treated it far too seriously.

Cort stars as Ted Whitley, a 35-year-old hippie on disability. A virginal, pathetically earnest nerd, Ted has a vision of a gorgeous young lady emerging from the sea, and when she turns out to be Linda (Kim Adams), the community service worker helping him find an apartment, he feels compelled to pursue her.

Egged on by his buddy (Jim Brolin) and encouraged by her enthusiasm for his poetry and general friendliness, Ted begins a romantic campaign that quickly degenerates into obscene phone calls and other antisocial acts.

Aside from telling an actively offputting story [by Paul Ciotti], Cort the director hasn't done a bad job of putting it up on the screen. He has packed the cast with a lively assortment of actor friends, and newcomer Adams is a stunner with a winning personality. Pic so impressively suggests the look and attitude of the time of the action (1974) that it almost could have been shot then.

● ●

■ TEENAGE MUTANT NINJA TURTLES

1990, 93 MINS, US ◇ ▽ ⊙
Dir Steve Barron   *Prod* Kim Dawson, Simon Fields,
David Chan   *Scr* Todd W. Langen, Bobby Herbeck
Ph John Fenner   *Ed* William Gordean, Sally Menke,
James Symons   *Mus* John Du Prez   *Art Dir* Roy Forge
Smith
● Judith Hoag, Elias Koteas, Raymond Serra, Michael
Turney, James Saito, Jay Patterson (Golden Harvest/
Limelight)

While visually rough around the edges, sometimes sluggish in its plotting and marred by

T

overtones of racism in its use of Oriental villains, the wacky live-action screen version of the *Teenage Mutant Ninja Turtles* cartoon characters [created by Kevin Eastman and Peter Laird] scores with its generally engaging tongue-in-cheek humor.

Supposedly mutated by radioactive goop, the turtles live in the sewers, eat pizza, dance to rock music, play Trivial Pursuit and casually toss around such words as 'awesome', 'bodacious' and 'gnarly'.

The screenplay makes all four of the green guys seem like clones, differentiated mostly by their variegated colored headbands. The plot is nothing more than some nonsense about the turtles and a handful of human sidekicks trying to stop the Foot Clan from terrorizing NY streets.

A bit too much time is devoted to the peculiar romance of unbelievably funky TV newswoman Judith Hoag and her off-the-wall vigilante b.f. Elias Koteas, who join forces with the creatures and misunderstood j.d. Michael Turney.

The martial-arts setpieces are amusingly outlandish, with the screen populated by hordes of attackers whom the nonchalant, graceful turtles have little trouble vanquishing as they toss off streams of surfer-lingo wisecracks.

■ **TEENAGE MUTANT NINJA TURTLES II THE SECRET OF OOZE**

1991, 88 MINS, US ◇ ⓦ ⊙
Dir Michael Pressman   *Prod* Thomas K. Gray, Kim Dawson, David Chan   *Scr* Todd W. Langen   *Ph* Shelly Johnson   *Ed* John Wright, Steve Mirkovich   *Mus* John Du Prez   *Art Dir* Roy Forge Smith
● Paige Turco, David Warner, Michelan Sisti, Leif Tilden, Kenn Troum, Mark Caso (Golden Harvest/Propper)

Though *Turtles II* suffers from a lack of novelty and an aimless screenplay, the bottom line is that the pic won't disappoint its core subteen audience. It gives more footage to Michelangelo, Donatello, Raphael, Leonardo and their giant rat master Splinter than the original did, and adds two hilarious childlike monsters, Rahzar and Tokka, who virtually steal the show.

The murky lighting, uninteresting human characters and violence of the original have been modified in the more amiable sequel, mostly to good effect.

Subtitle's promise that the ooze secret will be revealed doesn't pay off. David Warner, as the sympathetic and eccentric scientist who invented the stuff and now is trying to dispose of it, doesn't have much to do.

Paige Turco takes over the lead human role of Gotham TV newswoman April O'Neil from Judith Hoag, and while Turco is more glamorous, the character still seems unfocused and overly ditzy.

Ernie Reyes Jr has a winning role as a youthful pizza deliveryman/martial arts expert who wangles his way into the turtles' company and helps them in their neverending battle with the Foot Clan.

■ **TEENAGE MUTANT NINJA TURTLES III THE TURTLES ARE BACK . . . IN TIME**

1993, 95 MINS, US ◇ ⓦ ⊙
Dir Stuart Gillard   *Prod* Thomas Gray, Kim Dawson, David Chan   *Scr* Stuart Gillard   *Ph* David Gurfinkel   *Ed* William Gordean, James Symons   *Mus* John Du Prez   *Art Dir* Roy Forge Smith
● Elias Koteas, Paige Turco, Stuart Wilson, Vivian Wu, Sab Shimono, Henry Hayashi (Golden Harvest)

Bow-wow-abunga! The third installment of *Teenage Mutant Ninja Turtles* is a decided case of diminishing returns. On a story and craft level it borders on the unforgivably bad.

The new episode is a time travel yarn in

which the four amphibian heroes and their pal, reporter April O'Neill (Paige Turco), switch places with five 17th century samurai warriors. This is all effected with questionable scientific aplomb and a device that resembles a vintage street lamp.

In feudal Japan, they become embroiled in a struggle between two dynasties: Lord Norinaga (Sab Shimono) seeks to quash the rebel faction led by Mitsu (Vivian Wu) by enlisting the aid of the English mercenary and gunrunner Walker (Stuart Wilson).

Writer-director Stuart Gillard inappropriately paces the action at tortoise speed. Virtually every department fires wide. Performances range from competent to just plain embarrassing.

■ **TEEN AGENT**
See: If Looks Could Kill

■ **TEEN WOLF**

1985, 91 MINS, US ◇ ⓦ ⊙
Dir Rod Daniel   *Prod* Mark Levinson, Scott Rosenfelt   *Scr* Joseph Loeb III, Matthew Weisman   *Ph* Tim Suhrstedt   *Ed* Lois Freeman-Fox   *Mus* Miles Goodman   *Art Dir* Rosemary Brandenberg
● Michael J. Fox, James Hampton, Scott Paulin, Susan Ursitti, Jerry Levine, Jim Mackrell (Wolfkill/Atlantic)

Lightweight item is innocuous and well-intentioned but terribly feeble, another example of a decent idea yielding the least imaginative results conceivable.

The Beacontown Beavers have the most pathetic basketball team in high school history, and pint-sized Michael J. Fox is on the verge of quitting when he notices certain biological changes taking place. Heavy hair is growing on the backs of his hands, his ears and teeth are elongating.

Instead of turning into a horrific teen werewolf, however, Fox takes to trucking around school halls in full furry regalia, becoming more successful with the ladies and, most importantly, winning basketball games.

Fox is likeable enough in the lead, something that cannot be said for the remainder of the lackluster cast.

■ **TELL ME LIES**

1968, 118 MINS, UK/US ◇
Dir Peter Brook   *Prod* Peter Brook   *Scr* Denis Cannan   *Ph* Ian Wilson   *Ed* Ralph Sheldon   *Mus* Richard Peaslee
● Mark Jones, Pauline Munro, Robert Lloyd, Glenda Jackson, Paul Scofield, Kingsley Amis (Continental/Brook)

Tell Me Lies depicts a wide range of attitudes toward the war in Vietnam. It's loosely based on Peter Brook's theatrical success-de-scandale *US*.

While Brook's emotional concern about the war seems unquestionable, his artistic sincerity is open to examination. *Tell Me Lies* suggests an aesthetic bankruptcy resulting from the director's debts to Bertolt Brecht, Joan Littlewood (*Oh, What a Lovely War*) and Jean-Luc Godard.

Color and black-and-white footage is haphazardly alternated to no effect. Musical numbers are shouted-sung in a cacophonic manner that only underscores the lyrics' vacuity. Staged discussions are juxtaposed with cinema-verite encounters with British parliamentarians, Maoists and black-power advocate Stokeley Carmichael.

Verbal material is splayed in subtitles at the bottom of the screen, overlapped on sequences or subliminally injected word by word within a continuous segment. It's all pretty ugly.

■ **TELL THEM WILLIE BOY IS HERE**

1969, 97 MINS, US ◇ ⓦ
Dir Abraham Polonsky   *Prod* Jennings Lang   *Scr* Abraham Polonsky   *Ph* Conrad Hall   *Ed* Melvin Shapiro   *Mus* Dave Grusin   *Art Dir* Alexander Golitzen, Henry Bumstead
● Robert Redford, Katharine Ross, Robert Blake, Susan Clark, Barry Sullivan, John Vernon (Universal)

A powerful unfoldment of a particular incident in US history, the film becomes, by extension, a deeply personal and radical vision of the past and future.

Film [from the book *Willie Boy . . . A Desert Manhunt* by Harry Lawton] tells the story of the tracking-down of a renegade Indian in California in 1909. Although Robert Blake is the title character, the film is really about Robert Redford, Coop, the deputy sheriff whose assignment it is to track down Willie.

Abraham Polonsky, who was blacklisted for 20 years, is not a director who works through his actors. Thesps are simple tools of his vision – their presences more than their abilities are used. Nobody's going to win any acting awards for their work herein. Still, Redford's 'presence' is magnificent, always suggesting the classically-structured, powerful-but-weak American.

■ **TEMP, THE**

1993, 95 MINS, US ◇ ⓦ ⊙
Dir Tom Holland   *Prod* David Permut, Tom Engelman   *Scr* Kevin Falls   *Ph* Steve Yaconelli   *Ed* Scott Conrad   *Mus* Frederic Talgorn   *Art Dir* Joel Schiller
● Timothy Hutton, Lara Flynn Boyle, Dwight Schultz, Oliver Platt, Steven Weber, Faye Dunaway (Columbus Circle)

If this *Temp* were applying for a full-time position, she wouldn't get the job. Moronic, derivative, artificial and pointless are just the first adjectives that come to mind to describe this concoction [screen story by Kevin Falls and Tom Engelman].

Lara Flynn Boyle temps for Timothy Hutton, a junior executive at the Mrs Appleby baked goods firm in Portland, run by the sleekly ruthless Faye Dunaway. Job uncertainty pits worker against worker, but provides room for Boyle to slither up the corporate ladder through stealth and, depending upon what you choose to believe, murder. Boyle doesn't disguise her interest in Hutton.

Tom Holland's directorial style consists of making everyone appear busy by moving them around at twice normal speed and shoving Steadicams down every available hallway. Every cast member has been seen to better effect.

■ **TEMPEST, THE**

1979, 96 MINS, UK ◇ ⓦ
Dir Derek Jarman   *Prod* Guy Ford   *Scr* Derek Jarman   *Ph* Peter Middleton   *Ed* Leslie Walker   *Mus* Wavemaker   *Art Dir* Yolanda Sonnaband
● Heathcote Williams, Karl Johnson, Jack Birkett, Toyah Wilcox, Elisabeth Welch (Boyd's)

British helmer Derek Jarman's third feature, a film version of Shakespeare's most fanciful play, is definitely one of a kind. Its greatest strength is its 'look'. That offsets the director-adaptor's generally limp control of the narrative.

Although heavily cut and reorganized, the Bard's lines are used virtually throughout. The plot remains intact. Jarman's biggest liberty is the insertion of a wedding feast at the end, complete with dancing sailor boys, and blues singer Elisabeth Welch crooning 'Stormy Weather' as a kind of diva ex machina.

Most successful innovation is Toyah Wilcox's assault on the usually vacuous role of Miranda. Plump and punkish, her reaction to the first eligible male she has ever seen is more lusty than wide-eyed, and thoroughly believable.

••••••••••••••••••••••••••••••••••••

■ 10

1979, 122 MINS, US ◇ ⑨ ⊙
Dir Blake Edwards   *Prod* Blake Edwards, Tony Adams
Scr Blake Edwards   *Ph* Frank Stanley   *Ed* Ralph E. Winters   *Mus* Henry Mancini   *Art Dir* Rodger Maus
● Dudley Moore, Julie Andrews, Bo Derek, Brian Dennehy, Dee Wallace, Robert Webber (Orion/Geoffrey)

Blake Edwards' *10* is a shrewdly observed and beautifully executed comedy of manners and morals.

10 is theoretically the top score on Dudley Moore's female ranking system, although he raves that his dream girl is an '11' after he first spots her. Frustrated in his song writing and in his relationship with g.f. Julie Andrews, diminutive Moore, 40-ish, four-time Oscar winner, decides to pursue the vision incarnated by Bo Derek despite fact that she's on her honeymoon with a jock type seemingly twice Moore's size.

Long build-up to Moore's big night with Derek is spiced with plenty of physical comedy which displays both Moore and Edwards in top slapstick form.

□ 1979: Nominations: Best Original Score, Song ('It's Easy To Say')

••••••••••••••••••••••••••••••••••••

■ TENANT, THE

1976, 125 MINS, FRANCE ◇ ⑨
Dir Roman Polanski   *Scr* Roman Polanski, Gerard Brach
Ph Sven Nykvist   *Ed* Francoise Bonnot   *Mus* Philippe Sarde   *Art Dir* Pierre Guffroy
● Roman Polanski, Isabelle Adjani, Melvyn Douglas, Jo Van Fleet, Bernard Fresson, Lila Kedrova (Marianne)

A tale of a paranoid breakdown of a little bureaucratic clerk that wastes no time in trying to be clinical. It has a humorous tang, underlying the macabre.

Director Roman Polanski plays the little man himself, a naturalized Frenchman of Polish origin, that expertly combines a deceptive internal resiliency to his outward timidity that makes him pathetic.

He goes to look at an apartment he has heard of. A girl who has it threw herself out the window. He is told he may have it only if she does not come back. Polanski calls the hospital and learns the girl is dead. He moves in but mysterious things begin to happen.

There is an effective atmosphere and it does create a feeling of personal anguish. Thus not achieving a balance of humor and suspense.

••••••••••••••••••••••••••••••••••••

■ TEN COMMANDMENTS, THE

1923, 160 MINS, US ◇ ⊗ ⊙
Dir Cecil B. DeMille   *Prod* Cecil B. DeMille   *Scr* Jeanie MacPherson   *Ph* Bert Glennon, Peverell Marley, Archie Stout, J.F. Westerberg, Ray Rennahan   *Ed* Anne Bauchens   *Mus* Hugo Riesenfeld   *Art Dir* Paul Iribe
● Theodore Roberts, Charles De Roche, Estelle Taylor, Richard Dix, Rod La Rocque, Edythe Chapman (Paramount)

The opening Biblical scenes of *The Ten Commandments* are irresistible in their assembly, breadth, color and direction; they are enormous and just as attractive. Cecil B. DeMille puts in a thrill here with the opening of the Red Sea for Moses to pass through with the Children of Israel.

This section is in color, and there are often big scenes besides that one. They are immense and stupendous, so big the modern tale after that seems puny. The story is of two sons, one his mother's boy and the other a harum-scarum atheist. Cheating as a contractor, the atheist's defects in building material

result in the collapse of a partly built church's wall, with the mother killed by the falling debris.

The best performance is given by Rod La Rocque as the atheist son, Dan McTavish. La Rocque really doesn't get properly started until called upon for plenty of emotion toward the finish. Theodore Roberts as Moses is but required to stride majestically, something he can do perhaps a little better than any one else, while Charles De Roche as Rameses (Pharaoh) always appears in a genteel, thoughtful mood as though wondering what it is all about.

The women do no better. Leatrice Joy wears a hat that may have been of the period of Moses; anyway it is an awful hat and her acting is strong enough to make you forget it.

••••••••••••••••••••••••••••••••••••

■ TEN COMMANDMENTS, THE

1956, 219 MINS, US ◇ ⑨ ⊙
Dir Cecil B. DeMille   *Prod* Cecil B. DeMille
Scr Aeneas MacKenzie, Jesse L. Lasky Jr, Fredric M. Frank, Jack Gariss   *Ph* Loyal Griggs   *Ed* Anne Bauchens   *Mus* Elmer Bernstein   *Art Dir* Hal Pereira, Walter Tyler, Albert Nozaki
● Charlton Heston, Yul Brynner, Anne Baxter, Edward G. Robinson, Yvonne De Carlo, Debra Paget (Paramount)

Cecil B. DeMille's super-spectacular about the Children of Israel held in brutal bondage until Moses, prodded by the God of Abraham, delivers them from Egyptian tyranny is a statistically intimidating production: the negative cost was $13.5 million and 25,000 extras were employed.

DeMille remains conventional with the motion picture as an art form. The eyes of the onlooker are filled with spectacle. Emotional tug is sometimes lacking.

Commandments is too long. More than two hours pass before the intermission and the break is desperately welcome. Scenes of the greatness that was Egypt, and Hebrews by the thousands under the whip of the taskmasters, are striking. But bigness wearies. There's simply too much.

Commandments hits the peak of beauty with a sequence that is unelaborate, this being the Passover supper wherein Moses is shown with his family while the shadow of death falls on Egyptian first-borns.

The creeping shadow of darkness that destroyed the Egyptian first-borns, the transcomposition of Moses' staff into a serpent, the changeover of the life-giving water into blood, flames to engulf the land and the parting of the Red Sea – these are shown. The effect of all these special camera devices is varying, however, and does not escape a certain theatricality.

Performances meet requirements all the way but exception must be made of Anne Baxter as the Egyptian princess Nefretiri. Baxter leans close to old-school siren histrionics and this is out of sync with the spiritual nature of *Commandments*.

Charlton Heston is an adaptable performer as Moses, revealing inner glow as he is called by God to remove the chains of slavery that hold his people. Yvonne De Carlo is Sephora, the warm and understanding wife of Moses. Yul Brynner is expert as Rameses, who inherits the Egyptian throne and seeks to battle Moses and his God until he's forced to acknowledge that 'Moses' God is the real God'.

□ 1956: Best Special Effects.
□ Nominations: Best Picture, Color Cinematography, Color Costume Design, Color Art Direction, Editing, Sound

••••••••••••••••••••••••••••••••••••

■ TENDER COMRADE

1943, 103 MINS, US ⑨
Dir Edward Dmytryk   *Prod* David Hempstead
Scr Dalton Trumbo   *Ph* Russell Metty   *Ed* Roland Gross
Mus Leigh Harline

● Ginger Rogers, Robert Ryan, Ruth Hussey, Kim Hunter, Jane Darwell, Mady Christians (RKO)

Centered around five women, all of whom have their men in the services and all of whom are contributing to the war effort in one way or another, *Tender Comrade* is a preachment for all that democracy stands for.

It is a picture of considerable charm despite its terrific emotional effects. And if the emotional impact is sometimes achieved with what may seem to be overdone dramatics, then it's to be marked off to what one can assume to be an enactment of what is actually real-life drama.

Ginger Rogers gives an unrestrained performance throughout, and where several scenes are almost dawdling she perks it up with neat bits of business. Ruth Hussey, Kim Hunter and Patricia Collinge also give excellent portrayals.

Dalton Trumbo contributes a screenplay compact and replete with plenty of excellent dialog. A notably big factor in the film's pace is Edward Dmytryk's direction of the sometimes slow but never tedious story.

••••••••••••••••••••••••••••••••••••

■ TENDER IS THE NIGHT

1962, 146 MINS, US ◇
Dir Henry King   *Prod* Henry T. Weinstein   *Scr* Ivan Moffat   *Ph* Leon Shamroy   *Ed* William Reynolds
Mus Bernard Herrmann   *Art Dir* Jack Martin Smith, Malcolm Brown
● Jennifer Jones, Jason Robards, Joan Fontaine, Tom Ewell, Cesare Danova, Jill St John (20th Century-Fox)

A combination of attractive, intelligent performances and consistently interesting, De Luxecolorful photography of interiors and exteriors – mostly the French Riviera – provide big plus qualities in this 20th-Fox adaptation of *Tender Is The Night*. This may not be a 100 proof distillation of F. Scott Fitzgerald. But *Tender Is The Night* is nonetheless on its own filmic terms a thoughtful, disturbing and at times absorbing romantic drama.

Novel and film depict the decay and deterioration of a brilliant and idealistic psychiatrist (Jason Robards), whose love for and marriage to a wealthy patient (Jennifer Jones) ultimately consumes, dissipates and destroys him by engulfing him in the meaningless motives and glamorous leisure of upper social class Americans adrift in Europe in the prosperous 1920s. Moffat's screenplay emphasizes the point of transference of strength from doctor to patient, traces the reverse process in which heroine and hero travel in emotionally opposite directions as a result of their tragic relationship.

Jones emerges a crisply fresh, intriguing personality and creates a striking character as the schizophrenic Nicole, Robards, whose non-matinee-idol masculinity makes him an ideal choice for the role of the ill-fated doctor-husband, Dick Diver, plays with intelligence and conviction. Joan Fontaine is convincing as Nicole's shallow, older sister, performing with the right manifestation of frivolity and bite that her part requires.

□ 1962: Nomination: Best Song ('Tender is the Night')

••••••••••••••••••••••••••••••••••••

■ TENDER MERCIES

1983, 89 MINS, US/UK ◇ ⑨ ⊙
Dir Bruce Beresford   *Prod* Philip S. Hobel, Mary Ann Hobel   *Scr* Horton Foote   *Ph* Russell Boyd
Ed William Anderson   *Mus* George Dreyfus
Art Dir Jeannine Claudia Oppewall
● Robert Duvall, Tess Harper, Allan Hubbard, Betty Buckley, Ellen Barkin, Wilford Brimley (Antron Media/EMI)

Robert Duvall is Mac Sledge, a down-and-out ex-country and western singer on the skids since his marriage to fellow C&W warbler Dixie (Betty Buckley) broke up.

Out on a drunken binge one night, he winds up in a small motel in Texas prairie country, and next morning accepts an offer of work from Rosa Lee (Tess Harper), the young widow who runs the place. Rosa Lee's husband had been killed in Vietnam, and she is having trouble keeping the motel and gas station going, and at the same time looking after her small son (Allan Hubbard).

Sledge stays on, the couple fall in love and marry. When tragedy unexpectedly touches his life, he finds he now has the strength to keep going and achieves new peace of mind. *Tender Mercies* is, in the best sense, an old-fashioned film. There's no sex, no violence. Duvall is dignified and moving as Sledge; Harper is most affecting as the widow he loves and marries; Hubbard almost steals the film as her inquiring son.

☐ 1983: Best Actor (Robert Duvall), Original Screenplay.

☐ Nominations: Best Picture, Director, Original Song ('Over You')

••••••••••••••••••••••••••••••••

■ TENDER TRAP, THE

1955, 110 MINS, US ◇ ⊙
Dir Charles Walters   *Prod* Lawrence Weingarten
Scr Julius Epstein   *Ph* Paul C. Vogel   *Ed* Jack Dunning
Mus Jeff Alexander
● Frank Sinatra, Debbie Reynolds, David Wayne, Celeste Holm, Lola Albright, Carolyn Jones (M-G-M)

This film version of the legit comedy [by Max Shulman and Robert Paul Smith] is a fairly diverting, but considerably overlong, takeoff on the romantic didoes of bachelors and gals. Picture has been given a plushy look.

Into the lives of Frank Sinatra, bachelor theatrical agent, and David Wayne, his married friend from Indiana, visiting Manhattan sans spouse, enters Debbie Reynolds, a determined girl who already has set the date for her wedding even without having found the right man. After some preliminaries she decides Sinatra is it.

Remainder of the footage details his capture, but not before he finds himself engaged to both her and Celeste Holm, an impossible situation that rights itself following a humdinger of a drunken party that segues into the morning-after comedy highlight of the footage.

The title tune gets some consistent plugging in the film. It's good cleffing by Sammy Cahn and James Van Heusen.

☐ 1955: Nomination: Best Song ('(Love Is) The Tender Trap')

••••••••••••••••••••••••••••••••

■ TEN LITTLE INDIANS

1966, 92 MINS, UK ⊛
Dir George Pollock   *Prod* Harry Alan Towers
Scr Peter Yeldham   *Ph* Ernest Steward   *Ed* Peter Boita
Mus Malcolm Lockyer   *Art Dir* Frank White
● Hugh O'Brian, Shirley Eaton, Fabian, Leo Genn, Stanley Holloway, Wilfrid Hyde White (Tenlit)

Second film version [after *Aned Then There Were None*] of Agatha Christie's endurable variation on the old idea of putting a group of disparate characters into a confined situation and letting them be killed one by one shapes up as good suspenser. The film was made entirely in Ireland although the setting has been changed to what appears to be a solitary schloss in the Austrian Alps.

Director George Pollock, despite a script with complicated credits (screenplay by Peter Yeldham, based on a script by Dudley Nichols, and adapted by Peter Welbeck, based on the Christie novel and play, *Ten Little Niggers*), works quite a bit of suspense into the restricted action, successfully hiding identity of the tenth Indian without resorting to too many 'red herrings'.

One major switch, an unfortunate one, has the first victim, originally an eccentric prince,

changed to an American rock 'n' roll singer (Fabian, in an embarrassingly bad performance).

A one-minute 'whodunit break' is inserted near the end when the action is suspended while the audience is encouraged to guess the murderer's identity.

••••••••••••••••••••••••••••••••

■ TEN LITTLE INDIANS

1975, 105 MINS, ITALY/W. GERMANY/FRANCE/
SPAIN ◇ ⊛
Dir Peter Collinson   *Scr* Enrique Llovet, Erich Krohnke
Ph Fernando Arritas   *Mus* Bruno Nicolai   *Art Dir* Jose
Maria Tapiador
● Oliver Reed, Elke Sommer, Richard Attenborough, Gert Frobe, Stephane Audran, Herbert Lom (Talia/Coralta/Corona/Comeci)

Remake of Agatha Christie's whodunit classic, in which ten suspects find themselves incommunicado 300 kilometers from the nearest town in a luxurious hotel in the middle of a desert in Iran. The invitees accept this, and thereupon make only the feeblest of efforts to seek a way of escaping. Dressed in tuxedos and evening gowns, they resign themselves to being eliminated one by one.

The murders are all committed in the most discreet, unspectacular ways, and cause only the mildest of trepidations among the remaining 'Indians'.

Thesping consists of the usual cameos typical of the co-pro genre. Charles Aznavour manages to get in a song before nonchalantly drinking his poison and the others dutifully plod through their parts.

••••••••••••••••••••••••••••••••

■ TEN NORTH FREDERICK

1958, 102 MINS, US ⊛
Dir Philip Dunne   *Prod* Charles Brackett   *Scr* Philip
Dunne   *Ph* Joe MacDonald   *Ed* David Bretherton
Mus Leigh Harline   *Art Dir* Lyle R. Wheeler, Addison Hehr
● Gary Cooper, Diane Varsi, Geraldine Fitzgerald, Tom Tully, Suzy Parker, Stuart Whitman (20th Century-Fox)

Ten North Frederick is a fairly interesting study of a man who is the victim of his own virtues. But because of the psychological intricacies involved, the screen telling of the John O'Hara novel sacrifices detail and explanation at some loss to audience satisfaction.

The politics section has been so telescoped as to be puzzling. The question of whether the protagonist actually entertains the dream of the presidency or jollies his wife on the point is never clear. And it is crucial to conviction. Joe Chapin (Gary Cooper) is a regional lawyer, rich but not apparently otherwise distinguished. Most of all he is a gentleman and from this fact flows his troubles.

The vaguest part of the screen version is the home town attitude toward the hero although at his 50th birthday party he is twitted by a philanderer with being a dull and slow fellow. Nonetheless the story gets on and after his series of disillusionments, including his beloved daughter's forced marriage, subsequent miscarriage, annullment and leaving home, the lawyer moves to his bitter-sweet romance in New York with a younger woman.

Told in flashback, the story opens at the 1945 funeral of the lawyer and shows the hypocrites gathered afterwards in his home. The greatest hypocrite of all is the widow, played with iceberg selfishness by Geraldine Fitzgerald.

By the time the story is played out the thesis makes sense – Joe Chapin has indeed been hopelessly handicapped in life by being a gentleman. It is convincing in the end and in Cooper's performance, and it is also sad.

••••••••••••••••••••••••••••••••

■ 10 RILLINGTON PLACE

1971, 111 MINS, UK ◇ ⊛ ⊙
Dir Richard Fleischer   *Prod* Martin Ransohoff, Leslie

Linder   *Scr* Clive Exton   *Ph* Denys Coop   *Ed* Ernest
Walter   *Mus* John Dankworth   *Art Dir* Martin Cooper
● Richard Attenborough, Judy Geeson, John Hurt, Pat Heywood, Isobel Black, Robert Hardy (Columbia)

In 1944, a woman was gassed, strangled and ravished by John Christie, the first of several victims of a seemingly quiet, respectable man living in a drab London district.

Richard Fleischer has turned out an authenticated documentary-feature which is an absorbing and disturbing picture. But the film has the serious flaw of not even attempting to probe the reasons that turned a man into a necrological and monstrous pervert.

Could be that Fleischer, like most other people, found more interest in the other central figure in the case, Timothy Evans. He was an illiterate who, with his young wife and baby, was Christie's lodger. Mrs Evans and their daughter became death victims of Christie. The bewildered lad, duped by Christie, confessed and was executed. Several years later Christie was arrested for the murder of his own wife, confessed to the murder of seven women, including Mrs Evans, but vigorously denied strangling the child. Some 12 years later Evans was pardoned. All this is dealt with in the Ludovic Kennedy book from which Clive Exton has written a factual, interesting but not particularly moving or emotional screenplay.

Though Richard Attenborough, playing the killer, is the central character, the acting honors are firmly wrapped up by John Hurt as Evans. He gives a remarkably subtle and fascinating performance as the bewildered young man who plays into the hands of both the murderer and the police.

••••••••••••••••••••••••••••••••

■ TEN SECONDS TO HELL

1959, 93 MINS, UK
Dir Robert Aldrich   *Prod* Michael Carreras   *Scr* Robert
Aldrich, Teddi Sherman   *Ph* Ernest Laszlo   *Ed* James
Needs, Henry Richardson   *Mus* Kenneth V. Jones
Art Dir Ken Adam
● Jeff Chandler, Jack Palance, Martine Carol, Wesley Addy, Virginia Baker, Richard Wattis (Hammer)

Hazardous job of deactivating dud bombs after World War II appears sound material for a melodramatic and suspenseful film. But curiously *Ten Seconds to Hell* emerges as a downbeat picture.

Based on Lawrence P. Bachmann's novel, *The Phoenix*, the screenplay seldom draws sympathy for any of its characters. Of six former German soldiers who form a bomb disposal unit in Berlin at the war's end, three are quickly killed in performance of their duties.

Jack Palance, self-styled leader of the unit, is a man of courage and conviction. But he's a moody individual who appears to be continually wrestling with inner problems. Ruthless and egotistical is Jeff Chandler who has regard for no one except himself. Martine Carol, in an unglamorous role, runs a boarding house, where Palance and Chandle reside.

With the film shot on location in Berlin, cameraman Ernest Laszlo has provided some realistic backgrounds.

••••••••••••••••••••••••••••••••

■ TENSION

1950, 91 MINS, US
Dir John Berry   *Prod* Robert Sisk   *Scr* Allen Rivkin
Ph Harry Stradling   *Ed* Albert Akst   *Mus* Andre Previn
Art Dir Cedric Gibbons, Leonid Vasian
● Richard Basehart, Audrey Totter, Cyd Charisse, Barry Sullivan, Tom D'Andrea (M-G-M)

Tension lives up to its title. It's a tight, tersely stated melodrama that holds the attention.

Plot has Richard Basehart, drugstore manager married to wicked Audrey Totter, plotting a perfect murder to do away with his wife's lover (Lloyd Gough). He creates himself a new identity and carefully shapes his crime so that no suspicion will be cast on him.

Script [from a story by John Klorer] wraps smart dialog and situations around the plot to make it play very well and Berry's direction keeps it always on the move and the cast showing to advantage.

Cyd Charisse is charming as the girl whom Basehart meets during the establishment of his new identity.

■ TENSION AT TABLE ROCK

1956, 93 MINS, US
Dir Charles Marquis Warren   *Prod* Sam Wiesenthal   *Scr* Winston Miller   *Ph* Joseph Biroc   *Ed* Harry Marker, Dean Harrison   *Mus* Dimitri Tiomkin   *Art Dir* Albert S. D'Agostino, John B. Mansbridge
● Richard Egan, Dorothy Malone, Cameron Mitchell, Billy Chapin, Royal Dano, Angie Dickinson (RKO)

There's more 'mood' than pace in this western entry, but it comes off with a fair classification for the regular outdoor situation because of a number of good action scenes. Script from the Frank Gruber novel *Bitter Sage* abets the slow moodiness and takes quite awhile to set the characters.

Wes Tancred (Richard Egan) is on the run after having killed in self-defense the leader of a robber gang he is riding with. Main action takes place in Table Rock, where Egan brings a small boy (Billy Chapin) after the latter's dad has been killed by some holdup men. He finds the town prepping for the arrival of rough-and-ready Texas trailherders and the sheriff (Cameron Mitchell) frightened. The sheriff's wife (Dorothy Malone) could go for Egan.

Performances are all competent. Dimitri Tiomkin provides an okay background score. Malone and Angie Dickinson seem a bit too well-dressed for the prairie femmes they play.

■ TEN TALL MEN

1951, 97 MINS, US ◇
Dir Willis Goldbeck   *Prod* Harold Hecht   *Scr* Roland Kibbee, Frank Davis   *Ph* William Snyder   *Ed* William Lyon   *Mus* David Buttolph   *Art Dir* Carl Anderson
● Burt Lancaster, Jody Lawrance, Gilbert Roland, Kieron Moore, George Tobias, John Dehner (Norma/Columbia)

Yarn [from a story by James Warner Bellah and Willis Goldbeck] is tailor-made for the burly Burt Lancaster. Cast as a Foreign Legion sergeant, he picks up a tip while in jail that the Riffs plan an invasion of the city. With nine fellow prisoners he volunteers to harass the would-be invaders.

Mission succeeds all expectations when the group manages to seize a sheik's daughter (Jody Lawrance), a key to the whole attack.

Proceedings come off at a crisp pace under Willis Goldbeck's breezy direction. Lancaster, Lawrance and a lengthy list of supporting players handle their roles broadly, which at times aachieves almost a satiric effect. Whether that was intentional or not is tough to determine.

■ 10:30 P.M. SUMMER

1966, 85 MINS, US ◇
Dir Jules Dassin   *Prod* Jules Dassin, Anatole Litvak   *Scr* Jules Dassin, Marguerite Duras   *Ph* Gabor Pogany   *Ed* Roger Dwyre   *Mus* Christobal Halffter   *Art Dir* Enrique Alarcon
● Melina Mercouri, Romy Schneider, Peter Finch, Julian Mateos, Isabel Maria Perez, Beatriz Savon (Dassin-Litvak)

Jules Dassin's *10:30 P.M. Summer* is only 85 minutes long but seems longer. Dassin's direction is uncertain, frequently illogical and, for the most part, plodding; Melina Mercouri's thesping is in a similar vein. There's reason to believe that the major fault is in the script of Dassin and novelist Marguerite Duras and, beyond that, in the

novella of Duras on which the script is based.

The thread of a plot (a married couple and a female friend, traveling together in Spain, are under a mounting tension that is touched off by an incident with a fugitive in a village) may have made a moody and effective short story but as the basis of an intelligent screenplay it is less than satisfactory.

There's some possibility of exploitation in the frankly erotic scenes of lovemaking between Romy Schneider (the reluctant guest) and Peter Finch (the husband).

An even more grievous shortcoming is the absence of any explanation as to the reason for her condition. Alcoholism is, evidently, only a part of her tragedy, as is a suggested latent homosexual feeling towards Schneider.

Gabor Pogany's camerawork overcomes the necessary low-key lighting (most of the film takes place at night) to give a technical gloss to the proceedings.

■ 10 TO MIDNIGHT

1983, 100 MINS, US ◇ Ⓥ ⊙
Dir J. Lee Thompson   *Prod* Pancho Kohner, Lance Hool   *Scr* William Roberts   *Ph* Adam Greenberg   *Ed* Peter Lee-Thompson   *Mus* Robert O. Ragland   *Art Dir* Jim Freiburger
● Charles Bronson, Lisa Eilbacher, Gene Davis, Andrew Stevens, Geoffrey Lewis, Wilford Brimley (Golan-Globus/City)

A sexually deranged killer slices up five young women like melons. The killer (well enough played by Gene Davis) is literally getting away with murder because of bureaucratic red tape and a pending insanity plea. As cop Charles Bronson puts it: 'I remember when legal meant lawful. Now it means loophole'. So Bronson takes matters into his own hands.

William Roberts' screenplay, while it sags in the middle, is damnably clever at dropping in its vicious vigilante theme without being didactic, and J. Lee Thompson's direction, borrowing from Hitchcock's editing in *Psycho*, creates the full horror of blades thrusting into naked bellies without the viewer ever actually seeing it happen.

Lisa Eilbacher plays Bronson's daughter and the beautiful, major target of the killer. Geoffrey Lewis is very good as a self-serving defense attorney who tells his warped client to be cool because 'you'll walk out of a crazy house alive'.

■ TEQUILA SUNRISE

1988, 116 MINS, US ◇ Ⓥ ⊙
Dir Robert Towne   *Prod* Thom Mount   *Scr* Robert Towne   *Ph* Conrad L. Hall   *Ed* Claire Simpson   *Mus* Danny Bramson, Dave Grusin   *Art Dir* Richard Sylbert
● Mel Gibson, Kurt Russell, Michelle Pfeiffer, Raul Julia, J.T. Walsh, Arliss Howard (Mount/Warner)

There's not much kick in this cocktail, despite its mix of quality ingredients. Casually glamorous South Bay is the setting for a story of little substance as writer-director Robert Towne attempts a study of friendship and trust but gets lost in a clutter of drug dealings and police operations.

Mel Gibson plays Dale 'Mac' McKussic, a former bigtime drug operator who's attempting to go straight just about the time his high school pal, cop Nick Frescia (Kurt Russell), is required to bust him. Frescia tries to dodge the duty by pressuring his friend to get out, but Mac owes one last favor to an old friend who's a Mexican cocaine dealer (Raul Julia).

Russell and Gibson are pushed into a cat-and-mouse game, complicated by their attraction to high-class restaurant owner Jo Ann Vallenari (Michelle Pfeiffer).

Gibson projects control skating atop paranoia, and is appealing as a man you'd want to

trust. Russell is fine as the slick cop who's confused by his own shifting values, and Pfeiffer achieves a rather touching quality with her gun-shy girl beneath the polished professional.

☐ 1988: Nomination: Best Cinematography

■ TERESA

1951, 101 MINS, US
Dir Fred Zinnemann   *Prod* Arthur M. Loew   *Scr* Stewart Stern   *Ph* William J. Miller   *Ed* Frank Sullivan   *Mus* Louis Applebaum   *Art Dir* Leo Kerz
● Pier Angeli, John Ericson, Patricia Collinge, Richard Bishop, Peggy Ann Garner, Ralph Meeker (M-G-M)

Bright news of *Teresa* is the American introduction of Pier Angeli, as the Italian war bride of the mixed-up John Ericson. There's enough of the waif in her appearance to generate a tremendous audience sympathy.

Fred Zinnemann is too consciously documentary in the directorial handling of the story, and the Stewart Stern screenplay [from an original story by him and Alfred Hayes] does not support such treatment. Opening finds Ericson muddling his way through postwar life, resisting all aid, although wanting it. A flashback takes the plot to Italy, where he is a green replacement GI. During a stay in a small mountain village he meets and falls in love with Angeli.

On his first patrol, Ericson cracks up even before combat when the sergeant on whom he leans is absent. After a hospital confinement for treatment, he returns to the village, marries Angeli then goes to the States to await her arrival. When she does arrive, they make their home in cramped tenement quarters with his parents, and it is gradually brought out that his trouble is caused by a dominant mother and a false conception of his father.

☐ 1951: Nomination: Best Motion Picture Story

■ TERMINATOR, THE

1984, 108 MINS, US ◇ Ⓥ ⊙
Dir James Cameron   *Prod* Gale Anne Hurd   *Scr* James Cameron, Gale Anne Hurd   *Ph* Adam Greenberg   *Ed* Mark Goldblatt   *Mus* Brad Fiedel   *Art Dir* George Costello
● Arnold Schwarzenegger, Michael Biehn, Linda Hamilton, Paul Winfield, Lance Henriksen, Rick Rossovich (Hemdale)

The Terminator is a blazing, cinematic comic book, full of virtuoso moviemaking, terrific momentum, solid performances and a compelling story.

The clever script, cowritten by director James Cameron and producer Gale Anne Hurd, opens in a post-holocaust nightmare, A.D.2029, where brainy machines have crushed most of the human populace. From that point, Arnold Schwarzenegger as the cyborg Terminator is sent back to the present to assassinate a young woman named Sarah Connor (Linda Hamilton) who is, in the context of a soon-to-be-born son and the nuclear war to come, the mother of mankind's salvation.

A human survivor in that black future (Michael Biehn), also drops into 1984 to stop the Terminator and save the woman and the future.

The shotgun-wielding Schwarzenegger is perfectly cast in a machine-like portrayal that requires only a few lines of dialog.

■ TERMINATOR 2 JUDGMENT DAY

1991, 136 MINS, US ◇ Ⓥ ⊙
Dir James Cameron   *Prod* James Cameron   *Scr* James Cameron, William Wisher   *Ph* Adam Greenberg   *Ed* Conrad Buff, Mark Goldblatt, Richard A. Harris

Mus Brad Fiedel   *Art Dir* Joseph Nemec III
● Arnold Schwarzenegger, Linda Hamilton, Edward Furlong, Robert Patrick, Earl Boen, Joe Morton (Carolco/Pacific Western)

As with *Aliens*, director James Cameron has again taken a firstrate science fiction film and crafted a sequel that's in some ways more impressive – expanding on the original rather than merely remaking it. This time he's managed the trick by bringing two cyborgs back from the future into the sort-of present (the math doesn't quite work out) to respectively menace and defend the juvenile John Connor (Edward Furlong) – leader of the human resistance against machines that rule the war devastated world of 2029.

Arnold Schwarzenegger is more comfortable and assured here than the first time around, reprising a role so perfectly suited to the voice and physique that have established him as a larger-than-life film persona.

The story finds Connor living with foster parents, his mother Sarah (Linda Hamilton) having been captured and committed to an asylum for insisting on the veracity of events depicted in the first film. The machines who rule the future dispatch a new cyborg to slay him while the human resistance sends its own reprogrammed Terminator back – this one bearing a remarkable resemblance to the evil one that appeared in 1984.

The film's great innovation involves the second cyborg: an advanced model composed of a liquid metal alloy that can metamorphose into the shape of any person it contacts and sprout metal appendages to skewer its victims.

Script by Cameron and William Wisher at times gets lost amid all the carnage. Hamilton's heavy-handed narration also is at times unintentionally amusing, though through her Cameron again offers the sci-fi crowd a fiercely heroic female lead, albeit one who looks like she's been going to Madonna's physical trainer.

If the reported $100 million budget is a study in excess, at least a lot of it ended up on the screen.
□ 1991: Best Sound, Visual Effects, Sound Effects Editing, Makeup
□ Nominations: Best Cinematography, Editing

● ●

■ **TERM OF TRIAL**

1962, 130 MINS, UK
Dir Peter Glenville   *Prod* James Woolf   *Scr* Peter Glenville   *Ph* Oswald Morris   *Ed* James Clark *Mus* Jean-Michel Demase   *Art Dir* Wilfrid Shingleton
● Laurence Olivier, Simone Signoret, Sarah Miles, Terence Stamp, Thora Hird, Hugh Griffith (Warner-Pathe/Romulus)

Here Olivier's an idealistic, but seedily unsuccessful schoolmaster in a small mixed school in the North of England. He has had to settle for this inferior teaching job because as a pacifist during the war he went to jail. He's afflicted with a sense of inferiority, a nagging scold of a wife and a taste for hard liquor.

He also suffers from a suspicious headmaster and a class which, inevitably, contains the school bully, played with remarkable assurance by Terence Stamp. Olivier is delighted when he sees a desire to learn in a young 15-year-old girl (Sarah Miles) but, rather naively, fails to see that she is precociously sexually aroused by him.

The 'crush' comes to a head when he takes some of the pupils on a school trip to Paris. She then feeds her mother with the tale that she has been indecently assaulted and he lands in the courtroom.

There are several loose ends, which could have emerged from the writing or the editing. But overall the characters are well drawn, the situations dramatic and the thesping all round is tops.

● ●

■ **TERMS OF ENDEARMENT**

1983, 130 MINS, US ◇ 🎦 ⊙
Dir James L. Brooks   *Prod* James L. Brooks   *Scr* James L. Brooks   *Ph* Andrzej Bartkowiak   *Ed* Richard Marks *Mus* Michael Gore   *Art Dir* Polly Platt
● Shirley MacLaine, Debra Winger, Jack Nicholson, Jeff Daniels, John Lithgow, Danny DeVito (Paramount)

Teaming of Shirley MacLaine and Jack Nicholson at their best makes *Terms of Endearment* an enormously enjoyable offering, adding bite and sparkle when sentiment and seamlessness threatens to sink other parts of the picture [from the novel by Larry McMurtry].

At the core is mother MacLaine and daughter Debra Winger, fondly at odds from the beginning over the younger's impending marriage to likeable, but limited, Jeff Daniels. Literally, it's just one cut to the next; then Winger is a mother and moving away from Texas to Iowa, where she becomes a mother a couple of more times; talks to MacLaine every day, carries on an affair with John Lithgow while Daniels dallies at college with Kate Charleson.

Plotwise, MacLaine and Nicholson are first introduced as she watches him come home next door drunk. Then it's several more years before the film finds them together again as he makes a stumbling pass at her over the fence. Then it's several more years before they're together again and she finally agrees to go out to lunch.

Early on, MacLaine tells Winger, 'You aren't special enough to overcome a bad marriage'. But *Terms of Endearment* is certainly special enough to overcome its own problems.
□ 1983: Best Picture, Director, Actress (Shirley MacLaine), Supp. Actor (Jack Nicholson), Adapted Screenplay
□ Nominations: Best Actress (Debra Winger), Actor (John Lithgow), Art Direction, Editing, Original Score, Sound

● ●

■ **TERRORISTS, THE**

See: Ransom

● ●

■ **TERROR TRAIN**

1980, 97 MINS, CANADA/US ◇ 🎦 ⊙
Dir Roger Spottiswoode   *Prod* Harold Greenberg *Scr* T.Y. Drake   *Ph* John Alcott   *Ed* Anne Henderson *Mus* John Mills-Cockell   *Art Dir* Glenn Bydwell
● Ben Johnson, Jamie Lee Curtis, Hart Bochner, David Copperfield (Astral-Bellevue-Pathe)

Roger Spottiswoode, vet editor who co-authored a respected book on the subject with Karel Reisz, makes a competent directing debut here.

As in Jamie Lee Curtis' other shocker pix, she limns the feisty survivor character in a group of young people menaced by a psychotic while having a wild party on a train. Her acting fits a narrow groove. But it must be said in young thesp's favor that she has not been given the most challenging material.

Efficient screenplay quickly sets up the premise by showing a repulsive sick joke being perpetrated by college med students on a sensitive youth who goes insane as a result. Three years later the kids all take a train excursion to celebrate their graduation, and the chickens come home to roost.

● ●

■ **TERRY FOX STORY, THE**

1983, 96 MINS, CANADA ◇ 🎦
Dir R. L. Thomas   *Prod* Robert Cooper   *Scr* Edward Hume   *Ph* Richard Ciupka   *Ed* Ron Wisman *Mus* Bill Conti   *Art Dir* Gavin Mitchell
● Robert Duvall, Eric Fryer, Michael Zelniker, Chris Makepeace, Rosalind Chao, Elva Mai Hoover (Astral)

The Terry Fox Story chronicles the heroic life of the young Canadian man whose 1980

Marathon of Hope resulted in raising more than $20 million for cancer research.

Eric Fryer plays the title role with tremendous conviction. The story [by John and Rose Kastner] opens in Vancouver in 1977, prior to the time Fox lost his right leg to cancer. In short order, the film dispenses with the diagnosed malignancy, Fox's convalescence, the fitting of a prosthetic leg and his decision to run across Canada to raise money for cancer research.

Despite initial parental and medical opposition, Fox's dream begins in April 1980. He enlists the aid of his friend, Doug Alward (Michael Zeiniker) to drive a camper and watch his progress but cannot convince his girlfriend, Rika (Rosalind Chao), to leave her job and join the marathon.

Fryer, an acting newcomer and himself an amputee, shows no rough edges in his performance. Robert Duvall as Vigars has another accomplished, gutsy role.

● ●

■ **TESS**

1979, 180 MINS, FRANCE/UK ◇ 🎦 ⊙
Dir Roman Polanski   *Prod* Claude Berri   *Scr* Roman Polanski, Gerard Brach, John Brownjohn   *Ph* Geoffrey Unsworth, Ghislain Cloquet   *Ed* Alastair McIntyre *Mus* Philippe Sarde   *Art Dir* Pierre Guffroy
● Nastassja Kinski, Leigh Lawson, Peter Firth, John Collin, David Markham, Carolyn Pickles (Renn/Burrill)

Tess is a sensitive, intelligent screen treatment of a literary masterwork. Roman Polanski has practiced no betrayal in filming Thomas Hardy's 1891 novel, *Tess of the d'Urbervilles*, and his adaptation often has that infrequent quality of combining fidelity and beauty.

Tess Durbeyfield is an uncommonly beautiful peasant girl whose dever derelict father learns of the family's descent from once noble Norman ancestry, the d'Urbervilles. Learning of the existence of a rich family bearing this name, Tess' parents induce the girl to present herself as a distant relation in the hope of reaping profit from the family tree.

The young rakish master of the d'Urbervilles, Alec, gives her employment and seduces her. Tess returns home and bears a child who dies after a short time.

She meets and falls in love with Angel Clare. They marry but, on the wedding night, Tess reveals her past. Angel reacts horribly and leaves here.

First-rate contributions are the color photography of Geoffrey Unsworth (who died during the shooting and was succeeded by Ghislain Cloquet) and the superb production design of Pierre Guffroy.
□ 1980: Best Cinematography, Art Direction, Costume Design (Anthony Powell)
□ Nominations: Best Picture, Director, Original Score

● ●

■ **TESS OF THE STORM COUNTRY**

1922, 110 MINS, US ⊗
Dir John S. Robertson   *Scr* Elmer Harris   *Ph* Charles Rosher   *Art Dir* Frank Ormston
● Mary Pickford, Lloyd Hughes, Gloria Hope, David Torrence, Forrest Robinson, Jean Hersholt (Pickford/United Artists)

Mary Pickford fans will revel with her in *Tess of the Storm Country* [based on the novel by Grace Miller White]. It's Mary Pickford all of the time. Pickford acts with her head, hands, and feet; she pantomimes and plays the part all of the while, with the titles often lending an additional but quiet though effective amusing touch.

Naught to be said against the least item in the film. Everything has been done well, particularly the photography by Charles Rosher and the direction.

After Pickford, the finest performance is

that of Ben Letts by Jean Hersholt. Hersholt makes his villainous character real, of the seafaring sort, shaggy and bearded, uncouth and rough. In contrast is the Teola Graves of Gloria Hope, carrying a miserable whining countenance that cannot bring her sympathy in a sympathetic role.

■ **TESTAMENT**

1983, 89 MINS, US ◇ ▣ ⊙
Dir Lynne Littman   *Prod* Jonathan Bernstein, Lynne Littman   *Scr* John Sacret Young   *Ph* Steven Poster   *Ed* Suzanne Pettit   *Mus* James Horner   *Art Dir* David Nichols
● Jane Alexander, William Devane, Ross Harris, Roxana Zal, Lukas Haas, Kevin Costner (Entertainment Events/American Playhouse)

Testament is an exceptionally powerful film dealing with the survivors of a nuclear war. Debuting director Lynne Littman brings an original approach to the grim material.

Based on Carol Amen's magazine story *The Last Testament*, pic depicts a normal, complacent community in the small California town of Hamlin.

The town's calm is shattered when a TV newscast announces that nuclear devices have exploded in New York and on the east coast, with the film proper suddenly going to yellow and whiteout, indicating blasts on the west coast as well. Ham radio operator Henry Abhart (Leon Ames) becomes Hamlin's communications link to the outside world.

Isolated, Hamlin's residents attempt to survive, but within a month over 1,000 people have died from radiation sickness. A young couple (Rebecca DeMornay and Kevin Costner), whose baby has died, drive off in search of 'a safe place'.

Holding it all together as a tower of strength is actress Jane Alexander as Carol Wetherby, coping with the deaths of her family and friends in truly heroic fashion via an understated performance.
□ 1983: Nomination: Best Actress (Jane Alexander)

■ **TESTIMONY**

1987, 157 MINS, UK ◇
Dir Tony Palmer   *Prod* Tony Palmer   *Scr* David Rudkin, Tony Palmer   *Ph* Nic Knowland   *Ed* Tony Palmer   *Art Dir* Tony Palmer
● Ben Kingsley, Sherry Baines, Magdalen Asquith, Mark Asquith, Terence Rigby, Ronald Pickup (Isolde/Film Four)

Testimony is quite an undertaking. Long, muddled, and abstract at times, but ultimately a beautifully conceived and executed art film with fine topline performances, it makes fascinating viewing.

In essence the pic [based on *The Memoirs of Dmitri Shostakovich*, edited by Solomon Volkov] follows the life of the Russian composer, played by Ben Kingsley sporting a dubious wig, but especially focuses on his relationship with Stalin.

Testimony traces the young Shostakovich who had success after success until Stalin took a dislike to the opera *Lady Macbeth*, and in a marvelous scene at the Extraordinary Conference of Soviet Musicians his work is denounced, but still he apologizes.

Later Stalin pours on further humiliation by sending him to an International Peace Congress in New York, where he is forced to denounce his fellow musicians, such as Stravinsky, who had fled Russia.

Ronald Pickup is excellent as Kingsley's friend Tukhachevsky and Robert Urquhart puts in a telling – though small – appearance as the journalist who quizzes Kingsley at the US peace conference.

Helmer Tony Palmer utilizes stunning technical skill to tell his story though at times seems to be a bit too clever for his own good.

Technical credits are excellent, and Shostakovich's music suitably stirring.

■ **TEST PILOT**

1938, 120 MINS, US ▣
Dir Victor Fleming   *Prod* Louis D. Lighton   *Scr* Vincent Lawrence, Waldemar Young   *Ph* Ray June   *Ed* Tom Held   *Mus* Franz Waxman (dir.)   *Art Dir* Cedric Gibbons
● Clark Gable, Myrna Loy, Spencer Tracy, Lionel Barrymore, Samuel S. Hinds, Marjorie Main (M-G-M)

Test Pilot is an actioner against a new approach to the aviation theme, fortified by a strong romance.

Spencer Tracy is Clark Gable's ground aide – the Gunner. Gable as a crack but arrogant pilot is forced down on a Kansas farm, where Myrna Loy is introduced as a romance interest. Ensuing action, backgrounded by ultra-modern aviation tests and experiments, plus a military note attendant to the US aviation service, vividly portrays the strong Loy-Gable romance.

Her disposition to understand the peculiar ways of the men with wings, and the pilot's appreciation of this understanding, have been artfully limned by director Victor Fleming. Three stars are capital in their assignments, particularly Gable, because it's a tailor-made role.

Story bespeaks authority in detail, obviously explained by the fact that Capt Frank Wead, who authored the original, has had practical aviation background.
□ 1938: Nominations: Best Picture, Original Story, Editing

■ **TEX**

1982, 103 MINS, US ◇ ▣ ⊙
Dir Tim Hunter   *Prod* Tim Zinnemann   *Scr* Charlie Haas, Tim Hunter   *Ph* Ric Waite   *Ed* Howard Smith   *Mus* Pino Donaggio   *Art Dir* Jack T. Collis
● Matt Dillon, Jim Metzler, Meg Tilly, Bill McKinney, Ben Johnson, Emilio Estevez (Walt Disney)

What *Tex* will probably best be remembered for is breaking new ground at Disney Studios in representing some of the real problems confronting today's young people. The teenagers are put in the milieu of drugs, alcohol, sex and violence. Family life is not necessarily rosy and well-scrubbed.

Where the picture ironically goes awry is in trying to tackle all of these problems in the space of 103 minutes. Writers Charlie Haas and Tim Hunter (latter making his directing debut) seem intent on incorporating every conceivable adolescent and adult trauma into their script [from the novel by S.E. Hinton], thus leaving the film with a very overdone, contrived feeling.

Story primarily centers on 15-year-old Oklahoma farm boy Tex, played admirably by Matt Dillon. Growing up with his older brother, while his father is 'traveling' with the rodeo, he must deal with family skeletons, school, friends, class distinctions, drugs, love, sex, death, responsibility, etc.

■ **TEXANS, THE**

1938, 92 MINS, US
Dir James Hogan   *Prod* Lucien Hubbard   *Scr* Bertram Millhauser, Paul Sloane, William Wister Haines   *Ph* Theodor Sparkuhl   *Ed* LeRoy Stone   *Mus* Gerard Carbonara
● Joan Bennett, Randolph Scott, May Robson, Walter Brennan, Robert Cummings, Robert Barrat (Paramount)

More western than anything else, basically *The Texans* is a story of the Reconstruction period and carpetbaggers following the Civil War. It is another of a long line of pictures which adopts a strong pro-Southern attitude in dealing with this period of American history.

Plot [story by Emerson Hough] deals with the plight of an old Texas family of ranchers which escapes from the homeland with 10,000 head of cattle to avoid onerous taxation levied by the landgrabbers, scalawags and carpetbaggers of the days following the war between the States. Most of the action covers the long and treacherous drive of the cattle through wild country up to the nearest railroad point in Kansas.

Camera crew get some beautiful outdoor shots on the cattle push from Texas to Kansas. Blizzard is realistically shot, also the prairie fire sequence and the night scene when the caravan is camping.

Joan Bennett is too much the Fifth Avenue debbie in a cow-hat to impart the desired touch. Someone should have mussed her up a little now and then. Randolph Scott, paired with Bennett for romantic interest, shepherds the flock (men and cattle) through to Kansas and finally edges out Robert Cummings, who also figures on the romantic end, but unsympathetically. Scott gives an even performance and looks much more the pioneer type than the star opposite him.

■ **TEXAS ACROSS THE RIVER**

1966, 100 MINS, US ◇ ▣
Dir Michael Gordon   *Prod* Harry Keller   *Scr* Wells Root, Harold Greene, Ben Starr   *Ph* Russell Metty   *Ed* Gene Milford   *Mus* Frank DeVol   *Art Dir* Alexander Golitzen, William D. DeCinces
● Dean Martin, Alain Delon, Rosemary Forsyth, Joey Bishop, Tina Marquand, Peter Graves (Universal)

Texas Across the River is a rootin', tootin' comedy western with no holds barred. It's a gagman's dream, an uninhibited spoof of the early frontier packed with a choice assemblage if laughs, many of the belly genre.

Writers have developed a situation of a gallant Spanish innocent set down in a world he can never quite understand. That he is a nobleman, too, with courtly ethics, makes him all the more improbable as a character who takes in stride wild Comanches and wilder longhorns, and finds Dean Martin, as a Texan, the most perplexing of all.

Michael Gordon's direction juggles the misadventures of Alain Delon, in Spanish role, and Martin with a mission of transporting guns across Comanche terrritory and Delon on his hands. Both Indians and the cavalry are satirized with countless slick touches.

■ **TEXAS CARNIVAL**

1951, 76 MINS, US ◇ ▣
Dir Charles Walters   *Prod* Jack Cummings   *Scr* Dorothy Kingsley   *Ph* Robert Planck   *Ed* Adrienne Fazan   *Mus* David Rose (dir.)   *Art Dir* Cedric Gibbons, William Ferrari
● Esther Williams, Red Skelton, Howard Keel, Ann Miller, Paula Raymond, Keenan Wynn (M-G-M)

Plenty of laugh diversion, dressed up to treat the eye and ear, is offered in *Texas Carnival*. Material provides Red Skelton with several surefire comedy sequences. In the eye department film offers Esther Williams in a bathing suit and one imaginative dream swim number, as well as the talented terping and physical charms of Ann Miller. For tunes it has Howard Keel as a virile cowpoke baritoning his way through the footage and two of the four Harry Warren-Dorothy Fields songs.

Williams and Skelton are a carnival team struggling along until proud Texan Keenan Wynn, in an alcoholic moment, takes a fancy to Skelton. Latter goes to a swank hotel to meet Wynn but, instead, is mistaken for the rich Texan himself. Life of ease being lived by Skelton during Wynn's absence wears easy on his conscience even though it troubles Williams plenty. Appearance of Keel, foreman of Wynn's ranch, adds some complications.

■ TEXAS CHAIN SAW MASSACRE, THE

1974, 83 MINS, US ◇ ▼ ⊙
Dir Tobe Hooper *Prod* Tobe Hooper *Scr* Kim Henkel,
Tobe Hooper *Ph* Daniel Pearl, Tobe Hooper
Ed Sallye Richardson, Larry Carroll *Mus* Tobe Hooper,
Wayne Bell *Art Dir* Robert A. Burns
● Marilyn Burns, Allen Danziger, Paul A. Partain,
William Vail, Teri McMinn, Gunnar Hansen (Vortex)

Despite the heavy doses of gore in *The Texas
Chain Saw Massacre*, Tobe Hooper's pic is well-
made for an exploiter of its type. The script
by Hooper and Kim Henkel is a take-off on
the same incident which inspired Robert
Bloch's novel (and later Alfred Hitchcock's
film) *Psycho*.

In 1957, Plainfield, Wis, authorities arrested handyman Ed Gein after finding dismembered bodies and disinterred corpses
strewn all over his farmhouse.

When a dozen graves are found violated in
a rural Texas cemetery, Marilyn Burns visits
her father's grave to make sure it is unmo-
lested. Disaster strikes on a side trip to her
deserted family home. A family of graverob-
bers, led by saw-wielding Gunnar Hansen,
butcher everyone but Burns, who makes a
narrow escape.

■ TEXAS CHAIN SAW MASSACRE PART 2, THE

1986, 95 MINS, US ◇ ▼ ⊙
Dir Tobe Hooper *Prod* Menahem Golan, Yoram Globus
Scr L.M. Kit Carson *Ph* Richard Kooris *Ed* Alain
Jakubowicz *Mus* Tobe Hooper, Jerry Lambert
Art Dir Cary White
● Dennis Hopper, Caroline Williams, Bill Johnson, Jim
Siedow, Bill Moseley, Lou Perry (Cannon)

Success of the lowbudget *Chain Saw* in 1974
spawned a generation of splatter films which
largely have lost the power to shock and entertain. Not so *Chain Saw 2*. Director Tobe
Hooper is back on the Texas turf he knows.

Also a big help is L.M. Kit Carson's tongue-
in-cheek script. In truth the story is basically
a setup for a series of gory confrontations.
The family is just an ordinary American hard
luck story – butchers who have fallen on hard
times and take their resentment out on the
human race.

Although Dennis Hopper gets top billing
his role is surprisingly limited, climaxing in a
chainsaw duel to the death with Leatherface
(Bill Johnson). Performances of the family
are fine, especially Jim Siedow and a crazed
Bill Moseley, but the real star here is carnage.

■ TEXASVILLE

1990, 123 MINS, US ◇ ▼ ⊙
Dir Peter Bogdanovich *Prod* Barry Spikings, Peter
Bogdanovich *Scr* Peter Bogdanovich *Ph* Nicholas
von Sternberg *Ed* Richard Fields *Art Dir* Phedon
Papamichael
● Jeff Bridges, Cybill Shepherd, Annie Potts, Timothy
Bottoms, Cloris Leachman, Randy Quaid (Nelson/
Cine-Source)

Peter Bogdanovich's sequel to *The Last Picture
Show* is long on folksy humor and short on
plot. In adapting Larry McMurtry's 1987 follow-up novel (predecessor was penned in
1965, filmed in 1971), Bogdanovich uses an
impending county centennial celebration as
the weak spine for this slice of small-town
Texas life.

Set in 1984, film revolves around the non-
adventures of oil tycoon Jeff Bridges. He's $12
million in debt and his loyal assistant (Cloris
Leachman) is ready to quit.

Bogdanovich has rounded up many of the
first film's players (notably absent are Oscar-
winner Ben Johnson, whose character died,
Ellen Burstyn, Clu Gulager, Sam Bottoms
and John Hillerman), but the plum role goes

to Annie Potts as Bridges' domineering wife.
Less successful is Cybill Shepherd, whose
career was launched with the 1971 pic.
Making a delayed entrance as Bridges' old
flame who's brooding over the death of her
son, Shepherd adopts a no-makeup look and
is unflatteringly photographed.

Apart from a few set pieces involving the
Archer County pageant parade celebrating
Texasville, pic is static and poorly lensed.

■ THANKS A MILLION

1935, 85 MINS, US ▼
Dir Roy Del Ruth *Prod* Darryl F. Zanuck *Scr* Nunnally
Johnson *Ph* Peverell Marley *Ed* Allen McNeil
Mus Arthur Lange (dir.) *Art Dir* Jack Otterson
● Dick Powell, Ann Dvorak, Fred Allen, Patsy Kelly,
Raymond Walburn, Paul Whiteman (20th Century-Fox)

Thanks A Million is corking entertainment.
Film unquestionably establishes Fred Allen
for the screen. It also takes Paul Whiteman
and his orchestra, including Ramona, the
Yacht Club Boys, and Rubinoff and his violin,
and shows 'em at their best.

Allen's radio rep as a pungent comedy de-
liverer is well capitalized here as the manager
of the near-stranded unit which includes Ann
Dvorak and Patsy Kelly as a sister team; an
anonymous band, presumaly maestroed by
Dave Rubinoff who gets in a couple of violin
solos (including a pash personality); the
Yacht Club Boys, who, like Rubinoff, also
have lines besides two corking specialties; and
Benny Baker who's an indeterminate stooge
throughout the footage.

Nunnally Johnson's script [from a story by
Melville Crossman, nom de plume of Darryl
F. Zanuck] deserves some sort of an award as
a sample of celluloid writing. It's made to order for Allen's dead-pan comedy. Punchy,
pithy, and punctuated with a flock of telling
nifties, the comedy wordage doesn't sacrifice
the story. The title song is the best of Gus
Kahn-Arthur Johnston's five numbers 'Pocket
Full of Sunshine' and 'High on A Hill Top',
along with 'Thanks A Million', are handled by
Dick Powell.

□ 1935: Nomination: Best Sound

■ THAT CERTAIN FEELING

1956, 102 MINS, US ◇ ▼
Dir Norman Panama, Melvin Frank *Prod* Norman
Panama, Melvin Frank *Scr* Norman Panama, Melvin
Frank, I.A.L. Diamond, William Altman *Ph* Loyal
Griggs *Ed* Tom McAdoo *Mus* Joseph J. Lilley
● Bob Hope, Eva Marie Saint, George Sanders, Pearl
Bailey, David Lewis, Al Capp (Paramount)

Overall what's fashioned here is amusingly
frothy, with a touch of heart occasionally to
add depth to the adaptation of legiter *The
King of Hearts* by Jean Kerr and Eleanor
Brooke.

Bob Hope's femme costar is Eva Marie
Saint in her first film since *On the Waterfront*.
What she does in the change of pace casting
is all to the good.

A big asset is Pearl Bailey, maid in the
household of renowned cartoonist George
Sanders, for whom Saint is secretary-fiancee
and Hope is ghost 'stripper'. Bailey's wow
personality adds a most engaging comedy
touch.

Sanders has himself a free-wheeling ball as
the sophisticated cartoonist who has lost the
common touch and calls in ghoster Hope, a
neurotic who wants to upchuck every time he
tries to stand up to the boss. Complicating his
employment is the fact that Saint's his ex-
wife.

There's a nepotism note to the uncredited
casting. One of Hope's sons does well as a
playmate to young Mathers; and three other
Hope offspring are in amusement park bits.

■ THAT CERTAIN WOMAN

1937, 91 MINS, US
Dir Edmund Goulding *Prod* Robert Lord *Scr* Edmund
Goulding *Ph* Ernest Haller *Ed* Jack Killifer
Mus Max Steiner *Art Dir* Max Parker
● Bette Davis, Henry Fonda, Ian Hunter, Anita Louise,
Donald Crisp, Hugh O'Donnell (Warner)

Appeal is aimed strictly at the emotions, as
the plot is another variation of self-sacrificing
mother love. The film is a remake of *The
Trespasser*, which Edmund Goulding earlier
wrote and directed for Gloria Swanson in
1929.

Film relates the adventures of a self-reliant
young woman (Bette Davis), who as a girl of
16 married a gangster, since deceased, after a
bootleg altercation. She becomes the secretary of a prominent lawyer, an unhappily
married man, who falls in love with her but
keeps his distance. She falls in love with a
wealthy young wastrel and marries him.

His father compels the young woman to reveal her past. The marriage is annulled, and
the girl returns to her job. A son is born.
Much later a scandal brings back the wastrel
youth, now reformed, to help his one-time
wife.

It's a synthetic tale that does not stand up
under too close analysis. The story deficiencies are not so important, however, because
the characters are made credible by Davis
and the cast, and by Goulding's smooth direction. Ian Hunter as the girl's employer, and
Henry Fonda as the boy in the case are excellent.

■ THAT COLD DAY IN THE PARK

1969, 115 MINS, CANADA ◇ ▼
Dir Robert Altman *Scr* Gillian Freeman *Ph* Laszlo
Kovacs *Mus* Johnny Mandel
● Sandy Dennis, Michael Burns, Susanne Benton, Luana
Anders, John Garfield Jr (Factor-Altman-Mirell)

A pretty, reserved, rich spinster in
Vancouver, BC, spots a teenager sitting in
the park in the rain. She invites the boy to
her apartment and a strange relationship
starts that ends in breakdown and tragedy.

Sandy Dennis is strikingly effective, if her
character's veering into madness is a bit
abrupt. Michael Burns is good as the cherubic
youth, with Susanne Benton displaying a fine
feel for character as his freewheeling, slightly
nympho sister.

This mixing of themes and social strata
[from the book by Richard Miles] is too literary to get a true insight into the many layers
involved. It tries to bring in too much and waters down the interesting personal relations,
turning the denouement into grand guignol,
rather than perceptive dramatic and psychological progression.

■ THAT FORSYTE WOMAN

1950, 112 MINS, US ◇ ▼
Dir Compton Bennett *Prod* Leon Gordon *Scr* Jan
Lustig, Ivan Tors, James B. Williams, Arthur Wimperis
Ph Joseph Ruttenberg *Ed* Frederick Y. Smith
Mus Bronislau Kaper
● Errol Flynn, Greer Garson, Walter Pidgeon, Robert
Young, Janet Leigh, Henry Davenport (M-G-M)

Metro has fashioned a long, elaborate and
costly class feature out of John Galsworthy's
writings about his Victorian family, the
Forsytes.

Compton Bennett's direction unfolds it at a
measured pace, in keeping with the quaintness of the Victorian English setting, as it
tells the story of an outsider femme who marries into the Forsyte family, then falls in love
with a man engaged to one of the Forsyte
women, bringing discord into an ordered, dull
way of life.

Greer Garson's playing, and that of her co-

769

stars Errol Flynn, the cold, proper Forsyte whom she marries; Walter Pidgeon, the Forsyte blacksheep, and Robert Young, the man with whom she falls in love, approach the characters with all the dignified stuffiness that distinguishes Galsworthy's people.

The script is based on Book One of Galsworthy's *The Forsyte Saga*.

□ 1950: Nomination: Best Color Costume Design

....

■ **THAT HAMILTON WOMAN!**
(UK: *Lady Hamilton*)

1941, 124 MINS, US 🎞 ⊙
Dir Alexander Korda   *Prod* Alexander Korda
Scr Walter Reisch, R.C. Sherriff   *Ph* Rudolph Mate
Ed William Hornbeck   *Mus* Miklos Rozsa
Art Dir Vincent Korda
● Vivien Leigh, Laurence Olivier, Alan Mowbray, Sara Allgood, Gladys Cooper, Henry Wilcoxon (United Artists/London)

Alexander Korda dips into the files of British history for this biographical drama of Lady Hamilton and her amorous affair with naval hero Lord Nelson.

Korda makes out a sympathetic case for the scandalous (of the period) romance between the wife of a British ambassador and the great Lord Nelson. Utilizing the retrospect story device, the haggish Lady Hamilton is tossed in the Calais jail for stealing, and tells her tale to a girl of the streets.

Vivien Leigh hits the peaks with her delineation of Lady Hamilton, a vivacious girl who is pictured as a victim of men but whose ingenuity in statecraft saves the Empire. She dominates the picture throughout with her reserved love for Nelson and her determination to aid his success. Laurence Olivier's characterization of Nelson carries the full dignity and reserve of the historical figure.

Picture shows plenty of production outlay with its series of elaborate settings. Battle of Trafalgar sequence carries intercut of cannon broadsides from the English men-of-war with too obvious miniatures of the two fleets in action.

□ 1941: Best Sound Recording.
□ Nominations: Best B&W Cinematography, B&W Art Direction, Special Effects

....

■ **THAT'LL BE THE DAY**

1973, 90 MINS, UK ◇ 🎞 ⊙
Dir Claude Whatham   *Prod* David Puttnam, Sandy Lieberson   *Scr* Ray Connolly   *Ph* Peter Suschitzky
Ed Michael Bradsell   *Mus* Neil Aspinall, Keith Moon (sup.)
● David Essex, Ringo Starr, Rosemary Leach, James Booth, Billy Fury, Keith Moon (Anglo-EMI/Goodtimes)

Here is a nice bit of nostalgia (late 1950s): a serious, loving, but not sticky-sweet probe of a youngster's torment in finding himself, complete with parental problems, friendships gained and lost (ditto jobs), puppy love hangups and first sex; in short, the lot.

Script is a big assist, and it rings true without being cloying. Another major asset is having David Essex as its star and key ingredient, as well as in being able to hark back to so colorful a period in which to have him grow up. Essex copes well enough with the few dramatic requirements of the role. Ringo Starr is excellent as his sometime sidekick.

Technically, pic is a superior job, nicely paced by director Claude Whatham with a superior period feel.

....

■ **THAT LUCKY TOUCH**

1975, 93 MINS, UK ◇ 🎞
Dir Christopher Miles   *Prod* Dimitri de Grunwald
Scr John Briley   *Ph* Douglas Slocombe   *Mus* John Scott
Art Dir Tony Masters

● Roger Moore, Susannah York, Shelley Winters, Lee J. Cobb, Jean-Pierre Cassel, Raf Vallone (Rank)

This contemporary light comedy of love-against-the-odds, which evokes the Hollywood genre of the 1930s, falls short of its target.

The film aims to extract some classy fun from the entanglements of an arms dealer (Roger Moore) and a leftist women's libber (Susannah York), covering NATO war games for the Washington Post.

Moore just about copes as the assertive, high-living gun merchant, but where moments of finesse are called for he is merely game and/or workmanlike. York makes the best of her chances as the aggressive, sex-shunning pacifist.

Lee J. Cobb's harassed and world-weary US Army general is a gem of resigned bewilderment when coping with his wife (Shelley Winters) or her prickly journalistic pal (York).

....

■ **THAT NIGHT**

1993, 89 MINS, US ◇ 🎞 ⊙
Dir Craig Bolotin   *Prod* Arnon Milchan, Steve Reuther
Scr Craig Bolotin   *Ph* Bruce Surtees   *Ed* Priscilla Nedd-Friendly   *Mus* David Newman   *Art Dir* Maher Ahmad
● C. Thomas Howell, Juliette Lewis, Helen Shaver, Eliza Dushku, John Dossett, J. Smith-Cameron (Regency/Alcor/Canal Plus)

That Night is a modestly affecting romantic drama set in the Long Island suburbs of the early 60s.

Craig Bolotin, co-scripter of Ridley Scott's *Black Rain*, hasn't stretched himself in his directorial debut, either in his screenplay, based on an autobiographical novel by Alice McDermott, or in his careful helming. He seems to have pinned his faith on casting and performances.

Bolotin is particularly well served by 12-year-old Eliza Dushku who, as Alice, is really the focus of the story. A shy, imaginative child, she lives with her parents across the street from her idol, Sheryl (Juliette Lewis), the seemingly sophisticated high school beauty.

When the father suddenly dies, Sheryl reacts by dating Rick (C. Thomas Howell), a boy from the wrong side of the tracks. The affair ends in Sheryl's pregnancy, and she's sent to a home for unwed mothers.

This isn't exactly riveting material, and the film's modest production values seem more suited to the small screen.

....

■ **THAT NIGHT IN RIO**

1941, 90 MINS, US ◇
Dir Irving Cummings   *Prod* Fred Kohlmar   *Scr* George Seaton, Bess Meredyth, Hal Long, Samuel Hoffenstein
Ph Leon Shamroy, Ray Rennahan   *Ed* Walter Thompson
Mus Alfred Newman
● Alice Faye, Don Ameche, Carmen Miranda, J. Carrol Naish, S.K. Sakall, Curt Bois (20th Century-Fox)

This successor to *Down Argentine Way* is a close carbon copy of *Folies Bergere* which 20th turned out six years earlier, but with locale switch from Paris to Rio de Janeiro. Embellished with lavish production, brilliant Technicolor, and several tuneful songs, it's peak entertainment.

Lightweight story [from a play by Rudolph Lothar and Hans Adler] provides Don Ameche with the dual role of a breezy American night club m.c. performing in Rio, and a native financier. Resemblance beween the pair is so close the former's sweetheart (Carmen Miranda) and the financier's wife (Alice Faye) cannot tell them apart. When a business crisis arrives, the tycoon's associates secure the entertainer to impersonate the absent Baron, with the stand-in innocently completing a deal that prevents financial ruin.

Ameche is very capable in a dual role, and

Faye is eye-appealing but it's the tempestuous Miranda who really gets away to a flying start from the first sequence.

....

■ **THAT'S DANCING!**

1985, 105 MINS, US ◇ 🎞 ⊙
Dir Jack Haley Jr.   *Prod* David Niven Jr., Jack Haley Jr.
Scr Jack Haley Jr.   *Ph* Andrew Laszlo, Paul Lohmann
Ed Bud Friedgen, Michael J. Sheridan   *Mus* Henry Mancini
● Gene Kelly, Sammy Davis Jr, Mikhail Baryshnikov, Liza Minnelli, Ray Bolger (M-G-M)

For anyone who wants to see big-screen terpsichorean art at its top, *Dancing* is definitive. M-G-M has not only dipped into its own generous collection, but borrowed judiciously from most of the other studios that were in brisk competition during the golden years of movie musicals.

For openers from the early days, there is a lot of Busby Berkeley, plus Ruby Keeler and Dick Powell, followed by the wonderful work of Fred Astaire and Ginger Rogers and on through an absolutely complete list of the greats.

Much is made of a Ray Bolger-Judy Garland dance number from *The Wizard of Oz*, omitted from the final cut of the original. It's interesting to see, but also easy to see (contrary to the gushing narration) why it was left out: the technique is a bit tacky and hardly up to the quality of what was released.

....

■ **THAT'S ENTERTAINMENT!**

1974, 132 MINS, US ◇ 🎞 ⊙
Dir Jack Haley Jr   *Prod* Jack Haley Jr   *Scr* Jack Haley Jr   *Ph* Gene Polito, Ernest Laszlo, Russell Metty, Ennio Guarnieri, Allan Green   *Ed* Bud Friedgen, David E. Blewitt   *Mus* Henry Mancini (adapt.)
● Fred Astaire, Bing Crosby, Gene Kelly, Frank Sinatra, Liza Minelli, Donald O'Connor (M-G-M)

Metro-Goldwyn-Mayer celebrated its 50th anniversary with *That's Entertainment!*, an outstanding, stunning, sentimental, exciting, colorful, enjoyable, spirit-lifting, tuneful, youthful, invigorating, zesty, respectful, dazzling, and richly satisfying feature documentary commemorating its filmusicals.

As Liza Minnelli puts it in her narrated segment (among 11 names appearing in new footage and film clip voiceover): 'Thank God for film. It can capture and hold a performance forever'.

From the musical library, about 100 films were selected from the 1929-58 era, enough to satisfy nearly every memory. Each segment has a particular theme (usually film highlights of a particular star); and each has its narrator. Minnelli appears in the portion devoted to her mother, Judy Garland.

....

■ **THAT'S ENTERTAINMENT, PART II**

1976, 133 MINS, US ◇ 🎞 ⊙
Dir Gene Kelly   *Prod* Saul Chaplin, Daniel Melnick
Scr Leonard Gershe   *Ph* George Folsey   *Ed* Bud Friedgen, David Blewitt, David Bretherton, Peter C. Johnson   *Mus* Nelson Riddle (sup.)   *Art Dir* John DeCuir
● Fred Astaire, Gene Kelly (M-G-M)

That's Entertainment, Part II is a knockout. The very handsome and polished sequel to *That's Entertainment!* transforms excerpts from perhaps $100 million worth of classic Metro library footage into a billion dollars worth of fun, excitement, amusement, escapism, fantasy, nostalgia and happiness.

In addition, Fred Astaire and Gene Kelly shine in sharp bridging footage, well directed by Kelly.

There are approximately 100 remembered players to be seen in segments of about 75 films.

Bulk of the footage is Metro musicals. However, in a good pace change there are periodic brief collages including The Marx Brothers, Spencer Tracy-Katharine Hepburn, Clark Gable, Laurel & Hardy, and Buster Keaton.

．．．．．．．．．．．．．．．．．．．．．．．．．．

■ **THAT SINKING FEELING**

1979, 80 MINS, UK ◇ ⧨
Dir Bill Forsyth   *Prod* Bill Forsyth   *Scr* Bill Forsyth
Ph Michael Coulter   *Ed* John Gow   *Mus* Colin Tully
Art Dir Adrienne Atkinson
● Robert Buchanan, John Hughes, Billy Greenlees, Douglas Sannachan, Alan Love, John Gordon Sinclair (Minor Miracle)

The first wholly Scottish feature for many a year proves debuting filmmaker Bill Forsyth has an entertaining touch.

Forsyth's screenplay, largely set in the city's dank demolition areas, plots a motley bunch of unemployed lads, amiably led by Robert Buchanan, who heist a hundred stainless steel sinks in a boisterous bid to embark on an essentially light-hearted life of crime.

The central joke – the absurdity of seeing sinks as likely hot sellers – is hardly strong enough to carry a full-length film. But Forsyth's incidental observations, and the generally high standard of playing by non-professionals, help to offset the fact that most scenes could be pruned to advantage. Technical credits are remarkable considering the almost invisible production budget.

．．．．．．．．．．．．．．．．．．．．．．．．．．

■ **THAT'S LIFE!**

1986, 102 MINS, US ◇ ⧨ ⊙
Dir Blake Edwards   *Prod* Tony Adams   *Scr* Milton Wexler, Blake Edwards   *Ph* Anthony Richmond
Ed Lee Rhoads   *Mus* Henry Mancini   *Art Dir* Tony Marando
● Jack Lemmon, Julie Andrews, Sally Kellerman, Robert Loggia, Jennifer Edwards, Rob Knepper (Paradise Cove/Ubilam)

Personal virtually to the point of being a home movie, film proves thoroughly absorbing and entertaining and benefits enormously from a terrific lead performance by Jack Lemmon.

Story opens with Lemmon's wife, played by director Blake Edwards' wife, Julie Andrews, leaving a hospital and knowing she'll have to wait all weekend to learn the results of a biopsy.

For his part, Lemmon dreads the arrival of his 60th birthday, can't face the big party planned for him over the weekend, is fretting because he can't perform sexually these days and can't stand the idea of becoming a grandfather.

Andrews responds beautifully to Lemmon's sweaty, nerve-racked state, betraying years of love and understanding of her mate, but doesn't receive equal dramatic opportunities.
□ 1986: Nomination: Best Song ('Life in a Looking Glass')

．．．．．．．．．．．．．．．．．．．．．．．．．．

■ **THAT TOUCH OF MINK**

1962, 99 MINS, US ◇ ⧨
Dir Delbert Mann   *Prod* Stanley Shapiro, Martin Melcher   *Scr* Stanley Shapiro, Nate Monaster
Ph Russell Metty   *Ed* Ted Kent   *Mus* George Duning
Art Dir Alexander Golitzen, Robert Clatworthy
● Cary Grant, Doris Day, Gig Young, Audrey Meadows, John Astin, Dick Sargent (Universal)

The recipe is potent: Cary Grant and Doris Day in the old cat-and-mouse game. The gloss of *That Touch of Mink* however, doesn't obscure an essentially threadbare lining. In seeming to throw off a sparkle, credit performance and pace as the key virtues. The rest of it is commonplace.

In this particular arrangement of coy *he-she*-*nanigans*, the comedy is premised on the conflict of her inexperience and his old prosuavity. He's a company-gobbling financier; she's a trim chick legging it through Manhattan canyons in search of a job. It starts when his limousine splatters her with puddle water. Fortuitous meeting and mating maneuvres follow, with the action shuttling between Gotham and Bermuda or Gotham and New Jersey suburbia.

Although Grant gives his tycoon the advantage of long seasoning at this sort of gamey exercise, he's clearly shaded in the laughgetting allotment. As written, Day's clowning has the better of it; and she, by the way, certifies herself an adept farceur with this outing. But not surprisingly, the featured bananas make the best comedic score.
□ 1962: Nominations: Best Original Sory & Screenplay, Color Art Direction, Sound

．．．．．．．．．．．．．．．．．．．．．．．．．．

■ **THAT UNCERTAIN FEELING**

1941, 89 MINS, US ⧨
Dir Ernst Lubitsch   *Prod* Sol Lesser, Ernst Lubitsch
Scr Walter Reisch   *Ph* George Barnes   *Ed* William Shen   *Mus* Werner Heymann
● Merle Oberon, Melvyn Douglas, Burgess Meredith, Alan Mowbray, Olive Blakeney, Harry Davenport (United Artists)

Premised on the assumption that when a husband doesn't pay his wife enough attention someone else is going to do it for him, Ernst Lubitsch's *That Uncertain Feeling* tackles the problem in a light and singularly satirical vein. The famed Lubitsch touch is there but the entertainment value isn't.

Merle Oberon and Melvyn Douglas are the apparently happily-married Bakers. Husband is a prosperous insurance man who is settled in his home life in a routine way, but unconsciously fails to fulfill the more romantic duties expected of a spouse. Lubitsch, with characteristic subtlety, suggests that this is what causes the hiccups from which the wife suffers and ultimately lands her in a psychoanalyst's office.

By stages she begins to have suspicions concerning the widespread impressions that they are the happy Bakers and into her life, under slightly absurd circumstances, comes a wacky pianist. He's Burgess Meredith, not the great lover type, and he has a strange, impudent dislike for a lot of things.

Taking the picture as a whole it is tiring, very slow generally and embraces numerous situations that are basically weak.
□ 1941: Nomination: Best Scoring of a Dramatic Picture

．．．．．．．．．．．．．．．．．．．．．．．．．．

■ **THAT WAS THEN . . . THIS IS NOW**

1985, 102 MINS, US ◇ ⧨ ⊙
Dir Christopher Cain   *Prod* Gary R. Lindberg, John M. Ondor   *Scr* Emilio Estevez   *Ph* Juan Ruiz-Anchia
Ed Ken Johnson   *Mus* Keith Olsen, Bill Cuomo
Art Dir Chester Kaczenski
● Emilio Estevez, Craig Sheffer, Kim Delaney, Jill Schoelen, Barbara Babcock, Frank Howard (Media Ventures/Belkin)

God save the kids who live in an S.E. Hinton novel. They're firecrackers waiting to go off. Hinton's is a very peculiar vision where adults are basically in the background and kids are left on their own to battle their way into an adulthood that promises them even less.

Most troubled of the kids here is Emilio Estevez as Mark Jennings, a lonely, brooding child anxious to be through with his adolescence. Title refers to his youthful bond with Bryon Douglas (Craig Sheffer). To Mark's dismay, the friendship is falling apart as Bryon takes on a girlfriend and starts to accept some adult responsibility.

Estevez also wrote the screenplay and as a writer he fails to raise the pronouncements and revelations of youth beyond the mundane. Dark tone is reinforced by cinematographer Juan Ruiz-Anchia who captures well the look of the street, but that's all one sees. It's an oppressive world without being particularly insightful.

Central relationship between Estevez and Sheffer does have some touching moments. Kim Delaney is perfectly likable as Sheffer's girlfriend.

．．．．．．．．．．．．．．．．．．．．．．．．．．

■ **THEATER OF BLOOD**

1973, 104 MINS, US/UK ◇ ⧨ ⊙
Dir Douglas Hickox   *Prod* John Kohn, Stanley Mann
Scr Anthony Greville-Bell   *Ph* Wolfgang Suschitzky
Ed Malcolm Cooke   *Mus* Michael J. Lewis
Art Dir Michael Seymour
● Vincent Price, Diana Rigg, Ian Hendry, Harry Andrews, Coral Browne, Robert Coote (Harbor/Cineman)

Theatre of Blood is black comedy played for chills and mood and emerges a macabre piece of wild melodramatics.

Douglas Hickox manages neatly in his direction to catch the spirit of a demented Shakespearean actor's (Vincent Price) revenge on eight members of the London Critics' Circle who he believes denied him a Best Actor of the Year award. Situation [from an idea by producers Stanley Mann and John Kohn] allows for some good old-fashioned suspense and high comedy, such as the sequence in which Price saws off the head of one critic while his spouse, needled into unconsciousness, sleeps beside him.

Price uses gory Shakespeare-inspired deaths to systematically murder each of the offending critics.

Price delivers with his usual enthusiasm and Diana Rigg is good as his daughter. Ian Hendry heads the list of critics, and Diana Dors is in briefly as Jack Hawkins' wife whom he smothers to death in a moment of jealousy.

．．．．．．．．．．．．．．．．．．．．．．．．．．

■ **THELMA & LOUISE**

1991, 128 MINS, US ◇ ⧨ ⊙
Dir Ridley Scott   *Prod* Ridley Scott, Mimi Polk
Scr Callie Khouri   *Ph* Adrian Biddle   *Ed* Thom Noble
Mus Hans Zimmer   *Art Dir* Norris Spencer
● Susan Sarandon, Geena Davis, Harvey Keitel, Michael Madsen, Christopher McDonald, Brad Pitt (Pathe/Main)

Thelma & Louise is a thumpingly adventurous road pic about two regular gals who shoot down a would-be rapist and wind up on the lam in their 1966 T-bird. Even those who don't rally to pic's fed-up feminist outcry will take to its comedy, momentum and dazzling visuals.

Arkansas housewife Thelma (Geena Davis) and waitress Louise (Susan Sarandon) set out for a weekend fishing trip away from the drudgery of their lives and the indifference of their men; they stop at a roadside honkytonk to blow off steam, and things turn ugly. A guy tries to rape Thelma; Louise can't take it so she plugs the creep with a .38. Then they hit the highway, dazed and in trouble.

Sarandon is the big sister, more feminine, more focused, smoldering with a quiet determination. Davis is more loosely wrapped; she goes with the flow, follows her whims into trouble. The journey into recklessness is exhilarating, which gives the film its buoyant pull. In an indelible final image, it maintains the sense of reckless exhilaration to the end.

Despite some delectably funny scenes between the sexes, Ridley Scott's pic isn't about women vs men. It's about freedom, like any good road picture. In that sense, and in many others, it's a classic.

California and southern Utah locales stand in for Arkansas, Oklahoma and Texas.
□ 1991: Best Original Screenplay

☐ Nominations: Best Director, Actress (Geena Davis, Susan Sarandon), Cinematography, Editing

■ THEM!

1954, 93 MINS, US ⑦ ⊙
Dir Gordon Douglas   *Prod* David Weisbart   *Scr* Ted Sherdeman   *Ph* Sid Hickox   *Ed* Thomas Reilly   *Mus* Bronislau Kaper   *Art Dir* Stanley Fleischer
● James Whitmore, Edmund Gwenn, Joan Weldon, James Arness, Onslow Stevens, Sean McClory (Warner)

This science-fiction shocker has a well-plotted story [by George Worthing Yates, adapted by Russell Hughes], expertly directed and acted in a matter-of-fact style.

The title monsters are mutations caused by radiation from the 1945 detonation of an atomic bomb in the desert. Over the intervening years the tiny insects affected by the lingering radiation have become fantastic creatures, ranging in size from nine to 12 feet. James Whitmore, sergeant in the New Mexico State Police, first gets on the track of the incredible beings. Into the picture then come Edmund Gwenn and Joan Weldon, entomologists, and James Arness, FBI man.

With the aid of air force officers Onslow Stevens and Sean McClory, the little group attempts to wipe out the nest of the mutated monsters with flame throwers and gas.
☐ 1954: Nomination: Best Special Effects

■ THEODORA GOES WILD

1936, 94 MINS, US
Dir Richard Boleslawski   *Prod* Everett Riskin   *Scr* Sidney Buchman   *Ph* Joseph Walker   *Mus* Morris Stoloff
● Irene Dunne, Melvyn Douglas, Thomas Mitchell, Spring Byington, Elisabeth Risdon, Margaret McWade (Columbia)

A comedy of steady tempo and deepening laughter. Irene Dunne takes the hurdle into comedy with versatile grace.

Theodora may superficially be compared to the *Mr Deeds Goes to Town* (1936) character in that both come from small New England villages. Quaint and eccentric figures and customs are exploited for laughs and background in both cases. And the experiences of the small-town character when hitting Manhattan form the main content of the story [from the novel by Mary McCarthy].

Painstaking direction of Richard Boleslawski brings out the nuances. His direction and Dunne's playing of the first New York escapade of Theodora in a dashing blade's apartment is a high point of light-and-shade farce. Melvyn Douglas is an excellent romantic partner for Dunne. She, rather than he, gets the real acting chances but he is consistently intelligent.
☐ 1936: Nominations: Best Actress (Irene Dunn), Editing

■ THERE'S A GIRL IN MY SOUP

1971, 94 MINS, UK ◇ ⑦
Dir Roy Boulting   *Prod* Mike Frankovich, John Boulting   *Scr* Terence Frisby   *Ph* Harry Waxman   *Ed* Martin Charles   *Mus* Mike D'Abo   *Art Dir* John Howell
● Peter Sellers, Goldie Hawn, Tony Britton, Nicky Henson, John Comer, Diana Dors (Columbia)

There's a Girl in My Soup is a delightful surprise: a rather simple legit sex comedy (by Terence Frisby) transformed into breezy and extremely tasteful screen fun.

Peter Sellers is a TV personality whose roving eye misses few femme specimens. Accidental encounter with Goldie Hawn, who is having some free-love domestic problems with mate Nicky Henson, blossoms into unexpected love and compassion between the unlikely pair.

Henson is excellent in giving depth to the limited part, and adds immeasurably to the general moral tone. In superior support also are Tony Britton as Sellers' publisher-confidante; John Comer as Sellers' envious doorman; and Diana Dors in a good offbeat character casting as Comer's shrewish wife.

■ THERE'S NO BUSINESS LIKE SHOW BUSINESS

1954, 117 MINS, US ◇ ⑦ ⊙
Dir Walter Lang   *Prod* Sol C. Siegel   *Scr* Phoebe Ephron, Henry Ephron   *Ph* Leon Shamroy   *Ed* Robert Simpson   *Mus* Alfred Newman, Lionel Newman (dirs.)   *Art Dir* Lyle Wheeler, John DeCuir
● Ethel Merman, Donald O'Connor, Marilyn Monroe, Dan Dailey, Johnnie Ray, Mitzi Gaynor (20th Century-Fox)

Lamar Trotti's original, from which Phoebe and Henry Ephron fashioned the screenplay, is palpably a script primed to point up the 'heart' of showfolk.

Ethel Merman and Dan Dailey are capital as the vaudeville Donahues who bring out first one, then two, then three of their offspring for that extra bow, with a running gag, as the vaude annunciator cards change to the three Donahues, the four and finally the five Donahues.

Robert Alton rates a big bend along with producer Sol C. Siegel and director Walter Lang on those lavish musical routines. From Irving Berlin's viewpoint, they're all a songplugger's delight.

Ethel Merman is boffo. She's a belter of a school of song stylists not to be found on every stage or before every mike. *Show Business* gets the works in every respect. The orchestral-vocal treatments of the Berlin standards are so richly endowed as to give them constantly fresh values.
☐ 1954: Nominations: Best Motion Picture Story, Color Costume Design, Scoring of a Musical Picture

■ THERE WAS A CROOKED MAN

1960, 90 MINS, UK
Dir Stuart Burge   *Prod* John Bryan   *Scr* Reuben Ship   *Ph* Arthur Ibbetson   *Ed* Peter Hunt   *Mus* Kenneth V. Jones
● Norman Wisdom, Alfred Marks, Andrew Cruickshank, Reginald Beckwith, Susannah York, Jean Clarke (Knightsbridge)

Stuart Burge, a TV director making his debut in feature films, does a good job, considering the many traps that Reuben Ship's ingenious, though far-fetched, screenplay lays. Ship has overloaded his story line but has produced an idea which holds interest.

Norman Wisdom is a down-and-out who runs into a gang of crooks who want his help because he is a demolitions expert. Rather naively he is conned into assisting the mob into cracking a bank vault. He alone is caught holding the loot, and goes to jail. When he's let out after five years, he goes to take up a job in a Northern seaside factory. He soon finds out that the town is under the control of a swindler (Andrew Cruickshank) who is persuading everybody to buy up shares in the town's future. Wisdom enlists the help of his crook friends on a wild enterprise to outwit Cruickshank.

There are so many holes in this yarn that it's like a fishing net, but the result is amiable comedy. The robbery, in which Wisdom and his pals pose as surgeons and tunnel from the operating theatre into the next door bank, is wildly funny. Wisdom getting caught up in a wool sorting machine, avoiding the cops, and finally blowing up the town has good clowning moments.

■ THERE WAS A CROOKED MAN . . .

1970, 128 MINS, US ◇ ⑦
Dir Joseph L. Mankiewicz   *Prod* Joseph L. Mankiewicz   *Scr* David Newman, Robert Benton   *Ph* Harry Stradling Jr   *Ed* Gene Milford   *Mus* Charles Strouse
● Kirk Douglas, Henry Fonda, Hume Cronyn, Warren Oates, Burgess Meredith, Arthur O'Connell (Warner)

There Was a Crooked Man . . . has a crooked plot that is neither comedy nor convincing drama. Kirk Douglas, Henry Fonda, Hume Cronyn, Warren Oates and Burgess Meredith are the formidable elements that don't jell in this picaresque tale set in a bleak western desert prison. It is the type of action drama in which neither the actors nor director appear to believe the script or characters.

Douglas is the crooked man of title who steals $500,000 from Arthur O'Connell and is caught in a bordello literally with his pants down when voyeur O'Connell recognizes him through the peephole.

Fonda plays it straight as the saintly sheriff who becomes an idealistic prison reformer, only to have his principles literally blow up in his face when Douglas organizes a riot and break-out.

■ THESE ARE THE DAMNED

See: The Damned

■ THESE THREE

1936, 90 MINS, US ⑦ ⊙
Dir William Wyler   *Prod* Samuel Goldwyn   *Scr* Lillian Hellman   *Ph* Gregg Toland   *Ed* Danny Mandell   *Mus* Alfred Newman   *Art Dir* Richard Day
● Miriam Hopkins, Merle Oberon, Joel McCrea, Catherine Doucet, Alma Kruger, Bonita Granville (Goldwyn/United Artists)

A thoroughly fine cinematic transmutation of Lillian Hellman's dramatic Broadway smash, *The Childrens Hour* is her own scenarization, reedited and retitled for Haysian purposes as *These Three*. Stripped of its original theme [of lesbianism], it is fortified by a socko trio in Miriam Hopkins, Merle Oberon and Joel McCrea.

Parring the tungsten threesome, however, are two adolescents, Bonita Granville as the hateful Mary Tilford, and Marcia Mae Jones as the subjected, inhibited child. Theirs are inspired performances.

Hellman, if anything, has improved upon the original in scripting the triangle as a dramatis personae of romantic frustration, three basically wholesome victims of an unwholesome combination of circumstance.

McCrea was never better in translating a difficult assignment intelligently and sympathetically. The well bred restraint of Hopkins and Oberon in their travail with the mixture of juvenile emotions at their boarding school is likewise impressive. Oberon is the sympathetic Karen; Hopkins has the assignment of unrequited love.
☐ 1936: Nomination: Best Supp. Actress (Bonita Granville)

■ THEY ALL KISSED THE BRIDE

1942, 84 MINS, US
Dir Alexander Hall   *Prod* Edward Kaufman   *Scr* P.J. Wolfson   *Ph* Joseph Walker   *Ed* Viola Lawrence   *Mus* Werner Heymann
● Joan Crawford, Melvyn Douglas, Roland Young, Billie Burke, Helen Parrish, Allen Jenkins (Columbia)

Picture is adult entertainment – liberally spotted with episodes and lines of explosive and intimate nature – that veers from the general run of pictures of its type sufficiently to get audience attention. Originally, Carole Lombard was set for the starring spot, but her untimely death projected Joan Crawford in as replacement.

Crawford is in command of the vast business interests left by her father, and shaken by the writings of Melvyn Douglas, a happy-go-lucky scribbler of sorts who takes a crack at the family personal and business skeletons.

In addition to a spotlight performance by Crawford, Douglas clicks solidly as the writer and principal romanticist. Script is studded with amusing dialog of most intimate and double entendre content.

Alexander Hall's direction is snappy and speedy all along the line, and he contrives laugh toppers to every episode.

••••••••••••••••••••••••••••••••

■ THEY ALL LAUGHED

1981, 115 MINS, US ◇ ⓥ ⊙
Dir Peter Bogdanovich   *Prod* George Morfogen, Blaine Novak   *Scr* Peter Bogdanovich   *Ph* Robby Muller   *Ed* Scott Vickrey   *Mus* Douglas Dilge   *Art Dir* Kert Lundell
● Audrey Hepburn, Ben Gazzara, John Ritter, Colleen Camp, Dorothy Stratten, Patti Hansen (20th Century-Fox/Time-Life)

Rarely does a film come along featuring such an extensive array of attractive characters with whom it is simply a pleasure to spend two hours. Nothing of great importance happens in a strict plot sense, but this *La Ronde*-like tale is intensely devoted to the sexual and amorous sparks struck among some unusually magnetic people.

In fact, pic could be considered a successful, non-musical remake of *At Long Last Love*, as the dynamics of the partner changes are virtually identical.

It takes a little while to figure out just where the story is headed, but basic framework has Ben Gazzara, John Ritter and Blaine Novak working for the Odyssey Detective Agency, which is truthfully advertised by the line 'We never sleep'. Gazzara's been assigned to track Gotham visitor Audrey Hepburn by her husband, while Ritter and Novak trail Dorothy Stratten as she slips away from her husband to rendezvous with young Sean Ferrer.

Hepburn doesn't have a line to speak for the entire first hour (much of the film is devoted to vaguely voyeuristic pursuit and observation on the part of the detectives), but ultimately she emerges winningly as the most mature and discreet character in the group.

Certain plot contrivances bear eerie resemblances to the cirumstances leading up to Stratten's real-life 1980 murder, as she too, had been followed by a detective hired by a husband suspicious of her fidelity. A palm reading sequence in which Ritter predicts that her marriage will come to a quick end – and she wonders if she has much time left – is chilling for those familiar with the Stratten case.

••••••••••••••••••••••••••••••••

■ THEY CALL ME MISTER TIBBS!

1970, 108 MINS, US ◇ ⓥ
Dir Gordon Douglas   *Prod* Herbert Hirschman   *Scr* Alan R. Trustman, James R. Webb   *Ph* Gerald Perry Finnerman   *Ed* Bud Molin   *Mus* Quincy Jones   *Art Dir* Addison Hehr
● Sidney Poitier, Martin Landau, Barbara McNair, Anthony Zerbe, Edward Asner, Jeff Corey (Mirisch)

A Nob Hill prostitute is murdered in her $300 a month apartment. Last seen leaving the apartment is Martin Landau, a politically-involved minister in the midst of an activist campaign to pass a ballot measure to reform local government. Landau is a close personal friend of Sidney Poitier, who is assigned to investigate the case.

The detective is a tough, ruthlessly efficient cop, and the portrayal, realistic as it is, might be dramatically deadly. However script switches back and forth between the case and the cop's everyday domestic problems with

wife Barbara McNair, 11-year-old son George Spell and six-year-old daughter Wanda Spell.

The father all too frequently must also be a cop to his son and it is in the relationship with the boy that Poitier's character paradoxically is given flesh and blood.

••••••••••••••••••••••••••••••••

■ THEY CAME FROM WITHIN

See: Shivers

••••••••••••••••••••••••••••••••

■ THEY CAME TO CORDURA

1959, 123 MINS, US ◇ ⓥ ⊙
Dir Robert Rossen   *Prod* William Goetz   *Scr* Ivan Moffat, Robert Rossen   *Ph* Burnett Guffey   *Ed* William A. Lyon   *Mus* Elie Siegmeister
● Gary Cooper, Rita Hayworth, Van Heflin, Tab Hunter, Richard Conte, Michael Callan (Columbia)

A bitter and realistic drama of the wry twists life can work on men when they are thrown into situations beyond their control – in this case the 1916 border action between US troops and Pancho Villa's Mexican rebels.

The screenplay, from Glendon Swarthout's book, takes its theme from the title. Cordura is the name of the Texas town the principals are bound for. It is also the Spanish word for courage. The moral is that what's called courage is sometimes a question of interpretation, of accident, or of momentary aberration.

Gary Cooper is the US Army officer detailed to lead five Medal of Honor candidates back from the front lines of the war. Cooper has been made Awards Officer after showing cowardice in battle. The son of an army general and himself a career officer, Cooper is desperately interested in the five heroes because they have what he lacks – or so he thinks. Also on the party is Rita Hayworth, the disillusioned and dissolute daughter of a disgraced politician.

Gary Cooper is very good as the central figure, although he is somewhat too old for the role. Hayworth, looking haggard, drawn and defeated, gives the best performance of her career. If she shows only half the beauty she usually does, she displays twice the acting.

Van Heflin does a brilliantly evil job as one of the 'heroes', and Richard Conte, as his malevolent sidekick, is almost equally impressive.

••••••••••••••••••••••••••••••••

■ THEY DIED WITH THEIR BOOTS ON

1941, 140 MINS, US ⓥ ⊙
Dir Raoul Walsh   *Prod* Hal B. Wallis (exec.)
Scr Wally Kline, Aeneas MacKenzie   *Ph* Bert Glennon   *Ed* William Holmes   *Mus* Max Steiner   *Art Dir* John Hughes
● Errol Flynn, Olivia de Havilland, Arthur Kennedy, Charley Grapewin, Gene Lockhart, Anthony Quinn (Warner)

They Died with Their Boots On is the Custer story, full of action, Indians and anachronisms, with Olivia de Havilland co-starred.

Warner studio provided generously for the picture, in terms of a good supporting cast, hundreds of horsemen, and outdoor locations. Raoul Walsh directed and brought to the screen all the pageantry and adventure that the biography provides.

They're a long time getting to the tragic engagement in the Black Hills when Custer (Errol Flynn) with a third of his command, numbering 264 members of the 7th Cavalry, fell into ambush and were slaughtered by the Sioux.

The liberties which the screen writers have taken with well established and authenticated facts are likely to be a bit trying in spots. But the test of the yarn is not its accuracy, but its speed and excitement. Of these it has plenty.

When Flynn is ordered to command of a frontier post, disorders with Indians require

immediate and drastic action. Custer is the man for the emergency. There is a period of armistice. Then the civilian traders and land grabbers move in. Trouble with the redskins ride with every covered wagon.

••••••••••••••••••••••••••••••••

■ THEY DRIVE BY NIGHT

1940, 93 MINS, US ⓥ ⊙
Dir Raoul Walsh   *Prod* Mark Hellinger   *Scr* Jerry Wald, Richard Macaulay   *Ph* Arthur Edeson   *Ed* Thomas Richards   *Mus* Adolph Deutsch   *Art Dir* John Hughes
● George Raft, Ann Sheridan, Humphrey Bogart, Ida Lupino, Gale Page, Alan Hale (Warner)

Fast moving and actionful melodrama of long-haul trucking biz, *They Drive* clicks with plenty of entertainment content. Story, off the beaten track, divides into two sections, but with a neat dovetail to weld it together. First half is adventure of George Raft and Humphrey Bogart as brothers operating a freelance highway truck, culminating with an asleep-at-the-wheel wreck in which Bogart loses an arm and his desire for further highway adventures. Second half is devoted to the triangle melodrama, with Raft on the receiving end of persistent amorous advances of the married Ida Lupino.

Raoul Walsh provides deft direction that accentuates dramatic moments and maintains a zippo tempo throughout. Script is decidedly workmanlike with numerous snappy and at times spicily double-entendre lines interwoven.

Raft holds the spotlight as the vigorous and determined trucking indie battling against adversities to consummate a dream of owning his own fleet. He turns in a topnotch performance. Equal in importance is Lupino who turns in her dramatic talents for an exceptionally outstanding portrayal, unsympathetic though it is. Bogart is excellent as the hardworking driver and Raft's brother. Anne Sheridan is okay, mainly for love interest, overshadowed by the stellar performance of Lupino.

••••••••••••••••••••••••••••••••

■ THEY LIVE

1988, 93 MINS, US ◇ ⓥ ⊙
Dir John Carpenter   *Prod* Larry Franco   *Scr* Frank Armitage [= John Carpenter]   *Ph* Gary B. Kibbe   *Ed* Gib Jaffe, Frank E. Jimenez   *Mus* John Carpenter, Alan Howarth   *Art Dir* William J. Durrell Jr, Daniel Lomino
● Roddy Piper, Keith David, Meg Foster, George 'Buck' Flower, Peter Jason (Carolco/Alive)

Conceived on 1950s B-movie sci-fi terms, *They Live* is a fantastically subversive film, a nifty little confection pitting us vs them, the haves vs the have-nots.

Screenplay by 'Frank Armitage' (presumably another Carpenter pseudonym as was 'Martin Quatermass'), based on a Ray Nelson short story [*Eight O'Clock in the Morning*], takes the clever premise that those in control of the global economic power structure are secretly other-worldly aliens.

His leading character, pretentiously named Nada (Roddy Piper), is a heavily muscled working Joe, a wanderer who makes his way to Justiceville, a shantytown settlement for the homeless in the shadows of downtown's skyscrapers.

Nada happens upon some sunglasses which, when worn, reveal a whole alternate existence, in which certain individuals – the ruling class – are instantly recognizable due to their hideously decomposed, skeletal faces.

Nada becomes an outlaw, picking off aliens wherever he can. He seeks an accomplice, first in Meg Foster, who unwillingly rescues him from the police, and then in black co-worker Keith David, another bodybuilder whom he has to fight seemingly forever before getting him to try on the glasses.

Pro wrestler Piper comes across quite adequately as the blue collar Everyman, and remainder of the cast is okay.

● ●

■ THEY LIVE BY NIGHT
(Aka: The Twisted Road)

1948, 95 MINS, US 🎭 ⊙
Dir Nicholas Ray   *Prod* John Houseman   *Scr* Charles Schnee   *Ph* George E. Diskant   *Ed* Sherman Todd   *Mus* Leigh Harline   *Art Dir* Albert S. D'Agostino, Al Herman
● Cathy O'Donnell, Farley Granger, Howard da Silva, Jay C. Flippen, Helen Craig, Will Wright (RKO)

Underneath *They Live By Night* is a moving, somber story of hopeless young love. There's no attempt at sugarcoating a happy ending, and yarn moves towards its inevitable, tragic climax without compromise.

A gifted team of young players stands out in making the performances thoroughly realistic. Farley Granger and Cathy O'Donnell are in the lead roles, selling the portrayals with a sock.

The script by Charles Schnee is based on Edward Anderson's novel, *Thieves Like Us*, and tells the story of a young escaped convict who falls in love and marries a girl whose circumstances are little better than his own.

Nicholas Ray adapted the novel and directed, demonstrating a complete understanding of the characters. It's a firstrate job of moody storytelling. Howard da Silva clicks as a ruthless, one-eyed bank robber, and Jay C. Flippen is equally topnotch for his delineation of a criminal.

● ●

■ THEY MIGHT BE GIANTS

1971, 91 MINS, US ◇ 🎭
Dir Anthony Harvey   *Prod* John Foreman   *Scr* James Goldman   *Ph* Victor J. Kemper   *Ed* Gerald Greenberg   *Mus* John Barry   *Art Dir* John Robert Lloyd
● George C. Scott, Joanne Woodward, Jack Gilford, Lester Rawlins, Rue McClanahan, Ron Weyand (Universal)

They Might Be Giants starts off splendidly and hilariously, with George C. Scott at his intense and imposing best as a former jurist who thinks he's Sherlock Holmes, and Joanne Woodward charmingly harried as the psychiatrist who's delighted to encounter a 'classic paranoid', and who just happens to be named Dr (Mildred) Watson.

After that it's all downhill. It's not only unfunny, but increasingly preachy and sentimental – hammering at the cliched tale of the good-hearted nut who's basically saner, and certainly nicer, than the pack of meanies who attempt to defeat him.

Scott and Woodward battle the script valiantly. Scott has the easier time of it by virtue of his character's self-contained system. But both are buried eventually under a pile of loose ends, and they're not helped much either by Anthony Harvey's visually unimaginative direction.

● ●

■ THEY'RE A WEIRD MOB

1966, 109 MINS, AUSTRALIA/UK ◇ 🎭
Dir Michael Powell   *Prod* Michael Powell   *Scr* Richard Imrie   *Ph* Arthur Grant   *Ed* Gerald Turney-Smith   *Mus* Laurence Leonard, Alan Boustead   *Art Dir* Dennis Gentle
● Walter Chiari, Clare Dunne, Chips Rafferty, Alida Chelli, Ed Devereaux, Slim de Grey (Williamson/Powell International)

Italian import Walter Chiari scores in a role that seems tailor-made – an Italian journalist who emigrates to Australia to write for an Italian journal in Sydney edited by his cousin. He arrives very green, and much amusement is caused by his taking too literally some of the Aussie slang.

Chiari finds his cousin has fled. He has left a very irate young lady, Clare Dunne, who has put money into the journal. Chiari gets a job as a bricklayer and ultimately makes the grade with his fellow Aussie workmen. Determined to repay his cousin's debts in installments, Chiari seeks Dunne on Sydney's beaches and elsewhere, but is rebuffed all the way.

Apart from Chiari, Chips Rafferty (who gives an outstanding performance as Dunne's father) and Ed Devereaux as the main bricklayer, most of the cast seems self-conscious before the cameras. For the first half, the film [from the bestselling novel *Down Under* by John O'Grady] strives too hard to be funny and concentrates too much upon the strange Aussie lingo. Once it settles down to telling a story and forgetting about this, it is stronger entertainment.

● ●

■ THEY SHOOT HORSES, DON'T THEY?

1969, 129 MINS, US ◇ 🎭
Dir Sydney Pollack   *Prod* Irwin Winkler, Robert Chartoff, Sydney Pollack   *Scr* James Poe, Robert E. Thompson   *Ph* Philip H. Lathrop   *Ed* Fredric Steinkamp   *Mus* John Green   *Art Dir* Harry Horner
● Jane Fonda, Michael Sarrazin, Susannah York, Gig Young, Red Buttons, Robert Fields (Palomar)

Horace McCoy's 1935 grimy novel of a depression era dance marathon, which sold a forgettable 3,000 copies as a book, is a film with Jane Fonda as a hard-as-nails babe. It becomes, in a recreated old ballroom, a sordid spectacle of hard times, a kind of existentialist allegory of life.

Gig Young is the promoter-emcee, the barker for a cheap sideshow attraction with an endless patter of cliches on pluck, luck, courage, true grit, and the American Way. Puffy-eyed, unshaven, reeking of stale liquor, sweat and cigarets, Young has never looked older or acted better.

Fonda, as the unremittingly cynical loser, the tough and bruised babe of the Dust Bowl, gives a dramatic performance that gives the film a personal focus and an emotionally gripping power.

Pollack turns the marathon into a vulgar, sleazy, black microcosm of life in 1932.
☐ 1969: Best Supp. Actor (Gig Young).
Nominations: Best Actress (Jane Fonda), Supp. Actress (Susannah York), Screenplay Adaptation, Costume Design, Art Direction, Editing, Adapted Music Score

● ●

■ THEY WERE EXPENDABLE

1945, 135 MINS, US 🎭 ⊙
Dir John Ford   *Prod* John Ford   *Scr* Frank Wead   *Ph* Joseph H. August   *Ed* Frank E. Hull, Douglass Biggs   *Mus* Herbert Stothart   *Art Dir* Cedric Gibbons, Malcolm F. Brown
● Robert Montgomery, John Wayne, Donna Reed, Cameron Mitchell, Ward Bond, Leon Ames (M-G-M)

They Were Expendable, dealing with the Japs' overrunning of the Philippines [from the book of the same name by William L. White], primarily concerns the part played by the US torpedo boats in their use against the Japs.

Robert Montgomery and his buddy (John Wayne) are naval lieutenants in command of P-T boats. Montgomery from the start has faith in the little destroyers but Wayne is slow to appreciate their value.

While the squadron of P-T tubs stationed at Manila Bay prior to Pearl Harbor were looked upon doubtfully by naval officers, invasion by the Japs gave them their chance to show what they could do. Most of the rest of the picture vividly portrays the big job the little boats did.

The battle scenes in which the P-Ts go after Jap cruisers and supply ships were exceptionally well directed, John Ford aided by James

C. Havens, captain of the US Marine Corps Reserves.

Love interest is built around Wayne and an army nurse, played appealingly by Donna Reed. It develops at an early stage but is dropped as Wayne and Reed lose each other through assignments that separate them.
☐ 1945: Nominations: Best Sound, Special Effects

● ●

■ THIEF, THE

1952, 85 MINS, US 🎭
Dir Russell Rouse   *Prod* Clarence Greene   *Scr* Russell Rouse, Clarence Greene   *Ph* Sam Leavitt   *Ed* Chester Schaeffer   *Mus* Herschel Burke Gilbert   *Art Dir* Joseph St Amand
● Ray Milland, Rita Gam, Martin Gabel, Harry Bronson, Rex O'Malley, Rita Vale (Fran/United Artists)

This has an offbeat approach to film storytelling (a complete absence of dialog), a good spy plot and a strong performance by Ray Milland.

The film is not soundless. The busy hum of a city is a cacophonous note, a strident-sounding telephone bell plays an important part and, overall, there's the topnotch musical score by Herschel Gilbert, sometimes used almost too insistently to build a melodramatic mood and in other spots softly emphasizing and making clear the dumb action of the players.

Missed in the story is the reason why Milland, a respected scientist in the field of nuclear physics, should turn traitor to his country and deliver its nuclear secrets to foreign agents.

Film introduces Rita Gam, NY actress, and in her three scenes as a temptress her personality impresses.
☐ 1952: Scoring of a Dramatic Picture

● ●

■ THIEF

1981, 122 MINS, US ◇ 🎭 ⊙
Dir Michael Mann   *Prod* Jerry Bruckheimer, Ronnie Caan   *Scr* Michael Mann   *Ph* Donald Thorin   *Ed* Dov Hoenig   *Mus* Tangerine Dream   *Art Dir* Mel Bourne
● James Caan, Tuesday Weld, Willie Nelson, James Belushi, Robert Prosky, Tom Signorelli (United Artists)

Michael Mann proves to be a potent triple threat as exec producer-director-writer on *Thief*. Although there are points where he gets bogged down in the technical aspects of thievery, the film is a slick Chicago crimedrama with a well-developed sense of pathos running throughout. James Caan comes up with a particularly convincing portrait of the central figure and superior soundtrack from Tangerine Dream adds immeasurably to the action.

Mann, who won awards for his work on the critically acclaimed telefilm, *The Jericho Mile*, has woven a fine story around a highly honorable man who just happens to be an expert thief with an extensive prison record. Caan plays the thief, a victim of an unfortunate childhood who lands in jail and is hardened with his unsavory environment, with an incredible vulnerability.

In terms of story, Caan is a highly successful crook who takes great pains to maintain his professional independence. Against his better judgment he gives in to 'godfather' type Robert Prosky's request to join forces, mostly in an effort to provide personal stability.

The basic story centers on Caan's work, which becomes increasingly complicated by his new association. Oddly enough, Mann's major flaw is being a bit too meticulous in delineating the process Caan must go through in order to make a big score.

● ●

T

■ THIEF OF BAGDAD, THE

1924, 155 MINS, US ◇ ⊗ ⓦ
Dir Raoul Walsh   *Prod* Douglas Fairbanks   *Scr* Lotta
Woods, Elton Thomas [= Douglas Fairbanks]   *Ph* Arthur
Edeson   *Ed* William Nolan   *Mus* Mortimer Wilson
Art Dir William Cameron Menzies
● Douglas Fairbanks, Snitz Edwards, Julanne Johnston,
Anna May Wong, Charles Belcher, Sojin (Fairbanks/
United Artists)

Douglas Fairbanks comes forth with an absorbing, interesting picture, totally different than any of its predecessors. Nearly all of it is fairytale-like or fantasy, and so well is it done that the picture carries its audience along in the spirit of the depiction. *The Arabian Nights* are classic stories in book form. *The Thief of Bagdad* is a classic in pictures.

There is a magic rope thrown into the air up which the thief climbs high walls. There is a magic carpet upon which he sails with his princess away into the land of happiness. There is a magic chest which the favored one retrieves after heroic struggles through the valley of fire, the vale of dragons, even to the depths of the seas. It is the thief, now a prince who returns at the coming of the seventh moon to win his princess against the wiles of Oriental potentates seeking her hand. He wraps her in his invisible cloak and whisks her away.

The cast has been brightly selected. At the head of those players is Sojin in the role of the Mongol prince, a really fine characterization. Anna May Wong as the little slave girl who is a spy for the Mongol prince, proves herself a fine actress. Julanne Johnston as the princess is languorous, being more decorative than inspiring.

■ THIEF OF BAGDAD, THE

1940, 106 MINS, UK/US ◇ ⓦ ⊙
Dir Ludwig Berger, Michael Powell, Tim Whelan, Geoffrey
Boothby, Charles David, [Zoltan Korda, William Cameron
Menzies, Alexander Korda]   *Prod* Alexander Korda
Scr Lajos Biro, Miles Malleson   *Ph* Georges Perinal,
Osmond Borradaile   *Ed* William Hornbeck, Charles
Crichton   *Mus* Miklos Rozsa   *Art Dir* Vincent Korda
● Conrad Veidt, Sabu, June Duprez, John Justin, Rex
Ingram, Miles Malleson (Korda)

The Thief of Bagdad is a colorful, lavish and eye-appealing spectacle. It's an expensive production accenting visual appeal, combining sweeping panoramas and huge sets, amazing special effects and process photography, and vivid magnificent Technicolor. These factors completely submerge the stolid, slow and rather disjointed fairy tale which lacks any semblance of spontaneity in its telling.

Alexander Korda retains only the Bagdadian background and title in presenting his version of the picture first turned out by Douglas Fairbanks in 1924. But while Fairbanks presented dash and movement to his story, to have the latter dominate his spectacular set- tings, Korda uses the reverse angle. As result, audience interest is focused on the production and technical displays of the picture, and the unimpressive story and stagey acting of the cast fail to measure up to the general production qualities.

The story combines many imaginative incidents culled from Arabian Nights fables. There's the mechanical horse that flies through the air; the giant genie of the bottle; the huge spider that guards the all-seeing eye; the six-armed dancing doll; the evil magic of the villain; and the famous magic carpet.

Korda spent two years in preparation and production of *Thief of Bagdad*. All of the large sets, including the city of Bagdad and seaport of Basra, were shot in England, in addition to most of the dramatic action. With the war stopping production in England Korda moved to Hollywood to complete the picture, substituting the American desert and the Grand Canyon for sequences that he originally intended to shoot in Arabia and Egypt.

Conrad Veidt is most impressive as the sinister grand vizier, sharing honors with Sabu, who capably carries off the title role.

□ 1940: Best Color Cinematography, Color Interior Decoration (Vincent Korda), Special Effects (Lawrence Butler, Jacl Whitney)
□ Nomination: Best Original Score

■ THIEF WHO CAME TO DINNER, THE

1973, 105 MINS, US ◇ ⓦ
Dir Bud Yorkin   *Prod* Bud Yorkin   *Scr* Walter Hill
Ph Philip Lathrop   *Ed* John C. Horger   *Mus* Henry
Mancini   *Art Dir* Polly Platt
● Ryan O'Neal, Jacqueline Bisset, Warren Oates, Jill
Clayburgh, Charles Cioffi, Ned Beatty (Tandem/Warner)

The Thief Who Came to Dinner has a good title and a helpful supporting cast. Otherwise it is a tepid caper comedy, starring Ryan O'Neal as a computer-age society gem burglar, Jacqueline Bisset as his girl, and Warren Oates as a befuddled insurance detective.

Using a Terrence Lore novel, adapter Walter Hill structured an episodic script focussing on O'Neal who blackmails magnate Charles Cioffi for entree into rich circles where he can plot his heists.

The film, which exudes the lethargy of a project where some talent commitments are being exercised, uses as a running gag O'Neal's heist signature of a chess move, leading to a newspaper promotion with chess editor Austin Pendleton becoming frustrated as the thief's computer-aided expertise.

■ THIEVES' HIGHWAY

1949, 93 MINS, US
Dir Jules Dassin   *Prod* Robert Bassler   *Scr* A.I.
Bezzerides   *Ph* Norbert Brodine   *Ed* Nick DeMaggio
Mus Alfred Newman   *Art Dir* Lyle Wheeler, Chester
Gore
● Richard Conte, Valentina Cortese, Lee J. Cobb, Jack
Oakie, Millard Mitchell (20th Century-Fox)

Script stresses realism and Jules Dassin's direction further carries out that emphasis in the no-holds-barred love sequences between Richard Conte and Hollywood newcomer Valentina Cortese, and the high action trucking scenes and barroom fight finale. A. I. Bezzerides did the screenplay from his novel, *Thieves' Market*. It's guttily dialoged and plays fast under Dassin's helming.

Conte depicts a trucker whose father has lost his legs in an accident staged by heavy Lee J. Cobb, produce commission man. Conte goes out for revenge, aided by Millard Mitchell, in an attempt to beat Cobb at his own game of thievery.

Cortese is introduced as a prostitute, hired by Cobb to lure Conte from his revenge game. She and Conte make the most of the meaty assignments.

■ THIEVES LIKE US

1974, 123 MINS, US ◇
Dir Robert Altman   *Prod* Jerry Bick   *Scr* Calder
Willingham, Joan Tewkesbury, Robert Altman   *Ph* Jean
Boffety   *Ed* Lou Lombardo
● Keith Carradine, Shelley Duvall, John Schuck, Bert
Remsen, Louise Fletcher, Tom Skerritt (United Artists)

Thieves Like Us proves that when Robert Altman has a solid story and script, he can make an exceptional film, one mostly devoid of clutter, auterist mannerism, and other cinema chic. It's a better film than Nicholas Ray's first jab at the story in 1948 [*They Live By Night*], the mid-1930s tale of lower-class young love and Dixie bank-robbing.

Edward Anderson's novel of the same name has, this time, been adapted into a no-nonsense screenplay. Keith Carradine heads the cast as a young prison trustee who escapes with John Schuck to join Bert Remsen in a spree of small-town bank heists. Shelley Duvall and Carradine fall in love, their romance clearly destined for tragedy as the robberies inevitably lead to murders and eventual police capture.

■ THIN BLUE LINE, THE

1988, 106 MINS, US ◇ ⓦ ⊙
Dir Errol Morris   *Prod* Mark Lipson   *Ph* Stefan
Czapsky, Robert Chappell   *Ed* Paul Barnes   *Mus* Philip
Glass   *Art Dir* Teddy Bafaloukos
● (American Playhouse/Third Floor)

Errol Morris' *The Thin Blue Line* constitutes a mesmerizing reconstruction and investigation of a senseless murder. It employs strikingly original formal devices to pull together diverse interviews, filmclips, photo collages and recreations of the crime from many points of view.

Case in question centers upon the 1976 murder of a Dallas policeman. Late one night, Officer Robert Wood and his partner pulled over a car that was traveling without its headlights on. When Wood approached the driver's window, he was shot five times and killed.

Some time later, David Harris, 16, was arrested in Vidor, Texas, after having bragged to friends that he'd killed a Dallas cop. Harris later insisted his boasting was only meant to impress his buddies, and that the real murderer was a hitchhiker he'd picked up earlier in the day, one Randall Adams.

Despite Harris' extensive criminall history and Adams' unblemished past, the teenager got off scot-free, while the older man was convicted and sentenced to death (later committed to life imprisonment).

Morris first introduces the two men via freshly filmed, straightforward interviews, then stages the crime for the camera from a variety of angles and at an assortment of speeds.

Title refers to the police, said by the judge here to be the only thing that separates the public from the rule of anarchy.

■ THING, THE

1982, 108 MINS, US ◇ ⓦ ⊙
Dir John Carpenter   *Prod* David Foster, Lawrence
Turman   *Scr* Bill Lancaster   *Ph* Dean Cundey
Ed Todd Ramsay   *Mus* Ennio Morricone   *Art Dir* John
J. Lloyd
● Kurt Russell, A. Wilford Brimley, T.K. Carter, David
Clennon, Keith David, Richard Dysart (Universal/
Turman-Foster)

If it's the most vividly guesome monster ever to stalk the screen that audiences crave, then *The Thing* is the thing. On all other levels, however, John Carpenter's remake of Howard Hawks' 1951 sci-fi classic comes as a letdown.

Strong premise as a group of American scientists and researchers posted at an isolated station in Antarctica. A visit to a decimated Norwegian encampment in the vicinity reveals that a space ship, which had remained buried in ice for as many as 100,000 years, has been uncovered, and that no survivors were left to tell what was found.

First manifestation of The Thing arrives in the form of an escaped dog from the Scandinavian camp. It soon becomes clear that The Thing is capable of ingesting, then assuming the bodily form of, any living being.

What the old picture delivered – and what Carpenter has missed – was a sense of intense dread, a fear that the loathed creature might be lurking around any corner or behind any door.

Kurt Russell is the nominal hero, although suicidal attitude adopted towards the end undercuts his status as a centerscreen force.

■ THING (FROM ANOTHER WORLD), THE

1951, 89 MINS, US 🔞 ⊙

Dir Christian Nyby   *Prod* Howard Hawks   *Scr* Charles
Lederer   *Ph* Russell Harlan   *Ed* Roland Gross
Mus Dimitri Tiomkin   *Art Dir* Albert S. D'Agostino, John
J. Hughes
● Margaret Sheridan, Kenneth Tobey, Robert
Cornthwaite, Douglas Spencer, Dewey Martin, James
Arness (Winchester/RKO)

Strictly offbeat subject matter centers
around a weird, outlandish interplanetary
space-hopper (see title) which descends upon
earth in what's referred to as a flying saucer.

Christian Nyby's direction sustains a mood
of tingling expectancy as a small group of US
airmen and scientists stationed near the
North Pole learn that a new, mysterious element is playing tricks with their compass-
readings, etc. Tension develops effectively as
the expedition takes off to reckon with the
unearthly intruder. Hawks' production also
scores in its depiction of the bleak, snow-
swept Arctic region. The background layout,
shot in Montana, conveys an air of frigid authenticity.

But the resourcefulness shown in building
the plot groundwork is lacking as the yarn
gets into full swing. Cast members, headed by
Margaret Sheridan and Kenneth Tobey, fail
to communicate any real terror as the 'Thing'
makes its appearance and its power potential
to destroy the world is revealed.

Screenplay, based on the story *Who Goes
There* by John W. Campbell Jr., shows strain in
the effort to come up with a cosmic shocker in
the name of science fiction.

■ THINGS CHANGE

1988, 100 MINS, US ◇ 🔞 ⊙

Dir David Mamet   *Prod* Michael Hausman   *Scr* David
Mamet, Shel Silverstein   *Ph* Juan Ruiz-Anchia   *Ed* Trudy
Ship   *Mus* Alaric Jans   *Art Dir* Michael Merritt
● Don Ameche, Joe Mantegna, Robert Prosky, J.J
Johnston, Ricky Jay, Mike Nussbaum
(Filmhaus/Columbia)

David Mamet's *Things Change* is a dry, funny
and extremely intelligent comedy about an
innocent mistaken for a Mafia don.

Pic opens in Chicago as the elderly Gino
(Don Ameche), a shoeshine boy, is 'invited' to
meet a Mafia boss whom he physically resembles. He wants Gino to confess to a murder
and take the rap and as a reward he can have
his heart's desire.

Gino is handed over to Jerry (Joe
Mantegna), a very junior member of the
Mafia clan. All Jerry has to do is coach Gino
in his story for two days, then deliver him to
the law. Instead, Jerry decides to give the oldster a final fling, and takes him to Lake
Tahoe where, unknown to him, a Mafia convention is about to take place.

Gino is instantly mistaken for a senior Don
and given royal treatment. He's also invited
to meet the local Mafia kingpin (Robert
Prosky) with whom he instantly strikes up a
close rapport while Jerry sees himself getting
into deeper and deeper trouble.

This comedy of mistaken identity centers
around a beautifully modulated starring performance from Ameche as the poor but
painfully upright and honest Gino. As the
dimwitted Jerry, Mantegna is consistently
funny and touching.

■ THINGS TO COME

1936, 97 MINS, UK 🔞

Dir William Cameron Menzies   *Prod* Alexander Korda
Scr H.G. Wells   *Ph* Georges Perinal   *Ed* William
Hornbeck, Charles Crichton, Francis Lyon   *Mus* Arthur
Bliss   *Art Dir* Vincent Korda
● Raymond Massey, Cedric Hardwicke, Edward
Chapman, Ralph Richardson, Margaretta Scott, Maurice
Braddell (London)

This is England's first $1 million picture. It's
an impressive but dull exposition of a bad
dream.

H.G. Wells' idea is that in 1946 there will
be a new and disastrous world war. It will last
for 30 years and, at the end of that time, civilization will be reduced to nothingness, disease having scourged the world. In exile a
group of engineers and aviators, however,
think things over and decide that the ravages
and wastes of war, properly harnessed and
channeled, can be used for the world's salvation.

They take things over, do away with the
petty little fascistic countries that have
sprung up, do away with their petty little
fascistic leaders, and create a new world of
steel and glass, radio and television, artificial
light and heat. It is all very pictorial, very
imaginative, very artificial and it runs on and
on.

William Cameron Menzies directs with a
firm hand and even manages to inject some
power into the fantasy. Where his characters
are allowed to live, he sees to it that they also
breathe. Georges Perinal's photography is
tops. Garlands are also due Harry Zech for
trick photography and Ned Mann for special
effects.

Raymond Massey is tops as John Cabal,
leader of the new world. Ralph Richardson
does a splendid job as the Boss, a sort of
combo Hitler-Mussolini.

■ THINK BIG

1990, 86 MINS, US ◇ 🔞

Dir Jon Turteltaub   *Prod* Brad Krevoy, Steven Stabler
Scr Edward Kovach, David Tausik, John Turteltaub
Ph Mark Morris   *Ed* Jeff Reiner   *Mus* Michael
Sembello, Hilary Bercovici, Stephen Graziano
Art Dir Robert Schullenberg
● Peter Paul, David Paul, Ari Meyers, Martin Mull, David
Carradine, Claudia Christian (Motion Picture/Concorde)

This undemanding physical comedy offers
okay gags for audiences waxing nostalgic for
the generally unlamented 1970s vehicular
comedies involving trucks and cars.

The Barbarian Bros, twins Peter and David
Paul, topline as a pair of affable but somewhat retarded truckers hauling a load of toxic
waste across country. Brainy but beautiful 16-
year-old Ari Meyers stows away in their vehicle, as she's on the lam with her secret
weapon developed at Martin Mull's think
tank for kids.

There's plenty of effective slapstick as cartoonish villains chase after the trio, who are
joined later by Meyers' school psychologist
(Claudia Christian). David Carradine, in particular, is fun (costumed to resemble his
brother Keith) as a nutty repo man.

Meyers is delightful as the precocious heroine and manages to maintain a straight face
opposite the cuddly but oversize non-actor
Paul brothers.

■ THIN MAN, THE

1934, 80 MINS, US 🔞 ⊙

Dir W. S. Van Dyke   *Prod* Hunt Stromberg   *Scr* Albert
Hackett, Frances Goodrich   *Ph* James Wong Howe
Ed Robert J. Kern   *Mus* William Axt   *Art Dir* Cedric
Gibbons, David Townsend, Edwin B. Willis
● William Powell, Myrna Loy, Maureen O'Sullivan, Nat
Pendleton, Minna Gombell, Porter Hall (M-G-M/
Cosmopolitan)

The Thin Man was an entertaining novel, and
now it's an entertaining picture. In the
Dashiell Hammett original there was considerable material not suited by nature to pictures. That this has been cut without
noticeable loss of story punch or merit is high
commendation for the adapters.

They capture the spirit of the jovial, com-
panionable relationship of the characters,

Nick, retired detective, and Nora, his wife.
Their very pleasant manner of loving each
other and showing it is used as a light comedy
structure upon which the screen doctors perform their operation on the Hammett novel.

The comedy as inserted, and also as directed by W. S. Van Dyke and played by
William Powell and Myrna Loy, carries the
picture along during its early moments and
gives it an impetus which sweeps the meat of
the mystery story through to a fast finish.

No changes made in the basic plot nor in
the murder mystery developments.

☐ 1934: Nominations: Best Picture, Director,
Actor (William Powell), Writing Adaptation

■ THIN MAN GOES HOME, THE

1944, 100 MINS, US 🔞 ⊙

Dir Richard Thorpe   *Prod* Everett Riskin   *Scr* Robert
Riskin, Dwight Taylor   *Ph* Karl Freund   *Ed* Ralph E.
Winters   *Mus* David Snell   *Art Dir* Cedric Gibbons,
Edward Carfagno
● William Powell, Myrna Loy, Gloria de Haven, Anne
Revere, Harry Davenport, Edward Brophy (M-G-M)

Based on the characterizations originally created by Dashiell Hammett, the story emerges
as a neatly-fashioned whodunit. Richard
Thorpe paces the plot nicely, overcoming, before too long, the hurdles of a rather slow
opening.

Production as a whole, however, lacks much
of the sophistication and smartness which
characterized the early *Thin Man* films.
Deficiency is mainly in the dialog and other
business provided for the two leads.

Yarn deals with an espionage ring working
for a foreign power. Involves a battle of wits
to secure a group of paintings which leads to
a couple of killings.

Myrna Loy, while graceful and piquant for
the most part, photographs unattractively in
a number of sequences.

■ THIN RED LINE, THE

1964, 90 MINS, US

Dir Andrew Marton   *Prod* Sidney Harmon
Scr Bernard Gordon   *Ph* Manuel Berenguer   *Ed* Derek
Parsons   *Mus* Malcolm Arnold   *Art Dir* Jose Alguero
● Keir Dullea, Jack Warden, James Philbrook, Ray
Daley, Robert Kanter, Merlyn Yordan (Allied Artists)

Aficionados of the action-packed war film will
savor the crackling, combat-centered approach of *The Thin Red Line*, an explosive
melodramatization of the Yank assault on
Guadalcanal in World War II.

Bernard Gordon's scenario, turbulently
gleaned from James Jones' novel, focuses its
characterization gaze at two figures prominently implicated in the taking of that small
but significant piece of Pacific real estate.
One is a resourceful private (Keir Dullea),
the other a war-wise, sadistic sergeant (Jack
Warden).

The two quickly become enemies but it is
no surprise when, ultimately, one dies in the
other's arms after saving the other's life.
Dullea and Warden are colorful antagonists,
former's intensity contrasting sharply with
the latter's easygoing air. In addition to this
pivotal intramural conflict, there are other
hostilities including the one between Japan
and the United States.

■ THIRD DAY, THE

1965, 119 MINS, US ◇

Dir Jack Smight   *Prod* Jack Smight   *Scr* Burton Wohl,
Robert Presnell Jr   *Ph* Robert Surtees   *Ed* Stefan
Arnsten   *Mus* Percy Faith   *Art Dir* Edward Carrere
● George Peppard, Elizabeth Ashley, Roddy McDowall,
Arthur O'Connell, Mona Washbourne, Herbert Marshall
(Warner)

The Third Day shapes up as an interesting and sometimes suspenseful drama revolving around a man fighting amnesia and faced with a manslaughter rap. The production is adapted from Joseph Hayes' novel.

A chief weakness lies in the lack of script development of how George Peppard, who has lost all recollection of a 24-hour period during which a young woman meets her death, regains his memory.

Film opens on Peppard climbing a steep bank from a river into which he obviously plunged, but he cannot remember what happened or who he is. He learns he's married to a beautiful aristocrat whom he's about to lose because he's a drunk, and is about to be talked into selling the family business.

Peppard delivers an expert enactment and Elizabeth Ashley, as his wife, lends a colorful note as she handles a well-played role. Roddy McDowall socks over a conniving character and a standout performance is offered by Mona Washbourne in a warm and understanding characterization, perhaps the most memorable delineation of the picture.

■ THIRD MAN, THE

1949, 93 MINS, UK [V] ⊙
Dir Carol Reed *Prod* Carol Reed *Scr* Graham Greene *Ph* Robert Krasker *Ed* Oswald Hafenrichter *Mus* Anton Karas *Art Dir* Vincent Korda, John Hawkesworth, Joseph Bato
● Joseph Cotten, Alida Valli, Orson Welles, Trevor Howard, Bernard Lee, Wilfrid Hyde White (London)

This is a full-blooded, absorbing story adapted from book by Graham Greene. Locale is postwar Vienna, which is controlled by combined military force of the four occupying powers, and revolves around the black market and all its unsavory ramifications.

Holly Martins, a young American writer, arrives to join his friend, Harry Lime, who has promised him a job. He just gets to him in time to attend his funeral. Suspicious of conflicting evidence and with a strong hunch that Harry was murdered, Holly decides to unravel the mystery.

Orson Welles manifests as the 'corpse' of the opening shots, and his contribution is mainly in dodging through back streets.

Joseph Cotten makes a pleasing personality of the loyal friend, and Trevor Howard, as the detached, cool British officer, displays just the right amount of human sympathy and understanding.

☐ 1950: Best B&W Cinematography.
☐ Nominations: Best Director, Editing

■ THIRD SECRET, THE

1964, 103 MINS, UK
Dir Charles Crichton *Prod* Robert L. Joseph *Scr* Robert L. Joseph *Ph* Douglas Slocombe *Ed* Freddie Wilson *Mus* Richard Arnell *Art Dir* Tom Morahan
● Stephen Boyd, Jack Hawkins, Richard Attenborough, Diane Cilento, Pamela Franklin, Paul Rogers (20th Century-Fox)

When a renowned psychoanalyst is deemed a suicide, the puzzle surrounding his sudden and unaccountable death, as it is put together piece by piece by one of his agitated patients, is the plot pursued by *The Third Secret*, an engrossing, if not altogether convincing, mystery melodrama of the weighty psychological school.

Stephen Boyd, as the inquisitive patient of the deceased analyst, conducts a private investigation to determine whether the death was actually a suicide (contradicting everything the noted doctor stood for) or a murder committed by one of his patients, of whom there were only four, according to the analyst's daughter (Pamela Franklin). The investigation leads Boyd – an American telenewscaster living in England – from patient to patient, a fruitless path until he unearths 'the third secret'.

A lack of animation in spots is evident in Boyd's performance, but there are moments when he catches the spark of the character. Franklin does a highly professional job as the daughter. The three ex-patients visited by Boyd are Jack Hawkins as a judge, Diane Cilento as a secretary and Richard Attenborough as an art gallery owner.

■ THIRTEEN CHAIRS, THE

See: 12 Plus 1

■ 13 RUE MADELEINE

1946, 95 MINS, US [V]
Dir Henry Hathaway *Prod* Louis de Rochemont *Scr* John Monks Jr, Sy Bartlett *Ph* Norbert Brodine *Ed* Harmon Jones *Mus* David Buttolph *Art Dir* James Basevi, Maurice Ransford
● James Cagney, Annabella, Richard Conte, Frank Latimore, Walter Abel, Sam Jaffe (20th Century-Fox)

Utilizing the same off-screen documentary exposition as he did in *The House on 92nd Street* producer Louis de Rochemont, himself an alumnus of the *Time-Life* technique, reemploys the stentorian *March of Time* commentary to set his theme. Thereafter it evolves into a Nazi-Allies cops-and-robbers tale of bravery and bravado, honest histrionics and hokum.

When he is one of the strategic services' masterminds, on US or British soil, James Cagney is effectively the mature training officer engaged in the important branch of the service having to do with strategy. When he essays the role of a brave young soldier-spy, to pit himself against Richard Conte, the crack Gestapo agent who had insinuated himself into the American espionage school as a means to learn our invasion plans, Cagney suffers comparison. Conte as Bill O'Connell, nee Wilhelm Kuncel of the Nazi espionage, emerges as the cast's outstander.

The training methods, as indoctrinated into the plot's development, are arresting stuff. *Madeleine* was shot wholly away from Hollywood, utilizing New England and Quebec sites in the main, but there is nothing about the film that doesn't indicate super-Hollywood standards.

■ 13TH LETTER, THE

1951, 85 MINS, US
Dir Otto Preminger *Prod* Otto Preminger *Scr* Howard Koch *Ph* Joseph LaShelle *Ed* Louis Loeffler *Mus* Alex North *Art Dir* Lyle Wheeler, Maurice Ransford
● Linda Darnell, Charles Boyer, Michael Rennie, Constance Smith, Francoise Rosay (20th Century-Fox)

Well-made and with an offbeat location site, film is an interesting account of the effects of poison pen letters on a small Quebec village [from a story and screenplay *Le corbeau* by Louis Chavance, directed by Henri-Georges Clouzot in 1943].

Plot deals principally with Michael Rennie, as a doctor; Charles Boyer, an older doctor, and his young wife (Constance Smith). The small Quebec village in which they live becomes a gossip mill when poison pen letters, indicating Rennie and Smith are having an affair, are widely distributed. Letters go on to bring in other people, eventually causing a wounded war hero to commit suicide.

Linda Darnell heads the star list as a crippled, romance-starved girl on whom suspicion falls briefly. However, cleared she and Rennie become the story's one valid romance. Her playing is excellent.

Charles Boyer slips into the character of the elderly French-Canadian doctor with wonderful ease. Smith, a British import, displays emotional talent.

■ 30 IS A DANGEROUS AGE, CYNTHIA

1968, 85 MINS, UK ◇ [V]
Dir Joseph McGrath *Prod* Walter Shenson *Scr* Dudley Moore, Joseph McGrath, John Wells *Ph* Billy Williams *Ed* Bill Blunden *Mus* Dudley Moore *Art Dir* Brian Eatwell
● Dudley Moore, Eddie Foy Jr, Suzy Kendall, John Bird, Duncan MacRae (Columbia)

Generously endowed with the better comedic elements of satire, knockabouts, subtleties, pie-in-the-face, etc, film is almost a virtuoso performance by Dudley Moore. He stars, is credited with the original story, composed and conducted music – played by the Dudley Moore Trio.

Close to his 30th birthday Moore, with an amazing spurt of energy, launches a desperation drive to achieve two ambitions, writing a successful musical comedy and getting married.

From this plot establishment, Moore and friends take off on a romp that involves a false broken arm, getting away from it all, losing girl, finishing musical and so on, with such a sense of camp that audiences are bound to be laughing long after the last frame.

Moore's versatility is central focus with a remarkably underplayed performance that sets pace and keeps it on track; his storyline is a single joke that undoubtedly grew during the filming, and his music and lyrics are like early Noel Coward set in rock idiom.

■ 39 STEPS, THE

1935, 86 MINS, UK [V] ⊙
Dir Alfred Hitchcock *Prod* Michael Balcon *Scr* Charles Bennett, Alma Reville, Ian Hay *Ph* Bernard Knowles *Ed* Derek Twist *Mus* Louis Levy (dir.) *Art Dir* Oscar Werndorff, Albert Jullion
● Robert Donat, Madeleine Carroll, Godfrey Tearle, Peggy Ashcroft, Lucie Mannheim, Wylie Watson (Gaumont-British)

Gaumont has a zippy, punchy, romantic melodrama in *The 39 Steps*. Story is by John Buchan. It's melodrama and at times far-fetched and improbable, but the story twists and spins artfully from one high-powered sequence to another while the entertainment holds like steel cable from start to finish.

Story places a Canadian rancher (Robert Donat) in the centre of an English military secrets plot. He is simultaneously flying from a false accusation of murder and hunting down the leader of the spies, of whom he has learned from a lady who becomes a corpse early in the story. In the course of his wanderings through Scotland's hills and moors he has a series of spectacular escapes and encounters.

It's a creamy role for Donat and his performance, ranging from humor to horror, reveals acting ability behind that good-looking facade. Teamed with Madeleine Carroll, who enters the footage importantly only toward the latter quarter section of the film, the romance is given a light touch which nicely colors an international spy chase.

■ 39 STEPS, THE

1959, 93 MINS, UK ◇ [V]
Dir Ralph Thomas *Prod* Betty Box, Ralph Thomas *Scr* Frank Harvey *Ph* Ernest Steward *Ed* Alfred Roome *Mus* Clifton Parker
● Kenneth More, Taina Elg, Brenda de Banzie, Barry Jones, Reginald Beckwith, James Hayter (Rank)

Though somewhat altered from Alfred Hitchcock's original, the main idea remains unchanged and the new version of John Buchan's novel stands up very well.

When a strange young woman is stabbed to

death in his flat, Kenneth More finds himself involved in a mysterious adventure involving espionage and murder. Before her death the girl tells him that she is a secret agent and gives him all the clues she knows about a spy organization seeking to smuggle some important plans out of the country. All he knows is that the top man is somewhere in Scotland and that the tangle is tied up with strange words told him by the victim – 'The 39 Steps.' Suspected of the murder of the girl, More has just 48 hours to find out the secret of the 39 Steps, expose the gang and so clear himself of the murder rap.

Film starts off brilliantly with tremendous tension and suitably sinister atmosphere. After a while that mood wears off as the pic settles down to an exciting and often amusing chase yarn, set amid some easy-on-the-eye Scottish scenery.

More's performance is a likeable mixture of humor and toughness while Taina Elg is appealing as the pretty schoolmistress who is dragged into the adventure against her will. Then there are Barry Jones, as a sinister professor; Brenda de Banzie, as a fake spiritualist who, with her eccentric husband (Reginald Beckwith) helps More's getaway; James Hayter as a vaude 'memory man' who is a tool of the gang; and Faith Brook, whose murder sparks off the drama, all pitch in splendidly in a well acted picture.

● ●

■ THIRTY NINE STEPS, THE

1978, 102 MINS, UK ◇ ▼ ⊙
Dir Don Sharp   *Prod* Greg Smith   *Scr* Michael Robson
Ph John Coquillon   *Ed* Eric Boyd-Perkins   *Mus* Ed Welch   *Art Dir* Harry Pottle
● Robert Powell, David Warner, Eric Porter, Karen Dotrice, John Mills, George Baker (Rank/Norfolk)

The Thirty Nine Steps is okay period suspense, directed with a smooth but unremarkable touch by Don Sharp.

For the short of memory, *Steps* is the melodramatic tale of a man on the run from Prussian assassins plotting World War I. It was first a classic novel by John Buchan, then a classic film by Alfred Hitchcock [1935], with Robert Donat as the elusive hero and Madeleine Carroll as the romantic interest. This third version has attractive young Robert Powell and Karen Dotrice, but nothing like the Donat-Carroll chemistry or flourish.

John Mills is very good as the British agent trying to persuade the government of the momentous plot and its dire consequences. Also effective are David Warner as the topmost villain and Eric Porter as a police official.

● ●

■ THIRTY SECONDS OVER TOKYO

1944, 138 MINS, US ▼
Dir Mervyn LeRoy   *Prod* Sam Zimbalist   *Scr* Dalton Trumbo   *Ph* Harold Rosson, Robert Surtees   *Ed* Frank Sullivan   *Mus* Herbert Stothart   *Art Dir* Cedric Gibbons, Paul Groesse
● Van Johnson, Robert Walker, Phyllis Thaxter, Tim Murdock, Robert Mitchum, Spencer Tracy (M-G-M)

Lt Col James Doolittle mapped his blitz on Japan 131 days after Pearl Harbor. There is suspense as the flyers prepare themselves for their long-range training in anticipation of the secret mission. More or less relegated but capital as the bulwark of the entire mission is Spencer Tracy's conception of Doolittle. Van Johnson is Ted Lawson and Phyllis Thaxter his wife. It's an inspired casting.

Prominent in Johnson's crew are Tim Murdock, a standout as the co-pilot; Don DeFore as the navigator; Gordon McDonald as the bombardier; and Robert Walker, who is particularly effective as the wistful gunner-mechanic.

Their plane, the *Ruptured Duck*, and its pleasant little family become the focal attention henceforth. After Doolittle finally tells them of their mission to bomb Japan, the war becomes a highly personalized thing through the actions of these crew members.
☐ 1944: Best Special Effects
☐ Nomination: Best B&W Cinematography

● ●

■ 36 CHOWRINGHEE LANE

1982, 122 MINS, INDIA ◇
Dir Aparna Sen   *Prod* Shashi Kapoor   *Scr* Aparna Sen   *Ph* Ashok Mehta   *Ed* Bhanudas Divakar   *Mus* Vanraj Bhatia
● Jennifer Kendall, Dhritiamn Chatterjee, Debashree Roy, Geoffrey Kendall (Kapoor/Vilas)

Aparna Sen appeared in two Satyajit Ray films (*Three Daughters* and *Pikoo*) and her father, Chidananda Das Gupta, is a noted film critic, so she came to her first directorial stint with a good background.

Jennifer Kendall (wife of producer Shashi Kapoor, a top commercial film actor) is effective as a lonely Anglo-Indian old lady. She teaches Shakespeare in a private girls' school and has befriended a couple. She does not realise they have been using her for the use of her apartment rather than for a friendship that has seemingly grown between them and warmed her lonely life.

The couple marries. She gives them an old phonograph they coveted, goes to the wedding, but then does not hear much. They gently put her off until she finds they do not need her at all any more.

Item is mostly in English, though the young lovers speak their native Indian lingo when alone. Full of visual ideas, film does not quite transcend them to achieve a more piercing insight into aging and loneliness.

● ●

■ 36 HOURS

1964, 115 MINS, US/W. GERMANY
Dir George Seaton   *Prod* William Perlberg
Scr George Seaton   *Ph* Philip Lathrop   *Ed* Adrienne Fazan   *Mus* Dimitri Tiomkin   *Art Dir* George W. Davis, Edward Carfagno
● James Garner, Eva Marie Saint, Rod Taylor, Werner Peters, John Banner, Alan Napier (M-G-M/Perlberg-Seaton/Cherokee)

36 Hours is a fanciful war melodrama limning an incident during that crucial number of hours immediately preceding D-Day. The production takes its title from the span of time allotted a German psychiatrist to learn from a captured US intelligence officer fully briefed on the oncoming Allied invasion the exact point of landing.

Based on Roald Dahl's *Beware of the Dog* and a story of Carl K. Hittleman and Luis H. Vance, it provides a behind-the-scenes glimpse of high military intelligence at work.

James Garner plays the American sent to Lisbon to confirm through a German contact that the Nazis expect the Allies to land in the Calais area rather than the secretly-planned Normandy beach. Drugged, he's flown under heavy sedation by the Germans to an isolated resort in Bavaria where upon regaining consciousness he's led to believe he has been an amnesia victim for six years.

Rod Taylor registers most effectively in the offbeat role of the German, playing it for sympathy and realistically. Garner in a derring-do part is okay and up to his usual sound brand of histrionics. Eva Marie Saint also delivers strongly as the nurse drafted by the Nazis from a concentration camp and promised help by Taylor if she plays her part well – in the masquerade with Garner.

● ●

■ THIS ABOVE ALL

1942, 110 MINS, US
Dir Anatole Litvak   *Prod* Darryl F. Zanuck   *Scr* R.C. Sherriff   *Ph* Arthur Miller   *Ed* Walter Thompson

Mus Alfred Newman   *Art Dir* Richard Day, Joseph Wright
● Tyrone Power, Joan Fontaine, Thomas Mitchell, Henry Stephenson, Nigel Bruce, Gladys Cooper (20th Century-Fox)

This Above All is a tale of England in that tense interval between Dunkirk and the London blitz of September 1940. It tells of the romance between a beauteous daughter of the aristocracy and a lowly-born soldier who has deserted after fighting honorably through the shattering battle of Flanders and the tragic evacuation of Dunkirk.

Although the screen adaptation softens certain aspects of Eric M. Knight's novel, such as toning down the love affair during the couple's stay at the Dover inn, or eliminating the complication of the soldier's brain injury, it has not weakened the story.

In some ways the yarn is even improved. For one thing, the whole involved subject of the democratic aims in the war, problem of the conflict of social classes, or the question of pacifism against duty to one's country are expertly focused in personal terms.
☐ 1942: Best B&W Art Direction (Richard Day, Joseph Wright)
☐ Nominations: Best B&W Cinematography, Editing, Sound

● ●

■ THIS BOY'S LIFE

1993, 115 MINS, US ◇ ▼ ⊙
Dir Michael Caton-Jones   *Prod* Art Linson   *Scr* Robert Getchell   *Ph* David Watkin   *Ed* Jim Clark
Mus Carter Burwell   *Art Dir* Stephen J. Lineweaver
● Robert De Niro, Ellen Barkin, Leonardo DiCaprio, Jonah Blechman, Eliza Dushku, Chris Cooper (Warner)

This Boy's Life is a nicely acted but excessively bland coming-of-age memoir about a young man's escape from domestic turmoil and abuse, with numerous potent scenes of conflict between the central teenager and his violent stepfather.

Tale is based on Tobias Wolff's acclaimed 1989 book of the same name and is duly narrated in writerly style by young Toby (Leonardo DiCaprio). Hitting the road in 1957 with his working class mother Caroline (Ellen Barkin), Toby begins hanging out with a bad crowd once they settle in Seattle.

Then mom meets Dwight (Robert De Niro), a man's man with a crewcut. Even before Dwight and Caroline marry, Toby is sent to live with Dwight in Concrete, Wash., where Dwight devotes himself to cutting the sullen 'hotshot' down to size.

Unfortunately, after a relatively promising warmup, pic actually proceeds to flatten out the characters in the latter sections. Film's strength lies in its portrait of the father-stepson struggle, how each pushes the other toward even worse behavior.

De Niro brings both a rough charm and ferocious power to Dwight. Centerscreen almost throughout, DiCaprio is excellent as Toby. Barkin weighs in with plenty of spirit until her character dries up.

● ●

■ THIS EARTH IS MINE

1959, 123 MINS, US ◇
Dir Henry King   *Prod* Casey Robinson, Claude Heilman   *Scr* Casey Robinson   *Ph* Winton Hoch, Russel Metty   *Ed* Ted J. Kent   *Mus* Hugo Friedhofer
● Rock Hudson, Jean Simmons, Dorothy McGuire, Claude Rains, Kent Smith, Anna Lee (Universal/Vintage)

This film is almost completely lacking in dramatic cohesion. It is verbose and contradictory, and its complex plot relationships from Alice Tisdale Hobart's novel, *The Cup and the Sword* begin with confusion and end in tedium.

The setting is the Napa Valley wine country in the waning years of Prohibition. The basic plot is a conflict between generations – the older, European-born vintners, headed by Claude Rains, with traditions of dedication to the craft, and the younger men, represented by Rock Hudson, who are interested in selling their crop to the highest bidders, even if it means their grapes will be made into bootleg liquor.

Some of the scenes are pure bathos, such as the one where Rock Hudson learns that he is actually the son of his uncle (Kent Smith). What's lacking mostly in the script, and not supplemented in the direction, is an overall intelligence that would have appraised these complexities.

Hudson gives a sympathetic portrayal, but not a satisfying one, because his characterization is riddled by inconsistencies. Jean Simmons achieves involvement but little sympathy because her motivations are so sketchy and superficial. Claude Rains fares best.

....

■ THIS GUN FOR HIRE

1942, 86 MINS, US ⓥ
Dir Frank Tuttle   *Prod* Richard M. Blumenthal
Scr Albert Maltz, W.R. Burnett   *Ph* John Seitz
Ed Archie Marshek   *Mus* David Buttolph
● Veronica Lake, Robert Preston, Laird Cregar, Alan Ladd, Tully Marshall, Mikhail Rasumny (Paramount)

The idea of presenting Veronica Lake as the heroine of an exciting melodrama has its merits. But the material selected is distinctly unsuited to her. It is a very involved yarn by Graham Greene which deals with international intrigue and treason, having to do with the sale of a secret chemical formula to the Japanese. Albert Maltz and W.R. Burnett wrote the screenplay, which is a succession of gunplay scenes in which Lake becomes the unwilling accomplice of a young killer. He is Alan Ladd.

Other players in the film had difficult assignment trying to give some credence to an improbable story. Robert Preston plays a policeman, who is too easily outwitted to deserve Lake in the end. Laird Cregar is an interesting heavy, and Tully Marshall a reprobate of the worst kind.

....

■ THIS HAPPY BREED

1944, 116 MINS, UK ◇ ⓥ
Dir David Lean   *Prod* Noel Coward, Anthony Havelock-Allan   *Scr* Ronald Neame, David Lean, Anthony Havelock-Allan   *Ph* Ronald Neame   *Ed* Jack Harris
Mus Muir Mathieson (dir.)   *Art Dir* C. P. Norman
● Robert Newton, Celia Johnson, John Mills, Kay Walsh, Stanley Holloway, Amy Veness (Two Cities/Cineguild)

Based on Noel Coward's London legit hit, film soundly captures the spirit of the 1920s and 1930s reviving the era of the British general strike, the jazz dress style, the Charleston, and the depression. It touches on the troubled sphere of the class struggle and labor strife, although it has a dubious note once or twice, such as in an apparent defense of strike-breaking. But it is so much more the history of an average British family, with its pleasures and pains, to make this the paramount interest.

Film is a bit episodic and choppy at the start, as it unwinds in cavalcadish fashion, but it settles down soon to an absorbing chronicle.

Film's excellence comes mainly in the performances. Celia Johnson, as the mother of three grown children and the rock around which the family revolves, presents a masterful, poignant portrayal.

Robert Newton, who has almost as important a role as the head of the house, is also a superb presentation as the steady, earthbound but intelligent Britisher. Kay Walsh, as the flighty daughter dissatisfied with her lot; John Mills as the loyal sailor in love with the errant daughter; and Stanley Holloway as the nextdoor neighbor, give fine support.

....

■ THIS IS ELVIS

1981, 88 MINS, US ◇ ⓥ
Dir Malcolm Leo, Andrew Solt   *Prod* Malcolm Leo, Andrew Solt   *Scr* Malcolm Leo, Andrew Solt   *Ph* Gil Hubbs   *Ed* Bud Friedgen, Glenn Farr   *Mus* Walter Scharf   *Art Dir* Charles Hughes
● Johnny Harra, David Scott, Paul Boensch III, Lawrence Koller, Rhonda Lyn (Warner)

A real curiosity item, *This Is Elvis* is a fast-paced gloss on Presley's life and career packed with enough fine music and unusual footage to satisfy anyone with an interest in the late singing idol. An imaginative combination of docu-footage, home movies and docu-drama recreations of more private moments has been bolstered with a double album's worth of top tunes to good effect.

Pic opens with day of Presley's death at 42 and subsequent funeral mob scene, and is thereafter narrated by uncanny Elvis soundalike Ral Donner in fashion of William Holden telling tale of *Sunset Boulevard*, even though character is dead.

Much of the docu-material has been kept under wraps by Col Tom Parker for years only to be released here through his participation as technical adviser.

Included are glimpses of the 1950s sensation in his earliest television appearance, some previously unseen press conference footage, harsh, often racist, anti-rock 'n' roll diatribes by bluenoses of the period, the celebrated Ed Sullivan performance, extensive coverage of his army indoctrination and stint in Germany, comeback appearance with Frank Sinatra, clips of a few feature films and a look at his smash 1968 TV special.

Elvis' bloated condition by 1977 is genuinely shocking, effect being akin to seeing Robert De Niro in middle-age in *Raging Bull*. Narration has Elvis from above intoning, 'If only I coulda seen what was happening to me, I mighta done something about it.'

....

■ THIS ISLAND EARTH

1955, 87 MINS, US ◇ ⓥ
Dir Joseph Newman   *Prod* William Alland
Scr Franklin Coen, Edward G. O'Callaghan   *Ph* Clifford Stine   *Ed* Virgil Vogel   *Mus* Herman Stein
Art Dir Alexander Golitzen, Richard H. Riedel
● Jeff Morrow, Faith Domergue, Rex Reason, Lance Fuller, Russell Johnson, Douglas Spencer (Universal)

Plot motivation in the screenplay is derived from the frantic efforts of the men of the interstellar planet, Metaluna, to find on Earth a new source of atomic energy. For the accomplishment of this goal, the outstanding scientists in the field have been recruited by a character named Exeter, who has set up a completely-equipped laboratory in Georgia.

One of the most thrilling sequences occurs as huge meteors attack the space ship as it is working its way to Metaluna. Ingeniously-constructed props and equipment, together with strange sound effects also are responsible for furthering interest, which is of the edge-of-the-seat variety during the latter half of the film. For an added fillip, there's a Mutant, half human, half insect, which boards the ship as it escapes from Metaluna.

....

■ THIS IS MY AFFAIR

See: I Can Get It for You Wholesale

....

■ THIS IS MY LIFE

1992, 105 MINS, US ◇ ⓥ
Dir Nora Ephron   *Prod* Lynda Obst   *Scr* Nora Ephron, Delia Ephron   *Ph* Bobby Byrne   *Ed* Robert Reitano
Mus Carly Simon   *Art Dir* Barbra Matis
● Julie Kavner, Samantha Mathis, Gaby Hoffmann, Carrie Fisher, Dan Aykroyd, Danny Zorn (20th Century-Fox)

A schlepper turns star but finds that when your kids still need you, success is all very complicated in *This Is My Life*, a deftly accomplished directorial debut from scripter Nora Ephron. Glib urban sensibility that informed Ephron's screenplay for *When Harry Met Sally . . .* is toned down this time in favor of humbler, texture-of-life comedy co-scripted with sister Delia.

Julie Kavner stars as a New Jersey divorcee who hams it up in her cosmetics counter selling placenta extract and exfoliating wax to Jewish mavens, then shares her excess comic energy with her 16- and 10-year-old daughters (Samantha Mathis, Gaby Hoffmann) as they dream of her comedy breakthrough.

When an aunt leaves Kavner some start-up money, she packs the kids up for Manhattan, and before long her dreams do start to come true. But it's more than the teenage daughter, who's introverted and dependent, can handle.

Based on a novel [of the same name] by Meg Wolitzer, pic moves along quite briskly. Comedienne Kavner gives a zesty and touching perf as the mom coming into her own, and both girls, particularly Mathis as the confused, hypercritical teen, are quite skillful. Carrie FIsher contributes a deft and savory turn as a glib and chummy agent.

....

■ THIS IS SPINAL TAP
A ROCKUMENTARY BY MARTIN DIBERGI

1984, 82 MINS, US ◇ ⓥ ⓦ
Dir Rob Reiner   *Prod* Karen Murphy   *Scr* Christopher Guest, Michael McKean, Harry Shearer, Rob Reiner
Ph Peter Smokler   *Ed* Kent Beyda, Kim Seerisf
Art Dir Dryan Jones
● Rob Reiner, Michael McKean, Christopher Guest, Harry Shearer, R.J. Parnell, David Kaff (Spinal Tap)

For music biz insiders, *This Is Spinal Tap* is a vastly amusing satire of heavy metal bands. Director Rob Reiner has cast himself as Marty DiBergi, a filmmaker intent upon covering the long-awaited American return of the eponymous, 17-year-old British rock band. Pic then takes the form of a cinema-verité documentary, as Reiner includes interviews with the fictional musicians, records their increasingly disastrous tour and captures the internal strife which leads to the separation of the group's two founders.

Reiner and cowriters have had loads of fun with the material, creating mock 1960s TV videotapes of early gigs and filling the fringes with hilariously authentic music-biz types, most notably Fran Drescher's label rep and Paul Shaffer's cameo as a Chicago promo man.

....

■ THIS IS THE ARMY

1943, 120 MINS, US ◇ ⓥ
Dir Michael Curtiz   *Prod* Jack L. Warner   *Scr* Casey Robinson, Claude Rinyon   *Ph* Bert Glennon, Sol Polito
Ed George Amy   *Mus* Ray Heindorf (arr.)
Art Dir John Hughes, John Koenig
● George Murphy, Joan Leslie, Ronald Reagan, George Tobias, Julie Oshins, Una Merkel (Warner)

It's a dynamic linking of World War I and II with its respective soldier shows – *Yip Yip Yaphank* and *This Is the Army*, both by Irving Berlin. It's showmanship and patriotism combined to a super-duper Yankee Doodle degree.

Skillfully linked are both generations, with George Murphy capital as the yesteryear musicomedy star who suffers a leg injury, which doesn't curb his skill as a theatrical impresario post-1918, and Ronald Reagan, as Johnny Jones, his son, who carries the romance interest in World War II. George Tobias and Julie Oshins are father-and-son to span both periods, and Joan Leslie is the 1943 femme offspring of Charles Butterworth, an-

779

other of the 'Yip Yip Yaphankers'. She is the romantic vis-a-vis to Reagan.

But putting the story aside, the socko Berlin songs – 17 of them – tie the whole package together.

Under the Jack Warner-Hal Wallis production supervision and with Mike Curtiz's expert direction – all of whom donated their services, along with the rest of it – *This Is the Army* looks like a $3 million Technicolor production instead of the $1.4 million it cost to bring it in.

☐ 1943: Best Scoring of a Musical Picture
☐ Nominations: Best Color Art Direction, Sound

••••••••••••••••••••••••••••••••••

■ **THIS LAND IS MINE**

1943, 103 MINS, US ⓥ ⊙
Dir Jean Renoir   *Prod* Jean Renoir, Dudley Nichols
Scr Dudley Nichols   *Ph* Frank Redman   *Ed* Frederic Knudtson   *Mus* Lothar Perl   *Art Dir* Eugene Lourie
● Charles Laughton, Maureen O'Hara, George Sanders, Walter Slezak, Kent Smith, Una O'Connor (RKO)

Turned out by the ace director-writer combination of Jean Renoir and Dudley Nichols, *This Land* is a steadily engrossing film based on the inner drama of character rather than the exciting physical action of some war films. Its theme is the invincibility of ideas over brute force, and its story is of how circumstances and the realization of responsibility turn a craven weakling into a heroic champion of freedom. That is epic subject matter and it is given sincere, dignified and eloquent treatment.

Not that the picture is by any means perfect. Some of its incidents tax belief, and the presentation at times is ultra-obvious, possibly to clarify the meaning for the broadest possible audience. Similarly, although such scenes as Charles Laughton's courtroom espousal of the cause of patriotism, civil disobedience and even of sabotage, or his defiant schoolroom reading of 'The Rights of Man', are suspiciously theatrical, the speeches themselves are magnificent.

As usual when a picture has such compulsion and distinction, the individual roles are rewarding and the performances impressive. As the blubbering coward who rises to heroism in a crisis, Charles Laughton gives a shrewdly conceived and developed portrayal, although he occasionally mugs a bit. Maureen O'Hara is believably intense as the lovely, tragic patriot school teacher. George Sanders proper projects the mental turmoil of the traitorous informer, while Walter Slezak turns in an acting gem in the rich role of the Nazi major.

☐ 1943: Best Sound Recording (Stephen Dunn)

••••••••••••••••••••••••••••••••••

■ **THIS PROPERTY IS CONDEMNED**

1966, 110 MINS, US ◇ ⓥ ⊙
Dir Sydney Pollack   *Prod* John Houseman   *Scr* Francis Coppola, Fred Coe, Edith Sommer   *Ph* James Wong Howe   *Ed* Adrienne Fazan   *Mus* Kenyon Hopkins
Art Dir Hal Pereira
● Natalie Wood, Robert Redford, Charles Bronson, Kate Reid, Mary Badham, Alan Baxter (Seven Arts/Stark)

This is a handsomely-mounted, well acted Depression era drama about the effect of railroad retrenchment on a group of boardinghouse people. Derived from a Tennessee Williams one-acter, the production is adult without being sensational, touching without being maudlin.

Francis Coppola, Fred Coe and Edith Sommer are credited with the script, 'suggested' from an earlier Williams play in which two young kids chat about the past.

Natalie Wood stars as the young Dixie belle, older daughter of Kate Reid, latter playing a sleazy landlady to some railroad

men. Wood dreams of another life while she flirts up a storm, acting as the shill for her mother.

Robert Redford gives an outstanding performance as the railroad efficiency expert sent to town to lay off most of the crew. Plotwise, the role is thankless and heavy, but Redford, through voice, expression and movement – total acting – makes the character sympathetic.

Charles Bronson is excellent as the earthy boarder.

••••••••••••••••••••••••••••••••••

■ **THIS SPORTING LIFE**

1963, 134 MINS, UK
Dir Lindsay Anderson   *Prod* Julian Wintle, Leslie Parkyn
Scr David Storey   *Ph* Denys Coop   *Ed* Peter Taylor
Mus Robert Gerhard
● Richard Harris, Rachel Roberts, Alan Badel, William Hartnell, Colin Blakely, Arthur Lowe (Independent Artists)

Set in the raw, earthy mood of *Saturday Night and Sunday Morning*, *Taste of Honey* and *Room at the Top* this has a gutsy vitality. Karel Reisz who directed *Saturday Night*, produced this one and his influence can clearly be seen. Lindsay Anderson, making his debut as a feature director, brings the keen, observant eye of a documentary man to many vivid episodes without sacrificing the story line.

Based on a click novel by David Storey, who also scribed the screenplay, the yarn has a sporting background in that it concerns professional rugby football. Richard Harris plays miner Frank Machin who, at first, resents the hero-worship heaped on players of the local football team. But he has second thoughts. He gets a trial and soon becomes the skillful, ruthless star of his team. He revels in his new prosperity, and preens at the adulation that's showered on his bullet head. He doesn't realize that he is being used by local businessmen opportunists.

Anderson has directed with fluid skill and sharp editing keeps the film moving, even at its more leisurely moments, Denys Coop's lensing is graphic and the atmosphere of a northern town is captured soundly.

Among the varied sequences which impress are a horrifying quarrel between Harris and Rachel Roberts, a hospital death scene, a poignant interlude at a wedding when Harris first approaches the moment of truth, a rowdy Christmas party and a countryside excursion when Harris plays with the widow's two youngsters. The football scenes have a live authenticity.

Harris gives a dominating, intelligent performance as the arrogant, blustering, fundamentally simple and insecure footballer. Roberts as a repressed widow, brings commendable light and shade as well as poignance to a role that might have been shadowy and overly downbeat.

☐ 1963: Nominations: Best Actor (Richard Harris), Actress (Rachel Roberts)

••••••••••••••••••••••••••••••••••

■ **THOMAS CROWN AFFAIR, THE**

1968, 102 MINS, US ◇ ⓥ
Dir Norman Jewison   *Prod* Norman Jewison   *Scr* Alan R. Trustman   *Ph* Haskell Wexler   *Ed* Hal Ashby, Ralph Winters, Byron Brandt   *Mus* Michel Legrand
Art Dir Robert Boyle
● Steve McQueen, Faye Dunaway, Paul Burke, Jack Weston, Yaphet Kotto, Biff McGuire (United Artists/Mirisch)

The Thomas Crown Affair is a refreshingly different film which concerns a Boston bank robbery, engineered by a wealthy man who is romantically involved with the femme insurance investigator sent to expose him.

Free of social-conscious pretensions, the Norman Jewison film tells a crackerjack story, well-tooled, professionally crafted and fashioned with obvious meticulous care.

Boston attorney Alan R. Trustman, who never before wrote for films, is responsible for an excellent story. Steve McQueen is a rich young industrialist who masterminds a bank heist. Paul Burke delivers an excellent performance as a detective who works with Faye Dunaway, an insurance company bounty hunter whose job is to trap McQueen.

Jewison adds a showmanly touch in the use of split- and multiple-screen images.

McQueen is neatly cast as the likeable, but lonely heavy. Dunaway makes an excellent detective who gradually develops a conflict of interests regarding her prey. The only message in this film is: enjoy it.

☐ 1968: Best Song ('The Windmills of Your Mind').
☐ Nomination: Best Original Score

••••••••••••••••••••••••••••••••••

■ **THOROUGHLY MODERN MILLIE**

1967, 138 MINS, US ◇ ⓥ ⊙
Dir George Roy Hill   *Prod* Ross Hunter   *Scr* Richard Morris   *Ph* Russell Metty   *Ed* Stuart Gilmore
Mus Elmer Bernstein   *Art Dir* Alexander Golitzen, George C. Webb
● Julie Andrews, Mary Tyler Moore, Carol Channing, James Fox, John Gavin, Beatrice Lillie (Universal)

The first half of *Thoroughly Modern Mille* is quite successful in striking and maintaining a gay spirit and pace. There are many recognizable and beguiling satirical recalls of the flapper age and some quite funny bits.

Liberties taken with reality, not to mention period, in the first half are redeemed by wit and characterization. But the sudden thrusting of the hero, played by James Fox in horn-rimmed glasses, into a skyscraper-climbing, flagpole-hanging acrobat, a la Harold Lloyd, has little of Lloyd but the myth. This sequence is forced all the way.

Musically *Millie* is a melange. Standards such as 'Baby Face' mingle with specials by Jimmy Van Heusen and Sammy Cahn. All is part of Elmer Bernstein's score, as arranged and conducted by Andre Previn.

Julie Andrews is very much like the leading lady of the story but hardly more than a bystander when Carol Channing commands the scene and at such times it is seldom that a star has been so static so long in a film. Mary Tyler Moore serves the plot in that she is essentially a prototype of a sweet, long curls and rather dumb rich girl.

☐ 1967: Best Original Score.
☐ Nomination: Best Supp. Actress (Carol Channing), Costume Design, Scoring of Music, Song ('Thoroughly Modern Millie'), Sound

••••••••••••••••••••••••••••••••••

■ **THOSE MAGNIFICENT MEN IN THEIR FLYING MACHINES
OR HOW I FLEW FROM LONDON TO PARIS IN 25 HOURS 11 MINUTES**

1965, 133 MINS, UK ◇ ⓥ ⊙
Dir Ken Annakin   *Prod* Stan Margulies   *Scr* Jack Davies, Ken Annakin   *Ph* Christopher Challis
Ed Gordon Stone   *Mus* Ron Goodwin   *Art Dir* Tom Morahan
● Stuart Whitman, Sarah Miles, James Fox, Alberto Sordi, Robert Morley, Gert Frobe (20th Century-Fox)

As fanciful and nostalgic a piece of clever picture-making as has hit the screen in recent years, this backward look into the pioneer days of aviation, when most planes were built with spit and bailing wire, is a warming entertainment experience.

A newspaper circulation gimmick serves nicely as the story premise, with a London newspaper publisher offering a £10,000 prize to winner of an event which will focus worldwide attention on the fledgling sport of flying – circa 1910 – subsequently attracting a flock of international contestants.

While there is naturally a plotline, and a

T

nice romance, the planes themselves, a startling collection of uniquely-designed oddities, which actually fly, probably merit the most attention.

Top characters are played by Stuart Whitman, as an American entrant; James Fox, an English flier who interests publisher Robert Morley in the race to promote aviation; Sarah Miles, publisher's daughter understood to be the intended of Fox (arrangement with father) but beloved by Whitman. Terry-Thomas is a dastardly English lord not above the most abject skullduggery to win the race. Alberto Sordi as an Italian count with a worrying wife and immense family, Gert Frobe a German cavalry officer intent upon bringing glory to the Fatherland, Jean-Pierre Cassel, a whimsical Frenchman, are the chief Continental contestants.

☐ 1965: Nomination: Best Story & Screenplay

. . . .

■ **THOUSAND CLOWNS, A**

1965, 117 MINS, US ⓥ

Dir Fred Coe   *Prod* Fred Coe   *Scr* Herb Gardner
Ph Arthur J. Ornitz   *Ed* Ralph Rosenblum   *Mus* Judy Holliday, Gerry Mulligan   *Art Dir* Burr Smidt
● Jason Robards, Barbara Harris, Martin Balsam, Gene Saks, William Daniels, Barry Gordon (Harrell/United Artists)

A Thousand Clowns depicts a happy-go-lucky non-conformist who attains some maturity when a child welfare board threatens to take away his young resident nephew.

Key personnel of the long-running 1962-3 Broadway legiter have followed through with the pic. They include playwright-adapter Herb Gardner, producer-director Coe, and Jason Robards as the ex-vidscripter living it up in a littered NY pad while trying to prevent nephew Barry Gordon (also encoring) from becoming one of the 'dead people', meaning conformists.

Terrif dialog to match Robards' scenery-chewing create a sock impact as he lectures the 12-year-old (a hip juve, wiser than unk), ignores the pleas of brother-agent Martin Balsam to return to work, and pierces the outstanding social worker bureaucratic shell of Barbara Harris and original cast member William Daniels, who've arrived to check the kid's home life.

All performances present three-dimensional, identifiable characters underneath the yocks.

☐ 1965: Best Supp. Actor (Martin Balsam). ☐ Nominations: Best Picture, Screenplay Adaptation, Adapted Music Score

. . . .

■ **THOUSANDS CHEER**

1943, 124 MINS, US ◇ ⓥ ⊙

Dir George Sidney   *Prod* Joseph Pasternak   *Scr* Paul Jarrico, Richard Collins   *Ph* George Folsey
Ed George Boemler   *Mus* Herbert Stothart (dir.)
● Kathryn Grayson, Gene Kelly, Mary Astor, John Boles, Jose Iturbi, Frances Rafferty (M-G-M)

Comparison of *Thousands Cheer* to *Stage Door Canteen* is inevitable and natural. Both have the same format. Kathryn Grayson is the colonel's (John Boles) daughter who puts on a super-duper camp show which not only re-introduces Jose Iturbi as part of the entertainment – the eminent pianist-maestro is already made part of the regular plot – but it brings forth Mickey Rooney, Judy Garland, Red Skelton, Eleanor Powell and others.

Paramount keynote of this expert filmusical is the tiptop manner in which young George Sidney has marshalled his multiple talents so that none trips over the other. It's a triumph for Sidney on his first major league effort.

Paul Jarrico and Richard Collins supplied a smooth story to carry the mammoth marquee

values. Casting Kathryn Grayson as herself, a click diva, making her longhair farewell at an Iturbi concert, is as plausible as it is appealing. Her idea to move with papa Boles to his camp, in an endeavor to reconcile him and Mary Astor (the mother), is well interlarded with romance and basic Americanism.

Judy Garland's 'Joint Is Jumpin' Down at Carnegie Hall' (unbilled specialty) is the cue for Iturbi to boogie-woogie; and his Steinwaying straight or barrelhouse, is something for the cats.

☐ 1943: Nominations: Best Color Cinematography, Color Art Direction, Scoring of a Musical Picture

. . . .

■ **THREE**

1969, 105 MINS, UK ◇

Dir James Salter   *Scr* James Salter   *Ph* Etienne Becker   *Ed* Edward Nielson   *Mus* Laurence Rosenthal
● Charlotte Rampling, Robie Porter, Sam Waterston, Pascale Roberts (United Artists/Obelisk)

Three is a rare pic [from a story by Irwin Shaw] about youth that deals with a romantic summer idyll sans sentimentality and with a freshness and easy charm that pinpoints character without affectation.

Two young men, Robie Porter and Sam Waterston set off in an old car one summer to tour Italy and France. They meet a pretty English girl (Charlotte Rampling) and make a pact to keep her a friend rather than a sexual or love game. But Waterston begins to fall for her and their triple idyll deteriorates as she succumbs to Porter.

The principals all perform with grace and ease. It has a fine feel for the European summer scene and neatly observes the growing complicated feelings between the three by visual means that are never forced for symbolical needs.

. . . .

■ **¡THREE AMIGOS!**

1986, 105 MINS, US ◇ ⓥ ⊙

Dir John Landis   *Prod* Lorne Michaels, George Folsey Jr.
Scr Steve Martin, Lorne Michaels, Randy Newman
Ph Ronald W. Browne   *Ed* Malcolm Campbell
Mus Elmer Bernstein   *Art Dir* Richard Sawyer
● Chevy Chase, Steve Martin, Martin Short, Patrice Martinez, Alfonso Arau, Joe Mantegna (LA Films/Orion)

A few choice morsels of brilliant humor can't save *¡Three Amigos!* from missing the whole enchilada.

Film is a takeoff of *The Magnificent Seven*, but also tries perhaps too hard to parody the style of a number of other classic westerns.

It also has three funny guys, Steve Martin, Chevy Chase and Martin Short, playing the three wimpy matinee idols known as the 'Three Amigos', each doing his particular brand of shtick that is priceless in some scenes but not at all amusing in others.

Martin does clever slapstick, Chase does goofy slapstick and Short doesn't do slapstick, but plays off the other two with a certain wide-eyed innocence.

These singing cowboy stars of the silent screen have just been fired by the flamboyant Goldsmith Studios mogul Harry Flugelman (Joe Mantegna) when they get a cryptic telegram from a Mexican woman (Patrice Martinez) offering them 100,000 pesos to come to her dusty desert town of Santa Poco. It turns out she's hired them under the mistaken belief that they are as macho in real life as on screen.

. . . .

■ **THREE BITES OF THE APPLE**

1967, 98 MINS, US ◇

Dir Alvin Ganzer   *Prod* Alvin Ganzer   *Scr* George Wells   *Ph* Gabor Pogany   *Ed* Norman Savage
Mus Eddy Manson   *Art Dir* Elliot Scott

● David McCallum, Sylva Koscina, Tammy Grimes, Harvey Korman, Domenico Modugno (M-G-M)

As a travelog, *Three Bites of the Apple* has certain merit; as a madcap comedy, its intended goal, it hasn't. Filmed in Italy and Switzerland, what emerges is an unimaginative piece of film making.

The screenplay is based on the flimsiest of premises. David McCallum, a mildmannered tour guide, wins £1,200 in a plush Italian gambling casino; then is faced with the question of how to save it from taxes so he'll be able to return to his native Britain with any more than a pittance. A pretty young adventuress, Sylva Koscina, out to get the coin for herself, sells him on allowing a 'friend' help him in this matter.

McCallum seems to stumble through most of his appearance. Koscina has a vapid look but is nice to look at.

. . . .

■ **THREE COINS IN THE FOUNTAIN**

1954, 101 MINS, US ◇ ⓥ ⊙

Dir Jean Negulesco   *Prod* Sol C. Siegel   *Scr* John Patrick   *Ph* Milton Krasner   *Ed* William Reynolds
Mus Victor Young   *Art Dir* Lyle Wheeler, John De Cuir
● Clifton Webb, Dorothy McGuire, Jean Peters, Louis Jourdan, Maggie McNamara, Rossano Brazzi (20th Century-Fox)

Once before, in *How to Marry a Millionaire*, director Jean Negulesco CinemaScoped a trio of feminine beauties into a lucrative attraction. In *Three Coins in the Fountain* he repeats this feat but obviously has gained some experience. The film has warmth, humor, a rich dose of romance and almost incredible pictorial appeal.

For those who aren't satisfied feasting their eyes on the stunning backgrounds and the plush interior sets, there is another trio of femme stars – Dorothy McGuire, Jean Peters and Maggie McNamara – in smart and expensive-looking clothes. As their male counterparts they have Clifton Webb, debonnaire and fun as always; Rossano Brazzi, an appealing young Italian and suave Louis Jourdan, appealing as the romantic lead.

Story [from a novel by John H. Secondari] introduces to Rome McNamara, an American coming to take a secretarial job. She's met by Peters and later introduced to her third room-mate in their sumptuous apartment, McGuire. They all toss a coin in the fountain, and it grants them their wish.

☐ 1954: Best Color Cinematography, Song ('Three Coins in the Fountain'). ☐ Nomination: Best Picture

. . . .

■ **THREE COMRADES**

1938, 100 MINS, US

Dir Frank Borzage   *Prod* Frank Borzage   *Scr* F. Scott Fitzgerald, Edward E. Paramore   *Ph* Joseph Ruttenberg
Ed Frank Sullivan   *Mus* Franz Waxman
● Robert Taylor, Margaret Sullavan, Franchot Tone, Robert Young, Guy Kibbee, Lionel Atwill (M-G-M)

There must have been some reason for making this picture, but it certainly isn't in the cause of entertainment. It provides a dull interlude, despite the draught of the star names.

Someone passed producer-director Frank Borzage a novel of postwar Germany by Erich Maria Remarque which deals with the psychological subtleties of German youth lately released from the World War armies; of the internal political struggle in establishing the republic; of the futility of the army-bred boys to cope with civilian connivance; and finally the tragedy of a love affair between one of the youths and a young woman dying of tuberculosis (Margaret Sullavan).

It is a film of characterization, rather than plot. Writers string together an interminable thread of unimportant incident to show the deep affection which exists among three young German officers. The titular comrades are Robert Taylor, Franchot Tone and Robert Young. After Young is killed in a street riot, the other two look forward to a dark, unhappy and lonely future.

That's it, and all the poetry in the dialog about falling leaves and the approaching winter only further confuses.

□ 1938: Nomination: Best Actress (Margaret Sullavan)

．．．．．．．．．．．．．．．．．．．．．．．．．．．．

■ **THREE DAYS OF THE CONDOR**

1975, 117 MINS, US ◇ ⦿ ⊙
Dir Sydney Pollock   *Prod* Stanley Schneider
Scr Lorenzo Semple Jr, David Rayfiel   *Ph* Owen Rolgman   *Ed* Fredric Steinkamp, Don Guidice
Mus Dave Grusin   *Art Dir* Stephen Grimes
● Robert Redford, Faye Dunaway, Cliff Robertson, Max von Sydow, John Houseman, Addison Powell (Paramount)

rJames Grady's book, *Six Days of the Condor*, underwent a time-compression title change in this adaptation by Lorenzo Semple Jr and David Rayfiel. Robert Redford, working in a CIA front, discovers all his associates massacred. He runs, pants, thinks, schemes, evades and ultimately exposes an agency insider who has been plotting on the side, so to spek. Disenchanted with the world as he wants it, Redford walks into a newspaper to expose the whole thing.

The film is a perfect contemporary example of an old studio formula approach to filmmaking. Basically a B, it has been elevated in form – but not in substance – via four bigger names, location shooting and more production values. Sometimes the trick works, but not here.

□ 1975: Nomination: Best Editing

．．．．．．．．．．．．．．．．．．．．．．．．．．．．

■ **THREE FACES OF EVE, THE**

1957, 91 MINS, US ⦿
Dir Nunnally Johnson   *Prod* Nunnally Johnson
Scr Nunnally Johnson   *Ph* Stanley Cortez   *Ed* Marjorie Fowler   *Mus* Robert Emmett Dolan   *Art Dir* Lyle R. Wheeler, Herman A. Blumethal
● Joanne Woodward, David Wayne, Lee J. Cobb, Edwin Jerome, Alena Murray, Nancy Kulp (20th Century-Fox)

Three Faces of Eve is based on a true-life case history recorded by two psychiatrists – Corbett H. Thigpen and Hervey M. Cleckley – and which was a popular-selling book. It is frequently an intriguing, provocative motion picture, but director Nunnally Johnson's treatment of the subject matter makes the film neither fish nor foul. Johnson shifts back and forth – striving for comedy at one point and presenting a documentary case history at another.

However, it is notable for the performance of Joanne Woodward as the woman with the triple personality. The three personalities Woodward is called on to play are (1) a drab, colorless Georgia housewife, (2) a mischievous, irresponsible sexy dish, and (3) a sensible, intelligent and balanced woman.

The psychiatric sessions, while possibly authentic, could readily confuse the layman. The manner in which the doctor (Lee J. Cobb) can hypnotize and alter his patient's personality seems so easy and pat as to appear hard to believe.

That Johnson had no intention of treating the film entirely seriously is tipped off in an opening tongue-in-cheek narration by the urbane and erudite Alistair Cooke.

□ 1957: Best Actress (Joanne Woodward)

．．．．．．．．．．．．．．．．．．．．．．．．．．．．

■ **THREE FUGITIVES**

1989, 96 MINS, US ◇ ⦿ ⊙
Dir Francis Veber   *Prod* Lauren Shuler-Donner
Scr Francis Veber   *Ph* Haskell Wexler   *Ed* Bruce Green   *Mus* David McHugh   *Art Dir* Rick Carter

● Nick Nolte, Martin Short, Sarah Rowland Doroff, James Earl Jones, Alan Ruck, Kenneth McMillan (Touchstone)

Three Fugitives marks the Hollywood helming debut of French director Francis Veber, remaking his own 1986 comedy *Les fugitifs* American-style. Clever premise starts pic off on a roll, as master bankrobber Lucas (Nick Nolte) gets out of the slammer determined to go straight, only to get involved in another heist in the very first bank he enters.

This time, he's an innocent bystander taken hostage by a hysterically inept gunman (Martin Short). But who's going to believe that?

Short, once he figures out Nolte's predicament, blackmails him into aiding and abetting his escape from the country. To make things even stickier, Short's got an emotionally withdrawn little girl (Sarah Rowland Doroff) who latches onto Nolte like a stray kitten.

As for the Nolte-Short pairing, it'll do, but it's no chemical marvel. Nolte, not really a comic natural, gruffs and grumbles his way through as hunky straight man to Short's calamitous comedian. Short runs with the slapstick style.

．．．．．．．．．．．．．．．．．．．．．．．．．．．．

■ **300 SPARTANS, THE**

1962, 108 MINS, US ◇
Dir Rudolph Mate   *Prod* George St. George, Rudolph Mate   *Scr* George St. George   *Ph* Geoffrey Unsworth   *Ed* Jerome Webb   *Mus* Manos Hadjidakis
Art Dir Arrigo Equini
● Richard Egan, Ralph Richardson, Diane Baker, Barry Coe, David Farrar, Donald Houston (20th-Century Fox)

The hopeless but ultimately inspiring defense of their country by a band of 300 Spartan soldiers against an immense army of Persian invaders in 480 B.C. – known to history as the Battle of Thermopylae – is the nucleus around which George St. George's screenplay is constructed [based on original story material of Ugo Liberatori, Remigio Del Grosso, Giovanni Deramo, Gian Paolo Callegari]. The inherent appeal and magnitude of the battle itself virtually dwarfs and sweeps aside all attempts at romantic byplay.

An international cast has been assembled for the enterprise, primarily populated with Britishers, Greeks and Americans. Richard Egan, as King Leonidas of Sparta, is physically suitable for the character, but the heroic mold of his performance is only skin deep – more muscle than corpuscle. Ralph Richardson, as might be expected, does the best acting in the picture, but no one is going to list this portrayal as one of the great achievements in his career.

Diane Baker is glaringly miscast. The fragile actress has been assigned the part of a Spartan girl who knocks two large men off their feet, bodily. As written, it's a role that required an actress of at least Lorenesque proportions.

．．．．．．．．．．．．．．．．．．．．．．．．．．．．

■ **3 INTO 2 WON'T GO**

1969, 93 MINS, UK ◇
Dir Peter Hall   *Prod* Julian Blaustein   *Scr* Edna O'Brien   *Ph* Walter Lassally   *Ed* Alan Osbiston   *Mus* Francis Lai
Art Dir Peter Murton
● Rod Steiger, Claire Bloom, Judy Geeson, Peggy Ashcroft, Paul Rogers (Universal)

Superb British film, *3 into 2 Won't Go* is an examination of a shattered marriage between career-oriented Rod Steiger, who is an appliance salesman, and his childless, schoolteacher-wife, Claire Bloom. Judy Geeson, 19-year-old hitchhiker with no particular social or moral ties, seduces Steiger on one of his overnight sales trips.

With dialog that has the banal sound of realistic human exchanges, Edna O'Brien's

script [from a novel by Andrea Newman] investigates all sorts of suggestions and shifts in audience reaction.

With all technical credits at top level and director Peter Hall getting top performances from all involved, especially the well-controlled Steiger, film is brisk and emotionally stirring.

．．．．．．．．．．．．．．．．．．．．．．．．．．．．

■ **THREE LITTLE WORDS**

1950, 100 MINS, US ◇ ⦿ ⊙
Dir Richard Thorpe   *Prod* Jack Cummings   *Scr* George Wells   *Ph* Harry Jackson   *Ed* Ben Lewis   *Mus* Andre Previn (dir.)
● Fred Astaire, Red Skelton, Vera-Ellen, Arlene Dahl, Keenan Wynn, Debbie Reynolds (M-G-M)

A biopic of the songwriting team of Harry Ruby and Bert Kalmar, the picture is a charmful, entertaining cavalcade of show business which spans their years together. Yarn, while doing the usual glossy job on its subjects, sticks closely to the Kalmar-Ruby careers.

Toplined by Fred Astaire as Kalmar and Red Skelton as Ruby, the entire cast does fine work under the skillful direction of Richard Thorpe.

Vera-Ellen matches Astaire tap for tap in their terping duets, which is no mean achievement, and looks to be possibly the best partner he's ever had. Her singing, too, gets by and, as Jessie Brown, Kalmar's vaude partner, she emotes competently.

Arlene Dahl plays Eileen Percy and also turns in a standout performance.

□ 1950: Nomination: Best Scoring of a Musical Picture

．．．．．．．．．．．．．．．．．．．．．．．．．．．．

■ **3 MEN AND A BABY**

1987, 102 MINS, US ◇ ⦿ ⊙
Dir Leonard Nimoy   *Prod* Ted Field, Robert W. Cort
Scr James Orr, Jim Cruickshank   *Ph* Adam Greenberg
Ed Michael A. Stevenson   *Mus* Marvin Hamlisch
Art Dir Peter Larkin
● Tom Selleck, Steve Guttenberg, Ted Danson, Nancy Travis, Margaret Colin, Celeste Holm (Touchstone/Interscope)

3 Men and a Baby is about as slight a feature comedy as is made – while at the same time it's hard to resist Tom Selleck, Ted Danson and Steve Guttenberg shamelessly going goo-goo over caring for an infant baby girl all swaddled in pink.

This is an Americanized version of the 1985 French sleeper hit *3 hommes et un couffin* and parallels the original's storyline almost exactly.

The lives of three confirmed bachelors – the studly sort who live, play and scheme on voluptuous women together – is thrown into confusion when a baby is left at their front door. As it happens, actor and suspected father of the infant (Danson) is conveniently out of town on a shoot, leaving architect and super pushover Peter (Selleck) and cartoonist Michael (Guttenberg) all in a quandary what to do with the precious little thing.

Big macho men tripping all over themselves trying to successfully feed, diaper and bathe a bundle of innocence and helplessness is ripe for comic development, and it certainly helps that these three are having a blast seeing it through.

Film is a good showcase for the comic abilities of this threesome, all of whom seem to have their one-liner timing down pat.

．．．．．．．．．．．．．．．．．．．．．．．．．．．．

■ **3 MEN AND A LITTLE LADY**

1990, 100 MINS, US ◇ ⦿ ⊙
Dir Emile Ardolino   *Prod* Ted Field, Robert W. Cort
Scr Charlie Peters   *Ph* Adam Greenberg   *Ed* Michael A. Stevenson   *Mus* James Newton Howard
Art Dir Stuart Wurtzel

T

● Tom Selleck, Steve Guttenberg, Ted Danson, Nancy Travis, Robin Weisman, Christopher Cazenove (Touchstone/Interscope)

Back in their places for this two-dimensional sequel are the three bachelor dads of the waif who landed on their doorstep in part one: vain actor Ted Danson and biological dad, and architect Tom Selleck and illustrator Steve Guttenberg, the honorary dads.

What's new is that Selleck has fallen in love with the baby's mom, Sylvia (Nancy Travis), the actress who shares their new apartment, though he hasn't admitted it to her or himself.

Crisis occurs when baby turns five and enrolls in preschool, thereby encountering other children. Mom decides she must marry. She accepts a proposal from her director friend, Edward (Christopher Cazenove), and plans to move to England with little Mary (Robin Weisman), all because bachelor No. 2 (Selleck) is too confused to pop the question.

Rest of the pic is standard romantic comedy. Script [story by Sara Parriott and Josann McGibbon] spoonfeeds the audience with a plodding script that seems based more on demographic research than on any wisp of a creative impulse. Emile Ardolino directs with the same degree of competent but calculated non-risk. As for the actors, they have nothing to play.

■ THREE MUSKETEERS, THE

1921, 140 MINS, US ⊗
Dir Fred Niblo *Prod* Douglas Fairbanks *Scr* Edward Knoblock, Lotta Woods *Ph* Arthur Edeson *Ed* Nellie Mason *Mus* Louis F. Gottschalk *Art Dir* Edward M. Langley
● Douglas Fairbanks, Leon Bary, George Siegmann, Eugene Pallette, Marguerite De La Motte, Adolphe Menjou (Fairbanks/United Artists)

The story of Dumas has been ideally approximated in this screen version. There is a flare and sweep about the film, with the assembling, cutting and continuity seeming spotlessly correct. Douglas Fairbanks and D'Artagnan are a happy combination.

Of the interpretations, that of Nigel de Brulier as Richelieu developed a real creation. Excepting only the star, he dominates the picture. Adolphe Menjou does excellently in a role not actor-proof by any manner of means. His Louis XIII evidences both sides of the king, gaining sympathetic response where in most instances the opposite is the case.

The companions of D'Artagnan, Athos, Porthos and Aramis find apt treatment by Leon Bary, George Siegmann and Eugene Pallette. Marguerite De La Motte is a sweet and winsome Constance.

■ THREE MUSKETEERS, THE

1931, 97 MINS, US ▼ ⊙
Dir Rowland V. Lee *Prod* Cliff Reid *Scr* Dudley Nichols, Rowland V. Lee *Ph* Peverell Marley *Mus* Max Steiner
● Walter Abel, Paul Lukas, Margot Grahame, Heather Angel, Ian Keith, Moroni Olsen (RKO)

The impotency of the sound medium in the field of romantic adventure comedy, when inexpertly handled, is revealed with melancholy effect in the unreeling of this famous Dumas story, remade with dialog. *The Three Musketeers* is dull entertainment.

Walter Abel, a young, competent, and well regarded player from Broadway, is unsuited in nearly every respect for the role of D'Artagnan. If the tempo of the film were faster and the acting more flamboyant in the spirit of the story, Abel might have fared better.

From the title to the final fade there is an almost continuous struggle between the dialog and the musical score as to which will finally capture the ear.

The three men in the title parts are Paul Lukas as Athos, Moroni Olsen as Porthos, and Onslow Stevens as Aramis. Nigel de Brulier is convincing as Richelieu, the same role he played in the 1921 Fairbanks picture. Ian Keith, as the villainous de Rochefort, is excellent, as always, in a costume role which requires acting in the grand manner.

■ THREE MUSKETEERS, THE

1939, 71 MINS, US
Dir Allan Dwan *Prod* Raymond Griffith *Scr* M.M. Musselman, William A. Drake, Sam Hellman *Ph* Peverell Marley *Ed* Jack Dennis *Mus* David Buttolph (dir.) *Art Dir* Bernard Herzbrun, David Hall
● Don Ameche, Ritz Brothers, Binnie Barnes, Lionel Atwill, Pauline Moore (20th Century-Fox)

Utilizing the broadest strokes of comedy technique, this version of Dumas' romantic adventure presents Don Ameche as a rather personable D'Artagnan, and the Ritz Bros as a helter-skelter trio hopping in and out frequently to perform their standard screwball antics.

There is little seriousness or suspense generated in the slender story, and not much interest in the adventures of D'Artagnan and his pals to regain the queen's brooch in the possession of the Duke of Buckingham. Main excuse for the yarn apparently is to provide Ameche with an opportunity to be a dashing hero while the freres Ritz clown through the footage as phoney musketeers.

Romance between Ameche and Pauline Moore is sketchily presented, developing little interest or sincerity.

■ THREE MUSKETEERS, THE

1948, 126 MINS, US ◇ ▼ ⊙
Dir George Sidney *Prod* Pandro S. Berman *Scr* Robert Ardrey *Ph* Robert Planck *Ed* Robert J. Kern, George Boemler *Mus* Herbert Stothart *Art Dir* Cedric Gibbons, Malcolm Brown
● Gene Kelly, Lana Turner, June Allyson, Van Heflin, Angela Lansbury, Vincent Price (M-G-M)

The Three Musketeers is a swaggering, tongue-in-cheek treatment of picturesque fiction, extravagantly presented.

The fanciful tale is launched with a laugh, and quickly swings into some colorful and exciting sword duels as the pace is set for the imaginative adventures that feature the lives and loves of D'Artagnan and his three cronies. It is the complete Dumas novel.

There are acrobatics by Gene Kelly that would give Douglas Fairbanks pause. His first duel with Richelieu's cohorts is almost ballet, yet never loses the feeling of swaggering swordplay. It is a masterful mixture of dancing grace, acro-agility and sly horseplay of sock comedic punch.

Lana Turner is a perfect visualization of the sexy, wicked Lady de Winter, sharply contrasting with the sweet charm of June Allyson as the maid Constance. The three king's musketeers of the title are dashingly portrayed by Van Heflin, Gig Young and Robert Coote as Athos, Porthos and Aramis. They belt over their parts in keeping with the style Kelly uses for D'Artagnan.

Another aid in making the film top commercial entertainment is the telling score by Herbert Stothart, using themes by Tchaikovsky. Score bridges any gap in movement without intruding itself.
□ 1948: Nomination: Best Color Cinematography

■ THREE MUSKETEERS, THE THE QUEEN'S DIAMONDS

1973, 105 MINS, PANAMA/SPAIN ◇ ▼
Dir Richard Lester *Prod* Alexander Salkind, Brian Eatwell *Scr* George MacDonald Fraser *Ph* David

Watkin *Ed* John Victor Smith *Mus* Michel Legrand
● Oliver Reed, Charlton Heston, Raquel Welch, Faye Dunaway, Richard Chamberlain, Michael York (Fox Film Trust)

The Three Musketeers take very well to Richard Lester's provocative version that does not send it up but does add comedy to this adventure tale [by Alexandre Dumas].

Here D'Artagnan, played with brio by Michael York, is a country bumpkin; the musketeers themselves are more interested in money, dames and friendship than undue fidelity to the King, a simple-minded type, and their fight scenes are full of flailing, kicks and knockabout. They are not above starting a fight at an inn to steal victuals when they run out of money.

Behind it, however, is a look at an era of poverty and virtual worker slavery to fulfill the King's flagrantly rich whims.

Musketeers are played with panache by Richard Chamberlain as the haughty ladies' man, Oliver Reed as the gusty one and Frank Finlay as the dandyish type. Raquel Welch has comedic timing as the maladroit girl of D'Artagnan while Faye Dunaway has less to do as the perfidious Milady, but makes up for the lack in the sequel [*The Four Musketeers*] quietly made at the same time.

■ 3 NINJAS

1992, 84 MINS, US ◇ ▼ ⊙
Dir Jon Turtletaub *Prod* Martha Chang *Scr* Edward Emanuel *Ph* Richard Michalak, Chris Faloona *Ed* David Rennie *Mus* Rick Marvin *Art Dir* Kirk Petruccelli
● Victor Wong, Michael Treanor, Max Elliott Slade, Chad Power, Rand Kingsley, Alan McRae (Touchstone/Global Venture Hollywood)

Though there aren't any name actors in the chopsocky comedy and the plot [from Kenny Kim's story] is thin and formulaic, the gracefully choreographed spectacle of three little boys outfighting hordes of evil adult ninjas is a surefire juve crowd-pleaser.

Borrowing liberally from *The Karate Kid* and *Home Alone*, the filmmakers tap knowingly into kid's fantasies by showing little guys Michael Treanor, Max Elliott Slade and Chad Power hurling baddies through the air and flattening the massive, seemingly invincible Toru Tanaka.

Director Jon Turtletaub and editor David Rennie keep things zipping along, wisely not wasting much time with the ninjas' arms dealer boss, sneering Steven Seagal clone Rand Kingsley, or with his antagonist, the boys' blandly inattentive FBI agent father (Alan McRae).

When taken hostage, the Southern California boys have to rely on the martial arts lessons learned from their grandfather (the charming Victor Wong), who has shadowy past connections with Kingsley but takes their side in the battle royal.

■ THREE OF HEARTS

1993, 102 MINS, US ◇ ▼
Dir Yurek Bogayevicz *Prod* Joel B. Michaels, Matthew Irmas *Scr* Adam Greenman, Mitch Glazer *Ph* Andrzej Sekula *Ed* Dennis M. Hill *Mus* Richard Gibbs *Art Dir* Nelson Coates
● William Baldwin, Kelly Lynch, Sherilyn Fenn, Joe Pantoliano, Gail Strickland, Cec Verrell (New Line)

Most American comic triangles involve two men in love with the same woman. But *Three of Hearts* offers a male prostitute and a lesbian nurse enamored of a seemingly bisexual woman. The film [from a screen story by Adam Greenman] gets off to a good start, when Sherilyn Fenn dumps g.f. Kelly Lynch in Washington Square Park. The heartbroken Lynch, who intended to officially come out at her sister's wedding by bringing Fenn, hires

William Baldwin, a good-looking hustler, to accompany her.

Before long – with the help of a silly suspense subplot – Baldwin moves into Lynch's apartment and a new friendship is formed to win Fenn back.

For viewers willing to suspend disbelief, this aspiring screwball is immensely likable. As he demonstrated in *Anna*, Yurek Bogayevicz is a director with sensitivity for texture. Baldwin delivers a knockout performance in film's richest role. Lynch also shines as a droll, slightly obsessive lesbian.

[Version reviewed was a work-in-progress shown at 1993 Sundance Film Festival.]

■ **THREE ON A WEEKEND**
See: Bank Holiday

■ **3 RING CIRCUS**

1954, 103 MINS, US ◇
Dir Joseph Pevney   *Prod* Hal B. Wallis   *Scr* Don McGuire   *Ph* Loyal Griggs   *Ed* Warren Low   *Mus* Walter Scharf   *Art Dir* Hal Pereira, Tambi Larsen
● Dean Martin, Jerry Lewis, Joanne Dru, Zsa Zsa Gabor, Elsa Lanchester, Wallace Ford (Paramount)

Circus background of this expensively-mounted Hal Wallis production gives Dean Martin and Jerry Lewis slick opportunity to disport themselves along familiar lines.

The script projects comics straight from army uniform to the circus, where Lewis reports as a lion tamer's assistant in the hope he'll get to be a clown. Martin tags along, catching the eye of the beautiful but temperamental trapeze artist (Zsa Zsa Gabor), who makes him her 'assistant'. He takes over circus owner Joanne Dru's place when she leaves the circus – she's in love and keeps fighting with him – but all is later happiness again.

Comics as a team are somewhat less zany than in previous productions. Dru and Gabor supply plenty of flash and femme splendor. Wallace Ford is tops as the barking but sympathetic circus manager.

■ **THREE STRANGERS**

1946, 91 MINS, US
Dir Jean Negulesco   *Prod* Wolfgang Reinhardt   *Scr* John Huston, Howard Koch   *Ph* Arthur Edeson   *Ed* George Amy   *Mus* Adolph Deutsch   *Art Dir* Ted Smith
● Sydney Greenstreet, Peter Lorre, Geraldine Fitzgerald, Joan Lorring, Robert Shayne, Marjorie Riordan (Warner)

Three Strangers carries a rather complicated episodic plot, depending mostly on the fine cast performances to carry it.

Not only the three stars, Sydney Greenstreet, Geraldine Fitzgerald and Peter Lorre, but various supporting players command special attention. Greenstreet overplays to some extent as the attorney who has raided a trust fund, but he still does a good job. Lorre is tops as a drunk who gets involved in a murder of which he's innocent, while Fitzgerald rates as the victim.

Along with Greenstreet and Lorre, Fitzgerald has an equal share in a sweepstakes ticket. They are strangers. All three win on the ticket but Greenstreet murders the girl in a fit of rage, in Lorre's presence, thus leaving latter, also a loser, since he cannot risk trying to cash the ticket because it would involve him in the killing.

Story jumps around uncertainly but Jean Negulesco's direction is satisfactory.

■ **3:10 TO YUMA**

1957, 92 MINS, US ⊛ ⊙
Dir Delmer Daves   *Prod* David Heilweil   *Scr* Halsted Welles   *Ph* Charles Lawton Jr   *Ed* Al Clarke   *Mus* George Duning   *Art Dir* Frank Hotaling

● Glenn Ford, Van Heflin, Felicia Farr, Leora Dana, Henry Jones, Richard Jaeckel (Columbia)

Aside from the fact that this is an upper-drawer western, *3:10 to Yuma* will strike many for its resemblance to *High Noon*. That the climax fizzles must be laid on doorstep of Halsted Welles, who adapts Elmore Leonard's story quite well until that point.

Glenn Ford portrays the deadly leader of a slickly professional outlaw gang, which holds up a stagecoach. Van Heflin, impoverished neighborhood rancher, helps capture Ford when the latter lags behind his gang, to dally with lovely, lonely town barmaid Felicia Farr.

But Ford's gang is too strong for local lawmen to handle. Stagecoach owner Robert Emhardt promises a large reward to Heflin and the town drunk (Henry Jones). Idea is to hold Ford in another town, unknown to his gang, until daily train (3:10 of title) can take him to Yuma for trial. Here, story cleaves closely to *High Noon* formula.

Ford's switch-casting, as the quietly sinister gang leader, is authoritative, impressive and successful. Heflin measures up fully and convincingly to the rewarding role of the proud and troubled rancher. Farr's contribution is a short one, but she registers with a touching poignancy and a delicate beauty.

Title song by Ned Washington and George Duning, sung by Frankie Lane under credits and by Norma Zimmer during the picture, is a well-written tune.

■ **THREE WOMEN**

1977, 122 MINS, US ◇
Dir Robert Altman   *Prod* Robert Altman   *Scr* Robert Altman   *Ph* Chuck Rosher   *Ed* Dennis Hill   *Mus* Gerald Busby   *Art Dir* James D. Vance
● Shelley Duvall, Sissy Spacek, Janice Rule, Robert Fortier, Ruth Nelson, John Cromwell (20th Century-Fox)

Absorbing moody and often compelling story about psychological dependence and transference.

Robert Altman had a dream which he used as the basis for his original screenplay, set in the desert where Shelley Duvall works as an attendant in an old-folks' health center and new staffer Sissy Spacek becomes her roommate.

Janice Rule is the mural-painting wife of retired stuntman Robert Fortier, the two of them being important catalysts to the changing relationship between Spacek and Duvall.

Duvall is magnificent as a girl whose inner unhappiness is masked by dialog straight out of smart-set magazines and fast-snack recipe folders. Spacek, at the outset adoring and subservient, gets all the sympathy.

Spacek matches in complementing excellence Duvall's performance. Rule registers well.

■ **THREE WORLDS OF GULLIVER, THE**

1960, 98 MINS, UK ◇ ⊛ ⊙
Dir Jack Sher   *Prod* Charles H. Schneer   *Scr* Arthur Ross, Jack Sher   *Ph* Wilkie Cooper   *Ed* Raymond Poulton   *Mus* Bernard Herrmann   *Art Dir* Gil Parrendo, Derek Barrington
● Kerwin Mathews, Jo Morrow, June Thorburn, Basil Sydney, Gregoire Aslan, Lee Patterson (Columbia)

Jonathan Swift's 18th-century stinging satire has been considerably softened and drastically romanticized, but enough of its telling caustic comment remains.

The original four-part work has been trimmed to the more familiar twosome of Lilliput, land of little people, and Brobdingnag, where the natives are as tall in proportion to Gulliver as the Lilliputians are short. The hero's wife and family of Swift's tome have been dropped in favor of a fiery fiancee who shares his misadventure in Brobdingnag. Gulliver, thankfully, still goes it alone in Lilliput, according to the film.

The picture is notable for its visuo-cinematic achievements and its bold, bright and sweeping score by Bernard Herrmann. Special visual effects expert Ray Harryhausen, whose Superdynamation process makes the motion-pictured Gulliver plausible and workable, rates a low bow for his painstaking, productive efforts.

Kerwin Mathews, generally reserved and persuasive, makes a first-rate Gulliver. Among the more arresting performances are those of Basil Sydney as the pompous emperor of Lilliput, Martin Benson as its conniving minister of finance, Marian Spencer as the vain empress, Mary Ellis and Gregoire Aslan as king and queen of Brobdingnag.

■ **THRESHOLD**

1981, 106 MINS, CANADA ◇ ⊛
Dir Richard Pearce   *Prod* Jon Slan, Michael Burns   *Scr* James Salter   *Ph* Michael Brault   *Ed* Susan Martin   *Mus* Mickey Erbe, Mary-beth Solomon
● Donald Sutherland, John Marley, Sharon Ackerman, Jeff Goldblum, Mare Winningham, Michael Lerner (Paragon)

Donald Sutherland takes the central role of a heart specialist involved in the development of a mechanical heart for transplant purposes. The device is the brainchild of medical biologist Jeff Goldblum, a fanatic who is certain his radical conception will revolutionize surgical techniques.

When all current practices fail on patient Mare Winningham, Sutherland decides to defy the board and bring out the miracle device. The controversial operation immediately generates media attention and Sutherland nervously waits out the consequence of his action.

Writer James Salter and director Richard Pearce have strenuously avoided taking a melodramatic approach to the material. What emerges is virtually a visualized medical journal filled with the tedium and monotony facing a dedicated surgeon incorporated along with the excitement of venturing into new medical frontiers. At times one wishes the film had opted for a more dramatic tone.

Sutherland gives a cooly effective performance. The stability of Sutherland's surgeon is in sharp contrast to Goldblum's erratic inventor, providing the film with a keen sense of humor.

■ **THRILL OF IT ALL, THE**

1963, 108 MINS, US ◇ ⊛
Dir Norman Jewison   *Prod* Ross Hunter, Martin Melcher   *Scr* Carl Reiner   *Ph* Russell Metty   *Ed* Milton Carruth   *Mus* Frank DeVol   *Art Dir* Alexander Golitzen, Robert Boyle
● Doris Day, James Garner, Arlene Francis, Edward Andrews, ZaSu Pitts, Reginald Owen (Universal/Arwin)

Carl Reiner's scenario, from a story he wrote in collaboration with Larry Gelbart, is peppered with digs at various institutions of American life. Among the targets of his fairly subtle but telling assault with the needle are television, Madison Avenue, the servant problem and such specific matters as the sharp points at the rear extremities of the modern Cadillac and the maitre d' who has immediate seating for celebrities only.

But these nuggets and pinpricks of satiric substance are primarily bonuses. Ultimately it is in the design and engineering of cumulative sight gag situations that *Thrill of It All* excels. In addition to a running gag about a suspiciously similar weekly series of live TV dramas, there is a scene in which a swimming pool saturated with soap gives birth to a two-story-high mountain of suds and another in which James Garner, coming home from work one evening, drives his convertible into his back yard and straight into a pool that wasn't there in the morning.

Doris Day scores as the housewife with two children who is suddenly thrust into an irresistible position as an $80,000-a-year pitch woman for an eccentric soap tycoon who is impressed by her unaffected quality. Bearing the brunt of these soap operatics is Garner as the gynecologist whose domestic tranquillity is shattered by his wife's sudden transition to career girl.

Arlene Francis and Edward Andrews are spirited in the key roles of a middle-aged couple suddenly expectant parents. ZaSu Pitts does all she can with some ridiculous shenanigans as a fretful maid.

．．．．．．．．．．．．．．．．．．．．．．．．．．

■ THROW MOMMA FROM THE TRAIN

1987, 88 MINS, US ◇ ⓥ ⊙
Dir Danny DeVito   *Prod* Larry Brezner   *Scr* Stu Silver
Ph Barry Sonnenfeld   *Ed* Michael Jablow   *Mus* David
Newman   *Art Dir* Ida Random
● Danny DeVito, Billy Crystal, Anne Ramsey, Kim Greist,
Kate Mulgrew, Annie Ross (Orion)

Throw Momma from the Train is a fun and delightfully venal comedy. Very clever and engaging from beginning to end, pic builds on the notion that nearly everyone – at least once in life – has the desire to snuff out a relative or nemesis, even if 99.9% of us let the urge pass without ever acting on it.

Here, it's the idle death threats of a frustrated writer and flunky junior college professor (Billy Crystal) against his ex-wife that are overheard by one of his dimwitted and very impressionable students (Danny DeVito).

DeVito's limited creative abilities are further stifled by his crazy, overbearing momma (Anne Ramsey), a nasty, jealous old bag whom he loathes and fears. He seeks out Crystal for help on his writing and instead is told to go see Alfred Hitchcock's *Strangers on a Train*, which he does – coming away with a ridiculous scheme on the film's plot to kill Crystal's wife and then ask for a like favor in return.

Crystal's talent as a standup comic comes through as it appears he got away with a fair amount of ad-libbing. His tirades on his ex-wife, a routine he does several times, get funnier with each delivery and are a good counterbalance to DeVito's equally comical dumb-impish schtick.

If there were to be a first place prize for scene stealing, however, it would to to Ramsey, whose horrible looks and surly demeanor are sick and humorous at the same time.
□ 1987: Nomination: Best Supp. Actress (Anne Ramsey)

．．．．．．．．．．．．．．．．．．．．．．．．．．

■ THUNDER AND LIGHTNING

1977, 93 MINS, US ◇ ⓥ
Dir Corey Allen   *Prod* Roger Corman   *Scr* William
Hjortsberg   *Ph* James Pergola   *Ed* Anthony Redman
Mus Andy Stein
● David Carradine, Kate Jackson, Roger C. Carmel,
Sterling Holloway, Ed Barth, Ron Feinberg (20th Century-
Fox)

Thunder and Lightning has just about everything in the action department but Dracula loping after Frankenstein's monster, packing thrills and fast movement as stunt drivers have their day in some wild pic mileage.

Film picks up in tempo and ends on a socko note as David Carradine, an irrepressible booze runner, competes with girl-friend Kate Jackson's pop in his chosen field.

Script laces comedy with the action, and director Corey Allen expertly maneuvers his chase sequences with stunting both with Everglade buggies and fast cars on the highways.

Carradine shows he has the stuff of which

action stars are made, and distaffer Jackson lends a distracting note as an actress who doesn't mind getting her hair mussed.

．．．．．．．．．．．．．．．．．．．．．．．．．．

■ THUNDERBALL

1965, 130 MINS, UK ◇ ⓥ ⊙
Dir Terence Young   *Prod* Kevin McClory   *Scr* Richard
Maibaum, John Hopkins   *Ph* Ted Moore   *Ed* Peter
Hunt   *Mus* John Barry   *Art Dir* Ken Adam
● Sean Connery, Claudine Auger, Adolfo Celi, Luciana
Paluzzi, Rik Van Nutter, Bernard Lee (McClory)

Sean Connery plays his indestructible James Bond for the fourth time in the manner born, faced here with a $280 million atomic bomb ransom plot. Action, dominating element of three predecessors, gets rougher before even the credits flash on. Richard Maibaum (who coscripted former entries) and John Hopkins' screenplay [based on an original screenplay by Jack Whittingham, from the original story by Kevin McClory, Whittingham and Ian Fleming] is studded with inventive play and mechanical gimmicks. There's visible evidence that the reported $5.5 million budget was no mere publicity figure; it's posh all the way.

Underwater weapon-carrying sea sleds provide an imaginative note, as does a one-man jet pack used by Bond in the opening sequence, reminiscent of the one-man moon vehicle utilized by Dick Tracy in the cartoon strip.

Connery is up to his usual stylish self as he lives up to past rep, in which mayhem is a casual affair.

Adolfo Celi brings dripping menace to part of the swarthy heavy who is nearly as ingenious – but not quite – as the British agent, whom, among other means, he tries to kill with man-eating sharks.

Terence Young takes advantage of every situation in his direction to maintain action at fever-pitch.
□ 1965: Best Visual Effects (John Stears)

．．．．．．．．．．．．．．．．．．．．．．．．．．

■ THUNDERBOLT AND LIGHTFOOT

1974, 114 MINS, US ◇ ⓥ ⊙
Dir Michael Cimino   *Prod* Robert Daley   *Scr* Michael
Cimino   *Ph* Frank Stanley   *Ed* Ferris Webster
Mus Dee Barton   *Art Dir* Tambi Larsen
● Clint Eastwood, Jeff Bridges, George Kennedy,
Geoffrey Lewis, Catherine Bach, Gary Busey (United
Artists)

Thunderbolt and Lightfoot is an overlong, sometimes hilariously vulgar comedy-drama, about the restaging of a difficult safecracking heist. Debuting director Michael Cimino obtains superior performances from Clint Eastwood, George Kennedy, Geoffrey Lewis and especially Jeff Bridges.

Cimino's story picks up Eastwood as a cowtown preacher, his longtime refuge from Kennedy, a survivor of an earlier caper where the loot was hidden and never found. A Kennedy henchman uncovers Eastwood, who meets Bridges (also on the lam from a car theft), then Kennedy and Lewis. The secret hiding place of the loot, an old schoolhouse, has been replaced by a new structure. Uneasily, the group decides to pull the job all over again.
□ 1974: Nomination: Best Supp. Actor (Jeff Bridges)

．．．．．．．．．．．．．．．．．．．．．．．．．．

■ THUNDERHEART

1992, 118 MINS, US ◇ ⓥ ⊙
Dir Michael Apted   *Prod* Robert De Niro, Jane
Rosenthal, John Fusco   *Scr* John Fusco   *Ph* Roger
Deakins   *Ed* Ian Crafford   *Mus* James Horner
Art Dir Dan Bishop
● Val Kilmer, Graham Greene, Sam Shepard, Sheila
Tousey, Fred Ward, Fred Dalton Thompson
(Tribeca/Waterhorse)

Dances with the Evidence could be the title of this pic about a young, part-Indian FBI hotdog whose loyalties are tested when he discovers the power of his roots during a murder probe on a Sioux reservation. Reasonably engrossing as a mystery-thriller despite its overburdened plot, *Thunderheart* succeeds most in its captivating portrayal of mystical Native American ways.

Val Kilmer stars as a sharp but surly and guarded young fed whose crewcut bristles when he learns he's expected to use his long-suppressed Indian heritage to help quell violence on a South Dakota reservation. Partnered with a crack FBI vet (Sam Shepard), he travels 'cross the lone prairie to the Res, where the two city sharpies excel at shockingly insensitive behavior.

Befriended by a wary but compassionate Sioux sheriff (Graham Greene, in a standout portrayal), he's introduced to tribal spiritual elder (Chief Ted Thin Elk), who points him toward his true self.

Set among the tinderbox tensions of the late 1970s, when militant Indians waged bloody battles to take back their culture and lands, pic finds a lively platform for its essential view that the old ways were far wiser and better. Kilmer holds the screen strongly in an intense young Turk role, but when script calls for him to transform into a mythical Indian savior, he doesn't quite fill the moccasins.

．．．．．．．．．．．．．．．．．．．．．．．．．．

■ THUNDER IN THE CITY

1937, 86 MINS, UK ⓥ
Dir Marion Gering   *Prod* Alexander Erway
Scr Robert Sherwood, Aben Kandel, Akos Tolnay   *Ph* Al
Gilks   *Ed* Arthur Hilton   *Mus* Miklos Rozsa
Art Dir David Ramon
● Edward G. Robinson, Luli Deste, Nigel Bruce,
Constance Collier, Ralph Richardson, Arthur Wontner
(Atlantic/Columbia)

For a long time, Edward G. Robinson wanted to do something lighter than eye-gouging racketeers and went to London for that purpose after getting an offer to appear in this picture. He wasn't so wrong in wanting to try his hand at something different such as this, except that, as a romantic lead opposite Luli Deste, he is a bit awkward.

Robinson plays an American ballyhoo artist who invades the staid calm of business methods in England and, backed by a lot of nerve, much luck and fictional situations, promotes a metal mine in Africa into a big proposition. Robinson's rival ties him up under patents and it looks as though the Horatio Algerian hero is stymied.

Three writers have written much smart dialog into the picture and provided numerous comedy situations which are ably maneuvered by director Marion Gering.

Deste is a Viennese with a pleasant but very slight accent. She looks to have the goods besides having the looks. Two who contribute much are Nigel Bruce and Constance Collier, who play a duke and duchess, respectively. Ralph Richardson renders a good job as a British banker.

．．．．．．．．．．．．．．．．．．．．．．．．．．

■ THUNDER IN THE DUST
See: The Sundowners

．．．．．．．．．．．．．．．．．．．．．．．．．．

■ THX 1138

1971, 88 MINS, US ◇ ⓥ ⊙
Dir George Lucas   *Prod* Lawrence Sturhahn
Scr George Lucas, Walter Murch   *Ph* Dave Meyers,
Albert Kihn   *Ed* George Lucas   *Mus* Lalo Schifrin
Art Dir Michael Haller
● Robert Duvall, Donald Pleasence, Don Pedro Colley,
Maggie McOmie, Ian Wolfe, Sid Haig (American
Zoetrope)

THX 1138 is a psychedelic science fiction horror story about some future civilization regimented into computer-programmed slavery.

Film is a feature-length expansion of George Lucas' student film. In that brief form, the story of one man's determination to crash out of his worldly prison was exciting; the expansion by director-editor Lucas with Walter Murch succeeds in fleshing out the environment, but falls behind in constructing a plot line to sustain interest. Robert Duvall heads cast as the defector after his mate Maggie McOmie is programmed into the cell of Donald Pleasence, a corrupt computer technician. Don Pedro Colley is another fugitive, who helps Duvall reach his freedom.

■ **TIARA TAHITI**

1962, 100 MINS, UK ◇ ⓦ
Dir Ted Kotcheff   *Prod* Ivan Foxwell   *Scr* Geofrey Cotterell, Ivan Foxwell   *Ph* Otto Heller   *Ed* Anthony Gibbs   *Mus* Phil Green   *Art Dir* Alex Vetchinsky
● James Mason, John Mills, Claude Dauphin, Herbert Lom, Rosenda Monteros, Jacques Marin (Rank)

Action stems from Germany, just after the war. A jumped up, pompous lieutenant-colonel with a king size inferiority complex (Mills) clashes with a sophisticated, carefree junior officer (Mason). Mills stops Mason when he tries to smuggle loot back to London, and Mason is cashiered.

He finds a life of dissolute ease and enchantment in Tahiti, with a native girl and no worries. Mills, well after the war, arrives to negotiate a deal to build a hotel in Tahiti, comes across Mason and finds to his intense irritation that Mason still has the same effect on him, that of reducing him to fumbling ineptitude and humility.

The two male stars in this pic have a field day. Mason is fine as the mocking wastrel while Mills is equally good in a more difficult role that could have lapsed into parody.

These two carry the main burden of the film but get affectionate alliance from a string of people. As Mason's girl friend, Monteros is attractive. Herbert Lom (skilfully made up as a Chinese) has a serio-comic role as the local tradesman who is the frustrated rival for the affections of Monteros, and does it up brown.

■ **TIGER AND THE PUSSYCAT, THE**

1967, 105 MINS, ITALY/US ◇ ⓦ
Dir Dino Risi   *Prod* Mario Cecchi Gori   *Scr* Incrocci Agenore, Furio Scarpelli, Dino Risi   *Ph* Sandro D'Eva   *Ed* Marcello Malvestiti   *Mus* Fred Buongusto   *Art Dir* Luciano Ricceri
● Vittorio Gassman, Ann-Margret, Eleanor Parker (Fair/Embassy)

Screenwriters take a timeworn three-point relationship and bulwark it with many physical gag situations and flash comic inserts. But they depend on the more basic cleavage between parents and offspring to underscore the extra-marital fling between a middle-age captain of industry (Vittorio Gassman) and a 20-year-old Bohemian ball of fire (Ann-Margret). Eleanor Parker plays the abused wife with suave dignity.

For about two-thirds of the film *The Tiger* is a swiftly-paced romp of gay deceit for the male partner and a purposeful drive for sexual plentitude on the distaff side. Slowdown occurs with Gassman's dilemma. Prodded by his young mistress to give up wife and family (his career by this time is practically shot anyway), the charm and tempo slacken while Gassman weighs a choice that distills the joy of a seven-inning stretch.

Gassman is on the scene almost every minute of the film. It's an unfair load to bear with such a slight story in support but he's first-rate until the action sags. Parker is standout as the attractive, understanding wife and mother of two grownup children.

■ **TIGER BAY**

1959, 105 MINS, UK ⓦ
Dir J. Lee Thompson   *Prod* Julian Wintle, Leslie Parkyn   *Scr* John Hawkesworth, Shelley Smith   *Ph* Eric Cross   *Ed* Sidney Hayers   *Mus* Laurie Johnson
● John Mills, Horst Buchholz, Hayley Mills, Yvonne Mitchell, Megs Jenkins, Anthony Dawson (Rank)

A disarming, snub-nosed youngster makes her debut in *Tiger Bay*, and registers a sock impact. She is Hayley Mills, 12-year-old daughter of actor John Mills, star of the film. Young Mills gives a lift to a pic which, anyway, stacks up as a lively piece of drama.

The story concerns a Polish seaman who, returning from a voyage, finds that his mistress has moved in with another man. In a burst of anger he kills her. The slaying is witnessed by the child, who also rescues the gun. She is a lonely youngster whose attachment for the killer seriously complicates police investigations.

Mills is authoritative as the detective while Horst Buchholz brings charm to a role which could easily have been played by British actor.

Lee Thompson and cameraman Eric Cross capture the dockland area of Cardiff arrestingly. The screenplay by John Hawkesworth and Shelley Smith is taut and literate.

■ **TIGER MAKES OUT, THE**

1967, 94 MINS, US ◇
Dir Arthur Hiller   *Prod* George Justin   *Scr* Murray Schisgal   *Ph* Arthur J. Ornitz   *Ed* Robert C. Jones   *Mus* Milton 'Shorty' Rogers   *Art Dir* Paul Sylbert
● Eli Wallach, Anne Jackson, Bob Dishy, John Harkins, Ruth White, Roland Wood (Columbia)

Beware of the one-act play with apparent screen possibilities. *The Tiger Makes Out* was adapted by Murray Schisgal from his 1963 two-character comedy-drama *The Tiger* into a distended, uneven pic.

Filmed in New York, the George Justin production stars Eli Wallach and Ann Jackson, encoring their legit roles. Good performances, production and yeoman directorial effort by Arthur Hiller buoy up interest.

The play concerned the (offstage) kidnapping of Jackson, a suburban housefrau, by frustrated mailman Wallach, after which some genuinely tender dialog brings together the two spirits.

The kidnapping itself is not detailed; on film, however, it is, and, while necessary, the act itself is not a laugh-getter.

■ **TIGER SHARK**

1932, 78 MINS, US
Dir Howard Hawks   *Scr* Wells Root   *Ph* Tony Gaudio   *Ed* Thomas Pratt   *Art Dir* Jack Okey
● Edward G. Robinson, Zita Johann, Richard Arlen, Leila Bennett, Vince Barnett, J. Carrol Naish (First National)

A strong and exceedingly well played and directed sea drama [from the story *Tuna* by Houston Branch]. After losing his hand to a tiger shark in a realistic underwater shot, Edward G. Robinson, as Capt Mike Mascareno, replaces the lost member with a steel hook. The shady lady who marries him bears no love, but only appreciation for his kindness.

It's to be expected that she should fall for the personable best friend of her husband (Richard Arlen). From friendship, the captain's feelings toward his first mate turn to hatred when the boy and the missus are caught in a clinch.

No human villains in the cast. All the dirty work is assigned to the sharks. When they're not biting off the captain's hand they're chewing up luckless fishermen who fall into the water.

The tuna fishing moments are the big

thrills. One big scene shows a haul of countless tunas by hook and line. Sharks enter the picture with each fishing sequence, and disaster to one of the crew always follows.

■ **TIGHT LITTLE ISLAND**
See: Whisky Galore!

■ **TIGHTROPE**

1984, 117 MINS, US ◇ ⓦ ⊙
Dir Richard Tuggle   *Prod* Clint Eastwood, Fritz Manes   *Scr* Richard Tuggle   *Ph* Bruce Surtees   *Ed* Joel Cox   *Mus* Lennie Niehaus   *Art Dir* Edward Carfagno
● Clint Eastwood, Genevieve Bujold, Dan Hedaya, Alison Eastwood, Jennifer Beck, Marco St John (Malpaso/Warner)

Tightrope sees Clint Eastwood comfortably in the role of a big city homicide cop, but also as a vulnerable, hunted man, a deserted husband, father of two daughters, a man whose taste for seamy sex nearly brings him down.

Written and directed by Richard Tuggle, pic trades extensively on the theme of guilt transference from killer to presumed hero which for so long was the special domain of Alfred Hitchcock.

Surface action is highly familiar, as an anonymous killer, stalks prostitutes and massage parlor girls in New Orleans' French Quarter. Eastwood has been accustomed to taking his pleasure with the very sort of women upon whom the murderer is preying.

A fair amount of running time is given over to Eastwood's relationship with his growing daughters (older of whom is played by his real-life offspring, Alison).

It all leads up to a rather predictable assault on the cop's home and daughters, and some sweating and soul-searching on his part.

Overall, however, action is well-handled, as Tuggle demonstrates ample storytelling talent and draws a multitude of nuances from his cast.

■ **TILLIE AND GUS**

1933, 58 MINS, US
Dir Francis Martin   *Prod* Douglas MacLean   *Scr* Walter DeLeon, Francis Martin   *Ph* Ben Reynolds   *Art Dir* Hans Dreier, Harry Oliver
● W. C. Fields, Alison Skipworth, Baby LeRoy, Jacqueline Wells, George Barbier, Clarence Wilson (Paramount)

This is an effort to stretch a brief idea to feature length with horseplay and mechanical punch which doesn't quite register. Chief handicap is a lack of spontaneity and swiftness of movement. Basic idea is good, the big time slickers who beat the country amateur, but this rich vein is scarcely uncovered.

W.C. Fields and Alison Skipworth are a married couple who have gone their separate ways but reunite when called to the old home for a presumed legacy. Local bad boy is trying to hog the fortune and oust the young couple from their inheritance. Last thing to be picked up is a ferry franchise, and that's whipped into a race between the old boat and the new contender.

In between it's some of Fields' old vaude gags, frequent references to wet babies and such bits as the $1,000 vase being dropped to catch the $1 cane. Comedy not helped any by efforts to inject a dramatic story.

■ **TILL THE CLOUDS ROLL BY**

1946, 120 MINS, US ◇ ⓦ ⊙
Dir Richard Whorf   *Prod* Arthur Freed   *Scr* Myles Connolly, Jean Holloway   *Ph* Harry Stradling, George J. Folsey   *Ed* Albert Akst   *Mus* Jerome Kern   *Art Dir* Cedric Gibbons, Daniel B. Cathcart
● Robert Walker, Judy Garland, Lucille Bremer, Joan Wells, Van Heflin, Dorothy Patrick (M-G-M)

Why quibble about the story? It's notable that the Jerome Kern saga reminds of the Cole Porter *Night and Day* – both apparently enjoyed a monotonously successful life. No early-life struggles, no frustrations, nothing but an uninterrupted string of Broadway and West End show success. Nearest thing to travail is Kern's contretemps with turn-of-the-century Broadway impresario Charles Frohman, who was apparently a rabid Anglophile – 'no good songsmith in America; the only good ones come from Europe.'

Of the basic cast, Robert Walker is completely sympathetic as Kern. Van Heflin plays Jim Hessler, the arranger-composer-confidante, whose life story parallels Kern's in a Damon- and-Pythias plot. (Some real-life counterpart may be the veteran arranger, Frank Sadler).

Picture actually opens with *Show Boat*, a 1927 whammo. There is virtually a tabloid version of that operetta utilized for the opener, a play-within-a-play and the rest of the story is virtually a success-story flashback.

. . . .

■ TILL THERE WAS YOU

1991, 93 MINS, AUSTRALIA ◇ ⓥ
Dir John Seale   *Prod* Jim McElroy   *Scr* Michael Thomas   *Ph* Geoffrey Simpson   *Ed* Jim Bilcock   *Mus* Graeme Revell   *Art Dir* George Liddle
● Mark Harmon, Deborah Unger, Jeroen Krabbe, Shane Briant (Ayer/Five Arrow/AFFC)

By Australian standards, top cinematographer John Seale's first pic as a director is an expensive, high-concept affair that falls between several categories.

The serviceable, if familiar, plot has Mark Harmon playing a New York sax player who wings off to a Pacific island on his brother's invitation. When he arrives he discovers his brother has been killed, and that he's not very welcome on the island.

Although Harmon does his best with his undemanding role, Canadian-born Aussie thesp Deborah Unger is miscast as the sultry wife of the dead brother's friend. Unger is far too down-to-earth for the role.

Furthermore, there's no chemistry between her and Harmon. As her seemingly charming husband, Jeroen Krabbe brings a touch of menace to a conventional character.

Camerawork on little-seen island locations is often spectacular. A plane crash in the jungle is superbly staged, and the local Vanuatans, mostly from Pentecost Island, prove to be natural actors.

. . . .

■ TILL WE MEET AGAIN

1944, 85 MINS, US
Dir Frank Borzage   *Prod* Frank Borzage   *Scr* Lenore Coffee   *Ph* Theodor Sparkuhl   *Ed* Elmo Veron   *Mus* David Buttolph   *Art Dir* Hans Dreier, Robert Usher
● Ray Milland, Barbara Britton, Walter Slezak, Mona Freeman, Lucile Watson, Vladimir Sokoloff (Paramount)

For all its underground intrigue, Nazi brutality and Machiavellian Gestapo methods, film is a different sort of war romance. For one thing, its heroine is a novitiate nun and Ray Milland is an almost too happily married albeit dashing American aviator, forced down in occupied France.

Sometimes Milland's love-hunger for his wife and child is a bit sticky, but it gets over a wholesome message of the American standard of love and marriage to the young French convent girl. To her it's a new-found litany of love that awakens a new perspective on the mundane world as she accompanies Milland – as his pseudo-wife – in order to aid his escape with valuable secret papers from the French Underground for London.

Barbara Britton, a newcomer, is compelling as the beauteous but unworldly church disciple.

. . . .

■ 'TIL WE MEET AGAIN

1940, 99 MINS, US
Dir Edmund Goulding   *Prod* Hal B. Wallis, David Lewis   *Scr* Warren Duff, Robert Lord   *Ph* Tony Gaudio   *Ed* Ralph Dawson
● Merle Oberon, George Brent, Pat O'Brien, Geraldine Fitzgerald, Binnie Barnes, Frank McHugh (Warner)

This remake of *One Way Passage* still has plenty of sock left. The WB original, back in 1932, had William Powell and Kay Francis in the top roles, but the present combination, George Brent and Merle Oberon, do an excellent job. Oberon's sincere and eye-filling performance equals that of her predecessor in the role, while Brent comes within at least a shade of Powell's superb portrayal. Frank McHugh repeats his performance as the conman passenger.

Warren Duff's screenplay varies little from the 1932 adaptation of Robert Lord's original by Wilson Mizner and Joseph Jackson. Story opens in Hong Kong with Oberon falling for Brent, a total stranger, in a bar. She meets him again on the ship bound for the United States and chases after him in a manner that is just as implausible as in their original meeting. Brent is being returned to San Quentin to hang for murder, while Oberon is in final stages of cardiac ailment.

Pat O'Brien is considerably superior to Warren Hymer who played the police officer returning the prisoner to the US in the original, although the part is built up somewhat in the present version. Geraldine Fitzgerald, strangely heavy, is an exuberant and sympathetic tourist while Binnie Barnes, with a French accent, is a phony countess who plays for O'Brien in an effort to help Brent escape. Eric Blore is as usual strong as the 'branch of the Bank of England' who falls for McHugh's wily ways.

. . . .

■ TIME AFTER TIME

1980, 112 MINS, UK ◇ ⓥ ☉
Dir Nicholas Meyer   *Prod* Herb Jaffe   *Scr* Nicholas Meyer   *Ph* Paul Lohmann   *Ed* Donn Cambern   *Mus* Miklos Rozsa   *Art Dir* Edward C. Carfagno
● Malcolm McDowell, David Warner, Mary Steenburgen, Charles Cioffi, Patti D'Arbanville, Corey Feldman (Warner/Orion)

Time after Time is a delightful, entertaining trifle of a film that shows both the possibilities and limitations of taking liberties with literature and history. Nicholas Meyer has deftly juxtaposed Victorian England and contemporary America in a clever story, irresistible due to the competence of its cast.

H.G. Wells and Jack The Ripper abandon London circa 1893 in Wells' famous time machine. Their arrival in 1979 San Francisco is played for all the inevitable anachronisms, with results that are both witty and pointed.

Thanks to Meyer's astute scripting and direction, and superb performances by Malcolm McDowell as Wells, David Warner as the mythical killer, and Mary Steenburgen as the woman in between, there's plenty of mileage in *Time*.

. . . .

■ TIME BANDITS

1981, 110 MINS, UK ◇ ⓥ ☉
Dir Terry Gilliam   *Prod* Terry Gilliam   *Scr* Michael Palin, Terry Gilliam   *Ph* Peter Biziou   *Ed* Julian Doyle   *Mus* Mike Moran   *Art Dir* Milly Burns
● John Cleese, Sean Connery, Shelley Duvall, Ralph Richardson, David Warner, Michael Palin (Handmade)

When you can count the laughs in a comedy on the fingers of one hand, it isn't so funny. *Time Bandits*, is a kind of potted history of man, myth and the eternal clash between good and evil as told in the inimitable idiom of Monty Python.

Not that the basic premise is bad, with an

English youngster and a group of dwarfs passing through time holes on assignment by the Maker to patch up the shoddier parts of His creation. What results, unfortunately, is a hybrid neither sufficiently hair-raising nor comical.

The plot's grand tour ranges from ancient Greece and other parts to the Titanic to the Fortress of Ultimate Darkness, the latter gothic region presided over by a costume-heavy David Warner as one of nine above-title and mostly cameo parts. Of which the funniest, near pic's conclusion, is the Maker Himself as none other than Ralph Richardson in business suit.

John Cleese as Robin Hood, Ian Holm as Napoleon, Sean Connery as a Greek warrior-ruler with a passion for magic, and Michael Palin as a plummy English upperclass type all acquit well enough in the limited circumstances.

. . . .

■ TIME FOR ACTION
See: Tip on a Dead Jockey

. . . .

■ TIME LOST AND TIME REMEMBERED
See: I Was Happy Here

. . . .

■ TIME MACHINE, THE

1960, 103 MINS, US ◇ ⓥ ☉
Dir George Pal   *Prod* George Pal   *Scr* David Duncan   *Ph* Paul C. Vogel   *Ed* George Tomasini   *Mus* Russell Garcia   *Art Dir* George W. Davis, William Ferrari
● Rod Taylor, Alan Young, Yvette Mimieux, Sebastian Cabot, Tom Helmore, Whit Bissell (M-G-M/Galaxy)

In utilizing contemporary knowledge to update H.G. Wells' durable novel, scenarist David Duncan has brought the work into modern focus. The point-of-view springs properly from 1960 rather than from the turn of the century. The social comment of the original has been historically refined to encompass such plausible eventualities as the physical manifestation of atomic war weapons. But the basic spirit of Wells' work has not been lost.

The film's chief flaw is its somewhat palsied pace. Forging its way through vital initial exposition, it perks to a fascinating peak when the Time Traveller (Rod Taylor) plants himself in his machine and begins his enviable tour of time. His 'visits' to World Wars I, II, and III, and the way in which the passage of time is depicted within these 'local' stops give the picture its most delightful moments.

But things slow down to a walk when Taylor arrives at the year 802,701 and becomes involved generally with a group of tame, antisocial towheads (the Eloi) and specifically with their loveliest and most sociable representative (Yvette Mimieux), with whom he falls in love.

Taylor's performance is a gem of straightforwardness, with just the proper sensitivity and animation. A standout in support is Alan Young, in a gentle, three-ply role. Mimieux is well cast. Innocent vacancy gleams beautifully in her eyes.
□ 1960: Best Special Effects

. . . .

■ TIME OF THEIR LIVES, THE

1946, 82 MINS, US ⓥ
Dir Charles Barton   *Scr* Val Burton, Walter De Leon, Bradford Ropes   *Ph* Charles Van Enger   *Ed* Philip Cahn   *Mus* Milton Rosen   *Art Dir* Jack Otterson, Richard Riedel
● Lou Costello, Bud Abbott, Marjorie Reynolds, Binnie Barnes, Gale Sondergaard (Universal)

This one's a picnic for Abbott & Costello fans, replete with trowelled-on slapstick, corned-up gags and farcical plot.

Shot by mistake as a traitor in the American Revolutionary War and doomed to remain an earthbound ghost until proved innocent, Costello turns up in 1946 still looking for the evidence. In a similar fix, Marjorie Reynolds floats through the film like a Sears-Roebuck model ghost, but Costello can't quite make the smoothie grade. It's good for laughs.

Abbott, who early in the picture plays a 1780 heel, turns up in modern times as a psychiatrist, house-guesting in the mansion Costello and his girl friend are haunting. Latter wreak their revenge via a series of invisible-man stunts that drive the brain specialist out of his mind. This gimmick is worked to the limit, and beyond.

....

■ TIME TO LOVE AND A TIME TO DIE, A

1958, 133 MINS, US ◇ ▼
Dir Douglas Sirk   *Prod* Robert Arthur   *Scr* Orin Jannings   *Ph* Russell Metty   *Mus* Miklos Rozsa
Art Dir Alexander Golitzen, Alfred Sweeney
● John Gavin, Lilo Pulver, Keenan Wynn, Erich Maria Remarque, Thayer David, Jock Mahoney (Universal)

A Time to Love and a Time to Die is less a panorama of the battle horrors of the Second World War, though these are implicit, than a poignant telling of the anguish of being in love while civilian bombings rage, and decency is held hostage to vicious character traits. In unfolding the Erich Maria Remarque novel, producer and director have been long on 'heart' and 'sentiment' and the result is a bitter-sweet love story.

The story is somewhat slow in development. Orin Jannings opens his screenplay with the hero (John Gavin) on the Russian front under the cloud of defeat in 1944. The wretchedness of modern war, the compassion and pity felt by the better type of German soldier, is established before the boy gets his long-delayed furlough and goes off to his native town, only to find his home is rubble and his parents disappeared.

Nearly all the action comprises the experiences of the furloughed soldier: with the townspeople, the Nazis and the Gestapo as counterpoint to his budding romance and hurry-up marriage to the girl (Lilo Pulver) and the denouement comes back at the Russian front.

The film may be remembered more for types than performances. There is a mad air-raid warden (Alexander Engel), a Jew hiding in a Catholic church tower (Charles Regnier) and a Teutonic hellion (Dorothea Wieck).
□ 1958: Nomination: Best Sound

....

■ TIN MEN

1987, 112 MINS, US ◇ ▼ ⊙
Dir Barry Levinson   *Prod* Mark Johnson   *Scr* Barry Levinson   *Ph* Peter Sova   *Ed* Stu Linder   *Mus* David Steele, Andy Cox   *Art Dir* Peter Jamison
● Richard Dreyfuss, Danny DeVito, Barbara Hershey, John Mahoney, Jackie Gayle, Stanley Brock (Touchstone)

The improbable tale of a pair of feuding aluminum siding salesmen, *Tin Men* winds up as bountiful comedy material in the skillful hands of writer-director Barry Levinson.

Film is packed with laughs, thanks to taut scripting and superb character depictions by Richard Dreyfuss, Danny DeVito and a fascinating troupe of sidekicks. These fast-buck hustlers collectively fashion a portrait of superficial greed so pathetic it soars to a level of black humor.

Central storyline finds Dreyfuss and DeVito tangling from the start after an accident damages both of their Cadillacs. Conflict between the two strangers – who don't find out until later they're both tin men – escalates to the point where Dreyfuss seeks to get even by wooing DeVito's unhappy wife (Barbara Hershey) into bed.

While each of the tin men is revealed as a compelling, off-center type in his own right, the one played by Jackie Gayle especially shines.

....

■ TIN PAN ALLEY

1940, 94 MINS, US
Dir Walter Lang   *Prod* Kenneth Macgowan
Scr Robert Ellis, Helen Logan   *Ph* Leon Shamroy
Ed Walter Thompson   *Mus* Alfred Newman
● Alice Faye, Betty Grable, Jack Oakie, John Payne, Allen Jenkins, Esther Ralston (20th Century-Fox)

Tyrone Power and Don Ameche were originally set for the top honors with Alice Faye, but casting assignments necessitated shifts of Jack Oakie and John Payne into the Power-Ameche slots, and addition of Betty Grable. Hays Office also stepped in and required extended cutting of the harem number, nixing what was claimed a too vivid display of showgirls' torsos. Particularly efficient job of cutting in this sequence retains all of the entertainment, and speeds things up in what might have developed into a slowdown spot.

Story carries background of the noisy but colorful stretch of 46th Street and 8th Avenue, headquartering successful and shoe-string song publishers in 1915. Oakie is a typical breezy ex-vaudevillian, teamed with tunesmith-ambitious Payne in a publishing venture. The impecunious pair hit the jackpot with a pop tune, and swing into swank offices, with main song-plugging end handled by Faye, half of a sister act who warms up to Payne. But there's the inevitable romantic split. Faye hopes to London to become a music hall sensation with Grable.

In addition to infectious and solid entertainment factors, *Tin Pan Alley* focuses attention on the Edgar Leslie-Archie Gottler hit of 1917, 'America I Love You'. Other old favorites brought back for renewed interest include 'Goodbye Broadway, Hello France', 'K-K-Katy', 'Moonlight Bay', 'Honeysuckle Rose' and 'Shiek of Araby'. New tune 'You Say the Sweetest Things (Baby)', by Mack Gordon and Harry Warren, is enhanced by extended production montage.

Oakie provides a standout characterization as the free-and-easy vaudevillian, generating plenty of laughs with his mugging lines and situations that highlight his abilities. Faye is highlighted as the senior member of the sister act, and carries most of the singing burden to topmost effect. Grable displays her shapeliness in a series of abbreviated and eyeful costumes, although the camera in other respects is sometimes none too flattering; and Payne catches attention with his serious-minded portrayal of the ambitious song publisher and suitor in the romantic sequences.
□ 1940: Best Score

....

■ TIN STAR, THE

1957, 92 MINS, US ▼
Dir Anthony Mann   *Prod* William Perlberg, George Seaton   *Scr* Dudley Nichols   *Ph* Loyal Griggs
Ed Alma Macrorie   *Mus* Elmer Bernstein   *Art Dir* Hal Pereira, J. MacMillan Johnson
● Henry Fonda, Anthony Perkins, Betsy Palmer, Michael Ray, Neville Brand, John McIntire (Perlsea/Paramount)

The Tin Star is a quality western that unfolds interestingly under the smooth direction of Anthony Mann, who draws top performances from cast. Screenplay [from a story by Barney Slater and Joel Kane] centers around Anthony Perkins' insistence upon keeping his sheriff's badge despite the pleading of his sweetheart to abandon hazards of the job, and Henry Fonda, a former lawman turned human bounty hunter, reluctantly teaching him the tricks of the trade.

Fonda gives his character telling authority as he waits in a small western town for a reward check, then stays on to help the over-

anxious young sheriff. Perkins asserts himself forcibly, his nemesis being Neville Brand, capable as a gun-handy bully who nearly forces him to back down in his authority.
□ 1957: Nomination: Best Original Story & Screenplay

....

■ TIP ON A DEAD JOCKEY

(UK: Time for Action)

1957, 98 MINS, US
Dir Richard Thorpe   *Prod* Edwin H. Knopf
Scr Charles Lederer   *Ph* George J. Folsey   *Ed* Ben Lewis   *Mus* Miklos Rozsa   *Art Dir* William A. Horning, Hans Peters
● Robert Taylor, Dorothy Malone, Gia Scala, Martin Gabel, Marcel Dalio, Jack Lord (M-G-M)

Once this *Jockey* spurs up momentum, film shapes as a solid, satisfactory action picture. However, plots dealing with war-weary pilots who have lost their nerve have an overfamiliar ring and smart, updated dialogue by Charles Lederer, in adapting Irwin Shaw's *New Yorker* tale, doesn't entirely dispel the familiar.

In brittle, cosmopolitan expatriate society of Madrid, Robert Taylor is an ex-pilot, afraid of emotional entanglements because his war job was sending pilots to their deaths. He's now eking out a precarious existence on the fringes of Spain's precarious economy. Offbeat title reflects this, when he loses his entire bankroll on a horse-race in which his jockey is killed in a spill.

Dorothy Malone is his wife, fighting to regain his love after he requests a divorce. To help raise coin for war buddy Jack Lord, and Lord's lovely Spanish wife (Gia Scala) Taylor undertakes a currency-smuggling caper proposed by sinister Martin Gabel. Here, film picks up tempo, especially in chase sequences involving various Mediterranean police authorities.

....

■ TITANIC

1953, 97 MINS, US
Dir Jean Negulesco   *Prod* Charles Brackett
Scr Charles Brackett, Walter Reisch, Richard Breen
Ph Joe MacDonald   *Ed* Louis Loeffler   *Mus* Sol Kaplan
Art Dir Lyle R. Wheeler, Maurice Ransford
● Clifton Webb, Barbara Stanwyck, Robert Wagner, Audrey Dalton, Brian Aherne, Richard Basehart (20th Century-Fox)

The sinking of HMS *Titanic* in 1912 provides a factual basis for this screen drama reenacting the tragic voyage. Story line is built around fictional characters aboard the supposedly unsinkable British luxury liner when it started its maiden voyage from Southampton to NY on April 11 1912.

During the first half the film is inclined to dawdle and talk, but by the time the initial 45 or 50 minutes are out of the way, the impending disaster begins to take a firm grip on the imagination and builds a compelling expectancy.

Jean Negulesco's direction and the script really shine after the ship's bottom is opened by a jagged iceberg spur, bringing out the drama that lies in the confusion of shipwreck and passengers' reaction to certain doom. The records show that of the 2,229 persons aboard, only 712 escaped before the ship plunged to the bottom of the North Atlantic at 2:30 a.m., April15 1912.

Barbara Stanwyck and Clifton Webb do well by the principal roles in the fictional story. She is a wife trying to take her two children (Audrey Dalton and Harper Carter) away from the spoiling influence of a husband interested only in a superficial society life. A shipboard romance between Robert Wagner, a student returning to the states, and Dalton offer some pleasant, touching moments. Brian Aherne is excellent as the ship's captain. Richard Basehart, a de-frocked priest

T

addicted to the bottle, makes his few moments stand out.
- [ ] 1953: Best Story & Screenplay.
- [ ] Nomination: Best B&W Art Direction

■ TITFIELD THUNDERBOLT, THE

1953, 84 MINS, UK ◇ ⑫
Dir Charles Crichton   *Prod* Michael Truman   *Scr* T.E.B. Clarke   *Ph* Douglas Slocombe   *Ed* Seth Holt   *Mus* Georges Auric   *Art Dir* C.P. Norman
● Stanley Holloway, George Relph, Naunton Wayne, John Gregson, Godfrey Tearle, Hugh Griffith (Ealing)

Titfield is a small English village which gets worked up when the government decides to close the unprofitable branch railway line. The vicar and the squire are both railway enthusiasts and are heartbroken at the news. The only ones cheered by the decision are the partners of a transport company who can see big profits by organizing a bus service. The railway enthusiasts, however, persuade the village tippler to provide the cash by telling him he will be able to start drinking far earlier if they install a buffet car on the train.

The *Thunderbolt* is the railway engine involved in the story. Once the basic situation is accepted, the entire yarn concentrates on the feuding between the rival factions with the opposition stopping at nothing to block the train service.

Stanley Holloway gives a polished performance as the village soak. George Relph does a fine job as the vicar, Naunton Wayne's contribution as the town clerk is in typical vein while John Gregson does nicely as the earnest squire. A gem from Godfrey Tearle as the bishop and a powerful performance by Hugh Griffith are among the strong characterizations.

■ T-MEN

1947, 91 MINS, US ⑫
Dir Anthony Mann   *Prod* Aubrey Schenck   *Scr* John C. Higgins   *Ph* John Alton   *Ed* Alfred De Gaetano, Fred Allen   *Mus* Paul Sawtell   *Art Dir* Edward C. Jewell
● Dennis O'Keefe, Mary Meade, Charles McGraw, Alfred Ryder, Wally Ford, June Lockhart (Reliance/Small)

Producer Edward Small has taken a closed case out of the Treasury Dept files, reenacted it in documentary fashion, and the result is *T-Men* – an entertaining action film. *March-of-Time* technique in the early reels flavors the footage with pungent realism that builds up to a suspenseful finish at the final fadeout.

Location scenes in Detroit, Los Angeles and several of its beach suburbs, may have cost a little more but the effect they achieve in verity can't be denied.

Preceded by a brief foreword delivered by a Treasury official, plot [suggested by a story by Virginia Kellogg] unfolds at a slow pace in its early stages. Later, however, it's obvious why the opening scenes were so carefully and meticulously outlined. Solution of every crime depends upon the most minute clues. When assembled in the proper sequence there's a crashing denouement. And so it is with *T-Men*. The final reel is a corker.

Dennis O'Keefe's characterization of the Treasury agent is finely drawn. He's almost Jimmy Cagneyish at times. Cast as his partner is Alfred Ryder. They're undercover agents assigned to break the 'Shanghai Paper Case'. Masquerading as mobsters they join a ring of liquor cutters in Detroit who are known to be using phony revenue stamps.
- [ ] 1947: Nomination: Best Sound

■ TOBACCO ROAD

1941, 91 MINS, US
Dir John Ford   *Prod* Darryl F. Zanuck   *Scr* Nunnally Johnson   *Ph* Arthur Miller   *Ed* Barbara McLean   *Mus* David Buttolph   *Art Dir* Richard Day, James Basevi

● Charles Grapewin, Marjorie Rambeau, Gene Tierney, Dana Andrews, Elizabeth Patterson, William Tracy (20th Century-Fox)

Tobacco Road as a motion picture falls far short of its promises. The sensational pulling elements of the 1933 play by Jack Kirkland from Erskine Caldwell's saga – the dialog and the low-life manners of its people – have been deleted, altered or attenuated to the point of dullness. What remains of the story is a back-in-the-hills comedy of shiftless folk.

Tobacco Road emerges with a trite comedy theme about the dubious efforts, chiefly larcenous, by which old Jeeter hopes, through act of Providence or dishonest opportunity, to raise $100 for the annual rent of the old farm.

For all of its dehydration *Tobacco Road* is told with a canny camera. Ford is more intent on story telling than in his recent productions.

Chief load of the acting falls on Charley Grapewin, whose Jeeter is a fine characterization within the revised limitations. He plays the old fellow for comedy and sympathy, revealing also a lazy shrewdness. Elizabeth Patterson is Ma Ada, and brings out the sullen hopelessness of the role.

■ TO BE OR NOT TO BE

1942, 99 MINS, US ⑫
Dir Ernst Lubitsch   *Prod* Ernst Lubitsch   *Scr* Edwin Justus Mayer   *Ph* Rudolph Mate   *Ed* Dorothy Spencer   *Mus* Werner R. Heymann   *Art Dir* Vincent Korda
● Carole Lombard, Jack Benny, Robert Stack, Lionel Atwill, Sig Ruman, Felix Bressart (Korda)

To Be or Not to Be, co-starring Carole Lombard and Jack Benny, under expert guidance of Ernst Lubitsch, is absorbing drama with farcical trimmings. It's an acting triumph for Lombard, who delivers an effortless and highly effective performance that provides memorable finale to her brilliant screen career.

To Be is typically Lubitsch in dramatic setup and satirical by-play. He's responsible for the producer-director and original writer chores [with Melchior Lengyel], dovetailing all into a solid piece of entertainment. Story recounts the adventures of a legit stock company in Warsaw, before and during the Nazi invasion, from August 1939 to December 1941. Lombard is the femme lead, with husband Jack Benny a hammy matinee idol with penchant for playing *Hamlet*.

Lubitsch's guidance provides a tense dramatic pace with events developed deftly and logically throughout. The farcical episodes display Lubitsch in best form.
- [ ] 1942: Nomination: Best Scoring of a Dramatic Picture

■ TO BE OR NOT TO BE

1983, 108 MINS, US ◇ ⑫ ⊙
Dir Alan Johnson   *Prod* Mel Brooks   *Scr* Thomas Meehan, Ronny Graham   *Ph* Gerald Hirschfeld   *Ed* Alan Balsam   *Mus* John Morris   *Art Dir* Terence Marsh
● Mel Brooks, Anne Bancroft, Tim Matheson, Charles Durning, Jose Ferrer, James Haake (Brooksfilms)

With the solid farcical underpinning of Ernst Lubitsch's 1942 *To Be or Not to Be*, Mel Brooks' glossy remake of the original Carole Lombard-Jack Benny starrer is very funny stuff indeed.

Maintaining some of the dramatic core of the original, but played mostly for Brooks-style laughs, the convoluted tale of a Warsaw theatrical troupe that winds up saving the Polish underground during the Nazi occupation does have some potential hurdles to clear. Cute Nazis and roly-poly Gestapo officers hardly have universal lure.

Brooks sustains, with varying success, a full-fledged role as Frederick Bronski, vainglorious head of a tawdry theatrical company whose shows run the spectrum from cheap vaudeville turns to *Highlights from Hamlet*. Mainstay of the film is a superbly sustained comic performance by Anne Bancroft, as Bronski's wife, in the real-life Brooks couple's first tandem co-starring acting job.

Charles Durning is a standout as the buffoonish Gestapo topper and Bancroft's pseudo-seduction of him, and Nazi hireling Jose Ferrer, are among the pic's highpoints. Bancroft's sustained delights are not matched by Brooks, who seems to be trying too hard.
- [ ] 1983: Nomination: Best Supp. Actor (Charles Durning)

■ TOBRUK

1966, 107 MINS, US ◇ ⑫
Dir Arthur Hiller   *Prod* Gene Corman   *Scr* Leo V. Gordon   *Ph* Russell Harlan   *Ed* Robert C. Jones   *Mus* Bronislau Kaper   *Art Dir* Alexander Golitzen, Henry Bumstead
● Rock Hudson, George Peppard, Nigel Green, Guy Stockwell, Jack Watson, Norman Rossington (Gibraltar/Universal)

Tobruk is a colorful, hard-hitting World War II melodrama with plenty of guts and suspense to hold the action buff. Rock Hudson heads the four-name star roster but actually comes out third best to George Peppard and Nigel Green in interesting characterizations.

Screenplay has a serviceable plot twist as it projects the protagonists on a suicidal mission in the North African war of 1942. Daring plan calls for a British column of 90, composed of commandos and German-born Jews who have come over to the Allies, to form a special attack unit to cross the Libyan Desert to Tobruk, Mediterranean seaport in the hands of 50,000 German and Italian troops. Once there, they are to hold its key fortified positions pending arrival of a British naval force, and blow up the gigantic German fuel bunkers upon which Rommel depends for his push to the Suez canal.

Arthur Hiller's realistic direction makes the most of the premise, both in the eight-day desert trek and approach and invasion of Tobruk.
- [ ] 1967: Nomination: Best Sound Effects

■ TO CATCH A THIEF

1955, 103 MINS, US ◇ ⑫ ⊙
Dir Alfred Hitchcock   *Prod* Alfred Hitchcock   *Scr* John Michael Hayes   *Ph* Robert Burks   *Ed* George Tomasini   *Mus* Lyn Murray   *Art Dir* Hal Pereira, Joseph MacMillan Johnson
● Cary Grant, Grace Kelly, Jessie Royce Landis, John Williams, Charles Vanel, Brigitte Auber (Paramount)

Cary Grant is a reformed jewel thief, once known as 'The Cat', but now living quietly in a Cannes hilltop villa. When burglaries occur that seem to bear his old trademark, he has to catch the thief to prove his innocence, a chore in which he is assisted by Grace Kelly, rich American girl, her mother, Jessie Royce Landis, and insurance agent John Williams. While a suspense thread is present, director Alfred Hitchcock doesn't emphasize it, letting the yarn play lightly for comedy more than thrills.

Grant gives his role his assured style of acting, meaning the dialog and situations benefit. Kelly, too, dresses up the sequences in more ways than one.

Support from Landis and Williams is firstrate, both being major assets to the entertainment in their way with a line or a look.
- [ ] 1955: Best Color Cinematography.
- [ ] Nominations: Best Color Costume Design, Color Art Direction

TO HAVE AND HAVE NOT

1944, 100 MINS, US ⓥ ⊙
Dir Howard Hawks   *Prod* Howard Hawks   *Scr* Jules
Furthman, William Faulkner   *Ph* Sidney Hickox
Ed Christian Nyby   *Mus* Leo Forbstein   *Art Dir* Charles
Novi
● Humphrey Bogart, Walter Brennan, Lauren Bacall,
Dolores Moran, Hoagy Carmichael, Marcel Dalio
(Warner)

With an eye to the lucrative box-office of its
Casablanca, the brothers Warner turned out an-
other epic of similar genre in a none-too-literal
adaptation of Ernest Hemingway's novel *To
Have and Have Not*. There are enough similari-
ties in both films to warrant more than cursory
attention, even to the fact that Humphrey
Bogart is starred in each, though this story of
Vichy France collaborationism is not up to
Warners' melodramatic story standards.

Though *Have Not* was one of Hemingway's
inferior novels – whose theme of rum-running
was certainly antithetical to the film's story of
French collaboration – it affords considerable
picture interest because of some neat characterizations. And it introduces Lauren Bacall,
in her first part. She's an arresting personality. She can slink, brother, and no fooling!

Yarn deals with the intrigue centering
around the Caribbean island of Martinique,
owned by France, and the plotting that ensued there prior to its ultimate capitulation
to Allied pressure. Bogart is an American
skipper there who hires out his boat to anyone who has the price. When he becomes involved in the local Free French movement,
the story's pattern becomes woven around
him, at times in cops-and-robbers fashion.

Warners give the pic its usually nifty productional accoutrements, and that includes
casting, musical scoring and Howard Hawks'
direction but the basic story is too unsteady.

Bogart is in his usual metier, a tough guy
who, no less, has the facility of making a
dame go for him, instead of he for her. That's
where Bacall comes in. Walter Brennan, as
Bogart's drunken sidekick; Dolores Moran, as
the film's second looker; and songwriter
Hoagy Carmichael have lesser roles that they
handle to advantage.

TO HELL AND BACK

1955, 106 MINS, US ◇ ⓥ
Dir Jesse Hibbs   *Prod* Aaron Rosenberg   *Scr* Gil Doud
Ph Maury Gertsman   *Ed* Edward Curtiss   *Mus* Joseph
Gershenson (sup.)
● Audie Murphy, Marshall Thompson, Charles Drake,
Gregg Palmer, Jack Kelly, Susan Kohner (Universal)

This biopic on the World War II exploits that
made Audie Murphy the most decorated soldier in American history is gripping drama
with the original playing himself. The picturization of Murphy's autobiography has no
blustering heroics for the sake of derring-do
and the action shown is that of a modest,
unassuming young man.

He gets into the army in 1942 at 18. In
1943, Murphy became a replacement in
Company B, 15th Infantry Regiment, Third
Division, 7th Army, in North Africa, and
served with the unit throughout the war in
Tunisia, Italy, France, Germany and Austria.
During that time he rose from PFC to company commander, was wounded three times,
personally killed 240 Germans, and was one
of the only two soldiers left in the original
company at the end of the war. His decorations total 24, from the Congressional Medal
of Honor on down.

Among some of the more outstanding sequences are the knocking out of a Nazi ma-
chinegun nest from a farmhouse near Anzio,
the crazed attack on another Nazi emplace-
ment in France after one of his buddies has
been killed, and Murphy's almost single-
handed blasting of a German tank group.

Aside from the fighting, footage works in
some touching moments between battles during too-short leaves.

TO KILL A MOCKINGBIRD

1962, 129 MINS, US ⓥ ⊙
Dir Robert Mulligan   *Prod* Alan J. Pakula   *Scr* Horton
Foote   *Ph* Russell Harlan   *Ed* Aaron Stell   *Mus* Elmer
Bernstein   *Art Dir* Henry Bumstead
● Gregory Peck, Mary Badham, Phillip Alford, John
Megna, Robert Duvall, Brock Peters (Universal)

Harper Lee's highly regarded first novel has
been artfully and delicately translated to the
screen. Horton Foote's trenchant screenplay,
Robert Mulligan's sensitive and instinctively
observant direction and a host of exceptional
performances are all essential threads in the
rich, provocative fabric.

As it unfolds on the screen, *To Kill a
Mockingbird* bears with it, oddly enough, alternating overtones of Faulkner, Twain, Steinbeck,
Hitchcock and an *Our Gang* comedy. A telling
indictment of racial prejudice in the Deep
South, it is also a charming tale of the emergence of two youngsters from the realm of wild
childhood fantasy to the horizon of maturity, responsibility, compassion and social insight.

It is the story of a wise, gentle, soft-spoken
Alabama lawyer (Gregory Peck) entrusted
with the formidable dual chore of defending a
Negro falsely accused of rape while raising his
own impressionable, imaginative, motherless
children in a hostile, terrifying environment
of bigotry and economic depression.

For Peck, it is an especially challenging
role, requiring him to project through a veneer of civilized restraint and resigned, rational compromise the fires of social indignation
and humanitarian concern that burn within
the character. He not only succeeds, but
makes it appear effortless, etching a portrayal of strength, dignity, intelligence.

But by no means is this entirely, or even
substantially, Peck's film. Two youngsters just
about steal it away, although the picture
marks their screen bows. Both nine-year-old
Mary Badham and 13-year-old Phillip Alford,
each of whom hails from the South, make
striking debuts as Peck's two irrepressible,
mischievous, ubiquitous, irresistibly childish
children.

There are some top-notch supporting performances. Especially sharp and effective are
Frank Overton, Estelle Evans, James
Anderson and Robert Duvall. Brock Peters
has an outstanding scene as the innocent, ill-
fated Negro on trial for his life.

☐ 1962: Best Actor (Gregory Peck), Adapted
Screenplay, B&W Art Direction.
☐ Nominations: Best Picture, Director, Supp.
Actress (Mary Badham), B&W
Cinematography, Original Music Score

TO KILL A PRIEST

1988, 116 MINS, FRANCE/US ◇ ⓥ ⊙
Dir Agnieszka Holland   *Prod* Jean-Pierre Alessandri
(exec.)   *Scr* Agnieszka Holland, Jean-Yves Pitoun
Ph Adam Holender   *Ed* Herve de Luze   *Mus* Georges
Delerue, Zbigniew Preisner   *Art Dir* Emile Ghigo
● Christopher Lambert, Ed Harris, Joanne Whalley, Joss
Ackland, David Suchet, Tim Roth (JP/FR3/Columbia)

Polish by subject and director, French by official production and shooting locations,
American by soundtrack and partial financing, and transatlantic in casting, *To Kill a
Priest* is an ambitious political thriller emp-
tied of substance by its heterogeneous components and hybrid dramaturgy.

Backed by Columbia under the brief David
Puttnam regime, this is a fictional recreation
of the murder of Polish priest Jerzy
Popieluszko by security police in 1984. But
exiled Polish helmer Agnieszka Holland's
recreation on French soil of her homeland under the banner of Solidarity and the boot of

martial law lacks a sense of time and place, a
socio-political density.

Central weakness is the casting of France's
linguistically versatile Christopher Lambert,
playing a rather bland 'charismatic' priest
and Solidarity apostle, and America's Ed
Harris, not quite the right stuff as the Polish
militia officer who engineers and executes the
plot to assassinate him. The Cain and Abel
theme is spelled out literally in Joan Baez'
bookending theme song.

Film picks up some steam and dramatic interest in the second half, though by this time
one's empathy or antipathy for the principals
of the story has been severely tried.

TOKYO JOE

1949, 87 MINS, US ⓥ ⊙
Dir Stuart Heisler   *Prod* Robert Lord   *Scr* Cyril Hume,
Bertram Millhauser   *Ph* Charles Lawton Jr   *Ed* Viola
Lawrence   *Mus* George Antheil
● Humphrey Bogart, Alexander Knox, Florence Marley,
Sessue Hayakawa (Columbia/Santana)

Tokyo Joe has been given a documentary flavor
by much process footage shot in Tokyo. This
authetic touch serves as an excellent background for the unfolding of the plot's meller
elements, and Stuart Heisler's direction develops a neat air of anticipation that climaxes
in a gripping, exciting fight finale.

Story [from one by Steve Fisher, adapted by
Walter Doniger] opens with Bogart returning
to Tokyo, where he owns a night club, after
service in the war. He finds the wife he had
left has married another. Out to win her
back, Bogart starts a small freight airline,
and soon becomes involved in smuggling war
criminals back into Japan.

Alexander Knox is quietly effective as the
man who replaces Bogart as Florence Marly's
husband. Marly does an adequate job of her
role.

TO LIVE AND DIE IN L.A.

1985, 116 MINS, US ◇ ⓥ ⊙
Dir William Friedkin   *Prod* Irving H. Levin
Scr William Friedkin, Gerald Petievich   *Ph* Robby Muller
Ed Scott Smith   *Mus* Wang Chung   *Art Dir* Lilly Kilvert
● William L. Petersen, Willem Dafoe, John Pankow,
Debra Feuer, John Turturro, Darlanne Fluegel (United
Artists/New Century/SLM)

To Live and Die in L.A. looks like a rich man's
Miami Vice. William Friedkin's evident attempt to fashion a West Coast equivalent of
his [1971] *The French Connection* is engrossing
and diverting enough on a moment-to-moment basis but is overtooled.

Friedkin leaves no doubt about his technical
abilities, as he has created another memorable car chase and, with the considerable assistance of cinematographer Robby Muller,
has offered up any number of startling and
original shots of the characters inhabiting
weirdly ugly-beautiful LA cityscapes.

William L. Petersen plays a highly capable
Secret Service agent who decides to nail a notorious counterfeiter responsible for the murder of his partner.

Petersen's search leads him into the kinky,
high-tech world of Willem Dafoe, a supremely
talented and self-confident artist whose
phony $20 bills look magnificent and whose
tentacles reach into surprising areas of the
criminal underworld, both high and low-class.

Friedkin keeps dialog to a minimum, but
what conversation there is proves wildly overloaded with streetwise obscenities, so much so
that it becomes something of a joke.

TOMB OF LIGEIA, THE

1965, 80 MINS, UK/US ◇ ⓥ ⊙
Dir Roger Corman   *Prod* Pat Green   *Scr* Robert Towne
Ph Arthur Grant   *Ed* Alfred Cox   *Mus* Kenneth V.

Jones   *Art Dir* Colin Southcott
● Vincent Price, Elizabeth Shepherd, John Westbrook, Oliver Johnston, Derek Francis, Richard Vernon (American International/Alta Vista)

More Poe but no go about sums up *The Tomb of Ligeia*, a tedious and talky addition to American International's series of chillpix based on tales by the 19th century US author. Roger Corman produced and directed a script that resists analysis and lacks credibility, with all performances blah monotones and color lensing of no help. Widescreen pic tries serious supernatural approach minimizing gore angles, but it doesn't jell.

Amid ruins of English abbey lives widower Vincent Price, near grave of first wife Ligeia buried under strange circumstances some years before.

Price disappoints in attempt to project character's inner struggle to escape spell since no one knows why he acts kooky. Elizabeth Shepherd vacillates between too-stiff patrician elegance and unconvincing terror in role of second wife who is subjected to endless repetitions of brief, ineffective horror bits involving black cat, saucer of milk, and dead fox.

....

■ **TOM BROWN'S SCHOOL DAYS**
(US: Adventures at Rugby)

1940, 88 MINS, US ⓥ
Dir Robert Stevenson   *Prod* Gene Towne, Graham Baker   *Scr* Walter Ferris, Frank Cavett, Gene Towne, Graham Baker   *Ph* Nicholas Musuraca   *Ed* William Hamilton   *Mus* Anthony Collins   *Art Dir* Van Nest Polglase
● Cedric Hardwicke, Freddie Bartholomew, Jimmy Lydon, Josephine Hutchinson, Billy Halop, Polly Moran (The Play's The Thing/RKO)

Much can be said for the treatment in this edition of the Thomas Hughes yarn. While remaining faithful to the spirit of the original, it contrives to vitalize the action and humanize the characters. Thus young Tom's confused terror among the milling cruelties of the young hellions on his first time away from home is understandable and compelling. The terrible seriousness of his scrapes, his fights and youthful crises are immediate and vivid.

Although *Tom Brown* is not a lavish production, it is sympathetically and skillfully made, with many touching moments and an excellent cast. It alters the emphasis somewhat from the development of the boy to the character of the headmaster, Arnold. But that should bother only a few purists. It probably results in a better picture, since Cedric Hardwicke, who plays the wise and kindly teacher, is much better qualified to carry a story than is any Hollywood prodigy.

Hardwicke's performance is one of the best he has ever given on the screen. While maintaining the schoolmaster's surface severity, he clearly indicates the underlying sympathy, tolerance, quiet humor and steadfast courage. In the title part, Jimmy Lydon is believable and moving in the early portions, but too young for the final moments. Freddie Bartholomew is sincere and convincing as Tom's sidekick, while Josephine Hutchinson's lustrous quality makes the role of the headmaster's wife seem too brief. Billy Halop is a properly sadistic bully.

....

■ **TOM BROWN'S SCHOOLDAYS**

1951, 96 MINS, UK
Dir Gordon Parry   *Prod* George Minter   *Scr* Noel Langley   *Ph* C. Pennington-Richards, Raymond Sturgess   *Ed* Kenneth Heeley-Ray   *Mus* Richard Addinsell   *Art Dir* Frederick Pusey
● John Howard Davies, Robert Newton, Diana Wynyard, Francis De Wolff, Kathleen Byron, Hermione Baddeley (Renown)

England's classic story of public school life is

acted with great sincerity by a name cast, but script and direction go all out to emphasize the obvious emotional tear-jerker angles.

Almost the entire script hinges on the popular angle of the new boy versus the bully. John Howard Davies makes Tom Brown a lovable and sympathetic youngster without a shade of priggishness. Robert Newton as the reforming headmaster, Dr Arnold, fills his role with commendable restraint.

The plot, of course, is dominated by the schoolboys, and there is a standout performance by John Forrest as the sneering, bullying Flashman.

Special facilities having been granted to film this in Rugby School, the authenticity of the background cannot be questioned.

....

■ **TOM HORN**

1980, 98 MINS, US ◇ ⓥ
Dir William Wiard, [James William Guercio]   *Prod* Fred Weintraub   *Scr* Thomas McGuane, Bud Shrake   *Ph* John Alonzo   *Ed* George Grenville   *Mus* Ernest Gold   *Art Dir* Ron Hobbs
● Steve McQueen, Richard Farnsworth, Linda Evans, Billy Green Bush, Slim Pickens, Elisha Cook (Warner/First Artists)

Steve McQueen's *Tom Horn* is a sorry ending to the once high hopes of the star-studded founding of First Artists Prods.

If rumor be true, McQueen did not want to do *Horn* as his third pic to fulfill his founder's commitment, but was forced into it. True or not, he certainly looks like he's walking through the part.

Imagine a film that opens up with dialog that can't be heard at all, then proceeds to build up to a fistfight that's never seen, that cuts away to sunsets to fill in other scenes that have no dramatic point, and you have just the beginning of what's wrong with *Tom Horn*.

Pic [from Horn's *Life of Tom Horn, Government Scout and Interpreter*] takes up in the final days of the life of the legendary Western hero. And the only plus at all is a couple of good, bloody shoot-out sequences.

....

■ **TOM JONES**

1963, 128 MINS, UK ◇ ⓥ ⊙
Dir Tony Richardson   *Prod* Tony Richardson   *Scr* John Osborne   *Ph* Walter Lassally   *Ed* Antony Gibbs   *Mus* John Addison   *Art Dir* Ralph Brinton
● Albert Finney, Susannah York, Hugh Griffith, Edith Evans, Joan Greenwood, Diane Cilento (Woodfall)

Based on Henry Fielding's enduring novel, story is set in Somerset, a West Country lush county, and in London during the 18th century. Hero is Tom Jones (Albert Finney), born in suspicious circumstances, with a maidservant dismissed because she is suspected of being his unwed mother. He is brought up by Squire Allworthy (George Devine) and leads a rollicking life in which women play a prominent part before he finally escapes the gallows after a frameup.

The somewhat sprawling, bawdy and vivid screenplay of John Osborne provides some meaty acting opportunities and the thesps grasp their chances with vigorous zest. Finney slips through his adventures with an ebullient gusto that keeps the overlong film on its toes for most of the time. Hugh Griffith and Edith Evans as Squire Western and his sister ham disarmingly. Evans has some of the choicer cameos in the film.

Director Tony Richardson has occasionally pressed his luck with some over-deliberate arty camera bits. The music of John Addison is a trifle obtrusive and lacking in period style. An added bonus is Micheal MacLiammoir putting over occasional narration with smooth wit and perception.

□ 1963: Best Picture, Director, Adapted

Screenplay, Original Music Score.
□ Nominations: Best Actor (Albert Finney), Supp. Actor (Hugh Griffith), Supp. Actress (Diane Cilento, Dame Edith Evans, Joyce Redman), Color Art Direction

....

■ **TOMMY**

1975, 111 MINS, UK ◇ ⓥ ⊙
Dir Ken Russell   *Prod* Robert Stigwood   *Scr* Ken Russell   *Ph* Dick Bush   *Ed* Stuart Baird   *Mus* Pete Townshend, John Entwistle, Keith Moon   *Art Dir* John Clark
● Ann-Margret, Oliver Reed, Roger Daltrey, Elton John, Eric Clapton, Jack Nicholson (Columbia)

Ken Russell's filmization of *Tommy* is spectacular in nearly every way. The enormous appeal of the original 1969 record album by The Who has been complemented in a superbly added visual dimension.

Young Tommy, traumatized when he sees his real father Robert Powell accidentally killed in an argument with stepfather Oliver Reed as mother Ann-Margret watches in horror, grows up amid an atmosphere of cruel exploitation and abuse. Even his miraculous recovery, and subsequent delusions of grandeur, simply extend the ripoff.

Among the cameo players, Elton John plays the pinball wizard and Eric Clapton is well featured as a preacher and Tina Turner virtually rips the screen apart with her animalistic Acid Queen.

□ 1975: Nominations: Best Actress (Ann-Margret), Adapted Score

....

■ **TOM SAWYER**

1930, 82 MINS, US ⓥ
Dir John Cromwell   *Prod* Louis D. Lighton   *Scr* Sam Mintz, Grover Jones, William Slavens McNutt   *Ph* Charles Lang   *Ed* Alyson Shaffer   *Art Dir* Bernard Herzbrun, Robert O'Dell
● Jackie Coogan, Junior Durkin, Mitzi Green, Lucien Littlefield, Tully Marshall, Clara Blandick (Paramount)

The Mark Twain classic has been shrewdly molded to the screen. It somehow crystallizes the essence of a work that is timeless in its human appeal.

The picture is a real achievement for its director, John Cromwell, one of the stage directors who crashed Hollywood. Cromwell had a wild desire to do *Tom Sawyer* and the finished work has all the marks of a labor of love.

Picture was originally designed as the first of a series to bring the younger generation back to the talking screen. Story is splendidly acted by a great group of youngsters. Young Jackie Coogan plays Tom to the life but the secondary role of Junior Durkin as Huckleberry Finn [is also appealing]. Little Mitzi Green is rather lost in the child part of Becky Thatcher, built up somewhat for the film.

....

■ **TOM SAWYER**

1973, 100 MINS, US ◇ ⓥ
Dir Don Taylor   *Prod* Arthur P. Jacobs   *Scr* Robert B. Sherman, Richard M. Sherman   *Ph* Frank Stanley   *Ed* Marion Rothman   *Mus* Robert B. Sherman, Richard M. Sherman   *Art Dir* Philip Jefferies
● Johnny Whitaker, Celeste Holm, Warren Oates, Jeff East, Jodie Foster, Lucille Benson (Reader's Digest/United Artists)

The strikingly handsome $2.5 million production, directed with discreet and appealing folksiness by Don Taylor, boasts an excellent cast, including Johnny Whitaker as Sawyer and Celeste Holm just sensational as Aunt Polly. Robert B. and Richard M. Sherman's script, music and lyrics maintain an all-age interest.

Jeff East is most effective as Huck Finn, making of that character an intriguing and contrasting personality. Jodie Foster is great as Becky Thatcher.

Holm returns to the screen in personal triumph. Few actresses project so well warmth-with-backbone, and a ladylike gentility not immune to kicking up the heels occasionally.

Also superbly cast is Warren Oates as Muff Potter, the likeable boozy philosopher. Oates and Holm keep the film together for older audiences.

□ 1973: Nominations: Best Costume Design, Art Direction, Adapted Score

....

■ TOM THUMB

1958, 92 MINS, US ◇ ⓦ
Dir George Pal   *Prod* George Pal   *Scr* Ladislas Fodor
Ph Georges Perinal   *Ed* Frank Clarke   *Mus* Douglas Gamley, Ken Jones   *Art Dir* Elliot Scott
● Russ Tamblyn, Alan Young, Terry-Thomas, Peter Sellers, Jessie Matthews, June Thorburn (M-G-M)

The only thing lower case about this production is the Metro spelling of *tom thumb*. Otherwise, film is top-drawer, a comic fairy tale with music that stacks up alongside some of the Disney classics. It is really a musical comedy. It has five good songs, two of them by Peggy Lee.

The screenplay, from the Grimm Bros fairy tale, is as simple as it can be. A childless couple (Bernard Miles and Jessie Matthews) get a miniature son (Russ Tamblyn) when woodcutter Miles spares a special tree in the forest surrounding their home, and is rewarded by the Forest Queen (June Thorburn).

Complications in the story come from tom's size, only five and one-half inches. There are villains (Terry-Thomas and Peter Sellers) attempting to use tom for their own evil purposes. There is romance between Alan Young, a neighbor, and Thorburn, finally unbewitched from a fairy queen to a real, live girl.

Highlights of the production are the musical numbers and the special effects. Alex Romero staged the dance numbers, in which Tamblyn does some of the most athletic and exciting dancing he has had a chance at since *Seven Brides for Seven Brothers*. Georges Perinal's photography, with special effects by Tom Howard, catches all the fun and liveliness of the staging. The miniature work was done in Hollywood, based on George Pal's Puppetoon figures, and the life-size work in London.

□ 1958: Best Special Effects

....

■ TONIGHT FOR SURE

1962, 69 MINS, US ◇ ⓦ
Dir Francis Coppola   *Prod* Francis Coppola
Scr Francis Coppola   *Ph* Jack Hill   *Mus* Carmine Coppola   *Art Dir* Albert Locatelli, Barbara Cooper
● Don Kenney, Karl Schanzer, Virginia Gordon, Marti Renfro, Sandy Silver, Linda Gibson (Searchlight)

Francis Coppola's first feature film effort, the nudie pic *Tonight for Sure*, was released by Premier Pictures in 1962, thus preceding director's 'official' first film, *Dementia 13*, by at least a year.

There are really only two ways to approach viewing such a piece of juvenalia: to look for precocious signs of talent in the then-22-year-old filmmaker, and to consider its position in the late, unlamented 'nudie' genre.

Surprisingly, unlike most of the long-forgotten 'adults only' features of the period, *Tonight for Sure* is chock full of nudity.

Storyline is ridiculous, to be sure. Two definitive dirty old men who fashion themselves as moral crusaders slip into a Hollywood burlesque house to plot the cessation of the lewd, indecent behavior transpiring therein.

In the meantime, they relate how they've each arrived at their righteous beliefs. Two yarns are cut in with stripteases being performed at the club. Predictably, it all ends with forces of puritanism raiding the joint.

....

■ TONY ROME

1967, 110 MINS, US ◇ ⓦ
Dir Gordon M. Douglas   *Prod* Aaron Rosenberg
Scr Richard L. Breen   *Ph* Joseph Biroc   *Ed* Robert Simpson   *Mus* Billy May   *Art Dir* Jack Martin Smith, James Roth
● Frank Sinatra, Jill St John, Richard Conte, Gena Rowlands, Simon Oakland, Jeffrey Lynn (20th Century-Fox/Arcola-Millfield)

Tony Rome is a flip gumshoe on the Miami scene, with a busy, heavily-populated script, zesty Gordon Douglas direction, and solid production values.

Marvin H. Albert's novel, *Miami Mayhem*, is scripted into a fast-moving whodunit which, per se, is far less intriguing than the individual scenes en route to climax. Credit Frank Sinatra's excellent style, and the production elements, for pulling it off.

Apart from some inside gags, including an overplugging of the beer with which Sinatra has a blurb tie-in, there is an abundance of double-entendre dialog which in reality can be taken only one way.

....

■ TOO FAR TO GO

1982, 100 MINS, US ◇ ⓦ
Dir Fielder Cook   *Prod* Chiz Schultz   *Scr* William Hanley   *Ph* Walter Lassally   *Ed* Eric Albertson
Mus Elizabeth Swados   *Art Dir* Leon Munier
● Michael Moriarty, Blythe Danner, Glenn Close, Ken Kercheval, Josef Sommer, Kathryn Walker (Sea Cliff/Polytel)

Produced for and originally broadcast in 1979 over network television, *Too Far to Go* is an affecting feature film dealing with marital breakup.

Scripted from stories by John Updike, pic utilizes witty, arch dialog in limning the separation and divorce of New England couple Richard and Joan Maple (Michael Moriarty and Blythe Danner). Flashbacks concisely detail happier times for the duo, with sexual matters ranging from infidelity to cessation of marital relations for several years.

Lead thesps shine, particularly Danner as the stronger of the couple. Moriarty is generally impressive within the limitations of a forced accent.

Outstanding in brief support are Josef Sommer as Richard's accountant, laying down the law on alimony, Kathryn Walker as a chatty, family friend, Doran Clark as the eldest daughter – a beautiful, very natural actress, and Thomas Hill, as Joan's psychiatrist.

....

■ TOO HOT TO HANDLE

See: The Marrying Man

....

■ TOO HOT TO HANDLE

1938, 106 MINS, US ⓦ
Dir Jack Conway   *Prod* Lawrence Weingarten
Scr Laurence Stallings, John Lee Mahin   *Ph* Harold Rosson   *Ed* Frank Sullivan   *Mus* Franz Waxman
Art Dir Cedric Gibbons, Daniel B. Cathcart, Edwin B. Willis
● Clark Gable, Myrna Loy, Walter Pidgeon, Walter Connolly, Leo Carrillo, Marjorie Main (M-G-M)

Adventures of a newsreel cameraman are the basis for this Clark Gable-Myrna Loy co-starrer. It's a blazing action thriller aimed as a follow-up to same pair's click in *Test Pilot* (1938). It has driving excitement, crackling dialog, glittering performances and inescapable romantic pull.

The story is one of those familiar Hollywood triangle affairs, with Gable and Walter Pidgeon as the sizzling rival newsreelers and Loy the he-man's ideal who entangles their already frenzied competition. When Gable hijacks Pidgeon's girl and they both land in the doghouse through Pidgeon's efforts to get even, the girl goes to South America to search for her long-lost aviator brother.

Strange angle of the picture's implausibilities is that the story was written by Len Hammond, an executive of Fox Movietone newsreel, while Laurence Stallings co-author of the screenplay, is a former employee of the same outfit.

Best parts are the early sequences, all the way up to the sequence of a shipload of dynamite exploding directly underneath a tiny plane. Metro gives the picture one of its typically slick productions. Gable and Loy zoom through the leading parts with glittering persuasion.

....

■ TOO LATE BLUES

1962, 100 MINS, US
Dir John Cassavetes   *Prod* John Cassavetes   *Scr* John Cassavetes, Richard Carr   *Ph* Lionel Lindon   *Ed* Frank Bracht   *Mus* David Raksin   *Art Dir* Tambi Larsen
● Bobby Darin, Stella Stevens, Everett Chambers, Cliff Carnell, Seymour Cassel, Marilyn Clark (Paramount)

John Cassavetes' first Hollywood-made project shows a tendency to force casebook psychology on the characters at a loss of spontaneity. Thus an idealistic small-time jazz pianist and composer (Bobby Darin) loses his way when he is left by his girl due to a physically cowardly act. Used in an explanatory way there may be something psychologically right in this but it is somewhat too flat and contrived for acceptance in a film. Same goes for the flashy, good looking would-be singer, Stella Stevens.

Darin's group is shown playing engagements in orphanages and in a park where nobody comes. A chance for a record date is blown sky-high when Darin's early insistence on doing what he wants is compromised by his girl's quitting him after his cowardly actions in a pool room brawl. He becomes the gigolo of an aging woman but finds his spark dampened. He finally seeks out his old girl, now a tramp.

Film never makes it clear whether the Darin character truly has talent or whether he should accept what he has and do his best at it. Ambiguity also robs the pic of a lot of punch. Cassavetes shows at his best in party scenes where characters are deftly blocked in good natured 'getting-to-love-you' scenes.

Too Late Blues includes a neat jazz score by David Raksin. Dubbing for the musician-impersonating actors are Shelly Manne, Red Mitchell, Benny Carter, Uan Ramsey, Jimmy Bowles.

....

■ TOO LATE THE HERO

1970, 133 MINS, US ◇ ⓦ
Dir Robert Aldrich   *Prod* Robert Aldrich   *Scr* Robert Aldrich, Lukas Heller   *Ph* Joseph Biroc   *Ed* Michael Luciano   *Mus* Gerald Fried
● Michael Caine, Cliff Robertson, Henry Fonda, Ian Bannen, Harry Andrews, Denholm Elliott (ABC/Palomar)

An okay World War II melodrama [from a story by Robert Aldrich and Robert Sherman], featuring Michael Caine and Cliff Robertson as antagonists who come to respect each other in the course of destroying a Jaanese radio transmitter.

Robertson is introduced as a lazy Navy officer, specializing in Japanese translation. The British group, somewhat battle-weary and jaded in spirit, is headed by Harry Andrews, who outlines the mission to Robertson. The patrol, which must cross a sort of no-man's land where both Japanese and Allied soldiers occasionally exchange fire, comprises Robertson plus Denholm Elliott, as a weak, stupid, but curiously brave officer when it counted, and 12 enlisted men.

. . . .

■ TOO MANY CHEFS
See: Who Is Killing the Great Chefs of Europe?

. . . .

■ TOOTSIE

1982, 116 MINS, US ◇ ⑰ ⊙
Dir Sydney Pollack   *Prod* Sydney Pollack, Dick Richards
Scr Larry Gelbart, Murray Schisgal, [Elaine May]
Ph Owen Roizman   *Ed* Fredric Steinkamp, William Steinkamp   *Mus* Dave Grusin   *Art Dir* Peter Larkin
● Dustin Hoffman, Jessica Lange, Teri Garr, Dabney Coleman, Charles Durning, Bill Murray
(Mirage/Punch/Columbia)

Tootsie is a lulu. Remarkably funny and entirely convincing, film pulls off the rare accomplishment of being an in-drag comedy [from a story by Don McGuire and Larry Gelbart] which also emerges with three-dimensional characters.

Dustin Hoffman portrays a long-struggling New York stage actor whose 'difficult' reputation has relegated him to employment as a waiter and drama coach.

Brash but appealing actor's solution: audition for a popular soap opera as a woman. Becoming a hit on the show, 'Dorothy Michaels' develops into a media celebrity thanks to her forthright manner and 'different' personality. Hoffman finds it hard to devote much time to sort-of-girlfriend Teri Garr, and all the while is growing more deeply attracted to soap costar Jessica Lange.

Hoffman triumphs in what must stand as one of his most brilliant performances. His Dorothy is entirely plausible and, physically, reasonably appealing. But much more importantly, he gets across the enormous guts and determination required of his character to go through with the charade.

☐ 1982: Best Supp. Actress (Jessica Lange).
☐ Nominations: Best Picture, Director, Actor (Dustin Hoffman), Supp. Actress (Teri Garr), Original Screenplay, Cinematography, Editing, Original Song ('It Might Be You'), Sound

. . . .

■ TOPAZ

1969, 126 MINS, US ◇ ⑰ ⊙
Dir Alfred Hitchcock   *Prod* Alfred Hitchcock
Scr Samuel Taylor   *Ph* Jack Hildyard   *Ed* William H. Ziegler   *Mus* Maurice Jarre   *Art Dir* Henry Bumstead
● Frederick Stafford, Dany Robin, John Vernon, Karin Dor, Michel Piccoli, Philippe Noiret (Universal)

Topaz tends to move more solidly and less infectiously than many of Alfred Hitchcock's best remembered pix. Yet Hitchcock brings in a full quota of twists and tingling moments.

Story, from Leon Uris' heavily-plotted novel, centres around high politics, with intrigue and trickery involving French, American, Russian and Cuban security. Action is triggered by defection of a Russian scientist in Copenhagen to the Americans.

The director has a comparatively little known, but impeccable cast, with Frederick Stafford scoring as the French security investigator and with neat work by Philippe Noiret and Michel Piccoli as two French Quislings. John Vernon is a powerful Cuban political leader.

Hitchcock concentrates less than usual on his cool, blonde heroine, and it's Karin Dor as a Cuban spy and mistress of Stafford who steals most of the thunder.

. . . .

■ TOP GUN

1986, 110 MINS, US ◇ ⑰ ⊙
Dir Tony Scott   *Prod* Don Simpson, Jerry Bruckheimer
Scr Jim Cash, Jack Epps Jr.   *Ph* Jeffrey Kimball

Ed Billy Weber   *Mus* Harold Faltermeyer   *Art Dir* John F. DeCuir
● Tom Cruise, Kelly McGillis, Val Kilmer, Anthony Edwards, Tom Skerritt, Meg Ryan (Paramount)

Set in the world of naval fighter pilots, pic has strong visuals and pretty young people in stylish clothes and a non-stop soundtrack.

Cinematographer Jeffery Kimball and his team have assembled some exciting flight footage.

Tom Cruise is Maverick, a hot-shot fighter pilot with a mind of his own and something to prove, assigned to the prestigious Top Gun training school.

Along for the ride as a romantic interest is Kelly McGillis, a civilian astrophysicist brought in to teach the boys about negative Gs and inverted flight tanks. Cruise, however, has his sights set on other targets.

McGillis is blessed with an intelligent and mature face that doesn't blend that well with Cruise's one-note grinning. There is nothing menacing or complex about his character. Tom Skerritt turns in his usual nice job as the hardened but not hard flight instructor.

☐ 1986: Best Song ('Take My Breath Away')
☐ Nominations: Best Editing, Sound, Sound Effects Editing

. . . .

■ TOP HAT

1935, 101 MINS, US ⑰ ⊙
Dir Mark Sandrich   *Prod* Pandro S. Berman
Scr Dwight Taylor, Allan Scott   *Ph* David Abel
Ed William Hamilton   *Mus* Max Steiner (dir.)
Art Dir Van Nest Polglase, Carroll Clark
● Fred Astaire, Ginger Rogers, Edward Everett Horton, Erik Rhodes, Helen Broderick, Eric Blore (RKO)

This one can't miss and the reasons are three – Fred Astaire, Irving Berlin's 11 songs and sufficient comedy between numbers to hold the film together.

Astaire's sock routines are up forward starting with 'No Strings'. He does this alone. It is the hot ditty of the batch, then 'Isn't it a Lovely Day?' with Ginger Rogers for probably the best dance they've ever done together, trailed in turn by the title item, 'Top Hat, White Tie and Tails', the boy number. It is the same number Astaire did in his Ziegfeld show *Smiles*, practically the only change being the melody.

But the danger sign is in the story and cast. Substitute Alice Brady for Helen Broderick and it's the same lineup of players as was in *The Gay Divorcee* (1934). Besides which the situations in the two scripts parallel each other closely.

For the rest of the cast, Edward Everett Horton bears the brunt and is the secondary pillar around which the story revolves. His is the comedy burden which he splits with Eric Blore, his valet, and Erik Rhodes as a dress designer.

Rogers never opens her mouth vocally until the concluding 'Piccolino'. She is again badly dressed while her facial makeup and various coiffeurs give her a hard appearance.

☐ 1935: Nominations: Best Picture, Art Direction, Song ('Cheek to Cheek'), Dance Direction ('Top Hat', 'Piccolino')

. . . .

■ TOPKAPI

1964, 120 MINS, US ◇ ⑰
Dir Jules Dassin   *Prod* Jules Dassin   *Scr* Monja Danischewsky   *Ph* Henri Alekan   *Ed* Roger Dwyre
Mus Manos Hadjidakis   *Art Dir* Max Douy
● Melina Mercouri, Peter Ustinov, Maximilian Schell, Robert Morley, Akim Tamiroff, Gilles Segal (United Artists/Filmways)

Jules Dassin has taken a minor novel by Eric Ambler [*The Light of Day*] and turned it into a delightful and suspenseful comedy spoof of his own *Rififi*.

The band of thieves whose adventures make

Topkapi are a motley crew indeed. Besides Melina Mercouri, it includes Maximilian Schell, master thief; Robert Morley, Gilles Segal and Jess Hahn. Added later, although it takes him some time and a bit of adventure to realize it, Peter Ustinov is an unwitting accomplice.

The basically simple plot, which is rich in detail and background, has the gang attempting to steal a fabulous jeweled dagger from the Topkapi Palace museum in Istanbul. The actual theft is depicted in a long sequence reminiscent of the one in *Rififi* but with a bit more levity.

Mercouri has a holiday in a role that asks her to be equally enamored of gems and males. Schell, surprisingly, plays his role somewhat tongue-in-cheek, never evidencing more than a surface interest in anything (including Mercouri), other than his work. Ustinov has probably the meatiest part in the film and one that allows him to use many of the unsubtleties in dominating scenes he has at his command.

☐ 1964: Best Supp. Actor (Peter Ustinov)

. . . .

■ TOPPER

1937, 98 MINS, US ⑰ ⊙
Dir Norman Z. McLeod   *Prod* Hal Roach   *Scr* Jack Jevne, Eric Hatch, Eddie Moran   *Ph* Norbert Brodine
Ed William Terhune   *Mus* Arthur Morton (arr.)
Art Dir Arthur I. Royce
● Constance Bennett, Cary Grant, Roland Young, Billie Burke, Alan Mowbray, Eugene Pallette (Roach/M-G-M)

With the assistance of Norman McLeod, as director, Hal Roach has produced a weird and baffling tale of spiritualism. It is entitled *Topper*, from a story by the late Thorne Smith. It is carefully made, excellently photographed, and adroitly employs mechanical illusions and trick sound effects.

Story is about the adventures, among living persons, of a young married couple, George and Marion Kerby, who are killed in an automobile smashup as the climax of a wild night of drinking and carousing. Their astral bodies rise from the ruins, and they agree that until they have done someone a good deed they are likely to remain indefinitely in a state of double exposure.

Reviewing the possibilities for charitable action, they decide that their friend, Cosmo Topper, a hen-pecked bank president, who has lived a dull, routine life, shall have the benefit of their assistance.

Performances are usually good. Cary Grant and Constance Bennett, as the reincarnated Kerbys, do their assignments with great skill. Roland Young carries the brunt of the story and does it well. In the title role, he is the docile, good citizen until the transformation of his personality changes him into a dashing man about town.

☐ 1937: Nomination: Best Sound

. . . .

■ TOPPER TAKES A TRIP

1938, 80 MINS, US ⑰
Dir Norman Z. McLeod   *Prod* Hal Roach   *Scr* Eddie Moran, Jack Jevne, Corey Ford   *Ph* Norbert Brodine
Ed William Terhune   *Mus* Edward Powell, Hugo Friedhofer   *Art Dir* Charles D. Hall
● Constance Bennett, Roland Young, Billie Burke, Alan Mowbray, Verree Teasdale, Franklin Pangborn (United Artists)

A delightful, very entertaining comedy [from the novel by Thorne Smith] built around several of the characters who appear in *Topper*, of which this is a sequel.

Roland Young, as Topper, is in court trying to offer a dubious defense in a divorce case Billie Burke has brought against him because he had a woman in his room. Thereafter, with the action shifting to Europe, where Burke has gone to get her divorce, the living spirit of

Constance Bennett and her dog Skippy remain to keep him company. Bennett is still trying to reconcile Young and Burke.

Norman McLeod's adroit direction throughout keeps the film at a nice pace. Pantomime takes care of much of the footage, with just the proper but pungent amount of dialog to suit for story-telling and comedy purposes.
□ 1939: Nomination: Best Special Effects

• •

■ **TOP SECRET!**

1984, 90 MINS, US ◇ ⑲ ⊙
Dir Jim Abrahams, David Zucker, Jerry Zucker
Prod Jon Davison, Hunt Lowry   *Scr* Jim Abrahams,
David Zucker, Jerry Zucker, Martyn Burke
Ph Christopher Challis   *Ed* Bernard Gribble
Mus Maurice Jarre   *Art Dir* Peter Lamont
● Val Kilmer, Lucy Gutteridge, Christopher Villiers,
Omar Sharif, Peter Cushing, Jeremy Kemp (Paramount)

Top Secret! is another bumptious tribute to all that was odd in old movies. Followers of the *Airplane!* trio will probably be happy and satisfied with this effort, yet short of overjoyed.

The attempted target this time is a combination of the traditional spy film and Elvis Presley musical romps, which in and of itself is funny to start with. And Val Kilmer proves a perfect blend of staunch hero and hothouse heartthrob.

But in a deliberate effort to do something different, the directors have unfortunately discarded the cast of matinee idols so closely identified with the originals.

Other than that, *Secret!* shares the same wonderful wacky attitude that allows just about any kind of gag to come flowing in and out of the picture at the strangest times.

• •

■ **TORA! TORA! TORA!**

1970, 144 MINS, US ◇ ⑲ ⊙
Dir Richard Fleischer, Toshio Masuda, Kinji Fukasaku
Prod Elmo Williams   *Scr* Larry Forrester, Hideo Oguni,
Ryuzo Kikushima   *Ph* Charles F. Wheeler, Sinsaku
Himeda, Masamichi Satch, Osami Furuya   *Ed* James E.
Newcom, Pembroke J. Herring, Inoue Chikaya
Mus Jerry Goldsmith   *Art Dir* Jack Martin Smith, Yoshiro
Muraki, Richard Day, Taizoh Kawashima
● Martin Balsam, Soh Yamamura, Joseph Cotten,
Tatsuya Mihashi, E.G. Marshall, Takahiro Tamura (20th
Century-Fox)

Lavish ($25 million) and meticulous restaging of the Japanese airborne attack on Pearl Harbor on December 7 1941 constitutes a brilliant logistics achievement which is not generally matched by the overall artistic handling of the accompanying dramatic narrative.

Effect of the story [from *Tora! Tora! Tora!* by Gordon W. Prange and *The Broken Seal* by Ladislas Farago] seems to prove that the Japanese government, while somewhat divided internally, at least had some unity of purpose in its expansion plans.

Both overall director Richard Fleischer and his Japanese counterparts do a dull job, and the monotonously low-key tone of scene after scene almost suggests that each was filmed without a sense of ultimate slotting in the finished form.
□ 1970: Best Special Visual Effects (A. D. Flowers, L. B. Abbot).
□ Nominations: Best Cinematography, Art Direction, Editing, Sound

• •

■ **TORCHLIGHT**

1984, 91 MINS, US ◇ ⑲ ⊙
Dir Tom Wright   *Prod* Joel Douglas   *Scr* Pamela Sue
Martin, Eliza Moorman   *Ph* Alex Phillips   *Mus* Michael
Cannon   *Art Dir* Craig Stearns
● Pamela Sue Martin, Steve Railsback, Ian McShane, Al
Corley, Rita Taggart, Arnie Moore (UCO)

Torchlight is largely a family affair. Pamela Sue Martin, who costars with Steve Railsback

and Ian McShane, is cowriter of the screenplay, as well as taking associate producer credit, while her husband, Manuel Rojas, is exec producer. Between them they've fashioned a film which opens on a deceptively light-hearted note but develops in downbeat style.

In its opening sequences, the plot depicts the love-at-first-sight romance and marriage of Martin and Railsback. Enter McShane, a sinister and larger than life pusher, and Railsback's downfall progresses until he becomes a physical and mental wreck, left without wife or home.

Martin has written for herself a role which allows her to reach the highs and lows of elation and despair. Railsback has a demanding role and mainly fills it convincingly, but McShane as the sinister pusher is a grossly overdrawn character.

• •

■ **TORCH SONG TRILOGY**

1988, 117 MINS, US ◇ ⑲ ⊙
Dir Paul Bogart   *Prod* Howard Gottfried   *Scr* Harvey
Fierstein   *Ph* Mikael Salomon   *Ed* Nicholas C. Smith
Mus Peter Matz   *Art Dir* Richard Hoover
● Anne Bancroft, Matthew Broderick, Harvey Fierstein,
Brian Kerwin, Karen Young, Charles Pierce (New Line)

Harvey Fierstein repeats his Tony Award-winning performance as Arnold Beckoff, a flamboyant drag queen looking for love and respect. Originated as separately staged one-acts, the play, when finally mounted as a unified work in 1982, proved bracing in its frank depiction of gay sex life, both promiscuous and committed.

Nervous, mannered, gravelly voiced, overly sensitive, campy and with a taste for eye-rolling rivaled only by Groucho Marx in modern showbiz annals, Arnold appears a bit gun-shy of romance, but allows himself to be picked up in a gay bar by Ed (Brian Kerwin), a good-looking, straight-seeming fellow who openly announces his bisexuality.

This doesn't stop Arnold from falling head over heels for his Middle American catch, but causes him endless pain when he discovers Ed with a young woman, Laurel (Karen Young).

In what is effectively Act Two, Arnold meets Alan (Matthew Broderick), to him an impossibly good-looking kid who used to be a hustler and actively seeks out Arnold for his human, as opposed to superficial, qualities.

Act Three, the most conventional of the sections, is given over to Arnold's efforts to handle an adopted teenage son and sort out his strained relations with his mother (Anne Bancroft).

• •

■ **TORN CURTAIN**

1966, 126 MINS, US ◇ ⑲ ⊙
Dir Alfred Hitchcock   *Prod* Alfred Hitchcock   *Scr* Brian
Moore   *Ph* John F. Warren   *Ed* Bud Hoffman
Mus John Addison   *Art Dir* Hein Heckroth
● Paul Newman, Julie Andrews, Lila Kedrova,
Hansjoerg Felmy, Tamara Toumanova, Wolfgang Kieling
(Universal)

Torn Curtain is an okay Cold War suspenser with Paul Newman as a fake defector to East Germany in order to obtain Communist defense secrets. Julie Andrews is his femme partner. Alfred Hitchcock's direction emphasizes suspense and ironic comedy flair but some good plot ideas are marred by routine dialog, and a too relaxed pace contributes to a dull overlength.

Brian Moore scripted from his original story about a top US physicist who essays a public defection in order to pick the brains of a Communist wizard. Writing, acting and direction make clear from the outset that Newman is loyal, although about one-third of pic passes before this is made explicit in dialog. This early telegraphing diminishes suspense.

Hitchcock freshens up his bag of tricks in a good potpourri which becomes a bit stale through a noticeable lack of zip and pacing.

• •

■ **TORRENT, THE**

1926, 68 MINS, US ⊗
Dir Monta Bell   *Scr* Dorothy Farnum, Katherine Hilliker,
H.H. Caldwell   *Ph* William Daniels   *Ed* Frank Sullivan
Art Dir Cedric Gibbons, Merrill Pye
● Ricardo Cortez, Greta Garbo, Gertrude Olmstead,
Edward Connelly, Martha Mattox (Cosmopolitan/MGM)

Greta Garbo, making her American debut as a screen star, has everything with looks, acting ability and personality. When one is a Scandinavian and can put over a Latin characterization with sufficient power to make it most convincing, need there be any more said regarding her ability? She makes *The Torrent* worthwhile.

The Torrent is a picturization of the Blasco Ibanez novel of the same name. It is evident that the great scene of the rush of waters was counted on to carry the picture, but a bursting dam doesn't mean anything in a picture except as an incident. It is the story itself that carries here. The tale of the unrequited love of the little Spanish peasant girl who develops into a great operatic star will hold because of its love twist.

• •

■ **TORTURE GARDEN**

1968, 92 MINS, UK ◇ ⑲
Dir Freddie Francis   *Prod* Max S. Rosenberg, Milton
Subotsky   *Scr* Robert Bloch   *Ph* Norman Warwick
Ed Peter Elliott   *Mus* Don Banks   *Art Dir* Bill Constable
● Jack Palance, Burgess Meredith, Beverly Adams, Peter
Cushing, Michael Bryant, Barbara Ewing (Amicus)

Robert Bloch penned the episodic script in which Burgess Meredith is a sideshow mystic, who gives a special after-hours show to five patrons. Jack Palance is an Edgar Allen Poe buff who, it turns out, will do almost anything to achieve eminence in his hobby.

Michael Bryant's sequence involves a man-eating house cat with whom he tangles after greed induces him to permit the death of a supposedly wealthy relative.

The situations are developed economically and inventively, both from script and Freddie Francis' very good direction. Cast is competent, considering the apparent fast shooting sked and limited productions coin. In latter regard, sets range from well-thought-out to skimpy.

• •

■ **TO SIR, WITH LOVE**

1967, 104 MINS, UK ◇ ⑲
Dir James Clavell   *Prod* James Clavell   *Scr* James
Clavell   *Ph* Paul Beeson   *Ed* Peter Thornton
Mus Ron Grainer   *Art Dir* Tony Woollard
● Sidney Poitier, Christian Roberts, Judy Geeson, Suzy
Kendall, Lulu, Faith Brook (Columbia)

To Sir, With Love is a well-made, sometimes poignant, drama [from the 1959 E.R. Braithwaite novel] about a Negro teacher, working in a London slum, who transforms an unruly class into a group of youngsters better prepared for adult life. Sidney Poitier stars in an excellent performance.

Poitier, after gauging the rebellious mood of his class, scraps the formal agenda and institutes what he rightly calls 'survival training'.

Students include Christian Roberts, very good as the natural class leader, Judy Geeson, a looker who gets a crush on teacher, Christopher Chittell, another reformed punk, and Lulu, an engaging personality with substantial acting ability.

• •

T

■ TOTAL RECALL

1990, 109 MINS, US ◇ ▼ ⊙

Dir Paul Verhoeven   *Prod* Buzz Feitshans, Ronald
Shusett   *Scr* Ronald Shusett, Dan O'Bannon, Gary
Oldman   *Ph* Jost Vacano   *Ed* Frank J. Urioste
Mus Jerry Goldsmith   *Art Dir* William Sandell
● Arnold Schwarzenegger, Rachel Ticotin, Sharon
Stone, Ronny Cox, Michael Ironside, Marshall Bell
(Carolco)

Estimates of the cost of this futuristic extravaganza range from $60 to $70 million making
it one of the most expensive pics ever made.
There are gargantuan sets repping Mars and
a futuristic Earth society, grotesque creatures
galore, genuinely weird and mostly seamless
visual effects, and enough gunshots, grunts
and explosions to keep anyone in a high state
of nervous exhilaration.

The story is actually a good one, taking off
from Phillip K. Dick's celebrated sci-fi tale *We
Can Remember It for You Wholesale.*

Arnold Schwarzenegger's character, a working stiff in the year 2084, keeps having these
strange nightmares about living on Mars, and
it transpires that he once worked in the
colony as an intelligence agent before rebelling against dictator Ronny Cox.
Schwarzenegger had most, but not quite all,
of his bad memories erased and was sent to
Earth to work on a construction crew, with a
sexy but treacherous wife (Sharon Stone).

A visit to a mind-altering travel agency
named Rekall Inc. alerts Schwarzenegger to
the truth, setting him off on a rampage
through Earth and Mars with the help of
equally tough female sidekick Rachel Ticotin.

The fierce and unrelenting pace, accompanied by a tongue-in-cheek strain of humor in
the roughhouse screenplay, keeps the film
moving like a juggernaut.

□ 1990: Special Achievement Award (visual
effects)
□ Nomination: Best Sound

■ TO THE DEVIL A DAUGHTER

1976, 92 MINS, UK/W. GERMANY ◇ ▼

Dir Peter Sykes   *Prod* Roy Skeggs   *Scr* Chris Wicking
Ph David Watkin   *Ed* John Trumper   *Art Dir* Don
Picton
● Richard Widmark, Christopher Lee, Honor Blackman,
Denholm Elliott, Michael Goodliffe, Nastassja Kinski
(Hammer/Terra)

To the Devil a Daughter is lacklustre occult
melodrama in which Christopher Lee is up to
his old tricks as an excommunicated priest
who takes up satan's cause in order to save
the world from its own decadent folly.

Based on a novel by English author Dennis
Wheatley, the picture makes a few too many
pretensions to serious exploration of the occult, that hamper the flow.

Lee is ever-dependable in this sort of menace routine, Richard Widmark turns in a serviceable job, ditto Honor Blackman and
Anthony Valentine as pals who aid and abet
him at mortal cost. Nastassja Kinski is moderately appealing as the child-woman novitiate and Denholm Elliott turns on the
requisite anguish as the fearful father who
originally signed the girl over to Lee in order
to spare his own hide.

■ TO TRAP A SPY

1966, 92 MINS, US ◇

Dir Don Medford   *Prod* Norman Felton   *Scr* Sam Rolfe
Ph Joseph Biroc   *Ed* Henry Berman   *Mus* Jerry
Goldsmith   *Art Dir* George W. Davis, Merrill Pye
● Robert Vaughn, Luciana Paluzzi, Patricia Crowley,
Fritz Weaver, Will Kuluva, David McCallum (M-G-M)

To Trap a Spy is an elaborated version of
MGM-TV's *The Man From U.N.C.L.E.* pilot,
originally lensed in color but telecast in
black-and-white to tee off series on

September 23 1964. Additional footage was
shot to bring total running time now to 92
minutes.

Patently released to cash in on current espionage mania, much of the new footage is devoted to build Robert Vaughn, the agent from
U.N.C.L.E., into a glamor boy with a roving
eye for beautiful femmes. Whatever plot
there is revolves around efforts to prevent the
assassination of a visiting African dignitary,
but the refurbished entry isn't much better
than the original.

Vaughn tries hard and with some success
through plot-holes, and gets capable support
from Patricia Crowley, Luciana Paluzzi and
Fritz Weaver. His sidekick in teleseries,
David McCallum, is in only two scenes.

■ TOUCH, THE

1971, 113 MINS, SWEDEN/US ◇ ▼

Dir Ingmar Bergman   *Prod* Ingmar Bergman
Scr Ingmar Bergman   *Ph* Sven Nykvist   *Ed* Siv Kanaly-
Lundgren   *Mus* Jan Johannson
● Bibi Andersson, Elliott Gould, Max von Sydow, Sheila
Reid, Steffan Hallerstram, Maria Nolgard (ABC/Persona)

Shot in English with occasional Swedish dialog and splendidly acted and lensed, *The
Touch* is both a romantic film of great
poignancy and strength and an example of
masterful cinema honed down to deceptively
simple near-perfection.

In telling what is basically a straight triangle tale (bored wife, busy husband, 'interesting' and available friend) Bergman seems to
be appealing to and aiming primarily at the
emotions rather than the intellect.

Not unexpectedly, Bergman's cast is superb. Bibi Andersson walks away with pic
thanks to one of those immense, bigger-than-
life performances. Rarely has the moving anguish of a trysting woman been so stirringly
caught. Elliott Gould is a perfect choice as
the somewhat neurotic foreign archeologist
who, despite oafish manners, selfishness and
instability, fascinates and attracts her. Max
von Sydow does expected wonders with the
normally unplayable role of the silently
strong husband.

■ TOUCH AND GO

1986, 101 MINS, US ◇ ▼ ⊙

Dir Robert Mandel   *Prod* Stephen Friedman   *Scr* Alan
Ormsby, Bob Sand, Harry Colomby   *Ph* Richard H.
Kline   *Ed* Walt Mulconery   *Mus* Sylvester Levay
Art Dir Charles Rosen
● Michael Keaton, Maria Conchita Alonso, Ajay Naidu,
Maria Tucci, Max Wright, Jere Burns (Tri-Star)

Touch and Go mixes humor, heart and considerable hokum in an engaging story matching
an unusually serious Michael Keaton and
zesty Latin star Maria Conchita Alonso as
lovers in spite of themselves.

Pic features Keaton as a hot-shot hockey
jock with the Chicago Eagles. His regimen
gets disrupted one night when a punk kid
(Ajay Naidu) acts as the innocent front for his
thug friends as they try to mug the sports
star. Keaton fends the rascals off and he's left
throttling the 11-year-old. But the kid's a
charmer and Keaton returns him home to his
slummy neighborhood and to Mom (Alonso)
for discipline, opening the way for romance.
Rapport between the disrespectful kid and
Keaton unfolds immediately.

■ TOUCH OF CLASS, A

1973, 106 MINS, UK ◇ ▼

Dir Melvin Frank   *Prod* Melvin Frank   *Scr* Melvin
Frank, Jack Rose   *Ph* Austin Dempster   *Ed* Bill Butler
Mus John Cameron   *Art Dir* Terry Marsh
● George Segal, Glenda Jackson, Paul Sorvino,
Hildegard Neil, Cec Linder, K. Callan (Brut)

A Touch of Class is sensational. Director, writer
and producer Melvin Frank has accomplished
precisely what Peter Bogdanovich did in
What's Up, Doc? – revitalizing, updating and
invigorating an earlier film genre to smash
results.

George Segal herein justifies superbly a
reputation for comedy ability while Glenda
Jackson's full-spectrum talent is again confirmed. An accidental London meeting between Segal and Jackson leads to a casual
pass by Segal, thence (through a series of hilarious complications, including wife, in-laws,
and old friends) to a frustrated rendezvous in
a Spanish resort. Pair's romance flourishes
into a full-blown affair at home, with Segal
wearing himself out dashing between two
beds.

The visual and verbal antics are supported
by just enough underlying character depth to
keep the film on a solid credible basis, setting
up the plot for its tender, bittersweet climax.

□ 1973: Best Actress (Glenda Jackson).
□ Nominations: Best Picture, Story &
Screenplay, Original Dramatic Score, Song
('All That Love Went to Waste')

■ TOUCH OF EVIL

1958, 95 MINS, US ▼ ⊙

Dir Orson Welles, Harry Keller   *Prod* Albert Zugsmith
Scr Orson Welles   *Ph* Russell Metty   *Ed* Virgil M.
Vogel, Aaron Stell, [Edward Curtiss]   *Mus* Henry
Mancini   *Art Dir* Alexander Golitzen, Robert Clatworthy
● Charlton Heston, Janet Leigh, Orson Welles, Joseph
Calleia, Akim Tamiroff, Joanna Moore (Universal)

Touch of Evil smacks of brilliance but ultimately flounders in it. Taken scene by scene,
there is much to be said for this filmization of
Whit Masterson's novel, *Badge of Evil.* Orson
Welles' script contains some hard-hitting dialog; his use of low key lighting is effective,
and Russell Metty's photography is fluid and
impressive; and Henry Mancini's music is
poignant. But *Touch of Evil* proves it takes
more than good scenes to make a good picture.

Welles portrays an American cop who has
the keen reputation of always getting his
man. Before you know it, he's hot on the trail
of those scoundrels who blew to smithereens
the wealthy 'owner' of a small Mexican border town. Charlton Heston, a bigwig in the
Mexican government, just happens to be
around with his new American bride (Janet
Leigh) and gets himself rather involved in the
proceedings, feeling the dynamiting has
something to do with a narcotics racket he's
investigating.

Off his rocker since his wife was murdered
years ago, Welles supposedly is deserving of a
bit of sympathy. At least, there's a hint of it in
dialog, even though it isn't seen in his characterization. Aside from this, he turns in a
unique and absorbing performance. Heston
keeps his plight the point of major importance,
combining a dynamic quality with a touch of
Latin personality. Leigh, sexy as all get-out,
switches from charm to fright with facility in a
capable portrayal. Dennis Weaver, as the night
man, is fine though exaggerated.

Spicing up the production are a single
closeup of Zsa Zsa Gabor as a non-stripped
stripper, a word or two from Joseph Cotten
who's slipped in without screen credit, and a
provocative few minutes with gypsy-looking
Marlene Dietrich. Dietrich is rather sultry
and fun to watch, even though it's somewhat
incongruous to see her walk into the Mexican
darkness at the picture's finish, turn to wave,
then wail, 'Adios.'

■ TOUCH OF LOVE, A

1969, 102 MINS, UK ◇ ▼

Dir Waris Hussein   *Prod* Max J. Rosenberg, Milton
Subotsky   *Scr* Margaret Drabble   *Ph* Peter Suschitzky

Ed Bill Blunden   *Mus* Michael Dress   *Art Dir* Tony Curtis
● Sandy Dennis, Ian McKellen, Michael Coles, John Standing, Eleanor Bron (Palomar)

Sharply scripted by Margaret Drabble from her novel [*The Millstone*], story deals with a well-educated philosophy student whose first all-the-way seduction by a chance acquaintance leaves her pregnant, while each of her steady but platonic suitors thinks his rival is the father.

Pic details girl's solo battle against society and herself to decide whether to keep the child and bring it up sans a father.

Key factor, aside from a fine script, trim direction by newcomer Waris Hussein and moody lensing, lies in the Sandy Dennis performance, which is pin-point accurate in conveying the tremendous inner strength which helps her character win through against hostile – or disinterested – society and family.

She gets very strong support here from Ian McKellen as the unknowing father.

●●●●●●●●●●●●●●●●●●●●●●●●●●●●●●

■ TOUGH GUYS

1986, 104 MINS, US ◇ Ⓥ ⊙
Dir Jeff Kanew   *Prod* Joe Wizan   *Scr* James Orr, Jim Cruickshank   *Ph* King Baggot   *Ed* Kaja Fehr
Mus James Newton Howard   *Art Dir* Todd Hallowell
● Burt Lancaster, Kirk Douglas, Charles Durning, Alexis Smith, Dana Carvey, Darlanne Fluegel (Touchstone)

Tough Guys is unalloyed hokum that proves a sad waste of talent on the parts of co-stars Burt Lancaster and Kirk Douglas.

The two venerable thesps, both 70-ish and looking fit and alert, turn up here as Harry Doyle and Archie Long, two gentleman crooks celebrated in the annals of American crime for having been the last outlaws to rob a train.

Pic pokes along with Lancaster provoking havoc at his old folks' home and Douglas quitting a series of jobs in disgust until scripters decide that perhaps a plot would be nice, so the guys get together and – surprise – decide to rob the train again.

It's all silly, meaningless and vaguely depressing, since the awareness lingers throughout that both actors are capable of much, much more than is demanded of them here.

●●●●●●●●●●●●●●●●●●●●●●●●●●●●●●

■ TOUGH GUYS DON'T DANCE

1987, 108 MINS, US ◇ Ⓥ ⊙
Dir Norman Mailer   *Prod* Menahem Golan, Yoram Globus   *Scr* Norman Mailer   *Ph* John Bailey
Ed Debra McDermott   *Mus* Angelo Badalamenti
Art Dir Armin Ganz
● Ryan O'Neal, Isabella Rossellini, Debra Sandlund, Wings Hauser, John Bedford Lloyd, Frances Fisher (Cannon/Zoetrope)

Tough Guys is part parody and part serious with a nasty streak running right down the middle.

Set in a small coastal town in Massachusetts in the sort of place where everyone knows everyone else's business, and for Tim Madden (Ryan O'Neal) business is bad, story has something to do with a bottched drug deal, men who love the wrong women and women who love the wrong men.

In the course of playing its hand, Madden's wealthy wife (Debra Sandlund), a washed up porno star (Frances Fisher), a suicidal southerner (John Bedford Lloyd), a gay sugar daddy (R. Patrick Sulliva) and a corrupt police chief (Wings Hauser) all get blown away.

Film is at its best when it's tongue-in-cheek and it's fun to listen to the guys talk tough. And the biggest, baddest, nastiest one of them all is Lawrence Tierney as O'Neal's father, a man who won't dance for anyone.

●●●●●●●●●●●●●●●●●●●●●●●●●●●●●●

■ TOVARICH

1937, 94 MINS, US
Dir Anatole Litvak   *Prod* Robert Lord   *Scr* Casey Robinson   *Ph* Charles Lang   *Ed* Henri Rust
Mus Max Steiner
● Claudette Colbert, Charles Boyer, Basil Rathbone, Anita Louise, Melville Cooper, Isabel Jeans (Warner)

With a distinguished record in legit theatres, both here and abroad, [Jacques Deval's play] *Tovarich* emerges from its Warner filming as a piece of popular entertainment, plus the very considerable drawing value of Claudette Colbert and Charles Boyer. Story changes are not radical (one or two modifications being prompted by censorship restrictions).

Boyer's diction is difficult to comprehend in several places. His accent is enhanced by the fact that only he, of all the players, speaks rapidly. Only in brief moments does Colbert convey the dignity, bearing and fine humor of a Russian imperial princess.

Litvak seems imbued with the idea that he had to make *Tovarich* look like a big picture, whereas the story of the royal refugee couple, who enter domestic service in the household of a Paris banker, is a yarn of charming and finely shaded characterizations.

Of the supporting cast Melville Cooper, as the banker, and Basil Rathbone as a commissar contribute splendid characterizations.

●●●●●●●●●●●●●●●●●●●●●●●●●●●●●●

■ TOWERING INFERNO, THE

1974, 165 MINS, US ◇ Ⓥ ⊙
Dir John Guillermin, Irwin Allen   *Prod* Irwin Allen
Scr Stirling Silliphant   *Ph* Fred Koenekamp, Joseph Biroc   *Ed* Harold F. Kress, Carl Kress   *Mus* John Williams
Art Dir William Creber
● Steve McQueen, Paul Newman, William Holden, Faye Dunaway, Robert Vaughn, Richard Chamberlain (20th Century-Fox/Warner)

The Towering Inferno is one of the greatest disaster pictures made, a personal and professional triumph for producer Irwin Allen. The $14 million cost has yielded a truly magnificent production which complements but does not at all overwhelm a thoughtful personal drama.

The strategy of casting expensive talent pays off handsomely. Steve McQueen, as the fireman in charge of extinguishing the runaway fire in a 130-story San Francisco building, Paul Newman, as the heroic and chagrined architect of the glass and concrete pyre, William Holden as its builder, and Faye Dunaway, as Newman's fiancee, get and deserve their star billing.

Both 20th and WB pooled their finances and their separate but similar book acquisitions – Richard Martin Stern's *The Tower* and *The Glass Inferno*, by Thomas N. Scortia and Frank M. Robinson – to effect a true example of synergy.

□ 1974: Best Cinematography, Song ('We May Never Love Like This Again'), Editing.
□ Nominations: Best Picture, Supp. Actor (Fred Astaire), Art Direction, Original Dramatic Score, Sound

●●●●●●●●●●●●●●●●●●●●●●●●●●●●●●

■ TOWN LIKE ALICE, A

(US: The Rape of Malaya)

1956, 117 MINS, UK Ⓥ ⊙
Dir Jack Lee   *Scr* W.P. Lipscomb, Richard Mason
Ph Geoffrey Unsworth   *Ed* Sidney Hayers
Mus Matyas Seiber
● Virginia McKenna, Peter Finch, Maureen Swanson, Renee Houston, Marie Lohr, Jean Anderson (Rank)

Filmed largely on location in Malaya and Australia, story is based on Neville Shute's novel of the same name. Film describes how a handful of women and children were forced-marched through Malaya at the hands of the Japanese. For months on end they tramped from one camp to another, through swamp and storm, through dust and heat. Many died on the roadside, but the few survivors eventually found refuge in a village after their guard had succumbed.

During the period of their cross-country march the women and kids are befriended by a couple of Australian POWs who have been assigned to truck driving duties for the Japs, and over a shared cigarette and an exchange of minor confidence, a bond develops between Virginia McKenna and Peter Finch.

The subject matter is necessarily grim, but wherever possible the script and direction endeavor to infuse a touch of lighter relief. The focus, however, is almost constantly on the trials of the women and children as they fight against famine and disease.

●●●●●●●●●●●●●●●●●●●●●●●●●●●●●●

■ TOWN WITHOUT PITY

1961, 112 MINS, US
Dir Gottfried Reinhardt   *Prod* Gottfried Reinhardt
Scr Silvia Reinhardt, Georg Hurdalek   *Ph* Kurt Hasse
Ed Hermann Haller   *Mus* Dimitri Tiomkin   *Art Dir* Rolf Zehetbauer
● Kirk Douglas, E.G. Marshall, Robert Blake, Richard Jaeckel, Christine Kaufmann, Frank Sutton (United Artists/Mirisch/Gloria)

At face value, *Town without Pity* appears to be a straight courtroom drama treatment of a gang rape case and its repercussions on a German community incensed over the fact that the rapists are American GIs and the victim a local girl. But the production attempts to go much deeper than that.

The screenplay, based on an adaptation by Jan Lustig of Manfred Gregor's novel *The Verdict*, dramatizes the story of a military defense attorney who, in attempting to properly perform his task, must against his will bring about the destruction of an innocent (the raped girl), victim of her own human fallibility and the fallibility of German witnesses whose pride, hatreds and insecurities lead them to lie, exaggerate or conceal on the stand.

A picture that raises important moral and judicial questions must do so in terms of rounded, dimensional characters if it is to register with impact. *Town without Pity* fails in this regard.

Kirk Douglas does an able job as the defense attorney. Likewise E.G. Marshall as the prosecutor. There is an especially earnest and intense portrayal of one of the defendants by Robert Blake. The others – less prominent – are skillfully delineated by Richard Jaeckel, Frank Sutton and Mal Sondock. Christine Kaufmann, a rare combination of sensual beauty and sensitivity, handles her assignment – the victim – with sincerity and animation.

□ 1961: Nomination: Best Song ('Town Without Pity')

●●●●●●●●●●●●●●●●●●●●●●●●●●●●●●

■ TOXIC AVENGER, THE

1985, 100 MINS, US ◇ Ⓥ ⊙
Dir Michael Herz, Samuel Weil   *Prod* Lloyd Kaufman, Michael Herz   *Scr* Joe Ritter, Lloyd Kaufman, Gay Terry, Stuart Strutin   *Ph* James London, Lloyd Kaufman
Ed Richard W. Haines   *Mus* Marc Katz (consult.)
Art Dir Barry Shapiro, Alexandra Mazur
● Andree Maranda, Mitchell Cohen, Jennifer Baptist, Cindy Manion, Robert Prichard, Mark Torgl (Troma)

This madcap spoof on *The Incredible Hulk* is an outlandish mix of gory violence and realistic special effects.

The story concerns Melvin, a 90-pound weakling who works in a body-building club pushing around a mop, and who is hated by the muscular and healthy types that flaunt their bodies before him and the audience.

Following some rather pointless shenanigans in which Melvin is humiliated by the bodybuilders, he jumps out of a window and lands in a truck carrying toxic waste. This transforms him into a hulking monster, but one seeking only to right wrongs in his town and persecute the meanies.

••••••••••••••••••••••••••••••••

■ TOXIC AVENGER, PART II, THE

1989, 95 MINS, US ◇ ⓥ ⊙
Dir Lloyd Kaufman, Michael Herz   *Prod* Lloyd Kaufman, Michael Herz   *Scr* Gay Partington Terry   *Ph* James London   *Ed* Michael Schweitzer   *Mus* Barrie Guard   *Art Dir* Alex Grey
● Ron Fazio, John Altamura, Phoebe Legere, Rick Collins, Rikiya Yasuoka, Lisa Gaye (Troma)

Even die-hard Troma fans will have a hard time stomaching *The Toxic Avenger, Part II*. A weak script [from a story by Lloyd Kaufman] and sluggish direction turn this sequel to the 1985 spoof into a seemingly endless, stultifying mess.

Toxic II finds 90-pound weakling Melvin suffering from emotional problems. It seems he was unable to save a home for the blind from an evil drug magnate who razed the center and killed its inhabitants in his march to conquer Tromaville. The only thing that will help his depression is a trip to Japan to find his father, Big Mac, who turns out to be a fish peddler who is really an underworld coke peddler.

Because each limited spoof is telegraphed and laboriously executed, this toxic sequel can be hazardous to your health.

••••••••••••••••••••••••••••••••

■ TOYS

1992, 121 MINS, US ◇ ⓥ ⊙
Dir Barry Levinson   *Prod* Barry Levinson, Mark Johnson   *Scr* Valerie Curtin, Barry Levinson   *Ph* Adam Greenberg   *Ed* Stu Linder   *Mus* Hans Zimmer, Trevor Horn   *Art Dir* Ferdinando Scarfiotti
● Robin Williams, Michael Gambon, Joan Cusack, Robin Wright, LL Cool J, Donald O'Connor (20th Century-Fox/Baltimore)

Only a filmmaker with Barry Levinson's clout would have been so indulged to create such a sprawling, seemingly unsupervised mess as *Toys*, a painful exercise that makes *Hudson Hawk* look like a modest throwaway.

The slow-developing story has aging toymaker Kenneth Zevo (a cameo by Donald O'Connor) leave his factory to his army-general brother (Michael Gambon), fearing that his two children (Robin Williams and Joan Cusack) are too immature for the job.

Rendered obsolete by the end of the Cold War, the General goes about converting the plant into a factory producing war toys and machines of war, sinisterly training toddlers to operate them through the use of videogames.

Levinson, a director most at home with slice-of-life portraits relating to his Baltimore roots, tries his hand here at a darkly satiric fable and ends up doing an extremely poor impression of Terry Gilliam.

Williams and Cusack, the supposed spirits of innocence, are for the most part annoying – particularly Cusack's adult-as-child antics. Through sheer energy Williams generates a few laughs. The movie's real star, production designer Ferdinando Scarfiotti (*The Last Emperor*), nevertheless deserves enormous credit.
□ 1992: Nominations: Best Art Direction, Costume Design

••••••••••••••••••••••••••••••••

■ TOYS IN THE ATTIC

1963, 88 MINS, US ⓥ
Dir George Roy Hill   *Prod* Walter Mirisch   *Scr* James Poe   *Ph* Joseph F. Biroc   *Ed* Stuart Gilmore   *Mus* George Duning   *Art Dir* Cary Odell
● Dean Martin, Geraldine Page, Yvette Mimieux, Wendy Hiller, Gene Tierney, Frank Silvera (United Artists)

Toys in the Attic is a somewhat watered-down version of Lillian Hellman's play, but enough of the original emotional savagery has been retained to satisfy those who prefer their melodramatic meat raw and chewy. *Toys* is laid in the Deep South and liberally crammed with such sick-sick cargo as incest, adultery, imbecility, lust and a few other popular folk pleasantries.

Principal tampering scenarist James Poe has done with Hellman's neatly constructed, momentum-gathering play about a New Orleans household shattered by latent incest and corrosive possessiveness is in altering the ending.

Hellman's heavyweight drama examines the tragedy that transpires as a result of a spinster sister's secret lust for her younger brother, whose monetarily-motivated marriage to a simple-minded girl sets in operation the mechanism for his ultimate disaster. The new ending is thoroughly artificial. Otherwise, Poe's additions and subtractions are sound.

George Roy Hill has made an error or two along the way, but generally his direction is taut, progressive and fastpaced considering this is a very talky, confined piece. The performances are fine.
□ 1963: Nomination: Best B&W Costume Design

••••••••••••••••••••••••••••••••

■ TOY SOLDIERS

1991, 112 MINS, US ◇ ⓥ ⊙
Dir Daniel Petrie Jr   *Prod* Jack E. Freedman, Wayne S. Williams, Patricia Herskovic   *Scr* David Koepp, Daniel Petrie Jr   *Ph* Thomas Burstyn   *Ed* Michael Kahn   *Mus* Robert Folk   *Art Dir* Chester Kaczenski
● Sean Astin, Wil Wheaton, Keith Coogan, Andrew Divoff, Louis Gossett Jr, Denholm Elliott (Tri-Star)

Toy Soldiers is a very entertaining action film that updates 1981's sleeper hit *Taps*. Pic is unrelated to the 1984 *Toy Soldiers*, wherein Jason Miller and Cleavon Little led a bunch of Beverly Hills kids (including Tim Robbins in an early role) on a hostage rescue mission against terrorists in Colombia.

The new picture [from William P. Kennedy's novel] presents the reverse situation of rich kids at a Virginia prep school who have to develop some backbone and defend themselves against Andrew Divoff's group of Colombian terrorists who take over their school and hold them hostage. Seeing Sean Astin (son of John Astin and Patty Duke) and his pranksters turn into commandos who wipe out the nasty invaders makes for purely escapist, crowd-pleasing pleasure.

In his feature directing debut, Daniel Petrie Jr gets maximum mileage out of the derring-do of the final reels while emphasizing comic relief earlier on. Young villain Divoff is terrific at creating a brutal figure of hate.

Remaining in the end credits is Tracy Brooks Swope, but she doesn't appear on screen; in fact there are no women's roles other than bit parts.

••••••••••••••••••••••••••••••••

■ TRACES OF RED

1992, 104 MINS, US ◇ ⓥ ⊙
Dir Andy Wolk   *Prod* Mark Gordon   *Scr* Jim Piddock   *Ph* Timothy Suhrstedt   *Ed* Trudy Ship   *Mus* Graeme Revell   *Art Dir* Dan Bishop, Dianna Freas
● James Belushi, Lorraine Bracco, Tony Goldwyn, William Russ, Faye Grant, Michelle Joiner (Goldwyn)

Unintentional laughs and goofy plot twists make *Traces of Red* a dramatic failure but an entertaining exercise in camp.

James Belushi brings his usual man of the people persona to a role that should have been a bit more uppercrust: a cop in Palm Beach, Fla, whose brother (William Russ) is running for Senate. Belushi is assigned to a murder case, and before long all the principal characters (himself and brother included) are key suspects in the serial slayings of prostitutes and B girls.

With a nod to genre films like *Body Heat*, *Traces of Red* initially holds the interest in a whodunit mode. Unfortunately, pic includes so many traces of red herrings in its attempt to make every Palm Beach denizen a suspect, one fears that Ted Kennedy will eventually be dragged in as the killer.

In particular, Lorraine Bracco, playing her femme fatale as a wannabe Melanie Griffith (right down to the voice), does many things for no reason other than to make the audience wonder about her.

To throw film buffs off the track, Belushi narrates the film as a corpse, a successfully misleading homage to Billy Wilder's *Sunset Blvd.* format.

••••••••••••••••••••••••••••••••

■ TRACK OF THE CAT

1954, 102 MINS, US ◇
Dir William A. Wellman   *Prod* Robert Fellows   *Scr* A. J. Bezzerides   *Ph* William H. Clothier   *Ed* Fred MacDowell   *Mus* Roy Webb
● Robert Mitchum, Teresa Wright, Diana Lynn, Tab Hunter, Beulah Bondi, Philip Tonge (Warner)

The novelty of lensing, in color, a picture designed to reproduce black-and-white is rather dissipated in this production. If there had been some entertainment impact to go with the photographic treatment, the combination might have paid off strongly.

William A. Wellman is responsible for the novelty idea and directs in a manner to achieve some rather startling effects. Only color seen is the flesh tones of the characters, the green of trees on the snow-covered Mt Rainier location site, a red and black mackinaw and a light-colored blouse. It gives the right 'mood' to the Walter Van Tilburg Clark novel, which is a 'moody' piece, at best.

Story deals with a farm family of three brothers, an old-maid sister, a drunken father and a Bible-reading mother, plus a girl from a neighboring farm. As the melodrama unfolds, first the older brother, William Hopper, is killed by a mountain lion. Then the middle brother, Robert Mitchum dies, while looking for the 'cat'.

The lion symbolizes the 'cat' every man must throw off before he is a man.

••••••••••••••••••••••••••••••••

■ TRACKS

1976, 90 MINS, US ◇ ⓥ ⊙
Dir Henry Jaglom   *Prod* Howard Zuker   *Scr* Henry Jaglom   *Ph* Paul Glickman   *Ed* George Folsey Jr
● Dennis Hopper, Taryn Power, Dean Stockwell, Topo Swope, Alfred Ryder, Michael Emil (Rainbow)

Henry Jaglom abandons the poseur excesses that marred his first film, *A Safe Place*. This time it's an incisive, revelatory film about a returning war veteran from Vietnam transporting the body of a friend across the US for burial.

Dennis Hopper gives an excellent rendering of this pro-soldier probably needing tenderness but hiding it until he finds it with a headstrong but knowing girl, played with authority by Tyrone Power's daughter, Taryn, who shows an offbeat beauty and presence.

Sometimes uneasy on its rails, film has perceptive personages and works on the level of reality and hallucination as they interact to give a feel of the US. Film takes place mostly on the train.

••••••••••••••••••••••••••••••••

■ TRACK 29

1988, 86 MINS, UK ◇ ⓥ
Dir Nicolas Roeg   *Prod* Rick McCallum   *Scr* Dennis Potter   *Ph* Alex Thomson   *Ed* Tony Lawson   *Mus* Stanley Myers   *Art Dir* David Brockhurst

● Theresa Russell, Gary Oldman, Sandra Bernhard, Christopher Lloyd, Colleen Camp, Seymour Cassel (HandMade)

Though clearly of above-average quality in direction, psychology and Theresa Russell's 3-D performance as a childless housewife with a dark secret in the closet, *Track 29* is connected closely to the classic American small-town horror film.

Screenplay is set in a Southern town where strange things happen every day. Linda (Russell) and husband Henry (Christopher Lloyd) are at odds over Linda's burning desire for a child and Henry's preference for his model trains. He also enjoys being spanked by Nurse Stein (Sandra Bernhard).

Into this world of normal absurdity arrives a stranger. Young Martin (Gary Oldman) convinces Linda he's her baby boy born out of wedlock and taken from her at birth, but viewer begins to have doubts that the appearing-disappearing weirdo isn't a figment of her imagination.

Perverse humor is the keynote of the Oedipal complexed duo, who spend a long day going to bars, exchanging unplatonic caresses, and acting out their traumas. Russell and Oldman are consummate thesps able to reach the edge of frenzy (and beyond) while remaining fun and original.

■ TRADER HORN

1931, 123 MINS, US
Dir W.S. Van Dyke   *Scr* Richard Schayer, Cyril Hume, Dale Van Every, J.T. Neville   *Ph* Clyde De Vinna
Ed Ben Lewis   *Mus* Charles Maxwell
● Harry Carey, Edwina Booth, Duncan Renaldo, Mutia Omoolu, Olive Golden, C. Aubrey Smith (M-G-M)

A good-looking animal picture. The story doesn't mean anything other than a connecting link for a series of sequences which, at one point, become nothing more than an out-and-out lecture tour, as various herds of animals are described by the voice of Harry Carey, in the title role. Studio has simply interpreted the original novel [by Aloysius Horn and Ethelreda Lewis] as it saw fit, lifting a couple of characters therefrom and putting them through a succession of narrow escapes from four-footed enemies and a cannibal tribe.

Light love vein is introduced between Carey's young companion, Duncan Renaldo, and Edwina Booth as the queen of a tribe from whom she and the men escape when her followers turn on her after she countermands an order of death by torture for Carey, Renaldo and Rencharo, the former's native gun boy.

Booth, very easy to look at, prances through the jungle in scanty raiment, knowing only the gutteral language of the blacks. The escape of the quartet immediately goes into a chase, during which Carey doubles back to act as decoy so the boy and girl can get away. Finish is the successful reaching of a river settlement where the youth and former tribal queen board a small river steamer bound for civilization, while Carey, as Trader Horn, prepares to go back into the jungle.

Sound effects are outstanding. Andy Anderson, the sound man, accompanied director W.S. Van Dyke's unit to Africa. The camera work is also swell marksmanship.
□ 1930/31: Nomination: Best Picture

■ TRADING PLACES

1983, 106 MINS, US ◇ ⦿ ⊙
Dir John Landis   *Prod* Aaron Russo   *Scr* Timothy Harris, Herschel Weingrod   *Ph* Robert Paynter
Ed Malcolm Campbell   *Mus* Elmer Bernstein
Art Dir Gene Rudolf
● Dan Aykroyd, Eddie Murphy, Ralph Bellamy, Don Ameche, Denholm Elliott, Jamie Lee Curtis (Paramount)

Trading Places is a light romp geared up by the schtick shifted by Dan Aykroyd and Eddie Murphy. Happily, it's a pleasure to report also that even those two popular young comics couldn't have brought this one off without the contributions of three veterans – Ralph Bellamy, Don Ameche and the droll Englishman, Denholm Elliott.

Aykroyd plays a stuffy young financial wizard who runs a Philadelphia commodities house for two continually scheming brothers, Bellamy and Ameche.

Conversely, Murphy has grown up in the streets and lives on the con, including posing as a blind, legless veteran begging outside Aykroyd's private club.

On a whim motivated by disagreement over the importance of environment vs breeding, Bellamy bets Ameche that Murphy could run the complex commodities business just as well as Aykroyd, given the chance. Conversely, according to the bet, Aykroyd would resort to crime and violence if suddenly all friends and finances were stripped away from him.

So their scheme proceeds and both Aykroyd and Murphy are in top form reacting to their new situations.

The only cost, however, is a mid-section stretch without laughs, still made enjoyable by the presence of Jamie Lee Curtis as a good-hearted hooker who befriends Aykroyd.
□ 1983: Nomination: Best Adapted Score

■ TRAIL OF THE LONESOME PINE, THE

1936, 100 MINS, US ◇
Dir Henry Hathaway   *Prod* Walter Wanger
Scr Grover Jones, Harvey Thew, Horace McCoy   *Ph* W. Howard Greene, Robert C. Bruce   *Ed* Robert Bischoff
Mus Hugo Friedhofer, Gerard Carbonara
Art Dir Alexander Toluboff
● Sylvia Sidney, Henry Fonda, Fred MacMurray, Fred Stone, Nigel Bruce, Beulah Bondi (Paramount)

The Trail of the Lonesome Pine is a good show, the first all-Technicolor feature produced 100% outdoors.

Director Henry Hathaway has sympathetically dealt with the ignorance of the mountaineer folk. His dialogicians, following the John Fox Jr original play – have faithfully preserved the reticent, curt mien of the feuding Tolliver and Falin clans.

Sylvia Sidney's performances as the 'billy looker is uncompromising in every detail. After a brief spell of schooling in Louisville, where Fred MacMurray has sent her, she reverts to type. Upon hearing how Buddy (Spanky McFarland) has been murdered, she too cries for a Falin's blood. Henry Fonda, as her mountaineer vis-a-vis, is equally consistent in his scowling hate for the Falin clan, as well as for the advent of the city engineer (MacMurray). Latter is capital in his dealings with the ignorant hillbillies and his affection for June Tolliver (Sidney).
□ 1936: Nomination: Best Song ('A Melody From The Sky')

■ TRAIL OF THE PINK PANTHER

1983, 97 MINS, UK ◇ ⦿ ⊡
Dir Blake Edwards   *Prod* Blake Edwards, Tony Adams
Scr Frank Waldman, Tom Waldman, Blake Edwards, Geoffrey Edwards   *Ph* Dick Bush   *Ed* Alan Jones
Mus Henry Mancini   *Art Dir* Peter Mullins
● Peter Sellers, David Niven, Herbert Lom, Richard Mulligan, Joanna Lumley, Capucine (Titan)

A patchwork of out-takes, reprised clips and new connective footage, *Trail of the Pink Panther* is a thin, peculiar picture unsupported by the number of laughs one is accustomed to in this series. Stitched together after Peter Sellers' death, this is by a long way the slightest of the six Inspector Clouseau efforts.

Story's structure is strange, to say the least.

The fabulous Pink Panther gem is stolen yet again from its vulnerable resting place in an Arab museum, which sparks immediate interest from the haplessly effective French detective.

Opening two reels are devoted to supposed out-take footage of Sellers trying on a disguise and on attempting to relieve himself in an airplane lavatory despite the encumbrance of an ungainly cast.

After about 40 minutes, Clouseau's Lugash-bound plane is reported missing. French television reporter Joanna Lumley sets out to interview many of those who had known the inspector in earlier pics, including David Niven, Capucine (looking great), Burt Kwouk, Graham Stark and Andre Maranne, as well as his father, Richard Mulligan, and a Mafia kingpin, Robert Loggia.

■ TRAIN, THE

1965, 140 MINS, US/FRANCE/ITALY ⦿
Dir John Frankenheimer   *Prod* Jules Bricken
Scr Franklin Coen, Frank Davis, [Walter Bernstein, Ned Young, Howard Infell]   *Ph* Walter Wottitz, Jean Tournier
Ed David Bretherton   *Mus* Maurice Jarre
Art Dir Willy Holt
● Burt Lancaster, Paul Scofield, Jeanne Moreou, Michel Simon, Suzanne Flon, Charles Millot (Artistes Associes/Ariane/Dear)

After a slow start, *The Train* picks up to become a colorful, actionful big-scale adventure opus. Made in French and English in France, it was entirely lensed in real exteriors with unlimited access to old French rolling stock of the last war.

Pic [from the novel *Le front de l'art* by Rose Valland] concerns an elaborate railroad resistance plot to keep a train full of French art treasures from being shipped to Germany near the end of the war.

An earthy station master (Burt Lancaster), if in the resistance, is reluctant to sacrifice men for paintings, especially with the war nearing its end. But he finally gives in when an old engineer, almost his foster father, is killed by the Germans for trying to hold up the art train. An elaborate plot is put into action. Lancaster himself is made to drive the train by the fanatic German colonel (Paul Scofield) to whom the art has become bigger than the war itself.

Jeanne Moreau has a small but telling cameo bit as does Michel Simon as the dedicated old engineer who swings Lancaster into line to go all out for saving the train. But above all it is the railroad bustle, the trains themselves and some bangup special effects of bombing attacks and accidents that give the pic its main points.
□ 1965: Best Original Story & Screenplay

■ TRAIN ROBBERS, THE

1973, 92 MINS, US ◇ ⦿ ⊙
Dir Burt Kennedy   *Prod* Michael Wayne   *Scr* Burt Kennedy   *Ph* William H. Clothier   *Ed* Frank Santillo
Mus Dominic Frontiere   *Art Dir* Ray Moyer, Alfred Sweeney
● John Wayne, Ann-Margret, Rod Taylor, Ben Johnson, Christopher George, Bobby Vinton (Batjac)

The Train Robbers is an above-average John Wayne actioner, written and directed by Burt Kennedy with suspense, comedy and humanism not usually found in the formula.

The plot peg is simple. Wayne recruits a group to recover gold stolen from a train by Ann-Margret's deceased outlaw husband, so her name and that of her child can be clear. However, Kennedy has provided a series of rich, deep individual characterizations, plus some intriguing red-herring plot twists.

Most important, for example, is the exposition of the Wayne character. Instead of the cardboard superman, he is given the added dimension of a man who actually could fall for a woman. Ann-Margret is most convincing in a role which requires that she be of her hardy environment, but above it enough to be credible as a lady-like, attractive widow.

••••••••••••••••••••••••••••••••••••

■ **TRANCERS**
(Aka: Future Cop)

1985, 85 MINS, US ◇ ⓥ ⊙
Dir Charles Band   *Prod* Charles Band   *Scr* Paul De Meo, Danny Bilson   *Ph* Mac Ahlberg   *Mus* Mark Ryder, Phil Davies
● Tim Thomerson, Helen Hunt, Michael Stefani, Art La Fleur, Biff Manard, Anne Seymour (Empire)

Trancers works out of a central idea closely akin to *The Terminator*. That is where resemblances end. This film in no way can match the Arnold Schwarzenegger vehicle – in gritty action, wit and technical knowhow.

Plot centers on Angel City 2247 AD. The ruins of LA, as it exists today, lie below the sea following a catastrophic earthquake. A sinister mystic, Martin Whistler (Michael Stefani), threatens the peace with his legion of controlled trancers.

Whistler retreats in time to LA 1985 with a plan to murder the ancestors of the rulers of Angel City, thus ensuring that the rulers cease to exist. Trooper Jack Deth (Tim Thomerson) is sent back to stop him. He is aided by Leena (Helen Hunt), his guide in the 'strange world' of today.

Only Hunt in the femme role breaks through a script that rarely rings new.

••••••••••••••••••••••••••••••••••••

■ **TRANSYLVANIA TWIST**

1989, 82 MINS, US ◇
Dir Jim Wynorski   *Prod* Alida Camp   *Scr* R.J. Robertson   *Ph* Zoran Hochstatter   *Ed* Nina Gilberti   *Mus* Chuck Cirino   *Art Dir* Gary Randall
● Robert Vaughn, Teri Copley, Steve Altman, Monique Gabrielle, Angus Scrimm, Ace Mask (Concorde)

Transylvania Twist is an occasionally hilarious horror spoof notable for the range of its comical targets. Filmmakers let all the stops out in silliness worthy of Mel Brooks.

Immediately with the teaser opening of perennial Jim Wynorski starlet Monique Gabrielle (uncredited though in a big role) being stalked through the woods by Jason, Freddy Krueger and Leatherface, pic applies a scattershot approach delving into other genres as well.

Robert Vaughn is delightful as a Dracula-styled vampire pronouncing the end of his last name Orlock with relish. His beautiful niece Teri Copley is an American singing star who travels to his castle in Transylvania upon the death of her father, accompanied by wise-cracking sidekick Steve Altman.

Mixed into the comic stew are many delightful reflexive bits: tracking camera that gets sidetracked on bodacious women passing by; a black & white sequence when star visits a set that looks left over from *The Honeymooners*; and a terrifically edited appearance by Boris Karloff.

••••••••••••••••••••••••••••••••••••

■ **TRAP, THE**

1966, 106 MINS, UK ◇ ⓥ
Dir Sidney Hayers   *Prod* George H. Brown   *Scr* David Osborn   *Ph* Robert Krasker   *Ed* Tristam Cones   *Mus* Ron Grainer   *Art Dir* Harry White
● Rita Tushingham, Oliver Reed, Rex Sevenoaks, Barbara Chilcott, Linda Goranson, Blain Fairman (Rank)

This Anglo-Canadian get together deals with an earthy adventure yarn, a struggle for survival, and an offbeat battle of the sexes.

Story is set in the mid-1890s when British Columbia was wild and untamed and only the strong came out on top. Jean La Bete (Oliver Reed), a huge, lusty French-Canadian trap-

per, returns to the trading post too late for the once-a-year 'auction' of harlots, thieves and femme riff-raff sent away from civilization for this purpose. So he settles for a young mute orphan, a servant in the trader's house, sold to him by the grasping wife.

He hauls the protesting girl into a canoe and sets off for the wastes. There follows an edgy Taming of the Shrew situation as the hunter tries to win her affection by cajoling, bullying, threatening, and occasionally sweet-talking.

Reed is larger-than-life as the crude, brawling trapper yet also has moments of great sensitivity with his co-star. Tushingham, sans benefit of dialog has to depend on her famous eyes, and wistful mouth to put over a tricky role embracing many emotions, from spitfire to waif, and she does marvels.

••••••••••••••••••••••••••••••••••••

■ **TRAPEZE**

1956, 106 MINS, US ◇ ⓥ
Dir Carol Reed   *Prod* James Hill   *Scr* James R. Webb   *Ph* Robert Krasker   *Ed* Bert Bates   *Mus* Malcolm Arnold   *Art Dir* Rino Mondellini
● Burt Lancaster, Tony Curtis, Gina Lollobrigida, Katy Jurado, Thomas Gomez, Minor Watson (Susan/United Artists)

Trapeze is a high-flying screen entertainment equipped with circus thrills and excitement, a well-handled romantic triangle, and a cast of potent marquee names. Cirque d'Hiver, Paris' famed one-ring circus, provides the authentic, colorful, exciting setting.

Reed's direction loads the aerial scenes with story suspense for even more thrill effect, and male stars Burt Lancaster and Tony Curtis simulate the bigtop aristocrats realistically.

The well-plotted script, from Liam O'Brien's adaptation of Max Catto's novel *The Killing Frost*, tells how Curtis, son of an aerialist, comes to Paris to learn from Lancaster, one of the few fliers able to achieve the triple somersault, a feat which had left him crippled. Together, they start to work up an act when the tumbler moves in, using her wiles on the young man but loving the older.

Gina Lollobrigida, justly famed for her curves, proves she can act, giving the necessary touch of flamboyance without going overboard. Katy Jurado lights up what scenes she has.

••••••••••••••••••••••••••••••••••••

■ **TRASH**

1970, 103 MINS, US ◇ ⓥ
Dir Paul Morrissey   *Prod* Andy Warhol   *Scr* Paul Morrissey   *Ph* Paul Morrissey   *Ed* Jed Johnson
● Joe Dallesandro, Holly Woodlawn, Jane Forth, Michael Sklar, Geri Miller, Andrea Feldman (Warhol)

Andy Warhol surfaces from the camp underground with *Trash*, the most comprehensible, and least annoying of a long line of quasi-porno features from *Chelsea Girls* to *Lonesome Cowboys*.

As with earlier *Flesh*, director here is Paul Morrissey who has the Warhol gift of attracting gregarious grotesque and eliciting no-holds improvisations within loosely structured dramatic situations.

Once again, stud-in-residence is Joe Dallesandro, this time as a strung-out heroin addict unable to function sexually despite numerous provocations. He displays both a forceful screen presence and ease in front of the camera that cannot be hastily dismissed.

••••••••••••••••••••••••••••••••••••

■ **TRAVELING EXECUTIONER, THE**

1970, 94 MINS, US ◇ ⓥ
Dir Jack Smight   *Prod* Jack Smight   *Scr* Garrie Bateson   *Ph* Philip Lathrop   *Ed* Neil Travis   *Mus* Jerry Goldsmith   *Art Dir* George W. Davis, Edward Carfagno

● Stacy Keach, Marianna Hill, Bud Cort, Graham Jarvis, James J. Sloyan, M. Emmett Walsh (M-G-M)

The Traveling Executioner is a macabre, tastefully seamy comedy-drama about bayou prison life, circa 1918. The original Garrie Bateson screenplay stars Stacy Keach in an outstanding performance as an infectious con-man.

Bateson's first screenplay, written as a U of Southern California student, is dominated by Keach, the professional executioner who makes $100 per client. He's a promoter from the word go, but an underlying, disarming sincerity about the job makes the character believable and sympathetic. Keach's talents convey the whole spectrum of his role.

A literal description of the story does injustice to the whole; there are some gritty elements and some broad comedy elements – earthy enough to anchor the story in its proper context.

••••••••••••••••••••••••••••••••••••

■ **TRAVELLING NORTH**

1987, 96 MINS, AUSTRALIA ◇ ⓥ
Dir Carl Schultz   *Prod* Ben Gannon   *Scr* David Williamson   *Ph* Julian Penny   *Ed* Henry Dangar   *Mus* Alan John   *Art Dir* Owen Paterson
● Leo McKern, Julia Blake, Graham Kennedy, Henri Szeps, Michelle Fawdon, Diane Craig (View)

This superbly crafted adaptation of David Williamson's popular stage play is a mature, frequently funny and ultimately most moving story of old age and retirement.

Leo McKern plays Frank, a rather cantankerous ex-Communist and civil engineer who retires from work at age 70. A widower, he has persuaded his close friend, Frances (Julia Blake), a widow but not as old as he, to accompany him north, to subtropical northern Queensland.

After many happy days fishing, reading and listening to music (and enjoying the sexual side of the relationship), Frank's health begins to deteriorate and Frances starts to yearn to see her family again.

Australian-born McKern, in his first Australian film, gives a remarkable performance as the crotchety, yet endearing, Frank. It's a hugely enjoyable portrayal. As Frances, Blake positively glows; she plays a patient, loving woman with a determination of her own, and it's a rich characterization.

••••••••••••••••••••••••••••••••••••

■ **TRAVELS WITH MY AUNT**

1972, 109 MINS, UK ◇
Dir George Cukor   *Prod* Robert Fryer, James Cresson   *Scr* Jay Presson Allen, Hugh Wheeler   *Ph* Douglas Slocombe   *Ed* John Bloom   *Mus* Tony Hatch   *Art Dir* John Box
● Maggie Smith, Alec McCowen, Lou Gossett, Robert Stephens, Cindy Williams, Robert Flemyng (M-G-M)

Travels with My Aunt is the story [based on the Graham Greene bestseller] of an outrageous femme of indeterminate years cavorting in a set of outrageous situations which spell high comedy. Of course, it may also be regarded as utter nonsense in a hammed-up set of overly-contrived circumstances.

Maggie Smith plays the title role in an overdrawn but thoroughly delightful manner. Film opens quietly enough at the funeral services of her nephew's mother, but the disrupting arrival of the over-dressed, over-cosmeticked Aunt Augusta sets the stage for a comedy spree.

George Cukor's direction is quite up to meeting the demands of the script, and he is responsible for a tempo attuned to his unusual characters. Alec McCowen's characterization of the nephew is subtle and expansive as he gradually withdraws from his former stuffy, priggish, ex-bank manager style.
☐ 1972: Best Costume Design (Anthony Powell).

□ Nominations: Best Actress (Maggie Smith), Cinematography, Art Direction

••••••••••••••••••••••••••••••

■ **T.R. BASKIN**

(UK: A Date With a Lonely Girl)

1971, 89 MINS, US ◇ ⓥ

Dir Herbert Ross   *Prod* Peter Hyams   *Scr* Peter Hyams   *Ph* Gerald Hirschfield   *Ed* Maury Winstrobe   *Mus* Jack Elliott   *Art Dir* Albert Brenner

● Candice Bergen, Peter Boyle, James Caan, Marcia Rodd, Erin O'Reilly, Howard Platt (Paramount)

T.R. Baskin makes a few good comedy-comments on modern urban existence, but these are bits of rare jewelry lost on a vast beach of strung-out, erratic storytelling. Candice Bergen is featured in title role of a rural girl who is, or is not, worth caring about in the big city. Told in flashback, Peter Hyams' debut production is handsomely mounted, but his screenplay is sterile, superficial and inconsistent. Peter Boyle is an out-of-towner who called Bergen for sex, but instead suffers through her equivocal talk-therapy.

Bergen's screen presence is too sophisticated for the role, and both her acting, direction and dialog result in confusion. One moment she is to be pitied; the next she is fouling up her own chances with people. Boyle, whose contribution is little more than a foil, tries to get some depth into the role of a square salesman.

James Caan, looking more mature, is another professional victim, as a divorced man who ends a perfect night with Bergen by offering her some money. He isn't the only one who isn't sure what she is.

••••••••••••••••••••••••••••••

■ **TREASURE ISLAND**

1934, 105 MINS, US ⓥ

Dir Victor Fleming   *Prod* Hunt Stromberg   *Scr* John Lee Mahin   *Ph* Ray June, Clyde De Vinna, Harold Rosson   *Ed* Blanche Sewell   *Mus* Herbert Stothart   *Art Dir* Cedric Gibbons, Merrill Pye

● Wallace Beery, Jackie Cooper, Lionel Barrymore, Otto Kruger, Lewis Stone, Nigel Bruce (M-G-M)

It's pretty dangerous to put an old classic as popular as this Robert Louis Stevenson yarn on the screen. It is hard to imagine anyone else in the Long John Silver role than Wallace Beery. It is hard to think of anyone who might have replaced Jackie Cooper as Jim Hawkins. Yet neither of the two completely convinces.

Best performance honors are really split between Lionel Barrymore and Chic Sale. Former, as Billy Bones, and latter as Ben Gunn, seem most thoroughly to have caught the Stevenson spirit. They overact almost to mugging but it's in keeping with the manner of the story.

Treasure Island as a story is a grand, blood-curdling adventure yarn. In portions where it is so played it's genuinely thrilling and good entertainment.

••••••••••••••••••••••••••••••

■ **TREASURE ISLAND**

1950, 96 MINS, UK ◇ ⓥ ⊙

Dir Byron Haskin   *Prod* Perce Pearce   *Scr* Lawrence E. Watkin   *Ph* Freddie Young   *Ed* Alan Jaggs   *Mus* Clifton Parker   *Art Dir* Tom Morahan

● Bobby Driscoll, Robert Newton, Basil Sydney, Walter Fitzgerald, Dennis O'Dea, Finlay Currie (RKO/Walt Disney)

Treasure Island, Robert Louis Stevenson's classic, has been handsomely mounted by Walt Disney. Settings are sumptuous and a British cast headed by American moppet Bobby Driscoll faithfully recaptures the bloodthirsty 18th-century era when pirates vied for the supremacy of the seas. It was made in Britain with Disney and RKO frozen pounds.

Stevenson yarn revolves around a squire and a doctor who fit out a ship to search for South Seas treasure on the strength of a chart obtained from a dying pirate.

Robert Newton racks up a virtual tour de force as Long John Silver. Likewise, Driscoll smashes across with a vital portrayal of Jim Hawkins, the saloonkeeper's son who falls heir to a map leading the way to pirate treasure.

There's no dearth of action in the footage.

••••••••••••••••••••••••••••••

■ **TREASURE OF THE GOLDEN CONDOR**

1953, 93 MINS, US ◇ ⓥ

Dir Delmer Daves   *Prod* Jules Buck   *Scr* Delmer Daves   *Ph* Edward Cronjager   *Ed* Robert Simpson   *Mus* Sol Kaplan   *Art Dir* Lyle R. Wheeler, Albert Hogsett

● Cornel Wilde, Constance Smith, Finlay Currie, Walter Hampden, Anne Bancroft, Fay Wray (20th Century-Fox)

A moderate round of entertainment is offered in this adventure-swashbuckler that lays its action against Technicolored backgrounds in early France and Guatemala. Ancient Mayan ruins, particularly the earthquake-wrecked city of Antigua, supply a picturesque touch to the phsyical values. Action scenes are good.

Plot, from a novel by Edison Marshall, deals with Wilde's efforts to oust a cruel uncle (George Macready) who has usurped his French estates and title. Needing money to prove his rights, Wilde joins forces with Finlay Currie, possessor of a map to a fabulous Mayan treasure, and his daughter (Constance Smith). Back in France his plans are exposed by Anne Bancroft, a selfish girl he hopes to wed.

Wilde is likeable as the dashing hero and has some good swashbuckling moments in the latter portions of the footage. Smith and Bancroft both look good in their costumes. Fay Wray has only a few brief scenes as Macready's suffering wife

••••••••••••••••••••••••••••••

■ **TREASURE OF THE SIERRA MADRE, THE**

1948, 124 MINS, US ⓥ ⊙

Dir John Huston   *Prod* Henry Blanke   *Scr* John Huston   *Ph* Ted McCord   *Ed* Owen Marks   *Mus* Max Steiner   *Art Dir* John Hughes

● Humphrey Bogart, Walter Huston, Tim Holt, Bruce Bennett, Barton MacLane (Warner)

Sierra Madre, adapted from the popular novel by B. Traven, is a story of psychological disintegration under the crushers of greed and gold. The characters here are probed and thoroughly penetrated, not through psychoanalysis but through a crucible of human conflict, action, gesture and expressive facial tones.

Huston, with an extraordinary assist in the thesping department from his father, Walter Huston, has fashioned this standout film with an unfailing sensitivity for the suggestive detail and an uncompromising commitment to reality, no matter how stark ugly it may be.

Except for some incidental femmes who have no bearing on the story, it's an all-male cast headed by Bogart, Huston and Tim Holt. They play the central parts of three gold prospectors who start out for pay dirt in the Mexican mountains as buddies, but wind up in a murderous tangle at the finish.

Lensed for most part on location, the film has, at least, a physical aspect of rugged beauty against which is contrasted the human sordidness.

Bogart comes through with a performance as memorable as his first major film role in *The Petrified Forest*. In a remarkable controlled portrait, he progresses to the edge of madness without losing sight of the subtle shadings needed to establish persuasiveness.

□ 1948: Best Director, Best Supp. Actor (Walter Huston), Screenplay.
□ Nomination: Best Picture

••••••••••••••••••••••••••••••

■ **TREE GROWS IN BROOKLYN, A**

1945, 132 MINS, US ⓥ ⊙

Dir Elia Kazan   *Prod* Louis D. Lighton   *Scr* Tess Slesinger, Frank Davis   *Ph* Leon Shamroy   *Ed* Dorothy Spencer   *Mus* Alfred Newman   *Art Dir* Lyle R. Wheeler

● Dorothy McGuire, Joan Blondell, James Dunn, Lloyd Nolan, Peggy Ann Garner (20th Century-Fox)

The earthy quality of Brooklyn tenement squalor, about which Betty Smith wrote so eloquently in the bestseller novel *A Tree Grows in Brooklyn*, has been given a literal translation to the screen by 20th-Fox to become an experiment in audience restraint. This is the story of the poverty-ridden Nolan family.

Tree recalls an absorbing period of a colorful tribe, of a Brooklyn neighborhood that was tough in its growing-up, where kids fought, where on Saturday nights fathers and husbands, loped uncertainly from the corner quenchery.

Some of this might have acquired the tinge of travesty in hands less skilled than those of Smith – or director Elia Kazan – but never does the serio-comic intrude on a false note; never does this story become maudlin.

To Dorothy McGuire went the prize part of Katie Nolan. It is a role that she makes distinctive by underplaying. James Dunn plays excellently. Peggy Ann Garner is the teenaged Francie, and the young actress performs capitally.

Where *Tree* is frequently slow, it is offset by the story's significance and pointed up notably by the direction of Elia Kazan.

□ 1945: Best Supp. Actor (James Dunn).
□ Nomination: Best Screenplay

••••••••••••••••••••••••••••••

■ **TREMORS**

1990, 96 MINS, US ◇ ⓥ ⊙

Dir Ron Underwood   *Prod* S.S. Wilson, Brent Maddock   *Scr* S.S. Wilson, Brent Maddock   *Ph* Alexander Gruszynski   *Ed* O. Nicholas Brown   *Mus* Ernest Troost   *Art Dir* Ivo Cristante

● Kevin Bacon, Fred Ward, Finn Carter, Michael Gross, Reba McEntire, Bobby Jacoby (No Frills)

An affectionate send-up of schlocky 1950s monster pics, but with better special effects, *Tremors* has a few clever twists but ultimately can't decide what it wants to be – flat-out funny, which it's not, or a scarefest.

In this case, the threat comes in the form of four house trailer-sized worm-creatures, with multiple serpent like tongues, that tunnel underground before bursting up to devour human prey.

All the conventions of the genre are here: a small town in the middle of nowhere isolated from outside help, with a scientist on hand to study strange seismic phenomena. After that, however, the scripters begin to play with those cliches. The scientist, for example, is a pretty young woman (Finn Carter) who doesn't know where the monsters come from or understand why everyone keeps asking her to explain, while the heroes – handyman types Kevin Bacon and Fred Ward – carry on like Curly and Larry in search of Moe.

The pacing and action improve considerably as the film goes on, maintaining a tongue-in-cheek approach while the situation becomes more dire.

••••••••••••••••••••••••••••••

■ **TRESPASS**

1992, 101 MINS, US ◇ ⓥ ⊙

Dir Walter Hill   *Prod* Neil Canton   *Scr* Bob Gale, Robert Zemeckis   *Ph* Lloyd Ahern   *Ed* Freeman Davies   *Mus* Ry Cooder   *Art Dir* Jon Hutman

● Bill Paxton, Ice T, William Sadler, Ice Cube, Art Evans, De'voreaux White (Universal)

Throw together *The Treasure of the Sierra Madre* and *Rio Bravo*, bring in the Ice crew, inject a noxious dose of racial hatred and stir in some sharp action direction and you've got *Trespass*.

Originally called *Looters*, pic underwent a title change, a delay and some alterations after the LA riots in spring '92. Understandably so: the level of racial tension depicted here is way past the boiling point.

After a brief prologue, the film is entirely set in one location, a huge abandoned factory in East St. Louis, Ill. Learning that a huge stash of gold is supposedly buried somewhere in the bombed-out building, good ol' boy firemen Bill Paxton and William Sadler drive to the eerily underpopulated area with the idea of recovering the loot.

Unfortunately for them, the two Arkansas crackers stumble on to a gangland murder and instantly become marked men. Pursued by some tough, well-armed blacks led by a resplendent Ice T, Paxton and Sadler manage to nab T's brother (De'voreaux White). Holed up in one room, the white guys squabble about what to do with that loot.

Director Walter Hill's handling of the action is fluid and kinetic, making the film a pleasure to watch for the expertness of its craft.

Ice T and Ice Cube strut their stuff in impressively forceful, if one-dimensional, fashion. Paxton and Sadler come off as decent but unremarkable. Technically, film is tops. Buildings in Atlanta and Memphis were employed for the single location.

• •

■ TRIAL, THE

1962, 115 MINS, FRANCE/W. GERMANY/ITALY ⊗
Dir Orson Welles   *Prod* Alexander Salkind   *Scr* Orson Welles   *Ph* Edmond Richard   *Ed* Fritz H. Mueller   *Mus* Jean Ledrut   *Art Dir* Jean Mandaroux
● Anthony Perkins, Jeanne Moreau, Romy Schneider, Elsa Martinelli, Akim Tamiroff, Orson Welles (Paris-Europa/Hisa/FICIT)

Written and directed by himself from the 'nightmare' novel by Franz Kafka, Orson Welles' film may well delight film buffs and startle or irritate many others.

A young white-collar worker, Joseph K, wakes up one morning to find a sinister police inspector and two seedy detectives in his room. He is technically under arrest but he is not told why. He accepts the fact after various attempts at rationalizing.

Then the film gets progressively more expressionistic and surreal as he is caught up completely in his impending trial and neglects work, one woman next door who promised adventure, and gets deeper into the complex setup of the law. The geography of the film becomes inextricably bound up with dusty file rooms, waiting rooms full of supposedly guilty men not knowing why they are there and K's final attempt to revolt.

Anthony Perkins as K is on screen practically all the time. His boyishness is oft pedaled to turn him into a timid but priggish type who faces up to an impersonal court. It shapes as a knowing, incisive screen performance.

Jeanne Moreau, Elsa Martinelli and others have fleeting parts that are adequately done. Most outstanding is Romy Schneider as the lawyer's nurse who is irresistibly drawn to accused men.

Welles has given slight intimations that this could be a totalitarian nation or one of over-automation. And it also may be a man's awakening to consciousness and finding himself alienated in the world and rejecting its aspects one by one.

So pic is uneven and sometimes filled with arid talk, but has enough visual vitality to keep it engrossing in its first part.

• •

■ TRIAL, THE

1993, 118 MINS, UK ◇ ⊗
Dir David Jones   *Prod* Louis Marks   *Scr* Harold Pinter   *Ph* Phil Meheux   *Ed* John Stothart   *Mus* Carl Davis   *Art Dir* Don Taylor

● Kyle MacLachlan, Anthony Hopkins, Jason Robards, Jean Stapleton, Polly Walker, Juliet Stevenson (BBC/Europanda)

The Trial is just that. Despite a fine cast, superior Prague locations and a faithful Harold Pinter screenplay, this second film adaptation of Kafka's landmark 1913 novel is dull, lifeless and strictly TV-bound in its aesthetics.

Up against the brick wall of an authoritarian regime and an unknowable Law, K (Kyle MacLachlan) has experiences that are positively illogical and evocative of modern man's absurd status in the universe.

There are sexual skirmishes with another boarder (Juliet Stevenson) and his lawyer's mistress (Polly Walker), encounters with various men who possess passing knowledge of aspects of the Law (uncle Robert Lang, attorney Jason Robards, court painter Alfred Molina) and assorted odd characters, such as a washerwoman (Catherine Neilson) who submits sexually to her detested boyfriend in front of hundreds of people at K's hearing.

But, as structured, the script evolves as a tedious series of mostly two-character scenes. Performances are perfectly acceptable without being at all electrifying.

• •

■ TRIAL AND ERROR

See: *The Dock Brief*

• •

■ TRIAL OF BILLY JACK, THE

1974, 170 MINS, US ◇ ⊗
Dir Frank Laughlin, [= Tom Laughlin]   *Prod* Joe Cramer   *Scr* Frank Christina [= Tom Laughlin], Teresa Christina [= Dolores Taylor]   *Ph* Jack A. Marta   *Ed* Tom Rolf, Michael Economou, George Grenville, Michael Karr, Jules Nayfack   *Mus* Elmer Bernstein   *Art Dir* George W. Troast
● Tom Laughlin, Delores Taylor, Victor Izay, Teresa Laughlin, William Wellman Jr, Russell Lane (Taylor-Laughlin)

The Trial of Billy Jack is a violent, sometimes-explosive, anti-Establishment sequel to *Billy Jack* [1971]. Like its predecessor, starring the same two principals, it pinpoints community prejudices against the refusal of many to accept the American Indian.

Trial takes up as *Billy* ended, when Tom Laughlin as the halfbreed Billy Jack was arrested for murder. Told in flashback by Delores Taylor, whose earlier rape was avenged by Billy Jack, and now he is sentenced to prison much of the footage unfolds at the Freedom School, a reservation institution headed by white femme.

The production enjoys extraordinary pictorial interest through having been photographed in Arizona's Monument Valley. But it is only when Laughlin is on-camera that the picture picks up.

• •

■ TRIAL OF SERGEANT RUTLEDGE

See: *Sergeant Rutledge*

• •

■ TRIAL OF THE CATONSVILLE NINE, THE

1972, 85 MINS, US ◇ ⊗
Dir Gordon Davidson   *Prod* Gregory Peck   *Scr* Daniel Berrigan, Saul Levitt   *Ph* Haskell Wexler   *Ed* Aaron Stell   *Mus* Shelley Manne   *Art Dir* Peter Wexler
● Gwen Arner, Ed Flanders, Barton Heyman, Richard Jordan, Nancy Malone, Donald Moffat (Melville)

Gregory Peck has produced a film version of *The Trial of the Catonsville Nine* which shapes intelligent, well-acted filmed theatre and is potent in its look at the reasons behind burning of draft records and the trial that followed.

Film begins with a reenactment of burning of the records and the nine waiting for the police, to call attention to their outlooks.

Though based on a play by Father Daniel Berrigan, and with highflown passages of talk, it reportedly draws heavily on the actual court proceedings. But Berrigan tries to delve into the backgrounds, reasons and outlooks of those involved, their attempts to explain their actions by what they thought was wrong with the participation in the Vietnam War.

Theatrical, but fluidly controlled, direction by Gordon Davidson gives this a dramatic impetus despite static qualities and literary dialog.

• •

■ TRIALS OF OSCAR WILDE, THE
(US: *The Man with the Green Carnation*)

1960, 123 MINS, UK ◇
Dir Ken Hughes   *Prod* Harold Huth   *Scr* Ken Hughes   *Ph* Ted Moore   *Ed* Geoffrey Foot   *Mus* Ron Goodwin
● Peter Finch, Yvonne Mitchell, James Mason, Nigel Patrick, Lionel Jeffries, John Fraser (Viceroy/Warwick)

Color and wide screen are a sock asset to *The Trials of Oscar Wilde* and, on balance, it has greater stellar appeal [than the b&w version, *Oscar Wilde*, released at virtually the same time].

Main difference in the two films is the color job starts where the scandalous friendship is well established and spends more time setting the atmosphere of the time of the turn of the century.

Trials [from John Fernald's play *The Stringed Lute* and Montgomery Hyde's *Trial of Oscar Wilde*] also introduces Wilde's re-trial and, in one brilliant scene at Brighton, shows Wilde's anguish when he first realizes that he is merely being used by his young friend as a weapon in his vindictive struggle with his brutal father.

Peter Finch gives a moving and subtle performance as the ill-starred playwright. Before his downfall he gives the man the charm that he undoubtedly had. The famous Wilde epigrams could well have been thought up by Finch.

John Fraser as handsome young Lord Alfred Douglas is suitably vain, selfish, vindictive and petulant and the relationship between the two is more understandable.

Where *Trials* suffers in comparison with the b&w film is in the remarkable impact of the libel case court sequence. James Mason never provides the strength adn bitter logic necessary for the dramatic cut-and-thrust when Wilde is in the witness box.

• •

■ TRIBUTE TO A BAD MAN

1956, 95 MINS, US ◇
Dir Robert Wise   *Prod* Sam Zimbalist   *Scr* Michael Blankfort   *Ph* Robert Surtees   *Ed* Ralph E. Winters   *Mus* Miklos Rozsa   *Art Dir* Cedric Gibbons, Paul Groesse
● James Cagney, Don Dubbins, Stephen McNally, Irene Papas, Vic Morrow, Lee Van Cleef (M-G-M)

A rugged frontier drama of the early west, played off against the scenically striking Colorado Rockies, *Tribute to a Bad Man* is a sight to behold, using the location sites for full visual worth. Irene Papas, Greek actress, in her Hollywood debut comes off well.

Critically, *Bad Man* is both fast and slow-paced. Latter, in part, results from a feeling of repetition in some of the story points as scripted from a Jack Schaefer short story, and in some scene-prolonging beyond the point of good dramatic return by Robert Wise's direction.

The title is somewhat of a misnomer. The man portrayed so well by Cagney is a hard-bitten pioneer who must enforce his own law on the limitless range he controls. The picture of him is seen through the eyes of young Don Dubbins, eastern lad come west to make his fortune and who tarries awhile in Cagney's employ.

The stay is long enough for him to fall in

love with Papas and almost win her away from Cagney when she rebels at the latter's arrogant justice of the rope for breakers of his laws.

••••••••••••••••••••••••••••••

■ **TRICK OR TREAT**

1986, 97 MINS, US ◇ ▽
Dir Charles Martin Smith   *Prod* Michael S. Murphey, Joel Soisson   *Scr* Michael S. Murphey, Joel Soisson, Rhet Topham   *Ph* Robert Elswit   *Ed* Jane Schwartz   *Mus* Christopher Young, Fastway   *Art Dir* Curt Schnell
● Marc Price, Tony Fields, Lisa Orgolini, Ozzy Osbourne (De Laurentiis)

Like a relatively dark street on Halloween night, *Trick or Treat* is ripe for howls and hoots, but only manages to deliver a choice handful of them when the festivities are just about over.

A recently killed rock star named Sammi Curr (Tony Fields, made up like a member of KISS), comes back to life when his last, awful unreleased record is played backwards. He's determined to seek revenge on his most ardent critics.

The thing is, the satanic rocker takes himself seriously in reincarnation and ends up acting out all those evil acts he's been singing about for years – drawing his power from the megawatts that surge through his guitar.

There's a geeky highschool kid, Eddie (Marc Price), who idolizes the rocker and is responsible for his appearances. Price is cast perfectly as the dismayed rock worshipper.

••••••••••••••••••••••••••••••

■ **TRIO**

1950, 91 MINS, UK ▽
Dir Ken Annakin, Harold French   *Prod* Antony Darnborough   *Scr* W. Somerset Maugham, R.C. Sherriff, Noel Langley   *Ph* Reginald Wyer, Geoffrey Unsworth   *Ed* Alfred Roome   *Mus* John Greenwood   *Art Dir* Maurice Carter
● James Hayter, Anne Crawford, Nigel Patrick, Jean Simmons, Michael Rennie, Kathleen Harrison (Gainsborough)

The success of *Quartet*, in which four unrelated Somerset Maugham short stories were strung together in a single picture, encouraged the producers to repeat the formula.

The only connecting link between the three yarns is a pithy Maugham foreword. The first two vignettes, *The Verger* and *Mr Know-All* [directed by Ken Annakin], between them occupy roughly half the screen time. *Sanatorium* [directed by Harold French] deals with the treatment of tuberculosis.

The first two are bright. The longer piece strikes a happy note between sentiment and laughter.

In *The Verger*, James Hayter is warm and colorful and Kathleen Harrison is typically cast.

Nigel Patrick dominates *Mr Knowall* while Jean Simmons and Michael Rennie in *Sanatorium* play their roles with distinctive charm.

□ 1950: Nomination: Best Sound

••••••••••••••••••••••••••••••

■ **TRIP, THE**

1967, 85 MINS, US ◇ ▽
Dir Roger Corman   *Prod* Roger Corman   *Scr* Jack Nicholson   *Ph* Arch Dalzell   *Ed* Ronald Sinclair   *Mus* American Music Band
● Peter Fonda, Susan Strasberg, Bruce Dern, Dennis Hopper, Salli Sachse, Katherine Walsh (American International)

Jack Nicholson script opens with Peter Fonda, a director of TV commercials, shooting on a beach and being confronted by wife, Susan Strasberg, who is about to divorce him. Distressed by his personal life, he goes off with friend Bruce Dern to the hippie, weirdly-painted house of a pusher, played by Dennis Hopper, to buy LSD.

Guarded by Dern, Fonda's trip begins. Scenes rapidly cut from Fonda climbing lofty sand dunes, being chased by two black hooded horsemen through forests, as well as being the sacrificial victim at a dark medieval rite in a torchlit cave. Unconnected scenes begin to spin off the screen with increasing speed and with no attempt at explanation.

Fonda comes across very well, establishing the various moods needed to further the visual effects. Strasberg is on only briefly, and Hopper is okay, except in a dream sequence in which he plays a weirdo high priest, but that whole scene is sophomoric.

••••••••••••••••••••••••••••••

■ **TRIPLE CROSS**

1966, 140 MINS, FRANCE/UK ◇ ▽
Dir Terence Young   *Prod* Jacques-Paul Bertrand   *Scr* Rene Hardy, William Marchant, Terence Young   *Ph* Henri Alekan   *Ed* Roger Dwyre   *Mus* Georges Gavarentz   *Art Dir* Tony Roman
● Christopher Plummer, Yul Brynner, Romy Schneider, Claudine Auger, Trevor Howard, Gert Frobe (Cineurop)

Though based on a true story of a British safe-cracker who worked as a double spy during the Second World War, *Triple Cross* is made in the standard spy pattern of having him a ladies' man, fast with his mitts, glib and shrewd, and with overloaded and obvious suspense bits thrown in to rob this of the verisimilitude needed to give it a more original fillip.

Director Terence Young plays this slightly tongue-in-cheek and it actually emerges as a sort of mini-Bond. Christopher Plummer is first seen cracking a series of safes and is finally arrested on Jersey. Along comes war and the Germans take over the island. He bluffs his way into getting a hearing with some top German undercover people.

He manages to gull them into letting him work for them and is finally entrusted with a mission. Once in Britain he goes to the British security people, finally convinces them and goes to work for them for a big sum and a promise to wipe out his criminal record.

Plummer walks through his role and does not quite have the impassive mask for the pro criminal or the needed lightness to give it a romantic dash it calls for.

••••••••••••••••••••••••••••••

■ **TRIPLE ECHO, THE**

1972, 102 MINS, UK ◇ ▽
Dir Michael Apted   *Prod* Graham Cottle   *Scr* Robin Chapman   *Ph* Mark Wilkinson   *Ed* Barrie Vince   *Mus* Denis Lewiston   *Art Dir* Edward Marshall
● Glenda Jackson, Oliver Reed, Brian Deacon, Anthony May, Gavin Richards, Jenny Lee Wright (Hemdale/Senta)

Story is set on an English farm in 1943. Alice (Glenda Jackson) has been living alone in the country, since her husband was taken a prisoner by the Japanese a half-year earlier. One day a young soldier, Barton (Brian Deacon), comes along and during a tender moment she invites him in for tea. When time comes for Barton to rejoin his regiment, he decides to go AWOL and stay with Alice. So as not to be discovered he starts donning female clothes.

Just as Barton is becoming tired of his equivocal role, a stray tank comes rolling down the hill with a sergeant (Oliver Reed) in it. Next day he's back again, trying to catch a glimpse of Barton, whom he believes to be Alice's sister. At length he does see the 'sister' and announces he's going to take her out dancing.

Aside from the contrived ending, the slow pacing through most of the pic up to the time Reed appears, one never really gets into the motivations of the two main characters.

••••••••••••••••••••••••••••••

■ **TRIP TO BOUNTIFUL, THE**

1985, 106 MINS, US ◇ ▽ ⊙
Dir Peter Masterson   *Prod* Sterling Van Wagenen, Horton Foote   *Scr* Horton Foote   *Ph* Fred Murphy

Ed Jay Freund   *Mus* J.A.C. Redford   *Art Dir* Neil Spisak
● Geraldine Page, John Heard, Carlin Glynn, Richard Bradford, Rebecca DeMornay, Kevin Cooney (FilmDallas/Bountiful Film Partners)

The Trip to Bountiful is a superbly crafted drama featuring the performance of a lifetime by Geraldine Page. She plays Mrs Watts, a woman whose determination to escape the confines of life in a small Houston apartment with her selfless son Ludie (John Heard) and his domineering wife Jessie Mae (Carlin Glynn) leads her on a moving and memorable journey across the Gulf Coast to return to Bountiful, the town where she was born and raised.

Adapted by Horton Foote from his 1953 teleplay that enjoyed theatrical success on Broadway, the 1947-set film recalls the days of scripts with real plots and dialog.

Life for Mrs Watts with Ludie and Jessie Mae is a claustrophobic and harsh existence of forced politeness, petty battles and demanded apologies. Heard is excellent as the downtrodden Ludie burdened with keeping the peace while contending with money problems and self doubts.

Glynn likewise puts in a strong performance, giving a human edge and depth to what could have been an otherwise nagging wife stereotype. Page's work is excellent throughout.

□ 1985: Best Actress (Geraldine Page).
□ Nomination: Best Screenplay Adaptation

••••••••••••••••••••••••••••••

■ **TRIUMPH OF THE SPIRIT**

1989, 120 MINS, US ◇ ▽ ⊙
Dir Robert M. Young   *Prod* Arnold Kopelson, Shimon Arama   *Scr* Andrzej Krakowski, Laurence Heath   *Ph* Curtis Clark   *Ed* Arthur Coburn   *Mus* Cliff Eidelman   *Art Dir* Jerzy Maslowski
● Willem Dafoe, Edward James Olmos, Robert Loggia, Wendy Gazelle, Kelly Wolf, Costas Mandylor (Nova/Arama/Kopelson)

An event as oft-dramatized as the Holocaust becomes difficult to portray anew, a circumstance that blunts the impact of *Triumph of the Spirit*. Film's *raison d'etre* – its true story of a Greek boxing champ who survived life-or-death bouts in the ring at Auschwitz – is murkily underplayed within the harrowing chronicle of death-camp suffering.

Producer Arnold Kopelson (*Platoon*), bucking indifference from the studios, spent seven years bringing the story [by Shimon Arama and Zion Haen] to the screen.

In conveying the experience of the Greek middleweight boxer Salamo Arouch (Willem Dafoe), writers were hamstrung by history, as Arouch did not take part in the film's climactic event – an uprising that leads to the blowing up of the crematorium (and the death of most of the conspirators). Focus is therefore spread among Arouch's family and friends, including his love interest, Allegra (Wendy Gazelle).

Arouch's fights don't commence until 45 minutes into a very slow film. For the most part, screen time is devoted to retelling the Holocaust story in a version that, lacking distinctive characters, relies heavily on images chosen by director Robert M. Young. Film is notably short on dialog. Dafoe finds little to do; like the others he just tries to exude sorrowful stamina.

••••••••••••••••••••••••••••••

■ **TROJAN WOMEN, THE**

1971, 111 MINS, GREECE/US ◇ ▽
Dir Michael Cacoyannis   *Prod* Michael Cacoyannis, Anis Nohra   *Scr* Michael Cacoyannis   *Ph* Alfio Contini   *Ed* Russell Woolnough   *Mus* Mikis Theodorakis   *Art Dir* Nicholas Georgiadis
● Katharine Hepburn, Genevieve Bujold, Vanessa Redgrave, Irene Papas, Brian Blessed, Patrick Magee (Shaftel)

T

Michael Cacoyannis has come up with a version of Euripides' *The Trojan Women*, which he did successfully off-Broadway in New York. Pic has a surface resonance and not enough of the tragic sweep and force its outcry against war and oppression call for.

It has a solid cast. There is Katharine Hepburn as the proud but fallen Queen of Troy, Hecuba, whose husband and sons have been killed. Only a daughter, mad Cassandra, and Andromache, the wife and child of her son, Hector, are alive. She valiantly tries to lament, dirge and stand up to the fates in dignity, but the force and the needed tragic depth elude her laudatory attempt.

Vanessa Redgrave is lacking in passion as Andromache. Her tragic lamentations do not get to the core of loss. Nor is Genevieve Bujold, as Cassandra, up to the frenzy and needed steely quality of her preachments on man's warring nature and her prophecies on her future demise.

Irene Papas, probably the true tragedienne among them, plays Helen, abducted by Paris, Hecuba's son, on a visit to Sparta, causing the Greeks to attack Troy, sack it, kill the men and send the women, including Hecuba, off to slavery, then burning the city.

....

■ TROLL

1986, 86 MINS, US ◇ ⑩ ⊙
Dir John Buechler   *Prod* Albert Band   *Scr* Ed Naha
Ph Romana Albani   *Ed* Lee Percy   *Mus* Richard Band
Art Dir Gayle Simon
● Noah Hathaway, Michael Moriarty, Shelley Hack, Jenny Beck, Sonny Bono, June Lockhart (Empire)

Troll is a predictable, dim-witted premise executed for the most part with surprising style. Horror fantasy of a universe of trolls taking over a San Francisco apartment house is far-fetched even for this genre. Creatures designed by John Buechler, who also directed, are a repulsive assortment of hairy, fanged, evil-looking elves but the plot is pure shlock.

No sooner does the Potter family move into an ordinary looking building than the young daughter (Jenny Beck) is possessed by the troll. Where the film rises above the ordinary is in the domestic scenes when, thanks to her acquired personality, young Beck can flout all the conventions of how a good girl should act. Performances by the kids are convincing.

....

■ TROLLENBERG TERROR, THE

(US: The Crawling Eye)

1958, 85 MINS, UK ⑩ ⊙
Dir Quentin Lawrence   *Prod* Robert S. Baker, Monty Berman   *Scr* Jimmy Sangster   *Ph* Monty Berman
Ed Henry Richardson   *Mus* Stanley Black
Art Dir Duncan Sutherland
● Forrest Tucker, Laurence Payne, Janet Munro, Jennifer Jayne, Warren Mitchell, Andrew Faulds (Eros)

Based on a successful TV serial by Peter Key, the yarn concerns a creature from outer space secreted in a radioactive cloud on the mountain of Trollenberg in Switzerland. The mysterious disappearance of various climbers brings Forrest Tucker to the scene as a science investigator for UNO. He and a professor at the local observatory set out to solve the problem.

During investigations, two headless corpses are discovered and a couple of ordinary citizens go berserk and turn killers. Main object of the two is Janet Munro who is one of a sister mind-reading act and obviously presents a threat to the sinister visitor.

The taut screenplay extracts the most from the situations and is helped by strong, resourceful acting from a solid cast. Tucker tackles the problem with commendable lack of histrionics and Munro adds considerably to the film's interest with an excellent portrayal of the girl whose mental telepathy threatens

the creature's activities and draws her into danger.

....

■ TRON

1982, 96 MINS, US ◇ ⑩ ⊙
Dir Steven Lisberger   *Prod* Donald Kushner
Scr Steven Lisberger   *Ph* Bruce Logan   *Ed* Jeff Gourson
Mus Wendy Carlos   *Art Dir* Dean Edward Mitzner
● Jeff Bridges, Bruce Boxleitner, David Warner, Cindy Morgan, Barnard Hughes, Dan Shor (Walt Disney)

Tron is loaded with visual delights but falls way short of the mark in story and viewer involvement. Screenwriter-director Steven Lisberger has adequately marshalled a huge force of technicians to deliver the dazzle, but even kids (and specifically computer game freaks) will have a difficult time getting hooked on the situations.

After an awkward 'teaser' intro the story unfolds concisely: computer games designer Kevin Flynn (Jeff Bridges) has had his series of fabulously successful programs stolen by Ed Dillinger (David Warner). Dillinger has consequently risen to position of corporate power and with his Master Control Program (MCP) has increasingly dominated other programmers and users.

Flynn must obtain the evidence stored in computer's memory proving that Dillinger has appropriated his work. His friend Alan Bradley (Bruce Boxleitner) is concurrently working on a watchdog program (called Tron) to thwart the MCP's growing control. The MCP scientifically transforms Flynn into a computer-stored program, bringing the viewer into the parallel world inside the computer.

Computer-generated visuals created by divers hands are impressive but pic's design work and execution consistently lack the warmth and humanity that classical animation provides.
□ 1982: Nominations: Best Costume Design, Sound

....

■ TROUBLE IN MIND

1985, 111 MINS, US ◇ ⑩ ⊙
Dir Alan Rudolph   *Prod* Carolyn Pfeiffer, David Blocker
Scr Alan Rudolph   *Ph* Toyomichi Kurita   *Ed* Tom Walls
Mus Mark Isham   *Art Dir* Steven Legler
● Kris Kristofferson, Keith Carradine, Lori Singer, Genevieve Bujold, Joe Morton, Divine (Island Alive)

Trouble in Mind is a stylish urban melodrama instantly recognizable as an Alan Rudolph picture. It is peopled by a strange collection of off-center characters living in a stylish, almost-real location.

Set in RainCity, action could be taking place in the 1950s, 1980s or 1990s, so stylized is the production design. The good people of RainCity are like a microcosm of the larger world seen through the lens of 1940s gangster pictures with several other influences thrown in for good measure.

At the core of the film is a not-so-classic romantic triangle involving Hawk (Kris Kristofferson), Georgia (Lori Singer) and her boyfriend, Coop (Keith Carradine).

Center of this emotional landscape is Wanda's cafe, owned and operated by Wanda (Genevieve Bujold), a former lover of Hawk's and the woman for whom he committed a murder.

Rudolph stirs all the ingredients around – love, crime, friendship, responsibility – and ties them together with a charged score by Mark Isham.

....

■ TROUBLE IN PARADISE

1932, 81 MINS, US
Dir Ernst Lubitsch   *Prod* Ernst Lubitsch   *Scr* Samson Raphaelson, Grover Jones   *Ph* Victor Milner   *Mus* W. Franke Harling

● Miriam Hopkins, Kay Francis, Herbert Marshall, Charlie Ruggles, Edward Everett Horton, C. Aubrey Smith (Paramount)

Despite the Lubitsch artistry, much of which is technically apparent, it's not good cinema in toto. For one thing, it's predicated on a totally meretricious premise. Herbert Marshall is the gentleman crook. Miriam Hopkins is a light-fingered lady. Kay Francis is a rich young widow who owns the largest parfumerie in Paris. She's decidedly on the make for Marshall, and his appointment as her 'secretary' inspires beaucoup gossip.

Rest becomes a proposition of cheating cheaters as the well-mannered rogue exposes C. Aubrey Smith, the parfumerie's general manager, at the same time climaxing into a triangle among the two attractive femmes and Marshall.

The dialog is bright [from the play *The Honest Finder* by Laszlo Aladar] and the Lubitsch montage is per usually tres artistique, but somehow the whole thing misses.

There's some good trouping by all concerned, plus the intriguing Continental atmosphere of the Grand Hotel on the Grand Canal, Venice, plus ultra-modern social deportment in smart Parisian society.

....

■ TROUBLE IN STORE

1953, 85 MINS, UK ⑩
Dir John Paddy Carstairs   *Prod* Maurice Cowan
Scr John Paddy Carstairs, Maurice Cowan, Ted Willis
Ph Ernest Steward   *Ed* Peter Seabourne, Geoffrey Foot
Mus Mischa Spoliansky   *Art Dir* Alex Vetchinsky, John Gow
● Norman Wisdom, Margaret Rutherford, Moira Lister, Derek Bond, Lana Morris, Jerry Desmonde (Two Cities)

This British piece of slapstick marks the debut of Norman Wisdom. He clowns his way through the whole thing, playing in his inimitable way the most humble member of a big department store who falls foul of his new boss. But he gets his girl and also rounds up some gangsters.

Apart from one or two brief exteriors, the entire action is in the department store, but there is plenty of movement and an ample slice of broad comedy. Margaret Rutherford has some nice comedy scenes as an inveterate shoplifter and Moira Lister is a very lush manageress who's in league with the gangsters led by Derek Bond. Lana Morris pleasantly offers the romantic interest. Jerry Desmonde is little more than a comedy stooge, as the boss, but plays the role for all it is worth.

....

■ TROUBLE WITH HARRY, THE

1955, 96 MINS, US ◇ ⑩
Dir Alfred Hitchcock   *Prod* Alfred Hitchcock   *Scr* John Michael Hayes   *Ph* Robert Burks   *Ed* Alma Macrorie
Mus Bernard Herrmann   *Art Dir* Hal Pereira, John Goodman
● Edmund Gwenn, John Forsythe, Shirley MacLaine, Mildred Natwick, Mildred Dunnock, Royal Dano (Paramount)

This is a blithe little comedy, produced and directed with affection by Alfred Hitchcock, about a bothersome corpse that just can't stay buried.

Edmund Gwenn is a delight as a retired 'sea' captain who stumbles on Harry's corpse while rabbit hunting. In the belief he did the killing, he decides to bury the cadaver on the spot. Harry goes in and out of the ground three or four times, is responsible for two romances and not a little consternation and physical exercise.

During the course of events Gwenn and Mildred Natwick, a middle-aged spinster who thinks she did Harry in, find love, as do John Forsythe, local artist, and Shirley MacLaine, young widow of the in-and-out Harry. Natwick pairs perfectly with Gwenn, and the script from the novel by Jack Trevor Story provides them with dialog and situations that click.

••••••••••••••••••••••••••••••

■ TRUCK STOP WOMEN

1974, 82 MINS, US ◇ ⊕
Dir Mark L. Lester   *Prod* Mark L. Lester   *Scr* Mark L. Lester, Paul Deason   *Ph* John A. Morrill   *Ed* Marvin Wallowitz   *Mus* Big Mack & The Truckstoppers   *Art Dir* Tom Hassen
● Claudia Jennings, Lieux Dressler, John Martino, Dennis Fimple, Dolores Dorn, Gene Drew (Lester)

Truck Stop Women spoofs the mindless sensationalism involved in films of its type while it also exploits sex and violence.

Localed in New Mexico, pic deals with bloody territorial warfare between Mafia hit man John Martino and indie gang leader Lieux Dressler over Dressler's lucrative theft and prostitution operation, conducted out of a highway truck stop with henchpersons including her daughter Claudia Jennings.

A ludicrous string of murders occurs as the rivalry unfolds, with Jennings lured to the opposite side by money-waving Martino. Plenty of flesh is on display.

Mark L. Lester's direction is highly uneven, with many scenes run through in perfunctory fashion and others handled with care and skill. There is a stunning semidocumentary montage of trucks on the highway half an hour into the film, and action scenes are done with flair.

••••••••••••••••••••••••••••••

■ TRUE COLORS

1991, 111 MINS, US ◇ ⊕ ⊙
Dir Herbert Ross   *Prod* Herbert Ross, Laurence Mark   *Scr* Kevin Wade   *Ph* Dante Spinotti   *Ed* Robert Reitano, Stephen A. Rotter   *Mus* Trevor Jones   *Art Dir* Edward Pisoni
● John Cusack, James Spader, Imogen Stubbs, Mandy Patinkin, Richard Widmark, Dina Merrill (Paramount)

True Colors represents a cloyingly schematic attempt to portray the political and moral bankruptcy of the 1980s in a neat little package. Pic condemns but doesn't begin to analyze the corrupted values of the Reagan years, leaving one feeling soiled but unenlightened.

Paired off at law school at the U of Virginia in 1983, James Spader is a rich boy with the daughter of US senator Richard Widmark as a girlfriend, while John Cusack is pretender, a social climber whose lower-class roots are quickly exposed.

Cusack, a bluffer and something of a charmer, resolves to be elected to Congress within 10 years. He launches a political career based upon trickery, blackmail and betrayal, and receives backing from interests represented by oily developer Mandy Patinkin.

Personal relationships fall by the wayside like roadkill. Having scooped Spader's g.f. (Imogen Stubbs) out from under him, Cusack then loses her when he stupidly threatens her powerful father.

Cusack does what he can, but the character is simply weighed down with too much symbolic baggage. Yet again playing a privileged preppie type, Spader is likable but suffers from his character being pushed to the side mid-stream.

••••••••••••••••••••••••••••••

■ TRUE CONFESSIONS

1981, 108 MINS, US ◇ ⊕ ⊙
Dir Ulu Grosbard   *Prod* Irwin Winkler, Robert Chartoff   *Scr* John Gregory Dunne, Joan Didion   *Ph* Owen Roizman   *Ed* Lynzee Klingman   *Mus* Georges Delerue   *Art Dir* Stephen S. Grimes
● Robert De Niro, Robert Duvall, Charles Durning, Burgess Meredith, Cyril Cusack, Rose Gregorio (United Artists)

Given the powerhouse topline casting combo and provocative theme, *True Confessions* has to be chalked up as something of a disappointment. Adaptation of John Gregory Dunne's bestseller, which was inspired by LA's legendary Black Dahlia murder case of the late 1940s, features corrupt cops, whores, pimps, sibling rivalry, pornography and political intrigue within the Roman Catholic Church, but still comes off as relatively mild fare which fails to pack a dramatic or emotional wallop.

For at least the first hour, it's hard to tell where the drama's headed. Bookended by years-later scenes in which brothers Robert De Niro and Robert Duvall, both white-haired, play out mutual climax to their radically different lives at the former's pathetic desert parish, main body of pic flip-flops between police detective Duvall handling two bizarre deaths and ambitious Monsignor De Niro negotiating the delicate waters of church diplomacy.

Unfortunately, nowhere near the full weight of these considerations is ever felt in Ulu Grosbard's muted, unmuscular telling of the sordid, fateful events. Script is deliberately structured to build to a big dramatic pay-off, but this never comes, leaving audience frustrated that careful groundwork has been laid to no avail.

Failings cannot be attributed to the actors, all of whom have clearly immersed themselves in their roles. Duvall is excellent as an unsentimental dick working a tough beat which irrevocably poisons his personal life. Charles Durning's portrait of a big-time phony is right on target.

••••••••••••••••••••••••••••••

■ TRUE GRIT

1969, 128 MINS, US ◇ ⊕ ⊙
Dir Henry Hathaway   *Prod* Hal B. Wallis   *Scr* Marguerite Roberts   *Ph* Lucien Ballard   *Ed* Warren Low   *Mus* Elmer Bernstein   *Art Dir* Walter Tyler
● John Wayne, Glen Campbell, Kim Darby, Jeremy Slate, Robert Duvall, Dennis Hopper (Paramount)

Story centers on young girl (Kim Darby) of the 1830s starting out from Arkansas to avenge the murder of her father with the aid of Wayne, whom she pays, and Texas Ranger Glen Campbell, who wants to claim the murderer (Jeff Corey) for a reward. Men develop instant mutual loathing, but girl recognizes they can get her father's murderer because they have grit, true grit.

Darby is refreshingly original. If at times she seems restrained, she sticks relentlessly to the strong character of Mattie.

Campbell, less successful as an actor than as a singer-performer, still holds his own as a foil for Wayne. But it's mostly Wayne all the way. He towers over everything in the film — actors, script [from Charles Portis' novel], even the magnificent Colorado mountains. He rides tall in the saddle in this character role of 'the fat old man.'

☐ 1969: Best Actor (John Wayne).
☐ Nomination: Best Song ('True Grit')

••••••••••••••••••••••••••••••

■ TRUE IDENTITY

1991, 93 MINS, US ◇ ⊕ ⊙
Dir Charles Lane   *Prod* Carol Baum, Teri Schwartz   *Scr* Andy Breckman   *Ph* Tom Ackerman   *Ed* Kent Beyda   *Mus* Marc Marder   *Art Dir* John DeCuir Jr
● Lenny Henry, Frank Langella, Charles Lane, J.T. Walsh, Anne-Marie Johnson, Andreas Katsoulis (Touchstone)

The sterling talents of comic actor Lenny Henry shine through even in the feebly formulaic context of *True Identity*. This master of impersonation cooks up a lot of laughs where they wouldn't otherwise exist, and pretty much single-handedly makes the picture worth a look.

Tale plunges New York actor Miles Pope

(Henry), whose great dream is to play Othello, into a whirlpool of jeopardy, as he has the misfortune of learning that a pillar of the community and arts patron (Frank Langella) is actually a gangster thought to have died several years earlier. With a hitman hot on his trail, Miles places himself in the hands of his buddy Duane (played by the director), a makeup artist who decides to protect his friend by disguising Miles as a white man.

Mild-mannered and sporting an impeccable American accent, Henry erupts into flashes of brilliance when mimicking various types, both black and white, and masterfully carries off the caricature of a lowlife thug when forced to pretend to be the man hired to kill him. Otherwise, performances are on the broad side, and Charles Lane directs the comedy in obvious, hard-to-miss fashion.

••••••••••••••••••••••••••••••

■ TRUE LOVE

1989, 104 MINS, US ◇ ⊕ ⊙
Dir Nancy Savoca   *Prod* Richard Guay, Shelley Houis   *Scr* Nancy Savoca, Richard Guay   *Ph* Lisa Rinzler   *Ed* John Tintori   *Art Dir* Lester W. Cohen
● Annabella Sciorra, Ron Eldard, Star Jasper, Aida Turturro, Roger Rignack, Michael J. Wolfe (Forward)

True Love is anything but traditional, even though it's solidly rooted in the Bronx working-class Italian community. The bride (wonderfully played by newcomer Annabella Sciorra) and her bridesmaids know enough four-letter words to easily supply all the 'something blue' needed for the wedding preparations.

Sciorra and her friends aren't too starry-eyed about the men available for matrimony. Certainly, her fiance (well-acted by Ron Eldard in his feature debut) is no bargain, except perhaps in bed. For most of the picture, Sciorra frets about why she's marrying the immature, self-centered lout and never comes up with a good reason, except he's good-looking and says he loves her even though he doesn't act like it.

True Love is very much a story about family and neighborhood and Nancy Savoca obviously has an eye for the several generations. This is Savoca's first feature, with first-rate perfomances out of neophytes.

••••••••••••••••••••••••••••••

■ TRUE STORIES
A FILM ABOUT A BUNCH OF PEOPLE IN VIRGIL TEXAS

1986, 90 MINS, US ◇ ⊕ ⊙
Dir David Byrne   *Prod* Gary Kurfirst   *Scr* David Byrne, Beth Henley, Stephen Tobolowsky   *Ph* Ed Lachman   *Ed* Caroline Biggerstaff   *Mus* David Byrne, Talking Heads   *Art Dir* Barbara Ling
● David Byrne, John Goodman, Swoosie Kurtz, Spalding Gray, Alix Elias, Annie McEnroe (True Stories)

In more than 10 years with the Talking Heads, David Byrne received well-earned if often slavishly uncritical praise for his distinctive marriage of polyrhythmic pop-rock with an archly skewed perspective on mechanistic modern life. *True Stories* was a natural progression into film.

In his feature directorial debut, Byrne takes a bemused and benevolent view of provincial America's essential goodness in a loosely connected string of vignettes that amount to sophisticated music video concepts dressed up as film-making.

Byrne uses the surreal, cartoonish conceit of examining life in the hypothetical town of Virgil, Texas with the human interest perspective of a supermarket tabloid feature. Affecting a trusting innocence as easily as he slips into natty Western duds, Byrne drives into Virgil during its sesquicentennial 'celebration of specialness' for a series of close encounters with the town's peculiar denizens.

••••••••••••••••••••••••••••••

T

■ TRUE STORY OF JESSE JAMES, THE
(UK: The James Brothers)

1957, 92 MINS, US ◇
Dir Nicholas Ray   *Prod* Herbert B. Swope Jr
Scr Walter Newman   *Ph* Joe MacDonald   *Ed* Robert
Simpson   *Mus* Leigh Harline   *Art Dir* Lyle R. Wheeler,
Addison Hehr
● Robert Wagner, Jeffrey Hunter, Hope Lange, Agnes
Moorehead, Alan Hale, John Carradine (20th Century-
Fox)

On celluloid Jesse James has had more lives
than a cat, and *The True Story of Jesse James*
suggests it's time screenwriters let him roll
over and play dead for real and reel. In past
reworkings of the 19th-century delinquent's
shoddy career just about every angle was covered. There's nothing new in this glorification.
It's a routine offering for the outdoor market.

The attempt to view the James character
through the eyes of pro and con contemporaries only makes for confusion, depriving an
audience of clear-cut plot line that might
keep it interested. Dialog, too, is poor, continually veering from period to modern idioms in
the script, based on Nunnally Johnson's
screenplay for the 1939 *Jesse James*.

Nicholas Ray directs in stock fashion,
adding little of substance to the picture. As
Jesse and Frank James, respectively, Robert
Wagner and Jeffrey Hunter go through the
motions of telling why the former took up the
gun when Northern sympathizers made it difficult for them to live in Missouri after the
War between States. Both are adequate to
the demands of script and direction, as is
Hope Lange, playing Zee, the girl who married Jesse.

■ TRULY MADLY DEEPLY
(Aka: Cello)

1991, 105 MINS, UK ◇ ⓥ
Dir Anthony Minghella   *Prod* Robert Cooper
Scr Anthony Minghella   *Ph* Remi Adefarasian
Ed John Stothart   *Mus* Barrington Pheloung
Art Dir Barbara Gosnold
● Juliet Stevenson, Alan Rickman, Bill Paterson, Michael
Maloney, Jenny Howe, Stella Maris (BBC)

This sharply scripted study of a bereaved
woman who literally wishes her partner back
from the grave is an impressive directorial
bow by British playwright Anthony
Minghella. Despite surface similarities with
Ghost pic has a different feel and theme.

Nina (Juliet Stevenson) is still cut up about
losing her longtime partner, virtuoso cellist
Jamie (Alan Rickman). She still feels his presence in her tiny London flat, where plumbing's gone bananas and rats are moving in.

One day, while she's doodling at the piano,
Jamie literally reappears and thereon it's a
matter of reliving their idyllic relationship
until it's time for both to move on – he to a
higher plane, she to a growing friendship with
young social worker Mark (Michael Maloney)
who can give her the child Jamie never wanted.

Sans special effects, pic manages to suspend
belief through fine ensemble playing and
sheer strength of the main performances. It's
Stevenson's movie through and through (project was in the works for some years and was
penned for her), and although she sometimes
overdoes the histrionics, as in scenes with her
shrink, it's a tour de force of sustained playing. Rickman gives subtle support, with a nice
line in po-faced comedy.

[Pic was reviewed in original 16mm version
premiered at 1990 London Film Festival as
Cello. For 35mm theatrical release, and subsequent TV airing, title was changed to *Truly
Madly Deeply*.]

■ TRUST

1990, 103 MINS, US/UK ◇ ⓥ
Dir Hal Hartley   *Prod* Bruce Weiss   *Scr* Hal Hartley

Ph Mark Spiller   *Ed* Hal Hartley   *Mus* Phil Reed
Art Dir Daniel Ovellette
● Adrienne Shelly, Martin Donovan, Merritt Nelson,
John McKay, Edie Falco, Marko Hunt (True Fiction/Zenith)

Long Island filmaker Hal Hartley progresses
from his debut feature, *The Unbelievable Truth*
to this bleak, off-center comedy about dysfunctional families in working class suburbia.

When Maria (Adrienne Shelly) gets pregnant by the high school quarterback, she's
dropped by her boyfriend, drops out of school,
and her father drops dead of a heart attack.
Maria's hard-bitten mother treats her like a
pariah.

Meanwhile, Matthew (Martin Donovan), an
intellectually inclined reform school graduate
with a talent for fixing things, quits his mind-
numbing job assembling computers. Matthew
wanders the streets, encounters Maria, and
takes the shattered girl to his home.

This sets the stage for a tale of uneasy love
and spiritual anomie in sterile precincts of
middle America. Donovan is excellent as the
brooding misfit, and Shelly is tangibly right as
the suburban brat. Also very good are Merritt
Nelson as Maria's emotionally alienated
mother and John MacKay as Matthew's bullying father.

■ TRUTH OR DARE
IN BED WITH MADONNA
(UK: In Bed with Madonna)

1991, 118 MINS, UK ◇ ⓥ ⊙
Dir Alek Keshishian   *Prod* Jay Roewe, Tim Clawson
Ph Robert Leacock, Doug Nichol, Christophe Lanzenberg,
Marc Reshovsky, Daniel Pearl, Toby Phillips   *Ed* Barry
Alexander Brown, John Murray
● (Propaganda)

Twenty-six-year-old musicvideo director Alek
Keshishian landed the documaker's dream
subject when CAA agents paired him with unfettered exhibitionist Madonna. 'I have nothing to hide' seems to be her credo, and she's
shown in acts ranging from humdrumly
unglamorous to recklessly provocative.

Having her throat examined, talking gen-
der-bent sex lives with pal Sandra Bernhard,
cuddling near-naked in bed with her gay
dancers (both black and white), or treating
Warren Beatty like an ageing girl toy to be
pushed around her dressing room: what does
she care who sees it?

It's the warily indulgent Beatty who prods
her with pic's most amusing jibe: 'Why say
anything if it's not on camera?'

Keshishian includes just enough concert
footage, all shot on the 1990 'Blond Ambition'
tour, to make the importance of the stage
time felt. Concert photography is dazzling,
with as many as 22 35mm cameras used at a
show in Paris, and editing by Barry Alexander
Brown (*Do the Right Thing*) is superb. Color is
used for onstage sequences (to express theatricality), and a combination of hard and
soft contrast black & white for offstage
footage (to convey reality, such as it is here).

■ TRYGON FACTOR, THE

1967, 87 MINS, UK ◇
Dir Cyril Frankel   *Prod* Brian Taylor   *Scr* Derry Quinn,
Stanley Munroe   *Ph* Harry Waxman   *Ed* Oswald
Hafenrichter   *Mus* Peter Thomas   *Art Dir* Roy
Stannard
● Stewart Granger, Susan Hampshire, Robert Morley,
Cathleen Nesbitt, Brigitte Horney, James Robertson Justice
(Warner/Seven Arts/Rialto)

The Trygon Factor, its title totally meaningless,
is a complicated Scotland Yard whodunit
which the spectator will find taxing to follow.

Stewart Granger, as the Yard superintendent investigating a rash of unsolved robberies, is assigned to a large country house
where a gang is operating under the cloak of

respectability; its mistress, a member of an
old English family who has turned to crime to
save her family estate from ruin.

She has installed in her house a phony order of nuns who actually are in on the various
crimes, and who receive and ship stolen goods
to Morley's warehouse.

Script is pocketed with story loopholes and
attempts to confuse, plus certain motivations
and bits of business impossible to fathom.

Granger still makes a good impression.

■ TUCKER
THE MAN AND HIS DREAM

1988, 111 MINS, US ◇ ⓥ ⊙
Dir Francis Coppola   *Prod* Fred Roos, Fred Fuchs
Scr Arnold Schulman, David Seidler   *Ph* Vittorio Storaro
Ed Priscilla Nedd   *Mus* Joe Jackson   *Art Dir* Dean
Tavoularis
● Jeff Bridges, Joan Allen, Martin Landau, Frederic
Forrest, Dean Stockwell, Lloyd Bridges (Lucasfilm/
Zeotrope)

The true story of a great American visionary
who was thwarted, if not destroyed, by the established order, *Tucker* represents the sunni-
est imaginable telling of an at least partly
tragic episode in recent history.

Tucker's life and career present so many
parallels to Coppola's own it is easy to see why
he coveted his project for so long. Industryites
will nod in recognition of this story of a self-
styled genius up against business interests
hostile to his innovative ideas, but also will
note the accepting, unbelligerent stance
adopted toward the terms of the struggle.

After World War II, seemingly on the
strength of his enthusiasm alone, Tucker got
a small core of collaborators to work on his
dream project, which he called 'the first completely new car in 50 years'.

With a factory in Chicago, Tucker managed
to turn out 50 of his beauties, but vested interests in Detroit and Washington dragged
him into court on fraud charges, shutting him
down and effectively ending his automobile
career. As his moneyman tells him, 'You build
the car too good.'

Flashing his charming smile and ouzing
cocky confidence, Jeff Bridge's Tucker is inspiring because he won't be depressed or defeated by anything.
□ 1988: Nominations: Best Supp. Actor
(Martin Mandau), Art Direction, Costume
Design

■ TUFF TURF

1985, 112 MINS, US ◇ ⓥ
Dir Fritz Kiersch   *Prod* Donald Borchers   *Scr* Jette
Rinck   *Ph* Willy Kurant   *Ed* Marc Grossman
Mus Jonathan Elias   *Art Dir* Craig Stearns
● James Spader, Kim Richards, Paul Mones, Robert
Downey, Matt Clark, Claudette Nevins (New World)

This modestly budgeted youth pic is a poor
man's and partially musicalized *Rebel without a
Cause* with a touch of *The Warriors* thrown in.
Rebellious newcomer James Spader is the
James Dean character and saucy gang moll
Kim Richards is the Natalie Wood character.

They go through social and romantic hell
for each other and, in the process, a large
slice of suburban LA and uncomprehending
parenthood embellish a story that is deceptively compelling despite, in this case, a distracting mix of comedy and music. Latter,
which includes on-screen appearances by the
LA band Jack Mack and Heart Attack and
rocker Jim Carroll, gives the production a
socking sound.

The on-screen music, however, lurches the
film off balance, especially combined with unexpected and dramatically jarring numbers
by the two stars (Spader materializing as a
balladeer in a country club and Richards

whirling into an aerodynamic disco dancer).

Robert Downey is a fresh surprise in a nice sidekick role, and Olivia Barash and Catya Sassoon (the daughter of Vidal Sassoon) lend able teen support

● ●

■ TUGBOAT ANNIE

1933, 85 MINS, US

Dir Mervyn LeRoy   *Prod* Harry Rapf   *Scr* Zelda Sears, Eve Greene, Norman Reilly Raine   *Ph* Gregg Toland   *Ed* Blanche Sewell   *Art Dir* Merrill Pye
● Marie Dressler, Wallace Beery, Robert Young, Maureen O'Sullivan, Willard Robertson, Tammany Young (M-G-M)

Tugboat Annie, while weak in many respects, is on the whole perfectly suited to the Dressler-Beery requirements. In the hands of the co-starring couple its deficiencies are barely noticeable.

Making Marie Dressler the femme skipper of a harbor tugboat, Wallace Beery her shift-less, soused but likeable husband, and giving them a son of which to be proud, was giving Dressler-Beery a blueprint and then going home.

Beery is always stewed and Dressler constantly trying to keep him dry. That provides the comedy. Beery is getting the family into all sorts of jams – stupidly, drunkenly, tragically, but unintentionally. That provides the pathos.

Robert Young and Maureen O'Sullivan are the juves, and just juves, with no chance to be anything more. It's a Dressler-Beery picture [from the *Saturday Evening Post* series by Norman Reilly Raine].

● ●

■ TUNE IN TOMORROW

(UK: Aunt Julia and the Scriptwriter)

1990, 102 MINS, US ◇ ⑨ ⊙

Dir Jon Amiel   *Prod* John Fielder, Mark Tarlov   *Scr* William Boyd   *Ph* Robert Stevens   *Ed* Peter boyle   *Mus* Wynton Marsalis   *Art Dir* Jim Clay
● Barbara Hershey, Keanu Reeves, Peter Falk, Hope Lange, Peter Gallagher, Elizabeth McGovern (Polar)

Tune in Tomorrow, Jon Amiel's screen version of Mario Vargas Llosa's acclaimed novel *Aunt Julia and the Scriptwriter*, is lusty and full of zany characters, but cluttered and overdone.

Aunt Julia (Barbara Hershey), a double divorcee, returns to New Orleans in 1951 at age 36 to find a rich third husband. Instead, she finds her 21-year-old nephew by marriage (Keanu Reeves), a local radio station newsrun, who falls in love with her. The aunt succumbs, incurring her family's anger. On top of that plot is the more complicated story of a disheveled writer (Peter Falk), who's new in town.

Falk's Pedro Carmichael creates a successful radio soap opera laced with incest and anti-Albanian sentiment. While actors read their lines on the air, different ones, including John Larroquette, Hope Lange, Peter Gallagher and Elizabeth McGovern, act out the scenes in dramatic soap style. Falk manipulates the nephew-aunt relationship, and, to Reeves' anger, reproduces the couple's arguments in his soap.

There's enough in William Boyd's sprawling script for three films. And while the action is fun for much of the first half, the storylines ultimately smother each other. Hershey and Reeves are outstanding and Falk is delightfully melodramatic.

● ●

■ TUNES OF GLORY

1960, 105 MINS, UK ◇ ⑨ ⊙

Dir Ronald Neame   *Prod* Colin Lesslie   *Scr* James Kennaway   *Ph* Arthur Ibbetson   *Ed* Anne V. Coates   *Mus* Malcolm Arnold

● Alec Guinness, John Mills, Dennis Price, John Fraser, Susannah York, Kay Walsh (United Artists)

Both Alec Guinness and John Mills are cast as colonels, the former a man of humble origin who has risen from the ranks, the other a product of Eton, Oxford and a classy military academy. It is the clash of personalities between the two that provides the main story thread.

Tunes is the story of a Scottish regiment in peacetime commanded by Guinness. He's reasonably popular with his fellow officers, though a few appear to resent his rough-and-ready behavior in the mess. His is only an acting command, and when he is superseded by Mills (whose grandfather had commanded the same regiment), the clash is inevitable.

The struggle between the two reaches its climax when Guinness finds his daughter in a public house with a young corporal, and strikes the soldier. That's a serious offense under military law, and though Mills has the power to deal with the case, he chooses to submit a report to higher authority, which would inevitably lead to a courtmartial.

Ronald Neame's crisp and vigorous direction keeps the main spotlight on the two central characters. Guinness, as always, is outstanding, and his performance is as forthright as it is subtle. He assumes an authentic Scottish accent naturally, and never misses a trick to win sympathy, even when he behaves foolishly. It's a tough assignment for Mills to play against Guinness, particularly in a fundamentally unsympathetic role, but he is always a match for his co-star.

☐ 1960: Nomination: Best Adapted Screenplay

● ●

■ TUNNEL OF LOVE, THE

1958, 98 MINS, US

Dir Gene Kelly   *Prod* Joseph Fields, Martin Melcher   *Scr* Joseph Fields   *Ph* Robert Bronner   *Ed* John McSweeney Jr   *Art Dir* William A. Horning, Randall Duell
● Doris Day, Richard Widmark, Gig Young, Gia Scala, Elisabeth Fraser, Elizabeth Wilson (M-G-M)

The Broadway hit on which this is based has been transferred virtually intact to the screen.

Richard Widmark is a would-be cartoonist for a *New Yorker*-type magazine, whose gags are good but whose drawings are not. He and his wife (Doris Day) want a child and cannot catch. They live in a remodeled barn (naturally) adjacent to the home of their best friends (Gig Young and Elisabeth Fraser) whom they envy in many ways. Young is an editor of the magazine Widmark aspires to crack, and is a parent. Young adds to his and Fraser's brood as regularly as the seasons, Widmark and Day are planning to adopt a baby.

Meantime, back at the barn, Young, whose homework has been stimulated by extracurricular activities, urges his system on Widmark. With this suggestion in the back of his mind, Widmark is visited by an adoption home investigator (Gia Scala). When he wakes up in a motel after a night on the town with her, he assumes the thought has been father to the deed in more ways than one. Just a little over nine months later, the adoption agency presents a baby to Day and Widmark.

The only important change Joseph Fields has made in the screenplay, from the play by him and Peter DeVries (based on DeVries' book), is to explain at the very end that the child is not actually Widmark's.

Day and Widmark make a fine comedy team, working as smoothly as if they had been trading gags for years. They are ably abetted by Young, one of the greatest fly-catchers in operation, and Scala, who displays a nice and unexpected gift for comedy.

This is the first time Gene Kelly has operated entirely behind the camera, and he

emerges as an inventive and capable comedy director.

● ●

■ TURK 182!

1985, 98 MINS, US ◇ ⑨

Dir Bob Clark   *Prod* Ted Field, Rene DuPont   *Scr* James Gregory Kingston, Denis Hamill, John Hamill   *Ph* Reginald H. Morris   *Ed* Stan Cole   *Mus* Paul Zaza   *Art Dir* Harry Pottle
● Timothy Hutton, Robert Urich, Kim Cattrall, Robert Culp, Darren McGavin, Steven Keats (20th Century-Fox)

Taking aim squarely at the popular theme of the working man's struggle against the inequities in the system, *Turk 182!*, a cleverly conceived story [by James Gregory Kingston] of a mystery rebel in New York City whose popularity reaches almost mythic proportions, convincingly hits its mark.

Timothy Hutton plays a 20-year-old who defends the honor of his older brother (Robert Urich), fireman who, when off-duty in a bar, responds to a plea for help and risks his life by going into a burning building to save a young girl. Urich is severely injured but the city refuses to come to his aid, maintaining that he should not have entered the premises in his intoxicated state.

That's when Hutton takes his plea on his brother's behalf through the city bureaucracy to no avail, including a forced confrontation with the mayor (Robert Culp). Hutton begins a one-man quest to embarrass and discredit the mayor.

Besides its compelling storyline, *Turk 182!* features outstanding performances across the board, with Hutton perfect in the role of the determined unassuming hero.

● ●

■ TURNER & HOOCH

1989, 100 MINS, US ◇ ⑨ ⊙

Dir Roger Spottiswoode   *Prod* Raymond Wagner   *Scr* Dennis Shryack, Michael Blodgett, Daniel Petrie Jr., Jim Cash, Jack Epps Jr.   *Ph* Adam Greenberg   *Ed* Garth Craven, Paul Seydor, Mark Conte, Kenneth Morrisey, Lois Freeman-Fox   *Mus* Charles Gross   *Art Dir* John DeCuir Jr.
● Tom Hanks, Mare Winningham, Craig T. Nelson, Reginald VelJohnson, Scott Paulin, J.C. Quinn (Touchstone)

Until its grossly miscalculated bummer of an ending, *Turner & Hooch* is a routine but amiable cop-and-dog comedy enlivened by the charm of Tom Hanks and his homely-as-sin canine partner.

Hanks plays a fussy smalltown California police investigator whose life is disrupted by a messy junkyard dog with a face only a furry mother could love.

In the numbingly unoriginal plot, the dog named Hooch (delightfully played by Beasley), witnesses a double murder and is Hanks' only means of catching the drug smugglers responsible for the slayings. The rather mechanical style of director Roger Spottiwoode (who took over the film after original director Henry Winkler departed) fails to enliven the stereotypical criminal proceedings.

● ●

■ TURNING POINT, THE

1977, 119 MINS, US ◇ ⑨

Dir Herbert Ross   *Prod* Herbert Ross, Arthur Laurents   *Scr* Arthur Laurents   *Ph* Robert Surtees   *Ed* William Reynolds   *Mus* John Lanchbery   *Art Dir* Albert Brenner
● Anne Bancroft, Shirley MacLaine, Mikhail Baryshnikov, Leslie Browne, Tom Skerritt, Martha Scott (20th Century-Fox)

The Turning Point is one of the best films of its era. It's that rare example of synergy in which every key element is excellent and the ensemble is an absolute triumph.

Anne Bancroft and Shirley MacLaine, starring as longtime friends with unresolved problems, are magnificent.

The intricate plotting introduces Bancroft as a ballet star just reaching that uneasy age where a lot of Eve Harringtons (male and female) are beginning to move in.

MacLaine, her best friend, long ago abandoned a similar career to marry Tom Skerritt and now their teenage daughter (Leslie Browne) shows real promise as a dancer. This is the incident which triggers an explosion of new and old conflicts.

Pic ranks as one of MacLaine's career highlights, ditto for Bancroft. They have a climactic showdown scene which filmgoers will remember for decades.

□ 1977: Nominations: Best Picture, Director, Actress (Anne Bancroft, Shirley MacLaine), Supp. Actor (Mikhail Baryshnikov), Supp. Actress (Leslie Browne), Original Screenplay, Cinematography, Art Direction, Editing, Sound

••••••••••••••••••••••••••••••••••

■ 12 ANGRY MEN

1957, 95 MINS, US ⑫ ⊙
Dir Sidney Lumet   *Prod* Henry Fonda, Reginald Rose
Scr Reginald Rose   *Ph* Boris Kaufman   *Ed* Carl Lerner
Mus Kenyon Hopkins   *Art Dir* Robert Markel
● Henry Fonda, Lee J. Cobb, Ed Begley, E.G. Marshall, Jack Warden, Martin Balsam (Orion-Nova)

The *12 Angry Men* are a jury, a body of peers chosen to decide the guilt or innocence of a teenager accused of murdering his father. They have heard the arguments of the district attorney and the defense lawyer. They have received instructions from the presiding judge. Now they are on their own. What will they do?

Rose has a lot to say about the responsibility of citizens chosen to serve on a jury. He stresses the importance of taking into account the question of 'reasonable doubt'. It is soon evident that the majority of the men regard the assignment as a chore. To most of them, it is an open and shut case. The boy is guilty and they demand a quick vote. On the first ballot it is 11 to 1 for a conviction. Henry Fonda is the lone holdout.

Most of the action takes place in the one room on a hot summer day. The effect, rather than being confining, serves to heighten the drama. It's not static, however, for Sidney Lumet, making his bow as a film director, has cleverly maneuvered his players in the small area. Perhaps the motivations of each juror are introduced too quickly and are repeated too often before each changes his vote. However, the film leaves a tremendous impact.

□ 1957: Nominations: Best Picture, Director, Screenplay Adaptation

••••••••••••••••••••••••••••••••••

■ TWELVE CHAIRS, THE

1970, 94 MINS, US ◇ ⑫ ⊙
Dir Mel Brooks   *Prod* Michael Hertzberg   *Scr* Mel Brooks   *Ph* Djordje Nikolic   *Ed* Alan Heim
Mus John Morris   *Art Dir* Mile Nikolic
● Ron Moody, Frank Langella, Dom DeLouise, Mel Brooks, Andreas Voutsinas, David Lander (UMC/Crossbow)

The Twelve Chairs is a nutty farce, frequently slapstick and often tongue-in-cheek. Mel Brooks, who directed, scripted, plays a leading role and authored a song, has turned a search for jewels into a cornpop – circa 1927, Russia, when all men were comrades – and the result is a delightful adventure-comedy.

Based on the novel by Ilf & Petrov, exteriors were lensed in Yugoslavia, which provides some novel and picturesque backdrops. The steps in Dubrovnik, vistas of the Dalmatian coast and mountains in the interior lend fascinating atmosphere.

Simple story thread is of three men trying to locate 12 dining-room chairs, once owned by a wealthy woman who confesses separately to her son-in-law and village priest on her

deathbed that years before she had secreted all her jewels in the upholstery of one of them. Voila, the plot.

••••••••••••••••••••••••••••••••••

■ TWELVE O'CLOCK HIGH

1949, 132 MINS, US ⑫ ⊙
Dir Henry King   *Prod* Darryl F. Zanuck   *Scr* Sy Bartlett, Beirne Lay Jr   *Ph* Leon Shamroy   *Ed* Barbara McLean   *Mus* Alfred Newman   *Art Dir* Lyle Wheeler, Maurice Ransford
● Gregory Peck, Hugh Marlowe, Gary Merrill, Millard Mitchell, Dean Jagger, Robert Arthur (20th Century-Fox)

Picture treats its story [from the novel by Beirne Lay Jr and Sy Bartlett] from the high brass level, i.e. a general's concern for his men's morale while establishing the man-killing daylight bombing raids back in 1942.

As a drama, *High* deals soundly and interestingly with its situations. It gets close to the emotions in unveiling its plot and approaches it from a flashback angle so expertly presented that the emotional pull is sharpened.

Gregory Peck heads up the operations of a bombing squadron from a base in Chelveston, England. Peck gives the character much credence as he suffers and sweats with his men.

There are a number of what amount to 'surprise' performances in the male cast. Standout among them is Dean Jagger as a retread still determined to do his bit. Story comes to life through his eyes as he revisits the Chelveston base in 1948.

□ 1949: Best Supp. Actor (Dean Jagger), Sound Recording (20th Century-Fox Sound Dept).
□ Nominations: Best Picture, Actor (Gregory Peck)

••••••••••••••••••••••••••••••••••

■ 12 PLUS 1

(US: The Thirteen Chairs)
1970, 95 MINS, ITALY/FRANCE ◇ ⑫
Dir Nicholas Gessner   *Prod* Claude Giroux   *Scr* Marc Behm, Nicholas Gessner   *Ph* Giuseppe Ruzzolini
Ed Giancarlo Cappelli   *Mus* Piero Poletto, David Whitaker
● Vittorio Gassman, Sharon Tate, Orson Welles, Vittorio De Sica, Terry-Thomas, Mylene Demongeot (CEF/COFCI)

Film is mainly of interest as being the last of the tragically fated Sharon Tate. It is a sort of madcap romantico comedy in the form of a chase for treasure hidden in a chair left by a recluse, with some added fashionable sex tidbits and some way-out extravagant interludes by such stalwarts as Orson Welles and Vittorio De Sica.

Tate has charm and grace as a rather hard-bitten American girl abroad who puts money before romance. Gassman is a Yank barber who is supposedly left an estate in Britain by an eccentric aunt. But he finds only a run-down house and some antique chairs that he immediately sells to get the fare back.

He finds a note from his aunt saying a fortune is hidden in one of the chairs. So the chase begins. Tate, who works in the gallery he sold the chairs to, teams up with him for a share of the loot. The chase leads to a bordello, an Afro embassy in Paris and a villa in Rome plus a zany interlude in a grand guignol theater run by Welles.

Pic has some good moments, but overall misses the light touch and forward propelling zest to keep this comedy from lagging. Producer Claude Giroux changed title from original *13 Chairs* (from the old Russo tale) after the Tate murder.

••••••••••••••••••••••••••••••••••

■ TWENTIETH CENTURY

1934, 91 MINS, US ⑫
Dir Howard Hawks   *Prod* Howard Hawks   *Scr* Ben Hecht, Charles MacArthur   *Ph* Joseph August
Ed Gene Havlick

● John Barrymore, Carole Lombard, Walter Connolly, Roscoe Karns, Etienne Girardot, Ralph Forbes (Columbia)

John Barrymore, who stars, is quoted as saying, 'I've never done anything I like as well . . . a role that comes once in an actor's lifetime.' It's Barrymore's picture, no doubt of that, with something left over for Carole Lombard, who manages to shine despite practically stooging.

Lily Garland (Lombard) walks out on producer Oscar Jaffe (Barrymore) to go Hollywood shortly after he makes her, double, and that happens early in the picture [from the play *Napoleon of Broadway* by Charles Bruce Milholland]. From then on it's a chase. Jaffe goes broke trying to land another Lily Garland and Lily goes big in Hollywood. The way Jaffe and his boys try to frame Lily into coming back into the legit fold paves the road for some crazy trouping.

Lombard, looking very well, must take Barrymore's abuse as his mistress and handmade star for the first few hundred feet, but when she goes temperamental herself she's permitted to do some head-to-head temperament punching with him.

••••••••••••••••••••••••••••••••••

■ TWENTY-ONE

1991, 101 MINS, US ◇ ⑫ ⊙
Dir Don Boyd   *Prod* Morgan Mason, John Hardy
Scr Zoe Heller, Don Boyd   *Ph* Keith Goddard
Ed David Spiers   *Mus* Phil Sawyer   *Art Dir* Roger Murray Leach
● Patsy Kensit, Jack Shepherd, Patrick Ryecart, Rufus Sewell, Sophie Thompson, Maynard Eziashi (Anglo International)

Twenty-One mirrors the character of its cheeky protagonist: bored, cynical and operating chiefly for self-amusement. Director/co-writer Don Boyd [who also wrote the screen story] depicts the uncensored experience of a worldly young Brit (Patsy Kensit) who ankles her life in London for a fresh start in New York.

Boyd employs a direct-to-camera technique in which the frank, salty-tongued heroine talks while having her facial, tending to nature's call and so on. If only she were more compelling. This rather vapid lass hasn't much on her mind, and her intimate revelations are forgettable.

Kensit tells the audience she was doing all right in London, bouncing from job to job and having an affair with a married man (Patrick Ryecart) until she fell for a lovely Scot (Rufus Sewell). He proved to be a junkie.

Camera also operates in pic's spirit (with flash and style, and no real purpose). Fans of Kensit get plenty of her; her lovely face and form are always the center of attention. The cool control with which she executes the role is admirable.

••••••••••••••••••••••••••••••••••

■ 20,000 LEAGUES UNDER THE SEA

1954, 120 MINS, US ◇ ⑫ ⊙
Dir Richard Fleischer   *Prod* Walt Disney   *Scr* Earl Fenton   *Ph* Franz Planer   *Ed* Elmo Williams
Mus Paul Smith   *Art Dir* John Meehan
● Kirk Douglas, James Mason, Paul Lukas, Peter Lorre, Robert J. Wilke, Carleton Young (Walt Disney)

Walt Disney's production of *20,000 Leagues under the Sea* is very special kind of picture, combining photographic ingenuity, imaginative story telling and fiscal daring. Disney went for a bundle (say $5 million in negative costs) in fashioning the Jules Verne classic.

The story of the 'monster' ship *Nautilus*, astounding as it may be, is so astutely developed that the audience immediately accepts its part on the excursion through Captain Nemo's underseas realm.

James Mason is the captain, a genius who had fashioned and guides the out-of-this-world craft. Kirk Douglas is a free-wheeling, roguish harpoon artist. Paul Lukas is a kind and gentle man of science and Peter Lorre is Lukas' fretting apprentice.

But it is the production itself that is the star. Technical skill was lavished in fashioning the fabulous *Nautilus* with its exquisitely appointed interior. The underwater lensing is remarkable on a number of counts, among them being the special designing of aqualungs and other equipment to match Verne's own illustrations.

Story opens in San Francisco where maritime men have been terrorized by reports of a monstrous denizen of the seas which has been sinking their ships. An armed frigate sets out in pursuit and is itself destroyed, with Lukas, Douglas and Lorre the survivors.

☐ 1954: Best Color Art Direction, Special Effects
☐ Nomination: Best Editing

· ·

■ 20,000 YEARS IN SING SING

1932, 78 MINS, US

Dir Michael Curtiz   *Prod* [uncredited]   *Scr* Wilson Mizner, Brown Holmes   *Ph* Barney McGill   *Ed* George Amy   *Mus* [Bernhard Kaun]   *Art Dir* Anton Grot
● Spencer Tracy, Bette Davis, Arthur Byron, Lyle Talbot, Warren Hymer, Louis Calhern (First National)

Interesting film material comes from warden Lewis E. Lawes' book of memoirs of prison administration [adapted by Courtenay Terrett and Robert Lord]. While it may take some liberties and overstep bounds of conviction, it's still good entertainment.

Sing Sing's warden can have no complaint against the Warner picture. He extended WB every co-operation in the filming and permitted cameras within his prison for actual scenes, including prisoners in the mob scenes.

Of pictures having inside of penal institutions as their locale, this one is the best. It builds up its interest strongly through that alone, covering a lot of routine that's unknown to most outsiders. Finally, it begins to appear Sing Sing wouldn't be a bad place at all to spend a vacation over the Depression. Arthur Byron's paternal smile as the warden, his anxiety to create reform and allow plenty of leeway even to tuff ones among his charges, would make it quite a resort.

Though let out to visit the dying gal friend and committing murder meanwhile, convict Tom Connors (Spencer Tracy) returns, putting the warden's honor system to the strongest test imaginable. In the end it's the chair for the reformed bad boy whose only regret seems to be his parting from the warden's shelter and benevolence.

Far-fetched, but it sells. Considerable comedy dots the action. Tracy and Warren Hymer, teamed in *Up the River* for Fox, are again together. Bette Davis is the convict's moll who does him dirt in one breath and shoots to kill for him in another. She's not particularly impressive here.

· ·

■ TWICE IN A LIFETIME

1985, 117 MINS, US ◇ ⓦ ⊙

Dir Bud Yorkin   *Prod* Bud Yorkin   *Scr* Colin Welland   *Ph* Nick McLean   *Ed* Robert Jones   *Mus* Pat Metheny   *Art Dir* William Creber
● Gene Hackman, Ann-Margret, Ellen Burstyn, Amy Madigan, Ally Sheedy, Stephen Lang (Yorkin)

An edgy, shifty-eyed 50th birthday tribute for hero Harry Mackenzie gets this midlife-crisis film off to a risky, sentimental start, and from there on out it's Ellen Burstyn, the abandoned wife, versus Gene Hackman, the not-unsympathetic-but-risk-taking husband, vying for audience affections.

Burstyn claims the film as Kate, who has to cope with her own life and family, and some rather mediocre lines. Hackman is stalwart and determined in his resolve to make a new

life with Ann-Margret, but she is far too sexy and he far too underdeveloped for anybody to understand what she sees in him.

The pic is loaded with jock humor and incidental comments that allow the characters' frustrations to seep out. Audiences will love Burstyn's warm wrinkles and visit with her daughters to a male strip joint, as well as Hackman's workmanlike heroism.
☐ 1985: Nomination: Best Supp. Actress (Amy Madigan)

· ·

■ TWILIGHT FOR THE GODS

1958, 120 MINS, US ◇

Dir Joseph Pevney   *Prod* Gordon Kay   *Scr* Ernest K. Gann   *Ph* Irving Glassberg   *Ed* Tony Martinelli   *Mus* David Raksin   *Art Dir* Alexander Golitzen, Eric Orborn
● Rock Hudson, Cyd Charisse, Arthur Kennedy, Leif Erickson, Charles McGraw, Richard Haydn (Universal)

Twilight for the Gods emerges as a routine sea adventure drama, bolstered by the marquee names of Rock Hudson and Cyd Charisse. Novelist Ernest Gann, who also wrote the screenplay, has employed the familiar technique [from his successful *The High and the Mighty*] of assembling a group of passengers of different personalities and backgrounds, including several with shady pasts, and studies their reactions to the dangers encountered during a long sea voyage.

There's Hudson, a court-martialed ship's captain fighting alcoholism, as the skipper of the battered sailing ship; Charisse as a Honolulu call girl running away from the authorities; Arthur Kennedy as a bitter and treacherous second mate; Leif Erickson as a down-and-out showman; Judith Evelyn as a has-been opera singer; Vladimir Sokoloff and Celia Lovsky as an elderly refugee couple; Ernest Truex as a missionary, and Richard Haydn as a British beachcomber.

Filmed on location in the Hawaiian islands, the photography is a delight to the eyes as it captures the sailing ship in motion, a sea village, various beaches and sites on a chain of islands, Honolulu harbor, and Waikalulu Falls.

· ·

■ TWILIGHT OF HONOR

1963, 105 MINS, US

Dir Boris Sagal   *Prod* William Perlberg, George Seaton   *Scr* Henry Denker   *Ph* Philip Lathrop   *Ed* Hugh S. Fowler   *Mus* John Green   *Art Dir* George W. Davis, Paul Groesse
● Richard Chamberlain, Joey Heatherton, Nick Adams, Claude Rains, Joan Blackman, James Gregory (M-G-M)

Twilight of Honor casts Richard Chamberlain in his first starring role, as a court-appointed defense attorney who takes on an entire New Mexico town, at the risk of his career, to save his client from the gas chamber.

Frank and often startling treatment is made of a section in New Mexico's criminal code – No. 12-24 – which provides that a husband is innocent if he kills another man whom he discovers in the act of adultery with his wife. Henry Denker's polished script, based upon the novel by Al Dewlen, brings out that Chamberlain's client killed the town's most respected citizen after he found him in bed with his trampish teenage spouse.

Dexterity which writer displays is matched by the shrewd, moving direction of Boris Sagal, who is particularly proficient in his realistic courtroom sequences. Chamberlain turns in a smooth and persuasive performance. He is surrounded by a thoroughly experienced cast to help him over the rough spots. One of highlights of pic is introduction of Joey Heatherton, a sexpot from the eastern stage and television making her film bow. In the part of the twotiming wife of the man up for murder she registers impressively.

☐ 1963: Nominations: Best Supp. Actor (Nick Adams), B&W Art Direction

· ·

■ TWILIGHT'S LAST GLEAMING

1977, 146 MINS, US/W. GERMANY ◇ ⓦ ⊙

Dir Robert Aldrich   *Prod* Merv Adelson   *Scr* Ronald M. Cohen, Edward Huebsch   *Ph* Robert Hauser   *Ed* Michael Luciano   *Mus* Jerry Goldsmith   *Art Dir* Rolf Zehetbauer
● Burt Lancaster, Richard Widmark, Charles Durning, Melvyn Douglas, Paul Winfield, Burt Young (Lorimar-Bavaria/Geria)

Robert Aldrich's *Twilight's Last Gleaming* is intricate, intriguing and intelligent drama. Filmed in Munich, the setting is the US.

Burt Lancaster stars as a cashiered US Air Force officer who seizes a nuclear missile site to force public disclosure of secret Vietnam war policy goals. Charles Durning is outstanding as a US president who must respond to the challenge.

A Walter Wager novel, *Viper Three*, has been adapted into a suspenseful and taut confrontation.

Outside, Richard Widmark mobilizes for the forcible recapture of the base, while in the White House, Durning assembles his top military and Cabinet advisors to ponder Lancaster's demands.

· ·

■ TWILIGHT ZONE
THE MOVIE

1983, 102 MINS, US ◇ ⓦ ⊙

Dir John Landis, Steven Spielberg, Joe Dante, George Miller   *Prod* Steven Spielberg, John Landis   *Scr* John Landis, George Clayton Johnson, Richard Matheson, Josh Rogan   *Ph* Steve Larner, Allen Daviau, John Hora   *Ed* Malcolm Campbell, Michael Kahn, Tina Hirsch, Howard Smith   *Mus* Jerry Goldsmith   *Art Dir* James D. Bissell
● Dan Aykroyd, Albert Brooks, Vic Morrow, Scatman Crothers, Kathleen Quinlan, John Lithgow (Warner)

Twilight Zone, feature film spinoff from Rod Serling's perennially popular 1960s TV series, plays much like a traditional vaudeville card, what with its tantalizing teaser opening followed by three sketches of increasing quality, all building up to a socko headline act.

Pic consists of prolog by John Landis as well as vignettes, none running any longer than original TV episodes, by Landis, Steven Spielberg, Joe Dante and George Miller. Dante and Miller manage to shine the brightest in this context.

Landis gets things off to a wonderful start with a comic prolog starring Dan Aykroyd and Albert Brooks.

Landis' principal episode, however, is a downbeat, one-dimensional fable about racial and religious intolerance. An embittered, middle-aged man who has just been passed over for a job promotion, Vic Morrow sports a torrent of racial epithets aimed at Jews, Blacks and Orientals while drinking with buddies at a bar. Upon exiting, he finds himself in Nazi-occupied Paris as a suspected Jew on the run from the Gestapo.

This is the only sequence in the film not derived from an actual TV episode, although it does bear a thematic resemblance to a 1961 installment titled *A Quality of Mercy*.

Spielberg's entry is the most down-to-earth of all the stories. In a retirement home filled with oldsters living in the past, spry Scatman Crothers encourages various residents to think young and, in organizing a game of kick the can, actually transforms them into their childhood selves again.

Most bizarre contribution comes from Dante. Outsider Kathleen Quinlan enters the Twilight Zone courtesy of little Jeremy Licht, who lords it over a Looney-Tune household by virtue of his power to will anything into existence except happiness.

But wisely, the best has been saved for last. Miller's re-working of *Nightmare at 20,000 Feet*, about a man who sees a gremlin tearing up an engine wing of an airplane, is electrifying from beginning to end.

TWIN PEAKS
FIRE WALK WITH ME

1992, 135 MINS, US ◇ ⓥ ⊙
Dir David Lynch   *Prod* Gregg Fienberg   *Scr* David Lynch, Robert Engels   *Ph* Ron Garcia   *Ed* Mary Sweeney   *Mus* Angelo Badalamenti   *Art Dir* Patricia Norris
● Sheryl Lee, Moira Kelly, Chris Isaak, Ray Wise, Kyle MacLachlan, Kiefer Sutherland (Lynch-Frost/CIBY)

A feature prequel to the celebrated but short-lived TV series, pic is like an R-rated episode embodying both the pros and cons of the intriguingly offbeat TV program. It's a detailing of the final week in the life of the quasi-legendary Laura Palmer, with plenty of digressions and artistic doodlings, as well as the occasional striking sequence.

After a 33-minute prologue detailing the FBI's investigation of the Portland murder of a woman named Teresa Banks, action then cuts to one year later in Twin Peaks, where Laura (Sheryl Lee) prepares for class by snorting some coke. Events largely center on Laura's downward spiral of drug use, promiscuity and crime, up to the moment of her killing, which leaves things off where they started on TV.

Suspense is clearly lacking in this story with a preordained outcome. Another significant drawback is that long before the climax Laura has become a tiresome teen.

Many of the show's familiar performers (Lara Flynn Boyle, Sherilyn Fenn, Richard Beymer and Joan Chen just for starters) aren't on view here. Performances are solid but unremarkable across the board, and craft contributions are very attractively similar to what was accomplished on the small screen.

TWINS

1988, 112 MINS, US ◇ ⓥ ⊙
Dir Ivan Reitman   *Prod* Ivan Reitman   *Scr* William Davies, William Osborne, Timothy Harris, Herschel Weingrad   *Ph* Andrzej Bartkowiak   *Ed* Sheldon Kahn, Donn Cambern   *Mus* Georges Delerue   *Art Dir* James D. Bissell
● Arnold Schwarzenegger, Danny DeVito, Kelly Preston, Chloe Webb, Bonnie Bartlett, Trey Wilson (Universal)

Director Ivan Reitman more than delivers on the wacky promise of *Twins* in this nutty, storybook tale of siblings separated at birth and reunited at age 35.

Arnold Schwarzenegger plays Julius Benedict, a perfect specimen of a man in both body and soul, raised as an orphan in pristine innocence on a tropical isle. Created in a genetic experiment, he has a twin brother on the mainland. Lionhearted Julius, filled with familiar longing, rushes off to LA to search for bro – only to discover he'd have found him faster by looking under rocks.

Danny DeVito's Vincent Benedict is a major creep, a guy you wouldn't mind seeing get hit by a car. To him, Julius is a dopey nut who makes a good bodyguard. They finally set out to locate their mother, but Vincent still is on his incorrigible path.

Schwarzenegger is a delightful surprise in this perfect transitional role to comedy. So strongly does he project the tenderness, nobility and puppy-dog devotion that make Julius tick that one is nearly hypnotized into suspending disbelief.

DeVito is a blaze of energy and body language as Vince, articulating the part as though he's written it himself.

TWINS OF EVIL

1971, 87 MINS, UK ◇ ⓥ
Dir John Hough   *Prod* Harry Fine, Michael Style   *Scr* Tudor Gates   *Ph* Dick Bush   *Ed* Spencer Reeve   *Mus* Harry Robinson   *Art Dir* Roy Stannard
● Madeleine Collinson, Mary Collinson, Peter Cushing, Kathleen Byron, Dennis Price, Damien Thomas (Hammer)

Blood flows and thunder roars as Mary and Madeleine Collinson, attractive identical twins playing orphans, come to live with their witch-hunting, godfearing uncle (Peter Cushing), in the shadow of dreaded Karnstein Castle.

One is good and timid while the other is bold and brazen. The latter cannot wait to find out more about the castle and the handsome young count (Damien Thomas). He is one of the undead and soon she is his victim. The question becomes, which twin is the vampire?

John Hough has given Tudor Gates' script a good pace and directed so that audiences can take it as straight horror or as a slight send-up. Settings, production values, camerawork and acting are all of a high standard.

TWISTED NERVE

1968, 118 MINS, UK ◇ ⓥ
Dir Roy Boulting   *Prod* George W. George, Frank Granat   *Scr* Roy Boulting, Leo Marks   *Ph* Harry Waxman   *Ed* Martin Charles   *Mus* Bernard Herrmann   *Art Dir* Albert Witherick
● Hayley Mills, Hywel Bennett, Billie Whitelaw, Phyllis Calvert, Frank Finlay, Barry Foster (British Lion)

Twisted Nerve has Hayley Mills involved in some fairly gruesome *Psycho*-like proceedings.

She's a bit shocked when the young antihero (Hywel Bennett) catches her off guard and kisses her fiercely; she's sweetly reasonable when he suddenly turns to her stark naked; and she eventually faces near-rape and imminent murder with displeasure, but non-Disney-like aplomb.

There's a firm, if unwitting, implication of a link between Down's Syndrome and homicidal madness. This dangerous untruth is likely to be offensive to many.

This angle was not necessary. Stripped of it the film could still stand up as a reasonably tough chilling suspenser giving a compelling study of a warped young psychopath. Bennett, with his babyface and pageboy-bobbed hairstyle, is compelling, his performance being an effectively blended piece of menace.

Roy Boulting lacks the subtleties of a Hitchcock but manages to bring some brooding menace into his direction, woven with some neat dialog and brash humor.

TWISTED ROAD, THE
See: They Live By Night

TWISTER

1989, 94 MINS, US ◇ ⓥ ⊙
Dir Michael Almereyda   *Prod* Wieland Schulz-Keil   *Scr* Michael Almereyda   *Ph* Renato Berta   *Ed* Roberto Silvi   *Mus* Hans Zimmer   *Art Dir* David Waso
● Harry Dean Stanton, Suzy Amis, Crispin Glover, Dylan McDermott, Jenny Wright, Lois Chiles (Vestron)

Twister is an oddball family drama about some Kansas nuts who bounce off the walls of their mansion while a storm brews outside. Appealing for its ambition to achieve a unique tone and for its wildly disparate cast, pic never entirely comes together.

Harry Dean Stanton is a retired soda pop tycoon who casually presides over a brood consisting of his layabout daughter Suzy Amis, the latter's eight-year-old daughter, his pretentious would-be *artiste* son Crispin Glover, the latter's fiancee Jenny Wright, unconventional black maid Charlaine Woodard

and his own fiancee, children's TV evangelist Lois Chiles.

Trying to work his way back under the same roof is Dylan McDermott, father of Amis's child, a ne'er-do-well who seems like too nice a guy for the fruitcakes populating Stanton's family.

Although it's impossible to see what first-time writer-director Michael Almereyda, working from a novel [*OH!*] by Mary Robison, is trying to get at, he doesn't at this point display the powers to unify the set of performances or to consistently control the tone. Novelist William Burroughs puts in a brief appearance.

TWO-FACED WOMAN

1941, 94 MINS, US ⓥ
Dir George Cukor   *Prod* Gottfried Reinhardt   *Scr* S.N. Behrman, Salka Viertel, George Oppenheimer   *Ph* Joseph Ruttenberg   *Ed* George Boemler   *Mus* Bronislau Kaper   *Art Dir* Cedric Gibbons, Daniel B. Cathcart
● Greta Garbo, Melvyn Douglas, Constance Bennett, Ruth Gordon, Roland Young, Frances Carson (M-G-M)

In a daring piece of showmanship, Metro presents the one-time queen of mystery in a wild, and occasionally very risque, slap farce entitled *Two-Faced Woman*. That the experiment of converting Greta Garbo into a comedienne is not entirely successful is no fault of hers. Had the script writers and the director, George Cukor, entered into the spirit of the thing with as much enthusiasm, lack of self-consciousness and abandon as the star, the result would have been a smash hit.

There is no holding back Garbo when she steps down from the serious dramatic pedestal and has her fling with broad comedy. Melvyn Douglas is an excellent foil. Much of the action takes place in bedrooms, boudoirs and the psychological proximities of both.

The story, which was taken from a play by Ludwig Fulda, is one of those naturalized importations from the Continent wherein the wife masquerades during most of the film as her own twin-sister just to test the fibre of her husband's adoration. There's a double entendre to nearly everything that is said between the two, and nearly everything is said.

TWO FLAGS WEST

1950, 92 MINS, US
Dir Robert Wise   *Prod* Casey Robinson   *Scr* Casey Robinson   *Ph* Leon Shamroy   *Ed* Louis Loeffler   *Mus* Hugo Friedhofer
● Joseph Cotten, Linda Darnell, Jeff Chandler, Cornel Wilde, Dale Robertson, Jay C. Flippen (20th Century-Fox)

The Civil War is carried into the west for Indian-fighting, giving *Two Flags West* an interesting premise for solid action and fast pace.

Factual basis for the plot [from a story by Frank S. Nugent and Curtis Kenyon], laid in 1864, is the recruiting of Confederate prisoners to man western army outposts under the Union flag. Joseph Cotten, Confederate colonel, and a group of his soldiers accept the deal to escape prison existence and because they see in it an opportunity eventually to get back to fighting for the south.

The motley crew is taken west under the guidance of Cornel Wilde, Union officer, to the fort commanded by Jeff Chandler, a bitter, brooding man crippled in his first clash of arms.

TWO FOR THE ROAD

1967, 112 MINS, UK ◇ ⓥ
Dir Stanley Donen   *Prod* Stanley Donen   *Scr* Frederic Raphael   *Ph* Christopher Challis   *Ed* Richard Marden, Madeleine Gug   *Mus* Henry Mancini   *Art Dir* Willy Holt

● Audrey Hepburn, Albert Finney, Eleanor Bron, William Daniels, Claude Dauphin, Georges Descrieres (20th Century-Fox)

As far as producer, director, femme lead and screenwriter are concerned, this attempt to visually analyze the bits and pieces that go into making a marriage, and then making it work, is successful. If it drags a bit here and there, blame it on the stodgy performance of actor Albert Finney who is unable to convey the lightness, gaiety and romanticism needed.

In the story, the same married couple make basically the same trip, from London to the Riviera, at three different stages of their life with continual crosscutting and flashing backwards and forwards from one period to the other.

The credibility of the changes in periods is left, except for changes of costume and vehicular equipment, to the two leads. Finney remains the same throughout but Audrey Hepburn is amazing in her ability to portray a very young girl, a just pregnant wife of two years, and a beginning-to-be-bored wife of five years.
☐ 1967: Nomination: Best Original Story & Screenplay

■ TWO FOR THE SEESAW

1962, 119 MINS, US
Dir Robert Wise   *Prod* Walter Mirisch   *Scr* Isobel Lennart   *Ph* Ted McCord   *Ed* Stuart Gilmore   *Mus* Andre Previn   *Art Dir* Boris Leven
● Robert Mitchum, Shirley MacLaine, Edmon Ryan, Elisabeth Fraser, Eddie Firestone, Billy Gray (United Artists)

There is a fundamental torpor about *Seesaw* that is less troublesome on stage that it is on screen, a medium of motion that exaggerates its absence, that emphasizes the slightest hint of listlessness. On film, it drags. It drags in spite of the charm, insight, wit and compassion of William Gibson's play, the savvy and sense of scenarist Isobel Lennart's mild revisions and additions, the infectious friskiness of Shirley MacLaine's performance and the consummate care taken by those who shaped and mounted the film reproduction.

The basic flaws appear to be the play's innate talkiness and the unbalance of the two-way 'see-saw'. The selection of Robert Mitchum for the role of Jerry Ryan proves not to have a been a wise one. The strong attraction Gittel is supposed to feel for Jerry becomes less plausible because of Mitchum's lethargic, droopy-eyed enactment. Something more appealing and magnetic is needed to make this love affair ring true.

MacLaine's performance in the meaty role of the disarmingly candid, stupendously kind-hearted Gittel Mosca, is a winning one. Her handling of the Yiddish dialect and accompanying mannerisms is sufficiently reserved so that it does not lapse into a kind of gittal-gitterless caricature.
☐ 1962: Nominations: Best B&W Cinematography, Song ('Second Chance')

■ TWO GENTLEMEN SHARING

1969, 106 MINS, UK ◇
Dir Ted Kotcheff   *Prod* J. Barry Kulick   *Scr* Evan Jones   *Ph* Billy Williams   *Mus* Stanley Myers
● Robin Phillips, Judy Geeson, Esther Anderson, Hal Frederick, Norman Rossington, Rachel Kempson (American-International)

Film boasts a solid and well-chosen cast, strong physical values for such a medium-scaled item, and a racial story [from a novel by David Stuart Leslie] delivered with unhysterical acumen and, at times, with considerable barbed humor.

The two 'gentlemen' who share the London pad in question are a young white ad exec with a liberal outlook and a certain disgust – or mistrust – for his middle-class background, and a black lawyer with a youthfully un-blunted hope of making a go of things in his profession on his own merits.

Robin Phillips has just the right naive physique as the well-meaner who bears the major brunt of film's thematics and manages to convince as the white member of the temporary duo, while Hal Frederick is generally very good.

■ TWO GIRLS AND A SAILOR

1944, 124 MINS, US ⊙
Dir Richard Thorpe   *Prod* Joe Pasternak   *Scr* Richard Connell, Gladys Lehman   *Ph* Robert Surtees   *Ed* George Boemler   *Mus* George Stoll   *Art Dir* Cedric Gibbons, Paul Groesse
● Van Johnson, June Allyson, Gloria DeHaven, Jimmy Durante, Lena Horne, Jose Iturbi (M-G-M)

Weakness of story, a very thin one in this instance, reduces *Two Girls and a Sailor* to little more than a salmagundi of band numbers by Harry James and Xavier Cugat, with their soloists, plus Jimmy Durante, of whom there isn't enough, and various other specialties ranging from Lena Horne to the concert pianist Jose Iturbi. It is too long and generally slow.

June Allyson and Gloria DeHaven play a sister act, featured in a few short numbers. Headliners at a nightclub with the James and Cugat orchestras, they turn their home into a place where servicemen may be entertained after they're through with their nitery chores.

Allyson turns in a very fine performance despite the poorness of the script, which also is true of Van Johnson, opposite her as the sailor boy.
☐ 1944: Nomination: Best Original Screenplay

■ TWO-HEADED SPY, THE

1958, 93 MINS, UK
Dir Andre de Toth   *Prod* Bill Kirby   *Scr* James O'Donnell   *Ph* Ted Scaife   *Ed* Raymond Poulton   *Mus* Gerard Schurmann   *Art Dir* Ivan King
● Jack Hawkins, Gia Scala, Erik Schumann, Alexander Knox, Felix Aylmer, Donald Pleasence (Sabre)

Based on a real-life story, this pursues a fairly pedestrian beat but it builds its tension excellently and without too blatant use of the usual cloak-and-dagger methods. Director Andre de Toth has sought to get his effects by showing the mental strain of Jack Hawkins in his dilemma rather than by stress on too much physical danger.

Hawkins, a British spy in both wars, and therefore an exile in Germany between the two conflicts, has built up confidence as an astute, loyal and resourceful member of the Nazi machine. At the same time he is feeding the Allies invaluable information through a British agent, neatly played by Felix Aylmer, disguised as an antique clock seller. When Aylmer is arrested and murdered, suspicion falls on Hawkins through his aide, a member of the Gestapo. But he manages to brush off this suspicion and continues his espionage through his new contact, a beautiful singer.

Hawkins plays the role of the general with his usual reliability.

■ 200 MOTELS

1971, 98 MINS, UK ◇ ⓥ
Dir Frank Zappa, Tony Palmer   *Prod* Jerry Good, Herb Cohen   *Scr* Frank Zappa, Tony Palmer   *Ph* Tony Palmer   *Ed* Rich Harrison   *Mus* Frank Zappa   *Art Dir* Leo Austin
● The Mothers of Invention, Theodore Bikel, Ringo Starr, Janet Ferguson, Lucy Offerall, Pamela Miller (United Artists)

Frank Zappa's *200 Motels*, featuring his group, The Mothers Of Invention, plus Theodore Bikel and Ringo Starr, is the zaniest. The film is a series of surrealistic sequences allegedly inspired by the experiences of a rock group on the road. The incidents are often outrageously irreverent. The comedy is fast and furious, both sophisticated and sophomoric.

The story proceeds on many different levels. Bikel appears to superior advantage in several characterizations: a TV m.c., an officious military bureaucrat, and something resembling a British secret agent or banker. Starr's okay cameo has him dressed up like Zappa. Group member Jimmy Carl Black is excellent as a redneck cowboy, Keith Moon is in nun's drag; Janet Ferguson and Lucy Offerall (it says here) are smash as two jaded groupies; and leather-costumed Pamela Miller scores as an underground newshen.

Film is the first theatrical release to have been shot in the color vidtape-to-film process of Technicolor's vidtronics subsid. The seven-day shooting sked (on a reported $600,000 budget) was followed by 11 days of editing.

■ TWO JAKES, THE

1990, 138 MINS, US ◇ ⓥ ⊙
Dir Jack Nicholson   *Prod* Robert Evans, Harold Schneider   *Scr* Robert Towne   *Ph* Vilmos Zsigmond   *Ed* Anne Goursaud   *Mus* Van Dyke Parks   *Art Dir* Jeremy Railton, Richard Sawyer
● Jack Nicholson, Harvey Keitel, Meg Tilly, Madeleine Stowe, Eli Wallach, Frederic Forrest (Paramount)

Following a trek to the bigscreen almost as convoluted as its plot, this oft-delayed sequel proves a jumbled, obtuse yet not entirely unsatisfying follow-up to *Chinatown*, rightly considered one of the best films of the 1970s. Like much of the film noir of the 1940s, *Jakes* simply spins a web of intrigue so thick its origins become imperceptible.

Picking up in 1948, 11 years after the events in *Chinatown*, Jake Gittes (Jack Nicholson) has become a prosperous and respected private investigator, though he still makes his living spying on an unfaithful wife (Meg Tilly) for her suspicious husband, Jake Berman (Harvey Keitel).

When the name of Katherine Mulwray turns up on an audiotape of the couple in bed together, it revives Gittes' ghosts of events that occurred in *Chinatown*, linking sex, murder and deceit to the role of precious resources – *Chinatown*, water; here, oil – in a developing Southern California. The film then takes on a dual structure, with Gittes in the eye of the hurricane as holder of the incriminating tape while seeking to unravel its connection to Mulwray, the memorable product of the coupling of father and daughter in Roman Polanski's earlier film.

A few scenes do carry tremendous power, especially Gittes' confrontation with detective Loach (David Keith) and, from a comic standpoint, his encounter with the murdered man's not-so-grieving widow Lillian (Madeleine Stowe). Still, Nicholson the director (working from Robert Towne's script) provides too few moments of that stripe for Nicholson the star.

■ TWO-LANE BLACKTOP

1971, 102 MINS, US ◇
Dir Monte Hellman   *Prod* Michael S. Laughlin   *Scr* Rudolph Wurlitzer, Will Corry   *Ph* Jack Deerson   *Ed* Monte Hellman   *Mus* Bill James (sup.)
● James Taylor, Warren Oates, Laurie Bird, Dennis Wilson, David Drake, Richard Ruth (Universal)

The strange and sometimes pathetic world of barnstorming, hustling street-racing is explored with feeling by director-editor Monte Hellman in *Two-Lane Blacktop*. The production, shot on cross-country locations, shapes up as an excellent combination of in-depth contemporary story-telling and personality casting.

Will Corry's story, scripted by Rudolph Wurlitzer and Corry, establishes James Taylor as a modern dropout, living on winnings from impromptu pavement racing challenges. Dennis Wilson is his expert mechanic. En route to nowhere in particular, they are latched onto by Laurie Bird.

The strong and compelling plot fibre is supplied by the writing, direction and performing of Warren Oates' role. He's an older man, a failure in some Establishment profession, now roaming the country in a souped-up Detroit vehicle. When Oates challenges Taylor to a cross-country run, with vehicle ownership the payoff, the story becomes a superior interplay of basic human nature.

Much of the story's import is on Oates' back, and he carries it like a champion in an outstanding performance.

■ TWO LEFT FEET

1965, 93 MINS, UK
Dir Roy Baker   Prod Roy Baker, Leslie Gilliat   Scr Roy Baker, John Hopkins   Ph Wilkie Cooper   Ed Michael Hart   Mus Phil Green
● Michael Crawford, Nyree Dawn Porter, Julia Foster, Michael Craze, David Hemmings, Dilys Watling (British Lion)

Whatever attracted producers in David Stuart Leslie's novel must have been lost in the transition to the screen because this is a very flyweight trite pic. It explores in only the most superficial terms the dilemma of a gauche youth whose ham-handed attempts to cope with his early sex problems are not highly satisfactory.

A callow youth is infatuated with a teasing waitress but his attempt to seduce her ends in disaster. She turns to brighter young men at a jazz club and he finds consolation in a naive young shop assistant.

Undertones of homosexuality between two of the youths are only hinted at and the sex lark is more talked about than acted upon. An attempt to satirize an appalling suburban wedding party becomes more of a caricature. Director Baker seems to have been unable to pull together a limp script.

Nyree Dawn Porter plays the waitress with exaggerated sex appeal. Michael Crawford handles the role of the gauche lad likeably. But much of the dialog is out of step with the minus-confidence character he is playing. Julia Foster, as the simple, goodhearted wench with whom he feels at ease, is pleasant, but unexciting.

■ TWO LOVES

(UK: Spinster)
1961, 100 MINS, US
Dir Charles Walters   Prod Julian Blaustein   Scr Ben Maddow   Ph Joseph Ruttenberg   Ed Fredric Steinkamp   Mus Bronislau Kaper   Art Dir George W. Davis, Urie McCleary
● Shirley MacLaine, Laurence Harvey, Jack Hawkins, Juano Hernandez, Norah Howard, Nobu McCarthy (M-G-M)

Frigidity is the subject broached by Two Loves, a story of the reawakening of a spinster American schoolteacher in New Zealand. Based on Sylvia Ashton-Warner's novel Spinster, it also takes a passing swipe at US morality, examines the vigorous spontaneous way-of-life of the Maori natives and utilizes the 'civilized' point-of-view of western-white values as a frame of reference. Unfortunately, the personal story emerges less lucid than its broader overtones.

Shirley MacLaine plays a dedicated schoolteacher who has found her way to an isolated settlement in northern New Zealand from Pennsylvania, although how and why is never clearly established. Her dogged innocence is threatened by the amorous advances of Laurence Harvey, a rather irrational and immature fellow teacher unhappy with his lot but unable to rise above it. Influenced by the primitive but practical morality of the Maoris, she seems on the verge of giving her all to Harvey when he (rather conveniently) comes to a violentend in a motorcycle mishap. On the rebound, she is coaxed out of self-guilt pangs by senior school inspector Jack Hawkins.

MacLaine, although not ideally suited to the role, manages for the most part to rise above the miscasting and deliver an earnest, interesting portrayal. But there is a degree of gravity and warmth missing in her delineation, making it slightly difficult to understand Harvey's passion and Hawkins' tender affection for her. Nobu McCarthy comes through with flying colors as a 15-year-old Maori girl delighted to bear Harvey's children out of wedlock.

■ TWO-MINUTE WARNING

1976, 115 MINS, US
Dir Larry Peerce   Prod Edward S. Feldman
Scr Edward Hume   Ph Gerald Hirschfeld   Ed Eve Newman, Walter Hannemann   Mus Charles Fox
Art Dir Herman A. Blumenthal
● Charlton Heston, John Cassavetes, Martin Balsam, Beau Bridges, Marilyn Hassett, David Janssen (Universal)

An off-the-beaten-track story [based on the novel by George La Fountaine] of a football stadium crowd menaced by a sniper, combined with above-average plotting, acting and direction.

The sniper is introduced intriguingly via subjective camera, but later is seen (Warren Miller) in teasing long shots, blurred closed-circuit pans and other clever devices which keep him all the more menacing.

Among the prominent players, all of whom take seriously their roles, are stadium manager Martin Balsam and assistant Brock Peters; unmarried but longtime lovers David Janssen and Gena Rowlands (she can convey a reel of characterization in 10 seconds of film); and unemployed young father Beau Bridges, trying to show his and wife Pamela Bellwood's children a good time.
□ 1976: Nomination: Best Editing

■ TWO MOON JUNCTION

1988, 104 MINS, US
Dir Zalman King   Prod Donald P. Borchers
Scr Zalman King   Ph Mark Plummer   Ed Marc Grossman   Mus Jonathan Elias   Art Dir Michelle Minch
● Sherilyn Fenn, Richard Tyson, Louise Fletcher, Kristy McNichol, Martin Hewitt, Burl Ives (DDM/Lorimar)

Two Moon Junction is a bad hick version of Last Tango in Paris down to the poor imitative scoring by Jonathan Elias. Sexual obsession might be the aim, but the result is anything but hot.

In the Maria Schneider role is Madonna-clone Sherilyn Fenn who decides to give her virginity to a guy who works at the traveling midway (Richard Tyson) instead of her fiance (Martin Hewitt). She wears white all the time and acts pure when on her home turf.

Plot has all the ingredients of a 1940s meller with the obvious exception that poor little rich girl Fenn unabashedly defrocks at the drop of a hat while Tyson manages to never bare much more than his chest.

Kristy McNichol appears as a midway groupie whose subtle bisexual scenes dancing with Fenn have more electricity than Fenn's encounters with Tyson.

Shot in and around Los Angeles pic seldom looks like Alabama.

■ TWO MRS CARROLLS, THE

1947, 100 MINS, US
Dir Peter Godfrey   Prod Mark Hellinger   Scr Thomas Job   Ph Peverell Marley   Ed Frederick Richards   Mus Franz Waxman   Art Dir Anton Grot
● Humphrey Bogart, Barbara Stanwyck, Alexis Smith, Nigel Bruce, Isobel Elsom (Warner)

The Two Mrs Carrolls, adapted from the Martin Vale legiter, is more stage play than motion picture. Overladen with dialog as action substitute, it talks itself out of much of the suspense that should have developed. There is some femme appeal, however, in the Humphrey Bogart character as hero-villain.

Production format hugs stage technique in settings and carrying out story. Backgrounds never seem realistic but rather appear as grouped on stage. Bogart, Barbara Stanwyck and Alexis Smith feel the burden of dialog and unnatural characters but, under Peter Godfrey's direction, manage to give material an occasional lift.

Plot deals with married artist who meets a new love while vacationing in Scotland. He returns to London, murders his wife by methodical poisoning and marries the new flame. Second marriage works okay until another attractive girl appears.

■ TWO MULES FOR SISTER SARA

1970, 116 MINS, US
Dir Don Siegel   Prod Martin Rackin, Carroll Case
Scr Albert Maltz   Ph Gabriel Figueroa   Ed Robert F. Shugrue   Mus Ennio Morricone   Art Dir Jose Rodriguez Granada
● Shirley MacLaine, Clint Eastwood, Manolo Fabregas, Alberto Morin, Armando Silvestre, John Kelly (Universal/Malpaso)

Two Mules for Sister Sara might have worked. But with Clint Eastwood as one of the mules, an American mercenary looking for a fast peso in old French-occupied Mexico, Shirley MacLaine as a scarlet sister disguised in a nun's habit, and Don Siegel's by-the-old-book direction, it doesn't.

Screenplay based on a story by Budd Boetticher, needed a Lee Marvin, or a portrayal like Humphrey Bogart's in The African Queen to work. MacLaine is literally unbelievable as a nun, and the story's main thread of tension, the relationship between her and Eastwood, simply dissipates.

Siegel and Mexican cameraman Gabriel Figueroa use the Mexican locations to great advantage, with sweeping panoramics of the brutal countryside and intriguing settings.

■ TWO OF A KIND

1983, 87 MINS, US
Dir John Herzfeld   Prod Roger M. Rothstein, Joe Wizan
Scr John Herzfeld   Ph Fred Koenekamp   Ed Jack Hofstra   Mus Patrick Williams   Art Dir Albert Brenner
● John Travolta, Olivia Newton-John, Charles Durning, Beatrice Straight, Scatman Crothers, Oliver Reed (20th Century-Fox)

Aside from the presence of the two stars, Two of a Kind has all the earmarks of a bargain-basement job. Sets are as constricted as those for live, three-camera sitcoms, and many of the so-called New York location scenes possess an obvious back-lot look.

Script's only vaguely amusing conceit presents itself at the beginning, when God returns from a vacation and, finding the world gone to seed in the interim, announces to four of his angels that he's going to wipe out the human race and start over again. The angels urge Him to reconsider His decision based on whether or not a random man can prove himself possible of genuine goodness.

So John Travolta, a self-styled inventor of such inane items as edible sunglasses, is selected as the guinea pig, just in time to find him robbing a bank in order to pay off a debt to the mob. Bank teller Olivia Newton-John, fired for flirting with the stick-up man, actually makes off with the dough. She is saved by Travolta after being taken hostage by a gunman.

■ TWO PEOPLE

1973, 100 MINS, US ◇
Dir Robert Wise   *Prod* Robert Wise   *Scr* Richard DeRoy   *Ph* Henri Decae   *Ed* William Reynolds
Mus David Shire   *Art Dir* Henry Michelson
● Peter Fonda, Lindsay Wagner, Estelle Parsons, Alan Fudge, Philippe March, Frances Sternhagen (Filmakers/ Universal)

Two People is a major disappointment. Producer-director Robert Wise's film clearly aimed to develop a love-at-first-sight romance, in the form of a 'road' film, between two characters whose different life styles parallel in brief encounter. However, sluggish pacing and ludicrous dialog turn the film into a travesty of its own form.

Script finds Peter Fonda, a repentant Vietnam field deserter, tired of running and ready to return to the US to face his court martial and punishment. In Marrakech, Fonda meets Lindsay Wagner, a fashion model in the tow of her editor (Estelle Parsons) and her live-in lover (Geoffrey Horne), father of their child (Brian Lima) stashed in Manhattan with her mother Frances Sternhagen.

The film's pacing turns the desired audience wish – that the couple make physical love – into barely concealed impatience.

■ TWO RODE TOGETHER

1961, 108 MINS, US ◇ Ⓥ ⊙
Dir John Ford   *Prod* Stan Shpetner   *Scr* Frank Nugent
Ph Charles Lawton Jr   *Ed* Jack Murray   *Mus* George Duning   *Art Dir* Robert Peterson
● James Stewart, Richard Widmark, Shirley Jones, Linda Cristal, Andy Devine, John McIntire (Columbia)

John Ford's western is a story [from the novel by Will Cook] of the ill-advised attempt to haul white prisoners back to civilized society in the 1880s after they have spent a decade or more suffering the slings and arrows of Comanche Indian captivity. This is fairly fresh sagebrush fiction, invading and surveying a relatively untapped corner of American history. But somehow the production misfires in the process.

Whereas parts of the film zoom into the heavy, psychological sphere of the modern western, others revert to the outmoded innocence and directness of a 1930s sagebrush style, as if intended as parody.

There are, however, compensations. Not the least is the unusually practical, non-heroic nature of the central character, most disarmingly and authoritatively enacted by James Stewart. He far and away cops histrionic honors.

■ TWO SISTERS FROM BOSTON

1946, 112 MINS, US
Dir Henry Koster   *Prod* Joe Pasternak   *Scr* Myles Connolly   *Ph* Robert Surtees   *Ed* Douglas Biggs
Mus Sammy Fain, Ralph Freed   *Art Dir* Cedric Gibbons, Daniel B. Cathcart
● Kathryn Grayson, June Allyson, Lauritz Melchior, Jimmy Durante, Peter Lawford (M-G-M)

Two Sisters from Boston is both an operatic and a low comedy treat, Kathryn Grayson and Lauritz Melchior carry the straight chirping, Jimmy Durante is at his peak with an equally legit role in that he's an integral character in the plot. June Allyson is the other sister from Hubtown, good running mate to her impetuous cinematic kin, Grayson.

Latter tees off as 'High C Susie', a hotsy chirper who's quite a click in a Bowery joint until her staid Back Bay family descends on NY and with the somewhat outlandish assistance of Spike (Durante), the diamond-in-the-rough pianist-impressario of the Bowery bistro, does make the Met.

Starting in the Bowery atmosphere it segues into staid Boston. Thence the pyrotechnics to keep Grayson's shame from her family, until she makes good on her own in the Met. In between Melchior indulges in temperamental outbursts. There's a closeup on the prehistoric method of His Master's Voice recording (old phonograph horn, etc), a great sequence; and also some good turn-of-the-century song hokum, viz, 'There Are Two Sides to Every Girl' to carry the action along.

■ 2001: A SPACE ODYSSEY

1968, 160 MINS, UK ◇ Ⓥ ⊙
Dir Stanley Kubrick   *Prod* Stanley Kubrick   *Scr* Stanley Kubrick, Arthur C. Clarke   *Ph* Geoffrey Unsworth, John Alcott   *Ed* Ray Lovejoy   *Art Dir* Tony Masters, Harry Lange, Ernest Archer
● Keir Dullea, Gary Lockwood, William Sylvester, Daniel Richter, Douglas Rain, Leonard Rossiter (M-G-M)

When Stanley Kubrick and sci-fi specialist Arthur C. Clarke first conceived the idea of making a Cinerama film, neither had any idea that it would run into a project of several years.

A major achievement in cinematography and special effects, *2001* lacks dramatic appeal and only conveys suspense after the halfway mark; Kubrick must receive all the praise – and take all the blame.

The plot, so-called, uses up almost two hours in exposition of scientific advances in space travel and communications, before anything happens.

The little humor is provided by introducing well-known commercial names which are presumably still operational during the space age – the Orbiter Hilton hotel and Pan Am space ships.

Keir Dullea and Gary Lockwood, as the two principal astronauts, are not introduced until well along in the film. Their complete lack of emotion becomes rather implausible during scenes where they discuss the villainy of HAL, the talking computer [voiced by Douglas Rain].

Kubrick and Clarke have kept dialog to a minimum, frequently inserting lengthy passages where everything is told visually. The tremendous centrifuge which makes up the principal set (in which the two astronauts live and travel) reportedly cost $750,000 and looks every bit of it.

[Pic was cut to 139 mins by Kubrick after the premiere.]
□ 1968: Special Visual Effects
□ Nominations: Best Director, Original Story & Screenplay, Art Direction

■ 2010

1984, 114 MINS, US ◇ Ⓥ ⊙
Dir Peter Hyams   *Prod* Peter Hyams   *Scr* Peter Hyams
Ph Peter Hyams   *Ed* James Mitchell   *Mus* David Shire
Art Dir Albert Brenner
● Roy Scheider, John Lithgow, Helen Mirren, Bob Balaban, Keir Dullea, Douglas Rain (M-G-M)

As the title proclaims, *2010* begins nine years after something went wrong with the Jupiter voyage of Discovery. On earth, politicians have brought the US and Russia to the brink of war, but their scientists have united in a venture to return to Jupiter to seek an answer to Discovery's fate and the significance of the huge black monolith that orbits near it.

American crew is headed by Roy Scheider, John Lithgow and Bob Balaban. The Soviets want them along mainly for their understanding of HAL 9000, whose mutiny remains un-

explained. If revived in the salvage effort, can HAL still be trusted?

In Peter Hyams' hands [working from a novel by Arthur C. Clarke], the HAL mystery is the most satisfying substance of the film and handled the best. Unfortunately, it lies amid a hodge-podge of bits and pieces.
□ 1984: Nominations: Best Costume Design, Art Direction, Sound, Visual Effects, Makeup

■ TWO-WAY STRETCH

1960, 87 MINS, UK Ⓥ
Dir Robert Day   *Prod* George Black, Alfred Black
Scr John Warren, Len Heath, Alan Hackney
Ph Geoffrey Faithfull   *Ed* Bert Rule   *Mus* Ken Jones
● Peter Sellers, Wilfrid Hyde White, David Lodge, Bernard Cribbins, Maurice Denham, Lionel Jeffries (British Lion)

Peter Sellers gives another deft, very funny performance in *Two-Way Stretch*. The thin story line concerns a free-and-easy prison run by a governor who is more interested in gardening than discipline. Occupying a cell, which is far more like a luxury bed-sitting room, are three partners in crime – Sellers, David Lodge and Bernard Cribbins. They have the prison completely sewn up.

Posing as a clergyman, an outside partner arrives with a scheme for stealing $5 million in diamonds. It needs the trio to break jail the night before their release, pull off the job, return to prison with their loot, and next morning walk out free men and with a perfect alibi. The arrival of a tough new chief warden frustrates their plans.

Much of the dialog was supplied by Alan Hackney and, almost certainly, by Sellers himself. Success of this film depends largely on the actors and Robert Day's brisk direction. Sellers has himself a ball as the leader of the crafty trio of crooks while Lodge and Cribbins make perfectly contrasted partners. A long list of tried, handpicked performers chip in when required.

■ TWO WEEKS IN ANOTHER TOWN

1962, 106 MINS, US ◇ Ⓥ ⊙
Dir Vincente Minnelli   *Prod* John Houseman
Scr Charles Schnee   *Ph* Milton Krasner   *Ed* Adrienne Fazan, Robert J. Kern Jr   *Mus* David Raksin
Art Dir George W. Davis, Urie McCleary
● Kirk Douglas, Edward G. Robinson, Cyd Charisse, George Hamilton, Dahlia Lavi, Claire Trevor (M-G-M)

Two Weeks in Another Town [from the novel by Irwin Shaw] is not an achievement about which any of its creative people are apt to boast.

Kirk Douglas stars as an unstable actor, fresh off a three-year hitch in sanitariums, who goes to Rome to rejoin the director (Edward G. Robinson) with whom, years earlier, he's scored his greatest triumphs. In the course of a series of shattering incidents, Douglas comes to discover that it is upon himself alone that he must rely for the stability and strength of character with which he can fulfill his destiny.

Douglas emotes with his customary zeal and passion, but labors largely in vain to illuminate an unbelievable character. Even less believable is the character of his ex-wife, a black-as-night, hard-as-nails seductress exotically overplayed by Cyd Charisse.

Only remotely lifelike characters in the story are Robinson and Claire Trevor as an ambiguous married couple whose personalities transform under the secretive cover of night.

There is a haunting score by David Raksin. A considerable amount of footage from *The Bad and the Beautiful* is cleverly incorporated into the drama. As a matter of fact, the portion of the film-within-a-film is livelier than just about anything else in the film.

■ TWO YEARS BEFORE THE MAST

1946, 96 MINS, US
Dir John Farrow   *Prod* Seton I. Miller (assoc.)
Scr Seton I. Miller, George Bruce   *Ph* Ernest Laszlo
Ed Eda Warren   *Mus* Victor Young   *Art Dir* Hans
Dreier, Franz Bachelin
● Alan Ladd, Brian Donlevy, William Bendix, Barry
Fitzgerald, Howard da Silva, Esther Fernandez
(Paramount)

Chief credit for this one [based on Richard
Henry Dana Jr's famous book] belongs to director John Farrow. With the emphasis on action throughout, Farrow keeps his cast
thesping to the hilt and achieves several little
bits of suspense.

Although Alan Ladd and the other stars top
the cast, it's Howard da Silva, as the pitiless
ship's captain, who walks off with the blue
ribbon.

Rest of cast, from leads to minor bit parts
perform excellently. Ladd does a nice job as
the fop who finds his regeneration while fighting to get human treatment for the merchant
seamen of that day. Bendix gives a restrained
reading to his role as the tough but necessarily sympathetic first mate, and Barry
Fitzgerald adds the comedy touches as the
ship's cook.

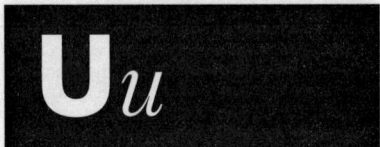

■ U-BOAT 29

See: The Spy in Black

■ UGLY AMERICAN, THE

1963, 120 MINS, US ◇ ⑩
Dir George Englund   *Prod* George Englund
Scr Stewart Stern   *Ph* Clifford Stine   *Ed* Ted J. Kent
Mus Frank Skinner   *Art Dir* Alexander Golitzen, Alfred
Sweeney
● Marlon Brando, Eiji Okada, Sandra Church, Arthur
Hill, Pat Hingle, Jocelyn Brando (Universal)

Some of the ambiguities, hypocrisies and perplexities of cold war politics are observed,
dramatized and, to a degree, analyzed in *The
Ugly American*. It is a thought-provoking but
uneven screen translation taken from, but not
in a literal sense based upon, the popular
novel by William J. Lederer and Eugene
Burdick.

Focal figure of the story is an American ambassador (Marlon Brando) to a Southeast
Asian nation who, after jumping to conclusions in the course of dealing with an uprising
of the natives of that country against the existing regime and what they interpret as
Yankee imperialism comes to understand
that there is more to modern political revolution than meets the casual or jaundiced bystander's eye. As a result of his experience, he
senses that Americans 'can't hope to win the
cold war unless we remember what we're for
as well as what we're against'.

Although skillfully and often explosively directed by George Englund and well played by
Brando and others in the cast, the film tends
to be overly talkative and lethargic in certain
areas, vague and confusing in others.
Probably the most jarring single flaw is the
failure to clarify the exact nature of events
during the ultimate upheaval.

Brando's performance is a towering one; restrained, intelligent and always masculine.
Japanese actor Eiji Okada of *Hiroshima, mon
amour* renown, makes a strong impression.

Mass riot scene near the outset of the picture is frighteningly realistic. Art direction is
outstanding, with a convincing replica of a
Southeast Asian village on the Universal
backlot.

■ UGLY DACHSHUND, THE

1965, 93 MINS, US ◇ ⑩
Dir Norman Tokar   *Prod* Walt Disney, Winston Hibley
Scr Albert Aley   *Ph* Edward Colman   *Ed* Robert Stafford
Mus George Bruns   *Art Dir* Carroll Clark, Marvin
Aubrey Davis
● Dean Jones, Suzanne Pleshette, Charlie Ruggles, Kelly
Thordsen, Farley Baer, Robert Kino (Walt Disney)

Walt Disney, who knows his way with a dog as
well as a family, has turned out a rollicking
piece of business in this comedy about a
Great Dane which thinks he's a dachshund.

Dean Jones and Suzanne Pleshette are the
two principals, a young married couple faced
with the fancy cut-ups of four Dachs and a
Dane raised with the low-slung pups. The
Fritzels are hers, the Dane his, and actually
the Albert Aley screenplay builds to trying to
sell the Dane – named Brutus – that he actually is a Dane.

Action is light and airy as the couple go their
own way with their respective pets, Suzanne insisting that Dean rid himself of the clumsy big-
foot while her spouse stoutly maintains that his
Dane has a rightful place in the household.

■ ULTIMATE SOLUTION OF GRACE QUIGLEY, THE

(UK: Grace Quigley)

1984, 102 MINS, US ◇ ⑩
Dir Anthony Harvey   *Prod* Menahem Golan, Yoram
Globus   *Scr* A. Martin Zweiback   *Ph* Larry Pizer
Ed Bob Raetano   *Mus* John Addison
● Katharine Hepburn, Nick Nolte, Elizabeth Wilson,
Chip Zien, Kit Le Fever, William Duell (Cannon/
Northbrook)

In this black comedy dealing with voluntary
euthanasia by the Geritol set, casting
Katharine Hepburn as the spry, entrepre-
neurial mother figure who arranges for her
peers' demise and Nick Nolte as the gruff,
hard-bitten and sarcastic hitman she hires,
the two actors impart a light-hearted and
whimsical tone to otherwise unpleasant subject matter.

Pic opens with Hepburn as a lonely and economically strapped pensioner who lost her
immediate family in a pre-war auto accident,
but who has a zestful embrace for life
nonetheless. Sitting across from her apartment one day, she inadvertently witnesses
Nolte put a bullet into her money-grubbing
land- lord, and subsequently enlists him in
her scheme to provide a 'service' for her aging compatriots who wish to meet the hereafter ahead of schedule.

There are some marvelous supporting performances by Elizabeth Wilson as the spinster who can't get arrested trying to get Nolte
to put her out of her misery, William Duell as
the nerdy neighbor of Hepburn, and Kit Le
Fever as Nolte's girlfriend hooker.

■ ULYSSES

1954, 104 MINS, ITALY ◇ ⑩
Dir Mario Camerini   *Prod* Carlo Ponti, Dino De
Laurentiis   *Scr* Mario Camerini, Franco Brusati, Ben
Hecht, Irwin Shaw, Hugh Gray, Ennio De Concini
Ph Harold Rosson   *Ed* Leo Catozzo   *Mus* Alessandro
Cicognini   *Art Dir* Flavio Mogherini
● Kirk Douglas, Silvana Mangano, Anthony Quinn,
Rossana Podesta, Jaques Dumesnil (Lux/Ponti-De
Laurentiis)

A lot, perhaps too much, money went into the
making of *Ulysses*, but expense shows. Besides
the epic Homeric peg, pic has an internationally balanced cast, with Yank, French and
Italian elements predominant.

Only a few of the w.k. Homeric episodes
have been included in the already lengthy pic,
and are told in flashback form as remembered by the hero. Featured are his love for
Nausicaa; the cave of Polyphemus, the one-
eyed monster; the Siren Rocks; the visit to
Circe's Island cave and the return to
Penelope. But material covered makes for
plenty of action, dominated by a virile performance by Kirk Douglas.

Others include costar Silvana Mangano, a
looker, as both Circe and Penelope, but unfortunately limited by both parts to expressing monotonous unhappiness until the finale.
Anthony Quinn handles his bits well. For a
spectacle, the pic runs too many closeups,
with longish stretches of dialog between the
two principals, or soliloquized.

■ ULYSSES

1967, 140 MINS, IRELAND ◇ ⑩ ⊙
Dir Joseph Strick   *Prod* Joseph Strick   *Scr* Joseph Strick,
Fred Haines   *Ph* Wolfgang Suschitzky   *Ed* Reginald
Mills   *Mus* Stanley Myers   *Art Dir* Graham Probst
● Barbara Jefford, Milo O'Shea, Maurice Roeves,, T.P.
McKenna, Martin Dempsey, Sheila O'Sullivan
(Continental/Walter Reade)

Ulysses [from James Joyce's novel] is a
healthy, promising cinematic piece of flora,
nightblooming and carnivorous. Filmed entirely in Ireland, with a cast almost entirely

Irish, the picture concentrates on the trio of primary characters – Leopold and Molly Bloom and student Stephen Dedalus. Although their tales overlap, the primary emphasis is on the two males leaving the last 20 or 30 minutes to Molly's famous libidinous soliloquy.

Barbara Jefford's Molly is handsomely overblown, a wasted garden of a woman who yearns for a man with a passion that almost causes the screen to pulsate yet depriving Leopold of his marital rights because she so abhors another possibility of pregnancy. Milo O'Shea's Leopold Bloom is a realised example of the degraded, dejected husband – his dignity rapidly fading, but still capable of dreaming of lost sexual prowess.

Maurice Roeves' Stephen Dedalus might have been more impressive had some of the many flashbacks been used to better fill in his past – viewers are only told that he comes from an unhappy home, with a failure of a father.

□ 1967: Nomination: Best Adapted Screenplay

••••••••••••••••••••••••••••••••

■ ULZANA'S RAID

1972, 103 MINS, US ◇ Ⓥ ⊙
Dir Robert Aldrich   *Prod* Carter De Haven   *Scr* Alan Sharp   *Ph* Joseph Biroc   *Ed* Michael Luciano   *Mus* Frank DeVol   *Art Dir* James D. Vance
● Burt Lancaster, Bruce Davison, Jorge Luke, Richard Jaeckel, Joaquin Martinez, Lloyd Bochner (Universal)

Ulzana's Raid is the sort of pretentious US Army-vs-Indians period potboiler that invites derision from its own dialog and situations. However, suffice it to say that the production is merely ponderous in its formula action-sociology-violence, routine in its acting and direction, and often confusing in its hokey storytelling.

Screenplay finds a weathered old frontier scout (Burt Lancaster) saddled with a super-naive greenhorn young army officer-who-matures-under-pressure-etc (Bruce Davison) as the patrol attempts to round up some marauding Apaches.

Whatever the film's aspirations, the effect is simply another exploitation western which crassly exploits the potentials in physical abuse, and in which plot suspense is not what is going to happen, but how bestial it can be.

••••••••••••••••••••••••••••••••

■ UNBEARABLE LIGHTNESS OF BEING, THE

1988, 171 MINS, US ◇ Ⓥ ⊙
Dir Philip Kaufman   *Prod* Saul Zaentz   *Scr* Jean-Claude Carriere, Philip Kaufman   *Ph* Sven Nykvist   *Ed* Walter Murch, B.J. Sears, Vivien Hillgrove Gilliam, Stephen A. Rotter   *Art Dir* Pierre Guffroy
● Daniel Day Lewis, Juliette Binoche, Lena Olin, Derek de Lint, Erland Josephson, Donald Moffat (Zaentz)

Milan Kundera's 1984 international bestseller of love and erotica set against the Russian invasion of Czechoslovakia has been regarded as essentially unfilmable by many observers, so Philip Kaufman has pulled off a near-miracle in creating this richly satisfying adaptation.

Tomas, a top surgeon and compulsive ladies' man in Prague, takes in and eventually marries a lovely country girl, Tereza. He continues his womanizing, however, particularly with his voluptuous mistress Sabina, an artist who takes off for Geneva as soon as Russian tanks put a halt to the Prague Spring of 1968.

The sexuality which drenches the entire film possesses a great buoyancy and spirit in the first act, set during the exciting liberalization of communism under Alexander Dubcek. Second act, in Geneva, is comparatively somber and spare, but is punctuated by Sabina's new affair with a married man and by the growing friendship between Sabina and Tereza.

As played by Juliette Binoche and Lena Olin, the two women are absolutely enchanting; Binoche is adorably doll-like while Olin is simply striking as a woman who lives her sexual and artistic lives just as she pleases.

Attractive in some ways, Tomas is irritatingly uncommunicative and opaque at others, and Daniel Day Lewis at times overdoes the self-consciously smug projection of his own appeal.

□ 1988: Nominations: Best Adapted Screenplay, Cinematography

••••••••••••••••••••••••••••••••

■ UNBECOMING AGE

1992, 90 MINS, US ◇ Ⓥ
Dir Alfredo Ringel, Deborah Ringel   *Prod* Alfredo Ringel, Deborah Ringel   *Scr* Meridith Baer, Geoff Prysirr   *Ph* Harry Mathias   *Ed* Alan Geik   *Mus* Jeff Lass   *Art Dir* Phil Dagort
● Diane Salinger, John Calvin, Priscilla Pointer, George Clooney, Colleen Camp, Wallace Shawn (Ringelvision)

The spirit is winning but the inspiration is missing in *Unbecoming Age*, an unbecoming comedy about a woman who would rather act like a child than mature gracefully.

First feature by the husband-and-wife team of Alfredo and Deborah Ringel takes its central device from Howard Hawks' 1962 farce *Monkey Business*, in which Cary Grant and company started behaving like teens after ingesting rejuvenation serum.

Here, suburban housewife Diane Salinger finds herself notably depressed on her 40th birthday. Some magic bubbles keep her the same physically but cause her to transform into an eight-year-old mentally. Hubby John Calvin sends her to shrink Wallace Shawn, but Salinger continues to rebel by indulging in a heavy flirtation with young hipster George Clooney and carting Calvin's ailing mother, Priscilla Pointer, off to Las Vegas, where she promptly dies at the blackjack table.

Comic approach throughout leans toward the brash and garish, with subtlety nowhere to be found. A number of talented thesps brighten up the supporting cast.

••••••••••••••••••••••••••••••••

■ UNBELIEVABLE TRUTH, THE

1989, 98 MINS, US ◇ Ⓥ
Dir Hal Hartley   *Prod* Bruce Weiss, Hal Hartley   *Scr* Hal Hartley   *Ph* Michael Spiller   *Ed* Hal Hartley   *Mus* Jim Coleman   *Art Dir* Carla Gerona
● Adrienne Shelly, Robert Burke, Christopher Cooke, Julia McNeal, Gary Saver, Mark Bailey (Action)

The Unbelievable Truth is a promising, reasonably engaging first feature of the art school film variety. Very consciously designed and stylized in all departments, pic has a minor-key feel to it.

Narrative has Josh, a good-looking, taciturn guy, showing up in his small New York home town after a spell in the slammer. Josh manages to land a job in a garage owned by Vic, whose daughter Audry is a 17-year-old sexpot due to enter Harvard at summer's end. Audry drops her longtime boyfriend, moans about the impending end of the world, resists going to college, then shocks everyone by going materialistic and hitting it big as a model in Manhattan, where she shacks up with a photographer she detests. She also makes passes at Josh, and the eventual sexual suspicions and permutations nearly take on the dimensions of a French farce.

All this is told by way of an acting style that could be described as heightened naturalism, the broadness of which constantly provokes a tickling humor while simultaneously emphasizing the banality of what is being said.

Framing the middle-class melodrama is director Hal Hartley's manipulative artistry, which uses such devices as orchestrated color

schemes, highly unrealistic sound, Godardian intertitles, repeated motifs and careful scoring.

••••••••••••••••••••••••••••••••

■ UNCENSORED

1944, 82 MINS, UK Ⓥ
Dir Anthony Asquith   *Prod* Edward Black   *Scr* Rodney Ackland, Terence Rattigan   *Ph* Arthur Crabtree   *Ed* R.E. Dearing   *Mus* Hanns May   *Art Dir* Alex Vetchinsky
● Eric Portman, Phyllis Calvert, Griffith Jones, Irene Handl, Peter Glenville, Walter Hudd (Gainsborough)

Efforts of the Belgian underground to thwart the Nazi grip form the basis for this thrilling melodrama, which often reaches the melodramatic heights of *39 Steps*. Picture contains about an hour of suspenseful action.

Director Anthony Asquith has done much to develop the yarn. Whole action centers about the efforts of Belgium's patriots to maintain regular publication of an underground paper as a constant thorn to the Nazi occupational troops. Scripters have taken Wolfgang Wilhelm's story and framed it around the apparently unpatriotic Eric Portman, who quietly continues his underground operations while entertaining nightly at a cabaret for Nazi toppers. Walter Hudd is the editor of paper while at the same time turning out material for the Nazi publication, at a fee.

Portman, slightly reminiscent of Cary Grant, contributes a standout performance. Phyllis Calvert, as the wistful, but faithful Belgian worker, provides several romantic interludes with Portman.

••••••••••••••••••••••••••••••••

■ UNCERTAIN GLORY

1944, 102 MINS, US Ⓥ
Dir Raoul Walsh   *Prod* Robert Buckner   *Scr* Laszlo Vadnay, Max Brand   *Ph* Sid Hickox   *Ed* George Amy   *Mus* Adolph Deutsch   *Art Dir* Robert M. Haas
● Errol Flynn, Paul Lukas, Jean Sullivan, Lucile Watson, Faye Emerson, Douglass Dumbrille (Warner)

France under the Nazis is again being portrayed in *Uncertain Glory*, a psychological, melodramatic study that is lengthy and frequently tedious.

Glory is more a yarn of two people than any group of people, it is scattered in its development of both narrative and characters; it is slow-paced and possessive of little action. Lack of action, perhaps, might be excusable in melodrama – providing that there is the omniscient thought of impending action. Story is involved, dealing with a Surete inspector and the object of his longtime chase (Errol Flynn).

The film's opening finds Flynn being led to the guillotine for murder. A British flying squadron bombs the prison, upsetting the execution and leading to Flynn's escape. Then follows once again the chase by Paul Lukas, the capture and the subsequent plan by Flynn, at first for escape reasons, to give himself up as a saboteur so that 100 French hostages could go free. The idea is that thus he would be doing the only redeeming thing in his life.

••••••••••••••••••••••••••••••••

■ UNCLE, THE

1966, 87 MINS, UK
Dir Desmond Davis   *Prod* Leonard Davis, Robert Goldston   *Scr* Desmond Davis, Margaret Abrams   *Ph* Manny Wynn   *Ed* Brian Smedley-Aston
● Rupert Davies, Brenda Bruce, Robert Duncan, William Marlowe, Ann Lynn, Maurice Denham (British Lion/Lenart)

A dispute ensued after completion of this excellent British film [based on the book by Margaret Abrams] between director Desmond Davis and producer Leonard Davis (no relation), because of editing and other changes made by the producer without the 'permission' of the director. The producer's version indicates that the changes were not sufficient to damage the film.

The director creates a cinematic essay on the life of a seven-year-old who finds himself in a catastrophic situation. Totally unprepared for the position, he finds being an uncle of a nephew the same age presents many difficulties. The entire film is done from the attitude of the pint-sized hero.

Most of *The Uncle* deals with the 'loss of innocence' of a small boy, Gus (Robert Duncan), over one summer.

Although the firm control of director Davis is evident throughout, he has been fortunate in having a cast that is entirely excellent, particularly young Robert Duncan as Gus (only a British child could look so profound at seven) and Rupert Davies and Brenda Bruce as his parents.

● ●

■ UNCLE BUCK

1989, 100 MINS, US ◇ ⓥ ⊙
Dir John Hughes   *Prod* John Hughes, Tom Jacobson
Scr John Hughes   *Ph* Ralf D. Bode   *Ed* Lou Lombardo, Tony Lombardo, Peck Prior   *Mus* Ira Newborn
Art Dir John W. Corso
● John Candy, Amy Madigan, Jean Louisa Kelly, Gaby Hoffman, Macaulay Culkin, Elaine Bromka (Universal)

John Hughes unsuccessfully tries to mix a serious generation gap message between the belly laughs in *Uncle Buck*, a warm-weather John Candy vehicle.

On paper the rotund Second City veteran seems ideal for the title role: a ne'er-do-well, coarse black sheep of the family suddenly pressed into service when his relatives (Elaine Bromka, Garrett M. Brown), a suburban Chicago family, have to rush off to visit Bromka's dad, stricken with a heart attack.

Enter Uncle Buck, put in charge of the three youngsters for an indefinite period. The kids wear down Buck's rough edges and he teaches them some seat-of-the-pants lessons about life.

Unfortunately, Candy is too likable to give the role any edge. When called upon to be tough or mean he's unconvincing, as in the slapstick dealings with the precociously oversexed boyfriend Bug (Jay Underwood) of eldest daughter Jean Louisa Kelly.

● ●

■ UNCOMMON VALOR

1983, 105 MINS, US ◇ ⓥ ⊙
Dir Ted Kotcheff   *Prod* John Milius, Buzz Feitshans
Scr Joe Gayton   *Ph* Stephen H. Burum   *Ed* Thom Noble, Mark Melnick   *Mus* James Horner   *Art Dir* James L. Schoppe
● Gene Hackman, Robert Stack, Fred Ward, Reb Brown, Randall 'Tex' Cobb, Patrick Swayze (Paramount)

All of the top talent involved – especially Gene Hackman – is hardly needed to make *Uncommon Valor* what it is, a very common action picture.

Hackman does as much as he can as a grieving father obsessed with the idea that his son remains a prisoner 10 years after he was reported missing-in-action in Vietnam. Financed by oil tycoon Robert Stack, whose son is also missing, Hackman puts together his small invasion force and two-thirds of *Valor* is consumed introducing the characters and putting them through various practice drills for the rescue which will predictably be tougher than they planned on.

True to a long tradition of war films, by the time the tough really get going it's only a question of who won't come back from the dangerous mission. But at least each of the main characters in *Valor* does his best to make you care whether it's him.

● ●

■ UNCONQUERED

1947, 135 MINS, US ◇
Dir Cecil B. DeMille   *Prod* Cecil B. DeMille   *Scr* Charles Bennett, Fredric M. Frank, Jesse Lasky Jr   *Ph* Ray Rennahan   *Ed* Anne Bauchens   *Mus* Victor Young
Art Dir Hans Dreier, Walter Tyler
● Gary Cooper, Paulette Goddard, Howard da Silva, Boris Karloff, Ward Bond, Cecil Kellaway (Paramount)

Cecil B. DeMille's *Unconquered* is a $4 million Technicolor spectacle; it's a pre-Revolutionary western with plenty of Injun stuff which, for all the vacuousness and shortcomings, has its gripping moments.

The redskins are ruthless scalpers and the British colonials alternatively naive and brave, patriotic and full of skullduggery to give substance to the melodramatic heroics and knavery of the most derring-do school.

Howard da Silva is the arch-knave whose marriage to Injun chief Boris Karloff's daughter (Katherine DeMille) puts him plenty in the black with the redskins on fur-trading and the like. Paulette Goddard is the proud slave-girl whose freedom Gary Cooper purchases on the British slaveship, only to cross paths with the heavy (da Silva) and his No. 2 menace (Mike Mazurki).

It's not generally known that in that 1763 period English convicts had the alternative of being sold into limited slavery in the American colonies. Although a bond slave, Goddard spurns da Silva and sufficiently attracts Cooper to make for a romantic angle.

Despite the ten-twent-thirt meller-dramatics and the frequently inept script [based on Neil H. Swanson's novel], the performances are convincing, and a great tribute to the cast because that dialog and those situations try the best of troupers.
□ 1947: Nomination: Best Special Effects

● ●

■ UNDEFEATED, THE

1969, 118 MINS, US ◇ ⓥ ⊙
Dir Andrew V. McLaglen   *Prod* Robert L. Jacks
Scr James Lee Barrett   *Ph* William Clothier   *Ed* Robert Simpson   *Mus* Hugo Montenegro   *Art Dir* Carl Anderson
● John Wayne, Rock Hudson, Tony Aguilar, Roman Gabriel, Marian McCargo, Lee Meriwether (20th Century-Fox)

John Wayne plays Old-Tall-In-The-Saddle in a film based on a story by Stanley L. Hough. Film has a basic storyline, character elements and dialog for what might have been a superior drama and possibly a great western. But Andrew McLaglen's direction, seems to consist of splicing together cliches, static camera work and Central Casting of the bit parts.

Wayne is the leader of the ragtail remnants of a troop of Union cavalry who make a bloody charge against a thin line of Confederate soldiers, only to find after the massacre that the war has been over for three days.

Basically wrong is the whole uneven mood of the film. Neither Wayne or Hudson seems to know whether they are in a light comedy or a serious drama. They are, to use the word in an exact sense, simply unbelievable.

● ●

■ UNDER CAPRICORN

1949, 116 MINS, UK ◇ ⓥ ⊙
Dir Alfred Hitchcock   *Prod* Alfred Hitchcock, Sidney Bernstein   *Scr* James Bridie   *Ph* Jack Cardiff, Paul Beeson   *Ed* A.S. Bates   *Mus* Richard Addinsell
● Ingrid Bergman, Joseph Cotten, Michael Wilding, Margaret Leighton, Cecil Parker (Transatlantic)

Under Capricorn is overlong and talky, with scant measure of the Alfred Hitchcock thriller tricks.

Time of the plot is 1831, in Sydney, NSW, during that period when a convict, after serving his time, could start life anew with a clean

slate. Such a man is Joseph Cotten, former groom and now Ingrid Bergman's husband. Cotten has become a man of wealth, but is not accepted socially.

That fact, along with his past crime – the killing of his wife's brother, a deed committed by Bergman but for which he took the blame – are the motives stressed as causing the wife's addiction to the bottle.

● ●

■ UNDERCOVER GIRL

1950, 83 MINS, US
Dir Joseph Pevney   *Prod* Aubrey Schenck   *Scr* Harry Essex   *Ph* Carl Guthrie   *Ed* Russell Schoengarth
Mus Joseph Gershenson (dir.)
● Alexis Smith, Scott Brady, Richard Egan, Gladys George, Royal Dano, Regis Toomey (Universal)

Undercover Girl, by its very title, suggests a conventional melodrama with a twist in that a girl is the gangsters' foil. Which is exactly what it is.

Alexis Smith has the part of Christine Miller, who interrupts her police training in New York to go to California to avenge the death of her policeman father, killed by a narcotics ring. Working with the Los Angeles police, she gets into the confidence of the gang, posing as a dope-buyer.

Love interest is provided by Smith and Scott Brady, who is in charge of the police detail working on the case, and there is an exciting windup in a hide-and-seek sequence in a deserted house.

Smith's role is routine but she makes the most of it, especially in a couple of sequences dealing with the small-fry of the gang.

● ●

■ UNDERCOVER MAN, THE

1949, 80 MINS, US
Dir Joseph H. Lewis   *Prod* Robert Rossen   *Scr* Sydney Boehm, Malvin Wald   *Ph* Burnett Guffey   *Ed* Al Clark
Mus George Duning   *Art Dir* Walter Holscher
● Glenn Ford, Nina Foch, James Whitmore, Barry Kelley, David Wolfe, Frank Tweddell (Columbia)

Narrated in a straightforward, hardhitting documentary style, *The Undercover Man* is a good crime-busting saga. Standout features are the pic's sustained pace and its realistic quality. Fresh, natural dialog help to cover up the formula yarn, while topnotch performances down the line carry conviction. Joseph H. Lewis's direction also mutes the melodramatic elements but manages to keep the tension mounting through a series of violent episodes [based on an article, *Undercover Man: He Trapped Capone*, by Frank J. Wilson and a story outline by Jack Rubin].

Glenn Ford plays a Government Treasury agent on the trail of an underworld czar. Aiming to nail the racketeer on a tax-evasion rap, Ford attempts to contact some stoolpigeons but the syndicate knocks them off before they can squeal.

Ford bolsters his conventional part with a sincere, matter-of-fact performance.

● ●

■ UNDERCURRENT

1946, 111 MINS, US ⓥ
Dir Vincente Minnelli   *Prod* Pandro S. Berman
Scr Edward Chodorov, Marguerite Roberts, [George Oppenheim]   *Ph* Karl Freund   *Ed* Ferris Webster
Mus Herbert Stothart   *Art Dir* Cedric Gibbons, Randall Duell
● Katharine Hepburn, Robert Taylor, Robert Mitchum, Edmund Gwenn, Marjorie Main, Jayne Meadows (M-G-M)

Undercurrent is heavy drama with femme appeal. Picture [from Thelma Strabel's novel *You Were There* deals with psychology angle in which a weak, uncertain man uses lies, theft and even murder to obtain power and acclaim.

Appeal lies in romance between Katharine Hepburn and Robert Taylor and uncertainty as to how it will work out. Taylor, war-made industrialist, marries Hepburn, daughter of a scientist, after a whirlwind courtship. After marriage, the bride begins to discover odd incidents in her husband's past, including his brother's mysterious disappearance and the fear that dogs and other animals have for the man.

Hepburn sells her role with usual finesse and talent. Robert Mitchum, as the missing brother, has only three scenes but makes them count for importance.

■ UNDER FIRE

1983, 100 MINS, US ◇ ⓥ ⊙
Dir Roger Spottiswoode   *Prod* Jonathan Taplin
Scr Ronald Shelton, Clayton Frohman   *Ph* John Alcott
Ed John Bloom, Mark Conte   *Mus* Jerry Goldsmith
Art Dir Agustin Ytuarte, Toby Rafelson
● Nick Nolte, Gene Hackman, Joanna Cassidy, Jean-Louis Trintignant, Ed Harris, Richard Masur (Lion's Gate)

The American media are strongly taken to task in *Under Fire*. This is the story of two correspondents (one working for *Time*, the other Public Radio) and an on-the-scenes war photographer. The action [story by Clayton Frohman] begins in the African bush of Chad, then moves on to Nicaragua – and a feature-film rehearsal of that tragic televised killing of the ABC correspondent by a Somoza government soldier in the late 1970s as he was covering the fighting with the winning Sandinista rebels.

Three individuals cover the Chad conflict in the late 1970s: the 30-year-old photog Russell Price (Nick Nolte), the 50-year-old senior correspondent for *Time* mag Alex Grazier (Gene Hackman), and the circa 40-year-old radio newslady Claire Stryder (Joanna Cassidy). All are tough professionals.

There's a fourth individual who surfaces now and then: he's a hired mercenary, a killer by trade, whom lenser Nolte meets from time to time, first in Chad and later in Nicaragua.

In the course of covering the events Nolte and Cassidy opt to search for a certain rebel leader named Rafael among the revolutionary Sandinistas, for Rafael has never been photographed nor interviewed by the American press.

Further, Nolte's photos of the rebels play into the hands of a double-agent, the Frenchman (Jean-Louis Trintignant), who uses them to hunt down and kill the key Sandinista leaders. Moral factors like these are the core of the action.
□ 1983: Nomination: Best Original Score

■ UNDER MILK WOOD

1971, 90 MINS, UK ◇ ⓥ
Dir Andrew Sinclair   *Prod* Jules Buck, Hugh French
Scr Andrew Sinclair   *Ph* Bob Huke   *Ed* Willy Kemplen
Mus Brian Gascoigne
● Richard Burton, Elizabeth Taylor, Peter O'Toole, Glynis Johns, Vivien Merchant, Sian Philips (Timon)

Screen adaptations of hard-to-slot items such as Dylan Thomas' *Under Milk Wood*, have long been tricky affairs, so it's a tribute to the makers of this pic that it's come off this well.

Writer-director Andrew Sinclair has a wonderful feel for his material, and a happy hand in matching it to its setting. Normal screen conventions are broken as Sinclair chooses to follow Thomas instead in his dissection of a Welsh seaside village and its inhabitants, done with caustically keen and boisterously, earthily humorous pen.

Peter O'Toole plays the blind but still all-seeing Captain Cat, with a (sometimes distracting) assist from makeup on the surface and a fine and oft-moving limn underneath. Richard Burton is fully at ease in a physical

walk-through of a village day, and he speaks the bulk of Thomas' voice-over lines with feeling and obvious love. Through him principally, the purr and the occasional soar of the poet's phrase flows and satisfies. Elizabeth Taylor, glimpsed all too briefly, has rarely been more beautiful. A very distinguished roster of featured players.

■ UNDER SIEGE

1992, 102 MINS, US ◇ ⓥ ⊙
Dir Andrew Davis   *Prod* Arnon Milchan, Steven Seagal, Steven Reuther   *Scr* J.F. Lawton   *Ph* Frank Tidy
Ed Robert A. Ferretti, Denis Virkler, Don Brochu, Dov Hoenig   *Mus* Gary Chang   *Art Dir* Bill Kenney
● Steven Seagal, Tommy Lee Jones, Gary Busey, Erika Eleniak, Patrick O'Neal, Nick Mancuso (Warner)

Warners has the right stuff with *Under Siege*, an immensely slick, if also old-fashioned and formulaic, entertainment. Steven Seagal fans and action buffs should eat this up.

Seagal plays a cook on the USS *Missouri*, the Navy's largest and most powerful battleship. En route to decommission, a quiet, calm journey turns out to be volatile and dangerous when two corrupt psychopaths, both top military experts, hijack the ship and steal its nuclear arsenal.

Seagal's rebellious cook is actually a decorated Navy Seal. He is contrasted with the lethal and hot-tempered William Strannix (Tommy Lee Jones), a former covert CIA operative, and Commander Krill (Gary Busey), a frustrated officer. Motivated by revenge, both men feel they have good reasons to execute their diabolical plot.

An attractive actress (*Playboy* and *Baywatch* alum Erika Eleniak), hired to perform at a farewell party, is thrown into the all-male adventure, and later functions as Seagal's resourceful mate and quasi-romantic interest.

In between battles, blasts and explosions, scripter J.F. Lawton (*Pretty Woman*) has shrewdly placed the funny one-liners, delivered by Seagal in his customary cool, tongue-in-cheek style.
□ 1992: Nomination: Best Sound, Sound Effects Editing

■ UNDER SUSPICION

1991, 99 MINS, UK ◇ ⓥ ⊙
Dir Simon Moore   *Prod* Brian Eastman   *Scr* Simon Moore   *Ph* Vernon Layton   *Ed* Tariq Anwar
Mus Christopher Gunning   *Art Dir* Tim Hutchinson
● Liam Neeson, Laura San Giacomo, Kenneth Cranham, Alphonsia Emmanuel, Stephen Moore, Maggie O'Neill (Carnival)

Writer-director Simon Moore makes a stylish bow with *Under Suspicion*, an old-fashioned murder mystery flawed by wobbly playing from Irish actor Liam Neeson.

Tense prolog, set in Brighton, 1957, has a cop (Neeson) caught with his pants down when he's trailing. Two years later, Neeson is a down-at-the-heels private investigator arranging phoney divorce evidence. O'Neill, now his wife, poses as the other woman in hotel setups to get photographic court evidence. During one of these setups, she ends up with her brain splattered on the sheets next to an equally dead client.

Enter the hotel stiff's mysterious American mistress (Laura San Giacomo) who quickly heads the police list of suspects. She hires Neeson to investigate her lover's murder.

Pic plays like a loving tribute to every film noir in the book. But despite vague parallels to Fritz Lang's *Beyond a Reasonable Doubt*, it's more like a rainy-day Brit cross between *Jagged Edge* and *Body Heat*. Former TV scripter Moore, keeps the dialog taut and the red herrings coming, but he skimps on electricity between the two leads. Production design is

polished, exactly catching the story's setting on the borderline of the more liberated 1960s.

■ UNDER THE CHERRY MOON

1986, 98 MINS, US ⓥ ⊙
Dir Prince   *Prod* Robert Cavallo, Joseph Ruffalo, Steven Fargnoli   *Scr* Becky Johnston   *Ph* Michael Ballhaus
Ed Eva Gardos   *Mus* Clare Fischer   *Art Dir* Richard Sylbert
● Prince, Steven Berkoff, Francesca Annis, Kristin Scott Thomas, Jerome Benton, Alexandra Stewart (Warner)

In *Under the Cherry Moon*, Prince tries to direct too, giving himself a lot of closeups kissing but hardly any of him singing. What is left is a trite story about a rich girl and a poor musician (Prince) that's set on the Riviera and shot in, of all things, black and white.

Before shooting began, Prince reportedly fired director Mary Lambert (who has retained the dubious distinction of having credit as 'creative consultant' and took over the set.

Story has less plot than the average music video, featuring Prince as a pianist at a Nice hotel and Revolution back-up singer, Jerome Benton, as his friend Tricky. After a half-hearted rendezvous with a wealthy woman (Francesca Annis), Prince sets his sights on meeting a young, wealthy woman.

Through the newspaper, he finds out that young, beautiful Mary Sharon (Kristin Scott Thomas) is about to turn 21 and come into her $50 million trust fund. He meets her, they fall in love, and Dad (Steven Berkoff) gets his thugs to rid his sheltered daughter of Prince.

Film was shot in color (at the insistence of Warner Bros.) with prints in black and white (at the insistence of Prince) on location in Nice, and comes out looking about as flat and uninteresting as a newsreel from the 1930s about vacationing in the south of France.

■ UNDER THE CLOCK
See: The Clock

■ UNDER THE VOLCANO

1984, 109 MINS, US ◇ ⓥ ⊙
Dir John Huston   *Prod* Moritz Borman, Wieland Schulz-Kiel   *Scr* Guy Gallo   *Ph* Gabriel Figueroa   *Ed* Roberto Silvi   *Mus* Alex North   *Art Dir* Gunther Gerzso
● Albert Finney, Jacqueline Bisset, Anthony Andrews, Ignacio Lopez Tarzo, Katy Jurado, James Villiers (Ithaca-Conacine)

Although it's said John Huston has wanted to film British author Malcolm Lowry's autobiographical masterpiece *Under the Volcano* for some 30 years, it was always a project fraught with difficulties.

Story unfolds over a 24-hour period in November 1938 in the Mexican village of Cuernavaca where the former British Consul, Geoffrey Firmin (Albert Finney), guilt-ridden over the past and abandoned by his wife, is drinking himself to death. It's a time of celebration, the Day of the Dead, a day when death is celebrated.

After a drunken night, Firmin returns home to discover that Yvonne (Jacqueline Bisset), the wife he so desperately yearned for, has unexpectedly returned. The occasion provides only a momentary interval from hard liquor, however.

Although this voyage into self-destruction won't be to the taste of many, there will be few unmoved by Finney's towering performance as the tragic Britisher, his values irretrievably broken down, drowning himself in alcohol and practically inviting his own death.
□ 1984: Nominations: Best Actor (Albert Finney), Original Score

U

■ UNDER THE YUM YUM TREE

1963, 110 MINS, US ◇

Dir David Swift Prod Frederick Brisson Scr Lawrence
Roman, David Swift Ph Joseph Biroc Ed Charles
Nelson Mus Frank DeVol Art Dir Dale Hennesy
● Jack Lemmon, Carol Lynley, Dean Jones, Edie Adams,
Imogen Coca, Paul Lynde (Columbia)

The screen version of Lawrence Roman's hit
stage play is concerned with an experiment
wherein two young people in love (Carol
Lynley and Dean Jones) agree to determine
their 'character compatibility' prior to marriage by living together platonically. The project is complicated by the intrusion of the
lecherous landlord (Jack Lemmon) of the
apartment building in which they have chosen to reside.

As engineered by director David Swift, the
film's cardinal error is its lack of restraint.
There is a tendency to embellish, out of all
proportion, devices and situations that, kept
simple, would have served the comic purposes
far more effectively.

Exaggeration has also spilled over into the
area of production design. Having Lemmon's
apartment fully equipped for romantic pursuits is one thing, but some of the props, notably a pair of pop-up, mechanical violins,
strain credulity.

For Lemmon, the role of amorous landlord
is a tour-de-farce, and he plays it to the hilt.
Lynley is a visual asset and does a satisfactory
job as the somewhat ingenuous ingenue.
Jones, who played the rather gullible boy
friend on Broadway, effectively repeats his
characterization on screen.

■ UNDER TWO FLAGS

1936, 111 MINS, US

Dir Frank Lloyd Prod Darryl F. Zanuck Scr W.P.
Lipscomb, Walter Ferris Ph Ernest Palmer Ed Ralph
Dietrich Mus Louis Silvers (dir.) Art Dir William
Darling
● Ronald Colman, Claudette Colbert, Victor McLaglen,
Rosalind Russell, Gregory Ratoff, Nigel Bruce (20th
Century-Fox)

The classic Under Two Flags, in book [by
Ouida], play and through two silent filmiza-
tions [1916 and 1922], is still sturdy fare,
talkerized. A pioneer saga of the Foreign
Legion, Darryl Zanuck and 20th-Fox have further fortified it by a four-ply marquee ensemble (Ronald Colman, Claudette Colbert,
Victor McLaglen and Rosalind Russell).

Not the tempestuous Cigarette of the
Theda Bara vintage [1916 version] when
Under Two Flags was a highlight in that silent
film vamp's career, Colbert nonetheless
makes the somewhat bawdy cafe hostess
stand up. It's not exactly in her metier. Twixt
the native Cigarette and Rosalind Russell as
the English lady, Colman does all right on the
romance interest, with the desert as a setting.

Victor McLaglen turns in an expert chore
as the scowling Major Doyle, lovesick for and
jealous of Cigarette's two-timing. Gregory
Ratoff is planted well for comedy relief with
his plaint that he's already forgotten just
what he joined the Legion to forget.

The production highlight is the pitched battle on the desert [directed by Otto Brower,
photographed by Sidney Wagner] between
the marauding Arabs and the handful of legionnaires defending the fort.

■ UNDERWATER!

1955, 98 MINS, US ◇

Dir John Sturges Prod Harry Tatelman Scr Walter
Newman Ph Harry J. Wild Ed Stuart Gilmore,
Frederic Knudtson Mus Roy Webb Art Dir Albert S.
D'Agostino, Carroll Clark
● Jane Russell, Gilbert Roland, Richard Egan, Lori
Nelson, Robert Keigh, Joseph Calleia (RKO)

While Jane Russell is the main cast attraction as far as name value goes, the story (by
Hugh King and Robert C. Bailey) is slanted
towards Richard Egan, her husband, and
Gilbert Roland, adventurer, who are diving
for the treasure aboard a sunken galleon.
Russell is a fetching sight, whether plumbing
the depths or lounging comfortably aboard
ship.

Egan and Roland handle the masculine
spots easily, both having the kind of muscles
that look good when bared. Robert Keith,
good as a priest with a knowledge of sunken
treasure, and Lori Nelson, scantly used but
good to look at, are the other principals in the
treasure-questing group. On the surface the
treasure-hunters are threatened by Cuban
shark fisherman (Joseph Calleia) and his
crew.

Sturges' direction is hampered for the first
half by more dialog than the picture's pace
can comfortably assimilate, but once the unnecessary talk and extraneous sequences are
out of the way, the pace tightens and thrills
are consistent.

Film is RKO's first SuperScope release. The
2-to-1 aspect ratio produces a big picture excellently proportioned to show off the pictorial splendors achieved by Harry J. Wild's
lensing above the water and Lamar Boren's
under the ocean.

■ UNDERWORLD INFORMERS

See: The Informers

■ UNDERWORLD, U.S.A.

1961, 98 MINS, US

Dir Samuel Fuller Prod Samuel Fuller Scr Samuel
Fuller Ph Hal Mohr Ed Jerome Thoms Mus Harry
Sukman Art Dir Robert Peterson
● Cliff Robertson, Dolores Dorn, Beatrice Kay, Paul
Dubov, Richard Rust, Larry Gates (Globe/Columbia)

Underworld, U.S.A. is a slick gangster melodrama made to order for filmgoers who prefer
screen fare explosive and uncomplicated. In
this picture, the 'hero' sets out on a four-ply
vendetta of staggering proportions and accomplishes his mission with the calculation
and poise of a pro bowler racking up a simple
four-way spare.

The yarn follows the wicked career of
supposedly decent but hate-motivated,
revenge-consumed fellow who, as a
youngster, witnessed in horror the gangland
slaying of his father by four budding racketeers.

As the central figure, Cliff Robertson delivers a brooding, virile, finely balanced portrayal. It's a first-rate delineation atop a cast
that performs expertly. Dolores Dorn supplies romantic interest with sufficient sincerity, and Beatrice Kay is persuasive as the
decent, compassionate woman whose fervent,
but unfulfilled, desire for motherhood gives
rise to a vague mother-son relationship with
Robertson.

Director Samuel Fuller's screenplay [from
the Saturdat Evening Post articles by Joseph F.
Dinneen] has its lags, character superficialities and unlikelihoods, but it is crisp with
right-sounding gangster jargon and remains
absorbing.

■ UNFAITHFULLY YOURS

1948, 105 MINS, US

Dir Preston Sturges Prod Preston Sturges Scr Preston
Sturges Ph Victor Milner Ed Robert Fritch
Mus Alfred Newman Art Dir Lyle R. Wheeler, Joseph C.
Wright
● Rex Harrison, Linda Darnell, Barbara Lawrence, Rudy
Vallee, Lionel Stander, Edgar Kennedy (20th Century-Fox)

Unfaithfully Yours misses that stamp of originality which marked the scripting and direc-

tion of Preston Sturges' previous films. The
fabric of stale ideas and antique gags out of
which this pic was spun is just barely hidden
by its glossy production casing.

The yarn is too slight to carry the long running time. It's a takeoff on the suspicious hus-
band-beautiful wife formula, which is stirred
up into a frothy pastry only on occasion. With
Rex Harrison playing a symphony orch
leader, Sturges executes some amusing high-
jinks with serious music, but the humor is
mild and unsustained.

The yarn unfolds via three long revenge fantasies which race through Harrison's brain
while he batons his way through a concert.
During a frenzied number by Rosini, there's a
gruesome sequence in which Harrison slashes
his wife, Linda Darnell, with a razor and then
pins the rap on her supposed lover. Against a
background of Wagnerian music, he daydreams of nobly renouncing his wife in favor of
the other man. Finally, against a Tchaikovsky
number, he imagines playing Russian roulette
with his rival in a test of passion.

Stylization of the fantasies would have
given these sequences that comic energy
which is lacking.

■ UNFAITHFULLY YOURS

1984, 96 MINS, US ◇ ⊙

Dir Howard Zieff Prod Marvin Worth, Joe Wizan
Scr Valerie Curtin, Barry Levinson, Robert Klane
Ph David M. Walsh Ed Sheldon Kahn Mus Bill Conti
Art Dir Albert Brenner
● Dudley Moore, Nastassja Kinski, Armand Assante,
Albert Brooks, Cassie Yates, Richard Libertini (20th
Century-Fox)

Unfaithfully Yours is a moderately amusing remake of Preston Sturges' wonderful comedy
which, it might be remembered, was a commercial bust upon its release in 1948.

Lavishly mounted and astutely cast farce
features Dudley Moore in the role of a big-
time orchestra conductor who has just taken
a much younger Italian screen star, Nastassja
Kinski, as his bride. Moore suspects her of
fooling around with dashing concert violinist
Armand Assante, and core of the film consists
of a fantasy in which Moore murders his wife,
but makes it look as though Assante did it.
He then tries to pull off such a scheme, with
predictably incompetent results.

Moore is right at home on the podium or
behind the piano, and his comic invention results in a delightful performance.

■ UNFINISHED BUSINESS

1984, 99 MINS, CANADA ◇

Dir Don Owen Prod Annette Cohen, Don Owen
Scr Don Owen Ph Douglas Kiefer Ed Peter Dale,
David Nicholson Mus Patricia Cullen Art Dir Barbara
Tranter, Ann Pepper
● Isabelle Mejias, Peter Spence, Leslie Toth, Peter
Kastner, Julie Biggs, Chuck Shamata (Zebra Films/NFBC)

Don Owen's Unfinished Business continues the
story the filmmaker began in Nobody Waved
Goodbye [1964], a ground-breaking Canadian
feature. Sequel picks up with the original
young couple, now divorced, experiencing the
travails of parents with a rebellious 17-year-
old daughter.

A high school senior, Izzy (Isabelle Mejias)
is days away from her finals yet balks at the
prospect of completing her education. She
finds diversions in dope, friends, a rock club
and a group of anti-nuke activists. The clash
between pressures from her parents and the
seemingly more meaningful pursuits of the
radicals sends her into the streets for a different kind of education.

Although a common enough story,
Unfinished Business has a raw energy which is
touching and deeply felt.

UNFINISHED SYMPHONY, THE

1934, 90 MINS, UK/GERMANY
Dir Willy Forst, Anthony Asquith   *Prod* Arnold
Pressburger   *Scr* Walter Reisch, Benn W. Levy
Ph Franz Planer   *Mus* Willy Schmidt-Gentner (adapt.)
● Helen Chandler, Marta Eggerth, Hans Jaray, Ronald
Squire, Beryl Laverick, Brember Wills (Gaumont-British/
UFA)

A thing of arresting beauty in pictorial and musical conception, *The Unfinished Symphony* should garner attention from the musically appreciative. Particularly those for whom the melodies of Franz Schubert have always been in the upper brackets of their enjoyment.

What emotional appeal there is is not derived from the acting but from the instrumentation of Schubert's *Unfinished Symphony*, and the reproduction in voice and orchestra of a number of his other compositions. They're all brilliantly woven into the fine costume mosaic turned out by director Willy Forst.

Story has been aptly cast, even if the players constitute a babel of dialects. Striking case in point is that of Marta Eggerth and Beryl Laverick, who are cast as sisters. The former's accent is German and the latter's a precise Oxonian. Like Hans Jaray, Eggerth did the same part in the UFA version of *Unfinished Symphony* which Forst also directed.

UNFORGIVEN, THE

1960, 125 MINS, US ◇ ⓥ
Dir John Huston   *Prod* James Hill   *Scr* Ben Maddow
Ph Franz Planer   *Ed* Hugh Russell Lloyd   *Mus* Dimitri
Tiomkin
● Burt Lancaster, Audrey Hepburn, Audie Murphy, John
Saxon, Charles Bickford, Lillian Gish (James/United
Artists)

There are many aspects of *The Unforgiven* that elicit comparison with *Shane*, particularly in regard to the composition of the scenes and the photography. Director John Huston and cameraman Franz Planer have teamed to provide an intelligent use of the medium for eye-pleasing effects, filmed in Mexico.

The screenplay from a novel by Alan Le May – although many parts are better than the whole – provides a good framework for the talents of Huston and his performers. Audrey Hepburn gives a shining performance as the foundling daughter of a frontier family. As her foster brother, obviously desperately in love with his 'sister', Burt Lancaster is fine as the strong-willed, heroic family spokesman and community leader.

The scene is the Texas Panhandle immediately after the Civil War at a time of unbending hatred between the white settlers and the local Kiowa Indians. The antagonism is marked by senseless massacres and excesses on the part of both sides. In the midst of this tension, it's discovered that Hepburn is actually a full-blooded Indian. The desire of the Indians to recover their own 'blood', the resentment of the settlers in having an 'enemy' in their midst, and the determination to hold on to the girl who has been a member of the family almost since birth provides the crux of the conflict.

Lillian Gish, a silent film favorite, is okay as the mother who guards the secret of her foundling daughter. However, she has a tendency to over-react emotionally. There are good performances by Charles Bickford, as the head of another frontier family; June Walker, as his wife; Albert Salmi, as his son who courts Hepburn; Kipp Hamilton, as his daughter, and Doug McClure, as Lancaster's youngest brother. Audie Murphy is surprisingly good as Lancaster's hot-headed brother whose hatred of Indians causes him to abandon his family.

UNFORGIVEN

1992, 130 MINS, US ◇ ⓥ ⊙
Dir Clint Eastwood   *Prod* Clint Eastwood   *Scr* David
Webb Peoples   *Ph* Jack N. Green   *Ed* Joel Cox
Mus Lenny Niehaus   *Art Dir* Henry Bumstead
● Clint Eastwood, Gene Hackman, Morgan Freeman,
Richard Harris, Jaimz Woolvett, Saul Rubinek (Warner/
Malpaso)

Unforgiven is a classic Western for the ages. In his 10th excursion into the genre that made him a star more than 25 years earlier, Clint Eastwood has crafted a tense, hard-edged, superbly dramatic yarn that is also an exceedingly intelligent meditation on the West, its myths and heroes.

Eastwood has dedicated the film 'to Sergio and Don,' references to Sergio Leone and Don Siegel. The salute signals Eastwood's intention to reflect upon the sort of terse, tough, hard-bitten characters he became famous for in his pictures, a man described here as being 'as cold as the snow.'

Eastwood's Bill Munny can be seen as a hypothetical portrait of the Man With No Name in his sunset years. When a hotshot named the 'Schofield Kid' (Jaimz Woolvett) turns up offering to split a $1,000 reward being offered for the hides of two men who gruesomely sliced up a prostitute, Munny reluctantly straps on his holster for the first time in more than a decade.

To the kid's annoyance, Munny insists upon bringing along his former partner in crime (Morgan Freeman). Beating this group to their destination of Big Whiskey is railroad gunman English Bob (Richard Harris), an arrogant mythomaniac traveling with a biographer (Saul Rubinek) who memorializes his bloody accomplishments in dime novels.

Outlaws and bounty hunters around Big Whiskey face a problem by the name of Sheriff Little Bill Daggett (Gene Hackman), a brutal ex-badman who allows no one to carry guns in town. Resolution comes not in an expected, standard showdown, but much more complexly, in a series of alternately tragic and touching confrontations.

Recurring Eastwood themes involving humiliation and physical pain are present, and a strong feminist streak runs through the center of the story. A close-knit group of hookers defy Sheriff Daggett in the first place and put up the reward money for their mutilated co-worker.

Playing a stubbly, worn-out, has-been outlaw who can barely mount his horse at first, Eastwood, unafraid to show his age, is outstanding in his best clipped, understated manner. Hackman deliciously realizes the two sides of the sheriff's quicksilver personality, the folksy raconteur and the vicious sadist.

Lenser Jack Green's widescreen images have a natural, unforced beauty that imaginatively make use of the mostly flat expanses of the Alberta locations.
☐ 1992: Best Picture, Director, Supp. Actor
(Gene Hackman), Editing.
☐ Nominations: Best Director, Actor (Clint
Eastwood), Original Screenplay,
Cinematography, Art Direction, Sound

UNION CITY

1980, 87 MINS, US ◇ ⓥ ⊙
Dir Mark Reichert   *Prod* Graham Belin   *Scr* Mark
Reichert   *Ph* Ed Lachman   *Ed* Lana Tokel, J. Michaels
Mus Chris Stein   *Art Dir* George Stavrinos
● Dennis Lipscomb, Deborah Harry, Irina Maleeva,
Everett McGill, Sam McMurray, Pat Benatar (Kinesis)

Cornell Woolrich's dark and fetishistic [1937 story *The Corpse Next Door*] is both a source of strength and the undoing of *Union City*. His story is similar to Poe's *The Telltale Heart* in structure and while indie helmer Mark Reichert exploits its strangeness very well, he fails to flesh out the short, one actor sketch into a full-length feature.

Pic concerns a paranoid businessman (Dennis Lipscomb), obsessed with catching the mysterious culprit who steals a drink out of his milk bottle that is delivered every morning. His plain, vapid wife Lillian (Deborah Harry, in her screen debut) puts up with his increasingly bizarre behavior.

Ultimately, he captures a young war vet vagrant (Sam McMurray) in the act and releases his pent-up anger and frustration by beating the man's head bloodily on the floor. The Hitchcockian body removal footage provides fine black humor as Lipscomb hides the corpse in a Murphy bed in the vacant apartment next door.

UNION PACIFIC

1939, 133 MINS, US ⓥ
Dir Cecil B. DeMille   *Prod* Cecil B. DeMille   *Scr* Walter
DeLeon, C. Gardner Sullivan, Jesse Lasky Jr   *Ph* Victor
Milner, Dewey Wrigley   *Ed* Anne Bauchens
Mus George Antheil
● Barbara Stanwyck, Joel McCrea, Akim Tamiroff,
Robert Preston, Brian Donlevy, Anthony Quinn
(Paramount)

Basically, the production a super-western, cowboys and Injuns backgrounded by the epochal building of the Union Pacific. It's a post-Civil War saga [from an adaptation by Jack Cunningham of an original by Ernest Haycox], with Henry Kolker enacting the banker menace who foments the sabotage that would favor the competitive Central Pacific.

Joel McCrea comes on the scene as a trouble-shooter. Barbara Stanwyck sustains the femme interest in a sometimes unprepossessing manner, which is chiefly the script's fault rather than her own. Basically she more than impresses as the railroad engineer's daughter.

The clash in realistic values comes through the pauses in the melodramatics between genial badman Preston and trouble-shooter McCrea. Preston does a standout job through a consistently affable albeit frankly renegade role.
☐ 1939: Nomination: Best Special Effects

UNION STATION

1950, 81 MINS, US ⓥ
Dir Rudolph Mate   *Prod* Jules Schermer   *Scr* Sydney
Boehm   *Ph* Daniel L. Fapp   *Ed* Ellsworth Hoagland
Mus Irvin Talbot   *Art Dir* Hans Dreier, Earl Hedrick
● William Holden, Nancy Olson, Barry Fitzgerald, Lyle
Bettger, Jan Sterling, Allene Roberts (Paramount)

Union Station [from a story by Thomas Walsh] is a melodrama that locales its thrills in a big city railway terminal and spins off a tale of kidnapping.

William Holden, while youthful in appearance to head up the railway policing department of a metropolitan terminal, is in good form. Kidnapping is revealed when a femme passenger arriving at the terminal reports two suspicious characters. The passenger is Nancy Olson, secretary to a rich man and his blind daughter (Allene Roberts). Events prove Roberts has been kidnapped and the terminal is to be used as the payoff location.

The production catches the feel of a large terminal and its constantly shifting scenes of people arriving and departing.

UNIVERSAL SOLDIER

1992, 104 MINS, US ◇ ⓥ ⊙
Dir Roland Emmerich   *Prod* Allen Shapiro, Craig
Baumgarten, Joel B. Michaels   *Scr* Richard Rothstein,
Christopher Leitch, Dean Devlin   *Ph* Kark Walter
Lindenlaub   *Ed* Michael J. Duthie   *Mus* Christopher
Franke   *Art Dir* Holger Gross

● Jean-Claude Van Damme, Dolph Lundgren, Ally Walker, Ed O'Ross, Jerry Orbach, Leon Rippy (Carolco/IndieProd)

Despite its not-insignificant production values, the story feels like a late-night sci-fi movie patched together with a mix of elements from *Robocop* and *The Terminator*, with a dash of Captain America comic books. The result is almost as many derisive laughs as dead bodies.

A crazed Vietnam platoon leader (Dolph Lundgren) and his thickly accented subordinate (Jean-Claude Van Damme) waste each other prior to the opening credits during a 1969 My Lai-type massacre, only to pop up 23 years later as re-animated corpses, brought back by the Defense Dept. to act as an elite terrorism-fighting unit.

Something goes wrong, however, and Van Damme begins to recover his memory, taking off accompanied by a pretty reporter (Ally Walker), with Lundgren, his mind still addled with 'Nam hysteria, and other brigade members in hot pursuit.

The film is on the wrong foot from the get-go, since it's difficult to have much empathy for walking corpses with superhuman strength whose flesh regenerates when punctured.

After his rendition of twin brothers in *Double Impact*, Van Damme offers nothing new here other than baring a little more of his physique than had been his norm. Lundgren remains an imposing presence who hasn't been properly used since *Rocky IV*, though he'll probably score points with some moviegoers thanks to his character's morbid penchant for collecting victims' ears. Walker is the modern damsel-in-distress blend of tomboy tough and conveniently available.

• •

■ UNLAWFUL ENTRY

1992, 111 MINS, US ◇ ⊛ ⊙
Dir Jonathan Kaplan   *Prod* Charles Gordon   *Scr* Lewis Colick   *Ph* Jamie Anderson   *Ed* Curtiss Clayton
Mus James Horner   *Art Dir* Lawrence G. Paull
● Kurt Russell, Ray Liotta, Madeleine Stowe, Roger E. Mosley, Ken Lerner, Deborah Offner (Largo/20th Century-Fox)

Although it exists primarily to send an audience into a bloodthirsty frenzy, and has major credibility problems in the bargain, *Unlawful Entry* still works as an effective victimization thriller.

Tense opening scene has a black intruder breaking into the lovely L.A. home of attractive married couple Kurt Russell and Madeleine Stowe. The man escapes after a scuffle with Russell and holding a knife to Stowe's throat; the policemen (Ray Liotta and Roger E. Mosley) are the picture of helpfulness and encouragement.

Problem is that Liotta becomes excessively solicitous, arranging for the installation of topnotch security system in the couple's home and eagerly accepting an invitation to dinner. After speaking nicely to a class at the elementary school where Stowe and her friend Deborah Offner teach, Liotta comes on to Stowe in a quiet but insidious way, and from this point will stop at nothing to get Russell out of the way and have Stowe for himself.

Had the Liotta character been presented as an essentially decent cop gone wrong, story [by George D. Putnam, John Katchmer and Lewis Colick] might have achieved genuinely chilling dimensions. Instead, fact that he's clearly off-base and demented from the beginning gets everyone off the hook.

Liotta effectively conveys both the nice and nasty sides of his character but true sexual tension between him and Stowe is absent, and he tips his hand too early regarding the man's instability. Russell is solid as the husband, while Stowe is opaque as the wife.

• •

■ UNMAN, WITTERING AND ZIGO

1971, 100 MINS, UK ◇
Dir John Mackenzie   *Prod* Gareth Wigan   *Scr* Simon Raven   *Ph* Geoffrey Unsworth   *Ed* Fergus McDonnell
Mus Michael J. Lewis   *Art Dir* Bill McCrow
● David Hemmings, Carolyn Seymour, Douglas Wilmer, Hamilton Dyce, Anthony Haygarth, Donald Gee (Mediarts)

Unman, Wittering and Zigo are on the roster at Chantry, a British school for teenage boys, which looks down treacherously on ocean-splashed rocks. The three are students, but Zigo is constantly marked absent, for reasons unexplained.

Unman, Wittering and the rest of the class are present and they make for a sinister lot, blatantly threatening their new teacher, David Hemmings, with the same kind of death-on-the-rocks that has befallen his predecessor, unless he eases up on the scholastic schedule and runs their bets with the local bookmaker. The viewer may be both intrigued and puzzled, for while film is a compelling piece of dramatics about innocent-looking terrorists, it asks a great deal of credence.

Director John Mackenzie, working with a screenplay by Simon Raven, which in turn was fashioned from a television show by Giles Cooper, has in large part captured the viciousness. But why these youths are this way goes unexplained.

• •

■ UNMARRIED WOMAN, AN

1978, 124 MINS, US ◇ ⊛
Dir Paul Mazursky   *Prod* Paul Mazursky, Tony Ray
Scr Paul Mazursky   *Ph* Arthur Ornitz   *Ed* Stuart H. Pappe   *Mus* Bill Conti   *Art Dir* Pato Guzman
● Jill Clayburgh, Alan Bates, Michael Murphy, Cliff Gorman, Pat Quinn, Kelly Bishop (20th Century-Fox)

Paul Mazursky's excellent screenplay presents Jill Clayburgh in a most demanding role where she is torn between conflicting forces following the surprise confession of weak-willed husband Michael Murphy that he has fallen in love with another woman.

Daughter Lisa Lucas needs her mother's support just as she herself is coming on to adolescent love; Clayburgh's girlfriends, Pat Quinn, Kelly Bishop and Linda Miller, offer well-meaning advice not necessarily of the best calibre; blind date Andrew Duncan's premature pass falls flat; therapist Penelope Russianoff's probing strikes raw nerves; neighborhood stud Cliff Gorman, in an excellent though brief role, comes to realize that the only thing worse than not getting what you want can be getting it.

Finally, artist Alan Bates arrives in Clayburgh's life. A thoughtful and deep attachment evolves which survives the early resentment of the daughter and the lover's increasing demands on her time. Resolution avoids the pat but portents for happiness are strong.

☐ 1978: Nominations: Best Picture, Actress (Jill Clayburgh), Original Screenplay

• •

■ UNSINKABLE MOLLY BROWN, THE

1964, 128 MINS, US ◇ ⊛ ⊙
Dir Charles Walters   *Prod* Lawrence Weingarten
Scr Helen Deutsch   *Ph* Daniel L. Fapp   *Ed* Fredric Steinkamp   *Mus* Robert Armbruster (dir.)
Art Dir George W. Davis, Preston Ames
● Debbie Reynolds, Harve Presnell, Ed Begley, Jack Kruschen, Hermione Baddeley, Martita Hunt (M-G-M)

The Unsinkable Molly Brown is a rowdy and sometimes rousing blend of song and sentiment, a converted stage tuner.

The film is adorned with the music and lyrics of Meredith Willson, although a number of his songs for the legiter have been excised and one new production number (He's

My Friend') has been added. The dramatic story remains virtually intact.

It relates the adventures of Molly Brown, a hillbilly heroine who rises from poverty to become one of the richest and most celebrated women of her time. Shortly after her marriage to Leadville Johnny Brown he strikes it rich, and the rest of the picture depicts her feverish efforts to cut the mustard with snooty Denver society.

In essence, it's a pretty shallow story since the title character, when you get right down to it, is obsessed with a very superficial, egotistical problem beneath her generous, razzmatazz facade. On top of that, Wilson's score is rather undistinguished.

Debbie Reynolds thrusts herself into the role with an enormous amount of verve and vigor. At times her approach to the character seems more athletic than artful.

Harve Presnell, who created the role on Broadway in 1960, makes a generally auspicious screen debut as the patient Johnny. His fine, booming voice and physical stature make him a valuable commodity for Hollywood.

☐ 1964: Nominations: Best Actress (Debbie Reynolds), Color Cinematography, Color Costume Design, Color Art Direction, Adapted Music Score

• •

■ UNSUITABLE JOB FOR A WOMAN, AN

1982, 94 MINS, UK ◇ ⊛
Dir Christopher Petit   *Scr* Elizabeth McKay, Brian Scobie, Christopher Petit   *Ph* Martin Schafer   *Ed* Mick Audsley
Mus Chas Jankel, Philip Bagenal, Peter Van Hooke
Art Dir Anton Furst
● Pippa Guard, Billie Whitelaw, Paul Freeman, Dominic Guard, Dawn Archibald, David Horovitch (Boyd's/NFE)

Cordelia Gray (Pippa Guard) comes to work one day where she is assistant to a shabby gumshoe. She finds him in his office with his veins cut and a big bowl of blood next to him. A posthumous tape asks her to take over. After the burial an intense middleaged woman (Billie Whitelaw) asks her to take on a case, the suicide of her boss's son.

Obsession is the keynote of this case. Gray slowly is fascinated by the dead boy as she finds out more about him. It develops he was first found hanging dressed and made up as a woman but someone had changed that.

She almost hangs herself imitating the way the dead boy did it, gets thrown into a well but muddles through as the English do. Perhaps it is unfair to unravel this tale [from the novel by P.D. James] which is handled from a distance by director Christopher Petit robbing it of a more forceful narration, timing and revelation.

• •

■ UNSUSPECTED, THE

1947, 103 MINS, US
Dir Michael Curtiz   *Prod* Charles Hoffman   *Scr* Ranald MacDougall   *Ph* Woody Bredell   *Ed* Frederick Richards
Mus Franz Waxman   *Art Dir* Anton Grot
● Joan Caulfield, Claude Rains, Audrey Totter, Constance Bennett, Hurd Hatfield, Michael North (Warner)

Director Michael Curtiz packs yarn with plenty of rugged action thrills, despite society setting. Two chase sequences are especially humdingers for audience chills. Story deals with suave mayhem, with murderer Claude Rains known from the opening crime.

Plot workings are not as clear as they could have been but motivation of principal characters is followable, as scripted from a Bess Meredyth adaptation of the Charlotte Armstrong story. Rains is seen as radio narrator of murder mysteries who's not above making his stories actually true. An apparently suave, kindly soul, he's unsuspected in the death of his secretary, niece and latter's husband.

Rains pulls out all his thesping tricks to sustain the character, and makes it believable. Joan Caulfield is good as the rich, troubled niece who believes in her uncle's goodness. Audrey Totter and Hurd Hatfield show up well as the murdered pair, and Constance Bennett peps up assignment as a radio producer.

....

■ **UNTAMED HEART**

1993, 102 MINS, US ◇ ⒲ ⊙
Dir Tony Bill   *Prod* Tony Bill, Helen Buck Bartlett
Scr Tom Sierchio   *Ph* Jost Vacano   *Ed* Mia Goldman
Mus Cliff Eidelman   *Art Dir* Steven Jordan
● Christian Slater, Marisa Tomei, Rosie Perez, Kyle Secor, Willie Garson (M-G-M)

Appealing lead performances elevate this modestly scaled romantic tearjerker, from a first script by Tom Sierchio. Marisa Tomei plays a Minneapolis waitress who is assaulted one night by two creeps from the local diner, only to be rescued by Christian Slater, an introverted, almost nonverbal busboy enamored of her.

An awkward and unlikely romance develops, Tomei slowly penetrating Slater's protective shell, put up due to the orphaned youth's congenital heart ailment, which has kept him at arm's distance from people throughout his life. He also clings to a fairy tale about his heart coming from a baboon king after the death of his father (the pic's working title was *Baboon Heart*).

The story sometimes seems like an excuse to get out the can opener and serve up the corn. But Sierchio's script possesses some strong romantic flourishes and director Tony Bill takes advantage of them. The perfs prove so earnest the movie largely works on its own terms, particularly for those looking for a traditional 'good cry.'

....

■ **UNTIL SEPTEMBER**

1984, 95 MINS, US ◇ ⒲
Dir Richard Marquand   *Prod* Michael Gruskoff
Scr Janice Lee Graham   *Ph* Philippe Welt   *Ed* Sean Barton   *Mus* John Barry   *Art Dir* Hilton McConnico
● Karen Allen, Thierry Lhermitte, Christopher Cazenove, Marie Catherine Conti, Hutton Cobb, Michael Mellinger (M-G-M/United Artists)

Set in Paris, plot centers on a young American woman stranded in the City of Lights when she becomes separated from a tour group headed for Eastern Bloc countries. Frustrated by airline and diplomatic red tape, Mo Alexander (Karen Allen), takes refuge in a modest hotel.

Temporary setback is put aright when a neighbor, suave banker Xavier de la Perouse (Thierry Lhermitte), checks on the woman's story for verification. It doesn't take much to guess that the two tenants are destined to hit it off romantically, even if there are some initial awkward moments.

However, filmmakers are not intent on making another 'woman involved with a married man' or 'doomed love affair' saga. Instead a fanciful, unconvincing 'love conquers all' scenario emerges.

....

■ **UNTIL THE END OF THE WORLD**

1991, 158 MINS, GERMANY/FRANCE/AUSTRALIA ◇ ⒲ ⊙
Dir Wim Wenders   *Prod* Jonathan Taplin, Anatole Dauman   *Scr* Peter Carey, Wim Wenders   *Ph* Robby Muller   *Ed* Peter Przygodda   *Mus* Graeme Revell
Art Dir Thierry Flamand
● William Hurt, Solveig Dommartin, Sam Neill, Max von Sydow, Rudiger Vogler, Jeanne Moreau (Road Movies/Agos/Village Roadshow)

A dream project about allowing other people to see one's dreams, *Until the End of the World*

is a dream partly realized and partly still in the head of the director. Described by director Wim Wenders as 'the ultimate road movie,' the \$23 million production was intended to shoot in 65mm in 17 countries, but the format proved too unwieldy for all the location work and budget limitations forced a cutback to nine nations.

Film conveys the feeling of an abridgment, as narration by Sam Neill wallpapers the gaps in the globetrotting of William Hurt, Solveig Dommartin and other characters. Set in 1999, script by Wenders and Aussie writer Peter Carey [from an idea by Wenders and Dommartin] presents a world threatened by a nuclear satellite careening toward Earth. Party girl Claire Tourneur (Dommartin) is given stolen money by some bank robbers and, for kicks, she picks up a stranger, Trevor McPhee (Hurt), while transporting the loot to Paris.

Pursuing Trevor to Lisbon, Claire gets him into bed, but he takes off again. One step behind him to Berlin, Moscow, China and Japan, with the assistance of detective Philip Winter (Wenders regular Rudiger Vogler), Claire finally wins Trevor's trust and learns his true agenda. Detouring to San Francisco, pic comes to a rest after 78 minutes in Australia's outback.

In the logistically taxing effort to get all this on screen, Wenders has sacrificed some of his customary poetry. And the grand emotion and obsession needed to carry the two lovers around the world isn't apparent in Hurt and Dommartin. Pair strike no sparks, and Hurt seems blank most of the time.
[Pre-release version ran 178 mins.]

....

■ **UNTOUCHABLES, THE**

1987, 119 MINS, US ◇ ⒲ ⊙
Dir Brian De Palma   *Prod* Art Linson   *Scr* David Mamet
Ph Stephen H. Burum   *Ed* Jerry Greenberg, Bill Pankow
Mus Ennio Morricone   *Art Dir* William A. Elliott
● Kevin Costner, Sean Connery, Charles Martin Smith, Andy Garcia, Robert De Niro, Richard Bradford (Linson/Paramount)

The Untouchables is a beautifully crafted portrait of Prohibition-era Chicago.

Director Brian De Palma sets the tone in a lavish overhead opening shot in which Robert De Niro's Al Capone professes to be just 'a businessman' giving people the product they want. That such business often required violent methods is immediately depicted as prelude to arrival of idealistic law enforcer Eliot Ness (Kevin Costner).

While the dichotomy of values is thus established between these two adversaries, it is the introduction of street cop Jim Malone (Sean Connery) that truly gives the film its momentum.

Connery delivers one of his finest performances. It is filled with nuance, humor and abundant self-confidence. Connery's depth strongly complements the youthful Costner, who does grow appreciably as Ness overcomes early naivete to become just hard-bitten enough without relinquishing the innocence of his personal life.

De Palma has brought his sure and skilled hand to a worthy enterprise. His signature for this film is an intense scene involving a baby carriage. Filmmakers liken it to the Odessa Steps montage from 1925's *The Battleship Potemkin* by Sergei Eisenstein.
□ 1987: Best Supp. Actor (Sean Connery).
□ Nominations: Best Costume Design, Art Direction, Original Music Score

....

■ **UP!**

1976, 80 MINS, US ◇
Dir Russ Meyer   *Prod* Russ Meyer   *Scr* B. Callum
Ph Russ Meyer   *Ed* Russ Meyer   *Mus* William Loose, Paul Ruhland   *Art Dir* Michele Levesque

● Robert McLane, Edward Schaaf, Mary Gavin, Elaine Collins, Su Ling, Janet Wood (RHM)

Director Russ Meyer's trademark is the casting of the most incredibly endowed actresses who bounce and jiggle through a primitive world, driving men to violence and murder for their favors.

The men in Meyer pix are rarely a match for the women, though Meyer has equipped his actors with 'marital aids' (to be polite) so they can compete with the ladies in long shots.

The violence, like much of the sex, is too outrageous to be believable. At one point, an axe is buried in a man's back, but he pulls it out and buries it in turn in his attacker's chest who then pulls it out and finishes the job with a buzzsaw to the groin. Fun stuff.

....

■ **UP IN SMOKE**

1978, 86 MINS, US ◇ ⒲ ⊙
Dir Lou Adler   *Prod* Lou Adler, Lou Lombardo
Scr Tommy Chong, Cheech Marin   *Ph* Gene Polito
Ed Lou Lombardo, Scott Conrad   *Art Dir* Leon Ericksen
● Cheech Marin, Tommy Chong, Stacy Keach, Edie Adams, Tom Skerritt, Strother Martin (Paramount)

Up in Smoke is essentially a drawn-out version of the drug-oriented comedy routines of Tommy Chong and Cheech Marin.

Script by the two comedians has hippie rich kid Chong teaming up with barrio boy Cheech in a confused search for some pot to puff on, presumably to aid them in putting together a rock band. Pursuit takes them to Tijuana, where they end up driving back a van constructed out of treated marijuana called 'fibreweed.'

In diligent pursuit is narcotics detective Stacy Keach, saddled with the usual crew of incompetent assistants. The trail eventually leads to popular LA nitery, The Roxy, (in which Adler is partnered) where the dopers' band engages in a punk rock marathon. They take top prize when the high-grade van, catching on fire, inundates the club with potent smoke.

What's lacking in *Up in Smoke* is a cohesiveness in both humor and characterization. Once the more obvious drug jokes are exhausted, director Lou Adler lets the film degenerate into a mixture of fitful slapstick and toilet humor.

....

■ **UP THE DOWN STAIRCASE**

1967, 120 MINS, US ◇ ⒲
Dir Robert Mulligan   *Prod* Alan J. Pakula   *Scr* Tad Mosel   *Ph* Joseph Coffey   *Ed* Folmar Blangsted
Mus Fred Karlin   *Art Dir* George Jenkins
● Sandy Dennis, Patrick Bedford, Eileen Heckart, Ruth White, Jean Stapleton (Warner)

Based on the novel of the same title by Bel Kaufman, *Up the Down Staircase* concerns troubles of a beginning teacher in a tough city high school. And it is very good, almost in spite of itself.

With only one major star (Sandy Dennis) and virtually a single setting, this pic is nevertheless thoroughly cinematic and completely engrossing. This is mainly because it is well acted, carefully scripted and directed and finely photographed. Director Robert Mulligan has for the most part avoided sentimentalism and presents his story honestly and directly.

As pretty young Miss Barrett, fresh from a purely theoretical college training as an English teacher, Dennis is plopped into impersonal Calvin Coolidge High School, a multiracial institution where most of the teachers feel they are successful if they manage to keep their classrooms fairly civilized. Though many of the characters are familiar stock ones their treatment is generally successful.

....

■ UP THE JUNCTION

1968, 119 MINS, UK ◇

Dir Peter Collinson *Prod* Anthony Havelock-Allan, John Brabourne *Scr* Roger Smith *Ph* Arthur Lavis *Ed* John Trumper *Mus* Mike Hugg, Manfred Mann *Art Dir* Ken Jones
● Suzy Kendall, Dennis Waterman, Adrienne Posta, Maureen Lipman, Michael Gothard, Alfie Bass (British Home Entertainment)

Up the Junction began its much-publicized life as a TV play which caused a flurry of controversy about its outspokenness. This feature pic is no sense a film version of the tele adaptation [of the book by Nell Dunn].

Story concerns an affluent girl (Suzy Kendall) who goes to live in Battersea, [then] a seedy area of London. There she works in a factory and falls for a goodlooking van driver.

The irony implicit in this relationship is that the boy wants the lush life she's left behind, and she is quite unsympathetic, feeling that life is more real when it is underprivileged.

But, in practically every respect, pic fails. The treatment introduces an air of patronage into what was honest reportage, and turns it into a condescending class-conscious view of the British working classes.

Kendall, while a looker, hasn't the versatility to encompass a role that demands a plus of personality to make it convincing. She is continuously blank and subdued. Dennis Waterman is quite pleasing as the boy friend.

■ UP THE RIVER

1930, 90 MINS, US

Dir John Ford *Scr* Maurine Watkins *Ph* Joseph August *Ed* Frank E. Hull *Art Dir* Duncan Cramer
● Spencer Tracy, Claire Luce, Warren Hymer, Humphrey Bogart, William Collier Sr, Joan Lawes (Fox)

A comedy prison picture. The love portion of this Maurine Watkins story is played underneath the comedy. Spencer Tracy and Warren Hymer, as the laugh team, take the picture all of the time, along with William Collier Sr, though much of their comic material is based on the love plot.

Funny idea has two escaped prisoners returning of their own volition just in time to save the big ball game against an opposition jail. Thought is said to have come from a Fox studio publicity man, Joe Shea.

Humphrey Bogart and Claire Luce are also in the prison, but really don't belong. The boy's respectable New England folks think he's in China. The girl was framed by a crooked stock salesman. The way the couple romance is interesting. They must do it with their backs turned and the prison fence between them.

This is Tracy's first talker, and he easily makes the grade. Joan Lawes, daughter of the noted warden of Sing Sing, plays just that part in this picture, and competently.

■ UP THE SANDBOX

1972, 97 MINS, US ◇ ⊚

Dir Irvin Kershner *Prod* Robert Chartoff, Irwin Winkler *Scr* Paul Zindel *Ph* Gordon Willis *Ed* Robert Lawrence *Mus* Billy Goldenberg *Art Dir* Harry Horner
● Barbra Streisand, David Selby, Jane Hoffman, John C. Becher, Jacobo Morales, Iris Brooks (First Artists)

Forget the euphemisms, *Up the Sandbox* is an untidy melange of overproduced, heavyhanded fantasy concerning a married woman's identity crisis, and laced with boring gallows humor about how bad life is in Manhattan.

The novel by Anne Richardson Roiphe has been adapted into a screenplay with very few genuine laughs but an awful lot of straining for cheap guffaws. Barbara Streisand, married to Prof David Selby, is harried by two

children and fears the effect on herself and her marriage of accommodating the birth of a third child.

Resolution is as inarticulate as the development. Were Streisand to have been working off some old contractual commitment, there would be much sympathy. But this is not the case, since the star is the producer.

■ UPTOWN SATURDAY NIGHT

1974, 104 MINS, US ◇ ⊚

Dir Sidney Poitier *Prod* Melville Tucker *Scr* Richard Wesley *Ph* Fred J. Koenekamp *Ed* Pembroke J. Herring *Mus* Tom Scott *Art Dir* Alfred Sweeney
● Sidney Poitier, Bill Cosby, Harry Belafonte, Flip Wilson, Richard Pryor, Rosalind Cash (First Artists)

Uptown Saturday Night is an uneven black melodramatic comedy. Its assets include an unwavering ragamuffin charm and some amusing bits by Bill Cosby, Harry Belafonte, Flip Wilson, Richard Pryor and Roscoe Lee Browne. Its debits stem from (1) a helterskelter screenplay; (2) Sidney Poitier's lifeless performance; and (3) Poitier's unimaginative comic direction.

Factory worker Poitier and cabdriver Cosby take a night off from their wives (Rosalind Cash, Ketty Lester) to visit ah after-hours gambling club, where the customers are held up by four stocking-hooded thieves.

When Poitier later realizes that a $50,000 winning lottery ticket was in his stolen wallet, he and Cosby decide to track down the holdup men. They seek help from gumshoe Pryor.

■ URBAN COWBOY

1980, 135 MINS, US ◇ ⊚ ⊙

Dir James Bridges *Prod* Robert Evans, Irving Azoff *Scr* James Bridges, Aaron Latham *Ph* Ray Villalobos *Ed* Dave Rawlins *Mus* Ralph Burns *Art Dir* Stephen Grimes
● John Travolta, Debra Winger, Scott Glenn, Madolyn Smith, Barry Corbin, Bonnie Raitt (Paramount)

Director James Bridges has ably captured the atmosphere of one of the most famous chipkicker hangouts of all: Gilley's Club on the outskirts of Houston.

Enter John Travolta, fresh from a West Texas farm and working his first job in an oil refinery, quickly learning that Gilley's is where everybody heads after work. Try as you might, it's hard to completely accept Travolta as a redneck and his Texas accent is not quite right.

Debra Winger is outstanding as a fetching little slut who marries Travolta only to lose him almost to Madolyn Smith.

Winger leaves Travolta to move in with Scott Glenn while Smith moves in with Travolta.

In one way or another, the quadrangle revolves around Gilley's mechanical bucking bull, a menacing device that tests the courage of all the would-be cowboys.

■ USED CARS

1980, 113 MINS, US ◇ ⊚ ⊙

Dir Robert Zemeckis *Prod* Bob Gale *Scr* Robert Zemeckis, Bob Gale *Ph* Donald M. Morgan *Ed* Michael Kahn *Mus* Patrick Williams *Art Dir* Peter M. Jamison
● Kurt Russell, Jack Warden, Frank McRae, Gerrit Graham, Deborah Harmon, Joseph P. Flaherty (Columbia)

What might have looked like a great idea on paper has been tackled by filmmakers who haven't expanded it much beyond the one joke inherent in the premise.

Plot has fat cat car dealer Jack Warden desperate to knock out competition provided by a brother also portrayed by Warden.

Latter dies early on but operator Kurt Russell and partners Gerrit Graham and Frank McRae disguise the fact to prevent their slimey neighbor from inheriting the property.

Scripters have provided very little context or societal texture for their unmodulated tale, which disagreeably seeks to find humor in characters' humiliation, embarrassment and even death.

Nonetheless Robert Zemeckis directs with undeniable vigor, if insufficient control and discipline.

■ USED PEOPLE

1992, 115 MINS, US ◇ ⊚ ⊙

Dir Beeban Kidron *Prod* Peggy Rajski *Scr* Todd Graff *Ph* David Watkin *Ed* John Tintori *Mus* Rachel Portman *Art Dir* Stuart Wurtzel
● Shirley MacLaine, Kathy Bates, Jessica Tandy, Marcello Mastroianni, Marcia Gay Harden, Sylvia Sidney (Largo/20th Century-Fox)

A modern, absurdist sensibility informs the soap opera *Used People* [from Todd Graff's *The Grandma Plays*], which harks back to '50s weepies.

Set in 1969 in the Sunnyside section of Queens, NY, film limns the colorful family life of a Jewish matriarchy centered around Shirley MacLaine, whose husband (Bob Dishy) has just died. Key characters include her protective mom (Jessica Tandy), dysfunctional children (Kathy Bates and Marcia Gay Harden), both of whom have been divorced, and Tandy's best friend (Sylvia Sidney).

Enter Marcello Mastroianni, MacLaine's secret admirer who uses the family's sitting shiva after Dishy's funeral as his occasion to make his platonic affections for her manifest.

The family's rejection of Mastroianni and cross-cultural antics between them and Mastroianni's Italian-American clan make for some effective comedy in the middle reels but Graff's work is built around highly dramatic confrontation scenes, in particular, a heartrending fight between MacLaine and daughter Bates.

MacLaine's precise acting is laudatory and balanced by a very sympathetic turn by twinkle-eyed Mastroianni, in his best English-language role by far. The support ensemble is excellent.

■ U.S.S. TEAKETTLE

1951, 92 MINS, US

Dir Henry Hathaway *Prod* Fred Kohlmar *Scr* Richard Murphy *Ph* Joe MacDonald *Ed* James B. Clark *Mus* Cyril Mockridge *Art Dir* Lyle Wheeler, J. Russell Spencer
● Gary Cooper, Jane Greer, Millard Mitchell, Eddie Albert, John McIntire, Ray Collins (20th Century-Fox)

The misadventures of a group of landlubbers in charge of a navy craft is rib-tickling filmfare as presented in *U.S.S. Teakettle*. Richard Murphy concocted his screenplay from a *New Yorker* article by John W. Hazard.

Gary Cooper is a 90-day wonder assigned to a craft to conduct trials with an experimental steam engine. He's given the chore simply because he studied engineering in college years before, not because of any nautical knowledge, of which he has none. Crew of the craft, with the exception of Navy vet Millard Mitchell, is in the landlubber class.

String of incidents developed around such a situation are run off smartly and help to disguise fact that there's practically no plot.

Cooper does excellently by his assignment, sharpening up the entertainment values. Jane Greer, as his wife, who joins the WAVES, doesn't have much footage but makes what she does have very pleasant to view. Mitchell's boatswain's mate chore is chuckful of salty humor that he plays to the hilt. Eddie

Albert, Jack Webb, Richard Erdman, Harvey Lembeck, Henry Slate, Charles Bronson, Lee Marvin and Jack Warden are among the motley crew.

■ **UTU**

1983, 120 MINS, NEW ZEALAND ◇ ⊛
Dir Geoff Murphy *Prod* Geoff Murphy *Scr* Geoff Murphy, Keith Aberdein *Ph* Graeme Cowley *Ed* Michael Horton *Mus* John Charles *Art Dir* Ron Highfield
● Anzac Wallace, Bruno Lawrence, Kelly Johnson, Wi Kuki Kaa, Tim Eliot, Ilona Rodgers (Murphy)

In a NZ western of the North American Indian-white settler school, Geoff Murphy has fashioned a fast-moving visual tale of archetypal passion and action. 'Utu' is the Maori word for 'revenge'.

Central figure is rebel leader Te Wheke (Anzac Wallace) during the wars between European settlers and the native Maoris in the late 19th century.

At first sympathetic to the European (pakeha) cause, Te Wheke turns guerrilla when his village is wiped out by British soldiers protecting the settlers. He retaliates in kind while recruiting supporters. As his actions become more despotic and cruel, he is hunted, captured and finally shot.

Murphy has produced powerful images and strong performances, particularly from Wallace, Wi Kuki Kaa (as Wirimu) and a big cast of Maori actors. Action sequences, special effects, and visual exploitation of a rugged, high country location in central New Zealand are superb.

■ **U2 RATTLE AND HUM**

1988, 99 MINS, US ◇ ⊛
Dir Phil Joanou *Prod* Michael Hamlyn *Ph* Robert Brinkmann, Jordan Cronenweth *Ed* Phil Joanou
● (Midnight)

Visionary Irish rock band U2 has not sold itself short with *U2 Rattle and Hum*, a deeply felt cinematic treatment of band's music and concern infused with striking visual style and electric momentum.

Film follows the band throughout the landscape of American-roots music, encountering street musicians in Harlem, collaborating with a gospel choir, performing with bluesmaster B. B. King and recording 'Angel of Harlem', a poignant remembrance of Billie Holiday at Sun Studios in Memphis.

There also is plenty of homage paid to the 1960s, with covers of Bob Dylan, the Beatles and Jimi Hendrix. None of it takes away from the riveting performances of U2's own music, captured mostly at concert venues in Denver, Fort Worth and Arizona.

Director Phil Joanou films mostly in black & white save one color concert sequence, using grainy blowups of 16mm footage to create a gritty texture for the 'street' segs and a startling mixture of silhouette and shadow for the concert footage.

■ **VAGABOND KING, THE**

1930, 100 MINS, US ◇
Dir Ludwig Berger *Scr* Herman J. Mankiewicz *Ph* Henry Gerrard *Ed* Merrill White *Mus* Rudolph Friml *Art Dir* Hans Dreier
● Dennis King, Jeanette MacDonald, O.P. Heggie, Lillian Roth, Warner Oland (Paramount)

This ornate operetta, a pageant of bright fabrics, big sets and milling mobs, is founded upon *If I Were King*, a story [by Justin Huntly McCarthy] which has been done three or four times earlier in pictures. Protagonist this time of Francois Villon is Englishman Dennis King.

Musically, only the one number, 'Song of the Vagabonds', stands out. *Vagabond King*, as an operetta, retards itself as a melodrama. Touches of grim realism are sapped of their power by girls in tights as pages in the royal court and dwarfs turning cartwheels.

At least one case of miscasting is also a handicap. Lillian Roth has neither the necessary age nor emotional maturity to play the passionate Huguette.

Despite its weaknesses, *Vagabond King* is always interesting. It's a treat for the optics with some of the color effects of arresting beauty. Jeanette MacDonald's performance supplies the requisite aroma of glamor.
□ 1929/30: Nomination: Best Art Direction

■ **VALACHI PAPERS, THE**

1972, 123 MINS, ITALY ◇ ⊛
Dir Terence Young *Prod* Dino De Laurentiis *Scr* Stephen Geller *Ph* Aldo Tonti *Ed* Johnny Dwyre *Mus* Riz Ortolani *Art Dir* Mario Garbuglia
● Charles Bronson, Lino Ventura, Jill Ireland, Walter Chiari, Joseph Wiseman, Gerald S. O'Loughlin (Columbia/De Laurentiis)

The Valachi Papers, based upon the revelations of the mobster [and a book by Peter Maas] who disclosed details of Cosa Nostra organized crime in the US, is a hard-hitting, violence-ridden documented melodrama of the underworld covering more than three decades.

Joseph Valachi was the Brooklyn gangster who, while serving a life sentence for his crimes, was induced by a Federal agent to reveal the inside structure of the Cosa Nostra.

Flashback technique is utilized as Charles Bronson, as Valachi, recounts to the Federal agent the innermost secrets of the mob, of which he was a constant but unimportant 'soldier'.

Terence Young, who directs forcefully, hits a shock note in this latter sequence which climaxes numerous scenes of brutality, including Anastasia's famed cutdown in Park Central Hotel barber shop chair.

■ **VALDEZ IS COMING**

1971, 90 MINS, US ◇ ⊛
Dir Edwin Sherin *Prod* Ira Steiner *Scr* Roland Kibbee, David Rayfiel *Ph* Gabor Pogany *Ed* James T. Heckart *Mus* Charles Gross *Art Dir* Jose Maria Tapiador
● Burt Lancaster, Susan Clark, Jon Cypher, Barton Heyman, Richard Jordan, Hector Elizondo (United Artists)

Valdez Is Coming is a sluggish [Spanish-shot western] meller starring Burt Lancaster. Story collapses from premise of a man attempting to right a wrong, to reels of boring mayhem. Legit stager Edwin Sherin's film directorial debut is unimpressive.

The Elmore Leonard novel is about an ethnic southwestern constable (Lancaster) who accidentally kills suspected murderer Lex Monson.

Latter has been tracked into a corner by Jon Cypher, who also happens to have stolen away Susan Clark, wife of the man Monson is wrongfully suspected of having killed. Cypher has Lancaster brutally beaten. Latter's vengeance comprises the main story thrust.

In supporting parts are Richard Jordan, flashy but shallow as a young psychotic killer; Barton Heyman as Cypher's gang boss who comes to respect Lancaster's guts; and the late Frank Silvera as a friend to Lancaster and therefore hassled by Cypher.

■ **VALENTINO**

1977, 132 MINS, UK ◇ ⊛
Dir Ken Russell *Prod* Robert Chartoff, Irwin Winkler *Scr* Ken Russell, John Byrum *Ph* Peter Suschitzky *Ed* Stuart Baird *Art Dir* Philip Harrison
● Rudolf Nureyev, Leslie Caron, Michelle Phillips, Carol Kane, Felicity Kendal, Seymour Cassel (United Artists)

Director Ken Russell seems less interested in nostalgia and early Hollywood days than in trying to find the essence of a certain charisma that can be turned into a sort of world sex symbol. Casting of Kirov defector ballet dancer Rudolf Nureyev as Valentino works despite the elimination of the Latino darkness and smoldering looks.

Nureyev's pic bow is impressive as he manages to avoid being ridiculous in certain scenes by sheer grace and aplomb. And using him also excuses the film a slavish need to hue to Valentino's factual life. Yet Russell has now and then opted for the lyric, even the outrageous.

Early part of the pic does not quite come alive but with the start of his film career it perks up for some bravura scenes that capture the strength, vulnerability and appeal of this tragic figure.

■ **VALERIE**

1957, 81 MINS, US
Dir Gerd Oswald *Prod* Hal R. Makelim *Scr* Leonard Heideman, Emmett Murphy *Ph* Ernest Laszlo *Ed* David Bretherton *Mus* Albert Glasser *Art Dir* Frank Smith
● Sterling Hayden, Anita Ekberg, Anthony Steel, Peter Walker (United Artists)

Tale, briskly and imaginatively directed by Gerd Oswald, is laid in the west, but is by no means a western. Rather, it is a gothic and sombre psychological tale which repeats the same theme three times, each time from the viewpoint of a different character. Save for a preposterously melodramatic finale, which doesn't fit, it's a well-told tale and a work of solid craftsmanship.

Story starts with bloody shooting fray, in which Sterling Hayden and his henchmen wipe out the family of his estranged wife (Anita Ekberg) and seriously wounds her. At the trial, sympathy is on his side, since he's a leading citizen, a war hero (Civil War), and Ekberg supposedly was running away with handsome preacher Anthony Steel.

But Steel's testimony, related in backflash, relates another version – that he was helping an ill and neglected parishioner by taking her to her parents. Hayden's story, also told in flashback, is that she was a loose wanton, only interested in his money, who had seduced his younger brother (Peter Walker) and was carrying on an affair with Steel.

But Ekberg, supposedly near death, regains consciousness and gives her testimony.

Hayden turns in one of his best chores in years, while Ekberg impresses as an actress as well as a scenic wonder.

■ **VALLEY GIRL**

1983, 95 MINS, US ◇ ⊛ ⊙
Dir Martha Coolidge *Prod* Wayne Crawford, Andrew Lane *Scr* Wayne Crawford, Andrew Lane

Ph Frederick Elmes   *Ed* Eva Gardos, Scott Wolk, Marc Levinthal   *Art Dir* Marya Delia Javier
● Nicolas Cage, Deborah Foreman, Elizabeth Daily, Michelle Meyrink, Colleen Camp, Frederic Forrest (Valley 9000/Atlantic)

Valley is very good simply because director Martha Coolidge obviously cares about her two lead characters and is privileged to have a couple of fine young performers, Nicolas Cage and Deborah Foreman, to make the audience care.

As the title suggests, she's a definitive valley girl, mouthing all the nonsensical catch phrases recently popularized in song and book. He's a Hollywood punker who normally wouldn't venture over the hills into the square valley, except to crash a party where they meet.

Their blazing romance, which shocks her high-school friends, ultimately becomes too socially threatening for Foreman and she cuts it off.

For a change, there aren't any cartoon problem adults on hand as there often are in these pictures.

■ **VALLEY OF THE DOLLS**

1967, 123 MINS, US ◇ Ⓥ ⊙
Dir Mark Robson   *Prod* David Weisbart   *Scr* Helen Deutsch, Dorothy Kingsley   *Ph* William H. Daniels   *Ed* Dorothy Spencer   *Mus* John Williams   *Art Dir* Jack Martin Smith, Richard Day
● Barbara Parkins, Patty Duke, Paul Burke, Sharon Tate, Tony Scotti, Martin Milner (20th Century-Fox/Red Lion)

Plot meanders between New England country girl Barbara Parkins, who comes to the big city and eventually is seduced by urban social patterns; Patty Duke, rising young singing star who gets hung up on pills, and Sharon Tate, playing a big-breasted, untalented, but basically sensitive girl who never finds happiness. Parkins and Tate, the latter particularly good, suffer from under-emphasis in early reels, and corny plot resolution.

Main body of the story [from Jacqueline Susann's novel] concerns the rise, plateau and erratic performance of Duke's character. For her, this is a very good role.

Susan Hayward, who replaced Judy Garland in cast, does an excellent job in giving acting depth to the role of the older legit star, ever alert to remove threats to her supremacy.

Five songs, including title theme, by Andre and Dory Previn are interpolated nicely, and logically, into plot. Dionne Warwick regularly warbles title tune.
□ 1967: Nomination: Best Adapted Music Score

■ **VALLEY OF THE KINGS**

1954, 85 MINS, US ◇
Dir Robert Pirosh   *Prod* [uncredited]   *Scr* Robert Pirosh, Karl Tunberg   *Ph* Robert Surtees   *Ed* Harold F. Kress   *Mus* Miklos Rozsa   *Art Dir* Cedric Gibbons, Jack Martin Smith
● Robert Taylor, Eleanor Parker, Carlos Thompson, Samia Gamal, Kurt Kasznar, Victor Jory (M-G-M)

Spectators are given a tour of the land of the Nile in this suspense drama, and the backgrounds offer more freshness to the film than does the routine story, dealing with robbers of the tombs of the Pharaohs, with a side angle having to do with the establishment that Old Testament accounts of Joseph in Egypt are literally true.

Robert Taylor plays a rugged American archaeologist who agrees to help Eleanor Parker, married to Carlos Thompson, search for the tomb of the Pharaoh, Ra-hotep. She wants to prove that her late father was right in believing the tomb will prove his theory about Joseph in Egypt. A mysterious gang, seemingly headed by sinister Kurt Kasznar, puts obstacles in the way of the search.

Plot period is 1900 and ageless wonders of the land of the Nile fit perfectly. Parker and Taylor are a good lead team for the drama, but Thompson comes off only fair. The script was suggested by historical data in *Gods, Graves and Scholars* by C.W. Ceram.
□ 1989: Nomination: Best Costume Design

■ **VALMONT**

1989, 137 MINS, FRANCE/UK ◇ Ⓥ ⊙
Dir Milos Forman   *Prod* Paul Rassam, Michael Hausman   *Scr* Jean-Claude Carriere   *Ph* Miroslav Ondricek   *Ed* Alan Heim, Nena Danevic   *Art Dir* Pierre Guffroy
● Colin Firth, Annette Bening, Meg Tilly, Fairuza Balk, Sian Phillips, Fabia Drake (Renn/Burrill)

Milos Forman's meticulously produced *Valmont* is an extremely well-acted period piece that suffers from stately pacing and lack of dramatic high points.

Plot of Choderlos de Laclos' 1782 novel is quite familiar due to Stephen Frears' 1988 hit film, *Dangerous Liaisons*, from Christopher Hampton's 1987 play. Forman has met the challenge of breathing new life into the material, but key plot twists and revelations are robbed of their novelty.

Basic story revolves around a bet by two 18th-century French aristocrats, Valmont (Colin Firth) and his old flame Marquise de Merteuil (Annette Bening). She wants Valmont to seduce 15-year-old Cecile (Fairuza Balk) to cuckold Cecile's fiance, Gercourt (Jeffrey Jones), who is Merteuil's unfaithful lover.

Valmont counters with the bet that he can bed timid married lady Madame de Tourvel (Meg Tilly). If he wins Merteuil must submit to his lust as well.

What keeps the film interesting, if not riveting, is the generally on target casting and resulting topnotch interpretations.

■ **VAMP**

1986, 94 MINS, US ◇ Ⓥ ⊙
Dir Richard Wenk   *Prod* Donald P. Borchers   *Scr* Richard Wenk   *Ph* Elliot Davis   *Ed* Marc Grossman   *Mus* Jonathan Elias   *Art Dir* Alan Roderick-Jones
● Chris Makepeace, Sandy Baron, Robert Rusler, Dedee Pfeiffer, Gedde Watanabe, Grace Jones (Balcor/Borchers)

Vamp is an extremely imaginative horror film styled as jet black comedy.

Richard Wenk opens the film deceptively with the format of a teenage sex comedy. Fraternity pledges Keith (Chris Makepeace) and A.J. (Robert Rusler) agree to find a stripper for the frat party that night. They team up with Duncan (Gedde Watanabe), who significantly has a car.

Upon their arrival in the big city, film quickly makes a permanent detour into *The Twilight Zone* when their car skids and comes out of a lengthy spin with bright daylight suddenly turned to spooky night-time. Trio heads for the After Dark Club, which turns out to be a den of vampires.

Picture benefits immensely from the casting of disco star turned actress Grace Jones as the leader of the vampires. She has no dialog in the film, but expresses herself sexily in several scary scenes.

■ **VAMPIRA**

(US: Old Dracula)

1975, 89 MINS, UK ◇ Ⓥ
Dir Clive Donner   *Prod* Jack H. Wiener   *Scr* Jeremy Lloyd   *Ph* Tony Richmond   *Ed* Bill Butler   *Mus* David Whittaker   *Art Dir* Phillip Harrison
● David Niven, Teresa Groves, Peter Bayliss, Jennie Linden, Nicky Henson, Linda Hayden (World)

David Niven goes the way of Vincent Price in *Vampira*. Screenplay is set in the present day, and has Dracula reading *Playboy*, sleeping in

an automated coffin, and giving tours of his castle as a means of luring fresh victims.

Niven smoothly incarnates the old-style rake, while magazine writer Nicky Henson, one of his victims, repellently typifies the hip young stud.

All of this might have made a good high-comedy satire, instead of sporadically amusing camp, if the dialog were sharper and if the plot didn't revolve around Niven's attempts to revive his long-dead mate Vampira, played witlessly by Teresa Graves.

■ **VAMPIRE LOVERS, THE**

1970, 91 MINS, UK/US ◇ Ⓥ
Dir Roy Ward Baker   *Prod* Harry Fine, Michael Style   *Scr* Tudor Gates   *Ph* Moray Grant   *Ed* James Needs   *Mus* Harry Robinson   *Art Dir* Scott MacGregor
● Ingrid Pitt, Pippa Steel, Madeleine Smith, Peter Cushing, Dawn Addams, Kate O'Mara (Hammer/American International)

The vampire-anti-heroine, played by Ingrid Pitt, has distinct lesbian tendencies. She prefers sinking her fangs into the bosoms of comely young women, though when required she's not averse to giving the works to an interfering local doctor and a manservant.

Not much of a story, but the screenplay [from an adaptation by Harry Fine, Tudor Gates and Michael Style of J. Sheridan Le Fanu's story *Carmilla*] has all the needed ingredients. Dank interiors, eerie exteriors and stagecoaches, plenty of blood, a couple of unconvincing decapitations, stakes in the vampire's heart, the sign of the Cross, etc. Fairly flat dialog doesn't provide much of the unconscious humor that usually gives a lift to this type of entertainment.

■ **VAMPIRE'S KISS**

1988, 103 MINS, US ◇ Ⓥ
Dir Robert Bierman   *Prod* Barry Shils, Barbara Zitwer   *Scr* Joseph Minion   *Ph* Stefan Czapsky   *Ed* Angus Newton   *Mus* Colin Towns   *Art Dir* Christopher Nowak
● Nicolas Cage, Maria Conchita Alonso, Jennnifer Beals, Elizabeth Ashley, Kasi Lemmons, Bob Lujan (Magellan)

Nicolas Cage is Peter Loew, a New York literary agent who works hard and plays hard. Only indication that all is not OK are his sessions with his shrink (Elizabeth Ashley). One night his latest pickup (Jennifer Beals) exposes her fangs. She keeps him alive so that she may continue to feed. As a result he starts getting the urge for blood himself, becoming even more manic at work and taking it out on his beleaguered secretary (Maria Conchita Alonso).

The film then takes a major U-turn, suddenly getting deadly serious as it appears that Loew is not turning into a vampire at all, but is becoming a full-blown psychotic. Latter portion of the film shows him raping, murdering and pleading with people to kill him.

Problem is that Cage's over-the-top performance generates little sympathy for the character, so it's tough to be interested in him as his personality disorder worsens. The supporting cast is given little to work with, as Alonso mostly cowers and Beals mostly bites Cage. Ashley fares best as the psychiatrist, particularly in a fantasy sequence at the end in which she tells Cage's character what he wants to hear.

■ **VANISHING, THE**

1993, 110 MINS, US ◇ Ⓥ ⊙
Dir George Sluizer   *Prod* Larry Brezner, Paul Schiff   *Scr* Todd Graff   *Ph* Peter Suschitzky   *Ed* Bruce Green   *Mus* Jerry Goldsmith   *Art Dir* Jeannine C. Oppewall
● Jeff Bridges, Kiefer Sutherland, Nancy Travis, Sandra Bullock, Maggie Linderman, Lisa Eichhorn (20th Century-Fox)

Some last-reel thrills and cathartic violence provide commercial oomph to the otherwise tedious thriller *The Vanishing*. Dutch director George Sluizer had the rare chance to re-make his own 1988 *Spoorloos* in America. Unfortunately this version, scripted by Todd Graff, is schematic and unconvincing.

Film introduces Jeff Bridges as the villain at the outset, rehearsing methods of chloro-forming victims and plotting kidnappings. He's a happily married school teacher but with a Nietszchean complex.

Parallel story has Kiefer Sutherland and g.f. Sandra Bullock on vacation from Seattle driving past Mount St. Helens when, after a row that hints at possibilities of a break-up, she suddenly disappears from a rest stop. Sutherland goes crazy looking for her; the police don't help as there's no evidence of foul play. Fade out to three years later and Sutherland's obsession with finding her has continued.

The ultimate chilling climax of the original is repeated in the remake, but with 25 min-utes to go and with very little impact. Unlike the subtle acting of Bernard-Pierre Donnadieu in the original, Bridges adopts an odd gait, curious manner, and an on-and-off accent that are distracting and spoil his per-formance. Sutherland comes off as a wimp.

■ VANISHING POINT

1971, 107 MINS, US ◇ ⊛ ⊙
Dir Richard C. Sarafian *Prod* Norman Spencer
Scr Guillermo Cain *Ph* John A. Alonzo *Ed* Stefan
Arnsten *Mus* Jimmy Bowen *Art Dir* Glen Daniels
● Barry Newman, Cleavon Little, Charlotte Rampling, Dean Jagger, Victoria Medlin, Paul Koslo (Cupid)

If the viewer believes what Guillermo Cain's screenplay is trying to say in this lowercase action effort, the 'wasteland' between Denver and the California border is peopled only with uniformed monsters, aided and abetted by an antagonistic citizenry with the only 'good' people the few hippies, motorcycle gangs and dope pushers.

The action is almost entirely made up of one man driving a car at maximum speed from Denver to, hopefully, San Francisco, against various odds, from the police who try to intercept him, to the oddball individuals he meets along the way.

Barry Newman is the ex-marine who tack-les the 15-hour drive sans rest or reason, kept awake by pep pills. A Negro disk jockey (Cleavon Little), tucked away on a tiny radio station in what is close to being a ghost town becomes his collaborator, warning him over the radio when he's near a police trap. This leads, naturally, to the now screen cliche of his being attacked and beaten by racists.

Also seen briefly is Dean Jagger as a Death Valley prospector who tries to befriend Newman and, very briefly, Charlotte Rampling, as a hitchhiker with whom Newman beds down for the night.

■ VENETIAN AFFAIR, THE

1967, 92 MINS, US ◇
Dir Jerry Thorpe *Prod* Jerry Thorpe, E. Jack Neuman
Scr E. Jack Neuman *Ph* Milton Krasner, Enzo Serafin
Ed Henry Berman *Mus* Lalo Schifrin *Art Dir* George
W. Davis, Leroy Coleman
● Robert Vaughn, Elke Sommer, Felicia Farr, Karl
Boehm, Ed Asner, Boris Karloff (M-G-M)

The Venetian Affair is a tepid programmer about international espionage in Venice. Pacing is tedious and plotting routine, but the production is enlivened by some actual footage of Venice.

E. Jack Neuman adapted a Helen MacInnes novel into a routine script, dotted generally with prototype spy types. Vaughn, ex-CIAgent now a reporter, is sent to Venice af-ter a diplomatic meeting has been bombed.

Ed Asner, CIA boss there, once canned Vaughn because latter's then wife, Elke Sommer, was a Communist agent. Now she has disappeared.

Pot boils slowly under Thorpe's casual di-rection. What was meant as an underplayed approach becomes awkward, meaningless pause, reinforced by dull dialog.

■ VENICE/VENICE

1992, 92 MINS, US ◇ ⊛
Dir Henry Jaglom *Prod* Judith Wolinsky *Scr* Henry
Jaglom *Ph* Hanania Baer *Ed* Henry Jaglom
● Nelly Alard, Henry Jaglom, Melissa Leo, Suzanne
Bertish, Daphna Kastner, David Duchovny (International
Rainbow)

Venice/Venice represents the definition of a vanity production. Sliding way over the line between personal cinema and egotism, Henry Jaglom's ninth feature lacks either the color-ful characters or innately interesting subject matter of his better films, telling essentially a non-story in slight, schematic fashion.

Portraying the director of the only American film in competition at the Venice Film Festival, Jaglom announces at the outset that he is a maverick: 'I am the representa-tive of the anti-establishment.'

Jaglom builds a fragile little story about his curious relationship with attractive French journalist Nelly Alard, who is obsessed with his work. Jaglom gives her a sort-of interview that allows him to expound upon his own tal-ents, pursue her a bit at lunch and around the pool and finally make out with her during a scenic gondola ride.

After an hour, setting shifts to Venice, Calif., as Alard wanders in on a party Jaglom is throwing. Nothing much happens here ex-cept for some auditions in which Jaglom is looking for a woman to play his wife in an up-coming film, *Happy Endings*.

Seemingly given their heads in the dialogue department, thesps seem at a loss where to take the scenes.

■ VENOM

1982, 93 MINS, UK ◇ ⊛
Dir Piers Haggard *Prod* Martin Bregman *Scr* Robert
Carrington *Ph* Gil Taylor *Ed* Michael Bradsell
Mus Michael Kamen *Art Dir* Tony Curtis
● Klaus Kinski, Oliver Reed, Nicol Williamson, Sarah
Miles, Sterling Hayden, Susan George (Venom/
Paramount)

Venom is an engrossing traditional suspense thriller [from a novel by Alan Scholefield] about a kidnapping, hyped by the genuinely frightening plot gimmick of a deadly black mamba snake on the loose.

Klaus Kinski toplines as Jacmel, a German criminal who kidnaps a young American boy (Lance Holcomb) living in London, aided in the inside job by the boy's servants (Oliver Reed and Susan George). Unbeknownst, the boy has accidentally acquired a poisonous snake intended for toxicologist Dr Marion Stowe (Sarah Miles) and the lethal reptile gets loose in the house.

With old-fashioned lines beween good guys and bad guys sharply drawn, film satisfyingly metes out snake-delivered justice to the evil-doers. Combo of Kinski's quiet, dominant menace and Reed's explosive, brutish vio-lence makes for a memorable ensemble of vil-lains.

■ VENUS PETER

1989, 92 MINS, UK ◇ ⊛
Dir Ian Sellar *Prod* Christopher Young *Scr* Ian Sellar,
Christopher Rush *Ph* Gabriel Beristain *Ed* David
Spiers *Mus* Jonathan Dove *Art Dir* Andy Harris
● Gordon R. Strachan, Ray McAnally, David Hayman,
Sinead Cusack, Caroline Paterson, Peter Caffrey (BFI)

Ian Sellar's first feature, shot in the wind-swept Orkney Islands, north of Scotland, is a film about childhood which moves very slowly to a quite moving climax.

Central character is young Peter who lives with his mother and fisherman grandfather; he's not certain where his father is, but imag-ines him to be a ship's captain. Much of the film is taken up with Peter's observations: family scenes, scenes in a church and at school, the discovery of a stranded whale. Then the father returns, and it seems he'd simply tired of island life and gone to the mainland.

The evocative background of the Orkneys is a major asset to the film, as is the unaffected performance of young Gordon R. Strachan, an Orkney schoolboy, as Peter. Professional players, like Ray McAnally as the grandfather and David Hayman as the local priest, work generously alongside the youthful tyro.

■ VERA CRUZ

1954, 94 MINS, US ◇ ⊛
Dir Robert Aldrich *Prod* James Hill *Scr* Roland Kibbee,
James R. Webb *Ph* Ernest Laszlo *Ed* Alan Crosland Jr
Mus Hugo Friedhofer
● Gary Cooper, Burt Lancaster, Denise Darcel, Cesar
Romero, Sarita Montiel, George Macready (United
Artists)

Vera Cruz, the first release in SuperScope, stresses mostly the violence and suspenseful action bred during Mexico's revolutionary pe-riod when the Juaristas were trying to free the country of the French-supported Emperor Maximilian.

Gary Cooper, ex-Confederate major from New Orleans, joins forces with Burt Lancaster, western outlaw, and his gang of choice pug-uglies to escort a countess from the court of Maximilian in Mexico City to the port at Vera Cruz. It's more than the simple guard job indicated, since secretly the count-ess has a load of gold to be used in Europe to bring more troops to Maximilian's aid.

Besides the more obvious advantages of their star teaming, Cooper and Lancaster come through with actionful and colorful per-formances. Sarita Montiel, of the Mexican film industry, is film-introduced stateside in this, and shows up well in her US debut.

■ VERDICT, THE

1946, 86 MINS, US
Dir Don Siegel *Prod* William Jacobs *Scr* Peter Milne
Ph Ernest Haller *Ed* Thomas Reilly *Mus* Frederick
Hollander *Art Dir* Ted Smith
● Sydney Greenstreet, Peter Lorre, Joan Lorring, George
Coulouris, Arthur Shields, Rosalind Ivan (Warner)

Stock mystery tale with period background, *The Verdict* aims at generating suspense and thrills, succeeding modestly. Sydney Greenstreet creates character of a Scotland Yard superintendent who is fired when he convicts and hangs a man on circumstantial evidence. To show up the Yard and the man who replaced him, Greenstreet commits the perfect crime. Only the conviction of an inno-cent man for the murder makes Greenstreet reveal how the killing was done and the rea-son for it.

Script by Peter Milne, from a novel by Israel Zangwill, is peopled with the usual number of suspects in order to divert suspi-cion from the real killer and Don Siegel's di-rection does well with his material. Peter Lorre, macabre artist friend of Greenstreet's is the prime suspect and turns in a good job to match latter's performance.

■ VERDICT, THE

1982, 122 MINS, US ◇ ⊛ ⊙
Dir Sidney Lumet *Prod* Richard D. Zanuck, David Brown

V

Scr David Mamet   Ph Andrzej Bartkowiak   Ed Peter Frank   Mus Johnny Mandel   Art Dir Edward Pisoni
● Paul Newman, Charlotte Rampling, Jack Warden, James Mason, Milo O'Shea, Edward Binns (20th Century-Fox/Zanuck-Brown)

There are many fine performances and sensitive moral issues contained in *The Verdict* but somehow that isn't enough to make it the compelling film it should be. David Mamet's script [from a novel by Barry Reed] offers little out of the ordinary.

Paul Newman is a cloudy-headed boozer who was at one time clearly a top junior lawyer but has been reduced to soliciting clients at funerals. Colleague Jack Warden hands him the case that could put him back on the straight and narrow.

A young woman lies in a respected Boston hospital – a vegetable thanks to a dose of anesthesia she received from doctors while delivering a baby. Her sister wants to sue the hospital and Catholic Church (which owns the facility) for a sum of money large enough to enable her to start a new life.

Newman becomes convinced the church and hospital have conspired to cover up medical malpractice.

While Newman's drunk is a little difficult to take at the outset, he manages to weave an extraordinarily realistic portrayal by the film's completion. He gets especially solid support from Warden and James Mason.
□ 1982: Nominations: Best Picture, Director, Actor (Paul Newman), Supp. Actor (James Mason), Screenplay Adaptation

....

■ VERTIGO

1958, 126 MINS, US ◇ ⑩ ⊙
Dir Alfred Hitchcock   Prod Alfred Hitchcock   Scr Alec Coppel, Samuel Taylor   Ph Robert Burks   Ed George Tomasini   Mus Bernard Herrmann   Art Dir Hal Pereira, Henry Bumstead
● James Stewart, Kim Novak, Barbara Bel Geddes, Tom Helmore, Henry Jones, Ellen Corby (Paramount)

Vertigo is prime though uneven Hitchcock. James Stewart, on camera almost constantly, comes through with a startlingly fine performance as the lawyer-cop who suffers from acrophobia. Kim Novak, shopgirl who involves Stewart in what turns out to be a clear case of murder, is interesting under Hitchcock's direction and nearer an actress than in the earlier *Pal Joey* or *Jeanne Eagles*.

Unbilled is the city of San Francisco, photographed extensively and in exquisite color. Through all of this runs Alfred Hitchcock's directorial hand, cutting, angling and gimmicking with mastery. Unfortunately, even that mastery is not enough to overcome one major fault – that the film's first half is too slow and too long. This may be because: (1) Hitchcock became overly enamored with the vertiginous beauty of Frisco; or (2) the screenplay (from the novel *D'entre les morts* by Pierre Boileau and Thomas Narcejac) just takes too long to get off the ground.

Film opens with a rackling scene in which Stewart's acrophobia is explained: he hangs from top of a building in midst of chasing a robber over rooftops and watches a police buddy plunge to his death. But for the next hour the action is mainly psychic, with Stewart hired by a rich shipbuilder to watch the shipowner's wife (Novak) as she loses her mental moorings, attempts suicide and immerses herself in the gloomy maunderings of her mad great-grandmother. Stewart goes off his rocker and winds up in a mental institution. When he comes out, still a trifle unbalanced, he keeps hunting for girl who resembles Novak.

Supporting players are all excellent, with Barbara Bel Geddes, in limited role of Stewart's down-to-earth girl friend, standout for providing early dashes of humor.

Frisco location scenes – whether of Nob Hill, interior of Ernie's restaurant, Land's End, downtown, Muir Woods, Mission Dolores or San Juan Bautista – are absolutely authentic and breathtaking.
□ 1958: Nominations: Best Art Direction, Sound

....

■ VERY SPECIAL FAVOR, A

1965, 105 MINS, US ◇
Dir Michael Gordon   Prod Stanley Shapiro   Scr Stanley Shapiro, Nate Monaster   Ph Leo Tover   Ed Russell F. Schoengarth   Mus Vic Mizzy   Art Dir Alexander Golitzen, Walter Simonds
● Rock Hudson, Leslie Caron, Charles Boyer, Walter Slezak, Dick Shawn, Larry Storch (Universal)

The beautifully-mounted feature draws its title from Rock Hudson, as American oilman who bests French lawyer Charles Boyer in a Paris court case simply by romancing the femme judge, admitting to Boyer on a plane en route back to US that he feels he owes him a favor by beating him at his own national sport, which he'll grant anytime latter requests.

Boyer, in NY to see a daughter for first time in 25 years, sees in her, although a highly successful psychologist, a spinster with the spirit of an old maid, a woman nearly 30 who has never tasted the life her French father thinks every femme should know. He calls on Hudson to make good his offer.

Script develops along expected lines, with Hudson posing to Leslie Caron, the psychologist, as a man with a disturbing problem – he's irresistible to women who pursue him and he's a love toy.

Hudson delivers one of his customary light characterizations, and Boyer as usual is suave. Most outstanding work in pic, however, is contributed by Nita Talbot, a switchboard operator infatuated with Hudson, and Larry Storch, a hardboiled taxi-driver.

....

■ VICE SQUAD

1953, 88 MINS, US
Dir Arnold Laven   Prod Jules V. Levy, Arthur Gardner   Scr Lawrence Roman   Ph Joseph F. Biroc   Ed Arthur H. Nadel   Mus Herschel Burke Gilbert   Art Dir Carroll Clark
● Edward G. Robinson, Paulette Goddard, K.T. Stevens, Porter Hall, Adam Williams, Mary Ellen Kay (United Artists/Sequoia)

The workaday world of a police captain, complete with murder, bank robbery and sundry other major and minor crimes, is basis for this okay melodrama. Because of the semi-documentary style, the picture has a tendency to be repetitious in detailing police work.

Edward G. Robinson does the expected competent job of playing the police captain who arrives at work one morning to find his men looking for the gunmen who killed a cop during the early hours. The killing is tied in with a planned bank robbery, a scheme thwarted by police vigilance, but which doesn't prevent the desperate kidnaping of a femme bank clerk as a shield.

Paulette Goddard is used as the head of an escort bureau whose girls sometimes furnish the police valuable leads. She plays it colorfully. Pic is based on Leslie T. White's novel, *Harness Bull*, and Los Angeles is the scene of the action.

....

■ VICE VERSA

1988, 98 MINS, US ◇ ⑩ ⊙
Dir Brian Gilbert   Prod Dick Clement, Ian La Frenais   Scr Dick Clement, Ian La Frenais   Ph King Baggot   Ed David Garfield   Mus David Shire   Art Dir Jim Schoppe
● Judge Reinhold, Fred Savage, Corinne Bohrer, Swoosie Kurtz, David Proval, Jane Kaczmerek (Columbia)

Vice Versa finds Judge Reinhold, a tony Chicago department store exec named Marshall, and his junior high school age son, Charlie (Fred Savage), ending up with each other's personalities after they both touch a mystical oriental skull.

Reinhold is in his element acting like an 11-year-old more interested in heavy metal rock and his pet frog than girls and other yucky things. The store's chief honcho is ready to fire him, but his fellow execs, all coveting his job, are relishing his antics.

Things get a bit too sappy, though, with his lovestruck girlfriend, Sam (Corinne Bohner); the more immature he acts, the more enamored she becomes.

It is really Savage, best known for his role as the little boy in *The Princess Bride*, who is particularly winsome as the smart-alecky Dad stuck in his kid's pint-size body. Except for the overuse of profanity for Savage's character, this is fun family fare.

....

■ VICTIM

1961, 100 MINS, UK ⑩
Dir Basil Dearden   Prod Michael Relph   Scr Janet Green, John McCormick   Ph Otto Heller   Ed John D. Guthridge   Mus Philip Green   Art Dir Alex Vetchinsky
● Dirk Bogarde, Sylvia Syms, Dennis Price, Anthony Nicholls, Peter McEnery, Nigel Stock (Allied Film Makers)

Producer Michael Relph, director Basil Dearden and writers Janet Green and John McCormick (the team which produced *Sapphire*, involving racial prejudice) adopt a similar technique with *Victim*. They provide a taut, holding thriller about blackmailers latching on to homosexuals and at the same time take several critical swipes at the British law which encourages the blackmailing by making homos criminal outcasts.

Dirk Bogarde plays a successful barrister who is on the verge of becoming a Queen's Counsel. He is happily married to a wife (Sylvia Syms) who knew of his homo leanings when she married him but has successfully helped him to lead a normal life. He refuses to see a youth (Peter McEnery) with whom he previously has had association because he fears possible blackmail. Instead the boy is trying to protect the barrister from blackmail. The youth commits suicide, Bogarde is caught up in enquiries by the cops and, from remorse, sets out to break the blackmailers even though he knows that if the facts come out it will ruin his marriage and his career.

The homosexuals involved are not caricatures but are shown as varying human beings. There are a philanthropist peer, an actor, an aging barber, a hearty car salesman from a good family, a photographer, a bookseller and a factory clerk.

Bogarde is subtle, sensitive and strong. Syms handles a difficult role with delicacy and there is one memorable scene when the two quarrel after she forces him to admit what she doesn't want to hear. This is telling, moving stuff.

....

■ VICTORIA THE GREAT

1937, 112 MINS, UK ◇
Dir Herbert Wilcox   Prod Herbert Wilcox   Scr Miles Malleson, Charles de Grandcourt   Ph Freddie Young, William V. Skall   Ed James Elmo Williams, Jill Irving   Mus Anthony Collins   Art Dir L.P. Williams
● Anna Neagle, Anton Walbrook, Walter Rilla, Mary Morris, H.B. Warner, Felix Aylmer (Imperator)

Not cloak-and-cocked-hat historical tedium of pageantry and fancy dramatics, *Victoria the Great* travels a long way toward a full and clarified explanation of the most popular ruler England ever had. Her career, both public and private, is traced from 20 June 1837 when she ascended the throne, until the day of her 60th anniversary as queen, shortly before her demise.

Anna Neagle, in the title role, gives an un-wavering performance throughout. Anton Walbrook as Albert, the Prince Consort, is superb.

The film wisely puts its prime focus on the private life of Victoria, her romance, marriage, and personal characteristics. Backgrounded is her public life, and her gradual rise to such high estimation of her people.

Victoria the Great is done with a lavish hand – the closing sequence is in Technicolor [shot by William V. Skall]. The tinting isn't too good, but serves effectively as a pointer-up for the climax.

This is the very first pic made after the Crown permitted a dramatization to be presented within the Empire dealing with Victoria.

▪▪▪▪▪▪▪▪▪▪▪▪▪▪▪▪▪▪▪▪▪▪▪▪▪▪▪

■ **VICTORS, THE**

1963, 175 MINS, US

Dir Carl Foreman   *Prod* Carl Foreman   *Scr* Carl Foreman   *Ph* Christopher Challis   *Ed* Alan Osbiston   *Mus* Sol Kaplan   *Art Dir* Geoffrey Drake
● George Hamilton, George Peppard, Eli Wallach, James Mitchum, Romy Schneider, Jeanne Moreau (Highroad/Columbia)

Carl Foreman tells his tale of war in terms of vignettes, concentrating on homesickness, woman-hunger, civilian starvation, the 'nice' girls who shack up with the GI smoothies for food, cigarettes and kicks. One of these is played by Romy Schneider. Her indifference to the decent soldier (George Hamilton) and ultimate bumming around with the slicker is underplayed, but it's part of the mosaic of the decent GI's own ultimate hardening.

The story is properly told in black and white photography. Foreman has incorporated a lot of newsreel footage. He has designed his narrative with great filmmaking skill and considerable daring, recalling the early 1940s both for nostalgia and irony.

In general Foreman has had the wisdom to underplay his scenes, leave many an incident without the sequel which seems, but is not, mandatory. In his alter ego as adaptor he has taken his story from [the book *The Human Factor* by] an English writer, Alexander Baron, to whom all proper honor. There will be a plausible temptation to call this a director's picture, which it is, but all is made possible in the end by a good script.

▪▪▪▪▪▪▪▪▪▪▪▪▪▪▪▪▪▪▪▪▪▪▪▪▪▪▪

■ **VICTOR/VICTORIA**

1982, 133 MINS, UK ◇ ⑫ ⊙

Dir Blake Edwards   *Prod* Blake Edwards, Tony Adams   *Scr* Blake Edwards   *Ph* Dick Bush   *Ed* Ralph E. Winters   *Mus* Henry Mancini   *Art Dir* Rodger Maus
● Julie Andrews, James Garner, Robert Preston, Lesley Ann Warren, Alex Karras, John Rhys-Davies (M-G-M/ Peerford/Artista)

Victor/Victoria is a sparkling, ultra-sophisticated entertainment from Blake Edwards. Based on a 1933 German film comedy [*Viktor und Viktoria*, written and directed by Rheinhold Schunzel] which was a big hit in its day, pic sees Edwards working in the Lubitsch-Wilder vein of sly wit and delightful sexual innuendo.

Set in Paris of 1934, gorgeously represented by Rodger Maus' studio-constructed settings, tale introduces Julie Andrews as a down-on-her-luck chanteuse. Also suffering a temporary career lapse is tres gai nightclub entertainer Robert Preston, who remakes her as a man who in short order becomes celebrated as Paris' foremost female impersonator.

Enter Windy City gangster James Garner, with imposing bodyguard Alex Karras and dizzy sexpot Lesley Ann Warren in tow. Not knowing he's in one of 'those' clubs, the tough guy falls hard for Andrews, only to experience a severe blow to his macho ego when it become's apparent she's a he.

While the central thrust of the story rests in Andrews-Garner covergence, everyone in the cast is given the chance to shine. Most impressive of all is Preston, with a shimmering portrait of a slightly decadent 'old queen'. Andrews is able to reaffirm her musical talents. Garner is quizzically sober as the story's straight man, in more ways than one.
□ 1982: Best Original Song Score.
□ Nominations: Best Actress (Julie Andrews), Supp. Actor (Robert Preston), Aupp. Actress (Lesley Ann Warren), Screenplay Adaptation, Costume Design, Art Direction

▪▪▪▪▪▪▪▪▪▪▪▪▪▪▪▪▪▪▪▪▪▪▪▪▪▪▪

■ **VICTORY**

1940, 77 MINS, US

Dir John Cromwell   *Prod* Anthony Veiller   *Scr* John L. Balderston   *Ph* Leo Tover   *Ed* William Shea   *Mus* Frederick Hollander
● Fredric March, Betty Field, Cedric Hardwicke, Jerome Cowan, Sig Rumann, Rafaela Ottiano (Paramount)

This film version of Joseph Conrad's novel impresses with several strongly individual performances rather than with the basic movement of the story itself.

Story unfolds at a most leisurely pace, script deviating from regulation picture formula and tempo, and filled with long stretches of dialog to highlight development of characters displayed. Fredric March is the recluse living on a small East Indian Island seeking happiness away from the world. Under his protection comes Betty Field, a stranded musician, and when March finds himself falling in love with the girl he prepares to ship her away on a trading schooner. Cedric Hardwicke and his outlaw companions arrive to rob and kill March for his buried fortune.

March capably carries the lead with restrained action to put over transformation of his original weakling, golden-rule character to one of strength, physically and mentally. Field registers with an unusual performance as the English girl musician who falls in love with the recluse. Jerome Cowan clicks with a meritorious performance as Hardwicke's Cockney assistant in outlawry; while Hardwicke handles his assignment with usual ability.

Direction by John Cromwell, in retaining all of the character etchings displayed in Conrad's book, employs a stagey technique with burdensome dialog and slow pace until the final episodes, which pick up dramatic interest.

▪▪▪▪▪▪▪▪▪▪▪▪▪▪▪▪▪▪▪▪▪▪▪▪▪▪▪

■ **VICTORY**

(UK: Escape to Victory)

1981, 117 MINS, US ◇ ⑫

Dir John Huston   *Prod* Freddie Fields   *Scr* Evan Jones, Yabo Yablonsky   *Ph* Gerry Fisher   *Ed* Roberto Silvi   *Mus* Bill Conti   *Art Dir* J. Dennis Washington
● Sylvester Stallone, Michael Caine, Max von Sydow, Pele, Daniel Massey, Carole Laure (Lorimar/Victory)

Victory amounts to a frankly oldfashioned World War II morality play, hinging on soccer as a civilized metaphor for the game of War.

Though set in a German p.o.w. camp in 1943, *Victory* is barely a 'war movie' by any stretch. Plot hinges on a morality-building ploy by a genteel propaganda officer (Max von Sydow) who once played for Germany to pit a team of Allied prisoners (including officer Michael Caine, a onetime British soccer pro, Brazil's legendary Pele, and Yank badboy Sylvester Stallone) against the local German troops.

When his superiors get wind of the plan, they quickly see the worldwide propaganda potential and insist on expanding the plan to square off a p.o.w. 'all star' team drawn from imprisoned footballers throughout Europe, against the German national team.

Script [from a story by Yabo Yablonsky, Djordje Milicevic and Jeff Maguire] spends so much effort extolling man's basic goodness and the values of selflessness, teamwork and fair play, that it frequently softens the action. Fortunately, director John Huston has such a firm grip on the dramatic line that does exist – and works some very good performances from the cast, particularly Caine – that the pic (lensed entirely in Hungary) survives intact.

▪▪▪▪▪▪▪▪▪▪▪▪▪▪▪▪▪▪▪▪▪▪▪▪▪▪▪

■ **VICTORY AT SEA**

1954, 97 MINS, US ⑫

Scr Henry Salomon, Richard Hanser   *Ed* Isaac Kleinerman   *Mus* Richard Rodgers
● (NBC Film Division)

Originally presented on NBC as a 26-part filmed documentary of World War II naval history, the television *Victory at Sea* was compressed to 97 minutes for theatrical release. But despite the loss of many fine scenes of the original the edited print is still a forceful pictorial chronicle of the Allies' global sea campaigns against the Axis Powers.

Sea covers the period from the Axis' 1939 ascendancy to its defeat in 1945. Among key points captured by the cameras are the Japanese attack on Pearl Harbor, the Allied invasion of Normandy, the sweep of the US fleets through the Pacific, the North African invasion, the atomic bombing of Japan and the liberation of the prisoners of Dachau, Buchenwald and other infamous concentration camps.

Alexander Scourby's narration of the commentary written by Henry Salomon and Richard Hanser is unobtrusive and never detracts from the screen movement. Quality of the print is good considering the varied origin and age of the footage.

▪▪▪▪▪▪▪▪▪▪▪▪▪▪▪▪▪▪▪▪▪▪▪▪▪▪▪

■ **VICTORY THROUGH AIR POWER**

1943, 65 MINS, US ◇

Dir H.C. Potter, Clyde Geronimi, Jack Kinney, James Algar   *Prod* Walt Disney   *Scr* Alexander P. de Seversky, T. Hee, Erdman Penner, William Cottrell, Jim Bodrero, George Stallings, Jose Rodriguez   *Ph* Ray Rennahan   *Ed* Jack Dennis   *Mus* Edward Plumb, Paul J. Smith, Oliver Wallace   *Art Dir* Richard Irvine
● Alexander P. de Seversky (Walt Disney)

Historically, albeit kaleidoscopically, Disney and Major Alexander P. de Seversky trace the progress of aviation in 65 snappy minutes, a combination of super-animation, all in color, plus Technicolored photography with the major himself participating.

It flashes back from the prophetic Gen. Billy Mitchell – to whom the film is dedicated – to 1903 when the Wright Bros first succeeded in lifting a heavier-than-air craft off the ground.

In cartoon and narration is traced the Luftwaffe's exploits, plus the concluding arguments by de Seversky of how to beat Hitler in his Fortress Europa and how to overcome the Japs' air-based advantages.

Disney and his battalion of artists, animators and backgrounders have not permitted the seriousness of the theme to completely dwarf their humor. There are the usual imaginative complement of Disneyisms in his cartoonics, and an excellent musical score to point it up.
□ 1943: Nomination: Best Scoring of a Dramatic Picture

▪▪▪▪▪▪▪▪▪▪▪▪▪▪▪▪▪▪▪▪▪▪▪▪▪▪▪

■ **VIDEODROME**

1983, 88 MINS, CANADA ◇ ⑫

Dir David Cronenberg   *Prod* Claude Heroux   *Scr* David Cronenberg   *Ph* Mark Irwin   *Ed* Ronald Sanders   *Mus* Howard Shore   *Art Dir* Carol Spier
● James Woods, Sonja Smits, Deborah Harry, Peter Dvorsky, Les Carlson, Jack Creley (Filmplan)

V

Story concerns a small-time cable TV outlet in Toronto. The quasi-clandestine operation is run by Max Renn (James Woods) who's ever on the lookout for offbeat and erotic material.

He becomes fascinated with a program called Videodrome, picked up from a satellite by a station technician. The show appears to be little more than a series of torture sequences, primarily involving women.

Renn pursues the program but is blocked at every turn. One of his suppliers warns him that the activities on the show are not staged. However, he perseveres, making contact with a McLuhanesque media guru named Brian O'Blivion (Jack Creley).

Film is dotted with video jargon and ideology which proves more fascinating than distancing. And Cronenberg amplifies the freaky situation with a series of stunning visual effects.

Woods aptly conveys Renn's obsession and eventual bondage to the television nightmare. Sonja Smits is an alluring and mysterious femme fatale and Deborah Harry seems just right as Renn's girlfriend who thrives on and is undone by Videodrome's games cruelty.

■ **VIETNAM, TEXAS**

1990, 85 MINS, US ◇ ▽
Dir Robert Ginty *Prod* Robert Ginty, Ron Joy *Scr* Tom Badal, C. Courtney Joyner *Ph* Robert M. Baldwin Jr *Ed* Jonathan P. Shaw *Mus* Richard Stone *Art Dir* Kate J. Sullivan
● Robert Ginty, Haing S. Ngor, Tim Thomersen, Kiev Chinh, Tamlyn Tomita (Epic)

Good intentions are roughly served in this uneven actioner that displays some compassion for the stateside Vietnam community while exploiting its violent elements.

Robert Ginty, who also directed, stars as Father Thomas McCain, a Vietnam vet turned priest who still suffers guilt about the Vietnamese woman he abandoned – pregnant with his child – when he returned to the States. Fifteen years later, he tracks them down in Houston's Little Saigon and forces himself into their lives, despite the fact that his former flame Mailan (Kieu Chinh) is now comfortably established as the wife of a vicious drug runner, Wong (Haing S. Ngor).

Ginty hooks up with his old soldier buddy Max (Tim Thomerson), now a dissolute bar owner, and they set out to reach Mailan and her teenage daughter Lan (Tamlyn Tomita), setting off beatings and murders as they run up against Wong's henchmen.

Among its plusses, pic features numerous Asian roles, with Tomita a standout as the spirited teenage daughter. Ngor (*The Killing Fields*) is suitable chilling as Wong.

■ **VIEW TO A KILL, A**

1985, 131 MINS, UK ◇ ▽ ⊙
Dir John Glen *Prod* Albert R. Broccoli, Michael G. Wilson *Scr* Richard Maibaum, Michael G. Wilson *Ph* Alan Hume *Ed* Peter Davies *Mus* John Barry *Art Dir* Peter Lamont
● Roger Moore, Christopher Walken, Tanya Roberts, Grace Jones, Patrick Macnee, Patrick Bauchan (Eon/United Arists)

Bond's adversary this time is the international industrialist Max Zorin (Christopher Walken) and his love-hate interest, May Day (Grace Jones). Bond tangles with them at their regal horse sale and uncovers a profitable scheme in which microchips are surgically implanted in the horse to assure an easy victory.

Horse business is moderately entertaining, particularly when Patrick Macnee is on screen as Bond's chauffeur accomplice. Action, however, jumps abruptly to San Francisco to reveal Zorin's true motives. He's hatching some master plan to pump water

from the sea into the San Andreas fault causing a major earthquake, destroying the Silicon Valley and leaving him with the world's microchip monopoly.

While Bond pics have always traded heavily on the camp value of its characters, *A View to a Kill* almost attacks the humor, practically winking at the audience with every move.

As for Roger Moore, making his seventh appearance as Bond, he is right about half the time. He still has the suave and cool for the part, but on occasion he looks a bit old and his womanizing seems dated when he does.

■ **VIGIL**

1984, 90 MINS, NEW ZEALAND ◇ ▽
Dir Vincent Ward *Prod* John Maynard *Scr* Vincent Ward, Graeme Tetley *Ph* Alun Bollinger *Ed* Simon Reece *Mus* Jack Body *Art Dir* Kai Hawkins
● Penelope Stewart, Frank Whitten, Bill Kerr, Fiona Kay (Film Investment/NZFC)

Central figure is 11-year-old Toss (Fiona Kay), on the threshold of womanhood and caught in the tragedy of the death of her father and the coincidental arrival of a stranger, Ethan (Frank Whitten). It is primarily through her eyes, actions and interpretation of events, that the impact of Ethan's presence upon the household is registered.

While Toss is fascinated by Ethan's mysterious aura, her mother Elizabeth (Penelope Stewart) is reawakened from a joyless marriage, and her grandfather Birdie (Bill Kerr) finds a comrade for his eccentric pranks and grandiose mechanical inventions.

The remarkable quality of the film is the way it gives fresh resonance to universal themes.

■ **VIKINGS, THE**

1958, 114 MINS, US ◇ ▽
Dir Richard Fleischer *Prod* Jerry Bresler *Scr* Calder Willingham *Ph* Jack Cardiff *Ed* Elmo Williams *Mus* Mario Nascimbene *Art Dir* Harper Goff
● Kirk Douglas, Tony Curtis, Ernest Borgnine, Janet Leigh, Alexander Knox, Frank Thring (United Artists/Bryna)

The Vikings is spectacular, rousing and colorful. Blood flows freely as swords are crossed and arrows meet their mark in barbarian combat. And there's no hesitance about throwing a victim into a wolf pit or a pool of crabs.

There is some complication at the start, however, as the various characters are brought into view – as the Viking army of 200 raids the Kingdom of Northumbria, in England, and elements of mystery and intrigue are brought into the story. But it is not too long before the screenplay [from the novel by Edison Marshall] and director Richard Fleischer have their people in clear focus.

History is highly fictionalized. It starts with the raid, the death of the English leader, the succession to the throne of Frank Thring who's strictly the heavy. The queen is with child, the father being Ernest Borgnine, head of the marauding Vikings. To escape the new king's wrath she flees to another land and with the proper passage of time the child, now a young man (Tony Curtis), turns up in the Viking village as a slave whose identity is not known.

It is at this point that Curtis encounters Kirk Douglas, latter as heir to the Viking throne. Neither is aware of the fact that the other is his brother. They clash. Janet Leigh participates as daughter of the king of Wales who is to be taken as a bride by the sadistic English king. Douglas falls for Leigh in a big way but she comes to favor Curtis, and thus is established the romantic triangle.

It's the production that counts and producer Jerry Bresler, working with Douglas' indie outfit, has done it up big and with apparent authenticity. Lensing was in the Norse fjord area and various parts of Europe, including the Bavarian Studios.

Douglas, doing a bangup, freewheeling job as the ferocious and disfigured Viking fighter, fits the part splendidly. Borgnine's Viking chief is a conqueror of authority.

■ **VILLAGE OF THE DAMNED**

1960, 77 MINS, US ▽
Dir Wolf Rilla *Prod* Ronald Kinnoch *Scr* Stirling Silliphant, Wolf Rilla, George Barclay *Ph* Geoffrey Faithfull *Ed* Gordon Hales *Mus* Ron Goodwin *Art Dir* Ivan King
● George Sanders, Barbara Shelley, Michael Gwynn, Laurence Naismith, John Phillips, Richard Vernon (M-G-M)

Plot kicks around what is not an uninteresting idea. A little British village comes under the spell of some strange, supernatural force which first puts everybody out for the count. Then the villagers come to and find that every woman capable of being pregnant is.

Snag is that all the children are little monsters. They all look alike – fair haired, unblinking stare and with intellects the equivalent of adults, plus the knack of mental telepathy. George Sanders, a physicist, is intimately involved, since his wife is the mother of the leader of the little gang of abnormal moppets. Sanders decides to probe the mystery.

If there had happend to be any hint of why this remarkable business should have occurred, the film [from the novel *The Midwich Cuckoos* by John Wyndham] would have been slightly more plausible. As it is, this just tapers off from a taut beginning into soggy melodrama. Wolf Rilla's direction is adequate, but no more.

■ **VILLAIN**

1971, 98 MINS, UK ◇ ▽
Dir Michael Tuchner *Prod* Alan Ladd Jr, Jay Kanter *Scr* Dick Clement, Ian La Frenais *Ph* Christopher Challis *Ed* Ralph Sheldon *Mus* Jonathan Hodge *Art Dir* Maurice Carter
● Richard Burton, Ian McShane, Nigel Davenport, Donald Sinden, Fiona Lewis, T.P. McKenna (Anglo-EMI)

Dick Clement and Ian La Frenais's screenplay, adapted by Al Lettieri, and based on a James Barlow novel [*The Burden of Proof*], uses a frayed shoestring plot of a payroll stickup to flesh out the sadistic actions of Richard Burton as a onetime nightclub bouncer with a handy razor who has become one of the major figures of the London underworld. It isn't just a penchant for cutting and slicing that makes our man tick. He has an entire assortment of quirks.

Tied to a dying mother (Cathleen Nesbitt) by a silver cord stronger than steel cable, he also is a homosexual but no run-of-the-subway version. He has a thing about a petty criminal (Ian McShane) that makes him beat him up, then bed down with him. His bete noir, however, is a dedicated police inspector (Nigel Davenport) whose sole duty is to pin something on him.

Support is strong with top honors going to Joss Ackland as a thief with an ulcer; Donald Sinden, as a Member of Parliament with not quite standard sexual demands which, naturally, makes him an ideal blackmail prospect; and T.P. McKenna, as another gang leader.

■ **VILLAIN, THE**

1979, 93 MINS, US ◇ ▽
Dir Hal Needham *Prod* Mort Engelberg *Scr* Robert G. Kane *Ph* Bobby Byrne *Ed* Walter Hannemann *Mus* Bill Justis *Art Dir* Carl Anderson

VILLA RIDES

● Kirk Douglas, Ann-Margret, Arnold Schwarzenegger, Paul Lynde, Ruth Buzzi, Jack Elam (Columbia/Rastar)

Idea for the satire must have looked great on paper. Why not take all the standard sagebrush types – the handsome stranger, the decollete femme, the evil outlaw, etc. – and put them through a parody of their usual paces?

The answer no one came up with was that without any depth of characterization, and only the flimsiest plot structure, a take-off has nowhere to go. Hal Needham, again dazzles audiences with some eye-popping stunts but the film gets lost in the dust.

With Kirk Douglas in the title role, Arnold Schwarzenegger as the good guy, and Ann-Margret as the lascivious girl who loves being fought over, *The Villain* becomes even more of a disappointment. Rarely has so much talent been used to so little purpose.

••••••••••••••••••••••••••••••

■ VILLA RIDES

1968, 125 MINS, US ◇ ⓦ
Dir Buzz Kulik   *Prod* Ted Richmond   *Scr* Robert Towne, Sam Peckinpah   *Ph* Jack Hildyard   *Ed* David Bretherton   *Mus* Maurice Jarre   *Art Dir* Ted Haworth
● Yul Brynner, Robert Mitchum, Grazia Buccella, Charles Bronson, Robert Viharo, Herbert Lom (Paramount)

Villa Rides is a pseudo-biopic of a portion of the bandit career of Mexico's folk hero, Pancho Villa, with Yul Brynner in title role.

Ted Richmond's handsome exterior production, filmed in 1967 in Spain, is competently, if leisurely and routinely, directed with the accent on violent death.

Script [based on the book *Pancho Villa* by William Douglas Lansford, adapted by the author] fails to establish clearly the precise political framework, while over-developing some lesser details. This, plus overlength, adds up to dramatic tedium.

Film concerns itself with Villa's own aggressive acts. With the aid of Charles Bronson and Robert Viharo, Brynner is responsible for the on-screen deaths of literally dozens of men, most explicitly detailed.

Brynner makes Villa sympathetic at times, as a man fighting for human rights, though that's a bit hard to swallow since his philosophy does not get spelled out for 105 minutes into the film. His rationalization is rather facile and specious: those he killed were 'traitors,' by his convenient self-excusing definition.

••••••••••••••••••••••••••••••

■ VINCENT AND THEO

1990, 138 MINS, UK/FRANCE/NETHERLANDS/ITALY ◇ ⓦ
Dir Robert Altman   *Prod* Ludi Boeken   *Scr* Julian Mitchell   *Ph* Jean Lepine   *Ed* Francoise Auger   *Mus* Gabriel Yared   *Art Dir* Stephen Altman
● Tim Roth, Paul Rhys, Jip Wijngaarden, Johanna Ter Steege, Jean-Pierre Cassel, Anna Covas (Belbo/Central/La Sept/Telepool/RAI Uno/Vara/Sofica Valor)

A study of Van Gogh's last years as seen through his tortured relationship with his brother, *Vincent and Theo* paradoxically is one of Robert Altman's most cinematically conventional films as well as one of his most deeply personal. Bearing little resemblance to the glamorized, overheated Vincente Minnelli 1956 biopic *Lust for Life*, this masterwork operates in the intimate, thoughtful vein of the great BBC bios of artistic figures.

Altman and his incisive scripter Julian Mitchell focus on Vincent's obsessive devotion to his craft and the failure of his overly timid art dealer-brother to win him acceptance in an art world that scorned his idiosyncratic genius.

The heart of the film is its exploration of the destructive, unacknowledged but important relationship between artist and patron.

Paul Rhys skillfully inhabits a character even more wretchedly unhappy than his brother, who at least has the consolation of his art, and Theo's own incipient madness gives the film much of its unsettling tone.

Tim Roth powerfully conveys Vincent's heroic, obsessive concentration on his work, and then resultant loneliness and isolation.

••••••••••••••••••••••••••••••

■ VINCENT
THE LIFE AND DEATH OF VINCENT VAN GOGH

1987, 103 MINS, AUSTRALIA/NETHERLANDS ◇ ⓦ
Dir Paul Cox   *Prod* Tony Llewellyn-Jones   *Scr* Paul Cox   *Ph* Paul Cox   *Ed* Paul Cox   *Mus* Norman Kaye   *Art Dir* Neil Angwin
● (Illumination/Look/Ozfilms/Dasha)

This very special art film is neither documentary nor fiction. Paul Cox, one of Australia's foremost directors, was born in Holland and has made an exquisite, timeless tribute to Vincent Van Gogh using as his text simply the letters Vincent wrote to his brother Theo, letters beautifully read by John Hurt.

Van Gogh worked as a painter for only 10 years, and during that period produced about 1,800 works, but when he killed himself at 37 in 1890 he had only sold one of them, and was unknown and impoverished. Cox' film covers those last 10 years but, save for one brief moment at the end, when Van Gogh's funeral is depicted, the central character of the drama is never seen. His thoughts and philosophies are enunciated superbly on the soundtrack.

Cox traveled to the places Van Gogh knew, lived and worked. The images accompanying the text are of trees and fields and birds in flight, and the inevitable sunflowers. And, of course, there are the paintings themselves.

••••••••••••••••••••••••••••••

■ VIOLENT PLAYGROUND

1958, 108 MINS, UK
Dir Basil Dearden   *Prod* Michael Relph   *Scr* James Kennaway   *Ph* Reginald Wyer   *Ed* Arthur Stevens   *Mus* Philip Green   *Art Dir* Maurice Carter
● Stanley Baker, Anne Heywood, David McCallum, Peter Cushing, John Slater, Clifford Evans (Rank)

Violent Playground brings a sincere semi-documentary touch to the matter of juve delinquency. James Kennaway's human and literate screenplay is convincingly acted against authentic Liverpool backgrounds. Result is an absorbing film that works up to an overlong but tense climax.

Film concerns an experiment made in Liverpool in 1949. Policemen have become Juvenile Liaison Officers whose job is to keep an eye on mischievous youngsters and steer them away from crime. Stanley Baker gives a vigorous and sympathetic performance as a cop who is taken off the investigation of a series of unexplained fires for this work. He becomes particularly involved with one family and discovers who is responsible for the arson.

There are a number of other very creditable performances, notably David McCallum as the young delinquent, Peter Cushing as a very serious but wholehearted priest, Clifford Evans as a schoolmaster and in her first big chance, as David McCallum's elder sister, Anne Heywood.

••••••••••••••••••••••••••••••

■ VIOLENT SATURDAY

1955, 90 MINS, US ◇
Dir Richard Fleischer   *Prod* Buddy Adler   *Scr* Sydney Boehm   *Ph* Charles G. Clarke   *Ed* Louis Loeffler   *Mus* Hugo Friedhofer
● Victor Mature, Richard Egan, Stephen McNally, Virginia Leith, Lee Marvin, Sylvia Sidney (20th Century-Fox)

Lensed on location in Arizona in a modern-day setting, the film concerns the bank rob-

bery planned by a cool trio played by Stephen McNally, Lee Marvin and J. Carrol Naish.

As their preparations for the holdup unfold, several subplots are set up.

Purpose of all the subplots is to set the stage for the holdup, where they all fall into place and are solved by the events of the holdup and what follows. They're highly contrived and unconvincing, but they do serve the purpose of giving the film a greater sense of scope and power.

Climax comes with the robbery itself and the getaway. It's here that the screen version of the William L. Heath novel strips the action of the non-essentials and turns on the heat in a powerful windup that's worth the waiting.

••••••••••••••••••••••••••••••

■ VIPER

1988, 94 MINS, US ◇
Dir Peter Maris   *Prod* Peter Maris   *Scr* Frank Kerr   *Ph* Gerald Wolfe   *Ed* Jack Tucker   *Mus* Scott Roewe
● Linda Purl, James Tolkan, Jeff Kober, Ken Force, Chris Robinson, David M. Sterling (Maris)

Viper is a well-crafted, riveting action drama which gets the job done efficiently and entertainingly. Pic is a companion piece to filmmaker Peter Maris' previous action *Terror Squad*, which dealt with a group of Libyan terrorists who invade America via Indiana (!) and hold a classroom of kids hostage. In *Viper*, it is a special US military unit that pretends to be Middle Eastern terrorists and takes over a building at a university in Indiana, in order to fake an incident that will allow the government to launch a reprisal mission. The plan goes awry quickly and our hero Jim McCalla (Chris Robinson) steals evil mission commander Col Tanzer's (James Tolkan) top-secret file on the project in order to go public, but is killed ruthlessly by a car bomb.

This leaves his mousy wife Laura (Linda Purl, very well cast) as a target for the heavies who want the file back. Ultimately, she's given a backbone and taught how to fight back (with hand grenades and automatic weaponry) by her husband's army buddy Trueblood (Ken Foree).

Vivid chase scenes and tech credits are fine.

••••••••••••••••••••••••••••••

■ V.I.P.S, THE

1963, 119 MINS, UK ◇
Dir Anthony Asquith   *Prod* Anatole de Grunwald   *Scr* Terence Rattigan   *Ph* Jack Hildyard   *Ed* Frank Clarke   *Mus* Miklos Rozsa
● Elizabeth Taylor, Richard Burton, Louis Jourdan, Margaret Rutherford, Maggie Smith, Rod Taylor (M-G-M)

This has suspense, conflict, romance, comedy and drama. Its main fault is that some of the characters and the by-plots are not developed enough. But that is a risk inevitable in any film in which a number of strangers are flung together, each with problems and linked by a single circumstance.

In this case the setting is London Airport and the basic problem is the necessity for at least four of the Very Important Passengers bound for the States to get out of the country pronto. Their plans go haywire when a thick fog grounds all planes overnight.

Terence Rattigan's screenplay juggles these situations and does not neglect many of the star performers. The script has literate, witty and sometimes touching dialog and Anthony Asquith has directed skillfully, in that though there is the sense of bustle inseparable from any international airport he has retained a sympathetic feeling of intimacy for all his characters.

Principal story, that of the business tycoon who has taken his wife for granted and now looks set to lose her, is played out by Elizabeth Taylor, Richard Burton and Louis Jourdan as the lover. Maybe Taylor needs a sabbatical but there is a feeling of ordinariness about her thesping.

Burton, however, gives a top-league performance as the business chief who eventually regains his wife but only after a few hours of taut misery, humiliating and self-enlightenment. Jourdan is also excellent as the would-be lover and he has one scene with Burton which is a little masterpiece of dual virtuosity.

□ 1963: Best Supp. Actress (Margaret Rutherford)

● ●

■ **VIRGIN AND THE GYPSY, THE**

1970, 95 MINS, UK ◇ ⊛
Dir Christopher Miles   *Prod* Kenneth Harper   *Scr* Alan Plater   *Ph* Bob Huke   *Ed* Paul Davies   *Mus* Patrick Gowers   *Art Dir* Terence Knight
● Joanna Shimkus, Franco Nero, Honor Blackman, Mark Burns, Maurice Denham, Fay Compton (De Grunwald)

D. H. Lawrence's last unpolished novella, *The Virgin and the Gypsy* is about a young English girl's awakening to adult life in northern England, circa 1921. While faithful perhaps to the author, film is a stilted period piece.

Joanna Shimkus and Harriett Harper are two rural sisters returning from a French school to a provincial environment, ruled by grandmother Fay Compton. Puppets in the household include rector-father Maurice Denham, aunt Kay Walsh, uncle Norman Bird, and maid Janet Chappell.

Shimkus (whose mother abandoned her family's stultifying influence) grows restive, and finds a sexual stirring under Franco Nero's gaze, plus sympathetic adult companionship from Honor Blackman and Mark Burns, who are living together and evoking prissy clucks from the townsfolk.

● ●

■ **VIRGINIA CITY**

1940, 123 MINS, US ⊛
Dir Michael Curtiz   *Prod* Hal B. Wallis (exec.)
Scr Robert Buckner   *Ph* Sol Polito   *Ed* George Amy   *Mus* Max Steiner   *Art Dir* Ted Smith
● Errol Flynn, Miriam Hopkins, Randolph Scott, Humphrey Bogart, Frank McHugh, Alan Hale (Warner)

On the theory, perhaps, that one good western deserves another, Warner Bros follows up *Dodge City*, starring Errol Flynn, with another saga of the land of the blazing sunsets entitled *Virginia City*. As a shoot 'em up, the picture is first class; as a bit of cinematic history telling, it is far short of the possibilities indicated by the title and cast.

It's about the cache of $5 million in gold bullion which Confederate sympathizers are reported to have offered to the cause of the Southern states during the Civil War. The catch, of course, is how to get the gold out of Nevada and through Union scouting lines.

Flynn is first shown as a Union captive in Libby prison, from which he and companions escape, later to be assigned to travel across the plains and thwart the conspiracy by which the Confederacy hoped to come in possession of all that gold from the Nevada hills. Miriam Hopkins is a singer in a Virginia City saloon and travels west on the stage with Flynn. She is a rebel spy, fresh from a meeting with Jeff Davis. There's the romance.

En route, the stage is held up by John Murrell, outlaw, who is really Humphrey Bogart behind a slick-waxed mustache. There's the chase.

And in Virginia City is Randolph Scott, secretly planning the removal of the gold, which is to be taken south in a wagon train. Scott also is much in love with Hopkins, who leans heavily towards Flynn. She betrays Flynn into a trap, thus placing patriotism ahead of love. There's the drama.

Michael Curtiz, the director, has taken all this and steamed it up with some noisy trigger work, charging cavalry, dance-hall intima-

cies and the burning sands of the desert to concoct a bustling western, which is replete with action, although short on credulity.

● ●

■ **VIRGINIAN, THE**

1929, 92 MINS, US ⊛
Dir Victor Fleming   *Scr* Howard Estabrook
● Gary Cooper, Walter Huston, Mary Brian, Chester Conklin, Eugene Pallette, E.H. Calvert (Paramount)

This Paramount production takes the old play dirt of ancient plains pictures, shuffles it around a bit, and makes of the Owen Wister and Kirk La Shelle story 92 minutes of drama and comedy.

There's an anti-climax toward the middle, one of the most harrowing and vivid sequences ever before the lenses. It is when the silent and lanky Virginian (Gary Cooper) is forced to give the signal which sends his pal, Steve (Richard Arlen), along with three other cattle rustlers, galloping to their death in nooses.

Trampas (Walter Huston), the menace, is saved from the hanging to bait along the story for the vengeance climax.

The school mam, played by the pretty Mary Brian, doesn't fly at the neck of the tall backwoodsman. She teases him, letting him use the old gag of rescuing her from a frightened cow and then promptly bawling him out. This provides Cooper with a chance for a bit of by-play and wise-cracking with Arlen as a sincere but out-for-easy-dough Steve.

● ●

■ **VIRGINIAN, THE**

1946, 83 MINS, US ◇
Dir Stuart Gilmore   *Prod* Paul Jones   *Scr* Frances Goodrich, Albert Hackett   *Ph* Harry Hallenberger   *Ed* Everett Douglas   *Mus* Daniele Amfitheatrof   *Art Dir* Hans Dreier, John Meehan
● Joel McCrea, Brian Donlevy, Sonny Tufts, Barbara Britton, Fay Bainter, Henry O'Neill (Paramount)

The Virginian stands up pretty well over the years. First filmed in 1914 for the silents, then in 1929 (by Par), the present version of the Owen Wister novel is still a pleasant, flavorsome western, with much of the old charm of a daguerreotype.

Although story is a little dated as well as a mite slow, the yarn is still a satisfactory romance, with enough shooting and suspense to offset the plodding pace. Yarn hasn't been changed much, still being the story of the little schoolmarm from Vermont and the cowboy from Virginia, who meet in Montana and wed, after the hero has disposed of a few troublesome cow rustlers.

Costumes of the eastern 1870s, the early-type railroads, the horse riding and cow roundups, the rolling Montana hills, all help in the nostalgic flavor.

Joel McCrea follows soundly in footsteps of Dustin Farnum and Gary Cooper as The ('When You Call Me That, Smile') Virginian, with a straightforward characterization. Barbara Britton is pert and pretty as the schoolteacher. Brian Donlevy, as the rustler, and Sonny Tufts, in his first western role as a misguided cowhand, head an okay supporting cast.

● ●

■ **VIRGIN SOLDIERS, THE**

1969, 96 MINS, UK ◇ ⊛
Dir John Dexter   *Prod* Leslie Gilliat, Ned Sherrin   *Scr* John Hopkins, Ian La Frenais   *Ph* Ken Higgins   *Ed* Thelma Connell   *Mus* Peter Greenwell   *Art Dir* Frank White
● Lynn Redgrave, Hywel Bennett, Nigel Davenport, Nigel Patrick, Rachel Kempson, Jack Shepherd (Columbia/Foreman)

Much of the irony and subtlety of Leslie Thomas's novel have been ironed out in favor

of a broader approach to the humor. Nevertheless, *The Virgin Soldiers* comes out as a bright and affectionate peek at the trials and tribulations of young National Service rookies.

Though the writers have concentrated mainly on making the film ruefully funny, the serious side has not been neglected. The smell of death is often just around the corner and violence in the jungle and streets of terrorist-infested Malaya is in striking, effective contrast to the boisterous, bawdy, barrack-room atmosphere.

Acting all around is first rate, though only a few characters are allowed to develop.

Redgrave as the sulky heroine has her moments but creates no sympathy and, in fact, is mainly dull, but Tsai Chin makes joyful capital out of her small but lively role as the local prostie.

● ●

■ **VISIONS OF EIGHT**

1973, 110 MINS, US ◇ ⊛
Dir Milos Forman, Kon Ichikawa, Claude Lelouch, Yuri Ozerov, Arthur Penn, Michael Pfleghar, John Schlesinger, Mai Zetterling   *Prod* Stan Margulies   *Ph* Arthur Wooster, Igor Slabnevich, Rune Ericson, Ernst Wild, Walter Lassally, Masuo Yamaguchi, Daniel Bocly, Jorgen Persson   *Ed* Robert Lambert, Jim Clark, Edward Roberts, Dede Allen, Margot von Schlieffen, Catherine Bernard, Lars Hagstrom   *Mus* Henry Mancini
● (Wolper)

Producer David Wolper recruited eight (originally 10) name directors to choose a segment of the 1972 Munich Olympics and give his / her view of the event on a smaller plane.

The problem is that many of the sketches sometimes forget the idea of sport and competition itself, to indulge in ideas. But the flurry, crowds and human endeavor are there, and in the background the tragic terrorist events that led to the massacre of Israeli athletes by Arab terrorists.

Russo film maker Yuri Ozerov starts the ball rolling with *The Beginning*. Mai Zetterling looks at weightlifters in *The Strongest*, a mannered seg but quite funny and well edited. Arthur Penn has a stylized look at pole-vaulting in *The Highest*. Michael Pfleghar devoted himself to women in various events.

Kon Ichikawa, who helmed the remarkable *Tokyo Olympiad* [1965], delves into the 300-meter dash, stretching it in time. Claude Lelouch concentrates on losers, and gets some laughable and even pathetic insights at times. Milos Forman lenses the harsh decathlon to milk comic relief from it. John Schlesinger winds it with a sentimental homage to a British marathon runner who loses.

● ●

■ **VITAL SIGNS**

1990, 103 MINS, US ◇ ⊛ ☉
Dir Marisa Silver   *Prod* Laurie Perlman, Cathleen Summers   *Scr* Larry Ketron, Jeb Stuart   *Ph* John Lindley   *Ed* Robert Brown, Danford B. Greene   *Mus* Miles Goodman   *Art Dir* Todd Hallowell
● Adrian Pascar, Diane Lane, Jimmy Smits, Norma Aleandro, Jack Gwaltney, Laura San Giacomo (20th Century-Fox)

Vital Signs is a strikingly well-done ensemble piece about a pivotal year in the lives of a group of medical students, with polished script, direction and performances.

As a gifted doctor-to-be who oozes charm and good looks, Adrian Pasdar is the focus of this group of serious strivers navigating their tough third year at LA Central's med school. Diane Lane is the crisp but compassionate fellow student he falls in love with. Jack Gwaltney plays the blander, grimmer fellow from a less-advantaged background who's determined not to let Pasdar surpass him.

Interesting subplots are played out in the relationship of Gwaltney and his neglected wife (Laura San Giacomo, in an effective but unexciting plain-jane turn), and the amusing discomfort of best pals Jane Adams and Tim Ransom after they cross into romantic involvement.

Director Marisa Silver does a good job of getting across characters' emotional lives, making these mainstream twentysomething types absorbing, and fashions a crisply moving story.

....

■ VIVACIOUS LADY

1938, 90 MINS, US Ⓥ
Dir George Stevens *Prod* George Stevens *Scr* P.J. Wolfson, Ernest Pagano *Ph* Robert de Grasse *Ed* Henry Berman *Mus* Roy Webb (dir.) *Art Dir* Van Nest Polglase
● Ginger Rogers, James Stewart, James Ellison, Beulah Bondi, Charles Coburn, Frances Mercer (RKO)

Vivacious Lady is entertainment of the highest order and broadest appeal. Story by I.A.R. Wylie tells the romantic adventures and tribulations of a New York cabaret singer and a youthful college professor.

It is a case of love at first sight, a speedy wooing and hasty marriage. Then the young man takes his bride to the small town and introduces her to his family and associates. Prejudice and stern respectability resist the invasion. Manner in which approval of the marriage is won from the boy's parents is amusingly accomplished.

In their predicament of living apart until the conventional amenities of proper introduction into society are observed, Ginger Rogers and James Stewart undergo a series of connubial disappointments, interruptions ad interferences.

Beulah Bondi is the understanding mother-in-law and Charles Coburn is excellent as the father of the bridegroom.
☐ 1938: Nominations: Best Cinematography, Sound

....

■ VIVA KNIEVEL!

1977, 104 MINS, US ◇ Ⓥ
Dir Gordon Douglas *Prod* Stan Hough *Scr* Antonio Santillan *Ph* Fred Jackman *Ed* Harold Kress *Mus* Charles Bernstein
● Evel Knievel, Gene Kelly, Marjoe Gortner, Lauren Hutton, Leslie Nielsen, Red Buttons (Warner/Corwin)

In the most daring feat of his career, Evel Knievel leaps over a mountain of blazing cliches and a cavernous plot, somehow landing upright to the predictable cheers of his legions of fans.

Actually, Evel the actor emerges from the wreck in better shape than the bent careers of his veteran co-stars, Gene Kelly, Marjoe Gortner, Red Buttons, Lauren Hutton and Leslie Nielsen. For him, it's a chance to show he can be fairly natural in front of the camera when the demands are minimal; for them, it's a credit best forgotten.

Plot: evil Leslie Nielsen will lure the leaper to Mexico where he'll kill Knievel and steal his red-white-and-blue truck, substituting an identical red-white-and-blue truck whose sides are packed with illegal white powder.

....

■ VIVA LAS VEGAS

1964, 85 MINS, US ◇ Ⓥ ☉
Dir George Sidney *Prod* Jack Cummings, George Sidney *Scr* Sally Benson *Ph* Joseph Biroc *Ed* John McSweeney *Mus* George Stoll *Art Dir* George W. Davis, Edward Carfagno
● Elvis Presley, Ann-Margret, Cesare Danova, William Demarest, Nicky Blair, Jack Carter (M-G-M)

The sizzling combination of Elvis Presley and Ann-Margret is enough to carry *Viva Las Vegas* over the top. The picture is fortunate in having two such commodities for bait, be-

cause beyond several flashy musical numbers, a glamorous locale and one electrifying auto race sequence, the production is a pretty trite and heavyhanded affair, puny in story development and distortedly preoccupied with anatomical oomph.

The film is designed to dazzle the eye, assault the ear and ignore the brain. Vegas, of course, is the setting of Sally Benson's superficial contrivance about an auto racing buff (Presley) trying to raise funds to purchase an engine for the racer with which he hopes to win the Grand Prix. His main obstacle is a swimming instructress (A-M) who doesn't approve of his goal, but ultimately softens.

Hackneyed yarn provides the skeletal excuse for about 10 musical interludes, a quick tour of the US gambling capital and that one slam-bang climactic sequence that lifts the film up by its bootstraps just when it is sorely in need of a lift.

....

■ VIVA MAX

1969, 92 MINS, US/UK ◇ Ⓥ
Dir Jerry Paris *Prod* Mark Carliner *Scr* Elliott Baker *Ph* Henri Persin *Ed* Bud Molin, David Berlatsky *Mus* Hugo Montenegro, Ralph Dino, John Sembello *Art Dir* James Hulsey
● Peter Ustinov, Pamela Tiffin, Jonathan Winters, John Astin, Keenan Wynn, Harry Morgan (Commonwealth United)

This satirical saga of a ragtail platoon of Mexican soldiers who recapture the Alamo in 1969 is a captivatingly original idea, well produced but questionably cast with Peter Ustinov in the lead. Screenplay, based on James Lehrer's novel, carries a perfectly plausible but inherently comic idea to its logical absurdities.

Ustinov is the Mexican general who leads his small band of grousing, shuffling troops across the border on the pretext of marching in a Washington Birthday parade in Laredo. Both he and John Astin, as his tough sergeant, do yeoman work, but have that vague aura of embarrassment of good actors who wonder what the director has wrought.

The film has a little something to offend a wide variety of groups – Texans, the National Guard, right-wing para-military groups, and even the Alamo defender, John Wayne.

Cameraman Henri Persin makes excellent use of the locations in San Antonio, and his matching of shots makes it impossible to tell at first viewing what was shot in Texas and what at Rome's Cinecitta Studios.

....

■ VIVA VILLA!

1934, 112 MINS, US
Dir Jack Conway *Prod* David O. Selznick *Scr* Ben Hecht *Ph* James Wong Howe, Charles G. Clarke *Ed* Robert J. Kern *Mus* Herbert Stothart *Art Dir* Harry Oliver
● Wallace Beery, Leo Carrillo, Fay Wray, Donald Cook, Joseph Schildkraut, Stuart Erwin (M-G-M)

Viva Villa! is a corking western. It's a big, impressive production which sets out to make Wallace Beery's Pancho Villa appear as a somewhat sympathetic and quasi-patriotic bandit.

But Beery's characterization, apart from the basic screen material [suggested by the book by Edgcumb Pinchon and O. B. Stade], lets Pancho down too much. His Villa is a hybrid dialectician, neither Mex nor gringo, with a vacillating accent that suffers alongside of Leo Carrillo's charming dialect or the contra-renegade version as done by Joseph Schildkraut as Pascal. Both impart an unction and a style to their cruelties that makes Beery's boorish Villa show up too sadly.

The two principal femmes are well handled by Fay Wray as the sympathetic aristocrat who is brutally assaulted and assassinated by

Villa; and Katherine DeMille (Cecil's daughter, who manifests much talent) likewise stands out. Latter's s.a. personality registers as one of Villa's casual 'brides' whom sotted newspaperman Johnny Sykes (Stuart Erwin) abracadabras in mock-marriage ritual in order to appease the requirements for ceremonials by both principals.

There is no denying the mass-movement impressiveness of the production in toto. The handling of the mob scenes on field of battle was no mean task.
☐ 1934: Best Assistant Director.
☐ Nominations: Best Picture, Writing Adaptation, Sound

....

■ VIVA ZAPATA!

1952, 112 MINS, US Ⓥ ☉
Dir Elia Kazan *Prod* Darryl F. Zanuck *Scr* John Steinbeck *Ph* Joe MacDonald *Ed* Barbara McLean *Mus* Alex North *Art Dir* Lyle Wheeler, Leland Fuller
● Marlon Brando, Jean Peters, Anthony Quinn, Joseph Wiseman, Arnold Moss, Margo (20th Century-Fox)

The story of Emiliano Zapata, a lesser-known Mexican revolutionary, is a picture that records a hard, cruel, curiously unemotional account of Mexican banditry and revolt against oppressive government. Elia Kazan's direction strives for a personal intimacy but neither he nor the John Steinbeck scripting achieves in enough measure.

Convenient use is made of historical fact as the script plays hop-skip-and-jump in spanning the nine years that Zapata was a controversial figure in Mexican political life just prior to and during the earlier part of World War I.

Marlon Brando brings to the Zapata character the same type of cold objectivity noted in script and direction. Jean Peters is the girl who becomes his bride and forsees his violent end.

There's a stark quality to the photography by Joe MacDonald that suggests the raw, hot atmosphere of Mexico.
☐ 1952: Best Supp. Actor (Anthony Quinn).
☐ Nominations: Best Actor (Marlon Brando), Story & Screenplay, Art Direction, Scoring of a Dramatic Picture

....

■ V.I. WARSHAWSKI

1991, 89 MINS, US ◇ Ⓥ ☉
Dir Jeff Kanew *Prod* Jeffrey Lurie *Scr* Edward Taylor, David Aaron Cohen, Nick Thiel *Ph* Jan Kiesser *Ed* C.Timothy O'Meara, Debra Neil *Mus* Randy Edelman *Art Dir* Barbara Ling
● Kathleen Turner, Jay O. Saunders, Charles Durning, Angela Goethals, Nancy Paul, Frederick Coffin (Hollywood/Chestnut Hill)

You can't be much worse-offski than to sit through *V.I. Warshawski*. Klutzy murder mystery [from a screen story by Edward Taylor] was obviously intended to be the first in a hoped-for series about the eponymous femme detective impersonated by Kathleen Turner.

Somewhere behind the vast underachievement here, one can discern that there was screen promise in the blue collar female dick of Sara Paretsky's novels. The daughter of a cop and a habitue of sports bars on Chicago's North Side, this salty, sexy, streetwise straight-shooter clearly could have represented a refreshing new twist on the standard issue private investigator.

The story has Warshawski getting involved in dirty business among three warring brothers. One brother, the good-looking Boom-Boom Grafalk, a former hockey player for whom V.I. has eyes, is killed in a suspicious dockside explosion. Warshawski also is responsible for Boom-Boom's 13-year-old daughter Kat (Angela Goethals), for whom she was babysitting when the girl's father was sent into permanent slumber.

From a filmmaking point of view, it is all uninspired and perfunctory, utterly lacking in a sense of style that might have made this punchy fun. Centerscreen throughout, Turner would seem to have been perfectly cast in such a sassy, confident part, but even she can't drive a totally rusty vehicle.

[For pic's UK release the handles *Detective in High Heels* were added to posters.]

. . . .

■ VIXEN!

1968, 71 MINS, US ◇

Dir Russ Meyer   *Prod* Russ Meyer   *Scr* Robert Rudelson
Ph Russ Meyer   *Ed* Russ Meyer   *Mus* Igo Kantor
Art Dir Wilfred Kues
● Erica Gavin, Harrison Page, Garth Pillsbury, Michael O'Donnell, Vincene Wallace, Robert Aiken (Eve/Coldstream)

Russ Meyer's film is another of his technically polished sexplicit dramas, this time free of physical violence and brutality, and hyped with some awkwardly developed draft-dodging and patriotism angles.

Vixen is a girl who can't say no, and she proves it every seven minutes. She finds time for her husband, too.

There is a frankness to Meyer's sex scenes, in that they are unabashed in their frequent amorality, motivated without hypocrisy, and executed with dispatch. No tortured rationalizing here (Meyer's budget – $70,000 – couldn't afford it anyway), nor any sophisticated gloss-over. His people simply meet, rut a bit, then move along. Often the sequences are hilarious in their unbelievability.

Erica Gavin is featured in title role, and besides the ample visual aspect, carries off the dramatic moments to okay effect. Garth Pillsbury is her square husband, Jon Evans her motorcycle hood brother, and Peter Carpenter the passing Mountie with whom she passes the first few minutes.

. . . .

■ VOICES

1979, 106 MINS, US ◇

Dir Robert Markowitz   *Prod* Joe Wizan   *Scr* John Herzfeld   *Ph* Alan Metzger   *Ed* Danford B. Green
Mus Jimmy Webb   *Art Dir* Richard Bianchi
● Michael Ontkean, Amy Irving, Alex Rocco, Viveca Lindfors, Barry Miller, Herbert Berghof (M-G-M)

The triumph of love, courage and determination over affliction is the theme in *Voices*, a nice enough little film with likable characters, acted well.

Michael Ontkean and Amy Irving pick up a couple of superior credits as the loving young couple. He's a rough-edged Hoboken truck driver who wants to sing, she a deaf girl who wants to dance. They're an unlikely couple, but that's the story.

John Herzfeld's script is straightforward but full of contrivances and overly obvious tugs at the heart-strings. Robert Markowitz' direction reflects the TV career that launched him into this film.

. . . .

■ VOLUNTEERS

1985, 106 MINS, US ◇

Dir Nicholas Meyer   *Prod* Richard Shepherd, Walter F. Parkes   *Scr* Ken Levine, David Isaacs   *Ph* Ric Waite
Ed Ronald Roose, Steven Polivka   *Mus* James Horner
Art Dir James Schoppe
● Tom Hanks, John Candy, Rita Wilson, Tim Thomerson, Gedde Watanabe, George Plimpton (HBO)

Volunteers is a very broad and mostly flat comedy [from a story by Keith Critchlow] about hijinx in the Peace Corps, circa 1962. Toplined Tom Hanks gets in a few good zingers as an upperclass snob doing time in Thailand, but promising premise and opening shortly descend into unduly protracted tedium.

Hanks plays Lawrence Bourne 3d, an arrogant, snide rich boy from Yale who trades places with an earnest Peace Corps designate when his gambling debts land him in danger at home. Once ensconced in a remote village, contentious couple Hanks and cohort Rita Wilson and ultra do-gooder John Candy set out to build a bridge across a river. Kidnapped and brainwashed by the commies, the gung-ho Candy disappears for a long stretch.

With Candy absent most of the time, Hanks' one-note, if sometimes clever, attitudinizing wears out its welcome after a while. He also is deprived of anyone effective to play off.

Lensed in Mexico, pic features a muddy, truly ugly look. Also present is the most offensively blatant plug for Coca-Cola yet seen in the new era of Coke-owned entertainment companies.

. . . .

■ VON RYAN'S EXPRESS

1965, 114 MINS, US ◇ ⊕

Dir Mark Robson   *Prod* Saul David   *Scr* Wendell Mayes, Joseph Landon   *Ph* William H. Daniels
Ed Dorothy Spencer   *Mus* Jerry Goldsmith   *Art Dir* Jack Martin Smith, Hilyard Brown
● Frank Sinatra, Trevor Howard, Raffaella Carra, Brad Dexter, Sergio Fantoni, John Leyton (20th Century-Fox)

Mass escape of 600 American and British prisoners-of-war across 1943 Nazi-controlled Italy lends colorful backing to this fast, suspenseful and exciting Second World War tale. Mark Robson has made realistic use of the actual Italian setting of the David Westheimer novel in garmenting his action in hard-hitting direction and sharply-drawn performances.

Frank Sinatra and Trevor Howard co-star as leaders of the escape, who, under former's initiative, seize a freight train which is bearing prisoners for delivery to the Germans in Austria and divert it across northern Italy in an attempt to find haven in Switzerland. Sinatra plays a hardboiled American Air Force colonel named Ryan, shot down by Italians and imprisoned in the camp where Howard, an equally tough British major, is senior officer.

Robson depends heavily on suspense and accompanying thrills after Sinatra and Howard take over the train.

☐ 1965: Nomination: Best Sound Effects

. . . .

■ VOYAGE OF THE DAMNED

1976, 155 MINS, UK ◇ ⊕

Dir Stuart Rosenberg   *Prod* Robert Fryer   *Scr* Steve Shagan, David Butler   *Ph* Billy Williams   *Ed* Tom Priestley   *Mus* Lalo Schifrin   *Art Dir* Wilfrid Shingleton
● Faye Dunaway, Max Von Sydow, Oskar Werner, Malcolm McDowell, Orson Welles, James Mason (ITC/Associated General)

Voyage of the Dammed is a sluggish melodrama, loaded with familiar film names who flesh out the diverse formula characters involved in this story about a ship carrying Jews away from Nazi Germany.

Based on the book by Gordon Thomas and Max Morgan-Witts, screenplay follows the form of a prototype 'ark' film, introducing the specimen couples, herein Jews deliberately loaded aboard a ship to which Cuba will deny entry permit, thereby fulfilling a Nazi propaganda plan. Max Von Sydow, a non-Nazi German, is skipper of the ship.

Fact that the story is based on an actual, and shocking, incident makes all the more disappointing its transfer to the screen. The action zigs and zags between the cluttered set of characters.

☐ 1976: Nominations: Best Supp. Actress (Lee Grant), Adapted Screenplay, Original Score

. . . .

■ VOYAGER

1991, 117 MINS, GERMANY/FRANCE ◇ ⊕

Dir Volker Schlondorff   *Prod* Eberhard Junkersdorf
Scr Volker Schlondorff, Rudy Wurlitzer   *Ph* Yorgos Arvanitis, Pierre Lhomme   *Ed* Dagmar Hirtz
Mus Stanley Myers   *Art Dir* Nicos Perakis
● Sam Shepard, Julie Delpy, Barbara Sukowa, Dieter Kirchlechner, Traci Lind, Debora-Lee Furness (Bioskop/Action)

Equal parts road movie and Greek tragedy, Volker Schlondorff's latest literary adaptation (of Max Frisch's German classic *Homo Faber*) makes good use of fine material.

In this moral tale without a moral, Walter Faber (Swiss in the book, Yank in pic) is an inveterate traveler, an engineer and pragmatist approaching middle age in the not-yet-defined postwar Europe of the 1950s. Sam Shepard is ideal as Faber, the quintessentially cool cowboy-loner-businessman.

Via black & white flashbacks, Faber recalls his days as a student in Zurich before the war: he was in love with Hanna, a German Jew pregnant with his child. Waiting for a flight to Venezuela, Faber learns that his friend Joachim married Hanna, and they had a daughter but divorced shortly afterward.

Back in New York, he decides to travel to Paris by ship. On board he meets Sabeth (Julie Delpy), 20ish and returning home after studying in the States. Faber initially ignores her until her charm and almost unbearably fragile beauty begin to take effect. Is it love or a protective, paternal instinct?

A well-told tale, with a fine cast and good tech credits.

. . . .

■ VOYAGE TO ITALY

(US: *Strangers*)

1954, 75 MINS, ITALY ⊕

Dir Roberto Rossellini   *Scr* Roberto Rossellini, Vitaliano Brancati   *Ph* Enzo Serafin   *Ed* Jolanda Benvenuti
Mus Renzo Rossellini   *Art Dir* Piero Filippone
● Ingrid Bergman, George Sanders, Leslie Daniels, Natalia Ray, Anna Proclemer, Maria Mauban (Sveva/Junior)

Story tells of an English couple, coldly moving close to divorce because of mutual incomprehension, who inherit a house near Naples. Planning to sell it, they begin suddenly to warm to the southern climate and the boisterous humanity about them. Film as a whole alternates brilliant bits with long stretches of so-so. [Version reviewed was 100-minute Italian-language one.]

Rapid change from grit to grin, especially in George Sanders, who plays Ingrid Bergman's husband, mars the effect of the warmup process by overspeeding. Tale is unevenly told, has some unhappy bits of dialog and sometimes shows the roughout form, which for its director is the final version.

Editing, for example, is characteristically abrupt. Whereas Bergman's character, given more footage, appears much clearer in delineation, Sanders lacks the needed definition enabling proper audience participation. For instance, his interlude with a prostitute begins promisingly, but the idea is not followed through. Others in cast fill in well.

. . . .

■ VOYAGE TO THE BOTTOM OF THE SEA

1961, 105 MINS, US ◇ ⊕

Dir Irwin Allen   *Prod* Irwin Allen   *Scr* Irwin Allen, Charles Bennett   *Ph* Winton C. Hoch   *Ed* George Boemler   *Mus* Paul Sawtell, Bert Shefter   *Art Dir* Jack Martin Smith, Herman A. Blumenthal
● Walter Pidgeon, Joan Fontaine, Barbara Eden, Peter Lorre, Michael Ansara, Frankie Avalon (20th Century-Fox)

Voyage is a crescendo of mounting jeopardy, an effervescent adventure in an anything-but-Pacific Ocean.

The way the story goes, this brilliant admiral (Walter Pidgeon), commander of a marvelous atomic sub that resembles a smiling Moby Dick, devises a scheme to save mankind when life on earth is suddenly threatened by a girdle of fire caused when the Van Allen Belt of Radiation encircling the globe goes berserk and erupts. Trouble is mankind does not seem to want to be saved and unable to contact the US prez (golfing?), skipper Pidgeon heads for a spot near the Marianas where he plans to orbit a Polaris and explode the heavenly blaze out into space.

Actually the title is somewhat misleading. Customers who expect a kind of advanced course in oceanography will discover only an occasional giant squid and a lot of rubbery vegetation. For the most part, *The Bottom* of director Irwin Allen's *Sea* is merely the setting for the kind of emotional calisthenics that might just as easily break out 100 feet from the tip of Mount Everest.

The acting is generally capable, about the best it can be under the trying dramatic circumstances.

■ WAGES OF FEAR
See: Sorcerer

■ WAGNER

1983, 300 MINS, UK/AUSTRIA/HUNGARY ◇ ▼
Dir Tony Palmer *Prod* Alan Wright *Scr* Charles Wood
Ph Vittorio Storaro, Nic Knowland
Graham Bunn *Art Dir* Kenneth E. Carey
● Richard Burton, Vanessa Redgrave, Gemma Craven, Marthe Keller, John Gielgud, Ralph Richardson (London Trust Cultural)

There's nothing particularly intimate or revelatory about this five-hour (plus intermission) biopic of the German 19th-century composer.

The film begins in Dresden in 1848 when Richard Wagner (Richard Burton) was beginning to gain notoriety for his compositions and grand, heroic operas. He was also actively involved in the movement for a unified Germany.

So begins a 40-year trek across Europe for the most part as a stateless artist. Brunt of the first part deals with his self-imposed exile with part two beginning with his introduction to Ludwig II who becomes his patron. Along the way there are mounting bills, political scandals and Faustian pursuits.

Burton's performance as Wagner presents an almost entirely unsympathetic picture. Vanessa Redgrave and Gemma Craven as Wagner's wives have largely thankless roles. For buffs, the film's biggest draw is watching England's acting knights – Laurence Olivier, John Gielgud, Ralph Richardson – working together for the first time on screen.

Chief attraction remains the visual components of the film which beautifully capture the era.

■ WAGON MASTER

1950, 85 MINS, US ▼ ☉
Dir John Ford *Prod* John Ford, Merian C. Cooper
Scr Frank Nugent, Patrick Ford *Ph* Bert Glennon
Ed Jack Murray *Mus* Richard Hageman *Art Dir* James Basevi
● Ben Johnson, Harry Carey Jr, Ward Bond, Joanne Dru, Alan Mowbray, Jane Darwell (RKO/Argosy)

Wagon Master is a good outdoor action film, done in the best John Ford manner. That means careful character development and movement, spiced with high spots of action, good drama and leavening comedy moments. Pic has some of the best cross-country chases.

Site of the story and the filming is Utah, and the rugged locale supplies fresh backgrounds for the action. The story deals with a wagontrain of Mormons seeking a rich valley in which to locate. They are led by Ward Bond and he hires horsetraders Ben Johnson and Harry Carey Jr to guide the pioneers to the new land.

Johnson sits his saddle mighty easily and gives the same kind of a performance, natural and likeable. Carey and Bond also come over in fine style.

■ WAIT UNTIL DARK

1967, 107 MINS, US ◇ ▼
Dir Terence Young *Prod* Mel Ferrer *Scr* Robert Carrington, Jane-Howard Carrington *Ph* Charles Lang
Ed Gene Milford *Mus* Henry Mancini *Art Dir* George Jenkins
● Audrey Hepburn, Alan Arkin, Richard Crenna, Efrem Zimbalist Jr, Jack Weston, Samantha Jones (Warner/Seven Arts)

Wait until Dark, based on Frederick Knott's legit hit, emerges as an excellent suspense drama, effective in casting, scripting, direction and genuine emotional impact. Audrey Hepburn stars as the not-so-helpless blind heroine, in a superior performance.

Plot turns on a supposedly hapless femme protagonist, an accident-blinded Hepburn. Hubby Efrem Zimbalist Jr has made his wife self-sufficient and reasonably able to fend for herself in their apartment home.

Zimbalist accidentally plays into the hands of heroin-smuggling Samantha Jones who plants a dope-loaded doll in his possession. Alan Arkin disposes of Jones, then hires Richard Crenna and Jack Weston to intimidate Hepburn into surrendering the doll.
□ 1967: Nomination: Best Actress (Audrey Hepburn)

■ WAKE ISLAND

1942, 87 MINS, US ▼
Dir John Farrow *Prod* Joseph Sistrom *Scr* W.R. Burnett, Frank Butler *Ph* Theodor Sparkuhl *Ed* LeRoy Stone *Mus* David Buttolph
● Brian Donlevy, Robert Preston, Macdonald Carey, Albert Dekker, Barbara Britton, William Bendix (Paramount)

The heroic defense of Wake Island in December 1941 by some 385 US marines has not only been reproduced as a screen feature almost minutely faithful to the facts but without stooping to cheapness in any way.

Wake Island makes it clear those men didn't fight and die in vain. True, the Japs took Wake, but the Marines took the Japs for at least four warships and hundreds of men.

Brian Donlevy is excellent as the ever-going and unexcitable major who commanded the post, while coming nearest to stealing personal glory away from the story itself are Robert Preston and William Bendix as a kind of Quirt and Flagg combination. Albert Dekker overdoes things just a bit as a tough construction superintendent, while Macdonald Carey shows fine restraint as a flier who is trying to even the score for the death of his wife in the Pearl Harbor attack.

Par obtained a very faithful reproduction of Wake on the shores of the Salton Sea in the California desert. It has all the desolateness of the real thing.
□ 1942: Nominations: Best Picture, Director, Supp. Actor (William Bendix), Original Screenplay

■ WAKE OF THE RED WITCH

1949, 106 MINS, US ▼
Dir Edward Ludwig *Prod* Edmund Grainger *Scr* Harry Brown, Kenneth Gamet *Ph* Reggie Lanning *Ed* Richard L. Van Enger *Mus* Nathan Scott
● John Wayne, Gail Russell, Gig Young, Luther Adler, Adele Mara, Eduard Franz (Republic)

Wake of the Red Witch, with its Polynesian locale, is replete with action, drama and adventure. Story is a gripping account of deadly rivalry between two men. Struggle between John Wayne, an impetuous sea captain, and his employer – shipping tycoon Luther Adler – should have been stressed more fully.

As master of the square rigger, *Red Witch*, Wayne has a score to settle with the ship's owner, Adler. He chooses to do it by scuttling the bullion-laden vessel on an uncharted reef.

Gail Russell appears miscast among the South Pacific flora and fauna. Her romantic scenes with Wayne never achieve an aura of realism.

■ WALKABOUT

1971, 95 MINS, UK ◇ ▼
Dir Nicolas Roeg *Prod* Si Litvinoff *Scr* Edward Bond
Ph Nicolas Roeg *Ed* Antony Gibbs, Alan Patillo
Mus John Barry *Art Dir* Brian Eatwell

● Jenny Agutter, Lucien John, David Gulpilil, John Meillon, John Illingsworth (Raab-Litvinoff)

Walkabout is a tepid artistic effort about two children, lost in the Australian wilds, who are befriended by an aborigine. Nicolas Roeg directed and photographed on authentic locations. Roeg's bag is photography, but pretty pictures alone cannot sustain – and, in fact, inhibit – this fragile and forced screen adaptation of a James Vance Marshall novel.

Apparent intent was to begin the film with jarring montage of urban life, so as to contrast better with the later wasteland footage. Jenny Agutter and Lucien John (Roeg's own son) find themselves alone in the desert after father John Meillon tries to kill the boy and then shoots himself after setting fire to his car.

On the kids' long trek in search of civilization, they encounter David Gulpilil, an aborigine who guides them towards rescue.

In an effort to pump up the plot, Roeg resorts to ad nauseam inserts of insects, reptiles and assorted wild beasts, in varying stages of life and decay.

■ WALK A CROOKED MILE

1948, 90 MINS, US
Dir Gordon M. Douglas *Prod* Edward Small
Scr George Bruce *Ph* George Robinson *Ed* James E. Newcom *Mus* Paul Sawtell *Art Dir* Rudolph Sternad
● Louis Hayward, Dennis O'Keefe, Louise Allbritton, Raymond Burr, Onslow Stephens (Columbia)

The documentary technique gives a factual gloss to the high melodramatics of *Walk a Crooked Mile*. A Southern California atomplant is losing its top secrets and the FBI and Scotland Yard, in the respective persons of Dennis O'Keefe and Louis Hayward, join forces to run down the criminals. Action swings to San Francisco and back to the southland, punching hard all the time under the knowledgeable direction of Gordon Douglas. On-the-site filming of locales adds authenticity.

George Bruce has loaded his script with nifty twists that add air of reality to the meller doings in the Bertram Millhauser story. Dialog is good and situations believably developed, even the highly contrived melodramatic finale. Documentary flavor is forwarded by Reed Hadley's credible narration chore.

■ WALK DON'T RUN

1966, 114 MINS, US
Dir Charles Walters *Prod* Sol C. Siegel *Scr* Sol Saks
Ph Harry Stradling *Ed* Walter Thompson, James Wells
Mus Quincy Jones *Art Dir* Joe Wright
● Cary Grant, Samantha Eggar, Jim Hutton, John Standing, Miiko Taka, Ted Hartley (Columbia/Granley)

Walk Don't Run is a completely entertaining, often hilarious romantic comedy spotlighting as a matchmaker a deliberately mature Cary Grant at the peak of his comedy prowess. The fast-moving and colorful production pegs its laughs on a Tokyo housing shortage during the 1964 Olympics [from a screen story by Robert Russell and Frank Ross].

Grant is outstanding as the middle-aged and distinguished English industrialist who arrives two days before his Tokyo hotel suite will be available. Noting an apartment-to-share sign, he finds it to be the diggings of prim, schedule-conscious Samantha Eggar. She is engaged to a stuffy embassy functionary, played by John Standing, with whom Grant has already had a run-in.

Jim Hutton, a member of the US Olympic walking team (hence the title), is also awaiting quarters, so he, too, winds up in Eggar's pad.

■ WALKER

1987, 95 MINS, US
Dir Alex Cox *Prod* Lorenzo O'Brien *Scr* Rudy Wurlitzer *Ph* David Bridges *Ed* Carlos Puente Ortega, Alex Cox *Mus* Joe Strummer *Art Dir* Bruno Rubeo
● Ed Harris, Marlee Matlin, Peter Boyle, Bianca Guerra, Richard Masur, Rene Auberjonois (Incine/Universal)

The potentially fascinating story of an American adventurer who installed himself as president of Nicaragua 132 years ago, *Walker* unfortunately exists for one reason and one reason only – for director Alex Cox to vent his spleen about continued American interference with the Central American country. The comic, idiosyncratic approach has merit in theory, but the result onscreen is a virtual fiasco.

With the financial backing of tycoon Cornelius Vanderbilt, Walker led a mercenary band of 58 men to Nicaragua in 1855 and ruled the tiny nation with an increasingly heavy hand for two years until being kicked out.

Cox makes a muddled attempt at the outset to paint Walker as an idealist who becomes fatally twisted after the premature death of his strong-willed fiancee (played in a very brief appearance by Marlee Matlin). From then on, however, Walker is ramrod stiff and impenetrable, a man given to self-seriously strutting about and delivering platitudes such as, 'One must act with severity, or perish.'

■ WALKING STICK, THE

1970, 100 MINS, UK
Dir Eric Till *Prod* Alan Ladd Jr *Scr* George Bluestone
Ph Arthur Ibbetson *Ed* John Jympson *Mus* Stanley Myers *Art Dir* John Howell
● David Hemmings, Samantha Eggar, Emlyn Williams, Phyllis Calvert, Ferdy Mayne, Dudley Sutton (Winkast/M-G-M)

The Walking Stick is notable for outstanding performances by David Hemmings and Samantha Eggar, and excellent direction by Eric Till. Story concerns a physically handicapped girl who finds love, then betrayal in a jewel robbery involvement.

George Bluestone adapted the Winston Graham novel about an introverted girl who blossoms under the patient love of a vagabond artist.

Hemmings suddenly emerges as a tool of Emlyn Williams, an art dealer whose night acquisitions come via robbery. Eggar, who works in a gallery, is pressured into the heist.

Her dilemma – should she give up her happiness by reporting to the police, or keep a gnawing silence? – is resolved in a somewhat melodramatic way.

■ WALK IN THE SHADOW

See: *Life for Ruth*

■ WALK IN THE SPRING RAIN, A

1970, 98 MINS, US
Dir Guy Green *Prod* Sterling Silliphant *Scr* Sterling Silliphant, [Frank Hummert, Anne Hummert] *Ph* Charles B. Lang *Ed* Ferris Webster *Mus* Elmer Bernstein *Art Dir* Malcolm C. Bert
● Anthony Quinn, Ingrid Bergman, Fritz Weaver, Katherine Crawford, Tom Fielding, Virginia Gregg (Columbia)

Rachel Maddux wrote the basic novella, adapted by Sterling Silliphant, with an uncredited bow to Frank and Anne Hummert. Ingrid Bergman and story hubby Fritz Weaver go on sabbatical from campus to the Tennessee mountain country so he can write a law text. Between the frigid winter and the verdant spring rains, Bergman finds love beating again in her bosom. The reason is

Anthony Quinn a Spanish desdendant, Zorba-like hillbilly.

Quinn is not without his own responsibilities. He has a cackling wife, played terribly by Virginia Gregg. He also has a son, played by Tom Fielding in the style of a Method ctor satire. At least he doesn't even bother faking a Dixie accent.

Cast is rounded out by Katherine Crawford, the selfish daughter.

■ WALK IN THE SUN, A

1945, 117 MINS, US
Dir Lewis Milestone *Prod* Lewis Milestone *Scr* Robert Rossen *Ph* Russell Harlan *Ed* Duncan Mansfield
Mus Frederic Efrem Rich *Art Dir* Max Bertisch
● Dana Andrews, Richard Conte, John Ireland, Norman Lloyd, Lloyd Bridges, Huntz Hall (20th Century-Fox)

As a film *Walk* is not so sunny. It is distinguished for some excellent, earthy GI dialog, but the author has failed to achieve a proper fusing of dialog and situation. Too frequently he is given to spieling the colorful talk of the enlisted man, and thus allows his yarn to flounder. He is content, seemingly, to allow GI talk to encompass all else.

Film [from a novel by Harry Brown] concerns an operation by a platoon of American soldiers after they hit the beach at Salerno. They're detailed to wipe out a farmhouse and its Nazi occupants. That's the major element of the story, such as it is, and the rest of the pic is mostly concerned with reactions of the GIs to the conditions under which they're fighting, their thoughts, and so forth.

Dana Andrews gives one of his invariably forthright performances as a sergeant, and the rest of the impressive cast know their way around a script. And that holds particularly true of Richard Conte, who, perhaps, has the best lines.

■ WALK LIKE A DRAGON

1960, 95 MINS, US
Dir James Clavell *Prod* James Clavell *Scr* James Clavell, David Mainwaring *Ph* Loyal Griggs
Ed Howard Smith *Mus* Paul Dunlop *Art Dir* Hal Pereira, Ronald Anderson
● Jack Lord, Nobu McCarthy, James Shigeta, Mel Torme, Benson Fong (Paramount)

In attempting to dramatize the unarguable doctrine that slavery is an ugly, unwelcome visitor in a free society, producer-director-writer James Clavell has somehow wound up with the curious message that clannish conformity is the logical path to peaceful coexistence for foreigners to pursue in America. Since Clavell wisely has set his story in the conveniently unprovocative and usefully primitive atmosphere of the old west, and has utilized some interesting, offbeat historical data in the process, the film fits snugly into the 'adult western' genre.

A maze of incomplete, often contradictory, character motivations gnaws away destructively at the roots of the screenplay. It is based on a three-ply conflict, an interracial romantic triangle consisting of one tall, strapping American (Jack Lord); one proud, rebellious Chinaman (James Shigeta); and one frail, would-be Chinese slave girl (Nobu McCarthy). Rescuing the latter from the perils of enforced prostitution, Lord promptly bumps into mass discrimination and an emotional duel with Shigeta when he brings the girl to live in his home.

Although shackled with a superficially-drawn role, Lord constructs a sympathetic characterization. McCarthy, an attractive actress, lacks the subtle variety required for her role. Shigeta, too, manages only a shallow, one-note portrayal of the defiant Oriental. Mel Torme, cast as a gun-totin', scripture-spoutin' 'deacon', plays the offbeat role with a flourish, but appears bewildered by the nebulous nature of the character.

As director, Clavell is adept in his handling of the film's more provocative moments, notably a scene where the heroine is stripped to the waist in the slave market. But his overall approach tends to form predictably repetitive patterns such as following each soft, tender sequence with an explosion of gunfire to open the next one.

● ●

■ WALK ON THE WILD SIDE

1962, 114 MINS, US Ⓥ
Dir Edward Dmytryk   *Prod* Charles K. Feldman
Scr John Fante, Edmund Morris   *Ph* Joe MacDonald
Ed Harry Gerstad   *Mus* Elmer Bernstein
Art Dir Richard Sylbert
● Laurence Harvey, Capucine, Jane Fonda, Anne Baxter, Barbara Stanwyck, Joanna Moore (Columbia)

It's obvious that in their treating of prostitution and lesbianism the filmmakers did not want to be offensive to anyone. The result is a somewhat watered-downing of the Nelson Algren story of the Doll House in New Orleans and the madame's affection for one of the girls.

Laurence Harvey plays a drifter in search of his lady, Capucine. He does it well but not strikingly. Capucine, it turns out, is a member of the Doll House, showing a classic, Garbo-type beauty but somehow limited as to range in emotionality via script and/or direction.

Jane Fonda cops the show with her hoydenish behavior as another member of the House and Just-Lucky-I-Guess Alumnus of the freighter transportation circuit. Barbara Stanwyck is steely as the madame who looks to Capucine for the 'affection' she cannot find in her maimed husband.

Dmytryk maintains a nice pace in direction – that is, a steady pace – but more forcefulness in both his direction and the writing might have provided more dramatic impact.
□ 1962: Nomination: Best Song ('Walk on the Wild Side')

● ●

■ WALK WITH LOVE AND DEATH, A

1969, 90 MINS, US ◊
Dir John Huston   *Prod* Carter De Haven   *Scr* Dale Wasserman   *Ph* Ted Scaife   *Ed* Russell Lloyd
Mus Georges Delerue   *Art Dir* Wolfgang Witzemann
● Anjelica Huston, Assaf Dayan, Anthony Corlan, John Hallam, Robert Lang, Michael Gough (20th Century-Fox)

A Walk with Love and Death, set in the framework of the Middle Ages, is an unrelenting examination of France when human life was valueless, social order unbending and individual outloook bleak. Filmed in Austria, director John Huston tells his story [from a novel by Hans Koningsberger] unhurriedly, lingering over details of style and torture with equal unsparing lenses.

His young hero, Assaf Dayan, obeying a mystic call from the sea, leaving Paris and studies behind, begins journey on foot through the war-scarred French countryside. His meeting with Anjelica Huston, daughter of a nobleman, is the beginning of the end for the scholar and the lady.

The slow pace and gloomy atmosphere tend to dull viewer interest. High flown speech, confusion of action undermine even as Huston builds.

● ●

■ WALL STREET

1987, 124 MINS, US ◊ Ⓥ ⊙
Dir Oliver Stone   *Prod* Edward R. Pressman   *Scr* Oliver Stone, Stanley Weiser   *Ph* Robert Richardson   *Ed* Claire Simpson   *Mus* Stewart Copeland   *Art Dir* Stephen Hendrickson
● Michael Douglas, Charlie Sheen, Daryl Hannah, Martin Sheen, Terence Stamp, Sean Young (Pressman/American Entertainment/20th Century-Fox)

Watching Oliver Stone's *Wall Street* is about as wordy and dreary as reading the financial papers accounts of the rise and fall of an Ivan Boesky-type arbitrageur.

The lure of making a bundle on Wall Street by the young broker (Charlie Sheen) totally seduced by the power and financial stature of such a megalomaniacal arbitrageur as Gordon Gekko (Michael Douglas) is as good a contemporary story as there is in the real world of takeovers and mergers.

Douglas is a nasty enough manipulator barking orders to buy, sell and run his competitors into the ground or delivering declamatory speeches on how greed is what makes America great.

Trouble is, Sheen comes off as a pawn in Douglas' corporate raider game and as the easily duped sort doesn't elicit much sympathy. Martin Sheen as his father, the airplane mechanic, is the only person worth caring about.
□ 1987: Best Actor (Michael Douglas)

● ●

■ WALTZ OF THE TOREADORS

1962, 104 MINS, UK ◊ Ⓥ
Dir John Guillermin   *Prod* Peter de Savigny   *Scr* Wolf Mankowitz   *Ph* John Wilcox   *Ed* Peter Taylor
Mus Richard Addinsell   *Art Dir* Wilfrid Shingleton
● Peter Sellers, Dany Robin, Margaret Leighton, John Fraser, Cyril Cusack, Prunella Scales (Rank/Independent Artists)

A considerably broadened version of Jean Anouilh's ironic stage comedy results in a capital acting opportunity for Peter Sellers. Pic is handsomely mounted, and it's directed with zest and pace by John Guillermin. But too many moods jostle for it to be a complete success. Slapstick, farce, high comedy, drama and tragedy are all there but they don't always make easy companions.

Mankowitz has transferred the yarn from France to Sussex. Briefly, it concerns an elderly general, about to retire before World War I. He is a man with a roving eye for the girls, trapped by a neurotic, shrewish, sham-invalid of a wife and two unprepossessing daughters. For 17 years, he has had a platonic romance with a French woman, never having a real opportunity to consummate their love. She turns up at his castle determined that this sad state of affairs should end.

Sellers extracts laughs and compassionate pity with equal ease, whether he is being caught up in a drunken party at a tavern, conducting a riotous mock duel with his local doctor (Cyril Cusack), taking charge of a court martial, leching after his maids, facing up to the fact that he is a failure or, in the more tragic moments, stripping his soul bare as he struggles in his hateful scenes with his wife.

● ●

■ WANDA

1970, 105 MINS, US ◊
Dir Barbara Loden   *Prod* Harry Shuster   *Scr* Barbara Loden   *Ph* Nicholas T. Proferes   *Ed* Nicholas T. Proferes
● Barbara Loden, Michael Higgins (Foundation for Filmakers)

Wanda is a wanderer, a loser somewhere in a heavily industrialized part of the US. Barbara Loden shows a calm, dispassionate feel for direction and an insight into the psyche of an inarticulate, ill-educated but non-despairing woman as the protagonist of this probing pic about a cultural wasteland alongside affluence. Loden dramatizes an oft-treated social theme about people drifting into crime and prostitution and does not force blame on anyone but denotes the growing conflicts between puritanism and promiscuity, poverty within plenty and ignorance alongside the more educated that grows in observation, insight and impact as it goes along.

Loden has the vulnerability, negation and yet inner resiliency that keeps her character from being a drudge.

● ●

■ WANDERERS, THE

1979, 113 MINS, US ◊ Ⓥ
Dir Philip Kaufman   *Prod* Martin Ransohoff   *Scr* Rose Kaufman, Philip Kaufman   *Ph* Michael Chapman
Ed Ronald Roose, Stuart H. Pappe   *Art Dir* Jay Moore
● Ken Wahl, John Friedrich, Karen Allen, Linda Manz, Toni Kalem, Tony Ganios (Orion)

Despite an uneasy blend of nostalgia and violence, *The Wanderers* is a well-made and impressive film. Philip Kaufman, who also co-scripted with his wife, Rose [from the novel by Richard Price], has accurately captured the urban angst of growing up in the 1960s.

Thesping is first-rate from the largely unknown cast, with Ken Wahl, John Friedrich and especially Tony Ganios delivering well-rounded and believable characterizations. Also outstanding are Toni Kalem as a gum-popping flirt, and Karen Allen as her more serious, soulful counterpart.

Disturbing elements in *The Wanderers* crop up in the explicitly violent episodes, including those involving the symbolic Ducky Boys, a murderous pint-sized gang, and the Fordham Baldies, bald behemoths.

● ●

■ WANDERING JEW, THE

1933, 110 MINS, UK
Dir Maurice Elvey   *Prod* Julius Hagen   *Scr* H. Fowler Mear   *Ph* Sydney Blythe   *Ed* Jack Harris
Art Dir James Carter
● Conrad Veidt, Marie Ney, Anne Grey, Joan Maude, Peggy Ashcroft (Twickenham/Gaumont-British)

The film is based on Temple Thurston's play of the same name, and the adaptation is divided into four episodes. The first is Jerusalem on the day of the Crucifixion; the second, Antioch in the time of the first crusade; third, Palermo, Sicily, in 1290; and fourth, Seville in 1560, during the Inquisition.

It is a massive, artistic and well-acted filming, flavored perhaps by an overplus of scenes, and more detail than is necessary.

Conrad Veidt in the first half of the picture is guilty of scene-chewing. All this is counteracted before the finish by a restrained, moving dignity which he contributes to the wanderer of centuries.

Maria Ney, Anne Grey and Joan Maude are the three women in the first three episodes, and do nothing to distinguish themselves; Peggy Ashcroft as the Magdalene in the fourth phase, who is converted by the Christ-like nobility of Battadios (Veidt), offers a fine characterization rich in feeling. The inquisitors are Francis L. Sullivan, Felix Aylmer and Ivor Barnard, all of them vividly Machiavellian.

● ●

■ WAR AND PEACE

1956, 208 MINS, US/ITALY ◊ Ⓥ ⊙
Dir King Vidor   *Prod* Dino De Laurentiis   *Scr* Bridget Boland, Robert Westerby, King Vidor, Mario Camerini, Ennio De Concini, Ivo Perilli, [Irwin Shaw]   *Ph* Jack Cardiff, Aldo Tonti   *Ed* Stuart Gilmore, Leo Catozzo
Mus Nino Rota   *Art Dir* Mario Chiari, Franz Bachelin
● Audrey Hepburn, Henry Fonda, Mel Ferrer, Vittorio Gassman, John Mills, Anita Ekberg (Ponti-De Laurentiis/Paramount)

Hollywood and Italian know-how, some $6 million capital investment, and between 5,000 and 6,000 Italian troops doubling as celluloid soldiers, have produced a visual epic.

The classic Tolstoy novel which requires weeks and, more often, months to read is digested into three-and-a-half hours of vivid cinematic magic.

The wonder of the production is that it has maintained cohesiveness and fluidity of story and also has given fullest accent to the size and sweep of Bonaparte's armies at Austerlitz and Borodino. Life among the Russian aristocracy with its passion for good living and innate respect for the church in time of stress is brought into sharp focus.

Audrey Hepburn is the epitome of wholesome young love under benevolent aristocratic rearing. Henry Fonda, the confused young liberal who apes the French as so many Russians did, is perhaps sometimes too literally the confused character.

Other than the above and the moody but compelling performance by Mel Ferrer, the rest are lesser roles but almost wholly effective.

The film's scripting credits are a strangely multiple thing in light of Irwin Shaw's request to remove his billing when director Vidor reportedly rewrote so many scenes on his own.

☐ 1956: Nominations: Best Director, Color Cinematography, Color Costume Design

••••••••••••••••••••••••••••••••••••••

■ **WAR GAME, THE**

1966, 50 MINS, UK 👁
Dir Peter Watkins   *Scr* Peter Watkins   *Ph* Peter Bartlett
Art Dir Michael Bradsell
● (BBC-TV)

The War Game was originally made by BBC-TV for showing on TV, but corporation brass had second thoughts after it had been completed, decided it was unsuitable for mass audiences, and ordered it to be kept off the airwaves. As a result of political and press agitation, it was eventually agreed to make it available for theatrical release through the British Film Institute.

A wholly imaginary picture of what could happen immediately before, during and after a nuclear attack on Britain, *The War Game* is grim, gruesome, horrific and realistic. It is not a pleasant picture to watch, but yet it is one that needs to be shown as widely as possible.

The attack itself is predictably grim, but the most telling part is the aftermath of the bomb – the severely burned are killed off and their bodies burned, and looters face the firing squad.

Watkins, who left the BBC in protest when it was banned, does an excellent and imaginative job, based on considerable research.

☐ 1966: Best Feature Documentary

••••••••••••••••••••••••••••••••••••••

■ **WARGAMES**

1983, 110 MINS, US ◇ 👁 ⊙
Dir John Badham   *Prod* Harold Schneider
Scr Lawrence Lasker, Walter F. Parkes   *Ph* William A. Fraker   *Ed* Tom Rolf   *Mus* Arthur B. Rubinstein
Art Dir Angelo P. Graham
● Matthew Broderick, Dabney Coleman, John Wood, Ally Sheedy, Barry Corbin, Dennis Lipscomb (United Artists)

Although the script has more than its share of short circuits, director John Badham solders the pieces into a terrifically exciting story charged by an irresistible idea: an extra-smart kid can get the world into a whole lot of trouble that it also takes the same extra-smart kid to rescue it from.

Matthew Broderick is on the mark as the bright teenager, bored by traditional high school subjects like biology, but brilliant with computers. Unfortunately, thinking he's sneaking an advance look at a new line of video games, he taps into the country's Norad missile-defense system to challenge its computer to a game of global thermonuclear warfare.

WarGames' weakness, sad to say, is that the adult side of the yarn is not peopled with very realistic characters, although the performances are fine.

Ally Sheedy is perfectly perky as Broderick's girlfriend; Dabney Coleman brings his usual dissonance to the role of the computer-reliant defense specialist; but John Wood's large talents aren't fully used in a somewhat confusing part as the misanthropic eccentric who designed the computer.

☐ 1983: Nominations: Best Original Screenplay, Cinematography, Sound

••••••••••••••••••••••••••••••••••••••

■ **WARLOCK**

1989, 102 MINS, US ◇ 👁 ⊙
Dir Steve Miner   *Prod* Steve Miner   *Scr* David Twohy
Ph David Eggby   *Ed* David Finfer   *Mus* Jerry Goldsmith
Art Dir Roy Forge Smith
● Richard E. Grant, Julian Sands, Lori Singer, Kevin O'Brien, Richard Kuse, Mary Woronov (New World)

Warlock is an attempt to concoct a pic from a pinch of occult chiller, a dash of fantasy thriller and a splash of 'stalk 'n' slash'. But what could have been a heady brew falls short, despite some gusto thesping from Richard E. Grant and Lori Singer.

Pic opens in the Massachusetts Bay colony in 1691 where a contemptuous warlock (Julian Sands) is being readied for execution. But with a bit of nifty hocus-pocus, both he and witch-hunter Grant are sent to 1988 LA.

Sands soon gets back to his nasty habits – including chopping off a finger, gouging out eyes and skinning a child – as he pursues the magical *Grand Grimoire*.

Waitress Lori Singer meets Sands when he crashes through a window into her house. After he puts an ageing spell on her, she teams up with Grant to try to kill the warlock.

Director Steve Miner directs ably but doesn't pull away from some of the horror cliches.

••••••••••••••••••••••••••••••••••••••

■ **WAR LORD, THE**

1965, 120 MINS, US ◇
Dir Franklin J. Schaffner   *Prod* Walter Seltzer   *Scr* John Collier, Millard Kaufman   *Ph* Russell Metty   *Ed* Folmar Blangsted   *Mus* Jerome Moross   *Art Dir* Alexander Golitzen, Henry Bumstead
● Charlton Heston, Richard Boone, Rosemary Forsyth, Maurice Evans, Guy Stockwell, Niall MacGinnis (Universal)

The War Lord digs back into the 11th century against a Druid setting in ancient Normandy for unfoldment of its generally fast action. Producer Walter Seltzer has given his picturization of Leslie Stevens' play *The Lovers* – finely lensed to lend realism and pictorial beauty – elaborate mounting and clash battle movement.

Franklin Schaffner's direction, while not always overcoming deficiencies of convincing dialog and Charlton Heston's sometimes vacillating characterization, in the main projects the proper spirit of a derring-do, days-of-yore melodrama. His battle scenes, utilizing the weapons and tactics of the period are particularly well handled.

Script presents Heston as war lord of the Duke of Normandy, detailed to oversee a primitive Druid village on a barren shore of the North Sea, whose inhabitants are constantly harassed by invaders from the north. With him are his brother (Guy Stockwell) and Richard Boone, his faithful aide in 20 years of warring. Plottage dwells on his mad passion for a village girl, claiming her on her wedding night according to custom of 'droit de seigneur' – a lord's right of the first night.

Heston is more convincing in his battle scenes than in romancing Rosemary Forsyth, but nevertheless delivers a hard-hitting performance. Top acting honors, however, go to Stockwell, as the young knight.

••••••••••••••••••••••••••••••••••••••

■ **WARLORDS OF ATLANTIS**

1978, 96 MINS, UK ◇ 👁
Dir Kevin Connor   *Prod* John Dark   *Scr* Brian Hayles
Ph Alan Hume   *Ed* Bill Blunden   *Mus* Mike Vickers
Art Dir Elliot Scott
● Doug McClure, Peter Gilmore, Shane Rimmer, Lea Brodie, Michael Gothard, Cyd Charisse (EMI)

In *Warlords of Atlantis*, Doug McClure and several other earthlings suffer a close encounter with Cyd Charisse and Daniel Massey who rule over the legendary lost city. More terrifying are their brushes with various species of marine monsters on periodic rampages. And a good thing, too, in an otherwise skimpy reworking of the hoary Atlantis legend.

Donald Bisset and Peter Gilmore are appealing as a British father-son scientific team in quest of Atlantis. McClure is the Yank who made the diving bell that plumbs the sea and implausibly manages to resurface.

The one not inconsiderable virtue of the script is that it keeps the pot boiling. Direction by Kevin Connor and the editing keep the eye-filling pace brisk. The cliched characters are played in workmanlike fashion by all hands.

••••••••••••••••••••••••••••••••••••••

■ **WARLORDS OF THE 21ST CENTURY**
See: *Battletruck*

••••••••••••••••••••••••••••••••••••••

■ **WAR LOVER, THE**

1962, 105 MINS, US ◇ ⊙
Dir Philip Leacock   *Prod* Arthur Hornblow Jr
Scr Howard Koch   *Ph* Bob Huke   *Ed* Gordon Hales
Mus Richard Addinsell   *Art Dir* Bill Andrews
● Steve McQueen, Robert Wagner, Shirley Anne Field, Gary Cockrell, Michael Crawford, Jerry Stovin (Columbia)

This production of John Hersey's novel *The War Lover* is accomplished in all respects save one: lack of proper penetration into the character referred to by the title. The scenario seems reluctant to come to grips with the issue of this character's unique personality – a 'war lover' whose exaggerated shell of heroic masculinity covers up a psychopathic inability to love or enjoy normal relationships with women.

The story transpires in 1943 England and focuses on B-17 bombing raids over Germany, with the title character (Steve McQueen) a pilot of one of the planes.

That the central character emerges more of an unappealing symbol than a sympathetic flesh-and-blood portrait is no fault of McQueen, who plays with vigor and authority, although occasionally with two much eye-ball emotion. Robert Wagner and Shirley Anne Field share the film's secondary, but interesting, romantic story. Wagner does quite well, and Field has a fresh, natural quality.

Outside of his central failure director Philip Leacock does a sound job. Scenes of the bombing raids and accompanying aerial incidents are adroitly and authentically executed.

••••••••••••••••••••••••••••••••••••••

■ **WARNING SHOT**

1967, 100 MINS, US ◇
Dir Buzz Kulik   *Prod* Buzz Kulik   *Scr* Mann Rubin
Ph Joseph Biroc   *Ed* Archie Marshek   *Mus* Jerry Goldsmith   *Art Dir* Hal Pereira, Roland Anderson
● David Janssen, Ed Begley, Keenan Wynn, Sam Wanamaker, Lillian Gish, Stefanie Powers (Paramount)

Warning Shot is a police drama in which fine production, direction and performances overcome a sometimes flawed script. David Janssen toplines as a cop accused of being trigger-happy.

Mann Rubin has adapted Whit Masterson's novel, *711 – Officer Needs Help*, in which a cop is accused of poor judgment in killing an apparently innocent medic. His superiors, the DA and the public turn on him, and only hope of vindication is proving the existence of a missing gun, and the discovery of evidence to prove the medic was breaking the law.

Filmed smoothly on LA locations, with technical assist from the Police Department, pic has the immediacy of headlines about police brutality, irresponsibility, etc. Scripting incorporates some cliche, unnecessary angles which detract from a very viable story line; namely, that cops are fallible human beings who drink, smoke, make mistakes – just like every one else.

. . . .

■ WAR OF THE ROSES, THE

1989, 116 MINS, US ◇ ⓥ ⊙
Dir Danny DeVito   *Prod* James L. Brooks, Arnon Milchan   *Scr* Michael Leeson   *Ph* Stephen H. Burum   *Ed* Lynzee Klingman   *Mus* David Newman   *Art Dir* Ida Random
● Michael Douglas, Kathleen Turner, Danny DeVito, Marianne Sagebrecht, Sean Astin, Heather Fairfield (Gracie/20th Century-Fox)

Entry in the Charlie Chan Chinese sleuth series provides an opportunity for the Oriental Sherlock to perform his deductions while a guest of the NY police force. Chan uncovers the killer of two people mixed up in the big city's mob.

Some of the plausible deductions lend more credulity than usual to this typical yarn. Art Arthur, Robert Ellis and Helen Logan combined forces on the original story.

Chan is again faithfully personated Warner Oland, with just as much interest as ever being shown in his clever portrayal. Keye Luke again is the effervescent son, with the lad even better than before if only because he does more things in his usual enthusiastic style. Joan Marsh makes a pert, candid-camera freelancer among the dailies, though the slight love interest she shows for the columnist is blotted out at the close. Harold Huber's conception of a police inspector is crisp and characteristic if a little too brusque.

. . . .

■ WAR OF THE WORLDS, THE

1953, 85 MINS, US ◇ ⓥ
Dir Byron Haskin   *Prod* George Pal   *Scr* Barre Lyndon   *Ph* George Barnes   *Ed* Everett Douglas   *Mus* Leith Stevens   *Art Dir* Hal Pereira, Albert Nozaki
● Gene Barry, Ann Robinson, Les Tremayne, Lewis Martin, Bob Cornthwaite, Jack Kruschen (Paramount)

War of the Worlds is a socko science-fiction feature, as fearsome as a film as was the Orson Welles 1938 radio interpretation of the H.G. Wells novel. Gene Barry, as a scientist, is the principal in this story of an invasion of the earth by weird, spider-like characters from Mars, against whom the world's most potent weapons, even the atom bomb are of no avail.

Into this setup, the special effects group headed by Gordon Jennings loosens a reign of screen terror, of futile defense, demolished cities, charred landscapes and people burned to ashes by the invaders' weapons.

While following closely the plot laid down in Wells' novel, the film transfers the first invasion to a small town in Southern California. What is believed to be a huge meteor lands near a small town but it turns out to be a Martian machine that raises itself on pulsating beams and promptly turns deadly heat-waves on humans, buildings and anything else that comes within range.

In the siege of terror, the story finds opportunity to develop a logical love story between Barry and Ann Robinson. Both are good and others seen to advantage include Les Tremayne as a general; Lewis Martin, a pastor who faces the invaders with a prayer and is struck down. An ominous commentary is spoken by Cedric Hardwicke.
☐ 1953: Best Special Effects
☐ Nominations: Best Editing, Sound

. . . .

■ WAR PARTY

1988, 99 MINS, US ◇ ⓥ ⊙
Dir Franc Roddam   *Prod* John Daly, Derek Gibson, Bernard Williams   *Scr* Spencer Eastman   *Ph* Brian Tufano   *Ed* Sean Barton   *Art Dir* Michael Bingham
● Billy Wirth, Kevin Dillon, Tim Sampson, Jimmy Ray Wales, Kevin M. Howard, M. Emmet Walsh (Hemdale)

A lethal contemporary game of Cowboys and Indians is played out in this revisionist western whose thesis is that, deep down, old hatreds never die. British director Franc Roddam comes down firmly on the side of the Native Americans in this downbeat action pic.

Opening scene is the aftermath of a massacre that took place 100 years ago: a camera pan, following runaway horses, brings us, without a cut, to present-day Montana and a small town with a large Indian population. The (white) Mayor has planned, as a Labor Day tourist attraction, a re-enactment of that old battle; but racial hatreds run deep, and a drunken white boy shoots and kills an Indian youth whose pals quickly avenge him. Pic then develops into a manhunt as five Indian youths take off on horseback.

It's to the credit of Roddam, and the late screenwriter Spencer Eastman (to whom the pic is dedicated), that the present-day world of the West's Indians is so thoughtfully and seriously presented. Yet despite its interesting depiction of modern Indian life, *War Party* is basically just another pursuit movie, no better or worse than the average. Billy Worth and Kevin Dillon impress as the two young Indian leaders.

. . . .

■ WARRENDALE

1967, 105 MINS, CANADA ◇
Dir Allan King   *Prod* Allan King   *Scr* Allan King   *Ph* William Brayne   *Ed* Peter Moseley
● (King)

This pic is a shattering documentary look at a home, Warrendale, for disturbed children and adolescents in Canada. It deals with a group of young, dedicated workers who stay with these emotionally mixed-up youngsters and emerges as engrossing, stark film.

The people involved seem unaware of the camera except when the filmmaker is mentioned by one of the workers. It is the treatment in this institution that is the thing in this psychologically absorbing, well made and incisive truth pic. Death of a beloved cook is one of the main segs of the film as it details the reactions of the patients who had become attached to her.

. . . .

■ WAR REQUIEM

1988, 85 MINS, UK ◇ ⓥ
Dir Derek Jarman   *Prod* Don Boyd   *Scr* Derek Jarman   *Ph* Richard Greatrex   *Ed* Rick Elgood   *Art Dir* Lucy Morahan
● Nathaniel Parker, Tilda Swinton, Laurence Olivier, Patricia Hayes, Rohan McCullough, Nigel Terry (Anglo International/BBC)

As well as being a stunning visual and serious music treat, *War Requiem* is probably avant garde British director Derek Jarman's most mature effort. Pic is a visualization of Benjamin Britten's oratorio and was financed through the BBC's Independent Planning Unit on a budget of just £650,000. It was shot and released in the UK within a staggeringly short three-month period.

War Requiem has no dialog, though it opens with Laurence Olivier reciting Wilfred Owen's poem 'Strange Meeting'. Olivier also appears in cameo as an old soldier tended by a young nurse (Tilda Swinton). The live-action footage is intercut with documentary footage from the Imperial War Museum.

Pic uses the story of Owen's experiences in World War I, up to his death by a sniper bul-

let one week before the war ended, as its structure, while a nurse and unknown soldier are introduced to supplement Britten's musical scenarios. Nathaniel Parker as tortured poet Owen and Swinton (a Jarman regular) as the nurse are excellent. The soundtrack is the original recording of the work, composed for the re-opening of Coventry Cathedral in 1962.

. . . .

■ WARRIORS, THE

1979, 90 MINS, US ◇ ⓥ ⊙
Dir Walter Hill   *Prod* Lawrence Gordon   *Scr* David Shaber, Walter Hill   *Ph* Andrew Laszlo   *Ed* David Holden   *Mus* Barry DeVorzon   *Art Dir* Don Swanagan, Bob Wightman
● Michael Beck, James Remar, David Patrick Kelly, Deborah Van Valkenburgh, Mercedes Ruehl, Brian Tyler (Paramount)

Theme of the pic, based on Sol Yurick's 1965 novel, is a variation on countless westerns and war films.

Update the setting to modern-day New York, and the avenues of escape to graffiti-emblazoned subway cars, and that's *The Warriors*.

The slaying of a hood (Roger Hill) is pinned on a Coney Island gang, the Warriors of the title, and the word soon goes out that the group's members are to be eliminated. It's a long subway ride to Coney Island, so for at least 70 of the film's 90 minutes, the boys in this band experience a variety of macho passage rites.

As with his previous pix, *Hard Times* and *The Driver*, director Walter Hill demonstrates an outstanding visual sense here, with the gaudy 'colors' of the gang members, the desolation of nighttime NY, and the cavernous subway platforms where much of the action takes place.

. . . .

■ WAR WAGON, THE

1967, 100 MINS, US ◇ ⓥ ⊙
Dir Burt Kennedy   *Prod* Marvin Schwartz   *Scr* Clair Huffaker   *Ph* William H. Clothier   *Ed* Harry Gerstad   *Mus* Dimitri Tiomkin   *Art Dir* Alfred Sweeney
● John Wayne, Kirk Douglas, Howard Keel, Robert Walker, Keenan Wynn, Bruce Cabot (Universal)

The War Wagon is an entertaining, exciting western drama of revenge, laced with action and humor. Strong scripting, performances and direction are evident, enhanced by terrif exterior production values. Kirk Douglas also stars in an excellent performance.

Clair Huffaker's novel, *Badman*, has been adapted by the author into a very fine screenplay which is a neat blend of always-advancing plot, the right amount of good-natured grousing, and two-fisted action, all building to a strong climax. Burt Kennedy directs with an eye for panorama, as well as intimate, personal interaction.

John Wayne, framed into prison by Bruce Cabot who then seized his land to make a fortune in gold, returns for revenge. He teams with Kirk Douglas, a hired gun used earlier by Cabot. Together they plan a heist of Cabot's armored gold wagon.

. . . .

■ WATCHER IN THE WOODS, THE

1980, 100 MINS, UK ◇ ⓥ
Dir John Hough   *Prod* Ron Miller   *Scr* Brian Clemens, Harry Spalding, Rosemary Anne Sisson   *Ph* Alan Hume   *Ed* Geoffrey Foot   *Mus* Stanley Myers   *Art Dir* Alan Cassie
● Bette Davis, Carroll Baker, David McCallum, Ian Bannen, Lynn-Holly Johnson, Kyle Richards (Walt Disney)

Although Bette Davis has star billing there's not much reason for it as the film revolves around teenager Lynn-Holly Johnson who just happens to resemble the long-lost daughter of Davis.

Johnson's family (Carroll Baker, David McCallum and Kyle Richards) rent the huge country house belonging to Davis, who lives in a nearby cottage and depends on the big-house rentals for income. The pretitle sequences establish the house and woods (which actually appear to encroach on the house at times) with being something less than fun city. Whatever is out there, however, remains undiscovered even after the film has ended.

The acting and writing are barely professional but the art direction, especially Alan Hume's stunning camerawork, gives the pic a gloss.

● ●

■ WATCH IT

1993, 102 MINS, US ◇

Dir Tom Flynn *Prod* Thomas J. Mangan IV, J. Christopher Burch, John C. McGinley *Scr* Tom Flynn *Ph* Stephen M. Katz *Ed* Dorian Harris *Mus* Stanley Clarke *Art Dir* Jeff Steven Ginn
● Peter Gallagher, Suzy Amis, John C. McGinley, Jon Tenney, Cynthia Stevenson, Lili Taylor (Island World/River One)

Male bonding receives a comic thrashing in *Watch It*, an entertaining diversion with a few serious things on its mind. First-time writer-director Tom Flynn does a nice little number on men in their late 20s who persist in behaving as if they were still living in freshman dorm.

Ladies' man Jon Tenney, goofball salesman John C. McGinley and decidedly unbrilliant auto mechanic Tom Sizemore live in a state of macho bliss in a Chicago suburb. Joined by Tenney's itinerant cousin Peter Gallagher, the boys particularly get off on a game from their college years called 'Watch It,' involving putting something over on one of the guys so he is utterly suckered.

Gallagher becomes fond of lovely veterinarian Suzy Amis and courts her charmingly. McGinley gets something promising going with bright, vulnerable Cynthia Stevenson.

Flynn the writer's sharp, observant dialogue acquits him more than Flynn the director's uncertain pacing and lackluster visual style.

● ●

■ WATCH ON THE RHINE

1943, 109 MINS, US Ⓥ

Dir Herman Shumlin *Prod* Hal B. Wallis *Scr* Dashiell Hammett *Ph* Merritt Gerstad, Hal Mohr *Ed* Rudi Fehr *Mus* Max Steiner
● Bette Davis, Paul Lukas, Geraldine Fitzgerald, George Coulouris, Lucile Watson, Beulah Bondi (Warner)

Watch on the Rhine is a distinguished picture. It is even better than its powerful original stage version. It expresses the same urgent theme, but with broader sweep and in more affecting terms of personal emotion.

The film more than retains the vital theme of the original play. It actually carries the theme further and deeper, and it does so with passionate conviction and enormous skill. There is no compromise on controversial matters. Fascists are identified as such and, although the point is not brought home as it might have been, the industrial-financial support that makes fascism possible is also mentioned.

Just as he was in the play, Paul Lukas is the outstanding star of the film. Anything his part may have lost in the transfer of key lines to Bette Davis is offset by the projective value of the camera for closeups. His portrayal of the heroic German has the same quiet strength and the slowly gathering force that it had on the stage, but it now seems even better defined and carefully detailed, and it has much more vitality.

In the lesser starring part of the wife Davis gives a performance of genuine distinction.
☐ 1943: Best Actor (Paul Lukas).
☐ Nominations: Best Picture, Supp. Actress (Lucile Watson), Screenplay

● ●

■ WATCH YOUR STERN

1960, 88 MINS, UK

Dir Gerald Thomas *Prod* Peter Rogers *Scr* Alan Hackney, Vivian A. Cox *Ph* Ted Scaife *Ed* John Shirley *Mus* Bruce Montgomery *Art Dir* Carmen Dillon
● Kenneth Connor, Eric Barker, Leslie Phillips, Joan Sims, Hattie Jacques, Spike Milligan (Anglo Amalgamated)

The team responsible for the clicko *Carry On* series are up to their profitable yock-raising larks with *Watch Your Stern*. There is a stronger story line [from Earle Couttie's play *Something about a Sailor*], characters are developed more roundly and director Gerald Thomas does not rely on a string of largely disconnected gags and situations.

The yarn concerns a top secret test on an acoustic torpedo which, when fired, upsets arrangements by doubling in its tracks, missing the target raft and blowing up the firing ship. An Admiralty boffin is detailed to modify the torpedo, the plan gets destroyed, a copy mislaid and the destroyer's officers manage to bluff the admiral with the plans of the ship's refrigeration plant.

Acting is on a firstclass farcical comedy level, with Kenneth Connor scoring heavily in his two disguises, especially when as a 'woman scientist,' he has to cope with the attentions of the amorous admiral. Sidney James, guest-starring as a chief petty officer, enlivens his scenes as always and there are standout cameos by Spike Milligan and Eric Sykes as a couple of gabby electricians.

● ●

■ WATER

1985, 95 MINS, UK ◇ Ⓥ

Dir Dick Clement *Prod* Ian La Frenais *Scr* Dick Clement, Ian La Frenais *Ph* Douglas Slocombe *Ed* John Victor Smith *Mus* Mike Moran *Art Dir* Norman Garwood
● Michael Caine, Valerie Perrine, Brenda Vaccaro, Billy Connolly, Leonard Rossiter, Maureen Lipman (HandMade)

A British satire of political muddle in Caribbean island, *Water* is a frenetic mishmash. Michael Caine is fine as a laidback British governor who is aptly described as 'the Patty Hearst of the British diplomatic corps,' but he can't salvage a production that's top heavy with multinational plots threatening the island's harmony.

Those include a singing revolutionary (Billy Connolly) backed by Cubans, mindless British officials (a nice turn by the late Leonard Rossiter and a Margaret Thatcher send-up by Maureen Lipman), some fuzzy French-German intruders, and a US industrialist (Fred Gwynne) who's exploiting the island's underground reserves of mineral water.

The British filmmakers, who shot on the West Indies island of St Lucia, obviously were targeting the invasions of Grenada and the Falkland Islands as subjects of cinematic satire.

Playing Caine's hysterical South American wife, Brenda Vaccaro hits the nadir of her career in a performance that is one unrelieved shriek. Valerie Perrine, as a green environmentalist, is generally wasted.

● ●

■ WATER BABIES, THE

1979, 93 MINS, UK ◇ Ⓥ

Dir Lionel Jeffries *Prod* Peter Shaw *Scr* Michael Robson *Ph* Ted Scaife *Ed* Peter Weatherley *Mus* Phil Coulter, Bill Martin *Art Dir* Herbert Westbrook
● James Mason, Billie Whitelaw, Bernard Cribbins, Joan Greenwood, David Tomlinson, Samantha Gates (Pethurst/Production Associates/Ariadne)

The musical screen version of *The Water Babies*, Charles Kingsley's children's novel, tells the story of innocence-versus-evil more or less straight. The slim $2 million

production budget combines live action footage and – for the underwater sequences – animation.

Screenplay plots the adventures of a 12-year-old apprentice chimneysweep, wrongly accused of theft, who dives into a pool to escape his pursuers. Trapped below the surface, he meets a succession of human stereotypes, jokily animated as underwater creatures, and has a battle to free the water babies, who normally inhabit an eternal playground in mid-ocean but have been captured by a shark and an electric eel.

Animated sequences by Cuthbert Cartoons in London, and movement synchronized by Miroslaw Kijowicz in Poland to a prerecorded soundtrack, are garish but effective.

● ●

■ WATERDANCE, THE

1992, 106 MINS, US ◇ Ⓥ ⊙

Dir Neal Jimenez, Michael Steinberg *Prod* Gale Anne Hurd, Marie Cantin *Scr* Neal Jimenez *Ph* Mark Plummer *Ed* Jeff Freeman *Mus* Michael Convertino *Art Dir* Bob Ziembicki
● Eric Stolz, Helen Hunt, William Forsythe, Wesley Snipes, Elizabeth Pena (JBW)

Co-directing debut of writer Neal Jimenez (*River's Edge*, *For the Boys*) with Michael Steinberg is a smashing success, the writer's semi-autobiographical story of a young man's struggle to avoid despair after a crippling accident.

Set in a hospital for paralyzed men where a young novelist (Eric Stolz) lands after a hiking accident, pic is about his coming to terms with the fate he shares with others in the ward; among them, a hostile white redneck biker (William Forsythe) and a restless, fast-talking black man (Wesley Snipes).

Script unfolds with a spirit and sparkle devoid of self-indulgence, and Stolz plays the lead with lightness, wit and balance, as well as a measure of despair and denial. Much of the pic concerns the anguish of these young men at losing sexual ability, and this aspect of paralysis is covered with a frankness heretofore unseen.

● ●

■ WATERHOLE #3

1967, 95 MINS, US ◇ Ⓥ

Dir William Graham *Prod* Joseph T. Steck *Scr* Joseph T. Steck, R.R. Young *Ph* Robert Burks *Ed* Warren Low *Mus* Dave Grusin *Art Dir* Fernando Carrere
● James Coburn, Carroll O'Connor, Margaret Blye, Claude Akins, Timothy Carey, Bruce Dern (Paramount)

Waterhole #3 is a slow-building, deliberate oater comedy blending satire, slapstick and double entendre dialog for laughs.

Distended story line turns on two gags: gold heist by crooked army sergeant Claude Akins, grounting outlaw Timothy Carey and unwilling hostage Harry Davis; and casual seduction by gambler James Coburn of Carroll O'Connor's daughter, Margaret Blye. O'Connor is far more interested in Coburn's theft of a prize horse, and this gag is milked for all it is worth. Joan Blondell has a bright role as a madame, ditto James Whitmore as a cliche frontier Army officer.

Coburn, O'Connor and Blye (whose voice and projection are perfect) handle their roles in very good fashion, while rest of cast offers good support.

● ●

■ WATERLAND

1992, 95 MINS, UK/US ◇ Ⓥ ⊙

Dir Stephen Gyllenhaal *Prod* Katy McGuinness, Patrick Cassavetti *Scr* Peter Prince *Ph* Robert Elswit *Ed* Lesley Walker *Mus* Carter Burwell *Art Dir* Hugo Luczyc-Wyhowski
● Jeremy Irons, Ethan Hawke, Sinead Cusack, John Heard, Cara Buono, Grant Warnock (Palace/Fine Line)

High school teacher Jeremy Irons walks his students through the physical and emotional landscapes of his troubled life in *Waterland*, a talented but terminally parched piece of literary cinema [from the novel by Graham Swift].

This twisted, inbred yarn is not the sort of thing normally associated with British accents, scarfed pipe-smokers and memory flashbacks. At heart, tale is a Southern gothic of sordid family secrets.

Seeing that his Pittsburgh students find little relevance in his lectures about the French Revolution, teacher Tom Crick (Irons) begins telling them about his own upbringing in the odd area called the Fens, bleak, flat marshlands in East Anglia on the North Sea.

At 16, he and his sweetheart Mary used to have feverish sex in private train compartments. Mary in the present is a barren woman in her 40s with a pathological desire for a child, someone clearly off the deep end who finally kidnaps a baby, insisting, 'I got him from God.'

Irons does his best to carry the project through thick and thin, but he can't entirely break through its fundamental reediness. As his wife, Irons' real-life mate Sinead Cusack seems utterly possessed.

●●●●●●●●●●●●●●●●●●●●●●●●●●●●●●●●●●●●●

■ WATERLOO

1970, 132 MINS, ITALY/USSR ◇ ⓦ

Dir Sergei Bondarchuk   *Prod* Dino De Laurentiis
Scr H.A.L. Craig, Sergei Bondarchuk, Vittorio Bonicelli   *Ph* Armando Nannuzzi   *Ed* Rachel C. Meyer, E.V. Michajlova   *Mus* Nino Rota   *Art Dir* Mario Garbuglia
● Rod Steiger, Christopher Plummer, Orson Welles, Jack Hawkins, Virginia McKenna, Dan O'Herlihy (De Laurentiis/Mosfilm)

Directed by Russia's Sergei Bondarchuk, who made *War and Peace*, and filmed on location in Italy and Russia, with interiors at De Laurentiis's Rome studios, the long-nursed Dino De Laurentiis project has an international flavor. Despite the fact that the battle is the focal point, and a striking din-laden affair it is, the film is raised from being just another historical war epic by the performances of Rod Steiger as Napoleon and Christopher Plummer as Wellington.

Story begins with Europe entirely opposed to the ambitious, flamboyant Napoleon and the French, scared of overwhelming odds, forcing him to abdicate and retire to the island of Elba. But barely has the film started than he's back again.

Steiger gives a remarkably powerful portrayal of Napoleon. It's a Method performance, with his sudden blazes of rage highlighting his moody introspection.

Others stand out, too. Dan O'Herlihy as Marshal Ney, devoted, loyalist to Napoleon, and Orson Welles, making much of two minor but memorable moments as Louis XVIII.

●●●●●●●●●●●●●●●●●●●●●●●●●●●●●●●●●●●●●

■ WATERLOO BRIDGE

1940, 103 MINS, US ⓦ ☉

Dir Mervyn LeRoy   *Prod* Sidney Franklin   *Scr* S.N. Behrman, Hans Rameau, George Froeschel   *Ph* Joseph Ruttenberg   *Ed* George Boemler   *Mus* Herbert Stothart
Art Dir Cedric Gibbons, Urie McCleary
● Vivien Leigh, Robert Taylor, Lucile Watson, Virginia Field, Maria Ouspenskaya, C. Aubrey Smith (M-G-M)

Elaborating on the basic premise of Robert Sherwood's play, and doing a slick job of cleansing to conform to present regulations of the Hays code, this is a persuasive and compelling romantic tragedy.

Story steers a leisurely path in delineating the romantic tragedy of a love affair which is launched on Waterloo Bridge during World War I. Vivien Leigh, a sweet, vivacious and unsophisticated ballet dancer, meets and falls in love with British officer Robert Taylor on eve of his departure for the front. There's a

whirlwind romance with immediate marriage delayed until his first furlough. Fate intervenes, and erroneous report of his death eventually sends her onto the streets, but Taylor returns, meets her at the station where she is soliciting, and the romance flares again for an instant.

Leigh demonstrates outstanding ability as an actress. Her transition from the virginal ingenue of the early passages to the hardened prostie later is a standout performance. Taylor, in a straight romantic role, provides an arresting characterization.

There's plenty of strength in the supporting cast. Virignia Field is excellent as Leigh's chum, who takes the first step along the easiest way to provide food for the pair. Lucile Watson is a perfect grand dame as the aristocratic mother of Taylor; Maria Ouspenskaya is a stern ballet mistress; and C. Aubrey Smith is an army colonel.
□ 1940: Nominations: Best B&W Cinematography, Original Score

●●●●●●●●●●●●●●●●●●●●●●●●●●●●●●●●●●●●●

■ WATERLOO ROAD

1945, 76 MINS, UK

Dir Sidney Gilliat   *Prod* Edward Black   *Scr* Sidney Gilliat   *Ph* Arthur Crabtree   *Ed* Alfred Roome
Mus Bob Busby   *Art Dir* Alex Vetchinsky
● John Mills, Stewart Granger, Alastair Sim, Joy Shelton, Beatrice Varley, George Carney (Gainsborough)

Played against the drab, bomb-shattered background of a London slum, story is the familiar triangle theme with use of the flashback technique not adding to its originality. But it's acted with such sincerity and is so true-to-life in its characterization that the picture grips throughout. There is a terrific climax in which the two men (John Mills and Stewart Granger) fight for one woman as the bombs thunder down.

A soldier deserts when he learns his wife is receiving attentions from another man. Story depicts his day spent in pursuit of the pair, finally confronting them in a sports arcade.

Entire cast is adequate, but particular praise goes to Alastair Sim as the neighborhood doctor and George Carney's role of pigeon fancier.

Picture [from a story by Val Valentine] is a striking example of how sound an English production can be if it keeps to the medium it interprets best, that of the middle-class character.

●●●●●●●●●●●●●●●●●●●●●●●●●●●●●●●●●●●●●

■ WATERMELON MAN

1970, 100 MINS, US ◇ ⓦ ☉

Dir Melvin Van Peebles   *Prod* John B. Bennett
Scr Herman Raucher   *Ph* W. Wallace Kelley   *Ed* Carl Kress   *Mus* Melvin Van Peebles   *Art Dir* Malcolm C. Bert
● Godfrey Cambridge, Estelle Parsons, Howard Caine, D'Urville Martin, Mantan Moreland, Kay Kimberly (Columbia)

Godfrey Cambridge heads cast as a white suburbanite who overnight turns black in biological accident. A few chuckles are evident, but as entertainment, *Watermelon Man* is a trifle; as an interracial social document, it's nothing.

Film's development involves the rather predictable reactions of friends, neighbors and business associates. Estelle Parson's duty is to segue from shock and sympathy to eventual alienation, scramming to her mother with kids (Scott Garrett and Erin Moran).

Employer Howard Caine, after a check with his optometrist about his contact lenses, immediately turns Cambridge to cultivating the black insurance-market potential.

As the film progresses, more plaintive and serious plot angles are suggested, but by this time it is too late.

●●●●●●●●●●●●●●●●●●●●●●●●●●●●●●●●●●●●●

■ WATERSHIP DOWN

1978, 92 MINS, UK ◇ ⓦ

Dir Martin Rosen   *Prod* Martin Rosen   *Scr* Martin Rosen   *Ed* Terry Rawlings   *Mus* Angela Morley, Malcolm Williamson
● (Nepenthe)

Employing fair-to-excellent animation and an array of fine voices drawn heavily from the English stage and screen, *Watership* traces the odyssey of a brave band of rabbits in search of a peaceful new home.

But this is not Bugs Bunny house-hunting. Producer-director Martin Rosen has taken author Richard Adams' concept of real rabbits – doomed by nature to be victims of those they cannot escape or outwit – and projected them into a fearful ordeal.

Along the way, the cottontails are shot-gunned, bitten, gnawed, scratched, hawked and torn apart by dogs and meaner rabbits, with no skimping on red ink. In one particularly gruesome scene, one of the heroes is snared around the neck by a wire, gushing and gurgling blood quite realistically.

This is too much, some would say, for tender eyes (if intended for them). Hooey. It's just what kids imagine their ghost stories and fairy tales would look like. Besides, it's got an overall positive theme with inspirational and ecological overtones to go with the suspense and excitement.

●●●●●●●●●●●●●●●●●●●●●●●●●●●●●●●●●●●●●

■ WAY AHEAD, THE

(US: Immortal Battalion)

1944, 115 MINS, UK ⓦ

Dir Carol Reed   *Prod* Norman Walker, John Sutro
Scr Eric Ambler, Peter Ustinov   *Ph* Guy Green
Ed Fergus McDonell   *Mus* William Alwyn
Art Dir David Rawnsley
● David Niven, Raymond Huntley, Billy Hartnell, Stanley Holloway, James Donald, Leo Genn (Two Cities)

There is no story in the accepted sense, and no love interest. There are momentary shots of femmes, chiefly wives, but no pin-up girls. This heightens the documentary value of this wartime slice of English life. Slickness of cutting should be enough to put this among notable British films, but there is additional cleverness in keeping David Niven far less obtrusive than his star's status might seem to justify. He's a subaltern in command of a platoon.

Covering the period from early 1939 to the Tunisian campaign of 1943, *The Way Ahead* shows how a totally unprepared, peace-loving people were suddenly catapulted into war; how a score of widely different individuals reacted to it.

Direction by Carol Reed is competent, and undoubtedly accounts for the underlying genuineness of the picture as a semi-documentary. Reed's job was made relatively easy by the solid script turned in by Eric Ambler and Peter Ustinov [from Ambler's original story].

●●●●●●●●●●●●●●●●●●●●●●●●●●●●●●●●●●●●●

■ WAY DOWN EAST

1920, 150 MINS, US ⊗ ⓦ

Dir D.W. Griffith   *Prod* D.W. Griffith   *Scr* Anthony Paul Kelly, Joseph R. Grismer, D.W. Griffith   *Ph* Billy Bitzer, Hendrik Sartov   *Ed* James E. Smith, Rose Smith
Mus William Frederick Peters   *Art Dir* Charles O. Sessel, Clifford Pember
● Lillian Gish, Richard Barthelmess, Lowell Sherman, Burr McIntosh, Creighton Hale, Kate Bruce (Griffith/United Artists)

Way down East by D.W. Griffith is a film poem. Without the aid of any especially spectacular or stupendous mechanical effects such as were utilized in *Intolerance*, or the employment of a large ensemble of mob scenes as in the same picture and *The Birth of a Nation*, *Judith of Bethulia*, etc., with the gathering together of a relatively small cast and less than half a

W

dozen stellar film artists, D.W. has taken a simple, elemental, old-fashioned, bucolic melodrama and milked it for 12 reels of absorbing entertainment.

First honors for acting belong to Lillian Gish, who had to court comparison with the preconceived characterization of Anna Moore, which had always been played by a much larger woman in the spoken productions [of the play by Lottie Blair Parker]. Hers is a materially different conception of the role, and she reveals hitherto unsuspected emotional powers. Richard Barthelmess, as David, has little to do until almost the finish, when he rescues Anna from an ice floe about to be precipitated over a rapidly-moving, seething waterfall.

. . . .

■ WAYNE'S WORLD

1992, 95 MINS, US ◇ ⑲ ⊙
Dir Penelope Spheeris   *Prod* Lorne Michaels   *Scr* Mike Myers, Bonnie Turner, Terry Turner   *Ph* Theo Van de Sande   *Ed* Malcolm Campbell   *Mus* J. Peter Robinson
Art Dir Gregg Fonseca
● Mike Myers, Dana Carvey, Rob Lowe, Tia Carrere, Lara Flynn Boyle, Colleen Camp (Paramount)

Wayne'ss World weakly transfers the popular *Saturday Night Live* TV sketch to the big screen. SNL regular Mike Myers created the characters of two overage heavy metal teens fronting a cable access TV show in Aurora, Ill. Like Weird Al Yankovic's flop pic *UHF*, the film satirizes various genres using TV as a starting point.

Ostensible plot has Rob Lowe as a slimy opportunist who buys the heroes' *Wayne's World* show and re-structures it to plug Brian Doyle-Murray's video arcade business. Wayne (Myers) falls in love with beautiful Hong Kong rock singer Tia Carrere and has to worry about womanizer Lowe stealing her away.

Director Penelope Spheeris, with her first major studio assignment (and eight-figure budget), delivers a colorful but uneventful picture. As with *Clue*, picture features three alternate endings, played back to back like the *Clue* video.

Guest stars add almost nothing to the proceedings, including Dan Aykroyd's wife Donna Dixon as Carvey's beautiful dream girl, Ione Skye as Lowe's girlfriend, Meat Loaf as a bouncer and Ed O'Neill as a nutty donut shop manager.

. . . .

■ WAY OF ALL FLESH, THE

1927, 90 MINS, US ⊗
Dir Victor Fleming   *Scr* Jules Furthman   *Ph* Victor Milner
● Emil Jannings, Belle Bennett, Phyllis Haver, Donald Keith, Fred Kohler (Paramount)

No specific punch to this initial made-in-the-USA Emil Jannings release. It really amounts to a study by the star of a middle class character who succumbs, just once, to the feminine and must forever after live in hiding while his family believes him dead and enjoys prosperity through one of the sons' violin concerts. Starting in 1910, the story weaves its way up to the present year, giving opportunity to display three characterizations in as many makeups.

First as the bewhiskered gruff and trusted cashier of a Milwaukee bank, second as under the influence of a demi-mondaine, thereby shorn of his facial growth, and finally as a broken example of indiscretion cleaning up park playgrounds and peddling chestnuts.

In substance the story revolves around the incident of Schilling (Jannings) being entrusted with valuable bonds to be sold in Chicago. On the train he meets Mayme (Phyllis Haver), obviously attired for the character, who ultimately leads him to a drunken sleep in a hotel where she rifles him of his consignment.

Most of the production is studio made, although there are theatre and amusement park sequences, the last named inviting various camera angles, one or two of which stand out.

As regards Jannings, this, is first domestic made picture, is assuredly creditable.
☐ 1927/28: Best Actor (Emil Jannings).
☐ Nomination: Best Picture

. . . .

■ WAY OUT WEST

1937, 64 MINS, US ⑲ ⊙
Dir James W. Horne   *Prod* Hal Roach, Stan Laurel
Scr Charles Rogers, Felix Adler, James Parrott   *Ph* Art Lloyd, Walter Lundin   *Ed* Bert Jordan   *Mus* Marvin Hatley (dir.)   *Art Dir* Arthur I. Royce
● Stan Laurel, Oliver Hardy, Sharon Lynne, James Finlayson, Stanley Fields, Vivian Oakland (M-G-M)

Manner in which this comedy falters and stumbles along is probably due both to formula direction and scripting. Three are credited with the scenario and two [Jack Jevne and Charles Rogers] for the original story. Seemingly too many took a hand; plot reads that way.

In general pattern the Laurel & Hardy entry follows closely the old methods used on their feature shorts. There's too much driving home of gags.

They sing and dance in this one, both to neat returns. The two boys are commissioned to deliver a deed to a gold mine. They find out, after handing it over, that the valuable paper has been given to the wrong girl. Hence, the mad race to readjust matters. On this thin framework hang all of the quips. And Oliver Hardy falls into a pool of water for the third time as the eventual fadeout arrives.

James Finlayson again is cast as villain-straight man, which further slows up the action. Rosina Lawrence, heroine who's supposed to inherit the gold mine, appears only for fleeting glimpses.
☐ 1937: Nomination: Best Score

. . . .

■ WAY TO THE STARS, THE

(US: Johnny in the Clouds)

1945, 107 MINS, UK
Dir Anthony Asquith   *Prod* Anatole de Grunwald
Scr Terence Rattigan   *Ph* Derrick Williams   *Ed* Fergus McDonell   *Mus* Nicholas Brodzsky   *Art Dir* Paul Sheriff, Carmen Dillon
● John Mills, Michael Redgrave, Douglass Montgomery, Trevor Howard, Rosamund John, Stanley Holloway (Two Cities)

This straight tale of what happened to an RAF airdrome when it was taken over by the 8th USAAF is outstanding. It's the nearest thing to a Yank's letter home from wartime England ever to reach the screen.

Not the least interesting thing is the camera technique. Instead of many aerial shots, the camera is grounded entirely. Except for a few necessary runway shots and snatches of formation flying as seen from the ground, the camera concentrates on how the forces lived on terra firma.

Despite technically perfect performances by the three male principals – Michael Redgrave, John Mills and Douglass Montgomery – Rosamund John actually walks away with the acting honors in a part as devoid of glamor as it is rich in femme charm.

Several sequences showing the British aces imitating the Yanks, and the Yanks imitating the Englishmen, are guaranteed belly laughs.

Direction by Anthony Asquith is underlined with sincerity and imagination while the script by Terence Rattigan [based on a scenario by him and Richard Sherman] is strong.

. . . .

■ WAY WEST, THE

1967, 122 MINS, US ◇ ⑲
Dir Andrew V. McLaglen   *Prod* Harold Hecht   *Scr* Ben Maddow, Mitch Lindemann   *Ph* William H. Clothier

Ed Otho Lovering   *Mus* Bronislau Kaper   *Art Dir* Ted Haworth
● Kirk Douglas, Robert Mitchum, Richard Widmark, Lola Albright, Jack Elam, Sally Field (United Artists)

A.B. Guthrie Jr wrote the Pulitzer Prize novel on which Ben Maddow and Mitch Lindemann have based a rambling screenplay. Story takes a group of Missouri farmers, under martinet Kirk Douglas, to the promised land of Oregon. Robert Mitchum is the trail scout who leads them despite fading eyesight, and Richard Widmark an irascible member of the party.

Project probably looked good on paper, but washed out in scripting, direction and pacing. Incidents do not build to any climax; excepting the first and last reels, any others could be shown out of order with no apparent discontinuity.

The three male stars all could have phoned in their acting. Douglas, the stern disciplinarian, at one point orders Negro slave Roy Glenn to whip him; this incident, as written, is crude, and instead of indicating a Spartan attempt at selfcontrol, it comes across as unmotivated masochism.

. . . .

■ WAY WE WERE, THE

1973, 118 MINS, US ◇ ⑲ ⊙
Dir Sydney Pollack   *Prod* Ray Stark, Sydney Pollack
Scr Arthur Laurents   *Ph* Harry Stradling   *Ed* Margaret Booth   *Mus* Marvin Hamlisch   *Art Dir* Stephen Grimes
● Barbra Streisand, Robert Redford, Bradford Dillman, Patrick O'Neal, Viveca Lindfors, Lois Chiles (Columbia/Rastar)

The film version of Arthur Laurents' book is a distended, talky, redundant and moody melodrama, combining young love, relentless 1930s and 1940s nostalgia, and spiced artifically with Hollywood Red-hunt pellets. The major positive achievement is Barbra Streisand's superior dramatic versatility, but Robert Redford has too little to work with in the script.

The story follows the stars from the late 1930s – on a college campus where Streisand is a young Communist activist, and Redford a casual, shallow type – through World War II civilian and military service, finally to Hollywood where liberal activities lead to blacklisting and marriage breakup.

The overemphasis on Streisand makes the film just another one of those Streisand vehicles where no other elements ever get a chance. Redford's role is another instance of waste of his talent. Supporting players are virtual cameos.
☐ 1973: Best Original Score, Song ('The Way We Were').
☐ Nominations: Best Actress (Barbra Streisand), Cinematography, Costume Design, Art Direction

. . . .

■ WEB, THE

1947, 87 MINS, US
Dir Michael Gordon   *Prod* Jerry Bresler   *Scr* William Bowers, Bertram Milhauser   *Ph* Irving Glassberg
Ed Russell Schoengarth   *Mus* Hans J. Salter
Art Dir Bernard Herzbrun, James Sullivan
● Ella Raines, Edmund O'Brien, William Bendix, Vincent Price, Maria Palmer (Universal-International)

There are no Freudian angles cluttering up *The Web's* melodrama. Picture presents a crook who kills because he wants money and power and not because of some psycho-quirk springing from a past incident.

Topnotch performances by majority of cast carry the melodramatics along in forthright style. The pace is tight and fast, accentuating intrigue and excitement. Standout is Edmond O'Brien as the hero who becomes enmeshed in Vincent Price's scheme to hold on to a stolen million dollars. Another honor-garnerer is William Bendix as an honest cop whose lack of faith in things being as they appear is responsible for eventual downfall of Price. Latter gives a compelling reading to the role of a treacherous, suave big-business man. Ella Raines co-stars as heroine and secretary to Price who awakens romantic interest in O'Brien.

Plot deals with efforts of a young attorney and the police to trap Price into confession of two murders and theft of the million bucks. As his first screen directing chore, former stage director Michael Gordon makes an effective first try that gets the best from the suspense ingredients.

■ **WEDDING, A**

1978, 125 MINS, US ◇ ⓥ
Dir Robert Altman   *Prod* Robert Altman   *Scr* John Considine, Patricia Resnik, Allan Nicholls, Robert Altman   *Ph* Charles Rosher   *Ed* Tony Lombardo   *Mus* Tom Walls
● Carol Burnett, Mia Farrow, Lillian Gish, Howard Duff, Geraldine Chaplin, Lauren Hutton (Lion's Gate)

If *Nashville* is ensemble Altman at its best – and it is – then *A Wedding* is the other extreme. Altman's loose, seemingly unstructured style backfires in this comedy-drama.

The title is self-descriptive: the picture is a day in the life of a wedding between the daughter of a nouveau rich southern family and the son of old midwestern money. The setting is rife with conventions – marriage, religion, wealth.

Unlike *Nashville*, the film lacks a core. Nothing builds; the characters, except for Lillian Gish as the old money matriarch and Mia Farrow as the silent sister of the bride, are uninteresting and unsympathetic. They pop in and out of the film and when they pop out, who cares if they return?

Altman's idea of humor comes off as puerile and dated. John Cromwell plays a senile bishop who performs the wedding ceremony. He forgets how to conduct the service and is too near sighted to know that at one point he's talking to a corpse. That's hardly sharp edged satire.

■ **WEDDING BELLS**
See: Royal Wedding

■ **WEDDING MARCH, THE**

1928, 115 MINS, US ◇ ⓥ
Dir Erich von Stroheim   *Prod* Pat Powers   *Scr* Erich von Stroheim, Harry Carr   *Ph* Ben Reynolds, Hal Mohr   *Ed* Josef von Sternberg   *Mus* J.B. Zamencnik, Louis de Francesco   *Art Dir* Erich von Stroheim, Richard Day
● Erich von Stroheim, Fay Wray, George Fawcett, George Nichols, ZaSu Pitts, Maude George (Paramount)

Left of all the footage on *Wedding March* are 10 reels, with the finish where intermission would have been had the picture come in for $2 with the rest of it. Also are remaining is a ponderous slow moving production and some beautiful photography telling a very familiar story, the tip off on which is the lead title, 'Vienna 1914'. It's fair but hardly brilliant program material which the boys salvaged from a regiment of reels.

Scissors to the right and left, leaving most of the picture still in cans, cut the story to the well-known blue-blooded Austrian army officer having his fling with the country maiden and then wedding a limping heiress as the seduced rural miss promises marriage to pacify the brow-beating butcher who has threatened the life of the hit-and-run lieutenant.

Fay Wray appeals and convinces as the shy, pretty-faced and innocent victim, while Stroheim's scoundrel is interesting, despite the half-hearted attempt to soften the character. George Fawcett and George Nichols make conventional fathers. Maude George

will startle the peasants with her cigar-smoking mother of Nicki. ZaSu Pitts is the crippled princess, giving the role legitimate interpretation.

Getting *Wedding March* to a screen took something like two years and over $1 million. Main defect is that deletion has not added pace. Synchronized score is excellent and shows judgment in the use of minor effects.

■ **WEDDING NIGHT, THE**

1935, 81 MINS, US
Dir King Vidor   *Prod* Samuel Goldwyn   *Scr* Edith Fitzgerald   *Ph* Gregg Toland   *Ed* Stuart Heisler   *Mus* Alfred Newman   *Art Dir* Richard Day
● Gary Cooper, Anna Sten, Helen Vinson, Ralph Bellamy, Siegfried Rumann, Esther Dale (Goldwyn/United Artists)

Story [by Edwin Knopf] is irritating in many ways. Gary Cooper is a young author who sells a piece of his land to a Polish tobacco grower, who wants it as a dowry for his daughter. He goes to the farmhouse to make the sale. He is received with hospitality and made welcome at the meal which turns out to be a betrothal feast.

Author returns home, announcing that he has found the theme for his new book in the family he has just left. The Polish girl becomes first interested in the man and then flattered by the novel in which she, the heroine, works the spiritual regeneration of the author, who frankly divorces his wife – on paper – to take on the new love.

King Vidor, in his direction, handles the incidents with fine touch, keeping each character whole and consistent and developing a fluid action which moves easily from the American to the Polish home and back again.

Anna Sten is more fortunately cast than in *Nana* (1934). She is exotic, but her still-marked accent fits the character and she gives a finely sensitive performance.

She is handicapped in a way by the more showy personality of Helen Vinson as the author's wife; hard as nails, but realizing eventually she loves her man and is willing to fight for him. Cooper contibutes an easy character drawing which by its charm almost blinds to the havoc he works. Ralph Bellamy is capital as the destined husband.

■ **WEDDING PARTY, THE**

1969, 90 MINS, US ⓥ
Dir Cynthia Munroe, Brian De Palma, Wilford Leach   *Prod* Cynthia Munroe, Brian De Palma, Wilford Leach   *Scr* Cynthia Munroe, Brian De Palma, Wilford Leach   *Ph* Peter Powell   *Ed* Cynthia Munroe, Brian De Palma, Wilford Leach   *Mus* John Herbert McDowell
● Jill Clayburgh, Charles Pflugar, Valda Setterfield, Ray McNally, Robert De Niro, Judy Thomas (Ondine)

Story dwells on a young man who, accompanied by two friends, arrives at the island estate of his soon-to-be-bride.

The individual scenes come off as a kind of practiced improvisation. Apparently a script was employed but the dialogue itself was produced by taping ad-libbed scenes.

The film suffers from this technique. Each scene is only loosely connected with what went before and what comes after. And tightness and direction of the dialogue is sacrificed for a certain spontaneity that is seldom forthcoming.

The cast includes professional actors combined with Sarah Lawrence College workshop students.

Film was actually completed [in 1963]. De Palma worked in collaboration with then fellow student Cynthia Munroe and faculty member Wilford Leach when all three were at Sarah Lawrence College.

■ **WE DIVE AT DAWN**

1943, 92 MINS, UK ⓥ
Dir Anthony Asquith   *Prod* Maurice Ostrer   *Scr* J.R. Williams, Val Valentine   *Ph* Jack Cox
● John Mills, Eric Portman, Jack Watling, Leslie Weston, Reginald Purdell, Niall MacGinnis (Gainsborough)

The submarine *Sea Tiger* is sent out to sink a Nazi battleship which is due to leave Bremerhaven for the Kiel Canal, en route to the Baltic. The sub's instructions are to intercept her off the German coast before she enters the canal. Too late for this, the lieutenant in charge decides to brave the dangers of the Baltic and attack the battleship when she emerges at the other end of the canal. Owing to depth charges from accompanying destroyers, the attack results in a leakage in the sub's oil tanks and the Britisher decides to blow her up and escape to Denmark.

One of the seamen remembers there is a port on a nearby Danish island where there may be a tanker in dock. Donning the uniform of a dead German airman, he lands on the island, finds a tanker and signals to his ship to come in shore. They refuel and return home, and only then discover they have sunk the German vessel they were after.

John Mills enacts the lieutenant with not only requisite dignity, but with a human touch. But it is Eric Portman, as the seaman, who has the outstanding role and scores best. Rest of the cast gives excellent performances, while direction and production are above par.

■ **WEEKEND AT BERNIE'S**

1989, 97 MINS, US ◇ ⓥ ⊙
Dir Ted Kotcheff   *Prod* Victor Drai   *Scr* Robert Klane   *Ph* Francois Protat   *Ed* Joan E. Chapman   *Mus* Andy Summers   *Art Dir* Peter Jamison
● Andrew McCarthy, Jonathan Silverman, Catherine Mary Stewart, Terry Kiser, Don Calfa, Catherine Parks (Gladden)

As shiepping-the-stiff pics go, *Weekend at Bernie's* ranks below the classic black comedy of *The Trouble with Harry* and *S.O.B.*, but there's enough farcical fun. Terry Kiser steals the show as the corpse hauled around by frantic Andrew McCarthy and Jonathan Silverman.

When Gotham insurance company go-getters McCarthy and Silverman show up for a weekend in the Hamptons with slimy boss Kiser, only to find him bumped off by the mob, it's a scream for a few minutes before the gags become repetitive.

Gross caricatures abound as Kiser's decadent party guests fail to notice their host is much more laid-back than usual. For reasons which are not made totally credible, the boys feel they have to keep Bernie's demise a secret from everyone, and only their hilarious attempts to get the stiff off the island put the film back on track.

Script comes up with the occasional outrageous invention, such as a scene in which Kiser's sex-crazed mistress engages him in strenuous lovemaking, causing McCarthy to lament that Bernie does better dead than he's been doing alive.

■ **WEEKEND AT BERNIE'S II**

1993, 90 MINS, ITALY/US ◇ ⓥ ⊙
Dir Robert Klane   *Prod* Victor Drai   *Scr* Robert Klane   *Ph* Edward Morry III   *Ed* Peck Prior   *Mus* Peter Wolf   *Art Dir* Michael Bolton
● Andrew McCarthy, Jonathan Silverman, Terry Kiser, Tom Wright, Steve James, Troy Beyer (Artimm/Drai)

Hitching a routine rehash of the first installment's cavorting cadaver antics to a frantic hunt for the defunct's cash stash, writer-director Robert Klane delivers a mildly diverting farcical caper in *Weekend at Bernie's II*.

Story picks up ambitious insurance company stooges Andrew McCarthy and Jonathan

Silverman, back in Gotham to check boss Bernie (Terry Kiser) into the morgue and return to work as heroes after uncovering his $2 million plunder. But instead of a promotion, they get fired, with company snoop Barry Bostwick tailing them to track down the missing loot.

Also after the cash are Kiser's mob cohorts, now in cahoots with a Virgin Islands voodoo queen. She dispatches a bumbling duo (Tom Wright and Steve James) to NY to resurrect Kiser and bring him back.

Plot complications are troweled on with varying degrees of plausibility, but serve mainly as a stage for Klane's endless succession of well-timed setups. But Klane pays scant attention to connecting scenes, which despite the affable mugging of McCarthy and Silverman, fail to keep things buoyant.

....

■ WEEKEND WITH KATE

1990, 95 MINS, AUSTRALIA ◇ ⑩

Dir Arch Nicholson   *Prod* Phillip Emanuel   *Scr* Henry Tefay, Kee Young   *Ph* Dan Burstall   *Ed* Rose Evans   *Mus* Bruce Rowland   *Art Dir* Larry Eastwood
● Colin Friels, Catherine McClements, Jerome Ehlers, Helen Mutkins (Emanuel)

The well constructed script indicates a knowledge of romantic comedies of another era. Setup has journalist turned rock music promoter Colin Friels torn between beautiful wife Catherine McClements, who wants to have a baby, and his ambitious mistress Helen Mutkins, who wants Friels.

He decides to tell his wife he's leaving her during a weekend they plan to spend alone at her family's beach house. She has decided to use the intimacy of the weekend to get pregnant. Both plans go astray when British rock idol Jerome Ehlers arrives and moves in for a peaceful weekend of fishing.

The sexual adventures are exuberantly captured on screen. Dialog is sharp and witty, direction is brisk and well-timed, and performances are top notch. Friels is fine as the errant, ambitious husband, and is nicely contrasted with Ehlers as the lanky, self-centered rock star. McClements is a joy as Kate.

Principal photography was completed by spring 1989, with additional shooting taking place several months later to provide a new ending and bridging scenes.

....

■ WEIRD SCIENCE

1985, 94 MINS, US ◇ ⑩ ⊙

Dir John Hughes   *Prod* Joel Silver   *Scr* John Hughes   *Ph* Matthew F. Leonetti   *Ed* Mark Warner, Christopher Lebenzon, Scott Wallace   *Mus* Ira Newborn   *Art Dir* John W. Corso
● Anthony Michael Hall, Kelly LeBrock, Ilan Mitchell-Smith, Bill Paxton, Suzanne Snyder, Robert Downey Jr (Universal)

Starting with the delectable premise of two high school nerds who create a woman through some inexplicable computer hocus-pocus, *Weird Science* veers off into a typical coming-of-age saga without exploring any of the psychological territory it lightly sails over in the early going.

Helplessly horny chums Gary (Anthony Michael Hall) and Wyatt (Ilan Mitchell-Smith), in an act of creative frustration, put their brains together and create the answer to their fantasies – the beautiful and very available Lisa (Kelly LeBrock). The trouble is the boys hardly use her.

Although clearly not grounded in reality, the film really goes nowhere with its central conceit, opting instead for a more ordinary approach . Director John Hughes never capitalizes on the idea that Lisa is a creation of 15-year-old psyches or examines the intriguing question of who controls whom in this relationship.

Hughes' true gift is at capturing the naturalistic rhythms and interaction between the boys with a great ear for dialog. LeBrock is just right as the film's calm but commanding center.

....

■ WELCOME HOME

1989, 87 MINS, US ◇ ⑩

Dir Franklin J. Schaffner   *Prod* Martin Ransohoff   *Scr* Maggie Kleinman   *Ph* Fred J. Koenekamp   *Ed* Bob Swink   *Mus* [uncredited]   *Art Dir* Dan Yarhi
● Kris Kristofferson, JoBeth Williams, Brian Keith, Sam Waterston, Trey Wilson, Thomas Wilson Brown (Columbia/Rank)

A fine opportunity to explore the emotional conflict and military-political hush-hush regarding the unexpected reappearance of US soldiers recorded as dead in Vietnam and Cambodia is missed almost totally in Franklin J. Schaffner's *Welcome Home*.

Kris Kristofferson looks suitably haggard and tired as Lt Jake Robbins, who returns to Vermont after 17 years in Cambodia. He was shot down there and put in POW camp. Jake later settled down to married village life with Cambodian Leang (Kieu Chinh Nguyen) who bore him two children.

It is not until he wakes up in a New York State Air Force hospital that Jake remembers that he had just married his American sweethert Sarah (mournfully played by JoBeth Williams) before he set out on his Far East tour of duty. He is told that she is now remarried and lives happily in Vermont with her second husband (Sam Waterston) and 17-year-old son (Thomas Wilson Brown), who is actually Jake's.

Jake, however, feels he must at least see his son, so he bungles on to the Vermont scene where he upsets everybody.

An uninspired screenplay does not help Schaffner in making the film move forward more than sluggishly. The plot flounders in shallow waters.

....

■ WELCOME HOME ROXY CARMICHAEL

1990, 98 MINS, US ◇ ⑩ ⊙

Dir Jim Abrahams   *Prod* Penney Finkelman Cox   *Scr* Karen Leigh Hopkins   *Ph* Paul Elliott   *Ed* Bruce Green   *Mus* Thomas Newman   *Art Dir* Dena Roth
● Winona Ryder, Jeff Daniels, Laila Robins, Thomas Wilson Brown, Joan McMurtrey, Frances Fisher (ITC)

Fans of Winona Ryder will definitely want to catch her in an offbeat role as the town rebel in this teen-oriented smalltown saga; unfortunately, the rest of the production doesn't quite match up.

Ryder plays 15-year-old Dinky Bossetti, a moody, glowering misfit who scribbles poetry, wears baggy black clothes and doesn't comb her hair. Her nowhereville hometown of Clyde, Ohio, is all in a dither about the impending return of legendary local Roxy Carmichael, and Dinky, being adopted, decides that Roxy must have been her real mother.

Also certain that Roxy is coming back for him is Jeff Daniels as Denton, formerly the teenaged boyfriend with whom she had a baby, now a married man with a family. As all gossip turns to Roxy and her precocious local deeds, Denton's wife (Joan McMurtrey) gets fed up with the situation and leaves him.

Meanwhile the socially reviled Dinky is being pursued by a nerdy guidance counselor who wants to put her in a school for misfits, and a rather blank-slated surfer-looking dude (Thomas Wilson Brown) who wants to be her boyfriend.

Ryder's performance has a subtle glow and maturity that mesmerizes. Her keenly observed creation of the spooky, androgynous Dinky, with her low voice and deadpan delivery, injects her scenes with a natural comedy far more satisfying than the more hysterical efforts being made around her.

....

■ WELCOME TO BLOOD CITY

1977, 96 MINS, UK/CANADA ◇ ⑩

Dir Peter Sasdy   *Prod* Marilyn Stonehouse   *Scr* Stephen Schneck, Michael Winder   *Ph* Reginald Morris C.S.C.   *Ed* Keith Palmer   *Mus* Roy Budd   *Art Dir* Tony Hall
● Jack Palance, Keir Dullea, Samantha Eggar, Barry Morse, Hollis McLaren, Chris Wiggins (EMI/Herberman)

An anonymous totalitarian organization kidnaps Keir Dullea. Via computer electronics, he is mentally transported to a fantasized oater settlement (Blood City) where a person's status accrues according to the number of people he/she can murder. Sheriff Jack Palance is classified as Immortal, having 20 killings to his score.

Dullea's progress through the city is monitored by program technicians Samantha Eggar (who also inexplicably lives in Blood City) and John Evans.

Although the film's initial conception may have held traces of intelligence, swiss-cheese script strains coherence and interest with each development. Consequently, neither in their interdependence or individuality do the film's sci-fi or western elements emerge as generically satisfying.

....

■ WELCOME TO HARD TIMES

1967, 103 MINS, US ◇

Dir Burt Kennedy   *Prod* Max E. Youngstein, David Karr   *Scr* Burt Kennedy   *Ph* Harry Stradling Jr   *Ed* Aaron Stell   *Mus* Harry Sukman   *Art Dir* George W. Davis, Carl Anderson
● Henry Fonda, Janice Rule, Keenan Wynn, Janis Paige, Warren Oates, Fay Spain (M-G-M)

Welcome to Hard Times is more than an oater title; it is a pretty fair evaluation of this production. Burt Kennedy's direction is as inept as his script, an adaptation of E.L. Doctorow's novel about sadistic tough Aldo Ray who burns down a western town. Cowardly (or is he?) mayor Henry Fonda inspires town to rebuild.

Janice Rule is unsatisfactory as the woman who taunts Fonda for a whole year, then cues a bloody climax. She plays it with an Irish accent, effect being a sort of Method school version of Maureen O'Hara.

Keenan Wynn, with wife Janis Paige and three saloon babes, offer some low comedy relief. Edgar Buchanan comes off best as a territorial officer. Presence of many pro names – Lon Chaney, Elisha Cook, Paul Fix, etc – only serves to emphasize the lack of depth and perception in script and direction.

....

■ WELCOME TO L.A.

1976, 103 MINS, US ◇ ⑩

Dir Alan Rudolph   *Prod* Robert Altman   *Scr* Alan Rudolph   *Ph* Dave Myers   *Ed* William A. Sawyer, Tom Walls   *Mus* Richard Baskin
● Keith Carradine, Sally Kellerman, Geraldine Chaplin, Harvey Keitel, Lauren Hutton, Viveca Lindfors (United Artists)

The banal point of *Welcome to L.A.* is pretty much summed up in the closing song by Richard Baskin, in which Keith Carradine sings of the city 'where the air is thick and yellow with the stale taste of decay'. The film has a studied, calculated, over-designed look that drains the vitality from the cast as director Alan Rudolph puts them through their predictable paces in a *Nashville*-like amorphous story which has something to do with the music industry.

Welcome to L.A. has lots of aimless driving around town, gloomy sex encounters, mumbled dialog, and showy camera movements.

Carradine sings a few songs, guzzles booze without feeling it, and exerts a mysterious attraction on every woman in sight.

....

■ WE LIVE AGAIN

1934, 85 MINS, US
Dir Rouben Mamoulian   *Prod* Samuel Goldwyn
Scr Maxwell Anderson, Leonard Praskins, Preston Sturges
Ph Gregg Toland   *Ed* Otho Lovering   *Mus* Alfred
Newman (dir.)   *Art Dir* Richard Day, Sergei Soudeikin
● Anna Sten, Fredric March, Jane Baxter, C. Aubrey
Fish, Sam Jaffe, Jessie Ralph (Goldwyn)

We Live Again is a fine, artistic production
which further impresses Anna Sten as a celluloid satellite, vividly displaying her histrionic
talents, with Fredric March equally effective.
It is Tolstoy's *Resurrection* beautifully re-created in dialog and endowed with lavish
Goldwynesque artistry.

The film itself opens almost as a scenic,
showing the peasants tilling the soil for benefit of a tyrannical nobility, and winds up
something of a spec, with the orgy of secular
splendor at the 8-10 minute Easter service
and the extra-curricular maneuvers between
the student officers and the ballerinas from
the czar's subsidized ballet.

The nobleman March portrays is well depicted to illustrate how the youth's natural
instincts are sated by power and pleasure to
the degree that he betrays the peasant girl
(Sten) with whom he had been reared in
equal companship.

March's resurrection and regeneration is
handled with unusual restraint. Director
Rouben Mamoulian has held him in fine
check, at the same time not sacrificing Sten.
Her blonde beauty is enhanced by a highly effective native histrionism which the camera
angles and the lighting further emphasize.

■ WENT THE DAY WELL?
(US: 48 Hours)

1942, 93 MINS, UK
Dir Alberto Cavalcanti   *Prod* Michael Balcon   *Scr* John
Dighton, Diana Morgan, Angus MacPhail   *Ph* Wilkie
Cooper   *Ed* Sidney Cole   *Mus* William Walton
Art Dir Tom Morahan
● Leslie Banks, Basil Sydney, Frank Lawton, Elizabeth
Allan, Valerie Taylor, John Slater (Ealing)

This Ealing Studios tale [from a story by
Graham Greene] of 72 hours of the life of
Bramley End, a tiny hamlet in the heart of
the English countryside, is introduced by an
old grave-digger playing straight into the
camera. Dealing with an attempt at an airborne invasion of a sparsely peopled part of
England, as contrasted with the well-de-
fended key cities, this picture achieves considerable interest.

Settings, exterior and interior, smack of the
real thing, from the 13th-century church to
the village grocery whose proprietress is also
postmistress and telephone exchange operator.

Direction by Alberto Cavalcanti is workmanlike, but to the men of the
Gloucestershire Regiment (cast as both
German invaders and members of the local
Home Guard) must go chief credit for the realistic note underlying the film, which is almost as factual as a propaganda short.

■ WE OF THE NEVER NEVER

1982, 136 MINS, AUSTRALIA ◇ ⦾
Dir Igor Auzins   *Prod* Greg Tepper   *Scr* Peter Schreck
Ph Gary Hansen   *Ed* Clifford Hayes   *Mus* Peter Best
Art Dir Josephine Ford
● Angela Punch McGregor, Arthur Dignam, Tony Barry,
Tommy Lewis, Lewis Fitz-Gerald, Martin Vaughan (Adams
Packer/FCWA)

We of the Never Never is a stirring historical
drama which explores a number of themes –
racism, women's emancipation, and man's
struggle to come to terms with an alien environment.

Pic is hindered, although not severely, by

the casting of Arthur Dignam in the lead
role. He lacks the authority and ruggedness
to be credible as a turn-of-the-century explorer and adventurer who can run a 4,000-
acre cattle station and control unruly stock-
men and nomadic Aborigines. Compensating
for that weakness is the topline performance
of Angela Punch McGregor, an actress with a
commanding presence.

Based on a classic Australian novel [by Mrs
Aeneas Gunn], film concerns a 30-year-old
city-bred woman, Jeannie, who is forced to
make the transition from civilized Melbourne
to the barren outback of the Northern
Territory when she marries station owner
Aeneas Gunn.

Director Igor Auzins, helming only his second feature, has created a big, bold and magnificently scenic picture. Gary Hansen's
photography eloquently captures the paradoxical beauty and harshness of the outback.

■ WE'RE NO ANGELS

1955, 103 MINS, US ◇ ⦿ ⦾
Dir Michael Curtiz   *Prod* Pat Duggan   *Scr* Ranald
MacDougall   *Ph* Loyal Griggs   *Ed* Arthur Schmidt
Mus Frederick Hollander   *Art Dir* Hal Pereira, Roland
Anderson
● Humphrey Bogart, Aldo Ray, Peter Ustinov, Joan
Bennett, Basil Rathbone, Leo G. Carroll (Paramount)

Paramount has fashioned a breezy 105-
minute VistaVision feature. Light antics
swing around three convicts of Devil's Island
who find themselves playing Santa Claus to a
family they came to rob.

At times proceedings are too consciously
cute and stage origin of material [a play by
Albert Husson] still clings since virtually all
scenes are interiors with characters constantly
entering and exiting. However, Michael
Curtiz' directorial pacing and topflight performances from Humphrey Bogart, Aldo Ray and
Peter Ustinov help minimize the few flaws.

Screenplay uses great deal of conversation,
mostly amusingly flavored, to tell how convicts descend on store-home operated by Leo
G. Carroll and his wife (Joan Bennett), planning robbery that would finance journey to
France. Trio, all lifers, Bogart for forgery,
others for murder, find family in difficulties
unbecoming Christmas Eve spirit.

■ WE'RE NO ANGELS

1989, 108 MINS, US ◇ ⦿ ⦾
Dir Neil Jordan   *Prod* Art Linson   *Scr* David Mamet
Ph Philippe Rousselot   *Ed* Mick Audsley, Jake Van Wuk
Mus George Fenton   *Art Dir* Wolf Kroeger
● Robert De Niro, Sean Penn, Demi Moore, Wallace
Shawn, Ray McAnally, James Russo (Paramount)

Described by its producer as 'very loosely
based on some of the ideas' in the eponymous
1955 movie about convicts on the lam, *We're
No Angels* is precisely about a pair of jailbirds
on the run. The year is 1935 and Robert De
Niro and Sean Penn are hard-timers in a hellish north country penitentiary that may be a
metaphor for Depression-era America.

The late, great Ray McAnally, reduced here
to a caricature of cruelty as the Big House
warden, forces the heroes to witness the elec-
tocution of a remorseless murderer. But the
condemned con and two heroes pull an improbable breakout and head for the Canadian
border.

De Niro and Penn reach a remote border
town renowned for a shrine of 'the weeping
Madonna' and a monastery. The town is
swarming with police on their trail, but the
cons are happily mistaken for visiting ecclesiastical scholars. Director Neil Jordan and
screenwriter David Mamet thus set the stage
for a parable about virtue, wisdom, faith and
redemption.

Pug-faced, slack-jawed and marble-
mouthed, De Niro and Penn mug their semi-
articulate proles with relish, but as religioso
fish out of water their con game becomes a
tiresome joke.

■ WEST 11

1963, 93 MINS, UK
Dir Michael Winner   *Prod* Daniel M. Angel   *Scr* Keith
Waterhouse, Willis Hall   *Ph* Otto Heller   *Ed* Bernard
Gribble   *Mus* Stanley Black, Acker Bilk
● Alfred Lynch, Kathleen Breck, Eric Portman, Diana
Dors, Harold Lang (Associated-British)

The writing team of Keith Waterhouse and
Willis Hall have done little to uplift this
adaptation of a novel called *The Furnished
Room*.

This is only hackneyed drama about a
young man (Alfred Lynch) who is a layabout,
a misfit, a self-pitier ('I'm an emotional leer,'
he says, profoundly). He gets involved with
chicks, can't keep a job and gets mixed up
with jazz clubs and seedy parties. Turning
point in his life is when he meets up with
Richard Dyce (Eric Portman), an ex-army
con-man. He is talked into an association
with Portman, who wants his aunt bumped
off.

It has its merits. The sleazy London locations are very authentically shown. Perhaps
too authentically. Lynch is an intelligent actor but, in this instance, he fails to induce any
pity. Probably the fault of the script.
Kathleen Breck, his girl friend, copes reasonably. It's her first film part after a small experience in stock.

■ WESTERNER, THE

1940, 97 MINS, US ⦿ ⦾
Dir William Wyler   *Prod* Samuel Goldwyn   *Scr* Jo
Swerling, Niven Busch   *Ph* Gregg Toland   *Ed* Daniel
Mandell   *Mus* Dimitri Tiomkin   *Art Dir* James Basevi
● Gary Cooper, Walter Brennan, Doris Davenport, Fred
Stone, Forrest Tucker, Lillian Bond (Goldwyn/United
Artists)

Although Gary Cooper is starred, Walter
Brennan commands major attention with a
slick characterization of Judge Roy Bean, the
dispenser of law at Vinegaroon – west of the
Pecos. Supplied with a particularly meaty
role, of which he takes fullest advantage,
Brennan turns in a socko job that does much
to hold together a not too impressive script.

The story [by Stuart N. Lake], of cattlemen's resentment against the migration of
settlers to Texas in the post-Civil War days, is
a rather familiar one cinematically. But producer Samuel Goldwyn has invested his version with plenty of production assets – good
cast topped by Cooper; extended shooting
schedule under direction of William Wyler;
and eye-filling scenic backgrounds that are
accentuated by expert photography.

Cooper is a wandering cowhand who comes
before the two-gun judge charged with horse-
stealing, and convicted by the jury that brings
in verdicts according to the ideas of Brennan.
But the latter is a worshipper of actress Lily
Langtry, and when Cooper professes intimate
acquaintance with the lady, sentence is suspended while the judge gets some anecdotes
about the beauteous 'Jersey Lily'.

A strange friendship develops between the
cantankerous old judge and the cowboy. In
the midst of the battle between the homesteaders and the cattlemen, Cooper mediates
the trouble by convincing the judge to declare
peace between the factions. Then Cooper
falls in love with Doris Davenport, daughter
of a rancher, to cement him closer to the settlers.

Cooper provides a satisfactory portrayal of
the roaming westerner; although he has handled the same type of roles many times.

Davenport, a newcomer from the extra field, delivers satisfactorily as the rancher's daughter.

☐ 1940: Best Supp. Actor (Walter Brennan).

☐ Nominations: Best Original Story, B&W Art Direction

....

■ WESTERN UNION

1941, 93 MINS, US ◇ ⊕

Dir Fritz Lang   *Prod* Harry Joe Brown   *Scr* Robert Carson   *Ph* Edward Cronjager   *Ed* Robert Bischoff   *Mus* David Buttolph

● Robert Young, Randolph Scott, Dean Jagger, Virginia Gilmore, Barton MacLane, John Carradine (20th Century-Fox)

Western Union is another epic of the early American frontier. This time the stringing of telephone lines in the 1860s, between Omaha and Salt Lake City, provides the background for adventures and excitement in empire building. Hewing to a straight line in telling the story of pioneering the west, *Western Union* is a lusty and actionful offering.

Mounted with expansiveness as a super-western of upper-budget proportions, picture displays some eyeful exterior panoramas. The tinting photography has some of the finest outdoor scenes which were photographed in the colorful Utah park country.

Randolph Scott, an ex-outlaw who joins the expedition as a scout turns in a strongly persuasive characterization. Dean Jagger is the company engineer in charge of construction; Robert Young a dudish easterner who toughens up under western ways; and Barton MacLane is the renegade outlaw whose band continually harasses the camp. Virginia Gilmore is minor as the romantic interest for conflict between Scott and Young in the early reels.

....

■ WEST POINT STORY, THE

(UK: Fine and Dandy)

1950, 106 MINS, US

Dir Roy Del Ruth   *Prod* Louis F. Edelman   *Scr* John Monks Jr, Charles Hoffmann, Irving Wallace   *Ph* Sid Hickox   *Ed* Owen Marks   *Mus* Ray Heindorf (dir.)

● James Cagney, Virginia Mayo, Doris Day, Gordon MacRae, Gene Nelson, Alan Hale Jr (Warner)

Fresh treatment and new twists to the musical formula make *The West Point Story* worthwhile entertainment.

James Cagney sparkplugs the fun and frolic among a group of players who press him hard for top honors. Another big assist in putting this one over is Virginia Mayo. She bolsters the comedy and wallops the eyes with her array of s.a.

There are several production numbers in keeping with the cadet background of the story.

The story has Cagney as a brash Broadway director down on his luck who accepts the assignment to stage the annual West Point show, '100th Night'. Gordon MacRae, a cadet, wrote the show's book and tunes, and his producer uncle wants it and the young man for a Broadway staging.

☐ 1950: Nomination: Best Score of a Musical Picture

....

■ WEST SIDE STORY

1961, 153 MINS, US ◇ ⊕ ⊙

Dir Robert Wise, Jerome Robbins   *Prod* Robert Wise   *Scr* Ernest Lehman   *Ph* Daniel L. Fapp   *Ed* Thomas Stanford   *Mus* Johnny Green (dir.)   *Art Dir* Boris Leven

● Natalie Wood, Richard Beymer, Russ Tamblyn, Rita Moreno, George Chakiris, Simon Oakland (Mirisch/Beta)

West Side Story is a beautifully-mounted, impressive, emotion-ridden and violent musical. This powerful and sometimes fascinating translation of the [1957] Broadway musical is

said to have cost $6 million.

The Romeo and Juliet theme, propounded against the seething background of rival Puerto Rican and American gangs (repping the Montagues and the Capulets) on the upper West Side of Manhattan, makes for both a savage and tender admixture of romance and war-to-the-death.

Even more notable, however, is the music of Leonard Bernstein and most of all the breathtaking choreography of Jerome Robbins. Bernstein's score, with Stephen Sondheim's expressive lyrics, accentuates the tenseness that constantly builds.

Ernest Lehman's screenplay, based upon Arthur Laurents' solid and compelling book in the Broadway production, is a faithful adaptation in which he reflects the brutality of the juve gangs which vent upon each other the hatred they feel against the world. Plottage focuses on the romance of a young Puerto Rican girl with a mainland boy, which fans the enmity between the two gangs and ultimately leads to the 'rumble' which leaves both gang leaders dead of knife wounds.

Natalie Wood offers an entrancing performance as the Puerto Rican who falls in love with Richard Beymer, forbidden by strict neighborhood ban against group intermingling, and latter impresses with his singing. Most colorful performance, perhaps, is by George Chakiris, leader of Puerto Rican gang the Sharks and brother of femme lead, who appeared in London company in same role portrayed here by Russ Tamblyn, leader of the white Jets gang. Tamblyn socks over his portrayal and scores particularly with his acrobatic terping. Rita Moreno, in love with Chakiris, presents a fiery characterization and also scores hugely.

Singer Marni Nixon dubs Wood's voice. Film, opening with a three-minute orchestral overture, has been expertly lensed by Daniel L. Fapp, whose aerial prolog, looking straight down upon Gotham as camera flies from the Battery uptown and swings to West Side, provides impressive views. Johnny Green conducts music score, which runs 51½ minutes; Saul Bass is responsible for novel presentation of titles and credits; Irene Sharaff, who designed costumes for Broadway, repeats here.

☐ 1961: Best Picture, Directors, Supp. Actor (George Chakiris), Supp. Actress (Rita Moreno), Color Cinematography, Color Art Direction, Sound (Todd-AO Sound Dept, Samuel Goldwyn Sound Dept), Scoring of a Musical Picture, Editing, Color Costume Design

☐ Nomination: Best Adapted Screenplay

....

■ WESTWORLD

1973, 88 MINS, US ◇ ⊕ ⊙

Dir Michael Crichton   *Prod* Paul N. Lazarus III   *Scr* Michael Crichton   *Ph* Gene Polito   *Ed* David Bretherton   *Mus* Fred Karlin   *Art Dir* Herman Blumenthal

● Yul Brynner, Richard Benjamin, James Brolin, Alan Oppenheimer, Victoria Shaw, Dick Van Patten (M-G-M)

Westworld is an excellent film, which combines solid entertainment, chilling topicality, and superbly intelligent serio-comic story values. Michael Crichton's original script is as superior as his direction.

Crichton's Westworld is one of three gigantic theme parks built in what is left of the American outdoors; the others are 'Romanworld' and 'Medievalworld'. For $1,000 a day, flown in tourists may indulge their highest and lowest appetites. Automated robots move about as real people. These automatons may be raped, shot to death, befriended, betrayed, etc. They never strike back.

To this world come Richard Benjamin and James Brolin. They have picked the western-themed park, where they switch to levis, pack

revolvers and live out the screen life depicted by John Wayne, Clint Eastwood, and other actioner stars. Yul Brynner plays a black-clothed bad guy whom Benjamin kills in a saloon confrontation. All the while supervisor Alan Oppenheimer oversees the entire world and its creatures.

But suddenly things begin to go wrong. An unidentified computer casualty begins to spread like a plague. The automatons strike back.

....

■ WETHERBY

1985, 97 MINS, UK ◇ ⊕

Dir David Hare   *Prod* Simon Relph   *Scr* David Hare   *Ph* Stuart Harris   *Ed* Chris Wimble   *Mus* Nick Bicat   *Art Dir* Hayden Griffin

● Vanessa Redgrave, Ian Holm, Judi Dench, Stuart Wilson, Tim McInnerny, Suzanna Hamilton (Greenpoint/Film Four)

The title refers to a small town in the northeastern county of Yorkshire. Jean Travers (Vanessa Redgrave) has lived here all her life; she's a lonely schoolteacher, tormented by the memory of a teenage love affair with a boy who was senselessly murdered while on air force duty in Malaya.

The film opens with a dinner party hosted by Jean in her little cottage. Present are two couples, close friends, and a young stranger John Morgan, whom Jean assumes came with one of the couples, while they in turn assume he is her guest. Next day, Morgan returns to the cottage, and while Jean is making tea, he pulls out a gun and kills himself.

The skill of Hare's approach is that he initially allows us to assume, via normal cinema techniques, that what we saw of the dinner party was the whole story. Gradually, however, we realize we only saw a highly selected part of that evening, and as we return to it again and again, the whole story takes on a different complexion.

Performances are uniformly excellent. Joely Richardson (real-life daughter of Redgrave and Tony Richardson) portrays Redgrave in her youth with great conviction.

....

■ WHALES OF AUGUST, THE

1987, 90 MINS, US ◇ ⊕ ⊙

Dir Lindsay Anderson   *Prod* Carolyn Pfeiffer, Mike Kaplan   *Scr* David Berry   *Ph* Mike Fash   *Ed* Nicolas Gaster   *Mus* Alan Price   *Art Dir* Jocelyn Herbert

● Bette Davis, Lillian Gish, Vincent Price, Ann Sothern, Harry Carey Jr, Frank Grimes (Alive)

Muted but engrossing tale about the balance of power between two elderly sisters boasts superior lead performances from two of the screen's most legendary actresses, Bette Davis and Lillian Gish.

Adapted by David Berry from his 1981 play, story has two sisters living alone in a comfortable but basic home they have occupied for decades on the striking coast of Maine. Sarah (Gish) is a doting busybody who is obliged to care for her sister Libby (Davis), because the latter is blind.

Trouble rears its head in the form of Vincent Price, a White Russian of considerable charm and gentlemanliness who for decades has lived as a 'houseguest' of numerous ladies.

Wearing long, pure white hair Davis looks gaunt, grim and disturbed, but her performance is restrained in such a way that may even increase its power. Gish is a delight throughout.

A black-&-white prolog, in which Mary Steenburgen, Tisha Sterling and Margaret Ladd appear as the women in their youth, gets the film off to a nice start.

☐ 1987: Nomination: Best Supp. Actress (Ann Sothern)

....

WHAT ABOUT BOB?

1991, 99 MINS, US ◇ Ⓥ ⊙
Dir Frank Oz   *Prod* Laura Ziskin   *Scr* Tom Schulman
Ph Michael Ballhaus   *Ed* Anne V. Coates   *Mus* Miles
Goodman   *Art Dir* Les Dilley
● Bill Murray, Richard Dreyfuss, Julie Hagerty, Charlie
Korsmo, Kathryn Erbe, Tom Aldredge (Touchstone Pacific
Partners I)

Bill Murray finds a real showcase for his oft-
shackled talent in this manic comedy.
Originally discussed as a pairing of Murray
and Woody Allen, pic ended up with Richard
Dreyfuss in the role of the tightly wound, egotistical psychiatrist whose life is disrupted by
'multiphobic' new patient Bob Wiley
(Murray), the human equivalent of gum on
the bottom of one's shoe.

Dreyfuss' Dr Leo Marvin gets irked when
the persistent patient follows him to a rustic
New Hampshire retreat, then grows increasingly outraged as Bob proceeds to win over
his family. He helps the doc's death-obsessed
son (Charlie Korsmo, kid in *Dick Tracy*) to
learn to enjoy life and shows compassion to
his daughter (Kathryn Erbe) and unappreciated wife (Julie Hagerty).

Murray has a field day with the character,
which allows him to act like a little kid while
occasionally lapsing into other aspects from
his *Saturday Night Life* days, from his smarmy
lounge singer to the nerd. Dreyfuss generally
reprises the role he played in *Down and Out in
Beverly Hills*: domineering, nouveau riche family man whose stolid existence is turned upside down by unwelcome intruder.

WHAT A MAN

See: Never Give a Sucker an Even Break

WHAT A WAY TO GO!

1964, 111 MINS, US ◇
Dir J. Lee Thompson   *Prod* Arthur P. Jacobs   *Scr* Betty
Comden, Adolph Green   *Ph* Leon Shamroy
Ed Marjorie Fowler   *Mus* Nelson Riddle   *Art Dir* Jack
Martin Smith, Ted Haworth
● Shirley MacLaine, Paul Newman, Robert Mitchum,
Dean Martin, Gene Kelly, Dick Van Dyke (Apjac/
Orchard/20th Century-Fox)

What a Way to Go! is a big, gaudy, gimmicky
comedy which continually promises more
than it delivers by way of wit and/or bellylaffs.

The screenplay, based on a story by Gwen
Davis, is, at its very promising basis, the sad,
sad story of a little poor girl from Ohio who,
though she wants only true love, is married and
widowed in succession by four diverse types
who eventually make her the richest woman in
the world. It's a sort of ironic *True Story*, related
in flashbacks from a psychiatrist's couch.

Essentially, the film is a series of blackout
sketches, enlivened from time to time as
Shirley MacLaine tells of her marriages in
styles of various types of films. Thus, in recalling her life with a Thoreau-reading idealist
(Dick Van Dyke), she sees it in the jerky, exaggerated terms of a silent movie romance;
her life with a beatnik, abstract-impressionist
painter (Paul Newman), in Paris, is viewed as
sexy French film complete with English subtitles; and her life with tycoon Robert Mitchum
is remembered as an overdressed Ross
Hunter production.

Some of these parodies are very funny but,
there often isn't much difference between the
style of the parody and that of the encasing
flashback.

Picture is gaudily, expensively mounted.
There are a couple of songs by Jule Styne, including an hilarious production number
(choreographed by Gene Kelly) which might
have come out of *Follow the Fleet*.
☐ 1964: Nominations: Best Color Costume
Design, Best Color Art Direction

WHAT DID YOU DO IN THE WAR, DADDY?

1966, 115 MINS, US
Dir Blake Edwards   *Prod* Blake Edwards   *Scr* William
Peter Blatty   *Ph* Philip Lathrop   *Ed* Ralph E. Winters
Mus Henry Mancini   *Art Dir* Fernando Carrere
● James Coburn, Dick Shawn, Sergio Fantoni, Aldo Ray,
Giovanna Ralli, Carroll O'Connor (United Artists/Mirisch)

What Did You Do in the War, Daddy? carries an
engaging title but after dreaming it up the
writers promptly forgot all about it and
launched into a thinly-devised comedy without much substance.

Blake Edwards, who directs, also collabed
on original story with Maurice Richlin. Set
against a World War II backdrop – Sicily,
1943 – one's theme. The screenplay dwells on a single situation which holds promise but is never sufficiently realized.

Basic idea has a war-weary American company, commanded by a by-the-book officer,
being detailed to take a town held by a large
Italian force, and their welcome reception by
the Italians who are agreeable to surrendering willingly. But first, they must hold their
wine festival. No festival, no surrender.

Edwards has packed his action with a flock
of individual gags and routines but frequently
the viewer isn't too certain what's happening.
Director draws good comedy portrayals from
a talented cast headed by James Coburn and
Dick Shawn, both delivering bangup performances.

WHATEVER HAPPENED TO AUNT ALICE?

1969, 101 MINS, US ◇ Ⓥ
Dir Lee H. Katzin   *Prod* Robert Aldrich   *Scr* Theodore
Apstein   *Ph* Joseph Biroc   *Ed* Frank J. Urioste
Mus Gerald Fried   *Art Dir* William Glasgow
● Geraldine Page, Ruth Gordon, Rosemary Forsyth,
Robert Fuller, Mildred Dunnock (Palomar/Associates &
Aldrich)

Fresh story, using old-hat scare tricks combined with highly skillful acting.

Widow Geraldine Page hits upon ingenious
method of building up unencumbered women
as companions, to take their life savings and
then bash their heads in. Trouble starts when
she eliminates wistful Mildred Dunnock.
Suspicious Ruth Gordon, former employer of
Dunnock, appears on the scene in the guise of
yet another housekeeper.

Page as a high and mighty wealthy eccentric delivers a bravura performance. Gordon,
working crisply, offers a remarkable portrait
of a brave woman. The two ladies play off
each other relentlessly and audience reaps
the rewards.

Grim humor and superior dialog, as well as
night prowling, barred doors, disconnected
phones, an unexplained wheelchair, wigs and
maniacal laughter total up to fine tale [from
the novel *The Forbidden Garden* by Ursula
Curtiss] of suspense rounded off with a twist
ending.

WHAT EVER HAPPENED TO BABY JANE?

1962, 132 MINS, US Ⓥ ⊙
Dir Robert Aldrich   *Prod* Robert Aldrich   *Scr* Lukas
Heller   *Ph* Ernest Haller   *Ed* Michael Luciano
Mus Frank DeVol   *Art Dir* William Glasgow
● Bette Davis, Joan Crawford, Victor Buono, Marjorie
Bennett, Anna Lee (Seven Arts-Associates)

Teaming Bette Davis and Joan Crawford now
seems like a veritable prerequisite to putting
Henry Farrell's slight tale of terror on the
screen. Although the results heavily favor
Davis (and she earns the credit), it should be
recognized that the plot, of necessity, allows
her to run unfettered through all the stages
of oncoming insanity.

Crawford gives a quiet, remarkably fine interpretation of the crippled Blanche, held in

emotionally by the nature and temperament
of the role. Physically confined to a wheelchair and bed through the picture, she has to
act from the inside and has her best scenes
(because she wisely underplays with Davis)
with a maid and those she plays alone.

The slight basic tale is of two sisters, complete opposites. As children, Jane is *Baby Jane*,
a vaudeville star and the idol of the public.
Offstage, she's a vicious brat, domineering
her plain, inhibited sister and preening parents. Eventually both girls go into films,
where the dark, mousey Blanche blossoms
into a beauty and fine actress, and becomes
Hollywood's top star.

As a result of an accident, hazily presented,
Blanche is permanently crippled. Jane, dependent on her sister for her livelihood, is
forced to care for her, her hate growing with
the years. So, also, does the 'Baby Jane' illusion until, living it daily, she determines to
get rid of Blanche and return to vaudeville.

Advertising for an accompanist, the sole applicant is a huge, ungainly lout (a superb offbeat performance by Victor Buono), who sizes
up the situation's opportunities and goes
along, planning to get enough money to enable him to break the tarnished-silver cord
binding him to a possessive mother.

The chain of circumstances grows, violence
creating violence. Once the inept, draggy
start is passed, the film's pace builds with
ever-growing favor.
☐ 1962: Best B&W Costume Design.
☐ Nominations: Best Actress (Bette Davis),
Supp. Actor (Victor Buono), B&W
Cinematography, Sound

WHAT EVERY WOMAN KNOWS

1934, 90 MINS, US
Dir Gregory La Cava   *Scr* Monckton Hoffe, John
Meehan, James Kevin McGuinness   *Ph* Charles Rosher
Mus Herbert Stothart
● Helen Hayes, Brian Aherne, Madge Evans, Lucile
Watson, Dudley Digges, Donald Crisp (M-G-M)

The theme is by no means new, but the idea
is ever popular. Paramount first presented it
as a silent back in 1921. In 1926 Helen Hayes
and Kenneth MacKenna made a season of
the same James M. Barrie play on Broadway.
It's the 'lil woman' all over again, the help-
meet who humbly does her quiet bit in balancing impulsive man's judgments or, rather,
misjudgments.

This Barrie version brings the egotistical
but knowledge-hungry young barrister (Brian
Aherne) out of Scotland into Parliament,
where he thinks he finds new romance with
power, but is actually catapulted into even
greater glory by the brainy Maggie (Hayes),
who types and edits his MP speeches.

Aherne is a vigorous zealot who makes his
upstartishness respected and even liked by
the Scots community (and the audience), for
none can deny his sincerity.

Madge Evans is out of her usual groove as a
light menace, but she makes it as likeable as
circumstances warrant. Lucile Watson as the
comtesse is a gallant lady, while Dudley
Digges is particularly impressive as the somewhat numb Jamie.

WHAT LOLA WANTS

See: Damn Yankees

WHAT PRICE GLORY?

1926, 116 MINS, US ⊗
Dir Raoul Walsh   *Prod* William Fox   *Scr* James T.
O'Donohoe, Malcolm Stuart Boylan   *Ph* Barney McGill,
Jack Marta, John Smith   *Ed* Rose Smith   *Art Dir* William
Darling
● Victor McLaglen, Edmund Lowe, Dolores Del Rio,
William V. Mong, Phyllis Haver, Leslie Fenton (Fox)

It's a picture [from the play by Maxwell Anderson and Laurence Stallings] that has everything except an out-and-out love story of the calibre of the one in *The Big Parade*. But where it lacks in that it certainly makes up in sex stuff and comedy.

There is a wallop right at the beginning in the two short sequences showing both Flagg and Quirt as sergeants of the marines in China and the Philippines. Right here the conflict between the two men, whose trade is soldiering, over women is set down, yet with a light touch of comedy.

Victor McLaglen stands out bigger than he ever has. He is the hardboiled Capt Flagg, and his role gets far greater sympathy than that of Sergeant Quirt, which Edmund Lowe plays.

As for the Charmaine of Dolores Del Rio, she registers like a house afire. It is no wonder that she had the whole army after her.

To Raoul Walsh a great deal of credit will have to go. His handling of the war stuff is little short of marvelous.

....

■ WHAT PRICE GLORY

1952, 110 MINS, US ◇ ℗

Dir John Ford *Prod* Sol C. Siegel *Scr* Phoebe Ephron, Henry Ephron *Ph* Joe MacDonald *Ed* Dorothy Spencer *Mus* Alfred Newman *Art Dir* Lyle Wheeler, George W. Davis

● James Cagney, Dan Dailey, Corinne Calvet, William Demarest, Robert Wagner, Marisa Pavan (20th Century-Fox)

The durable heroics of *What Price Glory* undergo a comedic treatment in Technicolor for this fresh version of the Maxwell Anderson-Laurence Stallings stage drama.

James Cagney, a corpulent Captain Flagg who looks like he'll bust out of his britches any minute, and Dan Dailey, the braggard Sergeant Quirt, enact the top male roles as rivals for gals and glory with amusing emphasis on frenetics. Both are inclined to mumble or shout their dialog.

Corinne Calvet's charms are freely displayed as the ever-loving Charmaine, ready and willing to give any masculine ally of France aid and comfort.

Story scatters itself among episodes dealing with the marines in World War I and the professional and amatory rivalry of Cagney and Dailey.

Over the entire production is a feeling that any second the picture will break into a musical number. This doesn't happen, but it still serves as a subconscious distraction.

....

■ WHAT PRICE HOLLYWOOD

1932, 87 MINS, US ℗ ⊙

Dir George Cukor *Scr* Gene Fowler, Rowland Brown, Jane Murfin, Ben Markson *Ph* Charles Rosher *Ed* Jack Kitchen *Mus* Max Steiner

● Constance Bennett, Lowell Sherman, Neil Hamilton, Gregory Ratoff, Brooks Benedict (RKO-Pathe)

It's a fan magazine-ish interpretation of Hollywood plus a couple of twists. A waitress becomes a picture star, marries a wealthy playboy, loses him and gets him back when her screen career founders on the suicide of the director who gave her a start.

Director George Cukor tells it interestingly. Story [by Adela Rogers St John] has its exaggerations, but they can sneak under the line as theatrical license. In any case, there's Constance Bennett floating around smartly costumed for street or boudoir; Neil Hamilton is more pleasant than usual as the juvenile; Gregory Ratoff is closer to some film producers in his portrayal than the average audience will realize; and Lowell Sherman is again to the front with a fine interpretation of a derelict director.

□ 1931/32: Nomination: Best Original Story

....

■ WHAT'S LOVE GOT TO DO WITH IT

1993, 118 MINS, US ◇ ℗ ⊙

Dir Brian Gibson *Prod* Doug Chapin, Barry Krost *Scr* Kate Lanier *Ph* Jamie Anderson *Ed* Stuart Pappe *Mus* Stanley Clarke *Art Dir* Stephen Altman

● Angela Bassett, Laurence Fishburne, Vanessa Bell Calloway, Jenifer Lewis, Phyllis Yvonne Stickney, Khandi Alexander (Touchstone)

This immensely enjoyable biography of songstress Tina Turner [from her and Kurt Loder's book *I, Tina*] is a passionate personal and professional drama that hits both the high and low notes of an extraordinary career.

Young Tina, a.k.a. Anna Mae Bullock (Angela Bassett), is first seen as a precocious youngster. She is left in the care of her grandmother after her mother (Jenifer Lewis) goes off to the big city.

It's also in St. Louis, circa 1958, that she encounters charismatic R&B singer-songwriter Ike Turner (Laurence Fishburne). Part of his act involves coaxing comely women to the mike. When Anna Mae lets loose, Ike sees a potent meal ticket.

Nothing in Bassett's earlier repertoire suggested the consummate skill she brings to the part. It is a full-bodied, nuanced portrayal. Fishburne as Ike Turner is also pitch perfect.

....

■ WHAT'S NEW PUSSYCAT

1965, 108 MINS, US ◇ ℗

Dir Clive Donner *Prod* Charles K. Feldman *Scr* Woody Allen *Ph* Jean Badal *Ed* Fergus McDonnell *Mus* Burt Bacharach *Art Dir* Jacques Saulnier

● Peter Sellers, Peter O'Toole, Romy Schneider, Capucine, Paula Prentiss, Woody Allen (United Artists)

What's New Pussycat is designed as a zany farce, as wayout as can be reached on the screen. It's all that, and more . . . it goes overboard in pressing for its goal and consequently suffers from over-contrived treatment.

The Charles K. Feldman production is peopled exclusively by mixed-up characters. Peter Sellers is a Viennese professor to whom Peter O'Toole, editor of a Parisian fashion magazine, goes for psychiatric help in solving his women problems, which keep piling up as he finds more pretty girls. On his part, Sellers has a jealous wife and a roving eye which keeps getting him into trouble.

Original screenplay by Woody Allen, who plays an un-dresser for strippers at the Crazy Horse Saloon and similarly afflicted with girl troubles – provides a field day for gagmen, who seldom miss a trick in inserting a sight gag.

Two top stars come off none too happily in their characterizations. Sellers' nuttiness knows no bounds as he speaks with a thick German accent, and O'Toole proves his forte in drama rather than comedy.

Trio of femmes who chase O'Toole have the proper looks and furnish as much glamor as any one man can take.

□ 1965: Nomination: Best Song ('What's New Pussycat')

....

■ WHAT'S THE MATTER WITH HELEN?

1971, 101 MINS, US ◇

Dir Curtis Harrington *Prod* George Edwards *Scr* Henry Farrell *Ph* Lucien Ballard *Ed* William H. Reynolds *Mus* David Raksin *Art Dir* Eugene Lourie

● Debbie Reynolds, Shelley Winters, Dennis Weaver, Agnes Moorehead, Micheal MacLiammoir, Sammee Lee Jones (Filmways/Raymax)

What's the Matter with Helen? is an okay exploitation shocker starring Debbie Reynolds and Shelley Winters as two Hollywood types of the early sound era caught up in mayhem and mutual suspicion. The good red-herring script is hindered from maximum impact by

director Curtis Harrington, who raises the interest and excitement level too early and lets the film coast to less-than-tense resolution.

Film opens with an excellent title sequence using period newsreel clips winding with a midwest Loeb-Leopold-type juve murder trial, where the femmes are mothers of the two slayers. Threatening phone calls spur pair to Hollywood, where they open a terp studio for would-be Shirley Temple carbons.

Reynolds finds romance with Dennis Weaver, the father of one of her pupils (Sammee Lee Jones). His Texas millionaire accent is a few feet too thick. Winters, mentally hassled by mysterious strangers across the street and unnerved by friends, turns more to the radio preachings of Agnes Moorehead, excellent in hard-sell evangelist role.

....

■ WHAT'S UP, DOC?

1972, 94 MINS, US ◇ ℗ ⊙

Dir Peter Bogdanovich *Prod* Peter Bogdanovich *Scr* Buck Henry, Robert Benton, David Newman *Ph* Laszlo Kovacs *Ed* Verna Fields *Mus* Artie Butler *Art Dir* Polly Platt

● Barbra Streisand, Ryan O'Neal, Kenneth Mars, Austin Pendleton, Sorrell Booke, Stefan Gierasch (Saticoy/Warner)

Peter Bogdanovich's *What's Up, Doc?* is a contemporary comedy [from his own original story] in the screwball 1930s style, with absolutely no socially relevant values. This picture is a total smash.

The script and cast are excellent; the direction and comedy staging are outstanding; and there are literally reels of pure, unadulterated and sustained laughs.

Gimmick is a quartet of identical suitcases which of course get into the wrong hands. Barbra Streisand is discovered conning some food out of a hotel, where Ryan O'Neal and fiancee (Madeline Kahn) are attending a musicologists' convention. There is an unending stream of opening and closing doors, perilous balcony walks, and two terrific chases through San Francisco streets.

The humor derives much from the tradition of Warner Bros. cartoons, with broad visuals amid sophisticated ideas. One of the hilarious car chases is virtually a *Road Runner* storyboard, and there's absolutely nothing wrong about that.

....

■ WHAT'S UP, TIGER LILY?

1966, 79 MINS, US ◇ ℗ ⊙

Dir Woody Allen *Prod* Henry G. Saperstein (exec.) *Scr* Woody Allen *Ph* Kazuo Yamada *Ed* Richard Krown *Mus* The Lovin' Spoonful

● Woody Allen, Tatsuya Mihashi, Mie Hama, Akiko Wakabayashi, Tadao Nakamura, Susumu Korobe (American International/Benedict)

Take a Toho Films (Japan) crime meller [directed by Senkichi Taniguchi], fashioned in the James Bond tradition for the domestic market there, then turn loose Woody Allen and associates to dub and re-edit in campcomedy vein, and the result is *What's Up, Tiger Lily?* The production has one premise – deliberately mismatched dialog – which is sustained reasonably well through its brief running time.

Film opens cold with over three minutes of straightforward Japanese meller and chase footage until Allen pops up, explaining the format to follow. The Samurai posturing, to the non-sequitur dialog, is relieved regularly by stop-motion and other effects.

Allen's cohorts, both in writing and dubbing, are Frank Buxton, Len Maxwell, Louise Lasser, Mickey Rose, Julie Bennett and Bryna Wilson.

....

■ WHEN A STRANGER CALLS

1979, 97 MINS, US ◇ Ⓥ ⊙
Dir Fred Walton   *Prod* Doug Chapin, Steve Feke
Scr Steve Feke, Fred Walton   *Ph* Don Peterman
Ed Sam Vitale   *Mus* Dana Kaproff   *Art Dir* Elayne
Barbara Ceder
● Carol Kane, Charles Durning, Colleen Dewhurst, Tony
Beckley, Rachel Roberts, Ron O'Neal (Columbia/Simon-
Krost)

Thanks to a fine cast, a rich and atmospheric
score by Dana Kaproff, and astute direction
by co-writer Fred Walton, *Stranger* is unquestionably a scary film. Bridging two distinct
storylines, one the standard frightened
babysitter alone in a dark house, and the
other the subsequent manhunt for an escaped
killer, script has chills a-plenty.

But something seems lacking overall. By
the film's end, the deficiency seems clear –
key actions and motivations just don't make
sense.

Carol Kane, who disappears for almost 70
of the film's 97 minutes, is quite good as the
terrified sitter who grows up to have the same
chilling chain of events begin all over again.

More than anything else, *When a Stranger
Calls* resembles a good, old-fashioned grade B
thriller.

■ WHEN DINOSAURS RULED THE EARTH

1970, 100 MINS, UK ◇ Ⓥ ⊙
Dir Val Guest   *Prod* Aida Young   *Scr* Val Guest
Ph Dick Bush   *Ed* Peter Curran   *Mus* Mario Nascimbene
Art Dir John Blezard
● Victoria Vetri, Robin Hawdon, Patrick Allen, Sean
Caffrey, Magda Konopka, Imogen Hassall (Hammer)

This is one of those simple sci-fi prehistoric
films which do no harm. Normally, they're
taken either dead seriously or as send-ups.
This one quite deftly combines the two angles.

What the story (mainly shot in the Canary
Islands) is all about is subject to doubt since
Val Guest, who both directed and wrote the
original screenplay, has elected to invent a
'prehistoric' lingo for the dialog.

Story concerns a huge upheaval in the Sun
at the Dawn of History, resulting in a fiery,
sullen appearance of the Moon. A blonde
(Victoria Vetri) is blamed for this, her golden
tresses having suspectedly insulted the Sun.
She's condemned to death, but is rescued by a
neighboring Sand Tribe. The rest consists
largely of fisherman Tara (Robin Hawdon)
falling for the cutie, which irritates his girl
friend (Imogen Hassall).

Amid the animals, special effects, and tribal
rituals (and saddled with non-communicative
language) the human thesps don't stand
much chance of scoring. There are a lot of
very nubile, scantily-clad dames.

■ WHEN EIGHT BELLS TOLL

1971, 94 MINS, UK ◇ Ⓥ
Dir Etienne Perier   *Prod* Elliott Kastner   *Scr* Alistair
MacLean   *Ph* Arthur Ibbetson   *Ed* John Shirley
Art Dir Jack Maxsted
● Anthony Hopkins, Robert Morley, Nathalie Delon,
Jack Hawkins, Corin Redgrave, Derek Bond (Gershwin-
Kastner)

Alistair MacLean's two-fisted, no-holds-
barred adventure yarns are a natural for the
screen. *When Eight Bells Toll* brings in more
slugging, quick action twists, sharp dialog,
amusing acting than many pix twice its
length.

Anthony Hopkins has a role that creates a
character full of resource, courage, cheek and
personality. A kind of James Bond, without
the latter's trademarks. Character is a naval
secret service agent assigned to find out how
millions of pounds in gold bullion are being
pirated. He starts his explorations in the

bleakness of the Western Highlands of
Scotland. Hopkins and his pal (Corin
Redgrave) posing as marine biologists find
mystery and hostility among the natives and
the obvious suspect is a suave, rich Greek tycoon (Jack Hawkins) whose luxury yacht
guests some odd characters.

Main femme appeal comes from Nathalie
Delon as the mystery woman who is allegedly
Hawkins' wife but apparently goes over to the
Hopkins camp. Hawkins, himself, as the
Greek tycoon retains his usual stature and his
voice (lost to throat cancer) is very shrewdly
dubbed. Comedy relief comes from Robert
Morley, as Hopkins' snobbish, stuffy chief.

■ WHEN HARRY MET SALLY. . .

1989, 95 MINS, US ◇ Ⓥ ⊙
Dir Rob Reiner   *Prod* Rob Reiner, Andrew Scheinman
Scr Nora Ephron   *Ph* Barry Sonnenfeld   *Ed* Robert
Leighton   *Mus* Marc Shaiman   *Art Dir* Jane Musky
● Billy Crystal, Meg Ryan, Carrie Fisher, Bruno Kirby,
Steven Ford, Lisa Jane Persky (Castle Rock/Nelson)

Can a man be friends with a woman he finds
attractive? Can usually acerbic scripter Nora
Ephron sustain 95 minutes of unrelenting
cuteness? Can the audience sit through 11
years of emotional foreplay between adorable
Billy Crystal and Meg Ryan?

Abandoning the sour, nasty tone of some of
her previous writing about contemporary sexual relationships, Ephron cuddles up to the
audience in this number about the joys and
woes of (mostly) platonic friendship.

Two characters who seem to have nothing
on their minds but each other (even though
they won't admit it), Harry and Sally are supposed to be a political consultant and a journalist, but it's hard to tell from the evidence
presented.

Rob Reiner directs with deftness and sincerity, making the material seem more engaging than it is, at least until the plot
machanics begin to unwind and the film
starts to seem shapeless. The only thing
that's unpredictable about the story is how
long it takes Harry and Sally to realize
they're perfect for each other.
□ 1989: Nomination: Best Original
Screenplay

■ WHEN I FALL IN LOVE

See: *Everybody's All-American*

■ WHEN LADIES MEET

1933, 73 MINS, US
Dir Harry Beaumont   *Prod* Lawrence Weingarten
Scr John Meehan, Leon Gordon   *Ph* Ray June   *Ed* Hugh
Wynn
● Ann Harding, Robert Montgomery, Myrna Loy, Alice
Brady, Frank Morgan, Luis Alberni (M-G-M)

Few stage plays reach the screen with the author's idea. But here the adapters have preserved the savor of the original [by Rachel
Crothers] while producing a generally mobile
atmosphere.

Story gets off to a typical picture start,
which will lead those unfamiliar with the
drama to fear another of those wild-life-in-so-
ciety yarns, but it soon steadies down into
nicely-paced action punctuated by plenty of
laughs that arise from the lines instead of
horseplay.

When the big scene between the two
women (Ann Harding and Myrna Loy) does
arrive, the spectator is so intrigued by the
characters that it is not necessary to frantically angle to conceal the fact that the chat
runs which might be overlong. It's interesting
and holds quiet attention, which is unusual.

The script is nicely planned with much of
the original dialog apparently preserved, and

Harry Beaumont does an exceptional job of
direction.

In addition to Harding's fine playing, Loy
does an excellent chore with the nominal
heroine as the ambitious young writer who
has fallen in love with her publisher. She
plays sincerely and naturally. Robert
Montgomery does not quite get into his character. On the other hand Alice Brady, in a fat
part as a socialite is dangerously close to running away with the film now and then, and is
responsible for the major portion of laughs.
□ 1932/33: Nomination: Best Art Direction

■ WHEN THE BOYS MEET THE GIRLS

1965, 97 MINS, US ◇
Dir Alvin Ganzer   *Prod* Sam Katzman   *Scr* Robert E.
Kent   *Ph* Paul C. Vogel   *Ed* Ben Lewis   *Mus* Fred
Karger
● Connie Francis, Harve Presnell, Herman's Hermits,
Louis Armstrong, Sam The Sham and the Pharoahs, Sue
Ane Langdon (Four Leaf/M-G-M)

When The Boys Meet The Girls is the third film
to be based specifically on the 1930-1 legituner, *Girl Crazy*. This production is a spotty
comedy film, loaded with often extraneous
tunes, also limited to some okay performances and gags.

Top-featured Connie Francis and Harve
Presnell (seemingly cast more from contractual commitments than suitability) are adequate; she as the backwoods Nevada US
mail-woman saddled with pop Frank Faylen, a
chronic gambler, while Presnell is the bigcity
playboy exiled to the boondocks to avoid a
breach-of-promise suit by chorine Sue Ane
Langdon.

Joby Baker is Presnell's buddy who eventually pairs with a rather mute Susan Holloway
and Fred Clark is good as the neighboring
rancher who hitches up with Hortense Petra.
Langdon remains the most impressive of the
principals; she makes a firstrate shrew.

Among the 11 tunes are five vintage
Gershwin numbers, including 'I Got Rhythm',
subject of what is the big production number.

■ WHEN THE WHALES CAME

1989, 99 MINS, UK ◇ Ⓥ ⊙
Dir Clive Rees   *Prod* Simon Channing Williams
Scr Michael Morpurgo   *Ph* Robert Paynter   *Ed* Andrew
Boulton   *Mus* Christopher Gunning   *Art Dir* Bruce
Grimes
● Paul Scofield, David Thelfall, Helen Mirren, David
Suchet, Helen Pearce, Jeremy Kemp (Golden Swan/
Central)

When The Whales Came is a slight story beautifully dressed to give the appearance of more
substance. Performances, direction and design are all first-rate, but there is the overwhelming sensation that there is a lot less
there then meets the eye.

Film [from the novel *Why the Whales Came*
by Michael Morpurgo] opens on the island of
Samson in the Scilly Isles in 1844 where locals
leave the island they believe cursed. Then in
1914 on the neighbouring island of Bryher
youngsters Daniel (Max Rennie) and Gracie
(Helen Pearce) play on the beach, watched by
the mysterious Birdman (Paul Scofield).

Though warned against Birdman by other
villagers they make friends with him and he
warns them about never going to Samson.
When a tusked whale (a narwhal) is beached
on the shore it seems the curse of Samson will
strike Bryher.

Paul Scofield's portrayal of the deaf
Birdman has the quality of sadness and pride
that only he can give a role. Most endearing
performance is by radiant young Pearce. A
non-actor, she is a resident of Bryher (where
pic is set) and was only found when she
turned up for work as an extra.

WHEN WORLDS COLLIDE

1951, 81 MINS, US ◇ ⊚ ⊙
Dir Rudolph Mate   *Prod* George Pal   *Scr* Sydney Boehm   *Ph* John F. Seitz, W. Howard Greene   *Ed* Doane Harrison, Arthur Schmidt   *Mus* Leith Stevens   *Art Dir* Hal Pereira, Albert Nozaki
● Richard Derr, Barbara Rush, Peter Hanson, John Hoyt, Larry Keating, Judith Ames (Paramount)

Top honors for this inter-planetary fantasy rest with the cameramen and special effects technicians rather than with performances of the non-name cast. Process photography and optical illusions are done with an imaginativeness that vicariously sweeps the spectator into space.

Story is predicated upon the findings of a scientist (Hayden Rorke) that a planet, Zyra, will pass so close to the earth a year hence that oceans will be pulled from their beds. Moreover, 19 days after this catastrophe, the star, Bellus, will collide with whatever remains of the world.

Unfortunately, scripter Sydney Boehm who fashioned the screenplay [from a novel by Edwin Balmer and Philip Wylie], chose to work in a romance between Barbara Rush, daughter of astronomer Larry Keating, and Richard Derr, a plane pilot. His love rival is Peter Hanson, a doctor.

Departure, actual flight and landing upon Zyra represent the highpoint of the picture. Somewhat of a puzzle, however, is the fact that although the ship lands upon an ice-covered valley, its occupants step out into a verdant paradise when opening the craft's door.
□ 1951: Best Special Effects
□ Nomination: Best Color Cinematography

WHERE ANGELS FEAR TO TREAD

1991, 112 MINS, UK ◇ ⊚
Dir Charles Sturridge   *Prod* Derek Granger   *Scr* Tim Sullivan, Derek Granger, Charles Sturridge   *Ph* Michael Coulter   *Ed* Peter Coulson   *Mus* Rachel Portman   *Art Dir* Simon Holland
● Helena Bonham Carter, Judy Davis, Rupert Graves, Giovanni Guidelli, Barbara Jefford, Helen Mirren (Sovereign)

A turn-of-the-century costumer about cold-blooded Brits thawing out in sunny Italy, *Where Angels Fear to Tread* is a far more rewarding dip into the E.M. Forster tub than some of its predecessors. Paralleling the 1905 book's light, serio-comic tone, pic has none of the top-heaviness of David Lean's *A Passage to India* or the starchiness of Merchant-Ivory's *A Room with a View*.

Feisty widow Lilia (Helen Mirren) goes to Italy for some r&r with younger companion Caroline (Helena Bonham Carter) and tangles with Tuscan boytoy Gino (Giovanni Guidelli). When news reaches home, Lilia's bossy mother-in-law, Mrs Herriton (Barbara Jefford), dispatches milquetoast son Philip (Rupert Graves) to buy off the hot-blooded Italo. That idea goes down the tubes when the pair reveal they're already hitched.

Pic's strength is the way in which characters come in and out of focus. Lilia, it turns out, is simply a catalyst: true love affair is a sexually blurred triangle of Philip, Caroline and Gino.

Helmer Charles Sturridge tweaks what could have been a talky telepic into a proper theatrical product. Like his previous *A Handful of Dust*, pic plays well on the big screen, with tasty Italian vistas, sharp pacing and (apart from a few static interiors) sequences that really move.

Bonham Carter, who gives her strongest performance to date as the repressed Caroline, is ably supported by Graves. Duo's final scene, a *Brief Encounter*-like meet in a station, packs real emotional clout.

WHERE EAGLES DARE

1969, 158 MINS, UK/US ◇ ⊚ ⊙
Dir Brian G. Hutton   *Prod* Elliott Kastner   *Scr* Alistair MacLean   *Ph* Arthur Ibbetson   *Ed* John Jympson   *Mus* Ron Goodwin   *Art Dir* Peter Mullins
● Richard Burton, Clint Eastwood, Mary Ure, Michael Hordern, Patrick Wymark, Anton Diffring (M-G-M/Winkast)

Alistair MacLean wrote an original screenplay that was treated with respect for the writer's unusual abilities as a master of actionful suspense. The resulting film is highly entertaining, thrilling and rarely lets down for a moment.

It's basically a tale of rescuing a captured American general from a German stronghold in Bavaria during World War II by a hand-picked team of experts. There are so many twists and turns that the viewer is seldom able to predict the next scene.

Richard Burton, a British agent, and Clint Eastwood, an OSS 'assassin', head the crew which includes femme agent Mary Ure, who works at the spy bit.

Although the film is replete with killings and explosions, they're so integrated into the story that they never appear overdone. It's more of a saga of cool, calculated courage, than any glorification of war.

Burton never treats his role, though full of cliches, as anything less than *Hamlet*. Eastwood seems rather wooden in the early scenes, but snaps out of it when action starts piling up.

WHERE LOVE HAS GONE

1964, 111 MINS, US ⊚
Dir Edward Dmytryk   *Prod* Joseph E. Levine   *Scr* John Michael Hayes   *Ph* Joseph MacDonald   *Ed* Frank Bracht   *Mus* Walter Scharf   *Art Dir* Hal Pereira, Walter Tyler
● Susan Hayward, Bette Davis, Michael Connors, Joey Heatherton, Jane Greer, DeForest Kelley (Paramount)

Sooner or later it was bound to happen – a film based on the celebrated onetime Hollywood scandal of the daughter of a film star stabbing to death her mother's paramour. Picture takes its cue in close detail from this incident and patently was inspiration for the Harold Robbins novel. Scene is changed from Hollywood to San Francisco, and the mother now is a society woman witth a bent for sculpture.

Sufficient ingenuity and shock value in character delineation have been interwoven into the screenplay to maintain high-tempoed interest as the yarn revolves around a bitter divorced couple come together again briefly to save their daughter after the 15-year-old girl kills her mother's lover.

Susan Hayward and Bette Davis share top honors in impressive performances, former as the daughter whose life is a story of indiscretions. Davis, smart in a white wig, plays the autocratic mother, who always sees that the family name is protected at any price, a scheming woman of unscrupulous methods and seemingly inexhaustible means. Picture is a brilliant showcase for both actresses and projects them in roles which will find much comment. As the mixed-up teenager who never knew domestic happiness, Joey Heatherton is ideally cast and delivers a compelling portrayal.
□ 1964: Nomination: Best Song ('Where Love Has Gone')

WHERE NO VULTURES FLY

(US: Ivory Hunter)

1951, 106 MINS, UK ◇
Dir Harry Watt   *Prod* Michael Balcon, Leslie Norman   *Scr* W.P. Lipscomb, Ralph Smart, Leslie Norman   *Ph* Paul Beeson   *Ed* Gordon Stone   *Mus* Alan Rawsthorne

● Anthony Steel, Dinah Sheridan, Harold Warrender, Meredith Edwards, William Simons, Orlando Martins (Ealing)

Excellent Technicolor photography and a few thrilling wild animal sequences are the highlights of *Where No Vultures Fly*. On the whole, it's a soundly made film, lensed in the attractive East African setting of the Kenya National Park.

Merely as a peg for the fine location work, there is tagged on an insignificant though basically true story of a game warden who starts the National Park after fighting local prejudice, hunters and ivory poachers. Plot is of little consequence. Main entertainment is derived from some of the exciting animal sequences.

Harry Watt's direction of the game sequences is top grade, but he tends to flounder when handling human characters. Notwithstanding this, Anthony Steel, does an excellent and spirited job as the warden, but Dinah Sheridan is never anything but demure as his wife.

WHERE'S JACK?

1969, 113 MINS, UK ◇
Dir James Clavell   *Prod* Stanley Baker   *Scr* Rafe Newhouse, David Newhouse   *Ph* John Wilcox   *Ed* Peter Thornton   *Mus* Elmer Bernstein
● Tommy Steele, Stanley Baker, Fiona Lewis, Alan Badel, Dudley Foster, Noel Purcell (Paramount/Oakhurst)

Where's Jack, story of Jack Sheppard, notorious 18th-century London highwayman, does not move speedily or with tremendous dramatic climaxes, but it has an authentic sense of atmosphere, and provides a holding battle of wits between the two leading protagonists.

Tommy Steele an Stanley Baker are supported by a competent cast of character actors.

Steele turns in a good acting performance. Unfortunately, the script does not give him much chance to give the role any depth.

Where's Jack? could well have been a more impressive picture about a colorful era in bawdy, criminal, corrupt London. But film has settled for a single adventure and, despite occasional lagging in inventiveness, is a simple and holding yarn.

WHERE SLEEPING DOGS LIE

1992, 89 MINS, US ◇ ⊚
Dir Charles Finch   *Prod* Mario Sotela   *Scr* Yolande Turner, Charles Finch   *Ph* Monty Rowan   *Ed* B.J. Sears, Gene M. Gemaine   *Mus* Hans Zimmer, Mark Mancina   *Art Dir* Eve Cauley
● Dylan McDermott, Tom Sizemore, Sharon Stone, Mary Woronov, David Combs, Shawne Rowe (Sotela)

A clash of two dissimilar personalities is examined with mixed success in the thriller *Where Sleeping Dogs Lie*. Dylan McDermott portrays an unsuccessful writer in Hollywood who's frustrated by the commercial need to write blood-and-guts stories. His agent Sharon Stone puts on the pressure, and he decides to write a detailed novel about a mass killer.

McDermott moves into the creepy old mansion his day-job real estate boss (Ron Karabatsos) has ordered him to sell. Gimmick is that he uses the house for inspiration, basing his novel on a notorious murder case that took place there. Before the film can turn into a haunted house suspenser, Tom Sizemore shows up as a twitchy boarder.

Director Charles Finch (son of the late actor Peter Finch) and his mother, co-scripter Yolande Turner, get good mileage from the insidious relationship that develops between the two protagonists, reminiscent of the classic *The Servant*. Stone is perfect in a small role as the bitchy agent. Rest of the cast has mere walk-ons in a film that reportedly was heavily trimmed to reach its release version.

••••••••••••••••••••••••••••••

■ WHERE'S POPPA?

1970, 83 MINS, US ◇ ⑰ ⊙
Dir Carl Reiner *Prod* Jerry Tokofsky, Marvin Worth *Scr* Robert Klane *Ph* Jack Priestly *Ed* Bud Molin, Chic Ciccolini *Mus* Jack Elliott *Art Dir* Warren Clymer
● George Segal, Ruth Gordon, Ron Liebman, Trish Van Devere, Barnard Hughes, Vincent Gardenia (United Artists)

Where's Poppa? is an insane movie, a black comedy with George Segal as a young lawyer with an active death wish for his old Jewish mother, played by Ruth Gordon, whose senile eccentricities are ruining his career, sex life and health.

Robert Klane's screenplay, adapted from his novel, is very close to tragedy, except that he, director Carl Reiner and an exceptional cast work from the firm conviction that everyone, at least everyone living in New York city, is insane.

Gordon, as the widowed mother, is in senile dementia constantly asking 'Where's Poppa?' and scaring off nurses and Segal's girlfriends with her bawdy eccentricities.

In her mental lapses she can't remember her son is a grown man, and when he brings home Trish Van Devere the mother suddenly describes the size of her son's sex organs as if he were a child.

Van Devere as a prospective nurse looks like the Angel of Mercy with her sweet pure face framed in a white cap, but she is also a little insane.

••••••••••••••••••••••••••••••

■ WHERE THE BOYS ARE

1960, 99 MINS, US ◇ ⑰ ⊙
Dir Henry Levin *Prod* Joe Pasternak *Scr* George Wells *Ph* Robert Bronner *Ed* Fredric Steinkamp *Mus* George Stoll *Art Dir* George W. Davis, Preston Ames
● Dolores Hart, George Hamilton, Yvette Mimieux, Jim Hutton, Barbara Nichols, Paula Prentiss (M-G-M)

The Boys of today, according to the screenplay out of Glendon Swarthout's novel, are generally in irresponsible sexual orbit and it is up to the girls of today to bring them down to earth.

The scenario is set in Fort Lauderdale, Florida, site of an annual spring invasion by Easter-vacationing collegians from all over the East and Midwest, most of the males apparently from the Halls of Ivy (or 'Yalies', as they are precociously referrred to once too often here). Most of the girls manage to avoid the primitive passion, but there is an occasional casualty, in this case Yvette Mimieux who winds up walking the white line on a Florida highway after getting in too deep with a pair of these unscrupulous 'Yalies'.

Mimieux, in a demanding role, gets by dramatically. Visually she is a knockout, and has a misty quality. Paula Prentiss, making her screen debut, is of the Rosalind Russell-Eve Arden mold. Recording star Connie Francis also makes her screen debut.

Jim Hutton is affable, Barbara Nichols flashy (as a dumb blonde in an exaggerated swimming-tank sequence), Frank Gorshin animated and amusing, and Chill Wills effective. Dolores Hart and George Hamilton make beautiful music together.

••••••••••••••••••••••••••••••

■ WHERE THE BUFFALO ROAM

1980, 96 MINS, US ◇ ⑰
Dir Art Linson *Prod* Art Linson *Scr* John Kaye *Ph* Tak Fujimoto *Ed* Christopher Greenbury *Mus* Neil Young *Art Dir* Richard Sawyer
● Peter Boyle, Bill Murray, Bruno Kirby, Rene Auberjonois, R.G. Armstrong, Leonard Frey (Universal)

Where the Buffalo Roam is based on the self-described antics of flip journalist Hunter S.

Thompson, who cooperated as 'executive consultant'. Pic features a number of amusing set-pieces of irreverent lunacy, but lack of serious substance renders film too frivolous and detached from reality.

Film establishes its tone in the opening scene, as writer tries to finish a piece while downing full glasses of Wild Turkey.

Only things fortifying Thompson here are drink, drugs and the search for the insane in American culture.

Sole exceptional element is Bill Murray's clearly studied but provocatively off-beat performance as Thompson, which rings absolutely true.

••••••••••••••••••••••••••••••

■ WHERE THE DAY TAKES YOU

1992, 92 MINS, US ◇ ⑰ ⊙
Dir Marc Rocco *Prod* Paul Hertzberg *Scr* Michael Hitchcock, Kurt Voss, Marc Rocco *Ph* King Baggott *Ed* Russel Livingstone *Art Dir* Kirk Petrucelli
● Dermont Mulroney, Lara Flynn Boyle, Balthazar Getty, Sean Astin, James LeGros, Kyle MacLachlan (Cintel)

Attempting a hard-hitting pic on the grimy realities of Hollywood Boulevard street life, and blessed with a cast bursting with up-and-comer names and a technically adept cameraman, *Where the Day Takes You* inevitably winds up giving the runaway's life the kind of romantic-tragic scope that appeals to troubled teens.

A goateed and tattooed Dermot Mulroney, in a very charismatic turn, plays King, a 21-year-old parolee who returns to his position as a natural leader of street dwellers. He has his hands full watching a gun-happy youth (Balthazar Getty) with an itch for violence and a middle-class runaway (Sean Astin) who stays totally 'tweaked' on speed.

In between profiling himself in social work sessions with a sultry-voiced interviewer (Laura San Giacomo), King takes up with the newest and prettiest chick off the bus from Chicago (a bra-less Lara Flynn Boyle), and shows her off round the streets.

Director Mark Rocco shapes some very fine performances, particularly from Mulroney, Boyle and Getty, while Steven Tobolowsky turns in a memorably chilly perf as a wealthy gay man who pays Getty for titillation. An uncredited Christian Slater turns up in a brief cameo as a social worker.

••••••••••••••••••••••••••••••

■ WHERE THE HEART IS

1990, 94 MINS, US ◇ ⑰ ⊙
Dir John Boorman *Prod* John Boorman *Scr* John Boorman, Telsche Boorman *Ph* Peter Suschitzky *Ed* Ian Crafford *Mus* Peter Martin *Art Dir* Carol Spier
● Dabney Coleman, Uma Thurman, Joanna Cassidy, David Hewlett, Suzy Amis, Christopher Plummer (Touchstone/Silver Screen Partners IV)

Film is a companion piece to John Boorman's little-seen *Leo the Last*, in which Marcello Mastroianni was an aristocrat who learns about life from ghetto denizens in London. This time it's tycoon Dabney Coleman who gets the message when he and his family end up in a Brooklyn tenement.

Predictable plotting has tyrannical buildings demolitions expert Coleman getting fed up with his spoiled, grown-up kids. He throws them out of the mansion and (unconvincingly) orders them to live in a Brooklyn tenement.

Kids, led by Uma Thurman, are determined to make it on their own. Her sister (Suzy Amis) gets a gig doing a calendar for an insurance company, with Thurman the chief nude model for her body-painting and photography artwork.

Film's most successful element is the series of spectacular *trompe d'oeil* artworks by Timna Woollard, personified by Thurman.
Combined with the all-nighter atmosphere of

the delapidated Brooklyn house, pic succeeds in capturing a 1960s ambience.

Beside Thurman, who is perfectly cast as a sexy kook, Amis makes a very good impression as her artistic, romantic sister.

••••••••••••••••••••••••••••••

■ WHERE THE RIVER BENDS

See: Bend of the River

••••••••••••••••••••••••••••••

■ WHERE THE RIVER RUNS BLACK

1986, 100 MINS, US ◇ ⑰
Dir Christopher Cain *Prod* Joe Roth *Scr* Peter Silverman, Neal Jimenez *Ph* Juan Ruiz-Anchia *Ed* Richard Chew *Mus* James Horner *Art Dir* Marcos Flaksman
● Charles Durning, Alessandro Rabelo, Ajay Naidu, Peter Horton, Conchata Ferrell, Marcelo Rabelo (M-G-M)

Where the River Runs Black is a beautifully simple film that celebrates an innocent boy's peaceful co-existence with nature while subtly despairing about man's abuse of it.

Film revolves around a boy with roots in modern civilization being raised by Amazon tribespeople without the knowledge he is the child of two very distinct worlds.

Scripters Peter Silverman and Neal Jimenez have taken David Kendall's novel, *Lazaro*, and crafted a screenplay where the few words of dialog spoken speak worlds of meaning.

Much is said in silence and most effectively told through the movements of 10-year-old Rabelo, a waif-like Brazilian swimmer perfectly cast to portray the physically and emotionally confused dolphin boy traumatized by competing forces. Charles Durning is a natural as a fatherly Irish priest, letting his heart – not the fact that he wears a collar – determine the ultimate fate of the orphan boy.

••••••••••••••••••••••••••••••

■ WHERE THE SIDEWALK ENDS

1950, 95 MINS, US
Dir Otto Preminger *Prod* Otto Preminger *Scr* Ben Hecht *Ph* Joseph LaShelle *Ed* Louis Loeffler *Mus* Cyril J. Mockridge *Art Dir* Lyle Wheeler, J. Russell Spencer
● Dana Andrews, Gene Tierney, Gary Merrill, Karl Malden, Tom Tully, Ruth Donnelly (20th Century-Fox)

Story, by Ben Hecht [adapted by Victor Trivas, Frank P. Rosenberg and Robert E. Kent from the novel *Night City* by William Stuart], unwinds with a maximum of suspense and swiftly-paced action and is featured by an excellent performance by Dana Andrews. Picture is also notable for better-than-average character portrayals and co-star Gene Tierney.

Andrews, while he is on the carpet for slugging too many hoodlums before he has criminal evidence against them, accidentally kills a man in a fistic battle, in self-defense. Victim is Craig Stevens, former war hero and ne'er-do-well estranged husband of Gene Tierney, a lush model.

Otto Preminger, director, does an excellent job of pacing the story and of building sympathy for Andrews.

••••••••••••••••••••••••••••••

■ WHERE THE SPIES ARE

1966, 113 MINS, UK ◇
Dir Val Guest *Prod* Val Guest, Steven Pallos *Scr* Wolf Mankowitz, Val Guest *Ph* Arthur Grant *Ed* Bill Lenny *Mus* Mario Nascimbene *Art Dir* John Howell
● David Niven, Francoise Dorleac, Cyril Cusack, John Le Mesurier, Nigel Davenport, Eric Pohlmann (M-G-M)

David Niven stars as a mild-mannered English doctor pressed into Middle East espionage. The production carries suspense, after a slow and talky start, and action, even if a bit on the contrived side, is fast-paced once story gets underway. Locale is Beirut where troupe locationed to come up with interesting authenticity of background.

Based on James Leasor's thriller, *Passport to Oblivion*, Guest, who also directs and collabed with Wolf Mankowitz on script, concentrates on the dangers confronting a secret agent. Niven, who once figured in some fancy undercover work for British Intelligence, is sent to Lebanon to try to learn what urgent information the agent there had uncovered before he was bumped off by the Russians.

Niven delivers one of his customary competent performances, stuffy at times but able to cope with the melodramatic demands of the character. Teaming with Niven as a French mam'selle playing both sides as a secret agent and supposedly his contact is Francoise Dorleac, lushly effective.

● ●

■ WHERE WERE YOU WHEN THE LIGHTS WENT OUT?

1968, 90 MINS, US ◇

Dir Hy Averback   *Prod* Everett Freeman, Martin Melcher   *Scr* Everett Freeman, Karl Tunberg   *Ph* Ellsworth Fredricks   *Ed* Rita Roland   *Mus* Dave Grusin   *Art Dir* George W. Davis, Urie McCleary
● Doris Day, Robert Morse, Terry-Thomas, Patrick O'Neal, Lola Albright, Jim Backus, Jim Backus (M-G-M)

An okay Doris Day comedy, well cast with Robert Morse and Terry-Thomas. On 9 November 1965, large parts of the eastern US were blacked out. Almost six months later, this film was announced. Some 15 months later, it rolled. And over 30 months after the event, it was released. How's that for reacting to events?

In this script [based on a play by Claude Magnier], the blackout is less than a prop for a routine marital mixup. Day, as a legit actress employed by producer Thomas, is married to architect Patrick O'Neal. Latter lingers a bit too long with sexy magazine interviewer Lola Albright, cueing Day's stormy exit to Connecticut hideaway. Simultaneously, Morse, aced out of being made president of his company by nepotism, steals a pile of money.

Averback's comedy direction lifts things a bit out of a well-plowed rut, making for an amusing, while never hilarious, film.

● ●

■ WHILE THE CITY SLEEPS

1956, 99 MINS, US ⦿

Dir Fritz Lang   *Prod* Bert E. Friedlob   *Scr* Casey Robinson   *Ph* Ernest Laszlo   *Ed* Gene Fowler Jr   *Mus* Herschel Burke Gilbert   *Art Dir* Carroll Clark
● Dana Andrews, Ida Lupino, Rhonda Fleming, George Sanders, Vincent Price, Howard Duff (RKO)

The old-fashioned 'stop the presses' newspaper yarn has been updated with intelligence and considerable authenticity, and further brightened with crisp dialog from the pen of Casey Robinson. His screen adaptation of Charles Einstein's novel [*The Bloody Spur*] weaves several story lines together.

Among them are the murderous activities of a homicidal maniac, played by John Barrymore Jr; a scramble for power among the top brass of a newspaper empire; and a good-natured love story between the paper's top reporter, played by Dana Andrews, and Sally Forrest, the secretary of one of the contestants.

When the empire's chieftain, played by Robert Warwick, dies, his son, Vincent Price, decides to set up a new top exec post for grabs. Contenders are: Thomas Mitchell, editor of the keystone paper; George Sanders, head of the empire's wire service; and James Craig, dapper photo bureau chief.

Price lets it be known that the one to crack the wave of murders being committed by Barrymore gets the job. Sanders and Mitchell commence heartily to cut each other's throats, while Craig puts the pressure, literally and figuratively, on Fleming.

Plot intricacies are deftly interwoven, with

director Fritz Lang doing a topflight job of balancing the ingredients without dragging the pace.

● ●

■ WHIRLPOOL

1949, 97 MINS, US

Dir Otto Preminger   *Prod* Otto Preminger   *Scr* Ben Hecht, Andrew Solt   *Ph* Arthur Miller   *Ed* Louis Loeffler   *Mus* David Raksin
● Gene Tierney, Richard Conte, Jose Ferrer, Charles Bickford, Barbara O'Neil, Fortunio Bonanova (20th Century-Fox)

Whirlpool is a highly entertaining, exciting melodrama that combines the authentic features of hypnosis.

Ben Hecht and Andrew Solt have tightly woven a screenplay [from a novel by Guy Endore] about the effects of hypnosis on the subconscious, but they, and Otto Preminger in his direction, have eliminated the phoney characteristics that might easily have allowed the picture to slither into becoming just another eerie melodrama.

Their subject is a young wife of a prominent psychiatrist who, since adolescence, has been plagued by kleptomania.

As the young wife, Gene Tierney gives a plausible performance, though at times she fails to achieve the intensity that the entranced woman should have. Richard Conte, as her husband, is a little out of his metier here. The acting honors go to Jose Ferrer as the blackguard hypnotist.

● ●

■ WHISKY GALORE!
(US: *Tight Little Island*)

1949, 82 MINS, UK ⦿

Dir Alexander Mackendrick   *Prod* Michael Balcon   *Scr* Compton Mackenzie, Angus MacPhail   *Ph* Gerald Gibbs, Chick Waterson   *Ed* Joseph Sterling   *Mus* Ernest Irving   *Art Dir* Jim Morahan
● Basil Radford, Joan Greenwood, Gordon Jackson, James Robertson Justice, Bruce Seaton, Gabrielle Blunt (Ealing)

Compton Mackenzie's novel, on which the pic is based, is unfolded on a Hebridean island in 1943. Only sign of the war is the local Home Guard, but a major disaster occurs when the island runs out of whisky. After some days a freighter with 50,000 cases of Scotch runs aground off the island. The natives organize a midnight expedition and lay in a tremendous store for future consumption.

Sustained comedy treatment successfully carries the film forward to the point where the islanders outwit the Home Guard captain who regards the adventure as the worst type of looting.

Basil Radford gives a flawless performance of the misunderstood Home Guard chief whose zealousness leads to trouble in high quarters. Bruce Seton and Joan Greenwood as well as Gabrielle Blunt and Gordon Jackson provide the slight romances of the film.

● ●

■ WHISPERERS, THE

1966, 103 MINS, UK

Dir Bryan Forbes   *Prod* Michael S. Laughlin, Ronald Shedlo   *Scr* Bryan Forbes   *Ph* Gerry Turpin   *Ed* Anthony Harvey   *Mus* John Barry   *Art Dir* Ray Sims
● Edith Evans, Eric Portman, Nanette Newman, Gerald Sim, Avis Bunnage, Ronald Fraser (United Artists)

Low-budgeter [from a novel by Robert Nicolson] centers around an old woman, estranged from her husband, who lives alone in a broken-down, tiny flat in a slummy outskirt of a British town. Her imaginary dream of sudden riches due her from a relative unexpectedly comes true one day when her son hides the haul of a robbery in her spare room, and she finds it.

Few other films have attacked the unglam-

orous but poignant theme of old-age loneliness with such understated feeling and unsentimental taste and discretion.

It has in Edith Evans' great performance an invaluable asset. Her portrayal of the ageing woman, now living on the near edge of insanity but unbowed by other physical hazards, determinedly struggling ahead in her waning fight for life, but head high, without complaints, makes the film.

□ 1967: Nomination: Best Actress (Edith Evans)

● ●

■ WHISPERS IN THE DARK

1992, 102 MINS, US ◇ ⦿ ⊙

Dir Christopher Crowe   *Prod* Martin Bregman, Michael S. Bregman   *Scr* Christopher Crowe   *Ph* Michael Chapman   *Ed* Bill Pankow   *Mus* Thomas Newman   *Art Dir* John Jay Moore
● Annabella Sciorra, Jamey Sheridan, Anthony LaPaglia, Jill Clayburgh, John Leguizamo, Deborah Unger (Paramount)

A turn-off psycho-sexual thriller, *Whispers in the Dark* grows steadily more absurd by the reel until literally stumbling into the ocean at its climax.

Looking pale and vulnerable, Annabella Sciorra essays a meek Gotham shrink who begins getting turned on by tales of bondage and great sex confided by her patient Deborah Unger, a disturbing development she confides to her professional mentor (Alan Alda).

Ending a relationship with b.f. Anthony Heald, Sciorra begins falling for straight-arrow pilot Jamey Sheridan, but then discovers Sheridan is the sex partner Unger so deliciously describes. In a tiff, Unger makes off with some of Sciorra's private files and tapes but, before you can say ropes and handcuffs, Sciorra finds Unger murdered in her gallery.

Detective Anthony LaPaglia develops a thing for Sciorra while investigating the case, and it all devolves into a guessing game over which of these men killed Unger and may or may not be threatening Sciorra.

Some initial interest is generated by the intensely erotic performance of Unger, and by the unavoidable voyeuristic appeal of the numerous private sexual revelations. But a succession of psychiatric sessions do not a plot make, and writer-director Christopher Crowe nudges the picture along a very narrow track without coupling the viewer to the train.

● ●

■ WHISTLE BLOWER, THE

1987, 104 MINS, UK ◇ ⦿ ⊙

Dir Simon Langton   *Prod* Geoffrey Reeve   *Scr* Julian Bond   *Ph* Fred Tammes   *Ed* Robert Morgan   *Mus* John Scott   *Art Dir* Morley Smith
● Michael Caine, James Fox, Nigel Havers, Felicity Dean, John Gielgud, Gordon Jackson (Portreeve)

The Whistle Blower [from John Hale's novel] is a highly charged conspiracy theory drama. A murdered man, played by Nigel Havers, worked as a Russian translator at the top-secret listening center, GCHQ, in Cheltenham.

Michael Caine is excellent as his father, a role rather similar to that played by Jack Lemmon in *Missing* – a non-political, middle-aged man who's driven to radical action as a result of what the government he once trusted has done to his son.

The central sections, as Caine doggedly insists on finding out who killed his son and why, are tautly handled, creating considerable tension. Unfortunately, the film ends rather lamely, almost as if the writer wasn't sure how to finish it.

● ●

■ WHISTLE DOWN THE WIND

1961, 99 MINS, UK ⦿

Dir Bryan Forbes   *Prod* Richard Attenborough, Bryan Forbes   *Scr* Keith Waterhouse, Willis Hall   *Ph* Arthur

Ibbetson   *Ed* Max Benedict   *Mus* Malcolm Arnold
Art Dir Ray Simm
● Hayley Mills, Alan Bates, Bernard Lee, Norman Bird,
Elsie Wagstaff, John Arnatt (Rank/Allied Film Makers)

Whistle down the Wind takes a modern, senti-
mental-religious subject and treats it with
care, taste, sincerity, imagination and good
humor. The film was shot entirely on location
in the bleak, raw countryside around Burnley
in Lancashire, superbly caught by Arthur
Ibbetson's camerawork.

Based on Mary Hayley Bell's novel, it is a
slight but human story of faith seen through
the eyes of children. Three small children,
leading a lonely life on their father's farm,
stumble on a ragged, unshaven man taking
refuge in their barn. Startled when a terrified
Hayley Mills asks who he is, the stranger is so
relieved at finding the intruder is merely a
child that he involuntarily swears 'Jesus . . .
Christ.' The children take the remark literally. In fact, the man is a murderer on the
run.

There are many pieces of New Testament
symbolism but they arise naturally from the
action. For instance, the betrayal is innocently done by a child at a birthday party.
The local bully twists a smaller boy's arm and
three times makes him deny that the fugitive
is, indeed, Jesus Christ. Finally, when the police close in and frisk him, he stands with
arms raised quite naturally, but the implication of the Crucifixion is clear in the pose.

Bryan Forbes in his debut as a director
coaxes some outstanding performances from
a bunch of local kids. Only their leader, young
Mills, ever saw a script before. Result is complete authenticity. Alan Bates as the mysterious stranger handles a very difficult role
brilliantly.

■ **WHITE BUFFALO, THE**

1977, 97 MINS, US ◇ ⦾

Dir J. Lee Thompson   *Prod* Pancho Kohner   *Scr* Richard
Sale   *Ph* Paul Lohmann   *Ed* Michael F. Anderson
Mus John Barry   *Art Dir* Tambi Larsen
● Charles Bronson, Jack Warden, Will Sampson, Kim
Novak, Clint Walker, Stuart Whitman (De Laurentiis)

Charles Bronson stars as Wild Bill Hickok,
returned to the West to hunt down an albino
buffalo that haunts his dreams. Will Sampson
is an Indian who also must purge himself of
some dishonor.

Production features arch scripting by
Richard Sale (from his novel), stilted acting
by the cast and forced direction by J. Lee
Thompson.

The title beast looks like a hung-over carnival prize despite attempts at camouflage via
hokey sound track noise, busy John Barry
scoring, murky photography and fast editing.

The buffalo trackdown is actually more of a
cheap writing hook, on which to hang a lot of
dubious sociological gab between the players,
than an outdoor adventure story.

■ **WHITE CARGO**

1942, 89 MINS, US

Dir Richard Thorpe   *Prod* Victor Saville   *Scr* Leon
Gordon   *Ph* Harry Stradling   *Ed* Frederick Y. Smith
Mus Bronislau Kaper
● Hedy Lamarr, Walter Pidgeon, Frank Morgan,
Richard Carlson, Reginald Owen (M-G-M)

This is the first American-made version of the
sensational stage hit produced in 1923 by
Earl Carroll in Greenwich Village, NY. From
that downtown area Carroll moved the Leon
Gordon play [from a novel by Ida Vera
Simonton] to Broadway for a boxoffice
mopup. The very fact that the entire action
revolved around the passion of a white man,
disintegrating in a tropical English colony, for
a half-breed made it surefire for the then jazz
and flapper era.

Playwright Leon Gordon adapted his own
play for the screen and he hews closely to the
original, even to holding off Tondelayo's first
entrance until the film is 30 minutes old.

Walter Pidgeon plays well the part of the
tough English magistrate of the colony who
has to wet-nurse a succession of novices from
the home country. Hedy Lamarr as the only
femme in the film does her best acting to date.

■ **WHITE CHRISTMAS**

1954, 120 MINS, US ◇ ⦾ ⊙

Dir Michael Curtiz   *Prod* Robert Emmett Dolan
Scr Norman Krasna, Norman Panama, Melvin Frank
Ph Loyal Griggs   *Ed* Frank Bracht   *Mus* Joseph J. Lilley
Art Dir Hal Pereira, Roland Anderson
● Bing Crosby, Danny Kaye, Rosemary Clooney, Vera-
Ellen, Dean Jagger, Mary Wickes (Paramount)

Bing Crosby and Danny Kaye, along with
Vista Vision, keep the entertainment going in
this fancifully staged production, clicking
well.

The directorial handling by Michael Curtiz
gives a smooth blend of music (13 numbers
plus snatches of others) and drama, and in
the climax creates a genuine heart tug that
will squeeze tears.

The plot holding the entire affair together
has Crosby and Kaye, two Army buddies, joining forces after the war and becoming a big
musical team. They get together with the
girls and trek to Vermont for a white
Christmas. The inn at which they stay is run
by Dean Jagger, their old general, and the
boys put on a show to pull him out of a financial hole.

Crosby wraps up his portion of the show
with deceptive ease, shuffling a mean hoof in
the dances and generally acquitting himself
like a champion. Kaye takes in his stride the
dance, song and comedy demands of his assignment, keeping Crosby on his toes at all
times.

□ 1954: Nomination: Best Song ('Count Your
Blessings Instead of Sheep')

■ **WHITE DAWN, THE**

1974, 109 MINS, US ◇ ⦾ ⊙

Dir Philip Kaufman   *Prod* Martin Ransohoff   *Scr* James
Houston, Tom Rickman   *Ph* Michael Chapman
Ed Douglas Stewart   *Mus* Henry Mancini
● Warren Oates, Timothy Bottoms, Lou Gossett, Simonie
Kopapik, Joanasie Salomone, Pilitak (Paramount)

James Houston's 1971 book, subtitled *An
Eskimo Saga*, is the springboard for this production. Both limn the tale of how a trio of
whaleboaters, stranded in the late 1890s near
the North Pole, interact with and nearly destroy the band of Eskimos who saved their
lives. But while the book had a logic and sensitivity of its own, the film version emerges as
a static narrative.

Essentially, the three whalers bring familiar
baggage to the pristine setting of the Eskimo
village – they find ways of making booze, they
gamble, they take advantage of village
women, they steal, etc. Although each member of the trio is by no means uniform in his
misconduct – Billy (Warren Oates) is easily
the most nefarious – collective behaviour is at
first accepted by the Eskimos, then tolerated
and then viewed with a deepseated displeasure.

Oates is properly blustery as the roistering
older sea hand.

■ **WHITE DOG**

1982, 90 MINS, US ◇ ⦾

Dir Samuel Fuller   *Prod* Jon Davison   *Scr* Samuel Fuller,
Curtis Hanson   *Ph* Bruce Surtees   *Ed* Bernard Gribble
Mus Ennio Morricone   *Art Dir* Brian Eatwell
● Kristy McNichol, Paul Winfield, Burl Ives, Jameson
Parker, Lynne Moody, Marshall Thompson (Paramount)

White Dog is an unusual, often powerful study
of racism in the guise of a man vs animal suspenser. Too unevenly balanced and single-
minded to work completely, Samuel Fuller's
first Hollywood picture in 18 years nevertheless packs a provocative punch.

Curtis Hanson and Fuller have fashioned
an intense yarn about an up-and-coming LA
actress (Kristy McNichol) who takes in a
German shepherd after she hits it with her
car, only to discover that her new pet is a
deadly White Dog, trained from birth to hate
anyone with black skin.

Pic really gets down to business when
McNichol takes the dog to Burl Ives' Noah's
Ark animal compound, where scientist-
trainer Paul Winfield quickly becomes obsessed with the idea of curing the beast of its
racism. Set in an enormous cage reminiscent
of a gladiatorial arena, Winfield's very physical attempts to wear the dog down are effectively elemental.

McNichol is very fine as a modern gal who
becomes devoted to the dog, as well as
Winfield's cause, in a totally unsentimental
way.

■ **WHITE HEAT**

1949, 114 MINS, US ⦾ ⊙

Dir Raoul Walsh   *Prod* Louis F. Edelman   *Scr* Ivan Goff,
Ben Roberts   *Ph* Sid Hickox   *Ed* Owen Marks
Mus Max Steiner   *Art Dir* Edward Carrere
● James Cagney, Virginia Mayo, Edmond O'Brien,
Steve Cochran, Margaret Wycherly, John Archer
(Warner)

The tight-lipped scowl, the hunched shoulders that rear themselves for the kill, the gargoyle speech, the belching gunfire of a
trigger-happy paranoiac – one with a mother
complex, no less – these are the standard and
still-popular ingredients that constitute the
James Cagney of *White Heat*. All that is missing is the grapefruit in a dame's physiog.

White Heat [suggested by a story by Virginia
Kellogg],specifically is about a killer over
whom only his mother can wield any influence.
He heads a western gang, with his mother and
his double-dealing wife along for company.

Cagney has an excellent supporting cast.
Steve Cochran makes a good-looking, double-
crossing mobster's aide whose ambition for
the gang leadership, and the leader's wife,
ends in a rain of bullets. It's a capable performance. Virginia Mayo has little to do except
look sexy as the wife.

□ 1949: Nomination: Best Motion Picture
Story

■ **WHITE HUNTER, BLACK HEART**

1990, 110 MINS, US ◇ ⦾ ⊙

Dir Clint Eastwood   *Prod* Clint Eastwood   *Scr* Peter
Viertel, James Bridges, Burt Kennedy   *Ph* Jack N. Green
Ed Joel Cox   *Mus* Lennie Niehaus   *Art Dir* John
Graysmark
● Clint Eastwood, Jeff Fahey, George Dzundza, Alun
Armstrong, Marisa Berenson, Richard Vanstone
(Malpaso/Rastar)

Clint Eastwood's film isn't an African adventure epic, as those unaware of Peter Viertel's
1953 book may surmise from the title. It's an
intelligent, affectionate study of an obsessive
American film director who, while working on
a film in colonial Africa, becomes sidetracked
by his compulsion to hunt elephants.

Though the end credits note that this is 'a
work of fiction' this is clearly a story about
John Huston and the preproduction period
for *The African Queen* (called *The African Trader*
here). Eastwood plays the Huston character
with obvious appreciation of the man: he
wears Huston clothes and hats, assumes
Huston mannerisms, smokes Huston cigars
and speaks with the characteristic Huston
timbre.

The first 20 minutes of the pic unfold in England, where Wilson is living in a splendid old stately home as if he were a country squire. It's here that Wilson welcomes Pete Verrell (Jeff Fahey), his biographer, and it's from Verrell's perspective that the events unfold. Once the film crew moves to Africa, it becomes clear that Wilson's interest in making the film takes second place to his impractical passion for big-game hunting.

....

■ WHITE LIGHTNING

1973, 100 MINS, US ◇ ⊚

Dir Joseph Sargent   *Prod* Arthur Gardner, Jules V. Levy
Scr William Norton   *Ph* Edward Rosson   *Ed* George
Nicholson   *Mus* Charles Bernstein   *Art Dir* [uncredited]
● Burt Reynolds, Jennifer Billingsley, Ned Beatty, Bo
Hopkins, Matt Clark, Diane Ladd (United Artists)

Cast as an expert auto driver doing time in a Southern state prison for running bootleg whiskey, Burt Reynolds makes a deal with US Treasury agents to help them trap a gang of bootleggers on income tax evasion. Pitch for his freedom to act as an undercover man is made after he learns that a sheriff on the take is the probable murderer of his brother.

He's helped by another undercover man (Matt Clark) and a daredevil driver (Bo Hopkins) from whom Reynolds proceeds to steal his gal (Jennifer Billingsley).

Joseph Sargent's direction is particularly effective in the light and auto-chasing sequences, latter a field day for stunt drivers and occasionally incorporating humorous bits of biz. Reynolds is quite up to all the demands of his smashing role.

....

■ WHITE LINE FEVER

1975, 89 MINS, US/CANADA ◇ ⊚ ⊙

Dir Jonathan Kaplan   *Prod* John Kemeny   *Scr* Ken
Friedman, Jonathan Kaplan   *Ph* Fred Koenekamp
Ed O. Nicholas Brown   *Mus* David Nichtern
Art Dir Sydney Litwack
● Jan-Michael Vincent, Kay Lenz, Slim Pickens, L.Q.
Jones, Don Porter, Sam Laws (Columbia/International
Cinemedia)

White Line Fever is a good action drama starring Jan-Michael Vincent as a young truck driver fighting corruption.

Air Force vet Vincent returns home to marriage with Kay Lenz and starting in as an independent trucker. He soon finds smuggling to be endemic to the career, and is repeatedly and violently hassled when he refuses to go along.

What seems missing from the film is more depth and logical transition: Vincent passes too rapidly from a stubborn honest lone wolf to practically a union leader.

With stunt experts Carey Loftin, Nate Long and Joe Hooker creating some powerful action footage, Vincent and Lenz experience assaults, fires, beatings and other troubles sent their way by L.Q. Jones and others, all under orders from Don Porter.

....

■ WHITE MISCHIEF

1987, 107 MINS, UK ◇ ⊚ ⊙

Dir Michael Radford   *Prod* Simon Perry   *Scr* Michael
Radford, Jonathan Gems   *Ed* Tom
Priestley   *Mus* George Fenton   *Art Dir* Roger Hall
● Greta Scacchi, Charles Dance, Sarah Miles, Joss
Ackland, John Hurt, Trevor Howard (Nelson/Goldcrest/
Umbrella)

White Mischief goes back into Africa with a vengeance. It glossily portrays the flip side of colonial life, exposing the opulent and lush – but downright debauched – lifestyle of the British 'Happy Valley' crowd in Kenya during the war years [from the book by James Fox].

Pic opens in 1940 with newlyweds 'Jock' Broughton (Joss Ackland) and Diana (Greta Scacchi) about to leave England for the British colony in Nairobi. He needs a wife and she wants the money and a title, but when Diana meets handsome Erroll (Charles Dance) in Nairobi the scene is set for some philandering.

With stoical British reserve Broughton seemingly accepts the affair, even suggesting a celebratory dinner for the couple when they announce their plans to go away together. Later that night Erroll is shot through the head while in his car. Suspects for the murder are plentiful and the scandal means the end of the Happy Valley set and their dalliances. In real life the Erroll murderer was never found.

Dance and Scacchi are fine in the lead roles, with Scacchi certainly looking desirable and elegant bedecked in stunning costumes and sporting a seemingly endless collection of sunglasses.

....

■ WHITE NIGHTS

1985, 135 MINS, US ◇ ⊚ ⊙

Dir Taylor Hackford   *Prod* Taylor Hackford, William S.
Gilmore   *Scr* James Goldman, Eric Hughes   *Ph* David
Watkin   *Ed* Fredric Steinkamp, William Steinkamp
Mus Michel Colombier   *Art Dir* Philip Harrison
● Mikhail Baryshnikov, Gregory Hines, Jerzy
Skolimowski, Helen Mirren, Geraldine Page, Isabella
Rossellini (Columbia-Delphi V/New Visions)

At its core *White Nights* is a political thriller about the dilemma of a famous Russian defector who, after a plane crash, finds himself trapped back in his mother country. However, pic shies away from the world of classical dance, personified by leading man Mikhail Baryshnikov, in favor of Gregory Hines' 'improvography' and assorted modern stuff in blatant music video contexts.

Mix all this in with KGB intrigue, racial tensions, numerous emotional breakdowns and several suspense sequences, all played at the broadest levels of melodrama, and one has quite a mish-mash indeed.

Without so much as an interrogation by the KGB, Baryshnikov is moved to the dingy Siberian residence of Hines, a black American tap dancer who jumped to the other side during Vietnam, and his Russian wife Isabella Rossellini.

The trio is installed in Baryshnikov's luxurious old apartment in Leningrad, and the dancer is expected to begin preparations for a triumphant homecoming at the Kirov. Inevitably, an escape attempt is the climax.

Hines plays a bitter, ornery man with a quick trigger. Rossellini, in her Hollywood film debut, has disappointingly little to do.

☐ 1985: Best Song ('Say You, Say Me')
☐ Nomination: Best Song ('Separate Lives')

....

■ WHITE OF THE EYE

1987, 110 MINS, UK ◇ ⊚

Dir Donald Cammell   *Prod* Cassian Elwes, Brad Wyman
Scr Donald Cammell, China Cammell   *Ph* Alan Jones,
Larry McConkey   *Ed* Terry Rawlings   *Mus* George
Fenton (sup.), Nick Mason, Rick Fenn
● David Keith, Cathy Moriarty, Art Evans, Alan
Rosenberg, Alberta Watson, Michael Greene (Kastner/
Cannon)

White of the Eye is an intriguing thriller [from the novel *Mrs White* by Margaret Tracy].

Beneath the layers of flashbacks and at times almost subliminal imagery is a conventional storyline. Sound expert Paul White (David Keith), living in a small Arizona town, is having marital problems with frau Joan (Cathy Moriarty). Circumstantial evidence points strongly at Keith, with cop Mendoza (Art Evans) in from Phoenix to hound him in the case of a serial murder who mutilates the corpses of his wealthy housewife victims.

With lots of clues and red herrings introduced in the early reels (including a heavy emphasis on 10 years earlier 16mm blow up flashbacks of Moriarty first meeting Keith while trekking westward with her boyfriend Alan Rosenberg), picture maintains considerable suspense.

Moriarty is quite forceful here. Keith likewise creates a powerful figure, until the mystery is fully out of the bag.

....

■ WHITE PALACE

1990, 104 MINS, US ◇ ⊚ ⊙

Dir Luis Mandoki   *Prod* Mark Rosenberg, Amy Robinson,
Griffin Dunne   *Scr* Ted Tally, Alvin Sargent   *Ph* Lajos
Koltai   *Ed* Carol Littleton   *Mus* George Fenton
Art Dir Jeannine Claudia Oppewall
● Susan Sarandon, James Spader, Jason Alexander,
Kathy Bates, Eileen Brennan, Steven Hill (Universal/Mirage)

Outstanding performances by Susan Sarandon and James Spader, working from a relentlessly witty script, make *White Palace* one of the best films of its kind since *The Graduate* (1967).

Sarandon is Nora, a 43-year-old fast-food worker who gets involved with a 27-year-old advertising exec – the same sort of character Spader played in *Pretty in Pink*, now mellowed and matured. Both have experienced terrible loss – Max (Spader) is a widower; Nora's child has died – and they share a magnetic sexual attraction.

Their *Odd Couple* differences, however, include class, religion and hygiene (he's a buttoned-down neat freak; she's a gregarious slob) in addition to the Mrs Robinson-esque age discrepancy.

The ferocity that director Luis Mandoki brings to the pair's early love scenes helps establish how two people can fall into lust and worry about love later.

Raunchy yet vulnerable, Sarandon carefully avoids the cliches that might have been associated with Nora. Spader continues to establish himself as star material, especially when it comes to playing self-conscious yuppies.

....

■ WHITE PARADE, THE

1934, 80 MINS, US

Dir Irving Cummings   *Prod* Jesse L. Lasky   *Scr* Sonya
Levien, Ernest Pascal   *Ph* Arthur Miller
● Loretta Young, John Boles, Dorothy Wilson, Muriel
Kirkland, Astrid Allwyn, Frank Conroy (Fox)

The White Parade is a woman's picture, but also for general appeal. The stern curriculum which goes towards the moulding of the 'white parade', the present-day Florence Nightingales who are dedicated to the service of humankind, and all the other details that go towards the schooling of the modern nurse are deftly, graphically, punchily and sometimes heart-throbbingly depicted [from the novel by Rian James, adapted by James and Jesse L. Lasky Jr].

Loretta Young is altogether convincing as the sympathetic femme novitiate who has consecrated herself to her profession. Dorothy Wilson is a fine little actress. Muriel Kirkland in a more hoydenish role registers, as do Astrid Allwyn as a light heavy, and Joyce Compton in one of those Una Merkel Dixie drawleries.

Frank Conroy is given the toughest male assignment as the mature medico of stern mien who must make some of his hyper-solemnous lines read convincingly. John Boles, though the featured vis-a-vis, is handicapped and limited by his role. Polo-playing Boston playboys who fall for nurses are tough to make real, but he manages quite well.

☐ 1934: Nomination: Best Picture

....

■ WHITE SANDS

1992, 101 MINS, US ◇ ⊚ ⊙

Dir Roger Donaldson   *Prod* William Sackheim, Scott
Rudin   *Scr* Daniel Pyne   *Ph* Peter Menzies Jr

Ed Nicholas Beauman   *Mus* Patrick O'Hearn
Art Dir John Graysmark
● Willem Dafoe, Mary Elizabeth Mastrantonio, Mickey Rourke, Samuel L. Jackson, M. Emmet Walsh, Mimi Rogers (Morgan Creek)

The plot shifts as often as the desert in *White Sands*, an absorbing, tightly coiled thriller not always easy to follow, with a fine cast, no-fat direction by Roger Donaldson, and nasties belonging to the all-purpose CIA-FBI consortium of evil.

Willem Dafoe sets himself up for plenty of abuse when, after finding a dead Indian with $500,000 in cash in the middle of nowhere, he takes on the victim's identity in an effort to solve the case. He is quickly beaten and robbed of the loot by two babes and then abducted by the FBI. Latter demands that the stash be recovered and Dafoe keeps an appointment in Santa Fe with mysterious Mickey Rourke, who introduces him to another shadowy character, spoiled rich girl Mary Elizabeth Mastrantonio.

Pic builds tautly to a powerful first act peak. Intensity dwindles a bit, however, when Dafoe pairs off with Mastrantonio, to whom he appeals for the extra coin.

Some thrillers have gone down as classics despite the lack of total narrative coherence, and while *White Sands* doesn't rate that high, it can hold its own with Donaldson's *No Way Out* as an audience-pleasing cliffhanger. An uncredited Mimi Rogers appears briefly at the outset as Dafoe's wife.

• •

■ WHO?

1974, 93 MINS, UK/W. GERMANY ◇ ⑫
Dir Jack Gold   *Prod* Barry Levinson, Kurt Berthold
Scr John Gould   *Ph* Petrus Schloemp   *Ed* Norman Wanstall   *Mus* John Cameron   *Art Dir* Peter Scharff
● Elliott Gould, Trevor Howard, Joe Bova, Ed Grover, James Noble, Lyndon Brook (Lion International/Hemisphere)

Adapted from Algis Budrys' novel by British playwright John Gould, *Who?* is an action-espionage thriller examining, from a science fiction perspective, the nature of identity.

Joe Bova gives a beautiful, underplayed performance as diminutive US scientist Martino, whose face and arm are remade in metal after an accident in Berlin. The film's mystery-suspense plot derives from iterated flashbacks showing Martino grilled and / or indoctrinated by East German intelligence officer Azarin (Trevor Howard).

Once back in the US, Martino is subjected to gruelling questioning and investigation by FBI operative Rogers (Elliott Gould) to check his new security clearance for continuing a top secret research project in Florida. Gould examines the reactions of Martino's old associates to his transformed, robot-like appearance.

Gould brings humor to the assignment. Howard is seen only in the flashbacks.

• •

■ WHO DARES WINS

1982, 125 MINS, UK ◇ ⑫
Dir Ian Sharp   *Prod* Euan Lloyd   *Scr* Reginald Rose
Ph Phil Meheux   *Ed* John Grover   *Mus* Roy Budd
Art Dir Syd Cain
● Lewis Collins, Judy Davis, Richard Widmark, Edward Woodward, Robert Webber, Tony Doyle (Rank)

Who Dares Wins is pulp fare about the politics of terrorism in which the anti-war movement is discredited as prone to reckless murder in the ironic name of peace. In this case, provocative premise is no substitute for classy drama.

The simple-minded plot [from an original story by George Markstein] has a militant anti-nuke organization take over a US diplomatic facility in London with its glitzy bunch of hostages and demanding the wipeout of a US sub base in Scotland by a nuclear missile. Wiped out instead, by a crack British commando team, are the peaceniks. All characters are stereotyped rather than cliched.

Performing standout is Judy Davis as the 'terrorist' leader. Lewis Collins offers pleasing virile projection as an undercover agent who shacks up with Davis.

• •

■ WHO FRAMED ROGER RABBIT

1988, 103 MINS, US ◇ ⑫ ⊙
Dir Robert Zemeckis   *Prod* Robert Watts, Frank Marshall
Scr Jeffrey Price, Peter S. Seaman   *Ph* Dean Cundey
Ed Arthur Schmidt   *Mus* Alan Silvestri   *Art Dir* Elliot Scott, Roger Cain
● Bob Hoskins, Christopher Lloyd, Joanna Cassidy, Stubby Kaye, Alan Tilvern (Touchstone/Amblin/Silver Screen Partners III)

Years in the planning and making, *Who Framed Roger Rabbit* is an unparalleled technical achievement where animation is brilliantly integrated into live action. Yet the story amounts to little more than inspired silliness about the filmmaking biz where cartoon characters face off against cartoonish humans.

Pic opens appropriately enough with a cartoon, a hilarious, overblown, calamitous scene where Roger Rabbit, a famous contract Toon player (as in *cartoon*) for Maroon Studios, is failing in his attempt to keep Baby Herman (voice by Lou Hirsch) from the cookie jar.

Things aren't going well for poor Roger. Ever since he became estranged from his voluptuous human character Toon wife Jessica (sultry, uncredited voice courtesy of Kathleen Turner, and Amy Irving for the singing) he just can't act.

This is the context from which scripters, in adapting Gary Wolf's story, try to work up a Raymond Chandler-style suspenser where Roger becomes an innocent murder suspect, with a disheveled, alcoholic private eye (Bob Hoskins) being his only hope to help him beat the rap.

The real stars are the animators, under British animation director Richard Williams, who pull off a technically amazing feat of having humans and Toons seem to be interacting with one another. It is clear from how well the imagery syncs that a lot of painstaking work [two years] went into this production – and clearly a lot of money [$35 million].

☐ 1988: Best Editing, Sound Effects Editing, Visual Effects
☐ Nominations: Best Cinematography, Art Direction, Sound

• •

■ WHO IS KILLING THE GREAT CHEFS OF EUROPE?
(UK: Too Many Chefs)

1978, 112 MINS, US/W. GERMANY ◇ ⑫
Dir Ted Kotcheff   *Prod* William Aldrich   *Scr* Peter Stone
Ph John Alcott   *Ed* Thom Noble   *Mus* Henry Mancini
Art Dir Rolf Zehetbauer
● George Segal, Jacqueline Bisset, Robert Morley, Jean-Pierre Cassel, Philippe Noiret, Jean Rochefort (Aldrich/Lorimar)

Who Is Killing the Great Chefs of Europe? is a happy combination of the macabre and the merry. It's a fast-moving, witty film, beautifully cast with a large group of international professionals who give full justice to Peter Stone's adaptation of Nan and Ivan Lyons' novel, *Someone Is Killing the Great Chefs of Europe.*

While George Segal and Jacqueline Bisset carry star billing and, indeed, provide the romantic and plot evolution, it is Robert Morley as a massive, dedicated gourmet, who provides the film's finest moments.

The series of murders is made the responsibility of some of France and Italy's most outstanding character actors. It's touch and go who excels but Philippe Noiret underplays in a manner that gives him a slight edge over the more voluble Italians although Stefano Satta Flores' unabashed description of how he'll romance Bisset, given the opportunity, is Italian macho comedy at its finest.

The other endangered chef is Jean-Pierre Cassel, while Jean Rochefort is a red herring who'll fool no one. These are the principal roles but Madge Ryan as Morley's dedicated secretary is also a key figure.

• •

■ WHOLE TOWN'S TALKING, THE
(UK: Passport to Fame)

1935, 95 MINS, US
Dir John Ford   *Prod* Lester Cowan   *Scr* Jo Swerling, Robert Riskin   *Ph* Joseph H. August   *Ed* Viola Lawrence
● Edward G. Robinson, Jean Arthur, Wallace Ford, Arthur Hohl, Donald Meek, Etienne Girardot (Columbia)

Robert Riskin and Jo Swerling put the scenario together [from a story by W.R. Burnett]. It's a model in the expert manipulation of such hokum as the office worm thrust into danger by coincidence and emerging with fame, fortune and the girl.

Edward G. Robinson plays a dual role. He is a softie in one part and tough in the other. Plot twist to the worm-turning is that the softie bookkeeper is a dead ringer for a gangster wanted by the police. Police have orders to shoot on sight, and when picking up the hoodlum's counterpart, and third-degreeing him, they are confronted with a dilemma: what to do to protect an innocent citizen from the police. So the bookkeeper gets a pass identifying him as okay. Real criminal, of course, shows up and quietly takes over the passport as a shield to continue his activities.

Robinson's characterization of the submerged, over-polite and indecisive office worker is human and believable.

Second in unusualness among the cast is Jean Arthur. She's gone blonde and fresh. She's more individualistic, more typically the young American, self-reliant, rather sassy, stenog.

• •

■ WHO'LL STOP THE RAIN
(UK: Dog Soldiers)

1978, 125 MINS, US ◇ ⑫ ⊙
Dir Karel Reisz   *Prod* Herb Jaffe, Gabriel Katzka
Scr Judith Roscoe, Robert Stone   *Ph* Richard H. Kline
Ed John Bloom   *Mus* Laurence Rosenthal
● Nick Nolte, Tuesday Weld, Michael Moriarty, Anthony Zerbe, Richard Masur, Ray Sharkey (United Artists)

British film-maker Karel Reisz for his second American film has come up with a corking couple-on-the-run adventure pic, given depth in its focus on the personal disarray, the growing governmental corruption and the effects of that most unpopular, divisive Vietnam war on America.

Michael Moriarty, a journalist and photog during the Vietnam War, suffers a trauma under a deadly enemy barrage and the mayhem around him. He decides to try to smuggle heroin to the US.

Moriarty brings in an old Marine buddy (Nick Nolte), who is now in the Merchant Marine. Nolte is to get in touch with Moriarty's wife (Tuesday Weld) and wait for him, Moriarty, to get back. But back in the US Nolte is followed. He and Weld go on the lam after sending Weld's little girl off to relatives for safekeeping.

Based on a bestseller by Robert Stone, film has a hardnose progression and solidity in its characterizations. Nolte earns his star stripes here, displaying presence and perceptiveness in socking home his character, while Weld and Moriarty are also effective.

• •

W

■ WHORE

1991, 84 MINS, US ◇ ⓦ ⊙

Dir Ken Russell   *Prod* Dan Ireland, Ronaldo Vasconcellos
Scr Ken Russell, Deborah Dalton   *Ph* Amir Mokri
Ed Brian Tagg   *Mus* Michael Gibbs   *Art Dir* Richard
Lewis

● Theresa Russell, Benjamin Mouton, Antonio Fargas,
Sanjay, Elizabeth Moorehead, Michael Crabtree
(Trimark)

Given the infinite possibilities afforded by the
subject matter, *Whore* features little of the
kinkiness and bravura stylistics one normally
expects from director Ken Russell, and no
compensating psychological or documentary
insight into the lead character or her
lifestyle.

Project is based on a British play by David
Hines, a London cabbie who nightly picked up
prostitutes in Kings Cross and began writing
down their stories they told him about their
work. Due to financing requirements, the setting is shifted to Los Angeles, where the consummately vulgar Liz (Theresa Russell) plies
her trade on thinly populated downtown
streets.

Flashbacks make up a substantial portion of
the brief running time, as Liz covers her initial tricks, hook-up with her pimp and sometime boyfriend, Blake (Benjamin Mouton),
and failed marriage and hopeless stint as a
mother.

Overriding problem is a pervasive feeling of
utter inauthenticity. Russell's strident, stops-
out performance sets the tone for the entire
picture. She's all over the place, occasionally
hitting a responsive note but more often
flailing about. Director puts in an unbilled
cameo appearance as a waiter in a snooty
restaurant.

■ WHO'S AFRAID OF VIRGINIA WOOLF?

1966, 131 MINS, US ⓦ ⊙

Dir Mike Nichols   *Prod* Ernest Lehman   *Scr* Ernest
Lehman   *Ph* Haskell Wexler   *Ed* Sam O'Steen
Mus Alex North   *Art Dir* Richard Sylbert

● Elizabeth Taylor, Richard Burton, George Segal,
Sandy Dennis (Warner)

The naked power and oblique tenderness of
Edward Albee's incisive, inhuman drama
have been transformed from legit into a brilliant motion picture. Keen adaptation and
handsome production by Ernest Lehman, outstanding direction by Mike Nichols in his feature debut, and four topflight performances
score an artistic bullseye.

Elizabeth Taylor earns every penny of her
reported $1 million plus. Her chacterization
is at once sensual, spiteful, cynical, pitiable,
loathsome, lustful and tender.

Richard Burton delivers a smash portrayal.
He evokes sympathy during the public degra-
dations to which his wife subjects him, and
his outrage, as well as his deliberate
vengeance, are totally believable.

Provoking the exercise in exorcism is the
late-night visit of Dennis and Segal. Latter is
the all-American boy type who, in the course
of one night, is seduced by his hostess, exposed by his host, but enlightened as to more
mature aspects of love and marriage. Segal is
able to evoke sympathy, then hatred, then
pity, in a first-rate performance.

Dennis makes an impressive screen debut
as the young bride, her delivery rounded
with the intended subtlety of a not-so-Dumb
Dora.

□ 1966: Best Actress (Elizabeth Taylor),
Supp. Actress (Sandy Dennis), B&W
Cinematography, B&W Art Direction, B&W
Costume Design (Irene Sharaff).

□ Nominations: Best Picture, Director, Actor
(Richard Burton), Supp. Actor (George
Segal), Screenplay Adaptation, Editing,
Original Music Score, Sound

■ WHO'S BEEN SLEEPING IN MY BED?

1963, 103 MINS, US ◇

Dir Daniel Mann   *Prod* Jack Rose   *Scr* Jack Rose
Ph Joseph Ruttenberg   *Ed* George Tomasini
Mus George Duning

● Dean Martin, Elizabeth Montgomery, Martin Balsam,
Jill St John, Carol Burnett, Macha Meril (Paramount)

Dean Martin is seemingly right for the part
of an actor who appears on television as a
doctor, such as Kildare or Ben Casey, and
then moonlights into the field of psychiatric
advice (and perhaps romantic stimulation)
for the glamorous dames married to his TV-
business associates.

But there's the slip between cup and lip.
The slip makes the difference between what
might have been mischievous, zesty comedy
and what is a sometimes laughable frolic that
in a couple of instances is permitted to sink in
its quest for sophisticated hilarity.

This is unfortunate because a substantial
part of *Who's Been Sleeping in My Bed?* plays
sparkingly well. Martin is an amiable performer in light comedy and does fine with the
material at hand.

■ WHOSE LIFE IS IT ANYWAY?

1981, 118 MINS, US ◇ ⓦ

Dir John Badham   *Prod* Lawrence P. Bachmann
Scr Brian Clark, Reginald Rose   *Ph* Mario Tosi
Ed Frank Morriss   *Mus* Arthur B. Rubinstein
Art Dir Gene Gallahan

● Richard Dreyfuss, John Cassavetes, Christine Lahti,
Bob Balaban, Kenneth McMillan, Kaki Hunter (M-G-M)

Director and scripters have done a masterly
job in the rather difficult screen adaptation of
Brian Clark's legit drama. Richard Dreyfuss
delivers a sensitive portrait of the animated
young sculptor who is cut down in an automobile accident at the height of his life and recovers only to be paralysed from the neck down.

Although John Badham directed Dreyfuss
in an actual stage version in Massachusetts
for two weeks, he succeeds in opening up the
story far beyond the confines of a proscenium.
There is an opening sequence establishing his
idyllic relationship with dancer Janet Eilber;
scenes throughout the hospital with hard-
crusted chief of staff John Cassavetes, soft-
hearted doctor Christine Lahti and
light-hearted, humane nurse trainee and orderly Kaki Hunter and Thomas Carter: and
glimpses at Dreyfuss' 'former' life, most particularly through his artist's studio.

All the action leads to the unresolvable issue of who has the power to decide the fate of
the patient – the hospital or the patient.
Dreyfuss demands a legal hearing in his fight
to be rid of all life-sustaining methods.

■ WHO'S HARRY CRUMB?

1989, 98 MINS, US ◇ ⓦ ⊙

Dir Paul Flaherty   *Prod* Arnon Milchan   *Scr* Robert
Conte, Peter Martin Wortmann   *Ph* Stephen M. Katz
Ed Danford B. Greene   *Mus* Michel Colombier
Art Dir Trevor Williams

● John Candy, Jeffrey Jones, Annie Potts, Tim
Thomerson, Barry Corbin, Shawnee Smith (Tri-Star/NBC/
Frostbacks)

Foolishness in the right hands can be sub-
limely funny, and combo of star John Candy
and director Paul Flaherty (former SCTV cohorts) puts the perfect spin on *Who's Harry
Crumb?*, a *Naked Gun*-style farce about a bumbling private eye who succeeds in spite of
himself.

Candy plays Crumb, a complete idiot who's
related by birth to a line of crack detectives
and finally gets assigned to a lucrative kidnapping case – but only because his beady-
eyed boss (Jeffrey Jones), who's the
kidnapper, doesn't want it solved.

At stake is Jones' lust for the golddigging

newlywed wife (maliciously and deliciously
played by Annie Potts) of a benign, trusting
multimillionaire (Barry Corbin). The plot is
to get $10 million ransom for the return of
Corbin's slinky daughter (Renee Coleman),
and use the riches to pry Potts away from her
main meal-ticket.

Candy seems to have picked up some tricks
from Dan Aykroyd and Steve Martin (both
former costars) that he applies to good effect
to achieve the attitude of a winning but moronic wiseguy in this pic. Director Flaherty
peppers the action with goofy business.

■ WHO'S MINDING THE STORE?

1963, 90 MINS, US ◇

Dir Frank Tashlin   *Prod* Paul Jones   *Scr* Frank Tashlin,
Harry Tugend   *Ph* W. Wallace Kelley   *Ed* John
Woodcock   *Mus* Joseph J. Lilley   *Art Dir* Hal Pereira,
Roland Anderson

● Jerry Lewis, Jill St John, Agnes Moorehead, John
McGiver, Ray Walston, Francesca Bellini (Paramount/
York/Lewis)

Frank Tashlin directs with full emphasis on
the madcap nonsense [from a screen story by
Harry Tugend] and Jerry Lewis has a field
day playing it all out in his uninhibited
(meaning zany) style. It's fun.

The filmmaker also has gotten in an abundance of commercial display for appliances,
other household items, as Lewis goes to work
in a department store and wrecks it department by department.

He has an especially attractive romantic
vis-a-vis in Jill St John who takes a job as elevator operator to hide the fact she's really the
daughter of the store's owner. Agnes
Moorehead plays the owner's domineering
wife, who regards Lewis as an idiot, Frank
McGiver is the owner, and Ray Walston is a
dame-chasing manager.

They all romp through with accent on the
broad comedy and, of course, with the spotlight mainly on havoc-wreaking Lewis.

■ WHO'S THAT GIRL

1987, 94 MINS, US ◇ ⓦ ⊙

Dir James Foley   *Prod* Rosilyn Heller, Bernard Williams
Scr Andrew Smith, Ken Finkleman   *Ph* Jan De Bont
Ed Pembroke Herring   *Mus* Stephen Bray, Patrick
Leonard   *Art Dir* Ida Random

● Madonna, Griffin Dunne, Haviland Morris, John
McMartin, Bibi Besch, John Mills (Warner)

Griffin Dunne reprises his role as the crazed,
overwrought straight man while Madonna
lays on a thick New Yawk bimbette act in this
frenetic and ridiculously re-worked *After
Hours-Arthur* combination.

The Material Girl plays a just-out-of-jail
back-talking petty thief who's bent on avenging the thugs who made her take the rap for a
murder she didn't commit. Weak-kneed
lawyer type Dunne is sent by his megabucks
soon-to-be-father-in-law (John McMartin) to
pick her up and make sure she's on the next
bus home. All this occurs on the eve of his
wedding to McMartin's ice princess daughter
(Haviland Morris).

Madonna bamboozles Dunne into doing
what she wants to do, turning him into a near
nut case bashing up his future mother-in-law's
Corniche, buying stolen goods in Harlem,
stealing right and left, and so on. Fortunately,
Dunne's playful personality eventually
counter-balances Madonna's shrillness, and
their adventures together, while completely
farfetched, finally become involving. What's
lacking is pure and simple good humor.

■ WHO'S THAT KNOCKING AT MY DOOR

1968, 90 MINS, US ⓦ

Dir Martin Scorsese   *Prod* Joseph Weill, Betzi
Manoogian, Haig Manoogian   *Scr* Martin Scorsese,

Betzi Manoogian   Ph Michael Wadley, Richard Coll
Ed Thelma Schoonmaker   Mus [uncredited]   Art Dir Vic
Magnotte
● Zina Bethune, Harvey Keitel, Lennard Kuras, Ann
Collette, Michael Scala, Harry Northup (Trimod)

This independent effort, two years in the
making, is the handiwork of, for the most
part, film teacher Haig Manoogian and his
students. These include Martin Scorsese
who's reponsible for both the script and the
direction (with some 'additional dialog' credited to Betzi (Mrs Haig) Manoogian). In
addition, Joseph Weill, a practising attorney
who's also a student, is listed as one of the
producers.
    The tale, apparently, is the inner struggle
of a young Italian-American, J.R., torn between a Roman Catholic upbringing and the
temptations of modern life. Unfortunately,
he's portrayed as a crude, carousing lout who
seemingly never works but devotes most of
his time to drinking and drifting or spending
time with a 'good' girl (until he finds that
she's not the virgin he imagined. Zina
Bethune, as the girl, is believable but Harvey
Keitel, as the anti-hero, is alternatively boorish or bewildered.
    Scorsese occasionally brings the film to life,
as in a weekend drive by J.R. and two buddies
to an upstate village where the camera shows
up their 'big city' shallowness in comparison
to the townspeople. Generally, however, his
script and direction lack any dramatic value
and give far too much exposure to sexual fantasies on the part of the boy.

....

■ WICKED LADY, THE

1945, 102 MINS, UK ⓥ
Dir Leslie Arliss   Prod R.J. Minney   Scr Leslie Arliss,
Gordon Glennon, Aimee Stuart   Ph Jack Cox
Ed Terence Fisher   Mus Hans May   Art Dir John Bryan
● Margaret Lockwood, James Mason, Patricia Roc,
Griffith Jones, Michael Rennie, Felix Aylmer
(Gainsborough)

Producers claim that this story is 'set in the
days of Charles II'. Sets, costumes and a
comely bunch of femmes bear out the claim.
But the period atmosphere is not convincing.
    James Mason as a Robin Hood type high-
wayman manages to suggest the swaggering
love-'em-and-leave-'em rascal of an earlier
day. He scores in spite of the weak script
[from the novel The Life and Death of the Wicked
Lady Skelton by Magdalen King-Hall]. The
other performance lending credibility to the
period comes from Felix Aylmer as an old retainer who tumbles to the villainy of
Margaret Lockwood in the title role, and dies
at her fair hands.
    The Wicked Lady as a title is a characteristic
English understatement. The way Lockwood
shoots, poisons and betrays all who get in her
way makes that taboo name a modest one.
Between murders she steals the fiance of her
best girl friend and then grabs the bridal
chamber for herself.

....

■ WICKED LADY, THE

1983, 98 MINS, US ◇ ⓥ
Dir Michael Winner   Prod Menahem Golan, Yoram
Globus   Scr Michael Winner, Leslie Arliss   Ph Jack
Cardiff   Ed Arnold Crust [= Michael Winner]
Mus Tony Banks   Art Dir John Blezard
● Faye Dunaway, Alan Bates, John Gielgud, Denholm
Elliott, Prunella Scales, Oliver Tobias (Cannon)

Sex, humor and even a facsimile of style distinguish Michael Winner's entertaining remake of The Wicked Lady as a comedy-drama
of rogue-ridden 17th-century England with
Faye Dunaway an effective title star.
    Winner, who coauthored the piece with [di-
rector of the 1945 version], Leslie Arliss
[based on The Life and Death of the Wicked Lady

Skelton by Magdalen King-Hall], has pumped
some amusing life and typically brisk pace
into a basically tired old (and even campy)
story about an alluring high society dame for
whom seduction, highway robbery and even
murder are all in a day's work.
    After marrying Denholm Elliott for his
money, Dunaway turns to a life of nocturnal
crime, solo at first, but later in cahoots with
legendary stagecoach robber Alan Bates.
    Dunaway performs her dominating role
with satisfying conviction, straight face and
all. Ditto Elliott as her scorned and cuckolded
husband. Bates makes for a charming but all-
too-brief rogue, while John Gielgud as a God-
fearing retainer has a marvelous deadpan
time of it kidding himself.

....

■ WICKER MAN, THE

1973, 87 MINS, UK ◇ ⓥ
Dir Robin Hardy   Prod Peter Snell   Scr Anthony Shaffer
Ph Harry Waxman   Ed Eric Boyd-Perkins   Mus Paul
Giovanni   Art Dir Seamus Flannery
● Edward Woodward, Britt Ekland, Diane Cilento,
Ingrid Pitt, Christopher Lee, Roy Boyd (British Lion/Brut)

The Wicker Man was lensed entirely on location in Scotland and is possessed of a weird
and paganistic story. Anthony Shaffer penned
the screenplay which, for sheer imagination
and near-terror, has seldom been equalled.
    Frightening aspects build one upon the
other as a Scottish police sergeant arrives on
a little offshore island to investigate the disappearance of a young girl. He finds, under
the regime of an all-powerful, benevolent and
suave despot, a sinister situation dating back
to the days of pagan practices and fertility
rites.
    Edward Woodward plays role of the
sergeant who arrives to find a conspiracy of silence and is forced into a fatal part in the paganistic rituals. Christopher Lee is the
cultured feudal Lord Summerisle, lord of the
island. Both score in their roles.

....

■ WIDE SARGASSO SEA

1993, 96 MINS, AUSTRALIA ◇ ⓥ ⊙
Dir John Duigan   Prod Jan Sharp   Scr Jan Sharp,
Carole Angier, John Duigan   Ph Geoff Burton, Gabriel
Beristain   Ed Anne Goursaud, Jimmy Sandoval
Mus Stewart Copeland   Art Dir Frankie D
◉ Karina Lombard, Nathaniel Parker, Rachel Ward,
Michael York, Martine Beswicke, Claudia Robinson
(Laughing Kookaburra)

An exotic and erotic melodrama bearing notable literary pedigrees, Wide Sargasso Sea is
an uneven but ultimately engrossing feature.
Aussie director John Duigan has filmed
British novelist Jean Rhys' novel with
stunning location photography in Jamaica
and the north of England, but the editing
looks like the film was put through a shred-
der.
    The initially confusing storyline concerns a
mad French woman (Rachel Ward) in
Jamaica who marries an Englishman
(Michael York). Her daughter (lovely model
Karina Lombard) is stuck in a marriage
arranged by her uncle to Englishman Edward
Rochester (Nathaniel Parker), the brooding
hero of Charlotte Bronte's Jane Eyre.
    The couple's erotic tangles in and out of
love are set against a backdrop of superstition
in which the local form of voodoo seems to
hold each of them in thrall.
    Lombard is a hauntingly beautiful heroine
well-matched to shirt-ad handsome Parker.
Their acting is not really up to some dramatic
scenes, particularly those in which they may
be operating under the influence of voodoo.
Thesping honors go to Claudia Robinson as
Lombard's sharp-tonged black nanny.

....

■ WIFE VS. SECRETARY

1936, 88 MINS, US
Dir Clarence Brown   Prod Hunt Stromberg
Scr Norman Krasna, Alice Duer Miller, John Lee Mahin
Ph Ray June   Ed Frank E. Hull   Mus Herbert Stothart,
Edward Ward   Art Dir Cedric Gibbons, William A.
Horning
● Clark Gable, Jean Harlow, Myrna Loy, May Robson,
Hobart Cavanaugh, James Stewart (M-G-M)

Here Jean Harlow is no siren. She is a perfectly competent secretary, very much in love
with her job and her boss, but she does not go
on the make for him. Myrna Loy, as the wife,
is much in love with Clark Gable, and he with
her. They are an ideal couple until his mother
plants the seeds of suspicion, which are watered and fertilized by other women friends.
    The blow-off comes when Gable refuses to
take his wife to Havana on a business trip,
but has his secretary fly down with some important data on the deal he has gone to close.
Loy calls up and Harlow answers the phone.
Loy decides to go to Europe and forget it all.
    The script has been excellently handled,
with the dialog held to a naturalness seldom
achieved on the screen.
    Gable gets a part which might have been
tailored to his order and differentiates skillfully between his impulsive love for his wife
and his friendly appreciation of his stenographer's merits. Loy gets a part which suits her,
but it is Harlow who profits most. She clicks
in every scene without going spectacular as to
costume.

....

■ WILBY CONSPIRACY, THE

1975, 101 MINS, UK ◇ ⓥ
Dir Ralph Nelson   Prod Martin Baum   Scr Rod
Amateau, Harold Nebenzal   Ph John Coquillon
Ed Ernest Walter   Mus Stanley Myers   Art Dir Harold
Pottle
● Sidney Poitier, Michael Caine, Nicol Williamson,
Prunella Gee, Persis Khambatta, Saeed Jaffrey (United
Artists)

The Wilby Conspiracy [from Peter Driscoll's
novel] is a good action melodrama about
apartheid in South Africa. It was made in
Kenya. The stars Sidney Poitier and Michael
Caine are relentlessly stalked by Nicol
Williamson, superb as a coldly dedicated and
brutal policeman out after racial agitators.
    Poitier is linked by fate with Caine, an
Englishman accidently enmeshed in South
African segregation discrimination through
his girl (Prunella Gee) who as Poitier's lawyer
has him Freed from a decade in prison for
racial agitation.
    Williamson, almost too chillingly realistic
as a bigot, permits the two to escape an early
police confrontation, so as to let Poitier lead
him to Joseph De Fraf, the title character and
a political guerrilla partner to Poitier. En
route to the good climax, one encounters
Persis Khambatta, a most attractive Indian
actress, and Rutger Hauer, Gee's playboy-
type husband.
    But somehow the story comes out too much
of a potboiler undeserving of the fine work
that Williamson, Caine and Poitier put into
it.

....

■ WILD AND THE WILLING, THE

(US: Young and Willing)

1962, 123 MINS, UK
Dir Ralph Thomas   Prod Betty E. Box   Scr Nicholas
Phipps, Mordecai Richler   Ph Ernest Steward   Ed Alfred
Roome   Mus Norrie Paramor   Art Dir Alex Vetchinsky
● Virginia Maskell, Paul Rogers, Ian McShane,
Samantha Eggar, John Hurt, Richard Warner (Rank)

The Wild and the Willing, adapted from The
Tinker, a play by Laurence Dobie and Robert
Sloman which didn't make the grade in the
West End, has nothing much new to say on its

chosen theme – youth trying to find its place in society – the screenplay is lucid and the background of a provincial university authentic.

It concerns a brilliant young student from a poor working class family who is acutely class-conscious and rebels against the university, its professors and the opportunities they offer. He does not know where he is going and is arrogantly content to drift along raising Cain, drinking beer, playing football and pawing his girl friend, another student. He is a leading light in the university with a particular influence on his roommate, a shyer, more introspective lad.

Throughout there is a complete air of realism. The students, the professors and the townsfolk are real people about whose problems audiences will care. Ralph Thomas has directed with tact and has brought out some surprisingly sure performances from his inexperienced actors.

Ian McShane, with a broad Manchester accent, came straight from drama school to play this leading role. He is a virile, goodlooking young man with authority who is a real discovery, as is John Hurt, also a first timer, who plays his sensitive roommate.

■ WILD ANGELS, THE

1966, 83 MINS, US ◇ ⓥ
Dir Roger Corman *Prod* Roger Corman *Scr* Charles B. Griffith *Ph* Richard Moore *Ed* Monte Hellman *Mus* Mike Curb *Art Dir* Leon Ericksen
● Peter Fonda, Nancy Sinatra, Bruce Dern, Diane Ladd, Michael J. Pollard, Gayle Hunnicutt (American International)

The foreword to this well-turned-out Roger Corman production is its tipoff: 'The picture you are about to see will shock and perhaps anger you. Although the events and characters are fictitious, the story is a reflection of our times'.

For thematic motivation, Corman, who produces in almost documentary style, chooses the marauding of the Hell's Angels. Pinpointed here, the Angels, in vicious stride and without regard for law and order, operate in a Southern California beach community, and it is upon this particular segment that Corman directs his clinical eye in dissecting their philosophical (?) rebellion.

Corman tackles assignment with realism, taking apart the cult and giving its members an indepth study as he follows a gang headed by Peter Fonda in their defiance of common decencies.

Fonda lends credence to character, voicing the creed of the Angels in 'wanting to do what we want to do' without interference, and is well-cast in part.

■ WILD AT HEART

1990, 127 MINS, US ◇ ⓥ ⊙
Dir David Lynch *Prod* Monty Montgomery, Steve Golin, Joni Sighvatsson *Scr* David Lynch *Ph* Fred Elmes *Ed* Duwayne Dunham *Mus* Angelo Badalamenti *Art Dir* Patricia Norris
● Nicolas Cage, Laura Dern, Diane Ladd, Willem Dafoe, Isabella Rossellini, Harry Dean Stanton (Polygram/Propaganda)

Joltingly violent, wickedly funny and rivetingly erotic, David Lynch's *Wild at Heart* [based on the novel by Barry Gifford] is a rollercoaster ride to redemption through an American gothic heart of darkness.

The brutal opening signals that this film is not for the faint of heart. Sailor (Nicolas Cage), an Elvis-acolyte whose snakeskin jacket proclaims his 'duality and individuality', and his seethingly sexy 18-year-old girlfriend Lula (Laura Dern) are waylaid leaving a dance hall somewhere in the Carolinas. Sailor literally cracks open the assassin with his bare hands. He does two years for manslaughter in 'Pee Dee' state pen.

Sailor breaks parole and absconds with Lula to New Orleans, pursued by private eye Johnnie Farragut (Harry Dean Stanton) who's hired by Lula's insanely obsessive mother Marietta (Dern's real-life mother, Diane Ladd) his sometime lover.

His rival for this psychotic witch's affections are mobster Marcello Santos (J.R. Freeman), also unleashed on the lovers' trail as a precaution by mamma. Santos tabs a bordello-dwelling hit-man to annihilate Stanton in a bayou-style ritual murder. It's not the story-line's first or last doublecross.
□ 1990: Nomination: Best Supp. Actress (Diane Ladd)

■ WILD BUNCH, THE

1969, 145 MINS, US ◇ ⓥ ⊙
Dir Sam Peckinpah *Prod* Phil Feldman *Scr* Walon Green, Sam Peckinpah *Ph* Lucien Ballard *Ed* Louis Lombardo *Mus* Jerry Fielding *Art Dir* Edward Carrere
● William Holden, Ernest Borgnine, Robert Ryan, Edmond O'Brien, Warren Oates, Jaime Sanchez (Warner/Seven Arts)

Plot concerns a small band of outlaws headed by William Holden who hijack a US ammunition train crossing the border into Mexico in 1913 to supply the revolutionary army of Pancho Villa.

Actually, the story is two-pronged. Holden and his men go their way of outlawry and Robert Ryan, former member of Holden's gang and temporarily-released convict, tracks down his former chief to 'buy' his freedom from jail.

Screenplay, based on a story by Walon Green and Roy N. Sickner, builds suspensefully when action finally starts about the middle of film. Sam Peckinpah's forceful direction is a definite asset, particularly in later sequences in which Holden deals with a vicious Mexican general over the hijacked guns and ammo.

Holden goes into character for his role and handles assignment expertly. Ernest Borgnine delivers his usual brand of acting as former's aide.
□ 1969: Nominations: Best Original Story & Screenplay, Original Music Score

■ WILDCATS

1986, 107 MINS, US ◇ ⓥ ⊙
Dir Michael Ritchie *Prod* Anthea Sylbert *Scr* Ezra Sacks *Ph* Donald E. Thorin *Ed* Richard A. Harris *Mus* Hawk Wolinski, James Newton Howard *Art Dir* Boris Leven
● Goldie Hawn, James Keach, Swoosie Kurtz, Nipsey Russell, Bruce McGill, M. Emmet Walsh (Warner)

When Goldie Hawn tangles with high school varsity coach Bruce McGill, anyone can foresee the final confrontation.

Sure enough, when McGill has her appointed football coach at the unspeakable ghetto school, Central High, it's an inevitable collision course. Along the way crises pop up at carefully placed intervals, the first being winning the confidence of the rag-tag collection of players.

Michael Ritchie's direction lacks his usual bite and eye for detail. There is nothing spontaneous about the action and football footage is also surprisingly dull.

Hawn, seemingly on screen for the entire film, is fun to watch as she runs her team through aerobics and mugs for the camera, but even better is Nipsey Russell as the rough-hewn high school principal with a word for all occasions.

■ WILD GEESE, THE

1978, 132 MINS, UK ◇ ⓥ ⊙
Dir Andrew V. McLaglen *Prod* Euan Lloyd *Scr* Reginald Rose *Ph* Jack Hildyard *Ed* John Glen *Mus* Roy Budd

● Richard Burton, Roger Moore, Richard Harris, Hardy Kruger, Stewart Granger, Jack Watson (Rank)

Euan Lloyd's uppercase actioner, centered on a caper by mercenaries in Africa, attempts to be a cornucopia of tried boxoffice hooks but ultimately fails to meld its comedy, adventure, pathos, violence, heroics – or even its political message – into a credible whole.

Reginald Rose's adaptation of Daniel Carney's story – about mercenary toughguys who parachute into the African bush to snatch a deposed African president for reinstatement to suit British business interests – is routinely predictable and, in the end, cornily incredible.

Roger Moore's shootouts with the Mafia in London and Hardy Kruger's neat killing of three sentries with cyanide-tipped arrows is good 'traditional' escapism. Then, as if to contemporize the film, Peckinpah-fashion, the screen's suddenly filled with bloody graphics and four-letter words.

Winston Ntshona is well cast as the deposed president Limbani though much of his 'message' dialog is unnecessary and unpalatably heavy for what's presumably designed as a riproaring blood and guts actioner.

■ WILD GEESE II

1985, 125 MINS, UK ◇ ⓥ ⊙ ⊙
Dir Peter Hunt *Prod* Euan Lloyd *Scr* Reginald Rose *Ph* Michael Reed *Ed* Keith Palmer *Mus* Roy Budd *Art Dir* Syd Cain
● Scott Glenn, Barbara Carrera, Edward Fox, Laurence Olivier, Robert Webber, Robert Freitag (Thorn-EMI/Frontier)

Script [from the book *The Square Circle* by Daniel Carney] has a promising basic premise. An American TV station commissions mercenary John Haddad (Scott Glenn) to kidnap the nonagenarian Nazi leader Rudolf Hess from the impregnable Spandau prison in Berlin, but the follow-through never arrives. A routine car ambush is substituted for the impossible jailbreak. The liberated Hess just doesn't want to play games with history by revealing the Watergate-style story supposedly underlying Hitler's rise to power.

Despite these structural problems, film contains a wealth of incident. Haddad is the object of numerous assassination attempts organized by the German Heinrich Stroebling (Robert Freitag), who is in league with the Russians and Palestinian terrorists. The British are after Hess too. There's also a supporting role for members of the Irish Republican Army and the kidnap of Yank journalist Kathy Lukas (Barbara Carrera) occasions a major shootout.

Edward Fox plays Colonel Faulkner with comic zest. Unintentionally, perhaps, Laurence Olivier also extracts laughs from his Hess cameo. By contrast, Glenn and Carrera take their parts more seriously than the script merits.

■ WILD HEART, THE
See: Gone to Earth

■ WILD IN THE COUNTRY

1961, 112 MINS, US ◇ ⓥ
Dir Philip Dunne *Prod* Jerry Wald *Scr* Clifford Odets *Ph* William C. Mellor *Ed* Dorothy Spencer *Mus* Kenyon Hopkins *Art Dir* Jack Martin Smith, Preston Ames
● Elvis Presley, Hope Lange, Tuesday Weld, Millie Perkins, John Ireland, Gary Lockwood (20th Century-Fox)

Dramatically, there simply isn't substance, novelty or spring to this wobbly and artificial tale of a maltreated country boy (Elvis Presley) who, supposedly, has the talent to become a great writer, but lacks the means, the emotional stability and the encouragement until he comes in contact with a beautiful psychiatric consultant (Hope Lange) who develops traumas of her own in the process.

The complications occur when the two spend an innocent night in a motel, innocent on the strength of their May (he)-December (she) respect for each other. The gap in romantic seasons is quickly bridged when their one-night relationship is misinterpreted by some of the incredibly foul and mischievous people who live in the town. Clifford Odets penned the screenplay, from the novel *The Lost Country* by J.R. Salamanca. The writing has its occasional rewards.

Presley, subdued, uses what dramatic resources he has to best advantage in this film. Lange, for the most part, plays intelligently and sensitively. Tuesday Weld contributes a flashy and arresting portrait of a sexy siren enamored of Mr P.

Story, set in the Shenandoah Valley, was filmed in the Napa Valley. Sans wiggle, Presley croons four or five songs. Guitars rather mysteriously keep turning up on the premises, but E.P. leaves the plunking to Weld.

. . . .

■ WILD IN THE STREETS

1968, 96 MINS, US ◇ ⓦ
Dir Barry Shear   *Prod* Burt Topper   *Scr* Robert Thom
Ph Richard Moore   *Ed* Fred Feitshans, Eve Newman
Mus Les Baxter
● Shelley Winters, Christopher Jones, Diane Varsi, Ed Begley, Hal Halbrook, Millie Perkins (American International)

An often chilling political science fiction drama, with comedy, the production considers the takeover of American government by the preponderant younger population. Good writing and direction enhance the impact of a diversified cast headed by Shelley Winters.

Christopher Jones plays a rock 'n' roll hero who, as a result of a request from would-be US Senator Hal Holbrook, exceeds the bounds of electioneering help by mobilizing teenagers into legalized voters.

Winters plays his sleazy, selfish mother, whose purported emasculation of dad Bert Freed years before cued Jones' running away from home.

Holbrook projects perfectly the bright young politico who exploits the young crowd, only to be turned on by those whose help he seeks.

Actual footage from real-life demonstrations was shot for pic, some of it matched quite well with internal drama. What comes off as a partial documentary flavor makes for a good artistic complement to the not-so-fictional hypothesis, the logical result of an over-accent on youth.
□ 1968: Nomination: Best Editing
. . . .

■ WILD IS THE WIND

1957, 110 MINS, US
Dir George Cukor   *Prod* Hal Wallis   *Scr* Arnold Schulman   *Ph* Charles Lang Jr   *Ed* Warren Low
Mus Dimitri Tiomkin   *Art Dir* Hal Pereira, Tambi Larsen
● Anna Magnani, Anthony Quinn, Anthony Franciosa, Dolores Hart, Joseph Calleia, Lili Valenty (Paramount)

Top grade performances, some unusual film sequences and expert production highlight *Wild Is the Wind*, a story of earthy passion.

Screenplay, from a story by Vittorio Nino Novarese, is a good one, particularly in its delineation of the characters. It's an unusual switch in that it starts off on a comedy level before abruptly switching to the dramatic problem and long early portions of it are almost entirely in Italian.

Anthony Quinn is a wealthy sheep rancher in Nevada and goes back to the old country to wed the sister of his long-dead wife. He brings her home to a promise of happiness,

but the shadow of the first wife is constantly between them. Her urgent need to be loved makes her mistake the growing attraction between herself and Anthony Franciosa, young Basque sheepherder who had been raised by Quinn.

George Cukor directs with taste and imagination and his skilful handling is evident in many scenes, particularly the sequence showing a film audience how a lamb is dropped, or one in which Franciosa trains sheep dogs, and in his handling of the affair between Magnani and Franciosa.
□ 1957: Nominations: Best Actor (Anthony Quinn), Actress (Anna Magnani), Song ('Wild is the Wind')
. . . .

■ WILD ONE, THE

1953, 79 MINS, US ⓦ ⊙
Dir Laslo Benedek   *Prod* Stanley Kramer   *Scr* John Paxton   *Ph* Hal Mohr   *Ed* Al Clark   *Mus* Leith Stevens
Art Dir Walter Holscher
● Marlon Brando, Mary Murphy, Robert Keith, Lee Marvin, Jay C. Flippen, Hugh Sanders (Columbia)

Inspired by an episode when a mob of youths on motorcycles terrorized a Californian town for an entire evening, this feature is long on suspense, brutality and sadism. Marlon Brando contributes another hard-faced 'hero' who never knew love as a boy and is now plainly in need of psychoanalysis.

The young cyclists are a motley mob of jivesters, some carrying their own female cargo. Much giving to showoff antics and mimicry, they also drink beer in vast quantities and incessantly deposit nickels in jukeboxes. Reckless, impudent, cruel and knife-carrying, they break and borrow things and drive motorcycles into and through saloons.

However intolerable and barbarian the cyclists are, nothing they do is as vicious and vindictive as the 'vigilante' spirit which develops among the merchants of the village. Big bruisers twice the size of the young cyclists, these adults readily and joyously beat Brando to a pulp and then later try to frame him by their silence for a manslaughter rap.

Picture [from a story by Frank Rooney] was made some time [before its release] and had three titles in succession, *Cyclists Raid*, *The Wild One* and *Hot Blood*. All performances are highly competent. A second band of ruffians comes along later led by a colorful young character named Lee Marvin.

The femme interest is intelligently managed by Mary Murphy. Robert Keith is excellent as the mush-soft village constable. The county sheriff is the nicest guy in the film, and nearly the only one. He's impersonated with professional sincerity by the old vaudeman Jay C. Flippen.
. . . .

■ WILD ORCHID

1990, 100 MINS, US ◇ ⓦ ⊙
Dir Zalman King   *Prod* Mark Damon, Tony Anthony, Howard North   *Scr* Zalman King, Patricia Louisianna Knop   *Ph* Gale Tattersall   *Mus* Geoff MacCormack, Simon Goldenberg
● Mickey Rourke, Jacqueline Bisset, Carre Otis (Vision)

If *Wild Orchid* aims to grab audiences with a hot-house atmosphere of erotica, it mainly teases until a pay-off in the last sequence.

Claudia (Jacqueline Bisset) is a wired jet-set businesswoman who hires tyro lawyer Emily (Carre Otis) to help her close a deal. Prim Emily, a Midwest farm girl still wet under the collar – but highly attractive – is dazed to find herself on a plane to Rio. There she meets Claudia's old flame Wheeler (Mickey Rourke), a self-made millionaire with perverse sexual tastes. Hypnotizing Emily with his original personality (?), he forces her to forget her good-girl upbringing and do liberating things.

What doesn't work is the hold Rourke is supposed to have over Otis. Looking pudgy and puffy-faced, with a little gold earring, he is anything but an appetizing sex object.

As Emily, Otis really is hypnotically attractive, but she plays the still-waters-run-deep country beauty with expressionless immobility. Bisset, always a class act, here bubbles over with caricatured joie de vivre.

As for eros, only when Emily breaks through Wheeler's reserve/importence in the last sequence does pic deliver in a torrid, highly choreographed but equally explicit bedroom session between the two.
. . . .

■ WILD PARTY, THE

1975, 100 MINS, US ◇ ⓦ
Dir James Ivory   *Prod* Ismail Merchant   *Scr* Walter Marks   *Ph* Walter Lassally   *Ed* Kent McKinney
Mus Laurence Rosenthal   *Art Dir* David Nichols
● James Coco, Raquel Welch, Perry King, Tiffany Bolling, Royal Dano, David Dukes (American International)

The Wild Party is an extremely handsome, overly talky musical drama starring James Coco as a faded 1920s film comic whose disastrous premiere houseparty for a comeback film leads to murder.

Based on a long-ago poem by Joseph Moncure March, the film is a magnificent showpiece for Coco's talents. He successfully covers a spectrum from silly comedy, warm humor, sober anger, maddening frustration and drunken psychosis. Holding her own as his mistress is Raquel Welch, registering very strongly.

Key featured players include Perry King, very good as a current film heartthrob; Tiffany Bolling, his femme counterpart; and Royal Dano, quite good as Coco's loyal valet.
. . . .

■ WILD RIVER

1960, 115 MINS, US ◇
Dir Elia Kazan   *Prod* Elia Kazan   *Scr* Paul Osborn
Ph Ellsworth Fredericks   *Ed* William Reynolds
Mus Kenyon Hopkins   *Art Dir* Lyle R. Wheeler, Herman A. Blumenthal
● Montgomery Clift, Lee Remick, Jo Van Fleet, Albert Salmi, Jay C. Flippen, Barbara Loden (20th Century-Fox)

Wild River is an important motion picture. In studying a slice of national socio-economic progress (the Tennessee Valley Authority of the early 1930s) in terms of people (those who enforced vs those who resisted), it catches something timeless and essential in the human spirit and shapes it in the American image.

Sturdy foundation for director Elia Kazan's artistic indulgences and a number of exceptional performances is Paul Osborn's thought-provoking screenplay, erected out of two novels, *Mud on the Stars* by William Bradford Huie, and *Dunbar's Cove* by Borden Deal. It is the tragic tale of an 80-year-old 'rugged individualist' (Jo Van Fleet) who refuses to give ground (a small island on the Tennessee River smack dab in TVA's dambuilding path) to an understanding, but equally firm, TV agent (Montgomery Clift).

In the process of successfully separating the grand old lady from her precious, but doomed, slice of real estate, Clift gets into several scrapes with the local Tennessee bigots over his decent treatment of Negroes and squeezes sufficient romance into his tight schedule to wind up the spouse of the old woman's pretty granddaughter (Lee Remick).

Where the film soars is in its clean, objective approach to the basic conflict between progress and tradition ('electricity and souls,' as Osborn puts it). Through this gentle veil of objectivity, a point-of-view unmistakably stirs, but never emerges to the point where it takes sides just to be taking sides. The result is that rare element of tragedy, in the truly classical sense of the word, where an indomitable individual eventually must fall helpless prey to an irresistible, but impersonal edict designed for universal good.

WILD ROVERS

1971, 110 MINS, US ◇ ⊛
Dir Blake Edwards *Prod* Blake Edwards, Ken Wales
Scr Blake Edwards *Ph* Philip Lathrop *Ed* John F. Burnett *Mus* Jerry Goldsmith *Art Dir* George W. Davis, Addison Hehr
● William Holden, Ryan O'Neal, Karl Malden, Lynn Carlin, Tom Skerritt, Joe Don Baker (M-G-M)

William Holden and Ryan O'Neal, two cowboys who decide to rob a bank, and Karl Malden, their employer, star in a technically superior film.

Film tells a sentimental story about an aging cowpoke and a younger buddy whose dreams of crashing out of their rut lead to violence and death.

Emphasis is on Holden and O'Neal, and there are a few touching moments as the older man imparts some wisdom to the younger. The mood is broken regularly with pratfall humor, also some dehumanizing slow-motion ballets of death. O'Neal's character is not always well defined, since the boyish naivete also exhibits some jarring evidence of cruelty, thereby limiting empathy for his ultimate downfall.

Large supporting cast is lost in throwaway parts. Even Malden has little to do except plot-motivate the dispatch of sons Tom Skerritt and Joe Don Baker to join the posse. Skerritt overacts, and Baker's abilities are smothered in a second banana line-throwing part.

WILLARD

1971, 95 MINS, US ◇ ⊛ ⊙
Dir Daniel Mann *Prod* Mort Briskin *Scr* Gilbert A. Ralston *Ph* Robert B. Hauser *Ed* Warren Low
Mus Alex North *Art Dir* Howard Hollander
● Bruce Davison, Ernest Borgnine, Elsa Lanchester, Sondra Locke, Michael Dante, Jody Gilbert (BCO)

Neat little horror tale, shrewdly organized from Stephen Gilbert's novel, *Ratman's Notebooks*, capitalizes on human repugnance for rodents as Bruce Davison unleashes his trained rats on obstacles. Some good jump moments and at least two stomach-churning murders committed by the rats with tight direction of Daniel Mann develop pic into sound nail-chewer.

Davison, working for wheeler-dealer Ernest Borgnine, who took foundry over from Davison's dead father, lives with invalid, unrelenting mother Elsa Lanchester. Their old mansion gone to seed, loner Davison makes friends with resident rats, who learn to obey his commands. Davison, after death of his mother, killing of one of chief rats at Borgnine's hands, and receipt of pink slip from Borgnine, begins to fight back.

Davison supplies nicely controlled characterization as he fiddles with his rats, puts up with his mother and her friends and finally loses patience. Borgnine is first rate as he confronts subordinates. Lanchester is highly credible as the demanding mama.

WILLIE & PHIL

1980, 116 MINS, US ◇ ⊛
Dir Paul Mazursky *Prod* Paul Mazursky, Tony Ray
Scr Paul Mazursky *Ph* Sven Nykvist *Ed* Donn Cambern *Mus* Claude Bolling, Georges Delerue
Art Dir Pato Guzman
● Michael Ontkean, Margot Kidder, Ray Sharkey, Jerry Hall, Natalie Wood, Tom Brennan (20th Century-Fox)

Willie & Phil is an amiable and humane film about a menage-a-trois spanning the 1970s.

Director Paul Mazursky's compassionate eye for character and his wry wit, balance out a tendency to overromanticize and sentimentalize his characters.

Michael Ontkean and Ray Sharkey play the title characters (roles once intended for Woody Allen and Al Pacino) and Margot Kidder completes the romantic triangle, which forms in Greenwich Village at the beginning of the 1970s and winds up in Malibu nine years later. Along the way, Mazursky deftly traces changing sexual mores and other social values while portraying the trio as typical representatives of their generation's hopes and confusions.

Beginning rather coyly with the two men meeting at a Blecker Street Cinema screening of Truffaut's classic 1962 film about a menage-a-trois, *Jules et Jim*, Mazursky then has the two become friends so inseparable that they have trouble deciding who should board with Kidder.

It's all handled in very civilized and low-key fashion by Mazursky and his characters.

WILLOW

1988, 125 MINS, US ◇ ⊛ ⊙ ⊙
Dir Ron Howard *Prod* Nigel Wooll *Scr* Bob Dolman *Ph* Adrian Biddle *Ed* Daniel Hanley, Michael Hill *Mus* James Horner *Art Dir* Allan Cameron
● Val Kilmer, Joanne Whalley-Kilmer, Warwick Davis, Patricia Hayes, Jean Marsh, Billy Barty (Lucasfilm)

Willow is medieval mishmash from George Lucas [executive producer who wrote the original story], a sort of 10th-century *Star Wars* tossed together with a plethora of elements taken from numerous classic fables. There's a baby princess, an evil queen, trolls, fairies, little people, warriors, sorcerers and a community of midgets called Nelwyns. Willow is a Nelwyn.

They are saving their kingdom from an evil queen (Jean Marsh) who makes her crusade to kill every newborn in the land to ensure that baby Elora Danan, a princess, never ascends to the throne. Willow gets a loving send-off, baby on his back papoose-style. Along the way, he teams up with a wisecracking Han Solo renegade warrior named Madmartigan (read: Mad Max), played well enough by Val Kilmer.

Dialog waivers from the truly banal – Willow himself is very earnest and boring – to some very clever interplay between the secondary characters, including a delightful scene between Madmartigan, dusted with love sparkles, and the object of his desire, Sorsha (real-life wife, Joanne Whalley), the evil queen's daughter.

Ron Howard directed, but only Lucasness shows up on the screen, particularly towards the end when the special effects start to come on at full bore. *Willow* was lensed in England, Wales and New Zealand. It's not surprising the overall flavor of the production looks familiar. Production designer Allan Cameron (*Aliens*) and cinematographer Adrian Biddle (*Aliens, The Princess Bride*) have put their stamp on the film. Industrial Light & Magic wizards, too numerous to mention, are up to usual Lucasfilm standards of excellence.
□ 1988: Nominations: Best Sound Effects Editing, Visual Effects

WILL PENNY

1968, 108 MINS, US ◇ ⊛ ⊙
Dir Tom Gries *Prod* Fred Engel, Walter Seltzer
Scr Tom Gries *Ph* Lucien Ballard *Ed* Warren Low *Mus* David Raksin *Art Dir* Hal Pereira, Roland Anderson
● Charlton Heston, Joan Hackett, Donald Pleasence, Lee Majors, Bruce Dern, Ben Johnson (Paramount)

Will Penny is not a straight out-and-out western but more a character study of an aging cowpoke who for the first time feels the stirrings of romance.

There is beautiful range and mountain scenery but basically interest rests on the man, and his gropings which at times aren't overly clear, rather than on western action all too often slowed by characterization.

Charlton Heston in title role is persuasively effective as the cowpoke who finally rides away from romance. Joan Hackett as the woman travelling across the plains with her young son to join her farmer-husband in Oregon, willing to renounce that marriage to wed the penniless range rider, is quietly commanding.

Donald Pleasence is a scavenging rawhider who with his three sons would rather murder than not. Given these elements, a story takes form which displays thoughtful conception. This is not a story of the wild West but the West as lived in by real-life characters.

WILL SUCCESS SPOIL ROCK HUNTER?
(UK: Oh! For a Man)

1957, 94 MINS, US ◇
Dir Frank Tashlin *Prod* Frank Tashlin *Scr* Frank Tashlin *Ph* Joseph MacDonald *Ed* Hugh Fowler *Mus* Cyril J. Mockridge *Art Dir* Lyle R. Wheeler, Leland Fuller
● Jayne Mansfield, Tony Randall, Betsy Drake, Joan Blondell, Mickey Hargitay, Groucho Marx (20th Century-Fox)

In converting the stageplay *Will Success Spoil Rock Hunter?* to his purposes, Frank Tashlin turns out a vastly amusing comedy. Picture bears comparatively little resemblance to the George Axelrod original.

Tony Randall's second excursion into the bigscreen realm from TV and the stage shows he's a fellow who knows timing, and his clowning has a slightly sophisticated touch that hits bullseye. Jayne Mansfield does a sock job as the featherbrained sex-motivated movie star.

Tashlin fashions a funny credit for the credits, which are introed by Randall. There's also an 'intermission', with Randall coming out to comfort those who are used to TV commercials. In the end, Groucho Marx comes on for a briefy.

Story has Randall as a TV commercial writer about to be fired because his agency is threatened with the loss of its big lipstick account. He saves the situation by getting the endorsement from a famous movie star.

Supporting roles are all very well cast. Betsy Drake is cute and displays a strong sense for comedy as Randall's fiancee; Henry Jones, ad-agency v.p., coaxes from the sidelines and delivers some rather lengthy speeches; Joan Blondell is standout in a small part and Mickey Hargitay is properly pompous as the Tarzan he-man who triggers Randall's troubles.

WILLY/MILLY

1986, 90 MINS, US ◇ ⊛
Dir Paul Schneider *Prod* M. David Chilewich
Scr Walter Carbonne, Carla Reuben *Ph* Dominique Chapuis *Ed* Michael Miller *Mus* David McHugh *Art Dir* Nora Chavooshian
● Pamela Segall, Eric Gurry, Mary Tanner, Patty Duke, John Glover, Seth Green (Cinema)

The rather silly title *Willy / Milly* caps this charming and substantial kidpic about sex roles.

Rather than face the trauma of crossing the threshold of womanhood, 14-year-old Milly (Pamela Segall) turns into a boy under the effect of a magic spell she tries out during an eclipse. The matter-of-fact reaction of Milly is captured when she spins the first letter of her name upside-down and decides to try out Willy, effectively turning her entire world upside down.

The effects of the kid's crossover are explored on all fronts, going beyond locker room humor and capturing the kinds of expectations that spark the war between the sexes at all ages.

Film's biggest asset is in the performances of the unknown adolescent actors.

● ●

■ WILLY WONKA & THE CHOCOLATE FACTORY

1971, 98 MINS, US ◇ ⓥ ⊙
Dir Mel Stuart   *Prod* Stan Margulies, David L. Wolper
Scr Roald Dahl   *Ph* Arthur Ibbetson   *Ed* David Saxon
Mus Walter Scharf (arr.)   *Art Dir* Harper Goff
● Gene Wilder, Jack Albertson, Peter Ostrum, Roy Kinnear, Julie Dawn Cole, Leonard Stone (Wolper/Quaker)

Based on a Roald Dahl children's book, *Willy Wonka & the Chocolate Factory* is an okay family musical fantasy featuring Gene Wilder as an eccentric candymaker who makes a boy's dreams come true. Handsomely produced in partnership with Quaker Oats, the film has a fair score by Leslie Bricusse and Anthony Newley.

Dahl himself adapted his book, *Charlie and the Chocolate Factory*, and his dialog is better than the structure. Plot hook is a merchandising gimmick by Wilder who puts five golden tickets into a candy bar run, and tests the honesty of the winners. Inhibiting the sustenance of interest among those who are not familiar with the book is that Wilder's character is rather cynical and sadistic until virtually the end of the film. Ultimately Peter Ostrum, the kids' hero, and grandpa Jack Albertson pass the honesty test.

Sidebar incidents and dialog are the sharpest elements, particularly the running satire on TV news programming cliche.
□ 1971: Nomination: Best Adapted Score

● ●

■ WILSON

1944, 136 MINS, US ◇
Dir Henry King   *Prod* Darryl F. Zanuck   *Scr* Lamar Trotti
Ph Leon Shamroy   *Ed* Barbara McLean   *Mus* Alfred Newman   *Art Dir* Wiard B. Ihnen, James Basevi
● Alexander Knox, Charles Coburn, Geraldine Fitzgerald, Thomas Mitchell, Cedric Hardwicke, Vincent Price (20th Century-Fox)

The production is said to cost over $3 million and looks it. When there are crowds in the Senate, at the sundry political conventions, in the Palmer Stadium, on the campus, they are there in staggering, sizable numbers.

When the period of 1912-20 is recreated in Technicolor it is as authentic as it is splendiferous. All the detail of the White House decor of the Wilson administration; all the local color of the era and the day are faithfully brought to the canvas in a nostalgic, authentic fashion.

In fact, that is the keynote of *Wilson* – authority, warmth, idealism, a search for a better world. Through it all stalks a potent personality in Alexander Knox, a newborn star, supported by a flawless cast.
□ 1944: Best Original Screenplay, Color Cinematography, Color Art Direction, Editing, Sound.
□ Nominations: Best Picture, Director, Actor (Alexander Knox), Scoring of a Dramatic Picture, Special Effects

● ●

■ WILT

1989, 91 MINS, UK ◇ ⓥ
Dir Michael Tuchner   *Prod* Brian Eastman   *Scr* Andrew Marshall, David Renwick   *Ph* Norman Langley
Ed Chris Blunden   *Mus* Anne Dudley   *Art Dir* Leo Austin
● Griff Rhys Jones, Mel Smith, Alison Steadman, Diana Quick, Jeremy Clyde (Carnival/LWT)

There is a good deal of enjoyment to be derived from *Wilt* [based on Tom Sharpe's novel], mainly thanks to a uniformly excel-

lent cast and unpretentious, straightforward direction by Michael Tuchner, as well as the charmingly honest urban provincial settings.

Griff Rhys Jones is the title character, a disillusioned college lecturer, who spends his spare time walking his dog and dreaming about murdering his domineering wife (Alison Steadman).

She has made friends with upwardly mobile couple Diana Quick and Jeremy Clyde. When Steadman and Rhys Jones attend a party at their posh country home Rhys Jones gets dead-drunk, and due to Quick's machinations finds himself locked in a naked passionate embrace with a life-size inflatable doll named Angelique.

He drunkenly roams the town trying to get rid of the doll. The next day, Steadman goes missing and Rhys Jones' nocturnal activities are noted – especially by ambitious inspector Mel Smith.

The most amusing scenes are those with Rhys Jones and Smith indulging in the banter they are known for from their TV appearances.

● ●

■ WINCHESTER '73

1950, 92 MINS, US ⓥ ⊙
Dir Anthony Mann   *Prod* Aaron Rosenberg   *Scr* Robert L. Richards, Borden Chase   *Ph* William Daniels
Ed Edward Curtiss   *Mus* Joseph Gershenson
● James Stewart, Shelley Winters, Dan Duryea, Stephen McNally, Rock Hudson, Tony Curtis (Universal)

Story [by Stuart N. Lake] is centered on a manhunt, the search of Lin McAdam (James Stewart) for the cowardly murderer of his father. Film opens with Lin and his friend, High Spade (Millard Mitchell), riding into Dodge City in time for a 4 July celebration. Big event is a rifle match, with first prize a priceless 'one of a 1,000' 1873 model Winchester rifle.

Lin's brother Dutch (Stephen McNally), however, makes off with the precious rifle.

Stewart brings real flavor and appeal to the role of Lin, in a lean, concentrated portrayal. McNally is hard and unbending as the runaway brother. Mitchell lends warmth as Stewart's loyal henchman and friend. Shelley Winters is just sufficiently hard-bitten and cynical as the dancehall girl.

● ●

■ WIND, THE

1928, 70 MINS, US ⓥ ⊙
Dir Victor Seastrom   *Scr* Frances Marion, John Colton
Ph John Arnold   *Ed* Conrad A. Nervig   *Art Dir* Cedric Gibbons, Edward Withers
● Lillian Gish, Lars Hanson, Montagu Love, Dorothy Cumming, Edward Earle, William Orlamond (M-G-M)

Some stories are just naturally poison for screen purposes and Dorothy Scarborough's novel here shows itself a conspicuous example. Everything a high pressure, lavishly equipped studio, expert director and reputable star could contribute was showered on this production. Everything about the picture breathes quality. Yet it flops dismally.

Tragedy on the high winds, on the desolate desert prairies, unrelieved by that sparkling touch of life that spells human interest, is what this picture has to offer. It may be a true picturization of life on the prairie but it still remains lifeless: and unentertaining.

The story opens with an unknown girl, Letty (Lillian Gish), from Virginia, trainbound for her cousin's ranch, which she describes as beautiful to the stranger, Roddy (Montagu Love), who has made her acquaintance informally.

Roaring, blinding wind and sandstorms immediately frighten the girl. She remains in a semi-conscious state of fright throughout, excepting at the close of the picture.

At Beverly's (Edward Earle) ranch the girl

becomes too popular with Cora's (Dorothy Cummings) children and is forced to leave. The girl then accepts a proposal from Lige (Lars Hanson), whom she had laughed at the night before. During a round-up of wild horses, brought down by a fierce northern gale, Roddy forces his way into Lige's home and stays there for the night with Letty.

● ●

■ WIND

1992, 125 MINS, US ◇ ⓥ ⊙
Dir Carroll Ballard   *Prod* Mata Yamamoto, Tom Luddy
Scr Rudy Wurlitzer, Mac Gudgeon   *Ph* John Toll
Ed Michael Chandler   *Mus* Basil Poledouris
Art Dir Laurence Eastwood
● Matthew Modine, Jennifer Grey, Stellan Skarsgard, Rebecca Miller, Cliff Robertson, Jack Thompson (Filmlink/American Zoetrope)

The elements prove far more stimulating than the people in *Wind*, a sail-racing saga that could have used a great deal more dramatic rigging.

In his two previous narrative pics (*The Black Stallion*, *Never Cry Wolf*), maverick director Carroll Ballard had subjects that suited his tendency to make Mother Nature the main character. Unfortunately, the crew members here are stick figures of no emotional or psychological interest.

Three-act script is credited to the distinctive writer Rudy Wurlitzer and Aussie scribe Mac Gudgeon, with three others [Jeff Benjamin, Roger Vaughan, Kimball Livingston] receiving story credit. But several other scenarists reportedly had a hand in this unimaginatively fictional telling of the U.S. losing, for the first time, then winning back the America's Cup.

Uncompelling protagonists are Matthew Modine, a young sailor with a knack for choking when things get tough, and Jennifer Grey, his spunky g.f., who is seemingly a sailing genius but is kept off the crew due to sexism.

Having lost the race and his lady, Modine turns up six months later at Deadman's Flat, Nev, where Grey and new b.f./engineering whiz Stellan Skarsgard are designing aircraft. Modine convinces them to develop a new yacht to compete in the next America's Cup race, more than three months hence.

Final 40 minutes go Down Under and downhill, with a *Rocky* underdog mood taking hold.

● ●

■ WIND ACROSS THE EVERGLADES

1958, 91 MINS, US ◇
Dir Nicholas Ray   *Prod* Stuart Schulberg   *Scr* Budd Schulberg   *Ph* Joseph Brun   *Ed* George Klotz, Joseph Zigman   *Art Dir* Richard Sylbert
● Burl Ives, Christopher Plummer, Gypsy Rose Lee, George Voskovec, Emmett Kelly, Peter Falk (Warner)

Wind across the Everglades is a worthy attempt to make a picture about early efforts of the Audubon Society to preserve the bird wild life of Florida. It is an 'interesting' picture, with some impressive backgrounds of the Everglades country (where it was shot), but it is not consistently engrossing. It should have been far better.

The screenplay fictionalizes the struggle of the Audubon Society to end the slaughter of Florida's plume birds, whose feathers were so highly prized around the turn of the century for women's hats. The action revolves around the almost single-handed efforts of an agent (Christopher Plummer) to stop the mass killings, and in particular his battle with the leader of one band of bird-hunters (Burl Ives).

There are some good shots of the egrets and other fowl, some with spectacular effect, and satisfactory simulated scenes of the birds' slaughter. Plummer does a good job as the idealistic bird warden, although not much motivation is ever given for his dedication.

Ives, looking remarkably like Henry VIII in a red beard, eyebrows and hair, does a characteristically intense job, and his character, as a free-booting, civilization-hating rugged individualist, makes sense if not sympathy. Gypsy Rose Lee has some good comedy scenes which she handles adroitly while displaying some startling cleavage.

■ **WIND AND THE LION, THE**

1975, 119 MINS, US ◇ ⓦ
Dir John Milius   *Prod* Herb Jaffe   *Scr* John Milius
Ph Billy Williams   *Ed* Robert L. Wolfe   *Mus* Jerry Goldsmith   *Art Dir* Gil Parrondo
● Sean Connery, Candice Bergen, Brian Keith, John Huston, Geoffrey Lewis, Steve Kanaly (M-G-M)

Sean Connery stars as an upstart independent Berber chieftain who in 1904 kidnaps Candice Bergen and children, provoking Brian Keith (as Theodore Roosevelt) into dramatic power politics, which confound European moves into North Africa.

The quasi-fictional story gives full exposition to the black, white and gray personal and political elements involved, providing focal points of empathy and criticism for all.

Connery scores one of his major screen impressions, while Bergen handles with assured excellence the subtleties of a woman first outraged at her captor, later his benefactor after a multinational doublecross.

Milius, armed with an expert crew of action specialists, has crafted a superior film, enhanced even further by Jerry Goldsmith's outstanding score.

□ 1975: Nomination: Best Original Score, Sound

■ **WIND CANNOT READ, THE**

1958, 115 MINS, UK ◇
Dir Ralph Thomas   *Prod* Betty E. Box   *Scr* Richard Mason   *Ph* Ernest Steward   *Ed* Freddie Wilson
Mus Angelo Lavagnino   *Art Dir* Maurice Carter
● Dirk Bogarde, Yoko Tani, Ronald Lewis, John Fraser, Anthony Bushell, Michael Medwin (Rank)

Richard Mason's novel shapes up as a useful romantic drama. The pic is a love story told against a Burma war background. Scenery pluses include the doll-like good looks of the young Japanese actress, Yoko Tani. She and Dirk Bogarde hold the acting side together in what is an almost uninterrupted Cupid duolog.

Bogarde is a grounded flyer sent to learn Japanese in order to be able to interrogate Japanese POWs. He falls for Tani, one of the instructors, marries her in secret and is then sent off to the front where he is captured, tortured and humiliated before escaping.

The gradual falling in love of the two stars is written with trite dialog but is directed charmingly. Then, when the action moves to the front, the prison torture scenes are put over with stark realism.

■ **WINDOM'S WAY**

1957, 108 MINS, UK ◇ ⓦ
Dir Ronald Neame   *Prod* John Bryan   *Scr* Jill Craigie
Ph Christopher Challis   *Ed* Reginald Mills   *Mus* James Bernard   *Art Dir* Michael Stringer
● Peter Finch, Mary Ure, Natasha Parry, Robert Flemyng, Michael Hordern, Gregoire Aslan (Rank) ˙˙

Peter Finch is a dedicated doctor working in the village of Selim, on a Far East island. He is loved and trusted by the villagers and finds himself involved in their political problems. Mary Ure is his estranged wife who comes out for a trial reconciliation at a time when the locality is in a state of unrest. Finch's ideals are such that he tries to prevent the villagers from getting up in arms against the local police and plantation manager.

The acting throughout this drama is first class, with Finch particularly convincing. Ure has little chance in the colorless role of his wife, but Natasha Parry as a native nursing sister, in love with Finch, is warm, sensitive and technically very sound.

Jill Craigie has provided a slow moving, but literate script, from a novel by James Ramsey Ullman. Ronald Neame's direction brings out qualities of dignity and credibility.

■ **WINDOW IN THE SKY**
See: The Other Side of the Mountain

■ **WINDY CITY**

1984, 102 MINS, US ◇ ⓦ
Dir Armyan Bernstein   *Prod* Alan Greisman
Scr Armyan Bernstein   *Ph* Reynaldo Villalobos
Ed Clifford Jones   *Mus* Jack Nitzsche   *Art Dir* Bill Kenney
● John Shea, Kate Capshaw, Josh Mostel, Jim Borrelli, Jeffrey DeMunn, Eric Pierpoint (CBS)

Windy City marks writer Armyan Bernstein's (*One from The Heart*) maiden voyage as director of his own tales, and while the endeavor isn't always smooth sailing, the heart-felt nature of his subject is generally strong enough to weather the awkwardness of this story of romance, friendship and shattered dreams.

Focus is Danny Morgan (John Shea), the most obvious victim of failed ambition among a group of seven men. He's a writer forced to take odd jobs including delivering mail. In the latter capacity he meets Emily (Kate Capshaw), the woman who finally accelerates his maturation which ironically forces their estrangement.

Cast is very strong although Shea is saddled with too much voice-over narration at top of picture.

■ **WINGED SERPENT, THE**
See: Q

■ **WINGED VICTORY**

1944, 130 MINS, US
Dir George Cukor   *Prod* Darryl F. Zanuck   *Scr* Moss Hart   *Ph* Glen MacWilliams   *Ed* Barbara McLean
Mus David Rose   *Art Dir* Lyle R. Wheeler, Lewis Creber
● Mark Daniels, Lon McCallister, Don Taylor, Red Buttons, Edmond O'Brien, Jeanne Crain (20th Century-Fox)

This is no story of any specific segment of Americana; it is, rather, the tale of Main Street and Broadway, of Texas and Brooklyn, of Christian and Jew — of American youth fighting for the preservation of American ideals. This is a documentation of American youth learning to fly for victory – a winged victory – and though it's fashioned in the manner of fictional entertainment, all the boys listed are bona fide members of the AAF – acting real-life roles.

The story of six boys from diverse parts of America, and how they leave behind wives and sweethearts and mothers to join the AAF, *Victory* is an honest understanding of American youth with the insatiable urge to ride the clouds.

The narrative follows them through basic training, the rigorous aptitude tests, and then the news on whether they had passed or were washed out. The solo flights – from which one of the sextet fails to return – and, ultimately, graduation day, followed by their assignments as either pilots, navigators or bombardiers, are all significantly told.

■ **WINGS**

1927, 139 MINS, US ◇ ⊗ ⓦ ⊙
Dir William A. Wellman   *Prod* Lucien Hubbard
Scr Hope Loring, Louis D. Lighton, Julian Johnson, John

Monk Saunders   *Ph* Harry Perry   *Ed* Lucien Hubbard
Mus (sound version) J.S. Zamecnik
● Clara Bow, Charles 'Buddy' Rogers, Richard Arlen, Jobyna Ralston, Gary Cooper, El Brendel (Paramount)

When the action settles on terra firma there is nothing present that other war supers haven't had, some to a greater degree. But nothing has possessed the graphic descriptive powers of aerial flying and combat that have been poured into this effort.

Some of the Magnascope battle scenes in the air are in color. Not natural but with sky and clouds deftly tinted plus spouts of flame shooting from planes that dive, spiral and even zoom as they supposedly plunge to earth in a final collapse.

Richard Arlen goes through the picture minus make-up. At least the cameras register him that way. Consequently he looks the high bred, high strung youngster who would dote on aviation and backs it up with a splendid performance that never hints of the actor. Charles Rogers' effort is also first rate, the important point here being that these two boys team well together. There not being so much of Clara Bow in the picture, she gives an all around corking performance. El Brendel's comedy is spasmodic and mostly early in the first half, while Gary Cooper is on and off within half a reel.

The most planes counted in the air at once are 18. But there are the pursuit and bombing machines, captive balloons, smashes and crashes of all types, with some of the shots of these 'crack-ups' remarkable. Fake stuff and double photography, too, although no miniatures in regard to the air action are discernible if used.

□ 1927/28: Best Picture, Engineering Effects

■ **WINGS OF THE APACHE**
See: Fire Birds

■ **WINNING**

1969, 123 MINS, US ◇ ⓦ
Dir James Goldstone   *Prod* John Foreman   *Scr* Howard Rodman   *Ph* Richard Moore   *Ed* Edward A. Biery, Richard C. Meyer   *Mus* Dave Grusin
Art Dir Alexander Golitzen, John J. Lloyd, Joe Alves
● Paul Newman, Joanne Woodward, Robert Wagner, Richard Thomas, David Sheiner, Clu Gulager (Universal)

Winning, a love story set against an auto racing background, stars Paul Newman and Joanne Woodward. Overly-long, it nevertheless carries sock appeal in suspenseful racing sequences and its principals in a realistically-developed marital romance score strongly.

Newman underplays his part throughout, resulting in one of his better performances. He is ideally cast as the racer, and those sequences in which he is racing are convincingly portrayed. There is a compelling authority, too, about his scenes with his femme costar.

Woodward, who makes no attempt at glamor or any other goal except as Newman's earthy wife, turns in a ringingly effective characterization, lacking in color but packing dramatic punch. Robert Wagner, who costars with other two, is the heavy, lending credibility to role.

■ **WINSLOW BOY, THE**

1948, 117 MINS, UK ⓦ
Dir Anthony Asquith   *Prod* Anatole de Grunwald
Scr Terence Rattigan, Anatole de Grunwald   *Ph* Freddie Young   *Ed* Gerald Turney Smith   *Mus* William Alwyn
Art Dir Andre Andrejew
● Robert Donat, Margaret Leighton, Cedric Hardwicke, Basil Radford, Kathleen Harrison, Francis L. Sullivan (British Lion/London)

Terence Rattigan's story, based on an actual incident that occurred just before the First World War, is a simple story of a 13-year-old naval cadet, expelled from school for the alleged theft of a postal order. The boy's father is certain of his innocence and when he fails to have the case reopened, invokes the whole machinery of British democracy by arranging a full-scale parliamentary debate and subsequently bringing a successful action against the King.

It's more the father's conviction of his son's innocence, rather than the incident itself, which forms the background of this well-knit story, with sufficient emphasis on the emotional angles to make it a sure tearjerker. From its brisk opening the plot quickly develops the main theme, building up the fight for justice through a series of incidents which are highlighted by the interview between Robert Morton, MP and famous attorney, and the boy before he decides to accept the brief.

A flawless cast portrays the principal characters to perfection, and minor roles have been painstakingly filled.

■ **WINSTANLEY**

1975, 95 MINS, UK

Dir Kevin Brownlow, Andrew Mollo   *Scr* Kevin Brownlow, Andrew Mollo   *Ph* Ernest Vincze   *Ed* Sarah Ellis   *Art Dir* Andrew Mollo
● Miles Halliwell, Jerome Wills (BFI)

The very opposite of the typical, commercial costume drama, *Winstanley* [based on the novel *Comrade Jacob* by David Caute] depicts the hardships and political turmoil in 17th-century England following the Civil War and the victory of the Puritans.

Winstanley was a leader of one of those dissident religious sects which sprang up in plentitude after the first wave of the Protestant Reformation. His was known as the Diggers, a commune set up in Surrey to proclaim equality and the right to work 'free' land.

The parson, upon whose land the Diggers squatted, takes a different view and sends ruffians to destroy their crops, beat them and burn down the makeshift hovels. Winstanley's writing and preaching wins him favor but the arrival of less idealistic members of the commune undermines the movement.

■ **WINTER KILLS**

1979, 97 MINS, US ◇ ⓥ ⊙

Dir William Richert   *Prod* Fred Caruso   *Scr* William Richert   *Ph* Vilmos Zsigmond   *Ed* David Bretherton   *Mus* Maurice Jarre   *Art Dir* Robert Boyle
● Jeff Bridges, John Huston, Anthony Perkins, Sterling Hayden, Eli Wallach, Elizabeth Taylor (Avco Embassy)

If there's a decent film lurking somewhere in *Winter Kills*, writer-director William Richert doesn't want anyone to see it in his Byzantine version of a presidential assassination conspiracy [from a book by Richard Condon].

Tale of wealthy family patriarch John Huston, whose elder son was a president slain 19 years before the pic's beginning, and younger sibling Jeff Bridges, now after his brother's killer(s), is an exercise in methodical obfuscation.

Huston gives a powerhouse performance, and Bridges, always likeable, runs through his repertoire of facial expressions and grimaces, but it's a lost cause.

Elizabeth Taylor has a worldless cameo as a procuress for the late president, but contractual provisions prevent her name from being used in connection with *Winter Kills*. The rest of the cast should have been so lucky.

[Pic was re-released in 1983 in a re-edited version and with original ending.]

■ **WINTER PEOPLE**

1989, 110 MINS, US ◇ ⓥ ⊙

Dir Ted Kotcheff   *Prod* Robert H. Solo   *Scr* Carol Sobieski   *Ph* Francois Protat   *Ed* Thom Noble   *Mus* John Scott   *Art Dir* Ron Foreman

● Kurt Russell, Kelly McGillis, Lloyd Bridges, Mitchell Ryan, Amelia Burnette (Nelson/Columbia)

The wages of sin are forever up in the old North Carolina hills, especially when they concern clans carrying on a blood feud. That's the backdrop for *Winter People*, a grimly unappetizing melodrama that forwards themes and concerns as remote as its time and place.

Adaptation of John Ehle's novel is set in 1934. Widower Kurt Russell decamps from his native town with little daughter in tow and alights at the remote cabin of Kelly McGillis, who has an illegitimate baby son.

An old-fashioned, unassertive type, Russell has to prove himself to McGillis' three brothers by joining them on a bear hunt, and wins the approval of her pa (Lloyd Bridges) by designing and building a clock tower for the little community.

But the demented Campbell clan lives across the river, and McGillis' dark secret is then revealed.

Continual histrionic demands are placed upon McGillis, who is not necessarily always up to them, and Russell is stuck with the Richard Barthlemess role of the earnest do-gooder forced to lower himself to the occasion of taking on brutal thugs.

■ **WIRED**

1989, 108 MINS, US ◇ ⓥ ⊙

Dir Larry Peerce   *Prod* Edward S. Feldman, Charles P. Meeker   *Scr* Earl Mac Rauch   *Ph* Tony Imi   *Ed* Eric Sears   *Mus* Basil Poledouris   *Art Dir* Brian Eatwell
● Michael Chiklis, Ray Sharkey, J. T. Walsh, Patti D'Arbanville, Lucinda Jenney, Alex Rocco (F/M/Lion)

In a brief but outstanding career on TV and in pics, John Belushi was an engaging personality. His drug overdose death further enthralled the public. *Wired*, however, told in episodes, flashbacks and dream sequences, is relentlessly offputting.

In a fanciful, less-than-successful effort to string together the events in Belushi's tragicomic life, *Wired* begins after Belushi (Michael Chiklis) has died. He rises, dressed in an autopsy gown to join another 'spirit', Angel Valesquez (Ray Sharkey), in a cab ride down memory lane.

The professional benchmarks in Belushi's life are there: the Blues Bros, the comic performances on *Saturday Night Live*, his Hollywood films. One episode is interrupted by others, including graphic glimpses of Belushi's cocaine habit and the devastating effect it has on his confidantes and colleagues.

Somehow, Chiklis ekes out an estimable performance as the doomed comic actor, sweating flashes of Belushi's intensity and vulnerability.

■ **WISE BLOOD**

1979, 108 MINS, US/W. GERMANY ◇ ⓥ

Dir John Huston   *Prod* Michael Fitzgerald, Kathy Fitzgerald   *Scr* Benedict Fitzgerald, Michael Fitzgerald   *Ph* Gerry Fisher   *Ed* Roberto Silvi   *Mus* Alex North
● Brad Dourif, Ned Beatty, Harry Dean Stanton, Amy Wright, John Huston, Dan Shor (Ithaca/Anthea)

John Huston, with uncluttered direction and expert handling of actors, has fashioned a disturbing tale of the fringe side of overzealous religious preachers in the deep South.

Taken from a short novel by Flannery O'Connor, film is grim and Gothic in feeling, but balanced by an underlying tenderness for these fringe people.

Brad Dourif is effective as a young man home from the wars, probably World War II. He visits his now boarded-up house in the country and then doffs his uniform to buy clothes making him look like a preacher.

He goes to a city where he is attracted by a blind preacher with a teenage daughter who

gives him lubricious looks. Flashbacks reveal Dourif as the grandson of a fire and brimstone preacher, played by Huston himself.

■ **WISH YOU WERE HERE**

1987, 91 MINS, UK ◇ ⓥ ⊙

Dir David Leland   *Prod* Sara Radclyffe   *Scr* David Leland   *Ph* Ian Wilson   *Mus* Stanley Myers   *Art Dir* Caroline Amies
● Emily Lloyd, Tom Bell, Clare Clifford, Barbara Durkin, Geoffrey Hutchings, Jesse Birdsall (Zenith/Working Title)

Set in a thoroughly uptight, provincial British seaside resort in the 1950s, this touching account of a girl's growing pains marks the directorial debut of director-scripter David Leland.

What makes it interesting is the character of the heroine; her refreshing rudeness disconcerts those around her. By focusing on a spunky but troubled 16-year-old girl named Lynda (played with exasperating charm by newcomer Emily Lloyd), Leland squeezes out more poignancy than would have been possible had the central character been the typical gawky male youth of most films about sexual awakening.

What makes the girl troubled is the fact that her mother died when she was 11 – and no one has replaced that essential loss. Lynda's reaction to her plight is to shock people with her rudeness and to taunt the opposite sex. This makes for some verbally sharp and occasionally visually eloquent scenes.

Lynda's rebelliousness eventually leads to a potentially sinister liaison with a seedy older man (played with taciturn intensity by Tom Bell), as much a misfit as she is. Their scenes together, though quite limited, are highly charged.

■ **WITCH DOCTOR**

See: Men of Two Worlds

■ **WITCHES, THE**

1966, 91 MINS, UK ◇

Dir Cyril Frankel   *Prod* Anthony Nelson Keys   *Scr* Nigel Kneale   *Ph* Arthur Grant   *Ed* James Needs, Chris Barnes   *Mus* Richard Rodney Bennett   *Art Dir* Bernard Robinson
● Joan Fontaine, Kay Walsh, Alec McCowen, Ann Bell, Gwen Ffrangcon-Davies, Ingrid Brett (Hammer)

Despite a very professional cast, this Nigel Kneale script [from Peter Curtis' novel *The Devil's Own*] doesn't spark off enough horror and tension to make the picture more than routine entertainment. This one has the air of a film that has lost its way.

Joan Fontaine is a schoolmistress who endures a horrible traumatic witch-doctor experience in an African mission. She seeks a new, peaceful life in a British village as headmistress of the local school, but she realizes that the village is under some strange spell.

Cyril Frankel has directed the slightly phony script with skill. But, mainly, it is the acting that keeps this pic alive. Fontaine brings a sensitive air to her thesping, but there's not enough fiber in her role to give her full scope. Kay Walsh is excellent as an enigmatic journalist and Gwen Ffrangcon-Davies, making one of her rare screen appearances, is dominating as the grandmother.

■ **WITCHES, THE**

1990, 92 MINS, US ◇ ⓥ ⊙

Dir Nicolas Roeg   *Prod* Mark Shivas   *Scr* Allan Scott   *Ph* Harvey Harrison   *Ed* Tony Lawson   *Mus* Stanley Myers   *Art Dir* Andrew Sanders
● Anjelica Huston, Mai Zetterling, Jasen Fisher, Rowan Atkinson, Bill Paterson, Jane Horrocks (Lorimar/Henson)

The wizardry of Jim Henson's Creature Shop and a superbly over-the-top performance by

Angelica Huston gives *The Witches* a good deal of charm and enjoyment.

Pic opens in Norway where grandmother Helga (Mai Zetterling) is telling her nine-year-old grandson Luke (Jasen Fisher) about witches and their wicked ways. His parents die in a car crash, and Luke and grandmother travel to England for a holiday.

They go to a stark Cornish hotel. Also checking in is the annual ladies meeting of the Royal Society for the Prevention of Cruelty to Children; in actual fact a meeting of the British witches, due to be addressed by the Grand High Witch, Huston. Young Luke accidentally overhears the meeting where Huston announces her grand plan to feed poisoned chocolate to all British children, which will turn them into mice.

In a tight black dress and vampish haircut, Huston seems to enjoy herself as the evil chief witch, and the pic seems to be merely plodding along until she arrives on the scene.

．．．．．．．．．．．．．．．．．．．．．．．．．．．

■ WITCHES OF EASTWICK, THE

1987, 118 MINS, US ◇ ⓦ ⊙
Dir George Miller   *Prod* Neil Canton, Peter Gruber, Jon Peters   *Scr* Michael Cristofer   *Ph* Vilmos Zsigmond   *Ed* Richard Francis-Bruce, Hubert C. de la Bouillerie   *Mus* John Williams   *Art Dir* Polly Platt
● Jack Nicholson, Cher, Susan Sarandon, Michelle Pfeiffer, Veronica Cartwright, Richard Jenkins (Warner/Guber-Peters/Kennedy Miller)

The Witches of Eastwick [from the novel by John Updike] is a brilliantly conceived metaphor for the battle between the sexes that literally poses the question must a woman sell her soul to the devil to have a good relationship?

With a no-holds-barred performance by Jack Nicholson as the horny Satan, it's a very funny and irresistible set-up for anyone who has ever been baffled by the opposite sex.

Sukie Ridgemont (Michelle Pfeiffer), a writer for the local newspaper, is the intellectual; Jane Spofford (Susan Sarandon), a high school music teacher, is the woman of feeling; and Alexandra Medford (Cher), a sculptress, represents the sensuous side. They're all divorced and they're all looking for a Mr Right.

Enter Daryl Van Horn (Jack Nicholson), the answer to their collective longing for a man of wit, charm and intelligence. For Nicholson it's the role of a lifetime, the chance to seduce these women and be cock of the roost.

Spectacle of the film is really Nicholson. Dressed in eccentric flowing robes, odd hats and installed in a lush mansion, he is larger than life, as indeed the devil should be. The witches, lovely though they are, exist more as types than distinct personalities.
□ 1987: Nominations: Best Original Score, Sound

．．．．．．．．．．．．．．．．．．．．．．．．．．．

■ WITCHFINDER GENERAL
(US: The Conqueror Worm)

1968, 88 MINS, UK ◇ ⓦ ⊙
Dir Michael Reeves   *Prod* Louis M. Heyward, Philip Waddilove, Arnold Miller   *Scr* Michael Reeves, Tom Baker, Louis M. Heyward   *Ph* John Coquillon   *Ed* Howard Lanning   *Mus* Paul Ferris   *Art Dir* Jim Morahan
● Vincent Price, Ian Ogilvy, Rupert Davies, Hilary Dwyer, Robert Russell, Nicky Henson (Tigon)

Story [from Ronald Bassett's novel] is all about witchcraft, inquisitions and executions as performed by Vincent Price and his thuggish henchman (Robert Russell) during the days when Cromwell was deposing the King of England. Ian Ogilvy is the soldier-hero who stops them after lots of bloody executions and the rape of his sweetheart (Hilary Dwyer).

Price is an excellent heavy, but while sometimes he seems to piously believe he is rooting out witches, most of the time he's simply killing for the fun of it, and some money.

Russell's character is similarly ambiguous. He's brutal, but isn't properly set up to display cowardice while fighting with Ogilvy in the film's only really good action scene.

Ogilvy is somewhat dashing, but has a one-note hero's role to play. Dwyer gives evidence of acting talent, but she and all principals are hampered by Michael Reeve's mediocre script and ordinary direction.

．．．．．．．．．．．．．．．．．．．．．．．．．．．

■ WITH A SONG IN MY HEART

1952, 116 MINS, US ◇
Dir Walter Lang   *Prod* Lamar Trotti   *Scr* Lamar Trotti   *Ph* Leon Shamroy   *Ed* J. Watson Webb Jr   *Mus* Alfred Newman (dir.)   *Art Dir* Lyle Wheeler, Joseph C. Wright
● Susan Hayward, Rory Calhoun, David Wayne, Thelma Ritter, Robert Wagner, Helen Westcott (20th Century-Fox)

The story of one of show business' courageous figures – Jane Froman – comes to the screen. Froman, a songbird who started her rise to fame in 1936 as a penny-ante singer of radio commercials, does her own chirping on 23 songs in this film version of her career.

In the first half, the pattern is the rather pat one of an unknown coming into prominence. The next 60 minutes, however, have the ring of sincere dramatics from the time Froman was nearly fatally injured in the Lisbon plane crash of February 23 1943, while enroute to entertain servicemen overseas. Her fight back to life and only partial recovery of the use of her limbs, the birth of a new love, the resumption of a career to pay the enormous medical bills, come over on the screen as heartening drama.

While not entirely at home in the dancing accompaniment to some of the production numbers [staged by Billy Daniel], Susan Hayward punches over the straight vocal-simulation and deftly handles the dramatic phases.
□ 1952: Best Scoring of a Musical Picture.
□ Nominations: Best Actress (Susan Hayward), Supp. Actress (Thelma Ritter), Color Costume Design, Sound

．．．．．．．．．．．．．．．．．．．．．．．．．．．

■ WITHNAIL & I

1986, 108 MINS, UK ◇ ⓦ ⊙
Dir Bruce Robinson   *Prod* Paul M. Heller   *Scr* Bruce Robinson   *Ph* Bob Smith   *Ed* Alan Strachan   *Mus* David Dundas   *Art Dir* Michael Pickwood
● Richard E. Grant, Paul McGann, Richard Griffiths, Ralph Brown, Michael Elphick (HandMade)

Withnail & I is about the end of an era. Set in 1969 England, it portrays the last throes of a friendship mirroring the seedy demise of the hippie period, delivering some comic gems along the way.

Pic is the tale of two city boys stuck in a dilapidated country cottage in the middle of nowhere. The humor is both brutal and clever, and the acting uniformly excellent.

Pic opens with a pan round the disgusting London flat of out-of-work actors Withnail and Marwood (the 'I' of the title). Marwood (Paul McGann) is the nervous type trying to look John Lennon, while Withnail (Richard E. Grant) is gaunt, acerbic, and never without a drink in his hand.

Marwood declares the need to 'get into the countryside and rejuvenate.' A visit to Withnail's Uncle Monty secures them the loan of his country cottage, and the two head off into the night. They eventually arrive at the remote cottage, only to discover there is no light, no heat, and no water.

Uncle Monty (a standout performance by the portly Richard Griffiths) arrives with a twinkle in his eye when he is sidling up closer to Marwood. Monty's ardor and a telegram from his agent with news of a job are enough to convince Marwood that home is where the heart is, and he and Withnail retreat back to

London. The two realize their friendship is coming to an end.

．．．．．．．．．．．．．．．．．．．．．．．．．．．

■ WITHOUT A TRACE

1983, 120 MINS, US ◇ ⓦ
Dir Stanley R. Jaffe   *Prod* Stanley R. Jaffe   *Scr* Beth Gutcheon   *Ph* John Bailey   *Ed* Cynthia Schneider   *Mus* Jack Nitzsche   *Art Dir* Paul Sylbert
● Kate Nelligan, Judd Hirsch, David Dukes, Stockard Channing, Jacqueline Brookes, Keith McDermott (20th Century-Fox)

A muted melodrama about a woman whose young son simply disappears one day, *Without a Trace* seems to be of two minds about its own emotional content.

Kate Nelligan plays an English teacher at Columbia whose six-year-old son vanishes from the Brooklyn streets while on his two-block walk to school.

Her husband (David Dukes) has left three months earlier to shack up with a girl in Greenwich Village. But she retains her composure to an admirable degree, even when the cops and the media invade and virtually take over her home to work on the case. Leading the investigation team is Judd Hirsch, almost too perfectly cast as an over-worked detective.

Stanley R. Jaffe, directing for the first time, could have bathed Beth Gutcheon's novel *Still Missing* in undiluted sentimentality from beginning to end, but has instead shied away from some of the most obvious potential dramatic developments. Nelligan's fundamental humorlessness keeps viewer at arm's length.

．．．．．．．．．．．．．．．．．．．．．．．．．．．

■ WITHOUT *YOU* I'M NOTHING

1990, 90 MINS, US ◇ ⓦ
Dir John Boskovich   *Prod* Jonathan D. Krane   *Scr* Sandra Bernhard, John Boskovich   *Ph* Joseph Yacoe   *Ed* Pamela Malouf-Cundy   *Mus* Patrice Rushen   *Art Dir* Kevin Rupnik
● Sandra Bernhard, Steve Antin, Lu Leonard (MCEG)

Sandra Bernhard's screen adaptation of her one-woman show is a rigorous, experimental examination of performance art. Stepping back from comedy per se, Bernhard and her collaborator, director John Boskovich, have fashioned a remote, self-absorbed and often cryptic picture.

Most ambitious device here is a failure: except for brief interstitial footage of 'witnesses' such as Steve Antin (as himself) or Lu Leonard (portraying Bernhard's manager) addressing the camera, film unfolds in performance on stage at a large, ersatz night club before a predominantly black audience. Crowd reacts only with silent, quizzical expressions or files out apparently not enjoying the show.

Pic's highlight underscores the material's emphasis on roleplaying and androgyny: a 1978-set 'I Feel Real' monolog/song with Bernhard pretending to be two guys in a disco, one of whom gets turned on by a black man and comes out of the closet. With helmer Boskovich letting loose his camera for once from its slow, monotonous pirouetting, scene is a showstopper.

．．．．．．．．．．．．．．．．．．．．．．．．．．．

■ WITNESS

1985, 112 MINS, US ◇ ⓦ ⊙
Dir Peter Weir   *Prod* Edward S. Feldman   *Scr* Earl W. Wallace, William Kelley   *Ph* John Seale   *Ed* Thom Noble   *Mus* Maurice Jarre   *Art Dir* Stan Jolley
● Harrison Ford, Kelly McGillis, Josef Sommer, Lukas Haas, Danny Glover, Alexander Godunov (Paramount)

Witness is at times a gentle, affecting story of star-crossed lovers limited within the fascinating Amish community. Too often, however, this fragile romance is crushed by a thoroughly absurd shoot-em-up, like ketchup poured over a delicate Pennsylvania Dutch dinner.

Australian director Peter Weir is obviously awed by the Amish, the quaint agrarian sect which maintains a 17th-century lifestyle, forsaking all modern conveniences while maintaining intense religious vows, including a pacifism most pertinent therein.

Venturing outside the community on a trip to see her sister, recently widowed Kelly McGillis is drawn unfortunately into the 20th century when her young son (Lukas Haas), witnesses a murder in the men's room at the train station.

Enter gruff, foul-mouthed, streetwise detective Harrison Ford, whom the writers [story by William Kelley, Pamela Wallace, Earl W. Wallace] must somehow get out into the countryside as soon as possible so the cross-cultural romance can begin.

Witness warms up as the attraction builds between Ford, McGillis and Haas – all performing excellently through this portion. Admirable, too, is Ford's growing admiration for the people he's been thrown among.
□ 1985: Best Original Screenplay, Editing.
□ Nominations: Best Picture, Director, Actor (Harrison Ford), Cinematography, Art Direction, Original Score

••••••••••••••••••••••••••••••••

■ WITNESS FOR THE PROSECUTION

1957, 114 MINS, US ⑲ ⊙
Dir Billy Wilder *Prod* Arthur Hornblow *Scr* Billy Wilder, Harry Kurnitz *Ph* Russell Harlan *Ed* Daniel Mandell *Mus* Matty Malneck *Art Dir* Alexandre Trauner
● Tyrone Power, Marlene Dietrich, Charles Laughton, Elsa Lanchester, Una O'Connor, Ian Wolfe (United Artists)

A courtroom meller played engagingly and building evenly to a surprising and arousing, albeit tricked-up, climax, *Witness for the Prosecution* has been transferred to the screen (from the Agatha Christie click play) with competence [adaptation by Larry Marcus].

Under Billy Wilder's direction, *Prosecution* unfolds realistically, generating a quiet and steady excitement.

Cleverly worked out is the story line which has defense attorney Charles Laughton, along with the audience, wholly convinced that the likeable chap played by Tyrone Power is innocent, that he couldn't have murdered the rich widow who had taken a fancy to him. A disturbing note, however, is the unexpected attitude taken by Power's wife (Marlene Dietrich) who, as it turns out, is not legally married to him and thus is not restrained from testifying against him.

Laughton, sage of the courtroom and cardiac patient who's constantly disobeying his nurse's orders, plays out the part flamboyantly and colorfully. His reputation for scenery chewing is unmarred via this outing.
□ 1957: Nominations: Best Picture, Director, Actor (Charles Laughton), Supp. Actress (Elsa Lanchester), Editing, Sound

••••••••••••••••••••••••••••••••

■ WITTGENSTEIN

1993, 71 MINS, UK ◇ ⑲
Dir Derek Jarman *Prod* Tariq Ali *Scr* Derek Jarman, Terry Eagleton, Ken Butler *Ph* James Welland *Ed* Budge Tremlett *Mus* Jan Latham-Koenig *Art Dir* Annie Lapaz
● Karl Johnson, Michael Gough, Tilda Swinton, John Quentin, Kevin Collins, Clancy Chassay (Channel 4/BFI/Bandung)

Shot on legit-like minimalist sets, this gabby but sophisticated riff on the tortured life of Austrian-born philosopher Ludwig Wittgenstein is an immaculately lensed, intellectual jape that's more a divertissement than a substantial addition to Derek Jarman's quirky oeuvre.

Pic's opening, with young Ludwig (confi-

dently played by 12-year-old Clancy Chassay) introducing the members of his ill-fated family, promises a Ken Russell-like irreverence that never really develops. With the appearance of the adult Wittgenstein (Karl Johnson), things settle down into a series of talky tableaux against black backdrops. Born into a rich Viennese family in 1889, Wittgenstein quickly fled to Britain, establishing his rep at Cambridge, where he fell in with other thinkers like Bertrand Russell (Michael Gough) and economist John Maynard Keynes (John Quentin). He died in 1951 of cancer.

Philosophical sparring between the trio takes up much of the running time, with light relief provided by Russell's snooty mistress, Lady Ottoline Morrell (Jarman regular Tilda Swinton in top histrionic form).

Running parallel with the intellectual stuff is an exploration of Wittgenstein's repressed homosexuality, per his friendship with a handsome, working-class student (Kevin Collins) and Keynes, portrayed as a flouncing gay.

••••••••••••••••••••••••••••••••

■ WIVES AND LOVERS

1963, 102 MINS, US
Dir John Rich *Prod* Hal Wallis *Scr* Edward Anhalt *Ph* Lucien Ballard *Ed* Warren Low *Mus* Lyn Murray *Art Dir* Hal Pereira, Walter Tyler
● Janet Leigh, Van Johnson, Shelley Winters, Martha Hyer, Ray Walston, Claire Wilcox (Paramount)

Failure to be consistent with itself mars *Wives and Lovers*, an otherwise highly polished and pleasurable sophisticated comedy about a couple whose happy marriage is nearly shattered in the wake of the husband's sudden professional success.

The film excels in one area. Edward Anhalt's scenario, from Jay Presson's stage play, *The First Wife* contains some of the sharpest, wittiest, most perceptive comedy dialog to pop out of a soundtrack in some time.

Story relates the marital misadventure that materializes when an unsuccessful writer (Van Johnson), who for three years has been lovingly and uncomplainingly supported by his wife (Janet Leigh) while he pens a novel, suddenly hits the book-of-the-month jackpot. In a flash, the couple and their precocious tot have moved from a cramped Gotham cold-water flat to the luxury living of the fashionable Connecticut suburbs.

In the process of converting his prose into a Broadway play, Johnson becomes entangled in an affair with his glamorous agent (Martha Hyer), in retaliation Leigh apparently gets herself voluntarily seduced by the star (Jeremy Slate) of her husband's play.

The acting is pleasing and skillful. Occasional mechanical inconsistencies tarnish John Rich's otherwise bright and breezy direction in his first major feature assignment.
□ 1963: Nomination: Best B&W Costume Design

••••••••••••••••••••••••••••••••

■ WIZ, THE

1978, 133 MINS, US ◇ ⑲ ⊙
Dir Sidney Lumet *Prod* Rob Cohen *Scr* Joel Schumacher *Ph* Oswald Morris *Ed* Dede Allen *Mus* Quincy Jones (adapt.) *Art Dir* Tony Walton
● Diana Ross, Michael Jackson, Nipsey Russell, Lena Horne, Richard Pryor, Ted Ross (Motown)

Frank Baum [author of book *The Wonderful Wizard of Oz*] would never recognize his simple little story in this fantastically blown-up version [of William F. Brown's play], but the heart of his tale – that a person must find what he's searching for within himself – is still there.

The cast is virtually flawless but, when all is said and done, it's the combination of Oswald

Morris's cinematography, the special visual effects of Albert Whitlock and Tony Walton's production design and costumes that linger longest in the memory.

Director Sidney Lumet has created what amounts to a love letter to the city of New York, which he equates with Oz.

Diana Ross, believable as a 24-year-old Harlem school teacher, is always in key with the mood, whether it calls for shyness, gaiety, courage or simply cutting up. Vocally, she's superb but, surprise, she also dances with all the abandon of an Alvin Ailey protege.

Of the supporting players and, despite their billing, that's what they amount to – Richard Pryor's Wiz (very briefly seen), Ted Ross's Lion and Mabel King's Evillene make the heaviest impressions. Nipsey Russell is fun as the Tin Man but Michael Jackson, though vocally great, needs more acting exposure.
□ 1978: Nominations: Best Cinematography, Costume Design, Art Direction, Adapted Score

••••••••••••••••••••••••••••••••

■ WIZARD OF OZ, THE

1939, 100 MINS, US ◇ ⑲ ⊙
Dir Victor Fleming, [George Cukor, King Vidor, Richard Thorpe, Lewis Milestone] *Prod* Mervyn LeRoy *Scr* Noel Langley, Florence Ryerson, Edgar Allan Woolf *Ph* Harold Rosson, Allen Davey *Ed* Blanche Sewell *Mus* Herbert Stothart (adapt.) *Art Dir* Cedric Gibbons, William A. Horning
● Judy Garland, Frank Morgan, Ray Bolger, Bert Lahr, Jack Haley, Billie Burke (M-G-M)

The Wizard of Oz springs from Metro's golden bowl (production cost reported close to $3 million). Except for opening and closing stretches of prolog and epilog, which are visioned in a rich sepia, the greater portion of the film is in Technicolor.

Such liberties that have been taken with the original story [from the book by L. Frank Baum, adaptation by Noel Langley] vest the yarn with constructive dramatic values. Underlying theme of conquest of fear is subtly thrust through the action. Fairy stories must teach simple truths.

What is on the screen is an adventure story about a small girl who lives on a Kansas farm. She and her dog, Toto, are caught in twister and whisked into an eerie land in which she encounters strange beings, good and evil fairies, and prototypes of some of the adults who comprised her farm world.

Then ensues the long trek to the mighty wizard's castle, where she and her companions, seek fulfillment of desire. Dorothy wishes only to return home. The plot is as thin as all that.

In the playing of it, however, Judy Garland as the little girl is an appealing figure as the wandering waif. Her companions are Ray Bolger, as the Scarecrow; Jack Haley, as the Woodman; and Bert Lahr as the cringing lion. Frank Morgan appears in sundry roles as the wizard, and the good and evil fairies are Billie Burke and Margaret Hamilton.
□ 1939: Best Original Score, Song ('Over the Rainbow').
□ Nominations: Best Picture, Art Direction, Special Effects

••••••••••••••••••••••••••••••••

■ WOLFEN

1981, 114 MINS, US ◇ ⑲
Dir Michael Wadleigh *Prod* Rupert Hitzig *Scr* David Eyre, Michael Wadleigh *Ph* Garry Fisher *Ed* Chris Lebenson, Dennis Dolan, Martin Bram, Marshall M. Borden *Mus* James Horner *Art Dir* Paul Sylbert
● Albert Finney, Diane Venora, Edward James Olmos, Gregory Hines, Tom Noonan, Dick O'Neill (Orion)

Wolfen is consistently more interesting than it is thrilling. Policeman Albert Finney is confronted with a series of baffling, grisly murders, gradually realizing they are not the

W

work of mere mortals. As always in the best of pictures like this, the buildup is the most fun.

Initially, director Michael Wadleigh creates an exceedingly chilling atmosphere, especially as Finney and Gregory Hines, excellent as a space-case coroner, deal matter-of-factly with the dismembered dead.

Wadleigh creates a surreal point-of-view for the killers that works effectively, accented by handy digital sound. Overall, Paul Sylbert's production design is also a major plus. Add to that a splendid performance by Finney and a solid film debut for Diane Venora as his psychologist sidekick.

Film [from a novel by Whitley Strieber] was reportedly recut several times (four editors are credited) and a couple of bad cuts are clearly evident; a few scenes are awkward, too.

● ●

■ WOLF MAN, THE

1941, 69 MINS, US 🎬 ⊙

Dir George Waggner *Prod* George Waggner
Scr Curt Siodmak *Ph* Joseph Valentine *Ed* Ted Kent
Mus Charles Previn
● Lon Chaney, Claude Rains, Ralph Bellamy, Bela
Lugosi, Maria Ouspenskaya (Universal)

The English legendary werewolf provides basis for another cinematic adventure into the horrific chiller-diller realm. *The Wolf Man* is a compactly-knit tale of its kind, with good direction and performances by an above par assemblage of players, but dubious entertainment.

Young Lon Chaney (who drops the Jr in films for the first time here) returns to the family's English castle after long absence in America, to stand in line as heir to the estate. According to legend, a person bitten by a werewolf assumes the dual personality of the latter – and Chaney is the victim of a bite.

Young Chaney gives a competent performance both straight and under makeup for the dual role. Script stresses the tenseness of the fabled tale in both action and dialog, with George Waggner piloting in okay manner.

● ●

■ WOLVES OF WILLOUGHBY CHASE, THE

1989, 93 MINS, UK ◇ 🎬 ⊙

Dir Stuart Orme *Prod* Mark Forstater *Scr* William M.
Akers *Ph* Paul Beeson *Ed* Martin Walsh *Mus* Colin
Towns *Art Dir* Christopher Hobbs
● Stephanie Beacham, Mel Smith, Emily Hudson, Aleks
Darowska, Geraldine James, Richard O'Brien (Zenith)

The Wolves of Willoughby Chase is a thoroughly enjoyable children's fantasy-adventure.

Pic has a suitable Dickensian feel, set during the imaginary reign of King James III some time in the last century in a snowbound part of North Yorkshire where wolves seem to rule the countryside. Based on Joan Aiken's children's novel, it has an attractively sinister quality and centers on the fight by two young girls to foil a dastardly plot hatched by the their evil governess, Slighcarp.

Tyro theatrical helmer Stuart Orme handles his chore well; they must have been doubly hard since pic was shot at the Barrandov Studios in Prague and on location around snowy Czechoslovakia in early 1988.

Emily Hudson and Aleks Darowska are excellent as the plucky youngsters, but best of all is Stephanie Beacham who outdoes herself as the wicked Slighcarp. The excellent cast is boosted by tongue-in-cheek performances from Mel Smith and Geraldine James.

● ●

■ WOMAN IN RED, THE

1984, 87 MINS, US ◇ 🎬 ⊙

Dir Gene Wilder *Prod* Victor Drai *Scr* Gene Wilder
Ph Fred Schuler *Ed* Christopher Greenburg *Mus* John
Morris *Art Dir* David L. Snyder
● Gene Wilder, Charles Grodin, Joseph Bologna, Judith
Ivey, Michael Huddleston, Kelly Le Brock (Orion)

The woman in red is simply a very sexy contemporary (Kelly Le Brock), hired as a model by a San Francisco city agency, bringing her into contact with a mundane bureaucrat, Gene Wilder, heretofore a contented family man.

But one look at Le Brock, and Wilder is ready to risk all for illicit romance: he is not very adept at adultery.

The laughs roll along readily as Wilder tries one idea after another to sneak out on wife Judith Ivey and family to rendevous with Le Brock.

A wonderful diversion through all of this is Gilda Radner, a relatively plain fellow office worker who initially thinks she's the object of Wilder's wanderlust and is bitterly – and vigorously – disappointed when she finds out she isn't. [Pic is based on 1976 French film, *Pardon Mon Affaire*, directed by Yves Robert.]
□ 1984: Best Song ('I Just Called to Say I Love You')

● ●

■ WOMAN IN THE WINDOW, THE

1945, 90 MINS, US 🎬

Dir Fritz Lang *Prod* Nunnally Johnson *Scr* Nunnally
Johnson *Ph* Milton Krasner *Ed* Marjorie Johnson
Mus Arthur Lange *Art Dir* Duncan Cramer
● Edward G. Robinson, Joan Bennett, Raymond Massey,
Dan Duryea, Edmond Breon, Robert Blake, Thomas E.
Jackson (RKO/International)

Nunnally Johnson whips up a strong and decidedly suspenseful murder melodrama in *Woman in the Window*. Producer, who also prepared the screenplay [from the novel *Once off Guard* by J.H. Wallis] continually punches across the suspense for constant and maximum audience reaction. Added are especially fine timing in the direction by Fritz Lang and outstanding performances by Edward G. Robinson, Joan Bennett, Raymond Massey and Dan Duryea.

Opening sequence suggests that tragedies spring from little things, and anyone can become involved in a murder or criminal action. That's just what happens to Robinson, a staid and middle-aged college professor whose wife and children depart for vacation in Maine. He pauses and admires a painting on exhibition in store window adjoining his club. Later he again glances at the girl's portrait and finds the model standing beside him.

Robinson visits her apartment to look over other sketches; a stranger breaks in to accuse the girl of infidelity and attacks Robinson, who stabs the visitor in self-protection. Sidetracking initial impulse to call the police, he connives with the girl to dispose of the body in the country woods. Finish is a surprise for smash climax.
□ 1945: Nomination: Best Scoring of a Dramatic Picture

● ●

■ WOMAN OF AFFAIRS, A

1929, 90 MINS, US 🎬

Dir Clarence Brown *Scr* Bess Meredyth, Hugh Wynn
Ph William Daniels *Art Dir* Cedric Gibbons
● Greta Garbo, John Gilbert, Lewis Stone, John Mack
Brown, Douglas Fairbanks Jr, Dorothy Sebastian (M-G-M)

A sensational array of screen names and the intriguing nature of the story (*The Green Hat*) from which it was made, together with some magnificent acting by Greta Garbo, carries through this vague and sterilized version of Michael Arlen's erotic play. Superb technical production counts in its favor.

But the kick is out of the material, and, worse still, John Gilbert has an utterly blah role. Most of the footage he merely stands around rather sheepishly.

So here is a woman who, disappointed in her first love, plunges into an orgy of amorous adventures from Calais to Cairo.

Garbo saves an unfortunate situation throughout by a subtle something in her play-

ing that suggests just the erotic note that is essential to the whole theme and story.

Production is noteworthy for its beauty of setting and atmosphere.

Lewis Stone plays a wise and kindly old counsellor of the madcap heroine that is made to order for his suave and sophisticated style of playing. Dorothy Sebastian manages to register real personality as the wife.

● ●

■ WOMAN OF DISTINCTION, A

1950, 89 MINS, US 🎬 ⊙

Dir Edward Buzzell *Prod* Buddy Adler *Scr* Charles
Hoffman *Ph* Joseph Walker *Ed* Charles Nelson
Mus Werner R. Heymann
● Ray Milland, Rosalind Russell, Edmund Gwenn, Janis
Carter, Mary Jane Saunders, Francis Lederer (Columbia)

A Woman of Distinction is a loosely-tied grab-bag of screwball and nonsensical doings about two warring-but-loving pedagogues. Sans much logic, the Rosalind Russell-Ray Milland teamwork is good for more laughs than not and the gags overcome a yarn [by Hugo Butler and Ian McLellan Hunter] that lacks sound motivation.

Featured is a running duel between Russell, the woman of distinction too busy for romance, and Prof Milland, who is dragged into a faked news-headlined affair with the dean of a woman's college through the connivings of an overly-diligent press agent.

Russell pitches in with nice change of pace. Milland pieces together the necessary ingredients of genteel sobriety, confusion and indignation.

● ●

■ WOMAN OF PARIS, A

1923, 84 MINS, US ⊗ 🎬

Dir Charles Chaplin *Prod* Charles Chaplin *Scr* Charles
Chaplin *Ph* Rollie Totheroh, Jack Wilson *Ed* Monta
Bell *Art Dir* Arthur Stibolt
● Edna Purviance, Adolphe Menjou, Carl Miller, Lydia
Knott, Charles K. French, Clarence Geldert (United Artists)

A Woman of Paris is a serious, sincere effort, with a bang story subtlely of idea-expression.

If the sentimental Charlie Chaplin made one outstanding error he did it in casting Edna Purviance, his leading woman of many classic comedies, for the central and stellar role in his first legitimate picture. She is not a sensation. She looks and acts well enough, but she falls short of the fine pace set by the rest of the endeavor.

However, this is not a conspicuous drag on *A Woman of Paris*. Chaplin, on the other hand, straying far from his haunts of yore, comes forth as a new genius both as a producer and a director.

The finish is as brilliant and as memorable as the Mexico-line finale of *The Pilgrim*. After the girl has gone through all the vicissitudes of Paris high and low life, her rich ex-lover, driving in the country passes her on the road as she sits on the back of a farmer's cart with a little orphan. He just whizzes by – that's all. And it tells more than if he had the conventional breakdown.

● ●

■ WOMAN OF STRAW

1964, 117 MINS, UK ◇

Dir Basil Dearden *Prod* Michael Relph *Scr* Robert
Muller, Stanley Mann *Ph* Otto Heller *Ed* John D.
Gutheridge *Mus* Muir Mathieson (arr.) *Art Dir* Ken
Adam
● Gina Lollobrigida, Sean Connery, Ralph Richardson,
Johnny Sekka, Laurence Hardy, Danny Daniels (United
Artists)

Director Basil Dearden seems, here, to have temporarily misplaced the vigorous insight that has earned him some top credits. Best that can be said of *Straw* [from the novel by Catherine Arley] is that it looks handsome.

But the film gets bogged down by stilted dialog and by the situations.

Ralph Richardson is a multimillionaire, an illmannered, sour tycoon condemned to spend his life in a wheelchair. He takes it out on anybody handy. These include his nephew-secretary (Sean Connery), his major-domo, colored houseboy, his yacht skipper and his dogs.

He even tosses some well considered snarls in the direction of Gina Lollobrigida who is hired by the nephew as the old man's nurse. As a result of all this humiliation there are several people who are not unhappy when he is found dead in the bunk of his yacht.

Interplay in the relationship and emotions of the characters involved make fair picture-going in the early stages. But when the plot gets down to the mystery of whether he died from natural causes or whether he was the victim of mayhem then it descends into under-average mishmash.

Richardson manages to extract what fun there is out of the desultory proceedings. Lollobrigida is out of her depth, while the welldressed Connery wanders around with the air of a man who can't wait to get back to being James Bond again.

● ●

■ WOMAN OF SUMMER
See: The Stripper

● ●

■ WOMAN OF THE YEAR

1942, 112 MINS, US ♥ ☉
Dir George Stevens   *Prod* Joseph L. Mankiewicz
Scr Ring Lardner Jr, Michael Kanin   *Ph* Joseph Ruttenberg   *Ed* Frank Sullivan   *Mus* Franz Waxman
Art Dir Cedric Gibbons, Randall Duell
● Spencer Tracy, Katharine Hepburn, Fay Bainter, Reginald Owen, William Bendix, Dan Tobin (M-G-M)

Woman of the Year is an entertaining film with superb work by Katharine Hepburn and Spencer Tracy. There are very few palms due writers Ring Lardner Jr and Michael Kanin, who reputedly received the sum of $100,000 for the original screenplay. Director George Stevens likewise merits small praise.

Lardner and Kanin had an amusing starting point – a sports writer and a young and beautiful counterpart of Dorothy Thompson spatting, then falling in love and marrying – but wend it tortuously through every hackneyed and expected plot device without a surprise at any turn. Director Stevens lets it get out of hand completely with minutes on end devoted to a few tired situation gags. Picture runs 112 minutes and frequently seems every moment of that. Tracy and Hepburn go a long way toward pulling the chestnut out of the fire.
□ 1942: Best Original Screenplay.
□ Nomination: Best Actress (Katharine Hepburn)

● ●

■ WOMAN ON PIER 13, THE
See: I Married a Communist

● ●

■ WOMAN ON THE BEACH, THE

1947, 71 MINS, US
Dir Jean Renoir   *Prod* Jack J. Gross   *Scr* Frank Davis, Jean Renoir   *Ph* Leo Tover, Harry Wild   *Ed* Roland Gross, Lyle Boyer   *Mus* Hanns Eisler   *Art Dir* Albert S. D'Agostino, Walter E. Keller
● Joan Bennett, Robert Ryan, Charles Bickford (RKO)

Film is more mood than meaning. On the surface, it is a confusion of logic, a narrative drawn with invisible lines around characters without motivation in a plot only shadowily defined. But beneath, the cinematic elements are brilliantly fused by Jean Renoir into an intense and compelling emotional experience.

Thesping is uniformly excellent with the cast from top to bottom responding to Renoir's controlling need for a surcharged atmosphere. In subtle counterpoint to the film's surface vagueness, the settings are notably realistic in their size and quality. Choice camerawork sustains the film's overall impact while sweeping through the entire production is a magnificent score b Hanns Eisler which heightens all of the film's pictorial values.

Basically, the yarn [based on the novels, *None So Blind* by Mitchell Wilson] is a variation of the eternal triangle theme but it unfolds elusively through implication and suggestion, only occasionally emerging to the level of full clarity. In the film's center, Charles Bickford plays the role of a blind artist, brutally strong and madly jealous of his wife. As the latter, Joan Bennett is a callous tart tied to her husband only through an obsession of guilt arising from their accidental blinding of Bickford early in their marriage.

Third part is played by Robert Ryan, a coast guard officer stationed near the blind man's home in a desolate spot on the ocean front. He is recovering from a mental shock obtained in naval combat during the war.

● ●

■ WOMAN'S FACE, A

1941, 105 MINS, US ♥
Dir George Cukor   *Prod* Victor Saville   *Scr* Donald Ogden Stewart, Elliot Paul   *Ph* Robert Planck   *Ed* Frank Sullivan   *Mus* Bronislau Kaper   *Art Dir* Cedric Gibbons, Wade B. Rubottom
● Joan Crawford, Melvyn Douglas, Conrad Veidt, Osa Massen, Reginald Owen, Albert Bassermann (M-G-M)

There's a rather intriguing dramatic quality to this American version of an original Swedish production [from a French play, Francis de Croisset's *Il etait une fois*] which had Ingrid Bergman as star. In a story of a woman's handicap and final regeneration.

Opening with the court trial of Joan Crawford for murder, the story is developed through various stages by testimony of the several witnesses – and finally the defendant herself. Dramatic suspense is maintained by keeping the victim's identity well hidden for a surprise climax.

Crawford is the victim of a childhood accident which left her face distorted and disfigured. Case-hardened and calloused, shunning people generally, she drops into a criminal career. Romantic approach of Conrad Veidt is the first she has had and she accepts his flattery with love-hungry adoration.

She meets plastic surgeon Melvyn Douglas whose offer of an operation is gladly accepted. Veidt then persuades her to take a job as governess on his uncle's estate – and to murder the child-heir that stands in his path to wealth inheritance.

Crawford has a strongly dramatic and sympathetic role, despite her hardened attitude, which she handles in topnotch fashion.

● ●

■ WOMAN'S SECRET, A

1949, 84 MINS, US ♥
Dir Nicholas Ray   *Prod* Herman J. Mankiewicz
Scr Herman J. Mankiewicz   *Ph* George Diskant
Ed Sherman Todd   *Mus* Frederick Hollander
Art Dir Albert S. D'Agostino, Carroll Clark
● Maureen O'Hara, Melvyn Douglas, Gloria Grahame, Bill Williams, Victor Jory, Jay C. Flippen (RKO)

There's too much unintended mystery about *A Woman's Secret* for it to be anything but spotty entertainment.

Story [from Vicki Baum's novel *Mortagage on Life*] opens with Maureen O'Hara confessing to the shooting of Gloria Grahame, a trollop-minded chirp she has coached into the bigtime. O'Hara's friend (Melvyn Douglas) doesn't believe she did the shooting, and picture then goes into a confusing flashback account of her life as told by Douglas to a police detective (Jay C. Flippen). Footage moves constantly from the present to the past as Douglas tries to justify his belief in Miss O'Hara's innocence.

O'Hara gives a straightforward account of herself. Grahame carries handicap of bad makeup and unbecoming hairdress, and Douglas is too coy as the piano-playing friend. Flippen is topnotch as the detective, lifting his scenes, as does Mary Phillips as his amateur private-eye wife.

● ●

■ WOMAN'S TALE, A

1991, 93 MINS, AUSTRALIA ◇ ♥
Dir Paul Cox   *Prod* Paul Cox, Sanantha Naidu
Scr Paul Cox, Barry Dickens   *Ph* Nino G. Martinetti
Ed Russell Hurley   *Mus* Paul Grabowski   *Art Dir* Neil Angwin
● Sheila Florance, Gosia Dobrowolska, Norman Kaye, Chris Haywood, Myrtle Woods, Ernest Gray (Illumination)

Sensitive and controversial themes about treatment of the aged and terminally ill are tackled with distinction in Paul Cox' *A Woman's Tale* which bears all the director's hallmarks. Pic is structured around one of Cox' favourite actresses, veteran Sheila Florance, who carries the film on her frail shoulders. Her Martha is terminally ill yet fiercely determined to hold on to her independence. She lives alone in a small city apartment with her cat, canary and memories.

A nurse, Anna, visits her every day and Martha even lets her use her apartment for afternoon trysts with her married lover. Gosia Dobrowolska plays the nurse with sweetness and sensitivity.

Living in the next-door apartment is the equally old and even frailer Billy (Norman Kaye, in a tremendously touching performance). Anna also visits Billy, but is unamused when he makes pathetic sexual advances towards her.

These characters, and others, are, however, marginal. As Martha, Florance dominates the film and is in almost every scene. It's no secret Florance was seriously ill during production.

● ●

■ WOMAN'S WORLD

1954, 94 MINS, US ◇
Dir Jean Negulesco   *Prod* Charles Brackett   *Scr* Claude Binyon, Mary Loos, Richard Sale, Howard Lindsay, Russel Crouse   *Ph* Joe MacDonald   *Ed* Louis Loeffler
Mus Cyril J. Mockridge   *Art Dir* Lyle Wheeler, Mark-Lee Kirk
● Clifton Webb, June Allyson, Van Heflin, Lauren Bacall, Fred MacMurray, Arlene Dahl (20th Century-Fox)

Woman's World is Hollywood at its commercial best, a highly-polished product, technically and story-wise. Basic story premise is the behind-the-scenes scramble for the top job of a gigantic industrial firm.

Clifton Webb, as president of Gifford Motors, brings three of his district managers to New York for a firsthand observation to select a successor to the recently-deceased sales manager. He invites their wives along since he believes that the right wife is just as important as the right man for the job.

There's June Allyson and Cornel Wilde from Kansas City, Lauren Bacall and Fred MacMurray from Philadelphia, and Arlene Dahl and Van Heflin from Dallas. All the men in Webb's estimation are equally capable of handling the No. 1 post. The final decision rests on their wives.

Allyson is a hayseed from K.C., extremely devoted to her husband and three children. Bacall is bitter and disillusioned and at the point of separation from her ambitious husband. Dahl is a pushy glamor gal, not unwilling to throw her sex around to gain her aims.

The choice, of course, is left to the very end and will come as a surprise to many. Unlike

Metro's *Executive Suite*, in which the audience could quickly put its finger on the chosen man, *World* keeps 'em guessing. The entire cast, under Jean Negulesco's fine direction, contribute a performance as polished as the entire production.

....

■ WOMAN TIMES SEVEN

1967, 99 MINS, US ◇ ⑫
Dir Vittorio De Sica   *Prod* Arthur Cohn   *Scr* Cesare Zavattini   *Ph* Christian Matras   *Ed* Teddy Darvas, Victoria Spiri-Mercanton   *Mus* Riz Ortolani
● Shirley MacLaine, Peter Sellers, Alan Arkin, Rossano Brazzi, Michael Caine, Vittorio Gassman (Embassy)

Woman Times Seven means a seven-segment showcase for the talents of Shirley MacLaine, playing in tragicomedy and dramatic fashion a variety of femme types. MacLaine is spotted in many different adult situations, and largely convinces with each switcheroo.

With Peter Sellers, she is the bereaved widow, trailing her late husband in funeral procession, as Sellers puts the make on her. Then, as a wife who surprises hubby Rossano Brazzi in bed with a neighbor, MacLaine shifts to the enraged female, determined on revenge. The major tour de force segment finds MacLaine and Alan Arkin alone in a flophouse room, plotting suicide together.

....

■ WOMAN UNDER THE INFLUENCE, A

1974, 155 MINS, US ◇
Dir John Cassavetes   *Scr* John Cassavetes   *Ph* Mitch Breit   *Ed* Bob Heffernan   *Mus* Bo Harwood   *Art Dir* Phedon Papamichael
● Peter Falk, Gena Rowlands, Matthew Cassel, Matthew Laborteaux, Christina Grisanti, Katherine Cassavetes (Faces International)

This is a disturbing portrait of a slightly-mad housewife. Its serious treament of a downbeat subject is hypoed by a fine performance from Peter Falk and a bravura one from Gena Rowlands.

Rowlands plays a lower middle-class LA housewife whose sense of identity is so impoverished she defines herself only in terms of her husband's love and the devotion of her children.

Rowlands' performance in the title role is one of those tour de force numbers available only to screen players of alcoholics and lunatics.

Falk is outstanding in a role which calls for him to be loving and callous at the same time. He, too, retains audience sympathy.

Film is technically superior to any of John Cassavetes' previous works.
□ 1974: Nominations: Best Director, Actress (Gena Rowlands)

....

■ WOMEN, THE

1939, 132 MINS, US ◇ ⑫ ⊙
Dir George Cukor   *Prod* Hunt Stromberg   *Scr* Anita Loos, Jane Murfin   *Ph* Oliver T. Marsh, Joseph Ruttenberg   *Ed* Robert J. Kern   *Mus* Edward Ward, David Snell   *Art Dir* Cedric Gibbons, Wade B. Rubottom
● Norma Shearer, Joan Crawford, Rosalind Russell, Paulette Goddard, Joan Fontaine, Hedda Hopper (M-G-M)

As in the play [by Clare Boothe], no man appears – it's a field day for the gals to romp intimately in panties, scanties and gorgeous gowns. Most of the members of the cast (studio claims 135 speaking parts) deport themselves in a manner best described by Joan Crawford at the end. 'There's a name for you ladies, but it's not used in high society outside of kennels.'

Story is essentially lightweight and trivial, and covers a wide range of fem conversations – barbed shafts at friends, whisperings of husbands' indiscretions, maligning gossip and

catty asides. Script basically maintains structure of the play but directs more sympathetic appeal to the marital problem of Norma Shearer.

Picture however holds passages that slow movement down to a walk.

....

■ WOMEN IN LOVE

1969, 130 MINS, UK ◇ ⑫ ⑰ ⊙
Dir Ken Russell   *Prod* Larry Kramer, Martin Rosen   *Scr* Larry Kramer   *Ph* Billy Williams   *Ed* Michael Bradsell   *Mus* Georges Delerue   *Art Dir* Luciana Arrighi
● Alan Bates, Oliver Reed, Glenda Jackson, Jennie Linden, Eleanor Bron, Vladek Sheybal (United Artists)

Directed with style and punch by Ken Russell this is an episodic but challenging and holding pic. D.H. Lawrence's pungent thoughts about love and marriage, and the attitudes of the two sexes toward them, are not highly original but are shrewdly put over.

Russell's direction dominates the film, but he has the benefit of four excellent performances. The rough, tough coalmining area of the Midlands is effectively evoked.

The story is fragmentary. Two sisters are wooed and won by two men and the film concerns their relationship. One settles down to a marriage on happy but uneasy terms. The other, more questing, has an equally uneasy yet gleeful romance which ends in tragedy.

Glenda Jackson gives a vital performance with punch and intelligence. Jennie Linden, settles for married life with Alan Bates.
□ 1970: Best Actress (Glenda Jackson).
□ Nominations: Best Director, Screenplay Adaptation, Cinematography

....

■ WONDERFUL LIFE

1964, 113 MINS, UK ◇
Dir Sidney J. Furie   *Prod* Kenneth Harper   *Scr* Peter Myers, Ronald Cass   *Ph* Kenneth Higgins   *Ed* Jack Slade   *Mus* Stanley Black   *Art Dir* Stanley Dorfman
● Cliff Richard, Walter Slezak, Susan Hampshire, The Shadows, Una Stubbs, Melvyn Hayes (Elstree/Ivy)

Film musicals often get by on shaky storylines but these are usually decked out with lively jokes and badinage and Peter Myers and Ronald Cass [who wrote the songs], prove themselves somewhat sparing in this department. It puts an unfair onus on Cliff Richard, to expect his personality to buck several slack passages and remarkably unwitty wordage.

Richard, the Shadows group and comedians Melvyn Hayes and Richard O'Sullivan are merchant sailors stranded in the Canaries where they come across Walter Slezak directing a diabolical *Beau Geste* epic. Caught up in this mish mash, leading lady Susan Hampshire is having a rough time. For love of the young lady the lads decide to boost her confidence by making an off-the-cuff musical version of the director's film.

The happiest flight of fancy is a sequence which sends up films down the ages. Richard, Hampshire, and the rest show a pleasing sense of mimicry and satire as they josh such favorites as Valentino, the Marx Brothers, the Mack Sennett Cops, Shirley Temple, Garbo, Grable, Boyer, Fairbanks Sr, Bogart, Dick Powell, Tarzan and others right up to James Bond.

....

■ WONDERFUL WORLD OF THE BROTHERS GRIMM, THE

1962, 135 MINS, US ◇ ⑫
Dir Henry Levin, George Pal   *Prod* George Pal   *Scr* David P. Harmon, Charles Beaumont, William Roberts   *Ph* Paul C. Vogel   *Ed* Walter Thompson   *Mus* Leigh Harline   *Art Dir* George W. Davis, Edward Carfagno
● Laurence Harvey, Karl Boehm, Claire Bloom, Walter Slezak, Yvette Mimieux, Russ Tamblyn (M-G-M/Cinerama)

Grimm is a delightful, refreshing entertainment. Pal himself shares dirctorial credit with Levin, as the producer also is responsible for directing the Fairy Tales sequences. Pal and Grimm are sympatico, although he permitted Jim Backus as the King to sound too much like Mr. Magoo in *The Dancing Princess* sequence.

This traditional fairy tale of the princess who finds her true love in the humble woodsman is interestingly choreographed by Alex Romero and charmingly interpreted by Yvette Mimieux and Russ Tamblyn.

As far as acting honors go, Harvey is dominant, for in addition to playing Wilhem Grimm he also enacts, and with touching warmth offset by a trace of irrascibility, the title role in *The Cobbler and the Elves*. This sequence, with its Christmas setting and assortment of orphans and puppets which performs a miracle in the cobbler's shop overnight, is entirely enchanting.

The Singing Bone dealing with a titanic encounter involving a supercilious aspiring knight and his servant with a fire-spouting dragon, is full of exaggerated chills and wry humor. Buddy Hackett (who reminds of the late Lou Costello) as the humble servant who finally emerges as the shining knight over his dastardly master, is enchanting. And Terry-Thomas also is excellent as the master whose cowardice ultimately strips him of honor and glory.
□ 1962: Best Color Costume Design 9Mary Wills).
□ Nominations: Best Color Cinematography, Color Art Direction, Scoring of Music

....

■ WONDER MAN

1945, 95 MINS, US ◇ ⑫
Dir H. Bruce Humberstone   *Prod* Samuel Goldwyn   *Scr* Don Hartman, Melville Shavelson, Philip Rapp   *Ph* Victor Milner, William Snyder   *Ed* Daniel Mandell   *Mus* Ray Heindorf (arr.)   *Art Dir* Ernst Fegte, McClure Capps
● Danny Kaye, Virginia Mayo, Vera-Ellen, Steve Cochran, Huntz Hall, Donald Woods (RKO/Goldwyn)

Niftily Technicolored and expensive-looking all the way, *Wonder Man* finds Kaye in a dual role, as twins, one being a nitery performer bumped off by yeggs because of information he was going to give the district attorney; the other as a mild-mannered, studious type who, after his brother's slaying, is belabored by the latter's 'spirit' into taking his place and thus help run down the thugs.

The complications, notably on the romance, frequently get too unwieldy for comfort. Several of the comedy situations are rewrites of oldies, but Kaye makes them capital. There is, in particular, a final-reel scene in which Kaye seeks refuge as a costumed singer during the midst of an operatic performance. It's boilerplate comedy but Kaye makes it belly-laugh fun.

If this sounds like all Kaye, there's no mistaking that without him this film would be decidedly commonplace. He has a good supporting cast, namely the beauteous Virginia Mayo, as the main romantic link, and Vera-Ellen, out of the Broadway musicals, who is the secondary love interest. The blonde Mayo screens like the couple of millions that are indicated to have been spent by Goldwyn on the pic; and Vera-Ellen is a fine young hoofer who can handle lines well, too.
□ 1945: Best Special Effects
□ Nominations: Best Scoring of a Musical Picture, Song ('So in Love'), Sound

....

■ WOODEN HORSE, THE

1950, 101 MINS, UK ⑫
Dir Jack Lee   *Prod* Ian Dalrymple   *Scr* Eric Williams   *Ph* C. Pennington-Richards   *Ed* John Seabourne Sr, Peter Seabourne   *Mus* Clifton Parker   *Art Dir* William Kellner

● Leo Genn, David Tomlinson, Anthony Steel, Bryan Forbes, David Greene, Peter Finch (London/Wessex)

A commendable degree of documentary fidelity is established in this picturization of the escape of three prisoners-of-war from a German camp. The long and torturous period of preparation is faithfully recaptured.

Yarn traces the exploits of three officers who, after receiving approval from the camp's 'escape committee', cover up their tunnel-digging by means of a vaulting horse.

Some of the best drama in the film comes after the prison break, where the two ex-airmen, with forged papers, make for a port and finally board a boat for Copenhagen on their last drive for freedom.

Thesping standard is universally good all round. Eric Williams' screenplay from his own novel is a workman-like job.

■ WOODSTOCK

1970, 183 MINS, US ◇ ⑰

Dir Michael Wadleigh   *Prod* Bob Maurice   *Ph* Michael Wadleigh, David Myers, Richard Pearce, Donald Lenzer, Al Wertheimer   *Ed* Thelma Schoonmaker, Martin Scorsese, Stan Warnow, Jere Huggins, Yeu-Bun Yee
● (Warner)

Woodstock, brilliantly made by Michael Wadleigh, is a virtually perfect record of the music festival held in Bethel, NY, in summer 1969.

As a documentary feature, the film is a milestone in artistic collation of raw footage into a multipanel, variable-frame, dazzling montage that engages the senses with barely a let-up.

From countless thousands of feet of exposed stock, Wadleigh has superbly orchestrated on film the mass intimacy of pop music and its latter-day relationship to self and environment. *Woodstock* is an absolute triumph in its marriage of cinematic technology to reality.

Of no mean help, of course, are the outstanding musical talents. They do their own things, while the individual and collective effect is spine-tingling.
□ 1970: Best Feature Documentary
□ Nominations: Best Editing, Sound

■ WORDS AND MUSIC

1948, 119 MINS, US ◇ ⑰ ⊙

Dir Norman Taurog   *Prod* Arthur Freed   *Scr* Fred Finklehoffe   *Ph* Charles Rosher, Harry Stradling   *Ed* Albert Akst, Ferris Webster   *Mus* Lennie Hayton (dir.)   *Art Dir* Cedric Gibbons, Jack Martin Smith
● Tom Drake, Mickey Rooney, Betty Garrett, Ann Sothern, Janet Leigh, Marshall Thompson (M-G-M)

The saga of Rodgers and Hart itself is neither very interesting nor exceptional, unless it be in their early and continued success at turning out words and music for one top Broadway and Hollywood musical hit after another. Fred Finklehoffe, therefore, in preparing his screenplay [from a story by Guy Bolton and Jean Holloway, adapted by Ben Feiner Jr], acted wisely in reducing the biographical aspects to almost a minimum, using them only as a rack around which to weave production numbers, terp routines and lyric assignments [staged and directed by Robert Alton].

Tom Drake plays the serious, businesslike and homeloving Rodgers, the melodist of the pair. Mickey Rooney plays Hart, giving the role at least some partial physical veri-similitude in that his tiny stature was a near-tragedy in the lyricist's life.

Biog, as a matter of fact, sticks to truth about as closely as can be presented on the screen. While details are freely reshuffled, the yarn is strikingly sound from an overall psychological view, catching Hart's early zest for life and its gradual change to a tragic

chase after a happiness he couldn't achieve, a chase that led to his death in 1943 at the age of 47.

Hart, who never married, but bounded about the world, was, of course, the more colorful of the pair and the camera faithfully catches that. Rooney plays Rooney, however, rather than Hart, almost turning the role into a burlesque. Drake imbues Rodgers with the dignity and modesty of a Rodgers – if not with the spark. Film doesn't go into the break between the pair, two years before Hart's death. It was at this time Rodgers teamed with Oscar Hammerstein II.

■ WORKING GIRL

1988, 113 MINS, US ◇ ⑰ ⊙

Dir Mike Nichols   *Prod* Douglas Wick   *Scr* Kevin Wade   *Ph* Michael Ballhaus   *Ed* Sam O'Steen   *Mus* Carly Simon   *Art Dir* Patrizia Von Brandenstein
● Sigourney Weaver, Harrison Ford, Melanie Griffith, Joan Cusack, Alec Baldwin, Philip Bosco (20th Century-Fox)

Working Girl is enjoyable largely due to the fun of watching scrappy, sexy, unpredictable Melanie Griffith rise from Staten Island secretary to Wall Street whiz. She's the kind with an eye for stock figures – the numeral kind and the real kind (Harrison Ford).

Griffith stands apart, both for her eagerness to break out of her clerical rut and her tenacity dealing with whomever seems to be thwarting her, at first a lecherous brokerage house exec, whom she very cleverly and humorously exposes, and then a much more formidable and disarming opponent, femme boss Sigourney Weaver.

Just because they're both 'girls' trying to make their way amidst a sea of men doesn't, however, make them friends.

This is not a laugh-out-loud film, though there is a lighthearted tone that runs consistently throughout, Griffith's innocent, breathy voice being a major factor.
□ 1988: Best Song ('Let the River Run').
□ Nominations: Best Picture, Director, Actress (Melanie Griffith), Supp. Actress (Joan Cusack), Sigourney Weaver)

■ WORKING GIRLS

1986, 90 MINS, US ◇ ⑰

Dir Lizzie Borden   *Prod* Lizzie Borden, Andi Gladstone   *Scr* Lizzie Borden   *Ph* Judy Irola   *Ed* Lizzie Borden   *Mus* David Van Tiegham   *Art Dir* Kurt Ossenfort
● Louise Smith, Ellen McEldruff, Amanda Goodwin, Marusia Zach, Janne Peters, Helen Nicholas (Alternative Current)

Working Girls is a simulated docu-style feature that allows audiences to be invisible guests for one day and part of the evening in a Manhattan brothel staffed by about 10 whores working two shifts and charging $50 per half hour when special services of limited scope ('mild dominance' is undertaken by some of the girls) are not required. When their shifts are over, the girls go home to private life with or without husbands or boyfriends.

Centering on Molly (Louise Smith), director Lizzie Borden neither glamorizes, romanticizes nor condemns anything or anybody connected to the brothel.

Borden sugars her pill with clean, crisp, often witty recording of brothel action and shop-talk. All acting is credible and the camerawork is smooth, the non-action a bit on the long winded side.

■ WORK IS A 4-LETTER WORD

1968, 93 MINS, UK ◇

Dir Peter Hall   *Prod* Thomas Clyde   *Scr* Jeremy Summers   *Ph* Gil Taylor   *Ed* Keith Green   *Mus* Guy Woolfenden   *Art Dir* Philip Harrison

● David Warner, Cilla Black, Elizabeth Spriggs, Zia Mohyeddin, Joe Gladiyn (Rank/Universal-Cavalcade)

Work Is a 4-Letter Word is based on Henry Livings' unconventional and not wholly satisfactory play *Eh?* A difficult theme for a film, *Work* is a wayout comedy fantasy.

There is an irritating air of improvisation about much of the picture which shows up particularly in the editing, Keith Green clearly having difficulty in keeping Jeremy Summers' wayward screenplay within coherent bounds.

The thin storyline visualizes man's struggle against automation, something of a harkback to Chaplin's *Modern Times*. Overwhelmed by the DICE organization which makes such horrors as plastic daffodils and whose skyscraper offices and factories are automated to a point of frenzy one young man holds out against the system.

The plot and message are merely hooks for a series of off-beat situations, some very funny and others over-reminiscent and over-stressed. Director Peter Hall often hangs on to a point just long enough to blunt it.

■ WORLD ACCORDING TO GARP, THE

1982, 136 MINS, US ◇ ⑰

Dir George Roy Hill   *Prod* George Roy Hill, Robert L. Crawford   *Scr* Steve Tesich   *Ph* Miroslav Ondricek   *Ed* Stephen A. Rotter   *Mus* David Shire (adapt.)   *Art Dir* Henry Bumstead
● Robin Williams, Mary Beth Hurt, Glenn Close, John Lithgow, Hume Cronyn, Jessica Tandy (Pan Arts)

George Roy Hill's film adaptation of [John Irving's novel] *The World According to Garp* has taste, intelligence, craft and numerous other virtues going for it.

Tale is that of young Garp, bastard son of independent-minded nurse Jenny Fields, who, at midlife, becomes a media celebrity upon the publication of her autobiographical tome, *A Sexual Suspect*.

Garp grows up in a placid academic environment, and the grown man in the person of Robin Williams appears only after 25 minutes. He meets and marries Mary Beth Hurt, raises his family, fitfully pursues his writing while she teaches, has skirmishes with the feminists at his mother's mansion, and all the while tries to avoid the 'undertoad', the unseen, pervasive threat which lurks everywhere and strikes without warning.

Physically, Williams is fine, but much of the performance is hit-and-miss. Otherwise, casting is superior. Hurt is excellent as Garp's wife. Glenn Close proves a perfect choice as Jenny Fields, a woman of almost ethereal simplicity. Best of all, perhaps, is John Lithgow as Roberta Muldoon, a former football player, now a transsexual.
□ 1982: Nominations: Best Supp. Actor (John Lithgow), Supp. Actress (Glenn Close)

■ WORLD AND HIS WIFE, THE

See: State of the Union

■ WORLD APART, A

1988, 113 MINS, UK ◇ ⑰ ⊙

Dir Chris Menges   *Prod* Sarah Radclyffe   *Scr* Shawn Slovo   *Ph* Peter Biziou   *Ed* Nicolas Gaster   *Mus* Hans Zimmer   *Art Dir* Brian Morris
● Barbara Hershey, Jodhi May, David Suchet, Jeroen Krabbe, Paul Freeman, Tim Roth (British Screen/Working Title)

A World Apart provides a sharp glimpse of what it was like to be politically contrary in the early 1960s in South Africa. It is mostly told from the p.o.v. of a 13-year-old girl, Molly (Jodhi May), whose life becomes dramatically disrupted as a result of her parents' subversive activities.

Set in 1963, story is described as a fictionalized account of what happened to young Shawn Slovo, the writer, and her family when the authorities began cracking down on them. Pic traces the growing emotional and political awareness of the youngster, but also represents a daughter's critique of what she perceives as her mother's selfish absorption in concerns she condescendingly considers above her offspring's head.

The casual cruelties and injustices of the South African system are displayed as part of life's fabric, but what's really going on with Molly's parents, as well as the friendly blacks who often visit the house, remains unclear and out of reach to the girl.

Barbara Hershey (as the mother) represents a solid central figure for the film. Nevertheless, the limited, daughter's-eye viewpoint restricts one's access to the woman's inner self, the source of her political beliefs and her self-image.

Happily, May is at all times engaging as Molly, sustaining the film with no problem. Performances throughout are uniformly naturalistic and believable, and pic, which was shot in Zimbabwe, possesses a rich, luminous look despite a limited budget.

••••••••••••••••••••••••••••

■ WORLD IS FULL OF MARRIED MEN, THE

1979, 107 MINS, UK ◇ ⊛
Dir Robert Young *Prod* Malcolm Fancey *Scr* Jackie Collins, Terry Howard *Ph* Ray Parslow *Ed* David Campling *Mus* Frank Musker, Dominic Bugatti *Art Dir* Tony Curtis
● Anthony Franciosa, Carroll Baker, Sherrie Cronn, Paul Nicholas, Gareth Hunt, Georgina Hale (New Realm/ Married Men)

Set in a glossy world of penthouses and charge accounts, the medium for Jackie Collins' first (1968) novel's message is sexploitation melodrama which, cunningly, will titillate both sexes.

Anthony Franciosa brings a mercifully light touch to the central antihero, an errant advertising executive who trips over one floozie too many and falls in love. Carroll Baker works creditably hard as Franciosa's oft-betrayed spouse who – in a suspiciously convenient dramatic move – finds affection in the back of a limousine with a teen-idol some 15 years his junior. Paul Nicholas in that role is uncharismatic.

Collins' manipulative technique does not allow for in-depth characterization, so cameos tend to come off best. Georgina Hale is routine (for her) but effective as a laconic wife who's come to terms with the sexcess scene.

••••••••••••••••••••••••••••

■ WORLD OF SUZIE WONG, THE

1960, 130 MINS, US ◇ ⊛ ⊙
Dir Richard Quine *Prod* Ray Stark *Scr* John Patrick *Ph* Geoffrey Unsworth *Ed* Bert Bates *Mus* George Duning *Art Dir* John Box
● William Holden, Nancy Kwan, Sylvia Syms, Michael Wilding, Jacqui Chan, Laurence Naismith (Paramount)

The advantage of on-the-spot geography does a great deal for the screen version of *The World of Suzie Wong*. The ultra-picturesque environment of teeming Hong Kong brings a note of ethnic charm to the production, and amounts to a major improvement over the legit translation by Paul Osborn of Richard Mason's novel.

Suzie Wong is the story of an artist (William Holden) who has come to Hong Kong to devote one year to 'learning something about painting and something about myself'. Before long, he is also learning a great deal about Suzie (Nancy Kwan), a kind of titular leader of a band of lovable, warmhearted prostitutes (are there any other kinds?). After resisting temptations of the flesh and giving her the brush for an admirable period, Holden eventually succumbs to the yen. Complications en-

sue when it develops Kwan has a child.

The love story makes much more sense with the substitution of the mature Holden for the younger hero of the play. That and the scenery are the major improvements.

On the decidedly negative side are three passages in which realism is virtually abandoned for theatrical effect. (1) Kwan, beaten up by a sailor, proudly displays her bloody lip to the girls as a token of Holden's jealousy, (2) Kwan and Holden dine on salad dressing so as not to reveal her illiteracy to a 'stuckup' waiter, and (3) Holden impulsively tears Kwan's dress off when she turns up in his room looking like the western version of what she is.

Holden gives a first-class performance, restrained and sincere. He brings authority and compassion to the role. Kwan is not always perfect in her timing of lines (she has a tendency to anticipate) and appears to lack a full range of depth or warmth, but on the whole she manages a fairly believable portrayal. Michael Wilding is capable in a role that has been trimmed down. Jacqui Chan is convincing as a B-girl sans sex appeal, only one of the group (outside of the heroine) left with an identity in the screen translation.

••••••••••••••••••••••••••••

■ WORLD'S GREATEST ATHLETE, THE

1973, 92 MINS, US ◇ ⊛
Dir Robert Scheerer *Prod* Bill Walsh *Scr* Gerald Gardner, Dee Caruso *Ph* Frank Phillips *Ed* Cotton Warburton *Mus* Marvin Hamlisch *Art Dir* John B. Mansbridge, Walter Tyler
● Tim Conway, Jan-Michael Vincent, John Amos, Roscoe Lee Browne, Dayle Haddon, Billy De Wolfe (Walt Disney)

The World's Greatest Athlete features Jan-Michael Vincent in title role of a jungle boy transplanted to an American campus where he becomes a one-man track squad. Emphasis is on visual comedy, from the sublime to the camp.

Coach John Amos and assistant Tim Conway, with a terrible record behind them in all sports and alumnus Billy De Wolfe on their backs, discover Vincent during a trip to Africa. Vincent's godfather, witchdoctor Roscoe Lee Browne, is tricked into letting him go back with Amos and Conway, who proceed to enter Vincent as the solo contender for a slew of inter-college field awards.

Vincent provides beefcake and little else, since the script keeps him in the status of the bewildered alien.

••••••••••••••••••••••••••••

■ WORLD'S GREATEST LOVER, THE

1977, 89 MINS, US ◇ ⊛
Dir Gene Wilder *Prod* Gene Wilder *Scr* Gene Wilder *Ph* Gerald Hirschfeld *Ed* Anthony A. Pellegrino *Mus* John Morris *Art Dir* Steve Sardanis
● Gene Wilder, Carol Kane, Dom DeLuise, Fritz Feld, Carl Ballantine, Michael Huddleston (20th Century-Fox)

The World's Greatest Lover is a good period comedy starring Gene Wilder competing in a Hollywood studio talent search of 50 years ago to be a rival of Rudolph Valentino. Wilder also functions as writer-producer-director on his second personal film project, ably assisted by Carol Kane, as his wife, and Dom DeLuise, as a prototype madhatter studio czar.

The individual sketchpieces – Wilder trapped on a bakery assembly line; swimming in a flooded sunken livingroom, seducing his own wife in Valentino disguise after tutoring by the great lover himself, freaking out at his screen test, emerge as varyingly humorous episodes strung out on a skimpy story line.

DeLuise and Michael Huddleston repeatedly bring up the laugh level.

••••••••••••••••••••••••••••

■ WORLD TEN TIMES OVER, THE

(US: Pussycat Alley)

1963, 93 MINS, UK
Dir Wolf Rilla *Prod* Michael Luke *Scr* Wolf Rilla *Ph* Larry Pizer *Ed* Jack Slade *Mus* Edwin Astley *Art Dir* Peggy Gick
● Sylvia Syms, Edward Judd, June Ritchie, William Hartnell (Cyclops/Associated-British)

Wolf Rilla's screenplay explores in one day's fairly busy activity the aimlessness, insecurity and heartaches of nightclub hostesses. The result is overdramatic but provides opportunities for deft thesping. Nightclub and location sequences in London have a brisk authenticity.

Story concerns two girls, euphemistically called nightclub hostesses, who share an apartment. One (June Ritchie) is a flighty, young extrovert who is having an affair with the married son of a property tycoon. The other (Sylvia Syms) is an older girl, daughter of a country schoolmaster, who is disgusted with her job but cannot break away from it.

Syms gives an intelligent and often moving performance. Her scenes with her father (William Hartnell) are excellent. Hartnell, playing the unworldly, scholarly father, who has no contact with his daughter, also gives an observant study. The other two principals are more phonily drawn characters. Edward Judd seems strangely uneasy in his role and Ritchie, despite many firstrate moments, sometimes appears as if she is simply jumping through paper hoops.

••••••••••••••••••••••••••••

■ WORLD, THE FLESH AND THE DEVIL, THE

1959, 95 MINS, US ⊛
Dir Ranald MacDougall *Prod* Sol C. Siegel *Scr* Ranald MacDougall *Ph* Harold J. Marzorati *Ed* Harold F. Kress *Mus* Miklos Rozsa
● Harry Belafonte, Inger Stevens, Mel Ferrer (M-G-M/ HarBel)

This is a provocative three-character story dealing with some pertinent issues (racism, atomic destruction) in a frame of suspense melodrama. Ranald MacDougall, who directed his own screenplay (based on an ancient novel by M.P. Shiel), leaves a few holes in his story, but deliberately.

Harry Belafonte is a coal miner who fights his way out of a wrecked Pennsylvania shaft to find himself apparently alone in a devastated world. After about a third of the film, Inger Stevens turns up, spared because she was in a decompression chamber when the bombs burst. Near the ending, in the last half-hour or so, Mel Ferrer arrives in a small power boat from a fishing expedition.

Although overall the film is engrossing, it gets curiously less effective as additional survivors turn up. When Belafonte is entirely alone on the screen for the first one-third of the film, and virtually alone for the first half, the semi-documentary style keeps the film crisp and credible.

It is not clear in the relationship between Belafonte and Stevens whether they are kept apart by her prejudice or his unfounded fear that such an attitude might exist. Ferrer's character is unsatisfying. He seems to be a racist of sorts, but how virulent isn't entirely clarified.

MacDougall shot a great deal of the film in Manhattan, and the realism (and the pains taken to achieve it) pay off. New Yorkers might complain that their geography is a little mixed up, but this is of small consequence.

••••••••••••••••••••••••••••

■ WRECKING CREW, THE

1969, 105 MINS, US ◇ ⊛
Dir Phil Karlson *Prod* Irving Allen *Scr* William McGivern *Ph* Sam Leavitt *Ed* Maury Winetrobe *Mus* Hugo Montenegro *Art Dir* Joe Wright

867

● Dean Martin, Elke Sommer, Sharon Tate, Nancy Kwan, Nigel Green, Tina Louise (Columbia/Meadway-Claude)

Fourth in the Matt Helm series, *The Wrecking Crew* emerges as a very entertaining, relaxed spy comedy. It features Dean Martin, Elke Sommer, Nancy Kwan and Sharon Tate, the latter in a delightful comedy performance.

Nigel Green is the heavy, as mastermind of a gold theft. Sommer and Kwan are his principal aides, while Tate is a British agent in support of Martin's work. You wouldn't know it, though, because Tate keeps aborting Martin's plans and intimate rendezvous.

Film rolls along pleasantly for its 105 minutes, featuring the recurring music of Hugo Montenegro and a song by Mack David and Frank DeVol.

. . . .

■ WRECK OF THE MARY DEARE, THE

1959, 105 MINS, US ◇
Dir Michael Anderson *Prod* Julian Blaustein *Scr* Eric Ambler *Ph* Joseph Ruttenberg *Ed* Eda Warren *Mus* George Duning
● Gary Cooper, Charlton Heston, Michael Redgrave, Emlyn Williams, Richard Harris, Ben Wright (M-G-M)

The mystery of a 'ghost' ship looming suddenly out of the night, with only a crazed and battered captain aboard, is solved skillfully and with a good deal of suspense in The Wreck of the Mary Deare, from the Hammond Innes novel originally published in the Saturday Evening Post in 1956. It's the kind of adventure yarn which, thanks to intelligent treatment and topnotch photography, comes off with a bang.

Gary Cooper is Gideon Patch, the captain who's been the victim of foul play but stands accused himself of negligence. And Charlton Heston plays the skipper of a salvage boat who becomes innocently involved in the mystery of the Mary Deare and, in the end, helps solve it. Both men are perfectly cast in rugged roles and Cooper particularly conveys a surprising range of emotion and reaction.

In the smaller (almost bit) parts, Michael Redgrave and Emlyn Williams are very British as they participate in the London Court of Inquiry. Richard Harris is the snarling villain. Ben Wright is comfortable as Heston's partner.

There's a letdown in pace at the middle of the film when the Court of Inquiry appears stacked against Cooper. But the climax comes off with bangup effects.

. . . .

■ WRITTEN ON THE WIND

1956, 99 MINS, US ◇ ⓥ
Dir Douglas Sirk *Prod* Albert Zugsmith *Scr* George Zuckerman *Ph* Russell Metty *Ed* Russell F. Schoengarth *Mus* Frank Skinner *Art Dir* Alexander Golitzen, Robert Clatworthy
● Rock Hudson, Lauren Bacall, Robert Stack, Dorothy Malone, Robert Keith, Grant Williams (Universal)

This outspoken drama probes rather startlingly into the morals and passions of an uppercrust Texas oil family. Intelligent use of the flashback technique before and during the titles credits runoff builds immediate interest and expectancy without diminishing plot punch. Tiptop scripting from the Robert Wilder novel, dramatically deft direction by Douglas Sirk and sock performances by the cast give the story development a followthrough.

Rock Hudson, Lauren Bacall, Robert Stack and Dorothy Malone, aptly cast in the star roles, add a zing to the characters that pays off in audience interest. Hudson scores as the normal, lifelong friend of profligate Stack. The latter, in one of his best performances, draws a compelling portrait of a psychotic man ruined by wealth and character weaknesses.

Bacall registers strongly as a sensible girl swept into the madness of the oil family when she marries Stack, while Malone hits a career high as the completely immoral sister.
□ 1956: Best Supp. Actress (Dorothy Malone).
□ Nominations: Best Supp. Actor (Robert Stack), Song ('Written on the Wind')

. . . .

■ WRONG ARM OF THE LAW, THE

1963, 94 MINS, UK ⓥ
Dir Cliff Owen *Prod* Aubrey Baring *Scr* Ray Galton, Alan Simpson, John Antrobus *Ph* Ernest Steward *Ed* Tristam Cones *Mus* Richard Rodney Bennett *Art Dir* Harry White
● Peter Sellers, Lionel Jeffries, Bernard Cribbins, Bill Kerr, Davy Kaye, Nanette Newman (Romulus)

A slightweight cops and robbers idea is pepped up into a briskly amusing farce thanks to a combo of deft direction, thesping and writing. Written by the authors of Tony Hancock's original TV series, with the assistance of 'Goon' writer John Antrobus, the screenplay [from a screenplay by John Warren and Len Heath; original story by Ivor Jay and William Whistance Smith], has a fair turn of wit and a number of excellent whacky situations.

Peter Sellers runs a top league West End dress salon as Monsieur Jules. But that's only a front. As Pearly Gates, he is the Cockney King of the Underworld. His own gang he runs onWelfare State lines, with free luncheon vouchers, bubbly on Sundays, holidays with pay on the Costa Brava.

Everything's going fine until the police swoop on the gang job after job. Sellers realizes that an IPO (Impersonating Police Officers) mob is in town. He calls an extraordinary general meeting of London's crime syndicates, negotiates with Scotland Yard and arranges for a 24-hour crime truce so that the police can concentrate on running in the IPO gang.

Sellers has a fat part as the gangster with modern methods (for instance, he makes his gang attend evenings of educational films such as *Rififi*). And he brings his usual alert intelligence to the role. He is surrounded with some sharp talent.

. . . .

■ WRONG BOX, THE

1966, 110 MINS, UK ◇ ⓥ
Dir Bryan Forbes *Prod* Bryan Forbes *Scr* Larry Gelbart, Burt Shevelove *Ph* Gerry Turpin *Ed* Alan Osbiston *Mus* John Barry *Art Dir* Ray Simm
● John Mills, Ralph Richardson, Michael Caine, Peter Cook, Dudley Moore, Peter Sellers (Columbia/Salamander)

Robert Louis Stevenson's macabre Victorian yarn has been impressively mounted by producer-director Bryan Forbes. He has lined up an impeccable cast of Britain's character comedian actors and brought his usual intelligent flourish to the film. But it might have improved this Columbia release had he written the script for *The Wrong Box* himself, instead of using the uneven work of Larry Gelbart and Burt Shevelove.

Storyline concerns a macabre lottery in which 20 parents each toss some money into a kitty for their children, the last survivor to draw the loot. Eventual survivors are two brothers who haven't seen each other for 40 years. One of them (John Mills) makes ineffective attempts to bump off his brother (Ralph Richardson), and their offspring take a more than casual interest in the proceedings.

Mills amusingly hams his way through two or three sequences as one of the dying brothers. Richardson, bland, imperturable old bore, is superb. He and Wilfrid Lawson, portraying a decrepit butler, virtually carry away the acting honors.

. . . .

■ WRONG IS RIGHT

(UK: The Man With the Deadly Lens)

1982, 117 MINS, US ◇ ☉
Dir Richard Brooks *Prod* Richard Brooks *Scr* Richard Brooks *Ph* Fred J. Koenekamp *Ed* George Grenville *Mus* Artie Kane *Art Dir* Edward Carfagno
● Sean Connery, George Grizzard, Robert Conrad, Katharine Ross, G.D. Spradlin, John Saxon (Columbia)

Wrong Is Right represents Richard Brooks' shriek of protest at what he sees as the insane, downward spiral of world history over the past decade. Part political satire, part doomsday melodrama and part intellectual graffiti scribbled on the screen, film is impossible to pigeon-hole.

In a style simultaneously literal and surreal, Brooks takes potshots at the CIA, the FBI, presidents Nixon, Carter and Reagan, the military, the Arabs, the oil crisis, international terrorists and television, among many targets.

Sean Connery plays a sort of combination Edward R. Murrow and James Bond, a globe-trotting television commentator who enjoys total access to world leaders of all persuasions.

Basic situation involves an Arab king who seems ready to turn over two mini-atom bombs to a Khaddafi-like revolutionary leader, with the devices to be detonated in Israel, and later New York, unless the US president, who has admitted ordering the killing of the king, resigns from office.

Wild proceedings are packed with convoluted intrigue involving such characters as CIA agents John Saxon and Katharine Ross, maniacal Pentagon rep Robert Conrad, international arms dealer Hardy Kruger and an array of suicidal terrorists who delight in blowing themselves up, as long as it's covered on television.

. . . .

■ WRONG MAN, THE

1958, 110 MINS, US ⓥ ☉
Dir Alfred Hitchcock *Prod* Alfred Hitchcock *Scr* Maxwell Anderson, Angus MacPhail *Ph* Robert Burks *Ed* George Tomasini *Mus* Bernard Herrmann *Art Dir* Paul Sylbert, William L. Kuehl
● Henry Fonda, Vera Miles, Anthony Quayle, Harold J. Stone, Charles Cooper, Richard Robbins (Warner)

Alfred Hitchcock draws upon real-life drama for this gripping piece of realism [from the *Life* magazine story *The True Story of Christopher Emmanuel Balestrero* by Maxwell Anderson]. He builds the case of a NY Stork Club musician falsely accused of a series of holdups to a powerful climax, the events providing director a field day in his art of characterization and suspense.

Subject here is Manny Balestrero, the bass fiddle player whose story hit Gotham headlines in 1953 when he was arrested for crimes he did not commit. In a case of mistaken identity, he was not freed until the actual culprit was found during his trial. Not, however, before the musician, a family man with a wife and two young sons, went through the harrowing ordeal of being unable to prove his innocence.

Hitchcock drains the dramatic possibilities with often frightening overtones, as the spectator comes to realize that the very same could happen to him, if he fell into such a situation. The musician, played with a stark kind of impersonation by Fonda, is positively identified by several of the holdup victims, and other circumstances arise which seem to prove his guilt.

. . . .

■ WRONG MAN, THE

1993, 110 MINS, US ◇ ⓥ ☉
Dir Jim McBride *Prod* Alan Beattie, Chris Chesser *Scr* Michael Thoma *Ph* Affonso Beato *Ed* Lisa Churgin *Mus* Los Lobos *Art Dir* Jeannine Oppewall

● Rosanna Arquette, Kevin Anderson, John Lithgow, Jorge Cervera Jr, Ernesto Laguardia, Robert Harper (Viacom)

A sultry sex-suspenser about gringos on the run south of the border, *The Wrong Man* teeters back and forth over the line between good, dirty, genre fun and outright silliness.

A blue-eyed Yank in a white suit (Kevin Anderson) is in the wrong place at the wrong time, standing in a grubby room with a gun in his hand over a dead man who robbed him of his wallet. Rosanna Arquette and older hubby John Lithgow agree to let him hitch a ride, and Arquette immediately gets their guest heated up by frolicking topless in the surf. It's only a matter of time until they ignite.

Michael Thoma's script, from a story by Roy Carlson, is low on believability and high on goofy contrivance; there's so little realistically at stake that no tension is generated.

These deficiencies make it incumbent upon director Jim McBride to goose up matters however he can, which he does through a heavy dose of colorfully seedy atmosphere.

● ●

■ W USA

1970, 114 MINS, US ◇

Dir Stuart Rosenberg   *Prod* Paul Newman, John Foreman   *Scr* Robert Stone   *Ph* Richard Moore   *Ed* Bob Wyman   *Mus* Lalo Schifrin   *Art Dir* Philip Jefferies

● Paul Newman, Joanne Woodward, Anthony Perkins, Laurence Harvey, Pat Hingle, Don Gordon (Paramount)

W USA has some serious liabilities, but for all of them it's a breath of fresh air.

Title derives from call letters of New Orleans radio station which spews forth the type propaganda regularly disciplined in real life by the Federal Communications Commission.

Script is not always lucid and director Stuart Rosenberg's pacing is numbed by needless Newman-Woodward scenes which drag pic.

The cynical profession of crowd manipulation and psychology is the primary plot line of Robert Stone's adaptation of his novel, *A Hall of Mirrors*, original title of film. Newman is a drifter with radio experience. His buddy, Laurence Harvey, a con-man mission preacher, sends him to the radio station dedicated to exposing 'welfare chiselers' and other social evils.

As Newman's star rises his affair with Woodward becomes strained; she, too, is a drifter but there was a chance of some happiness between the two.

● ●

■ WUTHERING HEIGHTS

1939, 103 MINS, US Ⓥ ⊙

Dir William Wyler   *Prod* Samuel Goldwyn   *Scr* Ben Hecht, Charles MacArthur   *Ph* Gregg Toland   *Ed* Daniel Mandell   *Mus* Alfred Newman   *Art Dir* James Basevi

● Merle Oberon, Laurence Olivier, David Niven, Flora Robson, Geraldine Fitzgerald, Donald Crisp (United Artists/Goldwyn)

Emily Bronte's novel tells a haunting tale of love and tragedy. Samuel Goldwyn's film version retains all of the grim drama of the book. It's heavy fare throughout.

Merle Oberon has two loves – a pash for stableboy Laurence Olivier and love of the worldly things David Niven can provide. After unsuccessfully goading Olivier to make something of himself, girl turns to Niven. Olivier disappears, to return several years later with a moderate fortune. Oberon keeps her smouldering passions under control, and Olivier marries Niven's sister (Geraldine Fitzgerald) for spite.

Story is unfolded through retrospect narration by Flora Robson, housekeeper in the early-Victorian mansion of Yorkshire.

Direction by William Wyler is slow and deliberate, accenting the tragic features of the piece.

□ 1939: Best B&W Cinematography.
□ Nominations: Best Picture, Director, Actor (Laurence Olivier), Supp. Actress (Geraldine Fitzgerald), Screenplay, Art Direction, Original Score

● ●

■ WUTHERING HEIGHTS

1971, 105 MINS, UK/US ◇ ◐

Dir Robert Fuest   *Prod* James H. Nicholson, Samuel Z. Arkoff   *Scr* Patrick Tilley   *Ph* John Coquillon   *Ed* Ann Chegwidden   *Mus* Michel Legrand   *Art Dir* Philip Harrison

● Anna Calder-Marshall, Timothy Dalton, Julian Glover, Ian Ogilvy, Hilary Dwyer, Judy Cornwell (American International)

Wuthering Heights is a competent, tasteful, frequently even lovely re-adaption of Emily Bronte's Gothic, mystical love story. But the brooding tension, the electric passion of two lovers compelled to an inevitable tragedy is not generated.

Anna Calder-Marshall as Catherine is quite good, giving the role a wild young animal look and spirit. Timothy Dalton is also a technically capable actor, with a dark gypsy brooding look that is appropriate for Heathcliff. But his sullen, almost sulking portrayal is often that of a hurt boy rather than a man seething with resentment and a frustrated passion, a powder keg ready to explode.

Director Robert Fuest and cameraman John Coquillon compose striking and beautiful pictures, but without creating the sort of mood and tension the film needs.

● ●

■ WUTHERING HEIGHTS

1992, 105 MINS, UK/US ◇ Ⓥ ⊙ ⊙

Dir Peter Kosminsky   *Prod* Mary Selway   *Scr* Anne Devlin   *Ph* Mike Southon   *Ed* Tony Lawson   *Mus* Ryuichi Sakamoto   *Art Dir* Brian Morris

● Juliette Binoche, Ralph Fiennes, Janet McTeer, Sophie Ward, Simon Shepherd, Simon Ward (Paramount)

UK-lensed *Wuthering Heights* is a by-the-numbers telling of the Emily Bronte classic that's as cool as a Yorkshire moor, weakened by a wobbly central perf by Gallic thesp Juliette Binoche.

Third big-screen outing of the yarn lacks the visual stylization and intense performances of the 1939 classic, and the believability of the 1970 British remake. It serves up the full work (unlike the truncated 1939 version) but misses out on atmosphere and passion.

Halting in her delivery, and with an accent that's every which way, Binoche misses the spontaneity and feeling at the heart of the twin roles. Screen newcomer Ralph Fiennes makes a good stab at the Heathcliff part, more successful in the later scenes as the embittered power player than in the early ones as the glowering bad boy.

Sprawling story, set across two generations, moves at quite a clip to get everything in. Pacing, as well as look, is more akin to an edited-down TV miniseries than a developed feature. Filmmakers seem over-bound by fidelity to the novel and unwilling to take risks: a late-on fantasy sequence of Heathcliff reunited with the dead Cathy has some of the romantic panache badly missing elsewhere.

● ●

■ W.W. AND THE DIXIE DANCEKINGS

1975, 91 MINS, US ◇

Dir John G. Avildsen   *Prod* Steve Shagan   *Scr* Thomas Rickman   *Ph* James Crabe   *Ed* Richard Halsey, Robbe Roberts   *Mus* Dave Grusin   *Art Dir* Larry Paull

● Burt Reynolds, Conny Van Dyke, Jerry Reed, Ned Beatty, James Hampton, Don Williams (20th Century-Fox)

Burt Reynolds stars as a 1950s con artist who turns straight through an odyssey with a country music band. The script establishes Reynolds as a footloose character, generating money by suave robberies of gas stations where he divides the loot with the underpaid attendants in return for their giving phony descriptions.

Sherman G. Lloyd, redneck oil magnate, concludes that a devil is amok, so he recruits Art Carney, a lawman turned fundamentalist preacher, to find the evil spirit. This plot angle alternates with Reynolds' growing attachment to the Dixie Dancekings, a c&w band headed by Jerry Reed.

● ●

X

(UK: The Man With the X-Ray Eyes)

1963, 80 MINS, US ◇ ▽
Dir Roger Corman   *Prod* Roger Corman   *Scr* Robert
Dillon, Ray Russell   *Ph* Floyd Crosby   *Ed* Anthony
Carras   *Mus* Les Baxter   *Art Dir* Daniel Haller
● Ray Milland, Diana van der Vlis, Harold J. Stone, Don
Rickles, John Hoyt (American International/Alta Vista)

Basically it's the plot where the scientist tampers with the unknown and is severely punished in the end. Ray Milland is a doctor who has devised a drug that he thinks will allow men's eyes to see infinitely more.

He tries it on himself when he is refused a grant to continue experiments on animals. He at first is put out of commission by a blinding light but then can see inside human tissue and through clothes. This permits him to visit a party where the women are nude to him.

Things get worse as he kills a friend inadvertently, forcing the doctor to hide out in a carnival as a mindreader. A girl who believes in him tries to help and they go off to work on some antidote.

There are many interesting comic, dramatic and philosophical ideas are touched on but treated only on the surface. However, director Roger Corman keeps this moving and Ray Milland is competent as the doomed man. Special effects on his prism-eye world, called Spectarama, are good if sometimes repetitive.

••••••••••••••••••••••••••••••

XANADU

1980, 92 MINS, US ◇ ▽ ⊙
Dir Robert Greenwald   *Prod* Lawrence Gordon
Scr Richard Christian Danus, Marc Reid Rubel   *Ph* Victor
J. Kemper   *Ed* Dennis Virkler   *Mus* Barry DeVorzon
Art Dir John W. Corso
● Olivia Newton-John, Gene Kelly, Michael Beck
(Universal)

Xanadu is truly a stupendously bad film whose only salvage is the music. Olivia Newton-John plays a muse, first seen with her eight sisters painted on a wall. Suddenly, they all come alive, with glowing stuff all around them, singing and zipping hither and yon, apparently looking for a script that will never be found.

Newton-John's task is to inspire Michael Beck in his work as an artist. For this she stops glowing and he thinks she's a real girl, despite the sun dress she wears with roller skates and rags around both ankles.

But love is threatening and Newton-John decides it's best if she goes back into the painting on the wall, so she starts glowing again and bids Beck farewell. But he gets up a head of steam and skates into the wall after her and winds up somewhere near Mount Olympus.

••••••••••••••••••••••••••••••

X, Y AND ZEE

See: Zee & Co.

••••••••••••••••••••••••••••••

YAKUZA, THE

1975, 112 MINS, US ◇ ▽ ⊙
Dir Sydney Pollack   *Prod* Sydney Pollack   *Scr* Paul
Schrader, Robert Towne   *Ph* Okazaki Kozo, Duke
Callaghan   *Ed* Fredric Steinkamp, Thomas Stamford,
Don Guidice   *Mus* Dave Grusin   *Art Dir* Stephen
Grimes
● Robert Mitchum, Ken Takakura, Brian Keith, Herb
Edelman, Richard Jordan, Kishi Keiko (Warner)

The Yakuza is a confused and diffused film which bites off more than it can artfully chew. Robert Mitchum stars as a private eye returning to Japan to unravel some international crime matters, as well as his long-ago love affair.

The result is an uneasy and incohesive combination of an oriental Mafia story overlaid on a formula international business swindle, mixed up with a 20-years-later update of *Sayonara*.

Mitchum is hired by old World War II army buddy Brian Keith, now a successful shipping executive, to rescue daughter Lee Chirillo from some Japanese hoods holding her for an alleged default on a business deal.

Ken Takakura, who owes Mitchum a favor from a generation back, must honor the request to infiltrate the mob.

••••••••••••••••••••••••••••••

YANGTSE INCIDENT

(US: Battle Hell)

1957, 113 MINS, UK ▽
Dir Michael Anderson   *Prod* Herbert Wilcox   *Scr* Eric
Ambler   *Ph* Gordon Diner   *Ed* Basil Warren
Mus Leighton Lucas   *Art Dir* Ralph Brinton
● Richard Todd, William Hartnell, Akim Tamiroff,
Donald Houston, Keye Luke, Sophie Stewart (British Lion)

Story [based on the book by Laurence Earl] is of the *Amethyst*, which, battered though not beaten, broke the Chinese Communist blockade and rejoined the British fleet. The *Amethyst* is shown sailing up the Yangtse, headed for Nanking on a lawful mission delivering supplies to the British Embassy. Suddenly, without warning, the Red shore batteries open fire and the frigate, after a heavy engagement, is grounded in the mud.

All his attempts to persuade the British to issue an apology for 'unprovoked aggression' are resolutely turned down and both sides play a waiting game until the British commander decides to run for it.

Vivid battle scenes have been magnificently handled. The on-board scenes are genuine enough too, as the *Amethyst* was reprieved from the breaker's yard to allow producer Herbert Wilcox to use it in the film.

There's a high standard of acting by an all-round cast, led by Richard Todd as the commander who takes over after the captain is killed in the first engagement.

••••••••••••••••••••••••••••••

YANK AT OXFORD, A

1938, 100 MINS, UK
Dir Jack Conway   *Prod* Michael Balcon   *Scr* Malcolm
Stuart Boylan, Walter Ferris, George Oppenheimer
Ph Harold Rosson   *Ed* Margaret Booth, Charles Frend
Mus Hubert Bath, Edward Ward
● Robert Taylor, Maureen O'Sullivan, Lionel Barrymore,
Vivien Leigh, Edmund Gwenn, Griffith Jones (M-G-M)

Robert Taylor brings back from Oxford an entertaining rah-rah film which is full of breathless quarter-mile dashes, heartbreaking boat race finishes and surefire sentiment – Metro's first British-made film under Hollywood supervision and with Hollywood principals and director.

Some of the opening sequennces were made on the west coast and pasted to what was shot in England. Taylor, Lionel Barrymore, Maureen O'Sullivan, Harold Rosson, cameraman, and Jack Conway and his directorial crew crossed the Atlantic. Their efforts were supported by British film and stage players, and Michael Balcon, formerly production head of Gaumont-British, acted as producer.

It is reported that the film players never were permitted within the sacred precincts of Oxford university which is unimportant from a picture viewpoint as the architectural reproductions have been carefully and effectively photographed.

What Conway has caught is the humor of student life at the university. This is the background for Taylor's adventures, the wall against which a cocky Yank bounces his somewhat enlarged head, eventually regaining his poise a better and tamed human being. [Original story by Leon Gordon, Sidney Gilliatt and Michael Hogan, based on an idea by John Monk Saunders.]

Teamed to these sometimes hilarious adventures is a sentimental story which tells of Taylor's liking for O'Sullivan, whose brother is a rival in undergraduate affairs.

Edmund Gwenn as the Dean of Cardinal College, one of the Oxford group, does a standout. Griffith Jones is an English boy, and gives a sincere and earnest performance. O'Sullivan and her diction fit nicely into ensemble, and Vivien Leigh, as a college vamp, has looks and a way about her.

••••••••••••••••••••••••••••••

YANKEE DOODLE DANDY

1942, 126 MINS, US ▽ ⊙
Dir Michael Curtiz   *Prod* Hal B. Wallis (exec.)
Scr Robert Buckner, Edmund Joseph   *Ph* James Wong
Howe   *Ed* George Amy   *Mus* Ray Heindorf (arr)
Art Dir Carl Jules Weyl
● James Cagney, Joan Leslie, Walter Huston, Richard
Whorf, Irene Manning, Jeanne Cagney (Warner)

Yankee Doodle Dandy is rah-rah, no matter how you slice it. It's a tribute to a grand American gentleman of the theatre – George M. Cohan – whose life and songs are glorified by Warner Bros; and it's a tribute, perhaps even more so, to all show business.

James Cagney does a Cohan of which the original George M. might well be proud.

That [original story writer] Robert Buckner, and his co-scripter, Edmund Joseph, jazzed up a little of the latter-day chronology is beside the point. That Cohan was cocky and conceited as the kid star of *Peck's Bad Boy*, in which he clicked at 13; that he remained close to Jerry Cohan, Nellie Cohan and sister Josie (so well played by the star's real-life sister, Jeanne Cagney); that his string of successes never upset this lovely and loving picture, are all part of a human, appealing story of one of the great theatrical families of all times.

☐ 1942: Best Actor (James Cagney), Scoring of a Musical Picture, Sound Recording.
☐ Nominations: Best Picture, Director, Supp. Actor (Walter Huston), Original Story, Editing

••••••••••••••••••••••••••••••

YANKEE IN KING ARTHUR'S COURT, A

See: A Connecticut Yankee in King Arthur's Court

••••••••••••••••••••••••••••••

YANK IN LONDON, A

See: I Live in Grosvenor Square

••••••••••••••••••••••••••••••

YANK IN THE R.A.F., A

1941, 97 MINS, US ▽
Dir Henry King   *Prod* Darryl F. Zanuck   *Scr* Darrell
Ware, Karl Tunberg   *Ph* Leon Shamroy   *Ed* Barbara
McLean   *Mus* Alfred Newman (dir.)   *Art Dir* Richard
Day, James Basevi

● Tyrone Power, Betty Grable, John Sutton, Reginald Gardiner, Donald Stuart, Morton Lowry (20th Century-Fox)

Picture neatly mixes the adventures of cocky and carefree Tyrone Power, former airline pilot, with the inner workings and flights of the RAF squadrons during the hectic times of the German blitz against the Low countries and France. Producer Darryl F. Zanuck (who also authored the original as 'Melville Crossman') sidesteps overloading the picture with flying sequences and bombing expeditions [photographed in England by Ronald Neame, Jack Whitehead and Otto Kanturek; directed by Herbert Mason].

In flying a training ship to Canada, Power enlists as pilot to ferry bombers to England. On his first trip, he meets former sweetheart (Betty Grable) a Texas girl performing in a night club and member of the ambulance reserve. Power pursues his former attention, and enlists in the RAF for fighter duty.

Power clicks solidly as the happy-go-lucky American pilot sure of his abilities with both planes and women. He handles the role with a lightly nonchalant attitude which will catch wide audience attention. Grable grooves excellently as the girl who fully realizes Power's inconsistencies, but finally breaks down.

☐ 1941: Nomination: Best Special Effects

■ YANKS

1979, 141 MINS, UK ◇ Ⓥ ⊙

Dir John Schlesinger *Prod* Joseph Janni, Lester Persky *Scr* Colin Welland, Walter Bernstein *Ph* Dick Bush *Ed* Jim Clark *Mus* Richard Rodney Bennett *Art Dir* Brian Morris

● Richard Gere, Lisa Eichhorn, Vanessa Redgrave, William Devane, Rachel Roberts, Annie Ross (CIP/Universal)

Director John Schlesinger has done a beautiful job with both cast and craft in *Yanks*, a multiple love story set in England in World War II. Yet little that's exciting ever happens in the picture.

The British director, working with his own and the personal recollections of writers Colin Welland [original story writer] and Walter Bernstein, vividly recreates the atmosphere in a small English village inundated by thousands of American troops prepping for the invasion of Europe.

At one end of the extreme, Vanessa Redgrave and William Devane struggle to maintain a platonic friendship while both are deprived of their spouses. At the other, Chick Vennera and Wendy Morgan rush to bed immediately, with little initial concern for what lies beyond the war.

The six lovers and both parents are played excellently and Schlesinger and crew have created an extravagantly authentic period setting.

■ YEARLING, THE

1946, 134 MINS, US ◇ Ⓥ ⊙

Dir Clarence Brown *Prod* Sidney Franklin *Scr* Paul Osborn *Ph* Charles Rosher, Leonard Smith, Arthur Arling *Ed* Harold F. Kress *Mus* Herbert Stothart *Art Dir* Cedric Gibbons, Paul Groesse

● Gregory Peck, Jane Wyman, Claude Jarman Jr, Chill Wills, Forrest Tucker, June Lockhart (M-G-M)

Marjorie Kinnan Rawlings' 1938 Pulitzer prizewinning novel is the heart-warming story of good earth, family ties and the love of the 11-year-old Jody Baxter for the faun which he is compelled to put out of his life as it becomes a yearling.

The Florida scrub country is the locale of the Baxters, and the story focuses on Gregory Peck and Jane Wyman in the fight for their very existence, while raising meagre patches of crops and also their offspring Jody (Claude Jarman Jr). The lad becomes a man, for all his meagre years, in a great love and effort to ward off destruction of his pet yearling, albeit it be at the kindly hands of his parents.

All done in a minor key, the underplaying is sometimes too static but, just as the interest lags, director Clarence Brown injects another highlight. The underlying power is impressive.

☐ 1946: Best Color Cinematography, Art Direction, Honorary (Claude Jarman Jr, outstanding child actor).

☐ Nominations: Best Picture, Director, Actor (Gregory Peck), Actress (Jane Wyman), Editing

■ YEAR MY VOICE BROKE, THE

1987, 103 MINS, AUSTRALIA ◇ Ⓥ ⊙

Dir John Duigan *Prod* George Miller, Doug Mitchell, Terry Hayes *Scr* John Duigan *Ph* Geoff Burton *Ed* Neil Thumpston *Mus* Christine Woodruff (co-ord.) *Art Dir* Roger Ford

● Noah Taylor, Loene Carmen, Ben Mendelsohn, Graeme Blundell, Lynette Curran, Bruce Spence (Kennedy Miller)

Setting is a small country town (pic was shot in Braidwood, NSW) in 1962. Danny (Noah Taylor) and Freya (Loene Carmen) have been friends from childhood: his parents run the local pub, hers the local cafe. Danny is confused and troubled because Freya, though she's the same age he is, is maturing far more rapidly. She falls heavily for Trev (Ben Mendelsohn), an older, hyperactive football coach.

Things turn out badly: Freya gets pregnant, Trev gets into trouble with the law. Danny tries to help his friends, but an old scandal involving Freya's mother, who died giving birth to her, surfaces causing more distress.

All of this is handled by John Duigan, who penned the original screenplay, with insight and under-statement. The characters are memorable ones, and beautifully played by the three young newcomers, with Noah Taylor especially effective as the lovesick Danny. Supporting roles are played by a fine roster of familiar Aussie thesps.

■ YEAR OF LIVING DANGEROUSLY, THE

1982, 114 MINS, AUSTRALIA/US ◇ Ⓥ ⊙

Dir Peter Weir *Prod* Jim McElroy *Scr* David Williamson, Peter Weir, C.J. Koch *Ph* Russell Boyd *Ed* Bill Anderson *Mus* Maurice Jarre *Art Dir* Herbert Pinter

● Mel Gibson, Sigourney Weaver, Linda Hunt, Michael Murphy, Bill Kerr, Noel Ferrier (McElroy & McElroy/M-G-M)

Peter Weir's *The Year of Living Dangerously*, is a $6 million adaptation of Christopher Koch's novel, set in Indonesia in 1965 in the turbulent months leading to the fall of the Sukarno government.

Mel Gibson limns a young Australian journalist on his first posting as a foreign correspondent. Wide-eyed and innocent, he is befriended by an astute Chinese-Australian cameraman, a dwarf who seeks to manipulate people as deftly as he handles shadow puppets.

Here is an astonishing feat of acting by New Yorker Linda Hunt, cast by Weir because he could not locate a short male actor to fit the bill. A bizarre, yet touching, romantic triangle develops between Gibson, Hunt, and Sigourney Weaver as a British Embassy official.

Having laid the groundwork, Weir hits the action button. Gibson learns that the Communists are bringing in arms for a coup against Sukarno and in broadcasting the story blows a confidence from Weaver, who rejects him.

Filming in the Philippines, and then Sydney, where the crew was forced to repair after receiving threats from the Islamic community, Weir and his crew expertly recreate the squalor, poverty, noise, heat and emotion of the pressure cooker that was Indonesia in 1965.

☐ 1983: Best Supp. Actress (Linda Hunt)

■ YEAR OF THE COMET

1992, 89 MINS, US ◇ Ⓥ ⊙

Dir Peter Yates *Prod* Peter Yates, Nigel Wooll *Scr* William Goldman *Ph* Roger Pratt *Ed* Ray Lovejoy *Mus* Hummie Mann *Art Dir* Anthony Pratt

● Penelope Ann Miller, Tim Daly, Louis Jourdan, Art Malik, Ian Richardson, Ian McNeice (Castle Rock)

Harvested from the same field as *Romancing the Stone*, this wine-soaked comedy-adventure never really ferments, in part due to a lack of chemistry between its romantic leads. William Goldman's first original script since *Butch Cassidy and the Sundance Kid* and his first collaboration with director Peter Yates since the 1972 *Hot Rock*, the film's problems begin with its title, a reference to the vintage of an invaluable 150-year-old bottle of wine that sounds more like a sci-fi thriller.

That bottle brings together a wine auctioneer's daughter (Penelope Ann Miller), who discovers it, and a Texan millionaire's troubleshooter (Tim Daly), assigned to bring it back to his boss. Unfortunately, Miller has the bad luck of finding the bottle in a Scottish castle where a trio of researchers, led by Louis Jourdan, are inconveniently torturing a scientist to obtain a secret formula, putting them in pursuit of the bottle.

Miller finds herself stranded by Goldman's screenplay, in which her character is a little bit of everything (spinster, repressed, ambitious) yet nothing in particular. Daly doesn't fare much better as a dapper leading man, who proves full of surprises.

■ YEAR OF THE DRAGON

1985, 136 MINS, US ◇ Ⓥ ⊙

Dir Michael Cimino *Prod* Dino De Laurentiis *Scr* Oliver Stone, Michael Cimino *Ph* Alex Thomson *Ed* Francoise Bonnot *Mus* David Mansfield *Art Dir* Wolf Kroeger

● Mickey Rourke, John Lone, Ariane, Leonard Termo, Ray Barry, Caroline Kava (De Laurentiis)

Year of the Dragon [based on the novel by Robert Daley] is never as important as director Michael Cimino thinks it is, but there's a fair amount of solid action and gunplay, all set securely in the intricate, mysterious enigma of New York's Chinatown and its ties to worldwide drug-dealing.

Unquestionably, Cimino's eye for detail and insistence thereon has paid off in his impressive recreation of Chinatown at producer Dino De Laurentiis' studios in North Carolina. Crammed with an array of interesting characters, including the extras in the background, *Dragon* brims with authenticity.

Assigned to Chinatown to clear up a problem of murderous youth gangs, Mickey Rourke quickly proves to be one of those lone renegade cops that fiction favors more than real-life. Beyond the teen toughs, Rourke wants to undo a criminal system rooted in a culture for thousands of years.

Beyond the color and the corpses, though, Cimino fails to focus on an idea and stick with it. He ends up playing with significant thoughts in between awkward lessons in Chinese history, losing most of them as they filter through half-baked resentments Rourke has left over from the Vietnam war. Performances, though, are generally excellent and *Dragon* certainly never drags.

■ YEAR OF THE GUN

1991, 111 MINS, US ◇ Ⓥ ⊙

Dir John Frankenheimer *Prod* Edward R. Pressman *Scr* David Ambrose *Ph* Blasco Giuarto *Ed* Lee Percy *Mus* Bill Conti *Art Dir* Aurelio Crugnola

● Andrew McCarthy, Valeria Golino, Sharon Stone, John Pankow, Mattia Sbragia, George Murcell (Pressman)

Year of the Gun is a competent but routine thriller [based on Michael Mewshaw's book] about a young American novelist in 1978 Rome who accidentally hits upon a terrorist kidnaping plot.

Andrew McCarthy plays an expatriate US journalist who's doing quite nicely in Rome with a rich Italian g.f. (Valeria Golino) and the insistent attentions of a beautiful and nervy American photojournalist (Sharon Stone). Trouble is, Stone wants in on a book she believes he's writing about the Red Brigades terrorists, and McCarthy knows he can't pull the book off unless it stays a secret. Stone leaks it to a mutual friend (John Pankow), a university prof who leaks it to the Red Brigades, and suddenly the two Yanks are imperiled.

Stone adds some interest as the provocative photographer, though one never knows what makes her character such a maniacal careerist. McCarthy is merely servicable in the lead. Director John Frankenheimer and cinematographer Blasco Giuarto do a standout job with the taut, hysterical action scenes.

● ●

■ **YEARS WITHOUT DAYS**
See: Castle on the Hudson

● ●

■ **YELLOW BALLOON, THE**

1953, 80 MINS, UK
Dir J. Lee Thompson   *Prod* Victor Skutezky   *Scr* Anne Burnaby, J. Lee Thompson   *Ph* Gilbert Taylor   *Ed* Richard Best   *Mus* Philip Green   *Art Dir* Robert Jones
● Andrew Ray, Kathleen Ryan, Kenneth More, Bernard Lee, William Sylvester, Sydney James (Associated British/Marble Arch)

This British pic is a depressing study of an innocent child who falls into the clutches of a modern Fagin and is forced to steal from his own parents before being used as a decoy in an holdup which leads to murder.

J. Lee Thompson directs, with entire dramatic content focussed on the youngster (Andrew Ray). The boy plays the part almost on a single key but his almost static expression captures the story's spirit.

With most of the screen time allotted to the youngster, the adult cast members have comparatively minor roles. The roles of the kid's parents are effectively sustained by Kathleen Ryan and Kenneth More, while William Sylvester does a smooth job as the crook. Lesser roles are distinctively filled, with Sydney James giving a rich performance as a cockney trader.

● ●

■ **YELLOW CANARY, THE**

1943, 95 MINS, UK
Dir Herbert Wilcox   *Prod* Herbert Wilcox   *Scr* Miles Malleson, DeWitt Bodeen   *Ph* Max Green
● Anna Neagle, Richard Greene, Nova Pilbeam, Albert Lieven, Margaret Rutherford (Imperator)

Direction, cast, production and camerawork are so good it is a pity the suspensive story [from an original by D.M. Bower] is not on the same plane of excellence. There is smart comedy dialog and plenty of action throughout. It has a 'mystery' start with red herring trails that lead up blind alleys, necessitating the return each time to a new start. The result is an overplus of the aforesaid 'mystery'.

Anna Neagle plays Sally Maitland, daughter of an aristocratic British family. She has achieved notoriety for her pre-war association with the Nazis. Public antagonism to her is so violent that she is practically forced to leave Britain. It is a role altogether different from her previous film appearances. Her co-star is Richard Greene, and principal support comes

from Nova Pilbeam, Lucie Mannheim and Albert Lieven.

● ●

■ **YELLOW CANARY, THE**

1963, 93 MINS, US
Dir Buzz Kulik   *Prod* Maury Dexter   *Scr* Rod Serling   *Ph* Floyd Crosby   *Ed* Jodie Copelan   *Mus* Kenyon Hopkins   *Art Dir* Walter Simmonds
● Pat Boone, Barbara Eden, Steve Forrest, Jack Klugman, Jesse White, Steve Harris (20th Century-Fox)

Hero of the piece is Pat Boone, a surly singing idol whose apparently loose ways have him on the brink of divorce with his wife (Barbara Eden), who remains only for the sake of their infant. The baby is suddenly kidnapped and three people are needlessly murdered by the kidnapper, who turns out to be one of Boone's sycophants, his psychotic bodyguard (Steve Forrest).

Rod Serling's screenplay, from Whit Masterson's novel, *Evil Come, Evil Go*, is reasonably strong in dramatic anatomy, but limp and fuzzy in character definition. The characters are thrust at the audience, with little or no attempt to illustrate the nature of their odd dispositions toward society and each other.

Boone warbles several old standards pleasantly. Eden is her usual curvaceous self, and gets off a number of very convincing screams and shrieks. Forrest is an okay heavy, Jack Klugman likable as a frustrated gendarme. Kenyon Hopkins has composed a racy, pulsating score to underline the action.

● ●

■ **YELLOW ROLLS-ROYCE, THE**

1964, 122 MINS, UK ◇
Dir Anthony Asquith   *Prod* Anatole de Grunwald   *Scr* Terence Rattigan   *Ph* Jack Hildyard   *Ed* Frank Clarke   *Mus* Riz Ortolani
● Rex Harrison, Jeanne Moreau, Shirley MacLaine, George C. Scott, Ingrid Bergman, Omar Sharif (M-G-M)

With a sizzling international cast, the team of Anatole de Grunwald, Anthony Asquith and Terence Rattigan have produced a sleek piece of entertainment in *The Yellow Rolls-Royce*. It is handsomely tinted, lushly lensed and though leisurely in its approach, this has style, humor and some effective thesping.

Film consists of three separate anecdotes, linked only by ownership of the elegant Phantom II Rolls-Royce auto.

First one concerns Lord Frinton (Rex Harrison), a Foreign Office big shot who buys the car as an anni gift for his wife (Jeanne Moreau) and discovers her and a Foreign Office minion (Edmund Purdom) in a passionate embrace in its back seat.

Much mileage later, in the 1930s, the car is bought in Italy by gangster George C. Scott as a present for his current moll, hatcheck gal Shirley MacLaine. The dame falls for a street photographer (Alain Delon) and again the comfortable, accommodating back seat of the Rolls is pressed into service for l'amour.

Finally, in 1942, the Phantom II is acquired by Ingrid Bergman playing a hectoring American woman. Hitler is attacking Yugoslavia and she becomes involved when she finds that she has smuggled an archpatriot (Omar Sharif) across the border.

● ●

■ **YELLOWSTONE KELLY**

1959, 91 MINS, US ◇
Dir Gordon Douglas   *Prod* [uncredited]   *Scr* Burt Kennedy   *Ph* Carl Guthrie   *Ed* William Ziegler   *Mus* Howard Jackson   *Art Dir* Stanley Fleischer
● Clint Walker, Edward Byrnes, John Russell, Ray Danton, Andra Martin, Claude Akins (Warner)

Yellowstone Kelly is a well-made western.
The story [from the book by Clay Fisher] concerns a fabled fur trapper, Kelly, who is on

good terms with the Sioux Indians. He refuses to help the US Cavalry's punitive expedition of 1876 but ultimately has to help the arrogant white men after they have been trounced by the righteous red men.

Director Gordon Douglas moves the story along with a speed sufficient to cover up weak plot points and extracts some solid characterizations not implicit in the script: Clint Walker, as Kelly the trapper, is a laconic, gargantuan woodsman: John Russell is a magnetically powerful and believable chief; Ray Danton's a handsome swine of a brave; Andra Martin is fetchingly and helplessly lovely as the Indian girl and Edward Byrnes enlists sympathy as the tenderfoot.

● ●

■ **YELLOW SUBMARINE**

1968, 89 MINS, UK ◇ ⓥ ⊙
Dir George Dunning   *Prod* Al Brodax   *Scr* Lee Minoff, Al Brodax, Jack Mendelsohn, Erich Segal   *Mus* The Beatles   *Art Dir* Heinz Edelmann
● (Apple/King/Subafilms)

This is a full length animated cartoon in which the prime factor is the appearance of the Beatles in caricature form. Here are all the ingredients of a novel entertainment.

Story consists of a fantastic voyage in a yellow submarine thru sky and sea, manned by the skipper, and The Beatles, to Pepperland where the inhabitants are up against thugs known as the Blue Meanies.

Time travel, science fiction, outer space, monsters, war and their own idiom of pop music are all taken for a ride in figments of fevered imaginations during which the Beatles come up against some odd specimens and situations.

The Beatles' flat Merseyside tones make good contrast to the surrounding frenzy.

Dialog is mostly puns and throwaway gags. It remains deliberately corny at times and never ventures out of its depth in flirtations with time, space and philosophy.

Unlike Disney the film makes no concession to sentiment. Characters are mostly matter-of-fact, grotesque and anti-heroic and tend to be harsh, angular and intro'd for shock effect rather than any winsome qualities.

● ●

■ **YENTL**

1983, 134 MINS, US ◇ ⓥ ⊙
Dir Barbra Streisand   *Prod* Barbra Streisand, Rusty Lemorande   *Scr* Jack Rosenthal, Barbra Streisand   *Ph* David Watkin   *Ed* Terry Rawlings   *Mus* Michel Legrand   *Art Dir* Roy Walker
● Barbra Streisand, Mandy Patinkin, Amy Irving, Nehemiah Persoff, Steven Hill, Allan Corduner (Barwood/United Artists)

Based on a short story by Isaac Bashevis Singer, *Yentl* tells the tale of a young Eastern European woman, circa 1904, who disguises herself as a boy in order to pursue her passion for studying holy scripture, an endeavor restricted exclusively to men in orthodox Jewish culture.

Moving from her native village and passing as a pubescent boy, Yentl has no problem in the scholarly world, but tragi-comic results stem from the romantic situation her presence creates. Befriended by her brash, attractive fellow student Avigdor, wonderfully played by Mandy Patinkin, Yentl falls in love with him.

When Avigdor is prevented from marrying his lovely fiancee Hadass (a china doll Amy Irving) through a technicality of religious law, Avigdor pushes Yentl to marry Hadass in his stead.

Songs by Michel Legrand, with lyrics by Alan and Marilyn Bergman, have been carefully planned as interior monologs for Yentl.

In league with ace cinematographer David Watkin, Streisand has created a fine-looking

period piece, working on Czech locations and in English studios.
☐ 1983: Best Original Song Score.
☐ Nominations: Best Supp. Actress (Amy Irving), Art Direction, Song ('Papa, Can You Hear Me?', 'The Way He Makes Me Feel')

....

■ YIELD TO THE NIGHT
(US: Blonde Sinner)

1956, 100 MINS, UK ⓦ
Dir J. Lee Thompson   *Scr* John Cresswell, Joan Henry   *Ph* Gilbert Taylor   *Ed* Richard Best   *Mus* Ray Martin   *Art Dir* Robert Jones
● Diana Dors, Yvonne Mitchell, Michael Craig, Marie Ney, Geoffrey Keen, Liam Redmond (Associated British)

Diana Dors plays a heavy dramatic role in *Yield to the Night*, which calls for a drastic de-glamorizing treatment.

The actual killing which leads the star to the death cell is depicted before the credit titles appear on the screen, but the events which led her to shoot at point blank range at the woman who forced her lover to suicide are shown in a series of flashbacks.

Main footage is concentrated inside the condemned cell and the script illustrates the anguish of mind of the girl, the wardresses who guard her night and day, the members of her family and the husband whom she deserted.

The script [from a novel by Joan Henry] succeeds in maintaining strong suspense.

In the main, Dors rises to the occasion and shows up as a dramatic actress better than anticipated. Yvonne Mitchell strikes the right sympathetic note as one of the wardresses, Michael Craig reveals a good presence as the lover and Marie Ney shows proper dignity and restraint as the prison governor.

....

■ YOLANDA AND THE THIEF

1945, 108 MINS, US ◇ ⓦ ⊙
Dir Vincente Minnelli   *Prod* Arthur Freed   *Scr* Irving Brecher   *Ph* Charles Rosher   *Ed* George White   *Mus* Lennie Hayton (dir.)   *Art Dir* Cedric Gibbons, Jack Martin Smith
● Fred Astaire, Lucille Bremer, Frank Morgan, Mildred Natwick, Mary Nash, Leon Ames (M-G-M)

Metro has a musical story of virtue and the Divine in *Yolanda and the Thief*, but the result is not all it might have been. Arthur Freed produced with lavishness, and the casting, topped by Fred Astaire, Lucille Bremer and Frank Morgan, has an eye towards marquee values, but the basic yarn doesn't lend itself toward the screen.

This is the story of a Latin-American heiress who, after being brought up in a convent, assumes charge of her fortune upon coming of age. Her childhood, naturally one that saw her sheltered from the outer world, makes her easy prey for a fraud that a young American and his elderly confederate would play upon her to relieve her of her millions.

There's an idea in this yarn, but it only suggests itself. It becomes too immersed in its musical background, and the story is too leisurely in pace. A musical production number attempts to be symbolic but only serves to waste too many moments of the over-long film. And the story itself, the way it's done, strains credibility.

....

■ YOU CAN'T SLEEP HERE
See: I Was a Male War Bride

....

■ YOU CAN'T TAKE IT WITH YOU

1938, 126 MINS, US ⓦ ⊙
Dir Frank Capra   *Prod* Frank Capra   *Scr* Robert Riskin   *Ph* Joseph Walker   *Ed* Gene Havlick   *Mus* Dimitri Tiomkin   *Art Dir* Stephen Goosson, Lionel Banks
● Jean Arthur, Lionel Barrymore, James Stewart, Edward Arnold, Mischa Auer, Ann Miller (Columbia)

A strong hit on Broadway, *You Can't Take It With You* [by George S. Kaufman and Moss Hart] is also a big hit on film. This is one of the highest priced plays to be bought in history, Columbia having taken the rights for $200,000. Production brought negative cost to around a reported $1.2 million.

The comedy is wholly American, wholesome, homespun, human, appealing, and touching in turn. The wackier comedy side contrasts with a somewhat serious, philosophical note which may seem a little overstressed on occasion.

The Vanderhoff tribe is played appealingly but screwily, the antics of the polyglot combination of grandpa, daughter, son-in-law, grandchildren and hangers-on, including a meek adding machine operator turned inventor, and a ballet teacher, being basically for creation of fun.

The romance between James Stewart and Jean Arthur is the keystone of the comedy. Other comedy elements are registered at the expense of Edward Arnold, the stuff-shirt banker, and his wife, played excellently by Mary Forbes. The link that is formed between the modest, homey Vanderhoff coterie and the very rich Kirbys, created principally through the romance of the Arthur-Stewart pair, is a bit unbelievable but for the purposes of entertainment has license.

Arthur acquits herself creditably. Stewart is not a strong romantic lead opposite her but does satisfactorily in the love scenes. Others are tops from Lionel Barrymore down.
☐ 1938: Best Picture, Director.
☐ Nominations: Best Supp. Actress (Spring Byington), Screenplay, Cinematography, Editing, Sound

....

■ YOU LIGHT UP MY LIFE

1977, 90 MINS, US ◇ ⓦ
Dir Joseph Brooks   *Prod* Joseph Brooks   *Scr* Joseph Brooks   *Ph* Eric Saarinen   *Ed* Lynzee Klingman   *Mus* Joseph Brook   *Art Dir* Tom Rasmussen
● Didi Conn, Joe Silver, Michael Zaslow, Stephan Nathan, Melanie Mayron, Amy Letterman (Brooks)

You Light Up My Life has all the virtues and all the liabilities of a low-budget effort. There's an earnest sincerity in the story of washed-up juvenile comedienne Didi Conn working out an adult identity. There's also a lot of cutesy, cornball, convenient and compacted plotting.

As the burnt-out child of stage-father Joe Silver (both of them doing very well in characterization), she is headed for a dull marriage to Stephan Nathan when film producer Michael Zaslow sponsors her first breakthrough into the field of pop music. She falls for Zaslow, but his mind is on his own career.

Along the way, there are some 'slices-of-life' scenes involving the teleblurb business (whence came producer-director Joseph Brooks), Jewish weddings, and also interactions between Conn and the men in her life which border on treacle. Production credits are okay.

....

■ YOU'LL NEVER GET RICH

1941, 87 MINS, US ⓦ ⊙
Dir Sidney Lanfield   *Prod* Samuel Bischoff   *Scr* Michael Fessier, Ernest Pagano   *Ph* Phillip Tannura   *Ed* Otto Meyer   *Mus* Morris Stoloff (dir.)
● Fred Astaire, Rita Hayworth, Robert Benchley, John Hubbard, Osa Massen, Frieda Inescort (Columbia)

Story has Fred Astaire as a stager of a musical show for producer Robert Benchley. Latter, in making a pitch for affections of Rita Hayworth, gets in a jam with his wife, and has Astaire get him out of the predicament. Girl, with a crush on Astaire, is somewhat disillusioned by the proceedings, and gives him the heave-ho.

When Astaire is inducted into the selective

service camp, Benchley makes a deal to conduct rehearsals and stage a show for the boys – in order to obtain services of Astaire in putting it on. There's plenty of serious and humorous by-play around the camp, with Astaire a permanent resident of the guardhouse, but it all works out when the show finally goes on.

Script is studded with humorous lines and situations, and despite a somewhat familiar ring it's all sufficiently refurbished by Sidney Lanfield's direction to get over in good style. Lanfield keeps things moving consistently, and the song and dance routines are neatly spotted.
☐ 1941: Nominations: Best Scoring of a Musical Picture, Song ('Since I Kissed My Baby Goodbye')

....

■ YOUNG AND WILLING
See: The Wild and the Willing

....

■ YOUNG BESS

1953, 111 MINS, US ◇
Dir George Sidney   *Prod* Sidney Franklin   *Scr* Jan Lustig, Arthur Wimperis   *Ph* Charles Rosher   *Ed* Ralph E. Winters   *Mus* Miklos Rozsa   *Art Dir* Cedric Gibbons, Urie McCleary
● Jean Simmons, Stewart Granger, Deborah Kerr, Charles Laughton, Kay Walsh, Guy Rolfe (M-G-M)

Margaret Irwin's fine book on the life and times of the girl who was to become England's Queen Elizabeth has been made into a remarkably engrossing motion picture. *Young Bess* is a romantic drama told against a Tudor setting. It is a human story, sensitively written, directed and played. Romance phases are rich in emotion; court intrigue conjures suspense, and there is a suggestion of action throughout.

The four-star bracketing of Jean Simmons, in the title role; Stewart Granger, the dashing, heroic Lord Admiral, Thomas Seymour; Deborah Kerr, the beautiful Catherine Parr; and Charles Laughton, the gross, pompous Henry VIII, insures splendid trouping.

Main story gets underway after opening sequence, a gem in itself, sets the stage for a flashback to the unhappy childhood of young Bess. It is not until gracious Catherine becomes queen that young Bess, now 15, takes up a more or less permanent residence in the palace, finding love and happiness with the queen and her little stepbrother, the sickly Edward. When Henry dies and the queen marries the Lord Admiral, young Bess conceals her own infatuation for the dashing hero, but her feelings are found out and used by the evil Ned Seymour, the admiral's brother.

Miklos Rozsa's music score is fine, never once intruding too strongly on a dramatic scene, and it is full of little identifying melodies for the humorous touches in the script.
☐ 1953: Nominations: Best Color Costume Design, Color Art Direction

....

■ YOUNG BILLY YOUNG

1969, 89 MINS, US ◇
Dir Burt Kennedy   *Prod* Max Youngstein   *Scr* Burt Kennedy   *Ph* Harry Stradling Jr   *Ed* Otho Lovering   *Mus* Shelly Manne   *Art Dir* Stan Jolley
● Robert Mitchum, Angie Dickinson, Robert Walker, David Carradine, Jack Kelly, John Anderson (United Artists)

Standard western plot undergoes generally good polishing in this production, costarring Robert Mitchum and Angie Dickinson. Plenty of gunplay heightens appeal and Robert Walker joins stars in turning in realistic performances.

Burt Kennedy, who directed and scripted

[from the novel *Who Rides with Wyatt* by Will Henry], could have tightened film for better effect. His climax lacks the suspense it should have carried and confrontation misses. On the whole, however, film progresses satisfactorily.

Narrative unfolds mostly in Lordsburg, where Mitchum takes on a marshal's job after he learns that his quarry may be found there. Walker, an ornery youngster who wants his way, is with him, leaving Mitchum to his own devices until he discovers that a dozen gunmen have arrived to mow down the marshal.

● ●

■ **YOUNGBLOOD**

1986, 109 MINS, US ◇ ⊽ ⊙
Dir Peter Markle   *Prod* Peter Bart, Patrick Wells
Scr Peter Markle   *Ph* Mark Irwin   *Ed* Stephen E. Rivkin, Jack Hofstra   *Mus* William Orbit, Torchsong
Art Dir Alicia Keywan
● Rob Lowe, Cynthia Gibb, Patrick Swayze, Ed Lauter, Jim Youngs, Fionnula Flannagan (United Artists/Guber-Peters)

Picture has a simple premise: Rob Lowe desperately wants to leave the hard life on his father's farm to join a minor league Canadian hockey team where he believes he will be the star player. His half-blind brother (Jim Youngs), who once played for the same team before he was injured, tells their Dad (Eric Nesterenko) he'll do double-duty so Lowe can be free to try and fulfill his dreams.

Dad agrees and Lowe takes off. He is an innocent who, after less than a week, is seduced by his landlady (Fionnula Flanagan), ridiculed by his teammates and enamored of the first girl he meets (Cynthia Gibb) – the coach's daughter who becomes his girlfriend. Scenes on the ice look great and Lowe truly looks like the fast and accurate son-of-a-gun hockey player he's supposed to be.

● ●

■ **YOUNG CASSIDY**

1965, 107 MINS, US ◇
Dir Jack Cardiff, John Ford   *Prod* Robert D. Graff, Robert Emmett Ginna   *Scr* John Whiting   *Ph* Ted Scaife
Ed Anne V. Coates   *Mus* Sean O'Riada
● Rod Taylor, Julie Christie, Edith Evans, Michael Redgrave, Flora Robson, Maggie Smith (M-G-M)

Young Cassidy, biopic of Irish playwright Sean O'Casey in his sprouting years based on his autobiography, *Mirror in My House*, is notable principally for the top-rating performance of Rod Taylor in title role. Story of a rebel who rises to literary greatness, like the majority of screen bio narratives, is episodic; in attempting to cover the many facets of career, film consequently lacks the cohesion necessary for a full dramatic enactment of a historic personality.

Originally started under John Ford's direction but taken over in mid-stream by Jack Cardiff when illness forced Ford to withdraw, pic opens in 1911 Dublin during the troubled times of opposition to the British. It is a period when Cassidy – name given himself by O'Casey in his third-person writing – was feeling the stirrings of a talent which was to elevate him ultimately to the position of one of Ireland's great playwrights.

Taylor delivers a fine, strongly-etched characterization, believable both in his romantic scenes and as the writer who comes up the hard way. Splendid support is afforded particularly by Maggie Smith, as his one love but who leaves him so he can progress better without her.

● ●

■ **YOUNG DOCTORS, THE**

1961, 103 MINS, US
Dir Phil Karlson   *Prod* Stuart Millar, Lawrence Turman
Scr Joseph Hayes   *Ph* Arthur J. Ornitz   *Ed* Robert Swink
Mus Elmer Bernstein   *Art Dir* Richard Sylbert

● Fredric March, Ben Gazzara, Dick Clark, Ina Balin, Eddie Albert, Phyllis Love (Drexel/Millar-Turman)

The Young Doctors is an enlightening motion picture executed with restraint and clinical authenticity.

The screenplay, based on a novel by Arthur Hailey, is a generally brisk, literate and substantial piece of writing marked by a few soaring bursts of thought-provoking philosophical wisdom as regards life, death and love.

Essentially the story represents an idealistic clash between two pathologists, one (Fredric March) the vet department head whose ideals and perspective have been mellowed and blunted somewhat by years of red tape and day-to-day frustration, the other (Ben Gazzara), his new assistant, young, aggressive, up-to-date and meticulous in his approach to the job. The conflict is dramatically illustrated via two critical cases in which both are pretty intimately involved.

Veteran March creates a character of dimension and compassion. Gazzara plays with great reserve and intensity, another fine portrayal. Dick Clark is persuasive as a young intern, Eddie Albert outstanding as a dedicated obstetrician. Ina Balin experiences a few uncertain moments as a gravely ill young nurse in love with life in general and Gazzara in particular, but she comes through in the more demanding passages. Camerawork by Arthur J. Ornitz is pretty bold stuff.

● ●

■ **YOUNG EINSTEIN**

1988, 89 MINS, AUSTRALIA ◇ ⊽ ⊙
Dir Yahoo Serious   *Prod* Yahoo Serious, Warwick Ross, David Roach   *Scr* David Roach, Yahoo Serious   *Ph* Jeff Darling   *Ed* Yahoo Serious   *Mus* William Motzing, Martin Armiger, Tommy Tycho   *Art Dir* Steve Marr, Laurie Faen, Colin Gibson, Ron Highfield
● Yahoo Serious, Odile Le Clezio, John Howard, Pee Wee Wilson, Su Cruickshank (Serious)

This wild, cheerful, off-the-wall comedy showcases the many talents of Australian satirist Yahoo Serious, who not only directed and plays the leading role, but also co-wrote (from his own original story), co-produced, edited and handled the stunts. Quite a lot to take on for a first-time filmmaker.

Pic posits young Einstein as the only son of eccentric apple farmers from Australia's southern island, Tasmania. He has a fertile mind, and is forever discovering things: it's not his fault that, by 1905 when the film's set, gravity has already been discovered by someone else.

According to the film, Einstein discovers accidentally how to split the atom while experimenting methods of injecting bubbles into home-brewed beer. He sets off for mainland Australia (a comically lengthy journey) to patent his invention, and meets French genius Marie Curie (Odile Le Clezio) on a train; he also meets villain and patents stealer Preston Preston (John Howard), scion of a family of Perth entrepreneurs.

The entire production rests on the shoulders of its director/star. Fortunately Serious (born Greg Pead), a long-haired gangly clown, exhibits a brash and confident sense of humor, endearing personality, and a fondness for sight gags.

● ●

■ **YOUNG FRANKENSTEIN**

1974, 108 MINS, US ⊽ ⊙
Dir Mel Brooks   *Prod* Michael Gruskoff   *Scr* Gene Wilder, Mel Brooks   *Ph* Gerald Hirschfeld   *Ed* John Howard   *Mus* John Morris   *Art Dir* Dale Hennesy
● Gene Wilder, Peter Boyle, Marty Feldman, Madeline Kahn, Cloris Leachman, Gene Hackman (20th Century-Fox)

Young Frankenstein emerges as a reverently satirical salute to the 1930s horror film genre.

The screenplay features Gene Wilder as the grandson of Baron Victor Frankenstein, creator of the monster. Wilder, an American medical college teacher, is lured back to Transylvania by old family retainer Richard Haydn. Wilder's assistant, the namesake descendant of Igor, is played by Marty Feldman.

Teri Garr is a curvaceous lab assistant, while Cloris Leachman is a mysterious housekeeper composite of Una O'Connor and Mrs Danvers. Wilder's fussy fiancee Madeline Kahn turns up importantly in the final reels. Peter Boyle is the monster, an artistically excellent blend of malice, pity and comedy.
☐ 1974: Nominations: Best Adapted Screenplay, Sound

● ●

■ **YOUNG GUNS**

1988, 107 MINS, US ◇ ⊽ ⊙
Dir Christopher Cain   *Prod* Joe Roth, Christopher Cain
Scr John Fusco   *Ph* Dean Semler   *Ed* Jack Hofstra
Mus Anthony Marinelli, Brian Banks   *Art Dir* Jane Musky
● Emilio Estevez, Kiefer Sutherland, Lou Diamond Phillips, Charlie Sheen, Jack Palance, Terence Stamp (Morgan Creek)

Young Guns is a lame attempt at a brat pack *Wild Bunch*, executed without style or feel for the genre.

Meager efforts at offbeat characterization are made at the outset, as British gang ringleader Terence Stamp seeks to better the lot of his renegade boys by encouraging them to read and call each other 'gentlemen.'

Stamp's early murder by town bigshots prompts quick retaliation by the trigger-happy kids, who are briefly deputized but whose irresponsibility and inclination toward gunplay brands them as outlaws and sets in motion an irreversible chain of violence that inevitably leads to a fateful confrontation.

What this film has that few, if any, Westerns ever have had before is a hard rock score. Music's every appearance on the scene throws one right out of the scene and serves to remind that this is a high-tech artifact of the late 1980s.

As Billy the Kid, Emilio Estevez is the nominal star here, but no one really shines.

● ●

■ **YOUNG GUNS II**

(UK: *Young Guns II – Blaze of Glory*)

1990, 103 MINS, US ◇ ⊽ ⊙
Dir Geoff Murphy   *Prod* Paul Schiff, Irby Smith
Scr John Fusco   *Ph* Dean Semler   *Ed* Bruce Green
Mus Alan Silvestri   *Art Dir* Gene Rudolf
● Emilio Estevez, Kiefer Sutherland, Lou Diamond Phillips, Christian Slater, William Petersen, James Coburn (Morgan Creek)

Although it's more ambitious than most sequels, *Young Guns II* exhausts its most inspired moment during the opening credits and fades into a copy of its 1988 predecessor – a slick, glossy MTV-style western.

Even the film's one surprise – a wizened horseman emerging from the desert, circa 1950, to recount the tale of Billy the Kid – feels lifted from Arthur Penn's 1970 classic *Little Big Man*, all the way down to Emilio Estevez' hoarse, whispering narration.

Oater follows a stripped-to-the-bone storyline that picks up the adventures of Billy Bonney's Lincoln County gang a few years after the events in 1988's *Young Guns*. Told in flashback, the story essentially involves the gang's hell-bent rush toward the perceived saftey of Mexico with a band of government men – headed by ally-turned-adversary Pat Garrett (William Petersen) – in hot pursuit.

Estevez, Kiefer Sutherland and Lou Diamond Phillips are back, but the rest of the gang is new, and the other characterizations prove disappointingly thin. Christian Slater has a nice recurring bit as a Gun with an inferiority complex over his lack of notoriety;

Petersen cuts a striking figure as Garrett without providing much insight into his motives.

☐ 1990: Nomination: Best Song ('Blaze of Glory')

. . . .

■ **YOUNG LIONS, THE**

1958, 167 MINS, US ⓥ ⊙
Dir Edward Dmytryk   *Prod* Al Lichtman   *Scr* Edward Anhalt   *Ph* Joe MacDonald   *Ed* Dorothy Spencer   *Mus* Hugo Friedhofer   *Art Dir* Lyle R. Wheeler, Addison Hehr
● Marlon Brando, Montgomery Clift, Dean Martin, Hope Lange, May Britt, Barbara Rush (20th Century-Fox)

The Young Lions is a canvas of the Second World War of scope and stature. It's a king-sized credit to all concerned, from Edward Anhalt's skillful adaptation of Irwin Shaw's novel to Edward Dmytryk's realistic direction, and the highly competent portrayals of virtually everyone in the cast.

Marlon Brando's interpretation of Anhalt's modified conception of the young Nazi officer; Montgomery Clift, the drafted GI of Jewish heritage; Dean Martin as a frankly would-be draft-dodger until the realities of war catch up with him are standout all the way.

Hope Lange gives a sensitive performance as the New England girl opposite Clift and Barbara Rush is properly more resourceful as Martin's romantic vis-a-vis. Even more vivid are the performances of Sweden's May Britt, making her US film debut in the role of the cheating wife of the Nazi officer, latter capitally played by Switzerland's Maximilian (young brother of Maria) Schell, also making his Hollywood bow.

Dmytryk effectively highlights the human values on both the German and American home-fronts. It gravitates from the boot-camp in the States to the fall of France, the North African campaign, the deterioration of the Third Reich, the smirking obsequiousness to the invading Yanks by the Bavarian town mayor when the GIs liberate the inhuman concentration camp, and the gradual disillusionment of the once ardent Nazi as symbolized by Brando.

The Anhalt screenplay captures shade and nuance of role in pithy, pungent dialog. The accent on romance is as strong as the war stuff. Underplaying is the keynote of virtually all the performances.

☐ 1958: Nominations: Best B&W Cinematography, Scoring of a Dramatic Picture, Sound

. . . .

■ **YOUNG LOVERS, THE**

1964, 110 MINS, US
Dir Samuel Goldwyn Jr   *Prod* Samuel Goldwyn Jr   *Scr* George Garrrett   *Ph* Joseph Biroc, Ellsworth Fredericks   *Ed* William A. Lyon   *Mus* Sol Kaplan   *Art Dir* Frank Wade
● Peter Fonda, Sharon Hugueny, Nick Adams, Deborah Walley, Beatrice Straight, Malachi Throne (M-G-M)

Samuel Goldwyn Jr's *The Young Lovers* has a lot of things going for it. While the story [from novel by Julian Halevy] about young, unwed parents-to-be is no shocker, the talk is frank and switch is on problems mainly on unwed father, rather than of mother.

Most awkward parts come during opening scenes, as love affair between college students Peter Fonda and Sharon Hugueny is slowly built up.

Fonda has uncomfortable moments as an art student who intends to live free, bachelor life, and his voice doesn't carry conviction in several scenes. How much of this is attributable to direction (film is producer Goldwyn's first as a director as well) rather than lack of acting experience is difficult to assess.

Hugueny also suffers acting lapses, but scores by making apparent her three-step

transition from shy teenager, to passionate lover, and on to wiser, more mature young adult.

. . . .

■ **YOUNG MAN OF MUSIC**

See: Young Man with a Horn

. . . .

■ **YOUNG MAN WITH A HORN**

(UK: Young Man of Music)

1950, 111 MINS, US ⓥ
Dir Michael Curtiz   *Prod* Jerry Wald   *Scr* Carl Foreman, Edmund H. North   *Ph* Ted McCord   *Ed* Alan Crosland Jr   *Mus* Ray Heindorf (dir.)
● Kirk Douglas, Lauren Bacall, Doris Day, Hoagy Carmichael, Juano Hernandez (Warner)

For the jazz devotee this is nearly two hours of top trumpet notes. For the regular film-goer, it is good drama.

Kirk Douglas' single-minded concentration on a horn and the notes that come from it sets the character up for an eventual downfall, but after events carry him down to alcoholic skidrow, a happy ending rounds out the film.

Topnotch scripting job adapts the Dorothy Baker novel, and Michael Curtiz' direction misses no bets in walloping over all the drama and heart-tugs.

Douglas falls for Lauren Bacall and the marriage that results falls apart, he hits the bottle and winds up a drunk, only to be saved by the wholesome affection that band canary Doris Day has had for him over the years.

. . . .

■ **YOUNG MR. LINCOLN**

1939, 101 MINS, US ⓥ ⊙
Dir John Ford   *Prod* Darryl F. Zanuck   *Scr* Lamar Trotti   *Ph* Bert Glennon   *Ed* Walter Thompson   *Mus* Alfred Newman   *Art Dir* Richard Day, Mark-Lee Kirk
● Henry Fonda, Alice Brady, Marjorie Weaver, Arleen Whelan, Richard Cromwell, Donald Meek (20th Century-Fox/Cosmopolitan)

As the title implies, this deals with the Great Emancipator's early days in New Salem Ill, emphasizing the Civil War president's then penchant for inherent honesty, fearlessness, shrewdness, plus such homely qualities as being a champ rail-splitter mixed with an avid hunger for book larnin'.

As motion picture entertainment, however, *Young Mr. Lincoln* is something else again. Fundamentally it resolves itself down to a courtroom drama. He's called upon to extricate Richard Cromwell and Eddie Quillan, as Matt and Adam Clay, following a murder rap.

Henry Fonda is capital in the highlight scenes where he languorously addresses the small group in front of the little Berry-Lincoln general store in New Salem, Ill.

With judicious eye to authenticity and dignity the major shortcoming of this Lincoln film is at the altar of faithfulness, hampered by the rather lethargic production and direction.

☐ 1939: Nomination: Best Original Story

. . . .

■ **YOUNG MR PITT, THE**

1942, 110 MINS, UK
Dir Carol Reed   *Prod* Edward Black   *Scr* Sidney Gilliatt, Frank Launder, Viscount Castlerosse   *Ph* Freddie Young   *Mus* Charles Williams
● Robert Donat, Robert Morley, Phyllis Calvert, John Mills, Max Adrian, Felix Aylmer (20th Century-Fox)

There is so much to acclaim and so little with which to find fault in this production. There are over 150 speaking parts, all of them praiseworthily handled, and the overly generous 18th-century period details have seldom been better reproduced. It's a costly production all the way.

Story is based on the political career of

William Pitt Jr (Robert Donat) who was Prime Minister of England at 24.

Robert Morley, who so frequently steals the show, again towers above the rest of the excellent cast. In the stellar role Donat acts with meticulous earnestness and sincerity, but seemingly lacks inspiration. One seems to detect the mechanics of fine acting – a sort of straining to be convincing. In sharp contrast, John Mills, in a relatively minor role, is impressive without resorting to heroics.

. . . .

■ **YOUNG ONE, THE**

1961, 94 MINS, US/MEXICO
Dir Luis Bunuel   *Prod* George P. Werker   *Scr* Luis Bunuel, H.B. Addis [= Hugo Butler]   *Ph* Gabriel Figueroa   *Ed* Carlos Savage   *Mus* Jesus Zarzosa   *Art Dir* Jesus Bracho
● Zachary Scott, Key Meersman, Bernie Hamilton, Crahan Denton, Claudio Brook (Werker/Olmeca)

The Young One is an odd, complicated and inconclusive attempt to interweave two sizzling themes – race prejudice in the deep South and an almost *Lolita*-like sex situation with Tennessee Williams overtones – into an engrossing melodramatic fabric. The offbeat project was lensed in Mexico.

Travelin' Man, a short story by Peter Matthiessen, is the origin of the screenplay. The story takes place on an island wild game preserve off South Carolina occupied by an unsavory gamekeeper (Zachary Scott) and a 13 or 14-year-old orphan girl whose handyman-grandfather has just expired. Into this potentially explosive scene drifts a hip-talking Negro (Bernie Hamilton) falsely accused of rape and on the run.

Scott is convincingly unpleasant, Hamilton equally believable and sympathetic. Kay Meersman cuts a rather pitiful figure as the innocent, nymphet-like nature girl creature involved helplessly in the emotional turmoil.

Luis Bunuel does an alert, perceptive job of directing, succeeding in getting the Carolina geographical flavor out of the Mexican location. But his vigorous efforts are lamentably diluted by the unsatisfactory nature of the story.

. . . .

■ **YOUNG ONES, THE**

1962, 108 MINS, UK ◇ ⓥ
Dir Sidney J. Furie   *Prod* Kenneth Harper   *Scr* Peter Myers, Ronald Cass   *Ph* Douglas Slocombe   *Ed* Jack Slade   *Mus* Stanley Black   *Art Dir* John Howell
● Cliff Richard, Robert Morley, Carole Gray, Richard O'Sullivan, Melvyn Hayes, The Shadows (Associated British)

Producer Kenneth Harper signed up a 28-year-old Canadian director, Sidney Furie; a slick choreographer, Herbert Ross; and Cliff Richard to play the hero.

The songs [mostly by Peter Myers and Ronald Cass], dancing and Furie's nimble direction keep the screenplay on zestful enough plane. Richard is the leader of a youth club whose humble little clubhouse is endangered when a millionaire property tycoon buys the land on which it is situated. Unbeknown to the other teenagers, the tycoon is Richard's father. They decide to fight him and this involves raising $4,000 to challenge the lease. It's decided the best way to do this is by taking over a derelict theatre to stage a show.

The choreography of Ross is agile and sharp. Musical supervisor Stanley Black has made best use of the musical side. Main fault of the film is that the screenplay and dialog are uneven.

However, Robert Morley, as the tycoon, does an impressive job in bringing some adult wit and irony to the screen. Richard is inexperienced as an actor but has a pleasant charm and sings well within his range.

New dancing girl Carole Gray is a youthful

delight, though she too is happier when enjoying the exuberance of the numbers than when having to act. Melvyn Hayes and Richard O'Sullivan offer some pleasantly shrewd comedy.

● ●

■ YOUNG SAVAGES, THE

1961, 103 MINS, US

Dir John Frankenheimer   *Prod* Pat Duggan   *Scr* Edward Anhalt, J.P. Miller   *Ph* Lionel Lindon   *Ed* Eda Warren   *Mus* David Amram   *Art Dir* Burr Smidt
● Burt Lancaster , Dina Merrill , Shelley Winters , Edward Andrews , Larry Gates , Telly Savalas (United Artists)

The Young Savages is a kind of non-musical east side variation on *West Side Story*. It is a socio-logical cussword puzzle, a twisted riddle aimed at detection of the true motivation for juvenile crime, as set against the backdrop of New York's teeming East Harlem district in which neighborhood nationalities mobilize into youthful raiding parties at the drop of a psychotic frustration.

The picture is inventively, arrestingly directed by John Frankenheimer with the aid of cameraman Lionel Lindon. Together they have manipulated the lens to catch the wild fury of gang pavement warfare; twisting, tilting, pulling way back, zeroing in and composing to follow and frame the excitement.

But there is nothing Frankenheimer can do to make the yarn itself – concocted out of a novel by Evan Hunter, *A Matter of Conviction* – stand tall as screen fiction. The story is that of three Italian lads (of 15, 16 and 17) who murder a blind Puerto Rican boy of 15 who is regarded as a top warlord of a rival gang. The case for the prosecution is taken over by scrupulous d.a.'s asst Burt Lancaster whose search for truth and justice and familiarity with the law of the asphalt jungle (he grew up there) leads him to make a valiant courtroom stand on behalf of the boys he is supposed to be trying to convict.

● ●

■ YOUNG SCARFACE

See: Brighton Rock

● ●

■ YOUNG SHERLOCK HOLMES

(UK: Young Sherlock Holmes and the Pyramid of Fear)

1985, 109 MINS, US ◇ ⓥ ⊙

Dir Barry Levinson   *Prod* Mark Johnson   *Scr* Chris Columbus   *Ph* Stephen Goldblatt   *Ed* Stu Linder   *Mus* Bruce Broughton   *Art Dir* Norman Reynolds
● Nicholas Rowe , Alan Cox , Sophie Ward , Anthony Higgins , Susan Fleetwood , Freddie Jones (Paramount)

Young Sherlock Holmes is another Steven Spielberg film corresponding to those lamps made from driftwood and coffee tables from redwood burl and hatchcovers. It's not art but they all serve their purpose and sell by the millions.

The formula this time is applied to the question of what might have happened had Sherlock Holmes and John Watson first met as teenage students.

As usual, Speilberg's team – this time led by director Barry Levinson – isn't really as interested in the answer as it is in fooling around with the visual effects possibilities conjured by George Lucas' Industrial Light & Magic shop.

Nicholas Rowe as Holmes and Alan Cox as Watson maturely carry off their roles, assisted by Sophie Ward as the necessary female accomplice. The adults are just there to fill in the spaces.
☐ 1985: Nomination: Best Visual Effects

● ●

■ YOUNG STRANGER, THE

1956, 83 MINS, US ⓥ ⊙

Dir John Frankenheimer   *Prod* Stuart Millar   *Scr* Robert Dozier   *Ph* Robert Planck   *Ed* Robert Swink, Edward

Biery Jr   *Mus* Leonard Rosenman   *Art Dir* Albert S. D'Agostino, John B. Mansbridge
● James MacArthur , Kim Hunter , James Daly , James Gregory , Whit Bissell , Jeff Silver (RKO)

A story of conflict between youth and parents, the plot indulges in 'one-note' dramatics that provide very little shading between the black and white of the problem, yet which are effective within the entertainment aim. Juvenile delinquency is not necessarily an issue. Rather, the plot purpose is to show how a father should give more time and understanding to his son.

Film marks the feature picture break-in of several younger talents. James MacArthur, teenage son of Helen Hayes and the late Charles MacArthur, gets his first prominent picture casting as the youthful star and delivers promisingly. He is seen as the rebellious son of picture producer James Daly and Kim Hunter. Film-making keeps the father too busy to give much time to his son, but he realizes the error after the son is arrested for socking a theatre manager and a cop.

Picture is young Stuart Millar's first full producership after production apprenticeship with William Whyler. Debuting as a theatrical film director is John Frankenheimer, from TV, and he handles the switch neatly. For Robert Dozier, son of RKO production veepee William Dozier, film is his first screenplay [from his TV play *Deal a Blow*].

● ●

■ YOUNG TOM EDISON

1940, 85 MINS, US

Dir Norman Taurog   *Prod* John W. Considine Jr   *Scr* Bradbury Foote, Dore Schary, Hugo Butler   *Ph* Sidney Wagner   *Ed* Elmo Vernon   *Mus* Edward Ward
● Mickey Rooney , Fay Bainter , George Bancroft , Virginia Weidler , Eugene Pallette (M-G-M)

When Metro originally planned to produce the biography of Thomas A. Edison, intention was to combine his boyhood and manhood in the one picture. But research provided so much material that two productions are necessary to adequately cover the life of the wizard of Menlo Park. *Young Tom Edison* covers the inventor's life as a boy in Port Huron, Michigan, around 1863. It details his inquisitiveness on chemicals and labor-saving gadgets, and his disregard for school curriculum and rules.

Splitup of the life of Edison into two parts marks the first time that such a procedure has been followed by any company. *Edison, The Man*, with Spencer Tracy starred as the inventor in his years of real accomplishment, is the second part [released three months later].

Story points up the courage and eventual triumph of a typical American youth. No attempt is made to paint him as a youthful genius. He's an all-American boy; an inventive opportunist.

Picture is rich in youthful adventure, and human, homey qualities. Mickey Rooney plays the young inventor with sympathetic restraint. There are no obvious stunts or gags; no overplaying of the dreamy, though deeply serious boy who is laying the foundation for his later achievements.

Story revolves around the home life of the Edison family. There's the lovable and protecting mother (Fay Bainter), the stern father (George Bancroft) who fails to understand his son, and a younger sister (Virginia Weidler) continually sympathetic to her brother and his problems.

● ●

■ YOUNG WINSTON

1972, 157 MINS, UK ◇ ⓥ

Dir Richard Attenborough   *Prod* Carl Foreman   *Scr* Carl Foreman   *Ph* Gerry Turpin   *Ed* Kevin Connor   *Mus* Alfred Ralston   *Art Dir* Geoffrey Drake, Don Ashton

● Simon Ward , Robert Shaw , Anne Bancroft , Jack Hawkins , Ian Holm , Anthony Hopkins (Columbia/Open Road)

Rate this biopic of Winston Churchill's early years as both a brilliant artistic achievement and a fascinating, highly enjoyable film – a combination not always obtained.

It's a richly multi-faced scrapbook [from Churchill's book *My Early Life*] which is unfolded, touching on his lonely childhood and only occasional contact with his politician father and a socially much-involved American mother, early school experience, first combat and war correspondent stints in India and the Sudan and on to first political defeat and ultimate vindication as – after a headline-grabbing Boer War exploit – he makes an early political mark in an impassioned House of Commons speech.

Far from a sycophantic paean to a great man in the bud, pic manages a believable portrait of an ambitious and sometimes arrogant young man.
☐ 1972: Nominations: Best Original Story & Screenplay, Costume Design, Art Direction

● ●

■ YOU ONLY LIVE ONCE

1937, 85 MINS, US ⓥ

Dir Fritz Lang   *Prod* Walter Wanger   *Scr* Gene Towne, Graham Baker   *Ph* Leon Shamroy   *Ed* Daniel Mandell   *Mus* Alfred Newman (dir.)   *Art Dir* Alexander Toluboff
● Sylvia Sidney , Henry Fonda , Barton MacLane , Jean Dixon , William Gargan , Warren Hymer (Wanger/United Artists)

Fritz Lang follows up his *Fury* (1936) with another wallop. *You Only Live Once* is full of stark and bitter moments, but these bite no more deeply than deftly wrought scenes of tenderness. The self-sacrificing love of the girl for the ex-convict reaches a high level of heart-tugging during their flight as fugitives from the law.

Lang's penchant for mob scenes receives indulgence in only one sequence staged outside the courthouse after Henry Fonda has been found guilty of causing the death of six men in a holdup. On the spectacular side are the gas bombing of money-truck guards in a one-man robbery, the guile used by Fonda in getting out of the deathhouse, and the bartering which goes on between the escaped convict and the warden just inside the prison gates.

Sylvia Sidney counts strongly. Turning in telling support are Barton MacLane, as the public defender, who, despite his love for Sidney, befriends Fonda, and Jean Dixon, as Sidney's critical but loyal sister.

● ●

■ YOU ONLY LIVE TWICE

1967, 117 MINS, UK ◇ ⓥ ⊙

Dir Lewis Gilbert   *Prod* Albert R. Broccoli, Harry Saltzman   *Scr* Roald Dahl   *Ph* Freddie Young   *Ed* Peter Hunt   *Mus* John Barry   *Art Dir* Ken Adam
● Sean Connery , Akiko Wakabayashi , Tetsuro Tamba, Mie Hama , Karin Dor , Donald Pleasence (United Artists/Eon)

Film begins with a prolog in which a US astronaut's spacewalk is interrupted by another spacecraft that, crocodile-style, opens its jaws and swallows the capsule. US government is peeved at what it assumes to be a Russian attempt to foil space exploration, and 007 is assigned by helpful British intelligence to locate the missing rocket before full-scale war breaks out between the two nuclear powers.

Sean Connery plays 007 with his usual finesse. Rest of cast in the $9.5 million film is strictly secondary, although Akiko Wakabayashi and Tetsuro Tamba register well as Bond's Japanese cohorts. Donald Pleasence makes a suitably menacing German heavy who appears in film's final scenes. [Additional story material by Harold Jack Bloom.]

● ●

■ YOU'RE A BIG BOY NOW

1966, 98 MINS, US ◇ Ⓥ
Dir Francis Coppola   *Prod* Phil Feldman   *Scr* Francis
Coppola   *Ph* Andy Laszlo   *Ed* Aram Avakian
Mus John Sebastian   *Art Dir* Vassieli Fotopoulos
● Elizabeth Hartman , Geraldine Page , Julie Harris ,
Peter Kastner , Rip Torn , Michael Dunn (Seven Arts)

You're a Big Boy Now [from the novel by David
Benedictus] has a simple premise – a virginal
young man growing into manhood, not so
much through his own efforts as those about
him – which has been expanded glowingly in
a sophisticated approach. Francis Coppola
has drawn topflight performances from his
talented cast.

Peter Kastner plays a roller-skating stack
boy in a NY public library, somewhat of a
dreamer. The father (Rip Torn) decides the
best way for his son to grow up would be to
move out of the family home on his own.
Straightaway, lad becomes ensconced in a
rooming house run by Julie Harris.

With the help of his library, dope-inclined
pal (Tony Bill) and a pretty library assistant
(Karen Black) the boy is launched on his road
to manhood, which takes him into the arms of
a sexy, way-out, Greenwich Village discotheque dish (Elizabeth Hartman).
Frequent laughs spark his career toward full-
blossomed virility, with amusing bumps along
the way.

Kastner turns in a slick portrayal, endowing
role with just the proper emphasis upon
youth in the wondering stage. Both Geraldine
Page as the mother and Harris as the landlady go all-out in hilarious roles and Torn,
too, delivers a sock performance as the father
who has difficulty understanding his son.
□ 1966: Nomination: Best Supp. Actress
(Geraldine Page)

■ YOU'RE IN THE ARMY NOW

See: O.H.M.S.

■ YOU'RE IN THE ARMY NOW

1941, 79 MINS, US
Dir Lewis Seiler   *Prod* Ben Stoloff   *Scr* Paul Gerard
Smith, George Beatty   *Ph* Arthur Todd   *Ed* Frank
Magee
● Jimmy Durante , Jane Wyman , Phil Silvers , Regis
Toomey , George Meeker , Donald MacBride (Warner)

Though it is a bit corny in spots and lays the
slapstick on heavily, with some gag sequences
stretched too far, here is a comedy of soldier
life that completely entertains.

Jimmy Durante goes to town on the clowning, slapstick and other means of comedy, but
while he's busy as a bee, many others contribute importantly to the numerous laugh-
producing sequences. Among these is Phil
Silvers.

Durante and Silvers, trying to interest a recruiting officer in a vacuum cleaner, accidentally get themselves enlisted. As buck
privates, they become guardhouse regulars as
result of getting themselves into one jam after another.

The story job by Paul Gerard Smith, an old
hand at the vaudeville-writing game, and
George Beatty is excellent and, if some of the
gag situations are stretched a little too far or
the slapstick gets out of hand, it may be the
fault of the director, Lewis Seiler. Dialog is
surefire all the way.

■ ZABRISKIE POINT

1970, 112 MINS, US ◇ Ⓥ ⊙
Dir Michelangelo Antonioni   *Prod* Carlo Ponti
Scr Michelangelo Antonioni, Fred Gardner, Sam
Shepard, Tonino Guerra, Clare Peploe   *Ph* Alfino Contini
Ed Franco Arcalli   *Art Dir* Dean Tavoularis
● Mark Frechette, Daria Halprin, Paul Fix, G.D.
Spradlin, Bill Garaway, Kathleen Cleaver (M-G-M)

Michelangelo Antonioni makes the US social
scene, and despite the imbalance in his concept, distills from his notes some arresting
photographic moments. Antonioni has sought
to bring into the focus of his own insights, the
student vs establishment conflict. He is on
foreign terrain. His off-camera presence is
sensed in each pictorial move.

Probably the most compelling footage of
Zabriskie Point is the finis wrapup, in which
things representative of the ultra 'haves' go
up in imagined explosions.

The special effects are magnificent as the
remnants of modern architectured big business, including mod edifices, and billboards
which had been planted by power corpora-
tions, hit the sky, piece by piece, and hang in
a dangling collage of symbolism.

■ ZANDY'S BRIDE

1974, 116 MINS, US ◇
Dir Jan Troell   *Prod* Harvey Matofsky   *Scr* Marc
Norman   *Ph* Jordan Cronenweth   *Ed* Gordon Scott
Mus Michael Franks   *Art Dir* Al Brenner
● Gene Hackman, Liv Ullmann, Eileen Heckart, Susan
Tyrrell, Sam Bottoms, Joe Santos (Warner)

Zandy's Bride is a good period frontier romantic melodrama starring Gene Hackman as a
gruff cattle rancher and Liv Ullmann as the
mail-order bride who softens him up. Star
performances sustain Jan Troell's delicate
but placid direction.

Marc Norman's spare screenplay was
adapted from a 1942 novel, *The Stranger*, by
Lillian Bos Ross. Set in 1870 in upstate
California's rugged Big Sur mountain and sea
interface, story takes Hackman from a crude,
thoughtless hermit to a loving husband and
father. The going is rough, however,
Ullmann's unexpectedly strong spirit overcomes his stiffness, learned at the back of the
hand of father Frank Cady, a cruel patriarch
who has reduced wife Eileen Heckart to serf
status.

The plot line is thin but sufficient.

■ ZARDOZ

1974, 104 MINS, UK ◇ Ⓥ ⊙
Dir John Boorman   *Prod* John Boorman   *Scr* John
Boorman   *Ph* Geoffrey Unsworth   *Ed* John Merritt
Mus David Munrow   *Art Dir* Anthony Pratt
● Sean Connery, Charlotte Rampling, Sara Kestelman,
John Alderton, Sally Anne Newton, Niall Buggy (20th
Century-Fox)

Zardoz is a futuristic, metaphysical and anthropological drama testing John Boorman in
three creative areas. The results: direction,
good; script, a brilliant premise which unfortunately washes out in climactic sound and
fury; and production, outstanding, particularly special visual effects which belie the
film's modest cost. Sean Connery heads the
cast as a 23rd-century Adam.

The story, set in 2293, postulates a world
society which this century's runaway technology forced into being. The highest order beings are an elitist group of effete aesthetics,

eternally youthful on a spiritual plane.
Connery rises from the lower ranks to overthrow the new order and recycle mankind
into its older pattern.

Connery manifests well the brooding duality of man's nature, emerging from mechanical breeding to eventually tear down the
system that created him.

■ ZED AND TWO NOUGHTS, A

1985, 115 MINS, UK/NETHERLANDS ◇ Ⓥ
Dir Peter Greenaway   *Prod* Kees Kasander, Peter
Sainsbury   *Scr* Peter Greenaway   *Ph* Sacha Vierny
Ed John Wilson   *Mus* Michael Nyman   *Art Dir* Ben
van Os
● Andrea Ferreol, Brian Deacon, Eric Deacon, Frances
Barber, Joss Ackland, Gerard Thoolen (Artificial Eye/BFI/
Channel Four/Allarts/VPRO)

Despite its visual pyrotechnics and an impressively woven texture of intellectual allusions,
Peter Greenaway's feature fails to engage the
audience's sympathies.

In the end, it remains the work of a highly
talented British eccentric who hasn't managed to thresh out his private fantasies and
obscurantist intellectual preoccupations to
connect with major concerns or touch the
emotions.

The action centers on a zoo (its letters making up the zed and two noughts of the title).
In this lurid arena Greenaway is intent on up-
turning the seamier, humiliating side of animal existence in captivity (including that of
homo sapiens).

Meanwhile, lots of pseudo-philosophical co-
nundrums are tossed at the audience like
peanuts to hungry caged animals. Is a zebra a
white horse with black stripes or a black one
with white? etc. Needless to say, the resulting
stilted dialog does not make the acting much
of a treat.

■ ZEE & CO.

(US: X, Y & Zee)

1972, 110 MINS, UK ◇ Ⓥ
Dir Brian G. Hutton   *Prod* Jay Kanter, Alan Ladd Jr
Scr Edna O'Brien   *Ph* Billy Williams   *Ed* Jim Clark
Mus Stanley Myers   *Art Dir* Peter Mullins
● Elizabeth Taylor, Michael Caine, Susannah York,
Margaret Leighton, John Standing, Mary Larkin
(Columbia)

Not in years have three people more deserved
the star billing they get in this *Love Story* for
adults. Elizabeth Taylor and Susannah York
both turn in performances that fully capture
the excellently conceived characters of Edna
O'Brien's original screenplay. Michael Caine
keeps up beautifully with the pace set by his
femme co-stars.

The script has Taylor, the 'Zee' of the title,
and Caine as a long-married couple, whose
relationship has turned into a love-hate affair
that leads into Caine's affair with York.

After a half-hearted suicide attempt Zee
recognizes the possibility of an actual break
but, by accident finding that her rival has her
own private Achilles heel, makes a final, desperate move which may answer one problem
but presents another.

■ ZELIG

1983, 84 MINS, US ◇ Ⓥ ⊙
Dir Woody Allen   *Prod* Robert Greenhut   *Scr* Woody
Allen   *Ph* Gordon Willis   *Ed* Susan E. Morse
Mus Dick Hyman   *Art Dir* Mel Bourne
● Woody Allen, Mia Farrow, Garreth Brown, Stephanie
Farrow, Will Holt, Sol Lomita (Rollins-Joffe/Orion)

Lampooning documentary tradition by structuring the entire film as a meticulously
crafted bogus docu, Woody Allen tackles
some serious stuff en route (namely the two-
edged sword of public and media celebrity-

hood) but manages to avoid the self-oriented seriousness that's alienated many of his onetime loyalist. More positively, *Zelig* is consistently funny, though more academic than boulevardier.

Allen plays the eponymous Leonard Zelig, subject of the 'documentary' that traces this onetime legend of the 1920s-30s whose weak personality and neurotic need to be liked caused him to become the ultimate conformist.

Through the use of doctored photos and staged black and white footage cannily – and usually undetectably – matched with authentic newsreels and stock footage of the period, Allen is seen intermingling with everyone from the Hearst crowd at San Simeon, Eugene O'Neill and Fanny Brice to the likes of Pope Pius XI and even Adolf Hitler.

The narrative that does emerge limns the efforts of a committed psychiatrist (played with tact and loveliness by Mia Farrow) to give Zelig a single self, a relationship that blossoms, predictably, to love by fadeout.
☐ 1983: Nomination: Best Cinematography, Costume Design

■ ZEPPELIN

1971, 97 MINS, UK ◇ ⓥ
Dir Etienne Perier *Prod* Owen Crump *Scr* Arthur Rowe, Donald Churchill *Ph* Alan Hume *Ed* John Shirley *Mus* Roy Budd *Art Dir* Bert Davey
● Michael York, Elke Sommer, Peter Carsten, Marius Goring, Anton Diffring, Andrew Keir (Getty & Fromkess/Warner)

Zeppelin settles for being just another wartime melodrama, with some good aerial sequences and a powerful, brisk raid sequence in the finale.

Story [by producer Owen Crump] deals with Britain's concern about German's new World War I weapon, the Zeppelin, the monstrous, looming aircraft that made Britain vulnerable. Indication that the Germans have perfected a new and even more effective Zeppelin jerks the British highups into swift action.

A young Scottish lieutenant, of Anglo-German parentage, who had left Germany and eventually joined the British Army (Michael York) looks the perfect spy. Worked on by an attractive German Mata Hari (Alexandra Stewart), he is softened up and when called on to 'volunteer' to 'defect' to the Germans and dig out the secrets of the new Zeppelin he reluctantly agrees.

Many Germans are suspicious of his sudden switch back to the homeland. But only one appears to be convinced that he's a spy. She (Elke Sommer) is the wife of the aircraft designer (Marius Goring) and she's more concerned with helping to prepare the Zepp for its final trial run than in exposing York.

■ ZIEGFELD FOLLIES

1945, 116 MINS, US ◇ ⓥ ⊙
Dir Vincente Minnelli, [George Sidney, Norman Taurog, Roy Del Ruth, Lemuel Ayers] *Prod* Arthur Freed *Scr* George White, William K. Wells, Al Lewis, Robert Alton, Kay Thompson, Roger Edens, Irving Brecher *Ph* George Folsey, Charles Rosher, Ray June *Ed* Albert Akst *Mus* Lennie Hayton (dir.) *Art Dir* Cedric Gibbons, Jack Martin Smith, Merrill Pye, Lemuel Ayers
● Fred Astaire, Lucille Ball, Fanny Brice, Judy Garland, Gene Kelly, William Powell (M-G-M)

Looking down from a very lush heaven, as Florenz Ziegfeld (William Powell) does in prolog of this film super, the Great Zieggy would be dazzled by color, sets and routines far above the capacities of his day. But despite the glory of Technicolor, Ziegfeld would have missed his nudes, his pleasantly risque interludes and a certain heart-warming which came with the old productions.

Those shining above all others in the generous cast of Metro stars are Fred Astaire, agile and gay; Judy Garland, who has perfected an ironic touch; sultry Lena Horne, graceful Esther Williams, comic Fanny Brice and sweet-warbling Lucille Bremer.

Pic opens with dreamland set out of which Powell emerges, apparently comfortably fixed in celestial heights a la Ziegfeld. As the great producer, he reflects on his successes – *Rosalie, Rio Rita, Show Boat*, the various *Follies*.

It's all stupendous, terrific, colossal, practically everyone would agree. Even Zieggy.

■ ZIEGFELD GIRL

1941, 135 MINS, US ⓥ ⊙
Dir Robert Z. Leonard, Busby Berkeley *Prod* Pandro S. Berman *Scr* Marguerite Roberts, Sonya Levien *Ph* Ray June *Ed* Blanche Sewell *Mus* Herbert Stothart
● James Stewart, Judy Garland, Hedy Lamarr, Lana Turner, Tony Martin, Dan Dailey (M-G-M)

The attempt to balance three parallel dramas of the lives of three Ziegfeld showgirls makes for continual switching from one tale to the other. Interpolation of two extended displays of Ziegfeldian production sequences, with parades of the glorified girls, prevents smooth unfolding of the piece and results in several dull passages.

Smart casting provides vivid contrast in the Ziegfeld selections for his showgirl ensemble. There's Judy Garland, youthful but veteran trouper, with showmanship, personality and talent; Hedy Lamarr, wife of a pecunious musical genius, with her striking and reserved beauty; and the sexy Lana Turner who succumbs to the easiest way for a brief fling at luxury.

Director Robert Z. Leonard provides a most capable directorial job. It's one of the top negative outlays of the studio, running approximately $1,900,000 in total outlay. The expenditure is apparent in every foot of unreeling.

■ ZOMBIES

See: *Dawn of the Dead*

■ ZOO IN BUDAPEST

1933, 82 MINS, US
Dir Rowland V. Lee *Prod* Jesse L. Lasky *Scr* Dan Totheroh, Louise Long, Rowland V. Lee *Ph* Lee Garmes *Mus* Hugo Friedhofer
● Loretta Young, Gene Raymond, O. P. Heggie, Wally Albright, Paul Fix (Fox)

Seemingly what producer Jesse Lasky has tried to do is to make a picture which has in it something of the strange fascination of romance and atmosphere of *Liliom* and at the same time an element of Hollywood punch. He has gotten both things and they don't blend.

Besides the warring elements of a *Liliom* theme and a dramatic finish, the story [by Melville Baker and Jack Kirkland] has still another facet, the development of a submotif of bitter social satire in symbolic suggestions of similarities between the animals in the zoo and some of the people that cross the screen. This slant is but vaguely suggested and is never worked out satisfactorily.

However, there can be no two views of the picture's pictorial beauty. There are several sequences of night falling over a lake in the zoo peopled with strange creatures, where an escaped orphan girl is hiding as the evening mists gather, that are a knockout.

Playing by the two leads is eminently good. Role of the terror-stricken orphanage refugee proves a happy one for Loretta Young's talents, while the opposite character, that of a wild youngster brought up in a big town menagerie, friend and play-fellow of the

beasts of the cages, turns out to be one of those once-in-a-blue-moon for Gene Raymond, a newcomer from legit of only one or two pictures.

■ ZORBA THE GREEK

1964, 142 MINS, US/GREECE ⓥ ⊙
Dir Michael Cacoyannis *Prod* Michael Cacoyannis *Scr* Michael Cacoyannis *Ph* Walter Lassally *Ed* Alex Archambault *Mus* Mikis Theodorakis *Art Dir* Vassili Fotopoulos
● Anthony Quinn, Alan Bates, Irene Papas, Lila Kedrova, George Foundas, Eleni Anousaki (International Classics)

To one who has not read Nikos Kazantzakis' widely praised novel it appears that producer-director-scenarist Michael Cacoyannis may have tried to be too faithful to the original.

Zorba the Greek is a paean to life in all its diverse aspects, ranging from the farcical to the tragic, and as epitomized by the lusty title character. This Zorba, beautifully played by Anthony Quinn, is a wise and aging peasant, a free soul who is totally committed to life no matter what it holds.

To dramatize this theme, Cacoyannis has written a screenplay which is so packed with incidents of varying moods that some of the more important ones cannot be developed fully. The story takes place in a remote section of the island of Crete where Zorba has come as the self-appointed aide-de-camp to a young, inhibited Englishman of Greek parentage, played by Alan Bates. Latter, who describes himself as a writer who hasn't written anything in a long, long time, intends to reopen an old lignite mine he has inherited. Their subsequent adventures – rather loosely connected and wherein Bates finally learns to live a la Zorba – comprise the body of the film.

Quinn is excellent, and Bates, in a less flamboyant role, is equally good. Irene Papas is strikingly effective as a doomed widow, a role without dialog. Lila Kedrova plays the aging courtesan with all stops out, always halfway between laughter and tears.
☐ 1964: Best Supp. Actress (Lila Kedrova), B&W Cinematography, B&W Art Direction.
☐ Nominations: Best Picture, Director, Actor (Anthony Quinn), Adapted Screenplay

■ ZORRO, THE GAY BLADE

1981, 93 MINS, US ◇ ⓥ
Dir Peter Medak *Prod* George Hamilton, C. O. Erickson *Scr* Hal Dresner *Ph* John A. Alonzo *Ed* Hillary Jane Kranze *Mus* Ian Fraser *Art Dir* Herman A. Blumenthal
● George Hamilton, Lauren Hutton, Brenda Vaccaro, Ron Leibman, Donovan Scott, James Booth (20th Century-Fox/Simon)

Despite an inspired, offbeat performance by George Hamilton, *Zorro, the Gay Blade* doesn't have nearly enough gags to sustain its 93 minutes. For the most part this is a Zorro with a very dull edge.

Although there is no time frame, film is obviously set years ago (in California) where Don Diego Vega, offspring of the legendary Zorro, is called upon to pick up his father's sword after the elder's death.

The hook here is that Hamilton's Vega, who is at first sight righting the wrongs of the poor villagers against leader Ron Leibman (who shouts unbearably through his entire role opposite equally brassy spouse Brenda Vaccaro), soon injures his foot and can no longer carry on his heroic deeds. Luckily his long-lost lookalike Englishman brother appears out of nowhere and takes on the Zorro persona.

The contrast between the two Zorros is initially quite funny but there is nothing intriguing or original through the rest of the action. Pic climaxes at a snail's pace to Hamilton

Z

getting the girl (Lauren Hutton as a rather
bland would-be political activist)
....

■ **ZULU**

1964, 135 MINS, UK ◇ ⓥ ⊙
Dir Cy Endfield   *Prod* Stanley Baker, Cy Endfield
Scr John Prebble, Cy Endfield   *Ph* Stephen Dade
Ed John Jympson   *Mus* John Barry   *Art Dir* Ernest
Archer
● Stanley Baker, Jack Hawkins, Ulla Jacobsson, James
Booth, Michael Caine, Nigel Green (Paramount/
Diamond)

Joseph E. Levine makes an impressive debut
in British film production with *Zulu*, a picture
that allows ample scope for his flamboyant
approach to showmanship.

Based on a famous heroic exploit, when a
handful of British soldiers withstood an onslaught by 4,000 Zulu warriors, the production is distinguished by its notable onscreen
values, which are enhanced by top-quality
lensing by Stephen Dade. It also has an intelligent screenplay which avoids most of the obvious cliches. It keeps the traditional British
stiff upper-lip attitudes down to the barest
minimum.

The defense of the garrison at Rorke's Drift
took place on 22 January 1879. At the time
the garrison heard the news that the 4,000
Zulu braves were on the way, reports had just
come in that a far larger garrison had been
completely wiped out, and there was no
prospect of help from any other source.

On of the more obvious cliches in this type
of yarn is apt to be the malingerer who displays great heroism in a moment of crisis.
There is such a situation in *Zulu*, but the
cliche is avoided, largely because of the excellent performance by James Booth. Indeed,
the high allround standard of acting is one of
the notable plus features. Stanley Baker, a
solid and reliable performer, turns in a thoroughly convincing portrayal as the resolute
Royal Engineers officer, with an effective contrasting study by Michael Caine as a supercilious lieutenant. Richard Burton contributes a
brief and dignified narration.

....

■ **ZULU DAWN**

1979, 117 MINS, UK ◇ ⓥ ⊙
Dir Douglas Hickox   *Prod* Nate Kohn   *Scr* Cy Enfield,
Anthony Storey   *Ph* Ousama Rawi   *Ed* Malcolm Cook
Mus Elmer Bernstein   *Art Dir* John Rosewarne
● Burt Lancaster, Peter O'Toole, Simon Ward, John
Mills, Nigel Davenport, Denholm Elliott (Lamitas/
Samarkand)

The subject of *Zulu Dawn* is the Battle of
Islandlhwana wherein some 1,500 redcoats
were slaughtered by 16 times their number of
Zulu warriors led by legendary chief
Cetshwayo.

The film is, in fact, a sort of 'prequel' to the
1964 picture *Zulu*, which dealt with an heroic
stand at Rorke's Drift by a small band of
British soldiers in 1879.

The action sequences are superbly handled,
as are the scenes in which the men and material are assembled and manoeuvered. For
sheer scope and numbers of people being manipulated for the cameras, *Zulu Dawn* is positively DeMillesque in scale.

Such banality as there is is, thankfully, confined to the expositional sequences which are
quickly gotten out of the way to allow the
army to get on the march.

....

Hutton, Brian G. *First Deadly Sin, The; High Road to China; Kelly's Heroes; Night Watch; Pad (and How to Use It), The; Sol Madrid; Where Eagles Dare; Zee & Co.*

Huyck, Willard *Howard the Duck*

Hyams, Peter *Busting; Capricorn One; Hanover Street; Narrow Margin; Outland; Peeper; Presidio, The; Running Scared; Star Chamber, The; Stay Tuned; 2010*

Ichikawa, Kon *Visions of Eight*

Ingram, Rex *Arab, The; Four Horsemen of the Apocalypse, The; Garden of Allah, The; Mare Nostrum; Prisoner of Zenda, The; Scaramouche*

Irvin, John *Dogs of War, The; Ghost Story; Hamburger Hill; Next of Kin; Raw Deal; Robin Hood*

Israel, Neal *Bachelor Party*

Ivory, James *Bostonians, The; Europeans, The; Guru, The; Heat and Dust; Howards End; Maurice; Mr. & Mrs. Bridge; Quartet; Room with a View, A; Roseland; Savages; Shakespeare Wallah; Wild Party, The*

Jackson, George *House Party 2*

Jackson, Mick *Bodyguard, The; Chattahoochee; L.A. Story*

Jackson, Pat *Encore*

Jackson, Peter *Braindead*

Jackson, Wilfred *Alice In Wonderland; Cinderella; Lady and the Tramp; Peter Pan*

Jaeckin, Just *Lady Chatterley's Lover*

Jaffe, Stanley R. *Without a Trace*

Jaglom, Henry *Always; Can She Bake a Cherry Pie?; Eating; New Year's Day; Safe Place, A; Sitting Ducks; Someone to Love; Tracks; Venice/Venice*

Jameson, Jerry *Airport '77; Raise the Titanic*

Jankel, Annabel *D.O.A.; Super Mario Bros.*

Jarman, Derek *Aria; Caravaggio; Edward II; Garden, The; Jubilee; Last of England, The; Tempest, The; War Requiem; Wittgenstein*

Jarmusch, Jim *Down by Law; Mystery Train; Night on Earth; Stranger Than Paradise*

Jarrott, Charles *Anne of the Thousand Days; Dove, The; Lost Horizon; Mary, Queen of Scots; Other Side of Midnight, The*

Jean, Vadim *Leon the Pig Farmer*

Jeffrey, Tom *Odd Angry Shot, The*

Jeffries, Lionel *Baxter!; Railway Children, The; Water Babies, The*

Jenkins, Michael *Heartbreak Kid, The*

Jewison, Norman *Agnes of God; … And Justice For All; Art of Love, The; Best Friends; Cincinnati Kid, The; Fiddler on the Roof; F.I.S.T.; Forty Pounds of Trouble; Gaily, Gaily; In Country; In the Heat of the Night; Jesus Christ Superstar; Moonstruck; Other People's Money; Rollerball; Russians Are Coming! The*

Russians Are Coming!, The; Send Me No Flowers; Soldier's Story, A; Thomas Crown Affair, The; Thrill of It All, The*

Jimenez, Neal *Waterdance, The*

Joanou, Phil *Final Analysis; State of Grace; U2 Rattle and Hum*

Joffe, Arthur *Harem*

Joffe, Roland *City of Joy; Fat Man and Little Boy; Killing Fields, The; Mission, The*

Johnson, Alan *To Be or Not to Be*

Johnson, Jed *Bad*

Johnson, Kenneth *Short Circuit 2*

Johnson, Lamont *Cattle Annie and Little Britches; Groundstar Conspiracy, The; Gunfight, A; Last American Hero, The; Lipstick; McKenzie Break, The; One On One; Spacehunter Adventures in the Forbidden Zone; You'll Like My Mother*

Johnson, Nunnally *How To Be Very, Very Popular; Man in the Gray Flannel Suit, The; Three Faces of Eve, The*

Johnston, Aaron Kim *Last Winter, The*

Johnston, Joe *Honey, I Shrunk the Kids; Rocketeer*

Jones, Amy *Love Letters; Slumber Party Massacre*

Jones, David *Betrayal; 84 Charing Cross Road; Jacknife; Trial, The*

Jones, F. Richard *Bulldog Drummond; Gaucho, The; Mickey*

Jones, Terry *Erik the Viking; Life of Brian; Monty Python and the Holy Grail; Monty Python's The Meaning Of Life; Personal Services*

Jordan, Neil *Angel; Company of Wolves, The; Crying Game, The; High Spirits; Miracle, The; Mona Lisa; We're No Angels*

Jordon, Glenn *Only When I Laugh*

Julian, Rupert *Phantom of the Opera, The*

Juran, Nathan *Drums Across the River; First Men in the Moon; 7th Voyage of Sinbad, The*

Kadar, Jan *Lies My Father Told Me*

Kagan, Jeremy Paul *Big Fix, The; By the Sword; Chosen, The; Heroes; Journey of Natty Gann, The; Scott Joplin; Sting II, The*

Kalatozov, Mikhail *Red Tent, The*

Kalin, Tom *Swoon*

Kampmann, Steven *Stealing Home*

Kane, Joseph *Flame of the Barbary Coast; Yellow Rose of Texas, The*

Kanew, Jeff *Eddie Macon's Run; Revenge of the Nerds; Tough Guys; V.I. Warshawski*

Kanievska, Marek *Another Country; Less Than Zero*

Kanin, Garson *Bachelor Mother; My Favorite Wife; Tom, Dick and Harry*

Kanter, Hal *Loving You*

Kaplan, Jonathan *Accused, The; Heart Like a Wheel; Immediate Family; Love Field; Mr. Billion;*

Project X; Unlawful Entry; White Line Fever*

Karbelnikoff, Michael *Mobsters*

Kardos, Leslie *Small Town Girl*

Karlson, Phil *Ben; Kansas City Confidential; Kid Galahad; Phenix City Story, The; Secret Ways, The; Silencers, The; Wrecking Crew, The; Young Doctors, The*

Karson, Eric *Octagon, The*

Kasdan, Lawrence *Accidental Tourist, The; Big Chill, The; Body Heat; Grand Canyon; I Love You to Death; Silverado*

Kastle, Leonard *Honeymoon Killers, The*

Katselas, Milton *Butterflies Are Free; Report to the Commissioner*

Katzin, Lee H. *Le Mans; Whatever Happened to Aunt Alice?*

Kaufman, George S. *Senator Was Indiscreet, The*

Kaufman, Lloyd *Class of Nuke 'em High; Toxic Avenger, The; Toxic Avenger, Part II, The*

Kaufman, Philip *Great Northfield, Minnesota Raid, The; Henry & June; Invasion of the Body Snatchers; Right Stuff, The; Unbearable Lightness of Being, The; Wanderers, The; White Dawn, The*

Kaurismaki, Mika *Amazon*

Kautner, Helmut *Restless Years, The*

Kaylor, Robert *Carny*

Kazan, Elia *America America; Arrangement, The; Baby Doll; Boomerang!; East of Eden; Face in the Crowd, A; Gentleman's Agreement; Last Tycoon, The; Man on a Tightrope; On the Waterfront; Panic in the Streets; Pinky; Sea of Grass, The; Splendor in the Grass; Streetcar Named Desire, A; Tree Grows in Brooklyn, A; Viva Zapata!; Wild River*

Keach, James *False Identity*

Keaton, Buster *Battling Butler; General, The; Go West; Navigator, The; Our Hospitality; Sherlock, Jr.; Three Ages, The*

Keaton, Diane *Heaven*

Keighley, William *Adventures of Robin Hood, The; Bride Came C.O.D., The; Bullets or Ballots; Each Dawn I Die; Fighting 69th, The; George Washington Slept Here; G-Men; Green Pastures; Man Who Came to Dinner, The; Master of Ballantrae, The; No Time for Comedy; Prince and the Pauper, The*

Keller, Harry *Touch of Evil*

Kellman, Barnet *Straight Talk*

Kellogg, Ray *Green Berets, The*

Kelly, Gene *Cheyenne Social Club, The; Guide for the Married Man, A; Hello, Dolly!; Invitation to the Dance; It's Always Fair Weather; On the Town; Singin' in the Rain; That's Entertainment, Part II; Tunnel of Love, The*

Kennedy, Burt *Dirty Dingus Magee; Good Guys and the Bad Guys, The;*

Hannie Caulder; Money Trap, The; Return of the Seven; Suburban Commando; Support Your Local Gunfighter; Support Your Local Sheriff; Train Robbers, The; War Wagon, The; Welcome to Hard Times; Young Billy Young*

Kenton, Erle C. *House of Dracula; House of Frankenstein; Island of Lost Souls; Pardon My Sarong; You're Telling Me*

Kershner, Irvin *Empire Strikes Back, The; Eyes of Laura Mars; Fine Madness, A; Flim-Flam Man, The; Hoodlum Priest, The; Loving; Luck of Ginger Coffey, The; Never Say Never Again; Return of a Man Called Horse, The; Robocop 2; Up the Sandbox*

Keshishian, Alek *Truth or Dare In Bed with Madonna*

Kibbee, Roland *Midnight Man, The*

Kidd, Michael *Merry Andrew*

Kidron, Beeban *Used People*

Kiely, Chris *Future Schlock*

Kiersch, Fritz *Children of the Corn; Into the Sun; Tuff Turf*

Kimmins, Anthony *Amorous Prawn, The; Captain's Paradise, The*

King, Allan *Warrendale*

King, Henry *Alexander's Ragtime Band; Bell for Adano, A; Black Swan, The; Captain from Castile; Carousel; Chad Hanna; David and Bathsheba; Fury; Gunfighter, The; I'd Climb the Highest Mountain; In Old Chicago; Jesse James; King of the Khyber Rifles; Love Is a Many-Splendored Thing; O. Henry's Full House; Prince of Foxes; Remember the Day; Seventh Heaven; Snows of Kilimanjaro, The; Song of Bernadette, The; Stanley and Livingstone; State Fair; Stella Dallas; Sun also Rises, The; Tender Is the Night; This Earth Is Mine; Twelve O'Clock High; Wilson; Winning of Barbara Worth, The; Yank in the R.A.F., A*

King, Louis *Charlie Chan in Egypt; Mrs. Mike; Thunderhead – Son of Flicka*

King, Stephen *Maximum Overdrive*

King, Zalman *Two Moon Junction; Wild Orchid*

Kinney, Jack *Make Mine Music; Victory Through Air Power*

Klane, Robert *Weekend at Bernie's II*

Kleiser, Randal *Big Top Pee-wee; Blue Lagoon, The; Flight of the Navigator; Getting It Right; Grease; Honey, I Blew Up the Kid*

Kloves, Steve *Fabulous Baker Boys, The*

Knopf, Edwin H. *Paramount on Parade*

Knowles, Bernard *Man Within, The*

Konchalovsky, Andrei *Duet For One; Homer and Eddie; Inner Circle, The; Maria's Lovers; Runaway Train; Shy People; Tango & Cash*

Kopple, Barbara *Harlan County, U.S.A.*